PETERSON'S GRADUATE PROGRAMS IN BUSINESS, EDUCATION, INFORMATION STUDIES, LAW & SOCIAL WORK

2015

About Peterson's

Peterson's provides the accurate, dependable, high-quality education content and guidance you need to succeed. No matter where you are on your academic or professional path, you can rely on Peterson's print and digital publications for the most up-to-date education exploration data, expert test-prep tools, and top-notch career success resources—everything you need to achieve your goals.

For more information, contact Peterson's Publishing, 3 Columbia Circle, Suite 205, Albany, NY 12203-5158; 800-338-3282 Ext. 54229; or find us on the World Wide Web at www.petersonsbooks.com.

CONTENTS

A Note from the Peterson's Editors   vii

THE GRADUATE ADVISER
The Admissions Process   3
Financial Support   5
Accreditation and Accrediting Agencies   9
How to Use These Guides   15

**DIRECTORY OF INSTITUTIONS WITH
PROGRAMS IN BUSINESS,
EDUCATION, INFORMATION
STUDIES, LAW & SOCIAL WORK**
**Directory of Institutions and Their
Offerings**   20

**ACADEMIC AND PROFESSIONAL
PROGRAMS IN BUSINESS**
**Section 1: Business Administration and
Management**   69
Program Directory
    Business Administration and
        Management—General   70
Close-Ups   181

Section 2: Accounting and Finance   199
Program Directories
    Accounting   200
    Finance and Banking   247
    Investment Management   291
    Taxation   293

**Section 3: Advertising and Public
Relations**   307
Program Directory
    Advertising and Public Relations   308

Section 4: Electronic Commerce   315
Program Directory
    Electronic Commerce   316

Section 5: Entrepreneurship   321
Program Directory
    Entrepreneurship   322

**Section 6: Facilities and Entertainment
Management**   339
Program Directories
    Entertainment Management   340
    Facilities Management   341

Section 7: Hospitality Management   343
Program Directories
    Hospitality Management   344
    Travel and Tourism   349

Section 8: Human Resources   355
Program Directories
    Human Resources Development   356
    Human Resources Management   362

**Section 9: Industrial and Manufacturing
Management**   391
Program Directory
    Industrial and Manufacturing
        Management   392

**Section 10: Insurance and Actuarial
Science**   401
Program Directories
    Actuarial Science   402
    Insurance   403

Section 11: International Business   407
Program Directory
    International Business   408

**Section 12: Management Information
Systems**   437
Program Directory
    Management Information Systems   438

**Section 13: Management Strategy
and Policy**   479
Program Directories
    Management Strategy and Policy   480
    Sustainability Management   491

Section 14: Marketing   499
Program Directories
    Marketing   500
    Marketing Research   533
Close-Ups   535

Section 15: Nonprofit Management 537
Program Directory
 Nonprofit Management 538

Section 16: Organizational Studies 555
Program Directories
 Organizational Behavior 556
 Organizational Management 560

Section 17: Project Management 583
Program Directory
 Project Management 584

Section 18: Quality Management 595
Program Directory
 Quality Management 596

Section 19: Quantitative Analysis 599
Program Directory
 Quantitative Analysis 600

Section 20: Real Estate 607
Program Directory
 Real Estate 608

**Section 21: Transportation Management,
Logistics, and Supply Chain Management** 615
Program Directories
 Aviation Management 616
 Logistics 617
 Supply Chain Management 622
 Transportation Management 632
Close-Ups 635

**ACADEMIC AND PROFESSIONAL
PROGRAMS IN EDUCATION**

Section 22: Education 639
Program Directory
 Education—General 640
Close-Ups 727

**Section 23: Administration, Instruction,
and Theory** 737
Program Directories
 Curriculum and Instruction 738
 Distance Education Development 777
 Educational Leadership and
  Administration 781
 Educational Measurement and
  Evaluation 861

Educational Media/Instructional
 Technology 871
Educational Policy 906
Educational Psychology 912
Foundations and Philosophy of
 Education 925
International and Comparative
 Education 933
Student Affairs 937

Section 24: Instructional Levels 949
Program Directories
 Adult Education 950
 Community College Education 960
 Early Childhood Education 963
 Elementary Education 997
 Higher Education 1042
 Middle School Education 1066
 Secondary Education 1082

Section 25: Special Focus 1127
Program Directories
 Education of Students with Severe/
  Multiple Disabilities 1128
 Education of the Gifted 1129
 English as a Second Language 1136
 Multilingual and Multicultural
  Education 1165
 Special Education 1179
 Urban Education 1241

Section 26: Subject Areas 1247
Program Directories
 Agricultural Education 1248
 Art Education 1252
 Business Education 1266
 Computer Education 1270
 Counselor Education 1273
 Developmental Education 1319
 English Education 1320
 Environmental Education 1340
 Foreign Languages Education 1343
 Health Education 1358
 Home Economics Education 1378
 Mathematics Education 1380
 Museum Education 1410
 Music Education 1411
 Reading Education 1433
 Religious Education 1477

Science Education   1483
Social Sciences Education   1512
Vocational and Technical Education   1530

ACADEMIC AND PROFESSIONAL PROGRAMS IN LAW

Section 27: Law   1541
Program Directories
    Environmental Law   1542
    Health Law   1543
    Intellectual Property Law   1545
    Law   1547
    Legal and Justice Studies   1567

ACADEMIC AND PROFESSIONAL PROGRAMS IN LIBRARY AND INFORMATION STUDIES

Section 28: Library and Information Studies   1577
Program Directories
    Archives/Archival Administration   1578
    Information Studies   1580
    Library Science   1586
Close-Ups   1597

ACADEMIC AND PROFESSIONAL PROGRAMS IN PHYSICAL EDUCATION, SPORTS, AND RECREATION

Section 29: Leisure Studies and Recreation   1605
Program Directories
    Leisure Studies   1606
    Recreation and Park Management   1608

Section 30: Physical Education and Kinesiology   1617
Program Directories
    Athletic Training and Sports Medicine   1618
    Exercise and Sports Science   1623
    Kinesiology and Movement Studies   1641
    Physical Education   1653

Section 31: Sports Management   1671
Program Directory
    Sports Management   1672

ACADEMIC AND PROFESSIONAL PROGRAMS IN SOCIAL WORK

Section 32: Social Work   1693
Program Directories
    Human Services   1694
    Social Work   1699
Close-Ups   1723

APPENDIXES

Institutional Changes Since the 2014 Edition   1731
Abbreviations Used in the Guides   1733

INDEXES

Displays and Close-Ups   1751
Directories and Subject Areas in This Book   1753
Directories and Subject Areas   1755

Science Education 1483
Social Sciences Education 1512
Vocational and Technical Education 1550

ACADEMIC AND PROFESSIONAL PROGRAMS IN LAW

Section 27. Law 1571
Program Directories
Environmental Law 1542
Health Law 1543
Intellectual Property Law 1545
Law 1547
Legal and Justice Studies 1567

ACADEMIC AND PROFESSIONAL PROGRAMS IN LIBRARY AND INFORMATION STUDIES

Section 28. Library and Information Studies 1577
Program Directories
Archives/Archival Administration 1578
Information Studies 1580
Library Science 1586
Close-Ups 1593

ACADEMIC AND PROFESSIONAL PROGRAMS IN HEALTH, PHYSICAL EDUCATION, SPORTS, AND RECREATION

Section 29. Leisure Studies and Recreation 1605
Program Directory
Leisure Studies 1606
Recreation and Park Management 1606

Section 30. Physical Education and Kinesiology 1619
Program Directories
Athletic Training and Sports Medicine 1628
Exercise and Sports Science 1635
Kinesiology and Movement Studies 1642
Physical Education 1653

Section 31. Sports Management 1674
Program Directory
Sports Management 1675

ACADEMIC AND PROFESSIONAL PROGRAMS IN SOCIAL WORK

Section 32. Social Work 1693
Program Directories
Human Services 1694
Social Work 1699
Close-Ups 1722

APPENDIXES

Institutional Changes Since the 2014 Edition 1731
Abbreviations Used in the Guides 1735

INDEXES

Displays and Close-Ups 1741
Directories and Subject Areas in This Book 1751
Directories and Subject Areas 1755

A Note from the Peterson's Editors

The six volumes of Peterson's *Graduate and Professional Programs*, the only annually updated reference work of its kind, provide wideranging information on the graduate and professional programs offered by accredited colleges and universities in the United States, U.S. territories, and Canada and by those institutions outside the United States that are accredited by U.S. accrediting bodies. Nearly 36,000 individual academic and professional programs at more than 2,200 institutions are listed. Peterson's *Graduate and Professional Programs* have been used for more than forty years by prospective graduate and professional students, placement counselors, faculty advisers, and all others interested in postbaccalaureate education.

Graduate & Professional Programs: An Overview contains information on institutions as a whole, while the other books in the series are devoted to specific academic and professional fields:

Graduate Programs in the Humanities, Arts & Social Sciences
Graduate Programs in the Biological/Biomedical Sciences & Health-Related Medical Professions
Graduate Programs in the Physical Sciences, Mathematics, Agricultural Sciences, the Environment & Natural Resources
Graduate Programs in Engineering & Applied Sciences
Graduate Programs in Business, Education, Information Studies, Law & Social Work

The books may be used individually or as a set. For example, if you have chosen a field of study but do not know what institution you want to attend or if you have a college or university in mind but have not chosen an academic field of study, it is best to begin with the Overview guide.

Graduate & Professional Programs: An Overview presents several directories to help you identify programs of study that might interest you; you can then research those programs further in the other books in the series by using the Directory of Graduate and Professional Programs by Field, which lists 500 fields and gives the names of those institutions that offer graduate degree programs in each.

For geographical or financial reasons, you may be interested in attending a particular institution and will want to know what it has to offer. You should turn to the Directory of Institutions and Their Offerings, which lists the degree programs available at each institution. As in the Directory of Graduate and Professional Programs by Field, the level of degrees offered is also indicated.

All books in the series include advice on graduate education, including topics such as admissions tests, financial aid, and accreditation. **The Graduate Adviser** includes two essays and information about accreditation. The first essay, "The Admissions Process," discusses general admission requirements, admission tests, factors to consider when selecting a graduate school or program, when and how to apply, and how admission decisions are made. Special information for international students and tips for minority students are also included. The second essay, "Financial Support," is an overview of the broad range of support available at the graduate level. Fellowships, scholarships, and grants; assistantships and internships; federal and private loan programs, as well as Federal Work-Study; and the GI bill are detailed. This essay concludes with advice on applying for need-based financial aid. "Accreditation and Accrediting Agencies" gives information on accreditation and its purpose and lists institutional accrediting agencies first and then specialized accrediting agencies relevant to each volume's specific fields of study.

With information on more than 44,000 graduate programs in more than 500 disciplines, Peterson's *Graduate and Professional Programs* give you all the information you need about the programs that are of interest to you in three formats: **Profiles** (capsule summaries of basic information), **Displays** (information that an institution or program wants to emphasize), and **Close-Ups** (written by administrators, with more expansive information than the **Profiles**, emphasizing different aspects of the programs). By using these various formats of program information, coupled with **Appendixes** and **Indexes** covering directories and subject areas for all six books, you will find that these guides provide the most comprehensive, accurate, and up-to-date graduate study information available.

Peterson's publishes a full line of resources with information you need to guide you through the graduate admissions process. Peterson's publications can be found at college libraries and career centers and your local bookstore or library—or visit us on the Web at www.petersonsbooks.com. Peterson's books are also available as ebooks.

Colleges and universities will be pleased to know that Peterson's helped you in your selection. Admissions staff members are more than happy to answer questions, address specific problems, and help in any way they can. The editors at Peterson's wish you great success in your graduate program search!

THE GRADUATE ADVISER

THE GRADUATE ADVISER

The Admissions Process

Generalizations about graduate admissions practices are not always helpful because each institution has its own set of guidelines and procedures. Nevertheless, some broad statements can be made about the admissions process that may help you plan your strategy.

Factors Involved in Selecting a Graduate School or Program

Selecting a graduate school and a specific program of study is a complex matter. Quality of the faculty; program and course offerings; the nature, size, and location of the institution; admission requirements; cost; and the availability of financial assistance are among the many factors that affect one's choice of institution. Other considerations are job placement and achievements of the program's graduates and the institution's resources, such as libraries, laboratories, and computer facilities. If you are to make the best possible choice, you need to learn as much as you can about the schools and programs you are considering before you apply.

The following steps may help you narrow your choices.

- Talk to alumni of the programs or institutions you are considering to get their impressions of how well they were prepared for work in their fields of study.
- Remember that graduate school requirements change, so be sure to get the most up-to-date information possible.
- Talk to department faculty members and the graduate adviser at your undergraduate institution. They often have information about programs of study at other institutions.
- Visit the websites of the graduate schools in which you are interested to request a graduate catalog. Contact the department chair in your chosen field of study for additional information about the department and the field.
- Visit as many campuses as possible. Call ahead for an appointment with the graduate adviser in your field of interest and be sure to check out the facilities and talk to students.

General Requirements

Graduate schools and departments have requirements that applicants for admission must meet. Typically, these requirements include undergraduate transcripts (which provide information about undergraduate grade point average and course work applied toward a major), admission test scores, and letters of recommendation. Most graduate programs also ask for an essay or personal statement that describes your personal reasons for seeking graduate study. In some fields, such as art and music, portfolios or auditions may be required in addition to other evidence of talent. Some institutions require that the applicant have an undergraduate degree in the same subject as the intended graduate major.

Most institutions evaluate each applicant on the basis of the applicant's total record, and the weight accorded any given factor varies widely from institution to institution and from program to program.

The Application Process

You should begin the application process at least one year before you expect to begin your graduate study. Find out the application deadline for each institution (many are provided in the **Profile** section of this guide). Go to the institution's website and find out if you can apply online. If not, request a paper application form. Fill out this form thoroughly and neatly. Assume that the school needs all the information it is requesting and that the admissions officer will be sensitive to the neatness and overall quality of what you submit. Do not supply more information than the school requires.

The institution may ask at least one question that will require a three- or four-paragraph answer. Compose your response on the assumption that the admissions officer is interested in both what you think and how you express yourself. Keep your statement brief and to the point, but, at the same time, include all pertinent information about your past experiences and your educational goals. Individual statements vary greatly in style and content, which helps admissions officers differentiate among applicants. Many graduate departments give considerable weight to the statement in making their admissions decisions, so be sure to take the time to prepare a thoughtful and concise statement.

If recommendations are a part of the admissions requirements, carefully choose the individuals you ask to write them. It is generally best to ask current or former professors to write the recommendations, provided they are able to attest to your intellectual ability and motivation for doing the work required of a graduate student. It is advisable to provide stamped, preaddressed envelopes to people being asked to submit recommendations on your behalf.

Completed applications, including references, transcripts, and admission test scores, should be received at the institution by the specified date.

Be advised that institutions do not usually make admissions decisions until all materials have been received. Enclose a self-addressed postcard with your application, requesting confirmation of receipt. Allow at least ten days for the return of the postcard before making further inquiries.

If you plan to apply for financial support, it is imperative that you file your application early.

ADMISSION TESTS

The major testing program used in graduate admissions is the Graduate Record Examinations (GRE®) testing program, sponsored by the GRE Board and administered by Educational Testing Service, Princeton, New Jersey.

The Graduate Record Examinations testing program consists of a General Test and eight Subject Tests. The General Test measures critical thinking, verbal reasoning, quantitative reasoning, and analytical writing skills. It is offered as an Internet-based test (iBT) in the United States, Canada, and many other countries.

The GRE® revised General Test's questions were designed to reflect the kind of thinking that students need to do in graduate or business school and demonstrate that students are indeed ready for graduate-level work.

- **Verbal Reasoning**—Measures ability to analyze and evaluate written material and synthesize information obtained from it, analyze relationships among component parts of sentences, and recognize relationships among words and concepts.
- **Quantitative Reasoning**—Measures problem-solving ability, focusing on basic concepts of arithmetic, algebra, geometry, and data analysis.
- **Analytical Writing**—Measures critical thinking and analytical writing skills, specifically the ability to articulate and support complex ideas clearly and effectively.

The computer-delivered GRE® revised General Test is offered year-round at Prometric™ test centers and on specific dates at testing locations outside of the Prometric test center network. Appointments are scheduled on a first-come, first-served basis. The GRE® revised General Test is also offered as a paper-based test three times a year in areas where computer-based testing is not available.

You can take the computer-delivered GRE® revised General Test once every twenty-one days, up to five times within any continuous rolling twelve-month period (365 days)—even if you canceled your

scores on a previously taken test. You may take the paper-delivered GRE® revised General Test as often as it is offered.

Three scores are reported on the revised General Test:

1. A **Verbal Reasoning score** is reported on a 130–170 score scale, in 1-point increments.

2. A **Quantitative Reasoning score** is reported on a 130–170 score scale, in 1-point increments.

3. An **Analytical Writing score** is reported on a 0–6 score level, in half-point increments.

The GRE® Subject Tests measure achievement and assume undergraduate majors or extensive background in the following eight disciplines:

- Biochemistry, Cell and Molecular Biology
- Biology
- Chemistry
- Computer Science
- Literature in English
- Mathematics
- Physics
- Psychology

The Subject Tests are available three times per year as paper-based administrations around the world. Testing time is approximately 2 hours and 50 minutes. You can obtain more information about the GRE® by visiting the ETS website at www.ets.org or consulting the *GRE® Information and Registration Bulletin*. The *Bulletin* can be obtained at many undergraduate colleges. You can also download it from the ETS website or obtain it by contacting Graduate Record Examinations, Educational Testing Service, P.O. Box 6000, Princeton, NJ 08541-6000; phone: 609-771-7670.

If you expect to apply for admission to a program that requires any of the GRE® tests, you should select a test date well in advance of the application deadline. Scores on the computer-based General Test are reported within ten to fifteen days; scores on the paper-based Subject Tests are reported within six weeks.

Another testing program, the Miller Analogies Test® (MAT®), is administered at more than 500 Controlled Testing Centers, licensed by Harcourt Assessment, Inc., in the United States, Canada, and other countries. The MAT® computer-based test is now available. Testing time is 60 minutes. The test consists of 120 partial analogies. You can obtain the *Candidate Information Booklet,* which contains a list of test centers and instructions for taking the test, from http://www.milleranalogies.com or by calling 800-328-5999 (toll-free).

Check the specific requirements of the programs to which you are applying.

How Admission Decisions Are Made

The program you apply to is directly involved in the admissions process. Although the final decision is usually made by the graduate dean (or an associate) or the faculty admissions committee, recommendations from faculty members in your intended field are important. At some institutions, an interview is incorporated into the decision process.

A Special Note for International Students

In addition to the steps already described, there are some special considerations for international students who intend to apply for graduate study in the United States. All graduate schools require an indication of competence in English. The purpose of the Test of English as a Foreign Language (TOEFL®) is to evaluate the English proficiency of people who are nonnative speakers of English and want to study at colleges and universities where English is the language of instruction. The TOEFL® is administered by Educational Testing Service (ETS) under the general direction of a policy board established by the College Board and the Graduate Record Examinations Board.

The TOEFL® iBT assesses the four basic language skills: listening, reading, writing, and speaking. It was administered for the first time in September 2005, and ETS continues to introduce the TOEFL® iBT in selected cities. The Internet-based test is administered at secure, official test centers. The testing time is approximately 4 hours. Because the TOEFL® iBT includes a speaking section, the Test of Spoken English (TSE) is no longer needed.

The TOEFL® is also offered in the paper-based format in areas of the world where Internet-based testing is not available. The paper-based TOEFL® consists of three sections—listening comprehension, structure and written expression, and reading comprehension. The testing time is approximately 3 hours. The Test of Written English (TWE®) is also given. The TWE® is a 30-minute essay that measures the examinee's ability to compose in English. Examinees receive a TWE® score separate from their TOEFL® score. The *Information Bulletin* contains information on local fees and registration procedures.

The TOEFL® paper-based test (TOEFL® PBT) began being phased out in mid-2012. For those who may have taken the TOEFL® PBT, scores remain valid for two years after the test date. The Test of Written English (TWE®) is also given. The TWE® is a 30-minute essay that measures the examinee's ability to compose in English. Examinees receive a TWE® score separate from their TOEFL® score. The Information Bulletin contains information on local fees and registration procedures.

Additional information and registration materials are available from TOEFL® Services, Educational Testing Service, P.O. Box 6151, Princeton, New Jersey 08541-6151. Phone: 609-771-7100. Website: www.toefl.org.

International students should apply especially early because of the number of steps required to complete the admissions process. Furthermore, many United States graduate schools have a limited number of spaces for international students, and many more students apply than the schools can accommodate.

International students may find financial assistance from institutions very limited. The U.S. government requires international applicants to submit a certification of support, which is a statement attesting to the applicant's financial resources. In addition, international students *must* have health insurance coverage.

Tips for Minority Students

Indicators of a university's values in terms of diversity are found both in its recruitment programs and its resources directed to student success. Important questions: Does the institution vigorously recruit minorities for its graduate programs? Is there funding available to help with the costs associated with visiting the school? Are minorities represented in the institution's brochures or website or on their faculty rolls? What campus-based resources or services (including assistance in locating housing or career counseling and placement) are available? Is funding available to members of underrepresented groups?

At the program level, it is particularly important for minority students to investigate the "climate" of a program under consideration. How many minority students are enrolled and how many have graduated? What opportunities are there to work with diverse faculty and mentors whose research interests match yours? How are conflicts resolved or concerns addressed? How interested are faculty in building strong and supportive relations with students? "Climate" concerns should be addressed by posing questions to various individuals, including faculty members, current students, and alumni.

Information is also available through various organizations, such as the Hispanic Association of Colleges & Universities (HACU), and publications such as *Diverse Issues in Higher Education* and *Hispanic Outlook* magazine. There are also books devoted to this topic, such as *The Multicultural Student's Guide to Colleges* by Robert Mitchell.

Financial Support

The range of financial support at the graduate level is very broad. The following descriptions will give you a general idea of what you might expect and what will be expected of you as a financial support recipient.

Fellowships, Scholarships, and Grants

These are usually outright awards of a few hundred to many thousands of dollars with no service to the institution required in return. Fellowships and scholarships are usually awarded on the basis of merit and are highly competitive. Grants are made on the basis of financial need or special talent in a field of study. Many fellowships, scholarships, and grants not only cover tuition, fees, and supplies but also include stipends for living expenses with allowances for dependents. However, the terms of each should be examined because some do not permit recipients to supplement their income with outside work. Fellowships, scholarships, and grants may vary in the number of years for which they are awarded.

In addition to the availability of these funds at the university or program level, many excellent fellowship programs are available at the national level and may be applied for before and during enrollment in a graduate program. A listing of many of these programs can be found at the Council of Graduate Schools' website: http://www. cgsnet.org. There is a wealth of information in the "Programs" and "Awards" sections.

Assistantships and Internships

Many graduate students receive financial support through assistantships, particularly involving teaching or research duties. It is important to recognize that such appointments should not be viewed simply as employment relationships but rather should constitute an integral and important part of a student's graduate education. As such, the appointments should be accompanied by strong faculty mentoring and increasingly responsible apprenticeship experiences. The specific nature of these appointments in a given program should be considered in selecting that graduate program.

TEACHING ASSISTANTSHIPS

These usually provide a salary and full or partial tuition remission and may also provide health benefits. Unlike fellowships, scholarships, and grants, which require no service to the institution, teaching assistantships require recipients to provide the institution with a specific amount of undergraduate teaching, ideally related to the student's field of study. Some teaching assistants are limited to grading papers, compiling bibliographies, taking notes, or monitoring laboratories. At some graduate schools, teaching assistants must carry lighter course loads than regular full-time students.

RESEARCH ASSISTANTSHIPS

These are very similar to teaching assistantships in the manner in which financial assistance is provided. The difference is that recipients are given basic research assignments in their disciplines rather than teaching responsibilities. The work required is normally related to the student's field of study; in most instances, the assistantship supports the student's thesis or dissertation research.

ADMINISTRATIVE INTERNSHIPS

These are similar to assistantships in application of financial assistance funds, but the student is given an assignment on a part-time basis, usually as a special assistant with one of the university's administrative offices. The assignment may not necessarily be directly related to the recipient's discipline.

RESIDENCE HALL AND COUNSELING ASSISTANTSHIPS

These assistantships are frequently assigned to graduate students in psychology, counseling, and social work, but they may be offered to students in other disciplines, especially if the student has worked in this capacity during his or her undergraduate years. Duties can vary from being available in a dean's office for a specific number of hours for consultation with undergraduates to living in campus residences and being responsible for both counseling and administrative tasks or advising student activity groups. Residence hall assistantships often include a room and board allowance and, in some cases, tuition assistance and stipends. Contact the Housing and Student Life Office for more information.

Health Insurance

The availability and affordability of health insurance is an important issue and one that should be considered in an applicant's choice of institution and program. While often included with assistantships and fellowships, this is not always the case and, even if provided, the benefits may be limited. It is important to note that the U.S. government requires international students to have health insurance.

The GI Bill

This provides financial assistance for students who are veterans of the United States armed forces. If you are a veteran, contact your local Veterans Administration office to determine your eligibility and to get full details about benefits. There are a number of programs that offer educational benefits to current military enlistees. Some states have tuition assistance programs for members of the National Guard. Contact the VA office at the college for more information.

Federal Work-Study Program (FWS)

Employment is another way some students finance their graduate studies. The federally funded Federal Work-Study Program provides eligible students with employment opportunities, usually in public and private nonprofit organizations. Federal funds pay up to 75 percent of the wages, with the remainder paid by the employing agency. FWS is available to graduate students who demonstrate financial need. Not all schools have these funds, and some only award them to undergraduates. Each school sets its application deadline and workstudy earnings limits. Wages vary and are related to the type of work done. You must file the Free Application for Federal Student Aid (FAFSA) to be eligible for this program.

Loans

Many graduate students borrow to finance their graduate programs when other sources of assistance (which do not have to be repaid) prove insufficient. You should always read and understand the terms of any loan program before submitting your application.

FEDERAL DIRECT LOANS

Federal Direct Stafford Loans. The Federal Direct Stafford Loan Program offers a variable-fixed interest rate loan to graduate students with the Department of Education acting as the lender. Students receive a new rate with each new loan, but that rate is fixed for the life of the loan. Beginning with loans made on or after July 1, 2013, the interest rate for loans made each July 1st to June 30th period are determined based on the last 10-year Treasury note auction prior to June 1st of that year,

plus an added percentage. The interest rate can be no higher than 9.5%.

Beginning July 1, 2012, the Federal Direct Stafford Loan for graduate students is an unsubsidized loan. Under the *unsubsidized* program, the grad borrower pays the interest on the loan from the day proceeds are issued and is responsible for paying interest during all periods. If the borrower chooses not to pay the interest while in school, or during the grace periods, deferment, or forbearance, the interest accrues and will be capitalized.

Graduate students may borrow up to $20,500 per year through the Direct Stafford Loan Program, up to a cumulative maximum of $138,500, including undergraduate borrowing. No more than $65,000 of the $138,500 can be from subsidized loans that the grad borrower may have received for periods of enrollment that began before July 1, 2012, or for prior undergraduate borrowing. You may borrow up to the cost of attendance at the school in which you are enrolled or will attend, minus estimated financial assistance from other federal, state, and private sources, up to a maximum of $20,500. Grad borrowers who reach the aggregate loan limit over the course of their education cannot receive additional loans; however, if they repay some of their loans to bring the outstanding balance below the aggregate limit, they could be eligible to borrow again, up to that limit.

For Unsubsidized loans first disbursed on or after July 1, 2013, and before July 1, 2014, the interest rate is 5.41%. For those first disbursed on or after July 1, 2014, and before July 1, 2015, the interest rate is 6.21%.

A fee is deducted from the loan proceeds upon disbursement. Loans with a first disbursement on or after July 1, 2010 but before July 1, 2012, have a borrower origination fee of 1 percent. For loans disbursed after July 1, 2012, these fee deductions no longer apply. The Budget Control Act of 2011, signed into law on August 2, 2011, eliminated Direct Subsidized Loan eligibility for graduate and professional students for periods of enrollment beginning on or after July 1, 2012 and terminated the authority of the Department of Education to offer most repayment incentives to Direct Loan borrowers for loans disbursed on or after July 1, 2012.

Under the *subsidized* Federal Direct Stafford Loan Program, repayment begins six months after your last date of enrollment on at least a half-time basis. Under the *unsubsidized* program, repayment of interest begins within thirty days from disbursement of the loan proceeds, and repayment of the principal begins six months after your last enrollment on at least a half-time basis. Some borrowers may choose to defer interest payments while they are in school. The accrued interest is added to the loan balance when the borrower begins repayment. There are several repayment options.

Federal Perkins Loans. The Federal Perkins Loan is available to students demonstrating financial need and is administered directly by the school. Not all schools have these funds, and some may award them to undergraduates only. Eligibility is determined from the information you provide on the FAFSA. The school will notify you of your eligibility.

Eligible graduate students may borrow up to $8,000 per year, up to a maximum of $60,000, including undergraduate borrowing (even if your previous Perkins Loans have been repaid). The interest rate for Federal Perkins Loans is 5 percent, and no interest accrues while you remain in school at least half-time. Students who are attending less than half-time need to check with their school to determine the length of their grace period. There are no guarantee, loan, or disbursement fees. Repayment begins nine months after your last date of enrollment on at least a half-time basis and may extend over a maximum of ten years with no prepayment penalty.

Federal Direct Graduate PLUS Loans. Effective July 1, 2006, graduate and professional students are eligible for Graduate PLUS loans. This program allows students to borrow up to the cost of attendance, less any other aid received. These loans have a fixed interest rate, and interest begins to accrue at the time of disbursement. Beginning with loans made on or after July 1, 2013, the interest rate for loans made each July 1st to June 30th period are determined based on the last 10-year Treasury note auction prior to June 1st of that year. The interest rate can be no higher than 10.5%. The PLUS loans do involve a credit check; a PLUS borrower may obtain a loan with a cosigner if his or her credit is not good enough. Grad PLUS loans may be deferred while a student is in school and for the six months following a drop below half-time

enrollment. For more information, you should contact a representative in your college's financial aid office.

Deferring Your Federal Loan Repayments. If you borrowed under the Federal Direct Stafford Loan Program, Federal Direct PLUS Loan Program, or the Federal Perkins Loan Program for previous undergraduate or graduate study, your payments may be deferred when you return to graduate school, depending on when you borrowed and under which program.

There are other deferment options available if you are temporarily unable to repay your loan. Information about these deferments is provided at your entrance and exit interviews. If you believe you are eligible for a deferment of your loan payments, you must contact your lender or loan servicer to request a deferment. The deferment must be filed prior to the time your payment is due, and it must be re-filed when it expires if you remain eligible for deferment at that time.

SUPPLEMENTAL (PRIVATE) LOANS

Many lending institutions offer supplemental loan programs and other financing plans, such as the ones described here, to students seeking additional assistance in meeting their education expenses. Some loan programs target all types of graduate students; others are designed specifically for business, law, or medical students. In addition, you can use private loans not specifically designed for education to help finance your graduate degree.

If you are considering borrowing through a supplemental or private loan program, you should carefully consider the terms and be sure to read the fine print. Check with the program sponsor for the most current terms that will be applicable to the amounts you intend to borrow for graduate study. Most supplemental loan programs for graduate study offer unsubsidized, credit-based loans. In general, a credit-ready borrower is one who has a satisfactory credit history or no credit history at all. A creditworthy borrower generally must pass a credit test to be eligible to borrow or act as a cosigner for the loan funds.

Many supplemental loan programs have minimum and maximum annual loan limits. Some offer amounts equal to the cost of attendance minus any other aid you will receive for graduate study. If you are planning to borrow for several years of graduate study, consider whether there is a cumulative or aggregate limit on the amount you may borrow. Often this cumulative or aggregate limit will include any amounts you borrowed and have not repaid for undergraduate or previous graduate study.

The combination of the annual interest rate, loan fees, and the repayment terms you choose will determine how much you will repay over time. Compare these features in combination before you decide which loan program to use. Some loans offer interest rates that are adjusted monthly, quarterly, or annually. Some offer interest rates that are lower during the in-school, grace, and deferment periods and then increase when you begin repayment. Some programs include a loan origination fee, which is usually deducted from the principal amount you receive when the loan is disbursed and must be repaid along with the interest and other principal when you graduate, withdraw from school, or drop below half-time study. Sometimes the loan fees are reduced if you borrow with a qualified cosigner. Some programs allow you to defer interest and/or principal payments while you are enrolled in graduate school. Many programs allow you to capitalize your interest payments; the interest due on your loan is added to the outstanding balance of your loan, so you don't have to repay immediately, but this increases the amount you owe. Other programs allow you to pay the interest as you go, which reduces the amount you later have to repay. The private loan market is very competitive, and your financial aid office can help you evaluate these programs.

Applying for Need-Based Financial Aid

Schools that award federal and institutional financial assistance based on need will require you to complete the FAFSA and, in some cases, an institutional financial aid application.

If you are applying for federal student assistance, you **must** complete the FAFSA. A service of the U.S. Department of Education, the FAFSA is free to all applicants. Most applicants apply online at www.fafsa.ed.gov. Paper applications are available at the financial aid office of your local college.

After your FAFSA information has been processed, you will receive a Student Aid Report (SAR). If you provided an e-mail address on the FAFSA, this will be sent to you electronically; otherwise, it will be mailed to your home address.

Follow the instructions on the SAR if you need to correct information reported on your original application. If your situation changes after you file your FAFSA, contact your financial aid officer to discuss amending your information. You can also appeal your financial aid award if you have extenuating circumstances.

If you would like more information on federal student financial aid, visit the FAFSA website or download the most recent version of *Funding Education Beyond High School: The Guide to Federal Student Aid* at http://studentaid.ed.gov/students/publications/student_guide/index.html. This guide is also available in Spanish.

The U.S. Department of Education also has a toll-free number for questions concerning federal student aid programs. The number is 1-800-4-FED AID (1-800-433-3243). If you are hearing impaired, call toll-free, 1-800-730-8913.

Summary

Remember that these are generalized statements about financial assistance at the graduate level. Because each institution allots its aid differently, you should communicate directly with the school and the specific department of interest to you. It is not unusual, for example, to find that an endowment vested within a specific department supports one or more fellowships. You may fit its requirements and specifications precisely.

Accreditation and Accrediting Agencies

Colleges and universities in the United States, and their individual academic and professional programs, are accredited by nongovernmental agencies concerned with monitoring the quality of education in this country. Agencies with both regional and national jurisdictions grant accreditation to institutions as a whole, while specialized bodies acting on a nationwide basis—often national professional associations—grant accreditation to departments and programs in specific fields.

Institutional and specialized accrediting agencies share the same basic concerns: the purpose an academic unit—whether university or program—has set for itself and how well it fulfills that purpose, the adequacy of its financial and other resources, the quality of its academic offerings, and the level of services it provides. Agencies that grant institutional accreditation take a broader view, of course, and examine university-wide or college-wide services with which a specialized agency may not concern itself.

Both types of agencies follow the same general procedures when considering an application for accreditation. The academic unit prepares a self-evaluation, focusing on the concerns mentioned above and usually including an assessment of both its strengths and weaknesses; a team of representatives of the accrediting body reviews this evaluation, visits the campus, and makes its own report; and finally, the accrediting body makes a decision on the application. Often, even when accreditation is granted, the agency makes a recommendation regarding how the institution or program can improve. All institutions and programs are also reviewed every few years to determine whether they continue to meet established standards; if they do not, they may lose their accreditation.

Accrediting agencies themselves are reviewed and evaluated periodically by the U.S. Department of Education and the Council for Higher Education Accreditation (CHEA). Recognized agencies adhere to certain standards and practices, and their authority in matters of accreditation is widely accepted in the educational community.

This does not mean, however, that accreditation is a simple matter, either for schools wishing to become accredited or for students deciding where to apply. Indeed, in certain fields the very meaning and methods of accreditation are the subject of a good deal of debate. For their part, those applying to graduate school should be aware of the safeguards provided by regional accreditation, especially in terms of degree acceptance and institutional longevity. Beyond this, applicants should understand the role that specialized accreditation plays in their field, as this varies considerably from one discipline to another. In certain professional fields, it is necessary to have graduated from a program that is accredited in order to be eligible for a license to practice, and in some fields the federal government also makes this a hiring requirement. In other disciplines, however, accreditation is not as essential, and there can be excellent programs that are not accredited. In fact, some programs choose not to seek accreditation, although most do.

Institutions and programs that present themselves for accreditation are sometimes granted the status of candidate for accreditation, or what is known as "preaccreditation." This may happen, for example, when an academic unit is too new to have met all the requirements for accreditation. Such status signifies initial recognition and indicates that the school or program in question is working to fulfill all requirements; it does not, however, guarantee that accreditation will be granted.

Institutional Accrediting Agencies—Regional

MIDDLE STATES ASSOCIATION OF COLLEGES AND SCHOOLS

Accredits institutions in Delaware, District of Columbia, Maryland, New Jersey, New York, Pennsylvania, Puerto Rico, and the Virgin Islands.

Dr. Elizabeth Sibolski, President
Middle States Commission on Higher Education
3624 Market Street, Second Floor West
Philadelphia, Pennsylvania 19104
Phone: 267-284-5000
Fax: 215-662-5501
E-mail: info@msche.org
Website: www.msche.org

NEW ENGLAND ASSOCIATION OF SCHOOLS AND COLLEGES

Accredits institutions in Connecticut, Maine, Massachusetts, New Hampshire, Rhode Island, and Vermont.

Dr. Barbara E. Brittingham, President/Director
Commission on Institutions of Higher Education
3 Burlington Woods Drive, Suite 100
Burlington, Massachusetts 01803-4531
Phone: 855-886-3272 or 781-425-7714
Fax: 781-425-1001
E-mail: cihe@neasc.org
Website: http://cihe.neasc.org

THE HIGHER LEARNING COMMISSION

Accredits institutions in Arizona, Arkansas, Colorado, Illinois, Indiana, Iowa, Kansas, Michigan, Minnesota, Missouri, Nebraska, New Mexico, North Dakota, Ohio, Oklahoma, South Dakota, West Virginia, Wisconsin, and Wyoming.

Dr. Barbara Gellman-Danley, President
The Higher Learning Commission
230 South LaSalle Street, Suite 7-500
Chicago, Illinois 60604-1413
Phone: 800-621-7440 or 312-263-0456
Fax: 312-263-7462
E-mail: info@hlcommission.org
Website: www.ncahlc.org

NORTHWEST COMMISSION ON COLLEGES AND UNIVERSITIES

Accredits institutions in Alaska, Idaho, Montana, Nevada, Oregon, Utah, and Washington.

Dr. Sandra E. Elman, President
8060 165th Avenue, NE, Suite 100
Redmond, Washington 98052
Phone: 425-558-4224
Fax: 425-376-0596
E-mail: selman@nwccu.org
Website: www.nwccu.org

SOUTHERN ASSOCIATION OF COLLEGES AND SCHOOLS

Accredits institutions in Alabama, Florida, Georgia, Kentucky, Louisiana, Mississippi, North Carolina, South Carolina, Tennessee, Texas, and Virginia.

Dr. Belle S. Wheelan, President
Commission on Colleges
1866 Southern Lane
Decatur, Georgia 30033-4097
Phone: 404-679-4500 Ext. 4504
Fax: 404-679-4558
E-mail: questions@sacscoc.org
Website: www.sacscoc.org

WESTERN ASSOCIATION OF SCHOOLS AND COLLEGES

Accredits institutions in California, Guam, and Hawaii.

Dr. Mary Ellen Petrisko, President
Accrediting Commission for Senior Colleges and Universities
985 Atlantic Avenue, Suite 100
Alameda, California 94501
Phone: 510-748-9001
Fax: 510-748-9797
E-mail: wasc@wascsenior.org
Website: http://www.wascsenior.org/

Institutional Accrediting Agencies—Other

ACCREDITING COUNCIL FOR INDEPENDENT COLLEGES AND SCHOOLS
Albert C. Gray, Ph.D., Executive Director and CEO
750 First Street, NE, Suite 980
Washington, DC 20002-4241
Phone: 202-336-6780
Fax: 202-842-2593
E-mail: info@acics.org
Website: www.acics.org

DISTANCE EDUCATION AND TRAINING COUNCIL (DETC)
Accrediting Commission
Leah Matthews, Executive Director
1601 18th Street, NW, Suite 2
Washington, DC 20009
Phone: 202-234-5100
Fax: 202-332-1386
E-mail: info@detc.org
Website: www.detc.org

Specialized Accrediting Agencies

ACUPUNCTURE AND ORIENTAL MEDICINE
Mark S. McKenzie, LAc MsOM DiplOM, Executive Director
Accreditation Commission for Acupuncture and Oriental Medicine
8941 Aztec Drive
Eden Prairie, Minnesota 55347
Phone: 952-212-2434
Fax: 301-313-0912
E-mail: coordinator@acaom.org
Website: www.acaom.org

ART AND DESIGN
Karen P. Moynahan, Executive Director
National Association of Schools of Art and Design (NASAD)
Commission on Accreditation
11250 Roger Bacon Drive, Suite 21
Reston, Virginia 20190-5248
Phone: 703-437-0700
Fax: 703-437-6312
E-mail: info@arts-accredit.org
Website: http://nasad.arts-accredit.org/

BUSINESS
Robert D. Reid, Executive Vice President and Chief Accreditation Officer
AACSB International—The Association to Advance Collegiate Schools of Business
777 South Harbour Island Boulevard, Suite 750
Tampa, Florida 33602
Phone: 813-769-6500
Fax: 813-769-6559
E-mail: bob@aacsb.edu
Website: www.aacsb.edu

CHIROPRACTIC
S. Ray Bennett, Director of Accreditation Services
Council on Chiropractic Education (CCE)
Commission on Accreditation
8049 North 85th Way
Scottsdale, Arizona 85258-4321
Phone: 480-443-8877 or 888-443-3506
Fax: 480-483-7333
E-mail: cce@cce-usa.org
Website: www.cce-usa.org

CLINICAL LABORATORY SCIENCES
Dianne M. Cearlock, Ph.D., Chief Executive Officer
National Accrediting Agency for Clinical Laboratory Sciences
5600 North River Road, Suite 720
Rosemont, Illinois 60018-5119
Phone: 773-714-8880 or 847-939-3597
Fax: 773-714-8886
E-mail: info@naacls.org
Website: www.naacls.org

CLINICAL PASTORAL EDUCATION
Trace Haythorn, Executive Director
Association for Clinical Pastoral Education, Inc.
1549 Clairmont Road, Suite 103
Decatur, Georgia 30033-4611
Phone: 404-320-1472
Fax: 404-320-0849
E-mail: acpe@acpe.edu
Website: www.acpe.edu

DANCE
Karen P. Moynahan, Executive Director
National Association of Schools of Dance (NASD)
Commission on Accreditation
11250 Roger Bacon Drive, Suite 21
Reston, Virginia 20190-5248
Phone: 703-437-0700
Fax: 703-437-6312
E-mail: info@arts-accredit.org
Website: http://nasd.arts-accredit.org

DENTISTRY
Dr. Sherin Tooks, Director
Commission on Dental Accreditation
American Dental Association
211 East Chicago Avenue, Suite 1900
Chicago, Illinois 60611
Phone: 312-440-4643 or 800-621-8099
E-mail: accreditation@ada.org
Website: www.ada.org

DIETETICS AND NUTRITION
Mary B. Gregoire, Ph.D., Executive Director; RD, FADA, FAND
Academy of Nutrition and Dietetics
Accreditation Council for Education in Nutrition and Dietetics (ACEND)
120 South Riverside Plaza, Suite 2000
Chicago, Illinois 60606-6995
Phone: 800-877-1600 Ext. 5400 or 312-899-0040
Fax: 312-899-4817
E-mail: acend@eatright.org
Website: www.eatright.org/ACEND

ENGINEERING
Michael Milligan, Ph.D., PE, Executive Director
Accreditation Board for Engineering and Technology, Inc. (ABET)
415 North Charles Street
Baltimore, Maryland 21201
Phone: 410-347-7700
E-mail: accreditation@abet.org
Website: www.abet.org

FORESTRY
Carol L. Redelsheimer
Director of Science and Education
Society of American Foresters
5400 Grosvenor Lane
Bethesda, Maryland 20814-2198
Phone: 301-897-8720 or 866-897-8720
Fax: 301-897-3690
E-mail: redelsheimerc@safnet.org
Website: www.safnet.org

HEALTH SERVICES ADMINISTRATION
Commission on Accreditation of Healthcare Management Education (CAHME)
Margaret Schulte, President and CEO
1700 Rockville Pike
Suite 400
Rockville, Maryland 20852
Phone: 301-998-6101
E-mail: info@cahme.org
Website: www.cahme.org

INTERIOR DESIGN
Holly Mattson, Executive Director
Council for Interior Design Accreditation
206 Grandview Avenue, Suite 350
Grand Rapids, Michigan 49503-4014
Phone: 616-458-0400
Fax: 616-458-0460
E-mail: info@accredit-id.org
Website: www.accredit-id.org

JOURNALISM AND MASS COMMUNICATIONS
Susanne Shaw, Executive Director
Accrediting Council on Education in Journalism and Mass Communications (ACEJMC)
School of Journalism
Stauffer-Flint Hall
University of Kansas
1435 Jayhawk Boulevard
Lawrence, Kansas 66045-7575
Phone: 785-864-3973
Fax: 785-864-5225
E-mail: sshaw@ku.edu
Website: http://www2.ku.edu/~acejmc/

LANDSCAPE ARCHITECTURE
Ronald C. Leighton, Executive Director
Landscape Architectural Accreditation Board (LAAB)
American Society of Landscape Architects (ASLA)
636 Eye Street, NW
Washington, DC 20001-3736
Phone: 202-898-2444 or 888-999-2752
Fax: 202-898-1185
E-mail: info@asla.org
Website: www.asla.org

LAW
Barry Currier, Managing Director of Accreditation & Legal Education
American Bar Association
321 North Clark Street, 21st Floor
Chicago, Illinois 60654
Phone: 312-988-6738
Fax: 312-988-5681
E-mail: legaled@americanbar.org
Website: http://www.americanbar.org/groups/legal_education/resources/accreditation.html

LIBRARY
Karen O'Brien, Director
Office for Accreditation
American Library Association
50 East Huron Street
Chicago, Illinois 60611-2795
Phone: 312-280-2432
Fax: 312-280-2433
E-mail: accred@ala.org
Website: www.ala.org/accreditation/

MARRIAGE AND FAMILY THERAPY
Tanya A. Tamarkin, Director of Educational Affairs
Commission on Accreditation for Marriage and Family Therapy Education
American Association for Marriage and Family Therapy
112 South Alfred Street
Alexandria, Virginia 22314-3061
Phone: 703-838-9808
Fax: 703-838-9805
E-mail: coamfte@aamft.org
Website: www.aamft.org

MEDICAL ILLUSTRATION
Commission on Accreditation of Allied Health Education Programs (CAAHEP)
Kathleen Megivern, Executive Director
1361 Park Street
Clearwater, Florida 33756
Phone: 727-210-2350
Fax: 727-210-2354
E-mail: mail@caahep.org
Website: www.caahep.org

MEDICINE
Liaison Committee on Medical Education (LCME)
Robert B. Hash, M.D., LCME Secretary
American Medical Association
Council on Medical Education
330 North Wabash Avenue, Suite 39300
Chicago, Illinois 60611-5885
Phone: 312-464-4933
E-mail: lcme@aamc.org
Website: www.ama-assn.org

Liaison Committee on Medical Education (LCME)
Heather Lent, M.A., Director
Accreditation Services
Association of American Medical Colleges
655 K Street, NW
Washington, DC 20001-2399
Phone: 202-828-0596
E-mail: lcme@aamc.org
Website: www.lcme.org

MUSIC
Karen P. Moynahan, Executive Director
National Association of Schools of Music (NASM)
Commission on Accreditation
11250 Roger Bacon Drive, Suite 21
Reston, Virginia 20190-5248
Phone: 703-437-0700
Fax: 703-437-6312
E-mail: info@arts-accredit.org
Website: http://nasm.arts-accredit.org/

NATUROPATHIC MEDICINE
Daniel Seitz, J.D., Ed.D., Executive Director
Council on Naturopathic Medical Education
P.O. Box 178
Great Barrington, Massachusetts 01230
Phone: 413-528-8877
E-mail: www.cnme.org/contact.html
Website: www.cnme.org

NURSE ANESTHESIA
Frank Gerbasi, Ph.D., CRNA, COA Executive Director
Council on Accreditation of Nurse Anesthesia Educational Programs
(COA)
American Association of Nurse Anesthetists
222 South Prospect Avenue, Suite 304
Park Ridge, Illinois 60068-4001
Phone: 847-655-1160
Fax: 847-692-7137
E-mail: accreditation@coa.us.com
Website: http://home.coa.us.com

NURSE EDUCATION
Jennifer L. Butlin, Executive Director
Commission on Collegiate Nursing Education (CCNE)
One Dupont Circle, NW, Suite 530
Washington, DC 20036-1120
Phone: 202-887-6791
Fax: 202-887-8476
E-mail: jbutlin@aacn.nche.edu
Website: www.aacn.nche.edu/accreditation

NURSE MIDWIFERY
Heather L. Maurer, M.A., Executive Director
Accreditation Commission for Midwifery Education (ACME)
American College of Nurse-Midwives
8403 Colesville Road, Suite 1550
Silver Spring, Maryland 20910
Phone: 240-485-1800
Fax: 240-485-1818
E-mail: info@acnm.org
Website: www.midwife.org/Program-Accreditation

NURSE PRACTITIONER
Gay Johnson, CEO
National Association of Nurse Practitioners in Women's Health
Council on Accreditation
505 C Street, NE
Washington, DC 20002
Phone: 202-543-9693 Ext. 1
Fax: 202-543-9858
E-mail: info@npwh.org
Website: www.npwh.org

NURSING
Nell Ard, Ph.D., RN, CNE, Associate Director
Accreditation Commission for Education in Nursing (ACEN)
3343 Peachtree Road, NE, Suite 850
Atlanta, Georgia 30326
Phone: 404-975-5000
Fax: 404-975-5020
E-mail: info@acenursing.org
Website: www.acenursing.org

OCCUPATIONAL THERAPY
Heather Stagliano, DHSc, OTR/L, Director of Accreditation
The American Occupational Therapy Association, Inc.
4720 Montgomery Lane, Suite 200
Bethesda, Maryland 20814-3449
Phone: 301-652-6611 Ext. 2914
TDD: 800-377-8555
Fax: 301-652-7711
E-mail: accred@aota.org
Website: www.aota.org

OPTOMETRY
Joyce L. Urbeck, Administrative Director
Accreditation Council on Optometric Education (ACOE)
American Optometric Association
243 North Lindbergh Boulevard
St. Louis, Missouri 63141-7881
Phone: 800-365-7881
Fax: 314-991-4101
E-mail: accredit@aoa.org
Website: www.theacoe.org

OSTEOPATHIC MEDICINE
Konrad C. Miskowicz-Retz, Ph.D., CAE
Director, Department of Accreditation
Commission on Osteopathic College Accreditation (COCA)
American Osteopathic Association
142 East Ontario Street
Chicago, Illinois 60611
Phone: 312-202-8097
Fax: 312-202-8397
E-mail: predoc@osteopathic.org
Website: www.osteopathic.org

PHARMACY
Peter H. Vlasses, PharmD, Executive Director
Accreditation Council for Pharmacy Education
135 South LaSalle Street, Suite 4100
Chicago, Illinois 60603-4810
Phone: 312-664-3575
Fax: 312-664-4652
E-mail: csinfo@acpe-accredit.org
Website: www.acpe-accredit.org

PHYSICAL THERAPY
Mary Jane Harris, M.S., PT, Director
Commission on Accreditation in Physical Therapy Education (CAPTE)
American Physical Therapy Association (APTA)
1111 North Fairfax Street
Alexandria, Virginia 22314-1488
Phone: 703-684-2782 or 800-999-2782
TDD: 703-683-6748
Fax: 703-684-7343
E-mail: accreditation@apta.org
Website: www.capteonline.org

PHYSICIAN ASSISTANT STUDIES
John E. McCarty, Executive Director
Accreditation Review Commission on Education for the Physician
Assistant, Inc. (ARC-PA)
12000 Findley Road, Suite 150
Johns Creek, Georgia 30097
Phone: 770-476-1224
Fax: 770-476-1738
E-mail: arc-pa@arc-pa.org
Website: www.arc-pa.org

PLANNING
Ms. Shonagh Merits, Executive Director
American Institute of Certified Planners/Association of Collegiate
Schools of Planning/American Planning Association
Planning Accreditation Board (PAB)
2334 West Lawrence Avenue, Suite 209
Chicago, Illinois 60625
Phone: 773-334-7200
E-mail: smerits@planningaccreditationboard.org
Website: www.planningaccreditationboard.org

PODIATRIC MEDICINE
Alan R. Tinkleman, M.P.A., Executive Director
Council on Podiatric Medical Education (CPME)
American Podiatric Medical Association (APMA)
9312 Old Georgetown Road
Bethesda, Maryland 20814-1621
Phone: 301-571-9200
Fax: 301-571-4903
Website: www.cpme.org

PSYCHOLOGY AND COUNSELING
Susan Zlotlow, Ph.D., Associate Executive Director
Office of Program Consultation and Accreditation
American Psychological Association
750 First Street, NE
Washington, DC 20002-4242
Phone: 202-336-5979 or 800-374-2721
TDD/TTY: 202-336-6123
Fax: 202-336-5978
E-mail: apaaccred@apa.org
Website: www.apa.org/ed/accreditation

Carol L. Bobby, Ph.D., Executive Director
Council for Accreditation of Counseling and Related Educational
    Programs (CACREP)
1001 North Fairfax Street, Suite 510
Alexandria, Virginia 22314
Phone: 703-535-5990
Fax: 703-739-6209
E-mail: cacrep@cacrep.org
Website: www.cacrep.org

PUBLIC AFFAIRS AND ADMINISTRATION
Crystal Calarusse, Chief Accreditation Officer
Commission on Peer Review and Accreditation
National Association of Schools of Public Affairs and Administration
1029 Vermont Avenue, NW, Suite 1100
Washington, DC 20005
Phone: 202-628-8965
Fax: 202-626-4978
E-mail: copra@naspaa.org
Website: www.naspaa.org

PUBLIC HEALTH
Laura Rasar King, M.P.H., MCHES, Executive Director
Council on Education for Public Health
1010 Wayne Avenue, Suite 220
Silver Spring, Maryland 20910
Phone: 202-789-1050
Fax: 202-789-1895
E-mail: Lking@ceph.org
Website: www.ceph.org

REHABILITATION EDUCATION
Frank Lane, Ph.D., Executive Director
Council on Rehabilitation Education (CORE)
Commission on Standards and Accreditation
1699 Woodfield Road, Suite 300
Schaumburg, Illinois 60173
Phone: 847-944-1345
Fax: 847-944-1346
E-mail: lane@iit.edu
Website: www.core-rehab.org

SOCIAL WORK
Jo Ann Regan, Ph.D., Director
Office of Social Work Accreditation
Council on Social Work Education
1701 Duke Street, Suite 200
Alexandria, Virginia 22314
Phone: 703-683-8080
Fax: 703-683-8099
E-mail: info@cswe.org
Website: www.cswe.org

SPEECH-LANGUAGE PATHOLOGY AND AUDIOLOGY
Patrima L. Tice, Director of Accreditation
American Speech-Language-Hearing Association
Council on Academic Accreditation in Audiology and
    Speech-Language Pathology
2200 Research Boulevard
Rockville, Maryland 20850-3289
Phone: 301-296-5796
Fax: 301-296-8750
E-mail: ptice@asha.org
Website: www.asha.org/academic/accreditation/default.htm

TECHNOLOGY
Michale S. McComis, Ed.D., Executive Director
Accrediting Commission of Career Schools and Colleges
2101 Wilson Boulevard, Suite 302
Arlington, Virginia 22201
Phone: 703-247-4212
Fax: 703-247-4533
E-mail: mccomis@accsc.org
Website: www.accsc.org

TEACHER EDUCATION
James G. Cibulka, Ph.D., President
Council for the Accreditation of Educator Preparation
1140 19th Street, NW, Suite 400
Washington, DC 20036
Phone: 202-223-0077
E-mail: caep@caepnet.org
Website: www.caepnet.org

THEATER
Karen P. Moynahan, Executive Director
National Association of Schools of Theatre Commission on
    Accreditation
11250 Roger Bacon Drive, Suite 21
Reston, Virginia 20190
Phone: 703-437-0700
Fax: 703-437-6312
E-mail: info@arts-accredit.org
Website: http://nast.arts-accredit.org/

THEOLOGY
Keith Sharfman, Director
Association of Advanced Rabbinical and Talmudic Schools (AARTS)
Accreditation Commission
11 Broadway, Suite 405
New York, New York 10004
Phone: 212-363-1991
Fax: 212-533-5335
E-mail: k.sharfman.aarts@gmail.com

Daniel O. Aleshire, Executive Director
Association of Theological Schools in the United States and Canada
    (ATS)
Commission on Accrediting
10 Summit Park Drive
Pittsburgh, Pennsylvania 15275
Phone: 412-788-6505
Fax: 412-788-6510
E-mail: ats@ats.edu
Website: www.ats.edu

Paul Boatner, President
Transnational Association of Christian Colleges and Schools (TRACS)
Accreditation Commission
15935 Forest Road
Forest, Virginia 24551
Phone: 434-525-9539
Fax: 434-525-9538
E-mail: info@tracs.org
Website: www.tracs.org

VETERINARY MEDICINE
David Granstrom, Executive Director
Education and Research Division
American Veterinary Medical Association (AVMA)
Council on Education
1931 North Meacham Road, Suite 100
Schaumburg, Illinois 60173-4360
Phone: 847-925-8070 Ext. 6674
Fax: 847-925-9329
E-mail: info@avma.org
Website: www.avma.org

How to Use These Guides

As you identify the particular programs and institutions that interest you, you can use both the *Graduate & Professional Programs: An Overview* volume and the specialized volumes in the series to obtain detailed information.

- *Graduate Programs in the Physical Sciences, Mathematics, Agricultural Sciences, the Environment & Natural Resources*
- *Graduate Programs in Engineering & Applied Sciences*
- *Graduate Programs the Humanities, Arts & Social Sciences*
- *Graduate Programs in the Biological/Biomedical Sciences & Health-Related Professions*
- *Graduate Programs in Business, Education, Information Studies, Law & Social Work*

Each of the specialized volumes in the series is divided into sections that contain one or more directories devoted to programs in a particular field. If you do not find a directory devoted to your field of interest in a specific volume, consult "Directories and Subject Areas" (located at the end of each volume). After you have identified the correct volume, consult the "Directories and Subject Areas in This Book" index, which shows (as does the more general directory) what directories cover subjects not specifically named in a directory or section title.

Each of the specialized volumes in the series has a number of general directories. These directories have entries for the largest unit at an institution granting graduate degrees in that field. For example, the general Engineering and Applied Sciences directory in the *Graduate Programs in Engineering & Applied Sciences* volume consists of **Profiles** for colleges, schools, and departments of engineering and applied sciences.

General directories are followed by other directories, or sections, that give more detailed information about programs in particular areas of the general field that has been covered. The general Engineering and Applied Sciences directory, in the previous example, is followed by nineteen sections with directories in specific areas of engineering, such as Chemical Engineering, Industrial/Management Engineering, and Mechanical Engineering.

Because of the broad nature of many fields, any system of organization is bound to involve a certain amount of overlap. Environmental studies, for example, is a field whose various aspects are studied in several types of departments and schools. Readers interested in such studies will find information on relevant programs in the *Graduate Programs in the Biological/Biomedical Sciences & Health-Related Professions* volume under Ecology and Environmental Biology and Environmental and Occupational Health; in the *Graduate Programs in the Physical Sciences, Mathematics, Agricultural Sciences, the Environment & Natural Resources* volume under Environmental Management and Policy and Natural Resources; and in the *Graduate Programs in Engineering & Applied Sciences* volume under Energy Management and Policy and Environmental Engineering. To help you find all of the programs of interest to you, the introduction to each section within the specialized volumes includes, if applicable, a paragraph suggesting other sections and directories with information on related areas of study.

Directory of Institutions with Programs in Business, Education, Information Studies, Law & Social Work

This directory lists institutions in alphabetical order and includes beneath each name the academic fields in which each institution offers graduate programs. The degree level in each field is also indicated, provided that the institution has supplied that information in response to Peterson's Annual Survey of Graduate and Professional Institutions.

An M indicates that a master's degree program is offered; a D indicates that a doctoral degree program is offered; an O signifies that other advanced degrees (e.g., certificates or specialist degrees) are offered; and an * (asterisk) indicates that a **Close-Up** and/or **Display** is located in this volume. See the index, "Close-Ups and Displays," for the specific page number.

Profiles of Academic and Professional Programs in the Specialized Volumes

Each section of **Profiles** has a table of contents that lists the Program Directories, **Displays**, and **Close-Ups**. Program Directories consist of the **Profiles** of programs in the relevant fields, with **Displays** following if programs have chosen to include them. **Close-Ups,** which are more individualized statements, are also listed for those graduate schools or programs that have chosen to submit them.

The **Profiles** found in the 500 directories in the specialized volumes provide basic data about the graduate units in capsule form for quick reference. To make these directories as useful as possible, **Profiles** are generally listed for an institution's smallest academic unit within a subject area. In other words, if an institution has a College of Liberal Arts that administers many related programs, the **Profile** for the individual program (e.g., Program in History), not the entire College, appears in the directory.

There are some programs that do not fit into any current directory and are not given individual **Profiles**. The directory structure is reviewed annually in order to keep this number to a minimum and to accommodate major trends in graduate education.

The following outline describes the **Profile** information found in the guides and explains how best to use that information. Any item that does not apply to or was not provided by a graduate unit is omitted from its listing. The format of the **Profiles** is constant, making it easy to compare one institution with another and one program with another.

Identifying Information. The institution's name, in boldface type, is followed by a complete listing of the administrative structure for that field of study. (For example, University of Akron, Buchtel College of Arts and Sciences, Department of Theoretical and Applied Mathematics, Program in Mathematics.) The last unit listed is the one to which all information in the **Profile** pertains. The institution's city, state, and zip code follow.

Offerings. Each field of study offered by the unit is listed with all postbaccalaureate degrees awarded. Degrees that are not preceded by a specific concentration are awarded in the general field listed in the unit name. Frequently, fields of study are broken down into subspecializations, and those appear following the degrees awarded; for example, "Offerings in secondary education (M.Ed.), including English education, mathematics education, science education." Students enrolled in the M.Ed. program would be able to specialize in any of the three fields mentioned.

Professional Accreditation. Some **Profiles** indicate whether a program is professionally accredited. Because it is possible for a program to receive or lose professional accreditation at any time, students entering fields in which accreditation is important to a career should verify the status of programs by contacting either the chairperson or the appropriate accrediting association.

Jointly Offered Degrees. Explanatory statements concerning programs that are offered in cooperation with other institutions are included in the list of degrees offered. This occurs most commonly on a regional basis (for example, two state universities offering a cooperative Ph.D. in special education) or where the specialized nature of the institutions encourages joint efforts (a J.D./M.B.A. offered by a law school at an institution with no formal business programs and an institution with a business school but lacking a law school). Only programs that are truly cooperative are listed; those involving only limited course work at

another institution are not. Interested students should contact the heads of such units for further information.

Part-Time and Evening/Weekend Programs. When information regarding the availability of part-time or evening/weekend study appears in the **Profile**, it means that students are able to earn a degree exclusively through such study.

Postbaccalaureate Distance Learning Degrees. A postbaccalaureate distance learning degree program signifies that course requirements can be fulfilled with minimal or no on-campus study.

Faculty. Figures on the number of faculty members actively involved with graduate students through teaching or research are separated into full- and part-time as well as men and women whenever the information has been supplied.

Students. Figures for the number of students enrolled in graduate and professional programs pertain to the semester of highest enrollment from the 2013–14 academic year. These figures are broken down into full- and part-time and men and women whenever the data have been supplied. Information on the number of matriculated students enrolled in the unit who are members of a minority group or are international students appears here. The average age of the matriculated students is followed by the number of applicants, the percentage accepted, and the number enrolled for fall 2013.

Degrees Awarded. The number of degrees awarded in the calendar year is listed. Many doctoral programs offer a terminal master's degree if students leave the program after completing only part of the requirements for a doctoral degree; that is indicated here. All degrees are classified into one of four types: master's, doctoral, first professional, and other advanced degrees. A unit may award one or several degrees at a given level; however, the data are only collected by type and may therefore represent several different degree programs.

Degree Requirements. The information in this section is also broken down by type of degree, and all information for a degree level pertains to all degrees of that type unless otherwise specified. Degree requirements are collected in a simplified form to provide some very basic information on the nature of the program and on foreign language, thesis or dissertation, comprehensive exam, and registration requirements. Many units also provide a short list of additional requirements, such as fieldwork or an internship. For complete information on graduation requirements, contact the graduate school or program directly.

Entrance Requirements. Entrance requirements are broken down into the four degree levels of master's, doctoral, first professional, and other advanced degrees. Within each level, information may be provided in two basic categories: entrance exams and other requirements. The entrance exams are identified by the standard acronyms used by the testing agencies, unless they are not well known. Other entrance requirements are quite varied, but they often contain an undergraduate or graduate grade point average (GPA). Unless otherwise stated, the GPA is calculated on a 4.0 scale and is listed as a minimum required for admission. Additional exam requirements/recommendations for international students may be listed here. Application deadlines for domestic and international students, the application fee, and whether electronic applications are accepted may be listed here. Note that the deadline should be used for reference only; these dates are subject to change, and students interested in applying should always contact the graduate unit directly about application procedures and deadlines.

Expenses. The typical cost of study for the 2013–14 academic year is given in two basic categories: tuition and fees. Cost of study may be quite complex at a graduate institution. There are often sliding scales for part-time study, a different cost for first-year students, and other variables that make it impossible to completely cover the cost of study for each graduate program. To provide the most usable information, figures are given for full-time study for a full year where available and for part-time study in terms of a per-unit rate (per credit, per semester hour, etc.). Occasionally, variances may be noted in tuition and fees for reasons such as the type of program, whether courses are taken during the day or evening, whether courses are at the master's or doctoral level, or other institution-specific reasons. Expenses are usually subject to change; for exact costs at any given time, contact your chosen schools and programs directly. Keep in mind that the tuition of Canadian institutions is usually given in Canadian dollars.

Financial Support. This section contains data on the number of awards administered by the institution and given to graduate students

during the 2013–14 academic year. The first figure given represents the total number of students receiving financial support enrolled in that unit. If the unit has provided information on graduate appointments, these are broken down into three major categories: fellowships give money to graduate students to cover the cost of study and living expenses and are not based on a work obligation or research commitment, research assistantships provide stipends to graduate students for assistance in a formal research project with a faculty member, and teaching assistantships provide stipends to graduate students for teaching or for assisting faculty members in teaching undergraduate classes. Within each category, figures are given for the total number of awards, the average yearly amount per award, and whether full or partial tuition reimbursements are awarded. In addition to graduate appointments, the availability of several other financial aid sources is covered in this section. Tuition waivers are routinely part of a graduate appointment, but units sometimes waive part or all of a student's tuition even if a graduate appointment is not available. Federal WorkStudy is made available to students who demonstrate need and meet the federal guidelines; this form of aid normally includes 10 or more hours of work per week in an office of the institution. Institutionally sponsored loans are low-interest loans available to graduate students to cover both educational and living expenses. Career-related internships or fieldwork offer money to students who are participating in a formal off-campus research project or practicum. Grants, scholarships, traineeships, unspecified assistantships, and other awards may also be noted. The availability of financial support to part-time students is also indicated here.

Some programs list the financial aid application deadline and the forms that need to be completed for students to be eligible for financial awards. There are two forms: FAFSA, the Free Application for Federal Student Aid, which is required for federal aid, and the CSS PROFILE®.

Faculty Research. Each unit has the opportunity to list several keyword phrases describing the current research involving faculty members and graduate students. Space limitations prevent the unit from listing complete information on all research programs. The total expenditure for funded research from the previous academic year may also be included.

Unit Head and Application Contact. The head of the graduate program for each unit may be listed with academic title, phone and fax numbers, and e-mail address. In addition to the unit head's contact information, many graduate programs also list a separate contact for application and admission information, followed by the graduate school, program, or department's website. If no unit head or application contact is given, you should contact the overall institution for information on graduate admissions.

Displays and Close-Ups

The **Displays** and **Close-Ups** are supplementary insertions submitted by deans, chairs, and other administrators who wish to offer an additional, more individualized statement to readers. A number of graduate school and program administrators have attached a **Display** ad near the **Profile** listing. Here you will find information that an institution or program wants to emphasize. The **Close-Ups** are by their very nature more expansive and flexible than the **Profiles**, and the administrators who have written them may emphasize different aspects of their programs. All of the **Close-Ups** are organized in the same way (with the exception of a few that describe research and training opportunities instead of degree programs), and in each one you will find information on the same basic topics, such as programs of study, research facilities, tuition and fees, financial aid, and application procedures. If an institution or program has submitted a **Close-Up**, a boldface cross-reference appears below its **Profile**. As with the **Displays**, all of the **Close-Ups** in the guides have been submitted by choice; the absence of a **Display** or **Close-Up** does not reflect any type of editorial judgment on the part of Peterson's, and their presence in the guides should not be taken as an indication of status, quality, or approval. Statements regarding a university's objectives and accomplishments are a reflection of its own beliefs and are not the opinions of the Peterson's editors.

Appendixes

This section contains two appendixes. The first, "Institutional Changes Since the 2014 Edition," lists institutions that have closed, merged, or changed their name or status since the last edition of the guides. The second, "Abbreviations Used in the Guides," gives abbreviations of degree names, along with what those abbreviations stand for. These appendixes are identical in all six volumes of *Peterson's Graduate and Professional Programs*.

Indexes

There are three indexes presented here. The first index, "Close-Ups and Displays," gives page references for all programs that have chosen to place **Close-Ups** and **Displays** in this volume. It is arranged alphabetically by institution; within institutions, the arrangement is alphabetical by subject area. It is not an index to all programs in the book's directories of **Profiles**; readers must refer to the directories themselves for **Profile** information on programs that have not submitted the additional, more individualized statements. The second index, "Directories and Subject Areas in Other Books in This Series", gives page references for the directories in the specialized volumes and also includes cross-references for subject area names not used in the directory structure, for example, "Computing Technology (see Computer Science)." The third index, "Directories and Subject Areas in This Book," gives page references for the directories in this volume and cross-references for subject area names not used in this volume's directory structure.

Data Collection Procedures

The information published in the directories and **Profiles** of all the books is collected through Peterson's Annual Survey of Graduate and Professional Institutions. The survey is sent each spring to nearly 2,400 institutions offering postbaccalaureate degree programs, including accredited institutions in the United States, U.S. territories, and Canada and those institutions outside the United States that are accredited by U.S. accrediting bodies. Deans and other administrators complete these surveys, providing information on programs in the 500 academic and professional fields covered in the guides as well as overall institutional information. While every effort has been made to ensure the accuracy and completeness of the data, information is sometimes unavailable or changes occur after publication deadlines. All usable information received in time for publication has been included. The omission of any particular item from a directory or **Profile** signifies either that the item is not applicable to the institution or program or that information was not available. **Profiles** of programs scheduled to begin during the 2014–15 academic year cannot, obviously, include statistics on enrollment or, in many cases, the number of faculty members. If no usable data were submitted by an institution, its name, address, and program name appear in order to indicate the availability of graduate work.

Criteria for Inclusion in This Guide

To be included in this guide, an institution must have full accreditation or be a candidate for accreditation (preaccreditation) status by an institutional or specialized accrediting body recognized by the U.S. Department of Education or the Council for Higher Education Accreditation (CHEA). Institutional accrediting bodies, which review each institution as a whole, include the six regional associations of schools and colleges (Middle States, New England, North Central, Northwest, Southern, and Western), each of which is responsible for a specified portion of the United States and its territories. Other institutional accrediting bodies are national in scope and accredit specific kinds of institutions (e.g., Bible colleges, independent colleges, and rabbinical and Talmudic schools). Program registration by the New York State Board of Regents is considered to be the equivalent of institutional accreditation, since the board requires that all programs offered by an institution meet its standards before recognition is granted. A Canadian institution must be chartered and authorized to grant degrees by the provincial government, affiliated with a chartered institution, or accredited by a recognized U.S. accrediting body. This guide also includes institutions outside the United States that are accredited by these U.S. accrediting bodies. There are recognized specialized or professional accrediting bodies in more than fifty different fields, each of which is authorized to accredit institutions or specific programs in its particular field. For specialized institutions that offer programs in one field only, we designate this to be the equivalent of institutional accreditation. A full explanation of the accrediting process and complete information on recognized institutional (regional and national) and specialized accrediting bodies can be found online at www.chea.org or at www.ed.gov/admins/finaid/accred/index.html.

DIRECTORY OF INSTITUTIONS WITH PROGRAMS IN BUSINESS, EDUCATION, INFORMATION STUDIES, LAW & SOCIAL WORK

ABILENE CHRISTIAN UNIVERSITY
Accounting M
Curriculum and Instruction M
Education—General M,O
Educational Leadership and Administration M,O
Educational Media/Instructional Technology M,O
Higher Education M
Human Resources Development M
Human Services M,O
Social Work M

ACACIA UNIVERSITY
Education—General M
Educational Leadership and Administration M
Elementary Education M
English as a Second Language M
Secondary Education M
Special Education M

ACADEMY OF ART UNIVERSITY
Advertising and Public Relations M
Art Education M

ACADIA UNIVERSITY
Counselor Education M
Curriculum and Instruction M
Education—General M,D
Educational Leadership and Administration M
Educational Media/Instructional Technology M
Mathematics Education M
Recreation and Park Management M
Science Education M
Social Sciences Education M
Special Education M

ADAMS STATE UNIVERSITY
Counselor Education M
Education—General M
Physical Education M
Special Education M

ADELPHI UNIVERSITY
Art Education M
Business Administration and Management—General M*
Education—General M,D,O*
Educational Leadership and Administration M,O
Educational Media/Instructional Technology M,O
Electronic Commerce M
Elementary Education M
English as a Second Language M,O
Finance and Banking M
Health Education M,O
Human Resources Management M,O
Management Information Systems M,O
Marketing M
Physical Education M,O
Reading Education M
Secondary Education M
Social Work M,D*
Special Education M,O

ADLER GRADUATE SCHOOL
Counselor Education M
Human Resources Development M

ADLER SCHOOL OF PROFESSIONAL PSYCHOLOGY
Nonprofit Management M,D,O

ADRIAN COLLEGE
Accounting M
Athletic Training and Sports Medicine M

AIR FORCE INSTITUTE OF TECHNOLOGY
Logistics M,D
Management Information Systems M

ALABAMA AGRICULTURAL AND MECHANICAL UNIVERSITY
Business Administration and Management—General M
Counselor Education M,O
Early Childhood Education M,O
Education—General M,O
Educational Leadership and Administration M,O
Elementary Education M,O
Human Resources Management M,O
Marketing M
Music Education M
Physical Education M
Secondary Education M,O
Social Work M
Special Education M,O
Vocational and Technical Education M

ALABAMA STATE UNIVERSITY
Accounting M
Business Administration and Management—General M
Counselor Education M,D,O
Early Childhood Education M,O
Education—General M,D,O
Educational Leadership and Administration M,D,O
Educational Media/Instructional Technology M,D,O
Educational Policy M,D,O
Elementary Education M,O
English Education M,O
Health Education M
Mathematics Education M,O
Music Education M,O
Physical Education M
Reading Education M,O
Science Education M,O
Secondary Education M,O
Social Sciences Education M,O
Special Education M,O

ALASKA PACIFIC UNIVERSITY
Business Administration and Management—General M
Education—General M
Elementary Education M
Environmental Education M
Investment Management M,O
Middle School Education M

ALBANY LAW SCHOOL
Law M,D

ALBANY STATE UNIVERSITY
Accounting M
Business Administration and Management—General M
Counselor Education M,O
Early Childhood Education M,O
Education—General M,O
Educational Leadership and Administration M,O
English Education M,O
Health Education M,O
Human Resources Management M
Mathematics Education M
Middle School Education M,O
Physical Education M,O
Science Education M
Social Work M
Special Education M,O

ALBERTUS MAGNUS COLLEGE
Business Administration and Management—General M
Education—General M
Human Services M
Organizational Management M

ALBRIGHT COLLEGE
Early Childhood Education M
Education—General M
Elementary Education M
English as a Second Language M
Special Education M

ALCORN STATE UNIVERSITY
Agricultural Education M,O
Business Administration and Management—General M
Counselor Education M,O
Education—General M,O
Elementary Education M,O
Health Education M,O
Physical Education M,O
Secondary Education M,O
Special Education M,O
Vocational and Technical Education M,O

ALFRED UNIVERSITY
Accounting M
Business Administration and Management—General M
Counselor Education M,D,O
Education—General M
Reading Education M

ALLEN COLLEGE
Health Education M,D,O

ALLIANT INTERNATIONAL UNIVERSITY–IRVINE
Educational Psychology M,D,O

ALLIANT INTERNATIONAL UNIVERSITY–LOS ANGELES
Business Administration and Management—General D
Education—General M,O
Educational Psychology M,D,O
Student Affairs M,D,O

ALLIANT INTERNATIONAL UNIVERSITY–MÉXICO CITY
Business Administration and Management—General M
Education—General M
International Business M

ALLIANT INTERNATIONAL UNIVERSITY–SACRAMENTO
Education—General M,O

ALLIANT INTERNATIONAL UNIVERSITY–SAN DIEGO
Business Administration and Management—General M
Education—General M,O
Educational Leadership and Administration M,D,O
Educational Psychology M,D,O
English as a Second Language M,D,O
Higher Education M,D,O
Student Affairs M,D,O

ALLIANT INTERNATIONAL UNIVERSITY–SAN FRANCISCO
Counselor Education M
Education—General M,O
Educational Leadership and Administration M,D,O
Educational Psychology M,D,O
English as a Second Language M,O
Higher Education M,D,O
Law D
Multilingual and Multicultural Education M,O
Special Education M,O

ALVERNIA UNIVERSITY
Business Administration and Management—General M
Education—General M
Organizational Management D
Urban Education M

ALVERNO COLLEGE
Adult Education M
Business Administration and Management—General M
Education—General M
Educational Leadership and Administration M
Educational Media/Instructional Technology M
Reading Education M
Science Education M

AMBERTON UNIVERSITY
Business Administration and Management—General M
Human Resources Development M
Human Resources Management M
Management Strategy and Policy M
Project Management M

THE AMERICAN COLLEGE
Business Administration and Management—General M
Finance and Banking M
Organizational Management M

AMERICAN COLLEGE OF EDUCATION
Curriculum and Instruction M
Education—General M
Educational Leadership and Administration M
Educational Media/Instructional Technology M
English as a Second Language M
Multilingual and Multicultural Education M

AMERICAN COLLEGE OF THESSALONIKI
Business Administration and Management—General M,O
Entrepreneurship M,O
Finance and Banking M,O
Marketing M,O

AMERICAN GRADUATE UNIVERSITY
Business Administration and Management—General M,O
Project Management M,O
Supply Chain Management M,O

AMERICAN INTERCONTINENTAL UNIVERSITY ATLANTA
International Business M
Management Information Systems M

AMERICAN INTERCONTINENTAL UNIVERSITY HOUSTON
Business Administration and Management—General M

AMERICAN INTERCONTINENTAL UNIVERSITY ONLINE
Accounting M
Business Administration and Management—General M
Curriculum and Instruction M
Education—General M
Educational Leadership and Administration M
Educational Measurement and Evaluation M
Educational Media/Instructional Technology M
Finance and Banking M
Human Resources Management M
Industrial and Manufacturing Management M
International Business M
Marketing M
Project Management M

AMERICAN INTERCONTINENTAL UNIVERSITY SOUTH FLORIDA
Accounting M
Business Administration and Management—General M
Educational Media/Instructional Technology M
Finance and Banking M
Human Resources Management M
International Business M
Marketing M

AMERICAN INTERNATIONAL COLLEGE
Accounting M
Business Administration and Management—General M
Counselor Education M,D,O
Early Childhood Education M,D,O
Education—General M,D,O
Educational Leadership and Administration M,D,O
Educational Psychology M,D
Elementary Education M,D,O
Middle School Education M,D,O
Reading Education M,D,O
Secondary Education M,D,O
Special Education M,D,O
Taxation M

AMERICAN JEWISH UNIVERSITY
Business Administration and Management—General M
Education—General M
Nonprofit Management M
Social Work M

AMERICAN NATIONAL UNIVERSITY
Business Administration and Management—General M

AMERICAN PUBLIC UNIVERSITY SYSTEM
Accounting M
Business Administration and Management—General M
Counselor Education M
Curriculum and Instruction M
Distance Education Development M
Educational Leadership and Administration M
Elementary Education M
English as a Second Language M
Entrepreneurship M
Exercise and Sports Science M
Finance and Banking M
Human Resources Management M
International Business M
Legal and Justice Studies M
Logistics M
Management Information Systems M
Management Strategy and Policy M
Marketing M
Nonprofit Management M
Organizational Management M
Project Management M
Reading Education M
Secondary Education M
Social Sciences Education M
Special Education M
Transportation Management M

AMERICAN SENTINEL UNIVERSITY
Business Administration and Management—General M
Management Information Systems M

AMERICAN UNIVERSITY
Accounting M,O
Business Administration and Management—General M,D,O
Curriculum and Instruction M,D,O
Early Childhood Education M,D,O
Education—General M,D,O
Elementary Education M,D,O
English as a Second Language M,D,O
Entrepreneurship M,D,O
Exercise and Sports Science M,D,O
Finance and Banking M,D,O
Health Education M,D,O
International and Comparative Education M,D,O
Law M,D,O
Legal and Justice Studies M,D,O
Management Information Systems M,D,O
Marketing M,O
Multilingual and Multicultural Education M,D,O
Nonprofit Management M,D,O
Organizational Management M,D,O
Quantitative Analysis M,D,O
Real Estate M,O
Secondary Education M,D,O
Special Education M,D,O
Sustainability Management M,O
Taxation M,O

THE AMERICAN UNIVERSITY IN CAIRO
Business Administration and Management—General M,O
English as a Second Language M,O
Foreign Languages Education M
Industrial and Manufacturing Management M
International and Comparative Education M
Law M
Management Information Systems M

THE AMERICAN UNIVERSITY IN DUBAI
Business Administration and Management—General M
Education—General M
Finance and Banking M
International Business M
Marketing M

AMERICAN UNIVERSITY OF ARMENIA
Business Administration and Management—General M
English as a Second Language M
Law M
Management Information Systems M

AMERICAN UNIVERSITY OF BEIRUT
Business Administration and Management—General M
Education—General M,D
Finance and Banking M,D
Human Resources Management M

THE AMERICAN UNIVERSITY OF PARIS
Business Administration and Management—General M
International Business M
Law M

AMERICAN UNIVERSITY OF PUERTO RICO
Art Education M
Education—General M
Elementary Education M
Physical Education M
Science Education M
Special Education M

AMERICAN UNIVERSITY OF SHARJAH
Accounting M
Business Administration and Management—General M
English as a Second Language M

AMRIDGE UNIVERSITY
Counselor Education M,D
Organizational Behavior M,D
Organizational Management M,D

ANAHEIM UNIVERSITY
Business Administration and Management—General M,D,O
English as a Second Language M,D,O
Entrepreneurship M,D,O
International Business M,D,O
Sustainability Management M,D,O

ANDERSON UNIVERSITY (IN)
Accounting	M,D
Business Administration and Management—General	M,D
Education—General	M

ANDERSON UNIVERSITY (SC)
Business Administration and Management—General	M
Education—General	M

ANDOVER NEWTON THEOLOGICAL SCHOOL
Religious Education	M,D

ANDREWS UNIVERSITY
Accounting	M
Curriculum and Instruction	M,D,O
Education—General	M,D,O
Educational Leadership and Administration	M,D,O
Educational Psychology	M,D
Elementary Education	M,D,O
English as a Second Language	M,D,O
English Education	M,D,O
Finance and Banking	M
Foreign Languages Education	M,D,O
Higher Education	M,D,O
Human Services	M
Religious Education	M,D,O
Science Education	M,D,O
Secondary Education	M,D,O
Social Sciences Education	M,D,O
Social Work	M
Special Education	M

ANGELO STATE UNIVERSITY
Accounting	M
Business Administration and Management—General	M
Counselor Education	M
Curriculum and Instruction	M
Education—General	M
Educational Leadership and Administration	M,O
Higher Education	M
Special Education	M
Sports Management	M

ANNA MARIA COLLEGE
Art Education	M
Business Administration and Management—General	M,O
Early Childhood Education	M,O
Education—General	M,O
Elementary Education	M,O
English Education	M,O

ANTIOCH UNIVERSITY LOS ANGELES
Business Administration and Management—General	M
Education—General	M
Human Resources Development	M
Nonprofit Management	M
Organizational Management	M

ANTIOCH UNIVERSITY MIDWEST
Business Administration and Management—General	M
Education—General	M
Management Strategy and Policy	M

ANTIOCH UNIVERSITY NEW ENGLAND
Business Administration and Management—General	M
Early Childhood Education	M
Education—General	M,O
Educational Leadership and Administration	M,O
Educational Media/Instructional Technology	M,O
Elementary Education	M,O
Environmental Education	M
Foundations and Philosophy of Education	M,O
Science Education	M
Special Education	M,O
Sustainability Management	M

ANTIOCH UNIVERSITY SANTA BARBARA
Education—General	M
Organizational Management	M

ANTIOCH UNIVERSITY SEATTLE
Counselor Education	M
Education—General	M
Organizational Management	M

APPALACHIAN SCHOOL OF LAW
Law	D

APPALACHIAN STATE UNIVERSITY
Accounting	M
Business Administration and Management—General	M
Counselor Education	M
Curriculum and Instruction	M
Educational Leadership and Administration	M,D,O
Educational Media/Instructional Technology	M,O
Elementary Education	M
English Education	M
Exercise and Sports Science	M
Foreign Languages Education	M
Higher Education	M,O
Library Science	M,O
Mathematics Education	M
Middle School Education	M
Music Education	M
Reading Education	M
Science Education	M
Social Sciences Education	M
Social Work	M

Special Education	M
Student Affairs	M
Taxation	M
Vocational and Technical Education	M

AQUINAS COLLEGE
Business Administration and Management—General	M
Education—General	M
Marketing	M
Organizational Management	M
Sustainability Management	M

ARCADIA UNIVERSITY
Art Education	M,D,O
Business Administration and Management—General	M
Computer Education	M,D,O
Curriculum and Instruction	M,D,O
Early Childhood Education	M,D,O
Education—General	M,D,O
Educational Leadership and Administration	M,D,O
Educational Media/Instructional Technology	M,D,O
Elementary Education	M,D,O
English Education	M,D,O
Environmental Education	M,D,O
Health Education	M
Mathematics Education	M,D,O
Music Education	M,D,O
Reading Education	M,D,O
Science Education	M,D,O
Secondary Education	M,D,O
Social Sciences Education	M,D,O
Special Education	M,D,O

ARGOSY UNIVERSITY, ATLANTA
Accounting	M,D
Business Administration and Management—General	M,D
Counselor Education	M,D,O
Education—General	M,D,O
Educational Leadership and Administration	M,D,O
Educational Media/Instructional Technology	M,D,O
Elementary Education	M,D
Finance and Banking	M,D
Higher Education	M,D,O
International Business	M,D
Management Information Systems	M,D
Marketing	M,D
Secondary Education	M,D,O

ARGOSY UNIVERSITY, CHICAGO
Accounting	M,D
Adult Education	M,D,O
Business Administration and Management—General	M,D
Community College Education	M,D,O
Counselor Education	D
Education—General	M,D,O
Educational Leadership and Administration	M,D,O
Elementary Education	M,D,O
Finance and Banking	M,D
Higher Education	M,D,O
International Business	M,D
Management Information Systems	M,D
Marketing	M,D
Organizational Behavior	D
Organizational Management	D
Secondary Education	M,D,O
Sustainability Management	M,D

ARGOSY UNIVERSITY, DALLAS
Accounting	M,D,O
Business Administration and Management—General	M,D,O
Counselor Education	D
Education—General	M,D
Educational Leadership and Administration	M,D
Finance and Banking	M,D,O
Higher Education	M,D
International Business	M,D,O
Management Information Systems	M,D,O
Marketing	M,D,O
Sustainability Management	M,D,O

ARGOSY UNIVERSITY, DENVER
Accounting	M,D
Business Administration and Management—General	M,D
Community College Education	M,D
Counselor Education	M,D
Education—General	M,D
Educational Leadership and Administration	M,D
Educational Media/Instructional Technology	M,D
Elementary Education	M,D
Finance and Banking	M,D
Higher Education	M,D
International Business	M,D
Management Information Systems	M,D
Marketing	M,D
Organizational Management	M,D
Sustainability Management	M,D

ARGOSY UNIVERSITY, HAWAI'I
Accounting	M,D,O
Adult Education	M,D
Business Administration and Management—General	M,D,O
Education—General	M,D
Educational Leadership and Administration	M,D
Elementary Education	M,D
Finance and Banking	M,D,O
Higher Education	M,D
International Business	M,D,O

Management Information Systems	M,D,O
Marketing	M,D,O
Organizational Management	D
Secondary Education	M,D
Sustainability Management	M,D,O

ARGOSY UNIVERSITY, INLAND EMPIRE
Accounting	M,D
Business Administration and Management—General	M,D
Community College Education	M,D
Education—General	M,D
Educational Leadership and Administration	M,D
Elementary Education	M,D
Finance and Banking	M,D
Higher Education	M,D
International Business	M,D
Management Information Systems	M,D
Marketing	M,D
Organizational Management	M,D
Secondary Education	M,D
Sustainability Management	M,D

ARGOSY UNIVERSITY, LOS ANGELES
Accounting	M,D
Business Administration and Management—General	M,D
Community College Education	M,D
Education—General	M,D
Educational Leadership and Administration	M,D
Elementary Education	M,D
Finance and Banking	M,D
Higher Education	M,D
International Business	M,D
Management Information Systems	M,D
Marketing	M,D
Organizational Management	M,D
Secondary Education	M,D
Sustainability Management	M,D

ARGOSY UNIVERSITY, NASHVILLE
Accounting	M,D
Business Administration and Management—General	M,D
Counselor Education	D
Education—General	M,D,O
Educational Leadership and Administration	M,D,O
Educational Media/Instructional Technology	M,D,O
Elementary Education	M,D,O
Finance and Banking	M,D
Higher Education	M,D,O
International Business	M,D
Management Information Systems	M,D
Marketing	M,D
Secondary Education	M,D,O

ARGOSY UNIVERSITY, ORANGE COUNTY
Accounting	M,D,O
Business Administration and Management—General	M,D,O
Community College Education	M,D
Education—General	M,D
Educational Leadership and Administration	M,D
Educational Media/Instructional Technology	M,D
Elementary Education	M,D
Finance and Banking	M,D
Higher Education	M,D
International Business	M,D
Management Information Systems	M,D
Marketing	M,D,O
Organizational Management	D
Secondary Education	M,D
Sustainability Management	M,D,O

ARGOSY UNIVERSITY, PHOENIX
Accounting	M,D
Adult Education	M,D
Business Administration and Management—General	M,D
Community College Education	M,D,O
Education—General	M,D,O
Educational Leadership and Administration	M,D,O
Educational Media/Instructional Technology	M,D,O
Elementary Education	M,D,O
Finance and Banking	M,D
Higher Education	M,D,O
International Business	M,D
Management Information Systems	M,D
Marketing	M,D,O
Secondary Education	M,D,O
Sustainability Management	M,D

ARGOSY UNIVERSITY, SALT LAKE CITY
Accounting	M,D
Business Administration and Management—General	M,D
Counselor Education	M,D
Education—General	M,D
Educational Leadership and Administration	M,D
Finance and Banking	M,D
International Business	M,D
Management Information Systems	M,D
Marketing	M,D
Sustainability Management	M,D

ARGOSY UNIVERSITY, SAN DIEGO
Accounting	M,D
Business Administration and Management—General	M,D
Community College Education	M,D
Education—General	M,D
Educational Leadership and Administration	M,D

Elementary Education	M,D
Finance and Banking	M,D
Higher Education	M,D
International Business	M,D
Management Information Systems	M,D
Marketing	M,D
Organizational Management	M,D
Secondary Education	M,D

ARGOSY UNIVERSITY, SAN FRANCISCO BAY AREA
Accounting	M,D
Business Administration and Management—General	M,D
Community College Education	M,D
Education—General	M,D
Educational Leadership and Administration	M,D
Educational Media/Instructional Technology	M,D
Elementary Education	M,D
Finance and Banking	M,D
Higher Education	M,D
International Business	M,D
Management Information Systems	M,D
Marketing	M,D
Organizational Management	M,D
Secondary Education	M,D
Sustainability Management	M,D

ARGOSY UNIVERSITY, SARASOTA
Accounting	M,D,O
Business Administration and Management—General	M,D,O
Counselor Education	M,D,O
Education—General	M,D,O
Educational Leadership and Administration	M,D,O
Educational Media/Instructional Technology	M,D,O
Elementary Education	M,D,O
Finance and Banking	M,D,O
Higher Education	M,D,O
International Business	M,D,O
Management Information Systems	M,D,O
Marketing	M,D,O
Organizational Management	M,D,O
Secondary Education	M,D,O
Sustainability Management	M,D,O

ARGOSY UNIVERSITY, SCHAUMBURG
Accounting	M,D,O
Business Administration and Management—General	M,D,O
Community College Education	M,D,O
Counselor Education	M,D,O
Education—General	M,D,O
Educational Leadership and Administration	M,D,O
Elementary Education	M,D,O
Finance and Banking	M,D,O
Higher Education	M,D,O
International Business	M,D,O
Management Information Systems	M,D,O
Marketing	M,D,O
Secondary Education	M,D,O
Sustainability Management	M,D,O

ARGOSY UNIVERSITY, SEATTLE
Accounting	M,D
Adult Education	M,D
Business Administration and Management—General	M,D
Community College Education	M,D
Education—General	M,D
Educational Leadership and Administration	M,D
Educational Media/Instructional Technology	M,D
Elementary Education	M,D
Finance and Banking	M,D
Higher Education	M,D
International Business	M,D
Management Information Systems	M,D
Marketing	M,D
Organizational Management	M,D
Secondary Education	M,D
Sustainability Management	M,D

ARGOSY UNIVERSITY, TAMPA
Accounting	M,D
Business Administration and Management—General	M,D
Community College Education	M,D,O
Counselor Education	M,D,O
Education—General	M,D,O
Educational Leadership and Administration	M,D,O
Elementary Education	M,D,O
Finance and Banking	M,D,O
Higher Education	M,D,O
International Business	M,D,O
Management Information Systems	M,D
Marketing	M,D
Organizational Management	M,D
Secondary Education	M,D
Sustainability Management	M,D

ARGOSY UNIVERSITY, TWIN CITIES
Accounting	M,D
Business Administration and Management—General	M,D
Education—General	M,D,O
Educational Leadership and Administration	M,D,O
Educational Media/Instructional Technology	M,D,O
Elementary Education	M,D,O
Finance and Banking	M,D,O
Higher Education	M,D,O
International Business	M,D,O
Management Information Systems	M,D
Marketing	M,D

M—masters degree; D—doctorate; O—other advanced degree; *—Close-Up and/or Display

Organizational Management — M,D
Secondary Education — M,D,O
Sustainability Management — M

ARGOSY UNIVERSITY, WASHINGTON DC
Accounting — M,D,O
Business Administration and Management—General — M,D,O
Community College Education — M,D,O
Counselor Education — M,D
Educator—General — M,D,O
Educational Leadership and Administration — M,D,O
Elementary Education — M,D,O
Finance and Banking — M,D,O
Higher Education — M,D,O
International Business — M,D,O
Management Information Systems — M,D,O
Marketing — M,D,O
Organizational Management — M,D,O
Secondary Education — M,D,O
Sustainability Management — M,D,O

ARIZONA STATE UNIVERSITY AT THE TEMPE CAMPUS
Accounting — M,D
Art Education — M,D
Aviation Management — M
Business Administration and Management—General — M,D
Counselor Education — M
Curriculum and Instruction — M,D
Education—General — M,D,O
Educational Leadership and Administration — M,D
Educational Media/Instructional Technology — M,D,O
Educational Policy — D
Elementary Education — M,D
English as a Second Language — M,D,O
Entrepreneurship — M
Exercise and Sports Science — M,D,O
Finance and Banking — M,D
Foreign Languages Education — M,D
Foundations and Philosophy of Education — M
Health Education — D
Higher Education — M
Kinesiology and Movement Studies — M,D,O
Law — M,D
Legal and Justice Studies — M,D,O
Management Information Systems — M,D
Marketing — M,D
Mathematics Education — M,D
Music Education — M,D
Nonprofit Management — M,D,O
Physical Education — M,D
Real Estate — M,D
Recreation and Park Management — M,D,O
Secondary Education — M,D
Social Work — M,D
Special Education — M,O
Supply Chain Management — M,D
Travel and Tourism — M,D,O

ARKANSAS STATE UNIVERSITY
Accounting — M
Agricultural Education — M,O
Business Administration and Management—General — M
Business Education — M,O
Community College Education — M,D,O
Counselor Education — M,O
Early Childhood Education — M,D,O
Education of the Gifted — M,D,O
Education—General — M,D,O
Educational Leadership and Administration — M,D,O
Elementary Education — M,D,O
English Education — M,O
Exercise and Sports Science — M,O
Foundations and Philosophy of Education — M,D,O
Health Education — M,D,O
Management Information Systems — M,O
Mathematics Education — M
Middle School Education — M,D,O
Music Education — M,O
Physical Education — M,O
Reading Education — M,D,O
Science Education — M,O
Social Sciences Education — M,O
Social Work — M,O
Special Education — M,D,O
Sports Management — M,O
Student Affairs — M,O

ARKANSAS TECH UNIVERSITY
Business Administration and Management—General — M
Counselor Education — M,O
Curriculum and Instruction — M
Education—General — M
Educational Leadership and Administration — M,O
Educational Media/Instructional Technology — M
Elementary Education — M
English as a Second Language — M
English Education — M
Physical Education — M
Student Affairs — M

ARLINGTON BAPTIST COLLEGE
Curriculum and Instruction — M
Education—General — M
Educational Leadership and Administration — M

ARMSTRONG STATE UNIVERSITY
Adult Education — M,O
Athletic Training and Sports Medicine — M,O
Business Administration and Management—General — M,O

Curriculum and Instruction — M,O
Early Childhood Education — M,O
Education—General — M,O
Exercise and Sports Science — M,O
Reading Education — M,O
Secondary Education — M,O
Special Education — M,O

ART ACADEMY OF CINCINNATI
Art Education — M

ASBURY THEOLOGICAL SEMINARY
Religious Education — M,D,O

ASBURY UNIVERSITY
Educational Leadership and Administration — M
English as a Second Language — M
Mathematics Education — M
Reading Education — M
Science Education — M
Social Sciences Education — M
Social Work — M
Special Education — M

ASHLAND THEOLOGICAL SEMINARY
Counselor Education — M,D,O

ASHLAND UNIVERSITY
Business Administration and Management—General — M
Curriculum and Instruction — M
Education of the Gifted — M
Education—General — M,D
Educational Leadership and Administration — M,D
Educational Media/Instructional Technology — M
Exercise and Sports Science — M
Foundations and Philosophy of Education — M
Physical Education — M
Reading Education — M
Special Education — M
Sports Management — M
Student Affairs — M

ASHWORTH COLLEGE
Business Administration and Management—General — M
Human Resources Management — M
International Business — M
Marketing — M

ASPEN UNIVERSITY
Business Administration and Management—General — M,O
Finance and Banking — M,O
Management Information Systems — M,O
Project Management — M,O

ASSUMPTION COLLEGE
Accounting — M,O
Business Administration and Management—General — M,O
Finance and Banking — M,O
Human Resources Management — M,O
International Business — M,O
Marketing — M,O
Nonprofit Management — M,O
Social Work — M,O
Special Education — M,O

ATHABASCA UNIVERSITY
Adult Education — M
Business Administration and Management—General — M,O
Counselor Education — M,O
Distance Education Development — M,O
Education—General — M,O
Organizational Management — M
Project Management — M,O

ATLANTA'S JOHN MARSHALL LAW SCHOOL
Law — M,D

A.T. STILL UNIVERSITY
Athletic Training and Sports Medicine — M,D
Health Education — M,D
Kinesiology and Movement Studies — M,D

AUBURN UNIVERSITY
Accounting — M
Adult Education — M,D,O
Business Administration and Management—General — M,D
Business Education — M,D,O
Curriculum and Instruction — M,D,O
Early Childhood Education — M,D,O
Education—General — M,D,O
Educational Leadership and Administration — M,D,O
Educational Media/Instructional Technology — M,D,O
Educational Psychology — M,D,O
Elementary Education — M,D,O
English Education — M,D,O
Exercise and Sports Science — M,D,O
Finance and Banking — M
Foreign Languages Education — M,D,O
Health Education — M,D,O
Higher Education — M,D,O
Hospitality Management — M,D,O
Human Resources Management — M,D,O
Kinesiology and Movement Studies — M,D,O
Management Information Systems — M,D,O
Mathematics Education — M,D,O
Music Education — M,D,O
Physical Education — M,D,O
Reading Education — M,D,O
Real Estate — M
Science Education — M,D,O
Secondary Education — M,D,O
Social Sciences Education — M,D,O
Special Education — M,D,O

AUBURN UNIVERSITY AT MONTGOMERY
Art Education — M,O
Business Administration and Management—General — M
Counselor Education — M,O
Early Childhood Education — M,O
Education—General — M,O
Educational Leadership and Administration — M,O
Educational Media/Instructional Technology — M,O
Elementary Education — M,O
English Education — M,O
Legal and Justice Studies — M,O
Management Information Systems — M
Mathematics Education — M,O
Nonprofit Management — M,D,O
Organizational Management — M,O
Science Education — M,O
Secondary Education — M,O
Social Sciences Education — M,O
Special Education — M,O

AUGSBURG COLLEGE
Business Administration and Management—General — M
Education—General — M
Organizational Management — M
Social Work — M

AUGUSTANA COLLEGE
Education—General — M
Educational Media/Instructional Technology — M
Reading Education — M
Special Education — M
Sports Management — M

AURORA UNIVERSITY
Business Administration and Management—General — M
Curriculum and Instruction — M,D
Early Childhood Education — M,D
Education—General — M,D
Educational Leadership and Administration — M,D
Educational Media/Instructional Technology — M
Elementary Education — M,D
Mathematics Education — M
Reading Education — M,D
Recreation and Park Management — M
Science Education — M
Social Work — M,D
Special Education — M

AUSTIN COLLEGE
Education—General — M

AUSTIN PEAY STATE UNIVERSITY
Business Administration and Management—General — M
Counselor Education — M
Curriculum and Instruction — M,O
Education—General — M,O
Educational Leadership and Administration — M,O
Elementary Education — M,O
Exercise and Sports Science — M
Health Education — M
Management Strategy and Policy — M
Music Education — M
Reading Education — M
Secondary Education — M,O
Social Work — M
Special Education — M,O

AVE MARIA SCHOOL OF LAW
Law — D

AVERETT UNIVERSITY
Art Education — M
Business Administration and Management—General — M
Curriculum and Instruction — M
Early Childhood Education — M
Education—General — M
Educational Leadership and Administration — M
English Education — M
Mathematics Education — M
Middle School Education — M
Reading Education — M
Science Education — M
Special Education — M

AVILA UNIVERSITY
Accounting — M
Business Administration and Management—General — M
Education—General — M,O
Educational Media/Instructional Technology — M
English as a Second Language — M,O
Finance and Banking — M
Human Resources Management — M
International Business — M
Management Information Systems — M
Marketing — M
Organizational Management — M
Project Management — M

AZUSA PACIFIC UNIVERSITY
Business Administration and Management—General — M
Counselor Education — M
Curriculum and Instruction — M
Education—General — M,D,O
Educational Leadership and Administration — M,D
Educational Media/Instructional Technology — M
English as a Second Language — M
Entrepreneurship — M
Finance and Banking — M

Foundations and Philosophy of Education — M
Higher Education — M,D,O
Human Resources Development — M
Human Resources Management — M
International Business — M
Library Science — M,O
Management Strategy and Policy — M
Marketing — M
Multilingual and Multicultural Education — M
Music Education — M
Nonprofit Management — M
Organizational Management — M
Physical Education — M
Religious Education — M
Social Work — M
Special Education — M
Student Affairs — M

BABSON COLLEGE
Accounting — M
Business Administration and Management—General — M,O
Entrepreneurship — M,O

BAINBRIDGE GRADUATE INSTITUTE
Business Administration and Management—General — M
Organizational Management — M

BAKER COLLEGE CENTER FOR GRADUATE STUDIES - ONLINE
Accounting — M,D
Business Administration and Management—General — M,D
Finance and Banking — M,D
Human Resources Management — M,D
Management Information Systems — M,D
Marketing — M,D

BAKER UNIVERSITY
Business Administration and Management—General — M
Education—General — M,D
Organizational Management — M

BAKKE GRADUATE UNIVERSITY
Business Administration and Management—General — M
Entrepreneurship — M,D
Urban Education — M,D

BALDWIN WALLACE UNIVERSITY
Accounting — M
Business Administration and Management—General — M
Education—General — M
Educational Leadership and Administration — M
Educational Media/Instructional Technology — M
Entrepreneurship — M
Human Resources Management — M
International Business — M
Reading Education — M
Special Education — M
Sustainability Management — M

BALL STATE UNIVERSITY
Accounting — M
Actuarial Science — M
Adult Education — M,D
Advertising and Public Relations — M
Business Administration and Management—General — M
Business Education — M
Curriculum and Instruction — M,O
Education—General — M,D,O
Educational Leadership and Administration — M,D,O
Educational Psychology — M,D,O
Elementary Education — M,D
English as a Second Language — M,D
Exercise and Sports Science — D
Foundations and Philosophy of Education — D
Higher Education — M,D
Mathematics Education — M
Music Education — M
Physical Education — M,D
Science Education — M,D
Secondary Education — M
Special Education — M,D,O
Vocational and Technical Education — M

BANK STREET COLLEGE OF EDUCATION
Early Childhood Education — M
Education—General — M
Educational Leadership and Administration — M
Elementary Education — M
Foundations and Philosophy of Education — M
Mathematics Education — M
Multilingual and Multicultural Education — M
Museum Education — M
Reading Education — M
Special Education — M

BAPTIST BIBLE COLLEGE OF PENNSYLVANIA
Counselor Education — M
Curriculum and Instruction — M
Educational Leadership and Administration — M
English as a Second Language — M
Organizational Management — M,D
Reading Education — M
Religious Education — M,D

BAPTIST THEOLOGICAL SEMINARY AT RICHMOND
Religious Education — M,D,O

BARD COLLEGE
Education—General — M
Sustainability Management — M,O

BARRY UNIVERSITY
Accounting — M
Athletic Training and Sports Medicine — M
Business Administration and Management—General — M,O
Counselor Education — M,D,O
Curriculum and Instruction — D,O
Distance Education Development — O
Early Childhood Education — M,D,O
Education of the Gifted — M
Education—General — M,D,O
Educational Leadership and Administration — M,D,O
Educational Media/Instructional Technology — M,D,O
Elementary Education — M,D,O
English as a Second Language — M,D,O
Exercise and Sports Science — M
Finance and Banking — O
Higher Education — M,D
Human Resources Development — M,D
Human Resources Management — O
International Business — O
Kinesiology and Movement Studies — D
Law — M
Management Information Systems — O,O
Marketing — O
Reading Education — M,D,O
Social Work — M
Special Education — M,D,O
Sports Management — M

BARTON COLLEGE
Elementary Education — M

BARUCH COLLEGE OF THE CITY UNIVERSITY OF NEW YORK
Accounting — M,D
Business Administration and Management—General — M,D,O
Educational Leadership and Administration — M,O
Entrepreneurship — M
Finance and Banking — M,D
Higher Education — M
Human Resources Management — M,D
Industrial and Manufacturing Management — M,D
International Business — M,D
Management Information Systems — M,D
Marketing — M,D
Nonprofit Management — M
Organizational Behavior — M
Quantitative Analysis — M
Real Estate — M
Sustainability Management — M,D
Taxation — M

BAYAMÓN CENTRAL UNIVERSITY
Accounting — M
Business Administration and Management—General — M
Counselor Education — M,O
Early Childhood Education — M,O
Education—General — M,O
Educational Leadership and Administration — M,O
Elementary Education — M,O
Finance and Banking — M
Marketing — M
Special Education — M,O

BAYLOR UNIVERSITY
Accounting — M
Business Administration and Management—General — M,D
Curriculum and Instruction — M,D
Education—General — M,D,O
Educational Leadership and Administration — M,O
Educational Measurement and Evaluation — M,D,O
Educational Psychology — M,D,O
Environmental Law — D
Exercise and Sports Science — M,D
Health Education — M,D
Health Law — D
Intellectual Property Law — D
Kinesiology and Movement Studies — M,D
Law — D
Management Information Systems — M,D
Physical Education — M,D
Real Estate — D
Social Work — M,D
Special Education — M,D,O
Sports Management — M,D

BAY PATH COLLEGE
Educational Leadership and Administration — M
Educational Media/Instructional Technology — M
Entrepreneurship — M
Higher Education — M
Management Information Systems — M
Nonprofit Management — M
Special Education — M,O

BELHAVEN UNIVERSITY (MS)
Business Administration and Management—General — M
Education—General — M
Educational Media/Instructional Technology — M
Elementary Education — M
Human Resources Management — M
Multilingual and Multicultural Education — M

Reading Education — M
Secondary Education — M
Sports Management — M

BELLARMINE UNIVERSITY
Business Administration and Management—General — M
Education—General — M,D,O
Educational Leadership and Administration — M,D,O
Elementary Education — M
Management Information Systems — M
Middle School Education — M,D,O
Reading Education — M,D,O
Secondary Education — M
Special Education — M,D,O

BELLEVUE UNIVERSITY
Business Administration and Management—General — M,D
Counselor Education — M
Educational Media/Instructional Technology — M
Finance and Banking — M,D
Human Resources Management — M,D
Human Services — M
Management Information Systems — M
Organizational Management — M
Project Management — M

BELMONT UNIVERSITY
Accounting — M
Business Administration and Management—General — M
Curriculum and Instruction — M
Education—General — M
Law — D
Music Education — M
Special Education — M
Sports Management — M

BEMIDJI STATE UNIVERSITY
Education—General — M
Mathematics Education — M
Special Education — M

BENEDICTINE COLLEGE
Business Administration and Management—General — M
Educational Leadership and Administration — M

BENEDICTINE UNIVERSITY
Accounting — M
Business Administration and Management—General — M
Curriculum and Instruction — M
Education—General — M
Educational Leadership and Administration — M,D
Elementary Education — M
Entrepreneurship — M
Exercise and Sports Science — M
Finance and Banking — M
Health Education — M
Higher Education — D
Human Resources Management — M
International Business — M
Logistics — M
Management Information Systems — M
Marketing — M
Organizational Behavior — M
Organizational Management — M,D
Reading Education — M
Science Education — M
Secondary Education — M
Special Education — M

BENEDICTINE UNIVERSITY AT SPRINGFIELD
Business Administration and Management—General — M
Elementary Education — M
Organizational Behavior — M
Organizational Management — M,D
Reading Education — M

BENNINGTON COLLEGE
Education—General — M
Foreign Languages Education — M
Multilingual and Multicultural Education — M

BENTLEY UNIVERSITY
Accounting — M,D
Business Administration and Management—General — M,D,O
Finance and Banking — M
Management Strategy and Policy — O
Marketing — M
Taxation — M

BERKLEE COLLEGE OF MUSIC
Entertainment Management — M

BERRY COLLEGE
Business Administration and Management—General — M
Curriculum and Instruction — O
Early Childhood Education — M
Education—General — M,O
Educational Leadership and Administration — O
Middle School Education — M
Reading Education — M
Secondary Education — M

BETHANY COLLEGE
Education—General — M

BETHEL COLLEGE
Business Administration and Management—General — M
Education—General — M

BETHEL UNIVERSITY (MN)
Business Administration and Management—General — M
Education—General — M,D,O
Educational Leadership and Administration — M,D,O
Elementary Education — M
Higher Education — M,D,O
Organizational Management — M,D,O
Reading Education — M,D,O
Secondary Education — M,D,O
Special Education — M,D,O

BETHEL UNIVERSITY (TN)
Business Administration and Management—General — M
Educational Leadership and Administration — M

BINGHAMTON UNIVERSITY, STATE UNIVERSITY OF NEW YORK
Accounting — M
Business Administration and Management—General — M,D
Early Childhood Education — M
Education—General — M,D,O
Educational Leadership and Administration — M,D,O
English Education — M
Finance and Banking — M
Foreign Languages Education — M
Foundations and Philosophy of Education — M,D,O
Legal and Justice Studies — M,D
Mathematics Education — M
Reading Education — M
Science Education — M
Secondary Education — M
Social Sciences Education — M
Social Work — M
Special Education — M
Student Affairs — M

BIOLA UNIVERSITY
Business Administration and Management—General — M
Curriculum and Instruction — M,O
Early Childhood Education — M,O
Education—General — M,O
English as a Second Language — M,D,O
Multilingual and Multicultural Education — M,O
Religious Education — M,O
Science Education — M
Special Education — M,O

BISHOP'S UNIVERSITY
Education—General — M,O
English as a Second Language — M,O

BLACK HILLS STATE UNIVERSITY
Business Administration and Management—General — M
Curriculum and Instruction — M
Management Strategy and Policy — M

BLOOMFIELD COLLEGE
Accounting — M

BLOOMSBURG UNIVERSITY OF PENNSYLVANIA
Accounting — M
Athletic Training and Sports Medicine — M
Business Administration and Management—General — M
Business Education — M
Counselor Education — M
Curriculum and Instruction — M,O
Early Childhood Education — M
Education—General — M,O
Educational Media/Instructional Technology — M,O
Elementary Education — M
English Education — M
Exercise and Sports Science — M
Mathematics Education — M
Middle School Education — M
Reading Education — M
Science Education — M
Secondary Education — M
Social Sciences Education — M
Special Education — M,O
Student Affairs — M
Urban Education — M

BLUE MOUNTAIN COLLEGE
Elementary Education — M
Reading Education — M

BLUFFTON UNIVERSITY
Business Administration and Management—General — M
Education—General — M
Organizational Management — M

BOB JONES UNIVERSITY
Accounting — M,D,O
Business Administration and Management—General — M,D,O
Counselor Education — M,D,O
Curriculum and Instruction — M,D,O
Educational Leadership and Administration — M,D,O
Elementary Education — M,D,O
English Education — M,D,O
Mathematics Education — M,D,O
Music Education — M,D,O
Secondary Education — M,D,O
Social Sciences Education — M,D,O
Special Education — M,D,O
Student Affairs — M,D,O

BOISE STATE UNIVERSITY
Accounting — M
Art Education — M
Business Administration and Management—General — M
Curriculum and Instruction — M,D
Early Childhood Education — M
Education—General — M,D,O
Educational Leadership and Administration — M,D
Educational Media/Instructional Technology — M,D,O
Exercise and Sports Science — M
Kinesiology and Movement Studies — M
Mathematics Education — M
Music Education — M
Physical Education — M
Reading Education — M
Science Education — M,D
Social Work — M
Special Education — M
Taxation — M

BORICUA COLLEGE
English as a Second Language — M
Human Services — M

BOSTON COLLEGE
Accounting — M
Business Administration and Management—General — M
Counselor Education — M,D
Curriculum and Instruction — M,D,O
Education—General — M,D,O
Educational Leadership and Administration — M,D,O
Educational Measurement and Evaluation — M,D
Educational Psychology — M,D
Elementary Education — M
Finance and Banking — M,D
Higher Education — M
Law — D
Organizational Behavior — D
Organizational Management — D
Reading Education — M,O
Religious Education — M
Science Education — M,D
Secondary Education — M
Social Work — M,D
Special Education — M

THE BOSTON CONSERVATORY
Music Education — M,O

BOSTON UNIVERSITY
Actuarial Science — M
Advertising and Public Relations — M
Art Education — M
Athletic Training and Sports Medicine — D
Business Administration and Management—General — M,D
Education—General — M,D,O
Electronic Commerce — M
Finance and Banking — M,D
Health Law — M,D
Intellectual Property Law — M,D
International Business — M,D
Investment Management — M
Law — M,D
Legal and Justice Studies — M
Management Information Systems — M,O
Management Strategy and Policy — M,O
Music Education — M,D
Organizational Management — M
Project Management — M,O
Social Work — M,D
Taxation — M,D
Travel and Tourism — M

BOWIE STATE UNIVERSITY
Business Administration and Management—General — M
Counselor Education — M
Education—General — M
Educational Leadership and Administration — M,D
Elementary Education — M
Human Resources Development — M
Management Information Systems — M,O
Reading Education — M
Secondary Education — M
Special Education — M

BOWLING GREEN STATE UNIVERSITY
Accounting — M
Art Education — M
Business Administration and Management—General — M
Business Education — M
Counselor Education — M
Curriculum and Instruction — M
Early Childhood Education — M
Education of the Gifted — M
Educational Leadership and Administration — M,D,O
Educational Media/Instructional Technology — M
Foreign Languages Education — M
Higher Education — D
International and Comparative Education — M
Kinesiology and Movement Studies — M
Leisure Studies — M
Mathematics Education — M,D
Music Education — M,D
Organizational Management — M,O
Reading Education — M
Recreation and Park Management — M
Science Education — M
Special Education — M
Sports Management — M

---

*M—masters degree; D—doctorate; O—other advanced degree; *—Close-Up and/or Display*

Student Affairs — M
Vocational and Technical Education — M

BRADLEY UNIVERSITY
Accounting — M
Business Administration and Management—General — M
Counselor Education — M
Curriculum and Instruction — M,O
Education—General — M,D,O
Educational Leadership and Administration — M

BRANDEIS UNIVERSITY
Business Administration and Management—General — M
Distance Education Development — M
Elementary Education — M
Finance and Banking — M
Health Education — D
Human Services — M
International Business — M,D
Management Information Systems — M
Management Strategy and Policy — M
Marketing — M,D
Nonprofit Management — M
Project Management — M
Real Estate — M,D
Religious Education — M
Secondary Education — M
Sustainability Management — M,D

BRANDMAN UNIVERSITY
Business Administration and Management—General — M
Counselor Education — M
Education—General — M
Educational Leadership and Administration — M
Human Resources Management — M
Organizational Management — M
Special Education — M

BRANDON UNIVERSITY
Counselor Education — M,O
Curriculum and Instruction — M,O
Education—General — M,O
Educational Leadership and Administration — M,O
Music Education — M
Special Education — M,O

BRENAU UNIVERSITY
Accounting — M
Business Administration and Management—General — M
Early Childhood Education — M,O
Education—General — M,O
Middle School Education — M,O
Organizational Management — M
Project Management — M
Secondary Education — M,O
Special Education — M,O

BRESCIA UNIVERSITY
Business Administration and Management—General — M
Curriculum and Instruction — M

BRIAR CLIFF UNIVERSITY
Human Resources Management — M

BRIDGEWATER STATE UNIVERSITY
Accounting — M
Art Education — M
Business Administration and Management—General — M,O
Counselor Education — M,O
Early Childhood Education — M
Education—General — M,O
Educational Leadership and Administration — M,O
Educational Media/Instructional Technology — M
Elementary Education — M
Finance and Banking — M
Mathematics Education — M
Physical Education — M
Reading Education — M,O
Science Education — M
Secondary Education — M
Social Sciences Education — M
Social Work — M
Special Education — M

BRIERCREST SEMINARY
Business Administration and Management—General — M
Organizational Management — M

BRIGHAM YOUNG UNIVERSITY
Accounting — M
Art Education — M
Athletic Training and Sports Medicine — M,D
Business Administration and Management—General — M
Education—General — M,D,O
Educational Leadership and Administration — M,D
Educational Media/Instructional Technology — M,D
Educational Psychology — M,D
English as a Second Language — M
Exercise and Sports Science — M,D
Finance and Banking — M
Foreign Languages Education — M
Foundations and Philosophy of Education — M,D
Health Education — M
Human Resources Management — M
Law — M,D
Management Information Systems — M
Mathematics Education — M
Music Education — M
Nonprofit Management — M
Physical Education — M
Reading Education — M

Recreation and Park Management — M
Religious Education — M
Science Education — M
Social Work — M
Special Education — M,D,O

BROADVIEW UNIVERSITY–WEST JORDAN
Business Administration and Management—General — M
Management Information Systems — M

BROCK UNIVERSITY
Accounting — M
Business Administration and Management—General — M
Education—General — M,D
English as a Second Language — M
Legal and Justice Studies — M

BROOKLYN COLLEGE OF THE CITY UNIVERSITY OF NEW YORK
Accounting — M
Art Education — M,O
Counselor Education — M,O
Early Childhood Education — M,O
Education—General — M,O
Educational Leadership and Administration — M
Elementary Education — M
English Education — M,O
Environmental Education — M
Exercise and Sports Science — M
Finance and Banking — M
Foreign Languages Education — M,O
Health Education — M,O
International Business — M
Mathematics Education — M,O
Middle School Education — M
Multilingual and Multicultural Education — M
Music Education — M,D,O
Organizational Behavior — M
Physical Education — M,O
Science Education — M,O
Secondary Education — M,O
Social Sciences Education — M,O
Special Education — M
Sports Management — M

BROOKLYN LAW SCHOOL
Law — M,D

BROWN UNIVERSITY
Education—General — M
Elementary Education — M
English as a Second Language — M,D
English Education — M
Multilingual and Multicultural Education — M,D
Science Education — M
Secondary Education — M
Social Sciences Education — M
Urban Education — M

BRYAN COLLEGE
Business Administration and Management—General — M

BRYANT UNIVERSITY
Accounting — M
Business Administration and Management—General — M
Finance and Banking — M
International Business — M
Supply Chain Management — M
Taxation — M

BRYN MAWR COLLEGE
Social Work — M,D

BUCKNELL UNIVERSITY
Education—General — M
Student Affairs — M

BUENA VISTA UNIVERSITY
Counselor Education — M
Curriculum and Instruction — M
Education—General — M
English as a Second Language — M

BUFFALO STATE COLLEGE, STATE UNIVERSITY OF NEW YORK
Adult Education — M,O
Art Education — M
Business Education — M
Early Childhood Education — M
Educational Leadership and Administration — O
Educational Media/Instructional Technology — M
Elementary Education — M
English Education — M
Human Resources Management — M,O
Mathematics Education — M
Multilingual and Multicultural Education — M
Reading Education — M
Science Education — M
Social Sciences Education — M
Special Education — M
Student Affairs — M
Vocational and Technical Education — M

BUTLER UNIVERSITY
Accounting — M
Business Administration and Management—General — M
Counselor Education — M
Education—General — M
Educational Leadership and Administration — M
Music Education — M

CABRINI COLLEGE
Accounting — M
Education—General — M
Organizational Management — M

CAIRN UNIVERSITY
Business Administration and Management—General — M,O
Education—General — M
Educational Leadership and Administration — M,O
Organizational Management — M,O

CALDWELL UNIVERSITY
Accounting — M
Business Administration and Management—General — M,O
Counselor Education — M,O
Curriculum and Instruction — M,O
Education—General — M,O
Educational Leadership and Administration — M,O
Reading Education — M,O
Special Education — M,O

CALIFORNIA BAPTIST UNIVERSITY
Accounting — M
Adult Education — M
Advertising and Public Relations — M
Athletic Training and Sports Medicine — M
Business Administration and Management—General — M
Counselor Education — M
Curriculum and Instruction — M
Education—General — M
Educational Leadership and Administration — M
Educational Media/Instructional Technology — M
English as a Second Language — M
English Education — M
Entrepreneurship — M
Exercise and Sports Science — M
International and Comparative Education — M
Music Education — M
Organizational Management — M
Physical Education — M
Reading Education — M
Science Education — M
Special Education — M
Sports Management — M
Vocational and Technical Education — M

CALIFORNIA COAST UNIVERSITY
Business Administration and Management—General — M
Curriculum and Instruction — M,D
Education—General — M,D
Educational Leadership and Administration — M,D
Educational Psychology — M
Human Resources Management — M
Marketing — M
Organizational Management — M,D

CALIFORNIA COLLEGE OF THE ARTS
Finance and Banking — M
Organizational Management — M

CALIFORNIA INTERCONTINENTAL UNIVERSITY
Business Administration and Management—General — M,D
Entertainment Management — M
Entrepreneurship — M,D
Finance and Banking — M,D
Human Resources Management — M,D
International Business — M
Management Information Systems — M,D
Marketing — M,D
Organizational Management — M,D
Project Management — M,D
Quality Management — M,D

CALIFORNIA INTERNATIONAL BUSINESS UNIVERSITY
Business Administration and Management—General — M,D

CALIFORNIA LUTHERAN UNIVERSITY
Business Administration and Management—General — M,O
Counselor Education — M,D
Education—General — M,D
Educational Leadership and Administration — M,D
Elementary Education — M,D
Entrepreneurship — M,O
Finance and Banking — M,O
Higher Education — M,D
International Business — M,O
Management Information Systems — M,O
Marketing — M,O
Middle School Education — M,D
Nonprofit Management — M,O
Organizational Behavior — M,O
Special Education — M

CALIFORNIA MARITIME ACADEMY
Transportation Management — M

CALIFORNIA MIRAMAR UNIVERSITY
Business Administration and Management—General — M
Management Strategy and Policy — M
Taxation — M

CALIFORNIA NATIONAL UNIVERSITY FOR ADVANCED STUDIES
Business Administration and Management—General — M

CALIFORNIA POLYTECHNIC STATE UNIVERSITY, SAN LUIS OBISPO
Agricultural Education — M
Business Administration and Management—General — M
Education—General — M
Industrial and Manufacturing Management — M

Kinesiology and Movement Studies — M
Taxation — M

CALIFORNIA STATE POLYTECHNIC UNIVERSITY, POMONA
Accounting — M
Business Administration and Management—General — M
Curriculum and Instruction — M
Education—General — M,D
Educational Leadership and Administration — M,D
Educational Media/Instructional Technology — M
Hospitality Management — M
Kinesiology and Movement Studies — M
Management Information Systems — M
Special Education — M

CALIFORNIA STATE UNIVERSITY, BAKERSFIELD
Business Administration and Management—General — M
Counselor Education — M
Curriculum and Instruction — M
Education—General — M
Educational Leadership and Administration — M
Mathematics Education — M
Middle School Education — M
Science Education — M
Secondary Education — M
Social Work — M
Special Education — M
Student Affairs — M

CALIFORNIA STATE UNIVERSITY CHANNEL ISLANDS
Business Administration and Management—General — M

CALIFORNIA STATE UNIVERSITY, CHICO
Business Administration and Management—General — M
Curriculum and Instruction — M
Educational Leadership and Administration — M
English as a Second Language — M
Foreign Languages Education — M
Kinesiology and Movement Studies — M
Mathematics Education — M
Recreation and Park Management — M
Social Sciences Education — M
Social Work — M
Special Education — M

CALIFORNIA STATE UNIVERSITY, DOMINGUEZ HILLS
Business Administration and Management—General — M
Computer Education — M,O
Counselor Education — M
Curriculum and Instruction — M
Education—General — M,O
Educational Leadership and Administration — M
Educational Media/Instructional Technology — M,O
English as a Second Language — M,O
International and Comparative Education — M
Mathematics Education — M
Multilingual and Multicultural Education — M
Physical Education — M
Quality Management — M
Science Education — M
Social Work — M
Special Education — M

CALIFORNIA STATE UNIVERSITY, EAST BAY
Accounting — M
Actuarial Science — M
Business Administration and Management—General — M
Counselor Education — M
Early Childhood Education — M
Education—General — M
Educational Leadership and Administration — M,D
Educational Media/Instructional Technology — M
English as a Second Language — M
Entrepreneurship — M
Finance and Banking — M
Human Resources Management — M
Industrial and Manufacturing Management — M
International Business — M
Management Information Systems — M
Management Strategy and Policy — M
Marketing — M
Mathematics Education — M
Organizational Management — M
Physical Education — M
Reading Education — M
Recreation and Park Management — M
Social Sciences Education — M
Social Work — M
Special Education — M
Supply Chain Management — M
Taxation — M
Travel and Tourism — M
Urban Education — M,D

CALIFORNIA STATE UNIVERSITY, FRESNO
Accounting — M
Business Administration and Management—General — M
Counselor Education — M
Curriculum and Instruction — M
Early Childhood Education — M
Education—General — M,D

Educational Leadership and Administration	M,D
English as a Second Language	M
Exercise and Sports Science	M
Kinesiology and Movement Studies	M
Mathematics Education	M
Music Education	M
Reading Education	M
Social Sciences Education	M
Social Work	M
Special Education	M

CALIFORNIA STATE UNIVERSITY, FULLERTON

Accounting	M
Advertising and Public Relations	M
Business Administration and Management—General	M
Community College Education	M,D
Counselor Education	M
Educational Leadership and Administration	M,D
Educational Media/Instructional Technology	M
Electronic Commerce	M
Elementary Education	M
English as a Second Language	M
Entertainment Management	M
Entrepreneurship	M
Finance and Banking	M
Higher Education	M,D
Insurance	M
International Business	M
Management Information Systems	M
Marketing	M
Mathematics Education	M
Multilingual and Multicultural Education	M
Music Education	M
Organizational Management	M
Physical Education	M
Reading Education	M
Science Education	M
Secondary Education	M
Social Work	M
Special Education	M
Taxation	M
Travel and Tourism	M

CALIFORNIA STATE UNIVERSITY, LONG BEACH

Art Education	M
Athletic Training and Sports Medicine	M
Business Administration and Management—General	M
Counselor Education	M
Education—General	M,D
Educational Leadership and Administration	M,D
Educational Psychology	M
Elementary Education	M
English as a Second Language	M
Exercise and Sports Science	M
Health Education	M
Higher Education	M
Hospitality Management	M
Kinesiology and Movement Studies	M
Leisure Studies	M
Logistics	M
Mathematics Education	M
Physical Education	M
Recreation and Park Management	M
Science Education	M
Secondary Education	M
Social Work	M
Special Education	M
Sports Management	M
Student Affairs	M

CALIFORNIA STATE UNIVERSITY, LOS ANGELES

Accounting	M
Art Education	M
Business Administration and Management—General	M
Counselor Education	M,D
Education—General	M,D
Elementary Education	M
Finance and Banking	M
Health Education	M
International Business	M
Kinesiology and Movement Studies	M
Management Information Systems	M
Marketing	M
Music Education	M
Physical Education	M
Reading Education	M
Secondary Education	M
Social Work	M
Special Education	M,D
Taxation	M

CALIFORNIA STATE UNIVERSITY, MONTEREY BAY

Business Administration and Management—General	M
Education—General	M
Educational Media/Instructional Technology	M
Management Information Systems	M
Social Work	M

CALIFORNIA STATE UNIVERSITY, NORTHRIDGE

Art Education	M
Business Administration and Management—General	M
Counselor Education	M
Curriculum and Instruction	M
Early Childhood Education	M
Education—General	M,D
Educational Leadership and Administration	M,D
Educational Media/Instructional Technology	M
Educational Psychology	M
Elementary Education	M
English Education	M
Entertainment Management	M,O
Health Education	M,O
Hospitality Management	M,O
Kinesiology and Movement Studies	M
Mathematics Education	M
Multilingual and Multicultural Education	M
Music Education	M
Nonprofit Management	O
Reading Education	M
Recreation and Park Management	M,O
Science Education	M
Secondary Education	M
Social Work	M,O
Special Education	M
Taxation	M,O
Travel and Tourism	M

CALIFORNIA STATE UNIVERSITY, SACRAMENTO

Accounting	M
Business Administration and Management—General	M
Community College Education	M
Counselor Education	M
Curriculum and Instruction	M
Education—General	M
Educational Leadership and Administration	M
Educational Media/Instructional Technology	M
English as a Second Language	M
Foreign Languages Education	M
Higher Education	M
Human Resources Development	M
Human Resources Management	M
Human Services	M
Multilingual and Multicultural Education	M
Physical Education	M
Reading Education	M
Real Estate	M
Recreation and Park Management	M
Social Work	M
Special Education	M
Student Affairs	M
Vocational and Technical Education	M

CALIFORNIA STATE UNIVERSITY, SAN BERNARDINO

Accounting	M
Business Administration and Management—General	M
Counselor Education	M
Curriculum and Instruction	M
Education—General	M,D
Educational Leadership and Administration	M,D
Educational Media/Instructional Technology	M
English as a Second Language	M,D
English Education	M,D
Entrepreneurship	M
Finance and Banking	M
Health Education	M
Management Information Systems	M
Marketing	M
Mathematics Education	M
Multilingual and Multicultural Education	M
Reading Education	M
Science Education	M
Secondary Education	M,D
Social Sciences Education	M,D
Social Work	M
Special Education	M
Supply Chain Management	M
Vocational and Technical Education	M

CALIFORNIA STATE UNIVERSITY, SAN MARCOS

Business Administration and Management—General	M
Education—General	M,D
Educational Leadership and Administration	M,D
Reading Education	M,D
Special Education	M,D

CALIFORNIA STATE UNIVERSITY, STANISLAUS

Business Administration and Management—General	M
Community College Education	D
Counselor Education	M
Curriculum and Instruction	M
Education—General	M,D,O
Educational Leadership and Administration	M,D
Educational Media/Instructional Technology	M
Elementary Education	M
English as a Second Language	M,O
Multilingual and Multicultural Education	M
Physical Education	M
Reading Education	M
Secondary Education	M
Social Work	M
Special Education	M

CALIFORNIA UNIVERSITY OF MANAGEMENT AND SCIENCES

Business Administration and Management—General	M,D
International Business	M,D
Management Information Systems	M,D
Sports Management	M,D

CALIFORNIA UNIVERSITY OF PENNSYLVANIA

Athletic Training and Sports Medicine	M
Business Administration and Management—General	M
Counselor Education	M
Education—General	M
Educational Leadership and Administration	M
Elementary Education	M
Exercise and Sports Science	M
Legal and Justice Studies	M
Reading Education	M
Secondary Education	M
Social Work	M
Special Education	M
Sports Management	M
Vocational and Technical Education	M

CALIFORNIA WESTERN SCHOOL OF LAW

Accounting	M,D
Law	M,D

CALUMET COLLEGE OF SAINT JOSEPH

Educational Leadership and Administration	M
Quality Management	M

CALVIN COLLEGE

Curriculum and Instruction	M
Education—General	M
Educational Leadership and Administration	M
Reading Education	M
Special Education	M

CALVIN THEOLOGICAL SEMINARY

Religious Education	M,D

CAMBRIDGE COLLEGE

Business Administration and Management—General	M
Counselor Education	M,D,O
Curriculum and Instruction	M,D,O
Early Childhood Education	M,D,O
Education—General	M,D,O
Educational Leadership and Administration	M,D,O
Educational Measurement and Evaluation	M,D,O
Educational Media/Instructional Technology	M,D,O
Elementary Education	M,D,O
English as a Second Language	M,D,O
Entrepreneurship	M
Health Education	M,D,O
Home Economics Education	M,D,O
Mathematics Education	M,D,O
Middle School Education	M,D,O
Nonprofit Management	M
Organizational Management	M
Reading Education	M,D,O
Science Education	M,D,O
Social Sciences Education	M,D,O
Special Education	M,D,O

CAMERON UNIVERSITY

Business Administration and Management—General	M
Education—General	M
Educational Leadership and Administration	M
Entrepreneurship	M

CAMPBELLSVILLE UNIVERSITY

Business Administration and Management—General	M
Counselor Education	M
Curriculum and Instruction	M
Education—General	M
Music Education	M
Organizational Management	M
Social Work	M
Special Education	M

CAMPBELL UNIVERSITY

Business Administration and Management—General	M
Counselor Education	M
Education—General	M
Educational Leadership and Administration	M
Elementary Education	M
English Education	M
Law	D
Mathematics Education	M
Middle School Education	M
Physical Education	M
Religious Education	M,D
Secondary Education	M
Social Sciences Education	M

CANISIUS COLLEGE

Accounting	M
Business Administration and Management—General	M
Business Education	M,O
Counselor Education	M
Early Childhood Education	M
Education of the Gifted	M,O
Education—General	M,O
Educational Leadership and Administration	M,O
Educational Media/Instructional Technology	M,O
Elementary Education	M,O
English as a Second Language	M,O
International Business	M
Kinesiology and Movement Studies	M
Middle School Education	M
Physical Education	M,O
Reading Education	M,O
Secondary Education	M,O
Special Education	M,O
Sports Management	M
Student Affairs	M,O

CAPE BRETON UNIVERSITY

Business Administration and Management—General	M

CAPELLA UNIVERSITY

Accounting	M,D
Adult Education	M,D
Business Administration and Management—General	M,D
Business Education	D
Counselor Education	M,D
Curriculum and Instruction	M,D
Distance Education Development	M,D
Early Childhood Education	M
Education—General	M,D
Educational Leadership and Administration	M,D
Educational Media/Instructional Technology	M,D
Educational Psychology	M,D
Elementary Education	M,D
Entrepreneurship	M,D
Finance and Banking	M,D
Higher Education	M,D
Human Resources Management	M,D
Human Services	M,D
Management Information Systems	M,D
Management Strategy and Policy	M,D
Marketing	M,D
Middle School Education	M,D
Nonprofit Management	D
Organizational Management	M,D
Project Management	M,D
Reading Education	M,D
Social Work	D
Special Education	M,D
Supply Chain Management	M,D
Vocational and Technical Education	D

CAPITAL UNIVERSITY

Business Administration and Management—General	M
Entrepreneurship	M
Finance and Banking	M
Law	M,D
Legal and Justice Studies	M
Marketing	M
Music Education	M
Taxation	M

CAPITOL COLLEGE

Business Administration and Management—General	M
Management Information Systems	M

CARDINAL STRITCH UNIVERSITY

Business Administration and Management—General	M
Computer Education	M
Education—General	M,D
Educational Leadership and Administration	M,D
Educational Media/Instructional Technology	M
English as a Second Language	M
Reading Education	M
Special Education	M
Sports Management	M
Urban Education	M

CARIBBEAN UNIVERSITY

Curriculum and Instruction	M,D
Early Childhood Education	M,D
Education—General	M,D
Educational Leadership and Administration	M,D
Educational Media/Instructional Technology	M,D
Elementary Education	M,D
English Education	M,D
Foreign Languages Education	M,D
Human Resources Management	M,D
Mathematics Education	M,D
Physical Education	M,D
Science Education	M,D
Social Sciences Education	M,D
Special Education	M,D

CARLETON UNIVERSITY

Business Administration and Management—General	M,D
Legal and Justice Studies	M,O
Social Work	M

CARLOS ALBIZU UNIVERSITY, MIAMI CAMPUS

Business Administration and Management—General	M,D
Education of the Gifted	M,D
English as a Second Language	M,D
Entrepreneurship	M,D
Human Services	M,D
Nonprofit Management	M,D
Organizational Management	M,D
Special Education	M,D

CARLOW UNIVERSITY

Art Education	M
Business Administration and Management—General	M
Counselor Education	M,O
Early Childhood Education	M,O
Education—General	M
International Business	M
Organizational Management	M,D,O

*M—masters degree; D—doctorate; O—other advanced degree; *—Close-Up and/or Display*

Project Management	M
Secondary Education	M
Special Education	M

CARNEGIE MELLON UNIVERSITY

Accounting	D
Business Administration and Management—General	M,D
Education—General	M,D
Electronic Commerce	M
Entertainment Management	M
Entrepreneurship	D
Finance and Banking	D
Industrial and Manufacturing Management	M,D
Management Information Systems	M,D
Marketing	D
Music Education	M
Organizational Behavior	D

CAROLINA CHRISTIAN COLLEGE

Religious Education	M

CARROLL UNIVERSITY

Business Administration and Management—General	M
Education—General	M

CARSON-NEWMAN UNIVERSITY

Business Administration and Management—General	M
Counselor Education	M
Curriculum and Instruction	M
Education—General	M
Educational Leadership and Administration	M
Elementary Education	M
English as a Second Language	M
Secondary Education	M

CARTHAGE COLLEGE

Art Education	M,O
Counselor Education	M,O
Education of the Gifted	M,O
Education—General	M,O
Educational Leadership and Administration	M,O
English Education	M,O
Reading Education	M,O
Science Education	M,O
Social Sciences Education	M,O

CASE WESTERN RESERVE UNIVERSITY

Accounting	M,D
Art Education	M
Business Administration and Management—General	M,D
Finance and Banking	M,D
Human Resources Management	M
Industrial and Manufacturing Management	M,D
Intellectual Property Law	M,D
Law	M,D
Legal and Justice Studies	M,D
Logistics	M,D
Management Information Systems	M,D
Management Strategy and Policy	M
Marketing	M,D
Music Education	M,D
Nonprofit Management	M,D,O
Organizational Behavior	M,D
Quality Management	M,D
Social Work	M,D
Supply Chain Management	M

CASTLETON STATE COLLEGE

Curriculum and Instruction	M
Education—General	M,O
Educational Leadership and Administration	M,O
Reading Education	M,O
Special Education	M,O

CATAWBA COLLEGE

Education—General	M
Elementary Education	M

THE CATHOLIC UNIVERSITY OF AMERICA

Accounting	M
Business Administration and Management—General	M
Education—General	M,D,O
Educational Leadership and Administration	M,D,O
Educational Policy	M,D,O
Educational Psychology	M,D,O
Human Resources Management	M
Information Studies	M
Law	D
Legal and Justice Studies	D,O
Library Science	M
Secondary Education	M,D,O
Social Work	M,D
Special Education	M,D,O

CEDAR CREST COLLEGE

Education—General	M

CEDARVILLE UNIVERSITY

Business Administration and Management—General	M,D
Curriculum and Instruction	M,D
Education—General	M,D
Educational Leadership and Administration	M,D

CENTENARY COLLEGE

Accounting	M
Business Administration and Management—General	M
Education—General	M
Educational Leadership and Administration	M
Special Education	M

CENTENARY COLLEGE OF LOUISIANA

Business Administration and Management—General	M
Curriculum and Instruction	M
Education—General	M
Educational Leadership and Administration	M
Elementary Education	M
Secondary Education	M

CENTRAL CONNECTICUT STATE UNIVERSITY

Actuarial Science	M,O
Advertising and Public Relations	M,O
Art Education	M,O
Counselor Education	M,O
Early Childhood Education	M
Education—General	M,D,O
Educational Leadership and Administration	M,D,O
Educational Media/Instructional Technology	M
Elementary Education	M,O
English as a Second Language	M,O
Exercise and Sports Science	M,O
Foreign Languages Education	M,O
Foundations and Philosophy of Education	M
Industrial and Manufacturing Management	M,O
Information Studies	M
Logistics	M,O
Music Education	M,O
Physical Education	M,O
Reading Education	M,O
Science Education	M,O
Secondary Education	M
Special Education	M,O
Supply Chain Management	M,O
Vocational and Technical Education	M,O

CENTRAL EUROPEAN UNIVERSITY

Business Administration and Management—General	M
Finance and Banking	M
International Business	M,D
Law	M,D
Legal and Justice Studies	M,D
Management Information Systems	M
Marketing	M

CENTRAL METHODIST UNIVERSITY

Counselor Education	M
Education—General	M
Music Education	M

CENTRAL MICHIGAN UNIVERSITY

Accounting	M,O
Business Administration and Management—General	M,O
Community College Education	M,O
Counselor Education	M
Curriculum and Instruction	M,D,O
Early Childhood Education	M,D,O
Education—General	M,D,O
Educational Leadership and Administration	M,D,O
Educational Media/Instructional Technology	M,D,O
Elementary Education	M,D
English as a Second Language	M,O
Exercise and Sports Science	M,D
Finance and Banking	M
Higher Education	M,D,O
Human Resources Management	M
Industrial and Manufacturing Management	M
International Business	M,O
Logistics	M,O
Management Information Systems	M,O
Marketing	M,O
Mathematics Education	M,D
Music Education	M
Nonprofit Management	M,O
Reading Education	M,O
Recreation and Park Management	M,O
Science Education	M,O
Secondary Education	M,O
Special Education	M,O
Sports Management	M,O
Student Affairs	M,D,O

CENTRAL PENN COLLEGE

Management Information Systems	M
Organizational Management	M

CENTRAL WASHINGTON UNIVERSITY

Accounting	M
Counselor Education	M
Curriculum and Instruction	M
Education—General	M
Educational Leadership and Administration	M
English as a Second Language	M
Exercise and Sports Science	M
Foundations and Philosophy of Education	M
Health Education	M
Home Economics Education	M
Physical Education	M
Reading Education	M
Special Education	M
Sports Management	M
Vocational and Technical Education	M

CHADRON STATE COLLEGE

Business Administration and Management—General	M,O
Business Education	M,O
Counselor Education	M,O
Education—General	M,O
Educational Leadership and Administration	M,O
Elementary Education	M,O
English Education	M,O
Secondary Education	M,O
Social Sciences Education	M,O

CHAMINADE UNIVERSITY OF HONOLULU

Accounting	M
Business Administration and Management—General	M
Early Childhood Education	M
Education—General	M
Educational Leadership and Administration	M
Elementary Education	M
English Education	M
Mathematics Education	M
Nonprofit Management	M
Science Education	M
Secondary Education	M
Social Sciences Education	M
Special Education	M

CHAMPLAIN COLLEGE

Business Administration and Management—General	M
Early Childhood Education	M
Law	M

CHAPMAN UNIVERSITY

Business Administration and Management—General	M
Counselor Education	M,D,O
Curriculum and Instruction	M,D,O
Education—General	M,D,O
Educational Leadership and Administration	M,D,O
Educational Psychology	M,D,O
Elementary Education	M,D,O
Environmental Law	M,D
Law	M,D
Secondary Education	M,D,O
Special Education	M,D,O
Taxation	M,D

CHARLESTON SOUTHERN UNIVERSITY

Accounting	M
Business Administration and Management—General	M
Education—General	M
Educational Leadership and Administration	M
Elementary Education	M
Finance and Banking	M
Management Information Systems	M

CHARLOTTE SCHOOL OF LAW

Law	D

CHATHAM UNIVERSITY

Accounting	M
Art Education	M
Business Administration and Management—General	M
Early Childhood Education	M
Education—General	M
Elementary Education	M
English Education	M
Environmental Education	M
Mathematics Education	M
Science Education	M
Secondary Education	M
Social Sciences Education	M
Special Education	M
Sustainability Management	M

CHESTNUT HILL COLLEGE

Distance Education Development	M,O
Early Childhood Education	M,O
Education—General	M,O
Educational Leadership and Administration	M,O
Educational Media/Instructional Technology	M,O
Elementary Education	M,O
Human Services	M,O
Middle School Education	M,O
Reading Education	M,O
Secondary Education	M,O
Special Education	M,O

CHEYNEY UNIVERSITY OF PENNSYLVANIA

Education—General	M
Educational Leadership and Administration	M,O
Elementary Education	M
Special Education	M
Urban Education	M

THE CHICAGO SCHOOL OF PROFESSIONAL PSYCHOLOGY

Organizational Management	M,D

CHICAGO STATE UNIVERSITY

Counselor Education	M
Early Childhood Education	M
Education—General	M,D
Educational Leadership and Administration	M,D
Educational Media/Instructional Technology	M
Elementary Education	M
Foundations and Philosophy of Education	M
Higher Education	M,D
Library Science	M
Middle School Education	M
Multilingual and Multicultural Education	M
Physical Education	M
Reading Education	M
Secondary Education	M
Social Work	M
Special Education	M
Vocational and Technical Education	M

CHOWAN UNIVERSITY

Education—General	M

CHRISTIAN BROTHERS UNIVERSITY

Accounting	M,O
Business Administration and Management—General	M,O
Education—General	M
Educational Leadership and Administration	M
International Business	M,O
Project Management	M,O

CHRISTOPHER NEWPORT UNIVERSITY

Art Education	M
Computer Education	M
Education—General	M
Elementary Education	M
English as a Second Language	M
English Education	M
Foreign Languages Education	M
Mathematics Education	M
Music Education	M
Science Education	M
Secondary Education	M
Social Sciences Education	M

THE CITADEL, THE MILITARY COLLEGE OF SOUTH CAROLINA

Business Administration and Management—General	M,O
Counselor Education	M,O
Education—General	M,O
Educational Leadership and Administration	M,O
Elementary Education	M
English Education	M
Health Education	M
Mathematics Education	M
Physical Education	M
Project Management	M
Reading Education	M
Science Education	M
Secondary Education	M
Social Sciences Education	M
Student Affairs	M

CITY COLLEGE OF THE CITY UNIVERSITY OF NEW YORK

Early Childhood Education	M
Education—General	M,O
Educational Leadership and Administration	M,O
English Education	M,O
Marketing	M
Mathematics Education	M,O
Middle School Education	M,O
Multilingual and Multicultural Education	M
Reading Education	M
Science Education	M
Secondary Education	M,O
Social Sciences Education	M,O
Special Education	M,O

CITY UNIVERSITY OF NEW YORK SCHOOL OF LAW

Law	D

CITY UNIVERSITY OF SEATTLE

Accounting	M,O
Business Administration and Management—General	M,O
Curriculum and Instruction	M,D,O
Education—General	M,D,O
Educational Leadership and Administration	M,D,O
Elementary Education	M,D,O
Finance and Banking	M,O
Higher Education	M,D,O
Human Resources Management	M,O
International Business	M,O
Management Information Systems	M,O
Marketing	M,O
Organizational Management	M,D,O
Project Management	M,O
Reading Education	M,D,O
Special Education	M,D,O
Sustainability Management	M,O

CLAFLIN UNIVERSITY

Business Administration and Management—General	M

CLAREMONT GRADUATE UNIVERSITY

Archives/Archival Administration	M,D,O
Business Administration and Management—General	M,D,O
Education—General	M,D,O
Educational Leadership and Administration	M,D,O
Educational Measurement and Evaluation	M,D,O
Electronic Commerce	M,D,O
Higher Education	M,D,O
Human Resources Development	M,D,O
Human Resources Management	M
Management Information Systems	M,D,O
Management Strategy and Policy	M,D,O
Special Education	M,D,O
Student Affairs	M,D,O
Urban Education	M,D,O

CLAREMONT MCKENNA COLLEGE

Finance and Banking	M

CLAREMONT SCHOOL OF THEOLOGY

Religious Education	M,D

CLARION UNIVERSITY OF PENNSYLVANIA

Advertising and Public Relations	O
Business Administration and Management—General	M
Curriculum and Instruction	M
Early Childhood Education	M
Education—General	M
Library Science	M,O
Mathematics Education	M
Reading Education	M
Science Education	M

Special Education M
Vocational and Technical Education M

CLARK ATLANTA UNIVERSITY
Accounting M
Business Administration and
  Management—General M
Counselor Education M
Curriculum and Instruction M
Education—General M,D,O
Educational Leadership and
  Administration M,D,O
Educational Psychology M
Mathematics Education M
Science Education M
Social Work M,D
Special Education M

CLARKE UNIVERSITY
Business Administration and
  Management—General M
Early Childhood Education M
Education—General M
Educational Leadership and
  Administration M
Educational Media/Instructional
  Technology M
Reading Education M
Special Education M

CLARKSON UNIVERSITY
Business Administration and
  Management—General M

CLARK UNIVERSITY
Accounting M
Business Administration and
  Management—General M
Education—General M
Finance and Banking M
International Business M
Management Information Systems M
Marketing M
Sustainability Management M

CLAYTON STATE UNIVERSITY
Accounting M
Archives/Archival Administration M
Business Administration and
  Management—General M
Education—General M
English Education M
International Business M
Mathematics Education M
Supply Chain Management M

CLEARWATER CHRISTIAN COLLEGE
Educational Leadership and
  Administration M

CLEARY UNIVERSITY
Accounting M,O
Business Administration and
  Management—General M,O
Finance and Banking M,O
Nonprofit Management M,O
Organizational Management M,O
Sustainability Management M,O

CLEMSON UNIVERSITY
Accounting M
Agricultural Education M
Business Administration and
  Management—General M
Counselor Education M
Curriculum and Instruction D
Education—General M,D,O
Educational Leadership and
  Administration M,D,O
Elementary Education M
English Education M
Entrepreneurship M
Higher Education D
Human Resources Development M
Human Resources Management M
Marketing M
Mathematics Education M
Middle School Education M
Reading Education M
Real Estate M
Recreation and Park Management M,D
Science Education M
Secondary Education M
Social Sciences Education M
Special Education M
Student Affairs M
Travel and Tourism M,D

CLEVELAND STATE UNIVERSITY
Accounting M
Adult Education M,D,O
Art Education M
Business Administration and
  Management—General M,D
Counselor Education M,D,O
Early Childhood Education M
Education of Students with
  Severe/Multiple Disabilities M
Education—General M,D,O
Educational Leadership and
  Administration M,D,O
Educational Media/Instructional
  Technology D
Educational Policy D
English as a Second Language M
Exercise and Sports Science M
Finance and Banking M,D,O
Foreign Languages Education M
Health Education M
Health Law M,D,O
Higher Education D
Human Resources Management M
Industrial and Manufacturing
  Management D

International Business M,D,O
Law M,D,O
Management Information Systems M,D
Marketing M
Mathematics Education M
Middle School Education M
Music Education M
Nonprofit Management M,O
Organizational Management M,O
Physical Education M
Real Estate M,O
Science Education M
Social Work M
Special Education M
Sports Management M
Taxation M,O
Urban Education M,D

COASTAL CAROLINA UNIVERSITY
Accounting M,O
Business Administration and
  Management—General M
Education—General M
Educational Leadership and
  Administration M
Management Information Systems M,O

COGSWELL POLYTECHNICAL COLLEGE
Entrepreneurship M

COKER COLLEGE
Sports Management M

COLGATE UNIVERSITY
Secondary Education M

THE COLLEGE AT BROCKPORT, STATE UNIVERSITY OF NEW YORK
Accounting M
Counselor Education M,O
Curriculum and Instruction M
Early Childhood Education M
Education—General M,O
Educational Leadership and
  Administration M,O
English Education M
Foreign Languages Education M
Health Education M
Leisure Studies M
Mathematics Education M
Middle School Education M
Multilingual and Multicultural
  Education M,O
Nonprofit Management M,O
Physical Education M,O
Reading Education M,O
Recreation and Park Management M
Science Education M
Social Sciences Education M
Social Work M,O
Sports Management M,O

COLLEGE FOR FINANCIAL PLANNING
Finance and Banking M

COLLEGE OF CHARLESTON
Accounting M
Business Administration and
  Management—General M
Early Childhood Education M
Education—General M,O
Elementary Education M
English as a Second Language O
Foreign Languages Education M
Management Information Systems M
Mathematics Education M
Music Education M
Science Education M
Special Education M

THE COLLEGE OF IDAHO
Curriculum and Instruction M
Education—General M

COLLEGE OF MOUNT SAINT VINCENT
Education—General M,O
Educational Media/Instructional
  Technology M,O
Middle School Education M,O
Multilingual and Multicultural
  Education M,O
Urban Education M,O

THE COLLEGE OF NEW JERSEY
Counselor Education M
Early Childhood Education M
Education—General M,O
Educational Leadership and
  Administration M,O
Elementary Education M
English as a Second Language M,O
Health Education M
International and Comparative
  Education M,O
Physical Education M,O
Reading Education M,O
Secondary Education M,O
Special Education M,O

THE COLLEGE OF NEW ROCHELLE
Art Education M
Early Childhood Education M
Education of the Gifted M
Education—General M,O
Educational Leadership and
  Administration M,O
Elementary Education M
English as a Second Language M,O
Human Resources Development M
Multilingual and Multicultural
  Education M,O
Reading Education M
Special Education M

COLLEGE OF SAINT ELIZABETH
Business Administration and
  Management—General M
Education—General M,D,O
Educational Leadership and
  Administration M,D,O
Educational Media/Instructional
  Technology M,D,O
Exercise and Sports Science M,O
Higher Education M,O
Human Resources Management M
Organizational Management M
Special Education M,D,O
Student Affairs M,O

COLLEGE OF ST. JOSEPH
Business Administration and
  Management—General M
Counselor Education M
Education—General M
Elementary Education M
English Education M
Reading Education M
Secondary Education M
Social Sciences Education M
Special Education M

COLLEGE OF SAINT MARY
Education—General M
Educational Leadership and
  Administration M
Educational Measurement and
  Evaluation M
English as a Second Language M
Health Education D
Organizational Management M

THE COLLEGE OF SAINT ROSE
Accounting M
Art Education M,O
Business Administration and
  Management—General M
Counselor Education M,O
Curriculum and Instruction M
Early Childhood Education M
Education—General M,O
Educational Leadership and
  Administration M,O
Educational Media/Instructional
  Technology M,O
Educational Psychology M,O
Higher Education M
Music Education M
Nonprofit Management O
Reading Education M
Secondary Education M
Special Education M
Student Affairs M

THE COLLEGE OF ST. SCHOLASTICA
Athletic Training and Sports
  Medicine M
Business Administration and
  Management—General M,O
Education—General M,O
Exercise and Sports Science M
Management Information Systems M,O
Social Work M

COLLEGE OF STATEN ISLAND OF THE CITY UNIVERSITY OF NEW YORK
Accounting M
Business Administration and
  Management—General M
Education—General M,O
Educational Leadership and
  Administration O
Elementary Education M
Secondary Education M
Special Education M,O

THE COLLEGE OF WILLIAM AND MARY
Accounting M
Business Administration and
  Management—General M
Counselor Education M,D
Curriculum and Instruction M,D
Education of the Gifted M
Education—General M,D,O
Educational Leadership and
  Administration M,D
Educational Media/Instructional
  Technology M,D
Educational Policy M,D
Elementary Education M
English Education M
Foreign Languages Education M
Law M,D
Mathematics Education M
Reading Education M
Science Education M
Secondary Education M
Social Sciences Education M
Special Education M

COLORADO CHRISTIAN UNIVERSITY
Business Administration and
  Management—General M
Business Education M
Curriculum and Instruction M
Distance Education Development M
Early Childhood Education M
Education—General M
Educational Media/Instructional
  Technology M
Elementary Education M
Project Management M
Special Education M

THE COLORADO COLLEGE
Art Education M
Education—General M
Elementary Education M

English Education M
Foreign Languages Education M
Mathematics Education M
Music Education M
Science Education M
Secondary Education M
Social Sciences Education M

COLORADO MESA UNIVERSITY
Business Administration and
  Management—General M
Education—General M
Educational Leadership and
  Administration M
English as a Second Language M

COLORADO STATE UNIVERSITY
Accounting M
Adult Education M,D
Advertising and Public Relations M,D
Business Administration and
  Management—General M
Community College Education M,D
Counselor Education M,D
Education—General M,D
Educational Leadership and
  Administration M,D
Exercise and Sports Science M,D
Finance and Banking M
Foreign Languages Education M
Management Information Systems M
Organizational Management M
Recreation and Park Management M,D
Social Work M,D
Student Affairs M,D
Sustainability Management M
Vocational and Technical Education M,D

COLORADO STATE UNIVERSITY–PUEBLO
Art Education M
Business Administration and
  Management—General M
Education—General M
Educational Media/Instructional
  Technology M
Foreign Languages Education M
Health Education M
Music Education M
Physical Education M
Special Education M

COLORADO TECHNICAL UNIVERSITY COLORADO SPRINGS
Accounting M,D
Business Administration and
  Management—General M,D
Finance and Banking M,D
Human Resources Management M,D
Industrial and Manufacturing
  Management M,D
Logistics M,D
Marketing M,D
Project Management M,D

COLORADO TECHNICAL UNIVERSITY DENVER SOUTH
Accounting M
Business Administration and
  Management—General M
Finance and Banking M
Human Resources Management M
Industrial and Manufacturing
  Management M
Marketing M
Project Management M

COLUMBIA COLLEGE (MO)
Business Administration and
  Management—General M
Education—General M
Educational Leadership and
  Administration M

COLUMBIA COLLEGE (SC)
Education—General M
Educational Leadership and
  Administration M
Elementary Education M
Higher Education M
Organizational Behavior M,O

COLUMBIA COLLEGE CHICAGO
Education—General M
Entertainment Management M

COLUMBIA INTERNATIONAL UNIVERSITY
Counselor Education M,D,O
Curriculum and Instruction M,D,O
Early Childhood Education M,D,O
Education—General M,D,O
Educational Leadership and
  Administration M,D,O
Educational Media/Instructional
  Technology M,D,O
Elementary Education M,D,O
English as a Second Language M,D,O
Higher Education M,D,O
Multilingual and Multicultural
  Education M,D,O
Religious Education M,D,O
Special Education M,D,O

COLUMBIA SOUTHERN UNIVERSITY
Business Administration and
  Management—General M,D
Finance and Banking M
Human Resources Management M
Marketing M
Organizational Management M

COLUMBIA UNIVERSITY
Accounting M,D

Actuarial Science — M
Archives/Archival Administration — M
Business Administration and
  Management—General — M,D
Entrepreneurship — M
Finance and Banking — M,D
Foreign Languages Education — M,D
Foundations and Philosophy of
  Education — M,D
Human Resources Management — M
Information Studies — M
International Business — M,D
Kinesiology and Movement Studies — M,D
Law — M,D
Legal and Justice Studies — M,D
Marketing — M,D
Nonprofit Management — M
Quantitative Analysis — M,D
Real Estate — M
Science Education — M,D,O
Social Work — M
Sports Management — M
Sustainability Management — M

COLUMBUS STATE UNIVERSITY
Art Education — M
Business Administration and
  Management—General — M,O
Counselor Education — M,D,O
Curriculum and Instruction — M,D,O
Early Childhood Education — M,D,O
Education—General — M,D,O
Educational Leadership and
  Administration — M,D,O
Educational Media/Instructional
  Technology — M,O
English as a Second Language — M,O
English Education — M,O
Exercise and Sports Science — M
Health Education — M
Higher Education — M,D,O
Mathematics Education — M,O
Middle School Education — M,O
Music Education — M,O
Organizational Management — M,O
Physical Education — M
Science Education — M,O
Secondary Education — M,O
Social Sciences Education — M,O
Special Education — M,O

CONCORDIA COLLEGE
Education—General — M
Foreign Languages Education — M

CONCORDIA COLLEGE–NEW YORK
Organizational Management — M
Special Education — M

CONCORDIA UNIVERSITY (CA)
Business Administration and
  Management—General — M
Counselor Education — M
Curriculum and Instruction — M
Education—General — M
Educational Leadership and
  Administration — M
Educational Media/Instructional
  Technology — M
Physical Education — M
Sports Management — M

CONCORDIA UNIVERSITY (CANADA)
Adult Education — M,O
Art Education — M,D
Business Administration and
  Management—General — M,D,O
Education—General — M,D,O
Educational Media/Instructional
  Technology — M,D,O
English as a Second Language — M,O
Exercise and Sports Science — M
Finance and Banking — M,D,O
Investment Management — M,D,O
Marketing — M,D,O
Mathematics Education — M,D
Organizational Management — M

CONCORDIA UNIVERSITY (OR)
Business Administration and
  Management—General — M,D
Curriculum and Instruction — M,D
Early Childhood Education — M,D
Education—General — M,D
Educational Leadership and
  Administration — M,D
Educational Media/Instructional
  Technology — M,D
Elementary Education — M,D
English as a Second Language — M,D
Environmental Education — M,D
Mathematics Education — M,D
Reading Education — M,D
Science Education — M,D
Secondary Education — M,D
Special Education — M,D
Vocational and Technical Education — M,D

CONCORDIA UNIVERSITY ANN ARBOR
Curriculum and Instruction — M
Educational Leadership and
  Administration — M
Organizational Management — M

CONCORDIA UNIVERSITY CHICAGO
Business Administration and
  Management—General — M
Counselor Education — M,O
Curriculum and Instruction — M
Early Childhood Education — M
Education—General — M
Educational Leadership and
  Administration — M,D,O
Educational Media/Instructional
  Technology — M
Elementary Education — M
Exercise and Sports Science — M

Human Services — M
Reading Education — M
Religious Education — M
Secondary Education — M

CONCORDIA UNIVERSITY, NEBRASKA
Early Childhood Education — M
Education—General — M
Educational Leadership and
  Administration — M
Elementary Education — M
Reading Education — M
Religious Education — M
Secondary Education — M

CONCORDIA UNIVERSITY, ST. PAUL
Business Administration and
  Management—General — M
Curriculum and Instruction — M,O
Early Childhood Education — M,O
Education—General — M
Educational Leadership and
  Administration — M,O
Educational Media/Instructional
  Technology — M,O
Exercise and Sports Science — M,O
Human Resources Management — M
Organizational Management — M
Reading Education — M,O
Special Education — M,O
Sports Management — M,O

CONCORDIA UNIVERSITY TEXAS
Education—General — M

CONCORDIA UNIVERSITY WISCONSIN
Art Education — M
Business Administration and
  Management—General — M
Counselor Education — M
Curriculum and Instruction — M
Early Childhood Education — M
Education—General — M
Educational Leadership and
  Administration — M
Environmental Education — M
Finance and Banking — M
Human Resources Management — M
Human Services — M,D
International Business — M
Management Information Systems — M
Marketing — M
Reading Education — M
Special Education — M
Student Affairs — M

CONCORD LAW SCHOOL
Law — D

CONCORD UNIVERSITY
Education—General — M
Educational Leadership and
  Administration — M
Reading Education — M
Social Sciences Education — M
Special Education — M

CONSERVATORIO DE MUSICA DE PUERTO RICO
Music Education — M

CONVERSE COLLEGE
Art Education — M
Education of the Gifted — M
Education—General — M,O
Educational Leadership and
  Administration — M,O
Elementary Education — M
English Education — M
Mathematics Education — M
Middle School Education — M
Music Education — M
Reading Education — O
Science Education — M
Secondary Education — M
Social Sciences Education — M
Special Education — M

COPENHAGEN BUSINESS SCHOOL
Business Administration and
  Management—General — M,D
International Business — M,D
Logistics — M,D
Management Information Systems — M,D

COPPIN STATE UNIVERSITY
Adult Education — M
Curriculum and Instruction — M
Education—General — M
Human Services — M
Reading Education — M
Special Education — M

CORBAN UNIVERSITY
Business Administration and
  Management—General — M
Education—General — M
Nonprofit Management — M

CORNELL UNIVERSITY
Accounting — D
Adult Education — M,D
Agricultural Education — M,D
Business Administration and
  Management—General — M,D
Curriculum and Instruction — M,D
Education—General — M,D
Educational Policy — M,D
Facilities Management — M
Finance and Banking — D
Foreign Languages Education — M,D
Hospitality Management — M,D
Human Resources Management — M,D
Information Studies — D
Law — M,D
Marketing — D
Mathematics Education — M,D
Organizational Behavior — M,D

Quantitative Analysis — M,D
Real Estate — M
Secondary Education — M,D
Social Work — M,D

CORNERSTONE UNIVERSITY
Business Administration and
  Management—General — M,O
Education—General — M,O
English as a Second Language — M,O

COVENANT COLLEGE
Education—General — M

CREIGHTON UNIVERSITY
Business Administration and
  Management—General — M
Counselor Education — M
Education—General — M
Educational Leadership and
  Administration — M,D
Elementary Education — M
Law — M,D,O
Management Information Systems — M
Secondary Education — M
Special Education — M
Student Affairs — M

CUMBERLAND UNIVERSITY
Business Administration and
  Management—General — M
Education—General — M

CURRY COLLEGE
Business Administration and
  Management—General — M,O
Education—General — M,O
Elementary Education — M
Finance and Banking — M,O
Foundations and Philosophy of
  Education — M,O
Reading Education — M,O
Special Education — M,O

DAEMEN COLLEGE
Accounting — M
Business Administration and
  Management—General — M
Early Childhood Education — M
Education—General — M
International Business — M
Management Information Systems — M
Marketing — M
Middle School Education — M
Nonprofit Management — M
Special Education — M

DAKOTA STATE UNIVERSITY
Business Administration and
  Management—General — M,D
Education—General — M
Educational Media/Instructional
  Technology — M
Management Information Systems — M,D

DAKOTA WESLEYAN UNIVERSITY
Curriculum and Instruction — M
Education—General — M
Educational Leadership and
  Administration — M
Secondary Education — M

DALHOUSIE UNIVERSITY
Business Administration and
  Management—General — M,O
Electronic Commerce — M,D
Finance and Banking — M
Health Education — M
Information Studies — M
Kinesiology and Movement Studies — M
Law — M,D
Leisure Studies — M
Library Science — M
Management Information Systems — M
Social Work — M

DALLAS BAPTIST UNIVERSITY
Accounting — M
Business Administration and
  Management—General — M
Counselor Education — M,O
Curriculum and Instruction — M
Distance Education Development — M
Early Childhood Education — M
Education—General — M
Educational Leadership and
  Administration — M
Elementary Education — M
English as a Second Language — M
Entrepreneurship — M
Finance and Banking — M
Higher Education — M
Human Resources Management — M
International Business — M
Kinesiology and Movement Studies — M
Management Information Systems — M
Marketing — M
Multilingual and Multicultural
  Education — M
Nonprofit Management — M
Organizational Management — M
Project Management — M
Reading Education — M
Religious Education — M
Secondary Education — M
Special Education — M

DALLAS THEOLOGICAL SEMINARY
Adult Education — M,D,O
Educational Leadership and
  Administration — M,D,O
Religious Education — M,D,O

DANIEL WEBSTER COLLEGE
Aviation Management — M
Business Administration and
  Management—General — M

DARTMOUTH COLLEGE
Business Administration and
  Management—General — M

DAVENPORT UNIVERSITY
Accounting — M
Business Administration and
  Management—General — M
Finance and Banking — M
Human Resources Management — M
Management Strategy and Policy — M

DEFIANCE COLLEGE
Adult Education — M
Business Administration and
  Management—General — M
Education—General — M
Management Strategy and Policy — M
Secondary Education — M
Special Education — M
Sports Management — M

DELAWARE STATE UNIVERSITY
Adult Education — M
Art Education — M
Business Administration and
  Management—General — M
Curriculum and Instruction — M
Education—General — M,D
Educational Leadership and
  Administration — M,D
Exercise and Sports Science — M
Foreign Languages Education — M
Mathematics Education — M
Reading Education — M
Science Education — M,D
Social Work — M
Special Education — M

DELAWARE VALLEY COLLEGE
Accounting — M
Business Administration and
  Management—General — M
Curriculum and Instruction — M
Educational Leadership and
  Administration — M
Educational Media/Instructional
  Technology — M
Entrepreneurship — M
Finance and Banking — M
Human Resources Management — M
International Business — M
Supply Chain Management — M

DELTA STATE UNIVERSITY
Accounting — M
Aviation Management — M
Business Administration and
  Management—General — M
Counselor Education — M,D
Education—General — M,D,O
Educational Leadership and
  Administration — M,D,O
Elementary Education — M,D,O
English Education — M
Exercise and Sports Science — M
Health Education — M
Higher Education — D
Physical Education — M
Recreation and Park Management — M
Secondary Education — M
Social Sciences Education — M,O
Special Education — M

DEPAUL UNIVERSITY
Accounting — M
Adult Education — M,D
Advertising and Public Relations — M
Business Administration and
  Management—General — M
Counselor Education — M,D
Curriculum and Instruction — M,D
Early Childhood Education — M,D
Education—General — M,D
Educational Leadership and
  Administration — M,D
Electronic Commerce — M,D
Elementary Education — M,D
Entrepreneurship — M
Finance and Banking — M
Foreign Languages Education — M,D
Foundations and Philosophy of
  Education — M,D
Health Law — M,D
Hospitality Management — M
Human Resources Management — M
Industrial and Manufacturing
  Management — M
Intellectual Property Law — M,D
Investment Management — M
Law — M,D
Management Information Systems — M,D
Management Strategy and Policy — M
Marketing — M
Mathematics Education — M,D
Multilingual and Multicultural
  Education — M,D
Music Education — M,O
Nonprofit Management — M
Organizational Management — M
Reading Education — M,D
Real Estate — M
Science Education — M,D
Secondary Education — M,D
Social Work — M
Special Education — M,D
Sports Management — M
Student Affairs — M,D
Sustainability Management — M
Taxation — M,D

DEREE - THE AMERICAN COLLEGE OF GREECE
Marketing — M

DESALES UNIVERSITY
Accounting — M

Program	Degree
Business Administration and Management—General	M
Early Childhood Education	M
Education—General	M
Educational Media/Instructional Technology	M
English as a Second Language	M
Finance and Banking	M
Human Resources Management	M
Management Information Systems	M
Marketing	M
Project Management	M
Secondary Education	M
Special Education	M

DEVRY COLLEGE OF NEW YORK

Program	Degree
Business Administration and Management—General	M

DEVRY UNIVERSITY

Program	Degree
Business Administration and Management—General	M,O

DEVRY UNIVERSITY

Program	Degree
Accounting	M
Business Administration and Management—General	M
Education—General	M
Educational Media/Instructional Technology	M
Finance and Banking	M
Human Resources Management	M
Management Information Systems	M
Project Management	M

DEVRY UNIVERSITY ONLINE

Program	Degree
Business Administration and Management—General	M

DOANE COLLEGE

Program	Degree
Business Administration and Management—General	M
Counselor Education	M
Curriculum and Instruction	M
Education—General	M
Educational Leadership and Administration	M

DOMINICAN COLLEGE

Program	Degree
Business Administration and Management—General	M
Elementary Education	M
Special Education	M

DOMINICAN UNIVERSITY

Program	Degree
Accounting	M
Business Administration and Management—General	M
Curriculum and Instruction	M
Early Childhood Education	M
Education—General	M
Educational Leadership and Administration	M
Elementary Education	M
English as a Second Language	M
Information Studies	M,D,O
Library Science	M,D,O
Reading Education	M
Social Work	M
Special Education	M

DOMINICAN UNIVERSITY OF CALIFORNIA

Program	Degree
Business Administration and Management—General	M
International Business	M
Management Strategy and Policy	M
Special Education	M
Sustainability Management	M

DORDT COLLEGE

Program	Degree
Education—General	M

DOWLING COLLEGE

Program	Degree
Aviation Management	M,O
Business Administration and Management—General	M,O
Early Childhood Education	M,D,O
Education of the Gifted	M,D,O
Education—General	M,D,O
Educational Leadership and Administration	M,D,O
Educational Media/Instructional Technology	M,D,O
Educational Psychology	M,D,O
Elementary Education	M,D,O
Entertainment Management	M,O
Finance and Banking	M,O
Human Resources Management	M,O
Management Information Systems	M,O
Marketing	M,O
Middle School Education	M,D,O
Project Management	M,O
Reading Education	M,D,O
Special Education	M,D,O
Sports Management	M,D,O

DRAKE UNIVERSITY

Program	Degree
Business Administration and Management—General	M
Education—General	M,D,O
Law	M,D

DREW UNIVERSITY

Program	Degree
Education—General	M
Foreign Languages Education	M
Mathematics Education	M
Science Education	M
Social Sciences Education	M

DREXEL UNIVERSITY

Program	Degree
Accounting	M,D,O
Archives/Archival Administration	M
Business Administration and Management—General	M,D,O
Curriculum and Instruction	M,D
Education—General	M,D
Educational Leadership and Administration	M,D
Educational Media/Instructional Technology	M,D
Entrepreneurship	M
Finance and Banking	M,D,O
Higher Education	M,D
Hospitality Management	M
Human Resources Development	M,D
Information Studies	M
International and Comparative Education	M,D
Library Science	M,D,O
Management Strategy and Policy	M,D,O
Marketing	M,D,O
Organizational Behavior	M,D,O
Project Management	M
Quantitative Analysis	M,D,O
Real Estate	M
Special Education	M,D
Sports Management	M

DRURY UNIVERSITY

Program	Degree
Business Administration and Management—General	M
Education of the Gifted	M
Education—General	M
Educational Media/Instructional Technology	M
Elementary Education	M
Human Services	M
Mathematics Education	M
Middle School Education	M
Reading Education	M
Secondary Education	M
Special Education	M

DUKE UNIVERSITY

Program	Degree
Accounting	D
Business Administration and Management—General	M,D,O
Education—General	M
Entrepreneurship	M,O
Finance and Banking	M,D,O
Industrial and Manufacturing Management	M,D,O
International Business	M,O
Law	M,D
Management Strategy and Policy	M,D,O
Marketing	M,D,O
Organizational Management	M,D,O
Quantitative Analysis	M,D,O

DUQUESNE UNIVERSITY

Program	Degree
Accounting	M
Business Administration and Management—General	M
Counselor Education	M,D,O
Curriculum and Instruction	M,O
Early Childhood Education	M
Education—General	M,D,O
Educational Leadership and Administration	M,D,O
Educational Measurement and Evaluation	M
Educational Media/Instructional Technology	M,D,O
Elementary Education	M
English as a Second Language	M
English Education	M
Finance and Banking	M
Foreign Languages Education	M
Foundations and Philosophy of Education	M
International Business	M
Law	M,D
Management Information Systems	M
Management Strategy and Policy	M
Marketing	M
Mathematics Education	M
Middle School Education	M
Music Education	M,O
Organizational Management	M
Reading Education	M
Science Education	M
Secondary Education	M
Social Sciences Education	M
Special Education	M
Sports Management	M
Supply Chain Management	M
Sustainability Management	M

D'YOUVILLE COLLEGE

Program	Degree
Business Administration and Management—General	M
Education—General	M,D,O
Educational Leadership and Administration	M,D,O
Elementary Education	M,D,O
Health Education	M,D,O
International Business	M
Secondary Education	M,D,O
Special Education	M,D,O

EARLHAM COLLEGE

Program	Degree
Education—General	M

EAST CAROLINA UNIVERSITY

Program	Degree
Accounting	M
Adult Education	M,D
Art Education	M
Athletic Training and Sports Medicine	M
Business Administration and Management—General	M,D,O
Business Education	M
Community College Education	M,O
Computer Education	M,O
Counselor Education	M,D
Curriculum and Instruction	M,O
Distance Education Development	M,O
Early Childhood Education	M,D
Education—General	M,D,O
Educational Leadership and Administration	M,D,O
Educational Media/Instructional Technology	M,O
Elementary Education	M,D,O
English as a Second Language	M,D,O
English Education	M
Exercise and Sports Science	M
Health Education	M
Higher Education	M,D
Hospitality Management	M
Industrial and Manufacturing Management	M,D,O
Kinesiology and Movement Studies	M,D,O
Leisure Studies	M,O
Library Science	M,O
Logistics	M,D,O
Management Information Systems	M,D,O
Mathematics Education	M,O
Middle School Education	M,O
Music Education	M,O
Physical Education	M,O
Quality Management	M,D,O
Reading Education	M,O
Recreation and Park Management	M,O
Science Education	M,O
Social Sciences Education	M,O
Social Work	M,O
Special Education	M,O
Sports Management	M,D,O
Vocational and Technical Education	M

EAST CENTRAL UNIVERSITY

Program	Degree
Counselor Education	M
Education—General	M
Human Resources Management	M
Human Services	M

EASTERN CONNECTICUT STATE UNIVERSITY

Program	Degree
Early Childhood Education	M
Education—General	M
Educational Media/Instructional Technology	M
Elementary Education	M
Organizational Management	M
Reading Education	M
Science Education	M
Secondary Education	M

EASTERN ILLINOIS UNIVERSITY

Program	Degree
Accounting	M,O
Art Education	M
Business Administration and Management—General	M,O
Community College Education	M
Counselor Education	M
Early Childhood Education	M,O
Education—General	M,O
Educational Leadership and Administration	M,O
Elementary Education	M
Exercise and Sports Science	M
Kinesiology and Movement Studies	M
Mathematics Education	M
Middle School Education	M
Music Education	M
Special Education	M
Student Affairs	M

EASTERN KENTUCKY UNIVERSITY

Program	Degree
Agricultural Education	M
Art Education	M
Business Administration and Management—General	M
Business Education	M
Counselor Education	M
Curriculum and Instruction	M
Education—General	M
Educational Leadership and Administration	M
Elementary Education	M
English Education	M
Health Education	M
Higher Education	M
Home Economics Education	M
Library Science	M
Mathematics Education	M
Music Education	M
Physical Education	M
Recreation and Park Management	M
Science Education	M
Secondary Education	M
Social Sciences Education	M
Special Education	M
Sports Management	M
Vocational and Technical Education	M

EASTERN MENNONITE UNIVERSITY

Program	Degree
Business Administration and Management—General	M
Counselor Education	M
Education—General	M
Nonprofit Management	M
Organizational Management	M

EASTERN MICHIGAN UNIVERSITY

Program	Degree
Accounting	M
Art Education	M
Athletic Training and Sports Medicine	M,O
Business Administration and Management—General	M,O
Counselor Education	M,O
Curriculum and Instruction	M
Developmental Education	M
Early Childhood Education	M
Education—General	M,D,O
Educational Leadership and Administration	M,D,O
Educational Measurement and Evaluation	M,O
Educational Media/Instructional Technology	M,O
Educational Psychology	M,O
Electronic Commerce	M,O
Elementary Education	M
English as a Second Language	M,O
English Education	M,O
Entrepreneurship	M,O
Exercise and Sports Science	M
Finance and Banking	M,O
Foundations and Philosophy of Education	M
Health Education	M
Hospitality Management	M,O
Human Resources Management	M,O
Human Services	O
International Business	M
Kinesiology and Movement Studies	M
Management Information Systems	M,O
Marketing	M,O
Mathematics Education	M
Middle School Education	M
Multilingual and Multicultural Education	M,D,O
Museum Education	O
Music Education	M
Nonprofit Management	M,O
Organizational Management	M,O
Physical Education	M
Quality Management	M,O
Reading Education	M
Science Education	M
Secondary Education	M
Social Work	M
Special Education	M,O
Sports Management	M
Supply Chain Management	M,O
Travel and Tourism	M

EASTERN NAZARENE COLLEGE

Program	Degree
Business Administration and Management—General	M
Early Childhood Education	M,O
Education—General	M,O
Educational Leadership and Administration	M,O
Elementary Education	M,O
English as a Second Language	M,O
Middle School Education	M,O
Reading Education	M,O
Secondary Education	M,O
Special Education	M,O

EASTERN NEW MEXICO UNIVERSITY

Program	Degree
Business Administration and Management—General	M
Counselor Education	M
Curriculum and Instruction	M
Early Childhood Education	M
Education—General	M
Educational Leadership and Administration	M
Educational Media/Instructional Technology	M
Elementary Education	M
English as a Second Language	M
Exercise and Sports Science	M
Human Services	M
Multilingual and Multicultural Education	M
Physical Education	M
Reading Education	M
Secondary Education	M
Special Education	M
Sports Management	M
Vocational and Technical Education	M

EASTERN OREGON UNIVERSITY

Program	Degree
Business Administration and Management—General	M
Education—General	M
Elementary Education	M
Secondary Education	M

EASTERN UNIVERSITY

Program	Degree
Business Administration and Management—General	M
Counselor Education	M,O
Early Childhood Education	M,O
Education—General	M,O
Educational Leadership and Administration	M,O
Elementary Education	M,O
English as a Second Language	M,O
English Education	M,O
Foreign Languages Education	M,O
Health Education	M,O
Mathematics Education	M,O
Middle School Education	M,O
Multilingual and Multicultural Education	M,O
Nonprofit Management	M
Organizational Management	M,D
Physical Education	M,O
Reading Education	M,O
Science Education	M,O
Secondary Education	M,O
Social Sciences Education	M,O
Special Education	M,O

EASTERN WASHINGTON UNIVERSITY

Program	Degree
Adult Education	M
Business Administration and Management—General	M
Computer Education	M
Counselor Education	M
Curriculum and Instruction	M
Early Childhood Education	M
Education—General	M
Elementary Education	M

*M—masters degree; D—doctorate; O—other advanced degree; *—Close-Up and/or Display*

English as a Second Language — M
Exercise and Sports Science — M
Mathematics Education — M
Music Education — M
Physical Education — M
Reading Education — M
Recreation and Park Management — M
Secondary Education — M
Social Work — M
Special Education — M
Sports Management — M

EAST STROUDSBURG UNIVERSITY OF PENNSYLVANIA
Athletic Training and Sports Medicine — M
Education—General — M
Educational Media/Instructional Technology — M
Elementary Education — M
Exercise and Sports Science — M
Health Education — M
Physical Education — M
Reading Education — M
Science Education — M
Secondary Education — M
Social Sciences Education — M
Special Education — M
Sports Management — M

EAST TENNESSEE STATE UNIVERSITY
Accounting — M
Archives/Archival Administration — M,O
Business Administration and Management—General — M,O
Curriculum and Instruction — M,O
Early Childhood Education — M,D,O
Education—General — M,D,O
Educational Leadership and Administration — M,D,O
Educational Media/Instructional Technology — M,O
Elementary Education — M,O
English as a Second Language — M,O
Entrepreneurship — M,O
Exercise and Sports Science — M,D
Finance and Banking — M,O
Higher Education — M,O
Kinesiology and Movement Studies — M
Library Science — M,O
Management Information Systems — M
Management Strategy and Policy — M,O
Middle School Education — M,O
Nonprofit Management — M,O
Reading Education — M,O
Secondary Education — M,O
Social Work — M
Special Education — M,D,O
Sports Management — M

EAST TEXAS BAPTIST UNIVERSITY
Curriculum and Instruction — M
Education—General — M
Physical Education — M

ECOLE HÔTELIÈRE DE LAUSANNE
Hospitality Management — M

EDGEWOOD COLLEGE
Accounting — M
Adult Education — M,D,O
Business Administration and Management—General — M
Education—General — M,D,O
Educational Leadership and Administration — M,D,O
English as a Second Language — M,D,O
Finance and Banking — M
Marketing — M
Multilingual and Multicultural Education — M,D,O
Organizational Management — M
Reading Education — M,D,O
Special Education — M,D,O
Sustainability Management — M,D,O

EDINBORO UNIVERSITY OF PENNSYLVANIA
Counselor Education — M,O
Early Childhood Education — M
Education—General — M,O
Educational Leadership and Administration — M,O
Educational Psychology — M
Elementary Education — M
Middle School Education — M
Reading Education — M,O
Secondary Education — M
Social Work — M
Special Education — M

ELIZABETH CITY STATE UNIVERSITY
Community College Education — M
Education—General — M
Educational Leadership and Administration — M
Elementary Education — M
Mathematics Education — M
Science Education — M

ELMHURST COLLEGE
Accounting — M
Business Administration and Management—General — M
Educational Leadership and Administration — M
Management Information Systems — M
Special Education — M
Supply Chain Management — M

ELMS COLLEGE
Early Childhood Education — M,O
Education—General — M,O
Elementary Education — M,O
English as a Second Language — M,O
English Education — M,O
Foreign Languages Education — M,O

Reading Education — M,O
Science Education — M,O
Secondary Education — M,O
Special Education — M,O

ELON UNIVERSITY
Business Administration and Management—General — M
Education of the Gifted — M
Education—General — M
Elementary Education — M
Law — D
Special Education — M

EMBRY-RIDDLE AERONAUTICAL UNIVERSITY–DAYTONA
Aviation Management — M*
Business Administration and Management—General — M
Finance and Banking — M

EMBRY-RIDDLE AERONAUTICAL UNIVERSITY–WORLDWIDE
Aviation Management — M,O
Business Administration and Management—General — M
Education—General — M,D,O
Industrial and Manufacturing Management — M,O
Logistics — M,O
Project Management — M,O
Supply Chain Management — M,O
Transportation Management — M,O

EMERSON COLLEGE
Advertising and Public Relations — M
International Business — M
Marketing — M

EMMANUEL CHRISTIAN SEMINARY
Religious Education — M,D

EMMANUEL COLLEGE (UNITED STATES)
Business Administration and Management—General — M,O
Education—General — M,O
Educational Leadership and Administration — M,O
Elementary Education — M,O
Human Resources Management — M,O
Secondary Education — M,O

EMORY & HENRY COLLEGE
Education—General — M
Organizational Management — M
Reading Education — M

EMORY UNIVERSITY
Accounting — D
Business Administration and Management—General — M,D
Education—General — M,D
Finance and Banking — D
Health Education — M,D,O
Law — M,D,O
Management Information Systems — D
Marketing — D
Middle School Education — M,D
Organizational Management — D
Secondary Education — M,D

EMPORIA STATE UNIVERSITY
Archives/Archival Administration — M,D,O
Business Administration and Management—General — M
Business Education — M
Counselor Education — M
Curriculum and Instruction — M
Early Childhood Education — M
Education of the Gifted — M
Education—General — M
Educational Leadership and Administration — M
Educational Media/Instructional Technology — M
Elementary Education — M
English as a Second Language — M
Information Studies — M,D,O
Library Science — M,D,O
Music Education — M
Physical Education — M
Reading Education — M
Social Sciences Education — M
Special Education — M

ENDICOTT COLLEGE
Art Education — M
Business Administration and Management—General — M
Distance Education Development — M
Early Childhood Education — M
Educational Leadership and Administration — D
Elementary Education — M
Hospitality Management — M
Management Information Systems — M
Organizational Management — M
Reading Education — M
Secondary Education — M
Special Education — M
Sports Management — M
Travel and Tourism — M

ERIKSON INSTITUTE
Early Childhood Education — M,D
English as a Second Language — M,O

ESSEC BUSINESS SCHOOL
Business Administration and Management—General — M,D
Hospitality Management — M,D
International Business — M,D

EVANGEL UNIVERSITY
Counselor Education — M
Education—General — M

Educational Leadership and Administration — M
Music Education — M
Organizational Management — M
Reading Education — M
Secondary Education — M

EVEREST UNIVERSITY (TAMPA)
Accounting — M
Business Administration and Management—General — M
Human Resources Management — M
International Business — M

EVEREST UNIVERSITY (ORLANDO)
Business Administration and Management—General — M

EVEREST UNIVERSITY (JACKSONVILLE)
Business Administration and Management—General — M

EVEREST UNIVERSITY (MELBOURNE)
Accounting — M
Business Administration and Management—General — M
Human Resources Management — M
International Business — M

EVEREST UNIVERSITY (TAMPA)
Business Administration and Management—General — M

EVEREST UNIVERSITY (LARGO)
Accounting — M
Business Administration and Management—General — M
Human Resources Management — M
International Business — M

EVEREST UNIVERSITY (ORLANDO)
Business Administration and Management—General — M

EVEREST UNIVERSITY (POMPANO BEACH)
Business Administration and Management—General — M

THE EVERGREEN STATE COLLEGE
Education—General — M

EXCELSIOR COLLEGE
Business Administration and Management—General — M,O
Health Education — M,O

FACULTAD DE DERECHO EUGENIO MARÍA DE HOSTOS
Law — D

FAIRFIELD UNIVERSITY
Accounting — M,O
Business Administration and Management—General — M,O
Counselor Education — M,O
Early Childhood Education — M,O
Education—General — M,O
Educational Media/Instructional Technology — M,O
Elementary Education — M,O
English as a Second Language — M,O
Entrepreneurship — M,O
Finance and Banking — M,O
Foundations and Philosophy of Education — M,O
Human Resources Management — M,O
Management Information Systems — M,O
Marketing — M,O
Multilingual and Multicultural Education — M,O
Secondary Education — M,O
Special Education — M,O
Taxation — M,O

FAIRLEIGH DICKINSON UNIVERSITY, COLLEGE AT FLORHAM
Accounting — M
Business Administration and Management—General — M,O
Education—General — M
Educational Leadership and Administration — M
Educational Media/Instructional Technology — M,O
Entrepreneurship — M,O
Finance and Banking — M,O
Hospitality Management — M,O
Human Resources Management — M,O
International Business — M,O
Marketing — M,O
Organizational Behavior — M,O
Organizational Management — M,O
Reading Education — M,O
Sports Management — M
Sustainability Management — O
Taxation — M,O

FAIRLEIGH DICKINSON UNIVERSITY, METROPOLITAN CAMPUS
Accounting — M,O
Business Administration and Management—General — M,O
Curriculum and Instruction — M
Education—General — M,O
Educational Leadership and Administration — M
Educational Media/Instructional Technology — M,O
Electronic Commerce — M,O
Entrepreneurship — M,O
Finance and Banking — M,O
Foundations and Philosophy of Education — M
Hospitality Management — M
Human Resources Management — M,O
International Business — M
Management Information Systems — M,O
Marketing — M,O

Educational Leadership and Administration — M
Music Education — M
Organizational Management — M
Reading Education — M
Secondary Education — M

Multilingual and Multicultural Education — M
Nonprofit Management — M,O
Reading Education — M,O
Science Education — M
Special Education — M
Sports Management — M
Taxation — M

FAIRMONT STATE UNIVERSITY
Business Administration and Management—General — M
Distance Education Development — M
Education—General — M
Educational Media/Instructional Technology — M
Exercise and Sports Science — M
Reading Education — M
Special Education — M

FASHION INSTITUTE OF TECHNOLOGY
Business Administration and Management—General — M*
Marketing — M*

FAULKNER UNIVERSITY
Business Administration and Management—General — M
Counselor Education — M
Education—General — M
Law — D

FAYETTEVILLE STATE UNIVERSITY
Business Administration and Management—General — M
Educational Leadership and Administration — M,D
Elementary Education — M
Middle School Education — M
Reading Education — M
Secondary Education — M
Social Sciences Education — M
Social Work — M

FELICIAN COLLEGE
Business Administration and Management—General — M
Education—General — M,O
Educational Leadership and Administration — M
Entrepreneurship — M
Religious Education — M,O

FERRIS STATE UNIVERSITY
Business Administration and Management—General — M
Community College Education — D
Curriculum and Instruction — M
Developmental Education — M
Education—General — M
Educational Leadership and Administration — M,D
Human Services — M
Management Information Systems — M
Project Management — M
Reading Education — M
Special Education — M

FIELDING GRADUATE UNIVERSITY
Community College Education — M,D,O
Education—General — M,D,O
Educational Leadership and Administration — M,D,O
Legal and Justice Studies — M,D,O
Nonprofit Management — M,D,O
Organizational Management — M,D,O

FITCHBURG STATE UNIVERSITY
Accounting — M
Art Education — M,O
Business Administration and Management—General — M
Counselor Education — M
Curriculum and Instruction — M
Early Childhood Education — M
Educational Leadership and Administration — M,O
Educational Media/Instructional Technology — M,O
Elementary Education — M,O
English Education — M,O
Human Resources Management — M
Middle School Education — M
Science Education — M
Secondary Education — M
Social Sciences Education — M
Special Education — M
Vocational and Technical Education — M

FIVE TOWNS COLLEGE
Early Childhood Education — M,D
Music Education — M,D

FLORIDA AGRICULTURAL AND MECHANICAL UNIVERSITY
Accounting — M
Adult Education — M,D
Business Administration and Management—General — M
Business Education — M
Counselor Education — M,D
Early Childhood Education — M
Education—General — M,D
Educational Leadership and Administration — M,D
Elementary Education — M
English Education — M
Finance and Banking — M
Health Education — M
Law — D
Management Information Systems — M
Marketing — M
Mathematics Education — M
Physical Education — M
Recreation and Park Management — M
Science Education — M
Secondary Education — M

- Social Sciences Education M
- Social Work M
- Vocational and Technical Education M

FLORIDA ATLANTIC UNIVERSITY
- Accounting M,D
- Adult Education M,D,O
- Art Education M
- Business Administration and Management—General M
- Counselor Education M,D,O
- Curriculum and Instruction M,D,O
- Early Childhood Education M,D,O
- Education—General M,D,O
- Educational Leadership and Administration M,D,O
- Educational Media/Instructional Technology M
- Educational Psychology M
- Elementary Education M
- English as a Second Language M,D,O
- English Education M
- Entrepreneurship M,D
- Environmental Education M
- Exercise and Sports Science M
- Finance and Banking D
- Foundations and Philosophy of Education M
- Higher Education M,D,O
- International Business M,D
- Management Information Systems M,D
- Marketing D
- Mathematics Education M
- Multilingual and Multicultural Education M,D,O
- Music Education M
- Nonprofit Management M,D
- Reading Education M
- Science Education M,D
- Social Sciences Education M
- Social Work M
- Special Education M,D
- Sports Management M,D
- Taxation M,D
- Travel and Tourism M,O

FLORIDA COASTAL SCHOOL OF LAW
- Law D

FLORIDA GULF COAST UNIVERSITY
- Accounting M
- Business Administration and Management—General M
- Counselor Education M
- Curriculum and Instruction M,D,O
- Education—General M,D,O
- Educational Leadership and Administration M,D,O
- Educational Media/Instructional Technology M,D,O
- English Education M,D,O
- Reading Education M
- Social Work M
- Special Education M
- Taxation M

FLORIDA INSTITUTE OF TECHNOLOGY
- Accounting M
- Business Administration and Management—General M,D
- Computer Education M,D,O
- Electronic Commerce M,D
- Elementary Education M,D,O
- Entrepreneurship M
- Environmental Education M,D,O
- Finance and Banking M
- Human Resources Management M,D
- International Business M
- Logistics M,D
- Management Information Systems M,D
- Marketing M
- Mathematics Education M,D,O
- Organizational Behavior M,D
- Project Management M,D
- Quality Management M,D
- Science Education M,D,O
- Supply Chain Management M,D
- Transportation Management M,D

FLORIDA INTERNATIONAL UNIVERSITY
- Accounting M
- Adult Education M,D,O
- Art Education M,D,O
- Athletic Training and Sports Medicine M
- Business Administration and Management—General M,D
- Counselor Education M,D,O
- Curriculum and Instruction M,D,O
- Early Childhood Education M,D,O
- Education—General M,D,O
- Educational Leadership and Administration M,D,O
- Educational Media/Instructional Technology M,D,O
- Elementary Education M,D,O
- English as a Second Language M,D,O
- English Education M,D,O
- Finance and Banking M
- Foreign Languages Education M,D,O
- Higher Education M,D,O
- Hospitality Management M
- Human Resources Development M,D,O
- Human Resources Management M
- International and Comparative Education M,D,O
- International Business M,D
- Law D
- Management Information Systems M,D
- Mathematics Education M,D,O
- Multilingual and Multicultural Education M,D,O
- Music Education M
- Physical Education M,D,O
- Reading Education M,D,O
- Real Estate M
- Recreation and Park Management M,D,O
- Science Education M,D,O
- Social Sciences Education M,D,O
- Social Work M,D
- Special Education M,D,O
- Sports Management M,D,O
- Taxation M
- Urban Education M,D,O

FLORIDA MEMORIAL UNIVERSITY
- Business Administration and Management—General M
- Education—General M
- Elementary Education M
- Reading Education M
- Special Education M

FLORIDA NATIONAL UNIVERSITY
- Business Administration and Management—General M
- Finance and Banking M
- Marketing M

FLORIDA SOUTHERN COLLEGE
- Business Administration and Management—General M
- Education—General M

FLORIDA STATE UNIVERSITY
- Accounting M,D
- Art Education M,D,O
- Business Administration and Management—General M,D
- Community College Education M
- Curriculum and Instruction M,D,O
- Early Childhood Education M,D,O
- Education—General M,D,O
- Educational Leadership and Administration M,D,O
- Educational Measurement and Evaluation M,D,O
- Educational Media/Instructional Technology M,D
- Educational Policy M,D,O
- Educational Psychology M,D,O
- Elementary Education M,D,O
- English Education M,D,O
- Environmental Law M,D
- Exercise and Sports Science M,D
- Finance and Banking M,D
- Foreign Languages Education M,D,O
- Foundations and Philosophy of Education M,D
- Health Education M,D
- Higher Education M,D,O
- Human Resources Management M,D
- Information Studies M,D,O
- Insurance M,D
- International and Comparative Education M,D
- International Business M
- Law M,D
- Library Science M,D,O
- Management Information Systems M,D,O
- Management Strategy and Policy M,D
- Marketing M,D
- Mathematics Education M,D,O
- Music Education M,D
- Organizational Behavior M,D
- Physical Education M,D,O
- Reading Education M,D,O
- Recreation and Park Management M,D,O
- Science Education M,D,O
- Secondary Education M
- Social Sciences Education M,D,O
- Social Work M,D
- Special Education M,D,O
- Sports Management M,D,O
- Taxation M,D

FONTBONNE UNIVERSITY
- Accounting M
- Business Administration and Management—General M
- Computer Education M
- Education—General M
- Special Education M

FORDHAM UNIVERSITY
- Accounting M
- Adult Education M,D,O
- Business Administration and Management—General M
- Counselor Education M,D,O
- Curriculum and Instruction M,D,O
- Early Childhood Education M,D,O
- Education—General M,D,O
- Educational Leadership and Administration M,D,O
- Educational Psychology M,D,O
- Elementary Education M,D,O
- English as a Second Language M,D,O
- Finance and Banking M
- Human Resources Management M,D,O
- Intellectual Property Law M,D
- Law M,D
- Management Information Systems M
- Marketing M
- Multilingual and Multicultural Education M,D,O
- Reading Education M,D,O
- Religious Education M,D,O
- Secondary Education M,D,O
- Social Work M,D
- Special Education M,D,O
- Taxation M

FORT HAYS STATE UNIVERSITY
- Business Administration and Management—General M
- Counselor Education M
- Education—General M,O
- Educational Leadership and Administration M,O
- Educational Media/Instructional Technology M
- Health Education M
- Physical Education M
- Special Education M

FORT LEWIS COLLEGE
- Educational Leadership and Administration M,O

FORT VALLEY STATE UNIVERSITY
- Counselor Education M,O

FRAMINGHAM STATE UNIVERSITY
- Business Administration and Management—General M
- Curriculum and Instruction M
- Early Childhood Education M
- Educational Leadership and Administration M
- Educational Media/Instructional Technology M
- Elementary Education M
- English as a Second Language M
- English Education M
- Foreign Languages Education M
- Health Education M
- Human Resources Management M
- Mathematics Education M
- Reading Education M
- Social Sciences Education M
- Special Education M

FRANCISCAN UNIVERSITY OF STEUBENVILLE
- Business Administration and Management—General M
- Curriculum and Instruction M
- Education—General M
- Educational Leadership and Administration M

FRANCIS MARION UNIVERSITY
- Business Administration and Management—General M
- Early Childhood Education M
- Education—General M
- Elementary Education M
- Secondary Education M
- Special Education M

FRANKLIN PIERCE UNIVERSITY
- Business Administration and Management—General M,D,O
- Curriculum and Instruction M,D,O
- Human Resources Management M,D,O
- Management Information Systems M,D,O
- Management Strategy and Policy M,D,O
- Special Education M,D,O
- Sports Management M,D,O
- Sustainability Management M,D,O

FRANKLIN UNIVERSITY
- Accounting M
- Business Administration and Management—General M
- Educational Media/Instructional Technology M
- Marketing M

FRANKLIN UNIVERSITY SWITZERLAND
- International Business M

FREED-HARDEMAN UNIVERSITY
- Accounting M
- Business Administration and Management—General M
- Counselor Education M,O
- Curriculum and Instruction M,O
- Education—General M,O
- Educational Leadership and Administration M,O
- Management Strategy and Policy M
- Special Education M,O

FRESNO PACIFIC UNIVERSITY
- Business Administration and Management—General M
- Counselor Education M
- Curriculum and Instruction M
- Education—General M,O
- Educational Leadership and Administration M
- Educational Media/Instructional Technology M
- English as a Second Language M,O
- International Business M
- Kinesiology and Movement Studies M
- Mathematics Education M
- Reading Education M,O
- Science Education M
- Special Education M,O
- Student Affairs M,O

FRIENDS UNIVERSITY
- Accounting M
- Business Administration and Management—General M
- Education—General M
- Industrial and Manufacturing Management M
- Law M
- Logistics M
- Management Information Systems M
- Management Strategy and Policy M
- Supply Chain Management M

FROSTBURG STATE UNIVERSITY
- Business Administration and Management—General M
- Counselor Education M
- Curriculum and Instruction M
- Education—General M
- Educational Leadership and Administration M
- Educational Media/Instructional Technology M
- Elementary Education M
- Reading Education M
- Recreation and Park Management M
- Secondary Education M
- Special Education M

FULL SAIL UNIVERSITY
- Business Administration and Management—General M
- Educational Media/Instructional Technology M
- Entertainment Management M
- Marketing M

FURMAN UNIVERSITY
- Curriculum and Instruction M,O
- Early Childhood Education M,O
- Education—General M,O
- Educational Leadership and Administration M,O
- English as a Second Language M,O
- Reading Education M,O
- Special Education M,O

GALLAUDET UNIVERSITY
- Counselor Education M,D,O
- Early Childhood Education M,D,O
- Education—General M,D,O
- Elementary Education M,D,O
- International and Comparative Education M,D,O
- Multilingual and Multicultural Education M,D,O
- Secondary Education M,D,O
- Social Work M,D,O
- Special Education M,D,O

GANNON UNIVERSITY
- Athletic Training and Sports Medicine M
- Business Administration and Management—General M
- Curriculum and Instruction M,O
- Education—General M,O
- Educational Leadership and Administration D,O
- English as a Second Language O
- Exercise and Sports Science M
- Finance and Banking M
- Human Resources Management M
- Marketing M
- Organizational Management D,O
- Reading Education M,O
- Special Education O

GARDNER-WEBB UNIVERSITY
- Business Administration and Management—General M
- Curriculum and Instruction D
- Education—General M,D
- Educational Leadership and Administration M,D
- Elementary Education M
- English Education M
- Exercise and Sports Science M
- Middle School Education M
- Physical Education M
- Religious Education M,D

GARRETT-EVANGELICAL THEOLOGICAL SEMINARY
- Religious Education M,D

GENEVA COLLEGE
- Business Administration and Management—General M
- Counselor Education M
- Education—General M
- Educational Leadership and Administration M
- Finance and Banking M
- Higher Education M
- Marketing M
- Organizational Management M
- Reading Education M
- Special Education M

GEORGE FOX UNIVERSITY
- Business Administration and Management—General M,D
- Counselor Education M,D,O
- Curriculum and Instruction M,D,O
- Education—General M,D,O
- Educational Leadership and Administration M,D,O
- Educational Media/Instructional Technology M,D,O
- English as a Second Language M,D,O
- Finance and Banking M,D
- Higher Education M,D
- Human Resources Management M,D
- Marketing M,D
- Multilingual and Multicultural Education M
- Organizational Management M,D
- Reading Education M,D,O
- Religious Education M,D,O
- Secondary Education M,D,O
- Special Education M

GEORGE MASON UNIVERSITY
- Accounting M,O
- Actuarial Science M,D,O
- Advertising and Public Relations M,O

*M—masters degree; D—doctorate; O—other advanced degree; *—Close-Up and/or Display*

- Art Education M
- Business Administration and Management—General M
- Community College Education M,D,O
- Counselor Education M
- Curriculum and Instruction M
- Education—General M,D
- Educational Leadership and Administration M
- Educational Psychology M
- Electronic Commerce M,D,O
- English as a Second Language M,D,O
- Entrepreneurship M,O
- Exercise and Sports Science M
- Foreign Languages Education M
- Higher Education M,D,O
- Human Resources Management M
- International and Comparative Education M
- International Business M
- Law M,D
- Logistics M,D
- Management Information Systems M,D,O
- Music Education M,D,O
- Nonprofit Management M,D,O
- Organizational Management M
- Project Management M,O
- Real Estate M,O
- Recreation and Park Management M
- Social Work M
- Special Education M
- Sports Management M
- Sustainability Management M
- Transportation Management M,O

GEORGETOWN COLLEGE
- Education—General M
- Reading Education M
- Special Education M

GEORGETOWN UNIVERSITY
- Advertising and Public Relations M
- Business Administration and Management—General M
- English as a Second Language M,D,O
- Finance and Banking D
- Health Law M
- Human Resources Management M
- Industrial and Manufacturing Management D
- International Business M,D
- Law M,D
- Multilingual and Multicultural Education M,D,O
- Real Estate M,D
- Sports Management M,D
- Taxation M,D

THE GEORGE WASHINGTON UNIVERSITY
- Accounting M,D
- Adult Education O
- Art Education M
- Business Administration and Management—General M,D,O
- Counselor Education M,D,O
- Curriculum and Instruction M,D,O
- Distance Education Development O
- Early Childhood Education M
- Education—General M,D,O
- Educational Leadership and Administration M,D,O
- Educational Media/Instructional Technology M,O
- Educational Policy M,D
- Elementary Education M
- Exercise and Sports Science M
- Finance and Banking M,D
- Foundations and Philosophy of Education O
- Higher Education M,D,O
- Hospitality Management M,O
- Human Resources Development M,D,O
- Human Resources Management M,D
- International and Comparative Education M
- International Business M,D
- Investment Management M,D
- Law M,D
- Legal and Justice Studies M,O
- Management Information Systems M,D
- Management Strategy and Policy M,D
- Marketing M,D
- Multilingual and Multicultural Education M,O
- Museum Education M,O
- Nonprofit Management M,D,O
- Organizational Management M,D,O
- Project Management M,D
- Reading Education O
- Real Estate M,D
- Secondary Education M
- Special Education M,D,O
- Sports Management M,O
- Travel and Tourism M,O
- Vocational and Technical Education O

GEORGIA COLLEGE & STATE UNIVERSITY
- Accounting M
- Business Administration and Management—General M
- Curriculum and Instruction O
- Early Childhood Education M,O
- Education—General M,O
- Educational Leadership and Administration O
- Educational Media/Instructional Technology M
- Exercise and Sports Science M
- Health Education M
- Kinesiology and Movement Studies M
- Logistics M
- Management Information Systems M
- Middle School Education M
- Music Education M
- Physical Education M
- Reading Education M
- Recreation and Park Management M
- Secondary Education M,O
- Special Education M,O

GEORGIA INSTITUTE OF TECHNOLOGY
- Accounting M,D,O
- Business Administration and Management—General M,D,O
- Electronic Commerce M,O
- Entrepreneurship M,O
- Finance and Banking M,D,O
- International Business M,O
- Management Information Systems M,D,O
- Management Strategy and Policy M,D,O
- Marketing M,D,O
- Organizational Behavior M,D,O

GEORGIAN COURT UNIVERSITY
- Business Administration and Management—General M
- Counselor Education M,O
- Education—General M
- Educational Leadership and Administration M,O
- Religious Education M,O

GEORGIA REGENTS UNIVERSITY
- Business Administration and Management—General M
- Counselor Education M
- Curriculum and Instruction M
- Education—General M,O
- Educational Leadership and Administration M,O
- Health Education M
- Physical Education M
- Secondary Education M
- Special Education M,O

GEORGIA SOUTHERN UNIVERSITY
- Accounting M
- Business Administration and Management—General M
- Business Education M
- Counselor Education M,O
- Curriculum and Instruction M,O
- Early Childhood Education M,O
- Education—General M,D,O
- Educational Leadership and Administration M,D,O
- Educational Media/Instructional Technology M,O
- Elementary Education M
- English Education M
- Foreign Languages Education M
- Health Education M,D
- Higher Education M
- Kinesiology and Movement Studies M
- Logistics D
- Management Information Systems M,O
- Mathematics Education M
- Middle School Education M,O
- Nonprofit Management O
- Reading Education M,O
- Secondary Education M,O
- Social Sciences Education M
- Special Education M,O
- Sports Management M
- Supply Chain Management D

GEORGIA SOUTHWESTERN STATE UNIVERSITY
- Business Administration and Management—General M
- Early Childhood Education M,O
- Education—General M,O
- Health Education M,O
- Middle School Education M,O
- Physical Education M,O
- Reading Education M,O
- Secondary Education M,O
- Special Education M,O

GEORGIA STATE UNIVERSITY
- Accounting M
- Actuarial Science M
- Art Education M
- Athletic Training and Sports Medicine M
- Business Administration and Management—General M,D
- Counselor Education M,D
- Early Childhood Education M,D,O
- Education of Students with Severe/Multiple Disabilities M
- Education—General M,D,O
- Educational Leadership and Administration M,D,O
- Educational Measurement and Evaluation M,D
- Educational Media/Instructional Technology M,D
- Educational Policy M,D,O
- Educational Psychology M,D
- Elementary Education M,D,O
- English as a Second Language M,D
- English Education M,D
- Entrepreneurship M,D
- Exercise and Sports Science M
- Finance and Banking M,D,O
- Foreign Languages Education M
- Foundations and Philosophy of Education M,D
- Health Education M
- Human Resources Management M,D
- Human Services M,O
- Insurance M,D,O
- International Business M
- Kinesiology and Movement Studies D
- Law D
- Management Information Systems M,D,O
- Management Strategy and Policy M,D
- Marketing M,D
- Mathematics Education M,D,O
- Middle School Education M,D
- Music Education M,D,O
- Nonprofit Management M,D,O
- Organizational Management M,D
- Physical Education M
- Reading Education M,D
- Real Estate M,D,O
- Science Education M,D
- Secondary Education M,D
- Social Sciences Education M,D
- Social Work M,O
- Special Education M,D
- Sports Management M
- Taxation M
- Urban Education M,D,O

GLION INSTITUTE OF HIGHER EDUCATION
- Hospitality Management M

GLOBAL UNIVERSITY
- Religious Education M

GLOBE UNIVERSITY–WOODBURY
- Business Administration and Management—General M
- Management Information Systems M

GODDARD COLLEGE
- Business Administration and Management—General M
- Education—General M
- Sustainability Management M

GOLDEN GATE BAPTIST THEOLOGICAL SEMINARY
- Early Childhood Education M,D,O
- Educational Leadership and Administration M,D,O

GOLDEN GATE UNIVERSITY
- Accounting M,D,O
- Advertising and Public Relations M,D,O
- Business Administration and Management—General M,D,O
- Environmental Law M,D
- Finance and Banking M,D,O
- Human Resources Management M,D,O
- Intellectual Property Law M,D
- International Business M,D,O
- Law M,D
- Legal and Justice Studies M,D
- Management Information Systems M,D,O
- Marketing M,D,O
- Supply Chain Management M,D,O
- Taxation M,D,O

GOLDEY-BEACOM COLLEGE
- Business Administration and Management—General M
- Finance and Banking M
- Human Resources Management M
- International Business M
- Management Information Systems M
- Marketing M
- Taxation M

GONZAGA UNIVERSITY
- Accounting M
- Business Administration and Management—General M
- Education—General M
- Educational Leadership and Administration M,D
- English as a Second Language M
- Law D
- Organizational Management M
- Special Education M
- Sports Management M

GORDON COLLEGE
- Education—General M
- Educational Leadership and Administration M,O
- English as a Second Language M,O
- Mathematics Education M,O
- Music Education M,O
- Reading Education M,O

GOSHEN COLLEGE
- Environmental Education M

GOUCHER COLLEGE
- Education—General M

GOVERNORS STATE UNIVERSITY
- Accounting M
- Business Administration and Management—General M
- Early Childhood Education M
- Education—General M
- Educational Leadership and Administration M
- Educational Media/Instructional Technology M
- Legal and Justice Studies M
- Management Information Systems M
- Reading Education M
- Social Work M
- Special Education M

GRACELAND UNIVERSITY (IA)
- Education—General M
- Educational Leadership and Administration M
- Educational Media/Instructional Technology M
- Organizational Management M,D,O
- Reading Education M
- Special Education M

THE GRADUATE CENTER, CITY UNIVERSITY OF NEW YORK
- Accounting D
- Business Administration and Management—General D
- Educational Psychology D
- Finance and Banking D
- Management Information Systems D
- Organizational Behavior D
- Social Work D
- Urban Education D

GRADUATE INSTITUTE OF APPLIED LINGUISTICS
- Multilingual and Multicultural Education M,O

GRAMBLING STATE UNIVERSITY
- Counselor Education M,D,O
- Curriculum and Instruction M,D,O
- Developmental Education M,D,O
- Education—General M,D,O
- Educational Leadership and Administration M,D,O
- Educational Media/Instructional Technology M,D,O
- Higher Education M,D,O
- Human Resources Management M
- Mathematics Education M,D,O
- Reading Education M,D,O
- Science Education M,D,O
- Social Sciences Education M
- Social Work M
- Special Education M
- Sports Management M
- Student Affairs M,D,O

GRAND CANYON UNIVERSITY
- Accounting M
- Business Administration and Management—General M,D
- Curriculum and Instruction M
- Education—General M,D
- Educational Leadership and Administration M,D
- Elementary Education M
- Entrepreneurship M
- Finance and Banking M
- Health Education D
- Higher Education D
- Human Resources Management M
- Management Information Systems M
- Marketing M
- Organizational Management D
- Secondary Education M
- Special Education M

GRAND RAPIDS THEOLOGICAL SEMINARY OF CORNERSTONE UNIVERSITY
- Religious Education M

GRAND VALLEY STATE UNIVERSITY
- Accounting M
- Adult Education M,O
- Business Administration and Management—General M
- Curriculum and Instruction M
- Early Childhood Education M,O
- Education—General M,O
- Educational Leadership and Administration M,O
- Educational Media/Instructional Technology M,O
- Elementary Education M,O
- English as a Second Language M,O
- English Education M
- Higher Education M,O
- Management Information Systems M,O
- Middle School Education M,O
- Reading Education M
- Secondary Education M,O
- Social Work M
- Special Education M
- Taxation M

GRAND VIEW UNIVERSITY
- Business Administration and Management—General M
- Education—General M
- Organizational Management M

GRANITE STATE COLLEGE
- Business Administration and Management—General M
- Organizational Management M
- Project Management M

GRANTHAM UNIVERSITY
- Business Administration and Management—General M
- Human Resources Development M
- Management Information Systems M
- Management Strategy and Policy M
- Organizational Management M
- Project Management M

GRATZ COLLEGE
- Education—General M
- Educational Media/Instructional Technology O
- Nonprofit Management O
- Religious Education M,D,O
- Social Work M,O

GREEN MOUNTAIN COLLEGE
- Business Administration and Management—General M

GREENSBORO COLLEGE
- Education—General M
- Elementary Education M
- English as a Second Language M
- Special Education M

GREENVILLE COLLEGE
- Education—General M
- Elementary Education M
- Secondary Education M

GWYNEDD MERCY UNIVERSITY
- Business Administration and Management—General M
- Counselor Education M
- Education—General M

Educational Leadership and
   Administration — M
Reading Education — M
Special Education — M

HAMLINE UNIVERSITY
Business Administration and
   Management—General — M,D
Education—General — M,D
English as a Second Language — M,D
Environmental Education — M,D
Law — M,D
Nonprofit Management — M,D
Reading Education — M,D
Science Education — M,D

HAMPTON UNIVERSITY
Business Administration and
   Management—General — M,D
Counselor Education — M
Early Childhood Education — M
Education of the Gifted — M
Education—General — M
Educational Leadership and
   Administration — M,D
Elementary Education — M
Middle School Education — M
Music Education — M
Secondary Education — M
Special Education — M
Student Affairs — M

HANNIBAL-LAGRANGE UNIVERSITY
Education—General — M
Reading Education — M

HARDING UNIVERSITY
Art Education — M,O
Business Administration and
   Management—General — M
Counselor Education — M,O
Early Childhood Education — M,O
Education—General — M,O
Educational Leadership and
   Administration — M,O
Elementary Education — M,O
English as a Second Language — M,O
English Education — M,O
Foreign Languages Education — M,O
Health Education — M,O
International Business — M
Mathematics Education — M,O
Organizational Management — M
Reading Education — M,O
Secondary Education — M,O
Social Sciences Education — M,O
Special Education — M,O

HARDIN-SIMMONS UNIVERSITY
Business Administration and
   Management—General — M
Counselor Education — M
Education of the Gifted — M
Education—General — M,D
Educational Leadership and
   Administration — D
Kinesiology and Movement Studies — M
Music Education — M
Reading Education — M
Recreation and Park Management — M
Science Education — M,D
Sports Management — M

HARRISBURG UNIVERSITY OF SCIENCE AND TECHNOLOGY
Educational Media/Instructional
   Technology — M
Entrepreneurship — M
Management Information Systems — M
Project Management — M

HARRISON MIDDLETON UNIVERSITY
Education—General — M,D
Legal and Justice Studies — M,D
Science Education — M,D

HARVARD UNIVERSITY
Accounting — D
Art Education — M
Business Administration and
   Management—General — M,D,O
Curriculum and Instruction — M,D
Education—General — M,D
Educational Leadership and
   Administration — M,D
Educational Measurement and
   Evaluation — D
Educational Media/Instructional
   Technology — M,O
Educational Policy — M
Educational Psychology — M
Foundations and Philosophy of
   Education — M,O
Higher Education — D
Industrial and Manufacturing
   Management — D
International and Comparative
   Education — M
Law — M,D
Legal and Justice Studies — D
Management Strategy and Policy — D
Marketing — D
Mathematics Education — M,O
Multilingual and Multicultural
   Education — D
Organizational Behavior — D
Reading Education — M

HASTINGS COLLEGE
Education—General — M

HAWAI'I PACIFIC UNIVERSITY
Accounting —

Business Administration and
   Management—General — M
Electronic Commerce — M
Elementary Education — M
English as a Second Language — M
Finance and Banking — M
Human Resources Management — M
International Business — M
Management Information Systems — M
Marketing — M
Organizational Management — M
Secondary Education — M
Social Work — M
Travel and Tourism — M

HEBREW COLLEGE
Early Childhood Education — M,O
Education—General — M,O
Middle School Education — M,O
Music Education — M,O
Religious Education — M,O
Special Education — M,O

HEBREW UNION COLLEGE–JEWISH INSTITUTE OF RELIGION (NY)
Education—General — M
Nonprofit Management — M
Religious Education — M

HEC MONTREAL
Accounting — M,O
Business Administration and
   Management—General — M,D,O
Electronic Commerce — M
Finance and Banking — M,O
Human Resources Management — M
Industrial and Manufacturing
   Management — M
International Business — M
Logistics — M
Management Information Systems — M
Management Strategy and Policy — M
Marketing — M
Organizational Management — M
Supply Chain Management — M,O
Taxation — M,O

HEIDELBERG UNIVERSITY
Business Administration and
   Management—General — M
Education—General — M
Music Education — M

HENDERSON STATE UNIVERSITY
Business Administration and
   Management—General — M
Counselor Education — M,O
Curriculum and Instruction — M,O
Early Childhood Education — M,O
Education—General — M,O
Educational Leadership and
   Administration — M,O
English as a Second Language — M,O
Middle School Education — M,O
Physical Education — M,O
Reading Education — M,O
Special Education — M,O
Sports Management — M

HENDRIX COLLEGE
Accounting — M

HERITAGE UNIVERSITY
Counselor Education — M
Education—General — M
Educational Leadership and
   Administration — M
English as a Second Language — M
Multilingual and Multicultural
   Education — M
Reading Education — M
Science Education — M
Special Education — M

HERZING UNIVERSITY ONLINE
Accounting — M
Business Administration and
   Management—General — M
Human Resources Management — M
Marketing — M
Project Management — M

HIGH POINT UNIVERSITY
Business Administration and
   Management—General — M
Education—General — M
Educational Leadership and
   Administration — M
Elementary Education — M
Mathematics Education — M
Nonprofit Management — M
Secondary Education — M
Special Education — M

HODGES UNIVERSITY
Business Administration and
   Management—General — M
Education—General — M
Legal and Justice Studies — M
Management Information Systems — M

HOFSTRA UNIVERSITY
Accounting — M,O
Advertising and Public Relations — M
Art Education — M
Business Administration and
   Management—General — M,O
Business Education — M,O
Counselor Education — M,O
Early Childhood Education — M,O
Education of the Gifted — M
Education—General — M,D,O
Educational Leadership and
   Administration — M,D,O

Educational Media/Instructional
   Technology — M,O
Educational Policy — M,D,O
Elementary Education — M,O
English as a Second Language — M,O
English Education — M,O
Entertainment Management — M,O
Exercise and Sports Science — M,O
Finance and Banking — M,O
Foreign Languages Education — M,O
Foundations and Philosophy of
   Education — M,D,O
Health Education — M,O
Higher Education — M,D,O
Human Resources Management — M,O
International Business — M,O
Investment Management — M,O
Law — M,D
Legal and Justice Studies — M,D
Management Information Systems — M,O
Marketing Research — M,O
Marketing — M,O
Mathematics Education — M,O
Middle School Education — M,O
Multilingual and Multicultural
   Education — M,O
Music Education — M,O
Physical Education — M,O
Quality Management — M,O
Quantitative Analysis — M,O
Reading Education — M,D,O
Real Estate — M,O
Science Education — M,O
Secondary Education — M,D,O
Social Sciences Education — M,O
Special Education — M,D,O
Sports Management — M,O
Taxation — M,O

HOLLINS UNIVERSITY
Education—General — M
Legal and Justice Studies — M,O

HOLY FAMILY UNIVERSITY
Business Administration and
   Management—General — M
Early Childhood Education — M
Education—General — M,D
Educational Leadership and
   Administration — M,D
Elementary Education — M
English as a Second Language — M
Finance and Banking — M
Human Resources Management — M
Management Information Systems — M
Middle School Education — M
Reading Education — M
Secondary Education — M
Special Education — M

HOLY NAMES UNIVERSITY
Business Administration and
   Management—General — M
Education—General — M,O
Educational Psychology — M,O
English as a Second Language — M,O
Finance and Banking — M
Marketing — M
Music Education — M,O
Special Education — M,O
Sports Management — M
Urban Education — M,O

HOOD COLLEGE
Accounting — M
Business Administration and
   Management—General — M
Curriculum and Instruction — M,O
Early Childhood Education — M,O
Education—General — M
Educational Leadership and
   Administration — M,O
Elementary Education — M,O
Finance and Banking — M
Human Resources Management — M
Management Information Systems — M
Marketing — M
Mathematics Education — M,O
Middle School Education — M,O
Reading Education — M,O
Science Education — M,O
Secondary Education — M,O
Special Education — M,O

HOPE INTERNATIONAL UNIVERSITY
Education—General — M
Educational Leadership and
   Administration — M
Elementary Education — M
International Business — M
Marketing — M
Nonprofit Management — M
Secondary Education — M

HOUSTON BAPTIST UNIVERSITY
Accounting — M
Business Administration and
   Management—General — M
Counselor Education — M
Curriculum and Instruction — M
Education—General — M
Educational Leadership and
   Administration — M
Educational Measurement and
   Evaluation — M
English as a Second Language — M
Human Resources Management — M
Reading Education — M

HOWARD PAYNE UNIVERSITY
Business Administration and
   Management—General — M

Educational Leadership and
   Administration — M

HOWARD UNIVERSITY
Accounting — M
Business Administration and
   Management—General — M
Counselor Education — M
Education—General — M,D,O
Educational Leadership and
   Administration — M,D,O
Educational Policy — M,D,O
Educational Psychology — D
Elementary Education — M
Exercise and Sports Science — M
Finance and Banking — M
Health Education — M
Human Resources Management — M
International Business — M
Law — M,D
Leisure Studies — M
Management Information Systems — M
Marketing — M
Multilingual and Multicultural
   Education — M,D
Music Education — M
Physical Education — M
Secondary Education — M
Social Work — M,D
Special Education — M
Sports Management — M
Supply Chain Management — M

HULT INTERNATIONAL BUSINESS SCHOOL (UNITED STATES)
Business Administration and
   Management—General — M
Entrepreneurship — M
Finance and Banking — M
International Business — M
Marketing — M

HUMBOLDT STATE UNIVERSITY
Athletic Training and Sports
   Medicine — M
Business Administration and
   Management—General — M
Education—General — M
English as a Second Language — M
Exercise and Sports Science — M
Kinesiology and Movement Studies — M
Physical Education — M
Social Work — M

HUMPHREYS COLLEGE
Law — D

HUNTER COLLEGE OF THE CITY UNIVERSITY OF NEW YORK
Accounting — M
Counselor Education — M
Early Childhood Education — M,O
Education of Students with
   Severe/Multiple Disabilities — M
Education—General — M,O
Educational Leadership and
   Administration — O
Elementary Education — M
English as a Second Language — M
English Education — M
Foreign Languages Education — M
Mathematics Education — M
Multilingual and Multicultural
   Education — M
Music Education — M
Reading Education — M,O
Science Education — M,O
Secondary Education — M
Social Sciences Education — M
Social Work — M,D
Special Education — M

HUNTINGTON UNIVERSITY
Education—General — M

HUSSON UNIVERSITY
Business Administration and
   Management—General — M
Counselor Education — M
Hospitality Management — M
Nonprofit Management — M

IDAHO STATE UNIVERSITY
Business Administration and
   Management—General — M,O
Counselor Education — M,D,O
Curriculum and Instruction — M,O
Education—General — M,D,O
Educational Leadership and
   Administration — M,D,O
Educational Media/Instructional
   Technology — M,D,O
Elementary Education — M,D,O
English as a Second Language — M,D,O
Health Education — M
Management Information Systems — M,O
Mathematics Education — M,D
Physical Education — M
Reading Education — M,O
Secondary Education — M,O
Special Education — M,D,O
Vocational and Technical Education — M

ILLINOIS COLLEGE
Education—General — M

ILLINOIS INSTITUTE OF TECHNOLOGY
Business Administration and
   Management—General — M,D
Computer Education — M,D
Finance and Banking — M,D
Human Resources Development — M,D
Industrial and Manufacturing
   Management — M

M—masters degree; D—doctorate; O—other advanced degree; *—Close-Up and/or Display

Law M,D
Management Information Systems M,D
Marketing M
Mathematics Education M,D
Science Education M,D
Sustainability Management M
Taxation M,D

ILLINOIS STATE UNIVERSITY
Accounting M
Business Administration and
 Management—General M
Curriculum and Instruction M
Education—General M,D
Educational Leadership and
 Administration M,D
Educational Policy M,D
Educational Psychology M,D,O
Health Education M
Higher Education M,D
Management Information Systems M
Mathematics Education D
Physical Education M
Reading Education M
Social Work M
Special Education M
Student Affairs M

IMCA–INTERNATIONAL MANAGEMENT CENTRES ASSOCIATION
Business Administration and
 Management—General M

IMMACULATA UNIVERSITY
Counselor Education M,D,O
Educational Leadership and
 Administration M,D,O
Elementary Education M,D,O
Multilingual and Multicultural
 Education M
Organizational Management M
Secondary Education M,D,O
Special Education M,D,O

INDEPENDENCE UNIVERSITY
Business Administration and
 Management—General M

INDIANA STATE UNIVERSITY
Athletic Training and Sports
 Medicine M
Business Administration and
 Management—General M
Counselor Education M,D,O
Curriculum and Instruction M,D
Early Childhood Education M
Education—General M,D,O
Educational Leadership and
 Administration M,D,O
Educational Media/Instructional
 Technology M,D
Elementary Education M
English as a Second Language M,O
English Education M
Exercise and Sports Science M
Health Education M
Higher Education M,D,O
Home Economics Education M
Human Resources Development M
Mathematics Education M
Multilingual and Multicultural
 Education M,O
Physical Education M
Science Education M,D
Sports Management M
Student Affairs M,D,O
Vocational and Technical Education M

INDIANA TECH
Accounting M
Business Administration and
 Management—General M
Human Resources Development M
Human Resources Management M
International Business D
Marketing M
Organizational Management M
Science Education M

INDIANA UNIVERSITY BLOOMINGTON
Art Education M,D,O
Athletic Training and Sports
 Medicine M,D
Business Administration and
 Management—General M
Counselor Education M,D,O
Curriculum and Instruction M,D,O
Education—General M,D,O
Educational Leadership and
 Administration M,D,O
Educational Measurement and
 Evaluation M,D,O
Educational Media/Instructional
 Technology M,D
Educational Policy M,D,O
Educational Psychology M,D,O
Elementary Education M,D,O
English as a Second Language M,D
Exercise and Sports Science M,D
Finance and Banking M,D,O
Foreign Languages Education M,D
Foundations and Philosophy of
 Education M,D,O
Health Education M,D
Higher Education M,D,O
International and Comparative
 Education M,D,O
Kinesiology and Movement Studies M,D
Law M,D
Leisure Studies M,D
Library Science M,D
Management Information Systems M,D,O
Mathematics Education M,D,O
Multilingual and Multicultural
 Education M,D,O
Nonprofit Management M,D,O

Organizational Management M,D,O
Physical Education M,D
Reading Education M,D,O
Recreation and Park Management M,D
Science Education M,D,O
Secondary Education M,D,O
Social Sciences Education M,D,O
Special Education M,D,O
Sports Management M,D
Sustainability Management M,D,O
Travel and Tourism M,D

INDIANA UNIVERSITY EAST
Education—General M
Social Work M

INDIANA UNIVERSITY KOKOMO
Business Administration and
 Management—General M
Education—General M
Elementary Education M

INDIANA UNIVERSITY NORTHWEST
Business Administration and
 Management—General M,O
Education—General M
Educational Leadership and
 Administration M
Elementary Education M
Human Services M,O
Nonprofit Management M,O
Secondary Education M
Social Work M

INDIANA UNIVERSITY OF PENNSYLVANIA
Adult Education M,D
Business Administration and
 Management—General M
Business Education M
Counselor Education M
Curriculum and Instruction D
Education—General M,D,O
Educational Leadership and
 Administration D,O
Educational Media/Instructional
 Technology M,D
Educational Psychology M,O
English as a Second Language M,D
English Education M
Exercise and Sports Science M
Foreign Languages Education M
Health Education M
Higher Education M
Human Resources Development M
Mathematics Education M
Music Education M
Physical Education M
Reading Education M,O
Special Education M
Sports Management M
Student Affairs M
Vocational and Technical Education M

INDIANA UNIVERSITY–PURDUE UNIVERSITY FORT WAYNE
Business Administration and
 Management—General M
Counselor Education M,O
Education—General M,O
Educational Leadership and
 Administration M,O
Elementary Education M
English as a Second Language M,O
English Education M,O
Mathematics Education M,O
Organizational Management M
Secondary Education M
Special Education M

INDIANA UNIVERSITY–PURDUE UNIVERSITY INDIANAPOLIS
Accounting M
Art Education M
Business Administration and
 Management—General M
Computer Education M,O
Counselor Education M,O
Curriculum and Instruction M,O
Early Childhood Education M,O
Education—General M,O
Educational Leadership and
 Administration M,O
English as a Second Language M,O
Foreign Languages Education M,O
Health Education M,D
Higher Education M,O
Law M,O
Library Science M,O
Mathematics Education M,D
Nonprofit Management M,O
Organizational Management M,O
Physical Education M
Reading Education M,O
Social Work M,D,O
Special Education M,O
Student Affairs M,O

INDIANA UNIVERSITY SOUTH BEND
Accounting M
Art Education M
Business Administration and
 Management—General M
Counselor Education M
Education—General M
Elementary Education M
Management Information Systems M
Secondary Education M
Social Work M
Special Education M

INDIANA UNIVERSITY SOUTHEAST
Business Administration and
 Management—General M
Counselor Education M
Education—General M
Elementary Education M

Finance and Banking M
Secondary Education M

INDIANA WESLEYAN UNIVERSITY
Accounting M,O
Business Administration and
 Management—General M
Counselor Education M
Educational Leadership and
 Administration M,O
Higher Education M,O
Human Resources Management M,O
Organizational Management M

INSTITUTE FOR CHRISTIAN STUDIES
Education—General M,D

INSTITUTE FOR CLINICAL SOCIAL WORK
Social Work D

INSTITUTE FOR CREATION RESEARCH
Religious Education M

INSTITUTO CENTROAMERICANO DE ADMINISTRACIÓN DE EMPRESAS
Business Administration and
 Management—General M
Finance and Banking M
Real Estate M

INSTITUTO TECNOLOGICO DE SANTO DOMINGO
Accounting M,O
Adult Education M,O
Business Administration and
 Management—General M,O
Education—General M,O
Educational Leadership and
 Administration M,O
Educational Psychology M,O
Environmental Education M,D,O
Finance and Banking M,O
Human Resources Management M,O
Industrial and Manufacturing
 Management M,O
International Business M,O
Marketing M,O
Organizational Management M,O
Quality Management M,O
Quantitative Analysis M,O
Secondary Education M,O
Social Sciences Education M,O
Taxation M,O
Transportation Management M,O

INSTITUTO TECNOLÓGICO Y DE ESTUDIOS SUPERIORES DE MONTERREY, CAMPUS CENTRAL DE VERACRUZ
Business Administration and
 Management—General M
Education—General M
Educational Leadership and
 Administration M
Educational Media/Instructional
 Technology M
Electronic Commerce M
Finance and Banking M
International Business M
Management Information Systems M
Marketing M

INSTITUTO TECNOLÓGICO Y DE ESTUDIOS SUPERIORES DE MONTERREY, CAMPUS CHIHUAHUA
International Business M

INSTITUTO TECNOLÓGICO Y DE ESTUDIOS SUPERIORES DE MONTERREY, CAMPUS CIUDAD DE MÉXICO
Business Administration and
 Management—General M
Education—General M,D
Educational Media/Instructional
 Technology M,D
Finance and Banking M,D
International Business M,D
Law O
Management Information Systems M,D
Quality Management M,D

INSTITUTO TECNOLÓGICO Y DE ESTUDIOS SUPERIORES DE MONTERREY, CAMPUS CIUDAD JUÁREZ
Business Administration and
 Management—General M
Education—General M
Educational Leadership and
 Administration M
Educational Media/Instructional
 Technology M,D
Electronic Commerce M
Management Information Systems M
Quality Management M

INSTITUTO TECNOLÓGICO Y DE ESTUDIOS SUPERIORES DE MONTERREY, CAMPUS CIUDAD OBREGÓN
Business Administration and
 Management—General M
Developmental Education M
Education—General M
Finance and Banking M
Management Information Systems M
Marketing M
Mathematics Education M

INSTITUTO TECNOLÓGICO Y DE ESTUDIOS SUPERIORES DE MONTERREY, CAMPUS CUERNAVACA
Business Administration and
 Management—General M
Finance and Banking M

Human Resources Management M
International Business M
Marketing M

INSTITUTO TECNOLÓGICO Y DE ESTUDIOS SUPERIORES DE MONTERREY, CAMPUS ESTADO DE MÉXICO
Business Administration and
 Management—General M,D
Education—General M,D
Educational Leadership and
 Administration M,D
Educational Media/Instructional
 Technology M,D
Electronic Commerce M,D
Finance and Banking M,D
Industrial and Manufacturing
 Management M,D
Management Information Systems M,D
Marketing M,D
Quality Management M,D

INSTITUTO TECNOLÓGICO Y DE ESTUDIOS SUPERIORES DE MONTERREY, CAMPUS GUADALAJARA
Business Administration and
 Management—General M
Finance and Banking M

INSTITUTO TECNOLÓGICO Y DE ESTUDIOS SUPERIORES DE MONTERREY, CAMPUS IRAPUATO
Business Administration and
 Management—General M,D
Education—General M,D
Educational Leadership and
 Administration M,D
Educational Media/Instructional
 Technology M,D
Electronic Commerce M,D
Finance and Banking M,D
Industrial and Manufacturing
 Management M,D
International Business M,D
Library Science M,D
Management Information Systems M,D
Marketing Research M,D
Quality Management M,D

INSTITUTO TECNOLÓGICO Y DE ESTUDIOS SUPERIORES DE MONTERREY, CAMPUS LAGUNA
Business Administration and
 Management—General M
Management Information Systems M

INSTITUTO TECNOLÓGICO Y DE ESTUDIOS SUPERIORES DE MONTERREY, CAMPUS LEÓN
Business Administration and
 Management—General M

INSTITUTO TECNOLÓGICO Y DE ESTUDIOS SUPERIORES DE MONTERREY, CAMPUS MONTERREY
Business Administration and
 Management—General M,D
Finance and Banking M
International Business M
Marketing M
Science Education M,D

INSTITUTO TECNOLÓGICO Y DE ESTUDIOS SUPERIORES DE MONTERREY, CAMPUS QUERÉTARO
Business Administration and
 Management—General M

INSTITUTO TECNOLÓGICO Y DE ESTUDIOS SUPERIORES DE MONTERREY, CAMPUS SONORA NORTE
Business Administration and
 Management—General M
Education—General M

INSTITUTO TECNOLÓGICO Y DE ESTUDIOS SUPERIORES DE MONTERREY, CAMPUS TOLUCA
Business Administration and
 Management—General M

INTER AMERICAN UNIVERSITY OF PUERTO RICO, AGUADILLA CAMPUS
Accounting M
Business Administration and
 Management—General M
Educational Leadership and
 Administration M
Elementary Education M
Finance and Banking M
Human Resources Management M
Management Information Systems M
Marketing M

INTER AMERICAN UNIVERSITY OF PUERTO RICO, ARECIBO CAMPUS
Accounting M
Business Administration and
 Management—General M
Counselor Education M
Curriculum and Instruction M
Education—General M
Educational Leadership and
 Administration M
Elementary Education M
English as a Second Language M
Finance and Banking M
Foreign Languages Education M
Human Resources Management M
Mathematics Education M
Science Education M
Social Sciences Education M

INTER AMERICAN UNIVERSITY OF PUERTO RICO, BARRANQUITAS CAMPUS
- Accounting M
- Business Administration and Management—General M
- Curriculum and Instruction M
- Education—General M
- Educational Leadership and Administration M
- Elementary Education M
- English as a Second Language M
- Finance and Banking M
- Foreign Languages Education M
- Library Science M
- Mathematics Education M
- Science Education M
- Social Sciences Education M
- Special Education M

INTER AMERICAN UNIVERSITY OF PUERTO RICO, BAYAMÓN CAMPUS
- Human Resources Management M

INTER AMERICAN UNIVERSITY OF PUERTO RICO, GUAYAMA CAMPUS
- Business Administration and Management—General M
- Early Childhood Education M
- Elementary Education M
- Marketing M

INTER AMERICAN UNIVERSITY OF PUERTO RICO, METROPOLITAN CAMPUS
- Accounting M
- Athletic Training and Sports Medicine M
- Business Administration and Management—General M
- Business Education M
- Counselor Education M,D
- Curriculum and Instruction M,D
- Education—General M,D
- Educational Leadership and Administration M,D
- Educational Media/Instructional Technology M
- Elementary Education M
- English as a Second Language M
- Exercise and Sports Science M
- Finance and Banking M
- Foreign Languages Education M
- Health Education M
- Higher Education M
- Human Resources Development M
- Human Resources Management M
- Industrial and Manufacturing Management M
- International Business M,D
- Management Information Systems M
- Marketing M
- Mathematics Education M
- Music Education M
- Physical Education M
- Religious Education D
- Science Education M
- Social Sciences Education M
- Social Work M
- Special Education M
- Vocational and Technical Education M

INTER AMERICAN UNIVERSITY OF PUERTO RICO, PONCE CAMPUS
- Accounting M
- Elementary Education M
- English as a Second Language M
- Finance and Banking M
- Human Resources Management M
- Marketing M
- Mathematics Education M
- Science Education M
- Social Sciences Education M

INTER AMERICAN UNIVERSITY OF PUERTO RICO, SAN GERMÁN CAMPUS
- Accounting M,D
- Business Administration and Management—General M,D
- Business Education M
- Counselor Education M,D
- Curriculum and Instruction D
- Elementary Education M
- English as a Second Language M
- Finance and Banking M,D
- Health Education M
- Human Resources Development M,D
- Human Resources Management M,D
- Industrial and Manufacturing Management M
- International Business M,D
- Kinesiology and Movement Studies M
- Library Science M
- Management Information Systems M,D
- Marketing M,D
- Mathematics Education M
- Music Education M
- Physical Education M
- Science Education M
- Special Education M

INTER AMERICAN UNIVERSITY OF PUERTO RICO SCHOOL OF LAW
- Law D

INTERNATIONAL BAPTIST COLLEGE
- Education—General M

INTERNATIONAL COLLEGE OF THE CAYMAN ISLANDS
- Business Administration and Management—General M
- Business Education M
- Human Resources Management M

INTERNATIONAL INSTITUTE FOR RESTORATIVE PRACTICES
- Organizational Behavior M,O

INTERNATIONAL TECHNOLOGICAL UNIVERSITY
- Business Administration and Management—General M
- Industrial and Manufacturing Management M

THE INTERNATIONAL UNIVERSITY OF MONACO
- Business Administration and Management—General M
- Entrepreneurship M
- Finance and Banking M
- International Business M
- Marketing M

IONA COLLEGE
- Accounting M,O
- Advertising and Public Relations M,O
- Business Administration and Management—General M,O
- Early Childhood Education M
- Education—General M
- Educational Leadership and Administration M
- Elementary Education M
- English Education M
- Finance and Banking M,O
- Foreign Languages Education M
- Human Resources Management M,O
- International Business M,O
- Marketing M,O
- Mathematics Education M
- Nonprofit Management M,O
- Project Management M,O
- Reading Education M
- Recreation and Park Management M,O
- Science Education M
- Secondary Education M
- Social Sciences Education M
- Special Education M
- Sports Management M,O

IOWA STATE UNIVERSITY OF SCIENCE AND TECHNOLOGY
- Accounting M
- Agricultural Education M,D
- Counselor Education M,D
- Curriculum and Instruction M,D
- Educational Leadership and Administration M,D
- Educational Measurement and Evaluation M,D
- Educational Media/Instructional Technology M,D
- Elementary Education M,D
- English as a Second Language M
- Exercise and Sports Science M
- Finance and Banking M
- Foundations and Philosophy of Education M,D
- Higher Education M,D
- Home Economics Education M,D
- Hospitality Management M,D
- Human Resources Development M,D
- Kinesiology and Movement Studies M,D
- Management Information Systems M,D
- Mathematics Education M,D
- Science Education M,D
- Special Education M,D
- Student Affairs M,D
- Transportation Management M
- Vocational and Technical Education M,D

ITHACA COLLEGE
- Accounting M
- Business Administration and Management—General M
- Elementary Education M
- English Education M
- Exercise and Sports Science M
- Foreign Languages Education M
- Health Education M
- Mathematics Education M
- Music Education M
- Physical Education M
- Science Education M
- Secondary Education M
- Social Sciences Education M

ITT TECHNICAL INSTITUTE (IN)
- Business Administration and Management—General M

JACKSON STATE UNIVERSITY
- Accounting M
- Business Administration and Management—General M,D
- Counselor Education M
- Early Childhood Education M,D,O
- Education—General M,D,O
- Educational Leadership and Administration M,D,O
- Educational Media/Instructional Technology M,D,O
- Elementary Education M,D,O
- English Education M
- Health Education M
- Mathematics Education M
- Music Education M
- Physical Education M
- Science Education M
- Secondary Education M,D,O
- Social Work M,D
- Special Education M,O
- Vocational and Technical Education M

JACKSONVILLE STATE UNIVERSITY
- Business Administration and Management—General M
- Counselor Education M
- Early Childhood Education M
- Education—General M,O
- Educational Leadership and Administration M,O
- Educational Media/Instructional Technology M
- Elementary Education M
- Physical Education M,O
- Reading Education M
- Secondary Education M
- Special Education M

JACKSONVILLE UNIVERSITY
- Accounting M
- Business Administration and Management—General M
- Education—General M
- Educational Leadership and Administration M
- Finance and Banking M
- Organizational Management M
- Sports Management M

JAMES MADISON UNIVERSITY
- Accounting M
- Art Education M
- Business Administration and Management—General M
- Early Childhood Education M
- Educational Leadership and Administration M
- Educational Measurement and Evaluation D
- Elementary Education M
- Health Education M
- Kinesiology and Movement Studies M
- Middle School Education M
- Music Education M,D
- Reading Education M
- Secondary Education M
- Special Education M
- Vocational and Technical Education M

THE JEWISH THEOLOGICAL SEMINARY
- Religious Education M,D

JOHN BROWN UNIVERSITY
- Business Administration and Management—General M
- Counselor Education M
- Curriculum and Instruction M
- Education—General M
- Educational Leadership and Administration M
- Higher Education M

JOHN CARROLL UNIVERSITY
- Accounting M
- Business Administration and Management—General M
- Counselor Education M,O
- Early Childhood Education M
- Education—General M
- Educational Leadership and Administration M
- Educational Psychology M
- Middle School Education M
- Nonprofit Management M
- Science Education M
- Secondary Education M

JOHN F. KENNEDY UNIVERSITY
- Business Administration and Management—General M,O
- Education—General M
- Health Education M
- Human Resources Development M,O
- Law D
- Organizational Management M,O

JOHN HANCOCK UNIVERSITY
- Accounting M
- Business Administration and Management—General M
- Early Childhood Education M
- Education—General M
- Educational Leadership and Administration M
- Educational Media/Instructional Technology M
- Electronic Commerce M
- Finance and Banking M
- International Business M
- Management Information Systems M
- Marketing M
- Project Management M

JOHN JAY COLLEGE OF CRIMINAL JUSTICE OF THE CITY UNIVERSITY OF NEW YORK
- Legal and Justice Studies M,D
- Organizational Behavior M,D

JOHN MARSHALL LAW SCHOOL
- Intellectual Property Law M,D
- International Business M,D
- Law M,D
- Legal and Justice Studies M,D
- Management Information Systems M,D
- Real Estate M,D
- Taxation M,D

JOHNS HOPKINS UNIVERSITY
- Business Administration and Management—General M
- Counselor Education M,O
- Early Childhood Education M,O
- Education of the Gifted M,O
- Education—General M,D,O
- Educational Leadership and Administration M,D,O
- Educational Media/Instructional Technology M,O
- Educational Policy D
- Elementary Education M
- Finance and Banking M,D,O
- Health Education M,D,O
- Investment Management M,O
- Management Information Systems M,O
- Marketing M
- Mathematics Education O
- Nonprofit Management M,O
- Reading Education M
- Real Estate M
- Secondary Education M
- Special Education M,O
- Urban Education O

JOHNSON & WALES UNIVERSITY
- Business Administration and Management—General M
- Business Education M
- Education—General M
- Educational Leadership and Administration D
- Elementary Education M
- Hospitality Management M
- Secondary Education M
- Special Education M

JOHNSON STATE COLLEGE
- Counselor Education M
- Curriculum and Instruction M
- Education—General M
- Reading Education M
- Secondary Education M
- Special Education M

JOHNSON UNIVERSITY
- Counselor Education M,D
- Education—General M,D
- Educational Media/Instructional Technology M,D
- Higher Education M,D

JONES INTERNATIONAL UNIVERSITY
- Accounting M
- Adult Education M
- Business Administration and Management—General M
- Curriculum and Instruction M
- Distance Education Development M
- Education—General M
- Educational Leadership and Administration M
- Educational Media/Instructional Technology M
- Elementary Education M
- Entrepreneurship M
- Finance and Banking M
- Higher Education M
- Organizational Management M
- Project Management M
- Secondary Education M

JOSE MARIA VARGAS UNIVERSITY
- Early Childhood Education M

THE JUDGE ADVOCATE GENERAL'S SCHOOL, U.S. ARMY
- Law M

JUDSON UNIVERSITY
- Business Administration and Management—General M
- Organizational Management M
- Reading Education M,D

JUNIATA COLLEGE
- Accounting M

KANSAS STATE UNIVERSITY
- Accounting M
- Adult Education M,D
- Advertising and Public Relations M
- Agricultural Education M
- Business Administration and Management—General M
- Counselor Education M,D
- Curriculum and Instruction M,D
- Early Childhood Education M,D,O
- Education—General M,D
- Educational Leadership and Administration M,D
- Educational Media/Instructional Technology M,D
- Elementary Education M,D
- English as a Second Language M,D
- English Education M,D
- Finance and Banking M,D,O
- Higher Education M,D
- Hospitality Management M,D
- Human Services M,D,O
- Industrial and Manufacturing Management M
- Kinesiology and Movement Studies M,D
- Marketing M
- Mathematics Education M,D
- Middle School Education M,D
- Music Education M,D
- Reading Education M,D
- Science Education M,D
- Secondary Education M,D
- Social Sciences Education M,D
- Special Education M,D
- Student Affairs M,D
- Supply Chain Management M
- Vocational and Technical Education M,D

KANSAS WESLEYAN UNIVERSITY
- Business Administration and Management—General M
- Sports Management M

*M—masters degree; D—doctorate; O—other advanced degree; *—Close-Up and/or Display*

KAPLAN UNIVERSITY, DAVENPORT CAMPUS
Business Administration and Management—General M
Education—General M
Educational Leadership and Administration M
Educational Media/Instructional Technology M
Entrepreneurship M
Finance and Banking M
Higher Education M
Human Resources Management M
International Business M
Law M
Legal and Justice Studies M,O
Logistics M
Management Information Systems M
Marketing M
Mathematics Education M
Organizational Management M
Project Management M
Reading Education M
Science Education M
Secondary Education M
Special Education M
Student Affairs M
Supply Chain Management M

KEAN UNIVERSITY
Accounting M
Art Education M
Business Administration and Management—General M
Counselor Education M
Curriculum and Instruction M
Early Childhood Education M
Education—General M
Educational Leadership and Administration M,D
English as a Second Language M
Exercise and Sports Science M
Foreign Languages Education M
International Business M
Management Information Systems M
Mathematics Education M
Multilingual and Multicultural Education M
Nonprofit Management M
Science Education M
Social Work M
Special Education M

KEENE STATE COLLEGE
Counselor Education M,O
Curriculum and Instruction M,O
Education—General M,O
Educational Leadership and Administration M,O
Special Education M,O

KEISER UNIVERSITY
Accounting M
Business Administration and Management—General M,D
Distance Education Development M
Education—General M
Educational Leadership and Administration M,D,O
Educational Media/Instructional Technology D,O
Health Education M
International Business M,D
Management Information Systems M
Marketing M,D
Organizational Management D

KENNESAW STATE UNIVERSITY
Accounting M
Art Education M
Business Administration and Management—General M,D
Early Childhood Education M
Education—General M,D,O
Educational Leadership and Administration M,D,O
Educational Media/Instructional Technology M
Elementary Education M
English as a Second Language M
English Education M
Exercise and Sports Science M
Foreign Languages Education M
Mathematics Education M
Middle School Education M
Reading Education M
Secondary Education M
Social Work M
Special Education M

KENT STATE UNIVERSITY
Accounting M,D
Art Education M
Athletic Training and Sports Medicine M,D
Business Administration and Management—General M
Computer Education M
Counselor Education M,D,O
Curriculum and Instruction M,D,O
Early Childhood Education M,D,O
Education of the Gifted M,D,O
Education—General M,D,O
Educational Leadership and Administration M,D,O
Educational Measurement and Evaluation M,D
Educational Media/Instructional Technology M
Educational Psychology M,D
English as a Second Language M,D
English Education M,D
Exercise and Sports Science M,D
Finance and Banking D
Foreign Languages Education M,D
Foundations and Philosophy of Education M,D
Health Education M,D
Higher Education M,D,O
Hospitality Management M
Human Services M,D,O
Library Science M
Management Information Systems D
Marketing D
Middle School Education M
Music Education M,D
Physical Education M
Reading Education M
Recreation and Park Management M
Secondary Education M
Special Education M,D,O
Sports Management M
Student Affairs M
Travel and Tourism M
Vocational and Technical Education M

KENT STATE UNIVERSITY AT STARK
Business Administration and Management—General M
Curriculum and Instruction M
Education—General M

KENTUCKY STATE UNIVERSITY
Business Administration and Management—General M
Human Resources Development M
Management Information Systems M
Nonprofit Management M
Special Education M

KETTERING UNIVERSITY
Business Administration and Management—General M

KEUKA COLLEGE
Business Administration and Management—General M
Early Childhood Education M

KING'S COLLEGE
Reading Education M

KING UNIVERSITY
Business Administration and Management—General M

KUTZTOWN UNIVERSITY OF PENNSYLVANIA
Art Education M
Business Administration and Management—General M
Counselor Education M
Curriculum and Instruction M
Education—General M
Educational Leadership and Administration M
Educational Media/Instructional Technology M
Elementary Education M
English Education M
Library Science M
Mathematics Education M
Reading Education M
Science Education M
Secondary Education M
Social Sciences Education M
Social Work M

LAGRANGE COLLEGE
Curriculum and Instruction M,O
Education—General M,O
Middle School Education M,O
Organizational Management M
Secondary Education M,O

LAKE ERIE COLLEGE
Business Administration and Management—General M
Curriculum and Instruction M
Education—General M
Educational Leadership and Administration M
Reading Education M

LAKE ERIE COLLEGE OF OSTEOPATHIC MEDICINE
Health Education M,D,O

LAKE FOREST COLLEGE
Art Education M
Education—General M
Elementary Education M
English Education M
Mathematics Education M
Music Education M
Science Education M
Secondary Education M
Social Sciences Education M

LAKE FOREST GRADUATE SCHOOL OF MANAGEMENT
Business Administration and Management—General M
Finance and Banking M
International Business M
Marketing M
Organizational Behavior M

LAKEHEAD UNIVERSITY
Education—General M,D
Exercise and Sports Science M
Kinesiology and Movement Studies M
Social Work M

LAKEHEAD UNIVERSITY–ORILLIA
Business Administration and Management—General M

LAKELAND COLLEGE
Accounting M
Business Administration and Management—General M
Counselor Education M
Education—General M
Finance and Banking M
Project Management M

LAMAR UNIVERSITY
Accounting M
Business Administration and Management—General M
Counselor Education M,D,O
Education—General M,D,O
Educational Leadership and Administration M,D,O
Educational Media/Instructional Technology M,D,O
Entrepreneurship M
Finance and Banking M
Kinesiology and Movement Studies M
Management Strategy and Policy M
Music Education M
Special Education M,D,O
Student Affairs M,O

LANCASTER BIBLE COLLEGE
Counselor Education M,D
Elementary Education M,D
Secondary Education M,D
Special Education M,D

LANCASTER THEOLOGICAL SEMINARY
Religious Education M,D,O

LANDER UNIVERSITY
Curriculum and Instruction M
Education—General M
Elementary Education M

LANGSTON UNIVERSITY
Education—General M
Elementary Education M
English as a Second Language M
Multilingual and Multicultural Education M
Urban Education M

LA ROCHE COLLEGE
Accounting M
Human Resources Management M,O

LA SALLE UNIVERSITY
Accounting M,O
Advertising and Public Relations M,O
Business Administration and Management—General M,O
Early Childhood Education M,O
Education—General M,O
Educational Leadership and Administration M,O
Educational Media/Instructional Technology M,O
English as a Second Language M,O
English Education M,O
Finance and Banking M,O
Human Resources Development M,O
Human Resources Management M,O
International Business M,O
Marketing M,O
Middle School Education M,O
Multilingual and Multicultural Education M,O
Nonprofit Management M
Quantitative Analysis M,O
Reading Education M,O
Religious Education M,D,O
Secondary Education M,O
Social Sciences Education M,O
Special Education M,O

LASELL COLLEGE
Advertising and Public Relations M,O
Business Administration and Management—General M,O
Education—General M
Elementary Education M
Hospitality Management M,O
Human Resources Management M,O
Marketing M,O
Nonprofit Management M,O
Project Management M,O
Special Education M
Sports Management M,O

LA SIERRA UNIVERSITY
Accounting M,O
Advertising and Public Relations M
Business Administration and Management—General M,O
Counselor Education M,O
Curriculum and Instruction M,D,O
Education—General M,D,O
Educational Leadership and Administration M,D,O
Educational Psychology M,O
Finance and Banking M,O
Human Resources Management M,O
Marketing M,O
Religious Education M

LAUREL UNIVERSITY (NC)
Business Administration and Management—General M

LAURENTIAN UNIVERSITY
Business Administration and Management—General M
Science Education O
Social Work M

LAWRENCE TECHNOLOGICAL UNIVERSITY
Business Administration and Management—General M,D
Educational Media/Instructional Technology M
Management Information Systems M,D
Science Education M

LEBANESE AMERICAN UNIVERSITY
Business Administration and Management—General M

LEBANON VALLEY COLLEGE
Business Administration and Management—General M
Educational Leadership and Administration M
Music Education M
Science Education M

LEE UNIVERSITY
Business Administration and Management—General M
Counselor Education M
Curriculum and Instruction M,O
Education—General M,O
Educational Leadership and Administration M,O
Elementary Education M,O
Higher Education M,O
Middle School Education M,O
Music Education M
Secondary Education M,O
Special Education M,O
Student Affairs M,O

LEHIGH UNIVERSITY
Accounting M
Business Administration and Management—General M
Counselor Education M,D,O
Curriculum and Instruction M,D,O
Education—General M,D,O
Educational Leadership and Administration M,D,O
Educational Media/Instructional Technology M,D,O
English as a Second Language M,D,O
Entrepreneurship M
Environmental Law M,O
Finance and Banking M
Human Services M,D,O
International and Comparative Education M,D,O
International Business M
Marketing M
Project Management M
Quantitative Analysis M
Special Education M,D,O
Supply Chain Management M

LEHMAN COLLEGE OF THE CITY UNIVERSITY OF NEW YORK
Accounting M
Business Education M
Counselor Education M
Early Childhood Education M
Education—General M
Elementary Education M
English as a Second Language M
English Education M
Health Education M
Mathematics Education M
Multilingual and Multicultural Education M
Music Education M
Reading Education M
Recreation and Park Management M
Science Education M
Social Sciences Education M
Special Education M

LE MOYNE COLLEGE
Business Administration and Management—General M
Early Childhood Education M,O
Education—General M,O
Educational Leadership and Administration M,O
Elementary Education M,O
English as a Second Language M,O
English Education M,O
Foreign Languages Education M,O
Middle School Education M,O
Reading Education M,O
Secondary Education M,O
Social Sciences Education M,O
Special Education M,O

LENOIR-RHYNE UNIVERSITY
Accounting M
Athletic Training and Sports Medicine M
Business Administration and Management—General M
Counselor Education M
Early Childhood Education M
Education—General M
Entrepreneurship M

LESLEY UNIVERSITY
Adult Education M,D,O
Art Education M,D,O
Computer Education M,D,O
Curriculum and Instruction M,D,O
Distance Education Development M,D,O
Early Childhood Education M,D,O
Education—General M,D,O
Educational Leadership and Administration M,D,O
Educational Media/Instructional Technology M,D,O
Elementary Education M,D,O
English as a Second Language M,D,O
Mathematics Education M,D,O
Middle School Education M,D,O
Reading Education M,D,O
Science Education M,D,O
Secondary Education M,D,O
Special Education M,D,O

LES ROCHES INTERNATIONAL SCHOOL OF HOTEL MANAGEMENT
Hospitality Management M

LETOURNEAU UNIVERSITY
Business Administration and Management—General M

Education—General M
Management Strategy and Policy M

LEWIS & CLARK COLLEGE
Curriculum and Instruction M
Early Childhood Education M
Educational Leadership and
   Administration D,O
Elementary Education M
Environmental Law M,D
Law M,D
Middle School Education M
Secondary Education M
Special Education M

LEWIS UNIVERSITY
Accounting M
Aviation Management M
Business Administration and
   Management—General M
Counselor Education M
Early Childhood Education M,D,O
Education—General M,D,O
Educational Leadership and
   Administration M,D
Educational Media/Instructional
   Technology M
Electronic Commerce M
Elementary Education M
English as a Second Language M
Finance and Banking M
Higher Education M
Human Resources Management M
International Business M
Management Information Systems M
Marketing M
Mathematics Education M
Nonprofit Management M
Organizational Management M
Project Management M
Reading Education M
Science Education M
Secondary Education M
Social Sciences Education M
Special Education M
Sports Management M
Student Affairs M

LIBERTY UNIVERSITY
Accounting M,D
Advertising and Public Relations M,D
Business Administration and
   Management—General M,D
Counselor Education M,D,O
Curriculum and Instruction M,D,O
Distance Education Development M,D,O
Early Childhood Education M,D,O
Education of the Gifted M,D,O
Education—General M,D,O
Educational Leadership and
   Administration M,D,O
Educational Media/Instructional
   Technology M,D,O
Elementary Education M,D,O
Exercise and Sports Science M,D,O
Human Resources Management M
Human Services M,D
International Business M,D
Law D
Management Information Systems M,D
Marketing M
Mathematics Education M,D,O
Middle School Education M,D,O
Music Education M
Project Management M,D
Reading Education M,D,O
Recreation and Park Management M,D,O
Religious Education M,D
Secondary Education M,D,O
Special Education M,D,O
Sports Management M,D,O
Student Affairs M,D,O
Travel and Tourism M,D,O

LIFE UNIVERSITY
Exercise and Sports Science M

LIM COLLEGE
Business Administration and
   Management—General M
Entrepreneurship M
Marketing M

LIMESTONE COLLEGE
Business Administration and
   Management—General M

LINCOLN CHRISTIAN SEMINARY
Religious Education M,D

LINCOLN MEMORIAL UNIVERSITY
Business Administration and
   Management—General M
Counselor Education M,D,O
Curriculum and Instruction M,D,O
Education—General M,D,O
Educational Leadership and
   Administration M,D,O
English Education M,D,O
Higher Education M,D,O
Human Resources Development M,D,O
Law D

LINCOLN UNIVERSITY (CA)
Business Administration and
   Management—General M,D
Finance and Banking M,D
Human Resources Management M,D
International Business M,D
Investment Management M,D
Management Information Systems M,D

LINCOLN UNIVERSITY (MO)
Accounting M,O

Business Administration and
   Management—General M,O
Counselor Education M,O
Educational Leadership and
   Administration M,O
Elementary Education M,O
Entrepreneurship M,O
Secondary Education M,O
Special Education M,O

LINCOLN UNIVERSITY (PA)
Business Administration and
   Management—General M
Early Childhood Education M
Educational Leadership and
   Administration M
Finance and Banking M
Human Resources Management M
Human Services M
Reading Education M

LINDENWOOD UNIVERSITY
Accounting M
Business Administration and
   Management—General M,O
Education—General M,D,O
Educational Leadership and
   Administration M,D,O
Educational Media/Instructional
   Technology M,D,O
English as a Second Language M,D,O
Entrepreneurship M
Finance and Banking M
Human Resources Management M,O
Human Services M
International Business M
Management Information Systems M,O
Marketing M
Nonprofit Management M
Physical Education M,D,O
Sports Management M
Supply Chain Management M

**LINDENWOOD UNIVERSITY–
BELLEVILLE**
Business Administration and
   Management—General M
Counselor Education M
Education—General M
Educational Leadership and
   Administration M
Human Resources Management M

LIPSCOMB UNIVERSITY
Accounting M,O
Business Administration and
   Management—General M,O
Education—General M,D,O
Educational Leadership and
   Administration M,D,O
Educational Media/Instructional
   Technology M,D,O
English Education M,D,O
Exercise and Sports Science M
Finance and Banking M,O
Human Resources Management M,O
Mathematics Education M,D,O
Nonprofit Management M,O
Organizational Management M
Reading Education M,D,O
Special Education M,D,O
Sports Management M,O
Sustainability Management M,O

**LOCK HAVEN UNIVERSITY OF
PENNSYLVANIA**
Education—General M
Educational Leadership and
   Administration M
Elementary Education M
Sports Management M

LOGAN UNIVERSITY
Exercise and Sports Science M

LOMA LINDA UNIVERSITY
Counselor Education M,D,O
Health Education M,D
Social Work M,D

**LONG ISLAND UNIVERSITY–
BRENTWOOD CAMPUS**
Counselor Education M
Early Childhood Education M
Education—General M
Reading Education M
Special Education M

**LONG ISLAND UNIVERSITY–HUDSON
AT ROCKLAND**
Business Administration and
   Management—General M,O
Counselor Education M
Early Childhood Education M
Educational Leadership and
   Administration M,O
Elementary Education M,O
Entrepreneurship M,O
Finance and Banking M,O
Reading Education M
Secondary Education M,O
Special Education M

**LONG ISLAND UNIVERSITY–HUDSON
AT WESTCHESTER**
Business Administration and
   Management—General M
Counselor Education M
Early Childhood Education M,O
Education—General M,O
Educational Psychology M,O
Elementary Education M,O
English as a Second Language M,O
Information Studies M

Library Science M
Multilingual and Multicultural
   Education M,O
Reading Education M,O
Secondary Education M,O
Special Education M,O

**LONG ISLAND UNIVERSITY–LIU
BROOKLYN**
Accounting M
Athletic Training and Sports
   Medicine M
Business Administration and
   Management—General M,O
Counselor Education M,O
Education—General M,O
Educational Leadership and
   Administration M
Educational Media/Instructional
   Technology M
Elementary Education M
English as a Second Language M
English Education M
Exercise and Sports Science M
Health Education M
Human Resources Management M
Mathematics Education M
Multilingual and Multicultural
   Education M
Physical Education M
Reading Education M
Special Education M
Taxation M

LONG ISLAND UNIVERSITY–LIU POST
Accounting M,O
Archives/Archival Administration M,D,O
Art Education M
Business Administration and
   Management—General M,O
Computer Education M
Counselor Education M
Early Childhood Education M
Education—General M,D,O
Educational Leadership and
   Administration M,D,O
Educational Media/Instructional
   Technology M
Elementary Education M
English as a Second Language M
English Education M
Finance and Banking M
Foreign Languages Education M
Information Studies M,D,O
International Business M
Library Science M,D,O
Management Information Systems M,O
Marketing M
Mathematics Education M
Middle School Education M
Multilingual and Multicultural
   Education M
Music Education M,O
Nonprofit Management M,O
Reading Education M
Science Education M
Secondary Education M
Social Work M
Special Education M
Taxation M,O

**LONG ISLAND UNIVERSITY–
RIVERHEAD**
Early Childhood Education M
Education—General M,O
Elementary Education M
Reading Education M
Special Education M

LONGWOOD UNIVERSITY
Business Administration and
   Management—General M
Counselor Education M
Education—General M
Educational Media/Instructional
   Technology M
Elementary Education M
English Education M
Health Education M
Mathematics Education M
Middle School Education M
Physical Education M
Reading Education M
Real Estate M
Special Education M

LORAS COLLEGE
Educational Leadership and
   Administration M
Special Education M

LOUISIANA COLLEGE
Education—General M

**LOUISIANA STATE UNIVERSITY AND
AGRICULTURAL & MECHANICAL
COLLEGE**
Accounting M,D
Agricultural Education M,D
Business Administration and
   Management—General M,D
Business Education M,D
Counselor Education M,D,O
Education—General M,D,O
Educational Leadership and
   Administration M,D,O
Educational Measurement and
   Evaluation M,D,O
Educational Media/Instructional
   Technology M,D,O
Elementary Education M,D,O
Finance and Banking M,D
Higher Education M,D,O

Home Economics Education M,D
Human Resources Development M,D
Information Studies M
International and Comparative
   Education M,D
Kinesiology and Movement Studies M,D
Law M,D
Library Science M
Management Information Systems M,D
Marketing D
Music Education M
Secondary Education M,D,O
Social Work M,D
Vocational and Technical Education M,D

**LOUISIANA STATE UNIVERSITY IN
SHREVEPORT**
Business Administration and
   Management—General M
Counselor Education M
Curriculum and Instruction M
Education—General M
Educational Leadership and
   Administration M
Human Services M

LOUISIANA TECH UNIVERSITY
Accounting M,D
Adult Education M,D
Business Administration and
   Management—General M,D
Counselor Education M,D
Curriculum and Instruction M,D
Early Childhood Education M,D
Education—General M,D
Educational Leadership and
   Administration M,D
English Education M
Exercise and Sports Science M
Finance and Banking M
Management Information Systems M,D
Mathematics Education M,D
Physical Education M
Science Education M,D
Social Sciences Education M,D
Special Education M,D

LOURDES UNIVERSITY
Business Administration and
   Management—General M
Curriculum and Instruction M
Educational Leadership and
   Administration M
Organizational Management M
Reading Education M

LOYOLA MARYMOUNT UNIVERSITY
Accounting M
Business Administration and
   Management—General M
Counselor Education M
Early Childhood Education M
Education—General M,D
Educational Leadership and
   Administration M,D
Elementary Education M
Law M,D
Mathematics Education M
Multilingual and Multicultural
   Education M
Reading Education M
Recreation and Park Management M
Religious Education M
Secondary Education M
Special Education M
Taxation M,D
Urban Education M

LOYOLA UNIVERSITY CHICAGO
Accounting M
Business Administration and
   Management—General M
Counselor Education M,O
Curriculum and Instruction M,D,O
Education—General M,D,O
Educational Leadership and
   Administration M,D,O
Educational Measurement and
   Evaluation M,D
Educational Media/Instructional
   Technology M,D
Educational Policy M,D
Educational Psychology M,D
Elementary Education M,O
English as a Second Language M,O
Entrepreneurship M
Finance and Banking M,D
Health Law M,D
Higher Education M,D
Human Resources Management M
International Business M
Law M,D
Legal and Justice Studies M
Management Information Systems M
Marketing M
Mathematics Education M,O
Reading Education M,O
Religious Education M,O
Science Education M,O
Secondary Education M,O
Social Work M,D,O
Special Education M
Supply Chain Management M
Taxation M,D

LOYOLA UNIVERSITY MARYLAND
Accounting M,O
Business Administration and
   Management—General M
Counselor Education M,O
Curriculum and Instruction M,O
Early Childhood Education M,O
Education—General M,O

---

*M—masters degree; D—doctorate; O—other advanced degree; *—Close-Up and/or Display*

Educational Leadership and Administration — M,O
Educational Media/Instructional Technology — M
Elementary Education — M
English Education — M
Finance and Banking — M
International Business — M
Management Information Systems — M
Marketing — M
Mathematics Education — M,O
Middle School Education — M
Music Education — M,O
Reading Education — M,O
Science Education — M
Secondary Education — M,O
Special Education — M,O

LOYOLA UNIVERSITY NEW ORLEANS
Business Administration and Management—General — M
Counselor Education — M
Law — M,D

LYNCHBURG COLLEGE
Business Administration and Management—General — M
Counselor Education — M
Curriculum and Instruction — M
Education—General — M,D
Educational Leadership and Administration — M,D
Reading Education — M
Science Education — M
Special Education — M

LYNDON STATE COLLEGE
Counselor Education — M
Curriculum and Instruction — M
Education—General — M
Reading Education — M
Science Education — M
Special Education — M

LYNN UNIVERSITY
Aviation Management — M
Business Administration and Management—General — M
Education of the Gifted — M,D
Education—General — M,D
Educational Leadership and Administration — M,D
Hospitality Management — M
International Business — M
Investment Management — M
Marketing — M
Special Education — M,D
Sports Management — M

MAASTRICHT SCHOOL OF MANAGEMENT
Business Administration and Management—General — M,D
Facilities Management — M,D
Sustainability Management — M,D

MADONNA UNIVERSITY
Business Administration and Management—General — M
Education—General — M
Educational Leadership and Administration — M
English as a Second Language — M
International Business — M
Quality Management — M
Reading Education — M
Special Education — M

MAHARISHI UNIVERSITY OF MANAGEMENT
Accounting — M,D
Business Administration and Management—General — M,D
Education—General — M
Elementary Education — M
Secondary Education — M
Sustainability Management — M,D

MAINE MARITIME ACADEMY
International Business — M
Supply Chain Management — M
Transportation Management — M

MALONE UNIVERSITY
Business Administration and Management—General — M
Counselor Education — M
Curriculum and Instruction — M
Education—General — M
Educational Leadership and Administration — M
Organizational Management — M
Special Education — M

MANCHESTER UNIVERSITY
Athletic Training and Sports Medicine — M
Education—General — M

MANHATTAN COLLEGE
Counselor Education — M,O
Early Childhood Education — M,O
Education—General — M,O
Educational Leadership and Administration — M,O
Multilingual and Multicultural Education — M,O
Special Education — M,O
Student Affairs — M,O

MANHATTANVILLE COLLEGE
Art Education — M
Business Administration and Management—General — M,D*
Early Childhood Education — M
Education—General — M,D*
Educational Leadership and Administration —

Elementary Education — M
English as a Second Language — M
English Education — M
Exercise and Sports Science — M
Finance and Banking — M
Foreign Languages Education — M
Human Resources Management — M
International Business — M
Management Strategy and Policy — M
Marketing — M
Mathematics Education — M
Middle School Education — M
Music Education — M
Organizational Management — M
Reading Education — M
Science Education — M
Secondary Education — M
Social Sciences Education — M
Special Education — M
Sports Management — M

MANSFIELD UNIVERSITY OF PENNSYLVANIA
Art Education — M
Education—General — M
Elementary Education — M
Information Studies — M
Library Science — M
Organizational Management — M
Secondary Education — M
Special Education — M

MAPLE SPRINGS BAPTIST BIBLE COLLEGE AND SEMINARY
Religious Education — M,D,O

MARIAN UNIVERSITY (IN)
Education—General — M

MARIAN UNIVERSITY (WI)
Business Administration and Management—General — M
Education—General — M,D
Educational Leadership and Administration — M,D
Organizational Management — M
Quality Management — M

MARIST COLLEGE
Business Administration and Management—General — M,O
Education—General — M,O
Management Information Systems — M
Marketing — M

MARLBORO COLLEGE
Business Administration and Management—General — M
Computer Education — M,O
Education—General — M,O
Educational Media/Instructional Technology — M,O
English as a Second Language — M
Legal and Justice Studies — M
Nonprofit Management — M
Project Management — M,O
Sustainability Management — M

MARQUETTE UNIVERSITY
Accounting — M
Advertising and Public Relations — M,O
Business Administration and Management—General — M
Counselor Education — M,D
Curriculum and Instruction — M,D,O
Education—General — M,D,O
Educational Leadership and Administration — M,D,O
Educational Policy — M,D,O
Elementary Education — M,D,O
Entrepreneurship — M,O
Finance and Banking — M,O
Foreign Languages Education — M
Foundations and Philosophy of Education — M,D,O
Human Resources Development — M
Human Resources Management — M,O
Industrial and Manufacturing Management — M,O
International Business — M
Law — D
Management Information Systems — M,O
Marketing Research — M,O
Marketing — M,O
Mathematics Education — M,D
Nonprofit Management — M,O
Reading Education — M,D,O
Real Estate — M
Secondary Education — M,D,O
Sports Management — M,O
Student Affairs — M,D,O
Supply Chain Management — M,O

MARSHALL UNIVERSITY
Accounting — M
Adult Education — M
Athletic Training and Sports Medicine — M
Business Administration and Management—General — M
Counselor Education — M,O
Early Childhood Education — M
Education—General — M,D,O
Educational Leadership and Administration — M,D,O
Elementary Education — M
Exercise and Sports Science — M
Health Education — M
Human Resources Management — M
Reading Education — M,O
Secondary Education — M
Special Education — M
Sports Management — M
Vocational and Technical Education — M

MARS HILL UNIVERSITY
Elementary Education — M

MARTIN LUTHER COLLEGE
Curriculum and Instruction — M
Education—General — M
Educational Leadership and Administration — M
Special Education — M

MARY BALDWIN COLLEGE
Education—General — M
Elementary Education — M
Middle School Education — M

MARYGROVE COLLEGE
Education—General — M
Educational Leadership and Administration — M
Elementary Education — M
Human Resources Management — M
Legal and Justice Studies — M
Reading Education — M
Secondary Education — M
Urban Education — M

MARYLAND INSTITUTE COLLEGE OF ART
Art Education — M
Business Administration and Management—General — M

MARYLHURST UNIVERSITY
Business Administration and Management—General — M
Education—General — M
Finance and Banking — M
Marketing — M
Nonprofit Management — M
Organizational Behavior — M
Real Estate — M

MARYMOUNT UNIVERSITY
Business Administration and Management—General — M,O
Counselor Education — M,D,O
Education—General — M,D
Educational Leadership and Administration — M,O
Elementary Education — M,D
English as a Second Language — M,D
Health Education — M
Human Resources Management — M,O
Legal and Justice Studies — M,O
Management Information Systems — M,O
Nonprofit Management — M,O
Project Management — M,O
Secondary Education — M,D
Special Education — M,D

MARYVILLE UNIVERSITY OF SAINT LOUIS
Accounting — M,O
Actuarial Science — M
Art Education — M,D
Business Administration and Management—General — M,O
Early Childhood Education — M,D
Education of the Gifted — M,D
Education—General — M,D
Educational Leadership and Administration — M,D
Elementary Education — M,D
Entertainment Management — M,O
Higher Education — M,D
Marketing — M,O
Middle School Education — M,D
Organizational Management — M
Project Management — M,D
Reading Education — M,D
Secondary Education — M,D
Sports Management — M,O

MARYWOOD UNIVERSITY
Art Education — M
Business Administration and Management—General — M
Counselor Education — M
Early Childhood Education — M
Education—General — M
Educational Leadership and Administration — M,D
Elementary Education — M
Exercise and Sports Science — M
Finance and Banking — M
Health Education — D
Higher Education — M,D
Investment Management — M
Management Information Systems — M
Music Education — M
Reading Education — M
Secondary Education — M
Social Work — M
Special Education — M

MASSACHUSETTS COLLEGE OF ART AND DESIGN
Art Education — M,O

MASSACHUSETTS COLLEGE OF LIBERAL ARTS
Business Administration and Management—General — M,O
Curriculum and Instruction — M,O
Education—General — M,O
Educational Leadership and Administration — M,O
Educational Media/Instructional Technology — M,O
Health Education — M,O
Physical Education — M,O
Reading Education — M,O
Special Education — M,O

MASSACHUSETTS INSTITUTE OF TECHNOLOGY
Business Administration and Management—General — M,D
Logistics — M,D
Real Estate — M

MASSACHUSETTS MARITIME ACADEMY
Facilities Management — M

MASSACHUSETTS SCHOOL OF LAW AT ANDOVER
Law — D

MASSACHUSETTS SCHOOL OF PROFESSIONAL PSYCHOLOGY
Student Affairs — M,D,O

MCDANIEL COLLEGE
Counselor Education — M
Curriculum and Instruction — M
Educational Leadership and Administration — M
Educational Media/Instructional Technology — M
Elementary Education — M
English as a Second Language — M
Exercise and Sports Science — M
Human Resources Development — M
Human Services — M
Library Science — M
Physical Education — M
Reading Education — M
Secondary Education — M
Special Education — M

MCGILL UNIVERSITY
Accounting — M,D,O
Business Administration and Management—General — M,D,O
Curriculum and Instruction — M,D,O
Education—General — M,D,O
Educational Leadership and Administration — M,D,O
Educational Psychology — M,D,O
Entrepreneurship — M,D,O
Finance and Banking — M,D,O
Foreign Languages Education — M,D,O
Foundations and Philosophy of Education — M,D,O
Industrial and Manufacturing Management — M,D,O
Information Studies — M,D,O
International Business — M,D,O
Kinesiology and Movement Studies — M,D,O
Law — M,D,O
Library Science — M,D,O
Management Information Systems — M,D,O
Management Strategy and Policy — M,D,O
Marketing — M,D
Music Education — M,D,O
Physical Education — M,D,O
Social Work — M,D,O
Transportation Management — M,D

MCKENDREE UNIVERSITY
Business Administration and Management—General — M
Curriculum and Instruction — M,D,O
Education—General — M,D,O
Educational Leadership and Administration — M,D,O
Higher Education — M,D,O
Human Resources Management — M
International Business — M
Music Education — M,D,O
Reading Education — M,D,O
Special Education — M,D,O

MCMASTER UNIVERSITY
Business Administration and Management—General — M,D
Human Resources Management — M,D
Kinesiology and Movement Studies — M,D
Management Information Systems — D
Social Work — M

MCNEESE STATE UNIVERSITY
Business Administration and Management—General — M
Counselor Education — M,O
Curriculum and Instruction — M
Early Childhood Education — M,O
Education—General — O
Educational Leadership and Administration — M,O
Educational Measurement and Evaluation — M,O
Educational Media/Instructional Technology — M,O
Elementary Education — M,O
Exercise and Sports Science — M
Library Science — O
Middle School Education — O
Music Education — O
Reading Education — M,O
Science Education — M
Secondary Education — M,O
Special Education — M,O

MEDAILLE COLLEGE
Business Administration and Management—General — M
Curriculum and Instruction — M
Education—General — M
Elementary Education — M
Organizational Management — M
Reading Education — M
Secondary Education — M
Special Education — M

MELBOURNE BUSINESS SCHOOL
Business Administration and Management—General — M,D,O
Marketing — M,D,O

MEMORIAL UNIVERSITY OF NEWFOUNDLAND
Adult Education — M,D,O
Business Administration and Management—General — M
Curriculum and Instruction — M,D,O
Education—General — M,D,O

Educational Leadership and
  Administration — M,D,O
Educational Media/Instructional
  Technology — M,D,O
Educational Psychology — M,D,O
Exercise and Sports Science — M
Kinesiology and Movement Studies — M
Physical Education — M
Social Work — M

MEMPHIS COLLEGE OF ART
Art Education — M

MERCER UNIVERSITY
Accounting — M
Business Administration and
  Management—General — M
Counselor Education — M,D
Curriculum and Instruction — M,D,O
Early Childhood Education — M,D,O
Education—General — M,D,O
Educational Leadership and
  Administration — M,D,O
Higher Education — M
Law — D
Middle School Education — M,D,O
Organizational Management — M,D
Reading Education — M,D,O
Secondary Education — M,D,O

MERCY COLLEGE
Accounting — M
Business Administration and
  Management—General — M
Counselor Education — M,O
Early Childhood Education — M
Education—General — M,O
Educational Leadership and
  Administration — M,O
Elementary Education — M
English as a Second Language — M,O
Human Resources Management — M
Organizational Management — M
Reading Education — M,O
Secondary Education — M

MERCYHURST UNIVERSITY
Accounting — M,O
Educational Leadership and
  Administration — M,O
Entrepreneurship — M
Exercise and Sports Science — M
Higher Education — M,O
Human Resources Management — M,O
Multilingual and Multicultural
  Education — M,O
Nonprofit Management — M,O
Organizational Management — M,O
Secondary Education — M,O
Special Education — M,O
Sports Management — M

MEREDITH COLLEGE
Business Administration and
  Management—General — M
Education—General — M

MERRIMACK COLLEGE
Adult Education — M,O
Business Administration and
  Management—General — M
Early Childhood Education — M,O
Education—General — M,O
Educational Leadership and
  Administration — M,O
Elementary Education — M,O
English as a Second Language — M,O
Higher Education — M,O
Middle School Education — M,O
Reading Education — M,O
Secondary Education — M,O
Special Education — M,O
Student Affairs — M,O

MESSIAH COLLEGE
Counselor Education — M,O
Curriculum and Instruction — M
English as a Second Language — M
Higher Education — M
Special Education — M
Sports Management — M
Student Affairs — M

METHODIST UNIVERSITY
Business Administration and
  Management—General — M

METROPOLITAN COLLEGE OF NEW YORK
Business Administration and
  Management—General — M
Elementary Education — M

METROPOLITAN STATE UNIVERSITY
Business Administration and
  Management—General — M,D,O
Information Studies — M
Management Information Systems — M,D,O
Nonprofit Management — M,D,O
Project Management — M,D,O

METROPOLITAN STATE UNIVERSITY OF DENVER
Accounting — M
Education—General — M
Elementary Education — M
Social Work — M
Special Education — M

MGH INSTITUTE OF HEALTH PROFESSIONS
Reading Education — M,O

MIAMI UNIVERSITY
Accounting — M

Art Education — M
Business Administration and
  Management—General — M
Education—General — M,D,O
Educational Leadership and
  Administration — M,D
Educational Media/Instructional
  Technology — M,O
Educational Psychology — M,O
Elementary Education — M
Exercise and Sports Science — M
Higher Education — M
Mathematics Education — M
Middle School Education — M
Music Education — M
Reading Education — M
Secondary Education — M
Special Education — M,O
Student Affairs — M,D

MICHIGAN SCHOOL OF PROFESSIONAL PSYCHOLOGY
Educational Psychology — M,D

MICHIGAN STATE UNIVERSITY
Accounting — M,D
Adult Education — M,D,O
Advertising and Public Relations — M
Business Administration and
  Management—General — M,D
Counselor Education — M,D,O
Curriculum and Instruction — M,D,O
Education—General — M
Educational Leadership and
  Administration — M,D,O
Educational Measurement and
  Evaluation — M,D,O
Educational Media/Instructional
  Technology — M,D,O
Educational Policy — D
Educational Psychology — M,D,O
English as a Second Language — M,D
Finance and Banking — M,D
Foreign Languages Education — D
Higher Education — M
Hospitality Management — M
Human Resources Management — M
Kinesiology and Movement Studies — M,D
Logistics — M,D
Management Information Systems — M,D
Management Strategy and Policy — M,D
Marketing Research — M
Marketing — M,D
Mathematics Education — M,D
Music Education — M,D
Reading Education — M
Recreation and Park Management — M,D
Science Education — M,D
Social Sciences Education — M,D
Social Work — M,D
Special Education — M,D,O
Supply Chain Management — M,D
Taxation — M,D

MICHIGAN STATE UNIVERSITY COLLEGE OF LAW
Intellectual Property Law — M,D
Law — M,D
Legal and Justice Studies — M,D

MICHIGAN TECHNOLOGICAL UNIVERSITY
Business Administration and
  Management—General — M
Entrepreneurship — O
Science Education — M,D
Sustainability Management — O

MID-AMERICA CHRISTIAN UNIVERSITY
Business Administration and
  Management—General — M
Organizational Management — M

MIDAMERICA NAZARENE UNIVERSITY
Business Administration and
  Management—General — M
Education—General — M
Educational Media/Instructional
  Technology — M
English as a Second Language — M
Finance and Banking — M
International Business — M
Nonprofit Management — M
Organizational Management — M
Special Education — M

MIDDLE TENNESSEE STATE UNIVERSITY
Accounting — M
Archives/Archival Administration — M,D,O
Aviation Management — M
Business Administration and
  Management—General — M
Business Education — M
Counselor Education — M
Curriculum and Instruction — M,O
Early Childhood Education — M,D,O
Education—General — M,D,O
Educational Leadership and
  Administration — M,O
Educational Media/Instructional
  Technology — M,O
Educational Psychology — M,O
Elementary Education — M,O
English as a Second Language — M,O
Exercise and Sports Science — M,D
Foreign Languages Education — M
Health Education — M
Management Information Systems — M
Management Strategy and Policy — M,O
Mathematics Education — M,D
Middle School Education — M
Physical Education — M

Reading Education — M,D
Recreation and Park Management — M
Science Education — M,D
Secondary Education — M,O
Social Work — M
Special Education — M
Vocational and Technical Education — M

MIDWAY COLLEGE
Business Administration and
  Management—General — M
Education—General — M
Organizational Management — M

MIDWESTERN BAPTIST THEOLOGICAL SEMINARY
Religious Education — M,D,O

MIDWESTERN STATE UNIVERSITY
Business Administration and
  Management—General — M
Counselor Education — M
Curriculum and Instruction — M
Education—General — M
Educational Leadership and
  Administration — M
Educational Media/Instructional
  Technology — M
English as a Second Language — M
Exercise and Sports Science — M
Human Resources Development — M
Multilingual and Multicultural
  Education — M
Reading Education — M
Special Education — M

MILLENNIA ATLANTIC UNIVERSITY
Accounting — M
Business Administration and
  Management—General — M
Human Resources Management — M

MILLERSVILLE UNIVERSITY OF PENNSYLVANIA
Art Education — M
Early Childhood Education — M
Education of the Gifted — M
Education—General — M
Elementary Education — M
English as a Second Language — M
Foundations and Philosophy of
  Education — M
Mathematics Education — M
Reading Education — M
Social Work — M
Special Education — M
Sports Management — M
Vocational and Technical Education — M

MILLIGAN COLLEGE
Business Administration and
  Management—General — M
Education—General — M

MILLIKIN UNIVERSITY
Business Administration and
  Management—General — M

MILLSAPS COLLEGE
Accounting — M
Business Administration and
  Management—General — M

MILLS COLLEGE
Art Education — M,D
Business Administration and
  Management—General — M
Curriculum and Instruction — M,D
Early Childhood Education — M,D
Education—General — M,D
Educational Leadership and
  Administration — M,D
Elementary Education — M,D
English Education — M,D
Foreign Languages Education — M,D
Health Education — M,D
Mathematics Education — M,D
Science Education — M,D
Secondary Education — M,D
Social Sciences Education — M,D

MILWAUKEE SCHOOL OF ENGINEERING
Business Administration and
  Management—General — M
Industrial and Manufacturing
  Management — M
International Business — M
Marketing — M

MINNESOTA STATE UNIVERSITY MANKATO
Art Education — M
Business Administration and
  Management—General — M
Counselor Education — M,D,O
Curriculum and Instruction — M,O
Early Childhood Education — M,O
Education—General — M,D,O
Educational Leadership and
  Administration — M
Educational Media/Instructional
  Technology — M,O
Elementary Education — M,O
English as a Second Language — M,O
English Education — M
Health Education — M,O
Higher Education — M
Human Services — M
Management Information Systems — M,O
Mathematics Education — M
Multilingual and Multicultural
  Education — M,O
Physical Education — M

Science Education — M
Secondary Education — M,O
Social Sciences Education — M
Social Work — M
Special Education — M,O
Student Affairs — M,D,O

MINNESOTA STATE UNIVERSITY MOORHEAD
Counselor Education — M
Curriculum and Instruction — M
Education—General — M,O
Educational Leadership and
  Administration — M,O
Human Services — M,O
Reading Education — M
Special Education — M

MINOT STATE UNIVERSITY
Business Administration and
  Management—General — M
Early Childhood Education — M
Education of Students with
  Severe/Multiple Disabilities — M
Elementary Education — M
Management Information Systems — M
Mathematics Education — M
Music Education — M
Science Education — M
Special Education — M

MISERICORDIA UNIVERSITY
Accounting — M
Business Administration and
  Management—General — M
Curriculum and Instruction — M
Education—General — M
Educational Media/Instructional
  Technology — M
Human Resources Management — M
Management Information Systems — M
Nonprofit Management — M
Organizational Management — M
Reading Education — M
Special Education — M
Sports Management — M

MISSISSIPPI COLLEGE
Accounting — M,O
Advertising and Public Relations — M
Art Education — M,D,O
Business Administration and
  Management—General — M,O
Business Education — M,D,O
Computer Education — M,D,O
Counselor Education — M,O
Curriculum and Instruction — M,D,O
Education—General — M,D,O
Educational Leadership and
  Administration — M,D,O
Elementary Education — M,D,O
English as a Second Language — M
English Education — M,D,O
Finance and Banking — M,O
Higher Education — M,D,O
Kinesiology and Movement Studies — M
Law — D,O
Legal and Justice Studies — M,O
Mathematics Education — M,D,O
Music Education — M
Science Education — M,D,O
Secondary Education — M,D,O
Social Sciences Education — M,D,O
Special Education — M,D,O

MISSISSIPPI STATE UNIVERSITY
Accounting — M,D
Agricultural Education — M,D
Business Administration and
  Management—General — M,D
Business Education — M,D,O
Community College Education — M,D,O
Counselor Education — M,D,O
Curriculum and Instruction — M,D,O
Early Childhood Education — M,D,O
Education—General — M,D,O
Educational Leadership and
  Administration — M,D,O
Educational Measurement and
  Evaluation — M,D,O
Educational Media/Instructional
  Technology — M,D,O
Educational Psychology — M,D,O
Elementary Education — M,D,O
Exercise and Sports Science — M
Finance and Banking — M,D
Foreign Languages Education — M
Higher Education — M,D,O
Human Resources Development — M,D,O
Kinesiology and Movement Studies — M
Management Information Systems — M,D
Marketing — M,D
Middle School Education — M,D,O
Physical Education — M
Project Management — M,D
Reading Education — M,D,O
Science Education — M,D
Secondary Education — M,D,O
Special Education — M,D,O
Sports Management — M
Student Affairs — M,D,O
Taxation — M

MISSISSIPPI UNIVERSITY FOR WOMEN
Curriculum and Instruction — M
Education of the Gifted — M
Education—General — M
Educational Leadership and
  Administration — M
Health Education — M
Reading Education — M

MISSISSIPPI VALLEY STATE UNIVERSITY

Education—General	M
Elementary Education	M

MISSOURI BAPTIST UNIVERSITY

Business Administration and Management—General	M,O
Counselor Education	M,O
Education—General	M,O
Educational Leadership and Administration	M,O

MISSOURI SOUTHERN STATE UNIVERSITY

Business Administration and Management—General	M
Early Childhood Education	M
Education—General	M
Educational Media/Instructional Technology	M

MISSOURI STATE UNIVERSITY

Accounting	M
Athletic Training and Sports Medicine	M
Business Administration and Management—General	M
Counselor Education	M,O
Early Childhood Education	M
Educational Leadership and Administration	M,O
Educational Media/Instructional Technology	M
Elementary Education	M,O
Higher Education	M
Kinesiology and Movement Studies	M
Management Information Systems	M
Music Education	M
Physical Education	M
Project Management	M
Reading Education	M
Science Education	M
Secondary Education	M,O
Social Sciences Education	M
Social Work	M
Special Education	M,D
Sports Management	M
Student Affairs	M

MISSOURI UNIVERSITY OF SCIENCE AND TECHNOLOGY

Mathematics Education	M,D

MISSOURI WESTERN STATE UNIVERSITY

Business Administration and Management—General	M
Educational Measurement and Evaluation	M,O
English as a Second Language	M,O
Management Information Systems	M,O
Special Education	M,O
Sports Management	M

MOLLOY COLLEGE

Accounting	M
Business Administration and Management—General	M
Education—General	M,O
Finance and Banking	M
Marketing	M

MONMOUTH UNIVERSITY

Accounting	M,O
Advertising and Public Relations	M,O
Business Administration and Management—General	M,O*
Education—General	M,O
Educational Leadership and Administration	M,O
Elementary Education	M,O
English as a Second Language	M,O
Finance and Banking	M,O
Human Resources Management	M,O
Management Information Systems	M,O
Reading Education	M,O
Real Estate	M,O
Secondary Education	M,O
Social Work	M,O
Special Education	M,O
Student Affairs	M,O

MONROE COLLEGE

Business Administration and Management—General	M
Hospitality Management	M

MONTANA STATE UNIVERSITY

Accounting	M
Adult Education	M,D,O
Agricultural Education	M
Curriculum and Instruction	M,D,O
Education—General	M,D,O
Educational Leadership and Administration	M,D,O
Health Education	M
Higher Education	M,D,O
Home Economics Education	M
Mathematics Education	M,D
Vocational and Technical Education	M,D,O

MONTANA STATE UNIVERSITY BILLINGS

Advertising and Public Relations	M
Athletic Training and Sports Medicine	M
Counselor Education	M,O
Curriculum and Instruction	M
Education—General	M,O
Educational Media/Instructional Technology	M
Human Services	M
Reading Education	M,O
Special Education	M,O

MONTANA STATE UNIVERSITY–NORTHERN

Counselor Education	M
Education—General	M

MONTANA TECH OF THE UNIVERSITY OF MONTANA

Project Management	M

MONTCLAIR STATE UNIVERSITY

Accounting	M,O
Advertising and Public Relations	M
Archives/Archival Administration	M
Art Education	M
Business Administration and Management—General	M,O
Counselor Education	M,D,O
Curriculum and Instruction	M,D,O
Early Childhood Education	M
Education—General	M,D,O
Educational Leadership and Administration	M,D
Educational Media/Instructional Technology	O
Elementary Education	M
English as a Second Language	M,O
English Education	M,O
Environmental Education	M
Exercise and Sports Science	M,O
Finance and Banking	O
Foreign Languages Education	M
Foundations and Philosophy of Education	D,O
Health Education	M
Intellectual Property Law	M,O
International Business	M
Law	M,O
Legal and Justice Studies	O
Management Information Systems	O
Marketing	O
Mathematics Education	M,D
Music Education	M
Physical Education	M
Reading Education	M,O
Science Education	M,O
Special Education	M,O
Sports Management	M

MONTEREY INSTITUTE OF INTERNATIONAL STUDIES

Business Administration and Management—General	M
English as a Second Language	M
Foreign Languages Education	M
International and Comparative Education	M
International Business	M

MONTREAT COLLEGE

Business Administration and Management—General	M
Environmental Education	M

MOODY THEOLOGICAL SEMINARY• MICHIGAN

Religious Education	M,O

MOORE COLLEGE OF ART & DESIGN

Art Education	M

MORAVIAN COLLEGE

Accounting	M
Business Administration and Management—General	M
Curriculum and Instruction	M
Education—General	M
Human Resources Development	M
Human Resources Management	M
Supply Chain Management	M

MOREHEAD STATE UNIVERSITY

Adult Education	M,O
Art Education	M
Business Administration and Management—General	M
Business Education	M,O
Counselor Education	M,O
Curriculum and Instruction	M,O
Education of the Gifted	M,O
Education—General	M,O
Educational Leadership and Administration	M,O
Educational Media/Instructional Technology	M,O
Elementary Education	M,O
English Education	M,O
Exercise and Sports Science	M
Foreign Languages Education	M
Health Education	M
Higher Education	M,O
International and Comparative Education	M,O
Management Information Systems	M
Mathematics Education	M
Middle School Education	M,O
Music Education	M
Physical Education	M
Reading Education	M,O
Science Education	M,O
Secondary Education	M,O
Social Sciences Education	M,O
Special Education	M,O
Sports Management	M
Vocational and Technical Education	M

MOREHOUSE SCHOOL OF MEDICINE

Health Education	M

MORGAN STATE UNIVERSITY

Business Administration and Management—General	D
Community College Education	D
Education—General	M,D
Educational Leadership and Administration	M,D
Elementary Education	M
Higher Education	M,D
Mathematics Education	M,D
Middle School Education	M
Science Education	M,D
Secondary Education	M
Social Work	M,D
Transportation Management	M
Urban Education	D

MORNINGSIDE COLLEGE

Education—General	M
Special Education	M

MORRISON UNIVERSITY

Business Administration and Management—General	M

MOUNT ALOYSIUS COLLEGE

Business Administration and Management—General	M
Education—General	M

MOUNT IDA COLLEGE

Business Administration and Management—General	M

MOUNT MARTY COLLEGE

Business Administration and Management—General	M

MOUNT MARY UNIVERSITY

Business Administration and Management—General	M
Counselor Education	M,O
Education—General	M
Health Education	M

MOUNT MERCY UNIVERSITY

Business Administration and Management—General	M
Education—General	M
Reading Education	M
Special Education	M

MOUNT ST. JOSEPH UNIVERSITY

Business Administration and Management—General	M
Early Childhood Education	M,O
Education—General	M,O
Educational Leadership and Administration	M,O
Middle School Education	M,O
Multilingual and Multicultural Education	M,O
Organizational Management	M,O
Reading Education	M,O
Secondary Education	M,O
Special Education	M,O

MOUNT SAINT MARY COLLEGE

Business Administration and Management—General	M
Early Childhood Education	M,O
Education—General	M,O
Elementary Education	M,O
Finance and Banking	M,O
Middle School Education	M,O
Reading Education	M,O
Secondary Education	M,O
Special Education	M,O

MOUNT ST. MARY'S COLLEGE

Business Administration and Management—General	M,D,O
Education—General	M,D,O

MOUNT ST. MARY'S UNIVERSITY

Business Administration and Management—General	M
Education—General	M

MOUNT SAINT VINCENT UNIVERSITY

Adult Education	M
Curriculum and Instruction	M
Education—General	M
Educational Psychology	M
Elementary Education	M
English as a Second Language	M
Foundations and Philosophy of Education	M
Middle School Education	M
Reading Education	M
Special Education	M

MOUNT VERNON NAZARENE UNIVERSITY

Business Administration and Management—General	M
Education—General	M

MULTNOMAH UNIVERSITY

Counselor Education	M
Education—General	M
English as a Second Language	M

MURRAY STATE UNIVERSITY

Accounting	M
Agricultural Education	M
Business Administration and Management—General	M
Counselor Education	M,O
Early Childhood Education	M
Education—General	M,D,O
Educational Leadership and Administration	M,O
Elementary Education	M,O
English as a Second Language	M
Exercise and Sports Science	M
Human Services	M
Leisure Studies	M
Middle School Education	M,O
Music Education	M
Physical Education	M,O
Reading Education	M,O
Secondary Education	M,O
Special Education	M
Vocational and Technical Education	M

MUSKINGUM UNIVERSITY

Education—General	M

NAROPA UNIVERSITY

Counselor Education	M
Education—General	M
Recreation and Park Management	M

NATIONAL AMERICAN UNIVERSITY

Business Administration and Management—General	M

THE NATIONAL GRADUATE SCHOOL OF QUALITY MANAGEMENT

Quality Management	M,D

NATIONAL LOUIS UNIVERSITY

Adult Education	M,D,O
Business Administration and Management—General	M
Counselor Education	M,D,O
Curriculum and Instruction	M,D,O
Developmental Education	M,D,O
Early Childhood Education	M,D,O
Education—General	M,D,O
Educational Leadership and Administration	M,D,O
Educational Media/Instructional Technology	M,D,O
Educational Psychology	M,D,O
Elementary Education	M,D,O
English Education	M,D,O
Human Resources Development	M
Human Resources Management	M
Human Services	M,D,O
Mathematics Education	M,D,O
Reading Education	M,D,O
Science Education	M,D,O
Secondary Education	M,D,O
Special Education	M,D,O

NATIONAL UNIVERSITY

Accounting	M,O
Business Administration and Management—General	M,O
Counselor Education	M,O
Distance Education Development	M,O
Early Childhood Education	M,O
Education—General	M,O
Educational Leadership and Administration	M,O
Educational Media/Instructional Technology	M,O
Finance and Banking	M,O
Human Resources Management	M,O
Human Services	M,D,O
International and Comparative Education	M,O
International Business	M,O
Legal and Justice Studies	M
Management Information Systems	M,O
Marketing	M,O
Mathematics Education	M,O
Organizational Management	M,O
Project Management	M,O
Reading Education	M,O
Special Education	M,O
Sports Management	M,O
Sustainability Management	M,O

NAVAL POSTGRADUATE SCHOOL

Business Administration and Management—General	M
Finance and Banking	M
Logistics	M
Management Information Systems	M,D,O
Supply Chain Management	M
Transportation Management	M

NAZARETH COLLEGE OF ROCHESTER

Art Education	M
Business Administration and Management—General	M
Business Education	M
Early Childhood Education	M
Education—General	M
Educational Media/Instructional Technology	M
Elementary Education	M
English as a Second Language	M
Human Resources Management	M
Middle School Education	M
Music Education	M
Reading Education	M
Social Work	M

NEUMANN UNIVERSITY

Education—General	M
Educational Leadership and Administration	D
Management Strategy and Policy	M
Sports Management	M

NEW CHARTER UNIVERSITY

Business Administration and Management—General	M
Finance and Banking	M

NEW ENGLAND COLLEGE

Accounting	M
Business Administration and Management—General	M
Education—General	M,D
Educational Leadership and Administration	M,D
Higher Education	M,D
Human Services	M
Management Strategy and Policy	M
Marketing	M
Nonprofit Management	M
Project Management	M
Recreation and Park Management	M
Special Education	M,D
Sports Management	M

NEW ENGLAND COLLEGE OF BUSINESS AND FINANCE

Finance and Banking	M

NEW ENGLAND INSTITUTE OF TECHNOLOGY
- Management Information Systems M

NEW ENGLAND LAW–BOSTON
- Law M,D

NEW HAMPSHIRE INSTITUTE OF ART
- Art Education M

NEW JERSEY CITY UNIVERSITY
- Accounting M
- Art Education M
- Business Administration and Management—General M
- Counselor Education M
- Early Childhood Education M
- Education—General M,D
- Educational Leadership and Administration M
- Educational Media/Instructional Technology M,D
- Educational Psychology M,O
- Elementary Education M
- English as a Second Language M
- Finance and Banking M
- Health Education M
- Mathematics Education M
- Multilingual and Multicultural Education M
- Music Education M
- Reading Education M
- Secondary Education M
- Special Education M
- Urban Education M

NEW JERSEY INSTITUTE OF TECHNOLOGY
- Business Administration and Management—General M,D
- Management Information Systems M,D
- Transportation Management M,D

NEWMAN THEOLOGICAL COLLEGE
- Educational Leadership and Administration M,O
- Religious Education M,O

NEWMAN UNIVERSITY
- Business Administration and Management—General M
- Curriculum and Instruction M
- Education—General M
- Educational Leadership and Administration M
- English as a Second Language M
- Finance and Banking M
- International Business M
- Management Information Systems M
- Organizational Management M
- Reading Education M
- Social Work M

NEW MEXICO HIGHLANDS UNIVERSITY
- Business Administration and Management—General M
- Counselor Education M
- Curriculum and Instruction M
- Education—General M
- Educational Leadership and Administration M
- Exercise and Sports Science M
- Health Education M
- Human Resources Management M
- International Business M
- Management Information Systems M
- Nonprofit Management M
- Social Work M
- Special Education M
- Sports Management M

NEW MEXICO INSTITUTE OF MINING AND TECHNOLOGY
- Science Education M

NEW MEXICO STATE UNIVERSITY
- Accounting M
- Agricultural Education M
- Business Administration and Management—General M,D
- Counselor Education M,D,O
- Curriculum and Instruction M,D
- Distance Education Development O
- Education—General M,D,O
- Educational Leadership and Administration M,D
- Educational Measurement and Evaluation M,D,O
- Finance and Banking O
- Health Education M
- Marketing D
- Multilingual and Multicultural Education M,D
- Music Education M
- Social Work M
- Special Education M,D

NEW ORLEANS BAPTIST THEOLOGICAL SEMINARY
- Religious Education M,D

THE NEW SCHOOL
- English as a Second Language M
- Finance and Banking M,D
- Nonprofit Management M
- Organizational Management M
- Sustainability Management M

NEW YORK INSTITUTE OF TECHNOLOGY
- Accounting M
- Business Administration and Management—General M
- Counselor Education M
- Distance Education Development M,O
- Early Childhood Education M,O
- Education—General M,O
- Educational Leadership and Administration O
- Educational Media/Instructional Technology M,O
- Finance and Banking M,O
- Human Resources Management M,O
- Marketing M
- Mathematics Education M,O
- Middle School Education M,O
- Science Education M,O
- Secondary Education M,O

NEW YORK LAW SCHOOL
- Finance and Banking M,D
- Law M,D
- Taxation M,D

NEW YORK MEDICAL COLLEGE
- Health Education O

NEW YORK UNIVERSITY
- Accounting M,D
- Advertising and Public Relations M
- Archives/Archival Administration M,D,O
- Art Education M,D
- Business Administration and Management—General M,D,O
- Business Education M,O
- Counselor Education M,D,O
- Early Childhood Education M,D
- Education—General M,D,O
- Educational Leadership and Administration M,D,O
- Educational Media/Instructional Technology M,D,O
- Educational Policy M,D
- Educational Psychology M,D
- Electronic Commerce M,D,O
- Elementary Education M,D
- English as a Second Language M,D,O
- English Education M,D,O
- Entrepreneurship M,D,O
- Environmental Education M
- Finance and Banking M,D,O
- Foreign Languages Education M,D,O
- Foundations and Philosophy of Education M,D
- Higher Education M,D
- Hospitality Management M,D,O
- Human Resources Development M,O
- Human Resources Management M,D,O
- International and Comparative Education M,D,O
- International Business M,D
- Kinesiology and Movement Studies M,D,O
- Law M,D,O
- Legal and Justice Studies M,D,O
- Management Information Systems M,D,O
- Management Strategy and Policy M,D,O
- Marketing M,D,O
- Mathematics Education M,D
- Middle School Education M
- Multilingual and Multicultural Education M,D,O
- Music Education M,D,O
- Nonprofit Management M,D,O
- Organizational Behavior M,D,O
- Organizational Management M,D,O
- Project Management M,D,O
- Quantitative Analysis M,D,O
- Reading Education M
- Real Estate M,O
- Science Education M
- Secondary Education M,D,O
- Social Sciences Education M,D,O
- Social Work M,D
- Special Education M,D
- Sports Management M,O
- Student Affairs M,D
- Taxation M,D,O
- Transportation Management M
- Travel and Tourism M,O

NIAGARA UNIVERSITY
- Business Administration and Management—General M
- Counselor Education M,O
- Early Childhood Education M,O
- Education—General M,D,O
- Educational Leadership and Administration M,D,O
- Educational Policy M,D,O
- Elementary Education M,O
- English as a Second Language M,O
- Finance and Banking M
- Foundations and Philosophy of Education M
- Mathematics Education M
- Middle School Education M,O
- Reading Education M
- Science Education M
- Secondary Education M,O
- Special Education M,O
- Vocational and Technical Education M

NICHOLLS STATE UNIVERSITY
- Business Administration and Management—General M
- Counselor Education M
- Curriculum and Instruction M
- Education—General M
- Educational Leadership and Administration M
- Mathematics Education M

NICHOLS COLLEGE
- Business Administration and Management—General M
- Organizational Management M

NIPISSING UNIVERSITY
- Education—General M,O

NORFOLK STATE UNIVERSITY
- Early Childhood Education M
- Education of Students with Severe/Multiple Disabilities M
- Education—General M
- Educational Leadership and Administration M
- Music Education M
- Secondary Education M
- Social Work M,D
- Special Education M
- Urban Education M

NORTH AMERICAN UNIVERSITY
- Educational Leadership and Administration M

NORTH CAROLINA AGRICULTURAL AND TECHNICAL STATE UNIVERSITY
- Accounting M
- Adult Education M
- Agricultural Education M
- Business Administration and Management—General M
- Business Education M
- Counselor Education M
- Early Childhood Education M
- Education—General M
- Educational Leadership and Administration M
- Educational Media/Instructional Technology M
- Elementary Education M
- English Education M
- Health Education M
- Human Resources Management M
- Management Information Systems M
- Physical Education M
- Reading Education M
- Science Education M
- Secondary Education M
- Social Work M
- Supply Chain Management M
- Vocational and Technical Education M

NORTH CAROLINA CENTRAL UNIVERSITY
- Business Administration and Management—General M
- Counselor Education M
- Curriculum and Instruction M
- Education—General M
- Educational Leadership and Administration M
- Educational Media/Instructional Technology M
- Elementary Education M
- Information Studies M
- Law D
- Library Science M
- Mathematics Education M
- Middle School Education M
- Physical Education M
- Recreation and Park Management M
- Special Education M
- Sports Management M

NORTH CAROLINA STATE UNIVERSITY
- Accounting M
- Adult Education M,D
- Agricultural Education M,O
- Business Administration and Management—General M*
- Business Education M
- Community College Education M,D
- Counselor Education M,D
- Curriculum and Instruction M,D
- Developmental Education M,D,O
- Education—General M,D,O
- Educational Leadership and Administration M,D
- Educational Measurement and Evaluation D
- Educational Media/Instructional Technology M,D
- Elementary Education M
- English Education M
- Entrepreneurship M
- Higher Education M,D
- Human Resources Development M
- Mathematics Education M,D
- Middle School Education M
- Nonprofit Management M,D,O
- Recreation and Park Management M,D
- Science Education M,D
- Secondary Education M
- Social Sciences Education M
- Social Work M
- Special Education M
- Sports Management M,D
- Supply Chain Management M
- Travel and Tourism M,D

NORTH CENTRAL COLLEGE
- Business Administration and Management—General M
- Curriculum and Instruction M
- Education—General M
- Educational Leadership and Administration M
- Finance and Banking M
- Human Resources Management M
- International Business M
- Management Information Systems M
- Management Strategy and Policy M
- Marketing M
- Nonprofit Management M
- Organizational Management M
- Sports Management M

NORTHCENTRAL UNIVERSITY
- Business Administration and Management—General M,D,O
- Education—General M,D,O

NORTH DAKOTA STATE UNIVERSITY
- Adult Education M,D,O
- Agricultural Education M
- Athletic Training and Sports Medicine M
- Business Administration and Management—General M
- Counselor Education M,D
- Curriculum and Instruction M
- Education—General M,D,O
- Educational Leadership and Administration M,O
- Electronic Commerce M,D,O
- Exercise and Sports Science M,D
- Higher Education O
- Logistics M,D
- Mathematics Education M,D,O
- Music Education M,D,O
- Science Education M,D,O
- Social Sciences Education M,D,O
- Sports Management M
- Transportation Management M,D
- Vocational and Technical Education M,D,O

NORTHEASTERN ILLINOIS UNIVERSITY
- Accounting M
- Business Administration and Management—General M
- Counselor Education M
- Early Childhood Education M
- Education of the Gifted M
- Education—General M
- Educational Leadership and Administration M
- Elementary Education M
- English as a Second Language M
- Exercise and Sports Science M
- Finance and Banking M
- Human Resources Development M
- Marketing M
- Mathematics Education M
- Multilingual and Multicultural Education M
- Reading Education M
- Secondary Education M
- Special Education M
- Urban Education M

NORTHEASTERN STATE UNIVERSITY
- Accounting M
- Business Administration and Management—General M
- Counselor Education M
- Early Childhood Education M
- Education—General M
- Educational Leadership and Administration M
- Educational Media/Instructional Technology M
- Finance and Banking M
- Foundations and Philosophy of Education M
- Health Education M
- Kinesiology and Movement Studies M
- Mathematics Education M
- Reading Education M
- Science Education M

NORTHEASTERN UNIVERSITY
- Accounting M
- Business Administration and Management—General M,D,O
- Counselor Education M,D,O
- Curriculum and Instruction M,D
- Education—General M,D
- Educational Leadership and Administration M,D
- Elementary Education M,D
- Exercise and Sports Science M,D,O
- Finance and Banking M
- Higher Education M,D
- Hospitality Management M
- Human Services M
- International Business M
- Law D
- Legal and Justice Studies M,D
- Management Information Systems M,D
- Nonprofit Management M
- Organizational Management M,D
- Project Management M
- Religious Education M,D
- Secondary Education M,D
- Special Education M,D
- Taxation M

NORTHERN ARIZONA UNIVERSITY
- Business Administration and Management—General M
- Community College Education M,D,O
- Counselor Education M,D,O
- Early Childhood Education M
- Education—General M,D,O
- Educational Leadership and Administration M,D,O
- Educational Media/Instructional Technology M,O
- Educational Psychology M,D,O
- Elementary Education M
- English as a Second Language M,D,O
- English Education M,D,O
- Foreign Languages Education M
- Foundations and Philosophy of Education M,D,O
- Higher Education M,D,O
- Mathematics Education M,O
- Multilingual and Multicultural Education M,O

*M—masters degree; D—doctorate; O—other advanced degree; *—Close-Up and/or Display*

Science Education — M,O
Secondary Education — M
Special Education — M,O
Student Affairs — M,D,O
Vocational and Technical Education — M,O

NORTHERN ILLINOIS UNIVERSITY
Accounting — M
Adult Education — M,D
Business Administration and Management—General — M
Counselor Education — M,D
Curriculum and Instruction — M,D
Early Childhood Education — M,D
Education—General — M,D,O
Educational Leadership and Administration — M,D,O
Educational Media/Instructional Technology — M,D
Educational Psychology — M,D,O
Elementary Education — M,D
Foundations and Philosophy of Education — M,D,O
Higher Education — M,D
Industrial and Manufacturing Management — M
Law — D
Management Information Systems — M
Physical Education — M
Reading Education — M,D
Secondary Education — M,D
Special Education — M,D
Sports Management — M
Taxation — M

NORTHERN KENTUCKY UNIVERSITY
Accounting — M,O
Advertising and Public Relations — M,O
Business Administration and Management—General — M,O
Counselor Education — M
Education—General — M,D,O
Educational Leadership and Administration — M,D,O
Law — D
Nonprofit Management — M
Organizational Management — M
Social Work — M,O
Special Education — M
Taxation — M

NORTHERN MICHIGAN UNIVERSITY
Counselor Education — M
Curriculum and Instruction — M,O
Education—General — M,O
Educational Leadership and Administration — M
Elementary Education — M
English as a Second Language — M,O
Exercise and Sports Science — M
Human Resources Management — M
Reading Education — M
Science Education — M
Secondary Education — M
Special Education — M

NORTHERN STATE UNIVERSITY
Counselor Education — M
Curriculum and Instruction — M
Education—General — M
Educational Leadership and Administration — M
Educational Media/Instructional Technology — M
Finance and Banking — M
Music Education — M
Sports Management — M

NORTH GREENVILLE UNIVERSITY
Education—General — M,D
Finance and Banking — M,D
Human Resources Management — M,D

NORTH PARK UNIVERSITY
Business Administration and Management—General — M
Education—General — M
Nonprofit Management — M

NORTHWEST CHRISTIAN UNIVERSITY
Business Administration and Management—General — M
Counselor Education — M
Curriculum and Instruction — M
Education—General — M
Educational Media/Instructional Technology — M

NORTHWESTERN OKLAHOMA STATE UNIVERSITY
Adult Education — M
Counselor Education — M
Curriculum and Instruction — M
Education—General — M
Educational Leadership and Administration — M
Elementary Education — M
Reading Education — M
Secondary Education — M

NORTHWESTERN POLYTECHNIC UNIVERSITY
Business Administration and Management—General — M

NORTHWESTERN STATE UNIVERSITY OF LOUISIANA
Adult Education — M
Counselor Education — M,O
Curriculum and Instruction — M
Early Childhood Education — M,O
Education—General — M,O
Educational Leadership and Administration — M,O
Educational Media/Instructional Technology — M,O
Elementary Education — M,O

Health Education — M
Middle School Education — M
Reading Education — M,O
Secondary Education — M,O
Special Education — M,O
Student Affairs — M

NORTHWESTERN UNIVERSITY
Accounting — M,D
Business Administration and Management—General — M,D
Education—General — M,D*
Educational Leadership and Administration — M
Educational Media/Instructional Technology — M
Electronic Commerce — M
Elementary Education — M
Entrepreneurship — M
Finance and Banking — M,D
Human Resources Management — M,D
Industrial and Manufacturing Management — M,D
International Business — M,D
Kinesiology and Movement Studies — D
Law — M,D
Management Information Systems — M
Management Strategy and Policy — M,D
Marketing — M,D
Music Education — M,D
Organizational Behavior — M
Organizational Management — M
Project Management — M
Quality Management — M
Quantitative Analysis — M,D
Real Estate — M,D
Secondary Education — M
Sports Management — M
Taxation — M,D

NORTHWEST MISSOURI STATE UNIVERSITY
Agricultural Education — M
Business Administration and Management—General — M
Counselor Education — M
Early Childhood Education — M,O
Education—General — M,O
Educational Leadership and Administration — M,O
Educational Media/Instructional Technology — M
Elementary Education — M,O
English as a Second Language — M,O
English Education — M
Health Education — M
Management Information Systems — M
Mathematics Education — M
Middle School Education — M
Music Education — M
Physical Education — M
Reading Education — M
Recreation and Park Management — M
Science Education — M
Secondary Education — M,O
Social Sciences Education — M,O
Special Education — M

NORTHWEST NAZARENE UNIVERSITY
Business Administration and Management—General — M
Counselor Education — M
Curriculum and Instruction — M,D,O
Education—General — M,D,O
Educational Leadership and Administration — M,D,O
Reading Education — M,D,O
Social Work — M
Special Education — M,D,O

NORTHWEST UNIVERSITY
Business Administration and Management—General — M
Education—General — M
International Business — M
Organizational Management — M
Project Management — M

NORTHWOOD UNIVERSITY, MICHIGAN CAMPUS
Business Administration and Management—General — M

NORWICH UNIVERSITY
Business Administration and Management—General — M
Finance and Banking — M
International Business — M
Management Information Systems — M
Organizational Management — M
Project Management — M

NOTRE DAME COLLEGE (OH)
Reading Education — M,O
Special Education — M,O

NOTRE DAME DE NAMUR UNIVERSITY
Business Administration and Management—General — M
Curriculum and Instruction — M,O
Education—General — M,O
Educational Leadership and Administration — M,O
Educational Media/Instructional Technology — M,O
English as a Second Language — M,O
Entrepreneurship — M
Finance and Banking — M
Human Resources Management — M
Industrial and Manufacturing Management — M
Marketing — M
Special Education — M,O

NOTRE DAME OF MARYLAND UNIVERSITY
Business Administration and Management—General — M
Education—General — M
Educational Leadership and Administration — M,D
English as a Second Language — M
Nonprofit Management — M

NOVA SOUTHEASTERN UNIVERSITY
Accounting — M,D
Business Administration and Management—General — M
Counselor Education — M,D,O
Distance Education Development — M,D,O
Education—General — M,D,O
Educational Media/Instructional Technology — M,D,O
Health Law — M,D
Human Resources Management — M,D
Human Services — M,D
International Business — M,D
Law — M,D
Legal and Justice Studies — M,D
Management Information Systems — M,D
Real Estate — M,D
Student Affairs — M,D,O
Taxation — M,D

NYACK COLLEGE
Business Administration and Management—General — M
Counselor Education — M
Elementary Education — M
English as a Second Language — M
Organizational Management — M
Special Education — M

OAKLAND CITY UNIVERSITY
Business Administration and Management—General — M
Education—General — M,D
Educational Leadership and Administration — M,D

OAKLAND UNIVERSITY
Accounting — M,O
Business Administration and Management—General — M,O
Early Childhood Education — M,D,O
Education—General — M,D,O
Educational Leadership and Administration — M,D,O
Educational Media/Instructional Technology — M,D,O
English as a Second Language — M,O
Entrepreneurship — M,O
Exercise and Sports Science — M,O
Finance and Banking — M,O
Foundations and Philosophy of Education — M
Higher Education — M,D,O
Human Resources Development — M
Human Resources Management — M,O
Industrial and Manufacturing Management — M,O
International Business — M
Management Information Systems — M,O
Marketing — M,O
Mathematics Education — M,D,O
Music Education — M,D
Reading Education — M,D,O
Secondary Education — M,O
Special Education — M,O

OBERLIN COLLEGE
Music Education — M,O

OCCIDENTAL COLLEGE
Education—General — M
Elementary Education — M
English Education — M
Foreign Languages Education — M
Mathematics Education — M
Science Education — M
Secondary Education — M
Social Sciences Education — M

OGLALA LAKOTA COLLEGE
Business Administration and Management—General — M
Educational Leadership and Administration — M

OHIO DOMINICAN UNIVERSITY
Accounting — M
Business Administration and Management—General — M
Curriculum and Instruction — M
Education—General — M
Educational Leadership and Administration — M
English as a Second Language — M
Finance and Banking — M

OHIO NORTHERN UNIVERSITY
Law — M,D

THE OHIO STATE UNIVERSITY
Accounting — M,D
Agricultural Education — M,D
Art Education — M,D
Business Administration and Management—General — M,D
Education—General — M,D,O
Educational Leadership and Administration — M,D,O
Educational Policy — M,D,O
Human Resources Management — M,D
Kinesiology and Movement Studies — M,D
Law — M,D
Logistics — M
Management Information Systems — M,D
Marketing — M,D
Mathematics Education — M,D
Physical Education — M

Social Work — M,D
Special Education — D

THE OHIO STATE UNIVERSITY AT LIMA
Early Childhood Education — M
Education—General — M
Middle School Education — M
Social Work — M

THE OHIO STATE UNIVERSITY AT MARION
Early Childhood Education — M
Education—General — M
Middle School Education — M

THE OHIO STATE UNIVERSITY–MANSFIELD CAMPUS
Early Childhood Education — M
Education—General — M
Middle School Education — M
Social Work — M

THE OHIO STATE UNIVERSITY–NEWARK CAMPUS
Early Childhood Education — M
Education—General — M
Middle School Education — M
Social Work — M

OHIO UNIVERSITY
Athletic Training and Sports Medicine — M
Business Administration and Management—General — M
Computer Education — M,D
Counselor Education — M,D
Curriculum and Instruction — M,D
Education—General — M,D
Educational Leadership and Administration — M,D
Educational Measurement and Evaluation — M,D
Educational Media/Instructional Technology — M,D
Exercise and Sports Science — M,D
Finance and Banking — M
Higher Education — M,D
Mathematics Education — M,D
Middle School Education — M,D
Multilingual and Multicultural Education — M,D
Music Education — M,O
Physical Education — M,O
Reading Education — M,D
Recreation and Park Management — M
Science Education — M,D
Secondary Education — M,D
Social Sciences Education — M,D
Social Work — M
Special Education — M,D
Sports Management — M
Student Affairs — M,D

OHIO VALLEY UNIVERSITY
Curriculum and Instruction — M
Education—General — M

OKLAHOMA BAPTIST UNIVERSITY
Business Administration and Management—General — M

OKLAHOMA CHRISTIAN UNIVERSITY
Accounting — M
Business Administration and Management—General — M
Electronic Commerce — M
Finance and Banking — M
Human Resources Management — M
International Business — M
Marketing — M
Organizational Management — M
Project Management — M

OKLAHOMA CITY UNIVERSITY
Accounting — M
Business Administration and Management—General — M
Early Childhood Education — M
Education—General — M
Elementary Education — M
English as a Second Language — M
Exercise and Sports Science — M
Finance and Banking — M
Law — M,D
Legal and Justice Studies — M
Marketing — M
Nonprofit Management — M
Taxation — M

OKLAHOMA STATE UNIVERSITY
Accounting — M,D
Agricultural Education — M,D
Business Administration and Management—General — M,D
Curriculum and Instruction — M,D
Distance Education Development — M,D,O
Education—General — M,D,O
Educational Leadership and Administration — M,D
Educational Psychology — M,D,O
Entrepreneurship — M,D,O
Finance and Banking — M,D
Health Education — M,D,O
Higher Education — M,D
Hospitality Management — M,D
Management Information Systems — M,D
Marketing — M,D
Mathematics Education — M,D
Music Education — M,D
Nonprofit Management — M,D,O
Quantitative Analysis — M,D
Sustainability Management — M,D,O

OLD DOMINION UNIVERSITY
Accounting — M
Business Administration and Management—General — M,D
Business Education — M,D

- Community College Education M,D
- Counselor Education M,D,O
- Curriculum and Instruction M,D
- Early Childhood Education M,D
- Education—General M,D,O
- Educational Leadership and Administration M,D,O
- Educational Media/Instructional Technology M,D
- Elementary Education M
- Exercise and Sports Science M
- Finance and Banking M,D
- Higher Education M,D,O
- International Business M
- Kinesiology and Movement Studies D
- Library Science M
- Management Information Systems M
- Marketing D
- Middle School Education M
- Music Education M
- Physical Education M
- Reading Education M,D
- Science Education M
- Secondary Education M
- Special Education M,D
- Sports Management M
- Vocational and Technical Education M,D

OLIVET COLLEGE
- Education—General M

OLIVET NAZARENE UNIVERSITY
- Business Administration and Management—General M
- Curriculum and Instruction M
- Education—General M
- Educational Leadership and Administration M
- Elementary Education M
- Library Science M
- Organizational Management M
- Reading Education M
- Secondary Education M

ORAL ROBERTS UNIVERSITY
- Accounting M
- Business Administration and Management—General M
- Curriculum and Instruction M,D
- Education—General M,D
- Educational Leadership and Administration M,D
- Entrepreneurship M
- Finance and Banking M
- Higher Education M,D
- International Business M
- Marketing M
- Nonprofit Management M
- Religious Education M,D

OREGON STATE UNIVERSITY
- Accounting M
- Adult Education M
- Agricultural Education M
- Business Administration and Management—General M,D
- Counselor Education M,D
- Education—General M,D
- Educational Leadership and Administration M
- Exercise and Sports Science M,D
- Finance and Banking M
- Investment Management M
- Kinesiology and Movement Studies M,D
- Marketing M
- Mathematics Education M,D
- Music Education M
- Physical Education M,D
- Science Education M,D
- Student Affairs M
- Supply Chain Management M
- Sustainability Management M,D

OREGON STATE UNIVERSITY–CASCADES
- Education—General M

OTTAWA UNIVERSITY
- Business Administration and Management—General M
- Counselor Education M
- Curriculum and Instruction M
- Early Childhood Education M
- Education—General M
- Educational Leadership and Administration M
- Educational Media/Instructional Technology M
- Elementary Education M
- Finance and Banking M
- Human Resources Development M
- Human Resources Management M
- Marketing M
- Special Education M

OTTERBEIN UNIVERSITY
- Business Administration and Management—General M
- Education—General M

OUR LADY OF HOLY CROSS COLLEGE
- Counselor Education M
- Curriculum and Instruction M
- Education—General M
- Educational Leadership and Administration M

OUR LADY OF THE LAKE UNIVERSITY OF SAN ANTONIO
- Accounting M
- Business Administration and Management—General M
- Counselor Education M
- Curriculum and Instruction M
- Early Childhood Education M
- Education—General M,D
- Educational Leadership and Administration M
- Educational Media/Instructional Technology M
- Elementary Education M
- English as a Second Language M
- English Education M
- Finance and Banking M
- Management Information Systems M
- Mathematics Education M
- Middle School Education M
- Multilingual and Multicultural Education M
- Nonprofit Management M
- Organizational Management M,D
- Reading Education M
- Science Education M
- Secondary Education M
- Social Work M
- Special Education M

OXFORD GRADUATE SCHOOL
- Organizational Management M,D

PACE UNIVERSITY
- Accounting M
- Business Administration and Management—General M,D,O
- Early Childhood Education M,O
- Education—General M,O
- Educational Leadership and Administration M,O
- Educational Media/Instructional Technology M,O
- Elementary Education M,O
- Entrepreneurship M
- Environmental Law M,D
- Finance and Banking M
- Human Resources Management M
- International Business M
- Investment Management M
- Law M,D
- Legal and Justice Studies M,D
- Management Information Systems M
- Management Strategy and Policy M
- Marketing Research M
- Marketing M
- Nonprofit Management M
- Reading Education M,O
- Special Education M,O
- Taxation M

PACIFIC LUTHERAN UNIVERSITY
- Business Administration and Management—General M
- Curriculum and Instruction M
- Education—General M
- Educational Leadership and Administration M
- Finance and Banking M

PACIFIC STATES UNIVERSITY
- Accounting M,D
- Business Administration and Management—General M,D
- Finance and Banking M,D
- International Business M,D
- Management Information Systems M,D
- Real Estate M,D

PACIFIC UNION COLLEGE
- Education—General M
- Elementary Education M
- Secondary Education M

PACIFIC UNIVERSITY
- Early Childhood Education M
- Education—General M
- Elementary Education M
- Middle School Education M
- Secondary Education M
- Special Education M

PALM BEACH ATLANTIC UNIVERSITY
- Business Administration and Management—General M
- Counselor Education M
- Education—General M
- Organizational Management M

PARK UNIVERSITY
- Business Administration and Management—General M,O
- Curriculum and Instruction M,O
- Education—General M,O
- Educational Leadership and Administration M,O
- Finance and Banking M,O
- International Business M,O
- Management Information Systems M,O
- Nonprofit Management M,O
- Reading Education M,O
- Social Work M,O

PENN STATE DICKINSON SCHOOL OF LAW
- Law M,D

PENN STATE ERIE, THE BEHREND COLLEGE
- Business Administration and Management—General M
- Industrial and Manufacturing Management M
- Project Management M
- Quality Management M

PENN STATE GREAT VALLEY
- Business Administration and Management—General M
- Finance and Banking M
- Human Resources Development M

PENN STATE HARRISBURG
- Business Administration and Management—General M
- Curriculum and Instruction M,O
- Developmental Education M,O
- Education—General M,O
- Health Education M,O
- Management Information Systems M
- Reading Education M,O

PENN STATE UNIVERSITY PARK
- Accounting M,D
- Adult Education M,D,O
- Agricultural Education M,D,O
- Art Education M,D,O
- Business Administration and Management—General M,D
- Counselor Education M,D,O
- Curriculum and Instruction M,D,O
- Education—General M,D,O
- Educational Leadership and Administration M,D,O
- Educational Media/Instructional Technology M,D,O
- Educational Policy M,D,O
- Educational Psychology M,D,O
- English as a Second Language M,D
- Higher Education M,D,O
- Hospitality Management M,D
- Human Resources Development M,D,O
- Human Resources Management M
- Kinesiology and Movement Studies M,D,O
- Leisure Studies M,D
- Management Information Systems M,D
- Music Education M,D,O
- Organizational Management M,D,O
- Recreation and Park Management M,D
- Special Education M,D,O
- Student Affairs M,D,O
- Supply Chain Management M,D
- Travel and Tourism M,D
- Vocational and Technical Education M,D,O

PEPPERDINE UNIVERSITY
- Business Administration and Management—General M
- Education—General M
- Educational Leadership and Administration M,D
- Educational Media/Instructional Technology M,D
- Finance and Banking M
- International Business M
- Law D
- Organizational Management M

PERU STATE COLLEGE
- Curriculum and Instruction M
- Education—General M
- Entrepreneurship M
- Organizational Management M

PFEIFFER UNIVERSITY
- Business Administration and Management—General M
- Elementary Education M
- Organizational Management M
- Religious Education M

PHILADELPHIA UNIVERSITY
- Business Administration and Management—General M
- Management Strategy and Policy M
- Marketing M
- Taxation M

PHILLIPS GRADUATE INSTITUTE
- Counselor Education M
- Organizational Behavior D

PHILLIPS THEOLOGICAL SEMINARY
- Business Administration and Management—General M,D
- Higher Education M,D
- Religious Education M,D
- Social Work M,D

PIEDMONT COLLEGE
- Art Education M,D,O
- Business Administration and Management—General M
- Early Childhood Education M,D,O
- Education—General M,D,O
- Educational Leadership and Administration M,D,O
- Educational Media/Instructional Technology M,D,O
- Middle School Education M,D,O
- Music Education M,D,O
- Secondary Education M,D,O
- Special Education M,D,O

PITTSBURG STATE UNIVERSITY
- Accounting M
- Art Education M
- Business Administration and Management—General M
- Community College Education O
- Counselor Education M
- Early Childhood Education M
- Education—General M,O
- Educational Leadership and Administration M,O
- Educational Media/Instructional Technology M
- Elementary Education M
- Higher Education M,O
- Human Resources Development M
- Music Education M
- Physical Education M
- Reading Education M
- Secondary Education M
- Special Education M
- Vocational and Technical Education M,O

PLYMOUTH STATE UNIVERSITY
- Adult Education D
- Art Education M
- Athletic Training and Sports Medicine M
- Business Administration and Management—General M
- Counselor Education M
- Curriculum and Instruction M
- Education—General O
- Educational Leadership and Administration M,O
- Educational Media/Instructional Technology M
- Elementary Education M
- English Education M
- Foreign Languages Education M
- Health Education M
- Higher Education D,O
- Mathematics Education M
- Music Education M
- Physical Education M
- Reading Education M
- Science Education M
- Secondary Education M
- Social Sciences Education M
- Special Education M

POINT LOMA NAZARENE UNIVERSITY
- Business Administration and Management—General M
- Counselor Education M
- Education—General M
- Educational Leadership and Administration M
- Nonprofit Management M
- Organizational Management M
- Special Education M
- Sustainability Management M

POINT PARK UNIVERSITY
- Business Administration and Management—General M
- Curriculum and Instruction M
- Education—General M
- Educational Leadership and Administration M
- Organizational Management M
- Special Education M

POLYTECHNIC UNIVERSITY OF PUERTO RICO
- Business Administration and Management—General M
- Industrial and Manufacturing Management M
- International Business M
- Management Information Systems M

POLYTECHNIC UNIVERSITY OF PUERTO RICO, MIAMI CAMPUS
- Accounting M
- Business Administration and Management—General M
- Finance and Banking M
- Human Resources Management M
- Industrial and Manufacturing Management M
- International Business M
- Logistics M
- Marketing M
- Project Management M
- Supply Chain Management M

POLYTECHNIC UNIVERSITY OF PUERTO RICO, ORLANDO CAMPUS
- Accounting M
- Business Administration and Management—General M
- Finance and Banking M
- Human Resources Management M
- Industrial and Manufacturing Management M
- International Business M

PONTIFICAL CATHOLIC UNIVERSITY OF PUERTO RICO
- Accounting M,O
- Business Administration and Management—General M,D,O
- Business Education M,D
- Counselor Education M
- Curriculum and Instruction M,D
- Education—General M,D
- Educational Leadership and Administration D
- Educational Psychology M
- English as a Second Language M
- Finance and Banking M
- Human Resources Management M,O
- Human Services M,D
- International Business M
- Law D
- Logistics O
- Management Information Systems M,O
- Marketing M
- Religious Education M
- Social Work M
- Transportation Management O

PONTIFICIA UNIVERSIDAD CATOLICA MADRE Y MAESTRA
- Business Administration and Management—General M
- Early Childhood Education M
- Entrepreneurship M
- Finance and Banking M
- Hospitality Management M
- Human Resources Management M
- Insurance M
- International Business M
- Law M
- Logistics M

*M—masters degree; D—doctorate; O—other advanced degree; *—Close-Up and/or Display*

Management Strategy and Policy M
Marketing M
Real Estate M
Travel and Tourism M

PORTLAND STATE UNIVERSITY
Adult Education M,D
Business Administration and Management—General M,D,O
Counselor Education M,D
Curriculum and Instruction M,D
Early Childhood Education M,D
Education—General M,D
Educational Leadership and Administration M,D
Educational Media/Instructional Technology M,D
Elementary Education M,D
English as a Second Language M
Finance and Banking M
Foreign Languages Education M
Health Education M,O
Higher Education M,D
Industrial and Manufacturing Management M,D
International Business M
Mathematics Education M,D
Music Education M
Reading Education M,D
Science Education M,D
Secondary Education M,D
Social Sciences Education M,D
Social Work M,D
Special Education M,D
Supply Chain Management M

POST UNIVERSITY
Accounting M
Business Administration and Management—General M
Distance Education Development M
Education—General M
Educational Leadership and Administration M
Educational Media/Instructional Technology M
English as a Second Language M
Entrepreneurship M
Finance and Banking M
Human Services M
Marketing M
Nonprofit Management M
Project Management M

PRAIRIE VIEW A&M UNIVERSITY
Accounting M
Business Administration and Management—General M
Counselor Education M,D
Curriculum and Instruction M,D
Education—General M
Educational Leadership and Administration M,D
Health Education M
Legal and Justice Studies M,D
Management Information Systems M,D
Physical Education M
Special Education M

PRATT INSTITUTE
Archives/Archival Administration M,O
Art Education M
Facilities Management M
Information Studies M,O*
Library Science M,O
Special Education M

PRESCOTT COLLEGE
Counselor Education M,D
Early Childhood Education M,D
Education—General M,D
Educational Leadership and Administration M,D
Elementary Education M,D
Environmental Education M,D
Legal and Justice Studies M,D
Leisure Studies M
Secondary Education M,D
Special Education M,D

PRINCETON UNIVERSITY
Finance and Banking M

PROVIDENCE COLLEGE
Accounting M
Business Administration and Management—General M
Counselor Education M
Educational Leadership and Administration M
Elementary Education M
Finance and Banking M
International Business M
Marketing M
Mathematics Education M
Nonprofit Management M
Reading Education M
Secondary Education M
Special Education M
Urban Education M

PROVIDENCE UNIVERSITY COLLEGE & THEOLOGICAL SEMINARY
English as a Second Language M,D,O
Religious Education M,D,O
Student Affairs M,D,O

PURDUE UNIVERSITY
Agricultural Education M,D,O
Art Education M,D,O
Aviation Management M
Business Administration and Management—General M,D
Counselor Education M,D,O
Curriculum and Instruction M,D,O
Education of the Gifted M,D,O
Education—General M,D,O
Educational Leadership and Administration M,D,O
Educational Media/Instructional Technology M,D,O
Educational Psychology M,D,O
Elementary Education M,D,O
English Education M,D,O
Exercise and Sports Science M,D
Finance and Banking M
Foreign Languages Education M,D,O
Foundations and Philosophy of Education M,D,O
Health Education M,D,O
Higher Education M,D,O
Home Economics Education M,D,O
Hospitality Management M,D
Human Resources Management M,D
Industrial and Manufacturing Management M
International Business M
Kinesiology and Movement Studies M,D
Management Information Systems M
Mathematics Education M,D,O
Organizational Behavior D
Physical Education M,D
Quantitative Analysis M,D
Reading Education M,D,O
Recreation and Park Management M,D
Science Education M,D,O
Social Sciences Education M,D,O
Special Education M,D,O
Sports Management M,D
Travel and Tourism M,D
Vocational and Technical Education M,D,O

PURDUE UNIVERSITY CALUMET
Accounting M
Business Administration and Management—General M
Counselor Education M
Education—General M
Educational Leadership and Administration M
Educational Media/Instructional Technology M
Human Services M
Mathematics Education M
Science Education M
Special Education M

PURDUE UNIVERSITY NORTH CENTRAL
Education—General M
Elementary Education M

QUEENS COLLEGE OF THE CITY UNIVERSITY OF NEW YORK
Accounting M
Art Education M,O
Counselor Education M
Early Childhood Education M,O
Education—General M,O
Educational Leadership and Administration O
Elementary Education M,O
English as a Second Language M,O
English Education M,O
Exercise and Sports Science M
Foreign Languages Education M,O
Home Economics Education M
Information Studies M,O
Library Science M,O
Mathematics Education M,O
Multilingual and Multicultural Education M,O
Music Education M,O
Reading Education M,O
Science Education M,O
Secondary Education M,O
Social Sciences Education M,O
Special Education M,O

QUEEN'S UNIVERSITY AT KINGSTON
Business Administration and Management—General M
Education—General M,D
Entrepreneurship M
Exercise and Sports Science M,D
Finance and Banking M
Information Studies M,D
Law M,D
Legal and Justice Studies M,D
Marketing M
Project Management M

QUEENS UNIVERSITY OF CHARLOTTE
Business Administration and Management—General M
Education—General M
Educational Leadership and Administration M
Elementary Education M
Reading Education M

QUINCY UNIVERSITY
Business Administration and Management—General M
Counselor Education M
Curriculum and Instruction M
Education—General M
Educational Leadership and Administration M
English as a Second Language M
Industrial and Manufacturing Management M
Multilingual and Multicultural Education M
Organizational Management M
Reading Education M
Special Education M

QUINNIPIAC UNIVERSITY
Advertising and Public Relations M
Business Administration and Management—General M
Education—General M,O
Educational Leadership and Administration M,O
Elementary Education M
English Education M
Finance and Banking M
Foreign Languages Education M
Health Law M,D
Investment Management M
Law M,D
Management Information Systems M
Marketing M
Mathematics Education M
Middle School Education M
Organizational Management M
Science Education M
Secondary Education M
Social Sciences Education M
Social Work M
Supply Chain Management M

RADFORD UNIVERSITY
Business Administration and Management—General M
Counselor Education M
Curriculum and Instruction M
Early Childhood Education M,O
Education—General M,O
Educational Leadership and Administration M,O
Educational Media/Instructional Technology M
Mathematics Education M
Music Education M
Reading Education M
Social Work M
Special Education M,O

RAMAPO COLLEGE OF NEW JERSEY
Business Administration and Management—General M
Educational Leadership and Administration M
Educational Media/Instructional Technology M

RANDOLPH COLLEGE
Curriculum and Instruction M
Education—General M
Special Education M

REFORMED THEOLOGICAL SEMINARY–JACKSON CAMPUS
Religious Education M,D,O

REGENT'S UNIVERSITY LONDON
Business Administration and Management—General M
Finance and Banking M
Human Resources Management M
International Business M
Management Information Systems M
Marketing M

REGENT UNIVERSITY
Adult Education M,D,O
Business Administration and Management—General M,D,O
Counselor Education M,D,O
Curriculum and Instruction M,D,O
Distance Education Development M,D,O
Education—General M,D,O
Educational Leadership and Administration M,D,O
Educational Psychology M,D,O
Elementary Education M,D,O
English as a Second Language M,D,O
Entrepreneurship M,D,O
Higher Education M,D,O
Human Resources Development M,D,O
Law M,D
Legal and Justice Studies M,D
Management Strategy and Policy M,D,O
Mathematics Education M,D,O
Nonprofit Management M,D,O
Organizational Management M,D,O
Reading Education M,D,O
Religious Education M,D,O
Special Education M,D,O
Student Affairs M,D,O

REGIS COLLEGE (MA)
Education—General M,D
Educational Leadership and Administration M,D
Elementary Education M,D
Higher Education M,D
Quality Management M
Reading Education M,D
Special Education M,D

REGIS UNIVERSITY
Accounting M
Adult Education M,O
Business Administration and Management—General M
Curriculum and Instruction M,O
Education of the Gifted M,O
Education—General M,O
Educational Leadership and Administration M,O
Educational Media/Instructional Technology M,O
Electronic Commerce M,O
Finance and Banking M
Human Resources Management M,O
Management Information Systems M,O
Management Strategy and Policy M
Marketing M
Nonprofit Management M,O
Organizational Management M,O
Project Management M,O
Reading Education M,O
Science Education M,O
Special Education M,O

REINHARDT UNIVERSITY
Business Administration and Management—General M
Early Childhood Education M
Education—General M
Music Education M

RENSSELAER AT HARTFORD
Business Administration and Management—General M

RENSSELAER POLYTECHNIC INSTITUTE
Business Administration and Management—General M,D
Entrepreneurship M
Management Information Systems M
Supply Chain Management M

RHODE ISLAND COLLEGE
Accounting M,O
Art Education M
Counselor Education M,O
Early Childhood Education M
Education—General D
Educational Leadership and Administration M,O
Elementary Education M
English as a Second Language M
English Education M
Finance and Banking M,O
Foreign Languages Education M
Health Education M,O
Mathematics Education M
Music Education M
Physical Education M,O
Reading Education M
Secondary Education M
Social Sciences Education M
Social Work M
Special Education M,O

RHODE ISLAND SCHOOL OF DESIGN
Art Education M

RHODES COLLEGE
Accounting M

RICE UNIVERSITY
Business Administration and Management—General M
Education—General M
Science Education M,D

THE RICHARD STOCKTON COLLEGE OF NEW JERSEY
Business Administration and Management—General M
Education—General M
Educational Leadership and Administration M
Educational Media/Instructional Technology M
Social Work M

RICHMONT GRADUATE UNIVERSITY
Counselor Education M

RIDER UNIVERSITY
Accounting M
Business Administration and Management—General M
Business Education O
Counselor Education M,O
Curriculum and Instruction M,O
Education—General M,O
Educational Leadership and Administration M,O
Elementary Education O
English as a Second Language O
English Education O
Foreign Languages Education O
Mathematics Education O
Music Education M
Organizational Management M
Reading Education M,O
Science Education O
Social Sciences Education O
Special Education M,O

RIVIER UNIVERSITY
Business Administration and Management—General M
Counselor Education M,D,O
Curriculum and Instruction M,D,O
Early Childhood Education M,D,O
Education—General M,D,O
Educational Leadership and Administration M,D,O
Elementary Education M,D,O
Foreign Languages Education M
Management Information Systems M
Reading Education M,D,O
Social Sciences Education M
Special Education M,D,O

ROBERT MORRIS UNIVERSITY
Business Administration and Management—General M
Business Education M,D,O
Education—General M,D,O
Educational Leadership and Administration M,D,O
Human Resources Management M
Management Information Systems M,D
Nonprofit Management M
Organizational Management M,D
Project Management M,D
Sports Management M,D,O
Taxation M

ROBERT MORRIS UNIVERSITY ILLINOIS
Accounting M
Business Administration and Management—General M
Educational Leadership and Administration M

Educational Media/Instructional
   Technology — M
Finance and Banking — M
Higher Education — M
Human Resources Management — M
Management Information Systems — M
Management Strategy and Policy — M
Sports Management — M

ROBERTS WESLEYAN COLLEGE
Business Administration and
   Management—General — M
Counselor Education — M
Early Childhood Education — M,O
Education—General — M,O
Human Services — M
Management Strategy and Policy — M
Marketing — M
Middle School Education — M,O
Reading Education — M,O
Secondary Education — M,O
Social Work — M
Special Education — M,O

ROCHESTER COLLEGE
Religious Education — M

ROCHESTER INSTITUTE OF TECHNOLOGY
Accounting — M
Art Education — M
Business Administration and
   Management—General — M
Entrepreneurship — M
Finance and Banking — M
Hospitality Management — M
Human Resources Development — M
Industrial and Manufacturing
   Management — M
International Business — M
Management Information Systems — M
Project Management — O
Secondary Education — M
Special Education — M
Sustainability Management — M,D
Travel and Tourism — M

ROCKFORD UNIVERSITY
Business Administration and
   Management—General — M
Early Childhood Education — M
Education—General — M
Elementary Education — M
Reading Education — M
Secondary Education — M
Special Education — M

ROCKHURST UNIVERSITY
Business Administration and
   Management—General — M
Education—General — M

ROCKY MOUNTAIN COLLEGE
Accounting — M
Educational Leadership and
   Administration — M

ROCKY MOUNTAIN COLLEGE OF ART + DESIGN
Art Education — M

ROGER WILLIAMS UNIVERSITY
Education—General — M
Elementary Education — M
Law — D
Reading Education — M

ROLLINS COLLEGE
Business Administration and
   Management—General — M,D
Counselor Education — M
Education—General — M
Elementary Education — M
Entrepreneurship — M,D
Finance and Banking — M
Human Resources Development — M
Human Resources Management — M
International Business — M,D
Marketing — M,D

ROOSEVELT UNIVERSITY
Accounting — M
Actuarial Science — M
Business Administration and
   Management—General — M
Counselor Education — M
Early Childhood Education — M
Education—General — M,D
Educational Leadership and
   Administration — M
Elementary Education — M
Hospitality Management — M
Human Resources Development — M
Human Resources Management — M
International Business — M
Management Information Systems — M
Marketing — M
Music Education — M,O
Organizational Management — M,D
Reading Education — M
Real Estate — M,O
Secondary Education — M
Special Education — M

ROSALIND FRANKLIN UNIVERSITY OF MEDICINE AND SCIENCE
Health Education — M

ROSE-HULMAN INSTITUTE OF TECHNOLOGY
Management Information Systems — M

ROSEMAN UNIVERSITY OF HEALTH SCIENCES
Business Administration and
   Management—General — M,O

ROSEMONT COLLEGE
Business Administration and
   Management—General — M
Counselor Education — M
Education—General — M
Elementary Education — M
Human Services — M

ROWAN UNIVERSITY
Accounting — O
Advertising and Public Relations — M
Business Administration and
   Management—General — M,O
Counselor Education — M
Education—General — M,D,O
Educational Leadership and
   Administration — M,D,O
Educational Media/Instructional
   Technology — M,O
Elementary Education — M
English as a Second Language — O
English Education — O
Exercise and Sports Science — M
Foreign Languages Education — M,O
Higher Education — M
Library Science — M,O
Marketing — O
Mathematics Education — O
Middle School Education — O
Multilingual and Multicultural
   Education — M,O
Reading Education — M
Science Education — M
Secondary Education — M
Special Education — M,O

ROYAL MILITARY COLLEGE OF CANADA
Business Administration and
   Management—General — M

ROYAL ROADS UNIVERSITY
Advertising and Public Relations — O
Business Administration and
   Management—General — M,O
Environmental Education — M,O
Hospitality Management — M,O
Human Resources Management — M,O
Project Management — O
Travel and Tourism — M,O

RUTGERS, THE STATE UNIVERSITY OF NEW JERSEY, CAMDEN
Business Administration and
   Management—General — M
Educational Leadership and
   Administration — M
Educational Policy — M
Law — D
Mathematics Education — M

RUTGERS, THE STATE UNIVERSITY OF NEW JERSEY, NEWARK
Accounting — D
Business Administration and
   Management—General — M,D
Finance and Banking — D
Health Education — M,D
Human Resources Management — M,D
International Business — D
Law — D
Management Information Systems — D
Marketing — D
Organizational Management — D
Quantitative Analysis — M,O
Supply Chain Management — D

RUTGERS, THE STATE UNIVERSITY OF NEW JERSEY, NEW BRUNSWICK
Counselor Education — M
Developmental Education — M
Early Childhood Education — M,D
Education—General — M,D
Educational Leadership and
   Administration — M,D
Educational Measurement and
   Evaluation — M
Educational Policy — D
Educational Psychology — M,D
Elementary Education — M
English as a Second Language — M,D
English Education — M
Foreign Languages Education — M,D
Foundations and Philosophy of
   Education — M,D,O
Health Education — M,D
Human Resources Management — M,D
Information Studies — M,D
Legal and Justice Studies — D
Library Science — M,D
Mathematics Education — M,D
Multilingual and Multicultural
   Education — M,D
Music Education — M,D,O
Quality Management — M,D
Reading Education — M,D
Science Education — M,D
Social Sciences Education — M,D
Social Work — M,D
Special Education — M,D
Student Affairs — M

SACRED HEART UNIVERSITY
Accounting — M,O
Advertising and Public Relations — M
Business Administration and
   Management—General — M,D,O
Education—General — M

Educational Leadership and
   Administration — M,O
Educational Media/Instructional
   Technology — M,O
Elementary Education — M,O
English as a Second Language — M,O
Exercise and Sports Science — M
Finance and Banking — D,O
Human Resources Management — M,O
International Business — M,O
Management Information Systems — M,O
Marketing — M,O
Reading Education — O
Secondary Education — M,O

SAGE GRADUATE SCHOOL
Art Education — M
Business Administration and
   Management—General — M,O
Counselor Education — M,O
Education—General — M,D,O
Educational Leadership and
   Administration — D
Elementary Education — M
English Education — M
Finance and Banking — M
Health Education — M
Human Resources Management — M
Management Strategy and Policy — M
Marketing — M
Mathematics Education — M
Organizational Management — M
Reading Education — M
Social Sciences Education — M
Special Education — M

SAGINAW VALLEY STATE UNIVERSITY
Business Administration and
   Management—General — M
Distance Education Development — M
Early Childhood Education — M
Education—General — M
Educational Leadership and
   Administration — M,O
Educational Media/Instructional
   Technology — M
Elementary Education — M
Middle School Education — M
Reading Education — M
Science Education — M
Secondary Education — M
Special Education — M

ST. AMBROSE UNIVERSITY
Accounting — M
Business Administration and
   Management—General — M,D
Education—General — M
Educational Leadership and
   Administration — M
Human Resources Management — M,D
Organizational Management — M
Social Work — M
Special Education — M

ST. AUGUSTINE'S SEMINARY OF TORONTO
Religious Education — M,O

ST. BONAVENTURE UNIVERSITY
Business Administration and
   Management—General — M
Counselor Education — M,O
Early Childhood Education — M
Education of the Gifted — M,O
Education—General — M,O
Educational Leadership and
   Administration — M,O
Marketing — M
Middle School Education — M
Reading Education — M
Secondary Education — M
Special Education — M

ST. CATHARINE COLLEGE
Organizational Management — M

ST. CATHERINE UNIVERSITY
Curriculum and Instruction — M
Early Childhood Education — M
Education—General — M
Information Studies — M
Library Science — M
Organizational Management — M
Social Work — M

ST. CLOUD STATE UNIVERSITY
Business Administration and
   Management—General — M
Counselor Education — M
Curriculum and Instruction — M
Education—General — M,D
Educational Leadership and
   Administration — M,D
Educational Media/Instructional
   Technology — M
English as a Second Language — M
Exercise and Sports Science — M
Higher Education — M,D
Music Education — M
Nonprofit Management — M
Social Work — M
Special Education — M
Sports Management — M
Student Affairs — M

ST. EDWARD'S UNIVERSITY
Accounting — M,O
Business Administration and
   Management—General — M,O
Finance and Banking — M,O
International Business — M,O
Management Information Systems — M,O
Marketing — M,O

Organizational Management — M
Student Affairs — M

ST. FRANCIS COLLEGE
Accounting — M

SAINT FRANCIS UNIVERSITY
Business Administration and
   Management—General — M
Education—General — M
Educational Leadership and
   Administration — M
Health Education — M
Human Resources Management — M
Reading Education — M

ST. FRANCIS XAVIER UNIVERSITY
Adult Education — M
Curriculum and Instruction — M
Education—General — M
Educational Leadership and
   Administration — M

ST. JOHN FISHER COLLEGE
Business Administration and
   Management—General — M,D,O
Education—General — M,D,O
Educational Leadership and
   Administration — M,D
Elementary Education — M,O
English Education — M
Foreign Languages Education — M
Mathematics Education — M
Middle School Education — M
Reading Education — M
Science Education — M
Social Sciences Education — M
Special Education — M,O

ST. JOHN'S UNIVERSITY (NY)
Accounting — M,O
Actuarial Science — M
Business Administration and
   Management—General — M,O
Counselor Education — M,O
Early Childhood Education — M,O
Education of the Gifted — M,D,O
Education—General — M,D,O
Educational Leadership and
   Administration — M,D,O
Elementary Education — M,O
English as a Second Language — M,O
Finance and Banking — M,O
Information Studies — M,O
Insurance — M
International Business — M,O
Investment Management — M
Law — M,D
Legal and Justice Studies — M
Library Science — M
Management Information Systems — M,O
Management Strategy and Policy — M,O
Marketing — M,O
Middle School Education — M
Multilingual and Multicultural
   Education — M,O
Quantitative Analysis — M,O
Reading Education — M,D,O
Secondary Education — M,O
Special Education — M,D,O
Sports Management — M
Taxation — M

ST. JOSEPH'S COLLEGE, LONG ISLAND CAMPUS
Accounting — M
Business Administration and
   Management—General — M,O
Early Childhood Education — M
Human Resources Management — M,O
Organizational Management — M,O
Reading Education — M
Special Education — M

ST. JOSEPH'S COLLEGE, NEW YORK
Accounting — M
Business Administration and
   Management—General — M
Early Childhood Education — M
Education—General — M
Human Services — M
Reading Education — M
Special Education — M

SAINT JOSEPH'S COLLEGE OF MAINE
Accounting — M
Adult Education — M
Business Administration and
   Management—General — M
Education—General — M
Educational Leadership and
   Administration — M
Health Education — M

SAINT JOSEPH'S UNIVERSITY
Accounting — M,O
Adult Education — M,O
Business Administration and
   Management—General — M,O
Curriculum and Instruction — M,D,O
Education—General — M,D,O
Educational Leadership and
   Administration — M,D,O
Educational Media/Instructional
   Technology — M,D,O
Elementary Education — M,D,O
Finance and Banking — M,O
Health Education — M,O
Human Resources Management — M,O
International Business — M,O
Law — M
Management Information Systems — M
Management Strategy and Policy — M
Marketing — M,O

Middle School Education — M,D,O
Organizational Management — M,O
Reading Education — M,D,O
Secondary Education — M,D,O
Special Education — M,D,O

ST. LAWRENCE UNIVERSITY
Counselor Education — M,O
Education—General — M,O
Educational Leadership and Administration — M,O

SAINT LEO UNIVERSITY
Accounting — M
Business Administration and Management—General — M
Curriculum and Instruction — M
Education of the Gifted — M
Education—General — M
Educational Leadership and Administration — M
Educational Media/Instructional Technology — M
Human Resources Management — M
Legal and Justice Studies — M
Marketing Research — M
Marketing — M
Project Management — M
Reading Education — M
Social Work — M
Sports Management — M

SAINT LOUIS UNIVERSITY
Accounting — M
Athletic Training and Sports Medicine — M,D
Business Administration and Management—General — M
Counselor Education — M,D,O
Curriculum and Instruction — M,D
Education—General — M,D
Educational Leadership and Administration — M,D,O
Finance and Banking — M
Foundations and Philosophy of Education — M,D
Higher Education — M,D,O
International Business — M,D
Law — M,D
Organizational Management — M,D,O
Social Work — M
Special Education — M,D
Student Affairs — M,D,O

SAINT MARTIN'S UNIVERSITY
Business Administration and Management—General — M
Counselor Education — M
Education—General — M
Educational Leadership and Administration — M
English as a Second Language — M
Reading Education — M
Special Education — M

SAINT MARY-OF-THE-WOODS COLLEGE
Management Strategy and Policy — M

SAINT MARY'S COLLEGE OF CALIFORNIA
Business Administration and Management—General — M
Counselor Education — M
Curriculum and Instruction — M
Early Childhood Education — M
Education—General — M,D
Educational Leadership and Administration — M,D
Exercise and Sports Science — M
Finance and Banking — M
Investment Management — M
Kinesiology and Movement Studies — M
Reading Education — M
Special Education — M
Sports Management — M

ST. MARY'S COLLEGE OF MARYLAND
Education—General — M

SAINT MARY'S UNIVERSITY (CANADA)
Business Administration and Management—General — M,D

ST. MARY'S UNIVERSITY (UNITED STATES)
Accounting — M
Business Administration and Management—General — M
Counselor Education — D
Education—General — M,O
Educational Leadership and Administration — M,O
Finance and Banking — M
Human Services — M,D,O
International Business — M
Law — D
Reading Education — M

SAINT MARY'S UNIVERSITY OF MINNESOTA
Accounting — M
Business Administration and Management—General — M,D
Education of the Gifted — M,O
Education—General — M,O
Educational Leadership and Administration — M,D,O
Educational Media/Instructional Technology — M,O
Elementary Education — M,O
Human Resources Management — M
International Business — M
Multilingual and Multicultural Education — M,O
Organizational Management — M
Project Management — M,O

Reading Education — M,O
Religious Education — M
Secondary Education — M,O
Special Education — M,O

SAINT MICHAEL'S COLLEGE
Art Education — M,O
Business Administration and Management—General — M,O
Curriculum and Instruction — M,O
Education—General — M,O
Educational Leadership and Administration — M,O
Educational Media/Instructional Technology — M,O
English as a Second Language — M,O
Reading Education — M,O
Special Education — M,O

SAINT PETER'S UNIVERSITY
Accounting — M
Business Administration and Management—General — M
Counselor Education — M,O
Education—General — M,D,O
Educational Leadership and Administration — M,D
Elementary Education — M
Finance and Banking — M
Higher Education — D
Human Resources Management — M
International Business — M
Management Information Systems — M
Marketing — M
Mathematics Education — M,D,O
Middle School Education — M,O
Reading Education — M,O
Secondary Education — M,O
Special Education — M,O

SAINTS CYRIL AND METHODIUS SEMINARY
Religious Education — M

ST. THOMAS AQUINAS COLLEGE
Business Administration and Management—General — M
Education—General — M,O
Educational Leadership and Administration — M,O
Elementary Education — M,O
Finance and Banking — M
Marketing — M
Middle School Education — M,O
Reading Education — M,O
Secondary Education — M,O
Special Education — M,O

ST. THOMAS UNIVERSITY
Accounting — M,O
Business Administration and Management—General — M,O
Counselor Education — M,O
Education of the Gifted — M,D,O
Education—General — M,D,O
Educational Leadership and Administration — M,D,O
Educational Media/Instructional Technology — M,D,O
Elementary Education — M,D,O
English as a Second Language — M,D,O
Human Resources Management — M,O
International Business — M,D
Law — M,D
Reading Education — M,D,O
Special Education — M,D,O
Sports Management — M
Taxation — M,D

SAINT VINCENT COLLEGE
Curriculum and Instruction — M
Education—General — M
Educational Leadership and Administration — M
Educational Media/Instructional Technology — M
Environmental Education — M
Special Education — M

ST. VLADIMIR'S ORTHODOX THEOLOGICAL SEMINARY
Religious Education — M,D

SAINT XAVIER UNIVERSITY
Business Administration and Management—General — M,O
Counselor Education — M
Curriculum and Instruction — M
Early Childhood Education — M
Education—General — M
Educational Leadership and Administration — M
Educational Media/Instructional Technology — M,-
Elementary Education — M
English as a Second Language — M,O
Finance and Banking — M,O
Foreign Languages Education — M,O
Marketing — M,O
Music Education — M
Project Management — M,O
Reading Education — M
Science Education — M
Secondary Education — M
Special Education — M

SALEM COLLEGE
Art Education — M
Counselor Education — M
Education—General — M
Elementary Education — M
English as a Second Language — M
Middle School Education — M
Reading Education — M
Secondary Education — M
Special Education — M

SALEM INTERNATIONAL UNIVERSITY
Business Administration and Management—General — M
Curriculum and Instruction — M
Education—General — M
Educational Leadership and Administration — M
International Business — M

SALEM STATE UNIVERSITY
Art Education — M
Business Administration and Management—General — M
Counselor Education — M
Early Childhood Education — M
Educational Leadership and Administration — M
Educational Media/Instructional Technology — M
Elementary Education — M
English as a Second Language — M
Higher Education — M
Mathematics Education — M
Middle School Education — M
Physical Education — M
Reading Education — M
Science Education — M
Secondary Education — M
Social Work — M
Special Education — M

SALISBURY UNIVERSITY
Accounting — M
Business Administration and Management—General — M
Curriculum and Instruction — M
Education—General — M
Educational Leadership and Administration — M
English as a Second Language — M
Reading Education — M
Secondary Education — M
Social Work — M

SALUS UNIVERSITY
Special Education — M,O

SALVE REGINA UNIVERSITY
Business Administration and Management—General — M,O
Entrepreneurship — M
Management Strategy and Policy — M,O
Nonprofit Management — M,O

SAMFORD UNIVERSITY
Business Administration and Management—General — M
Early Childhood Education — M,D,O
Education of the Gifted — M,D,O
Education—General — M,D,O
Educational Leadership and Administration — M,D,O
Elementary Education — M,D,O
Law — M,D
Music Education — M
Secondary Education — M,D,O

SAM HOUSTON STATE UNIVERSITY
Accounting — M
Business Administration and Management—General — M,D
Counselor Education — M,D
Curriculum and Instruction — M
Developmental Education — M,D
Education—General — M,D
Educational Leadership and Administration — M,D
Educational Media/Instructional Technology — M
Finance and Banking — M
Higher Education — M,D
Kinesiology and Movement Studies — M
Library Science — M
Project Management — M
Reading Education — M,D
Special Education — M,D

SAN DIEGO STATE UNIVERSITY
Accounting — M
Advertising and Public Relations — M
Business Administration and Management—General — M
Counselor Education — M
Curriculum and Instruction — M
Education—General — M,D
Educational Leadership and Administration — M
Educational Media/Instructional Technology — M,D
Elementary Education — M
English as a Second Language — M,O
Entrepreneurship — M
Exercise and Sports Science — M
Finance and Banking — M
Higher Education — M
Human Resources Management — M
Kinesiology and Movement Studies — M
Management Information Systems — M
Marketing — M
Mathematics Education — M,D
Multilingual and Multicultural Education — M,D
Music Education — M
Reading Education — M
Science Education — M,D
Secondary Education — M
Social Work — M
Special Education — M
Sports Management — M

SAN FRANCISCO STATE UNIVERSITY
Accounting — M
Adult Education — M,O
Business Administration and Management—General — M
Counselor Education — M,O

Early Childhood Education — M,D,O
Education—General — M,D,O
Educational Leadership and Administration — M,D,O
Educational Media/Instructional Technology — M
Elementary Education — M
English as a Second Language — M
English Education — M,O
Exercise and Sports Science — M
Finance and Banking — M
Health Education — M
Industrial and Manufacturing Management — M
Kinesiology and Movement Studies — M
Legal and Justice Studies — M
Leisure Studies — M
Management Information Systems — M
Marketing — M
Mathematics Education — M
Music Education — M
Nonprofit Management — M
Quantitative Analysis — M
Reading Education — M,O
Recreation and Park Management — M
Secondary Education — M
Social Work — M
Special Education — M
Sustainability Management — M
Travel and Tourism — M

SAN JOAQUIN COLLEGE OF LAW
Law — D

SAN JOSE STATE UNIVERSITY
Accounting — M
Business Administration and Management—General — M
Counselor Education — M
Curriculum and Instruction — M,O
Education—General — M,O
Educational Leadership and Administration — M
Elementary Education — M,O
English as a Second Language — M,O
Health Education — M,O
Higher Education — M
Industrial and Manufacturing Management — M
Information Studies — M,D
Kinesiology and Movement Studies — M
Library Science — M,D
Management Information Systems — M
Mathematics Education — M
Quality Management — M
Reading Education — M,O
Recreation and Park Management — M
Science Education — M
Secondary Education — O
Social Work — M,O
Special Education — M
Student Affairs — M
Taxation — M
Transportation Management — M

SANTA CLARA UNIVERSITY
Business Administration and Management—General — M
Counselor Education — M,O
Education—General — M,O
Educational Leadership and Administration — M,O
Entrepreneurship — M
Finance and Banking — M
Intellectual Property Law — M,D,O
Law — M,D,O
Management Information Systems — M

SARAH LAWRENCE COLLEGE
Education—General — M
Kinesiology and Movement Studies — M

SAVANNAH COLLEGE OF ART AND DESIGN
Advertising and Public Relations — M
Travel and Tourism — M

SAVANNAH STATE UNIVERSITY
Business Administration and Management—General — M
Human Resources Management — M
Nonprofit Management — M
Social Work — M

SAYBROOK UNIVERSITY
Organizational Behavior — M,D
Organizational Management — M,D

SCHILLER INTERNATIONAL UNIVERSITY (GERMANY)
Business Administration and Management—General — M
International Business — M
Management Information Systems — M

SCHILLER INTERNATIONAL UNIVERSITY
Business Administration and Management—General — M
International Business — M

SCHILLER INTERNATIONAL UNIVERSITY (SPAIN)
Business Administration and Management—General — M
International Business — M

SCHILLER INTERNATIONAL UNIVERSITY (UNITED STATES)
Business Administration and Management—General — M
Finance and Banking — M
Hospitality Management — M
International Business — M
Management Information Systems — M
Travel and Tourism — M

SCHOOL OF THE ART INSTITUTE OF CHICAGO
Art Education — M

SCHOOL OF THE MUSEUM OF FINE ARTS, BOSTON
Art Education — M,O

SCHOOL OF VISUAL ARTS (NY)
Art Education — M

SCHREINER UNIVERSITY
Business Administration and Management—General — M
Education—General — M,O
Educational Leadership and Administration — M,O

SEATTLE PACIFIC UNIVERSITY
Business Administration and Management—General — M
Counselor Education — M,D,O
Curriculum and Instruction — M
Educational Leadership and Administration — M,D,O
English as a Second Language — M
Human Resources Management — M
Management Information Systems — M
Reading Education — M
Secondary Education — M
Sustainability Management — M

SEATTLE UNIVERSITY
Accounting — M
Adult Education — M,O
Business Administration and Management—General — M,O
Counselor Education — M,O
Education—General — M,D,O
Educational Leadership and Administration — M,D,O
English as a Second Language — M,O
Finance and Banking — M,O
International Business — M,O
Law — D
Organizational Management — M,O
Reading Education — M,O
Special Education — M,O
Sports Management — M

SETON HALL UNIVERSITY
Accounting — M,O
Athletic Training and Sports Medicine — M
Business Administration and Management—General — M,O
Education—General — M,D,O
Educational Leadership and Administration — D,O
Educational Measurement and Evaluation — M,D,O
Educational Media/Instructional Technology — M
Finance and Banking — M
Health Law — M,D
Higher Education — D
International Business — M,O
Law — M,D
Marketing — M
Museum Education — M
Nonprofit Management — M,O
Special Education — M
Sports Management — M
Student Affairs — M
Supply Chain Management — M
Taxation — M,O

SETON HILL UNIVERSITY
Accounting — M,O
Business Administration and Management—General — M,O
Education—General — M
Elementary Education — M,O
Entrepreneurship — M,O
Middle School Education — M,O
Special Education — M,O
Sports Management — M,O

SHASTA BIBLE COLLEGE
Educational Leadership and Administration — M
Religious Education — M

SHAWNEE STATE UNIVERSITY
Curriculum and Instruction — M
Education—General — M

SHAW UNIVERSITY
Curriculum and Instruction — M

SHENANDOAH UNIVERSITY
Athletic Training and Sports Medicine — M,O
Business Administration and Management—General — M,O
Education—General — M,D,O
Music Education — M,D,O

SHEPHERD UNIVERSITY
Curriculum and Instruction — M

SHIPPENSBURG UNIVERSITY OF PENNSYLVANIA
Business Administration and Management—General — M,O
Counselor Education — M,O
Curriculum and Instruction — M
Early Childhood Education — M
Education—General — M,O
Educational Leadership and Administration — M
Elementary Education — M
Foreign Languages Education — M
Higher Education — M
Management Information Systems — M

Mathematics Education — M
Middle School Education — M
Organizational Management — M
Reading Education — M
Science Education — M
Social Work — M
Special Education — M
Student Affairs — M,O

SHORTER UNIVERSITY
Accounting — M
Business Administration and Management—General — M
Curriculum and Instruction — M

SIENA HEIGHTS UNIVERSITY
Early Childhood Education — M,O
Education—General — M,O
Educational Leadership and Administration — M,O
Elementary Education — M,O
Higher Education — M,O
Organizational Management — M,O
Reading Education — M,O
Secondary Education — M,O
Special Education — M,O

SIERRA NEVADA COLLEGE
Education—General — M
Educational Leadership and Administration — M
Elementary Education — M
Secondary Education — M

SILICON VALLEY UNIVERSITY
Business Administration and Management—General — M

SILVER LAKE COLLEGE OF THE HOLY FAMILY
Business Administration and Management—General — M
Education—General — M
Educational Leadership and Administration — M
Music Education — M
Organizational Behavior — M
Special Education — M

SIMMONS COLLEGE
Archives/Archival Administration — M,D,O
Business Administration and Management—General — M
Education—General — M,D,O
Educational Media/Instructional Technology — M,D,O
Elementary Education — M,D,O
English as a Second Language — M,D,O
Entrepreneurship — M
Health Education — M,D,O
Information Studies — M,D,O
Library Science — M,D,O
Management Strategy and Policy — M
Marketing — M
Nonprofit Management — M
Organizational Management — M
Reading Education — M,D,O
Secondary Education — M,D,O
Social Sciences Education — M,D,O
Social Work — M,D,O
Special Education — M,D,O

SIMON FRASER UNIVERSITY
Actuarial Science — M,D
Art Education — M,D
Business Administration and Management—General — M,D,O
Counselor Education — M
Curriculum and Instruction — M,D
Education—General — M,D,O
Educational Leadership and Administration — M,D
Educational Media/Instructional Technology — M,D
Educational Psychology — M,D
English as a Second Language — M,D
English Education — M,D
Finance and Banking — M,D,O
Foundations and Philosophy of Education — M,D
Kinesiology and Movement Studies — M,D
Legal and Justice Studies — M,D
Mathematics Education — M,D
Reading Education — D

SIMPSON COLLEGE
Education—General — M
Secondary Education — M

SIMPSON UNIVERSITY
Curriculum and Instruction — M
Education—General — M
Educational Leadership and Administration — M
Organizational Management — M

SINTE GLESKA UNIVERSITY
Education—General — M
Elementary Education — M

SIT GRADUATE INSTITUTE
Business Administration and Management—General — M
English as a Second Language — M
Foreign Languages Education — M
International and Comparative Education — M
International Business — M

SLIPPERY ROCK UNIVERSITY OF PENNSYLVANIA
Business Administration and Management—General — M
Counselor Education — M
Education—General — M

Educational Leadership and Administration — M
Elementary Education — M
English Education — M
Environmental Education — M
Higher Education — M
Mathematics Education — M
Physical Education — M
Reading Education — M
Recreation and Park Management — M
Science Education — M
Secondary Education — M
Social Sciences Education — M
Special Education — M
Student Affairs — M

SMITH COLLEGE
Education—General — M
Elementary Education — M
English Education — M
Exercise and Sports Science — M
Foreign Languages Education — M
Mathematics Education — M
Middle School Education — M
Science Education — M
Secondary Education — M
Social Sciences Education — M
Social Work — M,D
Special Education — M

SOJOURNER-DOUGLASS COLLEGE
Human Services — M
Reading Education — M
Urban Education — M

SOKA UNIVERSITY OF AMERICA
English as a Second Language — O
Foreign Languages Education — O

SONOMA STATE UNIVERSITY
Business Administration and Management—General — M
Counselor Education — M
Curriculum and Instruction — M,D,O
Early Childhood Education — M,D,O
Education—General — M,D,O
Educational Leadership and Administration — M,D,O
International Business — M
Kinesiology and Movement Studies — M
Nonprofit Management — M,O
Physical Education — M
Reading Education — M
Special Education — M,D,O
Sports Management — M

SOUTH CAROLINA STATE UNIVERSITY
Business Education — M
Counselor Education — M
Early Childhood Education — M
Education—General — M
Elementary Education — M
English Education — M
Entrepreneurship — M
Home Economics Education — M
Human Services — M
Mathematics Education — M
Science Education — M
Secondary Education — M
Social Sciences Education — M
Special Education — M
Vocational and Technical Education — M

SOUTH DAKOTA STATE UNIVERSITY
Counselor Education — M
Curriculum and Instruction — M
Education—General — M,D
Educational Leadership and Administration — M
Health Education — M
Hospitality Management — M,D
Physical Education — M
Recreation and Park Management — M

SOUTHEASTERN BAPTIST THEOLOGICAL SEMINARY
Religious Education — M,D

SOUTHEASTERN LOUISIANA UNIVERSITY
Accounting — M
Business Administration and Management—General — M
Counselor Education — M
Curriculum and Instruction — M
Education—General — M,D
Educational Leadership and Administration — M,D
Educational Media/Instructional Technology — M,D
Elementary Education — M
English Education — M
Health Education — M
Kinesiology and Movement Studies — M
Reading Education — M
Special Education — M

SOUTHEASTERN OKLAHOMA STATE UNIVERSITY
Aviation Management — M
Business Administration and Management—General — M
Counselor Education — M
Education—General — M
Educational Leadership and Administration — M
Management Information Systems — M
Mathematics Education — M
Reading Education — M

SOUTHEASTERN UNIVERSITY (FL)
Business Administration and Management—General — M
Counselor Education — M

Education—General — M
Educational Leadership and Administration — M
Elementary Education — M
Human Services — M

SOUTHEAST MISSOURI STATE UNIVERSITY
Accounting — M
Business Administration and Management—General — M
Counselor Education — M,O
Educational Leadership and Administration — M,O
Educational Media/Instructional Technology — M
Elementary Education — M,O
English as a Second Language — M
Entrepreneurship — M
Exercise and Sports Science — M
Finance and Banking — M
Foundations and Philosophy of Education — M
Higher Education — M,O
Industrial and Manufacturing Management — M
International Business — M
Leisure Studies — M
Middle School Education — M
Organizational Management — M
Secondary Education — M,O
Special Education — M
Sports Management — M

SOUTHERN ADVENTIST UNIVERSITY
Accounting — M
Business Administration and Management—General — M
Counselor Education — M
Education—General — M
Educational Leadership and Administration — M
Finance and Banking — M
Marketing — M
Nonprofit Management — M
Reading Education — M
Recreation and Park Management — M
Religious Education — M
Social Work — M

SOUTHERN ARKANSAS UNIVERSITY–MAGNOLIA
Business Administration and Management—General — M
Counselor Education — M
Curriculum and Instruction — M
Education—General — M
Educational Leadership and Administration — M
Elementary Education — M
English as a Second Language — M
Kinesiology and Movement Studies — M
Library Science — M
Reading Education — M
Secondary Education — M

SOUTHERN BAPTIST THEOLOGICAL SEMINARY
Higher Education — M,D
Religious Education — M,D

SOUTHERN CONNECTICUT STATE UNIVERSITY
Art Education — M
Business Administration and Management—General — M
Counselor Education — M,O
Education—General — M,D,O
Educational Leadership and Administration — M,D,O
Educational Measurement and Evaluation — M,D,O
Elementary Education — M,O
English as a Second Language — M
Environmental Education — M
Exercise and Sports Science — M
Foreign Languages Education — M
Foundations and Philosophy of Education — M,D,O
Health Education — M
Information Studies — M
Leisure Studies — M
Library Science — M,O
Multilingual and Multicultural Education — M
Physical Education — M
Reading Education — M,O
Recreation and Park Management — M
Science Education — M,O
Social Work — M
Special Education — M

SOUTHERN EVANGELICAL SEMINARY
Religious Education — M,D,O

SOUTHERN ILLINOIS UNIVERSITY CARBONDALE
Accounting — M,D
Business Administration and Management—General — M,D
Counselor Education — M,D
Curriculum and Instruction — M,D
Education—General — M,D
Educational Leadership and Administration — M,D
Educational Measurement and Evaluation — M,D
Educational Psychology — M,D
English as a Second Language — M
Health Education — M,D
Health Law — M
Higher Education — M
Kinesiology and Movement Studies — M

Law M,D
Legal and Justice Studies M
Music Education M
Physical Education M
Recreation and Park Management M
Social Work M
Special Education M
Vocational and Technical Education M,D

SOUTHERN ILLINOIS UNIVERSITY EDWARDSVILLE
Accounting M
Advertising and Public Relations M
Business Administration and Management—General M
Curriculum and Instruction M
Education—General M,D,O
Educational Leadership and Administration M,D,O
Educational Media/Instructional Technology M,O
English as a Second Language M,O
English Education M,O
Exercise and Sports Science M
Finance and Banking M
Foundations and Philosophy of Education M
Health Education M
Higher Education M
Kinesiology and Movement Studies M
Management Information Systems M
Marketing Research M
Mathematics Education M,O
Music Education M
Physical Education M
Reading Education M,O
Social Work M
Special Education M,O
Taxation M

SOUTHERN METHODIST UNIVERSITY
Accounting M
Advertising and Public Relations M
Business Administration and Management—General M
Counselor Education M
Education of the Gifted M,D
Education—General M,D
Entrepreneurship M
Finance and Banking M
Law M,D
Management Information Systems M
Management Strategy and Policy M
Marketing M
Multilingual and Multicultural Education M,D
Music Education M,D
Reading Education M
Real Estate M
Special Education M,D
Sports Management M
Taxation M,D

SOUTHERN NAZARENE UNIVERSITY
Business Administration and Management—General M
Sports Management M

SOUTHERN NEW HAMPSHIRE UNIVERSITY
Accounting M,O
Business Administration and Management—General M,O
Business Education M,D,O
Curriculum and Instruction M,D,O
Education—General M,D,O
Educational Leadership and Administration M,D,O
Educational Media/Instructional Technology M,D,O
Elementary Education M,D,O
English as a Second Language M,D,O
English Education M,D,O
Entrepreneurship M,O
Finance and Banking M,O
Human Resources Management M,O
Industrial and Manufacturing Management M,O
International Business M,O
Investment Management M,O
Legal and Justice Studies M,O
Management Information Systems M,O
Marketing M,O
Nonprofit Management M,O
Organizational Management M,O
Project Management M,O
Quality Management M,O
Reading Education M,D,O
Secondary Education M,D,O
Special Education M,D,O
Sports Management M,O
Supply Chain Management M,O
Sustainability Management M,O
Taxation M,O

SOUTHERN OREGON UNIVERSITY
Accounting M,O
Business Administration and Management—General M,O
Early Childhood Education M
Education—General M
Educational Leadership and Administration M
Elementary Education M
Environmental Education M
Foreign Languages Education M
International Business M,O
Reading Education M
Secondary Education M
Special Education M

SOUTHERN POLYTECHNIC STATE UNIVERSITY
Accounting M,O
Business Administration and Management—General M,O

Educational Media/Instructional Technology M,O
Finance and Banking M,O
Industrial and Manufacturing Management M,O
Management Information Systems M,O
Marketing M,O
Quality Management M,O

SOUTHERN UNIVERSITY AND AGRICULTURAL AND MECHANICAL COLLEGE
Business Administration and Management—General M
Counselor Education M
Education—General M,D
Educational Leadership and Administration M
Educational Media/Instructional Technology M
Elementary Education M
Law D
Mathematics Education D
Recreation and Park Management M
Science Education D
Secondary Education M
Special Education M,D

SOUTHERN UNIVERSITY AT NEW ORLEANS
Management Information Systems M
Social Work M

SOUTHERN UTAH UNIVERSITY
Accounting M
Business Administration and Management—General M
Education—General M,O
Exercise and Sports Science M

SOUTHERN WESLEYAN UNIVERSITY
Business Administration and Management—General M
Education—General M

SOUTH TEXAS COLLEGE OF LAW
Law D

SOUTH UNIVERSITY (AL)
Business Administration and Management—General M
Management Information Systems M

SOUTH UNIVERSITY
Business Administration and Management—General M
Management Information Systems M

SOUTH UNIVERSITY (GA)
Business Administration and Management—General M
Entrepreneurship M
Hospitality Management M
Organizational Management M
Sustainability Management M

SOUTH UNIVERSITY (MI)
Business Administration and Management—General M

SOUTH UNIVERSITY (NC)
Business Administration and Management—General M

SOUTH UNIVERSITY (OH)
Business Administration and Management—General M

SOUTH UNIVERSITY (SC)
Business Administration and Management—General M
Organizational Management M

SOUTH UNIVERSITY (TX)
Business Administration and Management—General M
Management Information Systems M

SOUTH UNIVERSITY
Business Administration and Management—General M

SOUTH UNIVERSITY
Business Administration and Management—General M
Management Information Systems M
Organizational Management M

SOUTHWEST BAPTIST UNIVERSITY
Business Administration and Management—General M
Education—General M,O
Educational Leadership and Administration M,O

SOUTHWESTERN ADVENTIST UNIVERSITY
Accounting M
Business Administration and Management—General M
Curriculum and Instruction M
Education—General M
Educational Leadership and Administration M
Finance and Banking M
Reading Education M

SOUTHWESTERN BAPTIST THEOLOGICAL SEMINARY
Religious Education M,D,O

SOUTHWESTERN COLLEGE (KS)
Accounting M
Business Administration and Management—General M
Curriculum and Instruction M,D
Education—General M,D
Special Education M,D

SOUTHWESTERN LAW SCHOOL
Law M,D

SOUTHWESTERN OKLAHOMA STATE UNIVERSITY
Art Education M
Business Administration and Management—General M
Counselor Education M
Early Childhood Education M
Education—General M
Educational Leadership and Administration M
Educational Measurement and Evaluation M
Elementary Education M
English Education M
Kinesiology and Movement Studies M
Mathematics Education M
Music Education M
Recreation and Park Management M
Science Education M
Secondary Education M
Social Sciences Education M
Special Education M

SOUTHWEST MINNESOTA STATE UNIVERSITY
Business Administration and Management—General M
Early Childhood Education M
Education—General M
Educational Leadership and Administration M
English as a Second Language M
Marketing M
Mathematics Education M
Reading Education M
Special Education M

SOUTHWEST UNIVERSITY
Business Administration and Management—General M
Organizational Management M

SPALDING UNIVERSITY
Art Education M
Business Administration and Management—General M
Business Education M
Counselor Education M
Education—General M,D
Educational Leadership and Administration M,D
Elementary Education M
Foreign Languages Education M
Middle School Education M
Secondary Education M
Social Work M
Special Education M

SPERTUS INSTITUTE FOR JEWISH LEARNING AND LEADERSHIP
Nonprofit Management M
Religious Education M

SPRING ARBOR UNIVERSITY
Business Administration and Management—General M
Education—General M
Organizational Management M
Reading Education M
Special Education M

SPRINGFIELD COLLEGE
Athletic Training and Sports Medicine M,D
Counselor Education M,D,O
Early Childhood Education M
Education—General M
Educational Leadership and Administration M
Elementary Education M
Exercise and Sports Science M,D
Health Education M,D,O
Human Services M
Organizational Management M
Physical Education M,D,O
Recreation and Park Management M
Secondary Education M
Social Work M
Special Education M
Sports Management M,D,O
Student Affairs M,D,O

SPRING HILL COLLEGE
Business Administration and Management—General M
Early Childhood Education M
Education—General M
Elementary Education M
Foundations and Philosophy of Education M
Secondary Education M
Social Sciences Education M

STANFORD UNIVERSITY
Business Administration and Management—General M,D
Curriculum and Instruction M,D
Education—General M,D
Educational Leadership and Administration M
Educational Media/Instructional Technology M

Elementary Education M
International and Comparative Education M,D
Law M,D
Secondary Education M

STATE UNIVERSITY OF NEW YORK AT FREDONIA
Education—General M,O
Educational Leadership and Administration O
Elementary Education M
English as a Second Language M
Music Education M
Reading Education M
Science Education M
Secondary Education M

STATE UNIVERSITY OF NEW YORK AT NEW PALTZ
Accounting M
Art Education M
Business Administration and Management—General M
Counselor Education M,O
Early Childhood Education M
Education—General M,O
Educational Leadership and Administration M,O
Elementary Education M
English as a Second Language M,O
English Education M,O
Mathematics Education M
Multilingual and Multicultural Education M,O
Reading Education M
Science Education M,O
Secondary Education M,O
Social Sciences Education M,O
Special Education M

STATE UNIVERSITY OF NEW YORK AT OSWEGO
Agricultural Education M
Art Education M
Business Administration and Management—General M
Business Education M
Early Childhood Education M
Education—General M,O
Educational Leadership and Administration O
Elementary Education M
Middle School Education M
Reading Education M
Secondary Education M
Special Education M
Vocational and Technical Education M

STATE UNIVERSITY OF NEW YORK AT PLATTSBURGH
Counselor Education M,O
Curriculum and Instruction M,O
Early Childhood Education O
Educational Leadership and Administration O
Elementary Education M,O
English Education M
Foreign Languages Education M
Mathematics Education M
Reading Education M
Science Education M
Secondary Education M
Social Sciences Education M
Special Education M
Student Affairs M,O

STATE UNIVERSITY OF NEW YORK COLLEGE AT CORTLAND
Early Childhood Education M
Education—General M,O
Educational Leadership and Administration O
English as a Second Language M
English Education M
Exercise and Sports Science M
Foreign Languages Education M
Health Education M
Mathematics Education M
Physical Education M
Reading Education M
Recreation and Park Management M
Science Education M
Secondary Education M
Social Sciences Education M
Special Education M
Sports Management M

STATE UNIVERSITY OF NEW YORK COLLEGE AT GENESEO
Accounting M
Business Administration and Management—General M
Early Childhood Education M
Education—General M
Multilingual and Multicultural Education M
Reading Education M
Secondary Education M

STATE UNIVERSITY OF NEW YORK COLLEGE AT OLD WESTBURY
Accounting M
Business Administration and Management—General M
English Education M
Foreign Languages Education M
Mathematics Education M
Middle School Education M
Science Education M
Social Sciences Education M
Taxation M

STATE UNIVERSITY OF NEW YORK COLLEGE AT ONEONTA
Counselor Education M,O

Education—General M,O
Educational Media/Instructional
   Technology M,O
Educational Psychology M,O
Elementary Education M
Middle School Education M
Reading Education M
Secondary Education M
Special Education M,O

STATE UNIVERSITY OF NEW YORK COLLEGE AT POTSDAM
Curriculum and Instruction M
Early Childhood Education M
Educational Media/Instructional
   Technology M
Elementary Education M
English Education M
Mathematics Education M
Middle School Education M
Music Education M
Organizational Management M
Reading Education M
Science Education M
Secondary Education M
Social Sciences Education M
Special Education M

STATE UNIVERSITY OF NEW YORK COLLEGE OF ENVIRONMENTAL SCIENCE AND FORESTRY
Sustainability Management M,D,O

STATE UNIVERSITY OF NEW YORK EMPIRE STATE COLLEGE
Adult Education M
Business Administration and
   Management—General M
Education—General M
Educational Media/Instructional
   Technology M
International Business M

STATE UNIVERSITY OF NEW YORK INSTITUTE OF TECHNOLOGY
Accounting M
Business Administration and
   Management—General M
Finance and Banking M
Human Resources Management M
Marketing M

STATE UNIVERSITY OF NEW YORK MARITIME COLLEGE
Transportation Management M

STEPHEN F. AUSTIN STATE UNIVERSITY
Accounting M
Agricultural Education M
Athletic Training and Sports
   Medicine M
Business Administration and
   Management—General M
Counselor Education M
Early Childhood Education M
Education—General M,D
Educational Leadership and
   Administration M,D
Elementary Education M
Kinesiology and Movement Studies M
Marketing M
Mathematics Education M
Secondary Education M,D
Social Work M
Special Education M

STEPHENS COLLEGE
Business Administration and
   Management—General M
Counselor Education M,O
Curriculum and Instruction M

STETSON UNIVERSITY
Accounting M
Business Administration and
   Management—General M
Counselor Education M
Curriculum and Instruction O
Education—General M,O
Educational Leadership and
   Administration M
Law M,D

STEVENS INSTITUTE OF TECHNOLOGY
Business Administration and
   Management—General M
Electronic Commerce M,O
Entrepreneurship M,O
Finance and Banking M
Human Resources Management M
Industrial and Manufacturing
   Management M
International Business M
Logistics M,D,O
Management Information Systems M,D,O
Management Strategy and Policy M
Project Management M,O
Quality Management M,O

STONY BROOK UNIVERSITY, STATE UNIVERSITY OF NEW YORK
Business Administration and
   Management—General M,O
Computer Education M
Educational Leadership and
   Administration M,O
Educational Media/Instructional
   Technology M,O
English as a Second Language M
English Education M,D,O
Finance and Banking M,O
Foreign Languages Education M,O
Higher Education M,O
Human Resources Management M,O

Management Information Systems M,D,O
Marketing M,O
Mathematics Education M,O
Physical Education M,O
Science Education M,D,O
Social Sciences Education M,O
Social Work M,D

STRATFORD UNIVERSITY (MD)
Hospitality Management M

STRATFORD UNIVERSITY (VA)
Accounting M
Business Administration and
   Management—General M
Entrepreneurship M
Management Information Systems M

STRAYER UNIVERSITY
Accounting M
Business Administration and
   Management—General M
Education—General M
Educational Media/Instructional
   Technology M
Finance and Banking M
Hospitality Management M
Human Resources Management M
Management Information Systems M
Marketing M
Supply Chain Management M
Taxation M
Travel and Tourism M

SUFFOLK UNIVERSITY
Accounting M,O
Advertising and Public Relations M
Business Administration and
   Management—General M,O
Counselor Education M,D,O
Entrepreneurship M,O
Finance and Banking M,O
Health Law M,D
Intellectual Property Law M,O
International Business M,O
Law M,D
Management Strategy and Policy M,O
Marketing M,O
Nonprofit Management M,O
Organizational Behavior M,O
Supply Chain Management M,O
Taxation M,O

SULLIVAN UNIVERSITY
Business Administration and
   Management—General M,D

SUL ROSS STATE UNIVERSITY
Art Education M
Business Administration and
   Management—General M
Counselor Education M
Education—General M,O
Educational Leadership and
   Administration M
Educational Measurement and
   Evaluation M,O
Elementary Education M
Multilingual and Multicultural
   Education M
Physical Education M
Reading Education M,O
Secondary Education M

SWEET BRIAR COLLEGE
Education—General M

SYRACUSE UNIVERSITY
Accounting M,D
Advertising and Public Relations M
Art Education M
Business Administration and
   Management—General M,D
Counselor Education M,D
Curriculum and Instruction M,D,O
Early Childhood Education M
Education of Students with
   Severe/Multiple Disabilities M
Education—General M,D,O
Educational Leadership and
   Administration M,D,O
Educational Measurement and
   Evaluation M,D,O
Educational Media/Instructional
   Technology M,O
Educational Policy O
English as a Second Language M
English Education M
Entertainment Management M
Entrepreneurship M
Exercise and Sports Science M
Finance and Banking M,D
Foundations and Philosophy of
   Education M,D,O
Health Law O
Higher Education M,D
Human Resources Development D
Industrial and Manufacturing
   Management D
Information Studies M,D*
Law D
Library Science M
Management Information Systems M,D,O
Management Strategy and Policy M,D
Marketing M,D
Mathematics Education M,D
Music Education M
Organizational Behavior D
Organizational Management O
Quantitative Analysis D
Reading Education M
Science Education M,D
Secondary Education M,D
Social Sciences Education M

Social Work M
Special Education M,D
Sports Management M
Student Affairs M
Supply Chain Management M,D
Travel and Tourism M

TABOR COLLEGE
Accounting M
Business Administration and
   Management—General M

TAFT LAW SCHOOL
Law M,D
Legal and Justice Studies M,D
Taxation M,D

TARLETON STATE UNIVERSITY
Agricultural Education M
Business Administration and
   Management—General M
Counselor Education M,O
Curriculum and Instruction M
Education—General M,D,O
Educational Leadership and
   Administration M,D,O
Human Resources Management M
Management Information Systems M
Music Education M
Physical Education M,O
Secondary Education M
Special Education M

TAYLOR COLLEGE AND SEMINARY
English as a Second Language M,O

TAYLOR UNIVERSITY
Business Administration and
   Management—General M
Higher Education M
International Business M
Management Strategy and Policy M

TEACHERS COLLEGE, COLUMBIA UNIVERSITY
Adult Education D
Art Education M,D
Computer Education M
Curriculum and Instruction M,D
Early Childhood Education M,D
Education of Students with
   Severe/Multiple Disabilities M
Education of the Gifted M,D
Education—General M,D,O
Educational Leadership and
   Administration M,D
Educational Measurement and
   Evaluation M,D
Educational Media/Instructional
   Technology M,D
Educational Psychology M,D
English as a Second Language M,D
English Education M,D
Foundations and Philosophy of
   Education M,D
Health Education M,D
Higher Education M,D
International and Comparative
   Education M,D
Kinesiology and Movement Studies M,D
Mathematics Education M,D
Multilingual and Multicultural
   Education M
Music Education M,D
Organizational Management M
Physical Education M
Reading Education M
Science Education M,D
Social Sciences Education M,D
Special Education M,D,O

TÉLÉ-UNIVERSITÉ
Distance Education Development M,D
Finance and Banking M,D

TEMPLE BAPTIST SEMINARY
Religious Education M,D

TEMPLE UNIVERSITY
Accounting M,D
Actuarial Science M
Art Education M
Athletic Training and Sports
   Medicine M,D
Business Administration and
   Management—General M,D
Business Education M
Curriculum and Instruction M
Education—General M,D,O
Educational Leadership and
   Administration M,D
Educational Psychology M,D
Elementary Education M,D
English as a Second Language M
English Education M
Entrepreneurship M,D
Exercise and Sports Science M,D
Finance and Banking M,D
Health Education M,D
Higher Education M,D
Hospitality Management M,D
Human Resources Management M
Insurance D
International Business M,D
Kinesiology and Movement Studies M,D
Law M,D
Legal and Justice Studies M,D
Leisure Studies D
Management Information Systems M,D
Management Strategy and Policy D
Marketing M,D
Mathematics Education M
Middle School Education M
Music Education M,D

Physical Education M,D
Recreation and Park Management M
Science Education M
Secondary Education M
Social Sciences Education M
Social Work M
Special Education M,D
Sports Management M,D
Taxation M,D
Transportation Management M
Travel and Tourism M
Urban Education M
Vocational and Technical Education M

TENNESSEE STATE UNIVERSITY
Agricultural Education M,D
Business Administration and
   Management—General M,D
Counselor Education M,D
Curriculum and Instruction M,D
Education—General M,D,O
Educational Leadership and
   Administration M,D,O
Elementary Education M,D
Exercise and Sports Science M
Human Resources Management M,D
Management Strategy and Policy M,D
Music Education M
Physical Education M
Social Work M,D
Special Education M,D
Sports Management M

TENNESSEE TECHNOLOGICAL UNIVERSITY
Accounting M
Business Administration and
   Management—General M
Curriculum and Instruction M,O
Early Childhood Education M,O
Education of the Gifted D
Education—General M,D,O
Educational Leadership and
   Administration M,O
Educational Measurement and
   Evaluation D
Educational Media/Instructional
   Technology M,O
Educational Psychology M,O
Elementary Education M,O
Finance and Banking M
Health Education M
Human Resources Management M
International Business M
Kinesiology and Movement Studies M
Library Science M
Management Information Systems M
Management Strategy and Policy M
Middle School Education M
Music Education M
Physical Education M
Reading Education M,D,O
Secondary Education M,O
Special Education M,O
Sports Management M

TENNESSEE TEMPLE UNIVERSITY
Curriculum and Instruction M
Education—General M
Educational Leadership and
   Administration M

TENNESSEE WESLEYAN COLLEGE
Curriculum and Instruction M
Education—General M
Educational Leadership and
   Administration M

TEXAS A&M HEALTH SCIENCE CENTER
Health Education M

TEXAS A&M INTERNATIONAL UNIVERSITY
Accounting M
Business Administration and
   Management—General M,D
Counselor Education M
Curriculum and Instruction M
Education—General M
Educational Leadership and
   Administration M
Finance and Banking M
Foreign Languages Education M,D
International Business M,D
Management Information Systems M,D
Special Education M

TEXAS A&M UNIVERSITY
Accounting M,D
Agricultural Education M,D
Athletic Training and Sports
   Medicine M,D
Business Administration and
   Management—General M,D
Curriculum and Instruction M,D
Education—General M,D
Educational Leadership and
   Administration M,D
Educational Media/Instructional
   Technology M,D
Educational Psychology M,D
Finance and Banking M,D
Health Education M,D
Human Resources Development M,D
Kinesiology and Movement Studies M,D
Law D
Management Information Systems M
Marketing M,D
Multilingual and Multicultural
   Education M,D
Nonprofit Management M,D
Real Estate M,D
Recreation and Park Management M,D

---

*M—masters degree; D—doctorate; O—other advanced degree; *—Close-Up and/or Display*

Special Education — M,D
Sports Management — M,D

TEXAS A&M UNIVERSITY AT GALVESTON
Transportation Management — M

TEXAS A&M UNIVERSITY–COMMERCE
Accounting — M
Agricultural Education — M
Business Administration and Management—General — M
Counselor Education — M,D
Early Childhood Education — M,D
Education—General — M,D
Educational Leadership and Administration — M,D
Educational Media/Instructional Technology — M,D
Elementary Education — M,D
English as a Second Language — M,D
English Education — M,D
Exercise and Sports Science — M,D
Finance and Banking — M
Health Education — M,D
Higher Education — M,D
Kinesiology and Movement Studies — M,D
Marketing — M
Multilingual and Multicultural Education — M,D
Music Education — M
Physical Education — M,D
Reading Education — M,D
Secondary Education — M,D
Social Sciences Education — M
Social Work — M
Special Education — M,D

TEXAS A&M UNIVERSITY–CORPUS CHRISTI
Accounting — M
Business Administration and Management—General — M
Counselor Education — M,D
Curriculum and Instruction — M,D
Early Childhood Education — M,D
Education—General — M,D
Educational Leadership and Administration — M,D
Educational Media/Instructional Technology — M,D
Elementary Education — M
International Business — M
Kinesiology and Movement Studies — M,D
Mathematics Education — M
Reading Education — M,D
Secondary Education — M
Special Education — M

TEXAS A&M UNIVERSITY–KINGSVILLE
Adult Education — M
Business Administration and Management—General — M
Counselor Education — M
Early Childhood Education — M
Education—General — M
Educational Leadership and Administration — M,D
Educational Media/Instructional Technology — M
English as a Second Language — M
Foreign Languages Education — M,D
Health Education — M
Higher Education — D
Kinesiology and Movement Studies — M
Music Education — M
Reading Education — M
Special Education — M

TEXAS A&M UNIVERSITY–SAN ANTONIO
Accounting — M
Business Administration and Management—General — M
Counselor Education — M
Early Childhood Education — M
Educational Leadership and Administration — M
Educational Measurement and Evaluation — M
Finance and Banking — M
Human Resources Management — M
International Business — M
Kinesiology and Movement Studies — M
Management Information Systems — M
Multilingual and Multicultural Education — M
Project Management — M
Reading Education — M
Special Education — M
Supply Chain Management — M

TEXAS A&M UNIVERSITY–TEXARKANA
Accounting — M
Adult Education — M
Business Administration and Management—General — M
Curriculum and Instruction — M
Education—General — M
Educational Leadership and Administration — M
Educational Media/Instructional Technology — M
Special Education — M

TEXAS CHRISTIAN UNIVERSITY
Accounting — M
Business Administration and Management—General — M,D
Counselor Education — M,D,O
Curriculum and Instruction — M,D
Education—General — M,D,O
Educational Leadership and Administration — M,D,O
Educational Psychology — M,D,O
Elementary Education — M

Higher Education — D
Kinesiology and Movement Studies — D
Mathematics Education — M
Middle School Education — M
Music Education — M,D,O
Science Education — M,D
Secondary Education — M
Special Education — M

TEXAS SOUTHERN UNIVERSITY
Business Administration and Management—General — M
Counselor Education — M,D
Curriculum and Instruction — M,D
Education—General — M,D
Educational Leadership and Administration — M,D
Health Education — M
Higher Education — M,D
Human Services — M
Law — D
Management Information Systems — M
Multilingual and Multicultural Education — M,D
Physical Education — M
Secondary Education — M
Transportation Management — M

TEXAS STATE UNIVERSITY
Accounting — M
Adult Education — D
Agricultural Education — M
Athletic Training and Sports Medicine — M
Business Administration and Management—General — M
Counselor Education — M
Developmental Education — M,D
Education—General — M,D,O
Educational Leadership and Administration — M,D
Educational Media/Instructional Technology — M
Elementary Education — M
Exercise and Sports Science — M
Health Education — M
Higher Education — M
Human Resources Management — M
Legal and Justice Studies — M
Leisure Studies — M
Management Information Systems — M,D
Mathematics Education — M
Multilingual and Multicultural Education — M
Music Education — M
Physical Education — M
Reading Education — M
Recreation and Park Management — M
Science Education — M
Secondary Education — M
Social Work — M
Special Education — M
Student Affairs — M
Vocational and Technical Education — M

TEXAS TECH UNIVERSITY
Accounting — M,D
Agricultural Education — M,D
Art Education — M
Business Administration and Management—General — D
Counselor Education — M,D
Curriculum and Instruction — M,D
Education—General — M,D
Educational Leadership and Administration — M,D
Educational Media/Instructional Technology — M,D
Educational Psychology — M,D
Elementary Education — M,D
Exercise and Sports Science — M
Finance and Banking — M,D
Higher Education — M,D
Home Economics Education — M,D
Hospitality Management — M,D
Industrial and Manufacturing Management — M,D
Law — M,D
Management Information Systems — M,D
Marketing — D
Mathematics Education — M
Multilingual and Multicultural Education — M,D
Music Education — M,D
Quantitative Analysis — M
Reading Education — M,D
Science Education — M,D
Secondary Education — M,D
Special Education — M,D
Taxation — M,D

TEXAS TECH UNIVERSITY HEALTH SCIENCES CENTER
Athletic Training and Sports Medicine — M

TEXAS WESLEYAN UNIVERSITY
Business Administration and Management—General — M
Counselor Education — M,D
Education—General — M
Law — D

TEXAS WOMAN'S UNIVERSITY
Business Administration and Management—General — M
Counselor Education — M,D
Curriculum and Instruction — M
Early Childhood Education — M,D
Education—General — M,D
Educational Leadership and Administration — M,D
Exercise and Sports Science — M
Health Education — M
Kinesiology and Movement Studies — M,D
Library Science — M,D

Mathematics Education — M
Physical Education — M,D
Reading Education — M,D
Special Education — M,D
Sports Management — M,D

THOMAS COLLEGE
Business Administration and Management—General — M
Business Education — M
Computer Education — M
Human Resources Management — M

THOMAS EDISON STATE COLLEGE
Business Administration and Management—General — M
Distance Education Development — O
Educational Leadership and Administration — M
Educational Media/Instructional Technology — O
Human Resources Management — M,O
Organizational Management — O

THOMAS JEFFERSON SCHOOL OF LAW
Law — D

THOMAS JEFFERSON UNIVERSITY
Health Education — M,D,O

THOMAS M. COOLEY LAW SCHOOL
Environmental Law — M
Finance and Banking — M,D
Insurance — M,D
Intellectual Property Law — M,D
Law — M,D
Legal and Justice Studies — M,D
Taxation — M,D

THOMAS MORE COLLEGE
Business Administration and Management—General — M
Education—General — M

THOMAS UNIVERSITY
Business Administration and Management—General — M
Education—General — M
Human Services — M

THOMPSON RIVERS UNIVERSITY
Business Administration and Management—General — M
Education—General — M
Social Work — M

THUNDERBIRD SCHOOL OF GLOBAL MANAGEMENT
Business Administration and Management—General — M
International Business — M

TIFFIN UNIVERSITY
Business Administration and Management—General — M
Finance and Banking — M
Human Resources Management — M
International Business — M
Marketing — M
Sports Management — M

TOURO COLLEGE
Counselor Education — M
Education—General — M
Educational Leadership and Administration — M
Educational Media/Instructional Technology — M
English as a Second Language — M
Law — M,D
Legal and Justice Studies — M,D
Management Information Systems — M
Mathematics Education — M
Reading Education — M
Science Education — M
Social Work — M
Special Education — M

TOURO UNIVERSITY
Education—General — M,D

TOWSON UNIVERSITY
Accounting — M
Art Education — M,O
Early Childhood Education — M,O
Education—General — M
Educational Media/Instructional Technology — M,D
Electronic Commerce — M,O
Elementary Education — M
Human Resources Development — M
Kinesiology and Movement Studies — M
Management Information Systems — M,D,O
Management Strategy and Policy — O
Mathematics Education — M
Music Education — M,O
Organizational Behavior — O
Reading Education — M,O
Religious Education — M,O
Secondary Education — M
Special Education — M,O
Supply Chain Management — M,O

TREVECCA NAZARENE UNIVERSITY
Business Administration and Management—General — M,O
Counselor Education — M,D
Curriculum and Instruction — M,D
Education—General — M,D
Educational Leadership and Administration — M,D
Elementary Education — M,D
English as a Second Language — M,D
Library Science — M,D
Management Information Systems — M,O
Organizational Management — M,O
Project Management — M,O
Secondary Education — M,O
Special Education — M,D

TRIDENT UNIVERSITY INTERNATIONAL
Adult Education — M
Business Administration and Management—General — M,D
Early Childhood Education — M
Education—General — M,D
Educational Leadership and Administration — M,D
Educational Media/Instructional Technology — M,D
Finance and Banking — M,D
Health Education — M,D,O
Higher Education — M,D
Human Resources Management — M,D
International Business — M,D
Legal and Justice Studies — M,D,O
Logistics — M,D,O
Management Information Systems — M,D,O
Marketing — M,D
Project Management — M,D
Quality Management — M,D,O
Reading Education — M

TRINE UNIVERSITY
Law — M

TRINITY BAPTIST COLLEGE
Educational Leadership and Administration — M
Special Education — M

TRINITY CHRISTIAN COLLEGE
Special Education — M

TRINITY INTERNATIONAL UNIVERSITY
Business Administration and Management—General — M,D,O
Education—General — M
Educational Leadership and Administration — M
Law — D
Religious Education — M,D,O

TRINITY LUTHERAN SEMINARY
Religious Education — M

TRINITY UNIVERSITY
Accounting — M
Business Administration and Management—General — M
Education—General — M
Educational Leadership and Administration — M

TRINITY WASHINGTON UNIVERSITY
Business Administration and Management—General — M
Counselor Education — M
Curriculum and Instruction — M
Early Childhood Education — M
Education—General — M
Educational Leadership and Administration — M
Elementary Education — M
English Education — M
Human Resources Management — M
Nonprofit Management — M
Organizational Management — M
Reading Education — M
Secondary Education — M
Social Sciences Education — M
Special Education — M

TRINITY WESTERN UNIVERSITY
Business Administration and Management—General — M
Educational Leadership and Administration — M,O
English as a Second Language — M
International Business — M
Nonprofit Management — M,O
Organizational Management — M,O

TROPICAL AGRICULTURE RESEARCH AND HIGHER EDUCATION CENTER
Travel and Tourism — M,D

TROY UNIVERSITY
Accounting — M
Adult Education — M
Art Education — M
Business Administration and Management—General — M
Computer Education — M
Counselor Education — M,O
Early Childhood Education — M,O
Education of the Gifted — M
Education—General — M,O
Educational Leadership and Administration — M,O
Educational Media/Instructional Technology — M
Elementary Education — M
English Education — M
Exercise and Sports Science — M
Finance and Banking — M
Foundations and Philosophy of Education — M
Higher Education — M
Hospitality Management — M
Human Resources Management — M
International Business — M
Management Information Systems — M
Mathematics Education — M
Music Education — M
Nonprofit Management — M
Organizational Management — M
Physical Education — M
Reading Education — M
Science Education — M
Secondary Education — M
Social Sciences Education — M
Social Work — M,O
Sports Management — M
Taxation — M,O

TRUMAN STATE UNIVERSITY
Accounting M
Education—General M

TUFTS UNIVERSITY
Art Education M,D,O
Early Childhood Education M,D
Education—General M,D,O
Elementary Education M,D
International Business M,D
Law M,D
Management Strategy and Policy O
Mathematics Education M,D
Middle School Education M,D
Museum Education M,D
Nonprofit Management O
Science Education M,D
Secondary Education M,D

TULANE UNIVERSITY
Business Administration and Management—General M,D
Health Education M
Law M,D
Social Work M

TUSCULUM COLLEGE
Adult Education M
Education—General M
Organizational Management M

UNIFICATION THEOLOGICAL SEMINARY
Religious Education M,D

UNION COLLEGE (KY)
Education—General M
Educational Leadership and Administration M
Elementary Education M
Health Education M
Middle School Education M
Music Education M
Physical Education M
Reading Education M
Secondary Education M
Special Education M

UNION GRADUATE COLLEGE
Business Administration and Management—General M,O
Computer Education M,O
Education—General M,O
Educational Leadership and Administration M,O
English Education M,O
Foreign Languages Education M,O
Health Law M,O
Human Resources Management M,O
Mathematics Education M,O
Middle School Education M,O
Science Education M,O
Social Sciences Education M,O

UNION INSTITUTE & UNIVERSITY
Education—General D
Educational Leadership and Administration D
Higher Education D

UNION PRESBYTERIAN SEMINARY
Religious Education M,D

UNION UNIVERSITY
Business Administration and Management—General M
Education—General M,D,O
Educational Leadership and Administration M,D,O
Higher Education M,D,O

UNITED STATES INTERNATIONAL UNIVERSITY
Business Administration and Management—General M
Entrepreneurship M
Finance and Banking M
Human Resources Management M
International Business M
Management Information Systems M
Management Strategy and Policy M
Marketing M
Organizational Management M

UNITED STATES SPORTS ACADEMY
Athletic Training and Sports Medicine M
Exercise and Sports Science M
Physical Education M
Sports Management M,D

UNITED STATES UNIVERSITY
Business Administration and Management—General M
Early Childhood Education M
Education—General M
Educational Leadership and Administration M
Foreign Languages Education M
Health Education M
Higher Education M
Special Education M

UNIVERSIDAD ADVENTISTA DE LAS ANTILLAS
Curriculum and Instruction M
Educational Leadership and Administration M
Health Education M

UNIVERSIDAD AUTONOMA DE GUADALAJARA
Advertising and Public Relations M,D
Business Administration and Management—General M,D
Education—General M,D
Entertainment Management M,D
International Business M,D
Law M,D
Legal and Justice Studies M,D
Marketing Research M,D
Mathematics Education M,D

UNIVERSIDAD CENTRAL DEL ESTE
Finance and Banking M
Higher Education M
Human Resources Development M
Law D

UNIVERSIDAD DE IBEROAMERICA
Educational Psychology M,D

UNIVERSIDAD DE LAS AMERICAS, A.C.
Business Administration and Management—General M
Education—General M
Finance and Banking M
Marketing Research M
Organizational Behavior M
Quality Management M

UNIVERSIDAD DE LAS AMÉRICAS PUEBLA
Business Administration and Management—General M
Education—General M
Finance and Banking M
Industrial and Manufacturing Management M

UNIVERSIDAD DEL ESTE
Accounting M
Adult Education M
Business Administration and Management—General M
Electronic Commerce M
Elementary Education M
English as a Second Language M
Foreign Languages Education M
Human Resources Management M
Management Information Systems M
Management Strategy and Policy M
Social Work M
Special Education M

UNIVERSIDAD DEL TURABO
Accounting M
Athletic Training and Sports Medicine M
Business Administration and Management—General M,D
Counselor Education M
Curriculum and Instruction M,D
Early Childhood Education M
Education—General M,D,O
Educational Leadership and Administration M,D,O
English as a Second Language M
Human Resources Management M
Human Services M
Information Studies M
Library Science M,O
Logistics M
Management Information Systems D
Marketing M
Physical Education M
Project Management M
Quality Management M
Special Education M

UNIVERSIDAD IBEROAMERICANA
Business Administration and Management—General M,D
Educational Leadership and Administration M,D
Human Resources Development M,D
Law M,D
Marketing M,D
Real Estate M,D
Special Education M,D

UNIVERSIDAD METROPOLITANA
Accounting M
Adult Education M
Business Administration and Management—General M
Curriculum and Instruction M
Education—General M
Educational Leadership and Administration M
Elementary Education M
Finance and Banking M
Human Resources Management M
International Business M
Leisure Studies M
Management Information Systems M
Marketing M
Physical Education M
Recreation and Park Management M
Secondary Education M
Special Education M

UNIVERSIDAD NACIONAL PEDRO HENRIQUEZ URENA
Project Management M
Science Education M

UNIVERSITÉ DE MONCTON
Business Administration and Management—General M
Counselor Education M
Education—General M
Educational Leadership and Administration M
Educational Psychology M
Social Work M

UNIVERSITÉ DE MONTRÉAL
Curriculum and Instruction M,D,O
Education—General M,D,O
Educational Leadership and Administration M,D,O
Educational Psychology M,D,O
Electronic Commerce M,D,O
Human Services D
Information Studies M,D
Kinesiology and Movement Studies M,D,O
Law M,D,O
Library Science M,D
Physical Education M,D,O
Social Work O
Taxation M,D,O

UNIVERSITÉ DE SAINT-BONIFACE
Education—General M

UNIVERSITÉ DE SHERBROOKE
Accounting M
Business Administration and Management—General M,D,O
Education—General M,O
Educational Leadership and Administration M
Electronic Commerce M
Elementary Education M,O
Finance and Banking M
Health Law M,D,O
Higher Education M,O
International Business M
Kinesiology and Movement Studies M,O
Law M,D,O
Management Information Systems M,O
Marketing M
Organizational Behavior M
Physical Education M,O
Social Work M
Special Education M,O
Taxation M,O

UNIVERSITÉ DU QUÉBEC À CHICOUTIMI
Business Administration and Management—General M
Education—General M,D
Project Management M

UNIVERSITÉ DU QUÉBEC À MONTRÉAL
Accounting M,O
Actuarial Science O
Business Administration and Management—General M,D,O
Education—General M,D,O
Environmental Education M,D,O
Finance and Banking O
Kinesiology and Movement Studies M
Law O
Management Information Systems M,O
Project Management M
Social Work M,O

UNIVERSITÉ DU QUÉBEC À RIMOUSKI
Business Administration and Management—General M,O
Education—General M,D,O
Project Management M,O

UNIVERSITÉ DU QUÉBEC À TROIS-RIVIÈRES
Accounting M
Business Administration and Management—General M,D
Education—General M,D
Educational Leadership and Administration O
Educational Psychology M,D
Finance and Banking O
Leisure Studies M,O
Physical Education M,O
Travel and Tourism M,O

UNIVERSITÉ DU QUÉBEC, ÉCOLE NATIONALE D'ADMINISTRATION PUBLIQUE
International Business M,O

UNIVERSITÉ DU QUÉBEC EN ABITIBI-TÉMISCAMINGUE
Business Administration and Management—General M
Education—General M,D,O
Project Management M,O
Social Work M

UNIVERSITÉ DU QUÉBEC EN OUTAOUAIS
Accounting M,O
Education—General M,D,O
Educational Psychology M
Finance and Banking M,O
Foreign Languages Education O
Project Management M,O
Social Work M,O

UNIVERSITÉ LAVAL
Accounting M,O
Advertising and Public Relations O
Business Administration and Management—General M,D,O
Counselor Education M,D
Curriculum and Instruction M,D
Education—General M,D,O
Educational Leadership and Administration M,D,O
Educational Measurement and Evaluation M,D,O
Educational Media/Instructional Technology M,D
Educational Psychology M,D
Electronic Commerce M,O
Entrepreneurship M,O
Facilities Management M,O
Finance and Banking M,O
International Business M,O
Kinesiology and Movement Studies M,D
Law M,D,O
Legal and Justice Studies O
Management Information Systems M,O
Marketing M,O
Music Education M,D
Organizational Management M,O
Social Work M,D

UNIVERSITÉ SAINTE-ANNE
Education—General M

UNIVERSITY AT ALBANY, STATE UNIVERSITY OF NEW YORK
Accounting M
Business Administration and Management—General M
Counselor Education M,D,O
Curriculum and Instruction M,D,O
Education—General M,D,O
Educational Leadership and Administration M,D,O
Educational Measurement and Evaluation M,D,O
Educational Media/Instructional Technology M,D,O
Educational Psychology M,D,O
Human Resources Management M
Information Studies M,D,O
Mathematics Education M,D
Reading Education M,D,O
Science Education M,D
Social Work M,D
Special Education M,O
Taxation M

UNIVERSITY AT BUFFALO, THE STATE UNIVERSITY OF NEW YORK
Accounting M,D
Business Administration and Management—General M,D
Counselor Education M,D,O
Curriculum and Instruction M,D,O
Early Childhood Education M,D,O
Education of the Gifted M,D,O
Education—General M,D,O
Educational Leadership and Administration M,D,O
Educational Media/Instructional Technology M,D,O
Educational Psychology M,D,O
Electronic Commerce M,D,O
Elementary Education M,D,O
English as a Second Language M,D,O
English Education M,D,O
Exercise and Sports Science M,D,O
Finance and Banking M,D
Foreign Languages Education M,D,O
Foundations and Philosophy of Education M,D,O
Higher Education M,D,O
Human Resources Management M,D,O
Information Studies M,D,O
International Business M,D,O
Law M,D
Library Science M,O
Logistics M,D
Management Information Systems M,D,O
Mathematics Education M,D,O
Multilingual and Multicultural Education M,D,O
Music Education M,D,O
Quantitative Analysis M,D
Reading Education M,D,O
Science Education M,D,O
Social Sciences Education M,D,O
Social Work M,D*
Special Education M,D,O

THE UNIVERSITY OF AKRON
Accounting M
Business Administration and Management—General M
Counselor Education D
Education—General M,D
Educational Leadership and Administration M
Electronic Commerce M
Elementary Education M,D
Exercise and Sports Science M
Finance and Banking M
Higher Education M
Human Resources Management M
International Business M
Law M,D
Management Information Systems M
Marketing M
Music Education M
Physical Education M
Secondary Education M,D
Social Work M
Special Education M
Supply Chain Management M
Taxation M
Vocational and Technical Education M

THE UNIVERSITY OF ALABAMA
Accounting M,D
Advertising and Public Relations M
Business Administration and Management—General M,D
Counselor Education M,D,O
Education of the Gifted M,D,O
Educational Leadership and Administration M,D,O
Elementary Education M,D,O
English as a Second Language M,D
Exercise and Sports Science M,D
Finance and Banking M,D
Health Education M,D
Higher Education M,D
Hospitality Management M

*M—masters degree; D—doctorate; O—other advanced degree; *—Close-Up and/or Display*

- Industrial and Manufacturing Management M,D
- Information Studies M,D
- Kinesiology and Movement Studies M,D
- Law M,D
- Library Science M,D
- Marketing M,D
- Music Education M,D,O
- Physical Education M,D
- Quality Management M,D
- Secondary Education M,D,O
- Social Work M,D
- Special Education M,D,O
- Sports Management M,D
- Taxation M,D

THE UNIVERSITY OF ALABAMA AT BIRMINGHAM
- Accounting M
- Art Education M
- Business Administration and Management—General M
- Counselor Education M
- Curriculum and Instruction O
- Early Childhood Education M,D
- Education—General M,D,O
- Educational Leadership and Administration M,D,O
- Elementary Education M
- English as a Second Language M
- Exercise and Sports Science M
- Finance and Banking M
- Health Education M,D
- Management Information Systems M
- Marketing M
- Physical Education M
- Quantitative Analysis M,D
- Reading Education M
- Secondary Education M
- Special Education M

THE UNIVERSITY OF ALABAMA IN HUNTSVILLE
- Accounting M,O
- Business Administration and Management—General M,O
- English Education M,O
- Entrepreneurship M,O
- Finance and Banking M,O
- Human Resources Management M,O
- Logistics M,O
- Management Information Systems M,O
- Marketing M,O
- Mathematics Education M,D
- Project Management M,O
- Reading Education M,O
- Science Education M,O
- Social Sciences Education M
- Supply Chain Management M,O
- Taxation M

UNIVERSITY OF ALASKA ANCHORAGE
- Business Administration and Management—General M
- Counselor Education M
- Early Childhood Education M,O
- Education—General M,O
- Educational Leadership and Administration M,O
- Logistics M,O
- Project Management M
- Social Work M,O
- Special Education M,O

UNIVERSITY OF ALASKA FAIRBANKS
- Business Administration and Management—General M
- Counselor Education M
- Curriculum and Instruction M,O
- Education—General M,O
- Elementary Education M,O
- English Education M,O
- Finance and Banking M
- Multilingual and Multicultural Education M,O
- Music Education M
- Reading Education M,O
- Secondary Education M,O
- Special Education M,O

UNIVERSITY OF ALASKA SOUTHEAST
- Business Administration and Management—General M
- Early Childhood Education M
- Education—General M
- Educational Media/Instructional Technology M
- Elementary Education M
- Secondary Education M

UNIVERSITY OF ALBERTA
- Accounting D
- Adult Education M,D,O
- Business Administration and Management—General M,D
- Counselor Education M,D
- Educational Leadership and Administration M,D,O
- Educational Media/Instructional Technology M,D
- Educational Policy M,D,O
- Educational Psychology M,D
- Elementary Education M,D
- English as a Second Language M,D
- Exercise and Sports Science M,D
- Finance and Banking M,D
- Information Studies M,D
- International Business M
- Law M,D
- Library Science M
- Marketing D
- Multilingual and Multicultural Education M
- Organizational Management D
- Physical Education M,D
- Recreation and Park Management M,D
- Secondary Education M,D
- Special Education M,D
- Sports Management M

UNIVERSITY OF ANTELOPE VALLEY
- Business Administration and Management—General M

THE UNIVERSITY OF ARIZONA
- Accounting M,D
- Agricultural Education M
- Art Education M,D
- Business Administration and Management—General M,D
- Counselor Education M
- Education—General M,D,O
- Educational Leadership and Administration M,D,O
- Educational Psychology M,D,O
- Elementary Education M,D
- English as a Second Language M,D
- English Education M,D
- Finance and Banking M,D
- Higher Education M,D
- Information Studies M,D
- Law M,D
- Library Science M,D
- Management Information Systems M
- Management Strategy and Policy D
- Marketing M,D
- Mathematics Education M
- Middle School Education M
- Multilingual and Multicultural Education M,D,O
- Music Education M,D
- Reading Education M,D,O
- Secondary Education M,D
- Special Education M,D

UNIVERSITY OF ARKANSAS
- Accounting M
- Agricultural Education M
- Athletic Training and Sports Medicine M
- Business Administration and Management—General M,D
- Counselor Education M,D,O
- Curriculum and Instruction D
- Early Childhood Education M
- Education—General M,D,O
- Educational Leadership and Administration M,D,O
- Educational Measurement and Evaluation M,D
- Educational Media/Instructional Technology M
- Educational Policy D
- Health Education M,D
- Higher Education M,D,O
- Human Resources Development M,D
- Industrial and Manufacturing Management M
- Kinesiology and Movement Studies M,D
- Law M,D
- Management Information Systems M
- Mathematics Education M
- Middle School Education M,D,O
- Physical Education M,D
- Recreation and Park Management M,D
- Secondary Education M,O
- Social Work M
- Special Education M
- Sports Management M,D
- Vocational and Technical Education M,D

UNIVERSITY OF ARKANSAS AT LITTLE ROCK
- Accounting M,O
- Adult Education M
- Art Education M
- Business Administration and Management—General M,O
- Counselor Education M
- Early Childhood Education M
- Education of the Gifted M
- Education—General M,D,O
- Educational Leadership and Administration M,D,O
- Educational Media/Instructional Technology M
- English as a Second Language M
- Entrepreneurship O
- Foreign Languages Education M
- Higher Education D
- Law D
- Management Information Systems M,O
- Middle School Education M
- Nonprofit Management O
- Reading Education M,O
- Secondary Education M
- Social Work M
- Special Education M,O
- Taxation M,O

UNIVERSITY OF ARKANSAS AT MONTICELLO
- Education—General M
- Educational Leadership and Administration M

UNIVERSITY OF ARKANSAS AT PINE BLUFF
- Early Childhood Education M
- Education—General M
- English Education M
- Mathematics Education M
- Physical Education M
- Science Education M
- Secondary Education M
- Social Sciences Education M

UNIVERSITY OF ARKANSAS FOR MEDICAL SCIENCES
- Health Education M,D,O

UNIVERSITY OF BALTIMORE
- Accounting M,O
- Business Administration and Management—General M,O
- Finance and Banking M
- Human Services M
- Law M,D
- Legal and Justice Studies M
- Management Information Systems M,O
- Marketing M
- Taxation M,D

UNIVERSITY OF BRIDGEPORT
- Accounting M
- Business Administration and Management—General M
- Computer Education M,D,O
- Early Childhood Education M,D,O
- Education—General M,D,O
- Educational Leadership and Administration M,D,O
- Elementary Education M,D,O
- Entrepreneurship M
- Finance and Banking M
- Human Resources Development M
- Human Resources Management M
- Human Services M
- Industrial and Manufacturing Management M
- International and Comparative Education M,D,O
- International Business M
- Management Information Systems M
- Marketing M
- Middle School Education M,D,O
- Music Education M,D,O
- Reading Education M,D,O
- Secondary Education M,D,O
- Student Affairs M

THE UNIVERSITY OF BRITISH COLUMBIA
- Accounting D
- Adult Education M,D
- Archives/Archival Administration M,D
- Art Education M,D
- Business Administration and Management—General M,D
- Business Education M,D
- Curriculum and Instruction M,D
- Early Childhood Education M,D
- Education—General M,D,O
- Educational Leadership and Administration M,D
- Educational Measurement and Evaluation M,D,O
- Educational Policy M,D
- English as a Second Language M,D
- Finance and Banking D
- Foundations and Philosophy of Education M,D
- Higher Education M,D
- Home Economics Education M,D
- Information Studies M,D
- Kinesiology and Movement Studies M,D
- Law M,D
- Library Science M,D
- Management Information Systems D
- Management Strategy and Policy D
- Marketing D
- Mathematics Education M,D
- Music Education M,D
- Organizational Behavior D
- Physical Education M,D
- Quantitative Analysis M,D
- Reading Education M,D
- Science Education M,D
- Social Sciences Education M,D
- Social Work M,D
- Special Education M,D,O
- Transportation Management D
- Vocational and Technical Education M,D

UNIVERSITY OF CALGARY
- Adult Education M,D
- Business Administration and Management—General M,D
- Curriculum and Instruction M,D
- Educational Leadership and Administration M,D
- Educational Measurement and Evaluation M,D
- Environmental Law M,O
- Kinesiology and Movement Studies M,D
- Law M,D,O
- Legal and Justice Studies M,O
- Management Strategy and Policy M,D
- Multilingual and Multicultural Education M,D
- Project Management M,D
- Social Work M,D,O

UNIVERSITY OF CALIFORNIA, BERKELEY
- Accounting D,O
- Business Administration and Management—General M,D,O
- Education—General M,D,O
- English as a Second Language O
- Facilities Management O
- Finance and Banking D,O
- Human Resources Management O
- Industrial and Manufacturing Management D
- Information Studies M,D
- International Business O
- Law M,D
- Legal and Justice Studies D
- Management Information Systems O
- Marketing D,O
- Mathematics Education M,D
- Organizational Behavior D
- Project Management O
- Real Estate D
- Science Education M,D
- Social Work M,D
- Special Education M,D
- Sustainability Management O

UNIVERSITY OF CALIFORNIA, DAVIS
- Accounting M
- Business Administration and Management—General M
- Curriculum and Instruction M,D
- Education—General M,D
- Educational Psychology M,D
- Exercise and Sports Science M
- Law M,D
- Transportation Management M,D

UNIVERSITY OF CALIFORNIA, HASTINGS COLLEGE OF THE LAW
- Law M,D

UNIVERSITY OF CALIFORNIA, IRVINE
- Business Administration and Management—General M,D
- Education—General M,D
- Educational Leadership and Administration M,D
- Elementary Education M,D
- Foreign Languages Education M,D
- Law D
- Secondary Education M,D

UNIVERSITY OF CALIFORNIA, LOS ANGELES
- Accounting M,D
- Archives/Archival Administration M,D,O
- Business Administration and Management—General M,D
- Education—General M,D
- Educational Leadership and Administration D
- English as a Second Language M,D,O
- Finance and Banking M,D
- Human Resources Development M,D
- Industrial and Manufacturing Management M,D
- Information Studies M,D,O
- International Business M,D
- Law M,D
- Library Science M,D,O
- Management Information Systems M,D
- Management Strategy and Policy M,D
- Marketing M,D
- Organizational Behavior M,D
- Social Work M,D
- Special Education D

UNIVERSITY OF CALIFORNIA, RIVERSIDE
- Accounting M,D
- Archives/Archival Administration M,D
- Business Administration and Management—General M,D
- Education—General M,D,O
- Educational Leadership and Administration M,D,O
- Educational Psychology M,D,O
- English as a Second Language M,D,O
- Finance and Banking M,D
- Foundations and Philosophy of Education M,D,O
- Higher Education M,D,O
- Multilingual and Multicultural Education M,D,O
- Reading Education M,D,O
- Special Education M,D,O

UNIVERSITY OF CALIFORNIA, SAN DIEGO
- Business Administration and Management—General M,D
- Curriculum and Instruction M,D
- Education—General M,D
- Educational Leadership and Administration M,D
- Finance and Banking M,D
- Health Law M
- Law M
- Legal and Justice Studies M
- Mathematics Education D
- Multilingual and Multicultural Education M,D
- Science Education D

UNIVERSITY OF CALIFORNIA, SANTA BARBARA
- Education—General M,D,O
- Finance and Banking M,D
- Quantitative Analysis M,D
- Transportation Management M,D

UNIVERSITY OF CALIFORNIA, SANTA CRUZ
- Education—General M,D
- Finance and Banking M
- Management Information Systems M,D
- Social Sciences Education M

UNIVERSITY OF CENTRAL ARKANSAS
- Accounting M
- Adult Education M,O
- Business Administration and Management—General M
- Counselor Education M
- Curriculum and Instruction M,O
- Education of the Gifted M,O
- Education—General M,O
- Educational Leadership and Administration M,O
- Educational Media/Instructional Technology M
- Foreign Languages Education M
- Health Education M
- Kinesiology and Movement Studies M
- Library Science M
- Mathematics Education M
- Music Education M,O
- Organizational Management D
- Reading Education M

52 www.petersonsbooks.com
Peterson's Graduate Programs in Business, Education, Information Studies, Law & Social Work 2015

Special Education	M,O
Student Affairs	M

UNIVERSITY OF CENTRAL FLORIDA

Accounting	M
Actuarial Science	M,O
Art Education	M,O
Business Administration and Management—General	M,D,O
Community College Education	M,D,O
Counselor Education	M,D,O
Early Childhood Education	D
Education of the Gifted	M,O
Educational Leadership and Administration	M,D
Educational Media/Instructional Technology	M,D,O
Elementary Education	M,D
English as a Second Language	M,D,O
English Education	M,O
Entrepreneurship	M,O
Exercise and Sports Science	M,D
Higher Education	M,D
Hospitality Management	M,D,O
International and Comparative Education	M,O
Mathematics Education	M,D,O
Middle School Education	M
Nonprofit Management	M,O
Reading Education	M,D,O
Science Education	M,D,O
Social Sciences Education	M,D,O
Social Work	M,O
Special Education	M,D,O
Sports Management	M
Student Affairs	M,D
Taxation	M
Travel and Tourism	M,D,O
Urban Education	M,O
Vocational and Technical Education	M

UNIVERSITY OF CENTRAL MISSOURI

Accounting	M,D,O
Business Administration and Management—General	M,D,O
Counselor Education	M,D,O
Early Childhood Education	M,D,O
Education—General	M,D,O
Educational Leadership and Administration	M,D,O
Educational Media/Instructional Technology	M,D,O
Elementary Education	M,D,O
English as a Second Language	M,D,O
Finance and Banking	M,D,O
Human Services	M,D,O
Industrial and Manufacturing Management	M,D,O
Kinesiology and Movement Studies	M,D,O
Library Science	M,D,O
Management Information Systems	M,D,O
Marketing	M,D,O
Reading Education	M,D,O
Special Education	M,D,O
Student Affairs	M,D,O
Vocational and Technical Education	M,D,O

UNIVERSITY OF CENTRAL OKLAHOMA

Accounting	M
Adult Education	M
Athletic Training and Sports Medicine	M
Counselor Education	M
Early Childhood Education	M
Education—General	M
Educational Leadership and Administration	M
Educational Media/Instructional Technology	M
Elementary Education	M
English as a Second Language	M
Exercise and Sports Science	M
Health Education	M
Higher Education	M
Library Science	M
Reading Education	M
Secondary Education	M
Special Education	M
Student Affairs	M

UNIVERSITY OF CHARLESTON

Accounting	M
Business Administration and Management—General	M
Legal and Justice Studies	M
Management Strategy and Policy	M
Organizational Management	D

UNIVERSITY OF CHICAGO

Accounting	M,O
Business Administration and Management—General	M,D,O
Entrepreneurship	M,O
Finance and Banking	M,O
Human Resources Management	M,O
International Business	M,O
Law	M,D
Management Strategy and Policy	M,O
Marketing	M,O
Organizational Behavior	M,O
Science Education	D
Social Work	M,D
Urban Education	M

UNIVERSITY OF CINCINNATI

Accounting	M,D
Adult Education	M,D,O
Art Education	M
Business Administration and Management—General	M,D
Counselor Education	M,D,O
Curriculum and Instruction	M,D
Early Childhood Education	M
Education—General	M,D,O
Educational Leadership and Administration	M,D,O
Elementary Education	M
English as a Second Language	M,D,O
Finance and Banking	M,D
Foundations and Philosophy of Education	M,D
Health Education	M,D
Industrial and Manufacturing Management	D
Law	D
Management Information Systems	M,D
Marketing	M,D
Mathematics Education	M,D
Music Education	M
Organizational Management	M
Quantitative Analysis	M,D
Reading Education	M,D
Science Education	M,D,O
Secondary Education	M
Social Sciences Education	M,D,O
Social Work	M
Special Education	M,D
Taxation	M

UNIVERSITY OF COLORADO BOULDER

Accounting	M,D
Business Administration and Management—General	M
Curriculum and Instruction	M,D
Education—General	M,D
Educational Measurement and Evaluation	D
Educational Policy	M,D
Educational Psychology	M,D
Entrepreneurship	M,D
Finance and Banking	M,D
Kinesiology and Movement Studies	M,D
Law	D
Management Information Systems	M,D
Marketing	M,D
Multilingual and Multicultural Education	M,D
Music Education	M,D
Organizational Management	M,D

UNIVERSITY OF COLORADO COLORADO SPRINGS

Athletic Training and Sports Medicine	M
Business Administration and Management—General	M
Counselor Education	M,D
Curriculum and Instruction	M,D
Education—General	M,D
Educational Leadership and Administration	M,D
Human Services	M,D
Special Education	M,D

UNIVERSITY OF COLORADO DENVER

Accounting	M
Adult Education	M
Business Administration and Management—General	M
Counselor Education	M
Distance Education Development	M
Early Childhood Education	M,D
Education—General	M,D,O
Educational Leadership and Administration	M,D,O
Educational Measurement and Evaluation	M,D,O
Educational Media/Instructional Technology	M
Educational Policy	D
Educational Psychology	M,O
Electronic Commerce	M
Elementary Education	M
English Education	M
Entertainment Management	M
Entrepreneurship	M,D
Environmental Education	M
Environmental Law	M,D
Finance and Banking	M
Health Education	M
Human Resources Management	M
Insurance	M
International Business	M
Investment Management	M
Management Information Systems	M,D
Management Strategy and Policy	M
Marketing Research	M
Marketing	M
Mathematics Education	M,D
Multilingual and Multicultural Education	M
Nonprofit Management	M,D
Quantitative Analysis	M
Reading Education	M
Science Education	M,D
Secondary Education	M
Special Education	M,D
Sports Management	M
Sustainability Management	M

UNIVERSITY OF CONNECTICUT

Accounting	M,D
Actuarial Science	M,D
Adult Education	M,D
Agricultural Education	M,D,O
Business Administration and Management—General	M,D
Counselor Education	M,D,O
Education of the Gifted	M,D,O
Education—General	M,D,O
Educational Leadership and Administration	D,O
Educational Measurement and Evaluation	M,D,O
Educational Media/Instructional Technology	M,D,O
Educational Psychology	M,D,O
Elementary Education	M,D,O
English Education	M,D,O
Exercise and Sports Science	M,D
Finance and Banking	M,D,O
Foreign Languages Education	M,D,O
Foundations and Philosophy of Education	D
Higher Education	M
Human Resources Development	M
Human Resources Management	M
Law	D
Leisure Studies	M,D
Marketing	M,D
Mathematics Education	M,D,O
Multilingual and Multicultural Education	M,D,O
Music Education	M,D,O
Nonprofit Management	M,O
Quantitative Analysis	M,O
Reading Education	M,D,O
Science Education	M,D
Secondary Education	M,D,O
Social Sciences Education	M,D,O
Special Education	M,D,O

UNIVERSITY OF DALLAS

Accounting	M
Business Administration and Management—General	M
Entertainment Management	M
Finance and Banking	M
Human Resources Management	M
International Business	M
Logistics	M
Management Information Systems	M
Management Strategy and Policy	M
Marketing	M
Organizational Management	M
Project Management	M
Sports Management	M
Supply Chain Management	M

UNIVERSITY OF DAYTON

Accounting	M
Business Administration and Management—General	M
Counselor Education	M,O
Early Childhood Education	M
Educational Leadership and Administration	M,D,O
Educational Media/Instructional Technology	M
Exercise and Sports Science	M,D
Finance and Banking	M
Law	M,D
Marketing	M
Mathematics Education	M
Middle School Education	M
Music Education	M
Physical Education	M,D
Reading Education	M
Secondary Education	M
Special Education	M
Student Affairs	M,O

UNIVERSITY OF DELAWARE

Accounting	M
Agricultural Education	M
Business Administration and Management—General	M,D
Business Education	M,D
Curriculum and Instruction	M,D,O
Education—General	M,D,O
Educational Leadership and Administration	M,D,O
English as a Second Language	M,D,O
Entrepreneurship	M,D
Finance and Banking	M
Foreign Languages Education	M
Higher Education	M,D,O
Hospitality Management	M
Kinesiology and Movement Studies	M,D
Management Information Systems	M
Multilingual and Multicultural Education	M,D,O
Music Education	M

UNIVERSITY OF DENVER

Accounting	M
Advertising and Public Relations	M,O
Business Administration and Management—General	M
Curriculum and Instruction	M,D,O
Early Childhood Education	M,D,O
Education—General	M,D,O
Educational Leadership and Administration	M,D,O
Educational Policy	M,D,O
Finance and Banking	M
Health Law	M,O
Higher Education	M,D,O
Human Resources Development	M,O
Human Resources Management	M,O
International Business	M,D,O
Law	M,D,O
Legal and Justice Studies	M,O
Library Science	M,D,O
Management Information Systems	M,O
Management Strategy and Policy	M
Marketing	M
Music Education	M,O
Organizational Management	M,O
Project Management	M,O
Real Estate	M
Social Work	M,D,O
Special Education	M,D,O
Taxation	M

UNIVERSITY OF DETROIT MERCY

Business Administration and Management—General	M,O
Computer Education	M
Counselor Education	M
Curriculum and Instruction	M
Education—General	M
Educational Leadership and Administration	M
Law	D
Management Information Systems	M
Mathematics Education	M
Special Education	M

UNIVERSITY OF DUBUQUE

Business Administration and Management—General	M

THE UNIVERSITY OF FINDLAY

Athletic Training and Sports Medicine	M,D
Business Administration and Management—General	M,D
Early Childhood Education	M,D
Education—General	M,D
Educational Leadership and Administration	M,D
Educational Media/Instructional Technology	M,D
English as a Second Language	M,D
Hospitality Management	M,D
Multilingual and Multicultural Education	M,D
Organizational Management	M,D
Reading Education	M,D
Science Education	M,D

UNIVERSITY OF FLORIDA

Accounting	M,D
Advertising and Public Relations	M
Agricultural Education	M,D
Art Education	M,D
Athletic Training and Sports Medicine	M,D
Business Administration and Management—General	M,D
Counselor Education	M,D,O
Curriculum and Instruction	M,D,O
Early Childhood Education	M,D,O
Education—General	M,D,O
Educational Leadership and Administration	M,D,O
Educational Measurement and Evaluation	M,D,O
Educational Policy	M,D,O
Elementary Education	M,D,O
English as a Second Language	M,D,O
English Education	M,D,O
Entrepreneurship	M,D,O
Environmental Education	M,D,O
Environmental Law	M,D
Exercise and Sports Science	M,D
Finance and Banking	M,D,O
Health Education	M,D,O
Higher Education	M,D,O
Human Resources Management	M
Insurance	M,D,O
International Business	M,D
Kinesiology and Movement Studies	M,D
Law	M,D
Management Information Systems	M,D,O
Marketing	M,D
Mathematics Education	M,D,O
Multilingual and Multicultural Education	M,D,O
Music Education	M,D
Nonprofit Management	M
Physical Education	M,D
Quantitative Analysis	M,D,O
Reading Education	M,D,O
Real Estate	M,D,O
Recreation and Park Management	M,D
Science Education	M,D,O
Social Sciences Education	M,D,O
Special Education	M,D,O
Sports Management	M,D
Student Affairs	M,D,O
Supply Chain Management	M,D,O
Taxation	M,D
Travel and Tourism	M,D

UNIVERSITY OF GEORGIA

Accounting	M
Adult Education	M,D,O
Agricultural Education	M
Art Education	M,D,O
Business Administration and Management—General	M,D
Business Education	M,D,O
Counselor Education	M,D,O
Early Childhood Education	M,D,O
Education—General	M,D,O
Educational Leadership and Administration	M,D,O
Educational Media/Instructional Technology	M,D,O
Educational Policy	M,D,O
Educational Psychology	M,D,O
Elementary Education	M,D,O
English Education	M,D,O
Foreign Languages Education	M,D,O
Health Education	M,D,O
Higher Education	D
Home Economics Education	M,D,O
Human Resources Management	M,D,O
Kinesiology and Movement Studies	M,D
Law	M,D
Leisure Studies	M,D,O
Management Information Systems	D
Mathematics Education	M,D,O
Middle School Education	M,D,O
Music Education	M,D,O

*M—masters degree; D—doctorate; O—other advanced degree; *—Close-Up and/or Display*

- Nonprofit Management M,D,O
- Physical Education M,D
- Reading Education M,D,O
- Science Education M,D,O
- Social Sciences Education M,D,O
- Social Work M,D,O
- Special Education M,D,O
- Student Affairs M,D,O
- Vocational and Technical Education M,D,O

UNIVERSITY OF GREAT FALLS
- Education—General M
- Human Services M
- Secondary Education M

UNIVERSITY OF GUAM
- Business Administration and Management—General M
- Counselor Education M
- Education—General M
- Educational Leadership and Administration M
- English as a Second Language M
- Reading Education M
- Secondary Education M
- Social Work M
- Special Education M

UNIVERSITY OF GUELPH
- Business Administration and Management—General M,D
- Hospitality Management M
- Organizational Management M

UNIVERSITY OF HARTFORD
- Accounting M,O
- Business Administration and Management—General M
- Counselor Education M,O
- Early Childhood Education M
- Education—General M,D,O
- Educational Leadership and Administration D,O
- Educational Media/Instructional Technology M
- Elementary Education M
- Music Education M,D,O
- Organizational Behavior M
- Taxation M,O

UNIVERSITY OF HAWAII AT HILO
- Education—General M
- Foreign Languages Education M,D

UNIVERSITY OF HAWAII AT MANOA
- Accounting M,D
- Business Administration and Management—General M
- Curriculum and Instruction M,D
- Early Childhood Education M
- Education—General M,D,O
- Educational Leadership and Administration M,D
- Educational Media/Instructional Technology M,D
- Educational Policy D
- Educational Psychology M,D
- English as a Second Language M,D,O
- Entrepreneurship M,O
- Finance and Banking M,D
- Foreign Languages Education M,D,O
- Foundations and Philosophy of Education M,D
- Human Resources Management M
- Information Studies M,O
- International Business M,D
- Kinesiology and Movement Studies M,D
- Law M,D,O
- Library Science M,O
- Management Information Systems M,D,O
- Marketing M,D
- Organizational Behavior M
- Organizational Management M,D
- Real Estate M
- Social Work M,D
- Special Education M,D
- Taxation M
- Travel and Tourism M

UNIVERSITY OF HOUSTON
- Accounting M,D
- Advertising and Public Relations M
- Business Administration and Management—General M,D
- Curriculum and Instruction M,D
- Education—General M,D
- Educational Leadership and Administration M,D
- Educational Psychology M,D
- Environmental Law M,D
- Exercise and Sports Science M,D
- Finance and Banking M
- Foundations and Philosophy of Education M,D
- Health Education M,D
- Health Law M,D
- Higher Education M,D
- Hospitality Management M
- Human Resources Development M
- Intellectual Property Law M,D
- Kinesiology and Movement Studies M,D
- Law M,D
- Logistics M
- Marketing D
- Music Education M,D
- Physical Education M,D
- Project Management M
- Social Work M,D
- Special Education M,D
- Supply Chain Management M
- Taxation M,D

UNIVERSITY OF HOUSTON–CLEAR LAKE
- Accounting M
- Business Administration and Management—General M
- Counselor Education M
- Curriculum and Instruction M
- Early Childhood Education M
- Education—General M,D
- Educational Leadership and Administration M,D
- Educational Media/Instructional Technology M
- Exercise and Sports Science M
- Finance and Banking M
- Foundations and Philosophy of Education M
- Human Resources Management M
- Library Science M
- Management Information Systems M
- Multilingual and Multicultural Education M
- Reading Education M

UNIVERSITY OF HOUSTON–DOWNTOWN
- Business Administration and Management—General M
- Curriculum and Instruction M
- Elementary Education M
- Entrepreneurship M
- Finance and Banking M
- Human Resources Management M
- Middle School Education M
- Nonprofit Management M
- Secondary Education M
- Supply Chain Management M
- Urban Education M

UNIVERSITY OF HOUSTON–VICTORIA
- Accounting M
- Adult Education M
- Business Administration and Management—General M
- Counselor Education M
- Curriculum and Instruction M
- Education—General M
- Educational Leadership and Administration M
- Entrepreneurship M
- Finance and Banking M
- Higher Education M
- International Business M
- Management Information Systems M
- Marketing M
- Special Education M

UNIVERSITY OF IDAHO
- Accounting M
- Agricultural Education M
- Art Education M
- Athletic Training and Sports Medicine M,D
- Business Administration and Management—General M,D
- Counselor Education M,O
- Curriculum and Instruction M,O
- Education—General M,D,O
- Educational Leadership and Administration M,O
- English as a Second Language M
- Entrepreneurship D
- Environmental Law D
- Human Services M,O
- Law D
- Physical Education M,D
- Recreation and Park Management M,D
- Special Education M,O
- Vocational and Technical Education M,O

UNIVERSITY OF ILLINOIS AT CHICAGO
- Accounting M
- Business Administration and Management—General M,D
- Computer Education D
- Curriculum and Instruction M,D
- Early Childhood Education M,D
- Education—General M,D
- Educational Leadership and Administration M,D
- Educational Measurement and Evaluation M,D
- Educational Policy M,D
- Educational Psychology M,D
- Elementary Education M,D
- English as a Second Language M
- English Education M,D
- Foreign Languages Education M,D
- Health Education M
- Kinesiology and Movement Studies M,D
- Management Information Systems M,D
- Mathematics Education M,D
- Multilingual and Multicultural Education M,D
- Reading Education M,D
- Real Estate M
- Science Education M,D
- Secondary Education M,D
- Social Sciences Education D
- Social Work M,D
- Special Education M,D
- Urban Education M,D

UNIVERSITY OF ILLINOIS AT SPRINGFIELD
- Accounting M
- Business Administration and Management—General M
- Education—General M,O
- Educational Leadership and Administration M,O
- English as a Second Language M,O
- English Education M,O
- Human Services M,O
- Legal and Justice Studies M
- Management Information Systems M

UNIVERSITY OF ILLINOIS AT URBANA–CHAMPAIGN
- Accounting M,D
- Actuarial Science M,D
- Advertising and Public Relations M
- Agricultural Education M
- Art Education M,D
- Business Administration and Management—General M,D
- Counselor Education M,D,O
- Curriculum and Instruction M,D,O
- Education of Students with Severe/Multiple Disabilities M,D,O
- Education—General M,D,O
- Educational Leadership and Administration M,D,O
- Educational Policy M,D,O
- Educational Psychology M,D,O
- English as a Second Language M,D
- Finance and Banking M,D
- Foreign Languages Education M,D
- Human Resources Development M,D,O
- Human Resources Management M,D,O
- Human Services M,D
- Information Studies M,D,O
- Kinesiology and Movement Studies M,D
- Law M,D
- Leisure Studies M,D
- Library Science M,D,O
- Management Strategy and Policy M,D,O
- Mathematics Education M,D
- Music Education M,D
- Science Education M,D
- Social Work M,D
- Special Education M,D,O
- Taxation M,D
- Vocational and Technical Education M,D,O

UNIVERSITY OF INDIANAPOLIS
- Art Education M
- Business Administration and Management—General M,O
- Curriculum and Instruction M
- Education—General M
- Educational Leadership and Administration M
- Elementary Education M
- English Education M
- Foreign Languages Education M
- Mathematics Education M
- Physical Education M
- Science Education M
- Secondary Education M
- Social Sciences Education M

THE UNIVERSITY OF IOWA
- Accounting M,D
- Actuarial Science M,D
- Art Education M,D
- Athletic Training and Sports Medicine M,D
- Business Administration and Management—General M,D
- Counselor Education M,D
- Developmental Education M,D
- Education—General M,D,O
- Educational Leadership and Administration M,D,O
- Educational Measurement and Evaluation M,D,O
- Educational Policy M,D,O
- Educational Psychology M,D,O
- Elementary Education M,D
- English as a Second Language M,D
- English Education M,D
- Exercise and Sports Science M,D
- Finance and Banking M,D
- Foreign Languages Education M,D
- Foundations and Philosophy of Education M,D,O
- Higher Education M,D
- Information Studies M,D
- Investment Management M
- Law M,D
- Leisure Studies M,D
- Library Science M,D
- Management Strategy and Policy M
- Marketing M,D
- Mathematics Education M,D
- Music Education M,D
- Quantitative Analysis M,D,O
- Recreation and Park Management M,D
- Science Education M,D
- Secondary Education M,D
- Social Sciences Education M,D
- Social Work M,D
- Special Education M,D
- Sports Management M,D
- Student Affairs M,D
- Supply Chain Management M

UNIVERSITY OF JAMESTOWN
- Curriculum and Instruction M
- Education—General M

THE UNIVERSITY OF KANSAS
- Accounting M
- Art Education M
- Business Administration and Management—General M,D
- Curriculum and Instruction M,D
- Education—General M,D,O
- Educational Leadership and Administration M,D
- Educational Measurement and Evaluation M,D
- Educational Media/Instructional Technology M,D
- Educational Policy D
- Educational Psychology M,D
- Facilities Management M,D,O
- Foundations and Philosophy of Education M,D
- Health Education M,D,O
- Higher Education M,D
- Law D
- Management Information Systems M
- Music Education M,D
- Organizational Management M,D,O
- Physical Education M,D
- Project Management M
- Social Work M,D
- Special Education M,D

UNIVERSITY OF KENTUCKY
- Accounting M
- Art Education M
- Athletic Training and Sports Medicine M
- Business Administration and Management—General M,D
- Curriculum and Instruction M,D
- Early Childhood Education M,D
- Education—General M,D,O
- Educational Leadership and Administration M,D,O
- Educational Measurement and Evaluation M,D
- Educational Media/Instructional Technology M,D
- Educational Policy M,D
- Educational Psychology D,O
- Elementary Education M,D
- Exercise and Sports Science M,D
- Foreign Languages Education M
- Higher Education M,D
- Hospitality Management M
- International Business M
- Kinesiology and Movement Studies M,D
- Law D
- Library Science M*
- Middle School Education M,D
- Music Education M,D
- Reading Education M,D
- Secondary Education M,D
- Social Work M,D
- Special Education M,D

UNIVERSITY OF LA VERNE
- Accounting M
- Business Administration and Management—General M,D,O
- Counselor Education M,D,O
- Education—General M,O
- Educational Leadership and Administration M,D,O
- Elementary Education M,D,O
- Finance and Banking M
- Human Resources Management M,O
- International Business M
- Law D
- Management Information Systems M,O
- Marketing M
- Nonprofit Management M,O
- Organizational Management M,D,O
- Reading Education M,O
- Secondary Education M,D,O
- Special Education M,D,O
- Supply Chain Management M

UNIVERSITY OF LETHBRIDGE
- Accounting M,D
- Business Administration and Management—General M,D
- Counselor Education M,D
- Education—General M,D
- Educational Leadership and Administration M,D
- Exercise and Sports Science M,D
- Finance and Banking M,D
- Foreign Languages Education M,D
- Human Resources Management M,D
- International Business M,D
- Kinesiology and Movement Studies M,D
- Management Information Systems M,D
- Management Strategy and Policy M,D

UNIVERSITY OF LOUISIANA AT LAFAYETTE
- Business Administration and Management—General M
- Counselor Education M
- Curriculum and Instruction M
- Education of the Gifted M
- Education—General M,D
- Educational Leadership and Administration M,D
- Music Education M

UNIVERSITY OF LOUISIANA AT MONROE
- Art Education M,D
- Business Administration and Management—General M
- Counselor Education M
- Curriculum and Instruction M,D
- Early Childhood Education M,D
- Education of the Gifted M,D
- Educational Leadership and Administration M,D
- Educational Measurement and Evaluation M,D
- Elementary Education M,D
- English as a Second Language M,D
- English Education M,D
- Exercise and Sports Science M
- Foreign Languages Education M,D
- Mathematics Education M,D
- Middle School Education M,D
- Music Education M,D
- Reading Education M,D
- Science Education M,D
- Secondary Education M
- Social Sciences Education M,D
- Special Education M,D

UNIVERSITY OF LOUISVILLE
- Accounting M
- Art Education M,D
- Business Administration and Management—General M
- Counselor Education M,D
- Curriculum and Instruction M,D
- Early Childhood Education M,D
- Education—General M,D,O

Educational Leadership and Administration M,D,O
Educational Psychology M,D,O
Elementary Education M,D
Entrepreneurship M,D
Exercise and Sports Science M
Health Education M,D
Higher Education M,D,O
Human Resources Development M,D,O
Human Resources Management M,D
International Business M
Law D
Logistics M,D,O
Middle School Education M,D
Music Education M,D
Nonprofit Management M,D
Physical Education M
Secondary Education M,D
Social Work M,D,O
Special Education M,D
Sports Management M
Student Affairs M,D
Supply Chain Management M,D,O

UNIVERSITY OF MAINE
Accounting M,O
Business Administration and Management—General M,O
Counselor Education M,D,O
Early Childhood Education M,D,O
Education—General M,D,O
Educational Leadership and Administration M,D,O
Educational Media/Instructional Technology M,D,O
Elementary Education M,D,O
English Education M
Exercise and Sports Science M,D,O
Finance and Banking M,O
Foreign Languages Education M
Higher Education M,D,O
International Business M,O
Kinesiology and Movement Studies M,D,O
Management Information Systems M,D,O
Mathematics Education M,D,O
Music Education M
Physical Education M,D,O
Reading Education M,D,O
Science Education M,D,O
Secondary Education M,D,O
Social Sciences Education M,D
Social Work M
Special Education M,D,O
Sustainability Management M,O

UNIVERSITY OF MAINE AT FARMINGTON
Early Childhood Education M
Education—General M
Educational Leadership and Administration M

UNIVERSITY OF MANAGEMENT AND TECHNOLOGY
Business Administration and Management—General M,D,O
Management Information Systems M,D,O
Project Management M,D,O

THE UNIVERSITY OF MANCHESTER
Accounting M,D
Actuarial Science M,D
Business Administration and Management—General M,D
Education—General M,D
Educational Psychology M,D
English as a Second Language M,D
Health Law M,D
Industrial and Manufacturing Management M,D
Law M,D
Social Work M,D

UNIVERSITY OF MANITOBA
Adult Education M
Archives/Archival Administration M,D
Business Administration and Management—General M,D
Counselor Education M
Curriculum and Instruction M
Education—General M,D
Educational Leadership and Administration M
Educational Psychology M
English as a Second Language M
English Education M
Foundations and Philosophy of Education M
Higher Education M
Kinesiology and Movement Studies M
Law M
Physical Education M
Recreation and Park Management M
Social Work M,D
Special Education M

UNIVERSITY OF MARY
Accounting M
Business Administration and Management—General M
Curriculum and Instruction M
Early Childhood Education M
Education—General M
Educational Leadership and Administration M
Higher Education M
Human Resources Management M
Management Strategy and Policy M
Project Management M
Reading Education M
Special Education M
Student Affairs M

UNIVERSITY OF MARY HARDIN-BAYLOR
Accounting M
Business Administration and Management—General M
Computer Education M
Counselor Education M
Curriculum and Instruction M,D
Education—General M,D
Educational Leadership and Administration M,D
Elementary Education M,D
Exercise and Sports Science M
Higher Education M,D
International Business M
Management Information Systems M
Secondary Education M,D
Sports Management M

UNIVERSITY OF MARYLAND, BALTIMORE
Law M,D
Social Work M,D

UNIVERSITY OF MARYLAND, BALTIMORE COUNTY
Art Education M
Distance Education Development M,O
Early Childhood Education M
Education—General M,O
Educational Media/Instructional Technology M,O
Educational Policy M,D
Elementary Education M
English as a Second Language M,O
English Education M
Foreign Languages Education M,O
Health Education M,O
Human Services M,D
Mathematics Education M
Multilingual and Multicultural Education M,O
Music Education M
Science Education M
Secondary Education M
Social Sciences Education M

UNIVERSITY OF MARYLAND, COLLEGE PARK
Advertising and Public Relations M,D
Business Administration and Management—General M,D
Counselor Education M,D,O
Curriculum and Instruction M,D,O
Education—General M,D,O
Educational Leadership and Administration M,D,O
Educational Measurement and Evaluation M,D
Educational Media/Instructional Technology M,D,O
English as a Second Language M,D,O
Foreign Languages Education D
Foundations and Philosophy of Education M,D,O
Health Education M,D
Information Studies M,D
Kinesiology and Movement Studies M,D
Law
Library Science
Music Education M,D
Quantitative Analysis M,D
Reading Education M,D,O
Real Estate M
Secondary Education M,D,O
Social Work
Student Affairs M,D,O

UNIVERSITY OF MARYLAND EASTERN SHORE
Counselor Education M
Education—General M
Educational Leadership and Administration D
Organizational Management D
Special Education M
Vocational and Technical Education M

UNIVERSITY OF MARYLAND UNIVERSITY COLLEGE
Accounting M,O
Business Administration and Management—General M,D,O
Distance Education Development M,O
Education—General M
Finance and Banking M,O
International Business M,O
Management Information Systems M,O

UNIVERSITY OF MARY WASHINGTON
Business Administration and Management—General M
Education—General M
Elementary Education M
Management Information Systems M

UNIVERSITY OF MASSACHUSETTS AMHERST
Accounting M,D
Art Education M
Business Administration and Management—General M,D
Counselor Education M,D,O
Early Childhood Education M,D,O
Education—General M,D,O
Educational Leadership and Administration M,D,O
Educational Measurement and Evaluation M,D,O
Educational Media/Instructional Technology M,D,O
Educational Policy M,D,O
Elementary Education M,D,O
English as a Second Language M,D,O
Entertainment Management
Entrepreneurship M,D
Finance and Banking M,D
Foreign Languages Education M
Health Education M,D
Higher Education M,D,O
Hospitality Management M,D
International and Comparative Education M,D,O
Kinesiology and Movement Studies M,D
Management Strategy and Policy M,D
Marketing M,D
Multilingual and Multicultural Education M,D,O
Music Education M,D
Organizational Management M,D
Reading Education M,D,O
Science Education M,D,O
Secondary Education M,D,O
Special Education M,D,O
Sports Management M,D
Travel and Tourism M,D

UNIVERSITY OF MASSACHUSETTS BOSTON
Archives/Archival Administration M
Business Administration and Management—General M
Counselor Education M,O
Curriculum and Instruction M
Education—General M,D,O
Educational Leadership and Administration M,D,O
Elementary Education M,D,O
English as a Second Language M
Foreign Languages Education M
Higher Education M,D,O
Human Services M
Multilingual and Multicultural Education M
Secondary Education M,D,O
Special Education M
Urban Education M,D,O

UNIVERSITY OF MASSACHUSETTS DARTMOUTH
Accounting M,O
Art Education M
Business Administration and Management—General M,O
Education—General D,O
Educational Leadership and Administration D
Finance and Banking M,O
International Business M,O
Law D
Marketing M,O
Mathematics Education D
Middle School Education O
Organizational Management M,O
Secondary Education O
Supply Chain Management M,O

UNIVERSITY OF MASSACHUSETTS LOWELL
Accounting M,D,O
Business Administration and Management—General M,D,O
Curriculum and Instruction M,D,O
Education—General M,D,O
Educational Leadership and Administration M,D,O
Entrepreneurship M,D,O
Finance and Banking M,D,O
Legal and Justice Studies M,D,O
Mathematics Education M,D,O
Music Education M
Reading Education M,D,O
Science Education M,D,O
Supply Chain Management M,D,O

UNIVERSITY OF MEMPHIS
Accounting M,D
Adult Education M,D
Business Administration and Management—General M,D
Counselor Education M,D
Curriculum and Instruction M,D
Early Childhood Education M,D
Education—General M,D,O
Educational Leadership and Administration M,D
Educational Measurement and Evaluation M,D
Educational Media/Instructional Technology M,D
Educational Psychology M,D
Elementary Education M,D
English as a Second Language M,D,O
Exercise and Sports Science M
Finance and Banking M,D
Higher Education M,D
International Business M,D
Law D
Leisure Studies M
Management Information Systems M,D
Marketing M,D
Middle School Education M,D
Music Education M,D
Nonprofit Management M
Physical Education M
Reading Education M,D
Real Estate M,D
Secondary Education M,D
Special Education M,D
Supply Chain Management M,D
Taxation M

UNIVERSITY OF MIAMI
Accounting M
Advertising and Public Relations M,D
Athletic Training and Sports Medicine M,D
Business Administration and Management—General M
Counselor Education M,O
Early Childhood Education M,O
Education—General M,D,O
Educational Measurement and Evaluation M,D
Exercise and Sports Science M,D
Finance and Banking M
Higher Education M,D,O
International Business M
Law M,D,O
Management Information Systems M
Marketing M
Mathematics Education D
Multilingual and Multicultural Education D
Music Education M,D,O
Reading Education D
Real Estate M,D,O
Science Education D
Special Education M,D,O
Sports Management M
Taxation M,D,O

UNIVERSITY OF MICHIGAN
Accounting M,D
Archives/Archival Administration M,D
Business Administration and Management—General M,D
Education—General M,D
Educational Media/Instructional Technology M,D
English Education D
Foreign Languages Education M,D
Health Education M,D
Information Studies M,D
Kinesiology and Movement Studies M,D
Law M,D
Library Science M,D
Music Education M,D,O
Real Estate M,O
Social Work M,D
Sports Management M,D
Supply Chain Management M,D
Taxation M,D

UNIVERSITY OF MICHIGAN–DEARBORN
Accounting M
Business Administration and Management—General M
Curriculum and Instruction D
Early Childhood Education M
Education—General M,D
Educational Leadership and Administration M,D
Educational Media/Instructional Technology M
Finance and Banking M
Human Resources Management M
International Business M
Investment Management M
Management Information Systems M
Management Strategy and Policy M
Marketing M
Project Management M
Science Education M
Special Education M
Supply Chain Management M
Taxation M
Urban Education D

UNIVERSITY OF MICHIGAN–FLINT
Accounting M,O
Business Administration and Management—General M,O
Curriculum and Instruction M,D,O
Early Childhood Education M
Education—General M,D,O
Educational Leadership and Administration M,D,O
Educational Media/Instructional Technology M
Elementary Education M
Finance and Banking M,O
Health Education M
Industrial and Manufacturing Management M,O
International Business M,O
Management Information Systems M,O
Marketing M,O
Nonprofit Management M
Organizational Management M,O
Reading Education M
Secondary Education M,D,O
Special Education M

UNIVERSITY OF MINNESOTA, DULUTH
Business Administration and Management—General M
Education—General D
Music Education M
Social Work M

UNIVERSITY OF MINNESOTA, TWIN CITIES CAMPUS
Accounting M,D
Adult Education M,D,O
Agricultural Education M,D
Art Education M,D,O
Business Administration and Management—General M,D
Business Education M,D
Counselor Education M,D,O
Curriculum and Instruction M,D,O
Early Childhood Education M,D,O
Education of the Gifted M,D,O
Education—General M,D,O
Educational Leadership and Administration M,D

*M—masters degree; D—doctorate; O—other advanced degree; *—Close-Up and/or Display*

Educational Measurement and Evaluation	M,D
Educational Media/Instructional Technology	M,D,O
Educational Policy	M,D,O
Educational Psychology	M,D,O
Elementary Education	M,D,O
English as a Second Language	M
English Education	M
Entrepreneurship	D
Environmental Education	M,D,O
Exercise and Sports Science	M,D,O
Finance and Banking	M,D
Foreign Languages Education	M
Foundations and Philosophy of Education	M,D,O
Higher Education	M,D,O
Human Resources Development	M,D,O
Human Resources Management	M,D
Industrial and Manufacturing Management	D
International and Comparative Education	M,D
Kinesiology and Movement Studies	M,D,O
Law	M,D
Leisure Studies	M,D
Management Information Systems	M,D
Management Strategy and Policy	D
Marketing	M,D
Mathematics Education	M
Multilingual and Multicultural Education	M
Physical Education	M,D,O
Quantitative Analysis	M,D,O
Reading Education	M,D,O
Recreation and Park Management	M,D
Science Education	M
Social Sciences Education	M
Social Work	M,D
Special Education	M,D,O
Sports Management	M,D,O
Student Affairs	M,D,O
Supply Chain Management	M
Taxation	M
Travel and Tourism	M,D
Vocational and Technical Education	M,D,O

UNIVERSITY OF MISSISSIPPI

Accounting	M,D
Art Education	M
Business Administration and Management—General	M,D
Counselor Education	M,D,O
Curriculum and Instruction	M,D,O
Education—General	M,D,O
Educational Leadership and Administration	M,D,O
Elementary Education	M,D,O
Exercise and Sports Science	M,D
Health Education	M,D
Higher Education	M,D,O
Kinesiology and Movement Studies	M,D
Law	M,D
Legal and Justice Studies	M
Leisure Studies	M,D
Management Information Systems	M,D
Reading Education	M,D,O
Recreation and Park Management	M,D
Secondary Education	M,D,O
Social Work	M
Special Education	M,D,O
Student Affairs	M,D,O
Taxation	M,D

UNIVERSITY OF MISSOURI

Accounting	M,D,O
Adult Education	M,D,O
Agricultural Education	M,D,O
Art Education	M,D,O
Business Administration and Management—General	M,D
Business Education	M,D,O
Curriculum and Instruction	M,D,O
Early Childhood Education	M,D,O
Education of the Gifted	M,D
Education—General	M,D,O
Educational Leadership and Administration	M,D,O
Educational Media/Instructional Technology	M,D,O
Educational Psychology	M,D,O
Elementary Education	M,D,O
English Education	M,D,O
Exercise and Sports Science	M,D
Finance and Banking	M,D
Foreign Languages Education	M,D,O
Health Education	M,D,O
Higher Education	M,D,O
Hospitality Management	M,D
Information Studies	M,D,O
Law	M,D
Library Science	M,D,O
Marketing	M,D
Mathematics Education	M,D,O
Music Education	M,D,O
Nonprofit Management	M,D,O
Organizational Management	M,D,O
Reading Education	M,D,O
Recreation and Park Management	M
Science Education	M,D,O
Social Sciences Education	M,D,O
Social Work	M,D,O
Special Education	M,D
Taxation	M,D,O
Vocational and Technical Education	M,D,O

UNIVERSITY OF MISSOURI–KANSAS CITY

Accounting	M,D
Business Administration and Management—General	M,D
Counselor Education	M,D,O
Curriculum and Instruction	M,D,O
Education—General	M,D,O
Educational Leadership and Administration	M,D,O
Entrepreneurship	M,D
Finance and Banking	M,D
Health Education	M,D
Higher Education	M,D,O
Law	M,D
Music Education	M,D
Reading Education	M,D,O
Real Estate	M,D
Social Work	M
Special Education	M,D,O
Taxation	M,D

UNIVERSITY OF MISSOURI–ST. LOUIS

Accounting	M,D,O
Adult Education	M,D,O
Business Administration and Management—General	M,D,O
Counselor Education	M,D
Curriculum and Instruction	M,O
Early Childhood Education	M,O
Education—General	M,D,O
Educational Leadership and Administration	M,D,O
Educational Measurement and Evaluation	M,O
Educational Psychology	D
Elementary Education	M,O
English as a Second Language	M,O
Finance and Banking	M,D,O
Higher Education	M,D,O
Human Resources Development	M,O
Human Resources Management	M,D,O
Industrial and Manufacturing Management	M,D,O
Logistics	M,D,O
Management Information Systems	M,D,O
Management Strategy and Policy	M,D,O
Marketing	M,D,O
Middle School Education	M,O
Music Education	M
Nonprofit Management	M,O
Reading Education	M,O
Secondary Education	M,O
Social Work	M,O
Special Education	M,O
Supply Chain Management	M,D,O

UNIVERSITY OF MOBILE

Business Administration and Management—General	M
Education—General	M

THE UNIVERSITY OF MONTANA

Accounting	M
Business Administration and Management—General	M
Counselor Education	M,D,O
Curriculum and Instruction	M,D
Education—General	M,D,O
Educational Leadership and Administration	M,D,O
English Education	M
Exercise and Sports Science	M
Health Education	M
Law	D
Mathematics Education	M,D
Music Education	M
Physical Education	M
Recreation and Park Management	M,D
Social Work	M

UNIVERSITY OF MONTEVALLO

Business Administration and Management—General	M
Counselor Education	M
Education—General	M,O
Educational Leadership and Administration	M,O
Elementary Education	M
Secondary Education	M

UNIVERSITY OF MOUNT UNION

Educational Leadership and Administration	M

UNIVERSITY OF NEBRASKA AT KEARNEY

Accounting	M
Art Education	M
Business Administration and Management—General	M
Counselor Education	M,O
Curriculum and Instruction	M
Early Childhood Education	M
Education of the Gifted	M
Education—General	M,O
Educational Leadership and Administration	M,O
Educational Media/Instructional Technology	M
Elementary Education	M
English as a Second Language	M
Exercise and Sports Science	M
Foreign Languages Education	M
Human Resources Management	M
Human Services	M
Leisure Studies	M
Library Science	M
Management Information Systems	M
Marketing	M
Mathematics Education	M
Music Education	M
Physical Education	M
Reading Education	M
Science Education	M
Secondary Education	M
Special Education	M,O
Sports Management	M
Student Affairs	M,O

UNIVERSITY OF NEBRASKA AT OMAHA

Accounting	M
Athletic Training and Sports Medicine	M,D
Business Administration and Management—General	M,O
Counselor Education	M
Education—General	M,D,O
Educational Leadership and Administration	M,D,O
Elementary Education	M
English as a Second Language	M,O
Exercise and Sports Science	M,D
Foreign Languages Education	M
Health Education	M,D
Human Resources Development	M,O
Management Information Systems	M,D,O
Physical Education	M,D
Project Management	M,D,O
Reading Education	M
Recreation and Park Management	M,D
Secondary Education	M
Social Work	M
Special Education	M
Urban Education	M,O

UNIVERSITY OF NEBRASKA–LINCOLN

Accounting	M,D
Actuarial Science	M
Adult Education	M,D,O
Advertising and Public Relations	M,D
Agricultural Education	M
Business Administration and Management—General	M,D
Curriculum and Instruction	M,D,O
Early Childhood Education	M,D
Educational Leadership and Administration	M,D,O
Educational Measurement and Evaluation	M,D,O
Educational Psychology	M,D,O
Exercise and Sports Science	M,D
Finance and Banking	M,D
Home Economics Education	M,D
Law	M,D
Legal and Justice Studies	M
Management Information Systems	M
Marketing	M,D
Music Education	M,D
Special Education	M,D,O
Vocational and Technical Education	M,D,O

UNIVERSITY OF NEVADA, LAS VEGAS

Accounting	M,O
Business Administration and Management—General	M,O
Counselor Education	M,D,O
Curriculum and Instruction	M,D,O
Early Childhood Education	M,D,O
Education—General	M,D,O
Educational Leadership and Administration	M,D,O
Educational Media/Instructional Technology	M,D,O
Educational Psychology	M,D,O
Entrepreneurship	M,O
Exercise and Sports Science	M,D
Higher Education	M,D,O
Hospitality Management	M,D
Human Resources Development	M,D,O
Kinesiology and Movement Studies	M,D
Law	D
Management Information Systems	M,O
Nonprofit Management	M,D,O
Organizational Management	M,D,O
Social Work	M,O
Special Education	M,D,O

UNIVERSITY OF NEVADA, RENO

Accounting	M
Business Administration and Management—General	M
Counselor Education	M,D,O
Curriculum and Instruction	D
Education—General	M,D,O
Educational Leadership and Administration	M,D,O
Educational Psychology	M,D,O
Elementary Education	M
English as a Second Language	M
Finance and Banking	M
Foreign Languages Education	M
Legal and Justice Studies	M,D
Management Information Systems	M
Mathematics Education	M
Reading Education	M,D
Secondary Education	M
Social Work	M
Special Education	M,D

UNIVERSITY OF NEW BRUNSWICK FREDERICTON

Business Administration and Management—General	M
Education—General	M,D
Entrepreneurship	M
Exercise and Sports Science	M
Marketing	M,D
Physical Education	M
Recreation and Park Management	M
Sports Management	M

UNIVERSITY OF NEW BRUNSWICK SAINT JOHN

Business Administration and Management—General	M
Electronic Commerce	M
International Business	M

UNIVERSITY OF NEW ENGLAND

Curriculum and Instruction	M,O
Education—General	M,O
Educational Leadership and Administration	M,D,O
Educational Measurement and Evaluation	M,O
Health Education	M,O
Reading Education	M,O
Social Work	M
Special Education	M,O
Vocational and Technical Education	M,O

UNIVERSITY OF NEW HAMPSHIRE

Accounting	M
Business Administration and Management—General	M,O
Counselor Education	M,O
Early Childhood Education	M,O
Education—General	M,D,O
Educational Leadership and Administration	M,O
Elementary Education	M
English Education	M,D
Environmental Education	M
Higher Education	M,O
Kinesiology and Movement Studies	M,O
Law	M,D,O
Legal and Justice Studies	M,O
Logistics	M,D
Management Information Systems	M,O
Mathematics Education	M,D,O
Physical Education	M,O
Recreation and Park Management	M
Science Education	M,D
Secondary Education	M,O
Social Work	M,O
Special Education	M,O
Sustainability Management	M,O

UNIVERSITY OF NEW HAVEN

Accounting	M,O
Business Administration and Management—General	M,O
Education—General	M
Facilities Management	M,O
Finance and Banking	M,O
Higher Education	M,O
Human Resources Management	M,O
Industrial and Manufacturing Management	M,O
International Business	M,O
Management Strategy and Policy	M,O
Marketing	M,O
Organizational Management	M,O
Science Education	M,O
Sports Management	M,O
Taxation	M,O

UNIVERSITY OF NEW MEXICO

Accounting	M
Art Education	M
Business Administration and Management—General	M
Counselor Education	M,D
Curriculum and Instruction	O
Early Childhood Education	D
Education—General	M,D,O
Educational Leadership and Administration	M,D,O
Educational Media/Instructional Technology	M,D,O
Educational Psychology	M,D
Elementary Education	M
English as a Second Language	M,D
English Education	M,D
Entrepreneurship	M
Exercise and Sports Science	M,D
Finance and Banking	M
Foundations and Philosophy of Education	M,D
Health Education	M
Higher Education	O
Human Resources Management	M
International Business	M
Law	D
Management Information Systems	M
Management Strategy and Policy	M
Marketing	M
Multilingual and Multicultural Education	M,D
Music Education	M
Organizational Management	M
Physical Education	M,D
Quantitative Analysis	D
Reading Education	M,D
Science Education	O
Secondary Education	M
Special Education	M,D,O
Sports Management	M,D
Taxation	M

UNIVERSITY OF NEW ORLEANS

Accounting	M
Business Administration and Management—General	M
Counselor Education	M,D
Curriculum and Instruction	M,D
Education—General	M,D
Educational Leadership and Administration	M,D
Finance and Banking	M,D
Hospitality Management	M
Special Education	M,D
Taxation	M
Travel and Tourism	M

UNIVERSITY OF NORTH ALABAMA

Accounting	M
Business Administration and Management—General	M
Counselor Education	M
Education—General	M,O
Educational Leadership and Administration	M,O
Elementary Education	M,O
Exercise and Sports Science	M
Finance and Banking	M
Kinesiology and Movement Studies	M
Management Information Systems	M
Physical Education	M
Project Management	M
Secondary Education	M
Special Education	M

THE UNIVERSITY OF NORTH CAROLINA AT CHAPEL HILL
- Accounting M,D
- Athletic Training and Sports Medicine M
- Business Administration and Management—General M,D
- Counselor Education M
- Curriculum and Instruction M,D
- Early Childhood Education M,D
- Education—General M,D
- Educational Leadership and Administration M,D
- Educational Measurement and Evaluation M,D
- Educational Psychology M,D
- English as a Second Language M
- English Education M
- Exercise and Sports Science M
- Finance and Banking D
- Foreign Languages Education M
- Information Studies M,D,O
- Kinesiology and Movement Studies M,D
- Law D
- Library Science M,D,O
- Management Information Systems D
- Management Strategy and Policy D
- Marketing D
- Mathematics Education M
- Music Education M
- Organizational Behavior D
- Physical Education M
- Reading Education M,D
- Science Education M
- Secondary Education M
- Social Sciences Education M
- Social Work M,D
- Sports Management M

THE UNIVERSITY OF NORTH CAROLINA AT CHARLOTTE
- Accounting M
- Advertising and Public Relations M,O
- Art Education M,O
- Business Administration and Management—General M,D,O
- Counselor Education M,D,O
- Curriculum and Instruction M,D,O
- Education of the Gifted M,D,O
- Educational Leadership and Administration M,D,O
- Educational Media/Instructional Technology M,D,O
- Elementary Education M
- English as a Second Language M,O
- English Education M,O
- Exercise and Sports Science M,O
- Facilities Management M
- Finance and Banking M,O
- Foreign Languages Education M,O
- Industrial and Manufacturing Management M,D,O
- Kinesiology and Movement Studies M,O
- Logistics M,D,O
- Management Information Systems M,D,O
- Mathematics Education M,D
- Middle School Education M,D,O
- Music Education M,O
- Nonprofit Management M,O
- Reading Education M
- Real Estate M,D,O
- Secondary Education M,D,O
- Social Sciences Education M
- Social Work M
- Special Education M,D,O
- Supply Chain Management M,D,O

THE UNIVERSITY OF NORTH CAROLINA AT GREENSBORO
- Accounting M,O
- Adult Education M,D,O
- Business Administration and Management—General M,O
- Counselor Education M,D,O
- Curriculum and Instruction M,D,O
- Early Childhood Education M,D,O
- Education—General M,D,O
- Educational Leadership and Administration M,D,O
- Educational Measurement and Evaluation D
- Educational Media/Instructional Technology M,D,O
- Elementary Education D
- English as a Second Language M,D,O
- English Education M,D
- Exercise and Sports Science M,D
- Finance and Banking M,O
- Foreign Languages Education M,D,O
- Higher Education D
- Information Studies M
- Library Science M
- Management Information Systems M,D,O
- Marketing M,D
- Mathematics Education M,D,O
- Middle School Education M,D,O
- Multilingual and Multicultural Education M,D,O
- Music Education M,D
- Nonprofit Management M,O
- Reading Education M,D,O
- Recreation and Park Management M
- Science Education M,D,O
- Social Sciences Education M,D,O
- Social Work M
- Special Education M,D,O
- Supply Chain Management M,D,O

THE UNIVERSITY OF NORTH CAROLINA AT PEMBROKE
- Art Education M
- Business Administration and Management—General M
- Counselor Education M
- Education—General M
- Educational Leadership and Administration M
- Elementary Education M
- English Education M
- Kinesiology and Movement Studies M
- Mathematics Education M
- Middle School Education M
- Music Education M
- Physical Education M
- Reading Education M
- Science Education M
- Social Sciences Education M
- Social Work M

THE UNIVERSITY OF NORTH CAROLINA WILMINGTON
- Accounting M
- Business Administration and Management—General M
- Early Childhood Education M
- Education—General M,D
- Educational Leadership and Administration M,D
- Educational Media/Instructional Technology M
- Elementary Education M
- Environmental Education M
- Middle School Education M
- Reading Education M
- Secondary Education M
- Social Work M
- Special Education M

UNIVERSITY OF NORTH DAKOTA
- Accounting M
- Business Administration and Management—General M
- Early Childhood Education M
- Education—General M,D,O
- Educational Leadership and Administration M,D,O
- Educational Measurement and Evaluation D
- Educational Media/Instructional Technology M
- Elementary Education M,D
- Kinesiology and Movement Studies M
- Law D
- Music Education M,D
- Reading Education M
- Secondary Education D
- Social Work M
- Special Education M,D

UNIVERSITY OF NORTHERN BRITISH COLUMBIA
- Education—General M,D,O
- Social Work M,D,O

UNIVERSITY OF NORTHERN COLORADO
- Accounting M
- Counselor Education M,D
- Early Childhood Education M,D
- Education of the Gifted M,D
- Education—General M,D,O
- Educational Leadership and Administration M,D,O
- Educational Measurement and Evaluation M,D
- Educational Media/Instructional Technology M,D
- Educational Psychology M,D
- Exercise and Sports Science M,D
- Foreign Languages Education M
- Health Education M
- Higher Education D
- Library Science M
- Mathematics Education M,D
- Music Education M,D
- Physical Education M,D
- Reading Education M
- Science Education M,D
- Special Education M,D
- Sports Management M,D
- Student Affairs D

UNIVERSITY OF NORTHERN IOWA
- Accounting M
- Actuarial Science M
- Art Education M
- Athletic Training and Sports Medicine M
- Business Administration and Management—General M
- Community College Education M
- Counselor Education M
- Curriculum and Instruction D
- Early Childhood Education M
- Education—General M,D,O
- Educational Leadership and Administration M,D
- Educational Measurement and Evaluation M
- Educational Media/Instructional Technology M
- Educational Psychology M
- Elementary Education M
- English as a Second Language M
- English Education M
- Foreign Languages Education M
- Health Education M
- Higher Education M
- Human Services M,D
- Kinesiology and Movement Studies M,D
- Mathematics Education M
- Middle School Education M
- Music Education M
- Nonprofit Management M
- Physical Education M
- Reading Education M
- Science Education M
- Secondary Education M
- Social Work M
- Special Education M,D
- Student Affairs M
- Vocational and Technical Education M,D

UNIVERSITY OF NORTH FLORIDA
- Accounting M
- Adult Education M
- Business Administration and Management—General M
- Counselor Education M,D
- Education—General M,D
- Educational Leadership and Administration M,D
- Educational Media/Instructional Technology M,D
- Electronic Commerce M
- Elementary Education M
- English as a Second Language M
- Exercise and Sports Science M,D
- Finance and Banking M
- Human Resources Management M
- International Business M
- Logistics M
- Management Information Systems M
- Nonprofit Management M,O
- Reading Education M
- Secondary Education M
- Special Education M
- Sports Management M,D

UNIVERSITY OF NORTH GEORGIA
- Art Education M,O
- Business Administration and Management—General M
- Early Childhood Education M,O
- Education—General M,O
- Educational Leadership and Administration M,O
- English Education M,O
- Mathematics Education M,O
- Middle School Education M,O
- Physical Education M,O
- Secondary Education M,O
- Social Sciences Education M,O

UNIVERSITY OF NORTH TEXAS
- Accounting M,D,O
- Advertising and Public Relations M,D,O
- Art Education M,D,O
- Business Administration and Management—General M,D,O
- Counselor Education M,D,O
- Curriculum and Instruction M,D,O
- Early Childhood Education M,D,O
- Education of the Gifted M,D,O
- Education—General M,D,O
- Educational Leadership and Administration M,D,O
- Educational Measurement and Evaluation M,D,O
- Educational Media/Instructional Technology M,D,O
- Educational Psychology M,D,O
- Finance and Banking M,D,O
- Higher Education M,D,O
- Hospitality Management M,D,O
- Human Resources Management M,D,O
- Industrial and Manufacturing Management M,D,O
- Kinesiology and Movement Studies M,D,O
- Library Science M,D,O
- Logistics M,D,O
- Management Information Systems M,D,O
- Management Strategy and Policy M,D,O
- Marketing M,D,O
- Music Education M,D,O
- Nonprofit Management M,D,O
- Quantitative Analysis M,D,O
- Reading Education M,D,O
- Recreation and Park Management M,D,O
- Special Education M,D,O
- Sports Management M,D,O
- Supply Chain Management M,D,O
- Taxation M,D,O
- Travel and Tourism M,D,O
- Vocational and Technical Education M,D,O

UNIVERSITY OF NORTH TEXAS HEALTH SCIENCE CENTER AT FORT WORTH
- Science Education M,D

UNIVERSITY OF NORTHWESTERN–ST. PAUL
- Business Administration and Management—General M
- Education—General M
- Human Services M
- Organizational Management M,O

UNIVERSITY OF NOTRE DAME
- Accounting M
- Business Administration and Management—General M
- Education—General M
- Law M,D
- Nonprofit Management M
- Taxation M

UNIVERSITY OF OKLAHOMA
- Accounting M,D
- Adult Education M,D
- Archives/Archival Administration M,O
- Business Administration and Management—General M,D*
- Curriculum and Instruction M,D,O
- Early Childhood Education M,D,O
- Education—General M,D,O
- Educational Leadership and Administration M,D,O
- Educational Measurement and Evaluation M,D
- Educational Media/Instructional Technology M,D
- Educational Psychology M,D
- Elementary Education M,D,O
- English Education M,D,O
- Exercise and Sports Science M,D
- Higher Education M,D,O
- Human Resources Management M,O
- Human Services M,O
- Information Studies M,O
- Law M,D
- Library Science M,O
- Management Information Systems M,D,O
- Mathematics Education M,D,O
- Multilingual and Multicultural Education M,D,O
- Music Education M,D
- Nonprofit Management M
- Organizational Behavior M
- Project Management M
- Reading Education M,D,O
- Science Education M,D,O
- Secondary Education M,D,O
- Social Sciences Education M,D,O
- Social Work M
- Special Education M,D

UNIVERSITY OF OKLAHOMA HEALTH SCIENCES CENTER
- Health Education D
- Reading Education M,D,O
- Special Education M,D,O

UNIVERSITY OF OREGON
- Accounting M,D
- Business Administration and Management—General M,D
- Education—General M,D
- Finance and Banking D
- Law M,D
- Management Information Systems M
- Marketing D
- Music Education M,D
- Quantitative Analysis M

UNIVERSITY OF OTTAWA
- Business Administration and Management—General M*
- Education—General M,D,O
- Electronic Commerce M,D,O
- Finance and Banking D,O
- Kinesiology and Movement Studies M
- Law M,D
- Music Education M,O
- Project Management M,O
- Social Work M

UNIVERSITY OF PENNSYLVANIA
- Accounting M,D
- Business Administration and Management—General M,D
- Education—General M,D,O*
- Educational Leadership and Administration M,D
- Educational Measurement and Evaluation M,D
- Educational Media/Instructional Technology M
- Educational Policy M,D
- Elementary Education M
- English as a Second Language M,D
- English Education M,D
- Entrepreneurship M
- Finance and Banking M,D
- Foundations and Philosophy of Education M,D
- Higher Education M,D
- Insurance M,D
- International and Comparative Education M
- International Business M
- Law M,D
- Legal and Justice Studies M,D
- Management Information Systems M,D
- Marketing M,D
- Multilingual and Multicultural Education M
- Nonprofit Management M,O
- Organizational Management M,O
- Reading Education M
- Real Estate M,D
- Science Education M,O
- Secondary Education M
- Social Work M,D*
- Urban Education M

UNIVERSITY OF PHOENIX–ATLANTA CAMPUS
- Accounting M
- Business Administration and Management—General M
- Human Resources Management M
- International Business M
- Management Information Systems M
- Marketing M

UNIVERSITY OF PHOENIX–AUGUSTA CAMPUS
- Accounting M
- Business Administration and Management—General M
- Human Resources Management M
- International Business M
- Management Information Systems M
- Marketing M

UNIVERSITY OF PHOENIX–AUSTIN CAMPUS
- Accounting M

*M—masters degree; D—doctorate; O—other advanced degree; *—Close-Up and/or Display*

Business Administration and
    Management—General   M
Curriculum and Instruction   M
Education—General   M
Electronic Commerce   M
Human Resources Management   M
International Business   M
Management Information Systems   M
Marketing   M

UNIVERSITY OF PHOENIX–BAY AREA CAMPUS

Accounting   M,D
Adult Education   M,D,O
Business Administration and
    Management—General   M,D
Early Childhood Education   M,D,O
Education—General   M,D,O
Educational Leadership and
    Administration   M,D,O
Elementary Education   M,D,O
Higher Education   M,D,O
Human Resources Management   M,D
International Business   M,D
Management Information Systems   M,D
Marketing   M,D
Organizational Management   M,D
Project Management   M,D
Secondary Education   M,D,O
Special Education   M,D,O

UNIVERSITY OF PHOENIX–BIRMINGHAM CAMPUS

Accounting   M
Business Administration and
    Management—General   M
Human Resources Management   M
International Business   M
Management Information Systems   M
Marketing   M

UNIVERSITY OF PHOENIX–BOSTON CAMPUS

Business Administration and
    Management—General   M
International Business   M
Management Information Systems   M

UNIVERSITY OF PHOENIX–CENTRAL MASSACHUSETTS CAMPUS

Business Administration and
    Management—General   M
Education—General   M

UNIVERSITY OF PHOENIX–CENTRAL VALLEY CAMPUS

Accounting   M
Business Administration and
    Management—General   M
Computer Education   M
Curriculum and Instruction   M
Education—General   M
Elementary Education   M
Human Resources Management   M
International Business   M
Management Information Systems   M
Marketing   M
Secondary Education   M

UNIVERSITY OF PHOENIX–CHARLOTTE CAMPUS

Accounting   M
Business Administration and
    Management—General   M
Health Education   M
International Business   M
Management Information Systems   M

UNIVERSITY OF PHOENIX–CHATTANOOGA CAMPUS

Accounting   M
Business Administration and
    Management—General   M
Curriculum and Instruction   M
Education—General   M
Educational Leadership and
    Administration   M
Elementary Education   M
Human Resources Management   M
International Business   M
Management Information Systems   M
Marketing   M
Secondary Education   M

UNIVERSITY OF PHOENIX–CHEYENNE CAMPUS

Business Administration and
    Management—General   M
Human Resources Management   M
International Business   M
Management Information Systems   M
Marketing   M

UNIVERSITY OF PHOENIX–CHICAGO CAMPUS

Business Administration and
    Management—General   M
Electronic Commerce   M
Human Resources Management   M
International Business   M
Management Information Systems   M

UNIVERSITY OF PHOENIX–CINCINNATI CAMPUS

Accounting   M
Business Administration and
    Management—General   M
Electronic Commerce   M
Human Resources Management   M
International Business   M
Management Information Systems   M
Marketing   M

UNIVERSITY OF PHOENIX–CLEVELAND CAMPUS

Accounting   M

Business Administration and
    Management—General   M
Human Resources Management   M
International Business   M
Management Information Systems   M
Marketing   M

UNIVERSITY OF PHOENIX–COLUMBIA CAMPUS

Business Administration and
    Management—General   M

UNIVERSITY OF PHOENIX–COLUMBUS GEORGIA CAMPUS

Accounting   M
Business Administration and
    Management—General   M
Electronic Commerce   M
Human Resources Management   M
International Business   M
Management Information Systems   M
Marketing   M

UNIVERSITY OF PHOENIX–COLUMBUS OHIO CAMPUS

Accounting   M
Business Administration and
    Management—General   M
Human Resources Management   M
International Business   M
Management Information Systems   M
Marketing   M

UNIVERSITY OF PHOENIX–DALLAS CAMPUS

Accounting   M
Business Administration and
    Management—General   M
Curriculum and Instruction   M
Education—General   M
Electronic Commerce   M
Human Resources Management   M
International Business   M
Management Information Systems   M
Marketing   M

UNIVERSITY OF PHOENIX–DENVER CAMPUS

Accounting   M
Business Administration and
    Management—General   M
Curriculum and Instruction   M
Education—General   M
Educational Leadership and
    Administration   M
Electronic Commerce   M
Elementary Education   M
Human Resources Management   M
International Business   M
Management Information Systems   M
Marketing   M
Secondary Education   M

UNIVERSITY OF PHOENIX–DES MOINES CAMPUS

Accounting   M
Business Administration and
    Management—General   M
Health Education   M,D
Human Resources Management   M
International Business   M
Management Information Systems   M
Marketing   M

UNIVERSITY OF PHOENIX–EASTERN WASHINGTON CAMPUS

Accounting   M
Business Administration and
    Management—General   M
Human Resources Management   M
Management Information Systems   M
Marketing   M

UNIVERSITY OF PHOENIX–HAWAII CAMPUS

Accounting   M
Business Administration and
    Management—General   M
Curriculum and Instruction   M
Education—General   M
Educational Leadership and
    Administration   M
Elementary Education   M
Human Resources Management   M
International Business   M
Management Information Systems   M
Marketing   M
Secondary Education   M
Special Education   M

UNIVERSITY OF PHOENIX–HOUSTON CAMPUS

Accounting   M
Business Administration and
    Management—General   M
Curriculum and Instruction   M
Education—General   M
Electronic Commerce   M
Human Resources Management   M
International Business   M
Management Information Systems   M
Marketing   M

UNIVERSITY OF PHOENIX–IDAHO CAMPUS

Accounting   M
Business Administration and
    Management—General   M
Curriculum and Instruction   M
Education—General   M
Educational Leadership and
    Administration   M
Elementary Education   M
Human Resources Management   M
International Business   M
Management Information Systems

Marketing   M
Secondary Education   M

UNIVERSITY OF PHOENIX–INDIANAPOLIS CAMPUS

Accounting   M
Business Administration and
    Management—General   M
Education—General   M
Elementary Education   M
Human Resources Management   M
International Business   M
Management Information Systems   M
Marketing   M
Secondary Education   M

UNIVERSITY OF PHOENIX–JERSEY CITY CAMPUS

Accounting   M
Business Administration and
    Management—General   M
Human Resources Management   M
International Business   M
Management Information Systems   M
Marketing   M

UNIVERSITY OF PHOENIX–KANSAS CITY CAMPUS

Accounting   M
Business Administration and
    Management—General   M
Education—General   M
Educational Leadership and
    Administration   M
Human Resources Management   M
International Business   M
Marketing   M

UNIVERSITY OF PHOENIX–LAS VEGAS CAMPUS

Accounting   M
Business Administration and
    Management—General   M
Counselor Education   M
Curriculum and Instruction   M
Education—General   M
Educational Leadership and
    Administration   M
Elementary Education   M
Human Resources Management   M
International Business   M
Management Information Systems   M
Marketing   M

UNIVERSITY OF PHOENIX–LITTLE ROCK CAMPUS

Business Administration and
    Management—General   M

UNIVERSITY OF PHOENIX–LOUISIANA CAMPUS

Accounting   M
Business Administration and
    Management—General   M
Curriculum and Instruction   M
Early Childhood Education   M
Education—General   M
Human Resources Management   M
International Business   M
Management Information Systems   M
Marketing   M

UNIVERSITY OF PHOENIX–LOUISVILLE CAMPUS

Business Administration and
    Management—General   M

UNIVERSITY OF PHOENIX–MADISON CAMPUS

Accounting   M
Business Administration and
    Management—General   M
Curriculum and Instruction   D,O
Education—General   D,O
Educational Leadership and
    Administration   D,O
Electronic Commerce   M
Higher Education   D,O
Human Resources Management   M
International Business   M
Management Information Systems   M
Marketing   M

UNIVERSITY OF PHOENIX–MARYLAND CAMPUS

Business Administration and
    Management—General   M
International Business   M

UNIVERSITY OF PHOENIX–MEMPHIS CAMPUS

Accounting   M
Business Administration and
    Management—General   M
Curriculum and Instruction   M
Education—General   M
Educational Leadership and
    Administration   M
Electronic Commerce   M
Elementary Education   M
Human Resources Management   M
International Business   M
Management Information Systems   M
Marketing   M
Secondary Education   M

UNIVERSITY OF PHOENIX–MILWAUKEE CAMPUS

Accounting   M
Business Administration and
    Management—General   M
Human Resources Management   M
International Business   M
Management Information Systems   M
Marketing   M
Project Management   M

UNIVERSITY OF PHOENIX–MINNEAPOLIS/ST. LOUIS PARK CAMPUS

Accounting   M
Business Administration and
    Management—General   M
Human Resources Management   M
Human Services   M
International Business   M
Marketing   M

UNIVERSITY OF PHOENIX–NASHVILLE CAMPUS

Business Administration and
    Management—General   M
Curriculum and Instruction   M
Education—General   M
Educational Leadership and
    Administration   M
Elementary Education   M
Human Resources Management   M
Management Information Systems   M
Secondary Education   M

UNIVERSITY OF PHOENIX–NEW MEXICO CAMPUS

Accounting   M
Business Administration and
    Management—General   M
Counselor Education   M
Curriculum and Instruction   M
Education—General   M
Educational Leadership and
    Administration   M
Electronic Commerce   M
Elementary Education   M
Human Resources Management   M
International Business   M
Management Information Systems   M
Marketing   M
Secondary Education   M

UNIVERSITY OF PHOENIX–NORTH FLORIDA CAMPUS

Accounting   M
Business Administration and
    Management—General   M
Computer Education   M
Curriculum and Instruction   M
Early Childhood Education   M
Education—General   M
Educational Leadership and
    Administration   M
Elementary Education   M
Human Resources Management   M
International Business   M
Management Information Systems   M
Marketing   M
Mathematics Education   M
Secondary Education   M

UNIVERSITY OF PHOENIX–NORTHWEST ARKANSAS CAMPUS

Accounting   M
Business Administration and
    Management—General   M
Human Resources Management   M
International Business   M
Management Information Systems   M
Marketing   M

UNIVERSITY OF PHOENIX–OKLAHOMA CITY CAMPUS

Accounting   M
Business Administration and
    Management—General   M
Electronic Commerce   M
Human Resources Management   M
International Business   M
Management Information Systems   M
Marketing   M

UNIVERSITY OF PHOENIX–OMAHA CAMPUS

Accounting   M
Adult Education   M
Business Administration and
    Management—General   M
Computer Education   M
Curriculum and Instruction   M
Education—General   M
Educational Leadership and
    Administration   M
Elementary Education   M
English as a Second Language   M
English Education   M
Human Resources Management   M
International Business   M
Management Information Systems   M
Marketing   M
Mathematics Education   M
Secondary Education   M
Special Education   M

UNIVERSITY OF PHOENIX–ONLINE CAMPUS

Accounting   M,O
Adult Education   M,O
Business Administration and
    Management—General   M,D,O
Computer Education   M,O
Curriculum and Instruction   M,D,O
Early Childhood Education   M,O
Education—General   M,O
Educational Leadership and
    Administration   M,D,O
Educational Media/Instructional
    Technology   D,O
Elementary Education   M,O
English as a Second Language   M,O
English Education   M,O
Health Education   M,O
Higher Education   D,O
Human Resources Management   M,O
International Business   M,O
Management Information Systems

Marketing | M,O
Mathematics Education | M,O
Middle School Education | M,O
Organizational Management | D,O
Project Management | M,O
Reading Education | M,O
Science Education | M,O
Secondary Education | M,O
Special Education | M,O

UNIVERSITY OF PHOENIX–OREGON CAMPUS
Accounting | M
Business Administration and Management—General | M
Curriculum and Instruction | M
Early Childhood Education | M
Education—General | M
Elementary Education | M
Human Resources Management | M
International Business | M
Management Information Systems | M
Marketing | M
Middle School Education | M
Secondary Education | M

UNIVERSITY OF PHOENIX–PHILADELPHIA CAMPUS
Accounting | M
Business Administration and Management—General | M
Human Resources Management | M
International Business | M
Management Information Systems | M
Marketing | M

UNIVERSITY OF PHOENIX–PHOENIX CAMPUS
Accounting | M,O
Adult Education | M
Business Administration and Management—General | M,O
Counselor Education | M
Curriculum and Instruction | M
Early Childhood Education | M
Education—General | M
Educational Leadership and Administration | M
Elementary Education | M
Human Resources Management | M,O
International Business | M,O
Marketing | M,O
Project Management | M,O
Reading Education | M
Secondary Education | M
Special Education | M
Vocational and Technical Education | M

UNIVERSITY OF PHOENIX–PITTSBURGH CAMPUS
Accounting | M
Business Administration and Management—General | M
Electronic Commerce | M
Human Resources Management | M
International Business | M
Management Information Systems | M
Marketing | M

UNIVERSITY OF PHOENIX–PUERTO RICO CAMPUS
Accounting | M
Business Administration and Management—General | M
Early Childhood Education | M
Education—General | M
Educational Leadership and Administration | M
Entrepreneurship | M
Human Resources Management | M
Human Services | M
International Business | M
Marketing | M
Project Management | M

UNIVERSITY OF PHOENIX–RICHMOND–VIRGINIA BEACH CAMPUS
Accounting | M
Business Administration and Management—General | M
Curriculum and Instruction | M
Education—General | M
Educational Leadership and Administration | M
Human Resources Management | M
International Business | M
Management Information Systems | M
Marketing | M

UNIVERSITY OF PHOENIX–SACRAMENTO VALLEY CAMPUS
Accounting | M
Adult Education | M,O
Business Administration and Management—General | M
Curriculum and Instruction | M,O
Education—General | M,O
Elementary Education | M,O
Human Resources Management | M
International Business | M
Management Information Systems | M
Marketing | M
Secondary Education | M,O

UNIVERSITY OF PHOENIX–ST. LOUIS CAMPUS
Accounting | M
Business Administration and Management—General | M
Human Resources Management | M
International Business | M
Management Information Systems | M
Marketing | M

UNIVERSITY OF PHOENIX–SAN ANTONIO CAMPUS
Accounting | M
Business Administration and Management—General | M
Curriculum and Instruction | M
Electronic Commerce | M
Human Resources Management | M
International Business | M
Management Information Systems | M
Marketing | M

UNIVERSITY OF PHOENIX–SAN DIEGO CAMPUS
Accounting | M
Business Administration and Management—General | M
Computer Education | M
Curriculum and Instruction | M
Education—General | M
Elementary Education | M
English as a Second Language | M
Human Resources Management | M
International Business | M
Management Information Systems | M
Marketing | M
Secondary Education | M

UNIVERSITY OF PHOENIX–SAVANNAH CAMPUS
Accounting | M
Business Administration and Management—General | M
Human Resources Management | M
International Business | M
Management Information Systems | M
Marketing | M

UNIVERSITY OF PHOENIX–SOUTHERN ARIZONA CAMPUS
Accounting | M
Adult Education | M,O
Business Administration and Management—General | M
Counselor Education | M,O
Curriculum and Instruction | M,O
Education—General | M,O
Educational Leadership and Administration | M,O
Educational Psychology | M,O
Elementary Education | M,O
Human Resources Management | M
International Business | M
Management Information Systems | M
Marketing | M
Secondary Education | M,O
Special Education | M,O

UNIVERSITY OF PHOENIX–SOUTHERN CALIFORNIA CAMPUS
Accounting | M
Adult Education | M,O
Business Administration and Management—General | M
Counselor Education | M
Education—General | M,O
Educational Leadership and Administration | M,O
Elementary Education | M,O
English as a Second Language | M,O
Human Resources Management | M
International Business | M
Marketing | M
Project Management | M
Secondary Education | M,O

UNIVERSITY OF PHOENIX–SOUTHERN COLORADO CAMPUS
Accounting | M
Business Administration and Management—General | M
Curriculum and Instruction | M,O
Education—General | M,O
Educational Leadership and Administration | M,O
Elementary Education | M,O
Health Education | M
Human Resources Management | M
International Business | M
Management Information Systems | M
Marketing | M
Secondary Education | M,O

UNIVERSITY OF PHOENIX–SOUTH FLORIDA CAMPUS
Accounting | M
Business Administration and Management—General | M
Computer Education | M
Curriculum and Instruction | M
Early Childhood Education | M
Education—General | M
Educational Leadership and Administration | M
Elementary Education | M
Human Resources Management | M
International Business | M
Management Information Systems | M
Marketing | M
Mathematics Education | M
Secondary Education | M

UNIVERSITY OF PHOENIX–SPRINGFIELD CAMPUS
Accounting | M
Business Administration and Management—General | M
Computer Education | M
Curriculum and Instruction | M
Education—General | M
Educational Leadership and Administration | M

English as a Second Language | M
English Education | M
Human Resources Management | M
International Business | M
Management Information Systems | M
Marketing | M
Mathematics Education | M

UNIVERSITY OF PHOENIX–TULSA CAMPUS
Accounting | M
Business Administration and Management—General | M
Human Resources Management | M
International Business | M
Management Information Systems | M
Marketing | M

UNIVERSITY OF PHOENIX–UTAH CAMPUS
Accounting | M
Business Administration and Management—General | M
Curriculum and Instruction | M
Education—General | M
Educational Leadership and Administration | M
Elementary Education | M
Human Resources Management | M
International Business | M
Management Information Systems | M
Marketing | M
Secondary Education | M
Special Education | M

UNIVERSITY OF PHOENIX–WASHINGTON D.C. CAMPUS
Accounting | M,D
Adult Education | M,D,O
Business Administration and Management—General | M,D
Computer Education | M,D,O
Curriculum and Instruction | M,D,O
Early Childhood Education | M,D,O
Education—General | M,D,O
Educational Leadership and Administration | M,D,O
Educational Media/Instructional Technology | M,D,O
Elementary Education | M,D,O
English as a Second Language | M,D,O
English Education | M,D,O
Health Education | M,D,O
Higher Education | M,D,O
Human Resources Management | M,D
Management Information Systems | M,D
Mathematics Education | M,D,O
Organizational Management | M,D
Secondary Education | M,D
Special Education | M,D,O

UNIVERSITY OF PHOENIX–WESTERN WASHINGTON CAMPUS
Business Administration and Management—General | M

UNIVERSITY OF PHOENIX–WEST FLORIDA CAMPUS
Accounting | M
Business Administration and Management—General | M
Computer Education | M
Curriculum and Instruction | M
Early Childhood Education | M
Education—General | M
Educational Leadership and Administration | M
Educational Media/Instructional Technology | M
Elementary Education | M
Human Resources Management | M
International Business | M
Management Information Systems | M
Marketing | M
Mathematics Education | M
Secondary Education | M

UNIVERSITY OF PHOENIX–WICHITA CAMPUS
Business Administration and Management—General | M

UNIVERSITY OF PITTSBURGH
Accounting | M,D
Athletic Training and Sports Medicine | M
Business Administration and Management—General | M,D
Early Childhood Education | M,D
Education—General | M,D
Educational Leadership and Administration | M,D
Educational Measurement and Evaluation | M,D
Educational Policy | D
Elementary Education | M,D
English as a Second Language | O
English Education | M,D
Environmental Law | M
Exercise and Sports Science | M,D
Finance and Banking | M,D
Foreign Languages Education | M,D
Foundations and Philosophy of Education | M,D
Health Education | M,D,O
Health Law | M
Higher Education | M,D
Human Resources Management | M
Industrial and Manufacturing Management | M
Information Studies | M,D
Intellectual Property Law | M,O

International and Comparative Education | M,D
International Business | M
Law | M,D,O
Legal and Justice Studies | M,O
Library Science | M,D
Management Information Systems | M,D
Management Strategy and Policy | M
Marketing | M,D
Mathematics Education | M,D
Organizational Behavior | M,D
Quantitative Analysis | D
Reading Education | M,D
Science Education | M,D
Secondary Education | M,D
Social Sciences Education | M,D
Social Work | M,D,O
Special Education | M,D

UNIVERSITY OF PORTLAND
Business Administration and Management—General | M
Education—General | M,D
Educational Leadership and Administration | M,D
English as a Second Language | M,D
Entrepreneurship | M
Finance and Banking | M
Industrial and Manufacturing Management | M
Marketing | M
Nonprofit Management | M
Organizational Management | M,D
Reading Education | M,D
Special Education | M,D
Sustainability Management | M

UNIVERSITY OF PRINCE EDWARD ISLAND
Education—General | M
Educational Leadership and Administration | M

UNIVERSITY OF PUERTO RICO, MAYAGÜEZ CAMPUS
Agricultural Education | M
Business Administration and Management—General | M
English Education | M
Exercise and Sports Science | M
Finance and Banking | M
Human Resources Management | M
Industrial and Manufacturing Management | M
Kinesiology and Movement Studies | M
Physical Education | M

UNIVERSITY OF PUERTO RICO, MEDICAL SCIENCES CAMPUS
Health Education | M
Special Education | O

UNIVERSITY OF PUERTO RICO, RÍO PIEDRAS CAMPUS
Accounting | M,D
Business Administration and Management—General | M,D
Counselor Education | M,D
Curriculum and Instruction | M,D
Early Childhood Education | M
Education—General | M,D
Educational Leadership and Administration | M,D
Educational Measurement and Evaluation | M
English as a Second Language | M
Exercise and Sports Science | M
Finance and Banking | M,D
Foreign Languages Education | M,D
Human Resources Management | M,D
Industrial and Manufacturing Management | M,D
Information Studies | M,O
International Business | M,D
Law | M,D
Library Science | M,O
Marketing | M,D
Mathematics Education | M,D
Quantitative Analysis | M,D
Science Education | M,D
Social Sciences Education | M,D
Social Work | M,D
Special Education | M,D

UNIVERSITY OF PUGET SOUND
Counselor Education | M
Education—General | M
Elementary Education | M
Secondary Education | M

UNIVERSITY OF REDLANDS
Business Administration and Management—General | M
Education—General | M,D,O
Management Information Systems | M

UNIVERSITY OF REGINA
Adult Education | M
Business Administration and Management—General | M,O
Curriculum and Instruction | M
Education—General | M,D,O
Educational Leadership and Administration | M
Educational Psychology | M
Human Resources Development | M,O
Human Resources Management | M,O
International Business | M,O
Kinesiology and Movement Studies | M,D
Organizational Management | M,O
Project Management | M,O
Social Work | M

---

*M—masters degree; D—doctorate; O—other advanced degree; *—Close-Up and/or Display*

UNIVERSITY OF RHODE ISLAND

Accounting	M,D
Adult Education	M,D
Business Administration and Management—General	M,D
Education—General	M,D
Elementary Education	M,D
Exercise and Sports Science	M
Finance and Banking	M,D
Health Education	M
Human Resources Management	M
Industrial and Manufacturing Management	M,D
Information Studies	M
Library Science	M
Marketing	M,D
Music Education	M,D
Physical Education	M
Reading Education	M,D
Recreation and Park Management	M
Secondary Education	M,D
Special Education	M,D
Student Affairs	M
Supply Chain Management	M,D

UNIVERSITY OF RICHMOND

Business Administration and Management—General	M
Law	D

UNIVERSITY OF RIO GRANDE

Art Education	M
Education—General	M
Mathematics Education	M
Reading Education	M
Special Education	M

UNIVERSITY OF ROCHESTER

Accounting	M
Business Administration and Management—General	M,D
Counselor Education	M,D
Curriculum and Instruction	M,D
Education—General	M,D
Educational Leadership and Administration	M,D
Educational Policy	M,D
Electronic Commerce	M
Entrepreneurship	M
Finance and Banking	M
Foundations and Philosophy of Education	D
Higher Education	M,D
Industrial and Manufacturing Management	M
International Business	M
Management Information Systems	M
Management Strategy and Policy	M
Marketing	M
Music Education	M,D
Student Affairs	M

UNIVERSITY OF ST. AUGUSTINE FOR HEALTH SCIENCES

Health Education	D

UNIVERSITY OF ST. FRANCIS (IL)

Art Education	M,D
Business Administration and Management—General	M,O
Business Education	M,O
Curriculum and Instruction	M,D
Education—General	M,D
Educational Leadership and Administration	M,D
Elementary Education	M,D
English Education	M,D
Higher Education	M,D
Logistics	M,O
Mathematics Education	M,D
Reading Education	M,D
Science Education	M,D
Secondary Education	M,D
Social Sciences Education	M,D
Social Work	M,O
Special Education	M,D

UNIVERSITY OF SAINT FRANCIS (IN)

Business Administration and Management—General	M
Counselor Education	M,O
Education—General	M,O
Special Education	M,O
Sustainability Management	M

UNIVERSITY OF SAINT JOSEPH

Business Administration and Management—General	M
Counselor Education	M
Education—General	M
Special Education	M,O

UNIVERSITY OF SAINT MARY

Advertising and Public Relations	M
Business Administration and Management—General	M
Education—General	M
Elementary Education	M
Finance and Banking	M
Human Resources Management	M
Marketing	M
Special Education	M

UNIVERSITY OF ST. MICHAEL'S COLLEGE

Religious Education	M,D,O

UNIVERSITY OF ST. THOMAS (MN)

Accounting	M
Business Administration and Management—General	M
Curriculum and Instruction	M,O
Early Childhood Education	M,O
Education—General	M,D,O
Educational Leadership and Administration	M,D,O
Educational Media/Instructional Technology	M,D
Educational Policy	M,D,O
Elementary Education	M,O
English as a Second Language	M,O
Human Resources Development	M,D
Law	M,D
Management Information Systems	M,O
Mathematics Education	M,O
Multilingual and Multicultural Education	M,O
Music Education	M
Organizational Management	M,D
Reading Education	M,O
Real Estate	M
Religious Education	M
Secondary Education	M,O
Social Work	M
Special Education	M,O
Student Affairs	M,D,O

UNIVERSITY OF ST. THOMAS (TX)

Business Administration and Management—General	M
Counselor Education	M
Curriculum and Instruction	M
Education—General	M
Educational Leadership and Administration	M
Educational Measurement and Evaluation	M
Elementary Education	M
English as a Second Language	M
Multilingual and Multicultural Education	M
Reading Education	M
Religious Education	M
Secondary Education	M
Special Education	M

UNIVERSITY OF SAN DIEGO

Accounting	M
Business Administration and Management—General	M
Counselor Education	M
Curriculum and Instruction	M
Education—General	M,D,O
Educational Leadership and Administration	M,D,O
English as a Second Language	M
Higher Education	M,D,O
International Business	M
Law	M,D,O
Legal and Justice Studies	M,D,O
Nonprofit Management	M,D,O
Reading Education	M
Real Estate	M
Special Education	M
Supply Chain Management	M,O
Taxation	M,D,O

UNIVERSITY OF SAN FRANCISCO

Business Administration and Management—General	M
Counselor Education	M
Curriculum and Instruction	M,D
Education—General	M,D
Educational Leadership and Administration	M,D
Educational Media/Instructional Technology	M,D
English as a Second Language	M,D
Entrepreneurship	M
Finance and Banking	M
Health Education	M
Intellectual Property Law	M
International and Comparative Education	M,D
International Business	M
Investment Management	M
Law	M,D
Management Information Systems	M
Marketing	M
Multilingual and Multicultural Education	M,D
Nonprofit Management	M
Organizational Management	M
Reading Education	M,D
Religious Education	M,D
Special Education	M,D
Sports Management	M
Taxation	M,D

UNIVERSITY OF SASKATCHEWAN

Accounting	M
Business Administration and Management—General	M
Curriculum and Instruction	M,D,O
Education—General	M,D,O
Educational Leadership and Administration	M,D,O
Educational Psychology	M,D,O
Finance and Banking	M
Foundations and Philosophy of Education	M,D,O
International Business	M,D
Kinesiology and Movement Studies	M,D,O
Law	M,D
Marketing	M
Special Education	M,D,O
Sustainability Management	M

THE UNIVERSITY OF SCRANTON

Accounting	M
Business Administration and Management—General	M
Counselor Education	M
Curriculum and Instruction	M
Early Childhood Education	M
Education—General	M
Educational Leadership and Administration	M
Finance and Banking	M
Human Resources Development	M
Human Resources Management	M
International Business	M
Management Information Systems	M
Marketing	M
Organizational Management	M
Reading Education	M
Secondary Education	M

UNIVERSITY OF SIOUX FALLS

Business Administration and Management—General	M
Education—General	M,O
Educational Leadership and Administration	M,O
Educational Media/Instructional Technology	M,O
Entrepreneurship	M
Marketing	M
Reading Education	M,O

UNIVERSITY OF SOUTH AFRICA

Accounting	M,D
Adult Education	M,D
Business Administration and Management—General	M,D
Counselor Education	M,D
Curriculum and Instruction	M,D
Education—General	M,D
Educational Leadership and Administration	M,D
Educational Media/Instructional Technology	M,D
Educational Psychology	M,D
English as a Second Language	M,D
Environmental Education	M,D
Foundations and Philosophy of Education	M,D
Health Education	M,D
Human Resources Development	M,D
International and Comparative Education	M,D
Law	M,D
Logistics	M,D
Management Information Systems	M
Marketing	M,D
Mathematics Education	M,D
Quantitative Analysis	M,D
Real Estate	M,D
Science Education	M,D
Social Work	M,D
Travel and Tourism	M,D
Vocational and Technical Education	M,D

UNIVERSITY OF SOUTH ALABAMA

Accounting	M
Business Administration and Management—General	M
Early Childhood Education	M,O
Education—General	M,D,O
Educational Leadership and Administration	M,O
Elementary Education	M,O
Exercise and Sports Science	M
Health Education	M
Leisure Studies	M
Management Information Systems	M
Physical Education	M
Reading Education	M,O
Recreation and Park Management	M
Science Education	M,O
Secondary Education	M,O
Special Education	M,O

UNIVERSITY OF SOUTH CAROLINA

Accounting	M
Archives/Archival Administration	M,O
Art Education	M,D
Business Administration and Management—General	M,D
Business Education	M,D
Counselor Education	D,O
Curriculum and Instruction	D
Early Childhood Education	M,D
Education—General	M,D,O
Educational Leadership and Administration	M,D,O
Educational Measurement and Evaluation	M,D
Educational Media/Instructional Technology	M
Educational Psychology	M,D
Elementary Education	M,D
English as a Second Language	M,D,O
English Education	M,D
Entertainment Management	M
Exercise and Sports Science	M,D
Foreign Languages Education	M,D
Foundations and Philosophy of Education	D
Health Education	M,D,O
Higher Education	M
Hospitality Management	M
Human Resources Management	M
Information Studies	M,D,O
International Business	M
Law	D
Library Science	M,D,O
Mathematics Education	M,D
Music Education	M,D,O
Physical Education	M,D
Reading Education	M,D
Science Education	M,D
Secondary Education	M,D
Social Sciences Education	M,D
Social Work	M,D
Special Education	M,D
Sports Management	M
Student Affairs	M
Travel and Tourism	M

UNIVERSITY OF SOUTH CAROLINA AIKEN

Educational Media/Instructional Technology	M

UNIVERSITY OF SOUTH CAROLINA UPSTATE

Early Childhood Education	M
Education—General	M
Elementary Education	M
Special Education	M

THE UNIVERSITY OF SOUTH DAKOTA

Accounting	M
Business Administration and Management—General	M
Counselor Education	M,D,O
Curriculum and Instruction	M,D,O
Education—General	M,D,O
Educational Leadership and Administration	M,D,O
Educational Media/Instructional Technology	M
Educational Psychology	M,D,O
Elementary Education	M
Exercise and Sports Science	M
Human Resources Management	M
Kinesiology and Movement Studies	M
Law	D
Music Education	M
Organizational Management	M
Secondary Education	M
Social Work	M,D,O
Special Education	M

UNIVERSITY OF SOUTHERN CALIFORNIA

Accounting	M
Advertising and Public Relations	M
Business Administration and Management—General	M,D
Counselor Education	M
Education—General	M,D
Educational Leadership and Administration	D
Educational Policy	D
Educational Psychology	D
English as a Second Language	M
Health Education	M
Higher Education	D
Kinesiology and Movement Studies	M,D
Law	M,D
Multilingual and Multicultural Education	D
Music Education	M,D,O
Nonprofit Management	M,O
Organizational Management	M
Quantitative Analysis	M,D
Real Estate	M
Social Work	M,D
Student Affairs	M
Supply Chain Management	M,D,O
Taxation	M
Urban Education	D

UNIVERSITY OF SOUTHERN INDIANA

Business Administration and Management—General	M
Education—General	M
Elementary Education	M
Industrial and Manufacturing Management	M
Secondary Education	M
Social Work	M

UNIVERSITY OF SOUTHERN MAINE

Accounting	M
Adult Education	M,O
Business Administration and Management—General	M,O
Counselor Education	M,O
Early Childhood Education	M
Education of the Gifted	M,O
Education—General	M,D,O
Educational Leadership and Administration	M,O
Educational Psychology	M,O
English as a Second Language	M,O
Finance and Banking	M
Higher Education	M,O
Law	D
Music Education	M
Nonprofit Management	M,O
Reading Education	M,O
Social Work	M
Special Education	M,O
Sustainability Management	M

UNIVERSITY OF SOUTHERN MISSISSIPPI

Accounting	M
Adult Education	M,D,O
Advertising and Public Relations	M,D
Business Administration and Management—General	M
Community College Education	M,D,O
Counselor Education	M,D,O
Curriculum and Instruction	M,D,O
Education—General	M,D,O
Educational Leadership and Administration	M,D,O
Educational Measurement and Evaluation	M,D,O
Educational Media/Instructional Technology	M,D,O
Elementary Education	M,D,O
Exercise and Sports Science	M,D
Foreign Languages Education	M
Health Education	M
Higher Education	M,D,O
Leisure Studies	M,D
Library Science	M
Logistics	M
Management Information Systems	M
Mathematics Education	M,D
Music Education	M,D
Physical Education	M,D
Recreation and Park Management	M,D
Science Education	M,D
Secondary Education	M,D,O
Social Sciences Education	M,D,O
Social Work	M
Special Education	M,D,O
Sports Management	M,D

Student Affairs — M,D,O
Vocational and Technical Education — M

UNIVERSITY OF SOUTH FLORIDA

Accounting — M,D
Adult Education — M,D,O
Athletic Training and Sports Medicine — M,D
Business Administration and Management—General — M,O
Community College Education — M,O
Counselor Education — M,D,O
Curriculum and Instruction — M,D,O
Distance Education Development — O
Early Childhood Education — M,D
Education of the Gifted — M,D
Education—General — M,D,O
Educational Leadership and Administration — M,D,O
Educational Measurement and Evaluation — M,D,O
Educational Media/Instructional Technology — M,D,O
Elementary Education — M,D,O
English as a Second Language — M,D,O
English Education — M,D,O
Entrepreneurship — M
Exercise and Sports Science — M
Finance and Banking — M,D
Foreign Languages Education — M,D
Higher Education — M,D,O
Human Resources Development — O
Information Studies — M,O
Legal and Justice Studies — O
Library Science — M,O
Management Information Systems — M,D,O
Management Strategy and Policy — O
Marketing — M,D
Mathematics Education — M,D,O
Music Education — M,D
Nonprofit Management — O
Organizational Behavior — M
Physical Education — M
Reading Education — M,D,O
Real Estate — M,D
Science Education — M,D,O
Secondary Education — M,D,O
Social Sciences Education — M,D,O
Social Work — M,D,O
Special Education — M,D,O
Sports Management — M
Student Affairs — M,D,O
Sustainability Management — M
Taxation — M,D
Travel and Tourism — M
Vocational and Technical Education — M,D,O

UNIVERSITY OF SOUTH FLORIDA–ST. PETERSBURG CAMPUS

Business Administration and Management—General — M
Education—General — M
Educational Leadership and Administration — M
Elementary Education — M
English Education — M
Mathematics Education — M
Middle School Education — M
Reading Education — M
Science Education — M

UNIVERSITY OF SOUTH FLORIDA SARASOTA-MANATEE

Business Administration and Management—General — M
Curriculum and Instruction — M
Education—General — M
Educational Leadership and Administration — M
English as a Second Language — M
English Education — M
Hospitality Management — M

THE UNIVERSITY OF TAMPA

Accounting — M
Business Administration and Management—General — M
Curriculum and Instruction — M
Education—General — M
Educational Leadership and Administration — M
Entrepreneurship — M
Finance and Banking — M
International Business — M
Management Information Systems — M
Marketing — M
Nonprofit Management — M

THE UNIVERSITY OF TENNESSEE

Accounting — M,D
Adult Education — M,D
Advertising and Public Relations — M,D
Agricultural Education — M
Art Education — M,D,O
Athletic Training and Sports Medicine — M,D
Business Administration and Management—General — M,D
Counselor Education — M,D,O
Curriculum and Instruction — M,D,O
Early Childhood Education — M,D,O
Education—General — M,D,O
Educational Leadership and Administration — M,D,O
Educational Measurement and Evaluation — M,D,O
Educational Media/Instructional Technology — M,D,O
Educational Psychology — M,D,O
Elementary Education — M,D,O
English as a Second Language — M,D,O
English Education — M,D,O

Exercise and Sports Science — M,D,O
Finance and Banking — M,D
Foreign Languages Education — M,D,O
Foundations and Philosophy of Education — M,D,O
Health Education — M
Hospitality Management — M
Human Resources Development — M
Industrial and Manufacturing Management — M,D
Kinesiology and Movement Studies — M,D
Law — D
Leisure Studies — M,D
Logistics — M,D
Marketing — M,D
Mathematics Education — M,D,O
Multilingual and Multicultural Education — M,D,O
Music Education — M,D,O
Reading Education — M,D,O
Recreation and Park Management — M,D
Science Education — M,D,O
Secondary Education — M,D,O
Social Sciences Education — M,D,O
Social Work — M,D
Special Education — M,D,O
Sports Management — M,D
Student Affairs — M
Transportation Management — M,D
Travel and Tourism — M

THE UNIVERSITY OF TENNESSEE AT CHATTANOOGA

Accounting — M
Athletic Training and Sports Medicine — M
Business Administration and Management—General — M
Counselor Education — M,D,O
Education—General — M,D,O
Educational Leadership and Administration — M,D,O
Educational Media/Instructional Technology — M,D,O
Elementary Education — M,D,O
Logistics — M,O
Mathematics Education — M
Music Education — M
Nonprofit Management — M,O
Physical Education — M
Project Management — M,O
Quality Management — M,O
Secondary Education — M,D,O
Special Education — M,D,O
Supply Chain Management — M

THE UNIVERSITY OF TENNESSEE AT MARTIN

Business Administration and Management—General — M
Counselor Education — M
Curriculum and Instruction — M
Education—General — M
Educational Leadership and Administration — M
Elementary Education — M
Physical Education — M
Secondary Education — M
Special Education — M

THE UNIVERSITY OF TEXAS AT ARLINGTON

Accounting — M,D
Business Administration and Management—General — M,D
Curriculum and Instruction — M
Education—General — M,D
Educational Leadership and Administration — M,D
Educational Policy — M,D
English as a Second Language — M
Exercise and Sports Science — M
Finance and Banking — M,D
Higher Education — M
Human Resources Management — M
Industrial and Manufacturing Management — M,D
Logistics — M
Management Information Systems — M,D
Marketing Research — M,D
Marketing — M,D
Mathematics Education — M,D
Multilingual and Multicultural Education — M
Music Education — M
Quantitative Analysis — M,D
Real Estate — M
Social Work — M,D
Taxation — M

THE UNIVERSITY OF TEXAS AT AUSTIN

Accounting — M,D
Actuarial Science — M
Advertising and Public Relations — M,D
Art Education — M
Business Administration and Management—General — M,D
Counselor Education — M,D
Curriculum and Instruction — M,D
Early Childhood Education — M,D
Education—General — M,D
Educational Leadership and Administration — M,D
Educational Media/Instructional Technology — M,D
Educational Psychology — M,D
Entrepreneurship — M
Exercise and Sports Science — M,D
Finance and Banking — M,D
Health Education — M,D
Industrial and Manufacturing Management — M,D

Information Studies — M,D
Kinesiology and Movement Studies — M,D
Law — M,D
Management Information Systems — M,D
Marketing — M,D
Multilingual and Multicultural Education — M,D
Music Education — M,D
Organizational Behavior — M
Physical Education — M,D
Quantitative Analysis — M,D
Reading Education — M,D
Social Work — M,D
Special Education — M,D
Supply Chain Management — M,D

THE UNIVERSITY OF TEXAS AT BROWNSVILLE

Business Administration and Management—General — M
Counselor Education — M
Curriculum and Instruction — M
Early Childhood Education — M
Education—General — M
Educational Leadership and Administration — M
Educational Media/Instructional Technology — M
Exercise and Sports Science — M
Multilingual and Multicultural Education — M
Music Education — M
Special Education — M

THE UNIVERSITY OF TEXAS AT DALLAS

Accounting — M,D
Actuarial Science — M,D
Business Administration and Management—General — M,D*
Entrepreneurship — M
Finance and Banking — M,D
International Business — M,D
Investment Management — M
Law — M,D
Management Information Systems — M,D
Management Strategy and Policy — M,D
Marketing — M,D
Mathematics Education — M
Project Management — M,D
Real Estate — M
Science Education — M
Supply Chain Management — M

THE UNIVERSITY OF TEXAS AT EL PASO

Accounting — M
Art Education — M
Business Administration and Management—General — M,D,O
Counselor Education — M
Curriculum and Instruction — M,D
Education—General — M,D
Educational Leadership and Administration — M,D
Educational Measurement and Evaluation — M
Educational Psychology — M
English as a Second Language — M,O
English Education — M,D,O
International Business — M,D,O
Kinesiology and Movement Studies — M
Mathematics Education — M
Multilingual and Multicultural Education — M,D,O
Music Education — M
Reading Education — M,D
Science Education — M
Social Work — M
Special Education — M

THE UNIVERSITY OF TEXAS AT SAN ANTONIO

Accounting — M,D
Business Administration and Management—General — M,D
Counselor Education — M,D
Curriculum and Instruction — M,D
Early Childhood Education — M,D
Educational Leadership and Administration — M,D
Educational Media/Instructional Technology — M,D
English as a Second Language — M,D
Finance and Banking — M,D
Health Education — M,D
Higher Education — M,D
Kinesiology and Movement Studies — M
Marketing — M,D
Mathematics Education — M
Multilingual and Multicultural Education — M,D
Organizational Management — D
Reading Education — M,D
Social Work — M,D
Special Education — M,D

THE UNIVERSITY OF TEXAS AT TYLER

Business Administration and Management—General — M
Early Childhood Education — M
Educational Leadership and Administration — M
Health Education — M
Human Resources Development — M,D
Industrial and Manufacturing Management — M,D
Kinesiology and Movement Studies — M
Reading Education — M
Special Education — M
Vocational and Technical Education — M,D

THE UNIVERSITY OF TEXAS HEALTH SCIENCE CENTER AT SAN ANTONIO

Special Education — M,D

THE UNIVERSITY OF TEXAS OF THE PERMIAN BASIN

Accounting — M
Business Administration and Management—General — M
Counselor Education — M
Early Childhood Education — M
Education—General — M
Educational Leadership and Administration — M
English as a Second Language — M
Foundations and Philosophy of Education — M
Kinesiology and Movement Studies — M
Reading Education — M
Special Education — M

THE UNIVERSITY OF TEXAS–PAN AMERICAN

Accounting — M
Advertising and Public Relations — M,O
Business Administration and Management—General — M,D
Counselor Education — M
Early Childhood Education — M
Education of the Gifted — M
Education—General — M,D
Educational Leadership and Administration — M,D
Educational Measurement and Evaluation — M
Educational Psychology — M
Elementary Education — M
English as a Second Language — M
Finance and Banking — M,D
Kinesiology and Movement Studies — M
Management Information Systems — M
Marketing — M,D
Mathematics Education — M
Multilingual and Multicultural Education — M
Music Education — M
Reading Education — M
Science Education — M
Secondary Education — M
Social Work — M
Special Education — M

THE UNIVERSITY OF THE ARTS

Art Education — M
Museum Education — M
Music Education — M

UNIVERSITY OF THE CUMBERLANDS

Accounting — M
Business Administration and Management—General — M
Business Education — M,D,O
Counselor Education — M,D,O
Education—General — M,D,O
Educational Leadership and Administration — M,D,O
Elementary Education — M,D,O
Marketing — M
Middle School Education — M,D,O
Reading Education — M,D,O
Secondary Education — M,D,O
Special Education — M,D,O
Student Affairs — M,D,O

UNIVERSITY OF THE DISTRICT OF COLUMBIA

Business Administration and Management—General — M
Counselor Education — M
Early Childhood Education — M
Education—General — M
Law — M,D
Legal and Justice Studies — M,D
Mathematics Education — M
Special Education — M

UNIVERSITY OF THE FRASER VALLEY

Social Work — M

UNIVERSITY OF THE INCARNATE WORD

Accounting — M
Adult Education — M,D
Business Administration and Management—General — M,D
Early Childhood Education — M,D
Education—General — M,D
Educational Leadership and Administration — M,D
Educational Media/Instructional Technology — M,D
Educational Psychology — M
Elementary Education — M
Entrepreneurship — M,D
Higher Education — M,D
International Business — M
Kinesiology and Movement Studies — M,D
Marketing — M
Mathematics Education — M
Multilingual and Multicultural Education — M,D
Organizational Management — M,D
Reading Education — M,D
Secondary Education — M,D
Special Education — M,D
Sports Management — M

UNIVERSITY OF THE PACIFIC

Business Administration and Management—General — M
Curriculum and Instruction — M,D
Education—General — M,D,O
Educational Leadership and Administration — M,D

---

*M—masters degree; D—doctorate; O—other advanced degree; *—Close-Up and/or Display*

Educational Psychology M,D,O
Exercise and Sports Science M
Law M,D
Legal and Justice Studies M,D
Music Education M
Special Education M,D
Taxation M,D

UNIVERSITY OF THE POTOMAC
Business Administration and Management—General M

UNIVERSITY OF THE SACRED HEART
Accounting M,O
Advertising and Public Relations M
Business Administration and Management—General M,O
Early Childhood Education M,O
Education—General M,O
Educational Media/Instructional Technology M
English Education M,O
Foreign Languages Education M,O
Human Resources Management M
Legal and Justice Studies M
Management Information Systems M
Marketing M
Mathematics Education M,O
Nonprofit Management M
Taxation M

UNIVERSITY OF THE SOUTHWEST
Business Administration and Management—General M
Counselor Education M
Curriculum and Instruction M
Early Childhood Education M
Education—General M
Educational Leadership and Administration M
English as a Second Language M
Multilingual and Multicultural Education M
Special Education M
Sports Management M

UNIVERSITY OF THE VIRGIN ISLANDS
Business Administration and Management—General M
Education—General M
Mathematics Education M

UNIVERSITY OF THE WEST
Business Administration and Management—General M
Finance and Banking M
International Business M
Management Information Systems M
Nonprofit Management M

THE UNIVERSITY OF TOLEDO
Accounting M
Art Education M,D,O
Business Administration and Management—General M
Business Education M,D,O
Counselor Education M,D,O
Curriculum and Instruction M,D,O
Early Childhood Education M,D,O
Education of the Gifted M,D,O
Education—General M,D,O
Educational Leadership and Administration M,D,O
Educational Measurement and Evaluation M,D,O
Educational Media/Instructional Technology M,D,O
Educational Psychology M,D,O
Elementary Education M,D,O
English as a Second Language M,D,O
English Education M,D,O
Exercise and Sports Science M,D
Finance and Banking M
Foreign Languages Education M,D,O
Foundations and Philosophy of Education M,D,O
Health Education M,D,O
Higher Education M,D,O
International Business M
Law D
Leisure Studies M,D
Marketing M
Mathematics Education M,D,O
Middle School Education M,D,O
Music Education M,D,O
Nonprofit Management M,O
Physical Education M
Recreation and Park Management M,D
Science Education M,D,O
Secondary Education M,D,O
Social Sciences Education M,D,O
Social Work M,O
Special Education M,D,O
Vocational and Technical Education M,D,O

UNIVERSITY OF TORONTO
Business Administration and Management—General M,D
Education—General M,D
Finance and Banking M
Human Resources Management M,D
Information Studies M,D
Law M,D
Music Education M,D
Physical Education M,D
Social Work M,D

THE UNIVERSITY OF TULSA
Accounting M
Business Administration and Management—General M
Education—General M
Elementary Education M
English Education M
Environmental Law M,D,O
Finance and Banking M
Health Law M,D,O
International Business M
Investment Management M
Law M,D,O
Management Information Systems M
Mathematics Education M
Science Education M
Secondary Education M
Taxation M

UNIVERSITY OF UTAH
Accounting M,D
Art Education M
Business Administration and Management—General M,D,O
Counselor Education M,D
Early Childhood Education M,D
Education—General M,D
Educational Leadership and Administration M,D
Educational Media/Instructional Technology M,D
Educational Psychology M,D
Elementary Education M,D
Exercise and Sports Science M,D
Finance and Banking M,D
Foreign Languages Education M,D
Foundations and Philosophy of Education M,D
Health Education M,D
Higher Education M,D
Industrial and Manufacturing Management M,D,O
Law M,D
Leisure Studies M,D
Management Information Systems M,D,O
Management Strategy and Policy M,D,O
Marketing M,D
Music Education M,D
Organizational Behavior M,D
Reading Education M,D
Real Estate M
Recreation and Park Management M,D
Science Education M,D
Secondary Education M,D
Social Work M,D
Special Education M,D
Student Affairs M,D

UNIVERSITY OF VERMONT
Accounting M
Business Administration and Management—General M
Counselor Education M
Curriculum and Instruction M
Education—General M,D
Educational Leadership and Administration M,D
Foreign Languages Education M,D
Mathematics Education M,D
Science Education M,D
Social Work M,D
Special Education M,D

UNIVERSITY OF VICTORIA
Art Education M,D
Business Administration and Management—General M
Counselor Education M,D
Curriculum and Instruction M,D
Early Childhood Education M,D
Education—General M,D
Educational Leadership and Administration M,D
Educational Measurement and Evaluation M,D
Educational Psychology M,D
English Education M,D
Environmental Education M,D
Foreign Languages Education M
Foundations and Philosophy of Education M,D
Kinesiology and Movement Studies M,D
Law M,D
Leisure Studies M
Mathematics Education M,D
Music Education M,D
Physical Education M
Reading Education M,D
Science Education M,D
Social Sciences Education M,D
Social Work M
Special Education M,D
Vocational and Technical Education M,D

UNIVERSITY OF VIRGINIA
Accounting M
Business Administration and Management—General M,D
Counselor Education M,D,O
Curriculum and Instruction M,D,O
Early Childhood Education M,D,O
Education of the Gifted M,D,O
Education—General M,D,O
Educational Leadership and Administration M,D,O
Educational Measurement and Evaluation M,D,O
Educational Media/Instructional Technology M,D,O
Educational Psychology M,D,O
Elementary Education M,D,O
English Education M,D,O
Finance and Banking M
Foreign Languages Education M,D,O
Health Education M,D
Higher Education M,D,O
Kinesiology and Movement Studies M,D
Law M,D
Management Information Systems M
Marketing M
Mathematics Education M,D,O
Physical Education M,D
Reading Education M,D,O
Science Education M,D,O
Social Sciences Education M,D,O
Special Education M,D,O
Student Affairs M,D,O

UNIVERSITY OF WASHINGTON
Accounting M,D
Business Administration and Management—General M,D
Business Education M,D
Curriculum and Instruction M,D
Education—General M,D
Educational Leadership and Administration M,D
Educational Measurement and Evaluation M,D
Educational Media/Instructional Technology M,D
Educational Policy M,D
Educational Psychology M,D
English as a Second Language M,D
English Education M,D
Foundations and Philosophy of Education M,D
Higher Education M,D
Intellectual Property Law M,D
International Business M,D,O
Law M,D
Legal and Justice Studies M,D
Library Science M,D
Logistics O
Mathematics Education M,D
Multilingual and Multicultural Education M,D
Music Education M,D
Physical Education M,D
Reading Education M,D
Science Education M,D
Social Sciences Education M,D
Social Work M,D
Special Education M,D
Taxation M,D
Transportation Management O

UNIVERSITY OF WASHINGTON, BOTHELL
Business Administration and Management—General M
Education—General M
Educational Leadership and Administration M
Middle School Education M
Secondary Education M

UNIVERSITY OF WASHINGTON, TACOMA
Accounting M
Business Administration and Management—General M
Education—General M
Educational Leadership and Administration M
Elementary Education M
Finance and Banking M
Mathematics Education M
Science Education M
Social Work M
Special Education M

UNIVERSITY OF WATERLOO
Accounting M,D
Actuarial Science M,D
Business Administration and Management—General M
Entrepreneurship M
Finance and Banking M,D
Health Education M,D
Kinesiology and Movement Studies M,D
Leisure Studies M,D
Recreation and Park Management M,D
Taxation M,D
Travel and Tourism M

THE UNIVERSITY OF WEST ALABAMA
Adult Education M
Counselor Education M,O
Curriculum and Instruction M,O
Early Childhood Education M,O
Education—General M,O
Educational Leadership and Administration M,O
Educational Media/Instructional Technology M,O
Elementary Education M,O
English Education M
Mathematics Education M
Physical Education M
Science Education M
Secondary Education M
Social Sciences Education M
Special Education M,O
Student Affairs M

THE UNIVERSITY OF WESTERN ONTARIO
Business Administration and Management—General M,D
Curriculum and Instruction M
Education—General M
Educational Policy M
Educational Psychology M
Entrepreneurship M,D
Finance and Banking M,D
Information Studies M,D
International Business M,D
Kinesiology and Movement Studies M,D
Law M,D,O
Library Science M,D
Management Strategy and Policy M,D
Marketing M,D
Special Education M

UNIVERSITY OF WEST FLORIDA
Accounting M
Business Administration and Management—General M,O
Counselor Education M
Curriculum and Instruction M,D,O
Early Childhood Education M
Education—General D
Educational Leadership and Administration M,D,O
Educational Media/Instructional Technology M,D
Elementary Education M
Exercise and Sports Science M,O
Health Education M
Leisure Studies M
Management Strategy and Policy M,O
Middle School Education M,O
Multilingual and Multicultural Education D
Physical Education M,D
Reading Education M
Science Education M,D
Secondary Education M,O
Social Sciences Education D
Social Work M
Special Education M
Student Affairs M
Vocational and Technical Education M,D,O

UNIVERSITY OF WEST GEORGIA
Accounting M
Business Administration and Management—General M
Counselor Education M,D,O
Early Childhood Education M,O
Education—General M,D,O
Educational Leadership and Administration M,O
Educational Measurement and Evaluation D
Educational Media/Instructional Technology M,O
Foundations and Philosophy of Education M,O
Mathematics Education M
Music Education M
Reading Education M,O
Special Education M,O

UNIVERSITY OF WINDSOR
Business Administration and Management—General M
Education—General M,D
Kinesiology and Movement Studies M
Legal and Justice Studies M
Social Work M

UNIVERSITY OF WISCONSIN–EAU CLAIRE
Business Administration and Management—General M
Education—General M
Library Science M
Reading Education M
Secondary Education M
Special Education M

UNIVERSITY OF WISCONSIN–GREEN BAY
Business Administration and Management—General M
Education—General M
Social Work M
Sustainability Management M

UNIVERSITY OF WISCONSIN–LA CROSSE
Athletic Training and Sports Medicine M
Business Administration and Management—General M
Education—General M
Elementary Education M
Exercise and Sports Science M
Health Education M
Higher Education M
Physical Education M
Recreation and Park Management M
Secondary Education M
Special Education M
Sports Management M
Student Affairs M

UNIVERSITY OF WISCONSIN–MADISON
Accounting M,D
Art Education M,D
Business Administration and Management—General M
Counselor Education M,D
Curriculum and Instruction M,D
Education—General M,D,O
Educational Leadership and Administration M,D,O
Educational Policy M,D,O
Educational Psychology M,D
Finance and Banking M,D
Foreign Languages Education M,D
Higher Education M,D,O
Human Resources Management M,D
Information Studies M,D
Insurance M,D
International and Comparative Education M,D,O
Investment Management D
Kinesiology and Movement Studies M,D
Law M,D
Library Science M,D
Management Information Systems D
Marketing Research M
Marketing D
Mathematics Education M,D
Music Education M,D
Real Estate M,D
Science Education M,D
Social Work M,D
Special Education M,D
Supply Chain Management M
Taxation M

UNIVERSITY OF WISCONSIN–MILWAUKEE

Adult Education	D
Archives/Archival Administration	M,D,O
Art Education	M
Business Administration and Management—General	M,D,O
Counselor Education	M,D
Curriculum and Instruction	M,D
Early Childhood Education	M
Education—General	M,D,O
Educational Leadership and Administration	M,D,O
Educational Measurement and Evaluation	M,D
Educational Psychology	M,D
Elementary Education	M
English as a Second Language	M,D,O
Foundations and Philosophy of Education	M,D
Health Education	M,D,O
Higher Education	M,O
Human Resources Development	M,O
Information Studies	M,D,O
International Business	M,O
Investment Management	M
Kinesiology and Movement Studies	M
Library Science	M,D,O
Middle School Education	M
Multilingual and Multicultural Education	D
Music Education	M,O
Nonprofit Management	M,D,O
Reading Education	M
Real Estate	M,O
Recreation and Park Management	M,O
Secondary Education	M
Social Work	M,D,O
Special Education	M,D,O
Taxation	M
Urban Education	M,D

UNIVERSITY OF WISCONSIN–OSHKOSH

Business Administration and Management—General	M
Counselor Education	M
Curriculum and Instruction	M
Early Childhood Education	M
Education—General	M
Educational Leadership and Administration	M
International Business	M
Mathematics Education	M
Reading Education	M
Social Work	M
Special Education	M

UNIVERSITY OF WISCONSIN–PARKSIDE

Business Administration and Management—General	M

UNIVERSITY OF WISCONSIN–PLATTEVILLE

Adult Education	M
Counselor Education	M
Education—General	M
Elementary Education	M
English Education	M
Middle School Education	M
Project Management	M
Secondary Education	M

UNIVERSITY OF WISCONSIN–RIVER FALLS

Agricultural Education	M
Business Administration and Management—General	M
Counselor Education	M,O
Education—General	M
Elementary Education	M
English as a Second Language	M
Mathematics Education	M
Reading Education	M
Science Education	M
Social Sciences Education	M

UNIVERSITY OF WISCONSIN–STEVENS POINT

Advertising and Public Relations	M
Business Administration and Management—General	M
Counselor Education	M
Education—General	M
Educational Leadership and Administration	M
Elementary Education	M
Music Education	M
Reading Education	M
Science Education	M
Secondary Education	M
Special Education	M

UNIVERSITY OF WISCONSIN–STOUT

Education—General	M,O
Human Resources Development	M
Vocational and Technical Education	M,O

UNIVERSITY OF WISCONSIN–SUPERIOR

Art Education	M
Counselor Education	M
Curriculum and Instruction	M
Education—General	M
Educational Leadership and Administration	M,O
Reading Education	M
Special Education	M
Sustainability Management	M

UNIVERSITY OF WISCONSIN–WHITEWATER

Accounting	M
Business Administration and Management—General	M
Business Education	M
Counselor Education	M
Curriculum and Instruction	M
Education of the Gifted	M
Education—General	M
Educational Leadership and Administration	M
Exercise and Sports Science	M
Finance and Banking	M
Higher Education	M
Human Resources Management	M
International Business	M
Library Science	M
Marketing	M
Multilingual and Multicultural Education	M
Physical Education	M
Reading Education	M
Special Education	M
Supply Chain Management	M

UNIVERSITY OF WYOMING

Accounting	M
Business Administration and Management—General	M
Counselor Education	M,D
Curriculum and Instruction	M,D
Educational Leadership and Administration	M,D,O
Educational Media/Instructional Technology	M,D
Exercise and Sports Science	M
Finance and Banking	M
Health Education	M
Kinesiology and Movement Studies	M
Law	D
Mathematics Education	M,D
Music Education	M
Physical Education	M
Science Education	M
Social Work	M
Special Education	M,D,O
Student Affairs	M,D

UPPER IOWA UNIVERSITY

Accounting	M
Business Administration and Management—General	M
Education—General	M
Educational Leadership and Administration	M
Finance and Banking	M
Higher Education	M
Human Resources Management	M
Human Services	M
International Business	M
Organizational Management	M
Quality Management	M

URBANA UNIVERSITY

Business Administration and Management—General	M
Education—General	M

URSULINE COLLEGE

Art Education	M
Business Administration and Management—General	M
Early Childhood Education	M
Education—General	M
Educational Leadership and Administration	M
Mathematics Education	M
Middle School Education	M
Reading Education	M
Science Education	M
Social Sciences Education	M
Special Education	M

UTAH STATE UNIVERSITY

Accounting	M
Agricultural Education	M
Business Administration and Management—General	M
Business Education	M,D
Counselor Education	M,D
Curriculum and Instruction	D
Education—General	M,D,O
Educational Measurement and Evaluation	M,D
Educational Media/Instructional Technology	M,D,O
Elementary Education	M
Health Education	M
Home Economics Education	M
Human Resources Management	M
Management Information Systems	M,D
Multilingual and Multicultural Education	M
Physical Education	M
Recreation and Park Management	M,D
Secondary Education	M
Special Education	M,D,O
Vocational and Technical Education	M

UTAH VALLEY UNIVERSITY

Accounting	M
Business Administration and Management—General	M
Education—General	M
Educational Media/Instructional Technology	M
Elementary Education	M
English as a Second Language	M
Mathematics Education	M

UTICA COLLEGE

Accounting	M
Education—General	M,O

VALDOSTA STATE UNIVERSITY

Business Administration and Management—General	M
Counselor Education	M,O

Early Childhood Education	M,O
Educational Leadership and Administration	M,D,O
English Education	M
Higher Education	M,D,O
Information Studies	M
Library Science	M
Social Work	M
Special Education	M,O

VALLEY CITY STATE UNIVERSITY

Education—General	M
Educational Media/Instructional Technology	M
Elementary Education	M
English as a Second Language	M
English Education	M
Library Science	M
Vocational and Technical Education	M

VALPARAISO UNIVERSITY

Business Administration and Management—General	M
Counselor Education	M
Education—General	M
Educational Leadership and Administration	M
English as a Second Language	M,O
Entertainment Management	M
Entrepreneurship	M,O
Finance and Banking	M,O
International and Comparative Education	M
International Business	M
Law	M,D
Legal and Justice Studies	O
Management Information Systems	M
Management Strategy and Policy	M,O
Marketing	M,O
Sports Management	M
Sustainability Management	M,O

VANCOUVER ISLAND UNIVERSITY

Business Administration and Management—General	M
Finance and Banking	M
International Business	M
Marketing	M

VANDERBILT UNIVERSITY

Accounting	M
Business Administration and Management—General	M
Counselor Education	M
Education—General	M,D*
Educational Leadership and Administration	M,D
Educational Policy	M,D
Elementary Education	M
English Education	M
Finance and Banking	M
Foreign Languages Education	M,D
Higher Education	M,D
International and Comparative Education	M,D
Law	M,D
Management Strategy and Policy	M,D
Marketing	M
Multilingual and Multicultural Education	M,D
Organizational Management	M,D
Reading Education	M
Science Education	M,D
Secondary Education	M
Special Education	M,D
Urban Education	M

VANDERCOOK COLLEGE OF MUSIC

Music Education	M

VANGUARD UNIVERSITY OF SOUTHERN CALIFORNIA

Education—General	M

VAUGHN COLLEGE OF AERONAUTICS AND TECHNOLOGY

Aviation Management	M

VERMONT LAW SCHOOL

Environmental Law	M
Law	D
Legal and Justice Studies	M

VILLANOVA UNIVERSITY

Accounting	M
Business Administration and Management—General	M
Counselor Education	M
Education—General	M
Educational Leadership and Administration	M
Finance and Banking	M
Human Resources Development	M
International Business	M
Law	D
Management Information Systems	M
Management Strategy and Policy	M
Marketing	M
Real Estate	M
Secondary Education	M
Taxation	M

VIRGINIA COLLEGE IN BIRMINGHAM

Business Administration and Management—General	M

VIRGINIA COMMONWEALTH UNIVERSITY

Accounting	M,D
Adult Education	M
Advertising and Public Relations	M
Art Education	M
Athletic Training and Sports Medicine	M
Business Administration and Management—General	M,O
Counselor Education	M
Early Childhood Education	M,O
Education—General	M,D,O
Educational Leadership and Administration	D
Educational Measurement and Evaluation	D
Educational Media/Instructional Technology	M
Educational Policy	D
Educational Psychology	D
Elementary Education	M,O
Exercise and Sports Science	M
Finance and Banking	M
Health Education	M,O
Human Resources Development	M
Industrial and Manufacturing Management	M
Insurance	M
Management Information Systems	M,D
Management Strategy and Policy	M
Marketing	M
Music Education	M
Nonprofit Management	M,O
Physical Education	M,D,O
Quantitative Analysis	M
Reading Education	M,O
Real Estate	M,O
Recreation and Park Management	M
Secondary Education	M,O
Social Work	M,D
Special Education	M,D,O
Student Affairs	M
Urban Education	D

VIRGINIA INTERNATIONAL UNIVERSITY

Accounting	M,O
Business Administration and Management—General	M,O
English as a Second Language	M,O
Finance and Banking	M,O
Human Resources Management	M,O
International Business	M,O
Logistics	M,O
Management Information Systems	M,O
Marketing	M,O

VIRGINIA POLYTECHNIC INSTITUTE AND STATE UNIVERSITY

Accounting	M,D
Business Administration and Management—General	M,D
Counselor Education	M,D,O
Curriculum and Instruction	M,D,O
Distance Education Development	M,O
Education—General	M,O
Educational Leadership and Administration	M,D,O
Educational Measurement and Evaluation	M,D,O
Educational Media/Instructional Technology	M,O
Educational Policy	M,D,O
Exercise and Sports Science	M,D
Foreign Languages Education	M,D,O
Higher Education	M,D,O
Hospitality Management	M,D
Management Information Systems	M,D,O
Mathematics Education	M,D
Nonprofit Management	M,O
Quantitative Analysis	M,O
Social Sciences Education	M,D,O
Student Affairs	M,D,O
Travel and Tourism	M,D
Vocational and Technical Education	M,D,O

VIRGINIA STATE UNIVERSITY

Education—General	M,O
Educational Leadership and Administration	M
Health Education	M,D
Mathematics Education	M
Vocational and Technical Education	M,O

VITERBO UNIVERSITY

Business Administration and Management—General	M
Education—General	M
International Business	M
Organizational Management	M
Project Management	M

WAGNER COLLEGE

Accounting	M
Business Administration and Management—General	M
Early Childhood Education	M
Education—General	M,O
Educational Leadership and Administration	M
Elementary Education	M
English Education	M
Finance and Banking	M
Foreign Languages Education	M
International Business	M
Marketing	M
Mathematics Education	M
Middle School Education	M
Reading Education	M
Science Education	M
Secondary Education	M
Social Sciences Education	M
Special Education	M

WAKE FOREST UNIVERSITY

Accounting	M
Business Administration and Management—General	M
Counselor Education	M
Education—General	M
Exercise and Sports Science	M

M—masters degree; D—doctorate; O—other advanced degree; *—Close-Up and/or Display

Finance and Banking M
Industrial and Manufacturing Management M
Law M,D
Marketing M
Secondary Education M
Taxation M

WALDEN UNIVERSITY
Accounting M,D,O
Adult Education M,D,O
Business Administration and Management—General M,D,O
Community College Education M,D,O
Counselor Education M,D
Curriculum and Instruction M,D,O
Developmental Education M,D,O
Distance Education Development M,D,O
Early Childhood Education M,D,O
Education—General M,D,O
Educational Leadership and Administration M,D,O
Educational Measurement and Evaluation M,D,O
Educational Media/Instructional Technology M,D,O
Educational Policy M,D,O
Educational Psychology M,D,O
Elementary Education M,D,O
English as a Second Language M,D,O
Entrepreneurship M,D,O
Finance and Banking M,D,O
Health Education M,D,O
Higher Education M,D,O
Human Resources Management M,D,O
Human Services M,D
International and Comparative Education M,D,O
International Business M,D,O
Law M,D,O
Management Information Systems M,D,O
Management Strategy and Policy M,D,O
Marketing M,D,O
Mathematics Education M,D,O
Middle School Education M,D,O
Multilingual and Multicultural Education M,D,O
Nonprofit Management M,D,O
Organizational Management M,D,O
Project Management M,D,O
Reading Education M,D,O
Science Education M,D,O
Social Work M,D
Special Education M,D,O
Supply Chain Management M,D,O

WALLA WALLA UNIVERSITY
Curriculum and Instruction M
Education—General M
Educational Leadership and Administration M
Reading Education M
Social Work M
Special Education M

WALSH COLLEGE OF ACCOUNTANCY AND BUSINESS ADMINISTRATION
Accounting M
Business Administration and Management—General M
Finance and Banking M
Management Information Systems M
Taxation M

WALSH UNIVERSITY
Business Administration and Management—General M
Counselor Education M
Education—General M
Educational Leadership and Administration M
Educational Media/Instructional Technology M
Entrepreneurship M
Higher Education M
Marketing M
Reading Education M
Religious Education M
Student Affairs M

WARNER PACIFIC COLLEGE
Business Administration and Management—General M
Education—General M
Nonprofit Management M
Organizational Management M

WARNER UNIVERSITY
Business Administration and Management—General M
Education—General M

WASHBURN UNIVERSITY
Accounting M
Business Administration and Management—General M
Curriculum and Instruction M
Education—General M
Educational Leadership and Administration M
Health Education M
Human Services M
Law M,D
Legal and Justice Studies M,D
Reading Education M
Social Work M
Special Education M

WASHINGTON ADVENTIST UNIVERSITY
Business Administration and Management—General M

WASHINGTON AND LEE UNIVERSITY
Law M,D

WASHINGTON STATE UNIVERSITY
Accounting M,D
Business Administration and Management—General M
Business Education M,D
Counselor Education M
Curriculum and Instruction M
Education—General M,D
Educational Leadership and Administration M,D
Educational Psychology M,D
Elementary Education M
English as a Second Language M,D
English Education M,D
Exercise and Sports Science M,D
Finance and Banking M,D
Foreign Languages Education M,D
Hospitality Management D
Industrial and Manufacturing Management D
International Business D
Management Information Systems D
Marketing M,D
Mathematics Education M,D
Multilingual and Multicultural Education M,D
Music Education M
Organizational Management D
Project Management M,O
Quality Management M,O
Quantitative Analysis D
Reading Education M
Science Education D
Secondary Education M
Special Education M,D
Sports Management M
Taxation M,D
Travel and Tourism D
Vocational and Technical Education D

WASHINGTON STATE UNIVERSITY SPOKANE
Curriculum and Instruction M,O
Education—General M,O
Educational Leadership and Administration M,O
Elementary Education M,O
Facilities Management M,O
Industrial and Manufacturing Management M,O
Logistics M,O
Project Management M,O
Quality Management M,O
Secondary Education M,O
Supply Chain Management M,O

WASHINGTON STATE UNIVERSITY TRI-CITIES
Business Administration and Management—General M
Education—General M,D
Educational Leadership and Administration M,D
Reading Education M,D
Secondary Education M,D

WASHINGTON STATE UNIVERSITY VANCOUVER
Accounting M
Business Administration and Management—General M
Education—General M,D
Taxation M

WASHINGTON UNIVERSITY IN ST. LOUIS
Accounting M
Business Administration and Management—General M,D
Education—General M,D
Educational Measurement and Evaluation D
Elementary Education M
Finance and Banking M
Health Education M,O
Kinesiology and Movement Studies D
Law M,D
Secondary Education M
Social Work M,D
Special Education M,D
Supply Chain Management M

WAYLAND BAPTIST UNIVERSITY
Accounting M
Business Administration and Management—General M
Education—General M
Educational Leadership and Administration M
Educational Measurement and Evaluation M
Educational Media/Instructional Technology M
Elementary Education M
English as a Second Language M
English Education M
Higher Education M
Human Resources Management M
International Business M
Management Information Systems M
Organizational Management M
Project Management M
Science Education M
Secondary Education M
Social Sciences Education M
Special Education M

WAYNESBURG UNIVERSITY
Business Administration and Management—General M,D
Curriculum and Instruction M,D
Distance Education Development M,D
Education—General M,D
Educational Leadership and Administration M,D
Educational Media/Instructional Technology M,D
Finance and Banking M,D
Human Resources Management M,D
Organizational Management M,D
Special Education M,D

WAYNE STATE COLLEGE
Business Administration and Management—General M
Business Education M
Counselor Education M
Curriculum and Instruction M
Early Childhood Education M
Education—General M,O
Educational Leadership and Administration M,O
Elementary Education M
English as a Second Language M
English Education M
Exercise and Sports Science M
Home Economics Education M
Mathematics Education M
Music Education M
Organizational Management M
Physical Education M
Science Education M
Social Sciences Education M
Special Education M
Sports Management M
Vocational and Technical Education M

WAYNE STATE UNIVERSITY
Accounting M,D,O
Advertising and Public Relations M,D,O
Archives/Archival Administration M,D,O
Art Education M,D,O
Business Administration and Management—General M,D,O
Counselor Education M,D,O
Curriculum and Instruction M,D,O
Distance Education Development M,D,O
Early Childhood Education M,D,O
Education—General M,D,O
Educational Leadership and Administration M,D,O
Educational Measurement and Evaluation M,D,O
Educational Media/Instructional Technology M,D,O
Educational Policy M,D,O
Educational Psychology M,D,O
Elementary Education M,D,O
English as a Second Language M,D,O
English Education M,D,O
Exercise and Sports Science M,D,O
Finance and Banking M,D
Foreign Languages Education M,D,O
Foundations and Philosophy of Education M,D,O
Health Education M,D,O
Higher Education M,D,O
Human Resources Management M,D
Industrial and Manufacturing Management M,D
Information Studies M,O
Kinesiology and Movement Studies M,D,O
Law M,D,O
Library Science M,O
Management Information Systems M,O
Mathematics Education M,D,O
Multilingual and Multicultural Education M,D,O
Music Education M,O
Nonprofit Management M
Organizational Behavior M
Organizational Management M
Physical Education M,D,O
Quantitative Analysis M,O
Reading Education M,D,O
Science Education M,D,O
Secondary Education M,D,O
Social Sciences Education M,D,O
Social Work M,D,O
Special Education M,D,O
Sports Management M,D,O
Taxation M,D,O
Urban Education M,O
Vocational and Technical Education M,D,O

WEBBER INTERNATIONAL UNIVERSITY
Accounting M
Business Administration and Management—General M
Sports Management M

WEBER STATE UNIVERSITY
Accounting M
Athletic Training and Sports Medicine M
Business Administration and Management—General M
Curriculum and Instruction M
Education—General M
Legal and Justice Studies M
Taxation M

WEBSTER UNIVERSITY
Accounting M
Advertising and Public Relations M
Business Administration and Management—General M
Early Childhood Education M
Education—General M,O
Educational Leadership and Administration M,O
Educational Media/Instructional Technology M,O
Educational Psychology M,O
Elementary Education M
Finance and Banking M
Human Resources Development M
Human Resources Management M
International Business M
Legal and Justice Studies M
Management Information Systems M
Marketing M
Mathematics Education M,O
Middle School Education M
Music Education M
Nonprofit Management M
Organizational Management M
Social Sciences Education M,O
Special Education M,O

WENTWORTH INSTITUTE OF TECHNOLOGY
Facilities Management M

WESLEYAN COLLEGE
Business Administration and Management—General M
Early Childhood Education M
Education—General M

WESLEY BIBLICAL SEMINARY
Religious Education M

WESLEY COLLEGE
Business Administration and Management—General M
Education—General M

WEST CHESTER UNIVERSITY OF PENNSYLVANIA
Athletic Training and Sports Medicine M,O
Business Administration and Management—General M,O
Counselor Education M,O
Early Childhood Education M,O
Education—General M,O
Educational Media/Instructional Technology M,O
Elementary Education M,O
English as a Second Language M,O
Entrepreneurship M,O
Exercise and Sports Science M,O
Foreign Languages Education M,O
Health Education M,O
Higher Education M,O
Human Resources Management M,O
Kinesiology and Movement Studies M,O
Management Information Systems M,O
Middle School Education M,O
Music Education M,O
Nonprofit Management M,O
Physical Education M,O
Reading Education M,O
Science Education O
Secondary Education M,O
Social Work M
Special Education M,O
Student Affairs M,O

WESTERN CAROLINA UNIVERSITY
Accounting M
Business Administration and Management—General M
Community College Education M,D,O
Counselor Education M
Education—General M,D,O
Educational Leadership and Administration M,D,O
English as a Second Language M
Entrepreneurship M
Higher Education M,D,O
Human Resources Development M
Physical Education M,D,O
Project Management M
Social Work M

WESTERN CONNECTICUT STATE UNIVERSITY
Accounting M
Business Administration and Management—General M
Counselor Education M
Curriculum and Instruction M
Education—General M,D
Educational Leadership and Administration D
Educational Media/Instructional Technology M
English as a Second Language M
English Education M
Mathematics Education M
Music Education M
Reading Education M
Science Education M
Secondary Education M
Special Education M

WESTERN GOVERNORS UNIVERSITY
Business Administration and Management—General M
Education—General M,O
Educational Leadership and Administration M,O
Educational Measurement and Evaluation M,O
Educational Media/Instructional Technology M,O
Elementary Education M,O
English Education M,O
Higher Education M,O
Management Information Systems M
Management Strategy and Policy M
Mathematics Education M,O
Science Education M,O
Social Sciences Education M,O
Special Education M,O

WESTERN ILLINOIS UNIVERSITY
Accounting M
Business Administration and Management—General M,O
Counselor Education M
Distance Education Development M,O
Education—General M,D,O
Educational Leadership and Administration M,D,O
Educational Media/Instructional Technology M,O
Elementary Education M
English as a Second Language M,O

Foundations and Philosophy of Education M,O
Health Education M,O
Kinesiology and Movement Studies M
Reading Education M
Recreation and Park Management M
Special Education M
Sports Management M
Student Affairs M
Supply Chain Management M,O
Travel and Tourism M

WESTERN INTERNATIONAL UNIVERSITY
Business Administration and Management—General M
Finance and Banking M
International Business M
Management Information Systems M
Management Strategy and Policy M
Marketing M
Organizational Behavior M
Organizational Management M

WESTERN KENTUCKY UNIVERSITY
Adult Education M,D,O
Art Education M
Business Administration and Management—General M
Counselor Education M
Early Childhood Education M,O
Educational Leadership and Administration M,D,O
Educational Media/Instructional Technology M,O
Elementary Education M,O
English as a Second Language M
English Education M
Foreign Languages Education M
Higher Education M
Middle School Education M,O
Music Education M
Physical Education M
Reading Education M,O
Recreation and Park Management M
Secondary Education M,O
Social Work M
Special Education M,O
Sports Management M
Student Affairs M

WESTERN MICHIGAN UNIVERSITY
Accounting M
Art Education M
Athletic Training and Sports Medicine M
Business Administration and Management—General M
Counselor Education M,D
Education—General M,D,O
Educational Leadership and Administration M,D,O
Educational Measurement and Evaluation M,D,O
Educational Media/Instructional Technology M,D,O
English Education M,D
Exercise and Sports Science M
Finance and Banking M
Health Education D
Human Resources Development M,D
Mathematics Education M,D
Music Education M
Nonprofit Management M,D,O
Physical Education M
Reading Education M,D
Science Education M,D
Social Work M
Special Education M,D
Sports Management M
Vocational and Technical Education M

WESTERN NEW ENGLAND UNIVERSITY
Accounting M
Advertising and Public Relations M
Business Administration and Management—General M
Curriculum and Instruction M
Elementary Education M
English Education M
Law M,D
Mathematics Education M
Sports Management M

WESTERN NEW MEXICO UNIVERSITY
Business Administration and Management—General M
Counselor Education M
Education—General M
Educational Leadership and Administration M
Elementary Education M
English as a Second Language M
Multilingual and Multicultural Education M
Reading Education M
Secondary Education M
Social Work M
Special Education M

WESTERN OREGON UNIVERSITY
Early Childhood Education M
Education—General M
Educational Media/Instructional Technology M
Health Education M
Mathematics Education M
Multilingual and Multicultural Education M
Science Education M
Secondary Education M
Social Sciences Education M
Special Education M

WESTERN SEMINARY
Human Resources Development M

WESTERN STATE COLLEGE OF LAW AT ARGOSY UNIVERSITY
Law D

WESTERN STATE COLORADO UNIVERSITY
Education—General M
Educational Leadership and Administration M
Reading Education M

WESTERN UNIVERSITY OF HEALTH SCIENCES
Health Education M

WESTERN WASHINGTON UNIVERSITY
Adult Education M
Business Administration and Management—General M
Counselor Education M
Education of the Gifted M
Education—General M
Educational Leadership and Administration M
Elementary Education M
Environmental Education M
Exercise and Sports Science M
Higher Education M
Physical Education M
Science Education M
Secondary Education M

WESTFIELD STATE UNIVERSITY
Counselor Education M
Early Childhood Education M
Education—General M,O
Educational Leadership and Administration M,O
Educational Media/Instructional Technology M
Elementary Education M
Physical Education M
Reading Education M
Secondary Education M
Special Education M
Vocational and Technical Education M,O

WEST LIBERTY UNIVERSITY
Education—General M

WESTMINSTER COLLEGE (PA)
Counselor Education M,O
Education—General M,O
Educational Leadership and Administration M,O
Reading Education M,O

WESTMINSTER COLLEGE (UT)
Accounting M,O
Business Administration and Management—General M,O
Education—General M

WEST TEXAS A&M UNIVERSITY
Accounting M
Business Administration and Management—General M
Counselor Education M
Curriculum and Instruction M
Education—General M
Educational Leadership and Administration M
Educational Measurement and Evaluation M
Educational Media/Instructional Technology M
Exercise and Sports Science M
Finance and Banking M
Reading Education M
Social Work M
Special Education M
Sports Management M

WEST VIRGINIA UNIVERSITY
Accounting M
Agricultural Education M,D
Art Education M
Athletic Training and Sports Medicine M,D
Business Administration and Management—General M
Counselor Education M
Curriculum and Instruction M,D
Early Childhood Education M,D
Education of Students with Severe/Multiple Disabilities M,D
Education of the Gifted M,D
Education—General M,D
Educational Leadership and Administration M,D
Educational Media/Instructional Technology M,D
Educational Psychology M
Elementary Education M
English as a Second Language M
Environmental Education M,D
Exercise and Sports Science M,D
Health Education M,D
Higher Education M,D
Human Services M
Law D
Legal and Justice Studies M
Marketing M,O
Mathematics Education M,D
Music Education M,D
Physical Education M,D
Reading Education M
Recreation and Park Management M
Secondary Education M,D
Social Work M

Special Education M,D
Sports Management M,D

WEST VIRGINIA WESLEYAN COLLEGE
Athletic Training and Sports Medicine M
Business Administration and Management—General M
Education—General M

WHEATON COLLEGE
Education—General M
Elementary Education M
English as a Second Language M,O
Religious Education M
Secondary Education M

WHEELING JESUIT UNIVERSITY
Accounting M
Business Administration and Management—General M
Educational Leadership and Administration M
Organizational Management M

WHEELOCK COLLEGE
Early Childhood Education M
Education—General M
Educational Leadership and Administration M
Elementary Education M
Reading Education M
Social Work M
Special Education M

WHITTIER COLLEGE
Education—General M
Educational Leadership and Administration M
Elementary Education M
Law D
Secondary Education M

WHITWORTH UNIVERSITY
Business Administration and Management—General M
Counselor Education M
Education of the Gifted M
Education—General M
Educational Leadership and Administration M
Elementary Education M
International Business M
Secondary Education M
Special Education M

WHU - OTTO BEISHEIM SCHOOL OF MANAGEMENT
Business Administration and Management—General M

WICHITA STATE UNIVERSITY
Accounting M
Business Administration and Management—General M
Counselor Education M,D,O
Curriculum and Instruction M
Early Childhood Education M
Education of the Gifted M
Education—General M,D,O
Educational Leadership and Administration M,D,O
Educational Psychology M,D,O
Exercise and Sports Science M
Human Services M
Music Education M
Social Work M
Special Education M
Sports Management M

WIDENER UNIVERSITY
Accounting M
Adult Education M,D
Business Administration and Management—General M
Counselor Education M,D
Early Childhood Education M,D
Education—General M,D
Educational Leadership and Administration M,D
Educational Media/Instructional Technology M,D
Educational Psychology M,D
Elementary Education M,D
English Education M,D
Foundations and Philosophy of Education M,D
Health Education M,D
Health Law M,D
Human Resources Management M
Law M,D
Mathematics Education M,D
Middle School Education M,D
Reading Education M,D
Science Education M,D
Social Sciences Education M,D
Social Work M,D
Special Education M,D
Taxation M

WILFRID LAURIER UNIVERSITY
Accounting M,D
Business Administration and Management—General M,D
Finance and Banking M,D
Human Resources Management M,D
Kinesiology and Movement Studies M,D
Legal and Justice Studies D
Marketing M,D
Organizational Behavior M,D
Organizational Management M,D
Physical Education M
Social Work M,D
Supply Chain Management M,D

WILKES UNIVERSITY
Accounting M
Business Administration and Management—General M
Curriculum and Instruction M,D
Distance Education Development M,D
Early Childhood Education M,D
Education—General M,D
Educational Leadership and Administration M,D
Educational Measurement and Evaluation M,D
Educational Media/Instructional Technology M,D
English as a Second Language M,D
English Education M,D
Entrepreneurship M
Finance and Banking M
Higher Education M,D
Human Resources Management M
Industrial and Manufacturing Management M
International and Comparative Education M,D
International Business M
Marketing M
Mathematics Education M,D
Middle School Education M,D
Organizational Management M
Reading Education M,D
Science Education M,D
Secondary Education M,D
Social Sciences Education M,D
Special Education M,D

WILLAMETTE UNIVERSITY
Business Administration and Management—General M
Education—General M
Law M,D
Reading Education M
Special Education M

WILLIAM CAREY UNIVERSITY
Art Education M,O
Business Administration and Management—General M
Education of the Gifted M,O
Education—General M,O
Elementary Education M,O
English Education M,O
Secondary Education M,O
Social Sciences Education M,O
Special Education M,O

WILLIAM HOWARD TAFT UNIVERSITY
Education—General M
Taxation M

WILLIAM MITCHELL COLLEGE OF LAW
Law M,D

WILLIAM PATERSON UNIVERSITY OF NEW JERSEY
Business Administration and Management—General M
Counselor Education M
Education—General M
Educational Leadership and Administration M
Exercise and Sports Science M,D
Reading Education M
Special Education M

WILLIAM PENN UNIVERSITY
Organizational Management M

WILLIAM WOODS UNIVERSITY
Advertising and Public Relations M,D,O
Business Administration and Management—General M,D,O
Curriculum and Instruction M,D,O
Educational Leadership and Administration M,D,O
Educational Media/Instructional Technology M,D,O
Human Resources Development M,D,O
Marketing M,D,O
Physical Education M,D,O

WILMINGTON COLLEGE
Education—General M
Reading Education M
Special Education M

WILMINGTON UNIVERSITY
Accounting M,D
Business Administration and Management—General M,D
Counselor Education M,D
Education of the Gifted M,D
Education—General M,D
Educational Leadership and Administration M,D
Educational Media/Instructional Technology M,D
Elementary Education M,D
English as a Second Language M,D
Finance and Banking M,D
Higher Education M,D
Human Resources Management M,D
Human Services M
Management Information Systems M,D
Marketing M,D
Organizational Management M,D
Reading Education M,D
Secondary Education M,D
Special Education M,D
Vocational and Technical Education M,D

WILSON COLLEGE
Education—General M
Elementary Education M
Secondary Education M

*M—masters degree; D—doctorate; O—other advanced degree; *—Close-Up and/or Display*

WINGATE UNIVERSITY
Business Administration and Management—General	M
Community College Education	M,D
Education—General	M,D
Educational Leadership and Administration	M,D
Elementary Education	M,D
Health Education	M,D
Physical Education	M,D
Sports Management	M,D

WINONA STATE UNIVERSITY
Counselor Education	M
Education—General	M
Educational Leadership and Administration	M,O
Recreation and Park Management	M,O
Special Education	M
Sports Management	M,O

WINSTON-SALEM STATE UNIVERSITY
Business Administration and Management—General	M
Elementary Education	M
Management Information Systems	M

WINTHROP UNIVERSITY
Art Education	M
Business Administration and Management—General	M
Counselor Education	M
Education—General	M
Educational Leadership and Administration	M
Middle School Education	M
Music Education	M
Physical Education	M
Project Management	M,O
Reading Education	M
Secondary Education	M
Social Work	M
Special Education	M

WITTENBERG UNIVERSITY
Education—General	M

WOODBURY UNIVERSITY
Business Administration and Management—General	M
Organizational Management	M

WORCESTER POLYTECHNIC INSTITUTE
Business Administration and Management—General	M,O

Educational Media/Instructional Technology	M,D
Management Information Systems	M,O
Marketing	M,O
Organizational Management	M,O

WORCESTER STATE UNIVERSITY
Accounting	M
Business Administration and Management—General	M
Early Childhood Education	M
Education—General	M,O
Educational Leadership and Administration	M,O
Elementary Education	M
English as a Second Language	M
English Education	M
Foreign Languages Education	M
Health Education	M
Middle School Education	M,O
Nonprofit Management	M
Organizational Management	M
Reading Education	M,O
Secondary Education	M
Social Sciences Education	M
Special Education	M,O

WRIGHT STATE UNIVERSITY
Accounting	M
Adult Education	O
Business Administration and Management—General	M
Business Education	M
Computer Education	M
Counselor Education	M
Curriculum and Instruction	M,O
Early Childhood Education	M
Education of the Gifted	M
Education—General	M,O
Educational Leadership and Administration	M,O
Elementary Education	M
English as a Second Language	M
Finance and Banking	M
Health Education	M
Higher Education	M,O
International and Comparative Education	M
International Business	M
Library Science	M
Logistics	M
Management Information Systems	M
Marketing	M
Mathematics Education	M

Middle School Education	M
Music Education	M
Physical Education	M
Project Management	M
Recreation and Park Management	M
Science Education	M
Secondary Education	M
Special Education	M
Supply Chain Management	M
Vocational and Technical Education	M

XAVIER UNIVERSITY
Business Administration and Management—General	M
Counselor Education	M
Early Childhood Education	M
Education—General	M
Educational Leadership and Administration	M
Elementary Education	M
Finance and Banking	M
Health Law	M
Human Resources Development	M
International Business	M
Management Strategy and Policy	M
Marketing	M
Multilingual and Multicultural Education	M
Reading Education	M
Religious Education	M
Secondary Education	M
Special Education	M
Sports Management	M

XAVIER UNIVERSITY OF LOUISIANA
Counselor Education	M
Curriculum and Instruction	M
Education—General	M
Educational Leadership and Administration	M

YALE UNIVERSITY
Accounting	D
Business Administration and Management—General	M,D
Finance and Banking	D
Law	M,D
Marketing	D
Organizational Management	D

YESHIVA UNIVERSITY
Accounting	M
Educational Leadership and Administration	M,D,O

Intellectual Property Law	M,D
Law	M,D
Religious Education	M,D,O
Social Work	M,D

YORK COLLEGE OF PENNSYLVANIA
Business Administration and Management—General	M
Education—General	M
Educational Leadership and Administration	M
Finance and Banking	M
Marketing	M
Reading Education	M

YORK UNIVERSITY
Accounting	M,D
Business Administration and Management—General	M,D
Education—General	M,D
Finance and Banking	M,D
Human Resources Management	M,D
International Business	M,D
Kinesiology and Movement Studies	M,D
Law	M,D
Social Work	M,D

YOUNGSTOWN STATE UNIVERSITY
Accounting	M
Business Administration and Management—General	M,O
Counselor Education	M
Curriculum and Instruction	M
Early Childhood Education	M
Education of the Gifted	M
Education—General	M,D
Educational Leadership and Administration	M,D
Educational Media/Instructional Technology	M
Finance and Banking	M
Human Services	M
Marketing	M
Mathematics Education	M
Middle School Education	M
Music Education	M
Reading Education	M
Science Education	M
Secondary Education	M
Special Education	M

ACADEMIC AND PROFESSIONAL PROGRAMS IN BUSINESS

Section 1
Business Administration and Management

This section contains a directory of institutions offering graduate work in business administration and management, followed by in-depth entries submitted by institutions that chose to prepare detailed program descriptions. Additional information about programs listed in the directory but not augmented by an in-depth entry may be obtained by writing directly to the dean of a graduate school or chair of a department at the address given in the directory.

For programs offering related work, see also in this book Sections 2–18, Education (Business Education), and Sports Management. In the other guides in this series:

Graduate Programs in the Humanities, Arts & Social Sciences

See *Art and Art History (Arts Administration), Economics, Family and Consumer Sciences (Consumer Economics), Political Science and International Affairs, Psychology (Industrial and Organizational Psychology),* and *Public, Regional, and Industrial Affairs (Industrial and Labor Relations)*

Graduate Programs in the Biological/Biomedical Sciences & Health-Related Medical Professions

See *Health Services* and *Nursing (Nursing and Healthcare Administration)*

Graduate Programs in the Physical Sciences, Mathematics, Agricultural Sciences, the Environment & Natural Resources

See *Environmental Sciences and Management (Environmental Management and Policy)* and *Mathematical Sciences*

Graduate Programs in Engineering & Applied Sciences

See *Computer Science and Information Technology, Civil and Environmental Engineering (Construction Engineering and Management), Industrial Engineering,* and *Management of Engineering and Technology*

CONTENTS

Program Directory
Business Administration and Management—General   70

Displays and Close-Ups
Adelphi University   70, 181
Fashion Institute of Technology   96, 183
Manhattanville College   185
Monmouth University   116, 187
North Carolina State University   120, 189
University of California, Los Angeles   145, 191
University of Oklahoma   158, 193
University of Ottawa   159, 195
The University of Texas at Dallas   168, 197

See also:
Embry-Riddle Aeronautical University–Daytona—
    Business Administration/Aviation Management   616, 635

Business Administration and Management— General

Adelphi University, Robert B. Willumstad School of Business, MBA Program, Garden City, NY 11530-0701. Offers finance (MBA); management information systems (MBA); management/human resource management (MBA); marketing/e-commerce (MBA). *Accreditation:* AACSB. Part-time and evening/weekend programs available. *Students:* 254 full-time (129 women), 118 part-time (63 women); includes 60 minority (13 Black or African American, non-Hispanic/Latino; 18 Asian, non-Hispanic/Latino; 28 Hispanic/Latino; 1 Native Hawaiian or other Pacific Islander, non-Hispanic/Latino), 200 international. Average age 28. In 2013, 182 master's awarded. *Degree requirements:* For master's, capstone course. *Entrance requirements:* For master's, GMAT, 2 letters of recommendation. Additional exam requirements/recommendations for international students: Required—TOEFL (minimum score 550 paper-based; 80 iBT). *Application deadline:* For fall admission, 4/1 for international students; for spring admission, 11/1 for international students. Applications are processed on a rolling basis. Application fee: $50. Electronic applications accepted. *Expenses:* Tuition: Full-time $32,530; part-time $1010 per credit. *Required fees:* $1150. Tuition and fees vary according to degree level and program. *Financial support:* Research assistantships with partial tuition reimbursements, career-related internships or fieldwork, Federal Work-Study, institutionally sponsored loans, scholarships/grants, tuition waivers (partial), and unspecified assistantships available. Financial award application deadline: 3/1; financial award applicants required to submit FAFSA. *Faculty research:* Supply chain management, distribution channels, productivity benchmark analysis, data envelopment analysis, financial portfolio analysis. *Unit head:* Dr. Rakesh Gupta, Associate Dean, 516-877-4629. *Application contact:* Christine Murphy, Director of Admissions, 516-877-3050, Fax: 516-877-3039, E-mail: graduateadmissions@adelphi.edu. Website: http://business.adelphi.edu/degree-programs/graduate-degree-programs/m-b-a/.

See Display below and Close-Up on page 181.

Alabama Agricultural and Mechanical University, School of Graduate Studies, School of Business, Department of Management and Marketing, Huntsville, AL 35811. Offers MBA. Part-time and evening/weekend programs available. *Degree requirements:* For master's, comprehensive exam, thesis optional. *Entrance requirements:* For master's, GMAT, minimum undergraduate GPA of 2.5. Additional exam requirements/recommendations for international students: Required—TOEFL (minimum score 500 paper-based; 61 iBT). Electronic applications accepted. *Faculty research:* Consumer behavior of blacks, small business marketing, economics of education, China in transition, international economics.

Alabama State University, College of Business Administration, Montgomery, AL 36101-0271. Offers M Acc. *Accreditation:* ACBSP. Part-time programs available. *Faculty:* 4 full-time (0 women). *Students:* 22 full-time (13 women), 10 part-time (6 women); includes 28 minority (26 Black or African American, non-Hispanic/Latino; 1 Asian, non-Hispanic/Latino; 1 Two or more races, non-Hispanic/Latino), 3 international. Average age 28. 29 applicants, 69% accepted, 20 enrolled. In 2013, 9 master's awarded. *Degree requirements:* For master's, comprehensive exam. *Entrance requirements:* For master's, GMAT, graduate writing competency test. Additional exam requirements/recommendations for international students: Required—TOEFL (minimum score 500 paper-based). *Application deadline:* For fall admission, 7/15 for domestic students; for spring admission, 12/15 for domestic students. Applications are processed on a rolling basis. Application fee: $25. *Expenses:* Tuition, state resident: full-time $7958; part-time $343 per credit hour. Tuition, nonresident: full-time $14,132; part-time $686 per credit hour. *Required fees:* $446 per term. One-time fee: $1784 full-time; $892 part-time. Tuition and fees vary according to course load. *Financial support:* Research assistantships available. Financial award application deadline: 6/15; financial award applicants required to submit FAFSA. *Unit head:* Dr. Le-Quita Booth, Dean, 334-229-4124, E-mail: lbooth@alasu.edu. *Application contact:* Dr. William Person, Dean of Graduate Studies, 334-229-4274, Fax: 334-229-4928, E-mail: wperson@alasu.edu. Website: http://www.alasu.edu/academics/colleges—departments/college-of-business-administration/index.aspx.

Alaska Pacific University, Graduate Programs, Business Administration Department, Program in Business Administration, Anchorage, AK 99508-4672. Offers business administration (MBA); health services administration (MBA). Part-time and evening/weekend programs available. *Degree requirements:* For master's, capstone course. *Entrance requirements:* For master's, GMAT or GRE General Test, minimum GPA of 3.0.

Albany State University, College of Business, Albany, GA 31705-2717. Offers accounting (MBA); general (MBA); healthcare (MBA). *Accreditation:* ACBSP. Part-time and evening/weekend programs available. *Degree requirements:* For master's, comprehensive exam, internship, 3 hours of physical education. *Entrance requirements:* For master's, GMAT (minimum score of 450)/GRE (minimum score of 800) for those without earned master's degree or higher, minimum undergraduate GPA of 2.5, 2 letters of reference, official transcript, pre-entrance medical record and certificate of immunization. Electronic applications accepted. *Faculty research:* Diversity issues, ancestry, understanding finance through use of technology.

Albertus Magnus College, Master of Arts in Leadership Program, New Haven, CT 06511-1189. Offers MA. Part-time and evening/weekend programs available. *Faculty:* 3 full-time (0 women), 8 part-time/adjunct (5 women). *Students:* 15 full-time (11 women), 8 part-time (all women); includes 7 minority (6 Black or African American, non-Hispanic/Latino; 1 Hispanic/Latino). 30 applicants, 83% accepted, 23 enrolled. In 2013, 17 master's awarded. *Degree requirements:* For master's, thesis optional. *Entrance requirements:* For master's, interview, minimum GPA of 2.7. Additional exam requirements/recommendations for international students: Recommended—TOEFL. Application fee: $50. *Faculty research:* Leadership, quality management, employee motivation. *Unit head:* Dr. Howard Fero, Director, 203-773-4424, E-mail: hfero@albertus.edu. *Application contact:* Annette Bosley-Boyce, Enrollment and Administrative Director, 203-773-8512, Fax: 203-773-5257, E-mail: leadership@albertus.edu.

Albertus Magnus College, Master of Business Administration Program, New Haven, CT 06511-1189. Offers MBA. Program also offered in East Hartford, CT. Part-time and evening/weekend programs available. Postbaccalaureate distance learning degree programs offered (no on-campus study). *Faculty:* 7 full-time (2 women), 24 part-time/adjunct (6 women). *Students:* 228 full-time (131 women), 19 part-time (9 women); includes 74 minority (61 Black or African American, non-Hispanic/Latino; 2 American Indian or Alaska Native, non-Hispanic/Latino; 1 Asian, non-Hispanic/Latino; 10 Hispanic/Latino). Average age 35. 52 applicants, 100% accepted, 52 enrolled. In 2013, 112 master's awarded. *Degree requirements:* For master's, thesis, capstone project. *Entrance requirements:* For master's, 3 years of management or related experience, minimum GPA of 2.5. Additional exam requirements/recommendations for international students: Required—TOEFL. *Application deadline:* Applications are processed on a rolling basis. Application fee: $50. *Financial support:* Available to part-time students. *Faculty research:* Finance, project management, accounting, business administration. *Unit head:* Dr. Wayne Gineo, Director, MBA Programs, 203-777-7100, E-mail: wgineo@albertus.edu. *Application contact:* Dr. Irene Rios, Dean of New Dimensions, 203-777-7100, Fax: 203-777-9906, E-mail: irios@albertus.edu. Website: http://www.albertus.edu/index.html.

Alcorn State University, School of Graduate Studies, School of Business, Alcorn State, MS 39096-7500. Offers MBA. *Accreditation:* ACBSP.

Alfred University, Graduate School, School of Business, Alfred, NY 14802-1205. Offers accounting (MBA); business administration (MBA). *Accreditation:* AACSB. Part-time programs available. *Faculty:* 8 full-time (2 women). *Students:* 18 full-time (10 women), 19 part-time (5 women). Average age 28. 29 applicants, 66% accepted, 15 enrolled. In 2013, 31 master's awarded. *Entrance requirements:* For master's, GMAT. Additional exam requirements/recommendations for international students: Required—TOEFL (minimum score 590 paper-based; 90 iBT), IELTS (minimum score 6.5). *Application deadline:* For fall admission, 8/1 for domestic students, 3/15 for international students; for winter admission, 12/1 for domestic students; for spring admission, 10/1 for international students. Applications are processed on a rolling basis. Application fee: $60. Electronic applications accepted. *Expenses: Tuition:* Full-time $38,020; part-time $810 per credit hour. *Required fees:* $950; $160 per semester. Part-time tuition and fees vary according to campus/location and program. *Financial support:* In 2013–14, 18 research assistantships with partial tuition reimbursements (averaging $19,010 per year) were awarded; tuition waivers (partial) and unspecified assistantships also available. Financial award applicants required to submit FAFSA. *Unit head:* Dr. Nancy Evangelista, Dean of Graduate Programs, 607-871-2124, Fax: 607-871-2114, E-mail: fevangel@alfred.edu. *Application contact:* Sara Love, Coordinator of Graduate Admissions, 607-871-2115, Fax: 607-871-2198, E-mail: gradinquiry@alfred.edu. Website: http://business.alfred.edu/mba/.

Alliant International University–Los Angeles, Marshall Goldsmith School of Management, Business Division, Alhambra, CA 91803-1360. Offers DBA. *Unit head:* Dr. Jim Goodrich, Systemwide Dean, 866-825-5426, Fax: 858-552-1974, E-mail: admissions@alliant.edu. *Application contact:* Alliant International University Central Contact Center, 866-U-ALLIANT, Fax: 858-635-4555, E-mail: admissions@alliant.edu.

Alliant International University–México City, School of Management, Mexico City, Mexico. Offers business administration (MBA); international business administration (MIBA); international studies (MA), including international relations. Part-time and evening/weekend programs available. *Faculty:* 7 part-time/adjunct (3 women). *Students:* 10 full-time (3 women), 9 international. Average age 31. 8 applicants, 75% accepted, 5 enrolled. In 2013, 9 master's awarded. *Degree requirements:* For master's, thesis (for some programs). *Entrance requirements:* For master's, GMAT or GRE (depending on program), minimum GPA of 3.0, letters of recommendation. Additional exam requirements/recommendations for international students: Required—TOEFL (minimum score 550 paper-based; 80 iBT), TWE (minimum score 5). *Application deadline:* For fall admission, 8/1 priority date for domestic and international students; for spring admission, 12/1 priority date for domestic and international students. Applications are processed on a rolling basis. Application fee: $55. Electronic applications accepted. *Financial support:* Research assistantships, teaching assistantships, career-related internships or fieldwork, Federal Work-Study, institutionally sponsored loans, and scholarships/grants available. Support available to part-time students. Financial award application deadline: 2/15; financial award applicants required to submit FAFSA. *Faculty research:* Global economy, international relations. *Unit head:* Dr. Lee White, Dean, 858-635-4495, E-mail: contacto@alliantmexico.com. *Application contact:* Lesly Gutierrez Garcia, Coordinator of Admissions and Student Services, 525 5525-7651, E-mail: contacto@alliantmexico.com. Website: http://www.alliantmexico.com.

Alliant International University–San Diego, Alliant School of Management, Business and Management Division, San Diego, CA 92131-1799. Offers business administration (MBA); MBA/MA; MBA/PhD. Part-time and evening/weekend programs available. *Faculty:* 8 full-time (3 women), 7 part-time/adjunct (1 woman). *Students:* 46 full-time (17 women), 40 part-time (18 women); includes 16 minority (5 Black or African American, non-Hispanic/Latino; 4 Asian, non-Hispanic/Latino; 5 Hispanic/Latino; 2 Two or more races, non-Hispanic/Latino), 52 international. Average age 34. 88 applicants, 75% accepted, 41 enrolled. In 2013, 16 master's awarded. *Entrance requirements:* For master's, GMAT or GRE, minimum GPA of 2.75. Additional exam requirements/recommendations for international students: Required—TOEFL (minimum score 550 paper-based; 80 iBT), TWE (minimum score 5). *Application deadline:* For fall admission, 8/1 priority date for domestic and international students; for spring admission, 12/1 priority date for domestic and international students. Applications are processed on a rolling basis. Application fee: $55. Electronic applications accepted. *Financial support:* Research assistantships, teaching assistantships, career-related internships or fieldwork, Federal Work-Study, institutionally sponsored loans, scholarships/grants, and tuition waivers (partial) available. Support available to part-time students. Financial award application deadline: 2/15; financial award applicants required to submit FAFSA. *Faculty research:* Financial and commodity markets, market micro-structures, risk measurement, virtual teams, sustainable work environments. *Unit head:* Dr. Rachna Kumar, Program Director, 858-635-4551, Fax: 855-635-4739, E-mail: admissions@alliant.edu. *Application contact:* Alliant International University Central Contact Center, 866-U-ALLIANT, Fax: 858-635-4555, E-mail: admissions@alliant.edu. Website: http://www.alliant.edu/usicb.

Alvernia University, Graduate Studies, Department of Business, Reading, PA 19607-1799. Offers MBA. *Accreditation:* ACBSP. Part-time and evening/weekend programs available. *Degree requirements:* For master's, thesis optional. *Entrance requirements:* For master's, GMAT, GRE, or MAT. Electronic applications accepted.

Alverno College, School of Business, Milwaukee, WI 53234-3922. Offers MBA. Evening/weekend programs available. *Faculty:* 6 full-time (4 women), 1 (woman) part-time/adjunct. *Students:* 85 full-time (67 women), 1 part-time (0 women); includes 24 minority (10 Black or African American, non-Hispanic/Latino; 1 Asian, non-Hispanic/Latino; 13 Hispanic/Latino), 1 international. Average age 36. 24 applicants, 96% accepted, 19 enrolled. In 2013, 32 master's awarded. *Entrance requirements:* For master's, 3 or more years of relevant work experience. Additional exam requirements/recommendations for international students: Required—TOEFL. *Application deadline:* For fall admission, 7/15 priority date for domestic and international students; for spring admission, 12/15 priority date for domestic and international students. Applications are processed on a rolling basis. Application fee: $0. Electronic applications accepted. Application fee is waived when completed online. *Expenses:* Contact institution. *Financial support:* Federal Work-Study and scholarships/grants available. Support available to part-time students. Financial award application deadline: 4/15; financial award applicants required to submit FAFSA. *Unit head:* Patricia Jensen, MBA Program Director, 414-382-6321, E-mail: patricia.jensen@alverno.edu. *Application contact:* Christy Stone, Director of Admissions, 414-382-6108, Fax: 414-382-6354, E-mail: christy.stone@alverno.edu.

Amberton University, Graduate School, Department of Business Administration, Garland, TX 75041-5595. Offers general business (MBA); management (MBA); project management (MBA); strategic leadership (MBA). Part-time and evening/weekend programs available. *Entrance requirements:* For master's, minimum GPA of 3.0. *Expenses: Tuition:* Full-time $5808; part-time $242 per credit hour.

The American College, Graduate Programs, Bryn Mawr, PA 19010-2105. Offers financial services (MSFS); leadership (MSM). Part-time and evening/weekend programs available. Postbaccalaureate distance learning degree programs offered (minimal on-campus study). Electronic applications accepted. *Faculty research:* Retirement counseling, social security, aging, family composition, inflation.

American College of Thessaloniki, Department of Business Administration, Pylea-Thessaloniki, Greece. Offers banking and finance (MBA); entrepreneurship (MBA, Certificate); finance (Certificate); management (MBA, Certificate); marketing (MBA, Certificate). Part-time and evening/weekend programs available. *Degree requirements:* For master's, thesis. *Entrance requirements:* For master's, bachelor's degree. Additional exam requirements/recommendations for international students: Recommended—TOEFL. Electronic applications accepted.

American Graduate University, Program in Acquisition Management, Covina, CA 91724. Offers MAM, Certificate. Part-time programs available. Postbaccalaureate distance learning degree programs offered (no on-campus study). *Degree requirements:* For master's, comprehensive exam, thesis (for some programs). *Entrance requirements:* For master's, undergraduate degree from institution accredited by accrediting agency recognized by the U.S. Department of Education, photo identification, response to distance education survey. Additional exam requirements/recommendations for international students: Required—TOEFL. Electronic applications accepted.

American Graduate University, Program in Business Administration, Covina, CA 91724. Offers acquisition and contracting (MBA); general management (MBA); program/project management (MBA); supply chain management (MBA). Part-time programs available. Postbaccalaureate distance learning degree programs offered (no on-campus study). *Degree requirements:* For master's, thesis. *Entrance requirements:* For master's, undergraduate degree from institution accredited by accrediting agency recognized by the U.S. Department of Education, photo identification, response to distance education survey. Additional exam requirements/recommendations for international students: Required—TOEFL. Electronic applications accepted.

American Graduate University, Program in Contract Management, Covina, CA 91724. Offers MCM, Certificate. Part-time programs available. Postbaccalaureate distance learning degree programs offered (no on-campus study). *Degree requirements:* For master's, comprehensive exam (for some programs), thesis (for some programs). *Entrance requirements:* For master's, undergraduate degree from institution accredited by accrediting agency recognized by the U.S. Department of Education, photo identification, response to distance education survey. Additional exam requirements/recommendations for international students: Required—TOEFL. Electronic applications accepted.

American InterContinental University Houston, School of Business, Houston, TX 77042. Offers management (MBA).

American InterContinental University Online, Program in Business Administration, Schaumburg, IL 60173. Offers accounting and finance (MBA); finance (MBA); healthcare management (MBA); human resource management (MBA); international business (MBA); management (MBA); marketing (MBA); operations management (MBA); organizational psychology and development (MBA); project management (MBA). *Accreditation:* ACBSP. Evening/weekend programs available. Postbaccalaureate distance learning degree programs offered (no on-campus study). *Entrance requirements:* Additional exam requirements/recommendations for international students: Required—TOEFL (minimum score 550 paper-based). Electronic applications accepted.

American InterContinental University South Florida, Program in International Business, Weston, FL 33326. Offers accounting and finance (MBA); human resource management (MBA); management (MBA); marketing (MBA). Part-time and evening/weekend programs available. Postbaccalaureate distance learning degree programs offered. Electronic applications accepted.

American International College, Graduate Business Programs, MBA Program, Springfield, MA 01109-3189. Offers MBA. Part-time and evening/weekend programs available. *Faculty:* 6 part-time/adjunct (2 women). *Students:* 60 full-time (22 women), 2 part-time (1 woman); includes 26 minority (19 Black or African American, non-Hispanic/Latino; 2 Asian, non-Hispanic/Latino; 4 Hispanic/Latino; 1 Native Hawaiian or other Pacific Islander, non-Hispanic/Latino), 2 international. Average age 28. 42 applicants, 79% accepted, 25 enrolled. In 2013, 18 master's awarded. *Entrance requirements:* For master's, bachelor's degree, minimum GPA of 2.75. Additional exam requirements/recommendations for international students: Required—TOEFL or IELTS. *Application deadline:* Applications are processed on a rolling basis. Application fee: $50. Electronic applications accepted. *Expenses: Tuition:* Full-time $14,040; part-time $780 per credit. Tuition and fees vary according to course load, degree level and program. *Financial support:* Career-related internships or fieldwork available. Financial award application deadline: 4/1; financial award applicants required to submit FAFSA. *Unit head:* Thomas Barron, Director, 413-205-3305, Fax: 413-205-3943, E-mail: thomas.barron@aic.edu. *Application contact:* Kerry Barnes, Director of Graduate Admissions, 413-205-3703, Fax: 413-205-3051, E-mail: kerry.barnes@aic.edu.

American Jewish University, Graduate School of Nonprofit Management, Program in Business Administration, Bel Air, CA 90077-1599. Offers general nonprofit administration (MBA); Jewish nonprofit administration (MBA). Part-time and evening/weekend programs available. *Degree requirements:* For master's, thesis, internship. *Entrance requirements:* For master's, GMAT or GRE General Test, interview, minimum undergraduate GPA of 3.0. Additional exam requirements/recommendations for international students: Required—TOEFL (minimum score 550 paper-based).

American National University, Program in Business Administration, Salem, VA 24153. Offers MBA.

American Public University System, AMU/APU Graduate Programs, Charles Town, WV 25414. Offers accounting (MBA, MS); criminal justice (MA), including business administration, emergency and disaster management, general (MA, MS); educational leadership (M Ed); emergency and disaster management (MA); entrepreneurship (MBA); environmental policy and management (MS), including environmental planning,

environmental sustainability, fish and wildlife management, general (MA, MS), global environmental management; finance (MBA); general (MBA); global business management (MBA); history (MA), including American history, ancient and classical history, European history, global history, public history; homeland security (MA), including business administration, counter-terrorism studies, criminal justice, cyber, emergency management and public health, intelligence studies, transportation security; homeland security resource allocation (MBA); humanities (MA); information technology (MS), including digital forensics, enterprise software development, information assurance and security, IT project management; information technology management (MBA); intelligence studies (MA), including criminal intelligence, cyber, general (MA, MS), homeland security, intelligence analysis, intelligence collection, intelligence management, intelligence operations, terrorism studies; international relations and conflict resolution (MA), including comparative and security issues, conflict resolution, international and transnational security issues, peacekeeping; legal studies (MA); management (MA), including defense management, general (MA, MS), human resource management, organizational leadership, public administration; marketing (MBA); military history (MA), including American military history, American Revolution, civil war, war since 1945, World War II; military studies (MA), including joint warfare, strategic leadership; national security studies (MA), including general (MA, MS), homeland security, regional security studies, security and intelligence analysis, terrorism studies; nonprofit management (MBA); political science (MA), including American politics and government, comparative government and development, general (MA, MS), international relations, public policy; psychology (MA), including general (MA, MS), maritime engineering management, reverse logistics management; public administration (MPA), including disaster management, environmental policy, health policy, human resources, national security, organizational management, security management; public health (MPH); reverse logistics management (MA); school counseling (M Ed); security management (MA); space studies (MS), including aerospace science, general (MA, MS), planetary science; sports and health sciences (MS); teaching (M Ed), including curriculum and instruction for elementary teachers, elementary reading, English language learners, instructional leadership, online learning, special education; transportation and logistics management (MA), including general (MA, MS), maritime engineering management, reverse logistics management. Programs offered via distance learning only. Part-time and evening/weekend programs available. Postbaccalaureate distance learning degree programs offered (no on-campus study). *Faculty:* 432 full-time (242 women), 1,722 part-time/adjunct (829 women). *Students:* 511 full-time (241 women), 10,947 part-time (4,294 women); includes 3,760 minority (2,058 Black or African American, non-Hispanic/Latino; 88 American Indian or Alaska Native, non-Hispanic/Latino; 293 Asian, non-Hispanic/Latino; 876 Hispanic/Latino; 91 Native Hawaiian or other Pacific Islander, non-Hispanic/Latino; 354 Two or more races, non-Hispanic/Latino), 134 international. Average age 36. In 2013, 3,323 master's awarded. *Degree requirements:* For master's, comprehensive exam or practicum. *Entrance requirements:* For master's, official transcript showing earned bachelor's degree from institution accredited by recognized accrediting body. Additional exam requirements/recommendations for international students: Required—TOEFL (minimum score 550 paper-based), IELTS (minimum score 6.5). *Application deadline:* Applications are processed on a rolling basis. Application fee: $0. Electronic applications accepted. *Expenses: Tuition:* Part-time $325 per semester hour. *Financial support:* Applicants required to submit FAFSA. *Faculty research:* Military history, criminal justice, management performance, national security. *Unit head:* Dr. Karan Powell, Executive Vice President and Provost, 877-468-6268, Fax: 304-724-3780. *Application contact:* Terry Grant, Vice President of Enrollment Management, 877-468-6268, Fax: 304-724-3780, E-mail: info@apus.edu.
Website: http://www.apus.edu.

American Sentinel University, Graduate Programs, Aurora, CO 80014. Offers business administration (MBA); business intelligence (MS); computer science (MSCS); health information management (MS); healthcare (MBA); information systems (MSIS); nursing (MSN). Part-time and evening/weekend programs available. Postbaccalaureate distance learning degree programs offered (no on-campus study). *Entrance requirements:* Additional exam requirements/recommendations for international students: Required—TOEFL (minimum score 600 paper-based). Electronic applications accepted.

American University, Kogod School of Business, Washington, DC 20016-8044. Offers accounting (MS); business administration (MBA); business fundamentals (Certificate); entrepreneurship (Certificate); finance (MS); forensic accounting (Certificate); management (MS); marketing (MS); real estate (MS, Certificate); sustainability management (MS); tax (Certificate); taxation (MS). *Accreditation:* AACSB. Part-time and evening/weekend programs available. Postbaccalaureate distance learning degree programs offered. *Faculty:* 75 full-time (24 women), 36 part-time/adjunct (7 women). *Students:* 194 full-time (95 women), 370 part-time (184 women); includes 168 minority (69 Black or African American, non-Hispanic/Latino; 60 Asian, non-Hispanic/Latino; 33 Hispanic/Latino; 2 Native Hawaiian or other Pacific Islander, non-Hispanic/Latino; 4 Two or more races, non-Hispanic/Latino), 108 international. Average age 30. 940 applicants, 46% accepted, 193 enrolled. In 2013, 221 master's, 4 other advanced degrees awarded. *Entrance requirements:* For master's, GMAT, resume, personal statement, interview, 2 letters of recommendation, transcripts. Additional exam requirements/recommendations for international students: Required—TOEFL (minimum score 100 iBT). *Application deadline:* Applications are processed on a rolling basis. Application fee: $100. Electronic applications accepted. *Expenses:* Contact institution. *Financial support:* Fellowships, career-related internships or fieldwork, Federal Work-Study, institutionally sponsored loans, and tuition waivers (partial) available. Support available to part-time students. Financial award application deadline: 2/1. *Unit head:* Dr. Michael Ginzberg, Dean, 202-885-1985, E-mail: ginzberg@american.edu. *Application contact:* Jason Kennedy, Associate Director of Graduate Admissions, 202-885-1968, E-mail: jkennedy@american.edu.
Website: http://www.kogod.american.edu/.

American University, School of Public Affairs, Washington, DC 20016-8022. Offers justice, law and criminology (MS, PhD); leadership for organizational change (Certificate); nonprofit management (Certificate); organization development (MS); political communication (MA); political science (MA, PhD); public administration (MPA, PhD); public administration: key executive leadership (MPA); public financial management (Certificate); public management (Certificate); public policy (MPP); public policy analysis (Certificate); terrorism and homeland security policy (MS); women, policy and political leadership (Certificate). Part-time and evening/weekend programs available. *Faculty:* 82 full-time (36 women), 56 part-time/adjunct (16 women). *Students:* 364 full-time (220 women), 238 part-time (146 women); includes 158 minority (76 Black or African American, non-Hispanic/Latino; 7 American Indian or Alaska Native, non-Hispanic/Latino; 26 Asian, non-Hispanic/Latino; 40 Hispanic/Latino; 2 Native Hawaiian or other Pacific Islander, non-Hispanic/Latino; 7 Two or more races, non-Hispanic/Latino), 39 international. Average age 28. In 2013, 239 master's, 10 doctorates, 7 other advanced degrees awarded. Terminal master's awarded for partial completion of doctoral program. *Degree requirements:* For master's, comprehensive exam; for doctorate, comprehensive exam, thesis/dissertation. *Entrance requirements:* For master's, GRE, statement of purpose; 2 recommendations, resume, transcript; for doctorate, GRE, 3 recommendations, statement of purpose, resume, writing sample, transcript. Additional exam requirements/recommendations for international students: Required—TOEFL (minimum score 100 iBT). *Application deadline:* For fall admission, 2/1 for domestic and international students. Application fee: $55. Electronic applications accepted. *Expenses: Tuition:* Full-time $25,920; part-time $1482 per credit hour. *Required fees:* $430. Tuition and fees vary according to course load and program. *Financial support:* Fellowships with tuition reimbursements, research assistantships with tuition reimbursements, teaching assistantships with tuition reimbursements, career-related internships or fieldwork, Federal Work-Study, institutionally sponsored loans, scholarships/grants, and tuition waivers (full and partial) available. Financial award application deadline: 2/1. *Unit head:* Dr. Barbara Romzek, Dean, 202-885-2940, E-mail: bromzek@american.edu. *Application contact:* Brenda Manley, Director of Graduate Admissions, 202-885-6202, E-mail: bmanley@american.edu.
Website: http://www.american.edu/spa/.

The American University in Cairo, School of Business, New Cairo, Egypt. Offers business administration (MBA, Diploma); economics (MA); economics in international development (MA). Part-time programs available. *Faculty:* 24 full-time (4 women), 5 part-time/adjunct (0 women). *Students:* 98 full-time (33 women), 88 part-time (43 women), 10 international. 236 applicants, 37% accepted, 36 enrolled. In 2013, 62 master's awarded. *Degree requirements:* For master's, comprehensive exam (for some programs), thesis (for some programs). *Entrance requirements:* For master's, GMAT, GRE. Additional exam requirements/recommendations for international students: Required—TOEFL (minimum score 450 paper-based; 45 iBT), IELTS (minimum score 5). *Application deadline:* For fall admission, 1/30 priority date for domestic and international students; for spring admission, 11/1 priority date for domestic and international students. Applications are processed on a rolling basis. Application fee: $50. Electronic applications accepted. Tuition and fees vary according to course level, course load and program. *Financial support:* Fellowships with partial tuition reimbursements, scholarships/grants, and tuition waivers (partial) available. Financial award application deadline: 7/1; financial award applicants required to submit CSS PROFILE. *Faculty research:* Marketing and quality management, banking operations management, economics, finance. *Unit head:* Dr. Sherif Kamel, Dean, 20-2-2615-3290, E-mail: skamel@aucegypt.edu. *Application contact:* Anna Rejman, Admissions Counselor, 212-730-8800 Ext. 4528, E-mail: wclark@aucegypt.edu.
Website: http://www.aucegypt.edu/Business/Pages/default.aspx.

The American University in Dubai, Graduate Programs, Dubai, United Arab Emirates. Offers construction management (MS); education (M Ed); finance (MBA); generalist (MBA); marketing (MBA). Part-time and evening/weekend programs available. *Degree requirements:* For master's, thesis optional. *Entrance requirements:* For master's, GMAT (for MBA); GRE (for M Ed and MS), minimum undergraduate GPA of 3.0, official transcripts, two reference forms, curriculum vitae/resume, statement of career objectives, work experience. Additional exam requirements/recommendations for international students: Required—TOEFL (minimum score 550 paper-based; 79 iBT). Electronic applications accepted.

American University of Armenia, Graduate Programs, Yerevan, Armenia. Offers business administration (MBA); computer and information science (MS), including business management, design and manufacturing, energy (ME, MS), industrial engineering and systems management; economics (MS); industrial engineering and systems management (ME), including business, computer aided design/manufacturing, energy (ME, MS), information technology; law (LL M); political science and international affairs (MPSIA); public health (MPH); teaching English as a foreign language (MA). Part-time and evening/weekend programs available. *Faculty:* 30 full-time (10 women), 42 part-time/adjunct (13 women). *Students:* 398 full-time (272 women), 138 part-time (84 women). Average age 24. 351 applicants, 77% accepted, 247 enrolled. In 2013, 215 master's awarded. *Degree requirements:* For master's, thesis (for some programs), capstone/project. *Entrance requirements:* For master's, GRE, GMAT, or LSAT. Additional exam requirements/recommendations for international students: Recommended—TOEFL (minimum score 79 iBT), IELTS (minimum score 6.5). *Application deadline:* For fall admission, 3/31 for domestic and international students; for spring admission, 12/20 for domestic and international students. Applications are processed on a rolling basis. Application fee: $30 ($70 for international students). *Expenses: Tuition:* Full-time $2683; part-time $122 per credit. Full-time tuition and fees vary according to program. *Financial support:* In 2013–14, 199 students received support. Teaching assistantships with partial tuition reimbursements available, career-related internships or fieldwork, institutionally sponsored loans, scholarships/grants, unspecified assistantships, and tuition assistance, institutionally-sponsored work study available. Support available to part-time students. Financial award application deadline: 6/30. *Faculty research:* Microfinance, finance (rural/development, international, corporate), firm life cycle theory, TESOL, language proficiency testing, public policy, administrative law, economic development, cryptography, artificial intelligence, energy efficiency/renewable energy, computer-aided design/manufacturing, health financing, tuberculosis control, mother/child health, preventive ophthalmology, post-earthquake psychopathological investigations, tobacco control, environmental health risk assessments. *Total annual research expenditures:* $465,763. *Unit head:* Dr. Dennis Leavens, Provost, 374 10512526, E-mail: provost@aua.am. *Application contact:* Karine Satamyan, Admissions Coordinator, 374-10324040, E-mail: grad@aua.am.
Website: http://www.aua.am.

American University of Beirut, Graduate Programs, Suliman S. Olayan School of Business, Executive MBA Program, Beirut, Lebanon. Offers EMBA. *Faculty:* 10 full-time (3 women), 7 part-time/adjunct (1 woman). *Students:* 35 full-time (5 women). Average age 38. 37 applicants, 59% accepted, 12 enrolled. In 2013, 16 master's awarded. *Degree requirements:* For master's, one foreign language. *Entrance requirements:* For master's, analytical exam (developed and administered in-house), letters of recommendation, interview, at least 10 years of relevant work experience. Additional exam requirements/recommendations for international students: Required—TOEFL (minimum score 600 paper-based; 97 iBT), IELTS (minimum score 7). *Application deadline:* Applications are processed on a rolling basis. Application fee: $75. *Expenses: Tuition:* Full-time $14,724; part-time $818 per credit. *Required fees:* $692; $692. Tuition and fees vary according to course load and program. *Faculty research:* Capital acquisition/mergers and acquisition, corporate governance and financial reporting, corporate social responsibility. *Unit head:* Riad Dimechkie, EMBA Executive Director, 961-1350000 Ext. 3724, E-mail: rd28@aub.edu.lb. *Application contact:* Rula Murtada-Karam, Executive MBA Officer, 961-1-350000 Ext. 3946, E-mail: rm04@aub.edu.lb.
Website: http://www.aub.edu.lb/osb/osb_home/program/EMBA/Pages/index.aspx.

American University of Beirut, Graduate Programs, Suliman S. Olayan School of Business, MBA Program, Beirut, Lebanon. Offers MBA. Part-time and evening/weekend programs available. *Faculty:* 10 full-time (2 women), 1 part-time/adjunct (0 women). *Students:* 30 full-time (11 women), 46 part-time (23 women). Average age 28. 75 applicants, 56% accepted, 16 enrolled. In 2013, 31 master's awarded. *Degree requirements:* For master's, one foreign language, thesis optional, final project or equivalent coursework (2 courses). *Entrance requirements:* For master's, GMAT (minimum score of 570), minimum 2 years of relevant work experience; minimum undergraduate average of 80 or equivalent in any major; undergraduate degree from

recognized university. Additional exam requirements/recommendations for international students: Required—TOEFL (minimum score 600 paper-based; 97 iBT), IELTS (minimum score 7). *Application deadline:* For fall admission, 4/1 for domestic and international students; for spring admission, 11/1 for domestic and international students. Application fee: $50. *Expenses: Tuition:* Full-time $14,724; part-time $818 per credit. *Required fees:* $692; $692. Tuition and fees vary according to course load and program. *Financial support:* In 2013–14, 21 students received support, including 13 teaching assistantships with partial tuition reimbursements available (averaging $16,000 per year); scholarships/grants and unspecified assistantships also available. Support available to part-time students. Financial award application deadline: 2/20. *Faculty research:* Organizational behavior, entrepreneurship, corporate social responsibility, corporate finance, statistics, business intelligence. *Unit head:* Dr. Victor Araman, Director, 961-1374374 Ext. 3737, E-mail: va03@aub.edu.lb. *Application contact:* Dr. Rabih Talhouk, Graduate Council Chair, 96-1-135-0000 Ext. 3955, E-mail: rtalhouk@aub.edu.lb.
Website: http://www.aub.edu.lb/osb/osb_home/program/MBA/Pages/index.aspx.

The American University of Paris, Graduate Programs, Paris, France. Offers cross-cultural and sustainable business management (MA); cultural translation (MA); global communications (MA); global communications and civil society (MA); international affairs (MA); international affairs, conflict resolution and civil society development (MA); Middle East and Islamic studies (MA); Middle East and Islamic studies and international affairs (MA); public policy and international affairs (MA); public policy and international law (MA). *Faculty:* 17 full-time (4 women), 12 part-time/adjunct (4 women). *Students:* 86 full-time (70 women), 92 part-time (75 women). *Degree requirements:* For master's, thesis (for some programs). *Entrance requirements:* For master's, minimum undergraduate GPA of 3.0. Additional exam requirements/recommendations for international students: Recommended—TOEFL, IELTS. *Application deadline:* For fall admission, 4/15 priority date for international students; for spring admission, 11/15 priority date for international students. Applications are processed on a rolling basis. Application fee: $75. Electronic applications accepted. *Expenses: Tuition:* Full-time 12,990 euros; part-time 812 euros per credit. *Required fees:* 890 euros per year. One-time fee: 510 euros. *Financial support:* In 2013–14, 86 students received support. Scholarships/grants available. Financial award applicants required to submit FAFSA. *Unit head:* Oliver Feltham, Associate Dean of Graduate Studies, 33 1 40 62 06 67, E-mail: ofeltham@aup.edu. *Application contact:* International Admissions Counselor, 33 1 40 62 07 20, Fax: 33 1 47 05 34 32, E-mail: admissions@aup.edu.
Website: http://www.aup.edu/academics/graduate.

American University of Sharjah, Graduate Programs, Sharjah, United Arab Emirates. Offers accounting (MS); business (EMBA, MBA); chemical engineering (MS Ch E); civil engineering (MSCE); computer engineering (MS); electrical engineering (MSEE); engineering systems management (MS); mathematics (MS); mechanical engineering (MSME); mechatronics engineering (MS); teaching English to speakers of other languages (MA); translation and interpreting (MA); urban planning (MUP). Part-time and evening/weekend programs available. *Faculty:* 59 full-time (4 women), 5 part-time/adjunct (1 woman). *Students:* 127 full-time (50 women), 342 part-time (148 women). Average age 27. 184 applicants, 83% accepted, 92 enrolled. In 2013, 97 master's awarded. *Degree requirements:* For master's, thesis (for some programs). *Entrance requirements:* For master's, GMAT (for MBA). Additional exam requirements/recommendations for international students: Required—TOEFL (minimum score 550 paper-based; 80 iBT), TWE (minimum score 5); Recommended—IELTS (minimum score 6.5). *Application deadline:* For fall admission, 8/28 priority date for domestic students, 8/14 priority date for international students; for spring admission, 1/22 priority date for domestic students, 1/8 for international students; for summer admission, 5/21 for domestic and international students. Applications are processed on a rolling basis. Application fee: $350. Electronic applications accepted. *Expenses: Tuition:* Full-time 69,660 United Arab Emirates dirhams; part-time 3870 United Arab Emirates dirhams per credit. Tuition and fees vary according to course load and program. *Financial support:* In 2013–14, 63 students received support, including 28 research assistantships with full and partial tuition reimbursements available, 35 teaching assistantships with full and partial tuition reimbursements available; scholarships/grants also available. *Faculty research:* Water pollution, management and waste water treatment, energy and sustainability, air pollution, Islamic finance, family business and small and medium enterprises. *Unit head:* Rami Mahfouz, Director of Enrollment Services, 971-6515-1030, E-mail: mahfouzr@aus.edu. *Application contact:* Mona A. Mabrouk, Graduate Admissions/Office of Enrollment Management, 971-65151012, E-mail: graduateadmission@aus.edu.
Website: http://www.aus.edu/programs/graduate/.

Anaheim University, Programs in Business Administration, Anaheim, CA 92806-5150. Offers entrepreneurship (ME, DBA); global sustainable management (MBA); international business (MBA, DBA, Certificate, Diploma); management (DBA); sustainable management (DBA, Certificate, Diploma). Postbaccalaureate distance learning degree programs offered.

Anderson University, College of Business, Anderson, SC 29621-4035. Offers MBA. *Accreditation:* ACBSP.

Anderson University, Falls School of Business, Anderson, IN 46012-3495. Offers accountancy (MA); business administration (MBA, DBA). *Accreditation:* ACBSP.

Angelo State University, College of Graduate Studies, College of Business, Department of Management and Marketing, San Angelo, TX 76909. Offers business administration (MBA). *Accreditation:* ACBSP. Part-time and evening/weekend programs available. *Entrance requirements:* For master's, GMAT or GRE, essay, resume. Additional exam requirements/recommendations for international students: Required—TOEFL or IELTS. Electronic applications accepted.

Anna Maria College, Graduate Division, Program in Business Administration, Paxton, MA 01612. Offers MBA, AC. Part-time and evening/weekend programs available. *Degree requirements:* For master's, capstone project. *Entrance requirements:* For master's, minimum GPA of 2.7. Additional exam requirements/recommendations for international students: Required—TOEFL (minimum score 500 paper-based). Electronic applications accepted. *Faculty research:* Management organization.

Antioch University Los Angeles, Graduate Programs, Program in Organizational Management, Culver City, CA 90230. Offers human resource development (MA); leadership (MA); organizational development (MA). Part-time and evening/weekend programs available. *Entrance requirements:* For master's, interview. Additional exam requirements/recommendations for international students: Required—TOEFL. *Faculty research:* Systems thinking and chaos theory, technology and organizational structure, nonprofit management, power and empowerment.

Antioch University Midwest, Graduate Programs, Individualized Liberal and Professional Studies Program, Yellow Springs, OH 45387-1609. Offers liberal and professional studies (MA), including counseling, creative writing, education, liberal studies, management, modern literature, psychology, visual arts. Part-time and evening/weekend programs available. Postbaccalaureate distance learning degree programs offered (minimal on-campus study). *Degree requirements:* For master's, thesis or

alternative. *Entrance requirements:* For master's, resume, goal statement, interview. Electronic applications accepted. *Expenses:* Contact institution.

Antioch University Midwest, Graduate Programs, Program in Management and Leading Change, Yellow Springs, OH 45387-1609. Offers MA. Part-time and evening/weekend programs available. Postbaccalaureate distance learning degree programs offered (minimal on-campus study). *Entrance requirements:* For master's, resume, goal statement, interview. Electronic applications accepted. *Expenses:* Contact institution.

Antioch University New England, Graduate School, Department of Management, Program in Sustainability (Green MBA), Keene, NH 03431-3552. Offers MBA. Part-time programs available. *Entrance requirements:* For master's, GRE, resume, 3 letters of recommendation. Additional exam requirements/recommendations for international students: Required—TOEFL (minimum score 600 paper-based).

Appalachian State University, Cratis D. Williams Graduate School, Program in Business Administration, Boone, NC 28608. Offers general management (MBA). *Accreditation:* AACSB. Part-time programs available. Postbaccalaureate distance learning degree programs offered (no on-campus study). *Degree requirements:* For master's, comprehensive exam. *Entrance requirements:* For master's, GMAT, 3 letters of recommendation. Additional exam requirements/recommendations for international students: Required—TOEFL (minimum score 550 paper-based; 79 iBT), IELTS (minimum score 6.5). Electronic applications accepted.

Aquinas College, School of Management, Grand Rapids, MI 49506-1799. Offers health care administration (MM); marketing management (MM); organizational leadership (MM); sustainable business (MM, MSB). Part-time and evening/weekend programs available. *Students:* 13 full-time (10 women), 56 part-time (38 women); includes 10 minority (4 Black or African American, non-Hispanic/Latino; 1 American Indian or Alaska Native, non-Hispanic/Latino; 4 Hispanic/Latino; 1 Two or more races, non-Hispanic/Latino), 1 international. Average age 33. In 2013, 18 master's awarded. *Entrance requirements:* For master's, GMAT, minimum undergraduate GPA of 2.75, 2 years of work experience. Additional exam requirements/recommendations for international students: Required—TOEFL (minimum score 550 paper-based). *Application deadline:* Applications are processed on a rolling basis. Application fee: $0. *Expenses:* Contact institution. *Financial support:* Scholarships/grants available. Support available to part-time students. Financial award application deadline: 3/15; financial award applicants required to submit FAFSA. *Unit head:* Brian DiVita, Director, 616-632-2922, Fax: 616-732-4489. *Application contact:* Lynn Atkins-Rykert, Administrative Assistant, 616-632-2924, Fax: 616-732-4489, E-mail: atkinlyn@aquinas.edu.

Arcadia University, Graduate Studies, Program in Business Administration, Glenside, PA 19038-3295. Offers IMBA, MBA. *Accreditation:* ACBSP. *Expenses:* Contact institution.

Argosy University, Atlanta, College of Business, Atlanta, GA 30328. Offers accounting (DBA); corporate compliance (MBA); customized professional concentration (MBA, DBA); finance (MBA); healthcare administration (MBA); information systems (DBA); information systems management (MBA); international business (MBA, DBA); management (MBA, MSM, DBA); marketing (MBA, DBA).

Argosy University, Chicago, College of Business, Chicago, IL 60601. Offers accounting (DBA); customized professional concentration (MBA, DBA); finance (MBA); fraud examination (MBA); global business sustainability (DBA); healthcare administration (MBA); information systems (DBA); information systems management (MBA); international business (MBA, DBA); management (MBA, MSM, DBA); marketing (MBA, DBA); organizational leadership (Ed D); public administration (MBA); sustainable management (MBA). Postbaccalaureate distance learning degree programs offered (minimal on-campus study).

Argosy University, Dallas, College of Business, Farmers Branch, TX 75244. Offers accounting (DBA, AGC); corporate compliance (MBA, Graduate Certificate); customized professional concentration (MBA); finance (MBA, Graduate Certificate); fraud examination (MBA, Graduate Certificate); global business sustainability (DBA, AGC); healthcare administration (Graduate Certificate); healthcare management (MBA); information systems (MBA, DBA, AGC); information systems management (Graduate Certificate); international business (MBA, DBA, AGC, Graduate Certificate); management (MBA, DBA, AGC, Graduate Certificate); marketing (MBA, DBA, AGC, Graduate Certificate); public administration (MBA, Graduate Certificate); sustainable management (MBA, Graduate Certificate).

Argosy University, Denver, College of Business, Denver, CO 80231. Offers accounting (DBA); corporate compliance (MBA); customized professional concentration (MBA, DBA); finance (MBA); fraud examination (MBA); global business sustainability (DBA); healthcare administration (MBA); information systems (DBA); information systems management (MBA); international business (MBA, DBA); management (MBA, MSM, DBA); marketing (MBA, DBA); organizational leadership (Ed D); public administration (MBA); sustainable management (MBA).

Argosy University, Hawai`i, College of Business, Honolulu, HI 96813. Offers accounting (DBA); corporate compliance (MBA); customized professional concentration (MBA, DBA); finance (MBA, Certificate); fraud examination (MBA); global business sustainability (DBA); healthcare administration (MBA, Certificate); information systems (DBA); information systems management (MBA, Certificate); international business (MBA, DBA, Certificate); management (MBA, MSM, DBA); marketing (MBA, DBA, Certificate); organizational leadership (Ed D); public administration (MBA); sustainable management (MBA).

Argosy University, Inland Empire, College of Business, Ontario, CA 91761. Offers accounting (DBA); corporate compliance (MBA); customized professional concentration (MBA, DBA); finance (MBA); fraud examination (MBA); global business sustainability (DBA); healthcare administration (MBA); information systems (DBA); information systems management (MBA); international business (MBA, DBA); management (MBA, MSM, DBA); marketing (MBA, DBA); organizational leadership (Ed D); public administration (MBA); sustainable management (MBA).

Argosy University, Los Angeles, College of Business, Santa Monica, CA 90045. Offers accounting (DBA); corporate compliance (MBA); customized professional concentration (MBA, DBA); finance (MBA); fraud examination (MBA); global business sustainability (DBA); healthcare administration (MBA); information systems (DBA); information systems management (MBA); international business (MBA, DBA); management (MBA, MSM, DBA); marketing (MBA, DBA); organizational leadership (Ed D); public administration (MBA); sustainable management (MBA).

Argosy University, Nashville, College of Business, Nashville, TN 37214. Offers accounting (DBA); customized professional concentration (MBA, DBA); finance (MBA); healthcare administration (MBA); information systems (MBA, DBA); international business (MBA, DBA); management (MBA, MSM, DBA); marketing (MBA, DBA).

Argosy University, Orange County, College of Business, Orange, CA 92868. Offers accounting (DBA, Adv C); corporate compliance (MBA); customized professional concentration (MBA, DBA); finance (MBA, Certificate); fraud examination (MBA); global business sustainability (DBA); healthcare administration (MBA, Certificate); information systems (DBA, Adv C, Certificate); information systems management (MBA);

international business (MBA, DBA, Adv C, Certificate); management (MBA, MSM, DBA, Adv C); marketing (MBA, DBA, Adv C, Certificate); organizational leadership (Ed D); public administration (MBA, Certificate); sustainable management (MBA).

Argosy University, Phoenix, College of Business, Phoenix, AZ 85021. Offers accounting (DBA); corporate compliance (MBA); customized professional concentration (MBA, DBA); finance (MBA); fraud examination (MBA); global business sustainability (DBA); healthcare administration (MBA); information systems (DBA); information systems management (MBA); international business (MBA, DBA); management (MBA, DBA); marketing (MBA, DBA); public administration (MBA); sustainable management (MBA).

Argosy University, Salt Lake City, College of Business, Draper, UT 84020. Offers accounting (DBA); corporate compliance (MBA); customized professional concentration (MBA, DBA); finance (MBA); fraud examination (MBA); global business sustainability (DBA); healthcare administration (MBA); information systems (DBA); information systems management (MBA); international business (MBA, DBA); management (MBA, DBA); marketing (MBA, DBA); public administration (MBA); sustainable management (MBA).

Argosy University, San Diego, College of Business, San Diego, CA 92108. Offers accounting (DBA); corporate compliance (MBA); customized professional concentration (MBA, DBA); finance (MBA); fraud examination (MBA); global business sustainability (DBA); information systems (DBA); information systems management (MBA); international business (MBA, DBA); management (MBA, MSM, DBA); marketing (MBA, DBA); organizational leadership (Ed D); public administration (MBA).

Argosy University, San Francisco Bay Area, College of Business, Alameda, CA 94501. Offers accounting (DBA); corporate compliance (MBA); customized professional concentration (MBA, DBA); finance (MBA); fraud examination (MBA); global business sustainability (DBA); healthcare administration (MBA); information systems (DBA); information systems management (MBA); international business (MBA, DBA); management (MBA, MSM, DBA); marketing (MBA, DBA); organizational leadership (Ed D); public administration (MBA); sustainable management (MBA).

Argosy University, Sarasota, College of Business, Sarasota, FL 34235. Offers accounting (DBA, Adv C); corporate compliance (MBA, DBA, Certificate); customized professional concentration (MBA, DBA); finance (MBA, Certificate); fraud examination (MBA, Certificate); global business sustainability (DBA, Adv C); healthcare administration (MBA, Certificate); information systems (DBA, Adv C, Certificate); information systems management (MBA); international business (MBA, DBA, Adv C, Certificate); management (MBA, MSM, DBA, Adv C, Certificate); marketing (MBA, DBA, Adv C, Certificate); organizational leadership (Ed D); public administration (MBA, Certificate); sustainable management (MBA, Certificate).

Argosy University, Schaumburg, College of Business, Schaumburg, IL 60173-5403. Offers accounting (DBA, Adv C); customized professional concentration (MBA, DBA); finance (MBA, Certificate); fraud examination (MBA); global business sustainability (DBA); healthcare administration (MBA, Certificate); information systems (DBA, Adv C, Certificate); information systems management (MBA); international business (MBA, DBA, Adv C, Certificate); management (MBA, MSM, DBA, Adv C, Certificate); marketing (MBA, DBA, Adv C, Certificate); organizational leadership (Ed D); public administration (MBA); sustainable management (MBA).

Argosy University, Seattle, College of Business, Seattle, WA 98121. Offers accounting (DBA); corporate compliance (MBA); customized professional concentration (MBA, DBA); finance (MBA); fraud examination (MBA); global business sustainability (DBA); healthcare administration (MBA); information systems (DBA); information systems management (MBA); international business (MBA, DBA); management (MBA, MSM, DBA); marketing (MBA, DBA); organizational leadership (Ed D); public administration (MBA); sustainable management (MBA).

Argosy University, Tampa, College of Business, Tampa, FL 33607. Offers accounting (DBA); corporate compliance (MBA); customized professional concentration (MBA, DBA); finance (MBA); fraud examination (MBA); global business sustainability (DBA); healthcare administration (MBA); information systems (DBA); information systems management (MBA); international business (MBA, DBA); management (MBA, MSM, DBA); marketing (MBA, DBA); organizational leadership (Ed D); public administration (MBA); sustainable management (MBA).

Argosy University, Twin Cities, College of Business, Eagan, MN 55121. Offers accounting (DBA); customized professional concentration (MBA, DBA); finance (MBA); fraud examination (MBA); global business sustainability (DBA); healthcare administration (MBA); information systems (DBA); information systems management (MBA); international business (MBA, DBA); management (MBA, MSM, DBA); marketing (MBA, DBA); organizational leadership (Ed D); public administration (MBA); sustainable management (MBA).

Argosy University, Washington DC, College of Business, Arlington, VA 22209. Offers accounting (DBA); customized professional concentration (MBA, DBA); finance (MBA); fraud examination (MBA); global business sustainability (DBA); healthcare administration (MBA); information systems (DBA); information systems management (MBA); international business (MBA, DBA, Certificate); management (MBA, MSM, DBA); marketing (MBA, DBA, Certificate); organizational leadership (Ed D); public administration (MBA); sustainable management (MBA).

Arizona State University at the Tempe campus, W. P. Carey School of Business, Program in Business Administration, Tempe, AZ 85287-4906. Offers accountancy (PhD); agribusiness (PhD); business administration (MBA); finance (PhD); financial management and markets (MBA); information management (MBA); information systems (PhD); management (PhD); marketing (PhD); strategic marketing and services leadership (MBA); supply chain financial management (MBA); supply chain management (MBA, PhD); JD/MBA; MBA/M Acc; MBA/M Arch. *Accreditation:* AACSB. Part-time and evening/weekend programs available. Postbaccalaureate distance learning degree programs offered (minimal on-campus study). Terminal master's awarded for partial completion of doctoral program. *Degree requirements:* For master's, thesis or alternative, internship, interactive Program of Study (iPOS) submitted before completing 50 percent of required credit hours; for doctorate, comprehensive exam, thesis/dissertation, interactive Program of Study (iPOS) submitted before completing 50 percent of required credit hours. *Entrance requirements:* For master's, GMAT, minimum GPA of 3.0 in last 2 years of work leading to bachelor's degree, 2 letters of recommendation, professional resume, official transcripts, 3 essays; for doctorate, GMAT or GRE, minimum GPA of 3.0 in last 2 years of work leading to bachelor's degree, 3 letters of recommendation, resume, personal statement/essay. Additional exam requirements/recommendations for international students: Required—TOEFL (minimum score 550 paper-based; 80 iBT), IELTS (minimum score 6.5). Electronic applications accepted. *Expenses:* Contact institution.

Arkansas State University, Graduate School, College of Business, Department of Economics and Finance, Jonesboro, AR 72467. Offers business administration (MBA). *Accreditation:* AACSB. Part-time programs available. *Faculty:* 10 full-time (1 woman). *Students:* 92 full-time (32 women), 93 part-time (48 women); includes 18 minority (7 Black or African American, non-Hispanic/Latino; 6 Asian, non-Hispanic/Latino; 4 Hispanic/Latino; 1 Two or more races, non-Hispanic/Latino), 92 international. Average age 28. 189 applicants, 69% accepted, 83 enrolled. In 2013, 40 master's awarded. *Degree requirements:* For master's, comprehensive exam, thesis or alternative. *Entrance requirements:* For master's, GMAT, appropriate bachelor's degree, letters of reference, official transcripts, immunization records. Additional exam requirements/recommendations for international students: Required—TOEFL (minimum score 550 paper-based; 79 iBT), IELTS (minimum score 6), PTE (minimum score 56). *Application deadline:* For fall admission, 7/1 for domestic and international students; for spring admission, 11/15 for domestic students, 11/14 for international students. Applications are processed on a rolling basis. Application fee: $30 ($40 for international students). Electronic applications accepted. *Expenses:* Contact institution. *Financial support:* In 2013–14, 8 students received support. Career-related internships or fieldwork, scholarships/grants, and unspecified assistantships available. Financial award application deadline: 7/1; financial award applicants required to submit FAFSA. *Unit head:* Dr. Patricia Robertson, Chair, 870-972-2280, Fax: 870-972-3417, E-mail: probertson@astate.edu. *Application contact:* Vickey Ring, Graduate Admissions Coordinator, 870-972-3029, Fax: 870-972-3857, E-mail: vickeyring@astate.edu.
Website: http://www.astate.edu/college/business/faculty-staff/economics-finance/.

Arkansas Tech University, College of Business, Russellville, AR 72801. Offers MSBA. Part-time programs available. Postbaccalaureate distance learning degree programs offered (minimal on-campus study). *Students:* 15 full-time (8 women), 19 part-time (10 women); includes 8 minority (6 Black or African American, non-Hispanic/Latino; 1 American Indian or Alaska Native, non-Hispanic/Latino; 1 Hispanic/Latino), 3 international. Average age 33. *Degree requirements:* For master's, complete all required coursework with minimum cumulative GPA of 3.0 within six years. *Entrance requirements:* For master's, official bachelor's degree transcripts from regionally-accredited university; minimum cumulative undergraduate GPA of 2.5 or 3.0 on last 30 credit hours; business information systems course or equivalent with minimum C grade; business statistics course or its equivalent with minimum C grade. Additional exam requirements/recommendations for international students: Required—TOEFL (minimum score 550 paper-based; 79 iBT), IELTS (minimum score 6). *Application deadline:* For fall admission, 3/1 priority date for domestic students, 5/1 priority date for international students; for spring admission, 10/1 priority date for domestic and international students. Applications are processed on a rolling basis. Application fee: $25 ($75 for international students). Electronic applications accepted. *Expenses:* Tuition, state resident: full-time $5976; part-time $249 per credit hour. Tuition, nonresident: full-time $11,952; part-time $498 per credit hour. *Required fees:* $411 per semester. Tuition and fees vary according to course load. *Financial support:* Application deadline: 4/15; applicants required to submit FAFSA. *Unit head:* Dr. Ed Bashaw, Dean, 479-968-0490, E-mail: ebashaw@atu.edu. *Application contact:* Dr. Mary B. Gunter, Dean of Graduate College, 479-968-0398, Fax: 479-964-0542, E-mail: gradcollege@atu.edu.
Website: http://www.atu.edu/business/.

Armstrong State University, School of Graduate Studies, Program in Professional Communication and Leadership, Savannah, GA 31419-1997. Offers MA, Certificate. Part-time and evening/weekend programs available. *Faculty:* 13 full-time (8 women), 1 part-time/adjunct (0 women). *Students:* 10 full-time (6 women), 35 part-time (23 women); includes 16 minority (all Black or African American, non-Hispanic/Latino). Average age 35. 23 applicants, 78% accepted, 16 enrolled. *Degree requirements:* For master's, comprehensive exam, project. *Entrance requirements:* For master's, minimum GPA of 2.5, letters of recommendation, letter of intent, resume. Additional exam requirements/recommendations for international students: Required—TOEFL (minimum score 523 paper-based). *Application deadline:* For fall admission, 6/1 priority date for domestic students, 5/1 priority date for international students; for spring admission, 11/15 priority date for domestic students, 9/15 priority date for international students; for summer admission, 4/15 for domestic students, 9/15 priority date for international students. Application fee: $30. *Expenses:* Tuition, state resident: part-time $201 per credit hour. Tuition, nonresident: part-time $745 per credit hour. *Required fees:* $310 per semester. Tuition and fees vary according to course load, campus/location and program. *Financial support:* In 2013–14, research assistantships with full tuition reimbursements (averaging $5,000 per year) were awarded; scholarships/grants and unspecified assistantships also available. Financial award application deadline: 3/15; financial award applicants required to submit FAFSA. *Faculty research:* Organizational communication, conflict resolution and mediation, rhetoric and language identity, brand identity and marketing, communication theory. *Unit head:* Dr. Chris Hendricks, Assistant Dean of Liberal Arts, 912-344-2725, E-mail: chris.hendricks@armstrong.edu. *Application contact:* Jill Bell, Director, Graduate Enrollment Services, 912-344-2798, Fax: 912-344-3488, E-mail: graduate@armstrong.edu.
Website: http://www.armstrong.edu/Majors/degree/master_professional_communication_leadership.

Ashland University, Dauch College of Business and Economics, Ashland, OH 44805-3702. Offers MBA. *Accreditation:* ACBSP. Part-time and evening/weekend programs available. *Degree requirements:* For master's, thesis optional. *Entrance requirements:* For master's, 2 years of full-time work experience. Additional exam requirements/recommendations for international students: Required—TOEFL. Electronic applications accepted. *Expenses:* Contact institution. *Faculty research:* Human resource management, statistical analysis, global business issues, organizational development, government and business.

Ashworth College, Graduate Programs, Norcross, GA 30092. Offers business administration (MBA); criminal justice (MS); health care administration (MBA, MS); human resource management (MBA, MS); international business (MBA); management (MS); marketing (MBA, MS).

Aspen University, Program in Business Administration, Denver, CO 80246-1930. Offers business administration (MBA); finance (MBA); information management (MBA); project management (MBA, Certificate). Part-time and evening/weekend programs available. Postbaccalaureate distance learning degree programs offered (no on-campus study). *Entrance requirements:* Additional exam requirements/recommendations for international students: Required—TOEFL (minimum score 530 paper-based). Electronic applications accepted.

Assumption College, Graduate Studies, Department of Business Studies, Worcester, MA 01609-1296. Offers accounting (MBA); business administration (CAGS); finance/economics (MBA); frontline management (CGS); general business (MBA); human resources (MBA); international business (MBA); management (MBA); marketing (MBA); nonprofit leadership (MBA, CGS); organizational communication (CGS). Part-time and evening/weekend programs available. *Faculty:* 5 full-time (0 women), 20 part-time/adjunct (7 women). *Students:* 20 full-time (7 women), 130 part-time (68 women); includes 20 minority (8 Black or African American, non-Hispanic/Latino; 2 Asian, non-Hispanic/Latino; 8 Hispanic/Latino; 1 Native Hawaiian or other Pacific Islander, non-Hispanic/Latino; 1 Two or more races, non-Hispanic/Latino), 2 international. Average age 31. 63 applicants, 62% accepted, 22 enrolled. In 2013, 58 master's, 1 other advanced degree awarded. *Degree requirements:* For master's, thesis, capstone. *Entrance requirements:* For master's and other advanced degree, 3 letters of recommendation, resume, essay. Additional exam requirements/recommendations for international students: Required—TOEFL (minimum score 540 paper-based; 76 iBT),

IELTS (minimum score 6). *Application deadline:* For fall admission, 10/1 for domestic and international students; for winter admission, 2/1 for domestic and international students; for spring admission, 4/1 for domestic and international students. Applications are processed on a rolling basis. Application fee: $30. Electronic applications accepted. *Expenses: Tuition:* Full-time $10,098; part-time $561 per credit. *Required fees:* $20 per term. Full-time tuition and fees vary according to course load and program. *Financial support:* In 2013–14, 15 students received support. Tuition waivers (full and partial), unspecified assistantships, and institutional discounts available. Financial award application deadline: 5/1; financial award applicants required to submit FAFSA. *Faculty research:* Workplace diversity, dynamics of team interaction, utilization of leased employees, experiential learning project on due diligence market for prostheses. *Unit head:* Dr. J. Bart Morrison, Director, 508-767-7458, Fax: 508-767-7252, E-mail: jmorrison@assumption.edu. *Application contact:* Laura Lawrence, Graduate Programs Operations Manager, 508-767-7387, Fax: 508-767-7030, E-mail: graduate@assumption.edu.
Website: http://graduate.assumption.edu/mba/assumption-mba.

Athabasca University, Centre for Innovative Management, St. Albert, AB T8N 1B4, Canada. Offers business administration (MBA); information technology management (MBA), including policing concentration; management (GDM); project management (MBA, GDM). Part-time and evening/weekend programs available. Postbaccalaureate distance learning degree programs offered (no on-campus study). *Degree requirements:* For master's, thesis or alternative, applied project. *Entrance requirements:* For master's, 3-8 years of managerial experience, 3 years with undergraduate degree, 5 years managerial experience with professional designation, 8-10 years management experience (on exception). Electronic applications accepted. *Expenses:* Contact institution. *Faculty research:* Human resources, project management, operations research, information technology management, corporate stewardship, energy management.

Auburn University, Graduate School, College of Business, Department of Management, Auburn University, AL 36849. Offers human resource management (PhD); management (MS, PhD); management information systems (MS, PhD). *Accreditation:* AACSB. Part-time programs available. *Faculty:* 42 full-time (9 women), 10 part-time/adjunct (2 women). *Students:* 94 full-time (43 women), 329 part-time (61 women); includes 77 minority (40 Black or African American, non-Hispanic/Latino; 2 American Indian or Alaska Native, non-Hispanic/Latino; 22 Asian, non-Hispanic/Latino; 13 Hispanic/Latino), 46 international. Average age 34. 408 applicants, 55% accepted, 126 enrolled. In 2013, 173 master's, 6 doctorates awarded. *Degree requirements:* For master's, thesis (for some programs); for doctorate, thesis/dissertation. *Entrance requirements:* For master's, GMAT, GRE General Test (MS); for doctorate, GMAT, GRE General Test. Additional exam requirements/recommendations for international students: Required—TOEFL. *Application deadline:* For fall admission, 7/7 for domestic students; for spring admission, 11/24 for domestic students. Applications are processed on a rolling basis. Application fee: $50 ($60 for international students). Electronic applications accepted. *Expenses:* Tuition, state resident: full-time $8262; part-time $459 per credit hour. Tuition, nonresident: full-time $24,786; part-time $1377 per credit hour. Tuition and fees vary according to degree level and program. *Financial support:* Teaching assistantships and Federal Work-Study available. Support available to part-time students. Financial award application deadline: 3/15; financial award applicants required to submit FAFSA. *Unit head:* Dr. Christopher Shook, Head, 334-844-9565. *Application contact:* Dr. George Flowers, Dean of the Graduate School, 334-844-2125.
Website: http://business.auburn.edu/academics/departments/department-of-management/.

Auburn University, Graduate School, College of Business, Program in Business Administration, Auburn University, AL 36849. Offers MBA. *Accreditation:* AACSB. Part-time programs available. *Faculty:* 42 full-time (9 women), 10 part-time/adjunct (2 women). *Students:* 76 full-time (35 women), 306 part-time (58 women); includes 67 minority (34 Black or African American, non-Hispanic/Latino; 2 American Indian or Alaska Native, non-Hispanic/Latino; 19 Asian, non-Hispanic/Latino; 12 Hispanic/Latino), 35 international. Average age 35. 295 applicants, 55% accepted, 126 enrolled. In 2013, 153 master's awarded. *Entrance requirements:* For master's, GMAT. *Application deadline:* For fall admission, 7/7 for domestic students; for spring admission, 11/24 for domestic students. Applications are processed on a rolling basis. Application fee: $50 ($60 for international students). Electronic applications accepted. *Expenses:* Tuition, state resident: full-time $8262; part-time $459 per credit hour. Tuition, nonresident: full-time $24,786; part-time $1377 per credit hour. Tuition and fees vary according to degree level and program. *Financial support:* Federal Work-Study available. Support available to part-time students. Financial award application deadline: 3/15; financial award applicants required to submit FAFSA. *Unit head:* Dr. Christopher Shook, Head, 334-844-9565. *Application contact:* Dr. George Flowers, Dean of the Graduate School, 334-844-2125.
Website: http://www.auburn.edu/business/mbaprog.html.

Auburn University at Montgomery, School of Business, Montgomery, AL 36124-4023. Offers EMBA, MBA, MSISM. *Accreditation:* AACSB. Part-time and evening/weekend programs available. *Faculty:* 15 full-time (4 women). *Students:* 64 full-time (32 women), 85 part-time (41 women); includes 54 minority (24 Black or African American, non-Hispanic/Latino; 30 Asian, non-Hispanic/Latino), 3 international. In 2013, 54 master's awarded. *Degree requirements:* For master's, comprehensive exam. *Entrance requirements:* For master's, GMAT. Additional exam requirements/recommendations for international students: Required—TOEFL. *Application deadline:* Applications are processed on a rolling basis. Electronic applications accepted. *Expenses:* Tuition, state resident: full-time $5994; part-time $333 per credit hour. Tuition, nonresident: full-time $17,982; part-time $999 per credit hour. *Financial support:* Career-related internships or fieldwork and scholarships/grants available. Support available to part-time students. Financial award application deadline: 3/1; financial award applicants required to submit FAFSA. *Unit head:* Dr. Rhea Ingram, Dean, 334-244-3476, Fax: 334-244-3792, E-mail: wingram4@aum.edu. *Application contact:* Dr. Evan Moore, Associate Dean of Graduate Programs, 334-244-3364, Fax: 334-277-3792, E-mail: emoore1@aum.edu.
Website: http://www.aum.edu/schools/school-of-business.

Augsburg College, Program in Business Administration, Minneapolis, MN 55454-1351. Offers MBA. Evening/weekend programs available. Electronic applications accepted.

Aurora University, College of Professional Studies, Dunham School of Business, Aurora, IL 60506-4892. Offers MBA. Part-time and evening/weekend programs available. *Entrance requirements:* For master's, minimum GPA of 2.75, 2 years of work experience. Additional exam requirements/recommendations for international students: Required—TOEFL (minimum score 550 paper-based). Electronic applications accepted. *Expenses:* Contact institution.

Austin Peay State University, College of Graduate Studies, College of Business, Clarksville, TN 37044. Offers management (MS). Part-time and evening/weekend programs available. Postbaccalaureate distance learning degree programs offered (no on-campus study). *Faculty:* 11 full-time (2 women). *Students:* 22 full-time (8 women), 36 part-time (18 women); includes 8 minority (3 Black or African American, non-Hispanic/Latino; 1 Asian, non-Hispanic/Latino; 4 Hispanic/Latino). Average age 33. 27 applicants, 85% accepted, 17 enrolled. In 2013, 40 master's awarded. *Degree requirements:* For master's, comprehensive exam. *Entrance requirements:* For master's, GMAT. Additional exam requirements/recommendations for international students: Required—TOEFL (minimum score 500 paper-based). *Application deadline:* For fall admission, 8/5 priority date for domestic students. Applications are processed on a rolling basis. Application fee: $25. Electronic applications accepted. *Expenses:* Tuition, state resident: full-time $7500; part-time $375 per credit hour. Tuition, nonresident: full-time $20,800; part-time $1040 per credit hour. *Required fees:* $1284; $64.20 per credit hour. *Financial support:* In 2013–14, research assistantships with full tuition reimbursements (averaging $6,500 per year) were awarded; career-related internships or fieldwork, Federal Work-Study, institutionally sponsored loans, scholarships/grants, and unspecified assistantships also available. Support available to part-time students. Financial award application deadline: 3/1; financial award applicants required to submit FAFSA. *Unit head:* Dr. William Rupp, Dean, 931-221-7674, Fax: 931-221-7355, E-mail: ruppw@apsu.edu. *Application contact:* June D. Lee, Graduate Coordinator, 800-859-4723, Fax: 931-221-7641, E-mail: gradadmissions@apsu.edu.
Website: http://www.apsu.edu/business/.

Averett University, Master of Business Administration Program, Danville, VA 24541. Offers MBA. Part-time programs available. *Faculty:* 8 full-time (1 woman), 27 part-time/adjunct (5 women). *Students:* 96 full-time (52 women), 299 part-time (161 women); includes 65 minority (55 Black or African American, non-Hispanic/Latino; 1 American Indian or Alaska Native, non-Hispanic/Latino; 7 Hispanic/Latino; 2 Native Hawaiian or other Pacific Islander, non-Hispanic/Latino). *Degree requirements:* For master's, 41-credit core curriculum, minimum GPA of 3.0 throughout program, completion of degree requirements within six years from start of program. *Entrance requirements:* For master's, minimum cumulative GPA of 3.0 over the last 60 semester hours of undergraduate study toward a baccalaureate degree, official transcripts, three years of full-time work experience, three letters of recommendation, current resume. Additional exam requirements/recommendations for international students: Required—TOEFL (minimum score 600 paper-based; 100 iBT). *Application deadline:* Applications are processed on a rolling basis. *Financial support:* Institutionally sponsored loans available. Support available to part-time students. *Unit head:* Dr. Eugene Steadman, Jr., Chair, Business Department, 434-791-5727, E-mail: eugene.steadman@averett.edu. *Application contact:* Marietta Sanford, Director of Academic Services, 434-791-5892, E-mail: marietta.sanford@averett.edu.

Avila University, School of Business, Kansas City, MO 64145-1698. Offers accounting (MBA); finance (MBA); health care administration (MBA); international business (MBA); management (MBA); management information systems (MBA); marketing (MBA). Part-time and evening/weekend programs available. *Faculty:* 9 full-time (4 women), 12 part-time/adjunct (3 women). *Students:* 66 full-time (32 women), 46 part-time (27 women); includes 34 minority (22 Black or African American, non-Hispanic/Latino; 1 American Indian or Alaska Native, non-Hispanic/Latino; 4 Asian, non-Hispanic/Latino; 7 Hispanic/Latino), 27 international. Average age 32. 30 applicants, 80% accepted, 24 enrolled. In 2013, 61 master's awarded. *Degree requirements:* For master's, comprehensive exam, capstone course. *Entrance requirements:* For master's, GMAT (minimum score 420), minimum GPA of 3.0, interview. Additional exam requirements/recommendations for international students: Required—TOEFL (minimum score 550 paper-based). *Application deadline:* For fall admission, 7/30 priority date for domestic and international students; for winter admission, 11/30 priority date for domestic and international students; for spring admission, 2/28 priority date for domestic and international students; for summer admission, 6/1 priority date for domestic and international students. Applications are processed on a rolling basis. Application fee: $0. Electronic applications accepted. *Expenses:* Contact institution. *Financial support:* In 2013–14, 11 students received support. Career-related internships or fieldwork and scholarships/grants available. Support available to part-time students. Financial award applicants required to submit FAFSA. *Faculty research:* Leadership characteristics, financial hedging, group dynamics. *Unit head:* Dr. Richard Woodall, Dean, 816-501-3720, Fax: 816-501-2463, E-mail: richard.woodall@avila.edu. *Application contact:* Sarah Belanus, MBA Admissions Director, 816-501-3601, Fax: 816-501-2463, E-mail: sarah.belanus@avila.edu.
Website: http://www.avila.edu/mba.

Avila University, School of Professional Studies, Kansas City, MO 64145-1698. Offers executive leadership development (MS); fundraising (MA); instructional design and technology (MA); leadership coaching (MS); organizational development (MS); project management (MA); strategic human resources (MS). Part-time and evening/weekend programs available. Postbaccalaureate distance learning degree programs offered (no on-campus study). *Faculty:* 2 full-time (1 woman), 10 part-time/adjunct (7 women). *Students:* 73 full-time (50 women), 68 part-time (54 women); includes 46 minority (33 Black or African American, non-Hispanic/Latino; 1 Asian, non-Hispanic/Latino; 11 Hispanic/Latino; 1 Two or more races, non-Hispanic/Latino), 11 international. Average age 38. 47 applicants, 64% accepted, 27 enrolled. In 2013, 42 master's awarded. *Degree requirements:* For master's, thesis optional. *Entrance requirements:* For master's, 2 letters of recommendation, minimum GPA of 3.0 during last 60 hours, resume, statement of intent. Additional exam requirements/recommendations for international students: Required—TOEFL. *Application deadline:* Applications are processed on a rolling basis. Application fee: $0. Electronic applications accepted. *Expenses: Tuition:* Full-time $8430; part-time $468 per credit hour. *Required fees:* $648; $36 per credit hour. Tuition and fees vary according to program. *Financial support:* In 2013–14, 20 students received support. Unspecified assistantships available. Support available to part-time students. Financial award applicants required to submit FAFSA. *Unit head:* Dr. Steve Iliff, Dean, 816-501-3737, Fax: 816-941-4650, E-mail: advantage@avila.edu. *Application contact:* Linda Dubar, School of Professional Studies, 816-501-3737, Fax: 816-941-4650, E-mail: advantage@avila.edu.
Website: http://www.avila.edu/advantage.

Azusa Pacific University, School of Business and Management, Program in Business Administration, Azusa, CA 91702-7000. Offers MBA.

Babson College, F. W. Olin Graduate School of Business, Wellesley, MA 02457-0310. Offers accounting (MSA); advanced management (Certificate); business administration (MBA); global entrepreneurship (MS); technological entrepreneurship (MS). *Accreditation:* AACSB. Part-time and evening/weekend programs available. Postbaccalaureate distance learning degree programs offered (minimal on-campus study). *Entrance requirements:* For master's, GMAT, 2 years of work experience, resume, letters of recommendation. Additional exam requirements/recommendations for international students: Required—TOEFL (minimum score 100 iBT), IELTS (minimum score 6.5). Electronic applications accepted. *Faculty research:* Entrepreneurship, sustainability, global markets, process of innovation, social media and advertising.

Bainbridge Graduate Institute, MBA Programs, Bainbridge Island, WA 98110. Offers MBA.

Baker College Center for Graduate Studies - Online, Graduate Programs, Flint, MI 48507-9843. Offers accounting (MBA); business administration (DBA); finance (MBA); general business (MBA); health care management (MBA); human resources management (MBA); information management (MBA); leadership studies (MBA); management information systems (MSIS); marketing (MBA). Part-time and evening/weekend programs available. Postbaccalaureate distance learning degree programs

offered. *Degree requirements:* For master's, portfolio. *Entrance requirements:* For master's, 3 years of work experience, minimum undergraduate GPA of 2.5, writing sample, 3 letters of recommendation; for doctorate, MBA or acceptable related master's degree from accredited association, 5 years work experience, minimum graduate GPA of 3.25, writing sample, 3 professional references. Additional exam requirements/recommendations for international students: Required—TOEFL (minimum score 550 paper-based). Electronic applications accepted.

Baker University, School of Professional and Graduate Studies, Programs in Business, Baldwin City, KS 66006-0065. Offers MAOL, MBA, MSM. Programs also offered in Lee's Summit, MO; Overland Park, KS; Topeka, KS; and Wichita, KS. *Accreditation:* ACBSP. Part-time and evening/weekend programs available. Postbaccalaureate distance learning degree programs offered (minimal on-campus study). *Students:* 186 full-time (97 women), 283 part-time (130 women); includes 110 minority (61 Black or African American, non-Hispanic/Latino; 15 American Indian or Alaska Native, non-Hispanic/Latino; 6 Asian, non-Hispanic/Latino; 23 Hispanic/Latino; 1 Native Hawaiian or other Pacific Islander, non-Hispanic/Latino; 4 Two or more races, non-Hispanic/Latino). Average age 34. In 2013, 217 master's awarded. *Entrance requirements:* For master's, 2 years of full-time work experience. Additional exam requirements/recommendations for international students: Required—TOEFL (minimum score 600 paper-based; 100 iBT). *Application deadline:* Applications are processed on a rolling basis. Application fee: $45. *Financial support:* Applicants required to submit FAFSA. *Unit head:* Dr. Brian Messer, Vice President and Dean of the School of Professional and Graduate Studies, 913-491-4432, E-mail: brian.messer@bakeru.edu. *Application contact:* Piper Childs, Enrollment Representative, 913-491-4432, E-mail: piper.childs@learn.bakeru.edu.

Bakke Graduate University, Programs in Pastoral Ministry and Business, Seattle, WA 98104. Offers business administration (MBA); church and ministry multiplication (D Min); global urban leadership (MA); leadership (D Min); ministry in complex contexts (D Min); social and civic entrepreneurship (MA); theology of work (D Min); theology reflection (D Min); transformational leadership (DTL); urban youth ministry (D Min). Part-time programs available. Postbaccalaureate distance learning degree programs offered (minimal on-campus study). *Faculty:* 5 full-time (3 women), 19 part-time/adjunct (7 women). *Students:* 72 full-time (36 women), 129 part-time (51 women). *Degree requirements:* For master's, thesis; for doctorate, thesis/dissertation. *Entrance requirements:* For master's, 2 years of ministry experience, BA in Biblical studies or theology; for doctorate, 3 years of ministry experience, M Div. Additional exam requirements/recommendations for international students: Required—TOEFL. *Application deadline:* For fall admission, 7/1 priority date for domestic students; for winter admission, 12/1 for domestic students; for spring admission, 3/15 for domestic students. Applications are processed on a rolling basis. Application fee: $75. Electronic applications accepted. *Financial support:* Scholarships/grants and tuition waivers (partial) available. Financial award applicants required to submit FAFSA. *Faculty research:* Theological systems, church management, worship. *Unit head:* Dr. Gwen Dewey, Academic Dean, 206-264-9119, Fax: 206-264-8828, E-mail: gwend@bgu.edu. *Application contact:* Dr. Judith A. Melton, Registrar, 206-246-9114, Fax: 206-264-8828.
Website: http://www.bgu.edu/.

Baldwin Wallace University, Graduate Programs, Division of Business, MBA in Management - Hybrid Program, Berea, OH 44017-2088. Offers MBA. Postbaccalaureate distance learning degree programs offered (minimal on-campus study). *Students:* 28 full-time (10 women), 1 part-time (0 women); includes 4 minority (2 Black or African American, non-Hispanic/Latino; 2 Hispanic/Latino). Average age 34. 8 applicants, 75% accepted, 4 enrolled. In 2013, 15 master's awarded. *Entrance requirements:* For master's, GMAT or minimum undergraduate GPA of 3.0, bachelor's degree in any field, work experience. Additional exam requirements/recommendations for international students: Required—TOEFL (minimum score 79 iBT). *Application deadline:* For fall admission, 3/31 for domestic students. Applications are processed on a rolling basis. Electronic applications accepted. Application fee is waived when completed online. *Expenses:* Contact institution. *Financial support:* Application deadline: 5/1; applicants required to submit FAFSA. *Unit head:* Dale Kramer, Program Director, 440-826-3331, Fax: 440-826-3868, E-mail: dkramer@bw.edu. *Application contact:* Laura Spencer, Graduate Application Specialist, 440-826-2191, Fax: 440-826-3868, E-mail: lspencer@bw.edu.
Website: http://www.bw.edu/academics/bus/programs/mba-online/.

Baldwin Wallace University, Graduate Programs, Division of Business, Program in Business Administration - Management, Berea, OH 44017-2088. Offers MBA. Part-time and evening/weekend programs available. Postbaccalaureate distance learning degree programs offered (minimal on-campus study). *Students:* 88 full-time (40 women), 74 part-time (43 women); includes 15 minority (5 Black or African American, non-Hispanic/Latino; 5 Asian, non-Hispanic/Latino; 3 Hispanic/Latino; 2 Two or more races, non-Hispanic/Latino), 4 international. Average age 34. 45 applicants, 71% accepted, 29 enrolled. In 2013, 54 master's awarded. *Degree requirements:* For master's, minimum overall GPA of 3.0, completion of all required courses. *Entrance requirements:* For master's, GMAT or minimum GPA of 3.0, bachelor's degree in any field, work experience. Additional exam requirements/recommendations for international students: Required—TOEFL (minimum score 523 paper-based; 70 iBT). *Application deadline:* For fall admission, 7/25 priority date for domestic students, 4/30 priority date for international students; for spring admission, 12/15 priority date for domestic students, 9/30 priority date for international students. Applications are processed on a rolling basis. Application fee: $25. Electronic applications accepted. Application fee is waived when completed online. *Expenses:* Contact institution. *Financial support:* Application deadline: 5/1; applicants required to submit FAFSA. *Unit head:* Dale Kramer, MBA/EMBA Director, 440-826-2392, Fax: 440-826-3868, E-mail: dkramer@bw.edu. *Application contact:* Laura Spencer, Graduate Application Specialist, 440-826-2191, Fax: 440-826-3868, E-mail: lspencer@bw.edu.
Website: http://www.bw.edu/academics/bus/programs/mba/.

Baldwin Wallace University, Graduate Programs, Division of Business, Program in Executive Management, Berea, OH 44017-2088. Offers MBA. Part-time and evening/weekend programs available. *Students:* 16 full-time (7 women), 1 part-time (0 women); includes 2 minority (1 Black or African American, non-Hispanic/Latino; 1 Hispanic/Latino). Average age 41. 17 applicants, 88% accepted, 8 enrolled. In 2013, 15 master's awarded. *Degree requirements:* For master's, project, minimum overall GPA of 3.0, completion of all required courses. *Entrance requirements:* For master's, interview, 10 years of work experience, current professional or managerial position, bachelor's degree in any field. Additional exam requirements/recommendations for international students: Required—TOEFL (minimum score 523 paper-based; 70 iBT). *Application deadline:* For fall admission, 7/25 priority date for domestic students, 4/30 priority date for international students; for spring admission, 12/15 priority date for domestic students, 9/30 priority date for international students. Applications are processed on a rolling basis. Application fee: $25. Electronic applications accepted. Application fee is waived when completed online. *Expenses:* Contact institution. *Financial support:* Application deadline: 5/1; applicants required to submit FAFSA. *Unit head:* Dale Kramer, MBA/EMBA Director, 440-826-2392, Fax: 440-826-3868, E-mail: dkramer@bw.edu. *Application contact:* Laura Spencer, Graduate Application Specialist, 440-826-2191, Fax: 440-826-3868, E-mail: lspencer@bw.edu.
Website: http://www.bw.edu/academics/bus/programs/emba.

Ball State University, Graduate School, Miller College of Business, Interdepartmental Program in Business Administration, Muncie, IN 47306-1099. Offers MBA. *Accreditation:* AACSB. *Faculty:* 12 full-time (2 women). *Students:* 57 full-time (19 women), 173 part-time (61 women); includes 20 minority (5 Black or African American, non-Hispanic/Latino; 1 American Indian or Alaska Native, non-Hispanic/Latino; 10 Asian, non-Hispanic/Latino; 2 Hispanic/Latino; 2 Two or more races, non-Hispanic/Latino), 15 international. Average age 27. 154 applicants, 53% accepted, 39 enrolled. In 2013, 70 master's awarded. *Entrance requirements:* For master's, GMAT, resume. Application fee: $50. *Financial support:* In 2013–14, 24 students received support. Application deadline: 3/1. *Unit head:* Jennifer Bott, Graduate Coordinator, 765-285-5323, Fax: 765-285-8818, E-mail: jpbott@bsu.edu. *Application contact:* Tamara Estep, Graduate Coordinator, 765-285-8311, Fax: 765-285-8818, E-mail: testep@bsu.edu.
Website: http://www.bsu.edu/business/mba/.

Barry University, Andreas School of Business, Graduate Certificate Programs, Miami Shores, FL 33161-6695. Offers finance (Certificate); health services administration (Certificate); international business (Certificate); management (Certificate); management information systems (Certificate); marketing (Certificate).

Barry University, Andreas School of Business, Program in Business Administration, Miami Shores, FL 33161-6695. Offers MBA, DPM/MBA, MBA/MS, MBA/MSN.

Barry University, School of Adult and Continuing Education, Division of Nursing and Andreas School of Business, Program in Nursing Administration and Business Administration, Miami Shores, FL 33161-6695. Offers MSN/MBA. *Accreditation:* AACN. Part-time and evening/weekend programs available. Electronic applications accepted. *Faculty research:* Power/empowerment, health delivery systems, managed care, employee health well-being.

Barry University, School of Adult and Continuing Education, Program in Administrative Studies, Miami Shores, FL 33161-6695. Offers MA. Part-time and evening/weekend programs available. *Entrance requirements:* For master's, GMAT, GRE or MAT, recommendations. Electronic applications accepted.

Barry University, School of Human Performance and Leisure Sciences and Andreas School of Business, Program in Sport Management and Business Administration, Miami Shores, FL 33161-6695. Offers MS/MBA. Part-time and evening/weekend programs available. Electronic applications accepted. *Faculty research:* Economic impact of professional sports, sport marketing.

Barry University, School of Podiatric Medicine, Podiatric Medicine and Surgery Program and Andreas School of Business, Podiatric Medicine/Business Administration Option, Miami Shores, FL 33161-6695. Offers DPM/MBA.

Baruch College of the City University of New York, Zicklin School of Business, New York, NY 10010-5585. Offers MBA, MS, PhD, Certificate, JD/MBA. JD/MBA offered jointly with Brooklyn Law School and New York Law School. *Accreditation:* AACSB. Part-time and evening/weekend programs available. *Degree requirements:* For doctorate, comprehensive exam, thesis/dissertation. *Entrance requirements:* For master's, GMAT or GRE, 2 letters of recommendation, resume, 2 years of work experience; for doctorate, GMAT or GRE. Additional exam requirements/recommendations for international students: Required—TOEFL (minimum iBT score of 102) or PTE. Electronic applications accepted.

Baruch College of the City University of New York, Zicklin School of Business, Zicklin Executive Programs, Executive MBA Program, New York, NY 10010-5585. Offers MBA. *Accreditation:* AACSB. *Entrance requirements:* For master's, 5 years of management-level work experience, personal interview. Additional exam requirements/recommendations for international students: Required—TOEFL. *Expenses:* Contact institution. *Faculty research:* Entrepreneurship, corporate governance, international finance, mergers and acquisitions.

Bayamón Central University, Graduate Programs, Program in Business Administration, Bayamón, PR 00960-1725. Offers accounting (MBA); finance (MBA); general business (MBA); management (MBA); marketing (MBA). Part-time and evening/weekend programs available. *Degree requirements:* For master's, comprehensive exam (for some programs). *Entrance requirements:* For master's, EXADEP, bachelor's degree in business or related field.

Baylor University, Graduate School, Hankamer School of Business, Program in Business Administration, Waco, TX 76798. Offers MBA, JD/MBA, MBA/MSIS. *Accreditation:* AACSB. Part-time programs available. *Students:* 170 full-time (54 women), 9 part-time (3 women); includes 40 minority (11 Black or African American, non-Hispanic/Latino; 11 Asian, non-Hispanic/Latino; 13 Hispanic/Latino; 5 Two or more races, non-Hispanic/Latino), 9 international. 240 applicants, 52% accepted, 83 enrolled. In 2013, 116 master's awarded. *Entrance requirements:* For master's, GMAT, minimum AACSB index of 1050. *Application deadline:* For fall admission, 8/1 for domestic students; for spring admission, 12/1 for domestic students. Applications are processed on a rolling basis. Application fee: $0. *Expenses:* Contact institution. *Financial support:* Research assistantships, teaching assistantships, career-related internships or fieldwork, Federal Work-Study, and institutionally sponsored loans available. *Unit head:* Dr. Gary Carini, Associate Dean, 254-710-3718, Fax: 254-710-1092, E-mail: gary_carini@baylor.edu. *Application contact:* Laurie Wilson, Director, Graduate Business Programs, 254-710-4163, Fax: 254-710-1066, E-mail: laurie_wilson@baylor.edu.

Baylor University, School of Law, Waco, TX 76798-7288. Offers administrative practice (JD); business litigation (JD); business transactions (JD); criminal practice (JD); estate planning (JD); general civil litigation (JD); healthcare (JD); intellectual property (JD); law (JD); real estate and natural resources (JD); JD/M Tax; JD/MBA; JD/MPPA. *Accreditation:* ABA. *Faculty:* 30 full-time (7 women), 45 part-time/adjunct (5 women). *Students:* 371 full-time (163 women), 8 part-time (2 women); includes 71 minority (6 Black or African American, non-Hispanic/Latino; 9 American Indian or Alaska Native, non-Hispanic/Latino; 14 Asian, non-Hispanic/Latino; 28 Hispanic/Latino; 14 Two or more races, non-Hispanic/Latino). Average age 24. 2,226 applicants, 37% accepted, 86 enrolled. In 2013, 176 doctorates awarded. *Entrance requirements:* For doctorate, LSAT. Additional exam requirements/recommendations for international students: Recommended—TOEFL. *Application deadline:* For fall admission, 3/1 for domestic and international students; for spring admission, 11/1 for domestic and international students; for summer admission, 2/1 for domestic and international students. Applications are processed on a rolling basis. Application fee: $0. Electronic applications accepted. Application fee is waived when completed online. *Expenses:* Contact institution. *Financial support:* In 2013–14, 296 students received support. Career-related internships or fieldwork and scholarships/grants available. Financial award application deadline: 3/1; financial award applicants required to submit FAFSA. *Unit head:* Dr. Bradley J. B. Toben, Dean, 254-710-1911, Fax: 254-710-2316. *Application contact:* Nicole Neeley, Assistant Dean of Admissions, 254-710-1911, Fax: 254-710-2316, E-mail: nicole_neeley@baylor.edu.
Website: http://www.baylor.edu/law.

Belhaven University, School of Business, Jackson, MS 39202-1789. Offers business administration (MBA); health administration (MBA); human resources (MBA, MSL); leadership (MBA); public administration (MPA); sports administration (MBA). MBA program also offered in Houston, TX, Memphis, TN and Orlando, FL. Part-time and evening/weekend programs available. Postbaccalaureate distance learning degree programs offered. *Faculty:* 21 full-time (4 women), 34 part-time/adjunct (12 women). *Students:* 166 full-time (112 women), 688 part-time (460 women); includes 576 minority (540 Black or African American, non-Hispanic/Latino; 2 American Indian or Alaska Native, non-Hispanic/Latino; 2 Asian, non-Hispanic/Latino; 26 Hispanic/Latino; 6 Two or more races, non-Hispanic/Latino). Average age 36. 325 applicants, 72% accepted, 185 enrolled. In 2013, 189 master's awarded. *Degree requirements:* For master's, comprehensive exam (for some programs), thesis (for some programs). *Entrance requirements:* For master's, GMAT, GRE General Test or MAT, minimum GPA of 2.8. *Application deadline:* Applications are processed on a rolling basis. Application fee: $25. Electronic applications accepted. *Financial support:* Applicants required to submit FAFSA. *Unit head:* Dr. Ralph Mason, Dean, 601-968-8949, Fax: 601-968-8951, E-mail: cmason@belhaven.edu. *Application contact:* Dr. Audrey Kelleher, Vice President of Adult and Graduate Marketing and Development, 407-804-1424, Fax: 407-620-5210, E-mail: akelleher@belhaven.edu.
Website: http://www.belhaven.edu/campuses/index.htm.

Bellarmine University, W. Fielding Rubel School of Business, Louisville, KY 40205-0671. Offers EMBA, MBA, MST. *Accreditation:* AACSB. Part-time and evening/weekend programs available. *Faculty:* 15 full-time (5 women), 6 part-time/adjunct (2 women). *Students:* 81 full-time (30 women), 89 part-time (42 women); includes 20 minority (12 Black or African American, non-Hispanic/Latino; 1 Asian, non-Hispanic/Latino; 6 Hispanic/Latino; 1 Two or more races, non-Hispanic/Latino), 3 international. Average age 30. In 2013, 94 master's awarded. *Degree requirements:* For master's, comprehensive exam. *Entrance requirements:* For master's, GMAT, baccalaureate degree from accredited institution. Additional exam requirements/recommendations for international students: Required—TOEFL (minimum score 550 paper-based; 80 iBT). *Application deadline:* Applications are processed on a rolling basis. Application fee: $25. Electronic applications accepted. *Expenses:* Contact institution. *Financial support:* Career-related internships or fieldwork, scholarships/grants, and unspecified assistantships available. Support available to part-time students. Financial award application deadline: 7/1. *Faculty research:* Marketing, management, small business and entrepreneurship, finance, economics. *Unit head:* Dr. Daniel L. Bauer, Dean, 800-274-4723 Ext. 8026, Fax: 502-272-8013, E-mail: dbauer@bellarmine.edu. *Application contact:* Dr. Sara Pettingill, Dean of Graduate Admission, 800-274-4723 Ext. 8258, Fax: 502-272-8002, E-mail: spettingill@bellarmine.edu.
Website: http://www.bellarmine.edu/business.aspx.

Bellevue University, Graduate School, College of Business, Bellevue, NE 68005-3098. Offers acquisition and contract management (MS); business administration (MBA); finance (MS); human capital management (PhD); management (MSM).

Belmont University, Jack C. Massey Graduate School of Business, Nashville, TN 37212. Offers accelerated (MBA); accounting (M Acc); healthcare (MBA); professional (MBA). *Accreditation:* AACSB. Part-time and evening/weekend programs available. *Faculty:* 46 full-time (16 women), 27 part-time/adjunct (11 women). *Students:* 162 full-time (61 women), 50 part-time (25 women); includes 30 minority (14 Black or African American, non-Hispanic/Latino; 1 American Indian or Alaska Native, non-Hispanic/Latino; 7 Asian, non-Hispanic/Latino; 5 Hispanic/Latino; 3 Two or more races, non-Hispanic/Latino), 5 international. Average age 28. 148 applicants, 64% accepted, 77 enrolled. In 2013, 136 master's awarded. *Entrance requirements:* For master's, GMAT, 2 years of work experience (MBA). Additional exam requirements/recommendations for international students: Required—TOEFL (minimum score 550 paper-based). *Application deadline:* For fall admission, 7/1 for domestic and international students; for spring admission, 11/1 for domestic and international students. Applications are processed on a rolling basis. Application fee: $50. Electronic applications accepted. *Expenses:* Contact institution. *Financial support:* Scholarships/grants, tuition waivers (partial), and unspecified assistantships available. Financial award application deadline: 7/1; financial award applicants required to submit FAFSA. *Faculty research:* Music business, strategy, ethics, finance, accounting systems. *Unit head:* Dr. Patrick Raines, Dean, 615-460-6480, Fax: 615-460-6455, E-mail: pat.raines@belmont.edu. *Application contact:* Tonya Hollin, Admissions Assistant, 615-460-6480, Fax: 615-460-6353, E-mail: masseyadmissions@belmont.edu.
Website: http://www.belmont.edu/business/masseyschool/.

Benedictine College, Executive Master of Business Administration Program, Atchison, KS 66002-1499. Offers EMBA. Evening/weekend programs available. *Faculty:* 4 full-time (1 woman), 4 part-time/adjunct (all women). *Students:* 20 full-time (9 women). Average age 41. In 2013, 20 master's awarded. *Entrance requirements:* For master's, 5 years of management experience, interview. Additional exam requirements/recommendations for international students: Required—TOEFL (minimum score 533 paper-based). *Application deadline:* For fall admission, 7/15 priority date for domestic students, 7/1 for international students; for spring admission, 4/15 priority date for domestic students, 4/1 for international students. Applications are processed on a rolling basis. Application fee: $100. Electronic applications accepted. *Expenses:* Contact institution. *Financial support:* Scholarships/grants and tuition waivers (full and partial) available. Financial award application deadline: 4/15; financial award applicants required to submit FAFSA. *Faculty research:* Banking, strategic planning, ethics, leadership and entrepreneurship. *Unit head:* Dave Geenens, Executive Director, Graduate Business Programs, 913-367-5340 Ext. 7633, Fax: 913-360-7301, E-mail: emba@benedictine.edu. *Application contact:* Donna Bonnel, Administrator of Graduate Programs, 913-367-5340 Ext. 7589, Fax: 913-360-7301, E-mail: dbonnel@benedictine.edu.
Website: http://www.benedictine.edu/emba.

Benedictine College, Traditional Business Administration Program, Atchison, KS 66002. Offers MBA. Part-time and evening/weekend programs available. *Faculty:* 4 full-time (1 woman), 4 part-time/adjunct (all women). *Students:* 23 full-time (10 women). 13 applicants, 100% accepted, 13 enrolled. In 2013, 9 master's awarded. *Degree requirements:* For master's, comprehensive exam. *Entrance requirements:* For master's, GMAT. Additional exam requirements/recommendations for international students: Required—TOEFL (minimum score 533 paper-based; 72 iBT). *Application deadline:* For fall admission, 8/1 priority date for domestic students, 7/1 priority date for international students; for winter admission, 1/7 priority date for domestic students, 12/1 priority date for international students; for spring admission, 5/1 priority date for domestic students, 4/1 priority date for international students. Applications are processed on a rolling basis. Application fee: $50. Electronic applications accepted. *Expenses:* Contact institution. *Financial support:* In 2013–14, 7 students received support. Scholarships/grants and unspecified assistantships available. Support available to part-time students. Financial award application deadline: 3/15; financial award applicants required to submit FAFSA. *Faculty research:* Banking, strategic planning, ethics, leadership and entrepreneurship. *Unit head:* Dave Geenens, Executive Director, Graduate Business Programs, 913-367-5340 Ext. 7633, Fax: 913-360-7301, E-mail: emba@

benedictine.edu. *Application contact:* Donna Bonnel, Administrative Specialist, 913-360-7589, Fax: 913-360-7301, E-mail: dbonnel@benedictine.edu.
Website: http://www.benedictine.edu/mba.

Benedictine University, Graduate Programs, Program in Business Administration, Lisle, IL 60532-0900. Offers accounting (MBA); entrepreneurship and managing innovation (MBA); financial management (MBA); health administration (MBA); human resource management (MBA); information systems security (MBA); international business (MBA); management consulting (MBA); management information systems (MBA); marketing management (MBA); operations management and logistics (MBA); organizational leadership (MBA). Part-time and evening/weekend programs available. Postbaccalaureate distance learning degree programs offered (minimal on-campus study). *Faculty:* 4 full-time (2 women), 24 part-time/adjunct (3 women). *Students:* 144 full-time (83 women), 599 part-time (328 women); includes 189 minority (115 Black or African American, non-Hispanic/Latino; 5 American Indian or Alaska Native, non-Hispanic/Latino; 43 Asian, non-Hispanic/Latino; 24 Hispanic/Latino; 2 Native Hawaiian or other Pacific Islander, non-Hispanic/Latino), 14 international. Average age 34. 211 applicants, 89% accepted, 155 enrolled. In 2013, 376 master's awarded. *Entrance requirements:* For master's, GMAT. Additional exam requirements/recommendations for international students: Required—TOEFL (minimum score 550 paper-based). *Application deadline:* For fall admission, 9/1 for domestic students; for winter admission, 12/1 for domestic students; for spring admission, 2/15 for domestic students. Applications are processed on a rolling basis. Application fee: $40. Electronic applications accepted. *Expenses: Tuition:* Part-time $590 per credit hour. *Financial support:* Career-related internships or fieldwork and health care benefits available. Support available to part-time students. *Faculty research:* Strategic leadership in professional organizations, sociology of professions, organizational change, social identity theory, applications to change management. *Unit head:* Dr. Sharon Borowicz, Director, 630-829-6219, E-mail: sborowicz@ben.edu. *Application contact:* Kari Gibbons, Director, Admissions, 630-829-6200, Fax: 630-829-6584, E-mail: kgibbons@ben.edu.

Benedictine University, Graduate Programs, Program in Management and Organizational Behavior, Lisle, IL 60532-0900. Offers MS, MBA/MS, MPH/MS. Part-time and evening/weekend programs available. *Students:* 15 full-time (10 women), 113 part-time (79 women); includes 40 minority (27 Black or African American, non-Hispanic/Latino; 1 American Indian or Alaska Native, non-Hispanic/Latino; 4 Asian, non-Hispanic/Latino; 7 Hispanic/Latino; 1 Native Hawaiian or other Pacific Islander, non-Hispanic/Latino), 5 international. Average age 40. 45 applicants, 96% accepted, 28 enrolled. In 2013, 61 master's awarded. *Entrance requirements:* For master's, GMAT. Additional exam requirements/recommendations for international students: Required—TOEFL (minimum score 550 paper-based). *Application deadline:* For fall admission, 9/1 for domestic students; for winter admission, 12/1 for domestic students; for spring admission, 2/15 for domestic students. Applications are processed on a rolling basis. Application fee: $40. Electronic applications accepted. *Expenses: Tuition:* Part-time $590 per credit hour. *Financial support:* Career-related internships or fieldwork and health care benefits available. Support available to part-time students. *Faculty research:* Organizational change, transformation, development, learning organizations, career transitions for academics. *Unit head:* Dr. Peter F. Sorensen, Director, 630-829-6220, Fax: 630-960-1126, E-mail: psorensen@ben.edu. *Application contact:* Kari Gibbons, Associate Vice President, Enrollment Center, 630-829-6200, Fax: 630-829-6584, E-mail: kgibbons@ben.edu.

Benedictine University at Springfield, Program in Business Administration, Springfield, IL 62702. Offers health administration (MBA); organizational leadership (MBA). Part-time and evening/weekend programs available. *Entrance requirements:* For master's, GMAT.

Benedictine University at Springfield, Program in Management and Organizational Behavior, Springfield, IL 62702. Offers MS. Evening/weekend programs available. *Entrance requirements:* For master's, official transcripts, 2 letters of reference, essay, resume, interview.

Bentley University, McCallum Graduate School of Business, Business PhD Program, Waltham, MA 02452-4705. Offers PhD. Part-time programs available. *Faculty:* 91 full-time (29 women), 22 part-time/adjunct (4 women). *Students:* 19 full-time (9 women), 2 part-time (1 woman); includes 2 minority (1 Black or African American, non-Hispanic/Latino; 1 Hispanic/Latino), 11 international. Average age 34. 44 applicants, 25% accepted, 8 enrolled. In 2013, 7 doctorates awarded. *Degree requirements:* For doctorate, comprehensive exam, thesis/dissertation. *Entrance requirements:* For doctorate, GMAT or GRE General Test. Additional exam requirements/recommendations for international students: Required—TOEFL (minimum score 600 paper-based; 100 iBT) or IELTS (minimum score 7). Application fee: $0. *Expenses: Tuition:* Full-time $30,400; part-time $1267 per credit. *Required fees:* $404. Tuition and fees vary according to course load and program. *Financial support:* In 2013–14, 20 students received support. Scholarships/grants available. Financial award application deadline: 6/1; financial award applicants required to submit CSS PROFILE or FAFSA. *Faculty research:* Information systems, management (including organization behavior, strategy, entrepreneurship, business ethics), marketing, business analytics. *Unit head:* Dr. Sue Newell, Director, 781-891-2399, Fax: 781-891-3121, E-mail: snewell@bentley.edu. *Application contact:* Sharon Hill, Director of Graduate Admissions, 781-891-2108, Fax: 781-891-2464, E-mail: bentleygraduateadmissions@bentley.edu.
Website: http://www.bentley.edu/offices/phd/phd-business/.

Bentley University, McCallum Graduate School of Business, Graduate Business Certificate Program, Waltham, MA 02452-4705. Offers accounting (GBC); business analytics (GBC); business ethics (GBC); financial planning (GBC); fraud and forensic accounting (GBC); marketing analytics (GBC); taxation (GBC). *Accreditation:* AACSB. Part-time and evening/weekend programs available. *Faculty:* 91 full-time (29 women), 22 part-time/adjunct (4 women). *Students:* 29 part-time (15 women); includes 3 minority (2 Asian, non-Hispanic/Latino; 1 Hispanic/Latino), 3 international. Average age 36. 16 applicants, 94% accepted, 9 enrolled. *Entrance requirements:* For degree, GMAT or GRE General Test. Additional exam requirements/recommendations for international students: Required—TOEFL (minimum score 600 paper-based; 100 iBT) or IELTS (minimum score 7). *Application deadline:* For fall admission, 11/1 priority date for domestic and international students; for spring admission, 10/1 priority date for domestic and international students. Applications are processed on a rolling basis. Application fee: $50. Electronic applications accepted. *Expenses: Tuition:* Full-time $30,400; part-time $1267 per credit. *Required fees:* $404. Tuition and fees vary according to course load and program. *Financial support:* Application deadline: 6/1. *Unit head:* Dr. Roy A. Wiggins, III, Dean, 781-891-3166. *Application contact:* Sharon Hill, Director of Graduate Admissions, 781-891-2108, Fax: 781-891-2464, E-mail: bentleygraduateadmissions@bentley.edu.
Website: http://www.bentley.edu/graduate/degree-programs/special-programs/graduate-certificate-programs.

Bentley University, McCallum Graduate School of Business, MBA Program, Waltham, MA 02452-4705. Offers MBA. *Accreditation:* AACSB. *Faculty:* 91 full-time (29 women), 22 part-time/adjunct (4 women). *Students:* 147 full-time (61 women); includes 15 minority (3 Black or African American, non-Hispanic/Latino; 6 Asian, non-Hispanic/Latino; 4 Hispanic/Latino; 2 Two or more races, non-Hispanic/Latino), 78 international.

Average age 26. 255 applicants, 65% accepted, 33 enrolled. *Entrance requirements:* For master's, GMAT or GRE General Test. Additional exam requirements/recommendations for international students: Required—TOEFL (minimum score 600 paper-based; 100 iBT) or IELTS (minimum score 7). *Application deadline:* For fall admission, 12/1 priority date for domestic and international students. Application fee: $50. Electronic applications accepted. *Expenses: Tuition:* Full-time $30,400; part-time $1267 per credit. *Required fees:* $404. Tuition and fees vary according to course load and program. *Financial support:* In 2013–14, 105 students received support, including 28 research assistantships (averaging $20,330 per year); scholarships/grants and unspecified assistantships also available. Financial award application deadline: 6/1; financial award applicants required to submit CSS PROFILE or FAFSA. *Faculty research:* Strategy and innovation, business process management, corporate social responsibility, IT strategy, organizational change and leadership. *Unit head:* Dr. David Schwarzkopf, MBA Program Director, 781-891-2783, Fax: 781-891-2464, E-mail: dschwarzkopf@bentley.edu. *Application contact:* Sharon Hill, Director of Graduate Admissions, 781-891-2108, Fax: 781-891-2464, E-mail: bentleygraduateadmissions@bentley.edu.
Website: http://www.bentley.edu/graduate/degree-programs/mba-programs.

Bentley University, McCallum Graduate School of Business, MS+MBA Program, Waltham, MA 02452-4705. Offers MS/MBA. *Accreditation:* AACSB. *Faculty:* 91 full-time (29 women), 22 part-time/adjunct (4 women). *Students:* 20 full-time (10 women), 1 part-time (0 women), 16 international. Average age 25. 22 applicants, 86% accepted, 5 enrolled. *Entrance requirements:* Additional exam requirements/recommendations for international students: Required—TOEFL (minimum score 600 paper-based; 100 iBT) or IELTS (minimum score 7). *Application deadline:* For fall admission, 12/1 priority date for domestic and international students; for spring admission, 10/1 priority date for domestic and international students. Application fee: $50. Electronic applications accepted. *Expenses: Tuition:* Full-time $30,400; part-time $1267 per credit. *Required fees:* $404. Tuition and fees vary according to course load and program. *Financial support:* In 2013–14, 16 students received support, including 4 research assistantships (averaging $22,425 per year); scholarships/grants and unspecified assistantships also available. Financial award application deadline: 6/1; financial award applicants required to submit CSS PROFILE or FAFSA. *Faculty research:* Strategy and innovation, business process management, corporate social responsibility, IT strategy, organizational change and leadership. *Unit head:* Dr. David Schwarzkopf, MBA Program Director, 781-891-2783, Fax: 781-891-2464, E-mail: dschwarzkopf@bentley.edu. *Application contact:* Sharon Hill, Director of Graduate Admissions, 781-891-2108, Fax: 781-891-2464, E-mail: bentleygraduateadmissions@bentley.edu.
Website: http://www.bentley.edu/graduate/mba-programs/elmba/ms-mba.

Bentley University, McCallum Graduate School of Business, Professional MBA Program, Waltham, MA 02452-4705. Offers MBA. *Accreditation:* AACSB. Part-time and evening/weekend programs available. *Faculty:* 91 full-time (29 women), 22 part-time/adjunct (4 women). *Students:* 50 full-time (23 women), 248 part-time (104 women); includes 46 minority (8 Black or African American, non-Hispanic/Latino; 18 Asian, non-Hispanic/Latino; 15 Hispanic/Latino; 5 Two or more races, non-Hispanic/Latino), 18 international. Average age 29. 132 applicants, 86% accepted, 77 enrolled. *Entrance requirements:* For master's, GMAT or GRE General Test. Additional exam requirements/recommendations for international students: Required—TOEFL (minimum score 600 paper-based; 100 iBT) or IELTS (minimum score 7). *Application deadline:* For fall admission, 6/1 priority date for domestic and international students; for spring admission, 11/1 for domestic and international students. Application fee: $50. Electronic applications accepted. *Expenses: Tuition:* Full-time $30,400; part-time $1267 per credit. *Required fees:* $404. Tuition and fees vary according to course load and program. *Financial support:* In 2013–14, 25 students received support. Scholarships/grants available. Financial award application deadline: 6/1; financial award applicants required to submit CSS PROFILE or FAFSA. *Faculty research:* Strategy and innovation, corporate social responsibility, IT strategy, business process management, organizational change and leadership. *Unit head:* Dr. David Schwarzkopf, MBA Program Director, 781-891-2783, Fax: 781-891-2464, E-mail: dschwarzkopf@bentley.edu. *Application contact:* Sharon Hill, Director of Graduate Admissions, 781-891-2108, Fax: 781-891-2464, E-mail: bentleygraduateadmissions@bentley.edu.
Website: http://www.bentley.edu/graduate/degree-programs/mba-programs/pmba.

Berry College, Graduate Programs, Campbell School of Business, Mount Berry, GA 30149-0159. Offers MBA. *Accreditation:* AACSB. Part-time and evening/weekend programs available. *Faculty:* 6 part-time/adjunct (3 women). *Students:* 3 full-time (1 woman), 21 part-time (14 women); includes 1 minority (Two or more races, non-Hispanic/Latino), 1 international. Average age 29. In 2013, 13 master's awarded. *Degree requirements:* For master's, thesis. *Entrance requirements:* For master's, GMAT or GRE, minimum GPA of 3.0, essay/goals statement. Additional exam requirements/recommendations for international students: Required—TOEFL (minimum score 550 paper-based). *Application deadline:* For fall admission, 7/25 for domestic students; for spring admission, 12/1 for domestic students. Applications are processed on a rolling basis. Application fee: $25 ($30 for international students). Electronic applications accepted. *Expenses:* Contact institution. *Financial support:* In 2013–14, 18 students received support, including 8 research assistantships with full tuition reimbursements available (averaging $4,520 per year); scholarships/grants, tuition waivers (partial), and unspecified assistantships also available. Support available to part-time students. Financial award application deadline: 3/1; financial award applicants required to submit FAFSA. *Unit head:* Dr. John Grout, Dean, 706-236-2233, Fax: 706-802-6728, E-mail: jgrout@berry.edu. *Application contact:* Brett Kennedy, Assistant Vice President of Enrollment Management, 706-236-2215, Fax: 706-290-2178, E-mail: admissions@berry.edu.
Website: http://www.campbell.berry.edu/.

Bethel College, Adult and Graduate Programs, Program in Business Administration, Mishawaka, IN 46545-5591. Offers MBA. Part-time and evening/weekend programs available. *Faculty:* 6 part-time/adjunct (3 women). *Students:* 14 full-time (9 women), 36 part-time (13 women); includes 11 minority (8 Black or African American, non-Hispanic/Latino; 1 Hispanic/Latino; 1 Native Hawaiian or other Pacific Islander, non-Hispanic/Latino; 1 Two or more races, non-Hispanic/Latino), 1 international. 37 applicants, 97% accepted, 34 enrolled. In 2013, 18 master's awarded. *Entrance requirements:* For master's, GMAT. Additional exam requirements/recommendations for international students: Required—TOEFL (minimum score 540 paper-based). *Application deadline:* For fall admission, 5/1 for international students; for spring admission, 10/1 for international students. Applications are processed on a rolling basis. Application fee: $25. Electronic applications accepted. *Expenses: Required fees:* $75 per semester. Tuition and fees vary according to program. *Financial support:* Career-related internships or fieldwork available. Financial award applicants required to submit FAFSA. *Faculty research:* Marketing. *Unit head:* Dawn Goellner, Director, 574-257-3485, E-mail: goellnd2@bethelcollege.edu.
Website: http://www.bethelcollege.edu/academics/graduate/mba/.

Bethel University, Graduate Programs, McKenzie, TN 38201. Offers administration and supervision (MA Ed); business administration (MBA); conflict resolution (MA); physician assistant studies (MS). Part-time and evening/weekend programs available. *Degree requirements:* For master's, thesis (for some programs). *Entrance requirements:* For master's, GRE General Test or MAT, minimum undergraduate GPA of 2.5.

Bethel University, Graduate School, St. Paul, MN 55112-6999. Offers autism spectrum disorders (Certificate); business administration (MBA); communication (MA); counseling psychology (MA); educational leadership (Ed D); gerontology (MA); international baccalaureate education (Certificate); K-12 education (MA); literacy education (MA, Certificate); nurse educator (Certificate); nurse leader (Certificate); nurse-midwifery (MS); nursing (MS); physician assistant (MS); postsecondary teaching (Certificate); special education (MA); strategic leadership (MA); teaching (MA). Part-time and evening/weekend programs available. Postbaccalaureate distance learning degree programs offered (no on-campus study). *Faculty:* 13 full-time (7 women), 89 part-time/adjunct (43 women). *Students:* 692 full-time (457 women), 573 part-time (371 women); includes 170 minority (86 Black or African American, non-Hispanic/Latino; 1 American Indian or Alaska Native, non-Hispanic/Latino; 49 Asian, non-Hispanic/Latino; 20 Hispanic/Latino; 1 Native Hawaiian or other Pacific Islander, non-Hispanic/Latino; 13 Two or more races, non-Hispanic/Latino), 21 international. Average age 37. In 2013, 166 master's, 9 doctorates, 11 other advanced degrees awarded. *Degree requirements:* For master's, comprehensive exam (for some programs), thesis (for some programs); for doctorate, comprehensive exam, thesis/dissertation. *Entrance requirements:* Additional exam requirements/recommendations for international students: Required—TOEFL (minimum score 550 paper-based; 80 iBT). *Application deadline:* Applications are processed on a rolling basis. Electronic applications accepted. Tuition and fees vary according to course load, degree level and program. *Financial support:* Teaching assistantships, career-related internships or fieldwork, and scholarships/grants available. Support available to part-time students. Financial award applicants required to submit FAFSA. *Unit head:* Dick Crombie, Vice-President/Dean, 651-635-8000, Fax: 651-635-8004, E-mail: gs@bethel.edu. *Application contact:* Director of Admissions, 651-635-8000, Fax: 651-635-8004, E-mail: gs@bethel.edu.
Website: http://gs.bethel.edu/.

Binghamton University, State University of New York, Graduate School, School of Management, Program in Business Administration, Vestal, NY 13850. Offers business administration (MBA); corporate executive (MBA); executive business administration (MBA); health care professional executive (MBA); management (PhD); professional business administration (MBA). Executive and Professional MBA programs offered in Manhattan. *Accreditation:* AACSB. *Students:* 131 full-time (48 women), 16 part-time (8 women); includes 31 minority (7 Black or African American, non-Hispanic/Latino; 13 Asian, non-Hispanic/Latino; 8 Hispanic/Latino; 3 Native Hawaiian or other Pacific Islander, non-Hispanic/Latino), 57 international. Average age 27. 324 applicants, 49% accepted, 102 enrolled. In 2013, 85 master's, 1 doctorate awarded. *Degree requirements:* For doctorate, thesis/dissertation. *Entrance requirements:* For master's and doctorate, GMAT. Additional exam requirements/recommendations for international students: Required—TOEFL (minimum score 550 paper-based; 80 iBT). *Application deadline:* For fall admission, 3/1 priority date for domestic and international students; for spring admission, 10/15 priority date for domestic and international students. Applications are processed on a rolling basis. Application fee: $75. Electronic applications accepted. *Financial support:* In 2013–14, 37 students received support, including 9 teaching assistantships with full tuition reimbursements available (averaging $17,000 per year); career-related internships or fieldwork, Federal Work-Study, institutionally sponsored loans, scholarships/grants, health care benefits, tuition waivers (full and partial), and unspecified assistantships also available. Financial award application deadline: 2/15; financial award applicants required to submit FAFSA. *Unit head:* Dr. Upinder Dhillon, Dean, 607-777-2314, E-mail: dhillon@binghamton.edu. *Application contact:* Kishan Zuber, Recruiting and Admissions Coordinator, 607-777-2151, Fax: 607-777-2501, E-mail: kzuber@binghamton.edu.

Biola University, Crowell School of Business, La Mirada, CA 90639-0001. Offers MBA. *Accreditation:* ACBSP. Part-time and evening/weekend programs available. *Faculty:* 10. *Students:* 24 part-time (12 women); includes 9 minority (1 Black or African American, non-Hispanic/Latino; 8 Asian, non-Hispanic/Latino). In 2013, 15 master's awarded. *Entrance requirements:* For master's, GMAT, 3 years of professional experience, minimum undergraduate GPA of 3.0. Additional exam requirements/recommendations for international students: Required—TOEFL (minimum score 600 paper-based; 100 iBT). *Application deadline:* For fall admission, 4/30 priority date for domestic students; for spring admission, 12/1 for domestic students. Applications are processed on a rolling basis. Application fee: $55. Electronic applications accepted. *Financial support:* Scholarships/grants available. Support available to part-time students. Financial award applicants required to submit FAFSA. *Faculty research:* Integration of theology with business principles. *Unit head:* Dr. Gary Lindblad, Dean, 562-777-4015, Fax: 562-906-4545, E-mail: mba@biola.edu. *Application contact:* Christina Gramenz, MBA Coordinator, 562-777-4015, E-mail: mba@biola.edu.
Website: http://crowell.biola.edu.

Black Hills State University, Graduate Studies, Program in Business Administration, Spearfish, SD 57799. Offers MBA. Evening/weekend programs available. *Faculty:* 12 full-time (4 women). *Students:* 20 part-time (8 women). In 2013, 7 master's awarded. *Entrance requirements:* Additional exam requirements/recommendations for international students: Required—TOEFL (minimum score 500 paper-based; 60 iBT). *Application deadline:* Applications are processed on a rolling basis. Application fee: $35. *Expenses:* Tuition, state resident: full-time $3718; part-time $201.85 per credit hour. Tuition, nonresident: full-time $7686; part-time $427.30 per credit hour. Tuition and fees vary according to course load, program and reciprocity agreements. *Financial support:* In 2013–14, 1 teaching assistantship with partial tuition reimbursement was awarded. *Unit head:* Dr. Byron Hollowell, Coordinator of MBA Program, 605-642-6429, Fax: 605-642-6973, E-mail: byron.hollowell@bhsu.edu.

Bloomsburg University of Pennsylvania, School of Graduate Studies, College of Business, Program in Business Administration, Bloomsburg, PA 17815-1301. Offers MBA. *Accreditation:* AACSB. *Faculty:* 7 full-time (0 women). *Students:* 28 full-time (10 women), 18 part-time (9 women); includes 3 minority (2 Black or African American, non-Hispanic/Latino; 1 Hispanic/Latino), 5 international. Average age 29. 31 applicants, 65% accepted, 18 enrolled. In 2013, 30 master's awarded. *Degree requirements:* For master's, minimum QPA of 3.0, practicum. *Entrance requirements:* For master's, GMAT, resume, 3 letters of recommendation, personal statement. Additional exam requirements/recommendations for international students: Required—TOEFL (minimum score 550 paper-based). *Application deadline:* Applications are processed on a rolling basis. Application fee: $35 ($60 for international students). Electronic applications accepted. *Expenses:* Tuition, state resident: full-time $7956; part-time $442 per credit. Tuition, nonresident: full-time $11,934; part-time $663 per credit. *Required fees:* $95.50 per credit. $55 per semester. Tuition and fees vary according to course load. *Financial support:* Federal Work-Study and unspecified assistantships available. *Unit head:* Dr. Darrin Kass, Coordinator, 570-389-4394, Fax: 570-389-3892, E-mail: dkass@bloomu.edu. *Application contact:* Jennifer Richard, Administrative Assistant, 570-389-4015, Fax: 570-389-3054, E-mail: jrichard@bloomu.edu.
Website: http://www.bloomu.edu/gradschool/mba.

Bluffton University, Programs in Business, Bluffton, OH 45817. Offers business administration (MBA); organizational management (MA). Evening/weekend programs

available. *Entrance requirements:* Additional exam requirements/recommendations for international students: Required—TOEFL. Electronic applications accepted.

Bob Jones University, Graduate Programs, Greenville, SC 29614. Offers accountancy (MS); Bible (MA); Bible translation (MA); Biblical studies (Certificate); broadcast management (MS); business administration (MBA); church history (MA, PhD); church ministries (MA); church music (MM); cinema and video production (MA); counseling (MS); curriculum and instruction (Ed D); divinity (M Div); dramatic production (MA); educational leadership (MS, Ed D, Ed S); elementary education (M Ed, MAT); English (M Ed, MA, MAT); fine arts (MA); graphic design (MA); history (M Ed, MA); illustration (MA); interpretative speech (MA); mathematics (M Ed, MAT); medical missions (Certificate); ministry (MM, D Min); multi-categorical special education (M Ed, MAT); music (M Ed); New Testament interpretation (PhD); Old Testament interpretation (PhD); orchestral instrument performance (MM); organ performance (MM); pastoral studies (MA); personnel services (MS, Ed S); piano pedagogy (MM); piano performance (MM); platform arts (MA); radio and television broadcasting (MS); rhetoric and public address (MA); secondary education (M Ed); studio art (MA); teaching Bible (MA); theology (MA, PhD); voice performance (MM); youth ministries (MA); M Div/MM.

Boise State University, College of Business and Economics, Program in Business Administration, Boise, ID 83725-0399. Offers MBA. *Accreditation:* AACSB. Part-time programs available. *Entrance requirements:* For master's, GMAT, minimum GPA of 3.0. Additional exam requirements/recommendations for international students: Required—TOEFL. Electronic applications accepted.

Boston College, Carroll School of Management, Business Administration Program, Chestnut Hill, MA 02467-3800. Offers MBA, JD/MBA, MBA/MA, MBA/MS, MBA/MSA, MBA/MSF, MBA/MSW, MBA/PhD. *Accreditation:* AACSB. Part-time and evening/weekend programs available. *Faculty:* 58 full-time (14 women), 40 part-time/adjunct (6 women). *Students:* 200 full-time (61 women), 384 part-time (134 women); includes 83 minority (12 Black or African American, non-Hispanic/Latino; 1 American Indian or Alaska Native, non-Hispanic/Latino; 37 Asian, non-Hispanic/Latino; 26 Hispanic/Latino; 7 Two or more races, non-Hispanic/Latino), 82 international. Average age 29. 820 applicants, 46% accepted, 168 enrolled. In 2013, 242 master's awarded. *Entrance requirements:* For master's, GMAT, GRE, 2 letters of recommendation, resume, transcript. Additional exam requirements/recommendations for international students: Required—TOEFL (minimum score 600 paper-based, 100 iBT), IELTS (minimum score 7.5), or PTE (minimum score 68). *Application deadline:* For fall admission, 11/1 for domestic and international students; for winter admission, 1/15 for domestic and international students; for spring admission, 3/15 for domestic and international students; for summer admission, 4/15 for domestic and international students. Applications are processed on a rolling basis. Application fee: $100. Electronic applications accepted. *Financial support:* In 2013–14, 167 students received support, including 167 fellowships with full and partial tuition reimbursements available (averaging $14,102 per year), 92 research assistantships with partial tuition reimbursements available (averaging $3,970 per year); career-related internships or fieldwork, Federal Work-Study, scholarships/grants, tuition waivers (full and partial), and unspecified assistantships also available. Support available to part-time students. Financial award application deadline: 3/1. *Faculty research:* Investments, corporate finance, management of financial services, strategic management. *Unit head:* Dr. Jeffrey L. Ringuest, Associate Dean for Graduate Programs, 617-552-9100, Fax: 617-552-0514, E-mail: jeffrey.ringuest@bc.edu. *Application contact:* Shelley A. Burt, Director of Graduate Enrollment, 617-552-3920, Fax: 617-552-8078, E-mail: bcmba@bc.edu.
Website: http://www.bc.edu/mba/.

Boston University, Metropolitan College, Department of Administrative Sciences, Boston, MA 02215. Offers banking and financial management (MSM); business continuity in emergency management (MSM); economics development and tourism management (MSAS); electronic commerce, systems, and technology (MSAS); financial economics (MSAS); innovation and technology (MSAS); insurance management (MSM); international market management (MSM); multinational commerce (MSAS); project management (MS). *Accreditation:* AACSB. Part-time and evening/weekend programs available. Postbaccalaureate distance learning degree programs offered (no on-campus study). *Faculty:* 15 full-time (3 women), 22 part-time/adjunct (3 women). *Students:* 177 full-time (85 women), 560 part-time (293 women); includes 89 minority (31 Black or African American, non-Hispanic/Latino; 31 Asian, non-Hispanic/Latino; 25 Hispanic/Latino; 2 Two or more races, non-Hispanic/Latino), 242 international. Average age 31. 509 applicants, 71% accepted, 222 enrolled. In 2013, 158 master's awarded. *Degree requirements:* For master's, thesis optional. *Entrance requirements:* For master's, 1 year of work experience, minimum GPA of 3.0. Additional exam requirements/recommendations for international students: Required—TOEFL (minimum score 84 iBT). *Application deadline:* Applications are processed on a rolling basis. Application fee: $80. Electronic applications accepted. *Expenses: Tuition:* Full-time $43,970; part-time $1374 per credit hour. *Required fees:* $60 per semester. Tuition and fees vary according to class time, course level and program. *Financial support:* In 2013–14, 15 students received support, including 7 research assistantships (averaging $8,400 per year); career-related internships or fieldwork, Federal Work-Study, and unspecified assistantships also available. *Faculty research:* International business, innovative process. *Unit head:* Dr. Kip Becker, Chairman, 617-353-3016, E-mail: adminsc@bu.edu. *Application contact:* Fiona Niven, Administrative Sciences Department, 617-353-3016, E-mail: adminsc@bu.edu.
Website: http://www.bu.edu/met/academic-community/departments/administrative-sciences/.

Boston University, Metropolitan College, Program in Gastronomy, Boston, MA 02215. Offers business (MLA); communications (MLA); food policy (MLA); history and culture (MLA). Part-time and evening/weekend programs available. *Faculty:* 4 full-time (3 women), 11 part-time/adjunct (6 women). *Students:* 6 full-time (all women), 83 part-time (71 women); includes 15 minority (1 Black or African American, non-Hispanic/Latino; 1 American Indian or Alaska Native, non-Hispanic/Latino; 3 Asian, non-Hispanic/Latino; 5 Hispanic/Latino; 5 Two or more races, non-Hispanic/Latino), 6 international. Average age 29. 58 applicants, 76% accepted, 27 enrolled. In 2013, 40 master's awarded. *Degree requirements:* For master's, thesis optional. *Entrance requirements:* Additional exam requirements/recommendations for international students: Required—TOEFL. *Application deadline:* Applications are processed on a rolling basis. Application fee: $80. Electronic applications accepted. *Expenses: Tuition:* Full-time $43,970; part-time $1374 per credit hour. *Required fees:* $60 per semester. Tuition and fees vary according to class time, course level and program. *Financial support:* In 2013–14, 3 research assistantships (averaging $5,000 per year) were awarded; career-related internships or fieldwork, scholarships/grants, and unspecified assistantships also available. Support available to part-time students. Financial award applicants required to submit FAFSA. *Faculty research:* Food studies. *Unit head:* Dr. Rachel Black, Assistant Professor, 617-353-6291, Fax: 617-353-4130, E-mail: rblack@bu.edu.
Website: http://www.bu.edu/met/gastronomy.

Boston University, School of Management, Boston, MA 02215. Offers business administration (MBA); executive business administration (EMBA); investment management (MS); management (PhD); mathematical finance (MS, PhD); JD/MBA; MBA/MA; MBA/MPH; MBA/MS; MBA/MSIS; MD/MBA; MS/MBA. *Accreditation:* AACSB. Part-time and evening/weekend programs available. *Faculty:* 185 full-time (49 women), 60 part-time/adjunct (15 women). *Students:* 497 full-time (171 women), 723 part-time (269 women); includes 162 minority (16 Black or African American, non-Hispanic/Latino; 108 Asian, non-Hispanic/Latino; 29 Hispanic/Latino; 9 Two or more races, non-Hispanic/Latino), 278 international. Average age 29. 1,387 applicants, 28% accepted, 160 enrolled. In 2013, 486 master's, 2 doctorates awarded. *Degree requirements:* For doctorate, comprehensive exam, thesis/dissertation. *Entrance requirements:* For master's, GMAT (for MBA and MS in investment management); GMAT or GRE General Test (for MS in mathematical finance), resume, 2 letters of recommendation; for doctorate, GMAT or GRE General Test, resume, personal statement, 3 letters of recommendation, 3 essays, official transcripts. *Application deadline:* For fall admission, 1/5 for domestic and international students; for spring admission, 11/1 for domestic students. Application fee: $125. Electronic applications accepted. *Expenses: Tuition:* Full-time $43,970; part-time $1374 per credit hour. *Required fees:* $60 per semester. Tuition and fees vary according to class time, course level and program. *Financial support:* Career-related internships or fieldwork, Federal Work-Study, institutionally sponsored loans, scholarships/grants, and tuition waivers (partial) available. Financial award applicants required to submit FAFSA. *Faculty research:* Innovation policy and productivity, corporate social responsibility, risk management, information systems, entrepreneurship, clean energy, sustainability. *Unit head:* Kenneth W. Freeman, Professor/Dean, 617-353-9720, Fax: 617-353-5581, E-mail: kfreeman@bu.edu. *Application contact:* Patti Cudney, Assistant Dean, Graduate Admissions, 617-353-2670, Fax: 617-353-7368, E-mail: mba@bu.edu.
Website: http://management.bu.edu/.

Bowie State University, Graduate Programs, Program in Business Administration, Bowie, MD 20715-9465. Offers MBA. *Accreditation:* ACBSP. Part-time and evening/weekend programs available. *Degree requirements:* For master's, comprehensive exam. *Entrance requirements:* For master's, GMAT, minimum undergraduate GPA of 2.5. Electronic applications accepted. *Expenses:* Tuition, state resident: full-time $8665. Tuition, nonresident: full-time $16,007. *Required fees:* $1927.

Bowling Green State University, Graduate College, College of Business Administration, Graduate Studies in Business Program, Bowling Green, OH 43403. Offers MBA. *Accreditation:* AACSB. Part-time and evening/weekend programs available. *Degree requirements:* For master's, thesis or alternative, research project. *Entrance requirements:* For master's, GMAT. Additional exam requirements/recommendations for international students: Required—TOEFL. Electronic applications accepted. *Faculty research:* Management of change processes, supply chain management, impacts of money on society, corporate financing strategies, macro-marketing/management of sales staff and services.

Bradley University, Graduate School, Foster College of Business Administration, Executive MBA Program, Peoria, IL 61625-0002. Offers MBA. *Accreditation:* AACSB. Evening/weekend programs available. *Entrance requirements:* For master's, company sponsorship, 7 years of managerial experience, letters of recommendation. Additional exam requirements/recommendations for international students: Required—TOEFL (minimum score 550 paper-based; 79 iBT). *Expenses:* Contact institution.

Bradley University, Graduate School, Foster College of Business Administration, Program in Business Administration, Peoria, IL 61625-0002. Offers MBA. *Accreditation:* AACSB. Part-time and evening/weekend programs available. *Degree requirements:* For master's, comprehensive exam. *Entrance requirements:* For master's, GMAT, minimum undergraduate GPA of 2.75 in major, 2 letters of recommendation. Additional exam requirements/recommendations for international students: Required—TOEFL (minimum score 550 paper-based; 79 iBT). *Expenses: Tuition:* Full-time $14,580; part-time $810 per credit hour. Tuition and fees vary according to course load and program.

Brandeis University, The Heller School for Social Policy and Management, Program in Nonprofit Management, Waltham, MA 02454-9110. Offers child, youth, and family management (MBA); health care management (MBA); social impact management (MBA); social policy and management (MBA); sustainable development (MBA); MBA/MA; MBA/MD. MBA/MD program offered in conjunction with Tufts University School of Medicine. *Accreditation:* AACSB. Part-time programs available. *Degree requirements:* For master's, team consulting project. *Entrance requirements:* For master's, GMAT (preferred) or GRE, 2 letters of recommendation, problem statement analysis, 3-5 years of professional experience. Additional exam requirements/recommendations for international students: Required—TOEFL (minimum score 600 paper-based; 100 iBT). Electronic applications accepted. *Expenses:* Contact institution. *Faculty research:* Health care; children and families; elder and disabled services; social impact management; organizations in the non-profit, for-profit, or public sector.

Brandman University, School of Business and Professional Studies, Irvine, CA 92618. Offers business administration (MBA); human resources (MS); organizational leadership (MA); public administration (MPA).

Brenau University, Sydney O. Smith Graduate School, School of Business and Mass Communication, Gainesville, GA 30501. Offers accounting (MBA); business administration (MBA); healthcare management (MBA); organizational leadership (MS); project management (MBA). *Accreditation:* ACBSP. Part-time and evening/weekend programs available. Postbaccalaureate distance learning degree programs offered (no on-campus study). *Degree requirements:* For master's, comprehensive exam (for some programs). *Entrance requirements:* For master's, resume, minimum undergraduate GPA of 2.5. Additional exam requirements/recommendations for international students: Required—TOEFL (minimum score 500 paper-based; 61 iBT); Recommended—IELTS (minimum score 5). Electronic applications accepted. *Expenses:* Contact institution.

Brescia University, Program in Business Administration, Owensboro, KY 42301-3023. Offers MBA. Part-time and evening/weekend programs available. *Entrance requirements:* For master's, GMAT or GRE.

Brescia University, Program in Management, Owensboro, KY 42301-3023. Offers MSM. Part-time and evening/weekend programs available. *Entrance requirements:* For master's, GMAT, minimum GPA of 2.5.

Bridgewater State University, School of Graduate Studies, School of Business, Department of Management, Bridgewater, MA 02325-0001. Offers MSM. *Entrance requirements:* For master's, GMAT.

Briercrest Seminary, Graduate Programs, Program in Leadership and Management, Caronport, SK S0H 0S0, Canada. Offers organizational leadership (MA). Part-time programs available. *Degree requirements:* For master's, comprehensive exam, thesis optional. *Entrance requirements:* Additional exam requirements/recommendations for international students: Required—TOEFL (minimum score 550 paper-based).

Brigham Young University, Graduate Studies, Marriott School of Management, Executive Master of Business Administration Program, Provo, UT 84602. Offers MBA. *Accreditation:* AACSB. Part-time and evening/weekend programs available. *Entrance requirements:* For master's, GMAT, 5 years of management experience, minimum GPA of 3.0 in last 60 undergraduate hours. Additional exam requirements/recommendations for international students: Required—TOEFL (minimum score 590 paper-based; 94 iBT). Electronic applications accepted. *Expenses:* Contact institution.

Business Administration and Management—General

Brigham Young University, Graduate Studies, Marriott School of Management, Master of Business Administration Program, Provo, UT 84602. Offers MBA, JD/MBA, MBA/MS. *Accreditation:* AACSB. *Entrance requirements:* For master's, GMAT, minimum GPA of 3.0 in last 60 hours. Additional exam requirements/recommendations for international students: Required—TOEFL (minimum score 590 paper-based). Electronic applications accepted. *Expenses:* Contact institution. *Faculty research:* Finance, organizational behavior/human relations, marketing, supply chain management, strategy.

Broadview University–West Jordan, Graduate Programs, West Jordan, UT 84088. Offers business administration (MBA); health care management (MSM); information technology (MSM); managerial leadership (MSM).

Brock University, Faculty of Graduate Studies, Faculty of Business, Program in Business Administration, St. Catharines, ON L2S 3A1, Canada. Offers MBA. *Degree requirements:* For master's, thesis or alternative. *Entrance requirements:* For master's, honours degree. Additional exam requirements/recommendations for international students: Required—TOEFL (minimum score 575 paper-based; 89 iBT), IELTS (minimum score 7), TWE (minimum score 4.5). Electronic applications accepted.

Brock University, Faculty of Graduate Studies, Faculty of Business, Program in Management, St. Catharines, ON L2S 3A1, Canada. Offers M Sc. Part-time programs available. *Degree requirements:* For master's, thesis. *Entrance requirements:* For master's, GMAT, honors degree. Additional exam requirements/recommendations for international students: Required—TOEFL (minimum score 600 paper-based; 100 iBT), IELTS (minimum score 7), TWE (minimum score 4.5). Electronic applications accepted.

Bryan College, MBA Program, Dayton, TN 37321. Offers MBA. *Entrance requirements:* For master's, resume, 2 letters of recommendation.

Bryant University, Graduate School of Business, Master of Business Administration Program, Smithfield, RI 02917. Offers general business (MBA); global finance (MBA); global supply chain management (MBA); international business (MBA). *Accreditation:* AACSB. Part-time and evening/weekend programs available. *Entrance requirements:* For master's, GMAT, transcripts, recommendation, resume, statement of objectives. Additional exam requirements/recommendations for international students: Required—TOEFL (minimum score 580 paper-based; 90 iBT). *Application deadline:* For fall admission, 7/15 for domestic and international students; for spring admission, 11/15 for domestic and international students. Applications are processed on a rolling basis. Application fee: $80. Electronic applications accepted. *Expenses: Tuition:* Full-time $26,832; part-time $1118 per credit hour. *Financial support:* In 2013–14, 11 research assistantships (averaging $6,708 per year) were awarded; unspecified assistantships also available. Financial award application deadline: 7/15; financial award applicants required to submit FAFSA. *Faculty research:* International business, information systems security, leadership, financial markets microstructure, commercial lending practice. *Unit head:* Richard S. Cheney, Director of Operations for Graduate Programs, School of Business, 401-232-6707, Fax: 401-232-6494, E-mail: rcheney@bryant.edu. *Application contact:* Linda Denzer, Assistant Director of Graduate Admission, 401-232-6529, Fax: 401-232-6494, E-mail: ldenzer@bryant.edu.

Butler University, College of Business Administration, Indianapolis, IN 46208-3485. Offers business administration (MBA); professional accounting (MP Acc). *Accreditation:* AACSB. Part-time and evening/weekend programs available. *Faculty:* 12 full-time (3 women), 5 part-time/adjunct (1 woman). *Students:* 30 full-time (6 women), 185 part-time (60 women); includes 18 minority (5 Black or African American, non-Hispanic/Latino; 1 American Indian or Alaska Native, non-Hispanic/Latino; 7 Asian, non-Hispanic/Latino; 4 Hispanic/Latino; 1 Two or more races, non-Hispanic/Latino), 7 international. Average age 31. 146 applicants, 64% accepted, 34 enrolled. In 2013, 57 master's awarded. *Entrance requirements:* For master's, GMAT, minimum AACSB index of 950. *Application deadline:* For fall admission, 8/15 priority date for domestic students. Applications are processed on a rolling basis. Application fee: $35. Electronic applications accepted. *Financial support:* Career-related internships or fieldwork and institutionally sponsored loans available. Support available to part-time students. Financial award application deadline: 7/15; financial award applicants required to submit FAFSA. *Unit head:* Dr. Stephen Standifird, Dean. *Application contact:* Diane Dubord, Graduate Student Service Specialist, 317-940-8107, Fax: 317-940-8250, E-mail: ddubord@butler.edu.
Website: http://www.butler.edu/academics/graduate-cob/.

Cairn University, School of Business and Leadership, Langhorne, PA 19047-2990. Offers business administration (MBA); organizational leadership (MSOL, Postbaccalaureate Certificate). Part-time and evening/weekend programs available. *Faculty:* 2 full-time (0 women), 2 part-time/adjunct (0 women). *Students:* 4 full-time (3 women), 21 part-time (11 women); includes 11 minority (9 Black or African American, non-Hispanic/Latino; 1 Asian, non-Hispanic/Latino; 1 Hispanic/Latino), 1 international. Average age 33. 16 applicants, 81% accepted, 10 enrolled. In 2013, 13 master's awarded. *Entrance requirements:* Additional exam requirements/recommendations for international students: Required—TOEFL (minimum score 550 paper-based). *Application deadline:* Applications are processed on a rolling basis. Application fee: $25. Electronic applications accepted. *Expenses: Tuition:* Full-time $11,250; part-time $625 per credit. Tuition and fees vary according to program. *Financial support:* Scholarships/grants available. Support available to part-time students. Financial award applicants required to submit FAFSA. *Unit head:* Dr. William Bowles, Chair, Graduate Programs, 215-702-4871, Fax: 215-702-4248, E-mail: wbowles@cairn.edu. *Application contact:* Timothy Nessler, Assistant Director, Graduate Admissions, 800-572-2472, Fax: 215-702-4248, E-mail: tnessler@cairn.edu.
Website: http://cairn.edu/academics/business.

Caldwell University, Graduate Studies, Division of Business, Caldwell, NJ 07006-6195. Offers accounting (MS); business administration (MBA). *Accreditation:* ACBSP. Part-time programs available. *Faculty:* 7 full-time (2 women), 4 part-time/adjunct (3 women). *Students:* 14 full-time (2 women), 49 part-time (35 women); includes 22 minority (10 Black or African American, non-Hispanic/Latino; 3 Asian, non-Hispanic/Latino; 8 Hispanic/Latino; 1 Two or more races, non-Hispanic/Latino). Average age 35. 46 applicants, 46% accepted, 18 enrolled. In 2013, 11 master's awarded. *Entrance requirements:* For master's, GMAT, undergraduate accounting, marketing, and finance. Additional exam requirements/recommendations for international students: Required—TOEFL (minimum score 580 paper-based). *Application deadline:* Applications are processed on a rolling basis. Application fee: $40. Electronic applications accepted. *Unit head:* Bernard O'Rourke, Division Associate Dean, 973-618-3409, Fax: 973-618-3355, E-mail: borourke@caldwell.edu. *Application contact:* Vilma Mueller, Director of Graduate Studies, 973-618-3544, E-mail: graduate@caldwell.edu.
Website: http://www.caldwell.edu/graduate.

California Baptist University, Program in Business Administration, Riverside, CA 92504-3206. Offers accounting (MBA); construction management (MBA); healthcare management (MBA); management (MBA). *Accreditation:* ACBSP. Part-time and evening/weekend programs available. Postbaccalaureate distance learning degree programs offered (minimal on-campus study). *Faculty:* 14 full-time (5 women), 4 part-time/adjunct (1 woman). *Students:* 49 full-time (20 women), 53 part-time (20 women); includes 43 minority (8 Black or African American, non-Hispanic/Latino; 2 American Indian or Alaska Native, non-Hispanic/Latino; 4 Asian, non-Hispanic/Latino; 28 Hispanic/Latino; 1 Two or more races, non-Hispanic/Latino), 6 international. Average age 28. 119 applicants, 60% accepted, 43 enrolled. In 2013, 46 master's awarded. *Degree requirements:* For master's, interdisciplinary capstone project. *Entrance requirements:* For master's, GMAT, minimum GPA of 2.5; two recommendations; comprehensive essay; resume; interview; 4 prerequisite courses. Additional exam requirements/recommendations for international students: Required—TOEFL (minimum score 80 iBT). *Application deadline:* For fall admission, 8/1 priority date for domestic students, 7/1 for international students; for spring admission, 12/1 priority date for domestic students, 11/1 for international students. Applications are processed on a rolling basis. Application fee: $45. Electronic applications accepted. *Expenses:* Contact institution. *Financial support:* Institutionally sponsored loans available. Financial award applicants required to submit CSS PROFILE or FAFSA. *Faculty research:* Econometrics, Biblical financial principles, strategic management and corporate performance, shared leadership models, international culture and economics. *Unit head:* Dr. Franco Gandolfi, Dean, School of Business, 951-343-4968, Fax: 951-343-4361, E-mail: fgandolfi@calbaptist.edu. *Application contact:* Dr. Keanon Alderson, Director, Business Administration Program, 951-343-4768, E-mail: kalderson@calbaptist.edu.
Website: http://www.calbaptist.edu/mba/about/.

California Coast University, School of Administration and Management, Santa Ana, CA 92701. Offers business marketing (MBA); health care management (MBA); human resource management (MBA); management (MBA, MS). Postbaccalaureate distance learning degree programs offered (no on-campus study). Electronic applications accepted.

California Intercontinental University, School of Business, Diamond Bar, CA 91765. Offers banking and finance (MBA); entrepreneurship and business management (DBA); global business leadership (DBA); international management and marketing (MBA); organizational management and human resource management (MBA).

California International Business University, Graduate Programs, San Diego, CA 92101. Offers MBA, MSIM, DBA.

California Lutheran University, Graduate Studies, School of Management, Thousand Oaks, CA 91360-2787. Offers business (IMBA); computer science (MS); econometrics (MBA); economics (MS); entrepreneurship (MBA, Certificate); finance (MBA, Certificate); financial planning (MBA, Certificate); information systems and technology (MS); information technology management (MBA, Certificate); international business (MBA, Certificate); management and organization behavior (MBA); management and organizational behavior (Certificate); marketing (MBA, Certificate); microeconomics (MBA); nonprofit and social enterprise (MBA). Part-time and evening/weekend programs available. Postbaccalaureate distance learning degree programs offered (no on-campus study). *Faculty:* 26 full-time (9 women), 50 part-time/adjunct (11 women). *Students:* 426 full-time (175 women), 220 part-time (91 women); includes 114 minority (14 Black or African American, non-Hispanic/Latino; 30 Asian, non-Hispanic/Latino; 57 Hispanic/Latino; 13 Two or more races, non-Hispanic/Latino), 321 international. Average age 31. 495 applicants, 76% accepted, 119 enrolled. In 2013, 297 master's awarded. *Entrance requirements:* For master's, GMAT, interview, minimum GPA of 3.0. *Application deadline:* Applications are processed on a rolling basis. Application fee: $50. *Expenses:* Contact institution. *Unit head:* Dr. Gerhard Apfelthaler, Dean, 805-493-3360. *Application contact:* 805-493-3325, Fax: 805-493-3861, E-mail: clugrad@callutheran.edu.
Website: http://www.callutheran.edu/business/.

California Miramar University, Program in Business Administration, San Diego, CA 92126. Offers MBA.

California National University for Advanced Studies, College of Business Administration, Northridge, CA 91325. Offers MBA, MHRM. Part-time programs available. Postbaccalaureate distance learning degree programs offered (no on-campus study). *Entrance requirements:* For master's, minimum GPA of 3.0. Additional exam requirements/recommendations for international students: Required—TOEFL. Electronic applications accepted.

California Polytechnic State University, San Luis Obispo, Orfalea College of Business, Graduate Programs in Business, San Luis Obispo, CA 93407. Offers business (MBA); taxation (MSA). *Faculty:* 1 full-time (0 women), 5 part-time/adjunct (all women). *Students:* 33 full-time (14 women), 9 part-time (6 women); includes 8 minority (3 Asian, non-Hispanic/Latino; 5 Hispanic/Latino), 3 international. Average age 25. 75 applicants, 59% accepted, 30 enrolled. In 2013, 58 master's awarded. *Degree requirements:* For master's, comprehensive exam (for some programs), thesis or alternative. *Entrance requirements:* For master's, GMAT. Additional exam requirements/recommendations for international students: Required—TOEFL (minimum score 550 paper-based) or IELTS (minimum score 6). *Application deadline:* For fall admission, 7/1 for domestic students, 11/30 for international students. Applications are processed on a rolling basis. Application fee: $55. Electronic applications accepted. *Financial support:* Fellowships, career-related internships or fieldwork, Federal Work-Study, institutionally sponsored loans, scholarships/grants, and unspecified assistantships available. Support available to part-time students. Financial award application deadline: 3/2; financial award applicants required to submit FAFSA. *Faculty research:* International business, organizational behavior, graphic communication document systems management, commercial development of innovative technologies, effective communication skills for managers. *Unit head:* Vicki Walls, Graduate Coordinator, 805-756-2637, Fax: 805-756-0110, E-mail: vwalls@calpoly.edu. *Application contact:* Vicki Walls, Graduate Coordinator, 805-756-5637, Fax: 805-756-0110, E-mail: vwalls@calpoly.edu.
Website: http://mba.calpoly.edu/.

California State Polytechnic University, Pomona, Academic Affairs, College of Business Administration, Master of Science in Business Administration Program, Pomona, CA 91768-2557. Offers information systems auditing (MS). *Students:* 3 full-time (2 women), 8 part-time (4 women); includes 7 minority (6 Asian, non-Hispanic/Latino; 1 Hispanic/Latino), 1 international. Average age 28. 28 applicants, 32% accepted, 5 enrolled. In 2013, 5 master's awarded. *Application deadline:* Applications are processed on a rolling basis. Application fee: $55. Electronic applications accepted. *Expenses:* Tuition, state resident: full-time $6738. Tuition, nonresident: full-time $12,690. *Required fees:* $878; $248 per credit hour. *Unit head:* Dr. Richard S. Lapidus, Dean, 909-869-2400, Fax: 909-869-6799, E-mail: rslapidus@csupomona.edu. *Application contact:* Tricia Alicante, Graduate Coordinator, 909-869-4894, E-mail: taalicante@csupomona.edu.
Website: http://cba.csupomona.edu/graduateprograms/.

California State Polytechnic University, Pomona, Academic Affairs, College of Business Administration, MBA Program, Pomona, CA 91768-2557. Offers MBA. *Students:* 11 full-time (7 women), 74 part-time (37 women); includes 44 minority (2 Black or African American, non-Hispanic/Latino; 24 Asian, non-Hispanic/Latino; 14 Hispanic/Latino; 2 Native Hawaiian or other Pacific Islander, non-Hispanic/Latino; 2 Two or more races, non-Hispanic/Latino), 13 international. Average age 30. 112 applicants, 18% accepted, 10 enrolled. In 2013, 34 master's awarded. *Application deadline:* Applications are processed on a rolling basis. Application fee: $55. *Expenses:* Tuition, state resident: full-time $6738. Tuition, nonresident: full-time $12,690. *Required fees:* $878; $248 per credit hour. *Unit head:* Dr. Richard S. Lapidus, Dean, 909-869-2400, E-mail: rslapidus@

csupomona.edu. *Application contact:* Tricia Alicante, Graduate Coordinator, 909-869-4894, E-mail: taalicante@csupomona.edu.
Website: http://cba.csupomona.edu/graduateprograms/.

California State University, Bakersfield, Division of Graduate Studies, Extended University Programs, Bakersfield, CA 93311. Offers administration (MS); curriculum and instruction (MA Ed). *Accreditation:* AACSB. Postbaccalaureate distance learning degree programs offered. *Degree requirements:* For master's, capstone course. *Entrance requirements:* For master's, resume, 3 letters of reference. Additional exam requirements/recommendations for international students: Required—TOEFL (minimum score 550 paper-based). Application fee: $75. *Unit head:* Rhonda Dawson, Director, 661-654-3489, Fax: 661-664-2447, E-mail: rdawson@csub.edu. *Application contact:* Debbie Blowers, Assistant Director of Admissions, 661-664-3381, E-mail: dblowers@csub.edu.
Website: http://www.csub.edu/regional/index.html.

California State University, Bakersfield, Division of Graduate Studies, School of Business and Public Administration, Program in Business Administration, Bakersfield, CA 93311. Offers MBA. *Accreditation:* AACSB. *Entrance requirements:* For master's, GMAT or GRE, baccalaureate degree, minimum undergraduate GPA of 2.75. *Application deadline:* Applications are processed on a rolling basis. Application fee: $55. *Unit head:* Dr. Jean West, Director, 661-654-2780. *Application contact:* Kathy Carpenter, Advisor, 661-654-3404, E-mail: mba@csub.edu.
Website: http://www.csub.edu/mba/index.html.

California State University Channel Islands, Extended University and International Programs, Master of Business Administration Program, Camarillo, CA 93012. Offers MBA. Part-time and evening/weekend programs available. *Entrance requirements:* For master's, GMAT, 2 years of work experience. Additional exam requirements/recommendations for international students: Required—TOEFL (minimum score 550 paper-based; 80 iBT), IELTS (minimum score 6). Electronic applications accepted. *Expenses:* Contact institution.

California State University, Chico, Office of Graduate Studies, College of Behavioral and Social Sciences, Department of Political Science, Program in Public Administration, Chico, CA 95929-0722. Offers health administration (MPA); local government management (MPA). *Accreditation:* NASPAA. Part-time programs available. *Degree requirements:* For master's, thesis or culminating practicum. *Entrance requirements:* For master's, 2 letters of recommendation. Additional exam requirements/recommendations for international students: Required—TOEFL (minimum score 550 paper-based; 80 iBT), IELTS (minimum score 6.5). Electronic applications accepted.

California State University, Chico, Office of Graduate Studies, College of Business, Program in Business Administration, Chico, CA 95929-0722. Offers MBA. *Accreditation:* AACSB. Part-time programs available. *Degree requirements:* For master's, thesis, project, or comprehensive exam. *Entrance requirements:* For master's, GMAT or GRE, 2 letters of recommendation, statement of purpose, resume. Additional exam requirements/recommendations for international students: Required—TOEFL (minimum score 550 paper-based; 80 iBT), IELTS (minimum score 6.5), PTE (minimum score 59). Electronic applications accepted.

California State University, Dominguez Hills, College of Business Administration and Public Policy, Program in Business Administration, Carson, CA 90747-0001. Offers MBA. Part-time and evening/weekend programs available. Postbaccalaureate distance learning degree programs offered (no on-campus study). *Faculty:* 13 full-time (3 women), 6 part-time/adjunct (1 woman). *Students:* 43 full-time (19 women), 73 part-time (24 women); includes 49 minority (12 Black or African American, non-Hispanic/Latino; 16 Asian, non-Hispanic/Latino; 17 Hispanic/Latino; 1 Native Hawaiian or other Pacific Islander, non-Hispanic/Latino; 3 Two or more races, non-Hispanic/Latino), 1 international. Average age 35. 114 applicants, 51% accepted, 36 enrolled. In 2013, 61 master's awarded. *Entrance requirements:* For master's, GMAT, minimum GPA of 2.75. Additional exam requirements/recommendations for international students: Required—TOEFL (minimum score 570 paper-based; 88 iBT). *Application deadline:* For fall admission, 4/1 for domestic and international students; for spring admission, 11/1 for domestic students, 10/1 for international students. Application fee: $55. *Expenses:* Tuition, state resident: full-time $6738. Tuition, nonresident: full-time $13,434. *Required fees:* $622. *Faculty research:* Management. *Unit head:* Betty Vu, Director of MBA and MPA Programs, 310-243-3165, Fax: 310-516-4178, E-mail: bvu@csudh.edu. *Application contact:* Cathi Ryan, Academic Adviser, 310-243-3646, Fax: 310-516-4178, E-mail: cryan@csudh.edu.
Website: http://www4.csudh.edu/mba/.

California State University, East Bay, Office of Academic Programs and Graduate Studies, College of Business and Economics, MBA Program, Hayward, CA 94542-3000. Offers entrepreneurship (MBA); finance (MBA); global innovators (MBA); human resources and organizational behavior (MBA); information technology management (MBA); marketing management (MBA); operations and supply chain management (MBA); strategy and international business (MBA). Part-time and evening/weekend programs available. *Degree requirements:* For master's, comprehensive exam or thesis. *Entrance requirements:* For master's, GMAT (minimum 20th percentile verbal and quantitative section), bachelor's degree, minimum GPA of 2.75. Additional exam requirements/recommendations for international students: Required—TOEFL (minimum score 550 paper-based; 79 iBT). Electronic applications accepted. *Expenses:* Contact institution.

California State University, Fresno, Division of Graduate Studies, Craig School of Business, Program in Business Administration, Fresno, CA 93740-8027. Offers MBA. *Accreditation:* AACSB. Part-time programs available. *Degree requirements:* For master's, thesis or alternative. *Entrance requirements:* For master's, GMAT, minimum GPA of 2.53. Additional exam requirements/recommendations for international students: Required—TOEFL. Electronic applications accepted. *Faculty research:* International trade development, entrepreneurial outreach.

California State University, Fullerton, Graduate Studies, College of Business and Economics, Department of Management, Fullerton, CA 92834-9480. Offers entrepreneurship (MBA); management (MBA). *Accreditation:* AACSB. Part-time programs available. *Students:* 17 full-time (8 women), 32 part-time (14 women); includes 19 minority (1 Black or African American, non-Hispanic/Latino; 11 Asian, non-Hispanic/Latino; 7 Hispanic/Latino), 5 international. Average age 28. In 2013, 32 master's awarded. *Degree requirements:* For master's, project or thesis. *Entrance requirements:* For master's, GMAT, minimum AACSB index of 950. Application fee: $55. *Financial support:* Career-related internships or fieldwork, Federal Work-Study, institutionally sponsored loans, and scholarships/grants available. Support available to part-time students. Financial award application deadline: 3/1; financial award applicants required to submit FAFSA. *Unit head:* Dr. Gus Manoochehri, Chair, 657-278-3071. *Application contact:* Admissions/Applications, 657-278-2371.

California State University, Fullerton, Graduate Studies, College of Business and Economics, Program in Business Administration, Fullerton, CA 92834-9480. Offers business intelligence (MBA); general (MBA); international business (MBA); organizational leadership (MBA); risk management and insurance (MBA). *Accreditation:* AACSB. Part-time programs available. *Students:* 54 full-time (26 women), 119 part-time (48 women); includes 74 minority (46 Asian, non-Hispanic/Latino; 23 Hispanic/Latino; 5 Two or more races, non-Hispanic/Latino), 34 international. Average age 28. 500 applicants, 41% accepted, 78 enrolled. In 2013, 65 master's awarded. *Degree requirements:* For master's, project or thesis. *Entrance requirements:* For master's, GMAT. Application fee: $55. *Financial support:* Career-related internships or fieldwork, Federal Work-Study, institutionally sponsored loans, and scholarships/grants available. Support available to part-time students. Financial award application deadline: 3/1; financial award applicants required to submit FAFSA. *Unit head:* Dr. Anil Puri, Dean, 657-773-2592. *Application contact:* Admissions/Applications, 657-278-2371.

California State University, Long Beach, Graduate Studies, College of Business Administration, Long Beach, CA 90840. Offers MBA. *Accreditation:* AACSB. Part-time and evening/weekend programs available. *Entrance requirements:* For master's, GMAT. Electronic applications accepted. *Faculty research:* Attitude formation theory, consumer motivation, gift giving, derivative and synthetic securities, financial applications of artificial intelligence.

California State University, Los Angeles, Graduate Studies, College of Business and Economics, Department of Information Systems, Los Angeles, CA 90032-8530. Offers business information systems (MBA); management (MS); management information systems (MS); office management (MBA). Part-time and evening/weekend programs available. *Faculty:* 3 full-time (0 women), 3 part-time/adjunct (1 woman). *Students:* 16 full-time (5 women), 13 part-time (5 women); includes 7 minority (2 Black or African American, non-Hispanic/Latino; 4 Asian, non-Hispanic/Latino; 1 Hispanic/Latino), 16 international. Average age 30. 60 applicants, 43% accepted, 6 enrolled. In 2013, 5 master's awarded. *Degree requirements:* For master's, comprehensive exam (MBA), thesis (MS). *Entrance requirements:* For master's, GMAT, minimum GPA of 2.5 during previous 2 years of course work. Additional exam requirements/recommendations for international students: Required—TOEFL (minimum score 550 paper-based). *Application deadline:* For fall admission, 5/1 for domestic and international students. Applications are processed on a rolling basis. Application fee: $55. Electronic applications accepted. *Financial support:* Career-related internships or fieldwork and Federal Work-Study available. Support available to part-time students. Financial award application deadline: 3/1. *Unit head:* Dr. Nanda Ganesen, Chair, 323-343-2983, E-mail: nganesa@calstatela.edu. *Application contact:* Dr. Larry Fritz, Dean of Graduate Studies, 323-343-3820, Fax: 323-343-5653, E-mail: lfritz@calstatela.edu.

California State University, Los Angeles, Graduate Studies, College of Business and Economics, Department of Management, Los Angeles, CA 90032-8530. Offers health care management (MS); management (MBA, MS). *Accreditation:* AACSB. Part-time and evening/weekend programs available. *Faculty:* 1 full-time (0 women), 4 part-time/adjunct (0 women). *Students:* 10 full-time (6 women), 41 part-time (29 women); includes 26 minority (2 Black or African American, non-Hispanic/Latino; 10 Asian, non-Hispanic/Latino; 14 Hispanic/Latino), 11 international. Average age 35. 55 applicants, 55% accepted, 20 enrolled. In 2013, 33 master's awarded. *Entrance requirements:* For master's, GMAT, minimum GPA of 2.5 during previous 2 years of course work. Additional exam requirements/recommendations for international students: Required—TOEFL (minimum score 550 paper-based). *Application deadline:* For fall admission, 5/1 for domestic and international students. Applications are processed on a rolling basis. Application fee: $55. Electronic applications accepted. *Financial support:* Application deadline: 3/1. *Unit head:* Dr. Angela Young, Chair, 323-343-2890, Fax: 323-343-6461, E-mail: ayoung3@calstatela.edu. *Application contact:* Dr. Larry Fritz, Dean of Graduate Studies, 323-343-3827, Fax: 323-343-5653, E-mail: lfritz@calstatela.edu.
Website: http://cbe.calstatela.edu/mgmt/.

California State University, Monterey Bay, College of Professional Studies, School of Business, Seaside, CA 93955-8001. Offers EMBA. Part-time and evening/weekend programs available. Postbaccalaureate distance learning degree programs offered (no on-campus study). *Entrance requirements:* For master's, recommendation, resume, work experience, bachelor's degree from accredited university. Additional exam requirements/recommendations for international students: Recommended—TOEFL (minimum score 550 paper-based; 79 iBT). Electronic applications accepted.

California State University, Northridge, Graduate Studies, College of Business and Economics, Northridge, CA 91330. Offers MBA. *Accreditation:* AACSB. Part-time programs available. *Degree requirements:* For master's, thesis or alternative. *Entrance requirements:* For master's, GMAT, minimum GPA of 3.0 in last 60 units. Additional exam requirements/recommendations for international students: Required—TOEFL.

California State University, Northridge, Graduate Studies, The Tseng College of Extended Learning, Program in Public Sector Management and Leadership, Northridge, CA 91330. Offers MPA. Postbaccalaureate distance learning degree programs offered (no on-campus study).

California State University, Sacramento, Office of Graduate Studies, College of Business Administration, Sacramento, CA 95819. Offers accountancy (MS); business administration (IMBA, MBA); human resources (MBA); urban land development (MBA). *Accreditation:* AACSB. Part-time and evening/weekend programs available. *Degree requirements:* For master's, thesis or alternative, writing proficiency exam. *Entrance requirements:* For master's, GMAT. Additional exam requirements/recommendations for international students: Required—TOEFL. *Application deadline:* For fall admission, 2/1 for domestic students, 3/1 for international students; for spring admission, 9/15 for domestic students, 9/30 for international students. Applications are processed on a rolling basis. Application fee: $55. Electronic applications accepted. *Financial support:* Research assistantships, teaching assistantships, career-related internships or fieldwork, and Federal Work-Study available. Support available to part-time students. Financial award applicants required to submit FAFSA. *Unit head:* Dr. Sanjay Varshney, Dean, 916-278-6942, Fax: 916-278-5793, E-mail: cba@csus.edu. *Application contact:* Jose Martinez, Graduate Admissions Supervisor, 916-278-7871, E-mail: martinj@skymail.csus.edu.
Website: http://www.cba.csus.edu.

California State University, San Bernardino, Graduate Studies, College of Business and Public Administration, Master in Business Administration Program, San Bernardino, CA 92407. Offers accounting (MBA); cyber security (MBA); entrepreneurship (MBA); finance (MBA); information systems and technology (MBA); management (MBA); marketing management (MBA); supply chain management (MBA). MBA is also offered online. *Accreditation:* AACSB. Part-time and evening/weekend programs available. Postbaccalaureate distance learning degree programs offered (no on-campus study). *Faculty:* 27 full-time (6 women), 8 part-time/adjunct (1 woman). *Students:* 161 full-time (59 women), 47 part-time (18 women); includes 74 minority (12 Black or African American, non-Hispanic/Latino; 19 Asian, non-Hispanic/Latino; 42 Hispanic/Latino; 1 Two or more races, non-Hispanic/Latino), 74 international. Average age 29. 281 applicants, 38% accepted, 67 enrolled. In 2013, 79 master's awarded. *Degree requirements:* For master's, comprehensive exam, thesis, portfolio, 60 units, minimum GPA of 3.0. *Entrance requirements:* For master's, GMAT or GRE, minimum GPA of 2.5. Additional exam requirements/recommendations for international students: Required—TOEFL (minimum score 550 paper-based; 79 iBT). *Application deadline:* For fall admission, 7/20 for domestic and international students; for winter admission, 10/20 for domestic and international students; for spring admission, 1/20 for domestic and

international students. Applications are processed on a rolling basis. Application fee: $55. Electronic applications accepted. *Expenses:* Contact institution. *Financial support:* In 2013–14, 79 students received support, including 21 fellowships (averaging $4,867 per year), 29 research assistantships (averaging $2,748 per year), 6 teaching assistantships (averaging $5,162 per year); career-related internships or fieldwork, Federal Work-Study, institutionally sponsored loans, scholarships/grants, and unspecified assistantships also available. Support available to part-time students. Financial award application deadline: 3/1; financial award applicants required to submit FAFSA. *Faculty research:* Market reaction to Form 20-F, tax Constitutional questions in Obamacare, the performance of the faith and ethical investment products prior to and following the 2008 meltdown, capital appreciation bonds: a ruinous decision for an unborn generation, the effects of calorie count display on consumer eating behavior, local government bankruptcy. *Total annual research expenditures:* $2.3 million. *Unit head:* Dr. Lawrence C. Rose, Dean, 909-537-3703, Fax: 909-537-7026, E-mail: lrose@csusb.edu. *Application contact:* Dr. Vipin Gupta, Associate Dean/MBA Director, 909-537-7380, Fax: 909-537-7026, E-mail: vgupta@csusb.edu.
Website: http://mba.csusb.edu/.

California State University, San Marcos, College of Business Administration, San Marcos, CA 92096-0001. Offers MBA. Evening/weekend programs available. *Degree requirements:* For master's, project. *Entrance requirements:* For master's, GMAT, minimum GPA of 3.0 in last 60 units, 3 years of full-time work experience. Additional exam requirements/recommendations for international students: Required—TOEFL (minimum score 550 paper-based). *Expenses:* Contact institution.

California State University, Stanislaus, College of Business Administration, Program in Business Administration (Executive MBA), Turlock, CA 95382. Offers EMBA. *Accreditation:* AACSB. Part-time and evening/weekend programs available. *Degree requirements:* For master's, comprehensive exam, thesis or alternative. *Entrance requirements:* For master's, GMAT or GRE, minimum GPA of 2.5, 2 letters of reference, personal statement, interview. Additional exam requirements/recommendations for international students: Required—TOEFL (minimum score 550 paper-based). Electronic applications accepted. *Expenses:* Contact institution.

California State University, Stanislaus, College of Business Administration, Program in Business Administration (MBA), Turlock, CA 95382. Offers MBA. *Accreditation:* AACSB. Part-time and evening/weekend programs available. *Degree requirements:* For master's, comprehensive exam, thesis or alternative. *Entrance requirements:* For master's, GMAT or GRE, minimum GPA of 2.5, 3 letters of reference, personal statement. Additional exam requirements/recommendations for international students: Required—TOEFL (minimum score 550 paper-based). Electronic applications accepted. *Expenses:* Contact institution. *Faculty research:* Teaching creativity, graduate operations management, curricula data mining, foreign direct investment.

California University of Management and Sciences, Graduate Programs, Anaheim, CA 92801. Offers business administration (MBA, DBA); computer information systems (MS); economics (MS); international business (MS); sports management (MS).

California University of Pennsylvania, School of Graduate Studies and Research, Eberly College of Science and Technology, Program in Business Administration, California, PA 15419-1394. Offers MSBA. Part-time and evening/weekend programs available. *Degree requirements:* For master's, comprehensive exam. *Entrance requirements:* For master's, minimum QPA of 3.0. Additional exam requirements/recommendations for international students: Required—TOEFL (minimum score 550 paper-based). Electronic applications accepted. *Faculty research:* Economics, applied economics, consumer behavior, technology and business, impact of technology.

Cambridge College, School of Management, Cambridge, MA 02138-5304. Offers business negotiation and conflict resolution (M Mgt); general business (M Mgt); health care informatics (M Mgt); health care management (M Mgt); leadership in human and organizational dynamics (M Mgt); non-profit and public organization management (M Mgt); small business development (M Mgt); technology management (M Mgt). Part-time and evening/weekend programs available. *Degree requirements:* For master's, thesis, seminars. *Entrance requirements:* For master's, resume, 2 professional references. Additional exam requirements/recommendations for international students: Required—TOEFL (minimum score 550 paper-based; 79 iBT), Michigan English Language Assessment Battery (minimum score 85); Recommended—IELTS (minimum score 6). Electronic applications accepted. *Expenses:* Contact institution. *Faculty research:* Negotiation, mediation and conflict resolution; leadership; management of diverse organizations; case studies and simulation methodologies for management education, digital as a second language: social networking for digital immigrants, non-profit and public management.

Cameron University, Office of Graduate Studies, Program in Business Administration, Lawton, OK 73505-6377. Offers MBA. *Accreditation:* ACBSP. Part-time and evening/weekend programs available. Postbaccalaureate distance learning degree programs offered (no on-campus study). *Degree requirements:* For master's, comprehensive exam. *Entrance requirements:* Additional exam requirements/recommendations for international students: Required—TOEFL (minimum score 550 paper-based). Electronic applications accepted. *Faculty research:* Financial liberalization, right to work, recession, teaching evaluations, database management.

Campbellsville University, School of Business and Economics, Campbellsville, KY 42718-2799. Offers business administration (MBA); business organizational management (MAOL). Part-time and evening/weekend programs available. *Entrance requirements:* For master's, GRE or GMAT. Additional exam requirements/recommendations for international students: Required—TOEFL (minimum score 550 paper-based). Electronic applications accepted. *Expenses:* Contact institution.

Campbell University, Graduate and Professional Programs, Lundy-Fetterman School of Business, Buies Creek, NC 27506. Offers MBA, MTIM. *Accreditation:* ACBSP. Part-time and evening/weekend programs available. *Degree requirements:* For master's, comprehensive exam, thesis or alternative. *Entrance requirements:* For master's, GMAT, minimum GPA of 2.7, 3 letters of reference. Additional exam requirements/recommendations for international students: Required—TOEFL (minimum score 550 paper-based). *Faculty research:* Agricultural economics, investments, leadership, marketing, law and economics.

Canisius College, Graduate Division, Richard J. Wehle School of Business, Department of Management, Buffalo, NY 14208-1098. Offers business administration (MBA); international business (MS). *Accreditation:* AACSB. Part-time and evening/weekend programs available. *Faculty:* 30 full-time (7 women), 8 part-time/adjunct (1 woman). *Students:* 99 full-time (43 women), 139 part-time (63 women); includes 22 minority (11 Black or African American, non-Hispanic/Latino; 2 American Indian or Alaska Native, non-Hispanic/Latino; 5 Asian, non-Hispanic/Latino; 2 Hispanic/Latino; 2 Two or more races, non-Hispanic/Latino), 3 international. Average age 28. 146 applicants, 68% accepted, 66 enrolled. In 2013, 113 master's awarded. *Entrance requirements:* For master's, GMAT, GRE, official transcript from colleges attended, current resume. Additional exam requirements/recommendations for international students: Required—TOEFL (minimum score 550 paper-based, 80 iBT), IELTS (minimum score 6.5), or CAEL (minimum score 70). *Application deadline:* For fall admission, 7/1 priority date for domestic students; for spring admission, 11/1 priority date for domestic students. Applications are processed on a rolling basis. Application fee: $25. Electronic applications accepted. Application fee is waived when completed online. *Expenses: Tuition:* Part-time $750 per credit hour. *Financial support:* Research assistantships, career-related internships or fieldwork, Federal Work-Study, scholarships/grants, and unspecified assistantships available. Support available to part-time students. Financial award application deadline: 4/30; financial award applicants required to submit FAFSA. *Faculty research:* Global leadership effectiveness, global supply chain management, quality management. *Unit head:* Dr. Gordon W. Meyer, Chair of Management, Entrepreneurship and International Business, 716-888-2634, E-mail: meyerg@canisius.edu. *Application contact:* Julie A. Zulewski, Director, Graduate Programs, 716-888-2548, Fax: 716-888-3195, E-mail: zulewskj@canisius.edu.
Website: http://www.canisius.edu/graduate/.

Cape Breton University, Shannon School of Business, Sydney, NS B1P 6L2, Canada. Offers MBA. Part-time programs available. *Entrance requirements:* For master's, GMAT. Additional exam requirements/recommendations for international students: Required—TOEFL (minimum score 550 paper-based; 80 iBT), IELTS (minimum score 6.5). Electronic applications accepted.

Capella University, School of Business and Technology, Doctoral Programs in Business, Minneapolis, MN 55402. Offers accounting (DBA, PhD); business intelligence (DBA); finance (DBA, PhD); general business management (PhD); human resource management (DBA, PhD); leadership (DBA, PhD); management education (PhD); marketing (DBA, PhD); project management (DBA, PhD); strategy and innovation (DBA, PhD).

Capella University, School of Business and Technology, Master's Programs in Business, Minneapolis, MN 55402. Offers accounting (MBA); business analysis (MS); business intelligence (MBA); entrepreneurship (MBA); finance (MBA); general business administration (MBA); general human resource management (MS); general leadership (MS); health care management (MBA); human resource management (MBA); marketing (MBA); project management (MBA, MS).

Capital University, Law School, Program in Business Law and Taxation, Columbus, OH 43209-2394. Offers business (LL M); business and taxation (LL M); taxation (LL M); JD/LL M. Part-time and evening/weekend programs available. *Degree requirements:* For master's, thesis or alternative. *Entrance requirements:* For master's, previous course work in accounting, business law, and taxation. Additional exam requirements/recommendations for international students: Required—TOEFL (minimum score 600 paper-based). Electronic applications accepted.

Capital University, School of Management, Columbus, OH 43209-2394. Offers entrepreneurship (MBA); finance (MBA); leadership (MBA); marketing (MBA); MBA/JD; MBA/LL M; MBA/MSN; MBA/MT. *Accreditation:* ACBSP. Part-time and evening/weekend programs available. *Faculty:* 17 full-time (7 women), 23 part-time/adjunct (1 woman). *Students:* 192 (77 women). Average age 31. 34 applicants, 74% accepted, 20 enrolled. In 2013, 1 master's awarded. *Entrance requirements:* For master's, GMAT, 2 years of work experience. Additional exam requirements/recommendations for international students: Required—TOEFL (minimum score 550 paper-based); Recommended—IELTS (minimum score 6.5). *Application deadline:* For fall admission, 7/1 priority date for domestic students; for winter admission, 11/1 for domestic students; for spring admission, 11/1 priority date for domestic students; for summer admission, 4/1 priority date for domestic students. Applications are processed on a rolling basis. Electronic applications accepted. *Financial support:* Application deadline: 8/1; applicants required to submit FAFSA. *Faculty research:* Taxation, public policy, health care, management of non-profits. *Unit head:* Dr. David Schwantes, MBA Director, 614-236-6984, Fax: 614-236-6923, E-mail: dschwant@capital.edu. *Application contact:* Carli Isgrigg, Assistant Director of Adult and Graduate Education Recruitment, 614-236-6546, Fax: 614-236-6923, E-mail: cisgrigg@capital.edu.
Website: http://www.capital.edu/capital-mba/.

Capitol College, Graduate Programs, Laurel, MD 20708-9759. Offers business administration (MBA); computer science (MS); electrical engineering (MS); information and telecommunications systems management (MS); information architecture (MS); network security (MS). Part-time and evening/weekend programs available. Postbaccalaureate distance learning degree programs offered (no on-campus study). *Entrance requirements:* For master's, minimum GPA of 3.0. Electronic applications accepted.

Cardinal Stritch University, College of Business and Management, Milwaukee, WI 53217-3985. Offers MBA, MSM. Programs also offered in Madison, WI and Minneapolis-St. Paul, MN. *Accreditation:* ACBSP. Part-time and evening/weekend programs available. *Degree requirements:* For master's, thesis (for some programs), case study, faculty recommendation. *Entrance requirements:* For master's, 3 years management or related experience, minimum GPA of 2.5. Additional exam requirements/recommendations for international students: Required—TOEFL. *Expenses:* Contact institution.

Carleton University, Faculty of Graduate Studies, Faculty of Business, Eric Sprott School of Business, Ottawa, ON K1S 5B6, Canada. Offers business administration (MBA); management (PhD). *Degree requirements:* For master's, thesis optional; for doctorate, comprehensive exam, thesis/dissertation. *Entrance requirements:* For master's, GMAT, honors degree; for doctorate, GMAT. Additional exam requirements/recommendations for international students: Required—TOEFL. *Faculty research:* Business information systems, finance, international business, marketing, production and operations.

Carlos Albizu University, Miami Campus, Graduate Programs, Miami, FL 33172-2209. Offers clinical psychology (Psy D); entrepreneurship (MBA); exceptional student education (MS); human services (PhD); industrial/organizational psychology (MS); marriage and family therapy (MS); mental health counseling (MS); nonprofit management (MBA); organizational management (MBA); psychology (MS); school counseling (MS); teaching English as a second language (MS). *Accreditation:* APA. Part-time and evening/weekend programs available. *Faculty:* 26 full-time (20 women), 34 part-time/adjunct (16 women). *Students:* 416 full-time (335 women), 281 part-time (237 women); includes 604 minority (57 Black or African American, non-Hispanic/Latino; 1 American Indian or Alaska Native, non-Hispanic/Latino; 13 Asian, non-Hispanic/Latino; 533 Hispanic/Latino), 14 international. Average age 36. 176 applicants, 59% accepted, 96 enrolled. In 2013, 176 master's, 37 doctorates awarded. Terminal master's awarded for partial completion of doctoral program. *Degree requirements:* For master's, one foreign language, comprehensive exam, integrative project (MBA), research project (exceptional student education, teaching English as a second language); for doctorate, one foreign language, comprehensive exam, internship, project. *Entrance requirements:* For master's, 3 letters of recommendation, interview, minimum GPA of 3.0, resume, statement of purpose, official transcripts; for doctorate, 3 letters of recommendation, minimum GPA of 3.0, resume, interview, statement of purpose, official transcripts. Additional exam requirements/recommendations for international students: Required—Michigan Test of English Language Proficiency. *Application deadline:* For fall admission, 4/1 priority date for domestic students, 5/1 priority date for international students; for spring admission, 11/1 priority date for domestic students, 9/1 priority date for international students. Applications are processed on a rolling basis. Application fee:

$50. Electronic applications accepted. *Expenses: Tuition:* Full-time $9360; part-time $520 per credit. *Required fees:* $298 per term. Tuition and fees vary according to course load, degree level and program. *Financial support:* In 2013–14, 62 students received support. Federal Work-Study, scholarships/grants, and tuition discounts available. Financial award application deadline: 6/1; financial award applicants required to submit FAFSA. *Faculty research:* Psychotherapy, forensic psychology, neuropsychology, marketing strategy, entrepreneurship, special education. *Unit head:* Peter M. Rubio, Interim Chancellor, 305-593-1223 Ext. 3120, Fax: 305-592-7930, E-mail: prubio@albizu.edu. *Application contact:* Vanessa Almendarez, Administrative Assistant, 305-593-1223 Ext. 3137, Fax: 305-593-1854, E-mail: valmendarez@albizu.edu.

Carlow University, School of Management, MBA Program, Pittsburgh, PA 15213-3165. Offers business administration (MBA); global business (MBA); healthcare management (MBA); project management (MBA). Part-time and evening/weekend programs available. Postbaccalaureate distance learning degree programs offered (no on-campus study). *Students:* 121 full-time (96 women), 26 part-time (17 women); includes 30 minority (22 Black or African American, non-Hispanic/Latino; 3 Asian, non-Hispanic/Latino; 3 Hispanic/Latino; 2 Two or more races, non-Hispanic/Latino), 5 international. Average age 32. 53 applicants, 96% accepted, 38 enrolled. In 2013, 41 master's awarded. *Entrance requirements:* For master's, minimum undergraduate GPA of 3.0; essay; resume; transcripts; two recommendations. Additional exam requirements/recommendations for international students: Required—TOEFL (minimum score 550 paper-based). *Application deadline:* Applications are processed on a rolling basis. Application fee: $20. Electronic applications accepted. Application fee is waived when completed online. *Expenses: Tuition:* Full-time $9523; part-time $744 per credit. Tuition and fees vary according to course load, degree level and program. *Unit head:* Dr. Enrique Mu, Chair, MBA Program, 412-578-8729, E-mail: emu@carlow.edu. *Application contact:* Jo Danhires, Administrative Assistant, Admissions, 412-578-6088, Fax: 412-578-6321, E-mail: gradstudies@carlow.edu.
Website: http://gradstudies.carlow.edu/management/mba.html.

Carnegie Mellon University, Heinz College, School of Public Policy and Management, Master of Entertainment Industry Management Program, Pittsburgh, PA 15213-3891. Offers MEIM. *Accreditation:* AACSB. *Entrance requirements:* For master's, GRE or GMAT, college-level course in advanced algebra/pre-calculus; college-level courses in economics and statistics (recommended). Additional exam requirements/recommendations for international students: Required—TOEFL or IELTS.

Carnegie Mellon University, Heinz College, School of Public Policy and Management, Master of Science Program in Biotechnology and Management, Pittsburgh, PA 15213-3891. Offers MS. *Accreditation:* AACSB. *Entrance requirements:* For master's, GRE or GMAT, college-level course in advanced algebra/pre-calculus; college-level courses in economics and statistics (recommended). Additional exam requirements/recommendations for international students: Required—TOEFL or IELTS.

Carnegie Mellon University, Tepper School of Business, Pittsburgh, PA 15213-3891. Offers accounting (PhD); algorithms, combinatorics, and optimization (MS, PhD); business management and software engineering (MBMSE); civil engineering and industrial management (MS); computational finance (MSCF); economics (MS, PhD); electronic commerce (MS); environmental engineering and management (MEEM); finance (PhD); financial economics (PhD); industrial administration (MBA), including administration and public management; information systems (PhD); management of manufacturing and automation (PhD); marketing (PhD); mathematical finance (PhD); operations research (PhD); organizational behavior and theory (PhD); political economy (PhD); production and operations management (PhD); public policy and management (MS, MSED); software engineering and business management (MS); JD/MS; JD/MSIA; M Div/MS; MOM/MSIA; MSCF/MSIA. JD/MSIA offered jointly with University of Pittsburgh. Part-time programs available. Terminal master's awarded for partial completion of doctoral program. *Degree requirements:* For doctorate, thesis/dissertation. *Entrance requirements:* For master's, GMAT. Additional exam requirements/recommendations for international students: Required—TOEFL. *Expenses:* Contact institution.

Carroll University, Program in Business Administration, Waukesha, WI 53186-5593. Offers MBA. Part-time programs available. *Entrance requirements:* For master's, GRE, resume, transcripts. Additional exam requirements/recommendations for international students: Required—TOEFL. Electronic applications accepted.

Carson-Newman University, Program in Business Administration, Jefferson City, TN 37760. Offers MBA. *Faculty:* 6 full-time (3 women). *Students:* 9 full-time (2 women), 55 part-time (31 women); includes 3 minority (2 Black or African American, non-Hispanic/Latino; 1 Hispanic/Latino), 11 international. In 2013, 16 master's awarded. *Application deadline:* For fall admission, 7/15 priority date for domestic students. Application fee: $50. *Expenses: Tuition:* Part-time $390 per credit hour. *Unit head:* Dr. Clyde Herring, Director, 865-471-3587, E-mail: ceherring@cn.edu. *Application contact:* Graduate Admissions and Services Adviser, 865-473-3468, Fax: 865-472-3475.

Case Western Reserve University, Weatherhead School of Management, Department of Operations, Management Program, Cleveland, OH 44106. Offers operations research (MSM); supply chain (MSM); MBA/MSM. *Accreditation:* AACSB. Part-time and evening/weekend programs available. *Entrance requirements:* For master's, GMAT or GRE, 3 letters of recommendation, resume. Additional exam requirements/recommendations for international students: Required—TOEFL (minimum score 600 paper-based). *Faculty research:* Supply chain management, operations management, operations/finance interface optimization, scheduling.

Case Western Reserve University, Weatherhead School of Management, Executive Doctor of Management Program, Cleveland, OH 44106. Offers management (EDM). Part-time and evening/weekend programs available. *Degree requirements:* For doctorate, thesis/dissertation. *Entrance requirements:* For doctorate, GMAT. Electronic applications accepted. *Expenses:* Contact institution. *Faculty research:* Information technology and design, emotional intelligence and leadership, entrepreneurship, governing of NP organizations, social ethics.

Case Western Reserve University, Weatherhead School of Management, Executive MBA Program, Cleveland, OH 44106. Offers EMBA. *Accreditation:* AACSB. *Entrance requirements:* For master's, GMAT (if candidate does not have an undergraduate degree from an accredited institution), work experience, interview. Electronic applications accepted. *Expenses:* Contact institution.

Case Western Reserve University, Weatherhead School of Management, Full Time MBA Program, Cleveland, OH 44106. Offers MBA, MBA/JD, MBA/M Acc, MBA/MD, MBA/MIM, MBA/MNO, MBA/MSM, MBA/MSN, MBA/MSSA. *Accreditation:* AACSB. *Entrance requirements:* For master's, GMAT, letters of recommendation, interview, work experience. Additional exam requirements/recommendations for international students: Required—TOEFL (minimum score 600 paper-based). Electronic applications accepted.

Case Western Reserve University, Weatherhead School of Management, Part-time MBA Program, Cleveland, OH 44106. Offers MBA, MBA/M Acc, MBA/MSM, MBA/MSSA. *Accreditation:* AACSB. Part-time and evening/weekend programs available. *Entrance requirements:* For master's, GMAT, interview, work experience. Additional

exam requirements/recommendations for international students: Recommended—TOEFL (minimum score 600 paper-based). Electronic applications accepted.

The Catholic University of America, Metropolitan School of Professional Studies, Washington, DC 20064. Offers human resource management (MA); management (MSM). Part-time and evening/weekend programs available. *Faculty:* 54 part-time/adjunct (22 women). *Students:* 44 full-time (25 women), 206 part-time (141 women); includes 133 minority (92 Black or African American, non-Hispanic/Latino; 1 American Indian or Alaska Native, non-Hispanic/Latino; 8 Asian, non-Hispanic/Latino; 24 Hispanic/Latino; 1 Native Hawaiian or other Pacific Islander, non-Hispanic/Latino; 7 Two or more races, non-Hispanic/Latino), 13 international. Average age 37. 152 applicants, 77% accepted, 81 enrolled. In 2013, 67 master's awarded. *Degree requirements:* For master's, minimum GPA of 3.0, capstone course. *Entrance requirements:* For master's, statement of purpose, official copies of academic transcripts, three letters of recommendation, resume. Additional exam requirements/recommendations for international students: Required—TOEFL (minimum score 93 iBT). *Application deadline:* For fall admission, 8/1 priority date for domestic students, 7/15 for international students; for spring admission, 12/1 priority date for domestic students, 10/15 for international students. Application fee: $55. *Expenses: Tuition:* Full-time $38,500; part-time $1490 per credit hour. *Required fees:* $400; $1525 per credit hour. One-time fee: $425. Tuition and fees vary according to program. *Total annual research expenditures:* $183,115. *Unit head:* Dr. Sara Thompson, Dean, 202-319-5256, Fax: 202-319-6032, E-mail: thompsons@cua.edu. *Application contact:* Andrew Woodall, Director of Graduate Admissions, 202-319-5057, Fax: 202-319-6533, E-mail: cua-admissions@cua.edu. Website: http://metro.cua.edu/.

The Catholic University of America, School of Business and Economics, Washington, DC 20064. Offers accounting (MS); business analysis (MS); integral economic development management (MA); integral economic development policy (MA); international political economics (MA). Part-time programs available. *Faculty:* 14 full-time (6 women), 30 part-time/adjunct (7 women). *Students:* 34 full-time (16 women), 12 part-time (7 women); includes 15 minority (9 Black or African American, non-Hispanic/Latino; 1 Asian, non-Hispanic/Latino; 2 Hispanic/Latino; 3 Two or more races, non-Hispanic/Latino), 10 international. Average age 28. 91 applicants, 60% accepted, 35 enrolled. In 2013, 16 master's awarded. *Degree requirements:* For master's, comprehensive exam. *Entrance requirements:* For master's, GRE General Test, statement of purpose, official copies of academic transcripts, three letters of recommendation. Additional exam requirements/recommendations for international students: Required—TOEFL (minimum score 580 paper-based). *Application deadline:* For fall admission, 8/1 priority date for domestic students, 7/15 for international students; for spring admission, 12/1 priority date for domestic students, 10/15 for international students. Applications are processed on a rolling basis. Application fee: $55. Electronic applications accepted. *Expenses: Tuition:* Full-time $38,500; part-time $1490 per credit hour. *Required fees:* $400; $1525 per credit hour. One-time fee: $425. Tuition and fees vary according to program. *Financial support:* Fellowships, research assistantships, teaching assistantships, Federal Work-Study, scholarships/grants, tuition waivers (full and partial), and unspecified assistantships available. Financial award application deadline: 2/1; financial award applicants required to submit FAFSA. *Faculty research:* Integrity of the marketing process, economics of energy and the environment, emerging markets, social change, international finance and economic development. *Total annual research expenditures:* $170,819. *Unit head:* Dr. Andrew V. Abela, Chair, 202-319-5235, Fax: 202-319-4426, E-mail: abela@cua.edu. *Application contact:* Andrew Woodall, Director of Graduate Admissions, 202-319-5057, Fax: 202-319-6533, E-mail: cua-admissions@cua.edu.
Website: http://business.cua.edu/.

Cedarville University, Graduate Programs, Cedarville, OH 45314-0601. Offers business administration (MBA); curriculum (M Ed); educational administration (M Ed); family nurse practitioner (MSN); global health ministries (MSN); instruction (M Ed); pharmacy (Pharm D). Part-time programs available. Postbaccalaureate distance learning degree programs offered (no on-campus study). *Faculty:* 23 full-time (12 women), 12 part-time/adjunct (5 women). *Students:* 119 full-time (74 women), 103 part-time (73 women); includes 16 minority (11 Black or African American, non-Hispanic/Latino; 4 Asian, non-Hispanic/Latino; 1 Native Hawaiian or other Pacific Islander, non-Hispanic/Latino), 4 international. Average age 31. In 2013, 26 master's awarded. *Degree requirements:* For master's, thesis. *Entrance requirements:* For master's, GRE, 2 professional recommendations; for doctorate, PCAT, professional recommendation from a practicing pharmacist or current employer/supervisor, resume, essay, interview. Additional exam requirements/recommendations for international students: Required—TOEFL (minimum score 550 paper-based; 80 iBT). *Application deadline:* For fall admission, 5/1 priority date for domestic and international students; for spring admission, 11/1 priority date for domestic and international students. Applications are processed on a rolling basis. Application fee: $30. Electronic applications accepted. *Financial support:* Scholarships/grants and unspecified assistantships available. Support available to part-time students. Financial award applicants required to submit FAFSA. *Unit head:* Dr. Mark McClain, Dean of Graduate Studies, 937-766-7700, E-mail: mcclain@cedarville.edu. *Application contact:* Roscoe F. Smith, Associate Vice-President of Enrollment, 937-766-7700, Fax: 937-766-7575, E-mail: smithr@cedarville.edu.
Website: http://www.cedarville.edu/academics/graduate/.

Centenary College, Program in Business Administration, Hackettstown, NJ 07840-2100. Offers MBA. Part-time and evening/weekend programs available. Postbaccalaureate distance learning degree programs offered (minimal on-campus study). *Entrance requirements:* For master's, GMAT.

Centenary College of Louisiana, Graduate Programs, Frost School of Business, Shreveport, LA 71104. Offers MBA. Part-time and evening/weekend programs available. *Degree requirements:* For master's, thesis. *Entrance requirements:* For master's, GMAT, minimum 5 years of professional/managerial experience. *Faculty research:* Leadership, organizational change strategy, market behavior, executive compensation.

Central European University, CEU Business School, Budapest, Hungary. Offers executive business administration (EMBA); finance (MBA); general management (MBA); information technology management (M Sc); marketing (MBA). Part-time and evening/weekend programs available. *Faculty:* 18 full-time (5 women), 6 part-time/adjunct (1 woman). *Students:* 37 full-time (16 women), 82 part-time (20 women). Average age 32. 219 applicants, 34% accepted, 35 enrolled. In 2013, 69 master's awarded. *Degree requirements:* For master's, one foreign language. *Entrance requirements:* For master's, GMAT. Additional exam requirements/recommendations for international students: Required—TOEFL (minimum score 570 paper-based); Recommended—IELTS (minimum score 6.5). *Application deadline:* For fall admission, 5/15 for domestic students, 5/22 for international students; for winter admission, 11/15 for domestic students, 11/10 for international students. Applications are processed on a rolling basis. Application fee: $40. Electronic applications accepted. *Expenses: Tuition:* Full-time 62,700 Hungarian forints. *Financial support:* Tuition waivers (partial) available. *Faculty research:* Social and ethical business, marketing, international business, international trade and investment, management development in Central and East Europe, non-market strategies of emerging-market multinationals, macro and micro analysis of the

business environment, international competitive analysis, the transition process from emerging economies to established market economies and its social impact, the regulation of natural monopolies. *Unit head:* Dr. Mel Horwitch, Dean and Managing Director, 361-887-5050, E-mail: mhorwitch@ceubusiness.com. *Application contact:* Miao Tan, Recruitment Coordinator, 361-887-5061, Fax: 361-887-5133, E-mail: tanm@ceubusiness.org.
Website: http://business.ceu.hu/.

Central Michigan University, Central Michigan University Global Campus, Program in Business Administration, Mount Pleasant, MI 48859. Offers enterprise resource planning (MBA, Certificate); human resource management (MBA); logistics management (MBA, Certificate); marketing (MBA); value-driven organization (MBA). Part-time and evening/weekend programs available. *Entrance requirements:* For master's, GMAT. *Financial support:* Scholarships/grants available. Support available to part-time students. *Unit head:* Dr. Debasish Chakraborty, 989-774-3678, E-mail: chakt1d@cmich.edu. *Application contact:* Global Campus Student Services Call Center, 877-268-4636, E-mail: cmuglobal@cmich.edu.

Central Michigan University, College of Graduate Studies, College of Business Administration, MBA Program, Mount Pleasant, MI 48859. Offers accounting (MBA); business economics (MBA); consulting (MBA); finance (MBA); general business (MBA); human resource management (MBA); information systems (MBA); international business (MBA); logistics management (MBA); marketing (MBA); value-driven organization (MBA). Part-time and evening/weekend programs available. Postbaccalaureate distance learning degree programs offered (no on-campus study). Electronic applications accepted. *Faculty research:* Accounting, consulting, international business, marketing, information systems.

Central Michigan University, College of Graduate Studies, Interdisciplinary Administration Programs, Mount Pleasant, MI 48859. Offers acquisitions administration (MSA, Graduate Certificate); general administration (MSA, Graduate Certificate); health services administration (MSA, Graduate Certificate); human resource administration (Graduate Certificate); human resources administration (MSA); information resource management (MSA, Graduate Certificate); international administration (MSA, Graduate Certificate); leadership (MSA, Graduate Certificate); public administration (MSA, Graduate Certificate); research administration (Graduate Certificate); sport administration (MSA). *Accreditation:* AACSB. Part-time and evening/weekend programs available. Postbaccalaureate distance learning degree programs offered (no on-campus study). *Degree requirements:* For master's, thesis or alternative. *Entrance requirements:* For master's, bachelor's degree with minimum GPA of 2.7. Electronic applications accepted. *Faculty research:* Interdisciplinary studies in acquisitions administration, health services administration, sport administration, recreation and park administration, and international administration.

Chadron State College, School of Professional and Graduate Studies, Department of Business and Economics, Chadron, NE 69337. Offers MBA. *Accreditation:* ACBSP. Part-time and evening/weekend programs available. Postbaccalaureate distance learning degree programs offered (minimal on-campus study). *Degree requirements:* For master's, thesis optional. *Entrance requirements:* For master's, GMAT, minimum GPA of 2.75 or 12 graduate hours at CSC with minimum GPA of 3.25. Additional exam requirements/recommendations for international students: Required—TOEFL. Electronic applications accepted.

Chaminade University of Honolulu, Graduate Services, Program in Business Administration, Honolulu, HI 96816-1578. Offers accounting (MBA); business (MBA); not-for-profit (MBA); public sector (MBA). Part-time and evening/weekend programs available. *Entrance requirements:* For master's, minimum GPA of 3.0, resume. Additional exam requirements/recommendations for international students: Required—TOEFL (minimum score 650 paper-based). Electronic applications accepted. *Faculty research:* Total quality management, international finance, not-for-profit accounting, service-learning in business contexts.

Champlain College, Graduate Studies, Burlington, VT 05402-0670. Offers business (MBA); digital forensic management (MS); digital forensic science (MS); early childhood education (M Ed); emergent media (MFA, MS); health care administration (MS); law (MS); managing innovation and information technology (MS); mediation and applied conflict studies (MS). MS in emergent media program held in Shanghai. Part-time programs available. Postbaccalaureate distance learning degree programs offered (no on-campus study). *Faculty:* 13 full-time (2 women), 34 part-time/adjunct (14 women). *Students:* 303 full-time (191 women), 104 part-time (58 women); includes 38 minority (21 Black or African American, non-Hispanic/Latino; 8 Asian, non-Hispanic/Latino; 7 Hispanic/Latino; 2 Two or more races, non-Hispanic/Latino), 4 international. Average age 37. In 2013, 169 master's awarded. *Degree requirements:* For master's, capstone project. *Entrance requirements:* Additional exam requirements/recommendations for international students: Required—TOEFL (minimum score 550 paper-based; 80 iBT). *Application deadline:* For fall admission, 8/1 priority date for domestic and international students; for spring admission, 1/1 priority date for domestic and international students. Applications are processed on a rolling basis. Electronic applications accepted. *Expenses: Tuition:* Full-time $18,456; part-time $769 per credit. Tuition and fees vary according to program. *Financial support:* Applicants required to submit FAFSA. *Unit head:* Dr. Donald Haggerty, Associate Provost of Graduate Studies, 802-865-6496, Fax: 802-865-6447, E-mail: haggerty@champlain.edu. *Application contact:* Matt Manz, Assistant Director, Graduate Admission, 800-383-6603, E-mail: mmanz@champlain.edu.
Website: http://www.champlain.edu/academics/graduate-studies.

Chapman University, The George L. Argyros School of Business and Economics, Orange, CA 92866. Offers business administration (Exec MBA, MBA); economic systems design (MS); JD/MBA. *Accreditation:* AACSB. Part-time and evening/weekend programs available. *Faculty:* 58 full-time (11 women), 39 part-time/adjunct (6 women). *Students:* 147 full-time (54 women), 111 part-time (47 women); includes 91 minority (3 Black or African American, non-Hispanic/Latino; 2 American Indian or Alaska Native, non-Hispanic/Latino; 33 Asian, non-Hispanic/Latino; 40 Hispanic/Latino; 2 Native Hawaiian or other Pacific Islander, non-Hispanic/Latino; 11 Two or more races, non-Hispanic/Latino), 63 international. Average age 28. 287 applicants, 60% accepted, 90 enrolled. In 2013, 134 master's awarded. *Entrance requirements:* Additional exam requirements/recommendations for international students: Required—TOEFL. Application fee: $60. Electronic applications accepted. *Expenses:* Contact institution. *Financial support:* Fellowships, Federal Work-Study, and scholarships/grants available. Financial award applicants required to submit FAFSA. *Unit head:* Reginald Gilyard, Dean, 714-997-6684. *Application contact:* Debra Gonda, Associate Dean, 714-997-6894, E-mail: gonda@chapman.edu.
Website: http://www.chapman.edu/argyros.

Charleston Southern University, School of Business, Charleston, SC 29423-8087. Offers accounting (MBA); finance (MBA); general management (MBA); leadership (MBA); management information systems (MBA). Part-time and evening/weekend programs available. *Degree requirements:* For master's, thesis optional. *Entrance requirements:* For master's, GMAT. Additional exam requirements/recommendations for international students: Required—TOEFL (minimum score 550 paper-based; 79 iBT).

Chatham University, Program in Business Administration, Pittsburgh, PA 15232-2826. Offers business administration (MBA); healthcare management (MBA); sustainability (MBA); women's leadership (MBA). Part-time and evening/weekend programs available. *Faculty:* 11 part-time/adjunct (8 women). *Students:* 17 full-time (12 women), 43 part-time (30 women); includes 10 minority (6 Black or African American, non-Hispanic/Latino; 1 American Indian or Alaska Native, non-Hispanic/Latino; 1 Asian, non-Hispanic/Latino; 1 Hispanic/Latino; 1 Two or more races, non-Hispanic/Latino), 11 international. Average age 29. 34 applicants, 79% accepted, 17 enrolled. In 2013, 28 master's awarded. *Entrance requirements:* For master's, minimum GPA of 3.0, letters of recommendation. Additional exam requirements/recommendations for international students: Required—TOEFL (minimum score 600 paper-based; 100 iBT), IELTS (minimum score 7), TWE. *Application deadline:* For fall admission, 4/1 for domestic and international students; for spring admission, 11/1 for domestic students, 10/1 for international students. Applications are processed on a rolling basis. Application fee: $45. Electronic applications accepted. Application fee is waived when completed online. *Expenses: Tuition:* Full-time $14,886; part-time $827 per credit hour. One-time fee: $396 full-time. *Financial support:* Applicants required to submit FAFSA. *Unit head:* Dr. Rachel Chung, Director of Business and Entrepreneurship Program, 412-365-2433. *Application contact:* Katie Noel, Assistant Director of Graduate Admission, 412-365-2758, Fax: 412-365-1609, E-mail: gradadmissions@chatham.edu.
Website: http://www.chatham.edu/mba.

Christian Brothers University, School of Business, Memphis, TN 38104-5581. Offers accountancy (M Acc); business (MBA); international business (MIB); project management (Certificate); MBA/MIB. Part-time and evening/weekend programs available. *Entrance requirements:* For master's, GMAT, GRE. Additional exam requirements/recommendations for international students: Required—TOEFL.

The Citadel, The Military College of South Carolina, Citadel Graduate College, School of Business Administration, Charleston, SC 29409. Offers MBA. *Accreditation:* AACSB. Part-time and evening/weekend programs available. *Faculty:* 18 full-time (3 women), 2 part-time/adjunct (0 women). *Students:* 21 full-time (6 women), 199 part-time (82 women); includes 22 minority (12 Black or African American, non-Hispanic/Latino; 2 American Indian or Alaska Native, non-Hispanic/Latino; 2 Asian, non-Hispanic/Latino; 4 Hispanic/Latino; 2 Two or more races, non-Hispanic/Latino), 3 international. Average age 29. In 2013, 109 master's awarded. *Entrance requirements:* For master's, GMAT (minimum score 410), minimum undergraduate GPA of 3.0, 2 letters of reference, resume detailing previous work experience. Additional exam requirements/recommendations for international students: Required—TOEFL (minimum score 550 paper-based; 79 iBT). *Application deadline:* For fall admission, 7/20 for domestic students; for spring admission, 12/1 for domestic students. Application fee: $30. Electronic applications accepted. *Expenses: Tuition, area resident:* Part-time $525 per credit hour. Tuition, state resident: part-time $525 per credit hour. Tuition, nonresident: part-time $865 per credit hour. *Financial support:* Fellowships, career-related internships or fieldwork, health care benefits, and unspecified assistantships available. Support available to part-time students. Financial award application deadline: 7/1; financial award applicants required to submit FAFSA. *Faculty research:* Business statistics and regression analysis, mentoring university students, tax reform proposals, risk management data, teaching leadership, inventory costing methods, capitalism, ethics in behavioral accounting, ethics of neuro-marketing, European and Japanese business ethics, profit motives, team building, process costing, FIFO vs. weight average. *Unit head:* Dr. Ronald F. Green, Dean, 843-953-5056, Fax: 843-953-6764, E-mail: ron.green@citadel.edu. *Application contact:* Lt. Col. Kathy Jones, Director, MBA Program, 843-953-5257, Fax: 843-953-6764, E-mail: kathy.jones@citadel.edu.
Website: http://www.citadel.edu/csba/mba.html.

City University of Seattle, Graduate Division, School of Management, Bellevue, WA 98005. Offers accounting (Certificate); change leadership (MBA, Certificate); computer systems (MS); finance (Certificate); financial management (MBA); general management (MBA); general management-Europe (MBA); global marketing (MBA); human resources management (Certificate); individualized study (MBA); information security (MS); information systems (MBA); leadership (MA); marketing (MBA, Certificate); project management (MBA, MS, Certificate); sustainable business (Certificate); technology management (MBA, Certificate). Part-time and evening/weekend programs available. Postbaccalaureate distance learning degree programs offered (no on-campus study). *Degree requirements:* For master's, comprehensive exam (for some programs), thesis (for some programs). *Entrance requirements:* Additional exam requirements/recommendations for international students: Required—TOEFL (minimum score 567 paper-based; 87 iBT); Recommended—IELTS. Electronic applications accepted.

Claflin University, Graduate Programs, Orangeburg, SC 29115. Offers biotechnology (MS); business administration (MBA). Part-time programs available. *Students:* 40 full-time (23 women), 10 part-time (7 women); includes 40 minority (36 Black or African American, non-Hispanic/Latino; 2 American Indian or Alaska Native, non-Hispanic/Latino; 2 Asian, non-Hispanic/Latino), 10 international. Average age 34. In 2013, 25 master's awarded. *Degree requirements:* For master's, comprehensive exam, thesis. *Entrance requirements:* For master's, GRE, GMAT, baccalaureate degree, 3 letters of recommendation, resume, statement of purpose. Additional exam requirements/recommendations for international students: Recommended—TOEFL (minimum score 550 paper-based). *Application deadline:* For fall admission, 8/1 for domestic students; for spring admission, 12/1 for domestic students. Application fee: $50 ($75 for international students). *Expenses: Tuition:* Full-time $9720; part-time $540 per credit hour. *Required fees:* $350; $350. *Financial support:* Research assistantships and teaching assistantships available. Financial award application deadline: 4/15; financial award applicants required to submit FAFSA. *Unit head:* Michael Zeigler, Director of Admissions, 803-535-5340, Fax: 803-535-5385, E-mail: mike.zeigler@claflin.edu. *Application contact:* Michael Zeigler, Director of Admissions, 803-535-5340, Fax: 803-535-5385, E-mail: mike.zeigler@claflin.edu.
Website: http://www.claflin.edu.

Claremont Graduate University, Graduate Programs, Peter F. Drucker and Masatoshi Ito Graduate School of Management, Claremont, CA 91711-6160. Offers EMBA, MA, MBA, MS, PhD, Certificate, MBA/MA, MBA/PhD. Part-time programs available. *Faculty:* 15 full-time (5 women), 2 part-time/adjunct (0 women). *Students:* 105 full-time (55 women), 107 part-time (38 women); includes 84 minority (13 Black or African American, non-Hispanic/Latino; 32 Asian, non-Hispanic/Latino; 29 Hispanic/Latino; 1 Native Hawaiian or other Pacific Islander, non-Hispanic/Latino; 9 Two or more races, non-Hispanic/Latino), 45 international. Average age 34. In 2013, 86 master's, 3 doctorates, 105 other advanced degrees awarded. *Entrance requirements:* For doctorate, GMAT or GRE General Test. Additional exam requirements/recommendations for international students: Required—TOEFL (minimum score 550 paper-based; 80 iBT). *Application deadline:* For fall admission, 2/15 for domestic students. Applications are processed on a rolling basis. Application fee: $80. Electronic applications accepted. *Expenses:* Contact institution. *Financial support:* Fellowships, research assistantships, teaching assistantships, Federal Work-Study, institutionally sponsored loans, and scholarships/grants available. Support available to part-time students. Financial award application deadline: 2/15; financial award applicants required to submit FAFSA. *Faculty research:* Strategy and leadership, brand management, cost management and control,

organizational transformation, general management. *Unit head:* Larry Crosby, Dean, 909-607-9209, Fax: 909-621-8543, E-mail: larry.crosby@cgu.edu. *Application contact:* Loren Bryant, Admissions Coordinator, 909-621-8067, Fax: 909-607-9104, E-mail: loren.bryant@cgu.edu.
Website: http://www.cgu.edu/pages/130.asp.

Claremont Graduate University, Graduate Programs, School of Social Science, Policy and Evaluation, Program in Politics, Economics, and Business, Claremont, CA 91711-6160. Offers MA. Part-time programs available. *Students:* 3 full-time (2 women), 1 (woman) part-time, 2 international. Average age 26. In 2013, 6 master's awarded. *Entrance requirements:* For master's, GRE General Test. Additional exam requirements/recommendations for international students: Required—TOEFL (minimum score 550 paper-based; 80 iBT). *Application deadline:* For fall admission, 2/1 priority date for domestic and international students. Applications are processed on a rolling basis. Application fee: $80. Electronic applications accepted. *Expenses: Tuition:* Full-time $40,560; part-time $1690 per credit. *Required fees:* $275 per semester. Tuition and fees vary according to program. *Financial support:* Federal Work-Study, institutionally sponsored loans, and scholarships/grants available. Support available to part-time students. Financial award application deadline: 2/15; financial award applicants required to submit FAFSA. *Unit head:* Stewart Donaldson, Dean. *Application contact:* Annekah Hall, Assistant Director of Admissions, 909-607-3371, E-mail: annekah.hall@cgu.edu.
Website: http://www.cgu.edu/pages/543.asp.

Clarion University of Pennsylvania, Office of Transfer, Adult and Graduate Admissions, Master of Business Administration Program, Clarion, PA 16214. Offers MBA. *Accreditation:* AACSB. Part-time and evening/weekend programs available. Postbaccalaureate distance learning degree programs offered (no on-campus study). *Faculty:* 20 full-time (1 woman). *Students:* 29 full-time (8 women), 88 part-time (52 women); includes 18 minority (4 Black or African American, non-Hispanic/Latino; 11 Asian, non-Hispanic/Latino; 3 Hispanic/Latino), 14 international. Average age 32. 78 applicants, 86% accepted, 40 enrolled. In 2013, 29 master's awarded. *Degree requirements:* For master's, portfolio. *Entrance requirements:* For master's, GMAT, minimum QPA of 2.75. Additional exam requirements/recommendations for international students: Required—TOEFL (minimum score 550 paper-based; 79 iBT), IELTS (minimum score 7). *Application deadline:* For fall admission, 8/1 priority date for domestic students, 4/15 priority date for international students; for spring admission, 12/1 priority date for domestic students, 9/15 priority date for international students. Applications are processed on a rolling basis. Application fee: $40. Electronic applications accepted. *Expenses:* Tuition, state resident: part-time $442 per credit. Tuition, nonresident: part-time $451 per credit. *Required fees:* $142.40 per semester. One-time fee: $150 part-time. *Financial support:* In 2013–14, 12 research assistantships with full and partial tuition reimbursements (averaging $9,420 per year) were awarded; career-related internships or fieldwork also available. Support available to part-time students. Financial award application deadline: 3/1. *Unit head:* David Hartley, Interim Dean, 814-393-2600, Fax: 814-393-1910. *Application contact:* Susan Staub, Assistant Director, Graduate Programs, 814-393-2337, Fax: 814-393-2722, E-mail: gradstudies@clarion.edu.
Website: http://www.clarion.edu/1077/.

Clark Atlanta University, School of Business Administration, Department of Business Administration, Atlanta, GA 30314. Offers MBA. *Accreditation:* AACSB. Part-time programs available. *Faculty:* 12 full-time (4 women). *Students:* 51 full-time (27 women), 6 part-time (1 woman); includes 45 minority (all Black or African American, non-Hispanic/Latino), 7 international. Average age 26. 52 applicants, 100% accepted, 33 enrolled. In 2013, 38 master's awarded. *Degree requirements:* For master's, thesis (for some programs). *Entrance requirements:* For master's, GMAT. Additional exam requirements/recommendations for international students: Required—TOEFL (minimum score 500 paper-based; 61 iBT). *Application deadline:* For fall admission, 4/1 for domestic and international students; for spring admission, 11/1 for domestic and international students. Applications are processed on a rolling basis. Application fee: $40 ($55 for international students). Electronic applications accepted. *Expenses: Tuition:* Full-time $14,616; part-time $812 per credit hour. *Required fees:* $706; $353 per semester. *Financial support:* Career-related internships or fieldwork, Federal Work-Study, scholarships/grants, and unspecified assistantships available. Support available to part-time students. Financial award application deadline: 4/30; financial award applicants required to submit FAFSA. *Unit head:* Dr. Kasim Alli, Chairperson, 404-880-8740, E-mail: kalli@cau.edu. *Application contact:* Michelle Clark-Davis, Graduate Program Admissions, 404-880-6605, E-mail: cauadmissions@cau.edu.

Clarke University, Program in Business Administration, Dubuque, IA 52001-3198. Offers MBA. Part-time and evening/weekend programs available. *Faculty:* 4 full-time (1 woman), 3 part-time/adjunct (2 women). *Students:* 17 full-time (8 women), 30 part-time (16 women); includes 2 minority (1 Black or African American, non-Hispanic/Latino; 1 Asian, non-Hispanic/Latino). In 2013, 28 master's awarded. *Entrance requirements:* For master's, GMAT, GRE General Test or MAT, minimum GPA of 3.0 in last 60 hours, previous undergraduate course work in business. *Application deadline:* Applications are processed on a rolling basis. Application fee: $25. Electronic applications accepted. *Expenses: Tuition:* Part-time $660 per credit. *Required fees:* $15 per credit. *Financial support:* Available to part-time students. Application deadline: 6/1; applicants required to submit FAFSA. *Unit head:* B'Ann Ditmer, Coordinator, 563-588-8143, Fax: 563-588-6789, E-mail: bann.ditmer@clarke.edu. *Application contact:* Kara Shroeder, Information Contact, 563-588-6635, Fax: 563-588-6789, E-mail: graduate@clarke.edu.
Website: http://www.clarke.edu/academics/graduate/MBA/index.htm.

Clarkson University, Graduate School, School of Business, MBA Programs, Potsdam, NY 13699. Offers MBA. *Accreditation:* AACSB. Part-time and evening/weekend programs available. Postbaccalaureate distance learning degree programs offered (minimal on-campus study). *Faculty:* 37 full-time (9 women), 6 part-time/adjunct (2 women). *Students:* 86 full-time (42 women), 18 part-time (8 women); includes 9 minority (2 Black or African American, non-Hispanic/Latino; 2 Asian, non-Hispanic/Latino; 3 Hispanic/Latino; 2 Two or more races, non-Hispanic/Latino), 42 international. Average age 28. 205 applicants, 80% accepted, 64 enrolled. In 2013, 78 master's awarded. *Entrance requirements:* For master's, GMAT or GRE, transcripts of all college coursework, resume, personal statement, three letters of recommendation. Additional exam requirements/recommendations for international students: Required—TOEFL (minimum score 550 paper-based; 80 iBT), IELTS (minimum score 6.5). *Application deadline:* For fall admission, 1/30 priority date for domestic and international students; for spring admission, 9/1 priority date for domestic and international students. Applications are processed on a rolling basis. Application fee: $25 ($35 for international students). Electronic applications accepted. *Expenses: Tuition:* Full-time $15,888; part-time $1324 per credit. *Required fees:* $295 per semester. *Financial support:* In 2013–14, 83 students received support. Scholarships/grants available. *Faculty research:* Industrial organization and regulated industries, end-user computing, systems analysis and design, technological marketing, leadership development. *Unit head:* Dr. Stephen Sauer, Associate Dean of Graduate Business Programs, 315-268-6457, Fax: 315-268-3810, E-mail: ssauer@clarkson.edu. *Application contact:* Nicole Sharlow, Assistant to the Graduate Director, 315-268-4170, Fax: 315-268-3810, E-mail: nsharlow@clarkson.edu.
Website: http://www.clarkson.edu/business/graduate/.

Clark University, Graduate School, Graduate School of Management, Business Administration Program, Worcester, MA 01610-1477. Offers accounting (MBA); finance (MBA); global business (MBA); information systems (MBA); management (MBA); marketing (MBA); social change (MBA); sustainability (MBA). *Accreditation:* AACSB. Part-time and evening/weekend programs available. *Students:* 109 full-time (50 women), 151 part-time (67 women); includes 16 minority (9 Black or African American, non-Hispanic/Latino; 3 Asian, non-Hispanic/Latino; 4 Hispanic/Latino), 74 international. Average age 30. 359 applicants, 50% accepted, 81 enrolled. In 2013, 125 master's awarded. *Degree requirements:* For master's, thesis optional. *Application deadline:* For fall admission, 6/1 priority date for domestic students; for spring admission, 12/1 priority date for domestic students. Applications are processed on a rolling basis. Application fee: $50. Electronic applications accepted. *Expenses: Tuition:* Full-time $39,200; part-time $1225 per credit hour. *Financial support:* In 2013–14, research assistantships with partial tuition reimbursements (averaging $4,800 per year), teaching assistantships with partial tuition reimbursements (averaging $4,800 per year) were awarded; fellowships, career-related internships or fieldwork, Federal Work-Study, institutionally sponsored loans, and tuition waivers (partial) also available. Support available to part-time students. Financial award application deadline: 5/31. *Faculty research:* Marketing, accounting, human resource management, management information systems, business finance. *Unit head:* Dr. Catherine Usoff, Dean, 508-793-8822, Fax: 508-793-8822, E-mail: clarkmba@clarku.edu. *Application contact:* Patrick Oroszko, Enrollment and Marketing Director, 508-793-8822, Fax: 508-793-8822, E-mail: clarkmba@clarku.edu.
Website: http://www.clarku.edu/gsom/graduate/fulltime/.

Clayton State University, School of Graduate Studies, College of Business, Program in Business Administration, Morrow, GA 30260-0285. Offers accounting (MBA); international business (MBA); supply chain management (MBA). *Accreditation:* AACSB. Part-time and evening/weekend programs available. *Degree requirements:* For master's, thesis. *Entrance requirements:* For master's, GMAT, 3 letters of recommendation; statement of purpose; 2 official transcripts. Additional exam requirements/recommendations for international students: Required—TOEFL (minimum score 550 paper-based; 80 iBT). Electronic applications accepted. *Expenses:* Contact institution.

Cleary University, Online Program in Business Administration, Ann Arbor, MI 48105-2659. Offers accounting (MBA); financial planning (MBA); financial planning (Graduate Certificate); green business strategy (MBA, Graduate Certificate); health care leadership (MBA); management (MBA); nonprofit management (MBA, Graduate Certificate); organizational leadership (MBA). Part-time and evening/weekend programs available. Postbaccalaureate distance learning degree programs offered (no on-campus study). *Degree requirements:* For master's, thesis. *Entrance requirements:* For master's, bachelor's degree; minimum GPA of 2.5; professional resume indicating minimum of 2 years of management or related experience; undergraduate degree from accredited college or university with at least 18 quarter hours (or 12 semester hours) of accounting study (for MBA in accounting). Additional exam requirements/recommendations for international students: Required—TOEFL (minimum score 550 paper-based; 79 iBT), Michigan English Language Assessment Battery (minimum score 75). Electronic applications accepted.

Clemson University, Graduate School, College of Architecture, Arts, and Humanities, Department of Planning, Development and Preservation and College of Business and Behavioral Science, Program in Real Estate Development, Greenville, SC 29601. Offers MRED. *Faculty:* 6 full-time (1 woman), 2 part-time/adjunct (0 women). *Students:* 31 full-time (3 women), 1 (woman) part-time; includes 5 minority (2 Black or African American, non-Hispanic/Latino; 2 Asian, non-Hispanic/Latino; 1 Hispanic/Latino). Average age 26. 37 applicants, 62% accepted, 16 enrolled. In 2013, 14 master's awarded. *Entrance requirements:* For master's, GRE or GMAT, 3 letters of recommendation, resume, personal statement, transcripts. Additional exam requirements/recommendations for international students: Required—TOEFL (minimum score 600 paper-based). *Application deadline:* For fall admission, 2/15 priority date for domestic and international students. Applications are processed on a rolling basis. Application fee: $70 ($80 for international students). Electronic applications accepted. *Expenses:* Contact institution. *Financial support:* In 2013–14, 8 students received support, including 8 fellowships (averaging $1,719 per year); career-related internships or fieldwork, scholarships/grants, and health care benefits also available. *Faculty research:* Real estate education, real estate investment/finance, sustainability, public private partnership, historic preservation. *Unit head:* Dr. Robert C. Benedict, Director, 864-656-2476, Fax: 864-656-7519, E-mail: benedic@clemson.edu. *Application contact:* Amy Matthews, Program Coordinator, 864-656-4257, E-mail: matthe3@clemson.edu.
Website: http://www.clemson.edu/mred.

Clemson University, Graduate School, College of Business and Behavioral Science, Program in Business Administration, Clemson, SC 29634. Offers entrepreneurship and innovation (MBA). *Accreditation:* AACSB. Part-time and evening/weekend programs available. *Faculty:* 30 full-time (5 women). *Students:* 101 full-time (40 women), 214 part-time (74 women); includes 34 minority (16 Black or African American, non-Hispanic/Latino; 3 Asian, non-Hispanic/Latino; 14 Hispanic/Latino; 1 Two or more races, non-Hispanic/Latino), 31 international. Average age 31. 223 applicants, 70% accepted, 109 enrolled. In 2013, 120 master's awarded. *Entrance requirements:* For master's, GMAT. Additional exam requirements/recommendations for international students: Required—TOEFL. *Application deadline:* For fall admission, 6/1 priority date for domestic students, 4/15 for international students; for spring admission, 11/1 for domestic and international students. Applications are processed on a rolling basis. Application fee: $70 ($80 for international students). Electronic applications accepted. *Financial support:* In 2013–14, 5 students received support, including 3 fellowships with full and partial tuition reimbursements available (averaging $1,333 per year), 2 research assistantships with partial tuition reimbursements available (averaging $8,080 per year); teaching assistantships with partial tuition reimbursements available, institutionally sponsored loans, and scholarships/grants also available. Financial award application deadline: 5/1; financial award applicants required to submit FAFSA. *Unit head:* Dr. Gregory Pickett, Director, 864-656-3975, Fax: 864-656-0947. *Application contact:* Deanna Burns, Director of Admissions, 864-656-8173, E-mail: dchambe@clemson.edu.
Website: http://www.clemson.edu/cbbs/departments/mba/.

Cleveland State University, College of Graduate Studies, Monte Ahuja College of Business, Doctor of Business Administration Program, Cleveland, OH 44115. Offers finance (DBA); global business (DBA); information systems (DBA); marketing (DBA); operations management (DBA). *Accreditation:* AACSB. Part-time and evening/weekend programs available. *Faculty:* 50 full-time (11 women). *Students:* 36 part-time (18 women); includes 6 minority (2 Black or African American, non-Hispanic/Latino; 4 Asian, non-Hispanic/Latino), 8 international. Average age 39. 96 applicants, 27% accepted, 6 enrolled. In 2013, 1 doctorate awarded. *Degree requirements:* For doctorate, comprehensive exam, thesis/dissertation, oral dissertation defense. *Entrance requirements:* For doctorate, GMAT, MBA or equivalent. Additional exam requirements/recommendations for international students: Required—TOEFL (minimum score 550

paper-based; 79 iBT). *Application deadline:* For spring admission, 2/28 priority date for domestic and international students. Application fee: $30. Electronic applications accepted. *Expenses:* Tuition, state resident: full-time $8335; part-time $521 per credit hour. Tuition, nonresident: full-time $15,670; part-time $979 per credit hour. *Required fees:* $50; $25 per semester. *Financial support:* In 2013–14, 5 research assistantships with full tuition reimbursements (averaging $12,700 per year), 4 teaching assistantships with full tuition reimbursements (averaging $12,700 per year) were awarded; tuition waivers (full) and unspecified assistantships also available. *Faculty research:* Supply chain management, international business, strategic management, risk analysis, consumer behavior. *Unit head:* Dr. Raj Shekhar G. Javalgi, Director, 216-687-3786, Fax: 216-687-9354, E-mail: r.javalgi@csuohio.edu. *Application contact:* Melinda J. Arnold, Administrative Secretary, 216-687-6952, Fax: 216-687-9257, E-mail: m.arnold@csuohio.edu.
Website: http://www.csuohio.edu/business/academics/doctoral.html.

Cleveland State University, College of Graduate Studies, Monte Ahuja College of Business, MBA Programs, Cleveland, OH 44115. Offers business administration (AMBA, MBA); executive business administration (EMBA); health care administration (MBA); JD/MBA; MSN/MBA. Programs also offered at Progressive Insurance Corporation, The Cleveland Clinic, and MetroHealth Medical Center. *Accreditation:* AACSB. Part-time and evening/weekend programs available. Postbaccalaureate distance learning degree programs offered (no on-campus study). *Faculty:* 33 full-time (9 women), 16 part-time/adjunct (2 women). *Students:* 258 full-time (116 women), 467 part-time (198 women); includes 130 minority (69 Black or African American, non-Hispanic/Latino; 3 American Indian or Alaska Native, non-Hispanic/Latino; 25 Asian, non-Hispanic/Latino; 23 Hispanic/Latino; 10 Two or more races, non-Hispanic/Latino), 98 international. Average age 30. 674 applicants, 48% accepted, 139 enrolled. In 2013, 325 master's awarded. *Degree requirements:* For master's, variable foreign language requirement, comprehensive exam (for some programs), thesis (for some programs). *Entrance requirements:* For master's, GMAT or GRE, minimum cumulative GPA of 2.75 from bachelor's degree; resume, statement of purpose and two letters of reference (for health care administration MBA). Additional exam requirements/recommendations for international students: Required—TOEFL (minimum score 550 paper-based; 78 iBT). *Application deadline:* For fall admission, 7/15 priority date for domestic students, 5/15 for international students; for spring admission, 12/15 priority date for domestic students, 11/1 for international students. Applications are processed on a rolling basis. Application fee: $30. *Expenses:* Tuition, state resident: full-time $8335; part-time $521 per credit hour. Tuition, nonresident: full-time $15,670; part-time $979 per credit hour. *Required fees:* $50; $25 per semester. *Financial support:* In 2013–14, 594 students received support, including 45 research assistantships with full and partial tuition reimbursements available (averaging $6,960 per year), 1 teaching assistantship with full and partial tuition reimbursement available (averaging $7,800 per year); tuition waivers (full) and unspecified assistantships also available. Financial award application deadline: 5/15; financial award applicants required to submit FAFSA. *Faculty research:* Accounting and finance, management and organizational behavior, marketing, computer information systems, international business. *Total annual research expenditures:* $70,000. *Unit head:* Ronald John Mickler, Jr., Acting Assistant Director, Graduate Programs, 216-687-3730, Fax: 216-687-5311, E-mail: cbacsu@csuohio.edu. *Application contact:* Kenneth Dippong, Director, Student Services, 216-523-7545, Fax: 216-687-9354, E-mail: k.dippong@csuohio.edu.
Website: http://www.csuohio.edu/cba/.

Coastal Carolina University, E. Craig Wall, Sr. College of Business Administration, Conway, SC 29528-6054. Offers accounting (M Acc); business administration (MBA); fraud examination (Certificate). *Accreditation:* AACSB. Part-time and evening/weekend programs available. *Faculty:* 9 full-time (3 women). *Students:* 59 full-time (31 women), 45 part-time (27 women); includes 17 minority (14 Black or African American, non-Hispanic/Latino; 1 Hispanic/Latino; 2 Two or more races, non-Hispanic/Latino), 12 international. Average age 30. 72 applicants, 88% accepted, 54 enrolled. In 2013, 62 master's awarded. *Entrance requirements:* For master's, GMAT, official transcripts, 2 letters of recommendation, resume, completion of prerequisites with minimum B average grade, baccalaureate degree; for Certificate, GMAT, official transcripts, 2 letters of recommendation, baccalaureate degree or evidence of receiving a CPA certificate, law degree, or admittance to an accredited law school. Additional exam requirements/recommendations for international students: Required—TOEFL (minimum score 575 paper-based; 89 iBT). *Application deadline:* For fall admission, 6/15 priority date for domestic and international students; for spring admission, 11/15 priority date for domestic and international students; for summer admission, 4/15 priority date for domestic and international students. Applications are processed on a rolling basis. Application fee: $45. Electronic applications accepted. *Expenses:* Contact institution. *Financial support:* Application deadline: 3/1; applicants required to submit FAFSA. *Unit head:* Dr. Kenneth W. Small, Director, Graduate Business Programs, 843-349-2469, Fax: 843-349-2455, E-mail: ksmall@coastal.edu. *Application contact:* Dr. James O. Luken, Associate Provost/Director of Graduate Studies, 843-349-2235, Fax: 843-349-6444, E-mail: joluken@coastal.edu.
Website: http://www.coastal.edu/business/.

College of Charleston, Graduate School, School of Business, Program in Business Administration, Charleston, SC 29424-0001. Offers MBA. *Entrance requirements:* For master's, GMAT or GRE, transcripts, recommendations, goal statement, bachelor's degree. Additional exam requirements/recommendations for international students: Required—TOEFL (minimum score 81 iBT), IELTS. Electronic applications accepted.

College of Saint Elizabeth, Department of Business Administration and Management, Morristown, NJ 07960-6989. Offers human resource management (MS); organizational change (MS). Part-time programs available. *Faculty:* 1 full-time (0 women), 2 part-time/adjunct (1 woman). *Students:* 6 full-time (5 women), 33 part-time (25 women); includes 14 minority (8 Black or African American, non-Hispanic/Latino; 1 Asian, non-Hispanic/Latino; 5 Hispanic/Latino), 1 international. Average age 34. In 2013, 17 master's awarded. *Entrance requirements:* For master's, minimum GPA of 3.0, personal statement/self-assessment. Additional exam requirements/recommendations for international students: Required—TOEFL. *Application deadline:* Applications are processed on a rolling basis. Application fee: $35. Electronic applications accepted. *Expenses: Tuition:* Full-time $19,152; part-time $1064 per credit. *Financial support:* Career-related internships or fieldwork, tuition waivers (partial), and unspecified assistantships available. Support available to part-time students. Financial award application deadline: 3/15; financial award applicants required to submit FAFSA. *Unit head:* Dr. Jonathan H. Silver, Professor, Graduate Program in Management, 973-290-4113, E-mail: jsilver@cse.edu. *Application contact:* Deborah S. Cobo, Associate Director of Graduate Admission, 973-290-4194, Fax: 973-290-4710, E-mail: dscobo@cse.edu.
Website: http://www.cse.edu/academics/catalog/academic-programs/business-administration.dot.

College of St. Joseph, Graduate Programs, Division of Business, Program in Business Administration, Rutland, VT 05701-3899. Offers MBA. Part-time and evening/weekend programs available. *Entrance requirements:* For master's, two letters of reference from academic or professional sources; official transcripts of all graduate and undergraduate study; access to computer; computer literacy. Additional exam requirements/recommendations for international students: Required—TOEFL (minimum score 550 paper-based). Electronic applications accepted. *Expenses:* Contact institution.

The College of Saint Rose, Graduate Studies, School of Business, Department of Business Administration, Albany, NY 12203-1419. Offers MBA, JD/MBA. JD/MBA offered jointly with Albany Law School. *Accreditation:* ACBSP. Part-time and evening/weekend programs available. *Entrance requirements:* For master's, GMAT, graduate degree, or minimum undergraduate GPA of 3.0. Additional exam requirements/recommendations for international students: Required—TOEFL (minimum score 550 paper-based). Electronic applications accepted.

The College of St. Scholastica, Graduate Studies, Department of Management, Duluth, MN 55811-4199. Offers MA, Certificate. Part-time and evening/weekend programs available. Postbaccalaureate distance learning degree programs offered (minimal on-campus study). *Faculty:* 6 full-time (0 women), 2 part-time/adjunct (1 woman). *Students:* 118 full-time (69 women), 64 part-time (42 women); includes 17 minority (1 Black or African American, non-Hispanic/Latino; 3 American Indian or Alaska Native, non-Hispanic/Latino; 2 Asian, non-Hispanic/Latino; 3 Hispanic/Latino; 8 Two or more races, non-Hispanic/Latino), 7 international. Average age 36. 94 applicants, 90% accepted, 54 enrolled. In 2013, 61 master's awarded. *Degree requirements:* For master's, thesis. *Entrance requirements:* Additional exam requirements/recommendations for international students: Required—TOEFL (minimum score 550 paper-based; 79 iBT). *Application deadline:* For fall admission, 8/1 for domestic and international students; for spring admission, 11/15 for domestic and international students. Applications are processed on a rolling basis. Application fee: $0. Electronic applications accepted. Application fee is waived when completed online. *Expenses:* Contact institution. *Financial support:* In 2013–14, 53 students received support. Scholarships/grants available. Support available to part-time students. Financial award applicants required to submit FAFSA. *Faculty research:* Violence in higher education and workplace, screening and selection procedures in law enforcement, internet use in criminal justice, stress management in law enforcement. *Unit head:* Randal Zimmermann, Chair, 218-625-4929, Fax: 218-723-6290, E-mail: rzimmerm@css.edu. *Application contact:* Lindsay Lahti, Director of Graduate and Extended Studies Recruitment, 218-733-2240, Fax: 218-733-2275, E-mail: gradstudies@css.edu.
Website: http://www.css.edu/Graduate/Masters-Doctoral-and-Professional-Programs/Areas-of-Study/MA-Management.html.

College of Staten Island of the City University of New York, Graduate Programs, School of Business, Program in Business Management, Staten Island, NY 10314-6600. Offers MS. Part-time and evening/weekend programs available. *Faculty:* 2 full-time (1 woman). *Students:* 34 part-time (18 women). Average age 32. 46 applicants, 48% accepted, 13 enrolled. In 2013, 17 master's awarded. *Degree requirements:* For master's, significant written paper. *Entrance requirements:* For master's, GMAT, proficiency in business fundamentals, baccalaureate degree in business or related field, minimum overall GPA of 3.0, letter of intent, 2 letters of recommendation. Additional exam requirements/recommendations for international students: Required—TOEFL (minimum score 600 paper-based; 100 iBT), IELTS (minimum score 7). *Application deadline:* For fall admission, 4/25 priority date for domestic and international students. Applications are processed on a rolling basis. Application fee: $125. Electronic applications accepted. *Expenses:* Tuition, state resident: full-time $9240; part-time $385 per credit hour. Tuition, nonresident: full-time $17,040; part-time $710 per credit hour. *Required fees:* $428; $128 per term. *Financial support:* Federal Work-Study and scholarships/grants available. Support available to part-time students. Financial award applicants required to submit FAFSA. *Unit head:* Dr. Eugene Garaventa, Graduate Program Coordinator, 718-982-2963, E-mail: eugene.garaventa@csi.cuny.edu. *Application contact:* Sasha Spence, Assistant Director for Graduate Admissions, 718-982-2019, Fax: 718-982-2500, E-mail: sasha.spence@csi.cuny.edu.
Website: http://www.csi.cuny.edu/schoolofbusiness/programs_graduate.php.

The College of William and Mary, Mason School of Business, Williamsburg, VA 23185. Offers EMBA, M Acc, MBA, JD/MBA, MBA/MPP. *Accreditation:* AACSB. Part-time and evening/weekend programs available. *Faculty:* 55 full-time (16 women), 9 part-time/adjunct (0 women). *Students:* 288 full-time (107 women), 146 part-time (48 women); includes 62 minority (24 Black or African American, non-Hispanic/Latino; 5 American Indian or Alaska Native, non-Hispanic/Latino; 19 Asian, non-Hispanic/Latino; 11 Hispanic/Latino; 3 Two or more races, non-Hispanic/Latino), 105 international. Average age 29. 777 applicants, 41% accepted, 189 enrolled. In 2013, 282 master's awarded. *Degree requirements:* For master's, three domestic residencies and international trip (EMBA). *Entrance requirements:* For master's, GMAT or GRE. Additional exam requirements/recommendations for international students: Required—TOEFL (minimum score 600 paper-based; 100 iBT), IELTS (minimum score 6.5). *Application deadline:* For fall admission, 11/3 for domestic and international students; for winter admission, 1/12 for domestic and international students; for spring admission, 5/11 for domestic and international students. Application fee: $100. Electronic applications accepted. *Expenses:* Contact institution. *Financial support:* In 2013–14, 141 students received support, including 15 fellowships, 52 research assistantships with partial tuition reimbursements available; career-related internships or fieldwork, scholarships/grants, and unspecified assistantships also available. Financial award application deadline: 3/7; financial award applicants required to submit FAFSA. *Faculty research:* Saving and asset allocation decisions in retirement accounts, supply chain management, virtual and networked organizations, healthcare informatics, sustainable business operations. *Total annual research expenditures:* $44,301. *Unit head:* Dr. Lawrence Pulley, Dean, 757-221-2891, Fax: 757-221-2937, E-mail: larry.pulley@mason.wm.edu. *Application contact:* Amanda K. Barth, Director, Full-time MBA Admissions, 757-221-2944, Fax: 757-221-2958, E-mail: amanda.barth@mason.wm.edu.
Website: http://mason.wm.edu/.

Colorado Christian University, Program in Business Administration, Lakewood, CO 80226. Offers corporate training (MBA); information security (MA); leadership (MBA); project management (MBA). Part-time and evening/weekend programs available. Postbaccalaureate distance learning degree programs offered (minimal on-campus study). *Degree requirements:* For master's, thesis optional. *Entrance requirements:* For master's, GMAT, 2 letters of recommendation, resume. Additional exam requirements/recommendations for international students: Required—TOEFL. Electronic applications accepted. *Expenses:* Contact institution.

Colorado Mesa University, Department of Business, Grand Junction, CO 81501-3122. Offers MBA. Part-time and evening/weekend programs available. *Degree requirements:* For master's, thesis or research practicum, written comprehensive exams. *Entrance requirements:* For master's, GMAT, MAT, or GRE, minimum GPA of 3.0 for last 60 undergraduate hours, 2 letters of recommendation. Additional exam requirements/recommendations for international students: Required—TOEFL (minimum score 550 paper-based). Electronic applications accepted.

Colorado State University, Graduate School, College of Business, Early Career MBA Program, Fort Collins, CO 80523-0015. Offers MBA. *Students:* 1 (woman) full-time. Average age 23. *Degree requirements:* For master's, practicum or internship. *Entrance requirements:* For master's, GMAT (minimum score of 500), bachelor's degree from accredited university, minimum GPA of 3.0. *Expenses:* Tuition, state resident: full-time

$9075.40; part-time $504 per credit. Tuition, nonresident: full-time $22,248; part-time $1236 per credit. *Required fees:* $1819; $60 per credit. *Unit head:* Dr. Ajay Menon, Dean, 970-491-2398, Fax: 970-491-0596, E-mail: ajay.menon@colostate.edu. *Application contact:* Rachel Stoll, Admissions Coordinator, 970-491-3704, Fax: 970-491-3481, E-mail: rachel.stoll@colostate.edu.
Website: http://biz.colostate.edu/ecmba/.

Colorado State University, Graduate School, College of Business, Executive MBA Program - Denver, Fort Collins, CO 80523-0015. Offers EMBA. *Entrance requirements:* For master's, GMAT, interview, personal statement, resume, 3 references, transcripts. *Expenses:* Tuition, state resident: full-time $9075.40; part-time $504 per credit. Tuition, nonresident: full-time $22,248; part-time $1236 per credit. *Required fees:* $1819; $60 per credit. *Unit head:* Jill Terry, Director, 303-534-3191, Fax: 303-534-3194, E-mail: jill.terry@colostate.edu. *Application contact:* Rachel Stoll, Admissions Coordinator, 970-491-3704, Fax: 970-491-3481, E-mail: rachel.stoll@colostate.edu.
Website: http://biz.colostate.edu/denverExecutive/.

Colorado State University, Graduate School, College of Business, MBA Program, Fort Collins, CO 80523-1201. Offers MBA, MBA/DVM. *Accreditation:* AACSB. Part-time and evening/weekend programs available. *Faculty:* 16 full-time (5 women). *Students:* 28 full-time (15 women), 1,299 part-time (365 women); includes 311 minority (55 Black or African American, non-Hispanic/Latino; 9 American Indian or Alaska Native, non-Hispanic/Latino; 112 Asian, non-Hispanic/Latino; 101 Hispanic/Latino; 4 Native Hawaiian or other Pacific Islander, non-Hispanic/Latino; 30 Two or more races, non-Hispanic/Latino), 16 international. Average age 36. 455 applicants, 96% accepted, 361 enrolled. In 2013, 357 master's awarded. *Entrance requirements:* For master's, GMAT, minimum undergraduate GPA of 3.0, 4 years of post-undergraduate professional work experience. Additional exam requirements/recommendations for international students: Required—TOEFL (minimum score 565 paper-based; 86 iBT); Recommended—IELTS (minimum score 6.5). *Application deadline:* For fall admission, 5/1 for domestic and international students. Application fee: $50. Electronic applications accepted. *Expenses:* Contact institution. *Financial support:* In 2013–14, 2 students received support, including 1 research assistantship (averaging $10,106 per year), 1 teaching assistantship with partial tuition reimbursement available (averaging $8,344 per year); fellowships, career-related internships or fieldwork, and unspecified assistantships also available. Support available to part-time students. Financial award application deadline: 6/1; financial award applicants required to submit FAFSA. *Faculty research:* E-commerce, entrepreneurship, global leadership, corporate citizenship, marketing management. *Total annual research expenditures:* $53,329. *Unit head:* Dr. John Hoxmeier, Associate Dean, 970-491-2142, Fax: 970-491-0596, E-mail: john.hoxmeier@colostate.edu. *Application contact:* Matthew Leland, Admissions Coordinator, 970-491-1917, Fax: 970-491-3481, E-mail: matt.leland@colostate.edu.
Website: http://www.biz.colostate.edu/degreesCertificates/mbaPrograms/pages/default.aspx.

Colorado State University–Pueblo, Malik and Seeme Hasan School of Business, Pueblo, CO 81001-4901. Offers MBA. *Accreditation:* AACSB. Part-time and evening/weekend programs available. *Degree requirements:* For master's, thesis optional. *Entrance requirements:* For master's, GMAT, minimum GPA of 3.0. Additional exam requirements/recommendations for international students: Required—TOEFL (minimum score 550 paper-based). *Faculty research:* Total quality management, leadership, small business studies, case research and writing.

Colorado Technical University Colorado Springs, Graduate Studies, Program in Management, Colorado Springs, CO 80907-3896. Offers accounting (MBA, MSA); business administration (MBA); finance (MBA); human resources management (MBA); logistics/supply chain management (MBA); management (DM); marketing (MBA); mediation and dispute resolution (MBA); operations management (MBA); project management (MBA); technology management (MBA). Part-time and evening/weekend programs available. Postbaccalaureate distance learning degree programs offered. *Degree requirements:* For master's, thesis or alternative; for doctorate, thesis/dissertation. *Entrance requirements:* For doctorate, minimum graduate GPA of 3.0, 5 years of related work experience. *Faculty research:* Sexual harassment, performance evaluation, critical thinking.

Colorado Technical University Denver South, Programs in Business Administration and Management, Aurora, CO 80014. Offers accounting (MBA); business administration (MBA); business administration and management (EMBA); finance (MBA); human resource management (MBA); marketing (MBA); mediation and dispute resolution (MBA); operations management (MBA); project management (MBA); technology management (MBA). Part-time and evening/weekend programs available. *Degree requirements:* For master's, thesis or alternative. *Entrance requirements:* For master's, minimum undergraduate GPA of 3.0, resume.

Columbia College, Master of Business Administration Program, Columbia, MO 65216-0002. Offers MBA. Part-time and evening/weekend programs available. Postbaccalaureate distance learning degree programs offered (no on-campus study). *Faculty:* 8 full-time (2 women), 45 part-time/adjunct (20 women). *Students:* 72 full-time (42 women), 425 part-time (256 women); includes 124 minority (76 Black or African American, non-Hispanic/Latino; 5 American Indian or Alaska Native, non-Hispanic/Latino; 13 Asian, non-Hispanic/Latino; 27 Hispanic/Latino; 1 Native Hawaiian or other Pacific Islander, non-Hispanic/Latino; 2 Two or more races, non-Hispanic/Latino), 17 international. Average age 36. 213 applicants, 74% accepted, 141 enrolled. In 2013, 181 master's awarded. *Entrance requirements:* For master's, 3 letters of recommendation, minimum cumulative undergraduate GPA of 3.0, resume, goal statement. Additional exam requirements/recommendations for international students: Required—TOEFL (minimum score 550 paper-based; 79 iBT). *Application deadline:* For fall admission, 8/9 priority date for domestic and international students; for spring admission, 12/27 priority date for domestic and international students. Applications are processed on a rolling basis. Application fee: $55. Electronic applications accepted. *Expenses: Tuition:* Part-time $330 per credit hour. Tuition and fees vary according to campus/location and program. *Financial support:* In 2013–14, 7 students received support. Federal Work-Study and scholarships/grants available. Financial award application deadline: 3/1; financial award applicants required to submit FAFSA. *Unit head:* Dr. Tim Ireland, MBA Program Coordinator, 573-875-7587, Fax: 573-876-4493, E-mail: tireland@ccis.edu. *Application contact:* Stephanie Johnson, Director of Admissions, 573-875-7352, Fax: 573-875-7506, E-mail: sjohnson@ccis.edu.
Website: http://www.ccis.edu/graduate/academics/degrees.asp?MBA.

Columbia Southern University, DBA Program, Orange Beach, AL 36561. Offers DBA. Part-time and evening/weekend programs available. Postbaccalaureate distance learning degree programs offered (minimal on-campus study). *Entrance requirements:* For doctorate, 2 years professional experience, relevant academic experience. Electronic applications accepted.

Columbia Southern University, MBA Program, Orange Beach, AL 36561. Offers finance (MBA); health care management (MBA); human resource management (MBA); marketing (MBA); project management (MBA); public administration (MBA). Part-time and evening/weekend programs available. Postbaccalaureate distance learning degree programs offered (no on-campus study). *Entrance requirements:* For master's, bachelor's degree from accredited/approved institution. Additional exam requirements/recommendations for international students: Required—TOEFL. Electronic applications accepted.

Columbia University, Graduate School of Business, Berkeley-Columbia Executive MBA Program, New York, NY 10027. Offers EMBA. Offered jointly with University of California, Berkeley. Part-time programs available. *Entrance requirements:* For master's, GMAT, 2 letters of reference, interview, minimum 5 years of work experience, transcripts, resume, employee support, personal essays. Additional exam requirements/recommendations for international students: Required—TOEFL (minimum score 570 paper-based; 68 iBT). Electronic applications accepted. *Expenses:* Contact institution.

Columbia University, Graduate School of Business, Doctoral Program in Business, New York, NY 10027. Offers business (PhD), including accounting, decision, risk, and operations, finance and economics, management, marketing. *Accreditation:* AACSB. *Degree requirements:* For doctorate, comprehensive exam, thesis/dissertation, major field exam, research paper, thesis proposal. *Entrance requirements:* For doctorate, GMAT or GRE (finance), 2 letters of reference, resume. Additional exam requirements/recommendations for international students: Required—TOEFL. Electronic applications accepted. *Expenses:* Contact institution. *Faculty research:* Human decision making and behavioral research; real estate market and mortgage defaults; financial crisis and corporate governance; international business; security analysis and accounting.

Columbia University, Graduate School of Business, Executive MBA Global Program, New York, NY 10027. Offers EMBA. Program offered jointly with London Business School. *Entrance requirements:* For master's, GMAT, 2 letters of reference, interview, minimum 5 years of work experience, curriculum vitae or resume, employer support. Additional exam requirements/recommendations for international students: Recommended—TOEFL, IELTS. Electronic applications accepted. *Expenses:* Contact institution.

Columbia University, Graduate School of Business, Executive MBA Program, New York, NY 10027. Offers EMBA. *Entrance requirements:* For master's, GMAT, minimum 5 years of work experience, 2 letters of reference, interview, company sponsorship. Additional exam requirements/recommendations for international students: Recommended—TOEFL. Electronic applications accepted. *Expenses:* Contact institution. *Faculty research:* Human decision making and behavioral research; real estate market and mortgage defaults; financial crisis and corporate governance; international business; and security analysis and accounting.

Columbia University, Graduate School of Business, MBA Program, New York, NY 10027. Offers accounting (MBA); decision, risk, and operations (MBA); entrepreneurship (MBA); finance and economics (MBA); healthcare and pharmaceutical management (MBA); human resource management (MBA); international business (MBA); leadership and ethics (MBA); management (MBA); marketing (MBA); media (MBA); private equity (MBA); real estate (MBA); social enterprise (MBA); value investing (MBA); DDS/MBA; JD/MBA; MBA/MIA; MBA/MPH; MBA/MS; MD/MBA. *Entrance requirements:* For master's, GMAT, 2 letters of recommendation. Additional exam requirements/recommendations for international students: Required—TOEFL. Electronic applications accepted. *Expenses:* Contact institution. *Faculty research:* Human decision making and behavioral research; real estate market and mortgage defaults; financial crisis and corporate governance; international business; security analysis and accounting.

Columbus State University, Graduate Studies, D. Abbott Turner College of Business and Computer Science, Columbus, GA 31907-5645. Offers applied computer science (MS); business administration (MBA); information systems security (Certificate); modeling and simulation (Certificate); organizational leadership (MS). *Accreditation:* AACSB. *Faculty:* 16 full-time (2 women), 1 (woman) part-time/adjunct. *Students:* 94 full-time (28 women), 182 part-time (56 women); includes 79 minority (49 Black or African American, non-Hispanic/Latino; 13 Asian, non-Hispanic/Latino; 8 Hispanic/Latino; 1 Native Hawaiian or other Pacific Islander, non-Hispanic/Latino; 8 Two or more races, non-Hispanic/Latino), 22 international. Average age 32. 170 applicants, 49% accepted, 66 enrolled. In 2013, 82 master's awarded. *Entrance requirements:* For master's, GMAT, GRE, minimum undergraduate GPA of 2.75, letters of recommendation. Additional exam requirements/recommendations for international students: Required—TOEFL (minimum score 550 paper-based; 79 iBT). *Application deadline:* For fall admission, 6/30 for domestic students, 5/1 for international students; for spring admission, 11/1 for domestic and international students; for summer admission, 3/1 for domestic and international students. Applications are processed on a rolling basis. Application fee: $40. Electronic applications accepted. *Expenses:* Tuition, state resident: full-time $4572; part-time $382 per credit hour. Tuition, nonresident: full-time $18,292; part-time $1526 per credit hour. *Required fees:* $1800; $196 per credit hour. Tuition and fees vary according to campus/location and program. *Financial support:* In 2013–14, 111 students received support, including 19 research assistantships (averaging $3,000 per year). Financial award application deadline: 5/1; financial award applicants required to submit FAFSA. *Unit head:* Dr. Linda U. Hadley, Dean, 706-507-8153, Fax: 706-568-2184, E-mail: hadley_linda@columbusstate.edu. *Application contact:* Kristin Williams, Director of International and Graduate Recruitment, 706-507-8848, Fax: 706-568-5091, E-mail: thornton_katie@colstate.edu.
Website: http://turner.columbusstate.edu/.

Concordia University, School of Business and Professional Studies, Irvine, CA 92612-3299. Offers business administration: business practice (MBA); international studies (MA). Part-time and evening/weekend programs available. *Faculty:* 9 full-time (2 women), 25 part-time/adjunct (6 women). *Students:* 167 full-time (86 women), 81 part-time (40 women); includes 78 minority (27 Black or African American, non-Hispanic/Latino; 19 Asian, non-Hispanic/Latino; 20 Hispanic/Latino; 12 Two or more races, non-Hispanic/Latino), 27 international. Average age 28. 331 applicants, 46% accepted, 102 enrolled. In 2013, 74 master's awarded. *Degree requirements:* For master's, capstone project or thesis. *Entrance requirements:* For master's, official college transcript(s), signed statement of intent, resume, two references, interview (MBA); passport photo, photocopies of valid U.S. passport, and college diploma (MAIS). Additional exam requirements/recommendations for international students: Required—TOEFL. *Application deadline:* For fall admission, 8/1 for domestic students, 6/1 for international students; for spring admission, 1/1 for domestic students, 11/1 for international students. Application fee: $50 ($125 for international students). Electronic applications accepted. *Expenses:* Contact institution. *Financial support:* In 2013–14, 20 students received support. Tuition waivers (full and partial) and unspecified assistantships available. Financial award applicants required to submit FAFSA. *Unit head:* Dr. Timothy Peters, Dean, 949-214-3363, E-mail: tim.peters@cui.edu. *Application contact:* Sherry Powers, MBA Admissions Coordinator, 949-214-3032, Fax: 949-854-6894, E-mail: sherry.powers@cui.edu.
Website: http://www.cui.edu/.

Concordia University, School of Graduate Studies, John Molson School of Business, Montreal, QC H3G 1M8, Canada. Offers administration (M Sc), including finance, management, marketing; business administration (MBA, PhD, Certificate, Diploma); executive business administration (EMBA); investment management (MBA). PhD program offered jointly with HEC Montreal, McGill University, and Université du Québec à Montréal. *Accreditation:* AACSB. Part-time and evening/weekend programs available.

Business Administration and Management—General

Degree requirements: For master's, one foreign language, thesis (for some programs), research project; for doctorate, one foreign language, thesis/dissertation; for other advanced degree, one foreign language. *Entrance requirements:* For master's, GMAT, minimum 2 years of work experience (for MBA); letters of recommendation, bachelor's degree from recognized university with minimum GPA of 3.0, curriculum vitae; for doctorate, GMAT (minimum score of 600), official transcripts, curriculum vitae, 3 letters of reference, statement of purpose; for other advanced degree, minimum GPA of 2.7, 2 letters of reference, statement of purpose, resume. Additional exam requirements/recommendations for international students: Required—TOEFL (minimum score 90 iBT), IELTS (minimum score 7). Electronic applications accepted. *Expenses:* Contact institution. *Faculty research:* General business, capital markets, international business.

Concordia University, School of Management, Portland, OR 97211-6099. Offers MBA. Evening/weekend programs available. *Degree requirements:* For master's, thesis optional. *Entrance requirements:* For master's, GMAT or professional portfolio, minimum GPA of 3.0, 2 letters of recommendation, 5 years of work experience, resume. Additional exam requirements/recommendations for international students: Required—TOEFL (minimum score 525 paper-based). *Faculty research:* Leadership characteristics in internships, marketing of MBA programs, entrepreneurship.

Concordia University Chicago, College of Graduate and Innovative Programs, Program in Business Administration, River Forest, IL 60305-1499. Offers MBA.

Concordia University, St. Paul, College of Business and Organizational Leadership, St. Paul, MN 55104-5494. Offers business and organizational leadership (MBA); criminal justice leadership (MA); forensic mental health (MA); health care management (MBA); human resource management (MA); leadership and management (MA). *Accreditation:* ACBSP. Evening/weekend programs available. Postbaccalaureate distance learning degree programs offered (minimal on-campus study). *Faculty:* 10 full-time (3 women), 20 part-time/adjunct (9 women). *Students:* 336 full-time (222 women), 84 part-time (44 women); includes 82 minority (46 Black or African American, non-Hispanic/Latino; 1 American Indian or Alaska Native, non-Hispanic/Latino; 17 Asian, non-Hispanic/Latino; 9 Hispanic/Latino; 1 Native Hawaiian or other Pacific Islander, non-Hispanic/Latino; 8 Two or more races, non-Hispanic/Latino), 1 international. Average age 34. 405 applicants, 50% accepted, 187 enrolled. In 2013, 253 master's awarded. *Degree requirements:* For master's, thesis (for some programs). *Entrance requirements:* For master's, official transcripts from regionally-accredited institution stating the conferral of a bachelor's degree with minimum cumulative GPA of 3.0; personal statement; professional resume. Additional exam requirements/recommendations for international students: Recommended—TOEFL (minimum score 547 paper-based; 78 iBT), IELTS (minimum score 6). *Application deadline:* For fall admission, 8/1 for domestic and international students; for spring admission, 12/1 for domestic and international students; for summer admission, 5/1 for domestic and international students. Applications are processed on a rolling basis. Application fee: $50. Electronic applications accepted. *Expenses: Tuition:* Full-time $6200; part-time $425 per credit. Tuition and fees vary according to degree level and program. *Financial support:* Applicants required to submit FAFSA. *Unit head:* Lonn Maly, Dean, 651-641-8203, Fax: 651-641-8807, E-mail: maly@csp.edu. *Application contact:* Kimberly Craig, Director of Graduate and Cohort Admission, 651-603-6223, Fax: 651-603-6320, E-mail: craig@csp.edu.

Concordia University Wisconsin, Graduate Programs, School of Business and Legal Studies, MBA Program, Mequon, WI 53097-2402. Offers finance (MBA); health care administration (MBA); human resource management (MBA); international business (MBA); international business-bilingual English/Chinese (MBA); management (MBA); management information systems (MBA); managerial communications (MBA); marketing (MBA); public administration (MBA); risk management (MBA). Postbaccalaureate distance learning degree programs offered (minimal on-campus study). *Degree requirements:* For master's, comprehensive exam, thesis or alternative. *Entrance requirements:* Additional exam requirements/recommendations for international students: Required—TOEFL. *Expenses:* Contact institution.

Copenhagen Business School, Graduate Programs, Copenhagen, Denmark. Offers business administration (Exec MBA, MBA, PhD); business administration and information systems (M Sc); business, language and culture (M Sc); economics and business administration (M Sc); health management (MHM); international business and politics (M Sc); public administration (MPA); shipping and logistics (Exec MBA); technology, market and organization (MBA).

Corban University, Graduate School, The Corban MBA, Salem, OR 97301-9392. Offers management (MBA); non-profit management (MBA). Postbaccalaureate distance learning degree programs offered (no on-campus study).

Cornell University, Graduate School, Graduate Field of Management, Ithaca, NY 14853. Offers accounting (PhD); finance (PhD); marketing (PhD); organizational behavior (PhD); production and operations management (PhD). *Accreditation:* AACSB. *Faculty:* 54 full-time (7 women). *Students:* 37 full-time (13 women); includes 5 minority (4 Asian, non-Hispanic/Latino; 1 Two or more races, non-Hispanic/Latino), 24 international. Average age 29. 486 applicants, 4% accepted, 11 enrolled. In 2013, 8 doctorates awarded. *Degree requirements:* For doctorate, comprehensive exam, thesis/dissertation. *Entrance requirements:* For doctorate, GMAT or GRE General Test. Additional exam requirements/recommendations for international students: Required—TOEFL (minimum score 600 paper-based; 77 iBT). *Application deadline:* For fall admission, 1/3 for domestic students. Application fee: $95. Electronic applications accepted. *Expenses:* Contact institution. *Financial support:* In 2013–14, 33 students received support, including 31 research assistantships with full tuition reimbursements available, 2 teaching assistantships with full tuition reimbursements available; fellowships with full tuition reimbursements available, institutionally sponsored loans, scholarships/grants, health care benefits, tuition waivers (full and partial), and unspecified assistantships also available. Financial award applicants required to submit FAFSA. *Faculty research:* Operations and manufacturing. *Unit head:* Director of Graduate Studies, 607-255-3669. *Application contact:* Graduate Field Assistant, 607-255-9431, E-mail: js_phd@cornell.edu.
Website: http://www.gradschool.cornell.edu/fields.php?id-91&a-2.

Cornell University, Samuel Curtis Johnson Graduate School of Management, Ithaca, NY 14853. Offers Exec MBA, MBA, PhD, JD/MBA, M Eng/MBA, MBA/MD, MBA/MHA, MBA/MILR. *Accreditation:* AACSB. *Faculty:* 57 full-time (12 women), 42 part-time/adjunct (4 women). *Students:* 571 full-time (176 women); includes 169 minority (37 Black or African American, non-Hispanic/Latino; 92 Asian, non-Hispanic/Latino; 5 Hispanic/Latino; 1 Native Hawaiian or other Pacific Islander, non-Hispanic/Latino; 34 Two or more races, non-Hispanic/Latino), 161 international. Average age 27. 2,356 applicants, 22% accepted, 289 enrolled. In 2013, 281 master's awarded. *Entrance requirements:* For master's, GMAT or GRE, resume, two essays, two recommendations. Additional exam requirements/recommendations for international students: Required—TOEFL. *Application deadline:* For fall admission, 10/1 for domestic and international students; for winter admission, 1/7 for domestic and international students; for spring admission, 3/11 for domestic and international students. Application fee: $200. Electronic applications accepted. *Expenses:* Contact institution. *Financial support:* Fellowships, research assistantships, career-related internships or fieldwork, Federal Work-Study, institutionally sponsored loans, and tuition waivers (full and partial) available. Financial award application deadline: 2/15; financial award applicants required to submit FAFSA. *Unit head:* Dr. Soumitra Dutta, Dean, 607-255-6418, E-mail: dean@johnson.cornell.edu. *Application contact:* Admissions Office, 800-847-2082, Fax: 607-255-0065, E-mail: mba@johnson.cornell.edu.
Website: http://www.johnson.cornell.edu.

Cornerstone University, Graduate Programs, Grand Rapids, MI 49525-5897. Offers business administration (MBA); education (MA Ed); management (MSM); teaching English to speakers of other languages (MA, Graduate Certificate). Programs also offered at Holland, Kalamazoo, and Troy, MI campuses. Part-time programs available. Postbaccalaureate distance learning degree programs offered. *Degree requirements:* For master's, comprehensive exam (for some programs), thesis (for some programs). *Entrance requirements:* For master's, minimum GPA of 2.5, 2 letters of reference. Additional exam requirements/recommendations for international students: Required—TOEFL (minimum score 575 paper-based). Electronic applications accepted.

Creighton University, Graduate School, Eugene C. Eppley College of Business Administration, Omaha, NE 68178-0001. Offers business administration (MBA); information technology management (MS); securities and portfolio management (MSAPM); JD/MBA; MBA/MS-ITM; MBA/MSAPM; MD/MBA; MS ITM/JD; Pharm D/MBA. *Accreditation:* AACSB. Part-time and evening/weekend programs available. Postbaccalaureate distance learning degree programs offered (no on-campus study). *Faculty:* 37 full-time (7 women). *Students:* 17 full-time (6 women), 298 part-time (75 women); includes 45 minority (21 Black or African American, non-Hispanic/Latino; 2 American Indian or Alaska Native, non-Hispanic/Latino; 14 Asian, non-Hispanic/Latino; 7 Hispanic/Latino; 1 Native Hawaiian or other Pacific Islander, non-Hispanic/Latino), 23 international. Average age 32. 113 applicants, 88% accepted, 98 enrolled. In 2013, 138 master's awarded. *Degree requirements:* For master's, thesis optional. *Entrance requirements:* For master's, GMAT, resume, 2 letters of recommendation. Additional exam requirements/recommendations for international students: Required—TOEFL (minimum score 550 paper-based; 80 iBT). *Application deadline:* For fall admission, 7/1 priority date for domestic students, 3/1 for international students; for winter admission, 10/1 priority date for domestic students, 7/1 for international students; for spring admission, 4/1 priority date for domestic students, 10/1 for international students; for summer admission, 5/1 for domestic and international students. Applications are processed on a rolling basis. Application fee: $50. Electronic applications accepted. *Expenses: Tuition:* Full-time $13,608; part-time $756 per credit hour. *Required fees:* $149 per semester. Tuition and fees vary according to course load, campus/location, program, reciprocity agreements and student's religious affiliation. *Financial support:* In 2013–14, 10 fellowships with partial tuition reimbursements (averaging $8,448 per year) were awarded; career-related internships or fieldwork, tuition waivers (partial), and unspecified assistantships also available. Financial award application deadline: 3/1. *Faculty research:* Small business issues, economics. *Unit head:* Dr. Deborah Wells, Associate Dean for Graduate Programs, 402-280-2841, E-mail: deborahwells@creighton.edu. *Application contact:* Gail Hafer, Assistant Dean, 402-280-2829, Fax: 402-280-2172, E-mail: ghafer@creighton.edu.
Website: http://business.creighton.edu.

Cumberland University, Program in Business Administration, Lebanon, TN 37087. Offers MBA. *Accreditation:* ACBSP. Part-time and evening/weekend programs available. *Degree requirements:* For master's, comprehensive exam. *Entrance requirements:* For master's, GMAT or GRE General Test, 3 letters of recommendation. Additional exam requirements/recommendations for international students: Required—TOEFL (minimum score 500 paper-based). *Expenses:* Contact institution.

Curry College, Graduate Studies, Program in Business Administration, Milton, MA 02186-9984. Offers business administration (MBA); finance (Certificate). Part-time and evening/weekend programs available. *Degree requirements:* For master's, capstone applied project. *Entrance requirements:* For master's, resume, recommendations, interview, written statement. Additional exam requirements/recommendations for international students: Required—TOEFL (minimum score 550 paper-based; 80 iBT). *Expenses:* Contact institution.

Daemen College, Program in Executive Leadership and Change, Amherst, NY 14226-3592. Offers business (MS); health professions (MS); not-for-profit organizations (MS). Part-time and evening/weekend programs available. *Degree requirements:* For master's, thesis, cohort learning sequence (2 years for weekend cohort; 3 years for weeknight cohort). *Entrance requirements:* For master's, 2 letters of recommendation, interview, goal statement, official transcripts, resume. Additional exam requirements/recommendations for international students: Required—TOEFL (minimum score 500 paper-based; 63 iBT), IELTS (minimum score 5.5). Electronic applications accepted.

Dakota State University, College of Business and Information Systems, Madison, SD 57042-1799. Offers applied computer science (MSACS); general management (MBA); health informatics (MSHI); information assurance (MSIA); information systems (MSIS, D Sc IS). *Accreditation:* ACBSP. Part-time and evening/weekend programs available. Postbaccalaureate distance learning degree programs offered (minimal on-campus study). *Faculty:* 20 full-time (6 women), 1 part-time/adjunct (0 women). *Students:* 47 full-time (12 women), 146 part-time (31 women); includes 38 minority (10 Black or African American, non-Hispanic/Latino; 1 American Indian or Alaska Native, non-Hispanic/Latino; 12 Asian, non-Hispanic/Latino; 7 Hispanic/Latino; 1 Native Hawaiian or other Pacific Islander, non-Hispanic/Latino; 7 Two or more races, non-Hispanic/Latino), 48 international. Average age 37. 167 applicants, 58% accepted, 62 enrolled. In 2013, 57 master's, 4 doctorates awarded. *Degree requirements:* For master's, comprehensive exam, thesis optional, examination, integrative project; for doctorate, comprehensive exam, thesis/dissertation, portfolio. *Entrance requirements:* For master's, GRE General Test, demonstration of information systems skills, minimum GPA of 2.7; for doctorate, GRE General Test, demonstration of information systems skills. Additional exam requirements/recommendations for international students: Required—TOEFL (minimum score 550 paper-based; 79 iBT), IELTS (minimum score 6.5). *Application deadline:* For fall admission, 6/15 for domestic and international students; for spring admission, 11/15 for domestic and international students. Applications are processed on a rolling basis. Application fee: $35 ($85 for international students). *Financial support:* In 2013–14, 47 students received support, including 13 fellowships with partial tuition reimbursements available (averaging $32,782 per year), 10 research assistantships with partial tuition reimbursements available (averaging $12,956 per year), 1 teaching assistantship with partial tuition reimbursement available (averaging $12,956 per year); Federal Work-Study, scholarships/grants, unspecified assistantships, and administrative assistantships also available. Support available to part-time students. Financial award applicants required to submit FAFSA. *Faculty research:* E-commerce, data mining and data warehousing, effectiveness of hybrid learning environments, biometrics and information assurance, decision support systems. *Unit head:* Dr. Omar El-Gayar, Dean of Graduate Studies and Research, 605-256-5799, Fax: 605-256-5093, E-mail: omar.el-gayar@dsu.edu. *Application contact:* Erin Blankespoor, Secretary, Office of Graduate Studies and Research, 605-256-5799, Fax: 605-256-5093, E-mail: erin.blankespoor@dsu.edu.
Website: http://www.dsu.edu/bis/index.aspx.

Dalhousie University, Faculty of Management, Centre for Advanced Management Education, Halifax, NS B3H 3J5, Canada. Offers financial services (MBA); information management (MIM); management (MPA); natural resources (MBA). Part-time programs available. Postbaccalaureate distance learning degree programs offered. *Entrance requirements:* For master's, GMAT, minimum GPA of 3.0, resume. Additional exam requirements/recommendations for international students: Required—TOEFL, IELTS, CANTEST, CAEL, or Michigan English Language Assessment Battery. Electronic applications accepted.

Dalhousie University, Faculty of Management, School of Business Administration, Halifax, NS B3H 3J5, Canada. Offers business administration (MBA); financial services (MBA); LL B/MBA; MBA/MLIS. Part-time programs available. *Entrance requirements:* For master's, GMAT, letter of non-financial guarantee for non-Canadian students, resume, Corporate Residency Preference Form. Additional exam requirements/recommendations for international students: Required—TOEFL, IELTS, CANTEST, CAEL, or Michigan English Language Assessment Battery. Electronic applications accepted. *Faculty research:* International business, quantitative methods, operations research, MIS, marketing, finance.

Dalhousie University, Faculty of Management, School of Public Administration, Halifax, NS B3H 3J5, Canada. Offers management (MPA); public administration (MPA, GDPA); LL B/MPA; MLIS/MPA. Part-time programs available. *Entrance requirements:* For master's, GMAT. Additional exam requirements/recommendations for international students: Required—TOEFL, IELTS, CANTEST, CAEL, or Michigan English Language Assessment Battery. Electronic applications accepted. *Expenses:* Contact institution. *Faculty research:* Municipal management, policy and program management, environmental policy, economic and social policy, business and government.

Dallas Baptist University, College of Business, Business Administration Program, Dallas, TX 75211-9299. Offers accounting (MBA); business communication (MBA); conflict resolution management (MBA); entrepreneurship (MBA); finance (MBA); health care management (MBA); international business (MBA); leading the non-profit organization (MBA); management (MBA); management information systems (MBA); marketing (MBA); project management (MBA); technology and engineering (MBA). *Accreditation:* ACBSP. Part-time and evening/weekend programs available. *Entrance requirements:* For master's, GMAT, minimum GPA of 3.0. Additional exam requirements/recommendations for international students: Required—TOEFL, IELTS. *Application deadline:* Applications are processed on a rolling basis. Application fee: $25. Electronic applications accepted. *Expenses: Tuition:* Full-time $13,410; part-time $745 per credit hour. *Required fees:* $300; $150 per semester. Tuition and fees vary according to degree level. *Financial support:* Federal Work-Study, institutionally sponsored loans, scholarships/grants, and tuition waivers (full and partial) available. Support available to part-time students. Financial award applicants required to submit FAFSA. *Faculty research:* Sports management, services marketing, retailing, strategic management, financial planning/investments. *Unit head:* Dr. Sandra S. Reid, Chair, 214-333-5280, Fax: 214-333-5293, E-mail: graduate@dbu.edu. *Application contact:* Kit P. Montgomery, Director of Graduate Programs, 214-333-5242, Fax: 214-333-5579, E-mail: graduate@dbu.edu.
Website: http://www3.dbu.edu/graduate/mba.asp.

Dallas Baptist University, College of Business, Management Program, Dallas, TX 75211-9299. Offers conflict resolution management (MA); general management (MA); health care management (MA); human resource management (MA); organizational management (MA); performance management (MA); professional sales and management optimization (MA). Part-time and evening/weekend programs available. *Entrance requirements:* For master's, GRE General Test, minimum GPA of 3.0. Additional exam requirements/recommendations for international students: Required—TOEFL, IELTS. *Application deadline:* Applications are processed on a rolling basis. Application fee: $25. Electronic applications accepted. *Expenses: Tuition:* Full-time $13,410; part-time $745 per credit hour. *Required fees:* $300; $150 per semester. Tuition and fees vary according to degree level. *Financial support:* Federal Work-Study, institutionally sponsored loans, scholarships/grants, and tuition waivers (full and partial) available. Support available to part-time students. Financial award applicants required to submit FAFSA. *Faculty research:* Organizational behavior, conflict personalities. *Unit head:* Joanne Hix, Director, 214-333-5280, Fax: 214-333-5293, E-mail: graduate@dbu.edu. *Application contact:* Kit P. Montgomery, Director of Graduate Programs, 214-333-5242, Fax: 214-333-5579, E-mail: graduate@dbu.edu.
Website: http://www3.dbu.edu/graduate/maom.asp.

Dallas Baptist University, Gary Cook School of Leadership, Program in Christian Education, Dallas, TX 75211-9299. Offers adult ministry (MA); business ministry (MA); Christian studies (MA); collegiate ministry (MA); communication ministry (MA); counseling ministry (MA); family ministry (MA); general ministry (MA); leading the nonprofit organization (MA); missions ministry (MA); small group ministry (MA); student ministry (MA); worship ministry (MA); MA/MA. Part-time and evening/weekend programs available. *Entrance requirements:* For master's, minimum GPA of 3.0. Additional exam requirements/recommendations for international students: Required—TOEFL. *Application deadline:* Applications are processed on a rolling basis. Application fee: $25. Electronic applications accepted. *Expenses: Tuition:* Full-time $13,410; part-time $745 per credit hour. *Required fees:* $300; $150 per semester. Tuition and fees vary according to degree level. *Financial support:* Federal Work-Study, institutionally sponsored loans, scholarships/grants, and tuition waivers (full and partial) available. Support available to part-time students. Financial award applicants required to submit FAFSA. *Unit head:* Dr. Judy Morris, Director, 214-333-5246, Fax: 214-333-5115, E-mail: graduate@dbu.edu. *Application contact:* Kit P. Montgomery, Director of Graduate Programs, 214-333-5242, Fax: 214-333-5579, E-mail: graduate@dbu.edu.
Website: http://www3.dbu.edu/leadership/mace/.

Dallas Baptist University, Gary Cook School of Leadership, Program in Christian Education and Business Administration, Dallas, TX 75211-9299. Offers MA/MBA. Part-time and evening/weekend programs available. *Students:* 15 applicants, 80% accepted, 6 enrolled. *Entrance requirements:* Additional exam requirements/recommendations for international students: Required—TOEFL, IELTS. Application fee: $25. *Expenses: Tuition:* Full-time $13,410; part-time $745 per credit hour. *Required fees:* $300; $150 per semester. Tuition and fees vary according to degree level. *Financial support:* Federal Work-Study, institutionally sponsored loans, scholarships/grants, and tuition waivers available. Support available to part-time students. Financial award applicants required to submit FAFSA. *Unit head:* Dr. Judy Morris, Co-Director, 214-333-5246, Fax: 214-333-5115, E-mail: graduate@dbu.edu. *Application contact:* Kit P. Montgomery, Director of Graduate Programs, 214-333-5242, Fax: 214-333-5579, E-mail: graduate@dbu.edu.
Website: http://www3.dbu.edu/leadership/dual_degrees/mace_mba.asp.

Daniel Webster College, MBA Program, Nashua, NH 03063-1300. Offers applied management (MBA). Part-time and evening/weekend programs available. *Degree requirements:* For master's, capstone research project. *Entrance requirements:* Additional exam requirements/recommendations for international students: Required—TOEFL (minimum score 550 paper-based; 79 iBT). Electronic applications accepted.

Dartmouth College, Tuck School of Business at Dartmouth, Hanover, NH 03755. Offers MBA, MBA/MPH, MD/MBA, PhD/MBA. *Accreditation:* AACSB. *Faculty:* 47 full-time (11 women). *Students:* 560 full-time (188 women); includes 94 minority (21 Black or African American, non-Hispanic/Latino; 2 American Indian or Alaska Native, non-Hispanic/Latino; 47 Asian, non-Hispanic/Latino; 18 Hispanic/Latino; 6 Two or more races, non-Hispanic/Latino), 176 international. Average age 28. 2,680 applicants, 21% accepted, 277 enrolled. In 2013, 266 master's awarded. *Entrance requirements:* For master's, GMAT or GRE, 2 letters of recommendation, resume/curriculum vitae. Additional exam requirements/recommendations for international students: Required—TOEFL. *Application deadline:* For fall admission, 10/1 for domestic and international students; for winter admission, 1/1 for domestic and international students; for spring admission, 4/1 for domestic and international students. Application fee: $225. Electronic applications accepted. *Expenses:* Contact institution. *Financial support:* In 2013–14, 379 students received support. Institutionally sponsored loans and scholarships/grants available. Financial award application deadline: 4/1; financial award applicants required to submit FAFSA. *Faculty research:* Database marketing, mutual fund investment performance, dynamic capabilities of firms, return on marketing investment, tradeoff between risk and return in international financial markets, strategic innovation in established firms. *Unit head:* Paul Danos, Dean, 603-646-2460, Fax: 603-646-1308, E-mail: tuck.public.relations@dartmouth.edu. *Application contact:* Dawna Clarke, Director of Admissions, 603-646-3162, Fax: 603-646-1441, E-mail: tuck.admissions@dartmouth.edu.
Website: http://www.tuck.dartmouth.edu/.

Davenport University, Sneden Graduate School, Grand Rapids, MI 49512. Offers accounting (MBA); business administration (EMBA); finance (MBA); health care management (MBA); human resources (MBA); information assurance (MS); public health (MPH); strategic management (MBA). Evening/weekend programs available. *Entrance requirements:* For master's, GMAT, minimum undergraduate GPA of 2.75. Additional exam requirements/recommendations for international students: Required—TOEFL. Electronic applications accepted. *Faculty research:* Leadership, management, marketing, organizational culture.

Defiance College, Program in Business Administration, Defiance, OH 43512-1610. Offers criminal justice (MBA); health care (MBA); leadership (MBA); sport management (MBA). Part-time and evening/weekend programs available. *Degree requirements:* For master's, thesis. *Entrance requirements:* For master's, minimum GPA of 2.5. Additional exam requirements/recommendations for international students: Recommended—TOEFL.

Delaware State University, Graduate Programs, College of Business, Program in Business Administration, Dover, DE 19901-2277. Offers MBA. *Accreditation:* AACSB. Part-time and evening/weekend programs available. *Degree requirements:* For master's, exit exam. *Entrance requirements:* For master's, GMAT (minimum score 400), minimum GPA of 3.0 in major, 2.75 overall. Additional exam requirements/recommendations for international students: Required—TOEFL (minimum score 550 paper-based). Electronic applications accepted. *Faculty research:* Managerial economics, strategic management, qualitative effort, finance.

Delaware Valley College, MBA Program, Doylestown, PA 18901-2697. Offers accounting (MBA); entrepreneurship (MBA); finance (MBA); food and agribusiness (MBA); general business (MBA); global executive leadership (MBA); human resource management (MBA); supply chain management (MBA). Part-time and evening/weekend programs available. Postbaccalaureate distance learning degree programs offered (no on-campus study). *Students:* 32 full-time (17 women), 183 part-time (99 women). Average age 34. 97 applicants, 78% accepted, 74 enrolled. *Entrance requirements:* For master's, minimum undergraduate GPA of 3.0. *Application deadline:* Applications are processed on a rolling basis. Application fee: $50. Electronic applications accepted. *Expenses:* Contact institution. *Financial support:* Applicants required to submit FAFSA. *Unit head:* Mike Prushan, Director of MBA Program, 215-489-2322, E-mail: michael.prushan@delval.edu. *Application contact:* Robin Mathews, Graduate and Continuing Studies Enrollment Manager, 215-489-2955, Fax: 215-489-4832, E-mail: robin.mathews@delval.edu.
Website: http://www.delval.edu/academics/graduate/master-of-business-administration.

Delta State University, Graduate Programs, College of Business, Division of Management, Marketing, and Business Administration, Cleveland, MS 38733-0001. Offers business administration (MBA). Part-time and evening/weekend programs available. *Faculty:* 5 full-time (2 women). *Students:* 123 full-time (62 women), 20 part-time (16 women); includes 93 minority (85 Black or African American, non-Hispanic/Latino; 1 American Indian or Alaska Native, non-Hispanic/Latino; 1 Asian, non-Hispanic/Latino; 4 Hispanic/Latino; 2 Two or more races, non-Hispanic/Latino), 9 international. Average age 31. 72 applicants, 100% accepted, 55 enrolled. In 2013, 37 master's awarded. *Entrance requirements:* For master's, GMAT. *Application deadline:* For fall admission, 8/1 priority date for domestic students; for spring admission, 12/1 priority date for domestic students. Applications are processed on a rolling basis. Application fee: $0. *Expenses:* Tuition, state resident: full-time $3006; part-time $334 per credit hour. Tuition, nonresident: full-time $3006; part-time $334 per credit hour. *Financial support:* In 2013–14, research assistantships (averaging $4,000 per year) were awarded; career-related internships or fieldwork, Federal Work-Study, and institutionally sponsored loans also available. Support available to part-time students. Financial award application deadline: 6/1. *Unit head:* Dr. Cooper Johnson, Chair, 662-846-4190, Fax: 662-846-4232, E-mail: bcjohnsn@deltastate.edu. *Application contact:* Carla Johnson, Coordinator, College of Business Graduate Programs, 662-846-4234, Fax: 662-846-4215, E-mail: cjohnson@deltastate.edu.
Website: http://www.deltastate.edu/pages/4746.asp.

DePaul University, Charles H. Kellstadt Graduate School of Business, Chicago, IL 60604. Offers accountancy (M Acc, MS, MSA); applied economics (MBA); banking (MBA); behavioral finance (MBA); brand and product management (MBA); business development (MBA); business information technology (MS); business strategy and decision-making (MBA); computational finance (MS); consumer insights (MBA); corporate finance (MBA); economic policy analysis (MS); entrepreneurship (MBA, MS); finance (MBA, MS); financial analysis (MBA); general business (MBA); health sector management (MBA); hospitality leadership (MBA); hospitality leadership and operational performance (MS); human resource management (MBA); human resources (MS); investment management (MBA); leadership and change management (MBA); management accounting (MBA); marketing (MBA, MS); marketing analysis (MS); marketing strategy and planning (MBA); operations management (MBA); organizational diversity (MBA); real estate (MS); real estate finance and investment (MBA); revenue management (MBA); sports management (MBA); strategic global marketing (MBA); strategy, execution and valuation (MBA); sustainable management (MBA, MS); taxation (MS); wealth management (MS); JD/MBA. *Accreditation:* AACSB. Part-time and evening/weekend programs available. Postbaccalaureate distance learning degree programs offered (no on-campus study). *Faculty:* 81 full-time (20 women), 45 part-time/adjunct (8 women). *Students:* 1,238 full-time (605 women), 617 part-time (223 women); includes 295 minority (71 Black or African American, non-Hispanic/Latino; 129 Asian, non-Hispanic/Latino; 74 Hispanic/Latino; 4 Native Hawaiian or other Pacific Islander, non-Hispanic/Latino; 17 Two or more races, non-Hispanic/Latino), 462 international. Average age 29. In 2013, 911 master's awarded. *Entrance requirements:* For master's, GMAT, 2 letters of recommendation, resume, essay, official transcripts. Additional exam

requirements/recommendations for international students: Required—TOEFL (minimum score 550 paper-based; 80 iBT). *Application deadline:* For fall admission, 7/1 for domestic students, 6/1 for international students; for winter admission, 10/1 for domestic students, 9/1 for international students; for spring admission, 2/1 for domestic students, 1/1 for international students. Applications are processed on a rolling basis. Application fee: $60. Electronic applications accepted. *Expenses:* Contact institution. *Financial support:* Application deadline: 4/1; applicants required to submit FAFSA. *Unit head:* Robert T. Ryan, Assistant Dean and Director, 312-362-8810, Fax: 312-362-6677, E-mail: rryan1@depaul.edu. *Application contact:* James Parker, Director of Recruitment and Admission, 312-362-8810, Fax: 312-362-6677, E-mail: kgsb@depaul.edu. Website: http://kellstadt.depaul.edu.

DeSales University, Graduate Division, Division of Business, Center Valley, PA 18034-9568. Offers accounting (MBA); computer information systems (MBA); finance (MBA); health care systems management (MBA); human resources management (MBA); management (MBA); marketing (MBA); project management (MBA); self-design (MBA). *Accreditation:* ACBSP. Part-time and evening/weekend programs available. Postbaccalaureate distance learning degree programs offered (no on-campus study). *Students:* 444 part-time. Average age 37. In 2013, 1 master's awarded. *Entrance requirements:* For master's, GMAT, minimum GPA of 3.0, 2 years of work experience. Additional exam requirements/recommendations for international students: Required—TOEFL. *Application deadline:* Applications are processed on a rolling basis. Application fee: $50. Electronic applications accepted. *Expenses: Tuition:* Part-time $790 per credit. *Financial support:* Applicants required to submit FAFSA. *Faculty research:* Quality improvement, executive development, productivity, cross-cultural managerial differences, leadership. *Unit head:* Dr. David Gilfoil, Director, 610-282-1100 Ext. 1828, Fax: 610-282-2869, E-mail: david.gilfoil@desales.edu. *Application contact:* Abigail Wernicki, Director of Graduate Admissions, 610-282-1100 Ext. 1768, E-mail: gradadmissions@desales.edu.

DeVry College of New York, Keller Graduate School of Management, New York, NY 10016-5267. Offers MAFM, MBA, MISM.

DeVry University, Graduate Programs, Phoenix, AZ 85021-2995. Offers MAFM, MBA, MEE, MET, MHRM, MISM, MNCM, MPA, MPM, MSA.

DeVry University, Graduate Programs, Pomona, CA 91768-2642. Offers M Ed, MAFM, MBA, MHRM, MISM, MNCM, MPA, MPM, MSA.

DeVry University, Graduate Programs, Miramar, FL 33027-4150. Offers M Ed, MAFM, MBA, MHRM, MISM, MNCM, MPA, MPM, MSA.

DeVry University, Graduate Programs, Orlando, FL 32839. Offers M Ed, MAFM, MBA, MHRM, MISM, MNCM, MPA, MPM, MSA.

DeVry University, Graduate Programs, Federal Way, WA 98001. Offers MAFM, MBA, MHRM, MISM, MNCM, MPA, MPM, MS Ed, MSA. *Accreditation:* ACBSP.

DeVry University, Graduate Programs, Downers Grove, IL 60515. Offers accounting and financial management (MAFM); business administration (MBA); education (MS); educational technology (MS); electrical engineering (MS); human resources management (MHRM); information systems management (MISM); network and communications management (MNCM); project management (MPM); public administration (MPA).

DeVry University, Keller Graduate School of Management, Fremont, CA 94555. Offers MAFM, MBA, MHRM, MISM, MNCM, MPA, MPM. *Accreditation:* ACBSP.

DeVry University, Keller Graduate School of Management, Long Beach, CA 90806. Offers MAFM, MBA, MHRM, MISM, MNCM, MPA, MPM. *Accreditation:* ACBSP.

DeVry University, Keller Graduate School of Management, Palmdale, CA 93551. Offers MAFM, MBA, MHRM, MPM, Graduate Certificate. *Accreditation:* ACBSP.

DeVry University, Keller Graduate School of Management, Colorado Springs, CO 80920. Offers MAFM, MBA, MHRM, MISM, MNCM, MPA, MPM, Graduate Certificate. *Accreditation:* ACBSP.

DeVry University, Keller Graduate School of Management, Alpharetta, GA 30009. Offers MAFM, MBA, MHRM, MISM, MNCM, MPA, MPM. *Accreditation:* ACBSP.

DeVry University, Keller Graduate School of Management, Decatur, GA 30030-2556. Offers MAFM, MBA, MHRM, MISM, MNCM, MPA, MPM, MSA. *Accreditation:* ACBSP.

DeVry University, Keller Graduate School of Management, Chicago, IL 60618-5994. Offers MAFM, MBA, MHRM, MISM, MPM. *Accreditation:* ACBSP.

DeVry University, Keller Graduate School of Management, Tinley Park, IL 60477. Offers MAFM, MBA, MHRM, MISM, MNCM, MPA, MPM. *Accreditation:* ACBSP.

DeVry University, Keller Graduate School of Management, Columbus, OH 43209-2705. Offers MAFM, MBA, MHRM, MISM, MNCM, MPA, MPM. *Accreditation:* ACBSP.

DeVry University, Keller Graduate School of Management, Fort Washington, PA 19034. Offers MAFM, MBA, MHRM, MISM, MNCM, MPA, MPM. *Accreditation:* ACBSP.

DeVry University, Keller Graduate School of Management, Irving, TX 75063-2439. Offers MAFM, MBA, MHRM, MISM, MPM. *Accreditation:* ACBSP.

DeVry University, Keller Graduate School of Management, Arlington, VA 22202. Offers MAFM, MBA, MHRM, MISM, MNCM, MPA, MPM. *Accreditation:* ACBSP.

DeVry University, Keller Graduate School of Management, Mesa, AZ 85210-2011. Offers MAFM, MBA, MHRM, MISM, MNCM, MPA, MPM, Graduate Certificate. *Accreditation:* ACBSP.

DeVry University, Keller Graduate School of Management, Glendale, AZ 85305. Offers MAFM, MBA, MHRM, MISM, MNCM, MPA, MPM, Graduate Certificate. *Accreditation:* ACBSP.

DeVry University, Keller Graduate School of Management, Oxnard, CA 93036. Offers MAFM, MBA, MHRM, MISM, MNCM, MPA, MPM, Graduate Certificate. *Accreditation:* ACBSP.

DeVry University, Keller Graduate School of Management, Elk Grove, CA 95758. Offers MAFM, MBA, MHRM, MISM, MNCM, MPA, MPM, Graduate Certificate. *Accreditation:* ACBSP.

DeVry University, Keller Graduate School of Management, San Diego, CA 92108-1633. Offers MAFM, MBA, MHRM, MISM, MNCM, MPA, MPM, Graduate Certificate. *Accreditation:* ACBSP.

DeVry University, Keller Graduate School of Management, Miami, FL 33174-2535. Offers MAFM, MBA, MHRM, MISM, MNCM, MPA, MPM, Graduate Certificate. *Accreditation:* ACBSP.

DeVry University, Keller Graduate School of Management, Tampa, FL 33609. Offers MAFM, MBA, MHRM, MISM, MNCM, MPA, MPM, Graduate Certificate. *Accreditation:* ACBSP.

DeVry University, Keller Graduate School of Management, Atlanta, GA 30305-1543. Offers MAFM, MBA, MHRM, MISM, MNCM, MPA, MPM, Graduate Certificate. *Accreditation:* ACBSP.

DeVry University, Keller Graduate School of Management, Duluth, GA 30096-7671. Offers MAFM, MBA, MHRM, MISM, MNCM, MPA, MPM, Graduate Certificate. *Accreditation:* ACBSP.

DeVry University, Keller Graduate School of Management, Elgin, IL 60123. Offers MAFM, MBA, MHRM, MISM, MNCM, MPA, MPM, Graduate Certificate. *Accreditation:* ACBSP.

DeVry University, Keller Graduate School of Management, Schaumburg, IL 60173-5009. Offers MAFM, MBA, MHRM, MISM, MNCM, MPA, MPM, Graduate Certificate. *Accreditation:* ACBSP.

DeVry University, Keller Graduate School of Management, Gurnee, IL 60031-9126. Offers MAFM, MBA, MHRM, MISM, MNCM, MPA, MPM, Graduate Certificate. *Accreditation:* ACBSP.

DeVry University, Keller Graduate School of Management, Indianapolis, IN 46240-2158. Offers MAFM, MBA, MHRM, MISM, MNCM, MPA, MPM. *Accreditation:* ACBSP.

DeVry University, Keller Graduate School of Management, Merrillville, IN 46410-5673. Offers MAFM, MBA, MHRM, MISM, MNCM, MPA, MPM, Graduate Certificate. *Accreditation:* ACBSP.

DeVry University, Keller Graduate School of Management, Bethesda, MD 20814-3304. Offers MAFM, MBA, MHRM, MISM, MNCM, MPA, MPM. *Accreditation:* ACBSP.

DeVry University, Keller Graduate School of Management, Kansas City, MO 64105-2112. Offers MAFM, MBA, MHRM, MISM, MNCM, MPA, MPM. *Accreditation:* ACBSP.

DeVry University, Keller Graduate School of Management, St. Louis, MO 63146. Offers MAFM, MBA, MHRM, MISM, MNCM, MPA, MPM, Graduate Certificate. *Accreditation:* ACBSP.

DeVry University, Keller Graduate School of Management, Charlotte, NC 28273-4068. Offers MAFM, MBA, MHRM, MISM, MNCM, MPA, MPM. *Accreditation:* ACBSP.

DeVry University, Keller Graduate School of Management, Henderson, NV 89074-7120. Offers MAFM, MBA, MHRM, MISM, MNCM, MPA, MPM. *Accreditation:* ACBSP.

DeVry University, Keller Graduate School of Management, Seven Hills, OH 44131. Offers MAFM, MBA, MHRM, MISM, MNCM, MPA, MPM, Graduate Certificate. *Accreditation:* ACBSP.

DeVry University, Keller Graduate School of Management, Portland, OR 97225-6651. Offers MAFM, MBA, MHRM, MISM, MNCM, MPA, MPM. *Accreditation:* ACBSP.

DeVry University, Keller Graduate School of Management, Pittsburgh, PA 15222-2606. Offers MAFM, MBA, MHRM, MISM, MNCM, MPA, MPM, Graduate Certificate. *Accreditation:* ACBSP.

DeVry University, Keller Graduate School of Management, King of Prussia, PA 19406-2926. Offers MAFM, MBA, MHRM, MISM, MNCM, MPA, MPM, Graduate Certificate. *Accreditation:* ACBSP.

DeVry University, Keller Graduate School of Management, Richardson, TX 75080. Offers MBA, Graduate Certificate. *Accreditation:* ACBSP.

DeVry University, Keller Graduate School of Management, Houston, TX 77041. Offers MAFM, MBA, MISM, MPM. *Accreditation:* ACBSP.

DeVry University, Keller Graduate School of Management, Manassas, VA 20109-3173. Offers MAFM, MBA, MHRM, MISM, MNCM, MPA, MPM, Graduate Certificate. *Accreditation:* ACBSP.

DeVry University, Keller Graduate School of Management, Bellevue, WA 98004-5110. Offers MAFM, MBA, MHRM, MISM, MNCM, MPA, MPM, Graduate Certificate. *Accreditation:* ACBSP.

DeVry University, Keller Graduate School of Management, Milwaukee, WI 53202. Offers MAFM, MBA, MHRM, MISM, MNCM, MPA, MPM. *Accreditation:* ACBSP.

DeVry University, Keller Graduate School of Management, Waukesha, WI 53188-1157. Offers MAFM, MBA, MHRM, MISM, MNCM, MPA, MPM, Graduate Certificate. *Accreditation:* ACBSP.

DeVry University, Keller Graduate School of Management, Naperville, IL 60563-2361. Offers MAFM, MBA, MHRM, MISM, MNCM, MPA, MPM, Graduate Certificate. *Accreditation:* ACBSP.

DeVry University, Keller Graduate School of Management, Sandy, UT 84070. Offers MAFM, MBA, MHRM, MISM, MNCM, MPA, MPM. *Accreditation:* ACBSP.

DeVry University, Keller Graduate School of Management, North Brunswick, NJ 08902-3362. Offers MBA. *Accreditation:* ACBSP.

DeVry University, Keller Graduate School of Management, Memphis, TN 38119. Offers MAFM, MBA, MHRM, MISM, MNCM, MPA, MPM. *Accreditation:* ACBSP.

DeVry University, Keller Graduate School of Management, Jacksonville, FL 32256-6040. Offers MAFM, MBA, MHRM, MISM, MNCM, MPA, MPM. *Accreditation:* ACBSP.

DeVry University, Keller Graduate School of Management, Anaheim, CA 92806-6136. Offers MAFM, MBA, MHRM, MISM, MNCM, MPA, MPM. *Accreditation:* ACBSP.

DeVry University, Keller Graduate School of Management, Paramus, NJ 07652. Offers MBA. *Accreditation:* ACBSP.

DeVry University, Keller Graduate School of Management, Columbus, OH 43240. Offers MAFM, MBA, MHRM, MISM, MNCM, MPA, MPM. *Accreditation:* ACBSP.

DeVry University, Keller Graduate School of Management, Oakland, CA 94612. Offers MAFM, MBA, MHRM, MISM, MNCM, MPA, MPM. *Accreditation:* ACBSP.

DeVry University, Keller Graduate School of Management, Nashville, TN 37211-4147. Offers MAFM, MBA, MHRM, MISM, MNCM, MPA, MPM. *Accreditation:* ACBSP.

DeVry University, Keller Graduate School of Management, Chesapeake, VA 23320-3671. Offers MAFM, MBA, MHRM, MISM, MNCM, MPA, MPM. *Accreditation:* ACBSP.

DeVry University, Keller Graduate School of Management, Alhambra, CA 91803. Offers MAFM, MBA, MHRM, MISM, MNCM, MPA, MPM. *Accreditation:* ACBSP.

DeVry University, Keller Graduate School of Management, Daly City, CA 94014-3899. Offers MAFM, MBA, MHRM, MISM, MNCM, MPA, MPM. *Accreditation:* ACBSP.

DeVry University Online, Graduate Programs, Addison, IL 60101-6106. Offers M Ed, MAFM, MBA, MEE, MET, MHRM, MISM, MNCM, MPA, MPM.

Doane College, Program in Management, Crete, NE 68333-2430. Offers MA. Part-time and evening/weekend programs available. *Faculty:* 2 full-time (1 woman), 21 part-time/adjunct (9 women). *Students:* 144 full-time (87 women), 22 part-time (16 women); includes 23 minority (8 Black or African American, non-Hispanic/Latino; 2 American Indian or Alaska Native, non-Hispanic/Latino; 5 Asian, non-Hispanic/Latino; 8 Hispanic/Latino). Average age 35. In 2013, 50 master's awarded. *Degree requirements:* For master's, thesis. *Entrance requirements:* For master's, minimum GPA of 3.0. Additional exam requirements/recommendations for international students: Required—TOEFL. *Application deadline:* Applications are processed on a rolling basis. Application fee: $25. *Expenses:* Contact institution. *Financial support:* Application deadline: 6/1; applicants required to submit FAFSA. *Unit head:* Janice Hedfield, Dean, 880-333-6263, E-mail:

janice.hedfield@doane.edu. *Application contact:* Wilma Daddario, Assistant Dean, 402-466-4774, Fax: 404-466-4228, E-mail: wilma.daddario@doane.edu.

Dominican College, MBA Program, Orangeburg, NY 10962-1210. Offers MBA. Evening/weekend programs available. *Faculty:* 1 full-time (0 women), 4 part-time/adjunct (2 women). *Students:* 4 full-time (3 women), 9 part-time (all women). In 2013, 4 master's awarded. *Entrance requirements:* For master's, GMAT, 2 letters of recommendation. Additional exam requirements/recommendations for international students: Required—TOEFL. Electronic applications accepted. *Expenses:* Contact institution. *Unit head:* Ken Mias, MBA Director, 845-848-4102, E-mail: ken.mias@dc.edu. *Application contact:* Joyce Elbe, Director of Admissions, 845-848-7896 Ext. 15, Fax: 845-365-3150, E-mail: admissions@dc.edu.

Dominican University, Edward A. and Lois L. Brennan School of Business, River Forest, IL 60305-1099. Offers MBA, MSA, JD/MBA, MBA/MLIS, MBA/MSW. JD/MBA offered jointly with John Marshall Law School. *Accreditation:* ACBSP. Part-time and evening/weekend programs available. Postbaccalaureate distance learning degree programs offered (no on-campus study). *Faculty:* 20 full-time (8 women), 20 part-time/adjunct (4 women). *Students:* 97 full-time (65 women), 130 part-time (74 women); includes 63 minority (19 Black or African American, non-Hispanic/Latino; 1 American Indian or Alaska Native, non-Hispanic/Latino; 16 Asian, non-Hispanic/Latino; 26 Hispanic/Latino; 1 Native Hawaiian or other Pacific Islander, non-Hispanic/Latino), 22 international. Average age 30. 113 applicants, 73% accepted, 59 enrolled. In 2013, 85 master's awarded. *Entrance requirements:* For master's, GMAT. Additional exam requirements/recommendations for international students: Required—TOEFL (minimum score 550 paper-based; 79 iBT); Recommended—IELTS (minimum score 6). *Application deadline:* Applications are processed on a rolling basis. Application fee: $25. Electronic applications accepted. *Expenses:* Contact institution. *Financial support:* In 2013–14, 111 students received support. Career-related internships or fieldwork, Federal Work-Study, tuition waivers (partial), and unspecified assistantships available. Support available to part-time students. Financial award application deadline: 3/1; financial award applicants required to submit FAFSA. *Faculty research:* Entrepreneurship, small business finance, business ethics, marketing strategy. *Unit head:* Dr. Molly Burke, Dean, 708-524-6465, Fax: 708-524-6939, E-mail: burkemq@dom.edu. *Application contact:* Matthew Quilty, Assistant Dean, Brennan School of Business, 708-524-6507, Fax: 708-524-6939, E-mail: mquilty@dom.edu. Website: http://business.dom.edu/.

Dominican University of California, Barowsky School of Business, San Rafael, CA 94901-2298. Offers global business (MBA); strategic leadership (MBA); sustainable enterprise (MBA). Part-time and evening/weekend programs available. *Faculty:* 7 full-time (3 women), 13 part-time/adjunct (5 women). *Students:* 53 full-time (35 women), 80 part-time (48 women); includes 28 minority (4 Black or African American, non-Hispanic/Latino; 6 Asian, non-Hispanic/Latino; 17 Hispanic/Latino; 1 Native Hawaiian or other Pacific Islander, non-Hispanic/Latino), 16 international. Average age 36. 136 applicants, 43% accepted, 36 enrolled. *Degree requirements:* For master's, thesis, capstone (for MBA). *Entrance requirements:* For master's, minimum GPA of 3.0. Additional exam requirements/recommendations for international students: Required—TOEFL (minimum score 550 paper-based; 80 iBT), IELTS (minimum score 6.5). *Application deadline:* For fall admission, 5/15 priority date for domestic and international students; for spring admission, 11/15 priority date for domestic and international students. Applications are processed on a rolling basis. Electronic applications accepted. Application fee is waived when completed online. *Expenses:* Contact institution. *Financial support:* Scholarships/grants and tuition discounts available. Support available to part-time students. Financial award application deadline: 3/2; financial award applicants required to submit FAFSA. *Unit head:* Dr. Sam Beldona, Dean, 415-458-3786, E-mail: sriam.beldona@dominican.edu. *Application contact:* Shannon Lovelace-White, Assistant Vice President, 415-485-3287, Fax: 415-485-3214, E-mail: shannon.lovelace-white@dominican.edu. Website: http://www.dominican.edu/academics/barowskyschoolofbusiness.

Dowling College, School of Business, Oakdale, NY 11769. Offers aviation management (MBA, Certificate); corporate finance (MBA, Certificate); health care management (MBA); human resource management (Certificate); information systems management (MBA); management and leadership (MBA); marketing (Certificate); project management (Certificate); public management (MBA); school district business leader (MBA); sport, event and entertainment management (Certificate); JD/MBA. Part-time and evening/weekend programs available. Postbaccalaureate distance learning degree programs offered (minimal on-campus study). *Faculty:* 7 full-time (2 women), 43 part-time/adjunct (7 women). *Students:* 183 full-time (79 women), 299 part-time (142 women); includes 137 minority (84 Black or African American, non-Hispanic/Latino; 14 Asian, non-Hispanic/Latino; 20 Hispanic/Latino; 19 Native Hawaiian or other Pacific Islander, non-Hispanic/Latino). Average age 32. 360 applicants, 58% accepted, 127 enrolled. In 2013, 235 master's, 15 other advanced degrees awarded. *Degree requirements:* For master's, comprehensive exam, thesis optional. *Entrance requirements:* For master's, minimum GPA of 2.8, 2 letters of recommendation, courses or seminar in accounting and finance, resume. Additional exam requirements/recommendations for international students: Required—TOEFL (minimum score 550 paper-based). *Application deadline:* For fall admission, 9/1 priority date for domestic students; for winter admission, 1/1 priority date for domestic students; for spring admission, 2/1 priority date for domestic students. Applications are processed on a rolling basis. Application fee: $50. Electronic applications accepted. *Expenses: Tuition:* Full-time $22,731; part-time $1029 per credit. *Required fees:* $956; $956. *Financial support:* Career-related internships or fieldwork and Federal Work-Study available. Support available to part-time students. Financial award application deadline: 6/30; financial award applicants required to submit FAFSA. *Faculty research:* International finance, computer applications, labor relations, executive development. *Unit head:* Dr. Elana Zolfo, Dean, 631-244-3266, Fax: 631-244-1018, E-mail: zolfoe@dowling.edu. *Application contact:* Mary Boullianne, Dean of Admissions, 631-244-3274, Fax: 631-244-1059, E-mail: boulliam@dowling.edu.

Drake University, College of Business and Public Administration, Des Moines, IA 50311-4516. Offers M Acc, MBA, MFM, MPA, JD/MBA, JD/MPA, Pharm D/MBA, Pharm D/MPA. *Accreditation:* AACSB. Part-time and evening/weekend programs available. *Faculty:* 48 full-time (15 women), 2 part-time/adjunct (both women). *Students:* 31 full-time (17 women), 271 part-time (134 women); includes 23 minority (10 Black or African American, non-Hispanic/Latino; 5 Asian, non-Hispanic/Latino; 7 Hispanic/Latino; 1 Two or more races, non-Hispanic/Latino), 17 international. Average age 31. 60 applicants, 78% accepted, 47 enrolled. In 2013, 202 master's awarded. *Degree requirements:* For master's, comprehensive exam (for some programs), thesis (for some programs), internships. *Entrance requirements:* For master's, GMAT, letters of recommendation, resume. Additional exam requirements/recommendations for international students: Required—TOEFL (minimum score 550 paper-based). *Application deadline:* For fall admission, 8/15 priority date for domestic students; for winter admission, 12/20 priority date for domestic students; for spring admission, 12/1 priority date for domestic students. Applications are processed on a rolling basis. Application fee: $25. Electronic applications accepted. *Expenses:* Contact institution. *Financial support:* Fellowships with tuition reimbursements, teaching assistantships, career-related internships or fieldwork, and institutionally sponsored loans available.

Support available to part-time students. Financial award application deadline: 3/1; financial award applicants required to submit FAFSA. *Faculty research:* Venture capital, online commerce, professional ethics, process improvement, project management. *Unit head:* Dr. Charles Edwards, Dean, 515-271-2871, Fax: 515-271-4518, E-mail: charles.edwards@drake.edu. *Application contact:* Danette Kenne, Director of Graduate Programs, 515-271-2188, Fax: 515-271-4518, E-mail: cbpa.gradprograms@drake.edu. Website: http://www.cbpa.drake.edu/.

Drexel University, LeBow College of Business, Program in Business Administration, Philadelphia, PA 19104-2875. Offers business administration (MBA, PhD, APC), including accounting (MBA, PhD), decision sciences (PhD), economics (MBA, PhD), finance (MBA, PhD), legal studies (MBA), management (MBA), marketing (MBA, PhD), organizational sciences (PhD), quantitative methods (MBA), strategic management (PhD). *Accreditation:* AACSB. Part-time and evening/weekend programs available. Postbaccalaureate distance learning degree programs offered (minimal on-campus study). Terminal master's awarded for partial completion of doctoral program. *Entrance requirements:* For master's, GMAT, minimum GPA of 2.75; for doctorate, GMAT. Additional exam requirements/recommendations for international students: Required—TOEFL. Electronic applications accepted. *Faculty research:* Decision support systems, individual and group behavior, operations research, techniques and strategy.

Drury University, Breech School of Business Administration, Springfield, MO 65802. Offers MBA. *Accreditation:* AACSB; ACBSP. Part-time and evening/weekend programs available. *Entrance requirements:* For master's, GMAT. Additional exam requirements/recommendations for international students: Required—TOEFL. Electronic applications accepted. *Expenses:* Contact institution. *Faculty research:* Health care management, cross cultural management, philosophical orientation and decision making.

Duke University, The Fuqua School of Business, Cross Continent Executive MBA Program, Durham, NC 27708-0586. Offers business administration (MBA); energy and the environment (MBA); entrepreneurship and innovation (MBA); finance (MBA); health sector management (Certificate); marketing (MBA); strategy (MBA). *Faculty:* 91 full-time (15 women), 53 part-time/adjunct (9 women). *Students:* 121 full-time (34 women); includes 23 minority (3 Black or African American, non-Hispanic/Latino; 15 Asian, non-Hispanic/Latino; 4 Hispanic/Latino; 1 Native Hawaiian or other Pacific Islander, non-Hispanic/Latino), 31 international. Average age 30. In 2013, 147 master's awarded. *Degree requirements:* For master's, one foreign language. *Entrance requirements:* For master's, GMAT or GRE, transcripts, essays, resume, recommendation letters, interview. Additional exam requirements/recommendations for international students: Required—TOEFL, IELTS, PTE. *Application deadline:* For fall admission, 10/16 for domestic students, 10/6 for international students; for winter admission, 2/12 for domestic and international students; for spring admission, 5/6 for domestic and international students; for summer admission, 6/4 for domestic students. Application fee: $225. Electronic applications accepted. *Financial support:* In 2013–14, 16 students received support. Institutionally sponsored loans and scholarships/grants available. Financial award applicants required to submit FAFSA. *Unit head:* John Gallagher, Associate Dean for Executive MBA Programs, 919-660-7641, E-mail: johng@duke.edu. *Application contact:* Liz Riley Hargrove, Associate Dean for Admissions, 919-660-1956, Fax: 919-681-8026, E-mail: admissions-info@fuqua.duke.edu. Website: http://www.fuqua.duke.edu/programs/duke_mba/cross_continent/.

Duke University, The Fuqua School of Business, Daytime MBA Program, Durham, NC 27708-0586. Offers academic excellence in finance (Certificate); business administration (MBA); decision sciences (MBA); energy and environment (MBA); energy finance (MBA); entrepreneurship and innovation (MBA); finance (MBA); financial analysis (MBA); health sector management (Certificate); leadership and ethics (MBA); management (MBA); marketing (MBA); operations management (MBA); social entrepreneurship (MBA); strategy (MBA). *Faculty:* 91 full-time (15 women), 53 part-time/adjunct (9 women). *Students:* 862 full-time (283 women); includes 179 minority (34 Black or African American, non-Hispanic/Latino; 1 American Indian or Alaska Native, non-Hispanic/Latino; 92 Asian, non-Hispanic/Latino; 42 Hispanic/Latino; 2 Native Hawaiian or other Pacific Islander, non-Hispanic/Latino; 8 Two or more races, non-Hispanic/Latino), 342 international. Average age 29. In 2013, 437 master's awarded. *Entrance requirements:* For master's, GMAT or GRE, transcripts, essays, resume, recommendation letters, interview. Additional exam requirements/recommendations for international students: Required—TOEFL, IELTS, PTE. *Application deadline:* For fall admission, 9/18 for domestic and international students; for winter admission, 10/21 for domestic and international students; for spring admission, 1/6 for domestic and international students; for summer admission, 3/20 for domestic and international students. Application fee: $225. Electronic applications accepted. *Financial support:* In 2013–14, 331 students received support. Institutionally sponsored loans and scholarships/grants available. Financial award applicants required to submit FAFSA. *Unit head:* Russ Morgan, Associate Dean for the Daytime MBA Program, 919-660-2931, Fax: 919-684-8742, E-mail: ruskin.morgan@duke.edu. *Application contact:* Liz Riley Hargrove, Associate Dean of Admissions, 919-660-7705, Fax: 919-681-8026, E-mail: liz.riley@duke.edu. Website: http://www.fuqua.duke.edu/daytime-mba/.

Duke University, The Fuqua School of Business, Global Executive MBA Program, Durham, NC 27708-0586. Offers business administration (MBA); energy and the environment (MBA); entrepreneurship and innovation (MBA); finance (MBA); health sector management (Certificate); marketing (MBA); strategy (MBA). *Faculty:* 91 full-time (15 women), 53 part-time/adjunct (9 women). *Students:* 49 full-time (7 women); includes 7 minority (1 Black or African American, non-Hispanic/Latino; 3 Asian, non-Hispanic/Latino; 3 Hispanic/Latino), 17 international. Average age 39. In 2013, 51 master's awarded. *Entrance requirements:* For master's, transcripts, essays, resume, recommendation letters, interview. Additional exam requirements/recommendations for international students: Required—TOEFL, IELTS, PTE. *Application deadline:* For fall admission, 9/4 for domestic and international students; for winter admission, 10/16 for domestic and international students; for spring admission, 12/5 for domestic and international students; for summer admission, 1/13 for domestic and international students. Application fee: $225. *Financial support:* In 2013–14, 8 students received support. Institutionally sponsored loans and scholarships/grants available. Financial award applicants required to submit FAFSA. *Unit head:* John Gallagher, Associate Dean for Executive MBA Programs, 919-660-7728, E-mail: johng@duke.edu. *Application contact:* Liz Riley Hargrove, Director of EMBA Admissions, 919-660-7705, Fax: 919-681-8026, E-mail: admissions-info@fuqua.duke.edu. Website: http://www.fuqua.duke.edu/programs/duke_mba/global-executive/.

Duke University, The Fuqua School of Business, MMS Program: Foundations of Business, Durham, NC 27708-0586. Offers MMS. *Faculty:* 91 full-time (15 women), 53 part-time/adjunct (9 women). *Students:* 111 full-time (58 women); includes 20 minority (3 Black or African American, non-Hispanic/Latino; 14 Asian, non-Hispanic/Latino; 3 Hispanic/Latino), 47 international. Average age 23. In 2013, 108 master's awarded. *Entrance requirements:* For master's, GMAT or GRE, transcripts, essays, resume, recommendation letters. Additional exam requirements/recommendations for international students: Required—TOEFL, IELTS, PTE. *Application deadline:* For fall admission, 11/5 for domestic and international students; for winter admission, 1/30 for domestic and international students; for spring admission, 3/6 for domestic and

international students; for summer admission, 4/1 for domestic and international students. Application fee: $125. Electronic applications accepted. *Financial support:* In 2013–14, 54 students received support. Institutionally sponsored loans and scholarships/grants available. Financial award applicants required to submit FAFSA. *Unit head:* Russ Morgan, Associate Dean for the Daytime MBA Program, 919-660-2931, Fax: 919-684-8742, E-mail: ruskin.morgan@duke.edu. *Application contact:* Liz Riley Hargrove, Associate Dean of Admissions, 919-660-7705, Fax: 919-681-8026, E-mail: liz.riley@duke.edu.
Website: http://www.fuqua.duke.edu/mms-foundations-of-business/.

Duke University, The Fuqua School of Business, PhD Program, Durham, NC 27708-0586. Offers accounting (PhD); decision sciences (PhD); finance (PhD); management and organizations (PhD); marketing (PhD); operations management (PhD); strategy (PhD). *Faculty:* 91 full-time (15 women). *Students:* 78 full-time (27 women); includes 4 minority (1 Black or African American, non-Hispanic/Latino; 3 Asian, non-Hispanic/Latino), 49 international. 589 applicants, 5% accepted, 16 enrolled. In 2013, 26 doctorates awarded. *Degree requirements:* For doctorate, thesis/dissertation, major field requirement (exam or major paper, depending upon the area). *Entrance requirements:* For doctorate, GMAT or GRE, transcripts, essays, recommendation letters, statement of purpose. Additional exam requirements/recommendations for international students: Required—TOEFL (minimum score 577 paper-based; 90 iBT), IELTS (minimum score 7). *Application deadline:* For fall admission, 12/8 priority date for domestic and international students. Application fee: $80. Electronic applications accepted. *Financial support:* In 2013–14, 70 fellowships with full tuition reimbursements (averaging $25,300 per year), 56 research assistantships with full tuition reimbursements (averaging $7,000 per year) were awarded; institutionally sponsored loans, scholarships/grants, and tuition waivers (full) also available. Financial award applicants required to submit FAFSA. *Unit head:* William Boulding, Dean, 919-660-7822, Fax: 919-684-8742, E-mail: bb1@duke.edu. *Application contact:* Dr. James R. Bettman, Director of Graduate Studies, 919-660-7851, Fax: 919-681-6245, E-mail: jrb12@mail.duke.edu.

Duke University, The Fuqua School of Business, Weekend Executive MBA Program, Durham, NC 27708-0586. Offers business administration (MBA); energy and environment (MBA); entrepreneurship and innovation (MBA); finance (MBA); health sector management (Certificate); marketing (MBA); strategy (MBA). *Faculty:* 91 full-time (15 women), 53 part-time/adjunct (9 women). *Students:* 93 full-time (14 women); includes 33 minority (5 Black or African American, non-Hispanic/Latino; 24 Asian, non-Hispanic/Latino; 3 Hispanic/Latino; 1 Two or more races, non-Hispanic/Latino), 15 international. Average age 36. In 2013, 103 master's awarded. *Degree requirements:* For master's, one foreign language. *Entrance requirements:* For master's, GMAT (preferred) or GRE, transcripts, essays, resume, recommendation letters, interview. Additional exam requirements/recommendations for international students: Required—TOEFL, IELTS, PTE. *Application deadline:* For fall admission, 9/4 for domestic and international students; for winter admission, 10/16 for domestic and international students; for spring admission, 2/12 for domestic and international students; for summer admission, 4/2 for domestic and international students. Application fee: $225. Electronic applications accepted. *Financial support:* In 2013–14, 14 students received support. Institutionally sponsored loans and scholarships/grants available. Financial award applicants required to submit FAFSA. *Unit head:* John Gallagher, Associate Dean for Executive MBA Programs, 919-660-7728, E-mail: johng@duke.edu. *Application contact:* Liz Riley Hargrove, Director of EMBA Admissions, 919-660-7705, Fax: 919-681-8026, E-mail: admissions-info@fuqua.duke.edu.
Website: http://www.fuqua.duke.edu/programs/duke_mba/weekend_executive/.

Duke University, Graduate School, Department of Business Administration, Durham, NC 27708. Offers PhD. *Faculty:* 80. *Students:* 78 full-time (27 women); includes 7 minority (1 Black or African American, non-Hispanic/Latino; 6 Asian, non-Hispanic/Latino), 48 international. 587 applicants, 5% accepted, 15 enrolled. In 2013, 16 doctorates awarded. *Degree requirements:* For doctorate, thesis/dissertation. *Entrance requirements:* For doctorate, GMAT or GRE General Test. Additional exam requirements/recommendations for international students: Required—TOEFL (minimum score 577 paper-based; 90 iBT) or IELTS (minimum score 7). *Application deadline:* For fall admission, 12/8 for domestic and international students. Application fee: $80. Electronic applications accepted. *Financial support:* Fellowships with full tuition reimbursements, research assistantships, career-related internships or fieldwork, Federal Work-Study, and institutionally sponsored loans available. Financial award application deadline: 12/8; financial award applicants required to submit FAFSA. *Unit head:* James Bettman, Director of Graduate Studies, 919-660-7862, Fax: 919-681-6245, E-mail: bobbiec@mail.duke.edu. *Application contact:* Elizabeth Hutton, Director, Graduate Admissions, 919-684-3913, Fax: 919-684-2277, E-mail: grad-admissions@duke.edu.
Website: http://www.fuqua.duke.edu/programs/other_programs/phd_program/.

Duquesne University, John F. Donahue Graduate School of Business, Pittsburgh, PA 15282-0001. Offers accounting (M Acc); finance (MBA); information systems management (MBA, MSISM); management (MBA); marketing (MBA); supply chain management (MBA); sustainability (MBA); JD/MBA; MBA/M Acc; MBA/MA; MBA/MES; MBA/MHMS; MBA/MSN; MSISM/MBA; Pharm D/MBA. *Accreditation:* AACSB. Part-time and evening/weekend programs available. *Faculty:* 58 full-time (17 women), 40 part-time/adjunct (8 women). *Students:* 117 full-time (59 women), 147 part-time (54 women); includes 14 minority (7 Black or African American, non-Hispanic/Latino; 1 Asian, non-Hispanic/Latino; 6 Hispanic/Latino), 53 international. Average age 27. 418 applicants, 46% accepted, 109 enrolled. In 2013, 133 master's awarded. *Entrance requirements:* For master's, GMAT, undergraduate transcripts, 2 letters of recommendation, current resume, personal statement. Additional exam requirements/recommendations for international students: Required—TOEFL (minimum score 577 paper-based; 90 iBT), IELTS (minimum score 7). *Application deadline:* For fall admission, 7/1 priority date for domestic students, 6/1 for international students; for spring admission, 11/1 for domestic and international students. Applications are processed on a rolling basis. Application fee: $0. Electronic applications accepted. *Expenses: Tuition:* Full-time $18,162; part-time $1009 per credit. *Required fees:* $1728; $96 per credit. Tuition and fees vary according to program. *Financial support:* In 2013–14, 39 students received support, including 6 fellowships with partial tuition reimbursements available (averaging $4,541 per year), 33 research assistantships with partial tuition reimbursements available (averaging $9,081 per year); career-related internships or fieldwork, scholarships/grants, and unspecified assistantships also available. Support available to part-time students. Financial award application deadline: 7/1; financial award applicants required to submit FAFSA. *Faculty research:* International business, investment management, business ethics, technology management, supply chain management, business strategy, finance. *Unit head:* Thomas J. Nist, Director of Graduate Programs, 412-396-6276, Fax: 412-396-1726, E-mail: nist@duq.edu. *Application contact:* Maria W. DeCrosta, Enrollment Manager, 412-396-5529, Fax: 412-396-1726, E-mail: decrostam@duq.edu.
Website: http://www.duq.edu/business/grad.

Duquesne University, School of Leadership and Professional Advancement, Pittsburgh, PA 15282-0001. Offers leadership (MS), including business ethics, community leadership, global leadership, health care, information technology, leadership, liberal studies, professional administration, sports leadership. Part-time and evening/weekend programs available. Postbaccalaureate distance learning degree programs offered (no on-campus study). *Faculty:* 15 full-time (7 women), 64 part-time/adjunct (26 women). *Students:* 213 full-time (106 women), 170 part-time (86 women); includes 89 minority (59 Black or African American, non-Hispanic/Latino; 2 American Indian or Alaska Native, non-Hispanic/Latino; 7 Asian, non-Hispanic/Latino; 9 Hispanic/Latino; 1 Native Hawaiian or other Pacific Islander, non-Hispanic/Latino; 11 Two or more races, non-Hispanic/Latino), 9 international. Average age 36. 204 applicants, 56% accepted, 103 enrolled. In 2013, 140 master's awarded. *Degree requirements:* For master's, capstone course. *Entrance requirements:* For master's, professional work experience, 500-word essay, resume, interview. Additional exam requirements/recommendations for international students: Required—TOEFL (minimum score 80 iBT). *Application deadline:* Applications are processed on a rolling basis. Application fee: $0. Electronic applications accepted. Application fee is waived when completed online. *Expenses: Tuition:* Full-time $18,162; part-time $1009 per credit. *Required fees:* $1728; $96 per credit. Tuition and fees vary according to program. *Financial support:* Scholarships/grants available. Financial award applicants required to submit FAFSA. *Unit head:* Dr. Dorothy Bassett, Dean, 412-396-2141, Fax: 412-396-4711, E-mail: bassettd@duq.edu. *Application contact:* Marianne Leister, Director of Student Services, 412-396-4933, Fax: 412-396-5072, E-mail: leister@duq.edu.
Website: http://www.duq.edu/academics/schools/leadership-and-professional-advancement.

D'Youville College, Department of Business, Buffalo, NY 14201-1084. Offers business administration (MBA); international business (MS). Part-time and evening/weekend programs available. *Students:* 61 full-time (20 women), 15 part-time (11 women); includes 10 minority (6 Black or African American, non-Hispanic/Latino; 3 Hispanic/Latino; 1 Two or more races, non-Hispanic/Latino), 12 international. Average age 27. 57 applicants, 46% accepted, 21 enrolled. In 2013, 15 master's awarded. *Degree requirements:* For master's, one foreign language, project or thesis. *Entrance requirements:* For master's, minimum GPA of 3.0. Additional exam requirements/recommendations for international students: Required—TOEFL (minimum score 500 paper-based). *Application deadline:* For fall admission, 5/1 priority date for international students; for spring admission, 9/1 priority date for international students. Applications are processed on a rolling basis. Application fee: $25. Electronic applications accepted. *Financial support:* Career-related internships or fieldwork, Federal Work-Study, and scholarships/grants available. Support available to part-time students. Financial award application deadline: 3/1; financial award applicants required to submit FAFSA. *Faculty research:* Assessment, accreditation, supply chain, online learning, adult learning. *Unit head:* Dr. Susan Kowaleski, Chair, 716-829-7839. *Application contact:* Mark Pavone, Graduate Admissions Director, 716-829-8400, Fax: 716-829-7900, E-mail: graduateadmissions@dyc.edu.
Website: http://www.dyc.edu/academics/business/index.asp.

East Carolina University, Graduate School, College of Business, Greenville, NC 27858-4353. Offers MBA, MS. *Accreditation:* AACSB. Part-time and evening/weekend programs available. *Entrance requirements:* For master's, GMAT. Additional exam requirements/recommendations for international students: Required—TOEFL. Electronic applications accepted. *Expenses:* Tuition, state resident: full-time $4223. Tuition, nonresident: full-time $16,540. *Required fees:* $2184.

East Carolina University, Graduate School, College of Technology and Computer Science, Department of Technology Systems, Greenville, NC 27858-4353. Offers computer network professional (Certificate); industrial technology (MS), including computer networking management, digital communications, industrial distribution and logistics, information security, manufacturing, performance improvement, quality systems; information assurance (Certificate); Lean Six Sigma Black Belt (Certificate); occupational safety (MS); technology management (PhD); Website developer (Certificate). *Entrance requirements:* For master's and Certificate, GRE General Test or MAT, minimum GPA of 2.5; for doctorate, GRE General Test, related work experience. *Expenses:* Tuition, state resident: full-time $4223. Tuition, nonresident: full-time $16,540. *Required fees:* $2184.

Eastern Illinois University, Graduate School, Lumpkin College of Business and Applied Sciences, Program in Business Administration, Charleston, IL 61920-3099. Offers accountancy (MBA, Certificate); general management (MBA). *Accreditation:* AACSB. Part-time programs available. *Entrance requirements:* For master's, GMAT. *Expenses: Tuition, area resident:* Part-time $283 per credit hour. Tuition, state resident: part-time $283 per credit hour. Tuition, nonresident: part-time $679 per credit hour.

Eastern Kentucky University, The Graduate School, College of Business and Technology, Program in Business Administration, Richmond, KY 40475-3102. Offers MBA. *Accreditation:* AACSB.

Eastern Mennonite University, Program in Business Administration, Harrisonburg, VA 22802-2462. Offers business administration (MBA); health services administration (MBA); non-profit management (MBA). Part-time and evening/weekend programs available. *Degree requirements:* For master's, final capstone course. *Entrance requirements:* For master's, GMAT, minimum GPA of 2.5, 2 years of work experience, 2 letters of reference. Additional exam requirements/recommendations for international students: Required—TOEFL (minimum score 500 paper-based). Electronic applications accepted. *Expenses:* Contact institution. *Faculty research:* Information security, Anabaptist/Mennonite experiences and perspectives, limits of multi-cultural education, international development performance criteria.

Eastern Michigan University, Graduate School, College of Business, Department of Management, Ypsilanti, MI 48197. Offers human resources management and organizational development (MSHROD). Part-time and evening/weekend programs available. Postbaccalaureate distance learning degree programs offered (minimal on-campus study). *Faculty:* 19 full-time (9 women). *Students:* 41 full-time (24 women), 71 part-time (55 women); includes 19 minority (13 Black or African American, non-Hispanic/Latino; 2 Asian, non-Hispanic/Latino; 2 Hispanic/Latino; 2 Two or more races, non-Hispanic/Latino), 35 international. Average age 30. 65 applicants, 69% accepted, 32 enrolled. In 2013, 53 master's awarded. *Degree requirements:* For master's, thesis optional. *Entrance requirements:* For master's, GMAT. Additional exam requirements/recommendations for international students: Required—TOEFL. *Application deadline:* For fall admission, 5/15 priority date for domestic and international students; for winter admission, 10/15 priority date for domestic and international students; for spring admission, 3/15 priority date for domestic and international students. Applications are processed on a rolling basis. Application fee: $35. *Expenses:* Tuition, state resident: full-time $12,300; part-time $466 per credit hour. Tuition, nonresident: full-time $23,159; part-time $918 per credit hour. *Required fees:* $71 per credit hour. $46 per semester. One-time fee: $100. Tuition and fees vary according to course level and degree level. *Financial support:* Fellowships, research assistantships with full tuition reimbursements, teaching assistantships with full tuition reimbursements, career-related internships or fieldwork, Federal Work-Study, institutionally sponsored loans, scholarships/grants, tuition waivers (partial), and unspecified assistantships available. Support available to part-time students. Financial award applicants required to submit FAFSA. *Unit head:* Dr. Fraya Wagner-Marsh, Department Head, 734-487-3240, Fax: 734-487-4100, E-mail:

fraya.wagner@emich.edu. *Application contact:* K. Michelle Henry, Director, Academic Services, 734-487-4444, Fax: 734-483-1316, E-mail: mhenry1@emich.edu.

Eastern Michigan University, Graduate School, College of Business, Programs in Business Administration, Ypsilanti, MI 48197. Offers business administration (MBA, Graduate Certificate); computer information systems (Graduate Certificate); e-business (MBA, Graduate Certificate); enterprise business intelligence (MBA); entrepreneurship (MBA, Graduate Certificate); finance (MBA, Graduate Certificate); human resources (MBA); human resources management (Graduate Certificate); information systems (MBA); internal auditing (MBA); international business (MBA, Graduate Certificate); marketing management (Graduate Certificate); nonprofit management (MBA); organizational development (Graduate Certificate); supply chain management (MBA, Graduate Certificate). *Accreditation:* AACSB. Part-time programs available. Postbaccalaureate distance learning degree programs offered (no on-campus study). *Students:* 74 full-time (28 women), 342 part-time (183 women); includes 122 minority (84 Black or African American, non-Hispanic/Latino; 2 American Indian or Alaska Native, non-Hispanic/Latino; 19 Asian, non-Hispanic/Latino; 7 Hispanic/Latino; 10 Two or more races, non-Hispanic/Latino), 38 international. Average age 33. 305 applicants, 72% accepted, 131 enrolled. In 2013, 69 master's, 57 other advanced degrees awarded. *Entrance requirements:* For master's, GMAT (minimum score 450), minimum cumulative undergraduate GPA of 2.75. Additional exam requirements/recommendations for international students: Required—TOEFL. *Application deadline:* For fall admission, 5/15 for domestic students, 5/1 for international students; for winter admission, 10/15 for domestic students, 10/1 for international students; for spring admission, 3/15 for domestic students, 3/1 for international students. Applications are processed on a rolling basis. *Application fee:* $35. *Expenses:* Tuition, state resident: full-time $12,300; part-time $466 per credit hour. Tuition, nonresident: full-time $23,159; part-time $918 per credit hour. *Required fees:* $71 per credit hour. $46 per semester. One-time fee: $100. Tuition and fees vary according to course level and degree level. *Financial support:* Fellowships, research assistantships with full tuition reimbursements, teaching assistantships with full tuition reimbursements, career-related internships or fieldwork, Federal Work-Study, institutionally sponsored loans, scholarships/grants, tuition waivers (partial), and unspecified assistantships available. Support available to part-time students. Financial award applicants required to submit FAFSA. *Unit head:* K. Michelle Henry, Director, Academic Services, 734-487-4444, Fax: 734-483-1316, E-mail: mhenry1@emich.edu. *Application contact:* Beste Windes, Advisor, 734-487-4444, Fax: 734-483-1316, E-mail: bwindes@emich.edu.
Website: http://www.emich.edu/public/cob/gr/grad.html.

Eastern Nazarene College, Adult and Graduate Studies, Program in Management, Quincy, MA 02170. Offers MSM.

Eastern New Mexico University, Graduate School, College of Business, Portales, NM 88130. Offers MBA. *Accreditation:* ACBSP. Part-time and evening/weekend programs available. Postbaccalaureate distance learning degree programs offered (no on-campus study). *Degree requirements:* For master's, comprehensive exam, comprehensive integrative project and presentation. *Entrance requirements:* For master's, GMAT (minimum score 450), minimum undergraduate GPA of 3.0. Additional exam requirements/recommendations for international students: Required—TOEFL (minimum score 550 paper-based; 79 iBT), IELTS (minimum score 6). Electronic applications accepted.

Eastern Oregon University, Program in Business Administration, La Grande, OR 97850-2899. Offers MBA. Part-time programs available. Postbaccalaureate distance learning degree programs offered (minimal on-campus study). *Degree requirements:* For master's, thesis. *Entrance requirements:* For master's, GRE General Test.

Eastern University, School of Leadership and Development, St. Davids, PA 19087-3696. Offers economic development (MBA), including international development, urban development (MA, MBA); international development (MA), including global development, urban development (MA, MBA); nonprofit management (MS); organizational leadership (MA); M Div/MBA. Part-time and evening/weekend programs available. Postbaccalaureate distance learning degree programs offered (minimal on-campus study). *Faculty:* 6 full-time (3 women), 19 part-time/adjunct (8 women). *Students:* 131 full-time (77 women), 67 part-time (42 women); includes 43 minority (29 Black or African American, non-Hispanic/Latino; 1 American Indian or Alaska Native, non-Hispanic/Latino; 6 Asian, non-Hispanic/Latino; 6 Hispanic/Latino; 1 Two or more races, non-Hispanic/Latino), 13 international. Average age 34. 45 applicants, 100% accepted, 33 enrolled. In 2013, 91 master's awarded. *Degree requirements:* For master's, thesis (for some programs). *Entrance requirements:* For master's, GMAT (MBA), minimum GPA of 2.5. Additional exam requirements/recommendations for international students: Required—TOEFL (minimum score 550 paper-based; 79 iBT). *Application deadline:* For fall admission, 8/14 for domestic students. Applications are processed on a rolling basis. *Application fee:* $35. Application fee is waived when completed online. *Expenses:* Contact institution. *Financial support:* In 2013–14, 131 students received support, including 3 fellowships with partial tuition reimbursements available (averaging $2,500 per year), 7 research assistantships with partial tuition reimbursements available (averaging $1,500 per year); scholarships/grants and unspecified assistantships also available. Financial award application deadline: 3/15; financial award applicants required to submit FAFSA. *Faculty research:* Micro-level economic development, China welfare and economic development, macroethics, micro- and macro-level economic development in transitional economics, organizational effectiveness. *Unit head:* Beth Birmingham, Chair, 610-341-4380. *Application contact:* Lindsey Perry, Enrollment Counselor, 484-581-1311, Fax: 484-581-1276, E-mail: lperry@eastern.edu.
Website: http://www.eastern.edu/academics/programs/school-leadership-and-development.

Eastern University, School of Management Studies, St. Davids, PA 19087-3696. Offers health administration (MBA); health services management (MS); management (MBA). Part-time and evening/weekend programs available. Postbaccalaureate distance learning degree programs offered (no on-campus study). *Faculty:* 7 full-time (5 women), 40 part-time/adjunct (13 women). *Students:* 185 full-time (125 women), 66 part-time (44 women); includes 122 minority (100 Black or African American, non-Hispanic/Latino; 8 Asian, non-Hispanic/Latino; 13 Hispanic/Latino; 1 Two or more races, non-Hispanic/Latino), 38 international. Average age 35. 72 applicants, 99% accepted, 55 enrolled. In 2013, 96 master's awarded. *Entrance requirements:* Additional exam requirements/recommendations for international students: Required—TOEFL (minimum score 550 paper-based; 79 iBT). *Application deadline:* For fall admission, 8/16 for domestic students; for spring admission, 3/14 for domestic students. Applications are processed on a rolling basis. *Application fee:* $35. Application fee is waived when completed online. *Expenses:* Tuition: Full-time $15,600; part-time $650 per credit. *Required fees:* $27.50 per semester. One-time fee: $50. Tuition and fees vary according to course load, degree level and program. *Financial support:* In 2013–14, 34 students received support. Scholarships/grants available. Financial award applicants required to submit FAFSA. *Unit head:* Dr. Pat Bleil, Chair, 610-341-1468. *Application contact:* Nicholas Snyder, Enrollment Counselor, 610-225-5557, Fax: 610-341-1468, E-mail: nsnyder@eastern.edu.
Website: http://www.eastern.edu/academics/programs/school-management-studies.

Eastern Washington University, Graduate Studies, College of Business and Public Administration, Business Administration Program, Cheney, WA 99004-2431. Offers MBA, MBA/MPA. *Accreditation:* AACSB. *Faculty:* 17 full-time (6 women). *Students:* 33 full-time (17 women), 24 part-time (11 women); includes 10 minority (3 Black or African American, non-Hispanic/Latino; 1 American Indian or Alaska Native, non-Hispanic/Latino; 5 Asian, non-Hispanic/Latino; 1 Hispanic/Latino). Average age 32. 46 applicants, 30% accepted, 14 enrolled. In 2013, 47 master's awarded. *Degree requirements:* For master's, comprehensive exam, thesis optional. *Entrance requirements:* For master's, GMAT, minimum GPA of 3.0. *Application deadline:* For fall admission, 4/1 priority date for domestic students; for spring admission, 1/15 for domestic students. Applications are processed on a rolling basis. *Application fee:* $50. *Financial support:* In 2013–14, 5 teaching assistantships with partial tuition reimbursements (averaging $7,000 per year) were awarded; career-related internships or fieldwork, Federal Work-Study, institutionally sponsored loans, scholarships/grants, health care benefits, tuition waivers (partial), and unspecified assistantships also available. Support available to part-time students. Financial award application deadline: 2/1. *Unit head:* Roberta Brooke, Director, 509-358-2270, Fax: 509-358-2267, E-mail: rbrooke@ewu.edu. *Application contact:* Prof. M. David Gorton, MBA Director, 509-358-2241, Fax: 509-358-2267, E-mail: mgorton@mailserver.ewu.edu.
Website: http://www.ewu.edu/cbpa.xml.

East Tennessee State University, School of Graduate Studies, College of Business and Technology, Johnson City, TN 37614. Offers M Acc, MBA, MS, Postbaccalaureate Certificate. *Accreditation:* AACSB. *Faculty:* 79 full-time (11 women), 9 part-time/adjunct (2 women). *Students:* 170 full-time (54 women), 56 part-time (22 women); includes 26 minority (13 Black or African American, non-Hispanic/Latino; 3 Asian, non-Hispanic/Latino; 6 Hispanic/Latino; 4 Two or more races, non-Hispanic/Latino), 22 international. Average age 29. 275 applicants, 50% accepted, 124 enrolled. In 2013, 118 master's, 6 other advanced degrees awarded. *Entrance requirements:* Additional exam requirements/recommendations for international students: Required—TOEFL (minimum score 550 paper-based; 79 iBT). *Application fee:* $35 ($45 for international students). *Expenses:* Tuition, state resident: full-time $7900; part-time $395 per credit hour. Tuition, nonresident: full-time $21,960; part-time $1098 per credit hour. *Required fees:* $1345; $84 per credit hour. *Financial support:* In 2013–14, 117 students received support, including 52 research assistantships with full tuition reimbursements available, 19 teaching assistantships with full tuition reimbursements available. Financial award application deadline: 7/1; financial award applicants required to submit FAFSA. *Unit head:* Dr. Linda Garceau, Dean, 423-439-5314, Fax: 423-439-5274, E-mail: garceaul@etsu.edu. *Application contact:* School of Graduate Studies, 423-439-4221, Fax: 423-439-5624, E-mail: gradsch@etsu.edu.
Website: http://www.etsu.edu/cbat.

Edgewood College, Program in Business, Madison, WI 53711-1997. Offers accountancy (MS); accounting (MBA); business administration (MBA); finance (MBA); management (MBA); marketing (MBA); organization development (MS); sustainability leadership (MBA). *Accreditation:* ACBSP. Part-time and evening/weekend programs available. *Students:* 24 full-time (8 women), 136 part-time (82 women); includes 18 minority (5 Black or African American, non-Hispanic/Latino; 1 American Indian or Alaska Native, non-Hispanic/Latino; 4 Asian, non-Hispanic/Latino; 4 Hispanic/Latino; 4 Two or more races, non-Hispanic/Latino), 10 international. Average age 33. In 2013, 55 master's awarded. *Entrance requirements:* For master's, GMAT (minimum score 430), minimum GPA of 2.75, 2 letters of recommendation. Additional exam requirements/recommendations for international students: Required—TOEFL. *Application deadline:* For fall admission, 8/15 for domestic students, 5/1 for international students; for spring admission, 1/8 for domestic students, 11/1 for international students. Applications are processed on a rolling basis. *Application fee:* $30. Electronic applications accepted. *Financial support:* Career-related internships or fieldwork and scholarships/grants available. *Unit head:* Martin Preizler, Dean, 608-663-2898, Fax: 608-663-3291, E-mail: martinpreizler@edgewood.edu. *Application contact:* Joann Eastman, Admissions Counselor, 608-663-3250, Fax: 608-663-2214, E-mail: gps@edgewood.edu.
Website: http://www.edgewood.edu/Academics/School-of-Business.

Elmhurst College, Graduate Programs, Program in Business Administration, Elmhurst, IL 60126-3296. Offers MBA. Part-time and evening/weekend programs available. Postbaccalaureate distance learning degree programs offered (no on-campus study). *Faculty:* 11 part-time/adjunct (2 women). *Students:* 5 full-time (1 woman), 63 part-time (36 women); includes 20 minority (7 Black or African American, non-Hispanic/Latino; 6 Asian, non-Hispanic/Latino; 5 Hispanic/Latino; 2 Native Hawaiian or other Pacific Islander, non-Hispanic/Latino). Average age 35. 76 applicants, 71% accepted, 46 enrolled. In 2013, 29 master's awarded. *Entrance requirements:* For master's, 3 recommendations, resume, statement of purpose. Additional exam requirements/recommendations for international students: Required—TOEFL (minimum score 550 paper-based; 79 iBT). *Application deadline:* Applications are processed on a rolling basis. *Application fee:* $0. Electronic applications accepted. *Expenses:* Contact institution. *Financial support:* In 2013–14, 13 students received support. Federal Work-Study and scholarships/grants available. Support available to part-time students. Financial award application deadline: 6/1; financial award applicants required to submit FAFSA. *Unit head:* Director of Adult and Graduate Admission. *Application contact:* Timothy J. Panfil, Director of Enrollment Management, School for Professional Studies, 630-617-3300 Ext. 3256, Fax: 630-617-6471, E-mail: panfilt@elmhurst.edu.
Website: http://public.elmhurst.edu/mba.

Elon University, Program in Business Administration, Elon, NC 27244-2010. Offers MBA. *Accreditation:* AACSB. Part-time and evening/weekend programs available. *Faculty:* 20 full-time (7 women), 1 (woman) part-time/adjunct. *Students:* 122 part-time (48 women); includes 35 minority (13 Black or African American, non-Hispanic/Latino; 1 American Indian or Alaska Native, non-Hispanic/Latino; 17 Asian, non-Hispanic/Latino; 2 Hispanic/Latino; 2 Two or more races, non-Hispanic/Latino). Average age 33. 99 applicants, 78% accepted, 46 enrolled. *Entrance requirements:* For master's, GMAT. Additional exam requirements/recommendations for international students: Required—TOEFL (minimum score 550 paper-based; 79 iBT). *Application deadline:* For fall admission, 8/1 priority date for domestic students; for spring admission, 2/1 priority date for domestic students. Applications are processed on a rolling basis. *Application fee:* $50. Electronic applications accepted. *Financial support:* Federal Work-Study and scholarships/grants available. Support available to part-time students. Financial award application deadline: 3/15; financial award applicants required to submit FAFSA. *Faculty research:* Business ethics, international business and global economics, sales force management, sustainable business practices, consumer behavior. *Unit head:* Dr. William Burpitt, Director, 336-278-5949, Fax: 336-278-5952, E-mail: wburpitt@elon.edu. *Application contact:* Art Fadde, Director of Graduate Admissions, 800-334-8448 Ext. 3, Fax: 336-278-7699, E-mail: afadde@elon.edu.
Website: http://www.elon.edu/mba/.

Embry-Riddle Aeronautical University–Daytona, Daytona Beach Campus Graduate Program, Department of Business Administration, Daytona Beach, FL 32114-3900. Offers MBA, MBA-AM, MSAF. *Accreditation:* ACBSP. Part-time programs available. *Degree requirements:* For master's, thesis or alternative. *Entrance requirements:* For master's, GMAT, minimum GPA of 2.5. Additional exam requirements/recommendations

for international students: Required—TOEFL (minimum score 550 paper-based; 79 iBT). Electronic applications accepted. *Faculty research:* Aircraft safety operations analysis, energy consumption analysis, statistical analysis of general aviation accidents, airport funding strategies, industry assessment and marketing analysis for ENAER aerospace.

See Display on page 616 and Close-Up on page 635.

Embry-Riddle Aeronautical University–Worldwide, Worldwide Headquarters - Graduate Programs, Program in Business Administration and Management, Daytona Beach, FL 32114-3900. Offers air transportation management (Graduate Certificate); airport planning design and development (Graduate Certificate); aviation (MBAA); aviation enterprises in the global environment (Graduate Certificate); aviation-aerospace industrial management (Graduate Certificate); engineering management (MSEM); integrated logistics management (Graduate Certificate); leadership (MSL); logistics and supply chain management (MSLSCM); management (MSM); modeling and simulation management (Graduate Certificate); occupational safety management (MSOSM); project management (MSPM, Graduate Certificate). Part-time and evening/weekend programs available. Postbaccalaureate distance learning degree programs offered (no on-campus study). *Degree requirements:* For master's, comprehensive exam (for some programs), thesis (for some programs). *Entrance requirements:* Additional exam requirements/recommendations for international students: Recommended—TOEFL (minimum score 550 paper-based; 79 iBT). Electronic applications accepted. *Faculty research:* Healthcare operations management, humanitarian logistics, supply chain risk management, collaborative supply chain management, intersection of collaborative supply chain management and the learning organization, development of assessment tool measuring supply chain collaborative capacity, teaching effectiveness, teaching quality, management style effectiveness, aeronautics, small/medium-sized business leadership study, leadership factors, critical thinking, efficacy of ePortfolio.

Emmanuel College, Graduate Studies, Graduate Programs in Management, Boston, MA 02115. Offers biopharmaceutical leadership (MSM, Graduate Certificate); human resource management (MSM, Graduate Certificate); management (MSM); management and leadership (Graduate Certificate); research administration (MSM, Graduate Certificate). Part-time and evening/weekend programs available. Postbaccalaureate distance learning degree programs offered (no on-campus study). *Faculty:* 1 (woman) full-time, 41 part-time/adjunct (15 women). *Students:* 5 full-time (4 women), 152 part-time (123 women); includes 49 minority (31 Black or African American, non-Hispanic/Latino; 1 American Indian or Alaska Native, non-Hispanic/Latino; 4 Asian, non-Hispanic/Latino; 13 Hispanic/Latino). Average age 36. In 2013, 82 master's, 4 other advanced degrees awarded. *Degree requirements:* For master's, thesis or alternative, 36 credits, including 6-credit capstone project. *Entrance requirements:* For master's and Graduate Certificate, transcripts from all regionally-accredited institutions attended (showing proof of bachelor's degree completion), 2 letters of recommendation, essay, resume, interview. Additional exam requirements/recommendations for international students: Required—TOEFL (minimum score 600 paper-based; 106 iBT) or IELTS (minimum score 6.5). *Application deadline:* For fall admission, 7/31 priority date for domestic students; for spring admission, 11/30 priority date for domestic students. Applications are processed on a rolling basis. Application fee: $0. Electronic applications accepted. *Financial support:* Applicants required to submit FAFSA. *Unit head:* Sandy Robbins, Dean of Enrollment, 617-735-9700, Fax: 617-507-0434, E-mail: graduatestudies@emmanuel.edu. *Application contact:* Enrollment Counselor, 617-735-9700, Fax: 617-507-0434, E-mail: graduatestudies@emmanuel.edu.
Website: http://www.emmanuel.edu/graduate-studies-nursing/academics/management.html.

Emory University, Goizueta Business School, Doctoral Program in Business, Atlanta, GA 30322-1100. Offers accounting (PhD); finance (PhD); information systems (PhD); marketing (PhD); organization and management (PhD). *Faculty:* 53 full-time (12 women). *Students:* 41 full-time (15 women); includes 28 minority (all Asian, non-Hispanic/Latino). Average age 29. 195 applicants, 9% accepted, 9 enrolled. In 2013, 1 doctorate awarded. *Degree requirements:* For doctorate, comprehensive exam, thesis/dissertation. *Entrance requirements:* For doctorate, GMAT (strongly preferred) or GRE. Additional exam requirements/recommendations for international students: Required—TOEFL. *Application deadline:* For fall admission, 1/3 priority date for domestic and international students. Application fee: $75. Electronic applications accepted. *Financial support:* In 2013–14, 35 students received support, including 3 fellowships (averaging $1,166 per year). *Unit head:* Dr. Anand Swaminathan, Associate Dean, Doctoral Program, 404-727-2306, Fax: 404-727-5337, E-mail: anand.swaminathan@emory.edu. *Application contact:* Allison Gilmore, Director of Admissions and Student Services, 404-727-6353, Fax: 404-727-5337, E-mail: phd@bus.emory.edu.

Emory University, Goizueta Business School, Evening MBA Program, Atlanta, GA 30322-1100. Offers MBA. Part-time and evening/weekend programs available. *Faculty:* 64 full-time (8 women), 20 part-time/adjunct (3 women). *Students:* 263 part-time (81 women); includes 79 minority (23 Black or African American, non-Hispanic/Latino; 36 Asian, non-Hispanic/Latino; 18 Hispanic/Latino; 2 Two or more races, non-Hispanic/Latino), 25 international. Average age 31. 181 applicants, 67% accepted, 95 enrolled. In 2013, 84 master's awarded. *Entrance requirements:* For master's, GMAT/GRE, undergraduate degree, interview, essays, recommendation letters. Additional exam requirements/recommendations for international students: Required—TOEFL (minimum score 100 iBT), IELTS (minimum score 7), PTE (minimum score 68). *Application deadline:* For fall admission, 11/1 for domestic students; for winter admission, 2/21 for domestic students; for spring admission, 4/25 for domestic students; for summer admission, 7/9 for domestic students. Application fee: $150. Electronic applications accepted. *Financial support:* In 2013–14, 78 students received support. Application deadline: 6/6; applicants required to submit FAFSA. *Unit head:* Harold S. Lewis, Associate Dean, Evening MBA Program, 404-712-6649, Fax: 404-712-9648, E-mail: harold.lewis@emory.edu. *Application contact:* Julie Barefoot, Associate Dean, 404-727-6311, Fax: 404-727-4612, E-mail: mbaadmissions@emory.edu.

Emory University, Goizueta Business School, Full Time MBA Program, Atlanta, GA 30322. Offers MBA. *Faculty:* 64 full-time (8 women), 20 part-time/adjunct (3 women). *Students:* 353 full-time (86 women); includes 76 minority (30 Black or African American, non-Hispanic/Latino; 27 Asian, non-Hispanic/Latino; 15 Hispanic/Latino; 4 Two or more races, non-Hispanic/Latino), 128 international. Average age 30. 1,233 applicants, 30% accepted, 157 enrolled. In 2013, 186 master's awarded. *Degree requirements:* For master's, 3 leadership courses; 2 mid-semester module programs; global component. *Entrance requirements:* For master's, GMAT/GRE, essays; recommendation letters; undergraduate degree; interview. Additional exam requirements/recommendations for international students: Required—TOEFL (minimum score 100 iBT), IELTS (minimum score 7), PTE (minimum score 68). *Application deadline:* For fall admission, 10/11 for domestic and international students; for winter admission, 11/20 for domestic and international students; for spring admission, 1/10 for domestic and international students; for summer admission, 3/14 for domestic and international students. Application fee: $150. Electronic applications accepted. *Expenses:* Contact institution. *Financial support:* In 2013–14, 264 students received support. Career-related internships or fieldwork, institutionally sponsored loans, scholarships/grants, and unspecified assistantships available. Financial award application deadline: 1/10; financial award applicants required to submit FAFSA. *Unit head:* Brian Mitchell, Associate Dean, 404-727-4824, Fax: 404-712-9648, E-mail: brian.mitchell@emory.edu. *Application contact:* Julie Barefoot, Associate Dean, 404-727-6311, Fax: 404-727-4612, E-mail: mbaadmissions@emory.edu.
Website: http://www.goizueta.emory.edu.

Emory University, Goizueta Business School, Modular Executive MBA Program, Atlanta, GA 30322-2710. Offers MBA. *Faculty:* 64 full-time (8 women), 5 part-time/adjunct (0 women). *Students:* 60 full-time (11 women); includes 20 minority (9 Black or African American, non-Hispanic/Latino; 7 Asian, non-Hispanic/Latino; 3 Hispanic/Latino; 1 Two or more races, non-Hispanic/Latino), 12 international. Average age 38. 72 applicants, 82% accepted, 30 enrolled. In 2013, 31 master's awarded. *Degree requirements:* For master's, completion of lock-step program with minimum of 54 credit hours, one elective course, management practice component, global business practices with 10-day international colloquium. *Entrance requirements:* For master's, GMAT/GRE, interview, essays, letters of recommendation, bachelor's degree. Additional exam requirements/recommendations for international students: Required—TOEFL (minimum score 600 paper-based; 100 iBT), IELTS (minimum score 7), PTE (minimum score 68). *Application deadline:* For fall admission, 12/1 for domestic and international students; for winter admission, 2/1 for domestic and international students; for spring admission, 5/1 for domestic and international students; for summer admission, 7/15 for domestic students, 6/30 for international students. Application fee: $150. Electronic applications accepted. *Financial support:* In 2013–14, 45 students received support. Scholarships/grants available. Financial award applicants required to submit FAFSA. *Unit head:* Jonathan P. Darsey, Associate Dean, 404-727-9040, Fax: 404-727-4936, E-mail: jonathan.p.darsey@emory.edu. *Application contact:* Julie Barefoot, Associate Dean of Admissions, 404-727-6311, Fax: 404-727-4612, E-mail: mbaadmissions@emory.edu.
Website: http://goizueta.emory.edu/degree/emba/memba/.

Emory University, Goizueta Business School, Weekend Executive MBA Program, Atlanta, GA 30322-2710. Offers MBA. Evening/weekend programs available. *Faculty:* 64 full-time (8 women), 5 part-time/adjunct (0 women). *Students:* 82 full-time (20 women); includes 35 minority (20 Black or African American, non-Hispanic/Latino; 12 Asian, non-Hispanic/Latino; 2 Hispanic/Latino; 1 Two or more races, non-Hispanic/Latino), 7 international. Average age 37. 80 applicants, 81% accepted, 45 enrolled. In 2013, 68 master's awarded. *Degree requirements:* For master's, completion of lock-step program with minimum of 54 credit hours, one elective course, management practice component, global business practices with 10-day international colloquium. *Entrance requirements:* For master's, GMAT/GRE, interview, essays, letters of recommendation, bachelor's degree. Additional exam requirements/recommendations for international students: Required—TOEFL (minimum score 100 iBT), IELTS (minimum score 7), PTE (minimum score 68). *Application deadline:* For fall admission, 12/1 for domestic and international students; for winter admission, 2/1 for domestic and international students; for spring admission, 5/1 for domestic and international students; for summer admission, 7/15 for domestic students, 6/30 for international students. Application fee: $150. Electronic applications accepted. *Financial support:* In 2013–14, 24 students received support. Institutionally sponsored loans and scholarships/grants available. Financial award applicants required to submit FAFSA. *Unit head:* Jonathan P. Darsey, Associate Dean, 404-727-9040, Fax: 404-727-4936, E-mail: jonathan.p.darsey@emory.edu. *Application contact:* Julie Barefoot, Associate Dean of Admissions, 404-727-6311, Fax: 404-727-4612, E-mail: mbaadmissions@emory.edu.
Website: http://goizueta.emory.edu/degree/emba/wemba/.

Emporia State University, Program in Business Administration, Emporia, KS 66801-5415. Offers MBA. Part-time and evening/weekend programs available. Postbaccalaureate distance learning degree programs offered (no on-campus study). *Faculty:* 26 full-time (7 women), 1 part-time/adjunct (0 women). *Students:* 68 full-time (38 women), 46 part-time (25 women); includes 4 minority (1 Black or African American, non-Hispanic/Latino; 2 Hispanic/Latino; 1 Two or more races, non-Hispanic/Latino), 62 international. 55 applicants, 93% accepted, 21 enrolled. In 2013, 36 master's awarded. *Entrance requirements:* For master's, GRE, 15 undergraduate credits in business, minimum undergraduate GPA of 2.7 in last 60 hours. Additional exam requirements/recommendations for international students: Required—TOEFL (minimum score 520 paper-based; 68 iBT). *Application deadline:* For fall admission, 8/15 for domestic students. Application fee: $30 ($75 for international students). *Expenses: Tuition, area resident:* Part-time $220 per credit hour. Tuition, state resident: part-time $220 per credit hour. Tuition, nonresident: part-time $685 per credit hour. *Required fees:* $73 per credit hour. *Financial support:* In 2013–14, 3 research assistantships with full tuition reimbursements (averaging $7,200 per year), 16 teaching assistantships with full tuition reimbursements (averaging $7,361 per year) were awarded; career-related internships or fieldwork, health care benefits, and unspecified assistantships also available. *Unit head:* Dr. Bill Barnes, Director, MBA Program, 620-341-5456, E-mail: wbarnes@emporia.edu. *Application contact:* Mary Sewell, Admissions Coordinator, 800-950-GRAD, Fax: 620-341-5909, E-mail: msewell@emporia.edu.
Website: http://www.emporia.edu/business/programs/mba/.

Endicott College, Van Loan School of Graduate and Professional Studies, Program in Business Administration, Beverly, MA 01915-2096. Offers MBA. Part-time and evening/weekend programs available. *Faculty:* 9 full-time (5 women), 34 part-time/adjunct (10 women). *Students:* 110 full-time (54 women), 107 part-time (60 women); includes 35 minority (14 Black or African American, non-Hispanic/Latino; 2 American Indian or Alaska Native, non-Hispanic/Latino; 9 Asian, non-Hispanic/Latino; 7 Hispanic/Latino; 1 Native Hawaiian or other Pacific Islander, non-Hispanic/Latino; 2 Two or more races, non-Hispanic/Latino), 15 international. Average age 31. 162 applicants, 83% accepted, 111 enrolled. In 2013, 98 master's awarded. *Degree requirements:* For master's, thesis, project. *Entrance requirements:* For master's, letters of recommendation, resume. Additional exam requirements/recommendations for international students: Required—TOEFL. *Application deadline:* Applications are processed on a rolling basis. Application fee: $50. Electronic applications accepted. *Expenses:* Contact institution. *Financial support:* Tuition waivers (full) available. Financial award applicants required to submit FAFSA. *Faculty research:* Adult learning and development, supply chain management, marketing, ethics. *Unit head:* Richard Benedetto, Associate Dean of Graduate School, 978-232-2744, Fax: 978-232-3000, E-mail: rbenedet@endicott.edu. *Application contact:* Dr. Mary Huegel, Vice President and Dean of the School of Graduate and Professional Studies, 978-232-2084, Fax: 978-232-3000, E-mail: mhuegel@endicott.edu.
Website: http://www.endicott.edu/GradProf/GPSGrad/GPSGradMBA.aspx.

ESSEC Business School, Graduate Programs, Paris, France. Offers business administration (PhD); executive business administration (MBA); global business administration (MBA); hospitality management (MBA); international luxury brand management (MBA); management (MSM).

Everest University, Department of Business Administration, Tampa, FL 33614-5899. Offers accounting (MBA); human resources (MBA); international business (MBA). Part-time and evening/weekend programs available. *Degree requirements:* For master's, thesis optional. *Entrance requirements:* For master's, GMAT or GRE General Test, minimum GPA of 3.0.

Everest University, Division of Business Administration, Orlando, FL 32810-5674. Offers MBA. Part-time and evening/weekend programs available. *Degree requirements:* For master's, thesis or alternative.

Everest University, Graduate Programs, Jacksonville, FL 32256. Offers business (MBA); criminal justice (MS).

Everest University, Program in Business Administration, Melbourne, FL 32935-6657. Offers MBA.

Everest University, Program in Business Administration, Tampa, FL 33619. Offers MBA. Part-time and evening/weekend programs available. Postbaccalaureate distance learning degree programs offered (minimal on-campus study). *Entrance requirements:* Additional exam requirements/recommendations for international students: Required—TOEFL (minimum score 550 paper-based).

Everest University, Program in Business Administration, Largo, FL 33770. Offers accounting (MBA); human resources management (MBA); international business (MBA). *Faculty research:* Management fads, learning styles, effective use of technology.

Everest University, Program in Business Administration, Orlando, FL 32819. Offers accounting (MBA); general management (MBA); human resources (MBA); international management (MBA).

Everest University, School of Business, Pompano Beach, FL 33062. Offers MBA. Part-time and evening/weekend programs available. *Entrance requirements:* For master's, minimum GPA of 3.0. *Faculty research:* E-learning.

Everglades University, Graduate Programs, Program in Business Administration, Boca Raton, FL 33431. Offers MBA. *Entrance requirements:* Additional exam requirements/recommendations for international students: Recommended—TOEFL (minimum score 500 paper-based). Electronic applications accepted.

Excelsior College, School of Business and Technology, Albany, NY 12203-5159. Offers business administration (MBA); cybersecurity (MS); cybersecurity management (MBA, Graduate Certificate); health care management (MBA); human performance technology (MBA); information security (MBA); leadership (MBA); social media management (MBA); technology management (MBA). Part-time and evening/weekend programs available. Postbaccalaureate distance learning degree programs offered (no on-campus study). *Faculty:* 36 part-time/adjunct (15 women). *Students:* 1,040 part-time (332 women); includes 411 minority (234 Black or African American, non-Hispanic/Latino; 3 American Indian or Alaska Native, non-Hispanic/Latino; 42 Asian, non-Hispanic/Latino; 104 Hispanic/Latino; 3 Native Hawaiian or other Pacific Islander, non-Hispanic/Latino; 25 Two or more races, non-Hispanic/Latino). Average age 41. In 2013, 75 master's awarded. *Application deadline:* Applications are processed on a rolling basis. Application fee: $100. *Expenses: Tuition:* Part-time $565 per credit. *Unit head:* Dr. Murray Block, Interim Dean, 888-647-2388. *Application contact:* Admissions, 888-647-2388 Ext. 133, Fax: 518-464-8777, E-mail: admissions@excelsior.edu.

Fairfield University, Charles F. Dolan School of Business, Fairfield, CT 06824-5195. Offers accounting (MBA, MS, CAS); accounting information systems (MBA, CAS); entrepreneurship (MBA, CAS); finance (MBA, MS, CAS); general management (MBA, CAS); human resource management (MBA, CAS); information systems and operations (MBA); information systems and operations management (CAS); marketing (MBA, CAS); taxation (MBA, CAS). *Accreditation:* AACSB. Part-time and evening/weekend programs available. *Faculty:* 18 full-time (9 women), 15 part-time/adjunct (4 women). *Students:* 94 full-time (45 women), 72 part-time (26 women); includes 49 minority (7 Black or African American, non-Hispanic/Latino; 33 Asian, non-Hispanic/Latino; 8 Hispanic/Latino; 1 Two or more races, non-Hispanic/Latino), 9 international. Average age 29. 116 applicants, 43% accepted, 26 enrolled. In 2013, 100 master's awarded. *Degree requirements:* For master's, capstone course. *Entrance requirements:* For master's, GMAT (minimum score 500), 2 letters of reference, resume, minimum GPA of 3.0. Additional exam requirements/recommendations for international students: Required—TOEFL (minimum score 550 paper-based; 80 iBT) or IELTS (minimum score 6.5). *Application deadline:* For fall admission, 5/15 for international students; for spring admission, 10/15 for international students. Applications are processed on a rolling basis. Application fee: $60. Electronic applications accepted. *Expenses:* Contact institution. *Financial support:* In 2013–14, 28 students received support. Scholarships/grants, unspecified assistantships, and merit-based one-time entrance scholarships available. Financial award applicants required to submit FAFSA. *Faculty research:* International finance, leadership and careers, ethics in accounting, emotions in consumer behavior, supply chain analysis, organizational leadership attributes, emotions in the workplace, real estate finance, effect of social media on stock prices. *Unit head:* Dr. Donald Gibson, Dean, 203-254-4070, Fax: 203-254-4105, E-mail: dgibson@fairfield.edu. *Application contact:* Marianne Gumpper, Director of Graduate and Continuing Studies Admission, 203-254-4184, Fax: 203-254-4073, E-mail: gradadmis@fairfield.edu.
Website: http://fairfield.edu/mba.

Fairleigh Dickinson University, College at Florham, Anthony J. Petrocelli College of Continuing Studies, School of Administrative Science, Program in Administrative Science, Madison, NJ 07940-1099. Offers MAS.

Fairleigh Dickinson University, College at Florham, Silberman College of Business, Madison, NJ 07940-1099. Offers EMBA, MBA, MS, Certificate, MA/MBA, MBA/MA. *Accreditation:* AACSB. Part-time and evening/weekend programs available.

Fairleigh Dickinson University, College at Florham, Silberman College of Business, Departments of Management, Marketing, and Entrepreneurial Studies, Program in Management, Madison, NJ 07940-1099. Offers evolving technology (Certificate); management (MBA); MBA/MA.

Fairleigh Dickinson University, College at Florham, Silberman College of Business, Executive MBA Programs, Executive MBA Program in Management, Madison, NJ 07940-1099. Offers EMBA.

Fairleigh Dickinson University, Metropolitan Campus, Anthony J. Petrocelli College of Continuing Studies, School of Administrative Science, Program in Administrative Science, Teaneck, NJ 07666-1914. Offers MAS, Certificate.

Fairleigh Dickinson University, Metropolitan Campus, Silberman College of Business, Teaneck, NJ 07666-1914. Offers EMBA, MBA, MS, Certificate, MBA/MA. *Accreditation:* AACSB. *Entrance requirements:* For master's, GMAT.

Fairleigh Dickinson University, Metropolitan Campus, Silberman College of Business, Departments of Management, Marketing, and Entrepreneurial Studies, Program in Management, Teaneck, NJ 07666-1914. Offers management (MBA); management information systems (Certificate). *Accreditation:* AACSB.

Fairmont State University, Program in Business Administration, Fairmont, WV 26554. Offers MBA. *Accreditation:* ACBSP. Part-time and evening/weekend programs available. *Faculty:* 8 part-time/adjunct (1 woman). *Students:* 14 full-time (6 women), 26 part-time (16 women); includes 4 minority (3 Black or African American, non-Hispanic/Latino; 1 Hispanic/Latino), 1 international. Average age 31. 32 applicants, 81% accepted, 20 enrolled. In 2013, 24 master's awarded. *Entrance requirements:* For master's, GRE, MAT, or GMAT, minimum overall undergraduate GPA of 2.75 or 3.0 on the last 60 hours. Additional exam requirements/recommendations for international students: Required—TOEFL. *Application deadline:* For fall admission, 5/1 for domestic and international students. Application fee: $40. *Expenses:* Tuition, state resident: full-time $6404; part-time $349 per credit hour. Tuition, nonresident: full-time $13,694; part-time $754 per credit hour. Part-time tuition and fees vary according to course load. *Financial support:* In 2013–14, 11 students received support. Federal Work-Study, scholarships/grants, and tuition waivers (full and partial) available. Financial award applicants required to submit FAFSA. *Unit head:* Dr. Edward Gailey, Director, 304-367-4728, Fax: 304-367-4613, E-mail: edward.gailey@fairmontstate.edu. *Application contact:* Jack Kirby, Director of Graduate Studies, 304-367-4101, E-mail: jack.kirby@fairmontstate.edu.
Website: http://www.fairmontstate.edu/graduatestudies/MBA_program.asp.

Fashion Institute of Technology, School of Graduate Studies, Program in Global Fashion Management, New York, NY 10001-5992. Offers MPS. Offered in collaboration with Hong Kong Polytechnic University and Institut Francais de la Mode. *Entrance requirements:* Additional exam requirements/recommendations for international students: Required—TOEFL (minimum score 550 paper-based). Electronic applications accepted.

See Display on next page and Close-Up on page 183.

Faulkner University, Harris College of Business and Executive Education, Montgomery, AL 36109-3398. Offers management (MSM).

Fayetteville State University, Graduate School, Program in Business Administration, Fayetteville, NC 28301-4298. Offers MBA. *Accreditation:* AACSB. *Faculty:* 23 full-time (6 women), 3 part-time/adjunct (1 woman). *Students:* 27 full-time (17 women), 53 part-time (32 women); includes 43 minority (31 Black or African American, non-Hispanic/Latino; 3 American Indian or Alaska Native, non-Hispanic/Latino; 5 Asian, non-Hispanic/Latino; 3 Hispanic/Latino; 1 Two or more races, non-Hispanic/Latino). Average age 33. 10 applicants, 100% accepted, 10 enrolled. In 2013, 24 master's awarded. *Entrance requirements:* For master's, GMAT. *Application deadline:* For fall admission, 4/15 for domestic students; for spring admission, 10/15 for domestic students. *Faculty research:* Business ethics, optimization and business simulation, consumer behavior, e-commerce and supply chain management, financial institutions. *Total annual research expenditures:* $15,000. *Unit head:* Dr. Assad Tavakoli, MBA Director/Assistant Dean, 910-672-1527, Fax: 910-672-1849, E-mail: atavakoli@uncfsu.edu. *Application contact:* Katrina Hoffman, Graduate Admissions Officer, 910-672-1374, Fax: 910-672-1470, E-mail: khoffma1@uncfsu.edu.

Felician College, Program in Business, Lodi, NJ 07644-2117. Offers innovation and entrepreneurship (MBA). Part-time and evening/weekend programs available. *Students:* 30 part-time (12 women); includes 9 minority (3 Black or African American, non-Hispanic/Latino; 2 Asian, non-Hispanic/Latino; 4 Hispanic/Latino). *Entrance requirements:* For master's, GMAT. *Application deadline:* Applications are processed on a rolling basis. *Expenses: Tuition:* Part-time $945 per credit. *Required fees:* $317.50 per semester. *Unit head:* Dr. Beth Castiglia, Dean, Division of Business and Management Services, 201-559-6140, E-mail: mctaggartp@felician.edu. *Application contact:* Nicole Vitale, Assistant Director of Graduate Admissions, 201-559-6077, Fax: 201-559-6138, E-mail: graduate@felician.edu.
Website: http://www2.felician.edu/school-of-business/business-management-sciences/graduate/mba-innovation-entrepreneurial-leadership.

Ferris State University, College of Business, Big Rapids, MI 49307. Offers business intelligence (MBA); design and innovation management (MBA); incident response (MBA); information security and intelligence (MS), including business intelligence, incident response, project management; management tools and concepts (MBA); project management (MBA). *Accreditation:* ACBSP. Part-time and evening/weekend programs available. Postbaccalaureate distance learning degree programs offered (minimal on-campus study). *Faculty:* 9 full-time (3 women), 6 part-time/adjunct (2 women). *Students:* 30 full-time (9 women), 101 part-time (51 women); includes 18 minority (5 Black or African American, non-Hispanic/Latino; 1 American Indian or Alaska Native, non-Hispanic/Latino; 2 Asian, non-Hispanic/Latino; 6 Hispanic/Latino; 4 Two or more races, non-Hispanic/Latino), 13 international. Average age 34. 72 applicants, 82% accepted, 31 enrolled. In 2013, 47 master's awarded. *Degree requirements:* For master's, comprehensive exam, thesis (for MS). *Entrance requirements:* For master's, GRE or GMAT (waived if GPA is 3.5 or better), minimum GPA of 3.0 in junior/senior level classes, 2.75 overall; statement of purpose; 3 letters of reference; resume. Additional exam requirements/recommendations for international students: Required—TOEFL (minimum score 500 paper-based; 67 iBT). *Application deadline:* For fall admission, 7/1 priority date for domestic students, 6/15 for international students; for winter admission, 11/1 priority date for domestic students, 10/15 for international students; for spring admission, 3/1 priority date for domestic students, 2/15 for international students. Applications are processed on a rolling basis. Application fee: $0 ($30 for international students). Electronic applications accepted. Application fee is waived when completed online. *Financial support:* Career-related internships or fieldwork, Federal Work-Study, scholarships/grants, and unspecified assistantships available. Support available to part-time students. Financial award application deadline: 3/15; financial award applicants required to submit FAFSA. *Faculty research:* Quality improvement, client/server end-user computing, security and digital forensics, performance metrics and sustainability. *Unit head:* Dr. David Nicol, College of Business Dean, 231-591-2168, Fax: 231-591-3521, E-mail: davidnicol@ferris.edu. *Application contact:* Shannon Yost, Department Secretary, 231-591-2168, Fax: 231-591-3521, E-mail: yosts@ferris.edu.
Website: http://cbgp.ferris.edu/.

Fitchburg State University, Division of Graduate and Continuing Education, Program in Business Administration, Fitchburg, MA 01420-2697. Offers accounting (MBA); human resource management (MBA); management (MBA). Part-time and evening/weekend programs available. Postbaccalaureate distance learning degree programs offered (no on-campus study). *Entrance requirements:* Additional exam requirements/recommendations for international students: Required—TOEFL (minimum score 550 paper-based; 79 iBT). Electronic applications accepted.

Florida Agricultural and Mechanical University, Division of Graduate Studies, Research, and Continuing Education, School of Business and Industry, Tallahassee, FL 32307-3200. Offers accounting (MBA); finance (MBA); management information systems (MBA); marketing (MBA). *Accreditation:* ACBSP. *Degree requirements:* For master's, residency. *Entrance requirements:* For master's, GMAT, minimum GPA of 3.0.

Florida Atlantic University, College of Business, Program in Music Business Administration, Boca Raton, FL 33431-0991. Offers MS. *Expenses:* Tuition, state resident: full-time $6660; part-time $370 per credit hour. Tuition, nonresident: full-time $18,450; part-time $1025 per credit hour. Tuition and fees vary according to course load. *Unit head:* Dr. Daniel Gropper, Dean, 561-297-3629, Fax: 561-297-3686, E-mail: vhale4@fau.edu. *Application contact:* Dr. Marcy Krugel, Graduate Adviser, 561-297-3940, Fax: 561-297-0801, E-mail: krugel@fau.edu.

Florida Gulf Coast University, Lutgert College of Business, Master of Business Administration Program, Fort Myers, FL 33965-6565. Offers MBA. *Accreditation:* AACSB. Part-time and evening/weekend programs available. *Entrance requirements:* For master's, GMAT, minimum GPA of 3.0. Additional exam requirements/recommendations for international students: Required—TOEFL (minimum score 550 paper-based). Electronic applications accepted. *Faculty research:* Fraud in audits,

Business Administration and Management—General

production planning in cell manufacturing systems, collaborative learning in distance courses, characteristics of minority and women-owned businesses.

Florida Institute of Technology, Graduate Programs, Extended Studies Division, Melbourne, FL 32901-6975. Offers acquisition and contract management (MS); aerospace engineering (MS); business administration (MBA, DBA); computer information systems (MS); computer science (MS); electrical engineering (MS); engineering management (MS); human resources management (MS); logistics management (MS), including humanitarian and disaster relief logistics; management (MS), including acquisition and contract management, e-business, human resources management, information systems, logistics management, management, transportation management; material acquisition management (MS); mechanical engineering (MS); operations research (MS); project management (MS), including information systems, operations research; public administration (MPA); quality management (MS); software engineering (MS); space systems (MS); space systems management (MS); supply chain management (MS); systems management (MS), including information systems, operations research; technology management (MS). Part-time and evening/weekend programs available. Postbaccalaureate distance learning degree programs offered (no on-campus study). *Faculty:* 8 full-time (1 woman), 96 part-time/adjunct (25 women). *Students:* 94 full-time (46 women), 912 part-time (397 women); includes 436 minority (290 Black or African American, non-Hispanic/Latino; 18 American Indian or Alaska Native, non-Hispanic/Latino; 38 Asian, non-Hispanic/Latino; 62 Hispanic/Latino; 2 Native Hawaiian or other Pacific Islander, non-Hispanic/Latino; 26 Two or more races, non-Hispanic/Latino), 9 international. Average age 37. 591 applicants, 44% accepted, 220 enrolled. In 2013, 522 master's awarded. *Degree requirements:* For master's, comprehensive exam (for some programs), capstone course. *Entrance requirements:* For master's, GMAT or resume showing 8 years of supervised experience, minimum GPA of 3.0, 2 letters of recommendation, resume. Additional exam requirements/recommendations for international students: Required—TOEFL (minimum score 550 paper-based; 79 iBT). *Application deadline:* For fall admission, 4/1 for international students; for spring admission, 9/30 for international students. Applications are processed on a rolling basis. Electronic applications accepted. *Expenses:* Contact institution. *Financial support:* Application deadline: 3/1; applicants required to submit FAFSA. *Unit head:* Dr. Theodore R. Richardson, III, Senior Associate Dean, 321-674-8123, Fax: 321-674-7597, E-mail: trichardson@fit.edu. *Application contact:* Carolyn Farrior, Director of Graduate Admissions, Online Learning and Off-Campus Programs, 321-674-7118, Fax: 321-674-8216, E-mail: cfarrior@fit.edu.
Website: http://es.fit.edu.

Florida Institute of Technology, Graduate Programs, Nathan M. Bisk College of Business, Online Programs, Melbourne, FL 32901-6975. Offers accounting (MBA); accounting and finance (MBA); business administration (MBA); finance (MBA); healthcare management (MBA); information assurance and cybersecurity (MS); information technology (MS); information technology cybersecurity (MS); information technology management (MBA); international business (MBA); Internet marketing (MBA); management (MBA); marketing (MBA); project management (MBA); supply chain management (MS). Part-time and evening/weekend programs available. Postbaccalaureate distance learning degree programs offered (no on-campus study). *Faculty:* 3 full-time (1 woman), 41 part-time/adjunct (13 women). *Students:* 6 full-time (1 woman), 1,121 part-time (530 women); includes 424 minority (276 Black or African American, non-Hispanic/Latino; 10 American Indian or Alaska Native, non-Hispanic/Latino; 45 Asian, non-Hispanic/Latino; 88 Hispanic/Latino; 5 Native Hawaiian or other Pacific Islander, non-Hispanic/Latino), 32 international. Average age 36. 348 applicants, 42% accepted, 146 enrolled. In 2013, 475 master's awarded. *Entrance requirements:* For master's, GMAT or resume showing 8 years of supervised experience, 2 letters of recommendation, resume, competency in math past college algebra. Additional exam

requirements/recommendations for international students: Required—TOEFL (minimum score 550 paper-based; 79 iBT). *Application deadline:* For fall admission, 4/1 for international students; for spring admission, 9/30 for international students. Applications are processed on a rolling basis. Electronic applications accepted. *Expenses:* Contact institution. *Financial support:* Available to part-time students. Application deadline: 3/1; applicants required to submit FAFSA. *Unit head:* Brian Ehrlich, Associate Vice President/Director of Online Learning, 321-674-8202, E-mail: behrlich@fit.edu. *Application contact:* Carolyn Farrior, Director of Graduate Admissions, Online Learning and Off-Campus Programs, 321-674-7118.
Website: http://online.fit.edu.

Florida International University, Alvah H. Chapman, Jr. Graduate School of Business, Program in Business Administration, Miami, FL 33199. Offers EMBA, IMBA, MBA, PMBA, PhD. *Accreditation:* AACSB. Part-time and evening/weekend programs available. *Degree requirements:* For doctorate, comprehensive exam, thesis/dissertation. *Entrance requirements:* For master's, GMAT or GRE (depending on program), minimum GPA of 3.0 (upper-level coursework); for doctorate, GMAT or GRE, minimum GPA of 3.0 in post-secondary education; letter of intent; 3 letters of recommendation; resume. Additional exam requirements/recommendations for international students: Required—TOEFL (minimum score 550 paper-based; 80 iBT) or IELTS (minimum score 6.5). Electronic applications accepted. *Expenses:* Contact institution. *Faculty research:* Taxation, financial and managerial accounting, human resource management, multinational corporations, strategy, international business, auditing, artificial intelligence, international banking, investments, entrepreneurship.

Florida Memorial University, School of Business, Miami-Dade, FL 33054. Offers MBA. *Accreditation:* ACBSP. Part-time programs available. *Entrance requirements:* For master's, GMAT, 3 letters of recommendation.

Florida National University, Program in Business Administration, Hialeah, FL 33012. Offers finance (MBA); general management (MBA); marketing (MBA). Postbaccalaureate distance learning degree programs offered (no on-campus study). *Degree requirements:* For master's, capstone.

Florida Southern College, Program in Business Administration, Lakeland, FL 33801-5698. Offers MBA. Part-time and evening/weekend programs available. *Entrance requirements:* For master's, GMAT or GRE General Test, 3 letters of reference, resume, personal statement. Additional exam requirements/recommendations for international students: Required—TOEFL (minimum score 550 paper-based). *Expenses:* Contact institution.

Florida State University, The Graduate School, College of Business, Tallahassee, FL 32306-1110. Offers accounting (M Acc), including accounting information services, assurance services, corporate accounting, taxation; business administration (MBA, PhD), including accounting (PhD), finance (PhD), management information systems (PhD), marketing (PhD), organizational behavior and human resources (PhD), risk management and insurance (PhD), strategic management (PhD); finance (MS); insurance (MSM); management information systems (MS); marketing (MS); JD/MBA; MSW/MBA. *Accreditation:* AACSB. Part-time programs available. Postbaccalaureate distance learning degree programs offered (no on-campus study). *Faculty:* 102 full-time (31 women), 5 part-time/adjunct (0 women). *Students:* 280 full-time (117 women), 278 part-time (88 women); includes 127 minority (26 Black or African American, non-Hispanic/Latino; 7 American Indian or Alaska Native, non-Hispanic/Latino; 44 Asian, non-Hispanic/Latino; 50 Hispanic/Latino). Average age 30. 630 applicants, 28% accepted, 103 enrolled. In 2013, 265 master's, 11 doctorates awarded. Terminal master's awarded for partial completion of doctoral program. *Degree requirements:* For doctorate, comprehensive exam, thesis/dissertation. *Entrance requirements:* For master's, GMAT, work experience (MBA, MS), minimum GPA of 3.0, letters of

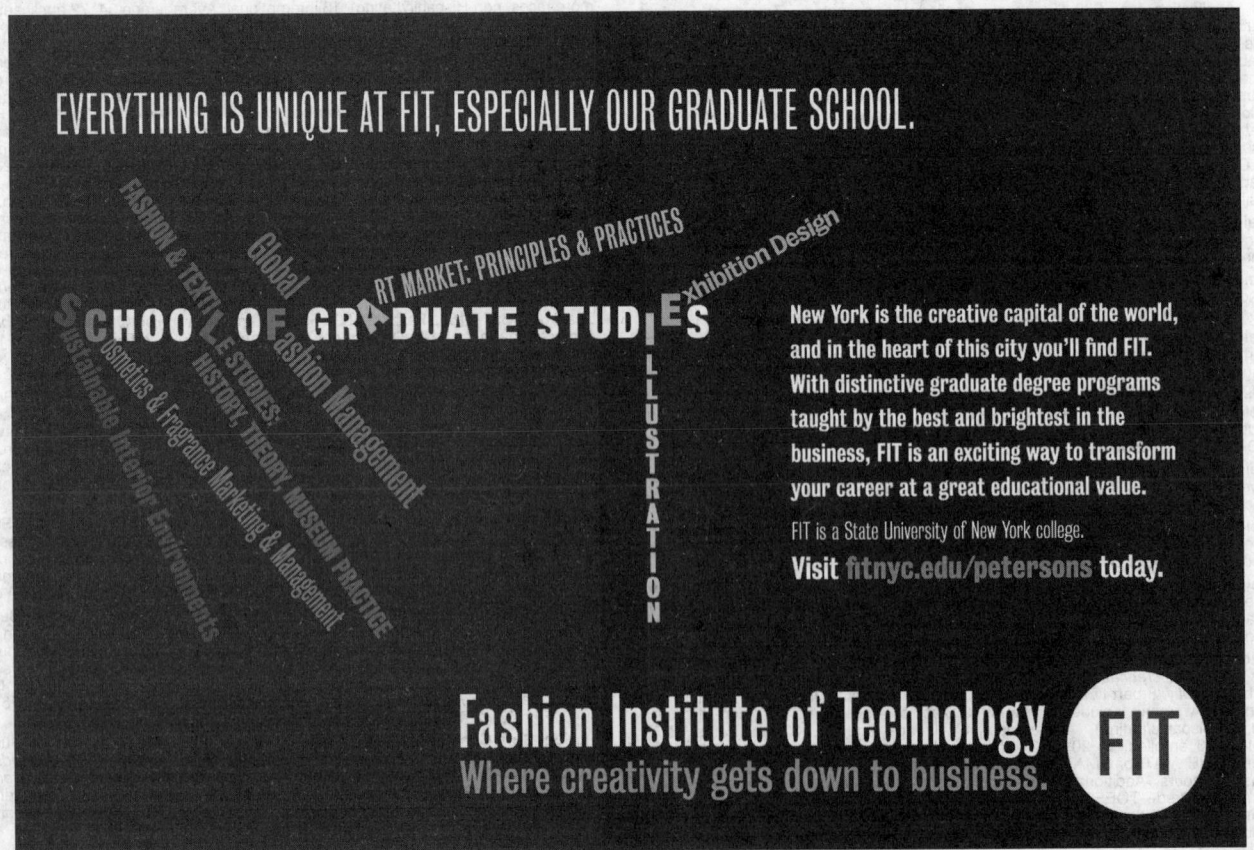

recommendation; for doctorate, GMAT, minimum graduate GPA of 3.5, letters of recommendation. Additional exam requirements/recommendations for international students: Required—TOEFL (minimum score 600 paper-based; 100 iBT); Recommended—IELTS (minimum score 6.5). *Application deadline:* For fall admission, 6/1 for domestic students, 5/1 for international students; for spring admission, 10/1 for domestic students, 9/1 for international students. Applications are processed on a rolling basis. Application fee: $30. Electronic applications accepted. *Expenses:* Tuition, state resident: part-time $403.51 per credit hour. Tuition, nonresident: part-time $1004.85 per credit hour. *Required fees:* $75.81 per credit hour. One-time fee: $20 part-time. Tuition and fees vary according to course load, campus/location and student level. *Financial support:* In 2013–14, 92 students received support, including 10 fellowships with full tuition reimbursements available (averaging $1,500 per year), 20 research assistantships with full tuition reimbursements available (averaging $20,000 per year), 35 teaching assistantships with full tuition reimbursements available (averaging $20,000 per year); career-related internships or fieldwork, scholarships/grants, health care benefits, and unspecified assistantships also available. Financial award application deadline: 1/1. *Unit head:* Dr. Caryn Beck-Dudley, Dean, 850-644-3090, Fax: 850-644-0915. *Application contact:* Lisa Beverly, Director, Graduate Programs Admissions, 850-644-6458, Fax: 850-644-0588, E-mail: lbeverly@cob.fsu.edu. Website: http://www.cob.fsu.edu/.

Fontbonne University, Graduate Programs, College of Global Business and Professional Studies, Options Program in Business Administration, St. Louis, MO 63105-3098. Offers MBA. *Accreditation:* ACBSP. Evening/weekend programs available. *Degree requirements:* For master's, applied management project. *Entrance requirements:* For master's, minimum GPA of 2.5. *Expenses:* Contact institution.

Fontbonne University, Graduate Programs, College of Global Business and Professional Studies, Options Program in Management, St. Louis, MO 63105-3098. Offers MM. *Accreditation:* ACBSP. Part-time and evening/weekend programs available. Postbaccalaureate distance learning degree programs offered. *Expenses:* Contact institution.

Fontbonne University, Graduate Programs, College of Global Business and Professional Studies, Program in Business Administration, St. Louis, MO 63105-3098. Offers MBA. *Accreditation:* ACBSP. Part-time and evening/weekend programs available. *Entrance requirements:* For master's, minimum GPA of 2.5. Additional exam requirements/recommendations for international students: Required—TOEFL (minimum score 450 paper-based; 45 iBT). *Expenses: Tuition:* Full-time $11,646; part-time $647 per credit hour. *Required fees:* $324; $18 per credit hour. Tuition and fees vary according to course load and program.

Fordham University, Graduate School of Business, New York, NY 10023. Offers accounting (MBA); communications and media management (MBA); executive business administration (EMBA); finance (MBA, MS); information systems (MBA, MS); management systems (MBA); marketing (MBA); media management (MS); taxation (MS); taxation and accounting (MTA); JD/MBA; MBA/MIM; MS/MBA. MBA/MIM offered jointly with Thunderbird School of Global Management. *Accreditation:* AACSB. Part-time and evening/weekend programs available. *Entrance requirements:* For master's, GMAT, 2 letters of recommendation, resume. Additional exam requirements/recommendations for international students: Required—TOEFL (minimum score 600 paper-based; 100 iBT). Electronic applications accepted. *Expenses:* Contact institution.

Fort Hays State University, Graduate School, College of Business and Leadership, Department of Management and Marketing, Hays, KS 67601-4099. Offers management (MBA). *Degree requirements:* For master's, thesis optional. *Entrance requirements:* For master's, GMAT. Additional exam requirements/recommendations for international students: Required—TOEFL (minimum score 550 paper-based). Electronic applications accepted. *Faculty research:* Organizational behavior and performance appraisal, data processing, international marketing.

Framingham State University, Continuing Education, Program in Business Administration, Framingham, MA 01701-9101. Offers MBA. Part-time and evening/weekend programs available. *Entrance requirements:* For master's, GMAT, GRE, or MAT.

Franciscan University of Steubenville, Graduate Programs, Department of Business, Steubenville, OH 43952-1763. Offers MBA. Part-time and evening/weekend programs available. *Degree requirements:* For master's, research paper. *Entrance requirements:* For master's, GMAT, minimum undergraduate GPA of 2.5. *Expenses:* Contact institution.

Francis Marion University, Graduate Programs, School of Business, Florence, SC 29502-0547. Offers business (MBA); health management (MBA). *Accreditation:* AACSB. Part-time and evening/weekend programs available. *Faculty:* 23 full-time (9 women). *Students:* 3 full-time (0 women), 26 part-time (13 women); includes 8 minority (5 Black or African American, non-Hispanic/Latino; 2 Asian, non-Hispanic/Latino; 1 Hispanic/Latino), 1 international. Average age 30. 18 applicants, 44% accepted, 7 enrolled. In 2013, 12 master's awarded. *Degree requirements:* For master's, comprehensive exam. *Entrance requirements:* For master's, GMAT. *Application deadline:* For fall admission, 3/15 for domestic students; for spring admission, 10/15 for domestic students. Applications are processed on a rolling basis. Application fee: $33. *Expenses:* Tuition, state resident: full-time $9184; part-time $459.20 per credit hour. Tuition, nonresident: full-time $18,368; part-time $918.40 per credit hour. *Required fees:* $13.50 per credit hour. $92 per semester. Tuition and fees vary according to program. *Financial support:* Available to part-time students. Application deadline: 3/1; applicants required to submit FAFSA. *Faculty research:* Ethics, directions of MBA, international business, regional economics, environmental issues. *Unit head:* Dr. M. Barry O'Brien, Dean, 843-661-1419, Fax: 843-661-1432, E-mail: mbobrien@fmarion.edu. *Application contact:* Rannie Gamble, Administrative Manager, 843-661-1286, Fax: 843-661-4688, E-mail: rgamble@fmarion.edu. Website: http://www.fmarion.edu/academics/schoolofbusiness.

Franklin Pierce University, Graduate Studies, Rindge, NH 03461-0060. Offers curriculum and instruction (M Ed); emerging network technologies (Graduate Certificate); energy and sustainability studies (MBA); health administration (MBA, Graduate Certificate); human resource management (MBA, Graduate Certificate); information technology (MBA); information technology management (MS); leadership (MBA, DA); nursing (MS); physical therapy (DPT); physician assistant studies (MPAS); special education (M Ed); sports management (MBA). *Accreditation:* APTA. Part-time programs available. Postbaccalaureate distance learning degree programs offered (no on-campus study). *Degree requirements:* For master's, concentrated original research projects; student teaching; fieldwork and/or internship; leadership project; PRAXIS I and II (for M Ed); for doctorate, concentrated original research projects, clinical fieldwork and/or internship, leadership project. *Entrance requirements:* For master's, minimum GPA of 2.5, 3 letters of recommendation; competencies in accounting, economics, statistics, and computer skills through life experience or undergraduate coursework (for MBA); certification/e-portfolio, minimum C grade in all education courses (for M Ed); license to practice as RN (for MS in nursing); for doctorate, GRE, BA/BS, 3 letters of recommendation, personal mission statement, interview, writing sample, minimum cumulative GPA of 2.8, master's degree (for DA); 80 hours of observation/work in PT

settings, completion of anatomy, chemistry, physics, and statistics, minimum GPA of 3.0 (for DPT). Additional exam requirements/recommendations for international students: Required—TOEFL (minimum score 550 paper-based; 61 iBT). Electronic applications accepted. *Faculty research:* Evidence-based practice in sports physical therapy, human resource management in economic crisis, leadership in nursing, innovation in sports facility management, differentiated learning and understanding by design.

Franklin University, MBA Program, Columbus, OH 43215-5399. Offers MBA. Part-time and evening/weekend programs available. Postbaccalaureate distance learning degree programs offered (no on-campus study). *Entrance requirements:* For master's, minimum undergraduate GPA of 2.75. Additional exam requirements/recommendations for international students: Required—TOEFL (minimum score 550 paper-based). Electronic applications accepted.

Freed-Hardeman University, Program in Business Administration, Henderson, TN 38340-2399. Offers accounting (MBA); corporate responsibility (MBA); leadership (MBA). *Accreditation:* ACBSP. Part-time and evening/weekend programs available. Postbaccalaureate distance learning degree programs offered (no on-campus study). *Entrance requirements:* For master's, GMAT. Additional exam requirements/recommendations for international students: Required—TOEFL (minimum score 500 paper-based).

Fresno Pacific University, Graduate Programs, Program in Leadership Studies, Fresno, CA 93702-4709. Offers MA. Part-time and evening/weekend programs available. *Faculty:* 2 full-time. *Students:* 2 full-time (1 woman), 59 part-time (40 women); includes 25 minority (3 Black or African American, non-Hispanic/Latino; 1 American Indian or Alaska Native, non-Hispanic/Latino; 21 Hispanic/Latino). Average age 38. In 2013, 23 master's awarded. *Degree requirements:* For master's, thesis. *Entrance requirements:* For master's, MAT, GRE or GMAT, interview, 2 writing samples. Additional exam requirements/recommendations for international students: Required—TOEFL (minimum score 550 paper-based). *Application deadline:* For fall admission, 7/15 for domestic and international students; for spring admission, 11/15 for domestic and international students. Applications are processed on a rolling basis. Application fee: $90. Electronic applications accepted. *Expenses:* Contact institution. *Financial support:* Scholarships/grants and tuition waivers (full and partial) available. Support available to part-time students. Financial award applicants required to submit FAFSA. *Faculty research:* Ethics, servant leadership, communication, creative problem solving. *Unit head:* Susan Cox, Program Director, 559-453-2026, E-mail: susan.cox@fresno.edu. *Application contact:* Amanda Krum-Stovall, Director of Graduate Admissions, 559-453-2016, E-mail: amanda.krum-stovall@fresno.edu. Website: http://grad.fresno.edu/programs/master-arts-leadership-studies.

Friends University, Graduate School, Wichita, KS 67213. Offers business law (MBL); Christian ministry (MACM); family therapy (MSFT); global (MBA), including accounting, business law, change management, health care leadership, management information systems, supply chain management and logistics; health care leadership (MHCL); management information systems (MMIS); operations management (MSOM); professional (MBA), including accounting, business law, change management, health care leadership, management information systems, supply chain management and logistics; teaching (MAT). Part-time and evening/weekend programs available. Postbaccalaureate distance learning degree programs offered (no on-campus study). *Faculty:* 18 full-time (8 women), 62 part-time/adjunct (28 women). *Students:* 161 full-time (111 women), 408 part-time (258 women); includes 157 minority (68 Black or African American, non-Hispanic/Latino; 7 American Indian or Alaska Native, non-Hispanic/Latino; 28 Asian, non-Hispanic/Latino; 18 Hispanic/Latino; 1 Native Hawaiian or other Pacific Islander, non-Hispanic/Latino; 35 Two or more races, non-Hispanic/Latino). Average age 36. 371 applicants, 90% accepted, 178 enrolled. In 2013, 432 master's awarded. *Degree requirements:* For master's, research project. *Entrance requirements:* For master's, bachelor's degree from accredited institution, official transcripts, interview with program director, letter(s) of recommendation. Additional exam requirements/recommendations for international students: Required—TOEFL (minimum score 560 paper-based). *Application deadline:* Applications are processed on a rolling basis. Application fee: $35 ($50 for international students). Electronic applications accepted. *Expenses: Tuition:* Part-time $631 per credit hour. Tuition and fees vary according to program. *Financial support:* In 2013–14, 30 students received support. Applicants required to submit FAFSA. *Unit head:* Dr. David Hofmeister, Dean of the Graduate School, 800-794-6945 Ext. 5858, Fax: 316-295-5040, E-mail: david_hofmeister@friends.edu. *Application contact:* Rachel Steiner, Manager, Graduate Recruiting Services, 800-794-6945, Fax: 316-295-5872, E-mail: rachel_steiner@friends.edu. Website: http://www.friends.edu/.

Frostburg State University, Graduate School, College of Business, Frostburg, MD 21532-1099. Offers MBA. *Accreditation:* AACSB. Part-time and evening/weekend programs available. *Faculty:* 13 full-time (5 women), 3 part-time/adjunct (0 women). *Students:* 62 full-time (23 women), 245 part-time (127 women); includes 53 minority (27 Black or African American, non-Hispanic/Latino; 1 American Indian or Alaska Native, non-Hispanic/Latino; 14 Asian, non-Hispanic/Latino; 6 Hispanic/Latino; 1 Native Hawaiian or other Pacific Islander, non-Hispanic/Latino; 4 Two or more races, non-Hispanic/Latino), 14 international. Average age 33. 116 applicants, 68% accepted, 46 enrolled. In 2013, 68 master's awarded. *Entrance requirements:* For master's, GMAT. Additional exam requirements/recommendations for international students: Required—TOEFL. *Application deadline:* For fall admission, 7/15 priority date for domestic students. Applications are processed on a rolling basis. Application fee: $30. Electronic applications accepted. *Expenses: Tuition, area resident:* Part-time $340 per credit hour. Tuition, state resident: part-time $340 per credit hour. Tuition, nonresident: part-time $437 per credit hour. *Financial support:* In 2013–14, 8 research assistantships with full tuition reimbursements (averaging $5,000 per year) were awarded; career-related internships or fieldwork and Federal Work-Study also available. Financial award application deadline: 4/1; financial award applicants required to submit FAFSA. *Faculty research:* Cooperative teaching methods, strategic change processes, political marketing. *Unit head:* Dr. Ahmad Tootoonchi, Interim Dean, 301-687-4019, E-mail: tootoonchi@frostburg.edu. *Application contact:* Vickie Mazer, Director, Graduate Services, 301-687-7053, Fax: 301-687-4597, E-mail: vmmazer@frostburg.edu. Website: http://www.frostburg.edu/colleges/cob/.

Full Sail University, Entertainment Business Master of Science Program - Online, Winter Park, FL 32792-7437. Offers MS. Postbaccalaureate distance learning degree programs offered. *Entrance requirements:* Additional exam requirements/recommendations for international students: Required—TOEFL (minimum score 550 paper-based; 79 iBT).

Gannon University, School of Graduate Studies, College of Engineering and Business, Dahlkemper School of Business, Program in Business Administration, Erie, PA 16541-0001. Offers business administration (MBA); finance (MBA); human resources management (MBA); marketing (MBA). *Accreditation:* ACBSP. Part-time and evening/weekend programs available. Postbaccalaureate distance learning degree programs offered (no on-campus study). *Students:* 44 full-time (20 women), 87 part-time (30 women); includes 7 minority (4 Black or African American, non-Hispanic/Latino; 1 Asian, non-Hispanic/Latino; 2 Hispanic/Latino), 22 international. Average age 28. 279 applicants, 84% accepted, 59 enrolled. In 2013, 40 master's awarded. *Degree*

requirements: For master's, comprehensive exam, thesis. *Entrance requirements:* For master's, GMAT, resume, transcripts, 3 letters of recommendation. Additional exam requirements/recommendations for international students: Required—TOEFL (minimum score 79 iBT). *Application deadline:* Applications are processed on a rolling basis. Application fee: $25. Electronic applications accepted. *Expenses: Tuition:* Full-time $15,930; part-time $885 per credit. *Required fees:* $430; $18 per credit. Tuition and fees vary according to course load, degree level and program. *Financial support:* Administrative assistantships available. Financial award application deadline: 7/1; financial award applicants required to submit FAFSA. *Unit head:* Dr. Donna Mottilla, Director, 814-871-7780, E-mail: mottilla001@gannon.edu. *Application contact:* Kara Morgan, Director of Graduate Admissions, 814-871-5831, Fax: 814-871-5827, E-mail: graduate@gannon.edu.

Gardner-Webb University, Graduate School of Business, Boiling Springs, NC 28017. Offers IMBA, M Acc, MBA. *Accreditation:* ACBSP. Part-time and evening/weekend programs available. Postbaccalaureate distance learning degree programs offered (no on-campus study). *Faculty:* 15 full-time (2 women), 1 (woman) part-time/adjunct. *Students:* 27 full-time (7 women), 352 part-time (216 women); includes 103 minority (84 Black or African American, non-Hispanic/Latino; 8 Asian, non-Hispanic/Latino; 11 Hispanic/Latino), 1 international. Average age 31. 332 applicants, 67% accepted, 183 enrolled. In 2013, 145 master's awarded. *Entrance requirements:* For master's, GMAT, GRE, 2 semesters of course work each in economics, statistics, and accounting. Additional exam requirements/recommendations for international students: Required—TOEFL (minimum score 500 paper-based; 61 iBT). *Application deadline:* For spring admission, 1/15 for domestic students. Applications are processed on a rolling basis. Application fee: $40. Electronic applications accepted. *Expenses:* Contact institution. *Financial support:* In 2013–14, 23 students received support. Unspecified assistantships available. Support available to part-time students. Financial award applicants required to submit FAFSA. *Unit head:* Dr. Anthony Negbenebor, Dean, 704-406-4622, E-mail: anegbenebor@gardner-webb.edu. *Application contact:* Mischia Taylor, Director of Admissions, 877-498-4723, Fax: 704-406-3895, E-mail: mataylor@gardner-webb.edu.
Website: http://gardner-webb.edu/academics/academic-publications/graduate-catalog/the-graduate-school-of-business/index.

Geneva College, Program in Business Administration, Beaver Falls, PA 15010-3599. Offers business administration (MBA); finance (MBA); marketing (MBA); operations (MBA). *Accreditation:* ACBSP. Part-time and evening/weekend programs available. *Faculty:* 5 full-time (1 woman), 1 part-time/adjunct (0 women). *Students:* 1 (woman) full-time, 19 part-time (8 women); includes 3 minority (1 Black or African American, non-Hispanic/Latino; 2 Asian, non-Hispanic/Latino). Average age 33. 9 applicants, 100% accepted, 6 enrolled. In 2013, 9 master's awarded. *Degree requirements:* For master's, 36 credit hours of course work (30 of which are required of all students). *Entrance requirements:* For master's, GMAT (if college GPA less than 2.5), undergraduate transcript, 2 letters of recommendation, resume, goals statement. Additional exam requirements/recommendations for international students: Required—TOEFL. *Application deadline:* For fall admission, 3/1 priority date for domestic students; for spring admission, 11/1 priority date for domestic students. Applications are processed on a rolling basis. Electronic applications accepted. *Expenses:* Contact institution. *Financial support:* In 2013–14, 1 student received support. Scholarships/grants available. Financial award application deadline: 8/1; financial award applicants required to submit FAFSA. *Unit head:* Dr. Gary Vander Plaats, Director of the MBA Program, 724-847-6619, E-mail: gpvander@geneva.edu. *Application contact:* Marina Frazier, Director of Graduate Enrollment, 724-847-6697, E-mail: mba@geneva.edu.
Website: http://www.geneva.edu/page/masters_business.

George Fox University, College of Business, Newberg, OR 97132-2697. Offers finance (MBA); management (DBA); management and leadership (MBA); marketing (DBA); organizational strategy (MBA); strategic human resource management (MBA). MBA offered in Newberg, OR and in Portland, OR. *Accreditation:* ACBSP. Part-time and evening/weekend programs available. Postbaccalaureate distance learning degree programs offered (minimal on-campus study). *Faculty:* 8 full-time (2 women), 5 part-time/adjunct (2 women). *Students:* 31 full-time (15 women), 194 part-time (76 women); includes 21 minority (6 Black or African American, non-Hispanic/Latino; 4 American Indian or Alaska Native, non-Hispanic/Latino; 6 Asian, non-Hispanic/Latino; 3 Hispanic/Latino; 2 Two or more races, non-Hispanic/Latino), 15 international. Average age 39. 98 applicants, 79% accepted, 62 enrolled. In 2013, 98 master's, 2 doctorates awarded. *Degree requirements:* For master's, capstone project; for doctorate, credit-applied research project. *Entrance requirements:* For master's, resume (5 years of professional experience); 3 professional references; interview; financial e-learning course, official transcripts; for doctorate, GRE or GMAT, resume; personal mission statement; academic research writing sample; official transcript from each college/university attended; three professional references. Additional exam requirements/recommendations for international students: Required—TOEFL (minimum score 577 paper-based; 90 iBT) or IELTS (minimum score 7). *Application deadline:* For fall admission, 8/1 for domestic and international students; for spring admission, 12/1 for domestic and international students. Applications are processed on a rolling basis. Application fee: $40. Electronic applications accepted. *Expenses:* Contact institution. *Financial support:* Applicants required to submit FAFSA. *Unit head:* Dr. Chris Meade, Professor/Dean, 800-631-0921. *Application contact:* Ty Sohlman, Admissions Counselor, 800-493-4937, Fax: 503-554-6111, E-mail: business@georgefox.edu.
Website: http://www.georgefox.edu/business/index.html.

George Mason University, School of Business, Program in Business Administration, Fairfax, VA 22030. Offers MBA. *Accreditation:* AACSB. *Faculty:* 73 full-time (20 women), 41 part-time/adjunct (12 women). *Students:* 196 full-time (73 women), 212 part-time (68 women); includes 93 minority (30 Black or African American, non-Hispanic/Latino; 2 American Indian or Alaska Native, non-Hispanic/Latino; 32 Asian, non-Hispanic/Latino; 21 Hispanic/Latino; 3 Native Hawaiian or other Pacific Islander, non-Hispanic/Latino; 5 Two or more races, non-Hispanic/Latino), 22 international. Average age 36. 354 applicants, 42% accepted, 87 enrolled. In 2013, 152 master's awarded. *Entrance requirements:* For master's, GMAT/GRE, resume; 2 official copies of transcripts; 2 professional letters of recommendation; personal career goals statement; professional essay; interview. Additional exam requirements/recommendations for international students: Required—TOEFL (minimum score 570 paper-based; 88 iBT), IELTS (minimum score 6.5), PTE. *Application deadline:* For fall admission, 1/15 priority date for domestic students, 3/15 priority date for international students; for spring admission, 10/15 priority date for domestic students. Application fee: $65 ($80 for international students). Electronic applications accepted. *Expenses:* Contact institution. *Financial support:* In 2013–14, 15 students received support, including 11 research assistantships with full and partial tuition reimbursements available (averaging $6,364 per year), 8 teaching assistantships with full and partial tuition reimbursements available (averaging $8,481 per year); career-related internships or fieldwork, Federal Work-Study, scholarships/grants, unspecified assistantships, and health care benefits (for full-time research or teaching assistantship recipients) also available. Support available to part-time students. Financial award application deadline: 3/1; financial award applicants required to submit FAFSA. *Faculty research:* Electronic commerce, marketing information systems, group decision-making, corporate governance, risk management. *Unit head:* Rebecca M. Diemer, Associate Director, 703-993-2216, Fax: 703-993-1778, E-mail: rdiemer@gmu.edu. *Application contact:* Nancy Doernhoefer, MBA Program Coordinator, 703-993-4128, Fax: 703-993-1778, E-mail: ndoernho@gmu.edu.
Website: http://business.gmu.edu/mba-programs/.

Georgetown University, Graduate School of Arts and Sciences, McDonough School of Business, Washington, DC 20057. Offers business administration (IEMBA, MBA). *Accreditation:* AACSB. *Entrance requirements:* For master's, GMAT. Additional exam requirements/recommendations for international students: Required—TOEFL. *Expenses:* Contact institution.

The George Washington University, School of Business, Washington, DC 20052. Offers M Accy, MBA, MS, MSF, MSIST, MTA, PMBA, PhD, Certificate, Professional Certificate, JD/MBA, MBA/MA. PMBA program also offered in Alexandria and Ashburn, VA. Part-time and evening/weekend programs available. Postbaccalaureate distance learning degree programs offered (no on-campus study). *Faculty:* 130 full-time (37 women). *Students:* 1,176 full-time (598 women), 916 part-time (428 women); includes 556 minority (253 Black or African American, non-Hispanic/Latino; 7 American Indian or Alaska Native, non-Hispanic/Latino; 169 Asian, non-Hispanic/Latino; 100 Hispanic/Latino; 2 Native Hawaiian or other Pacific Islander, non-Hispanic/Latino; 25 Two or more races, non-Hispanic/Latino), 634 international. Average age 32. 2,776 applicants, 57% accepted, 714 enrolled. In 2013, 849 master's, 11 doctorates awarded. *Degree requirements:* For doctorate, thesis/dissertation. *Entrance requirements:* For doctorate, GMAT or GRE. Additional exam requirements/recommendations for international students: Required—TOEFL. *Application deadline:* For fall admission, 4/1 priority date for domestic students; for spring admission, 10/1 for domestic students. Applications are processed on a rolling basis. Application fee: $75. Electronic applications accepted. *Financial support:* In 2013–14, 194 students received support. Fellowships with tuition reimbursements available, teaching assistantships with tuition reimbursements available, career-related internships or fieldwork, Federal Work-Study, institutionally sponsored loans, and tuition waivers (partial) available. Financial award application deadline: 4/1. *Unit head:* Dr. Linda Livingstone, Dean. *Application contact:* Christopher Storer, Executive Director, Graduate Admissions, 202-994-1212, E-mail: gwmba@gwu.edu.
Website: http://business.gwu.edu/grad.

Georgia College & State University, Graduate School, The J. Whitney Bunting School of Business, Program in Business Administration, Milledgeville, GA 31061. Offers MBA. Part-time programs available. *Students:* 27 full-time (13 women), 85 part-time (39 women); includes 27 minority (12 Black or African American, non-Hispanic/Latino; 2 American Indian or Alaska Native, non-Hispanic/Latino; 4 Asian, non-Hispanic/Latino; 4 Hispanic/Latino; 2 Native Hawaiian or other Pacific Islander, non-Hispanic/Latino; 3 Two or more races, non-Hispanic/Latino), 7 international. Average age 32. In 2013, 74 master's awarded. *Degree requirements:* For master's, minimum GPA of 3.0, complete program within 7 years of start date. *Entrance requirements:* For master's, GRE or GMAT. Additional exam requirements/recommendations for international students: Recommended—TOEFL (minimum score 500 paper-based; 61 iBT), IELTS (minimum score 6). *Application deadline:* For fall admission, 7/1 for domestic students; for spring admission, 11/15 for domestic students; for summer admission, 4/1 for domestic students. Application fee: $35. *Financial support:* Unspecified assistantships available. *Unit head:* Dr. Dale Young, Interim Dean, 478-445-5497, E-mail: dale.young@gcsu.edu. *Application contact:* Lynn Hanson, Director of Graduate Programs, 478-445-5115, E-mail: lynn.hanson@gcsu.edu.

Georgia Institute of Technology, Graduate Studies and Research, College of Management, Program in Business Administration, Atlanta, GA 30332-0001. Offers accounting (MBA); e-commerce (Certificate); engineering entrepreneurship (MBA); entrepreneurship (Certificate); finance (MBA); information technology management (MBA); international business (MBA, Certificate); management of technology (Certificate); marketing (MBA); operations management (MBA); organizational behavior (MBA); strategic management (MBA). *Accreditation:* AACSB.

Georgia Institute of Technology, Graduate Studies and Research, College of Management, Program in Management, Atlanta, GA 30332-0001. Offers accounting (PhD); finance (PhD); information technology management (PhD); marketing (PhD); operations management (PhD); organizational behavior (PhD); quantitative and computational finance (MS); strategic management (PhD). *Accreditation:* AACSB. *Degree requirements:* For doctorate, comprehensive exam, thesis/dissertation, oral exams. *Entrance requirements:* For master's and doctorate, GMAT. Additional exam requirements/recommendations for international students: Required—TOEFL. *Faculty research:* Management information systems, management of technology, international business, entrepreneurship, operations management.

Georgian Court University, School of Business, Lakewood, NJ 08701-2697. Offers MBA. *Accreditation:* ACBSP. Part-time and evening/weekend programs available. *Faculty:* 7 full-time (3 women), 5 part-time/adjunct (3 women). *Students:* 29 full-time (17 women), 43 part-time (26 women); includes 12 minority (4 Black or African American, non-Hispanic/Latino; 2 Asian, non-Hispanic/Latino; 6 Two or more races, non-Hispanic/Latino), 2 international. In 2013, 49 master's awarded. *Entrance requirements:* For master's, GMAT or CPA exam, 3 letters of recommendation. Additional exam requirements/recommendations for international students: Required—TOEFL (minimum score 550 paper-based). *Application deadline:* For fall admission, 8/1 priority date for domestic students, 4/1 for international students; for spring admission, 1/1 priority date for domestic students, 7/1 for international students. Applications are processed on a rolling basis. Application fee: $40. Electronic applications accepted. *Expenses: Tuition:* Full-time $18,912; part-time $788 per credit. *Required fees:* $906. *Financial support:* Scholarships/grants, health care benefits, and unspecified assistantships available. Financial award application deadline: 4/15; financial award applicants required to submit FAFSA. *Unit head:* Dr. Janice Warner, Dean, 732-987-2662, Fax: 732-987-2024, E-mail: warnerj@georgian.edu. *Application contact:* Patrick Givens, Director of Graduate Admissions, 732-987-2736, Fax: 732-987-2084, E-mail: graduateadmissions@georgian.edu.
Website: http://www.georgian.edu/business/gcu_business.htm.

Georgia Regents University, The Graduate School, Hull College of Business, Augusta, GA 30912. Offers MBA. *Accreditation:* AACSB. Part-time and evening/weekend programs available. *Entrance requirements:* For master's, GMAT.

Georgia Southern University, Jack N. Averitt College of Graduate Studies, College of Business Administration, The Georgia WebMBA, Statesboro, GA 30460. Offers MBA. Part-time and evening/weekend programs available. Postbaccalaureate distance learning degree programs offered. *Students:* 1 full-time (0 women), 82 part-time (22 women); includes 15 minority (11 Black or African American, non-Hispanic/Latino; 3 Asian, non-Hispanic/Latino; 1 Hispanic/Latino), 1 international. Average age 32. 80 applicants, 66% accepted, 30 enrolled. In 2013, 44 master's awarded. *Entrance requirements:* For master's, GMAT. Additional exam requirements/recommendations for international students: Required—TOEFL (minimum score 550 paper-based; 80 iBT). *Application deadline:* For fall admission, 3/1 priority date for domestic and international students. Applications are processed on a rolling basis. Application fee: $50. Electronic applications accepted. *Expenses:* Contact institution. *Financial support:* In 2013–14, 2

students received support. Application deadline: 4/15; applicants required to submit FAFSA. *Unit head:* Dr. Gordon Smith, Graduate Program Director, 912-478-2357, Fax: 912-478-0292, E-mail: gsmith@georgiasouthern.edu. *Application contact:* Amanda Gilliland, Coordinator for Graduate Student Recruitment, 912-478-5384, Fax: 912-478-0740, E-mail: gradadmissions@georgiasouthern.edu.
Website: http://cogs.georgiasouthern.edu/admission/GraduatePrograms/mbagaweb.php.

Georgia Southern University, Jack N. Averitt College of Graduate Studies, College of Business Administration, Program in Business Administration, Statesboro, GA 30460. Offers MBA. *Accreditation:* AACSB. Part-time and evening/weekend programs available. Postbaccalaureate distance learning degree programs offered. *Students:* 47 full-time (23 women), 54 part-time (20 women); includes 14 minority (6 Black or African American, non-Hispanic/Latino; 2 Asian, non-Hispanic/Latino; 3 Hispanic/Latino; 3 Two or more races, non-Hispanic/Latino), 4 international. Average age 29. 92 applicants, 53% accepted, 37 enrolled. In 2013, 83 master's awarded. *Entrance requirements:* For master's, GMAT. Additional exam requirements/recommendations for international students: Required—TOEFL (minimum score 550 paper-based; 80 iBT), IELTS (minimum score 6). *Application deadline:* For fall admission, 3/1 priority date for domestic students, 6/1 priority date for international students; for spring admission, 10/1 priority date for domestic students, 10/1 for international students. Applications are processed on a rolling basis. Application fee: $50. Electronic applications accepted. *Expenses:* Tuition, state resident: full-time $7068; part-time $270 per semester hour. Tuition, nonresident: full-time $26,446; part-time $1077 per semester hour. *Required fees:* $2092. *Financial support:* In 2013–14, 3 students received support, including research assistantships with partial tuition reimbursements available (averaging $7,200 per year), teaching assistantships with partial tuition reimbursements available (averaging $7,200 per year); career-related internships or fieldwork, Federal Work-Study, scholarships/grants, tuition waivers (partial), and unspecified assistantships also available. Support available to part-time students. Financial award application deadline: 4/15; financial award applicants required to submit FAFSA. *Faculty research:* Applied, discipline, pedagogical theory-based, empirical-based. *Unit head:* Gordon Smith, Graduate Program Director, 912-478-2357, Fax: 912-478-7480, E-mail: gsmith@georgiasouthern.edu. *Application contact:* Amanda Gilliland, Coordinator for Graduate Student Recruitment, 912-478-5384, Fax: 912-478-0740, E-mail: gradadmissions@georgiasouthern.edu.
Website: http://coba.georgiasouthern.edu/mba/.

Georgia Southwestern State University, Graduate Studies, School of Business Administration, Americus, GA 31709-4693. Offers MBA. *Accreditation:* AACSB. *Entrance requirements:* For master's, GMAT or GRE General Test, minimum GPA of 2.5. Electronic applications accepted.

Georgia State University, J. Mack Robinson College of Business, Department of Managerial Sciences, Atlanta, GA 30302-3083. Offers business analysis (MBA, MS); entrepreneurship (MBA); human resources management (MBA, MS); operations management (MBA, MS); organization behavior/human resource management (PhD); organization management (MBA); organizational change (MS); strategic management (PhD). *Accreditation:* AACSB. Part-time and evening/weekend programs available. *Faculty:* 18 full-time (6 women). *Students:* 31 full-time (15 women), 22 part-time (14 women); includes 20 minority (11 Black or African American, non-Hispanic/Latino; 1 American Indian or Alaska Native, non-Hispanic/Latino; 2 Asian, non-Hispanic/Latino; 2 Hispanic/Latino; 4 Two or more races, non-Hispanic/Latino), 16 international. Average age 31. 92 applicants, 20% accepted, 13 enrolled. In 2013, 45 master's, 2 doctorates awarded. *Degree requirements:* For doctorate, comprehensive exam, thesis/dissertation. *Entrance requirements:* For master's, GRE or GMAT, transcripts from all institutions attended, resume, essays; for doctorate, GMAT, three letters of recommendation, personal statement, transcripts from all institutions attended, resume. Additional exam requirements/recommendations for international students: Required—TOEFL (minimum score 610 paper-based; 101 iBT), IELTS (minimum score 7). *Application deadline:* For fall admission, 5/1 priority date for domestic students, 2/1 priority date for international students; for spring admission, 9/15 priority date for domestic students, 4/1 priority date for international students. Applications are processed on a rolling basis. Application fee: $50. Electronic applications accepted. *Expenses: Tuition, area resident:* Full-time $4176; part-time $348 per credit hour. Tuition, state resident: full-time $14,544; part-time $1212 per credit hour. Tuition, nonresident: full-time $14,544; part-time $1212 per credit hour. Tuition and fees vary according to course load and program. *Financial support:* Research assistantships, teaching assistantships, scholarships/grants, tuition waivers, and unspecified assistantships available. *Faculty research:* Entrepreneurship and Innovation; strategy process; workplace interactions, relationships, and processes; leadership and culture; supply chain management. *Unit head:* Dr. Pamela S. Barr, Interim Chair, 404-413-7525, Fax: 404-413-7571. *Application contact:* Toby McChesney, Assistant Dean for Graduate Recruiting and Student Services, 404-413-7167, Fax: 404-413-7162, E-mail: rcbgradadmissions@gsu.edu.
Website: http://mgmt.robinson.gsu.edu/.

Georgia State University, J. Mack Robinson College of Business, Executive Doctorate in Business Program, Atlanta, GA 30302-3083. Offers EDB. *Accreditation:* AACSB. Part-time and evening/weekend programs available. *Students:* Average age 0. *Entrance requirements:* Additional exam requirements/recommendations for international students: Required—TOEFL (minimum score 610 paper-based; 101 iBT), IELTS (minimum score 7). *Application deadline:* For fall admission, 5/1 priority date for domestic students, 2/1 priority date for international students. Applications are processed on a rolling basis. Application fee: $100. Electronic applications accepted. *Expenses: Tuition, area resident:* Full-time $4176; part-time $348 per credit hour. Tuition, state resident: full-time $14,544; part-time $1212 per credit hour. Tuition, nonresident: full-time $14,544; part-time $1212 per credit hour. Tuition and fees vary according to course load and program. *Financial support:* Scholarships/grants available. *Unit head:* Maury C. Kalnitz, Director of the Executive Doctorate in Business, 404-413-7178. *Application contact:* Heather Jacobs, Assistant Director of the Executive Doctorate in Business, 404-413-7178, E-mail: hjacob3@gsu.edu.
Website: http://robinson.gsu.edu/execdoctorate/index.html.

Georgia State University, J. Mack Robinson College of Business, Program in General Business Administration, Atlanta, GA 30302-3083. Offers business administration (MBA); executive business administration (EMBA); global business administration (GMBA); professional business administration (PMBA); PMBA/MHA. *Accreditation:* AACSB. Part-time and evening/weekend programs available. *Students:* Average age 0. *Entrance requirements:* For master's, GRE or GMAT, transcripts from all institutions attended, resume, essays. Additional exam requirements/recommendations for international students: Required—TOEFL (minimum score 610 paper-based; 101 iBT), IELTS (minimum score 7). *Application deadline:* For fall admission, 5/1 priority date for domestic students, 2/1 priority date for international students; for spring admission, 9/15 priority date for domestic students, 4/1 priority date for international students. Applications are processed on a rolling basis. Application fee: $50. Electronic applications accepted. *Expenses: Tuition, area resident:* Full-time $4176; part-time $348 per credit hour. Tuition, state resident: full-time $14,544; part-time $1212 per credit hour. Tuition, nonresident: full-time $14,544; part-time $1212 per credit hour. Tuition and fees vary according to course load and program. *Financial support:* Research assistantships, scholarships/grants, tuition waivers, and unspecified assistantships available. Financial award application deadline: 5/1. *Unit head:* Dr. Richard Phillips, Associate Dean for Academic Initiatives and Innovation, 404-413-7000, Fax: 404-413-7035. *Application contact:* Toby McChesney, Assistant Dean for Graduate Recruiting and Student Services, 404-413-7167, Fax: 404-413-7162, E-mail: rcbgradadmissions@gsu.edu.
Website: http://robinson.gsu.edu/mba/index.html.

Globe University–Woodbury, Minnesota School of Business, Woodbury, MN 55125. Offers business administration (MBA); health care management (MSM); information technology (MSM); managerial leadership (MSM).

Goddard College, Graduate Division, Master of Arts in Sustainable Business and Communities Program, Plainfield, VT 05667-9432. Offers MA. Postbaccalaureate distance learning degree programs offered (minimal on-campus study). *Degree requirements:* For master's, thesis. *Entrance requirements:* For master's, 3 letters of recommendation, study plan and resource list, interview.

Golden Gate University, Ageno School of Business, San Francisco, CA 94105-2968. Offers accounting (MBA); business administration (EMBA, MBA, PMBA, DBA); finance (MBA, MS, Certificate); financial planning (MS, Certificate); healthcare information systems (Certificate); human resource management (MBA, MS); human resources management (Certificate); information systems (MS); information technology (MBA); information technology management (Certificate); integrated marketing and communications (MS, Certificate); international business (MBA); management (MBA); marketing (MBA, MS, Certificate); operations supply chain management (Certificate); psychology (MA, Certificate); public administration (EMPA); public relations (MS, Certificate); technical market analysis (Certificate); JD/MBA. Part-time and evening/weekend programs available. *Degree requirements:* For doctorate, thesis/dissertation, qualifying examination. *Entrance requirements:* For master's, GMAT (MBA), minimum GPA of 2.5 (MS). Additional exam requirements/recommendations for international students: Required—TOEFL (minimum score 550 paper-based; 79 iBT). Electronic applications accepted. *Expenses:* Contact institution.

Goldey-Beacom College, Graduate Program, Wilmington, DE 19808-1999. Offers business administration (MBA); finance (MS); financial management (MBA); health care management (MBA); human resource management (MBA); information technology (MBA); international business management (MBA); major finance (MBA); major taxation (MBA); management (MM); marketing management (MBA); taxation (MBA, MS). *Accreditation:* ACBSP. Part-time and evening/weekend programs available. *Entrance requirements:* For master's, GMAT, MAT, GRE, minimum GPA of 3.0. Additional exam requirements/recommendations for international students: Required—TOEFL (minimum score 65 iBT); Recommended—IELTS (minimum score 6). Electronic applications accepted.

Gonzaga University, School of Business Administration, Spokane, WA 99258. Offers M Acc, MBA, JD/M Acc, JD/MBA. *Accreditation:* AACSB. Part-time and evening/weekend programs available. *Faculty:* 43 full-time (12 women), 6 part-time/adjunct (2 women). *Students:* 47 full-time (18 women), 106 part-time (51 women); includes 25 minority (8 American Indian or Alaska Native, non-Hispanic/Latino; 7 Asian, non-Hispanic/Latino; 8 Hispanic/Latino; 2 Two or more races, non-Hispanic/Latino), 10 international. Average age 29. 123 applicants, 50% accepted, 34 enrolled. In 2013, 97 master's awarded. *Entrance requirements:* For master's, GMAT. Additional exam requirements/recommendations for international students: Required—TOEFL. *Application deadline:* For fall admission, 7/20 priority date for domestic students; for spring admission, 11/1 for domestic students. Applications are processed on a rolling basis. Application fee: $50. Electronic applications accepted. *Expenses:* Contact institution. *Financial support:* Teaching assistantships and Federal Work-Study available. Support available to part-time students. Financial award application deadline: 2/1; financial award applicants required to submit FAFSA. *Unit head:* Dr. Ken Anderson, Interim Dean, 509-313-5991. *Application contact:* Stacey Chatman, Assistant Director for Admissions, 509-313-4622, Fax: 509-313-7044, E-mail: chatman@gonzaga.edu.
Website: http://www.gonzaga.edu/MBA.

Governors State University, College of Business and Public Administration, Program in Business Administration, University Park, IL 60484. Offers MBA. *Accreditation:* ACBSP. Evening/weekend programs available. *Degree requirements:* For master's, thesis optional, competency exams in elementary and intermediate algebra. *Entrance requirements:* For master's, GMAT.

The Graduate Center, City University of New York, Graduate Studies, Program in Business, New York, NY 10016-4039. Offers accounting (PhD); behavioral science (PhD); finance (PhD); management planning systems (PhD). *Degree requirements:* For doctorate, thesis/dissertation. *Entrance requirements:* For doctorate, GMAT, writing sample (15 pages). Additional exam requirements/recommendations for international students: Required—TOEFL. Electronic applications accepted.

Grand Canyon University, College of Business, Phoenix, AZ 85017-1097. Offers accounting (MBA); corporate business administration (MBA); disaster preparedness and crisis management (MBA); executive fire service leadership (MS); finance (MBA); general management (MBA); government and policy (MPA); health care management (MPA); health systems management (MBA); human resource management (MBA); innovation (MBA); leadership (MBA, MS); management of information system (MBA); marketing (MBA); project-based (MBA); six sigma (MBA); strategic human resource management (MBA). *Accreditation:* ACBSP. Part-time and evening/weekend programs available. Postbaccalaureate distance learning degree programs offered (no on-campus study). *Entrance requirements:* For master's, equivalent of two years full-time professional work experience. Additional exam requirements/recommendations for international students: Required—TOEFL (minimum score 575 paper-based; 90 iBT), IELTS (minimum score 7). Electronic applications accepted.

Grand Canyon University, College of Doctoral Studies, Phoenix, AZ 85017-1097. Offers business administration (DBA); general psychology (PhD), including cognition and instruction, industrial and organizational psychology; organizational leadership (Ed D, PhD), including behavioral health (PhD), education and effective schools (PhD), higher education (PhD), instructional leadership (PhD), organizational development (Ed D). *Degree requirements:* For doctorate, comprehensive exam, thesis/dissertation. *Entrance requirements:* For doctorate, minimum GPA of 3.4 on earned advanced degree from regionally-accredited institution; transcripts; goals statement.

Grand Valley State University, Seidman College of Business, Program in Business Administration, Allendale, MI 49401-9403. Offers MBA, MSN/MBA. *Accreditation:* AACSB. Part-time and evening/weekend programs available. *Entrance requirements:* For master's, GMAT. Additional exam requirements/recommendations for international students: Required—TOEFL. Electronic applications accepted. *Faculty research:* E-commerce, continuous improvement, currency futures, manufacturing flexibility.

Grand View University, Master of Science in Innovative Leadership Program, Des Moines, IA 50316-1599. Offers business (MS); education (MS); nursing (MS). Part-time and evening/weekend programs available. *Degree requirements:* For master's,

completion of all required coursework in common core and selected track with minimum cumulative GPA of 3.0 and no more than two grades of C. *Entrance requirements:* For master's, GRE, GMAT, or essay, minimum undergraduate GPA of 3.0, professional resume, 3 letters of recommendation, interview. Additional exam requirements/recommendations for international students: Required—TOEFL (minimum score 550 paper-based). Electronic applications accepted.

Granite State College, Program in Management, Concord, NH 03301. Offers MS. Part-time programs available. Postbaccalaureate distance learning degree programs offered (no on-campus study). *Faculty:* 1 (woman) full-time, 15 part-time/adjunct (9 women). *Degree requirements:* For master's, capstone. *Entrance requirements:* For master's, bachelor's degree with minimum GPA of 3.0 on last 60 credit hours, 500-1000 word statement, two letters of professional or academic reference, resume, official transcripts. Additional exam requirements/recommendations for international students: Required—TOEFL, IELTS. *Application deadline:* Applications are processed on a rolling basis. Electronic applications accepted. *Expenses:* Tuition, state resident: full-time $8910; part-time $495 per credit. Tuition, nonresident: full-time $9090; part-time $515 per credit. *Unit head:* Heidi Wilkes, Director, 855-228-3000, E-mail: heidi.wilkes@granite.edu. *Application contact:* Ana Gonzalez, Administrative Assistant, Office of Graduate Studies, 603-513-1334, Fax: 603-513-1387, E-mail: gsc.graduatestudies@granite.edu.
Website: http://www.granite.edu/academics/degrees/masters/management.php.

Grantham University, Mark Skousen School of Business, Lenexa, KS 66219. Offers business administration (MBA); business intelligence (MS); information management (MBA); information management technology (MS); information technology (MS); performance improvement (MS); project management (MBA, MS). Part-time and evening/weekend programs available. Postbaccalaureate distance learning degree programs offered (no on-campus study). *Faculty:* 3 full-time (2 women), 35 part-time/adjunct (11 women). *Students:* 233 full-time (75 women), 559 part-time (207 women); includes 399 minority (296 Black or African American, non-Hispanic/Latino; 6 American Indian or Alaska Native, non-Hispanic/Latino; 14 Asian, non-Hispanic/Latino; 58 Hispanic/Latino; 1 Native Hawaiian or other Pacific Islander, non-Hispanic/Latino; 24 Two or more races, non-Hispanic/Latino). Average age 40. 792 applicants, 100% accepted, 792 enrolled. In 2013, 404 master's awarded. *Degree requirements:* For master's, thesis, capstone project, simulation game. *Entrance requirements:* For master's, bachelor's degree from accredited degree-granting institution with minimum GPA of 2.5. Additional exam requirements/recommendations for international students: Required—TOEFL (minimum score 530 paper-based; 71 iBT). *Application deadline:* Applications are processed on a rolling basis. Application fee: $30. Electronic applications accepted. *Expenses: Tuition:* Full-time $3900; part-time $325 per credit hour. *Required fees:* $35 per term. One-time fee: $100. *Financial support:* In 2013–14, 792 students received support. Scholarships/grants available. *Faculty research:* Relationship between media choices and teaching experience in online courses, online best teaching practices, strategy for co-creation of value with consumers, political identity and party polarization in the American Electorate, political participation and Web 2.0. *Unit head:* Dr. Niccole Buckley, Dean, Mark Skousen School of Business, 800-955-2527, E-mail: admissions@grantham.edu. *Application contact:* Jared Parlette, Vice President of Admissions, 800-955-2527, E-mail: admissions@grantham.edu.
Website: http://www.grantham.edu/colleges-and-schools/school-of-business/.

Green Mountain College, Program in Business Administration, Poultney, VT 05764-1199. Offers MBA. Distance learning only. Postbaccalaureate distance learning degree programs offered (no on-campus study). *Entrance requirements:* For master's, GMAT or Quantitative Skills Assessment, 3 recommendations. Electronic applications accepted. *Faculty research:* Migrant farm workers and world systems theory ecosystem assessments.

Gwynedd Mercy University, Center for Lifelong Learning, Gwynedd Valley, PA 19437-0901. Offers education (MSE); educational administration (MS); management (MSM). Part-time and evening/weekend programs available. *Degree requirements:* For master's, thesis. *Entrance requirements:* For master's, minimum GPA of 3.0.

Hamline University, School of Business, St. Paul, MN 55104-1284. Offers business administration (MBA); nonprofit management (MA); public administration (MA, DPA); JD/MA; JD/MBA; LL M/MA; LL M/MBA; MBA/MA. Part-time and evening/weekend programs available. Postbaccalaureate distance learning degree programs offered (minimal on-campus study). *Faculty:* 13 full-time (4 women), 26 part-time/adjunct (7 women). *Students:* 114 full-time (55 women), 325 part-time (148 women); includes 39 minority (17 Black or African American, non-Hispanic/Latino; 2 American Indian or Alaska Native, non-Hispanic/Latino; 13 Asian, non-Hispanic/Latino; 5 Hispanic/Latino; 2 Two or more races, non-Hispanic/Latino), 26 international. Average age 32. 216 applicants, 80% accepted, 134 enrolled. In 2013, 203 master's, 3 doctorates awarded. *Degree requirements:* For master's, thesis (for some programs); for doctorate, comprehensive exam, thesis/dissertation. *Entrance requirements:* For master's, personal statement, official transcripts, curriculum vitae, letters of recommendation, writing sample; for doctorate, personal statement, curriculum vitae, official transcripts, letters of recommendation, writing sample. Additional exam requirements/recommendations for international students: Required—TOEFL (minimum score 550 paper-based; 80 iBT). *Application deadline:* Applications are processed on a rolling basis. Application fee: $0 ($100 for international students). Electronic applications accepted. *Financial support:* Career-related internships or fieldwork, Federal Work-Study, scholarships/grants, and unspecified assistantships available. Support available to part-time students. Financial award applicants required to submit FAFSA. *Faculty research:* Liberal arts-based business programs, experiential learning, organizational process/politics, gender differences, social equity. *Unit head:* Dr. Anne McCarthy, Dean, 651-523-2284, Fax: 651-523-3098, E-mail: amccarthy02@hamline.edu. *Application contact:* Shawn Skoog, Director of Graduate Recruitment and Admission, 651-523-2900, Fax: 651-523-3058, E-mail: sskoog03@hamline.edu.
Website: http://www.hamline.edu/business.

Hampton University, Graduate College, Program in Business Administration, Hampton, VA 23668. Offers MBA, PhD. Part-time and evening/weekend programs available. *Entrance requirements:* For master's, GRE General Test.

Hampton University, Hampton U Online, Hampton, VA 23668. Offers business administration (PhD); educational management (PhD); health administration (MHA); nursing (MSN, PhD).

Harding University, Paul R. Carter College of Business Administration, Searcy, AR 72149-0001. Offers health care management (MBA); information technology management (MBA); international business (MBA); leadership and organizational management (MBA). *Accreditation:* ACBSP. Part-time and evening/weekend programs available. Postbaccalaureate distance learning degree programs offered (no on-campus study). *Faculty:* 25 part-time/adjunct (5 women). *Students:* 55 full-time (36 women), 115 part-time (50 women); includes 22 minority (17 Black or African American, non-Hispanic/Latino; 2 American Indian or Alaska Native, non-Hispanic/Latino; 3 Asian, non-Hispanic/Latino), 27 international. Average age 34. 48 applicants, 100% accepted, 48 enrolled. In 2013, 88 master's awarded. *Degree requirements:* For master's, portfolio. *Entrance requirements:* For master's, GMAT (minimum score of 500) or GRE (minimum score of 300), minimum GPA of 3.0, 2 letters of recommendation, resume, 3 essays, all official transcripts. Additional exam requirements/recommendations for international students: Required—TOEFL (minimum score 550 paper-based; 79 iBT). *Application deadline:* For fall admission, 8/1 priority date for domestic and international students; for spring admission, 12/1 priority date for domestic and international students. Applications are processed on a rolling basis. Application fee: $40. *Expenses: Tuition:* Full-time $11,574; part-time $643 per credit hour. *Required fees:* $432; $24 per credit hour. Tuition and fees vary according to course load, degree level and program. *Financial support:* Unspecified assistantships available. Financial award application deadline: 7/30; financial award applicants required to submit FAFSA. *Unit head:* Glen Metheny, Director of Graduate Studies, 501-279-5851, Fax: 501-279-4805, E-mail: gmetheny@harding.edu. *Application contact:* Melanie Kiihnl, Recruiting Manager/Director of Marketing, 501-279-4523, Fax: 501-279-4805, E-mail: mba@harding.edu.
Website: http://www.harding.edu/mba.

Hardin-Simmons University, The Acton MBA in Entrepreneurship, Austin, TX 78701. Offers MBA. *Entrance requirements:* For master's, GMAT, letters of recommendation. Additional exam requirements/recommendations for international students: Required—TOEFL. *Application deadline:* For fall admission, 5/1 for domestic students, 2/25 for international students. Application fee: $150. *Expenses: Tuition:* Full-time $13,410; part-time $745 per credit hour. *Required fees:* $325; $110 per semester. Tuition and fees vary according to program. *Application contact:* Jessica Blanchard, Director of Recruiting, 512-703-1231, E-mail: jblanchard@actonmba.org.
Website: http://www.actonmba.org.

Hardin-Simmons University, Graduate School, Kelley College of Business, Abilene, TX 79698-0001. Offers business administration (MBA); sports management (MBA). *Accreditation:* ACBSP. Part-time and evening/weekend programs available. *Faculty:* 10 full-time (3 women). *Students:* 16 full-time (9 women), 13 part-time (6 women); includes 8 minority (2 Black or African American, non-Hispanic/Latino; 5 Hispanic/Latino; 1 Two or more races, non-Hispanic/Latino), 5 international. Average age 27. 5 applicants, 100% accepted, 5 enrolled. In 2013, 16 master's awarded. *Degree requirements:* For master's, thesis or alternative. *Entrance requirements:* For master's, GMAT, minimum GPA of 3.0 in upper-level course work, resume, interview. Additional exam requirements/recommendations for international students: Required—TOEFL (minimum score 600 paper-based; 75 iBT). *Application deadline:* For fall admission, 8/15 priority date for domestic students, 4/1 for international students; for spring admission, 1/5 priority date for domestic students, 9/1 for international students. Applications are processed on a rolling basis. Application fee: $50. *Expenses: Tuition:* Full-time $13,410; part-time $745 per credit hour. *Required fees:* $325; $110 per semester. Tuition and fees vary according to program. *Financial support:* In 2013–14, 16 students received support, including 1 fellowship (averaging $1,500 per year); scholarships/grants also available. Support available to part-time students. Financial award application deadline: 6/30; financial award applicants required to submit FAFSA. *Unit head:* Dr. Nancy Kucinski, Dean of Graduate Studies, 325-670-1298, Fax: 325-670-1564, E-mail: gradoff@hsutx.edu. *Application contact:* Dr. Nancy Kucinski, Dean of Graduate Studies, 325-670-1298, Fax: 325-670-1564, E-mail: gradoff@hsutx.edu.
Website: http://www.hsutx.edu/academics/kelley/graduate/mba.

Harvard University, Extension School, Cambridge, MA 02138-3722. Offers applied sciences (CAS); biotechnology (ALM); educational technologies (ALM); educational technology (CET); English for graduate and professional studies (DGP); environmental management (ALM, CEM); information technology (ALM); journalism (ALM); liberal arts (ALM); management (ALM, CM); mathematics for teaching (ALM); museum studies (ALM); premedical studies (Diploma); publication and communication (CPC). Part-time and evening/weekend programs available. *Degree requirements:* For master's, thesis. *Entrance requirements:* For master's, 3 completed graduate courses with grade of B or higher. Additional exam requirements/recommendations for international students: Required—TOEFL (minimum score 600 paper-based), TWE (minimum score 5). *Expenses:* Contact institution.

Harvard University, Harvard Business School, Doctoral Programs in Management, Boston, MA 02163. Offers accounting and management (DBA); business economics (PhD); health policy management (PhD); management (DBA); marketing (DBA); organizational behavior (PhD); science, technology and management (PhD); strategy (DBA); technology and operations management (DBA). *Degree requirements:* For doctorate, comprehensive exam (for some programs), thesis/dissertation. *Entrance requirements:* For doctorate, GRE General Test or GMAT. Additional exam requirements/recommendations for international students: Required—TOEFL. *Expenses: Tuition:* Full-time $38,888. *Required fees:* $958. Tuition and fees vary according to campus/location, program and student level.

Harvard University, Harvard Business School, Master's Program in Business Administration, Boston, MA 02163. Offers MBA, JD/MBA. *Entrance requirements:* For master's, GMAT. Additional exam requirements/recommendations for international students: Required—TOEFL. *Expenses: Tuition:* Full-time $38,888. *Required fees:* $958. Tuition and fees vary according to campus/location, program and student level.

Hawai`i Pacific University, College of Business Administration, Honolulu, HI 96813. Offers accounting/CPA (MBA); e-business (MBA); economics (MBA); finance (MBA); healthcare management (MBA); human resource management (MA, MBA); information systems (MBA, MSIS); international business (MBA); management (MBA); marketing (MBA); organizational change (MA, MBA); travel industry management (MBA). Part-time and evening/weekend programs available. *Faculty:* 22 full-time (9 women), 6 part-time/adjunct (0 women). *Students:* 232 full-time (100 women), 174 part-time (84 women); includes 241 minority (18 Black or African American, non-Hispanic/Latino; 112 Asian, non-Hispanic/Latino; 33 Hispanic/Latino; 11 Native Hawaiian or other Pacific Islander, non-Hispanic/Latino; 67 Two or more races, non-Hispanic/Latino). Average age 31. 240 applicants, 81% accepted, 102 enrolled. In 2013, 206 master's awarded. *Degree requirements:* For master's, thesis. *Entrance requirements:* For master's, GMAT. Additional exam requirements/recommendations for international students: Recommended—TOEFL (minimum score 550 paper-based; 80 iBT), TWE (minimum score 5). *Application deadline:* For fall admission, 2/15 priority date for domestic students; for spring admission, 10/15 priority date for domestic students. Applications are processed on a rolling basis. Application fee: $50. Electronic applications accepted. *Financial support:* In 2013–14, 90 students received support. Research assistantships, career-related internships or fieldwork, Federal Work-Study, scholarships/grants, tuition waivers, and unspecified assistantships available. Financial award application deadline: 3/1; financial award applicants required to submit FAFSA. *Faculty research:* Statistical control process as used by management, studies in comparative cross-cultural management styles, not-for-profit management. *Unit head:* Dr. Deborah Crown, Dean, 808-544-0275, Fax: 808-544-0283, E-mail: dcrown@hpu.edu. *Application contact:* Rumi Yoshida, Associate Director of Graduate Admissions, 808-543-8034, Fax: 808-544-0280, E-mail: grad@hpu.edu.
Website: http://www.hpu.edu/CBA/Graduate/index.html.

HEC Montreal, School of Business Administration, Doctoral Program in Administration, Montréal, QC H3T 2A7, Canada. Offers PhD. Program offered jointly with Concordia University, McGill University, and Université du Québec à Montréal. *Accreditation:* AACSB. *Students:* 137 full-time (58 women). 62 applicants, 39% accepted, 14 enrolled.

In 2013, 32 doctorates awarded. *Degree requirements:* For doctorate, one foreign language, thesis/dissertation. *Entrance requirements:* For doctorate, GMAT, GRE, master's degree in administration or related field. *Application deadline:* For fall admission, 1/15 for domestic and international students; for winter admission, 9/1 for domestic and international students. Application fee: $83. Electronic applications accepted. *Expenses: Tuition, area resident:* Part-time $74.14 per credit. Tuition, state resident: full-time $2669.04; part-time $201.83 per credit. Tuition, nonresident: full-time $7266; part-time $500.59 per credit. *International tuition:* $18,021.24 full-time. *Required fees:* $1529.70; $36.20 per credit. $65.50 per term. Tuition and fees vary according to degree level and program. *Financial support:* In 2013–14, 1,007 students received support. Research assistantships, teaching assistantships, and scholarships/grants available. Financial award application deadline: 9/2. *Faculty research:* Art management, business policy, entrepreneurship, new technologies, transportation. *Unit head:* Alain d'Astous, Director, 514-340-6416, Fax: 514-340-5690, E-mail: alain.dastous@hec.ca. *Application contact:* Marianne de Moura, Administrative Director, 514-340-7106, Fax: 514-340-6411, E-mail: marianne.de-moura@hec.ca.
Website: http://www.hec.ca/en/programs_training/phd/index.html.

HEC Montreal, School of Business Administration, Graduate Diplomas Programs in Administration, Program in Management, Montréal, QC H3T 2A7, Canada. Offers Graduate Diploma. All courses are given in French. *Accreditation:* AACSB. *Students:* 84 full-time (41 women), 416 part-time (244 women). 242 applicants, 74% accepted, 133 enrolled. In 2013, 106 Graduate Diplomas awarded. *Degree requirements:* For Graduate Diploma, one foreign language. *Entrance requirements:* For degree, bachelor's degree (not in administration). *Application deadline:* For fall admission, 4/1 for domestic and international students; for winter admission, 9/15 for domestic and international students; for spring admission, 2/15 for domestic and international students. Application fee: $83 Canadian dollars. Electronic applications accepted. *Expenses: Tuition, area resident:* Part-time $74.14 per credit. Tuition, state resident: full-time $2669.04; part-time $201.83 per credit. Tuition, nonresident: full-time $7266; part-time $500.59 per credit. *International tuition:* $18,021.24 full-time. *Required fees:* $1529.70; $36.20 per credit. $65.50 per term. Tuition and fees vary according to degree level and program. *Financial support:* In 2013–14, 1,007 students received support. Research assistantships, teaching assistantships, and scholarships/grants available. Financial award application deadline: 9/2. *Unit head:* Silvia Ponce, Director, 514-340-6393, Fax: 514-340-6915, E-mail: silvia.ponce@hec.ca. *Application contact:* Jo Anne Audet, Administrative Director, 514-340-1315, Fax: 514-340-6411, E-mail: joanne.audet@hec.ca.
Website: http://www.hec.ca/programmes_formations/des/dess/dess_gestion/index.html.

HEC Montreal, School of Business Administration, Graduate Diplomas Programs in Administration, Program in Management and Sustainable Development, Montréal, QC H3T 2A7, Canada. Offers Graduate Diploma. All courses are given in French. *Students:* 21 full-time (8 women), 55 part-time (31 women). 64 applicants, 78% accepted, 38 enrolled. In 2013, 28 Graduate Diplomas awarded. *Degree requirements:* For Graduate Diploma, one foreign language. *Entrance requirements:* For degree, bachelor's degree (not in administration). *Application deadline:* For fall admission, 4/15 for domestic and international students. Application fee: $83. Electronic applications accepted. *Expenses: Tuition, area resident:* Part-time $74.14 per credit. Tuition, state resident: full-time $2669.04; part-time $201.83 per credit. Tuition, nonresident: full-time $7266; part-time $500.59 per credit. *International tuition:* $18,021.24 full-time. *Required fees:* $1529.70; $36.20 per credit. $65.50 per term. Tuition and fees vary according to degree level and program. *Financial support:* In 2013–14, 1,007 students received support. Research assistantships, teaching assistantships, and scholarships/grants available. Financial award application deadline: 9/2. *Unit head:* Silvia Ponce, Director, 514-340-6393, Fax: 514-340-6915, E-mail: silvia.ponce@hec.ca. *Application contact:* Jo Anne Audet, Administrative Director, 514-340-1315, Fax: 514-340-6411, E-mail: joanne.audet@hec.ca.
Website: http://www.hec.ca/programmes_formations/des/dess/dess_gestion_developpement_durable/index.html.

HEC Montreal, School of Business Administration, Master of Science Programs in Administration, Montréal, QC H3T 2A7, Canada. Offers applied economics (M Sc); applied financial economics (M Sc); business analytics (M Sc); business intelligence (M Sc); cultural enterprises (MM); electronic commerce (M Sc); finance (M Sc); financial and strategic accounting (M Sc); financial engineering (M Sc); global supply chain management (M Sc); human resources management (M Sc); information technologies (M Sc); international business (M Sc); international logistics (M Sc); management (M Sc); management and social innovations (M Sc); management control (M Sc); marketing (M Sc); operations management (M Sc); organizational development (M Sc); public accounting (M Sc); strategy (M Sc); taxation (LL M). All courses are given in French, some also offered in English. *Accreditation:* AACSB. *Students:* 783 full-time (385 women), 304 part-time (164 women). 793 applicants, 65% accepted, 311 enrolled. In 2013, 403 master's awarded. *Degree requirements:* For master's, one foreign language, thesis. *Entrance requirements:* For master's, bachelor's degree in business administration or equivalent. *Application deadline:* For fall admission, 3/15 for domestic and international students; for winter admission, 9/15 for domestic and international students; for summer admission, 4/15 for domestic and international students. Application fee: $83 Canadian dollars. Electronic applications accepted. *Expenses: Tuition, area resident:* Part-time $74.14 per credit. Tuition, state resident: full-time $2669.04; part-time $201.83 per credit. Tuition, nonresident: full-time $7266; part-time $500.59 per credit. *International tuition:* $18,021.24 full-time. *Required fees:* $1529.70; $36.20 per credit. $65.50 per term. Tuition and fees vary according to degree level and program. *Financial support:* In 2013–14, 1,007 students received support. Research assistantships, teaching assistantships, and scholarships/grants available. Financial award application deadline: 9/2. *Unit head:* Dr. Anne Bourhis, Director, 514-340-6536, Fax: 514-340-6880, E-mail: anne.bourhis@hec.ca. *Application contact:* Marianne de Moura, Administrative Director, 514-340-7106, Fax: 514-340-6411, E-mail: marianne.de-moura@hec.ca.
Website: http://www.hec.ca/en/programs_training/msc/index.html.

HEC Montreal, School of Business Administration, Master's Program in Business Administration and Management, Montréal, QC H3T 2A7, Canada. Offers MBA. Offered in French or English. *Accreditation:* AACSB. *Students:* 168 full-time (57 women), 195 part-time (64 women). 530 applicants, 44% accepted, 182 enrolled. In 2013, 79 master's awarded. *Degree requirements:* For master's, one foreign language. *Entrance requirements:* For master's, GMAT, 3 years of related work experience. Additional exam requirements/recommendations for international students: Required—TOEFL (minimum score iBT 95 for program in French; 100 in English). *Application deadline:* For fall admission, 3/15 for domestic students, 2/1 for international students; for summer admission, 1/15 for domestic students, 10/15 for international students. Application fee: $83 Canadian dollars. Electronic applications accepted. *Expenses: Tuition, area resident:* Part-time $74.14 per credit. Tuition, state resident: full-time $2669.04; part-time $201.83 per credit. Tuition, nonresident: full-time $7266; part-time $500.59 per credit. *International tuition:* $18,021.24 full-time. *Required fees:* $1529.70; $36.20 per credit. $65.50 per term. Tuition and fees vary according to degree level and program. *Financial support:* In 2013–14, 1,007 students received support. Research assistantships, teaching assistantships, and scholarships/grants available. Financial award application deadline: 9/2. *Unit head:* Michael Wybo, Director, 514-340-6830, Fax: 514-340-6132, E-mail: michael.wybo@hec.ca. *Application contact:* Julie Benoit, Administrative Director, 514-340-6137, Fax: 514-340-5640, E-mail: julie.benoit@hec.ca.
Website: http://www.hec.ca/en/programs/mba/.

Heidelberg University, Program in Business Administration, Tiffin, OH 44883-2462. Offers MBA. Part-time and evening/weekend programs available. *Degree requirements:* For master's, thesis or alternative, internship, practicum. *Entrance requirements:* For master's, previous undergraduate course work in business, minimum GPA of 2.7. Additional exam requirements/recommendations for international students: Required—TOEFL. *Expenses:* Contact institution.

Henderson State University, Graduate Studies, School of Business Administration, Arkadelphia, AR 71999-0001. Offers MBA. *Accreditation:* AACSB. Part-time programs available. *Faculty:* 12 full-time (2 women), 1 part-time/adjunct (0 women). *Students:* 22 full-time (8 women), 14 part-time (11 women); includes 4 minority (all Black or African American, non-Hispanic/Latino), 6 international. Average age 28. 10 applicants, 100% accepted, 10 enrolled. In 2013, 34 master's awarded. *Entrance requirements:* For master's, GMAT (minimum score 400), minimum AACSB index of 1000, minimum GPA of 2.7. Additional exam requirements/recommendations for international students: Required—TOEFL (minimum score 600 paper-based); Recommended—IELTS (minimum score 6.5). *Application deadline:* For fall admission, 8/1 priority date for domestic students, 6/30 priority date for international students; for spring admission, 1/1 priority date for domestic students, 11/30 priority date for international students. Applications are processed on a rolling basis. Application fee: $25 ($75 for international students). *Expenses:* Tuition, state resident: full-time $4284; part-time $238 per credit hour. Tuition, nonresident: full-time $8802; part-time $489 per credit hour. Tuition and fees vary according to course load and campus/location. *Financial support:* In 2013–14, 7 teaching assistantships with partial tuition reimbursements (averaging $4,000 per year) were awarded; scholarships/grants and unspecified assistantships also available. *Unit head:* Dr. Brenda Ponsford, Dean, 870-230-5377, Fax: 870-230-5286, E-mail: ponsfob@hsu.edu. *Application contact:* Dr. Ken Taylor, Graduate Dean, 870-230-5126, Fax: 870-230-5479, E-mail: taylorke@hsu.edu.
Website: http://www.hsu.edu/SchoolofBusiness/.

Herzing University Online, Program in Business Administration, Milwaukee, WI 53203. Offers accounting (MBA); business administration (MBA); business management (MBA); healthcare management (MBA); human resources (MBA); marketing (MBA); project management (MBA); technology management (MBA). Postbaccalaureate distance learning degree programs offered (no on-campus study).

High Point University, Norcross Graduate School, High Point, NC 27262-3598. Offers business administration (MBA); educational leadership (M Ed); elementary education (M Ed); history (MA); nonprofit management (MA); secondary math (M Ed); special education (M Ed); strategic communication (MA); teaching elementary education k-6 (MAT); teaching secondary mathematics 9-12 (MAT). *Accreditation:* NCATE. Part-time and evening/weekend programs available. *Degree requirements:* For master's, comprehensive exam (for some programs), thesis (for some programs). *Entrance requirements:* For master's, GMAT (MBA), GRE, MAT, minimum GPA of 3.0. Additional exam requirements/recommendations for international students: Required—TOEFL (minimum score 550 paper-based). Electronic applications accepted.

Hodges University, Graduate Programs, Naples, FL 34119. Offers business administration (MBA); clinical mental health counseling (MS); criminal justice (MS); education (MPS); information systems management (MIS); legal studies (MS); management (MSM); public administration (MPA). Part-time and evening/weekend programs available. Postbaccalaureate distance learning degree programs offered (no on-campus study). *Faculty:* 17 full-time (5 women), 5 part-time/adjunct (3 women). *Students:* 20 full-time (13 women), 182 part-time (131 women); includes 75 minority (18 Black or African American, non-Hispanic/Latino; 1 American Indian or Alaska Native, non-Hispanic/Latino; 7 Asian, non-Hispanic/Latino; 48 Hispanic/Latino; 1 Two or more races, non-Hispanic/Latino). Average age 35. 58 applicants, 100% accepted, 58 enrolled. In 2013, 88 master's awarded. *Degree requirements:* For master's, comprehensive exam (for some programs), thesis (for some programs). *Entrance requirements:* For master's, in-house entrance exam. Additional exam requirements/recommendations for international students: Recommended—TOEFL. *Application deadline:* Applications are processed on a rolling basis. Application fee: $50. Electronic applications accepted. *Financial support:* In 2013–14, 153 students received support. Federal Work-Study and scholarships/grants available. Financial award application deadline: 7/9; financial award applicants required to submit FAFSA. *Unit head:* Dr. Jeanette Brock, President, 239-513-1122, Fax: 239-598-6253, E-mail: jbrock@hodges.edu. *Application contact:* Christy Saunders, Director of Admissions, 239-513-1122, Fax: 239-598-6253, E-mail: csaunders@hodges.edu.

Hofstra University, Frank G. Zarb School of Business, Executive Program in Management, Hempstead, NY 11549. Offers EMBA.

Hofstra University, Frank G. Zarb School of Business, Programs in Accounting and Taxation, Hempstead, NY 11549. Offers accounting (MS, Advanced Certificate); business administration (MBA), including accounting, professional accountancy, taxation; taxation (MS, Advanced Certificate).

Hofstra University, Frank G. Zarb School of Business, Programs in Finance, Hempstead, NY 11549. Offers business administration (MBA), including finance, real estate management; corporate finance (Advanced Certificate); finance (MS); investment management (Advanced Certificate); quantitative finance (MS).

Hofstra University, Frank G. Zarb School of Business, Programs in Information Technology, Hempstead, NY 11549. Offers business administration (MBA), including information technology, quality management; information technology (MS, Advanced Certificate).

Hofstra University, Frank G. Zarb School of Business, Programs in Management and General Business, Hempstead, NY 11549. Offers business administration (MBA), including health services management, management, sports and entertainment management; general management (Advanced Certificate); human resource management (MS, Advanced Certificate).

Hofstra University, Frank G. Zarb School of Business, Programs in Marketing and International Business, Hempstead, NY 11549. Offers business administration (MBA), including international business, marketing; international business (Advanced Certificate); marketing (MS, Advanced Certificate); marketing research (MS).

Holy Family University, Division of Extended Learning, Bensalem, PA 19020. Offers business administration (MBA); finance (MBA); health care administration (MBA); human resources management (MBA). *Accreditation:* ACBSP. Part-time and evening/weekend programs available. *Faculty:* 13 part-time/adjunct (3 women). *Students:* 116 part-time (59 women); includes 4 minority (2 Black or African American, non-Hispanic/Latino; 1 Asian, non-Hispanic/Latino; 1 Hispanic/Latino). Average age 34. 25 applicants, 96% accepted, 6 enrolled. In 2013, 52 master's awarded. *Entrance requirements:* For master's, minimum GPA of 3.0, interview, essay/professional statement, 2 recommendations, current resume, official transcripts of college or university work. Additional exam requirements/recommendations for international students: Required—

TOEFL (minimum score 550 paper-based; 79 iBT). *Application deadline:* For fall admission, 7/1 priority date for domestic and international students; for spring admission, 11/1 priority date for domestic and international students; for summer admission, 4/1 priority date for domestic and international students. Applications are processed on a rolling basis. Application fee: $50. Electronic applications accepted. *Expenses: Tuition:* Full-time $12,060. *Required fees:* $250. Tuition and fees vary according to degree level. *Financial support:* In 2013–14, 3 students received support. Available to part-time students. Applicants required to submit FAFSA. *Unit head:* Chris Quinn, Director of Academic Services, 267-341-5006, Fax: 215-633-0558, E-mail: cquinn1@holyfamily.edu. *Application contact:* Don Reinmold, Director of Admissions, 267-341-5001 Ext. 3230, Fax: 215-633-0558, E-mail: dreinmold@holyfamily.edu.

Holy Family University, Graduate School, School of Business Administration, Philadelphia, PA 19114. Offers human resources management (MS); information systems management (MS). *Accreditation:* ACBSP. Part-time and evening/weekend programs available. *Faculty:* 2 full-time (1 woman), 7 part-time/adjunct (4 women). *Students:* 5 full-time (2 women), 45 part-time (28 women); includes 19 minority (13 Black or African American, non-Hispanic/Latino; 2 Asian, non-Hispanic/Latino; 4 Hispanic/Latino). Average age 32. 12 applicants, 58% accepted, 5 enrolled. In 2013, 23 master's awarded. *Degree requirements:* For master's, comprehensive exam, thesis optional. *Entrance requirements:* For master's, minimum GPA of 3.0, interview, essay/personal statement, current resume, official transcript of all college or university work. Additional exam requirements/recommendations for international students: Required—TOEFL (minimum score 550 paper-based; 79 iBT), IELTS (minimum score 6), PTE (minimum score 54). *Application deadline:* For fall admission, 7/1 priority date for domestic and international students; for winter admission, 1/1 for domestic students; for spring admission, 11/1 priority date for domestic and international students; for summer admission, 4/1 priority date for domestic and international students. Applications are processed on a rolling basis. Application fee: $25. Electronic applications accepted. *Expenses: Tuition:* Full-time $12,060. *Required fees:* $250. Tuition and fees vary according to degree level. *Financial support:* In 2013–14, 2 students received support. Available to part-time students. Application deadline: 5/1; applicants required to submit FAFSA. *Unit head:* Dr. Barry Dickinson, Dean of the School of Business, 267-341-3440, Fax: 215-637-5937, E-mail: jdickinson@holyfamily.edu. *Application contact:* Gidget Marie Montelibano, Associate Director of Graduate Admissions, 267-341-3558, Fax: 215-637-1478, E-mail: gmontelibano@holyfamily.edu.
Website: http://www.holyfamily.edu/choosing-holy-family-u/academics/schools-of-study/school-of-business-administration.

Holy Names University, Graduate Division, Department of Business, Oakland, CA 94619-1699. Offers energy and environment management (MBA); finance (MBA); management and leadership (MBA); marketing (MBA); sports management (MBA). Part-time and evening/weekend programs available. *Faculty:* 4 full-time, 12 part-time/adjunct. *Students:* 23 full-time (14 women), 20 part-time (12 women); includes 30 minority (19 Black or African American, non-Hispanic/Latino; 4 Asian, non-Hispanic/Latino; 7 Hispanic/Latino), 4 international. Average age 32. 35 applicants, 31% accepted, 7 enrolled. In 2013, 30 master's awarded. *Entrance requirements:* For master's, minimum undergraduate GPA of 2.6 overall, 3.0 in major; two recommendations (letter or form) from previous professors or current or previous work supervisors, 1-3 page personal statement, resume. Additional exam requirements/recommendations for international students: Required—TOEFL (minimum score 550 paper-based; 79 iBT). *Application deadline:* For fall admission, 8/1 priority date for domestic students, 7/15 for international students; for spring admission, 12/1 priority date for domestic students, 12/1 for international students; for summer admission, 5/1 priority date for domestic students, 5/1 for international students. Applications are processed on a rolling basis. Application fee: $65. Electronic applications accepted. Application fee is waived when completed online. *Expenses: Tuition:* Part-time $866 per unit. *Financial support:* Career-related internships or fieldwork, Federal Work-Study, scholarships/grants, and unspecified assistantships available. Support available to part-time students. Financial award application deadline: 3/2; financial award applicants required to submit FAFSA. *Faculty research:* Business ethics, sustainable economics, accounting models, cross-cultural management, diversity in organizations. *Unit head:* Dr. Hector Saez, MBA Program Director, 510-436-1622, E-mail: saez@hnu.edu. *Application contact:* 800-430-1321, Fax: 510-436-1325, E-mail: graduateadmissions@hnu.edu.
Website: http://www.hnu.edu.

Hood College, Graduate School, Department of Economics and Business Administration, Frederick, MD 21701-8575. Offers accounting (MBA); administration and management (MBA); finance (MBA); human resource management (MBA); information systems (MBA); marketing (MBA); public management (MBA). *Accreditation:* ACBSP. Part-time and evening/weekend programs available. *Faculty:* 6 full-time (2 women), 7 part-time/adjunct (1 woman). *Students:* 31 full-time (21 women), 131 part-time (66 women); includes 36 minority (18 Black or African American, non-Hispanic/Latino; 7 Asian, non-Hispanic/Latino; 8 Hispanic/Latino; 3 Two or more races, non-Hispanic/Latino), 12 international. Average age 31. 78 applicants, 56% accepted, 33 enrolled. In 2013, 35 master's awarded. *Degree requirements:* For master's, capstone/final research project. *Entrance requirements:* For master's, minimum GPA of 2.75, resume, letters of recommendation. Additional exam requirements/recommendations for international students: Required—TOEFL (minimum score 575 paper-based; 89 iBT), IELTS (minimum score 6.5). *Application deadline:* For fall admission, 7/15 priority date for domestic students, 7/15 for international students; for spring admission, 12/1 priority date for domestic students, 12/1 for international students. Applications are processed on a rolling basis. Application fee: $35. Electronic applications accepted. Application fee is waived when completed online. *Expenses: Tuition:* Part-time $405 per credit. *Required fees:* $100 per semester. *Financial support:* In 2013–14, 11 students received support. Tuition waivers (partial) and unspecified assistantships available. Financial award applicants required to submit FAFSA. *Faculty research:* Corporate strategy and sustainable competitive advantages, business ethics, entrepreneurship, investments management, economic development. *Unit head:* Dr. Anita Jose, Program Director, 301-696-3691, Fax: 301-696-3597, E-mail: jose@hood.edu. *Application contact:* Dr. Maria Green Cowles, Dean of Graduate School, 301-696-3811, Fax: 301-696-3597, E-mail: gofurther@hood.edu.

Houston Baptist University, School of Business, Program in Business Administration, Houston, TX 77074-3298. Offers MBA, MIB, MSM. *Accreditation:* ACBSP. Part-time and evening/weekend programs available. *Entrance requirements:* For master's, GMAT, minimum GPA of 2.5. Additional exam requirements/recommendations for international students: Required—TOEFL (minimum score 550 paper-based). *Expenses:* Contact institution.

Howard Payne University, Program in Business Administration, Brownwood, TX 76801-2715. Offers MBA. Part-time and evening/weekend programs available. *Faculty:* 5 full-time (1 woman), 2 part-time/adjunct (1 woman). *Students:* 21 full-time (9 women), 16 part-time (5 women); includes 6 minority (all Hispanic/Latino). Average age 33. 11 applicants, 64% accepted, 4 enrolled. In 2013, 8 master's awarded. *Degree requirements:* For master's, comprehensive exam, research project. *Entrance requirements:* For master's, minimum undergraduate GPA of 3.0, 3.3 in first 9 hours of coursework; business foundation classes (for those without undergraduate business degree and no business-related coursework). Additional exam requirements/recommendations for international students: Required—TOEFL (minimum score 79 iBT). *Application deadline:* For fall admission, 7/1 for domestic students; for spring admission, 12/1 for domestic students. Applications are processed on a rolling basis. Application fee: $0. Electronic applications accepted. *Expenses: Tuition:* Full-time $8820; part-time $490 per credit hour. *Financial support:* Application deadline: 3/15; applicants required to submit FAFSA. *Unit head:* Dr. Lois Patton, Director, 325-649-8146, E-mail: lpatton@hputx.edu. *Application contact:* Mary Hill, Administrative Assistant, School of Business, 325-649-8704, E-mail: mhill@hputx.edu.
Website: http://www.hputx.edu/academics/schools/school-of-business/school-of-business-graduate-program/.

Howard University, School of Business, Graduate Programs in Business, Washington, DC 20059-0002. Offers accounting (MBA); entrepreneurship (MBA); finance (MBA); general management (MBA); human resources management (MBA); information systems (MBA); international business (MBA); marketing (MBA); supply chain management (MBA); JD/MBA. *Accreditation:* AACSB. Part-time and evening/weekend programs available. Postbaccalaureate distance learning degree programs offered (no on-campus study). *Entrance requirements:* For master's, GMAT, minimum 1 year post undergraduate work experience, resume, 3 letters of recommendation, advanced college algebra. Additional exam requirements/recommendations for international students: Required—TOEFL. *Faculty research:* Marketing research in multi-ethnic populations, U.S. trade policies and international relations, risk management (finance).

Hult International Business School, MBA Program, Cambridge, MA 02141. Offers MBA. *Entrance requirements:* For master's, GMAT, 3 years of management experience. Additional exam requirements/recommendations for international students: Required—TOEFL. Electronic applications accepted. *Faculty research:* Management for international development.

Hult International Business School, Program in Business Administration - Hult London Campus, London WC 1B 4JP, United Kingdom. Offers entrepreneurship (MBA); international business (MBA); international finance (MBA); marketing (MBA). Part-time programs available. *Degree requirements:* For master's, comprehensive exam, thesis, internship. *Entrance requirements:* Additional exam requirements/recommendations for international students: Required—TOEFL (minimum score 580 paper-based), TWE (minimum score 5). Electronic applications accepted.

Humboldt State University, Academic Programs, College of Professional Studies, School of Business, Arcata, CA 95521-8299. Offers MBA. Part-time and evening/weekend programs available. *Degree requirements:* For master's, thesis or alternative. *Entrance requirements:* For master's, GMAT or GRE, minimum GPA of 2.5. Additional exam requirements/recommendations for international students: Required—TOEFL (minimum score 500 paper-based). *Expenses:* Contact institution. *Faculty research:* International business development, small town entrepreneurship, international trade: Pacific Rim.

Husson University, Master of Business Administration Program, Bangor, ME 04401-2999. Offers general business administration (MBA); healthcare management (MBA); hospitality and tourism management (MBA); non-profit management (MBA). Part-time and evening/weekend programs available. *Faculty:* 7 full-time (4 women), 16 part-time/adjunct (3 women). *Students:* 91 full-time (55 women), 87 part-time (47 women); includes 21 minority (7 Black or African American, non-Hispanic/Latino; 11 Asian, non-Hispanic/Latino; 3 Two or more races, non-Hispanic/Latino), 4 international. 112 applicants, 88% accepted, 86 enrolled. In 2013, 163 master's awarded. *Degree requirements:* For master's, comprehensive exam (for some programs), thesis optional. *Entrance requirements:* For master's, GMAT or GRE, minimum GPA of 3.0. Additional exam requirements/recommendations for international students: Required—TOEFL (minimum score 550 paper-based). *Application deadline:* Applications are processed on a rolling basis. Application fee: $40. Electronic applications accepted. *Expenses:* Contact institution. *Financial support:* In 2013–14, 6 students received support. Career-related internships or fieldwork, Federal Work-Study, scholarships/grants, and unspecified assistantships available. Financial award application deadline: 4/15; financial award applicants required to submit FAFSA. *Unit head:* Prof. Stephanie Shayne, Director, Graduate and Online Programs, 207-404-5632, Fax: 207-992-4987, E-mail: shaynes@husson.edu. *Application contact:* Kristen Card, Director of Graduate Admissions, 207-404-5660, Fax: 207-941-7935, E-mail: cardk@husson.edu.
Website: http://www.husson.edu/mba.

Idaho State University, Office of Graduate Studies, College of Business, Pocatello, ID 83209-8020. Offers business administration (MBA, Postbaccalaureate Certificate); computer information systems (MS, Postbaccalaureate Certificate). *Accreditation:* AACSB. Part-time programs available. *Degree requirements:* For master's, comprehensive exam, thesis (for some programs), oral exam; for Postbaccalaureate Certificate, comprehensive exam, thesis (for some programs), 6 hours of clerkship. *Entrance requirements:* For master's, GMAT, GRE General Test, minimum GPA of 3.0, resume outlining work experience, 2 letters of reference; for Postbaccalaureate Certificate, GMAT, GRE General Test, minimum upper-level GPA of 3.0, resume of work experience. Additional exam requirements/recommendations for international students: Required—TOEFL (minimum score 550 paper-based; 80 iBT). Electronic applications accepted. *Faculty research:* Information assurance, computer information technology, finance management, marketing.

Illinois Institute of Technology, Stuart School of Business, Program in Business Administration, Chicago, IL 60661. Offers financial management (MBA); innovation and emerging enterprises (MBA); management science (MBA); marketing (MBA); sustainability (MBA); JD/MBA; M Des/MBA; MBA/MS. *Accreditation:* AACSB. Part-time and evening/weekend programs available. *Entrance requirements:* For master's, GRE (minimum score 1000) or GMAT (500). Additional exam requirements/recommendations for international students: Required—TOEFL (minimum score 600 paper-based; 85 iBT); Recommended—IELTS (minimum score 7). Electronic applications accepted. *Expenses:* Contact institution. *Faculty research:* Global management and marketing strategy, technological innovation, management science, financial management, knowledge management.

Illinois Institute of Technology, Stuart School of Business, Program in Management Science, Chicago, IL 60661. Offers PhD. *Accreditation:* AACSB. Part-time programs available. *Degree requirements:* For doctorate, comprehensive exam, thesis/dissertation. *Entrance requirements:* For doctorate, GRE (minimum score 1300) or GMAT (minimum score 650). Additional exam requirements/recommendations for international students: Required—TOEFL (minimum score 600 paper-based; 85 iBT). Electronic applications accepted. *Expenses:* Contact institution. *Faculty research:* Scheduling systems, queuing systems, optimization, quality systems, foreign exchange, enterprise risk management, credit risk modeling.

Illinois State University, Graduate School, College of Business, Program in Business Administration, Normal, IL 61790-2200. Offers MBA. *Accreditation:* AACSB. Part-time programs available. *Degree requirements:* For master's, thesis optional. *Entrance requirements:* For master's, GMAT, minimum GPA of 2.75 during previous 2 years of course work. Additional exam requirements/recommendations for international students:

Required—TOEFL. *Faculty research:* McLean County small business development center.

IMCA–International Management Centres Association, Programs in Business Administration, Buckingham, United Kingdom. Offers M Mgt, M Phil, MBA, MS. Postbaccalaureate distance learning degree programs offered (no on-campus study).

Independence University, Program in Business Administration, Salt Lake City, UT 84107. Offers MBA.

Indiana State University, College of Graduate and Professional Studies, College of Business, Terre Haute, IN 47809. Offers MBA. *Accreditation:* AACSB. Part-time and evening/weekend programs available. *Degree requirements:* For master's, thesis optional. *Entrance requirements:* For master's, GMAT. Electronic applications accepted. *Faculty research:* Small business and entrepreneurial sciences, production and operations management.

Indiana Tech, Program in Business Administration, Fort Wayne, IN 46803-1297. Offers accounting (MBA); health care administration (MBA); human resources (MBA); management (MBA); marketing (MBA). Part-time and evening/weekend programs available. Postbaccalaureate distance learning degree programs offered (no on-campus study). *Students:* 160 full-time (94 women), 97 part-time (53 women); includes 69 minority (58 Black or African American, non-Hispanic/Latino; 1 Asian, non-Hispanic/Latino; 8 Hispanic/Latino; 2 Two or more races, non-Hispanic/Latino), 11 international. Average age 36. *Entrance requirements:* For master's, GMAT, bachelor's degree from regionally-accredited university; minimum undergraduate GPA of 2.5; 2 years of significant work experience; 3 letters of recommendation. *Application deadline:* Applications are processed on a rolling basis. Application fee: $25. Electronic applications accepted. *Expenses: Tuition:* Full-time $8910; part-time $495 per credit. Tuition and fees vary according to course load, degree level and program. *Financial support:* Applicants required to submit FAFSA. *Unit head:* Dr. Andrew I. Nwanne, Associate Dean of Business/Academic Coordinator, 260-422-5561 Ext. 2214, E-mail: ainwanne@indianatech.edu.
Website: http://www.indianatech.edu/.

Indiana Tech, Program in Management, Fort Wayne, IN 46803-1297. Offers MSM. Part-time and evening/weekend programs available. *Students:* 27 full-time (16 women), 12 part-time (8 women); includes 20 minority (17 Black or African American, non-Hispanic/Latino; 1 Asian, non-Hispanic/Latino; 2 Hispanic/Latino), 4 international. Average age 39. *Entrance requirements:* For master's, bachelor's degree from regionally-accredited university; minimum undergraduate GPA of 2.5; 2 years of significant work experience; 3 letters of recommendation. *Application deadline:* Applications are processed on a rolling basis. Application fee: $25. Electronic applications accepted. *Expenses: Tuition:* Full-time $8910; part-time $495 per credit. Tuition and fees vary according to course load, degree level and program. *Financial support:* Applicants required to submit FAFSA. *Unit head:* Dr. Jeffrey A. Zimmerman, Dean of Business, 260-422-5561 Ext. 2117, E-mail: jazimmerman@indianatech.edu.
Website: http://www.indianatech.edu.

Indiana University Bloomington, Kelley School of Business, Bloomington, IN 47405-7000. Offers MBA, MPA, MS, DBA, PhD, DBA/MIS, JD/MBA, JD/MPA, MBA/MA, PhD/MIS. PhD offered through University Graduate School. *Accreditation:* AACSB. *Faculty:* 71 full-time (10 women). *Students:* 1,429 full-time (387 women), 720 part-time (182 women); includes 363 minority (69 Black or African American, non-Hispanic/Latino; 205 Asian, non-Hispanic/Latino; 60 Hispanic/Latino; 2 Native Hawaiian or other Pacific Islander, non-Hispanic/Latino; 27 Two or more races, non-Hispanic/Latino), 619 international. Average age 31. 2,681 applicants, 42% accepted, 808 enrolled. In 2013, 1,065 master's, 11 doctorates awarded. *Degree requirements:* For doctorate, thesis/dissertation. *Entrance requirements:* For master's, GMAT; for doctorate, GMAT, GRE General Test. Additional exam requirements/recommendations for international students: Required—TOEFL. *Application deadline:* For fall admission, 1/15 priority date for domestic students, 12/1 priority date for international students; for winter admission, 3/1 priority date for domestic students; for spring admission, 4/15 for domestic students, 9/1 for international students. Application fee: $55 ($65 for international students). Electronic applications accepted. *Expenses:* Contact institution. *Financial support:* Fellowships with full and partial tuition reimbursements, research assistantships, teaching assistantships, career-related internships or fieldwork, Federal Work-Study, institutionally sponsored loans, tuition waivers (full and partial), and unspecified assistantships available. Support available to part-time students. Financial award application deadline: 3/1; financial award applicants required to submit FAFSA. *Total annual research expenditures:* $1.1 million. *Unit head:* Idalene Kessler, Dean, E-mail: business@indiana.edu. *Application contact:* Flora Barker, Associate Director of Admissions and Financial Aid, 812-856-3145, E-mail: fbarker@indiana.edu.
Website: http://kelley.iu.edu/.

Indiana University Kokomo, School of Business, Kokomo, IN 46904-9003. Offers business administration (MBA). *Accreditation:* AACSB. Part-time and evening/weekend programs available. *Faculty:* 14 full-time (6 women). *Students:* 39 full-time (9 women), 45 part-time (21 women); includes 5 minority (3 Black or African American, non-Hispanic/Latino; 1 American Indian or Alaska Native, non-Hispanic/Latino; 1 Hispanic/Latino), 32 international. Average age 35. 84 applicants, 62% accepted, 40 enrolled. In 2013, 22 master's awarded. *Degree requirements:* For master's, thesis optional, research project. *Entrance requirements:* For master's, GMAT. Additional exam requirements/recommendations for international students: Required—TOEFL (minimum score 550 paper-based). *Application deadline:* For fall admission, 8/1 priority date for domestic and international students; for spring admission, 12/15 priority date for domestic and international students. Applications are processed on a rolling basis. *Expenses:* Contact institution. *Financial support:* Fellowships, research assistantships, teaching assistantships, career-related internships or fieldwork, and tuition waivers (partial) available. *Faculty research:* Investments, outsourcing, technology, adoption. *Unit head:* Dr. Erv Boschmann, Interim Dean, 756-455-9275, E-mail: erv@iu.edu. *Application contact:* Terri Butler, Administrative Secretary, 765-455-9275, Fax: 765-455-9348, E-mail: tbutler@iuk.edu.
Website: http://iuk.edu/academics/majors/business/graduate-programs/index.shtml.

Indiana University Northwest, School of Business and Economics, Gary, IN 46408-1197. Offers management (Certificate); management and administrative studies (MBA). *Accreditation:* AACSB. Part-time and evening/weekend programs available. *Faculty:* 5 full-time (0 women). *Students:* 61 full-time (21 women), 45 part-time (24 women); includes 39 minority (18 Black or African American, non-Hispanic/Latino; 6 Asian, non-Hispanic/Latino; 15 Hispanic/Latino). Average age 34. 54 applicants, 93% accepted, 45 enrolled. In 2013, 25 master's, 4 other advanced degrees awarded. *Entrance requirements:* For master's, GMAT, letter of recommendation. *Application deadline:* For fall admission, 7/15 priority date for domestic students; for spring admission, 11/15 for domestic students. Applications are processed on a rolling basis. *Expenses:* Contact institution. *Financial support:* Federal Work-Study, institutionally sponsored loans, and unspecified assistantships available. Support available to part-time students. Financial award application deadline: 7/15. *Faculty research:* International finance, wellness in the workplace, handicapped employment, management information systems, regional economic forecasting. *Unit head:* John Gibson, Director of Graduate and Undergraduate

Programs, 219-980-6635, E-mail: jagibson@iun.edu. *Application contact:* 219-980-6552, E-mail: iunbiz@iun.edu.
Website: http://www.iun.edu/business/graduate/index.htm.

Indiana University of Pennsylvania, School of Graduate Studies and Research, Eberly College of Business and Information Technology, MBA Executive Track Program, Indiana, PA 15705-1087. Offers MBA. Part-time and evening/weekend programs available. *Faculty:* 23 full-time (3 women), 3 part-time/adjunct (1 woman). *Students:* 64 full-time (20 women), 27 part-time (9 women); includes 21 minority (9 Black or African American, non-Hispanic/Latino; 8 Asian, non-Hispanic/Latino; 3 Hispanic/Latino; 1 Two or more races, non-Hispanic/Latino). Average age 34. 61 applicants, 74% accepted, 30 enrolled. In 2013, 49 master's awarded. *Entrance requirements:* Additional exam requirements/recommendations for international students: Required—TOEFL (minimum score 540 paper-based). *Application deadline:* Applications are processed on a rolling basis. Application fee: $50. Electronic applications accepted. *Expenses:* Tuition, state resident: full-time $3978; part-time $442 per credit. Tuition, nonresident: full-time $5967; part-time $663 per credit. *Required fees:* $2080; $115.55 per credit. $93 per semester. Tuition and fees vary according to degree level and program. *Financial support:* In 2013–14, 1 fellowship with full tuition reimbursement (averaging $1,250 per year), 1 research assistantship with full and partial tuition reimbursement (averaging $5,940 per year) were awarded; career-related internships or fieldwork, Federal Work-Study, scholarships/grants, and unspecified assistantships also available. Financial award application deadline: 4/15; financial award applicants required to submit FAFSA. *Unit head:* Dr. Krish Krishnan, Director, 724-357-2522, E-mail: krishnan@iup.edu.
Website: http://www.iup.edu/grad/mba/default.aspx.

Indiana University of Pennsylvania, School of Graduate Studies and Research, Eberly College of Business and Information Technology, Program in Business Administration, Indiana, PA 15705-1087. Offers MBA. *Accreditation:* AACSB. Part-time programs available. *Faculty:* 23 full-time (3 women), 3 part-time/adjunct (1 woman). *Students:* 167 full-time (63 women), 13 part-time (5 women); includes 1 minority (Black or African American, non-Hispanic/Latino), 154 international. Average age 23. 161 applicants, 58% accepted, 77 enrolled. In 2013, 90 master's awarded. *Degree requirements:* For master's, thesis optional. *Entrance requirements:* For master's, GMAT, 2 letters of recommendation. Additional exam requirements/recommendations for international students: Required—TOEFL (minimum score 540 paper-based). *Application deadline:* Applications are processed on a rolling basis. Application fee: $50. Electronic applications accepted. *Expenses:* Tuition, state resident: full-time $3978; part-time $442 per credit. Tuition, nonresident: full-time $5967; part-time $663 per credit. *Required fees:* $2080; $115.55 per credit. $93 per semester. Tuition and fees vary according to degree level and program. *Financial support:* In 2013–14, 1 fellowship with full tuition reimbursement (averaging $1,000 per year), 27 research assistantships with full and partial tuition reimbursements (averaging $2,279 per year) were awarded; career-related internships or fieldwork, Federal Work-Study, scholarships/grants, and unspecified assistantships also available. Support available to part-time students. Financial award application deadline: 4/15; financial award applicants required to submit FAFSA. *Unit head:* Dr. Krish Krishnan, Graduate Coordinator, 724-357-2522, E-mail: krishnan@iup.edu.
Website: http://www.iup.edu/grad/mba/default.aspx.

Indiana University–Purdue University Fort Wayne, Doermer School of Business, Fort Wayne, IN 46805-1499. Offers MBA. *Accreditation:* AACSB. Part-time programs available. *Faculty:* 26 full-time (10 women). *Students:* 47 full-time (14 women), 43 part-time (10 women); includes 14 minority (3 Black or African American, non-Hispanic/Latino; 2 American Indian or Alaska Native, non-Hispanic/Latino; 5 Asian, non-Hispanic/Latino; 3 Hispanic/Latino; 1 Two or more races, non-Hispanic/Latino), 8 international. Average age 32. 61 applicants, 100% accepted, 42 enrolled. In 2013, 67 master's awarded. *Entrance requirements:* For master's, GMAT, minimum GPA of 3.0, two letters of recommendation, essay, interview. Additional exam requirements/recommendations for international students: Required—TOEFL (minimum score 600 paper-based; 100 iBT). *Application deadline:* For fall admission, 7/15 for domestic students, 5/1 for international students; for spring admission, 11/15 for domestic students, 10/1 for international students. Applications are processed on a rolling basis. Application fee: $55. *Financial support:* In 2013–14, 8 teaching assistantships with partial tuition reimbursements (averaging $13,322 per year) were awarded; scholarships/grants and unspecified assistantships also available. Support available to part-time students. Financial award application deadline: 3/1; financial award applicants required to submit FAFSA. *Faculty research:* External loans and small businesses, student learning, business school graduates and employer perspectives. *Unit head:* Dr. Otto Chang, Dean, 260-481-0219, Fax: 260-481-6879, E-mail: chango@ipfw.edu. *Application contact:* Dr. Maneesh Sharma, Director/Associate Professor, 260-481-6484, Fax: 260-481-6879, E-mail: sharmam@ipfw.edu.
Website: http://www.ipfw.edu/business.

Indiana University–Purdue University Indianapolis, Kelley School of Business, Indianapolis, IN 46202-2896. Offers accounting (MSA); business (MBA). *Accreditation:* AACSB. Part-time and evening/weekend programs available. Postbaccalaureate distance learning degree programs offered (minimal on-campus study). *Faculty:* 20 full-time (4 women), 1 part-time/adjunct (0 women). *Students:* 150 full-time (52 women), 349 part-time (104 women); includes 89 minority (28 Black or African American, non-Hispanic/Latino; 44 Asian, non-Hispanic/Latino; 11 Hispanic/Latino; 6 Two or more races, non-Hispanic/Latino), 127 international. Average age 30. 302 applicants, 56% accepted, 141 enrolled. In 2013, 200 master's awarded. *Entrance requirements:* For master's, GMAT, previous course work in accounting and statistics. *Application deadline:* For fall admission, 4/15 priority date for domestic and international students; for spring admission, 11/1 priority date for domestic and international students. Applications are processed on a rolling basis. Application fee: $55 ($65 for international students). Electronic applications accepted. *Expenses:* Contact institution. *Financial support:* Fellowships, teaching assistantships, Federal Work-Study, institutionally sponsored loans, and scholarships/grants available. Support available to part-time students. Financial award application deadline: 3/1; financial award applicants required to submit FAFSA. *Unit head:* Susan L. Cauble, Director, Graduate Accounting Programs, 317-274-3451, E-mail: busugrad@iupui.edu. *Application contact:* Felicia Morris, Student Services Support, 317-274-0890, E-mail: mbaindy@iupui.edu.
Website: http://kelley.iupui.edu/evemba.

Indiana University South Bend, Judd Leighton School of Business and Economics, South Bend, IN 46634-7111. Offers accounting (MSA); business administration (MBA); management of information technologies (MS). Part-time and evening/weekend programs available. *Faculty:* 17 full-time (2 women), 3 part-time/adjunct (1 woman). *Students:* 34 full-time (18 women), 101 part-time (38 women); includes 13 minority (7 Black or African American, non-Hispanic/Latino; 3 Asian, non-Hispanic/Latino; 2 Hispanic/Latino; 1 Two or more races, non-Hispanic/Latino), 30 international. Average age 32. 48 applicants, 79% accepted, 18 enrolled. In 2013, 42 master's awarded. *Entrance requirements:* For master's, GMAT. Additional exam requirements/recommendations for international students: Required—TOEFL (minimum score 550 paper-based). *Application deadline:* For fall admission, 7/1 priority date for domestic and

international students; for spring admission, 11/1 priority date for domestic and international students. Applications are processed on a rolling basis. *Expenses:* Contact institution. *Financial support:* Fellowships, Federal Work-Study, and institutionally sponsored loans available. Support available to part-time students. Financial award applicants required to submit FAFSA. *Faculty research:* Financial accounting, consumer research, capital budgeting research, business strategy research. *Unit head:* Robert H. Ducoffe, Dean, 574-520-4228, Fax: 574-520-4866. *Application contact:* Tracy White, Assistant Director of Graduate Business Program, 574-520-4138, E-mail: whitet@iusb.edu.
Website: https://www.iusb.edu/buse/graduate_programs/.

Indiana University Southeast, School of Business, New Albany, IN 47150-6405. Offers business administration (MBA); strategic finance (MS). *Accreditation:* AACSB. *Faculty:* 11 full-time (2 women). *Students:* 7 full-time (0 women), 187 part-time (78 women); includes 17 minority (5 Black or African American, non-Hispanic/Latino; 7 Asian, non-Hispanic/Latino; 1 Hispanic/Latino; 2 Native Hawaiian or other Pacific Islander, non-Hispanic/Latino; 2 Two or more races, non-Hispanic/Latino), 6 international. Average age 31. 60 applicants, 75% accepted, 36 enrolled. In 2013, 76 master's awarded. *Degree requirements:* For master's, community service. *Entrance requirements:* For master's, GMAT, work experience. Additional exam requirements/recommendations for international students: Required—TOEFL. *Expenses:* Contact institution. *Financial support:* In 2013–14, 2 teaching assistantships (averaging $4,500 per year) were awarded. *Unit head:* Dr. Jay White, Dean, 812-941-2362, Fax: 812-941-2672. *Application contact:* Admissions Counselor, 812-941-2212, Fax: 812-941-2595, E-mail: admissions@ius.edu.
Website: http://www.ius.edu/mba.

Indiana Wesleyan University, College of Adult and Professional Studies, Graduate Studies in Business, Marion, IN 46953. Offers accounting (MBA, Graduate Certificate); applied management (MBA); business administration (MBA); health care (MBA, Graduate Certificate); human resources (MBA, Graduate Certificate); management (MS); organizational leadership (MA). Part-time and evening/weekend programs available. Postbaccalaureate distance learning degree programs offered (no on-campus study). *Degree requirements:* For master's, applied business or management project. *Entrance requirements:* For master's, minimum GPA of 2.5, 2 years of related work experience. Additional exam requirements/recommendations for international students: Required—TOEFL (minimum score 550 paper-based). Electronic applications accepted. *Expenses: Tuition:* Full-time $8712; part-time $484 per credit hour. *Required fees:* $1673; $105 per credit hour. Tuition and fees vary according to course load, degree level, campus/location and program.

Instituto Centroamericano de Administración de Empresas, Graduate Programs, La Garita, Costa Rica. Offers agribusiness management (MIAM); business administration (EMBA); finance (MBA); real estate management (MGREM); sustainable development (MBA); technology (MBA). *Degree requirements:* For master's, comprehensive exam, essay. *Entrance requirements:* For master's, GMAT or GRE General Test, fluency in Spanish, interview, letters of recommendation, minimum 1 year of work experience. Additional exam requirements/recommendations for international students: Recommended—TOEFL. Electronic applications accepted. *Faculty research:* Competitiveness, production.

Instituto Tecnologico de Santo Domingo, Graduate School, Area of Business, Santo Domingo, Dominican Republic. Offers banking and securities markets (M Mgmt); corporate finance (M Mgmt); human resources management (M Mgmt, Certificate); international trade management (M Mgmt); marketing (M Mgmt); organizational development (M Mgmt); quality and productivity management (Certificate); tax management and planning (M Mgmt); upper management (M Mgmt).

Instituto Tecnológico y de Estudios Superiores de Monterrey, Campus Central de Veracruz, Graduate Programs, Córdoba, Mexico. Offers administration (MA); administration of information technologies (MTI); computer sciences (MCC); education (MEE); educational institution administration (MAD); educational technology (MTE); electronic commerce (MCE); finance (MAF); humanistic studies (MEH); international business for Latin America (MNL); marketing (MMT); science (MCP). Part-time and evening/weekend programs available. Postbaccalaureate distance learning degree programs offered (minimal on-campus study). *Degree requirements:* For master's, thesis (for some programs). *Entrance requirements:* For master's, PAEP College Board. Electronic applications accepted.

Instituto Tecnológico y de Estudios Superiores de Monterrey, Campus Ciudad de México, School of Business Administration, Ciudad de Mexico, Mexico. Offers business administration (EMBA, MBA, PhD); economy (MBA); finance (MBA). EMBA program offered jointly with The University of Texas at Austin. Part-time and evening/weekend programs available. Postbaccalaureate distance learning degree programs offered (minimal on-campus study). *Entrance requirements:* For master's and doctorate, Instituto entrance exam. Additional exam requirements/recommendations for international students: Required—TOEFL.

Instituto Tecnológico y de Estudios Superiores de Monterrey, Campus Ciudad Juárez, Program in Business Administration, Ciudad Juárez, Mexico. Offers MBA. Part-time programs available. Postbaccalaureate distance learning degree programs offered. *Entrance requirements:* Additional exam requirements/recommendations for international students: Required—TOEFL (minimum score 500 paper-based).

Instituto Tecnológico y de Estudios Superiores de Monterrey, Campus Ciudad Obregón, Program in Administration, Ciudad Obregón, Mexico. Offers MA.

Instituto Tecnológico y de Estudios Superiores de Monterrey, Campus Cuernavaca, Programs in Business Administration, Temixco, Mexico. Offers finance (MA); human resources management (MA); international business (MA); marketing (MA).

Instituto Tecnológico y de Estudios Superiores de Monterrey, Campus Estado de México, Professional and Graduate Division, Estado de Mexico, Mexico. Offers administration of information technologies (MITA); architecture (M Arch); business administration (GMBA, MBA); computer sciences (MCS, PhD); education (M Ed); educational institution administration (MAD); educational technology and innovation (PhD); electronic commerce (MEC); environmental systems (MS); finance (MAF); humanistic studies (MHS); information sciences and knowledge management (MISKM); information systems (MS); manufacturing systems (MS); marketing (MEM); quality systems and productivity (MS); science and materials engineering (PhD); telecommunications management (MTM). Part-time programs available. Postbaccalaureate distance learning degree programs offered (minimal on-campus study). *Degree requirements:* For master's, one foreign language, thesis (for some programs); for doctorate, one foreign language, thesis/dissertation. *Entrance requirements:* For master's, E-PAEP 500, interview; for doctorate, E-PAEP 500, research proposal. Additional exam requirements/recommendations for international students: Required—TOEFL (minimum score 550 paper-based). *Faculty research:* Surface treatments by plasmas, mechanical properties, robotics, graphical computing, mechatronics security protocols.

Instituto Tecnológico y de Estudios Superiores de Monterrey, Campus Guadalajara, Program in Business Administration, Zapopan, Mexico. Offers IEMBA, M Ad. Part-time and evening/weekend programs available. Postbaccalaureate distance learning degree programs offered. *Degree requirements:* For master's, one foreign language. *Entrance requirements:* For master's, ITESM admission test. *Faculty research:* Strategic alliances in small business, family business practice in Mexico, competitiveness under NAFTA for Mexican firms.

Instituto Tecnológico y de Estudios Superiores de Monterrey, Campus Irapuato, Graduate Programs, Irapuato, Mexico. Offers administration (MBA); administration of information technology (MAIT); administration of telecommunications (MAT); architecture (M Arch); computer science (MCS); education (M Ed); educational administration (MEA); educational innovation and technology (DEIT); educational technology (MET); electronic commerce (MBA); environmental administration and planning (MEAP); environmental systems (MES); finances (MBA); humanistic studies (MHS); international management for Latin American executives (MIMLAE); library and information science (MLIS); manufacturing quality management (MMQM); marketing research (MBA).

Instituto Tecnológico y de Estudios Superiores de Monterrey, Campus Laguna, Graduate School, Torreón, Mexico. Offers business administration (MBA); industrial engineering (MIE); management information systems (MS). Part-time programs available. *Entrance requirements:* For master's, GMAT. *Faculty research:* Computer communications from home to the university.

Instituto Tecnológico y de Estudios Superiores de Monterrey, Campus León, Program in Business Administration, León, Mexico. Offers MBA. Part-time programs available.

Instituto Tecnológico y de Estudios Superiores de Monterrey, Campus Monterrey, Graduate School of Business Administration and Leadership, Program in Business Administration, Monterrey, Mexico. Offers business administration (MA, MBA); finance (M Sc); international business (M Sc); marketing (M Sc). *Accreditation:* AACSB. Part-time programs available. *Degree requirements:* For master's, one foreign language, thesis. *Entrance requirements:* For master's, GMAT. Additional exam requirements/recommendations for international students: Required—TOEFL. *Faculty research:* Technology management, quality management, organizational theory and behavior.

Instituto Tecnológico y de Estudios Superiores de Monterrey, Campus Monterrey, Graduate School of Business Administration and Leadership, Program in Management, Monterrey, Mexico. Offers PhD. *Accreditation:* AACSB. Part-time programs available. *Degree requirements:* For doctorate, one foreign language, thesis/dissertation. *Entrance requirements:* For doctorate, GMAT. Additional exam requirements/recommendations for international students: Required—TOEFL. *Faculty research:* Quality management, manufacturing and technology management, information systems, managerial economics, business policy.

Instituto Tecnológico y de Estudios Superiores de Monterrey, Campus Querétaro, School of Business, Santiago de Querétaro, Mexico. Offers MBA. *Entrance requirements:* For master's, GRE General Test. *Faculty research:* Organizational analysis, industrial marketing, international trade.

Instituto Tecnológico y de Estudios Superiores de Monterrey, Campus Sonora Norte, Program in Business, Hermosillo, Mexico. Offers MA. *Entrance requirements:* For master's, GMAT.

Instituto Tecnológico y de Estudios Superiores de Monterrey, Campus Toluca, Graduate Programs, Toluca, Mexico. Offers MBA. Part-time and evening/weekend programs available. *Degree requirements:* For master's, one foreign language. *Faculty research:* Management in the industrial valley of Toluca.

Inter American University of Puerto Rico, Aguadilla Campus, Graduate School, Aguadilla, PR 00605. Offers accounting (MBA); counseling psychology specializing in family (MS); criminal justice (MA); educative management and leadership (MA); elementary education (M Ed); finance (MBA); human resources (MBA); industrial management (MBA); management information systems (MBA); marketing (MBA). Part-time and evening/weekend programs available. *Degree requirements:* For master's, comprehensive exam. *Entrance requirements:* For master's, EXADEP, 2 letters of recommendation, minimum GPA of 2.5. Electronic applications accepted.

Inter American University of Puerto Rico, Arecibo Campus, Program in Business Administration, Arecibo, PR 00614-4050. Offers accounting (MBA); finance (MBA); human resources (MBA).

Inter American University of Puerto Rico, Barranquitas Campus, Program in Business Administration, Barranquitas, PR 00794. Offers accounting (IMBA); finance (IMBA).

Inter American University of Puerto Rico, Guayama Campus, Department of Business Administration, Guayama, PR 00785. Offers marketing (MBA).

Inter American University of Puerto Rico, Metropolitan Campus, Graduate Programs, Program in General Business, San Juan, PR 00919-1293. Offers MBA.

Inter American University of Puerto Rico, San Germán Campus, Graduate Studies Center, Program in Business Administration, San Germán, PR 00683-5008. Offers accounting (MBA); finance (MBA); general business administration (MBA); human resources (MBA, PhD); industrial relations (MBA); information systems (MBA); international and interregional business (PhD); management (MBA); marketing (MBA). Part-time and evening/weekend programs available. *Faculty:* 8 full-time (2 women), 4 part-time/adjunct (3 women). *Students:* 138 full-time (80 women), 35 part-time (21 women); includes 172 minority (all Hispanic/Latino). 60 applicants, 65% accepted, 38 enrolled. In 2013, 38 master's, 3 doctorates awarded. *Degree requirements:* For master's, comprehensive exam. *Entrance requirements:* For master's, GRE General Test or EXADEP, minimum GPA of 3.0. *Application deadline:* For fall admission, 4/30 priority date for domestic students; for spring admission, 11/15 for domestic students. Applications are processed on a rolling basis. Application fee: $31. *Expenses: Tuition:* Full-time $2424; part-time $202 per credit hour. *Required fees:* $260 per semester. Tuition and fees vary according to course level, course load, degree level and program. *Financial support:* Teaching assistantships, Federal Work-Study, and unspecified assistantships available. *Unit head:* Dr. Elba T. Irizarry, Director of Graduate Studies Center, 787-264-1912 Ext. 7357, Fax: 787-892-6350, E-mail: elbat@sg.inter.edu. *Application contact:* Dr. Ailin Padilla, Coordinator, 787-264-1912 Ext. 7355, E-mail: ailin_padilla@intersg.edu.

International College of the Cayman Islands, Graduate Program in Management, Newlands, Cayman Islands. Offers business administration (MBA); management (MS), including education, human resources. Part-time and evening/weekend programs available. *Degree requirements:* For master's, comprehensive exam. *Entrance requirements:* Additional exam requirements/recommendations for international students: Recommended—TOEFL. *Faculty research:* International human resources administration.

International Technological University, Program in Business Administration, San Jose, CA 95113. Offers MBA. Part-time and evening/weekend programs available. *Degree requirements:* For master's, thesis or alternative. *Entrance requirements:* For

master's, 1 semester of calculus, minimum GPA of 2.5. Additional exam requirements/recommendations for international students: Required—TOEFL. *Faculty research:* High tech management, business management, international marketing.

The International University of Monaco, Graduate Programs, Monte Carlo, Monaco. Offers entrepreneurship (EMBA, MBA); financial engineering (M Sc); hedge fund and private equity (M Sc); international marketing (EMBA, MBA); international wealth management (M Sc); luxury goods and services (EMBA, M Sc, MBA); wealth and asset management (EMBA, MBA). Part-time programs available. *Degree requirements:* For master's, comprehensive exam (for some programs), applied research project. *Entrance requirements:* Additional exam requirements/recommendations for international students: Required—TOEFL (minimum score 550 paper-based), IELTS. Electronic applications accepted. *Faculty research:* Gaming, leadership, disintermediation.

Iona College, Hagan School of Business, New Rochelle, NY 10801-1890. Offers MBA, MS, AC, PMC. *Accreditation:* AACSB. Part-time and evening/weekend programs available. *Faculty:* 28 full-time (6 women), 14 part-time/adjunct (3 women). *Students:* 128 full-time (59 women), 240 part-time (114 women); includes 52 minority (17 Black or African American, non-Hispanic/Latino; 7 Asian, non-Hispanic/Latino; 28 Hispanic/Latino), 31 international. Average age 29. 123 applicants, 94% accepted, 81 enrolled. In 2013, 224 master's, 192 other advanced degrees awarded. *Entrance requirements:* For master's, GMAT, 2 letters of recommendation. Additional exam requirements/recommendations for international students: Required—TOEFL (minimum score 550 paper-based; 80 iBT), IELTS (minimum score 6.5). *Application deadline:* For fall admission, 8/15 priority date for domestic students, 8/1 priority date for international students; for winter admission, 11/15 priority date for domestic students, 11/1 priority date for international students; for spring admission, 2/15 priority date for domestic students, 2/1 priority date for international students; for summer admission, 5/15 priority date for domestic students, 5/1 priority date for international students. Applications are processed on a rolling basis. Application fee: $50. Electronic applications accepted. *Expenses: Tuition:* Part-time $948 per credit. *Required fees:* $235 per term. *Financial support:* In 2013–14, 161 students received support. Scholarships/grants, tuition waivers (partial), and unspecified assistantships available. Support available to part-time students. Financial award application deadline: 4/15; financial award applicants required to submit FAFSA. *Faculty research:* Artificial intelligence, financial services, value-based management, public policy, business ethics. *Unit head:* Dr. Vincent Calluzzo, Dean, 914-633-2256, E-mail: vcalluzzo@iona.edu. *Application contact:* Cameron Hudson, Director of MBA Admissions, 914-633-2288, Fax: 914-637-2708, E-mail: chudson@iona.edu.
Website: http://www.iona.edu/Academics/Hagan-School-of-Business.aspx.

Ithaca College, School of Business, Program in Business Administration, Ithaca, NY 14850. Offers MBA. *Accreditation:* AACSB. Part-time programs available. *Faculty:* 16 full-time (6 women). *Students:* 11 full-time (4 women), 7 part-time (4 women); includes 2 minority (both Hispanic/Latino), 2 international. Average age 29. 43 applicants, 51% accepted, 12 enrolled. In 2013, 15 master's awarded. *Degree requirements:* For master's, thesis optional. *Entrance requirements:* For master's, GMAT, minimum GPA of 3.0. Additional exam requirements/recommendations for international students: Required—TOEFL (minimum score 550 paper-based; 80 iBT). *Application deadline:* For fall admission, 5/15 for domestic and international students; for spring admission, 11/1 for domestic and international students. Applications are processed on a rolling basis. Application fee: $40. Electronic applications accepted. *Expenses:* Contact institution. *Financial support:* In 2013–14, 12 students received support, including 7 fellowships (averaging $8,071 per year), 4 teaching assistantships (averaging $6,297 per year); career-related internships or fieldwork, Federal Work-Study, and scholarships/grants also available. Support available to part-time students. Financial award application deadline: 3/1; financial award applicants required to submit CSS PROFILE or FAFSA. *Unit head:* Dr. Barbara Howard, MBA Program Director, 607-274-1762, Fax: 607-274-1263, E-mail: bhoward@ithaca.edu. *Application contact:* Gerard Turbide, Director, Office of Admission, 607-274-3143, Fax: 607-274-1263, E-mail: gps@ithaca.edu.
Website: http://www.ithaca.edu/business/mba.

ITT Technical Institute, Online MBA Program, Indianapolis, IN 46268-1119. Offers MBA.

Jackson State University, Graduate School, College of Business, Department of Economics, Finance and General Business, Jackson, MS 39217. Offers business administration (MBA, PhD). *Accreditation:* AACSB. Part-time and evening/weekend programs available. *Degree requirements:* For master's, comprehensive exam, thesis. *Entrance requirements:* For master's, GRE General Test, GMAT; for doctorate, MAT, GMAT. Additional exam requirements/recommendations for international students: Required—TOEFL.

Jacksonville State University, College of Graduate Studies and Continuing Education, College of Commerce and Business Administration, Jacksonville, AL 36265-1602. Offers MBA. *Accreditation:* AACSB. Part-time and evening/weekend programs available. *Degree requirements:* For master's, comprehensive exam, thesis (for some programs). *Entrance requirements:* For master's, GMAT. Additional exam requirements/recommendations for international students: Required—TOEFL (minimum score 500 paper-based; 61 iBT). Electronic applications accepted.

Jacksonville University, Davis College of Business, Accelerated Day-time MBA Program, Jacksonville, FL 32211. Offers accounting and finance (MBA); management (MBA); management accounting (MBA). *Faculty:* 12 full-time (1 woman). *Students:* 35 full-time (19 women), 2 part-time (0 women); includes 6 minority (2 Black or African American, non-Hispanic/Latino; 1 Asian, non-Hispanic/Latino; 3 Hispanic/Latino), 21 international. Average age 26. 47 applicants, 66% accepted, 22 enrolled. In 2013, 59 master's awarded. *Entrance requirements:* For master's, GRE or GMAT (may be waived for 3.3 undergraduate GPA or higher from AACSB-accredited institution). Additional exam requirements/recommendations for international students: Required—TOEFL, IELTS. *Application deadline:* For fall admission, 8/1 priority date for domestic students, 7/15 priority date for international students; for spring admission, 12/1 priority date for domestic students, 11/15 priority date for international students. Application fee: $50. Electronic applications accepted. *Expenses:* Contact institution. *Financial support:* In 2013–14, 4 students received support. Scholarships/grants and unspecified assistantships available. Financial award applicants required to submit FAFSA. *Faculty research:* Behavioral finance, game theory, regional economic integration, information sabotage, public choice and public finance. *Unit head:* Dr. Mohamad Sepehri, Associate Dean and Graduate Programs Director, 904-256-7435, Fax: 904-256-7168, E-mail: msepehr@ju.edu. *Application contact:* AnnaMaria Murphy, Admissions Counselor, 904-256-7426, Fax: 904-256-7168, E-mail: mba@ju.edu.
Website: http://www.ju.edu/dcob/AcademicPrograms/Pages/Accelerated-MBA.aspx.

Jacksonville University, Davis College of Business, Executive Master of Business Administration Program, Jacksonville, FL 32211. Offers leadership development (MBA). *Accreditation:* AACSB. Evening/weekend programs available. *Faculty:* 15 full-time (4 women), 1 part-time/adjunct (0 women). *Students:* 27 full-time (6 women); includes 10 minority (5 Black or African American, non-Hispanic/Latino; 2 Asian, non-Hispanic/Latino; 3 Hispanic/Latino). Average age 39. 15 applicants, 100% accepted, 13 enrolled. In 2013, 11 master's awarded. *Entrance requirements:* For master's, 7 years of managerial or professional experience. Additional exam requirements/recommendations for international students: Required—TOEFL. *Application deadline:* For fall admission, 9/1 priority date for domestic students, 8/15 priority date for international students. Application fee: $50. Electronic applications accepted. *Expenses:* Contact institution. *Financial support:* Application deadline: 8/15; applicants required to submit FAFSA. *Faculty research:* Data analytics, emerging markets and economic development, high-performing teams, government deficit, learning from corporate failure. *Unit head:* Dr. Mohamad Sepehri, Associate Dean and Director of Graduate Studies, 904-256-7435, Fax: 904-256-7168, E-mail: msepehr@ju.edu. *Application contact:* AnnaMaria Murphy, Admissions Counselor, 904-256-7426, Fax: 904-256-7168, E-mail: mba@ju.edu.
Website: http://www.ju.edu/DCOB/AcademicPrograms/Pages/Executive-MBA.aspx.

Jacksonville University, Davis College of Business, FLEX Master of Business Administration Program, Jacksonville, FL 32211. Offers accounting and finance (MBA); management (MBA); management accounting (MBA). *Accreditation:* AACSB. Part-time and evening/weekend programs available. *Faculty:* 19 full-time (3 women). *Students:* 77 full-time (32 women), 35 part-time (16 women); includes 40 minority (23 Black or African American, non-Hispanic/Latino; 1 American Indian or Alaska Native, non-Hispanic/Latino; 7 Asian, non-Hispanic/Latino; 8 Hispanic/Latino; 1 Native Hawaiian or other Pacific Islander, non-Hispanic/Latino), 4 international. Average age 31. 77 applicants, 38% accepted, 24 enrolled. In 2013, 54 master's awarded. *Entrance requirements:* For master's, GMAT or GRE (may be waived for 3.3 or higher undergraduate GPA from AACSB-accredited institution). Additional exam requirements/recommendations for international students: Required—TOEFL, IELTS. *Application deadline:* For fall admission, 8/1 priority date for domestic students, 7/15 priority date for international students; for spring admission, 12/1 priority date for domestic students, 11/15 priority date for international students; for summer admission, 4/1 priority date for domestic students, 3/15 priority date for international students. Applications are processed on a rolling basis. Application fee: $50. Electronic applications accepted. *Expenses:* Contact institution. *Financial support:* Application deadline: 3/15; applicants required to submit FAFSA. *Faculty research:* Downsizing with integrity; impact of YouTube videos; game theory; analysis of effective tax rates; creativity innovation and change. *Unit head:* Dr. Mohamad Sepehri, Associate Dean and Director of Graduate Studies, 904-256-7435, Fax: 904-256-7168, E-mail: mba@ju.edu. *Application contact:* AnnaMaria Murphy, Admissions Counselor, 904-256-7426, Fax: 904-256-7168, E-mail: mba@ju.edu.

James Madison University, The Graduate School, College of Business, Program in Business Administration, Harrisonburg, VA 22807. Offers MBA. *Accreditation:* AACSB. Part-time and evening/weekend programs available. Postbaccalaureate distance learning degree programs offered (no on-campus study). *Students:* 30 full-time (15 women), 51 part-time (13 women); includes 19 minority (6 Black or African American, non-Hispanic/Latino; 9 Asian, non-Hispanic/Latino; 1 Hispanic/Latino; 3 Two or more races, non-Hispanic/Latino), 1 international. Average age 27. In 2013, 8 master's awarded. *Entrance requirements:* For master's, GMAT, resume, 2 letters of recommendation. Additional exam requirements/recommendations for international students: Required—TOEFL. *Application deadline:* For fall admission, 6/1 priority date for domestic students, 5/1 for international students; for spring admission, 6/1 for domestic students, 9/1 for international students. Applications are processed on a rolling basis. Application fee: $55. Electronic applications accepted. *Financial support:* In 2013–14, 3 students received support. Federal Work-Study and 1 athletic assistantship (averaging $8837), 2 graduate assistantships (averaging $7530) available. Financial award application deadline: 3/1; financial award applicants required to submit FAFSA. *Unit head:* Dr. Paul E. Bierly, Director, 540-568-3009. *Application contact:* Lynette M. Bible, Director of Graduate Admissions, 540-568-6395, Fax: 540-568-7860, E-mail: biblelm@jmu.edu.

John Brown University, Graduate Business Programs, Siloam Springs, AR 72761-2121. Offers global continuous improvement (MBA); higher education leadership (MS); international community development leadership (MS); leadership and ethics (MBA, MS). *Accreditation:* ACBSP. Part-time and evening/weekend programs available. Postbaccalaureate distance learning degree programs offered (minimal on-campus study). *Faculty:* 6 full-time (1 woman), 29 part-time/adjunct (8 women). *Students:* 23 full-time (13 women), 210 part-time (102 women); includes 41 minority (14 Black or African American, non-Hispanic/Latino; 5 American Indian or Alaska Native, non-Hispanic/Latino; 3 Asian, non-Hispanic/Latino; 11 Hispanic/Latino; 8 Two or more races, non-Hispanic/Latino), 3 international. Average age 34. 121 applicants, 98% accepted, 99 enrolled. *Entrance requirements:* For master's, MAT, GMAT or GRE if undergraduate GPA is less than 3.0, recommendation forms from three people, 200-word essay describing professional plans and reason for seeking acceptance. Additional exam requirements/recommendations for international students: Required—TOEFL (minimum score 550 paper-based; 70 iBT). *Application deadline:* Applications are processed on a rolling basis. Application fee: $35 ($100 for international students). Electronic applications accepted. *Expenses: Tuition:* Part-time $515 per credit hour. *Financial support:* Fellowships with full tuition reimbursements, scholarships/grants, and unspecified assistantships available. Financial award applicants required to submit FAFSA. *Unit head:* Dr. Joe Walenciak, Program Director, 479-524-7431, E-mail: jwalenci@jbu.edu. *Application contact:* Brent Young, Graduate Business Representative, 479-524-7450, E-mail: byoung@jbu.edu.
Website: http://www.jbu.edu/grad/business/.

John Carroll University, Graduate School, John M. and Mary Jo Boler School of Business, University Heights, OH 44118-4581. Offers accountancy (MS); business (MBA). *Accreditation:* AACSB. Part-time and evening/weekend programs available. *Entrance requirements:* For master's, GMAT, minimum GPA of 2.5. Additional exam requirements/recommendations for international students: Required—TOEFL (minimum score 550 paper-based). Electronic applications accepted. *Expenses:* Contact institution. *Faculty research:* Accounting, economics and finance, management, marketing and logistics.

John F. Kennedy University, School of Management, Program in Business Administration, Pleasant Hill, CA 94523-4817. Offers business administration (MBA); organizational leadership (Certificate). Part-time and evening/weekend programs available. *Degree requirements:* For master's, thesis or alternative. *Entrance requirements:* For master's, interview. Additional exam requirements/recommendations for international students: Required—TOEFL.

John Hancock University, MBA Program, Oakbrook Terrace, IL 60181. Offers e-commerce (MBA); finance (MBA); general business (MBA); global management (MBA); health care administration (MBA); leadership (MBA); management of information systems (MBA); marketing (MBA); professional accounting (MBA); project management (MBA); public accounting (MBA); risk management (MBA).

John Hancock University, Program in Management, Oakbrook Terrace, IL 60181. Offers MS. *Degree requirements:* For master's, capstone course.

Johns Hopkins University, Carey Business School, MBA Programs, Baltimore, MD 21218-2699. Offers Exec MBA, MBA, MBA/JD, MBA/MA, MBA/MD, MBA/MPH, MBA/MS, MBA/MSIS, MBA/MSN. Part-time and evening/weekend programs available. Postbaccalaureate distance learning degree programs offered (minimal on-campus study). *Faculty:* 29 full-time (6 women), 135 part-time/adjunct (29 women). *Students:*

282 full-time (120 women), 454 part-time (150 women); includes 219 minority (77 Black or African American, non-Hispanic/Latino; 94 Asian, non-Hispanic/Latino; 33 Hispanic/Latino; 2 Native Hawaiian or other Pacific Islander, non-Hispanic/Latino; 13 Two or more races, non-Hispanic/Latino), 144 international. Average age 33. 425 applicants, 73% accepted, 169 enrolled. In 2013, 271 master's awarded. *Degree requirements:* For master's, capstone project (MBA). *Entrance requirements:* For master's, GMAT or GRE, minimum GPA of 3.0, resume, work experience, two letters of recommendation. Additional exam requirements/recommendations for international students: Required—TOEFL (minimum score 600 paper-based; 100 iBT). *Application deadline:* For fall admission, 4/1 for international students; for spring admission, 8/15 for international students. Applications are processed on a rolling basis. Application fee: $100. Electronic applications accepted. *Financial support:* Scholarships/grants available. Support available to part-time students. Financial award application deadline: 4/15; financial award applicants required to submit FAFSA. *Unit head:* Dr. Dipankar Chakravarti, Vice Dean of Programs, 410-234-9311, Fax: 410-516-2033, E-mail: dipankar.chakravarti@jhu.edu. *Application contact:* Robin Greenberg, Admissions Coordinator, 410-234-9227, Fax: 443-529-1554, E-mail: carey.admissions@jhu.edu.
Website: http://carey.jhu.edu/academics/master-of-business-administration/.

Johns Hopkins University, School of Education, Master's Programs in Education, Baltimore, MD 21218-2699. Offers counseling (MS), including mental health counseling, school counseling; education (MS), including educational studies, gifted education, reading, school administration and supervision, technology for educators; elementary education (MAT); health professions (M Ed); intelligence analysis (MS); management (MS); secondary education (MAT); special education (MS), including early childhood special education, general special education studies, mild to moderate disabilities, severe disabilities. Part-time and evening/weekend programs available. Postbaccalaureate distance learning degree programs offered (no on-campus study). *Students:* 183 full-time (123 women), 1,001 part-time (757 women); includes 380 minority (160 Black or African American, non-Hispanic/Latino; 4 American Indian or Alaska Native, non-Hispanic/Latino; 91 Asian, non-Hispanic/Latino; 78 Hispanic/Latino; 4 Native Hawaiian or other Pacific Islander, non-Hispanic/Latino; 43 Two or more races, non-Hispanic/Latino), 28 international. Average age 28. 508 applicants, 90% accepted, 337 enrolled. In 2013, 565 degrees awarded. *Degree requirements:* For master's, comprehensive exam (for some programs), portfolio, capstone project and/or internship; PRAXIS II (for teacher preparation programs that lead to licensure). *Entrance requirements:* For master's, GRE (for full-time programs only); PRAXIS I or equivalent (for teacher preparation programs that lead to licensure), bachelor's degree from regionally- or nationally-accredited institution, minimum GPA of 3.0 in all previous programs of study, official transcripts from all post-secondary institutions attended, essay, curriculum vitae/resume, minimum of two letters of recommendation. Additional exam requirements/recommendations for international students: Required—TOEFL (minimum score 600 paper-based; 100 iBT) or IELTS (minimum score 7). *Application deadline:* For fall admission, 4/1 for domestic and international students; for spring admission, 10/1 for domestic and international students; for summer admission, 2/1 for domestic and international students. Application fee: $80. Electronic applications accepted. *Financial support:* Application deadline: 6/1; applicants required to submit FAFSA. *Unit head:* Dr. David A. Andrews, Dean, 410-516-7820, Fax: 410-516-6697, E-mail: davidandrews@jhu.edu. *Application contact:* Catherine Wilson, Associate Director of Admissions, 410-516-9797, Fax: 410-516-9799, E-mail: soe.info@jhu.edu.

Johnson & Wales University, Graduate School, MBA Program, Providence, RI 02903-3703. Offers MBA. Part-time programs available. *Entrance requirements:* For master's, minimum GPA of 2.75. Additional exam requirements/recommendations for international students: Required—TOEFL (minimum score 550 paper-based) or IELTS (recommended); Recommended—TWE. *Faculty research:* International banking, global economy, international trade, cultural differences.

Jones International University, School of Business, Centennial, CO 80112. Offers accounting (MBA); business communication (MABC); entrepreneurship (MABC, MBA); finance (MBA); global enterprise management (MBA); health care management (MBA); information security management (MBA); information technology management (MBA); leadership and influence (MABC); leading the customer-driven organization (MABC); negotiation and conflict management (MBA); project management (MABC, MBA). Program only offered online. Part-time and evening/weekend programs available. Postbaccalaureate distance learning degree programs offered (no on-campus study). *Degree requirements:* For master's, capstone project. *Entrance requirements:* For master's, minimum cumulative GPA of 2.5. Additional exam requirements/recommendations for international students: Recommended—TOEFL (minimum score 550 paper-based). Electronic applications accepted.

Judson University, Graduate Programs, Master of Business Administration Program, Elgin, IL 60123-1498. Offers MBA. Evening/weekend programs available. Postbaccalaureate distance learning degree programs offered (no on-campus study). *Faculty:* 1 (woman) full-time. *Students:* 23 full-time (10 women); includes 7 minority (6 Black or African American, non-Hispanic/Latino; 1 Hispanic/Latino). *Entrance requirements:* For master's, bachelor's degree from college or university; minimum overall undergraduate GPA of 3.0; two years of work experience; two letters of recommendation; professional resume; two letters of reference from pastors and/or other professionals in Christian ministry leadership; personal essay. *Application deadline:* Applications are processed on a rolling basis. Application fee: $35. Electronic applications accepted. *Financial support:* Applicants required to submit FAFSA. *Faculty research:* Ethics. *Unit head:* Dr. Michelle L. Kilbourne, Director, 847-268-1515, E-mail: mkilbourne@judsonu.edu. *Application contact:* Maria Aguirre, Assistant to the Registrar for Graduate Programs, 847-628-1160, E-mail: maguirre@judsonu.edu.
Website: http://www.judsonu.edu/Graduate/Master_of_Business_Administration/Overview/.

Kansas State University, Graduate School, College of Business Administration, Program in Business Administration, Manhattan, KS 66506. Offers enterprise information systems (MBA); entrepreneurial technology (MBA); finance (MBA); management (MBA); supply chain management (MBA). *Accreditation:* AACSB. Part-time programs available. *Faculty:* 1 full-time (0 women), 2 part-time/adjunct (0 women). *Students:* 54 full-time (25 women), 24 part-time (14 women); includes 9 minority (3 Black or African American, non-Hispanic/Latino; 2 Asian, non-Hispanic/Latino; 2 Hispanic/Latino; 2 Two or more races, non-Hispanic/Latino), 22 international. Average age 26. 121 applicants, 69% accepted, 23 enrolled. In 2013, 28 master's awarded. *Entrance requirements:* For master's, GMAT (minimum score of 500), minimum undergraduate GPA of 3.0. Additional exam requirements/recommendations for international students: Required—TOEFL (minimum score 550 paper-based; 79 iBT); Recommended—IELTS (minimum score 7). *Application deadline:* For fall admission, 2/1 priority date for domestic and international students; for spring admission, 10/1 priority date for domestic students, 8/1 priority date for international students. Applications are processed on a rolling basis. Application fee: $70 ($80 for international students). Electronic applications accepted. *Financial support:* In 2013–14, 1 research assistantship with partial tuition reimbursement (averaging $8,320 per year) was awarded; institutionally sponsored loans and scholarships/grants also available. Financial award application deadline: 3/1; financial award applicants required to submit FAFSA. *Faculty research:* Organizational citizenship behavior, service marketing, impression management, human resources management, lean manufacturing and supply chain management, financial market behavior and investment management. *Total annual research expenditures:* $11,288. *Unit head:* Dr. Ali Malekzadeh, Dean, 785-532-7227, Fax: 785-532-7216. *Application contact:* Dr. Stacy Kovar, Associate Dean for Academic Programs, 785-532-7190, Fax: 785-532-7809, E-mail: gradbusiness@ksu.edu.
Website: http://www.cba.k-state.edu/.

Kansas Wesleyan University, Program in Business Administration, Salina, KS 67401-6196. Offers business administration (MBA); sports management (MBA). Part-time and evening/weekend programs available. *Entrance requirements:* For master's, GMAT, minimum graduate GPA of 3.0 or undergraduate GPA of 3.25.

Kaplan University, Davenport Campus, School of Business, Davenport, IA 52807-2095. Offers business administration (MBA); change leadership (MS); entrepreneurship (MBA); finance (MBA); health care management (MBA, MS); human resource (MBA); international business (MBA); management (MS); marketing (MBA); project management (MBA, MS); supply chain management and logistics (MBA, MS). *Accreditation:* ACBSP. Part-time and evening/weekend programs available. Postbaccalaureate distance learning degree programs offered (no on-campus study). *Entrance requirements:* Additional exam requirements/recommendations for international students: Required—TOEFL (minimum score 550 paper-based; 80 iBT). Electronic applications accepted.

Kean University, Nathan Weiss Graduate College, Program in Educational Administration, Union, NJ 07083. Offers school business administration (MA); supervisors and principals (MA); supervisors, principals and school business administrators (MA). *Accreditation:* NCATE. Part-time programs available. *Faculty:* 7 full-time (4 women). *Students:* 4 full-time (2 women), 148 part-time (89 women); includes 46 minority (24 Black or African American, non-Hispanic/Latino; 4 Asian, non-Hispanic/Latino; 18 Hispanic/Latino), 1 international. Average age 36. 99 applicants, 99% accepted, 59 enrolled. In 2013, 49 master's awarded. *Degree requirements:* For master's, comprehensive exam (for some programs), portfolio, field experience, research component, internship, teaching experience. *Entrance requirements:* For master's, GRE General Test or MAT, minimum GPA of 3.0; New Jersey or out-of-state Standard Instructional or Educational Services Certificate; one year of experience under the appropriate certificate; official transcripts from all institutions attended; two letters of recommendation; personal statement; professional resume/curriculum vitae. Additional exam requirements/recommendations for international students: Required—TOEFL (minimum score 550 paper-based; 79 iBT). *Application deadline:* For fall admission, 6/1 for domestic and international students; for spring admission, 12/1 for domestic and international students. Applications are processed on a rolling basis. Application fee: $75 ($150 for international students). Electronic applications accepted. *Expenses:* Tuition, state resident: full-time $12,099; part-time $589 per credit. Tuition, nonresident: full-time $16,399; part-time $722 per credit. *Required fees:* $3050; $139 per credit. Part-time tuition and fees vary according to course level, course load, degree level and program. *Financial support:* In 2013–14, research assistantships with full tuition reimbursements (averaging $3,713 per year) were awarded; unspecified assistantships also available. Financial award applicants required to submit FAFSA. *Unit head:* Dr. Leila Sadeghi, Program Coordinator, 908-737-5977, E-mail: lsadeghi@kean.edu. *Application contact:* Ann-Marie Kay, Assistant Director of Graduate Admissions, 908-737-5922, Fax: 908-737-5925, E-mail: akay@kean.edu.
Website: http://grad.kean.edu/edleadership.

Keiser University, Doctor of Business Administration Program, Ft. Lauderdale, FL 33309. Offers global business (DBA); global organizational leadership (DBA); marketing (DBA).

Keiser University, Joint MS Ed/MBA Program, Ft. Lauderdale, FL 33309. Offers MS Ed/MBA.

Keiser University, Master of Business Administration Program, Ft. Lauderdale, FL 33309. Offers accounting (MBA); health services management (MBA); information security management (MBA); international business (MBA); leadership for managers (MBA); marketing (MBA). All concentrations except information security management also offered in Mandarin; leadership for managers and international business also offered in Spanish. Part-time programs available. Postbaccalaureate distance learning degree programs offered (minimal on-campus study).

Keiser University, MS in Management Program, Ft. Lauderdale, FL 33309. Offers MS. Program also offered in Spanish.

Kennesaw State University, Michael J. Coles College of Business, Doctor of Business Administration Program, Kennesaw, GA 30144-5591. Offers DBA. *Accreditation:* AACSB. Part-time programs available. *Students:* 14 full-time (7 women), 45 part-time (19 women); includes 11 minority (9 Black or African American, non-Hispanic/Latino; 2 Hispanic/Latino), 1 international. Average age 47. In 2013, 13 doctorates awarded. *Degree requirements:* For doctorate, thesis/dissertation. *Entrance requirements:* Additional exam requirements/recommendations for international students: Required—TOEFL (minimum score 550 paper-based; 80 iBT), IELTS (minimum score 6). *Application deadline:* For spring admission, 10/1 for domestic and international students. Applications are processed on a rolling basis. Application fee: $100. Electronic applications accepted. *Expenses:* Tuition, state resident: full-time $4806; part-time $267 per semester hour. Tuition, nonresident: full-time $17,298; part-time $961 per semester hour. *Required fees:* $1834; $784.50 per semester. *Financial support:* Application deadline: 4/1; applicants required to submit FAFSA. *Unit head:* Dr. Neal Mero, Director, 770-499-3306, E-mail: nmero@kennesaw.edu. *Application contact:* Susan Cochran, Administrative Coordinator, 678-797-2802, Fax: 770-423-6885, E-mail: scochran@kennesaw.edu.

Kennesaw State University, Michael J. Coles College of Business, Program in Business Administration, Kennesaw, GA 30144-5591. Offers MBA. *Accreditation:* AACSB. Part-time and evening/weekend programs available. Postbaccalaureate distance learning degree programs offered (no on-campus study). *Students:* 77 full-time (34 women), 266 part-time (103 women); includes 85 minority (55 Black or African American, non-Hispanic/Latino; 7 Asian, non-Hispanic/Latino; 18 Hispanic/Latino; 5 Two or more races, non-Hispanic/Latino), 12 international. Average age 34. 321 applicants, 46% accepted, 104 enrolled. In 2013, 209 master's awarded. *Entrance requirements:* For master's, GMAT (minimum score 530), minimum GPA of 2.8, 1 year of work experience. Additional exam requirements/recommendations for international students: Required—TOEFL (minimum score 550 paper-based; 80 iBT), IELTS (minimum score 6). *Application deadline:* For fall admission, 7/1 for domestic and international students; for spring admission, 12/1 for domestic and international students; for summer admission, 5/1 for domestic and international students. Applications are processed on a rolling basis. Application fee: $60. Electronic applications accepted. *Expenses:* Tuition, state resident: full-time $4806; part-time $267 per semester hour. Tuition, nonresident: full-time $17,298; part-time $961 per semester hour. *Required fees:* $1834; $784.50 per semester. *Financial support:* In 2013–14, 4 research assistantships with tuition reimbursements (averaging $8,000 per year) were awarded; unspecified assistantships also available. Financial award application deadline: 4/1; financial award applicants required to submit FAFSA. *Unit head:* Dr. Raj Veliyath, Director, 770-499-3329, E-mail:

rveliyat@kennesaw.edu. *Application contact:* Admissions Counselor, 770-420-4377, Fax: 770-423-6885, E-mail: ksugrad@kennesaw.edu.
Website: http://www.kennesaw.edu.

Kent State University, College of Business Administration, Master's Program in Business Administration, Kent, OH 44242-0001. Offers MBA. *Accreditation:* AACSB. Part-time and evening/weekend programs available. *Faculty:* 65 full-time (22 women). *Students:* 46 full-time (28 women), 80 part-time (33 women); includes 13 minority (7 Black or African American, non-Hispanic/Latino; 3 Asian, non-Hispanic/Latino; 2 Hispanic/Latino; 1 Two or more races, non-Hispanic/Latino), 10 international. Average age 29. 131 applicants, 59% accepted, 44 enrolled. In 2013, 63 master's awarded. *Entrance requirements:* For master's, GMAT, minimum GPA of 2.75. Additional exam requirements/recommendations for international students: Required—TOEFL (minimum score 550 paper-based; 79 iBT). *Application deadline:* For fall admission, 6/1 for domestic students, 4/1 for international students; for spring admission, 12/1 for domestic students. Application fee: $30 ($70 for international students). Electronic applications accepted. *Financial support:* In 2013–14, 16 students received support, including 16 research assistantships with full tuition reimbursements available (averaging $19,000 per year); fellowships, career-related internships or fieldwork, Federal Work-Study, and unspecified assistantships also available. Financial award application deadline: 4/1; financial award applicants required to submit FAFSA. *Unit head:* Louise M. Ditchey, Administrative Director, 330-672-2282, Fax: 330-672-7303, E-mail: gradbus@kent.edu. *Application contact:* Felecia A. Urbanek, Coordinator, Graduate Programs, 330-672-2282, Fax: 330-672-7303, E-mail: gradbus@kent.edu.

Kent State University at Stark, Professional MBA Program, Canton, OH 44720-7599. Offers MBA.

Kentucky State University, College of Business and Computer Science, Frankfort, KY 40601. Offers business administration (MBA); computer science technology (MS). *Accreditation:* ACBSP. Part-time and evening/weekend programs available. Postbaccalaureate distance learning degree programs offered. *Degree requirements:* For master's, comprehensive exam, thesis optional. *Entrance requirements:* For master's, GMAT, GRE. Additional exam requirements/recommendations for international students: Required—TOEFL (minimum score 525 paper-based). Electronic applications accepted.

Kettering University, Graduate School, Department of Business, Flint, MI 48504. Offers MBA, MS. *Accreditation:* ACBSP. Part-time and evening/weekend programs available. Postbaccalaureate distance learning degree programs offered (no on-campus study). *Faculty:* 7 full-time (3 women), 1 part-time/adjunct (0 women). *Students:* 15 full-time (4 women), 219 part-time (64 women); includes 40 minority (19 Black or African American, non-Hispanic/Latino; 9 Asian, non-Hispanic/Latino; 11 Hispanic/Latino; 1 Two or more races, non-Hispanic/Latino), 13 international. Average age 33. 152 applicants, 51% accepted, 40 enrolled. In 2013, 101 master's awarded. *Entrance requirements:* Additional exam requirements/recommendations for international students: Required—TOEFL (minimum score 550 paper-based; 79 iBT). *Application deadline:* For fall admission, 9/15 for domestic students, 6/15 for international students; for winter admission, 12/15 for domestic students, 9/15 for international students; for spring admission, 3/15 for domestic students, 12/15 for international students. Applications are processed on a rolling basis. Electronic applications accepted. *Expenses: Tuition:* Part-time $798 per credit hour. *Financial support:* Tuition waivers (partial) available. Financial award application deadline: 7/15; financial award applicants required to submit FAFSA. *Unit head:* Karen Cayo, Department Head, 810-762-7969, E-mail: kcayo@kettering.edu. *Application contact:* Bonnie Switzer, Admissions Representative, 810-762-7953, Fax: 810-762-9935, E-mail: bswitzer@kettering.edu.

Keuka College, Program in Management, Keuka Park, NY 14478-0098. Offers MS. Evening/weekend programs available. *Faculty:* 3 full-time (1 woman), 15 part-time/adjunct (5 women). *Students:* 13 full-time (10 women), 72 part-time (50 women); includes 11 minority (9 Black or African American, non-Hispanic/Latino; 1 American Indian or Alaska Native, non-Hispanic/Latino; 1 Asian, non-Hispanic/Latino). 31 applicants, 100% accepted, 31 enrolled. In 2013, 54 master's awarded. *Degree requirements:* For master's, thesis. *Entrance requirements:* For master's, 2 letters of reference, minimum GPA of 3.0. Additional exam requirements/recommendations for international students: Required—TOEFL (minimum score 550 paper-based). *Application deadline:* For fall admission, 8/15 priority date for domestic students; for winter admission, 12/15 priority date for domestic students; for spring admission, 4/15 priority date for domestic students. Applications are processed on a rolling basis. Application fee: $30. *Expenses:* Contact institution. *Faculty research:* Leadership, adult education, decision-making, strategic planning, business ethics. *Unit head:* Owen Borda, Chair, Division of Business and Management, 315-279-5352, E-mail: gsmith@mail.keuka.edu. *Application contact:* Jack Ferrel, Director of Admissions, 315-279-5413, Fax: 315-279-5386, E-mail: admissions@mail.keuka.edu.

King University, School of Business and Economics, Bristol, TN 37620-2699. Offers MBA. Part-time and evening/weekend programs available. Postbaccalaureate distance learning degree programs offered (no on-campus study). *Degree requirements:* For master's, comprehensive exam, thesis optional. *Entrance requirements:* For master's, GMAT, 2 years of work experience. Additional exam requirements/recommendations for international students: Required—TOEFL (minimum score 550 paper-based). Electronic applications accepted. *Faculty research:* Leadership, international monetary policy.

Kutztown University of Pennsylvania, College of Business, Program in Business Administration, Kutztown, PA 19530-0730. Offers MBA. Part-time and evening/weekend programs available. *Faculty:* 8 full-time (2 women). *Students:* 18 full-time (6 women), 25 part-time (10 women); includes 1 minority (Hispanic/Latino), 4 international. Average age 30. 38 applicants, 37% accepted, 8 enrolled. In 2013, 21 master's awarded. *Degree requirements:* For master's, comprehensive exam, thesis (for some programs). *Entrance requirements:* For master's, GMAT. Additional exam requirements/recommendations for international students: Required—TOEFL (minimum score 550 paper-based; 79 iBT). *Application deadline:* For fall admission, 8/1 for domestic students, 8/1 priority date for international students; for spring admission, 12/1 for domestic students, 12/1 priority date for international students. Applications are processed on a rolling basis. Application fee: $35. Electronic applications accepted. *Expenses: Tuition, area resident:* Part-time $442 per credit. Tuition, state resident: part-time $442 per credit. Tuition, nonresident: part-time $663 per credit. *Required fees:* $80 per credit. *Financial support:* Career-related internships or fieldwork, Federal Work-Study, scholarships/grants, tuition waivers (partial), and unspecified assistantships available. Financial award application deadline: 3/1; financial award applicants required to submit FAFSA. *Unit head:* Dr. William Dempsey, Interim Dean, 610-683-4575, Fax: 610-683-4573, E-mail: dempsey@kutztown.edu. *Application contact:* Kelly Hish, Admissions Clerk, 610-683-4200, Fax: 610-683-1393, E-mail: graduate@kutztown.edu.
Website: http://www.kutztown.edu/academics/business/mbaprograms/.

Lake Erie College, School of Business, Painesville, OH 44077-3389. Offers general management (MBA); health care administration (MBA). Part-time and evening/weekend programs available. *Faculty:* 8 full-time (3 women), 2 part-time/adjunct (0 women). *Students:* 23 full-time (12 women), 135 part-time (56 women); includes 19 minority (12 Black or African American, non-Hispanic/Latino; 5 Asian, non-Hispanic/Latino; 1 Hispanic/Latino; 1 Two or more races, non-Hispanic/Latino), 3 international. Average age 34. 100 applicants, 77% accepted, 65 enrolled. In 2013, 53 master's awarded. *Entrance requirements:* For master's, GMAT or minimum GPA of 3.0, resume, references. Additional exam requirements/recommendations for international students: Required—TOEFL (minimum score 550 paper-based). *Application deadline:* For fall admission, 8/1 priority date for domestic students, 6/1 for international students; for spring admission, 12/15 for domestic students, 10/1 for international students. Applications are processed on a rolling basis. Application fee: $30. Electronic applications accepted. Application fee is waived when completed online. Tuition and fees vary according to course load and program. *Financial support:* Career-related internships or fieldwork, tuition waivers (full and partial), and unspecified assistantships available. Financial award applicants required to submit FAFSA. *Unit head:* Prof. Robert Trebar, Dean of the School of Business, 440-375-7115, Fax: 440-375-7005, E-mail: rtrebar@lec.edu. *Application contact:* Milena Velez, Senior Admissions Counselor, 800-533-4996, Fax: 440-375-7000, E-mail: admissions@lec.edu.
Website: http://www.lec.edu/parkermba.

Lake Forest Graduate School of Management, The Leadership MBA Program, Lake Forest, IL 60045. Offers finance (MBA); global business (MBA); healthcare management (MBA); management (MBA); marketing (MBA); organizational behavior (MBA). Part-time and evening/weekend programs available. *Entrance requirements:* For master's, 4 years of work experience in field, interview, 2 letters of recommendation. Electronic applications accepted.

Lakehead University–Orillia, MBA Program, Orillia, ON L3V 0B9, Canada. Offers MBA. Part-time programs available.

Lakeland College, Graduate Studies Division, Program in Business Administration, Sheboygan, WI 53082-0359. Offers accounting (MBA); finance (MBA); healthcare management (MBA); project management (MBA). *Entrance requirements:* For master's, GMAT. *Expenses:* Contact institution.

Lamar University, College of Graduate Studies, College of Business, Beaumont, TX 77710. Offers accounting (MBA); experiential business and entrepreneurship (MBA); financial management (MBA); healthcare administration (MBA); information systems (MBA); management (MBA). *Accreditation:* AACSB. Part-time and evening/weekend programs available. *Degree requirements:* For master's, comprehensive exam (for some programs), thesis optional. *Entrance requirements:* For master's, GMAT. Additional exam requirements/recommendations for international students: Required—TOEFL (minimum score 525 paper-based). *Faculty research:* Marketing, finance, quantitative methods, management information systems, legal, environmental.

La Salle University, College of Professional and Continuing Studies, Philadelphia, PA 19141-1199. Offers MBA, MS, Certificate. Part-time and evening/weekend programs available. Postbaccalaureate distance learning degree programs offered (no on-campus study). *Faculty:* 9. *Students:* 1 (woman) full-time, 109 part-time (79 women); includes 48 minority (36 Black or African American, non-Hispanic/Latino; 3 Asian, non-Hispanic/Latino; 6 Hispanic/Latino; 2 Native Hawaiian or other Pacific Islander, non-Hispanic/Latino; 1 Two or more races, non-Hispanic/Latino). Average age 38. 27 applicants, 100% accepted, 15 enrolled. In 2013, 68 master's, 26 other advanced degrees awarded. *Entrance requirements:* Additional exam requirements/recommendations for international students: Required—TOEFL. *Application deadline:* For fall admission, 8/15 priority date for domestic students, 7/15 for international students; for spring admission, 12/15 priority date for domestic students, 6/15 for international students; for summer admission, 4/15 for domestic students, 3/15 for international students. Applications are processed on a rolling basis. Application fee: $35. Electronic applications accepted. Application fee is waived when completed online. *Expenses: Tuition:* Full-time $20,750; part-time $695 per credit hour. *Required fees:* $300; $200 per year. Tuition and fees vary according to program. *Financial support:* In 2013–14, 14 students received support. Federal Work-Study and scholarships/grants available. Support available to part-time students. Financial award application deadline: 8/31; financial award applicants required to submit FAFSA. *Unit head:* Dr. Joseph Y. Ugras, Dean, 215-951-5124, Fax: 215-951-1276. *Application contact:* Paul J. Reilly, Assistant Vice President, Enrollment Services, 215-951-1946, Fax: 215-951-1462, E-mail: reilly@lasalle.edu.
Website: http://www.lasalle.edu/schools/cpcs/.

La Salle University, School of Business, Philadelphia, PA 19141-1199. Offers accounting (MBA, Post-MBA Certificate); business systems and analytics (MBA, Post-MBA Certificate); finance (MBA, Post-MBA Certificate); general business administration (MBA); human resource management (MBA, Post-MBA Certificate); international business (Post-MBA Certificate); management (MBA, Post-MBA Certificate); marketing (MBA, Post-MBA Certificate); MSN/MBA. *Accreditation:* AACSB. Part-time and evening/weekend programs available. Postbaccalaureate distance learning degree programs offered (minimal on-campus study). *Faculty:* 27 full-time (13 women), 15 part-time/adjunct (4 women). *Students:* 81 full-time (30 women), 428 part-time (211 women); includes 109 minority (47 Black or African American, non-Hispanic/Latino; 39 Asian, non-Hispanic/Latino; 18 Hispanic/Latino; 5 Two or more races, non-Hispanic/Latino), 6 international. Average age 30. 215 applicants, 90% accepted, 120 enrolled. In 2013, 182 master's, 1 other advanced degree awarded. *Entrance requirements:* For master's, GMAT or GRE, two letters of reference; resume; for Post-MBA Certificate, MBA with minimum GPA of 3.0. Additional exam requirements/recommendations for international students: Required—TOEFL. *Application deadline:* For fall admission, 8/15 priority date for domestic students, 7/15 for international students; for spring admission, 12/15 priority date for domestic students, 11/15 for international students; for summer admission, 4/15 priority date for domestic students, 3/15 for international students. Applications are processed on a rolling basis. Application fee: $35. Electronic applications accepted. Application fee is waived when completed online. *Expenses:* Contact institution. *Financial support:* In 2013–14, 88 students received support. Career-related internships or fieldwork, Federal Work-Study, scholarships/grants, and unspecified assistantships available. Support available to part-time students. Financial award application deadline: 8/31; financial award applicants required to submit FAFSA. *Unit head:* Dr. Gary Giamartino, Dean, 215-951-1040, Fax: 215-951-1886, E-mail: giamartino@lasalle.edu. *Application contact:* Paul J. Reilly, Assistant Vice President, Enrollment Services, 215-951-1946, Fax: 215-951-1462, E-mail: reilly@lasalle.edu.
Website: http://www.lasalle.edu/grad/index.php?section-mba&page-index.

Lasell College, Graduate and Professional Studies in Management, Newton, MA 02466-2709. Offers business administration (PMBA); elder care management (MSM, Graduate Certificate); elder care marketing (MSM); human resource management (Graduate Certificate); human resources management (MSM); integrated marketing communication (Graduate Certificate); management (MSM, Graduate Certificate); marketing (MSM, Graduate Certificate); non-profit management (MSM, Graduate Certificate); project management (MSM, Graduate Certificate); public relations (Graduate Certificate). Part-time and evening/weekend programs available. Postbaccalaureate distance learning degree programs offered (no on-campus study). *Faculty:* 3 full-time (1 woman), 16 part-time/adjunct (9 women). *Students:* 46 full-time (33 women), 105 part-time (73 women); includes 35 minority (24 Black or African American, non-Hispanic/Latino; 1 American Indian or Alaska Native, non-Hispanic/Latino; 3 Asian, non-Hispanic/Latino; 7 Hispanic/Latino), 22 international. Average age 32. 88 applicants, 55% accepted, 29 enrolled. In 2013, 61 master's awarded. *Entrance*

requirements: For master's and Graduate Certificate, bachelor's degree from an accredited institution. Additional exam requirements/recommendations for international students: Required—TOEFL (minimum score 550 paper-based; 79 iBT). *Application deadline:* For fall admission, 8/31 priority date for domestic students, 6/30 priority date for international students; for spring admission, 12/31 priority date for domestic students, 10/31 priority date for international students. Applications are processed on a rolling basis. Electronic applications accepted. *Expenses: Tuition:* Part-time $575 per credit. *Required fees:* $80 per semester. *Financial support:* Available to part-time students. Application deadline: 8/31; applicants required to submit FAFSA. *Unit head:* Dr. Joan Dolamore, Dean of Graduate and Professional Studies, 617-243-2485, Fax: 617-243-2450, E-mail: gradinfo@lasell.edu. *Application contact:* Adrienne Franciosi, Director of Graduate Admission, 617-243-2214, Fax: 617-243-2450, E-mail: gradinfo@lasell.edu.
Website: http://www.lasell.edu/Academics/Graduate-and-Professional-Studies/MS-in-Management.html.

La Sierra University, School of Business and Management, Riverside, CA 92515. Offers accounting (MBA); finance (MBA); general management (MBA); human resources management (MBA); leadership, values, and ethics for business and management (Certificate); marketing (MBA). *Degree requirements:* For master's, research project. *Entrance requirements:* For master's, GMAT, minimum GPA of 3.0. Additional exam requirements/recommendations for international students: Required—TOEFL. *Faculty research:* Financial econometrics, institutional assessment and strategic planning, legal issues in management, behavioral finance, content of financial reports.

Laurel University, School of Management, High Point, NC 27265-3197. Offers MBA.

Laurentian University, School of Graduate Studies and Research, School of Commerce and Administration, Sudbury, ON P3E 2C6, Canada. Offers MBA. Part-time and evening/weekend programs available. *Entrance requirements:* For master's, GMAT, 2 years of work experience. *Faculty research:* Small business and entrepreneurship development, mutual fund performance, donorship behavior, stress and organizations, quality programs.

Lawrence Technological University, College of Management, Southfield, MI 48075-1058. Offers business administration (MBA, DBA); information systems (MS); management (PhD). *Accreditation:* ACBSP. Part-time and evening/weekend programs available. *Faculty:* 15 full-time (5 women), 19 part-time/adjunct (4 women). *Students:* 3 full-time (2 women), 406 part-time (147 women); includes 149 minority (70 Black or African American, non-Hispanic/Latino; 2 American Indian or Alaska Native, non-Hispanic/Latino; 63 Asian, non-Hispanic/Latino; 10 Hispanic/Latino; 1 Native Hawaiian or other Pacific Islander, non-Hispanic/Latino; 3 Two or more races, non-Hispanic/Latino), 25 international. Average age 36. 325 applicants, 51% accepted, 99 enrolled. In 2013, 174 master's, 14 doctorates awarded. *Degree requirements:* For master's, thesis (for some programs). *Entrance requirements:* Additional exam requirements/recommendations for international students: Required—TOEFL (minimum score 550 paper-based; 79 iBT). *Application deadline:* For fall admission, 8/1 priority date for domestic students, 5/29 for international students; for spring admission, 12/1 priority date for domestic students, 10/15 for international students. Applications are processed on a rolling basis. Application fee: $50. Electronic applications accepted. *Expenses: Tuition:* Full-time $14,112; part-time $1008 per credit hour. *Required fees:* $519. One-time fee: $519 part-time. *Financial support:* In 2013–14, 57 students received support, including 8 research assistantships (averaging $7,853 per year); Federal Work-Study and institutionally sponsored loans also available. Support available to part-time students. Financial award application deadline: 4/1; financial award applicants required to submit FAFSA. *Unit head:* Dr. Bahman Mirshab, Dean, 248-204-3050, E-mail: mgtdean@ltu.edu. *Application contact:* Jane Rohrback, Director of Admissions, 248-204-3160, Fax: 248-204-2228, E-mail: admissions@ltu.edu.
Website: http://www.ltu.edu/management/index.asp.

Lebanese American University, School of Business, Beirut, Lebanon. Offers MBA.

Lebanon Valley College, Program in Business Administration, Annville, PA 17003-1400. Offers business administration (MBA); healthcare management (MBA); school leadership (MBA). *Accreditation:* ACBSP. Part-time and evening/weekend programs available. *Faculty:* 3 full-time (0 women), 16 part-time/adjunct (2 women). *Students:* 14 full-time (6 women), 156 part-time (82 women); includes 12 minority (4 Black or African American, non-Hispanic/Latino; 1 American Indian or Alaska Native, non-Hispanic/Latino; 4 Asian, non-Hispanic/Latino; 3 Hispanic/Latino). Average age 38. In 2013, 48 master's awarded. *Entrance requirements:* For master's, 3 years of work experience. *Application deadline:* Applications are processed on a rolling basis. Application fee: $30. Electronic applications accepted. *Expenses:* Contact institution. *Financial support:* Application deadline: 5/1; applicants required to submit FAFSA. *Unit head:* Brenda Adams, Director of the MBA Program, 717-867-6335, Fax: 717-867-6018, E-mail: badams@lvc.edu. *Application contact:* Susan Greenawalt, Graduate Studies and Continuing Education Assistant/Records Coordinator, 717-867-6213, Fax: 717-867-6018, E-mail: greenawa@lvc.edu.
Website: http://www.lvc.edu/mba.

Lee University, MBA Program, Cleveland, TN 37320-3450. Offers MBA. Part-time programs available. *Faculty:* 3 full-time (0 women). *Students:* 4 full-time (3 women), 23 part-time (7 women); includes 5 minority (2 Black or African American, non-Hispanic/Latino; 1 American Indian or Alaska Native, non-Hispanic/Latino; 1 Asian, non-Hispanic/Latino; 1 Hispanic/Latino). Average age 27. 31 applicants, 100% accepted, 27 enrolled. *Degree requirements:* For master's, variable foreign language requirement, comprehensive exam, thesis, internship. *Entrance requirements:* For master's, GMAT (within last 5 years), minimum undergraduate cumulative GPA of 3.0. Additional exam requirements/recommendations for international students: Required—TOEFL (minimum score 450 paper-based). *Application deadline:* For fall admission, 4/1 priority date for domestic and international students; for spring admission, 10/1 priority date for domestic and international students. Applications are processed on a rolling basis. Application fee: $25. *Expenses: Tuition:* Full-time $9900; part-time $550 per credit hour. *Required fees:* $35 per term. One-time fee: $25. *Financial support:* In 2013–14, 18 students received support. Application deadline: 3/1. *Unit head:* Shane Griffith, Director, 423-614-8694, E-mail: mba@leeuniversity.edu. *Application contact:* Vicki Glasscock, Director of Graduate Enrollment, 423-614-8059, E-mail: vglasscock@leeuniversity.edu.
Website: http://www.leeuniversity.edu/academics/graduate/mba/.

Lehigh University, College of Business and Economics, Department of Management, Bethlehem, PA 18015. Offers business administration (MBA); corporate entrepreneurship (MBA); international business (MBA); marketing (MBA); project management (MBA); supply chain management (MBA); MBA/E; MBA/M Ed. *Accreditation:* AACSB. Part-time and evening/weekend programs available. Postbaccalaureate distance learning degree programs offered (minimal on-campus study). *Faculty:* 11 full-time (4 women), 13 part-time/adjunct (4 women). *Students:* 28 full-time (10 women), 171 part-time (54 women); includes 32 minority (2 Black or African American, non-Hispanic/Latino; 21 Asian, non-Hispanic/Latino; 6 Hispanic/Latino; 3 Two or more races, non-Hispanic/Latino), 21 international. Average age 33. 108 applicants, 63% accepted, 25 enrolled. In 2013, 79 master's awarded. *Entrance requirements:* For master's, GMAT or GRE. Additional exam requirements/recommendations for international students: Required—TOEFL (minimum score 600 paper-based; 94 iBT). *Application deadline:* For fall admission, 7/15 for domestic students, 5/1 for international students; for spring admission, 12/1 for domestic students. Applications are processed on a rolling basis. Application fee: $100. Electronic applications accepted. *Financial support:* In 2013–14, 33 students received support, including 10 teaching assistantships with full and partial tuition reimbursements available (averaging $14,200 per year); career-related internships or fieldwork, scholarships/grants, health care benefits, tuition waivers (full and partial), and unspecified assistantships also available. Support available to part-time students. Financial award application deadline: 1/15. *Faculty research:* Information systems, organizational behavior, supply chain management, strategic management, entrepreneurship. *Total annual research expenditures:* $77,886. *Unit head:* Dr. Robert J. Trent, Department Chair, 610-758-4952, Fax: 610-758-6941, E-mail: rjt2@lehigh.edu. *Application contact:* Jen Giordano, Director of Recruitment and Admissions, 610-758-3418, Fax: 610-758-5283, E-mail: jlg210@lehigh.edu.
Website: http://www4.lehigh.edu/business/academics/depts/management.

Le Moyne College, Madden School of Business, Syracuse, NY 13214. Offers MBA. *Accreditation:* AACSB. Part-time and evening/weekend programs available. *Faculty:* 13 full-time (2 women), 10 part-time/adjunct (4 women). *Students:* 20 full-time (8 women), 71 part-time (29 women); includes 4 minority (1 Black or African American, non-Hispanic/Latino; 2 Asian, non-Hispanic/Latino; 1 Hispanic/Latino). Average age 28. 64 applicants, 86% accepted, 50 enrolled. In 2013, 44 master's awarded. *Degree requirements:* For master's, capstone-level course. *Entrance requirements:* For master's, GMAT or GRE General Test, interview, bachelor's degree, minimum GPA of 3.0, resume, 2 letters of recommendation, personal statement, transcripts. Additional exam requirements/recommendations for international students: Required—TOEFL (minimum score 550 paper-based; 79 iBT). *Application deadline:* For fall admission, 7/1 priority date for domestic and international students; for spring admission, 11/1 priority date for domestic and international students; for summer admission, 4/1 priority date for domestic and international students. Applications are processed on a rolling basis. Application fee: $0. *Expenses: Tuition:* Full-time $13,194; part-time $733 per credit hour. *Required fees:* $25 per semester. *Financial support:* In 2013–14, 29 students received support. Career-related internships or fieldwork, scholarships/grants, health care benefits, and unspecified assistantships available. Support available to part-time students. Financial award applicants required to submit FAFSA. *Faculty research:* Performance evaluation outcomes assessment, technology outsourcing, international business, systems for Web-based information-seeking, non-profit business practices, business sustainability practices, management/leadership development, operations management optimization applications. *Unit head:* Dr. George Kulick, Associate Dean of Madden School of Business, 315-445-4786, Fax: 315-445-4787, E-mail: kulick@lemoyne.edu. *Application contact:* Kristen P. Trapasso, Senior Director of Enrollment Management, 315-445-4265, Fax: 315-445-6092, E-mail: trapaskp@lemoyne.edu.
Website: http://www.lemoyne.edu/mba.

Lenoir-Rhyne University, Graduate Programs, Charles M. Snipes School of Business, Hickory, NC 28601. Offers accounting (MBA); entrepreneurship (MBA); global leadership (MBA); leadership development (MBA). *Accreditation:* ACBSP. Part-time and evening/weekend programs available. *Degree requirements:* For master's, capstone course. *Entrance requirements:* For master's, GMAT, minimum undergraduate GPA of 2.7, graduate 3.0. Additional exam requirements/recommendations for international students: Required—TOEFL (minimum score 600 paper-based). Electronic applications accepted. *Expenses:* Contact institution.

LeTourneau University, Graduate Programs, Longview, TX 75607-7001. Offers business administration (MBA); counseling (MA); education (M Ed); engineering (MS); health care administration (MS); marriage and family therapy (MA); psychology (MA); strategic leadership (MSL). Part-time programs available. Postbaccalaureate distance learning degree programs offered (no on-campus study). *Faculty:* 15 full-time (7 women), 54 part-time/adjunct (23 women). *Students:* 58 full-time (45 women), 365 part-time (287 women); includes 106 minority (51 Black or African American, non-Hispanic/Latino; 3 American Indian or Alaska Native, non-Hispanic/Latino; 1 Asian, non-Hispanic/Latino; 45 Hispanic/Latino; 6 Two or more races, non-Hispanic/Latino), 4 international. Average age 38. 263 applicants, 68% accepted, 116 enrolled. In 2013, 112 master's awarded. *Degree requirements:* For master's, thesis (for some programs). *Entrance requirements:* For master's, GRE (for engineering programs), minimum GPA of 2.8 (3.0 for counseling and engineering programs). Additional exam requirements/recommendations for international students: Required—TOEFL. *Application deadline:* For fall admission, 8/22 for domestic students, 8/29 for international students; for winter admission, 10/10 for domestic students; for spring admission, 1/2 for domestic students, 1/10 for international students; for summer admission, 5/1 for domestic and international students. Applications are processed on a rolling basis. Electronic applications accepted. Application fee is waived when completed online. *Financial support:* In 2013–14, 11 students received support, including 13 research assistantships (averaging $9,122 per year); institutionally sponsored loans and unspecified assistantships also available. Financial award applicants required to submit FAFSA. *Unit head:* Dr. Robert Hudson, Vice President and Dean of the Graduate School, 903-233-1110, E-mail: roberthudson@letu.edu. *Application contact:* Chris Fontaine, Assistant Vice President for Global Campus Admissions, 903-233-4312, E-mail: chrisfontaine@letu.edu.
Website: http://www.adults.letu.edu/.

Lewis University, College of Business, Graduate School of Management, Romeoville, IL 60446. Offers business administration (MBA), including accounting, custom elective option, e-business, finance, healthcare management, human resources management, international business, management information systems, marketing, project management, technology and operations management; finance (MS); project management (MS). *Accreditation:* ACBSP. Part-time and evening/weekend programs available. Postbaccalaureate distance learning degree programs offered (no on-campus study). *Students:* 3 part-time (1 woman). Average age 32. Application fee: $40. *Financial support:* Applicants required to submit FAFSA. *Unit head:* Dr. Rami Khasawneh, Dean, 800-838-0500 Ext. 5360, E-mail: khasawra@lewisu.edu. *Application contact:* Michele Ryan, Director of Admission, 815-836-5384, E-mail: gsm@lewisu.edu.

Lewis University, College of Nursing and Health Professions and College of Business, Program in Nursing/Business, Romeoville, IL 60446. Offers MSN/MBA. Part-time and evening/weekend programs available. *Students:* 7 full-time (6 women), 18 part-time (17 women); includes 9 minority (4 Black or African American, non-Hispanic/Latino; 1 Asian, non-Hispanic/Latino; 3 Hispanic/Latino; 1 Native Hawaiian or other Pacific Islander, non-Hispanic/Latino). Average age 36. *Entrance requirements:* Additional exam requirements/recommendations for international students: Required—TOEFL (minimum score 550 paper-based; 80 iBT). *Application deadline:* For fall admission, 4/2 priority date for domestic students, 5/1 priority date for international students; for spring admission, 11/15 priority date for international students. Applications are processed on a rolling basis. Electronic applications accepted. *Financial support:* Scholarships/grants, tuition waivers (full and partial), and unspecified assistantships available. Financial award application deadline: 5/1; financial award applicants required to submit FAFSA. *Faculty research:* Cancer prevention, phenomenological methods, public policy analysis. *Total annual research expenditures:* $1,000. *Unit head:* Dr. Linda Niedringhaus, Interim Director, 815-838-0500 Ext. 5878, E-mail: niedrili@lewisu.edu.

Application contact: Nancy Wiksten, Adult Admission Counselor, 815-838-0500 Ext. 5628, Fax: 815-836-5578, E-mail: wikstena@lewisu.edu.

Liberty University, School of Business, Lynchburg, VA 24515. Offers accounting (MBA, MS, DBA); business administration (MBA); criminal justice (MBA); cyber security (MS); executive leadership (MA); healthcare (MBA); human resources (DBA); information systems (MS), including information assurance, technology management; international business (MBA, DBA); leadership (MBA, DBA); management and leadership (MA); marketing (MBA, MS, DBA), including digital marketing and advertising (MS), project management (MS), public relations (MS), sports marketing and media (MS); project management (MBA, DBA); public administration (MBA); public relations (MBA). Part-time programs available. Postbaccalaureate distance learning degree programs offered (minimal on-campus study). *Students:* 1,342 full-time (749 women), 3,704 part-time (1,820 women); includes 1,657 minority (1,221 Black or African American, non-Hispanic/Latino; 11 American Indian or Alaska Native, non-Hispanic/Latino; 74 Asian, non-Hispanic/Latino; 209 Hispanic/Latino; 13 Native Hawaiian or other Pacific Islander, non-Hispanic/Latino; 129 Two or more races, non-Hispanic/Latino), 40 international. Average age 35. 5,899 applicants, 48% accepted, 1716 enrolled. In 2013, 1,535 master's awarded. *Entrance requirements:* For master's, minimum undergraduate GPA of 3.0, 15 hours of upper-level business courses. Additional exam requirements/recommendations for international students: Required—TOEFL (minimum score 600 paper-based; 100 iBT). *Application deadline:* Applications are processed on a rolling basis. Application fee: $50. Electronic applications accepted. *Expenses:* Contact institution. *Unit head:* Dr. Scott Hicks, Dean, 434-592-4808, Fax: 434-582-2366, E-mail: smhicks@liberty.edu. *Application contact:* Jay Bridge, Director of Graduate Admissions, 800-424-9595, Fax: 800-628-7977, E-mail: gradadmissions@liberty.edu.
Website: http://www.liberty.edu/academics/business/index.cfm?PID-149.

LIM College, MBA Program, New York, NY 10022-5268. Offers entrepreneurship (MBA); fashion management (MBA). *Accreditation:* ACBSP. *Faculty:* 4 full-time (1 woman), 9 part-time/adjunct (4 women). *Students:* 44 full-time (43 women), 26 part-time (20 women). 46 applicants, 61% accepted, 21 enrolled. *Entrance requirements:* For master's, interview. Additional exam requirements/recommendations for international students: Required—TOEFL (minimum score 550 paper-based; 80 iBT), IELTS (minimum score 6.5). *Application deadline:* For fall admission, 7/1 for domestic students, 7/15 for international students; for spring admission, 1/15 for domestic and international students. *Expenses: Tuition:* Full-time $25,050; part-time $835 per credit hour. Tuition and fees vary according to course load. *Financial support:* Institutionally sponsored loans and scholarships/grants available. *Unit head:* Jacqueline Jenkins, Graduate Studies Director, 212-752-1530 Ext. 416, Fax: 212-750-3779, E-mail: mba@limcollege.edu. *Application contact:* Paul Mucciarone, Graduate Admission Coordinator, 646-218-4124, Fax: 212-750-3779, E-mail: paul.mucciarone@limcollege.edu.
Website: http://graduate.limcollege.edu/mba.

LIM College, MPS Program, New York, NY 10022-5268. Offers fashion marketing (MPS); fashion merchandising and retail management (MPS); visual merchandising (MPS). *Faculty:* 21. *Students:* 58 full-time (53 women), 8 part-time (all women). *Expenses: Tuition:* Full-time $25,050; part-time $835 per credit hour. Tuition and fees vary according to course load. *Application contact:* Paul Mucciarone, Associate Director of Graduate Admissions, 646-218-4124, Fax: 212-750-3779, E-mail: paul.mucciarone@limcollege.edu.

Limestone College, MBA Program, Gaffney, SC 29340-3799. Offers MBA. Part-time and evening/weekend programs available. Postbaccalaureate distance learning degree programs offered (minimal on-campus study). *Faculty:* 12 full-time (3 women), 2 part-time/adjunct (both women). *Students:* 32 full-time (22 women), 30 part-time (13 women); includes 23 minority (all Black or African American, non-Hispanic/Latino). Average age 40. 49 applicants, 59% accepted, 19 enrolled. *Degree requirements:* For master's, comprehensive exam, three weekend residency seminars (on campus). *Entrance requirements:* For master's, GMAT/GRE, two letters of recommendation, official transcript(s). Additional exam requirements/recommendations for international students: Required—TOEFL (minimum score 500 paper-based; 90 iBT). *Application deadline:* For fall admission, 8/1 priority date for domestic and international students; for winter admission, 12/12 priority date for domestic and international students; for spring admission, 4/1 priority date for domestic and international students. Applications are processed on a rolling basis. Application fee: $25. Electronic applications accepted. Application fee is waived when completed online. *Expenses: Tuition:* Full-time $22,800; part-time $625 per credit hour. *Required fees:* $300; $150 per semester. *Financial support:* In 2013–14, 8 students received support. Application deadline: 6/15; applicants required to submit FAFSA. *Faculty research:* Management. *Unit head:* Brandon Gibson, Director, MBA Program, 864-488-4371, Fax: 864-487-8706, E-mail: bgibson@limestone.edu. *Application contact:* Adair Haynes, Administrative Assistant, MBA Program, 800-795-7151 Ext. 4370, Fax: 864-467-8706, E-mail: ahaynes@limestone.edu.
Website: http://www.limestone.edu/mba-program.

Lincoln Memorial University, School of Business, Harrogate, TN 37752-1901. Offers MBA. *Accreditation:* ACBSP. Part-time and evening/weekend programs available. *Degree requirements:* For master's, comprehensive exam, thesis. *Entrance requirements:* For master's, GMAT, resume, letters of recommendation, interview. Additional exam requirements/recommendations for international students: Required—TOEFL (minimum score 500 paper-based).

Lincoln University, Graduate Programs, Philadelphia, PA 19104. Offers early childhood education (M Ed); educational leadership (M Ed); human resources (MSA), including finance, human resources management; human services (MHS); reading (MSR). Evening/weekend programs available. *Faculty:* 10 full-time (4 women), 34 part-time/adjunct (19 women). *Students:* 224 full-time (145 women), 115 part-time (74 women); includes 328 minority (311 Black or African American, non-Hispanic/Latino; 17 Hispanic/Latino). Average age 40. 237 applicants, 65% accepted, 64 enrolled. In 2013, 155 master's awarded. *Degree requirements:* For master's, thesis. *Entrance requirements:* For master's, working as full-time, paid staff member in the human services field, at least one year of paid experience in this field, and undergraduate degree in human services or a related field from an accredited institution (for MHS). *Application deadline:* For fall admission, 6/1 priority date for domestic and international students. Applications are processed on a rolling basis. Application fee: $50. *Expenses:* Tuition, state resident: full-time $10,106; part-time $567 per hour. Tuition, nonresident: full-time $17,636; part-time $949 per hour. *Financial support:* Application deadline: 8/1. *Unit head:* Dr. Cheryl Gooch, Dean, School of Humanities and Graduate Studies, 484-365-7664, E-mail: cgooch@lincoln.edu. *Application contact:* Jernice Lea, Director of Graduate Admissions, 215-590-8233, Fax: 215-387-3859, E-mail: jlea@lincoln.edu.
Website: http://www.lincoln.edu/academicaffairs/uc.html.

Lincoln University, Graduate Studies, Oakland, CA 94612. Offers finance and investments (DBA); finance management and investment banking (MBA); general business (MBA); human resource management (MBA, DBA); international business (MBA); management information systems (MBA). Part-time and evening/weekend programs available. *Faculty:* 8 full-time (2 women), 22 part-time/adjunct (7 women). *Students:* 372 full-time (171 women), 4 part-time (1 woman); includes 8 minority (2 Black or African American, non-Hispanic/Latino; 6 Asian, non-Hispanic/Latino), 363 international. Average age 26. 421 applicants, 71% accepted, 133 enrolled. *Degree requirements:* For master's, research project (thesis), internship report, or comprehensive exam; for doctorate, comprehensive exam, thesis/dissertation. *Entrance requirements:* For master's, minimum GPA of 2.7; for doctorate, GMAT (minimum score: 550), GRE (minimum score: 1000), or equivalent test results (waived for master's degree with minimum cumulative GPA of 3.3). Additional exam requirements/recommendations for international students: Required—TOEFL (minimum score 525 paper-based; 71 iBT) or IELTS (minimum score 5.5) for MBA; TOEFL (minimum score 550 paper-based; 79 iBT) or IELTS (minimum score 6) for DBA. *Application deadline:* For fall admission, 7/1 priority date for domestic and international students; for spring admission, 11/1 priority date for domestic and international students; for summer admission, 5/1 for domestic and international students. Applications are processed on a rolling basis. Application fee: $75. Electronic applications accepted. *Expenses: Tuition:* Full-time $7290; part-time $405 per unit. *Required fees:* $375; $405 per unit. $375 per year. Tuition and fees vary according to course level and degree level. *Financial support:* Teaching assistantships with tuition reimbursements, career-related internships or fieldwork, and scholarships/grants available. Financial award application deadline: 7/31; financial award applicants required to submit FAFSA. *Unit head:* Dr. Marshall Burak, Director of Graduate Programs, 510-628-8016, Fax: 510-628-8012, E-mail: mburak@lincolnuca.edu. *Application contact:* Reenu Shrestha, Admissions Officer, 510-628-8010 Ext. 8030, Fax: 510-628-8012, E-mail: admissions@lincolnuca.edu.
Website: http://www.lincolnuca.edu/.

Lincoln University, Graduate Studies, Jefferson City, MO 65101. Offers business administration (MBA), including accounting, entrepreneurship, management, public administration and policy; educational leadership (Ed S), including elementary leadership, secondary leadership, superintendency; guidance and counseling (M Ed), including community/agency counseling, elementary school, secondary school; history (MA); school administration and supervision (M Ed), including elementary school administration, secondary school administration, special education administration; school teaching (M Ed), including elementary school teaching, secondary school teaching; sociology (MA); sociology/criminal justice (MA). Part-time and evening/weekend programs available. Postbaccalaureate distance learning degree programs offered (minimal on-campus study). *Students:* 42 full-time (29 women), 109 part-time (66 women); includes 51 minority (37 Black or African American, non-Hispanic/Latino; 10 American Indian or Alaska Native, non-Hispanic/Latino; 1 Asian, non-Hispanic/Latino; 2 Hispanic/Latino; 1 Two or more races, non-Hispanic/Latino), 10 international. Average age 33. 84 applicants, 76% accepted, 51 enrolled. In 2013, 73 master's, 6 other advanced degrees awarded. *Degree requirements:* For master's and Ed S, comprehensive exam, thesis optional. *Entrance requirements:* For master's and Ed S, GRE, MAT or GMAT, minimum GPA of 2.75 in major, 2.5 overall; 3 letters of recommendation; minimum C average in English composition; personal statement of purpose. Additional exam requirements/recommendations for international students: Required—TOEFL (minimum score 500 paper-based; 61 iBT). *Application deadline:* For fall admission, 8/1 priority date for domestic and international students; for spring admission, 12/1 priority date for domestic and international students; for summer admission, 5/1 priority date for domestic and international students. Applications are processed on a rolling basis. Application fee: $30. *Expenses:* Tuition, state resident: full-time $6840; part-time $285 per credit hour. Tuition, nonresident: full-time $12,720; part-time $530 per credit hour. *Required fees:* $587; $587 per year. Tuition and fees vary according to course load. *Financial support:* Federal Work-Study and scholarships/grants available. Support available to part-time students. Financial award application deadline: 3/1; financial award applicants required to submit FAFSA. *Unit head:* Dr. Linda S. Bickel, Dean, 573-681-5247, Fax: 573-681-5106, E-mail: gradschool@lincolnu.edu. *Application contact:* Irasema Steck, Administrative Assistant, 573-681-5247, Fax: 573-681-5106, E-mail: gradschool@lincolnu.edu.
Website: http://www.lincolnu.edu/web/graduate-studies/graduate-studies.

Lindenwood University, Graduate Programs, College of Individualized Education, St. Charles, MO 63301-1695. Offers administration (MSA); business administration (MBA); communications (MA); criminal justice and administration (MS); gerontology (MA); healthcare administration (MS); human resource management (MS); information technology (MBA, Certificate); managing information technology (MS); writing (MFA). Part-time and evening/weekend programs available. *Faculty:* 20 full-time (7 women), 96 part-time/adjunct (36 women). *Students:* 928 full-time (587 women), 85 part-time (53 women); includes 394 minority (336 Black or African American, non-Hispanic/Latino; 2 American Indian or Alaska Native, non-Hispanic/Latino; 7 Asian, non-Hispanic/Latino; 24 Hispanic/Latino; 2 Native Hawaiian or other Pacific Islander, non-Hispanic/Latino; 23 Two or more races, non-Hispanic/Latino), 33 international. Average age 34. 569 applicants, 62% accepted, 331 enrolled. In 2013, 487 master's awarded. *Degree requirements:* For master's, thesis (for some programs). *Entrance requirements:* For master's, interview, minimum GPA of 3.0. Additional exam requirements/recommendations for international students: Required—TOEFL (minimum score 550 paper-based; 80 iBT). *Application deadline:* For fall admission, 10/5 priority date for domestic and international students; for winter admission, 1/6 priority date for domestic and international students; for spring admission, 4/7 priority date for domestic and international students. Applications are processed on a rolling basis. Application fee: $30 ($100 for international students). Electronic applications accepted. *Expenses: Tuition:* Full-time $14,800; part-time $428 per credit hour. *Required fees:* $350. Tuition and fees vary according to course level and course load. *Financial support:* In 2013–14, 654 students received support. Career-related internships or fieldwork, institutionally sponsored loans, scholarships/grants, tuition waivers (partial), and unspecified assistantships available. Financial award application deadline: 6/30; financial award applicants required to submit FAFSA. *Unit head:* Dan Kemper, Dean, 636-949-4501, Fax: 636-949-4505, E-mail: dkemper@lindenwood.edu. *Application contact:* Brett Barger, Dean of Evening Admissions and Extension Campuses, 636-949-4934, Fax: 636-949-4109, E-mail: adultadmissions@lindenwood.edu.

Lindenwood University, Graduate Programs, School of Business and Entrepreneurship, St. Charles, MO 63301-1695. Offers accountancy (MA); accounting (MBA); business administration (MBA); entrepreneurial studies (MBA); finance (MBA, MS); human resource management (MBA); international business (MBA); leadership (MA); management (MBA); marketing (MBA, MS); public management (MBA); sport management (MA); supply chain management (MBA). *Accreditation:* ACBSP. Part-time and evening/weekend programs available. Postbaccalaureate distance learning degree programs offered (no on-campus study). *Faculty:* 18 full-time (8 women), 33 part-time/adjunct (8 women). *Students:* 292 full-time (130 women), 111 part-time (46 women); includes 59 minority (42 Black or African American, non-Hispanic/Latino; 5 American Indian or Alaska Native, non-Hispanic/Latino; 1 Asian, non-Hispanic/Latino; 5 Hispanic/Latino; 6 Two or more races, non-Hispanic/Latino), 112 international. Average age 29. 212 applicants, 51% accepted, 102 enrolled. In 2013, 221 master's awarded. *Degree requirements:* For master's, comprehensive exam (for some programs), thesis (for some programs), minimum GPA of 3.0. *Entrance requirements:* For master's, interview, minimum GPA of 3.0, letter of recommendation. Additional exam requirements/recommendations for international students: Required—TOEFL (minimum score 550 paper-based; 80 iBT). *Application deadline:* For fall admission, 8/12 priority date for

domestic and international students; for winter admission, 1/6 priority date for domestic and international students; for spring admission, 3/10 priority date for domestic and international students; for summer admission, 5/27 priority date for domestic and international students. Applications are processed on a rolling basis. Application fee: $30 ($100 for international students). Electronic applications accepted. *Expenses: Tuition:* Full-time $14,800; part-time $428 per credit hour. *Required fees:* $350. Tuition and fees vary according to course level and course load. *Financial support:* In 2013–14, 268 students received support. Career-related internships or fieldwork, Federal Work-Study, institutionally sponsored loans, scholarships/grants, tuition waivers (partial), and unspecified assistantships available. Financial award application deadline: 6/30; financial award applicants required to submit FAFSA. *Unit head:* Roger Ellis, Dean, 636-949-4839, E-mail: rellis@lindenwood.edu. *Application contact:* Brett Barger, Dean of Evening Admissions and Extension Campuses, 636-949-4934, Fax: 636-949-4109, E-mail: adultadmissions@lindenwood.edu.
Website: http://www.lindenwood.edu.

Lindenwood University–Belleville, Graduate Programs, Belleville, IL 62226. Offers business administration (MBA); communications (MA), including digital and multimedia, media management, promotions, training and development; counseling (MA); criminal justice administration (MS); education (MA); healthcare administration (MS); human resource management (MS); school administration (MA); teaching (MAT).

Lipscomb University, Graduate School of Business, Nashville, TN 37204-3951. Offers accountancy (M Acc); accounting (MBA); conflict management (MBA); distributive (general) (MBA); financial services (MBA); health care informatics (MBA); healthcare management (MBA); human resources (MHR); information security (MBA); leadership (MBA); nonprofit management (MBA); professional accountancy (Certificate); sports management (MBA); strategic human resources (MBA); sustainability (MBA); MBA/MS. *Accreditation:* ACBSP. Part-time and evening/weekend programs available. *Faculty:* 12 full-time (1 woman), 12 part-time/adjunct (2 women). *Students:* 90 full-time (44 women), 104 part-time (51 women); includes 28 minority (24 Black or African American, non-Hispanic/Latino; 3 Hispanic/Latino; 1 Two or more races, non-Hispanic/Latino), 6 international. Average age 33. 145 applicants, 79% accepted, 69 enrolled. In 2013, 98 master's, 1 other advanced degree awarded. *Entrance requirements:* For master's, GMAT, transcripts, interview, 2 references, resume. Additional exam requirements/recommendations for international students: Required—TOEFL (minimum score 570 paper-based). *Application deadline:* For fall admission, 6/15 for domestic students, 2/1 for international students; for winter admission, 6/1 for international students; for spring admission, 11/15 for domestic students. Applications are processed on a rolling basis. Application fee: $50 ($75 for international students). Electronic applications accepted. *Expenses:* Contact institution. *Financial support:* Career-related internships or fieldwork, scholarships/grants, tuition waivers (partial), and unspecified assistantships available. Support available to part-time students. Financial award application deadline: 7/1; financial award applicants required to submit FAFSA. *Faculty research:* Impact of spirituality on organization commitment, women in corporate leadership, psychological empowerment, training. *Unit head:* Joe Ivey, Associate Dean of Graduate Business Programs, 615-966-6229, Fax: 615-966-1818, E-mail: joe.ivey@lipscomb.edu. *Application contact:* Lisa Shacklett, Assistant Dean of Enrollment and Marketing, 615-966-5968, E-mail: lisa.shacklett@lipscomb.edu.
Website: http://www.lipscomb.edu/business/Graduate-Programs.

Long Island University–Hudson at Rockland, Graduate School, Master of Business Administration Program, Orangeburg, NY 10962. Offers business administration (Post Master's Certificate); entrepreneurship (MBA); finance (MBA); healthcare sector management (MBA); management (MBA). Part-time and evening/weekend programs available. *Entrance requirements:* For master's, GMAT, college transcripts, two letters of recommendation, personal statement, resume.

Long Island University–Hudson at Westchester, Program in Business Administration, Purchase, NY 10577. Offers MBA. Part-time and evening/weekend programs available. *Entrance requirements:* For master's, GMAT. Additional exam requirements/recommendations for international students: Required—TOEFL (minimum score 500 paper-based).

Long Island University–LIU Brooklyn, School of Business, Public Administration and Information Sciences, Program in Business Administration, Brooklyn, NY 11201-8423. Offers MBA. Part-time and evening/weekend programs available. *Entrance requirements:* For master's, GMAT or GRE General Test, 2 letters of recommendation. Additional exam requirements/recommendations for international students: Required—TOEFL (minimum score 500 paper-based). Electronic applications accepted.

Long Island University–LIU Post, College of Management, Department of Management, Brookville, NY 11548-1300. Offers MBA.

Long Island University–LIU Post, College of Management, School of Business, Brookville, NY 11548-1300. Offers accounting and taxation (Certificate); business administration (Certificate); finance (MBA, Certificate); general business administration (MBA); international business (MBA, Certificate); management (MBA, Certificate); management information systems (MBA, Certificate); marketing (MBA, Certificate). *Accreditation:* AACSB. Part-time and evening/weekend programs available. *Entrance requirements:* For master's, GMAT, resume, minimum GPA of 3.0, 2 letters of recommendation. Additional exam requirements/recommendations for international students: Required—TOEFL (minimum score 527 paper-based). Electronic applications accepted. *Faculty research:* Financial markets, consumer behavior.

Longwood University, College of Graduate and Professional Studies, College of Business and Economics, Farmville, VA 23909. Offers general business (MBA); real estate (MBA); retail management (MBA). *Accreditation:* AACSB. Part-time programs available. Postbaccalaureate distance learning degree programs offered (minimal on-campus study). *Faculty:* 15 full-time (6 women). *Students:* 1 full-time (0 women), 16 part-time (9 women); includes 1 minority (Two or more races, non-Hispanic/Latino). 7 applicants, 71% accepted, 5 enrolled. In 2013, 13 master's awarded. *Degree requirements:* For master's, internship. *Entrance requirements:* For master's, GMAT. Additional exam requirements/recommendations for international students: Required—TOEFL (minimum score 570 paper-based), IELTS (minimum score 6.5). *Application deadline:* For fall admission, 5/1 priority date for domestic students; for summer admission, 2/1 priority date for domestic students. Applications are processed on a rolling basis. Application fee: $50. Electronic applications accepted. *Expenses:* Tuition, state resident: full-time $7506; part-time $327 per credit hour. Tuition, nonresident: full-time $17,100; part-time $837 per credit hour. Tuition and fees vary according to course load and campus/location. *Unit head:* Abigail H. O'Connor, Assistant Dean and MBA Program Coordinator, 434-395-2043, E-mail: oconnorah@longwood.edu. *Application contact:* College of Graduate and Professional Studies, 434-395-2380, Fax: 434-395-2750, E-mail: graduate@longwood.edu.
Website: http://www.longwood.edu/business/mba.htm.

Louisiana State University and Agricultural & Mechanical College, Graduate School, E. J. Ourso College of Business, Department of Finance, Baton Rouge, LA 70803. Offers business administration (PhD), including finance; finance (MS). *Faculty:* 13 full-time (4 women). *Students:* 24 full-time (9 women), 6 part-time (1 woman); includes 2 minority (1 Black or African American, non-Hispanic/Latino; 1 Asian, non-Hispanic/Latino), 11 international. Average age 25. 70 applicants, 21% accepted, 8 enrolled. In 2013, 21 master's, 2 doctorates awarded. *Degree requirements:* For master's, thesis or alternative; for doctorate, thesis/dissertation. *Entrance requirements:* For master's and doctorate, GMAT. Additional exam requirements/recommendations for international students: Required—TOEFL (minimum score 550 paper-based; 79 IBT), IELTS (minimum score 6.5), or PTE (minimum score 59). *Application deadline:* For fall admission, 1/25 priority date for domestic students, 5/15 for international students; for spring admission, 10/15 for international students. Applications are processed on a rolling basis. Application fee: $50 ($70 for international students). *Financial support:* In 2013–14, 19 students received support, including 5 research assistantships with full and partial tuition reimbursements available (averaging $19,000 per year), 5 teaching assistantships with full and partial tuition reimbursements available (averaging $9,600 per year); fellowships, career-related internships or fieldwork, Federal Work-Study, scholarships/grants, health care benefits, and unspecified assistantships also available. Support available to part-time students. Financial award application deadline: 4/1; financial award applicants required to submit FAFSA. *Faculty research:* Derivatives and risk management, capital structure, asset pricing, spatial statistics, financial institutions and underwriting. *Total annual research expenditures:* $56,155. *Unit head:* Dr. Vestor Carlos Slawson, Jr., Interim Chair, 225-578-6291, Fax: 225-578-6366, E-mail: cslawson@lsu.edu. *Application contact:* Dr. Rajesh Narayanan, Graduate Adviser, 225-578-6236, Fax: 225-578-6366, E-mail: rnarayan@lsu.edu.
Website: http://business.lsu.edu/finance.

Louisiana State University and Agricultural & Mechanical College, Graduate School, E. J. Ourso College of Business, Department of Management, Baton Rouge, LA 70803. Offers business administration (PhD), including management. *Accreditation:* AACSB. *Faculty:* 12 full-time (2 women). *Students:* 1 full-time (0 women). Average age 35. *Degree requirements:* For doctorate, thesis/dissertation. *Entrance requirements:* For doctorate, GMAT. Additional exam requirements/recommendations for international students: Required—TOEFL (minimum score 550 paper-based; 79 IBT), IELTS (minimum score 6.5), or PTE (minimum score 59). *Application deadline:* For fall admission, 1/25 priority date for domestic students, 5/15 for international students; for spring admission, 10/15 for international students. Applications are processed on a rolling basis. Application fee: $50 ($70 for international students). Electronic applications accepted. *Financial support:* In 2013–14, 1 student received support, including 1 teaching assistantship with full and partial tuition reimbursement available (averaging $16,000 per year); fellowships, research assistantships with full and partial tuition reimbursements available, Federal Work-Study, institutionally sponsored loans, scholarships/grants, health care benefits, and unspecified assistantships also available. Support available to part-time students. Financial award applicants required to submit FAFSA. *Faculty research:* Human resource management, organizational behavior, strategy. *Total annual research expenditures:* $12,242. *Unit head:* Dr. Timothy Chandler, Co-Chair, 225-578-6101, Fax: 225-578-6140, E-mail: mgchan@lsu.edu. *Application contact:* Dr. Jean McGuire, Co-Chair, 225-578-6101, Fax: 225-578-6140, E-mail: mcguire@lsu.edu.
Website: http://www.business.lsu.edu/management.

Louisiana State University and Agricultural & Mechanical College, Graduate School, E. J. Ourso College of Business, Department of Marketing, Baton Rouge, LA 70803. Offers business administration (PhD), including marketing. Part-time programs available. *Faculty:* 9 full-time (1 woman). *Students:* 1 (woman) part-time, all international. Average age 32. *Degree requirements:* For doctorate, thesis/dissertation. *Entrance requirements:* Additional exam requirements/recommendations for international students: Required—TOEFL (minimum score 550 paper-based; 79 IBT), IELTS (minimum score 6.5), or PTE (minimum score 59). *Application deadline:* For fall admission, 1/25 priority date for domestic students, 5/15 for international students; for spring admission, 10/15 for international students. Applications are processed on a rolling basis. Application fee: $50 ($70 for international students). Electronic applications accepted. *Financial support:* Fellowships, research assistantships with partial tuition reimbursements, teaching assistantships with full and partial tuition reimbursements, career-related internships or fieldwork, Federal Work-Study, institutionally sponsored loans, scholarships/grants, health care benefits, and unspecified assistantships available. Support available to part-time students. Financial award applicants required to submit FAFSA. *Faculty research:* Consumer behavior, marketing strategy, global marketing, e-commerce, branding/brand equity. *Total annual research expenditures:* $20,956. *Unit head:* Dr. Ronald Niedrich, Chair, 225-578-8684, Fax: 225-578-8616, E-mail: niedrich@lsu.edu. *Application contact:* Dr. Judith Garretson Folse, Graduate Adviser, 225-578-6539, Fax: 225-578-8616, E-mail: folse@lsu.edu.
Website: http://www.business.lsu.edu/marketing.

Louisiana State University and Agricultural & Mechanical College, Graduate School, E. J. Ourso College of Business, Flores MBA Program, Baton Rouge, LA 70803. Offers EMBA, MBA, PMBA, JD/IMBA. *Accreditation:* AACSB. *Students:* 242 full-time (84 women), 69 part-time (20 women); includes 48 minority (27 Black or African American, non-Hispanic/Latino; 11 Asian, non-Hispanic/Latino; 6 Hispanic/Latino; 4 Two or more races, non-Hispanic/Latino), 38 international. Average age 29. 333 applicants, 54% accepted, 129 enrolled. In 2013, 122 master's awarded. *Entrance requirements:* Additional exam requirements/recommendations for international students: Required—TOEFL (minimum score 550 paper-based; 79 IBT), IELTS (minimum score 6.5), or PTE (minimum score 59). *Application deadline:* For fall admission, 1/25 priority date for domestic students, 5/15 for international students; for spring admission, 10/15 for international students. Application fee: $50 ($70 for international students). Electronic applications accepted. *Financial support:* In 2013–14, 184 students received support, including 23 research assistantships with partial tuition reimbursements available (averaging $15,928 per year), 64 teaching assistantships with full and partial tuition reimbursements available (averaging $12,803 per year); fellowships, Federal Work-Study, institutionally sponsored loans, scholarships/grants, health care benefits, and unspecified assistantships also available. Support available to part-time students. Financial award applicants required to submit FAFSA. *Total annual research expenditures:* $327,431. *Unit head:* Dr. Dana Hart, Director, 225-578-8892, Fax: 225-578-2421, E-mail: dhart@lsu.edu. *Application contact:* Dr. Dana Hart, Director, 225-578-8892, Fax: 225-578-2421, E-mail: dhart@lsu.edu.
Website: http://mba.lsu.edu/.

Louisiana State University in Shreveport, College of Business, Education, and Human Development, Program in Business Administration, Shreveport, LA 71115-2399. Offers MBA. Part-time and evening/weekend programs available. *Students:* 16 full-time (7 women), 45 part-time (21 women); includes 13 minority (8 Black or African American, non-Hispanic/Latino; 3 Asian, non-Hispanic/Latino; 1 Hispanic/Latino; 1 Two or more races, non-Hispanic/Latino), 7 international. Average age 32. 47 applicants, 66% accepted, 14 enrolled. In 2013, 37 master's awarded. *Degree requirements:* For master's, comprehensive exam. *Entrance requirements:* For master's, GMAT, minimum undergraduate GPA of 2.5, 2.75 for last 60 credits. Additional exam requirements/recommendations for international students: Required—TOEFL (minimum score 550 paper-based; 80 iBT). *Application deadline:* For fall admission, 6/30 for domestic and international students; for spring admission, 11/30 for domestic and international students. Applications are processed on a rolling basis. Application fee: $10 ($20 for international students). *Expenses: Tuition, area resident:* Part-time $182 per credit hour.

Required fees: $51. *Financial support:* In 2013–14, 5 research assistantships (averaging $5,000 per year) were awarded; scholarships/grants also available. *Unit head:* Dr. Bill Bigler, Program Director, 318-797-5247, Fax: 318-797-5176, E-mail: bill.bigler@lsus.edu. *Application contact:* Christianne Wojcik, Secretary, Graduate Studies, 318-797-5247, Fax: 318-798-4120, E-mail: christianne.wojcik@lsus.edu.

Louisiana Tech University, Graduate School, College of Business, Ruston, LA 71272. Offers MBA, MPA, DBA. *Accreditation:* AACSB. Part-time programs available. *Degree requirements:* For doctorate, thesis/dissertation. *Entrance requirements:* For master's and doctorate, GMAT. *Application deadline:* For fall admission, 7/29 for domestic students; for spring admission, 2/3 for domestic students. Application fee: $20 ($30 for international students). *Financial support:* Fellowships, research assistantships, and teaching assistantships available. *Unit head:* Dr. Timothy O. Bisping, Interim Dean, 318-257-4526, Fax: 318-257-4253. *Application contact:* Marilyn J. Robinson, Assistant to the Dean, 318-257-2924, Fax: 318-257-4487.
Website: http://business.latech.edu/.

Lourdes University, Graduate School, Sylvania, OH 43560-2898. Offers business (MBA); leadership (M Ed); nurse anesthesia (MSN); nurse educator (MSN); nurse leader (MSN); organizational leadership (MOL); reading (M Ed); teaching and curriculum (M Ed); theology (MA). Evening/weekend programs available. *Entrance requirements:* Additional exam requirements/recommendations for international students: Required—TOEFL. *Application deadline:* For fall admission, 6/15 priority date for domestic students; for spring admission, 11/1 priority date for domestic students. Application fee: $25. *Application contact:* Melissa Bergfeld, Administrative Assistant, 419-824-3517, Fax: 419-824-3510, E-mail: mbergfeld2@lourdes.edu.
Website: http://www.lourdes.edu/gradschool.aspx.

Loyola Marymount University, College of Business Administration, Los Angeles, CA 90045-2659. Offers MBA, MS, MBA/JD, MBA/MS. *Accreditation:* AACSB. *Expenses:* Contact institution. *Unit head:* Dr. Jack Gregg, Associate Dean, Graduate Programs, 310-338-2848, Fax: 310-338-2899, E-mail: jack.gregg@lmu.edu. *Application contact:* Chake H Kouyoumjian, Associate Dean of Graduate Studies, 310-338-2721, E-mail: ckouyoum@lmu.edu.
Website: http://cba.lmu.edu/.

Loyola University Chicago, Quinlan School of Business, Chicago, IL 60610. Offers MBA, MSA, MSF, MSHR, MSIMC, MSSCM, JD/MBA, MBA/MSF, MBA/MSHR, MBA/MSN, MBA/MSP, MBA/MSSCM, MSA/MBA, MSIMC/MBA. *Accreditation:* AACSB. Part-time and evening/weekend programs available. *Faculty:* 76 full-time (20 women), 10 part-time/adjunct (4 women). *Students:* 731 (382 women); includes 135 minority (39 Black or African American, non-Hispanic/Latino; 2 American Indian or Alaska Native, non-Hispanic/Latino; 49 Asian, non-Hispanic/Latino; 34 Hispanic/Latino; 1 Native Hawaiian or other Pacific Islander, non-Hispanic/Latino; 10 Two or more races, non-Hispanic/Latino), 212 international. Average age 27. 1,040 applicants, 65% accepted, 267 enrolled. In 2013, 384 master's awarded. *Entrance requirements:* For master's, GMAT or GRE, official transcripts, two letters of recommendation, statement of purpose, resume. Additional exam requirements/recommendations for international students: Required—TOEFL (minimum score 90 iBT) or IELTS (minimum score 6.5). *Application deadline:* For fall admission, 7/15 for domestic and international students; for winter admission, 10/1 for domestic and international students; for spring admission, 1/15 for domestic and international students; for summer admission, 4/1 for domestic and international students. Applications are processed on a rolling basis. Application fee: $50. Electronic applications accepted. Application fee is waived when completed online. *Expenses: Tuition:* Full-time $16,740; part-time $930 per credit. *Required fees:* $135 per semester. *Financial support:* In 2013–14, 78 students received support. Scholarships/grants and unspecified assistantships available. *Faculty research:* Social enterprise and responsibility, emerging markets, supply chain management, risk management. *Unit head:* Jennifer Huntley, Assistant Dean for Graduate Programs, 312-915-6124, Fax: 312-915-7207, E-mail: jhuntle@luc.edu. *Application contact:* Jessica Gagle, Enrollment Advisor, Quinlan School of Business Graduate Programs, 312-915-8908, Fax: 312-915-7207, E-mail: jgagle@luc.edu.
Website: http://www.luc.edu/quinlan/mba/index.shtml.

Loyola University Maryland, Graduate Programs, Sellinger School of Business and Management, Emerging Leaders MBA Program, Baltimore, MD 21210-2699. Offers MBA. Part-time programs available. *Entrance requirements:* For master's, GMAT, essay, 2 letters of recommendation, resume, transcripts. Additional exam requirements/recommendations for international students: Required—TOEFL. Electronic applications accepted.

Loyola University Maryland, Graduate Programs, Sellinger School of Business and Management, Program in Business Administration, Baltimore, MD 21210-2699. Offers accounting (MBA); finance (MBA); general business (MBA); information systems operations management (MBA); international business (MBA); management (MBA); marketing (MBA). *Accreditation:* AACSB. Part-time and evening/weekend programs available. *Entrance requirements:* For master's, GMAT, letter of recommendation, resume, essay. Additional exam requirements/recommendations for international students: Required—TOEFL (minimum score 550 paper-based).

Loyola University Maryland, Graduate Programs, Sellinger School of Business and Management, Program in Executive Business Administration, Baltimore, MD 21210-2699. Offers MBA. *Accreditation:* AACSB. *Entrance requirements:* For master's, resume, letter of recommendation, essay, resume. Additional exam requirements/recommendations for international students: Required—TOEFL (minimum score 550 paper-based). Electronic applications accepted.

Loyola University New Orleans, Joseph A. Butt, S.J., College of Business, Program in Business Administration, New Orleans, LA 70118-6195. Offers MBA, JD/MBA. Application fee waived if attended open house. *Accreditation:* AACSB. Part-time and evening/weekend programs available. Postbaccalaureate distance learning degree programs offered (minimal on-campus study). *Faculty:* 6 full-time (1 woman), 4 part-time/adjunct (1 woman). *Students:* 15 full-time (7 women), 39 part-time (20 women); includes 6 minority (2 American Indian or Alaska Native, non-Hispanic/Latino; 1 Asian, non-Hispanic/Latino; 3 Hispanic/Latino), 3 international. Average age 29. 35 applicants, 83% accepted, 12 enrolled. In 2013, 28 master's awarded. *Entrance requirements:* For master's, GMAT or GRE, minimum GPA of 3.0, transcript, resume, 2 letters of recommendation, work experience in field. Additional exam requirements/recommendations for international students: Required—TOEFL (minimum score 550 paper-based). *Application deadline:* For fall admission, 6/15 priority date for domestic students, 5/15 priority date for international students; for spring admission, 11/15 priority date for domestic students, 10/15 priority date for international students. Applications are processed on a rolling basis. Application fee: $50. Electronic applications accepted. *Expenses: Tuition:* Part-time $818 per hour. Part-time tuition and fees vary according to program. *Financial support:* Research assistantships, scholarships/grants, tuition waivers (partial), and unspecified assistantships available. Financial award application deadline: 5/1; financial award applicants required to submit FAFSA. *Faculty research:* Ethics, international business, entrepreneurship, quality management, risk management. *Unit head:* Dr. William B. Locander, Dean, 504-864-7979, Fax: 504-864-7970, E-mail: mba@loyno.edu. *Application contact:* Dr. Jeffrey A. Krug, Associate Dean of Graduate Programs, 504-864-7953, Fax: 504-864-7970, E-mail: mba@loyno.edu.
Website: http://www.business.loyno.edu/mba/programs.

Lynchburg College, Graduate Studies, School of Business and Economics, Master of Business Administration Program, Lynchburg, VA 24501-3199. Offers MBA. Part-time and evening/weekend programs available. *Faculty:* 4 full-time (1 woman), 1 part-time/adjunct (0 women). *Students:* 6 full-time (3 women), 26 part-time (5 women); includes 1 minority (Two or more races, non-Hispanic/Latino), 2 international. Average age 32. In 2013, 22 master's awarded. *Degree requirements:* For master's, capstone course. *Entrance requirements:* For master's, GMAT (minimum score of 400) or GRE, personal essay, 3 letters of recommendation, official transcripts (bachelor's, others as relevant), career goals statement. Additional exam requirements/recommendations for international students: Required—TOEFL (minimum score 550 paper-based; 79 iBT), IELTS (minimum score 6.5). *Application deadline:* For fall admission, 7/31 for domestic students, 6/1 for international students; for spring admission, 11/30 for domestic students, 10/15 for international students. Applications are processed on a rolling basis. Application fee: $30. Electronic applications accepted. Application fee is waived when completed online. *Financial support:* Fellowships, Federal Work-Study, scholarships/grants, health care benefits, and unspecified assistantships available. Support available to part-time students. Financial award application deadline: 7/31; financial award applicants required to submit FAFSA. *Unit head:* Dr. Atul Gupta, Professor/Director of MBA Program, 434-522-8651, E-mail: gupta@lynchburg.edu. *Application contact:* Anne Pingstock, Executive Assistant, Graduate Studies, 434-544-8383, Fax: 434-544-8483, E-mail: gradstudies@lynchburg.edu.
Website: http://www.lynchburg.edu/master-business-administration.

Lynn University, College of Business and Management, Boca Raton, FL 33431-5598. Offers aviation management (MBA); financial valuation and investment management (MBA); hospitality management (MBA); international business (MBA); marketing (MBA); mass communication and media management (MBA); sports and athletics administration (MBA). Part-time and evening/weekend programs available. Postbaccalaureate distance learning degree programs offered. *Faculty:* 16 full-time (6 women), 8 part-time/adjunct (3 women). *Students:* 181 full-time (95 women), 83 part-time (37 women); includes 41 minority (22 Black or African American, non-Hispanic/Latino; 1 Asian, non-Hispanic/Latino; 17 Hispanic/Latino; 1 Two or more races, non-Hispanic/Latino), 77 international. Average age 28. 137 applicants, 100% accepted, 107 enrolled. In 2013, 149 master's awarded. *Degree requirements:* For master's, projects. *Entrance requirements:* For master's, GMAT or GRE, bachelor's degree from accredited institution, minimum undergraduate GPA of 2.5, resume, 2 letters of recommendation. Additional exam requirements/recommendations for international students: Required—TOEFL (minimum score 550 paper-based). *Application deadline:* Applications are processed on a rolling basis. Application fee: $45. Electronic applications accepted. *Expenses: Tuition:* Full-time $23,760; part-time $660 per credit. *Required fees:* $300; $50 per term. Tuition and fees vary according to degree level and program. *Financial support:* Career-related internships or fieldwork, Federal Work-Study, institutionally sponsored loans, scholarships/grants, tuition waivers (full and partial), and unspecified assistantships available. Support available to part-time students. Financial award application deadline: 8/1; financial award applicants required to submit FAFSA. *Faculty research:* Labor relations, dynamic balance in leisure-time skills, ethics in athletics, hotel development. *Unit head:* Dr. Ralph Norcio, Senior Associate Dean, 561-237-7010, Fax: 561-237-7014, E-mail: rnorcio@lynn.edu. *Application contact:* Steven Pruitt, Director of Graduate and Undergraduate Evening Admission, 561-237-7834, Fax: 561-237-7100, E-mail: spruitt@lynn.edu.
Website: http://www.lynn.edu/academics/colleges/business-and-management.

Maastricht School of Management, Graduate Programs, Maastricht, Netherlands. Offers business administration (MBA, DBA, PhD); facility management (Exec MBA); management (M Sc); sustainability (Exec MBA).

Madonna University, School of Business, Livonia, MI 48150-1173. Offers business administration (MBA); international business (MSBA); leadership studies (MSBA); leadership studies in criminal justice (MSBA); quality and operations management (MSBA). Part-time and evening/weekend programs available. Postbaccalaureate distance learning degree programs offered (minimal on-campus study). *Degree requirements:* For master's, thesis (for some programs), foreign language proficiency (international business). *Entrance requirements:* For master's, GMAT, GRE General Test, minimum GPA of 3.0. Electronic applications accepted. *Faculty research:* Management, women in management, future studies.

Maharishi University of Management, Graduate Studies, Program in Business Administration, Fairfield, IA 52557. Offers accounting (MBA); business administration (PhD); sustainability (MBA). Evening/weekend programs available. Postbaccalaureate distance learning degree programs offered (minimal on-campus study). *Degree requirements:* For doctorate, thesis/dissertation. *Entrance requirements:* For master's, GMAT, minimum GPA of 3.0; for doctorate, minimum GPA of 3.0. Additional exam requirements/recommendations for international students: Required—TOEFL. *Faculty research:* Leadership, effects of the group dynamics of consciousness on the economy, innovation, employee development, cooperative strategy.

Malone University, Graduate Program in Business, Canton, OH 44709. Offers MBA. *Accreditation:* ACBSP. Part-time and evening/weekend programs available. Postbaccalaureate distance learning degree programs offered (no on-campus study). *Faculty:* 8 full-time (3 women), 2 part-time/adjunct (1 woman). *Students:* 20 full-time (4 women), 68 part-time (32 women); includes 10 minority (5 Black or African American, non-Hispanic/Latino; 5 Hispanic/Latino), 2 international. Average age 35. In 2013, 36 master's awarded. *Entrance requirements:* For master's, minimum GPA of 3.0. Additional exam requirements/recommendations for international students: Required—TOEFL (minimum score 550 paper-based; 79 iBT). *Application deadline:* Applications are processed on a rolling basis. *Expenses:* Contact institution. *Financial support:* Tuition waivers (partial) available. Support available to part-time students. Financial award application deadline: 6/30. *Faculty research:* Leadership, business ethics, sustainability, globalization, non-profit financial management. *Unit head:* Dr. Dennis D. Kincaid, Director, 330-471-8186, Fax: 330-471-8563, E-mail: dkincaid@malone.edu. *Application contact:* Natalie D. Denholm, Graduate Recruiter, 330-471-8623, Fax: 330-471-8343, E-mail: ndenholm@malone.edu.
Website: http://www.malone.edu/admissions/graduate/mba/.

Manhattanville College, School of Business, Purchase, NY 10577-2132. Offers M Ed, MA, MAT, MPS, MS, Ed D. Part-time and evening/weekend programs available. *Entrance requirements:* Additional exam requirements/recommendations for international students: Required—TOEFL. *Application deadline:* Applications are processed on a rolling basis. Application fee: $75. *Financial support:* Career-related internships or fieldwork, Federal Work-Study, institutionally sponsored loans, scholarships/grants, tuition waivers (partial), and unspecified assistantships available. Support available to part-time students. Financial award application deadline: 3/1; financial award applicants required to submit FAFSA. *Unit head:* Anthony Davidson, Dean, 914-323-5315, E-mail: anthony.davidson@mville.edu.

Business Administration and Management—General

Application contact: Liz Brosseau, Enrollment Services Coordinator, 914-323-5418, E-mail: elizabeth.brosseau@mville.edu. Website: http://www.mville.edu/graduate.html.

See Close-Up on page 185.

Marian University, School of Business and Public Safety, Fond du Lac, WI 54935-4699. Offers criminal justice leadership (MS); organizational leadership and quality (MS). Part-time and evening/weekend programs available. *Faculty:* 1 full-time (0 women), 6 part-time/adjunct (2 women). *Students:* 1 full-time (0 women), 53 part-time (31 women); includes 7 minority (3 Black or African American, non-Hispanic/Latino; 1 American Indian or Alaska Native, non-Hispanic/Latino; 2 Asian, non-Hispanic/Latino; 1 Hispanic/Latino). Average age 37. In 2013, 45 master's awarded. *Degree requirements:* For master's, comprehensive group project. *Entrance requirements:* For master's, 3 years of managerial experience, minimum GPA of 2.75, letters of professional reference. Additional exam requirements/recommendations for international students: Required—TOEFL (minimum score 525 paper-based; 70 iBT). *Application deadline:* Applications are processed on a rolling basis. Application fee: $25. Electronic applications accepted. *Expenses:* Contact institution. *Financial support:* In 2013–14, 1 student received support. Institutionally sponsored loans available. Financial award application deadline: 3/1; financial award applicants required to submit FAFSA. *Faculty research:* Organizational values, statistical decision-making, learning organization, quality planning, customer research. *Unit head:* Dr. Jeffrey G. Reed, Dean, Marian School of Business, 920-923-8759, Fax: 920-923-7167, E-mail: jreed@marianuniversity.edu. *Application contact:* Jordan Baitinger, Admission Counselor, 920-923-8609, Fax: 920-923-7167, E-mail: jlbaitinger16@marianuniversity.edu. Website: http://www.marianuniversity.edu/Academic-Programs/School-of-Business-and-Public-Safety/School-of-Business-and-Public-Safety/.

Marist College, Graduate Programs, School of Management, Business Administration Program, Poughkeepsie, NY 12601-1387. Offers business administration (MBA); executive leadership (Adv C). *Accreditation:* AACSB. Part-time and evening/weekend programs available. *Entrance requirements:* For master's, GMAT, resume, 2 letters of recommendation. Additional exam requirements/recommendations for international students: Required—TOEFL (minimum score 550 paper-based; 80 iBT); Recommended—IELTS (minimum score 6.5). Electronic applications accepted. *Faculty research:* International trade law, process management, AIDS and the medical provider, mid-Hudson region economics, time quality management and organizational behavior.

Marist College, Graduate Programs, School of Management, Online MBA Program, Poughkeepsie, NY 12601-1387. Offers MBA. Postbaccalaureate distance learning degree programs offered (no on-campus study).

Marlboro College, Graduate and Professional Studies, Program in Business Administration, Marlboro, VT 05344. Offers managing for sustainability (MBA). Part-time and evening/weekend programs available. Postbaccalaureate distance learning degree programs offered (minimal on-campus study). *Faculty:* 14 part-time/adjunct (6 women). *Students:* 5 full-time (4 women), 11 part-time (9 women); includes 1 minority (Asian, non-Hispanic/Latino). Average age 35. 7 applicants, 71% accepted, 4 enrolled. In 2013, 7 master's awarded. *Degree requirements:* For master's, 60 credits including capstone project. *Entrance requirements:* For master's, letter of intent, essay, transcripts, 2 letters of recommendation. *Application deadline:* For fall admission, 7/1 priority date for domestic students; for winter admission, 11/1 priority date for domestic students. Applications are processed on a rolling basis. Application fee: $0. Electronic applications accepted. *Expenses:* Tuition: Part-time $685 per credit. Tuition and fees vary according to course load and program. *Financial support:* Applicants required to submit FAFSA. *Unit head:* Patricia Daniel, Degree Chair, 802-451-7511, Fax: 802-258-9201, E-mail: pdaniel@gradschool.marlboro.edu. *Application contact:* Matthew Livingston, Director of Graduate Admissions, 802-258-9209, Fax: 802-258-9201, E-mail: mlivingston@marlboro.edu. Website: https://www.marlboro.edu/academics/graduate/mba.

Marquette University, Graduate School of Management, Executive MBA Program, Milwaukee, WI 53201-1881. Offers economics (MBA); finance (MBA); human resources (MBA); international business (MBA); management information systems (MBA); marketing (MBA); operations and supply chain management (MBA); sports business (MBA). *Accreditation:* AACSB. *Students:* 38 full-time (12 women), 1 international. Average age 36. 36 applicants. In 2013, 21 master's awarded. *Degree requirements:* For master's, international trip. *Entrance requirements:* For master's, GMAT or GRE, two letters of recommendation, official transcripts from current and previous colleges/universities. Additional exam requirements/recommendations for international students: Required—TOEFL (minimum score 550 paper-based; 88 iBT), IELTS (minimum score 6.5), PTE. *Application deadline:* For fall admission, 2/15 for domestic and international students. Application fee: $50. Electronic applications accepted. *Expenses:* Contact institution. *Financial support:* Application deadline: 2/15. *Faculty research:* International trade and finance, customer relationship management, consumer satisfaction, customer service. *Unit head:* Dr. Mark Eppli, Dean, 414-288-5724. *Application contact:* Dr. Jeanne Simmons, Associate Dean, 414-288-7145. Website: http://www.busadm.mu.edu/emba/.

Marquette University, Graduate School of Management, Program in Business Administration, Milwaukee, WI 53201-1881. Offers business administration (MBA); economics (MBA); entrepreneurship (Certificate); finance (MBA); human resources (MBA); international business (MBA); management information systems (MBA); marketing (MBA); operations and supply chain management (MBA); sports business (MBA); JD/MBA; MBA/MA; MBA/MSN. *Accreditation:* AACSB. Part-time and evening/weekend programs available. *Students:* 28 full-time (13 women), 265 part-time (66 women); includes 20 minority (7 Black or African American, non-Hispanic/Latino; 8 Asian, non-Hispanic/Latino; 5 Hispanic/Latino), 11 international. Average age 31. 185 applicants. In 2013, 129 master's, 2 other advanced degrees awarded. *Degree requirements:* For Certificate, business plan. *Entrance requirements:* For master's, GMAT or GRE, letters of recommendation. Additional exam requirements/recommendations for international students: Required—TOEFL (minimum score 550 paper-based; 88 iBT), IELTS (minimum score 6.5), PTE. *Application deadline:* For fall admission, 2/15 for domestic and international students. Applications are processed on a rolling basis. Application fee: $50. Electronic applications accepted. *Financial support:* In 2013–14, 4 fellowships, 11 teaching assistantships were awarded; research assistantships, Federal Work-Study, institutionally sponsored loans, scholarships/grants, and tuition waivers (full and partial) also available. Support available to part-time students. Financial award application deadline: 2/15. *Faculty research:* Ethics in the professions, services marketing, technology impact on decision-making, mentoring. *Unit head:* Dr. Mark Eppli, Dean, 414-288-5724. *Application contact:* Dr. Jeanne Simmons, Associate Dean, 414-288-7145. Website: http://business.marquette.edu/academics/mba.

Marshall University, Academic Affairs Division, College of Business, Program in Business Administration, Huntington, WV 25755. Offers EMBA, MBA. Part-time and evening/weekend programs available. *Students:* 79 full-time (23 women), 37 part-time (15 women); includes 10 minority (6 Black or African American, non-Hispanic/Latino; 3 Asian, non-Hispanic/Latino; 1 Two or more races, non-Hispanic/Latino), 21 international.

Average age 27. In 2013, 41 master's awarded. *Degree requirements:* For master's, comprehensive assessment. *Entrance requirements:* For master's, GMAT. *Application deadline:* Applications are processed on a rolling basis. Application fee: $40. *Financial support:* Tuition waivers (full) available. Support available to part-time students. Financial award applicants required to submit FAFSA. *Unit head:* Dr. Margie McInerney, Associate Dean, 304-696-2675, E-mail: mcinerney@marshall.edu. *Application contact:* Wesley Spradlin, Information Contact, 304-746-8964, Fax: 304-746-1902, E-mail: spradlin2@marshall.edu.

Maryland Institute College of Art, Graduate Studies, The Business of Art and Design Program, Baltimore, MD 21217. Offers MPS. Part-time programs available. Postbaccalaureate distance learning degree programs offered (minimal on-campus study). *Degree requirements:* For master's, business plan presentation. *Entrance requirements:* For master's, essay, good academic standing, resume. Additional exam requirements/recommendations for international students: Required—TOEFL (minimum score 550 paper-based; 80 iBT). *Expenses:* Contact institution.

Maryland Institute College of Art, Graduate Studies, Program in Design Leadership, Baltimore, MD 21217. Offers MBA/MA. Program offered in collaboration with The Johns Hopkins University. *Entrance requirements:* Additional exam requirements/recommendations for international students: Required—TOEFL (minimum score 100 iBT) or IELTS (minimum score 7). *Expenses:* Contact institution.

Marylhurst University, Department of Business Administration, Marylhurst, OR 97036-0261. Offers finance (MBA); general management (MBA); government policy and administration (MBA); green development (MBA); health care management (MBA); marketing (MBA); natural and organic resources (MBA); nonprofit management (MBA); organizational behavior (MBA); real estate (MBA); renewable energy (MBA); sustainable business (MBA). Part-time and evening/weekend programs available. Postbaccalaureate distance learning degree programs offered (no on-campus study). *Degree requirements:* For master's, comprehensive exam, capstone course. *Entrance requirements:* For master's, GMAT (if GPA less than 3.0 and fewer than 5 years of work experience), interview, resume, 2 letters of recommendation. Additional exam requirements/recommendations for international students: Recommended—TOEFL (minimum score 550 paper-based; 80 iBT). Electronic applications accepted.

Marymount University, School of Business Administration, Program in Business Administration, Arlington, VA 22207-4299. Offers MBA, Certificate. *Accreditation:* ACBSP. Part-time and evening/weekend programs available. *Faculty:* 9 full-time (6 women), 3 part-time/adjunct (1 woman). *Students:* 39 full-time (23 women), 86 part-time (45 women); includes 40 minority (19 Black or African American, non-Hispanic/Latino; 1 American Indian or Alaska Native, non-Hispanic/Latino; 10 Asian, non-Hispanic/Latino; 8 Hispanic/Latino; 2 Two or more races, non-Hispanic/Latino), 14 international. Average age 31. 64 applicants, 84% accepted, 36 enrolled. In 2013, 65 master's awarded. *Degree requirements:* For master's, thesis or alternative. *Entrance requirements:* For master's, GMAT or GRE General Test, resume; for Certificate, resume. Additional exam requirements/recommendations for international students: Required—TOEFL (minimum score 600 paper-based; 96 iBT), IELTS (minimum score 6.5). *Application deadline:* For fall admission, 7/15 priority date for domestic students, 7/1 for international students; for spring admission, 11/15 priority date for domestic and international students. Applications are processed on a rolling basis. Application fee: $40. Electronic applications accepted. *Expenses:* Contact institution. *Financial support:* In 2013–14, 6 students received support, including 3 research assistantships with full and partial tuition reimbursements available; career-related internships or fieldwork, Federal Work-Study, scholarships/grants, and unspecified assistantships also available. Support available to part-time students. Financial award applicants required to submit FAFSA. *Unit head:* Dr. Terri Long, Director, 703-284-5918, E-mail: terri.long@marymount.edu. *Application contact:* Francesca Reed, Director, Graduate Admissions, 703-284-5901, Fax: 703-527-3815, E-mail: grad.admissions@marymount.edu. Website: http://www.marymount.edu/academics/programs/businessAdminMBA.

Marymount University, School of Business Administration, Program in Leadership and Management, Arlington, VA 22207-4299. Offers leadership (Certificate); management (MS); non-profit management (Certificate); project management (Certificate). Part-time and evening/weekend programs available. *Faculty:* 5 full-time (2 women), 1 (woman) part-time/adjunct. *Students:* 1 full-time (0 women), 22 part-time (16 women); includes 8 minority (4 Black or African American, non-Hispanic/Latino; 2 Asian, non-Hispanic/Latino; 2 Hispanic/Latino). Average age 37. 14 applicants, 93% accepted, 11 enrolled. In 2013, 7 master's, 13 other advanced degrees awarded. *Degree requirements:* For master's, thesis or alternative. *Entrance requirements:* For master's, GMAT or GRE General Test, resume, at least 3 years of managerial experience, essay; for Certificate, resume, at least 3 years of managerial experience. Additional exam requirements/recommendations for international students: Required—TOEFL (minimum score 600 paper-based; 96 iBT), IELTS (minimum score 6.5). *Application deadline:* For fall admission, 7/15 priority date for domestic students, 7/1 for international students; for spring admission, 11/15 priority date for domestic students, 11/15 for international students. Applications are processed on a rolling basis. Application fee: $40. Electronic applications accepted. *Expenses:* Tuition: Part-time $850 per credit. *Required fees:* $10 per credit. One-time fee: $200 part-time. Tuition and fees vary according to program. *Financial support:* Research assistantships with full and partial tuition reimbursements, career-related internships or fieldwork, Federal Work-Study, scholarships/grants, and unspecified assistantships available. Support available to part-time students. Financial award applicants required to submit FAFSA. *Unit head:* Dr. Lorri Cooper, Director, Master's in Management Program, 703-284-5950, Fax: 703-527-3830, E-mail: lorri.cooper@marymount.edu. *Application contact:* Francesca Reed, Director, Graduate Admissions, 703-284-5901, Fax: 703-527-3815, E-mail: grad.admissions@marymount.edu.

Maryville University of Saint Louis, The John E. Simon School of Business, St. Louis, MO 63141-7299. Offers accounting (MBA, PGC); management (MBA, PGC); marketing (MBA, PGC); process and project management (MBA, PGC); sport and entertainment management (MBA, PGC). *Accreditation:* ACBSP. Part-time and evening/weekend programs available. *Faculty:* 5 full-time (3 women), 14 part-time/adjunct (4 women). *Students:* 21 full-time (12 women), 85 part-time (41 women); includes 22 minority (8 Black or African American, non-Hispanic/Latino; 2 Asian, non-Hispanic/Latino; 7 Hispanic/Latino; 5 Two or more races, non-Hispanic/Latino), 3 international. Average age 31. In 2013, 39 master's awarded. *Entrance requirements:* For master's, GMAT (unless applicant possesses undergraduate business degree with minimum cumulative GPA of 3.0, or has completed master's degree from accredited university or one early access course prior to undergraduate degree). Additional exam requirements/recommendations for international students: Required—TOEFL (minimum score 85 iBT). *Application deadline:* Applications are processed on a rolling basis. Application fee: $40 ($60 for international students). Electronic applications accepted. Application fee is waived when completed online. *Expenses:* Tuition: Full-time $23,812; part-time $728 per credit hour. *Required fees:* $395 per year. Tuition and fees vary according to course load, degree level and program. *Financial support:* Career-related internships or fieldwork, Federal Work-Study, tuition waivers (partial), and campus employment available. Financial award application deadline: 3/1; financial award applicants required to submit FAFSA. *Faculty research:* International business, e-marketing, strategic

planning, interpersonal management skills, financial analysis. *Unit head:* Dr. Pamela Horwitz, Dean, 314-529-9418, Fax: 314-529-9975, E-mail: horwitz@maryville.edu. *Application contact:* Kathy Dougherty, Director of MBA Programs, 314-529-9382, Fax: 314-529-9975, E-mail: business@maryville.edu.
Website: http://www.maryville.edu/bu/business-administration-masters/.

Marywood University, Academic Affairs, College of Liberal Arts and Sciences, School of Business and Global Innovation, Scranton, PA 18509-1598. Offers financial information systems (MBA, MS); general management (MBA); management information systems (MBA, MS). *Accreditation:* ACBSP. *Entrance requirements:* Additional exam requirements/recommendations for international students: Required—TOEFL (minimum score 550 paper-based; 79 iBT). *Application deadline:* For fall admission, 4/1 priority date for domestic students, 3/31 priority date for international students; for spring admission, 11/1 priority date for domestic students, 8/31 priority date for international students. Applications are processed on a rolling basis. Application fee: $35. Electronic applications accepted. *Expenses: Tuition:* Part-time $775 per credit. Tuition and fees vary according to degree level. *Financial support:* Research assistantships, career-related internships or fieldwork, scholarships/grants, and unspecified assistantships available. Support available to part-time students. Financial award application deadline: 6/30; financial award applicants required to submit FAFSA. *Faculty research:* Problem formulation in ill-structured situations, corporate tax structures. *Unit head:* Dr. Arthur Comstock, Chairman, 570-348-6211 Ext. 2449, E-mail: comstock@marywood.edu. *Application contact:* Tammy Manka, Assistant Director of Graduate Admissions, 570-348-6211 Ext. 2322, E-mail: tmanka@marywood.edu.
Website: http://www.marywood.edu/business/.

Massachusetts College of Liberal Arts, Graduate Programs, North Adams, MA 01247-4100. Offers business (MBA); educational administration (M Ed); educational leadership (CAGS); instruction and curriculum (M Ed); instructional technology (M Ed); physical education and health (M Ed); reading (M Ed); special education (M Ed). Part-time and evening/weekend programs available. *Degree requirements:* For master's, thesis. *Entrance requirements:* For master's, writing sample.

Massachusetts Institute of Technology, MIT Sloan School of Management, Cambridge, MA 02142. Offers M Fin, MBA, MS, SM, PhD. *Accreditation:* AACSB. *Degree requirements:* For master's, thesis (for some programs); for doctorate, thesis/dissertation, exams. *Entrance requirements:* For master's, GMAT, previous course work in calculus and economics; for doctorate, GMAT, GRE, previous course work in calculus and economics. Electronic applications accepted. *Expenses:* Contact institution. *Faculty research:* Financial engineering, entrepreneurship, e-business, work and employment, leaders for manufacturing.

McGill University, Faculty of Graduate and Postdoctoral Studies, Desautels Faculty of Management, Montréal, QC H3A 2T5, Canada. Offers administration (PhD); entrepreneurial studies (MBA); finance (MBA); general management (Post Master's Certificate); information systems (MBA); international business (MBA); international practicing management (MM); management (MBA); management for development (MBA); manufacturing management (MMM); marketing (MBA); operations management (MBA); public accountancy (Diploma); strategic management (MBA); MBA/LL B; MD/MBA. MMM offered jointly with Faculty of Engineering; PhD with Concordia University, HEC Montreal, Université de Montréal, Université du Québec à Montréal.

McKendree University, Graduate Programs, Master of Business Administration Program, Lebanon, IL 62254-1299. Offers business administration (MBA); human resource management (MBA); international business (MBA). Part-time and evening/weekend programs available. Postbaccalaureate distance learning degree programs offered (no on-campus study). *Entrance requirements:* For master's, official transcripts from all institutions attended, essay, minimum GPA of 3.0, three references, resume. Additional exam requirements/recommendations for international students: Required—TOEFL. Electronic applications accepted.

McMaster University, School of Graduate Studies, Faculty of Business, Hamilton, ON L8S 4M2, Canada. Offers MBA, PhD. *Accreditation:* AACSB. Part-time programs available. *Degree requirements:* For doctorate, comprehensive exam, thesis/dissertation. *Entrance requirements:* For master's, GMAT; for doctorate, GMAT or GRE, master's degree. Additional exam requirements/recommendations for international students: Required—TOEFL (minimum score 580 paper-based). *Faculty research:* Mergers, acquisitions, and restructuring; business investment; capital structure and dividend policy; employee pay/reward systems; pay and employment equity.

McNeese State University, Doré School of Graduate Studies, College of Business, Master of Business Administration Program, Lake Charles, LA 70609. Offers MBA. *Accreditation:* AACSB. Evening/weekend programs available. *Degree requirements:* For master's, written exam. *Entrance requirements:* For master's, GMAT. *Faculty research:* Management development, integrating technology into the work force, union/management relations, economic development.

Medaille College, Program in Business Administration - Amherst, Amherst, NY 14221. Offers business administration (MBA); organizational leadership (MA). Evening/weekend programs available. *Faculty:* 20 full-time (17 women), 8 part-time/adjunct (6 women). *Students:* 116 full-time (72 women), 14 part-time (6 women); includes 42 minority (27 Black or African American, non-Hispanic/Latino; 1 American Indian or Alaska Native, non-Hispanic/Latino; 6 Asian, non-Hispanic/Latino; 8 Hispanic/Latino), 6 international. Average age 40. 92 applicants, 89% accepted, 29 enrolled. In 2013, 91 master's awarded. *Degree requirements:* For master's, thesis or alternative. *Entrance requirements:* For master's, GMAT, minimum undergraduate GPA of 2.7, 3 years of work experience. Additional exam requirements/recommendations for international students: Required—TOEFL (minimum score 550 paper-based). *Application deadline:* Applications are processed on a rolling basis. Application fee: $35. Electronic applications accepted. *Expenses:* Contact institution. *Financial support:* Federal Work-Study available. Financial award applicants required to submit FAFSA. *Unit head:* Jennifer Bavifard, Associate Dean for Special Programs, 716-631-1061 Ext. 150, Fax: 716-631-1380, E-mail: jbavifar@medaille.edu. *Application contact:* E-mail: sageadmissions@medaille.edu.
Website: http://www.medaille.edu/.

Medaille College, Program in Business Administration - Rochester, Rochester, NY 14623. Offers business administration (MBA); organizational leadership (MA). Evening/weekend programs available. *Students:* 16 full-time (12 women), 1 part-time (0 women); includes 10 minority (6 Black or African American, non-Hispanic/Latino; 1 Asian, non-Hispanic/Latino; 3 Hispanic/Latino). Average age 32. 19 applicants, 100% accepted, 13 enrolled. In 2013, 13 master's awarded. *Degree requirements:* For master's, thesis or alternative. *Entrance requirements:* For master's, GMAT, 3 years of work experience, minimum undergraduate GPA of 2.7. Additional exam requirements/recommendations for international students: Required—TOEFL (minimum score 550 paper-based). *Application deadline:* Applications are processed on a rolling basis. Application fee: $35. *Expenses:* Contact institution. *Financial support:* Federal Work-Study available. Financial award applicants required to submit FAFSA. *Unit head:* Jennifer Bavifard, Branch Campus Director, 716-932-2591, Fax: 716-631-1380, E-mail: jbavifard@medaille.edu. *Application contact:* E-mail: sageadmissions@medaille.edu.
Website: http://www.medaille.edu/.

Melbourne Business School, Graduate Programs, Carlton, Australia. Offers business administration (Exec MBA, MBA); management (PhD); management science (PhD); marketing (PhD); social impact (Graduate Certificate); JD/MBA.

Memorial University of Newfoundland, School of Graduate Studies, Faculty of Business Administration, St. John's, NL A1C 5S7, Canada. Offers EMBA, MBA. *Accreditation:* AACSB. Part-time programs available. *Degree requirements:* For master's, thesis (for some programs). *Entrance requirements:* For master's, GMAT. Additional exam requirements/recommendations for international students: Required—TOEFL (minimum score 580 paper-based), TWE (minimum score 4). Electronic applications accepted. *Faculty research:* International business, marketing, organizational theory and behavior, management science and information systems, small business.

Mercer University, Graduate Studies, Cecil B. Day Campus, Eugene W. Stetson School of Business and Economics (Atlanta), Atlanta, GA 30341. Offers accounting (M Acc); business administration (EMBA, PMBA); international business (MBA); MBA/M Acc; Pharm D/MBA. *Accreditation:* AACSB. Part-time and evening/weekend programs available. Postbaccalaureate distance learning degree programs offered (no on-campus study). *Faculty:* 20 full-time (9 women), 7 part-time/adjunct (2 women). *Students:* 207 full-time (112 women), 103 part-time (62 women); includes 143 minority (116 Black or African American, non-Hispanic/Latino; 2 American Indian or Alaska Native, non-Hispanic/Latino; 18 Asian, non-Hispanic/Latino; 6 Hispanic/Latino; 1 Native Hawaiian or other Pacific Islander, non-Hispanic/Latino), 43 international. Average age 32. 117 applicants, 97% accepted, 94 enrolled. In 2013, 150 master's awarded. *Entrance requirements:* For master's, GMAT or GRE. Additional exam requirements/recommendations for international students: Required—TOEFL (minimum score 550 paper-based; 80 iBT). *Application deadline:* For fall admission, 7/1 priority date for domestic students, 7/1 for international students; for spring admission, 11/1 priority date for domestic students, 11/1 for international students. Applications are processed on a rolling basis. Application fee: $50 ($100 for international students). Electronic applications accepted. *Financial support:* Federal Work-Study available. Financial award application deadline: 5/1; financial award applicants required to submit FAFSA. *Faculty research:* Entrepreneurship, market studies, international business strategy, financial analysis. *Unit head:* Dr. Michael Weber, Associate Dean, 678-547-6056, Fax: 678-547-6337, E-mail: weber_jm@mercer.edu. *Application contact:* Lael Whiteside, Admissions Counselor, 678-547-6147, Fax: 678-547-6160, E-mail: graduatessbe@mercer.edu.
Website: http://business.mercer.edu.

Mercer University, Graduate Studies, Macon Campus, Eugene W. Stetson School of Business and Economics (Macon), Macon, GA 31207-0003. Offers MBA. *Accreditation:* AACSB. Part-time and evening/weekend programs available. *Faculty:* 6 full-time (2 women), 3 part-time/adjunct (0 women). *Students:* 30 full-time (12 women), 38 part-time (15 women); includes 23 minority (18 Black or African American, non-Hispanic/Latino; 1 American Indian or Alaska Native, non-Hispanic/Latino; 3 Hispanic/Latino; 1 Two or more races, non-Hispanic/Latino), 1 international. Average age 31. In 2013, 43 master's awarded. *Entrance requirements:* For master's, GMAT/GRE. Additional exam requirements/recommendations for international students: Required—TOEFL (minimum score 550 paper-based). *Application deadline:* For fall admission, 8/1 for domestic students; for spring admission, 12/1 for domestic students. Applications are processed on a rolling basis. Application fee: $50 ($100 for international students). *Faculty research:* Federal Reserve System, management of nurses, sales promotion, systems for common stock selection, interest rate premiums. *Unit head:* Dr. Allen K. Lynch, Associate Dean, 478-301-4055, E-mail: lynch_ak@mercer.edu. *Application contact:* Robert Holland, Jr., Director/Academic Administrator, 478-301-2835, Fax: 478-301-2635, E-mail: holland_r@mercer.edu.
Website: http://business.mercer.edu/academics/.

Mercy College, School of Business, Program in Business Administration, Dobbs Ferry, NY 10522-1189. Offers MBA. Part-time and evening/weekend programs available. Postbaccalaureate distance learning degree programs offered (no on-campus study). *Students:* 170 full-time (93 women), 76 part-time (46 women); includes 160 minority (80 Black or African American, non-Hispanic/Latino; 1 American Indian or Alaska Native, non-Hispanic/Latino; 17 Asian, non-Hispanic/Latino; 54 Hispanic/Latino; 1 Native Hawaiian or other Pacific Islander, non-Hispanic/Latino; 7 Two or more races, non-Hispanic/Latino), 15 international. Average age 32. 264 applicants, 67% accepted, 103 enrolled. In 2013, 45 master's awarded. *Entrance requirements:* For master's, interview, two letters of recommendation, undergraduate transcripts. Additional exam requirements/recommendations for international students: Required—TOEFL (minimum score 600 paper-based; 100 iBT), IELTS (minimum score 8). *Application deadline:* For fall admission, 8/1 for international students. Applications are processed on a rolling basis. Application fee: $40. Electronic applications accepted. *Expenses: Tuition:* Full-time $19,344; part-time $806 per credit. *Required fees:* $580; $806 per credit. $145 per term. Tuition and fees vary according to course load, degree level and program. *Financial support:* Career-related internships or fieldwork, Federal Work-Study, scholarships/grants, and unspecified assistantships available. Support available to part-time students. Financial award applicants required to submit FAFSA. *Unit head:* Ed Weis, Dean, School of Business, 914-674-7490, E-mail: eweis@mercy.edu. *Application contact:* Allison Gurdineer, Senior Director of Admissions, 877-637-2946, Fax: 914-674-7382, E-mail: admissions@mercy.edu.
Website: https://www.mercy.edu/academics/school-of-business/department-of-business-administration/mba-in-business-administration/.

Meredith College, John E. Weems Graduate School, School of Business, Raleigh, NC 27607-5298. Offers business administration (MBA). *Accreditation:* AACSB. Part-time and evening/weekend programs available. *Degree requirements:* For master's, thesis optional. *Entrance requirements:* For master's, GMAT, interview, minimum GPA of 2.5, letters of recommendation. Additional exam requirements/recommendations for international students: Required—TOEFL. Electronic applications accepted.

Merrimack College, Girard School of Business, North Andover, MA 01845-5800. Offers management (MS). Part-time and evening/weekend programs available. *Faculty:* 6 full-time (3 women), 2 part-time/adjunct (0 women). *Students:* 45 full-time (22 women), 5 part-time (2 women); includes 1 minority (Hispanic/Latino), 6 international. Average age 25. 55 applicants, 75% accepted, 29 enrolled. In 2013, 18 master's awarded. *Degree requirements:* For master's, variable foreign language requirement, comprehensive exam (for some programs), thesis optional, capstone. *Entrance requirements:* For master's, official college transcripts, resume, personal statement, 2 recommendations. Additional exam requirements/recommendations for international students: Required—TOEFL (minimum score 84 iBT), IELTS (minimum score 6.5). *Application deadline:* For fall admission, 8/15 for domestic and international students; for winter admission, 12/1 for domestic students, 11/15 for international students; for spring admission, 1/10 for domestic and international students. Applications are processed on a rolling basis. Application fee: $0. Electronic applications accepted. Tuition and fees vary according to course load and program. *Financial support:* Career-related internships or fieldwork, scholarships/grants, health care benefits, and unspecified assistantships available. Support available to part-time students. Financial award application deadline: 5/1; financial award applicants required to submit FAFSA. *Faculty research:* Leadership,

teams, theories of behavior and behavior change, consumer behavior, marketing analytics. *Application contact:* Kristen English, Interim Director of Graduate Admission, 978-837-5073, E-mail: englishkr@merrimack.edu.
Website: http://www.merrimack.edu/academics/graduate/management/.

Methodist University, School of Graduate Studies, Program in Business Administration, Fayetteville, NC 28311-1498. Offers MBA. *Accreditation:* ACBSP. Part-time and evening/weekend programs available. *Entrance requirements:* For master's, GMAT or MAT. Additional exam requirements/recommendations for international students: Required—TOEFL (minimum score 500 paper-based; 60 iBT).

Metropolitan College of New York, Program in General Management, New York, NY 10013. Offers MBA. *Accreditation:* ACBSP. Evening/weekend programs available. *Degree requirements:* For master's, thesis, 10 day study abroad. *Entrance requirements:* For master's, GMAT. Additional exam requirements/recommendations for international students: Required—TOEFL (minimum score 600 paper-based). Electronic applications accepted. *Expenses:* Contact institution.

Metropolitan State University, College of Management, St. Paul, MN 55106-5000. Offers business administration (MBA, DBA); database administration (Graduate Certificate); healthcare information technology management (Graduate Certificate); information assurance security (Graduate Certificate); management information systems (MMIS); MIS generalist (Graduate Certificate); MIS systems analysis and design (Graduate Certificate); project management (Graduate Certificate); public and nonprofit administration (MPNA). Part-time and evening/weekend programs available. *Degree requirements:* For master's, thesis optional, computer language (MMIS). *Entrance requirements:* For master's, GMAT (for MBA), resume. Additional exam requirements/recommendations for international students: Required—TOEFL (minimum score 550 paper-based). Electronic applications accepted. *Expenses:* Tuition, state resident: full-time $5548. Tuition, nonresident: full-time $10,929. *Faculty research:* Yugoslav economic system, workers' cooperatives, participative management and job enrichment, global business systems.

Miami University, Farmer School of Business, Oxford, OH 45056. Offers M Acc, MA, MBA. *Accreditation:* AACSB. *Expenses:* Tuition, state resident: full-time $12,634; part-time $526 per credit hour. Tuition, nonresident: full-time $27,892; part-time $1162 per credit hour. Part-time tuition and fees vary according to course load, campus/location and program. *Unit head:* Dr. Raymond Gorman, Interim Dean and Professor of Finance, 513-529-3631, Fax: 513-529-6992, E-mail: deanofbusiness@miamioh.edu. *Application contact:* Admission Coordinator, 513-529-3734, E-mail: gradschool@miamioh.edu.
Website: http://www.fsb.miamioh.edu/.

Michigan State University, The Graduate School, Eli Broad College of Business, Department of Management, East Lansing, MI 48824. Offers management (PhD); management, strategy, and leadership (MS). Part-time programs available. Postbaccalaureate distance learning degree programs offered (no on-campus study). *Faculty:* 24. *Degree requirements:* For doctorate, comprehensive exam, thesis/dissertation. *Entrance requirements:* For master's, full-time managerial experience in a supervisory role; for doctorate, GMAT or GRE, letters of recommendation, experience in teaching and conducting research, work experience in business contexts, personal essay. Additional exam requirements/recommendations for international students: Required—TOEFL (minimum score 600 paper-based). Electronic applications accepted. *Financial support:* Research assistantships with tuition reimbursements and teaching assistantships with tuition reimbursements available. Financial award application deadline: 1/1; financial award applicants required to submit FAFSA. *Unit head:* Dr. Robert Wiseman, Chairperson, 517-355-1878, Fax: 517-432-1111, E-mail: wiseman@broad.msu.edu. *Application contact:* Program Information Contact, 517-355-1878, Fax: 517-432-1111, E-mail: mgt@msu.edu.
Website: http://management.broad.msu.edu/.

Michigan State University, The Graduate School, Eli Broad College of Business, Program in Business Administration, East Lansing, MI 48824. Offers finance (MBA); human resource management (MBA); integrative management (MBA); marketing (MBA); supply chain management (MBA). MBA in integrative management is through Weekend MBA Program; other 4 concentrations are through Full-Time MBA Program. Evening/weekend programs available. *Students:* 432. In 2013, 241 degrees awarded. *Degree requirements:* For master's, enrichment experience. *Entrance requirements:* For master's, GMAT or GRE, 4-year bachelor's degree; resume; work experience (minimum of 5 years for Weekend MBA); 2-3 personal essays; 2 letters of recommendation; personal interview. Additional exam requirements/recommendations for international students: Required—PTE (minimum score 70), TOEFL (minimum score 100 iBT) or IELTS (minimum score 7) for Full-Time MBA applicants. *Application deadline:* Applications are processed on a rolling basis. Application fee: $50. Electronic applications accepted. *Expenses:* Contact institution. *Financial support:* Fellowships with tuition reimbursements, research assistantships with tuition reimbursements, teaching assistantships with tuition reimbursements, scholarships/grants, unspecified assistantships, and non-resident tuition waivers (for all military veterans and their dependents in the Full-Time MBA Program) available. Financial award applicants required to submit FAFSA. *Unit head:* Dr. Sanjay Gupta, Associate Dean for MBA and Professional Master's Programs, 517-432-6488, Fax: 517-353-6395, E-mail: gupta@broad.msu.edu. *Application contact:* Program Information Contact, 517-355-7604, Fax: 517-353-1649, E-mail: mba@msu.edu.
Website: http://mba.broad.msu.edu.

Michigan Technological University, Graduate School, School of Business and Economics, Houghton, MI 49931. Offers applied natural resource economics (MS); business administration (MBA). *Accreditation:* AACSB. Part-time programs available. *Degree requirements:* For master's, comprehensive exam (for some programs), thesis (for some programs). *Entrance requirements:* For master's, GMAT (recommended minimum score in the 50th percentile), statement of purpose, official transcripts, 2 letters of recommendation, resume/curriculum vitae, prerequisites in statistics and economics. Additional exam requirements/recommendations for international students: Required—TOEFL (minimum score 95 iBT) or IELTS. Electronic applications accepted.

Mid-America Christian University, Program in Business Administration, Oklahoma City, OK 73170-4504. Offers MBA. *Entrance requirements:* For master's, bachelor's degree from regionally-accredited college or university, minimum overall cumulative GPA of 2.75 on undergraduate course work. Additional exam requirements/recommendations for international students: Required—TOEFL (minimum score 550 paper-based).

MidAmerica Nazarene University, Graduate Studies in Management, Olathe, KS 66062-1899. Offers management (MBA); organizational administration (MA), including finance, international business, leadership, non-profit. Evening/weekend programs available. *Entrance requirements:* For master's, mathematical assessment, minimum undergraduate GPA of 3.0, letters of recommendation. Additional exam requirements/recommendations for international students: Required—TOEFL. Electronic applications accepted. *Faculty research:* Economic development, international finance, business development, employee evaluation.

Middle Tennessee State University, College of Graduate Studies, Jennings A. Jones College of Business, Department of Management and Marketing, Murfreesboro, TN 37132. Offers business administration (MBA); management (MS). *Accreditation:* AACSB. Part-time and evening/weekend programs available. Postbaccalaureate distance learning degree programs offered. *Faculty:* 31 full-time (11 women), 2 part-time/adjunct (both women). *Students:* 116 full-time (34 women), 190 part-time (72 women); includes 69 minority (34 Black or African American, non-Hispanic/Latino; 24 Asian, non-Hispanic/Latino; 7 Hispanic/Latino; 4 Two or more races, non-Hispanic/Latino). 226 applicants, 65% accepted. In 2013, 140 master's awarded. *Degree requirements:* For master's, comprehensive exam. *Entrance requirements:* Additional exam requirements/recommendations for international students: Required—TOEFL (minimum score 525 paper-based; 71 iBT) or IELTS (minimum score 6). *Application deadline:* For fall admission, 6/1 for domestic and international students. Applications are processed on a rolling basis. Application fee: $25 ($30 for international students). Electronic applications accepted. *Financial support:* In 2013–14, 8 students received support. Tuition waivers available. Support available to part-time students. Financial award application deadline: 5/1; financial award applicants required to submit FAFSA. *Unit head:* Dr. Jill Austin, Chair, 615-898-2992, Fax: 615-898-5308, E-mail: jill.austin@mtsu.edu. *Application contact:* Dr. Michael D. Allen, Vice Provost for Research and Dean, 615-898-2840, Fax: 615-904-8020, E-mail: michael.allen@mtsu.edu.

Midway College, Graduate Programs, Midway, KY 40347-1120. Offers education (MAT); leadership (MBA). *Degree requirements:* For master's, capstone course. *Entrance requirements:* For master's, GMAT (for MBA); GRE or PRAXIS I (for MAT), bachelor's degree; interview; minimum GPA of 3.0 (for MBA), 2.75 (for MAT); 3 years of professional work experience (for MBA). Additional exam requirements/recommendations for international students: Required—TOEFL (minimum score 550 paper-based; 80 iBT).

Midwestern State University, Graduate School, Dillard College of Business Administration, Wichita Falls, TX 76308. Offers MBA. *Accreditation:* AACSB. Part-time and evening/weekend programs available. *Degree requirements:* For master's, comprehensive exam, thesis optional. *Entrance requirements:* For master's, GMAT. Additional exam requirements/recommendations for international students: Required—TOEFL (minimum score 550 paper-based). *Application deadline:* For fall admission, 7/1 priority date for domestic students, 4/1 for international students; for spring admission, 11/1 priority date for domestic students, 8/1 for international students. Applications are processed on a rolling basis. Application fee: $35 ($50 for international students). Electronic applications accepted. *Expenses:* Tuition, state resident: full-time $3627; part-time $201.50 per credit hour. Tuition, nonresident: full-time $10,899; part-time $605.50 per credit hour. *Required fees:* $1357. *Financial support:* Teaching assistantships with partial tuition reimbursements, career-related internships or fieldwork, Federal Work-Study, institutionally sponsored loans, tuition waivers (partial), and unspecified assistantships available. Support available to part-time students. Financial award application deadline: 3/1; financial award applicants required to submit FAFSA. *Faculty research:* Citizenship behavior, software solutions, mediations, sales force training, stock trading volume. *Unit head:* Dr. Terry Patton, Dean, 940-397-4088, Fax: 940-397-4280. *Application contact:* Dr. Bob Thomas, Graduate Coordinator, 940-397-6206, Fax: 940-397-4280, E-mail: bob.thomas@mwsu.edu.
Website: http://www.mwsu.edu/academics/business/.

Millennia Atlantic University, Graduate Programs, Doral, FL 33178. Offers accounting (MBA); business administration (MBA); health information management (MS); human resource management (MA). Postbaccalaureate distance learning degree programs offered (no on-campus study).

Milligan College, Program in Business Administration, Milligan College, TN 37682. Offers MBA. Postbaccalaureate distance learning degree programs offered (minimal on-campus study). *Degree requirements:* For master's, comprehensive exam (for some programs), thesis or alternative. *Entrance requirements:* For master's, GMAT if undergraduate GPA less than 3.0, 2 professional recommendations, 3 years related work experience. Additional exam requirements/recommendations for international students: Required—TOEFL. Electronic applications accepted.

Millikin University, Tabor School of Business, Decatur, IL 62522-2084. Offers MBA. *Accreditation:* ACBSP. Evening/weekend programs available. *Faculty:* 8 full-time (2 women), 9 part-time/adjunct (3 women). *Students:* 41 full-time (7 women), 1 part-time (0 women); includes 3 minority (all Black or African American, non-Hispanic/Latino), 2 international. Average age 37. 49 applicants, 90% accepted, 42 enrolled. In 2013, 24 master's awarded. *Entrance requirements:* For master's, GMAT, resume, 3 reference letters, interview. Additional exam requirements/recommendations for international students: Required—TOEFL (minimum score 550 paper-based; 79 iBT). *Application deadline:* For spring admission, 11/1 priority date for domestic students, 8/1 priority date for international students. Applications are processed on a rolling basis. Application fee: $0. Electronic applications accepted. *Expenses: Tuition:* Full-time $20,300; part-time $700 per credit hour. Tuition and fees vary according to program. *Financial support:* Applicants required to submit FAFSA. *Faculty research:* E-commerce, international marketing, pedagogy, total quality management, auditing. *Application contact:* Dr. Anthony Liberatore, Director of MBA Program, 217-424-6338, Fax: 217-424-6286, E-mail: aliberatore@millikin.edu.
Website: http://www.millikin.edu/ACADEMICS/TABOR/MBA/.

Millsaps College, Else School of Management, Jackson, MS 39210-0001. Offers accounting (M Acc); business administration (MBA). *Accreditation:* AACSB. Part-time programs available. *Entrance requirements:* For master's, GMAT. Additional exam requirements/recommendations for international students: Required—TOEFL. Electronic applications accepted. *Faculty research:* Ethics, audit independence, satisfaction with assurance services, political business cycles, economic development, commercialization of new products.

Mills College, Graduate Studies, Joint MBA/MPP Program, Oakland, CA 94613-1000. Offers MBA/MPP. *Faculty:* 5 full-time (4 women). *Students:* 5 full-time (3 women). Average age 28. 8 applicants, 75% accepted, 5 enrolled. *Application deadline:* For winter admission, 2/1 priority date for domestic students, 12/15 priority date for international students. Application fee: $50. Electronic applications accepted. *Expenses: Tuition:* Full-time $29,860. *Required fees:* $1134. Part-time tuition and fees vary according to course load, degree level and program. *Financial support:* In 2013–14, 5 students received support, including 5 fellowships (averaging $11,912 per year). Financial award application deadline: 2/1; financial award applicants required to submit FAFSA. *Faculty research:* Diversity and inclusion, applied econometrics, non-profit management, business communication and effective public speaking, social media, Internet marketing, organizational and cultural chance, economics of the family, urbanization and land conservation, gender and science, comparative race and ethnic relations. *Unit head:* Carol Chetkovich, Professor of Public Policy, 510-430-3370, Fax: 510-430-2159, E-mail: cchetkov@mills.edu. *Application contact:* Shrim Bathey, Director of Graduate Admission, 510-430-3309, Fax: 510-430-2159, E-mail: grad-admission@mills.edu.
Website: http://www.mills.edu/academics/graduate/ppol/program/joint_MPPMBA.php.

Mills College, Graduate Studies, Lorry I. Lokey Graduate School of Business, Oakland, CA 94613-1000. Offers management (MBA). Part-time programs available. *Faculty:* 2 full-time (1 woman), 2 part-time/adjunct (1 woman). *Students:* 57 full-time (51 women),

25 part-time (all women); includes 50 minority (18 Black or African American, non-Hispanic/Latino; 1 American Indian or Alaska Native, non-Hispanic/Latino; 8 Asian, non-Hispanic/Latino; 14 Hispanic/Latino; 1 Native Hawaiian or other Pacific Islander, non-Hispanic/Latino; 8 Two or more races, non-Hispanic/Latino), 5 international. Average age 33. 55 applicants, 78% accepted, 22 enrolled. In 2013, 57 master's awarded. *Entrance requirements:* For master's, GRE, SAT, or ACT, 3 letters of recommendation, 2 transcripts. Additional exam requirements/recommendations for international students: Required—TOEFL (minimum score 550 paper-based; 80 iBT) or IELTS (minimum score 6). *Application deadline:* For fall admission, 2/1 priority date for domestic students, 12/15 for international students; for spring admission, 10/1 for domestic students. Applications are processed on a rolling basis. Application fee: $50. *Expenses: Tuition:* Full-time $29,860. *Required fees:* $1134. Part-time tuition and fees vary according to course load, degree level and program. *Financial support:* In 2013–14, 79 students received support, including 79 fellowships with full and partial tuition reimbursements available (averaging $7,010 per year); scholarships/grants also available. Support available to part-time students. Financial award application deadline: 2/1; financial award applicants required to submit FAFSA. *Faculty research:* Diversity and inclusion, applied econometrics, non-profit management, business communication and effective public speaking, social media and Internet marketing. *Unit head:* Dr. Deborah Merrill-Sands, Dean, 510-430-3345, Fax: 510-430-2159, E-mail: dmerrillsands@mills.edu. *Application contact:* Shrim Bathey, Director of Graduate Admission, 510-430-3309, Fax: 510-430-2159, E-mail: grad-admission@mills.edu.
Website: http://www.mills.edu/mba.

Milwaukee School of Engineering, Rader School of Business, Program in Business Administration, Milwaukee, WI 53202-3109. Offers MBA. *Expenses: Tuition:* Full-time $6939; part-time $771 per credit.

Minnesota State University Mankato, College of Graduate Studies, College of Business, Mankato, MN 56001. Offers MBA. *Accreditation:* AACSB. *Students:* 4 full-time (1 woman), 48 part-time (12 women). *Entrance requirements:* For master's, GMAT, 2 letters of reference, resume. Additional exam requirements/recommendations for international students: Required—TOEFL. *Application deadline:* For fall admission, 7/1 for domestic students, 5/1 for international students; for spring admission, 11/1 for domestic students, 10/1 for international students. Electronic applications accepted. *Unit head:* Dr. Kevin Elliott, Graduate Coordinator, 507-389-5420. *Application contact:* 507-389-2321, E-mail: grad@mnsu.edu.
Website: http://cob.mnsu.edu/.

Minot State University, Graduate School, Program in Management, Minot, ND 58707-0002. Offers MS. *Degree requirements:* For master's, comprehensive exam (for some programs), thesis (for some programs). *Entrance requirements:* For master's, minimum GPA of 2.75. Additional exam requirements/recommendations for international students: Required—TOEFL. *Faculty research:* Distance education.

Misericordia University, College of Professional Studies and Social Sciences, Master of Business Administration Program, Dallas, PA 18612-1098. Offers accounting (MBA); human resources (MBA); management (MBA); sport management (MBA). Part-time and evening/weekend programs available. Postbaccalaureate distance learning degree programs offered (no on-campus study). *Faculty:* 4 full-time (2 women), 5 part-time/adjunct (2 women). *Students:* 100 part-time (53 women); includes 1 minority (Black or African American, non-Hispanic/Latino), 1 international. Average age 33. In 2013, 32 master's awarded. *Entrance requirements:* For master's, GMAT, MAT, GRE (50th percentile or higher), or minimum undergraduate GPA of 3.0, interview. Additional exam requirements/recommendations for international students: Required—TOEFL. *Application deadline:* Applications are processed on a rolling basis. Application fee: $35. Electronic applications accepted. Application fee is waived when completed online. *Expenses: Tuition:* Full-time 14,450; part-time $680 per credit. Tuition and fees vary according to degree level. *Financial support:* In 2013–14, 68 students received support. Scholarships/grants and unspecified assistantships available. Support available to part-time students. Financial award applicants required to submit FAFSA. *Unit head:* Dr. Timothy Kearney, Chair of Business Department, 570-674-1487, E-mail: tkearney@misericordia.edu. *Application contact:* David Pasquini, Assistant Director of Admissions, 570-674-8183, Fax: 570-674-6232, E-mail: dpasquin@misericordia.edu.
Website: http://www.misericordia.edu/mba.

Misericordia University, College of Professional Studies and Social Sciences, Program in Organizational Management, Dallas, PA 18612-1098. Offers human resource management (MS); information technology management (MS); management (MS); not-for-profit management (MS). Part-time and evening/weekend programs available. Postbaccalaureate distance learning degree programs offered (no on-campus study). *Faculty:* 3 full-time (0 women), 6 part-time/adjunct (0 women). *Students:* 82 part-time (53 women); includes 2 minority (1 Hispanic/Latino; 1 Native Hawaiian or other Pacific Islander, non-Hispanic/Latino). Average age 33. In 2013, 25 master's awarded. *Entrance requirements:* For master's, GRE General Test, MAT (35th percentile or higher), or minimum undergraduate GPA of 3.0. Additional exam requirements/recommendations for international students: Required—TOEFL. *Application deadline:* Applications are processed on a rolling basis. Application fee: $35. Electronic applications accepted. Application fee is waived when completed online. *Expenses:* Contact institution. *Financial support:* In 2013–14, 55 students received support. Scholarships/grants available. Support available to part-time students. Financial award application deadline: 6/30; financial award applicants required to submit FAFSA. *Unit head:* Dr. Timothy Kearney, Chair of Business Department, 570-674-1487, E-mail: tkearney@misericordia.edu. *Application contact:* David Pasquini, Assistant Director of Admissions, 570-674-8183, Fax: 570-674-6232, E-mail: dpasquin@misericordia.edu.
Website: http://www.misericordia.edu/om.

Mississippi College, Graduate School, School of Business, Clinton, MS 39058. Offers accounting (Certificate); business administration (MBA), including accounting; business education (M Ed); finance (MBA, Certificate); JD/MBA. Part-time and evening/weekend programs available. *Degree requirements:* For master's, comprehensive exam, thesis optional. *Entrance requirements:* For master's, GMAT, minimum GPA of 2.5, 24 hours of undergraduate course work in business. Additional exam requirements/recommendations for international students: Recommended—TOEFL, IELTS. Electronic applications accepted.

Mississippi State University, College of Business, Department of Management and Information Systems, Mississippi State, MS 39762. Offers business administration (MBA, PhD), including accounting, business administration (MBA), business information systems (PhD), finance (PhD), management (PhD), marketing (PhD); information systems (MSIS); project management (MBA). Part-time programs available. *Faculty:* 12 full-time (4 women). *Students:* 69 full-time (20 women), 245 part-time (69 women); includes 34 minority (9 Black or African American, non-Hispanic/Latino; 12 Asian, non-Hispanic/Latino; 7 Hispanic/Latino; 1 Native Hawaiian or other Pacific Islander, non-Hispanic/Latino; 5 Two or more races, non-Hispanic/Latino), 20 international. Average age 31. 367 applicants, 29% accepted, 73 enrolled. In 2013, 127 master's, 2 doctorates awarded. *Degree requirements:* For master's, comprehensive exam; for doctorate, comprehensive exam, thesis/dissertation. *Entrance requirements:* For master's, GMAT, minimum GPA of 3.0 in last 60 hours of undergraduate course work; for doctorate, GMAT (minimum score of 550), minimum GPA of 3.25 on all graduate work; BS with

minimum GPA of 3.0 cumulative and last 60 hours. Additional exam requirements/recommendations for international students: Required—TOEFL (minimum score 575 paper-based; 84 iBT); Recommended—IELTS (minimum score 7). *Application deadline:* For fall admission, 7/1 for domestic students, 5/1 for international students; for spring admission, 11/1 for domestic students, 9/1 for international students. Applications are processed on a rolling basis. Application fee: $60. Electronic applications accepted. *Financial support:* In 2013–14, 1 teaching assistantship (averaging $13,497 per year) was awarded; career-related internships or fieldwork, Federal Work-Study, institutionally sponsored loans, scholarships/grants, and unspecified assistantships also available. Financial award applicants required to submit FAFSA. *Faculty research:* Electronic commerce, management of information technology. *Unit head:* Dr. Tim Barnett, Department Chairperson and Professor of Management, 662-325-3928, Fax: 662-325-8651, E-mail: tim.barnett@msstate.edu. *Application contact:* Dr. Rebecca Long, Graduate Coordinator, 662-325-3928, E-mail: gsb@cobian.msstate.edu.
Website: http://www.business.msstate.edu/programs/mis/index.php.

Missouri Baptist University, Graduate Programs, St. Louis, MO 63141-8660. Offers business administration (MBA); Christian ministries (MACM); counseling (MAC); education (MSE); education administration (MEA); educational leadership (MSE, Ed S); teaching (MAT).

Missouri Southern State University, Program in Business Administration, Joplin, MO 64801-1595. Offers MBA. Program offered jointly with Northwest Missouri State University. *Accreditation:* ACBSP. Postbaccalaureate distance learning degree programs offered. *Degree requirements:* For master's, capstone seminar.

Missouri State University, Graduate College, College of Business Administration, Department of Computer Information Systems, Springfield, MO 65897. Offers computer information systems (MS); secondary education (MS Ed), including business. Part-time and evening/weekend programs available. Postbaccalaureate distance learning degree programs offered (no on-campus study). *Faculty:* 13 full-time (2 women), 6 part-time/adjunct (0 women). *Students:* 22 full-time (3 women); includes 4 minority (2 Black or African American, non-Hispanic/Latino; 1 Hispanic/Latino; 1 Two or more races, non-Hispanic/Latino), 21 international. Average age 38. 20 applicants, 70% accepted, 12 enrolled. In 2013, 15 master's awarded. *Degree requirements:* For master's, thesis optional. *Entrance requirements:* For master's, GMAT, 3 years of work experience in computer information systems, minimum GPA of 2.75 (MS), 9-12 teaching certification (MS Ed). Additional exam requirements/recommendations for international students: Required—TOEFL (minimum score 550 paper-based; 79 iBT). *Application deadline:* For fall admission, 7/20 priority date for domestic students, 5/1 for international students; for spring admission, 12/20 priority date for domestic students, 9/1 for international students. Applications are processed on a rolling basis. Application fee: $35 ($50 for international students). Electronic applications accepted. *Expenses:* Contact institution. *Financial support:* Federal Work-Study, institutionally sponsored loans, scholarships/grants, and unspecified assistantships available. Support available to part-time students. Financial award application deadline: 3/31; financial award applicants required to submit FAFSA. *Faculty research:* Decision support systems, algorithms in Visual Basic, end-user satisfaction, information security. *Unit head:* Dr. Jerry Chin, Head, 417-836-4131, Fax: 417-836-6907, E-mail: jerrychin@missouristate.edu. *Application contact:* Misty Stewart, Coordinator of Graduate Admissions and Recruitment, 417-836-6079, Fax: 417-836-6200, E-mail: mistystewart@missouristate.edu.
Website: http://cis.missouristate.edu/.

Missouri State University, Graduate College, College of Business Administration, Program in Business Administration, Springfield, MO 65897. Offers MBA. *Accreditation:* AACSB. Part-time and evening/weekend programs available. *Students:* 353 full-time (191 women), 150 part-time (72 women); includes 20 minority (8 Black or African American, non-Hispanic/Latino; 5 Asian, non-Hispanic/Latino; 3 Hispanic/Latino; 4 Two or more races, non-Hispanic/Latino), 284 international. Average age 27. 266 applicants, 91% accepted, 182 enrolled. In 2013, 364 master's awarded. *Degree requirements:* For master's, thesis optional. *Entrance requirements:* For master's, GMAT, minimum GPA of 2.75. Additional exam requirements/recommendations for international students: Required—TOEFL (minimum score 550 paper-based; 79 iBT). *Application deadline:* For fall admission, 7/20 priority date for domestic students, 5/1 for international students; for spring admission, 12/20 priority date for domestic students, 9/1 for international students. Applications are processed on a rolling basis. Application fee: $35 ($50 for international students). Electronic applications accepted. *Expenses:* Tuition, state resident: full-time $4500; part-time $250 per credit hour. Tuition, nonresident: full-time $9018; part-time $501 per credit hour. *Required fees:* $361 per semester. Tuition and fees vary according to course level, course load and program. *Financial support:* Federal Work-Study, institutionally sponsored loans, scholarships/grants, and unspecified assistantships available. Support available to part-time students. Financial award application deadline: 3/31; financial award applicants required to submit FAFSA. *Unit head:* Dr. Elizabeth Rozell, MBA Program Director, 417-836-5616, Fax: 417-836-4407, E-mail: mbaprogram@missouristate.edu. *Application contact:* Misty Stewart, Coordinator of Graduate Admissions and Recruitment, 417-836-6079, Fax: 417-836-6200, E-mail: mistystewart@missouristate.edu.
Website: http://mba.missouristate.edu.

Missouri Western State University, Program in Applied Science, St. Joseph, MO 64507-2294. Offers chemistry (MAS); engineering technology management (MAS); human factors and usability testing (MAS); industrial life science (MAS); information technology management (MAS); sport and fitness management (MAS). Part-time programs available. *Students:* 38 full-time (11 women), 24 part-time (10 women); includes 7 minority (4 Black or African American, non-Hispanic/Latino; 1 Asian, non-Hispanic/Latino; 1 Hispanic/Latino; 1 Two or more races, non-Hispanic/Latino), 21 international. Average age 28. 60 applicants, 90% accepted, 37 enrolled. In 2013, 15 master's awarded. *Entrance requirements:* Additional exam requirements/recommendations for international students: Recommended—TOEFL (minimum score 500 paper-based; 61 iBT), IELTS (minimum score 5.5). *Application deadline:* For fall admission, 7/15 for domestic students, 6/15 for international students; for spring admission, 10/1 for domestic students, 10/15 for international students. Applications are processed on a rolling basis. Application fee: $45 ($50 for international students). Electronic applications accepted. *Expenses:* Tuition, state resident: full-time $6019; part-time $300.96 per credit hour. Tuition, nonresident: full-time $11,194; part-time $559.71 per credit hour. *Required fees:* $542; $99 per credit hour. $176 per semester. Tuition and fees vary according to course load and program. *Financial support:* Scholarships/grants and unspecified assistantships available. Support available to part-time students. *Unit head:* Dr. Benjamin D. Caldwell, Dean of the Graduate School, 816-271-4394, Fax: 816-271-4525, E-mail: graduate@missouriwestern.edu. *Application contact:* Dr. Benjamin D. Caldwell, Dean of the Graduate School, 816-271-4394, Fax: 816-271-4525, E-mail: graduate@missouriwestern.edu.

Molloy College, Graduate Business Program, Rockville Centre, NY 11571-5002. Offers accounting (MBA); accounting and finance (MBA); accounting and management (MBA); finance (MBA); finance and management (MBA); finance and personal financial planning (MBA); healthcare administration (MBA); management (MBA); management and personal financial planning (MBA); marketing (MBA); personal financial planning (MBA). Part-time programs available. *Faculty:* 8 full-time (3 women), 7 part-time/adjunct

(1 woman). *Students:* 41 full-time (19 women), 104 part-time (36 women); includes 45 minority (21 Black or African American, non-Hispanic/Latino; 8 Asian, non-Hispanic/Latino; 14 Hispanic/Latino; 1 Native Hawaiian or other Pacific Islander, non-Hispanic/Latino; 1 Two or more races, non-Hispanic/Latino), 4 international. Average age 29. 48 applicants, 71% accepted, 27 enrolled. In 2013, 33 master's awarded. *Application deadline:* Applications are processed on a rolling basis. Application fee: $60. *Expenses: Tuition:* Full-time $16,920; part-time $940 per credit. *Required fees:* $880. *Faculty research:* Leadership, marketing, accounting, finance, international. *Unit head:* Dr. Daniel Cillis, Associate Dean and Director, MBA Program, 516-323-3080, E-mail: dcillis@molloy.edu. *Application contact:* Alina Haitz, Assistant Director of Graduate Admissions, 516-323-4008, E-mail: ahaitz@molloy.edu.

Monmouth University, The Graduate School, Leon Hess Business School, West Long Branch, NJ 07764-1898. Offers accounting (MBA, Post-Master's Certificate); business (MBA); finance (MBA); real estate (MBA). *Accreditation:* AACSB. Part-time and evening/weekend programs available. *Faculty:* 32 full-time (10 women), 5 part-time/adjunct (0 women). *Students:* 92 full-time (35 women), 98 part-time (45 women); includes 30 minority (9 Black or African American, non-Hispanic/Latino; 12 Asian, non-Hispanic/Latino; 6 Hispanic/Latino; 3 Two or more races, non-Hispanic/Latino), 9 international. Average age 27. 157 applicants, 82% accepted, 84 enrolled. In 2013, 134 master's awarded. *Degree requirements:* For master's, capstone course. *Entrance requirements:* For master's, GMAT, minimum GPA of 3.0 in major, 2.75 overall. Additional exam requirements/recommendations for international students: Required—TOEFL (minimum score 550 paper-based; 79 iBT), IELTS (minimum score 6), Michigan English Language Assessment Battery (minimum score 77). *Application deadline:* For fall admission, 7/15 priority date for domestic students, 6/1 for international students; for spring admission, 11/15 priority date for domestic students, 11/1 for international students. Applications are processed on a rolling basis. Application fee: $50. Electronic applications accepted. *Expenses: Tuition:* Part-time $1004 per credit hour. *Required fees:* $157 per semester. *Financial support:* In 2013–14, 119 students received support, including 281 fellowships (averaging $1,244 per year), 27 research assistantships (averaging $6,273 per year); career-related internships or fieldwork, scholarships/grants, and unspecified assistantships also available. Support available to part-time students. Financial award applicants required to submit FAFSA. *Faculty research:* Information technology and marketing, behavioral research in accounting, human resources, management of technology. *Unit head:* Dr. Susan Gupta, MBA Program Director, 732-571-3639, Fax: 732-263-5517, E-mail: sgupta@monmouth.edu. *Application contact:* Lauren Vento-Cifelli, Associate Vice President of Undergraduate and Graduate Admission, 732-571-3452, Fax: 732-263-5123, E-mail: gradadm@monmouth.edu. Website: http://www.monmouth.edu/mba.

See Display on this page and Close-Up on page 187.

Monroe College, King Graduate School, Bronx, NY 10468-5407. Offers business management (MBA); criminal justice (MS); executive leadership in hospitality management (MS); public health (MPH). Program also offered in New Rochelle, NY. Postbaccalaureate distance learning degree programs offered.

Montclair State University, The Graduate School, College of Humanities and Social Sciences, MA Program in Law and Governance, Montclair, NJ 07043-1624. Offers conflict management and peace studies (MA); governance, compliance and regulation (MA); intellectual property (MA); law and governance (MA); legal management (MA). Part-time and evening/weekend programs available. *Degree requirements:* For master's, thesis or comprehensive exam. *Entrance requirements:* For master's, GRE General Test, minimum cumulative GPA of 2.75 for undergraduate work, 2 letters of recommendation, essay. Additional exam requirements/recommendations for international students: Required—TOEFL (minimum score 83 iBT) or IELTS (minimum score 6.5). Electronic applications accepted.

Montclair State University, The Graduate School, School of Business, General MBA Program, Montclair, NJ 07043-1624. Offers MBA. Part-time and evening/weekend programs available. *Degree requirements:* For master's, culminating experience. *Entrance requirements:* For master's, GMAT or GRE General Test, 2 letters of recommendation, resume, essay. Additional exam requirements/recommendations for international students: Required—TOEFL (minimum score 83 iBT), IELTS (minimum score 6.5). Electronic applications accepted. *Faculty research:* Accounting, management, marketing.

Montclair State University, The Graduate School, School of Business, Saturday MBA Program, Montclair, NJ 07043-1624. Offers MBA. Part-time and evening/weekend programs available. Postbaccalaureate distance learning degree programs offered (no on-campus study). *Degree requirements:* For master's, culminating experience. *Entrance requirements:* For master's, GMAT or GRE General Test, 2 letters of recommendation, resume, essay. Additional exam requirements/recommendations for international students: Required—TOEFL (minimum score 83 iBT), IELTS (minimum score 6.5). Electronic applications accepted.

Monterey Institute of International Studies, Graduate School of International Policy and Management, Fisher International MBA Program, Monterey, CA 93940-2691. Offers MBA. *Accreditation:* AACSB. *Degree requirements:* For master's, one foreign language, thesis. *Entrance requirements:* For master's, GMAT, minimum GPA of 3.0, proficiency in a foreign language. Additional exam requirements/recommendations for international students: Required—TOEFL (minimum score 550 paper-based; 80 iBT). Electronic applications accepted. *Expenses: Tuition:* Full-time $34,970; part-time $1665 per credit. *Required fees:* $28 per semester. *Faculty research:* Cross-cultural consumer behavior, foreign direct investment, marketing and entrepreneurial orientation, political risk analysis and area studies, managing international human resources.

Montreat College, School of Professional and Adult Studies, Montreat, NC 28757-1267. Offers business administration (MBA); clinical mental health counseling (MA); environmental education (MS); management and leadership (MS). Evening/weekend programs available. Postbaccalaureate distance learning degree programs offered (minimal on-campus study). *Faculty:* 12 full-time (3 women), 14 part-time/adjunct (3 women). *Students:* 108 full-time (65 women), 179 part-time (111 women); includes 130 minority (116 Black or African American, non-Hispanic/Latino; 5 American Indian or Alaska Native, non-Hispanic/Latino; 2 Asian, non-Hispanic/Latino; 6 Hispanic/Latino; 1 Two or more races, non-Hispanic/Latino). Average age 34. 145 applicants, 41% accepted, 57 enrolled. In 2013, 142 master's awarded. *Degree requirements:* For master's, business consulting project (for MBA). *Entrance requirements:* For master's, GMAT. Additional exam requirements/recommendations for international students: Required—TOEFL (minimum score 550 paper-based; 80 iBT). *Application deadline:* Applications are processed on a rolling basis. *Financial support:* Available to part-time students. Application deadline: 7/1; applicants required to submit FAFSA. *Unit head:* Joseph Kirkland, Interim President, 828-669-8012, Fax: 828-669-0500, E-mail: jkirkland@montreat.edu. *Application contact:* Julia Pacilli, Director of Enrollment, 828-669-8012 Ext. 2756, Fax: 828-669-0500, E-mail: jpacilli@montreat.edu. Website: http://www.montreat.edu/.

Moravian College, Moravian College Comenius Center, Business and Management Programs, Bethlehem, PA 18018-6650. Offers accounting (MBA); business analytics (MBA); general management (MBA); health administration (MHA); healthcare

management (MBA); human resource management (MBA); leadership (MSHRM); learning and performance management (MSHRM); supply chain management (MBA). Part-time and evening/weekend programs available. *Entrance requirements:* For master's, GMAT. Additional exam requirements/recommendations for international students: Required—TOEFL (minimum score 550 paper-based; 90 iBT). Application fee is waived when completed online. *Expenses:* Contact institution. *Faculty research:* Leadership, change management, human resources.

Morehead State University, Graduate Programs, College of Business and Public Affairs, Morehead, KY 40351. Offers MA, MBA, MPA, MSIS. *Accreditation:* AACSB. Part-time and evening/weekend programs available. Postbaccalaureate distance learning degree programs offered (minimal on-campus study). *Entrance requirements:* For master's, GMAT, GRE General Test, minimum GPA of 2.5 on undergraduate work. Additional exam requirements/recommendations for international students: Required—TOEFL (minimum score 525 paper-based). Electronic applications accepted. *Faculty research:* Regional economic development, accounting systems, banking market structures, macroeconomics, distance learning.

Morgan State University, School of Graduate Studies, Earl G. Graves School of Business and Management, PhD Program in Business Administration, Baltimore, MD 21251. Offers PhD. *Degree requirements:* For doctorate, thesis/dissertation. *Entrance requirements:* For doctorate, GMAT. Additional exam requirements/recommendations for international students: Required—TOEFL (minimum score 550 paper-based).

Morrison University, Graduate School, Reno, NV 89521. Offers business administration (MBA). Part-time and evening/weekend programs available. *Degree requirements:* For master's, thesis. *Entrance requirements:* For master's, GMAT, minimum 3 years minimum work experience, interview, minimum GPA of 3.0. Additional exam requirements/recommendations for international students: Recommended—TOEFL. Electronic applications accepted.

Mount Aloysius College, Masters in Business Administration Program, Cresson, PA 16630. Offers MBA. Part-time and evening/weekend programs available. *Entrance requirements:* Additional exam requirements/recommendations for international students: Recommended—TOEFL. Electronic applications accepted.

Mount Ida College, Program in Management, Newton, MA 02459-3310. Offers MSM. Part-time and evening/weekend programs available. Postbaccalaureate distance learning degree programs offered (minimal on-campus study). *Entrance requirements:* Additional exam requirements/recommendations for international students: Required—TOEFL (minimum score 550 paper-based; 79 iBT); Recommended—IELTS (minimum score 5.5). Electronic applications accepted.

Mount Marty College, Graduate Studies Division, Yankton, SD 57078-3724. Offers business administration (MBA); nurse anesthesia (MS); nursing (MSN); pastoral ministries (MPM). *Accreditation:* AANA/CANAEP (one or more programs are accredited). *Degree requirements:* For master's, thesis or alternative. *Entrance requirements:* For master's, GRE General Test, minimum GPA of 3.0. Electronic applications accepted. *Faculty research:* Clinical anesthesia, professional characteristics, motivations of applicants.

Mount Mary University, Graduate Division, Program in Business Administration, Milwaukee, WI 53222-4597. Offers general management (MBA); health systems leadership (MBA). Part-time and evening/weekend programs available. *Faculty:* 1 (woman) full-time, 5 part-time/adjunct (1 woman). *Students:* 28 full-time (23 women), 11 part-time (9 women); includes 11 minority (5 Black or African American, non-Hispanic/Latino; 1 Asian, non-Hispanic/Latino; 4 Hispanic/Latino; 1 Two or more races, non-Hispanic/Latino). Average age 35. 12 applicants, 92% accepted, 5 enrolled. In 2013, 9 master's awarded. *Degree requirements:* For master's, terminal project. *Entrance requirements:* For master's, minimum GPA of 2.75. Additional exam requirements/recommendations for international students: Required—TOEFL (minimum score 80 iBT) or IELTS (minimum score 6.5). *Application deadline:* For fall admission, 7/15 for domestic and international students; for spring admission, 12/1 for domestic and international students. Applications are processed on a rolling basis. Application fee: $45 ($100 for international students). Electronic applications accepted. *Expenses:* Contact institution. *Financial support:* Career-related internships or fieldwork and Federal Work-Study available. Support available to part-time students. Financial award application deadline: 5/1; financial award applicants required to submit FAFSA. *Unit head:* Dr. Kristen Roche, Director, 414-258-4810, E-mail: rochek@mtmary.edu. *Application contact:* Dr. Douglas J. Mickelson, Dean for Graduate Education, 414-256-1252, Fax: 414-256-0167, E-mail: mickelsd@mtmary.edu. Website: http://www.mtmary.edu/majors-programs/graduate/mba/index.html.

Mount Mercy University, Program in Business Administration, Cedar Rapids, IA 52402-4797. Offers MBA. Evening/weekend programs available. *Entrance requirements:* For master's, minimum cumulative GPA of 3.0, 2 letters of recommendation, resume. Additional exam requirements/recommendations for international students: Required—TOEFL (minimum score 570 paper-based; 88 iBT). Electronic applications accepted.

Mount St. Joseph University, Master of Business Administration Program, Cincinnati, OH 45233-1670. Offers MBA. Part-time and evening/weekend programs available. *Faculty:* 7 full-time (3 women). *Students:* 12 full-time (1 woman), 1 part-time (0 women). Average age 24. 17 applicants, 88% accepted, 9 enrolled. *Degree requirements:* For master's, internship; portfolio. *Entrance requirements:* For master's, minimum GPA of 3.0; foundational course form; 2 letters of reference; essay; interview. Additional exam requirements/recommendations for international students: Required—TOEFL (minimum score 560 paper-based; 83 iBT). *Application deadline:* Applications are processed on a rolling basis. Application fee: $50. Electronic applications accepted. *Expenses: Tuition:* Full-time $18,400; part-time $575 per credit hour. *Required fees:* $450; $450 per year. Part-time tuition and fees vary according to course load, degree level and program. *Financial support:* Application deadline: 6/1; applicants required to submit FAFSA. *Unit head:* Dr. Nancy Waldeck, Professor, 513-244-4917, E-mail: nancy_waldeck@mail.msj.edu. *Application contact:* Mary Brigham, Assistant Director for Graduate Recruitment, 513-244-4333, Fax: 513-745-4629, E-mail: mary_brigham@mail.msj.edu. Website: http://www.msj.edu/academics/graduate-programs/master-of-business-administration/.

Mount Saint Mary College, Division of Business, Newburgh, NY 12550-3494. Offers business (MBA); financial planning (MBA). Part-time and evening/weekend programs available. *Faculty:* 7 full-time (2 women), 3 part-time/adjunct (1 woman). *Students:* 40 full-time (18 women), 51 part-time (22 women); includes 18 minority (6 Black or African American, non-Hispanic/Latino; 1 Asian, non-Hispanic/Latino; 11 Hispanic/Latino). Average age 30. 42 applicants, 69% accepted, 22 enrolled. In 2013, 25 master's awarded. *Degree requirements:* For master's, thesis or alternative. *Entrance requirements:* For master's, GMAT or minimum undergraduate GPA of 2.7. *Application deadline:* Applications are processed on a rolling basis. Application fee: $45. Application fee is waived when completed online. *Expenses: Tuition:* Full-time $13,356; part-time $742 per credit. *Required fees:* $70 per semester. *Financial support:* In 2013–14, 31 students received support. Unspecified assistantships available. Financial award application deadline: 4/15; financial award applicants required to submit FAFSA. *Faculty research:* Financial reform, entrepreneurship and small business development, global

business relations, technology's impact on business decision-making, college-assisted business education. *Unit head:* Dr. Andrew Weiss, Graduate Coordinator, 845-569-3121, Fax: 845-562-6762, E-mail: andrew.weiss@msmc.edu. *Application contact:* Lisa Gallina, Director of Admissions for Graduate Programs and Adult Degree Completion, 845-569-3166, Fax: 845-569-3450, E-mail: lisa.gallina@msmc.edu. Website: http://www.msmc.edu/Academics/Graduate_Programs/master_of_business_administration.be.

Mount St. Mary's College, Graduate Division, Los Angeles, CA 90049-1599. Offers business administration (MBA); counseling psychology (MS); creative writing (MFA); education (MS, Certificate); humanities (MA); nursing (MSN, Certificate); physical therapy (DPT); religious studies (MA); MFA/MA. Part-time and evening/weekend programs available. *Faculty:* 35 full-time (26 women), 112 part-time/adjunct (76 women). *Students:* 416 full-time (324 women), 233 part-time (184 women); includes 376 minority (64 Black or African American, non-Hispanic/Latino; 2 American Indian or Alaska Native, non-Hispanic/Latino; 57 Asian, non-Hispanic/Latino; 229 Hispanic/Latino; 8 Native Hawaiian or other Pacific Islander, non-Hispanic/Latino; 16 Two or more races, non-Hispanic/Latino), 4 international. Average age 33. 1,041 applicants, 22% accepted, 183 enrolled. In 2013, 168 master's, 29 doctorates awarded. *Entrance requirements:* Additional exam requirements/recommendations for international students: Required—TOEFL. *Application deadline:* Applications are processed on a rolling basis. Application fee: $50. Electronic applications accepted. *Expenses: Tuition:* Part-time $798 per unit. *Required fees:* $125 per semester. Tuition and fees vary according to program. *Financial support:* Career-related internships or fieldwork, Federal Work-Study, institutionally sponsored loans, and tuition waivers (full and partial) available. Support available to part-time students. Financial award application deadline: 3/15; financial award applicants required to submit FAFSA. *Unit head:* Dr. Linda Moody, Graduate Dean, 213-477-2800, E-mail: gradprograms@msmc.la.edu. *Application contact:* Natalie Dymchenko, Senior Graduate Admission Counselor, 213-477-2800, E-mail: gradprograms@msmc.la.edu. Website: http://www.msmc.la.edu/admission/graduate-admission.asp.

Mount St. Mary's University, Program in Business Administration, Emmitsburg, MD 21727-7799. Offers MBA. Part-time and evening/weekend programs available. *Faculty:* 11 full-time (3 women), 18 part-time/adjunct (3 women). *Students:* 75 full-time (38 women), 137 part-time (60 women); includes 37 minority (17 Black or African American, non-Hispanic/Latino; 1 American Indian or Alaska Native, non-Hispanic/Latino; 7 Asian, non-Hispanic/Latino; 5 Hispanic/Latino; 2 Native Hawaiian or other Pacific Islander, non-Hispanic/Latino; 5 Two or more races, non-Hispanic/Latino), 5 international. Average age 33. 225 applicants, 94% accepted, 77 enrolled. In 2013, 107 master's awarded. *Degree requirements:* For master's, thesis. *Entrance requirements:* For master's, minimum undergraduate GPA of 2.75, 5 years' relevant professional business experience, or GMAT (minimum score of 500). Additional exam requirements/recommendations for international students: Required—TOEFL (minimum score 550 paper-based). *Application deadline:* Applications are processed on a rolling basis. Application fee: $35. *Expenses: Tuition:* Full-time $9846; part-time $547 per credit hour. Tuition and fees vary according to program. *Financial support:* In 2013–14, 42 students received support. Career-related internships or fieldwork and unspecified assistantships available. Financial award applicants required to submit FAFSA. *Faculty research:* Corporate social responsibility and business ethics in China and India; changing revenue source as related to healthcare; behavioral economics; poverty, inequality and economic growth; neuroeconomics. *Unit head:* Deborah Powell, Director of Graduate and Adult Business Program, 301-447-5326, Fax: 301-447-5335, E-mail: mba@msmary.edu. *Application contact:* Director, Center for Professional and Continuing Studies. Website: http://www.msmary.edu/School_of_business/Graduate_Programs/mba/.

Mount Vernon Nazarene University, Program in Management, Mount Vernon, OH 43050-9500. Offers MSM. *Accreditation:* ACBSP. Part-time and evening/weekend programs available.

Murray State University, College of Business and Public Affairs, MBA Program, Murray, KY 42071. Offers MBA. *Accreditation:* AACSB. Part-time and evening/weekend programs available. *Entrance requirements:* For master's, GMAT. Additional exam requirements/recommendations for international students: Required—TOEFL.

National American University, Graduate Programs, Rapid City, SD 57701. Offers MBA, MM. Programs also offered in Wichita, KS; Albuquerque, NM; Bloomington, MN; Brooklyn Center, MN; Colorado Springs, CO; Denver, CO; Independence, MO; Overland Park, KS; Rio Rancho, NM; Roseville, MN; Zona Rosa, MO. Part-time and evening/weekend programs available. Postbaccalaureate distance learning degree programs offered. *Entrance requirements:* For master's, minimum undergraduate GPA of 2.75. Additional exam requirements/recommendations for international students: Required—TOEFL, TWE. Electronic applications accepted. *Faculty research:* Tourism, finance, marketing.

National Louis University, College of Management and Business, Chicago, IL 60603. Offers business administration (MBA); human resource management and development (MS); management (MS). Part-time and evening/weekend programs available. *Entrance requirements:* For master's, college-administered critical thinking and writing skills test, minimum GPA of 3.0, resume, 3 references. Additional exam requirements/recommendations for international students: Required—TOEFL (minimum score 550 paper-based; 79 iBT).

National University, Academic Affairs, School of Business and Management, La Jolla, CA 92037-1011. Offers accountancy (Certificate); business administration (GMBA, MBA), including financial management (MBA), human resource management (MBA), integrated marketing communications (MBA), international business (MBA), management accounting (MBA), marketing (MBA), mobile marketing and social media (MBA), organizational leadership (MA, MBA), professional golf management (MBA); global management (MGM); human resource management (MA), including organizational development and change, organizational leadership (MA, MBA); international business (Certificate); management information systems (MS); organizational leadership (MS), including community development; sustainability management (MS). Part-time and evening/weekend programs available. Postbaccalaureate distance learning degree programs offered (no on-campus study). *Faculty:* 30 full-time (8 women), 88 part-time/adjunct (25 women). *Students:* 688 full-time (357 women), 331 part-time (161 women); includes 453 minority (105 Black or African American, non-Hispanic/Latino; 2 American Indian or Alaska Native, non-Hispanic/Latino; 143 Asian, non-Hispanic/Latino; 162 Hispanic/Latino; 13 Native Hawaiian or other Pacific Islander, non-Hispanic/Latino; 28 Two or more races, non-Hispanic/Latino), 165 international. Average age 33. 286 applicants, 100% accepted, 217 enrolled. In 2013, 641 master's awarded. *Degree requirements:* For master's, thesis (for some programs). *Entrance requirements:* For master's, interview, minimum GPA of 2.5. Additional exam requirements/recommendations for international students: Required—TOEFL (minimum score 550 paper-based; 79 iBT), IELTS (minimum score 6). *Application deadline:* Applications are processed on a rolling basis. Application fee: $60 ($65 for international students). Electronic applications accepted. *Expenses: Tuition:* Full-time $13,824; part-time $1728 per course. One-time fee: $160. *Financial support:* Career-related internships or fieldwork, scholarships/grants, and tuition waivers (partial)

available. Support available to part-time students. Financial award application deadline: 6/30; financial award applicants required to submit FAFSA. *Unit head:* School of Business and Management, 800-628-8648, Fax: 858-642-8719, E-mail: sobm@nu.edu. *Application contact:* Louis Cruz, Interim Vice President for Enrollment Services, 800-628-8648, E-mail: advisor@nu.edu.
Website: http://www.nu.edu/OurPrograms/SchoolOfBusinessAndManagement.html.

Naval Postgraduate School, Departments and Academic Groups, Graduate School of Business and Public Policy, Monterey, CA 93943. Offers acquisition and contract management (MBA); business administration (EMBA, MBA); contract management (MS); defense business management (MBA); defense systems analysis (MS), including management; defense systems management (international) (MBA); financial management (MBA); information management (MBA); manpower systems analysis (MS); material logistics support management (MBA); program management (MS); resource planning and management for international defense (MBA); supply chain management (MBA); systems acquisition management (MBA); transportation management (MBA). Program only open to commissioned officers of the United States and friendly nations and selected United States federal civilian employees. *Accreditation:* AACSB; NASPAA. Part-time programs available. Postbaccalaureate distance learning degree programs offered (minimal on-campus study). *Degree requirements:* For master's, thesis (for some programs), terminal project/capstone (for some programs). *Faculty research:* U.S. and European public procurement policies for small and medium-sized enterprises, examining external validity criticisms in the choice of students as subjects in accounting experiment studies, assurance of learning in contract management education, contracting for cloud computing: opportunities and risks, NPS, Apple App Store as a business model supporting U. S. Navy requirements.

Nazareth College of Rochester, Graduate Studies, Department of Business, Program in Management, Rochester, NY 14618-3790. Offers MS. Part-time and evening/weekend programs available. *Entrance requirements:* For master's, minimum GPA of 3.0.

New Charter University, College of Business, San Francisco, CA 94105. Offers finance (MBA); health care management (MBA); management (MBA). Part-time and evening/weekend programs available. Postbaccalaureate distance learning degree programs offered (no on-campus study). *Entrance requirements:* For master's, course work in calculus, statistics, macroeconomics. Additional exam requirements/recommendations for international students: Required—TOEFL (minimum score 550 paper-based). Electronic applications accepted.

New England College, Program in Management, Henniker, NH 03242-3293. Offers accounting (MSA); healthcare administration (MS); international relations (MA); marketing management (MS); nonprofit leadership (MS); project management (MS); strategic leadership (MS). Part-time and evening/weekend programs available. *Degree requirements:* For master's, independent research project. Electronic applications accepted.

New Jersey City University, Graduate Studies and Continuing Education, College of Professional Studies, Department of Business Administration, Jersey City, NJ 07305-1597. Offers accounting (MS); finance (MBA, MS); marketing (MBA); organizational management and leadership (MBA). *Accreditation:* ACBSP. Part-time and evening/weekend programs available. *Faculty:* 16 full-time (7 women), 7 part-time/adjunct (2 women). *Students:* 47 full-time (28 women), 71 part-time (44 women); includes 75 minority (34 Black or African American, non-Hispanic/Latino; 13 Asian, non-Hispanic/Latino; 28 Hispanic/Latino), 13 international. Average age 33. In 2013, 10 master's awarded. *Entrance requirements:* Additional exam requirements/recommendations for international students: Required—TOEFL (minimum score 61 iBT). *Application deadline:* For fall admission, 8/1 priority date for domestic students; for spring admission, 12/1 for domestic students. Applications are processed on a rolling basis. Application fee: $0. *Expenses: Tuition, area resident:* Part-time $527.90 per credit. Tuition, nonresident: part-time $947.75 per credit. *Financial support:* Career-related internships or fieldwork and unspecified assistantships available. *Unit head:* Dr. Marilyn Ettinger, Head, 201-200-3353, E-mail: mettinger@njcu.edu. *Application contact:* Dr. William Bajor, Dean of Graduate Studies, 201-200-3409, Fax: 201-200-3411, E-mail: wbajor@njcu.edu.

New Jersey Institute of Technology, College of Computing Science, Newark, NJ 07102. Offers computer science (MS, PhD), including bioinformatics (MS), computer science, computing and business (MS), cyber security and privacy (MS), software engineering (MS); information systems (MS, PhD), including business and information systems (MS), emergency management and business continuity (MS), information systems; information technology administration and security (MS). Part-time and evening/weekend programs available. *Faculty:* 50 full-time (7 women), 22 part-time/adjunct (2 women). *Students:* 315 full-time (110 women), 317 part-time (86 women); includes 196 minority (53 Black or African American, non-Hispanic/Latino; 3 American Indian or Alaska Native, non-Hispanic/Latino; 78 Asian, non-Hispanic/Latino; 62 Hispanic/Latino), 605 international. Average age 30. 1,559 applicants, 63% accepted, 227 enrolled. In 2013, 239 master's, 4 doctorates awarded. Terminal master's awarded for partial completion of doctoral program. *Degree requirements:* For master's, thesis optional; for doctorate, thesis/dissertation. *Entrance requirements:* For master's, GRE General Test; for doctorate, GRE General Test, minimum graduate GPA of 3.5. Additional exam requirements/recommendations for international students: Required—TOEFL (minimum score 550 paper-based; 79 iBT). *Application deadline:* For fall admission, 6/1 priority date for domestic students, 5/1 priority date for international students; for spring admission, 11/15 priority date for domestic and international students. Applications are processed on a rolling basis. Application fee: $65. Electronic applications accepted. *Expenses:* Tuition, state resident: full-time $17,384; part-time $945 per credit. Tuition, nonresident: full-time $25,404; part-time $1341 per credit. *Required fees:* $2396; $118 per credit. *Financial support:* Fellowships with full and partial tuition reimbursements, research assistantships with full and partial tuition reimbursements, teaching assistantships with full and partial tuition reimbursements, career-related internships or fieldwork, Federal Work-Study, institutionally sponsored loans, and unspecified assistantships available. Financial award application deadline: 1/15. *Faculty research:* Computer systems, communications and networking, artificial intelligence, database engineering, systems analysis. *Total annual research expenditures:* $984,200. *Unit head:* Dr. Narain Gehani, Dean, 973-542-5488, Fax: 973-596-5777, E-mail: narain.gehani@njit.edu. *Application contact:* Kathryn Kelly, Director of Admissions, 973-596-3300, Fax: 973-596-3461, E-mail: admissions@njit.edu.
Website: http://ccs.njit.edu.

New Jersey Institute of Technology, School of Management, Newark, NJ 07102. Offers business administration (MBA); management (MS). Part-time and evening/weekend programs available. *Faculty:* 26 full-time (9 women), 21 part-time/adjunct (2 women). *Students:* 139 full-time (55 women), 148 part-time (46 women); includes 95 minority (28 Black or African American, non-Hispanic/Latino; 2 American Indian or Alaska Native, non-Hispanic/Latino; 36 Asian, non-Hispanic/Latino; 29 Hispanic/Latino), 114 international. Average age 31. 456 applicants, 66% accepted, 93 enrolled. In 2013, 88 master's awarded. Terminal master's awarded for partial completion of doctoral program. *Degree requirements:* For master's, thesis optional. *Entrance requirements:* Additional exam requirements/recommendations for international students: Required—TOEFL (minimum score 550 paper-based; 79 iBT). *Application deadline:* For fall admission, 6/1 priority date for domestic students, 5/1 priority date for international students; for spring admission, 11/15 priority date for domestic and international students. Applications are processed on a rolling basis. Application fee: $65. Electronic applications accepted. *Expenses:* Tuition, state resident: full-time $17,384; part-time $945 per credit. Tuition, nonresident: full-time $25,404; part-time $1341 per credit. *Required fees:* $2396; $118 per credit. *Financial support:* Fellowships with full and partial tuition reimbursements, research assistantships with full and partial tuition reimbursements, teaching assistantships with full and partial tuition reimbursements, career-related internships or fieldwork, Federal Work-Study, institutionally sponsored loans, and unspecified assistantships available. Financial award application deadline: 1/15. *Total annual research expenditures:* $1.1 million. *Unit head:* Dr. Pius Egbelu, Interim Dean, 973-596-3000, Fax: 973-596-3074, E-mail: pius.j.egbelu@njit.edu. *Application contact:* Stephen Eck, Director of Admissions, 973-596-3300, Fax: 973-596-3461, E-mail: admissions@njit.edu.
Website: http://management.njit.edu.

Newman University, MBA Program, Wichita, KS 67213-2097. Offers finance (MBA); international business (MBA); leadership (MBA); management (MBA); management information technology (MBA). Part-time programs available. *Faculty:* 7 full-time (1 woman), 7 part-time/adjunct (4 women). *Students:* 31 full-time (19 women), 56 part-time (24 women); includes 24 minority (6 Black or African American, non-Hispanic/Latino; 1 American Indian or Alaska Native, non-Hispanic/Latino; 9 Asian, non-Hispanic/Latino; 5 Hispanic/Latino; 3 Two or more races, non-Hispanic/Latino), 9 international. Average age 31. 83 applicants, 63% accepted, 32 enrolled. In 2013, 47 master's awarded. *Degree requirements:* For master's, thesis optional. *Entrance requirements:* For master's, minimum GPA of 3.0; 2 letters of recommendation; course work in algebra, statistics, macroeconomics, and financial accounting. Additional exam requirements/recommendations for international students: Required—TOEFL (minimum score 600 paper-based; 100 iBT). *Application deadline:* For fall admission, 8/1 priority date for domestic students, 7/15 priority date for international students; for winter admission, 1/1 priority date for domestic students; for spring admission, 1/1 priority date for domestic students, 11/15 priority date for international students. Applications are processed on a rolling basis. Application fee: $25 ($40 for international students). Electronic applications accepted. *Expenses:* Contact institution. *Financial support:* In 2013–14, 8 students received support. Scholarships/grants available. Financial award application deadline: 8/15; financial award applicants required to submit FAFSA. *Unit head:* Dr. Wendy Munday, Director of MBA Program, 316-942-4291 Ext. 2296, Fax: 316-942-4483, E-mail: mundayw@newmanu.edu. *Application contact:* Linda Kay Sabala, Director of Graduate Admissions, 316-942-4291 Ext. 2230, Fax: 316-942-4483, E-mail: sabalal@newmanu.edu.
Website: http://www.newmanu.edu.

New Mexico Highlands University, Graduate Studies, School of Business, Media and Technology, Las Vegas, NM 87701. Offers business administration (MBA), including government nonprofit management, human resource management, international business, management, management information systems; media arts and technology (MA), including media arts and computer science. *Accreditation:* ACBSP. *Faculty:* 13 full-time (5 women). *Students:* 65 full-time (34 women), 146 part-time (89 women); includes 137 minority (3 Black or African American, non-Hispanic/Latino; 9 American Indian or Alaska Native, non-Hispanic/Latino; 1 Asian, non-Hispanic/Latino; 120 Hispanic/Latino; 2 Native Hawaiian or other Pacific Islander, non-Hispanic/Latino; 2 Two or more races, non-Hispanic/Latino), 23 international. Average age 34. In 2013, 56 master's awarded. *Degree requirements:* For master's, comprehensive exam, thesis or alternative. *Entrance requirements:* For master's, minimum undergraduate GPA of 3.0. Additional exam requirements/recommendations for international students: Required—TOEFL (minimum score 540 paper-based). *Application deadline:* For fall admission, 8/1 priority date for domestic students. Applications are processed on a rolling basis. Application fee: $15. *Expenses:* Tuition, state resident: full-time $4278; part-time $178 per credit hour. Tuition, nonresident: full-time $6716; part-time $281 per credit hour. One-time fee: $15. *Financial support:* Career-related internships or fieldwork, Federal Work-Study, institutionally sponsored loans, scholarships/grants, tuition waivers (full and partial), and unspecified assistantships available. Support available to part-time students. Financial award application deadline: 3/1; financial award applicants required to submit FAFSA. *Faculty research:* Real estate valuation, studying expert judgments in complex accounting, decision environments, green marketing, environmentalism, marketing research methodology. *Unit head:* Dr. Margaret Young, Dean, 505-454-3522, Fax: 505-454-3354, E-mail: young_m@nmhu.edu. *Application contact:* Diane Trujillo, Administrative Assistant, Graduate Studies, 505-454-3266, Fax: 505-426-2117, E-mail: dtrujillo@nmhu.edu.

New Mexico State University, Graduate School, College of Arts and Sciences, Department of Biology, Las Cruces, NM 88003-8001. Offers biology (MS, PhD); biotechnology and business (MS). Part-time programs available. *Faculty:* 23 full-time (11 women). *Students:* 60 full-time (35 women), 11 part-time (7 women); includes 18 minority (1 Black or African American, non-Hispanic/Latino; 3 American Indian or Alaska Native, non-Hispanic/Latino; 13 Hispanic/Latino; 1 Two or more races, non-Hispanic/Latino), 19 international. Average age 30. 34 applicants, 50% accepted, 14 enrolled. In 2013, 9 master's, 11 doctorates awarded. *Degree requirements:* For master's, thesis (for some programs), defense or oral exam; for doctorate, comprehensive exam, thesis/dissertation, qualifying exam. *Entrance requirements:* Additional exam requirements/recommendations for international students: Required—TOEFL (minimum score 550 paper-based; 79 iBT), IELTS (minimum score 6.5). *Application deadline:* For fall admission, 1/15 priority date for domestic students, 1/15 for international students; for spring admission, 10/4 priority date for domestic students, 10/4 for international students. Applications are processed on a rolling basis. Application fee: $40 ($50 for international students). Electronic applications accepted. *Expenses:* Tuition, state resident: full-time $5398; part-time $224.90 per credit. Tuition, nonresident: full-time $18,821; part-time $784.20 per credit. *Required fees:* $1310; $54.60 per credit. *Financial support:* In 2013–14, 54 students received support, including 6 fellowships (averaging $4,050 per year), 10 research assistantships (averaging $15,919 per year), 36 teaching assistantships (averaging $16,098 per year); Federal Work-Study, scholarships/grants, health care benefits, and unspecified assistantships also available. Support available to part-time students. Financial award application deadline: 1/15. *Faculty research:* Microbiology, cell and organismal physiology, ecology and ethology, evolution, genetics, developmental biology. *Total annual research expenditures:* $3 million. *Unit head:* Dr. Ralph Preszler, Head, 575-646-3611, Fax: 575-646-5665, E-mail: rpreszle@nmsu.edu. *Application contact:* Gloria Valencia, Administrative Assistant, 575-646-3611, Fax: 575-646-5665, E-mail: gvalenci@nmsu.edu.
Website: http://biology-web.nmsu.edu/.

New Mexico State University, Graduate School, College of Business, Department of Management, Las Cruces, NM 88003. Offers PhD. Part-time and evening/weekend programs available. *Faculty:* 14 full-time (4 women), 1 part-time/adjunct (0 women). *Students:* 14 full-time (5 women), 1 part-time (0 women); includes 2 minority (both Hispanic/Latino), 5 international. Average age 34. 36 applicants, 8% accepted, 3 enrolled. In 2013, 5 doctorates awarded. *Degree requirements:* For doctorate, comprehensive exam, thesis/dissertation optional. *Entrance requirements:* Additional exam requirements/recommendations for international students: Required—TOEFL

(minimum score 550 paper-based; 79 iBT), IELTS (minimum score 6.5). *Application deadline:* For fall admission, 7/15 priority date for domestic students, 4/15 priority date for international students; for spring admission, 11/15 priority date for domestic students, 9/15 priority date for international students. *Expenses:* Tuition, state resident: full-time $5398; part-time $224.90 per credit. Tuition, nonresident: full-time $18,821; part-time $784.20 per credit. *Required fees:* $1310; $54.60 per credit. *Financial support:* In 2013–14, 12 students received support, including 3 fellowships (averaging $4,050 per year), 10 teaching assistantships (averaging $22,161 per year); Federal Work-Study, health care benefits, and unspecified assistantships also available. Financial award application deadline: 3/1. *Faculty research:* Small business/entrepreneurship, human resources, consumer behavior, economic development, finance. *Unit head:* Dr. Steven Elias, Academic Department Head, 575-646-1201, Fax: 575-646-1372, E-mail: selias@nmsu.edu. *Application contact:* Coordinator, 575-646-2736, Fax: 575-646-7721, E-mail: gradinfo@nmsu.edu.
Website: http://business.nmsu.edu/academics/management-gb/.

New Mexico State University, Graduate School, College of Business, MBA Program, Las Cruces, NM 88003-8001. Offers MBA. *Accreditation:* AACSB. Part-time and evening/weekend programs available. *Students:* 64 full-time (32 women), 74 part-time (36 women); includes 62 minority (1 Black or African American, non-Hispanic/Latino; 3 American Indian or Alaska Native, non-Hispanic/Latino; 2 Asian, non-Hispanic/Latino; 49 Hispanic/Latino; 2 Native Hawaiian or other Pacific Islander, non-Hispanic/Latino; 5 Two or more races, non-Hispanic/Latino), 22 international. Average age 30. 68 applicants, 68% accepted, 31 enrolled. In 2013, 60 master's awarded. *Degree requirements:* For master's, comprehensive exam, thesis optional. *Entrance requirements:* For master's, GMAT or GRE (depending upon undergraduate or graduate degree institution and GPA). Additional exam requirements/recommendations for international students: Required—TOEFL (minimum score 550 paper-based; 79 iBT), IELTS (minimum score 6.5). *Application deadline:* For fall admission, 7/15 priority date for domestic students, 5/15 priority date for international students; for spring admission, 11/15 priority date for domestic students, 10/15 priority date for international students; for summer admission, 4/15 for domestic students, 2/15 for international students. Applications are processed on a rolling basis. Application fee: $40 ($50 for international students). Electronic applications accepted. *Expenses:* Tuition, state resident: full-time $5398; part-time $224.90 per credit. Tuition, nonresident: full-time $18,821; part-time $784.20 per credit. *Required fees:* $1310; $54.60 per credit. *Financial support:* In 2013–14, 47 students received support, including 1 fellowship (averaging $4,050 per year), 16 teaching assistantships (averaging $12,467 per year); Federal Work-Study, institutionally sponsored loans, scholarships/grants, health care benefits, and unspecified assistantships also available. Financial award application deadline: 3/1. *Faculty research:* Small business/entrepreneurship, human resources, global marketing and management, supply chain management, financial management, investments, banking, insurance, regulated utilities, economic development, international business and finance. *Unit head:* Dr. Kathleen Brook, Interim Dean, 575-646-4083, Fax: 575-646-6155, E-mail: kbrook@nmsu.edu. *Application contact:* John Shonk, Coordinator, 575-646-8003, Fax: 575-646-7977, E-mail: mba@nmsu.edu.
Website: http://business.nmsu.edu/academics/mba/.

New York Institute of Technology, School of Management, Department of Business Administration, Old Westbury, NY 11568-8000. Offers management (MBA), including decision science, finance, management, marketing; professional accounting (MBA). Part-time and evening/weekend programs available. *Faculty:* 22 full-time (6 women), 17 part-time/adjunct (3 women). *Students:* 151 full-time (74 women), 120 part-time (47 women); includes 44 minority (13 Black or African American, non-Hispanic/Latino; 23 Asian, non-Hispanic/Latino; 4 Hispanic/Latino; 4 Two or more races, non-Hispanic/Latino), 177 international. Average age 27. 355 applicants, 66% accepted, 110 enrolled. In 2013, 151 master's awarded. *Degree requirements:* For master's, thesis (for some programs). *Entrance requirements:* For master's, minimum QPA of 2.85. Additional exam requirements/recommendations for international students: Required—TOEFL (minimum score 550 paper-based; 79 iBT), IELTS (minimum score 6). *Application deadline:* For fall admission, 7/1 priority date for domestic students, 6/1 for international students; for spring admission, 12/1 priority date for domestic students, 12/1 for international students. Applications are processed on a rolling basis. Application fee: $50. Electronic applications accepted. *Expenses: Tuition:* Full-time $18,900; part-time $1050 per credit. *Financial support:* Research assistantships with partial tuition reimbursements, career-related internships or fieldwork, scholarships/grants, health care benefits, tuition waivers (full and partial), and unspecified assistantships available. Support available to part-time students. Financial award applicants required to submit FAFSA. *Faculty research:* Accounting, economics, finance, management, marketing. *Unit head:* Dr. Diamando Afxentiou, Director, 212-261-1602, E-mail: dafxenti@nyit.edu. *Application contact:* Alice Dolitsky, Director, Graduate Admissions, 516-686-7520, Fax: 516-686-1116, E-mail: nyitgrad@nyit.edu.
Website: http://www.nyit.edu/management/mba.

New York University, Leonard N. Stern School of Business, Department of Marketing, New York, NY 10012-1019. Offers entertainment, media and technology (MBA); general marketing (MBA); marketing (PhD); product management (MBA). *Expenses: Tuition:* Full-time $35,856; part-time $1494 per unit. *Required fees:* $1408; $64 per unit. $473 per term. Tuition and fees vary according to course load and program.

New York University, Polytechnic School of Engineering, Department of Technology Management, New York, NY 10012-1019. Offers construction management (Advanced Certificate); electronic business management (Advanced Certificate); entrepreneurship (Advanced Certificate); human resources management (Advanced Certificate); industrial engineering (MS); information management (Advanced Certificate); management (MS); management of technology (MS); manufacturing engineering (MS); organizational behavior (MS, Advanced Certificate); project management (Advanced Certificate); technology management (MBA, PhD, Advanced Certificate); telecommunications management (Advanced Certificate). Part-time and evening/weekend programs available. *Faculty:* 7 full-time (1 woman), 41 part-time/adjunct (2 women). *Students:* 285 full-time (132 women), 116 part-time (45 women); includes 50 minority (10 Black or African American, non-Hispanic/Latino; 29 Asian, non-Hispanic/Latino; 11 Hispanic/Latino), 284 international. Average age 30. 726 applicants, 60% accepted, 140 enrolled. In 2013, 137 master's awarded. *Degree requirements:* For master's, comprehensive exam (for some programs), thesis (for some programs); for doctorate, comprehensive exam, thesis/dissertation. *Entrance requirements:* For master's, GMAT, minimum B average in undergraduate course work. Additional exam requirements/recommendations for international students: Required—TOEFL (minimum score 550 paper-based; 80 iBT); Recommended—IELTS (minimum score 6.5). *Application deadline:* For fall admission, 7/31 priority date for domestic students, 4/30 priority date for international students; for spring admission, 12/31 priority date for domestic students, 11/30 priority date for international students. Applications are processed on a rolling basis. Application fee: $75. Electronic applications accepted. *Expenses: Tuition:* Full-time $35,856; part-time $1494 per unit. *Required fees:* $1408; $64 per unit. $473 per term. Tuition and fees vary according to course load and program. *Financial support:* In 2013–14, 1 fellowship (averaging $26,400 per year) was awarded; research assistantships, teaching assistantships, institutionally sponsored loans, scholarships/grants, and unspecified assistantships also available. Support available to part-time students. *Faculty research:* Global innovation and research and development strategy, managing emerging technologies, technology and development, service design and innovation, tech entrepreneurship and commercialization, sustainable and clean-tech innovation, impacts of information technology upon individuals, organizations and society. *Total annual research expenditures:* $692,936. *Unit head:* Prof. Bharadwaj Rao, Head, 718-260-3617, Fax: 718-260-3874, E-mail: brao@poly.edu. *Application contact:* Raymond Lutzky, Director of Graduate Enrollment Management, 718-637-5984, Fax: 718-260-3624, E-mail: rlutzky@poly.edu.
Website: http://www.poly.edu/academics/departments/technology/.

New York University, School of Law, New York, NY 10012-1019. Offers law (LL M, JD, JSD); law and business (Advanced Certificate); taxation (MSL, Advanced Certificate); JD/JD; JD/LL B; JD/MA; JD/MBA; JD/MPA; JD/MPP; JD/MSW; JD/MUP; JD/PhD. *Accreditation:* ABA. Part-time programs available. Postbaccalaureate distance learning degree programs offered. *Faculty:* 137 full-time (44 women), 68 part-time/adjunct (18 women). *Students:* 1,418 full-time (619 women); includes 394 minority (80 Black or African American, non-Hispanic/Latino; 1 American Indian or Alaska Native, non-Hispanic/Latino; 165 Asian, non-Hispanic/Latino; 120 Hispanic/Latino; 28 Two or more races, non-Hispanic/Latino), 69 international. 5,730 applicants, 437 enrolled. In 2013, 532 master's, 537 doctorates awarded. *Entrance requirements:* For doctorate, LSAT (for JD). *Application deadline:* For fall admission, 2/15 for domestic students. Application fee: $85. Electronic applications accepted. *Expenses:* Contact institution. *Financial support:* Fellowships, research assistantships, teaching assistantships, career-related internships or fieldwork, Federal Work-Study, scholarships/grants, and loan repayment assistance available. Financial award application deadline: 4/15; financial award applicants required to submit FAFSA. *Faculty research:* International law, environmental law, corporate law, globalization of law, philosophy of law. *Unit head:* Trevor Morrison, Dean, 212-998-6000, Fax: 212-995-3150. *Application contact:* Kenneth J. Kleinrock, Assistant Dean for Admissions, 212-998-6060, Fax: 212-995-4527.
Website: http://www.law.nyu.edu/.

Niagara University, Graduate Division of Business Administration, Niagara Falls, NY 14109. Offers business (MBA); commerce (MBA); finance (MS). *Accreditation:* AACSB. Part-time and evening/weekend programs available. *Faculty:* 24 full-time (6 women), 17 part-time/adjunct (4 women). *Students:* 149 full-time (54 women), 92 part-time (46 women); includes 20 minority (6 Black or African American, non-Hispanic/Latino; 1 American Indian or Alaska Native, non-Hispanic/Latino; 4 Asian, non-Hispanic/Latino; 5 Hispanic/Latino; 4 Two or more races, non-Hispanic/Latino), 70 international. Average age 28. In 2013, 132 master's awarded. *Entrance requirements:* For master's, GMAT. Additional exam requirements/recommendations for international students: Required—TOEFL (minimum score 550 paper-based, 79 iBT) or IELTS (minimum score 6). *Application deadline:* For fall admission, 8/1 for domestic students; for spring admission, 11/1 for domestic students. Applications are processed on a rolling basis. Application fee: $30. Electronic applications accepted. Tuition and fees vary according to program. *Financial support:* Fellowships, research assistantships, career-related internships or fieldwork, and Federal Work-Study available. Support available to part-time students. Financial award application deadline: 4/15; financial award applicants required to submit FAFSA. *Faculty research:* Capital flows, Federal Reserve policy, human resource management, public policy, issues in marketing, auctions, economics of information, risk and capital markets, management strategy, consumer behavior, Internet and social media marketing. *Unit head:* Dr. Paul Richardson, Director, 716-286-8169, Fax: 716-286-8206, E-mail: psr@niagara.edu. *Application contact:* Evan Pierce, Associate Director for Graduate Recruitment, 716-286-8769, Fax: 716-286-8170, E-mail: epierce@niagara.edu.
Website: http://mba.niagara.edu.

Nicholls State University, Graduate Studies, College of Business Administration, Thibodaux, LA 70310. Offers MBA. *Accreditation:* AACSB. Part-time and evening/weekend programs available. *Degree requirements:* For master's, thesis optional. *Entrance requirements:* For master's, GMAT. Additional exam requirements/recommendations for international students: Required—TOEFL (minimum score 550 paper-based). Electronic applications accepted.

Nichols College, Graduate and Professional Studies, Dudley, MA 01571-5000. Offers business administration (MBA); organizational leadership (MSOL). Part-time and evening/weekend programs available. Postbaccalaureate distance learning degree programs offered (no on-campus study). *Degree requirements:* For master's, project (for MOL). *Entrance requirements:* For master's, 2 letters of recommendation, current resume, official transcripts, 800-word personal statement. Additional exam requirements/recommendations for international students: Required—TOEFL (minimum score 500 paper-based). Electronic applications accepted.

North Carolina Agricultural and Technical State University, School of Graduate Studies, School of Business and Economics, Greensboro, NC 27411. Offers accounting (MSM); business education (MAT); human resources management (MSM); supply chain systems (MSM).

North Carolina Central University, School of Business, Durham, NC 27707-3129. Offers MBA, JD/MBA. *Accreditation:* AACSB; ACBSP. Part-time and evening/weekend programs available. *Degree requirements:* For master's, thesis. *Entrance requirements:* For master's, GMAT. Additional exam requirements/recommendations for international students: Required—TOEFL. *Faculty research:* Small business issues, research of pedagogy, African business environment.

North Carolina State University, Graduate School, Poole College of Management, Program in Business Administration, Raleigh, NC 27695. Offers biosciences management (MBA); entrepreneurship and technology commercialization (MBA); financial management (MBA); innovation management (MBA); marketing management (MBA); services management (MBA); supply chain management (MBA). *Accreditation:* AACSB. Part-time programs available. *Degree requirements:* For master's, thesis optional. *Entrance requirements:* For master's, GMAT, interview, 3 letters of recommendation. Additional exam requirements/recommendations for international students: Required—TOEFL (minimum score 600 paper-based; 100 iBT). Electronic applications accepted. *Faculty research:* Manufacturing strategy, information systems, technology commercialization, managing research and development, historical stock returns.

See Display on next page and Close-Up on page 189.

North Central College, Graduate and Continuing Studies Programs, Department of Business, Program in Business Administration, Naperville, IL 60566-7063. Offers change management (MBA); finance (MBA); human resource management (MBA); international business administration (MIBA); management (MBA); marketing (MBA). Part-time and evening/weekend programs available. *Faculty:* 13 full-time (4 women), 8 part-time/adjunct (0 women). *Students:* 31 full-time (8 women), 67 part-time (32 women); includes 16 minority (6 Black or African American, non-Hispanic/Latino; 5 Asian, non-Hispanic/Latino; 5 Hispanic/Latino), 3 international. Average age 30. 99 applicants, 54% accepted, 29 enrolled. In 2013, 51 master's awarded. *Degree requirements:* For master's, thesis optional, project. *Entrance requirements:* For master's, interview. Additional exam requirements/recommendations for international students: Required—TOEFL (minimum score 577 paper-based; 90 iBT). *Application deadline:* For fall

Business Administration and Management—General

admission, 8/15 for domestic students; for winter admission, 12/1 for domestic students; for spring admission, 2/1 for domestic students. Application fee: $25. *Expenses: Tuition:* Full-time $4716; part-time $786 per credit hour. *Financial support:* Scholarships/grants available. Support available to part-time students. *Unit head:* Dr. Robert Moussetis, Program Coordinator, 630-637-5475, E-mail: rcmoussetis@noctrl.edu. *Application contact:* Wendy Kulpinski, Director of Graduate and Continuing Education Admission, 630-637-5808, Fax: 630-637-5844, E-mail: wekulpinski@noctrl.edu.

North Central College, Graduate and Continuing Studies Programs, Program in Leadership Studies, Naperville, IL 60566-7063. Offers higher education leadership (MLD); professional leadership (MLD); social entrepreneurship (MLD); sports leadership (MLD). Part-time and evening/weekend programs available. *Faculty:* 9 full-time (1 woman), 16 part-time/adjunct (9 women). *Students:* 42 full-time (24 women), 24 part-time (8 women); includes 16 minority (10 Black or African American, non-Hispanic/Latino; 6 Hispanic/Latino), 4 international. Average age 28. 104 applicants, 51% accepted, 23 enrolled. In 2013, 36 master's awarded. *Degree requirements:* For master's, thesis optional, project. *Entrance requirements:* For master's, interview. Additional exam requirements/recommendations for international students: Required—TOEFL (minimum score 570 paper-based; 90 iBT). *Application deadline:* For fall admission, 8/15 for domestic students; for winter admission, 12/1 for domestic students; for spring admission, 2/1 for domestic students. Applications are processed on a rolling basis. Application fee: $25. *Expenses:* Contact institution. *Financial support:* In 2013–14, 1 student received support. Scholarships/grants available. Support available to part-time students. *Unit head:* Dr. Thomas Cavenagh, Program Coordinator, Leadership Studies, 630-637-5285. *Application contact:* Wendy Kulpinski, Director of Graduate and Continuing Education Admission, 630-637-5808, Fax: 630-637-5844, E-mail: wekulpinski@noctrl.edu.

Northcentral University, Graduate Studies, Prescott Valley, AZ 86314. Offers business (MBA, DBA, PhD, Post-Master's Certificate, Postbaccalaureate Certificate); education (M Ed, Ed D, PhD, Ed S, Post-Master's Certificate, Postbaccalaureate Certificate); marriage and family therapy (MA, PhD, Post-Master's Certificate, Postbaccalaureate Certificate); psychology (MA, PhD, Post-Master's Certificate, Postbaccalaureate Certificate). Part-time and evening/weekend programs available. Postbaccalaureate distance learning degree programs offered (no on-campus study). *Faculty:* 94 full-time (58 women), 390 part-time/adjunct (164 women). *Students:* 7,902 full-time (4,776 women), 4,835 part-time (2,804 women); includes 3,752 minority (2,664 Black or African American, non-Hispanic/Latino; 82 American Indian or Alaska Native, non-Hispanic/Latino; 245 Asian, non-Hispanic/Latino; 476 Hispanic/Latino; 43 Native Hawaiian or other Pacific Islander, non-Hispanic/Latino; 242 Two or more races, non-Hispanic/Latino). Average age 44. 3,043 applicants, 69% accepted, 1734 enrolled. In 2013, 538 master's, 253 doctorates, 31 other advanced degrees awarded. *Entrance requirements:* For master's, bachelor's degree from regionally- or nationally-accredited institution, current resume or curriculum vitae, statement of intent, interview, and background check (for marriage and family therapy); for doctorate, post-baccalaureate master's degree and/or doctoral degree from nationally- or regionally-accredited academic institution; for other advanced degree, bachelor's-level or higher degree from accredited institution or university (for Post-Baccalaureate Certificate); master's and/or doctoral degree from regionally- or nationally-accredited academic institution (for Post-Master's Certificate). Additional exam requirements/recommendations for international students: Required—TOEFL (minimum score 95 iBT), IELTS (minimum score 6) or PTE (minimum score 65). *Application deadline:* Applications are processed on a rolling basis. Application fee: $0. Electronic applications accepted. *Expenses: Tuition:* Full-time $16,584; part-time $2764 per course. *Financial support:* Scholarships/grants available. *Faculty research:* Business management, curriculum and instruction, educational leadership, health psychology, organizational behavior. *Unit head:* Dr. Scott Burrus, Provost and Chief Academic Officer, 888-327-2877, Fax: 928-759-6381, E-mail: provost@ncu.edu. *Application contact:* Ken Boutelle, Vice President, Enrollment Services, 480-253-3535, E-mail: kboutelle@ncu.edu.

North Dakota State University, College of Graduate and Interdisciplinary Studies, College of Business, Fargo, ND 58108. Offers MBA. *Accreditation:* AACSB. Part-time and evening/weekend programs available. *Faculty:* 16 full-time (5 women). *Students:* 70 full-time (27 women), 27 part-time (11 women); includes 9 minority (3 Black or African American, non-Hispanic/Latino; 1 American Indian or Alaska Native, non-Hispanic/Latino; 2 Asian, non-Hispanic/Latino; 3 Two or more races, non-Hispanic/Latino), 22 international. Average age 31. 32 applicants, 94% accepted, 26 enrolled. In 2013, 43 master's awarded. *Entrance requirements:* For master's, GMAT. Additional exam requirements/recommendations for international students: Required—TOEFL (minimum score 550 paper-based; 79 iBT). *Application deadline:* For fall admission, 7/1 priority date for domestic students, 5/1 priority date for international students; for spring admission, 11/15 for domestic students, 8/1 priority date for international students. Applications are processed on a rolling basis. Application fee: $35. Electronic applications accepted. *Financial support:* In 2013–14, 14 students received support, including 13 research assistantships, 1 teaching assistantship; institutionally sponsored loans and tuition waivers (partial) also available. Support available to part-time students. Financial award application deadline: 5/15; financial award applicants required to submit FAFSA. *Faculty research:* Labor management, operations, international finance, agency, Internet marketing. *Unit head:* Dr. Ron Johnson, Dean, 701-231-8805. *Application contact:* Paul R. Brown, Director, 701-231-7681, Fax: 701-231-7508, E-mail: paul.brown@ndsu.edu.
Website: http://www.ndsu.edu/business/graduate_programs/.

Northeastern Illinois University, College of Graduate Studies and Research, College of Business and Management, MBA Program, Chicago, IL 60625-4699. Offers MBA.

Northeastern State University, College of Business and Technology, Master of Business Administration Program, Tahlequah, OK 74464-2399. Offers MBA. *Accreditation:* ACBSP. Part-time and evening/weekend programs available. *Faculty:* 9 full-time (1 woman), 1 part-time/adjunct (0 women). *Students:* 30 full-time (9 women), 46 part-time (24 women); includes 28 minority (8 Black or African American, non-Hispanic/Latino; 10 American Indian or Alaska Native, non-Hispanic/Latino; 2 Asian, non-Hispanic/Latino; 2 Hispanic/Latino; 6 Two or more races, non-Hispanic/Latino), 16 international. Average age 31. In 2013, 30 master's awarded. *Degree requirements:* For master's, comprehensive exam, thesis, business plan, oral exam. *Entrance requirements:* For master's, GMAT, minimum GPA of 2.5. Additional exam requirements/recommendations for international students: Required—TOEFL. *Application deadline:* For fall admission, 6/1 priority date for domestic students. Applications are processed on a rolling basis. Application fee: $25. Electronic applications accepted. *Expenses:* Tuition, state resident: full-time $3029; part-time $168.25 per credit hour. Tuition, nonresident: full-time $7709; part-time $428.25 per credit hour. *Required fees:* $35.90 per credit hour. *Financial support:* Teaching assistantships and Federal Work-Study available. Financial award application deadline: 3/1. *Unit head:* Dr. Sandra Edwards, Chair, 918-683-0400 Ext. 5219. *Application contact:* Margie Railey, Administrative Assistant, 918-456-5511 Ext. 2093, Fax: 918-458-2061, E-mail: railey@nsouk.edu.
Website: http://academics.nsuok.edu/businesstechnology/Graduate/MBA.aspx.

Northeastern State University, College of Business and Technology, Professional Master of Business Administration Program, Tahlequah, OK 74464-2399. Offers PMBA. *Faculty:* 6 full-time (2 women). *Students:* 1 (woman) full-time, 36 part-time (9 women); includes 8 minority (2 Black or African American, non-Hispanic/Latino; 4 American Indian or Alaska Native, non-Hispanic/Latino; 1 Hispanic/Latino; 1 Two or more races,

non-Hispanic/Latino), 1 international. Average age 35. In 2013, 30 master's awarded. *Degree requirements:* For master's, integrative project or research. *Expenses:* Tuition, state resident: full-time $3029; part-time $168.25 per credit hour. Tuition, nonresident: full-time $7709; part-time $428.25 per credit hour. *Required fees:* $35.90 per credit hour. *Unit head:* Dr. Sandra Edwards, Director, 918-449-6542, Fax: 918-449-6561, E-mail: edwar001@nsuok.edu. *Application contact:* Margie Railey, Administrative Assistant, 918-456-5511 Ext. 2093, Fax: 918-458-2061, E-mail: railey@nsouk.edu.
Website: http://academics.nsuok.edu/businesstechnology/Graduate/PMBA.aspx.

Northeastern University, Bouvé College of Health Sciences, Boston, MA 02115-5096. Offers audiology (Au D); biotechnology (MS); counseling psychology (MS, PhD, CAGS); counseling/school psychology (PhD); exercise physiology (MS), including exercise physiology, public health; health informatics (MS); nursing (MS, PhD, CAGS), including acute care (MS), administration (MS), anesthesia (MS), primary care (MS), psychiatric mental health (MS); pharmaceutical sciences (PhD); pharmaceutics and drug delivery systems (MS); pharmacology (MS); physical therapy (DPT); physician assistant (MS); school psychology (PhD, CAGS); school/counseling psychology (PhD); speech language pathology (MS); urban public health (MPH); MS/MBA. *Accreditation:* ACPE (one or more programs are accredited). Part-time and evening/weekend programs available. *Degree requirements:* For doctorate, thesis/dissertation (for some programs); for CAGS, comprehensive exam.

Northeastern University, D'Amore-McKim School of Business, Boston, MA 02115-5096. Offers accounting (MS); business administration (EMBA, MBA); finance (MS); international business (MS); taxation (MS); technological entrepreneurship (MS); JD/MBA; MBA/MSN; MS/MBA. Part-time and evening/weekend programs available. Postbaccalaureate distance learning degree programs offered (no on-campus study). *Entrance requirements:* For master's, GMAT or GRE, interview. Additional exam requirements/recommendations for international students: Required—TOEFL (minimum score 600 paper-based; 100 iBT). Electronic applications accepted. *Expenses:* Contact institution.

Northern Arizona University, Graduate College, NAU-Yuma, Master of Administration Program, Flagstaff, AZ 86011. Offers M Adm. *Accreditation:* ACBSP. Part-time programs available. Postbaccalaureate distance learning degree programs offered (no on-campus study). *Faculty:* 35 full-time (14 women), 13 part-time/adjunct (4 women). *Students:* 59 full-time (38 women), 318 part-time (177 women); includes 127 minority (12 Black or African American, non-Hispanic/Latino; 22 American Indian or Alaska Native, non-Hispanic/Latino; 9 Asian, non-Hispanic/Latino; 69 Hispanic/Latino; 1 Native Hawaiian or other Pacific Islander, non-Hispanic/Latino; 14 Two or more races, non-Hispanic/Latino). Average age 39. 96 applicants, 96% accepted, 70 enrolled. In 2013, 138 master's awarded. *Degree requirements:* For master's, projects. *Entrance requirements:* For master's, five years' related work experience, minimum GPA of 3.0. Additional exam requirements/recommendations for international students: Required—TOEFL (minimum score 550 paper-based; 80 iBT), IELTS (minimum score 7). *Application deadline:* For fall admission, 3/1 priority date for international students; for spring admission, 9/15 priority date for international students. Applications are processed on a rolling basis. Application fee: $65. Electronic applications accepted. *Financial support:* Federal Work-Study and scholarships/grants available. Support available to part-time students. Financial award applicants required to submit FAFSA. *Unit head:* Dr. Alex Steenstra, Chair, 928-317-6083, E-mail: alex.steenstra@nau.edu. *Application contact:* Pam Torbico, Coordinator, 928-523-6694, E-mail: m.admin@nau.edu.
Website: http://extended.nau.edu/madmin/.

Northern Arizona University, Graduate College, The W. A. Franke College of Business, Flagstaff, AZ 86011. Offers MBA. *Accreditation:* AACSB; ACBSP. Part-time programs available. *Faculty:* 59 full-time (22 women), 3 part-time/adjunct (2 women). *Students:* 34 full-time (7 women); includes 4 minority (2 Hispanic/Latino; 2 Two or more races, non-Hispanic/Latino), 5 international. Average age 25. 70 applicants, 64% accepted, 34 enrolled. In 2013, 28 master's awarded. *Entrance requirements:* For master's, GMAT/GRE. Additional exam requirements/recommendations for international students: Required—TOEFL (minimum score 550 paper-based; 80 iBT), IELTS (minimum score 7). *Application deadline:* For fall admission, 5/15 priority date for domestic students, 3/1 priority date for international students. Applications are processed on a rolling basis. Application fee: $65. Electronic applications accepted. *Expenses:* Contact institution. *Financial support:* In 2013–14, 7 research assistantships (averaging $4,587 per year) were awarded; Federal Work-Study, institutionally sponsored loans, scholarships/grants, health care benefits, tuition waivers (partial), and unspecified assistantships also available. Support available to part-time students. Financial award applicants required to submit FAFSA. *Faculty research:* Data processing applications for business situations and problems, accounting fraud, effects of sales tactics, self-efficacy and performance. *Unit head:* Dr. Eric Yordy, Associate Dean, 928-523-5633, Fax: 928-523-7331, E-mail: eric.yordy@nau.edu. *Application contact:* Natasha Silvestri, Administrative Associate, 928-523-7342, Fax: 928-523-6559, E-mail: fcb_gradprog@nau.edu.
Website: http://www.nau.edu/franke/.

Northern Illinois University, Graduate School, College of Business, MBA Program, De Kalb, IL 60115-2854. Offers MBA. *Accreditation:* AACSB. Part-time and evening/weekend programs available. *Faculty:* 53 full-time (17 women), 3 part-time/adjunct (0 women). *Students:* 136 full-time (41 women), 440 part-time (133 women); includes 161 minority (36 Black or African American, non-Hispanic/Latino; 70 Asian, non-Hispanic/Latino; 41 Hispanic/Latino; 1 Native Hawaiian or other Pacific Islander, non-Hispanic/Latino; 13 Two or more races, non-Hispanic/Latino), 28 international. Average age 33. 260 applicants, 76% accepted, 130 enrolled. In 2013, 228 master's awarded. *Degree requirements:* For master's, thesis optional, seminar. *Entrance requirements:* For master's, GMAT, minimum GPA of 2.75. Additional exam requirements/recommendations for international students: Required—TOEFL (minimum score 550 paper-based). *Application deadline:* For fall admission, 6/1 for domestic students, 5/1 for international students; for spring admission, 11/1 for domestic students, 10/1 for international students. Applications are processed on a rolling basis. Application fee: $40. Electronic applications accepted. *Financial support:* In 2013–14, 6 research assistantships with full tuition reimbursements, 5 teaching assistantships with full tuition reimbursements were awarded; fellowships with full tuition reimbursements, career-related internships or fieldwork, Federal Work-Study, scholarships/grants, tuition waivers (full), and unspecified assistantships also available. Support available to part-time students. Financial award applicants required to submit FAFSA. *Unit head:* Mona Salmon, Associate Dean of Graduate Affairs and Research, 815-753-1245, E-mail: mba@niu.edu. *Application contact:* Office of Graduate Studies in Business, 815-753-6301.
Website: http://www.cob.niu.edu/mbaprograms/.

Northern Kentucky University, Office of Graduate Programs, College of Business, Program in Business Administration, Highland Heights, KY 41099. Offers business administration (MBA, Certificate); JD/MBA. *Accreditation:* AACSB. Part-time programs available. *Faculty:* 4 full-time (3 women). *Students:* 1 (woman) full-time, 76 part-time (38 women); includes 3 minority (2 Black or African American, non-Hispanic/Latino; 1 Asian, non-Hispanic/Latino), 4 international. Average age 32. 67 applicants, 45% accepted, 23 enrolled. In 2013, 44 master's awarded. *Degree requirements:* For master's, thesis optional. *Entrance requirements:* For master's, GMAT (minimum score 525), minimum GPA of 2.5, resume, statement of purpose, three letters of recommendation. Additional exam requirements/recommendations for international students: Required—TOEFL (minimum score 550 paper-based; 79 iBT); Recommended—IELTS (minimum score 6.5). *Application deadline:* For fall admission, 6/1 for domestic students, 6/1 priority date for international students. Applications are processed on a rolling basis. Application fee: $40. Electronic applications accepted. *Expenses:* Contact institution. *Financial support:* In 2013–14, 10 students received support. Unspecified assistantships available. Financial award applicants required to submit FAFSA. *Faculty research:* Strategic management, business analytics, managing and leading organizations, business ethics and culture, global business operations. *Unit head:* Ned Jackson, Program Director, 859-572-6357, Fax: 859-572-6177, E-mail: jacksoned@nku.edu. *Application contact:* Dr. Christian Gamm, Director of Graduate Programs, 859-572-6364, Fax: 859-572-6177, E-mail: gammc1@nku.edu.
Website: http://cob.nku.edu/graduatedegrees/mba.html.

Northern Kentucky University, Office of Graduate Programs, College of Business, Program in Executive Leadership and Organizational Change, Highland Heights, KY 41099. Offers MS. Part-time and evening/weekend programs available. *Faculty:* 3 full-time (2 women), 1 part-time/adjunct (0 women). *Students:* 43 part-time (17 women); includes 8 minority (4 Black or African American, non-Hispanic/Latino; 2 Hispanic/Latino; 2 Two or more races, non-Hispanic/Latino). Average age 37. 40 applicants, 68% accepted, 24 enrolled. In 2013, 23 master's awarded. *Degree requirements:* For master's, field research project. *Entrance requirements:* For master's, minimum GPA of 2.5; essay on professional career objective; 3 letters of recommendation, 1 from a current organization; 3 years of professional or managerial work experience; full-time employment at time of entry. Additional exam requirements/recommendations for international students: Required—TOEFL (minimum score 600 paper-based; 79 iBT); Recommended—IELTS (minimum score 6.5). *Application deadline:* For fall admission, 6/15 for domestic students, 6/1 priority date for international students. Applications are processed on a rolling basis. Application fee: $40. Electronic applications accepted. *Expenses:* Contact institution. *Financial support:* In 2013–14, 9 students received support. Unspecified assistantships available. Financial award applicants required to submit FAFSA. *Faculty research:* Organizational change, assessment and development, strategy development and systems thinking, global leadership and sustainable changes. *Unit head:* Dr. Kenneth Rhee, Program Director, 859-572-6310, Fax: 859-572-5150, E-mail: rhee@nku.edu. *Application contact:* Amberly Hurst-Nutini, Coordinator, 859-572-5947, Fax: 859-572-5150, E-mail: hurstam@nku.edu.
Website: http://cob.nku.edu/graduatedegrees/eloc.html.

North Park University, School of Business and Nonprofit Management, Chicago, IL 60625-4895. Offers MBA, MHEA, MHRM, MM, MNA. Part-time and evening/weekend programs available. Postbaccalaureate distance learning degree programs offered (no on-campus study). *Entrance requirements:* For master's, GMAT, GRE. Additional exam requirements/recommendations for international students: Required—TOEFL. *Expenses:* Contact institution.

Northwest Christian University, School of Business and Management, Eugene, OR 97401-3745. Offers MBA. Part-time and evening/weekend programs available. *Degree requirements:* For master's, thesis. *Entrance requirements:* For master's, GMAT, GRE, MAT, minimum undergraduate GPA of 3.0, 500-word essay, resume. Electronic applications accepted.

Northwestern Polytechnic University, School of Business and Information Technology, Fremont, CA 94539-7482. Offers MBA. Part-time and evening/weekend programs available. *Degree requirements:* For master's, thesis optional. *Entrance requirements:* For master's, GMAT, minimum GPA of 3.0. Additional exam requirements/recommendations for international students: Required—TOEFL (minimum score 550 paper-based; 79 iBT). *Expenses:* Contact institution. *Faculty research:* Entrepreneurship, accounting, information technology.

Northwestern University, The Graduate School, Kellogg School of Management, Management Programs, Evanston, IL 60208. Offers accounting information and management (MBA, PhD); analytical finance (MBA); business administration (MBA); decision sciences (MBA); entrepreneurship and innovation (MBA); finance (MBA, PhD); health enterprise management (MBA); human resources management (MBA); international business (MBA); management and organizations (MBA, PhD); management and organizations and sociology (PhD); management and strategy (MBA); management studies (MS); managerial analytics (MBA); managerial economics (MBA); managerial economics and strategy (PhD); marketing (MBA, PhD); marketing management (MBA); media management (MBA); operations management (MBA, PhD); real estate (MBA); social enterprise at Kellogg (MBA); JD/MBA. Part-time and evening/weekend programs available. Terminal master's awarded for partial completion of doctoral program. *Degree requirements:* For doctorate, thesis/dissertation, 2 years of coursework, qualifying (field) exam and candidacy, summer research papers and presentations to faculty, proposal defense, final exam/defense. *Entrance requirements:* For master's, GMAT, GRE, interview, 2 letters of recommendation, college transcripts, resume, essays, Kellogg honor code; for doctorate, GMAT, GRE, statement of purpose, transcripts, 2 letters of recommendation, resume, interview. Additional exam requirements/recommendations for international students: Required—TOEFL, IELTS. Electronic applications accepted. *Expenses:* Contact institution. *Faculty research:* Business cycles and international finance, health policy, networks, non-market strategy, consumer psychology.

Northwestern University, McCormick School of Engineering and Applied Science, MMM Program, Evanston, IL 60208. Offers MBA/MEM. *Unit head:* Dr. Julio Ottino, Dean, 847-491-5220, E-mail: jm-ottino@northwestern.edu. *Application contact:* Dr. Bruce Alan Lindvall, Assistant Dean for Graduate Studies, 847-491-4547, Fax: 847-491-5341, E-mail: b-lindvall@northwestern.edu.
Website: http://www.mmm.northwestern.edu/.

Northwest Missouri State University, Graduate School, Melvin and Valorie Booth College of Business and Professional Studies, Program in Business Administration, Maryville, MO 64468-6001. Offers MBA. *Accreditation:* ACBSP. *Degree requirements:* For master's, comprehensive exam. *Entrance requirements:* For master's, GMAT/GRE, minimum GPA of 2.5. Additional exam requirements/recommendations for international students: Required—TOEFL (minimum score 550 paper-based). Electronic applications accepted.

Northwest Nazarene University, Graduate Studies, Program in Business Administration, Nampa, ID 83686-5897. Offers business administration (MBA); healthcare (MBA). *Accreditation:* ACBSP. Part-time and evening/weekend programs available. Postbaccalaureate distance learning degree programs offered (no on-campus study). *Faculty:* 12 full-time (4 women), 14 part-time/adjunct (2 women). *Students:* 103 full-time (31 women), 36 part-time (14 women); includes 17 minority (1 Black or African American, non-Hispanic/Latino; 1 American Indian or Alaska Native, non-Hispanic/Latino; 2 Asian, non-Hispanic/Latino; 9 Hispanic/Latino; 4 Two or more races, non-Hispanic/Latino), 5 international. Average age 34. 26 applicants, 62% accepted, 11 enrolled. In 2013, 41 master's awarded. *Degree requirements:* For master's,

comprehensive exam, thesis or alternative. *Entrance requirements:* For master's, minimum GPA of 3.0. *Application deadline:* Applications are processed on a rolling basis. Application fee: $50. Electronic applications accepted. *Expenses:* Contact institution. *Unit head:* Dr. Brenda Johnson, Director, 208-467-8415, Fax: 208-467-8440, E-mail: mba@nnu.edu. *Application contact:* Wendy Rhodes, MBA Program Coordinator, 208-467-8123, Fax: 208-467-8440, E-mail: nnu-mba@nnu.edu.
Website: http://nnu.edu/mba.

Northwest University, School of Business and Management, Kirkland, WA 98033. Offers business administration (MBA); international business (MBA); project management (MBA); social entrepreneurship (MBA). *Accreditation:* ACBSP. Part-time and evening/weekend programs available. *Degree requirements:* For master's, formalized research. *Entrance requirements:* For master's, GMAT. Additional exam requirements/recommendations for international students: Required—TOEFL (minimum score 550 paper-based; 75 iBT). *Application deadline:* For fall admission, 8/1 for domestic and international students; for spring admission, 12/1 for domestic and international students. Application fee: $75. Electronic applications accepted. *Expenses:* Contact institution. *Financial support:* Federal Work-Study, scholarships/grants, health care benefits, and tuition waivers (full and partial) available. Financial award applicants required to submit FAFSA. *Unit head:* Dr. Teresa Gillespie, Dean, 425-889-5290, E-mail: teresa.gillespie@northwestu.edu. *Application contact:* Aaron Oosterwyk, Director of Graduate and Professional Studies Enrollment, 425-889-7792, Fax: 425-803-3059, E-mail: aaron.oosterwyk@northwestu.edu.
Website: http://www.northwestu.edu/business/.

Northwood University, Michigan Campus, DeVos Graduate School, Midland, MI 48640-2398. Offers MBA, MSOL. MBA also offered on Florida and Texas campuses; MSOL offered online only. Part-time and evening/weekend programs available. Postbaccalaureate distance learning degree programs offered (no on-campus study). *Degree requirements:* For master's, capstone project. *Entrance requirements:* For master's, GMAT, interview, letters of recommendation, resume. Additional exam requirements/recommendations for international students: Required—TOEFL (minimum score 550 paper-based). Electronic applications accepted.

Norwich University, College of Graduate and Continuing Studies, Master of Business Administration Program, Northfield, VT 05663. Offers finance (MBA); organizational leadership (MBA); project management (MBA). *Accreditation:* ACBSP. Evening/weekend programs available. Postbaccalaureate distance learning degree programs offered (minimal on-campus study). *Faculty:* 16 part-time/adjunct (6 women). *Students:* 198 full-time (57 women); includes 33 minority (18 Black or African American, non-Hispanic/Latino; 9 Asian, non-Hispanic/Latino; 3 Hispanic/Latino; 3 Two or more races, non-Hispanic/Latino). Average age 36. 200 applicants, 41% accepted, 82 enrolled. In 2013, 89 master's awarded. *Degree requirements:* For master's, comprehensive exam, thesis optional. *Entrance requirements:* For master's, minimum undergraduate GPA of 2.75. Additional exam requirements/recommendations for international students: Required—TOEFL (minimum score 600 paper-based; 94 iBT). *Application deadline:* For fall admission, 8/1 for domestic and international students; for winter admission, 11/1 for domestic and international students; for spring admission, 2/1 for domestic and international students; for summer admission, 5/1 for domestic and international students. Applications are processed on a rolling basis. Application fee: $50. Electronic applications accepted. *Expenses:* Contact institution. *Financial support:* In 2013–14, 65 students received support. Scholarships/grants available. Financial award applicants required to submit FAFSA. *Unit head:* Dr. Jose Cordova, Program Director, 802-485-2567, Fax: 802-485-2533, E-mail: jcordova@norwich.edu. *Application contact:* Ashley Farren, Associate Program Director, 802-485-2748, Fax: 802-485-2533, E-mail: afarren@norwich.edu.
Website: http://online.norwich.edu/degree-programs/masters/master-business-administration/overview.

Notre Dame de Namur University, Division of Academic Affairs, School of Business and Management, Program in Business Administration, Belmont, CA 94002-1908. Offers business administration (MBA); entrepreneurship (MBA); finance (MBA); human resource management (MBA); marketing (MBA); media and promotion (MBA); technology and operations management (MBA). *Accreditation:* ACBSP. Part-time and evening/weekend programs available. *Entrance requirements:* For master's, minimum GPA of 2.5. Additional exam requirements/recommendations for international students: Required—TOEFL (minimum score 550 paper-based; 79 iBT). Electronic applications accepted.

Notre Dame de Namur University, Division of Academic Affairs, School of Business and Management, Program in Systems Management, Belmont, CA 94002-1908. Offers MSM. Part-time and evening/weekend programs available. Postbaccalaureate distance learning degree programs offered (no on-campus study). *Entrance requirements:* For master's, minimum GPA of 2.5. Additional exam requirements/recommendations for international students: Required—TOEFL (minimum score 550 paper-based; 79 iBT). Electronic applications accepted.

Notre Dame of Maryland University, Graduate Studies, Program in Management, Baltimore, MD 21210-2476. Offers MA. Part-time and evening/weekend programs available. *Degree requirements:* For master's, thesis optional. *Entrance requirements:* For master's, minimum GPA of 3.0. Additional exam requirements/recommendations for international students: Required—TOEFL (minimum score 500 paper-based; 61 iBT). Electronic applications accepted.

Nova Southeastern University, H. Wayne Huizenga School of Business and Entrepreneurship, Fort Lauderdale, FL 33314-7796. Offers accounting (M Acc); business administration (MBA, DBA); human resource management (MSHRM); international business administration (MIBA); leadership (MS); public administration (MPA, DPA); real estate development (MS); taxation (M Tax); JD/MBA; Pharm D/MBA. Part-time and evening/weekend programs available. Postbaccalaureate distance learning degree programs offered (minimal on-campus study). *Faculty:* 67 full-time (24 women), 135 part-time/adjunct (37 women). *Students:* 207 full-time (110 women), 3,069 part-time (1,888 women); includes 2,213 minority (1,077 Black or African American, non-Hispanic/Latino; 2 American Indian or Alaska Native, non-Hispanic/Latino; 108 Asian, non-Hispanic/Latino; 975 Hispanic/Latino; 2 Native Hawaiian or other Pacific Islander, non-Hispanic/Latino; 49 Two or more races, non-Hispanic/Latino), 190 international. Average age 33. 1,291 applicants, 68% accepted, 636 enrolled. In 2013, 1,146 master's, 17 doctorates awarded. *Degree requirements:* For master's, thesis optional; for doctorate, comprehensive exam, thesis/dissertation. *Entrance requirements:* For doctorate, GMAT. Additional exam requirements/recommendations for international students: Required—TOEFL (minimum score 550 paper-based; 79 iBT), IELTS (minimum score 6). *Application deadline:* Applications are processed on a rolling basis. Application fee: $50. Electronic applications accepted. *Financial support:* In 2013–14, 2 students received support. Federal Work-Study and scholarships/grants available. Support available to part-time students. Financial award applicants required to submit FAFSA. *Faculty research:* Reputation management, call centers, international social capital, corporate earnings guidance, corporate governance. *Unit head:* Dr. J. Preston Jones, Dean, 954-262-5127, E-mail: fieldsm@nova.edu. *Application contact:* Karen Goldberg, Associate Director of Recruitment and Special Events, 954-262-5039, Fax: 954-262-3822, E-mail: karen@nova.edu.
Website: http://www.huizenga.nova.edu.

Nyack College, School of Business and Leadership, Nyack, NY 10960-3698. Offers business administration (MBA); organizational leadership (MS). Evening/weekend programs available. Postbaccalaureate distance learning degree programs offered (no on-campus study). *Students:* 75 full-time (40 women), 53 part-time (29 women); includes 95 minority (65 Black or African American, non-Hispanic/Latino; 1 American Indian or Alaska Native, non-Hispanic/Latino; 2 Asian, non-Hispanic/Latino; 24 Hispanic/Latino; 3 Two or more races, non-Hispanic/Latino), 13 international. Average age 35. In 2013, 95 master's awarded. *Degree requirements:* For master's, thesis (for some programs). *Entrance requirements:* For master's, GMAT (for MBA only), transcripts, personal goals statement, recommendations, resume, interview. Additional exam requirements/recommendations for international students: Required—TOEFL (minimum score 550 paper-based; 83 iBT). *Application deadline:* Applications are processed on a rolling basis. Application fee: $50. Electronic applications accepted. *Expenses:* Contact institution. *Financial support:* Applicants required to submit FAFSA. *Unit head:* Dr. Anita Underwood, Dean, 845-675-4511, Fax: 845-353-5812. *Application contact:* Traci Piescki, Director of Admissions, 800-541-6891, Fax: 845-348-3912, E-mail: admissions.grad@nyack.edu.
Website: http://www.nyack.edu/sbl.

Oakland City University, School of Adult and Extended Learning, Oakland City, IN 47660-1099. Offers MBA. Part-time and evening/weekend programs available. *Degree requirements:* For master's, thesis or alternative. *Entrance requirements:* For master's, GMAT, GRE, or MAT, appropriate bachelor's degree, computer literacy. Additional exam requirements/recommendations for international students: Required—TOEFL. *Faculty research:* Leadership and management styles, international business, new technologies.

Oakland University, Graduate Study and Lifelong Learning, School of Business Administration, Rochester, MI 48309-4401. Offers M Acc, MBA, MS, Certificate. *Accreditation:* AACSB. Part-time and evening/weekend programs available. *Faculty:* 35 full-time (11 women), 11 part-time/adjunct (2 women). *Students:* 130 full-time (56 women), 286 part-time (91 women); includes 68 minority (21 Black or African American, non-Hispanic/Latino; 2 American Indian or Alaska Native, non-Hispanic/Latino; 36 Asian, non-Hispanic/Latino; 8 Hispanic/Latino; 1 Two or more races, non-Hispanic/Latino), 45 international. Average age 31. 367 applicants, 41% accepted, 138 enrolled. In 2013, 187 master's, 9 other advanced degrees awarded. *Entrance requirements:* For master's, GMAT, minimum GPA of 3.0 for unconditional admission. Additional exam requirements/recommendations for international students: Required—TOEFL (minimum score 550 paper-based). *Application deadline:* For fall admission, 8/15 priority date for domestic students, 5/1 priority date for international students; for winter admission, 12/1 priority date for domestic students, 9/1 priority date for international students; for spring admission, 4/15 priority date for domestic students. Applications are processed on a rolling basis. Application fee: $35. Electronic applications accepted. *Expenses:* Contact institution. *Financial support:* Career-related internships or fieldwork, Federal Work-Study, institutionally sponsored loans, and tuition waivers (full) available. Financial award application deadline: 3/1; financial award applicants required to submit FAFSA. *Unit head:* Dr. Jonathan Silberman, Dean, 248-370-3286, Fax: 248-370-4974. *Application contact:* Donna Free, Coordinator, 248-370-3281.
Website: http://www.sba.oakland.edu/grad/.

Oglala Lakota College, Graduate Studies, Program in Lakota Leadership and Management, Kyle, SD 57752-0490. Offers MA. Part-time and evening/weekend programs available. *Degree requirements:* For master's, thesis. *Entrance requirements:* For master's, minimum GPA of 2.5. *Faculty research:* Curriculum, values, retention of administrators, behavior, graduate follow-up.

Ohio Dominican University, Graduate Programs, Division of Business, Columbus, OH 43219-2099. Offers accounting (MBA); business administration (MBA); finance (MBA); leadership (MBA); public administration (MBA). *Accreditation:* ACBSP. Part-time and evening/weekend programs available. Postbaccalaureate distance learning degree programs offered (no on-campus study). *Degree requirements:* For master's, thesis or alternative. *Entrance requirements:* For master's, minimum GPA of 3.0, 3 letters of recommendation. Additional exam requirements/recommendations for international students: Required—TOEFL (minimum score 550 paper-based), IELTS (minimum score 6.5).

The Ohio State University, Graduate School, Max M. Fisher College of Business, Program in Business Administration, Columbus, OH 43210. Offers MA, MBA, PhD. *Accreditation:* AACSB. *Students:* 399 full-time (120 women), 187 part-time (55 women); includes 96 minority (21 Black or African American, non-Hispanic/Latino; 55 Asian, non-Hispanic/Latino; 15 Hispanic/Latino; 5 Two or more races, non-Hispanic/Latino), 123 international. Average age 31. In 2013, 272 master's, 7 doctorates awarded. *Degree requirements:* For doctorate, thesis/dissertation. *Entrance requirements:* For master's and doctorate, GMAT. Additional exam requirements/recommendations for international students: Required—TOEFL (minimum score 600 paper-based; 100 iBT), Michigan English Language Assessment Battery (minimum score 86); Recommended—IELTS (minimum score 7). *Application deadline:* For fall admission, 10/15 priority date for domestic and international students; for winter admission, 12/1 for domestic students, 11/1 for international students; for spring admission, 3/1 for domestic students, 2/1 for international students. Applications are processed on a rolling basis. Application fee: $60 ($70 for international students). Electronic applications accepted. *Financial support:* Fellowships, research assistantships, teaching assistantships, Federal Work-Study, institutionally sponsored loans, and unspecified assistantships available. Support available to part-time students. *Unit head:* Karen Wruck, Associate Dean for Graduate Programs, 614-688-5543, Fax: 614-292-9006, E-mail: wruck.1@osu.edu. *Application contact:* Graduate Admissions, 614-292-6031, Fax: 614-292-3656, E-mail: gradadmissions@osu.edu.
Website: http://fisher.osu.edu/ftmba.

The Ohio State University, Graduate School, Max M. Fisher College of Business, Program in Business Logistics Engineering, Columbus, OH 43210. Offers MBLE. *Students:* 75 full-time (49 women); includes 1 minority (Asian, non-Hispanic/Latino), 73 international. Average age 23. In 2013, 38 master's awarded. *Entrance requirements:* For master's, GRE or GMAT. Additional exam requirements/recommendations for international students: Required—TOEFL (minimum score 550 paper-based; 79 iBT), Michigan English Language Assessment Battery (minimum score 82); Recommended—IELTS (minimum score 7). *Application deadline:* For fall admission, 7/15 for domestic students, 5/1 for international students; for spring admission, 5/15 for domestic students, 4/1 for international students. Applications are processed on a rolling basis. Application fee: $60 ($70 for international students). Electronic applications accepted. *Unit head:* Walter Zinn, Chair, 614-292-0797, E-mail: zinn.13@osu.edu. *Application contact:* Graduate Admissions, 614-292-6031, Fax: 614-292-3656, E-mail: gradadmissions@osu.edu.
Website: http://fisher.osu.edu/mble.

Ohio University, Graduate College, College of Business, Program in Business Administration, Athens, OH 45701-2979. Offers executive management (MBA); finance (MBA); healthcare (MBA). *Accreditation:* AACSB. Part-time and evening/weekend programs available. Postbaccalaureate distance learning degree programs offered (minimal on-campus study). *Entrance requirements:* For master's, minimum GPA of 3.0. Additional exam requirements/recommendations for international students: Required—TOEFL (minimum score 600 paper-based). Electronic applications accepted. *Expenses:* Contact institution.

Oklahoma Baptist University, Program in Business Administration, Shawnee, OK 74804. Offers business administration (MBA); energy management (MBA). *Accreditation:* ACBSP. Postbaccalaureate distance learning degree programs offered (no on-campus study).

Oklahoma Christian University, Graduate School of Business, Oklahoma City, OK 73136-1100. Offers accounting (MBA); electronic business (MBA); financial services (MBA); health services management (MBA); human resources (MBA); international business (MBA); leadership and organizational development (MBA); marketing (MBA); project management (MBA). Postbaccalaureate distance learning degree programs offered (no on-campus study). *Entrance requirements:* For master's, bachelor's degree. Electronic applications accepted.

Oklahoma City University, Meinders School of Business, Program in Business Administration, Oklahoma City, OK 73106-1402. Offers accounting (MBA); finance (MBA); general (MBA); marketing (MBA); JD/MBA; MSN/MBA. *Accreditation:* ACBSP. Part-time and evening/weekend programs available. *Students:* 82 full-time (39 women), 101 part-time (41 women); includes 18 minority (7 Black or African American, non-Hispanic/Latino; 6 American Indian or Alaska Native, non-Hispanic/Latino; 3 Asian, non-Hispanic/Latino; 2 Two or more races, non-Hispanic/Latino), 50 international. Average age 31. 109 applicants, 61% accepted, 19 enrolled. In 2013, 114 master's awarded. *Degree requirements:* For master's, comprehensive exam. *Entrance requirements:* For master's, GRE or GMAT, bachelor's degree from accredited institution, minimum GPA of 3.0, essay, recommendation letters. Additional exam requirements/recommendations for international students: Required—TOEFL (minimum score 550 paper-based; 80 iBT). *Application deadline:* Applications are processed on a rolling basis. Application fee: $50. Electronic applications accepted. *Expenses: Tuition:* Full-time $16,848; part-time $936 per credit hour. Tuition and fees vary according to course load, degree level and program. *Financial support:* Career-related internships or fieldwork, Federal Work-Study, institutionally sponsored loans, scholarships/grants, and tuition waivers (partial) available. Support available to part-time students. Financial award application deadline: 6/1; financial award applicants required to submit FAFSA. *Faculty research:* Management information systems, international business strategies. *Unit head:* Dr. Steve Agee, Dean, 405-208-5130, Fax: 405-208-5098, E-mail: sagee@okcu.edu. *Application contact:* Heidi Puckett, Director of Graduate Admissions, 800-633-7242, Fax: 405-208-5916, E-mail: gadmissions@okcu.edu.
Website: http://msb.okcu.edu/graduate/.

Oklahoma City University, Petree College of Arts and Sciences, Program in Liberal Arts, Oklahoma City, OK 73106-1402. Offers general studies (MLA); leadership/management (MLA). Part-time and evening/weekend programs available. *Students:* 29 full-time (26 women), 8 part-time (6 women); includes 11 minority (5 Black or African American, non-Hispanic/Latino; 3 American Indian or Alaska Native, non-Hispanic/Latino; 3 Hispanic/Latino), 20 international. Average age 32. 20 applicants, 50% accepted, 2 enrolled. In 2013, 8 master's awarded. *Degree requirements:* For master's, comprehensive exam, thesis optional. *Entrance requirements:* For master's, bachelor's degree from accredited institution, minimum GPA of 3.0, essay, recommendation letters. Additional exam requirements/recommendations for international students: Required—TOEFL (minimum score 550 paper-based; 80 iBT). *Application deadline:* Applications are processed on a rolling basis. Application fee: $50. Electronic applications accepted. *Expenses: Tuition:* Full-time $16,848; part-time $936 per credit hour. Tuition and fees vary according to course load, degree level and program. *Financial support:* Career-related internships or fieldwork, Federal Work-Study, institutionally sponsored loans, scholarships/grants, and tuition waivers available. Support available to part-time students. Financial award application deadline: 6/1; financial award applicants required to submit FAFSA. *Unit head:* Dr. Regina Bennett, Director, 405-208-5178, Fax: 405-208-5451, E-mail: rbennett@okcu.edu. *Application contact:* Heidi Puckett, Director, Admissions, 800-633-7242, Fax: 405-208-5916, E-mail: gadmissions@okcu.edu.
Website: http://www.okcu.edu/mla.

Oklahoma State University, Spears School of Business, Department of Management, Stillwater, OK 74078. Offers MBA, MS, PhD. Part-time programs available. *Faculty:* 24 full-time (9 women), 12 part-time/adjunct (7 women). *Students:* 3 full-time (1 woman), 8 part-time (2 women); includes 1 minority (Asian, non-Hispanic/Latino), 3 international. Average age 32. 32 applicants, 6% accepted, 1 enrolled. In 2013, 2 doctorates awarded. *Degree requirements:* For master's, thesis or alternative; for doctorate, comprehensive exam, thesis/dissertation. *Entrance requirements:* For master's and doctorate, GRE or GMAT. Additional exam requirements/recommendations for international students: Required—TOEFL (minimum score 550 paper-based; 79 iBT). *Application deadline:* For fall admission, 3/1 priority date for international students; for spring admission, 8/1 priority date for international students. Applications are processed on a rolling basis. Application fee: $40 ($75 for international students). Electronic applications accepted. *Expenses:* Tuition, state resident: full-time $4272; part-time $178 per credit hour. Tuition, nonresident: full-time $17,472; part-time $709 per credit hour. *Required fees:* $2413.20; $100.55 per credit hour. One-time fee: $50 full-time. Part-time tuition and fees vary according to course load and campus/location. *Financial support:* In 2013–14, 11 research assistantships (averaging $13,540 per year), 6 teaching assistantships (averaging $15,418 per year) were awarded; career-related internships or fieldwork, Federal Work-Study, scholarships/grants, health care benefits, tuition waivers (partial), and unspecified assistantships also available. Support available to part-time students. Financial award application deadline: 3/1; financial award applicants required to submit FAFSA. *Faculty research:* Telecommunications management, innovative decision support techniques, knowledge networking, organizational research methods, strategic planning. *Unit head:* Dr. James Pappas, Department Head, 405-744-5201, Fax: 405-744-5180, E-mail: james.pappas@okstate.edu. *Application contact:* Dr. Rebecca Greenbaum, PhD Coordinator, 405-744-8655, Fax: 405-744-5180, E-mail: rebecca.greenbaum@okstate.edu.
Website: http://spears.okstate.edu/management.

Old Dominion University, College of Business and Public Administration, Doctoral Program in Business Administration, Norfolk, VA 23529. Offers finance (PhD); information technology (PhD); marketing (PhD); strategic management (PhD). *Accreditation:* AACSB. *Faculty:* 29 full-time (6 women). *Students:* 29 full-time (8 women), 29 part-time (13 women); includes 3 minority (1 Black or African American, non-Hispanic/Latino; 1 Asian, non-Hispanic/Latino; 1 Native Hawaiian or other Pacific Islander, non-Hispanic/Latino), 41 international. Average age 33. 77 applicants, 35% accepted, 12 enrolled. In 2013, 8 doctorates awarded. *Degree requirements:* For doctorate, comprehensive exam, thesis/dissertation. *Entrance requirements:* For doctorate, GMAT. Additional exam requirements/recommendations for international students: Required—TOEFL (minimum score 550 paper-based; 79 iBT). *Application deadline:* For fall admission, 3/1 priority date for domestic and international students. Application fee: $50. Electronic applications accepted. *Expenses:* Tuition, state resident: full-time $9888; part-time $412 per credit. Tuition, nonresident: full-time $25,152; part-time $1048 per credit. *Required fees:* $59 per semester. One-time fee: $50. *Financial support:* In 2013–14, 27 students received support, including 14 fellowships with full tuition reimbursements available (averaging $7,500 per year), 24 research assistantships with full tuition reimbursements available (averaging $7,500 per year), 16 teaching assistantships with full tuition reimbursements available (averaging $7,500 per year); scholarships/grants and unspecified assistantships also available. Financial award application deadline: 3/1; financial award applicants required to submit FAFSA. *Faculty research:* International business, buyer behavior, financial markets, strategy, operations research. *Unit head:* Dr. John B. Ford, Graduate Program Director, 757-683-3587, Fax: 757-683-4076, E-mail: jbford@odu.edu. *Application contact:* Katrina Davenport, Program Coordinator, 757-683-5138, Fax: 757-683-4076, E-mail: kdavenpo@odu.edu.
Website: http://bpa.odu.edu/bpa/academics/baphd.shtml.

Old Dominion University, College of Business and Public Administration, MBA Program, Norfolk, VA 23529. Offers business and economic forecasting (MBA); financial analysis and valuation (MBA); health sciences administration (MBA); information technology and enterprise integration (MBA); international business (MBA); maritime and port management (MBA); public administration (MBA). *Accreditation:* AACSB. Part-time and evening/weekend programs available. Postbaccalaureate distance learning degree programs offered (no on-campus study). *Faculty:* 83 full-time (19 women), 5 part-time/adjunct (2 women). *Students:* 42 full-time (20 women), 103 part-time (42 women); includes 18 minority (8 Black or African American, non-Hispanic/Latino; 4 Asian, non-Hispanic/Latino; 1 Hispanic/Latino; 1 Native Hawaiian or other Pacific Islander, non-Hispanic/Latino; 4 Two or more races, non-Hispanic/Latino), 16 international. Average age 30. 161 applicants, 71% accepted, 75 enrolled. In 2013, 61 master's awarded. *Entrance requirements:* For master's, GMAT, GRE, letter of reference, resume, essay. Additional exam requirements/recommendations for international students: Required—TOEFL (minimum score 550 paper-based; 80 iBT). *Application deadline:* For fall admission, 6/1 priority date for domestic students, 4/15 priority date for international students; for spring admission, 11/1 priority date for domestic students, 10/1 priority date for international students. Applications are processed on a rolling basis. Application fee: $50. Electronic applications accepted. *Expenses:* Tuition, state resident: full-time $9888; part-time $412 per credit. Tuition, nonresident: full-time $25,152; part-time $1048 per credit. *Required fees:* $59 per semester. One-time fee: $50. *Financial support:* In 2013–14, 47 students received support, including 94 research assistantships with partial tuition reimbursements available (averaging $8,900 per year); career-related internships or fieldwork, scholarships/grants, and unspecified assistantships also available. Support available to part-time students. Financial award application deadline: 2/15; financial award applicants required to submit FAFSA. *Faculty research:* International business, buyer behavior, financial markets, strategy, operations research, maritime and transportation economics. *Unit head:* Dr. Kiran Karaude, Graduate Program Director, 757-683-3585, Fax: 757-683-5750, E-mail: mbainfo@odu.edu. *Application contact:* Sandi Phillips, MBA Program Assistant, 757-683-3585, Fax: 757-683-5750, E-mail: mbainfo@odu.edu.
Website: http://www.odu.edu/mba/.

Olivet Nazarene University, Graduate School, Department of Business, Bourbonnais, IL 60914. Offers business administration (MBA). Evening/weekend programs available. *Degree requirements:* For master's, thesis or alternative. *Expenses:* Contact institution.

Oral Roberts University, School of Business, Tulsa, OK 74171. Offers accounting (MBA); entrepreneurship (MBA); finance (MBA); international business (MBA); management (MBA); marketing (MBA); non-profit management (MBA); not for profit management (MNM). *Accreditation:* ACBSP. Part-time programs available. Postbaccalaureate distance learning degree programs offered (minimal on-campus study). *Degree requirements:* For master's, thesis optional. *Entrance requirements:* For master's, minimum cumulative GPA of 3.0. Additional exam requirements/recommendations for international students: Required—TOEFL (minimum score 550 paper-based; 79 iBT). Electronic applications accepted. *Faculty research:* Social media, international business and marketing.

Oregon State University, College of Business, Corvallis, OR 97331. Offers MA, MAIS, MBA, MS, PhD. *Accreditation:* AACSB. Part-time programs available. Postbaccalaureate distance learning degree programs offered (minimal on-campus study). *Faculty:* 40 full-time (19 women), 2 part-time/adjunct (1 woman). *Students:* 186 full-time (89 women), 54 part-time (27 women); includes 23 minority (1 Black or African American, non-Hispanic/Latino; 14 Asian, non-Hispanic/Latino; 3 Hispanic/Latino; 1 Native Hawaiian or other Pacific Islander, non-Hispanic/Latino; 4 Two or more races, non-Hispanic/Latino), 114 international. Average age 29. 228 applicants, 60% accepted, 115 enrolled. In 2013, 75 master's, 4 doctorates awarded. *Degree requirements:* For master's, portfolio. *Application deadline:* For fall admission, 3/15 for domestic students. Application fee: $60. *Expenses:* Tuition, state resident: full-time $11,664; part-time $432 per credit hour. Tuition, nonresident: full-time $19,197; part-time $711 per credit hour. *Required fees:* $1446; $443 per quarter. One-time fee: $300. Tuition and fees vary according to course load and program. *Financial support:* Fellowships, teaching assistantships, career-related internships or fieldwork, Federal Work-Study, and institutionally sponsored loans available. Financial award application deadline: 2/1. *Faculty research:* Financial and account services, market analysis and planning, innovation, family business, tourism. *Unit head:* Dr. Ilene K. Kleinsorge, Dean, 541-737-6024, Fax: 541-737-3033, E-mail: ilene@bus.oregonstate.edu. *Application contact:* Dr. Jim Coakley, Associate Dean for Academic Programs, 541-737-5510, E-mail: jim.coakley@bus.oregonstate.edu.
Website: http://business.oregonstate.edu/.

Ottawa University, Graduate Studies-Arizona, Programs in Business, Ottawa, KS 66067-3399. Offers business administration (MBA); finance (MBA); human resources (MA, MBA); leadership (MBA); marketing (MBA). Programs offered in Mesa, Phoenix, Tempe and West Valley, AZ. Part-time and evening/weekend programs available. Postbaccalaureate distance learning degree programs offered. *Degree requirements:* For master's, thesis or alternative. *Entrance requirements:* For master's, minimum undergraduate GPA of 3.0. Additional exam requirements/recommendations for international students: Required—TOEFL (minimum score 550 paper-based). Electronic applications accepted.

Ottawa University, Graduate Studies-International, Ottawa, KS 66067-3399. Offers business administration (MBA). Postbaccalaureate distance learning degree programs offered (minimal on-campus study). *Degree requirements:* For master's, thesis or alternative. *Entrance requirements:* For master's, minimum undergraduate GPA of 3.0. Additional exam requirements/recommendations for international students: Required—TOEFL (minimum score 550 paper-based). Electronic applications accepted. *Expenses:* Contact institution.

Ottawa University, Graduate Studies-Kansas City, Overland Park, KS 66211. Offers business administration (MBA); human resources (MA). Part-time and evening/weekend programs available. Postbaccalaureate distance learning degree programs offered (minimal on-campus study). *Degree requirements:* For master's, thesis or alternative.

Entrance requirements: For master's, resume, 3 letters of recommendation. Additional exam requirements/recommendations for international students: Required—TOEFL (minimum score 550 paper-based). Electronic applications accepted. *Expenses:* Contact institution.

Ottawa University, Graduate Studies-Wisconsin, Brookfield, WI 53005. Offers business administration (MBA). Part-time and evening/weekend programs available. Postbaccalaureate distance learning degree programs offered. *Degree requirements:* For master's, thesis or alternative. *Entrance requirements:* For master's, resume, 3 letters of recommendation. Additional exam requirements/recommendations for international students: Required—TOEFL (minimum score 550 paper-based). Electronic applications accepted.

Otterbein University, Department of Business, Accounting and Economics, Westerville, OH 43081. Offers MBA. Part-time and evening/weekend programs available. *Degree requirements:* For master's, consulting project team. *Entrance requirements:* For master's, GMAT, 2 reference forms, resume. Additional exam requirements/recommendations for international students: Required—TOEFL (minimum score 550 paper-based; 79 iBT). *Expenses:* Contact institution. *Faculty research:* Organizational design, dispute resolution international trade, developing economies, marketing consumer goods, human resources development.

Our Lady of the Lake University of San Antonio, School of Business and Leadership, Program in Management, San Antonio, TX 78207-4689. Offers business administration (MBA); management (MBA). Part-time and evening/weekend programs available. Postbaccalaureate distance learning degree programs offered (minimal on-campus study). *Faculty:* 8 full-time (0 women), 5 part-time/adjunct (0 women). *Students:* 24 full-time (17 women), 1 (woman) part-time; includes 16 minority (2 Black or African American, non-Hispanic/Latino; 13 Hispanic/Latino; 1 Native Hawaiian or other Pacific Islander, non-Hispanic/Latino). Average age 36. 102 applicants, 80% accepted, 42 enrolled. In 2013, 53 master's awarded. *Entrance requirements:* For master's, GMAT, GRE General Test, or MAT. Additional exam requirements/recommendations for international students: Required—TOEFL. *Application deadline:* Applications are processed on a rolling basis. Application fee: $25 ($50 for international students). Electronic applications accepted. *Expenses: Tuition:* Full-time $9120; part-time $760 per credit. *Required fees:* $698; $334 per trimester. Tuition and fees vary according to course load, degree level, campus/location and program. *Financial support:* Fellowships, career-related internships or fieldwork, Federal Work-Study, institutionally sponsored loans, scholarships/grants, and tuition waivers (partial) available. Support available to part-time students. Financial award application deadline: 4/15. *Faculty research:* Decision-making and problem-solving behavior for professional administrators, integrating scientific and technological advances with proven principles of management. *Unit head:* Dr. Robert Bisking, Dean, 210-434-6711, E-mail: kmwinney@lake.ollusa.edu. *Application contact:* Graduate Admission, 210-431-3961, Fax: 210-431-4013, E-mail: gradadm@ollusa.edu.
Website: http://www.ollusa.edu/s/1190/ollu-3-column-noads.aspx?sid=1190&gid=1&pgid=1704.

Pace University, Lubin School of Business, New York, NY 10038. Offers MBA, MS, DPS, APC. *Accreditation:* AACSB. Part-time and evening/weekend programs available. Postbaccalaureate distance learning degree programs offered (minimal on-campus study). *Students:* 234 full-time (116 women), 1,046 part-time (550 women); includes 248 minority (77 Black or African American, non-Hispanic/Latino; 2 American Indian or Alaska Native, non-Hispanic/Latino; 130 Asian, non-Hispanic/Latino; 33 Hispanic/Latino; 6 Two or more races, non-Hispanic/Latino), 629 international. Average age 28. 1,621 applicants, 38% accepted, 400 enrolled. In 2013, 439 master's, 8 doctorates, 1 other advanced degree awarded. *Degree requirements:* For doctorate, thesis/dissertation, oral and written exams. *Entrance requirements:* For master's, GMAT, GRE; for doctorate, GMAT, MBA or master's in business program, 10 years of experience, interview; for APC, MBA or master's in business program, relevant professional experience. Additional exam requirements/recommendations for international students: Required—TOEFL. *Application deadline:* For fall admission, 8/1 priority date for domestic students, 6/1 for international students; for spring admission, 12/1 priority date for domestic students, 10/1 for international students. Applications are processed on a rolling basis. Application fee: $70. Electronic applications accepted. *Expenses:* Contact institution. *Financial support:* Research assistantships, career-related internships or fieldwork, Federal Work-Study, and tuition waivers (full and partial) available. Support available to part-time students. Financial award applicants required to submit FAFSA. *Faculty research:* Accounting standards and reporting, financial markets and instruments, strategy and entrepreneurship, management learning, marketing and customers. *Unit head:* Neil S. Braun, Dean, Lubin School of Business, 212-618-6600, E-mail: nbraun@pace.edu. *Application contact:* Susan Ford-Goldschein, Director of Graduate Admissions, 212-346-1531, Fax: 212-346-1585, E-mail: gradnyc@pace.edu.
Website: http://www.pace.edu/lubin.

Pacific Lutheran University, Graduate Programs and Continuing Education, School of Business, Tacoma, WA 98447. Offers business administration (MBA), including technology and innovation management; finance (MSF). *Accreditation:* AACSB. Part-time and evening/weekend programs available. *Faculty:* 13 full-time (6 women), 1 part-time/adjunct (0 women). *Students:* 27 full-time (5 women), 25 part-time (10 women); includes 11 minority (1 Black or African American, non-Hispanic/Latino; 3 Asian, non-Hispanic/Latino; 4 Hispanic/Latino; 3 Two or more races, non-Hispanic/Latino), 4 international. Average age 34. 37 applicants, 62% accepted, 19 enrolled. In 2013, 27 master's awarded. *Entrance requirements:* For master's, GMAT or GRE. Additional exam requirements/recommendations for international students: Required—TOEFL (minimum score 550 paper-based; 88 iBT). *Application deadline:* Applications are processed on a rolling basis. Application fee: $40. Electronic applications accepted. *Expenses: Tuition:* Full-time $18,560; part-time $1160. Tuition and fees vary according to program and student level. *Financial support:* In 2013–14, 15 students received support. Fellowships, career-related internships or fieldwork, Federal Work-Study, scholarships/grants, and unspecified assistantships available. Financial award application deadline: 3/1. *Unit head:* Dr. Nancy Albers-Miller, Dean, School of Business, 253-535-7251, Fax: 253-535-8723, E-mail: plumba@plu.edu. *Application contact:* Theresa Ramos, Director, MBA Program, 253-535-7330, Fax: 253-535-8723, E-mail: plumba@plu.edu.
Website: http://www.plu.edu/mba/.

Pacific States University, College of Business, Los Angeles, CA 90006. Offers accounting (MBA); finance (MBA); international business (MBA, DBA); management of information technology (MBA); real estate management (MBA). Part-time and evening/weekend programs available. Postbaccalaureate distance learning degree programs offered (no on-campus study). *Degree requirements:* For doctorate, comprehensive exam, thesis/dissertation. *Entrance requirements:* For master's, minimum undergraduate GPA of 2.5 during last 90 hours of course work. Additional exam requirements/recommendations for international students: Required—TOEFL (minimum score 500 paper-based; 61 iBT), IELTS (minimum score 5.5).

Palm Beach Atlantic University, Rinker School of Business, West Palm Beach, FL 33416-4708. Offers MBA. Part-time and evening/weekend programs available. *Faculty:* 1 full-time (0 women), 9 part-time/adjunct (2 women). *Students:* 45 full-time (27 women), 60 part-time (29 women); includes 41 minority (26 Black or African American, non-Hispanic/Latino; 5 Asian, non-Hispanic/Latino; 8 Hispanic/Latino; 2 Two or more races, non-Hispanic/Latino), 16 international. Average age 31. 48 applicants, 94% accepted, 35 enrolled. In 2013, 49 master's awarded. *Entrance requirements:* For master's, minimum GPA of 3.0. Additional exam requirements/recommendations for international students: Required—TOEFL (minimum score 550 paper-based; 79 iBT). *Application deadline:* For fall admission, 7/15 priority date for domestic students; for spring admission, 11/15 priority date for domestic students. Applications are processed on a rolling basis. Application fee: $45. Electronic applications accepted. *Expenses: Tuition:* Part-time $495 per credit hour. *Required fees:* $495 per credit hour. Part-time tuition and fees vary according to course load and program. *Financial support:* Application deadline: 5/1; applicants required to submit FAFSA. *Unit head:* Dr. Edgar Langlois, MBA Program Director, 561-803-2456, E-mail: edgar_langlois@pba.edu. *Application contact:* Graduate Admissions, 888-468-6722, Fax: 561-803-2115, E-mail: grad@pba.edu.
Website: http://www.pba.edu/bus-mba.

Park University, School of Graduate and Professional Studies, Kansas City, MO 54105. Offers adult education (M Ed); business and government leadership (Graduate Certificate); business, government, and global society (MPA); communication and leadership (MA); creative and life writing (Graduate Certificate); disaster and emergency management (MPA, Graduate Certificate); educational leadership (M Ed); finance (MBA, Graduate Certificate); general business (MBA); global business (Graduate Certificate); healthcare administration (MHA); healthcare services management and leadership (Graduate Certificate); international business (MBA); language and literacy (M Ed), including English for speakers of other languages, special reading teacher/literacy coach; leadership of international healthcare organizations (Graduate Certificate); management information systems (MBA, Graduate Certificate); music performance (ADP, Graduate Certificate), including cello (MM, ADP), piano (MM, ADP), viola (MM, ADP), violin (MM, ADP); nonprofit and community services management (MPA); nonprofit leadership (Graduate Certificate); performance (MM), including cello (MM, ADP), piano (MM, ADP), viola (MM, ADP), violin (MM, ADP); public management (MPA); social work (MSW); teacher leadership (M Ed), including curriculum and assessment, instructional leader. Part-time and evening/weekend programs available. Postbaccalaureate distance learning degree programs offered (no on-campus study). *Students:* 862 full-time (482 women); includes 55 minority (30 Black or African American, non-Hispanic/Latino; 2 American Indian or Alaska Native, non-Hispanic/Latino; 4 Asian, non-Hispanic/Latino; 14 Hispanic/Latino; 5 Two or more races, non-Hispanic/Latino), 141 international. Average age 34. 497 applicants, 62% accepted, 119 enrolled. In 2013, 281 master's, 14 other advanced degrees awarded. *Degree requirements:* For master's, comprehensive exam (for some programs), thesis (for some programs), internship (for some programs); exam (for some programs). *Entrance requirements:* For master's, GRE or GMAT (for some programs), teacher certification (for some M Ed programs), letters of recommendation, essay, resume (for some programs). Additional exam requirements/recommendations for international students: Required—TOEFL (minimum score 550 paper-based; 79 iBT), IELTS (minimum score 6). *Application deadline:* For fall admission, 8/1 priority date for domestic students, 7/15 priority date for international students; for spring admission, 1/1 priority date for domestic students, 11/1 priority date for international students. Applications are processed on a rolling basis. Application fee: $50 ($100 for international students). Electronic applications accepted. *Financial support:* In 2013–14, 2 research assistantships with full tuition reimbursements (averaging $15,760 per year) were awarded. Financial award applicants required to submit FAFSA. *Unit head:* Dr. Laurie Dipadova-Stocks, Dean of Graduate and Professional Studies, 816-559-5624, Fax: 816-472-1173, E-mail: ldipadovastocks@park.edu. *Application contact:* Judith Appollis, Director of Graduate Admissions and Internationalization, School of Graduate and Professional Studies, 816-559-5627, Fax: 816-472-1173, E-mail: gradschool@park.edu.
Website: http://www.park.edu/grad.

Penn State Erie, The Behrend College, Graduate School, Erie, PA 16563-0001. Offers business administration (MBA); project management (MPM); quality and manufacturing management (MMM). *Accreditation:* AACSB. Part-time programs available. *Students:* 31 full-time (10 women), 83 part-time (23 women); includes 8 minority (2 Black or African American, non-Hispanic/Latino; 3 Asian, non-Hispanic/Latino; 3 Hispanic/Latino), 3 international. Average age 29. 71 applicants, 79% accepted, 45 enrolled. In 2013, 52 master's awarded. *Entrance requirements:* Additional exam requirements/recommendations for international students: Required—TOEFL (minimum score 550 paper-based; 80 iBT). *Application deadline:* Applications are processed on a rolling basis. Application fee: $65. Electronic applications accepted. *Financial support:* Federal Work-Study available. Financial award application deadline: 2/15; financial award applicants required to submit FAFSA. *Unit head:* Dr. Donald L. Birx, Chancellor, 814-898-6160, Fax: 814-898-6461, E-mail: dlb69@psu.edu. *Application contact:* Ann M. Burbules, Assistant Director, Graduate Admissions, 866-374-3378, Fax: 814-898-6053, E-mail: psbehrendmba@psu.edu.
Website: http://psbehrend.psu.edu/.

Penn State Great Valley, Graduate Studies, Management Division, Malvern, PA 19355-1488. Offers business administration (MBA); finance (M Fin); leadership development (MLD). *Accreditation:* AACSB. *Unit head:* Dr. Craig S. Edelbrock, Chancellor, 610-648-3202, Fax: 610-889-1334, E-mail: cse1@psu.edu. *Application contact:* JoAnn Kelly, Director of Admissions, 610-648-3315, Fax: 610-725-5296, E-mail: jek2@psu.edu.
Website: http://www.sgps.psu.edu/Academics/Degrees/31885.htm.

Penn State Harrisburg, Graduate School, School of Business Administration, Program in Business Administration, Middletown, PA 17057-4898. Offers MBA. *Accreditation:* AACSB. *Entrance requirements:* For master's, GMAT. *Unit head:* Dr. Mukund S. Kulkarni, Chancellor, 717-948-6103, Fax: 717-948-6452, E-mail: msk5@psu.edu. *Application contact:* Robert W. Coffman, Jr., Director of Enrollment Management, Admissions, 717-948-6250, Fax: 717-948-6325, E-mail: ric1@psu.edu.

Penn State University Park, Graduate School, Intercollege Graduate Programs, Intercollege Graduate Program in Business Administration, State College, PA 16802. Offers MBA. Program offered via the PSU World Campus. Postbaccalaureate distance learning degree programs offered (no on-campus study). *Unit head:* Dr. Regina Vasilatos-Younken, Interim Dean, 814-865-2516, Fax: 814-863-4627, E-mail: rxv@psu.edu. *Application contact:* Cynthia E. Nicosia, Director, Graduate Enrollment Services, 814-865-1834, Fax: 814-863-4627, E-mail: cey1@psu.edu.

Penn State University Park, Graduate School, The Mary Jean and Frank P. Smeal College of Business Administration, State College, PA 16802. Offers accounting (M Acc); business administration (MBA, MS, PhD); supply chain management (MPS). *Accreditation:* AACSB. Part-time and evening/weekend programs available. *Students:* 297 full-time (94 women), 4 part-time (1 woman); includes 58 minority (19 Black or African American, non-Hispanic/Latino; 30 Asian, non-Hispanic/Latino; 9 Hispanic/Latino), 96 international. Average age 30. 1,153 applicants, 20% accepted, 141 enrolled. In 2013, 245 master's, 20 doctorates awarded. *Entrance requirements:* Additional exam requirements/recommendations for international students: Required—TOEFL (minimum score 550 paper-based; 80 iBT). *Application deadline:* Applications are processed on a rolling basis. Application fee: $65. Electronic applications accepted. *Financial support:*

Fellowships, research assistantships, teaching assistantships, career-related internships or fieldwork, Federal Work-Study, and unspecified assistantships available. Support available to part-time students. Financial award application deadline: 2/15; financial award applicants required to submit FAFSA. *Unit head:* Dr. Charles H. Whiteman, Dean, 814-863-0448, Fax: 814-865-7064, E-mail: chw17@psu.edu. *Application contact:* Cynthia E. Nicosia, Director, Graduate Enrollment Services, 814-865-1834, Fax: 814-863-4627, E-mail: cey1@psu.edu.
Website: http://www.smeal.psu.edu/.

Pepperdine University, Graziadio School of Business and Management, Executive MBA Program, Malibu, CA 90263. Offers Exec MBA. Part-time and evening/weekend programs available. *Students:* 127 full-time (46 women); includes 43 minority (10 Black or African American, non-Hispanic/Latino; 33 Asian, non-Hispanic/Latino), 1 international. 51 applicants, 84% accepted, 35 enrolled. In 2013, 67 master's awarded. *Entrance requirements:* For master's, two personal interviews; two letters of nomination; minimum of seven years professional experience, including two years at a significant level of management. *Application deadline:* For fall admission, 6/10 priority date for domestic students. Application fee: $75. Tuition and fees vary according to program. *Unit head:* Dr. Gary Mangiofico, Associate Dean of Fully-Employed and Executive Programs, Graziadio School of Business and Management, 310-568-5541, Fax: 310-568-5610, E-mail: gary.mangiofico@pepperdine.edu. *Application contact:* Regina Korossy, Deputy Director, EMBA and PKE Recruitment for Graziadio School of Business and Management, 310-568-5702, E-mail: regina.korossy@pepperdine.edu.
Website: http://bschool.pepperdine.edu/programs/executive/.

Pepperdine University, Graziadio School of Business and Management, Full-Time MBA Program, Malibu, CA 90263. Offers MBA. *Students:* 185 full-time (85 women), 4 part-time (1 woman); includes 26 minority (5 Black or African American, non-Hispanic/Latino; 1 American Indian or Alaska Native, non-Hispanic/Latino; 19 Asian, non-Hispanic/Latino; 1 Hispanic/Latino), 79 international. 248 applicants, 75% accepted, 105 enrolled. In 2013, 128 master's awarded. *Entrance requirements:* For master's, GMAT or GRE, two letters of recommendation. Additional exam requirements/recommendations for international students: Required—TOEFL. *Application deadline:* For fall admission, 5/1 for domestic students, 4/1 for international students. Application fee: $75. Electronic applications accepted. Tuition and fees vary according to program. *Financial support:* Applicants required to submit FAFSA. *Unit head:* Dr. Michael L. Williams, Associate Dean for Full-Time Programs, Graziadio School of Business and Management, 310-506-4100, Fax: 310-506-4126, E-mail: michael.williams@pepperdine.edu. *Application contact:* April Brickell, Recruiter, Full-Time MBA Programs, 310-506-4100, E-mail: april.brickell@pepperdine.edu.
Website: http://bschool.pepperdine.edu/programs/full-time-mba/.

Pepperdine University, Graziadio School of Business and Management, Fully-Employed MBA Program, Malibu, CA 90263. Offers MBA. Part-time and evening/weekend programs available. *Students:* 112 full-time (55 women), 321 part-time (141 women); includes 120 minority (25 Black or African American, non-Hispanic/Latino; 4 American Indian or Alaska Native, non-Hispanic/Latino; 41 Asian, non-Hispanic/Latino; 47 Hispanic/Latino; 2 Native Hawaiian or other Pacific Islander, non-Hispanic/Latino; 1 Two or more races, non-Hispanic/Latino), 6 international. *Entrance requirements:* For master's, GMAT or GRE, professional recommendation. Additional exam requirements/recommendations for international students: Required—TOEFL. *Application deadline:* For fall admission, 6/25 for domestic students. Application fee: $75. Electronic applications accepted. Tuition and fees vary according to program. *Unit head:* Dr. Linda A. Livingstone, Dean, Graziadio School of Business and Management, 310-568-5689, Fax: 310-568-5766, E-mail: linda.livingstone@pepperdine.edu. *Application contact:* Darrell Eriksen, Director of Admission and Student Accounts, Graziadio School of Business and Management, 310-568-5525, E-mail: darrell.eriksen@pepperdine.edu.
Website: http://bschool.pepperdine.edu/programs/mba/.

Pepperdine University, Graziadio School of Business and Management, MBA Program for Presidents and Key Executives, Malibu, CA 90263. Offers MBA. Part-time and evening/weekend programs available. *Students:* 44 full-time (18 women); includes 12 minority (5 Black or African American, non-Hispanic/Latino; 7 Asian, non-Hispanic/Latino), 1 international. *Entrance requirements:* For master's, two letters of nomination; two personal interviews; minimum of 10 years of organizational or professional experience, including at least one year in a senior executive position. Additional exam requirements/recommendations for international students: Required—TOEFL. *Application deadline:* For fall admission, 6/15 priority date for domestic students. Application fee: $75. Tuition and fees vary according to program. *Unit head:* Dr. Linda A. Livingstone, Dean, Graziadio School of Business and Management, 310-568-5689, Fax: 310-568-5766, E-mail: linda.livingstone@pepperdine.edu. *Application contact:* Darrell Eriksen, Director of Admission and Student Accounts, Graziadio School of Business and Management, 310-568-5525, E-mail: darrell.eriksen@pepperdine.edu.
Website: http://bschool.pepperdine.edu/programs/presidential-mba/.

Pepperdine University, Graziadio School of Business and Management, MS in Management and Leadership Program, Malibu, CA 90263. Offers MS. Part-time and evening/weekend programs available. *Students:* 11 full-time (4 women), 37 part-time (31 women); includes 19 minority (8 Black or African American, non-Hispanic/Latino; 2 American Indian or Alaska Native, non-Hispanic/Latino; 2 Asian, non-Hispanic/Latino; 7 Hispanic/Latino), 3 international. In 2013, 25 master's awarded. *Entrance requirements:* For master's, GMAT or GRE, two letters of recommendation. Additional exam requirements/recommendations for international students: Required—TOEFL. *Application deadline:* For fall admission, 6/25 for domestic students. Application fee: $75. Tuition and fees vary according to program. *Financial support:* Applicants required to submit FAFSA. *Unit head:* Dr. Gary Mangiofico, Associate Dean of Fully-Employed and Executive Programs, Graziadio School of Business and Management, 310-568-5512, Fax: 310-258-2855, E-mail: gary.mangiofico@pepperdine.edu. *Application contact:* Karen Riggione, Regional Director of Recruitment, Corporate and Community Relations for Graziadio School of Business and Management, 310-568-5555, Fax: 310-568-5727, E-mail: karen.reggione@pepperdine.edu.
Website: http://bschool.pepperdine.edu/programs/masters-management-leadership/.

Pfeiffer University, Program in Business Administration, Misenheimer, NC 28109-0960. Offers MBA, MBA/MHA. Part-time and evening/weekend programs available. Postbaccalaureate distance learning degree programs offered (minimal on-campus study). *Entrance requirements:* For master's, GMAT, minimum GPA of 3.0.

Philadelphia University, School of Business Administration, Program in Business Administration, Philadelphia, PA 19144. Offers general business (MBA); innovation (MBA); management (MBA); marketing (MBA); strategic design (MBA); MBA/MS. Part-time and evening/weekend programs available. Postbaccalaureate distance learning degree programs offered (no on-campus study). *Entrance requirements:* For master's, GMAT. Additional exam requirements/recommendations for international students: Required—TOEFL (minimum score 550 paper-based; 79 iBT).

Phillips Theological Seminary, Programs in Theology, Tulsa, OK 74116. Offers administration of church agencies (M Div); campus ministry (M Div); church-related social work (M Div); college and seminary teaching (M Div); global mission work (M Div); institutional chaplaincy (M Div); ministerial vocations in Christian education (M Div);

ministry (D Min), including parish ministry, pastoral counseling, practices of ministry; ministry and culture (MAMC), including Christian education, congregational leadership, history and practice of Christian spirituality, theology, ethics, and culture; ministry of music (M Div); pastoral care and counseling (M Div); pastoral ministry (M Div); theological studies (MTS). *Accreditation:* ATS. Part-time programs available. Postbaccalaureate distance learning degree programs offered (minimal on-campus study). *Degree requirements:* For master's, thesis (for some programs); for doctorate, thesis/dissertation. *Entrance requirements:* For master's, minimum GPA of 2.5; for doctorate, M Div, minimum GPA of 3.0. *Faculty research:* Biblical studies, historical studies, theology and culture, practical theology, theology and film.

Piedmont College, School of Business, Demorest, GA 30535-0010. Offers MBA. *Accreditation:* ACBSP. Part-time and evening/weekend programs available. *Students:* 58 full-time (27 women), 23 part-time (13 women); includes 18 minority (13 Black or African American, non-Hispanic/Latino; 5 Asian, non-Hispanic/Latino). Average age 28. 42 applicants, 95% accepted, 38 enrolled. In 2013, 41 master's awarded. *Degree requirements:* For master's, capstone. *Entrance requirements:* For master's, GMAT, GRE, minimum GPA of 2.75. Additional exam requirements/recommendations for international students: Required—TOEFL (minimum score 550 paper-based). *Application deadline:* For fall admission, 7/15 for domestic students; for spring admission, 12/1 for domestic students. Applications are processed on a rolling basis. Electronic applications accepted. *Expenses: Tuition:* Full-time $7992; part-time $444 per credit hour. *Financial support:* Federal Work-Study and unspecified assistantships available. Financial award applicants required to submit FAFSA. *Unit head:* Dr. John Misner, Dean, 706-778-3000 Ext. 1349, Fax: 706-778-0701, E-mail: jmisner@piedmont.edu. *Application contact:* Kathleen Anderson, Director of Graduate Enrollment Management, 706-778-8500 Ext. 1181, Fax: 706-778-0150, E-mail: kanderson@piedmont.edu.
Website: http://www.piedmont.edu.

Pittsburg State University, Graduate School, Kelce College of Business, Department of Management and Marketing, Pittsburg, KS 66762. Offers general administration (MBA). *Accreditation:* AACSB. *Degree requirements:* For master's, thesis or alternative. *Entrance requirements:* For master's, GMAT. *Faculty research:* Consumer behavior, productions management, forecasting interest rate swaps, strategy management.

Plymouth State University, College of Graduate Studies, Graduate Studies in Business, Plymouth, NH 03264-1595. Offers general management (MBA). *Accreditation:* ACBSP. Part-time and evening/weekend programs available. Postbaccalaureate distance learning degree programs offered (no on-campus study). *Entrance requirements:* For master's, minimum GPA of 2.5. Additional exam requirements/recommendations for international students: Required—TOEFL (minimum score 550 paper-based). *Expenses:* Contact institution.

Point Loma Nazarene University, Fermanian School of Business, San Diego, CA 92106-2899. Offers general business (MBA); healthcare (MBA); not-for-profit management (MBA); organizational leadership (MBA); sustainability (MBA). *Accreditation:* ACBSP. Part-time and evening/weekend programs available. *Students:* 37 full-time (12 women), 70 part-time (35 women); includes 33 minority (3 Black or African American, non-Hispanic/Latino; 9 Asian, non-Hispanic/Latino; 14 Hispanic/Latino; 1 Native Hawaiian or other Pacific Islander, non-Hispanic/Latino; 6 Two or more races, non-Hispanic/Latino), 1 international. Average age 29. 51 applicants, 65% accepted, 28 enrolled. In 2013, 59 master's awarded. *Entrance requirements:* For master's, GMAT, letters of recommendation, essay, interview. Additional exam requirements/recommendations for international students: Required—TOEFL. *Application deadline:* For fall admission, 8/4 priority date for domestic students; for spring admission, 12/8 priority date for domestic students; for summer admission, 4/13 priority date for domestic students. Applications are processed on a rolling basis. Application fee: $50. Electronic applications accepted. *Expenses: Tuition:* Full-time $6900; part-time $567 per credit hour. *Financial support:* Applicants required to submit FAFSA. *Unit head:* Dr. Ken Armstrong, Interim Dean, 619-849-2290, E-mail: kenarmstrong@pointloma.edu. *Application contact:* Laura Leinweber, Director of Graduate Admission, 866-692-4723, E-mail: lauraleinweber@pointloma.edu.
Website: http://www.pointloma.edu/discover/graduate-school-san-diego/san-diego-graduate-programs-masters-degree-san-diego/mba.

Point Park University, School of Business, Pittsburgh, PA 15222-1984. Offers business (MBA); organizational leadership (MA). Part-time and evening/weekend programs available. *Degree requirements:* For master's, comprehensive exam (for some programs), thesis or alternative. *Entrance requirements:* For master's, minimum QPA of 2.75; 2 letters of recommendation; resume (MA). Additional exam requirements/recommendations for international students: Required—TOEFL (minimum score 550 paper-based; 79 iBT). Electronic applications accepted. *Faculty research:* Technology issues, foreign direct investment, multinational corporate issues, cross-cultural international organizations/administrations, regional integration issues.

Polytechnic University of Puerto Rico, Graduate School, Hato Rey, PR 00919. Offers business administration (MBA), including computer information systems, general management, management of information systems, management of international enterprises; civil engineering (ME, MS); computer engineering (ME, MS); computer science (MCS, MS); electrical engineering (ME, MS); engineering management (MEM); environmental management (MEM); landscape architecture (M Land Arch); manufacturing competitiveness (MMC, MS); manufacturing engineering (ME, MS); mechanical engineering (M Mech E). Part-time and evening/weekend programs available. *Entrance requirements:* For master's, 3 letters of recommendation.

Polytechnic University of Puerto Rico, Miami Campus, Graduate School, Miami, FL 33166. Offers accounting (MBA); business administration (MBA); construction management (MEM); environmental management (MEM); finance (MBA); human resources management (MBA); logistics and supply chain management (MBA); management of international enterprises (MBA); manufacturing management (MEM); marketing management (MBA); project management (MBA). Part-time and evening/weekend programs available. Postbaccalaureate distance learning degree programs offered (no on-campus study). *Entrance requirements:* For master's, minimum GPA of 3.0. Electronic applications accepted.

Polytechnic University of Puerto Rico, Orlando Campus, Graduate School, Winter Park, FL 32792. Offers accounting (MBA); business administration (MBA); construction management (MEM); engineering management (MEM); environmental management (MEM); finance (MBA); human resources management (MBA); management of international enterprises (MBA); management of technology (MBA); manufacturing management (MEM). Part-time and evening/weekend programs available. Postbaccalaureate distance learning degree programs offered (no on-campus study). *Entrance requirements:* For master's, minimum GPA of 3.0. Additional exam requirements/recommendations for international students: Recommended—TOEFL. Electronic applications accepted.

Pontifical Catholic University of Puerto Rico, College of Business Administration, Ponce, PR 00717-0777. Offers MBA, DBA, PhD, Professional Certificate. Part-time and evening/weekend programs available. *Degree requirements:* For master's, thesis; for doctorate, comprehensive exam, thesis/dissertation. *Entrance requirements:* For

master's, GRE, interview, minimum GPA of 2.75; for doctorate, 2 letters of recommendation, 2 years experience in a related field, interview.

Pontificia Universidad Catolica Madre y Maestra, Graduate School, Faculty of Social and Administrative Sciences, Santiago, Dominican Republic. Offers business administration (MBA), including business development, finance, international business, management skills (M Mgmt, MBA), marketing, operations, strategic cost management, strategy, tourist destination planning and management; law (LL M), including civil law, corporate business law, criminal law, international relations, real estate law; management (M Mgmt), including higher financial management, insurance program administration, management skills (M Mgmt, MBA); psychology (MA), including clinical child and adolescent psychology, forensic psychology; strategic human resources (EMBA).

Portland State University, Graduate Studies, School of Business Administration, Program in Business Administration, Portland, OR 97207-0751. Offers MBA. Part-time and evening/weekend programs available. *Students:* 106 full-time (44 women), 118 part-time (38 women); includes 36 minority (1 Black or African American, non-Hispanic/Latino; 21 Asian, non-Hispanic/Latino; 10 Hispanic/Latino; 4 Two or more races, non-Hispanic/Latino), 24 international. Average age 33. 278 applicants, 44% accepted, 88 enrolled. In 2013, 106 master's awarded. *Degree requirements:* For master's, one foreign language, project. *Entrance requirements:* For master's, GMAT, minimum GPA of 3.0 in upper-division course work, 2 recommendations, resume, interview. Additional exam requirements/recommendations for international students: Required—TOEFL (minimum score 550 paper-based). *Application deadline:* For fall admission, 4/1 priority date for domestic students, 3/1 priority date for international students. Applications are processed on a rolling basis. Application fee: $50. *Expenses:* Tuition, state resident: full-time $9207; part-time $341 per credit. Tuition, nonresident: full-time $14,391; part-time $533 per credit. *Required fees:* $1263; $22 per credit. $98 per quarter. One-time fee: $150. Tuition and fees vary according to program. *Financial support:* Research assistantships with partial tuition reimbursements, teaching assistantships with partial tuition reimbursements, career-related internships or fieldwork, and Federal Work-Study available. Support available to part-time students. Financial award application deadline: 3/1; financial award applicants required to submit FAFSA. *Faculty research:* Quality management and organizational excellence, performance measurement, customer satisfaction, values, technology management and technology transfer. *Unit head:* Dr. Berrin Erdogan, Chair, 503-725-3798, Fax: 503-725-5850, E-mail: berrine@sba.pdx.edu. *Application contact:* Pam Mitchell, Administrator, 503-725-3730, Fax: 503-725-5850, E-mail: pamm@sba.pdx.edu.
Website: http://www.pdx.edu/gradbusiness/mba-portland-state-university.

Portland State University, Graduate Studies, Systems Science Program, Portland, OR 97207-0751. Offers computational intelligence (Certificate); computer modeling and simulation (Certificate); systems science (MS); systems science/anthropology (PhD); systems science/business administration (PhD); systems science/civil engineering (PhD); systems science/economics (PhD); systems science/engineering management (PhD); systems science/general (PhD); systems science/mathematical sciences (PhD); systems science/mechanical engineering (PhD); systems science/psychology (PhD); systems science/sociology (PhD). *Faculty:* 2 full-time (0 women), 1 part-time/adjunct (0 women). *Students:* 12 full-time (3 women), 33 part-time (9 women); includes 6 minority (1 Black or African American, non-Hispanic/Latino; 1 American Indian or Alaska Native, non-Hispanic/Latino; 1 Asian, non-Hispanic/Latino; 2 Hispanic/Latino; 1 Two or more races, non-Hispanic/Latino), 1 international. Average age 40. 5 applicants, 40% accepted, 2 enrolled. In 2013, 5 master's, 3 doctorates awarded. *Degree requirements:* For doctorate, variable foreign language requirement, thesis/dissertation. *Entrance requirements:* For master's, 2 letters of recommendation; for doctorate, GMAT, GRE General Test, minimum undergraduate GPA of 3.0. Additional exam requirements/recommendations for international students: Required—TOEFL. *Application deadline:* For fall admission, 2/1 for domestic students; for spring admission, 11/1 for domestic students. Application fee: $50. *Expenses:* Tuition, state resident: full-time $9207; part-time $341 per credit. Tuition, nonresident: full-time $14,391; part-time $533 per credit. *Required fees:* $1263; $22 per credit. $98 per quarter. One-time fee: $150. Tuition and fees vary according to program. *Financial support:* In 2013–14, 1 teaching assistantship with full tuition reimbursement (averaging $7,074 per year) was awarded; career-related internships or fieldwork, Federal Work-Study, scholarships/grants, and unspecified assistantships also available. Support available to part-time students. Financial award application deadline: 3/1; financial award applicants required to submit FAFSA. *Faculty research:* Systems theory and methodology, artificial intelligence neural networks, information theory, nonlinear dynamics/chaos, modeling and simulation. *Total annual research expenditures:* $171,104. *Unit head:* George Lendaris, Acting Director, 503-725-4988, E-mail: lendaris@sysc.pdx.edu. *Application contact:* Dawn Sharafi, Administrative Assistant, 503-725-4960, E-mail: dawn@sysc.pdx.edu.
Website: http://www.sysc.pdx.edu.

Post University, Program in Business Administration, Waterbury, CT 06723-2540. Offers accounting (MSA); business administration (MBA); corporate innovation (MBA); entrepreneurship (MBA); finance (MBA); healthcare (MBA); leadership (MBA); marketing (MBA); project management (MBA). *Accreditation:* ACBSP. Postbaccalaureate distance learning degree programs offered.

Prairie View A&M University, College of Business, Prairie View, TX 77446-0519. Offers accounting (MS); general business administration (MBA). *Accreditation:* AACSB. Part-time and evening/weekend programs available. *Faculty:* 7 full-time (0 women), 10 part-time/adjunct (3 women). *Students:* 61 full-time (38 women), 169 part-time (103 women); includes 207 minority (186 Black or African American, non-Hispanic/Latino; 13 Asian, non-Hispanic/Latino; 7 Hispanic/Latino; 1 Two or more races, non-Hispanic/Latino), 16 international. Average age 31. 268 applicants, 53% accepted, 105 enrolled. In 2013, 37 master's awarded. *Entrance requirements:* For master's, GMAT, minimum GPA of 2.45. Additional exam requirements/recommendations for international students: Required—TOEFL. *Application deadline:* For fall admission, 7/1 for domestic students, 7/1 priority date for international students; for spring admission, 11/1 for domestic students, 11/1 priority date for international students. Applications are processed on a rolling basis. Application fee: $50. Electronic applications accepted. *Expenses:* Tuition, state resident: full-time $3776; part-time $209.77 per credit hour. Tuition, nonresident: full-time $10,183; part-time $565.77 per credit hour. *Required fees:* $2037; $446.50 per credit hour. *Financial support:* In 2013–14, 9 research assistantships (averaging $6,240 per year), 7 teaching assistantships (averaging $6,240 per year) were awarded; career-related internships or fieldwork, Federal Work-Study, institutionally sponsored loans, and tuition waivers (partial) also available. Support available to part-time students. Financial award application deadline: 4/1; financial award applicants required to submit FAFSA. *Faculty research:* Operations, finance, marketing. *Total annual research expenditures:* $30,000. *Unit head:* Dr. Munir Quddus, Dean, 936-261-9200, Fax: 936-261-9241, E-mail: cob@pvamu.edu. *Application contact:* Dr. John Dyck, Director, Graduate Programs in Business, 936-261-9217, Fax: 936-261-9232, E-mail: cob@pvamu.edu.
Website: http://www.pvamu.edu.

Providence College, School of Business, Providence, RI 02918. Offers accounting (MBA); finance (MBA); international business (MBA); management (MBA); marketing (MBA); not-for-profit organizations (MBA). Part-time and evening/weekend programs available. *Faculty:* 14 full-time (5 women), 3 part-time/adjunct (1 woman). *Students:* 68 full-time (25 women), 54 part-time (25 women); includes 12 minority (3 Black or African American, non-Hispanic/Latino; 1 Asian, non-Hispanic/Latino; 6 Hispanic/Latino; 2 Two or more races, non-Hispanic/Latino), 7 international. Average age 25. 43 applicants, 95% accepted, 36 enrolled. In 2013, 38 master's awarded. *Degree requirements:* For master's, thesis optional. *Entrance requirements:* For master's, GMAT. Additional exam requirements/recommendations for international students: Required—TOEFL (minimum score 550 paper-based; 80 iBT). *Application deadline:* For fall admission, 7/15 priority date for domestic and international students; for spring admission, 11/15 priority date for domestic and international students; for summer admission, 4/15 priority date for domestic students. Applications are processed on a rolling basis. Application fee: $55. *Expenses:* Contact institution. *Financial support:* Federal Work-Study, institutionally sponsored loans, and unspecified assistantships available. Support available to part-time students. Financial award application deadline: 8/1; financial award applicants required to submit FAFSA. *Unit head:* Jacqueline Elcik, Director, 401-865-2131, E-mail: jelcik@providence.edu. *Application contact:* MBA Program, 401-865-2294, E-mail: mba@providence.edu.
Website: http://www.providence.edu/business/Pages/default.aspx.

Purdue University, Graduate School, Krannert School of Management, Doctoral Program in Management, West Lafayette, IN 47907-2056. Offers PhD. *Degree requirements:* For doctorate, comprehensive exam, thesis/dissertation, first-year summer paper, dissertation proposal, dissertation defense. *Entrance requirements:* For doctorate, GMAT or GRE. Additional exam requirements/recommendations for international students: Required—TOEFL (minimum score 575 paper-based); Recommended—TWE. Electronic applications accepted. *Faculty research:* Accounting, finance, marketing, management information systems, operations management, organizational behavior and human resource management, quantitative methods/management science, strategic management.

Purdue University, Graduate School, Krannert School of Management, Executive MBA Program, West Lafayette, IN 47907. Offers EMBA. *Entrance requirements:* For master's, letters of recommendation, essays, transcripts, resume. Electronic applications accepted. *Faculty research:* Trust in organizations, regulations and supply chain impact, carbon emissions and transportation costs.

Purdue University, Graduate School, Krannert School of Management, GISMA Program, 30169 Hannover, Germany. Offers general business (MBA). *Entrance requirements:* For master's, GMAT, letters of recommendation. Additional exam requirements/recommendations for international students: Required—TOEFL (minimum score 550 paper-based; 77 iBT). *Expenses:* Contact institution.

Purdue University, Graduate School, Krannert School of Management, Master of Business Administration Program, West Lafayette, IN 47907. Offers MBA. *Entrance requirements:* For master's, GMAT, four-year baccalaureate degree, minimum GPA of 3.0, essays, recommendation letters, work/internship experience. Additional exam requirements/recommendations for international students: Required—TOEFL (minimum score 550 paper-based; 77 iBT), IELTS (minimum score 6.5), or PTE. Electronic applications accepted. *Faculty research:* Capital market imperfections and the sensitivity of investment to stock prices, identifying beneficial collaboration in decentralized logistics systems, performance periods and the dynamics of the performance-risk relationship, applications of global optimization to process and molecular design.

Purdue University, Graduate School, Krannert School of Management, Weekend Master of Business Administration Program, West Lafayette, IN 47907. Offers MBA. Part-time and evening/weekend programs available. *Entrance requirements:* For master's, GMAT, minimum GPA of 3.0, four-year baccalaureate degree, essays, letters of recommendation. Additional exam requirements/recommendations for international students: Required—TOEFL (minimum score 550 paper-based; 77 iBT). Electronic applications accepted.

Purdue University Calumet, Graduate Studies Office, School of Management, Hammond, IN 46323-2094. Offers accountancy (M Acc); business administration (MBA); business administration for executives (EMBA). Part-time and evening/weekend programs available. *Entrance requirements:* For master's, GMAT. Additional exam requirements/recommendations for international students: Required—TOEFL. Electronic applications accepted.

Queen's University at Kingston, Queens School of Business, Program in Business Administration, Kingston, ON K7L 3N6, Canada. Offers consulting and project management (MBA); finance (MBA); innovation and entrepreneurship (MBA); marketing (MBA). *Accreditation:* AACSB. *Degree requirements:* For master's, thesis optional, research project. *Entrance requirements:* For master's, GMAT, minimum B+ average. Additional exam requirements/recommendations for international students: Required—TOEFL. Electronic applications accepted. *Faculty research:* Management fundamentals, strategic thinking, global business, innovation and change, leadership.

Queens University of Charlotte, McColl School of Business, Charlotte, NC 28274-0002. Offers business administration (EMBA, MBA). *Accreditation:* AACSB; ACBSP. Part-time and evening/weekend programs available. *Degree requirements:* For master's, capstone course. *Entrance requirements:* For master's, GMAT, minimum GPA of 2.5. Additional exam requirements/recommendations for international students: Required—TOEFL. Electronic applications accepted. *Expenses:* Contact institution.

Quincy University, Program in Business Administration, Quincy, IL 62301-2699. Offers general business administration (MBA); operations management (MBA); organizational leadership (MBA). Part-time and evening/weekend programs available. Postbaccalaureate distance learning degree programs offered (no on-campus study). *Faculty:* 5 full-time (3 women). *Students:* 5 full-time (0 women), 18 part-time (5 women), 1 international. In 2013, 20 master's awarded. *Entrance requirements:* For master's, GMAT, previous course work in accounting, economics, finance, management or marketing, and statistics. Additional exam requirements/recommendations for international students: Required—TOEFL (minimum score 550 paper-based; 79 iBT). *Application deadline:* Applications are processed on a rolling basis. Application fee: $25. Electronic applications accepted. *Expenses:* Contact institution. *Financial support:* Applicants required to submit FAFSA. *Faculty research:* Macroeconomic forecasting. *Unit head:* Dr. Cynthia Haliemun, Director, 217-228-5432 Ext. 3067, E-mail: haliecy@quincy.edu. *Application contact:* Office of Admissions, 217-228-5210, Fax: 217-228-5479, E-mail: admissions@quincy.edu.
Website: http://www.quincy.edu/academics/graduate-programs/business-administration.

Quinnipiac University, School of Business and Engineering, Program in Business Administration, Hamden, CT 06518-1940. Offers chartered financial analyst (MBA); finance (MBA); healthcare management (MBA); information systems management (MBA); marketing (MBA); supply chain management (MBA); JD/MBA. *Accreditation:* AACSB. Part-time and evening/weekend programs available. Postbaccalaureate distance learning degree programs offered (no on-campus study). *Faculty:* 33 full-time (10 women), 7 part-time/adjunct (3 women). *Students:* 109 full-time (48 women), 225 part-time (101 women); includes 44 minority (14 Black or African American, non-Hispanic/Latino; 2 American Indian or Alaska Native, non-Hispanic/Latino; 12 Asian, non-Hispanic/Latino; 15 Hispanic/Latino; 1 Two or more races, non-Hispanic/Latino), 17

international. 230 applicants, 80% accepted, 154 enrolled. In 2013, 124 master's awarded. *Entrance requirements:* For master's, GMAT or GRE, minimum GPA of 3.0. Additional exam requirements/recommendations for international students: Required—TOEFL (minimum score 575 paper-based; 90 iBT), IELTS (minimum score 6.5). *Application deadline:* For fall admission, 7/30 priority date for domestic students, 4/30 priority date for international students; for spring admission, 12/15 priority date for domestic students, 9/15 priority date for international students. Applications are processed on a rolling basis. Application fee: $45. Electronic applications accepted. *Expenses: Tuition:* Part-time $920 per credit. *Required fees:* $37 per credit. *Financial support:* In 2013–14, 41 students received support. Career-related internships or fieldwork, Federal Work-Study, scholarships/grants, and unspecified assistantships available. Support available to part-time students. Financial award application deadline: 6/1; financial award applicants required to submit FAFSA. *Faculty research:* Financial markets and investments, international business, supply chain management, health care management, corporate governance. *Unit head:* Lisa Braiewa, MBA Program Director, E-mail: lisa.braiewa@quinnipiac.edu. *Application contact:* Office of Graduate Admissions, 800-462-1944, Fax: 203-582-3443, E-mail: graduate@quinnipiac.edu.
Website: http://www.quinnipiac.edu/mba.

Radford University, College of Graduate and Professional Studies, College of Business and Economics, Program in Business Administration, Radford, VA 24142. Offers MBA. *Accreditation:* AACSB. Part-time and evening/weekend programs available. *Faculty:* 9 full-time (1 woman). *Students:* 33 full-time (14 women), 34 part-time (13 women); includes 11 minority (6 Black or African American, non-Hispanic/Latino; 2 Asian, non-Hispanic/Latino; 2 Hispanic/Latino; 1 Native Hawaiian or other Pacific Islander, non-Hispanic/Latino), 7 international. Average age 30. 34 applicants, 65% accepted, 14 enrolled. In 2013, 40 master's awarded. *Entrance requirements:* For master's, GMAT or GRE, minimum GPA of 2.75, 2 letters of reference, letter of intent, resume, official transcripts. Additional exam requirements/recommendations for international students: Required—TOEFL (minimum score 550 paper-based; 79 iBT). *Application deadline:* For fall admission, 2/15 priority date for domestic students, 12/1 for international students; for spring admission, 7/1 for international students. Applications are processed on a rolling basis. Application fee: $50. Electronic applications accepted. *Expenses:* Tuition, state resident: full-time $6800; part-time $283 per credit hour. Tuition, nonresident: full-time $15,610; part-time $627 per credit hour. *Required fees:* $2944; $123 per credit hour. Tuition and fees vary according to program. *Financial support:* In 2013–14, 23 students received support, including 17 research assistantships (averaging $7,544 per year), 5 teaching assistantships with partial tuition reimbursements available (averaging $10,000 per year); career-related internships or fieldwork, Federal Work-Study, institutionally sponsored loans, scholarships/grants, and unspecified assistantships also available. Financial award application deadline: 3/1; financial award applicants required to submit FAFSA. *Unit head:* Dr. George Santopietro, Interim Director, MBA Program, 540-831-6905, Fax: 540-831-6103, E-mail: rumba@radford.edu. *Application contact:* Rebecca Conner, Director, Graduate Enrollment, 540-831-6296, Fax: 540-831-6061, E-mail: gradcollege@radford.edu.
Website: http://www.radford.edu/content/cobe/home/programs/mba.html.

Ramapo College of New Jersey, Master of Business Administration Program, Mahwah, NJ 07430-1680. Offers MBA. *Accreditation:* AACSB. Part-time and evening/weekend programs available. *Faculty:* 3 full-time (2 women). *Students:* 49 part-time (22 women); includes 10 minority (4 Black or African American, non-Hispanic/Latino; 1 Asian, non-Hispanic/Latino; 4 Hispanic/Latino; 1 Two or more races, non-Hispanic/Latino), 4 international. Average age 32. *Degree requirements:* For master's, capstone course. *Entrance requirements:* For master's, GMAT or GRE within the past five years (waived if applicant has master's or higher degree), official transcript; written statement describing why applicant wishes to pursue an MBA at Ramapo College, including short and long term aspirations (500-word minimum); 2 letters of recommendation; resume. Additional exam requirements/recommendations for international students: Required—TOEFL (minimum score 550 paper-based; 79 iBT); Recommended—IELTS (minimum score 6). *Application deadline:* For fall admission, 8/1 for domestic and international students. Applications are processed on a rolling basis. Application fee: $60. Electronic applications accepted. *Expenses:* Contact institution. *Faculty research:* Ethical implications of taxation on society, organizational governance, applied labor economics, empirical market microstructure, foreign direct investment. *Unit head:* Dr. Lewis M. Chakrin, Dean of the Anisfield School of Business, 201-684-7377, E-mail: lchakrin@ramapo.edu. *Application contact:* Timothy Landers, Assistant Dean/Director of the MBA Program, 201-684-7771, E-mail: tlanders@ramapo.edu.
Website: http://www.ramapo.edu/mba/.

Regent's University London, Webster Graduate School, London, United Kingdom. Offers business (MBA); finance (MS); human resources (MA); information technology management (MA); international business (MA); international non-governmental organizations (MA); international relations (MA); management and leadership (MA); marketing (MA). Part-time programs available.

Regent University, Graduate School, School of Business and Leadership, Virginia Beach, VA 23464-9800. Offers business administration (MBA); leadership (Certificate); organizational leadership (MA, PhD), including ecclesial leadership (PhD), entrepreneurial leadership (PhD), human resource development (PhD); strategic foresight (MA); strategic leadership (DSL), including global consulting, leadership coaching, strategic foresight. Part-time and evening/weekend programs available. Postbaccalaureate distance learning degree programs offered (minimal on-campus study). *Faculty:* 11 full-time (4 women), 6 part-time/adjunct (3 women). *Students:* 34 full-time (19 women), 655 part-time (276 women); includes 222 minority (175 Black or African American, non-Hispanic/Latino; 2 American Indian or Alaska Native, non-Hispanic/Latino; 16 Asian, non-Hispanic/Latino; 29 Hispanic/Latino), 117 international. Average age 42. 384 applicants, 53% accepted, 120 enrolled. In 2013, 74 master's, 72 doctorates awarded. *Degree requirements:* For master's, thesis or alternative, 3 credit hour culminating experience; for doctorate, thesis/dissertation. *Entrance requirements:* For master's, GRE, GMAT, minimum undergraduate GPA of 2.75, computer literacy survey, 2 recommendations, resume, transcripts, essay; for doctorate, GRE, GMAT, sample of writing, minimum 3 years of relevant experience, computer literacy survey, 2 recommendations, resume, essay, transcripts; for Certificate, writing sample, resume, transcripts. Additional exam requirements/recommendations for international students: Required—TOEFL (minimum score 577 paper-based). *Application deadline:* For fall admission, 5/1 priority date for domestic students; for spring admission, 10/1 priority date for domestic students. Applications are processed on a rolling basis. Application fee: $50. Electronic applications accepted. *Expenses:* Contact institution. *Financial support:* Career-related internships or fieldwork, scholarships/grants, and tuition waivers (full and partial) available. Support available to part-time students. Financial award application deadline: 9/1. *Faculty research:* Servant leadership, ethics and values, telecommuting and family values, organizational communications, distance education. *Unit head:* Dr. Doris Gomez, Interim Dean, 757-352-4686, Fax: 757-352-4634, E-mail: dorigom@regent.edu. *Application contact:* Matthew Chadwick, Director of Enrollment Support Services, 800-373-5504, Fax: 757-352-4381, E-mail: admissions@regent.edu.
Website: http://www.regent.edu/acad/global/.

Regis University, College for Professional Studies, School of Management, MBA Program, Denver, CO 80221-1099. Offers finance and accounting (MBA); general business (MBA); health industry leadership (MBA); marketing (MBA); operations management (MBA); organizational performance management (MBA); strategic management (MBA). Part-time and evening/weekend programs available. Postbaccalaureate distance learning degree programs offered (no on-campus study). *Faculty:* 10 full-time (3 women), 74 part-time/adjunct (17 women). *Students:* 386 full-time (183 women), 269 part-time (134 women); includes 190 minority (38 Black or African American, non-Hispanic/Latino; 2 American Indian or Alaska Native, non-Hispanic/Latino; 30 Asian, non-Hispanic/Latino; 109 Hispanic/Latino; 1 Native Hawaiian or other Pacific Islander, non-Hispanic/Latino; 10 Two or more races, non-Hispanic/Latino), 11 international. Average age 42. 152 applicants, 91% accepted, 112 enrolled. In 2013, 318 master's awarded. *Degree requirements:* For master's, thesis (for some programs), final research project. *Entrance requirements:* For master's, official transcript reflecting baccalaureate degree awarded from regionally-accredited college or university, work experience, resume, letters of recommendation. Additional exam requirements/recommendations for international students: Required—TOEFL (minimum score 550 paper-based; 82 iBT). *Application deadline:* Applications are processed on a rolling basis. Application fee: $75. Electronic applications accepted. *Expenses:* Contact institution. *Financial support:* In 2013–14, 22 students received support. Federal Work-Study and scholarships/grants available. Financial award application deadline: 4/15; financial award applicants required to submit FAFSA. *Unit head:* Dr. Anthony Vrba, Interim Dean, 303-964-5384, Fax: 303-964-5538, E-mail: avrba@regis.edu. *Application contact:* Sarah Engel, Director of Admissions, 303-458-4900, Fax: 303-964-5534, E-mail: regisadm@regis.edu.
Website: http://www.regis.edu/CPS/Academics/Degrees-and-Programs/Graduate-Programs/MBA-College-for-Professional-Studies.aspx.

Regis University, College for Professional Studies, School of Management, MBA Program in Emerging Markets, Denver, CO 80221-1099. Offers MBA. Postbaccalaureate distance learning degree programs offered (no on-campus study). *Entrance requirements:* For master's, GMAT or essay, official transcript, resume, two recommendations, interview. Application fee: $75. Tuition and fees vary according to program. *Unit head:* Dr. Peter Bemski, Chair, 303-458-1805. *Application contact:* Information Contact, 303-458-4300, Fax: 303-964-5274, E-mail: masters@regis.edu.
Website: http://www.regis.edu/CPS/Academics/Degrees-and-Programs/Graduate-Programs/MBA-Emerging-Markets.aspx.

Reinhardt University, Reinhardt Advantage MBA Program, Alpharetta, GA 30005-4442. Offers MBA. Program offered at North Fulton Center in Alpharetta, GA and at The Chambers at City Center in Woodstock, GA. Part-time and evening/weekend programs available. *Degree requirements:* For master's, comprehensive exam. *Entrance requirements:* For master's, GRE (minimum score in upper-50th percentile) or GMAT (minimum score 500), bachelor's degree with minimum GPA of 2.75, current resume, interview, 3 professional references. Additional exam requirements/recommendations for international students: Required—TOEFL. Electronic applications accepted.

Rensselaer at Hartford, Lally School of Management and Technology, Hartford, CT 06120-2991. Offers MBA, MS. Part-time and evening/weekend programs available. Postbaccalaureate distance learning degree programs offered (no on-campus study). *Degree requirements:* For master's, capstone course. *Entrance requirements:* For master's, GMAT (MBA). Additional exam requirements/recommendations for international students: Required—TOEFL (minimum score 600 paper-based; 100 iBT). Electronic applications accepted.

Rensselaer Polytechnic Institute, Graduate School, Lally School of Management, Troy, NY 12180-3590. Offers EMBA, MBA, MS, PhD. *Accreditation:* AACSB. Part-time and evening/weekend programs available. *Faculty:* 53 full-time (13 women), 4 part-time/adjunct (0 women). *Students:* 187 full-time (99 women), 31 part-time (11 women); includes 11 minority (1 Black or African American, non-Hispanic/Latino; 5 Asian, non-Hispanic/Latino; 2 Hispanic/Latino; 3 Two or more races, non-Hispanic/Latino), 31 international. Average age 27. 744 applicants, 40% accepted, 140 enrolled. In 2013, 114 master's, 8 doctorates awarded. *Degree requirements:* For doctorate, thesis/dissertation. *Entrance requirements:* For master's and doctorate, GMAT or GRE. Additional exam requirements/recommendations for international students: Required—TOEFL (minimum score 570 paper-based; 88 iBT), IELTS (minimum score 6.5), PTE (minimum score 60). *Application deadline:* For fall admission, 1/1 priority date for domestic and international students; for spring admission, 8/15 priority date for domestic and international students. Applications are processed on a rolling basis. Application fee: $75. Electronic applications accepted. *Expenses: Tuition:* Full-time $45,100; part-time $1879 per credit hour. *Required fees:* $1983. *Financial support:* In 2013–14, 157 students received support, including research assistantships (averaging $18,500 per year), teaching assistantships (averaging $18,500 per year); fellowships and scholarships/grants also available. Financial award application deadline: 1/1; financial award applicants required to submit FAFSA. *Faculty research:* Business analytics; quantitative finance and risk analytics; management; supply chain management; technology commercialization and entrepreneurship. *Total annual research expenditures:* $727,740. *Application contact:* Office of Graduate Admissions, 518-276-6216, E-mail: gradadmissions@rpi.edu.
Website: http://lallyschool.rpi.edu/.

Rice University, Graduate Programs, Jesse H. Jones Graduate School of Management, Houston, TX 77251-1892. Offers business administration (EMBA, MBA, PMBA); MBA/M Eng; MD/MBA. *Accreditation:* AACSB. Evening/weekend programs available. *Entrance requirements:* For master's, GMAT. Additional exam requirements/recommendations for international students: Required—TOEFL (minimum score 600 paper-based). Electronic applications accepted. *Expenses:* Contact institution. *Faculty research:* Marketing strategy, technology transfer initiatives, management accounting, leadership and change management, financial management.

The Richard Stockton College of New Jersey, School of Graduate and Continuing Studies, Program in Business Administration, Galloway, NJ 08205-9441. Offers MBA. Part-time and evening/weekend programs available. *Faculty:* 8 full-time (4 women), 2 part-time/adjunct (1 woman). *Students:* 13 full-time (5 women), 42 part-time (22 women); includes 11 minority (5 Black or African American, non-Hispanic/Latino; 3 Asian, non-Hispanic/Latino; 1 Hispanic/Latino; 2 Two or more races, non-Hispanic/Latino), 1 international. Average age 31. 29 applicants, 79% accepted, 19 enrolled. In 2013, 16 master's awarded. *Degree requirements:* For master's, project. *Entrance requirements:* For master's, GMAT. Additional exam requirements/recommendations for international students: Required—TOEFL. *Application deadline:* For fall admission, 7/1 for domestic and international students; for spring admission, 12/1 for domestic students, 11/1 for international students. Applications are processed on a rolling basis. Application fee: $50. Electronic applications accepted. *Expenses: Tuition, area resident:* Part-time $559 per credit. Tuition, state resident: part-time $559 per credit. Tuition, nonresident: part-time $861 per credit. *Required fees:* $168.23 per credit. $75 per semester. Tuition and fees vary according to course load and degree level. *Financial support:* In 2013–14, 4 students received support, including 1 research assistantship with partial tuition reimbursement available; fellowships, career-related internships or fieldwork, Federal Work-Study, scholarships/grants, and unspecified assistantships also available. Support

available to part-time students. Financial award application deadline: 3/1; financial award applicants required to submit FAFSA. *Faculty research:* Business ethics, marketing channels development, event studies, total quality management. *Unit head:* Dr. Gurprit Chhatwal, Director, 609-626-3640, E-mail: mba@stockton.edu. *Application contact:* Tara Williams, Assistant Director of Graduate Enrollment Management, 609-626-3640, Fax: 609-626-6050, E-mail: gradschool@stockton.edu.

Rider University, College of Business Administration, Lawrenceville, NJ 08648-3001. Offers EMBA, M Acc, MBA. *Accreditation:* AACSB. Part-time and evening/weekend programs available. *Entrance requirements:* For master's, GMAT, minimum AACSB index of 1050, resume. Additional exam requirements/recommendations for international students: Required—TOEFL (minimum score 550 paper-based). Electronic applications accepted. *Expenses:* Contact institution.

Rivier University, School of Graduate Studies, Department of Business Administration, Nashua, NH 03060. Offers MBA. Part-time and evening/weekend programs available. *Entrance requirements:* Additional exam requirements/recommendations for international students: Recommended—TOEFL.

Robert Morris University, Graduate Studies, School of Business, Moon Township, PA 15108-1189. Offers business administration (MBA); human resource management (MS); nonprofit management (MS); taxation (MS). *Accreditation:* AACSB. Part-time and evening/weekend programs available. Postbaccalaureate distance learning degree programs offered (no on-campus study). *Faculty:* 25 full-time (10 women), 8 part-time/adjunct (2 women). *Students:* 247 part-time (99 women); includes 10 minority (1 Black or African American, non-Hispanic/Latino; 2 Asian, non-Hispanic/Latino; 7 Two or more races, non-Hispanic/Latino), 5 international. Average age 26. 214 applicants, 40% accepted, 62 enrolled. In 2013, 187 master's awarded. *Entrance requirements:* For master's, GMAT, letters of recommendation. Additional exam requirements/recommendations for international students: Required—TOEFL (minimum score 550 paper-based; 79 iBT). *Application deadline:* For fall admission, 7/1 priority date for domestic and international students; for spring admission, 11/1 priority date for domestic and international students. Applications are processed on a rolling basis. Application fee: $35. Electronic applications accepted. *Expenses: Tuition:* Part-time $825 per credit. Part-time tuition and fees vary according to degree level and program. *Financial support:* Research assistantships with partial tuition reimbursements, Federal Work-Study, institutionally sponsored loans, and unspecified assistantships available. Support available to part-time students. Financial award application deadline: 5/1; financial award applicants required to submit FAFSA. *Unit head:* Dr. John M. Beehler, Dean, 412-397-5445, Fax: 412-397-2172, E-mail: beehler@rmu.edu. *Application contact:* 412-397-5200, Fax: 412-397-5915, E-mail: graduateadmissions@rmu.edu.
Website: http://www.rmu.edu/web/cms/schools/sbus/Pages/default.aspx.

Robert Morris University Illinois, Morris Graduate School of Management, Chicago, IL 60605. Offers accounting (MBA); accounting/finance (MBA); business analytics (MIS); design and media (MM); educational technology (MM); health care administration (MM); higher education administration (MM); human resource management (MBA); information security (MIS); information systems (MIS); law enforcement administration (MM); management (MBA); management/finance (MBA); management/human resource management (MBA); mobile computing (MIS); sports administration (MM). Part-time and evening/weekend programs available. *Faculty:* 12 full-time (5 women), 18 part-time/adjunct (4 women). *Students:* 240 full-time (128 women), 195 part-time (127 women); includes 242 minority (147 Black or African American, non-Hispanic/Latino; 2 American Indian or Alaska Native, non-Hispanic/Latino; 24 Asian, non-Hispanic/Latino; 63 Hispanic/Latino; 1 Native Hawaiian or other Pacific Islander, non-Hispanic/Latino; 5 Two or more races, non-Hispanic/Latino), 26 international. Average age 33. 210 applicants, 63% accepted, 116 enrolled. In 2013, 278 master's awarded. *Entrance requirements:* For master's, official transcripts, two letters of recommendation. Additional exam requirements/recommendations for international students: Required—TOEFL (minimum score 550 paper-based). *Application deadline:* Applications are processed on a rolling basis. Application fee: $20 ($100 for international students). Electronic applications accepted. *Expenses: Tuition:* Full-time $14,400; part-time $2400 per course. *Financial support:* In 2013–14, 488 students received support. Federal Work-Study and scholarships/grants available. Support available to part-time students. Financial award applicants required to submit FAFSA. *Unit head:* Kayed Akkawi, Dean for Morris Graduate School of Management, 312-935-6050, Fax: 312-935-6020, E-mail: kakkawi@robertmorris.edu. *Application contact:* Fernando Villeda, Dean of Graduate Enrollment, 312-935-6050, Fax: 312-935-6020, E-mail: fvilleda@robertmorris.edu.

Roberts Wesleyan College, Graduate Business Programs, Rochester, NY 14624-1997. Offers strategic leadership (MS); strategic marketing (MS). Evening/weekend programs available. *Degree requirements:* For master's, thesis or alternative. *Entrance requirements:* For master's, GMAT, minimum GPA of 2.75, verifiable work experience. *Application deadline:* Applications are processed on a rolling basis. Application fee: $35. *Expenses:* Contact institution. *Financial support:* Applicants required to submit FAFSA. *Unit head:* Dr. Steven Bovee, Co-Director, 585-594-6763, Fax: 716-594-6316, E-mail: bovees@roberts.edu. *Application contact:* Office of Admissions, 800-777-4RWC, E-mail: admissions@roberts.edu.
Website: http://www.roberts.edu/graduate-business-programs.aspx.

Rochester Institute of Technology, Graduate Enrollment Services, Saunders College of Business, Executive MBA Program, Rochester, NY 14623-5603. Offers Exec MBA. *Accreditation:* AACSB. Part-time and evening/weekend programs available. Postbaccalaureate distance learning degree programs offered (minimal on-campus study). *Students:* 62 full-time (28 women), 22 part-time (11 women); includes 9 minority (3 Black or African American, non-Hispanic/Latino; 3 Asian, non-Hispanic/Latino; 3 Hispanic/Latino), 1 international. Average age 40. 44 applicants, 59% accepted, 16 enrolled. In 2013, 39 master's awarded. *Degree requirements:* For master's, thesis. *Entrance requirements:* For master's, GMAT, minimum of 6 years of work experience. Additional exam requirements/recommendations for international students: Required—TOEFL (minimum score 580 paper-based; 92 iBT) or IELTS (minimum score 7). *Application deadline:* For fall admission, 6/30 for domestic students, 2/15 for international students. Applications are processed on a rolling basis. Application fee: $60. Electronic applications accepted. *Expenses:* Contact institution. *Financial support:* In 2013–14, 41 students received support. Scholarships/grants available. Support available to part-time students. Financial award applicants required to submit FAFSA. *Faculty research:* Entrepreneurship, strategic growth in small business, leadership effectiveness, corporate environmental strategy and management, lean manufacturing and environmental performance. *Unit head:* Charles Ackley, Graduate Program Director, 585-475-6916, E-mail: cackley@saunders.rit.edu. *Application contact:* Diane Ellison, Assistant Vice President, Graduate Enrollment Services, 585-475-2229, Fax: 585-475-7164, E-mail: gradinfo@rit.edu.
Website: http://saunders.rit.edu/programs/executive/index.php.

Rochester Institute of Technology, Graduate Enrollment Services, Saunders College of Business, Program in Business Administration, Rochester, NY 14623-5603. Offers MBA. *Accreditation:* AACSB. Part-time programs available. *Students:* 72 full-time (25 women), 60 part-time (16 women); includes 18 minority (2 Black or African American, non-Hispanic/Latino; 3 Asian, non-Hispanic/Latino; 4 Hispanic/Latino; 9 Two or more races, non-Hispanic/Latino), 43 international. Average age 27. 296 applicants, 38% accepted, 43 enrolled. In 2013, 97 master's awarded. *Degree requirements:* For master's, comprehensive exam (for some programs), thesis (for some programs). *Entrance requirements:* For master's, GMAT or GRE. Additional exam requirements/recommendations for international students: Required—PTE (minimum score 63), TOEFL (minimum score 580 paper-based; 92 iBT) or IELTS (minimum score 7). *Application deadline:* For fall admission, 2/15 for domestic and international students; for winter admission, 11/1 for domestic students, 10/1 for international students; for spring admission, 2/1 for domestic students, 1/1 for international students. Applications are processed on a rolling basis. Application fee: $60. Electronic applications accepted. *Expenses: Tuition:* Full-time $37,236; part-time $1552 per credit hour. *Required fees:* $250. *Financial support:* Research assistantships with partial tuition reimbursements, teaching assistantships with partial tuition reimbursements, career-related internships or fieldwork, scholarships/grants, and unspecified assistantships available. Support available to part-time students. Financial award applicants required to submit FAFSA. *Faculty research:* Strategic use of information technology to gain a competitive advantage, developing new statistical quality control techniques and revising the existing techniques to improve their performance, corporate governance. *Unit head:* Charles Ackley, Graduate Program Director, 585-475-6916, E-mail: cackley@saunders.rit.edu. *Application contact:* Diane Ellison, Assistant Vice President, Graduate Enrollment Services, 585-475-2229, Fax: 585-475-7164, E-mail: gradinfo@rit.edu.
Website: http://saunders.rit.edu/.

Rockford University, Graduate Studies, Program in Business Administration, Rockford, IL 61108-2393. Offers MBA. Part-time and evening/weekend programs available. *Entrance requirements:* For master's, GMAT, 3 letters of recommendation. Additional exam requirements/recommendations for international students: Required—TOEFL (minimum score 550 paper-based; 79 iBT). Electronic applications accepted. *Faculty research:* Entrepreneurship, leadership, international business, services marketing, project management.

Rockhurst University, Helzberg School of Management, Kansas City, MO 64110-2561. Offers Executive Fellows MBA, MBA, DO/MBA, DPT/MBA. *Accreditation:* AACSB. Part-time and evening/weekend programs available. *Faculty:* 17 full-time (2 women), 16 part-time/adjunct (6 women). *Students:* 114 full-time (40 women), 152 part-time (58 women); includes 43 minority (17 Black or African American, non-Hispanic/Latino; 10 Asian, non-Hispanic/Latino; 15 Hispanic/Latino; 1 Two or more races, non-Hispanic/Latino), 7 international. Average age 30. 247 applicants, 62% accepted, 116 enrolled. In 2013, 117 master's awarded. *Entrance requirements:* For master's, GMAT or GRE. Additional exam requirements/recommendations for international students: Required—TOEFL (minimum score 550 paper-based; 79 iBT). *Application deadline:* For fall admission, 7/25 priority date for domestic students; for spring admission, 12/15 priority date for domestic students. Applications are processed on a rolling basis. Application fee: $0. Electronic applications accepted. Tuition and fees vary according to program. *Financial support:* Career-related internships or fieldwork available. Support available to part-time students. Financial award application deadline: 4/1; financial award applicants required to submit FAFSA. *Faculty research:* Offshoring/outsourcing, systems analysis/synthesis, work teams, multilateral trade, path dependencies/creation. *Unit head:* Cheryl McConnell, Dean, 816-501-4201, Fax: 816-501-4650, E-mail: cheryl.mcconnell@rockhurst.edu. *Application contact:* Valerie Wright, Director of MBA Advising, 816-501-4823, E-mail: valerie.wright@rockhurst.edu.
Website: http://www.rockhurst.edu/helzberg-school-of-management.

Rollins College, Crummer Graduate School of Business, Winter Park, FL 32789-4499. Offers business administration (EDBA); entrepreneurship (MBA); finance (MBA); international business (MBA); management (MBA); marketing (MBA); operations and technology management (MBA). *Accreditation:* AACSB. Part-time and evening/weekend programs available. Postbaccalaureate distance learning degree programs offered (minimal on-campus study). *Faculty:* 21 full-time (3 women), 2 part-time/adjunct (1 woman). *Students:* 157 full-time (86 women), 135 part-time (83 women); includes 60 minority (12 Black or African American, non-Hispanic/Latino; 1 American Indian or Alaska Native, non-Hispanic/Latino; 17 Asian, non-Hispanic/Latino; 23 Hispanic/Latino; 1 Native Hawaiian or other Pacific Islander, non-Hispanic/Latino; 6 Two or more races, non-Hispanic/Latino), 19 international. Average age 37. 264 applicants, 53% accepted, 105 enrolled. In 2013, 169 master's awarded. *Degree requirements:* For master's, minimum GPA of 2.85; for doctorate, thesis/dissertation, minimum GPA of 3.0. *Entrance requirements:* For master's, GMAT or GRE, official transcripts, two letters of recommendation, essay, current resume/curriculum vitae, interview; for doctorate, official transcripts, two letters of recommendation, essays, current resume/curriculum vitae, interview with EDBA academic committee. Additional exam requirements/recommendations for international students: Required—TOEFL (minimum score 100 iBT) or IELTS (minimum score 7). *Application deadline:* Applications are processed on a rolling basis. Application fee: $50. Electronic applications accepted. *Expenses:* Contact institution. *Financial support:* In 2013–14, 87 students received support. Federal Work-Study and scholarships/grants available. Support available to part-time students. Financial award applicants required to submit FAFSA. *Faculty research:* Sustainability, world financial markets, international business, market research, strategic marketing. *Unit head:* Dr. Craig M. McAllaster, Dean, 407-646-2249, Fax: 407-646-1550, E-mail: cmcallaster@rollins.edu. *Application contact:* Eva Gauthier Oleksiw, Admissions Coordinator, 407-646-2405, Fax: 407-646-1550, E-mail: mbaadmissions@rollins.edu.
Website: http://www.rollins.edu/mba/.

Roosevelt University, Graduate Division, Walter E. Heller College of Business Administration, Program in Business Administration, Chicago, IL 60605. Offers MBA. *Accreditation:* ACBSP. Part-time and evening/weekend programs available. *Entrance requirements:* For master's, GMAT.

Roseman University of Health Sciences, College of Dental Medicine - Henderson Campus, Henderson, NV 89014. Offers business administration (MBA); dental medicine (Post-Doctoral Certificate). *Faculty:* 3 full-time (1 woman), 11 part-time/adjunct (2 women). *Students:* 29 full-time (12 women); includes 13 minority (1 Black or African American, non-Hispanic/Latino; 11 Asian, non-Hispanic/Latino; 1 Two or more races, non-Hispanic/Latino). Average age 30. 110 applicants, 9% accepted, 10 enrolled. In 2013, 10 other advanced degrees awarded. *Degree requirements:* For master's, comprehensive exam, thesis or alternative. *Entrance requirements:* For master's, National Board Dental Examination 1 and 2, graduation from U.S. or Canadian dental school, Nevada dental license. *Application deadline:* For fall admission, 9/15 for domestic students. Applications are processed on a rolling basis. Application fee: $50. *Expenses:* Contact institution. *Financial support:* In 2013–14, 1 student received support. Scholarships/grants, health care benefits, and stipends available. Financial award application deadline: 3/2; financial award applicants required to submit FAFSA. *Unit head:* Dr. Jaleh Pourhamidi, Dean, 702-968-1652, Fax: 702-968-5277, E-mail: jpourhamidi@roseman.edu. *Application contact:* Maria Doleshal, Administrative Assistant to the Dean, 702-968-1682, E-mail: mdoleshal@roseman.edu.
Website: http://www.roseman.edu.

Roseman University of Health Sciences, MBA Program, Henderson, NV 89014. Offers MBA. Part-time and evening/weekend programs available. *Faculty:* 2 full-time (1 woman), 28 part-time/adjunct (11 women). *Students:* 5 full-time (4 women), 46 part-time (31 women); includes 25 minority (4 Black or African American, non-Hispanic/Latino; 14

Asian, non-Hispanic/Latino; 4 Hispanic/Latino; 3 Native Hawaiian or other Pacific Islander, non-Hispanic/Latino), 1 international. Average age 38. 13 applicants, 100% accepted, 13 enrolled. In 2013, 32 master's awarded. *Degree requirements:* For master's, comprehensive exam, entrepreneurial project, summative assessment and capstone. *Entrance requirements:* For master's, GMAT or leveling course for applicants whose overall GPA is below 3.0, bachelor's degree. Additional exam requirements/recommendations for international students: Required—TOEFL (minimum score 550 paper-based; 79 iBT). *Application deadline:* Applications are processed on a rolling basis. Application fee: $100. *Expenses:* Contact institution. *Financial support:* Federal Work-Study, scholarships/grants, and health care benefits available. Financial award application deadline: 3/1; financial award applicants required to submit FAFSA. *Faculty research:* Corporate leadership, economic development, dental practice management. *Unit head:* Dr. Okeleke Nzeogwu, Program Director, 702-968-1659, Fax: 702-968-1685, E-mail: onzeogwu@roseman.edu. *Application contact:* Dr. Okeleke Nzeogwu, Director, MBA Program, 702-968-1659, E-mail: onzeogwu@roseman.edu.
Website: http://www.roseman.edu.

Rosemont College, Schools of Graduate and Professional Studies, Graduate Business Programs, Rosemont, PA 19010-1699. Offers business administration (MBA); leadership (MS); management (MS). Part-time and evening/weekend programs available. Postbaccalaureate distance learning degree programs offered. *Degree requirements:* For master's, thesis (unless seeking certificate). *Entrance requirements:* For master's, minimum college GPA of 3.0, 3 letters of recommendation. Application fee is waived when completed online. *Expenses:* Contact institution.

Rowan University, Graduate School, William G. Rohrer College of Business, Department of Business Administration, Glassboro, NJ 08028-1701. Offers MBA. Part-time and evening/weekend programs available. *Faculty:* 13 full-time (8 women), 6 part-time/adjunct (2 women). *Students:* 25 full-time (7 women), 90 part-time (35 women); includes 12 minority (2 Black or African American, non-Hispanic/Latino; 5 Asian, non-Hispanic/Latino; 4 Hispanic/Latino; 1 Two or more races, non-Hispanic/Latino), 4 international. Average age 29. 54 applicants, 65% accepted, 24 enrolled. In 2013, 54 master's awarded. *Degree requirements:* For master's, comprehensive exam, thesis. *Entrance requirements:* For master's, GRE General Test. Additional exam requirements/recommendations for international students: Required—TOEFL. Application fee: $65. *Expenses: Tuition, area resident:* Part-time $638 per credit. Tuition, state resident: full-time $5742. *Required fees:* $142 per credit. Tuition and fees vary according to course level and program. *Financial support:* Career-related internships or fieldwork, Federal Work-Study, and unspecified assistantships available. Support available to part-time students. *Unit head:* Dr. Horacio Sosa, Dean, College of Graduate and Continuing Education, 856-256-4747, Fax: 856-256-5638, E-mail: sosa@rowan.edu. *Application contact:* Admissions and Enrollment Services, 856-256-5435, Fax: 856-256-5637, E-mail: cgceadmissions@rowan.edu.

Rowan University, Graduate School, William G. Rohrer College of Business, Department of Marketing and Business Information Systems, Program in Business, Glassboro, NJ 08028-1701. Offers CGS. Part-time and evening/weekend programs available. *Faculty:* 6 full-time (5 women). *Students:* 4 full-time (2 women), 25 part-time (12 women); includes 4 minority (1 Asian, non-Hispanic/Latino; 3 Hispanic/Latino), 1 international. Average age 32. 23 applicants, 78% accepted, 14 enrolled. *Entrance requirements:* Additional exam requirements/recommendations for international students: Required—TOEFL. *Application deadline:* Applications are processed on a rolling basis. Application fee: $65. Electronic applications accepted. *Expenses: Tuition, area resident:* Part-time $638 per credit. Tuition, state resident: full-time $5742. *Required fees:* $142 per credit. Tuition and fees vary according to course level and program. *Financial support:* Career-related internships or fieldwork, Federal Work-Study, and unspecified assistantships available. Support available to part-time students. *Unit head:* Dr. Horacio Sosa, Dean, College of Graduate and Continuing Education, 856-256-4747, Fax: 856-256-5638, E-mail: sosa@rowan.edu. *Application contact:* Admissions and Enrollment Services, 856-256-5435, Fax: 856-256-5637, E-mail: cgceadmissions@rowan.edu.

Royal Military College of Canada, Division of Graduate Studies and Research, Continuing Studies, Department of Business Administration, Kingston, ON K7K 7B4, Canada. Offers MBA. *Degree requirements:* For master's, thesis. *Entrance requirements:* For master's, GMAT, honours degree with second-class standing. Electronic applications accepted.

Royal Roads University, Graduate Studies, Applied Leadership and Management Program, Victoria, BC V9B 5Y2, Canada. Offers executive coaching (Graduate Certificate); health systems leadership (Graduate Certificate); project management (Graduate Certificate); public relations management (Graduate Certificate); strategic human resources management (Graduate Certificate).

Royal Roads University, Graduate Studies, Faculty of Management, Victoria, BC V9B 5Y2, Canada. Offers digital technologies management (MBA); executive management (MBA), including global aviation management, knowledge management, leadership; human resources management (MBA). Postbaccalaureate distance learning degree programs offered (minimal on-campus study). *Degree requirements:* For master's, thesis. *Entrance requirements:* For master's, 5-7 years of related work experience. Additional exam requirements/recommendations for international students: Required—TOEFL (paper-based 570) or IELTS (7) recommended. Electronic applications accepted. *Expenses:* Contact institution. *Faculty research:* Global venture analysis standards; computer assisted venture opportunity screening; teaching philosophies, instructions and methods.

Rutgers, The State University of New Jersey, Camden, School of Business, Camden, NJ 08102-1401. Offers MBA, JD/MBA. *Accreditation:* AACSB. Part-time and evening/weekend programs available. *Entrance requirements:* For master's, GMAT, 2 letters of recommendation. Additional exam requirements/recommendations for international students: Required—TOEFL (minimum score 89 iBT). Electronic applications accepted. *Expenses:* Contact institution. *Faculty research:* Efficiency in utility industry, management information systems development, management/labor relations.

Rutgers, The State University of New Jersey, Newark, Graduate School, Program in Management, Newark, NJ 07102. Offers accounting (PhD); accounting information systems (PhD); computer information systems (PhD); finance (PhD); information technology (PhD); international business (PhD); management science (PhD); marketing (PhD); organization management (PhD). Program offered jointly with New Jersey Institute of Technology. *Accreditation:* AACSB. *Degree requirements:* For doctorate, thesis/dissertation, cumulative exams. *Entrance requirements:* For doctorate, GMAT or GRE General Test, minimum undergraduate B average. Additional exam requirements/recommendations for international students: Required—TOEFL. Electronic applications accepted. *Faculty research:* Technology management, leadership and teams, consumer behavior, financial and markets, logistics.

Rutgers, The State University of New Jersey, Newark, Rutgers Business School–Newark and New Brunswick, Newark, NJ 07102. Offers MBA, MBA/MS, MD/MBA, MPH/MBA, MS/MBA. *Accreditation:* AACSB. Part-time and evening/weekend programs available. Terminal master's awarded for partial completion of doctoral program. *Degree requirements:* For master's, 60 total credits including capstone course. *Entrance requirements:* For master's, GMAT, GRE. Additional exam requirements/recommendations for international students: Required—TOEFL (minimum score 600 paper-based). Electronic applications accepted. *Expenses:* Contact institution. *Faculty research:* Finance/economics, accounting, international business, operations research, marketing, organizational behavior, supply chain management, pharmaceutical management.

Sacred Heart University, Graduate Programs, John F. Welch College of Business, Fairfield, CT 06825-1000. Offers accounting (MBA); business (MBA); finance (MBA, DBA, Certificate), including corporate finance (Certificate), finance (DBA), financial management (Certificate), global investments (Certificate); human resource management (MS); management (MBA); marketing (MBA, MS), including digital marketing (MS). *Accreditation:* AACSB. Part-time and evening/weekend programs available. Postbaccalaureate distance learning degree programs offered. *Faculty:* 15 full-time (4 women), 3 part-time/adjunct (2 women). *Students:* 30 full-time (11 women), 164 part-time (96 women); includes 36 minority (12 Black or African American, non-Hispanic/Latino; 5 Asian, non-Hispanic/Latino; 19 Hispanic/Latino), 4 international. Average age 32. 138 applicants, 80% accepted, 87 enrolled. In 2013, 81 master's awarded. *Degree requirements:* For master's, thesis or alternative. *Entrance requirements:* For master's, GMAT (preferred) or GRE General Test. Additional exam requirements/recommendations for international students: Required—PTE; Recommended—TOEFL (minimum score 570 paper-based; 80 iBT), IELTS (minimum score 6.5). *Application deadline:* Applications are processed on a rolling basis. Application fee: $60. Electronic applications accepted. *Expenses:* Contact institution. *Financial support:* Career-related internships or fieldwork, institutionally sponsored loans, and unspecified assistantships available. Support available to part-time students. Financial award applicants required to submit FAFSA. *Unit head:* Dr. John Chalykoff, Dean, 203-396-8084, Fax: 203-365-7538, E-mail: chalykoffj@sacredheart.edu. *Application contact:* Kathy Dilks, Executive Director of Graduate Admissions, 203-365-7619, Fax: 203-365-4732, E-mail: dilksk@sacredheart.edu.
Website: http://www.sacredheart.edu/academics/johnfwelchcollegeofbusiness/graduateprogramscertificates/.

Sage Graduate School, School of Management, Program in Business Administration, Troy, NY 12180-4115. Offers business strategy (MBA); finance (MBA); human resources (MBA); marketing (MBA); JD/MBA. Part-time and evening/weekend programs available. *Faculty:* 2 full-time (both women), 9 part-time/adjunct (2 women). *Students:* 10 full-time (5 women), 53 part-time (33 women); includes 14 minority (5 Black or African American, non-Hispanic/Latino; 6 Asian, non-Hispanic/Latino; 2 Hispanic/Latino; 1 Two or more races, non-Hispanic/Latino). Average age 30. 52 applicants, 54% accepted, 16 enrolled. In 2013, 22 master's awarded. *Entrance requirements:* For master's, minimum GPA of 2.75, resume, 2 letters of recommendation. Additional exam requirements/recommendations for international students: Required—TOEFL (minimum score 550 paper-based). *Application deadline:* Applications are processed on a rolling basis. Application fee: $40. *Expenses: Tuition:* Full-time $11,880; part-time $660 per credit hour. *Financial support:* Fellowships, research assistantships, Federal Work-Study, scholarships/grants, and unspecified assistantships available. Support available to part-time students. Financial award application deadline: 3/1; financial award applicants required to submit FAFSA. *Unit head:* Dr. Daniel Robeson, Dean, School of Management, 518-292-8657, Fax: 518-292-1964, E-mail: robesd@sage.edu. *Application contact:* Wendy D. Diefendorf, Director of Graduate and Adult Admission, 518-244-2443, Fax: 518-244-6880, E-mail: diefew@sage.edu.

Saginaw Valley State University, College of Business and Management, Program in Business Administration, University Center, MI 48710. Offers MBA. *Accreditation:* AACSB. Part-time and evening/weekend programs available. *Faculty:* 8 full-time (2 women), 6 part-time/adjunct (2 women). *Students:* 67 full-time (25 women), 64 part-time (31 women); includes 14 minority (5 Black or African American, non-Hispanic/Latino; 1 American Indian or Alaska Native, non-Hispanic/Latino; 2 Asian, non-Hispanic/Latino; 3 Hispanic/Latino; 3 Two or more races, non-Hispanic/Latino), 63 international. Average age 28. 105 applicants, 89% accepted, 30 enrolled. In 2013, 37 master's awarded. *Entrance requirements:* Additional exam requirements/recommendations for international students: Required—TOEFL (minimum score 550 paper-based; 79 iBT). *Application deadline:* For fall admission, 7/15 for international students; for winter admission, 11/15 for international students; for spring admission, 4/15 for international students. Applications are processed on a rolling basis. Application fee: $30 ($80 for international students). Electronic applications accepted. *Expenses:* Tuition, state resident: full-time $8933; part-time $496.30 per credit hour. Tuition, nonresident: full-time $16,806; part-time $933.65 per credit hour. *Required fees:* $263; $14.60 per credit hour. Tuition and fees vary according to degree level. *Financial support:* Federal Work-Study and scholarships/grants available. Support available to part-time students. Financial award application deadline: 4/15; financial award applicants required to submit FAFSA. *Unit head:* Dr. Mark McCartney, MBA Program Coordinator, 989-964-4064. *Application contact:* Jenna Briggs, Director, Graduate and International Admissions, 989-964-6096, Fax: 989-964-2788, E-mail: gradadm@svsu.edu.
Website: http://www.svsu.edu/mba/.

St. Ambrose University, College of Business, Program in Business Administration, Davenport, IA 52803-2898. Offers business administration (DBA); health care (MBA); human resources (MBA). *Accreditation:* ACBSP. Part-time and evening/weekend programs available. *Degree requirements:* For master's, comprehensive exam (for some programs), thesis or alternative, capstone seminar; for doctorate, comprehensive exam, thesis/dissertation, oral and written exams. *Entrance requirements:* For master's, GMAT; for doctorate, GMAT, master's degree. Additional exam requirements/recommendations for international students: Required—TOEFL. Electronic applications accepted. *Expenses:* Contact institution.

St. Bonaventure University, School of Graduate Studies, School of Business, St. Bonaventure, NY 14778-2284. Offers general business (MBA). *Accreditation:* AACSB. Part-time and evening/weekend programs available. *Faculty:* 12 full-time (4 women), 2 part-time/adjunct (0 women). *Students:* 72 full-time (25 women), 46 part-time (20 women); includes 4 minority (1 Black or African American, non-Hispanic/Latino; 2 Hispanic/Latino; 1 Two or more races, non-Hispanic/Latino), 6 international. Average age 28. 68 applicants, 93% accepted, 43 enrolled. In 2013, 106 master's awarded. *Entrance requirements:* For master's, GMAT or GRE, undergraduate degree, letters of recommendation, transcripts, current resume, personal statement. Additional exam requirements/recommendations for international students: Required—TOEFL (minimum score 550 paper-based; 79 iBT). *Application deadline:* For fall admission, 6/15 priority date for domestic students, 2/1 priority date for international students; for spring admission, 11/1 priority date for domestic students, 7/1 priority date for international students. Applications are processed on a rolling basis. Application fee: $0. Electronic applications accepted. *Financial support:* In 2013–14, 8 research assistantships with full and partial tuition reimbursements were awarded; career-related internships or fieldwork, Federal Work-Study, scholarships/grants, health care benefits, and unspecified assistantships also available. Support available to part-time students. Financial award application deadline: 4/15; financial award applicants required to submit FAFSA. *Unit head:* John B. Stevens, MBA Director, 719-375-7662, Fax: 716-372-2191.

Application contact: Bruce Campbell, Director of Graduate Admissions, 716-375-2429, Fax: 716-375-4015, E-mail: gradsch@sbu.edu.
Website: http://www.sbu.edu/academics/schools/business/graduate-degrees/master-of-business-administration-(mba).

St. Cloud State University, School of Graduate Studies, Herberger Business School, Program in Business Administration, St. Cloud, MN 56301-4498. Offers business administration (MBA); information assurance (MS). Part-time and evening/weekend programs available. *Degree requirements:* For master's, thesis or alternative. *Entrance requirements:* For master's, GMAT, minimum GPA of 2.75. Additional exam requirements/recommendations for international students: Required—Michigan English Language Assessment Battery; Recommended—TOEFL (minimum score 550 paper-based), IELTS (minimum score 6.5).

St. Edward's University, School of Management and Business, Austin, TX 78704. Offers M Ac, MA, MBA, MS, Certificate, MBA/MS. Part-time and evening/weekend programs available. *Students:* 93 full-time (38 women), 272 part-time (145 women); includes 145 minority (29 Black or African American, non-Hispanic/Latino; 2 American Indian or Alaska Native, non-Hispanic/Latino; 10 Asian, non-Hispanic/Latino; 96 Hispanic/Latino; 8 Two or more races, non-Hispanic/Latino), 18 international. Average age 33. 252 applicants, 66% accepted, 105 enrolled. In 2013, 138 master's awarded. *Degree requirements:* For master's, minimum of 24 hours in residence. *Entrance requirements:* For master's, GMAT or GRE General Test, minimum GPA of 2.75 in last 60 hours of course work. Additional exam requirements/recommendations for international students: Required—TOEFL (minimum score 79 iBT) or IELTS (minimum score 6). *Application deadline:* For fall admission, 6/1 priority date for domestic and international students; for spring admission, 10/1 priority date for domestic and international students; for summer admission, 3/1 priority date for domestic and international students. Applications are processed on a rolling basis. Application fee: $50. Electronic applications accepted. *Expenses: Tuition:* Full-time $20,664; part-time $1148 per credit hour. *Required fees:* $50 per trimester. Full-time tuition and fees vary according to course load and program. *Unit head:* Dr. Tom Sechrest, Interim Dean, 512-637-1954, Fax: 512-448-8492, E-mail: thomasls@stedwards.edu. *Application contact:* Office of Admission, 512-448-8500, Fax: 512-464-8877, E-mail: seu.admit@stedwards.edu.
Website: http://www.stedwards.edu.

Saint Francis University, School of Business, Loretto, PA 15640. Offers business administration (MBA); human resource management (MHRM). Part-time and evening/weekend programs available. *Faculty:* 8 full-time (2 women), 25 part-time/adjunct (12 women). *Students:* 25 full-time (10 women), 122 part-time (68 women); includes 11 minority (8 Black or African American, non-Hispanic/Latino; 2 Asian, non-Hispanic/Latino; 1 Hispanic/Latino). Average age 30. 25 applicants, 96% accepted, 20 enrolled. In 2013, 60 master's awarded. *Degree requirements:* For master's, comprehensive exam (for some programs), thesis (for some programs). *Entrance requirements:* For master's, GMAT (waived if undergraduate QPA is 3.3 or above), 2 letters of recommendation, minimum GPA of 2.75, two essays. Additional exam requirements/recommendations for international students: Required—TOEFL (minimum score 550 paper-based; 57 iBT). *Application deadline:* For fall admission, 8/15 priority date for domestic and international students; for spring admission, 12/1 priority date for domestic students, 12/1 for international students. Applications are processed on a rolling basis. Application fee: $30. *Expenses:* Contact institution. *Financial support:* Fellowships with partial tuition reimbursements, career-related internships or fieldwork, and unspecified assistantships available. Financial award application deadline: 8/15. *Unit head:* Dr. Randy L. Frye, Director, Graduate Business Programs, 814-472-3041, Fax: 814-472-3174, E-mail: rfrye@francis.edu. *Application contact:* Nicole Marie Bauman, Coordinator, Graduate Business Programs, 814-472-3026, Fax: 814-472-3369, E-mail: nbauman@francis.edu.
Website: http://francis.edu/school-of-business/.

St. John Fisher College, School of Business, MBA Program, Rochester, NY 14618-3597. Offers MBA. *Accreditation:* AACSB. Part-time and evening/weekend programs available. *Faculty:* 12 full-time (3 women), 5 part-time/adjunct (1 woman). *Students:* 67 full-time (29 women), 103 part-time (51 women); includes 16 minority (2 Black or African American, non-Hispanic/Latino; 1 American Indian or Alaska Native, non-Hispanic/Latino; 4 Asian, non-Hispanic/Latino; 5 Hispanic/Latino; 4 Two or more races, non-Hispanic/Latino), 4 international. Average age 27. 98 applicants, 84% accepted, 57 enrolled. In 2013, 70 master's awarded. *Degree requirements:* For master's, capstone project. *Entrance requirements:* For master's, GMAT, 2 letters of recommendation, personal statement, current resume, interview. Additional exam requirements/recommendations for international students: Required—TOEFL (minimum score 575 paper-based; 80 iBT). *Application deadline:* Applications are processed on a rolling basis. Application fee: $30. Electronic applications accepted. *Expenses: Tuition:* Part-time $795 per credit hour. *Required fees:* $10 per credit hour. Tuition and fees vary according to course load, degree level and program. *Financial support:* In 2013–14, 53 students received support. Scholarships/grants available. Financial award applicants required to submit FAFSA. *Faculty research:* Business strategy, consumer behavior, cross-cultural management practices, international finance, organizational trust. *Unit head:* Lori Hollenbeck, Assistant Dean of the School of Business, 585-899-3707, Fax: 585-385-8094, E-mail: lhollenbeck@sjfc.edu. *Application contact:* Jose Perales, Director of Graduate Admissions, 585-385-8067, E-mail: jperales@sjfc.edu.

St. John's University, The Peter J. Tobin College of Business, Queens, NY 11439. Offers MBA, MS, Adv C, JD/MBA, MS/JD. *Accreditation:* AACSB. Part-time and evening/weekend programs available. Postbaccalaureate distance learning degree programs offered (no on-campus study). *Faculty:* 104 full-time (24 women), 35 part-time/adjunct (4 women). *Students:* 509 full-time (287 women), 221 part-time (93 women); includes 166 minority (31 Black or African American, non-Hispanic/Latino; 87 Asian, non-Hispanic/Latino; 40 Hispanic/Latino; 2 Native Hawaiian or other Pacific Islander, non-Hispanic/Latino; 6 Two or more races, non-Hispanic/Latino), 343 international. Average age 26. 697 applicants, 77% accepted, 279 enrolled. In 2013, 361 master's, 1 other advanced degree awarded. *Degree requirements:* For master's, comprehensive exam (for some programs), thesis optional. *Entrance requirements:* For master's, GMAT, 2 letters of recommendation, resume, statement of goals, minimum GPA of 3.0; for Adv C, GMAT, 2 letters of recommendation, resume, undergraduate and graduate transcripts, essay, MBA. Additional exam requirements/recommendations for international students: Required—TOEFL (minimum score 600 paper-based; 100 iBT), IELTS (minimum score 7). *Application deadline:* For fall admission, 5/1 priority date for domestic and international students; for spring admission, 11/1 priority date for domestic and international students. Applications are processed on a rolling basis. Application fee: $50. Electronic applications accepted. *Expenses:* Contact institution. *Financial support:* In 2013–14, 1 fellowship (averaging $18,180 per year), 43 research assistantships with full and partial tuition reimbursements (averaging $16,475 per year), 1 teaching assistantship (averaging $21,210 per year) were awarded; scholarships/grants and unspecified assistantships also available. Support available to part-time students. Financial award application deadline: 3/1; financial award applicants required to submit FAFSA. *Unit head:* Dr. Victoria Shoaf, Dean, 718-990-6800, E-mail: shoafv@stjohns.edu. *Application contact:* Carol J. Swanberg, Assistant Dean/Director of Graduate Admissions, 718-990-1345, Fax: 718-990-5242, E-mail: tobingradnyc@stjohns.edu.
Website: http://www.stjohns.edu/academics/schools-and-colleges/peter-j-tobin-college-business.

St. Joseph's College, Long Island Campus, Executive MBA Program, Patchogue, NY 11772-2399. Offers EMBA.

St. Joseph's College, Long Island Campus, Program in Management, Patchogue, NY 11772-2399. Offers health care (AC); health care management (MS); human resource management (AC); human resources management (MS); organizational management (MS).

St. Joseph's College, New York, Graduate Programs, Programs in Business, Brooklyn, NY 11205-3688. Offers accounting (MBA); executive business administration (EMBA); management (MS).

Saint Joseph's College of Maine, Master of Business Administration in Leadership Program, Standish, ME 04084. Offers MBA. Part-time programs available. Postbaccalaureate distance learning degree programs offered (no on-campus study). *Entrance requirements:* For master's, two years of work experience.

Saint Joseph's University, Erivan K. Haub School of Business, Philadelphia, PA 19131-1395. Offers MBA, MS, Post Master's Certificate, Postbaccalaureate Certificate, DO/MBA. *Accreditation:* AACSB. Part-time and evening/weekend programs available. Postbaccalaureate distance learning degree programs offered (no on-campus study). *Faculty:* 53 full-time (12 women), 29 part-time/adjunct (4 women). *Students:* 342 full-time (175 women), 867 part-time (369 women); includes 197 minority (92 Black or African American, non-Hispanic/Latino; 2 American Indian or Alaska Native, non-Hispanic/Latino; 52 Asian, non-Hispanic/Latino; 32 Hispanic/Latino; 2 Native Hawaiian or other Pacific Islander, non-Hispanic/Latino; 17 Two or more races, non-Hispanic/Latino), 232 international. Average age 30. In 2013, 413 master's, 2 other advanced degrees awarded. *Degree requirements:* For master's and other advanced degree, minimum GPA of 3.0. *Entrance requirements:* For master's, GMAT, MAT, GRE, letters of recommendation, resume, personal statement, official undergraduate and graduate transcripts; for other advanced degree, official master's-level transcripts. Additional exam requirements/recommendations for international students: Required—TOEFL (minimum score 550 paper-based, 80 iBT), IELTS (minimum score 6.5), or PTE (minimum score 60). *Application deadline:* For fall admission, 7/15 priority date for domestic students, 5/15 priority date for international students; for spring admission, 11/15 priority date for domestic students, 10/15 priority date for international students; for summer admission, 4/15 priority date for domestic students, 2/15 priority date for international students. Applications are processed on a rolling basis. Application fee: $35. Electronic applications accepted. *Expenses: Tuition:* Part-time $786 per credit hour. Tuition and fees vary according to degree level and program. *Financial support:* In 2013–14, research assistantships with partial tuition reimbursements (averaging $4,000 per year) were awarded; scholarships/grants and unspecified assistantships also available. Support available to part-time students. Financial award application deadline: 5/1; financial award applicants required to submit FAFSA. *Faculty research:* Ethical business practices, sustainability, organic food marketing, managing the business value chain, leadership. *Total annual research expenditures:* $1.1 million. *Unit head:* Dr. Joseph A. DiAngelo, Dean, 610-660-1645, Fax: 610-660-1649, E-mail: jodiange@sju.edu. *Application contact:* Christine Hartmann, Director, MBA Program, 610-660-1659, Fax: 610-660-1599, E-mail: chartman@sju.edu.
Website: http://www.sju.edu/academics/hsb/grad.

Saint Leo University, Graduate Business Studies, Saint Leo, FL 33574-6665. Offers accounting (M Acc, MBA); business (MBA); health care management (MBA); human resource management (MBA); information security management (MBA); marketing (MBA); marketing research and social media analytics (MBA); project management (MBA); sport business (MBA). Part-time and evening/weekend programs available. Postbaccalaureate distance learning degree programs offered (no on-campus study). *Faculty:* 48 full-time (12 women), 61 part-time/adjunct (21 women). *Students:* 1,855 full-time (1,020 women); includes 810 minority (587 Black or African American, non-Hispanic/Latino; 7 American Indian or Alaska Native, non-Hispanic/Latino; 36 Asian, non-Hispanic/Latino; 161 Hispanic/Latino; 3 Native Hawaiian or other Pacific Islander, non-Hispanic/Latino; 16 Two or more races, non-Hispanic/Latino), 33 international. Average age 38. In 2013, 905 master's awarded. *Entrance requirements:* For master's, GMAT (minimum score 500 if applicant has less than 3.0 in the last two years of undergraduate study), bachelor's degree with minimum GPA of 3.0 in the last 60 hours of coursework from regionally-accredited college or university; 2 years of professional work experience; resume; 2 letters of recommendation. Additional exam requirements/recommendations for international students: Required—TOEFL (minimum score 550 paper-based; 80 iBT). *Application deadline:* For fall admission, 7/1 priority date for domestic and international students; for spring admission, 11/12 priority date for domestic students, 11/1 for international students. Applications are processed on a rolling basis. Application fee: $80. Electronic applications accepted. *Expenses: Tuition:* Full-time $12,114; part-time $673 per semester hour. Tuition and fees vary according to degree level, campus/location and program. *Financial support:* In 2013–14, 116 students received support. Career-related internships or fieldwork, Federal Work-Study, scholarships/grants, and health care benefits available. Financial award application deadline: 3/1; financial award applicants required to submit FAFSA. *Unit head:* Dr. Lorrie McGovern, Assistant Dean, Graduate Studies in Business, 352-588-7390, Fax: 352-588-8585, E-mail: mbaslu@saintleo.edu. *Application contact:* Joshua Stagner, Director of Graduate Admission, 800-707-8846, Fax: 352-588-7873, E-mail: grad.admissions@saintleo.edu.
Website: http://www.saintleo.edu/academics/graduate.aspx.

Saint Louis University, Graduate Education, John Cook School of Business, Program in Business Administration, St. Louis, MO 63103-2097. Offers MBA. *Accreditation:* AACSB. Part-time and evening/weekend programs available. *Entrance requirements:* For master's, GMAT, letter of recommendation, resume. Additional exam requirements/recommendations for international students: Required—TOEFL (minimum score 570 paper-based; 88 iBT). Electronic applications accepted. *Expenses:* Contact institution.

Saint Martin's University, Office of Graduate Studies, School of Business, Lacey, WA 98503. Offers MBA. Part-time and evening/weekend programs available. *Faculty:* 4 full-time (1 woman), 9 part-time/adjunct (2 women). *Students:* 75 full-time (31 women), 13 part-time (7 women); includes 21 minority (10 Black or African American, non-Hispanic/Latino; 1 American Indian or Alaska Native, non-Hispanic/Latino; 2 Asian, non-Hispanic/Latino; 4 Hispanic/Latino; 2 Native Hawaiian or other Pacific Islander, non-Hispanic/Latino; 2 Two or more races, non-Hispanic/Latino), 18 international. Average age 31. 80 applicants, 64% accepted, 38 enrolled. In 2013, 21 master's awarded. *Degree requirements:* For master's, thesis (for some programs). *Entrance requirements:* For master's, personal essay. Additional exam requirements/recommendations for international students: Required—TOEFL (minimum score 550 paper-based; 79 iBT); Recommended—IELTS (minimum score 6.5). *Application deadline:* For fall admission, 7/1 priority date for domestic and international students; for spring admission, 12/1 for domestic students, 12/1 priority date for international students. Applications are processed on a rolling basis. Application fee: $50. Electronic applications accepted.

Expenses: Tuition: Part-time $990 per credit hour. Tuition and fees vary according to course level and program. *Financial support:* Career-related internships or fieldwork and scholarships/grants available. Support available to part-time students. Financial award application deadline: 3/1; financial award applicants required to submit FAFSA. *Unit head:* Dr. Donald Conant, Director, MBA Program, 360-556-7359, E-mail: dconant@stmartin.edu. *Application contact:* Marie C. Boisvert, Director, Graduate Studies, 360-412-6145, E-mail: gradstudies@stmartin.edu.
Website: http://www.stmartin.edu/GradStudies/MBA.

Saint Mary's College of California, School of Economics and Business Administration, Executive MBA Program, Moraga, CA 94556. Offers MBA. Part-time and evening/weekend programs available. Postbaccalaureate distance learning degree programs offered (minimal on-campus study). *Entrance requirements:* For master's, 5 years of management experience. Additional exam requirements/recommendations for international students: Required—TOEFL. *Expenses:* Contact institution.

Saint Mary's College of California, School of Economics and Business Administration, Professional MBA Program, Moraga, CA 94556. Offers MBA. Part-time and evening/weekend programs available. *Degree requirements:* For master's, 4 half-day management practica. *Entrance requirements:* For master's, GMAT. Additional exam requirements/recommendations for international students: Required—TOEFL. *Expenses:* Contact institution.

Saint Mary's College of California, School of Liberal Arts, Leadership Studies Programs, Moraga, CA 94556. Offers MA. Part-time and evening/weekend programs available. Postbaccalaureate distance learning degree programs offered (minimal on-campus study). *Degree requirements:* For master's, research project. *Entrance requirements:* For master's, letters of recommendation, interview. Electronic applications accepted. *Expenses:* Contact institution. *Faculty research:* Leadership, organizational change, values, adult learning, transformative learning.

Saint Mary's University, Faculty of Commerce, Halifax, NS B3H 3C3, Canada. Offers MBA, MF, PhD. *Accreditation:* AACSB. Part-time and evening/weekend programs available. *Degree requirements:* For master's, research project; for doctorate, thesis/dissertation. *Entrance requirements:* For master's, GMAT, minimum B average; for doctorate, GMAT or GRE, MBA or other master's-level degree, minimum B+ average. *Expenses:* Contact institution.

St. Mary's University, Graduate School, Bill Greehey School of Business, San Antonio, TX 78228-8507. Offers accounting (MBA); business administration (MBA), including finance, international business, management; JD/MBA. *Accreditation:* AACSB. Part-time and evening/weekend programs available. Postbaccalaureate distance learning degree programs offered (minimal on-campus study). *Degree requirements:* For master's, comprehensive exam. *Entrance requirements:* For master's, GMAT. Additional exam requirements/recommendations for international students: Required—TOEFL (minimum score 550 paper-based; 80 iBT). Electronic applications accepted. *Faculty research:* International operations, job satisfaction, total quality management, taxation, stress management.

Saint Mary's University of Minnesota, Schools of Graduate and Professional Programs, Graduate School of Business and Technology, Business Administration Program, Winona, MN 55987-1399. Offers MBA, DBA. *Unit head:* Matthew Nowakowski, Director, 612-728-5142, Fax: 612-728-5121, E-mail: mnowakow@smumn.edu. *Application contact:* Russell Kreager, Director of Admissions for Graduate and Professional Programs, 612-728-5207, Fax: 612-728-5121, E-mail: rkreager@smumn.edu.
Website: http://www.smumn.edu/graduate-home/areas-of-study/graduate-school-of-business-technology/master-of-business-administration-mba.

Saint Mary's University of Minnesota, Schools of Graduate and Professional Programs, Graduate School of Business and Technology, Management Program, Winona, MN 55987-1399. Offers MA. *Degree requirements:* For master's, capstone course. *Entrance requirements:* For master's, undergraduate degree from regionally-accredited institution with minimum overall GPA of 2.75, official transcripts, personal statement, two letters of recommendation, resume. Additional exam requirements/recommendations for international students: Required—TOEFL, IELTS, or Michigan English Language Assessment Battery. Application fee: $25. Electronic applications accepted. *Unit head:* Paula Justich, Director, 612-728-5165, E-mail: pjustich@smumn.edu. *Application contact:* Russell Kreager, Director of Admissions for Graduate and Professional Programs, 612-728-5207, Fax: 612-728-5121, E-mail: rkreager@smumn.edu.
Website: http://www.smumn.edu/graduate-home/areas-of-study/graduate-school-of-business-technology/ma-in-management.

Saint Michael's College, Graduate Programs, Program in Administration and Management, Colchester, VT 05439. Offers MSA, CAMS. Part-time and evening/weekend programs available. *Degree requirements:* For master's, portfolio. *Entrance requirements:* For master's, GMAT or GRE or 3 years of work experience, minimum undergraduate GPA of 2.8. Additional exam requirements/recommendations for international students: Required—TOEFL (minimum score 550 paper-based; 80 iBT), IELTS (minimum score 6). Electronic applications accepted. *Faculty research:* Learnership/leadership, international banking, top-quality management and organizational changes, national health care, management and ethics.

Saint Peter's University, Graduate Business Programs, MBA Program, Jersey City, NJ 07306-5997. Offers finance (MBA); health care administration (MBA); human resource management (MBA); international business (MBA); management (MBA); management information systems (MBA); marketing (MBA); risk management (MBA); MBA/MS. Part-time and evening/weekend programs available. *Entrance requirements:* Additional exam requirements/recommendations for international students: Required—TOEFL. Electronic applications accepted. *Faculty research:* Finance, health care management, human resource management, international business, management, management information systems, marketing, risk management.

St. Thomas Aquinas College, Division of Business Administration, Sparkill, NY 10976. Offers business administration (MBA); finance (MBA); management (MBA); marketing (MBA). Part-time and evening/weekend programs available. *Entrance requirements:* For master's, GMAT. Additional exam requirements/recommendations for international students: Required—TOEFL. Electronic applications accepted.

St. Thomas University, School of Business, Department of Business Administration, Miami Gardens, FL 33054-6459. Offers M Acc, MBA, Certificate. Part-time and evening/weekend programs available. *Degree requirements:* For master's, comprehensive exam. *Entrance requirements:* Additional exam requirements/recommendations for international students: Required—TOEFL (minimum score 550 paper-based; 79 iBT). Electronic applications accepted.

St. Thomas University, School of Business, Department of Management, Miami Gardens, FL 33054-6459. Offers accounting (MBA); general management (MSM, Certificate); health management (MBA, MSM, Certificate); human resource management (MBA, MSM, Certificate); international business (MBA, MIB, MSM, Certificate); justice administration (MSM, Certificate); management accounting (MSM, Certificate); public management (MSM, Certificate); sports administration (MS). Part-time and evening/weekend programs available. *Degree requirements:* For master's, comprehensive exam. *Entrance requirements:* For master's, interview, minimum GPA of 3.0 or GMAT. Additional exam requirements/recommendations for international students: Required—TOEFL (minimum score 550 paper-based; 79 iBT). Electronic applications accepted.

St. Thomas University, School of Leadership Studies, Program in Professional Studies, Miami Gardens, FL 33054-6459. Offers executive management (MPS). *Entrance requirements:* Additional exam requirements/recommendations for international students: Required—TOEFL (minimum score 550 paper-based; 79 iBT).

Saint Xavier University, Graduate Studies, Graham School of Management, Chicago, IL 60655-3105. Offers employee health benefits (Certificate); finance (MBA); financial fraud examination and management (MBA, Certificate); financial planning (MBA, Certificate); generalist/individualized (MBA); health administration (MBA); managed care (Certificate); management (MBA); marketing (MBA); project management (MBA, Certificate); MBA/MS. *Accreditation:* ACBSP. Part-time and evening/weekend programs available. *Entrance requirements:* For master's, GMAT, minimum GPA of 3.0, 2 years of work experience. Electronic applications accepted. *Expenses:* Contact institution.

Salem International University, School of Business, Salem, WV 26426-0500. Offers information security (MBA); international business (MBA). Part-time programs available. Postbaccalaureate distance learning degree programs offered (no on-campus study). *Entrance requirements:* For master's, minimum undergraduate GPA of 2.5, course work in business, resume. Additional exam requirements/recommendations for international students: Recommended—TOEFL (minimum score 550 paper-based), IELTS (minimum score 6.5). Electronic applications accepted. *Expenses:* Contact institution. *Faculty research:* Organizational behavior strategy, marketing services.

Salem State University, School of Graduate Studies, Program in Business Administration, Salem, MA 01970-5353. Offers MBA. Part-time and evening/weekend programs available. *Students:* 11 full-time (3 women), 60 part-time (39 women); includes 4 minority (1 Black or African American, non-Hispanic/Latino; 1 American Indian or Alaska Native, non-Hispanic/Latino; 2 Hispanic/Latino), 13 international. 24 applicants, 83% accepted, 14 enrolled. In 2013, 20 master's awarded. *Entrance requirements:* For master's, GMAT. Additional exam requirements/recommendations for international students: Required—TOEFL (minimum score 550 paper-based; 80 iBT) or IELTS (minimum score 5.5). *Application deadline:* For fall admission, 5/1 for domestic students; for spring admission, 11/1 for domestic students. Applications are processed on a rolling basis. Application fee: $50. *Financial support:* Career-related internships or fieldwork, Federal Work-Study, scholarships/grants, and unspecified assistantships available. Support available to part-time students. Financial award application deadline: 5/1; financial award applicants required to submit FAFSA. *Unit head:* Dr. Duncan LaBay, Associate Dean, 978-542-2229, E-mail: dlabay@salemstate.edu. *Application contact:* Dr. Lee A. Brossoit, Assistant Dean of Graduate Admissions, 978-542-6673, Fax: 978-542-7215, E-mail: lbrossoit@salemstate.edu.
Website: http://www.salemstate.edu/academics/schools/2114.php.

Salisbury University, Program in Business Administration, Salisbury, MD 21801. Offers accounting (MBA); business administration (MBA). *Accreditation:* AACSB. Part-time and evening/weekend programs available. *Faculty:* 5 full-time (1 woman). *Students:* 18 full-time (10 women), 6 part-time (0 women); includes 1 minority (Black or African American, non-Hispanic/Latino), 2 international. Average age 26. 49 applicants, 37% accepted, 18 enrolled. In 2013, 26 master's awarded. *Entrance requirements:* For master's, GMAT, resume, 2 recommendations, essay, foundation course completions with minimum C grade. Additional exam requirements/recommendations for international students: Required—TOEFL (minimum score 550 paper-based; 79 iBT), IELTS (minimum score 6.5). *Application deadline:* For fall admission, 3/1 priority date for domestic and international students; for spring admission, 10/15 for domestic students. Application fee: $50. Electronic applications accepted. *Expenses: Tuition, area resident:* Part-time $342 per credit hour. Tuition, state resident: part-time $342 per credit hour. Tuition, nonresident: part-time $631 per credit hour. *Required fees:* $76 per credit hour. Tuition and fees vary according to program. *Financial support:* In 2013–14, 1 teaching assistantship with full tuition reimbursement (averaging $5,000 per year) was awarded; institutionally sponsored loans, scholarships/grants, and unspecified assistantships also available. Support available to part-time students. Financial award application deadline: 3/1; financial award applicants required to submit FAFSA. *Faculty research:* Supply chain management, accounting. *Unit head:* Yvonne Downie, Director of MBA Program, 410-548-3983, E-mail: yxdownie@salisbury.edu. *Application contact:* Kristi Horner, Administrative Assistant, MBA Program Office and Global Programs, 410-548-3377, E-mail: kmhorner@salisbury.edu.
Website: http://mba.salisbury.edu.

Salve Regina University, Program in Business Administration, Newport, RI 02840-4192. Offers cybersecurity issues in business (MBA); entrepreneurial enterprise (MBA); health care administration and management (MBA); social ventures (MBA). Part-time and evening/weekend programs available. Postbaccalaureate distance learning degree programs offered (no on-campus study). *Faculty:* 3 full-time (2 women), 12 part-time/adjunct (5 women). *Students:* 32 full-time (15 women), 67 part-time (31 women); includes 8 minority (4 Black or African American, non-Hispanic/Latino; 1 American Indian or Alaska Native, non-Hispanic/Latino; 2 Hispanic/Latino; 1 Two or more races, non-Hispanic/Latino), 2 international. Average age 29. 49 applicants, 82% accepted, 20 enrolled. In 2013, 68 master's awarded. *Entrance requirements:* For master's, GMAT, GRE General Test, or MAT, 6 undergraduate credits each in accounting, economics, quantitative analysis and calculus or statistics. Additional exam requirements/recommendations for international students: Required—TOEFL (minimum score 600 paper-based; 100 iBT) or IELTS. *Application deadline:* For fall admission, 3/15 priority date for domestic and international students; for spring admission, 9/15 priority date for domestic and international students. Applications are processed on a rolling basis. Application fee: $60. Electronic applications accepted. *Expenses: Tuition:* Full-time $8280; part-time $460 per credit. *Required fees:* $40 per term. Tuition and fees vary according to course level, course load, degree level and program. *Financial support:* Career-related internships or fieldwork and Federal Work-Study available. Support available to part-time students. Financial award application deadline: 3/1; financial award applicants required to submit FAFSA. *Unit head:* Dr. Arlene Nicholas, Director, 401-341-3280, E-mail: arlene.nicholas@salve.edu. *Application contact:* Kelly Alverson, Director of Graduate Admissions, 401-341-2153, Fax: 401-341-2973, E-mail: kelly.alverson@salve.edu.
Website: http://salve.edu/graduate-studies/business-administration-and-management.

Salve Regina University, Program in Management, Newport, RI 02840-4192. Offers law enforcement leadership (MS); nonprofit management (MS, Certificate). Part-time and evening/weekend programs available. Postbaccalaureate distance learning degree programs offered (no on-campus study). *Faculty:* 3 full-time (2 women), 12 part-time/adjunct (5 women). *Students:* 6 full-time (4 women), 24 part-time (13 women); includes 3 minority (1 Black or African American, non-Hispanic/Latino; 2 Hispanic/Latino). Average age 38. 7 applicants, 86% accepted, 4 enrolled. In 2013, 13 master's awarded. *Entrance requirements:* For master's, GMAT, GRE General Test, or MAT. Additional exam requirements/recommendations for international students: Required—TOEFL (minimum score 600 paper-based; 100 iBT). *Application deadline:* For fall admission, 3/15 priority

date for domestic students, 3/5 priority date for international students; for spring admission, 9/15 priority date for domestic and international students. Applications are processed on a rolling basis. Application fee: $60. Electronic applications accepted. *Expenses: Tuition:* Full-time $8280; part-time $460 per credit. *Required fees:* $40 per term. Tuition and fees vary according to course level, course load, degree level and program. *Financial support:* Career-related internships or fieldwork and Federal Work-Study available. Support available to part-time students. Financial award application deadline: 3/1; financial award applicants required to submit FAFSA. *Unit head:* Dr. Arlene Nicholas, Director, 401-341-3280, E-mail: arlene.nicholas@salve.edu. *Application contact:* Kelly Alverson, Director of Graduate Admissions, 401-341-2153, Fax: 401-341-2973, E-mail: kelly.alverson@salve.edu.
Website: http://salve.edu/graduate-studies/business-administration-and-management.

Samford University, Brock School of Business, Birmingham, AL 35229. Offers M Acc, MBA, JD/M Acc, JD/MBA, MBA/M Acc. *Accreditation:* AACSB. Part-time and evening/weekend programs available. *Faculty:* 12 full-time (2 women), 1 part-time/adjunct (0 women). *Students:* 123 full-time (48 women), 10 part-time (4 women); includes 8 minority (4 Black or African American, non-Hispanic/Latino; 3 Asian, non-Hispanic/Latino; 1 Hispanic/Latino), 32 international. Average age 25. 150 applicants, 72% accepted, 80 enrolled. In 2013, 55 master's awarded. *Degree requirements:* For master's, capstone course. *Entrance requirements:* For master's, GMAT. Additional exam requirements/recommendations for international students: Required—TOEFL (minimum score 90 iBT) or IELTS (minimum score 6.5). *Application deadline:* For fall admission, 8/31 priority date for domestic students, 7/1 for international students; for spring admission, 12/1 priority date for domestic students, 11/1 for international students. Applications are processed on a rolling basis. Application fee: $35. *Expenses: Tuition:* Full-time $11,552; part-time $722 per credit. *Required fees:* $500; $250 per term. *Financial support:* In 2013–14, 48 students received support. Career-related internships or fieldwork, institutionally sponsored loans, scholarships/grants, and tuition waivers (partial) available. Support available to part-time students. Financial award application deadline: 3/1; financial award applicants required to submit FAFSA. *Faculty research:* Entrepreneurship, accounting, finance, marketing, economics. *Total annual research expenditures:* $25,000. *Unit head:* Dr. Barbara Carttledge, Assistant Dean, 205-726-2935, Fax: 205-726-2540, E-mail: bhcartle@samford.edu. *Application contact:* Elizabeth Gambrell, Assistant Director of Academic Programs, 205-726-2040, Fax: 205-726-2540, E-mail: eagambre@samford.edu.
Website: http://www.samford.edu/business/.

Sam Houston State University, College of Business Administration, Department of General Business and Finance, Huntsville, TX 77341. Offers banking and financial institutions (EMBA); business administration (MBA); project management (MS). Part-time and evening/weekend programs available. Postbaccalaureate distance learning degree programs offered (minimal on-campus study). *Faculty:* 22 full-time (7 women). *Students:* 94 full-time (47 women), 283 part-time (122 women); includes 109 minority (39 Black or African American, non-Hispanic/Latino; 1 American Indian or Alaska Native, non-Hispanic/Latino; 17 Asian, non-Hispanic/Latino; 40 Hispanic/Latino; 2 Native Hawaiian or other Pacific Islander, non-Hispanic/Latino; 10 Two or more races, non-Hispanic/Latino), 29 international. Average age 35. 279 applicants, 89% accepted, 89 enrolled. In 2013, 92 master's awarded. *Degree requirements:* For master's, comprehensive exam. *Entrance requirements:* For master's, GMAT. Additional exam requirements/recommendations for international students: Required—TOEFL (minimum score 550 paper-based; 79 iBT), IELTS (minimum score 6.5). *Application deadline:* For fall admission, 8/1 for domestic students, 6/25 for international students; for spring admission, 12/1 for domestic students, 11/12 for international students. Applications are processed on a rolling basis. Application fee: $45 ($75 for international students). Electronic applications accepted. *Financial support:* Career-related internships or fieldwork, Federal Work-Study, institutionally sponsored loans, scholarships/grants, tuition waivers, and unspecified assistantships available. Support available to part-time students. Financial award application deadline: 5/31; financial award applicants required to submit FAFSA. *Unit head:* Dr. Kurt Jesswein, Chair, 936-294-4582, E-mail: kurt.jesswein@shsu.edu. *Application contact:* Rick Thaler, Associate Director, 936-294-1239, Fax: 936-294-3612, E-mail: busgrad@shsu.edu.
Website: http://www.shsu.edu/~gba_www/.

Sam Houston State University, College of Criminal Justice, Huntsville, TX 77341. Offers criminal justice (MS, PhD); criminal justice and criminology (MA); criminal justice leadership and management (MS); criminal justice management (MS); forensic science (MS); security studies (MS); victim services management (MS). Part-time and evening/weekend programs available. Postbaccalaureate distance learning degree programs offered (no on-campus study). *Faculty:* 33 full-time (11 women). *Students:* 114 full-time (69 women), 224 part-time (89 women); includes 96 minority (39 Black or African American, non-Hispanic/Latino; 3 American Indian or Alaska Native, non-Hispanic/Latino; 6 Asian, non-Hispanic/Latino; 45 Hispanic/Latino; 3 Two or more races, non-Hispanic/Latino), 24 international. Average age 34. 324 applicants, 83% accepted, 107 enrolled. In 2013, 81 master's, 9 doctorates awarded. *Degree requirements:* For master's, comprehensive exam (for some programs), thesis (for some programs); for doctorate, comprehensive exam, thesis/dissertation. *Entrance requirements:* For master's, GRE General Test; for doctorate, GRE General Test, master's degree. Additional exam requirements/recommendations for international students: Required—TOEFL (minimum score 550 paper-based; 79 iBT), IELTS (minimum score 6.5). *Application deadline:* For fall admission, 8/1 for domestic students, 6/25 for international students; for spring admission, 12/1 for domestic students, 11/12 for international students. Applications are processed on a rolling basis. Application fee: $45 ($75 for international students). Electronic applications accepted. *Financial support:* In 2013–14, 80 research assistantships (averaging $12,245 per year), 18 teaching assistantships (averaging $10,953 per year) were awarded; career-related internships or fieldwork, Federal Work-Study, institutionally sponsored loans, tuition waivers (partial), and unspecified assistantships also available. Support available to part-time students. Financial award application deadline: 5/31; financial award applicants required to submit FAFSA. *Unit head:* Dr. Vincent J. Webb, Dean, 936-294-1632, Fax: 936-294-1653, E-mail: vwebb@shsu.edu. *Application contact:* Doris Powell-Pratt, Graduate Advising Coordinator, 936-294-3637, Fax: 936-294-4055, E-mail: icc_dcp@shsu.edu.
Website: http://www.shsu.edu/cjcenter/.

San Diego State University, Graduate and Research Affairs, College of Business Administration, Department of Management, San Diego, CA 92182. Offers entrepreneurship (MS); human resources management (MS); management science (MS). Part-time and evening/weekend programs available. *Degree requirements:* For master's, thesis or alternative. *Entrance requirements:* For master's, GMAT, resume, letters of reference. Additional exam requirements/recommendations for international students: Required—TOEFL. Electronic applications accepted.

San Diego State University, Graduate and Research Affairs, College of Business Administration, Program in Business Administration, San Diego, CA 92182. Offers MBA. *Accreditation:* AACSB. Part-time programs available. *Degree requirements:* For master's, thesis or alternative. *Entrance requirements:* For master's, GMAT, resume, letters of reference. Additional exam requirements/recommendations for international students: Required—TOEFL. Electronic applications accepted.

San Francisco State University, Division of Graduate Studies, College of Business, San Francisco, CA 94132-1722. Offers MA, MBA, MSA. *Unit head:* Linda Oubre, Dean, 415-817-4300, E-mail: loubre@sfsu.edu. *Application contact:* Armaan Moatarri, Assistant Director, Graduate Programs, 415-817-4314, Fax: 415-817-4340, E-mail: amoatt@sfsu.edu.
Website: http://gbp.cob.sfsu.edu/.

San Jose State University, Graduate Studies and Research, Lucas Graduate School of Business, Programs in Business Administration, San Jose, CA 95192-0001. Offers MBA. *Accreditation:* AACSB. *Degree requirements:* For master's, comprehensive exam, thesis or alternative. *Entrance requirements:* For master's, GMAT, minimum GPA of 3.0. Electronic applications accepted.

Santa Clara University, Leavey School of Business, Santa Clara, CA 95053. Offers accelerated business administration (MBA); business administration (MBA); emerging professional business administration (MBA); entrepreneurship (MS); executive business administration (MBA); finance (MSF); information systems (MSIS); JD/MBA; MSIS/JD. *Accreditation:* AACSB. Part-time and evening/weekend programs available. *Faculty:* 85 full-time (21 women), 64 part-time/adjunct (20 women). *Students:* 292 full-time (154 women), 543 part-time (196 women); includes 262 minority (9 Black or African American, non-Hispanic/Latino; 203 Asian, non-Hispanic/Latino; 43 Hispanic/Latino; 2 Native Hawaiian or other Pacific Islander, non-Hispanic/Latino; 5 Two or more races, non-Hispanic/Latino), 260 international. Average age 30. 428 applicants, 77% accepted, 212 enrolled. In 2013, 345 master's awarded. *Degree requirements:* For master's, thesis or alternative. *Entrance requirements:* For master's, GMAT, GRE. Additional exam requirements/recommendations for international students: Required—TOEFL (minimum score 600 paper-based; 100 iBT). *Application deadline:* For fall admission, 6/1 for domestic and international students; for spring admission, 1/19 for domestic and international students. Applications are processed on a rolling basis. Application fee: $100 ($150 for international students). Electronic applications accepted. *Expenses:* Contact institution. *Financial support:* In 2013–14, 348 students received support. Career-related internships or fieldwork, Federal Work-Study, institutionally sponsored loans, and scholarships/grants available. Support available to part-time students. Financial award applicants required to submit FAFSA. *Faculty research:* Sovereign debt default, empire, and trade during the gold standard; CISE pathways to revitalized undergraduate computing education. *Unit head:* Elizabeth B. Ford, Senior Assistant Dean, 408-554-2752, Fax: 408-554-4571, E-mail: eford@scu.edu. *Application contact:* Tammy Fox, Director, Graduate Admissions and Financial Aid, 408-554-7858, E-mail: mbaadmissions@scu.edu.
Website: http://www.scu.edu/business/graduates.

Savannah State University, Master of Business Administration Program, Savannah, GA 31404. Offers MBA. *Accreditation:* AACSB. Part-time and evening/weekend programs available. *Faculty:* 6 full-time (1 woman). *Students:* 12 full-time (5 women), 26 part-time (15 women); includes 21 minority (20 Black or African American, non-Hispanic/Latino; 1 Asian, non-Hispanic/Latino), 9 international. Average age 29. 19 applicants, 100% accepted, 15 enrolled. *Entrance requirements:* For master's, GMAT, GRE, or successful completion of pre-MBA program, BA/BS from an accredited institution, official transcripts, essay, 3 letters of recommendation, immunization certificate, current resume. Additional exam requirements/recommendations for international students: Required—TOEFL. *Application deadline:* For fall admission, 6/15 for domestic students, 6/1 for international students; for spring admission, 10/1 for domestic and international students; for summer admission, 3/15 for domestic students, 3/1 for international students. Applications are processed on a rolling basis. Application fee: $25. Electronic applications accepted. *Expenses:* Tuition, state resident: full-time $4482; part-time $187 per credit hour. Tuition, nonresident: full-time $16,660; part-time $694 per credit hour. *Required fees:* $1716; $858 per term. *Financial support:* Career-related internships or fieldwork, Federal Work-Study, institutionally sponsored loans, scholarships/grants, health care benefits, and unspecified assistantships available. Financial award applicants required to submit FAFSA. *Unit head:* Dr. Mostafa Sarhan, Dean, 912-358-3389, E-mail: sarhanm@savannahstate.edu. *Application contact:* Cindy Murphy-Kelley, MBA Program Coordinator, 912-358-3393, E-mail: mba@savannahstate.edu.
Website: http://www.savannahstate.edu/coba/programs-mba.shtml.

Schiller International University, MBA Program, Madrid, Spain, Madrid, Spain. Offers international business (MBA). Part-time programs available. *Degree requirements:* For master's, comprehensive exam, thesis optional. *Entrance requirements:* Additional exam requirements/recommendations for international students: Required—TOEFL (minimum score 550 paper-based).

Schiller International University, MBA Program Paris, France, Paris, France. Offers international business (MBA). Bilingual French/English MBA available for native French speakers. Part-time and evening/weekend programs available. Postbaccalaureate distance learning degree programs offered (no on-campus study). *Degree requirements:* For master's, comprehensive exam, thesis or alternative. *Entrance requirements:* Additional exam requirements/recommendations for international students: Required—TOEFL (minimum score 550 paper-based).

Schiller International University, MBA Programs, Florida, Largo, FL 33771. Offers financial planning (MBA); information technology (MBA); international business (MBA); international hotel and tourism management (MBA). Part-time and evening/weekend programs available. Postbaccalaureate distance learning degree programs offered (no on-campus study). *Degree requirements:* For master's, thesis optional. *Entrance requirements:* Additional exam requirements/recommendations for international students: Required—TOEFL (minimum score 550 paper-based).

Schiller International University, MBA Programs, Heidelberg, Germany, Heidelberg, Germany. Offers international business (MBA, MIM); management of information technology (MBA). Part-time and evening/weekend programs available. *Degree requirements:* For master's, thesis optional. *Entrance requirements:* Additional exam requirements/recommendations for international students: Required—TOEFL (minimum score 550 paper-based). *Faculty research:* Leadership, international economy, foreign direct investment.

Schreiner University, MBA Program, Kerrville, TX 78028-5697. Offers ethical leadership (MBA). Part-time programs available. Postbaccalaureate distance learning degree programs offered (no on-campus study). *Faculty:* 7 full-time (2 women), 1 part-time/adjunct (0 women). *Students:* 26 full-time (11 women); includes 5 minority (all Hispanic/Latino). Average age 32. 19 applicants, 95% accepted, 17 enrolled. In 2013, 8 master's awarded. *Entrance requirements:* For master's, 3 recommendations; personal essay; transcripts; resume. Additional exam requirements/recommendations for international students: Required—TOEFL. *Application deadline:* For fall admission, 8/1 priority date for domestic students, 8/1 for international students; for spring admission, 12/1 priority date for domestic students, 12/1 for international students; for summer admission, 5/1 priority date for domestic students, 4/1 for international students. Applications are processed on a rolling basis. Application fee: $25. Electronic applications accepted. *Expenses:* Contact institution. *Financial support:* In 2013–14, 26 students received support. Application deadline: 8/1; applicants required to submit FAFSA. *Unit head:* Dr. Mark Woodhull, Director, 830-792-7479. *Application contact:*

Caroline Randall, Director of Admissions, 800-343-4919, Fax: 830-792-7226, E-mail: gradadmissions@schreiner.edu.
Website: http://www.schreiner.edu/online/default.aspx.

Seattle Pacific University, Master of Arts in Management Program, Seattle, WA 98119-1997. Offers faith and business (MA); human resources (MA); social and sustainable management (MA). *Entrance requirements:* For master's, GMAT or GRE (waived with cumulative GPA of 3.3 or above), bachelor's degree from accredited college or university, resume, essay, official transcript. *Application deadline:* For fall admission, 6/15 for domestic students. Application fee: $50. *Unit head:* Vicki Eveland, Program Director, 206-281-2088, E-mail: evelav@spu.edu. *Application contact:* John Glancy, Director, Graduate Admissions and Marketing, 206-281-2325, Fax: 206-281-2877, E-mail: jglancy@spu.edu.
Website: http://spu.edu/academics/school-of-business-and-economics/graduate-programs/ma-management/massm.

Seattle Pacific University, Master's Degree in Business Administration (MBA) Program, Seattle, WA 98119-1997. Offers business administration (MBA); social and sustainable enterprise (MBA). *Accreditation:* AACSB. Part-time programs available. *Students:* 24 full-time (15 women), 63 part-time (25 women); includes 26 minority (3 Black or African American, non-Hispanic/Latino; 14 Asian, non-Hispanic/Latino; 5 Hispanic/Latino; 4 Two or more races, non-Hispanic/Latino), 7 international. Average age 31. 35 applicants, 23% accepted, 8 enrolled. In 2013, 37 master's awarded. *Entrance requirements:* For master's, GMAT (minimum score of 500 preferred; 25 verbal, 30 quantitative, 4.4 analytical writing); GRE (minimum score of 295 preferred; 150 verbal/450 old scoring, 145 quantitative/525 old scoring), BA, resume as evidence of substantive work experience. Additional exam requirements/recommendations for international students: Required—TOEFL. *Application deadline:* For fall admission, 8/1 for domestic and international students; for winter admission, 11/1 for domestic and international students; for spring admission, 2/1 for domestic and international students. Applications are processed on a rolling basis. Application fee: $50. Electronic applications accepted. *Financial support:* Scholarships/grants available. Financial award applicants required to submit FAFSA. *Unit head:* Gary Karns, Associate Dean for Graduate Studies, 206-281-2948, Fax: 206-281-2733. *Application contact:* 206-281-2091.
Website: http://www.spu.edu/academics/school-of-business-and-economics/graduate-programs/mba.

Seattle University, Albers School of Business and Economics, Master of Business Administration Program, Seattle, WA 98122-1090. Offers MBA, Certificate, JD/MBA. *Accreditation:* AACSB. Part-time and evening/weekend programs available. *Faculty:* 16 full-time (4 women), 1 (woman) part-time/adjunct. *Students:* 109 full-time (58 women), 321 part-time (106 women); includes 116 minority (8 Black or African American, non-Hispanic/Latino; 1 American Indian or Alaska Native, non-Hispanic/Latino; 69 Asian, non-Hispanic/Latino; 21 Hispanic/Latino; 2 Native Hawaiian or other Pacific Islander, non-Hispanic/Latino; 15 Two or more races, non-Hispanic/Latino), 51 international. Average age 30. 206 applicants, 60% accepted, 77 enrolled. In 2013, 174 master's, 3 other advanced degrees awarded. *Entrance requirements:* For master's, GMAT, minimum GPA of 3.0, 2 years of related work experience. Additional exam requirements/recommendations for international students: Required—TOEFL (minimum score 580 paper-based; 92 iBT). *Application deadline:* For fall admission, 8/20 priority date for domestic students, 4/1 priority date for international students; for winter admission, 11/20 priority date for domestic students, 9/1 priority date for international students; for spring admission, 2/20 priority date for domestic students, 12/1 priority date for international students. Applications are processed on a rolling basis. Application fee: $55. Electronic applications accepted. *Financial support:* In 2013–14, 114 students received support. Career-related internships or fieldwork and Federal Work-Study available. Support available to part-time students. Financial award applicants required to submit FAFSA. *Unit head:* Dr. Greg Magnan, Director, 206-296-5700, Fax: 206-296-5795, E-mail: gmagnan@seattleu.edu. *Application contact:* Janet Shandley, Director of Graduate Admissions, 206-296-5900, Fax: 206-298-5656, E-mail: grad_admissions@seattleu.edu.
Website: http://www.seattleu.edu/albers/mba/.

Seton Hall University, Stillman School of Business, South Orange, NJ 07079-2697. Offers MBA, MS, Certificate. *Accreditation:* AACSB. Part-time and evening/weekend programs available. *Faculty:* 32 full-time (6 women), 20 part-time/adjunct (3 women). *Students:* 106 full-time (45 women), 265 part-time (107 women); includes 30 minority (7 Black or African American, non-Hispanic/Latino; 11 Asian, non-Hispanic/Latino; 8 Hispanic/Latino; 4 Native Hawaiian or other Pacific Islander, non-Hispanic/Latino). Average age 30. 361 applicants, 52% accepted, 93 enrolled. In 2013, 211 master's awarded. *Degree requirements:* For master's, 20 hours of community service (Social Responsibility Project). *Entrance requirements:* For master's, GMAT, GRE or CPA, advanced degree from AACSB institution, MS in a business discipline, professional degree (MD, JD, PhD, DVM, DDS, etc.), minimum undergraduate GPA of 3.0. Additional exam requirements/recommendations for international students: Required—TOEFL (minimum score 102 iBT), IELTS or PTE. *Application deadline:* For fall admission, 5/31 priority date for domestic students, 3/31 priority date for international students; for spring admission, 10/31 priority date for domestic students, 9/30 priority date for international students. Applications are processed on a rolling basis. Application fee: $75. Electronic applications accepted. *Expenses:* Contact institution. *Financial support:* In 2013–14, 24 students received support, including research assistantships with full tuition reimbursements available (averaging $23,956 per year); career-related internships or fieldwork, Federal Work-Study, scholarships/grants, and unspecified assistantships also available. Support available to part-time students. Financial award application deadline: 6/30; financial award applicants required to submit FAFSA. *Faculty research:* Sport, hedge funds, international business, legal issues, disclosure and branding. *Total annual research expenditures:* $68,000. *Unit head:* Dr. Joyce Strawser, Dean, 973-761-9013, Fax: 973-275-2465, E-mail: joyce.strawser@shu.edu. *Application contact:* Catherine Bianchi, Director of Graduate Admissions, 973-761-9262, Fax: 973-761-9208, E-mail: catherine.bianchi@shu.edu.
Website: http://www.shu.edu/academics/business/.

Seton Hill University, Program in Business Administration, Greensburg, PA 15601. Offers accounting (MBA); entrepreneurship (MBA, Certificate); management (MBA); sports management (MBA). Part-time and evening/weekend programs available. *Faculty:* 9 full-time (3 women), 6 part-time/adjunct (1 woman). *Students:* 37 full-time (15 women), 52 part-time (34 women); includes 4 minority (3 Black or African American, non-Hispanic/Latino; 1 Hispanic/Latino), 8 international. Average age 30. 93 applicants, 47% accepted, 28 enrolled. In 2013, 15 master's awarded. *Entrance requirements:* For master's, resume, 3 letters of recommendation, personal statement, transcripts. Additional exam requirements/recommendations for international students: Required—TOEFL (minimum score 600 paper-based; 100 iBT), IELTS (minimum score 6.5). *Application deadline:* Applications are processed on a rolling basis. Application fee: $0. Electronic applications accepted. *Expenses:* Tuition: Full-time $14,220; part-time $790 per credit. *Required fees:* $700; $34 per credit. $50 per semester. *Financial support:* Federal Work-Study, scholarships/grants, and tuition discounts available. Financial award application deadline: 8/15. *Faculty research:* Entrepreneurship, leadership and

strategy, knowledge management, sports management, human resources. *Unit head:* Dr. Douglas Nelson, Director, 724-830-4738, E-mail: dnelson@setonhill.edu. *Application contact:* Laurel Komarny, Program Counselor, 724-838-4209, E-mail: lkomarny@setonhill.edu.
Website: http://www.setonhill.edu/academics/graduate_programs/mba.

Shenandoah University, Harry F. Byrd, Jr. School of Business, Winchester, VA 22601-5195. Offers business administration (MBA); business administration essentials (Certificate). *Accreditation:* AACSB. Part-time and evening/weekend programs available. *Faculty:* 18 full-time (5 women), 3 part-time/adjunct (2 women). *Students:* 26 full-time (11 women), 50 part-time (21 women); includes 9 minority (2 Black or African American, non-Hispanic/Latino; 5 Asian, non-Hispanic/Latino; 1 Hispanic/Latino; 1 Native Hawaiian or other Pacific Islander, non-Hispanic/Latino), 19 international. Average age 31. 51 applicants, 51% accepted, 17 enrolled. In 2013, 43 master's, 4 other advanced degrees awarded. *Entrance requirements:* For master's, transcripts from all institutions of higher learning, minimum GPA of 2.0 in appropriate undergraduate coursework, 2 letters of recommendation, resume, interview, brief narrative; for Certificate, 2 letters of recommendation, resume, interview, brief narrative, transcripts from all institutions of higher learning attended. Additional exam requirements/recommendations for international students: Required—TOEFL (minimum score 550 paper-based; 79 iBT), IELTS (minimum score 6.5), Sakae Institute of Study Abroad (SISA) test (minimum score 15). *Application deadline:* For fall admission, 5/1 for domestic and international students; for spring admission, 11/1 for domestic and international students; for summer admission, 3/1 for domestic and international students. Application fee: $30. Electronic applications accepted. *Expenses: Tuition:* Full-time $19,176; part-time $799 per credit. *Required fees:* $365 per term. Tuition and fees vary according to course level, course load and program. *Financial support:* In 2013–14, 21 students received support, including 12 teaching assistantships with partial tuition reimbursements available (averaging $3,087 per year); career-related internships or fieldwork, institutionally sponsored loans, scholarships/grants, and unspecified assistantships also available. Support available to part-time students. Financial award application deadline: 3/15; financial award applicants required to submit FAFSA. *Faculty research:* Supply chain management, international business, micro and macro economics, organizational behavior and theory, marketing research, general accounting. *Unit head:* Miles K. Davis, PhD, Dean, 540-665-4572, Fax: 540-665-5437, E-mail: mdavi3@su.edu. *Application contact:* Andrew Woodall, Executive Director of Recruitment and Admissions, 540-665-4581, Fax: 540-665-4627, E-mail: admit@su.edu.
Website: http://www.su.edu/business/.

Shippensburg University of Pennsylvania, School of Graduate Studies, College of Arts and Sciences, Department of Sociology and Anthropology, Shippensburg, PA 17257-2299. Offers organizational development and leadership (MS), including business, communications, environmental management, higher education structure and policy, historical administration, individual and organizational development, management information systems, public organizations, social structures and organizations. Part-time and evening/weekend programs available. *Faculty:* 4 full-time (all women). *Students:* 19 full-time (11 women), 40 part-time (23 women); includes 7 minority (all Black or African American, non-Hispanic/Latino), 4 international. Average age 32. 63 applicants, 49% accepted, 19 enrolled. In 2013, 24 master's awarded. *Degree requirements:* For master's, capstone experience including internship. *Entrance requirements:* For master's, interview (if GPA less than 2.75), resume, personal goals statement. Additional exam requirements/recommendations for international students: Required—TOEFL (minimum score 580 paper-based); Recommended—IELTS (minimum score 6). *Application deadline:* For fall admission, 4/30 for international students; for spring admission, 9/30 for international students. Applications are processed on a rolling basis. Application fee: $45. Electronic applications accepted. *Expenses: Tuition, area resident:* Part-time $442 per credit. Tuition, state resident: part-time $442 per credit. Tuition, nonresident: part-time $663 per credit. *Required fees:* $127 per credit. *Financial support:* In 2013–14, 10 research assistantships with full tuition reimbursements (averaging $5,000 per year) were awarded; career-related internships or fieldwork, scholarships/grants, unspecified assistantships, and resident hall director and student payroll positions also available. Support available to part-time students. Financial award applicants required to submit FAFSA. *Unit head:* Dr. Barbara Denison, Program Coordinator, 717-477-1735, Fax: 717-477-4011, E-mail: bjdeni@ship.edu. *Application contact:* Jeremy R. Goshorn, Assistant Dean of Graduate Admissions, 717-477-1231, Fax: 717-477-4016, E-mail: jrgoshorn@ship.edu.
Website: http://www.ship.edu/odl/.

Shippensburg University of Pennsylvania, School of Graduate Studies, John L. Grove College of Business, Shippensburg, PA 17257-2299. Offers advanced studies in business (Certificate); business administration (MBA). *Accreditation:* AACSB. Part-time and evening/weekend programs available. Postbaccalaureate distance learning degree programs offered (minimal on-campus study). *Faculty:* 22 full-time (7 women), 2 part-time/adjunct (1 woman). *Students:* 34 full-time (11 women), 195 part-time (74 women); includes 24 minority (9 Black or African American, non-Hispanic/Latino; 1 American Indian or Alaska Native, non-Hispanic/Latino; 6 Asian, non-Hispanic/Latino; 8 Hispanic/Latino), 20 international. Average age 33. 229 applicants, 50% accepted, 74 enrolled. In 2013, 55 master's awarded. *Degree requirements:* For master's, thesis optional, practicum. *Entrance requirements:* For master's, GMAT (minimum score 450 if less than 5 years of post-graduate experience, including some mid-level management), resume; relevant work/classroom experience; personal goals statement; prerequisites of quantitative analysis, computer usage, and oral and written communications; laptop computer. Additional exam requirements/recommendations for international students: Required—TOEFL (minimum score 580 paper-based); Recommended—IELTS (minimum score 6). *Application deadline:* For fall admission, 4/30 for international students; for spring admission, 9/30 for international students. Applications are processed on a rolling basis. Application fee: $45. Electronic applications accepted. *Expenses: Tuition, area resident:* Part-time $442 per credit. Tuition, state resident: part-time $442 per credit. Tuition, nonresident: part-time $663 per credit. *Required fees:* $127 per credit. *Financial support:* In 2013–14, 14 research assistantships with full tuition reimbursements (averaging $5,000 per year) were awarded; career-related internships or fieldwork, scholarships/grants, unspecified assistantships, and resident hall director and student payroll positions also available. Support available to part-time students. Financial award application deadline: 3/1; financial award applicants required to submit FAFSA. *Unit head:* Dr. Robert D. Stephens, Director of MBA Program, 717-477-1483, Fax: 717-477-4003, E-mail: rdstep@ship.edu. *Application contact:* Jeremy R. Goshorn, Associate Dean of Graduate Admissions, 717-477-1231, Fax: 717-477-4016, E-mail: jrgoshorn@ship.edu.
Website: http://www.ship.edu/mba.

Shorter University, Professional Studies, Rome, GA 30165. Offers accountancy (MAC); business administration (MBA); curriculum and instruction (M Ed); leadership (MA). Evening/weekend programs available. *Degree requirements:* For master's, project. *Entrance requirements:* For master's, minimum undergraduate GPA of 2.75 in last 60 hours, 3 years of work experience. Additional exam requirements/recommendations for international students: Required—TOEFL (minimum score 550

paper-based; 79 iBT). *Faculty research:* Systems design, leadership, pedagogy using technology.

Silicon Valley University, Graduate Programs, San Jose, CA 95131. Offers business administration (MBA); computer engineering (MSCE); computer science (MSCS). *Degree requirements:* For master's, project (MSCS).

Silver Lake College of the Holy Family, Division of Graduate Studies, Program in Management and Organizational Development, Manitowoc, WI 54220-9319. Offers MS. Part-time and evening/weekend programs available. Postbaccalaureate distance learning degree programs offered (minimal on-campus study). *Faculty:* 27 part-time/adjunct (14 women). *Students:* 15 full-time (13 women), 52 part-time (31 women); includes 7 minority (6 American Indian or Alaska Native, non-Hispanic/Latino; 1 Asian, non-Hispanic/Latino). Average age 38. 33 applicants, 94% accepted, 18 enrolled. In 2013, 39 master's awarded. *Degree requirements:* For master's, thesis optional. *Entrance requirements:* For master's, minimum undergraduate GPA of 3.0, statement of purpose, three letters of recommendation, professional resume. Additional exam requirements/recommendations for international students: Required—TOEFL. *Application deadline:* For fall admission, 8/1 priority date for domestic students; for spring admission, 12/1 priority date for domestic students. Applications are processed on a rolling basis. Application fee: $0. Electronic applications accepted. *Expenses: Tuition:* Part-time $500 per credit. *Financial support:* Career-related internships or fieldwork, Federal Work-Study, and scholarships/grants available. Support available to part-time students. Financial award application deadline: 6/30; financial award applicants required to submit FAFSA. *Application contact:* Ryan Roberts, Assistant Director of Admissions, 920-686-6204, Fax: 920-686-6350, E-mail: ryan.roberts@sl.edu. Website: https://www.sl.edu/adult-education/academics/graduate-program/master-of-science-in-management-and-organizational-development/.

Simmons College, School of Management, Boston, MA 02115. Offers business administration (MBA); business and financial analytics (MBA); corporate social responsibility and sustainability (MBA); entrepreneurship (MBA); healthcare management (MBA); management (MS), including communications management, non-profit management; marketing (MBA); nonprofit management (MBA); organizational leadership (MBA); MBA/MSW; MS/MA. *Accreditation:* AACSB. Part-time and evening/weekend programs available. *Students:* 34 full-time (33 women), 233 part-time (214 women); includes 67 minority (41 Black or African American, non-Hispanic/Latino; 1 American Indian or Alaska Native, non-Hispanic/Latino; 9 Asian, non-Hispanic/Latino; 10 Hispanic/Latino; 2 Native Hawaiian or other Pacific Islander, non-Hispanic/Latino; 4 Two or more races, non-Hispanic/Latino), 7 international. In 2013, 133 master's awarded. *Entrance requirements:* For master's, GMAT or GRE. Additional exam requirements/recommendations for international students: Required—TOEFL. *Application deadline:* Applications are processed on a rolling basis. Application fee: $75. Electronic applications accepted. *Financial support:* Scholarships/grants and unspecified assistantships available. Financial award applicants required to submit FAFSA. *Faculty research:* Gender and organizations, leadership, health care management. *Unit head:* Cathy Minehan, Dean, 617-521-2846. *Application contact:* Melissa Terrio, Director of Graduate Admissions, 617-521-3840, Fax: 617-521-3880, E-mail: somadm@simmons.edu.
Website: http://www.simmons.edu/som.

Simon Fraser University, Office of Graduate Studies, Faculty of Business Administration, Vancouver, BC V5A 1S6, Canada. Offers business administration (EMBA, PhD, Graduate Diploma); finance (M Sc); management of technology (MBA); management of technology/biotechnology (MBA). *Accreditation:* AACSB. Postbaccalaureate distance learning degree programs offered. *Students:* 422 full-time (177 women), 120 part-time (48 women). 767 applicants, 43% accepted, 231 enrolled. In 2013, 219 master's, 9 doctorates, 65 other advanced degrees awarded. *Degree requirements:* For master's, thesis (for some programs); for doctorate, comprehensive exam, thesis/dissertation. *Entrance requirements:* For master's, GMAT, minimum GPA of 3.0 (on scale of 4.33), or 3.33 based on last 60 credits of undergraduate courses; for doctorate, minimum GPA of 3.5 (on scale of 4.33); for Graduate Diploma, minimum GPA of 2.5 (on scale of 4.33), or 2.67 based on the last 60 credits of undergraduate courses. Additional exam requirements/recommendations for international students: Recommended—TOEFL (minimum score 580 paper-based; 93 iBT), IELTS (minimum score 7), TWE (minimum score 5). *Application deadline:* For fall admission, 4/2 for domestic students; for winter admission, 10/1 for domestic students; for spring admission, 2/2 for domestic students. Application fee: $90 ($125 for international students). *Expenses:* Contact institution. *Financial support:* In 2013–14, 20 students received support, including 27 fellowships (averaging $6,250 per year), teaching assistantships (averaging $5,608 per year); research assistantships, career-related internships or fieldwork, and scholarships/grants also available. *Faculty research:* Accounting, management and organizational studies, technology and operations management, finance, international business. *Unit head:* Dr. Colleen Collins, Associate Dean, Graduate Programs, 778-782-5195, Fax: 778-782-4920, E-mail: grad-business@sfu.ca. *Application contact:* Graduate Secretary, 778-782-5013, Fax: 778-782-5122, E-mail: grad-business@sfu.ca.
Website: http://beedie.sfu.ca/segal/.

SIT Graduate Institute, Graduate Programs, Master's Programs in Intercultural Service, Leadership, and Management, Brattleboro, VT 05302-0676. Offers conflict transformation (MA); intercultural service, leadership, and management (MA); international education (MA); sustainable development (MA). Postbaccalaureate distance learning degree programs offered (minimal on-campus study). *Degree requirements:* For master's, one foreign language, thesis. *Entrance requirements:* For master's, 4 letters of reference. Additional exam requirements/recommendations for international students: Required—TOEFL, IELTS. *Faculty research:* Intercultural communication, conflict resolution, international education, world issues, international affairs.

Slippery Rock University of Pennsylvania, Graduate Studies (Recruitment), College of Business, Information and Social Sciences, School of Business, Slippery Rock, PA 16057-1383. Offers MBA. *Expenses:* Tuition, state resident: full-time $7956; part-time $442 per credit. Tuition, nonresident: full-time $11,934; part-time $663 per credit. *Required fees:* $2896; $148 per credit. Tuition and fees vary according to degree level and program. *Unit head:* Dr. David Culp, Chairperson, 724-738-2971, E-mail: david.culp@sru.edu. *Application contact:* Brandi Weber-Mortimer, Director of Graduate Admissions, 724-738-2051, Fax: 724-738-2146, E-mail: graduate.admissions@sru.edu. Website: http://www.sru.edu/academics/colleges/cbiss/business/Pages/index.aspx.

Sonoma State University, School of Business and Economics, Rohnert Park, CA 94928. Offers business administration (MBA), including contemporary business issues, international business and global issues, leadership and ethics; executive business administration (MBA); wine business (MBA), including contemporary business issues, international business and global issues, leadership and ethics. *Accreditation:* AACSB. Part-time and evening/weekend programs available. *Faculty:* 8 full-time (3 women). *Students:* 45 part-time (20 women); includes 10 minority (3 Black or African American, non-Hispanic/Latino; 2 Asian, non-Hispanic/Latino; 3 Hispanic/Latino; 2 Two or more races, non-Hispanic/Latino). Average age 31. 35 applicants, 83% accepted, 10 enrolled. In 2013, 49 master's awarded. *Degree requirements:* For master's, thesis or alternative. *Entrance requirements:* For master's, GMAT. Additional exam requirements/recommendations for international students: Required—TOEFL (minimum score 500 paper-based). *Application deadline:* For fall admission, 1/31 priority date for domestic students; for spring admission, 8/31 for domestic students. Applications are processed on a rolling basis. Application fee: $55. *Expenses:* Tuition, state resident: full-time $8500. Tuition, nonresident: full-time $12,964. *Required fees:* $1762. *Financial support:* Career-related internships or fieldwork, Federal Work-Study, institutionally sponsored loans, and scholarships/grants available. Support available to part-time students. Financial award application deadline: 3/2; financial award applicants required to submit FAFSA. *Unit head:* Dr. Terry Lease, Department Chair, 707-664-2377, E-mail: terry.lease@sonoma.edu. *Application contact:* Kris Wright, Associate Vice Provost, Academic Programs and Graduate Studies, 707-664-3954, E-mail: wright@sonoma.edu.
Website: http://www.sonoma.edu/busadmin/mba/.

Southeastern Louisiana University, College of Business, Hammond, LA 70402. Offers accounting (MBA); general (MBA). *Accreditation:* AACSB. *Faculty:* 12 full-time (1 woman). *Students:* 66 full-time (37 women), 20 part-time (12 women); includes 13 minority (8 Black or African American, non-Hispanic/Latino; 2 Asian, non-Hispanic/Latino; 3 Hispanic/Latino), 6 international. Average age 27. 37 applicants, 100% accepted, 23 enrolled. In 2013, 73 master's awarded. *Entrance requirements:* For master's, GMAT (minimum score 450), minimum cumulative GPA of 2.75 for all undergraduate work attempted or 3.0 all upper-division. Additional exam requirements/recommendations for international students: Required—TOEFL (minimum score 525 paper-based; 61 iBT), IELTS (minimum score 6). *Application deadline:* For fall admission, 7/15 priority date for domestic students, 6/1 priority date for international students; for spring admission, 12/1 priority date for domestic students, 10/1 priority date for international students. Applications are processed on a rolling basis. Application fee: $20 ($30 for international students). Electronic applications accepted. *Expenses:* Tuition, state resident: full-time $5047. Tuition, nonresident: full-time $17,066. *Required fees:* $1213. Tuition and fees vary according to degree level. *Financial support:* Career-related internships or fieldwork, Federal Work-Study, institutionally sponsored loans, and scholarships/grants available. Support available to part-time students. Financial award application deadline: 5/1; financial award applicants required to submit FAFSA. *Faculty research:* Ethical decision-making in accounting, entrepreneurship and emerging information, leadership and organizational performance. *Total annual research expenditures:* $18,824. *Unit head:* Dr. Antoinette Phillips, Interim Dean, 985-549-2258, Fax: 985-549-5038, E-mail: business@selu.edu. *Application contact:* Sandra Meyers, Graduate Admissions Analyst, 985-549-5620, Fax: 985-549-5882, E-mail: admissions@selu.edu.
Website: http://www.selu.edu/acad_research/colleges/bus/index.html.

Southeastern Oklahoma State University, School of Business, Durant, OK 74701-0609. Offers MBA. *Accreditation:* AACSB; ACBSP. Part-time and evening/weekend programs available. *Degree requirements:* For master's, thesis optional. *Entrance requirements:* For master's, GMAT, minimum GPA of 3.0 in last 60 hours or 2.75 overall. Additional exam requirements/recommendations for international students: Required—TOEFL (minimum score 550 paper-based; 79 iBT). Electronic applications accepted.

Southeastern University, College of Business and Legal Studies, Lakeland, FL 33801-6099. Offers business administration (MBA). Evening/weekend programs available. Postbaccalaureate distance learning degree programs offered. *Entrance requirements:* For master's, GMAT, minimum cumulative GPA of 3.0, writing sample. Electronic applications accepted.

Southeast Missouri State University, School of Graduate Studies, Harrison College of Business, Cape Girardeau, MO 63701-4799. Offers accounting (MBA); entrepreneurship (MBA); environmental management (MBA); financial management (MBA); general management (MBA); health administration (MBA); industrial management (MBA); international business (MBA); organizational management (MS); sport management (MBA). *Accreditation:* AACSB. Part-time and evening/weekend programs available. Postbaccalaureate distance learning degree programs offered (no on-campus study). *Faculty:* 27 full-time (7 women), 1 (woman) part-time/adjunct. *Students:* 59 full-time (27 women), 83 part-time (28 women); includes 10 minority (5 Black or African American, non-Hispanic/Latino; 3 Asian, non-Hispanic/Latino; 1 Hispanic/Latino; 1 Two or more races, non-Hispanic/Latino), 40 international. Average age 28. 77 applicants, 79% accepted, 48 enrolled. In 2013, 50 master's awarded. *Degree requirements:* For master's, variable foreign language requirement, comprehensive exam (for some programs), thesis or alternative, applied research project. *Entrance requirements:* For master's, GMAT or GRE, minimum undergraduate GPA of 2.5, C or better in prerequisite courses. Additional exam requirements/recommendations for international students: Required—TOEFL (minimum score 550 paper-based; 79 iBT), IELTS (minimum score 6), PTE (minimum score 53). *Application deadline:* For fall admission, 8/1 for domestic students, 6/1 for international students; for spring admission, 11/21 for domestic students, 10/1 for international students; for summer admission, 5/15 for domestic students. Applications are processed on a rolling basis. Application fee: $30 ($40 for international students). Electronic applications accepted. *Expenses:* Tuition, state resident: full-time $5139; part-time $285.50 per credit hour. Tuition, nonresident: full-time $9099; part-time $505.50 per credit hour. *Financial support:* In 2013–14, 52 students received support, including 12 teaching assistantships with full tuition reimbursements available (averaging $8,144 per year); career-related internships or fieldwork, Federal Work-Study, scholarships/grants, traineeships, tuition waivers (full), and unspecified assistantships also available. Financial award application deadline: 6/30; financial award applicants required to submit FAFSA. *Faculty research:* Ethics, corporate finance, generational difference, leadership, organizational justice. *Unit head:* Dr. Kenneth A. Heischmidt, Director, Graduate Business Studies, 573-651-2912, Fax: 573-651-5032, E-mail: kheischmidt@semo.edu. *Application contact:* Gail Amick, Admissions Specialist, 573-651-2590, Fax: 573-651-5936, E-mail: gamick@semo.edu.
Website: http://www.semo.edu/mba.

Southern Adventist University, School of Business and Management, Collegedale, TN 37315-0370. Offers accounting (MBA); church administration (MSA); church and nonprofit leadership (MBA); financial management (MFM); healthcare administration (MBA); management (MBA); marketing management (MBA); outdoor education (MSA). Part-time and evening/weekend programs available. Postbaccalaureate distance learning degree programs offered (no on-campus study). *Entrance requirements:* For master's, GMAT. Additional exam requirements/recommendations for international students: Required—TOEFL (minimum score 600 paper-based; 100 iBT). Electronic applications accepted.

Southern Arkansas University–Magnolia, Graduate Programs, Magnolia, AR 71753. Offers agriculture (MS); business administration (MBA); computer and information sciences (MS); education (M Ed), including counseling and development, curriculum and instruction, educational administration and supervision, elementary education, reading, secondary education, TESOL; kinesiology (M Ed); library media and information specialist (M Ed); mental health and clinical counseling (MS); public administration (MPA); school counseling (M Ed); teaching (MAT). *Accreditation:* NCATE. Part-time and evening/weekend programs available. Postbaccalaureate

distance learning degree programs offered. *Faculty:* 34 full-time (15 women), 8 part-time/adjunct (5 women). *Students:* 48 full-time (22 women), 269 part-time (167 women); includes 85 minority (78 Black or African American, non-Hispanic/Latino; 2 Asian, non-Hispanic/Latino; 2 Hispanic/Latino; 1 Native Hawaiian or other Pacific Islander, non-Hispanic/Latino; 2 Two or more races, non-Hispanic/Latino), 5 international. Average age 33. 149 applicants, 73% accepted, 109 enrolled. In 2013, 149 master's awarded. *Degree requirements:* For master's, comprehensive exam (for some programs), thesis optional. *Entrance requirements:* For master's, GRE, MAT or GMAT, minimum GPA of 2.5. Additional exam requirements/recommendations for international students: Required—TOEFL, IELTS. *Application deadline:* For fall admission, 7/10 for domestic and international students; for winter admission, 12/1 for domestic and international students; for spring admission, 12/1 for domestic and international students; for summer admission, 4/1 for domestic students. Applications are processed on a rolling basis. Application fee: $25 ($50 for international students). Electronic applications accepted. *Expenses:* Tuition, state resident: part-time $254 per credit hour. Tuition, nonresident: part-time $370 per credit hour. *Required fees:* $136 per credit hour. $259 per semester. Tuition and fees vary according to course load and program. *Financial support:* Career-related internships or fieldwork, Federal Work-Study, scholarships/grants, tuition waivers (full), and unspecified assistantships available. Financial award applicants required to submit FAFSA. *Faculty research:* Alternative certification for teachers, supervision of instruction, instructional leadership, counseling. *Unit head:* Dr. Kim Bloss, Dean, School of Graduate Studies, 870-235-4150, Fax: 870-235-5227, E-mail: kkbloss@saumag.edu. *Application contact:* Shrijana Malaka, Admissions Specialist, 870-235-4150, Fax: 870-235-5227, E-mail: smalakar@saumag.edu. Website: http://www.saumag.edu/graduate.

Southern Connecticut State University, School of Graduate Studies, School of Business, Program in Business Administration, New Haven, CT 06515-1355. Offers MBA. Part-time and evening/weekend programs available. *Entrance requirements:* For master's, GMAT, interview. Electronic applications accepted.

Southern Illinois University Carbondale, Graduate School, College of Business and Administration, Department of Business Administration, Carbondale, IL 62901-4701. Offers MBA, PhD, JD/MBA, MBA/MA, MBA/MS. *Accreditation:* AACSB. *Faculty:* 41 full-time (7 women), 6 part-time/adjunct (2 women). *Students:* 54 full-time (25 women), 141 part-time (59 women); includes 25 minority (13 Black or African American, non-Hispanic/Latino; 9 Asian, non-Hispanic/Latino; 3 Hispanic/Latino), 25 international. Average age 26. 98 applicants, 27% accepted, 21 enrolled. In 2013, 72 master's, 12 doctorates awarded. *Degree requirements:* For doctorate, thesis/dissertation. *Entrance requirements:* For master's, GMAT, minimum GPA of 2.7; for doctorate, GMAT, minimum graduate GPA of 3.25. Additional exam requirements/recommendations for international students: Required—TOEFL. *Application deadline:* For fall admission, 6/15 priority date for domestic students. Applications are processed on a rolling basis. Application fee: $50. *Financial support:* In 2013–14, 108 students received support, including 2 fellowships with full tuition reimbursements available, 42 research assistantships with full tuition reimbursements available, 49 teaching assistantships with full tuition reimbursements available; Federal Work-Study, institutionally sponsored loans, and tuition waivers (full) also available. Support available to part-time students. *Faculty research:* Marketing, corporate finance, organizational behavior, accounting, management information systems, international business. *Total annual research expenditures:* $200,000. *Unit head:* Dr. Suzanne Altobello, Director of Graduate Studies, 618-453-3030, E-mail: saltobello@business.siu.edu. *Application contact:* Jennie Janssen, Administrative Aide, 618-453-7559, Fax: 618-453-7961, E-mail: janssen@business.siu.edu.

Southern Illinois University Edwardsville, Graduate School, School of Business, Program in Business Administration, Edwardsville, IL 62026. Offers management information systems (MBA). *Accreditation:* AACSB. Part-time and evening/weekend programs available. *Students:* 22 full-time (10 women), 102 part-time (44 women); includes 11 minority (4 Black or African American, non-Hispanic/Latino; 2 Asian, non-Hispanic/Latino; 2 Hispanic/Latino; 3 Two or more races, non-Hispanic/Latino), 9 international. 50 applicants, 50% accepted. In 2013, 57 master's awarded. *Degree requirements:* For master's, comprehensive exam. *Entrance requirements:* For master's, GMAT. Additional exam requirements/recommendations for international students: Required—TOEFL (minimum score 550 paper-based, 79 iBT), IELTS (minimum score 6.5), Michigan Test of English Language Proficiency or PTE. *Application deadline:* For fall admission, 7/18 for domestic students, 6/1 for international students; for spring admission, 12/12 for domestic students, 10/1 for international students; for summer admission, 4/24 for domestic students, 3/1 for international students. Applications are processed on a rolling basis. Application fee: $30. Electronic applications accepted. *Expenses:* Tuition, state resident: full-time $3551. Tuition, nonresident: full-time $8378. *Financial support:* In 2013–14, 18 students received support, including fellowships with full tuition reimbursements available (averaging $8,370 per year), 4 research assistantships with full tuition reimbursements available (averaging $9,585 per year), 14 teaching assistantships with full tuition reimbursements available (averaging $9,585 per year); institutionally sponsored loans, scholarships/grants, and unspecified assistantships also available. Financial award application deadline: 3/1; financial award applicants required to submit FAFSA. *Unit head:* Dr. Janice Joplin, Director, 618-650-2485, E-mail: jjoplin@siue.edu. *Application contact:* Melissa K. Mace, Assistant Director of Graduate and International Recruitment, 618-650-2756, Fax: 618-650-3618, E-mail: mmace@siue.edu. Website: http://www.siue.edu/business/mba.

Southern Methodist University, Cox School of Business, Dallas, TX 75275. Offers accounting (MSA); business (Exec MBA); business administration (MBA), including accounting, finance, information technology and operations management, management, marketing, strategy and entrepreneurship; entrepreneurship (MS); finance (MSF); management (MSM); JD/MBA. *Accreditation:* AACSB. Part-time and evening/weekend programs available. *Entrance requirements:* For master's, GMAT. Additional exam requirements/recommendations for international students: Required—TOEFL, PTE. Electronic applications accepted. *Expenses:* Contact institution. *Faculty research:* Financial markets structure, international finance, accounting disclosure, corporate finance, leadership, change management, organizational behavior, entrepreneurship, strategic marketing, corporate strategy, product innovation, information systems, knowledge management, energy markets, customer relationship management.

Southern Nazarene University, College of Professional and Graduate Studies, School of Business, Bethany, OK 73008. Offers business administration (MBA); health care management (MBA); management (MS Mgt). *Accreditation:* ACBSP. Part-time and evening/weekend programs available. Postbaccalaureate distance learning degree programs offered (minimal on-campus study). *Degree requirements:* For master's, thesis optional. *Entrance requirements:* For master's, resume. Additional exam requirements/recommendations for international students: Required—TOEFL (minimum score 550 paper-based; 80 iBT), IELTS (minimum score 7). *Application deadline:* For fall admission, 8/1 priority date for domestic students. Applications are processed on a rolling basis. Application fee: $0. Electronic applications accepted. *Unit head:* Dr.

Randall Spindle, Chair, 405-491-6358, E-mail: rspindle@snu.edu. *Application contact:* Casey Cole, GSM Enrollment Coordinator, 405-491-6628, E-mail: cacole@snu.edu. Website: http://snu.edu/school-of-business.

Southern New Hampshire University, School of Business, Manchester, NH 03106-1045. Offers accounting (MBA, MS, Graduate Certificate); accounting finance (MS); accounting/auditing (MS); accounting/forensic accounting (MS); accounting/taxation (MS); athletic administration (MBA, Graduate Certificate); business administration (IMBA, MBA, Certificate, Graduate Certificate), including accounting (Certificate), business administration (MBA), business information systems (Graduate Certificate), human resource management (Certificate); corporate social responsibility (MBA); entrepreneurship (MBA); finance (MBA, MS, Graduate Certificate); finance/corporate finance (MS); finance/investments and securities (MS); forensic accounting (MBA); healthcare informatics (MBA); healthcare management (MBA); human resource management (Graduate Certificate); information technology (MS, Graduate Certificate); information technology management (MBA); international business (Graduate Certificate); international business and information technology (Graduate Certificate); international finance (Graduate Certificate); international sport management (Graduate Certificate); justice studies (MBA); leadership of nonprofit organizations (Graduate Certificate); marketing (MBA, MS, Graduate Certificate); operations and project management (MS); operations and supply chain management (MBA, Graduate Certificate); organizational leadership (MS); project management (MBA, Graduate Certificate); Six Sigma (MBA); Six Sigma quality (Graduate Certificate); social media marketing (MBA); sport management (MBA, MS, Graduate Certificate); sustainability and environmental compliance (MBA); workplace conflict management (MBA); MBA/Certificate. *Accreditation:* ACBSP. Part-time and evening/weekend programs available. Postbaccalaureate distance learning degree programs offered (no on-campus study). Terminal master's awarded for partial completion of doctoral program. *Degree requirements:* For master's, one foreign language, comprehensive exam (for some programs), thesis or alternative. *Entrance requirements:* For master's, minimum GPA of 2.5. Additional exam requirements/recommendations for international students: Required—TOEFL (minimum score 500 paper-based). Electronic applications accepted.

Southern Oregon University, Graduate Studies, School of Business, Ashland, OR 97520. Offers accounting (Postbaccalaureate Certificate); business administration (MBA); international management (MIM). *Accreditation:* ACBSP. Part-time and evening/weekend programs available. Postbaccalaureate distance learning degree programs offered (minimal on-campus study). *Faculty:* 19 full-time (5 women), 7 part-time/adjunct (2 women). *Students:* 37 full-time (16 women), 75 part-time (31 women); includes 11 minority (2 Black or African American, non-Hispanic/Latino; 2 American Indian or Alaska Native, non-Hispanic/Latino; 2 Hispanic/Latino; 5 Two or more races, non-Hispanic/Latino), 26 international. Average age 35. 83 applicants, 71% accepted, 34 enrolled. *Degree requirements:* For master's, comprehensive exam. *Entrance requirements:* For master's, GMAT, minimum cumulative GPA of 3.0 in the last 90 quarter credits (60 semester credits) of undergraduate coursework. Additional exam requirements/recommendations for international students: Required—TOEFL (minimum score 540 paper-based; 76 iBT), IELTS (minimum score 6), ELPT (minimum score 964) or ELS (minimum score 112). *Application deadline:* For fall admission, 7/31 priority date for domestic and international students; for winter admission, 11/15 priority date for domestic students, 11/14 priority date for international students; for spring admission, 1/7 priority date for domestic and international students. Applications are processed on a rolling basis. Application fee: $50. Electronic applications accepted. *Expenses:* Tuition, state resident: full-time $13,635; part-time $378.72 per credit hour. Tuition, nonresident: full-time $17,042; part-time $473.40 per credit hour. *Required fees:* $408 per quarter. *Financial support:* In 2013–14, 7 students received support, including 7 research assistantships with partial tuition reimbursements available; career-related internships or fieldwork, institutionally sponsored loans, scholarships/grants, and unspecified assistantships also available. *Unit head:* Dr. Mark Siders, Graduate Program Coordinator, 541-552-6709, E-mail: sidersm@sou.edu. *Application contact:* Kelly Moutsatson, Director of Admissions, 541-552-6411, Fax: 541-552-8403, E-mail: admissions@sou.edu. Website: http://www.sou.edu/business/graduate-programs.html.

Southern Polytechnic State University, School of Engineering Technology and Management, Department of Business Administration, Marietta, GA 30060-2896. Offers accounting (MBA, MSA); business administration (Graduate Transition Certificate); finance (MBA); general (MBA); management (MBA); management information systems (MBA); marketing (MBA); operations and technology management (MBA). *Accreditation:* ACBSP. Part-time and evening/weekend programs available. Postbaccalaureate distance learning degree programs offered (no on-campus study). *Degree requirements:* For master's, comprehensive exam (for some programs), capstone course and major field exam (for MBA); 30 semester hours of course work (for MSA). *Entrance requirements:* For master's, GMAT or GRE, letters of recommendation, statement of purpose, resume, minimum GPA of 2.75 or undergraduate degree in business with up to 6 transition courses; undergraduate degree in accounting from regionally-accredited school (for MSA). Additional exam requirements/recommendations for international students: Required—TOEFL (minimum score 550 paper-based; 79 iBT), IELTS (minimum score 6.5). Electronic applications accepted. *Faculty research:* Ethics, virtual reality, sustainability, management of technology, quality management, capacity planning, human-computer interaction/interface, enterprise integration planning, economic impact of educational institutions, behavioral accounting, accounting ethics, taxation, information security, visualization simulation, human-computer interaction, supply chain, logistics, economics.

Southern University and Agricultural and Mechanical College, College of Business, Baton Rouge, LA 70813. Offers MBA. *Accreditation:* AACSB. *Degree requirements:* For master's, comprehensive exam. *Entrance requirements:* For master's, GMAT. Additional exam requirements/recommendations for international students: Required—TOEFL (minimum score 525 paper-based). *Faculty research:* Accounting theory, auditing, governmental and non-profit accounting.

Southern Utah University, Master of Accountancy/MBA Dual Degree Program, Cedar City, UT 84720-2498. Offers MBA/M Acc. Part-time programs available. Postbaccalaureate distance learning degree programs offered. *Students:* 2 full-time (0 women). Average age 30. 7 applicants, 43% accepted, 4 enrolled. *Entrance requirements:* Additional exam requirements/recommendations for international students: Required—TOEFL (minimum score 550 paper-based, 79 iBT) or IELTS (minimum score 6). *Application deadline:* For fall admission, 3/1 for domestic and international students; for spring admission, 10/1 for domestic and international students; for summer admission, 3/1 for domestic and international students. Applications are processed on a rolling basis. Application fee: $60 ($65 for international students). Electronic applications accepted. *Expenses:* Contact institution. *Financial support:* Unspecified assistantships available. *Application contact:* Paula Alger, Advisor/Curriculum Coordinator, 435-865-8157, Fax: 435-586-5493, E-mail: alger@suu.edu. Website: http://www.suu.edu/business/grad.html.

Southern Utah University, Program in Business Administration, Cedar City, UT 84720-2498. Offers MBA. *Accreditation:* AACSB; ACBSP. Part-time programs available.

Business Administration and Management—General

Postbaccalaureate distance learning degree programs offered. *Students:* 20 full-time (6 women), 18 part-time (5 women); includes 2 minority (both American Indian or Alaska Native, non-Hispanic/Latino), 4 international. Average age 29. 50 applicants, 36% accepted, 32 enrolled. In 2013, 42 master's awarded. *Entrance requirements:* For master's, GMAT or GRE. Additional exam requirements/recommendations for international students: Required—TOEFL (minimum score 550 paper-based, 79 iBT) or IELTS (minimum score 6). *Application deadline:* For fall admission, 3/1 for domestic and international students; for spring admission, 10/1 for domestic and international students; for summer admission, 3/1 for domestic students, 2/1 for international students. Applications are processed on a rolling basis. Application fee: $60 ($65 for international students). Electronic applications accepted. *Expenses:* Contact institution. *Financial support:* Unspecified assistantships available. *Unit head:* Dr. Gerald Calvasina, MBA Program Director, 435-586-1976, Fax: 435-586-5493, E-mail: hamlin@suu.edu. *Application contact:* Paula Alger, Advisor/Curriculum Coordinator, 435-865-8157, Fax: 435-586-5493, E-mail: alger@suu.edu.
Website: http://suu.edu/prostu/majors/business/mba.html.

Southern Wesleyan University, Program in Business Administration, Central, SC 29630-1020. Offers MBA. Evening/weekend programs available. *Degree requirements:* For master's, comprehensive exam. *Entrance requirements:* For master's, GMAT, GRE, or MAT, minimum of 3 undergraduate semester credit hours each in accounting, economics, and statistics; minimum of 18 undergraduate semester credit hours in business administration; minimum of 2 years' significant work experience. Additional exam requirements/recommendations for international students: Required—TOEFL (minimum score 500 paper-based).

Southern Wesleyan University, Program in Management, Central, SC 29630-1020. Offers MSM. Evening/weekend programs available. *Entrance requirements:* For master's, GMAT, GRE, or MAT, minimum of 18 undergraduate semester credit hours in business administration; minimum of 2 years significant work experience. Additional exam requirements/recommendations for international students: Required—TOEFL (minimum score 500 paper-based). *Expenses:* Contact institution.

South University, Graduate Programs, College of Business, Savannah, GA 31406. Offers corrections (MBA); entrepreneurship and small business (MBA); healthcare administration (MBA); hospitality management (MBA); leadership (MS); public administration (MPA); sustainability (MBA).

South University, Program in Business Administration, Royal Palm Beach, FL 33411. Offers business administration (MBA); healthcare administration (MBA).

South University, Program in Business Administration, Montgomery, AL 36116-1120. Offers MBA.

South University, Program in Business Administration, Columbia, SC 29203. Offers MBA.

South University, Program in Business Administration, Glen Allen, VA 23060. Offers MBA.

South University, Program in Business Administration, Virginia Beach, VA 23452. Offers MBA.

South University, Program in Business Administration, Austin, TX 78729. Offers MBA.

South University, Program in Business Administration, Novi, MI 48377. Offers MBA.

South University, Program in Business Administration, Tampa, FL 33614. Offers MBA.

South University, Program in Business Administration, High Point, NC 27265. Offers MBA.

South University, Program in Business Administration, Cleveland, OH 44128. Offers MBA.

Southwest Baptist University, Program in Business, Bolivar, MO 65613-2597. Offers business administration (MBA); health administration (MBA). *Accreditation:* ACBSP. Part-time programs available. Postbaccalaureate distance learning degree programs offered (no on-campus study). *Degree requirements:* For master's, comprehensive exam. *Entrance requirements:* For master's, interviews, minimum GPA of 2.75. Additional exam requirements/recommendations for international students: Required—TOEFL (minimum score 550 paper-based).

Southwestern Adventist University, Business Administration Department, Keene, TX 76059. Offers accounting (MBA); finance (MBA); management/leadership (MBA). Part-time and evening/weekend programs available. *Degree requirements:* For master's, capstone course. *Entrance requirements:* For master's, GMAT, GRE General Test.

Southwestern College, Fifth-Year Graduate Programs, Winfield, KS 67156-2499. Offers management (MBA). Part-time programs available. *Faculty:* 3 full-time (0 women), 3 part-time/adjunct (0 women). *Students:* 12 full-time (6 women), 11 part-time (5 women); includes 2 minority (both Hispanic/Latino), 10 international. Average age 26. 17 applicants, 100% accepted, 14 enrolled. In 2013, 17 master's awarded. *Entrance requirements:* For master's, baccalaureate degree, minimum GPA of 3.0. Additional exam requirements/recommendations for international students: Required—TOEFL (minimum score 550 paper-based). *Application deadline:* For fall admission, 4/1 priority date for domestic students; for spring admission, 12/1 priority date for domestic students. Applications are processed on a rolling basis. Electronic applications accepted. *Expenses: Tuition:* Full-time $8968; part-time $498 per credit hour. Tuition and fees vary according to course level and program. *Financial support:* In 2013–14, 9 students received support. Federal Work-Study, tuition waivers (partial), and unspecified assistantships available. Financial award application deadline: 4/1; financial award applicants required to submit FAFSA. *Unit head:* Dr. James Sheppard, Vice President for Academic Affairs, 620-229-6227, Fax: 620-229-6224, E-mail: james.sheppard@sckans.edu. *Application contact:* Marla Sexson, Vice President for Enrollment Management, 800-846-1543 Ext. 6364, Fax: 620-229-6344, E-mail: marla.sexson@sckans.edu.
Website: http://www.sckans.edu/graduate.

Southwestern College, Professional Studies Programs, Wichita, KS 67207. Offers accountancy (MA); business administration (MBA); leadership (MS); management (MS); security administration (MS); specialized ministries (MA); theological studies (MA). Part-time and evening/weekend programs available. Postbaccalaureate distance learning degree programs offered (minimal on-campus study). *Faculty:* 33 part-time/adjunct (6 women). *Students:* 125 part-time (48 women); includes 28 minority (12 Black or African American, non-Hispanic/Latino; 1 American Indian or Alaska Native, non-Hispanic/Latino; 2 Asian, non-Hispanic/Latino; 7 Hispanic/Latino; 6 Two or more races, non-Hispanic/Latino). Average age 37. 95 applicants, 57% accepted, 29 enrolled. In 2013, 85 master's awarded. *Degree requirements:* For master's, practicum/capstone project. *Entrance requirements:* For master's, baccalaureate degree; minimum GPA of 2.5 (for MA and MS), 3.0 (for MBA). Additional exam requirements/recommendations for international students: Required—TOEFL (minimum score 550 paper-based). *Application deadline:* For fall admission, 8/1 for domestic students; for spring admission, 12/1 for domestic students. Applications are processed on a rolling basis. Application fee: $0. Electronic applications accepted. *Expenses: Tuition:* Full-time $8968; part-time $498 per credit hour. Tuition and fees vary according to course level and program. *Financial support:* In 2013–14, 8 students received support. Federal Work-Study, tuition waivers (partial), and unspecified assistantships available. Financial award application deadline: 4/1; financial award applicants required to submit FAFSA. *Unit head:* Susan Backofen, Vice President for Enrollment Management, 888-684-5335 Ext. 214, Fax: 316-688-5218, E-mail: susan.backofen@sckans.edu. *Application contact:* Elmer Patterson, Enrollment Manager, 888-684-5335 Ext. 131, Fax: 316-688-5218, E-mail: elmer.patterson@sckans.edu.
Website: http://www.southwesterncollege.org.

Southwestern Oklahoma State University, College of Professional and Graduate Studies, School of Business and Technology, Weatherford, OK 73096-3098. Offers MBA. MBA distance learning degree program offered to Oklahoma residents only. Part-time and evening/weekend programs available. Postbaccalaureate distance learning degree programs offered (minimal on-campus study). *Degree requirements:* For master's, comprehensive exam. *Entrance requirements:* For master's, GMAT, minimum GPA of 2.5. Additional exam requirements/recommendations for international students: Required—TOEFL.

Southwest Minnesota State University, Department of Business and Public Affairs, Marshall, MN 56258. Offers leadership (MBA); management (MBA); marketing (MBA). Part-time and evening/weekend programs available. Postbaccalaureate distance learning degree programs offered (no on-campus study). *Degree requirements:* For master's, thesis. *Entrance requirements:* For master's, GMAT (minimum score: 450). Additional exam requirements/recommendations for international students: Recommended—TOEFL (minimum score 550 paper-based; 79 iBT), IELTS. Electronic applications accepted.

Southwest University, MBA Program, Kenner, LA 70062. Offers business administration (MBA); management (MBA); organizational management (MBA).

Southwest University, Program in Management, Kenner, LA 70062. Offers MA.

Spalding University, Graduate Studies, College of Social Sciences and Humanities, School of Business, Louisville, KY 40203-2188. Offers business communication (MS). Part-time and evening/weekend programs available. *Faculty:* 6 full-time (4 women), 5 part-time/adjunct (2 women). *Students:* 60 full-time (39 women), 24 part-time (19 women); includes 25 minority (24 Black or African American, non-Hispanic/Latino; 1 Native Hawaiian or other Pacific Islander, non-Hispanic/Latino), 2 international. Average age 37. 37 applicants, 78% accepted, 20 enrolled. In 2013, 35 master's awarded. *Degree requirements:* For master's, project. *Entrance requirements:* For master's, GRE or GMAT, writing sample, interview, letters of recommendation, transcripts, resume. Additional exam requirements/recommendations for international students: Required—TOEFL (minimum score 535 paper-based). *Application deadline:* Applications are processed on a rolling basis. Application fee: $30. *Expenses: Tuition:* Full-time $21,450. *Required fees:* $810. Tuition and fees vary according to course load, degree level, program and student level. *Financial support:* Application deadline: 3/30; applicants required to submit FAFSA. *Faculty research:* Curriculum development, consumer behavior, interdisciplinary pedagogy. *Unit head:* Dr. Robin Hinkle, Director, 502-873-4244, E-mail: rhinkle@spalding.edu. *Application contact:* Claire Elder, Administrative Assistant, 502-873-7120, E-mail: celder@spalding.edu.

Spring Arbor University, School of Business and Management, Spring Arbor, MI 49283-9799. Offers MBA. Part-time and evening/weekend programs available. Postbaccalaureate distance learning degree programs offered. *Faculty:* 7 full-time (2 women), 9 part-time/adjunct (4 women). *Students:* 174 full-time (105 women), 26 part-time (13 women); includes 27 minority (22 Black or African American, non-Hispanic/Latino; 1 American Indian or Alaska Native, non-Hispanic/Latino; 3 Asian, non-Hispanic/Latino; 1 Hispanic/Latino), 1 international. Average age 37. In 2013, 30 master's awarded. *Degree requirements:* For master's, thesis. *Entrance requirements:* For master's, minimum overall GPA of 3.0 for all undergraduate coursework, bachelor's degree from regionally-accredited college or university, two recommendation forms from professional/academic individuals. Additional exam requirements/recommendations for international students: Required—TOEFL (minimum score 600 paper-based). *Application deadline:* Applications are processed on a rolling basis. Application fee: $40. *Financial support:* Career-related internships or fieldwork, scholarships/grants, and tuition waivers (partial) available. Support available to part-time students. Financial award application deadline: 8/25; financial award applicants required to submit FAFSA. *Unit head:* Dr. James Coe, Dean, 517-750-1200 Ext. 1569, Fax: 517-750-6624, E-mail: jcoe@arbor.edu. *Application contact:* Greg Bentle, Coordinator of Graduate Recruitment, 517-750-6763, Fax: 517-750-6624, E-mail: gbentle@arbor.edu.
Website: http://www.arbor.edu/academics/schools/gainey-school-of-business/.

Spring Hill College, Graduate Programs, Program in Business Administration, Mobile, AL 36608-1791. Offers MBA. Part-time and evening/weekend programs available. *Faculty:* 2 full-time (0 women), 1 part-time/adjunct (0 women). *Students:* 2 full-time (both women), 17 part-time (8 women); includes 3 minority (1 Black or African American, non-Hispanic/Latino; 1 Asian, non-Hispanic/Latino; 1 Hispanic/Latino). Average age 35. In 2013, 5 master's awarded. *Degree requirements:* For master's, comprehensive exam, capstone course, completion of program within 6 calendar years. *Entrance requirements:* For master's, GMAT, bachelor's degree. Additional exam requirements/recommendations for international students: Required—TOEFL (minimum score 550 paper-based; 80 iBT), IELTS (minimum score 6.5), CPE or CAE (minimum score C), Michigan English Language Assessment Battery (minimum score 90). *Application deadline:* For fall admission, 8/1 priority date for domestic and international students; for spring admission, 12/1 priority date for domestic and international students. Applications are processed on a rolling basis. Application fee: $25 ($35 for international students). Electronic applications accepted. *Expenses:* Contact institution. *Financial support:* Applicants required to submit FAFSA. *Unit head:* Dr. Sergio Castello, Director, 251-380-4123, Fax: 251-460-2178, E-mail: scastello@shc.edu. *Application contact:* Donna B. Tarasavage, Associate Director, Academic Affairs, 251-380-3067, Fax: 251-460-2182, E-mail: dtarasavage@shc.edu.
Website: http://www.shc.edu/grad/academics/business.

Stanford University, Graduate School of Business, Stanford, CA 94305-9991. Offers MBA, PhD, JD/MBA, MBA/MS. *Accreditation:* AACSB. Terminal master's awarded for partial completion of doctoral program. *Degree requirements:* For doctorate, thesis/dissertation. *Entrance requirements:* For master's, GMAT; for doctorate, GMAT, GRE. Electronic applications accepted. *Expenses:* Contact institution.

State University of New York at New Paltz, Graduate School, School of Business, New Paltz, NY 12561. Offers business administration (MBA); public accountancy (MBA). Part-time and evening/weekend programs available. *Faculty:* 20 full-time (7 women), 2 part-time/adjunct (1 woman). *Students:* 54 full-time (29 women), 18 part-time (13 women); includes 15 minority (2 Black or African American, non-Hispanic/Latino; 8 Asian, non-Hispanic/Latino; 4 Hispanic/Latino; 1 Two or more races, non-Hispanic/Latino), 22 international. Average age 27. 48 applicants, 90% accepted, 30 enrolled. In 2013, 45 master's awarded. *Degree requirements:* For master's, internship. *Entrance requirements:* For master's, GMAT or GRE, minimum GPA of 3.0. Additional exam requirements/recommendations for international students: Required—TOEFL (minimum score 550 paper-based; 80 iBT), IELTS (minimum score 6.5). *Application deadline:* For fall admission, 5/15 priority date for domestic students, 5/15 for international students; for spring admission, 11/15 for domestic and international students. Applications are

processed on a rolling basis. Application fee: $50. Electronic applications accepted. *Expenses:* Contact institution. *Financial support:* In 2013–14, 6 research assistantships with partial tuition reimbursements (averaging $5,000 per year), 1 teaching assistantship with partial tuition reimbursement (averaging $5,000 per year) were awarded; scholarships/grants, traineeships, and unspecified assistantships also available. Financial award application deadline: 8/1. *Faculty research:* Cognitive styles in management education, supporting SME e-commerce migration through e-learning, earnings management and board activity, trading future spread portfolio, global equity market correlation and volatility. *Unit head:* Dr. Chih-Yang Tsai, Interim Dean, 845-257-2930, E-mail: mba@newpaltz.edu. *Application contact:* Aaron Hines, Director of MBA Program, 845-257-2968, E-mail: mba@newpaltz.edu. Website: http://mba.newpaltz.edu.

State University of New York at Oswego, Graduate Studies, School of Business, Program in Business Administration, Oswego, NY 13126. Offers MBA. *Accreditation:* AACSB. Part-time and evening/weekend programs available. *Entrance requirements:* For master's, GMAT, minimum GPA of 2.6. Additional exam requirements/recommendations for international students: Required—TOEFL (minimum score 560 paper-based). *Faculty research:* Marketing, industrial finance, technology.

State University of New York College at Geneseo, Graduate Studies, School of Business, Geneseo, NY 14454. Offers accounting (MS). *Accreditation:* AACSB. *Faculty:* 4 full-time (1 woman), 1 part-time/adjunct (0 women). *Students:* 13 full-time (4 women); includes 1 minority (Asian, non-Hispanic/Latino), 1 international. Average age 25. 21 applicants, 100% accepted, 14 enrolled. In 2013, 13 master's awarded. *Entrance requirements:* For master's, GMAT, bachelor's degree in accounting. *Application deadline:* For fall admission, 2/1 priority date for domestic students; for spring admission, 9/1 for domestic students. Application fee: $50. *Expenses:* Tuition, state resident: full-time $8790; part-time $411 per credit hour. Tuition, nonresident: full-time $18,350; part-time $765 per credit hour. *Required fees:* $795; $32.90 per credit hour. *Financial support:* Application deadline: 4/1; applicants required to submit FAFSA. *Unit head:* Dr. Michael D. Schinski, Associate Professor, 585-245-5367, Fax: 585-245-5467, E-mail: schinski@geneseo.edu. *Application contact:* Dr. Harry Howe, Professor/Coordinator, 585-245-5465, Fax: 585-245-5467, E-mail: howeh@geneseo.edu.

State University of New York College at Old Westbury, School of Business, Old Westbury, NY 11568-0210. Offers accounting (MS); taxation (MS). Part-time and evening/weekend programs available. *Faculty:* 8 full-time (1 woman), 2 part-time/adjunct (0 women). *Students:* 39 full-time (19 women), 66 part-time (32 women); includes 31 minority (6 Black or African American, non-Hispanic/Latino; 12 Asian, non-Hispanic/Latino; 13 Hispanic/Latino). Average age 33. 65 applicants, 83% accepted, 36 enrolled. In 2013, 36 master's awarded. *Entrance requirements:* For master's, GMAT, 2 letters of recommendation. Additional exam requirements/recommendations for international students: Required—TOEFL (minimum score 550 paper-based). *Application deadline:* For fall admission, 6/15 priority date for domestic students; for spring admission, 11/15 priority date for domestic students. Applications are processed on a rolling basis. Application fee: $50. Electronic applications accepted. *Expenses:* Tuition, state resident: full-time $9370; part-time $390 per credit. Tuition, nonresident: full-time $16,680; part-time $695 per credit. *Required fees:* $45.85 per credit. $47 per term. *Faculty research:* Corporate governance, asset pricing, corporate finance, hedge funds, taxation. *Unit head:* Rita Buttermilch, Director of Graduate Business Programs, 516-876-3900, E-mail: buttermilchr@oldwestbury.edu. *Application contact:* Philip D'Angelo, Graduate Admissions Office, 516-876-3073, E-mail: enroll@oldwestbury.edu.

State University of New York Empire State College, School for Graduate Studies, Program in Business Administration, Saratoga Springs, NY 12866-4391. Offers global leadership (MBA); management (MBA). Part-time programs available. Postbaccalaureate distance learning degree programs offered (minimal on-campus study). *Degree requirements:* For master's, thesis or alternative. *Entrance requirements:* For master's, previous course work in statistics, macroeconomics, microeconomics, and accounting. Additional exam requirements/recommendations for international students: Required—TOEFL (minimum score 600 paper-based). Electronic applications accepted. *Expenses:* Contact institution. *Faculty research:* Corporate strategy, managerial competencies, decision analysis, economics in transition, organizational communication.

State University of New York Institute of Technology, Program in Business Administration in Technology Management, Utica, NY 13504-3050. Offers accounting and finance (MBA); business management (MBA); health services management (MBA); human resource management (MBA); marketing management (MBA). Part-time programs available. Postbaccalaureate distance learning degree programs offered (no on-campus study). *Faculty:* 10 full-time (2 women), 2 part-time/adjunct (1 woman). *Students:* 29 full-time (13 women), 89 part-time (26 women); includes 17 minority (5 Black or African American, non-Hispanic/Latino; 8 Asian, non-Hispanic/Latino; 3 Hispanic/Latino; 1 Two or more races, non-Hispanic/Latino), 1 international. Average age 33. 78 applicants, 54% accepted, 29 enrolled. In 2013, 57 master's awarded. *Degree requirements:* For master's, capstone course. *Entrance requirements:* For master's, GMAT, resume, one letter of reference. Additional exam requirements/recommendations for international students: Required—TOEFL (minimum score 550 paper-based; 79 iBT), IELTS (minimum score 6.5). *Application deadline:* For fall admission, 8/1 priority date for domestic students, 7/1 for international students; for spring admission, 12/1 for domestic students, 11/1 for international students. Applications are processed on a rolling basis. Application fee: $60. Electronic applications accepted. *Expenses:* Tuition, state resident: full-time $9870; part-time $411 per credit hour. Tuition, nonresident: full-time $20,150; part-time $765 per credit hour. *Required fees:* $1180; $50.73 per credit hour. *Financial support:* In 2013–14, 3 students received support, including 1 fellowship with full tuition reimbursement available (averaging $5,545 per year), 2 research assistantships with partial tuition reimbursements available (averaging $4,000 per year); unspecified assistantships also available. Financial award application deadline: 6/1; financial award applicants required to submit FAFSA. *Faculty research:* Technology management, writing schools, leadership, new products. *Unit head:* Dr. Rafael Romero, Program Coordinator and Associate Professor, 315-792-7337, Fax: 315-792-7138, E-mail: rafael.romero@sunyit.edu. *Application contact:* Maryrose Raab, Coordinator of Graduate Center, 315-792-7347, Fax: 315-792-7221, E-mail: maryrose.raab@sunyit.edu. Website: http://www.sunyit.edu/programs/graduate/mbatm/

Stephen F. Austin State University, Graduate School, College of Business, Program in Business Administration, Nacogdoches, TX 75962. Offers business (MBA); management and marketing (MBA). *Accreditation:* AACSB. Part-time and evening/weekend programs available. *Degree requirements:* For master's, comprehensive exam. *Entrance requirements:* For master's, GMAT, minimum AACSB index of 1000. Additional exam requirements/recommendations for international students: Required—TOEFL (minimum score 550 paper-based). *Faculty research:* Strategic implications, information search, multinational firms, philosophical guidance.

Stephens College, Division of Graduate and Continuing Studies, Graduate Business Programs, Columbia, MO 65215-0002. Offers MBA, MSL. Part-time programs available. Postbaccalaureate distance learning degree programs offered (minimal on-campus study). *Entrance requirements:* For master's, minimum GPA of 3.0 in last 60 hours.

Additional exam requirements/recommendations for international students: Required—TOEFL. Electronic applications accepted.

Stetson University, School of Business Administration, Program in Business Administration, DeLand, FL 32723. Offers MBA, JD/MBA. *Accreditation:* AACSB. Part-time and evening/weekend programs available. *Faculty:* 13 full-time (3 women), 6 part-time/adjunct (2 women). *Students:* 90 full-time (35 women), 35 part-time (19 women); includes 21 minority (4 Black or African American, non-Hispanic/Latino; 2 Asian, non-Hispanic/Latino; 15 Hispanic/Latino), 8 international. Average age 30. 98 applicants, 62% accepted, 56 enrolled. In 2013, 94 master's awarded. *Entrance requirements:* For master's, GMAT, GRE. Additional exam requirements/recommendations for international students: Required—TOEFL (minimum score 90 iBT), IELTS (minimum score 7.5). *Application deadline:* For fall admission, 7/21 for domestic students; for spring admission, 12/20 for domestic students; for summer admission, 4/14 for domestic students. Applications are processed on a rolling basis. Application fee: $50. Electronic applications accepted. *Financial support:* Application deadline: 3/15. *Unit head:* Kathy Hannon, Assistant Director for Graduate Business Programs, 386-822-7410. *Application contact:* John F. Moore, Jr., Assistant Director of Graduate Admissions, 386-822-7100, Fax: 386-822-7112, E-mail: jfmoore@stetson.edu.

Stevens Institute of Technology, Graduate School, Wesley J. Howe School of Technology Management, Program in Business Administration, Hoboken, NJ 07030. Offers engineering management (MBA); financial engineering (MBA); information management (MBA); information technology in financial services (MBA); information technology in the pharmaceutical industry (MBA); information technology outsourcing (MBA); pharmaceutical management (MBA); project management (MBA); technology management (MBA); telecommunications management (MBA).

Stevens Institute of Technology, Graduate School, Wesley J. Howe School of Technology Management, Program in Management, Hoboken, NJ 07030. Offers general management (MS); global innovation management (MS); human resource management (MS); information management (MS); project management (MS); technology commercialization (MS); technology management (MS). Part-time programs available. *Degree requirements:* For master's, thesis optional. *Entrance requirements:* For master's, GMAT, GRE General Test. Additional exam requirements/recommendations for international students: Required—TOEFL. Electronic applications accepted. *Faculty research:* Industrial economics.

Stony Brook University, State University of New York, Graduate School, College of Business, Program in Business Administration, Stony Brook, NY 11794. Offers finance (MBA, Certificate); health care management (MBA, Certificate); human resource management (Certificate); human resources (MBA); information systems management (MBA, Certificate); management (MBA); marketing (MBA). *Faculty:* 32 full-time (7 women), 29 part-time/adjunct (8 women). *Students:* 189 full-time (102 women), 111 part-time (40 women); includes 50 minority (10 Black or African American, non-Hispanic/Latino; 1 American Indian or Alaska Native, non-Hispanic/Latino; 25 Asian, non-Hispanic/Latino; 14 Hispanic/Latino), 114 international. 255 applicants, 53% accepted, 70 enrolled. In 2013, 157 master's, 1 other advanced degree awarded. *Entrance requirements:* For master's, GMAT, 3 letters of recommendation from current or former employers or professors, transcripts, personal statement, resume. Additional exam requirements/recommendations for international students: Required—TOEFL (minimum score 550 paper-based; 90 iBT), IELTS (minimum score 6.5). *Application deadline:* For fall admission, 6/1 for domestic students, 3/15 for international students; for spring admission, 12/1 for domestic students, 11/1 for international students. Application fee: $100. *Expenses:* Tuition, state resident: full-time $9870; part-time $411 per credit. Tuition, nonresident: full-time $18,350; part-time $765 per credit. *Financial support:* Teaching assistantships available. Total annual research expenditures: $53,718. *Unit head:* Dr. Manuel London, Dean and Director, Center for Human Resource Management, 631-632-7159, Fax: 631-632-8181, E-mail: manuel.london@stonybrook.edu. *Application contact:* Dr. Dmytro Holod, Interim Associate Dean/Graduate Program Director, 631-632-7183, Fax: 631-632-8181, E-mail: dmytro.holod@stonybrook.edu.

Stratford University, School of Graduate Studies, Falls Church, VA 22043. Offers accounting (MS); business administration (IMBA, MBA); enterprise business management (MS); entrepreneurial management (MS); information assurance (MS); information systems (MS); software engineering (MS); telecommunications (MS). Part-time and evening/weekend programs available. Postbaccalaureate distance learning degree programs offered (no on-campus study). *Degree requirements:* For master's, comprehensive exam, capstone project. *Entrance requirements:* For master's, GRE or GMAT, baccalaureate degree. Additional exam requirements/recommendations for international students: Required—TOEFL (minimum score 79 iBT) or IELTS (6.5). Electronic applications accepted.

Strayer University, Graduate Studies, Washington, DC 20005-2603. Offers accounting (MS); acquisition (MBA); business administration (MBA); communications technology (MS); educational management (M Ed); finance (MBA); health services administration (MHSA); hospitality and tourism management (MBA); human resource management (MBA); information systems (MS), including computer security management, decision support system management, enterprise resource management, network management, software engineering management, systems development management; management (MBA); management information systems (MS); marketing (MBA); professional accounting (MS), including accounting information systems, controllership, taxation; public administration (MPA); supply chain management (MBA); technology in education (M Ed). Programs also offered at campus locations in Birmingham, AL; Chamblee, GA; Cobb County, GA; Morrow, GA; White Marsh, MD; Charleston, SC; Columbia, SC; Greensboro, NC; Greenville, SC; Lexington, KY; Louisville, KY; Nashville, TN; North Raleigh, NC; Washington, DC. Part-time and evening/weekend programs available. Postbaccalaureate distance learning degree programs offered (minimal on-campus study). *Degree requirements:* For master's, thesis. *Entrance requirements:* For master's, GMAT, GRE General Test, bachelor's degree from an accredited college or university, minimum undergraduate GPA of 2.75. Electronic applications accepted.

Suffolk University, Sawyer Business School, Master of Business Administration Program, Boston, MA 02108-2770. Offers accounting (MBA); business administration (APC); entrepreneurship (MBA); executive business administration (EMBA); finance (MBA); global business administration (GMBA); health administration (MBA); international business (MBA); marketing (MBA); nonprofit management (MBA); organizational behavior (MBA); strategic management (MBA); supply chain management (MBA); taxation (MBA); JD/MBA; MBA/GDPA; MBA/MHA; MBA/MSA; MBA/MSF; MBA/MST. *Accreditation:* AACSB. Part-time and evening/weekend programs available. Postbaccalaureate distance learning degree programs offered (no on-campus study). *Faculty:* 29 full-time (9 women), 12 part-time/adjunct (2 women). *Students:* 106 full-time (44 women), 334 part-time (184 women); includes 57 minority (20 Black or African American, non-Hispanic/Latino; 1 American Indian or Alaska Native, non-Hispanic/Latino; 18 Asian, non-Hispanic/Latino; 14 Hispanic/Latino; 4 Two or more races, non-Hispanic/Latino), 61 international. Average age 30. 448 applicants, 61% accepted, 135 enrolled. In 2013, 217 master's awarded. *Entrance requirements:* For master's, GMAT, minimum undergraduate GPA of 2.75 (MBA), 5 years of managerial experience (EMBA). Additional exam requirements/recommendations for international

students: Required—TOEFL (minimum score 550 paper-based; 80 iBT). *Application deadline:* For fall admission, 6/15 priority date for domestic students, 6/15 for international students; for spring admission, 11/1 priority date for domestic students, 11/1 for international students. Applications are processed on a rolling basis. Application fee: $50. Electronic applications accepted. *Expenses: Tuition:* Full-time $38,374; part-time $1279 per credit. *Required fees:* $40; $20 per semester. Tuition and fees vary according to program. *Financial support:* In 2013–14, 107 students received support, including 91 fellowships with full and partial tuition reimbursements available (averaging $12,428 per year); career-related internships or fieldwork, Federal Work-Study, and institutionally sponsored loans also available. Support available to part-time students. Financial award application deadline: 4/1; financial award applicants required to submit FAFSA. *Faculty research:* Foreign investments; career strategies and boundaryless careers; corporate ethics codes; interest rates, inflation, and growth options; innovation and product development performance. *Unit head:* Heather Hewitt, Assistant Dean of Graduate Programs/Director of MBA Programs, 617-573-8306, E-mail: hhewitt@suffolk.edu. *Application contact:* Cory Meyers, Director of Graduate Admissions, 617-573-8302, Fax: 617-305-1733, E-mail: grad.admission@suffolk.edu.
Website: http://www.suffolk.edu/mba.

Sullivan University, School of Business, Louisville, KY 40205. Offers EMBA, MBA, MPM, MSCM, MSHRL, MSM, MSMIT, PhD, Pharm D. Part-time programs available. Postbaccalaureate distance learning degree programs offered (no on-campus study). *Degree requirements:* For doctorate, comprehensive exam, thesis/dissertation. *Entrance requirements:* Additional exam requirements/recommendations for international students: Required—TOEFL.

Sul Ross State University, Rio Grande College of Sul Ross State University, Alpine, TX 79832. Offers business administration (MBA); teacher education (M Ed), including bilingual education, counseling, educational diagnostics, elementary education, general education, reading, school administration, secondary education. Part-time and evening/weekend programs available. Postbaccalaureate distance learning degree programs offered (no on-campus study). *Degree requirements:* For master's, comprehensive exam, thesis optional, minimum GPA of 3.0. *Entrance requirements:* For master's, GMAT or GRE General Test, minimum GPA of 2.5 in last 60 hours of undergraduate work. Additional exam requirements/recommendations for international students: Required—TOEFL.

Sul Ross State University, School of Professional Studies, Department of Business Administration, Alpine, TX 79832. Offers EMBA, MBA. Two-year Executive MBA program in cooperation with La Universidad de Chihuahua, Mexico (UACH). Part-time and evening/weekend programs available. *Degree requirements:* For master's, thesis optional. *Entrance requirements:* For master's, GMAT or GRE General Test, minimum GPA of 2.5 in last 60 hours of undergraduate work. *Faculty research:* Cross-cultural comparisons, U.S.-Mexico management relations.

Syracuse University, Martin J. Whitman School of Management, Syracuse, NY 13244. Offers MBA, MS, MS Acct, PhD, JD/MBA, JD/MS Acct, JD/MSF. *Accreditation:* AACSB. Part-time programs available. Postbaccalaureate distance learning degree programs offered (minimal on-campus study). *Faculty:* 79 full-time (20 women), 25 part-time/adjunct (6 women). *Students:* 321 full-time (164 women), 220 part-time (68 women); includes 73 minority (22 Black or African American, non-Hispanic/Latino; 33 Asian, non-Hispanic/Latino; 12 Hispanic/Latino; 6 Two or more races, non-Hispanic/Latino), 231 international. Average age 29. 1,328 applicants, 38% accepted, 166 enrolled. In 2013, 230 master's, 15 doctorates awarded. *Degree requirements:* For doctorate, comprehensive exam, thesis/dissertation, summer research paper. *Entrance requirements:* For master's, GMAT, 2 letters of recommendation; for doctorate, GMAT or GRE, 3 letters of recommendation. Additional exam requirements/recommendations for international students: Required—TOEFL (minimum score 600 paper-based; 100 iBT). *Application deadline:* For fall admission, 1/30 priority date for domestic and international students. Applications are processed on a rolling basis. Application fee: $75. Electronic applications accepted. *Expenses:* Contact institution. *Financial support:* In 2013–14, 45 students received support. Fellowships with full tuition reimbursements available, research assistantships with full and partial tuition reimbursements available, and teaching assistantships with full and partial tuition reimbursements available. Financial award application deadline: 1/30; financial award applicants required to submit FAFSA. *Unit head:* Dr. Ken Kavajecz, Dean, 315-443-3751, E-mail: kakavaje@syr.edu. *Application contact:* Danielle Goodroe, Director, Graduate Enrollment, 315-443-3006, Fax: 315-443-9517, E-mail: mbainfo@syr.edu.
Website: http://whitman.syr.edu.

Tabor College, Graduate Program, Hillsboro, KS 67063. Offers accounting (MBA). Program offered at the Wichita campus only.

Tarleton State University, College of Graduate Studies, College of Business Administration, Stephenville, TX 76402. Offers MBA, MS. *Accreditation:* ACBSP. Part-time and evening/weekend programs available. Postbaccalaureate distance learning degree programs offered (minimal on-campus study). *Faculty:* 19 full-time (2 women), 12 part-time/adjunct (4 women). *Students:* 79 full-time (35 women), 375 part-time (203 women); includes 113 minority (53 Black or African American, non-Hispanic/Latino; 10 Asian, non-Hispanic/Latino; 46 Hispanic/Latino; 4 Two or more races, non-Hispanic/Latino), 6 international. Average age 33. 232 applicants, 78% accepted, 159 enrolled. In 2013, 137 master's awarded. *Degree requirements:* For master's, comprehensive exam, thesis optional. *Entrance requirements:* For master's, GMAT or GRE General Test, minimum GPA of 3.0. Additional exam requirements/recommendations for international students: Required—TOEFL (minimum score 550 paper-based; 80 iBT). *Application deadline:* For fall admission, 8/15 priority date for domestic students; for spring admission, 1/7 for domestic students. Applications are processed on a rolling basis. Application fee: $30 ($130 for international students). Electronic applications accepted. *Expenses:* Tuition, state resident: full-time $3312; part-time $184 per credit hour. Tuition, nonresident: full-time $9144; part-time $508 per credit hour. *Required fees:* $1916. Tuition and fees vary according to course load and campus/location. *Financial support:* Research assistantships, teaching assistantships, career-related internships or fieldwork, Federal Work-Study, and institutionally sponsored loans available. Support available to part-time students. Financial award application deadline: 5/1; financial award applicants required to submit FAFSA. *Unit head:* Dr. Adolfo Benavides, Dean, 254-968-9496, Fax: 254-968-9496, E-mail: benavides@tarleton.edu. *Application contact:* Information Contact, 254-968-9104, Fax: 254-968-9670, E-mail: gradoffice@tarleton.edu.
Website: http://www.tarleton.edu/COBAWEB/coba.

Taylor University, Master of Business Administration Program, Upland, IN 46989-1001. Offers emerging business strategies (MBA); global leadership (MBA). Part-time programs available.

Temple University, Fox School of Business, Doctoral Programs in Business, Philadelphia, PA 19122-6096. Offers accounting (PhD); entrepreneurship (PhD); finance (PhD); international business (PhD); management information systems (PhD); marketing (PhD); risk management and insurance (PhD); statistics (PhD); strategic management (PhD); tourism and sport (PhD). *Accreditation:* AACSB. *Degree requirements:* For doctorate, thesis/dissertation. *Entrance requirements:* For doctorate, GRE General Test, GMAT, minimum GPA of 3.0, master's degree. Additional exam requirements/recommendations for international students: Required—TOEFL (minimum score 600 paper-based; 100 iBT), IELTS (minimum score 7.5). Electronic applications accepted.

Temple University, Fox School of Business, MBA Programs, Philadelphia, PA 19122-6096. Offers accounting (MBA); business management (MBA); financial management (MBA); healthcare and life sciences innovation (MBA); human resource management (MBA); international business (IMBA); IT management (MBA); marketing management (MBA); pharmaceutical management (MBA); strategic management (EMBA, MBA). EMBA offered in Philadelphia, PA and Tokyo, Japan. *Accreditation:* AACSB. Part-time and evening/weekend programs available. Postbaccalaureate distance learning degree programs offered (minimal on-campus study). *Entrance requirements:* For master's, GMAT, minimum undergraduate GPA of 3.0. Additional exam requirements/recommendations for international students: Required—TOEFL (minimum score 600 paper-based; 100 iBT), IELTS (minimum score 7.5).

Temple University, Fox School of Business, Specialized Master's Programs, Philadelphia, PA 19122-6096. Offers accountancy (MS); actuarial science (MS); finance (MS); financial engineering (MS); human resource management (MS); innovation management and entrepreneurship (MS); marketing (MS); statistics (MS). MS in innovation management and entrepreneurship delivered jointly with College of Engineering. *Accreditation:* AACSB. Part-time programs available. *Entrance requirements:* For master's, GRE General Test or GMAT, minimum undergraduate GPA of 3.0. Additional exam requirements/recommendations for international students: Required—TOEFL (minimum score 600 paper-based; 100 iBT), IELTS (minimum score 7.5).

Tennessee State University, The School of Graduate Studies and Research, College of Business, Nashville, TN 37209-1561. Offers MBA. *Accreditation:* AACSB. Part-time and evening/weekend programs available. Postbaccalaureate distance learning degree programs offered. *Students:* 41 full-time (19 women), 41 part-time (17 women); includes 45 minority (40 Black or African American, non-Hispanic/Latino; 3 Asian, non-Hispanic/Latino; 2 Hispanic/Latino), 16 international. Average age 30. *Entrance requirements:* For master's, GMAT. Additional exam requirements/recommendations for international students: Required—TOEFL (minimum score 500 paper-based). *Application deadline:* For fall admission, 4/1 priority date for domestic and international students. Applications are processed on a rolling basis. Application fee: $25. Electronic applications accepted. *Financial support:* Research assistantships and teaching assistantships available. *Faculty research:* Supply chain management, health economics, accounting, e-commerce, international business. *Unit head:* Dr. Millicent Lownes-Jackson, Dean, 615-963-7127, Fax: 615-963-7139, E-mail: mlownes@tnstate.edu. *Application contact:* Anis Mnif, Director, 615-963-7295, Fax: 615-963-7139, E-mail: amnif@tnstate.edu.
Website: http://www.tnstate.edu/business/.

Tennessee Technological University, College of Graduate Studies, College of Business, Cookeville, TN 38505. Offers accounting (MBA); finance (MBA); human resource management (MBA); international business (MBA); management information systems (MBA). *Accreditation:* AACSB. Part-time and evening/weekend programs available. Postbaccalaureate distance learning degree programs offered (no on-campus study). *Faculty:* 28 full-time (5 women). *Students:* 54 full-time (22 women), 115 part-time (44 women); includes 11 minority (5 Black or African American, non-Hispanic/Latino; 1 Asian, non-Hispanic/Latino; 1 Hispanic/Latino; 4 Two or more races, non-Hispanic/Latino), 8 international. Average age 25. 171 applicants, 47% accepted, 50 enrolled. In 2013, 87 master's awarded. *Entrance requirements:* For master's, GMAT, GRE. Additional exam requirements/recommendations for international students: Required—TOEFL (minimum score 550 paper-based; 79 iBT), IELTS (minimum score 5.5), PTE (minimum score 53), or TOEIC (Test of English as an International Communication). *Application deadline:* For fall admission, 8/1 for domestic students, 5/1 for international students; for spring admission, 12/1 for domestic students, 10/1 for international students. Applications are processed on a rolling basis. Application fee: $35 ($40 for international students). Electronic applications accepted. *Expenses:* Tuition, state resident: full-time $9347; part-time $465 per credit hour. Tuition, nonresident: full-time $23,635; part-time $1152 per credit hour. *Financial support:* In 2013–14, 5 fellowships (averaging $10,000 per year), 18 research assistantships (averaging $4,000 per year), teaching assistantships (averaging $4,000 per year) were awarded. Support available to part-time students. Financial award application deadline: 4/1. *Unit head:* Amanda L. Brown, Interim Director, 931-372-3600, Fax: 931-372-6249, E-mail: albrown@tntech.edu. *Application contact:* Shelia K. Kendrick, Coordinator of Graduate Studies, 931-372-3808, Fax: 931-372-3497, E-mail: skendrick@tntech.edu.
Website: http://www.tntech.edu/mba.

Texas A&M International University, Office of Graduate Studies and Research, A.R. Sanchez School of Business, Laredo, TX 78041-1900. Offers MBA, MP Acc, MSIS, PhD. *Accreditation:* AACSB. Part-time and evening/weekend programs available. *Faculty:* 22 full-time (4 women), 2 part-time/adjunct (0 women). *Students:* 63 full-time (21 women), 219 part-time (100 women); includes 192 minority (11 Black or African American, non-Hispanic/Latino; 4 Asian, non-Hispanic/Latino; 177 Hispanic/Latino), 81 international. Average age 31. 233 applicants, 64% accepted, 98 enrolled. In 2013, 95 master's, 3 doctorates awarded. *Degree requirements:* For master's, thesis (for some programs). *Entrance requirements:* For master's, GMAT or GRE General Test. Additional exam requirements/recommendations for international students: Required—TOEFL (minimum score 550 paper-based; 79 iBT), IELTS (minimum score 6.5). *Application deadline:* For fall admission, 4/30 priority date for domestic students, 4/30 for international students; for spring admission, 11/30 for domestic students, 10/1 for international students. Applications are processed on a rolling basis. Application fee: $35 ($50 for international students). *Expenses:* Tuition, state resident: full-time $5184. *International tuition:* $11,556 full-time. *Financial support:* In 2013–14, 7 students received support, including 5 research assistantships, 2 teaching assistantships; fellowships, Federal Work-Study, institutionally sponsored loans, and scholarships/grants also available. Support available to part-time students. Financial award application deadline: 4/1; financial award applicants required to submit FAFSA. *Unit head:* Dr. Stephen R. Sears, Dean, 956-326-2480, E-mail: steve.sears@tamiu.edu. *Application contact:* Imelda Lopez, Graduate Admissions Counselor, 956-326-2485, Fax: 956-326-2459, E-mail: lopez@tamiu.edu.
Website: http://www.tamiu.edu/arssb/.

Texas A&M University, Mays Business School, Department of Management, College Station, TX 77843. Offers MS, PhD. *Faculty:* 31. *Students:* 89 full-time (56 women), 2 part-time (both women); includes 17 minority (3 Black or African American, non-Hispanic/Latino; 6 Asian, non-Hispanic/Latino; 8 Hispanic/Latino), 5 international. Average age 27. 157 applicants, 31% accepted, 42 enrolled. In 2013, 61 master's, 1 doctorate awarded. Terminal master's awarded for partial completion of doctoral program. *Degree requirements:* For master's, comprehensive exam; for doctorate, thesis/dissertation. *Entrance requirements:* For master's, GMAT or GRE; for doctorate, GMAT or GRE General Test. Additional exam requirements/recommendations for international students: Required—TOEFL. *Application deadline:* For fall admission, 3/1 priority date for domestic students; for spring admission, 8/1 for domestic students. Applications are processed on a rolling basis. Application fee: $50 ($75 for international

students). *Expenses:* Tuition, state resident: full-time $4078; part-time $226.55 per credit hour. Tuition, nonresident: full-time $10,450; part-time $580.55 per credit hour. *Required fees:* $2328; $278.50 per credit hour. $642.45 per semester. *Financial support:* Fellowships, research assistantships, teaching assistantships, career-related internships or fieldwork, and institutionally sponsored loans available. Financial award application deadline: 2/1. *Faculty research:* Strategic and human resource management, business and public policy, organizational behavior, organizational theory. *Unit head:* Dr. Ricky W. Griffin, Head, 979-862-3962, Fax: 979-845-9641, E-mail: rgriffin@mays.tamu.edu. *Application contact:* Kristi Mora, Senior Academic Advisor II, 979-845-6127, Fax: 979-845-9641, E-mail: kmora@mays.tamu.edu. Website: http://mays.tamu.edu/mgmt/.

Texas A&M University–Commerce, Graduate School, College of Business, MBA Program, Commerce, TX 75429-3011. Offers MBA. *Accreditation:* AACSB. Part-time programs available. *Degree requirements:* For master's, comprehensive exam, thesis (for some programs). *Entrance requirements:* For master's, GMAT. *Expenses:* Tuition, state resident: full-time $3630; part-time $2420 per year. Tuition, nonresident: full-time $9948; part-time $6632.16 per year. *Required fees:* $1006 per year. Tuition and fees vary according to course load.

Texas A&M University–Commerce, Graduate School, College of Business, MS Programs, Commerce, TX 75429-3011. Offers accounting (MS); economics (MA); finance (MS); management (MS); marketing (MS). Part-time programs available. *Degree requirements:* For master's, comprehensive exam, thesis (for some programs). *Entrance requirements:* For master's, GMAT or GRE General Test. Electronic applications accepted. *Expenses:* Tuition, state resident: full-time $3630; part-time $2420 per year. Tuition, nonresident: full-time $9948; part-time $6632.16 per year. *Required fees:* $1006 per year. Tuition and fees vary according to course load. *Faculty research:* Economic activity, forensic economics, volatility and finance, international economics.

Texas A&M University–Corpus Christi, Graduate Studies and Research, College of Business, Corpus Christi, TX 78412-5503. Offers accounting (M Acc); health care administration (MBA); international business (MBA). *Accreditation:* AACSB. Part-time and evening/weekend programs available. *Degree requirements:* For master's, comprehensive exam, thesis (for some programs). *Entrance requirements:* For master's, GMAT. Additional exam requirements/recommendations for international students: Required—TOEFL. Electronic applications accepted.

Texas A&M University–Kingsville, College of Graduate Studies, College of Business Administration, Kingsville, TX 78363. Offers MBA, MS. *Accreditation:* ACBSP. Part-time and evening/weekend programs available. *Faculty:* 6 full-time (5 women), 5 part-time/adjunct (1 woman). *Students:* 2 full-time (both women), 79 part-time (43 women); includes 49 minority (4 Black or African American, non-Hispanic/Latino; 4 Asian, non-Hispanic/Latino; 39 Hispanic/Latino; 1 Native Hawaiian or other Pacific Islander, non-Hispanic/Latino; 1 Two or more races, non-Hispanic/Latino), 1 international. Average age 31. *Degree requirements:* For master's, comprehensive exam, thesis or alternative. *Entrance requirements:* For master's, GMAT, minimum GPA of 2.5. Additional exam requirements/recommendations for international students: Required—TOEFL. *Application deadline:* For fall admission, 6/1 for domestic students; for spring admission, 11/15 for domestic students. Applications are processed on a rolling basis. Application fee: $35 ($50 for international students). *Financial support:* Federal Work-Study available. Support available to part-time students. Financial award application deadline: 5/15. *Faculty research:* Capital budgeting, international trade. *Unit head:* Dr. Darvin Hoffman, Graduate Coordinator, 361-593-3802. *Application contact:* Dr. Alberto M. Olivares, Dean, College of Graduate Studies, 361-593-2808, Fax: 361-593-3412, E-mail: a-olivares@tamuk.edu.
Website: http://www.cba.tamuk.edu.

Texas A&M University–San Antonio, School of Business, San Antonio, TX 78224. Offers business administration (MBA); enterprise resource planning systems (MBA); finance (MBA); healthcare management (MBA); human resources management (MBA); information assurance and security (MBA); international business (MBA); professional accounting (MPA); project management (MBA); supply chain management (MBA). Part-time and evening/weekend programs available. *Entrance requirements:* For master's, GMAT. Additional exam requirements/recommendations for international students: Required—TOEFL (minimum score 550 paper-based; 80 iBT), IELTS (minimum score 6). Electronic applications accepted.

Texas A&M University–Texarkana, Graduate Studies and Research, College of Business, Texarkana, TX 75505-5518. Offers accounting (MSA); business administration (MBA, MS). Part-time and evening/weekend programs available. *Degree requirements:* For master's, thesis or alternative. *Entrance requirements:* For master's, minimum GPA of 2.5 in last 60 hours of bachelor's degree. Additional exam requirements/recommendations for international students: Required—TOEFL. Electronic applications accepted.

Texas Christian University, College of Science and Engineering, Department of Physics and Astronomy, Fort Worth, TX 76129. Offers physics (MA, MS, PhD), including astrophysics (PhD); biophysics (PhD); business (PhD); physics (PhD); PhD/MBA. *Faculty:* 7 full-time (0 women). *Students:* 20 part-time (8 women); includes 2 minority (1 Asian, non-Hispanic/Latino; 1 Hispanic/Latino), 11 international. Average age 32. 27 applicants, 26% accepted, 6 enrolled. In 2013, 2 doctorates awarded. Terminal master's awarded for partial completion of doctoral program. *Degree requirements:* For master's, comprehensive exam, thesis; for doctorate, comprehensive exam, thesis/dissertation, paper submitted to scientific journal. *Entrance requirements:* For master's and doctorate, GRE General Test, minimum GPA of 3.0. Additional exam requirements/recommendations for international students: Required—TOEFL (minimum score 600 paper-based). *Application deadline:* For fall admission, 2/1 for domestic and international students; for spring admission, 10/1 for domestic and international students. Applications are processed on a rolling basis. Application fee: $60. Electronic applications accepted. *Expenses: Tuition:* Part-time $1270 per credit hour. Tuition and fees vary according to course load and program. *Financial support:* In 2013–14, 16 students received support, including 1 research assistantship with full tuition reimbursement available (averaging $20,500 per year), 11 teaching assistantships with full tuition reimbursements available (averaging $19,500 per year); scholarships/grants, tuition waivers, and unspecified assistantships also available. Financial award application deadline: 2/1. *Faculty research:* Biophysics, astrophysics, molecular physics, solid state physics, spectroscopy. Total annual research expenditures: $225,000. *Unit head:* Dr. William R. Graham, Professor and Chair, 817-257-7375 Ext. 6383, Fax: 817-257-7742, E-mail: w.graham@tcu.edu. *Application contact:* Dr. Yuri Strzhemechny, Associate Professor/Director, Graduate Program, 817-257-7375 Ext. 5793, Fax: 817-257-7742, E-mail: y.strzhemechny@tcu.edu.
Website: http://www.phys.tcu.edu/grad_program.asp.

Texas Christian University, Neeley School of Business at TCU, Executive MBA Program, Fort Worth, TX 76129-0002. Offers MBA. Evening/weekend programs available. *Students:* 53 full-time (12 women); includes 7 minority (3 Black or African American, non-Hispanic/Latino; 1 American Indian or Alaska Native, non-Hispanic/Latino; 1 Asian, non-Hispanic/Latino; 2 Hispanic/Latino). Average age 40. 34 applicants, 94% accepted, 28 enrolled. In 2013, 31 master's awarded. *Entrance requirements:* For

master's, minimum of 8 years of full-time work experience with 5 years of management experience. *Application deadline:* For winter admission, 2/1 priority date for domestic students; for spring admission, 7/19 for domestic students; for summer admission, 7/18 for domestic students. Applications are processed on a rolling basis. Application fee: $100. Electronic applications accepted. *Expenses:* Contact institution. *Financial support:* Tuition waivers (partial) available. Financial award application deadline: 7/18; financial award applicants required to submit FAFSA. *Unit head:* Dr. Suzanne Carter, Executive Director, 817-257-7543, E-mail: s.carter@tcu.edu. *Application contact:* Kevin Thomas Davis, Director, Executive MBA Recruiting and External Relations, 817-257-4681, Fax: 817-257-7719, E-mail: kevin.davis@tcu.edu.
Website: http://neeley.tcu.edu/Academics/Executive_MBA.aspx.

Texas Christian University, Neeley School of Business at TCU, Full-time Master's Program in Business Administration and Accelerated MBA, Fort Worth, TX 76129-0002. Offers MBA. *Accreditation:* AACSB. *Students:* 88 full-time (26 women), 2 part-time (0 women); includes 13 minority (3 Black or African American, non-Hispanic/Latino; 5 Asian, non-Hispanic/Latino; 5 Hispanic/Latino), 28 international. Average age 28. 187 applicants, 49% accepted, 53 enrolled. In 2013, 46 master's awarded. *Entrance requirements:* For master's, GMAT, 3 hours of course work in college algebra. Additional exam requirements/recommendations for international students: Required—TOEFL (minimum score 600 paper-based; 100 iBT). *Application deadline:* For fall admission, 11/1 priority date for domestic and international students; for winter admission, 1/15 priority date for domestic and international students; for spring admission, 4/15 priority date for domestic and international students. Applications are processed on a rolling basis. Application fee: $100. Electronic applications accepted. *Expenses: Tuition:* Part-time $1270 per credit hour. Tuition and fees vary according to course load and program. *Financial support:* Career-related internships or fieldwork, Federal Work-Study, institutionally sponsored loans, scholarships/grants, and unspecified assistantships available. Support available to part-time students. Financial award application deadline: 5/1; financial award applicants required to submit FAFSA. *Faculty research:* Emerging financial markets, derivative trading activity, salesforce deployment, examining sales activity, litigation against tax practitioners. Total annual research expenditures: $2.5 million. *Unit head:* Dr. Bill Wempe, Executive Director, Graduate Programs, 817-257-7531, Fax: 817-257-6431. *Application contact:* Peggy Conway, Director, MBA Admissions, 817-257-7531, Fax: 817-257-6431, E-mail: mbainfo@tcu.edu.
Website: http://www.neeley.tcu.edu/.

Texas Christian University, Neeley School of Business at TCU, Professional MBA Program, Fort Worth, TX 76129-0002. Offers MBA. Part-time and evening/weekend programs available. *Students:* 3 full-time (0 women), 119 part-time (34 women); includes 15 minority (2 Black or African American, non-Hispanic/Latino; 2 American Indian or Alaska Native, non-Hispanic/Latino; 1 Asian, non-Hispanic/Latino; 7 Hispanic/Latino; 2 Native Hawaiian or other Pacific Islander, non-Hispanic/Latino; 1 Two or more races, non-Hispanic/Latino), 2 international. Average age 29. 81 applicants, 83% accepted, 48 enrolled. In 2013, 54 degrees awarded. *Entrance requirements:* For master's, GMAT, 3 hours of course work in college algebra. Additional exam requirements/recommendations for international students: Required—TOEFL (minimum score 600 paper-based; 100 iBT). *Application deadline:* For fall admission, 11/1 priority date for domestic and international students; for winter admission, 1/15 priority date for domestic and international students; for spring admission, 4/15 priority date for domestic and international students. Applications are processed on a rolling basis. Application fee: $100. Electronic applications accepted. *Expenses: Tuition:* Part-time $1270 per credit hour. Tuition and fees vary according to course load and program. *Financial support:* Institutionally sponsored loans and scholarships/grants available. Financial award application deadline: 5/1; financial award applicants required to submit FAFSA. *Unit head:* Dr. Bill Wempe, Executive Director, Graduate Programs, 817-257-7531, Fax: 817-257-6431. *Application contact:* Peggy Conway, Director, MBA Admissions, 817-257-7531, Fax: 817-257-6431, E-mail: mbainfo@tcu.edu.
Website: http://www.neeley.tcu.edu/Professional_MBA.aspx.

Texas Southern University, Jesse H. Jones School of Business, Program in Business Administration, Houston, TX 77004-4584. Offers MBA. *Accreditation:* AACSB. Part-time and evening/weekend programs available. *Faculty:* 14 full-time (7 women), 8 part-time/adjunct (1 woman). *Students:* 93 full-time (47 women), 141 part-time (77 women); includes 218 minority (206 Black or African American, non-Hispanic/Latino; 9 Asian, non-Hispanic/Latino; 3 Hispanic/Latino), 9 international. Average age 33. 198 applicants, 43% accepted, 68 enrolled. In 2013, 87 master's awarded. *Degree requirements:* For master's, comprehensive exam. *Entrance requirements:* For master's, GMAT, minimum GPA of 2.5. *Application deadline:* For fall admission, 7/1 for domestic and international students; for spring admission, 11/1 for domestic and international students. Applications are processed on a rolling basis. Application fee: $50 ($75 for international students). Electronic applications accepted. *Financial support:* Fellowships, research assistantships, teaching assistantships, career-related internships or fieldwork, scholarships/grants, and unspecified assistantships available. Financial award application deadline: 5/1. *Unit head:* Dr. Mahesh Vanjani, Interim Chair, 713-313-7786, E-mail: vanjanim@tsu.edu. *Application contact:* Dr. Gregory Maddox, Dean of the Graduate School, 713-313-7011, E-mail: maddox_gh@tsu.edu.
Website: http://www.tsu.edu/academics/colleges__schools/Jesse_H_Jones_School_of_Business/mba.php.

Texas State University, Graduate School, Emmett and Miriam McCoy College of Business Administration, Program in Business Administration, San Marcos, TX 78666. Offers MBA. *Accreditation:* AACSB. Part-time programs available. *Faculty:* 24 full-time (8 women), 1 part-time/adjunct (0 women). *Students:* 83 full-time (35 women), 188 part-time (77 women); includes 76 minority (14 Black or African American, non-Hispanic/Latino; 1 American Indian or Alaska Native, non-Hispanic/Latino; 11 Asian, non-Hispanic/Latino; 45 Hispanic/Latino; 5 Two or more races, non-Hispanic/Latino), 13 international. Average age 30. 194 applicants, 53% accepted, 75 enrolled. In 2013, 123 master's awarded. *Degree requirements:* For master's, comprehensive exam, thesis optional. *Entrance requirements:* For master's, GMAT (minimum preferred score of 450 prior to admission decision), minimum GPA of 2.0 in last 60 hours of undergraduate work. Additional exam requirements/recommendations for international students: Required—TOEFL (minimum score 550 paper-based; 78 iBT). *Application deadline:* For fall admission, 6/1 for domestic and international students; for spring admission, 10/1 for domestic and international students. Applications are processed on a rolling basis. Application fee: $40 ($90 for international students). Electronic applications accepted. *Expenses:* Tuition, state resident: full-time $6663; part-time $278 per credit hour. Tuition, nonresident: full-time $15,159; part-time $632 per credit hour. *Required fees:* $1872; $54 per credit hour. $306 per term. Tuition and fees vary according to course load. *Financial support:* In 2013–14, 93 students received support, including 3 research assistantships (averaging $12,451 per year), 16 teaching assistantships (averaging $11,440 per year); Federal Work-Study, institutionally sponsored loans, scholarships/grants, health care benefits, and unspecified assistantships also available. Support available to part-time students. Financial award application deadline: 4/1; financial award applicants required to submit FAFSA. *Unit head:* Dr. William Chittenden, Graduate Advisor, 512-245-3591, Fax: 512-245-7973, E-mail: wc10@txstate.edu.

Application contact: Dr. Andrea Golato, Dean of Graduate School, 512-245-2581, Fax: 512-245-8365, E-mail: gradcollege@txstate.edu.
Website: http://www.business.txstate.edu/.

Texas Tech University, Graduate School, Rawls College of Business Administration, Area of Management, Lubbock, TX 79409. Offers PhD. *Accreditation:* AACSB. Part-time programs available. *Faculty:* 11 full-time (2 women). *Students:* 15 full-time (5 women). Average age 32. In 2013, 1 doctorate awarded. *Degree requirements:* For doctorate, comprehensive exam, thesis/dissertation, qualifying exams. *Entrance requirements:* For doctorate, GMAT, holistic profile of academic credentials. Additional exam requirements/recommendations for international students: Required—TOEFL (minimum score 550 paper-based; 79 iBT). *Application deadline:* For fall admission, 7/1 priority date for domestic students, 1/15 for international students. Applications are processed on a rolling basis. Application fee: $60. Electronic applications accepted. *Expenses:* Tuition, state resident: full-time $6062; part-time $252.57 per credit hour. Tuition, nonresident: full-time $14,558; part-time $606.57 per credit hour. *Required fees:* $2655; $35 per credit hour. $907.50 per semester. Tuition and fees vary according to course load. *Financial support:* In 2013–14, 5 research assistantships (averaging $14,550 per year), 4 teaching assistantships (averaging $18,000 per year) were awarded; career-related internships or fieldwork, Federal Work-Study, and scholarships/grants also available. Financial award applicants required to submit FAFSA. *Faculty research:* Entrepreneurship, leadership, health care, organization theory. *Unit head:* Dr. William Gardner, Area Coordinator, 806-742-1055, Fax: 806-742-2308, E-mail: william.gardner@ttu.edu. *Application contact:* Terri Boston, Applications Manager, Graduate and Professional Programs, 806-742-3184, Fax: 806-742-3958, E-mail: rawlsgrad@ttu.edu.
Website: http://management.ba.ttu.edu.

Texas Wesleyan University, Graduate Programs, Graduate Business Programs, Fort Worth, TX 76105-1536. Offers business administration (MBA); health services administration (MS); management (MiM). *Accreditation:* ACBSP. Part-time and evening/weekend programs available. *Degree requirements:* For master's, capstone course. *Entrance requirements:* For master's, GMAT, 3 letters of recommendation. *Expenses:* Contact institution.

Texas Woman's University, Graduate School, College of Arts and Sciences, School of Management, Denton, TX 76201. Offers business administration (MBA); health systems management (MHSM). *Accreditation:* ACBSP. Part-time programs available. *Faculty:* 12 full-time (5 women), 2 part-time/adjunct (0 women). *Students:* 660 full-time (556 women), 474 part-time (379 women); includes 758 minority (461 Black or African American, non-Hispanic/Latino; 14 American Indian or Alaska Native, non-Hispanic/Latino; 139 Asian, non-Hispanic/Latino; 142 Hispanic/Latino; 2 Native Hawaiian or other Pacific Islander, non-Hispanic/Latino), 30 international. Average age 34. 429 applicants, 77% accepted, 259 enrolled. In 2013, 600 master's awarded. *Degree requirements:* For master's, thesis optional. *Entrance requirements:* For master's, 2 letters of reference, resume, 5 years of relevant experience (EMBA only). Additional exam requirements/recommendations for international students: Required—TOEFL (minimum score 550 paper-based; 79 iBT). *Application deadline:* For fall admission, 8/1 priority date for domestic students, 3/1 for international students; for spring admission, 12/1 priority date for domestic students, 7/1 for international students. Applications are processed on a rolling basis. Application fee: $50 ($75 for international students). Electronic applications accepted. *Expenses:* Tuition, state resident: full-time $4182; part-time $233.32 per credit hour. Tuition, nonresident: full-time $10,716; part-time $595.32 per credit hour. *Financial support:* In 2013–14, 254 students received support, including 15 research assistantships (averaging $11,520 per year); career-related internships or fieldwork, Federal Work-Study, institutionally sponsored loans, scholarships/grants, traineeships, health care benefits, and unspecified assistantships also available. Support available to part-time students. Financial award application deadline: 3/1; financial award applicants required to submit FAFSA. *Faculty research:* Tax research, privacy issues in Web-based marketing, multitasking, leadership, women in management, global comparative studies, corporate sustainability and responsibility. *Unit head:* Ron Hovis, Interim Director, 940-898-2121, Fax: 940-898-2120, E-mail: rhovis@twu.edu. *Application contact:* Dr. Samuel Wheeler, Assistant Director of Admissions, 940-898-3188, Fax: 940-898-3081, E-mail: wheelersr@twu.edu.
Website: http://www.twu.edu/som/.

Thomas College, Graduate School, Programs in Business, Waterville, ME 04901-5097. Offers business (MBA); computer technology education (MS); education (MS); human resource management (MBA). Part-time and evening/weekend programs available. *Entrance requirements:* For master's, GMAT, GRE, MAT or minimum GPA of 3.3 in first 3 graduate-level courses. Additional exam requirements/recommendations for international students: Recommended—TOEFL.

Thomas Edison State College, School of Business and Management, Program in Management, Trenton, NJ 08608-1176. Offers MSM. Part-time programs available. Postbaccalaureate distance learning degree programs offered (minimal on-campus study). *Degree requirements:* For master's, final capstone project. *Entrance requirements:* For master's, bachelor's degree from a regionally-accredited college or university; minimum 2 letters of recommendation; 3-5 years of related working experience; current resume. Additional exam requirements/recommendations for international students: Required—TOEFL (minimum score 550 paper-based; 79 iBT). Electronic applications accepted.

Thomas More College, Program in Business Administration, Crestview Hills, KY 41017-3495. Offers MBA. *Faculty:* 13 full-time (4 women), 3 part-time/adjunct (0 women). *Students:* 80 full-time (30 women); includes 5 minority (4 Black or African American, non-Hispanic/Latino; 1 Native Hawaiian or other Pacific Islander, non-Hispanic/Latino). Average age 34. 31 applicants, 68% accepted, 21 enrolled. In 2013, 47 master's awarded. *Degree requirements:* For master's, comprehensive exam, final project. *Entrance requirements:* For master's, GMAT, minimum GPA of 2.7. Additional exam requirements/recommendations for international students: Required—TOEFL (minimum score 600 paper-based; 100 iBT). *Application deadline:* Applications are processed on a rolling basis. Application fee: $100. Electronic applications accepted. *Expenses: Tuition:* Full-time $13,807; part-time $460 per credit hour. Tuition and fees vary according to program. *Financial support:* In 2013–14, 5 students received support. Federal Work-Study, institutionally sponsored loans, and scholarships/grants available. Financial award application deadline: 3/15; financial award applicants required to submit FAFSA. *Faculty research:* Comparison level and consumer satisfaction, history of U.S. business development, share price reaction, quality and competition, personnel development. *Unit head:* Robert Arnold, JD, Chair of Business Administration, 859-344-3612, Fax: 859-344-3345, E-mail: arnoldr@thomasmore.edu. *Application contact:* Judy Bautista, Enrollment Manager, 859-341-4554, Fax: 859-578-3589, E-mail: judy.bautista@thomasmore.edu.
Website: http://www.thomasmore.edu.

Thomas University, Department of Business Administration, Thomasville, GA 31792-7499. Offers MBA. Part-time programs available. *Entrance requirements:* For master's, resume, 3 professional or academic references. Additional exam requirements/recommendations for international students: Required—TOEFL (minimum score 600 paper-based). Electronic applications accepted.

Thompson Rivers University, Program in Business Administration, Kamloops, BC V2C 0C8, Canada. Offers MBA. Part-time programs available. *Entrance requirements:* For master's, GMAT, undergraduate degree with minimum B- average in last 60 credits, personal resume. Additional exam requirements/recommendations for international students: Required—TOEFL (570 paper-based, 88 iBT), IELTS (6.5), or CAEL (70).

Thunderbird School of Global Management, Full-Time MBA Programs, Glendale, AZ 85306. Offers GMBA, MBA. Part-time and evening/weekend programs available. Postbaccalaureate distance learning degree programs offered (minimal on-campus study). *Degree requirements:* For master's, one foreign language. *Entrance requirements:* For master's, GMAT, 2 years work experience. Additional exam requirements/recommendations for international students: Required—TOEFL (minimum score 600 paper-based; 100 iBT). Electronic applications accepted. *Faculty research:* Management, social enterprise, cross-cultural communication, finance, marketing.

Thunderbird School of Global Management, Master's Programs in Global Management, Glendale, AZ 85306. Offers global affairs and management (MA); global management (MS). *Accreditation:* AACSB. *Degree requirements:* For master's, one foreign language. *Entrance requirements:* For master's, GMAT/GRE. Additional exam requirements/recommendations for international students: Required—TOEFL.

Tiffin University, Program in Business Administration, Tiffin, OH 44883-2161. Offers finance (MBA); general management (MBA); healthcare administration (MBA); human resources (MBA); international business (MBA); leadership (MBA); marketing (MBA); sports management (MBA). *Accreditation:* ACBSP. Part-time and evening/weekend programs available. Postbaccalaureate distance learning degree programs offered (no on-campus study). *Entrance requirements:* For master's, minimum undergraduate GPA of 2.5, work experience. Additional exam requirements/recommendations for international students: Required—TOEFL (minimum score 550 paper-based; 79 iBT). Electronic applications accepted. *Faculty research:* Small business, executive development operations, research and statistical analysis, market research, management information systems.

Trevecca Nazarene University, Graduate Business Programs, Nashville, TN 37210-2877. Offers business administration (MBA); healthcare administration (Certificate); information technology (MBA, MS, Certificate); management (MSM); management and leadership (Certificate); project management (Certificate). Evening/weekend programs available. Postbaccalaureate distance learning degree programs offered. *Faculty:* 7 full-time (0 women), 3 part-time/adjunct (0 women). *Students:* 101 full-time (55 women), 21 part-time (8 women); includes 30 minority (27 Black or African American, non-Hispanic/Latino; 2 Asian, non-Hispanic/Latino; 1 Hispanic/Latino), 3 international. Average age 36. In 2013, 33 master's awarded. *Entrance requirements:* For master's, minimum GPA of 2.75, resume, official transcript from regionally-accredited institution, minimum math grade of C, minimum English composition grade of C, MS-IT requires undergraduate computing degree. Additional exam requirements/recommendations for international students: Required—TOEFL (minimum score 550 paper-based; 80 iBT). *Application deadline:* Applications are processed on a rolling basis. Application fee: $25. *Expenses:* Contact institution. *Financial support:* Applicants required to submit FAFSA. *Unit head:* Dr. Rick Mann, Director of Graduate and Professional Programs for School of Business, 615-248-1529, E-mail: management@trevecca.edu. *Application contact:* 615-248-1529, E-mail: cll@trevecca.edu.

Trident University International, College of Business Administration, Program in Business Administration, Cypress, CA 90630. Offers business administration (PhD); conflict and negotiation management (MBA); criminal justice administration (MBA); entrepreneurship (MBA); finance (MBA); general management (MBA); government accounting (MBA); human resource management (MBA); information security and digital assurance management (MBA); information technology management (MBA); international business (MBA); logistics management (MBA); marketing (MBA); project management (MBA); public management (MBA); quality management (MBA); strategic leadership (MBA). Part-time and evening/weekend programs available. Postbaccalaureate distance learning degree programs offered (no on-campus study). *Degree requirements:* For doctorate, comprehensive exam, thesis/dissertation, defense of dissertation. *Entrance requirements:* For master's, minimum GPA of 2.5 (students with GPA 3.0 or greater may transfer up to 30% of graduate level credits); for doctorate, minimum GPA of 3.4, curriculum vitae, course work in research methods or statistics. Additional exam requirements/recommendations for international students: Required—TOEFL. Electronic applications accepted.

Trinity International University, Trinity Evangelical Divinity School, Deerfield, IL 60015-1284. Offers Biblical and Near Eastern archaeology and languages (MA); Christian studies (MA, Certificate); Christian thought (MA); church history (MA, Th M); congregational ministry: pastor-teacher (M Div); congregational ministry: team ministry (M Div); counseling ministries (MA); counseling psychology (MA); cross-cultural ministry (M Div); educational studies (PhD); evangelism (MA); history of Christianity in America (MA); intercultural studies (MA, PhD); leadership and ministry management (D Min); military chaplaincy (D Min); ministry (MA); mission and evangelism (Th M); missions and evangelism (D Min); New Testament (MA, Th M); Old Testament (Th M); Old Testament and Semitic languages (MA); pastoral care (M Div); pastoral care and counseling (D Min); pastoral counseling and psychology (Th M); pastoral theology (Th M); philosophy of religion (MA); preaching (D Min); religion (MA); research ministry (M Div); systematic theology (Th M); theological studies (PhD); urban ministry (MA). *Accreditation:* ATS (one or more programs are accredited). Part-time programs available. Postbaccalaureate distance learning degree programs offered (minimal on-campus study). *Degree requirements:* For master's, comprehensive exam, thesis, fieldwork; for doctorate, comprehensive exam (for some programs), thesis/dissertation; for Certificate, comprehensive exam, integrative papers. *Entrance requirements:* For master's, GRE, MAT, minimum cumulative undergraduate GPA of 3.0; for doctorate, GRE, minimum cumulative graduate GPA of 3.2; for Certificate, GRE, MAT, minimum undergraduate GPA of 2.5. Additional exam requirements/recommendations for international students: Required—TOEFL (minimum score 580 paper-based), TWE (minimum score 4). Electronic applications accepted.

Trinity University, Department of Business Administration, San Antonio, TX 78212-7200. Offers accounting (MS). *Accreditation:* AACSB. Part-time programs available. *Entrance requirements:* For master's, GMAT, minimum GPA of 3.0, course work in accounting and business law.

Trinity Washington University, School of Business and Graduate Studies, Washington, DC 20017-1094. Offers business administration (MBA); communication (MA); international security studies (MA); organizational management (MSA), including federal program management, human resource management, nonprofit management, organizational development, public and community health. Part-time and evening/weekend programs available. *Degree requirements:* For master's, thesis (for some programs), capstone project (MSA). *Entrance requirements:* For master's, minimum GPA of 2.5. Additional exam requirements/recommendations for international students: Required—TOEFL (minimum score 550 paper-based). *Application deadline:* For fall admission, 4/1 priority date for domestic students; for winter admission, 11/1 priority date for domestic students; for spring admission, 11/1 priority date for domestic students. Applications are processed on a rolling basis. Application fee: $40. *Expenses:*

Tuition: Part-time $715 per credit. *Financial support:* Career-related internships or fieldwork and unspecified assistantships available. Support available to part-time students. Financial award application deadline: 4/1; financial award applicants required to submit FAFSA. *Unit head:* Dr. Peggy Lewis, Associate Dean, 202-884-9204, E-mail: lewisp@trinitydc.edu. *Application contact:* Alesha Tyson, Director of Admissions for School of Business and Graduate Studies, 202-884-9400, Fax: 202-884-9229, E-mail: tysona@trinitydc.edu.
Website: http://www.trinitydc.edu/bgs/.

Trinity Western University, School of Graduate Studies, Program in Business Administration, Langley, BC V2Y 1Y1, Canada. Offers international business (MBA); management of the growing enterprise (MBA); non-profit and charitable organization management (MBA). Part-time programs available. Postbaccalaureate distance learning degree programs offered (minimal on-campus study). *Degree requirements:* For master's, thesis or alternative, applied project. *Entrance requirements:* For master's, GMAT (minimum score of 550 recommended). Additional exam requirements/ recommendations for international students: Required—TOEFL (minimum score 600 paper-based; 100 iBT), IELTS. Electronic applications accepted.

Troy University, Graduate School, College of Business, Program in Business Administration, Troy, AL 36082. Offers accounting (EMBA, MBA); criminal justice (EMBA); finance (MBA); general management (EMBA, MBA); healthcare management (EMBA); information systems (EMBA, MBA); international economic development (MBA). *Accreditation:* ACBSP. Part-time and evening/weekend programs available. *Faculty:* 56 full-time (20 women), 3 part-time/adjunct (0 women). *Students:* 142 full-time (89 women), 310 part-time (192 women); includes 265 minority (185 Black or African American, non-Hispanic/Latino; 3 American Indian or Alaska Native, non-Hispanic/ Latino; 62 Asian, non-Hispanic/Latino; 8 Hispanic/Latino; 1 Native Hawaiian or other Pacific Islander, non-Hispanic/Latino; 6 Two or more races, non-Hispanic/Latino). Average age 29. 472 applicants, 68% accepted, 51 enrolled. In 2013, 293 master's awarded. *Degree requirements:* For master's, minimum GPA of 3.0, capstone course, research course. *Entrance requirements:* For master's, GMAT (minimum score 500) or GRE General Test (minimum score 900 on old exam or 294 on new exam), bachelor's degree; minimum undergraduate GPA of 2.5 or 3.0 on last 30 semester hours, letter of recommendation. Additional exam requirements/recommendations for international students: Required—TOEFL (minimum score 523 paper-based; 70 iBT), IELTS (minimum score 6). *Application deadline:* Applications are processed on a rolling basis. Application fee: $50. *Expenses:* Tuition, state resident: full-time $6084; part-time $338 per credit hour. Tuition, nonresident: full-time $12,168; part-time $676 per credit hour. *Required fees:* $630; $35 per credit hour. $50 per semester. *Unit head:* Dr. Bob Wheatley, Director, Graduate Business Programs, 334-670-3194, Fax: 334-670-3599, E-mail: rwheat@troy.edu. *Application contact:* Brenda K. Campbell, Director of Graduate Admissions, 334-670-3178, Fax: 334-670-3733, E-mail: bcamp@troy.edu.

Troy University, Graduate School, College of Business, Program in Management, Troy, AL 36082. Offers applied management (MSM); healthcare management (MSM); human resources management (MSM); information systems (MSM); international hospitality management (MSM); international management (MSM); leadership and organizational effectiveness (MSM); public management (MS, MSM). *Accreditation:* ACBSP. Part-time and evening/weekend programs available. *Faculty:* 15 full-time (8 women), 3 part-time/adjunct (0 women). *Students:* 18 full-time (14 women), 148 part-time (86 women); includes 95 minority (75 Black or African American, non-Hispanic/ Latino; 1 American Indian or Alaska Native, non-Hispanic/Latino; 4 Asian, non-Hispanic/ Latino; 8 Hispanic/Latino; 7 Two or more races, non-Hispanic/Latino). Average age 35. 124 applicants, 79% accepted, 30 enrolled. In 2013, 75 master's awarded. *Degree requirements:* For master's, Graduate Educational Testing Service Major Field Test, capstone exam, minimum GPA of 3.0. *Entrance requirements:* For master's, GRE (minimum score of 900 on old exam or 294 on new exam) or GMAT (minimum score of 500), bachelor's degree; minimum undergraduate GPA of 2.5 or 3.0 on last 30 semester hours, letter of recommendation. Additional exam requirements/recommendations for international students: Required—TOEFL (minimum score 523 paper-based; 70 iBT), IELTS (minimum score 6). *Application deadline:* Applications are processed on a rolling basis. Application fee: $50. Electronic applications accepted. *Expenses:* Contact institution. *Unit head:* Dr. Bob Wheatley, Director, Graduate Business Programs, 334-670-3143, Fax: 334-670-3599, E-mail: rwheat@troy.edu. *Application contact:* Brenda K. Campbell, Director of Graduate Admissions, 334-670-3178, Fax: 334-670-3733, E-mail: bcamp@troy.edu.

Tulane University, A. B. Freeman School of Business, New Orleans, LA 70118-5669. Offers EMBA, M Acct, M Fin, MBA, PMBA, PhD, JD/M Acct, JD/MBA, MBA/M Acc, MBA/MA, MBA/MD, MBA/ME, MBA/MPH. *Accreditation:* AACSB. Part-time and evening/weekend programs available. Terminal master's awarded for partial completion of doctoral program. *Entrance requirements:* For master's, GMAT, interview. Additional exam requirements/recommendations for international students: Required—TOEFL. Electronic applications accepted. *Expenses:* Contact institution.

Union Graduate College, School of Management, Schenectady, NY 12308-3107. Offers business administration (MBA); general management (Certificate); health systems administration (MBA, Certificate); human resources (Certificate). *Accreditation:* AACSB. Part-time and evening/weekend programs available. Postbaccalaureate distance learning degree programs offered (minimal on-campus study). *Faculty:* 16 full-time (3 women), 9 part-time/adjunct (4 women). *Students:* 77 full-time (31 women), 70 part-time (31 women); includes 23 minority (2 Black or African American, non-Hispanic/ Latino; 19 Asian, non-Hispanic/Latino; 2 Two or more races, non-Hispanic/Latino), 5 international. Average age 27. In 2013, 94 master's, 11 other advanced degrees awarded. *Degree requirements:* For master's, internship, capstone course. *Entrance requirements:* For master's, GMAT, GRE, minimum GPA of 3.0, 3 letters of recommendation. Additional exam requirements/recommendations for international students: Required—TOEFL (minimum score 550 paper-based). *Application deadline:* Applications are processed on a rolling basis. Application fee: $60. *Financial support:* Research assistantships, career-related internships or fieldwork, Federal Work-Study, scholarships/grants, health care benefits, and tuition waivers (partial) available. Support available to part-time students. Financial award applicants required to submit FAFSA. *Unit head:* Bela Musits, Dean, 518-631-9890, Fax: 518-631-9902, E-mail: musitsb@uniongraduatecollege.edu. *Application contact:* Diane Trzaskos, Admissions Coordinator, 518-631-9837, Fax: 518-631-9901, E-mail: trzaskod@uniongraduatecollege.edu.
Website: http://www.uniongraduatecollege.edu.

Union University, McAfee School of Business Administration, Jackson, TN 38305-3697. Offers MBA. Also available at Germantown campus. Evening/weekend programs available. *Entrance requirements:* For master's, GMAT, minimum GPA of 2.5. Electronic applications accepted. *Expenses:* Contact institution. *Faculty research:* Personal financial management, strategy, accounting, marketing, economics.

United States International University, School of Business Administration, Nairobi, Kenya. Offers business administration (GEMBA); entrepreneurship (MBA); finance (MBA); human resource management (MBA); information technology management (MBA); integrated studies (MBA); international business administration (MBA); management and organizational development (MS); marketing (MBA); organizational development (EMS); strategic management (MBA). Part-time and evening/weekend programs available. *Degree requirements:* For master's, thesis. *Entrance requirements:* For master's, GMAT, 2 letters of reference, resume. Additional exam requirements/ recommendations for international students: Required—TOEFL (minimum score 550 paper-based). *Faculty research:* Marketing in small business enterprises, total quality management in Kenya.

United States University, School of Management, Cypress, CA 90630. Offers MBA. *Entrance requirements:* For master's, undergraduate degree from accredited institution, minimum cumulative GPA of 2.5, official transcripts.

Universidad Autonoma de Guadalajara, Graduate Programs, Guadalajara, Mexico. Offers administrative law and justice (LL M); advertising and corporate communications (MA); architecture (M Arch); business (MBA); computational science (MCC); education (Ed M, Ed D); English-Spanish translation (MA); entrepreneurship and management (MBA); integrated management of digital animation (MA); international business (MIB); international corporate law (LL M); internet technologies (MS); manufacturing systems (MMS); occupational health (MS); philosophy (MA, PhD); power electronics (MS); quality systems (MQS); renewable energy (MS); social evaluation of projects (MBA); strategic market research (MBA); tax law (MA); teaching mathematics (MA).

Universidad de las Americas, A.C., Program in Business Administration, Mexico City, Mexico. Offers finance (MBA); marketing research (MBA); production and quality (MBA).

Universidad de las Américas Puebla, Division of Graduate Studies, School of Business and Economics, Puebla, Mexico. Offers business administration (MBA); finance (M Adm). Part-time and evening/weekend programs available. *Degree requirements:* For master's, one foreign language, thesis. *Entrance requirements:* Additional exam requirements/recommendations for international students: Required—TOEFL. *Faculty research:* System dynamics, information technology, marketing, international business, strategic planning, quality.

Universidad del Este, Graduate School, Carolina, PR 00984. Offers accounting (MBA); adult education (M Ed); agribusiness (MBA); criminal justice and criminology (MA); curriculum and instruction - early education (M Ed); curriculum and instruction - elementary (M Ed); curriculum and instruction - English (M Ed); curriculum and instruction - Spanish (M Ed); human resources (MBA); information security management (MBA); information technology and Web business development (MBA); management (MBA); public policy (MPA); social work (MA), including clinical social work; special education (M Ed); strategic leadership (MBA). *Students:* 464 full-time (322 women), 669 part-time (499 women); all minorities (all Hispanic/Latino). Average age 35. 693 applicants, 61% accepted, 332 enrolled. In 2013, 228 master's awarded. *Unit head:* Jose R. Clintron, Dean, 787-257-7373 Ext. 3007, E-mail: ue_jcintron@suagm.edu. *Application contact:* Clotilde Santiago, Director of Admissions, 787-257-7373 Ext. 3400, E-mail: ue_csantiago@suagm.edu.

Universidad del Turabo, Graduate Programs, School in Business Administration, Program in Management, Gurabo, PR 00778-3030. Offers MBA, DBA. Part-time and evening/weekend programs available. *Entrance requirements:* For master's, GRE, EXADEP, interview.

Universidad Iberoamericana, Graduate School, Santo Domingo D.N., Dominican Republic. Offers business administration (MBA, PMBA); constitutional law (LL M); dentistry (DMD); educational management (MA); integrated marketing communication (MA); psychopedagogical intervention (M Ed); real estate law (LL M); strategic management of human talent (MM).

Universidad Metropolitana, School of Business Administration, San Juan, PR 00928-1150. Offers accounting (MBA); finance (MBA); human resources management (MBA); international business (MBA); management (MBA); management information systems (MBA); marketing (MBA). Part-time and evening/weekend programs available. *Degree requirements:* For master's, thesis or alternative. Electronic applications accepted. *Faculty research:* Latin American trade, international investments, central city business development, Hispanic consumer research, Caribbean and Asian trade cooperation.

Université de Moncton, Faculty of Administration, Moncton, NB E1A 3E9, Canada. Offers MBA, JD/MBA. Part-time and evening/weekend programs available. Postbaccalaureate distance learning degree programs offered (no on-campus study). *Faculty:* 24 full-time (11 women), 18 part-time/adjunct (3 women). *Students:* 36 full-time (19 women), 9 international. Average age 28. 160 applicants, 56% accepted, 48 enrolled. In 2013, 20 master's awarded. *Degree requirements:* For master's, one foreign language, thesis. *Entrance requirements:* For master's, minimum undergraduate GPA of 3.0. *Application deadline:* For fall admission, 6/1 for domestic students, 2/1 for international students; for winter admission, 11/15 for domestic students, 9/1 for international students; for spring admission, 3/31 for domestic students, 1/1 for international students; for summer admission, 3/31 for domestic students, 1/1 for international students. Applications are processed on a rolling basis. Application fee: $50. Electronic applications accepted. *Financial support:* In 2013–14, 7 fellowships (averaging $2,500 per year) were awarded; teaching assistantships and institutionally sponsored loans also available. Support available to part-time students. Financial award application deadline: 5/30. *Faculty research:* Service management, corporate reputation, financial management, accounting, supply chain. *Total annual research expenditures:* $150,000. *Unit head:* Dr. Nha Nguyen, Director, 506-858-4231, Fax: 506-858-4093, E-mail: nha.nguyen@umoncton.ca. *Application contact:* Natalie Allain, Admission Counselor, 506-858-4273, Fax: 506-858-4093, E-mail: natalie.allain@umoncton.ca.
Website: http://www.umoncton.ca/umcm-administration/.

Université de Sherbrooke, Faculty of Administration, Doctoral Program in Business Administration, Sherbrooke, QC J1K 2R1, Canada. Offers DBA. *Degree requirements:* For doctorate, one foreign language, comprehensive exam, thesis/dissertation. *Entrance requirements:* For doctorate, 3 years of related work experience, interview, fluency in French, advanced English, good oral and written French comprehension (tested with an interview). Electronic applications accepted. *Faculty research:* Change management, international business and finance, work organization, information technology implementation and impact on organizations, strategic management.

Université de Sherbrooke, Faculty of Administration, Master of Business Administration Program, Sherbrooke, QC J1K 2R1, Canada. Offers executive business administration (EMBA); general management (MBA). Part-time and evening/weekend programs available. *Entrance requirements:* For master's, bachelor's degree, minimum GPA of 2.7 (on 4.3 scale), minimum of two years of work experience, letters of recommendation. Electronic applications accepted.

Université de Sherbrooke, Faculty of Law, Sherbrooke, QC J1K 2R1, Canada. Offers alternative dispute resolution (LL M, Diploma); business law (Diploma); common law (JD); criminal and penal law (Diploma); health law (LL M, Diploma); international law (LL M); law (LL D); legal management (Diploma); notarial law (Diploma); transnational law (Diploma). Part-time and evening/weekend programs available. *Degree requirements:* For master's, thesis; for Diploma, one foreign language. *Entrance requirements:* For master's and Diploma, LL B. Electronic applications accepted.

Université du Québec à Chicoutimi, Graduate Programs, Program in Small and Medium-Sized Organization Management, Chicoutimi, QC G7H 2B1, Canada. Offers

Business Administration and Management—General

M Sc. Part-time programs available. *Degree requirements:* For master's, thesis. *Entrance requirements:* For master's, appropriate bachelor's degree, proficiency in French.

Université du Québec à Montréal, Graduate Programs, PhD Program in Business Administration, Montréal, QC H3C 3P8, Canada. Offers PhD. Part-time programs available. *Degree requirements:* For doctorate, thesis/dissertation. *Entrance requirements:* For doctorate, appropriate master's degree or equivalent, proficiency in French.

Université du Québec à Montréal, Graduate Programs, Program in Business Administration (Professional), Montréal, QC H3C 3P8, Canada. Offers business administration (MBA); management consultant (Diploma). Part-time programs available. *Entrance requirements:* For master's and Diploma, appropriate bachelor's degree or equivalent, proficiency in French.

Université du Québec à Montréal, Graduate Programs, Program in Business Administration (Research), Montréal, QC H3C 3P8, Canada. Offers MBA. Part-time programs available. *Entrance requirements:* For master's, appropriate bachelor's degree or equivalent and proficiency in French.

Université du Québec à Rimouski, Graduate Programs, Program in Business Administration, Rimouski, QC G5L 3A1, Canada. Offers MBA.

Université du Québec à Rimouski, Graduate Programs, Program in Management of People in Working Situation, Rimouski, QC G5L 3A1, Canada. Offers M Sc, Diploma.

Université du Québec à Trois-Rivières, Graduate Programs, Program in Business Administration, Trois-Rivières, QC G9A 5H7, Canada. Offers MBA, DBA. DBA offered jointly with Université de Sherbrooke. *Degree requirements:* For doctorate, thesis/dissertation.

Université du Québec en Abitibi-Témiscamingue, Graduate Programs, Program in Business Administration, Rouyn-Noranda, QC J9X 5E4, Canada. Offers MBA.

Université du Québec en Abitibi-Témiscamingue, Graduate Programs, Program in Organization Management, Rouyn-Noranda, QC J9X 5E4, Canada. Offers M Sc. Part-time programs available. *Degree requirements:* For master's, thesis. *Entrance requirements:* For master's, appropriate bachelor's degree, proficiency in French.

Université Laval, Faculty of Administrative Sciences, Program in Organizations Management and Development, Québec, QC G1K 7P4, Canada. Offers Diploma. Part-time programs available. *Entrance requirements:* For degree, knowledge of French. Electronic applications accepted.

Université Laval, Faculty of Administrative Sciences, Programs in Administrative Studies, Québec, QC G1K 7P4, Canada. Offers administrative studies (M Sc, PhD); financial engineering (M Sc). *Accreditation:* AACSB. Terminal master's awarded for partial completion of doctoral program. *Degree requirements:* For master's, thesis (for some programs); for doctorate, comprehensive exam, thesis/dissertation. *Entrance requirements:* For master's and doctorate, knowledge of French and English. Electronic applications accepted.

Université Laval, Faculty of Administrative Sciences, Programs in Business Administration, Québec, QC G1K 7P4, Canada. Offers accounting (MBA); agri-food management (MBA); electronic business (MBA, Diploma); factory management and logistics (MBA); finance (MBA); firm management (MBA); geomatic management (MBA); information technology management (MBA); international management (MBA); management (MBA); management accounting (MBA, Diploma); marketing (MBA); modeling and organizational decision (MBA); occupational health and safety management (MBA); pharmacy management (MBA); social and environmental responsibility (MBA); technological entrepreneurship (Diploma). *Accreditation:* AACSB. Part-time and evening/weekend programs available. Postbaccalaureate distance learning degree programs offered (no on-campus study). *Entrance requirements:* For master's and Diploma, knowledge of French and English. Electronic applications accepted.

University at Albany, State University of New York, School of Business, Albany, NY 12222-0001. Offers MBA, MS. *Accreditation:* AACSB. Part-time and evening/weekend programs available. Terminal master's awarded for partial completion of doctoral program. *Degree requirements:* For master's, project. *Entrance requirements:* For master's, GMAT. Additional exam requirements/recommendations for international students: Required—TOEFL (minimum score 550 paper-based). Electronic applications accepted.

University at Buffalo, the State University of New York, Graduate School, School of Management, Buffalo, NY 14260. Offers accounting (MS); business administration (EMBA, MBA, PMBA); finance (MS), including financial management, quantitative finance; management (PhD); management information systems (MS); supply chains and operations management (MS); Au D/MBA; DDS/MBA; JD/MBA; M Arch/MBA; MA/MBA; MD/MBA; MPH/MBA; MSW/MBA; Pharm D/MBA. *Accreditation:* AACSB. Part-time and evening/weekend programs available. *Faculty:* 72 full-time (23 women), 51 part-time/adjunct (13 women). *Students:* 627 full-time (266 women), 181 part-time (65 women); includes 50 minority (16 Black or African American, non-Hispanic/Latino; 5 American Indian or Alaska Native, non-Hispanic/Latino; 5 Asian, non-Hispanic/Latino; 3 Hispanic/Latino; 21 Native Hawaiian or other Pacific Islander, non-Hispanic/Latino), 332 international. Average age 28. 2,083 applicants, 52% accepted, 432 enrolled. In 2013, 476 master's, 10 doctorates awarded. *Degree requirements:* For master's, thesis (for some programs); for doctorate, comprehensive exam, thesis/dissertation. *Entrance requirements:* For master's, GMAT (for MS in accounting); GRE or GMAT (for MBA and all other MS concentrations), essays, letters of recommendation; for doctorate, GMAT or GRE, essays, writing sample, letters of recommendation. Additional exam requirements/recommendations for international students: Required—IELTS or PTE; Recommended—TOEFL (minimum score 95 iBT). *Application deadline:* For fall admission, 5/2 priority date for domestic students, 2/1 priority date for international students. Applications are processed on a rolling basis. Application fee: $100. Electronic applications accepted. *Expenses:* Contact institution. *Financial support:* In 2013–14, 115 students received support, including 40 fellowships (averaging $5,250 per year), 33 research assistantships with full and partial tuition reimbursements available (averaging $18,000 per year), 42 teaching assistantships with partial tuition reimbursements available (averaging $10,255 per year); career-related internships or fieldwork, Federal Work-Study, institutionally sponsored loans, scholarships/grants, health care benefits, and unspecified assistantships also available. Financial award application deadline: 2/15; financial award applicants required to submit FAFSA. *Faculty research:* Earnings management and electronic information assurance, supply chain and operations management, corporate financing and asset pricing, consumer behavior and quantitative modeling of marketing behavior, leadership and politics in organizations. *Total annual research expenditures:* $155,000. *Unit head:* Erin K. O'Brien, Assistant Dean and Director of Graduate Programs, 716-645-3204, Fax: 716-645-2341, E-mail: ekobrien@buffalo.edu. *Application contact:* Meghan Felser, Associate Director of Admissions and Recruiting, 716-645-3204, Fax: 716-645-2341, E-mail: mpwood@buffalo.edu.
Website: http://mgt.buffalo.edu/.

The University of Akron, Graduate School, College of Business Administration, Department of Management, Program in Management, Akron, OH 44325. Offers MBA. *Students:* 19 full-time (9 women), 47 part-time (17 women); includes 4 minority (2 Asian, non-Hispanic/Latino; 1 Hispanic/Latino; 1 Two or more races, non-Hispanic/Latino), 12 international. Average age 29. 40 applicants, 55% accepted, 16 enrolled. In 2013, 28 master's awarded. *Entrance requirements:* For master's, GMAT, minimum GPA of 2.75, two letters of recommendation, statement of purpose, resume. Additional exam requirements/recommendations for international students: Required—TOEFL (minimum score 550 paper-based; 79 iBT). *Application deadline:* For fall admission, 7/15 for domestic and international students; for spring admission, 11/15 for domestic and international students. Application fee: $40 ($60 for international students). Electronic applications accepted. *Expenses:* Tuition, state resident: full-time $7430; part-time $412.80 per credit hour. Tuition, nonresident: full-time $12,722; part-time $706.80 per credit hour. *Required fees:* $53 per credit hour. $12 per semester. Tuition and fees vary according to course load and program. *Unit head:* Dr. Steve Ash, Head, 330-972-6429, E-mail: ash@uakron.edu. *Application contact:* Dr. William Hauser, Director of Graduate Business Programs, 330-972-7043, Fax: 330-972-6588, E-mail: whauser@uakron.edu. Website: https://www.uakron.edu/cba/departments/management/management-programs.dot.

The University of Alabama, Graduate School, Manderson Graduate School of Business, Department of Management, Tuscaloosa, AL 35487. Offers MA, MS, PhD. *Accreditation:* AACSB. Part-time and evening/weekend programs available. Postbaccalaureate distance learning degree programs offered (no on-campus study). *Faculty:* 21 full-time (7 women). *Students:* 19 full-time (9 women), 56 part-time (17 women); includes 15 minority (9 Black or African American, non-Hispanic/Latino; 1 American Indian or Alaska Native, non-Hispanic/Latino; 3 Asian, non-Hispanic/Latino; 1 Hispanic/Latino; 1 Two or more races, non-Hispanic/Latino), 4 international. Average age 33. 60 applicants, 55% accepted, 24 enrolled. In 2013, 26 master's, 2 doctorates awarded. Terminal master's awarded for partial completion of doctoral program. *Degree requirements:* For master's, comprehensive exam (for some programs), thesis (for some programs), formal project paper; for doctorate, comprehensive exam, thesis/dissertation. *Entrance requirements:* For master's and doctorate, GMAT or GRE, minimum GPA of 3.0. Additional exam requirements/recommendations for international students: Required—TOEFL (minimum score 600 paper-based) or IELTS (minimum score 6.5). *Application deadline:* For fall admission, 6/30 priority date for domestic students, 1/31 for international students; for spring admission, 10/30 for domestic students. Applications are processed on a rolling basis. Application fee: $50 ($60 for international students). *Expenses:* Tuition, state resident: full-time $9450. Tuition, nonresident: full-time $23,950. *Financial support:* In 2013–14, 5 fellowships with full and partial tuition reimbursements (averaging $15,000 per year), 2 research assistantships (averaging $18,444 per year), 2 teaching assistantships (averaging $16,200 per year) were awarded; scholarships/grants, health care benefits, and unspecified assistantships also available. *Faculty research:* Leadership, entrepreneurship, health care management, organizational behavior, strategy. *Unit head:* Dr. Robert M. Morgan, Department Head, 205-348-6183, Fax: 205-348-6695, E-mail: rmorgan@cba.ua.edu. *Application contact:* Courtney Cox, Office Associate II, 205-348-6183, Fax: 205-348-6695, E-mail: crhodes@cba.ua.edu. Website: http://cba.ua.edu/mgt.

The University of Alabama, Graduate School, Manderson Graduate School of Business, Program in General Commerce and Business, Tuscaloosa, AL 35487. Offers EMBA, MBA. *Accreditation:* AACSB. Part-time programs available. *Students:* 205 full-time (67 women), 1 part-time (0 women); includes 23 minority (13 Black or African American, non-Hispanic/Latino; 1 American Indian or Alaska Native, non-Hispanic/Latino; 4 Asian, non-Hispanic/Latino; 1 Hispanic/Latino; 1 Native Hawaiian or other Pacific Islander, non-Hispanic/Latino; 3 Two or more races, non-Hispanic/Latino), 18 international. Average age 28. 179 applicants, 59% accepted, 87 enrolled. In 2013, 125 master's awarded. *Entrance requirements:* For master's, GMAT or GRE. Additional exam requirements/recommendations for international students: Required—TOEFL (minimum score 550 paper-based). *Application deadline:* For winter admission, 1/2 priority date for domestic students, 1/1 priority date for international students; for spring admission, 4/15 for domestic and international students. Applications are processed on a rolling basis. Application fee: $50 ($60 for international students). Electronic applications accepted. *Expenses:* Tuition, state resident: full-time $9450. Tuition, nonresident: full-time $23,950. *Financial support:* In 2013–14, 26 students received support, including 22 research assistantships (averaging $5,400 per year), 4 teaching assistantships; health care benefits also available. Financial award application deadline: 4/15. *Unit head:* Susan C. West, Assistant Dean and Director of MBA Programs, 205-348-0954, Fax: 205-348-0479, E-mail: swest@cba.ua.edu. *Application contact:* Blake Bedsole, Coordinator of Graduate Recruiting and Admissions, 205-348-9122, Fax: 205-348-4504, E-mail: bbedsole@cba.ua.edu.

The University of Alabama at Birmingham, School of Business, Birmingham, AL 35294-4460. Offers M Acct, MBA, MS. *Accreditation:* AACSB. Part-time programs available. Postbaccalaureate distance learning degree programs offered (no on-campus study). *Faculty:* 61 full-time (18 women). *Students:* 102 full-time (47 women), 311 part-time (177 women); includes 96 minority (67 Black or African American, non-Hispanic/Latino; 15 Asian, non-Hispanic/Latino; 11 Hispanic/Latino; 3 Two or more races, non-Hispanic/Latino), 23 international. Average age 31. In 2013, 167 master's awarded. *Entrance requirements:* For master's, GMAT. Additional exam requirements/recommendations for international students: Required—TOEFL. *Application deadline:* Applications are processed on a rolling basis. Electronic applications accepted. *Financial support:* Fellowships and career-related internships or fieldwork available. Financial award applicants required to submit FAFSA. *Unit head:* Dr. Eric Jack, Dean, 205-934-8800, Fax: 205-934-8886, E-mail: ejack@uab.edu. *Application contact:* Director, 205-934-8817.
Website: http://www.uab.edu/business/.

The University of Alabama in Huntsville, School of Graduate Studies, College of Business Administration, Programs in Business and Management, Huntsville, AL 35899. Offers federal contracting and procurement management (Certificate); management (MBA), including acquisition management, entrepreneurship, federal contract accounting, finance, human resource management, logistics and supply chain management, marketing, project management; supply chain management (Certificate); technology and innovation management (Certificate). *Accreditation:* AACSB. Part-time and evening/weekend programs available. *Faculty:* 13 full-time (3 women), 5 part-time/adjunct (0 women). *Students:* 41 full-time (19 women), 144 part-time (59 women); includes 35 minority (13 Black or African American, non-Hispanic/Latino; 1 American Indian or Alaska Native, non-Hispanic/Latino; 9 Asian, non-Hispanic/Latino; 11 Hispanic/Latino; 1 Two or more races, non-Hispanic/Latino), 13 international. Average age 33. 131 applicants, 78% accepted, 67 enrolled. In 2013, 83 master's, 5 other advanced degrees awarded. *Degree requirements:* For master's, comprehensive exam, thesis or alternative. *Entrance requirements:* For master's, GMAT (minimum score 500), minimum AACSB index of 1080. Additional exam requirements/recommendations for international students: Required—TOEFL (minimum score 550 paper-based; 80 iBT), IELTS (minimum score 6.5). *Application deadline:* For fall admission, 7/15 priority date for domestic students, 4/1 priority date for international students; for spring admission,

11/30 priority date for domestic students, 9/1 priority date for international students. Applications are processed on a rolling basis. Application fee: $50. Electronic applications accepted. *Expenses:* Tuition, state resident: full-time $8912; part-time $540 per credit hour. Tuition, nonresident: full-time $20,774; part-time $1252 per credit hour. *Required fees:* $148 per semester. One-time fee: $150. *Financial support:* In 2013–14, 10 students received support, including 4 research assistantships with full and partial tuition reimbursements available (averaging $7,750 per year), 5 teaching assistantships with full and partial tuition reimbursements available (averaging $9,000 per year); career-related internships or fieldwork, Federal Work-Study, institutionally sponsored loans, scholarships/grants, health care benefits, tuition waivers (full and partial), and unspecified assistantships also available. Support available to part-time students. Financial award application deadline: 4/1; financial award applicants required to submit FAFSA. *Faculty research:* Supply chain management, management of research and development, international marketing and branding, organizational behavior and human resource management, social networks and computational economics. *Total annual research expenditures:* $2.1 million. *Unit head:* Dr. Cynthia Gramm, Chair, 256-824-6913, Fax: 256-824-6328, E-mail: cynthia.gramm@uah.edu. *Application contact:* Jennifer Pettitt, Director of Graduate Programs, 256-824-6681, Fax: 256-824-7571, E-mail: jennifer.pettitt@uah.edu.

University of Alaska Anchorage, College of Business and Public Policy, Program in Business Administration, Anchorage, AK 99508. Offers MBA. *Accreditation:* AACSB. Part-time programs available. *Degree requirements:* For master's, comprehensive exam, thesis (for some programs), capstone projects. *Entrance requirements:* Additional exam requirements/recommendations for international students: Required—TOEFL (minimum score 550 paper-based). *Faculty research:* Complex global environments.

University of Alaska Fairbanks, School of Management, Department of Business Administration, Fairbanks, AK 99775-6080. Offers capital markets (MBA); general management (MBA). *Accreditation:* AACSB. Part-time programs available. *Faculty:* 10 full-time (4 women). *Students:* 29 full-time (18 women), 41 part-time (20 women); includes 13 minority (2 American Indian or Alaska Native, non-Hispanic/Latino; 2 Asian, non-Hispanic/Latino; 2 Hispanic/Latino; 7 Two or more races, non-Hispanic/Latino), 4 international. Average age 34. 36 applicants, 56% accepted, 19 enrolled. In 2013, 28 master's awarded. *Degree requirements:* For master's, comprehensive exam, thesis or alternative. *Entrance requirements:* For master's, GMAT. Additional exam requirements/recommendations for international students: Required—TOEFL (minimum score 550 paper-based; 80 iBT). *Application deadline:* For fall admission, 6/1 priority date for domestic students, 2/1 for international students; for spring admission, 10/15 priority date for domestic students, 9/1 for international students. Applications are processed on a rolling basis. Application fee: $60. Electronic applications accepted. *Expenses:* Tuition, state resident: full-time $7254; part-time $403 per credit. Tuition, nonresident: full-time $14,814; part-time $823 per credit. Tuition and fees vary according to course level, course load and reciprocity agreements. *Financial support:* In 2013–14, 6 teaching assistantships with tuition reimbursements (averaging $11,115 per year) were awarded; fellowships with tuition reimbursements, research assistantships with tuition reimbursements, career-related internships or fieldwork, Federal Work-Study, scholarships/grants, health care benefits, and unspecified assistantships also available. Support available to part-time students. Financial award application deadline: 2/15; financial award applicants required to submit FAFSA. *Faculty research:* Consumer behavior, marketing, international finance and business, strategic risk, organization theory. *Total annual research expenditures:* $116,000. *Unit head:* Dr. Liz Ross, Director, MBA Program, 907-474-7793, Fax: 907-474-5219, E-mail: bmross@alaska.edu. *Application contact:* Libby Eddy, Registrar and Director of Admissions, 907-474-7500, Fax: 907-474-7097, E-mail: admissions@uaf.edu.
Website: http://www.uaf.edu/som/degrees/graduate/.

University of Alaska Southeast, Graduate Programs, Program in Business Administration, Juneau, AK 99801. Offers MBA. Part-time and evening/weekend programs available. Postbaccalaureate distance learning degree programs offered (minimal on-campus study). *Degree requirements:* For master's, residential seminar. *Entrance requirements:* For master's, curriculum vitae, letters of reference, minimum GPA of 3.0. Additional exam requirements/recommendations for international students: Recommended—TOEFL. Electronic applications accepted. *Faculty research:* Services marketing; marketing and technology issues: social capital and entrepreneurship; motivation and managerial tactics.

University of Alberta, Faculty of Graduate Studies and Research, Doctoral Program in Business, Edmonton, AB T6G 2E1, Canada. Offers accounting (PhD); finance (PhD); human resources/industrial relations (PhD); management science (PhD); marketing (PhD); organizational analysis (PhD); MBA/PhD. *Accreditation:* AACSB. Part-time programs available. *Degree requirements:* For doctorate, comprehensive exam, thesis/dissertation. *Entrance requirements:* For doctorate, GMAT. Additional exam requirements/recommendations for international students: Required—TOEFL (minimum score 550 paper-based). Electronic applications accepted. *Faculty research:* Accounting, capital markets and corporate finance, organizational change and human resource management, marketing, strategic management.

University of Alberta, Faculty of Graduate Studies and Research, Executive MBA Program, Edmonton, AB T6G 2E1, Canada. Offers Exec MBA. Program offered jointly with University of Calgary. *Accreditation:* AACSB. *Entrance requirements:* For master's, GMAT. Additional exam requirements/recommendations for international students: Required—TOEFL. Electronic applications accepted. *Expenses:* Contact institution.

University of Alberta, Faculty of Graduate Studies and Research, Program in Business Administration, Edmonton, AB T6G 2E1, Canada. Offers international business (MBA); leisure and sport management (MBA); natural resources and energy (MBA); technology commercialization (MBA); MBA/LL B; MBA/M Ag; MBA/M Eng; MBA/MF; MBA/PhD. *Accreditation:* AACSB. Part-time and evening/weekend programs available. *Degree requirements:* For master's, thesis or alternative. *Entrance requirements:* For master's, GMAT. Additional exam requirements/recommendations for international students: Required—TOEFL (minimum score 600 paper-based). Electronic applications accepted. *Faculty research:* Natural resources and energy/management and policy/family enterprise/international business/healthcare research management.

University of Antelope Valley, Program in Business Management, Lancaster, CA 93534. Offers MS. *Degree requirements:* For master's, capstone. *Entrance requirements:* For master's, official transcripts documenting earned bachelor's degree from nationally- or regionally-accredited institution with minimum cumulative GPA of 2.0.

The University of Arizona, Eller College of Management, Tucson, AZ 85721. Offers M Ac, MA, MBA, MS, PhD, JD/MA, JD/MBA, JD/PhD. *Accreditation:* AACSB. Evening/weekend programs available. *Faculty:* 68 full-time (18 women), 7 part-time/adjunct (2 women). *Students:* 625 full-time (202 women), 174 part-time (48 women); includes 117 minority (15 Black or African American, non-Hispanic/Latino; 5 American Indian or Alaska Native, non-Hispanic/Latino; 35 Asian, non-Hispanic/Latino; 41 Hispanic/Latino; 1 Native Hawaiian or other Pacific Islander, non-Hispanic/Latino; 20 Two or more races, non-Hispanic/Latino), 317 international. Average age 31. 1,865 applicants, 40% accepted, 296 enrolled. In 2013, 335 master's, 23 doctorates awarded. *Degree requirements:* For doctorate, thesis/dissertation. *Entrance requirements:* Additional exam requirements/recommendations for international students: Required—TOEFL (minimum score 550 paper-based; 79 iBT). *Application deadline:* Applications are processed on a rolling basis. Application fee: $75. Electronic applications accepted. *Expenses:* Contact institution. *Financial support:* In 2013–14, 39 research assistantships with full tuition reimbursements (averaging $22,989 per year), 179 teaching assistantships with full tuition reimbursements (averaging $23,305 per year) were awarded; career-related internships or fieldwork, Federal Work-Study, scholarships/grants, health care benefits, tuition waivers (partial), and unspecified assistantships also available. Financial award application deadline: 3/15. *Total annual research expenditures:* $6.5 million. *Unit head:* Dr. Len Jessup, Dean, 520-621-2125, Fax: 520-621-8105. *Application contact:* Information Contact, 520-621-2165, Fax: 520-621-8105, E-mail: mbaadmissions@eller.arizona.edu.
Website: http://www.eller.arizona.edu/.

University of Arkansas, Graduate School, Sam M. Walton College of Business Administration, Program in Business Administration, Fayetteville, AR 72701-1201. Offers MBA, PhD. *Accreditation:* AACSB. Part-time and evening/weekend programs available. Postbaccalaureate distance learning degree programs offered (minimal on-campus study). *Degree requirements:* For doctorate, thesis/dissertation. *Entrance requirements:* For master's and doctorate, GMAT.

University of Arkansas at Little Rock, Graduate School, College of Business Administration, Little Rock, AR 72204-1099. Offers accountancy (M Acc, Graduate Certificate); business administration (MBA); construction management (Graduate Certificate); management (Graduate Certificate); management information system (MIS); management information systems (Graduate Certificate); management information systems leadership (Graduate Certificate); taxation (MS, Graduate Certificate). *Accreditation:* AACSB. Part-time and evening/weekend programs available. *Entrance requirements:* For master's, GMAT, minimum undergraduate GPA of 2.7. Additional exam requirements/recommendations for international students: Required—TOEFL (minimum score 525 paper-based). *Expenses:* Tuition, state resident: full-time $5690; part-time $284.50 per credit hour. Tuition, nonresident: full-time $13,030; part-time $651.50 per credit hour. *Required fees:* $1121; $672 per term. One-time fee: $40 full-time.

University of Baltimore, Graduate School, Merrick School of Business, Baltimore, MD 21201-5779. Offers MBA, MS, Graduate Certificate, JD/MBA, MBA/MSN, MBA/Pharm D. *Accreditation:* AACSB. Part-time and evening/weekend programs available. Postbaccalaureate distance learning degree programs offered (no on-campus study). *Entrance requirements:* For master's, GMAT. Additional exam requirements/recommendations for international students: Required—TOEFL (minimum score 550 paper-based). Electronic applications accepted. *Faculty research:* Finance, economics, accounting, health care, management information systems.

University of Baltimore, Joint University of Baltimore/Towson University (UB/Towson) MBA Program, Baltimore, MD 21201-5779. Offers MBA, JD/MBA, MBA/MSN, MBA/Pharm D. MBA/MSN, MBA/PhamrD offered jointly with University of Maryland, Baltimore. *Accreditation:* AACSB. Part-time and evening/weekend programs available. Postbaccalaureate distance learning degree programs offered (no on-campus study). *Entrance requirements:* For master's, GMAT. Additional exam requirements/recommendations for international students: Required—TOEFL (minimum score 550 paper-based).

University of Bridgeport, School of Business, Bridgeport, CT 06604. Offers accounting (MBA); finance (MBA); general business (MBA); global financial services (MBA); human resource management (MBA); information systems and knowledge management (MBA); international business (MBA); management (MBA); marketing (MBA); operations management (MBA); small business and entrepreneurship (MBA); specialized business (MBA). *Accreditation:* ACBSP. Part-time and evening/weekend programs available. *Faculty:* 11 full-time (2 women), 39 part-time/adjunct (8 women). *Students:* 162 full-time (90 women), 69 part-time (45 women); includes 44 minority (20 Black or African American, non-Hispanic/Latino; 7 Asian, non-Hispanic/Latino; 15 Hispanic/Latino; 2 Two or more races, non-Hispanic/Latino), 163 international. Average age 28. 492 applicants, 48% accepted, 55 enrolled. In 2013, 144 master's awarded. *Degree requirements:* For master's, thesis optional. *Entrance requirements:* For master's, GMAT. Additional exam requirements/recommendations for international students: Recommended—TOEFL (minimum score 550 paper-based; 80 iBT), IELTS (minimum score 6.5). *Application deadline:* For fall admission, 8/1 priority date for domestic and international students; for spring admission, 12/1 priority date for domestic and international students. Applications are processed on a rolling basis. Application fee: $50. Electronic applications accepted. *Expenses:* Contact institution. *Financial support:* In 2013–14, 69 students received support. Fellowships, research assistantships, teaching assistantships, career-related internships or fieldwork, Federal Work-Study, institutionally sponsored loans, and tuition waivers (partial) available. Support available to part-time students. Financial award application deadline: 6/1; financial award applicants required to submit FAFSA. *Unit head:* Dr. Lloyd G. Gibson, Dean, 203-576-4384, Fax: 203-576-4388, E-mail: llgibson@bridgeport.edu. *Application contact:* Leanne Proctor, Director of Graduate Admissions, 203-576-4552, Fax: 203-576-4941, E-mail: mba@bridgeport.edu.
Website: http://www.bridgeport.edu.

The University of British Columbia, Sauder School of Business, Doctoral Program in Commerce and Business Administration, Vancouver, BC V6T 1Z1, Canada. Offers accounting (PhD); finance (PhD); management information systems (PhD); management science (PhD); marketing (PhD); organizational behavior (PhD); strategy and business economics (PhD); transportation and logistics (PhD); urban land economics (PhD). *Faculty:* 91 full-time (22 women). *Students:* 66 full-time (24 women). Average age 30. 418 applicants, 2% accepted, 8 enrolled. In 2013, 7 doctorates awarded. *Degree requirements:* For doctorate, comprehensive exam, thesis/dissertation. *Entrance requirements:* For doctorate, GMAT or GRE. Additional exam requirements/recommendations for international students: Required—TOEFL (minimum score 600 paper-based; 100 iBT). *Application deadline:* For fall admission, 1/31 for domestic students, 12/31 for international students. Applications are processed on a rolling basis. Application fee: $95 Canadian dollars ($153 Canadian dollars for international students). Electronic applications accepted. *Expenses: Tuition, area resident:* Full-time $8000 Canadian dollars. *Financial support:* In 2013–14, fellowships with full tuition reimbursements (averaging $17,500 per year), research assistantships with full tuition reimbursements (averaging $8,500 per year), teaching assistantships with full tuition reimbursements (averaging $17,500 per year) were awarded. Financial award application deadline: 12/31. *Unit head:* Dr. Ralph Winter, Director, 604-822-8366, Fax: 604-822-8755. *Application contact:* Elaine Cho, Administrator, PhD and M Sc Programs, 604-822-8366, Fax: 604-822-8755, E-mail: phd.program@sauder.ubc.ca.
Website: http://www.sauder.ubc.ca/.

The University of British Columbia, Sauder School of Business, MBA Program, Vancouver, BC V6T 1Z1, Canada. Offers IMBA, MBA. *Accreditation:* AACSB. *Expenses: Tuition, area resident:* Full-time $8000 Canadian dollars.

University of Calgary, Faculty of Graduate Studies, Haskayne School of Business, Alberta/Haskayne Executive MBA Program, Calgary, AB T2N 1N4, Canada. Offers

EMBA. Program offered with School of Business at University of Alberta. *Accreditation:* AACSB. Part-time programs available. *Entrance requirements:* For master's, GMAT, minimum GPA of 3.0, minimum 7 years of work experience, 3 letters of reference. Additional exam requirements/recommendations for international students: Required—TOEFL (minimum score 600 paper-based; 100 iBT). *Expenses:* Contact institution. *Faculty research:* Accounting, data analysis and modeling, strategy, entrepreneurship, negotiations.

University of Calgary, Faculty of Graduate Studies, Haskayne School of Business, Program in Business Administration, Calgary, AB T2N 1N4, Canada. Offers MBA, MBA/LL B, MBA/MBT, MBA/MD, MBA/MSW. *Accreditation:* AACSB. Part-time and evening/weekend programs available. *Degree requirements:* For master's, comprehensive exam, thesis optional. *Entrance requirements:* For master's, GMAT (minimum score 550), minimum GPA of 3.0, resume, 3 years of work experience, 3 letters of reference, 4 year bachelor degree. Additional exam requirements/recommendations for international students: Required—TOEFL (minimum score 600 paper-based). Electronic applications accepted. *Expenses:* Contact institution. *Faculty research:* Entrepreneurship, ethics, strategy, finance energy management and sustainability.

University of Calgary, Faculty of Graduate Studies, Haskayne School of Business, Program in Management, Calgary, AB T2N 1N4, Canada. Offers MBA, PhD. *Accreditation:* AACSB. Terminal master's awarded for partial completion of doctoral program. *Degree requirements:* For master's, one foreign language, comprehensive exam, thesis; for doctorate, one foreign language, comprehensive exam, thesis/dissertation, written and oral exams. *Entrance requirements:* For master's, GMAT, GRE, minimum GPA of 3.3 in last 2 years of course work, 2 letters of ref.; for doctorate, GMAT, GRE, minimum GPA of 3.5 in last 2 years of course work, 2 letters of reference. Additional exam requirements/recommendations for international students: Required—TOEFL (minimum score 600 paper-based; 100 iBT), IELTS (minimum score 7). Electronic applications accepted. *Faculty research:* Operations management, international business, management information systems, accounting, finance, sustainable development.

University of California, Berkeley, Graduate Division, Haas School of Business and School of Law, Concurrent JD/MBA Program, Berkeley, CA 94720-1500. Offers JD/MBA. *Accreditation:* AACSB; ABA. *Students:* 1 (woman) full-time; minority (Two or more races, non-Hispanic/Latino). Average age 29. *Entrance requirements:* Required—Additional exam requirements/recommendations for international students: Required—TOEFL (minimum score 570 paper-based; 68 iBT). *Application deadline:* For fall admission, 10/16 for domestic and international students; for winter admission, 1/8 for domestic and international students; for spring admission, 3/12 for domestic and international students. Application fee: $200. Electronic applications accepted. *Financial support:* Application deadline: 3/1; applicants required to submit FAFSA. *Faculty research:* Accounting, business and public policy, economic analysis and public policy, entrepreneurship, finance, management of organizations, marketing, operations and information technology management, real estate. *Unit head:* Julia Hwang, Director, MBA Program, 510-642-1405, Fax: 510-643-6659, E-mail: julia_hwang@haas.berkeley.edu. *Application contact:* Office of Admissions, 510-642-1405, Fax: 510-643-6659, E-mail: admissions@boalt.berkeley.edu.
Website: http://mba.haas.berkeley.edu/academics/concurrentdegrees.html.

University of California, Berkeley, Graduate Division, Haas School of Business and School of Public Health, Concurrent MBA/MPH Program, Berkeley, CA 94720-1500. Offers MBA/MPH. *Accreditation:* AACSB; CEPH. *Students:* 35 full-time (22 women); includes 9 minority (8 Asian, non-Hispanic/Latino; 1 Hispanic/Latino), 9 international. Average age 28. *Entrance requirements:* Additional exam requirements/recommendations for international students: Required—TOEFL. *Application deadline:* For fall admission, 10/16 for domestic and international students; for winter admission, 1/8 for domestic and international students; for spring admission, 3/12 for domestic and international students. Application fee: $200. Electronic applications accepted. *Financial support:* Fellowships with tuition reimbursements, teaching assistantships with tuition reimbursements, career-related internships or fieldwork, scholarships/grants, and unspecified assistantships available. Financial award application deadline: 6/12. *Faculty research:* Accounting, business and public policy, economic analysis and public policy, entrepreneurship, finance, management of organizations, marketing, operations and information technology management, real estate. *Unit head:* Prof. Kristi Raube, Director, Health Services Management Program, 510-642-5023, Fax: 510-643-6659, E-mail: raube@haas.berkeley.edu. *Application contact:* Lee Forgue, Student Affairs Officer, 510-642-5023, Fax: 510-643-6659, E-mail: eilis@haas.berkeley.edu.
Website: http://www.haas.berkeley.edu/.

University of California, Berkeley, Graduate Division, Haas School of Business, Evening and Weekend MBA Program, Berkeley, CA 94720-1500. Offers MBA. *Accreditation:* AACSB. Part-time and evening/weekend programs available. *Students:* 803 part-time (212 women); includes 200 minority (11 Black or African American, non-Hispanic/Latino; 1 American Indian or Alaska Native, non-Hispanic/Latino; 152 Asian, non-Hispanic/Latino; 13 Hispanic/Latino; 1 Native Hawaiian or other Pacific Islander, non-Hispanic/Latino; 22 Two or more races, non-Hispanic/Latino), 324 international. Average age 33. 712 applicants, 251 enrolled. In 2013, 227 master's awarded. *Degree requirements:* For master's, comprehensive exam, academic retreat, experiential learning course. *Entrance requirements:* For master's, GMAT or GRE, BA or BS. Additional exam requirements/recommendations for international students: Required—TOEFL (minimum score: paper-based 570, iBT 68) or IELTS. *Application deadline:* For fall admission, 11/20 for domestic and international students; for winter admission, 1/21 for domestic and international students; for spring admission, 3/20 for domestic and international students; for summer admission, 5/1 for domestic and international students. Application fee: $200. Electronic applications accepted. *Expenses:* Contact institution. *Financial support:* In 2013–14, 54 students received support, including 54 fellowships (averaging $6,561 per year); research assistantships and teaching assistantships also available. Financial award application deadline: 6/5. *Faculty research:* Accounting, business and public policy, economic analysis and public policy, finance, management of organizations, marketing, operations and information technology management, real estate. *Unit head:* Jonathan Kaplan, Executive Director, 510-643-0434, Fax: 510-643-5902, E-mail: ewmbaadm@haas.berkeley.edu. *Application contact:* Evening and Weekend MBA Admissions Office, 510-642-0292, Fax: 510-643-5902, E-mail: ewmbaadm@haas.berkeley.edu.
Website: http://ewmba.haas.berkeley.edu/.

University of California, Berkeley, Graduate Division, Haas School of Business, Full-Time MBA Program, Berkeley, CA 94720-1902. Offers MBA. *Accreditation:* AACSB. *Students:* 461 full-time (130 women); includes 112 minority (14 Black or African American, non-Hispanic/Latino; 58 Asian, non-Hispanic/Latino; 24 Hispanic/Latino; 16 Two or more races, non-Hispanic/Latino), 170 international. Average age 29. 3,422 applicants, 251 enrolled. In 2013, 227 master's awarded. *Degree requirements:* For master's, 51 units, one Innovative Leader Curriculum experiential learning course. *Entrance requirements:* For master's, GMAT or GRE, BA/BS. Additional exam requirements/recommendations for international students: Required—TOEFL (minimum score 570 paper-based; 68 iBT), IELTS (minimum score 7). *Application deadline:* For fall admission, 10/16 for domestic and international students; for winter admission, 1/8 for domestic and international students; for spring admission, 3/12 for domestic and international students. Application fee: $200. Electronic applications accepted. *Expenses:* Contact institution. *Financial support:* In 2013–14, 283 students received support, including 230 fellowships with full and partial tuition reimbursements available (averaging $23,147 per year), 107 teaching assistantships with partial tuition reimbursements available (averaging $10,415 per year); tuition waivers (full and partial) and non-resident waivers (for some students, such as military veterans) also available. Financial award application deadline: 6/12. *Unit head:* Julia Hwang, Executive Director, 510-642-1407, Fax: 510-643-6659, E-mail: julia_hwang@haas.berkeley.edu. *Application contact:* Stephanie Fujii, Executive Director, Full-Time MBA Admissions, 510-642-1405, Fax: 510-643-6659, E-mail: mbaadm@haas.berkeley.edu.
Website: http://mba.haas.berkeley.edu/.

University of California, Berkeley, Graduate Division, Haas School of Business and Program in International and Area Studies, MBA/MA Program in International and Area Studies, Berkeley, CA 94720-1500. Offers MBA/MA. *Accreditation:* AACSB. *Entrance requirements:* Additional exam requirements/recommendations for international students: Required—TOEFL (minimum score 570 paper-based; 68 iBT). Application fee: $200. *Financial support:* Fellowships with full tuition reimbursements, research assistantships, teaching assistantships with partial tuition reimbursements, career-related internships or fieldwork, scholarships/grants, and unspecified assistantships available. Financial award application deadline: 6/6; financial award applicants required to submit FAFSA. *Unit head:* Julia Hwang, Director, MBA Program, 510-642-1405, Fax: 510-643-6659, E-mail: julia_hwang@haas.berkeley.edu. *Application contact:* 510-642-1405, Fax: 510-643-6659.

University of California, Berkeley, Graduate Division, Haas School of Business, PhD in Business Administration Program, Berkeley, CA 94720-1500. Offers accounting (PhD); business and public policy (PhD); finance (PhD); management of organizations (PhD); marketing (PhD); operations management (PhD); real estate (PhD). *Accreditation:* AACSB. *Students:* 74 full-time (28 women); includes 11 minority (9 Asian, non-Hispanic/Latino; 2 Hispanic/Latino), 38 international. Average age 27. 490 applicants, 6% accepted, 14 enrolled. In 2013, 14 doctorates awarded. *Degree requirements:* For doctorate, comprehensive exam, thesis/dissertation, written preliminary exams, oral qualifying exam. *Entrance requirements:* For doctorate, GMAT or GRE, minimum GPA of 3.0 in undergraduate and graduate coursework. Additional exam requirements/recommendations for international students: Required—TOEFL (minimum score 570 paper-based; 70 iBT), IELTS (minimum score 7). *Application deadline:* For fall admission, 12/10 for domestic and international students. Application fee: $80 ($100 for international students). Electronic applications accepted. *Financial support:* In 2013–14, 74 students received support, including 62 fellowships with full and partial tuition reimbursements available (averaging $30,000 per year), research assistantships with full and partial tuition reimbursements available (averaging $12,000 per year), teaching assistantships with full and partial tuition reimbursements available (averaging $13,000 per year); scholarships/grants, health care benefits, tuition waivers (full), unspecified assistantships, and transit passes, travel grants also available. Financial award application deadline: 12/10; financial award applicants required to submit FAFSA. *Faculty research:* Accounting, business and public policy, entrepreneurship, finance, management of organizations, marketing, operations and information technology management, real estate. *Unit head:* Dr. Martin Lettau, Director, 510-643-6349, Fax: 510-643-4255, E-mail: kimg@haas.berkeley.edu. *Application contact:* Kim Guilfoyle, Director, Student Affairs, 510-642-3944, Fax: 510-643-4255, E-mail: kimg@haas.berkeley.edu.
Website: http://www.haas.berkeley.edu/Phd/.

University of California, Berkeley, UC Berkeley Extension, Certificate Programs in Business, Berkeley, CA 94720-1500. Offers accounting (Certificate); business administration (Certificate); finance (Certificate); human resource management (Certificate); management (Certificate); marketing (Certificate); project management (Certificate). *Accreditation:* AACSB. Postbaccalaureate distance learning degree programs offered.

University of California, Berkeley, UC Berkeley Extension, International Diploma Programs, Berkeley, CA 94720-1500. Offers business administration (Certificate); finance (Certificate); global business management (Certificate); marketing (Certificate); project management (Certificate). *Accreditation:* AACSB.

University of California, Davis, Graduate School of Management, Daytime MBA Program, Davis, CA 95616. Offers MBA, JD/MBA, M Engr/MBA, MBA/MPH, MBA/MS, MD/MBA, MSN/MBA. *Faculty:* 32 full-time (13 women), 25 part-time/adjunct (0 women). *Students:* 97 full-time (36 women); includes 18 minority (2 Black or African American, non-Hispanic/Latino; 9 Asian, non-Hispanic/Latino; 5 Hispanic/Latino; 2 Two or more races, non-Hispanic/Latino), 34 international. Average age 29. 341 applicants, 18% accepted, 48 enrolled. In 2013, 48 master's awarded. *Degree requirements:* For master's, thesis or alternative, Integrated Management Project. *Entrance requirements:* For master's, GMAT or GRE, letters of recommendation, resume, essays, equivalent of a 4-year U.S. undergraduate degree. Additional exam requirements/recommendations for international students: Required—TOEFL (minimum score 600 paper-based; 100 iBT), IELTS (minimum score 7), PTE (minimum score 68). *Application deadline:* For fall admission, 11/6 priority date for domestic and international students. Application fee: $125. Electronic applications accepted. *Financial support:* In 2013–14, 67 students received support. Fellowships, teaching assistantships with partial tuition reimbursements available, career-related internships or fieldwork, Federal Work-Study, institutionally sponsored loans, scholarships/grants, tuition waivers (partial), and unspecified assistantships available. Financial award application deadline: 3/1; financial award applicants required to submit FAFSA. *Faculty research:* Technology management, finance, marketing, corporate governance and investor welfare, organizational behavior. *Unit head:* James Stevens, Assistant Dean of Student Affairs, 530-752-7658, Fax: 530-754-9355, E-mail: admissions@gsm.ucdavis.edu. *Application contact:* Kathy Gleed, Senior Director of Admission, 530-752-7658, Fax: 530-754-9355, E-mail: admissions@gsm.ucdavis.edu.
Website: http://gsm.ucdavis.edu/daytime-mba-program.

University of California, Davis, Graduate School of Management, MBA Programs in Sacramento and San Francisco Bay Area, Davis, CA 95616. Offers MBA. Part-time and evening/weekend programs available. *Faculty:* 32 full-time (13 women), 25 part-time/adjunct (0 women). *Students:* 460 part-time (155 women); includes 210 minority (9 Black or African American, non-Hispanic/Latino; 1 American Indian or Alaska Native, non-Hispanic/Latino; 147 Asian, non-Hispanic/Latino; 35 Hispanic/Latino; 3 Native Hawaiian or other Pacific Islander, non-Hispanic/Latino; 15 Two or more races, non-Hispanic/Latino), 40 international. Average age 31. 237 applicants, 70% accepted, 134 enrolled. In 2013, 113 master's awarded. *Degree requirements:* For master's, Integrated Management Project. *Entrance requirements:* For master's, GMAT or GRE, letters of recommendation, resume, equivalent of a 4-year undergraduate degree. Additional exam requirements/recommendations for international students: Required—TOEFL (minimum score 600 paper-based; 100 iBT), IELTS (minimum score 7), PTE (minimum score 68). *Application deadline:* For fall admission, 11/13 priority date for domestic students, 10/13 priority date for international students. Application fee: $125. Electronic applications accepted. *Expenses:* Contact institution. *Financial support:* In 2013–14, 22

students received support. Fellowships and scholarships/grants available. Financial award application deadline: 3/31; financial award applicants required to submit FAFSA. *Faculty research:* Technology management, finance, marketing, corporate governance and investor welfare, organizational behavior. *Unit head:* James Stevens, Assistant Dean of Student Affairs, 530-752-7658, Fax: 530-754-9355, E-mail: admissions@gsm.ucdavis.edu. *Application contact:* Kathy Gleed, Senior Director of Admissions, 530-752-7658, Fax: 530-754-9355, E-mail: admissions@gsm.ucdavis.edu.
Website: http://gsm.ucdavis.edu/mba-programs.

University of California, Irvine, The Paul Merage School of Business, Doctoral Program in Management, Irvine, CA 92697. Offers PhD. *Students:* 45 full-time (23 women); includes 10 minority (9 Asian, non-Hispanic/Latino; 1 Hispanic/Latino), 27 international. Average age 31. 230 applicants, 6% accepted, 12 enrolled. In 2013, 9 doctorates awarded. Application fee: $80 ($100 for international students). *Unit head:* Dr. Terry Shevlin, Director, 949-824-6149, E-mail: tshevlin@uci.edu. *Application contact:* Noel Negrete, Associate Director, 949-824-8318, Fax: 949-824-1592, E-mail: nnegrete@uci.edu.
Website: http://merage.uci.edu/PhD/Default.aspx.

University of California, Irvine, The Paul Merage School of Business, Executive MBA Program, Irvine, CA 92697. Offers EMBA. *Students:* 56 full-time (13 women), 26 part-time (7 women); includes 36 minority (3 American Indian or Alaska Native, non-Hispanic/Latino; 32 Asian, non-Hispanic/Latino; 1 Hispanic/Latino), 3 international. Average age 40. 86 applicants, 72% accepted, 42 enrolled. In 2013, 35 master's awarded. Application fee: $80 ($100 for international students). *Unit head:* Anthony Hansford, Senior Assistant Dean, 949-824-3801, E-mail: hansfora@uci.edu. *Application contact:* Sofia Trinidad Dang, Associate Director, Student Affairs, 949-824-5374, Fax: 949-824-0522, E-mail: sofia.dang@uci.edu.
Website: http://merage.uci.edu/ExecutiveMBA/.

University of California, Irvine, The Paul Merage School of Business, Full-Time MBA Program, Irvine, CA 92697. Offers MBA. *Students:* 184 full-time (77 women), 9 part-time (3 women); includes 42 minority (3 American Indian or Alaska Native, non-Hispanic/Latino; 36 Asian, non-Hispanic/Latino; 3 Hispanic/Latino), 97 international. Average age 29. 874 applicants, 24% accepted, 91 enrolled. In 2013, 107 master's awarded. Application fee: $80 ($100 for international students). *Unit head:* Gary Lindblad, Assistant Dean and Director, 949-824-9654, Fax: 949-824-2235, E-mail: lindblad@uci.edu. *Application contact:* Sarah Gill, Director of Recruitment and Admissions, 949-824-0462, Fax: 949-824-2235, E-mail: srgill@uci.edu.
Website: http://merage.uci.edu/FullTimeMBA/default.aspx.

University of California, Irvine, The Paul Merage School of Business, Fully Employed MBA Program, Irvine, CA 92697. Offers MBA. Part-time programs available. *Students:* 112 full-time (41 women), 266 part-time (89 women); includes 159 minority (6 Black or African American, non-Hispanic/Latino; 10 American Indian or Alaska Native, non-Hispanic/Latino; 127 Asian, non-Hispanic/Latino; 15 Hispanic/Latino; 1 Native Hawaiian or other Pacific Islander, non-Hispanic/Latino), 25 international. Average age 30. 164 applicants, 78% accepted, 85 enrolled. In 2013, 155 master's awarded. *Application deadline:* For fall admission, 7/11 for domestic students. Application fee: $80 ($100 for international students). *Unit head:* Mary Clark, Assistant Dean, 949-824-4207, Fax: 949-824-2235, E-mail: mary.clark@uci.edu. *Application contact:* Melanie Coburn, Senior Associate Director, Admissions, 949-824-7505, E-mail: mcoburn@uci.edu.
Website: http://merage.uci.edu/FullyEmployedMBA/default.aspx.

University of California, Los Angeles, Graduate Division, UCLA Anderson School of Management, Los Angeles, CA 90095-1481. Offers accounting (PhD); Americas (EMBA); Asia Pacific (EMBA); business administration (EMBA, MBA); decisions, operations and technology management (PhD); finance (PhD); financial engineering (MFE); global economics and management (PhD); management and organizations (PhD); marketing (PhD); strategy and policy (PhD); DDS/MBA; MBA/JD; MBA/MD; MBA/MLAS; MBA/MLIS; MBA/MPH; MBA/MPP; MBA/MSCS; MBA/MSN; MBA/MUP. *Accreditation:* AACSB. Part-time programs available. *Faculty:* 104 full-time (20 women), 28 part-time/adjunct (4 women). *Students:* 1,069 full-time (324 women), 879 part-time (251 women); includes 664 minority (37 Black or African American, non-Hispanic/Latino; 1 American Indian or Alaska Native, non-Hispanic/Latino; 470 Asian, non-Hispanic/Latino; 34 Hispanic/Latino; 2 Native Hawaiian or other Pacific Islander, non-Hispanic/Latino; 120 Two or more races, non-Hispanic/Latino), 444 international. Average age 30. 5,084 applicants, 27% accepted, 845 enrolled. In 2013, 801 master's, 14 doctorates awarded. *Degree requirements:* For master's, comprehensive exam, field study consulting project (for MBA); thesis (for MFE); for doctorate, comprehensive exam, thesis/dissertation, oral and written qualifying exams. *Entrance requirements:* For master's, GMAT (for MBA); GMAT or GRE General Test (for MFE), 4-year bachelor's degree or equivalent; recommendation letters (1 for MBA, 2 for MFE); two essays; interview (by invitation only for MBA); for doctorate, GMAT or GRE General Test, bachelor's degree from college or university of fully-recognized standing; minimum B average in undergraduate coursework or B+ average in prior graduate work; statement of purpose; three recommendation letters. Additional exam requirements/recommendations for international students: Required—TOEFL (minimum score 560 paper-based; 87 iBT). *Application deadline:* For fall admission, 10/22 priority date for domestic and international students; for winter admission, 1/7 for domestic and international students; for spring admission, 4/15 for domestic and international students. Applications are processed on a rolling basis. Application fee: $200. Electronic applications accepted. *Expenses:* Contact institution. *Financial support:* In 2013–14, 522 students received support. Fellowships, research assistantships with partial tuition reimbursements available, teaching assistantships with partial tuition reimbursements available, career-related internships or fieldwork, institutionally sponsored loans, scholarships/grants, health care benefits, and tuition waivers (partial) available. Financial award application deadline: 4/15; financial award applicants required to submit FAFSA. *Faculty research:* Asset pricing, decision-making, behavioral finance, international finance and economics, global macroeconomics. *Total annual research expenditures:* $368,086. *Unit head:* Dr. Judy D. Olian, Dean/Chair in Management, 310-825-7982, Fax: 310-206-2073, E-mail: judy.olian@anderson.ucla.edu. *Application contact:* Alex Lawrence, Assistant Dean, MBA Admissions and Financial Aid, 310-825-6944, Fax: 310-825-8582, E-mail: mba.admissions@anderson.ucla.edu.
Website: http://www.anderson.ucla.edu/.
See Display on this page and Close-Up on page 191.

University of California, Riverside, Graduate Division, A. Gary Anderson Graduate School of Management, Riverside, CA 92521-0102. Offers accountancy (MPAC); business administration (MBA, PhD); finance (M Fin). *Accreditation:* AACSB. Part-time and evening/weekend programs available. *Faculty:* 24 full-time (6 women), 11 part-time/adjunct (3 women). *Students:* 295 full-time (161 women), 1 part-time (0 women); includes 38 minority (2 Black or African American, non-Hispanic/Latino; 31 Asian, non-Hispanic/Latino; 5 Hispanic/Latino), 237 international. Average age 24. 565 applicants, 82% accepted, 186 enrolled. In 2013, 89 master's awarded. Terminal master's awarded for partial completion of doctoral program. *Degree requirements:* For master's, thesis optional; for doctorate, comprehensive exam, thesis/dissertation. *Entrance requirements:* For master's, GMAT or GRE, minimum GPA of 3.2; for doctorate, GMAT

or GRE. Additional exam requirements/recommendations for international students: Required—TOEFL (minimum score 550 paper-based; 80 iBT), IELTS. *Application deadline:* For fall admission, 9/1 for domestic students, 5/1 for international students; for winter admission, 12/1 for domestic students, 9/1 for international students; for spring admission, 3/1 for domestic students, 10/1 for international students. Applications are processed on a rolling basis. Application fee: $100 ($125 for international students). *Expenses:* Contact institution. *Financial support:* In 2013–14, 58 fellowships with partial tuition reimbursements (averaging $22,848 per year), 46 teaching assistantships with partial tuition reimbursements (averaging $20,000 per year) were awarded; research assistantships with full tuition reimbursements, career-related internships or fieldwork, institutionally sponsored loans, scholarships/grants, and tuition waivers (full) also available. Financial award application deadline: 5/1; financial award applicants required to submit FAFSA. *Faculty research:* Option pricing, marketing, decision modeling, new technologies in cost accounting, supply chain management, operations, production and inventory systems, entrepreneurial finance, e-commerce. *Unit head:* Dr. Yunzeng Wang, Dean, 951-827-6329, Fax: 951-827-3970, E-mail: mba@ucr.edu. *Application contact:* Dr. Rami Zwick, Associate Dean/Graduate Adviser, 951-827-7766, Fax: 951-827-3970, E-mail: mba@ucr.edu.
Website: http://agsm.ucr.edu/.

University of California, San Diego, Office of Graduate Studies, Rady School of Management, La Jolla, CA 92093. Offers business administration (MBA); finance (MF); management (PhD). Part-time and evening/weekend programs available. *Students:* 218 full-time (152 women), 51 part-time (35 women); includes 78 minority (5 Black or African American, non-Hispanic/Latino; 53 Asian, non-Hispanic/Latino; 20 Hispanic/Latino), 63 international. 532 applicants, 31% accepted, 99 enrolled. In 2013, 112 master's awarded. *Degree requirements:* For doctorate, thesis/dissertation. *Entrance requirements:* For master's, GMAT (for MBA); GMAT or GRE General Test (for MF); for doctorate, GMAT or GRE General Test. Additional exam requirements/recommendations for international students: Required—TOEFL, IELTS. Application fee: $80 ($100 for international students). Electronic applications accepted. *Expenses:* Tuition, state resident: full-time $11,220; part-time $1870 per quarter. Tuition, nonresident: full-time $26,322; part-time $4387 per quarter. *Required fees:* $519.50 per quarter. Part-time tuition and fees vary according to course load and program. *Financial support:* Fellowships, teaching assistantships, and scholarships/grants available. Financial award applicants required to submit FAFSA. *Unit head:* Robert Sullivan, Dean, 858-822-0830, E-mail: rss@ucsd.edu. *Application contact:* Laurel Nelson, Graduate Coordinator, 858-822-4279, E-mail: lrnelson@ucsd.edu.
Website: http://rady.ucsd.edu/.

University of Central Arkansas, Graduate School, College of Business Administration, Program in Business Administration, Conway, AR 72035-0001. Offers MBA. *Accreditation:* AACSB. Part-time and evening/weekend programs available. *Entrance requirements:* For master's, GMAT or GRE, minimum GPA of 2.7. Additional exam requirements/recommendations for international students: Required—TOEFL (minimum score 550 paper-based).

University of Central Florida, College of Business Administration, Department of Management, Orlando, FL 32816. Offers entrepreneurship (Graduate Certificate); management (MSM); technology ventures (Graduate Certificate). *Accreditation:* AACSB. *Faculty:* 27 full-time (10 women), 6 part-time/adjunct (2 women). *Students:* 36 part-time (30 women); includes 15 minority (7 Black or African American, non-Hispanic/Latino; 2 Asian, non-Hispanic/Latino; 6 Hispanic/Latino). Average age 33. 19 applicants, 84% accepted, 12 enrolled. In 2013, 14 other advanced degrees awarded. *Entrance requirements:* For master's, GMAT, minimum GPA of 3.0 in last 60 hours. *Application deadline:* For fall admission, 2/1 priority date for domestic students; for spring admission, 11/1 priority date for domestic students. Application fee: $30. Electronic applications accepted. *Financial support:* Fellowships, research assistantships, and teaching assistantships available. *Unit head:* Dr. Stephen Goodman, Chair, 407-823-2675, Fax: 407-823-3725, E-mail: sgoodman@bus.ucf.edu. *Application contact:* Judy Ryder, Director, Graduate Admissions, 407-823-2364, Fax: 407-823-0219, E-mail: jryder@bus.ucf.edu.
Website: http://www.graduatecatalog.ucf.edu/programs/program.aspx?id-1080&program-Management MS.

University of Central Florida, College of Business Administration, Program in Business Administration, Orlando, FL 32816. Offers MBA, PhD. *Accreditation:* AACSB. Part-time and evening/weekend programs available. *Students:* 191 full-time (83 women), 283 part-time (115 women); includes 136 minority (32 Black or African American, non-Hispanic/Latino; 1 American Indian or Alaska Native, non-Hispanic/Latino; 29 Asian, non-Hispanic/Latino; 64 Hispanic/Latino; 1 Native Hawaiian or other Pacific Islander, non-Hispanic/Latino; 9 Two or more races, non-Hispanic/Latino), 25 international. Average age 30. 234 applicants, 50% accepted, 101 enrolled. In 2013, 248 master's, 6 doctorates awarded. *Degree requirements:* For master's, exam; for doctorate, thesis/dissertation, departmental candidacy exam. *Entrance requirements:* For master's and doctorate, GMAT, minimum GPA of 3.0 in last 60 hours. Additional exam requirements/recommendations for international students: Required—TOEFL. *Application deadline:* For fall admission, 2/1 priority date for domestic students; for spring admission, 11/1 priority date for domestic students. Application fee: $30. Electronic applications accepted. *Financial support:* In 2013–14, 45 students received support, including 12 fellowships with partial tuition reimbursements available (averaging $7,600 per year), 2 research assistantships with partial tuition reimbursements available (averaging $13,300 per year), 45 teaching assistantships with partial tuition reimbursements available (averaging $12,100 per year); career-related internships or fieldwork, Federal Work-Study, institutionally sponsored loans, tuition waivers (partial), and unspecified assistantships also available. Financial award application deadline: 3/1; financial award applicants required to submit FAFSA. *Unit head:* Dr. Paul Jarley, Dean, 407-823-2183, E-mail: pjarley@bus.ucf.edu. *Application contact:* Judy Ryder, Director, Graduate Admissions, 407-823-2364, Fax: 407-823-0219, E-mail: judy.ryder@bus.ucf.edu.
Website: http://www.bus.ucf.edu.

University of Central Missouri, The Graduate School, Warrensburg, MO 6409. Offers accountancy (MA); accounting (MBA); applied mathematics (MS); aviation safety (MA); biology (MS); business administration (MBA); career and technical education leadership (MS); college student personnel administration (MS); communication (MA); computer science (MS); counseling (MS); criminal justice (MS); educational leadership (Ed D); educational technology (MS); elementary and early childhood education (MSE); English (MA); environmental studies (MA); finance (MBA); history (MA); human services/educational technology (Ed S); human services/learning resources (Ed S); human services/professional counseling (Ed S); industrial hygiene (MS); industrial management (MS); information systems (MBA); information technology (MS); kinesiology (MS); library science and information services (MS); literacy education (MSE); marketing (MBA); mathematics (MS); music (MA); occupational safety management (MS); psychology (MS); rural family nursing (MS); school administration (MSE); social gerontology (MS); sociology (MA); special education (MSE); speech language pathology (MS); superintendency (Ed S); teaching (MAT); teaching English as a second language (MA); technology (MS); technology management (PhD); theatre (MA). Part-time programs available. *Faculty:* 233. *Students:* 890 full-time (396 women), 1,486 part-time (1,001 women); includes 192 minority (97 Black or African American, non-Hispanic/Latino; 9 American Indian or Alaska Native, non-Hispanic/Latino; 32 Asian, non-Hispanic/Latino; 40 Hispanic/Latino; 3 Native Hawaiian or other Pacific Islander, non-Hispanic/Latino; 11 Two or more races, non-Hispanic/Latino), 539 international. Average age 31. 1,953 applicants, 75% accepted. In 2013, 719 master's, 58 other advanced degrees awarded. *Degree requirements:* For master's and Ed S, comprehensive exam (for some programs), thesis (for some programs). *Entrance requirements:* Additional exam requirements/recommendations for international students: Required—TOEFL (minimum score 550 paper-based; 79 iBT). *Application deadline:* For fall admission, 6/1 for domestic students; for spring admission, 10/1 for domestic and international students. Applications are processed on a rolling basis. Application fee: $30 ($75 for international students). Electronic applications accepted. *Expenses:* Tuition, state resident: full-time $7326; part-time $276.25 per credit hour. Tuition, nonresident: full-time $13,956; part-time $552.50 per credit hour. *Required fees:* $29 per credit hour. *Financial support:* In 2013–14, 118 students received support, including 271 research assistantships with full and partial tuition reimbursements available (averaging $7,500 per year), 109 teaching assistantships with full and partial tuition reimbursements available (averaging $7,500 per year); career-related internships or fieldwork, Federal Work-Study, scholarships/grants, and administrative and laboratory assistantships also available. Support available to part-time students. Financial award application deadline: 3/1; financial award applicants required to submit FAFSA. *Unit head:* Dr. Joseph Vaughn, Assistant Provost for Research/Dean, 660-543-4092, Fax: 660-543-4778, E-mail: vaughn@ucmo.edu. *Application contact:* Brittany Lawrence, Graduate Student Services Coordinator, 660-543-4621, Fax: 660-543-4778, E-mail: gradinfo@ucmo.edu.
Website: http://www.ucmo.edu/graduate/.

University of Charleston, Executive Master of Business Administration Program, Charleston, WV 25304-1099. Offers EMBA. Part-time and evening/weekend programs available. *Students:* 55 full-time (20 women). Average age 37. In 2013, 51 degrees awarded. *Degree requirements:* For master's, international practicum, capstone, minimum cumulative GPA of 3.0. *Entrance requirements:* For master's, GMAT, undergraduate degree with minimum GPA of 3.0 or documented outstanding executive experience, 3-5 years' work experience since graduation (may be waived by program director), one employer letter of recommendation. Additional exam requirements/recommendations for international students: Required—TOEFL, IELTS. *Application deadline:* Applications are processed on a rolling basis. Application fee: $50. Electronic applications accepted. *Financial support:* Scholarships/grants and unspecified assistantships available. Financial award application deadline: 3/1; financial award applicants required to submit FAFSA. *Unit head:* Dr. Scott Bellamy, Dean of the School of Business, 304-357-4373, E-mail: scottbellamy@ucwv.edu. *Application contact:* Rick Ferris, Program Coordinator, 304-357-4373, E-mail: emba@ucwv.edu.
Website: http://www.ucwv.edu/business/emba/.

University of Charleston, Master of Business Administration and Leadership Program, Charleston, WV 25301. Offers MBA. *Students:* 19 full-time (7 women); includes 1 minority (Black or African American, non-Hispanic/Latino), 8 international. Average age 23. In 2013, 14 master's awarded. *Degree requirements:* For master's, thesis, international study practicum, professional mentoring, capstone seminar. *Entrance requirements:* For master's, official transcripts for all undergraduate work; minimum GPA of 3.0; personal interview. Additional exam requirements/recommendations for international students: Required—TOEFL, IELTS. *Application deadline:* Applications are processed on a rolling basis. Application fee: $0. Electronic applications accepted. *Financial support:* Career-related internships or fieldwork and scholarships/grants available. Financial award application deadline: 3/1; financial award applicants required to submit FAFSA. *Unit head:* Dr. Scott Bellamy, Dean of the School of Business, 304-357-4373, E-mail: scottbellamy@ucwv.edu. *Application contact:* Ashley Wheeler, Admissions Representative, 304-357-4866, E-mail: ashleywheeler@ucwv.edu.
Website: http://www.ucwv.edu/business/mbal/.

University of Chicago, Booth School of Business, Doctoral Program in Business, Chicago, IL 60637-1513. Offers PhD. *Accreditation:* AACSB. *Degree requirements:* For doctorate, thesis/dissertation, workshops, curriculum paper. *Entrance requirements:* For doctorate, GMAT or GRE, resume, transcripts, letters of referral, essay, interview. Additional exam requirements/recommendations for international students: Required—TOEFL, IELTS. Electronic applications accepted. *Faculty research:* Accounting, finance, marketing, economics, econometrics and statistics.

University of Chicago, Booth School of Business, Full-Time MBA Program, Chicago, IL 60637. Offers accounting (MBA); analytic finance (MBA); analytic management (MBA); econometrics and statistics (MBA); economics (MBA); entrepreneurship (MBA); finance (MBA); general management (MBA); health administration and policy (Certificate); human resource management (MBA); international business (MBA); managerial and organizational behavior (MBA); marketing management (MBA); operations management (MBA); strategic management (MBA); MBA/AM; MBA/JD; MBA/MA; MBA/MD; MBA/MPP. *Accreditation:* AACSB. Part-time and evening/weekend programs available. Terminal master's awarded for partial completion of doctoral program. *Entrance requirements:* For master's, GMAT, 2 letters of recommendation, 3 essays, resume, interview. Additional exam requirements/recommendations for international students: Required—TOEFL (minimum score 600 paper-based; 104 iBT), IELTS. Electronic applications accepted. *Expenses:* Contact institution. *Faculty research:* Finance, marketing, economics, entrepreneurship, strategy, management.

University of Chicago, Booth School of Business, Part-Time Evening MBA Program, Chicago, IL 60611. Offers MBA. *Accreditation:* AACSB. Part-time and evening/weekend programs available. *Entrance requirements:* For master's, GMAT, 2 letters of recommendation, interview. Additional exam requirements/recommendations for international students: Required—TOEFL (minimum score 600 paper-based), IELTS. Electronic applications accepted. *Expenses:* Contact institution. *Faculty research:* Finance, entrepreneurship, strategy, marketing, international business.

University of Chicago, Booth School of Business, Part-Time Weekend MBA Program, Chicago, IL 60611. Offers MBA. *Accreditation:* AACSB. Part-time and evening/weekend programs available. *Entrance requirements:* For master's, GMAT, 2 letters of recommendation, interview, resume. Additional exam requirements/recommendations for international students: Required—TOEFL or IELTS. *Faculty research:* Finance, marketing, international business, strategy, entrepreneurship.

University of Cincinnati, Graduate School, Carl H. Lindner College of Business, MBA Program, Cincinnati, OH 45221. Offers MBA. Part-time and evening/weekend programs available. Postbaccalaureate distance learning degree programs offered (no on-campus study). *Faculty:* 39 full-time (11 women), 11 part-time/adjunct (3 women). *Students:* 111 full-time (41 women), 158 part-time (57 women); includes 28 minority (12 Black or African American, non-Hispanic/Latino; 5 Asian, non-Hispanic/Latino; 2 Hispanic/Latino; 1 Native Hawaiian or other Pacific Islander, non-Hispanic/Latino; 8 Two or more races, non-Hispanic/Latino), 44 international. Average age 26. 224 applicants, 74% accepted, 104 enrolled. In 2013, 111 master's awarded. *Degree requirements:* For master's, capstone project. *Entrance requirements:* For master's, GMAT, resume, letters of recommendation, essays, official transcripts. Additional exam requirements/recommendations for international students: Required—TOEFL (minimum score 600

paper-based; 100 iBT), IELTS (minimum score 6.5). *Application deadline:* For fall admission, 3/15 priority date for domestic students, 3/15 for international students; for spring admission, 12/15 for domestic students, 9/15 for international students; for summer admission, 4/15 for domestic students. Application fee: $65 ($70 for international students). Electronic applications accepted. *Expenses:* Contact institution. *Financial support:* In 2013–14, 72 students received support. Scholarships/grants, tuition waivers (full and partial), and unspecified assistantships available. Financial award application deadline: 3/15; financial award applicants required to submit FAFSA. *Unit head:* Dr. David Szymanski, Dean, 513-556-7001, Fax: 513-556-4891, E-mail: david.szymanski@uc.edu. *Application contact:* Dona Clary, Director, Graduate Programs, 513-556-3546, Fax: 513-558-7006, E-mail: dona.clary@uc.edu.
Website: http://www.business.uc.edu/mba.

University of Cincinnati, Graduate School, Carl H. Lindner College of Business, PhD Programs, Cincinnati, OH 45221. Offers accounting (PhD); economics (PhD); finance (PhD); information systems (PhD); management (PhD); marketing (PhD); operations and business analytics (PhD). *Faculty:* 62 full-time (13 women). *Students:* 27 full-time (15 women), 9 part-time (1 woman); includes 2 minority (1 Asian, non-Hispanic/Latino; 1 Hispanic/Latino), 16 international. Average age 29. 86 applicants, 13% accepted, 6 enrolled. In 2013, 8 doctorates awarded. *Degree requirements:* For doctorate, comprehensive exam, thesis/dissertation. *Entrance requirements:* For doctorate, GMAT, GRE, transcripts, essays, resume, letters of recommendation. Additional exam requirements/recommendations for international students: Required—TOEFL (minimum score 600 paper-based; 100 iBT), IELTS (minimum score 6.5). *Application deadline:* For fall admission, 1/15 for domestic and international students. Application fee: $65 ($70 for international students). Electronic applications accepted. *Expenses:* Contact institution. *Financial support:* In 2013–14, 33 students received support, including 25 research assistantships with full and partial tuition reimbursements available (averaging $23,250 per year); scholarships/grants, tuition waivers (full and partial), and unspecified assistantships also available. Financial award application deadline: 1/15; financial award applicants required to submit FAFSA. *Unit head:* Dr. Suzanne Masterson, Director, 513-556-7125, Fax: 513-556-5499, E-mail: suzanne.masterson@uc.edu. *Application contact:* Angel Elvin, Assistant Director, 513-556-7190, Fax: 513-558-7006, E-mail: angel.elvin@uc.edu.
Website: http://www.business.uc.edu/phd.

University of Colorado Boulder, Leeds School of Business, Division of MBA, Boulder, CO 80309. Offers MBA. *Accreditation:* AACSB. *Students:* 245 full-time (69 women), 7 part-time (2 women); includes 22 minority (3 Black or African American, non-Hispanic/Latino; 2 American Indian or Alaska Native, non-Hispanic/Latino; 8 Asian, non-Hispanic/Latino; 6 Hispanic/Latino; 1 Native Hawaiian or other Pacific Islander, non-Hispanic/Latino; 2 Two or more races, non-Hispanic/Latino), 32 international. Average age 30. 277 applicants, 60% accepted, 74 enrolled. In 2013, 136 master's awarded. *Entrance requirements:* For master's, GMAT, minimum undergraduate GPA of 2.75. *Application deadline:* Applications are processed on a rolling basis. Application fee: $50 ($60 for international students). Electronic applications accepted. *Financial support:* In 2013–14, 180 students received support, including 143 fellowships (averaging $4,627 per year), 2 teaching assistantships with full and partial tuition reimbursements available (averaging $9,550 per year); institutionally sponsored loans, scholarships/grants, health care benefits, and unspecified assistantships also available. Financial award applicants required to submit FAFSA.
Website: http://leeds.colorado.edu/mba/#welcome.

University of Colorado Colorado Springs, College of Business, Colorado Springs, CO 80933-7150. Offers MBA. *Accreditation:* AACSB. Part-time and evening/weekend programs available. Postbaccalaureate distance learning degree programs offered (minimal on-campus study). *Faculty:* 36 full-time (13 women), 35 part-time/adjunct (9 women). *Students:* 49 full-time (22 women), 274 part-time (115 women); includes 49 minority (6 Black or African American, non-Hispanic/Latino; 12 Asian, non-Hispanic/Latino; 24 Hispanic/Latino; 7 Two or more races, non-Hispanic/Latino), 11 international. Average age 33. 110 applicants, 87% accepted, 58 enrolled. In 2013, 110 master's awarded. *Entrance requirements:* For master's, GMAT or GRE. Additional exam requirements/recommendations for international students: Recommended—TOEFL. *Application deadline:* For fall admission, 6/1 for domestic and international students; for spring admission, 11/1 for domestic and international students; for summer admission, 4/1 for domestic and international students. Application fee: $60 ($75 for international students). Electronic applications accepted. *Expenses:* Contact institution. *Financial support:* In 2013–14, 21 students received support, including 21 fellowships (averaging $1,978 per year); career-related internships or fieldwork, Federal Work-Study, and scholarships/grants also available. Support available to part-time students. Financial award application deadline: 3/1; financial award applicants required to submit FAFSA. *Faculty research:* Quality financial reporting, investments and corporate governance, group support systems, environmental and project management, customer relationship management. *Unit head:* Dr. Venkateshwar Reddy, Dean, 719-255-3113, Fax: 719-255-3100, E-mail: vreddy@uccs.edu. *Application contact:* Jolene Schauland, MBA Admissions Specialist, 719-255-3112, Fax: 719-255-3100, E-mail: jschaula@uccs.edu.
Website: http://www.uccs.edu/mba.

University of Colorado Denver, Business School, Master of Business Administration Program, Denver, CO 80217. Offers bioinnovation and entrepreneurship (MBA); business intelligence (MBA); business strategy (MBA); business to business marketing (MBA); business to consumer marketing (MBA); change management (MBA); corporate financial management (MBA); enterprise technology management (MBA); entrepreneurship (MBA); health administration (MBA), including financial management, health administration, health information technologies, international health management and policy; human resources management (MBA); international business (MBA); investment management (MBA); managing for sustainability (MBA); sports and entertainment management (MBA). *Accreditation:* AACSB. Part-time and evening/weekend programs available. Postbaccalaureate distance learning degree programs offered (no on-campus study). *Students:* 611 full-time (246 women), 144 part-time (58 women); includes 102 minority (14 Black or African American, non-Hispanic/Latino; 2 American Indian or Alaska Native, non-Hispanic/Latino; 38 Asian, non-Hispanic/Latino; 42 Hispanic/Latino; 6 Two or more races, non-Hispanic/Latino), 26 international. Average age 32. 330 applicants, 64% accepted, 125 enrolled. In 2013, 398 master's awarded. *Degree requirements:* For master's, 48 semester hours, including 30 of core courses, 3 in international business, and 15 in electives from over 50 other graduate business courses. *Entrance requirements:* For master's, GMAT, resume, official transcripts, essay, two letters of recommendation, financial statements (for international applicants). Additional exam requirements/recommendations for international students: Required—TOEFL (minimum score 560 paper-based; 83 iBT); Recommended—IELTS (minimum score 6.5). *Application deadline:* For fall admission, 4/15 priority date for domestic students, 3/15 priority date for international students; for spring admission, 10/15 priority date for domestic students, 9/15 priority date for international students. Applications are processed on a rolling basis. Application fee: $50 ($75 for international students). Electronic applications accepted. *Expenses:* Contact institution. *Financial support:* In 2013–14, 62 students received support. Fellowships, research assistantships, teaching assistantships, Federal Work-Study, institutionally sponsored loans, scholarships/grants, traineeships, and unspecified assistantships available. Financial award application deadline: 4/1; financial award applicants required to submit FAFSA. *Faculty research:* Marketing, management, entrepreneurship, finance, health administration. *Unit head:* Elizabeth Cooperman, Professor of Finance and Managing for Sustainability/MBA Program Director, 303-315-8422, E-mail: elizabeth.cooperman@ucdenver.edu. *Application contact:* Shelly Townley, Admissions Director, Graduate Programs, 303-315-8202, E-mail: shelly.townley@ucdenver.edu.
Website: http://www.ucdenver.edu/academics/colleges/business/degrees/mba/Pages/MBA.aspx.

University of Colorado Denver, Business School, Program in Management and Organization, Denver, CO 80217. Offers business strategy (MS); change and innovation (MS); enterprise technology management (MS); entrepreneurship and innovation (MS); global management (MS); human resources management (MS); leadership and management (MS); quantitative decision methods (MS); sports and entertainment management (MS); sustainability management (MS). *Accreditation:* AACSB. Part-time and evening/weekend programs available. Postbaccalaureate distance learning degree programs offered (no on-campus study). *Students:* 27 full-time (19 women), 14 part-time (7 women); includes 4 minority (1 Black or African American, non-Hispanic/Latino; 2 Hispanic/Latino; 1 Two or more races, non-Hispanic/Latino), 6 international. Average age 29. 38 applicants, 45% accepted, 8 enrolled. In 2013, 28 master's awarded. *Degree requirements:* For master's, 30 semester hours (12 of required courses, 12 of management electives, and 6 of free electives). *Entrance requirements:* For master's, GMAT, resume, two letters of recommendation, essay, financial statements (for international applicants). Additional exam requirements/recommendations for international students: Required—TOEFL (minimum score 537 paper-based; 75 iBT); Recommended—IELTS (minimum score 6.5). *Application deadline:* For fall admission, 4/15 for domestic students, 3/15 for international students; for spring admission, 10/15 for domestic students, 9/15 for international students. Applications are processed on a rolling basis. Application fee: $50 ($75 for international students). Electronic applications accepted. *Expenses:* Contact institution. *Financial support:* In 2013–14, 5 students received support. Fellowships, research assistantships, teaching assistantships, Federal Work-Study, institutionally sponsored loans, scholarships/grants, and traineeships available. Financial award application deadline: 4/1; financial award applicants required to submit FAFSA. *Faculty research:* Human resource management, management of catastrophe, turnaround strategies. *Unit head:* Dr. Kenneth Bettenhausen, Associate Professor/Director of MS in Management, 303-315-8425, E-mail: kenneth.bettenhausen@ucdenver.edu. *Application contact:* Shelly Townley, Admissions Director, Graduate Programs, 303-315-8202, E-mail: shelly.townley@ucdenver.edu.
Website: http://www.ucdenver.edu/academics/colleges/business/degrees/ms/management/Pages/Management.aspx.

University of Connecticut, Graduate School, School of Business, Storrs, CT 06269. Offers accounting (MS, PhD); business administration (Exec MBA, MBA, PhD); finance (PhD); health care management and insurance studies (MBA); management (PhD); management consulting (MBA); marketing (PhD); marketing intelligence (MBA); MA/MBA; MBA/MSW. *Accreditation:* AACSB. *Degree requirements:* For master's, comprehensive exam; for doctorate, thesis/dissertation. *Entrance requirements:* For master's and doctorate, GMAT. Additional exam requirements/recommendations for international students: Required—TOEFL (minimum score 550 paper-based). Electronic applications accepted.

University of Dallas, Graduate School of Management, Irving, TX 75062-4736. Offers accounting (MBA, MM, MS); business management (MBA, MM); corporate finance (MBA, MM); financial services (MBA); global business (MBA, MM); health services management (MBA, MM); human resource management (MBA, MM); information assurance (MBA, MM, MS); information technology (MBA, MM, MS); information technology service management (MBA, MM, MS); marketing management (MBA, MM); organization development (MBA, MM); project management (MBA, MM); sports and entertainment management (MBA, MM); strategic leadership (MBA, MM); supply chain management (MBA); supply chain management and market logistics (MM). *Accreditation:* ACBSP. Part-time and evening/weekend programs available. Postbaccalaureate distance learning degree programs offered (no on-campus study). *Entrance requirements:* Additional exam requirements/recommendations for international students: Required—TOEFL. Electronic applications accepted. *Expenses:* Contact institution.

University of Dayton, School of Business Administration, Dayton, OH 45469-1300. Offers accounting (MBA); cyber security (MBA); finance (MBA); marketing (MBA); JD/MBA. *Accreditation:* AACSB. Part-time and evening/weekend programs available. *Faculty:* 20 full-time (7 women), 8 part-time/adjunct (1 woman). *Students:* 166 full-time (76 women), 85 part-time (43 women); includes 10 minority (4 Black or African American, non-Hispanic/Latino; 4 Asian, non-Hispanic/Latino; 2 Hispanic/Latino), 96 international. Average age 27. 437 applicants, 44% accepted, 53 enrolled. In 2013, 119 master's awarded. *Entrance requirements:* For master's, GMAT or GRE. Additional exam requirements/recommendations for international students: Required—TOEFL (minimum score 550 paper-based; 80 iBT); Recommended—IELTS (minimum score 6.5). *Application deadline:* For fall admission, 5/1 priority date for international students; for winter admission, 7/1 for international students; for spring admission, 11/1 priority date for international students. Applications are processed on a rolling basis. Application fee: $0 ($50 for international students). Electronic applications accepted. *Expenses:* Contact institution. *Financial support:* In 2013–14, 10 research assistantships with partial tuition reimbursements (averaging $7,020 per year) were awarded; institutionally sponsored loans, health care benefits, and unspecified assistantships also available. Financial award application deadline: 3/1; financial award applicants required to submit FAFSA. *Faculty research:* Management information systems, economics, finance, entrepreneurship, marketing, accounting and cyber security. *Unit head:* John M. Gentner, Director, MBA Program, 937-229-3733, Fax: 937-229-3882, E-mail: jgentner1@udayton.edu. *Application contact:* Mandy Schrank, Assistant Director, MBA Program, 937-229-3733, Fax: 937-229-3882, E-mail: mschrank2@udayton.edu.
Website: http://business.udayton.edu/mba/.

University of Delaware, Alfred Lerner College of Business and Economics, Program in Business Administration, Newark, DE 19716. Offers MBA, MA/MBA, MBA/MIB, MBA/MS. *Accreditation:* AACSB. Part-time and evening/weekend programs available. *Entrance requirements:* For master's, GMAT, 2 letters of recommendation, resume. Additional exam requirements/recommendations for international students: Required—TOEFL (minimum score 600 paper-based; 79 iBT). Electronic applications accepted. *Expenses:* Contact institution. *Faculty research:* Finance, corporate governance, information systems, leadership, marketing.

University of Delaware, College of Agriculture and Natural Resources, Department of Entomology and Wildlife Ecology, Newark, DE 19716. Offers entomology and applied ecology (MS, PhD), including avian ecology, evolution and taxonomy, insect biological control, insect ecology and behavior (MS), insect genetics, pest management, plant-insect interactions, wildlife ecology and management. Part-time programs available. *Degree requirements:* For master's, comprehensive exam, thesis, oral exam, seminar; for doctorate, comprehensive exam, thesis/dissertation, qualifying exam, seminar. *Entrance requirements:* For master's, GRE General Test, minimum GPA of 3.0 in field, 2.8 overall; for doctorate, GRE General Test, GRE Subject Test (biology), minimum

GPA of 3.0 in field, 2.8 overall. Additional exam requirements/recommendations for international students: Required—TOEFL. Electronic applications accepted. *Faculty research:* Ecology and evolution of plant-insect interactions, ecology of wildlife conservation management, habitat restoration, biological control, applied ecosystem management.

University of Denver, Daniels College of Business, Denver, CO 80208. Offers IMBA, M Acc, MBA, MS. *Accreditation:* AACSB. Part-time and evening/weekend programs available. *Faculty:* 115 full-time (35 women), 44 part-time/adjunct (13 women). *Students:* 541 full-time (244 women), 427 part-time (200 women); includes 91 minority (13 Black or African American, non-Hispanic/Latino; 26 Asian, non-Hispanic/Latino; 37 Hispanic/Latino; 15 Two or more races, non-Hispanic/Latino), 367 international. Average age 28. 2,007 applicants, 63% accepted, 443 enrolled. In 2013, 593 master's awarded. *Entrance requirements:* For master's, GRE General Test or GMAT, bachelor's degree, transcripts, essays, resume, two letters of recommendation, interview. Additional exam requirements/recommendations for international students: Required—TOEFL (minimum score 570 paper-based; 88 iBT). *Application deadline:* For fall admission, 1/15 for domestic students. Applications are processed on a rolling basis. Application fee: $100. Electronic applications accepted. *Financial support:* In 2013–14, 452 students received support, including 92 teaching assistantships with full and partial tuition reimbursements available (averaging $8,886 per year); career-related internships or fieldwork, Federal Work-Study, institutionally sponsored loans, scholarships/grants, and unspecified assistantships also available. Support available to part-time students. Financial award application deadline: 2/15; financial award applicants required to submit FAFSA. *Unit head:* Dr. Charles H. Patti, Interim Dean, 303-871-6858, E-mail: charles.patti@du.edu. *Application contact:* Information Contact, 303-871-3416, Fax: 303-871-4466, E-mail: daniels@du.edu.
Website: http://daniels.du.edu/.

University of Detroit Mercy, College of Business Administration, Program in Business Administration, Detroit, MI 48221. Offers MBA, JD/MBA. *Accreditation:* AACSB. Part-time and evening/weekend programs available. *Degree requirements:* For master's, thesis or alternative. *Entrance requirements:* For master's, GMAT, minimum GPA of 2.75.

University of Detroit Mercy, College of Business Administration, Program in Business Turnaround Management, Detroit, MI 48221. Offers MS, Certificate.

University of Detroit Mercy, College of Business Administration, Program in Executive MBA, Detroit, MI 48221. Offers EMBA.

University of Dubuque, Program in Business Administration, Dubuque, IA 52001-5099. Offers MBA. Part-time and evening/weekend programs available. *Entrance requirements:* For master's, 2 letters of recommendation. Electronic applications accepted.

The University of Findlay, Office of Graduate Admissions, Findlay, OH 45840-3653. Offers athletic training (MAT); business (MBA), including health care management, hospitality management, organizational leadership, public management; education (MA Ed), including administration, children's literature, early childhood, human resource development, reading, science, special education, technology; environmental, safety and health management (MSEM); health informatics (MS); occupational therapy (MOT); pharmacy (Pharm D); physical therapy (DPT); physician assistant (MPA); rhetoric and writing (MA); teaching English to speakers of other languages (TESOL) and bilingual education (MA). Part-time and evening/weekend programs available. Postbaccalaureate distance learning degree programs offered (no on-campus study). *Faculty:* 209 full-time (98 women), 69 part-time/adjunct (38 women). *Students:* 551 full-time (332 women), 457 part-time (276 women); includes 77 minority (37 Black or African American, non-Hispanic/Latino; 1 American Indian or Alaska Native, non-Hispanic/Latino; 15 Asian, non-Hispanic/Latino; 23 Hispanic/Latino; 1 Native Hawaiian or other Pacific Islander, non-Hispanic/Latino), 135 international. Average age 28. 637 applicants, 66% accepted, 241 enrolled. In 2013, 267 master's, 91 doctorates awarded. *Degree requirements:* For master's, thesis, cumulative project, capstone project. *Entrance requirements:* For master's, GRE/GMAT, bachelor's degree from accredited institution, minimum undergraduate GPA of 2.5 in last 64 hours of course work; for doctorate, GRE, minimum cumulative GPA of 3.0. Additional exam requirements/recommendations for international students: Required—TOEFL (minimum score 80 iBT). *Application deadline:* Applications are processed on a rolling basis. Application fee: $25. Electronic applications accepted. *Expenses: Required fees:* $146 per semester. Tuition and fees vary according to degree level and program. *Financial support:* In 2013–14, 11 research assistantships with full and partial tuition reimbursements (averaging $4,000 per year), 10 teaching assistantships with full and partial tuition reimbursements (averaging $3,600 per year) were awarded; career-related internships or fieldwork, Federal Work-Study, health care benefits, and unspecified assistantships also available. Financial award application deadline: 4/1; financial award applicants required to submit FAFSA. *Unit head:* Christopher M. Harris, Director of Admissions, 419-434-4347, E-mail: harrisc1@findlay.edu. *Application contact:* Emily Ickes, Graduate Admissions Counselor, 419-434-6933, Fax: 419-434-4898, E-mail: ickese@findlay.edu.
Website: http://www.findlay.edu/admissions/graduate/Pages/default.aspx.

University of Florida, Graduate School, Warrington College of Business Administration, Hough Graduate School of Business, Department of Management, Gainesville, FL 32611. Offers health care risk management (MS); international business (MA); management (MS, PhD). *Accreditation:* AACSB. Postbaccalaureate distance learning degree programs offered. *Faculty:* 8 full-time (3 women), 1 part-time/adjunct (0 women). *Students:* 114 full-time (67 women), 40 part-time (9 women); includes 45 minority (10 Black or African American, non-Hispanic/Latino; 2 American Indian or Alaska Native, non-Hispanic/Latino; 9 Asian, non-Hispanic/Latino; 24 Hispanic/Latino), 42 international. Average age 25. 211 applicants, 33% accepted, 43 enrolled. In 2013, 212 master's, 3 doctorates awarded. *Degree requirements:* For master's, comprehensive exam, thesis; for doctorate, comprehensive exam, thesis/dissertation. *Entrance requirements:* For master's and doctorate, GMAT (minimum score of 465) or GRE General Test, minimum GPA of 3.0. Additional exam requirements/recommendations for international students: Required—TOEFL (minimum score 550 paper-based; 80 iBT), IELTS (minimum score 6). *Application deadline:* For fall admission, 1/1 for domestic and international students. Applications are processed on a rolling basis. Application fee: $30. Electronic applications accepted. *Expenses:* Tuition, state resident: full-time $12,640. Tuition, nonresident: full-time $30,000. *Financial support:* In 2013–14, 10 students received support, including 10 teaching assistantships (averaging $21,605 per year); unspecified assistantships also available. Financial award applicants required to submit FAFSA. *Faculty research:* Job attitudes, personality and individual differences, organizational entry and exit, knowledge management, competitive dynamics. *Unit head:* Robert E. Thomas, PhD, Chair, 352-392-0136, Fax: 352-392-6020, E-mail: rethomas@ufl.edu. *Application contact:* Office of Admissions, 352-392-1365, E-mail: webrequests@admissions.ufl.edu.
Website: http://www.cba.ufl.edu/mang/.

University of Florida, Graduate School, Warrington College of Business Administration, Hough Graduate School of Business, Programs in Business Administration, Gainesville, FL 32611. Offers business administration (MBA); competitive strategy (MBA); entrepreneurship (MBA); finance (MBA); global management (MBA); Graham-Buffett security analysis (MBA); human resource management (MBA); information systems and operations management (MBA); international studies (MBA); Latin American business (MBA); management (MBA); marketing (MBA); real estate (MBA); sports administration (MBA); JD/MBA; MBA/MS; MBA/PhD; MBA/Pharm D; MD/MBA. *Accreditation:* AACSB. Part-time and evening/weekend programs available. Postbaccalaureate distance learning degree programs offered. *Faculty:* 72 full-time (10 women), 29 part-time/adjunct (7 women). *Students:* 440 full-time (122 women), 472 part-time (159 women); includes 203 minority (43 Black or African American, non-Hispanic/Latino; 3 American Indian or Alaska Native, non-Hispanic/Latino; 64 Asian, non-Hispanic/Latino; 92 Hispanic/Latino; 1 Native Hawaiian or other Pacific Islander, non-Hispanic/Latino), 39 international. Average age 32. 568 applicants, 58% accepted, 261 enrolled. In 2013, 405 master's awarded. *Degree requirements:* For master's, capstone course. *Entrance requirements:* For master's, GMAT (minimum score 465), minimum GPA of 3.0, interview. Additional exam requirements/recommendations for international students: Required—TOEFL (minimum score 550 paper-based; 80 iBT), IELTS (minimum score 6). *Application deadline:* For fall admission, 7/1 for domestic students, 1/1 for international students; for spring admission, 12/1 for domestic and international students. Applications are processed on a rolling basis. Application fee: $30. Electronic applications accepted. *Expenses:* Tuition, state resident: full-time $12,640. Tuition, nonresident: full-time $30,000. *Financial support:* In 2013–14, 24 students received support, including 24 teaching assistantships (averaging $6,143 per year); career-related internships or fieldwork, scholarships/grants, and unspecified assistantships also available. Support available to part-time students. Financial award applicants required to submit FAFSA. *Faculty research:* Accounting, finance, insurance, management, real estate, urban analysis marketing. *Unit head:* Alexander D. Sevilla, Assistant Dean/Director of MBA Program, 352-273-3252, Fax: 352-392-8791, E-mail: alex.sevilla@warrington.ufl.edu. *Application contact:* Andrew S. Lord, Senior Director of Admissions, 352-273-3241, Fax: 352-392-8791, E-mail: andrew.lord@warrington.ufl.edu.
Website: http://www.floridamba.ufl.edu/.

University of Georgia, Terry College of Business, Program in Business Administration, Athens, GA 30602. Offers MA, MBA, PhD, JD/MBA. *Accreditation:* AACSB. *Degree requirements:* For master's, thesis (MA); for doctorate, thesis/dissertation. *Entrance requirements:* For master's, GMAT (MBA), GRE General Test (MA); for doctorate, GMAT or GRE General Test. Electronic applications accepted.

University of Guam, Office of Graduate Studies, School of Business and Public Administration, Business Administration Program, Mangilao, GU 96923. Offers PMBA. *Entrance requirements:* For master's, GMAT. Additional exam requirements/recommendations for international students: Required—TOEFL.

University of Guelph, Graduate Studies, College of Management and Economics, Guelph, ON N1G 2W1, Canada. Offers M Sc, MA, MBA, PhD.

University of Hartford, Barney School of Business, Program in Business Administration, West Hartford, CT 06117-1599. Offers MBA, MBA/M Eng. *Accreditation:* AACSB. Part-time and evening/weekend programs available. *Entrance requirements:* For master's, GMAT, 2 letters of recommendation, resume. Additional exam requirements/recommendations for international students: Required—TOEFL (minimum score 550 paper-based). Electronic applications accepted.

University of Hartford, College of Education, Nursing, and Health Professions, Program in Nursing, West Hartford, CT 06117-1599. Offers community/public health nursing (MSN); nursing education (MSN); nursing management (MSN). *Accreditation:* AACN. Part-time and evening/weekend programs available. *Degree requirements:* For master's, research project. *Entrance requirements:* For master's, BSN, Connecticut RN license. Additional exam requirements/recommendations for international students: Required—TOEFL (minimum score 550 paper-based). Electronic applications accepted. *Expenses:* Contact institution. *Faculty research:* Child development, women in doctoral study, applying feminist theory in teaching methods, near death experience, grandmothers as primary care providers.

University of Hawaii at Manoa, Graduate Division, Shidler College of Business, Executive MBA Programs, Honolulu, HI 96822. Offers executive business administration (EMBA); Vietnam focused business administration (EMBA). *Accreditation:* AACSB. Part-time programs available. *Entrance requirements:* For master's, GMAT, minimum GPA of 3.0.

University of Hawaii at Manoa, Graduate Division, Shidler College of Business, Program in Business Administration, Honolulu, HI 96822. Offers Asian business studies (MBA); Chinese business studies (MBA); decision sciences (MBA); entrepreneurship (MBA); finance (MBA); finance and banking (MBA); human resources management (MBA); information management (MBA); information technology (MBA); international business (MBA); Japanese business studies (MBA); marketing (MBA); organizational behavior (MBA); organizational management (MBA); real estate (MBA); student-designed track (MBA). *Accreditation:* AACSB. Part-time and evening/weekend programs available. *Degree requirements:* For master's, thesis optional. *Entrance requirements:* For master's, GMAT, minimum GPA of 3.0. Additional exam requirements/recommendations for international students: Required—TOEFL (minimum score 600 paper-based; 100 iBT), IELTS (minimum score 7). *Expenses:* Contact institution.

University of Houston, Bauer College of Business, Houston, TX 77204. Offers MBA, MS, MS Accy, PhD. *Accreditation:* AACSB. Part-time and evening/weekend programs available. *Degree requirements:* For master's, 30 hours completed in residence, minimum cumulative GPA of 3.0 at UH, no more than 11 semester hours of 'C' grades or below in graduate courses taken at UH; for doctorate, comprehensive exam, thesis/dissertation, minimum GPA of 3.25, continuous full time enrollment, dissertation defense within 6 years of entering the program. *Entrance requirements:* For master's, GMAT or GRE (MBA), official transcripts from all higher education institutions attended, resume, letters of recommendation, self appraisal and goal statement (MBA); for doctorate, GMAT or GRE, letter of financial backing, statement of understanding, reference letters, statement of academic and research interests. Additional exam requirements/recommendations for international students: Required—TOEFL (minimum score 603 paper-based; 100 iBT), IELTS (minimum score 6.5), PTE (minimum score 70). Electronic applications accepted. *Faculty research:* Accountancy and taxation, finance, international business, management.

University of Houston–Clear Lake, School of Business, Program in Business Administration, Houston, TX 77058-1002. Offers MBA. *Accreditation:* AACSB. Part-time and evening/weekend programs available. *Degree requirements:* For master's, thesis optional. *Entrance requirements:* For master's, GMAT. Additional exam requirements/recommendations for international students: Required—TOEFL (minimum score 550 paper-based). Electronic applications accepted.

University of Houston–Downtown, College of Business, Houston, TX 77002. Offers finance (MBA); general management (MBA); human resource management (MBA); leadership (MBA); sales management and business development (MBA); supply chain management (MBA). Evening/weekend programs available. *Faculty:* 18 full-time (7 women). *Students:* 1 (woman) full-time, 88 part-time (32 women); includes 60 minority (18 Black or African American, non-Hispanic/Latino; 10 Asian, non-Hispanic/Latino; 30

Hispanic/Latino; 1 Native Hawaiian or other Pacific Islander, non-Hispanic/Latino; 1 Two or more races, non-Hispanic/Latino), 2 international. Average age 33. 41 applicants, 63% accepted, 24 enrolled. *Entrance requirements:* For master's, GMAT, official transcripts, bachelor's degree. or equivalent, resume, 2 professional references. Additional exam requirements/recommendations for international students: Required—TOEFL (minimum score 81 iBT). *Application deadline:* For fall admission, 7/15 for domestic and international students. Applications are processed on a rolling basis. Application fee: $35 ($60 for international students). Electronic applications accepted. *Expenses:* Contact institution. *Financial support:* In 2013–14, 2 fellowships (averaging $6,000 per year) were awarded. Financial award application deadline: 4/1; financial award applicants required to submit FAFSA. *Faculty research:* Corporate finance, sustainability, recruitment and selection, international strategic management, gender and race discrimination. *Unit head:* Dr. D. Michael Fields, Dean, College of Business, 713-221-8179, Fax: 713-221-8675, E-mail: fieldsd@uhd.edu. *Application contact:* Ceshia Love, Assistant Director of Graduate Admissions, 713-221-8093, Fax: 713-223-7408, E-mail: gradadmissions@uhd.edu.
Website: http://mba.uhd.edu/.

University of Houston–Victoria, School of Business Administration, Victoria, TX 77901-4450. Offers accounting (MBA); economic development and entrepreneurship (MS); finance (GMBA, MBA); general business (MBA); international business (MBA); management (GMBA, MBA); marketing (MBA). *Accreditation:* AACSB. Part-time and evening/weekend programs available. Postbaccalaureate distance learning degree programs offered (minimal on-campus study). *Faculty:* 45 full-time (15 women). *Students:* 193 full-time (93 women), 673 part-time (325 women); includes 489 minority (185 Black or African American, non-Hispanic/Latino; 169 Asian, non-Hispanic/Latino; 114 Hispanic/Latino; 1 Native Hawaiian or other Pacific Islander, non-Hispanic/Latino; 20 Two or more races, non-Hispanic/Latino), 94 international. *Entrance requirements:* For master's, GMAT. Additional exam requirements/recommendations for international students: Required—TOEFL (minimum score 550 paper-based). *Application deadline:* For fall admission, 6/1 for international students; for spring admission, 10/1 for international students. Applications are processed on a rolling basis. Application fee: $0. Electronic applications accepted. *Expenses:* Tuition, state resident: full-time $4534; part-time $251 per credit hour. Tuition, nonresident: full-time $10,906; part-time $606 per contact hour. *Required fees:* $68 per semester hour. Tuition and fees vary according to course load. *Financial support:* In 2013–14, research assistantships with partial tuition reimbursements (averaging $2,000 per year), teaching assistantships with partial tuition reimbursements (averaging $2,000 per year) were awarded; Federal Work-Study, scholarships/grants, and unspecified assistantships also available. Support available to part-time students. Financial award application deadline: 4/15; financial award applicants required to submit FAFSA. *Faculty research:* Economic development, marketing, finance. *Unit head:* Dr. Farhang Niroomand, Dean, 361-570-4230, Fax: 361-580-5599, E-mail: niroomandf@uhv.edu. *Application contact:* Admissions and Records, 361-570-4359, Fax: 361-580-5500, E-mail: admissions@uhv.edu.
Website: http://www.uhv.edu/bus/.

University of Idaho, College of Graduate Studies, College of Business and Economics, Department of Business and Economics, Moscow, ID 83844-3161. Offers general management (MBA). *Faculty:* 8 full-time. *Students:* 12 full-time, 14 part-time. Average age 38. In 2013, 17 master's awarded. *Entrance requirements:* Additional exam requirements/recommendations for international students: Required—TOEFL (minimum score 550 paper-based). *Application deadline:* For fall admission, 8/1 for domestic students; for spring admission, 12/15 for domestic students. Applications are processed on a rolling basis. Application fee: $60. Electronic applications accepted. *Expenses:* Tuition, state resident: full-time $5596; part-time $363 per credit hour. Tuition, nonresident: full-time $18,672; part-time $1089 per credit hour. *Financial support:* Applicants required to submit FAFSA. *Unit head:* Dr. Metlen Scott, Department Head, 208-885-6295, E-mail: cbe@uidaho.edu. *Application contact:* Stephanie Thomas, Graduate Recruitment Coordinator, 208-885-4001, Fax: 208-885-4406, E-mail: gadms@uidaho.edu.
Website: http://www.uidaho.edu/cbe/business.

University of Idaho, College of Law, Moscow, ID 83844-2321. Offers business law and entrepreneurship (JD); law (JD); litigation and alternative dispute resolution (JD); Native American law (JD); natural resources and environmental law (JD). *Accreditation:* ABA. *Faculty:* 31 full-time, 7 part-time/adjunct. *Students:* 314 full-time, 8 part-time. Average age 29. *Entrance requirements:* For doctorate, LSAT, Law School Admission Council Credential Assembly Service (CAS) Report. Additional exam requirements/recommendations for international students: Required—TOEFL. *Application deadline:* For fall admission, 2/15 for domestic students. Applications are processed on a rolling basis. Application fee: $50 ($60 for international students). Electronic applications accepted. *Expenses:* Tuition, state resident: full-time $5596; part-time $363 per credit hour. Tuition, nonresident: full-time $18,672; part-time $1089 per credit hour. *Financial support:* Career-related internships or fieldwork, Federal Work-Study, and institutionally sponsored loans available. Financial award applicants required to submit FAFSA. *Faculty research:* Transboundary river governance, tribal protection and stewardship, regional water issues, environmental law. *Unit head:* Michael Satz, Jr., Dean, 208-885-4977, E-mail: uilaw@uidaho.edu. *Application contact:* Carole Wells, Interim Director of Admissions, 208-885-2300, Fax: 208-885-2252, E-mail: lawadmit@uidaho.edu.
Website: http://www.uidaho.edu/law/.

University of Illinois at Chicago, Graduate College, Liautaud Graduate School of Business, Program in Business Administration, Chicago, IL 60607-7128. Offers MBA, PhD, MBA/MA, MBA/MD, MBA/MPH, MBA/MS. *Accreditation:* AACSB. Part-time programs available. *Students:* 280 full-time (153 women), 171 part-time (58 women); includes 67 minority (20 Black or African American, non-Hispanic/Latino; 27 Asian, non-Hispanic/Latino; 18 Hispanic/Latino; 2 Two or more races, non-Hispanic/Latino), 222 international. Average age 30. 461 applicants, 53% accepted, 194 enrolled. In 2013, 283 master's, 9 doctorates awarded. *Entrance requirements:* For master's, GMAT, minimum GPA of 2.75; for doctorate, GMAT. Additional exam requirements/recommendations for international students: Required—TOEFL. *Application deadline:* For fall admission, 2/1 for domestic and international students. Applications are processed on a rolling basis. Application fee: $40 ($50 for international students). Electronic applications accepted. *Expenses:* Tuition, state resident: full-time $11,066; part-time $3689 per term. Tuition, nonresident: full-time $23,064; part-time $7688 per term. *Required fees:* $3004; $1190 per term. Tuition and fees vary according to course level and program. *Financial support:* In 2013–14, 5 fellowships were awarded; research assistantships, teaching assistantships, career-related internships or fieldwork, Federal Work-Study, institutionally sponsored loans, and tuition waivers (full) also available. Support available to part-time students. Financial award application deadline: 2/15. *Unit head:* Michele Sexton Dorvil, Assistant Dean and Director, 312-996-4573, Fax: 312-413-0338, E-mail: mdorvil@uic.edu. *Application contact:* Ann Rosi, Information Contact, 312-996-4751, E-mail: agrosi@uic.edu.
Website: http://business.uic.edu/programs-and-degrees/liautaud-programs/mba/.

University of Illinois at Springfield, Graduate Programs, College of Business and Management, Program in Business Administration, Springfield, IL 62703-5407. Offers MBA. *Accreditation:* AACSB. Part-time and evening/weekend programs available.

Faculty: 5 full-time (0 women), 1 part-time/adjunct (0 women). *Students:* 62 full-time (24 women), 74 part-time (31 women); includes 18 minority (6 Black or African American, non-Hispanic/Latino; 5 Asian, non-Hispanic/Latino; 5 Hispanic/Latino; 2 Two or more races, non-Hispanic/Latino), 11 international. Average age 33. 125 applicants, 48% accepted, 40 enrolled. In 2013, 56 master's awarded. *Degree requirements:* For master's, closure course. *Entrance requirements:* For master's, GMAT or substantial supervisory experience and managerial responsibility, minimum cumulative GPA of 2.5; 3 letters of reference; resume; single-spaced essay, no more than two pages, discussing career goals and/or professional aspirations. Additional exam requirements/ recommendations for international students: Required—TOEFL (minimum score 550 paper-based; 61 iBT). *Application deadline:* Applications are processed on a rolling basis. Application fee: $60 ($75 for international students). Electronic applications accepted. *Expenses:* Tuition, state resident: full-time $7440. Tuition, nonresident: full-time $15,744. *Required fees:* $2985.60. *Financial support:* In 2013–14, fellowships with full tuition reimbursements (averaging $9,900 per year), research assistantships with full tuition reimbursements (averaging $9,550 per year), teaching assistantships with full tuition reimbursements (averaging $9,700 per year) were awarded; career-related internships or fieldwork, Federal Work-Study, scholarships/grants, health care benefits, and unspecified assistantships also available. Support available to part-time students. Financial award application deadline: 11/15; financial award applicants required to submit FAFSA. *Unit head:* Dr. Jorge Villegas, Program Administrator, 217-206-6780, Fax: 217-206-7541, E-mail: jvill2@uis.edu. *Application contact:* Dr. Lynn Pardie, Office of Graduate Studies, 800-252-8533, Fax: 217-206-7623, E-mail: lpard1@uis.edu.
Website: http://www.uis.edu/mba/.

University of Illinois at Urbana–Champaign, Graduate College, College of Business, Department of Business Administration, Champaign, IL 61820. Offers business administration (MS, PhD); technology management (MS). *Accreditation:* AACSB. *Students:* 193 (73 women). Application fee: $75 ($90 for international students). *Expenses:* Contact institution. *Unit head:* Aric P. Rindfleisch, Interim Head, 217-333-4240, Fax: 217-244-7969, E-mail: aric@illinois.edu. *Application contact:* Diana K. Gonzalez, Coordinator of Graduate Programs, 217-300-8484, Fax: 217-244-7969, E-mail: dgonzal2@illinois.edu.
Website: http://www.business.illinois.edu/ba/.

University of Illinois at Urbana–Champaign, Graduate College, College of Business, Program in Business Administration, Champaign, IL 61820. Offers MBA, Ed M/MBA, JD/MBA, M Arch/MBA, MCS/MBA, MHRIR/MBA, MS/MBA. *Accreditation:* AACSB. *Students:* 398 (116 women). Application fee: $75 ($90 for international students). *Unit head:* Darcy A. Sementi, Assistant Dean, 217-333-7412, Fax: 217-333-1156, E-mail: dsementi@illinois.edu. *Application contact:* Jackie Wilson, Admissions Director, 217-244-2953, Fax: 217-333-1156, E-mail: jjwilson@illinois.edu.
Website: http://www.mba.illinois.edu/.

University of Indianapolis, Graduate Programs, School of Business, Indianapolis, IN 46227-3697. Offers EMBA, MBA, Graduate Certificate. *Accreditation:* ACBSP. Part-time and evening/weekend programs available. *Faculty:* 3 full-time (1 woman), 4 part-time/adjunct (1 woman). *Students:* 37 full-time (15 women), 161 part-time (64 women); includes 24 minority (7 Black or African American, non-Hispanic/Latino; 7 Asian, non-Hispanic/Latino; 6 Hispanic/Latino; 4 Two or more races, non-Hispanic/Latino), 13 international. Average age 31. In 2013, 74 master's awarded. *Entrance requirements:* For master's, GMAT, interview, minimum GPA of 2.8, 2 letters of recommendation, resume. Additional exam requirements/recommendations for international students: Required—TOEFL (minimum score 550 paper-based). *Application deadline:* Applications are processed on a rolling basis. Application fee: $50. *Expenses:* Tuition: Full-time $5436; part-time $810 per credit hour. *Financial support:* Tuition waivers (full and partial) and unspecified assistantships available. Support available to part-time students. Financial award application deadline: 5/1; financial award applicants required to submit FAFSA. *Unit head:* Dr. Sheela Yadav, Dean, 317-788-3232, E-mail: syadav@uindy.edu. *Application contact:* Stephen A. Tokar, Sr., Director of Graduate Business Programs, 317-788-4905, E-mail: tokarsa@uindy.edu.
Website: http://www.uindy.edu/business/mba.

The University of Iowa, Henry B. Tippie College of Business, Department of Finance, Iowa City, IA 52242-1316. Offers PhD. *Faculty:* 22 full-time (4 women), 11 part-time/adjunct (2 women). *Students:* 15 full-time (5 women), 1 part-time (0 women); includes 2 minority (both Asian, non-Hispanic/Latino), 9 international. Average age 32. 74 applicants, 7% accepted, 4 enrolled. *Degree requirements:* For doctorate, comprehensive exam, thesis/dissertation, thesis defense. *Entrance requirements:* For doctorate, GMAT or GRE. Additional exam requirements/recommendations for international students: Recommended—TOEFL (minimum score 100 iBT), IELTS (minimum score 7). *Application deadline:* For fall admission, 1/15 for domestic and international students. Applications are processed on a rolling basis. Application fee: $60 ($100 for international students). Electronic applications accepted. *Financial support:* In 2013–14, 15 students received support, including 2 fellowships with full tuition reimbursements available (averaging $17,680 per year), 13 teaching assistantships with full tuition reimbursements available (averaging $17,680 per year); institutionally sponsored loans, scholarships/grants, health care benefits, and unspecified assistantships also available. Financial award application deadline: 1/15. *Faculty research:* International finance, real estate finance, theoretical and empirical corporate finance, theoretical and empirical asset pricing bond pricing and derivatives. *Unit head:* Prof. Erik Lie, Department Executive Officer, 319-335-0929, Fax: 319-335-3690, E-mail: erik-lie@uiowa.edu. *Application contact:* Renea L. Jay, PhD Program Coordinator, 319-335-0830, Fax: 319-335-1956, E-mail: renea-jay@uiowa.edu.
Website: http://tippie.uiowa.edu/finance/.

The University of Iowa, Henry B. Tippie College of Business, Department of Management and Organizations, Iowa City, IA 52242-1316. Offers PhD. *Accreditation:* AACSB. *Faculty:* 24 full-time (7 women), 37 part-time/adjunct (10 women). *Students:* 17 full-time (9 women); includes 1 minority (Hispanic/Latino), 2 international. Average age 32. 48 applicants, 8% accepted, 3 enrolled. In 2013, 1 doctorate awarded. *Degree requirements:* For doctorate, comprehensive exam, thesis/dissertation, thesis defense. *Entrance requirements:* For doctorate, GMAT or GRE. Additional exam requirements/ recommendations for international students: Recommended—TOEFL (minimum score 100 iBT), IELTS (minimum score 7). *Application deadline:* For fall admission, 1/15 for domestic and international students. Applications are processed on a rolling basis. Application fee: $60 ($100 for international students). Electronic applications accepted. *Financial support:* In 2013–14, 17 students received support, including 8 fellowships with full tuition reimbursements available (averaging $17,680 per year), 1 research assistantship with full tuition reimbursement available (averaging $17,680 per year), 8 teaching assistantships with full tuition reimbursements available (averaging $17,680 per year); institutionally sponsored loans, scholarships/grants, health care benefits, and unspecified assistantships also available. Financial award application deadline: 1/15; financial award applicants required to submit FAFSA. *Faculty research:* Decision-making, human resources, personal selection, organizational behavior, training. *Unit head:* Prof. Amy Kristof-Brown, Department Executive Officer, 319-335-0927, Fax: 319-335-1956, E-mail: amy-kristofbrown@uiowa.edu. *Application contact:* Renea L. Jay,

PhD Program Coordinator, 319-335-0830, Fax: 319-335-1956, E-mail: renea-jay@uiowa.edu.
Website: http://tippie.uiowa.edu/management-organizations/.

The University of Iowa, Henry B. Tippie College of Business, Department of Management Sciences, Iowa City, IA 52242-1316. Offers business administration (PhD), including management sciences. *Accreditation:* AACSB. *Faculty:* 16 full-time (2 women), 8 part-time/adjunct (1 woman). *Students:* 15 full-time (8 women); includes 1 minority (Asian, non-Hispanic/Latino), 12 international. Average age 31. 17 applicants, 12% accepted, 1 enrolled. *Degree requirements:* For doctorate, comprehensive exam, thesis/dissertation, thesis defense. *Entrance requirements:* For doctorate, GRE General Test or GMAT. Additional exam requirements/recommendations for international students: Recommended—TOEFL (minimum score 100 iBT), IELTS (minimum score 7). *Application deadline:* For fall admission, 1/15 for domestic and international students. Applications are processed on a rolling basis. Application fee: $60 ($100 for international students). Electronic applications accepted. *Financial support:* In 2013–14, 15 students received support, including 1 research assistantship with full tuition reimbursement available (averaging $17,680 per year), 14 teaching assistantships with full tuition reimbursements available (averaging $17,680 per year); institutionally sponsored loans, scholarships/grants, health care benefits, and unspecified assistantships also available. Financial award application deadline: 1/15. *Faculty research:* Optimization, supply chain management, data mining, logistics, database management. *Unit head:* Prof. Nick Street, Department Executive Officer, 319-335-0858, Fax: 319-335-1956, E-mail: nick-street@uiowa.edu. *Application contact:* Renea L. Jay, PhD Program Coordinator, 319-335-0830, Fax: 319-335-1956, E-mail: renea-jay@uiowa.edu.
Website: http://tippie.uiowa.edu/management-sciences/.

The University of Iowa, Henry B. Tippie College of Business, Henry B. Tippie School of Management, Iowa City, IA 52242-1316. Offers corporate finance (MBA); investment management (MBA); marketing (MBA); strategic management and innovation (MBA); supply chain and analytics (MBA); JD/MBA; MBA/MA; MBA/MD; MBA/MHA; MBA/MSN. *Accreditation:* AACSB. Part-time and evening/weekend programs available. *Faculty:* 113 full-time (27 women), 89 part-time/adjunct (23 women). *Students:* 110 full-time (28 women), 786 part-time (236 women); includes 51 minority (13 Black or African American, non-Hispanic/Latino; 3 American Indian or Alaska Native, non-Hispanic/Latino; 23 Asian, non-Hispanic/Latino; 12 Hispanic/Latino), 162 international. Average age 33. 622 applicants, 73% accepted, 383 enrolled. In 2013, 333 master's awarded. *Degree requirements:* For master's, minimum GPA of 2.75. *Entrance requirements:* For master's, GMAT, GRE, quality work experience and leadership as shown through resume, references, and essays. Additional exam requirements/recommendations for international students: Required—TOEFL (minimum score 600 paper-based; 100 iBT), IELTS (minimum score 7). *Application deadline:* For fall admission, 7/30 for domestic students, 4/1 for international students; for spring admission, 12/30 for domestic and international students. Applications are processed on a rolling basis. Application fee: $60 ($100 for international students). Electronic applications accepted. *Expenses:* Contact institution. *Financial support:* In 2013–14, 96 students received support, including 102 fellowships (averaging $9,519 per year), 83 research assistantships with partial tuition reimbursements available (averaging $8,893 per year), 14 teaching assistantships with partial tuition reimbursements available (averaging $17,049 per year); career-related internships or fieldwork, scholarships/grants, health care benefits, and unspecified assistantships also available. Financial award application deadline: 7/30; financial award applicants required to submit FAFSA. *Faculty research:* Capital markets, econometrics, optimization, investments and empirical corporate finance, Iowa electronic markets. *Unit head:* Prof. David W. Frasier, Associate Dean, Tippie School of Management, 800-622-4692, Fax: 319-335-3604, E-mail: david-frasier@uiowa.edu. *Application contact:* Jodi Schafer, Director, MBA Admissions and Financial Aid, 319-335-0864, Fax: 319-335-3604, E-mail: jodi-schafer@uiowa.edu.
Website: http://tippie.uiowa.edu/mba.

The University of Kansas, Graduate Studies, School of Business, Program in Business, Lawrence, KS 66045. Offers PhD. *Accreditation:* AACSB. *Faculty:* 116. *Students:* 90 full-time (27 women), 7 part-time (4 women); includes 16 minority (6 Black or African American, non-Hispanic/Latino; 4 Asian, non-Hispanic/Latino; 2 Native Hawaiian or other Pacific Islander, non-Hispanic/Latino; 4 Two or more races, non-Hispanic/Latino), 25 international. Average age 33. 265 applicants, 36% accepted, 70 enrolled. In 2013, 8 doctorates awarded. *Degree requirements:* For doctorate, comprehensive exam, thesis/dissertation, departmental qualifying exam. *Entrance requirements:* For doctorate, GMAT or GRE. Additional exam requirements/recommendations for international students: Required—TOEFL (minimum score 600 paper-based; 100 iBT). *Application deadline:* For fall admission, 1/10 for domestic and international students. Applications are processed on a rolling basis. Application fee: $65. Electronic applications accepted. *Financial support:* Fellowships with full tuition reimbursements, research assistantships with full tuition reimbursements, teaching assistantships with full tuition reimbursements, scholarships/grants, health care benefits, tuition waivers (full), and unspecified assistantships available. *Faculty research:* Financial and auditing accounting; mergers and acquisitions, corporate finance and investments, banking; strategic human resource management, business ethics, organizational theory/behavior, corporate strategy, international business; supply chain management, Bayesian networks, game theory, decision analysis and time/series analysis; pricing, consumer effects, advertising and emotion. *Unit head:* Charly Edmonds, Director, 785-864-3841, Fax: 785-864-5376, E-mail: bschoolphd@ku.edu. *Application contact:* Dee Steinle, Administrative Director of Master's Programs, 785-864-3795, Fax: 785-864-5328, E-mail: bschoolgrad@ku.edu.
Website: http://www.business.ku.edu/.

The University of Kansas, Graduate Studies, School of Business, Program in Business Administration and Management, Lawrence, KS 66045. Offers finance (MBA); human resources management (MBA); information systems (MBA); international business (MBA); management (MBA); marketing (MBA); strategic management (MBA); JD/MBA; MBA/MA; MBA/MM; MBA/MS; MBA/Pharm D. *Accreditation:* AACSB. Part-time programs available. *Faculty:* 116. *Students:* 78 full-time (19 women), 175 part-time (46 women); includes 39 minority (2 Black or African American, non-Hispanic/Latino; 3 American Indian or Alaska Native, non-Hispanic/Latino; 20 Asian, non-Hispanic/Latino; 9 Hispanic/Latino; 1 Native Hawaiian or other Pacific Islander, non-Hispanic/Latino; 4 Two or more races, non-Hispanic/Latino), 27 international. Average age 31. 149 applicants, 61% accepted, 67 enrolled. In 2013, 111 master's awarded. *Degree requirements:* For master's, comprehensive exam (for some programs), thesis optional. *Entrance requirements:* For master's, GMAT, 2 years of professional work experience. Additional exam requirements/recommendations for international students: Required—TOEFL (minimum score 53 paper-based); Recommended—IELTS (minimum score 6). *Application deadline:* For fall admission, 6/1 priority date for domestic students, 5/1 priority date for international students; for spring admission, 11/1 for domestic students, 10/1 for international students. Application fee: $65. Electronic applications accepted. *Financial support:* Research assistantships, career-related internships or fieldwork, Federal Work-Study, institutionally sponsored loans, scholarships/grants, and unspecified assistantships available. Financial award application deadline: 6/1; financial award applicants required to submit FAFSA. *Faculty research:* Advanced audit technologies, real options and asset pricing, corporate governance, foreign direct investment, CEO characteristics and organizational innovation. *Unit head:* Dr. Cathy Shenoy, Director of MBA Programs, 785-864-7519, E-mail: cshenoy@ku.edu. *Application contact:* Dee Steinle, Administrative Director of Master's Programs, 785-864-7596, Fax: 785-864-5376, E-mail: dsteinle@ku.edu.
Website: http://www.business.ku.edu/.

University of Kentucky, Graduate School, Gatton College of Business and Economics, Program in Business Administration, Lexington, KY 40506-0032. Offers MBA, PhD. *Accreditation:* AACSB. *Degree requirements:* For master's, comprehensive exam; for doctorate, comprehensive exam, thesis/dissertation. *Entrance requirements:* For master's, GMAT, minimum undergraduate GPA of 2.75; for doctorate, GMAT, minimum undergraduate GPA of 3.0. Additional exam requirements/recommendations for international students: Required—TOEFL (minimum score 550 paper-based). Electronic applications accepted. *Faculty research:* Expert systems in manufacturing, knowledge acquisition and management, financial institutions, market in service organizations, strategic planning.

University of La Verne, College of Business and Public Management, Graduate Programs in Business Administration, La Verne, CA 91750-4443. Offers accounting (MBA); executive management (MBA-EP); finance (MBA, MBA-EP); health services management (MBA); information technology (MBA, MBA-EP); international business (MBA, MBA-EP); leadership (MBA-EP); managed care (MBA); management (MBA, MBA-EP); marketing (MBA, MBA-EP). Part-time and evening/weekend programs available. *Faculty:* 22 full-time (9 women), 37 part-time/adjunct (10 women). *Students:* 793 full-time (356 women), 164 part-time (80 women); includes 153 minority (17 Black or African American, non-Hispanic/Latino; 21 Asian, non-Hispanic/Latino; 110 Hispanic/Latino; 5 Two or more races, non-Hispanic/Latino), 691 international. Average age 27. In 2013, 514 master's awarded. *Entrance requirements:* For master's, GMAT, MAT, or GRE, minimum undergraduate GPA of 3.0, 2 letters of recommendation, resume, statement of purpose. Additional exam requirements/recommendations for international students: Required—TOEFL (minimum score 550 paper-based; 85 iBT). *Application deadline:* Applications are processed on a rolling basis. Application fee: $50. *Expenses:* Contact institution. *Financial support:* Career-related internships or fieldwork, institutionally sponsored loans, and scholarships/grants available. Financial award application deadline: 3/2; financial award applicants required to submit FAFSA. *Unit head:* Dr. Abe Helou, Chairperson, 909-593-3511 Ext. 4211, Fax: 909-392-2704, E-mail: ihelou@laverne.edu. *Application contact:* Rina Lazarian-Chehab, Senior Associate Director of Graduate Admissions, 909-593-3511 Ext. 4317, Fax: 909-392-2704, E-mail: rlazarian@laverne.edu.

University of La Verne, College of Business and Public Management, Program in Gerontology, La Verne, CA 91750-4443. Offers business administration (MS); gerontology (MS, Certificate); gerontology administration (MS); health services management (MS). Part-time programs available. *Faculty:* 1 (woman) full-time, 3 part-time/adjunct (2 women). *Students:* 15 full-time (all women), 16 part-time (12 women); includes 18 minority (5 Black or African American, non-Hispanic/Latino; 13 Hispanic/Latino), 3 international. Average age 40. In 2013, 10 master's awarded. *Entrance requirements:* For master's, minimum GPA of 2.5, 2 recommendations, personal statement. Additional exam requirements/recommendations for international students: Required—TOEFL (minimum score 550 paper-based). *Application deadline:* Applications are processed on a rolling basis. Application fee: $50. *Expenses:* Contact institution. *Financial support:* Institutionally sponsored loans available. Financial award application deadline: 3/2; financial award applicants required to submit FAFSA. *Unit head:* Dr. Kathy Duncan, Program Director, 909-593-3511 Ext. 4796, E-mail: tford@laverne.edu. *Application contact:* Barbara Cox, Program and Admissions Specialist, 909-593-3511 Ext. 4004, Fax: 909-392-2761, E-mail: bcox@laverne.edu.
Website: http://www.laverne.edu/business-and-public-administration/healthadmin-gerontology/.

University of La Verne, College of Business and Public Management, Program in Health Administration, La Verne, CA 91750-4443. Offers financial management (MHA); health information systems (MHA); human resource management (MHA); managed care (MHA); management and leadership (MHA); marketing and business development (MHA). Part-time programs available. *Faculty:* 3 full-time (1 woman), 5 part-time/adjunct (1 woman). *Students:* 43 full-time (31 women), 35 part-time (20 women); includes 29 minority (9 Black or African American, non-Hispanic/Latino; 9 Asian, non-Hispanic/Latino; 11 Hispanic/Latino), 13 international. Average age 31. In 2013, 31 master's awarded. *Entrance requirements:* For master's, minimum undergraduate GPA of 2.5, 3 letters of reference, curriculum vitae or resume, writing sample. Additional exam requirements/recommendations for international students: Required—TOEFL (minimum score 550 paper-based). *Application deadline:* Applications are processed on a rolling basis. Application fee: $50. *Expenses:* Contact institution. *Financial support:* Application deadline: 3/2; applicants required to submit FAFSA. *Unit head:* Dr. Kathy Duncan, Program Chairperson, 909-593-3511 Ext. 4415, E-mail: kduncan2@laverne.edu. *Application contact:* Barbara Cox, Program and Admissions Specialist, 909-593-3511 Ext. 4004, Fax: 909-392-2761, E-mail: bcox@laverne.edu.
Website: http://www.laverne.edu/business-and-public-administration/healthadmin-gerontology/.

University of La Verne, College of Business and Public Management, Program in Organizational Management and Leadership, La Verne, CA 91750-4443. Offers leadership and management (MS), including human resource management, nonprofit management, organizational development; nonprofit management (Certificate); organizational leadership (Certificate). Part-time programs available. *Faculty:* 2 full-time (1 woman), 8 part-time/adjunct (6 women). *Students:* 77 full-time (39 women), 67 part-time (47 women); includes 69 minority (7 Black or African American, non-Hispanic/Latino; 3 Asian, non-Hispanic/Latino; 55 Hispanic/Latino; 2 Native Hawaiian or other Pacific Islander, non-Hispanic/Latino; 2 Two or more races, non-Hispanic/Latino), 38 international. Average age 32. In 2013, 183 master's awarded. *Degree requirements:* For master's, thesis or research project. *Entrance requirements:* For master's, minimum undergraduate GPA of 2.75, 2 letters of recommendation, interview, resume. Additional exam requirements/recommendations for international students: Required—TOEFL (minimum score 550 paper-based). *Application deadline:* Applications are processed on a rolling basis. Application fee: $50. *Expenses:* Contact institution. *Financial support:* Institutionally sponsored loans available. Financial award application deadline: 3/2; financial award applicants required to submit FAFSA. *Unit head:* Dr. Kathy Duncan, Program Director, 909-593-3511 Ext. 4415, E-mail: kduncan2@laverne.edu. *Application contact:* Rina Lazarian-Chehab, Senior Associate Director of Graduate Admissions, 909-593-3511 Ext. 4317, Fax: 909-392-2761, E-mail: rlazarian@laverne.edu.
Website: http://www.laverne.edu/business-and-public-administration/org-mgmt/.

University of La Verne, Regional and Online Campuses, Graduate Programs, Central Coast/Vandenberg Air Force Base Campuses, La Verne, CA 91750-4443. Offers business administration for experienced professionals (MBA), including health services management, information technology; education (special emphasis) (M Ed); educational counseling (MS); educational leadership (M Ed); multiple subject (elementary) (Credential); preliminary administrative services (Credential); pupil personnel services (Credential); single subject (secondary) (Credential). Part-time programs available. *Faculty:* 11 part-time/adjunct (2 women). *Students:* 17 full-time (7 women), 34 part-time

(22 women); includes 15 minority (1 Black or African American, non-Hispanic/Latino; 1 American Indian or Alaska Native, non-Hispanic/Latino; 1 Asian, non-Hispanic/Latino; 10 Hispanic/Latino; 2 Two or more races, non-Hispanic/Latino). Average age 38. In 2013, 25 master's awarded. *Application deadline:* Applications are processed on a rolling basis. Application fee: $50. *Expenses:* Contact institution. *Financial support:* Institutionally sponsored loans available. Financial award application deadline: 3/2; financial award applicants required to submit FAFSA. *Unit head:* Kitt Vincent, Director, Central Coast Campus, 805-788-6202, Fax: 805-788-6201, E-mail: kvincent@laverne.edu. *Application contact:* Gene Teal, Admissions, 805-788-6205, Fax: 805-788-6201, E-mail: eteal@laverne.edu.
Website: http://www.laverne.edu/locations.

University of La Verne, Regional and Online Campuses, Graduate Programs, High Desert Campus, Victorville, CA 92392. Offers business administration for experienced professionals (MBA); educational counseling (MS); educational leadership (M Ed); multiple subject (elementary) (Credential); preliminary administrative services (Credential); pupil personnel services (Credential); single subject (secondary) (Credential). *Faculty:* 3 part-time/adjunct (0 women). *Students:* 10 full-time (6 women), 17 part-time (12 women); includes 14 minority (3 Black or African American, non-Hispanic/Latino; 3 Asian, non-Hispanic/Latino; 6 Hispanic/Latino; 1 Native Hawaiian or other Pacific Islander, non-Hispanic/Latino; 1 Two or more races, non-Hispanic/Latino). Average age 38. In 2013, 6 master's awarded. *Application deadline:* Applications are processed on a rolling basis. Application fee: $50. *Expenses:* Contact institution. *Financial support:* Application deadline: 3/2; applicants required to submit FAFSA. *Unit head:* Juli Roberts, Regional Campus Director, 760-955-6448, Fax: 760-843-9505, E-mail: jroberts@laverne.edu. *Application contact:* Donald Parker, Associate Director of Admissions, 760-955-6477, E-mail: dparker@laverne.edu.
Website: http://www.laverne.edu/locations/victorville/.

University of La Verne, Regional and Online Campuses, Graduate Programs, Inland Empire Campus, Ontario, CA 91761. Offers business administration (MBA, MBA-EP), including accounting (MBA), finance (MBA), health services management (MBA-EP), information technology (MBA-EP), international business (MBA), managed care (MBA), management and leadership (MBA-EP), marketing (MBA-EP), supply chain management (MBA); leadership and management (MS), including human resource management, nonprofit management, organizational development. Part-time and evening/weekend programs available. *Faculty:* 1 full-time (0 women), 14 part-time/adjunct (6 women). *Students:* 26 full-time (15 women), 106 part-time (65 women); includes 92 minority (15 Black or African American, non-Hispanic/Latino; 29 Asian, non-Hispanic/Latino; 43 Hispanic/Latino; 1 Native Hawaiian or other Pacific Islander, non-Hispanic/Latino; 4 Two or more races, non-Hispanic/Latino). Average age 37. In 2013, 49 master's awarded. *Application deadline:* Applications are processed on a rolling basis. Application fee: $50. *Expenses:* Contact institution. *Financial support:* Institutionally sponsored loans available. Financial award application deadline: 3/2; financial award applicants required to submit FAFSA. *Unit head:* Allen Stout, Campus Director, Inland Empire Regional Campus in Ontario, 909-937-6987, E-mail: astout@laverne.edu. *Application contact:* Karen Schumann, Senior Associate Director of Admissions, Inland Empire Regional Campus in Ontario, 909-937-6991, E-mail: kschumann@laverne.edu.
Website: http://laverne.edu/locations/inland-empire/.

University of La Verne, Regional and Online Campuses, Graduate Programs, Kern County Campus, Bakersfield, CA 93301. Offers business administration for experienced professionals (MBA-EP); education (special emphasis) (M Ed); educational counseling (MS); educational leadership (M Ed); health administration (MHA); leadership and management (MS); mild/moderate education specialist preliminary (Credential); multiple subject (elementary) (Credential); organizational leadership (Ed D); preliminary administrative services (Credential); single subject (secondary) (Credential); special education studies (MS). Part-time and evening/weekend programs available. *Faculty:* 2 part-time/adjunct (1 woman). *Students:* 1 (woman) full-time, 5 part-time (3 women); includes 4 minority (3 Hispanic/Latino; 1 Two or more races, non-Hispanic/Latino). Average age 36. In 2013, 4 master's awarded. *Application deadline:* Applications are processed on a rolling basis. Application fee: $50. *Expenses:* Contact institution. *Financial support:* Institutionally sponsored loans available. Financial award application deadline: 3/2; financial award applicants required to submit FAFSA. *Unit head:* Nora Dominguez, Regional Campus Director, 661-861-6802, E-mail: ndominguez@laverne.edu. *Application contact:* Regina Benavides, Associate Director of Admissions, 661-861-6807, E-mail: rbenavides@laverne.edu.
Website: http://laverne.edu/locations/bakersfield/.

University of La Verne, Regional and Online Campuses, Graduate Programs, Orange County Campus, Irvine, CA 92606. Offers business administration for experienced professionals (MBA); educational counseling (MS); educational leadership (M Ed); health administration (MHA); leadership and management (MS); preliminary administrative services (Credential); pupil personnel services (Credential). Part-time programs available. *Faculty:* 3 full-time (all women), 12 part-time/adjunct (3 women). *Students:* 38 full-time (21 women), 78 part-time (36 women); includes 69 minority (7 Black or African American, non-Hispanic/Latino; 1 American Indian or Alaska Native, non-Hispanic/Latino; 19 Asian, non-Hispanic/Latino; 40 Hispanic/Latino; 1 Native Hawaiian or other Pacific Islander, non-Hispanic/Latino; 1 Two or more races, non-Hispanic/Latino). Average age 37. In 2013, 30 master's awarded. *Application deadline:* Applications are processed on a rolling basis. Application fee: $50. *Expenses:* Contact institution. *Financial support:* Institutionally sponsored loans available. Financial award application deadline: 3/2; financial award applicants required to submit FAFSA. *Unit head:* Pam Bergovoy, Director, Center for Educators, 909-448-4953, E-mail: pbergovoy@laverne.edu. *Application contact:* Alison Rodriguez-Balles, Associate Director of Admissions, 714-505-6943, E-mail: arodriguez2@laverne.edu.
Website: http://laverne.edu/locations/irvine/.

University of La Verne, Regional and Online Campuses, Graduate Programs, San Fernando Valley Campus, Burbank, CA 91505. Offers business administration for experienced professionals (MBA-EP); educational counseling (MS); educational leadership (M Ed); leadership and management (MS); preliminary administrative services (Credential); pupil personnel services (Credential). Part-time and evening/weekend programs available. *Faculty:* 2 full-time (1 woman), 12 part-time/adjunct (5 women). *Students:* 46 full-time (20 women), 128 part-time (76 women); includes 121 minority (29 Black or African American, non-Hispanic/Latino; 19 Asian, non-Hispanic/Latino; 66 Hispanic/Latino; 1 Native Hawaiian or other Pacific Islander, non-Hispanic/Latino; 6 Two or more races, non-Hispanic/Latino). Average age 38. In 2013, 79 master's awarded. *Application deadline:* Applications are processed on a rolling basis. Application fee: $50. *Expenses:* Contact institution. *Financial support:* Institutionally sponsored loans available. Financial award application deadline: 3/2; financial award applicants required to submit FAFSA. *Unit head:* Dr. Nelly Kazman, Senior Executive Director, 818-295-6502, E-mail: nkazman@laverne.edu. *Application contact:* Debi Hrboka, Associate Director of Admissions, 818-295-6508, E-mail: dhrboka@laverne.edu.
Website: http://laverne.edu/locations/burbank/.

University of La Verne, Regional and Online Campuses, Graduate Programs, Ventura County/Point Mugu Naval Air Station Campuses, Oxnard, CA 93036. Offers business administration for experienced professionals (MS); educational counseling (MS); educational leadership (M Ed); leadership and management (MS); multiple subject (elementary) (Credential); pupil personnel services (Credential); single subject (secondary) (Credential). Part-time and evening/weekend programs available. *Faculty:* 12 part-time/adjunct (2 women). *Students:* 34 full-time (13 women), 37 part-time (20 women); includes 39 minority (3 Black or African American, non-Hispanic/Latino; 2 American Indian or Alaska Native, non-Hispanic/Latino; 3 Asian, non-Hispanic/Latino; 29 Hispanic/Latino; 2 Two or more races, non-Hispanic/Latino). Average age 38. In 2013, 31 master's awarded. Application fee: $50. *Expenses:* Contact institution. *Financial support:* Institutionally sponsored loans available. Financial award application deadline: 3/2; financial award applicants required to submit FAFSA. *Unit head:* Jamie Dempsey, Director, Point Mugu, 661-986-6902, E-mail: jdempsey@laverne.edu. *Application contact:* Kevin Laack, Regional Campus Director, Ventura, 805-981-6022, E-mail: klaack@laverne.edu.
Website: http://laverne.edu/locations/oxnard/.

University of La Verne, Regional and Online Campuses, Graduate Program, ULV Online, La Verne, CA 91750-4443. Offers business administration for experienced professionals (MBA). Part-time and evening/weekend programs available. Postbaccalaureate distance learning degree programs offered (no on-campus study). *Faculty:* 8 full-time (3 women), 2 part-time/adjunct (0 women). *Students:* 35 full-time (19 women), 108 part-time (59 women); includes 72 minority (16 Black or African American, non-Hispanic/Latino; 1 American Indian or Alaska Native, non-Hispanic/Latino; 14 Asian, non-Hispanic/Latino; 38 Hispanic/Latino; 3 Two or more races, non-Hispanic/Latino). Average age 37. In 2013, 42 master's awarded. *Entrance requirements:* For master's, GMAT, MAT, or GRE, minimum undergraduate GPA of 3.0, 2 letters of recommendation, resume, statement of purpose. *Application deadline:* Applications are processed on a rolling basis. Application fee: $50. *Expenses: Tuition:* Part-time $690 per credit hour. *Required fees:* $30 per course. *Financial support:* Application deadline: 3/2; applicants required to submit FAFSA. *Unit head:* Barbara Colley, Coordinator, ULV Online, 909-448-4944, E-mail: bcolley@ulv.edu. *Application contact:* Jesse S. Martinez, Associate Director of Admission, 909-448-4961, E-mail: jmartinez@laverne.edu.
Website: http://laverne.edu/admission/online/.

University of Lethbridge, School of Graduate Studies, Lethbridge, AB T1K 3M4, Canada. Offers accounting (MScM); addictions counseling (M Sc); agricultural biotechnology (M Sc); agricultural studies (M Sc, MA); anthropology (MA); archaeology (M Sc, MA); art (MA, MFA); biochemistry (M Sc); biological sciences (M Sc); biomolecular science (PhD); biosystems and biodiversity (PhD); Canadian studies (MA); chemistry (M Sc); computer science (M Sc); computer science and geographical information science (M Sc); counseling (MC); counseling psychology (M Ed); dramatic arts (MA); earth, space, and physical science (PhD); economics (MA); education (MA); educational leadership (M Ed); English (MA); environmental science (M Sc); evolution and behavior (PhD); exercise science (M Sc); finance (MScM); French (MA); French/German (MA); French/Spanish (MA); general education (M Ed); general management (MScM); geography (M Sc, MA); German (MA); health sciences (M Sc); human resource management and labour relations (MScM); individualized multidisciplinary (M Sc, MA); information systems (MScM); international management (MScM); kinesiology (M Sc, MA); marketing (MScM); mathematics (M Sc); modern languages (MA); music (M Mus, MA); Native American studies (MA); neuroscience (M Sc, PhD); new media (MA, MFA); nursing (M Sc); philosophy (MA); physics (M Sc); policy and strategy (MScM); political science (MA); psychology (M Sc, MA); religious studies (MA); sociology (MA); theatre and dramatic arts (MFA); theoretical and computational science (PhD); urban and regional studies (MA); women and gender studies (MA). Part-time and evening/weekend programs available. *Degree requirements:* For doctorate, comprehensive exam, thesis/dissertation. *Entrance requirements:* For master's, GMAT (for M Sc in management), bachelor's degree in related field, minimum GPA of 3.0 during previous 20 graded semester courses, 2 years teaching or related experience (M Ed); for doctorate, master's degree, minimum graduate GPA of 3.5. Additional exam requirements/recommendations for international students: Required—TOEFL. Application fee: $60 Canadian dollars. *Financial support:* Fellowships, research assistantships, teaching assistantships, scholarships/grants, health care benefits, and unspecified assistantships available. *Faculty research:* Movement and brain plasticity, gibberellin physiology, photosynthesis, carbon cycling, molecular properties of main-group ring components. *Application contact:* School of Graduate Studies, 403-329-2793, Fax: 403-332-5239, E-mail: sgsinquiries@uleth.ca.
Website: http://www.uleth.ca/graduatestudies/.

University of Louisiana at Lafayette, BI Moody III College of Business Administration MBA Program, Lafayette, LA 70504. Offers MBA. *Accreditation:* AACSB. Part-time and evening/weekend programs available. *Entrance requirements:* For master's, GRE General Test. Additional exam requirements/recommendations for international students: Required—TOEFL (minimum score 550 paper-based).

University of Louisiana at Monroe, Graduate School, College of Business and Social Sciences, Monroe, LA 71209-0001. Offers MA, MBA, MS. *Accreditation:* AACSB. Part-time and evening/weekend programs available. Postbaccalaureate distance learning degree programs offered. *Degree requirements:* For master's, comprehensive exam. *Entrance requirements:* For master's, GMAT, minimum GPA of 2.5, minimum AACSB index of 950. Additional exam requirements/recommendations for international students: Required—TOEFL (minimum score 500 paper-based). *Application deadline:* For fall admission, 8/24 for domestic students, 7/1 for international students; for winter admission, 12/14 for domestic students; for spring admission, 1/19 for domestic students, 11/1 for international students. Applications are processed on a rolling basis. Application fee: $20 ($30 for international students). Electronic applications accepted. *Expenses:* Tuition, state resident: full-time $6607. Tuition, nonresident: full-time $17,179. Full-time tuition and fees vary according to program. *Financial support:* Research assistantships, career-related internships or fieldwork, Federal Work-Study, and unspecified assistantships available. Financial award application deadline: 4/1; financial award applicants required to submit FAFSA. *Faculty research:* Information assurance framework, bias in balanced scorecard. *Unit head:* Dr. Ronald Berry, Dean, 318-342-1103, E-mail: rberry@ulm.edu. *Application contact:* Dr. Donna Luse, MBA Director, 318-342-1106, Fax: 318-342-1101, E-mail: luse@ulm.edu.
Website: http://www.ulm.edu/cbss/.

University of Louisville, Graduate School, College of Business, MBA Programs, Louisville, KY 40292-0001. Offers entrepreneurship (MBA); global business (MBA); health sector management (MBA). *Accreditation:* AACSB. Part-time and evening/weekend programs available. *Students:* 202 full-time (65 women), 42 part-time (15 women); includes 21 minority (9 Black or African American, non-Hispanic/Latino; 1 American Indian or Alaska Native, non-Hispanic/Latino; 7 Asian, non-Hispanic/Latino; 3 Hispanic/Latino; 1 Two or more races, non-Hispanic/Latino), 38 international. Average age 29. 314 applicants, 42% accepted, 116 enrolled. In 2013, 61 master's awarded. *Degree requirements:* For master's, international learning experience. *Entrance requirements:* For master's, GMAT, 2 letters of reference, personal interview, resume, personal statement, college transcript(s). Additional exam requirements/

recommendations for international students: Required—TOEFL (minimum score 83 iBT). *Application deadline:* For fall admission, 7/1 for domestic students; for spring admission, 12/1 for domestic students. Applications are processed on a rolling basis. Application fee: $60. *Expenses:* Tuition, state resident: full-time $10,788; part-time $599 per credit hour. Tuition, nonresident: full-time $22,446; part-time $1247 per credit hour. *Required fees:* $196. Tuition and fees vary according to program and reciprocity agreements. *Financial support:* Fellowships with full tuition reimbursements, research assistantships with full tuition reimbursements, health care benefits, and unspecified assistantships available. Financial award application deadline: 3/31; financial award applicants required to submit FAFSA. *Faculty research:* Entrepreneurship, venture capital, retailing/franchising, corporate governance and leadership, supply chain management. *Unit head:* Dr. Carolyn M. Callahan, Dean, 502-852-6440, Fax: 502-852-7557, E-mail: cmcall04@louisville.edu. *Application contact:* Susan E. Hildebrand, Program Director, 502-852-7257, Fax: 502-852-4901, E-mail: s.hildebrand@louisville.edu.
Website: http://business.louisville.edu/mba.

University of Maine, Graduate School, The Maine Business School, Orono, ME 04469. Offers accounting (MBA); business administration (CGS); business and sustainability (MBA); finance (MBA); international business (MBA); management (MBA). *Accreditation:* AACSB. Part-time and evening/weekend programs available. Postbaccalaureate distance learning degree programs offered. *Faculty:* 23 full-time (7 women). *Students:* 31 full-time (12 women), 12 part-time (9 women); includes 5 minority (1 Black or African American, non-Hispanic/Latino; 3 Asian, non-Hispanic/Latino; 1 Hispanic/Latino), 4 international. Average age 29. 41 applicants, 71% accepted, 24 enrolled. In 2013, 28 master's awarded. *Entrance requirements:* For master's, GMAT. Additional exam requirements/recommendations for international students: Required—TOEFL (minimum score 550 paper-based). *Application deadline:* For fall admission, 6/1 priority date for domestic and international students; for spring admission, 11/15 priority date for domestic and international students. Applications are processed on a rolling basis. Application fee: $65. Electronic applications accepted. *Expenses:* Contact institution. *Financial support:* In 2013–14, 14 students received support, including 3 teaching assistantships with full tuition reimbursements available (averaging $14,100 per year); career-related internships or fieldwork, Federal Work-Study, institutionally sponsored loans, scholarships/grants, tuition waivers (full and partial), and unspecified assistantships also available. Financial award application deadline: 3/1. *Faculty research:* Entrepreneurship, investment management, international markets, decision support systems, strategic planning. *Total annual research expenditures:* $5,089. *Unit head:* Carol Mandzik, Manager of MBA Programs, Executive Education and Internships, 207-581-1971, Fax: 207-581-1930, E-mail: carol.mandzik@maine.edu. *Application contact:* Scott G. Delcourt, Associate Dean of the Graduate School, 207-581-3291, Fax: 207-581-3232, E-mail: graduate@maine.edu.
Website: http://www.umaine.edu/business/.

University of Management and Technology, Program in Business Administration, Arlington, VA 22209. Offers acquisition management (DBA); general management (MBA, DBA); project management (MBA, DBA). Part-time and evening/weekend programs available. Postbaccalaureate distance learning degree programs offered (no on-campus study). *Degree requirements:* For master's, comprehensive exam. *Entrance requirements:* For master's, 3 recommendations, resume. Additional exam requirements/recommendations for international students: Required—TOEFL (minimum score 530 paper-based; 71 iBT). Electronic applications accepted.

University of Management and Technology, Program in Management, Arlington, VA 22209. Offers acquisition management (MS, AC); criminal justice administration (MPA, MS); general management (MS); project management (MS, AC); public administration (MPA, MS, AC). Part-time and evening/weekend programs available. Postbaccalaureate distance learning degree programs offered (no on-campus study). *Entrance requirements:* For master's, 3 recommendations, resume. Additional exam requirements/recommendations for international students: Required—TOEFL (minimum score 530 paper-based; 71 iBT). Electronic applications accepted.

The University of Manchester, Manchester Business School, Manchester, United Kingdom. Offers accounting (M Phil, PhD); business (M Ent, D Ent); business and management (M Phil); business management (PhD).

University of Manitoba, Faculty of Graduate Studies, Asper School of Business, Winnipeg, MB R3T 2N2, Canada. Offers M Sc, MBA, PhD. *Accreditation:* AACSB.

University of Mary, Gary Tharaldson School of Business, Bismarck, ND 58504-9652. Offers accountancy (MBA); business administration (MBA); health care (MBA); human resource management (MBA); management (MBA); project management (MPM); strategic leadership (MSSL). Part-time and evening/weekend programs available. *Degree requirements:* For master's, strategic planning seminar. *Entrance requirements:* For master's, minimum GPA of 2.5. Additional exam requirements/recommendations for international students: Required—TOEFL (minimum score 500 paper-based; 71 iBT).

University of Mary Hardin-Baylor, Graduate Studies in Business Administration, Belton, TX 76513. Offers accounting (MBA); information systems management (MBA); international business (MBA); management (MBA). Part-time and evening/weekend programs available. *Faculty:* 10 full-time (4 women), 2 part-time/adjunct (1 woman). *Students:* 26 full-time (11 women), 52 part-time (19 women); includes 20 minority (7 Black or African American, non-Hispanic/Latino; 3 Asian, non-Hispanic/Latino; 9 Hispanic/Latino; 1 Two or more races, non-Hispanic/Latino), 21 international. Average age 30. 55 applicants, 75% accepted, 27 enrolled. In 2013, 23 master's awarded. *Degree requirements:* For master's, comprehensive exam. *Entrance requirements:* For master's, minimum GPA of 3.0, interview. Additional exam requirements/recommendations for international students: Required—TOEFL (minimum score 550 paper-based; 80 iBT), IELTS (minimum score 6). *Application deadline:* For fall admission, 6/1 for domestic students, 6/15 priority date for international students; for spring admission, 11/1 for domestic students, 10/15 priority date for international students. Applications are processed on a rolling basis. Application fee: $35 ($135 for international students). Electronic applications accepted. *Expenses: Tuition:* Full-time $14,130; part-time $785 per credit hour. *Required fees:* $1350; $75 per credit hour. $50 per term. *Financial support:* Federal Work-Study, unspecified assistantships, and scholarships (for some active duty military personnel only) available. Financial award applicants required to submit FAFSA. *Unit head:* Dr. Nancy Bonner, Assistant Professor/Program Director, 254-295-5405, E-mail: nbonner@umhb.edu. *Application contact:* Melissa Ford, Director of Graduate Admissions, 254-295-4020, Fax: 254-295-5038, E-mail: mford@umhb.edu.
Website: http://www.graduate.umhb.edu/mba.

University of Maryland, College Park, Academic Affairs, Joint Program in Business and Management/Public Policy, College Park, MD 20742. Offers MBA/MPM. *Accreditation:* AACSB. *Students:* 16 full-time (6 women), 2 part-time (1 woman); includes 8 minority (5 Black or African American, non-Hispanic/Latino; 1 Asian, non-Hispanic/Latino; 2 Hispanic/Latino). 32 applicants, 31% accepted, 6 enrolled. *Application deadline:* For fall admission, 4/1 for domestic students, 2/1 for international students; for spring admission, 10/15 for domestic students, 6/1 for international students. Applications are processed on a rolling basis. Application fee: $75. Electronic applications accepted. *Expenses:* Tuition, state resident: full-time $10,314; part-time $573 per credit hour. Tuition, nonresident: full-time $22,248; part-time $1236 per credit. *Required fees:* $1446; $403.15 per semester. Tuition and fees vary according to program. *Financial support:* In 2013–14, 5 fellowships with full and partial tuition reimbursements (averaging $46,450 per year) were awarded. Financial award applicants required to submit FAFSA. *Unit head:* Dr. Charles A. Caramello, Dean of the Graduate School, 301-405-0358, Fax: 301-314-9305. *Application contact:* Dr. Charles A. Caramello, Dean of Graduate School, 301-405-0358, Fax: 301-314-9305, E-mail: ccaramel@umd.edu.

University of Maryland, College Park, Academic Affairs, Robert H. Smith School of Business, Combined MSW/MBA Program, College Park, MD 20742. Offers MSW/MBA. *Accreditation:* AACSB. *Students:* 2 full-time (both women). 8 applicants, 38% accepted, 1 enrolled. *Entrance requirements:* Additional exam requirements/recommendations for international students: Required—TOEFL. *Application deadline:* For fall admission, 12/15 priority date for domestic students, 12/15 for international students; for spring admission, 11/30 for domestic students, 6/1 for international students. Application fee: $75. *Expenses:* Tuition, state resident: full-time $10,314; part-time $573 per credit hour. Tuition, nonresident: full-time $22,248; part-time $1236 per credit. *Required fees:* $1446; $403.15 per semester. Tuition and fees vary according to program. *Financial support:* In 2013–14, 1 fellowship (averaging $79,151 per year) was awarded; research assistantships and teaching assistantships also available. *Unit head:* Dr. Anand Anandalingam, Dean, 301-405-2308, E-mail: ganand@umd.edu. *Application contact:* Dr. Charles A. Caramello, Dean of Graduate School, 301-405-0358, Fax: 301-314-9305, E-mail: ccaramel@umd.edu.

University of Maryland, College Park, Academic Affairs, Robert H. Smith School of Business, Executive MBA Program, College Park, MD 20742. Offers EMBA. *Accreditation:* AACSB. *Students:* 74 full-time (23 women); includes 15 minority (7 Black or African American, non-Hispanic/Latino; 5 Asian, non-Hispanic/Latino; 1 Hispanic/Latino; 2 Two or more races, non-Hispanic/Latino), 35 international. 3 applicants. In 2013, 69 master's awarded. *Entrance requirements:* For master's, minimum GPA of 3.0, 7-12 years of professional experience. Additional exam requirements/recommendations for international students: Required—TOEFL. *Application deadline:* For fall admission, 12/15 priority date for domestic students, 12/15 for international students; for spring admission, 11/30 for domestic students, 6/1 for international students. Application fee: $75. *Expenses:* Tuition, state resident: full-time $10,314; part-time $573 per credit hour. Tuition, nonresident: full-time $22,248; part-time $1236 per credit. *Required fees:* $1446; $403.15 per semester. Tuition and fees vary according to program. *Financial support:* In 2013–14, 20 fellowships with full and partial tuition reimbursements (averaging $18,980 per year) were awarded. *Unit head:* Dr. Anand Anandalingam, Dean, 301-405-2306, E-mail: ganand@umd.edu. *Application contact:* Dr. Charles A. Caramello, Dean of Graduate School, 301-405-0358, Fax: 301-314-9305, E-mail: ccaramel@umd.edu.

University of Maryland, College Park, Academic Affairs, Robert H. Smith School of Business, Joint Program in Business and Management, College Park, MD 20742. Offers MBA/MS. *Accreditation:* AACSB. *Students:* 40 full-time (7 women), 13 part-time (3 women); includes 14 minority (4 Black or African American, non-Hispanic/Latino; 5 Asian, non-Hispanic/Latino; 3 Hispanic/Latino; 2 Two or more races, non-Hispanic/Latino), 9 international. 78 applicants, 24% accepted, 16 enrolled. *Entrance requirements:* Additional exam requirements/recommendations for international students: Required—TOEFL. *Application deadline:* For fall admission, 12/15 for domestic and international students; for spring admission, 11/30 for domestic students, 6/1 for international students. Applications are processed on a rolling basis. Application fee: $75. Electronic applications accepted. *Expenses:* Tuition, state resident: full-time $10,314; part-time $573 per credit hour. Tuition, nonresident: full-time $22,248; part-time $1236 per credit. *Required fees:* $1446; $403.15 per semester. Tuition and fees vary according to program. *Financial support:* In 2013–14, 2 teaching assistantships (averaging $14,772 per year) were awarded. *Unit head:* Dr. Anand Anandalingam, Dean, 301-405-2308, E-mail: ganand@umd.edu. *Application contact:* Dr. Charles A. Caramello, Dean of Graduate School, 301-405-0358, Fax: 301-314-9305, E-mail: ccaramel@umd.edu.

University of Maryland, College Park, Academic Affairs, Robert H. Smith School of Business, Program in Business Administration, College Park, MD 20742. Offers MBA. *Accreditation:* AACSB. Part-time and evening/weekend programs available. Postbaccalaureate distance learning degree programs offered. *Students:* 723 full-time (230 women), 145 part-time (47 women); includes 249 minority (77 Black or African American, non-Hispanic/Latino; 1 American Indian or Alaska Native, non-Hispanic/Latino; 118 Asian, non-Hispanic/Latino; 36 Hispanic/Latino; 1 Native Hawaiian or other Pacific Islander, non-Hispanic/Latino; 16 Two or more races, non-Hispanic/Latino), 98 international. 920 applicants, 55% accepted, 314 enrolled. In 2013, 408 master's awarded. *Entrance requirements:* For master's, GMAT, minimum GPA of 3.0, resume, 3 letters of recommendation. Additional exam requirements/recommendations for international students: Required—TOEFL. *Application deadline:* For fall admission, 5/1 for domestic students, 2/1 for international students; for spring admission, 11/30 for domestic students, 6/1 for international students. Applications are processed on a rolling basis. Application fee: $75. Electronic applications accepted. *Expenses:* Tuition, state resident: full-time $10,314; part-time $573 per credit hour. Tuition, nonresident: full-time $22,248; part-time $1236 per credit. *Required fees:* $1446; $403.15 per semester. Tuition and fees vary according to program. *Financial support:* In 2013–14, 31 fellowships with full tuition reimbursements (averaging $62,656 per year), 105 teaching assistantships (averaging $15,149 per year) were awarded. Financial award applicants required to submit FAFSA. *Faculty research:* Accounting, entrepreneurship, finance management and organization, management server and statistical information systems. *Unit head:* Dr. Anand Anandalingam, Dean, 301-405-2308, E-mail: ganand@umd.edu. *Application contact:* Dr. Charles A. Caramello, Dean of Graduate School, 301-405-0358, Fax: 301-314-9305, E-mail: ccaramel@umd.edu.

University of Maryland, College Park, Academic Affairs, Robert H. Smith School of Business, Program in Business and Management, College Park, MD 20742. Offers MS, PhD. *Accreditation:* AACSB. Part-time programs available. *Students:* 763 full-time (453 women), 255 part-time (170 women); includes 67 minority (31 Black or African American, non-Hispanic/Latino; 28 Asian, non-Hispanic/Latino; 4 Hispanic/Latino; 4 Two or more races, non-Hispanic/Latino), 853 international. 3,543 applicants, 36% accepted, 485 enrolled. In 2013, 324 master's, 26 doctorates awarded. *Degree requirements:* For master's, thesis optional; for doctorate, comprehensive exam, thesis/dissertation. *Entrance requirements:* For master's, GMAT, minimum GPA of 3.0, resume, 2 letters of recommendation; for doctorate, GMAT or GRE General Test, minimum GPA of 3.0, resume, 2 letters of recommendation. Additional exam requirements/recommendations for international students: Required—TOEFL. *Application deadline:* For fall admission, 12/15 for domestic and international students. Applications are processed on a rolling basis. Application fee: $75. Electronic applications accepted. *Expenses:* Tuition, state resident: full-time $10,314; part-time $573 per credit hour. Tuition, nonresident: full-time $22,248; part-time $1236 per credit. *Required fees:* $1446; $403.15 per semester. Tuition and fees vary according to program. *Financial support:* In 2013–14, 11 fellowships with full and partial tuition reimbursements (averaging $31,490 per year), 82

teaching assistantships with tuition reimbursements (averaging $22,885 per year) were awarded; research assistantships with tuition reimbursements also available. Financial award applicants required to submit FAFSA. *Unit head:* Dr. Anand Anandalingam, Dean, 301-405-2308, E-mail: ganand@umd.edu. *Application contact:* Dr. Charles A. Caramello, Dean of Graduate School, 301-405-0358, Fax: 301-314-9305, E-mail: ccaramel@umd.edu.

University of Maryland, College Park, Academic Affairs, Robert H. Smith School of Business, Program in Business Management/Law, College Park, MD 20742. Offers JD/MBA. *Accreditation:* AACSB. *Students:* 3 full-time (0 women), 1 part-time (0 women); includes 2 minority (1 Black or African American, non-Hispanic/Latino; 1 Hispanic/Latino). 6 applicants, 33% accepted, 1 enrolled. *Entrance requirements:* Additional exam requirements/recommendations for international students: Required—TOEFL. *Application deadline:* For fall admission, 12/15 for domestic and international students; for spring admission, 11/30 for domestic students, 6/1 for international students. Applications are processed on a rolling basis. Application fee: $75. *Expenses:* Tuition, state resident: full-time $10,314; part-time $573 per credit hour. Tuition, nonresident: full-time $22,248; part-time $1236 per credit. *Required fees:* $1446; $403.15 per semester. Tuition and fees vary according to program. *Financial support:* In 2013–14, 1 fellowship (averaging $10,000 per year), 1 teaching assistantship (averaging $16,078 per year) were awarded. Financial award applicants required to submit FAFSA. *Unit head:* Dr. Anand Anandalingam, Dean, 301-405-2308, E-mail: ganand@umd.edu. *Application contact:* Dr. Charles A. Caramello, Dean of Graduate School, 301-405-0358, Fax: 301-314-9305, E-mail: ccaramel@umd.edu.

University of Maryland University College, Graduate School of Management and Technology, Doctoral Program in Management, Adelphi, MD 20783. Offers DM. *Accreditation:* AACSB. Part-time programs available. *Students:* 161 part-time (88 women); includes 66 minority (56 Black or African American, non-Hispanic/Latino; 6 Asian, non-Hispanic/Latino; 2 Hispanic/Latino; 2 Two or more races, non-Hispanic/Latino), 6 international. Average age 47. 78 applicants, 100% accepted, 7 enrolled. In 2013, 81 doctorates awarded. *Degree requirements:* For doctorate, comprehensive exam, thesis/dissertation. *Application deadline:* Applications are processed on a rolling basis. Application fee: $100. Electronic applications accepted. *Financial support:* Federal Work-Study and scholarships/grants available. Support available to part-time students. Financial award application deadline: 6/1; financial award applicants required to submit FAFSA. *Unit head:* Dr. Bryan Booth, Executive Director, 240-684-2400, Fax: 240-684-2401, E-mail: bryan.booth@umuc.edu. *Application contact:* Admissions Coordinator, 800-888-8682, Fax: 240-684-2151, E-mail: newgrad@umuc.edu.
Website: http://www.umuc.edu/grad/dm/dm_home.shtml.

University of Maryland University College, Graduate School of Management and Technology, Program in Business Administration, Adelphi, MD 20783. Offers MBA, Certificate. *Accreditation:* AACSB. Part-time and evening/weekend programs available. Postbaccalaureate distance learning degree programs offered (no on-campus study). *Students:* 1,154 full-time (622 women), 863 part-time (495 women); includes 1,163 minority (870 Black or African American, non-Hispanic/Latino; 10 American Indian or Alaska Native, non-Hispanic/Latino; 117 Asian, non-Hispanic/Latino; 117 Hispanic/Latino; 5 Native Hawaiian or other Pacific Islander, non-Hispanic/Latino; 44 Two or more races, non-Hispanic/Latino), 30 international. Average age 35. 880 applicants, 100% accepted, 335 enrolled. In 2013, 1,314 master's, 13 other advanced degrees awarded. *Degree requirements:* For master's, thesis or alternative, capstone course. *Application deadline:* Applications are processed on a rolling basis. Application fee: $50. Electronic applications accepted. *Financial support:* Federal Work-Study and scholarships/grants available. Support available to part-time students. Financial award application deadline: 6/1; financial award applicants required to submit FAFSA. *Unit head:* Anita Baker, Program Director, 240-684-2960, Fax: 240-684-2960, E-mail: anita.baker@umuc.edu. *Application contact:* Coordinator, Graduate Admissions, 800-888-8682, Fax: 240-684-2151, E-mail: newgrad@umuc.edu.
Website: http://www.umuc.edu/grad/mba.

University of Maryland University College, Graduate School of Management and Technology, Program in Management, Adelphi, MD 20783. Offers MS, Certificate. Program offered evenings and weekends only. Part-time programs available. Postbaccalaureate distance learning degree programs offered (no on-campus study). *Students:* 69 full-time (42 women), 3,448 part-time (2,291 women); includes 2,081 minority (1,654 Black or African American, non-Hispanic/Latino; 7 American Indian or Alaska Native, non-Hispanic/Latino; 124 Asian, non-Hispanic/Latino; 197 Hispanic/Latino; 11 Native Hawaiian or other Pacific Islander, non-Hispanic/Latino; 88 Two or more races, non-Hispanic/Latino), 33 international. Average age 36. 977 applicants, 100% accepted, 594 enrolled. In 2013, 839 master's, 233 other advanced degrees awarded. *Degree requirements:* For master's, thesis or alternative. *Application deadline:* Applications are processed on a rolling basis. Application fee: $50. Electronic applications accepted. *Financial support:* Federal Work-Study and scholarships/grants available. Support available to part-time students. Financial award application deadline: 6/1; financial award applicants required to submit FAFSA. *Unit head:* Al Raider, Chair, 240-684-2400, Fax: 240-684-2401, E-mail: al.raider@umuc.edu. *Application contact:* Coordinator, Graduate Admissions, 888-888-8682, Fax: 240-684-2151, E-mail: newgrad@umuc.edu.
Website: http://www.umuc.edu/grad/msm/msm_home.shtml.

University of Mary Washington, College of Business, Fredericksburg, VA 22401-5300. Offers business administration (MBA); management information systems (MSMIS). Part-time and evening/weekend programs available. *Faculty:* 12 full-time (4 women), 5 part-time/adjunct (0 women). *Students:* 45 full-time (19 women), 125 part-time (64 women); includes 48 minority (30 Black or African American, non-Hispanic/Latino; 2 American Indian or Alaska Native, non-Hispanic/Latino; 8 Asian, non-Hispanic/Latino; 8 Hispanic/Latino), 47 international. Average age 36. 51 applicants, 73% accepted, 21 enrolled. In 2013, 104 master's awarded. *Entrance requirements:* For master's, GMAT or GRE, minimum GPA of 3.0. Additional exam requirements/recommendations for international students: Required—TOEFL (minimum score 570 paper-based; 88 iBT), IELTS (minimum score 6.5). *Application deadline:* For fall admission, 6/1 priority date for domestic students, 6/1 for international students; for spring admission, 10/1 for domestic and international students. Application fee: $50. Electronic applications accepted. *Expenses: Tuition, area resident:* Part-time $444 per credit hour. Tuition, state resident: part-time $444 per credit hour. Tuition, nonresident: part-time $883 per credit hour. *Required fees:* $30 per semester. *Financial support:* Available to part-time students. Application deadline: 3/15; applicants required to submit FAFSA. *Faculty research:* Power laws/CEO compensation, sustainable competitive advantage, resistance to security implementation, profiling sustainable curriculums, perceived customer value. *Unit head:* Dr. Lynne D. Richardson, Dean, 540-654-2470, Fax: 540-654-2430, E-mail: lynne.richardson@umw.edu. *Application contact:* Dre N. Anthes, Associate Dean of Admissions, 540-286-8086, Fax: 540-286-8085, E-mail: aanthes@umw.edu.
Website: http://business.umw.edu/.

University of Massachusetts Amherst, Graduate School, Interdisciplinary Programs, Dual Degree Program in Business Administration and Civil Engineering, Amherst, MA 01003. Offers MSCE/MBA. Part-time programs available. *Entrance requirements:* Additional exam requirements/recommendations for international students: Required—TOEFL (minimum score 600 paper-based; 100 iBT), IELTS (minimum score 7). *Application deadline:* For fall admission, 1/2 for domestic and international students. Applications are processed on a rolling basis. Application fee: $75. Electronic applications accepted. *Financial support:* Career-related internships or fieldwork, Federal Work-Study, scholarships/grants, traineeships, health care benefits, tuition waivers (full), and unspecified assistantships available. Support available to part-time students. Financial award application deadline: 1/2. *Unit head:* Dr. Sanjay Arwade, Graduate Program Director, 413-545-0686, Fax: 413-545-2840, E-mail: muriel@ecs.umass.edu. *Application contact:* Lindsay DeSantis, Supervisor of Admissions, 413-545-0722, Fax: 413-577-0010, E-mail: gradadm@grad.umass.edu.
Website: http://www-new.ecs.umass.edu/dual-degrees.

University of Massachusetts Amherst, Graduate School, Interdisciplinary Programs, Dual Degree Program in Business Administration and Environmental Engineering, Amherst, MA 01003. Offers MBA/MS. Part-time programs available. *Entrance requirements:* Additional exam requirements/recommendations for international students: Required—TOEFL (minimum score 600 paper-based; 100 iBT), IELTS (minimum score 7). *Application deadline:* For fall admission, 1/2 for domestic and international students. Applications are processed on a rolling basis. Application fee: $75. Electronic applications accepted. *Financial support:* Career-related internships or fieldwork, Federal Work-Study, scholarships/grants, traineeships, health care benefits, tuition waivers (full), and unspecified assistantships available. Support available to part-time students. Financial award application deadline: 1/2. *Unit head:* Dr. Sanjay Arwade, Graduate Program Director, 413-545-0686, Fax: 413-545-2840. *Application contact:* Lindsay DeSantis, Supervisor of Admissions, 413-545-0722, Fax: 413-577-0010, E-mail: gradadm@grad.umass.edu.
Website: http://www-new.ecs.umass.edu/dual-degrees.

University of Massachusetts Amherst, Graduate School, Interdisciplinary Programs, Dual Degree Program in Business Administration and Public Policy and Administration, Amherst, MA 01003. Offers MPPA/MBA. *Accreditation:* AACSB. Part-time programs available. *Students:* 6 full-time (4 women). Average age 28. 6 applicants, 83% accepted, 4 enrolled. *Entrance requirements:* Additional exam requirements/recommendations for international students: Required—TOEFL (minimum score 600 paper-based; 100 iBT), IELTS (minimum score 7). *Application deadline:* For fall admission, 2/1 for domestic and international students. Applications are processed on a rolling basis. Application fee: $75. Electronic applications accepted. *Financial support:* Career-related internships or fieldwork, Federal Work-Study, scholarships/grants, traineeships, health care benefits, tuition waivers (full), and unspecified assistantships available. Support available to part-time students. Financial award application deadline: 2/1. *Unit head:* Dr. Kathryn McDermott, Graduate Program Director, 413-545-3956, Fax: 413-545-1108, E-mail: szoller@pubpol.umass.edu. *Application contact:* Lindsay DeSantis, Supervisor of Admissions, 413-545-0722, Fax: 413-577-0010, E-mail: gradadm@grad.umass.edu.
Website: http://www.masspolicy.org/acad_mppa_mba.html.

University of Massachusetts Amherst, Graduate School, Interdisciplinary Programs, Dual Degree Program in Business Administration and Sport Management, Amherst, MA 01003. Offers MBA/MS. Part-time programs available. *Students:* 22 full-time (9 women), 1 part-time (0 women); includes 1 minority (Two or more races, non-Hispanic/Latino), 7 international. Average age 25. 60 applicants, 30% accepted, 13 enrolled. *Entrance requirements:* Additional exam requirements/recommendations for international students: Required—TOEFL (minimum score 600 paper-based; 100 iBT), IELTS (minimum score 7). *Application deadline:* For fall admission, 2/1 for domestic and international students; for spring admission, 10/1 for domestic and international students. Applications are processed on a rolling basis. Application fee: $75. Electronic applications accepted. *Financial support:* Career-related internships or fieldwork, Federal Work-Study, scholarships/grants, traineeships, health care benefits, tuition waivers (full), and unspecified assistantships available. Support available to part-time students. Financial award application deadline: 2/1. *Unit head:* Dr. Stephen McKelvey, Graduate Program Director, 413-545-0471, Fax: 413-545-0642. *Application contact:* Lindsay DeSantis, Supervisor of Admissions, 413-545-0722, Fax: 413-577-0010, E-mail: gradadm@grad.umass.edu.
Website: http://www.isenberg.umass.edu/sportmgt/Dual_Degree/.

University of Massachusetts Amherst, Graduate School, Isenberg School of Management, Program in Management, Amherst, MA 01003. Offers accounting (PhD); business administration (MBA); entrepreneurship (MBA); finance (MBA, PhD); healthcare administration (MBA); hospitality and tourism management (PhD); management science (PhD); marketing (MBA, PhD); organization studies (PhD); sport management (PhD); strategic management (PhD); MBA/MS. *Accreditation:* AACSB. Part-time and evening/weekend programs available. Postbaccalaureate distance learning degree programs offered. *Faculty:* 68 full-time (14 women). *Students:* 140 full-time (59 women), 1,127 part-time (319 women); includes 229 minority (24 Black or African American, non-Hispanic/Latino; 2 American Indian or Alaska Native, non-Hispanic/Latino; 135 Asian, non-Hispanic/Latino; 51 Hispanic/Latino; 6 Native Hawaiian or other Pacific Islander, non-Hispanic/Latino; 11 Two or more races, non-Hispanic/Latino), 131 international. Average age 36. 828 applicants, 56% accepted, 351 enrolled. In 2013, 361 master's, 12 doctorates awarded. Terminal master's awarded for partial completion of doctoral program. *Degree requirements:* For doctorate, comprehensive exam, thesis/dissertation. *Entrance requirements:* For master's and doctorate, GMAT or GRE General Test. Additional exam requirements/recommendations for international students: Required—TOEFL (minimum score 550 paper-based; 80 iBT), IELTS (minimum score 6.5). *Application deadline:* For fall admission, 1/20 for domestic and international students. Applications are processed on a rolling basis. Application fee: $75. Electronic applications accepted. *Financial support:* Fellowships with full and partial tuition reimbursements, research assistantships with full and partial tuition reimbursements, teaching assistantships with full and partial tuition reimbursements, career-related internships or fieldwork, Federal Work-Study, scholarships/grants, traineeships, health care benefits, tuition waivers (full and partial), and unspecified assistantships available. Support available to part-time students. Financial award application deadline: 1/20; financial award applicants required to submit FAFSA. *Unit head:* Dr. John Wells, Chair, 413-545-7609, Fax: 413-577-2234. *Application contact:* Lindsay DeSantis, Supervisor of Admissions, 413-545-0722, Fax: 413-577-0010, E-mail: gradadm@grad.umass.edu.
Website: http://www.isenberg.umass.edu/.

University of Massachusetts Boston, Office of Graduate Studies, College of Management, Program in Business Administration, Boston, MA 02125-3393. Offers MBA, MS/MBA. *Accreditation:* AACSB. Part-time and evening/weekend programs available. *Degree requirements:* For master's, capstone project. *Entrance requirements:* For master's, GMAT, minimum GPA of 3.0. *Faculty research:* International finance, human resource management, management information systems, investment and corporate finance, international marketing.

University of Massachusetts Dartmouth, Graduate School, Charlton College of Business, Program in Business Administration, North Dartmouth, MA 02747-2300. Offers accounting (Postbaccalaureate Certificate); business administration (MBA); business foundations (Graduate Certificate); finance (Postbaccalaureate Certificate); international business (Graduate Certificate); management (Postbaccalaureate

Certificate); marketing (Postbaccalaureate Certificate); organizational leadership (Graduate Certificate); supply chain management (Postbaccalaureate Certificate). *Accreditation:* AACSB. Part-time programs available. Postbaccalaureate distance learning degree programs offered (no on-campus study). *Faculty:* 36 full-time (12 women), 27 part-time/adjunct (10 women). *Students:* 154 full-time (73 women), 120 part-time (55 women); includes 28 minority (2 Black or African American, non-Hispanic/Latino; 1 American Indian or Alaska Native, non-Hispanic/Latino; 6 Asian, non-Hispanic/Latino; 11 Hispanic/Latino; 8 Two or more races, non-Hispanic/Latino), 129 international. Average age 29. 204 applicants, 82% accepted, 112 enrolled. In 2013, 71 master's, 15 other advanced degrees awarded. *Degree requirements:* For master's, portfolio of MBA course work. *Entrance requirements:* For master's, GMAT, statement of purpose (minimum of 300 words), resume, 2 letters of recommendation, official transcripts; for other advanced degree, statement of purpose (minimum of 300 words), resume, official transcripts. Additional exam requirements/recommendations for international students: Required—TOEFL (minimum score 500 paper-based; 72 iBT), IELTS (minimum score 6). *Application deadline:* For fall admission, 8/1 priority date for domestic students, 5/1 priority date for international students; for spring admission, 1/1 priority date for domestic students, 10/1 priority date for international students. Applications are processed on a rolling basis. Application fee: $60. Electronic applications accepted. *Expenses:* Tuition, state resident: full-time $2071; part-time $86.29 per credit. Tuition, nonresident: full-time $8099; part-time $337.46 per credit. Tuition and fees vary according to course load and reciprocity agreements. *Financial support:* Federal Work-Study and unspecified assistantships available. Support available to part-time students. Financial award application deadline: 3/1; financial award applicants required to submit FAFSA. *Faculty research:* E-commerce, managing diversity, agile manufacturing, green business, activity-based management, build-to-order supply chain management. *Total annual research expenditures:* $330,000. *Unit head:* Toby Stapleton, Assistant Dean for Graduate Studies, 508-999-8543, Fax: 508-999-8646, E-mail: tstapleton@umassd.edu. *Application contact:* Steven Briggs, Director of Marketing and Recruitment for Graduate Studies, 508-999-8604, Fax: 508-999-8183, E-mail: graduate@umassd.edu.
Website: http://www.umassd.edu/charlton/.

University of Massachusetts Lowell, Manning School of Business, Lowell, MA 01854-2881. Offers accounting (MSA); business administration (MBA, PhD); financial management (Graduate Certificate); foundations of business (Graduate Certificate); healthcare innovation and entrepreneurship (MS); innovation and technological entrepreneurship (MS); new venture creation (Graduate Certificate); supply chain and operations management (Graduate Certificate). *Accreditation:* AACSB. Part-time and evening/weekend programs available. *Entrance requirements:* For master's, GMAT.

University of Memphis, Graduate School, Fogelman College of Business and Economics, Program in Business Administration, Memphis, TN 38152. Offers accounting (MBA, PhD); economics (MBA, PhD); executive business administration (MBA); finance (PhD); finance, insurance, and real estate (MBA, MS); international business administration (IMBA); management (MBA, MS, PhD); management information systems (MBA, MS, PhD); management science (MBA); marketing (MBA, MS); marketing and supply chain management (PhD); real estate development (MS); JD/MBA. *Accreditation:* AACSB. *Faculty:* 44 full-time (9 women), 5 part-time/adjunct (0 women). *Students:* 238 full-time (101 women), 315 part-time (113 women); includes 146 minority (80 Black or African American, non-Hispanic/Latino; 1 American Indian or Alaska Native, non-Hispanic/Latino; 46 Asian, non-Hispanic/Latino; 13 Hispanic/Latino; 2 Native Hawaiian or other Pacific Islander, non-Hispanic/Latino; 4 Two or more races, non-Hispanic/Latino), 104 international. Average age 32. 343 applicants, 62% accepted, 102 enrolled. In 2013, 140 master's, 17 doctorates awarded. *Degree requirements:* For master's, comprehensive exam; for doctorate, comprehensive exam, thesis/dissertation. *Entrance requirements:* For master's, GMAT, resume; for doctorate, GMAT, interview, minimum GPA of 3.4, resume, letter of recommendation. Additional exam requirements/recommendations for international students: Required—TOEFL (minimum score 550 paper-based). *Application deadline:* For fall admission, 8/1 for domestic students; for spring admission, 12/1 for domestic students. Application fee: $35 ($60 for international students). *Financial support:* In 2013–14, 164 students received support. Research assistantships with full tuition reimbursements available, teaching assistantships with full tuition reimbursements available, career-related internships or fieldwork, Federal Work-Study, scholarships/grants, and unspecified assistantships available. Financial award application deadline: 2/15; financial award applicants required to submit FAFSA. *Faculty research:* Competitive business strategy, finance microstructures, supply chain management innovations, health care economics, litigation risks and corporate audits. *Unit head:* Rajiv Grover, Dean, 901-678-3759, E-mail: rgrover@memphis.edu. *Application contact:* Dr. Carol V. Danehower, Associate Dean, 901-678-5402, Fax: 901-678-3579, E-mail: fcbegp@memphis.edu.
Website: http://www.memphis.edu/fcbe/grad_programs.php.

University of Miami, Graduate School, School of Business Administration, Program in Business Administration, Coral Gables, FL 33124. Offers accounting (MBA); computer information systems (MBA); executive and professional (MBA), including international business, management; finance (MBA); international business (MBA); management (MBA); management science (MBA); marketing (MBA); professional management (MSPM); JD/MBA; MBA/MSIE. *Accreditation:* AACSB. Evening/weekend programs available. *Degree requirements:* For master's, comprehensive exam. *Entrance requirements:* For master's, GMAT. Additional exam requirements/recommendations for international students: Required—TOEFL (minimum score 550 paper-based; 59 iBT). Electronic applications accepted. *Faculty research:* Leadership, e-commerce, supply chain management.

University of Michigan, Ross School of Business, Ann Arbor, MI 48109-1234. Offers accounting (M Acc); business (MBA); business administration (PhD); supply chain management (MSCM); JD/MBA; MBA/M Arch; MBA/M Eng; MBA/MA; MBA/MEM; MBA/MHSA; MBA/MM; MBA/MPP; MBA/MS; MBA/MSE; MBA/MSI; MBA/MSW; MBA/MUP; MD/MBA; MHSA/MBA. Part-time and evening/weekend programs available. *Degree requirements:* For doctorate, comprehensive exam, thesis/dissertation, oral defense of dissertation, preliminary exam. *Entrance requirements:* For master's, GMAT or GRE, completion of equivalent of four-year U.S. bachelor's degree, two letters of recommendation, essays, resume; for doctorate, GMAT or GRE. Additional exam requirements/recommendations for international students: Required—TOEFL (minimum score 600 paper-based; 100 iBT). Electronic applications accepted. Tuition and fees vary according to course level, course load, degree level, program and student level. *Faculty research:* Finance and accounting, marketing, technology and operations management, corporate strategy, management and organizations.

University of Michigan–Dearborn, College of Business, Dearborn, MI 48128-1491. Offers accounting (MBA, MS); business analytics (MS); finance (MBA, MS); human resource management (MBA); information systems (MS); international business (MBA); investment (MBA); management (MBA); management information systems (MBA); marketing (MBA); supply chain management (MBA, MS); taxation (MBA); MBA/MHSA; MBA/MSE; MBA/MSF; MBA/MSIS; MBA/MSSCM; MSF/MSA. *Accreditation:* AACSB. Part-time and evening/weekend programs available. Postbaccalaureate distance learning degree programs offered (no on-campus study). *Faculty:* 24 full-time (8 women), 5 part-time/adjunct (2 women). *Students:* 82 full-time (31 women), 323 part-time (116 women); includes 72 minority (17 Black or African American, non-Hispanic/Latino; 2 American Indian or Alaska Native, non-Hispanic/Latino; 30 Asian, non-Hispanic/Latino; 15 Hispanic/Latino; 8 Two or more races, non-Hispanic/Latino), 65 international. Average age 32. 290 applicants, 44% accepted, 99 enrolled. In 2013, 143 master's awarded. *Entrance requirements:* For master's, GMAT or GRE, pre-calculus or finite mathematics; 18 credits of accounting course work beyond introductory courses (MS in accounting). Additional exam requirements/recommendations for international students: Required—TOEFL (minimum score 560 paper-based; 84 iBT), IELTS. *Application deadline:* For fall admission, 8/1 priority date for domestic students, 5/1 priority date for international students; for winter admission, 12/1 priority date for domestic students, 9/1 priority date for international students; for spring admission, 4/1 priority date for domestic students, 1/1 priority date for international students. Applications are processed on a rolling basis. Application fee: $60. Electronic applications accepted. *Expenses:* Contact institution. *Financial support:* Career-related internships or fieldwork, Federal Work-Study, and scholarships/grants available. Support available to part-time students. Financial award application deadline: 9/1; financial award applicants required to submit FAFSA. *Faculty research:* Cultural diversity, buyer-supplier relations, error detection in data, economic evolution. *Unit head:* Dr. Raju Balakrishnan, Dean, 313-593-5248, Fax: 313-271-9835, E-mail: rajub@umich.edu. *Application contact:* Joan Doherty, Academic Advisor/Counselor, 313-593-5460, Fax: 313-271-9838, E-mail: umd-gradbusiness@umich.edu.
Website: http://www.cob.umd.umich.edu.

University of Michigan–Flint, School of Management, Flint, MI 48502-1950. Offers accounting (MBA, MSA); business (Graduate Certificate); computer information systems (MBA); finance (MBA); health care management (MBA); international business (MBA); lean manufacturing (MBA); marketing (MBA); organizational leadership (MBA). *Accreditation:* AACSB. Part-time and evening/weekend programs available. Postbaccalaureate distance learning degree programs offered (minimal on-campus study). *Faculty:* 13 full-time (3 women), 4 part-time/adjunct (0 women). *Students:* 19 full-time (6 women), 234 part-time (72 women); includes 50 minority (21 Black or African American, non-Hispanic/Latino; 5 American Indian or Alaska Native, non-Hispanic/Latino; 12 Asian, non-Hispanic/Latino; 5 Hispanic/Latino; 7 Two or more races, non-Hispanic/Latino), 30 international. Average age 32. 195 applicants, 56% accepted, 88 enrolled. In 2013, 73 master's awarded. *Degree requirements:* For master's, thesis or alternative. *Entrance requirements:* For master's, GMAT or GRE, minimum GPA of 3.0. Additional exam requirements/recommendations for international students: Required—TOEFL (minimum score 560 paper-based; 84 iBT), IELTS (minimum score 6.5). *Application deadline:* For fall admission, 8/1 for domestic students, 5/1 for international students; for winter admission, 11/1 for domestic students, 9/1 for international students; for spring admission, 2/15 for domestic students, 1/15 for international students. Applications are processed on a rolling basis. Application fee: $55. Electronic applications accepted. *Financial support:* Federal Work-Study, scholarships/grants, and unspecified assistantships available. Support available to part-time students. Financial award application deadline: 3/1; financial award applicants required to submit FAFSA. *Unit head:* Dr. Scott Johnson, Dean, School of Management, 810-762-3164, Fax: 810-237-6685, E-mail: scotjohn@umflint.edu. *Application contact:* Jeremiah Cook, Marketing Communications Specialist, 810-424-5583, Fax: 810-766-6789, E-mail: jecook@umflint.edu.
Website: http://www.umflint.edu/som/.

University of Minnesota, Duluth, Graduate School, Labovitz School of Business and Economics, Program in Business Administration, Duluth, MN 55812-2496. Offers MBA. *Accreditation:* AACSB. Part-time and evening/weekend programs available. *Entrance requirements:* For master's, GMAT, minimum GPA of 3.0; course work in accounting, business administration, and economics. Additional exam requirements/recommendations for international students: Required—TOEFL (minimum score 550 paper-based; 79 iBT). *Expenses:* Contact institution. *Faculty research:* Regional economic analysis, marketing, management, human resources, organizational behavior.

University of Minnesota, Twin Cities Campus, Carlson School of Management, Minneapolis, MN 55455. Offers EMBA, M Acc, MA, MBA, MBT, PhD, JD/MBA, MBA/MPP, MD/MBA, MHA/MBA, Pharm D/MBA. *Accreditation:* AACSB. Part-time and evening/weekend programs available. *Faculty:* 137 full-time (42 women), 19 part-time/adjunct (4 women). *Students:* 533 full-time (220 women), 1,327 part-time (467 women); includes 187 minority (32 Black or African American, non-Hispanic/Latino; 5 American Indian or Alaska Native, non-Hispanic/Latino; 121 Asian, non-Hispanic/Latino; 17 Hispanic/Latino; 1 Native Hawaiian or other Pacific Islander, non-Hispanic/Latino; 11 Two or more races, non-Hispanic/Latino), 272 international. Average age 28. In 2013, 634 master's, 12 doctorates awarded. Terminal master's awarded for partial completion of doctoral program. *Degree requirements:* For doctorate, comprehensive exam, thesis/dissertation. Electronic applications accepted. *Expenses:* Contact institution. *Financial support:* Fellowships with full and partial tuition reimbursements, research assistantships with full tuition reimbursements, teaching assistantships with full and partial tuition reimbursements, career-related internships or fieldwork, Federal Work-Study, institutionally sponsored loans, scholarships/grants, health care benefits, tuition waivers (full and partial), and unspecified assistantships available. Support available to part-time students. Financial award application deadline: 4/1; financial award applicants required to submit FAFSA. *Faculty research:* Finance and accounting: financial reporting, asset pricing models and corporate finance; information and decision sciences: on-line auctions, information transparency and recommender systems; marketing: psychological influences on consumer behavior, brand equity, pricing and marketing channels; operations: lean manufacturing, quality management and global supply chains; strategic management and organization: global strategy, networks, entrepreneurship and innovation, sustainability. *Unit head:* Prof. George John, Dean, 612-626-1402, Fax: 612-624-6374, E-mail: johnx001@umn.edu. *Application contact:* Information Contact, 612-625-3014, Fax: 612-625-6002, E-mail: gsquest@umn.edu.
Website: http://www.carlsonschool.umn.edu.

University of Mississippi, Graduate School, School of Business Administration, Oxford, MS 38677. Offers business administration (MBA, PhD); systems management (MS); JD/MBA. *Accreditation:* AACSB. *Faculty:* 53 full-time (16 women), 5 part-time/adjunct (1 woman). *Students:* 87 full-time (34 women), 105 part-time (37 women); includes 23 minority (7 Black or African American, non-Hispanic/Latino; 4 Asian, non-Hispanic/Latino; 5 Hispanic/Latino; 1 Native Hawaiian or other Pacific Islander, non-Hispanic/Latino; 6 Two or more races, non-Hispanic/Latino), 15 international. In 2013, 71 master's, 7 doctorates awarded. *Degree requirements:* For doctorate, thesis/dissertation. *Entrance requirements:* For master's, GMAT, minimum GPA of 3.0; for doctorate, GMAT. Additional exam requirements/recommendations for international students: Required—TOEFL. *Application deadline:* For fall admission, 2/1 for domestic students; for spring admission, 10/1 for domestic students. Applications are processed on a rolling basis. Application fee: $40. Electronic applications accepted. *Financial support:* Fellowships, career-related internships or fieldwork, scholarships/grants, tuition waivers (full), and unspecified assistantships available. Financial award application deadline: 3/1; financial award applicants required to submit FAFSA. *Unit head:* Dr. Ken Cyree, Dean, 662-915-5820, Fax: 662-915-5821, E-mail: info@

bus.olemiss.edu. *Application contact:* Dr. Christy M. Wyandt, Associate Dean, 662-915-7474, Fax: 662-915-7577, E-mail: cwyandt@olemiss.edu.
Website: http://www.olemissbusiness.com/.

University of Missouri, Graduate School, Robert J. Trulaske, Sr. College of Business, Program in Business Administration, Columbia, MO 65211. Offers business administration (MBA); executive (MBA); finance (PhD); management (PhD); marketing (PhD); MBA/JD; MBA/MHA; MBA/MSIE. *Accreditation:* AACSB. *Faculty:* 42 full-time (9 women), 4 part-time/adjunct (2 women). *Students:* 208 full-time (69 women), 16 part-time (6 women); includes 9 minority (2 Black or African American, non-Hispanic/Latino; 1 Asian, non-Hispanic/Latino; 4 Hispanic/Latino; 2 Two or more races, non-Hispanic/Latino), 63 international. Average age 29. 435 applicants, 30% accepted, 86 enrolled. In 2013, 101 master's, 6 doctorates awarded. *Degree requirements:* For doctorate, thesis/dissertation. *Entrance requirements:* For master's and doctorate, GMAT, minimum GPA of 3.0. Additional exam requirements/recommendations for international students: Required—TOEFL (minimum score 500 paper-based; 61 iBT). *Application deadline:* For fall admission, 2/1 priority date for domestic and international students. Applications are processed on a rolling basis. Application fee: $55 ($75 for international students). Electronic applications accepted. *Financial support:* Fellowships with full and partial tuition reimbursements, research assistantships with full and partial tuition reimbursements, teaching assistantships with full and partial tuition reimbursements, institutionally sponsored loans, scholarships/grants, health care benefits, and unspecified assistantships available. Support available to part-time students. *Faculty research:* International relations, management, finance, marketing, entrepreneurship, organization and process theory, mentoring and networking processes, capital market regulation, corporate governance, bankruptcy. *Unit head:* Joan T.A. Gabel, Dean, 573-882-6688, E-mail: gabelj@missouri.edu. *Application contact:* Jan Curry, Administrative Assistant, 573-882-2750, E-mail: curryja@missouri.edu.
Website: http://business.missouri.edu/.

University of Missouri–Kansas City, Henry W. Bloch School of Management, Kansas City, MO 64110-2499. Offers accounting (MS); business administration (MBA); entrepreneurial real estate (MERE); entrepreneurship and innovation (PhD); finance (MS); public affairs (MPA, PhD); JD/MBA; LL M/MPA. PhD (interdisciplinary) offered through the School of Graduate Studies. *Accreditation:* AACSB; NASPAA. Part-time and evening/weekend programs available. *Faculty:* 57 full-time (15 women), 32 part-time/adjunct (10 women). *Students:* 309 full-time (151 women), 377 part-time (163 women); includes 100 minority (39 Black or African American, non-Hispanic/Latino; 2 American Indian or Alaska Native, non-Hispanic/Latino; 27 Asian, non-Hispanic/Latino; 24 Hispanic/Latino; 1 Native Hawaiian or other Pacific Islander, non-Hispanic/Latino; 7 Two or more races, non-Hispanic/Latino), 93 international. Average age 30. 489 applicants, 54% accepted, 252 enrolled. In 2013, 252 master's, 1 doctorate awarded. Terminal master's awarded for partial completion of doctoral program. *Entrance requirements:* For master's, GMAT, GRE, 2 essays, 2 references, support of employer; for doctorate, GRE, minimum GPA of 3.0. Additional exam requirements/recommendations for international students: Required—TOEFL (minimum score 550 paper-based; 80 iBT). *Application deadline:* For fall admission, 5/1 priority date for domestic and international students; for spring admission, 10/1 priority date for domestic and international students. Applications are processed on a rolling basis. Application fee: $45 ($50 for international students). Electronic applications accepted. *Expenses:* Tuition, state resident: full-time $6073; part-time $337.40 per credit hour. Tuition, nonresident: full-time $15,680; part-time $871.10 per credit hour. *Required fees:* $97.59 per credit hour. Full-time tuition and fees vary according to program. *Financial support:* In 2013–14, 38 research assistantships with partial tuition reimbursements (averaging $10,499 per year), 6 teaching assistantships with partial tuition reimbursements (averaging $13,380 per year) were awarded; career-related internships or fieldwork, Federal Work-Study, institutionally sponsored loans, scholarships/grants, tuition waivers (full and partial), and unspecified assistantships also available. Support available to part-time students. Financial award application deadline: 3/1; financial award applicants required to submit FAFSA. *Faculty research:* Entrepreneurship, finance, non-profit, risk management. *Unit head:* Dr. David Donnelly, Dean, 816-235-1333, Fax: 816-235-2206, E-mail: donnellyd@umkc.edu. *Application contact:* 816-235-1111, E-mail: admit@umkc.edu.
Website: http://www.bloch.umkc.edu.

University of Missouri–St. Louis, College of Business Administration, Program in Business Administration, St. Louis, MO 63121. Offers accounting (MBA); business administration (Certificate); business intelligence (Certificate); finance (MBA); human resource management (Certificate); information systems (MBA); logistics and supply chain management (MBA, PhD, Certificate); marketing (MBA); marketing management (Certificate); operations management (MBA). *Accreditation:* AACSB. Part-time and evening/weekend programs available. *Faculty:* 30 full-time (5 women), 20 part-time/adjunct (8 women). *Students:* 114 full-time (51 women), 269 part-time (100 women); includes 43 minority (16 Black or African American, non-Hispanic/Latino; 14 Asian, non-Hispanic/Latino; 11 Hispanic/Latino; 1 Native Hawaiian or other Pacific Islander, non-Hispanic/Latino; 1 Two or more races, non-Hispanic/Latino), 56 international. Average age 31. 153 applicants, 91% accepted, 110 enrolled. In 2013, 136 master's, 7 other advanced degrees awarded. *Degree requirements:* For doctorate, thesis/dissertation. *Entrance requirements:* For master's, GMAT, 2 letters of recommendation. Additional exam requirements/recommendations for international students: Recommended—TOEFL (minimum score 550 paper-based; 79 iBT), IELTS (minimum score 6.5). *Application deadline:* For fall admission, 7/1 for domestic and international students; for spring admission, 12/1 for domestic and international students. Applications are processed on a rolling basis. Application fee: $50 ($40 for international students). Electronic applications accepted. *Expenses:* Tuition, state resident: full-time $7364; part-time $409.10 per credit hour. Tuition, nonresident: full-time $19,162; part-time $1008.50 per credit hour. *Financial support:* In 2013–14, 14 research assistantships with full and partial tuition reimbursements (averaging $5,625 per year), 6 teaching assistantships with full and partial tuition reimbursements (averaging $9,403 per year) were awarded; career-related internships or fieldwork, Federal Work-Study, and institutionally sponsored loans also available. Support available to part-time students. Financial award application deadline: 4/1; financial award applicants required to submit FAFSA. *Faculty research:* Human resources, strategic management, marketing strategy, consumer behavior product development, advertising. *Unit head:* Francesca Ferrari, Assistant Director, 314-516-5885, Fax: 314-516-6420, E-mail: mba@umsl.edu. *Application contact:* 314-516-5458, Fax: 314-516-6996, E-mail: gradadm@umsl.edu.
Website: http://mba.umsl.edu/Degree%20Programs/index.html.

University of Missouri–St. Louis, Graduate School, Program in Public Policy Administration, St. Louis, MO 63121. Offers local government management (MPPA, Certificate); managing human resources and organization (MPPA); nonprofit organization management (MPPA); nonprofit organization management and leadership (Certificate); policy research and analysis (MPPA). *Accreditation:* NASPAA. Part-time and evening/weekend programs available. *Faculty:* 9 full-time (4 women), 13 part-time/adjunct (9 women). *Students:* 19 full-time (12 women), 59 part-time (36 women); includes 20 minority (17 Black or African American, non-Hispanic/Latino; 1 Asian, non-Hispanic/Latino; 1 Hispanic/Latino; 1 Two or more races, non-Hispanic/Latino), 4 international. Average age 33. 39 applicants, 74% accepted, 16 enrolled. In 2013, 25 master's, 27 Certificates awarded. *Degree requirements:* For master's, exit project. *Entrance requirements:* For master's, 3 letters of recommendation. Additional exam requirements/recommendations for international students: Recommended—TOEFL (minimum score 550 paper-based), IELTS (minimum score 6.5). *Application deadline:* For fall admission, 7/1 priority date for domestic and international students; for spring admission, 12/1 priority date for domestic and international students. Applications are processed on a rolling basis. Application fee: $50 ($40 for international students). Electronic applications accepted. *Expenses:* Tuition, state resident: full-time $7364; part-time $409.10 per credit hour. Tuition, nonresident: full-time $19,162; part-time $1008.50 per credit hour. *Financial support:* In 2013–14, 2 research assistantships with full and partial tuition reimbursements (averaging $12,000 per year) were awarded; career-related internships or fieldwork also available. Financial award application deadline: 4/1; financial award applicants required to submit FAFSA. *Faculty research:* Urban policy, public finance, evaluation. *Unit head:* Dr. Deborah Balser, Director, 314-516-5145, Fax: 314-516-5210, E-mail: balserd@msx.umsl.edu. *Application contact:* 314-516-5458, Fax: 314-516-6996, E-mail: gradadm@umsl.edu.
Website: http://www.umsl.edu/divisions/graduate/mppa/.

University of Mobile, Graduate Programs, Program in Business Administration, Mobile, AL 36613. Offers MBA. *Accreditation:* ACBSP. Part-time and evening/weekend programs available. *Faculty:* 4 full-time (all women), 2 part-time/adjunct (0 women). *Students:* 2 full-time (1 woman), 15 part-time (9 women); includes 8 minority (all Black or African American, non-Hispanic/Latino), 1 international. Average age 36. 5 applicants, 100% accepted, 4 enrolled. In 2013, 11 master's awarded. *Degree requirements:* For master's, comprehensive exam. *Entrance requirements:* For master's, GMAT. Additional exam requirements/recommendations for international students: Required—TOEFL (minimum score 550 paper-based; 80 iBT). *Application deadline:* For fall admission, 8/3 for domestic students; for spring admission, 12/23 for domestic students. Applications are processed on a rolling basis. Application fee: $40 ($50 for international students). *Financial support:* Application deadline: 8/1. *Faculty research:* Management, personnel management, small business, diversity. *Unit head:* Dr. Jane Finley, Dean, School of Business, 251-442-2219, Fax: 251-442-2523, E-mail: jfinley@umobile.edu. *Application contact:* Danielle M. Riley, Administrative Assistant to Dean of Graduate Programs, 251-442-2270, Fax: 251-442-2523, E-mail: driley@umobile.edu.
Website: http://www.umobile.edu/.

The University of Montana, Graduate School, School of Business Administration, MBA Professional Program, Missoula, MT 59812-0002. Offers MBA, JD/MBA, MBA/Pharm D. *Accreditation:* AACSB. Part-time and evening/weekend programs available. Postbaccalaureate distance learning degree programs offered (minimal on-campus study). *Degree requirements:* For master's, thesis optional. *Entrance requirements:* For master's, GMAT. Additional exam requirements/recommendations for international students: Required—TOEFL. *Faculty research:* Information systems, research methods, international business, human resource management, marketing.

University of Montevallo, Stephens College of Business, Montevallo, AL 35115. Offers MBA. *Accreditation:* AACSB. Part-time and evening/weekend programs available. *Students:* 11 full-time (7 women), 33 part-time (13 women); includes 13 minority (12 Black or African American, non-Hispanic/Latino; 1 Two or more races, non-Hispanic/Latino). In 2013, 17 master's awarded. *Degree requirements:* For master's, comprehensive exam. *Entrance requirements:* Additional exam requirements/recommendations for international students: Required—TOEFL (minimum score 550 paper-based). *Application deadline:* For fall admission, 7/15 for domestic students; for spring admission, 11/15 for domestic students. Application fee: $25. *Unit head:* Dr. Stephen H. Craft, Dean, 205-665-6540. *Application contact:* Kevin Thornthwaite, Director, Graduate Admissions and Records, 205-665-6350, E-mail: graduate@montevallo.edu.
Website: http://www.montevallo.edu/scob/.

University of Nebraska at Kearney, Graduate Programs, College of Business and Technology, Department of Business, Kearney, NE 68849-0001. Offers accounting (MBA); generalist (MBA); human resources (MBA); human services (MBA); marketing (MBA). *Accreditation:* AACSB. Part-time and evening/weekend programs available. *Degree requirements:* For master's, thesis optional. *Entrance requirements:* For master's, GMAT or GRE, letters of recommendation, work history, letter of interest, resume. Additional exam requirements/recommendations for international students: Required—TOEFL (minimum score 550 paper-based; 79 iBT). Electronic applications accepted. *Faculty research:* Small business financial management, employment law, expert systems, international trade and marketing, environmental economics.

University of Nebraska at Omaha, Graduate Studies, College of Business Administration, Program in Business Administration, Omaha, NE 68182. Offers business administration (MBA); business for bioscientists (Certificate); executive business administration (EMBA). *Accreditation:* AACSB. Part-time and evening/weekend programs available. *Faculty:* 25 full-time (9 women). *Students:* 80 full-time (24 women), 227 part-time (80 women); includes 33 minority (5 Black or African American, non-Hispanic/Latino; 12 Asian, non-Hispanic/Latino; 13 Hispanic/Latino; 3 Two or more races, non-Hispanic/Latino), 28 international. Average age 30. 157 applicants, 59% accepted, 78 enrolled. In 2013, 101 master's, 1 other advanced degree awarded. *Degree requirements:* For master's, thesis (for some programs), capstone course. *Entrance requirements:* For master's, GMAT or GRE, minimum GPA of 3.0, official transcripts, resume; for Certificate, minimum GPA of 3.0, official transcripts, resume, letter of recommendation, statement of purpose. Additional exam requirements/recommendations for international students: Required—TOEFL, IELTS, PTE. *Application deadline:* For fall admission, 7/1 for domestic students; for spring admission, 11/1 for domestic students; for summer admission, 4/1 for domestic students. Applications are processed on a rolling basis. Application fee: $45. Electronic applications accepted. *Financial support:* In 2013–14, 11 students received support, including 9 research assistantships with tuition reimbursements available, 2 teaching assistantships with tuition reimbursements available; Federal Work-Study, institutionally sponsored loans, scholarships/grants, tuition waivers (partial), and unspecified assistantships also available. Support available to part-time students. Financial award application deadline: 3/1; financial award applicants required to submit FAFSA. *Application contact:* Lex Kaczmarek, Director, 402-554-2303, E-mail: graduate@unomaha.edu.

University of Nebraska–Lincoln, Graduate College, College of Business Administration, Interdepartmental Area of Business, Lincoln, NE 68588. Offers accountancy (PhD); business (MBA); finance (MA, PhD), including business; management (MA, PhD), including business; marketing (MA, PhD), including business; JD/MBA; M Arch/MBA. *Accreditation:* AACSB. Part-time programs available. Postbaccalaureate distance learning degree programs offered. *Degree requirements:* For doctorate, comprehensive exam, thesis/dissertation. *Entrance requirements:* For master's and doctorate, GMAT. Additional exam requirements/recommendations for international students: Required—TOEFL (minimum score 550 paper-based). Electronic applications accepted.

University of Nevada, Las Vegas, Graduate College, College of Business, Department of Management, Entrepreneurship and Technology, Las Vegas, NV 89154-6034. Offers management (Certificate); management information systems (MS, Certificate); new venture management (Certificate); MS/MS. Part-time and evening/weekend programs

available. *Faculty:* 9 full-time (1 woman), 1 (woman) part-time/adjunct. *Students:* 30 full-time (8 women), 19 part-time (6 women); includes 11 minority (2 Black or African American, non-Hispanic/Latino; 3 Asian, non-Hispanic/Latino; 4 Hispanic/Latino; 1 Native Hawaiian or other Pacific Islander, non-Hispanic/Latino; 1 Two or more races, non-Hispanic/Latino), 18 international. Average age 31. 55 applicants, 82% accepted, 19 enrolled. In 2013, 21 master's, 1 other advanced degree awarded. *Entrance requirements:* For master's and Certificate, GMAT or GRE. Additional exam requirements/recommendations for international students: Required—TOEFL (minimum score 550 paper-based; 80 iBT), IELTS (minimum score 7). *Application deadline:* For fall admission, 8/1 for domestic students, 5/1 for international students; for spring admission, 11/15 for domestic students, 10/1 for international students. Application fee: $60 ($95 for international students). Electronic applications accepted. *Expenses:* Tuition, state resident: full-time $4752; part-time $264 per credit. Tuition, nonresident: full-time $18,662; part-time $554.50 per credit. *International tuition:* $18,952 full-time. *Required fees:* $532; $12 per credit. $266 per semester. One-time fee: $35. Tuition and fees vary according to course load and program. *Financial support:* In 2013–14, 8 students received support, including 5 research assistantships with partial tuition reimbursements available (averaging $8,000 per year), 3 teaching assistantships with partial tuition reimbursements available (averaging $8,333 per year); institutionally sponsored loans, scholarships/grants, health care benefits, and unspecified assistantships also available. Financial award application deadline: 3/1. *Faculty research:* Decision-making, publish or perish, ethical issues in information systems, IT-enabled decision making, business ethics. *Unit head:* Alan Miller, Chair/Associate Professor, 702-895-1724, E-mail: alan.miller@unlv.edu. *Application contact:* Graduate College Admissions Evaluator, 702-895-3320, Fax: 702-895-4180, E-mail: gradcollege@unlv.edu.
Website: http://business.unlv.edu/met/.

University of Nevada, Las Vegas, Graduate College, College of Business, Program in Business Administration, Las Vegas, NV 89154-6031. Offers Exec MBA, MBA, DMD/MBA, MBA/JD, MBA/MS. *Accreditation:* AACSB. Part-time and evening/weekend programs available. *Faculty:* 16 full-time (3 women), 2 part-time/adjunct (1 woman). *Students:* 99 full-time (40 women), 65 part-time (21 women); includes 36 minority (7 Black or African American, non-Hispanic/Latino; 17 Asian, non-Hispanic/Latino; 5 Hispanic/Latino; 7 Two or more races, non-Hispanic/Latino), 17 international. Average age 31. 97 applicants, 69% accepted, 52 enrolled. In 2013, 83 master's awarded. *Entrance requirements:* For master's, GMAT. Additional exam requirements/recommendations for international students: Required—TOEFL (minimum score 550 paper-based; 80 iBT), IELTS (minimum score 7). *Application deadline:* For fall admission, 6/1 for domestic students, 5/1 for international students; for spring admission, 11/15 for domestic students, 10/1 for international students. Application fee: $60 ($95 for international students). Electronic applications accepted. *Expenses:* Contact institution. *Financial support:* In 2013–14, 13 students received support, including 3 research assistantships with partial tuition reimbursements available (averaging $10,417 per year), 10 teaching assistantships with partial tuition reimbursements available (averaging $8,500 per year); institutionally sponsored loans, scholarships/grants, health care benefits, and unspecified assistantships also available. Financial award application deadline: 3/1. *Faculty research:* Economic effects on wages, benefits and economic effects of risk, uncertainty; asymmetric information: adverse selection, moral hazard; business processes. *Unit head:* Keong Leong, Department Chair/Professor/Associate Dean, 702-895-3960, E-mail: keong.leong@unlv.edu. *Application contact:* Graduate College Admissions Evaluator, 702-895-3320, Fax: 702-895-4180, E-mail: gradcollege@unlv.edu.
Website: http://business.unlv.edu/mba/.

University of Nevada, Reno, Graduate School, College of Business Administration, Department of Business Administration, Reno, NV 89557. Offers MBA. *Accreditation:* AACSB. Part-time and evening/weekend programs available. Postbaccalaureate distance learning degree programs offered. *Entrance requirements:* For master's, GMAT, minimum GPA of 2.75. Additional exam requirements/recommendations for international students: Required—TOEFL (minimum score 500 paper-based; 61 iBT), IELTS (minimum score 6). Electronic applications accepted.

University of New Brunswick Fredericton, School of Graduate Studies, Faculty of Business Administration, Fredericton, NB E3B 5A3, Canada. Offers business administration (MBA); engineering management (MBA); entrepreneurship (MBA); sports and recreation management (MBA); MBA/LL B. Part-time programs available. *Faculty:* 23 full-time (3 women), 5 part-time/adjunct (2 women). *Students:* 48 full-time (15 women), 31 part-time (12 women), 1 international. In 2013, 30 master's awarded. *Degree requirements:* For master's, thesis optional. *Entrance requirements:* For master's, GMAT (minimum score 550), minimum GPA of 3.0; 3-5 years of work experience; 3 letters of reference with at least one academic reference. Additional exam requirements/recommendations for international students: Required—TOEFL (minimum score 580 paper-based; 92 iBT) or IELTS (minimum score 7). *Application deadline:* For fall admission, 10/31 priority date for domestic and international students; for spring admission, 3/31 priority date for domestic and international students. Application fee: $50 Canadian dollars. Electronic applications accepted. *Financial support:* In 2013–14, 6 fellowships, 3 research assistantships (averaging $4,500 per year), 22 teaching assistantships (averaging $2,250 per year) were awarded. *Faculty research:* Entrepreneurship, finance, law, sport and recreation management, and engineering management. *Unit head:* Judy Roy, Director of Graduate Studies, 506-458-7307, Fax: 506-453-3561, E-mail: jroy@unb.ca. *Application contact:* Marilyn Davis, Acting Graduate Secretary, 506-453-4766, Fax: 506-453-3561, E-mail: mbacontact@unb.ca.
Website: http://go.unb.ca/gradprograms.

University of New Brunswick Saint John, Faculty of Business, Saint John, NB E2L 4L5, Canada. Offers administration (MBA); electronic commerce (MBA); international business (MBA); natural resource management (MBA). Part-time programs available. *Faculty:* 7 full-time (3 women), 2 part-time/adjunct (1 woman). *Students:* 72 full-time (28 women), 100 part-time (47 women). In 2013, 102 master's awarded. *Entrance requirements:* For master's, GMAT (minimum score of 550) or GRE (minimum 54th percentile), minimum GPA of 3.0. Additional exam requirements/recommendations for international students: Required—TOEFL (minimum score 580 paper-based; 93 iBT), TWE (minimum score 4.5). *Application deadline:* For fall admission, 5/31 for domestic students, 7/15 for international students. Application fee: $100. Electronic applications accepted. *Expenses:* Contact institution. *Financial support:* In 2013–14, 4 students received support. Career-related internships or fieldwork and scholarships/grants available. *Faculty research:* International business, project management, innovation and technology management; business use of Weblogs and podcasts to communicate; corporate governance; high-involvement work systems; international competitiveness; supply chain management and logistics. *Unit head:* Dr. Shelley Rinehart, Director of Graduate Studies, 506-648-5902, Fax: 506-648-5574, E-mail: rinehart@unb.ca. *Application contact:* Tammy Morin, Secretary, 506-648-5746, Fax: 506-648-5574, E-mail: tmorin@unbsj.ca.
Website: http://go.unb.ca/gradprograms.

University of New Hampshire, Graduate School Manchester Campus, Manchester, NH 03101. Offers business administration (MBA); counseling (M Ed); education (M Ed, MAT); educational administration and supervision (M Ed, Ed S); information technology (MS); management of technology (MS); public administration (MPA); public health (MPH, Certificate); social work (MSW); software systems engineering (Certificate). Part-time and evening/weekend programs available. *Students:* 2 full-time (0 women), 5 part-time (0 women), 2 international. Average age 38. 6 applicants, 17% accepted, 1 enrolled. In 2013, 1 master's awarded. *Degree requirements:* For master's, thesis or alternative. *Entrance requirements:* Additional exam requirements/recommendations for international students: Required—TOEFL (minimum score 550 paper-based; 80 iBT). *Application deadline:* For fall admission, 6/1 for domestic students, 4/1 for international students; for spring admission, 12/1 for domestic students. Applications are processed on a rolling basis. Application fee: $65. Electronic applications accepted. *Expenses:* Tuition, state resident: full-time $13,500; part-time $750 per credit hour. Tuition, nonresident: full-time $26,200; part-time $1100 per credit hour. *Required fees:* $1741; $435.25 per term. Tuition and fees vary according to course level, course load, campus/location and program. *Financial support:* Fellowships, research assistantships, teaching assistantships, Federal Work-Study, scholarships/grants, health care benefits, and unspecified assistantships available. Support available to part-time students. Financial award application deadline: 3/1; financial award applicants required to submit FAFSA. *Unit head:* Candice Brown, Director, 603-641-4313, E-mail: unhm.gradcenter@unh.edu. *Application contact:* Graduate Admissions Office, 603-862-3000, Fax: 603-862-0275, E-mail: grad.school@unh.edu.
Website: http://www.gradschool.unh.edu/manchester/.

University of New Hampshire, Graduate School, Peter T. Paul College of Business and Economics, Department of Business Administration, Durham, NH 03824. Offers business administration (MBA); executive business administration (MBA); health management (MBA). *Accreditation:* AACSB. Part-time and evening/weekend programs available. Postbaccalaureate distance learning degree programs offered. *Faculty:* 17 full-time (4 women). *Students:* 109 full-time (37 women), 105 part-time (33 women); includes 9 minority (4 Asian, non-Hispanic/Latino; 4 Hispanic/Latino; 1 Two or more races, non-Hispanic/Latino), 15 international. Average age 33. 200 applicants, 63% accepted, 88 enrolled. In 2013, 78 master's awarded. *Entrance requirements:* For master's, GMAT. Additional exam requirements/recommendations for international students: Required—TOEFL (minimum score 550 paper-based; 80 iBT). *Application deadline:* For fall admission, 7/1 priority date for domestic students, 4/1 for international students; for spring admission, 11/1 for domestic students. Applications are processed on a rolling basis. Application fee: $65. Electronic applications accepted. *Expenses:* Contact institution. *Financial support:* In 2013–14, 36 students received support, including 1 research assistantship; fellowships, teaching assistantships, career-related internships or fieldwork, Federal Work-Study, scholarships/grants, and tuition waivers (full and partial) also available. Financial award application deadline: 2/15. *Unit head:* Mike Merenda, Chairperson, 603-862-3352. *Application contact:* Wendy Harris, Administrative Assistant, 603-862-3326, E-mail: mba.info@unh.edu.
Website: http://paulcollege.unh.edu/academics/graduate-programs/mba.

University of New Haven, Graduate School, College of Business, Executive Program in Business Administration, West Haven, CT 06516-1916. Offers EMBA. Part-time and evening/weekend programs available. *Students:* 14 full-time (6 women); includes 1 minority (Black or African American, non-Hispanic/Latino), 1 international. In 2013, 2 master's awarded. *Entrance requirements:* Additional exam requirements/recommendations for international students: Required—TOEFL (minimum score 80 iBT), IELTS, PTE (minimum score 53). *Application deadline:* For fall admission, 5/31 for international students; for winter admission, 10/15 for international students; for spring admission, 1/15 for international students. Applications are processed on a rolling basis. Application fee: $75. Electronic applications accepted. Application fee is waived when completed online. *Expenses:* Contact institution. *Financial support:* Application deadline: 5/1. *Unit head:* Dr. Kamal Upadhyaya, Chair, 203-932-7487, E-mail: kupadhyaya@newhaven.edu. *Application contact:* Eloise Gormley, Director of Graduate Admissions, 203-932-7440, E-mail: gradinfo@newhaven.edu.
Website: http://www.newhaven.edu/6465/.

University of New Haven, Graduate School, College of Business, Program in Business Administration, West Haven, CT 06516-1916. Offers accounting (MBA, Certificate), including CPA (MBA); business administration (MBA); business management (Certificate); business policy and strategic leadership (MBA); finance (MBA), including CFA; global marketing (MBA); human resource management (Certificate); human resources management (MBA); international business (Certificate); marketing (MBA, Certificate); sports management (MBA). Part-time and evening/weekend programs available. *Students:* 125 full-time (55 women), 88 part-time (30 women); includes 31 minority (16 Black or African American, non-Hispanic/Latino; 1 American Indian or Alaska Native, non-Hispanic/Latino; 8 Asian, non-Hispanic/Latino; 5 Hispanic/Latino; 1 Native Hawaiian or other Pacific Islander, non-Hispanic/Latino), 72 international. 196 applicants, 89% accepted, 72 enrolled. In 2013, 143 master's, 24 other advanced degrees awarded. *Degree requirements:* For master's, thesis optional. *Entrance requirements:* For master's, GMAT. Additional exam requirements/recommendations for international students: Required—TOEFL (minimum score 80 iBT), IELTS, PTE (minimum score 53). *Application deadline:* For fall admission, 5/31 for international students; for winter admission, 10/15 for international students; for spring admission, 1/15 for international students. Applications are processed on a rolling basis. Application fee: $75. Electronic applications accepted. Application fee is waived when completed online. *Expenses: Tuition:* Full-time $21,600; part-time $800 per credit hour. *Required fees:* $45 per trimester. *Financial support:* Research assistantships with partial tuition reimbursements, teaching assistantships with partial tuition reimbursements, career-related internships or fieldwork, Federal Work-Study, scholarships/grants, and unspecified assistantships available. Support available to part-time students. Financial award applicants required to submit FAFSA. *Unit head:* Dr. Armando Rodriguez, Director, 203-932-7372, E-mail: arodriguez@newhaven.edu. *Application contact:* Eloise Gormley, Director of Graduate Admissions, 203-932-7440, E-mail: gradinfo@newhaven.edu.
Website: http://www.newhaven.edu/7433/.

University of New Mexico, Anderson Graduate School of Management, Albuquerque, NM 87131. Offers EMBA, M Acct, MBA, JD/M Acct, JD/MBA, MBA/MA, MBA/MEME, MBA/Pharm D. *Accreditation:* AACSB. Part-time and evening/weekend programs available. *Faculty:* 53 full-time (14 women), 26 part-time/adjunct (10 women). *Students:* 353 full-time (185 women), 289 part-time (134 women); includes 297 minority (12 Black or African American, non-Hispanic/Latino; 13 American Indian or Alaska Native, non-Hispanic/Latino; 32 Asian, non-Hispanic/Latino; 227 Hispanic/Latino; 13 Two or more races, non-Hispanic/Latino), 28 international. Average age 31. 310 applicants, 62% accepted, 145 enrolled. In 2013, 283 master's awarded. *Entrance requirements:* For master's, GMAT or GRE (minimum score of 500), minimum GPA of 3.0 on last 60 hours of coursework. Additional exam requirements/recommendations for international students: Required—TOEFL (minimum score 550 paper-based; 79 iBT). *Application deadline:* For fall admission, 4/1 priority date for domestic and international students; for spring admission, 10/1 priority date for domestic and international students. Applications are processed on a rolling basis. Application fee: $50. Electronic applications accepted. *Expenses:* Contact institution. *Financial support:* In 2013–14, 50 students received support, including 50 fellowships (averaging $1,000 per year), 55 research

assistantships with partial tuition reimbursements available (averaging $6,300 per year); career-related internships or fieldwork, Federal Work-Study, scholarships/grants, and unspecified assistantships also available. Support available to part-time students. Financial award application deadline: 6/1; financial award applicants required to submit FAFSA. *Faculty research:* Organizational and social aspects of accounting, international management of technology and entrepreneurship, business ethics and corporate social responsibility, marketing, information assurance and fraud. *Unit head:* Douglas M. Brown, Dean, 505-277-6471, Fax: 505-277-0344, E-mail: browndm@unm.edu. *Application contact:* Tracy Wilkey, Manager, Academic Advisement, 505-277-3290, Fax: 505-277-8436, E-mail: andersonadvising@unm.edu.
Website: http://www.mgt.unm.edu.

University of New Orleans, Graduate School, College of Business Administration, Program in Business Administration, New Orleans, LA 70148. Offers MBA. *Accreditation:* AACSB. *Degree requirements:* For master's, thesis optional. *Entrance requirements:* For master's, GMAT. Additional exam requirements/recommendations for international students: Required—TOEFL (minimum score 550 paper-based; 79 iBT). Electronic applications accepted.

University of North Alabama, College of Business, Florence, AL 35632-0001. Offers accounting (MBA); enterprise resource planning systems (MBA); finance (MBA); health care management (MBA); information systems (MBA); professional (MBA); project management (MBA). *Accreditation:* ACBSP. Part-time and evening/weekend programs available. *Faculty:* 20 full-time (2 women). *Students:* 118 full-time (50 women), 273 part-time (130 women); includes 115 minority (37 Black or African American, non-Hispanic/Latino; 4 American Indian or Alaska Native, non-Hispanic/Latino; 68 Asian, non-Hispanic/Latino; 4 Hispanic/Latino; 2 Two or more races, non-Hispanic/Latino), 36 international. Average age 34. 296 applicants, 82% accepted, 149 enrolled. In 2013, 179 master's awarded. *Entrance requirements:* For master's, GMAT, GRE, minimum GPA of 2.75 in last 60 hours, 2.5 overall on a 3.0 scale; 27 hours of course work in business and economics. Additional exam requirements/recommendations for international students: Required—TOEFL (minimum score 500 paper-based; 79 iBT), IELTS (minimum score 6). *Application deadline:* For fall admission, 7/1 priority date for domestic students, 7/1 for international students; for spring admission, 12/1 for domestic and international students. Applications are processed on a rolling basis. Application fee: $25 ($50 for international students). Electronic applications accepted. *Expenses:* Tuition, state resident: full-time $4968; part-time $3312 per year. Tuition, nonresident: full-time $9936; part-time $6624 per year. *Required fees:* $970; $60.33 per credit. $362 per semester. *Financial support:* Federal Work-Study available. Support available to part-time students. Financial award application deadline: 4/1; financial award applicants required to submit FAFSA. *Unit head:* Dr. Kerry Gatlin, Dean, 256-765-4261, Fax: 256-765-4170, E-mail: kpgatlin@una.edu. *Application contact:* Russ Darracott, Graduate Admissions Counselor, 256-765-4447, E-mail: erdarracott@una.edu.
Website: http://www.una.edu/business/.

The University of North Carolina at Chapel Hill, Kenan-Flagler Business School, Doctoral Program in Business Administration, Chapel Hill, NC 27599. Offers accounting (PhD); finance (PhD); marketing (PhD); operations management (PhD); organizational behavior (PhD); strategy (PhD). *Accreditation:* AACSB. *Degree requirements:* For doctorate, thesis/dissertation. *Entrance requirements:* For doctorate, GMAT or GRE General Test. Electronic applications accepted. *Expenses:* Contact institution.

The University of North Carolina at Chapel Hill, Kenan-Flagler Business School, Executive MBA Programs, Chapel Hill, NC 27599. Offers MBA. *Accreditation:* AACSB. Evening/weekend programs available. Postbaccalaureate distance learning degree programs offered (minimal on-campus study). *Degree requirements:* For master's, exams, project. *Entrance requirements:* For master's, GMAT, 5 years of full-time work experience, interview. Electronic applications accepted. *Expenses:* Contact institution.

The University of North Carolina at Chapel Hill, Kenan-Flagler Business School, MBA Program, Chapel Hill, NC 27599. Offers MBA, MBA/JD, MBA/MHA, MBA/MRP, MBA/MSIS. *Accreditation:* AACSB. *Degree requirements:* For master's, exams, practicum. *Entrance requirements:* For master's, GMAT, interview, minimum 2 years of work experience. Additional exam requirements/recommendations for international students: Required—TOEFL. Electronic applications accepted.

The University of North Carolina at Charlotte, The Graduate School, Belk College of Business, Department of Management, Charlotte, NC 28223-0001. Offers business administration (MBA, PhD); real estate finance and development (Graduate Certificate). Part-time and evening/weekend programs available. *Faculty:* 11 full-time (4 women), 1 part-time/adjunct (0 women). *Students:* 114 full-time (43 women), 266 part-time (86 women); includes 64 minority (28 Black or African American, non-Hispanic/Latino; 2 American Indian or Alaska Native, non-Hispanic/Latino; 11 Asian, non-Hispanic/Latino; 13 Hispanic/Latino; 10 Two or more races, non-Hispanic/Latino), 132 international. Average age 31. 286 applicants, 51% accepted, 98 enrolled. In 2013, 169 master's, 2 doctorates, 2 other advanced degrees awarded. Terminal master's awarded for partial completion of doctoral program. *Degree requirements:* For master's, thesis or alternative; for doctorate, thesis/dissertation. *Entrance requirements:* For master's, GMAT or GRE, 3 letters of recommendation, essay; for doctorate, GMAT (minimum score of 650), letters of recommendation, minimum GPA of 3.25. Additional exam requirements/recommendations for international students: Required—TOEFL (minimum score 557 paper-based; 83 iBT). *Application deadline:* For fall admission, 1/15 priority date for domestic and international students; for spring admission, 10/1 priority date for domestic and international students. Applications are processed on a rolling basis. Application fee: $75. Electronic applications accepted. *Expenses:* Tuition, state resident: full-time $3522. Tuition, nonresident: full-time $16,051. *Required fees:* $2585. Tuition and fees vary according to course load and program. *Financial support:* In 2013–14, 2 students received support, including 1 research assistantship (averaging $18,000 per year), 1 teaching assistantship (averaging $18,000 per year); career-related internships or fieldwork, institutionally sponsored loans, scholarships/grants, and unspecified assistantships also available. Support available to part-time students. Financial award application deadline: 4/1; financial award applicants required to submit FAFSA. *Total annual research expenditures:* $104,426. *Unit head:* Dr. Christie Amato, Associate Dean, 704-687-7712, Fax: 704-687-5309, E-mail: chamato@uncc.edu. *Application contact:* Kathy B. Giddings, Director of Graduate Admissions, 704-687-5503, Fax: 704-687-1668, E-mail: gradadm@uncc.edu.
Website: http://belkcollege.uncc.edu/about-college/departments/management.

The University of North Carolina at Greensboro, Graduate School, Bryan School of Business and Economics, Department of Business Administration, Greensboro, NC 27412-5001. Offers MBA, PMC, Postbaccalaureate Certificate, MS/MBA, MSN/MBA. *Accreditation:* AACSB. *Entrance requirements:* For master's, GMAT, GRE General Test, managerial experience. Additional exam requirements/recommendations for international students: Required—TOEFL. Electronic applications accepted.

The University of North Carolina at Pembroke, Graduate Studies, School of Business, Program in Business Administration, Pembroke, NC 28372-1510. Offers MBA. Part-time and evening/weekend programs available. *Degree requirements:* For master's, thesis optional. *Entrance requirements:* For master's, GMAT, minimum GPA of 3.0 in major or 2.5 overall. Additional exam requirements/recommendations for international students: Required—TOEFL.

The University of North Carolina Wilmington, School of Business, Business Administration Program, Wilmington, NC 28403-3297. Offers MBA. *Accreditation:* AACSB. Part-time and evening/weekend programs available. *Faculty:* 9 full-time (5 women). *Students:* 2 full-time (0 women), 28 part-time (11 women); includes 2 minority (both Black or African American, non-Hispanic/Latino). Average age 30. 31 applicants, 77% accepted, 17 enrolled. In 2013, 58 master's awarded. *Degree requirements:* For master's, comprehensive exam, thesis (for some programs), final project. *Entrance requirements:* For master's, GMAT, 1 year of appropriate work experience. Additional exam requirements/recommendations for international students: Required—TOEFL (minimum score 550 paper-based; 79 iBT), IELTS (minimum score 6.5). *Application deadline:* For fall admission, 2/1 for domestic students. Applications are processed on a rolling basis. Application fee: $60. *Expenses:* Tuition, state resident: full-time $4163. Tuition, nonresident: full-time $16,098. *Financial support:* In 2013–14, 1 teaching assistantship with full and partial tuition reimbursement (averaging $9,000 per year) was awarded; career-related internships or fieldwork and Federal Work-Study also available. Support available to part-time students. Financial award application deadline: 3/15. *Unit head:* Dr. Vince Howe, Coordinator, 910-962-3882, E-mail: howe@uncw.edu. *Application contact:* Karen Barnhill, Graduate Coordinator, 910-962-3903, E-mail: barnhillk@uncw.edu.
Website: http://www.csb.uncw.edu/mba/.

University of North Dakota, Graduate School, College of Business and Public Administration, Business Administration Program, Grand Forks, ND 58202. Offers MBA. *Accreditation:* AACSB. Part-time and evening/weekend programs available. Postbaccalaureate distance learning degree programs offered (minimal on-campus study). *Degree requirements:* For master's, comprehensive exam, thesis or alternative, project. *Entrance requirements:* For master's, GMAT, minimum GPA of 3.25. Additional exam requirements/recommendations for international students: Required—TOEFL (minimum score 550 paper-based; 79 iBT), IELTS (minimum score 6.5). Electronic applications accepted.

University of Northern Iowa, Graduate College, College of Business Administration, MBA Program in Business Administration, Cedar Falls, IA 50614. Offers MBA. *Accreditation:* AACSB. Part-time and evening/weekend programs available. *Students:* 16 full-time (4 women), 53 part-time (23 women); includes 2 minority (both Asian, non-Hispanic/Latino), 25 international. 73 applicants, 66% accepted, 39 enrolled. In 2013, 28 master's awarded. *Entrance requirements:* For master's, GMAT (minimum score 500), minimum GPA of 3.0. Additional exam requirements/recommendations for international students: Required—TOEFL (minimum score 500 paper-based; 61 iBT). *Application deadline:* For fall admission, 8/1 priority date for domestic students. Applications are processed on a rolling basis. Application fee: $50 ($70 for international students). Electronic applications accepted. *Financial support:* Career-related internships or fieldwork, Federal Work-Study, scholarships/grants, and tuition waivers (full and partial) available. Support available to part-time students. Financial award application deadline: 2/1. *Unit head:* Dr. Leslie K. Wilson, Coordinator, 319-273-6240, Fax: 319-273-2922, E-mail: leslie.wilson@uni.edu. *Application contact:* Laurie S. Russell, Record Analyst, 319-273-2623, Fax: 319-273-2885, E-mail: laurie.russell@uni.edu.
Website: http://business.uni.edu/web/pages/academics/mba.cfm.

University of North Florida, Coggin College of Business, MBA Program, Jacksonville, FL 32224. Offers accounting (MBA); construction management (MBA); e-commerce (MBA); economics (MBA); finance (MBA); human resource management (MBA); international business (MBA); logistics (MBA); management applications (MBA). *Accreditation:* AACSB. Part-time and evening/weekend programs available. *Faculty:* 14 full-time (6 women), 1 part-time/adjunct (0 women). *Students:* 90 full-time (41 women), 231 part-time (84 women); includes 47 minority (18 Black or African American, non-Hispanic/Latino; 8 Asian, non-Hispanic/Latino; 16 Hispanic/Latino; 5 Two or more races, non-Hispanic/Latino), 29 international. Average age 29. 222 applicants, 47% accepted, 80 enrolled. In 2013, 152 master's awarded. *Entrance requirements:* For master's, GMAT or GRE, U.S. bachelor's degree from regionally-accredited university or equivalent foreign degree. Additional exam requirements/recommendations for international students: Required—TOEFL (minimum score 550 paper-based; 79 iBT). *Application deadline:* For fall admission, 7/1 priority date for domestic students, 5/1 for international students; for spring admission, 11/1 priority date for domestic students, 10/1 for international students. Application fee: $30. *Expenses:* Tuition, state resident: full-time $9794; part-time $408.10 per credit hour. Tuition, nonresident: full-time $22,383; part-time $932.61 per credit hour. *Required fees:* $2020; $84.20 per credit hour. Tuition and fees vary according to course load and program. *Financial support:* In 2013–14, 35 students received support, including 1 research assistantship (averaging $2,700 per year); teaching assistantships, Federal Work-Study, and tuition waivers (partial) also available. Support available to part-time students. Financial award application deadline: 4/1; financial award applicants required to submit FAFSA. *Faculty research:* Performance measures, costing, and inventory issues in logistics and supply chain management; inter-organizational systems; international management and marketing practices; e-commerce; organizational learning and socialization processes. *Total annual research expenditures:* $12,025. *Application contact:* Cheryl Campbell, Graduate Advisor, 904-620-2575, Fax: 904-620-2832, E-mail: ccampbell@unf.edu.
Website: http://www.unf.edu/coggin/academics/graduate/mba.aspx.

University of North Georgia, Mike Cottrell School of Business, Dahlonega, GA 30597. Offers MBA. *Accreditation:* AACSB. Part-time and evening/weekend programs available. *Entrance requirements:* For master's, GRE or GMAT, references, resume. Additional exam requirements/recommendations for international students: Required—TOEFL (minimum score 550 paper-based; 79 iBT), IELTS (minimum score 6.5). Electronic applications accepted. *Faculty research:* Leadership development, psychological contract and cynicism, positive organizational behavior, service quality, economic opportunity cost, mood and likeability, proactive socialization, attitudes, perceived technology policy, task significance in teams.

University of North Texas, Robert B. Toulouse School of Graduate Studies, Denton, TN 76203-5017. Offers accounting (MS, PhD); applied anthropology (MA, MS); applied behavior analysis (Certificate); applied technology and performance improvement (M Ed, MS, PhD); art education (MA, PhD); art history (MA); art museum education (Certificate); arts leadership (Certificate); audiology (Au D); behavior analysis (MS); biochemistry and molecular biology (MS, PhD); biology (MA, MS, PhD); business (PhD); business computer information systems (PhD); chemistry (MS, PhD); clinical psychology (PhD); communication studies (MA, MS); computer engineering (MS); computer science (MS); computer science and engineering (PhD); counseling (M Ed, MS, PhD), including clinical mental health counseling (MS), college and university counseling (M Ed, MS), elementary school counseling (M Ed, MS), secondary school counseling (M Ed, MS); counseling psychology (PhD); creative writing (MA); criminal justice (MS); curriculum and instruction (M Ed, PhD), including curriculum studies (PhD), early childhood studies (PhD), language and literacy studies (PhD); decision sciences (MBA); design (MA, MFA), including fashion design (MFA), innovation studies, interior design (MFA); early childhood studies (MS); economics (MS); educational leadership (M Ed, Ed D, PhD); educational psychology (MS), including family studies, gifted and talented (MS, PhD),

Business Administration and Management—General

human development, learning and cognition, research, measurement and evaluation; educational research (PhD), including gifted and talented (MS, PhD), human development and family studies, psychological aspects of sports and exercise, research, measurement and statistics; electrical engineering (MS); emergency management (MPA); engineering systems (MS); English (MA, PhD); environmental science (MS, PhD); experimental psychology (PhD); finance (MBA, MS, PhD); financial management (MPA); French (MA); health psychology and behavioral medicine (PhD); health services management (MBA); higher education (M Ed, Ed D, PhD); history (MA, MS, PhD), including European history (PhD), military history (PhD), United States history (PhD); hospitality management (MS); human resources management (MPA); information science (MS, PhD); information technologies (MBA); information technology and decision sciences (MS); interdisciplinary studies (MA, MS); international sustainable tourism (MS); jazz studies (MM); journalism (MA, MJ, Graduate Certificate), including interactive and virtual digital communication (Graduate Certificate), narrative journalism (Graduate Certificate), public relations (Graduate Certificate); kinesiology (MS); learning technologies (MS, PhD); library science (MS); local government management (MPA); logistics and supply chain management (MBA, PhD); long-term care, senior housing, and aging services (MA, MS); management science (PhD); marketing (MBA, PhD); materials science and engineering (MS, PhD); mathematics (MS); merchandising (MS); music (MA, MM Ed, PhD), including ethnomusicology (MA), music education (MM Ed, PhD), music theory (MA, PhD), musicology (MA, PhD), performance (MA); nonprofit management (MPA); operations and supply chain management (MBA); performance (MM, DMA); philosophy (MA, PhD); physics (MS, PhD); political science (MA, MS, PhD); public administration and management (PhD), including emergency management, nonprofit management, public financial management, urban management; radio, television and film (MA, MFA); recreation, event and sport management (MS); rehabilitation counseling (MS, Certificate); sociology (MA, MS, PhD); Spanish (MA); special education (M Ed, PhD), including autism intervention (PhD), emotional/behavioral disorders (PhD), mild/moderate disabilities (PhD); speech-language pathology (MA, MS); strategic management (MBA); studio art (MFA); taxation (MS); teaching (M Ed); MBA/MS; MS/MPH; MSES/MBA. Part-time and evening/weekend programs available. Postbaccalaureate distance learning degree programs offered. *Faculty:* 661 full-time (213 women), 240 part-time/adjunct (144 women). *Students:* 3,106 full-time (1,620 women), 3,543 part-time (2,221 women); includes 1,740 minority (533 Black or African American, non-Hispanic/Latino; 15 American Indian or Alaska Native, non-Hispanic/Latino; 286 Asian, non-Hispanic/Latino; 746 Hispanic/Latino; 3 Native Hawaiian or other Pacific Islander, non-Hispanic/Latino; 157 Two or more races, non-Hispanic/Latino), 1,145 international. Average age 32. 6,289 applicants, 43% accepted, 1751 enrolled. In 2013, 1,778 master's, 239 doctorates, 10 other advanced degrees awarded. Terminal master's awarded for partial completion of doctoral program. *Degree requirements:* For master's, variable foreign language requirement, comprehensive exam (for some programs), thesis (for some programs); for doctorate, variable foreign language requirement, comprehensive exam (for some programs), thesis/dissertation; for other advanced degree, variable foreign language requirement, comprehensive exam (for some programs). *Entrance requirements:* For master's and doctorate, GRE, GMAT. Additional exam requirements/recommendations for international students: Required—TOEFL (minimum score 550 paper-based; 79 iBT). *Application deadline:* For fall admission, 7/15 for domestic students, 3/15 for international students; for spring admission, 11/15 for domestic students, 9/15 for international students; for summer admission, 5/1 for domestic students. Applications are processed on a rolling basis. Application fee: $60. Electronic applications accepted. *Financial support:* Fellowships with partial tuition reimbursements, research assistantships with partial tuition reimbursements, teaching assistantships, career-related internships or fieldwork, Federal Work-Study, institutionally sponsored loans, scholarships/grants, health care benefits, and library assistantships available. Support

available to part-time students. Financial award applicants required to submit FAFSA. *Unit head:* Mark Wardell, Dean, 940-565-2383, E-mail: mark.wardell@unt.edu. *Application contact:* Toulouse School of Graduate Studies, 940-565-2383, Fax: 940-565-2141, E-mail: gradsch@unt.edu. Website: http://tsgs.unt.edu/.

University of Northwestern–St. Paul, Program in Business Administration, St. Paul, MN 55113-1598. Offers MBA. Part-time and evening/weekend programs available. Postbaccalaureate distance learning degree programs offered (no on-campus study). *Expenses: Tuition:* Full-time $8820; part-time $490 per credit. Website: http://www.unwsp.edu/web/grad-studies/master-of-business-administration.

University of Notre Dame, Mendoza College of Business, Executive Master of Business Administration Program, Notre Dame, IN 46556. Offers MBA. Program also offered at Notre Dame Chicago Commons in downtown Chicago, IL. *Accreditation:* AACSB. *Students:* 2 applicants. *Entrance requirements:* For master's, 5 years of work experience in management. *Application deadline:* For fall admission, 6/1 for domestic students; for winter admission, 11/1 for domestic students. Applications are processed on a rolling basis. Application fee: $100. Electronic applications accepted. *Expenses:* Contact institution. *Financial support:* Fellowships available. Financial award application deadline: 6/1; financial award applicants required to submit FAFSA. *Faculty research:* Exchange rates, compensation, market microstructure or volatility in foreign currency, ethical negotiation/decision-making. *Unit head:* Suzanne T. Waller, Director of Degree Programs, 574-631-2717, Fax: 574-631-6783, E-mail: suzanne.waller@nd.edu. *Application contact:* Nicholas A. Farmer, Senior Associate Director, 574-631-8351, Fax: 574-631-6783, E-mail: nfarmer@nd.edu. Website: http://emba.nd.edu.

University of Notre Dame, Mendoza College of Business, Master of Business Administration Program, Notre Dame, IN 46556. Offers MBA. *Accreditation:* AACSB. *Faculty:* 61 full-time (10 women), 19 part-time/adjunct (3 women). *Students:* 313 full-time (83 women); includes 48 minority (10 Black or African American, non-Hispanic/Latino; 15 Asian, non-Hispanic/Latino; 3 Hispanic/Latino; 20 Two or more races, non-Hispanic/Latino), 64 international. Average age 27. 740 applicants, 40% accepted, 136 enrolled. In 2013, 192 master's awarded. *Entrance requirements:* For master's, GMAT, GRE, work experience. Additional exam requirements/recommendations for international students: Required—TOEFL, IELTS or PTE. *Application deadline:* For fall admission, 9/9 for domestic and international students; for winter admission, 11/4 for domestic students, 11/4 priority date for international students; for spring admission, 1/6 for domestic and international students; for summer admission, 3/3 for domestic and international students. Applications are processed on a rolling basis. Application fee: $175. Electronic applications accepted. *Financial support:* In 2013–14, 211 students received support, including fellowships with full and partial tuition reimbursements available (averaging $28,474 per year), research assistantships (averaging $3,000 per year), teaching assistantships (averaging $3,000 per year); career-related internships or fieldwork, Federal Work-Study, institutionally sponsored loans, scholarships/grants, and unspecified assistantships also available. Financial award application deadline: 3/31; financial award applicants required to submit FAFSA. *Faculty research:* Market microstructure, marketing and public policy, corporate finance and accounting, corporate governance and ethical behavior, high performing organizations. *Unit head:* Dr. Jeffrey Bergstrand, Associate Dean, Graduate Programs, 574-631-3759, Fax: 574-631-4825, E-mail: bergstrand.1@nd.edu. *Application contact:* Kristin McAndrew, Director of MBA Admissions, 574-631-8488, Fax: 574-631-8800, E-mail: kmcadre@nd.edu. Website: http://business.nd.edu/mba/.

University of Notre Dame, Mendoza College of Business, Master of Science in Management Program, Notre Dame, IN 46556. Offers MSM. *Faculty:* 16 full-time (3

women). *Students:* 28 full-time (10 women); includes 3 minority (1 Asian, non-Hispanic/Latino; 2 Two or more races, non-Hispanic/Latino), 2 international. Average age 22. 77 applicants, 58% accepted, 28 enrolled. *Entrance requirements:* For master's, GMAT, GRE. Additional exam requirements/recommendations for international students: Required—TOEFL, IELTS or PTE. *Application deadline:* For fall admission, 9/9 for domestic and international students; for winter admission, 10/4 for domestic and international students; for spring admission, 1/6 for domestic and international students; for summer admission, 3/3 for domestic and international students. Applications are processed on a rolling basis. Application fee: $50. Electronic applications accepted. *Financial support:* In 2013–14, 18 students received support, including 18 fellowships (averaging $12,000 per year); scholarships/grants and unspecified assistantships also available. Financial award application deadline: 3/31; financial award applicants required to submit FAFSA. *Unit head:* Dr. Jeffrey Bergstrand, Associate Dean, Graduate Programs, 574-631-3759, E-mail: bergstrand.1@nd.edu. *Application contact:* Kristin McAndrew, Director of Admissions, 574-631-8488, Fax: 574-631-8800, E-mail: kmcadre@nd.edu.
Website: http://business.nd.edu/msm/.

University of Oklahoma, Michael F. Price College of Business, Program in Business Administration, Norman, OK 73019. Offers MBA, PhD, JD/MBA, MBA/MS. *Accreditation:* AACSB. Part-time and evening/weekend programs available. *Students:* 136 full-time (42 women), 128 part-time (27 women); includes 50 minority (6 Black or African American, non-Hispanic/Latino; 10 American Indian or Alaska Native, non-Hispanic/Latino; 16 Asian, non-Hispanic/Latino; 11 Hispanic/Latino; 7 Two or more races, non-Hispanic/Latino), 28 international. Average age 28. 294 applicants, 39% accepted, 100 enrolled. In 2013, 91 master's, 5 doctorates awarded. Terminal master's awarded for partial completion of doctoral program. *Degree requirements:* For master's, comprehensive exam; for doctorate, comprehensive exam, thesis/dissertation. *Entrance requirements:* For master's, GMAT or GRE; for doctorate, GMAT. Additional exam requirements/recommendations for international students: Required—TOEFL (minimum score 100 iBT). *Application deadline:* For fall admission, 2/1 for domestic and international students; for spring admission, 11/1 for domestic students, 9/1 for international students. Application fee: $50 ($100 for international students). Electronic applications accepted. *Expenses:* Tuition, state resident: full-time $4205; part-time $175.20 per credit hour. Tuition, nonresident: full-time $16,205; part-time $675.20 per credit hour. *Required fees:* $2745; $103.85 per credit hour. $126.50 per semester. *Financial support:* In 2013–14, 110 students received support, including 9 fellowships with full tuition reimbursements available (averaging $4,626 per year); career-related internships or fieldwork, scholarships/grants, health care benefits, and unspecified assistantships also available. Support available to part-time students. Financial award application deadline: 6/1; financial award applicants required to submit FAFSA. *Faculty research:* Corporate finance issues (capital structure, dividend policy and privatization), IT and organizational behavior, entrepreneurship and venture capital, corporate governance and risk management, relationship marketing and distribution channels, human technology interactions, corporate finance and governance, earnings management. *Unit head:* Dr. Robert Dauffenbach, Associate Dean, Research and Graduate Programs, 405-325-2934, Fax: 405-325-7688, E-mail: rdauffen@ou.edu. *Application contact:* Callen Brehm, Academic Counselor, 405-325-2074, Fax: 405-325-7753, E-mail: cbrehm@ou.edu. Website: http://www.ou.edu/content/price/divisions/graduate.html.
See Display on previous page and Close-Up on page 193.

University of Oregon, Graduate School, Charles H. Lundquist College of Business, Department of Management, Eugene, OR 97403. Offers PhD. *Accreditation:* AACSB. Part-time programs available. Terminal master's awarded for partial completion of doctoral program. *Degree requirements:* For doctorate, thesis/dissertation, 2

comprehensive exams. *Entrance requirements:* For doctorate, GMAT. Additional exam requirements/recommendations for international students: Required—TOEFL.

University of Oregon, Graduate School, Charles H. Lundquist College of Business, Department of Management: General Business, Eugene, OR 97403. Offers MBA. *Accreditation:* AACSB. *Entrance requirements:* For master's, GMAT. Additional exam requirements/recommendations for international students: Required—TOEFL.

University of Ottawa, Faculty of Graduate and Postdoctoral Studies, Telfer School of Management, Executive Business Administration Program, Ottawa, ON K1N 6N5, Canada. Offers EMBA. *Accreditation:* AACSB. Evening/weekend programs available. *Entrance requirements:* For master's, bachelor's degree or equivalent, minimum B average, business experience. Additional exam requirements/recommendations for international students: Recommended—TOEFL. Electronic applications accepted. *Expenses:* Contact institution.

University of Ottawa, Faculty of Graduate and Postdoctoral Studies, Telfer School of Management, MBA Program, Ottawa, ON K1N 6N5, Canada. Offers MBA. *Accreditation:* AACSB. Part-time and evening/weekend programs available. *Degree requirements:* For master's, thesis optional. *Entrance requirements:* For master's, GMAT, bachelor's degree or equivalent, minimum B average, minimum 2 years of work experience. Additional exam requirements/recommendations for international students: Recommended—TOEFL. Electronic applications accepted.
See Display below and Close-Up on page 195.

University of Pennsylvania, Wharton School, Management Department, Philadelphia, PA 19104. Offers MBA, PhD. *Accreditation:* AACSB. *Entrance requirements:* For master's, GMAT; for doctorate, GMAT or GRE. *Faculty research:* Cross-cultural leadership, international technology transfers, human resource management, financial services.

University of Pennsylvania, Wharton School, Wharton Doctoral Programs, Philadelphia, PA 19104. Offers accounting (PhD); applied economics (PhD); ethics and legal studies (PhD); finance (PhD); health care management and economics (PhD); management (PhD); marketing (PhD); operations and information management (PhD); statistics (PhD). *Accreditation:* AACSB. *Degree requirements:* For doctorate, thesis/dissertation. *Entrance requirements:* For doctorate, GMAT or GRE, letters of recommendation. Additional exam requirements/recommendations for international students: Required—TOEFL, TWE. Electronic applications accepted.

University of Pennsylvania, Wharton School, The Wharton MBA Program, Philadelphia, PA 19104. Offers MBA, DMD/MBA, JD/MBA, MBA/MA, MBA/MS, MBA/MSN, MBA/MSW, MBA/PhD, MD/MBA, VMD/MBA. *Accreditation:* AACSB. *Entrance requirements:* For master's, GMAT, interview, 2 letters of recommendation, resume/curriculum vitae. Additional exam requirements/recommendations for international students: Required—TOEFL. Electronic applications accepted. *Faculty research:* Entrepreneurial studies, finance, management of technology.

University of Pennsylvania, Wharton School, The Wharton MBA Program for Executives, Wharton Executive MBA East, Philadelphia, PA 19104. Offers MBA. *Accreditation:* AACSB. Evening/weekend programs available. *Entrance requirements:* For master's, GMAT. Additional exam requirements for international students: Recommended—TOEFL.

University of Pennsylvania, Wharton School, The Wharton MBA Program for Executives, Wharton Executive MBA West, Philadelphia, PA 19104. Offers MBA. *Accreditation:* AACSB. Evening/weekend programs available. *Entrance requirements:* For master's, GMAT. Additional exam requirements/recommendations for international students: Recommended—TOEFL.

Business Administration and Management—General

University of Phoenix–Atlanta Campus, School of Business, Sandy Springs, GA 30350-4153. Offers accounting (MBA); business administration (MBA); global management (MBA); human resources management (MBA, MM); management (MM); marketing (MBA); public administration (MM). Evening/weekend programs available. Postbaccalaureate distance learning degree programs offered. *Degree requirements:* For master's, thesis (for some programs). *Entrance requirements:* For master's, minimum undergraduate GPA of 3.0, 3 years of work experience. Additional exam requirements/recommendations for international students: Required—TOEFL (minimum score 550 paper-based; 79 iBT).

University of Phoenix–Augusta Campus, School of Business, Augusta, GA 30909-4583. Offers accounting (MBA); business administration (MBA); business and management (MBA, MM); global management (MBA); human resources management (MBA, MM); management (MM); marketing (MBA); public administration (MBA, MM). Postbaccalaureate distance learning degree programs offered.

University of Phoenix–Austin Campus, School of Business, Austin, TX 78759. Offers accounting (MBA); business administration (MBA); business and management (MBA); e-business (MBA); global management (MBA); human resources management (MBA, MM); management (MM); marketing (MBA); public administration (MBA). Postbaccalaureate distance learning degree programs offered.

University of Phoenix–Bay Area Campus, School of Business, San Jose, CA 95134-1805. Offers accountancy (MS); accounting (MBA); business administration (MBA, DBA); energy management (MBA); global management (MBA); health care management (MBA); human resource management (MBA); human resources management (MM); management (MM); marketing (MBA); organizational leadership (DM); project management (MBA); public administration (MPA); technology management (MBA). Evening/weekend programs available. Postbaccalaureate distance learning degree programs offered (no on-campus study). *Degree requirements:* For master's, thesis (for some programs). *Entrance requirements:* For master's, minimum undergraduate GPA of 3.0, 3 years of work experience. Additional exam requirements/recommendations for international students: Required—TOEFL (minimum score 550 paper-based; 79 iBT). Electronic applications accepted.

University of Phoenix–Birmingham Campus, College of Graduate Business and Management, Birmingham, AL 35242. Offers accounting (MBA); business administration (MBA); global management (MBA); human resources management (MBA, MM); management (MM); marketing (MBA); public administration (MM).

University of Phoenix–Boston Campus, School of Business, Braintree, MA 02184. Offers administration (MBA); global management (MBA). Evening/weekend programs available. *Degree requirements:* For master's, thesis (for some programs). *Entrance requirements:* For master's, 3 years of work experience, minimum undergraduate GPA of 3.0. Additional exam requirements/recommendations for international students: Required—TOEFL (minimum score 550 paper-based; 79 iBT).

University of Phoenix–Central Massachusetts Campus, School of Business, Westborough, MA 01581-3906. Offers business administration (MBA); global management (MBA). Evening/weekend programs available. *Degree requirements:* For master's, thesis (for some programs). *Entrance requirements:* For master's, minimum undergraduate GPA of 3.0, 3 years of work experience. Additional exam requirements/recommendations for international students: Required—TOEFL (minimum score 550 paper-based; 79 iBT). Electronic applications accepted.

University of Phoenix–Central Valley Campus, School of Business, Fresno, CA 93720-1562. Offers accounting (MBA); business administration (MBA); global management (MBA); human resources management (MBA, MM); management (MM); marketing (MBA); public administration (MBA, MM).

University of Phoenix–Charlotte Campus, School of Business, Charlotte, NC 28273-3409. Offers accounting (MBA); business administration (MBA); global management (MBA). Evening/weekend programs available. *Degree requirements:* For master's, thesis (for some programs). *Entrance requirements:* For master's, minimum undergraduate GPA of 3.0, 3 years work experience. Additional exam requirements/recommendations for international students: Required—TOEFL (minimum score 550 paper-based; 79 iBT). Electronic applications accepted.

University of Phoenix–Chattanooga Campus, School of Business, Chattanooga, TN 37421-3707. Offers accounting (MBA); business administration (MBA); business and management (MBA); global management (MBA); human resources management (MBA, MM); management (MM); marketing (MBA); public administration (MBA, MM). Postbaccalaureate distance learning degree programs offered.

University of Phoenix–Cheyenne Campus, School of Business, Cheyenne, WY 82009. Offers global management (MBA); human resources management (MBA, MM); management (MM); marketing (MBA); public administration (MBA, MM). Postbaccalaureate distance learning degree programs offered.

University of Phoenix–Chicago Campus, School of Business, Schaumburg, IL 60173-4399. Offers business administration (MBA); global management (MBA); human resources management (MBA); information systems (MIS); management (MM). Evening/weekend programs available. *Degree requirements:* For master's, thesis (for some programs). *Entrance requirements:* For master's, minimum undergraduate GPA of 3.0, 3 years of work experience. Additional exam requirements/recommendations for international students: Required—TOEFL (minimum score 550 paper-based; 79 iBT). Electronic applications accepted.

University of Phoenix–Cincinnati Campus, School of Business, West Chester, OH 45069-4875. Offers accounting (MBA); business administration (MBA); global management (MBA); human resources management (MBA, MM); management (MM); marketing (MBA); public administration (MM). Evening/weekend programs available. *Degree requirements:* For master's, thesis (for some programs). *Entrance requirements:* For master's, minimum undergraduate GPA of 3.0, 3 years of work experience. Additional exam requirements/recommendations for international students: Required—TOEFL (minimum score 550 paper-based; 79 iBT). Electronic applications accepted.

University of Phoenix–Cleveland Campus, School of Business, Independence, OH 44131-2194. Offers accounting (MBA); business administration (MBA); global management (MBA); human resources management (MBA, MM); management (MM); marketing (MBA); public administration (MBA, MM). Evening/weekend programs available. Postbaccalaureate distance learning degree programs offered (no on-campus study). *Degree requirements:* For master's, thesis (for some programs). *Entrance requirements:* For master's, minimum undergraduate GPA of 3.0, 3 years of work experience. Additional exam requirements/recommendations for international students: Required—TOEFL (minimum score 550 paper-based; 79 iBT). Electronic applications accepted.

University of Phoenix–Columbia Campus, School of Business, Columbia, SC 29223. Offers MBA. Postbaccalaureate distance learning degree programs offered.

University of Phoenix–Columbus Georgia Campus, School of Business, Columbus, GA 31909. Offers accounting (MBA); business administration (MBA); global management (MBA); human resources management (MBA, MM); management (MM); marketing (MBA); public administration (MBA). Evening/weekend programs available. *Degree requirements:* For master's, thesis (for some programs). *Entrance requirements:* For master's, minimum undergraduate GPA of 3.0, 3 years of work experience. Additional exam requirements/recommendations for international students: Required—TOEFL (minimum score 550 paper-based; 79 iBT). Electronic applications accepted.

University of Phoenix–Columbus Ohio Campus, School of Business, Columbus, OH 43240-4032. Offers accounting (MBA); business administration (MBA); global management (MBA); human resources management (MBA, MM); management (MM); marketing (MBA); public administration (MM). Evening/weekend programs available. Postbaccalaureate distance learning degree programs offered. *Degree requirements:* For master's, thesis (for some programs). *Entrance requirements:* For master's, minimum undergraduate GPA of 3.0, 3 years of work experience. Additional exam requirements/recommendations for international students: Required—TOEFL (minimum score 550 paper-based; 79 iBT). Electronic applications accepted.

University of Phoenix–Dallas Campus, School of Business, Dallas, TX 75251. Offers accounting (MBA); business administration (MBA); global management (MBA); human resources management (MBA, MM); management (MM); marketing (MBA); public administration (MBA, MM). Evening/weekend programs available. Postbaccalaureate distance learning degree programs offered. *Degree requirements:* For master's, thesis (for some programs). *Entrance requirements:* For master's, 3 years of work experience, minimum undergraduate GPA of 3.0. Additional exam requirements/recommendations for international students: Required—TOEFL (minimum score 550 paper-based; 79 iBT). Electronic applications accepted.

University of Phoenix–Denver Campus, College of Information Systems and Technology, Lone Tree, CO 80124-5453. Offers e-business (MBA); management (MIS); technology management (MBA). Evening/weekend programs available. Postbaccalaureate distance learning degree programs offered. *Degree requirements:* For master's, thesis (for some programs). *Entrance requirements:* For master's, minimum undergraduate GPA of 3.0, 3 years of work experience. Additional exam requirements/recommendations for international students: Required—TOEFL (minimum score 550 paper-based; 79 iBT). Electronic applications accepted.

University of Phoenix–Denver Campus, School of Business, Lone Tree, CO 80124-5453. Offers accountancy (MSA); accounting (MBA); business administration (MBA); e-business (MBA); global management (MBA); human resources management (MBA, MM); management (MM); marketing (MBA); public administration (MBA, MM). Evening/weekend programs available. Postbaccalaureate distance learning degree programs offered. *Degree requirements:* For master's, thesis (for some programs). *Entrance requirements:* For master's, minimum undergraduate GPA of 3.0, 3 years work experience. Additional exam requirements/recommendations for international students: Required—TOEFL (minimum score 550 paper-based; 79 iBT). Electronic applications accepted.

University of Phoenix–Des Moines Campus, School of Business, Des Moines, IA 50309. Offers accounting (MBA); business administration (MBA); global management (MBA); human resources management (MBA, MM); management (MM); marketing (MBA); public administration (MBA, MM). Postbaccalaureate distance learning degree programs offered.

University of Phoenix–Eastern Washington Campus, School of Business, Spokane, WA 99212-2531. Offers accounting (MBA); business administration (MBA); human resources management (MBA); marketing (MBA); public administration (MBA). Evening/weekend programs available. *Degree requirements:* For master's, thesis (for some programs). *Entrance requirements:* For master's, minimum undergraduate GPA of 3.0, 3 years of work experience. Additional exam requirements/recommendations for international students: Required—TOEFL (minimum score 550 paper-based; 79 iBT). Electronic applications accepted.

University of Phoenix–Hawaii Campus, School of Business, Honolulu, HI 96813-4317. Offers accounting (MBA); business administration (MBA); global management (MBA); human resources management (MBA, MM); management (MM); marketing (MBA); public administration (MBA, MM). Evening/weekend programs available. *Degree requirements:* For master's, thesis (for some programs). *Entrance requirements:* For master's, minimum undergraduate GPA of 3.0, 3 years of work experience. Additional exam requirements/recommendations for international students: Required—TOEFL (minimum score 550 paper-based; 79 iBT). Electronic applications accepted.

University of Phoenix–Houston Campus, School of Business, Houston, TX 77079-2004. Offers accounting (MBA); business administration (MBA); global management (MBA); human resources management (MBA, MM); management (MM); marketing (MBA); public administration (MBA, MM). Evening/weekend programs available. Postbaccalaureate distance learning degree programs offered. *Degree requirements:* For master's, thesis (for some programs). *Entrance requirements:* For master's, 3 years of work experience, minimum undergraduate GPA of 3.0. Additional exam requirements/recommendations for international students: Required—TOEFL (minimum score 550 paper-based; 79 iBT). Electronic applications accepted.

University of Phoenix–Idaho Campus, School of Business, Meridian, ID 83642-5114. Offers accounting (MBA); administration (MBA); global management (MBA); human resources management (MBA, MM); management (MM); marketing (MBA); public administration (MM). Evening/weekend programs available. Postbaccalaureate distance learning degree programs offered. *Degree requirements:* For master's, thesis (for some programs). *Entrance requirements:* For master's, 3 years of work experience, minimum undergraduate GPA of 3.0. Additional exam requirements/recommendations for international students: Required—TOEFL (minimum score 550 paper-based). Electronic applications accepted.

University of Phoenix–Indianapolis Campus, School of Business, Indianapolis, IN 46250-932. Offers accounting (MBA); business administration (MBA); global management (MBA); human resources management (MBA, MM); management (MM); marketing (MBA); public administration (MM). Evening/weekend programs available. *Degree requirements:* For master's, thesis (for some programs). *Entrance requirements:* For master's, minimum undergraduate GPA of 3.0, 3 years of work experience. Additional exam requirements/recommendations for international students: Required—TOEFL (minimum score 550 paper-based). Electronic applications accepted.

University of Phoenix–Jersey City Campus, School of Business, Jersey City, NJ 07310. Offers accounting (MBA); business administration (MBA); global management (MBA); human resources management (MBA, MM); management (MM); marketing (MBA); public administration (MBA, MM).

University of Phoenix–Kansas City Campus, School of Business, Kansas City, MO 64131. Offers accounting (MBA); business administration (MBA); global management (MBA); human resources management (MBA, MM); management (MM); marketing (MBA); public administration (MBA). Evening/weekend programs available. *Degree requirements:* For master's, thesis (for some programs). *Entrance requirements:* For master's, minimum undergraduate GPA of 3.0, 3 years of work experience. Additional exam requirements/recommendations for international students: Required—TOEFL (minimum score 550 paper-based). Electronic applications accepted.

University of Phoenix–Las Vegas Campus, School of Business, Las Vegas, NV 89135. Offers accounting (MBA); business administration (MBA); global management

(MBA); human resources management (MBA, MM); management (MM); marketing (MBA); public administration (MM). Evening/weekend programs available. Postbaccalaureate distance learning degree programs offered (no on-campus study). *Degree requirements:* For master's, thesis (for some programs). *Entrance requirements:* For master's, minimum undergraduate GPA of 3.0, 3 years of work experience. Additional exam requirements/recommendations for international students: Required—TOEFL (minimum score 550 paper-based; 79 iBT). Electronic applications accepted.

University of Phoenix–Little Rock Campus, School of Business, Little Rock, AR 72211-3500. Offers MBA, MM. Evening/weekend programs available. *Degree requirements:* For master's, thesis (for some programs). *Entrance requirements:* For master's, minimum undergraduate GPA of 3.0, 3 years of work experience. Additional exam requirements/recommendations for international students: Required—TOEFL (minimum score 550 paper-based). Electronic applications accepted.

University of Phoenix–Louisiana Campus, School of Business, Metairie, LA 70001-2082. Offers accounting (MBA); business administration (MBA); global management (MBA); human resources management (MBA, MM); management (MM); marketing (MBA); public administration (MBA). Evening/weekend programs available. *Degree requirements:* For master's, thesis (for some programs). *Entrance requirements:* For master's, minimum undergraduate GPA of 3.0, 3 years work experience. Additional exam requirements/recommendations for international students: Required—TOEFL (minimum score 550 paper-based; 79 iBT). Electronic applications accepted.

University of Phoenix–Louisville Campus, School of Business, Louisville, KY 40223-3839. Offers MBA. Evening/weekend programs available. Postbaccalaureate distance learning degree programs offered. *Entrance requirements:* Additional exam requirements/recommendations for international students: Required—TOEFL, TOEIC (Test of English as an International Communication), Berlitz Online English Proficiency Exam, PTE, or IELTS. Electronic applications accepted.

University of Phoenix–Madison Campus, School of Business, Madison, WI 53718-2416. Offers accounting (MBA); business and management (MBA); e-business (MBA); global management (MBA); human resources management (MBA, MM); management (MM); marketing (MBA); public administration (MBA).

University of Phoenix–Maryland Campus, School of Business, Columbia, MD 21045-5424. Offers business administration (MBA); global management (MBA); technology management (MBA). Evening/weekend programs available. Postbaccalaureate distance learning degree programs offered. *Entrance requirements:* Additional exam requirements/recommendations for international students: Required—TOEFL, TOEIC (Test of English as an International Communication), Berlitz Online English Proficiency Exam, PTE, or IELTS. Electronic applications accepted. *Expenses:* Contact institution.

University of Phoenix–Memphis Campus, School of Business, Cordova, TN 38018. Offers accounting (MBA); business and management (MBA); e-business (MBA); global management (MBA); human resources management (MBA, MM); management (MM); marketing (MBA); public administration (MBA, MM).

University of Phoenix–Milwaukee Campus, School of Business, Milwaukee, WI 53224. Offers accounting (MBA); business administration (MBA); energy management (MBA); global management (MBA); health care management (MBA); human resource management (MBA); management (MM); marketing (MBA); project management (MBA); technology management (MBA). Evening/weekend programs available. Postbaccalaureate distance learning degree programs offered. *Entrance requirements:* Additional exam requirements/recommendations for international students: Required—TOEFL, TOEIC (Test of English as an International Communication), Berlitz Online English Proficiency Exam, PTE, or IELTS. Electronic applications accepted. *Expenses:* Contact institution.

University of Phoenix–Minneapolis/St. Louis Park Campus, School of Business, St. Louis Park, MN 55426. Offers accounting (MBA); business administration (MBA); global management (MBA); human resources management (MBA); management (MM); marketing (MBA); public administration (MBA).

University of Phoenix–Nashville Campus, School of Business, Nashville, TN 37214-5048. Offers business administration (MBA); human resources management (MBA); management (MM). Evening/weekend programs available. *Degree requirements:* For master's, thesis (for some programs). *Entrance requirements:* For master's, minimum undergraduate GPA of 3.0, 3 years of work experience. Additional exam requirements/recommendations for international students: Required—TOEFL (minimum score 550 paper-based; 79 iBT). Electronic applications accepted.

University of Phoenix–New Mexico Campus, School of Business, Albuquerque, NM 87113-1570. Offers accounting (MBA); business administration (MBA); global management (MBA); human resources management (MBA, MM); management (MM); marketing (MBA). Evening/weekend programs available. *Degree requirements:* For master's, thesis (for some programs). *Entrance requirements:* For master's, 3 years of work experience, minimum undergraduate GPA of 3.0. Additional exam requirements/recommendations for international students: Required—TOEFL (minimum score 550 paper-based; 79 iBT). Electronic applications accepted.

University of Phoenix–North Florida Campus, College of Information Systems and Technology, Jacksonville, FL 32216-0959. Offers information systems (MIS); management (MIS). Evening/weekend programs available. *Degree requirements:* For master's, thesis (for some programs). *Entrance requirements:* For master's, minimum undergraduate GPA of 3.0, 3 years work experience. Additional exam requirements/recommendations for international students: Required—TOEFL (minimum score 550 paper-based; 79 iBT). Electronic applications accepted.

University of Phoenix–North Florida Campus, School of Business, Jacksonville, FL 32216-0959. Offers accounting (MBA); business administration (MBA); global management (MBA); human resources management (MBA, MM); management (MM); marketing (MBA); public administration (MBA, MM). Evening/weekend programs available. *Degree requirements:* For master's, thesis (for some programs). *Entrance requirements:* For master's, minimum undergraduate GPA of 3.0, 3 years work experience. Additional exam requirements/recommendations for international students: Required—TOEFL (minimum score 550 paper-based; 79 iBT). Electronic applications accepted.

University of Phoenix–Northwest Arkansas Campus, School of Business, Rogers, AR 72756-9615. Offers accounting (MBA); business and management (MBA); global management (MBA); human resources management (MBA, MM); management (MM); marketing (MBA); public administration (MBA, MM).

University of Phoenix–Oklahoma City Campus, School of Business, Oklahoma City, OK 73116-8244. Offers accounting (MBA); business administration (MBA); global management (MBA); human resource management (MBA); management (MM); marketing (MBA). Evening/weekend programs available. *Degree requirements:* For master's, thesis (for some programs). *Entrance requirements:* For master's, minimum undergraduate GPA of 3.0, 3 years of work experience. Additional exam requirements/recommendations for international students: Required—TOEFL (minimum score 550 paper-based; 79 iBT). Electronic applications accepted.

University of Phoenix–Omaha Campus, School of Business, Omaha, NE 68154-5240. Offers accounting (MBA); business and management (MBA); global management (MBA); human resources management (MBA, MM); management (MM); marketing (MBA); public administration (MBA, MM).

University of Phoenix–Online Campus, School of Advanced Studies, Phoenix, AZ 85034-7209. Offers business administration (DBA); education (Ed S); educational leadership (Ed D), including curriculum and instruction, education technology, educational leadership; health administration (DHA); higher education administration (PhD); industrial/organizational psychology (PhD); nursing (PhD); organizational leadership (DM), including information systems and technology, organizational leadership. Evening/weekend programs available. Postbaccalaureate distance learning degree programs offered. *Degree requirements:* For doctorate, thesis/dissertation. *Entrance requirements:* Additional exam requirements/recommendations for international students: Required—TOEFL, TOEIC (Test of English as an International Communication), Berlitz Online English Proficiency Exam, PTE, or IELTS. Electronic applications accepted. *Expenses:* Contact institution.

University of Phoenix–Online Campus, School of Business, Phoenix, AZ 85034-7209. Offers accountancy (MS); accounting (MBA, Certificate); business administration (MBA); energy management (MBA); global management (MBA); health care management (MBA); human resource management (MBA, Certificate); human resources management (MM); management (MM); marketing (MBA, Certificate); project management (MBA, Certificate); public administration (MBA, MM); technology management (MBA). Evening/weekend programs available. Postbaccalaureate distance learning degree programs offered. *Entrance requirements:* Additional exam requirements/recommendations for international students: Required—TOEFL, TOEIC (Test of English as an International Communication), Berlitz Online English Proficiency Exam, PTE, or IELTS. Electronic applications accepted. *Expenses:* Contact institution.

University of Phoenix–Oregon Campus, School of Business, Tigard, OR 97223. Offers accounting (MBA); business administration (MBA); global management (MBA); human resource management (MM); human resources management (MBA); management (MM); marketing (MBA); public administration (MM). Evening/weekend programs available. *Degree requirements:* For master's, thesis (for some programs). *Entrance requirements:* For master's, minimum undergraduate GPA of 3.0, 3 years of work experience. Additional exam requirements/recommendations for international students: Required—TOEFL (minimum score 550 paper-based; 79 iBT). Electronic applications accepted.

University of Phoenix–Philadelphia Campus, School of Business, Wayne, PA 19087-2121. Offers accounting (MBA); business administration (MBA); global management (MBA); human resources management (MBA, MM); management (MM); marketing (MBA); public administration (MM). Evening/weekend programs available. *Degree requirements:* For master's, thesis (for some programs). *Entrance requirements:* For master's, minimum undergraduate GPA of 3.0, 3 years work experience. Additional exam requirements/recommendations for international students: Required—TOEFL (minimum score 550 paper-based; 79 iBT). Electronic applications accepted.

University of Phoenix–Phoenix Campus, School of Business, Tempe, AZ 85282-2371. Offers accounting (MBA, MS, Certificate); business administration (MBA); energy management (MBA); global management (MBA); health care management (MBA); human resource management (MBA, Certificate); management (MM); marketing (MBA); project management (MBA); technology management (MBA). Evening/weekend programs available. Postbaccalaureate distance learning degree programs offered. *Entrance requirements:* Additional exam requirements/recommendations for international students: Required—TOEFL, TOEIC (Test of English as an International Communication), Berlitz Online English Proficiency Exam, PTE, or IELTS. Electronic applications accepted. *Expenses:* Contact institution.

University of Phoenix–Pittsburgh Campus, School of Business, Pittsburgh, PA 15276. Offers accounting (MBA); business administration (MBA); global management (MBA); human resources management (MBA, MM); management (MM); marketing (MBA); public administration (MBA, MM). Evening/weekend programs available. *Degree requirements:* For master's, thesis (for some programs). *Entrance requirements:* For master's, minimum undergraduate GPA of 3.0, 3 years work experience. Additional exam requirements/recommendations for international students: Required—TOEFL (minimum score 550 paper-based; 79 iBT). Electronic applications accepted.

University of Phoenix–Puerto Rico Campus, School of Business, Guaynabo, PR 00968. Offers accounting (MBA); energy management (MBA); global management (MBA); human resource management (MBA); marketing (MBA); project management (MBA); small business administration (MBA). Evening/weekend programs available. *Degree requirements:* For master's, thesis (for some programs). *Entrance requirements:* For master's, minimum undergraduate GPA of 3.0, 3 years work experience. Additional exam requirements/recommendations for international students: Required—TOEFL (minimum score 550 paper-based; 79 iBT). Electronic applications accepted.

University of Phoenix–Richmond-Virginia Beach Campus, School of Business, Glen Allen, VA 23060. Offers accounting (MBA); business administration (MBA); global management (MBA); human resources management (MBA, MM); management (MM); marketing (MBA); public administration (MBA, MM). Evening/weekend programs available. *Degree requirements:* For master's, thesis (for some programs). *Entrance requirements:* For master's, minimum undergraduate GPA of 3.0, 3 years work experience. Additional exam requirements/recommendations for international students: Required—TOEFL (minimum score 550 paper-based; 79 iBT). Electronic applications accepted.

University of Phoenix–Sacramento Valley Campus, College of Information Systems and Technology, Sacramento, CA 95833-3632. Offers management (MIS); technology management (MBA). Evening/weekend programs available. *Degree requirements:* For master's, thesis (for some programs). *Entrance requirements:* For master's, minimum undergraduate GPA of 3.0, 3 years work experience. Additional exam requirements/recommendations for international students: Required—TOEFL (minimum score 550 paper-based; 79 iBT). Electronic applications accepted.

University of Phoenix–Sacramento Valley Campus, School of Business, Sacramento, CA 95833-3632. Offers accounting (MBA); business administration (MBA); global management (MBA); human resources management (MBA, MM); management (MM); marketing (MBA); public administration (MBA, MM). Evening/weekend programs available. *Degree requirements:* For master's, thesis (for some programs). *Entrance requirements:* For master's, minimum undergraduate GPA of 3.0, 3 years work experience. Additional exam requirements/recommendations for international students: Required—TOEFL (minimum score 550 paper-based; 79 iBT). Electronic applications accepted.

University of Phoenix–St. Louis Campus, School of Business, St. Louis, MO 63043. Offers accounting (MBA); business administration (MBA); global management (MBA); human resources management (MBA, MM); management (MM); marketing (MBA); public administration (MM). Evening/weekend programs available. *Degree requirements:* For master's, thesis (for some programs). *Entrance requirements:* For master's, 3 years of work experience, minimum undergraduate GPA of 3.0. Additional

exam requirements/recommendations for international students: Required—TOEFL (minimum score 550 paper-based; 79 iBT). Electronic applications accepted.

University of Phoenix–San Antonio Campus, School of Business, San Antonio, TX 78230. Offers accounting (MBA); business administration (MBA); e-business (MBA); global management (MBA); human resources management (MBA, MM); management (MM); marketing (MBA); public administration (MBA, MM).

University of Phoenix–San Diego Campus, College of Information Systems and Technology, San Diego, CA 92123. Offers management (MIS); technology management (MBA). Evening/weekend programs available. *Degree requirements:* For master's, thesis (for some programs). *Entrance requirements:* For master's, minimum undergraduate GPA of 3.0, 3 years work experience. Additional exam requirements/recommendations for international students: Required—TOEFL (minimum score 550 paper-based; 79 iBT). Electronic applications accepted.

University of Phoenix–San Diego Campus, School of Business, San Diego, CA 92123. Offers accounting (MBA); business administration (MBA); global management (MBA); human resources management (MBA, MM); management (MM); marketing (MBA); public administration (MBA). Evening/weekend programs available. *Degree requirements:* For master's, thesis (for some programs). *Entrance requirements:* For master's, 3 years of work experience, minimum undergraduate GPA of 3.0. Additional exam requirements/recommendations for international students: Required—TOEFL (minimum score 550 paper-based; 79 iBT). Electronic applications accepted.

University of Phoenix–Savannah Campus, School of Business, Savannah, GA 31405-7400. Offers accounting (MBA); business administration (MBA); global management (MBA); human resources management (MBA, MM); management (MM); marketing (MBA); public administration (MBA, MM).

University of Phoenix–Southern Arizona Campus, School of Business, Tucson, AZ 85711. Offers accountancy (MS); accounting (MBA); business administration (MBA); global management (MBA); human resources management (MBA); management (MM); marketing (MBA). Evening/weekend programs available. *Degree requirements:* For master's, thesis (for some programs). *Entrance requirements:* For master's, minimum undergraduate GPA of 3.0, 3 years of work experience. Additional exam requirements/recommendations for international students: Required—TOEFL (minimum score 550 paper-based; 79 iBT). Electronic applications accepted.

University of Phoenix–Southern California Campus, School of Business, Costa Mesa, CA 92626. Offers accounting (MBA); business administration (MBA); energy management (MBA); global management (MBA); health care management (MBA); human resource management (MBA); management (MM); marketing (MBA); project management (MBA); technology management (MBA). Evening/weekend programs available. Postbaccalaureate distance learning degree programs offered. *Entrance requirements:* Additional exam requirements/recommendations for international students: Required—TOEFL, TOEIC (Test of English as an International Communication), Berlitz Online English Proficiency Exam, PTE, or IELTS. Electronic applications accepted. *Expenses:* Contact institution.

University of Phoenix–Southern Colorado Campus, School of Business, Colorado Springs, CO 80903. Offers accounting (MBA); business administration (MBA); global management (MBA); human resources management (MBA, MM); management (MM); marketing (MBA); public administration (MM). Evening/weekend programs available. *Degree requirements:* For master's, thesis (for some programs). *Entrance requirements:* For master's, minimum undergraduate GPA of 3.0, 3 years of work experience. Additional exam requirements/recommendations for international students: Required—TOEFL (minimum score 550 paper-based; 79 iBT). Electronic applications accepted.

University of Phoenix–South Florida Campus, College of Information Systems and Technology, Miramar, FL 33030. Offers management (MIS); technology management (MBA). Evening/weekend programs available. *Degree requirements:* For master's, thesis (for some programs). *Entrance requirements:* For master's, minimum undergraduate GPA of 3.0, 3 years of work experience. Additional exam requirements/recommendations for international students: Required—TOEFL (minimum score 550 paper-based; 79 iBT). Electronic applications accepted.

University of Phoenix–South Florida Campus, School of Business, Miramar, FL 33030. Offers accounting (MBA); business administration (MBA); global management (MBA); human resource management (MBA); human resources management (MM); management (MM); marketing (MBA); public administration (MBA, MM). Evening/weekend programs available. *Degree requirements:* For master's, thesis (for some programs). *Entrance requirements:* For master's, minimum undergraduate GPA of 3.0, 3 years work experience. Additional exam requirements/recommendations for international students: Required—TOEFL (minimum score 550 paper-based; 79 iBT). Electronic applications accepted.

University of Phoenix–Springfield Campus, School of Business, Springfield, MO 65804-7211. Offers accounting (MBA); business administration (MBA); global management (MBA); human resources management (MBA, MM); management (MM); marketing (MBA); public administration (MBA, MM).

University of Phoenix–Tulsa Campus, School of Business, Tulsa, OK 74134-1412. Offers accounting (MBA); business (MM); business administration (MBA); global management (MBA); human resources management (MBA); marketing (MBA). Evening/weekend programs available. *Degree requirements:* For master's, thesis (for some programs). *Entrance requirements:* For master's, minimum undergraduate GPA of 3.0, 3 years work experience. Additional exam requirements/recommendations for international students: Required—TOEFL (minimum score 550 paper-based; 79 iBT).

University of Phoenix–Utah Campus, School of Business, Salt Lake City, UT 84123-4617. Offers accounting (MBA); business administration (MBA); global management (MBA); human resource management (MBA, MM); management (MM); marketing (MBA); technology management (MBA). Evening/weekend programs available. *Degree requirements:* For master's, thesis (for some programs). *Entrance requirements:* For master's, minimum undergraduate GPA of 3.0, 3 years of work experience. Additional exam requirements/recommendations for international students: Required—TOEFL (minimum score 550 paper-based; 79 iBT). Electronic applications accepted.

University of Phoenix–Washington D.C. Campus, School of Business, Washington, DC 20001. Offers accountancy (MS); business administration (MBA, DBA); human resources management (MM); management (MM); organizational leadership (DM); public administration (MPA).

University of Phoenix–Western Washington Campus, School of Business, Tukwila, WA 98188. Offers MBA. Evening/weekend programs available. *Degree requirements:* For master's, thesis (for some programs). *Entrance requirements:* For master's, minimum undergraduate GPA of 3.0, 3 years of work experience. Additional exam requirements/recommendations for international students: Required—TOEFL (minimum score 550 paper-based; 79 iBT). Electronic applications accepted.

University of Phoenix–West Florida Campus, School of Business, Temple Terrace, FL 33637. Offers accounting (MBA); business administration (MBA); global management (MBA); human resources management (MBA, MM); management (MM); marketing (MBA); public administration (MBA, MM). Evening/weekend programs available. *Degree requirements:* For master's, thesis (for some programs). *Entrance requirements:* For master's, 3 years of work experience, minimum undergraduate GPA of 3.0. Additional exam requirements/recommendations for international students: Required—TOEFL (minimum score 550 paper-based; 79 iBT). Electronic applications accepted.

University of Phoenix–Wichita Campus, School of Business, Wichita, KS 67226-4011. Offers MBA. Evening/weekend programs available. *Degree requirements:* For master's, thesis (for some programs). *Entrance requirements:* For master's, minimum undergraduate GPA of 3.0, 3 years of work experience. Additional exam requirements/recommendations for international students: Required—TOEFL (minimum score 550 paper-based; 79 iBT). Electronic applications accepted.

University of Pittsburgh, Katz Graduate School of Business, Doctoral Program in Business Administration, Pittsburgh, PA 15260. Offers accounting (PhD); finance (PhD); information systems (PhD); marketing (PhD); operations/decision sciences/artificial intelligence (PhD); organizational behavior and human resource management (PhD); strategic planning (PhD). *Accreditation:* AACSB. *Faculty:* 60 full-time (17 women). *Students:* 50 full-time (22 women); includes 4 minority (2 Black or African American, non-Hispanic/Latino; 2 Asian, non-Hispanic/Latino), 27 international. 321 applicants, 7% accepted, 14 enrolled. In 2013, 10 doctorates awarded. *Degree requirements:* For doctorate, comprehensive exam, thesis/dissertation. *Entrance requirements:* For doctorate, GMAT or GRE, 3 recommendations, statement of purpose, transcripts of all previous course work and degrees. Additional exam requirements/recommendations for international students: Required—TOEFL. *Application deadline:* For fall admission, 1/1 priority date for domestic and international students. Applications are processed on a rolling basis. Application fee: $50. Electronic applications accepted. *Expenses:* Tuition, state resident: full-time $19,964; part-time $807 per credit. Tuition, nonresident: full-time $32,686; part-time $1337 per credit. *Required fees:* $740; $200. Tuition and fees vary according to program. *Financial support:* In 2013–14, 40 students received support, including 30 research assistantships with full tuition reimbursements available (averaging $23,045 per year), 10 teaching assistantships with full tuition reimbursements available (averaging $26,055 per year); fellowships, Federal Work-Study, scholarships/grants, health care benefits, and unspecified assistantships also available. Financial award application deadline: 1/1. *Faculty research:* Accounting systems/financial reporting, corporate finance, shopper marketing/consumer behavior, management information systems, organizational behavior and entrepreneurship. *Unit head:* Dr. Dennis Galletta, Director, 412-648-1699, Fax: 412-624-3633, E-mail: galletta@katz.pitt.edu. *Application contact:* Carrie Woods, Assistant Director, 412-648-1525, Fax: 412-624-3633, E-mail: cawoods@katz.pitt.edu.
Website: http://www.business.pitt.edu/katz/phd/.

University of Pittsburgh, Katz Graduate School of Business, Executive MBA Program, Pittsburgh, PA 15260. Offers EMBA. *Accreditation:* AACSB. *Faculty:* 21 full-time (4 women), 4 part-time/adjunct (1 woman). *Students:* 71 full-time (11 women); includes 9 minority (2 Black or African American, non-Hispanic/Latino; 5 Asian, non-Hispanic/Latino; 2 Hispanic/Latino). Average age 37. 75 applicants, 99% accepted, 71 enrolled. In 2013, 55 master's awarded. *Entrance requirements:* For master's, GMAT (for candidates with less than 10 years experience, GPA less than 3.0, or limited quantitative background), 3 credits of course work in college-level calculus, minimum 5 years of management experience, resume, 2 letters of recommendations, essay, interview. Additional exam requirements/recommendations for international students: Required—TOEFL or IELTS. *Application deadline:* For winter admission, 12/1 for domestic students, 3/1 for international students; for spring admission, 4/1 priority date for domestic and international students. Application fee: $0. *Expenses:* Contact institution. *Financial support:* Scholarships/grants available. Financial award application deadline: 12/1; financial award applicants required to submit FAFSA. *Faculty research:* Accounting systems/financial reporting, corporate finance, shopper marketing/consumer behavior, management information systems, organizational behavior and entrepreneurship. *Unit head:* William T. Valenta, Jr., Assistant Dean, 412-648-1610, Fax: 412-648-1787, E-mail: wtvalenta@katz.pitt.edu. *Application contact:* Christine Kush, Director of Operations, 412-648-1806, Fax: 412-648-1787, E-mail: embaprogram@katz.pitt.edu.
Website: http://www.business.pitt.edu/katz/emba/.

University of Pittsburgh, Katz Graduate School of Business, Master of Business Administration Programs, Pittsburgh, PA 15260. Offers finance (MBA); information systems (MBA); marketing (MBA); operations management (MBA); organizational behavior and human resource management (MBA); strategy, environment and organizations (MBA); MBA/JD; MBA/MIB; MBA/MPIA; MBA/MSE; MBA/MSIS; MID/MBA. *Accreditation:* AACSB. Part-time and evening/weekend programs available. *Faculty:* 60 full-time (14 women), 21 part-time/adjunct (5 women). *Students:* 107 full-time (31 women), 428 part-time (155 women); includes 55 minority (15 Black or African American, non-Hispanic/Latino; 26 Asian, non-Hispanic/Latino; 10 Hispanic/Latino; 4 Two or more races, non-Hispanic/Latino), 83 international. Average age 30. 449 applicants, 23% accepted, 63 enrolled. In 2013, 279 master's awarded. *Degree requirements:* For master's, minimum GPA of 3.0. *Entrance requirements:* For master's, GMAT, recommendations, undergraduate transcripts, essay, resume, interview, bachelor's degree. Additional exam requirements/recommendations for international students: Required—TOEFL (minimum score 600 paper-based; 100 iBT) or IELTS. *Application deadline:* For fall admission, 4/1 priority date for domestic students, 2/1 priority date for international students. Application fee: $50. Electronic applications accepted. *Expenses:* Tuition, state resident: full-time $19,964; part-time $807 per credit. Tuition, nonresident: full-time $32,686; part-time $1337 per credit. *Required fees:* $740; $200. Tuition and fees vary according to program. *Financial support:* In 2013–14, 60 students received support. Career-related internships or fieldwork and scholarships/grants available. Financial award application deadline: 2/1. *Faculty research:* Accounting systems/financial reporting, corporate finance, shopper marketing/consumer behavior, management information systems, organizational behavior and entrepreneurship. *Unit head:* Tim Robison, Assistant Dean, 412-648-1700, Fax: 412-648-1659, E-mail: trobison@katz.pitt.edu. *Application contact:* Thomas Keller, Director of MBA Admissions, 412-648-1700, Fax: 412-648-1659, E-mail: mba@katz.pitt.edu.
Website: http://www.business.pitt.edu/katz/mba/.

University of Pittsburgh, Katz Graduate School of Business, MBA/Juris Doctor Program, Pittsburgh, PA 15260. Offers MBA/JD. *Faculty:* 61 full-time (15 women), 21 part-time/adjunct (5 women). *Students:* 23 full-time (10 women), 1 (woman) part-time; includes 3 minority (2 Black or African American, non-Hispanic/Latino; 1 Hispanic/Latino), 4 international. Average age 37. 17 applicants, 88% accepted, 10 enrolled. *Entrance requirements:* Additional exam requirements/recommendations for international students: Required—TOEFL (minimum score 600 paper-based; 100 iBT) or IELTS. *Application deadline:* For fall admission, 4/1 priority date for domestic students, 2/1 priority date for international students. Application fee: $50. Electronic applications accepted. *Expenses:* Tuition, state resident: full-time $19,964; part-time $807 per credit. Tuition, nonresident: full-time $32,686; part-time $1337 per credit. *Required fees:* $740; $200. Tuition and fees vary according to program. *Financial support:* In 2013–14, 11 students received support. Career-related internships or fieldwork and scholarships/grants available. Financial award application deadline: 2/1. *Faculty research:* Accounting

systems/financial reporting, corporate finance, shopper marketing/consumer behavior, management information systems, organizational behavior and entrepreneurship. *Unit head:* Tim Robison, Assistant Dean, 412-648-1700, Fax: 412-648-1659, E-mail: trobison@katz.pitt.edu. *Application contact:* Thomas Keller, Director of MBA Admissions, 412-648-1700, Fax: 412-648-1659, E-mail: mba@katz.pitt.edu.
Website: http://www.business.pitt.edu/katz/mba/academics/programs/mba-jd.php.

University of Pittsburgh, Katz Graduate School of Business, MBA/Master of International Business Dual Degree Program, Pittsburgh, PA 15260. Offers MBA/MIB. Part-time and evening/weekend programs available. *Faculty:* 61 full-time (15 women), 21 part-time/adjunct (5 women). *Students:* 1 full-time (0 women), 6 part-time (3 women). Average age 29. 15 applicants, 20% accepted, 1 enrolled. *Entrance requirements:* Additional exam requirements/recommendations for international students: Required—TOEFL (minimum score 600 paper-based; 100 iBT) or IELTS. *Application deadline:* For fall admission, 4/1 priority date for domestic students, 2/1 priority date for international students. Application fee: $50. Electronic applications accepted. *Expenses:* Tuition, state resident: full-time $19,964; part-time $807 per credit. Tuition, nonresident: full-time $32,686; part-time $1337 per credit. *Required fees:* $740; $200. Tuition and fees vary according to program. *Financial support:* In 2013–14, 1 student received support. Career-related internships or fieldwork and scholarships/grants available. Financial award application deadline: 2/1. *Faculty research:* Accounting systems/financial reporting, corporate finance, shopper marketing/consumer behavior, management information systems, organizational behavior and entrepreneurship. *Unit head:* Tim Robison, Assistant Dean/Director, 412-648-1700, Fax: 412-648-1659, E-mail: trobison@katz.pitt.edu. *Application contact:* Thomas Keller, Director of MBA Admissions, 412-648-1700, Fax: 412-648-1659, E-mail: mba@katz.pitt.edu.
Website: http://www.business.pitt.edu/katz/mba/academics/programs/mba-mib.php.

University of Pittsburgh, Katz Graduate School of Business, MBA/Master of International Development Joint Degree Program, Pittsburgh, PA 15260. Offers MID/MBA. *Accreditation:* AACSB. Part-time and evening/weekend programs available. *Faculty:* 61 full-time (15 women), 21 part-time/adjunct (5 women). *Students:* 1 (woman) full-time; minority (Asian, non-Hispanic/Latino). Average age 30. 1 applicant, 100% accepted, 1 enrolled. *Entrance requirements:* Additional exam requirements/recommendations for international students: Required—TOEFL (minimum score 600 paper-based; 100 iBT) or IELTS. *Application deadline:* For fall admission, 4/1 priority date for domestic students, 2/1 priority date for international students. Application fee: $50. Electronic applications accepted. *Expenses:* Tuition, state resident: full-time $19,964; part-time $807 per credit. Tuition, nonresident: full-time $32,686; part-time $1337 per credit. *Required fees:* $740; $200. Tuition and fees vary according to program. *Financial support:* In 2013–14, 1 student received support. Career-related internships or fieldwork and scholarships/grants available. Financial award application deadline: 2/1. *Faculty research:* Accounting systems/financial reporting, corporate finance, shopper marketing/consumer behavior, management information systems, organizational behavior and entrepreneurship. *Unit head:* Tim Robison, Assistant Dean, 412-648-1700, Fax: 412-648-1659, E-mail: trobison@katz.pitt.edu. *Application contact:* Thomas Keller, Director of MBA Admissions, 412-648-1700, Fax: 412-648-1659, E-mail: mba@katz.pitt.edu.
Website: http://www.business.pitt.edu/katz/mba/academics/programs/mba-mid.php.

University of Pittsburgh, Katz Graduate School of Business, MBA/Master of Public and International Affairs Dual-Degree Program, Pittsburgh, PA 15260. Offers MBA/MPIA. *Accreditation:* AACSB. Part-time and evening/weekend programs available. *Faculty:* 61 full-time (15 women), 21 part-time/adjunct (5 women). *Students:* 2 full-time (1 woman). Average age 27. 2 applicants, 50% accepted, 1 enrolled. *Entrance requirements:* Additional exam requirements/recommendations for international students: Required—TOEFL (minimum score 600 paper-based; 100 iBT) or IELTS. *Application deadline:* For fall admission, 4/1 priority date for domestic students, 2/1 priority date for international students. Application fee: $50. Electronic applications accepted. *Expenses:* Tuition, state resident: full-time $19,964; part-time $807 per credit. Tuition, nonresident: full-time $32,686; part-time $1337 per credit. *Required fees:* $740; $200. Tuition and fees vary according to program. *Financial support:* In 2013–14, 1 student received support. Career-related internships or fieldwork and scholarships/grants available. Financial award application deadline: 2/1. *Faculty research:* Accounting systems/financial reporting, corporate finance, shopper marketing/consumer behavior, management information systems, organizational behavior and entrepreneurship. *Unit head:* Tim Robison, Assistant Dean/Director, 412-648-1700, Fax: 412-648-1659, E-mail: trobison@katz.pitt.edu. *Application contact:* Thomas Keller, Director of MBA Admissions, 412-648-1700, Fax: 412-648-1659, E-mail: mba@katz.pitt.edu.
Website: http://www.business.pitt.edu/katz/mba/academics/programs/mba-mpia.php.

University of Pittsburgh, Katz Graduate School of Business, MBA/Master of Science in Engineering Joint Degree Program, Pittsburgh, PA 15260. Offers MBA/MSE. *Accreditation:* AACSB. Part-time and evening/weekend programs available. *Faculty:* 61 full-time (15 women), 21 part-time/adjunct (5 women). *Students:* 9 full-time (2 women), 25 part-time (3 women); includes 7 minority (1 Black or African American, non-Hispanic/Latino; 1 Asian, non-Hispanic/Latino; 3 Hispanic/Latino; 2 Two or more races, non-Hispanic/Latino), 3 international. Average age 29. 16 applicants, 50% accepted, 6 enrolled. *Entrance requirements:* Additional exam requirements/recommendations for international students: Required—TOEFL (minimum score 600 paper-based; 100 iBT) or IELTS. *Application deadline:* For fall admission, 4/1 priority date for domestic students, 2/1 priority date for international students. Application fee: $50. Electronic applications accepted. *Expenses:* Tuition, state resident: full-time $19,964; part-time $807 per credit. Tuition, nonresident: full-time $32,686; part-time $1337 per credit. *Required fees:* $740; $200. Tuition and fees vary according to program. *Financial support:* In 2013–14, 6 students received support. Career-related internships or fieldwork and scholarships/grants available. Financial award application deadline: 2/1. *Faculty research:* Accounting systems/financial reporting, corporate finance, shopper marketing/consumer behavior, management information systems, organizational behavior and entrepreneurship. *Unit head:* Tim Robison, Assistant Dean/Director, 412-648-1700, Fax: 412-648-1659, E-mail: trobison@katz.pitt.edu. *Application contact:* Thomas Keller, Director of MBA Admissions, 412-648-1700, Fax: 412-648-1659, E-mail: mba@katz.pitt.edu.
Website: http://www.business.pitt.edu/katz/mba/academics/programs/mba-msengineering.php.

University of Portland, Dr. Robert B. Pamplin, Jr. School of Business, Portland, OR 97203-5798. Offers entrepreneurship (MBA); finance (MBA, MS); health care management (MBA); marketing (MBA); nonprofit management (EMBA); operations and technology management (MBA, MS); sustainability (MBA). *Accreditation:* AACSB. Part-time and evening/weekend programs available. *Faculty:* 26 full-time (5 women), 8 part-time/adjunct (1 woman). *Students:* 37 full-time (11 women), 93 part-time (44 women); includes 15 minority (1 Black or African American, non-Hispanic/Latino; 7 Asian, non-Hispanic/Latino; 5 Hispanic/Latino; 2 Two or more races, non-Hispanic/Latino), 21 international. Average age 32. In 2013, 68 master's awarded. *Entrance requirements:* For master's, GMAT, minimum GPA of 3.0, resume, 2 letters of recommendation. Additional exam requirements/recommendations for international students: Required—TOEFL (minimum score 570 paper-based; 89 iBT), IELTS (minimum score 7). *Application deadline:* For fall admission, 7/15 priority date for domestic and international

students; for spring admission, 12/15 priority date for domestic and international students. Applications are processed on a rolling basis. Application fee: $50. *Expenses:* Contact institution. *Financial support:* Federal Work-Study, scholarships/grants, and tuition waivers (partial) available. Support available to part-time students. Financial award application deadline: 3/1; financial award applicants required to submit FAFSA. *Unit head:* Melissa McCarthy, Director, 503-943-7224, E-mail: mba-up@up.edu.
Website: http://business.up.edu/mba/default.aspx?cid-1179&pid-6450.

University of Puerto Rico, Mayagüez Campus, Graduate Studies, College of Business Administration, Mayagüez, PR 00681-9000. Offers business administration (MBA); finance (MBA); human resources (MBA); industrial management (MBA). Part-time and evening/weekend programs available. *Faculty:* 42 full-time (26 women), 1 part-time/adjunct (0 women). *Students:* 36 full-time (18 women), 15 part-time (11 women). 26 applicants, 50% accepted, 10 enrolled. In 2013, 7 master's awarded. *Degree requirements:* For master's, comprehensive exam. *Entrance requirements:* For master's, GMAT or EXADEP, bachelor's degree with courses in calculus, microeconomics, accounting and statistics. Additional exam requirements/recommendations for international students: Required—TOEFL (minimum score 500 paper-based). *Application deadline:* For fall admission, 2/15 for domestic and international students; for spring admission, 9/15 for domestic and international students. Applications are processed on a rolling basis. Application fee: $25. *Expenses:* Tuition, area resident: Full-time $2466; part-time $822 per year. *International tuition:* $6371 full-time. *Required fees:* $1095; $1095. Tuition and fees vary according to course level, course load and reciprocity agreements. *Financial support:* In 2013–14, 7 students received support, including 2 research assistantships (averaging $8,725 per year), 5 teaching assistantships (averaging $4,106 per year); fellowships with full tuition reimbursements available, Federal Work-Study, institutionally sponsored loans, and unspecified assistantships also available. *Faculty research:* Organizational studies, management, accounting. *Total annual research expenditures:* $20,000. *Unit head:* Dr. Ana Martin, Graduate Student Coordinator, 787-832-4040 Ext. 3800, Fax: 787-832-5320, E-mail: ana.martin@upr.edu. *Application contact:* Milagros Soto, Student Administrator, 787-265-3887, Fax: 787-832-5320, E-mail: milagros.soto1@upr.edu.
Website: http://enterprise.uprm.edu/.

University of Puerto Rico, Río Piedras Campus, College of Business Administration, San Juan, PR 00931-3300. Offers accounting (MBA); finance (MBA, PhD); general business (MBA); human resources management (MBA); international trade and business (MBA, PhD); marketing (MBA); operations management (MBA); quantitative methods (MBA). Part-time programs available. *Degree requirements:* For master's, comprehensive exam, thesis or alternative, research project. *Entrance requirements:* For master's, GMAT or PAEG, minimum GPA of 3.0, letter of recommendation; for doctorate, GMAT, PAEG, minimum GPA of 3.0, master degree. *Faculty research:* Management.

University of Redlands, School of Business, Redlands, CA 92373-0999. Offers business (MBA); information technology (MS); management (MA). Evening/weekend programs available. *Entrance requirements:* For master's, minimum GPA of 3.0, 2 letters of recommendation. *Faculty research:* Human resources management, educational leadership, humanities, teacher education.

University of Regina, Faculty of Graduate Studies and Research, Kenneth Levene Graduate School of Business, Regina, SK S4S 0A2, Canada. Offers EMBA, M Admin, MBA, MHRM, Master's Certificate, PGD. Part-time and evening/weekend programs available. *Faculty:* 39 full-time (14 women), 7 part-time/adjunct (0 women). *Students:* 107 full-time (39 women), 79 part-time (43 women). 184 applicants, 22% accepted. In 2013, 58 master's, 23 other advanced degrees awarded. *Degree requirements:* For master's, project (for some programs). *Entrance requirements:* For master's, two years of relevant work experience (MHRM, M Admin); three years relevant work experience (MBA); for other advanced degree, two years of relevant work experience (Master's Certificate); three years relevant work experience (PGD). Additional exam requirements/recommendations for international students: Required—TOEFL (minimum score 580 paper-based; 80 iBT), IELTS (minimum score 6.5). *Application deadline:* Applications are processed on a rolling basis. Application fee: $100. Electronic applications accepted. *Expenses:* Contact institution. *Financial support:* In 2013–14, 8 fellowships (averaging $6,000 per year), 1 research assistantship (averaging $5,500 per year), 8 teaching assistantships (averaging $2,356 per year) were awarded; scholarships/grants also available. Financial award application deadline: 6/15. *Faculty research:* Management of public and private sector organizations. *Unit head:* Dr. Andrew Gaudes, Dean, 306-585-4162, Fax: 306-585-4805, E-mail: andrew.gaudes@uregina.ca. *Application contact:* Dr. Ronald Camp, Associate Dean, Research and Graduate Programs/Director of Kenneth Levene Graduate School, 306-337-2387, Fax: 306-585-5361, E-mail: ronald.camp@uregina.ca.
Website: http://www.uregina.ca/business/levene/.

University of Rhode Island, Graduate School, College of Business Administration, Kingston, RI 02881. Offers accounting (MS); business administration (MBA, PhD), including finance and insurance (PhD), management (PhD), marketing (PhD), operations and supply chain management (MBA); finance (MBA); general business (MBA); management (MBA); marketing (MBA); supply chain management (MBA). *Accreditation:* AACSB. Part-time and evening/weekend programs available. *Faculty:* 43 full-time (16 women). *Students:* 103 full-time (37 women), 196 part-time (82 women); includes 42 minority (6 Black or African American, non-Hispanic/Latino; 1 American Indian or Alaska Native, non-Hispanic/Latino; 16 Asian, non-Hispanic/Latino; 13 Hispanic/Latino; 6 Two or more races, non-Hispanic/Latino), 29 international. In 2013, 119 master's, 3 doctorates awarded. *Degree requirements:* For master's, comprehensive exam (for some programs), thesis optional; for doctorate, comprehensive exam, thesis/dissertation. *Entrance requirements:* For master's, GMAT or GRE, 2 letters of recommendation, resume; for doctorate, GMAT or GRE, 3 letters of recommendation, resume. Additional exam requirements/recommendations for international students: Required—TOEFL (minimum score 575 paper-based; 91 iBT). *Application deadline:* For fall admission, 4/15 for domestic students, 2/15 for international students. Application fee: $65. Electronic applications accepted. *Expenses:* Tuition, state resident: full-time $11,532; part-time $641 per credit. Tuition, nonresident: full-time $23,606; part-time $1311 per credit. *Required fees:* $1388; $36 per credit. $35 per semester. One-time fee: $130. *Financial support:* In 2013–14, 14 teaching assistantships with full and partial tuition reimbursements (averaging $15,220 per year) were awarded. Financial award application deadline: 4/15; financial award applicants required to submit FAFSA. *Total annual research expenditures:* $66,948. *Unit head:* Dr. Mark Higgins, Dean, 401-874-4244, Fax: 401-874-4312, E-mail: markhiggins@uri.edu. *Application contact:* Lisa Lancellotta, Coordinator, MBA Programs, 401-874-4241, Fax: 401-874-4312, E-mail: mba@uri.edu.
Website: http://www.cba.uri.edu/.

University of Richmond, Robins School of Business, Richmond, VA 23173. Offers MBA, JD/MBA. *Accreditation:* AACSB. Part-time and evening/weekend programs available. *Faculty:* 32 full-time (6 women), 5 part-time/adjunct (1 woman). *Students:* 96 full-time (34 women); includes 11 minority (5 Black or African American, non-Hispanic/Latino; 4 Asian, non-Hispanic/Latino; 2 Hispanic/Latino), 2 international. Average age 27. 57 applicants, 79% accepted, 37 enrolled. In 2013, 28 degrees awarded. *Degree*

requirements: For master's, capstone project. *Entrance requirements:* For master's, GMAT, 2 years of work experience. Additional exam requirements/recommendations for international students: Required—TOEFL (minimum score 600 paper-based; 100 iBT). *Application deadline:* For fall admission, 5/12 for domestic and international students; for spring admission, 11/17 for domestic and international students; for summer admission, 1/1 for international students. Application fee: $50. Electronic applications accepted. *Financial support:* In 2013–14, 75 students received support. Scholarships/grants available. Support available to part-time students. Financial award application deadline: 6/1; financial award applicants required to submit FAFSA. *Faculty research:* Entrepreneurship, investments, auditing, consumer behavior, strategic management. *Unit head:* Dr. Nancy Bagranoff, Dean, Robins School of Business, 804-289-8549, Fax: 804-287-6544, E-mail: nbagrano@richmond.edu. *Application contact:* Dr. Richard Coughlan, Senior Associate Dean/MBA Program Director, 804-289-8553, Fax: 804-287-1228, E-mail: rcoughla@richmond.edu.
Website: http://robins.richmond.edu/.

University of Rochester, Simon Business School, Doctoral Program in Business Administration, Rochester, NY 14627. Offers PhD. *Accreditation:* AACSB. *Faculty:* 60 full-time (11 women), 23 part-time/adjunct (3 women). *Students:* 47 full-time (18 women), 31 international. Average age 26. 329 applicants, 9% accepted, 5 enrolled. In 2013, 9 doctorates awarded. *Degree requirements:* For doctorate, comprehensive exam, thesis/dissertation, qualifying exam. *Entrance requirements:* For doctorate, GMAT or GRE. Additional exam requirements/recommendations for international students: Required—TOEFL. *Application deadline:* For fall admission, 1/10 for domestic and international students. Application fee: $100. Electronic applications accepted. *Expenses:* Contact institution. *Financial support:* Fellowships, research assistantships, teaching assistantships, and tuition waivers (full and partial) available. Financial award application deadline: 1/10. *Unit head:* Dr. Ron Kaniel, Committee Chair, 585-275-2959. *Application contact:* Sue Harris, PhD Administrator, 585-275-2959, E-mail: phdoffice@simon.rochester.edu.

University of Rochester, Simon Business School, Full-Time Master's Program in Business Administration, Rochester, NY 14627. Offers accounting and information systems (MBA); business environment and public policy (MBA); business systems consulting (MBA); competitive and organizational strategy - pricing (MBA); computers and information systems (MBA); corporate accounting (MBA); electronic commerce (MBA); entrepreneurship (MBA); finance (MBA); health sciences management (MBA); international management (MBA); marketing - brand management and pricing (MBA); operations management - manufacturing (MBA); operations management - services (MBA); public accounting (MBA). *Accreditation:* AACSB. Part-time and evening/weekend programs available. *Faculty:* 60 full-time (11 women), 23 part-time/adjunct (3 women). *Students:* 282 full-time (74 women); includes 55 minority (29 Black or African American, non-Hispanic/Latino; 1 American Indian or Alaska Native, non-Hispanic/Latino; 11 Asian, non-Hispanic/Latino; 12 Hispanic/Latino; 2 Two or more races, non-Hispanic/Latino), 144 international. 673 applicants, 33% accepted, 65 enrolled. In 2013, 176 master's awarded. *Entrance requirements:* For master's, GMAT/GRE, previous course work in calculus. Additional exam requirements/recommendations for international students: Required—TOEFL. *Application deadline:* For fall admission, 10/15 for domestic and international students; for winter admission, 1/5 for domestic and international students; for spring admission, 3/15 for domestic and international students; for summer admission, 5/15 for domestic students. Applications are processed on a rolling basis. Application fee: $150. Electronic applications accepted. *Expenses: Tuition:* Full-time $44,580; part-time $1394 per credit hour. *Required fees:* $492. *Financial support:* In 2013–14, 72 students received support. Fellowships, research assistantships, teaching assistantships, institutionally sponsored loans, scholarships/grants, and tuition waivers (partial) available. Financial award application deadline: 3/1; financial award applicants required to submit CSS PROFILE or FAFSA. *Unit head:* Mark Zupan, Dean, 585-275-3316. *Application contact:* Rebekah S. Lewin, Assistant Dean of Admissions and Student Engagement, 585-275-3533, E-mail: admissions@simon.rochester.edu.

University of Rochester, Simon Business School, MS Program in Management, New York City, Rochester, NY 14627. Offers MS. Part-time and evening/weekend programs available. *Faculty:* 60 full-time (11 women), 23 part-time/adjunct (3 women). *Students:* 15 part-time (4 women); includes 3 minority (1 Black or African American, non-Hispanic/Latino; 1 Asian, non-Hispanic/Latino; 1 Hispanic/Latino), 3 international. Average age 31. 21 applicants, 100% accepted, 16 enrolled. *Entrance requirements:* For master's, GRE or GMAT. *Application deadline:* For summer admission, 6/1 for domestic students. Applications are processed on a rolling basis. Application fee: $150. Electronic applications accepted. *Expenses: Tuition:* Full-time $44,580; part-time $1394 per credit hour. *Required fees:* $492. *Financial support:* In 2013–14, 14 students received support. Scholarships/grants available. Financial award application deadline: 6/1. *Unit head:* Janet Anderson, Executive Director of NYC-Based Programs, 585-275-3439, Fax: 585-244-3612, E-mail: janet.anderson@simon.rochester.edu.
Website: http://www.simon.rochester.edu/programs/ms-in-management-in-new-york-city/index.aspx.

University of Rochester, Simon Business School, Part-Time MBA Program, Rochester, NY 14627. Offers accounting and information systems (MBA); business environment and public policy (MBA); business systems consulting (MBA); competitive and organizational strategy (MBA); computers and information systems (MBA); corporate accounting (MBA); electronic commerce (MBA); entrepreneurship (MBA); finance (MBA); health sciences management (MBA); international management (MBA); manufacturing management (MBA); marketing (MBA); operations management - services (MBA); public accounting (MBA). Part-time and evening/weekend programs available. *Faculty:* 59 full-time (10 women), 23 part-time/adjunct (3 women). *Students:* 270 part-time (75 women); includes 38 minority (5 Black or African American, non-Hispanic/Latino; 1 American Indian or Alaska Native, non-Hispanic/Latino; 24 Asian, non-Hispanic/Latino; 5 Hispanic/Latino; 3 Two or more races, non-Hispanic/Latino). Average age 32. 56 applicants, 98% accepted, 51 enrolled. In 2013, 77 master's awarded. *Entrance requirements:* For master's, GRE or GMAT, resume, recommendation letters, essays, transcipts. *Application deadline:* For fall admission, 8/15 for domestic students; for winter admission, 11/15 for domestic students; for spring admission, 2/15 for domestic students; for summer admission, 5/15 for domestic students. Applications are processed on a rolling basis. Application fee: $150. Electronic applications accepted. *Expenses: Tuition:* Full-time $44,580; part-time $1394 per credit hour. *Required fees:* $492. *Financial support:* Scholarships/grants and tuition waivers available. Financial award applicants required to submit CSS PROFILE. *Unit head:* Mark Zupan, Dean, 585-275-3316, E-mail: mark.zupan@simon.rochester.edu. *Application contact:* Jennifer Mossotti, Associate Director of Part-Time Programs, 585-275-3803, E-mail: jennifer.mossotti@simon.rochester.edu.
Website: http://www.simon.rochester.edu/programs/part-time-mba-programs/index.aspx.

University of St. Francis, College of Business and Health Administration, School of Business, Joliet, IL 60435-6169. Offers business administration (MBA); logistics (Certificate); management (MSM). Part-time and evening/weekend programs available. Postbaccalaureate distance learning degree programs offered (no on-campus study). *Faculty:* 8 full-time (4 women), 17 part-time/adjunct (9 women). *Students:* 32 full-time (16 women), 106 part-time (55 women); includes 38 minority (24 Black or African American, non-Hispanic/Latino; 3 Asian, non-Hispanic/Latino; 10 Hispanic/Latino; 1 Two or more races, non-Hispanic/Latino), 7 international. Average age 35. 118 applicants, 60% accepted, 53 enrolled. In 2013, 54 master's, 3 other advanced degrees awarded. *Entrance requirements:* For master's, GMAT or 2 years of managerial experience, minimum GPA of 2.75, 2 letters recommendation, personal essay, computer proficiency. Additional exam requirements/recommendations for international students: Required—TOEFL (minimum score 550 paper-based; 79 iBT), IELTS (minimum score 6.5). *Application deadline:* Applications are processed on a rolling basis. Application fee: $30. Electronic applications accepted. Application fee is waived when completed online. *Expenses: Tuition:* Part-time $710 per credit hour. *Required fees:* $125 per semester. Part-time tuition and fees vary according to degree level and program. *Financial support:* In 2013–14, 47 students received support. Scholarships/grants, tuition waivers (partial), and unspecified assistantships available. Support available to part-time students. Financial award applicants required to submit FAFSA. *Unit head:* Dr. Christopher Clott, Dean, 815-740-3395, Fax: 815-740-3537, E-mail: cclott@stfrancis.edu. *Application contact:* Sandra Sloka, Director of Admissions for Graduate and Degree Completion Programs, 800-735-7500, Fax: 815-740-3431, E-mail: ssloka@stfrancis.edu.
Website: http://www.stfrancis.edu/academics/college-of-business-health-administration/

University of Saint Francis, Graduate School, Keith Busse School of Business and Entrepreneurial Leadership, Fort Wayne, IN 46808-3994. Offers business administration (MBA); environmental health (MEH); healthcare administration (MHA); sustainability (MBA). *Accreditation:* ACBSP. Part-time and evening/weekend programs available. Postbaccalaureate distance learning degree programs offered (no on-campus study). *Faculty:* 8. *Students:* 74 full-time (38 women), 69 part-time (35 women); includes 22 minority (12 Black or African American, non-Hispanic/Latino; 2 Asian, non-Hispanic/Latino; 7 Hispanic/Latino; 1 Two or more races, non-Hispanic/Latino), 3 international. Average age 34. 73 applicants, 97% accepted, 71 enrolled. In 2013, 12 master's awarded. *Entrance requirements:* For master's, minimum undergraduate GPA of 2.75. *Application deadline:* For fall admission, 7/1 priority date for domestic students; for spring admission, 11/1 priority date for domestic students. Applications are processed on a rolling basis. Application fee: $20. Application fee is waived when completed online. *Financial support:* Federal Work-Study, scholarships/grants, and unspecified assistantships available. Support available to part-time students. Financial award application deadline: 3/10; financial award applicants required to submit FAFSA. *Unit head:* Dr. Karen Palumbo, Professor/Graduate Program Director, 260-399-7700 Ext. 8312, Fax: 260-399-8174, E-mail: kpalumbo@sf.edu. *Application contact:* James Cashdollar, Admissions Counselor, 260-399-7700 Ext. 6302, Fax: 260-399-8152, E-mail: jcashdollar@sf.edu.
Website: http://www.sf.edu/sf/graduate/business.

University of Saint Joseph, Department of Business, West Hartford, CT 06117-2700. Offers management (MS). Part-time and evening/weekend programs available. *Entrance requirements:* For master's, 2 letters of recommendation. Electronic applications accepted. Application fee is waived when completed online.

University of Saint Mary, Graduate Programs, Program in Business Administration, Leavenworth, KS 66048-5082. Offers enterprise risk management (MBA); finance (MBA); general management (MBA); health care management (MBA); human resource management (MBA); marketing and advertising management (MBA). Part-time and evening/weekend programs available. Postbaccalaureate distance learning degree programs offered (no on-campus study). *Students:* 151 full-time (87 women), 61 part-time (39 women); includes 60 minority (38 Black or African American, non-Hispanic/Latino; 1 American Indian or Alaska Native, non-Hispanic/Latino; 10 Asian, non-Hispanic/Latino; 11 Hispanic/Latino). *Degree requirements:* For master's, thesis. *Entrance requirements:* For master's, minimum undergraduate GPA of 2.75, official transcripts, two letters of recommendation. *Application deadline:* Applications are processed on a rolling basis. Application fee: $25. *Expenses: Tuition:* Part-time $550 per credit hour. *Unit head:* Rick Gunter, Director, 913-319-3007. *Application contact:* Patrick Smith, Coordinator of Business Programs, 913-319-3007, E-mail: smithp@stmary.edu.

University of St. Thomas, Cameron School of Business, Houston, TX 77006-4696. Offers EMBA, MBA, MSA, MSF. Part-time and evening/weekend programs available. *Faculty:* 20 full-time (7 women), 8 part-time/adjunct (4 women). *Students:* 187 full-time (85 women), 260 part-time (144 women); includes 158 minority (43 Black or African American, non-Hispanic/Latino; 27 Asian, non-Hispanic/Latino; 79 Hispanic/Latino; 2 Native Hawaiian or other Pacific Islander, non-Hispanic/Latino; 7 Two or more races, non-Hispanic/Latino), 172 international. Average age 31. 244 applicants, 67% accepted, 108 enrolled. In 2013, 191 master's awarded. *Degree requirements:* For master's, capstone (for some programs), additional course requirements for those sitting for state accountancy exam. *Entrance requirements:* For master's, GMAT or GRE, minimum GPA of 2.5, 3 letters of recommendation. Additional exam requirements/recommendations for international students: Required—TOEFL (minimum score 550 paper-based; 79 iBT), IELTS (minimum score 6). *Application deadline:* For fall admission, 7/15 for domestic and international students; for winter admission, 7/15 for domestic and international students; for spring admission, 11/15 for domestic students, 10/15 for international students. Applications are processed on a rolling basis. Application fee: $35. Electronic applications accepted. *Expenses: Tuition:* Full-time $19,530; part-time $1085 per credit hour. *Required fees:* $258; $82 per term. One-time fee: $100. Part-time tuition and fees vary according to course level, course load, campus/location and program. *Financial support:* In 2013–14, 43 students received support, including research assistantships with partial tuition reimbursements available (averaging $3,000 per year); Federal Work-Study, scholarships/grants, unspecified assistantships, and state work-study, institutional employment also available. Support available to part-time students. Financial award application deadline: 4/15; financial award applicants required to submit FAFSA. *Unit head:* Dr. Beena George, Dean, 713-525-2100, Fax: 713-525-2110, E-mail: cameron@stthom.edu. *Application contact:* Jon Vague, Assistant Director, 713-525-2100, Fax: 713-525-2110, E-mail: cameron@stthom.edu.
Website: http://www.stthom.edu/Academics/Cameron_School_of_Business/Index.aqf.

University of St. Thomas, Graduate Studies, Opus College of Business, Evening UST MBA Program, Minneapolis, MN 55403. Offers MBA. Part-time and evening/weekend programs available. *Students:* 774 part-time (308 women); includes 99 minority (23 Black or African American, non-Hispanic/Latino; 1 American Indian or Alaska Native, non-Hispanic/Latino; 45 Asian, non-Hispanic/Latino; 18 Hispanic/Latino; 2 Native Hawaiian or other Pacific Islander, non-Hispanic/Latino; 10 Two or more races, non-Hispanic/Latino), 19 international. Average age 32. 185 applicants, 97% accepted, 127 enrolled. In 2013, 237 master's awarded. *Entrance requirements:* For master's, GMAT. Additional exam requirements/recommendations for international students: Required—TOEFL (minimum score 80 iBT), IELTS, or Michigan English Language Assessment Battery. *Application deadline:* For fall admission, 5/1 priority date for domestic students; for spring admission, 11/1 priority date for domestic students. Applications are processed on a rolling basis. Application fee: $60. Electronic applications accepted. *Financial support:* In 2013–14, 61 students received support. Scholarships/grants available. Financial award application deadline: 6/1. *Unit head:* Corey Eakins, Program

Director, 651-962-4200, Fax: 651-962-4129, E-mail: eveningmba@stthomas.edu. *Application contact:* Tiffany Cork, Director of Admissions, 651-962-4200, Fax: 651-962-4129, E-mail: eveningmba@stthomas.edu. Website: http://www.stthomas.edu/eveningmba.

University of St. Thomas, Graduate Studies, Opus College of Business, Executive UST MBA Program, Minneapolis, MN 55403. Offers MBA. Part-time programs available. *Students:* 36 part-time (11 women); includes 1 minority (Hispanic/Latino), 1 international. Average age 43. 25 applicants, 100% accepted, 20 enrolled. In 2013, 23 master's awarded. *Entrance requirements:* For master's, five years of significant management or leadership experience. *Application deadline:* For fall admission, 10/7 for domestic and international students. Applications are processed on a rolling basis. Application fee: $100. Electronic applications accepted. *Expenses:* Contact institution. *Unit head:* Dr. John McVea, Program Director, 651-962-4230, Fax: 651-962-4235, E-mail: execmba@stthomas.edu. *Application contact:* Katherine Johnson, Manager, 651-962-4230, Fax: 651-962-4235, E-mail: execmba@stthomas.edu. Website: http://www.stthomas.edu/execmba.

University of St. Thomas, Graduate Studies, Opus College of Business, Full-time UST MBA Program, Minneapolis, MN 55403. Offers MBA. *Students:* 91 full-time (35 women); includes 25 minority (10 Black or African American, non-Hispanic/Latino; 7 Asian, non-Hispanic/Latino; 5 Hispanic/Latino; 3 Two or more races, non-Hispanic/Latino), 11 international. Average age 28. 93 applicants, 78% accepted, 47 enrolled. In 2013, 37 master's awarded. *Entrance requirements:* For master's, GMAT, GRE. Additional exam requirements/recommendations for international students: Required—TOEFL (minimum score 90 iBT), IELTS (minimum score 7), or Michigan English Language Assessment Battery. *Application deadline:* For fall admission, 12/15 for domestic and international students; for winter admission, 2/15 for domestic and international students; for spring admission, 4/15 for domestic and international students; for summer admission, 6/15 for domestic students. Applications are processed on a rolling basis. Application fee: $60. Electronic applications accepted. *Financial support:* Scholarships/grants, tuition waivers (full and partial), and unspecified assistantships available. Financial award application deadline: 4/15. *Unit head:* Tiffany Cork, Director of Admissions, 651-962-8800, Fax: 651-962-4129, E-mail: ustmba@stthomas.edu. *Application contact:* Tiffany Cork, Director of Admissions, 651-962-8800, Fax: 651-962-4129, E-mail: ustmba@stthomas.edu. Website: http://www.stthomas.edu/mba.

University of San Diego, School of Business Administration, MBA Program, San Diego, CA 92110-2492. Offers IMBA, MBA, JD/IMBA, JD/MBA. Part-time and evening/weekend programs available. *Students:* 97 full-time (37 women), 102 part-time (38 women); includes 36 minority (1 Black or African American, non-Hispanic/Latino; 1 American Indian or Alaska Native, non-Hispanic/Latino; 18 Asian, non-Hispanic/Latino; 16 Hispanic/Latino), 43 international. Average age 29. In 2013, 92 master's awarded. *Degree requirements:* For master's, community service, capstone project. *Entrance requirements:* For master's, GMAT, minimum GPA of 3.0, minimum 2 years of full-time professional experience. Additional exam requirements/recommendations for international students: Required—TOEFL (minimum score 580 paper-based; 92 iBT), TWE. *Application deadline:* For fall admission, 11/15 priority date for domestic students, 3/15 for international students; for spring admission, 12/15 for domestic students. Applications are processed on a rolling basis. Application fee: $80. Electronic applications accepted. *Expenses:* Tuition: Full-time $23,580; part-time $1310 per credit. *Required fees:* $350. *Financial support:* In 2013–14, 141 students received support. Career-related internships or fieldwork, Federal Work-Study, institutionally sponsored loans, scholarships/grants, and unspecified assistantships available. Support available to part-time students. Financial award application deadline: 4/1; financial award applicants required to submit FAFSA. *Faculty research:* Exchange rate forecasting, corporate governance, performance of private equity funds, economic geography, food banking. *Unit head:* Dr. Manzur Rahman, Academic Director, MBA Programs, 619-260-2388, E-mail: mba@sandiego.edu. *Application contact:* Monica Mahon, Associate Director of Graduate Admissions, 619-260-4524, Fax: 619-260-4158, E-mail: grads@sandiego.edu. Website: http://www.sandiego.edu/business/programs/graduate/MBA/.

University of San Diego, School of Business Administration, Program in Executive Leadership, San Diego, CA 92110-2492. Offers MS. Evening/weekend programs available. *Students:* 39 full-time (18 women), 3 part-time (1 woman); includes 12 minority (2 Black or African American, non-Hispanic/Latino; 1 Asian, non-Hispanic/Latino; 8 Hispanic/Latino; 1 Two or more races, non-Hispanic/Latino), 1 international. Average age 42. In 2013, 23 master's awarded. *Entrance requirements:* Additional exam requirements/recommendations for international students: Required—TOEFL (minimum score 580 paper-based; 92 iBT), TWE. *Application deadline:* For fall admission, 5/15 for domestic students. Applications are processed on a rolling basis. Application fee: $80. Electronic applications accepted. *Expenses:* Tuition: Full-time $23,580; part-time $1310 per credit. *Required fees:* $350. *Financial support:* In 2013–14, 6 students received support. Scholarships/grants available. Financial award application deadline: 4/1; financial award applicants required to submit FAFSA. *Unit head:* Christina De Vaca, Director, MS in Executive Leadership, 619-260-4828, Fax: 619-260-4891, E-mail: msel@sandiego.edu. *Application contact:* Monica Mahon, Associate Director of Graduate Admissions, 619-260-4524, Fax: 619-260-4158, E-mail: grads@sandiego.edu. Website: http://www.sandiego.edu/business/programs/ms-executive-leadership/.

University of San Francisco, School of Management, Executive Master of Business Administration Program, San Francisco, CA 94105. Offers MBA. *Accreditation:* AACSB. Part-time and evening/weekend programs available. *Faculty:* 5 full-time (1 woman), 3 part-time/adjunct (1 woman). *Students:* 22 full-time (7 women); includes 7 minority (1 Black or African American, non-Hispanic/Latino; 6 Asian, non-Hispanic/Latino), 1 international. Average age 39. 19 applicants, 95% accepted, 14 enrolled. In 2013, 15 master's awarded. *Entrance requirements:* For master's, GMAT (for applicants with less than eight years of post-undergraduate professional experience), resume demonstrating minimum of eight years of professional work experience, transcripts from each college or university attended, two letters of recommendation, essays, interview. Additional exam requirements/recommendations for international students: Required—TOEFL (minimum score 600 paper-based, 100 iBT), IELTS (minimum score 7) or PTE (minimum score 68). *Application deadline:* Applications are processed on a rolling basis. Application fee: $55. Electronic applications accepted. *Expenses:* Contact institution. *Financial support:* In 2013–14, 2 students received support. Scholarships/grants available. Financial award application deadline: 3/2; financial award applicants required to submit FAFSA. *Unit head:* Jane Gleason, Program Director, 415-422-6936, E-mail: emba@usfca.edu. *Application contact:* Secretary. Website: http://www.usfca.edu/emba.

University of San Francisco, School of Management, Master of Business Administration Program, San Francisco, CA 94105. Offers entrepreneurship and innovation (MBA); finance (MBA); international business (MBA); marketing (MBA); organization development (MBA); DDS/MBA; JD/MBA; MBA/MAPS. *Accreditation:* AACSB. Part-time and evening/weekend programs available. *Faculty:* 18 full-time (4 women), 20 part-time/adjunct (10 women). *Students:* 157 full-time (69 women), 14 part-

time (7 women); includes 57 minority (7 Black or African American, non-Hispanic/Latino; 31 Asian, non-Hispanic/Latino; 14 Hispanic/Latino; 5 Two or more races, non-Hispanic/Latino), 30 international. Average age 29. 345 applicants, 68% accepted, 79 enrolled. In 2013, 131 master's awarded. *Entrance requirements:* For master's, GMAT or GRE, resume (two years of professional work experience required for Part-Time MBA, preferred for Full-Time MBA), transcripts from each college or university attended, two letters of recommendation, a personal statement and an interview. Additional exam requirements/recommendations for international students: Required—TOEFL (minimum score 600 paper-based, 100 iBT), IELTS (minimum score 7) or PTE (minimum score 68). *Application deadline:* For fall admission, 6/5 for domestic students, 5/15 for international students; for spring admission, 11/30 for domestic students. Application fee: $55. Electronic applications accepted. *Expenses:* Tuition: Full-time $21,150; part-time $1175 per unit. Tuition and fees vary according to course load, campus/location and program. *Financial support:* In 2013–14, 42 students received support. Fellowships and scholarships/grants available. Financial award application deadline: 3/2; financial award applicants required to submit FAFSA. *Faculty research:* International financial markets, technology transfer licensing, international marketing, strategic planning. *Total annual research expenditures:* $50,000. *Unit head:* Dr. John Veitch, Associate Dean and Program Director, 415-422-2221, Fax: 415-422-6315, E-mail: management@usfca.edu. *Application contact:* Office of Graduate Recruiting and Admissions, 415-422-2221, Fax: 415-422-6315, E-mail: management@usfca.edu. Website: http://www.usfca.edu/mba.

University of Saskatchewan, College of Graduate Studies and Research, Edwards School of Business, Saskatoon, SK S7N 5A2, Canada. Offers M Sc, MBA, MP Acc. Part-time programs available. *Degree requirements:* For master's, thesis (for some programs). *Entrance requirements:* For master's, GMAT. Additional exam requirements/recommendations for international students: Required—TOEFL. *Expenses: Tuition, area resident:* Full-time $3585 Canadian dollars; part-time $585 Canadian dollars per course. Tuition, nonresident: part-time $877 Canadian dollars per course. *International tuition:* $5377 Canadian dollars full-time. *Required fees:* $889.51 Canadian dollars.

The University of Scranton, College of Graduate and Continuing Education, Program in Business Administration, Scranton, PA 18510. Offers accounting (MBA); finance (MBA); general business administration (MBA); health care management (MBA); international business (MBA); management information systems (MBA); marketing (MBA); operations management (MBA). *Accreditation:* AACSB. Part-time and evening/weekend programs available. Postbaccalaureate distance learning degree programs offered (no on-campus study). *Faculty:* 34 full-time (8 women). *Students:* 316 full-time (134 women), 241 part-time (94 women); includes 104 minority (43 Black or African American, non-Hispanic/Latino; 3 American Indian or Alaska Native, non-Hispanic/Latino; 29 Asian, non-Hispanic/Latino; 27 Hispanic/Latino; 2 Two or more races, non-Hispanic/Latino), 47 international. Average age 34. 249 applicants, 85% accepted. In 2013, 200 master's awarded. *Degree requirements:* For master's, capstone experience. *Entrance requirements:* For master's, GMAT, minimum GPA of 3.0. Additional exam requirements/recommendations for international students: Required—TOEFL (minimum score 500 paper-based), IELTS (minimum score 6). *Application deadline:* Applications are processed on a rolling basis. Application fee: $0. *Financial support:* In 2013–14, 13 students received support, including 13 teaching assistantships with full and partial tuition reimbursements available (averaging $8,800 per year); fellowships, career-related internships or fieldwork, Federal Work-Study, and unspecified assistantships also available. Support available to part-time students. Financial award application deadline: 3/1. *Faculty research:* Financial markets, strategic impact of total quality management, internal accounting controls, consumer preference, information systems and the Internet. *Unit head:* Dr. Murli Rajan, Director, 570-941-4043, Fax: 570-941-4342. *Application contact:* Joseph M. Roback, Director of Admissions, 570-941-4385, Fax: 570-941-5928, E-mail: robackj2@scranton.edu. Website: http://www.scranton.edu/academics/cgce/busad.shtml.

University of Sioux Falls, Vucurevich School of Business, Sioux Falls, SD 57105-1699. Offers entrepreneurial leadership (MBA); general management (MBA); health care management (MBA); marketing (MBA). Part-time and evening/weekend programs available. *Degree requirements:* For master's, project. *Entrance requirements:* For master's, minimum GPA of 3.0. Additional exam requirements/recommendations for international students: Required—TOEFL. *Expenses:* Contact institution.

University of South Africa, College of Economic and Management Sciences, Pretoria, South Africa. Offers accounting (D Admin, D Com); accounting science (DA); auditing (D Admin, D Com); business administration (M Tech); business economics (D Admin); business leadership (DBL); business management (D Admin, D Com); economic management analysis (M Tech); economics (D Admin, D Com, PhD); human resource development (M Tech); industrial psychology (D Admin, D Com, PhD); logistics (D Com); marketing (M Tech); public administration (D Admin, D Com, DPA, PhD); public management (M Tech); quantitative management (D Admin, D Com); real estate (M Tech); statistics (D Admin, PhD); tourism management (D Admin, D Com); transport economics (D Admin, D Com).

University of South Africa, Graduate School of Business Leadership, Pretoria, South Africa. Offers MBA, MBL, DBL.

University of South Alabama, Graduate School, Mitchell College of Business, Program in Business Management, Mobile, AL 36688-0002. Offers general management (MBA). *Accreditation:* AACSB. Part-time and evening/weekend programs available. *Faculty:* 7 full-time (1 woman). *Students:* 66 full-time (25 women), 6 part-time (2 women); includes 9 minority (3 Black or African American, non-Hispanic/Latino; 1 American Indian or Alaska Native, non-Hispanic/Latino; 4 Hispanic/Latino; 1 Two or more races, non-Hispanic/Latino), 8 international. 68 applicants, 51% accepted, 32 enrolled. In 2013, 23 master's awarded. *Degree requirements:* For master's, comprehensive exam. *Entrance requirements:* For master's, GMAT, minimum undergraduate GPA of 3.0. *Application deadline:* For fall admission, 7/15 priority date for domestic students, 6/15 priority date for international students; for spring admission, 12/1 priority date for domestic students, 11/1 priority date for international students. Applications are processed on a rolling basis. Application fee: $35. *Expenses:* Tuition, state resident: full-time $8976; part-time $374 per credit hour. Tuition, nonresident: full-time $17,952; part-time $748 per credit hour. *Financial support:* Research assistantships available. Support available to part-time students. Financial award application deadline: 4/1. *Unit head:* Dr. Carl Moore, Dean, College of Business, 251-460-6310. *Application contact:* Dr. John Gamble, Director of Graduate Studies, 251-460-6418.

University of South Carolina, The Graduate School, Darla Moore School of Business, Columbia, SC 29208. Offers accountancy (M Acc), including business measurement and assurance; business administration (MBA, PhD), including business administration (PhD), economics (PhD); economics (MA); human resources (MHR); international business administration (IMBA); JD/M Acc; JD/MA; JD/MHR. *Accreditation:* AACSB. Part-time and evening/weekend programs available. Postbaccalaureate distance learning degree programs offered (minimal on-campus study). *Degree requirements:* For doctorate, one foreign language, thesis/dissertation. *Entrance requirements:* For master's, GMAT, GRE, minimum GPA of 3.0; for doctorate, GMAT or GRE. Additional exam requirements/recommendations for international students: Required—TOEFL

(minimum score 600 paper-based). Electronic applications accepted. *Expenses:* Contact institution. *Faculty research:* Finance, marketing, strategic management, international management, operations.

The University of South Dakota, Graduate School, College of Arts and Sciences, Program in Administrative Studies, Vermillion, SD 57069-2390. Offers alcohol and drug studies (MSA); criminal justice (MSA); health services administration (MSA); human resource management (MSA); interdisciplinary (MSA); long term care administration (MSA); organizational leadership (MSA). Part-time and evening/weekend programs available. Postbaccalaureate distance learning degree programs offered (no on-campus study). *Degree requirements:* For master's, thesis or alternative. *Entrance requirements:* For master's, 3 years of work or experience, minimum GPA of 2.7, resume. Additional exam requirements/recommendations for international students: Required—TOEFL (minimum score 550 paper-based; 79 iBT). Electronic applications accepted.

The University of South Dakota, Graduate School, School of Business, Department of Business Administration, Vermillion, SD 57069-2390. Offers business administration (MBA); health services administration (MBA); JD/MBA. *Accreditation:* AACSB. Part-time and evening/weekend programs available. Postbaccalaureate distance learning degree programs offered (no on-campus study). *Degree requirements:* For master's, thesis or alternative. *Entrance requirements:* For master's, GMAT, minimum GPA of 2.7, resume. Additional exam requirements/recommendations for international students: Required—TOEFL (minimum score 550 paper-based; 79 iBT). Electronic applications accepted. *Expenses:* Contact institution.

University of Southern California, Graduate School, Marshall School of Business, Los Angeles, CA 90089. Offers M Acc, MBA, MBT, MBV, MMM, MS, PhD, DDS/MBA, JD/MBT, MBA/Ed D, MBA/M Pl, MBA/MD, MBA/MRED, MBA/MS, MBA/MSW, MBA/Pharm D. *Accreditation:* AACSB. *Degree requirements:* For doctorate, thesis/dissertation. *Entrance requirements:* For master's, GMAT and/or CPA Exam; for doctorate, GMAT or GRE. Additional exam requirements/recommendations for international students: Required—TOEFL. Electronic applications accepted.

University of Southern Indiana, Graduate Studies, College of Business, Program in Business Administration, Evansville, IN 47712-3590. Offers MBA. *Accreditation:* AACSB. Part-time and evening/weekend programs available. *Faculty:* 21 full-time (4 women), 1 part-time/adjunct (0 women). *Students:* 14 full-time (6 women), 84 part-time (32 women); includes 4 minority (1 Black or African American, non-Hispanic/Latino; 1 American Indian or Alaska Native, non-Hispanic/Latino; 1 Asian, non-Hispanic/Latino; 1 Two or more races, non-Hispanic/Latino), 4 international. Average age 29. 64 applicants, 72% accepted, 36 enrolled. In 2013, 22 master's awarded. *Entrance requirements:* For master's, GMAT or GRE, minimum GPA of 2.5, resume. Additional exam requirements/recommendations for international students: Required—TOEFL (minimum score 550 paper-based; 79 iBT), IELTS (minimum score 6). *Application deadline:* For fall admission, 8/15 for domestic students, 3/1 priority date for international students. Applications are processed on a rolling basis. Application fee: $40. Electronic applications accepted. *Expenses:* Tuition, state resident: full-time $5567; part-time $309 per credit hour. Tuition, nonresident: full-time $10,977; part-time $610 per credit. *Required fees:* $23 per semester. *Financial support:* In 2013–14, 10 students received support. Federal Work-Study, scholarships/grants, tuition waivers (full and partial), and unspecified assistantships available. Financial award application deadline: 3/1; financial award applicants required to submit FAFSA. *Unit head:* Dr. Ernest H. Hall, Program Director, 812-465-7038, E-mail: ehall@usi.edu. *Application contact:* Michelle Simmons, IMBA Program Assistant, 812-464-1926, Fax: 812-465-1044, E-mail: masimmons3@usi.edu.
Website: http://business.usi.edu/mba/.

University of Southern Maine, College of Management and Human Service, School of Business, Portland, ME 04104-9300. Offers accounting (MBA); business administration (MBA); finance (MBA); health management and policy (MBA); sustainability (MBA); JD/MBA; MBA/MSA; MBA/MSN; MS/MBA. *Accreditation:* AACSB. Part-time and evening/weekend programs available. *Faculty:* 10 part-time/adjunct (2 women). *Students:* 89 part-time (37 women); includes 4 minority (3 American Indian or Alaska Native, non-Hispanic/Latino; 1 Asian, non-Hispanic/Latino), 2 international. Average age 31. 36 applicants, 56% accepted, 16 enrolled. In 2013, 34 master's awarded. *Entrance requirements:* For master's, GMAT or GRE, minimum AACSB index of 1100. Additional exam requirements/recommendations for international students: Required—TOEFL (minimum score 550 paper-based; 79 iBT). *Application deadline:* For fall admission, 8/1 priority date for domestic students, 5/1 priority date for international students; for spring admission, 12/1 priority date for domestic students, 9/1 priority date for international students. Applications are processed on a rolling basis. Application fee: $65. Electronic applications accepted. *Expenses:* Tuition, state resident: part-time $380 per credit. Tuition, nonresident: part-time $1026 per credit. Part-time tuition and fees vary according to program. *Financial support:* In 2013–14, 3 research assistantships with partial tuition reimbursements (averaging $9,000 per year), 3 teaching assistantships with partial tuition reimbursements (averaging $9,000 per year) were awarded; career-related internships or fieldwork, Federal Work-Study, scholarships/grants, tuition waivers (full and partial), and unspecified assistantships also available. Support available to part-time students. Financial award application deadline: 2/15; financial award applicants required to submit FAFSA. *Faculty research:* Economic development, management information systems, real options, system dynamics, simulation. *Unit head:* Joseph W. McDonnell, Dean, 207-228-8002, Fax: 207-780-4060, E-mail: jmcdonnell@usm.maine.edu. *Application contact:* Alice B. Cash, Assistant Director for Student Affairs, 207-780-4184, Fax: 207-780-4662, E-mail: acash@usm.maine.edu.
Website: http://www.usm.maine.edu/sb.

University of Southern Maine, Lewiston-Auburn College, Program in Leadership Studies, Portland, ME 04104-9300. Offers creative leadership/global strategies (CGS); leadership studies (MA). Part-time programs available. Postbaccalaureate distance learning degree programs offered (minimal on-campus study). *Faculty:* 5 full-time (3 women). *Students:* 5 full-time (3 women), 31 part-time (20 women); includes 2 minority (1 Hispanic/Latino; 1 Two or more races, non-Hispanic/Latino). Average age 38. 19 applicants, 84% accepted, 14 enrolled. In 2013, 7 master's awarded. *Application deadline:* Applications are processed on a rolling basis. Application fee: $65. *Expenses:* Tuition, state resident: part-time $380 per credit. Tuition, nonresident: part-time $1026 per credit. Part-time tuition and fees vary according to program. *Financial support:* Federal Work-Study available. *Unit head:* Dr. Tara Coste, Director, 207-753-6596, Fax: 207-753-6555, E-mail: tcoste@usm.maine.edu. *Application contact:* Mary Sloan, Assistant Dean of Graduate Studies and Director of Graduate Admissions, 207-780-4386, E-mail: gradstudies@usm.maine.edu.

University of Southern Mississippi, Graduate School, College of Business, Department of Business Administration, Hattiesburg, MS 39406-0001. Offers MBA. *Accreditation:* AACSB. Part-time and evening/weekend programs available. *Faculty:* 61 full-time (27 women). *Students:* 13 full-time (8 women), 26 part-time (15 women); includes 6 minority (3 Black or African American, non-Hispanic/Latino; 2 Hispanic/Latino; 1 Two or more races, non-Hispanic/Latino), 3 international. Average age 33. 25 applicants, 84% accepted, 14 enrolled. In 2013, 15 master's awarded. *Degree requirements:* For master's, comprehensive exam. *Entrance requirements:* For master's, GMAT, minimum GPA of 2.75 on last 60 hours. Additional exam requirements/recommendations for international students: Required—TOEFL, IELTS. *Application deadline:* For fall admission, 7/15 priority date for domestic students, 7/15 for international students; for spring admission, 11/15 priority date for domestic students, 11/15 for international students. Application fee: $50. Electronic applications accepted. *Financial support:* In 2013–14, 14 research assistantships with full and partial tuition reimbursements (averaging $7,200 per year), 1 teaching assistantship with full tuition reimbursement (averaging $7,200 per year) were awarded; Federal Work-Study, institutionally sponsored loans, scholarships/grants, health care benefits, and unspecified assistantships also available. Support available to part-time students. Financial award application deadline: 3/15; financial award applicants required to submit FAFSA. *Faculty research:* Inflation accounting, self-esteem training, international trade policy, health care marketing, ethics in strategic planning. *Unit head:* Dr. Elizabeth LaFleur, Chair, 601-266-4659. *Application contact:* Dr. Joseph Peyrefitte, Assistant Dean, 601-266-4664, Fax: 601-266-5814.
Website: http://www.usm.edu/graduateschool/table.php.

University of South Florida, College of Business, Department of Business Administration, Tampa, FL 33620-9951. Offers business administration (MBA); executive business administration (EMBA); sport and entertainment management (MBA); MBA/MS. *Accreditation:* AACSB. Part-time and evening/weekend programs available. *Students:* 65 full-time (13 women); includes 21 minority (7 Black or African American, non-Hispanic/Latino; 4 Asian, non-Hispanic/Latino; 9 Hispanic/Latino; 1 Native Hawaiian or other Pacific Islander, non-Hispanic/Latino), 2 international. Average age 31. 46 applicants, 80% accepted, 33 enrolled. In 2013, 18 master's awarded. *Degree requirements:* For master's, comprehensive exam, thesis (for some programs). *Entrance requirements:* For master's, GMAT (preferred), GRE or MCAT, minimum GPA of 3.0 in upper-level bachelor's degree course work from regionally-accredited institution; recommendation letters; statement of purpose. Additional exam requirements/recommendations for international students: Required—TOEFL (minimum score 550 paper-based; 79 iBT) or IELTS (minimum score 6.5). *Application deadline:* For fall admission, 6/1 for domestic students, 1/2 for international students; for spring admission, 10/15 for domestic students, 6/1 for international students. Application fee: $30. *Financial support:* Scholarships/grants, health care benefits, and unspecified assistantships available. Financial award applicants required to submit FAFSA. *Faculty research:* Business communications; business intelligence; business process improvement; corporate governance; sustainability, ethics, and environmentally-friendly business practices; small business development; graduate education; women/minority business development; business planning; leadership. *Unit head:* Dr. Jacqueline Reck, Professor and Interim Dean, 813-974-6721, Fax: 813-974-6528, E-mail: jreck@usf.edu. *Application contact:* Irene Hurst, Director, MBA and EMBA Programs, 813-974-3335, Fax: 813-974-4518, E-mail: ihurst@usf.edu.
Website: http://business.usf.edu/.

University of South Florida, College of Business, Department of Management and Organization, Tampa, FL 33620-9951. Offers management (MS). *Accreditation:* AACSB. Part-time programs available. Postbaccalaureate distance learning degree programs offered (minimal on-campus study). *Faculty:* 11 full-time (3 women). *Students:* 14 full-time (5 women), 11 part-time (4 women); includes 4 minority (1 Black or African American, non-Hispanic/Latino; 3 Hispanic/Latino), 8 international. Average age 29. 28 applicants, 54% accepted, 11 enrolled. In 2013, 9 master's awarded. Terminal master's awarded for partial completion of doctoral program. *Degree requirements:* For master's, comprehensive exam. *Entrance requirements:* For master's, GMAT, letters of recommendation, resume, statement of purpose, relevant work experience. Additional exam requirements/recommendations for international students: Required—TOEFL (minimum score 550 paper-based; 79 iBT) or IELTS (minimum score 6.5). *Application deadline:* For fall admission, 6/1 for domestic students, 1/2 for international students. Application fee: $30. Electronic applications accepted. *Financial support:* In 2013–14, 4 students received support, including 1 research assistantship with tuition reimbursement available (averaging $9,002 per year), 3 teaching assistantships with tuition reimbursements available (averaging $9,002 per year); tuition waivers also available. Financial award applicants required to submit FAFSA. *Faculty research:* Leadership and employment relations, time management, personal motivation, crew resource management in aviation, psychology of gambling, organizational culture, issues of fairness, employment law, marketing strategy/implementation, organizational diversity, ethics, environmentally-friendly business practices, green business, sustainable business plans, institutional theory, social movement theory, diffusion of innovations, stakeholder human resources management, social responsibility. *Unit head:* Dr. Sally Fuller, Interim Department Chair and Associate Professor, 813-974-1766, Fax: 813-905-9964, E-mail: sfuller@usf.edu. *Application contact:* Carrie Fischer, Office Manager, 813-974-1714, Fax: 813-974-9964, E-mail: cfischer1@usf.edu.
Website: http://business.usf.edu/departments/management/.

University of South Florida, University College/Distance Education, Tampa, FL 33620-9951. *Unit head:* Kathy Barnes, Interdisciplinary Programs Coordinator, 813-974-8031, Fax: 813-974-7061, E-mail: barnesk@usf.edu. *Application contact:* Karen Tylinski, Metro Initiatives, 813-974-9943, Fax: 813-974-7061, E-mail: ktylinsk@usf.edu.
Website: http://uc.usf.edu/.

University of South Florida–St. Petersburg Campus, College of Business, St. Petersburg, FL 33701. Offers MBA. *Accreditation:* AACSB. Part-time programs available. *Entrance requirements:* For master's, GMAT (minimum score of 500), bachelor's degree with minimum GPA of 3.0 overall or in upper two years from regionally-accredited institution; resume. Additional exam requirements/recommendations for international students: Required—TOEFL (minimum score 550 paper-based; 79 iBT); Recommended—IELTS. Electronic applications accepted.

University of South Florida Sarasota-Manatee, College of Business, Sarasota, FL 34243. Offers MBA. *Accreditation:* AACSB. Part-time and evening/weekend programs available. *Faculty:* 6 full-time (0 women). *Students:* 12 full-time (3 women), 24 part-time (13 women); includes 8 minority (3 Black or African American, non-Hispanic/Latino; 1 Asian, non-Hispanic/Latino; 2 Hispanic/Latino; 1 Native Hawaiian or other Pacific Islander, non-Hispanic/Latino; 1 Two or more races, non-Hispanic/Latino), 2 international. Average age 33. 50 applicants, 30% accepted, 10 enrolled. In 2013, 18 master's awarded. *Degree requirements:* For master's, capstone project. *Entrance requirements:* For master's, GRE or GMAT, minimum upper-division GPA of 3.0, two letters of recommendation, statement of purpose. Additional exam requirements/recommendations for international students: Required—TOEFL (minimum score 550 paper-based; 79 iBT), IELTS (minimum score 6.5). *Application deadline:* For fall admission, 3/1 priority date for domestic students, 3/1 for international students; for spring admission, 10/1 priority date for domestic students, 10/1 for international students. Applications are processed on a rolling basis. Application fee: $30. Electronic applications accepted. *Expenses:* Tuition, state resident: full-time $10,029; part-time $418 per credit. Tuition, nonresident: full-time $20,727; part-time $863 per credit. *Required fees:* $10; $5. Tuition and fees vary according to program. *Financial support:* Federal Work-Study, scholarships/grants, health care benefits, and unspecified assistantships available. Support available to part-time students. Financial award application deadline: 3/1; financial award applicants required to submit FAFSA. *Faculty research:* Mergers and acquisitions, customer loyalty, employment discrimination,

measurement of quality, efficiency of markets. *Unit head:* Dr. Robert L. Anderson, Dean, 941-359-4274, Fax: 941-359-4367, E-mail: randerson@sar.usf.edu. *Application contact:* Andy Telatovich, Director, Admissions, 941-359-4330, E-mail: atelatovich@sar.usf.edu.
Website: http://usfsm.edu/college-of-business/.

The University of Tampa, John H. Sykes College of Business, Tampa, FL 33606-1490. Offers accounting (MS); entrepreneurship (MBA); finance (MBA, MS); information systems management (MBA); innovation management (MBA); international business (MBA); marketing (MBA, MS); nonprofit management (MBA). *Accreditation:* AACSB. Part-time and evening/weekend programs available. *Faculty:* 41 full-time (15 women), 5 part-time/adjunct (1 woman). *Students:* 406 full-time (171 women), 152 part-time (61 women); includes 104 minority (18 Black or African American, non-Hispanic/Latino; 1 American Indian or Alaska Native, non-Hispanic/Latino; 20 Asian, non-Hispanic/Latino; 59 Hispanic/Latino; 6 Two or more races, non-Hispanic/Latino), 154 international. Average age 33. 1,341 applicants, 37% accepted, 256 enrolled. In 2013, 218 master's awarded. *Degree requirements:* For master's, capstone. *Entrance requirements:* For master's, GMAT or GRE, 4-year undergraduate degree, minimum GPA of 3.0, professional experience (for Executive MBA). Additional exam requirements/ recommendations for international students: Required—TOEFL (minimum score 577 paper-based; 90 iBT); Recommended—IELTS (minimum score 7.5). *Application deadline:* Applications are processed on a rolling basis. Application fee: $40. Electronic applications accepted. *Expenses: Tuition:* Full-time $8928; part-time $558 per credit hour. *Required fees:* $80; $80 $40 per term. Tuition and fees vary according to program. *Financial support:* In 2013–14, 110 students received support. Career-related internships or fieldwork, scholarships/grants, and unspecified assistantships available. Financial award applicants required to submit FAFSA. *Faculty research:* Job market signaling, on-line shopping behaviors and social media, the Tampa Bay economy, digital literacy, entrepreneurship in small businesses. *Unit head:* Dr. Stephanie Thomason, Associate Dean, 813-253-6289, E-mail: sthomason@ut.edu. *Application contact:* Charlene Tobie, Associate Director of Admissions, 813-257-3566, E-mail: ctobie@ut.edu.
Website: http://www.ut.edu/business/.

The University of Tennessee, Graduate School, College of Business Administration, Program in Business Administration, Knoxville, TN 37996. Offers accounting (PhD); finance (MBA, PhD); logistics and transportation (MBA, PhD); management (PhD); marketing (MBA, PhD); operations management (MBA); professional business administration (MBA); statistics (PhD); JD/MBA; MS/MBA; Pharm D/MBA. Pharm D/ MBA offered jointly with The University of Tennessee Health Science Center. *Accreditation:* AACSB. Postbaccalaureate distance learning degree programs offered. *Degree requirements:* For master's, thesis or alternative; for doctorate, thesis/ dissertation. *Entrance requirements:* For master's and doctorate, GMAT, minimum GPA of 2.7. Additional exam requirements/recommendations for international students: Required—TOEFL. Electronic applications accepted. *Expenses:* Tuition, state resident: full-time $9540; part-time $531 per credit hour. Tuition, nonresident: full-time $27,728; part-time $1542 per credit hour. *Required fees:* $1404; $67 per credit hour.

The University of Tennessee, Graduate School, College of Business Administration, Program in Management Science, Knoxville, TN 37996. Offers MS, PhD. *Accreditation:* AACSB. *Degree requirements:* For master's, thesis or alternative; for doctorate, thesis/ dissertation. *Entrance requirements:* For master's and doctorate, GMAT or GRE General Test, minimum GPA of 2.7. Additional exam requirements/recommendations for international students: Required—TOEFL. Electronic applications accepted. *Expenses:* Tuition, state resident: full-time $9540; part-time $531 per credit hour. Tuition, nonresident: full-time $27,728; part-time $1542 per credit hour. *Required fees:* $1404; $67 per credit hour.

The University of Tennessee at Chattanooga, Graduate School, College of Business, Program in Business Administration, Chattanooga, TN 37403. Offers EMBA, MBA. *Accreditation:* AACSB. Part-time and evening/weekend programs available. *Faculty:* 15 full-time (1 woman), 3 part-time/adjunct (2 women). *Students:* 83 full-time (34 women), 150 part-time (63 women); includes 32 minority (14 Black or African American, non-Hispanic/Latino; 6 Asian, non-Hispanic/Latino; 5 Hispanic/Latino; 7 Two or more races, non-Hispanic/Latino), 7 international. Average age 30. 97 applicants, 71% accepted, 48 enrolled. In 2013, 107 master's awarded. *Entrance requirements:* For master's, GMAT (minimum score 450) or GRE General Test (minimum score 1000). Additional exam requirements/recommendations for international students: Required—TOEFL (minimum score 550 paper-based; 79 iBT), IELTS (minimum score 6). *Application deadline:* For fall admission, 6/13 priority date for domestic students, 6/1 for international students; for spring admission, 10/15 priority date for domestic students, 10/1 for international students. Applications are processed on a rolling basis. Application fee: $30 ($35 for international students). Electronic applications accepted. *Financial support:* In 2013–14, 10 research assistantships with tuition reimbursements (averaging $6,639 per year), 4 teaching assistantships with tuition reimbursements (averaging $6,210 per year) were awarded; career-related internships or fieldwork, scholarships/grants, tuition waivers (partial), and unspecified assistantships also available. Support available to part-time students. *Faculty research:* Diversity, operations/production management, entrepreneurial processes, customer satisfaction and retention, branding. *Unit head:* Dr. Robert Dooley, Dean, 423-425-4403, Fax: 423-425-5255, E-mail: robert-dooley@utc.edu. *Application contact:* Dr. J. Randy Walker, Interim Dean of Graduate Studies, 423-425-4478, Fax: 423-425-5223, E-mail: randy-walker@utc.edu.
Website: http://www.utc.edu/Academic/BusinessGraduatePrograms/MBA.php.

The University of Tennessee at Martin, Graduate Programs, College of Business and Global Affairs, Program in Business, Martin, TN 38238-1000. Offers MBA. *Accreditation:* AACSB. Part-time programs available. *Faculty:* 31. *Students:* 17 full-time (6 women), 45 part-time (19 women); includes 8 minority (6 Black or African American, non-Hispanic/ Latino; 1 Hispanic/Latino; 1 Two or more races, non-Hispanic/Latino), 9 international. 47 applicants, 23% accepted, 9 enrolled. In 2013, 46 master's awarded. *Degree requirements:* For master's, comprehensive exam. *Entrance requirements:* For master's, GMAT, minimum GPA of 2.5, resume. Additional exam requirements/ recommendations for international students: Required—TOEFL (minimum score 525 paper-based; 71 iBT). *Application deadline:* For fall admission, 7/29 priority date for domestic students, 7/29 for international students; for spring admission, 12/12 priority date for domestic students, 12/12 for international students. Applications are processed on a rolling basis. Application fee: $30 ($130 for international students). Electronic applications accepted. *Financial support:* In 2013–14, 16 students received support, including 6 research assistantships with full tuition reimbursements available (averaging $7,917 per year), 10 teaching assistantships (averaging $8,158 per year); career-related internships or fieldwork, scholarships/grants, and unspecified assistantships also available. Support available to part-time students. Financial award application deadline: 3/1. *Unit head:* Dr. Kevin Hammond, Coordinator, 731-881-7236, Fax: 731-881-7241, E-mail: bagrad@utm.edu. *Application contact:* Jolene L. Cunningham, Student Services Specialist, 731-881-7012, Fax: 731-881-7499, E-mail: jcunningham@utm.edu.

The University of Texas at Arlington, Graduate School, College of Business, Program in Business Administration, Arlington, TX 76019. Offers accounting (PhD); business statistics (PhD); finance (MBA, PhD); information systems (MBA, PhD); management (MBA, PhD); marketing (MBA, PhD); operations management (MBA, PhD); real estate (MBA). *Accreditation:* AACSB. Part-time and evening/weekend programs available. *Degree requirements:* For master's, thesis optional; for doctorate, comprehensive exam, thesis/dissertation. *Entrance requirements:* For master's, GMAT or GRE; for doctorate, GMAT, minimum GPA of 3.0 (undergraduate), 3.4 (graduate); 30 hours of graduate course work. Additional exam requirements/recommendations for international students: Required—TOEFL (minimum score 550 paper-based; 79 iBT). Electronic applications accepted.

The University of Texas at Austin, Graduate School, McCombs School of Business, Department of Management, Austin, TX 78712-1111. Offers PhD. *Accreditation:* AACSB. *Degree requirements:* For doctorate, thesis/dissertation. *Entrance requirements:* For doctorate, GMAT or GRE. Electronic applications accepted.

The University of Texas at Austin, Graduate School, McCombs School of Business, Executive MBA Program at Mexico City, Austin, TX 78712-1111. Offers MBA. Program offered jointly with Instituto Tecnológico y de Estudios Superiores de Monterrey, Campus Ciudad de México. *Accreditation:* AACSB. *Entrance requirements:* For master's, GMAT, 5 years of work experience. Additional exam requirements/ recommendations for international students: Required—TOEFL.

The University of Texas at Austin, Graduate School, McCombs School of Business, MBA Programs, Austin, TX 78712-1111. Offers MBA, JD/MBA, MBA/MA, MBA/MP Aff, MBA/MSN. *Accreditation:* AACSB. Part-time programs available. *Entrance requirements:* For master's, GMAT, minimum 2 years of full-time work experience. Additional exam requirements/recommendations for international students: Required—TOEFL. Electronic applications accepted.

The University of Texas at Brownsville, Graduate Studies, School of Business, Brownsville, TX 78520-4991. Offers MBA. *Accreditation:* AACSB. Part-time and evening/weekend programs available. Postbaccalaureate distance learning degree programs offered (no on-campus study). *Faculty:* 23 full-time (4 women). *Students:* 40 full-time (26 women), 117 part-time (63 women); includes 115 minority (3 Black or African American, non-Hispanic/Latino; 11 Asian, non-Hispanic/Latino; 101 Hispanic/ Latino), 19 international. 46 applicants, 57% accepted, 24 enrolled. In 2013, 33 master's awarded. *Degree requirements:* For master's, capstone courses. *Entrance requirements:* For master's, GRE General Test. Additional exam requirements/ recommendations for international students: Required—TOEFL (minimum score 550 paper-based; 77 iBT). *Application deadline:* For fall admission, 7/1 priority date for domestic students, 7/1 for international students; for spring admission, 12/1 priority date for domestic students, 12/1 for international students. Applications are processed on a rolling basis. Application fee: $30. Electronic applications accepted. *Expenses:* Tuition, state resident: full-time $3444; part-time $1148 per semester. Tuition, nonresident: full-time $9816. *Required fees:* $1018; $221 per credit hour. $401 per semester. *Financial support:* In 2013–14, 14 students received support, including 3 research assistantships (averaging $10,000 per year); Federal Work-Study, scholarships/grants, tuition waivers (partial), and unspecified assistantships also available. Support available to part-time students. Financial award application deadline: 4/3; financial award applicants required to submit FAFSA. *Unit head:* Dr. Mark Kroll, Dean, 956-882-5803, Fax: 956-982-0159, E-mail: mark.kroll@utb.edu. *Application contact:* Mari Montelongo, Graduate Studies Specialist, 956-882-7787, Fax: 956-882-7279, E-mail: mari.montelongo@utb.edu.
Website: http://www.utb.edu/vpaa/cob/Pages/default.aspx.

The University of Texas at Dallas, Naveen Jindal School of Management, Richardson, TX 75080. Offers EMBA, MBA, MS, PhD, MSEE/MBA. Part-time and evening/weekend programs available. Postbaccalaureate distance learning degree programs offered. *Faculty:* 100 full-time (21 women), 52 part-time/adjunct (18 women). *Students:* 2,301 full-time (1,159 women), 1,388 part-time (597 women); includes 640 minority (98 Black or African American, non-Hispanic/Latino; 7 American Indian or Alaska Native, non-Hispanic/Latino; 354 Asian, non-Hispanic/Latino; 146 Hispanic/Latino; 1 Native Hawaiian or other Pacific Islander, non-Hispanic/Latino; 34 Two or more races, non-Hispanic/Latino), 2,099 international. Average age 28. 5,522 applicants, 50% accepted, 1420 enrolled. In 2013, 1,535 master's, 19 doctorates awarded. *Degree requirements:* For doctorate, thesis/dissertation. *Entrance requirements:* For master's and doctorate, GMAT. Additional exam requirements/recommendations for international students: Required—TOEFL (minimum score 550 paper-based). *Application deadline:* For fall admission, 7/15 for domestic students, 5/1 priority date for international students; for spring admission, 11/15 for domestic students, 9/1 priority date for international students. Applications are processed on a rolling basis. Application fee: $50 ($100 for international students). Electronic applications accepted. *Expenses:* Tuition, state resident: full-time $11,940; part-time $663.33 per credit hour. Tuition, nonresident: full-time $21,606; part-time $1200.33 per credit hour. *Financial support:* In 2013–14, 927 students received support, including 3 research assistantships with partial tuition reimbursements available (averaging $13,750 per year), 18 teaching assistantships with partial tuition reimbursements available (averaging $10,340 per year); career-related internships or fieldwork, Federal Work-Study, institutionally sponsored loans, scholarships/grants, and unspecified assistantships also available. Support available to part-time students. Financial award application deadline: 4/30; financial award applicants required to submit FAFSA. *Faculty research:* Finance, marketing and organization, strategy, management education for physicians. *Total annual research expenditures:* $1.8 million. *Unit head:* Dr. Hasan Pirkul, Dean, 972-883-2705, Fax: 972-883-2799, E-mail: hpirkul@utdallas.edu. *Application contact:* David B. Ritchey, Director of Advising, 972-883-2750, Fax: 972-883-6425, E-mail: davidr@utdallas.edu.
Website: http://jindal.utdallas.edu/.

See Display on next page and Close-Up on page 197.

The University of Texas at El Paso, Graduate School, College of Business Administration, Programs in Business Administration, El Paso, TX 79968-0001. Offers business administration (MBA, Certificate); international business (PhD). *Accreditation:* AACSB. Part-time and evening/weekend programs available. Postbaccalaureate distance learning degree programs offered (no on-campus study). *Degree requirements:* For master's, comprehensive exam. *Entrance requirements:* For master's and doctorate, GMAT. Additional exam requirements/recommendations for international students: Required—TOEFL. Electronic applications accepted. *Faculty research:* Cross-border modeling, human resources, and outsourcing and manufacturing; global information technology transfer; international investments and risk management.

The University of Texas at San Antonio, College of Business, Department of Information Systems and Cyber Security, San Antonio, TX 78249-0617. Offers business (MBA), including information systems; business administration (PhD), including information technology; information technology (MS, MSIT), including information assurance (MS). Part-time and evening/weekend programs available. *Faculty:* 9 full-time (3 women), 2 part-time/adjunct (0 women). *Students:* 36 full-time (12 women), 37 part-time (7 women); includes 21 minority (1 Black or African American, non-Hispanic/Latino; 3 Asian, non-Hispanic/Latino; 14 Hispanic/Latino; 1 Native Hawaiian or other Pacific Islander, non-Hispanic/Latino; 2 Two or more races, non-Hispanic/Latino), 14 international. Average age 31. 60 applicants, 47% accepted, 11 enrolled. In 2013, 34 master's awarded. *Degree requirements:* For master's, thesis or alternative; for doctorate, comprehensive exam, thesis/dissertation. *Entrance requirements:* For master's, GMAT, bachelor's degree with 18 credit hours in the field of study or another

Business Administration and Management—General

appropriate field of study, statement of purpose; for doctorate, GMAT or GRE, resume or curriculum vitae, three letters of recommendation from academic or professional sources familiar with the applicant's background. Additional exam requirements/ recommendations for international students: Required—TOEFL (minimum score 550 paper-based; 79 iBT), IELTS (minimum score 6.5). *Application deadline:* For fall admission, 7/1 for domestic students, 4/1 for international students; for spring admission, 11/1 for domestic students, 9/1 for international students. Applications are processed on a rolling basis. Application fee: $45 ($80 for international students). Electronic applications accepted. *Expenses:* Tuition, state resident: full-time $4671. Tuition, nonresident: full-time $8708. *International tuition:* $17,415 full-time. *Required fees:* $1924.60. Tuition and fees vary according to course load and degree level. *Financial support:* Scholarships/grants, health care benefits, and unspecified assistantships available. *Faculty research:* Economics of information systems, information security, digital forensics, information systems strategy, adoption and diffusion. *Unit head:* Dr. Au Yoris, Chair/Associate Professor, 210-458-6337, Fax: 210-458-6305, E-mail: yoris.au@utsa.edu. *Application contact:* Katherine Pope, Graduate Advisor of Record, 210-458-7316, Fax: 210-458-4398, E-mail: katherine.pope@utsa.edu.
Website: http://business.utsa.edu/it/.

The University of Texas at San Antonio, College of Business, Department of Management, San Antonio, TX 78249-0617. Offers management and organization studies (PhD). *Students:* 17 full-time (6 women); includes 5 minority (3 Black or African American, non-Hispanic/Latino; 1 American Indian or Alaska Native, non-Hispanic/ Latino; 1 Hispanic/Latino), 1 international. Average age 24. 5 applicants, 80% accepted, 4 enrolled. In 2013, 17 doctorates awarded. Terminal master's awarded for partial completion of doctoral program. *Degree requirements:* For doctorate, comprehensive exam, thesis/dissertation. *Entrance requirements:* For doctorate, GMAT, GRE. Additional exam requirements/recommendations for international students: Required— TOEFL (minimum score 550 paper-based; 79 iBT), IELTS (minimum score 6.5). *Application deadline:* For fall admission, 7/1 for domestic students, 4/1 for international students; for spring admission, 11/1 for domestic students, 9/1 for international students. Application fee: $45 ($80 for international students). Electronic applications accepted. *Expenses:* Tuition, state resident: full-time $4671. Tuition, nonresident: full-time $8708. *International tuition:* $17,415 full-time. *Required fees:* $1924.60. Tuition and fees vary according to course load and degree level. *Financial support:* In 2013–14, 9 students received support, including 14 research assistantships with tuition reimbursements available (averaging $22,000 per year), 14 teaching assistantships with tuition reimbursements available (averaging $22,000 per year); fellowships with full tuition reimbursements available also available. Financial award application deadline: 3/31. *Total annual research expenditures:* $35. *Unit head:* Dr. William Gerard Sanders, Dean, 210-458-4317, Fax: 210-458-4308, E-mail: gerry.sanders@utsa.edu. *Application contact:* Caron Kiley, Assistant Director of Graduate Fiscal Services/PhD Program Manager, 210-458-7324, Fax: 210-458-4398, E-mail: caron.kiley@utsa.edu.
Website: http://business.utsa.edu/mgt/.

The University of Texas at San Antonio, College of Business, Department of Management Science and Statistics, San Antonio, TX 78249-0617. Offers applied statistics (MS, PhD); management science (MBA). *Accreditation:* AACSB. Part-time and evening/weekend programs available. *Faculty:* 14 full-time (2 women), 2 part-time/ adjunct (1 woman). *Students:* 36 full-time (14 women), 35 part-time (8 women); includes 18 minority (1 Black or African American, non-Hispanic/Latino; 2 Asian, non-Hispanic/ Latino; 15 Hispanic/Latino), 21 international. Average age 30. 63 applicants, 62% accepted, 31 enrolled. In 2013, 14 master's, 2 doctorates awarded. *Degree requirements:* For master's, comprehensive exam (for some programs), thesis or alternative; for doctorate, comprehensive exam, thesis/dissertation. *Entrance*

requirements: For master's, GMAT, minimum of 36 semester credit hours of coursework beyond any hours acquired in the MBA-leveling courses; statement of purpose; for doctorate, GRE, minimum cumulative GPA of 3.3 in the last 60 hours of coursework; transcripts from all colleges and universities attended; curriculum vitae; statement of academic work experiences, interests, and goals; three letters of recommendation; BA, BS, or MS in mathematics, statistics, or closely-related field. Additional exam requirements/recommendations for international students: Required—TOEFL (minimum score 550 paper-based; 79 iBT), IELTS (minimum score 6.5). *Application deadline:* For fall admission, 7/1 for domestic students, 4/1 for international students; for spring admission, 11/1 for domestic students, 9/1 for international students. Applications are processed on a rolling basis. Application fee: $45 ($80 for international students). Electronic applications accepted. *Expenses:* Tuition, state resident: full-time $4671. Tuition, nonresident: full-time $8708. *International tuition:* $17,415 full-time. *Required fees:* $1924.60. Tuition and fees vary according to course load and degree level. *Financial support:* Scholarships/grants, health care benefits, and unspecified assistantships available. *Faculty research:* Statistical signal processing, reliability and life-testing experiments, modeling decompression sickness using survival analysis. *Unit head:* Dr. Raydel Tullous, Chair, 210-458-6345, Fax: 210-458-6350, E-mail: raydel.tullous@utsa.edu. *Application contact:* Katherine Pope, Graduate Assistant of Record, 210-458-7316, Fax: 210-458-4398, E-mail: katherine.pope@utsa.edu.
Website: http://business.utsa.edu/mss/.

The University of Texas at Tyler, College of Business and Technology, School of Business Administration, Tyler, TX 75799-0001. Offers business administration (MBA); general management (MBA); health care (MBA). Part-time programs available. Postbaccalaureate distance learning degree programs offered (no on-campus study). *Entrance requirements:* Additional exam requirements/recommendations for international students: Required—TOEFL (minimum score 550 paper-based). *Faculty research:* General business, inventory control, institutional markets, service marketing, product distribution, accounting fraud, financial reporting and recognition.

The University of Texas of the Permian Basin, Office of Graduate Studies, School of Business, Program in Management, Odessa, TX 79762-0001. Offers MBA. *Accreditation:* AACSB. *Entrance requirements:* For master's, GMAT. Additional exam requirements/recommendations for international students: Required—TOEFL (minimum score 550 paper-based).

The University of Texas–Pan American, College of Business Administration, Edinburg, TX 78539. Offers M Acc, MBA, MS, PhD. *Accreditation:* AACSB. Part-time and evening/weekend programs available. *Degree requirements:* For master's, thesis optional; for doctorate, one foreign language, thesis/dissertation, internship. *Entrance requirements:* For master's, GMAT, minimum AACSB index of 1000 (based on last 60 semester hours); for doctorate, GMAT. Additional exam requirements/recommendations for international students: Required—TOEFL. *Expenses:* Tuition, state resident: full-time $5986; part-time $333 per credit hour. Tuition, nonresident: full-time $12,358; part-time $687 per credit hour. *Required fees:* $782. Tuition and fees vary according to program.

University of the Cumberlands, Hutton School of Business, Williamsburg, KY 40769-1372. Offers accounting (MBA); business (MBA). Part-time programs available. Postbaccalaureate distance learning degree programs offered (no on-campus study). *Entrance requirements:* For master's, GMAT, GRE. Additional exam requirements/ recommendations for international students: Required—TOEFL. Electronic applications accepted.

University of the District of Columbia, School of Business and Public Administration, Program in Business Administration, Washington, DC 20008-1175. Offers MBA. *Accreditation:* ACBSP. *Degree requirements:* For master's, comprehensive exam, thesis

optional. *Entrance requirements:* For master's, GMAT, writing proficiency exam. *Expenses: Tuition, area resident:* Full-time $7883.28; part-time $437.96 per credit hour. Tuition, state resident: full-time $8923.14. Tuition, nonresident: full-time $15,163; part-time $842.40 per credit hour. *Required fees:* $620; $30 per credit hour.

University of the Incarnate Word, Extended Academic Programs, Program in Administration, San Antonio, TX 78209-6397. Offers applied administration (MAA); organizational development (MAA). Part-time and evening/weekend programs available. *Faculty:* 12 part-time/adjunct (2 women). *Students:* 2 full-time (both women), 325 part-time (193 women); includes 215 minority (54 Black or African American, non-Hispanic/Latino; 3 American Indian or Alaska Native, non-Hispanic/Latino; 13 Asian, non-Hispanic/Latino; 143 Hispanic/Latino; 2 Native Hawaiian or other Pacific Islander, non-Hispanic/Latino). Average age 37. 138 applicants, 99% accepted, 98 enrolled. In 2013, 96 master's awarded. *Degree requirements:* For master's, capstone experience. *Entrance requirements:* For master's, GRE (minimum score of 800) or GMAT (minimum score of 450) if GPA is between 2.0 - 2.5. Additional exam requirements/recommendations for international students: Required—TOEFL (minimum score 560 paper-based; 83 iBT). *Expenses: Tuition:* Part-time $815 per credit hour. *Required fees:* $86 per credit hour. One-time fee: $40 part-time. Tuition and fees vary according to degree level and program. *Unit head:* Dr. Cyndi Porter, Vice President, 877-603-1130, E-mail: porter@uiwtx.edu. *Application contact:* Julie Weber, Director of Marketing and Recruitment, 210-832-2100, Fax: 210-829-2756, E-mail: eapadmission@uiwtx.edu.
Website: http://adcap.uiw.edu/academics/graduate_degrees/ma_administration.

University of the Incarnate Word, Extended Academic Programs, Program in Business Administration, San Antonio, TX 78209-6397. Offers business administration (MS); general business (MBA); international business (MBA). Part-time and evening/weekend programs available. Postbaccalaureate distance learning degree programs offered (minimal on-campus study). *Faculty:* 3 full-time (0 women), 20 part-time/adjunct (8 women). *Students:* 221 part-time (113 women); includes 138 minority (17 Black or African American, non-Hispanic/Latino; 1 American Indian or Alaska Native, non-Hispanic/Latino; 10 Asian, non-Hispanic/Latino; 109 Hispanic/Latino; 1 Two or more races, non-Hispanic/Latino). Average age 35. 105 applicants, 86% accepted, 66 enrolled. In 2013, 74 master's awarded. *Entrance requirements:* For master's, GMAT (minimum score of 450), baccalaureate degree with minimum GPA of 3.0. Additional exam requirements/recommendations for international students: Required—TOEFL (minimum score 560 paper-based; 83 iBT). *Application deadline:* Applications are processed on a rolling basis. Electronic applications accepted. *Expenses: Tuition:* Part-time $815 per credit hour. *Required fees:* $86 per credit hour. One-time fee: $40 part-time. Tuition and fees vary according to degree level and program. *Financial support:* Applicants required to submit FAFSA. *Unit head:* Dr. Cyndi Porter, Vice President, 877-603-1130, E-mail: porter@uiwtx.edu. *Application contact:* Julie Weber, Director of Marketing and Recruitment, 210-832-2100, Fax: 210-829-2756, E-mail: eapadmission@uiwtx.edu.

University of the Incarnate Word, School of Graduate Studies and Research, H-E-B School of Business and Administration, DBA Program, San Antonio, TX 78209-6397. Offers DBA. *Faculty:* 20 full-time (10 women), 14 part-time/adjunct (6 women). *Students:* 8 full-time (3 women), 4 part-time (1 woman); includes 6 minority (2 Black or African American, non-Hispanic/Latino; 2 Asian, non-Hispanic/Latino; 2 Hispanic/Latino), 1 international. Average age 45. 21 applicants, 67% accepted, 12 enrolled. *Entrance requirements:* For doctorate, GRE, official transcripts, master's degree in business administration or equivalent, statement of purpose, two years of full-time professional employment and meaningful management experience within the past five years, three letters of recommendation, interview. Additional exam requirements/recommendations for international students: Required—TOEFL (minimum score 560 paper-based; 83 iBT). *Expenses: Tuition:* Part-time $815 per credit hour. *Required fees:* $86 per credit hour. One-time fee: $40 part-time. Tuition and fees vary according to degree level and program. *Unit head:* Dr. Annette Craven, Director, 210-829-3190, E-mail: craven@uiwtx.edu. *Application contact:* Andrea Cyterski-Acosta, Dean of Enrollment, 210-829-6005, Fax: 210-829-3921, E-mail: admis@uiwtx.edu.
Website: http://www.uiw.edu/dba/.

University of the Incarnate Word, School of Graduate Studies and Research, H-E-B School of Business and Administration, Programs in Administration, San Antonio, TX 78209-6397. Offers adult education (MAA); communication arts (MAA); healthcare administration (MAA); instructional technology (MAA); nutrition (MAA); organizational development (MAA); sports management (MAA). Part-time and evening/weekend programs available. Postbaccalaureate distance learning degree programs offered (no on-campus study). *Faculty:* 20 full-time (10 women), 14 part-time/adjunct (6 women). *Students:* 31 full-time (22 women), 54 part-time (36 women); includes 61 minority (14 Black or African American, non-Hispanic/Latino; 1 Asian, non-Hispanic/Latino; 46 Hispanic/Latino), 6 international. Average age 31. 63 applicants, 68% accepted, 21 enrolled. In 2013, 35 master's awarded. *Degree requirements:* For master's, capstone. *Entrance requirements:* For master's, GRE, GMAT, undergraduate degree, minimum GPA of 2.5. Additional exam requirements/recommendations for international students: Required—TOEFL (minimum score 560 paper-based; 83 iBT). *Application deadline:* Applications are processed on a rolling basis. Application fee: $20. Electronic applications accepted. *Expenses: Tuition:* Part-time $815 per credit hour. *Required fees:* $86 per credit hour. One-time fee: $40 part-time. Tuition and fees vary according to degree level and program. *Financial support:* Federal Work-Study and scholarships/grants available. Financial award applicants required to submit FAFSA. *Unit head:* Dr. Mark Teachout, MAA Programs Director, 210-829-3177, Fax: 210-805-3564, E-mail: teachout@uiwtx.edu. *Application contact:* Andrea Cyterski-Acosta, Dean of Enrollment, 210-829-6005, Fax: 210-829-3921, E-mail: admis@uiwtx.edu.
Website: http://www.uiw.edu/maa/.

University of the Incarnate Word, School of Graduate Studies and Research, H-E-B School of Business and Administration, Programs in Business Administration, San Antonio, TX 78209-6397. Offers general business (MBA); international business (MBA); marketing (MBA); sports management (MBA). *Accreditation:* ACBSP. Part-time and evening/weekend programs available. Postbaccalaureate distance learning degree programs offered. *Faculty:* 20 full-time (10 women), 14 part-time/adjunct (6 women). *Students:* 95 full-time (33 women), 74 part-time (40 women); includes 93 minority (11 Black or African American, non-Hispanic/Latino; 1 American Indian or Alaska Native, non-Hispanic/Latino; 4 Asian, non-Hispanic/Latino; 71 Hispanic/Latino; 2 Native Hawaiian or other Pacific Islander, non-Hispanic/Latino; 4 Two or more races, non-Hispanic/Latino), 41 international. Average age 28. 183 applicants, 66% accepted, 51 enrolled. In 2013, 75 master's awarded. *Degree requirements:* For master's, capstone. *Entrance requirements:* For master's, GMAT (minimum score 450), undergraduate degree with minimum overall GPA of 2.5. Additional exam requirements/recommendations for international students: Required—TOEFL (minimum score 560 paper-based; 83 iBT). *Application deadline:* Applications are processed on a rolling basis. Application fee: $20. Electronic applications accepted. *Expenses: Tuition:* Part-time $815 per credit hour. *Required fees:* $86 per credit hour. One-time fee: $40 part-time. Tuition and fees vary according to degree level and program. *Financial support:* Federal Work-Study and scholarships/grants available. Financial award applicants required to submit FAFSA. *Unit head:* Dr. Jeannie Scott, Acting Dean, 210-283-5002, Fax: 210-805-3564, E-mail: scott@uiwtx.edu. *Application contact:* Andrea Cyterski-Acosta, Dean of Enrollment, 210-829-6005, Fax: 210-829-3921, E-mail: admis@uiwtx.edu.
Website: http://www.uiw.edu/mba/index.htm and http://www.uiw.edu/mba/admission.html.

University of the Pacific, Eberhardt School of Business, Stockton, CA 95211-0197. Offers M Acc, MBA, JD/MBA. *Accreditation:* AACSB. Part-time programs available. *Faculty:* 25 full-time (11 women), 2 part-time/adjunct (0 women). *Students:* 35 full-time (18 women), 3 part-time (1 woman); includes 11 minority (1 Black or African American, non-Hispanic/Latino; 1 American Indian or Alaska Native, non-Hispanic/Latino; 7 Asian, non-Hispanic/Latino; 2 Hispanic/Latino), 10 international. Average age 24. 346 applicants, 20% accepted, 29 enrolled. In 2013, 18 master's awarded. *Entrance requirements:* For master's, GMAT. Additional exam requirements/recommendations for international students: Required—TOEFL (minimum score 475 paper-based). *Application deadline:* For fall admission, 7/31 priority date for domestic students; for spring admission, 11/30 for domestic students. Applications are processed on a rolling basis. Application fee: $75. *Financial support:* Fellowships, research assistantships, Federal Work-Study, and institutionally sponsored loans available. Support available to part-time students. Financial award application deadline: 3/1; financial award applicants required to submit FAFSA. *Unit head:* Dr. Lewis R. Gale, Dean, 209-946-2466, Fax: 209-946-7710, E-mail: business@pacific.edu. *Application contact:* Dr. Christopher Lozano, MBA Recruiting Director, 209-946-2629, Fax: 209-946-2586, E-mail: clozano@pacific.edu.
Website: http://www.pacific.edu/mba/.

University of the Potomac, Program in Business Administration, Washington, DC 20005. Offers MBA. Program also offered at Vienna, VA campus. Postbaccalaureate distance learning degree programs offered (no on-campus study).

University of the Sacred Heart, Graduate Programs, Department of Business Administration, San Juan, PR 00914-0383. Offers human resource management (MBA); information systems auditing (MS); information technology (Certificate); international marketing (MBA); management information systems (MBA); production and marketing of special events (Certificate); taxation (MBA). Part-time and evening/weekend programs available. *Degree requirements:* For master's, thesis. *Entrance requirements:* For master's, EXADEP, minimum undergraduate GPA of 2.75, interview.

University of the Southwest, Graduate Programs, Hobbs, NM 88240-9129. Offers business administration (MBA); curriculum and instruction (MSE); curriculum and instruction: bilingual (MSE); curriculum and instruction: TESOL (MSE); early childhood education (MSE); educational administration (MSE); mental health counseling (MSE); school counseling (MSE); special education (MSE); sports management (MBA). Part-time and evening/weekend programs available. Postbaccalaureate distance learning degree programs offered (no on-campus study). *Degree requirements:* For master's, comprehensive exam, thesis (for some programs). *Entrance requirements:* Additional exam requirements/recommendations for international students: Recommended—TOEFL. Electronic applications accepted.

University of the Virgin Islands, Graduate Programs, Division of Business Administration, Saint Thomas, VI 00802-9990. Offers MBA. Part-time and evening/weekend programs available. *Degree requirements:* For master's, comprehensive exam or thesis. *Entrance requirements:* For master's, GMAT, minimum GPA of 2.5. Additional exam requirements/recommendations for international students: Required—TOEFL (minimum score 550 paper-based). *Faculty research:* Management information systems.

University of the West, Department of Business Administration, Rosemead, CA 91770. Offers business administration (EMBA); computer information systems (MBA); finance (MBA); international business (MBA); nonprofit organization management (MBA). Part-time and evening/weekend programs available. *Entrance requirements:* Additional exam requirements/recommendations for international students: Required—TOEFL. *Application deadline:* For fall admission, 6/15 for domestic and international students; for winter admission, 4/1 for domestic and international students; for spring admission, 11/15 for domestic and international students. Applications are processed on a rolling basis. Application fee: $50 ($100 for international students). *Expenses: Tuition:* Full-time $7200; part-time $400 per credit hour. *Required fees:* $750; $400 per credit hour. $275 per semester. One-time fee: $75. Tuition and fees vary according to course level and program. *Financial support:* Career-related internships or fieldwork, Federal Work-Study, scholarships/grants, and tuition waivers (partial) available. Financial award applicants required to submit FAFSA. *Unit head:* Dr. Bill Y. Chen, Chair, 626-656-2125, Fax: 626-571-1413, E-mail: billchen@uwest.edu. *Application contact:* Jason Kosareff, Enrollment Counselor, 626-571-8811 Ext. 311, Fax: 626-571-1413, E-mail: jasonk@uwest.edu.

The University of Toledo, College of Graduate Studies, College of Business and Innovation, Department of Management, Toledo, OH 43606-3390. Offers MBA. Part-time and evening/weekend programs available. *Faculty:* 8. *Students:* 23 full-time (13 women), 110 part-time (51 women); includes 20 minority (13 Black or African American, non-Hispanic/Latino; 2 American Indian or Alaska Native, non-Hispanic/Latino; 2 Asian, non-Hispanic/Latino; 2 Hispanic/Latino; 1 Two or more races, non-Hispanic/Latino), 23 international. Average age 30. 44 applicants, 91% accepted, 32 enrolled. In 2013, 97 master's awarded. *Entrance requirements:* For master's, GMAT, GRE, or LSAT, minimum GPA of 2.7 for all prior academic work, three letters of recommendation, statement of purpose, transcripts from all prior institutions attended. Additional exam requirements/recommendations for international students: Required—TOEFL (minimum score 550 paper-based; 80 iBT). *Application deadline:* For fall admission, 8/1 priority date for domestic students, 5/1 priority date for international students; for spring admission, 11/15 for domestic students, 10/1 for international students; for summer admission, 4/15 for domestic students, 3/1 for international students. Applications are processed on a rolling basis. Application fee: $45 ($75 for international students). Electronic applications accepted. *Financial support:* In 2013–14, 12 research assistantships with full and partial tuition reimbursements (averaging $4,844 per year) were awarded; career-related internships or fieldwork, Federal Work-Study, institutionally sponsored loans, scholarships/grants, tuition waivers (full and partial), unspecified assistantships, and administrative assistantships also available. Support available to part-time students. *Faculty research:* Stress, deviation, workplace, globalization, recruitment. *Unit head:* Dr. Sonny Ariss, Chair, 419-530-2366. *Application contact:* Graduate School Office, 419-530-4723, Fax: 419-530-4724, E-mail: grdsch@utnet.utoledo.edu.
Website: http://www.utoledo.edu/business/MGMT/MGMTCCD/MGMT.html.

University of Toronto, School of Graduate Studies, Rotman School of Management, Toronto, ON M5S 1A1, Canada. Offers MBA, MF, PhD, JD/MBA. *Accreditation:* AACSB. Part-time and evening/weekend programs available. *Degree requirements:* For doctorate, thesis/dissertation. *Entrance requirements:* For master's, GMAT (MBA), minimum mid-B average in final undergraduate year; minimum 2 years of full-time work experience; 2-3 letters of reference; for doctorate, GMAT or GRE, minimum B+ average, master's degree in business administration, 2-3 letters of reference. *Expenses:* Contact

institution. *Faculty research:* Natural resources, organizational behavior, finance, marketing, strategic management.

The University of Tulsa, Graduate School, Collins College of Business, Business Administration/Computer Science Program, Tulsa, OK 74104-3189. Offers MBA/MS. Part-time programs available. *Students:* 1 full-time (0 women), all international. Average age 23. 1 applicant. *Entrance requirements:* Additional exam requirements/recommendations for international students: Required—TOEFL (minimum score 577 paper-based; 91 iBT), IELTS (minimum score 6.5). *Application deadline:* Applications are processed on a rolling basis. Application fee: $40. Electronic applications accepted. *Expenses: Tuition:* Full-time $19,566; part-time $1087 per credit hour. *Required fees:* $1690; $5 per credit hour. $160 per semester. Tuition and fees vary according to course load. *Financial support:* In 2013–14, 1 student received support, including 1 research assistantship with full and partial tuition reimbursement available (averaging $16,200 per year); fellowships with full and partial tuition reimbursements available, teaching assistantships with full and partial tuition reimbursements available, career-related internships or fieldwork, Federal Work-Study, institutionally sponsored loans, scholarships/grants, health care benefits, tuition waivers, and unspecified assistantships also available. Support available to part-time students. Financial award application deadline: 2/1; financial award applicants required to submit FAFSA. *Unit head:* Dr. Linda Nichols, Associate Dean, 918-631-2242, Fax: 918-631-2142, E-mail: linda-nichols@utulsa.edu. *Application contact:* Information Contact, 918-631-2242, E-mail: graduate-business@utulsa.edu.

The University of Tulsa, Graduate School, Collins College of Business, Master of Business Administration Program, Tulsa, OK 74104-3189. Offers accounting (MBA); business administration (MBA); energy management (MBA); finance (MBA); international business (MBA); management information systems (MBA); taxation (MBA); JD/MBA; MBA/MSCS; MBA/MSF. *Accreditation:* AACSB. Part-time and evening/weekend programs available. *Faculty:* 32 full-time (6 women). *Students:* 59 full-time (28 women), 29 part-time (9 women); includes 11 minority (1 Black or African American, non-Hispanic/Latino; 5 American Indian or Alaska Native, non-Hispanic/Latino; 3 Asian, non-Hispanic/Latino; 1 Hispanic/Latino; 1 Two or more races, non-Hispanic/Latino), 16 international. Average age 27. 53 applicants, 81% accepted, 28 enrolled. In 2013, 39 master's awarded. *Entrance requirements:* For master's, GMAT. Additional exam requirements/recommendations for international students: Required—TOEFL (minimum score 577 paper-based; 91 iBT), IELTS (minimum score 6.5). *Application deadline:* Applications are processed on a rolling basis. Application fee: $40. Electronic applications accepted. *Expenses: Tuition:* Full-time $19,566; part-time $1087 per credit hour. *Required fees:* $1690; $5 per credit hour. $160 per semester. Tuition and fees vary according to course load. *Financial support:* In 2013–14, 31 students received support, including 1 research assistantship (averaging $1,500 per year), 30 teaching assistantships (averaging $10,112 per year); fellowships, career-related internships or fieldwork, institutionally sponsored loans, scholarships/grants, health care benefits, tuition waivers (full and partial), and unspecified assistantships also available. Support available to part-time students. Financial award application deadline: 2/1; financial award applicants required to submit FAFSA. *Faculty research:* Accounting, energy management, finance, international business, management information systems, taxation. *Unit head:* Dr. Linda Nichols, Associate Dean of the Collins College of Business, 918-631-2242, Fax: 918-631-2142, E-mail: linda-nichols@utulsa.edu. *Application contact:* Information Contact, 918-631-2242, E-mail: graduate-business@utulsa.edu.
Website: http://www.utulsa.edu/academics/colleges/collins-college-of-business/bus-dept-schools/graduate-business-programs/degree-programs/MBA-Programs.aspx.

University of Utah, Graduate School, David Eccles School of Business, Salt Lake City, UT 84112. Offers EMBA, M Acc, MBA, MHA, MRED, MS, PMBA, PhD, Graduate Certificate, MBA/JD, MBA/MHA, MBA/MS, MHA/MPA, MPH/MHA, PMBA/MHA. *Accreditation:* AACSB. Part-time and evening/weekend programs available. *Faculty:* 58 full-time (21 women), 37 part-time/adjunct (7 women). *Students:* 746 full-time (173 women), 257 part-time (47 women); includes 78 minority (5 Black or African American, non-Hispanic/Latino; 29 Asian, non-Hispanic/Latino; 35 Hispanic/Latino; 1 Native Hawaiian or other Pacific Islander, non-Hispanic/Latino; 8 Two or more races, non-Hispanic/Latino), 118 international. Average age 31. 887 applicants, 66% accepted, 486 enrolled. In 2013, 564 master's, 10 doctorates awarded. *Degree requirements:* For master's, comprehensive exam (for some programs), thesis (for some programs); for doctorate, comprehensive exam (for some programs), thesis/dissertation. *Entrance requirements:* Additional exam requirements/recommendations for international students: Required—TOEFL. Application fee: $55 ($65 for international students). Electronic applications accepted. *Expenses:* Contact institution. *Financial support:* Fellowships with partial tuition reimbursements, research assistantships with partial tuition reimbursements, teaching assistantships with full and partial tuition reimbursements, scholarships/grants, tuition waivers (full and partial), and unspecified assistantships available. Financial award applicants required to submit FAFSA. *Faculty research:* Information systems, investment, financial accounting, international strategy. *Unit head:* Dr. Taylor Randall, Dean, 801-581-3074, E-mail: dean@business.utah.edu. *Application contact:* Andrea Miller, Director of Graduate Admissions, 801-585-7366, E-mail: andrea.miller@business.utah.edu.
Website: http://www.business.utah.edu/.

University of Vermont, Graduate College, School of Business Administration, Burlington, VT 05405. Offers M Acc, MBA. *Accreditation:* AACSB. Part-time programs available. *Faculty:* 25. *Students:* 23 (7 women); includes 1 minority (Two or more races, non-Hispanic/Latino), 2 international. 19 applicants, 58% accepted, 2 enrolled. In 2013, 27 master's awarded. *Entrance requirements:* For master's, GMAT, resume. Additional exam requirements/recommendations for international students: Required—TOEFL (minimum score 550 paper-based; 80 iBT). *Application deadline:* For fall admission, 1/15 for domestic and international students. Applications are processed on a rolling basis. Application fee: $65. Electronic applications accepted. *Financial support:* Fellowships, teaching assistantships, and Federal Work-Study available. Financial award application deadline: 3/1. *Unit head:* Dr. Sanjay Sharma, Dean, 802-656-4119. *Application contact:* Prof. William Cats-Baril, Coordinator, 802-656-4119.

University of Victoria, Faculty of Graduate Studies, Faculty of Business, Victoria, BC V8W 2Y2, Canada. Offers MBA, MBA/LL B. *Accreditation:* AACSB. Part-time programs available. *Entrance requirements:* For master's, GMAT, minimum B average. Additional exam requirements/recommendations for international students: Required—TOEFL (minimum score 575 paper-based), IELTS (minimum score 7). Electronic applications accepted. *Expenses:* Contact institution. *Faculty research:* Organizational design and analysis, negotiation and conflict management, human resources management, entrepreneurship, international marketing and tourism.

University of Virginia, Darden Graduate School of Business Administration, Charlottesville, VA 22903. Offers MBA, PhD, MBA/JD, MBA/M Ed, MBA/MA, MBA/MD, MBA/ME, MBA/MPP, MBA/MSN. *Accreditation:* AACSB. *Faculty:* 65 full-time (14 women), 4 part-time/adjunct (2 women). *Students:* 835 full-time (237 women), 2 part-time (0 women); includes 140 minority (30 Black or African American, non-Hispanic/Latino; 3 American Indian or Alaska Native, non-Hispanic/Latino; 51 Asian, non-Hispanic/Latino; 44 Hispanic/Latino; 12 Two or more races, non-Hispanic/Latino), 191 international. Average age 29. 2,997 applicants, 31% accepted, 416 enrolled. In 2013, 382 master's, 2 doctorates awarded. *Degree requirements:* For doctorate, thesis/dissertation. *Entrance requirements:* For master's, GMAT, resume; 2 letters of recommendation; interview; for doctorate, GMAT, resume; essay; 2 letters of recommendation; interview. Additional exam requirements/recommendations for international students: Required—TOEFL. *Application deadline:* For fall admission, 3/1 for domestic students, 3/2 for international students. Applications are processed on a rolling basis. Application fee: $200. Electronic applications accepted. *Expenses:* Contact institution. *Financial support:* Career-related internships or fieldwork available. Financial award applicants required to submit FAFSA. *Unit head:* Robert F. Bruner, Dean, 434-924-3900, E-mail: darden@virginia.edu. *Application contact:* Sara Neher, Assistant Dean of MBA Admissions, 434-924-3900, E-mail: darden@virginia.edu.
Website: http://www.darden.virginia.edu/html/default.aspx.

University of Virginia, McIntire School of Commerce, Charlottesville, VA 22903. Offers accounting (MS); commerce (MSC), including financial services, marketing and management; management of information technology (MS); JD/MS. *Accreditation:* AACSB. *Faculty:* 67 full-time (22 women), 2 part-time/adjunct (1 woman). *Students:* 233 full-time (96 women), 2 part-time (1 woman); includes 52 minority (11 Black or African American, non-Hispanic/Latino; 1 American Indian or Alaska Native, non-Hispanic/Latino; 23 Asian, non-Hispanic/Latino; 11 Hispanic/Latino; 1 Native Hawaiian or other Pacific Islander, non-Hispanic/Latino; 5 Two or more races, non-Hispanic/Latino), 40 international. Average age 27. 683 applicants, 51% accepted, 237 enrolled. In 2013, 183 master's awarded. *Entrance requirements:* For master's, GMAT, 2 letters of recommendation. Additional exam requirements/recommendations for international students: Required—TOEFL (minimum score 600 paper-based; 100 iBT), IELTS (minimum score 7). *Application deadline:* Applications are processed on a rolling basis. Application fee: $75. Electronic applications accepted. *Expenses:* Contact institution. *Financial support:* Fellowships, research assistantships, teaching assistantships, career-related internships or fieldwork, and Federal Work-Study available. Financial award applicants required to submit FAFSA. *Unit head:* Carl Zeithaml, Dean, 434-924-3110, Fax: 434-924-7074, E-mail: mcs@virginia.edu. *Application contact:* Emma Candalier, Associate Director of Graduate Recruiting, 434-243-4992, Fax: 434-924-4511, E-mail: ecandalier@virginia.edu.
Website: http://www.commerce.virginia.edu/Pages/default.aspx.

University of Washington, Graduate School, Michael G. Foster School of Business, Seattle, WA 98195-3200. Offers auditing and assurance (MP Acc); business administration (MBA, PhD); executive business administration (MBA); global executive business administration (MBA); taxation (MP Acc); technology management (MBA); JD/MBA; MBA/MAIS; MBA/MHA. *Accreditation:* AACSB. Part-time and evening/weekend programs available. *Faculty:* 100 full-time (28 women), 55 part-time/adjunct (22 women). *Students:* 407 full-time (130 women), 369 part-time (110 women); includes 199 minority (16 Black or African American, non-Hispanic/Latino; 5 American Indian or Alaska Native, non-Hispanic/Latino; 139 Asian, non-Hispanic/Latino; 25 Hispanic/Latino; 7 Native Hawaiian or other Pacific Islander, non-Hispanic/Latino; 7 Two or more races, non-Hispanic/Latino), 178 international. Average age 32. 2,474 applicants, 40% accepted, 776 enrolled. In 2013, 468 master's, 8 doctorates awarded. Terminal master's awarded for partial completion of doctoral program. *Degree requirements:* For doctorate, comprehensive exam, thesis/dissertation. *Entrance requirements:* For master's, GMAT; for doctorate, GMAT, GRE. Additional exam requirements/recommendations for international students: Required—TOEFL (minimum score 600 paper-based; 100 iBT). *Application deadline:* For fall admission, 3/15 for domestic students, 1/20 for international students. Application fee: $85. Electronic applications accepted. *Expenses:* Contact institution. *Financial support:* Fellowships with partial tuition reimbursements, research assistantships with partial tuition reimbursements, teaching assistantships with partial tuition reimbursements, Federal Work-Study, institutionally sponsored loans, and scholarships/grants available. Financial award application deadline: 2/28; financial award applicants required to submit FAFSA. *Faculty research:* Finance, marketing, organizational behavior, information technology, strategy. *Unit head:* Dr. James Jiambalvo, Dean, 206-543-4750. *Application contact:* Erin Town, Director of Admissions, 206-543-4661, Fax: 206-616-7351, E-mail: mba@uw.edu.
Website: http://www.foster.washington.edu/.

University of Washington, Bothell, School of Business, Bothell, WA 98011-8246. Offers leadership (MBA); technology (MBA). *Accreditation:* AACSB. Part-time and evening/weekend programs available. *Degree requirements:* For master's, 72 credits, minimum cumulative GPA of 3.0. *Entrance requirements:* For master's, GMAT or GRE General Test. Additional exam requirements/recommendations for international students: Required—TOEFL (minimum score 580 paper-based; 92 iBT), IELTS (minimum score 7). Electronic applications accepted. *Expenses:* Contact institution. *Faculty research:* Leadership, supply chain management, entrepreneurship, game theory, corporate finance, marketing innovation.

University of Washington, Tacoma, Graduate Programs, MBA Programs, Tacoma, WA 98402-3100. Offers accounting (MBA); business administration (MBA); certified financial analyst (MBA). *Accreditation:* AACSB. Part-time and evening/weekend programs available. *Entrance requirements:* For master's, GMAT, minimum GPA of 3.0 in final graded 90 quarter credits or 60 graded semester credits; at least 2 years of professional/management work experience. Additional exam requirements/recommendations for international students: Required—TOEFL (minimum score 580 paper-based; 92 iBT). Electronic applications accepted. *Expenses:* Contact institution. *Faculty research:* International accounting, marketing, change management, investments, corporate social responsibility.

University of Waterloo, Graduate Studies, Centre for Business, Entrepreneurship and Technology, Waterloo, ON N2L 3G1, Canada. Offers MBET. *Entrance requirements:* For master's, honors degree. Additional exam requirements/recommendations for international students: Required—TOEFL (minimum score 550 paper-based), TWE. Electronic applications accepted.

The University of Western Ontario, Richard Ivey School of Business, London, ON N6A 3K7, Canada. Offers business (EMBA, PhD); corporate strategy and leadership elective (MBA); entrepreneurship elective (MBA); finance elective (MBA); health sector stream (MBA); international management elective (MBA); marketing elective (MBA); JD/MBA. *Degree requirements:* For master's, thesis (for some programs); for doctorate, thesis/dissertation. *Entrance requirements:* For master's, GMAT, 2 years of full-time work experience, interview. Additional exam requirements/recommendations for international students: Required—TOEFL (minimum score 100 iBT) or IELTS (minimum score 6). Electronic applications accepted. *Faculty research:* Strategy, organizational behavior, international business, finance, operations management.

University of West Florida, College of Business, Program in Business Administration, Pensacola, FL 32514-5750. Offers MBA. *Accreditation:* AACSB. Part-time and evening/weekend programs available. *Degree requirements:* For master's, industry portfolio project based on information from five of the core MBA courses. *Entrance requirements:* For master's, GMAT or GRE, official transcripts; minimum undergraduate GPA of 3.0; bachelor's degree; business course academic preparation; graduate-level motivation and writing abilities as noted in essay responses; two letters of recommendation; appropriate employment at increasing levels of responsibility via resume. Additional

exam requirements/recommendations for international students: Required—TOEFL (minimum score 550 paper-based). *Faculty research:* Robotics, corporate behavior, international trade, franchising, counterfeiting.

University of West Florida, College of Professional Studies, Department of Research and Advanced Studies, Pensacola, FL 32514-5750. Offers administration (MSA), including acquisition and contract administration, biomedical/pharmaceutical, criminal justice administration, database administration, education leadership, healthcare administration, human performance technology, leadership, nursing administration, public administration, software engineering and administration; college student personnel administration (M Ed), including college personnel administration, guidance and counseling; curriculum and instruction (M Ed, Ed S); educational leadership (M Ed); middle and secondary level education and ESOL (M Ed). Part-time and evening/weekend programs available. *Entrance requirements:* For master's, GRE or MAT, official transcripts; minimum undergraduate GPA of 3.0; letter of intent; three letters of recommendation; resume. Additional exam requirements/recommendations for international students: Required—TOEFL (minimum score 550 paper-based).

University of West Florida, College of Professional Studies, Program in Administration, Pensacola, FL 32514-5750. Offers acquisition and contract administration (MSA); database administration (MSA); health care administration (MSA); human performance technology (MSA); leadership (MSA); public administration (MSA); software engineering administration (MSA). Part-time and evening/weekend programs available. Postbaccalaureate distance learning degree programs offered (no on-campus study). *Entrance requirements:* For master's, GRE General Test, letter of intent, names of references. Additional exam requirements/recommendations for international students: Required—TOEFL (minimum score 550 paper-based).

University of West Georgia, Richards College of Business, Program of Business Administration, Carrollton, GA 30118. Offers MBA. *Accreditation:* AACSB. Part-time and evening/weekend programs available. *Faculty:* 12 full-time (5 women). *Students:* 47 full-time (22 women), 92 part-time (44 women); includes 50 minority (37 Black or African American, non-Hispanic/Latino; 2 American Indian or Alaska Native, non-Hispanic/Latino; 4 Asian, non-Hispanic/Latino; 6 Hispanic/Latino; 1 Two or more races, non-Hispanic/Latino), 10 international. Average age 31. 64 applicants, 94% accepted, 43 enrolled. In 2013, 53 master's awarded. *Degree requirements:* For master's, comprehensive exam. *Entrance requirements:* For master's, GMAT, minimum GPA of 2.5. Additional exam requirements/recommendations for international students: Required—TOEFL (minimum score 550 paper-based; 79 iBT); Recommended—IELTS (minimum score 6.5). *Application deadline:* For fall admission, 7/15 for domestic students, 6/1 for international students; for spring admission, 11/15 for domestic students, 10/15 for international students. Applications are processed on a rolling basis. Application fee: $40. Electronic applications accepted. *Expenses:* Contact institution. *Financial support:* In 2013–14, 11 students received support, including 15 research assistantships with full tuition reimbursements available (averaging $5,333 per year); career-related internships or fieldwork, tuition waivers (partial), and unspecified assistantships also available. Support available to part-time students. Financial award application deadline: 4/1; financial award applicants required to submit FAFSA. *Faculty research:* Distance learning, small business development, e-commerce, computer self-efficacy. *Unit head:* Dr. Douglas Turner, Associate Dean, 678-839-5252, E-mail: dturner@westga.edu. *Application contact:* Dr. Hope Udombon, Administrative Director of Graduate Business Programs, 678-839-5355, Fax: 678-839-5040, E-mail: udombon@westga.edu.
Website: http://www.westga.edu/business/mba_business_administration.php.

University of Windsor, Faculty of Graduate Studies, Odette School of Business, Windsor, ON N9B 3P4, Canada. Offers MBA, MM, MBA/LL B. Evening/weekend programs available. *Degree requirements:* For master's, thesis or alternative. *Entrance requirements:* For master's, GMAT, minimum B average. Additional exam requirements/recommendations for international students: Required—TOEFL (minimum score 600 paper-based). Electronic applications accepted. *Faculty research:* Accounting, administrative studies, finance, marketing, business policy and strategy.

University of Wisconsin–Eau Claire, College of Business, Program in Business Administration, Eau Claire, WI 54702-4004. Offers MBA. *Accreditation:* AACSB. Part-time and evening/weekend programs available. Postbaccalaureate distance learning degree programs offered (no on-campus study). *Faculty:* 9 full-time (5 women). *Students:* 7 full-time (1 woman), 223 part-time (101 women); includes 19 minority (4 Black or African American, non-Hispanic/Latino; 1 American Indian or Alaska Native, non-Hispanic/Latino; 9 Asian, non-Hispanic/Latino; 3 Hispanic/Latino; 2 Two or more races, non-Hispanic/Latino), 9 international. Average age 33. 102 applicants, 87% accepted, 36 enrolled. In 2013, 65 master's awarded. Terminal master's awarded for partial completion of doctoral program. *Degree requirements:* For master's, thesis optional, applied field project. *Entrance requirements:* For master's, GMAT or GRE, minimum GPA of 2.75 overall. Additional exam requirements/recommendations for international students: Required—TOEFL (minimum score 79 iBT). *Application deadline:* For fall admission, 7/1 priority date for domestic students, 6/1 priority date for international students; for spring admission, 12/1 priority date for domestic students, 11/1 priority date for international students. Applications are processed on a rolling basis. Application fee: $56. *Expenses:* Contact institution. *Financial support:* In 2013–14, 4 students received support. Federal Work-Study and unspecified assistantships available. Financial award application deadline: 3/1; financial award applicants required to submit FAFSA. *Unit head:* Dr. Robert Erffmeyer, Director, 715-836-5509, Fax: 715-836-4014, E-mail: erffmerc@uwec.edu. *Application contact:* Nancy Amdahl, Graduate Dean Assistant, 715-836-2721, Fax: 715-836-2902, E-mail: graduate@uwec.edu.
Website: http://www.uwec.edu/cob/graduate/index.htm.

University of Wisconsin–Green Bay, Graduate Studies, Program in Management, Green Bay, WI 54311-7001. Offers MS. Part-time programs available. *Faculty:* 6 full-time (0 women). *Students:* 7 full-time (2 women), 17 part-time (7 women); includes 2 minority (1 Black or African American, non-Hispanic/Latino; 1 American Indian or Alaska Native, non-Hispanic/Latino), 4 international. Average age 34. 23 applicants, 52% accepted, 8 enrolled. In 2013, 7 master's awarded. *Degree requirements:* For master's, thesis or alternative. *Entrance requirements:* For master's, GMAT or GRE General Test, minimum GPA of 3.0. *Application deadline:* For fall admission, 8/1 for domestic students; for spring admission, 11/1 for domestic students. Applications are processed on a rolling basis. Application fee: $56. Electronic applications accepted. *Expenses:* Tuition, state resident: full-time $7640; part-time $424 per credit. Tuition, nonresident: full-time $16,772; part-time $932 per credit. *Required fees:* $1378. Full-time tuition and fees vary according to course load and reciprocity agreements. *Financial support:* Career-related internships or fieldwork, Federal Work-Study, and institutionally sponsored loans available. Financial award application deadline: 7/15; financial award applicants required to submit FAFSA. *Faculty research:* Planning methods, budgeting, decision-making, organizational behavior and theory, management. *Unit head:* Dr. David Radosevich, Chair, 920-465-2051, E-mail: radosevd@uwgb.edu. *Application contact:* Mary Valitchka, Graduate Studies Coordinator, 920-465-2123, Fax: 920-465-2043, E-mail: valitchm@uwgb.edu.
Website: http://www.uwgb.edu/management/.

University of Wisconsin–La Crosse, Graduate Studies, College of Business Administration, La Crosse, WI 54601-3742. Offers MBA. *Accreditation:* AACSB. Part-time and evening/weekend programs available. *Faculty:* 8 full-time (2 women). *Students:* 20 full-time (9 women), 23 part-time (7 women), 19 international. Average age 27. 58 applicants, 64% accepted, 28 enrolled. In 2013, 33 master's awarded. *Degree requirements:* For master's, thesis optional. *Entrance requirements:* For master's, GMAT. Additional exam requirements/recommendations for international students: Required—TOEFL (minimum score 550 paper-based; 79 iBT). *Application deadline:* For fall admission, 6/15 priority date for domestic and international students; for spring admission, 11/15 priority date for domestic and international students. Applications are processed on a rolling basis. Electronic applications accepted. *Expenses:* Contact institution. *Financial support:* Research assistantships with partial tuition reimbursements, Federal Work-Study, scholarships/grants, health care benefits, and tuition waivers (partial) available. Support available to part-time students. Financial award application deadline: 3/15; financial award applicants required to submit FAFSA. *Faculty research:* Tax regulation, accounting standards, public sector information technology, corporate social responsibility, economics of sports. *Unit head:* Dr. Bruce May, Associate Dean, 608-785-8095, Fax: 608-785-6700, E-mail: may.bruce@uwlax.edu. *Application contact:* Martina Skobic, Director of MBA and International Programs, 608-785-8371, Fax: 608-785-6700, E-mail: mskobic@uwlax.edu.
Website: http://www.uwlax.edu/ba/graduate/gradstudents.htm.

University of Wisconsin–Madison, Graduate School, Wisconsin School of Business, Wisconsin Evening MBA Program, Madison, WI 53706-1380. Offers general management (MBA). Part-time and evening/weekend programs available. *Faculty:* 11 full-time (1 woman), 8 part-time/adjunct (0 women). *Students:* 145 part-time (45 women); includes 15 minority (2 Black or African American, non-Hispanic/Latino; 1 American Indian or Alaska Native, non-Hispanic/Latino; 9 Asian, non-Hispanic/Latino; 2 Hispanic/Latino; 1 Native Hawaiian or other Pacific Islander, non-Hispanic/Latino), 9 international. Average age 30. 66 applicants, 88% accepted, 50 enrolled. In 2013, 52 master's awarded. *Entrance requirements:* For master's, GMAT, bachelor's degree, 2 years of work experience. Additional exam requirements/recommendations for international students: Required—TOEFL (minimum score 600 paper-based; 100 iBT). *Application deadline:* For fall admission, 5/1 priority date for domestic and international students. Applications are processed on a rolling basis. Application fee: $56. Electronic applications accepted. *Expenses:* Contact institution. *Financial support:* Scholarships/grants available. Support available to part-time students. Financial award application deadline: 5/1; financial award applicants required to submit FAFSA. *Faculty research:* Regulation, housing economy, environmental issues on supply chain management, marketing strategy, cost management. *Unit head:* Dr. Don Hausch, Associate Dean, 608-263-1169, Fax: 608-262-3607, E-mail: emba@bus.wisc.edu. *Application contact:* Linda Uitvlugt, Director of Admissions, 608-263-1169, Fax: 608-262-3607, E-mail: emba@bus.wisc.edu.
Website: http://www.bus.wisc.edu/evemba/.

University of Wisconsin–Madison, Graduate School, Wisconsin School of Business, Wisconsin Executive MBA Program, Madison, WI 53706-1380. Offers general management (MBA). Part-time and evening/weekend programs available. *Faculty:* 15 full-time (1 woman), 7 part-time/adjunct (2 women). *Students:* 67 part-time (19 women); includes 11 minority (2 Black or African American, non-Hispanic/Latino; 7 Asian, non-Hispanic/Latino; 1 Hispanic/Latino; 1 Two or more races, non-Hispanic/Latino), 3 international. Average age 42. 47 applicants, 89% accepted, 34 enrolled. In 2013, 37 master's awarded. *Entrance requirements:* For master's, 8 years of professional work experience, 5 years of leadership experience, minimum GPA of 3.0. Additional exam requirements/recommendations for international students: Recommended—TOEFL. *Application deadline:* For fall admission, 5/1 priority date for domestic and international students. Applications are processed on a rolling basis. Application fee: $56. Electronic applications accepted. *Expenses:* Tuition, state resident: full-time $10,728; part-time $790 per credit. Tuition, nonresident: full-time $24,054; part-time $1623 per credit. *Required fees:* $1130; $119 per credit. *Financial support:* Scholarships/grants available. Support available to part-time students. Financial award application deadline: 5/1; financial award applicants required to submit FAFSA. *Faculty research:* Marketing strategy, housing markets, corporate governance, healthcare fiscal management, management in cross-cultural boundaries. *Unit head:* Dr. Don Hausch, Associate Dean, 608-263-1169, Fax: 608-262-3607, E-mail: emba@bus.wisc.edu. *Application contact:* Linda Uitvlugt, Director of Admissions, 608-263-1169, Fax: 608-262-3607, E-mail: emba@bus.wisc.edu.
Website: http://www.bus.wisc.edu/execmba/.

University of Wisconsin–Madison, Graduate School, Wisconsin School of Business, Wisconsin Full-Time MBA Program, Madison, WI 53706. Offers applied security analysis (MBA); arts administration (MBA); brand and product management (MBA); corporate finance and investment banking (MBA); marketing research (MBA); operations and technology management (MBA); real estate (MBA); risk management and insurance (MBA); strategic human resource management (MBA); supply chain management (MBA). *Faculty:* 34 full-time (5 women), 30 part-time/adjunct (15 women). *Students:* 193 full-time (61 women); includes 37 minority (10 Black or African American, non-Hispanic/Latino; 14 Asian, non-Hispanic/Latino; 12 Hispanic/Latino; 1 Native Hawaiian or other Pacific Islander, non-Hispanic/Latino), 37 international. Average age 28. 460 applicants, 33% accepted, 101 enrolled. In 2013, 110 master's awarded. *Degree requirements:* For master's, thesis (for arts administration specialization). *Entrance requirements:* For master's, GMAT or GRE, bachelor's or equivalent degree, 2 years of work experience, letters of recommendation, resume. Additional exam requirements/recommendations for international students: Required—TOEFL (minimum score 600 paper-based; 100 iBT), IELTS. *Application deadline:* For fall admission, 11/5 for domestic and international students; for winter admission, 2/4 for domestic and international students; for spring admission, 4/28 for domestic students, 4/2 for international students. Applications are processed on a rolling basis. Application fee: $56. Electronic applications accepted. *Expenses:* Contact institution. *Financial support:* In 2013–14, 176 students received support, including 12 fellowships with full tuition reimbursements available (averaging $37,956 per year), 42 research assistantships with full tuition reimbursements available (averaging $28,175 per year), 43 teaching assistantships with full tuition reimbursements available (averaging $28,175 per year); scholarships/grants, health care benefits, and unspecified assistantships also available. Financial award application deadline: 4/26; financial award applicants required to submit FAFSA. *Faculty research:* Market consequences of International Financial Reporting Standards (IFRS), inter-firm relationships and strategic partnerships, application of Bayesian statistical methods and applied probability models to understanding individuals' behaviors in the context of customer relationship management (CRM) applications, liquidity provision and the structure of financial markets, strategic management of global startups. *Unit head:* Prof. Larry W. Hunter, Associate Dean of Master's Programs, 608-265-3494, Fax: 608-265-4192, E-mail: lhunter@bus.wisc.edu. *Application contact:* William H. Wait, Assistant Director of MBA Marketing and Recruiting, 608-262-4000, Fax: 608-265-4192, E-mail: wwait@bus.wisc.edu.
Website: http://www.bus.wisc.edu/mba.

University of Wisconsin–Milwaukee, Graduate School, Sheldon B. Lubar School of Business, Milwaukee, WI 53201. Offers business administration (MBA); enterprise

resource planning (Certificate); investment management (Certificate); management science (MS, PhD); nonprofit management and leadership (MS, Certificate); state and local taxation (Certificate); MS/MBA. *Accreditation:* AACSB. Part-time and evening/weekend programs available. *Faculty:* 50 full-time (11 women), 4 part-time/adjunct (2 women). *Students:* 282 full-time (123 women), 322 part-time (126 women); includes 87 minority (30 Black or African American, non-Hispanic/Latino; 2 American Indian or Alaska Native, non-Hispanic/Latino; 28 Asian, non-Hispanic/Latino; 3 Hispanic/Latino; 24 Two or more races, non-Hispanic/Latino), 93 international. Average age 32. 517 applicants, 54% accepted, 154 enrolled. In 2013, 245 master's, 10 doctorates awarded. *Degree requirements:* For master's, comprehensive exam (for some programs); for doctorate, comprehensive exam, thesis/dissertation. *Entrance requirements:* For master's and doctorate, GMAT or GRE General Test. Additional exam requirements/recommendations for international students: Required—TOEFL (minimum score 550 paper-based; 79 iBT), IELTS (minimum score 6.5). *Application deadline:* For fall admission, 1/1 priority date for domestic students; for spring admission, 9/1 for domestic students. Applications are processed on a rolling basis. Application fee: $56 ($96 for international students). Electronic applications accepted. *Expenses:* Contact institution. *Financial support:* In 2013–14, 5 fellowships with full tuition reimbursements, 2 research assistantships with full tuition reimbursements, 41 teaching assistantships with full tuition reimbursements were awarded; career-related internships or fieldwork, Federal Work-Study, health care benefits, unspecified assistantships, and project assistantships also available. Support available to part-time students. Financial award application deadline: 4/15; financial award applicants required to submit FAFSA. *Faculty research:* Applied management research in finance, management information systems, marketing, operations research, organizational sciences. *Total annual research expenditures:* $616,761. *Unit head:* Timothy L. Smunt, Dean, 414-229-6256, Fax: 414-229-2372, E-mail: tsmunt@uwm.edu. *Application contact:* Matthew Jensen, Administrative Program Manager III, 414-229-5403, E-mail: mba-ms@uwm.edu.
Website: http://www4.uwm.edu/business.

University of Wisconsin–Oshkosh, Graduate Studies, College of Business, Program in Business Administration, Oshkosh, WI 54901. Offers MBA. *Accreditation:* AACSB. Part-time programs available. *Degree requirements:* For master's, integrative seminar. *Entrance requirements:* For master's, GMAT, GRE, minimum undergraduate GPA of 2.75. Additional exam requirements/recommendations for international students: Required—TOEFL (minimum score 550 paper-based; 79 iBT). Electronic applications accepted.

University of Wisconsin–Parkside, School of Business and Technology, Kenosha, WI 53141-2000. Offers MBA, MSCIS. *Accreditation:* AACSB. Part-time and evening/weekend programs available. *Entrance requirements:* For master's, GMAT. Additional exam requirements/recommendations for international students: Required—TOEFL (minimum score 550 paper-based; 79 iBT). Electronic applications accepted. *Expenses:* Contact institution. *Faculty research:* Business strategy, ethics in accounting and finance, mutual funds, decision analysis and neural networks, management skills.

University of Wisconsin–River Falls, Outreach and Graduate Studies, College of Business and Economics, River Falls, WI 54022. Offers MBA, MM. *Accreditation:* AACSB. *Degree requirements:* For master's, thesis or alternative. *Entrance requirements:* Additional exam requirements/recommendations for international students: Required—TOEFL (minimum score 550 paper-based; 79 iBT). Electronic applications accepted.

University of Wisconsin–Stevens Point, College of Letters and Science, Division of Business and Economics, Stevens Point, WI 54481-3897. Offers MBA. Program offered jointly with University of Wisconsin–Oshkosh.

University of Wisconsin–Whitewater, School of Graduate Studies, College of Business and Economics, Program in Business Administration, Whitewater, WI 53190-1790. Offers finance (MBA); human resource management (MBA); information technology management (MBA); international business (MBA); management (MBA); marketing (MBA); operations and supply chain management (MBA). *Accreditation:* AACSB. Part-time and evening/weekend programs available. Postbaccalaureate distance learning degree programs offered (no on-campus study). *Entrance requirements:* For master's, GMAT or GRE, minimum AACSB index of 1000, minimum GPA of 2.75. Additional exam requirements/recommendations for international students: Required—TOEFL (minimum score 550 paper-based; 80 iBT), IELTS (minimum score 6). Electronic applications accepted. *Faculty research:* Interface between social institutions and individual behavior, technology and innovation management, occupational mental health, workplace deviance and workplace romance.

University of Wyoming, College of Business, Program in Business Administration, Laramie, WY 82071. Offers MBA. *Accreditation:* AACSB. Part-time and evening/weekend programs available. Postbaccalaureate distance learning degree programs offered (minimal on-campus study). *Degree requirements:* For master's, comprehensive exam, thesis or alternative. *Entrance requirements:* For master's, GMAT, GRE General Test, minimum GPA of 3.0. Additional exam requirements/recommendations for international students: Required—TOEFL (minimum score 550 paper-based; 80 iBT). Electronic applications accepted. *Faculty research:* Natural resource marketing and product development, work place violence.

Upper Iowa University, Online Master's Programs, Fayette, IA 52142-1857. Offers accounting (MBA); corporate financial management (MBA); global business (MBA); health and human services (MPA); higher education administration (MHEA); homeland security (MPA); human resources management (MBA); justice administration (MPA); organizational development (MBA); public personnel management (MPA); quality management (MBA). MBA also available at Madison, WI campus. Part-time programs available. Postbaccalaureate distance learning degree programs offered (no on-campus study). *Degree requirements:* For master's, research project. *Entrance requirements:* For master's, GMAT, GRE, or minimum GPA of 2.7 during last 60 hours. Additional exam requirements/recommendations for international students: Required—TOEFL (minimum score 570 paper-based). Electronic applications accepted. *Faculty research:* Total quality management, CQI, teams, organization culture and climate, management.

Urbana University, Division of Business Administration, Urbana, OH 43078-2091. Offers MBA. Part-time and evening/weekend programs available. *Degree requirements:* For master's, comprehensive exam, thesis or alternative. *Entrance requirements:* For master's, GMAT, minimum GPA of 2.7, BS in business, 3 letters of recommendation, work experience. Additional exam requirements/recommendations for international students: Required—TOEFL (minimum score 550 paper-based). *Faculty research:* Organizational behavior, taxation, segmentation, information systems, retail gravitation.

Ursuline College, School of Graduate Studies, Program in Business Administration, Pepper Pike, OH 44124-4398. Offers MBA. Part-time programs available. Postbaccalaureate distance learning degree programs offered (minimal on-campus study). *Faculty:* 5 full-time (3 women), 10 part-time/adjunct (2 women). *Students:* 22 full-time (19 women), 52 part-time (35 women); includes 24 minority (22 Black or African American, non-Hispanic/Latino; 1 Hispanic/Latino; 1 Two or more races, non-Hispanic/Latino), 1 international. Average age 38. 42 applicants, 71% accepted, 20 enrolled. In 2013, 57 master's awarded. *Expenses: Tuition:* Full-time $16,920; part-time $940 per credit. *Required fees:* $270. *Financial support:* In 2013–14, 17 students received support. *Unit head:* Dr. Debra Fleming, Executive Director, 440-684-6041, Fax: 440-684-6088, E-mail: dfleming@ursuline.edu. *Application contact:* Stehanie Pratt, Graduate Admission Coordinator, 440-646-8119, Fax: 440-684-6138, E-mail: graduateadmissions@ursuline.edu.

Utah State University, School of Graduate Studies, College of Business, Program in Business Administration, Logan, UT 84322. Offers MBA. *Accreditation:* AACSB. Part-time and evening/weekend programs available. Postbaccalaureate distance learning degree programs offered (minimal on-campus study). *Degree requirements:* For master's, comprehensive exam. *Entrance requirements:* For master's, GMAT or GRE, minimum GPA of 3.0. Additional exam requirements/recommendations for international students: Required—TOEFL. Electronic applications accepted. *Faculty research:* Marketing strategy, technology and innovation, public utility finance, international competitiveness.

Utah Valley University, MBA Program, Orem, UT 84058-5999. Offers accounting (MBA); management (MBA). *Accreditation:* AACSB. Part-time and evening/weekend programs available. *Students:* 79 part-time (16 women). *Entrance requirements:* For master's, GMAT, official transcripts, current resume, three letters of recommendation. Additional exam requirements/recommendations for international students: Required—TOEFL (minimum score 79 iBT). *Application deadline:* For fall admission, 2/1 priority date for domestic students. Applications are processed on a rolling basis. Application fee: $45. Electronic applications accepted. *Expenses:* Tuition, state resident: full-time $8520; part-time $355 per credit. Tuition, nonresident: full-time $21,232; part-time $885 per credit. *Required fees:* $700; $350 per semester. Tuition and fees vary according to program. *Unit head:* Trisha Alexander, Director, 801-863-5504, E-mail: trishan@uvu.edu.
Website: http://www.uvu.edu/mba/.

Valdosta State University, Program in Business Administration, Valdosta, GA 31698. Offers business administration (MBA); healthcare administration (MBA). Program is also a member of the Georgia WebMBA®. *Accreditation:* AACSB. Part-time and evening/weekend programs available. Postbaccalaureate distance learning degree programs offered (no on-campus study). *Faculty:* 8 full-time (1 woman). *Students:* 13 full-time (3 women), 59 part-time (34 women); includes 22 minority (19 Black or African American, non-Hispanic/Latino; 1 Hispanic/Latino; 2 Two or more races, non-Hispanic/Latino), 5 international. Average age 25. 38 applicants, 82% accepted, 29 enrolled. In 2013, 39 master's awarded. *Degree requirements:* For master's, comprehensive written and/or oral exams. *Entrance requirements:* For master's, GMAT or GRE, minimum GPA of 2.75. Additional exam requirements/recommendations for international students: Required—TOEFL (minimum score 523 paper-based). *Application deadline:* For fall admission, 7/1 for domestic and international students; for spring admission, 11/1 for domestic students. Applications are processed on a rolling basis. Application fee: $35. Electronic applications accepted. *Expenses:* Tuition, state resident: full-time $4140; part-time $230 per credit hour. Tuition, nonresident: full-time $14,904; part-time $828 per credit hour. *Required fees:* $995 per semester. Tuition and fees vary according to course load. *Financial support:* In 2013–14, 5 students received support, including 5 research assistantships with full tuition reimbursements available (averaging $3,652 per year); institutionally sponsored loans and scholarships/grants also available. Support available to part-time students. Financial award application deadline: 7/1; financial award applicants required to submit FAFSA. *Unit head:* Dr. Mel Schnake, Director, 229-245-2233, Fax: 229-245-2795, E-mail: mschnake@valdosta.edu. *Application contact:* Jessica Powers, Coordinator of Graduate Admissions, 229-333-5694, Fax: 229-245-3853, E-mail: jldevane@valdosta.edu.
Website: http://www.valdosta.edu/academics/graduate-school/our-programs/business-administration.php.

Valparaiso University, Graduate School, College of Business, Valparaiso, IN 46383. Offers business administration (MBA); business intelligence (Certificate); engineering management (Certificate); entrepreneurship (Certificate); finance (Certificate); general business (Certificate); management (Certificate); marketing (Certificate); sustainability (Certificate); JD/MBA; MSN/MBA. *Accreditation:* AACSB. Part-time and evening/weekend programs available. Postbaccalaureate distance learning degree programs offered (minimal on-campus study). *Faculty:* 11 part-time/adjunct (2 women). *Students:* 13 full-time (3 women), 48 part-time (21 women); includes 6 minority (3 Black or African American, non-Hispanic/Latino; 2 Hispanic/Latino; 1 Two or more races, non-Hispanic/Latino), 5 international. Average age 33. In 2013, 19 master's, 3 other advanced degrees awarded. *Entrance requirements:* For master's, GMAT, GRE, minimum GPA of 3.0. Additional exam requirements/recommendations for international students: Required—TOEFL (minimum score 550 paper-based; 80 iBT), IELTS (minimum score 6). *Application deadline:* Applications are processed on a rolling basis. Application fee: $30 ($50 for international students). Electronic applications accepted. *Expenses:* Contact institution. *Financial support:* Available to part-time students. Applicants required to submit FAFSA. *Unit head:* Bruce MacLean, Director of Graduate Programs in Management, 219-465-7952, Fax: 219-464-5789, E-mail: bruce.maclean@valpo.edu. *Application contact:* Cindy Scanlan, Assistant Director of Graduate Programs in Management, 219-465-7952, Fax: 219-464-5789, E-mail: cindy.scanlan@valpo.edu.
Website: http://www.valpo.edu/mba/.

Vancouver Island University, Master of Business Administration Program, Nanaimo, BC V9R 5S5, Canada. Offers international business (MBA), including finance, marketing. Program offered jointly with University of Hertfordshire. *Accreditation:* ACBSP. Part-time programs available. *Degree requirements:* For master's, thesis. *Entrance requirements:* Additional exam requirements/recommendations for international students: Required—TOEFL (minimum score 550 paper-based). Electronic applications accepted. *Faculty research:* Tourism development, entrepreneurship, organizational development, strategic planning, international business strategy, intercultural team work.

Vanderbilt University, Vanderbilt Graduate School of Management, Vanderbilt Executive MBA and Americas MBA for Executives Programs, Nashville, TN 37203. Offers EMBA, MBA. *Accreditation:* AACSB. Evening/weekend programs available. *Students:* 111 full-time (24 women); includes 16 minority (2 Black or African American, non-Hispanic/Latino; 1 American Indian or Alaska Native, non-Hispanic/Latino; 5 Asian, non-Hispanic/Latino; 3 Hispanic/Latino; 5 Two or more races, non-Hispanic/Latino), 7 international. Average age 36. 97 applicants, 68% accepted, 53 enrolled. In 2013, 55 master's awarded. *Entrance requirements:* For master's, GMAT, minimum of 5 years of professional work experience. *Application deadline:* For fall admission, 6/1 for domestic and international students; for winter admission, 1/31 for domestic students; for spring admission, 3/31 priority date for domestic students; for summer admission, 5/31 for domestic students. Applications are processed on a rolling basis. Application fee: $150. Electronic applications accepted. *Expenses:* Contact institution. *Financial support:* In 2013–14, 14 students received support. Scholarships/grants available. Financial award application deadline: 5/31; financial award applicants required to submit FAFSA. *Unit head:* Juli Bennett, Executive Director, 615-322-3120, Fax: 615-343-2293, E-mail: juli.bennett@owen.vanderbilt.edu. *Application contact:* Sarah Fairbank, Director, 615-322-0745, Fax: 615-343-2293, E-mail: sarah.fairbank@owen.vanderbilt.edu.
Website: http://www.owen.vanderbilt.edu.

Vanderbilt University, Vanderbilt Graduate School of Management, Vanderbilt MBA Program (Full-time), Nashville, TN 37203. Offers accounting (MBA); finance (MBA); general management (MBA); human and organizational performance (MBA); marketing (MBA); operations (MBA); strategy (MBA); MBA/JD; MBA/M Div; MBA/MD; MBA/MTS; MBA/PhD. *Accreditation:* AACSB. *Students:* 341 full-time (119 women); includes 42 minority (20 Black or African American, non-Hispanic/Latino; 12 Asian, non-Hispanic/Latino; 5 Hispanic/Latino; 5 Two or more races, non-Hispanic/Latino), 73 international. Average age 28. 1,059 applicants, 38% accepted, 166 enrolled. In 2013, 161 master's awarded. *Entrance requirements:* For master's, GMAT (preferred) or GRE, 2 years of work experience (recommended). Additional exam requirements/recommendations for international students: Required—TOEFL. *Application deadline:* For fall admission, 10/1 priority date for domestic and international students; for winter admission, 1/6 priority date for domestic and international students; for spring admission, 3/3 priority date for domestic students, 3/5 priority date for international students; for summer admission, 4/5 for domestic students, 5/5 for international students. Applications are processed on a rolling basis. Application fee: $75 ($175 for international students). Electronic applications accepted. *Financial support:* In 2013–14, 237 students received support. Scholarships/grants and tuition waivers (full and partial) available. Financial award application deadline: 5/15; financial award applicants required to submit FAFSA. *Unit head:* Nancy Lea Hyer, Associate Dean, 615-322-2530, Fax: 615-343-7110, E-mail: nancy.lea.hyer@owen.vanderbilt.edu. *Application contact:* Dinah Webster, Administrative Assistant, 615-322-6469, Fax: 615-343-1175, E-mail: mba@owen.vanderbilt.edu.
Website: http://www.owen.vanderbilt.edu.

Villanova University, Villanova School of Business, Executive MBA Program, Radnor, PA 19087. Offers EMBA. *Accreditation:* AACSB. Evening/weekend programs available. *Faculty:* 101 full-time (33 women), 36 part-time/adjunct (3 women). *Students:* 57 part-time (13 women); includes 12 minority (4 Black or African American, non-Hispanic/Latino; 6 Asian, non-Hispanic/Latino; 1 Hispanic/Latino; 1 Two or more races, non-Hispanic/Latino). Average age 37. In 2013, 30 master's awarded. *Degree requirements:* For master's, minimum cumulative GPA of 3.0. *Entrance requirements:* For master's, significant managerial or executive work experience, employer approval. Additional exam requirements/recommendations for international students: Required—TOEFL (minimum score 550 paper-based; 90 iBT). *Application deadline:* For fall admission, 6/30 for domestic and international students. Applications are processed on a rolling basis. Application fee: $50. Electronic applications accepted. *Expenses:* Contact institution. *Financial support:* Scholarships/grants available. Financial award application deadline: 6/30; financial award applicants required to submit FAFSA. *Faculty research:* Business analytics; creativity, innovation and entrepreneurship; global leadership; real estate; church management; business ethics. *Unit head:* Eileen Cassidy, Director of Executive Programs, 610-523-1739, E-mail: eileen.cassidy@villanova.edu. *Application contact:* Laurie Cato, Recruiting Manager, Executive Programs, 610-523-1749, E-mail: laurie.cato@villanova.edu.
Website: http://www.emba.villanova.edu/.

Villanova University, Villanova School of Business, MBA - The Fast Track Program, Villanova, PA 19085. Offers finance (MBA); health care management (MBA); international business (MBA); management information systems (MBA); marketing (MBA); real estate (MBA); strategic management (MBA). *Accreditation:* AACSB. Part-time and evening/weekend programs available. *Faculty:* 101 full-time (33 women), 36 part-time/adjunct (3 women). *Students:* 140 part-time (44 women); includes 22 minority (1 Black or African American, non-Hispanic/Latino; 17 Asian, non-Hispanic/Latino; 3 Hispanic/Latino; 1 Two or more races, non-Hispanic/Latino), 3 international. Average age 29. 127 applicants, 72% accepted, 75 enrolled. In 2013, 61 master's awarded. *Degree requirements:* For master's, minimum GPA of 3.0. *Entrance requirements:* For master's, GMAT or GRE, work experience. Additional exam requirements/recommendations for international students: Required—TOEFL (minimum score 550 paper-based; 90 iBT). *Application deadline:* For fall admission, 6/30 for domestic and international students. Application fee: $50. Electronic applications accepted. *Financial support:* Scholarships/grants available. Financial award application deadline: 6/30; financial award applicants required to submit FAFSA. *Faculty research:* Business analytics; creativity, innovation and entrepreneurship; global leadership; real estate; church management; business ethics. *Unit head:* Zelon Crawford, Director of Graduate Business Programs, 610-519-6283, Fax: 610-519-6273, E-mail: zelon.crawford@villanova.edu. *Application contact:* Meredith L. Lockyer, Manager of Recruiting, 610-519-7016, Fax: 610-519-6273, E-mail: meredith.lockyer@villanova.edu.
Website: http://www1.villanova.edu/villanova/business/graduate/mba/fasttrack.html.

Villanova University, Villanova School of Business, MBA - The Flex Track Program, Villanova, PA 19085. Offers finance (MBA); health care management (MBA); international business (MBA); management information systems (MBA); marketing (MBA); real estate (MBA); strategic management (MBA); JD/MBA. *Accreditation:* AACSB. Part-time and evening/weekend programs available. Postbaccalaureate distance learning degree programs offered (minimal on-campus study). *Faculty:* 101 full-time (33 women), 36 part-time/adjunct (3 women). *Students:* 13 full-time (5 women), 413 part-time (127 women); includes 63 minority (13 Black or African American, non-Hispanic/Latino; 1 American Indian or Alaska Native, non-Hispanic/Latino; 29 Asian, non-Hispanic/Latino; 14 Hispanic/Latino; 1 Native Hawaiian or other Pacific Islander, non-Hispanic/Latino; 5 Two or more races, non-Hispanic/Latino), 9 international. Average age 29. 84 applicants, 83% accepted, 66 enrolled. In 2013, 133 master's awarded. *Degree requirements:* For master's, minimum GPA of 3.0. *Entrance requirements:* For master's, GMAT or GRE, work experience. Additional exam requirements/recommendations for international students: Required—TOEFL (minimum score 550 paper-based; 90 iBT). *Application deadline:* For fall admission, 6/30 for domestic and international students; for winter admission, 11/15 for domestic and international students; for spring admission, 11/15 for domestic and international students; for summer admission, 3/31 for domestic and international students. Applications are processed on a rolling basis. Application fee: $50. Electronic applications accepted. *Financial support:* In 2013–14, 13 research assistantships with full tuition reimbursements (averaging $13,100 per year) were awarded; scholarships/grants and unspecified assistantships also available. Financial award application deadline: 6/30; financial award applicants required to submit FAFSA. *Faculty research:* Business analytics; creativity, innovation and entrepreneurship; global leadership; real estate; church management; business ethics. *Unit head:* Zelon Crawford, Director of Graduate Business Programs, 610-610-6283, Fax: 610-519-6273, E-mail: zelon.crawford@villanova.edu. *Application contact:* Meredith L. Lockyer, Manager of Recruiting, 610-519-7016, Fax: 610-519-6273, E-mail: meredith.lockyer@villanova.edu.
Website: http://www1.villanova.edu/villanova/business/graduate/mba/flextrack.html.

Virginia College in Birmingham, Program in Business Administration, Birmingham, AL 35209. Offers healthcare (MBA); management (MBA). Part-time and evening/weekend programs available. Postbaccalaureate distance learning degree programs offered (no on-campus study). *Entrance requirements:* For master's, bachelor's degree in related academic area.

Virginia College in Birmingham, Virginia College Online, Birmingham, AL 35209. Offers business administration (MBA); criminal justice (MCJ); cybersecurity (MC). Part-time and evening/weekend programs available. Postbaccalaureate distance learning degree programs offered (no on-campus study).

Virginia Commonwealth University, Graduate School, School of Business, Program in Business Administration, Richmond, VA 23284-9005. Offers MBA, Postbaccalaureate Certificate. *Entrance requirements:* For master's, GMAT. Additional exam requirements/recommendations for international students: Required—TOEFL (minimum score 600 paper-based; 100 iBT). Electronic applications accepted.

Virginia Commonwealth University, Graduate School, School of Business, Program in Management, Richmond, VA 23284-9005. Offers Certificate.

Virginia International University, School of Business, Fairfax, VA 22030. Offers accounting (MBA); executive management (Graduate Certificate); global logistics (MBA); health care management (MBA); human resources management (MBA); international business management (MBA); international finance (MBA); marketing management (MBA). Part-time programs available. *Entrance requirements:* For master's and Graduate Certificate, bachelor's degree. Additional exam requirements/recommendations for international students: Required—TOEFL (minimum score 550 paper-based; 80 iBT), IELTS (minimum score 6). Electronic applications accepted.

Virginia Polytechnic Institute and State University, Graduate School, Pamplin College of Business, Blacksburg, VA 24061. Offers accounting and information systems (MACIS); business (PhD); business administration (MBA, MS); hospitality and tourism management (MS, PhD). *Faculty:* 118 full-time (35 women), 1 part-time/adjunct (0 women). *Students:* 333 full-time (149 women), 129 part-time (47 women); includes 75 minority (14 Black or African American, non-Hispanic/Latino; 42 Asian, non-Hispanic/Latino; 12 Hispanic/Latino; 7 Two or more races, non-Hispanic/Latino), 115 international. Average age 30. 520 applicants, 38% accepted, 157 enrolled. In 2013, 199 master's, 12 doctorates awarded. *Degree requirements:* For master's, comprehensive exam (for some programs), thesis (for some programs); for doctorate, comprehensive exam (for some programs), thesis/dissertation (for some programs). *Entrance requirements:* For master's and doctorate, GRE/GMAT (may vary by department). Additional exam requirements/recommendations for international students: Required—TOEFL (minimum score 550 paper-based). *Application deadline:* For fall admission, 8/1 for domestic students, 4/1 for international students; for spring admission, 1/1 for domestic students, 9/1 for international students. Applications are processed on a rolling basis. Application fee: $75. Electronic applications accepted. *Expenses:* Tuition, state resident: full-time $11,185; part-time $621.50 per credit hour. Tuition, nonresident: full-time $22,146; part-time $1230.25 per credit hour. *Required fees:* $2442; $449.25 per semester. Tuition and fees vary according to course load, campus/location and program. *Financial support:* In 2013–14, 5 fellowships with full tuition reimbursements (averaging $19,435 per year), 61 teaching assistantships with full tuition reimbursements (averaging $15,805 per year) were awarded. Financial award application deadline: 3/1; financial award applicants required to submit FAFSA. *Total annual research expenditures:* $2.5 million. *Unit head:* Dr. Robert T. Sumichrast, Dean, 540-231-6601, Fax: 540-231-4487, E-mail: busdean@vt.edu. *Application contact:* Martha Hilton, Executive Assistant to the Dean, 540-231-9647, Fax: 540-231-4487, E-mail: cartermc@vt.edu.
Website: http://www.pamplin.vt.edu/.

Viterbo University, Master of Business Administration Program, La Crosse, WI 54601-4797. Offers general business administration (MBA); health care management (MBA); international business (MBA); leadership (MBA); project management (MBA). *Accreditation:* ACBSP. Part-time and evening/weekend programs available. *Faculty:* 3 full-time (2 women), 4 part-time/adjunct (2 women). *Students:* 86 full-time (47 women), 11 part-time (8 women); includes 5 minority (1 Black or African American, non-Hispanic/Latino; 3 Asian, non-Hispanic/Latino; 1 Hispanic/Latino), 11 international. Average age 34. In 2013, 59 master's awarded. *Degree requirements:* For master's, 34 credits. *Entrance requirements:* For master's, BS, transcripts, minimum undergraduate cumulative GPA of 3.0, 2 letters of reference, 3-5 page essay. Additional exam requirements/recommendations for international students: Recommended—TOEFL (minimum score 550 paper-based). Application fee: $50. Electronic applications accepted. *Expenses: Tuition:* Full-time $7140; part-time $444 per credit hour. *Required fees:* $100. *Unit head:* Dr. Barbara Gayle, Dean of Graduate Studies, 608-796-3080, E-mail: bmgayle@viterbo.edu. *Application contact:* Tiffany Morey, MBA Coordinator, 608-796-3379, E-mail: tlmorey@viterbo.edu.

Wagner College, Division of Graduate Studies, Department of Business Administration, Staten Island, NY 10301-4495. Offers accelerated business administration (MBA); accounting (MS); finance (MBA); health care administration (MBA); international business (MBA); management (Exec MBA, MBA); marketing (MBA). *Accreditation:* ACBSP. Part-time and evening/weekend programs available. *Faculty:* 8 full-time (3 women), 17 part-time/adjunct (5 women). *Students:* 84 full-time (38 women), 32 part-time (14 women); includes 23 minority (12 Black or African American, non-Hispanic/Latino; 1 American Indian or Alaska Native, non-Hispanic/Latino; 2 Asian, non-Hispanic/Latino; 7 Hispanic/Latino; 1 Native Hawaiian or other Pacific Islander, non-Hispanic/Latino), 3 international. Average age 26. 62 applicants, 97% accepted, 45 enrolled. In 2013, 68 master's awarded. *Degree requirements:* For master's, thesis optional. *Entrance requirements:* For master's, GMAT, minimum GPA of 2.75, proficiency in computers and math. Additional exam requirements/recommendations for international students: Required—TOEFL (minimum score 550 paper-based; 79 iBT). *Application deadline:* For fall admission, 5/1 priority date for domestic students, 3/1 priority date for international students; for spring admission, 12/1 for domestic students, 11/1 for international students. Applications are processed on a rolling basis. Application fee: $50. *Expenses: Tuition:* Full-time $17,496; part-time $972 per credit. Tuition and fees vary according to course load. *Financial support:* In 2013–14, 89 students received support. Career-related internships or fieldwork, unspecified assistantships, and alumni fellowship grants available. Financial award application deadline: 4/1; financial award applicants required to submit FAFSA. *Unit head:* Dr. Donald Crooks, Director, 718-390-3429, Fax: 718-390-3429, E-mail: dcrooks@wagner.edu. *Application contact:* Patricia Clancy, Administrative Assistant, 718-420-4464, Fax: 718-390-3105, E-mail: patricia.clancy@wagner.edu.
Website: http://www.wagner.edu/departments/mba/main.

Wake Forest University, School of Business, Charlotte Evening MBA Program, Charlotte, NC 28211. Offers MBA. *Accreditation:* AACSB. Evening/weekend programs available. *Faculty:* 77 full-time (21 women), 32 part-time/adjunct (8 women). *Students:* 114 full-time (30 women); includes 17 minority (11 Black or African American, non-Hispanic/Latino; 3 Asian, non-Hispanic/Latino; 3 Hispanic/Latino), 4 international. Average age 32. In 2013, 45 master's awarded. *Degree requirements:* For master's, 54 total credit hours. *Entrance requirements:* For master's, GMAT or GRE, letters of recommendation, official transcripts, current resume or curriculum vitae, three years of work experience. Additional exam requirements/recommendations for international students: Required—TOEFL (minimum score 600 paper-based; 100 iBT), PTE. *Application deadline:* For fall admission, 6/1 for domestic and international students. Applications are processed on a rolling basis. Application fee: $100. Electronic applications accepted. *Expenses:* Contact institution. *Financial support:* In 2013–14, 48 students received support. Scholarships/grants available. Financial award application deadline: 4/1; financial award applicants required to submit FAFSA. *Faculty research:*

Business Administration and Management—General

The influence of personal relationships on business decision-making and management of change; drivers of perceived value and consumer behavior; impact of accounting on auditing, financial, managerial, systems and taxation stakeholders; corporate governance and executive compensation; impact of operations strategies on competitiveness. *Unit head:* Matthew Phillips, Associate Dean of Working Professional Programs, 704-365-1717, Fax: 704-365-3511, E-mail: cltbusadmissions@wfu.edu. *Application contact:* Judi Affeldt, Administrative Assistant, 704-365-1717, Fax: 704-365-3511, E-mail: cltbusadmissions@wfu.edu.
Website: http://business.wfu.edu/charlotte-evening-mba/.

Wake Forest University, School of Business, Evening MBA Program–Winston-Salem, Winston-Salem, NC 27106. Offers MBA, PhD/MBA. *Accreditation:* AACSB. Evening/weekend programs available. *Faculty:* 77 full-time (21 women), 32 part-time/adjunct (8 women). *Students:* 89 full-time (32 women); includes 20 minority (11 Black or African American, non-Hispanic/Latino; 3 Asian, non-Hispanic/Latino; 3 Hispanic/Latino; 3 Two or more races, non-Hispanic/Latino), 3 international. Average age 32. In 2013, 40 master's awarded. *Degree requirements:* For master's, 54 total credit hours. *Entrance requirements:* For master's, GMAT or GRE, letters of recommendation, official transcripts, current resume or curriculum vitae, three years of work experience. Additional exam requirements/recommendations for international students: Required—TOEFL (minimum score 600 paper-based; 100 iBT), PTE. *Application deadline:* For fall admission, 7/15 for domestic and international students. Applications are processed on a rolling basis. Application fee: $100. Electronic applications accepted. *Expenses:* Contact institution. *Financial support:* In 2013–14, 48 students received support. Scholarships/grants available. Financial award applicants required to submit FAFSA. *Faculty research:* The influence of personal relationships on business decision-making and management of change; drivers of perceived value and consumer behavior; impact of accounting on auditing, financial, managerial, systems and taxation stakeholders; corporate governance and executive compensation; impact of operations strategies on competitiveness. *Unit head:* Matthew Phillips, Associate Dean of Working Professional Programs, 336-758-5422, Fax: 336-758-5830, E-mail: busadmissions@wfu.edu. *Application contact:* Tamara Paquee, Administrative Assistant, 336-758-5422, Fax: 336-758-5830, E-mail: busadmissions@wfu.edu.
Website: http://www.business.wfu.edu/.

Wake Forest University, School of Business, Full-time MBA Program, Winston-Salem, NC 27106. Offers finance (MBA); marketing (MBA); operations management (MBA); JD/MBA; MD/MBA; MSA/MBA. *Accreditation:* AACSB. *Faculty:* 77 full-time (21 women), 32 part-time/adjunct (8 women). *Students:* 107 full-time (33 women); includes 22 minority (11 Black or African American, non-Hispanic/Latino; 4 Asian, non-Hispanic/Latino; 3 Hispanic/Latino; 4 Two or more races, non-Hispanic/Latino), 21 international. Average age 30. In 2013, 66 master's awarded. *Degree requirements:* For master's, 65.5 credit hours. *Entrance requirements:* For master's, GMAT or GRE, letters of recommendation, official transcripts, current resume or curriculum vitae, 2 years of work experience. Additional exam requirements/recommendations for international students: Required—TOEFL (minimum score 600 paper-based; 100 iBT), PTE. *Application deadline:* For fall admission, 4/15 for domestic and international students. Applications are processed on a rolling basis. Application fee: $100. Electronic applications accepted. *Expenses:* Contact institution. *Financial support:* In 2013–14, 90 students received support. Career-related internships or fieldwork, scholarships/grants, and unspecified assistantships available. Financial award application deadline: 2/15; financial award applicants required to submit FAFSA. *Faculty research:* The influence of personal relationships on business decision-making and management of change; drivers of perceived value and consumer behavior; impact of accounting on auditing, financial, managerial, systems and taxation stakeholders; corporate governance and executive compensation; impact of operations strategies on competitiveness. *Unit head:* Scott Schaffer, Associate Dean, 336-758-5422, Fax: 336-758-5830, E-mail: busadmissions@wfu.edu. *Application contact:* Tamara Paquee, Administrative Assistant, 336-758-5422, Fax: 336-758-5830, E-mail: busadmissions@wfu.edu.
Website: http://www.business.wfu.edu/.

Wake Forest University, School of Business, MA in Management Program, Winston-Salem, NC 27106. Offers MA. *Faculty:* 77 full-time (21 women), 32 part-time/adjunct (8 women). *Students:* 138 full-time (64 women); includes 56 minority (40 Black or African American, non-Hispanic/Latino; 4 Asian, non-Hispanic/Latino; 10 Hispanic/Latino; 2 Two or more races, non-Hispanic/Latino), 5 international. Average age 24. In 2013, 102 master's awarded. *Degree requirements:* For master's, 41.5 credit hours. *Entrance requirements:* For master's, GMAT or GRE, letters of recommendation, official transcripts, current resume or curriculum vitae. Additional exam requirements/recommendations for international students: Required—TOEFL (minimum score 600 paper-based; 100 iBT), PTE. *Application deadline:* For fall admission, 6/15 for domestic and international students. Applications are processed on a rolling basis. Application fee: $100. Electronic applications accepted. *Financial support:* In 2013–14, 113 students received support. Scholarships/grants available. Financial award application deadline: 4/1; financial award applicants required to submit FAFSA. *Faculty research:* The influence of personal relationships on business decision-making and management of change; drivers of perceived value and consumer behavior; impact of accounting on auditing, financial, managerial, systems and taxation stakeholders; corporate governance and executive compensation; impact of operations strategies on competitiveness. *Unit head:* Derrick Boone, Director, MA in Management Program, 336-758-5422, Fax: 336-758-5830, E-mail: busadmissions@wfu.edu. *Application contact:* Tamara Paquee, Administrative Assistant, 336-758-5422, Fax: 336-758-5830, E-mail: busadmissions@wfu.edu.
Website: http://www.business.wfu.edu/.

Wake Forest University, School of Business, Saturday MBA Program–Charlotte, Charlotte, NC 28211. Offers MBA. *Accreditation:* AACSB. Evening/weekend programs available. *Faculty:* 77 full-time (21 women), 32 part-time/adjunct (8 women). *Students:* 84 full-time (28 women); includes 23 minority (10 Black or African American, non-Hispanic/Latino; 1 American Indian or Alaska Native, non-Hispanic/Latino; 7 Asian, non-Hispanic/Latino; 4 Hispanic/Latino; 1 Two or more races, non-Hispanic/Latino), 6 international. Average age 35. In 2013, 36 master's awarded. *Degree requirements:* For master's, 54 total credit hours. *Entrance requirements:* For master's, GMAT or GRE, letters of recommendation, official transcripts, current resume or curriculum vitae, three years of work experience. Additional exam requirements/recommendations for international students: Required—TOEFL (minimum score 600 paper-based; 100 iBT), PTE. *Application deadline:* For spring admission, 11/1 for domestic and international students. Applications are processed on a rolling basis. Application fee: $100. Electronic applications accepted. *Expenses:* Contact institution. *Financial support:* In 2013–14, 51 students received support. Scholarships/grants available. Financial award application deadline: 9/1; financial award applicants required to submit FAFSA. *Faculty research:* The influence of personal relationships on business decision-making and management of change; drivers of perceived value and consumer behavior; impact of accounting on auditing, financial, managerial, systems and taxation stakeholders; corporate governance and executive compensation; impact of operations strategies on competitiveness. *Unit head:* Matthew Phillips, Associate Dean of Working Professional Programs, 704-365-1717, Fax: 704-365-3511, E-mail: cltbusadmissions@wfu.edu.

Application contact: Judi Affeldt, Administrative Assistant, 704-365-1717, Fax: 704-365-3511, E-mail: cltbusadmissions@wfu.edu.
Website: http://www.mba.wfu.edu/.

Walden University, Graduate Programs, School of Management, Minneapolis, MN 55401. Offers accounting (MBA, MS, DBA), including accounting for the professional (MS), accounting with CPA emphasis (MS), self-designed (MS, PhD); accounting and management (MS), including accountants as strategic managers, self-designed (MS, PhD); advanced project management (Graduate Certificate); applied project management (Graduate Certificate); bridge to business administration (Post-Doctoral Certificate); bridge to management (Post-Doctoral Certificate); business administration (EMBA); business management (Graduate Certificate); communication (MS, Graduate Certificate); corporate finance (MBA); entrepreneurship (DBA); entrepreneurship and small business (MBA); finance (DBA); global supply chain management (DBA); healthcare management (MBA, DBA); human resource management (MBA, MS, Graduate Certificate), including functional human resource management (MS), general program (MS), integrating functional and strategic human resource management (MS), organizational strategy (MS); human resources management (DBA); information systems management (DBA); international business (MBA, DBA); leadership (MBA, MS, DBA), including general program (MS), human resources leadership (MS), leader development (MS), self-designed (MS, PhD); management (MS, PhD), including accounting (PhD), engineering management (PhD), finance (PhD), general program (MS), healthcare management (MS), human resource management (MS), human resources management (PhD), information systems management (PhD), leadership (MS), leadership and organizational change (PhD), marketing (MS), operations research (PhD), project management (MS), self-designed, strategy and operations (MS); marketing (MBA, DBA); project management (MBA, MS, DBA); self-designed (MBA, DBA); social impact management (DBA); technology entrepreneurship (DBA). Part-time and evening/weekend programs available. Postbaccalaureate distance learning degree programs offered (minimal on-campus study). *Faculty:* 24 full-time (9 women), 337 part-time/adjunct (127 women). *Students:* 4,369 full-time (2,379 women), 2,181 part-time (1,304 women); includes 3,669 minority (3,020 Black or African American, non-Hispanic/Latino; 22 American Indian or Alaska Native, non-Hispanic/Latino; 156 Asian, non-Hispanic/Latino; 331 Hispanic/Latino; 11 Native Hawaiian or other Pacific Islander, non-Hispanic/Latino; 129 Two or more races, non-Hispanic/Latino), 107 international. Average age 41. 2,030 applicants, 94% accepted, 1436 enrolled. In 2013, 757 master's, 128 doctorates, 32 other advanced degrees awarded. *Degree requirements:* For master's, residency (for some programs); for doctorate, thesis/dissertation (for some programs), residency. *Entrance requirements:* For master's, bachelor's degree or higher; minimum GPA of 2.5; official transcripts; goal statement (for some programs); access to computer and Internet; for doctorate, master's degree or higher; three years of related professional or academic experience (preferred); minimum GPA of 3.0; goal statement and current resume (select programs); official transcripts; access to computer and Internet; for other advanced degree, relevant work experience; access to computer and Internet. Additional exam requirements/recommendations for international students: Required—TOEFL (minimum score 550 paper-based; 79 iBT), IELTS (minimum score 6.5), Michigan English Language Assessment Battery (minimum score 82), or PTE. *Application deadline:* Applications are processed on a rolling basis. Application fee: $0. Electronic applications accepted. *Expenses: Tuition:* Full-time $11,813.55; part-time $500 per credit. *Required fees:* $618.76. *Financial support:* Fellowships, Federal Work-Study, scholarships/grants, unspecified assistantships, and family tuition reduction, active duty/veteran tuition reduction, group tuition reduction, interest-free payment plans, employee tuition reduction available. Support available to part-time students. Financial award applicants required to submit FAFSA. *Unit head:* Dr. Ward Ulmer, III, Associate Dean, 800-925-3368. *Application contact:* Jennifer Hall, Vice President of Enrollment Management, 866-4-WALDEN, E-mail: info@waldenu.edu.
Website: http://www.waldenu.edu/programs/colleges-schools/management.

Walden University, Graduate Programs, School of Public Policy and Administration, Minneapolis, MN 55401. Offers criminal justice (MPA, MPP, MS, Graduate Certificate), including emergency management (MS, PhD), general program (MS, PhD), homeland security and policy coordination (MS, PhD), law and public policy (MS, PhD), policy analysis (MS, PhD), public management and leadership (MS, PhD), self-designed (MS), terrorism, mediation, and peace (MS, PhD); criminal justice leadership and executive management (MS), including emergency management (MS, PhD), general program (MS, PhD), homeland security and policy coordination (MS, PhD), law and public policy (MS, PhD), policy analysis (MS, PhD), public management and leadership (MS, PhD), self-designed, terrorism, mediation, and peace (MS, PhD); emergency management (MPA, MPP, MS), including criminal justice (MS, PhD), general program (MS, PhD), homeland security (MS), public management and leadership (MS, PhD), terrorism and emergency management (MS); general program (MPA, MPP); government management (Graduate Certificate); health policy (MPA, MPP); homeland security (Graduate Certificate); homeland security and policy coordination (MPA, MPP); international nongovernmental organizations (MPA, MPP); law and public policy (MPA, MPP); local government management for sustainable communities (MPA, MPP); nonprofit management (Graduate Certificate); nonprofit management and leadership (MPA, MPP, MS); policy analysis (MPA); public management and leadership (MPA, MPP, Graduate Certificate); public policy (Graduate Certificate); public policy and administration (PhD), including criminal justice (MS, PhD), emergency management (MS, PhD), general program (MS, PhD), health policy, homeland security and policy coordination (MS, PhD), international nongovernmental organizations, law and public policy (MS, PhD), local government management for sustainable communities, nonprofit management and leadership, policy analysis (MS, PhD), public management and leadership (MS, PhD), terrorism, mediation, and peace (MS, PhD); strategic planning and public policy (Graduate Certificate); terrorism, mediation, and peace (MPA, MPP). Part-time and evening/weekend programs available. Postbaccalaureate distance learning degree programs offered (minimal on-campus study). *Faculty:* 10 full-time (4 women), 123 part-time/adjunct (55 women). *Students:* 1,029 full-time (640 women), 1,601 part-time (981 women); includes 1,579 minority (1,326 Black or African American, non-Hispanic/Latino; 18 American Indian or Alaska Native, non-Hispanic/Latino; 39 Asian, non-Hispanic/Latino; 127 Hispanic/Latino; 3 Native Hawaiian or other Pacific Islander, non-Hispanic/Latino; 66 Two or more races, non-Hispanic/Latino), 27 international. Average age 42. 566 applicants, 93% accepted, 412 enrolled. In 2013, 257 master's, 44 doctorates, 18 other advanced degrees awarded. *Degree requirements:* For doctorate, thesis/dissertation, residency. *Entrance requirements:* For master's, bachelor's degree or higher; minimum GPA of 2.5; official transcripts; goal statement (for some programs); access to computer and Internet; for doctorate, master's degree or higher; three years of related professional or academic experience (preferred); minimum GPA of 3.0; goal statement and current resume (select programs); official transcripts; access to computer and Internet; for Graduate Certificate, relevant work experience; access to computer and Internet. Additional exam requirements/recommendations for international students: Required—TOEFL (minimum score 550 paper-based; 79 iBT), IELTS (minimum score 6.5), Michigan English Language Assessment Battery (minimum score 82), or PTE. *Application deadline:* Applications are processed on a rolling basis. Application fee: $0. Electronic applications accepted. *Expenses: Tuition:* Full-time $11,813.55; part-time $500 per credit. *Required fees:* $618.76. *Financial support:*

Fellowships, Federal Work-Study, scholarships/grants, unspecified assistantships, and family tuition reduction, active duty/veteran tuition reduction, group tuition reduction, interest-free payment plans, employee tuition reduction available. Support available to part-time students. Financial award applicants required to submit FAFSA. *Unit head:* Dr. Mark Gordon, Associate Dean, 800-925-3368. *Application contact:* Jennifer Hall, Vice President of Enrollment Management, 866-4-WALDEN. E-mail: info@waldenu.edu. Website: http://www.waldenu.edu/programs/colleges-schools/public-policy-and-administration.

Walsh College of Accountancy and Business Administration, Graduate Programs, Program in Business Administration, Troy, MI 48007-7006. Offers MBA. *Accreditation:* ACBSP. *Entrance requirements:* For master's, GMAT, minimum GPA of 2.75, previous course work in business. Additional exam requirements/recommendations for international students: Required—TOEFL. Electronic applications accepted.

Walsh College of Accountancy and Business Administration, Graduate Programs, Program in Management, Troy, MI 48007-7006. Offers MSIB, MSSL. Part-time and evening/weekend programs available. *Entrance requirements:* For master's, minimum GPA of 2.75, previous course work in business. Additional exam requirements/recommendations for international students: Required—TOEFL. Electronic applications accepted.

Walsh University, Graduate Studies, MBA Program, North Canton, OH 44720-3396. Offers entrepreneurship (MBA); healthcare management (MBA); management (MBA); marketing (MBA). Part-time and evening/weekend programs available. Postbaccalaureate distance learning degree programs offered (no on-campus study). *Faculty:* 5 full-time (1 woman), 16 part-time/adjunct (4 women). *Students:* 29 full-time (15 women), 147 part-time (77 women); includes 6 minority (5 Black or African American, non-Hispanic/Latino; 1 American Indian or Alaska Native, non-Hispanic/Latino), 2 international. Average age 34. 69 applicants, 94% accepted, 31 enrolled. In 2013, 63 master's awarded. *Degree requirements:* For master's, capstone course in strategic management. *Entrance requirements:* For master's, GMAT (minimum score of 490), minimum GPA of 3.0. Additional exam requirements/recommendations for international students: Required—TOEFL (minimum score 500 paper-based; 61 iBT). *Application deadline:* For fall admission, 7/15 priority date for domestic students. Applications are processed on a rolling basis. Application fee: $25. Electronic applications accepted. *Expenses:* Tuition: Full-time $10,890; part-time $605 per credit hour. *Required fees:* $100; $100. *Financial support:* In 2013–14, 91 students received support, including 4 research assistantships with partial tuition reimbursements available (averaging $8,088 per year), 4 teaching assistantships (averaging $6,806 per year); scholarships/grants, tuition waivers (partial), unspecified assistantships, and tuition discounts also available. Support available to part-time students. Financial award application deadline: 12/31; financial award applicants required to submit FAFSA. *Faculty research:* Patient and physician satisfaction, advancing and improving learning with information technology, consumer-driven healthcare, branding and the service industry, service provider training and customer satisfaction, entrepreneurship, business strategy, social media, curriculum redesign, leadership, educational funding. *Total annual research expenditures:* $3,100. *Unit head:* Dr. Michael A. Petrochuk, Director of the MBA Program/Assistant Professor, 330-244-4764, Fax: 330-490-7359, E-mail: mpetrochuk@walsh.edu. *Application contact:* Audra Dice, Graduate and Transfer Admissions Counselor, 330-490-7181, Fax: 330-244-4925, E-mail: adice@walsh.edu. Website: http://www.walsh.edu/mba-program.

Warner Pacific College, Graduate Programs, Portland, OR 97215-4099. Offers Biblical and theological studies (MA); Biblical studies (M Rel); education (M Ed); management and organizational leadership (MS); not-for-profit leadership (MSM); pastoral ministries (M Rel); religion and ethics (M Rel); teaching (MAT); theology (M Rel). Part-time programs available. *Faculty:* 20 part-time/adjunct (6 women). *Students:* 57 full-time (26 women), 4 part-time (2 women); includes 5 minority (4 Black or African American, non-Hispanic/Latino; 1 Asian, non-Hispanic/Latino). *Degree requirements:* For master's, thesis or alternative, presentation of defense. *Entrance requirements:* For master's, interview, minimum GPA of 2.5, letters of recommendation. *Application deadline:* Applications are processed on a rolling basis. *Expenses:* Tuition: Part-time $630 per credit hour. *Financial support:* Application deadline: 7/1; applicants required to submit FAFSA. *Faculty research:* New Testament studies, nineteenth-century Wesleyan theology, preaching and church growth, Christian ethics. *Unit head:* Dr. Andrea P. Cook, President, 503-517-1045, Fax: 503-517-1350. *Application contact:* Dr. John Fazio, Professor, 503-517-1043, Fax: 503-517-1350, E-mail: jfazio@warnerpacific.edu.

Warner University, School of Business, Lake Wales, FL 33859. Offers MBA. Part-time and evening/weekend programs available. Postbaccalaureate distance learning degree programs offered. *Degree requirements:* For master's, comprehensive exam, thesis. *Entrance requirements:* For master's, minimum GPA of 3.0, letters of recommendation (2). Additional exam requirements/recommendations for international students: Required—TOEFL. Electronic applications accepted.

Washburn University, School of Business, Topeka, KS 66621. Offers accountancy (M Acc). *Accreditation:* AACSB. Part-time and evening/weekend programs available. *Entrance requirements:* For master's, GMAT, minimum GPA of 2.75. Additional exam requirements/recommendations for international students: Required—TOEFL (minimum score 550 paper-based; 80 iBT); Recommended—IELTS (minimum score 6.5). *Application deadline:* For fall admission, 7/1 priority date for domestic and international students; for spring admission, 11/15 priority date for domestic and international students. Applications are processed on a rolling basis. Application fee: $40 ($70 for international students). Electronic applications accepted. *Expenses:* Tuition, state resident: full-time $5850; part-time $325 per credit hour. Tuition, nonresident: full-time $11,916; part-time $662 per credit hour. *Required fees:* $86; $43 per semester. Tuition and fees vary according to program. *Financial support:* Available to part-time students. Application deadline: 2/15; applicants required to submit FAFSA. *Faculty research:* Ethics in information technology, forecasting for shareholder value creation, model for measuring expected losses from litigation contingencies, business vs. family commitment in family businesses, calculated intangible value and brand recognition. *Unit head:* Dr. David L. Sollars, Dean, 785-670-2045, Fax: 785-670-1063, E-mail: david.sollars@washburn.edu. *Application contact:* Dr. Robert J. Boncella, MBA Director, 785-670-1308, Fax: 785-670-1063, E-mail: bob.boncella@washburn.edu.

Washington Adventist University, MBA Program, Takoma Park, MD 20912. Offers MBA. Part-time and evening/weekend programs available. Postbaccalaureate distance learning degree programs offered (no on-campus study). *Entrance requirements:* For master's, minimum undergraduate GPA of 2.75, curriculum vitae, interview, essay, personal statement. Additional exam requirements/recommendations for international students: Required—TOEFL (minimum score 550 paper-based), IELTS (minimum score 5).

Washington State University, Graduate School, College of Business, Business Administration Program, Pullman, WA 99164. Offers MBA. *Accreditation:* AACSB. *Degree requirements:* For master's, comprehensive exam (for some programs), thesis (for some programs), final presentation. *Entrance requirements:* For master's, GMAT. Additional exam requirements/recommendations for international students: Required—

TOEFL (minimum score 580 paper-based), IELTS, PTE (minimum score 93). Electronic applications accepted.

Washington State University, Graduate School, College of Business, Executive MBA Online Program, Pullman, WA 99164. Offers Exec MBA. Postbaccalaureate distance learning degree programs offered (no on-campus study).

Washington State University, Graduate School, College of Business, Online MBA Program, Pullman, WA 99164. Offers finance (MBA); general business (MBA); international business (MBA); marketing (MBA). Postbaccalaureate distance learning degree programs offered (no on-campus study).

Washington State University Tri-Cities, Graduate Programs, College of Business, Richland, WA 99352-1671. Offers business management (MBA). Part-time and evening/weekend programs available. *Degree requirements:* For master's, thesis (for some programs), oral presentation exam. *Entrance requirements:* For master's, GMAT, minimum GPA of 3.0, 3 letters of recommendation. Additional exam requirements/recommendations for international students: Required—TOEFL. Electronic applications accepted. *Faculty research:* Strategy, organizational transformation, technology and instructional effectiveness, market research effects of type (fonts), optimization of price structure, accounting ethic.

Washington State University Vancouver, Graduate Programs, Program in Business Administration, Vancouver, WA 98686. Offers MBA. *Degree requirements:* For master's, comprehensive exam (for some programs), thesis (for some programs), final presentation, portfolio. *Entrance requirements:* For master's, GMAT, minimum GPA of 3.0, 3 letters of recommendation, resume. Additional exam requirements/recommendations for international students: Required—TOEFL. *Faculty research:* Responses to injustice, business ethics, finance and nonfinancial performance measurement, interorganizational marketing relationships, market volatility.

Washington University in St. Louis, Olin Business School, St. Louis, MO 63130-4899. Offers EMBA, M Acc, MBA, MS, PhD, JD/MBA, M Arch/MBA, M Eng/MBA, MBA/MA, MBA/MSW. *Accreditation:* AACSB. *Faculty:* 82 full-time (18 women), 38 part-time/adjunct (8 women). *Students:* 560 full-time (224 women), 662 part-time (181 women); includes 347 minority (67 Black or African American, non-Hispanic/Latino; 2 American Indian or Alaska Native, non-Hispanic/Latino; 221 Asian, non-Hispanic/Latino; 22 Hispanic/Latino; 8 Native Hawaiian or other Pacific Islander, non-Hispanic/Latino; 27 Two or more races, non-Hispanic/Latino), 305 international. *Entrance requirements:* Additional exam requirements/recommendations for international students: Required—TOEFL. Electronic applications accepted. *Unit head:* Dr. Mahendra Gupta, Dean, 314-935-6344.
Website: http://www.olin.wustl.edu/.

Wayland Baptist University, Graduate Programs, Programs in Business Administration/Management, Plainview, TX 79072-6998. Offers accounting (MBA); general business (MBA); health care administration (MAM, MBA); healthcare administration (MBA); human resource management (MAM, MBA); international management (MBA); management (MBA); management information systems (MBA); organization management (MAM); project management (MBA). Part-time and evening/weekend programs available. Postbaccalaureate distance learning degree programs offered (no on-campus study). *Faculty:* 30 full-time (5 women), 38 part-time/adjunct (9 women). *Students:* 44 full-time (20 women), 702 part-time (315 women); includes 348 minority (149 Black or African American, non-Hispanic/Latino; 4 American Indian or Alaska Native, non-Hispanic/Latino; 23 Asian, non-Hispanic/Latino; 139 Hispanic/Latino; 9 Native Hawaiian or other Pacific Islander, non-Hispanic/Latino; 24 Two or more races, non-Hispanic/Latino), 5 international. Average age 40. 147 applicants, 94% accepted, 73 enrolled. In 2013, 296 master's awarded. *Degree requirements:* For master's, capstone course. *Entrance requirements:* For master's, GMAT, GRE or MAT. Additional exam requirements/recommendations for international students: Required—TOEFL (minimum score 500 paper-based; 61 iBT). *Application deadline:* Applications are processed on a rolling basis. Application fee: $50. Electronic applications accepted. *Expenses:* Tuition: Full-time $8190; part-time $455 per credit hour. *Required fees:* $970; $455 per credit hour. $485 per semester. *Financial support:* Federal Work-Study, institutionally sponsored loans, and scholarships/grants available. Support available to part-time students. Financial award application deadline: 5/1; financial award applicants required to submit FAFSA. *Unit head:* Dr. Otto Schacht, Chairman, 806-291-1020, Fax: 806-291-1957, E-mail: schachto@wbu.edu. *Application contact:* Amanda Stanton, Graduate Studies, 806-291-3423, Fax: 806-291-1950, E-mail: stanton@wbu.edu.

Waynesburg University, Graduate and Professional Studies, Canonsburg, PA 15370. Offers business (MBA), including energy management, finance, health systems, human resources, leadership, market development; counseling (MA), including addictions counseling, clinical mental health; education (M Ed, MAT), including autism (M Ed), curriculum and instruction (M Ed), educational leadership (M Ed), online teaching (M Ed); nursing (MSN), including administration, education, informatics; nursing practice (DNP); special education (M Ed); technology (M Ed); MSN/MBA. *Accreditation:* AACN. Part-time and evening/weekend programs available. *Faculty:* 11 full-time (5 women), 136 part-time/adjunct (80 women). *Students:* 146 full-time (99 women), 419 part-time (268 women). In 2013, 290 master's, 7 doctorates awarded. *Degree requirements:* For doctorate, thesis/dissertation. *Entrance requirements:* Additional exam requirements/recommendations for international students: Required—TOEFL. *Application deadline:* For fall admission, 8/1 priority date for domestic students. Applications are processed on a rolling basis. Electronic applications accepted. *Financial support:* Available to part-time students. Application deadline: 5/1. *Unit head:* David Mariner, Dean, 724-743-4420, Fax: 724-743-4425, E-mail: dmariner@waynesburg.edu. *Application contact:* Dr. Michael Bednarski, Director of Enrollment, 724-743-4420, Fax: 724-743-4425, E-mail: mbednars@waynesburg.edu.
Website: http://www.waynesburg.edu/.

Wayne State College, School of Business and Technology, Wayne, NE 68787. Offers MBA. Part-time and evening/weekend programs available. Postbaccalaureate distance learning degree programs offered (minimal on-campus study). *Entrance requirements:* For master's, GMAT, minimum overall GPA of 3.0. Additional exam requirements/recommendations for international students: Required—TOEFL (minimum score 550 paper-based).

Wayne State University, School of Business Administration, Detroit, MI 48202. Offers accounting (MS, Postbaccalaureate Certificate); business (Graduate Certificate); business administration (MBA, PhD); taxation (MST); JD/MBA. *Accreditation:* AACSB. Part-time and evening/weekend programs available. Postbaccalaureate distance learning degree programs offered (no on-campus study). *Students:* 143 full-time (67 women), 539 part-time (211 women); includes 179 minority (80 Black or African American, non-Hispanic/Latino; 2 American Indian or Alaska Native, non-Hispanic/Latino; 67 Asian, non-Hispanic/Latino; 22 Hispanic/Latino; 8 Two or more races, non-Hispanic/Latino), 71 international. Average age 31. 648 applicants, 26% accepted, 107 enrolled. In 2013, 281 master's, 3 doctorates, 1 other advanced degree awarded. *Degree requirements:* For doctorate, thesis/dissertation. *Entrance requirements:* For master's, GMAT; for doctorate, GMAT (minimum score of 600), minimum undergraduate GPA of 3.0, 3.5 upper-division or graduate; three letters of recommendation; brief essay. Additional exam requirements/recommendations for international students: Required—

TOEFL (minimum score 550 paper-based; 79 iBT), Michigan English Language Assessment Battery (minimum score 85); Recommended—IELTS (minimum score 6.5), TWE (minimum score 5.5). *Application deadline:* For fall admission, 6/1 priority date for domestic students, 5/1 priority date for international students; for winter admission, 10/1 priority date for domestic students, 9/1 priority date for international students; for spring admission, 2/1 priority date for domestic students, 1/1 priority date for international students. Applications are processed on a rolling basis. Application fee: $0. Electronic applications accepted. *Expenses:* Contact institution. *Financial support:* In 2013–14, 105 students received support, including 2 fellowships with tuition reimbursements available (averaging $18,000 per year), 2 teaching assistantships with tuition reimbursements available (averaging $9,000 per year); scholarships/grants, health care benefits, and unspecified assistantships also available. Support available to part-time students. Financial award application deadline: 3/31; financial award applicants required to submit FAFSA. *Faculty research:* Executive compensation and stock performance, consumer reactions to pricing strategies, communication across the automotive supply chain, performance of firms in sub-Saharan Africa, implementation issues with ERP software. *Unit head:* Margaret Williams, Interim Dean, School of Business Administration, 313-577-4501, Fax: 313-577-4557, E-mail: margaret.l.williams@wayne.edu. *Application contact:* Amber Conway, Director, Graduate Programs Office, 313-577-4511, Fax: 313-577-9442, E-mail: ck8173@wayne.edu.
Website: http://business.wayne.edu/.

Webber International University, Graduate School of Business, Babson Park, FL 33827-0096. Offers accounting (MBA); management (MBA); security management (MBA); sports management (MBA). Part-time and evening/weekend programs available. *Degree requirements:* For master's, thesis or alternative. *Entrance requirements:* For master's, previous course work in financial and managerial accounting. Additional exam requirements/recommendations for international students: Required—TOEFL. *Faculty research:* Finance strategy, market research, investments, intranet.

Weber State University, John B. Goddard School of Business and Economics, Program in Business Administration, Ogden, UT 84408-1001. Offers MBA. *Accreditation:* AACSB. Part-time and evening/weekend programs available. *Faculty:* 13 full-time (2 women), 4 part-time/adjunct (0 women). *Students:* 60 full-time (12 women), 84 part-time (14 women); includes 7 minority (2 Black or African American, non-Hispanic/Latino; 1 Asian, non-Hispanic/Latino; 3 Hispanic/Latino; 1 Two or more races, non-Hispanic/Latino), 8 international. Average age 31. 92 applicants, 66% accepted, 59 enrolled. In 2013, 81 master's awarded. *Entrance requirements:* For master's, GMAT, resume, letters of recommendation. Additional exam requirements/recommendations for international students: Required—TOEFL (minimum score 550 paper-based). *Application deadline:* For fall admission, 5/9 priority date for domestic and international students; for spring admission, 11/7 for domestic and international students. Applications are processed on a rolling basis. Application fee: $60 ($90 for international students). Electronic applications accepted. *Expenses:* Tuition, state resident: full-time $7118; part-time $253 per credit hour. Tuition, nonresident: full-time $12,480; part-time $634 per credit hour. *Required fees:* $34.33; $34.33 per credit hour. $257 per semester. Full-time tuition and fees vary according to course load. *Financial support:* In 2013–14, 8 students received support. Institutionally sponsored loans, scholarships/grants, and tuition waivers (partial) available. Support available to part-time students. Financial award application deadline: 6/15; financial award applicants required to submit FAFSA. *Unit head:* Dr. Rolf David Dixon, Director, 801-626-7542, Fax: 801-626-7423, E-mail: rddixon@weber.edu. *Application contact:* Dr. Mark A. Stevenson, MBA Enrollment Director, 801-395-3528, Fax: 801-395-3525, E-mail: mba@weber.edu.

Webster University, George Herbert Walker School of Business and Technology, Department of Business, St. Louis, MO 63119-3194. Offers business and organizational security management (MBA); decision support systems (MBA); environmental management (MBA); finance (MBA, MS); forensic accounting (MS); gerontology (MBA); human resources development (MBA); human resources management (MBA); information technology management (MBA); international business (MA, MBA); international relations (MBA); management and leadership (MBA); marketing (MBA); media communications (MBA); procurement and acquisitions management (MBA); Web services (MBA). *Accreditation:* ACBSP. Part-time and evening/weekend programs available. Postbaccalaureate distance learning degree programs offered (no on-campus study). *Degree requirements:* For master's, comprehensive exam (for some programs), thesis (for some programs). *Entrance requirements:* Additional exam requirements/recommendations for international students: Required—TOEFL. *Expenses: Tuition:* Full-time $11,610; part-time $645 per credit hour. Tuition and fees vary according to campus/location and program.

Webster University, George Herbert Walker School of Business and Technology, Department of Management, St. Louis, MO 63119-3194. Offers business and organizational security management (MA); health administration (MHA); health care management (MA); health services management (MA); human resources development (MA); human resources management (MA); information technology management (MS); management and leadership (MA); marketing (MA); nonprofit leadership (MA); procurement and acquisitions management (MA); public administration (MPA); space systems operations management (MS). Part-time and evening/weekend programs available. Postbaccalaureate distance learning degree programs offered (no on-campus study). *Degree requirements:* For master's, thesis (for some programs). *Entrance requirements:* Additional exam requirements/recommendations for international students: Required—TOEFL. *Expenses: Tuition:* Full-time $11,610; part-time $645 per credit hour. Tuition and fees vary according to campus/location and program.

Wesleyan College, Department of Business and Economics, EMBA Program, Macon, GA 31210-4462. Offers EMBA. Evening/weekend programs available. *Entrance requirements:* For master's, GMAT, LSAT, GRE or MAT, 5 years of work experience, 5 years of management experience. Additional exam requirements/recommendations for international students: Required—TOEFL (minimum score 550 paper-based). Electronic applications accepted.

Wesley College, Business Program, Dover, DE 19901-3875. Offers environmental management (MBA); executive leadership (MBA); management (MBA). Executive leadership concentration also offered at New Castle, DE location. Part-time and evening/weekend programs available. *Entrance requirements:* For master's, GMAT or GRE, minimum undergraduate GPA of 2.75.

West Chester University of Pennsylvania, College of Business and Public Affairs, The School of Business, West Chester, PA 19383. Offers MBA, Certificate. *Accreditation:* AACSB. Part-time and evening/weekend programs available. Postbaccalaureate distance learning degree programs offered (minimal on-campus study). *Faculty:* 9 full-time (4 women), 1 part-time/adjunct (0 women). *Students:* 14 full-time (4 women), 97 part-time (30 women); includes 17 minority (8 Black or African American, non-Hispanic/Latino; 8 Asian, non-Hispanic/Latino; 1 Hispanic/Latino), 2 international. Average age 31. 75 applicants, 72% accepted, 33 enrolled. In 2013, 24 master's, 5 other advanced degrees awarded. *Degree requirements:* For master's and Certificate, minimum GPA of 3.0. *Entrance requirements:* For master's, GMAT or GRE, statement of professional goals, resume, two letters of recommendation, transcripts. Additional exam requirements/recommendations for international students: Required—TOEFL (minimum score 550 paper-based; 80 iBT). *Application deadline:* For fall admission, 4/15 priority date for domestic students, 3/15 for international students; for spring admission, 10/15 priority date for domestic students, 9/1 for international students. Applications are processed on a rolling basis. Application fee: $45. Electronic applications accepted. *Expenses:* Tuition, state resident: full-time $7956; part-time $442 per credit. Tuition, nonresident: full-time $11,934; part-time $663 per credit. *Required fees:* $2134.20; $106.24 per credit. Tuition and fees vary according to campus/location and program. *Financial support:* Unspecified assistantships available. Support available to part-time students. Financial award application deadline: 2/15; financial award applicants required to submit FAFSA. *Unit head:* Dr. Paul Christ, MBA Director and Graduate Coordinator, 610-425-5000, E-mail: mba@wcupa.edu. *Application contact:* Office of Graduate Studies, 610-436-2943, Fax: 610-436-2763, E-mail: gradstudy@wcupa.edu.
Website: http://www.wcumba.org/.

Western Carolina University, Graduate School, College of Business, Program in Business Administration, Cullowhee, NC 28723. Offers MBA. *Accreditation:* AACSB. Part-time and evening/weekend programs available. *Entrance requirements:* For master's, GMAT, appropriate undergraduate degree, 3 letters of recommendation. Additional exam requirements/recommendations for international students: Required—TOEFL (minimum score 550 paper-based; 79 iBT). *Faculty research:* Marketing strategy, biotechnology, executive education, business statistics, supply chain management, innovation.

Western Connecticut State University, Division of Graduate Studies, Ancell School of Business, Program in Business Administration, Danbury, CT 06810-6885. Offers accounting (MBA); business administration (MBA). Part-time programs available. *Degree requirements:* For master's, comprehensive exam, completion of program within 8 years. *Entrance requirements:* For master's, GMAT. Additional exam requirements/recommendations for international students: Recommended—TOEFL (minimum score 550 paper-based; 79 iBT), IELTS (minimum score 6). *Faculty research:* Global strategic marketing planning, project management and team coordination; email, discussion boards that act as blogs and videoconferencing.

Western Governors University, College of Business, Salt Lake City, UT 84107. Offers information technology management (MBA); management and strategy (MBA); strategic leadership (MBA). Evening/weekend programs available. *Degree requirements:* For master's, capstone project. *Entrance requirements:* For master's, Readiness Assessment, transcripts. Additional exam requirements/recommendations for international students: Required—TOEFL (minimum score 450 paper-based; 80 iBT). Electronic applications accepted.

Western Illinois University, School of Graduate Studies, College of Business and Technology, Program in Business Administration, Macomb, IL 61455-1390. Offers business administration (MBA, Certificate); supply chain management (Certificate). *Accreditation:* AACSB. Part-time programs available. *Students:* 42 full-time (23 women), 54 part-time (28 women); includes 6 minority (5 Black or African American, non-Hispanic/Latino; 1 Hispanic/Latino), 16 international. Average age 28. In 2013, 36 master's awarded. *Degree requirements:* For master's, thesis or alternative. *Entrance requirements:* For master's, GMAT. Additional exam requirements/recommendations for international students: Required—TOEFL (minimum score 550 paper-based; 80 iBT). *Application deadline:* Applications are processed on a rolling basis. Application fee: $30. Electronic applications accepted. *Financial support:* In 2013–14, 19 students received support, including 3 research assistantships with full tuition reimbursements available (averaging $7,544 per year), 16 teaching assistantships with full tuition reimbursements available (averaging $8,688 per year). Financial award applicants required to submit FAFSA. *Unit head:* Dr. John Drea, Associate Dean, 309-298-2442. *Application contact:* Dr. Nancy Parsons, Associate Provost and Director of Graduate Studies, 309-298-1806, Fax: 309-298-2345, E-mail: grad-office@wiu.edu.
Website: http://wiu.edu/cbt.

Western International University, Graduate Programs in Business, Master of Business Administration Program, Phoenix, AZ 85021-2718. Offers MBA. Part-time and evening/weekend programs available. Postbaccalaureate distance learning degree programs offered (no on-campus study). *Entrance requirements:* For master's, minimum GPA of 2.75. Additional exam requirements/recommendations for international students: Required—TOEFL (minimum score 550 paper-based; 79 iBT), TWE (minimum score 5), or IELTS (minimum score 6.5). Electronic applications accepted.

Western International University, Graduate Programs in Business, Master of Business Administration Program in Management, Phoenix, AZ 85021-2718. Offers MBA. Part-time and evening/weekend programs available. Postbaccalaureate distance learning degree programs offered (no on-campus study). *Entrance requirements:* For master's, minimum GPA of 2.75. Additional exam requirements/recommendations for international students: Required—TOEFL (minimum score 550 paper-based; 79 iBT), TWE (minimum score 5), or IELTS (minimum score 6.5). Electronic applications accepted.

Western Kentucky University, Graduate Studies, Gordon Ford College of Business, MBA Program, Bowling Green, KY 42101. Offers MBA. *Accreditation:* AACSB. Part-time and evening/weekend programs available. *Degree requirements:* For master's, comprehensive exam, thesis optional. *Entrance requirements:* For master's, GMAT, minimum GPA of 2.5. Additional exam requirements/recommendations for international students: Required—TOEFL (minimum score 555 paper-based; 79 iBT). *Faculty research:* Business and international education, web page development, management training, international studies, globalization.

Western Michigan University, Graduate College, Haworth College of Business, Department of Finance and Commercial Law, Kalamazoo, MI 49008. Offers finance (MBA). *Accreditation:* AACSB. *Entrance requirements:* For master's, GMAT.

Western New England University, College of Business, Program in Business Administration, Springfield, MA 01119. Offers general business (MBA); sport management (MBA); JD/MBA; Pharm D/MBA. *Accreditation:* AACSB. Part-time and evening/weekend programs available. Postbaccalaureate distance learning degree programs offered (no on-campus study). *Faculty:* 20 full-time (7 women). *Students:* 123 part-time (51 women); includes 8 minority (2 Black or African American, non-Hispanic/Latino; 3 Asian, non-Hispanic/Latino; 2 Hispanic/Latino; 1 Two or more races, non-Hispanic/Latino), 7 international. Average age 31. 585 applicants. In 2013, 45 master's awarded. *Entrance requirements:* For master's, GMAT, official transcript, two letters of recommendation, essay, resume. Additional exam requirements/recommendations for international students: Required—TOEFL. *Application deadline:* Applications are processed on a rolling basis. Application fee: $30. Electronic applications accepted. Tuition and fees vary according to program. *Financial support:* Application deadline: 4/15; applicants required to submit FAFSA. *Unit head:* Dr. Julie Siciliano, Dean, 413-782-1224, E-mail: julie.siciliano@wne.edu. *Application contact:* Matthew Fox, Director of Recruiting and Marketing for Adult Learners, 413-782-1517, Fax: 413-782-1779, E-mail: study@wne.edu.

Western New Mexico University, Graduate Division, Department of Business Administration and Criminal Justice, Silver City, NM 88062-0680. Offers business administration (MBA). *Accreditation:* ACBSP. Part-time and evening/weekend programs available. *Entrance requirements:* For master's, GMAT. Additional exam requirements/

recommendations for international students: Required—TOEFL (minimum score 550 paper-based). Electronic applications accepted.

Western Washington University, Graduate School, College of Business and Economics, Bellingham, WA 98225-5996. Offers MBA, MP Acc. *Accreditation:* AACSB. Part-time and evening/weekend programs available. *Degree requirements:* For master's, comprehensive exam. *Entrance requirements:* For master's, GMAT, minimum GPA of 3.0 in last 60 semester hours or last 90 quarter hours. Additional exam requirements/recommendations for international students: Required—TOEFL (minimum score 567 paper-based). Electronic applications accepted. *Faculty research:* Enterprise strategy/corporate social performance, sustainability/environmental management/ nonprofit marketing, managerial/environmental accounting, organizational applications of collaborative technology, environmental and resource economics.

Westminster College, The Bill and Vieve Gore School of Business, Salt Lake City, UT 84105-3697. Offers accountancy (M Acc); business administration (MBA, Certificate); technology management (MBATM). *Accreditation:* ACBSP. Part-time and evening/ weekend programs available. Postbaccalaureate distance learning degree programs offered (minimal on-campus study). *Faculty:* 24 full-time (5 women), 12 part-time/adjunct (6 women). *Students:* 245 full-time (83 women), 156 part-time (57 women); includes 60 minority (3 Black or African American, non-Hispanic/Latino; 3 American Indian or Alaska Native, non-Hispanic/Latino; 21 Asian, non-Hispanic/Latino; 28 Hispanic/Latino; 1 Native Hawaiian or other Pacific Islander, non-Hispanic/Latino; 4 Two or more races, non-Hispanic/Latino), 17 international. Average age 33. 256 applicants, 59% accepted, 77 enrolled. In 2013, 201 master's, 46 other advanced degrees awarded. *Degree requirements:* For master's, international trip, minimum grade of C in all classes. *Entrance requirements:* For master's, GMAT, 2 professional recommendations, employer letter of support, personal resume, essay, official transcripts. Additional exam requirements/recommendations for international students: Required—TOEFL (minimum score 600 paper-based; 100 iBT), IELTS (minimum score 7.5). *Application deadline:* For fall admission, 8/31 for domestic students, 5/31 for international students; for spring admission, 1/1 for domestic students; for summer admission, 5/1 for domestic students. Applications are processed on a rolling basis. Application fee: $50. Electronic applications accepted. *Expenses:* Contact institution. *Financial support:* In 2013–14, 46 students received support. Career-related internships or fieldwork, unspecified assistantships, and tuition reimbursements, tuition remission available. Support available to part-time students. Financial award applicants required to submit FAFSA. *Faculty research:* Innovation and entrepreneurship, business strategy and change, financial analysis and capital budgeting, leadership development, knowledge management. *Unit head:* Dr. Jin Wang, Dean, Gore School of Business, 801-832-2600, Fax: 801-832-3106, E-mail: jwang@westminstercollege.edu. *Application contact:* Dr. John Baworowsky, Vice President of Enrollment Management, 801-832-2200, Fax: 801-832-3101, E-mail: admission@westminstercollege.edu.
Website: http://www.westminstercollege.edu/mba/.

West Texas A&M University, College of Business, Department of Management, Marketing, and General Business, Canyon, TX 79016-0001. Offers business administration (MBA). *Accreditation:* AACSB. Part-time and evening/weekend programs available. Postbaccalaureate distance learning degree programs offered (minimal on-campus study). *Entrance requirements:* For master's, GMAT. Additional exam requirements/recommendations for international students: Required—TOEFL (minimum score 550 paper-based). Electronic applications accepted. *Faculty research:* Human resources, international business, southern Asian markets, global strategies, international trade composition.

West Virginia University, College of Business and Economics, Program in Business Administration, Morgantown, WV 26506. Offers MBA, JD/MBA. *Accreditation:* AACSB. Part-time and evening/weekend programs available. *Entrance requirements:* For master's, GMAT. Additional exam requirements/recommendations for international students: Required—TOEFL. Electronic applications accepted. *Faculty research:* Financial management, managerial accounting, marketing, planning, corporate finance.

West Virginia Wesleyan College, MBA Program, Buckhannon, WV 26201. Offers MBA. Part-time and evening/weekend programs available. *Degree requirements:* For master's, exit evaluation. *Entrance requirements:* For master's, GMAT. Additional exam requirements/recommendations for international students: Required—TOEFL.

Wheeling Jesuit University, Department of Business, Wheeling, WV 26003-6295. Offers accounting (MSA); business administration (MBA). *Accreditation:* ACBSP. Part-time and evening/weekend programs available. *Entrance requirements:* For master's, minimum undergraduate GPA of 2.8. Additional exam requirements/recommendations for international students: Required—TOEFL (minimum score 600 paper-based; 100 iBT). Electronic applications accepted. *Faculty research:* Forensic economics, consumer behavior, economic development, capitalism, leadership.

Whitworth University, School of Business, Spokane, WA 99251-0001. Offers international management (MBA). Part-time and evening/weekend programs available. *Faculty:* 5 full-time (1 woman), 9 part-time/adjunct (2 women). *Students:* 5 full-time (1 woman), 30 part-time (17 women); includes 5 minority (2 Black or African American, non-Hispanic/Latino; 1 American Indian or Alaska Native, non-Hispanic/Latino; 2 Asian, non-Hispanic/Latino). Average age 29. 33 applicants, 67% accepted, 20 enrolled. In 2013, 12 master's awarded. *Degree requirements:* For master's, foreign language (for MBA in international management). *Entrance requirements:* For master's, GMAT or GRE, minimum GPA of 3.0; two letters of recommendation; resume; completion of prerequisite courses in micro-economics, macro-economics, financial accounting, finance, and marketing, interview with director. Additional exam requirements/ recommendations for international students: Required—TOEFL (minimum score 88 iBT), TWE. *Application deadline:* For fall admission, 8/1 priority date for domestic and international students; for spring admission, 1/6 priority date for domestic students, 1/6 for international students. Applications are processed on a rolling basis. Application fee: $35. Electronic applications accepted. *Financial support:* In 2013–14, 9 students received support. Scholarships/grants available. Financial award applicants required to submit FAFSA. *Faculty research:* International business (European, Central America and Asian topics), entrepreneurship and business plan development. *Unit head:* John Hengesh, Director, Graduate Studies in Business, 509-777-4455, Fax: 509-777-3723, E-mail: jhengesh@whitworth.edu. *Application contact:* Susan Cook, Admissions Manager, Graduate Studies, 509-777-4298, Fax: 509-777-3723, E-mail: scook@ whitworth.edu.
Website: http://www.whitworth.edu/schoolofbusiness.

WHU - Otto Beisheim School of Management, Graduate Programs, Vallendar, Germany. Offers EMBA, MBA, MS. EMBA offered jointly with Kellogg School of Management.

Wichita State University, Graduate School, W. Frank Barton School of Business, Department of Business, Wichita, KS 67260. Offers EMBA, MBA. *Accreditation:* AACSB. Part-time and evening/weekend programs available. *Unit head:* Angela Jones, Director, 316-978-3230, E-mail: angela.jones@wichita.edu. *Application contact:* Jordan Oleson, Admissions Coordinator, 316-978-3095, Fax: 316-978-3253, E-mail: jordan.oleson@wichita.edu.
Website: http://www.wichita.edu/.

Widener University, School of Business Administration, Chester, PA 19013-5792. Offers MBA, MHA, MHR, MS, JD/MBA, MD/MBA, MD/MHA, ME/MBA, Psy D/MBA, Psy D/MHA, Psy D/MHR. *Accreditation:* AACSB. Part-time and evening/weekend programs available. *Faculty:* 14 full-time (6 women), 6 part-time/adjunct (2 women). *Students:* 26 full-time (8 women), 74 part-time (30 women); includes 22 minority (13 Black or African American, non-Hispanic/Latino; 1 American Indian or Alaska Native, non-Hispanic/Latino; 5 Asian, non-Hispanic/Latino; 2 Hispanic/Latino; 1 Two or more races, non-Hispanic/Latino), 6 international. Average age 34. 254 applicants, 91% accepted. In 2013, 85 master's awarded. *Entrance requirements:* For master's, minimum GPA of 2.5. *Application deadline:* For fall admission, 8/1 priority date for domestic students; for spring admission, 12/1 for domestic students. Applications are processed on a rolling basis. Application fee: $25 ($300 for international students). Electronic applications accepted. *Expenses:* Contact institution. *Financial support:* In 2013–14, 11 research assistantships with full tuition reimbursements were awarded; career-related internships or fieldwork, Federal Work-Study, and traineeships also available. Support available to part-time students. Financial award application deadline: 5/1. *Faculty research:* Cost containment in health care, human resource management, productivity, globalization. *Unit head:* Dr. Savas Ozatalay, Dean, 610-499-4300, Fax: 610-499-4615. *Application contact:* Ann Seltzer, Graduate Enrollment Administrator, 610-499-4305, E-mail: apseltzer@widener.edu.
Website: http://www.widener.edu.

Wilfrid Laurier University, Faculty of Graduate and Postdoctoral Studies, School of Business and Economics, Business Administration Program, Waterloo, ON N2L 3C5, Canada. Offers co-op (MBA); full-time (MBA); part-time (MBA). *Accreditation:* AACSB. Part-time and evening/weekend programs available. *Degree requirements:* For master's, thesis. *Entrance requirements:* For master's, GMAT, minimum 2 years of business experience (for 12-month or part-time MBA formats), minimum B average in 4-year BA program. Additional exam requirements/recommendations for international students: Required—TOEFL (minimum score 89 iBT). Electronic applications accepted.

Wilfrid Laurier University, Faculty of Graduate and Postdoctoral Studies, School of Business and Economics, Department of Business, Waterloo, ON N2L 3C5, Canada. Offers accounting (PhD); finance (M Fin); financial economics (PhD); marketing (PhD); operations and supply chain management (PhD); organizational behavior and human resource management (M Sc); organizational behaviour and human resource management (PhD); supply chain management (M Sc); technology management (EMTM). *Accreditation:* AACSB. Part-time and evening/weekend programs available. *Degree requirements:* For master's, thesis optional; for doctorate, comprehensive exam, thesis/dissertation. *Entrance requirements:* For master's, GMAT, 4-year honors degree with minimum B+ average; for doctorate, GMAT, master's degree, minimum B+ average. Additional exam requirements/recommendations for international students: Required—TOEFL (minimum score 89 iBT). Electronic applications accepted. *Faculty research:* Financial economics, management and organizational behavior, operations and supply chain management.

Wilkes University, College of Graduate and Professional Studies, Jay S. Sidhu School of Business and Leadership, Wilkes-Barre, PA 18766-0002. Offers accounting (MBA); entrepreneurship (MBA); finance (MBA); health care administration (MBA); human resource management (MBA); international business (MBA); marketing (MBA); operations management (MBA); organizational leadership and development (MBA). *Accreditation:* ACBSP. Part-time and evening/weekend programs available. *Students:* 41 full-time (20 women), 119 part-time (48 women); includes 20 minority (5 Black or African American, non-Hispanic/Latino; 3 Asian, non-Hispanic/Latino; 7 Hispanic/Latino; 5 Two or more races, non-Hispanic/Latino), 7 international. Average age 31. In 2013, 55 master's awarded. *Entrance requirements:* For master's, GMAT. Additional exam requirements/recommendations for international students: Required—TOEFL (minimum score 550 paper-based; 79 iBT). *Application deadline:* Applications are processed on a rolling basis. Application fee: $45 ($65 for international students). Electronic applications accepted. *Expenses:* Contact institution. *Financial support:* Federal Work-Study and unspecified assistantships available. Financial award application deadline: 3/1; financial award applicants required to submit FAFSA. *Unit head:* Dr. Jeffrey Alves, Dean, 570-408-4702, Fax: 570-408-7846, E-mail: jeffrey.alves@wilkes.edu. *Application contact:* Joanne Thomas, Interim Director of Graduate Enrollment, 570-408-4234, Fax: 570-408-7846, E-mail: joanne.thomas1@wilkes.edu.
Website: http://www.wilkes.edu/pages/457.asp.

Willamette University, George H. Atkinson Graduate School of Management, Salem, OR 97301-3931. Offers MBA, JD/MBA. *Accreditation:* AACSB; NASPAA. Part-time and evening/weekend programs available. *Faculty:* 20 full-time (4 women), 20 part-time/ adjunct (8 women). *Students:* 198 full-time (75 women), 77 part-time (31 women); includes 38 minority (9 Black or African American, non-Hispanic/Latino; 2 American Indian or Alaska Native, non-Hispanic/Latino; 13 Asian, non-Hispanic/Latino; 9 Hispanic/ Latino; 2 Native Hawaiian or other Pacific Islander, non-Hispanic/Latino; 3 Two or more races, non-Hispanic/Latino), 82 international. Average age 28. 230 applicants, 89% accepted, 114 enrolled. In 2013, 158 master's awarded. *Degree requirements:* For master's, minimum cumulative GPA of 3.0. *Entrance requirements:* For master's, GMAT or GRE, essays, transcripts, references, resume, interview. Additional exam requirements/recommendations for international students: Required—TOEFL (minimum score 570 paper-based; 88 iBT), IELTS (minimum score 6.5). *Application deadline:* For fall admission, 5/1 priority date for domestic and international students; for winter admission, 5/1 for domestic and international students; for spring admission, 5/1 for domestic and international students. Applications are processed on a rolling basis. Application fee: $100. Electronic applications accepted. Application fee is waived when completed online. *Expenses:* Contact institution. *Financial support:* In 2013–14, 209 students received support, including 12 research assistantships with tuition reimbursements available (averaging $2,000 per year); career-related internships or fieldwork, Federal Work-Study, scholarships/grants, and unspecified assistantships also available. Financial award application deadline: 5/1; financial award applicants required to submit FAFSA. *Faculty research:* Entrepreneurship, organizational behavior, social networks, general management, finance, marketing, public management, human resources, duty of care, angel investing, public budgeting, operations, sustainability. *Unit head:* Dr. Debra J. Ringold, Dean/Professor of Free Enterprise, 503-370-6440, Fax: 503-370-3011, E-mail: dringold@willamette.edu. *Application contact:* Aimee Akimoff, Director of Recruitment, 503-370-6167, Fax: 503-370-3011, E-mail: aakimoff@ willamette.edu.
Website: http://www.willamette.edu/mba/.

William Carey University, School of Business, Hattiesburg, MS 39401-5499. Offers MBA. Part-time programs available. *Entrance requirements:* For master's, GMAT. Additional exam requirements/recommendations for international students: Required—TOEFL (minimum score 500 paper-based).

William Paterson University of New Jersey, Christos M. Cotsakos College of Business, Wayne, NJ 07470-8420. Offers MBA. *Accreditation:* AACSB. Part-time and evening/weekend programs available. *Faculty:* 16 full-time (12 women), 2 part-time/ adjunct (both women). *Students:* 32 full-time (19 women), 75 part-time (29 women); includes 32 minority (7 Black or African American, non-Hispanic/Latino; 14 Asian, non-Hispanic/Latino; 9 Hispanic/Latino; 2 Two or more races, non-Hispanic/Latino). Average

age 31. 106 applicants, 62% accepted, 45 enrolled. In 2013, 54 master's awarded. *Entrance requirements:* For master's, GMAT (minimum score 500), minimum AACSB index of 1000, minimum GPA of 3.0. Additional exam requirements/recommendations for international students: Required—TOEFL (minimum score 550 paper-based; 79 iBT), IELTS (minimum score 6). *Application deadline:* For fall admission, 6/1 for domestic students, 5/1 for international students; for spring admission, 11/1 for domestic students, 10/1 for international students. Applications are processed on a rolling basis. Application fee: $50. Electronic applications accepted. *Financial support:* Research assistantships with full tuition reimbursements and unspecified assistantships available. Support available to part-time students. Financial award application deadline: 4/1; financial award applicants required to submit FAFSA. *Faculty research:* Sustainable energy, multinational corporations and global capital, tax reform, human capital and innovation, emerging markets. *Unit head:* Dr. Siamack Shojai, Dean, 973-720-2964, E-mail: shojais@wpunj.edu. *Application contact:* Tinu Adeniran, Assistant Director, Graduate Admissions, 973-720-2764, Fax: 973-720-2035, E-mail: adenirant@wpunj.edu.
Website: http://www.wpunj.edu/ccob.

William Woods University, Graduate and Adult Studies, Fulton, MO 65251-1098. Offers administration (M Ed, Ed S); athletic/activities administration (M Ed); curriculum and instruction (M Ed, Ed S); educational leadership (Ed D); equestrian education (M Ed); health management (MBA); human resources (MBA); leadership (MBA); marketing, advertising, and public relations (MBA); teaching and technology (M Ed). Part-time and evening/weekend programs available. *Faculty:* 231 part-time/adjunct (87 women). *Students:* 418 full-time (276 women), 716 part-time (433 women); includes 51 minority (34 Black or African American, non-Hispanic/Latino; 4 American Indian or Alaska Native, non-Hispanic/Latino; 5 Asian, non-Hispanic/Latino; 3 Hispanic/Latino; 5 Two or more races, non-Hispanic/Latino), 4 international. Average age 35. In 2013, 507 master's, 8 doctorates, 143 other advanced degrees awarded. *Degree requirements:* For master's, capstone course (MBA), action research (M Ed); for Ed S, field experience. *Entrance requirements:* Additional exam requirements/recommendations for international students: Required—TOEFL (minimum score 550 paper-based). *Application deadline:* Applications are processed on a rolling basis. Application fee: $0. Electronic applications accepted. *Expenses:* Contact institution. *Financial support:* Institutionally sponsored loans available. Financial award applicants required to submit FAFSA. *Unit head:* Dr. Michael Westerfield, Vice President and Dean of the Graduate College, 573-592-4383, Fax: 573-592-1164. *Application contact:* Jessica Brush, Director of Operations, 573-592-4227, Fax: 573-592-1164, E-mail: jessica.brush@williamwoods.ede.
Website: http://www.williamwoods.edu/evening_programs/index.asp.

Wilmington University, College of Business, New Castle, DE 19720-6491. Offers accounting (MBA, MS); business administration (MBA, DBA); environmental stewardship (MBA); finance (MBA); health care administration (MBA, MSM); homeland security (MBA, MSM); human resource management (MSM); management information systems (MBA, MSN); marketing (MSM); marketing management (MBA); military leadership (MSM); organizational leadership (MBA, MSM); public administration (MSM). Part-time and evening/weekend programs available. *Entrance requirements:* Additional exam requirements/recommendations for international students: Required—TOEFL (minimum score 500 paper-based). Electronic applications accepted.

Wingate University, Byrum School of Business, Wingate, NC 28174-0159. Offers MAC, MBA. *Accreditation:* ACBSP. Part-time and evening/weekend programs available. *Entrance requirements:* For master's, GMAT, work experience, 2 letters of recommendation. Electronic applications accepted. *Expenses:* Contact institution. *Faculty research:* Stochastic processes, business ethics, regional economic development, municipal finance, consumer behavior.

Winston-Salem State University, Program in Business Administration, Winston-Salem, NC 27110-0003. Offers MBA. *Accreditation:* AACSB. Part-time and evening/weekend programs available. Postbaccalaureate distance learning degree programs offered (minimal on-campus study). *Entrance requirements:* For master's, GMAT, resume, 3 letters of recommendation. Electronic applications accepted. *Faculty research:* Innovative entrepreneurship and customer service, econometrics and operations research.

Winthrop University, College of Business Administration, Program in Business Administration, Rock Hill, SC 29733. Offers MBA. *Accreditation:* AACSB. *Entrance requirements:* For master's, GMAT.

Woodbury University, School of Business and Management, Burbank, CA 91504-1099. Offers business administration (MBA); organizational leadership (MA). *Accreditation:* ACBSP. Part-time and evening/weekend programs available. *Faculty:* 8 full-time (5 women), 9 part-time/adjunct (1 woman). *Students:* 92 full-time (51 women), 10 part-time (5 women); includes 22 minority (5 Black or African American, non-Hispanic/Latino; 3 Asian, non-Hispanic/Latino; 14 Hispanic/Latino), 10 international. Average age 31. 166 applicants, 79% accepted, 82 enrolled. In 2013, 50 master's awarded. *Entrance requirements:* For master's, GMAT, transcripts, resume. Additional exam requirements/recommendations for international students: Required—TOEFL (minimum score 550 paper-based; 83 iBT), IELTS (minimum score 6.5). *Application deadline:* For fall admission, 8/1 priority date for domestic students; for spring admission, 12/1 for domestic and international students. Applications are processed on a rolling basis. Application fee: $35 ($50 for international students). *Expenses: Tuition:* Full-time $30,120; part-time $1004 per unit. *Required fees:* $8 per unit. $195 per term. Tuition and fees vary according to course load and program. *Financial support:* In 2013–14, 59 students received support. Scholarships/grants available. Financial award applicants required to submit FAFSA. *Faculty research:* Total quality management, leadership. *Unit head:* Dr. Andre Van Niekerk, Dean, 818-767-0888 Ext. 264, Fax: 818-767-0032. *Application contact:* Ani Khukoyan, Assistant Director, Graduate Admissions, 818-767-0888 Ext. 224, Fax: 818-767-7520, E-mail: ani.khukoyan@woodbury.edu.
Website: http://woodbury.edu/school-of-business.

Worcester Polytechnic Institute, Graduate Studies and Research, School of Business, Worcester, MA 01609-2280. Offers information technology (MS), including information security management; management (Graduate Certificate); marketing and technological innovation (MS); operations design and leadership (MS); technology (MBA, MS). *Accreditation:* AACSB. Part-time and evening/weekend programs available. Postbaccalaureate distance learning degree programs offered (minimal on-campus study). *Faculty:* 28 full-time (12 women), 17 part-time/adjunct (3 women). *Students:* 123 full-time (77 women), 282 part-time (88 women); includes 34 minority (3 Black or African American, non-Hispanic/Latino; 15 Asian, non-Hispanic/Latino; 10 Hispanic/Latino; 6 Two or more races, non-Hispanic/Latino), 146 international. 747 applicants, 56% accepted, 111 enrolled. In 2013, 110 master's awarded. *Degree requirements:* For master's, thesis optional. *Entrance requirements:* For master's, GMAT (MBA); GMAT or GRE General Test (MS), statement of purpose, 3 letters of recommendation, resume; for Graduate Certificate, GMAT or GRE General Test, statement of purpose, 3 letters of recommendation. Additional exam requirements/recommendations for international students: Required—TOEFL (minimum score 563 paper-based; 84 iBT), IELTS (minimum score 7). *Application deadline:* For fall admission, 6/1 priority date for domestic and international students; for spring admission, 11/1 priority date for domestic students, 10/1 priority date for international students. Applications are processed on a rolling basis. Application fee: $70. Electronic applications accepted. *Financial support:* Career-related internships or fieldwork, institutionally sponsored loans, scholarships/grants, and unspecified assistantships available. Financial award application deadline: 6/1; financial award applicants required to submit FAFSA. *Unit head:* Dr. Paul Mack, Dean, 508-831-4665, Fax: 508-831-4665, E-mail: biz@wpi.edu. *Application contact:* Eileen Dagostino, Recruiting Operations Coordinator, 508-831-4665, Fax: 508-831-5720, E-mail: edag@wpi.edu.
Website: http://www.wpi.edu/academics/business/about.html.

Worcester State University, Graduate Studies, Program in Management, Worcester, MA 01602-2597. Offers accounting (MS); managerial leadership (MS). Part-time and evening/weekend programs available. *Faculty:* 4 full-time (3 women), 3 part-time/adjunct (0 women). *Students:* 6 full-time (4 women), 29 part-time (15 women); includes 12 minority (4 Black or African American, non-Hispanic/Latino; 3 Asian, non-Hispanic/Latino; 4 Hispanic/Latino; 1 Two or more races, non-Hispanic/Latino), 4 international. Average age 31. 30 applicants, 60% accepted, 7 enrolled. In 2013, 6 master's awarded. *Degree requirements:* For master's, comprehensive exam (for some programs), thesis optional. *Entrance requirements:* For master's, GMAT. Additional exam requirements/recommendations for international students: Required—TOEFL (minimum score 500 paper-based; 61 iBT). *Application deadline:* For fall admission, 6/15 for domestic and international students; for spring admission, 4/1 for domestic and international students. Applications are processed on a rolling basis. Application fee: $40. Electronic applications accepted. *Expenses: Tuition, area resident:* Part-time $150 per credit. Tuition, state resident: part-time $150 per credit. Tuition, nonresident: part-time $150 per credit. *Required fees:* $114.50 per credit. *Financial support:* In 2013–14, 2 students received support, including 2 research assistantships with full tuition reimbursements available (averaging $4,800 per year); career-related internships or fieldwork, scholarships/grants, and unspecified assistantships also available. Financial award application deadline: 3/1; financial award applicants required to submit FAFSA. *Unit head:* Dr. Rodney Oudan, Coordinator, 508-929-8751, Fax: 508-929-8048, E-mail: roudan@worcester.edu. *Application contact:* Sara Grady, Assistant Dean of Continuing Education, 508-929-8787, Fax: 508-929-8100, E-mail: sara.grady@worcester.edu.

Wright State University, School of Graduate Studies, Raj Soin College of Business, Program in Business Administration, Dayton, OH 45435. Offers MBA.

Xavier University, Williams College of Business, Master of Business Administration Program, Cincinnati, OH 45207-3221. Offers business administration (Exec MBA, MBA); business intelligence (MBA); finance (MBA); health industry (MBA); international business (MBA); marketing (MBA); values-based leadership (MBA); MBA/MHSA; MSN/MBA. *Accreditation:* AACSB. Part-time and evening/weekend programs available. *Faculty:* 39 full-time (17 women), 12 part-time/adjunct (2 women). *Students:* 163 full-time (47 women), 483 part-time (162 women); includes 91 minority (28 Black or African American, non-Hispanic/Latino; 3 American Indian or Alaska Native, non-Hispanic/Latino; 42 Asian, non-Hispanic/Latino; 14 Hispanic/Latino; 4 Two or more races, non-Hispanic/Latino), 33 international. Average age 30. 190 applicants, 86% accepted, 110 enrolled. In 2013, 319 master's awarded. *Degree requirements:* For master's, capstone course. *Entrance requirements:* For master's, GMAT or GRE. Additional exam requirements/recommendations for international students: Required—TOEFL (minimum score 550 paper-based; 79 iBT). *Application deadline:* For fall admission, 8/1 priority date for domestic students, 5/1 for international students; for spring admission, 12/1 priority date for domestic students, 9/1 for international students. Applications are processed on a rolling basis. Application fee: $0. Electronic applications accepted. *Expenses:* Contact institution. *Financial support:* In 2013–14, 115 students received support. Scholarships/grants, tuition waivers (partial), and unspecified assistantships available. Financial award application deadline: 3/1; financial award applicants required to submit FAFSA. *Unit head:* Jennifer Bush, Assistant Dean of Graduate Programs, Williams College of Business, 513-745-3527, Fax: 513-745-2929, E-mail: bush@xavier.edu. *Application contact:* Lauren Parcell, MBA Advisor, 513-745-1014, Fax: 513-745-2929, E-mail: parcelll@xavier.edu.
Website: http://www.xavier.edu/williams/mba/.

Yale University, Yale School of Management and Graduate School of Arts and Sciences, Doctoral Program in Management, New Haven, CT 06520. Offers accounting (PhD); financial economics (PhD); marketing (PhD); organizations and management (PhD). *Accreditation:* AACSB. *Degree requirements:* For doctorate, comprehensive exam, thesis/dissertation. *Entrance requirements:* For doctorate, GMAT or GRE General Test. Additional exam requirements/recommendations for international students: Required—TOEFL or IELTS. Electronic applications accepted. *Expenses:* Contact institution. *Faculty research:* Pricing of options and futures, term structure of interest rates, use of accounting numbers in debt contracts, product differentiation, e-commerce and marketing, behavioral finance.

Yale University, Yale School of Management, Program in Business Administration, New Haven, CT 06520. Offers MBA, MBA/JD, MBA/M Arch, MBA/M Div, MBA/MA, MBA/MEM, MBA/MF, MBA/MFA, MBA/MPH, MBA/PhD, MD/MBA. *Accreditation:* AACSB. Terminal master's awarded for partial completion of doctoral program. *Degree requirements:* For master's, international experience. *Entrance requirements:* For master's, GMAT or GRE. Additional exam requirements/recommendations for international students: Required—TOEFL, PTE, or IELTS. Electronic applications accepted. *Expenses:* Contact institution. *Faculty research:* Finance, strategy, marketing, leadership, operations.

York College of Pennsylvania, Graham School of Business, York, PA 17405-7199. Offers continuous improvement (MBA); financial management (MBA); health care management (MBA); management (MBA); marketing (MBA); self-designed focus (MBA). *Accreditation:* ACBSP. Part-time and evening/weekend programs available. *Faculty:* 13 full-time (3 women), 2 part-time/adjunct (0 women). *Students:* 6 full-time (all women), 109 part-time (40 women); includes 8 minority (2 Black or African American, non-Hispanic/Latino; 1 Asian, non-Hispanic/Latino; 1 Hispanic/Latino; 4 Two or more races, non-Hispanic/Latino), 3 international. Average age 30. 62 applicants, 63% accepted, 23 enrolled. In 2013, 24 master's awarded. *Entrance requirements:* For master's, GMAT. Additional exam requirements/recommendations for international students: Required—TOEFL (minimum score 530 paper-based; 72 iBT). *Application deadline:* For fall admission, 7/15 priority date for domestic students; for spring admission, 12/15 priority date for domestic students. Applications are processed on a rolling basis. Application fee: $50. Electronic applications accepted. *Expenses: Tuition:* Full-time $12,870; part-time $715 per credit. *Required fees:* $1660; $360 per semester. Tuition and fees vary according to degree level. *Financial support:* In 2013–14, 4 students received support. Scholarships/grants available. Financial award application deadline: 4/15; financial award applicants required to submit FAFSA. *Unit head:* Dr. David Greisler, MBA Director, 717-815-6410, Fax: 717-600-3999, E-mail: dgreisle@ycp.edu. *Application contact:* Brenda Adams, Assistant Director, MBA Program, 717-815-1749, Fax: 717-600-3999, E-mail: badams@ycp.edu.
Website: http://www.ycp.edu/mba.

York University, Faculty of Graduate Studies, Schulich School of Business, Toronto, ON M3J 1P3, Canada. Offers accounting (M Acc); administration (PhD); business (MBA); business analytics (MBA); finance (MF); international business (IMBA); MBA/JD; MBA/MA; MBA/MFA. Part-time and evening/weekend programs available. *Students:*

683 full-time (255 women), 407 part-time (125 women). Average age 29. 1,498 applicants, 30% accepted, 409 enrolled. In 2013, 587 master's, 96 doctorates awarded. *Median time to degree:* Of those who began their doctoral program in fall 2005, 55% received their degree in 8 years or less. *Degree requirements:* For master's, advanced proficiency in a second language, work term (IMBA); for doctorate, comprehensive exam, thesis/dissertation. *Entrance requirements:* For master's, GMAT or GRE, minimum GPA of 3.0 (3.3 for MF, MBA in business analytics, and IMBA); for doctorate, GMAT or GRE, minimum GPA of 3.3. Additional exam requirements/recommendations for international students: Required—TOEFL (minimum score 600 paper-based; 100 iBT), IELTS (minimum score 7), York English Language Test (minimum score 1); PearsonVUE (minimum score 64). *Application deadline:* For fall admission, 4/30 for domestic students, 2/28 for international students; for winter admission, 9/1 for domestic and international students. Applications are processed on a rolling basis. Application fee: $150. Electronic applications accepted. *Financial support:* In 2013–14, 800 students received support, including fellowships (averaging $5,000 per year), research assistantships (averaging $3,000 per year), teaching assistantships (averaging $7,000 per year); career-related internships or fieldwork, scholarships/grants, and bursaries (for part-time students) also available. Financial award application deadline: 2/1. *Faculty research:* Accounting, finance, marketing, operations management and information systems, organizational studies, strategic management. *Unit head:* Dezso Horvath, Dean, 416-736-5070, E-mail: dhorvath@schulich.yorku.ca. *Application contact:* Graduate Admissions, 416-736-5060, Fax: 416-650-8174, E-mail: admissions@schulich.yorku.ca.
Website: http://www.schulich.yorku.ca.

Youngstown State University, Graduate School, Williamson College of Business Administration, Youngstown, OH 44555-0001. Offers MBA, Certificate. *Accreditation:* AACSB. Part-time and evening/weekend programs available. *Degree requirements:* For master's, thesis optional. *Entrance requirements:* For master's, GMAT, minimum GPA of 2.7. Additional exam requirements/recommendations for international students: Required—TOEFL. *Faculty research:* Taxation and compliance, business ethics, operations management, organizational behavior, gender issues.

ADELPHI UNIVERSITY
Robert B. Willumstad School of Business

Programs of Study

Adelphi University's Robert B. Willumstad School of Business creates managers, leaders, and entrepreneurs who can flourish amid unprecedented change. The Willumstad School's philosophy is that the best business leaders are those who enjoy intellectual challenge, have a deep appreciation of the theoretical and the practical, understand today's realities and tomorrow's possibilities, and see the link between the skills they learn and the character they display.

Adelphi's M.B.A. program requires a minimum of 33 and a maximum of 66 credits, accommodating students with varied academic backgrounds. It meets state, regional, and national accreditation standards and serves middle-level professionals seeking advancement in management careers. The curriculum integrates contemporary management issues and business fundamentals, enabling students to perform with distinction in the global environment. Its mission is to produce intellectually well-rounded, effective communicators who are aware of societal issues and responsibilities, and have a thorough understanding of the legal, environmental, technological, and social issues that affect an organization's operation. Candidates are required to fulfill or waive graduate prerequisites in financial accounting, computer applications, and mathematics for managers.

The curriculum begins with a 24-credit foundation core consisting of studies in the legal and ethical environment, macroeconomics, microeconomics, corporate finance, management theory, marketing management, management information systems, and statistical methods. The 21-credit advanced core includes accounting for managerial analysis, entrepreneurship/intrapreneurship, communication and negotiations, building shareholder value, leadership and innovation, technology management, and total quality management. Specializations are available in accounting, finance, health services administration, human resources management, management information systems, marketing, and sport management.

Students with four years' managerial experience may elect the G.O.A.L. M.B.A. program. This accelerated program requires 14 courses; students take two courses per term over seven eight-week terms. Courses are held on Saturdays only. Post-master's certificates are available in accounting, finance, and human resource management.

Most graduate students in the Willumstad School of Business attend part time and are working full time. Qualified students may also select the fast-track G.O.A.L. M.B.A. program option.

Research Facilities

The University's primary research holdings are at Swirbul Library and include 603,000 volumes (including bound periodicals and government publications); 786,000 items in microformats; 35,000 audiovisual items; and online access to more than 80,000 e-book titles, 76,000 electronic journal titles, and 265 research databases.

Financial Aid

Financial aid counseling is available. Students may qualify for federal and state aid programs, scholarships, and fellowship programs, including a limited number of graduate assistantships.

Value

Earning an Adelphi degree means joining a growing network of more than 90,000 alumni. For the eighth straight year, Adelphi was designated a Best Buy by the *Fiske Guide to Colleges*, one of only twenty private universities nationwide to earn that distinction. *The Princeton Review* also named Adelphi a Best College in the Northeast

and *Forbes* magazine named Adelphi a Top College. According to payscale.com's 2013 College Education ROI rankings, Adelphi ranks in the top 15 percent of colleges and universities nationwide for return on investment. The numbers speak for themselves—91 percent of Adelphi undergraduates receive financial aid or scholarships.

Cost of Study

The 2014–15 tuition rate is $1,055 per credit hour. University fees range from about $330 to $575 per semester. Students should also plan for expenditures associated with books, travel, and personal items.

Living and Housing Costs

The University assists single and married students in finding suitable accommodations whenever possible. The cost of living depends on the location and number of rooms rented.

Student Group

The Willumstad School's 375 graduate students form a diverse and vibrant community. They come from across the United States and 53 percent come from other countries. Undergraduate majors range from anthropology and economics to nursing and fine arts, and students' professional backgrounds range from bank officers and senior accountants to government officials and entrepreneurs. There are 121 part-time students. Students' average age is 28, and 52 percent are women. Guest speakers, internship opportunities, and the Distinguished Executive Lecture Series further enhance the learning environment. Professional clubs and organizations provide forums to exchange ideas. The Willumstad School has been granted a charter for the Beta Xi chapter of Delta Mu Delta, one of the oldest national honor societies in business administration. Delta Mu Delta is a member of the Association of College Honor Societies.

Location

Located in historic Garden City, New York, just 23 miles from Manhattan, where students can take advantage of numerous cultural and internship opportunities, Adelphi's 75-acre suburban campus is known for the beauty of its landscape and architecture. The campus is a short walk from the Long Island Rail Road and convenient to New York's major airports and several major highways. Off-campus centers are located in Manhattan, the Hudson Valley, and Suffolk County. Students enjoy the benefits of being close to the financial, medical, and technological centers and cultural and sporting facilities of Manhattan and Long Island. The campus is close to fine restaurants and shopping, and only 15 miles from Long Island's beautiful beaches.

The University

Founded in 1896, Adelphi is a fully accredited, private university with nearly 8,000 undergraduate, graduate, and returning-adult students in the arts and sciences, business, clinical psychology, education, nursing, and social work. Students come from 40 states and 45 countries.

Applying

Applicants must have a bachelor's degree from an accredited college or university and provide official academic transcripts, an essay, GMAT scores, and two letters of recommendation from academic or professional sources. Additional requirements for international students may be found online at admissions.adelphi.edu/international.

Adelphi University

The Robert B. Willumstad School of Business accepts applicants on a rolling basis. The application deadlines for international students are May 1 for the fall semester and November 1 for the spring semester.

Correspondence and Information

Adelphi University
One South Avenue
Garden City, New York 11530
United States
800-ADELPHI (toll-free)
business.adelphi.edu

The Robert B. Willumstad School of Business is focused on developing ethical, effective leaders in the field.

THE FACULTY AND THEIR RESEARCH

There are 42 full-time faculty members in the Robert B. Willumstad School of Business, all with advanced degrees. The faculty is known for its teaching excellence. Over the past few years, the Willumstad School has hired a number of new faculty members with specialties in management, marketing, and decision sciences; accounting and law; and finance and economics. Students should visit business.adelphi.edu/our-faculty for complete faculty information.

Adelphi's professors are industry leaders themselves and the Willumstad School of Business classroom experience is only the beginning.

FASHION INSTITUTE OF TECHNOLOGY

State University of New York

M.P.S. in Global Fashion Management

Programs of Study

The Fashion Institute of Technology (FIT), a State University of New York (SUNY) college of art and design, business, and technology, is home to a mix of innovative achievers, creative thinkers, and industry pioneers. FIT fosters interdisciplinary initiatives, advances research, and provides access to an international network of professionals. With a reputation for excellence, FIT offers its diverse student body access to world-class faculty, dynamic and relevant curricula, and a superior education at an affordable cost. It offers seven programs of graduate study. The programs in Art Market: Principles and Practices; Exhibition Design; Fashion and Textile Studies: History, Theory, Museum Practice; and Sustainable Interior Environments lead to the Master of Arts (M.A.) degree. The Illustration program leads to the Master of Fine Arts (M.F.A.) degree. The Master of Professional Studies (M.P.S.) degree programs are Cosmetics and Fragrance Marketing and Management, and Global Fashion Management.

Global Fashion Management is a 36-credit, full-time Master of Professional Studies program offered in collaboration with Hong Kong Polytechnic University in Hong Kong and the Institut Français de la Mode in Paris. The program is designed to prepare current apparel industry managers for senior- and executive-level positions. The course of study is completed in three semesters and brings students from all three institutions together for intensive seminars held at each of the three participating institutions, thus providing a unique international experience for those involved. The curriculum includes courses in production and supply chain management, global marketing and fashion brand management, international retail management, business policy, international culture and business, finance, politics, and world trade. Students devote a year to research in preparation for delivering a capstone project that is judged by industry executives.

Research Facilities

The School of Graduate Studies is primarily located in the campus's Shirley Goodman Resource Center, which also houses the Gladys Marcus Library and The Museum at FIT. School of Graduate Studies facilities include conference rooms; a fully equipped conservation laboratory; a multipurpose laboratory for conservation projects and the dressing of mannequins; storage facilities for costume and textile materials; a graduate student lounge with computer and printer access; a graduate student library reading room with computers, reference materials, and copies of past classes' qualifying and thesis papers; specialized wireless classrooms; traditional and digital illustration studios; and classrooms equipped with model stands, easels, and drafting tables.

The Gladys Marcus Library houses more than 300,000 volumes of print, nonprint, and digital resources. Specialized holdings include industry reference materials, manufacturers' catalogues, original fashion sketches and scrapbooks, photographs, portfolios of plates, and sample books. The FIT Digital Library provides access to over 90 searchable online databases.

The Museum at FIT houses one of the world's most important collections of clothing and textiles and is the only museum in New York City dedicated to the art of fashion. The permanent collection encompasses more than 50,000 garments and accessories dating from the eighteenth century to the present, with particular strength in twentieth-century fashion, as well as 30,000 textiles and 100,000 textile swatches. Each year, nearly 100,000 visitors are drawn to the museum's award-winning exhibitions and public programs.

Financial Aid

FIT directly administers its institutional grants, scholarships, and loans. Federal funding administered by the college may include Federal Perkins Loans, federally subsidized and unsubsidized Direct Loans for students, Grad PLUS loans, and the Federal Work-Study Program. Priority for institutionally administered funds is given to students enrolled and designated as full-time.

Cost of Study

Tuition for New York State residents is $5,185 per semester, or $432 per credit. Out-of-state residents' tuition is $10,095 per semester, or $841 per credit. Tuition and fees are subject to change at the discretion of FIT's Board of Trustees. Additional expenses—for class materials, textbooks, and travel—may apply and vary per program.

Living and Housing Costs

On-campus housing is available to graduate students. Traditional residence hall accommodations (including meal plan) cost from $6,485 to $6,688 per semester. Apartment-style housing options (not including meal plan) cost from $6,060 to $10,095 per semester.

Student Group

Enrollment in the School of Graduate Studies is approximately 200 students per academic year, allowing considerable individualized advisement. Students come to FIT from throughout the country and around the world.

Student Outcomes

Students in the Global Fashion Management program maintain full-time employment in the industry while working toward their degree, which provides the basis for advancement to positions of upper-level managerial responsibility.

Location

FIT is located in Manhattan's Chelsea neighborhood, at the heart of the advertising, visual arts, marketing, fashion, business, design, and communications industries. Students are connected to New York City and gain unparalleled exposure to their field through guest lectures, field trips, internships, and sponsored competitions. The location provides access to major museums, galleries, and auction houses as well as dining, entertainment, and shopping options. The campus is near subway, bus, and commuter rail lines.

Applying

Applicants to all School of Graduate Studies programs must hold a baccalaureate degree in an appropriate major from a college or university, with a cumulative GPA of 3.0 or higher. International students from non-English-speaking countries are required to submit minimum TOEFL scores of 550 on the written test, 213 on the computer test, or 80 on the Internet test. Students applying to

Fashion Institute of Technology

the Global Fashion Management program must submit GRE scores. Each major has additional, specialized prerequisites for admission; for detailed information, students should visit the School of Graduate Studies on FIT's website.

Domestic and international students use the same application when seeking admission. The deadline for completed applications with transcripts and supplemental materials is February 15 for the Global Fashion Management program. After the deadline date, applicants are considered on a rolling admissions basis. Candidates may apply online at fitnyc.edu/gradstudies.

Correspondence and Information

School of Graduate Studies
Shirley Goodman Resource Center, Room E315
Fashion Institute of Technology
227 West 27 Street
New York, New York 10001-5992
Phone: 212-217-4300
Fax: 212-217-4301
E-mail: gradinfo@fitnyc.edu
Website: http://www.fitnyc.edu/gradstudies
          http://www.fitnyc.edu/GFM

THE FACULTY
The faculty members listed below constitute a partial listing. Guest lecturers are not included.

Pamela Ellsworth, Associate Chairperson; M.P.S., Fashion Institute of Technology.
Brooke Carlson, Sc.D., New Haven.
Praveen K. Chaudhry, Ph.D., Pennsylvania.
Robin Lewis, B.S., Northwestern.
Tom Nastos, B.S., Fashion Institute of Technology.
Jeanette Nostra, B.A., Goddard.
Judith Ryba, Ph.D., Paris Dauphine (France).

MANHATTANVILLE COLLEGE
School of Business

Programs of Study

The Manhattanville School of Business (MSB) offers six industry-driven and newly designed Master of Science degrees in business leadership, finance, human resource management and organizational effectiveness, international management, marketing communications management, and sport business management, along with advanced certificates in business leadership, finance, human resources, and marketing communications. Master's degree programs are offered in an accelerated format, and can be completed in as little as 18 months of part-time study. Advanced certificates can be completed in six months and each course may be applied toward its respective graduate degree. In addition, MSB offers three accelerated Bachelor of Science degrees (including adult retry) in behavioral studies, communications, and organization management; and executive and professional education. Students can upgrade their skills and earn a professional credential in as little as 1½ years.

There are also dual-degree options, in which students can work toward their master's degree while completing their undergraduate studies, offering a savings of both time and money.

The School of Business is in the process of launching an executive leadership and development center for women as well as a certificate program in nonprofit leadership.

All faculty members within the School of Business are experienced in their respective fields and bring their business perspective into the classroom, an important distinction when compared to other graduate business programs. Students learn from these leading business professionals in small and highly interactive classes. The School of Business also hosts professional development events, career fairs, and industry panels to keep students and alumni up-to-date on the latest developments and practices in their professions. Classes are scheduled at night or on weekends to accommodate busy lifestyles and working professionals. With industry-driven content, and an extensive faculty and alumni network, the School of Business offers students the skills, best practices, and real-world knowledge necessary to excel in their chosen industry.

Manhattanville College has received specialized accreditation for its business programs through the International Assembly of Collegiate Business Education (IACBE), located in Olathe, Kansas. The following business programs are accredited by the IACBE:

- Business Leadership
- Human Resource Management and Organizational Effectiveness
- International Management
- Marketing Communication Management
- Sport Business Management

Research Facilities

The Manhattanville College Library offers impressive collections and outstanding services to assist students with their research needs. The library provides a wide range of subscription databases, electronic journals, and electronic books along with over 200,000 books, over 100 current periodical subscriptions, an outstanding media collection, and a scholarly rare book collection.

The library website serves the college community with extensive research tools. The library catalog provides access to the library's holdings, patron information, and the holdings of the other academic libraries in Westchester County. The library subscribes to 143 databases linking to over 45,000 electronic journals, 12,000+ electronic books, and a large selection of periodical indexes in a broad range of disciplines. All of these resources are available off-campus to members of the Manhattanville community. The library supports teaching and learning by providing 24/7 online access to course reserve materials, ranging from text assignments to audio and video files. The library offers alumni and community memberships. Members enjoy special borrowing privileges and hours of access.

Reference service is available both in person during the day and evening hours, and online at anytime from anywhere in the world. Students and faculty members may also text questions to a librarian. A library mobile app delivers services to users. Librarians work with each student to integrate traditional print materials and the newest electronic forms of information into their research. Manhattanville graduates are capable searchers and users of these resources.

Manhattanville College supports instruction in French, Spanish, Russian, Italian, German, Chinese, Japanese, Hindi, Marathi, modern Hebrew, and English as a second language. The College provides tutoring in every academic subject, customized services for students with special needs, audiovisual facilities, and a leading Information Literacy instruction program. The library building is open 24 hours a day, 7 days a week through most of the fall and spring semesters, and it offers computer labs, quiet study areas, group-study rooms, and a café where students and faculty members can meet informally.

Financial Aid

Federal Family Educational Loans are available to graduate students. A deferred payment plan is also available. For further information, prospective students should contact the Office of Financial Aid, Reid Hall, Purchase, New York 10577; phone: 914-323-5357.

Cost of Study

Tuition is $895 per credit for 2014–15. There is a semester registration fee of $60.

Living and Housing Costs

Most School of Business graduate students live and work in their own homes and communities throughout Westchester and the surrounding counties. For campus housing information, students can contact Residence Life at 914-323-5217.

Student Group

There are approximately 250 students in the School of Business at Manhattanville College. Most are making career changes. Their average age is 30.

Location

Manhattanville's campus, 100 acres of suburban countryside, is located in New York's Westchester County, just minutes from White Plains to the west and Greenwich, Connecticut, to the east. It is 30 minutes from Manhattan. The campus is accessible via public transportation.

Manhattanville College

The College

Manhattanville College is a coeducational, independent liberal arts college whose mission is to educate ethically and socially responsible leaders for the global community. Founded in 1841, the College has 1,600 undergraduate students and about 1,200 graduate students. Of the graduate students, approximately 300 are enrolled in the School of Business. Manhattanville offers bachelor's, master's, and doctoral degrees in more than fifty academic concentrations in the arts and sciences. Its curriculum nurtures intellectual curiosity and independent thinking.

Applying

Applications are processed on a rolling basis. Application requirements include submission of a completed application form, a fee of $75, two letters of recommendation, a personal statement, and official transcripts of all previous college work (undergraduate). Study as a nonmatriculated student is permitted.

Correspondence and Information

Elizabeth (Liz) Brosseau
Enrollment Services Coordinator
School of Business
Manhattanville College
2900 Purchase Street
Purchase, New York 10577
Phone: 914-323-5300
Fax: 914-694-3488
E-mail: business@mville.edu
Website: http://www.mville.edu/business

SCHOOL OF BUSINESS ADMINISTRATION

Anthony Davidson, Dean.
Steve Albanese, Assistant Dean.
Jean Mann, Director of Marketing and Enrollment Services.
David Torromeo, Program Director, Sport Business Management.
Art Berke, Internship Advisor.
Laura Persky, Program Director, Business Leadership, Finance, Human Resource Management, International Management, and Marketing Communication Management.
Scott Walsh, Assistant Director.
David Borker, Accounting and Corporate Finance Advisor.
Bozidar Jovanovic, Investment Management Advisor.
Rhonna Goodman, Director, Certificate in Nonprofit Leadership.
Denise Cain, Assistant Director.
Ruth Diamond, Executive Assistant to the Dean.
Liz Brosseau, Enrollment Services Coordinator.

MONMOUTH UNIVERSITY
Leon Hess Business School

Programs of Study

Monmouth University is a leading private institution that helps students of all ages to increase their professional skills and enhance their intellectual development. Graduate programs are offered within six academic schools: the Leon Hess Business School (M.B.A.), the Wayne D. McMurray School of Humanities and Social Sciences (M.A., M.S.), the Marjorie K. Unterberg School of Nursing and Health Studies (M.S.N., M.S., D.N.P.), the School of Education (M.A.T., M.S.Ed.), the School of Science (M.S.), and the School of Social Work (M.S.W.).

Monmouth provides high-quality graduate, doctoral, and certificate programs in areas that are in demand in the workplace, including software engineering (M.S.), homeland security (M.S.), and physician assistant (M.S.). The University also offers a Doctor of Nursing Practice (D.N.P.) program, as well as a new program in information systems (M.S.). Monmouth's programs offer hands-on, personalized attention to improve students' leadership qualities and prepare them for career advancement, career changes, or further study. Graduate students also have opportunities to engage in scholarly research with the University's innovative faculty.

Many of Monmouth's graduate students work or intern on a full-time basis and attend classes in the evening. To provide flexibility, some programs offer courses in hybrid format, consisting of face-to-face classes interspersed with online sessions on alternate weeks. The online component is asynchronous, allowing students to participate when it is most convenient for them. The University encourages students to accelerate their program by taking summer course work and also offers an accelerated program (the accelerated M.B.A.) that allows students to complete their degree in only 12 months.

Research Facilities

The Monmouth University Library holds approximately 340,000 print and electronic monographs, 49,000 print and electronic periodicals, and 155 databases (including journals, videos, and e-books). All academic programs are amply supported by state-of-the-art computer hardware and software and classroom/laboratory facilities. The major components supporting Monmouth's academic programs include Windows, Mac OS, and Unix systems connected via an expansive wired and wireless network, which spans twenty-three buildings and encompasses more than 2,400 workstations in general and specialty labs and classrooms.

Financial Aid

Financial aid is available in the form of scholarships, assistantships, and loans. Fellowships are awarded to qualified students on the basis of undergraduate cumulative grade point average. A limited number of assistantships are available to continuing students, with preference given to those maintaining a high grade point average. To obtain federal loans, applicants must file the FAFSA form, which is available online at http://www.fafsa.ed.gov. Monmouth University participates in the Federal Direct Student Loan Program, which makes loans available to all students who file the FAFSA. Alternative loan funding sources are available to those students who might not otherwise qualify for federal funding or need additional funding above and beyond the amount that has already been provided.

Cost of Study

Tuition for study in 2014–15 is $1,004 per credit. A University fee is assessed each semester.

Living and Housing Costs

Due to Monmouth's proximity to the beach, there are ample off-campus housing opportunities that are conveniently located near the University. These accommodations are relatively inexpensive since the academic year is also the off-season for tourism. A rental listing website is maintained by the Office of Off-Campus and Commuter Services and can be found at http://www.monmouth.edu/commuter. Graduate students may also apply for University housing; these apartment-style accommodations are located in University-owned or -sponsored housing.

Student Group

Monmouth University enrolls approximately 6,300 students, roughly 1,800 of whom are enrolled in the Graduate School. The diverse student body includes international students representing thirty-six different countries.

Location

Monmouth University is located less than a mile from the Atlantic Ocean on a 159-acre campus in the safe, suburban town of West Long Branch, New Jersey. The campus is approximately an hour from New York City and Philadelphia. The University's proximity to high-technology firms, financial institutions, and a thriving business-industrial sector provides Monmouth students and graduates with a wide variety of employment possibilities. The surrounding area also has numerous activities, theaters, restaurants, and cultural events.

The University

Monmouth University provides a learning environment that enables students to pursue their educational goals and realize their full potential as leaders. Small classes allow for individual attention and student-faculty dialogue, and the Center for Student Success offers a hub of academic and career counseling services.

At Monmouth, students enjoy one of the most beautiful campuses in New Jersey. The centerpiece of campus is Woodrow Wilson Hall, a National Historic Landmark, which was used as Daddy Warbucks' mansion in the film *Annie*. Other unique buildings include the Jules L. Plangere Jr. Center for Communication, which provides state-of-the-art studios and editing facilities, and Bey Hall, which houses the financial markets lab.

Throughout the year, students and employees cheer on Monmouth's Division I athletic teams. The school fields 21 teams for men and women. The University's basketball and track and field teams compete in the 153,200-square-foot Multipurpose Activity Center (MAC), which features a 4,100-seat arena with premium suites, as well as a fitness center and a 200-meter, six-lane indoor track.

Applying

An application for graduate admission includes a completed application form with fee, official transcripts of the undergraduate record, score reports from the appropriate entrance examination, and transcripts of any graduate work done elsewhere. Students should contact the Office of Graduate Admission for details, or visit http://www.monmouth.edu/gradbook. International students must also provide evidence of English proficiency.

The application deadlines are July 15 for the fall term, December 1 for the spring term, and May 1 for the summer sessions. (Please note that some programs have different application deadlines and only accept students once per year.) An initial review of the complete application for admission is conducted by the Office of Graduate Admission; the file is then forwarded to the faculty director of the program for an admission decision. All correspondence should be directed to the Office of Graduate Admission.

Correspondence and Information

Office of Graduate Admission
Monmouth University
400 Cedar Avenue
West Long Branch, New Jersey 07764-1898
United States
Phone: 732-571-3452
Fax: 732-263-5123
E-mail: gradadm@monmouth.edu
Website: http://www.monmouth.edu/gradbook

THE FACULTY AND THEIR RESEARCH AREAS

Faculty members at Monmouth University are committed teachers with extensive academic and professional experience who have established themselves as important scholars in their respective fields. Their work has been published in a variety of major journals, the proceedings of national and international conferences, books, and other outlets.

Students at Monmouth learn in small classes that promote close interaction with this knowledgeable faculty. Each faculty member strives to provide students with the foundation to succeed. Teaching and learning are not just confined to the classroom; professors and students often continue their discussions in the hallways, faculty offices, and dining facilities on campus.

NORTH CAROLINA STATE UNIVERSITY

Jenkins Graduate School of Management
Program in Business Administration

Programs of Study

The guiding principle of the North Carolina State Jenkins MBA program is *We think and do*. The School works hand-in-hand with the University and business communities to prepare professionals to effectively lead people and organizations in a technology-rich, global marketplace.

The MBA program provides full-time, part-time for working professionals, and online options.

Rankings organizations have taken note of NC State's innovative approach to business education, which emphasizes applied learning opportunities in addition to top-notch academics. The program is ranked as high as 20 among part-time programs, 36 among online programs, and 65 among full-time M.B.A. programs nationwide.

Several features set the program apart:

Innovative—Building upon the expertise of noted faculty and extensive partnerships with industry, the program delivers a highly experiential academic program focused on issues and challenges faced by technology-drive businesses today. In some courses, students work alongside students from NC State's highly regarded graduate programs in computer science, engineering, design, and the sciences.

Real projects and partnerships—Through partnerships with other disciplines on NC State's campus and working on project teams with companies, students put learning into practice and gain valuable real-world experience.

Flexibility—The Professional MBA offers the option of choosing an accelerated or flexible program, which can take as little as 21 months or up to six years.

Students begin the program by taking core courses. Students in the full-time program may then choose from six concentrations: biosciences management, entrepreneurship, financial management, marketing management, innovation management, or supply chain management. Students in the Professional MBA program may choose an optional area of emphasis. NC State also offers a number of dual-degree programs: Doctorate of Veterinary Medicine/MBA, Master of Biomanufacturing/MBA, Juris Doctor at Campbell University/MBA, Master of Accounting/MBA, Master of Industrial Engineering/MBA, Master of Global Innovation Management/MBA, and Master of Microbial Biotechnology/MBA.

Biosciences management is an exciting area of specialization at NC State. One of today's fastest-growing business sectors, life sciences offers new opportunities for those who can provide managerial leadership in a technology-focused environment. This concentration was designed and is taught by faculty members with extensive experience in biotechnology and pharmaceuticals, working closely with industry leaders located in the nearby Research Triangle Park.

The **entrepreneurship concentration** teaches students how to commercialize technologies, using real case studies. Supported by the National Science Foundation, the Kenan Institute, and several other organizations, graduate students and faculty members work closely in interdisciplinary teams to identify, evaluate, and commercialize promising technologies. Students gain evaluation skills for commercializing new technologies, along with an understanding of what it takes to start and run a high-technology business. Students also interact with business experts and entrepreneurs from outside the University.

Research Facilities

The NC State Jenkins MBA program is part of the Poole College of Management, headquartered in Nelson Hall, featuring state-of-the-art with tiered seating and multimedia facilities. There is also a campus in Research Triangle Park, which is convenient to many working professionals.

Students have access to one of the most innovative libraries in the world, the James B. Hunt, Jr. library located on NC State's Centennial Campus. NC State is also home to D. H. Hill Library, which is located near the center of the campus and offers access to millions of volumes of books and journals and an extensive and growing collection of CD-ROM and electronic databases. Graduate students also have borrowing privileges at Duke University, North Carolina Central University, and the University of North Carolina at Chapel Hill.

Financial Aid

Graduate assistantships and scholarships are available to full-time students through the MBA program. Grants and loan programs are available through the Graduate School and the University's Financial Aid Office.

Cost of Study

The estimated total tuition for full-time MBA students beginning in the 2014–15 school year is approximately $42,535 for North Carolina residents and $70,881 for nonresidents. More detailed tuition and financial aid information can be found online at mba.ncsu.edu.

Graduate assistantships are available to full-time students. Graduate assistantships cover full or partial tuition, health insurance, and a monthly stipend. Grants and loan programs are available through the Graduate School and the University's Financial Aid Office.

Living and Housing Costs

On-campus dormitory facilities are provided for unmarried graduate students. The 2014–15 rates for double-occupancy rooms start at $2,740 per semester. Accommodations in Wolf Village, the newest residence hall for graduate students, cost $2,995 per semester. Apartments for married students in King Village rent for as low as $600 per month.

Student Group

NC State Jenkins MBA students graduate ready to hit the ground running, and recruiters have consistently given the program high marks, ranking NC State grads among the best nationwide. The average full-time MBA student has four years of work experience. The age range of students is between 22 and 45. Women comprise approximately 35 percent of each entering class; members of minority groups, approximately 10 percent; and international students, 30 percent.

Student Outcomes

The NC State Jenkins MBA Career Management team takes a customized approach, providing education, resources, and coaching centered around leadership development, job search, internal career advancement, and entrepreneurship. The program's team of career

coaches and specialists works one-on-one with each MBA student to build an Individualized Career Management Plan (ICM). Creating this plan includes assessing strengths and interests, building a brand and developing marketing documents, identifying target industries and employers or entrepreneurial endeavors, networking with advocates, interviewing, and negotiating.

Recent employers include SAS Institute, IBM, Progress Energy, Red Hat, John Deere, GlaxoSmithKline, and Cisco Systems. In 2014, 88 percent of full-time MBA graduates had at least one job offer at the time of graduation. The 2013 graduates of the Professional MBA program realized a greater than 30 percent average salary increase over the duration of the program.

Location

The NC State Jenkins MBA offers the best of all worlds: a top MBA program, a nationally ranked research university, and one of the country's best places to live and work. A top five emerging tech hub internationally, Raleigh is part of the Research Triangle, a world-renowned center of research, industry, technology, culture, and education. Both are home to over 170 tech startups and established powerhouses that want to hire Jenkins talent.

The University

NC State was founded in 1889 as a land-grant institution. Within 100 years, it became one of the nation's leading research universities. Located in the Research Triangle, a world-renowned center of research, industry, technology, and education, the College of Management is housed on the 623-acre main campus of NC State, which lies just west of downtown Raleigh, the state capital. NC State comprises eleven colleges and schools serving a total student population of more than 30,000. More than 5,000 of those students are in graduate programs.

Applying

Admission to the MBA program is competitive. Applicants need to demonstrate the following personal accomplishments and attributes:

1. Strong intellectual performance and academic promise, evidenced by previous undergraduate and graduate work as well as GMAT or GRE scores.

2. An employment history demonstrating management potential.

3. Leadership skills, maturity, creativity, initiative, and teamwork orientation.

4. A desire and willingness to learn about technology and the management challenges it creates.

MBA students must have a baccalaureate degree from an accredited college or university. Admissions decisions are based on previous academic performance, GMAT or GRE scores (those with graduate degrees should contact the MBA office for information on waivers), essays, letters of reference, and previous work experience. Applicants whose native language is other than English, regardless of citizenship, must also submit TOEFL or IELTS scores (professional program applicants may qualify for a waiver and should inquire with the MBA office). Interviews are required for applicants for both the full-time and professional MBA programs.

Correspondence and Information

Ms. Jen Arthur, Director
MBA Program
North Carolina State University
Box 8114
Raleigh, North Carolina 27695
United States
Phone: 919-515-5584
Fax: 919-515-5073
E-mail: mba@ncsu.edu
Website: http://www.mba.ncsu.edu

THE FACULTY AND THEIR RESEARCH

The NC State Jenkins MBA program is "not your grandfather's MBA." The program has built a faculty rich in technology-related business expertise, management experience, and practical research. Professors have a passion for teaching and a commitment to working closely with industry to solve real-world problems. Faculty members excel in both traditional scholarly pursuits and practical, corporate-sponsored research. The program is home to a number of extensively published scholars, and editors and editorial board members of prestigious research journals.

Since the day of its creation—March 7, 1887—NC State has been moving forward.

NC State Jenkins MBA students during fall 2013 orientation.

UNIVERSITY OF CALIFORNIA, LOS ANGELES

UCLA Anderson School of Management
Master of Business Administration Program

UCLAAnderson
SCHOOL *of* MANAGEMENT

Programs of Study

UCLA Anderson School of Management recently implemented fundamental changes to its curriculum to better prepare M.B.A. students to succeed in the marketplace. This new curriculum focuses on four key components designed to help students quickly build the knowledge and skills necessary to realize their career goals.

First, UCLA Anderson works with students to enhance crucial leadership skills through the Leadership Foundations program. Next, the School offers a customized core curriculum that builds general management prowess across a variety of fields while also providing students with the flexibility to develop depth of expertise in their chosen area. This is used as a foundation for the third component: a set of discipline-based tracks in which students can choose to pursue advanced skills in marketing, finance, consulting, or an individually customized area. These tracks may also be complemented by industry-based specializations in fields such as technology management, real estate, entertainment, and entrepreneurship.

The final step is the capstone Applied Management Research program. This is a twenty-week experiential learning process in which students work as a team, allowing them to apply the knowledge they gained in the classroom to solve the challenges of a real-world client. This sharpens their teamwork, written, and verbal communication skills via a final report and oral presentation to the client.

Research Facilities

UCLA Anderson's Rosenfeld Library seeks to offer superior customer service to its clientele. Rosenfeld Library provides access to more than 100 specialized databases, as well as to an expanding array of electronic journals and texts supporting all areas of business and management, such as accounting, business economics, strategy and policy, finance, human resources, marketing, and organizational behavior. It also delivers robust reference, consultation, course outreach, course reserves, facilities management, document delivery, and information fluency programs. The library's digital and print collections support the UCLA Anderson curriculum in all areas of business and management and comprise 180,600 volumes, extensive serial subscriptions, 633,000 microforms, and access to more than 269,000 historical corporate reports. While the Rosenfeld Library's information sources are of particular value to the M.B.A. curriculum, Rosenfeld Library is one of ten UCLA campus libraries, all with vast resources that are also available to the M.B.A. student. In addition, UCLA students, including Anderson M.B.A. students, are part of the University of California (UC) Library system and have access to UC–wide information resources through a variety of programs ranging from licensed databases to interlibrary loan to borrowing print materials. The Rosenfeld Library also participates in an international interlibrary loan program that allows it to borrow materials M.B.A. students may need from libraries beyond the UC system.

Research programs and study centers associated with the School and its faculty include the Harold and Pauline Price Center for Entrepreneurial Studies, the Center for Global Management, the Richard S. Ziman Center for Real Estate, the UCLA Anderson Forecast, the Laurence D. and Lori W. Fink Center for Finance & Investments, and the Center for Management of Enterprise in Media, Entertainment, and Sports.

Financial Aid

Merit and donor fellowships are available. Private education loans are available for international students who do not have a U.S. cosigner. A limited number of research and teaching assistantship positions are also available.

Cost of Study

For 2014–15, program charges per academic year total $51,159 for California residents and $56,159 for nonresidents. These costs are subject to change.

Living and Housing Costs

Room and board for the 2014–15 academic year are estimated at $17,719. Books and supplies will be $3,494 (including a $2,000 laptop computer allowance.) These costs are for students living off campus in shared housing. Additional costs may include support of dependents and medical expenses. Married students should budget additional costs from personal resources as financial aid only covers the student's costs.

Student Group

UCLA Anderson has a vibrant student body with members whose extraordinary intellectual, cultural, social, and athletic energies spill out of the classroom into a plethora of nonacademic activities. The average age of the most recent entering class for the Full-Time M.B.A. program (class of 2015) is 28 and the average number of years postgraduate work experience is five years. Of this class, 33 percent of the students are female and 33 percent are international students.

Location

Los Angeles is among the world's most vibrant and exciting cities. In addition to being the entertainment capital of the world, businesses in Los Angeles create four times the gross domestic product and diversity of the Silicon Valley. The city is home to Fortune 500 companies and major industries, ranging from financial services and health care to manufacturing and aerospace. The city hosts even more small businesses, which are a significant source of U.S. economic growth. From its location in Southern California, Los Angeles serves as a gateway to both Asia and Latin America.

UCLA Anderson students enjoy access to extensive cultural and recreational opportunities with museums, sporting events, theaters, and countless other activities offered both on campus and throughout the city. Because the location is such a cultural crossroads, there are always opportunities to engage with people from various backgrounds and points of view. Students benefit from this interaction both professionally and personally, learning as they share cultural traditions with each other.

The School

UCLA Anderson's management education complex is a testament to the School's vision for superior management education. Continuing the School's reputation as a national leader in the use of technology in M.B.A. instruction, the eleven specially designed case-study rooms have power, wireless, and wired network data ports at each seat, as well as a custom teaching lectern with state-of-the-art audiovisual and instructional technologies that support, enhance, and extend the School's active learning environment.

The Rosenfeld Library houses three computer labs for M.B.A. students, one of which includes twenty-three desktop computers and two networked printers. The other two collaborative labs also provide wired and wireless network access and printing and can seat up to fifteen teams of 5 students. In addition, the Bloomberg Lab houses a suite of Bloomberg Professional terminals. The library also contains a professional audiovisual presentation facility, known as the Board Room, twenty additional collaborative pods for teamwork, and eight individual quiet study spaces.

Applying

Applicants may apply for fall 2015 admission starting August 1, 2014. More information and updates are available online at www.mba.anderson.ucla.edu.

Correspondence and Information

Alex Lawrence
Assistant Dean and Director, M.B.A. Admissions and Financial Aid
UCLA Anderson School of Management
110 Westwood Plaza, Suite B201
Los Angeles, California 90095-1481
United States
Phone: 310-825-6944
E-mail: mba.admissions@anderson.ucla.edu
Website: http://www.anderson.ucla.edu

THE FACULTY

Judy D. Olian, Dean and John E. Anderson Chair in Management, UCLA Anderson School of Management; Ph.D. (industrial relations), Wisconsin–Madison.

Accounting

David Aboody, Professor; Ph.D., Berkeley. Shlomo Benartzi, Professor and Co-Chair of the Behavioral Decision-Making Group; Ph.D., Cornell. Maria Boss, Lecturer; J.D., California, Hastings Law. Henry Friedman, Assistant Professor; Ph.D., Pennsylvania (Wharton). Gonzalo Freixes, Lecturer and Associate Dean; J.D., Loyola Law School. Jane Guerin, Continuing Lecturer; J.D., Denver. Carla Hayn, Professor; Ph.D., Michigan. John S. Hughes, Ernst and Young Chair in Accounting; Ph.D., Purdue. Gordon Klein, Lecturer; J.D., Michigan. Danny Litt, Lecturer; M.B.A., UCLA. Beatrice Michaeli, Assistant Professor; Ph.D., Columbia.

University of California, Los Angeles

Bruce Miller, Professor Emeritus; Ph.D., Stanford. Bugra Ozel, Assistant Professor; Ph.D., Columbia. Suhas Sridharan, Assistant Professor; Ph.D., Stanford. Eric Sussman, Senior Lecturer; M.B.A., Stanford. Brett Trueman, Professor and Area Chair; Ph.D., Columbia.

Decisions, Operations, and Technology Management
Reza Ahmadi, Professor; Ph.D., Texas at Austin. Christiane Barz, Assistant Professor; Dr. rer. pol., Karlsruhe (Germany). Sushil Bikhchandani, Professor and Faculty Vice-Chairman; Ph.D., Stanford. Felipe Caro, Associate Professor; Ph.D., MIT. Charles J. Corbett, Professor; Ph.D., INSEAD. Donald Erlenkotter, Professor Emeritus; Ph.D., Stanford. Robert Foster, Adjunct Professor; M.B.A., UCLA. Arthur Geoffrion, Professor Emeritus and James A. Collins Chair in Management Emeritus; Ph.D., Stanford. F. A. Hagigi, Adjunct Professor and Director, Global Health Initiatives; Ph.D., UCLA. Ariella Herman, Senior Lecturer; Ph.D., Paris. Uday S. Karmarkar, Distinguished Professor and L. A. Times Chair in Technology and Strategy; Ph.D., MIT. Elisa Long, Assistant Professor; Ph.D., Stanford. John W. Mamer, Professor and Senior Associate Dean of the EMBA Programs; Ph.D., Berkeley. Kevin McCardle, Professor; Ph.D., UCLA. Donald Morrison, Professor Emeritus; Ph.D., Stanford. William Pierskalla, Distinguished Professor Emeritus and Dean Emeritus; Ph.D., Stanford. Kumar Rajaram, Professor; Ph.D., Pennsylvania (Wharton). Guillaume Roels, Associate Professor; Ph.D., MIT. Rakesh Sarin, Distinguished Professor and Paine Chair in Management; Ph.D., UCLA. Christopher S. Tang, Distinguished Professor and Edward W. Carter Chair in Business Administration; Ph.D., Yale.

Finance
Daniel Andrei, Assistant Professor; Ph.D., Lausanne (Switzerland). Antonio Bernardo, Professor and Robert D. Beyer '83 Term Chair in Management and Area Chair; Ph.D., Stanford. Michael Brennan, Professor Emeritus; Ph.D., MIT. Bruce I. Carlin, Associate Professor; Ph.D., Duke. Mikhail Chernov, Professor; Ph.D., Penn State. Bhagwan Chowdhry, Professor; Ph.D., Chicago. William Cockrum, Adjunct Professor; M.B.A., Harvard. Andrea Eisfeldt, Professor; Ph.D., Chicago. Stuart Gabriel, Professor and Arden Realty Chair and Director of the Richard S. Ziman Center for Real Estate at UCLA; Ph.D., Berkeley. Mark J. Garmaise, Professor and Senior Associate Dean of the M.B.A. program; Ph.D., Stanford. Robert Geske, Associate Professor Emeritus; Ph.D., Berkeley. Mark Grinblatt, Professor and Japan Alumni Chair in International Finance; Ph.D., Yale. Barney Hartman-Glaser, Assistant Professor; Ph.D., Berkeley. Jason Hsu, Adjunct Professor; Ph.D., UCLA. Francis Longstaff, Professor, Allstate Chair of Insurance and Finance, and Senior Associate Dean of the Ph.D. Program; Ph.D., Chicago. Hanno Lustig, Professor and Faculty Director of the MFE Program; Ph.D., Stanford. William Mann, Assistant Professor; Ph.D., Pennsylvania (Wharton). Richard Roll, Distinguished Professor Emeritus and Joel Fried Chair in Applied Finance; Ph.D., Chicago. Eduardo Schwartz, Distinguished Professor and California Chair in Real Estate and Land Economics; Ph.D., British Columbia. Avanidhar (Subra) Subrahmanyam, Professor and Goldyne and Irwin Hearsh Chair in Money and Banking; Ph.D., UCLA. Walter Torous, Professor Emeritus; Ph.D., Pennsylvania. Ivo Welch, Distinguished Professor, J. Fred Weston Professor of Finance, and Director of Fink Center; Ph.D., Chicago.

Global Economics and Management
Antonio Bernardo, Professor and Robert D. Beyer '83 Term Chair in Management; Ph.D., Stanford. Leonardo Bursztyn, Assistant Professor; Ph.D., Harvard. Christian Dippel, Assistant Professor; Ph.D., Toronto. Sebastian Edwards, Distinguished Professor, Henry Ford II Chair in International Management, and Associate Dean of Center for Global Management; Ph.D., Chicago. Mark J. Garmaise, Professor and Senior Associate Dean of the M.B.A. program; Ph.D., Stanford. Paola Giuliano, Assistant Professor; Ph.D., Berkeley. Edward Leamer, Distinguished Professor, Chauncey J. Medberry Chair in Management and Director of the UCLA Anderson Forecast; Ph.D., Michigan. Hanno Lustig, Professor and Faculty Director of the MFE Program; Ph.D., Stanford. Alfred E. Osborne Jr., Senior Associate Dean, Harold and Pauline Price Center for Entrepreneurial Studies; Ph.D. Hans Schollhammer, Professor Emeritus; D.B.A., Indiana. Robert Spich, Senior Lecturer; Ph.D., Washington (Seattle). Victor Tabbush, Adjunct Professor Emeritus; Ph.D., UCLA. Nico Voigtlander, Assistant Professor; Ph.D., Pompeu Fabra (Spain). Romain Wacziarg, Professor and Area Chair; Ph.D., Harvard.

Management and Organizations
Corinne Bendersky, Associate Professor; Ph.D., MIT. Samuel Culbert, Professor; Ph.D., UCLA. Christopher Erickson, Professor; Ph.D., MIT. Iris Firstenberg, Adjunct Associate Professor; Ph.D., UCLA. Eric Flamholtz, Professor Emeritus; Ph.D., Michigan. Noah Goldstein, Associate Professor and Area Chair; Ph.D., Arizona State. Sanford M. Jacoby, Distinguished Professor and Howard Noble Chair of Management; Ph.D., Berkeley. Keyvan Kashkooli, Assistant Professor; Ph.D., Berkeley. Barbara S. Lawrence, Professor Emeritus; Ph.D., MIT. Robert M. McCann, Adjunct Professor; Ph.D., California, Santa Barbara. Daniel J. B. Mitchell, Professor Emeritus; Ph.D., MIT. Judy D. Olian, Dean and John E. Anderson Chair in Management; Ph.D., Wisconsin–Madison. William G. Ouchi, Distinguished Professor and Sanford and Betty Sigoloff Chair in Corporate Renewal; Ph.D., Chicago. Jenessa Shapiro, Associate Professor; Ph.D., Arizona State. Margaret Shih, Professor and Senior Associate Dean of the FEMBA program; Ph.D., Harvard. John Ullmen, Continuing Lecturer; Ph.D., UCLA. Miguel M. Unzueta, Associate Professor; Ph.D., Stanford. Maia Young, Associate Professor; Ph.D., Stanford.

Information Systems
George Geis, Adjunct Professor; Ph.D., USC. Bennet P. Lientz, Professor Emeritus; Ph.D., Washington (Seattle). E. B. Swanson, Professor Emeritus; Ph.D., Berkeley.

Marketing
Anke Audenaert, Adjunct Assistant Professor; M.A., Catholic University Leuven, (Belgium). Anand V. Bodapati, Associate Professor; Ph.D., Stanford. Randolph E. Bucklin, Professor, Peter W. Mullin Chair in Management, Faculty Chairman and Deputy Dean of Academic Affairs; Ph.D., Stanford. Lee Cooper, Professor Emeritus; Ph.D., Illinois. Aimee Drolet Rossi, Professor; Ph.D., Stanford. Dominique Hanssens, Distinguished Professor and Bud Knapp Chair in Marketing; Ph.D., Purdue. Hal Hershfield, Assistant Professor; Ph.D., Stanford. Brett Hollenbeck, Assistant Professor; Ph.D., Texas at Austin. Sanjog Misra, Professor; Ph.D., Buffalo, SUNY. Daniel Oppenheimer, Associate Professor; Ph.D., Stanford. Peter Rossi, Distinguished Professor and James Collins, Professor of Marketing and Area Chair, Statistics, and Economics; Ph.D., Chicago. Carol Scott, Professor Emeritus; Ph.D., Northwestern. Suzanne Shu, Associate Professor; Ph.D., Chicago. Sanjay Sood, Professor, Faculty Director of MEMES; Ph.D., Stanford. Stephen Spiller, Assistant Professor; Ph.D., Duke. Jim Stengel, Adjunct Professor; M.B.A., Penn State. Andres Terech, Adjunct Assistant Professor; Ph.D., UCLA. Robert Zeithammer, Associate Professor; Ph.D., MIT. Shi (Shir) Zhang, Associate Professor; Ph.D., Columbia.

Strategy
Sushil Bikhchandani, Professor and Faculty Vice Chairman; Ph.D., Stanford. M. Keith Chen, Associate Professor; Ph.D., Harvard. Michael Darby, Distinguished Professor and Warren C. Cordner Professor of Money and Financial Markets; Ph.D., Chicago. Craig Fox, Professor and Ho-Su Wu Term Chair in Management; Ph.D., Stanford. Ian Larkin, Assistant Professor; Ph.D., Berkeley. Phillip Leslie, Associate Professor; Ph.D., Yale. Marvin Lieberman, Professor; Ph.D., Harvard. Steven Lippman, Distinguished Professor, Area Chair and George W. Robbins Chair in Management; Ph.D., Stanford. John McDonough, Professor Emeritus; D.B.A., Harvard. Richard P. Rumelt, Harry and Elsa Kunin Chair in Business and Society; D.B.A., Harvard. Mariko Sakakibara, Professor; Ph.D., Harvard. Jason Snyder, Assistant Professor; Ph.D., Berkeley.

Photograph of UCLA Anderson School of Management Complex by Peden+Munk.

UNIVERSITY OF OKLAHOMA
Price College of Business

Programs of Study

The Price College of Business at the University of Oklahoma (OU) offers the following graduate programs: the Master of Business Administration (MBA), the Master of Accountancy (MAcc), the Master of Science in Management Information Systems (MS in MIS), and the Doctor of Philosophy (Ph.D.). Dual-degree programs offered include the MBA/MS in MIS, JD/MBA, MAcc/MBA, MAcc/MS in MIS, and generic dual degrees, which combine any other graduate program available at OU with the MBA. For the dual-degree programs, applicants must apply and be admitted to each program separately. Programs in the Price College of Business are fully accredited by AACSB International–The Association to Advance Collegiate Schools of Business.

The University of Oklahoma MBA degree program prepares students to fulfill their potential as business leaders through the development of core managerial competencies with emphasis on the global business perspective and practical application. Course topics include business ethics, corporate finance, financial markets and securities, marketing management, negotiation and leadership, strategic management, and supply chain management. The University of Oklahoma MBA degree program is delivered in three formats: the Full-time MBA, the Professional/Part-time MBA, and the Executive MBA in Energy. Both the Full-time and Professional MBA programs allow students to pursue their interests and develop a competitive edge through customized elective specializations. Specializations include energy, entrepreneurship, finance, management information systems (MIS), and risk management. Putting theories to test in the field is an important part of higher education. Full-time MBA students have the opportunity to make hands-on connections through internships, while the professionals enrolled in the part-time format can make direct, practical connections between their current jobs and what they learn in class.

The Full-time MBA is a 47-credit hour, sixteen-month program, with all courses taken at the graduate level. The full-time program facilitates the development of professional skills and broad business perspectives through opportunities such as unique summer internships in New York (Price Scholars), London (Dunham Scholars), Houston (Energy Scholars), and Dallas (Corporate Scholars) along with other domestic and international internships, case competitions, and working in teams on real-life cases. Interacting with excellent faculty members keeps Full-time MBA students on the cutting edge of knowledge. A customized program in one of five specializations—finance, risk management, energy, entrepreneurship, or MIS—allows personal attention for each student. Students specializing in energy can spend a spring semester abroad, study at the Institute of French Petroleum, and receive an M.S. in energy economics, in addition to their OU MBA. Low tuition costs plus significant scholarship and assistantship opportunities make the OU Full-time MBA an outstanding program for those looking to improve their professional opportunities and create a pathway to business leadership.

The Professional Part-time MBA requires 37 credit hours, with all courses taken at the graduate level. Designed for the working professional, the majority of courses are offered in the evening and are based in downtown Oklahoma City at the University of Oklahoma Health Sciences Center. Classes are typically held Monday through Thursday from 6–9:40 p.m. In this program, each class usually meets one night per week for eight weeks. Most students will take two courses at a time, which allows them to graduate within two years. However, the program is flexible and students have up to five years to finish.

The Executive MBA in Energy is a fifteen-month, 36-credit-hour program that is delivered primarily online with on-site events in Norman and international locations. Applicants need to have a minimum of three years energy industry experience and eight years of overall work experience. Ideal candidates have a bachelor's degree from an accredited institution, eight or more years of progressive management experience, and are currently employed by an energy company.

The joint Master of Accountancy (MAcc)/MBA program allows students to develop in-depth accounting and financial management expertise along with a broader general business perspective. Graduates meet the educational requirement to sit for the CPA exam and are particularly well suited for successful careers in corporate accounting and finance.

The joint MBA/MS in Management Information Systems program allows students to develop a broad general business background along with a deeper understanding of information technology. Students are given the information needed to manage information technology firms as well as other areas of business.

The joint Juris Doctor/MBA degree is designed to provide professionals with legal training and managerial skills to achieve high success in an increasingly complex world. With the benefits of degrees from two of Oklahoma's top programs, JD/MBA graduates go on to be corporate lawyers or run their own law firms.

Research Facilities

Research facilities that are available to graduate students include an extensive university library, the Amoco Business Resource Information Center, a graduate computer lab, the Bass Business History Collection, the Oklahoma University Research Institute, the Center for Economic and Management Research, and extensive computer facilities including a new trading floor lab.

Financial Aid

Graduate assistantships of up to $18,700 a year, special instructorships, fellowships and scholarships, and tuition-waiver scholarships are available for qualified graduate students. Graduate assistantships may include a full waiver of resident or nonresident tuition.

Cost of Study

For the 2013–14 academic year, the tuition rate was $175.20 per credit hour for an Oklahoma resident, or $675.20 per credit hour for a non-Oklahoma resident. With fees, Full-time MBA students who are Oklahoma resident students can expect to pay approximately $7,700 per semester, based on current figures. Books and supplies are estimated at $1,000 per academic year.

Living and Housing Costs

Many graduate students live on campus in one of the University's three apartment complexes or in the residence halls. Prices for apartments vary from $475 to $1,000 per month. Room and board rates for the residence halls are approximately $4,191 for one semester. For more information, students can call 405-325-2511 or visit the website at https://www.ou.edu/content/housingandfood/aud/graduate_student.html.

Student Group

Typically, the Full-time MBA class consists of 45 percent business majors, 24 percent engineering majors, and the remainder science and humanities majors. More than 40 percent have two years or more of professional work experience. The average age is 25 and approximately 30 percent are women.

University of Oklahoma

Location

Although part of the Oklahoma City metropolitan area, Norman began as and continues to be an independent community with a permanent population of approximately 113,000. It has extensive parks and recreation programs, a 10,000-acre lake and park area, a community theater, an art center and art league, and other amenities of a university town. Norman is minutes from downtown Oklahoma City and a 3-hour drive from the Dallas/Fort Worth metroplex.

The University

The University of Oklahoma, which was founded in 1890, is a doctoral degree-granting research university. The Norman campus serves as home to all of the University's academic programs, except health-related fields. Both the Norman and Health Sciences Center colleges offer programs at the Schusterman Center, the site of OU-Tulsa. OU enrolls more than 31,000 students, has more than 2,400 full-time faculty members, and has twenty colleges offering 163 majors at the baccalaureate level, 166 majors at the master's level, eighty-one majors at the doctoral level, twenty-seven majors at the first-professional level, and twenty-six graduate certificates.

Applying

A complete application for the Full-time and Professional MBA programs requires an application with the University of Oklahoma and then a separate application with the MBA program at the Price College of Business. The University of Oklahoma requires an online application, a nonrefundable application fee ($50 for U.S. residents), and the submission of official transcripts from all previous colleges. The Price College of Business also requires a GRE or GMAT scores taken within the last five years, a resume and a statement of goals, all of which can be uploaded to the online application.

Correspondence and Information

Student Support Center
Price College of Business
1003 Asp Avenue, Suite 3050
University of Oklahoma
Norman, Oklahoma 73019-4302
United States
Phone: 405-325-5623
E-mail: oklahomamba@ou.edu
Website: http://price.ou.edu/mba/

THE FACULTY AND THEIR RESEARCH

Faculty members in the Price College of Business are dedicated to students. As researchers in their respective fields, they bring real-world knowledge and experience to the classroom. Recognized nationally and internationally, Oklahoma MBA faculty members demonstrate extensive knowledge in their diverse teaching and research interests.

Michael F. Price Hall, home to the OU Price College of business. This 55,000-square-foot building is dedicated entirely to student learning.

Michael F. Price Hall provides students with a collaborative learning environment, complete with a business communication center, study rooms, conference rooms, Student Services offices, a large commons area, and this relaxing courtyard.

UNIVERSITY OF OTTAWA

Telfer School of Management
Master of Business Administration

Programs of Study

The Telfer School of Management is a leading international centre of management education and research, and the proud academic, research, and professional home of some 4,200 students, 200 full- and part-time faculty members, and 25,000 alumni.

The School has earned accreditations from the three most demanding organizations in the world: AACSB, AMBA, and EQUIS. Achieving the highly coveted triple crown of accreditations places the Telfer School of Management in the top 1 percent of the world's business schools and validates its success in surpassing the highest-possible standards for management education.

The School is a rich learning environment that provides students with the leadership training and global perspective required to excel in the changing and competitive worlds of business, technology, healthcare, government, and industry associations.

The Telfer M.B.A. program provides students with an exceptional academic foundation in the disciplines of management along with superior opportunities for experiential learning through unparalleled access to business and political leaders.

The Telfer M.B.A. enhances students' management skills; strengthens their ability to lead high-performance organizations; and provides them with the knowledge and training they need to focus on results, value, and outcomes with discipline and adaptability. Graduates will have the power to accelerate their career, rise above the competition, and realize their full potential in any sector, any industry, anywhere. Armed with the Telfer M.B.A., they will have the power to outperform.

The School offers an intensive and integrated program that features small class sizes, high interaction, and peer learning, all conducted in world-class facilities.

In addition, the Telfer M.B.A. provides students with opportunities to work directly with business-intelligence tools and closely examine methods and processes used by organizations to create integrated performance management systems. The curriculum covers the fundamental skills needed by leaders to achieve high performance in any industry or sector.

Using the extensive network within the local business community and the public sector, students must complete a major project under the supervision of a faculty member, the mentorship of a Certified Management Consultant from the Canadian Association of Management (CMC–Canada), and the direction of an executive from the host organization. While completing the project, students apply their newly acquired knowledge and skills, balance theory and practice, and gain valuable management experience. Students have completed projects for numerous firms, including Adobe, Alcatel Lucent, Bank of Canada, Canada Post, Cirque du Soleil, Foreign Affairs Canada, International Trade Canada, Live Work Learn Play LLP, Lumenera Corporation, March Networks, National Research Council (NRC), PAI Medical Group, Pricewaterhouse Coopers, Ottawa Senators, RBC, SNC-Lavalin, the *Ottawa Citizen,* and Volvo Cars of Canada.

Program delivery is flexible. Full- and part-time study options allow students to complete the degree requirements in as little as twelve months or as long as sixty months. Courses are offered in a variety of formats ranging from day, evening, or weekend classes. The program is available in either English or French.

The Telfer M.B.A. draws students from around the world, from a variety of educational backgrounds and diverse professional experiences. The program is designed to build on the diversity and wealth of its students' profiles. A cohort environment allows students to work and learn together, benefiting from each other's strengths, capabilities, and experiences. Students participate in national and international case competitions annually. The strong performance of the Telfer School's M.B.A. teams over the years is a clear reflection of its talented students and the high quality of the program.

Other graduate management programs offered at the Telfer School include the Executive M.B.A. (EMBA), a twenty-one month program with classes one day a week; the Master of Health Administration (M.H.A.), a sixteen-month program that includes a four-month administrative residency; the Master of Science in Management (M.Sc.); the Master of Science in Health Systems (M.Sc.); graduate diplomas in management, e-commerce, and e-business; and a Ph.D. in management (subject to funding approval by the province).

Research Facilities

The Telfer School fosters the development of the students' high-tech skills by providing them with state-of-the-art computing and teaching facilities. From private rooms to multimedia labs and teaching rooms, students can prepare their assignments using common and specialized software, advanced financial and accounting databases, electronic mail, and the computerized libraries of the University.

A dedicated Management Library ensures that students can access—directly and easily—indispensable learning materials, such as the latest academic journals and trade publications and the increasing number of online databases and electronic resources.

The Telfer School of Management proudly promotes its Career Centre, which is dedicated exclusively to management students. The Career Centre provides a wide array of first-class services, programs, events, and resources to help students and alumni succeed professionally. It also cultivates strong relationships with employers in all business and government sectors, creating employment opportunities, enhancing student value, and facilitating employer recruitment.

The new Financial Research and Learning Lab is a high-quality learning environment and data resource centre used to support research and experiential learning. The Lab is designed to emulate a professional trading lab and houses real-time industry-standard products from public and private sector environments where finance is practiced.

The University also offers a variety of services and resources that contribute to students' professional development and success in achieving career goals.

Financial Aid

The Telfer School of Management's goal is to attract top quality candidates to its M.B.A. program. Numerous scholarships are awarded, which reflects the Telfer School's ongoing commitment to reward exceptional students for their academic successes and achievements. Students can visit the website at www.telfer.uOttawa.ca/mba to learn more about scholarships and awards.

Canadian citizens and permanent residents in need of financial aid can apply for government assistance. The Telfer School of Management provides funding for teaching assistants and research assistants.

Cost of Study

In 2013–14, tuition for a full-time M.B.A. program (three semesters) was Can$23,987 for Canadian students and Can$36,177 for international students. For part-time students, tuition was Can$617 per credit, with 54 credits needed.

Living and Housing Costs

Other estimated costs for the academic year include housing (off campus), Can$7,500; food, Can$4,800; books, Can$1,500; and for non-Canadians, health insurance, Can$750.

Location

Located in the heart of the nation's capital, the Telfer School of Management at the University of Ottawa is at the center of an extensive group of government and private organizations that drive most of Canada's business and trade nationally and internationally. The main campus is located in the downtown core and is within walking distance of shopping malls, restaurants, cinemas, and museums.

The University of Ottawa and the Telfer School

The University of Ottawa is a cosmopolitan campus where more than 40,000 students from a variety of cultural heritages live and learn in an atmosphere of tolerance and understanding. International students benefit from the University's long tradition of excellence in teaching and research while learning about the multicultural Canadian social mosaic. The Telfer School of Management provides a rich educational experience—both inside and outside the classroom—that prepares students to be leaders in the new global, knowledge-based economy. The Telfer School's graduates are in demand by high-technology companies, leading consulting firms, financial institutions, and public-sector organizations in Canada and abroad.

Applying

Admission to the Telfer M.B.A. program is competitive and granted to candidates who clearly demonstrate high promise of success. The admission requirements are: a baccalaureate degree with at least a B or a 70 percent overall standing, at least three years of full-time work experience, and at least a 50th percentile score on the GMAT. The most recent average score

University of Ottawa

was 627 and the range was 550–780. Application deadlines are February 1 for international students and April 1 for students from the United States and Canada. Students should allow four to six weeks for notification. Preference is given to candidates who have greater work experience, particularly where there is evidence of career progression.

Correspondence and Information

M.B.A. Program
University of Ottawa Telfer School of Management
55 Laurier Avenue East, Room 4160
Ottawa, Ontario K1N 6N5
Canada
Phone: 613-562-5884
      800-965-5512 (toll-free)
Fax: 613-562-5912
E-mail: mba@telfer.uOttawa.ca
Website: http://www.telfer.uOttawa.ca/mba

THE FACULTY

Many of the Telfer School's faculty members serve as consultants to major corporations and government organizations around the world. Holders of numerous teaching and research awards, the professors combine excellence in teaching with outstanding scholarship.

Administration

Dean: François Julien, Associate Professor; Ph.D., Waterloo.
Vice-Dean and Associate Dean (Programs): Julie Beauchamp, Associate Professor; Ph.D., McGill.
Vice-Dean (Career Development): Barbara Orser, Full Professor, Deloitte Professor in the Management of Growth Enterprises; Ph.D., Bradford.
Associate Dean (Academic) and Secretary: Martine Spence, Full Professor; M.B.A., Concordia (Montréal); Ph.D., Middlesex.
Accreditation Team Leader, Associate Professor: Michel Nedzela, Associate Professor; M.S., Stanford.
Director of the Master of Business Administration (M.B.A.) Program: Greg Richards; Ph.D., Carleton.
Director of the Executive M.B.A. (EMBA) Program: Sophia Leong; M.B.A., Ottawa.
Director of the Master of Health Administration (M.H.A.) Program: Brian Malcolmson; M.H.A., Ottawa.
Director of the Master of Science in Health Systems (M.Sc.): Craig Kuziemsky; Associate Professor; Ph.D., Victoria (British Columbia).
Director of the Master of Science in Management (M.Sc.): Leila Hamzaoui Essoussi, Associate Professor; Ph.D., Université d'Aix-Marseille III.
Director, Undergraduate Program: Dana Hyde; Ph.D., INSEAD

Professors

Fodil Adjaoud, Full Professor; M.B.A., Ph.D., Laval.
Sadrudin Ahmed, Professor Emeritus; M.B.A., Ph.D., Western Ontario.
Pavel Andreev, Assistant Professor; Ph.D., Israel.
Douglas Angus, Full Professor; M.A., Ottawa.
Jacques Barrette, Vice Dean and Associate Dean (Programs), Full Professor; Ph.D., Montréal.
Walid Ben Amar, Assistant Professor; Ph.D., HEC Montréal.
Sarah Ben Amor, Assistant Professor; Ph.D., Laval.
Morad Benyoucef, Associate Professor; Ph.D., Montréal.
Silvia Bonaccio, Associate Professor; Ph.D., Purdue.
Ameur Boujenoui, Assistant Professor; Ph.D., HEC Montréal.
James E. Bowen, Adjunct Professor; Ph.D., Carleton.
Richard Bozec, Full Professor; Ph.D., Montréal.
Kevin Brand, Associate Professor; S.M., Sc.D., Harvard.
Jonathan Calof, Associate Professor; M.B.A., Ph.D., Western Ontario.
Denis H. J. Caro, Full Professor; M.B.A., Ph.D., Minnesota.
Jules Carrière, Associate Professor; Ph.D., Montréal.
Tyler Chamberlin, Assistant Professor; Ph.D., Manchester.
Imed Eddine Chkir, Associate Professor; Ph.D., Laval.
Lamia Chourou, Assistant Professor; Ph.D., University of Tunis; Ph.D., Queen's (Kingston).
Samia Chreim, Associate Professor; Ph.D., HEC Montréal.
Robert Collier, Lecturer; B.A., Carleton; CMA.
Brian Conheady, Assistant Professor; M.B.A., McGill; CMA.
Jean Couillard, Associate Professor; M.B.A., Ph.D., Laval.
David H. J. Delcorde, Lecturer; M.B.A., Heriot-Watt (Edinburgh); Ph.D., London South Bank (UK).
Shujun Ding, Associate Professor; Ph.D, Calgary.
Anna Dodonova, Associate Professor; Ph.D., Michigan.
David Doloreux, Full Professor; Ph.D., Waterloo.
Magda Donia, Assistant Professor; Ph.D., Concordia (Montréal).
Sylvain Durocher, Associate Professor; Ph.D., Quebec at Montréal.

Ronald Eden, Associate Professor; M.B.A., Dalhousie; Ph.D., NYU; CA.
Bruce M. Firestone, Entrepreneur-in-Residence; Ph.D., Australian National.
Mark Freel, Full Professor; Ph.D., Aberdeen.
Devinder Gandhi, Full Professor; Ph.D., Pennsylvania.
Chen Guo, Associate Professor; M.B.A., Ph.D., Queen's (Kingston).
Michael Guolla, Teaching Associate; Ph.D., Michigan.
Lavagnon Ika, Assistant Professor; Ph.D., UQAM.
Mirou Jaana, Associate Professor; Ph.D., Iowa.
Yuri Khoroshilov, Associate Professor; Ph.D., Michigan.
Gurprit S. Kindra, Full Professor; M.B.A., Northwest Missouri State; Ph.D., Iowa.
Kaouthar Lajili, Associate Professor; Ph.D., Illinois.
Daniel E. Lane, Full Professor; Ph.D., British Columbia.
Laurent Lapierre, Associate Professor; Ph.D., McMaster.
David Large, Assistant Professor; M.B.A., Ph.D., Western Ontario.
Joanne Leck, Full Professor; M.B.A., Ph.D., McGill.
Jonathan Linton, Full Professor; Ph.D., York.
Judith Madill, Full Professor; Ph.D., Western Ontario.
Michael Maingot, Full Professor; Ph.D., Queen's (Belfast).
Pranlal Manga, Full Professor; Ph.D., Toronto.
Philip McIlkenny, Associate Professor; Ph.D., Essex.
Cheryl McWatters, Full Professor; M.B.A., Ph.D., Queen's (Kingston).
Wojtek Michalowski, Full Professor; Ph.D., Warsaw.
Muriel Mignerat, Assistant Professor; Ph.D., HEC Montréal.
Michael Miles, Assistant Professor; Ph.D., Fielding Institute.
Laurent Mirabeau, Assistant Professor; Ph.D., McGill.
Michael Mulvey, Assistant Professor; Ph.D., Penn State.
John Nash, Adjunct Professor; D.Phil., Oxford.
Miwako Nitani, Assistant Professor; Ph.D., Carleton.
Alan O'Sullivan, Assistant Professor; M.B.A., Dublin; Ph.D., McGill.
Sharon O'Sullivan, Associate Professor; M.B.A., McGill; Ph.D. Toronto.
Gilles Paquet, Full Professor; doctoral studies, Queen's (Kingston).
Jonathan Patrick, Assistant Professor; Ph.D., British Columbia.
Kathryn Pedwell, Assistant Professor; M.B.A., Ph.D., Calgary.
Ajax Persaud, Associate Professor, Ph.D., Carleton.
Rhonda Pyper, Assistant Professor; M.B.A., Laurentian; CMA.
Tony Quon, Associate Professor; Ph.D., Princeton.
Bijan Raajemi, Associate Professor; Ph.D., Waterloo.
François-Éric Racicot, Associate Professor; Ph.D., Montréal.
William Rentz, Associate Professor; Ph.D., Rochester.
Greg Richards, Professor of Performance Management; M.B.A., Ottawa; Ph.D., Carleton.
Allan Riding, Full Professor; Ph.D., McGill.
Umar Ruhi, Assistant Professor; M.B.A., Ph.D., McMaster.
Samir Saadi, Assistant Professor; Ph.D., Queen's (Kingston).
Sandra Schillo, Assistant Professor; Ph.D., Kiel.
Jeffrey Sidney, Full Professor; Ph.D., Michigan.
Martine Spence, Associate Dean (Academic) and Secretary, Full Professor; M.B.A., Concordia (Montréal); Ph.D., Middlesex.
Patrick Woodcock, Assistant Professor; M.B.A., Ph.D., Western Ontario.
David J. Wright, Full Professor; Ph.D., Cambridge.
Mehdi Zahaf, Associate Professor; Ph.D., HEC Montréal.
Daniel Zéghal, Full Professor; M.B.A., Ph.D., Laval; CGA.

THE UNIVERSITY OF TEXAS AT DALLAS
Naveen Jindal School of Management

Programs of Study

The Naveen Jindal School of Management's 11 dynamic master's programs answer the challenges facing today's business leaders. The curriculum for each of these degrees is built around a strong core of classes with detailed study addressing specific industry issues. These master's programs—accounting, business analytics, finance, healthcare management, information technology and management, innovation and entrepreneurship, international management studies, management and administrative sciences, marketing, supply chain management, and systems engineering and management—also prepare students to take national certification exams, including CPA, CFA, CFP, Certified Internal Auditor, and others.

Master's degrees require 36 credit hours for completion. Jindal School of Management classes are offered year-round, with a full schedule of courses offered in the evening to accommodate working professionals. Full-time graduate students could complete a master's degree in three semesters; most graduate students complete their degree programs within three calendar years by taking a blend of on-campus and online programs. Several master's degrees, including accounting, information technology and management, and supply chain management may be earned either fully or almost completely with online classes.

Those seeking a greater breadth of study may enroll in a dual master's/M.B.A. degree program at the Jindal School. While earning the two degrees would typically require 89 credit hours, with careful planning the degrees can be earned in a total of 63 credit hours. Additional information is available online at jindal.utdallas.edu/msmba or from a Jindal School of Management graduate adviser (jindal.utdallas.edu/advising).

The Jindal School also offers five M.B.A. programs with concentrations in accounting, finance, healthcare administration, healthcare management for physicians, information systems, innovation and entrepreneurship, internal audit, international management, leadership in organizations, marketing, operations management, product lifecycle and supply chain management, project management, strategic management, and supply chain management. Employers particularly like the strong analytical skills University of Texas at Dallas (UT Dallas) students develop during their M.B.A. studies, and students may focus their course work to match their individual career goals. The Jindal School offers an M.B.A. that can be earned completely online.

These programs are nationally recognized and offer a terrific tuition value for in-state students. Several of these 53-hour programs include an international study trip, most offer opportunities to take classes online, and all develop cross-disciplinary skills sought by the most competitive employers in the nation and around the world. Unique areas of specialization, including internal audit and executive and professional coaching, are offered.

Representatives from many corporations—ranging from retail to transportation to banking, finance, healthcare and communications—partner with the Jindal School of Management. These industry executives sit on various advisory panels, provide financial and research support, and serve as mentors to students. Faculty members seek these outside professionals as classroom speakers, adding real-life perspective to textbook learning.

Research Facilities

The Jindal School of Management faculty has been recognized globally for its research productivity. The faculty ranks sixteenth in North America and seventeenth globally based on research contributions to major journals, according to *The UTD Top 100 Business School Research Rankings*, and ranks eighteenth worldwide according to *Financial Times*. Research by the information systems faculty and operations management faculty ranks in the top three nationally in those respective fields. The Jindal School also hosts twelve Centers of Excellence where faculty and students join to tackle real-world issues faced by local businesses. Students also have the opportunity to apply for internships with these centers and participate in the meetings and lectures they sponsor for industry professionals.

Financial Aid

The Naveen Jindal School of Management Scholarship Committee makes awards based on merit, need, or a combination of the two. The School's annual Scholarship Breakfast most recently generated more than $100,000 in scholarships for its students at all levels. Students may also apply for the Dean's Excellence Scholarships, several of which are awarded each year. Full-time M.B.A. students with strong academic potential are eligible for significant scholarship and grant assistance. Last year, the Jindal School awarded more than $725,000 in scholarships to graduate students. The University participates in most federal and state aid programs. Short-term loans are also available. Prospective students should visit the Jindal School of Management's website at http://jindal.utdallas.edu/scholarships for more information.

Cost of Study

Tuition for in-state full-time graduate students (9 hours) for fall 2014 is $5,970. For graduate students attending school part-time, tuition is $2,654 for 3 hours and $4,238 for 6 hours. These prices exclude fees and other charges. The cost of obtaining a master's degree depends upon how many hours a student completes each semester. The Full-Time M.B.A. costs about $31,000 for students entering in fall 2013, although generous scholarships are available to well-qualified students.

Living and Housing Costs

UT Dallas' on-campus apartments, Waterview Park, offer a variety of floorplans, are competitively priced, and fill quickly. Interested students should visit http://www.utdallas.edu/housing for on-campus housing information.

The surrounding metropolitan area offers off-campus housing options in a wide range of prices and amenities. An array of shopping and dining establishments, representing everything from large chains to small, single proprietor–run shops, are within bicycling distance of campus.

The Comet Cruiser, a Dallas Area Rapid Transit (DART) bus route, connects the campus with nearby shopping, apartment complexes, and the DART light rail line that goes to downtown Dallas for additional easy-access housing, shopping, and entertainment options. The Comet Cruiser operates seven days a week and is free to students.

Student Groups

About 60 percent of Naveen Jindal School of Management graduate students are working professionals seeking an advanced degree; they often take classes online, in the evening, and during the summer semester. The Jindal School's environment is both challenging and naturally diverse. About a third of the graduate students take 9 or more hours a semester. With about 7,000 students, Naveen Jindal School of Management is the largest of UT Dallas' seven schools. Jindal School students are equally split between undergraduate and graduate studies.

Most graduate students have at least five years of work experience. Women make up about 40 percent of master's students, and minorities represent almost 30 percent of the student population. About 30 percent of the students are from another country. Students range in age from 20 to more than 70; the average age is 30.

Location

The University of Texas at Dallas campus is in Richardson, a close suburb to the vibrant and diverse city of Dallas. The median age in the Dallas-Fort Worth area is about 33, younger than the national average of almost 37. The region is home to five professional sports teams: the Dallas Cowboys, Dallas Stars, FC Dallas, the two-time American League pennant-winning Texas Rangers, and the 2011 NBA champion Dallas Mavericks. Dallas is the only city in the world with buildings designed by four Prizker Prize–winning architects in one block and is also home to the nation's largest state fair—the State Fair of Texas—which runs from late September through October. Dallas and Fort Worth both have a wide spectrum of cultural activities, from world-class museums and opera to internationally recognized symphony performances and the best in pop, folk, and country music.

Because of Dallas' central location in the U.S., air travel to either coast is as short as three hours and many major cities in Europe and the Far East are a nonstop flight away. The campus, about 18 miles north of downtown Dallas, is convenient to the George Bush Turnpike, U.S. Highway 75 and the Dallas North Tollway.

The University and The School

The University of Texas at Dallas was established in 1969 by the Texas Legislature as a response to the developing high-tech industry in North Texas. Originally conceived by Cecil Green, J. Erik Jonsson, and Eugene McDermott—founders of Texas Instruments—the University initially offered only master's degrees in engineering and science. A little more than four decades later, the University more than 20,000 students in undergraduate, graduate, and doctoral programs.

The University of Texas at Dallas

The two largest alumni gifts in University history, with a combined value of $30 million, were made in October 2011 to the Naveen Jindal School of Management. Gifts from Naveen Jindal (M.B.A. '92) and Charles (M.S. '80) and Nancy (B.S. '80) Davidson endow professorial chairs, provide scholarships, and fund research.

Construction has begun on the Jindal School's 108,000-square-foot addition to provide space for the growing faculty (currently more than 200) and student populations. The Jindal School is fully accredited by AACSB International (The Association to Advance Collegiate Schools of Business) and currently occupies a 204,000-square-foot building that opened in 2003.

Applying

Prerequisites for all graduate admissions include a bachelor's degree from an accredited institution; most also require calculus and spreadsheet proficiency. Undergraduate work in business-related courses is not required. Additional requirements include GMAT or GRE scores, a complete application, an essay of educational intent, and three recent letters of reference. A TOEFL score is required from those for whom English is not the native language. Applicants are evaluated on personal qualities and academic backgrounds, following admission formula guidelines of the International Association for Management Education. Personal interviews are not required. Admission deadlines vary by program and according to the applicant's citizenship status. Application requirements and deadlines are available on the School's website at http://jindal.utdallas.edu.

Master's programs in healthcare management, international management studies, innovation and entrepreneurship, and marketing do not require calculus. Applicants who do not meet the calculus requirement may be admitted but must make up the deficiency in the first semester at UT Dallas.

Most programs enroll students in the next semester after acceptance. Certain programs, including the Full-Time M.B.A., Executive M.B.A., and Global Leadership Executive M.B.A. admit students only once each year.

Correspondence and Information

Joanna Fowler, Associate Director
Naveen Jindal School of Management, SM21
The University of Texas at Dallas
800 West Campbell Road
Richardson, Texas 75080
Phone: 972-883-6282
Fax: 972-883-6823
E-mail: joanna.fowler@utdallas.edu
Website: http://jindal.utdallas.edu

The strong North Texas economy provides many job opportunities in fields such as healthcare, finance, transportation, and information technology for graduates of the Naveen Jindal School of Management.

THE FACULTY

Faculty research at the Naveen Jindal School of Management covers a range of topics, from findings of corruption in Asia to developing models for predicting the timing and frequency of future patient re-admissions related to congestive heart failure. Jindal School faculty members are globally ranked for their research productivity. They are well-represented in professional associations and publications and speak at events worldwide. A complete list of faculty members and their research publications is available online at jindal.utdallas.edu/faculty.

ACADEMIC AREAS

Accounting: Area Coordinator, Dr. William Cready. In the accounting programs at The University of Texas at Dallas, students learn to prepare, analyze, and communicate relevant information for making business decisions. Accounting focuses on an organization's resources and how efficiently it performs. The discipline of accounting can be subdivided into career paths that align with the Jindal School's graduate-degree concentrations: corporate accounting, auditing, tax accounting, and internal auditing. More information is available at www.jindal.utdallas.edu/accounting.

Finance and Managerial Economics: Area Coordinator, Dr. Robert Kieschnick. Students who earn a Bachelor of Science in finance degree will have the skills to do rigorous analysis of financial information. These skills are in high demand across the corporate world and prized in government and nonprofit sectors. The Personal Financial Planning track is registered with the Certified Financial Planner Board of Standards, which means that students completing that track meet the educational requirements to sit for the CFP® certification exam. The Master of Science in Finance degree, which has six areas of concentration, is offered for graduate students who have an interest in such areas as corporate finance, investment banking, venture capital, investment management, private equity, commercial banking, insurance, or real estate. One of the concentrations is designed to meet the educational requirements to sit for level 1 of the Chartered Financial Analyst (CFA) examination, and another concentration is designed to meet the requirements of the Financial Risk Manager (FRM) examination. An undergraduate degree in finance or a related area is not required. The Finance and Managerial Economics area's doctoral program offers students the opportunity to develop strong research skills that are especially relevant for students interested in an academic career. Additional information can be found online at www.jindal.utdallas.edu/finance.

Information Systems and Operations Management: Area Coordinators, Dr. Milind Dawande and Dr. Srinivasan Raghunathan. The Jindal School's Information Systems and Operations Management (ISOM) programs allow students to customize and supplement their general business degree with courses from information systems or operations management. ISOM bridges the gap between technologies and business through high-quality research and disseminates knowledge through relevant academic programs. Additional details can be found at www.jindal.utdallas.edu/isom.

Marketing: Area Coordinator, Dr. Ernan Haruvy. The marketing academic area in the Naveen Jindal School of Management is committed to creating a practical and applied learning environment for the study, research, and practice of marketing. The school has designed a number of courses to meet the needs of students who choose general management careers as well as those who choose a marketing concentration. The school's marketing faculty are highly regarded as experts in marketing science, which is an approach to marketing characterized by an analytical orientation and employing quantitative methods to solve practical problems. Students interested in studying the marketing discipline may pursue the following degrees: Bachelor of Science in marketing, Master of Science in marketing, M.B.A. with focus in marketing, or a Ph.D. in management science with concentration in marketing. More information is available at www.jindal.utdallas.edu/marketing.

Organizations, Strategy and International Management: Area Coordinator, Dr. Mike Peng. The Organizations, Strategy, and International Management (OSIM) area features a multidisciplinary group of management scholars engaged in cutting edge research and teaching activities. OSIM faculty research covers domains such as: entrepreneurship, international business/international management, organizational behavior, organization theory, and strategic management.

The OSIM area offers (1) a B.S. in global business, (2) an M.S. in international management studies, (3) an M.S. in management and administrative sciences, and (4) a Ph.D. in international management studies with concentrations in strategy, organization behavior/organization theory, and international management. In addition, the area offers a variety of elective courses for the Bachelor of Science in business administration, M.B.A., and M.S. programs that reflect the challenges of managing in a dynamic, global environment. More details are available at www.jindal.utdallas.edu/osim.

Section 2
Accounting and Finance

This section contains a directory of institutions offering graduate work in accounting and finance. Additional information about programs listed in the directory but not augmented by an in-depth entry may be obtained by writing directly to the dean of a graduate school or chair of a department at the address given in the directory.

For programs offering related work, see also in this book *Business Administration and Management, International Business,* and *Nonprofit Management.* In the other guides in this series:

Graduate Programs in the Humanities, Arts & Social Sciences
See *Economics* and *Family and Consumer Sciences (Consumer Economics)*

Graduate Programs in the Physical Sciences, Mathematics, Agricultural Sciences, the Environment & Natural Resources
See *Mathematical Sciences*

Graduate Programs in Engineering & Applied Sciences
See *Computer Science and Information Technology*

CONTENTS

Program Directories

Accounting	200
Finance and Banking	247
Investment Management	291
Taxation	293

Displays and Close-Ups

See:

Adelphi University—Business Administration and Management	70, 181
Embry-Riddle Aeronautical University–Daytona—Business Administration/Aviation Management	616, 635
Monmouth University	116, 187
University of California, Los Angeles—Business Administration and Management	145, 191
University of Oklahoma—Business Administration and Management	158, 193

Accounting

Abilene Christian University, Graduate School, College of Business Administration, Abilene, TX 79699-9100. Offers M Acc. *Accreditation:* AACSB. Part-time programs available. *Faculty:* 7 part-time/adjunct (0 women). *Students:* 38 full-time (14 women), 8 part-time (4 women); includes 5 minority (1 Black or African American, non-Hispanic/Latino; 1 Asian, non-Hispanic/Latino; 2 Hispanic/Latino; 1 Two or more races, non-Hispanic/Latino), 15 international. 63 applicants, 44% accepted, 24 enrolled. In 2013, 31 master's awarded. *Entrance requirements:* For master's, GMAT. Additional exam requirements/recommendations for international students: Required—TOEFL (minimum score 550 paper-based; 90 iBT), IELTS (minimum score 6.5), PTE. *Application deadline:* For fall admission, 4/1 priority date for domestic students; for spring admission, 11/1 for domestic students. Applications are processed on a rolling basis. Application fee: $50. Electronic applications accepted. *Expenses: Tuition:* Full-time $17,100; part-time $950 per credit hour. *Financial support:* In 2013–14, 20 students received support. Federal Work-Study and scholarships/grants available. Support available to part-time students. Financial award application deadline: 4/1; financial award applicants required to submit FAFSA. *Faculty research:* Organizational structure, financial management, cost accounting, unit analysis management. *Unit head:* Bill Fowler, Department Chair, 325-674-2080, Fax: 325-674-2564, E-mail: bill.fowler@coba.acu.edu. *Application contact:* Corey Patterson, Director of Graduate Admission and Recruiting, 325-674-6566, Fax: 325-674-6717, E-mail: gradinfo@acu.edu.
Website: http://www.acu.edu/academics/coba/index.html.

Adrian College, Graduate Programs, Adrian, MI 49221-2575. Offers accounting (MS); athletic training (MS); criminal justice (MA). *Faculty:* 11 part-time/adjunct (3 women). *Students:* 9 full-time (3 women); includes 1 minority (Black or African American, non-Hispanic/Latino). Average age 23. 9 applicants, 100% accepted, 6 enrolled. In 2013, 2 master's awarded. *Degree requirements:* For master's, comprehensive exam (for some programs), thesis (for some programs), thesis, internship or practicum with corresponding in-depth paper and/or presentation. *Entrance requirements:* For master's, appropriate undergraduate degree, minimum cumulative and major GPA of 3.0, personal statement. *Application deadline:* For fall admission, 8/1 priority date for domestic and international students. Applications are processed on a rolling basis. Application fee: $0. *Expenses: Tuition:* Full-time $5880; part-time $490 per credit hour. *Required fees:* $550; $275 per semester. *Financial support:* Scholarships/grants and tuition waivers (full and partial) available. Financial award application deadline: 3/1; financial award applicants required to submit FAFSA. *Unit head:* Dr. Paul Rupert, Dean, Graduate Studies, 517-264-3931, E-mail: prupert@adrian.edu. *Application contact:* Melissa Woolsey, Admissions Counselor, 800-877-2246, E-mail: mwoolsey@adrian.edu.

Alabama State University, College of Business Administration, Department of Accounting and Finance, Montgomery, AL 36101-0271. Offers accountancy (M Acc). *Faculty:* 4 full-time (0 women). *Students:* 22 full-time (13 women), 10 part-time (6 women); includes 28 minority (26 Black or African American, non-Hispanic/Latino; 1 Asian, non-Hispanic/Latino; 1 Two or more races, non-Hispanic/Latino), 3 international. Average age 28. 29 applicants, 69% accepted, 20 enrolled. In 2013, 9 master's awarded. *Entrance requirements:* For master's, GMAT, writing competency test. Additional exam requirements/recommendations for international students: Required—TOEFL (minimum score 500 paper-based). *Application deadline:* For fall admission, 7/15 for domestic students; for spring admission, 12/15 for domestic students. Applications are processed on a rolling basis. Application fee: $25. *Expenses:* Tuition, state resident: full-time $7958; part-time $343 per credit hour. Tuition, nonresident: full-time $14,132; part-time $686 per credit hour. *Required fees:* $446 per term. One-time fee: $1784 full-time; $892 part-time. Tuition and fees vary according to course load. *Financial support:* In 2013–14, 2 research assistantships (averaging $9,450 per year) were awarded. *Unit head:* Dr. Dave Thompson, Chair, 334-229-4134, Fax: 334-229-4870, E-mail: dthompson@asunet.alasu.edu. *Application contact:* Dr. William Person, Dean of Graduate Studies, 334-229-4274, Fax: 334-229-4928, E-mail: wperson@alasu.edu.
Website: http://www.alasu.edu/academics/colleges—departments/college-of-business-administration/college-of-business-academics/accounting—finance/index.aspx.

Albany State University, College of Business, Albany, GA 31705-2717. Offers accounting (MBA); general (MBA); healthcare (MBA). *Accreditation:* ACBSP. Part-time and evening/weekend programs available. *Degree requirements:* For master's, comprehensive exam, internship, 3 hours of physical education. *Entrance requirements:* For master's, GMAT (minimum score of 450)/GRE (minimum score of 800) for those without earned master's degree or higher, minimum undergraduate GPA of 2.5, 2 letters of reference, official transcript, pre-entrance medical record and certificate of immunization. Electronic applications accepted. *Faculty research:* Diversity issues, ancestry, understanding finance through use of technology.

Alfred University, Graduate School, School of Business, Alfred, NY 14802-1205. Offers accounting (MBA); business administration (MBA). *Accreditation:* AACSB. Part-time programs available. *Faculty:* 8 full-time (2 women). *Students:* 18 full-time (10 women), 19 part-time (5 women). Average age 28. 29 applicants, 66% accepted, 15 enrolled. In 2013, 31 master's awarded. *Entrance requirements:* For master's, GMAT. Additional exam requirements/recommendations for international students: Required—TOEFL (minimum score 590 paper-based; 90 iBT), IELTS (minimum score 6.5). *Application deadline:* For fall admission, 8/1 for domestic students, 3/15 for international students; for winter admission, 12/1 for domestic students; for spring admission, 10/1 for international students. Applications are processed on a rolling basis. Application fee: $60. Electronic applications accepted. *Expenses: Tuition:* Full-time $38,020; part-time $810 per credit hour. *Required fees:* $950; $160 per semester. Part-time tuition and fees vary according to campus/location and program. *Financial support:* In 2013–14, 18 research assistantships with partial tuition reimbursements (averaging $19,010 per year) were awarded; tuition waivers (partial) and unspecified assistantships also available. Financial award applicants required to submit FAFSA. *Unit head:* Dr. Nancy Evangelista, Dean of Graduate Programs, 607-871-2124, Fax: 607-871-2114, E-mail: fevangel@alfred.edu. *Application contact:* Sara Love, Coordinator of Graduate Admissions, 607-871-2115, Fax: 607-871-2198, E-mail: gradinquiry@alfred.edu.
Website: http://business.alfred.edu/mba/.

American InterContinental University Online, Program in Business Administration, Schaumburg, IL 60173. Offers accounting and finance (MBA); finance (MBA); healthcare management (MBA); human resource management (MBA); international business (MBA); management (MBA); marketing (MBA); operations management (MBA); organizational psychology and development (MBA); project management (MBA). *Accreditation:* ACBSP. Evening/weekend programs available. Postbaccalaureate distance learning degree programs offered (no on-campus study). *Entrance requirements:* Additional exam requirements/recommendations for international

students: Required—TOEFL (minimum score 550 paper-based). Electronic applications accepted.

American InterContinental University South Florida, Program in International Business, Weston, FL 33326. Offers accounting and finance (MBA); human resource management (MBA); management (MBA); marketing (MBA). Part-time and evening/weekend programs available. Postbaccalaureate distance learning degree programs offered. Electronic applications accepted.

American International College, Graduate Business Programs, Master of Science in Accounting and Taxation Program, Springfield, MA 01109-3189. Offers MSAT. Part-time and evening/weekend programs available. *Faculty:* 4 part-time/adjunct (0 women). *Students:* 1 full-time (0 women), 18 part-time (5 women); includes 5 minority (3 Black or African American, non-Hispanic/Latino; 1 Asian, non-Hispanic/Latino; 1 Hispanic/Latino). Average age 30. 9 applicants, 89% accepted, 5 enrolled. In 2013, 6 master's awarded. *Entrance requirements:* For master's, bachelor's degree, minimum GPA of 2.75. Additional exam requirements/recommendations for international students: Required—TOEFL or IELTS. *Application deadline:* Applications are processed on a rolling basis. Application fee: $50. Electronic applications accepted. *Expenses: Tuition:* Full-time $14,040; part-time $780 per credit. Tuition and fees vary according to course load, degree level and program. *Financial support:* Career-related internships or fieldwork available. Financial award applicants required to submit FAFSA. *Unit head:* Thomas Barron, Director, 413-205-3305, Fax: 413-205-3943, E-mail: thomas.barron@aic.edu. *Application contact:* Kerry Barnes, Director of Graduate Admissions, 413-205-3703, Fax: 413-205-3051, E-mail: kerry.barnes@aic.edu.

American Public University System, AMU/APU Graduate Programs, Charles Town, WV 25414. Offers accounting (MBA, MS); criminal justice (MA), including business administration, emergency and disaster management, general (MA, MS); educational leadership (M Ed); emergency and disaster management (MA); entrepreneurship (MBA); environmental policy and management (MS), including environmental planning, environmental sustainability, fish and wildlife management, general (MA, MS), global environmental management; finance (MBA); general (MBA); global business management (MBA); history (MA), including American history, ancient and classical history, European history, global history, public history; homeland security (MA), including business administration, counter-terrorism studies, criminal justice, cyber, emergency management and public health, intelligence studies, transportation security; homeland security resource allocation (MBA); humanities (MA); information technology (MS), including digital forensics, enterprise software development, information assurance and security, IT project management; information technology management (MBA); intelligence studies (MA), including criminal intelligence, cyber, general (MA, MS), homeland security, intelligence analysis, intelligence collection, intelligence management, intelligence operations, terrorism studies; international relations and conflict resolution (MA), including comparative and security issues, conflict resolution, international and transnational security issues, peacekeeping; legal studies (MA); management (MA), including defense management, general (MA, MS), human resource management, organizational leadership, public administration; marketing (MBA); military history (MA), including American military history, American Revolution, civil war, war since 1945, World War II; military studies (MA), including joint warfare, strategic leadership; national security studies (MA), including general (MA, MS), homeland security, regional security studies, security and intelligence analysis, terrorism studies; nonprofit management (MBA); political science (MA), including American politics and government, comparative government and development, general (MA, MS), international relations, public policy; psychology (MA), including general (MA, MS), maritime engineering management, reverse logistics management; public administration (MPA), including disaster management, environmental policy, health policy, human resources, national security, organizational management, security management; public health (MPH); reverse logistics management (MA); school counseling (M Ed); security management (MA); space studies (MS), including aerospace science, general (MA, MS), planetary science; sports and health sciences (MS); teaching (M Ed), including curriculum and instruction for elementary teachers, elementary reading, English language learners, instructional leadership, online learning, special education; transportation and logistics management (MA), including general (MA, MS), maritime engineering management, reverse logistics management. Programs offered via distance learning only. Part-time and evening/weekend programs available. Postbaccalaureate distance learning degree programs offered (no on-campus study). *Faculty:* 432 full-time (242 women), 1,722 part-time/adjunct (829 women). *Students:* 511 full-time (241 women), 10,947 part-time (4,294 women); includes 3,760 minority (2,058 Black or African American, non-Hispanic/Latino; 88 American Indian or Alaska Native, non-Hispanic/Latino; 293 Asian, non-Hispanic/Latino; 876 Hispanic/Latino; 91 Native Hawaiian or other Pacific Islander, non-Hispanic/Latino; 354 Two or more races, non-Hispanic/Latino), 134 international. Average age 36. In 2013, 3,323 master's awarded. *Degree requirements:* For master's, comprehensive exam or practicum. *Entrance requirements:* For master's, official transcript showing earned bachelor's degree from institution accredited by recognized accrediting body. Additional exam requirements/recommendations for international students: Required—TOEFL (minimum score 550 paper-based), IELTS (minimum score 6.5). *Application deadline:* Applications are processed on a rolling basis. Application fee: $0. Electronic applications accepted. *Expenses: Tuition:* Part-time $325 per semester hour. *Financial support:* Applicants required to submit FAFSA. *Faculty research:* Military history, criminal justice, management performance, national security. *Unit head:* Dr. Karan Powell, Executive Vice President and Provost, 877-468-6268, Fax: 304-724-3780. *Application contact:* Terry Grant, Vice President of Enrollment Management, 877-468-6268, Fax: 304-724-3780, E-mail: info@apus.edu.
Website: http://www.apus.edu.

American University, Kogod School of Business, Washington, DC 20016-8044. Offers accounting (MS); business administration (MBA); business fundamentals (Certificate); entrepreneurship (Certificate); finance (MS); forensic accounting (Certificate); management (MS); marketing (MS); real estate (MS, Certificate); sustainability management (MS); tax (Certificate); taxation (MS). *Accreditation:* AACSB. Part-time and evening/weekend programs available. Postbaccalaureate distance learning degree programs offered. *Faculty:* 75 full-time (24 women), 36 part-time/adjunct (7 women). *Students:* 194 full-time (95 women), 370 part-time (184 women); includes 168 minority (69 Black or African American, non-Hispanic/Latino; 60 Asian, non-Hispanic/Latino; 33 Hispanic/Latino; 2 Native Hawaiian or other Pacific Islander, non-Hispanic/Latino; 4 Two or more races, non-Hispanic/Latino), 108 international. Average age 30. 940 applicants, 46% accepted, 193 enrolled. In 2013, 221 master's, 4 other advanced degrees awarded. *Entrance requirements:* For master's, GMAT, resume, personal statement, interview, 2 letters of recommendation, transcripts. Additional exam requirements/recommendations for international students: Required—TOEFL (minimum score 100 iBT). *Application*

deadline: Applications are processed on a rolling basis. Application fee: $100. Electronic applications accepted. *Expenses:* Contact institution. *Financial support:* Fellowships, career-related internships or fieldwork, Federal Work-Study, institutionally sponsored loans, and tuition waivers (partial) available. Support available to part-time students. Financial award application deadline: 2/1. *Unit head:* Dr. Michael Ginzberg, Dean, 202-885-1985, E-mail: ginzberg@american.edu. *Application contact:* Jason Kennedy, Associate Director of Graduate Admissions, 202-885-1968, E-mail: jkennedy@american.edu.
Website: http://www.kogod.american.edu/.

American University of Sharjah, Graduate Programs, Sharjah, United Arab Emirates. Offers accounting (MS); business (EMBA, MBA); chemical engineering (MS Ch E); civil engineering (MSCE); computer engineering (MS); electrical engineering (MSEE); engineering systems management (MS); mathematics (MS); mechanical engineering (MSME); mechatronics engineering (MS); teaching English to speakers of other languages (MA); translation and interpreting (MA); urban planning (MUP). Part-time and evening/weekend programs available. *Faculty:* 59 full-time (4 women), 5 part-time/adjunct (1 woman). *Students:* 127 full-time (50 women), 342 part-time (148 women). Average age 27. 184 applicants, 83% accepted, 92 enrolled. In 2013, 97 master's awarded. *Degree requirements:* For master's, thesis (for some programs). *Entrance requirements:* For master's, GMAT (for MBA). Additional exam requirements/recommendations for international students: Required—TOEFL (minimum score 550 paper-based; 80 iBT), TWE (minimum score 5); Recommended—IELTS (minimum score 6.5). *Application deadline:* For fall admission, 8/28 priority date for domestic students, 8/14 priority date for international students; for spring admission, 1/22 priority date for domestic students, 1/8 for international students; for summer admission, 5/21 for domestic and international students. Applications are processed on a rolling basis. Application fee: $350. Electronic applications accepted. *Expenses:* Tuition: Full-time 69,660 United Arab Emirates dirhams; part-time 3870 United Arab Emirates dirhams per credit. Tuition and fees vary according to course load and program. *Financial support:* In 2013–14, 63 students received support, including 28 research assistantships with full and partial tuition reimbursements available, 35 teaching assistantships with full and partial tuition reimbursements available; scholarships/grants also available. *Faculty research:* Water pollution, management and waste water treatment, energy and sustainability, air pollution, Islamic finance, family business and small and medium enterprises. *Unit head:* Rami Mahfouz, Director of Enrollment Services, 971-6515-1030, E-mail: mahfouzr@aus.edu. *Application contact:* Mona A. Mabrouk, Graduate Admissions/Office of Enrollment Management, 971-65151012, E-mail: graduateadmission@aus.edu.
Website: http://www.aus.edu/programs/graduate/.

Anderson University, Falls School of Business, Anderson, IN 46012-3495. Offers accountancy (MA); business administration (MBA, DBA). *Accreditation:* ACBSP.

Andrews University, School of Graduate Studies, School of Business, Graduate Programs in Business, Berrien Springs, MI 49104. Offers MBA, MSA. *Faculty:* 10 full-time (4 women). *Students:* 21 full-time (16 women), 39 part-time (22 women); includes 25 minority (10 Black or African American, non-Hispanic/Latino; 4 Asian, non-Hispanic/Latino; 10 Hispanic/Latino; 1 Native Hawaiian or other Pacific Islander, non-Hispanic/Latino), 20 international. Average age 32. 90 applicants, 44% accepted, 24 enrolled. In 2013, 13 master's awarded. *Entrance requirements:* For master's, GMAT. Additional exam requirements/recommendations for international students: Required—TOEFL (minimum score 550 paper-based). Application fee: $40. *Unit head:* Dr. Leonard K. Gashugi, Chair, 769-471-3429, E-mail: gashugi@andrews.edu. *Application contact:* Monica Wringer, Supervisor of Graduate Admission, 800-253-2874, Fax: 269-471-6321, E-mail: graduate@andrews.edu.

Angelo State University, College of Graduate Studies, College of Business, Department of Accounting, Economics, and Finance, San Angelo, TX 76909. Offers professional accountancy (MPAC). Part-time and evening/weekend programs available. *Degree requirements:* For master's, comprehensive exam. *Entrance requirements:* For master's, GMAT, essay. Additional exam requirements/recommendations for international students: Required—TOEFL or IELTS. Electronic applications accepted.

Appalachian State University, Cratis D. Williams Graduate School, Department of Accounting, Boone, NC 28608. Offers taxation (MS). Part-time programs available. *Degree requirements:* For master's, comprehensive exam, thesis optional. *Entrance requirements:* For master's, GMAT, 3 letters of recommendation. Additional exam requirements/recommendations for international students: Required—TOEFL (minimum score 550 paper-based; 79 iBT), IELTS (minimum score 6.5). Electronic applications accepted. *Faculty research:* Audit assurance risk, state taxation, financial accounting inconsistencies, management information systems, charitable contribution taxation.

Argosy University, Atlanta, College of Business, Atlanta, GA 30328. Offers accounting (DBA); corporate compliance (MBA); customized professional concentration (MBA, DBA); finance (MBA); healthcare administration (MBA); information systems (DBA); information systems management (MBA); international business (MBA, DBA); management (MBA, MSM, DBA); marketing (MBA, DBA).

Argosy University, Chicago, College of Business, Chicago, IL 60601. Offers accounting (DBA); customized professional concentration (MBA, DBA); finance (MBA); fraud examination (MBA); global business sustainability (DBA); healthcare administration (MBA); information systems (DBA); information systems management (MBA); international business (MBA, DBA); management (MBA, MSM, DBA); marketing (MBA, DBA); organizational leadership (Ed D); public administration (MBA); sustainable management (MBA). Postbaccalaureate distance learning degree programs offered (minimal on-campus study).

Argosy University, Dallas, College of Business, Farmers Branch, TX 75244. Offers accounting (DBA, AGC); corporate compliance (MBA, Graduate Certificate); customized professional concentration (MBA); finance (MBA, Graduate Certificate); fraud examination (MBA, Graduate Certificate); global business sustainability (DBA, AGC); healthcare administration (Graduate Certificate); healthcare management (MBA); information systems (MBA, DBA, AGC); information systems management (Graduate Certificate); international business (MBA, DBA, AGC, Graduate Certificate); management (MBA, DBA, AGC, Graduate Certificate); marketing (MBA, DBA, AGC, Graduate Certificate); public administration (MBA, Graduate Certificate); sustainable management (MBA, Graduate Certificate).

Argosy University, Denver, College of Business, Denver, CO 80231. Offers accounting (DBA); corporate compliance (MBA); customized professional concentration (MBA, DBA); finance (MBA); fraud examination (MBA); global business sustainability (DBA); healthcare administration (MBA); information systems (DBA); information systems management (MBA); international business (MBA, DBA); management (MBA, MSM, DBA); marketing (MBA, DBA); organizational leadership (Ed D); public administration (MBA); sustainable management (MBA).

Argosy University, Hawai`i, College of Business, Honolulu, HI 96813. Offers accounting (DBA); corporate compliance (MBA); customized professional concentration (MBA, DBA); finance (MBA, Certificate); fraud examination (MBA); global business sustainability (DBA); healthcare administration (MBA, Certificate); information systems (DBA); information systems management (MBA, Certificate); international business

(MBA, DBA, Certificate); management (MBA, MSM, DBA); marketing (MBA, DBA, Certificate); organizational leadership (Ed D); public administration (MBA); sustainable management (MBA).

Argosy University, Inland Empire, College of Business, Ontario, CA 91761. Offers accounting (DBA); corporate compliance (MBA); customized professional concentration (MBA, DBA); finance (MBA); fraud examination (MBA); global business sustainability (DBA); healthcare administration (MBA); information systems (DBA); information systems management (MBA); international business (MBA, DBA); management (MBA, MSM, DBA); marketing (MBA, DBA); organizational leadership (Ed D); public administration (MBA); sustainable management (MBA).

Argosy University, Los Angeles, College of Business, Santa Monica, CA 90045. Offers accounting (DBA); corporate compliance (MBA); customized professional concentration (MBA, DBA); finance (MBA); fraud examination (MBA); global business sustainability (DBA); healthcare administration (MBA); information systems (DBA); information systems management (MBA); international business (MBA, DBA); management (MBA, MSM, DBA); marketing (MBA, DBA); organizational leadership (Ed D); public administration (MBA); sustainable management (MBA).

Argosy University, Nashville, College of Business, Nashville, TN 37214. Offers accounting (DBA); customized professional concentration (MBA, DBA); finance (MBA); healthcare administration (MBA); information systems (MBA, DBA); international business (MBA, DBA); management (MBA, MSM, DBA); marketing (MBA, DBA).

Argosy University, Orange County, College of Business, Orange, CA 92868. Offers accounting (DBA, Adv C); corporate compliance (MBA); customized professional concentration (MBA, DBA); finance (MBA, Certificate); fraud examination (MBA); global business sustainability (DBA); healthcare administration (MBA, Certificate); information systems (DBA, Adv C, Certificate); information systems management (MBA); international business (MBA, DBA, Adv C, Certificate); management (MBA, MSM, DBA, Adv C); marketing (MBA, DBA, Adv C, Certificate); organizational leadership (Ed D); public administration (MBA, Certificate); sustainable management (MBA).

Argosy University, Phoenix, College of Business, Phoenix, AZ 85021. Offers accounting (DBA); corporate compliance (MBA); customized professional concentration (MBA, DBA); finance (MBA); fraud examination (MBA); global business sustainability (DBA); healthcare administration (MBA); information systems (DBA); information systems management (MBA); international business (MBA, DBA); management (MBA, DBA); marketing (MBA, DBA); public administration (MBA); sustainable management (MBA).

Argosy University, Salt Lake City, College of Business, Draper, UT 84020. Offers accounting (DBA); corporate compliance (MBA); customized professional concentration (MBA, DBA); finance (MBA); fraud examination (MBA); global business sustainability (DBA); healthcare administration (MBA); information systems (DBA); information systems management (MBA); international business (MBA, DBA); management (MBA, DBA); marketing (MBA, DBA); public administration (MBA); sustainable management (MBA).

Argosy University, San Diego, College of Business, San Diego, CA 92108. Offers accounting (DBA); corporate compliance (MBA); customized professional concentration (MBA, DBA); finance (MBA); fraud examination (MBA); global business sustainability (DBA); information systems (DBA); information systems management (MBA); international business (MBA, DBA); management (MBA, MSM, DBA); marketing (MBA, DBA); organizational leadership (Ed D); public administration (MBA).

Argosy University, San Francisco Bay Area, College of Business, Alameda, CA 94501. Offers accounting (DBA); corporate compliance (MBA); customized professional concentration (MBA, DBA); finance (MBA); fraud examination (MBA); global business sustainability (DBA); healthcare administration (MBA); information systems (DBA); information systems management (MBA); international business (MBA, DBA); management (MBA, MSM, DBA); marketing (MBA, DBA); organizational leadership (Ed D); public administration (MBA); sustainable management (MBA).

Argosy University, Sarasota, College of Business, Sarasota, FL 34235. Offers accounting (DBA, Adv C); corporate compliance (MBA, DBA, Certificate); customized professional concentration (MBA, DBA); finance (MBA, Certificate); fraud examination (MBA, Certificate); global business sustainability (DBA, Adv C); healthcare administration (MBA, Certificate); information systems (DBA, Adv C, Certificate); information systems management (MBA); international business (MBA, DBA, Adv C, Certificate); management (MBA, MSM, DBA, Adv C, Certificate); marketing (MBA, DBA, Adv C, Certificate); organizational leadership (Ed D); public administration (MBA, Certificate); sustainable management (MBA, Certificate).

Argosy University, Schaumburg, College of Business, Schaumburg, IL 60173-5403. Offers accounting (DBA, Adv C); customized professional concentration (MBA, DBA); finance (MBA, Certificate); fraud examination (MBA); global business sustainability (DBA); healthcare administration (MBA, Certificate); information systems (DBA, Adv C, Certificate); information systems management (MBA); international business (MBA, DBA, Adv C, Certificate); management (MBA, MSM, DBA, Adv C, Certificate); marketing (MBA, DBA, Adv C, Certificate); organizational leadership (Ed D); public administration (MBA); sustainable management (MBA).

Argosy University, Seattle, College of Business, Seattle, WA 98121. Offers accounting (DBA); corporate compliance (MBA); customized professional concentration (MBA, DBA); finance (MBA); fraud examination (MBA); global business sustainability (DBA); healthcare administration (MBA); information systems (DBA); information systems management (MBA); international business (MBA, DBA); management (MBA, MSM, DBA); marketing (MBA, DBA); organizational leadership (Ed D); public administration (MBA); sustainable management (MBA).

Argosy University, Tampa, College of Business, Tampa, FL 33607. Offers accounting (DBA); corporate compliance (MBA); customized professional concentration (MBA, DBA); finance (MBA); fraud examination (MBA); global business sustainability (DBA); healthcare administration (MBA); information systems (DBA); information systems management (MBA); international business (MBA, DBA); management (MBA, MSM, DBA); marketing (MBA, DBA); organizational leadership (Ed D); public administration (MBA); sustainable management (MBA).

Argosy University, Twin Cities, College of Business, Eagan, MN 55121. Offers accounting (DBA); customized professional concentration (MBA, DBA); finance (MBA); fraud examination (MBA); global business sustainability (DBA); healthcare administration (MBA); information systems (DBA); information systems management (MBA); international business (MBA, DBA); management (MBA, MSM, DBA); marketing (MBA, DBA); organizational leadership (Ed D); public administration (MBA); sustainable management (MBA).

Argosy University, Washington DC, College of Business, Arlington, VA 22209. Offers accounting (DBA); customized professional concentration (MBA, DBA); finance (MBA); fraud examination (MBA); global business sustainability (DBA); healthcare administration (MBA); information systems (DBA); information systems management (MBA); international business (MBA, DBA, Certificate); management (MBA, MSM,

DBA); marketing (MBA, DBA, Certificate); organizational leadership (Ed D); public administration (MBA); sustainable management (MBA).

Arizona State University at the Tempe campus, W. P. Carey School of Business, Program in Business Administration, Tempe, AZ 85287-4906. Offers accountancy (PhD); agribusiness (PhD); business administration (MBA); finance (PhD); financial management and markets (MBA); information management (MBA); information systems (PhD); management (PhD); marketing (PhD); strategic marketing and services leadership (MBA); supply chain financial management (MBA); supply chain management (MBA, PhD); JD/MBA; MBA/M Acc; MBA/M Arch. *Accreditation:* AACSB. Part-time and evening/weekend programs available. Postbaccalaureate distance learning degree programs offered (minimal on-campus study). Terminal master's awarded for partial completion of doctoral program. *Degree requirements:* For master's, thesis or alternative, internship, interactive Program of Study (iPOS) submitted before completing 50 percent of required credit hours; for doctorate, comprehensive exam, thesis/dissertation, interactive Program of Study (iPOS) submitted before completing 50 percent of required credit hours. *Entrance requirements:* For master's, GMAT, minimum GPA of 3.0 in last 2 years of work leading to bachelor's degree, 2 letters of recommendation, professional resume, official transcripts, 3 essays; for doctorate, GMAT or GRE, minimum GPA of 3.0 in last 2 years of work leading to bachelor's degree, 3 letters of recommendation, resume, personal statement/essay. Additional exam requirements/recommendations for international students: Required—TOEFL (minimum score 550 paper-based; 80 iBT), IELTS (minimum score 6.5). Electronic applications accepted. *Expenses:* Contact institution.

Arizona State University at the Tempe campus, W. P. Carey School of Business, School of Accountancy, Tempe, AZ 85287-3606. Offers accountancy (M Acc, M Tax); business administration (accountancy) (PhD). *Accreditation:* AACSB. Part-time and evening/weekend programs available. *Degree requirements:* For master's, thesis optional, interactive Program of Study (iPOS) submitted before completing 50 percent of required credit hours. *Entrance requirements:* For master's, GMAT (waivers may apply for ASU accountancy undergraduates), minimum GPA of 3.0 in last 2 years of work leading to bachelor's degree, 2 letters of recommendation, professional resume, official transcripts, responses to 3 essay questions. Additional exam requirements/recommendations for international students: Required—TOEFL (minimum score 550 paper-based; 80 iBT), IELTS (minimum score 6.5). Electronic applications accepted. *Expenses:* Contact institution.

Arkansas State University, Graduate School, College of Business, Department of Accounting, Jonesboro, AR 72467. Offers accountancy (M Acc). Part-time programs available. *Faculty:* 6 full-time (2 women). *Students:* 29 full-time (18 women), 12 part-time (11 women); includes 2 minority (1 Black or African American, non-Hispanic/Latino; 1 Asian, non-Hispanic/Latino), 27 international. Average age 29. 30 applicants, 70% accepted, 18 enrolled. In 2013, 12 master's awarded. *Degree requirements:* For master's, comprehensive exam, thesis or alternative. *Entrance requirements:* For master's, GMAT, appropriate bachelor's degree, letters of reference, official transcript, immunization records. Additional exam requirements/recommendations for international students: Required—TOEFL (minimum score 550 paper-based; 79 iBT), IELTS (minimum score 6), PTE (minimum score 56). *Application deadline:* For fall admission, 7/1 for domestic and international students; for spring admission, 11/15 for domestic students, 11/14 for international students. Applications are processed on a rolling basis. Application fee: $30 ($40 for international students). Electronic applications accepted. *Expenses:* Contact institution. *Financial support:* Career-related internships or fieldwork, scholarships/grants, and unspecified assistantships available. Financial award application deadline: 7/1; financial award applicants required to submit FAFSA. *Unit head:* Dr. John Robertson, Chair, 870-972-3038, Fax: 870-972-3868, E-mail: jfrobert@astate.edu. *Application contact:* Vickey Ring, Graduate Admissions Coordinator, 870-972-3029, Fax: 870-972-3857, E-mail: vickeyring@astate.edu.
Website: http://www.astate.edu/college/business/faculty-staff/accounting/.

Assumption College, Graduate Studies, Department of Business Studies, Worcester, MA 01609-1296. Offers accounting (MBA); business administration (CAGS); finance/economics (MBA); frontline management (CGS); general business (MBA); human resources (MBA); international business (MBA); management (MBA); marketing (MBA); nonprofit leadership (MBA, CGS); organizational communication (CGS). Part-time and evening/weekend programs available. *Faculty:* 5 full-time (0 women), 20 part-time/adjunct (7 women). *Students:* 20 full-time (7 women), 130 part-time (68 women); includes 20 minority (8 Black or African American, non-Hispanic/Latino; 2 Asian, non-Hispanic/Latino; 8 Hispanic/Latino; 1 Native Hawaiian or other Pacific Islander, non-Hispanic/Latino; 1 Two or more races, non-Hispanic/Latino), 2 international. Average age 31. 63 applicants, 62% accepted, 22 enrolled. In 2013, 58 master's, 1 other advanced degree awarded. *Degree requirements:* For master's, thesis, capstone. *Entrance requirements:* For master's and other advanced degree, 3 letters of recommendation, resume, essay. Additional exam requirements/recommendations for international students: Required—TOEFL (minimum score 540 paper-based; 76 iBT), IELTS (minimum score 6). *Application deadline:* For fall admission, 10/1 for domestic and international students; for winter admission, 2/1 for domestic and international students; for spring admission, 4/1 for domestic and international students. Applications are processed on a rolling basis. Application fee: $30. Electronic applications accepted. *Expenses: Tuition:* Full-time $10,098; part-time $561 per credit. *Required fees:* $20 per term. Full-time tuition and fees vary according to course load and program. *Financial support:* In 2013–14, 15 students received support. Tuition waivers (full and partial), unspecified assistantships, and institutional discounts available. Financial award application deadline: 5/1; financial award applicants required to submit FAFSA. *Faculty research:* Workplace diversity, dynamics of team interaction, utilization of leased employees, experiential learning project on due diligence market for prostheses. *Unit head:* Dr. J. Bart Morrison, Director, 508-767-7458, Fax: 508-767-7252, E-mail: jmorrison@assumption.edu. *Application contact:* Laura Lawrence, Graduate Programs Operations Manager, 508-767-7387, Fax: 508-767-7030, E-mail: graduate@assumption.edu.
Website: http://graduate.assumption.edu/mba/assumption-mba.

Auburn University, Graduate School, College of Business, School of Accountancy, Auburn University, AL 36849. Offers M Acc. *Accreditation:* AACSB. Part-time programs available. *Faculty:* 17 full-time (8 women), 3 part-time/adjunct (1 woman). *Students:* 43 full-time (26 women), 49 part-time (23 women); includes 6 minority (1 Black or African American, non-Hispanic/Latino; 1 American Indian or Alaska Native, non-Hispanic/Latino; 3 Asian, non-Hispanic/Latino; 1 Hispanic/Latino). Average age 28. 128 applicants, 49% accepted, 57 enrolled. In 2013, 74 master's awarded. *Entrance requirements:* For master's, GMAT, GRE General Test. Additional exam requirements/recommendations for international students: Required—TOEFL. *Application deadline:* For fall admission, 7/7 for domestic students; for spring admission, 11/24 for domestic students. Applications are processed on a rolling basis. Application fee: $50 ($60 for international students). Electronic applications accepted. *Expenses:* Tuition, state resident: full-time $8262; part-time $459 per credit hour. Tuition, nonresident: full-time $24,786; part-time $1377 per credit hour. Tuition and fees vary according to degree level and program. *Financial support:* Teaching assistantships and Federal Work-Study available. Support available to part-time students. Financial award application deadline: 3/15; financial award applicants required to submit FAFSA. *Unit head:* Dewayne Searcy, Director, 334-844-5827. *Application contact:* Dr. George Flowers, Dean of the Graduate School, 334-844-2125.
Website: http://business.auburn.edu/academics/departments/school-of-accountancy.

Avila University, School of Business, Kansas City, MO 64145-1698. Offers accounting (MBA); finance (MBA); health care administration (MBA); international business (MBA); management (MBA); management information systems (MBA); marketing (MBA). Part-time and evening/weekend programs available. *Faculty:* 9 full-time (4 women), 12 part-time/adjunct (3 women). *Students:* 66 full-time (32 women), 46 part-time (27 women); includes 34 minority (22 Black or African American, non-Hispanic/Latino; 1 American Indian or Alaska Native, non-Hispanic/Latino; 4 Asian, non-Hispanic/Latino; 7 Hispanic/Latino), 27 international. Average age 32. 30 applicants, 80% accepted, 24 enrolled. In 2013, 61 master's awarded. *Degree requirements:* For master's, comprehensive exam, capstone course. *Entrance requirements:* For master's, GMAT (minimum score 420), minimum GPA of 3.0, interview. Additional exam requirements/recommendations for international students: Required—TOEFL (minimum score 550 paper-based). *Application deadline:* For fall admission, 7/30 priority date for domestic and international students; for winter admission, 11/30 priority date for domestic and international students; for spring admission, 2/28 priority date for domestic and international students; for summer admission, 6/1 priority date for domestic and international students. Applications are processed on a rolling basis. Application fee: $0. Electronic applications accepted. *Expenses:* Contact institution. *Financial support:* In 2013–14, 11 students received support. Career-related internships or fieldwork and scholarships/grants available. Support available to part-time students. Financial award applicants required to submit FAFSA. *Faculty research:* Leadership characteristics, financial hedging, group dynamics. *Unit head:* Dr. Richard Woodall, Dean, 816-501-3720, Fax: 816-501-2463, E-mail: richard.woodall@avila.edu. *Application contact:* Sarah Belanus, MBA Admissions Director, 816-501-3601, Fax: 816-501-2463, E-mail: sarah.belanus@avila.edu.
Website: http://www.avila.edu/mba.

Babson College, F. W. Olin Graduate School of Business, Wellesley, MA 02457-0310. Offers accounting (MSA); advanced management (Certificate); business administration (MBA); global entrepreneurship (MS); technological entrepreneurship (MS). *Accreditation:* AACSB. Part-time and evening/weekend programs available. Postbaccalaureate distance learning degree programs offered (minimal on-campus study). *Entrance requirements:* For master's, GMAT, 2 years of work experience, resume, letters of recommendation. Additional exam requirements/recommendations for international students: Required—TOEFL (minimum score 100 iBT), IELTS (minimum score 6.5). Electronic applications accepted. *Faculty research:* Entrepreneurship, sustainability, global markets, process of innovation, social media and advertising.

Baker College Center for Graduate Studies - Online, Graduate Programs, Flint, MI 48507-9843. Offers accounting (MBA); business administration (DBA); finance (MBA); general business (MBA); health care management (MBA); human resources management (MBA); information management (MBA); leadership studies (MBA); management information systems (MSIS); marketing (MBA). Part-time and evening/weekend programs available. Postbaccalaureate distance learning degree programs offered. *Degree requirements:* For master's, portfolio. *Entrance requirements:* For master's, 3 years of work experience, minimum undergraduate GPA of 2.5, writing sample, 3 letters of recommendation; for doctorate, MBA or acceptable related master's degree from accredited association, 5 years work experience, minimum graduate GPA of 3.25, writing sample, 3 professional references. Additional exam requirements/recommendations for international students: Required—TOEFL (minimum score 550 paper-based). Electronic applications accepted.

Baldwin Wallace University, Graduate Programs, Division of Business, Program in Accounting, Berea, OH 44017-2088. Offers MBA. Part-time and evening/weekend programs available. *Students:* 14 full-time (10 women), 9 part-time (2 women); includes 3 minority (2 Black or African American, non-Hispanic/Latino; 1 Hispanic/Latino), 2 international. Average age 33. 11 applicants, 64% accepted, 4 enrolled. In 2013, 45 master's awarded. *Degree requirements:* For master's, minimum overall GPA of 3.0, completion of all required courses. *Entrance requirements:* For master's, GMAT or minimum undergraduate GPA of 3.0, minimum GPA of 3.0, work experience, bachelor's degree in any field, undergraduate accounting coursework. Additional exam requirements/recommendations for international students: Required—TOEFL (minimum score 523 paper-based; 70 iBT). *Application deadline:* For fall admission, 7/25 priority date for domestic students, 4/30 priority date for international students; for spring admission, 12/15 priority date for domestic students, 9/30 priority date for international students. Applications are processed on a rolling basis. Application fee: $25. Electronic applications accepted. Application fee is waived when completed online. *Expenses:* Contact institution. *Financial support:* Application deadline: 5/1; applicants required to submit FAFSA. *Unit head:* Thomas Garvey, Director, 440-826-2438, Fax: 440-826-3868, E-mail: tgarvey@bw.edu. *Application contact:* Laura Spencer, Graduate Application Specialist, 440-826-2191, Fax: 440-826-3868, E-mail: lspencer@bw.edu.
Website: http://www.bw.edu/academics/bus/programs/amba/.

Ball State University, Graduate School, Miller College of Business, Department of Accounting, Muncie, IN 47306-1099. Offers MS. *Accreditation:* AACSB. *Faculty:* 5 full-time (1 woman). *Students:* 18 full-time (8 women), 1 part-time (0 women); includes 3 minority (1 Black or African American, non-Hispanic/Latino; 2 Asian, non-Hispanic/Latino), 5 international. Average age 25. 38 applicants, 76% accepted, 8 enrolled. In 2013, 26 master's awarded. Application fee: $50. *Financial support:* In 2013–14, 15 students received support, including 5 teaching assistantships with full tuition reimbursements available (averaging $9,762 per year). Financial award application deadline: 3/1. *Unit head:* Dr. Lucinda Van Alst, Head, 765-285-5105, E-mail: lvanalst@bsu.edu. *Application contact:* Dr. Mark Myring, Information Contact, 765-285-5100, Fax: 765-285-8024, E-mail: mmyring@bsu.edu.
Website: http://cms.bsu.edu/Academics/CollegesandDepartments/MCOB/Programs/Depts/Accounting.aspx.

Barry University, Andreas School of Business, Program in Accounting, Miami Shores, FL 33161-6695. Offers MSA.

Baruch College of the City University of New York, Zicklin School of Business, Department of Accounting, Program in Accounting, New York, NY 10010-5585. Offers MBA, MS, PhD. PhD offered jointly with Graduate School and University Center of the City University of New York. *Accreditation:* AACSB. Part-time and evening/weekend programs available. *Degree requirements:* For doctorate, comprehensive exam, thesis/dissertation. *Entrance requirements:* For master's, GMAT, 2 letters of recommendation, resume, 2 years of work experience; for doctorate, GMAT. Additional exam requirements/recommendations for international students: Required—TOEFL (minimum score 590 paper-based), TWE (minimum score 5).

Bayamón Central University, Graduate Programs, Program in Business Administration, Bayamón, PR 00960-1725. Offers accounting (MBA); finance (MBA); general business (MBA); management (MBA); marketing (MBA). Part-time and evening/weekend programs available. *Degree requirements:* For master's, comprehensive exam

(for some programs). *Entrance requirements:* For master's, EXADEP, bachelor's degree in business or related field.

Baylor University, Graduate School, Hankamer School of Business, Department of Accounting and Business Law, Waco, TX 76798. Offers M Acc, MT, JD/MT. *Accreditation:* AACSB. Part-time programs available. *Faculty:* 11 full-time (2 women). *Students:* 64 full-time (33 women), 8 part-time (6 women); includes 14 minority (3 Black or African American, non-Hispanic/Latino; 10 Hispanic/Latino; 1 Two or more races, non-Hispanic/Latino), 3 international. In 2013, 66 master's awarded. *Entrance requirements:* For master's, GMAT. *Application deadline:* For fall admission, 8/1 for domestic students; for spring admission, 12/1 for domestic students. Applications are processed on a rolling basis. Application fee: $25. *Expenses: Tuition:* Full-time $25,866; part-time $1437 per credit hour. *Required fees:* $2736; $152 per credit hour. Tuition and fees vary according to course load and program. *Financial support:* Research assistantships, career-related internships or fieldwork, Federal Work-Study, and institutionally sponsored loans available. *Faculty research:* Continuing professional education (CPE), accounting education, retirement plans. *Unit head:* Dr. Jane Baldwin, Adviser, 254-710-3536, Fax: 254-710-2421, E-mail: jane_baldwin@baylor.edu. *Application contact:* Vicky Todd, Administrative Assistant, 254-710-3718, Fax: 254-710-1066, E-mail: mba@hsb.baylor.edu.

Belmont University, Jack C. Massey Graduate School of Business, Nashville, TN 37212. Offers accelerated (MBA); accounting (M Acc); healthcare (MBA); professional (MBA). *Accreditation:* AACSB. Part-time and evening/weekend programs available. *Faculty:* 46 full-time (16 women), 27 part-time/adjunct (11 women). *Students:* 162 full-time (61 women), 50 part-time (25 women); includes 30 minority (14 Black or African American, non-Hispanic/Latino; 1 American Indian or Alaska Native, non-Hispanic/Latino; 7 Asian, non-Hispanic/Latino; 5 Hispanic/Latino; 3 Two or more races, non-Hispanic/Latino), 5 international. Average age 28. 148 applicants, 64% accepted, 77 enrolled. In 2013, 136 master's awarded. *Entrance requirements:* For master's, GMAT, 2 years of work experience (MBA). Additional exam requirements/recommendations for international students: Required—TOEFL (minimum score 550 paper-based). *Application deadline:* For fall admission, 7/1 for domestic and international students; for spring admission, 11/1 for domestic and international students. Applications are processed on a rolling basis. Application fee: $50. Electronic applications accepted. *Expenses:* Contact institution. *Financial support:* Scholarships/grants, tuition waivers (partial), and unspecified assistantships available. Financial award application deadline: 7/1; financial award applicants required to submit FAFSA. *Faculty research:* Music business, strategy, ethics, finance, accounting systems. *Unit head:* Dr. Patrick Raines, Dean, 615-460-6480, Fax: 615-460-6455, E-mail: pat.raines@belmont.edu. *Application contact:* Tonya Hollin, Admissions Assistant, 615-460-6480, Fax: 615-460-6353, E-mail: masseyadmissions@belmont.edu.
Website: http://www.belmont.edu/business/masseyschool/.

Benedictine University, Graduate Programs, Program in Accountancy, Lisle, IL 60532-0900. Offers MS. Evening/weekend programs available. *Students:* 8 full-time (3 women), 39 part-time (23 women); includes 14 minority (6 Black or African American, non-Hispanic/Latino; 6 Asian, non-Hispanic/Latino; 2 Hispanic/Latino), 5 international. 19 applicants, 68% accepted, 6 enrolled. In 2013, 23 master's awarded. *Entrance requirements:* For master's, official transcripts, 2 letters of reference, resume. Additional exam requirements/recommendations for international students: Required—TOEFL. *Application deadline:* Applications are processed on a rolling basis. Electronic applications accepted. *Expenses: Tuition:* Part-time $590 per credit hour. *Unit head:* Dr. Sharon Borowicz, Director, 630-829-6219, E-mail: sborowicz@ben.edu. *Application contact:* Kari Gibbons, Associate Vice President, Enrollment Center, 630-829-6200, Fax: 630-829-6584, E-mail: kgibbons@ben.edu.

Benedictine University, Graduate Programs, Program in Business Administration, Lisle, IL 60532-0900. Offers accounting (MBA); entrepreneurship and managing innovation (MBA); financial management (MBA); health administration (MBA); human resource management (MBA); information systems security (MBA); international business (MBA); management consulting (MBA); management information systems (MBA); marketing management (MBA); operations management and logistics (MBA); organizational leadership (MBA). Part-time and evening/weekend programs available. Postbaccalaureate distance learning degree programs offered (minimal on-campus study). *Faculty:* 4 full-time (2 women), 24 part-time/adjunct (3 women). *Students:* 144 full-time (83 women), 599 part-time (328 women); includes 189 minority (115 Black or African American, non-Hispanic/Latino; 5 American Indian or Alaska Native, non-Hispanic/Latino; 43 Asian, non-Hispanic/Latino; 24 Hispanic/Latino; 2 Native Hawaiian or other Pacific Islander, non-Hispanic/Latino), 14 international. Average age 34. 211 applicants, 89% accepted, 155 enrolled. In 2013, 376 master's awarded. *Entrance requirements:* For master's, GMAT. Additional exam requirements/recommendations for international students: Required—TOEFL (minimum score 550 paper-based). *Application deadline:* For fall admission, 9/1 for domestic students; for winter admission, 12/1 for domestic students; for spring admission, 2/15 for domestic students. Applications are processed on a rolling basis. Application fee: $40. Electronic applications accepted. *Expenses: Tuition:* Part-time $590 per credit hour. *Financial support:* Career-related internships or fieldwork and health care benefits available. Support available to part-time students. *Faculty research:* Strategic leadership in professional organizations, sociology of professions, organizational change, social identity theory, applications to change management. *Unit head:* Dr. Sharon Borowicz, Director, 630-829-6219, E-mail: sborowicz@ben.edu. *Application contact:* Kari Gibbons, Director, Admissions, 630-829-6200, Fax: 630-829-6584, E-mail: kgibbons@ben.edu.

Bentley University, McCallum Graduate School of Business, Accountancy PhD Program, Waltham, MA 02452-4705. Offers PhD. Part-time programs available. *Faculty:* 91 full-time (29 women), 22 part-time/adjunct (4 women). *Students:* 11 full-time (6 women). Average age 35. 19 applicants, 26% accepted, 4 enrolled. In 2013, 4 doctorates awarded. *Degree requirements:* For doctorate, comprehensive exam, thesis/dissertation. *Entrance requirements:* For doctorate, GMAT or GRE General Test. Additional exam requirements/recommendations for international students: Required—TOEFL (minimum score 650 paper-based; 100 iBT) or IELTS (minimum score 7). Application fee: $0. *Expenses: Tuition:* Full-time $30,400; part-time $1267 per credit. *Required fees:* $404. Tuition and fees vary according to course load and program. *Financial support:* In 2013–14, 11 students received support. Scholarships/grants available. Financial award applicants required to submit CSS PROFILE or FAFSA. *Faculty research:* Accounting information systems, financial fraud, forensic accounting, enterprise risks and controls, managerial incentive systems. *Unit head:* Dr. Sue Newell, Director, 781-891-2399, Fax: 781-891-3121, E-mail: snewell@bentley.edu. *Application contact:* Sharon Hill, Director of Graduate Admissions, 781-891-2108, Fax: 781-891-2464, E-mail: bentleygraduateadmissions@bentley.edu.
Website: http://www.bentley.edu/offices/phd/phd-accountancy/.

Bentley University, McCallum Graduate School of Business, Master's Program in Accounting, Waltham, MA 02452-4705. Offers MSA. *Accreditation:* AACSB. Part-time and evening/weekend programs available. *Faculty:* 91 full-time (29 women), 22 part-time/adjunct (4 women). *Students:* 212 full-time (146 women), 80 part-time (44 women); includes 34 minority (4 Black or African American, non-Hispanic/Latino; 1 American Indian or Alaska Native, non-Hispanic/Latino; 22 Asian, non-Hispanic/Latino; 5 Hispanic/Latino; 2 Two or more races, non-Hispanic/Latino), 125 international. Average age 25. 599 applicants, 47% accepted, 151 enrolled. In 2013, 208 master's awarded. *Entrance requirements:* For master's, GMAT or GRE General Test. Additional exam requirements/recommendations for international students: Required—TOEFL (minimum score 600 paper-based; 100 iBT) or IELTS (minimum score 7). *Application deadline:* For fall admission, 12/1 priority date for domestic and international students. Application fee: $50. Electronic applications accepted. *Expenses: Tuition:* Full-time $30,400; part-time $1267 per credit. *Required fees:* $404. Tuition and fees vary according to course load and program. *Financial support:* In 2013–14, 44 students received support. Scholarships/grants and unspecified assistantships available. Financial award application deadline: 6/1; financial award applicants required to submit CSS PROFILE or FAFSA. *Faculty research:* Audit risk assessment, ethics in accounting, corporate governance, accounting information systems and management control, tax policy, forensic accounting. *Unit head:* Dr. Donna McConville, Director, 781-891-2108, E-mail: dmcconville@bentley.edu. *Application contact:* Sharon Hill, Director of Graduate Admissions, 781-891-2108, Fax: 781-891-2464, E-mail: bentleygraduateadmissions@bentley.edu.
Website: http://www.bentley.edu/graduate/degree-programs/ms-programs/accountancy.

Binghamton University, State University of New York, Graduate School, School of Management, Program in Accounting, Vestal, NY 13850. Offers MS. Evening/weekend programs available. *Students:* 193 full-time (105 women), 13 part-time (6 women); includes 36 minority (32 Asian, non-Hispanic/Latino; 3 Hispanic/Latino; 1 Native Hawaiian or other Pacific Islander, non-Hispanic/Latino), 102 international. Average age 24. 525 applicants, 45% accepted, 144 enrolled. In 2013, 144 master's awarded. *Entrance requirements:* For master's, GMAT. Additional exam requirements/recommendations for international students: Required—TOEFL (minimum score 550 paper-based; 80 iBT). *Application deadline:* For fall admission, 3/1 priority date for domestic and international students; for spring admission, 10/15 priority date for domestic and international students. Applications are processed on a rolling basis. Application fee: $75. Electronic applications accepted. *Financial support:* In 2013–14, 9 students received support. Career-related internships or fieldwork, Federal Work-Study, institutionally sponsored loans, scholarships/grants, health care benefits, and unspecified assistantships available. Financial award application deadline: 2/15; financial award applicants required to submit FAFSA. *Unit head:* Dr. Upinder Dhillon, Dean of School of Management, 607-777-2314, E-mail: dhillon@binghamton.edu. *Application contact:* Kishan Zuber, Recruiting and Admissions Coordinator, 607-777-2151, Fax: 607-777-2501, E-mail: kzuber@binghamton.edu.

Bloomfield College, Program in Accounting, Bloomfield, NJ 07003-9981. Offers MS.

Bloomsburg University of Pennsylvania, School of Graduate Studies, College of Business, Program in Accounting, Bloomsburg, PA 17815-1301. Offers M Acc. *Faculty:* 4 full-time (0 women). *Students:* 1 full-time (0 women), 16 part-time (7 women); includes 2 minority (1 Black or African American, non-Hispanic/Latino; 1 Hispanic/Latino), 1 international. Average age 24. 24 applicants, 71% accepted, 13 enrolled. In 2013, 8 master's awarded. *Degree requirements:* For master's, minimum QPA of 3.0. *Entrance requirements:* For master's, GRE, GMAT, 2 letters of recommendation, resume. Additional exam requirements/recommendations for international students: Required—TOEFL. *Application deadline:* Applications are processed on a rolling basis. Application fee: $35 ($60 for international students). Electronic applications accepted. *Expenses:* Tuition, state resident: full-time $7956; part-time $442 per credit. Tuition, nonresident: full-time $11,934; part-time $663 per credit. *Required fees:* $95.50 per credit. $55 per semester. Tuition and fees vary according to course load. *Unit head:* Dr. Gary Robson, Chair, 570-389-4519, Fax: 570-389-3892, E-mail: grobson@bloomu.edu. *Application contact:* Jennifer Richard, Administrative Assistant, 570-389-4015, Fax: 570-389-3054, E-mail: jrichard@bloomu.edu.
Website: http://www.bloomu.edu/accounting.

Bob Jones University, Graduate Programs, Greenville, SC 29614. Offers accountancy (MS); Bible (MA); Bible translation (MA); Biblical studies (Certificate); broadcast management (MS); business administration (MBA); church history (MA, PhD); church ministries (MA); church music (MM); cinema and video production (MA); counseling (MS); curriculum and instruction (Ed D); divinity (M Div); dramatic production (MA); educational leadership (MS, Ed D, Ed S); elementary education (M Ed, MAT); English (M Ed, MA, MAT); fine arts (MA); graphic design (MA); history (M Ed, MA); illustration (MA); interpretative speech (MA); mathematics (M Ed, MAT); medical missions (Certificate); ministry (MM, D Min); multi-categorical special education (M Ed, MAT); music (M Ed); New Testament interpretation (PhD); Old Testament interpretation (PhD); orchestral instrument performance (MM); organ performance (MM); pastoral studies (MA); personnel services (MS, Ed S); piano pedagogy (MM); piano performance (MM); platform arts (MA); radio and television broadcasting (MS); rhetoric and public address (MA); secondary education (M Ed); studio art (MA); teaching Bible (MA); theology (MA, PhD); voice performance (MM); youth ministries (MA); M Div/MM.

Boise State University, College of Business and Economics, Program in Accountancy, Boise, ID 83725-0399. Offers accountancy (MSA); taxation (MSA). *Accreditation:* AACSB. Part-time programs available. *Entrance requirements:* For master's, GMAT, minimum GPA of 3.0. Additional exam requirements/recommendations for international students: Required—TOEFL. Electronic applications accepted.

Boston College, Carroll School of Management, Programs in Accounting, Chestnut Hill, MA 02467-3800. Offers MSA. *Faculty:* 10 full-time (2 women), 8 part-time/adjunct (1 woman). *Students:* 88 full-time (61 women); includes 10 minority (8 Asian, non-Hispanic/Latino; 2 Hispanic/Latino), 47 international. Average age 23. 458 applicants, 19% accepted, 44 enrolled. In 2013, 100 master's awarded. *Entrance requirements:* For master's, GMAT, GRE, recommendations, resume, transcript. Additional exam requirements/recommendations for international students: Required—TOEFL (minimum score 600 paper-based, 100 iBT), IELTS (minimum score 7.5), or PTE (minimum score 68). *Application deadline:* For fall admission, 2/1 for domestic and international students; for spring admission, 2/15 for domestic and international students. Applications are processed on a rolling basis. Application fee: $100. Electronic applications accepted. *Financial support:* In 2013–14, 46 students received support, including 46 fellowships with full and partial tuition reimbursements available (averaging $4,663 per year); tuition waivers (partial) also available. *Faculty research:* Financial reporting, auditing, tax planning, financial statement analysis. *Unit head:* Dr. Jeffrey L. Ringuest, Associate Dean, Graduate Programs, 617-552-9100, Fax: 617-552-0514, E-mail: gsomdean@bc.edu. *Application contact:* Shelley A. Burt, Director of Graduate Enrollment, 617-552-3920, Fax: 617-552-8078, E-mail: bcmba@bc.edu.
Website: http://www.bc.edu/schools/csom/graduate/msa.html/.

Bowling Green State University, Graduate College, College of Business Administration, Program in Accountancy, Bowling Green, OH 43403. Offers M Acc. *Accreditation:* AACSB. Part-time programs available. *Degree requirements:* For master's, thesis or alternative. *Entrance requirements:* For master's, GMAT. Additional exam requirements/recommendations for international students: Required—TOEFL. Electronic applications accepted. *Faculty research:* Financial reporting and auditing, accounting information systems, taxation.

Accounting

Bradley University, Graduate School, Foster College of Business Administration, Program in Accounting, Peoria, IL 61625-0002. Offers MSA. *Accreditation:* AACSB. Part-time and evening/weekend programs available. *Degree requirements:* For master's, comprehensive exam. *Entrance requirements:* For master's, GMAT, minimum undergraduate GPA of 2.75 in major, 2 letters of recommendation. Additional exam requirements/recommendations for international students: Required—TOEFL (minimum score 550 paper-based; 79 iBT). *Expenses: Tuition:* Full-time $14,580; part-time $810 per credit hour. Tuition and fees vary according to course load and program.

Brenau University, Sydney O. Smith Graduate School, School of Business and Mass Communication, Gainesville, GA 30501. Offers accounting (MBA); business administration (MBA); healthcare management (MBA); organizational leadership (MS); project management (MBA). *Accreditation:* ACBSP. Part-time and evening/weekend programs available. Postbaccalaureate distance learning degree programs offered (no on-campus study). *Degree requirements:* For master's, comprehensive exam (for some programs). *Entrance requirements:* For master's, resume, minimum undergraduate GPA of 2.5. Additional exam requirements/recommendations for international students: Required—TOEFL (minimum score 500 paper-based; 61 iBT); Recommended—IELTS (minimum score 5). Electronic applications accepted. *Expenses:* Contact institution.

Bridgewater State University, School of Graduate Studies, School of Business, Department of Accounting and Finance, Bridgewater, MA 02325-0001. Offers MSM. Part-time and evening/weekend programs available. *Entrance requirements:* For master's, GMAT.

Brigham Young University, Graduate Studies, Marriott School of Management, Master of Accountancy Program, Provo, UT 84602. Offers M Acc, JD/M Acc. *Accreditation:* AACSB. *Entrance requirements:* For master's, GMAT, minimum GPA of 3.0 in last 60 hours. Additional exam requirements/recommendations for international students: Required—TOEFL (minimum score 580 paper-based). Electronic applications accepted. *Expenses:* Contact institution.

Brock University, Faculty of Graduate Studies, Faculty of Business, Program in Accountancy, St. Catharines, ON L2S 3A1, Canada. Offers M Acc. *Degree requirements:* For master's, thesis or alternative. *Entrance requirements:* For master's, honours degree. Additional exam requirements/recommendations for international students: Required—TOEFL (minimum score 550 paper-based; 80 iBT), IELTS (minimum score 6.5), TWE (minimum score 4.5). Electronic applications accepted.

Brooklyn College of the City University of New York, Division of Graduate Studies, Department of Economics, Brooklyn, NY 11210-2889. Offers accounting (MS); business economics (MS), including economic analysis, global business and finance; economics (MA). Part-time and evening/weekend programs available. *Degree requirements:* For master's, comprehensive exam, thesis or alternative. *Entrance requirements:* For master's, GMAT (for MS), 2 letters of recommendation. Additional exam requirements/recommendations for international students: Required—TOEFL (minimum score 550 paper-based; 79 iBT). Electronic applications accepted. *Faculty research:* Econometrics, environmental economics, microeconomics, macroeconomics, taxation.

Bryant University, Graduate School of Business, Master of Professional Accountancy Program, Smithfield, RI 02917. Offers accounting (MPAC); tax (MPAC). *Entrance requirements:* For master's, GMAT, waived for students with a minimum cumulative GPA of 3.5 from an AACSB-accredited institution), transcripts, resume, recommendation, statement of objectives. Additional exam requirements/recommendations for international students: Required—TOEFL (minimum score 580 paper-based; 90 iBT). *Application deadline:* For fall admission, 7/15 for domestic and international students; for spring admission, 11/15 for domestic and international students; for summer admission, 4/1 for domestic and international students. Applications are processed on a rolling basis. Application fee: $80. Electronic applications accepted. *Expenses: Tuition:* Full-time $26,832; part-time $1118 per credit hour. *Financial support:* In 2013–14, 10 students received support, including 10 fellowships with partial tuition reimbursements available (averaging $11,289 per year); scholarships/grants also available. Financial award application deadline: 2/15; financial award applicants required to submit FAFSA. *Faculty research:* Director compensation, public sector auditing, employee stock options, financial disclosure. *Unit head:* Richard S. Cheney, Director of Operations for Graduate Programs, School of Business, 401-232-6707, Fax: 401-232-6494, E-mail: rcheney@bryant.edu. *Application contact:* Nancy Terry, Assistant Director of Graduate Admission, 401-232-6205, Fax: 401-232-6494, E-mail: nterry@bryant.edu.
Website: http://gradschool.bryant.edu/business/mpac.htm.

Butler University, College of Business Administration, Indianapolis, IN 46208-3485. Offers business administration (MBA); professional accounting (MP Acc). *Accreditation:* AACSB. Part-time and evening/weekend programs available. *Faculty:* 12 full-time (3 women), 5 part-time/adjunct (1 woman). *Students:* 30 full-time (6 women), 185 part-time (60 women); includes 18 minority (5 Black or African American, non-Hispanic/Latino; 1 American Indian or Alaska Native, non-Hispanic/Latino; 7 Asian, non-Hispanic/Latino; 4 Hispanic/Latino; 1 Two or more races, non-Hispanic/Latino), 7 international. Average age 31. 146 applicants, 64% accepted, 34 enrolled. In 2013, 57 master's awarded. *Entrance requirements:* For master's, GMAT, minimum AACSB index of 950. *Application deadline:* For fall admission, 8/15 priority date for domestic students. Applications are processed on a rolling basis. Application fee: $35. Electronic applications accepted. *Financial support:* Career-related internships or fieldwork and institutionally sponsored loans available. Support available to part-time students. Financial award application deadline: 7/15; financial award applicants required to submit FAFSA. *Unit head:* Dr. Stephen Standifird, Dean. *Application contact:* Diane Dubord, Graduate Student Service Specialist, 317-940-8107, Fax: 317-940-8250, E-mail: ddubord@butler.edu.
Website: http://www.butler.edu/academics/graduate-cob/.

Cabrini College, Graduate Studies, Radnor, PA 19087-3698. Offers accounting (M Acc); education (M Ed); leadership (MS). Part-time and evening/weekend programs available. *Faculty:* 9 full-time (7 women), 81 part-time/adjunct (64 women). *Students:* 75 full-time (53 women), 1,031 part-time (789 women); includes 135 minority (95 Black or African American, non-Hispanic/Latino; 13 Asian, non-Hispanic/Latino; 24 Hispanic/Latino; 3 Two or more races, non-Hispanic/Latino). Average age 33. 417 applicants, 73% accepted, 261 enrolled. In 2013, 717 master's awarded. *Degree requirements:* For master's, thesis optional. *Entrance requirements:* For master's, GRE and/or MAT (in some cases), bachelor's degree with minimum GPA of 3.0, one-page personal essay/statement, professional letter of recommendation. Additional exam requirements/recommendations for international students: Required—TOEFL. *Application deadline:* For fall admission, 7/29 priority date for domestic students, 7/29 for international students; for spring admission, 12/9 for domestic and international students. Applications are processed on a rolling basis. Application fee: $50. Electronic applications accepted. *Expenses: Tuition:* Part-time $595 per credit hour. *Financial support:* Career-related internships or fieldwork and unspecified assistantships available. Support available to part-time students. Financial award applicants required to submit FAFSA. *Unit head:* Dr. Jeffrey P. Gingerich, Vice Provost/Dean for Academic Affairs, 610-902-8302, Fax: 610-902-8552, E-mail: jeffrey.p.gingerich@cabrini.edu.

Application contact: Bruce D. Bryde, Director of Enrollment and Recruiting, 610-902-8291, Fax: 610-902-8522, E-mail: bruce.d.bryde@cabrini.edu.
Website: http://cabrini.edu/graduate.

Caldwell University, Graduate Studies, Division of Business, Caldwell, NJ 07006-6195. Offers accounting (MS); business administration (MBA). *Accreditation:* ACBSP. Part-time programs available. *Faculty:* 7 full-time (2 women), 4 part-time/adjunct (3 women). *Students:* 14 full-time (2 women), 49 part-time (35 women); includes 22 minority (10 Black or African American, non-Hispanic/Latino; 3 Asian, non-Hispanic/Latino; 8 Hispanic/Latino; 1 Two or more races, non-Hispanic/Latino). Average age 35. 46 applicants, 46% accepted, 18 enrolled. In 2013, 11 master's awarded. *Entrance requirements:* For master's, GMAT, undergraduate accounting, marketing, and finance. Additional exam requirements/recommendations for international students: Required—TOEFL (minimum score 580 paper-based). *Application deadline:* Applications are processed on a rolling basis. Application fee: $40. Electronic applications accepted. *Unit head:* Bernard O'Rourke, Division Associate Dean, 973-618-3409, Fax: 973-618-3355, E-mail: borourke@caldwell.edu. *Application contact:* Vilma Mueller, Director of Graduate Studies, 973-618-3544, E-mail: graduate@caldwell.edu.
Website: http://www.caldwell.edu/graduate.

California Baptist University, Program in Business Administration, Riverside, CA 92504-3206. Offers accounting (MBA); construction management (MBA); healthcare management (MBA); management (MBA). *Accreditation:* ACBSP. Part-time and evening/weekend programs available. Postbaccalaureate distance learning degree programs offered (minimal on-campus study). *Faculty:* 14 full-time (5 women), 4 part-time/adjunct (1 woman). *Students:* 49 full-time (20 women), 53 part-time (20 women); includes 43 minority (8 Black or African American, non-Hispanic/Latino; 2 American Indian or Alaska Native, non-Hispanic/Latino; 4 Asian, non-Hispanic/Latino; 28 Hispanic/Latino; 1 Two or more races, non-Hispanic/Latino), 6 international. Average age 28. 119 applicants, 60% accepted, 43 enrolled. In 2013, 46 master's awarded. *Degree requirements:* For master's, interdisciplinary capstone project. *Entrance requirements:* For master's, GMAT, minimum GPA of 2.5; two recommendations; comprehensive essay; resume; interview; 4 prerequisite courses. Additional exam requirements/recommendations for international students: Required—TOEFL (minimum score 80 iBT). *Application deadline:* For fall admission, 8/1 priority date for domestic students, 7/1 for international students; for spring admission, 12/1 priority date for domestic students, 11/1 for international students. Applications are processed on a rolling basis. Application fee: $45. Electronic applications accepted. *Expenses:* Contact institution. *Financial support:* Institutionally sponsored loans available. Financial award applicants required to submit CSS PROFILE or FAFSA. *Faculty research:* Econometrics, Biblical financial principles, strategic management and corporate performance, shared leadership models, international culture and economics. *Unit head:* Dr. Franco Gandolfi, Dean, School of Business, 951-343-4968, Fax: 951-343-4361, E-mail: fgandolfi@calbaptist.edu. *Application contact:* Dr. Keanon Alderson, Director, Business Administration Program, 951-343-4768, E-mail: kalderson@calbaptist.edu.
Website: http://www.calbaptist.edu/mba/about/.

California State Polytechnic University, Pomona, Academic Affairs, College of Business Administration, Master of Science in Business Administration Program, Pomona, CA 91768-2557. Offers information systems auditing (MS). *Students:* 3 full-time (2 women), 8 part-time (4 women); includes 7 minority (6 Asian, non-Hispanic/Latino; 1 Hispanic/Latino), 1 international. Average age 28. 28 applicants, 32% accepted, 5 enrolled. In 2013, 5 master's awarded. *Application deadline:* Applications are processed on a rolling basis. Application fee: $55. Electronic applications accepted. *Expenses:* Tuition, state resident: full-time $6738. Tuition, nonresident: full-time $12,690. *Required fees:* $878; $248 per credit hour. *Unit head:* Dr. Richard S. Lapidus, Dean, 909-869-2400, Fax: 909-869-6799, E-mail: rslapidus@csupomona.edu. *Application contact:* Tricia Alicante, Graduate Coordinator, 909-869-4894, E-mail: taalicante@csupomona.edu.
Website: http://cba.csupomona.edu/graduateprograms/.

California State Polytechnic University, Pomona, Academic Affairs, College of Business Administration, Program in Accountancy, Pomona, CA 91768-2557. Offers MS. *Students:* Average age 32. In 2013, 1 master's awarded. *Application deadline:* Applications are processed on a rolling basis. Application fee: $55. Electronic applications accepted. *Expenses:* Tuition, state resident: full-time $6738. Tuition, nonresident: full-time $12,690. *Required fees:* $878; $248 per credit hour. *Unit head:* Dr. Richard S. Lapidus, Dean, 909-869-2363, E-mail: rslapidus@csupomona.edu. *Application contact:* Tricia Alicante, Associate Dean, 909-869-4894, E-mail: taalicante@csupomona.edu.
Website: http://cba.csupomona.edu/cba/news/.

California State University, East Bay, Office of Academic Programs and Graduate Studies, College of Business and Economics, Department of Accounting and Finance, Option in Accounting/Finance, Hayward, CA 94542-3000. Offers MBA. *Degree requirements:* For master's, comprehensive exam or thesis. *Entrance requirements:* For master's, GMAT, minimum GPA of 2.75. Additional exam requirements/recommendations for international students: Required—TOEFL (minimum score 550 paper-based). Electronic applications accepted.

California State University, Fresno, Division of Graduate Studies, Craig School of Business, Department of Accountancy, Fresno, CA 93740-8027. Offers MS. Part-time programs available. *Degree requirements:* For master's, comprehensive exam. *Entrance requirements:* For master's, GMAT, minimum GPA of 2.75. Additional exam requirements/recommendations for international students: Required—TOEFL. Electronic applications accepted.

California State University, Fullerton, Graduate Studies, College of Business and Economics, Department of Accounting, Fullerton, CA 92834-9480. Offers accounting (MBA, MS); taxation (MS). *Accreditation:* AACSB. Part-time programs available. *Students:* 138 full-time (85 women), 75 part-time (43 women); includes 104 minority (3 Black or African American, non-Hispanic/Latino; 79 Asian, non-Hispanic/Latino; 20 Hispanic/Latino; 2 Two or more races, non-Hispanic/Latino), 71 international. Average age 27. 275 applicants, 60% accepted, 75 enrolled. In 2013, 74 master's awarded. *Degree requirements:* For master's, thesis or alternative, project. *Entrance requirements:* For master's, GMAT, minimum AACSB index of 950. *Application deadline:* Applications are processed on a rolling basis. Application fee: $55. Electronic applications accepted. *Financial support:* Career-related internships or fieldwork, Federal Work-Study, institutionally sponsored loans, and scholarships/grants available. Support available to part-time students. Financial award application deadline: 3/1; financial award applicants required to submit FAFSA. *Unit head:* Dr. Betty Chavis, Chair, 657-278-2225. *Application contact:* Admissions/Applications, 657-278-2371.

California State University, Los Angeles, Graduate Studies, College of Business and Economics, Department of Accounting, Los Angeles, CA 90032-8530. Offers accountancy (MS), including business taxation, financial accounting, information systems, management accounting; accounting (MBA). Part-time and evening/weekend programs available. *Faculty:* 4 full-time (0 women), 4 part-time/adjunct (2 women). *Students:* 35 full-time (23 women), 48 part-time (23 women); includes 38 minority (5 Black or African American, non-Hispanic/Latino; 26 Asian, non-Hispanic/Latino; 7

Hispanic/Latino), 33 international. Average age 31. 155 applicants, 48% accepted, 37 enrolled. In 2013, 36 master's awarded. *Degree requirements:* For master's, comprehensive exam (MBA), thesis (MS). *Entrance requirements:* For master's, GMAT, minimum GPA of 2.5 during previous 2 years of course work. Additional exam requirements/recommendations for international students: Required—TOEFL (minimum score 550 paper-based). *Application deadline:* For fall admission, 5/1 for domestic and international students. Applications are processed on a rolling basis. Application fee: $55. Electronic applications accepted. *Financial support:* Career-related internships or fieldwork and Federal Work-Study available. Support available to part-time students. Financial award application deadline: 3/1. *Unit head:* Dr. Kathryn Hansen, Chair, 323-343-2830, Fax: 323-343-6439, E-mail: khansen3@calstatela.edu. *Application contact:* Dr. Larry Fritz, Dean of Graduate Studies, 323-343-3820, Fax: 323-343-5653, E-mail: lfritz@calstatela.edu.
Website: http://cbe.calstatela.edu/acct/.

California State University, Sacramento, Office of Graduate Studies, College of Business Administration, Sacramento, CA 95819. Offers accountancy (MS); business administration (IMBA, MBA); human resources (MBA); urban land development (MBA). *Accreditation:* AACSB. Part-time and evening/weekend programs available. *Degree requirements:* For master's, thesis or alternative, writing proficiency exam. *Entrance requirements:* For master's, GMAT. Additional exam requirements/recommendations for international students: Required—TOEFL. *Application deadline:* For fall admission, 2/1 for domestic students, 3/1 for international students; for spring admission, 9/15 for domestic students, 9/30 for international students. Applications are processed on a rolling basis. Application fee: $55. Electronic applications accepted. *Financial support:* Research assistantships, teaching assistantships, career-related internships or fieldwork, and Federal Work-Study available. Support available to part-time students. Financial award applicants required to submit FAFSA. *Unit head:* Dr. Sanjay Varshney, Dean, 916-278-6942, Fax: 916-278-5793, E-mail: cba@csus.edu. *Application contact:* Jose Martinez, Graduate Admissions Supervisor, 916-278-7871, E-mail: martinj@skymail.csus.edu.
Website: http://www.cba.csus.edu.

California State University, San Bernardino, Graduate Studies, College of Business and Public Administration, Master in Business Administration Program, San Bernardino, CA 92407. Offers accounting (MBA); cyber security (MBA); entrepreneurship (MBA); finance (MBA); information systems and technology (MBA); management (MBA); marketing management (MBA); supply chain management (MBA). MBA is also offered online. *Accreditation:* AACSB. Part-time and evening/weekend programs available. Postbaccalaureate distance learning degree programs offered (no on-campus study). *Faculty:* 27 full-time (6 women), 8 part-time/adjunct (1 woman). *Students:* 161 full-time (59 women), 47 part-time (18 women); includes 74 minority (12 Black or African American, non-Hispanic/Latino; 19 Asian, non-Hispanic/Latino; 42 Hispanic/Latino; 1 Two or more races, non-Hispanic/Latino), 74 international. Average age 29. 281 applicants, 38% accepted, 67 enrolled. In 2013, 79 master's awarded. *Degree requirements:* For master's, comprehensive exam, thesis, portfolio, 60 units, minimum GPA of 3.0. *Entrance requirements:* For master's, GMAT or GRE, minimum GPA of 2.5. Additional exam requirements/recommendations for international students: Required—TOEFL (minimum score 550 paper-based; 79 iBT). *Application deadline:* For fall admission, 7/20 for domestic and international students; for winter admission, 10/20 for domestic and international students; for spring admission, 1/20 for domestic and international students. Applications are processed on a rolling basis. Application fee: $55. Electronic applications accepted. *Expenses:* Contact institution. *Financial support:* In 2013–14, 79 students received support, including 21 fellowships (averaging $4,867 per year), 29 research assistantships (averaging $2,748 per year), 6 teaching assistantships (averaging $5,162 per year); career-related internships or fieldwork, Federal Work-Study, institutionally sponsored loans, scholarships/grants, and unspecified assistantships also available. Support available to part-time students. Financial award application deadline: 3/1; financial award applicants required to submit FAFSA. *Faculty research:* Market reaction to Form 20-F, tax Constitutional questions in Obamacare, the performance of the faith and ethical investment products prior to and following the 2008 meltdown, capital appreciation bonds: a ruinous decision for an unborn generation, the effects of calorie count display on consumer eating behavior, local government bankruptcy. *Total annual research expenditures:* $2.3 million. *Unit head:* Dr. Lawrence C. Rose, Dean, 909-537-3703, Fax: 909-537-7026, E-mail: lrose@csusb.edu. *Application contact:* Dr. Vipin Gupta, Associate Dean/MBA Director, 909-537-7380, Fax: 909-537-7026, E-mail: vgupta@csusb.edu.
Website: http://mba.csusb.edu.

California Western School of Law, Graduate and Professional Programs, San Diego, CA 92101-3090. Offers law (LL M, JD); JD/MBA; JD/MSW; JD/PhD; MCL/LL M. JD/MSW and JD/MBA offered jointly with San Diego State University; JD/PhD with University of California, San Diego. *Accreditation:* ABA. Part-time programs available. *Entrance requirements:* For doctorate, LSAT. Additional exam requirements/recommendations for international students: Required—TOEFL. Electronic applications accepted. *Faculty research:* Biotechnology, child and family law, international law, labor and employment law, sports law.

Canisius College, Graduate Division, Richard J. Wehle School of Business, Department of Accounting, Buffalo, NY 14208-1098. Offers accounting (MBA); forensic accounting (MS); professional accounting (MBA). Part-time and evening/weekend programs available. *Faculty:* 8 full-time (1 woman), 1 (woman) part-time/adjunct. *Students:* 35 full-time (14 women), 33 part-time (14 women); includes 10 minority (3 Black or African American, non-Hispanic/Latino; 4 Asian, non-Hispanic/Latino; 1 Hispanic/Latino; 2 Two or more races, non-Hispanic/Latino), 3 international. Average age 29. 46 applicants, 70% accepted, 23 enrolled. In 2013, 33 master's awarded. *Entrance requirements:* For master's, GMAT, GRE, official transcript from colleges attended, current resume. Additional exam requirements/recommendations for international students: Required—TOEFL (minimum score 550 paper-based, 80 iBT), IELTS (minimum score 6.5), or CAEL (minimum score 70). *Application deadline:* For fall admission, 7/1 priority date for domestic students; for spring admission, 11/1 priority date for domestic students. Applications are processed on a rolling basis. Application fee: $25. Electronic applications accepted. Application fee is waived when completed online. *Expenses: Tuition:* Part-time $750 per credit hour. *Financial support:* Career-related internships or fieldwork, Federal Work-Study, scholarships/grants, tuition waivers (partial), and unspecified assistantships available. Support available to part-time students. Financial award application deadline: 4/30; financial award applicants required to submit FAFSA. *Faculty research:* Auditing (process and operational factors), fraud from a global perspective, managing risk in software development, valuation of intellectual property. *Unit head:* Dr. Joseph B. O'Donnell, Chair/Professor, 716-888-2868, E-mail: odonnelj@canisius.edu. *Application contact:* Julie A. Zulewski, Director, Graduate Admissions, 716-888-2548, Fax: 716-888-3195, E-mail: zulewskj@canisius.edu.
Website: http://www.canisius.edu/graduate/.

Capella University, School of Business and Technology, Doctoral Programs in Business, Minneapolis, MN 55402. Offers accounting (DBA, PhD); business intelligence (DBA); finance (DBA, PhD); general business management (PhD); human resource management (DBA, PhD); leadership (DBA, PhD); management education (PhD); marketing (DBA, PhD); project management (DBA, PhD); strategy and innovation (DBA, PhD).

Capella University, School of Business and Technology, Master's Programs in Business, Minneapolis, MN 55402. Offers accounting (MBA); business analysis (MS); business intelligence (MBA); entrepreneurship (MBA); finance (MBA); general business administration (MBA); general human resource management (MS); general leadership (MS); health care management (MBA); human resource management (MBA); marketing (MBA); project management (MBA, MS).

Carnegie Mellon University, Tepper School of Business, Program in Accounting, Pittsburgh, PA 15213-3891. Offers PhD. *Accreditation:* AACSB. *Degree requirements:* For doctorate, thesis/dissertation. *Entrance requirements:* For doctorate, GRE.

Case Western Reserve University, Weatherhead School of Management, Department of Accountancy, Cleveland, OH 44106. Offers M Acc, PhD, MBA/M Acc. *Accreditation:* AACSB. Evening/weekend programs available. *Degree requirements:* For doctorate, thesis/dissertation. *Entrance requirements:* For master's and doctorate, GMAT. *Faculty research:* Auditing, regulation, financial reporting, public interest, efficient markets.

The Catholic University of America, School of Business and Economics, Washington, DC 20064. Offers accounting (MS); business analysis (MS); integral economic development management (MA); integral economic development policy (MA); international political economics (MA). Part-time programs available. *Faculty:* 14 full-time (6 women), 30 part-time/adjunct (7 women). *Students:* 34 full-time (16 women), 12 part-time (7 women); includes 15 minority (9 Black or African American, non-Hispanic/Latino; 1 Asian, non-Hispanic/Latino; 2 Hispanic/Latino; 3 Two or more races, non-Hispanic/Latino), 10 international. Average age 28. 91 applicants, 60% accepted, 35 enrolled. In 2013, 16 master's awarded. *Degree requirements:* For master's, comprehensive exam. *Entrance requirements:* For master's, GRE General Test, statement of purpose, official copies of academic transcripts, three letters of recommendation. Additional exam requirements/recommendations for international students: Required—TOEFL (minimum score 580 paper-based). *Application deadline:* For fall admission, 8/1 priority date for domestic students, 7/15 for international students; for spring admission, 12/1 priority date for domestic students, 10/15 for international students. Applications are processed on a rolling basis. Application fee: $55. Electronic applications accepted. *Expenses: Tuition:* Full-time $38,500; part-time $1490 per credit hour. *Required fees:* $400; $1525 per credit hour. One-time fee: $425. Tuition and fees vary according to program. *Financial support:* Fellowships, research assistantships, teaching assistantships, Federal Work-Study, scholarships/grants, tuition waivers (full and partial), and unspecified assistantships available. Financial award application deadline: 2/1; financial award applicants required to submit FAFSA. *Faculty research:* Integrity of the marketing process, economics of energy and the environment, emerging markets, social change, international finance and economic development. *Total annual research expenditures:* $170,819. *Unit head:* Dr. Andrew V. Abela, Chair, 202-319-5235, Fax: 202-319-4426, E-mail: abela@cua.edu. *Application contact:* Andrew Woodall, Director of Graduate Admissions, 202-319-5057, Fax: 202-319-6533, E-mail: cua-admissions@cua.edu.
Website: http://business.cua.edu/.

Centenary College, Program in Professional Accounting, Hackettstown, NJ 07840-2100. Offers MS. Part-time and evening/weekend programs available. Postbaccalaureate distance learning degree programs offered (minimal on-campus study).

Central Michigan University, College of Graduate Studies, College of Business Administration, Department of Business Information Systems, Mount Pleasant, MI 48859. Offers business computing (Graduate Certificate); information systems (MS), including accounting information systems, business informatics, enterprise systems using SAP software, information systems. Part-time and evening/weekend programs available. *Degree requirements:* For master's, thesis or alternative. Electronic applications accepted. *Faculty research:* Enterprise software, electronic commerce, decision support systems, ethical issues in information systems, information technology management and teaching issues.

Central Michigan University, College of Graduate Studies, College of Business Administration, MBA Program, Mount Pleasant, MI 48859. Offers accounting (MBA); business economics (MBA); consulting (MBA); finance (MBA); general business (MBA); human resource management (MBA); information systems (MBA); international business (MBA); logistics management (MBA); marketing (MBA); value-driven organization (MBA). Part-time and evening/weekend programs available. Postbaccalaureate distance learning degree programs offered (no on-campus study). Electronic applications accepted. *Faculty research:* Accounting, consulting, international business, marketing, information systems.

Central Washington University, Graduate Studies and Research, College of Business, Department of Accounting, Ellensburg, WA 98926. Offers MPA. *Accreditation:* AACSB. Part-time programs available. *Degree requirements:* For master's, comprehensive exam. *Entrance requirements:* For master's, GMAT, minimum GPA of 3.0. Additional exam requirements/recommendations for international students: Required—TOEFL (minimum score 550 paper-based; 79 iBT), IELTS (minimum score 6.5). Electronic applications accepted.

Chaminade University of Honolulu, Graduate Services, Program in Business Administration, Honolulu, HI 96816-1578. Offers accounting (MBA); business (MBA); not-for-profit (MBA); public sector (MBA). Part-time and evening/weekend programs available. *Entrance requirements:* For master's, minimum GPA of 3.0, resume. Additional exam requirements/recommendations for international students: Required—TOEFL (minimum score 650 paper-based). Electronic applications accepted. *Faculty research:* Total quality management, international finance, not-for-profit accounting, service-learning in business contexts.

Charleston Southern University, School of Business, Charleston, SC 29423-8087. Offers accounting (MBA); finance (MBA); general management (MBA); leadership (MBA); management information systems (MBA). Part-time and evening/weekend programs available. *Degree requirements:* For master's, thesis optional. *Entrance requirements:* For master's, GMAT. Additional exam requirements/recommendations for international students: Required—TOEFL (minimum score 550 paper-based; 79 iBT).

Chatham University, Program in Accounting, Pittsburgh, PA 15232-2826. Offers M Acc, MAC. Part-time and evening/weekend programs available. *Faculty:* 1 full-time (0 women), 3 part-time/adjunct (1 woman). *Students:* 20 full-time (10 women), 21 part-time (12 women); includes 6 minority (4 Black or African American, non-Hispanic/Latino; 1 Asian, non-Hispanic/Latino; 1 Hispanic/Latino), 12 international. Average age 30. 30 applicants, 60% accepted, 11 enrolled. In 2013, 17 master's awarded. *Entrance requirements:* Additional exam requirements/recommendations for international students: Required—TOEFL (minimum score 600 paper-based; 100 iBT), IELTS (minimum score 7), TWE. *Application deadline:* For fall admission, 4/1 for domestic and international students; for spring admission, 11/1 for domestic students, 10/1 for international students. Applications are processed on a rolling basis. Application fee: $45. Electronic applications accepted. Application fee is waived when completed online.

Accounting

Expenses: Tuition: Full-time $14,886; part-time $827 per credit hour. One-time fee: $396 full-time. *Financial support:* Applicants required to submit FAFSA. *Unit head:* Dr. Rachel Chung, Director of Business and Entrepreneurship Program, 412-365-2433, E-mail: rchung@chatham.edu. *Application contact:* 412-365-1141, Fax: 412-365-1609, E-mail: gradadmissions@chatham.edu.
Website: http://www.chatham.edu/macc.

Christian Brothers University, School of Business, Memphis, TN 38104-5581. Offers accountancy (M Acc); business (MBA); international business (MIB); project management (Certificate); MBA/MIB. Part-time and evening/weekend programs available. *Entrance requirements:* For master's, GMAT, GRE. Additional exam requirements/recommendations for international students: Required—TOEFL.

City University of Seattle, Graduate Division, School of Management, Bellevue, WA 98005. Offers accounting (Certificate); change leadership (MBA, Certificate); computer systems (MS); finance (Certificate); financial management (MBA); general management (MBA); general management-Europe (MBA); global marketing (MBA); human resources management (Certificate); individualized study (MBA); information security (MS); information systems (MBA); leadership (MA); marketing (MBA, Certificate); project management (MBA, MS, Certificate); sustainable business (Certificate); technology management (MBA, Certificate). Part-time and evening/weekend programs available. Postbaccalaureate distance learning degree programs offered (no on-campus study). *Degree requirements:* For master's, comprehensive exam (for some programs), thesis (for some programs). *Entrance requirements:* Additional exam requirements/recommendations for international students: Required—TOEFL (minimum score 567 paper-based; 87 iBT); Recommended—IELTS. Electronic applications accepted.

Clark Atlanta University, School of Business Administration, Department of Accounting, Atlanta, GA 30314. Offers MA. Part-time programs available. *Faculty:* 2 full-time (both women). *Students:* 10 full-time (5 women); includes 4 minority (all Black or African American, non-Hispanic/Latino), 3 international. Average age 25. 9 applicants, 100% accepted, 9 enrolled. In 2013, 7 master's awarded. *Entrance requirements:* For master's, GMAT, minimum undergraduate GPA of 2.5. Additional exam requirements/recommendations for international students: Required—TOEFL (minimum score 500 paper-based; 61 iBT). *Application deadline:* For fall admission, 4/1 for domestic and international students; for spring admission, 11/1 for domestic and international students. Applications are processed on a rolling basis. Application fee: $40 ($55 for international students). Electronic applications accepted. *Expenses: Tuition:* Full-time $14,616; part-time $812 per credit hour. *Required fees:* $706; $353 per semester. *Financial support:* Career-related internships or fieldwork, Federal Work-Study, scholarships/grants, and unspecified assistantships available. Support available to part-time students. Financial award application deadline: 4/30; financial award applicants required to submit FAFSA. *Unit head:* Dr. Kasim Alli, Chairperson, 404-880-8740, E-mail: kalli@cau.edu. *Application contact:* Michelle Clark-Davis, Graduate Program Admissions, 404-880-6605, E-mail: cauadmissions@cau.edu.

Clark University, Graduate School, Graduate School of Management, Business Administration Program, Worcester, MA 01610-1477. Offers accounting (MBA); finance (MBA); global business (MBA); information systems (MBA); management (MBA); marketing (MBA); social change (MBA); sustainability (MBA). *Accreditation:* AACSB. Part-time and evening/weekend programs available. *Students:* 109 full-time (50 women), 151 part-time (67 women); includes 16 minority (9 Black or African American, non-Hispanic/Latino; 3 Asian, non-Hispanic/Latino; 4 Hispanic/Latino), 74 international. Average age 30. 359 applicants, 50% accepted, 81 enrolled. In 2013, 125 master's awarded. *Degree requirements:* For master's, thesis optional. *Application deadline:* For fall admission, 6/1 priority date for domestic students; for spring admission, 12/1 priority date for domestic students. Applications are processed on a rolling basis. Application fee: $50. Electronic applications accepted. *Expenses: Tuition:* Full-time $39,200; part-time $1225 per credit hour. *Financial support:* In 2013–14, research assistantships with partial tuition reimbursements (averaging $4,800 per year), teaching assistantships with partial tuition reimbursements (averaging $4,800 per year) were awarded; fellowships, career-related internships or fieldwork, Federal Work-Study, institutionally sponsored loans, and tuition waivers (partial) also available. Support available to part-time students. Financial award application deadline: 5/31. *Faculty research:* Marketing, accounting, human resource management, management information systems, business finance. *Unit head:* Dr. Catherine Usoff, Dean, 508-793-8822, Fax: 508-793-8822, E-mail: clarkmba@clarku.edu. *Application contact:* Patrick Oroszko, Enrollment and Marketing Director, 508-793-8822, Fax: 508-793-8822, E-mail: clarkmba@clarku.edu.
Website: http://www.clarku.edu/gsom/graduate/fulltime/.

Clark University, Graduate School, Graduate School of Management, Program in Accounting, Worcester, MA 01610-1477. Offers MSA. Part-time programs available. *Entrance requirements:* For master's, GMAT or GRE, statement of purpose, resume, two letters of recommendation. Additional exam requirements/recommendations for international students: Required—TOEFL (minimum score 577 paper-based; 90 iBT) or IELTS (minimum score 6.5). Application fee: $100. Electronic applications accepted. *Expenses: Tuition:* Full-time $39,200; part-time $1225 per credit hour. *Unit head:* Dr. Catherine Usoff, Dean, 508-793-8822, Fax: 508-793-8822, E-mail: cusoff@clarku.edu. *Application contact:* Patrick Oroszko, Enrollment and Marketing Director, 508-793-8822, Fax: 508-793-8822, E-mail: clarkmba@clarku.edu.
Website: http://www.clarku.edu/gsom/graduate/accounting/.

Clayton State University, School of Graduate Studies, College of Business, Program in Business Administration, Morrow, GA 30260-0285. Offers accounting (MBA); international business (MBA); supply chain management (MBA). *Accreditation:* AACSB. Part-time and evening/weekend programs available. *Degree requirements:* For master's, thesis. *Entrance requirements:* For master's, GMAT, 3 letters of recommendation; statement of purpose; 2 official transcripts. Additional exam requirements/recommendations for international students: Required—TOEFL (minimum score 550 paper-based; 80 iBT). Electronic applications accepted. *Expenses:* Contact institution.

Cleary University, Online Program in Business Administration, Ann Arbor, MI 48105-2659. Offers accounting (MBA); financial planning (MBA); financial planning (Graduate Certificate); green business strategy (MBA, Graduate Certificate); health care leadership (MBA); management (MBA); nonprofit management (MBA, Graduate Certificate); organizational leadership (MBA). Part-time and evening/weekend programs available. Postbaccalaureate distance learning degree programs offered (no on-campus study). *Degree requirements:* For master's, thesis. *Entrance requirements:* For master's, bachelor's degree; minimum GPA of 2.5; professional resume indicating minimum of 2 years of management or related experience; undergraduate degree from accredited college or university with at least 18 quarter hours (or 12 semester hours) of accounting study (for MBA in accounting). Additional exam requirements/recommendations for international students: Required—TOEFL (minimum score 550 paper-based; 79 iBT), Michigan English Language Assessment Battery (minimum score 75). Electronic applications accepted.

Clemson University, Graduate School, College of Business and Behavioral Science, School of Accountancy and Finance, Clemson, SC 29634. Offers MP Acc. *Accreditation:* AACSB. Part-time programs available. *Faculty:* 7 full-time (2 women), 3 part-time/adjunct (0 women). *Students:* 68 full-time (35 women), 2 part-time (0 women); includes 7 minority (5 Hispanic/Latino; 2 Two or more races, non-Hispanic/Latino), 11 international. Average age 22. 120 applicants, 71% accepted, 64 enrolled. In 2013, 63 master's awarded. *Entrance requirements:* For master's, GMAT, BS in accounting or equivalent, minimum GPA of 3.0. Additional exam requirements/recommendations for international students: Required—TOEFL. *Application deadline:* For fall admission, 1/1 priority date for domestic students, 4/15 for international students; for spring admission, 10/1 priority date for domestic students, 9/15 for international students. Applications are processed on a rolling basis. Application fee: $70 ($80 for international students). Electronic applications accepted. *Financial support:* In 2013–14, 23 students received support, including 9 fellowships with full and partial tuition reimbursements available (averaging $1,556 per year), 14 teaching assistantships with partial tuition reimbursements available (averaging $7,830 per year); research assistantships with partial tuition reimbursements available, career-related internships or fieldwork, institutionally sponsored loans, scholarships/grants, health care benefits, and unspecified assistantships also available. Support available to part-time students. Financial award applicants required to submit FAFSA. *Unit head:* Dr. Frances Kennedy, Director, 864-656-4712, Fax: 864-656-4892, E-mail: fkenned@clemson.edu. *Application contact:* Dr. Carl W. Hollingsworth, Program Coordinator, 864-656-4883, Fax: 864-656-4892, E-mail: chollin@clemson.edu.
Website: http://business.clemson.edu/departments/acct/acct_about.htm.

Cleveland State University, College of Graduate Studies, Monte Ahuja College of Business, Department of Accounting, Cleveland, OH 44115. Offers financial accounting/audit (M Acc); taxation (M Acc). *Accreditation:* AACSB. Part-time and evening/weekend programs available. *Faculty:* 13 full-time (3 women), 11 part-time/adjunct (3 women). *Students:* 118 full-time (63 women), 166 part-time (77 women); includes 42 minority (17 Black or African American, non-Hispanic/Latino; 18 Asian, non-Hispanic/Latino; 5 Hispanic/Latino; 2 Two or more races, non-Hispanic/Latino), 111 international. Average age 29. 182 applicants, 63% accepted, 54 enrolled. In 2013, 91 master's awarded. *Entrance requirements:* For master's, GMAT, minimum GPA of 2.75. Additional exam requirements/recommendations for international students: Required—TOEFL (minimum score 525 paper-based). *Application deadline:* For fall admission, 7/15 priority date for domestic students; for spring admission, 12/15 priority date for domestic students. Applications are processed on a rolling basis. Application fee: $30. *Expenses:* Tuition, state resident: full-time $8335; part-time $521 per credit hour. Tuition, nonresident: full-time $15,670; part-time $979 per credit hour. *Required fees:* $50; $25 per semester. *Financial support:* In 2013–14, 3 research assistantships with full and partial tuition reimbursements (averaging $6,960 per year) were awarded; career-related internships or fieldwork, Federal Work-Study, scholarships/grants, and unspecified assistantships also available. Financial award applicants required to submit FAFSA. *Faculty research:* Internal auditing, computer auditing, accounting education, managerial accounting. *Unit head:* Bruce W. McClain, Chair, 216-687-3652, Fax: 216-687-9212, E-mail: b.mcclain@csuohio.edu. *Application contact:* Bruce Gottschalk, MBA Programs Administrator, 216-687-3730, Fax: 216-687-5311, E-mail: cbacsu@csuohio.edu.
Website: http://www.csuohio.edu/business/academics/act/macc.html.

Coastal Carolina University, E. Craig Wall, Sr. College of Business Administration, Conway, SC 29528-6054. Offers accounting (M Acc); business administration (MBA); fraud examination (Certificate). *Accreditation:* AACSB. Part-time and evening/weekend programs available. *Faculty:* 9 full-time (3 women). *Students:* 59 full-time (31 women), 45 part-time (27 women); includes 17 minority (14 Black or African American, non-Hispanic/Latino; 1 Hispanic/Latino; 2 Two or more races, non-Hispanic/Latino), 12 international. Average age 30. 72 applicants, 88% accepted, 54 enrolled. In 2013, 62 master's awarded. *Entrance requirements:* For master's, GMAT, official transcripts, 2 letters of recommendation, resume, completion of prerequisites with minimum B average grade, baccalaureate degree; for Certificate, GMAT, official transcripts, 2 letters of recommendation, baccalaureate degree or evidence of receiving a CPA certificate, law degree, or admittance to an accredited law school. Additional exam requirements/recommendations for international students: Required—TOEFL (minimum score 575 paper-based; 89 iBT). *Application deadline:* For fall admission, 6/15 priority date for domestic and international students; for spring admission, 11/15 priority date for domestic and international students; for summer admission, 4/15 priority date for domestic and international students. Applications are processed on a rolling basis. Application fee: $45. Electronic applications accepted. *Expenses:* Contact institution. *Financial support:* Application deadline: 3/1; applicants required to submit FAFSA. *Unit head:* Dr. Kenneth W. Small, Director, Graduate Business Programs, 843-349-2469, Fax: 843-349-2455, E-mail: ksmall@coastal.edu. *Application contact:* Dr. James O. Luken, Associate Provost/Director of Graduate Studies, 843-349-2235, Fax: 843-349-6444, E-mail: joluken@coastal.edu.
Website: http://www.coastal.edu/business/.

The College at Brockport, State University of New York, School of Business Administration and Economics, Brockport, NY 14420-2997. Offers forensic accounting (MS). Part-time programs available. *Faculty:* 4 full-time (1 woman), 1 part-time/adjunct (0 women). *Students:* 13 full-time (5 women), 8 part-time (5 women); includes 4 minority (3 Black or African American, non-Hispanic/Latino; 1 Asian, non-Hispanic/Latino). 14 applicants, 57% accepted, 7 enrolled. In 2013, 13 master's awarded. *Entrance requirements:* For master's, GMAT or GRE General Test. Additional exam requirements/recommendations for international students: Required—TOEFL (minimum score 550 paper-based; 79 iBT), IELTS (minimum score 6.5). *Application deadline:* For fall admission, 7/1 priority date for domestic and international students; for spring admission, 12/1 priority date for domestic and international students. Application fee: $50. Electronic applications accepted. *Expenses:* Tuition, state resident: full-time $9870. Tuition, nonresident: full-time $18,350. *Required fees:* $1848. *Financial support:* Career-related internships or fieldwork, Federal Work-Study, scholarships/grants, and unspecified assistantships available. Financial award application deadline: 3/15; financial award applicants required to submit FAFSA. *Unit head:* Dr. James Cordeiro, Department Chair, 585-395-5793, Fax: 585-395-2542. *Application contact:* Dr. Donald A. Kent, Graduate Director, 585-395-5521, Fax: 585-395-2515, E-mail: dkent@brockport.edu.
Website: http://www.brockport.edu/bus-econ/.

College of Charleston, Graduate School, School of Business, Program in Accountancy, Charleston, SC 29424-0001. Offers MS. *Accreditation:* AACSB. Evening/weekend programs available. *Entrance requirements:* For master's, GMAT, minimum GPA of 3.0 in last 60 hours of undergraduate course work, 24 hours of course work in accounting, 2 letters of reference. Additional exam requirements/recommendations for international students: Required—TOEFL (minimum score 81 iBT). Electronic applications accepted.

The College of Saint Rose, Graduate Studies, School of Business, Department of Accounting, Albany, NY 12203-1419. Offers MS. Part-time and evening/weekend programs available. *Entrance requirements:* For master's, GMAT, graduate degree, or minimum undergraduate GPA of 3.0. Additional exam requirements/recommendations for international students: Required—TOEFL (minimum score 550 paper-based). Electronic applications accepted.

College of Staten Island of the City University of New York, Graduate Programs, School of Business, Program in Accounting, Staten Island, NY 10314-6600. Offers MS. *Faculty:* 3 full-time (2 women). *Students:* 23 (9 women). Average age 32. 29 applicants, 48% accepted, 12 enrolled. *Degree requirements:* For master's, significant written assignment in capstone course. *Entrance requirements:* For master's, GMAT or College of Staten Island degree with minimum GPA of 3.2 in accounting or business pre-major and major, baccalaureate degree in accounting or related field; letter of intent; minimum GPA of 3.0; two letters of recommendation from instructors or employers; proficiency in business fundamentals and in-depth knowledge of accounting through undergraduate coursework. Additional exam requirements/recommendations for international students: Required—TOEFL (minimum score 600 paper-based; 100 iBT), IELTS (minimum score 7). *Application deadline:* For fall admission, 4/25 priority date for domestic and international students; for spring admission, 11/25 priority date for domestic and international students. Applications are processed on a rolling basis. Application fee: $125. Electronic applications accepted. *Expenses:* Tuition, state resident: full-time $9240; part-time $385 per credit hour. Tuition, nonresident: full-time $17,040; part-time $710 per credit hour. *Required fees:* $428; $128 per term. *Financial support:* Career-related internships or fieldwork, Federal Work-Study, and scholarships/grants available. Support available to part-time students. Financial award applicants required to submit FAFSA. *Unit head:* Prof. John Sandler, Graduate Program Coordinator, 718-982-2921, E-mail: john.sandler@csi.cuny.edu. *Application contact:* Sasha Spence, Assistant Director for Graduate Recruitment and Admissions, 718-982-2019, Fax: 718-982-2500, E-mail: sasha.spence@csi.cuny.edu.
Website: http://www.csi.cuny.edu/schoolofbusiness/programs_graduate.php.

The College of William and Mary, Mason School of Business, Master of Accounting Program, Williamsburg, VA 23185. Offers M Acc. *Accreditation:* AACSB. *Faculty:* 10 full-time (3 women), 7 part-time/adjunct (0 women). *Students:* 69 full-time (40 women); includes 11 minority (1 Black or African American, non-Hispanic/Latino; 8 Asian, non-Hispanic/Latino; 2 Hispanic/Latino), 22 international. Average age 24. 422 applicants, 23% accepted, 59 enrolled. In 2013, 78 master's awarded. *Degree requirements:* For master's, 30 credit hours. *Entrance requirements:* For master's, GMAT, 2 written recommendations, interview, transcripts. Additional exam requirements/recommendations for international students: Required—TOEFL (minimum score 620 paper-based; 102 iBT) or IELTS (minimum score 7). *Application deadline:* Applications are processed on a rolling basis. Application fee: $80. Electronic applications accepted. *Expenses:* Contact institution. *Financial support:* In 2013–14, 70 students received support, including 12 research assistantships (averaging $4,000 per year); fellowships, scholarships/grants, and unspecified assistantships also available. Financial award application deadline: 3/15; financial award applicants required to submit FAFSA. *Faculty research:* Valuation, voluntary disclosure, auditing, taxation, executive compensation. *Unit head:* Linda Espahbodi, Director, 757-221-2953, Fax: 757-221-7862, E-mail: linda.espahbodi@mason.wm.edu. *Application contact:* Beth McGraw, Associate Director, 757-221-2879, Fax: 757-221-7862, E-mail: beth.mcgraw@mason.wm.edu.
Website: http://mason.wm.edu/programs/macc/index.php.

Colorado State University, Graduate School, College of Business, Department of Accounting, Fort Collins, CO 80523-1271. Offers M Acc. Part-time programs available. *Faculty:* 11 full-time (3 women). *Students:* 38 full-time (23 women), 13 part-time (6 women); includes 6 minority (2 Black or African American, non-Hispanic/Latino; 3 Asian, non-Hispanic/Latino; 1 Hispanic/Latino), 9 international. Average age 29. 76 applicants, 67% accepted, 30 enrolled. In 2013, 47 master's awarded. *Degree requirements:* For master's, thesis or alternative. *Entrance requirements:* For master's, GMAT (minimum score of 600), minimum GPA of 3.0, BA/BS, 3 letters of reference, transcripts. Additional exam requirements/recommendations for international students: Required—TOEFL (minimum score 565 paper-based; 86 iBT). *Application deadline:* For fall admission, 7/15 for domestic students, 6/1 for international students; for spring admission, 11/15 for domestic students, 11/1 for international students. Applications are processed on a rolling basis. Application fee: $50. Electronic applications accepted. *Expenses:* Tuition, state resident: full-time $9075.40; part-time $504 per credit. Tuition, nonresident: full-time $22,248; part-time $1236 per credit. *Required fees:* $1819; $60 per credit. *Financial support:* In 2013–14, 1 student received support, including 1 research assistantship with partial tuition reimbursement available (averaging $9,265 per year); unspecified assistantships also available. Financial award application deadline: 3/1; financial award applicants required to submit FAFSA. *Faculty research:* Financial accounting and reporting, managerial accounting, earnings management, stock options, corporate social responsibility. *Total annual research expenditures:* $11,297. *Unit head:* Dr. Bill Rankin, Department Head, 970-491-2422, Fax: 970-491-2676, E-mail: bill.rankin@business.colostate.edu. *Application contact:* Janet Estes, Graduate Contact, 970-491-4612, Fax: 970-491-2676, E-mail: janet.estes@colostate.edu.
Website: http://www.biz.colostate.edu/accounting/Pages/default.aspx.

Colorado Technical University Colorado Springs, Graduate Studies, Program in Management, Colorado Springs, CO 80907-3896. Offers accounting (MBA, MSA); business administration (MBA); finance (MBA); human resources management (MBA); logistics/supply chain management (MBA); management (DM); marketing (MBA); mediation and dispute resolution (MBA); operations management (MBA); project management (MBA); technology management (MBA). Part-time and evening/weekend programs available. Postbaccalaureate distance learning degree programs offered. *Degree requirements:* For master's, thesis or alternative; for doctorate, thesis/dissertation. *Entrance requirements:* For doctorate, minimum graduate GPA of 3.0, 5 years of related work experience. *Faculty research:* Sexual harassment, performance evaluation, critical thinking.

Colorado Technical University Denver South, Programs in Business Administration and Management, Aurora, CO 80014. Offers accounting (MBA); business administration (MBA); business administration and management (EMBA); finance (MBA); human resource management (MBA); marketing (MBA); mediation and dispute resolution (MBA); operations management (MBA); project management (MBA); technology management (MBA). Part-time and evening/weekend programs available. *Degree requirements:* For master's, thesis or alternative. *Entrance requirements:* For master's, minimum undergraduate GPA of 3.0, resume.

Columbia University, Graduate School of Business, Doctoral Program in Business, New York, NY 10027. Offers business (PhD), including accounting, decision, risk, and operations, finance and economics, management, marketing. *Accreditation:* AACSB. *Degree requirements:* For doctorate, comprehensive exam, thesis/dissertation, major field exam, research paper, thesis proposal. *Entrance requirements:* For doctorate, GMAT or GRE (finance), 2 letters of reference, resume. Additional exam requirements/recommendations for international students: Required—TOEFL. Electronic applications accepted. *Expenses:* Contact institution. *Faculty research:* Human decision making and behavioral research; real estate market and mortgage defaults; financial crisis and corporate governance; international business; security analysis and accounting.

Columbia University, Graduate School of Business, MBA Program, New York, NY 10027. Offers accounting (MBA); decision, risk, and operations (MBA); entrepreneurship (MBA); finance and economics (MBA); healthcare and pharmaceutical management (MBA); human resource management (MBA); international business (MBA); leadership and ethics (MBA); management (MBA); marketing (MBA); media (MBA); private equity

(MBA); real estate (MBA); social enterprise (MBA); value investing (MBA); DDS/MBA; JD/MBA; MBA/MIA; MBA/MPH; MBA/MS; MD/MBA. *Entrance requirements:* For master's, GMAT, 2 letters of recommendation. Additional exam requirements/recommendations for international students: Required—TOEFL. Electronic applications accepted. *Expenses:* Contact institution. *Faculty research:* Human decision making and behavioral research; real estate market and mortgage defaults; financial crisis and corporate governance; international business; security analysis and accounting.

Cornell University, Graduate School, Graduate Field of Management, Ithaca, NY 14853. Offers accounting (PhD); finance (PhD); marketing (PhD); organizational behavior (PhD); production and operations management (PhD). *Accreditation:* AACSB. *Faculty:* 54 full-time (7 women). *Students:* 37 full-time (13 women); includes 5 minority (4 Asian, non-Hispanic/Latino; 1 Two or more races, non-Hispanic/Latino), 24 international. Average age 29. 486 applicants, 4% accepted, 11 enrolled. In 2013, 8 doctorates awarded. *Degree requirements:* For doctorate, comprehensive exam, thesis/dissertation. *Entrance requirements:* For doctorate, GMAT or GRE General Test. Additional exam requirements/recommendations for international students: Required—TOEFL (minimum score 600 paper-based; 77 iBT). *Application deadline:* For fall admission, 1/3 for domestic students. Application fee: $95. Electronic applications accepted. *Expenses:* Contact institution. *Financial support:* In 2013–14, 33 students received support, including 31 research assistantships with full tuition reimbursements available, 2 teaching assistantships with full tuition reimbursements available; fellowships with full tuition reimbursements available, institutionally sponsored loans, scholarships/grants, health care benefits, tuition waivers (full and partial), and unspecified assistantships also available. Financial award applicants required to submit FAFSA. *Faculty research:* Operations and manufacturing. *Unit head:* Director of Graduate Studies, 607-255-3669. *Application contact:* Graduate Field Assistant, 607-255-9431, E-mail: js_phd@cornell.edu.
Website: http://www.gradschool.cornell.edu/fields.php?id-91&a-2.

Daemen College, Department of Accounting/Information Systems, Amherst, NY 14226-3592. Offers global business (MS), including accounting, global business, management information systems, marketing. Part-time and evening/weekend programs available. *Degree requirements:* For master's, minimum GPA of 3.0. *Entrance requirements:* For master's, GMAT if undergraduate GPA is less than 3.0, 2 letters of recommendation; goal statement; transcripts; demonstration of satisfactory oral and written English. Additional exam requirements/recommendations for international students: Required—TOEFL (minimum score 500 paper-based; 63 iBT), IELTS (minimum score 5.5). Electronic applications accepted. *Faculty research:* Internationalization of small business, cultural influences on business practices, international human resource practices.

Dallas Baptist University, College of Business, Business Administration Program, Dallas, TX 75211-9299. Offers accounting (MBA); business communication (MBA); conflict resolution management (MBA); entrepreneurship (MBA); finance (MBA); health care management (MBA); international business (MBA); leading the non-profit organization (MBA); management (MBA); management information systems (MBA); marketing (MBA); project management (MBA); technology and engineering (MBA). *Accreditation:* ACBSP. Part-time and evening/weekend programs available. *Entrance requirements:* For master's, GMAT, minimum GPA of 3.0. Additional exam requirements/recommendations for international students: Required—TOEFL, IELTS. *Application deadline:* Applications are processed on a rolling basis. Application fee: $25. Electronic applications accepted. *Expenses:* Tuition: Full-time $13,410; part-time $745 per credit hour. *Required fees:* $300; $150 per semester. Tuition and fees vary according to degree level. *Financial support:* Federal Work-Study, institutionally sponsored loans, scholarships/grants, and tuition waivers (full and partial) available. Support available to part-time students. Financial award applicants required to submit FAFSA. *Faculty research:* Sports management, services marketing, retailing, strategic management, financial planning/investments. *Unit head:* Dr. Sandra S. Reid, Chair, 214-333-5280, Fax: 214-333-5293, E-mail: graduate@dbu.edu. *Application contact:* Kit P. Montgomery, Director of Graduate Programs, 214-333-5242, Fax: 214-333-5579, E-mail: graduate@dbu.edu.
Website: http://www3.dbu.edu/graduate/mba.asp.

Davenport University, Sneden Graduate School, Grand Rapids, MI 49512. Offers accounting (MBA); business administration (EMBA); finance (MBA); health care management (MBA); human resources (MBA); information assurance (MS); public health (MPH); strategic management (MBA). Evening/weekend programs available. *Entrance requirements:* For master's, GMAT, minimum undergraduate GPA of 2.75. Additional exam requirements/recommendations for international students: Required—TOEFL. Electronic applications accepted. *Faculty research:* Leadership, management, marketing, organizational culture.

Delaware Valley College, MBA Program, Doylestown, PA 18901-2697. Offers accounting (MBA); entrepreneurship (MBA); finance (MBA); food and agribusiness (MBA); general business (MBA); global executive leadership (MBA); human resource management (MBA); supply chain management (MBA). Part-time and evening/weekend programs available. Postbaccalaureate distance learning degree programs offered (no on-campus study). *Students:* 32 full-time (17 women), 183 part-time (99 women). Average age 34. 97 applicants, 78% accepted, 74 enrolled. *Entrance requirements:* For master's, minimum undergraduate GPA of 3.0. *Application deadline:* Applications are processed on a rolling basis. Application fee: $50. Electronic applications accepted. *Expenses:* Contact institution. *Financial support:* Applicants required to submit FAFSA. *Unit head:* Mike Prushan, Director of MBA Program, 215-489-2322, E-mail: michael.prushan@delval.edu. *Application contact:* Robin Mathews, Graduate and Continuing Studies Enrollment Manager, 215-489-2955, Fax: 215-489-4832, E-mail: robin.mathews@delval.edu.
Website: http://www.delval.edu/academics/graduate/master-of-business-administration.

Delta State University, Graduate Programs, College of Business, Division of Accounting, Computer Information Systems, and Finance, Cleveland, MS 38733-0001. Offers accountancy (MPA). *Faculty:* 12 full-time (5 women). *Students:* 9 full-time (5 women), 3 part-time (1 woman); includes 5 minority (all Black or African American, non-Hispanic/Latino), 1 international. Average age 26. 7 applicants, 100% accepted, 6 enrolled. In 2013, 6 master's awarded. *Expenses:* Tuition, state resident: full-time $3006; part-time $334 per credit hour. Tuition, nonresident: full-time $3006; part-time $334 per credit hour. *Unit head:* Dr. Billy Moore, Dean, 662-846-4200, Fax: 662-846-4215, E-mail: bcmoore@deltastate.edu. *Application contact:* Carla Johnson, Coordinator, College of Business Graduate Programs, 662-846-4234, Fax: 662-846-4215, E-mail: cjohnson@deltastate.edu.
Website: http://www.deltastate.edu/pages/4747.asp.

DePaul University, Charles H. Kellstadt Graduate School of Business, Chicago, IL 60604. Offers accountancy (M Acc, MS, MSA); applied economics (MBA); banking (MBA); behavioral finance (MBA); brand and product management (MBA); business development (MBA); business information technology (MS); business strategy and decision-making (MBA); computational finance (MS); consumer insights (MBA); corporate finance (MBA); economic policy analysis (MS); entrepreneurship (MBA, MS); finance (MBA, MS); financial analysis (MBA); general business (MBA); health sector management (MBA); hospitality leadership (MBA); hospitality leadership and operational

performance (MS); human resource management (MBA); human resources (MS); investment management (MBA); leadership and change management (MBA); management accounting (MBA); marketing (MBA, MS); marketing analysis (MS); marketing strategy and planning (MBA); operations management (MBA); organizational diversity (MBA); real estate (MS); real estate finance and investment (MBA); revenue management (MBA); sports management (MBA); strategic global marketing (MBA); strategy, execution and valuation (MBA); sustainable management (MBA, MS); taxation (MS); wealth management (MS); JD/MBA. *Accreditation:* AACSB. Part-time and evening/weekend programs available. Postbaccalaureate distance learning degree programs offered (no on-campus study). *Faculty:* 81 full-time (20 women), 45 part-time/adjunct (8 women). *Students:* 1,238 full-time (605 women), 617 part-time (223 women); includes 295 minority (71 Black or African American, non-Hispanic/Latino; 129 Asian, non-Hispanic/Latino; 74 Hispanic/Latino; 4 Native Hawaiian or other Pacific Islander, non-Hispanic/Latino; 17 Two or more races, non-Hispanic/Latino), 462 international. Average age 29. In 2013, 911 master's awarded. *Entrance requirements:* For master's, GMAT, 2 letters of recommendation, resume, essay, official transcripts. Additional exam requirements/recommendations for international students: Required—TOEFL (minimum score 550 paper-based; 80 iBT). *Application deadline:* For fall admission, 7/1 for domestic students, 6/1 for international students; for winter admission, 10/1 for domestic students, 9/1 for international students; for spring admission, 2/1 for domestic students, 1/1 for international students. Applications are processed on a rolling basis. Application fee: $60. Electronic applications accepted. *Expenses:* Contact institution. *Financial support:* Application deadline: 4/1; applicants required to submit FAFSA. *Unit head:* Robert T. Ryan, Assistant Dean and Director, 312-362-8810, Fax: 312-362-6677, E-mail: rryan1@depaul.edu. *Application contact:* James Parker, Director of Recruitment and Admission, 312-362-8810, Fax: 312-362-6677, E-mail: kgsb@depaul.edu.
Website: http://kellstadt.depaul.edu.

DeSales University, Graduate Division, Division of Business, Center Valley, PA 18034-9568. Offers accounting (MBA); computer information systems (MBA); finance (MBA); health care systems management (MBA); human resources management (MBA); management (MBA); marketing (MBA); project management (MBA); self-design (MBA). *Accreditation:* ACBSP. Part-time and evening/weekend programs available. Postbaccalaureate distance learning degree programs offered (no on-campus study). *Students:* 444 part-time. Average age 37. In 2013, 1 master's awarded. *Entrance requirements:* For master's, GMAT, minimum GPA of 3.0, 2 years of work experience. Additional exam requirements/recommendations for international students: Required—TOEFL. *Application deadline:* Applications are processed on a rolling basis. Application fee: $50. Electronic applications accepted. *Expenses: Tuition:* Part-time $790 per credit. *Financial support:* Applicants required to submit FAFSA. *Faculty research:* Quality improvement, executive development, productivity, cross-cultural managerial differences, leadership. *Unit head:* Dr. David Gilfoil, Director, 610-282-1100 Ext. 1828, Fax: 610-282-2869, E-mail: david.gilfoil@desales.edu. *Application contact:* Abigail Wernicki, Director of Graduate Admissions, 610-282-1100 Ext. 1768, E-mail: gradadmissions@desales.edu.

DeVry University, Graduate Programs, Downers Grove, IL 60515. Offers accounting and financial management (MAFM); business administration (MBA); education (MS); educational technology (MS); electrical engineering (MS); human resources management (MHRM); information systems management (MISM); network and communications management (MNCM); project management (MPM); public administration (MPA).

Dominican University, Edward A. and Lois L. Brennan School of Business, River Forest, IL 60305-1099. Offers MBA, MSA, JD/MBA, MBA/MLIS, MBA/MSW. JD/MBA offered jointly with John Marshall Law School. *Accreditation:* ACBSP. Part-time and evening/weekend programs available. Postbaccalaureate distance learning degree programs offered (no on-campus study). *Faculty:* 20 full-time (8 women), 20 part-time/adjunct (4 women). *Students:* 97 full-time (65 women), 130 part-time (74 women); includes 63 minority (19 Black or African American, non-Hispanic/Latino; 1 American Indian or Alaska Native, non-Hispanic/Latino; 16 Asian, non-Hispanic/Latino; 26 Hispanic/Latino; 1 Native Hawaiian or other Pacific Islander, non-Hispanic/Latino), 22 international. Average age 30. 113 applicants, 73% accepted, 59 enrolled. In 2013, 85 master's awarded. *Entrance requirements:* For master's, GMAT. Additional exam requirements/recommendations for international students: Required—TOEFL (minimum score 550 paper-based; 79 iBT); Recommended—IELTS (minimum score 6). *Application deadline:* Applications are processed on a rolling basis. Application fee: $25. Electronic applications accepted. *Expenses:* Contact institution. *Financial support:* In 2013–14, 111 students received support. Career-related internships or fieldwork, Federal Work-Study, tuition waivers (partial), and unspecified assistantships available. Support available to part-time students. Financial award application deadline: 3/1; financial award applicants required to submit FAFSA. *Faculty research:* Entrepreneurship, small business finance, business ethics, marketing strategy. *Unit head:* Dr. Molly Burke, Dean, 708-524-6465, Fax: 708-524-6939, E-mail: burkemq@dom.edu. *Application contact:* Matthew Quilty, Assistant Dean, Brennan School of Business, 708-524-6507, Fax: 708-524-6939, E-mail: mquilty@dom.edu.
Website: http://business.dom.edu/.

Drexel University, LeBow College of Business, Department of Accounting, Program in Accounting, Philadelphia, PA 19104-2875. Offers MS. *Entrance requirements:* For master's, GMAT, minimum GPA of 2.75. Additional exam requirements/recommendations for international students: Required—TOEFL. Electronic applications accepted.

Drexel University, LeBow College of Business, Program in Business Administration, Philadelphia, PA 19104-2875. Offers business administration (MBA, PhD, APC), including accounting (MBA, PhD), decision sciences (PhD), economics (MBA, PhD), finance (MBA, PhD), legal studies (MBA), management (MBA), marketing (MBA, PhD), organizational sciences (PhD), quantitative methods (MBA), strategic management (PhD). *Accreditation:* AACSB. Part-time and evening/weekend programs available. Postbaccalaureate distance learning degree programs offered (minimal on-campus study). Terminal master's awarded for partial completion of doctoral program. *Entrance requirements:* For master's, GMAT, minimum GPA of 2.75; for doctorate, GMAT. Additional exam requirements/recommendations for international students: Required—TOEFL. Electronic applications accepted. *Faculty research:* Decision support systems, individual and group behavior, operations research, techniques and strategy.

Duke University, The Fuqua School of Business, PhD Program, Durham, NC 27708-0586. Offers accounting (PhD); decision sciences (PhD); finance (PhD); management and organizations (PhD); marketing (PhD); operations management (PhD); strategy (PhD). *Faculty:* 91 full-time (15 women). *Students:* 78 full-time (27 women); includes 4 minority (1 Black or African American, non-Hispanic/Latino; 3 Asian, non-Hispanic/Latino), 49 international. 589 applicants, 5% accepted, 16 enrolled. In 2013, 26 doctorates awarded. *Degree requirements:* For doctorate, thesis/dissertation, major field requirement (exam or major paper, depending upon the area). *Entrance requirements:* For doctorate, GMAT or GRE, transcripts, essays, recommendation letters, statement of purpose. Additional exam requirements/recommendations for international students: Required—TOEFL (minimum score 577 paper-based; 90 iBT), IELTS (minimum score 7). *Application deadline:* For fall admission, 12/8 priority date for domestic and international students. Application fee: $80. Electronic applications accepted. *Financial support:* In 2013–14, 70 fellowships with full tuition reimbursements (averaging $25,300 per year), 56 research assistantships with full tuition reimbursements (averaging $7,000 per year) were awarded; institutionally sponsored loans, scholarships/grants, and tuition waivers (full) also available. Financial award applicants required to submit FAFSA. *Unit head:* William Boulding, Dean, 919-660-7822, Fax: 919-684-8742, E-mail: bb1@duke.edu. *Application contact:* Dr. James R. Bettman, Director of Graduate Studies, 919-660-7851, Fax: 919-681-6245, E-mail: jrb12@mail.duke.edu.

Duquesne University, John F. Donahue Graduate School of Business, Pittsburgh, PA 15282-0001. Offers accounting (M Acc); finance (MBA); information systems management (MBA, MSISM); management (MBA); marketing (MBA); supply chain management (MBA); sustainability (MBA); JD/MBA; MBA/M Acc; MBA/MA; MBA/MES; MBA/MHMS; MBA/MSN; MSISM/MBA; Pharm D/MBA. *Accreditation:* AACSB. Part-time and evening/weekend programs available. *Faculty:* 58 full-time (17 women), 40 part-time/adjunct (8 women). *Students:* 117 full-time (59 women), 147 part-time (54 women); includes 14 minority (7 Black or African American, non-Hispanic/Latino; 1 Asian, non-Hispanic/Latino; 6 Hispanic/Latino), 53 international. Average age 27. 418 applicants, 46% accepted, 109 enrolled. In 2013, 133 master's awarded. *Entrance requirements:* For master's, GMAT, undergraduate transcripts, 2 letters of recommendation, current resume, personal statement. Additional exam requirements/recommendations for international students: Required—TOEFL (minimum score 577 paper-based; 90 iBT), IELTS (minimum score 7). *Application deadline:* For fall admission, 7/1 priority date for domestic students, 6/1 for international students; for spring admission, 11/1 for domestic and international students. Applications are processed on a rolling basis. Application fee: $0. Electronic applications accepted. *Expenses: Tuition:* Full-time $18,162; part-time $1009 per credit. *Required fees:* $1728; $96 per credit. Tuition and fees vary according to program. *Financial support:* In 2013–14, 39 students received support, including 6 fellowships with partial tuition reimbursements available (averaging $4,541 per year), 33 research assistantships with partial tuition reimbursements available (averaging $9,081 per year); career-related internships or fieldwork, scholarships/grants, and unspecified assistantships also available. Support available to part-time students. Financial award application deadline: 7/1; financial award applicants required to submit FAFSA. *Faculty research:* International business, investment management, business ethics, technology management, supply chain management, business strategy, finance. *Unit head:* Thomas J. Nist, Director of Graduate Programs, 412-396-6276, Fax: 412-396-1726, E-mail: nist@duq.edu. *Application contact:* Maria W. DeCrosta, Enrollment Manager, 412-396-5529, Fax: 412-396-1726, E-mail: decrostam@duq.edu.
Website: http://www.duq.edu/business/grad.

East Carolina University, Graduate School, College of Business, Department of Accounting, Greenville, NC 27858-4353. Offers MS. *Expenses:* Tuition, state resident: full-time $4223. Tuition, nonresident: full-time $16,540. *Required fees:* $2184.

Eastern Illinois University, Graduate School, Lumpkin College of Business and Applied Sciences, Program in Business Administration, Charleston, IL 61920-3099. Offers accountancy (MBA, Certificate); general management (MBA). *Accreditation:* AACSB. Part-time programs available. *Entrance requirements:* For master's, GMAT. *Expenses: Tuition, area resident:* Part-time $283 per credit hour. Tuition, state resident: part-time $283 per credit hour. Tuition, nonresident: part-time $679 per credit hour.

Eastern Michigan University, Graduate School, College of Business, Department of Accounting and Finance, Ypsilanti, MI 48197. Offers accounting (MS); accounting information systems (MS). Part-time and evening/weekend programs available. Postbaccalaureate distance learning degree programs offered (minimal on-campus study). *Faculty:* 24 full-time (9 women). *Students:* 67 full-time (39 women), 38 part-time (21 women); includes 18 minority (6 Black or African American, non-Hispanic/Latino; 7 Asian, non-Hispanic/Latino; 3 Hispanic/Latino; 1 Native Hawaiian or other Pacific Islander, non-Hispanic/Latino; 1 Two or more races, non-Hispanic/Latino), 26 international. Average age 28. 66 applicants, 74% accepted, 27 enrolled. In 2013, 55 master's awarded. *Entrance requirements:* For master's, GMAT. Additional exam requirements/recommendations for international students: Required—TOEFL. *Application deadline:* Applications are processed on a rolling basis. Application fee: $35. *Expenses:* Tuition, state resident: full-time $12,300; part-time $466 per credit hour. Tuition, nonresident: full-time $23,159; part-time $918 per credit hour. *Required fees:* $71 per credit hour. $46 per semester. One-time fee: $100. Tuition and fees vary according to course level and degree level. *Financial support:* Fellowships, research assistantships with full tuition reimbursements, teaching assistantships with full tuition reimbursements, career-related internships or fieldwork, Federal Work-Study, institutionally sponsored loans, scholarships/grants, tuition waivers (partial), and unspecified assistantships available. Support available to part-time students. Financial award applicants required to submit FAFSA. *Unit head:* Dr. Zafar Khan, Interim Department Head, 734-487-3320, Fax: 734-487-0806, E-mail: zafar.khan@emich.edu. *Application contact:* Dr. Phil Lewis, Advisor, 734-487-1311, Fax: 734-482-0806, E-mail: phil.lewis@emich.edu.
Website: http://www.accfin.emich.edu.

East Tennessee State University, School of Graduate Studies, College of Business and Technology, Department of Accountancy, Johnson City, TN 37614. Offers M Acc. *Accreditation:* AACSB. Part-time and evening/weekend programs available. *Faculty:* 11 full-time (2 women), 1 (woman) part-time/adjunct. *Students:* 43 full-time (22 women), 8 part-time (5 women); includes 2 minority (1 Black or African American, non-Hispanic/Latino; 1 Asian, non-Hispanic/Latino), 3 international. Average age 25. 52 applicants, 60% accepted, 26 enrolled. In 2013, 29 master's awarded. *Degree requirements:* For master's, comprehensive exam, capstone, professional accounting experience. *Entrance requirements:* For master's, GMAT, minimum GPA of 2.5. Additional exam requirements/recommendations for international students: Required—TOEFL (minimum score 550 paper-based; 79 iBT). *Application deadline:* For fall admission, 6/1 for domestic students, 4/30 for international students; for spring admission, 11/1 for domestic students, 9/30 for international students. Application fee: $35 ($45 for international students). Electronic applications accepted. *Expenses:* Tuition, state resident: full-time $7900; part-time $395 per credit hour. Tuition, nonresident: full-time $21,960; part-time $1098 per credit hour. *Required fees:* $1345; $84 per credit hour. *Financial support:* In 2013–14, 33 students received support, including 15 research assistantships with full tuition reimbursements available (averaging $6,000 per year); career-related internships or fieldwork, institutionally sponsored loans, scholarships/grants, and unspecified assistantships also available. Financial award application deadline: 7/1; financial award applicants required to submit FAFSA. *Faculty research:* Smaller firm practice management, personal financial planning, accounting education, taxation issues. *Unit head:* Dr. Gary Burkette, Chair, 423-439-4432, Fax: 423-439-8659, E-mail: burkette@etsu.edu. *Application contact:* Cindy Hill, Graduate Specialist, 423-439-6590, Fax: 423-439-5624, E-mail: hillcc@etsu.edu.
Website: http://www.etsu.edu/acct/Academics/MAcc/Index.htm.

Edgewood College, Program in Business, Madison, WI 53711-1997. Offers accountancy (MS); accounting (MBA); business administration (MBA); finance (MBA); management (MBA); marketing (MBA); organization development (MS); sustainability leadership (MBA). *Accreditation:* ACBSP. Part-time and evening/weekend programs

available. *Students:* 24 full-time (8 women), 136 part-time (82 women); includes 18 minority (5 Black or African American, non-Hispanic/Latino; 1 American Indian or Alaska Native, non-Hispanic/Latino; 4 Asian, non-Hispanic/Latino; 4 Hispanic/Latino; 4 Two or more races, non-Hispanic/Latino), 10 international. Average age 33. In 2013, 55 master's awarded. *Entrance requirements:* For master's, GMAT (minimum score 430), minimum GPA of 2.75, 2 letters of recommendation. Additional exam requirements/recommendations for international students: Required—TOEFL. *Application deadline:* For fall admission, 8/15 for domestic students, 5/1 for international students; for spring admission, 1/8 for domestic students, 11/1 for international students. Applications are processed on a rolling basis. Application fee: $30. Electronic applications accepted. *Financial support:* Career-related internships or fieldwork and scholarships/grants available. *Unit head:* Martin Preizler, Dean, 608-663-2898, Fax: 608-663-3291, E-mail: martinpreizler@edgewood.edu. *Application contact:* Joann Eastman, Admissions Counselor, 608-663-3250, Fax: 608-663-2214, E-mail: gps@edgewood.edu. Website: http://www.edgewood.edu/Academics/School-of-Business.

Elmhurst College, Graduate Programs, Program in Professional Accountancy, Elmhurst, IL 60126-3296. Offers MPA. Part-time and evening/weekend programs available. *Faculty:* 1 full-time (0 women), 1 (woman) part-time/adjunct. *Students:* 2 full-time (1 woman), 22 part-time (11 women); includes 4 minority (2 Black or African American, non-Hispanic/Latino; 2 Hispanic/Latino), 1 international. Average age 28. 12 applicants, 67% accepted, 6 enrolled. In 2013, 4 master's awarded. *Entrance requirements:* For master's, 3 recommendations, resume, statement of purpose. Additional exam requirements/recommendations for international students: Required—TOEFL (minimum score 550 paper-based; 79 iBT). *Application deadline:* Applications are processed on a rolling basis. Application fee: $0. Electronic applications accepted. *Expenses:* Contact institution. *Financial support:* In 2013–14, 2 students received support. Federal Work-Study and scholarships/grants available. Support available to part-time students. Financial award application deadline: 6/1; financial award applicants required to submit FAFSA. *Application contact:* Timothy J. Panfil, Director of Enrollment Management, School for Professional Studies, 630-617-3300 Ext. 3256, Fax: 630-617-6471, E-mail: panfilt@elmhurst.edu.

Emory University, Goizueta Business School, Doctoral Program in Business, Atlanta, GA 30322-1100. Offers accounting (PhD); finance (PhD); information systems (PhD); marketing (PhD); organization and management (PhD). *Faculty:* 53 full-time (12 women). *Students:* 41 full-time (15 women); includes 28 minority (all Asian, non-Hispanic/Latino). Average age 29. 195 applicants, 9% accepted, 9 enrolled. In 2013, 1 doctorate awarded. *Degree requirements:* For doctorate, comprehensive exam, thesis/dissertation. *Entrance requirements:* For doctorate, GMAT (strongly preferred) or GRE. Additional exam requirements/recommendations for international students: Required—TOEFL. *Application deadline:* For fall admission, 1/3 priority date for domestic and international students. Application fee: $75. Electronic applications accepted. *Financial support:* In 2013–14, 35 students received support, including 3 fellowships (averaging $1,166 per year). *Unit head:* Dr. Anand Swaminathan, Associate Dean, Doctoral Program, 404-727-2306, Fax: 404-727-5337, E-mail: anand.swaminathan@emory.edu. *Application contact:* Allison Gilmore, Director of Admissions and Student Services, 404-727-6353, Fax: 404-727-5337, E-mail: phd@bus.emory.edu.

Everest University, Department of Business Administration, Tampa, FL 33614-5899. Offers accounting (MBA); human resources (MBA); international business (MBA). Part-time and evening/weekend programs available. *Degree requirements:* For master's, thesis optional. *Entrance requirements:* For master's, GMAT or GRE General Test, minimum GPA of 3.0.

Everest University, Program in Business Administration, Largo, FL 33770. Offers accounting (MBA); human resources management (MBA); international business (MBA). *Faculty research:* Management fads, learning styles, effective use of technology.

Everest University, Program in Business Administration, Orlando, FL 32819. Offers accounting (MBA); general management (MBA); human resources (MBA); international management (MBA).

Fairfield University, Charles F. Dolan School of Business, Fairfield, CT 06824-5195. Offers accounting (MBA, MS, CAS); accounting information systems (MBA, CAS); entrepreneurship (MBA, CAS); finance (MBA, MS, CAS); general management (MBA, CAS); human resource management (MBA, CAS); information systems and operations (MBA); information systems and operations management (CAS); marketing (MBA, CAS); taxation (MBA, CAS). *Accreditation:* AACSB. Part-time and evening/weekend programs available. *Faculty:* 18 full-time (9 women), 15 part-time/adjunct (4 women). *Students:* 94 full-time (45 women), 72 part-time (26 women); includes 49 minority (7 Black or African American, non-Hispanic/Latino; 33 Asian, non-Hispanic/Latino; 8 Hispanic/Latino; 1 Two or more races, non-Hispanic/Latino), 9 international. Average age 29. 116 applicants, 43% accepted, 26 enrolled. In 2013, 100 master's awarded. *Degree requirements:* For master's, capstone course. *Entrance requirements:* For master's, GMAT (minimum score 500), 2 letters of reference, resume, minimum GPA of 3.0. Additional exam requirements/recommendations for international students: Required—TOEFL (minimum score 550 paper-based; 80 iBT) or IELTS (minimum score 6.5). *Application deadline:* For fall admission, 5/15 for international students; for spring admission, 10/15 for international students. Applications are processed on a rolling basis. Application fee: $60. Electronic applications accepted. *Expenses:* Contact institution. *Financial support:* In 2013–14, 28 students received support. Scholarships/grants, unspecified assistantships, and merit-based one-time entrance scholarships available. Financial award applicants required to submit FAFSA. *Faculty research:* International finance, leadership and careers, ethics in accounting, emotions in consumer behavior, supply chain analysis, organizational leadership attributes, emotions in the workplace, real estate finance, effect of social media on stock prices. *Unit head:* Dr. Donald Gibson, Dean, 203-254-4070, Fax: 203-254-4105, E-mail: dgibson@fairfield.edu. *Application contact:* Marianne Gumpper, Director of Graduate and Continuing Studies Admission, 203-254-4184, Fax: 203-254-4073, E-mail: gradadmis@fairfield.edu. Website: http://fairfield.edu/mba.

Fairleigh Dickinson University, College at Florham, Silberman College of Business, Department of Accounting, Law, and Tax, Program in Accounting, Madison, NJ 07940-1099. Offers MS. *Entrance requirements:* For master's, GMAT.

Fairleigh Dickinson University, Metropolitan Campus, Silberman College of Business, Department of Accounting, Law, and Tax, Program in Accounting, Teaneck, NJ 07666-1914. Offers MBA, MS, Certificate. *Faculty research:* Corporate accounting, legal issues.

Fitchburg State University, Division of Graduate and Continuing Education, Program in Business Administration, Fitchburg, MA 01420-2697. Offers accounting (MBA); human resource management (MBA); management (MBA). Part-time and evening/weekend programs available. Postbaccalaureate distance learning degree programs offered (no on-campus study). *Entrance requirements:* Additional exam requirements/recommendations for international students: Required—TOEFL (minimum score 550 paper-based; 79 iBT). Electronic applications accepted.

Florida Agricultural and Mechanical University, Division of Graduate Studies, Research, and Continuing Education, School of Business and Industry, Tallahassee, FL

32307-3200. Offers accounting (MBA); finance (MBA); management information systems (MBA); marketing (MBA). *Accreditation:* ACBSP. *Degree requirements:* For master's, residency. *Entrance requirements:* For master's, GMAT, minimum GPA of 3.0.

Florida Atlantic University, College of Business, School of Accounting, Boca Raton, FL 33431-0991. Offers accounting (MAC, MBA, PhD); accounting information systems (MAC); business valuation (Exec MAC); forensic accounting (Exec MAC); taxation (MAC). *Accreditation:* AACSB. Part-time and evening/weekend programs available. Postbaccalaureate distance learning degree programs offered (minimal on-campus study). *Faculty:* 18 full-time (8 women), 10 part-time/adjunct (4 women). *Students:* 105 full-time (35 women), 365 part-time (200 women); includes 154 minority (50 Black or African American, non-Hispanic/Latino; 30 Asian, non-Hispanic/Latino; 68 Hispanic/Latino; 6 Two or more races, non-Hispanic/Latino), 9 international. Average age 33. 284 applicants, 42% accepted, 92 enrolled. In 2013, 201 master's awarded. *Degree requirements:* For master's, comprehensive exam, thesis optional. *Entrance requirements:* For master's, GMAT with minimum score 500 (preferred) or GRE (minimum score 1000 old test, 153 Verbal, 144 Quantitative, 4 Writing) taken within last 5 years, BS in accounting or equivalent, minimum GPA of 3.0 in last 60 hours of undergraduate study. Additional exam requirements/recommendations for international students: Required—TOEFL (minimum score 600 paper-based; 61 iBT), IELTS (minimum score 6). *Application deadline:* For fall admission, 7/1 priority date for domestic students, 2/15 priority date for international students; for spring admission, 11/1 priority date for domestic students, 7/15 priority date for international students. Applications are processed on a rolling basis. Application fee: $30. *Expenses:* Tuition, state resident: full-time $6660; part-time $370 per credit hour. Tuition, nonresident: full-time $18,450; part-time $1025 per credit hour. Tuition and fees vary according to course load. *Financial support:* Fellowships, research assistantships with partial tuition reimbursements, teaching assistantships, career-related internships or fieldwork, Federal Work-Study, institutionally sponsored loans, scholarships/grants, and tuition waivers (partial) available. Support available to part-time students. Financial award application deadline: 3/1. *Faculty research:* Systems and computer applications, accounting theory, information systems. *Unit head:* Dr. Kimberly Dunn, Director, 561-297-3638, Fax: 561-297-7023, E-mail: kdunn@fau.edu. *Application contact:* Dr. Marcy Krugel, Graduate Adviser, 561-297-3940, Fax: 561-297-1315, E-mail: krugel@fau.edu. Website: http://business.fau.edu/departments/accounting/index.aspx.

Florida Gulf Coast University, Lutgert College of Business, Program in Accounting and Taxation, Fort Myers, FL 33965-6565. Offers MS. Part-time and evening/weekend programs available. *Degree requirements:* For master's, thesis or alternative. *Entrance requirements:* For master's, GMAT, minimum GPA of 3.0. Additional exam requirements/recommendations for international students: Required—TOEFL (minimum score 550 paper-based). Electronic applications accepted. *Faculty research:* Stock petitions, mergers and acquisitions, deferred taxes, fraud and accounting regulations, graphical reporting practices.

Florida Institute of Technology, Graduate Programs, Nathan M. Bisk College of Business, Online Programs, Melbourne, FL 32901-6975. Offers accounting (MBA); accounting and finance (MBA); business administration (MBA); finance (MBA); healthcare management (MBA); information assurance and cybersecurity (MS); information technology (MS); information technology cybersecurity (MS); information technology management (MBA); international business (MBA); Internet marketing (MBA); management (MBA); marketing (MBA); project management (MBA); supply chain management (MS). Part-time and evening/weekend programs available. Postbaccalaureate distance learning degree programs offered (no on-campus study). *Faculty:* 3 full-time (1 woman), 41 part-time/adjunct (13 women). *Students:* 6 full-time (1 woman), 1,121 part-time (530 women); includes 424 minority (276 Black or African American, non-Hispanic/Latino; 10 American Indian or Alaska Native, non-Hispanic/Latino; 45 Asian, non-Hispanic/Latino; 88 Hispanic/Latino; 5 Native Hawaiian or other Pacific Islander, non-Hispanic/Latino), 32 international. Average age 36. 348 applicants, 42% accepted, 146 enrolled. In 2013, 475 master's awarded. *Entrance requirements:* For master's, GMAT or resume showing 8 years of supervised experience, 2 letters of recommendation, resume, competency in math past college algebra. Additional exam requirements/recommendations for international students: Required—TOEFL (minimum score 550 paper-based; 79 iBT). *Application deadline:* For fall admission, 4/1 for international students; for spring admission, 9/30 for international students. Applications are processed on a rolling basis. Electronic applications accepted. *Expenses:* Contact institution. *Financial support:* Available to part-time students. Application deadline: 3/1; applicants required to submit FAFSA. *Unit head:* Brian Ehrlich, Associate Vice President/Director of Online Learning, 321-674-8202, E-mail: behrlich@fit.edu. *Application contact:* Carolyn Farrior, Director of Graduate Admissions, Online Learning and Off-Campus Programs, 321-674-7118. Website: http://online.fit.edu.

Florida International University, Alvah H. Chapman, Jr. Graduate School of Business, School of Accounting, Program in Accounting, Miami, FL 33199. Offers M Acc. *Accreditation:* AACSB. Part-time and evening/weekend programs available. *Entrance requirements:* For master's, GMAT or GRE, minimum GPA of 3.0 (upper-level coursework); resume. Additional exam requirements/recommendations for international students: Required—TOEFL (minimum score 550 paper-based; 80 iBT) or IELTS (minimum score 6.5). Electronic applications accepted. *Expenses:* Contact institution. *Faculty research:* Financial and managerial accounting.

Florida State University, The Graduate School, College of Business, Tallahassee, FL 32306-1110. Offers accounting (M Acc), including accounting information services, assurance services, corporate accounting, taxation; business administration (MBA, PhD), including accounting (PhD), finance (PhD), management information systems (PhD), marketing (PhD), organizational behavior and human resources (PhD), risk management and insurance (PhD), strategic management (PhD); finance (MS); insurance (MSM); management information systems (MS); marketing (MS); JD/MBA; MSW/MBA. *Accreditation:* AACSB. Part-time programs available. Postbaccalaureate distance learning degree programs offered (no on-campus study). *Faculty:* 102 full-time (31 women), 5 part-time/adjunct (0 women). *Students:* 280 full-time (117 women), 278 part-time (88 women); includes 127 minority (26 Black or African American, non-Hispanic/Latino; 7 American Indian or Alaska Native, non-Hispanic/Latino; 44 Asian, non-Hispanic/Latino; 50 Hispanic/Latino). Average age 30. 630 applicants, 28% accepted, 103 enrolled. In 2013, 265 master's, 11 doctorates awarded. Terminal master's awarded for partial completion of doctoral program. *Degree requirements:* For doctorate, comprehensive exam, thesis/dissertation. *Entrance requirements:* For master's, GMAT, work experience (MBA, MS), minimum GPA of 3.0, letters of recommendation; for doctorate, GMAT, minimum graduate GPA of 3.5, letters of recommendation. Additional exam requirements/recommendations for international students: Required—TOEFL (minimum score 600 paper-based; 100 iBT); Recommended—IELTS (minimum score 6.5). *Application deadline:* For fall admission, 6/1 for domestic students, 5/1 for international students; for spring admission, 10/1 for domestic students, 9/1 for international students. Applications are processed on a rolling basis. Application fee: $30. Electronic applications accepted. *Expenses:* Tuition, state resident: part-time $403.51 per credit hour. Tuition, nonresident: part-time $1004.85 per credit hour. *Required fees:* $75.81 per credit hour. One-time fee: $20 part-time. Tuition

and fees vary according to course load, campus/location and student level. *Financial support:* In 2013–14, 92 students received support, including 10 fellowships with full tuition reimbursements available (averaging $1,500 per year), 20 research assistantships with full tuition reimbursements available (averaging $20,000 per year), 35 teaching assistantships with full tuition reimbursements available (averaging $20,000 per year); career-related internships or fieldwork, scholarships/grants, health care benefits, and unspecified assistantships also available. Financial award application deadline: 1/1. *Unit head:* Dr. Caryn Beck-Dudley, Dean, 850-644-3090, Fax: 850-644-0915. *Application contact:* Lisa Beverly, Director, Graduate Programs Admissions, 850-644-6458, Fax: 850-644-0588, E-mail: lbeverly@cob.fsu.edu.
Website: http://www.cob.fsu.edu/.

Fontbonne University, Graduate Programs, College of Global Business and Professional Studies, Program in Accounting, St. Louis, MO 63105-3098. Offers MS. Part-time programs available. *Entrance requirements:* For master's, GMAT. Additional exam requirements/recommendations for international students: Required—TOEFL (minimum score 71 iBT). *Expenses: Tuition:* Full-time $11,646; part-time $647 per credit hour. *Required fees:* $324; $18 per credit hour. Tuition and fees vary according to course load and program.

Fordham University, Graduate School of Business, New York, NY 10023. Offers accounting (MBA); communications and media management (MBA); executive business administration (EMBA); finance (MBA, MS); information systems (MBA, MS); management systems (MBA); marketing (MBA); media management (MS); taxation (MS); taxation and accounting (MTA); JD/MBA; MBA/MIM; MS/MBA. MBA/MIM offered jointly with Thunderbird School of Global Management. *Accreditation:* AACSB. Part-time and evening/weekend programs available. *Entrance requirements:* For master's, GMAT, 2 letters of recommendation, resume. Additional exam requirements/recommendations for international students: Required—TOEFL (minimum score 600 paper-based; 100 iBT). Electronic applications accepted. *Expenses:* Contact institution.

Franklin University, Accounting Program, Columbus, OH 43215-5399. Offers MSA. Postbaccalaureate distance learning degree programs offered (minimal on-campus study).

Freed-Hardeman University, Program in Business Administration, Henderson, TN 38340-2399. Offers accounting (MBA); corporate responsibility (MBA); leadership (MBA). *Accreditation:* ACBSP. Part-time and evening/weekend programs available. Postbaccalaureate distance learning degree programs offered (no on-campus study). *Entrance requirements:* For master's, GMAT. Additional exam requirements/recommendations for international students: Required—TOEFL (minimum score 500 paper-based).

Friends University, Graduate School, Wichita, KS 67213. Offers business law (MBL); Christian ministry (MACM); family therapy (MSFT); global (MBA), including accounting, business law, change management, health care leadership, management information systems, supply chain management and logistics; health care leadership (MHCL); management information systems (MMIS); operations management (MSOM); professional (MBA), including accounting, business law, change management, health care leadership, management information systems, supply chain management and logistics; teaching (MAT). Part-time and evening/weekend programs available. Postbaccalaureate distance learning degree programs offered (no on-campus study). *Faculty:* 18 full-time (8 women), 62 part-time/adjunct (28 women). *Students:* 161 full-time (111 women), 408 part-time (258 women); includes 157 minority (68 Black or African American, non-Hispanic/Latino; 7 American Indian or Alaska Native, non-Hispanic/Latino; 28 Asian, non-Hispanic/Latino; 18 Hispanic/Latino; 1 Native Hawaiian or other Pacific Islander, non-Hispanic/Latino; 35 Two or more races, non-Hispanic/Latino). Average age 36. 371 applicants, 90% accepted, 178 enrolled. In 2013, 432 master's awarded. *Degree requirements:* For master's, research project. *Entrance requirements:* For master's, bachelor's degree from accredited institution, official transcripts, interview with program director, letter(s) of recommendation. Additional exam requirements/recommendations for international students: Required—TOEFL (minimum score 560 paper-based). *Application deadline:* Applications are processed on a rolling basis. Application fee: $35 ($50 for international students). Electronic applications accepted. *Expenses: Tuition:* Part-time $631 per credit hour. Tuition and fees vary according to program. *Financial support:* In 2013–14, 30 students received support. Applicants required to submit FAFSA. *Unit head:* Dr. David Hofmeister, Dean of the Graduate School, 800-794-6945 Ext. 5858, Fax: 316-295-5040, E-mail: david_hofmeister@friends.edu. *Application contact:* Rachel Steiner, Manager, Graduate Recruiting Services, 800-794-6945, Fax: 316-295-5872, E-mail: rachel_steiner@friends.edu.
Website: http://www.friends.edu/.

George Mason University, School of Business, Program in Accounting, Fairfax, VA 22030. Offers forensic accounting (Certificate). *Accreditation:* AACSB. *Faculty:* 18 full-time (9 women), 1 part-time/adjunct (0 women). *Students:* 30 full-time (18 women), 7 part-time (4 women); includes 12 minority (1 Black or African American, non-Hispanic/Latino; 5 Asian, non-Hispanic/Latino; 3 Hispanic/Latino; 3 Two or more races, non-Hispanic/Latino), 12 international. Average age 27. 77 applicants, 64% accepted, 20 enrolled. In 2013, 26 master's awarded. *Entrance requirements:* For master's, GMAT/GRE, resume; official transcripts; 2 letters of recommendation; personal statement; professional essay; interview. Additional exam requirements/recommendations for international students: Required—TOEFL (minimum score 570 paper-based; 88 iBT), IELTS (minimum score 6.5), PTE. *Application deadline:* For fall admission, 1/15 priority date for domestic students; for spring admission, 10/15 priority date for domestic students, 10/1 priority date for international students. Application fee: $65 ($80 for international students). Electronic applications accepted. *Expenses:* Contact institution. *Financial support:* In 2013–14, 13 students received support, including 11 research assistantships with full and partial tuition reimbursements available (averaging $7,785 per year), 4 teaching assistantships (averaging $8,411 per year); career-related internships or fieldwork, Federal Work-Study, scholarships/grants, unspecified assistantships, and health care benefits (for full-time research or teaching assistantship recipients) also available. Support available to part-time students. Financial award application deadline: 3/1; financial award applicants required to submit FAFSA. *Faculty research:* Current leading global business issues, including offshore outsourcing, international financial risk, and comparative systems of innovation; business management/practices; emerging technology and generating new business. *Unit head:* Dr. Gnanakumar Visvanathan, Chair, 703-993-4236, Fax: 703-993-1809, E-mail: gvisvana@gmu.edu. *Application contact:* Nancy Doernhoefer, Admissions Specialist, 703-993-4128, Fax: 703-993-1778, E-mail: ndoernho@gmu.edu.
Website: http://business.gmu.edu/masters-in-accounting/.

The George Washington University, School of Business, Department of Accountancy, Washington, DC 20052. Offers M Accy, MBA, PhD. *Accreditation:* AACSB. Part-time and evening/weekend programs available. *Faculty:* 17 full-time (6 women). *Students:* 185 full-time (144 women), 59 part-time (34 women); includes 22 minority (5 Black or African American, non-Hispanic/Latino; 2 American Indian or Alaska Native, non-Hispanic/Latino; 8 Asian, non-Hispanic/Latino; 6 Hispanic/Latino; 1 Two or more races, non-Hispanic/Latino), 168 international. Average age 26. 301 applicants, 88% accepted, 133 enrolled. In 2013, 85 master's awarded. *Degree requirements:* For doctorate, thesis/dissertation. *Entrance requirements:* For master's, GMAT; for doctorate, GMAT or GRE. Additional exam requirements/recommendations for international students: Required—TOEFL. *Application deadline:* For fall admission, 4/1 priority date for domestic students; for spring admission, 10/1 for domestic students. Applications are processed on a rolling basis. Application fee: $75. *Financial support:* In 2013–14, 50 students received support. Fellowships, teaching assistantships, career-related internships or fieldwork, Federal Work-Study, and institutionally sponsored loans available. Financial award application deadline: 4/1. *Faculty research:* Management accounting and capital markets, financial accounting and the analytic hierarchy process, ethics and accounting, accounting information systems. *Unit head:* Dr. Angela Gore, Chair, 202-994-5164, E-mail: agore@gwu.edu. *Application contact:* Louba Hatoum, Program Director, 202-994-4450, E-mail: lhatoum@gwu.edu.
Website: http://business.gwu.edu/about-us/departments/department-of-accountancy/.

Georgia College & State University, Graduate School, The J. Whitney Bunting School of Business, Program in Accounting, Milledgeville, GA 31061. Offers M Acc. Part-time programs available. *Students:* 17 full-time (11 women), 22 part-time (11 women); includes 6 minority (4 Black or African American, non-Hispanic/Latino; 1 Asian, non-Hispanic/Latino; 1 Two or more races, non-Hispanic/Latino), 6 international. Average age 29. In 2013, 21 master's awarded. *Degree requirements:* For master's, minimum GPA of 3.0, complete program within 7 years of start date. *Entrance requirements:* For master's, GRE or GMAT. Additional exam requirements/recommendations for international students: Recommended—TOEFL (minimum score 500 paper-based; 61 iBT), IELTS (minimum score 6). *Application deadline:* For fall admission, 7/1 for domestic students; for spring admission, 11/15 for domestic students; for summer admission, 4/1 for domestic students. Applications are processed on a rolling basis. Application fee: $35. Electronic applications accepted. *Financial support:* Unspecified assistantships available. *Unit head:* Dr. Dale Young, Interim Dean, 478-445-5497, E-mail: dale.young@gcsu.edu. *Application contact:* Lynn Hanson, Director of Graduate Programs, 478-445-5115, E-mail: lynn.hanson@gcsu.edu.
Website: http://www.gcsu.edu/business/graduateprograms/maac.htm.

Georgia Institute of Technology, Graduate Studies and Research, College of Management, Program in Business Administration, Atlanta, GA 30332-0001. Offers accounting (MBA); e-commerce (Certificate); engineering entrepreneurship (MBA); entrepreneurship (Certificate); finance (MBA); information technology management (MBA); international business (MBA, Certificate); management of technology (Certificate); marketing (MBA); operations management (MBA); organizational behavior (MBA); strategic management (MBA). *Accreditation:* AACSB.

Georgia Institute of Technology, Graduate Studies and Research, College of Management, Program in Management, Atlanta, GA 30332-0001. Offers accounting (PhD); finance (PhD); information technology management (PhD); marketing (PhD); operations management (PhD); organizational behavior (PhD); quantitative and computational finance (MS); strategic management (PhD). *Accreditation:* AACSB. *Degree requirements:* For doctorate, comprehensive exam, thesis/dissertation, oral exams. *Entrance requirements:* For master's and doctorate, GMAT. Additional exam requirements/recommendations for international students: Required—TOEFL. *Faculty research:* Management information systems, management of technology, international business, entrepreneurship, operations management.

Georgia Southern University, Jack N. Averitt College of Graduate Studies, College of Business Administration, School of Accountancy, Statesboro, GA 30460. Offers accounting (M Acc). *Accreditation:* AACSB. Part-time and evening/weekend programs available. *Students:* 51 full-time (32 women), 37 part-time (26 women); includes 13 minority (11 Black or African American, non-Hispanic/Latino; 1 Hispanic/Latino; 1 Two or more races, non-Hispanic/Latino), 7 international. Average age 28. 62 applicants, 52% accepted, 26 enrolled. In 2013, 58 master's awarded. *Entrance requirements:* For master's, GMAT. Additional exam requirements/recommendations for international students: Required—TOEFL (minimum score 550 paper-based; 80 iBT), IELTS (minimum score 6). *Application deadline:* For fall admission, 3/1 priority date for domestic and international students; for spring admission, 10/1 priority date for domestic students, 10/1 for international students. Applications are processed on a rolling basis. Application fee: $50. Electronic applications accepted. *Expenses:* Contact institution. *Financial support:* In 2013–14, 14 students received support, including research assistantships with partial tuition reimbursements available (averaging $7,200 per year), teaching assistantships with partial tuition reimbursements available (averaging $7,200 per year); career-related internships or fieldwork, Federal Work-Study, scholarships/grants, tuition waivers (partial), and unspecified assistantships also available. Support available to part-time students. Financial award application deadline: 4/15; financial award applicants required to submit FAFSA. *Faculty research:* Consolidation of fraud in the financial statement, reasons why firms switch auditions for the financial audit, internalization of accounting standards, pedagogy issues in accounting and law courses. *Unit head:* Dr. Gordon Smith, Graduate Program Director, 912-478-2357, Fax: 912-478-0292, E-mail: gsmith@georgiasouthern.edu. *Application contact:* Amanda Gilliland, Coordinator for Graduate Student Recruitment, 912-478-5384, Fax: 912-478-0740, E-mail: gradadmissions@georgiasouthern.edu.
Website: http://coba.georgiasouthern.edu/soa/graduate/.

Georgia State University, J. Mack Robinson College of Business, School of Accountancy, Program in Professional Accountancy, Atlanta, GA 30303. Offers MPA. *Accreditation:* AACSB. Part-time and evening/weekend programs available. *Students:* Average age 0. *Entrance requirements:* For master's, GRE or GMAT, transcripts from all institutions attended, resume, essays. Additional exam requirements/recommendations for international students: Required—TOEFL (minimum score 610 paper-based; 101 iBT), IELTS (minimum score 7). *Application deadline:* For fall admission, 5/1 priority date for domestic students, 2/1 priority date for international students; for spring admission, 9/15 priority date for domestic students, 4/1 priority date for international students. Applications are processed on a rolling basis. Application fee: $50. Electronic applications accepted. *Expenses: Tuition, area resident:* Full-time $4176; part-time $348 per credit hour. Tuition, state resident: full-time $14,544; part-time $1212 per credit hour. Tuition, nonresident: full-time $14,544; part-time $1212 per credit hour. Tuition and fees vary according to course load and program. *Financial support:* In 2013–14, 50 students received support. Research assistantships, scholarships/grants, tuition waivers, and unspecified assistantships available. *Unit head:* Dr. Galen R. Sevcik, Director of the School of Accountancy, 404-413-7200, Fax: 404-413-7203. *Application contact:* Toby McChesney, Assistant Dean for Graduate Recruiting and Student Services, 404-413-7167, Fax: 404-413-7162, E-mail: rcbgradadmissions@gsu.edu.
Website: http://robinson.gsu.edu/accountancy/mpa.html.

Golden Gate University, Ageno School of Business, San Francisco, CA 94105-2968. Offers accounting (MBA); business administration (EMBA, MBA, PMBA, DBA); finance (MBA, MS, Certificate); financial planning (MS, Certificate); healthcare information systems (Certificate); human resource management (MBA, MS); human resources management (Certificate); information systems (MS); information technology (MBA); information technology management (Certificate); integrated marketing and communications (MS, Certificate); international business (MBA); management (MBA); marketing (MBA, MS, Certificate); operations supply chain management (Certificate); psychology (MA, Certificate); public administration (EMPA); public relations (MS, Certificate); technical market analysis (Certificate); JD/MBA. Part-time and evening/

weekend programs available. *Degree requirements:* For doctorate, thesis/dissertation, qualifying examination. *Entrance requirements:* For master's, GMAT (MBA), minimum GPA of 2.5 (MS). Additional exam requirements/recommendations for international students: Required—TOEFL (minimum score 550 paper-based; 79 iBT). Electronic applications accepted. *Expenses:* Contact institution.

Golden Gate University, School of Accounting, San Francisco, CA 94105-2968. Offers accounting (M Ac, MSA, Graduate Certificate); forensic accounting (M Ac, MSA, Graduate Certificate); taxation (M Ac). Part-time and evening/weekend programs available. *Entrance requirements:* For master's, minimum GPA of 3.0. Additional exam requirements/recommendations for international students: Required—TOEFL. Electronic applications accepted. *Faculty research:* Forensic accounting, audit, tax, CPA exam.

Gonzaga University, School of Business Administration, Spokane, WA 99258. Offers M Acc, MBA, JD/M Acc, JD/MBA. *Accreditation:* AACSB. Part-time and evening/weekend programs available. *Faculty:* 43 full-time (12 women), 6 part-time/adjunct (2 women). *Students:* 47 full-time (18 women), 106 part-time (51 women); includes 25 minority (8 American Indian or Alaska Native, non-Hispanic/Latino; 7 Asian, non-Hispanic/Latino; 8 Hispanic/Latino; 2 Two or more races, non-Hispanic/Latino), 10 international. Average age 29. 123 applicants, 50% accepted, 34 enrolled. In 2013, 97 master's awarded. *Entrance requirements:* For master's, GMAT. Additional exam requirements/recommendations for international students: Required—TOEFL. *Application deadline:* For fall admission, 7/20 priority date for domestic students; for spring admission, 11/1 for domestic students. Applications are processed on a rolling basis. Application fee: $50. Electronic applications accepted. *Expenses:* Contact institution. *Financial support:* Teaching assistantships and Federal Work-Study available. Support available to part-time students. Financial award application deadline: 2/1; financial award applicants required to submit FAFSA. *Unit head:* Dr. Ken Anderson, Interim Dean, 509-313-5991. *Application contact:* Stacey Chatman, Assistant Director for Admissions, 509-313-4622, Fax: 509-313-7044, E-mail: chatman@gonzaga.edu. Website: http://www.gonzaga.edu/MBA.

Governors State University, College of Business and Public Administration, Program in Accounting, University Park, IL 60484. Offers MS. *Entrance requirements:* For master's, GMAT.

The Graduate Center, City University of New York, Graduate Studies, Program in Business, New York, NY 10016-4039. Offers accounting (PhD); behavioral science (PhD); finance (PhD); management planning systems (PhD). *Degree requirements:* For doctorate, thesis/dissertation. *Entrance requirements:* For doctorate, GMAT, writing sample (15 pages). Additional exam requirements/recommendations for international students: Required—TOEFL. Electronic applications accepted.

Grand Canyon University, College of Business, Phoenix, AZ 85017-1097. Offers accounting (MBA); corporate business administration (MBA); disaster preparedness and crisis management (MBA); executive fire service leadership (MS); finance (MBA); general management (MBA); government and policy (MPA); health care management (MPA); health systems management (MBA); human resource management (MBA); innovation (MBA); leadership (MBA, MS); management of information system (MBA); marketing (MBA); project-based (MBA); six sigma (MBA); strategic human resource management (MBA). *Accreditation:* ACBSP. Part-time and evening/weekend programs available. Postbaccalaureate distance learning degree programs offered (no on-campus study). *Entrance requirements:* For master's, equivalent of two years full-time professional work experience. Additional exam requirements/recommendations for international students: Required—TOEFL (minimum score 575 paper-based; 90 iBT), IELTS (minimum score 7). Electronic applications accepted.

Grand Valley State University, Seidman College of Business, Program in Accounting, Allendale, MI 49401-9403. Offers MSA. *Accreditation:* AACSB. Part-time and evening/weekend programs available. *Degree requirements:* For master's, comprehensive exam. *Entrance requirements:* For master's, GMAT. Additional exam requirements/recommendations for international students: Required—TOEFL. *Faculty research:* Public trust, capacity measurement, theoretical capacity, economic order quantity.

Harvard University, Harvard Business School, Doctoral Programs in Management, Boston, MA 02163. Offers accounting and management (DBA); business economics (PhD); health policy management (PhD); management (DBA); marketing (DBA); organizational behavior (PhD); science, technology and management (PhD); strategy (DBA); technology and operations management (DBA). *Degree requirements:* For doctorate, comprehensive exam (for some programs), thesis/dissertation. *Entrance requirements:* For doctorate, GRE General Test or GMAT. Additional exam requirements/recommendations for international students: Required—TOEFL. *Expenses: Tuition:* Full-time $38,888. *Required fees:* $958. Tuition and fees vary according to campus/location, program and student level.

Hawai'i Pacific University, College of Business Administration, Honolulu, HI 96813. Offers accounting/CPA (MBA); e-business (MBA); economics (MBA); finance (MBA); healthcare management (MBA); human resource management (MA, MBA); information systems (MBA, MSIS); international business (MBA); management (MBA); marketing (MBA); organizational change (MA, MBA); travel industry management (MBA). Part-time and evening/weekend programs available. *Faculty:* 22 full-time (9 women), 6 part-time/adjunct (0 women). *Students:* 232 full-time (100 women), 174 part-time (84 women); includes 241 minority (18 Black or African American, non-Hispanic/Latino; 112 Asian, non-Hispanic/Latino; 33 Hispanic/Latino; 11 Native Hawaiian or other Pacific Islander, non-Hispanic/Latino; 67 Two or more races, non-Hispanic/Latino). Average age 31. 240 applicants, 81% accepted, 102 enrolled. In 2013, 206 master's awarded. *Degree requirements:* For master's, thesis. *Entrance requirements:* For master's, GMAT. Additional exam requirements/recommendations for international students: Recommended—TOEFL (minimum score 550 paper-based; 80 iBT), TWE (minimum score 5). *Application deadline:* For fall admission, 2/15 priority date for domestic students; for spring admission, 10/15 priority date for domestic students. Applications are processed on a rolling basis. Application fee: $50. Electronic applications accepted. *Financial support:* In 2013–14, 90 students received support. Research assistantships, career-related internships or fieldwork, Federal Work-Study, scholarships/grants, tuition waivers, and unspecified assistantships available. Financial award application deadline: 3/1; financial award applicants required to submit FAFSA. *Faculty research:* Statistical control process as used by management, studies in comparative cross-cultural management styles, not-for-profit management. *Unit head:* Dr. Deborah Crown, Dean, 808-544-0275, Fax: 808-544-0283, E-mail: dcrown@hpu.edu. *Application contact:* Rumi Yoshida, Associate Director of Graduate Admissions, 808-543-8034, Fax: 808-544-0280, E-mail: grad@hpu.edu. Website: http://www.hpu.edu/CBA/Graduate/index.html.

HEC Montreal, School of Business Administration, Graduate Diplomas Programs in Administration, Program in Public Accounting, Montréal, QC H3T 2A7, Canada. Offers Graduate Diploma. All courses are given in French. *Students:* 231 full-time (137 women), 15 part-time (11 women). 320 applicants, 83% accepted, 238 enrolled. In 2013, 174 Graduate Diplomas awarded. *Degree requirements:* For Graduate Diploma, one foreign language. *Entrance requirements:* For degree, bachelor's degree in accounting. *Application deadline:* For spring admission, 2/15 for domestic and international students.

Application fee: $83 Canadian dollars. Electronic applications accepted. *Expenses: Tuition, area resident:* Part-time $74.14 per credit. Tuition, state resident: full-time $2669.04; part-time $201.83 per credit. Tuition, nonresident: full-time $7266; part-time $500.59 per credit. *International tuition:* $18,021.24 full-time. *Required fees:* $1529.70; $36.20 per credit. $65.50 per term. Tuition and fees vary according to degree level and program. *Financial support:* In 2013–14, 1,007 students received support. Research assistantships, teaching assistantships, and scholarships/grants available. Financial award application deadline: 9/2. *Unit head:* Silvia Ponce, Director, 514-340-6393, Fax: 514-340-6915, E-mail: silvia.ponce@hec.ca. *Application contact:* Jo Anne Audet, Administrative Director, 514-340-1315, Fax: 514-340-6411, E-mail: joanne.audet@hec.ca.
Website: http://www.hec.ca/programmes_formations/msc/options/comptabilite_publique/index.html.

HEC Montreal, School of Business Administration, Master of Science Programs in Administration, Program in Management Control, Montréal, QC H3T 2A7, Canada. Offers M Sc. All courses are given in French. *Students:* 21 full-time (8 women), 14 part-time (8 women). 24 applicants, 58% accepted, 5 enrolled. In 2013, 15 master's awarded. *Degree requirements:* For master's, one foreign language, thesis. *Entrance requirements:* For master's, Test de francais international (TFI) with minimum score of 850 (for those who have never studied in French), BBA, undergraduate degree in another field, degree deemed equivalent by program director and minimum GPA of 3.0 on 4.3 scale. *Application deadline:* For fall admission, 3/15 for domestic and international students; for winter admission, 9/15 for domestic and international students. Application fee: $83 Canadian dollars. Electronic applications accepted. *Expenses: Tuition, area resident:* Part-time $74.14 per credit. Tuition, state resident: full-time $2669.04; part-time $201.83 per credit. Tuition, nonresident: full-time $7266; part-time $500.59 per credit. *International tuition:* $18,021.24 full-time. *Required fees:* $1529.70; $36.20 per credit. $65.50 per term. Tuition and fees vary according to degree level and program. *Financial support:* In 2013–14, 1,007 students received support. Research assistantships, teaching assistantships, and scholarships/grants available. Financial award application deadline: 9/2. *Unit head:* Dr. Anne Bourhis, Director, 514-340-6873, Fax: 514-340-6880, E-mail: anne.bourhis@hec.ca. *Application contact:* Marianne de Moura, Administrative Director, 514-340-7106, Fax: 514-340-6411, E-mail: marianne.de-moura@hec.ca.
Website: http://www.hec.ca/programmes_formations/msc/options/controle_gestion/index.html.

HEC Montreal, School of Business Administration, Master of Science Programs in Administration, Program in Public Accounting, Montréal, QC H3T 2A7, Canada. Offers M Sc. All courses are given in French. *Students:* 5 full-time (3 women), 17 part-time (10 women). 29 applicants, 100% accepted, 15 enrolled. In 2013, 14 master's awarded. *Degree requirements:* For master's, one foreign language, thesis. *Entrance requirements:* For master's, short graduate program in public accounting from HEC Montreal, minimum GPA of 3.0 on 4.3 scale. *Application deadline:* For fall admission, 3/15 for domestic and international students; for winter admission, 9/15 for domestic and international students; for spring admission, 4/15 for domestic and international students. Application fee: $83. Electronic applications accepted. *Expenses: Tuition, area resident:* Part-time $74.14 per credit. Tuition, state resident: full-time $2669.04; part-time $201.83 per credit. Tuition, nonresident: full-time $7266; part-time $500.59 per credit. *International tuition:* $18,021.24 full-time. *Required fees:* $1529.70; $36.20 per credit. $65.50 per term. Tuition and fees vary according to degree level and program. *Financial support:* In 2013–14, 1,007 students received support. Research assistantships, teaching assistantships, and scholarships/grants available. Financial award application deadline: 9/2. *Unit head:* Dr. Anne Bourhis, Director, 514-340-6873, Fax: 514-340-6880, E-mail: anne.bourhis@hec.ca. *Application contact:* Marianne de Moura, Administrative Director, 514-340-7106, Fax: 514-340-6411, E-mail: marianne.de-moura@hec.ca.
Website: http://www.hec.ca/programmes_formations/msc/options/comptabilite_publique/index.html.

Hendrix College, Program in Accounting, Conway, AR 72032-3080. Offers MA. Part-time programs available. *Entrance requirements:* For master's, GMAT. Additional exam requirements/recommendations for international students: Required—TOEFL. *Faculty research:* Meta-analysis, utility regulatory entities.

Herzing University Online, Program in Business Administration, Milwaukee, WI 53203. Offers accounting (MBA); business administration (MBA); business management (MBA); healthcare management (MBA); human resources (MBA); marketing (MBA); project management (MBA); technology management (MBA). Postbaccalaureate distance learning degree programs offered (no on-campus study).

Hofstra University, Frank G. Zarb School of Business, Programs in Accounting and Taxation, Hempstead, NY 11549. Offers accounting (MS, Advanced Certificate); business administration (MBA), including accounting, professional accountancy, taxation; taxation (MS, Advanced Certificate).

Hood College, Graduate School, Department of Economics and Business Administration, Frederick, MD 21701-8575. Offers accounting (MBA); administration and management (MBA); finance (MBA); human resource management (MBA); information systems (MBA); marketing (MBA); public management (MBA). *Accreditation:* ACBSP. Part-time and evening/weekend programs available. *Faculty:* 6 full-time (2 women), 7 part-time/adjunct (1 woman). *Students:* 31 full-time (21 women), 131 part-time (66 women); includes 36 minority (18 Black or African American, non-Hispanic/Latino; 7 Asian, non-Hispanic/Latino; 8 Hispanic/Latino; 3 Two or more races, non-Hispanic/Latino), 12 international. Average age 31. 78 applicants, 56% accepted, 33 enrolled. In 2013, 35 master's awarded. *Degree requirements:* For master's, capstone/final research project. *Entrance requirements:* For master's, minimum GPA of 2.75, resume, letters of recommendation. Additional exam requirements/recommendations for international students: Required—TOEFL (minimum score 575 paper-based; 89 iBT), IELTS (minimum score 6.5). *Application deadline:* For fall admission, 7/15 priority date for domestic students, 7/15 for international students; for spring admission, 12/1 priority date for domestic students, 12/1 for international students. Applications are processed on a rolling basis. Application fee: $35. Electronic applications accepted. Application fee is waived when completed online. *Expenses: Tuition:* Part-time $405 per credit. *Required fees:* $100 per semester. *Financial support:* In 2013–14, 11 students received support. Tuition waivers (partial) and unspecified assistantships available. Financial award applicants required to submit FAFSA. *Faculty research:* Corporate strategy and sustainable competitive advantages, business ethics, entrepreneurship, investments management, economic development. *Unit head:* Dr. Anita Jose, Program Director, 301-696-3691, Fax: 301-696-3597, E-mail: jose@hood.edu. *Application contact:* Dr. Maria Green Cowles, Dean of Graduate School, 301-696-3811, Fax: 301-696-3597, E-mail: gofurther@hood.edu.

Houston Baptist University, School of Business, Program in Accounting, Houston, TX 77074-3298. Offers MACCT. *Entrance requirements:* For master's, GMAT. Additional exam requirements/recommendations for international students: Required—TOEFL (minimum score 550 paper-based).

Accounting

Howard University, School of Business, Graduate Programs in Business, Washington, DC 20059-0002. Offers accounting (MBA); entrepreneurship (MBA); finance (MBA); general management (MBA); human resources management (MBA); information systems (MBA); international business (MBA); marketing (MBA); supply chain management (MBA); JD/MBA. *Accreditation:* AACSB. Part-time and evening/weekend programs available. Postbaccalaureate distance learning degree programs offered (no on-campus study). *Entrance requirements:* For master's, GMAT, minimum 1 year post undergraduate work experience, resume, 3 letters of recommendation, advanced college algebra. Additional exam requirements/recommendations for international students: Required—TOEFL. *Faculty research:* Marketing research in multi-ethnic populations, U.S. trade policies and international relations, risk management (finance).

Hunter College of the City University of New York, Graduate School, School of Arts and Sciences, Department of Economics, Program in Accounting, New York, NY 10065-5085. Offers MS. *Faculty:* 2 full-time (0 women), 3 part-time/adjunct (1 woman). *Students:* 9 full-time (6 women), 41 part-time (21 women); includes 27 minority (7 Black or African American, non-Hispanic/Latino; 1 American Indian or Alaska Native, non-Hispanic/Latino; 14 Asian, non-Hispanic/Latino; 5 Hispanic/Latino), 6 international. Average age 27. 57 applicants, 65% accepted, 16 enrolled. In 2013, 37 master's awarded. *Application deadline:* For fall admission, 4/1 for domestic students, 2/1 for international students; for spring admission, 11/1 for domestic students, 9/1 for international students. Application fee: $125. *Unit head:* Dr. Fatma Cebenoyan, Director of the Accounting Program/Associate Professor, 212-772-5393, E-mail: fatma.cebenoyan@hunter.cuny.edu. *Application contact:* Milena Solo, Graduate Admissions Director, 212-772-4480, E-mail: admissions@hunter.cuny.edu.

Illinois State University, Graduate School, College of Business, Department of Accounting, Normal, IL 61790-2200. Offers MPA, MS. *Accreditation:* AACSB. *Degree requirements:* For master's, comprehensive exam. *Entrance requirements:* For master's, GMAT, minimum GPA of 2.75 in last 60 hours of course work. Additional exam requirements/recommendations for international students: Required—TOEFL.

Indiana Tech, Program in Business Administration, Fort Wayne, IN 46803-1297. Offers accounting (MBA); health care administration (MBA); human resources (MBA); management (MBA); marketing (MBA). Part-time and evening/weekend programs available. Postbaccalaureate distance learning degree programs offered (no on-campus study). *Students:* 160 full-time (94 women), 97 part-time (53 women); includes 69 minority (58 Black or African American, non-Hispanic/Latino; 1 Asian, non-Hispanic/Latino; 8 Hispanic/Latino; 2 Two or more races, non-Hispanic/Latino), 11 international. Average age 36. *Entrance requirements:* For master's, GMAT, bachelor's degree from regionally-accredited university; minimum undergraduate GPA of 2.5; 2 years of significant work experience; 3 letters of recommendation. *Application deadline:* Applications are processed on a rolling basis. Application fee: $25. Electronic applications accepted. *Expenses: Tuition:* Full-time $8910; part-time $495 per credit. Tuition and fees vary according to course load, degree level and program. *Financial support:* Applicants required to submit FAFSA. *Unit head:* Dr. Andrew I. Nwanne, Associate Dean of Business/Academic Coordinator, 260-422-5561 Ext. 2214, E-mail: ainwanne@indianatech.edu.
Website: http://www.indianatech.edu/.

Indiana University–Purdue University Indianapolis, Kelley School of Business, Indianapolis, IN 46202-2896. Offers accounting (MSA); business (MBA). *Accreditation:* AACSB. Part-time and evening/weekend programs available. Postbaccalaureate distance learning degree programs offered (minimal on-campus study). *Faculty:* 20 full-time (4 women), 1 part-time/adjunct (0 women). *Students:* 150 full-time (52 women), 349 part-time (104 women); includes 89 minority (28 Black or African American, non-Hispanic/Latino; 44 Asian, non-Hispanic/Latino; 11 Hispanic/Latino; 6 Two or more races, non-Hispanic/Latino), 127 international. Average age 30. 302 applicants, 56% accepted, 141 enrolled. In 2013, 200 master's awarded. *Entrance requirements:* For master's, GMAT, previous course work in accounting and statistics. *Application deadline:* For fall admission, 4/15 priority date for domestic and international students; for spring admission, 11/1 priority date for domestic and international students. Applications are processed on a rolling basis. Application fee: $55 ($65 for international students). Electronic applications accepted. *Expenses:* Contact institution. *Financial support:* Fellowships, teaching assistantships, Federal Work-Study, institutionally sponsored loans, and scholarships/grants available. Support available to part-time students. Financial award application deadline: 3/1; financial award applicants required to submit FAFSA. *Unit head:* Susan L. Cauble, Director, Graduate Accounting Programs, 317-274-3451, E-mail: busugrad@iupui.edu. *Application contact:* Felicia Morris, Student Services Support, 317-274-0890, E-mail: mbaindy@iupui.edu.
Website: http://kelley.iupui.edu/evemba.

Indiana University South Bend, Judd Leighton School of Business and Economics, South Bend, IN 46634-7111. Offers accounting (MSA); business administration (MBA); management of information technologies (MS). Part-time and evening/weekend programs available. *Faculty:* 17 full-time (2 women), 3 part-time/adjunct (1 woman). *Students:* 34 full-time (18 women), 101 part-time (38 women); includes 13 minority (7 Black or African American, non-Hispanic/Latino; 3 Asian, non-Hispanic/Latino; 2 Hispanic/Latino; 1 Two or more races, non-Hispanic/Latino), 30 international. Average age 32. 48 applicants, 79% accepted, 18 enrolled. In 2013, 42 master's awarded. *Entrance requirements:* For master's, GMAT. Additional exam requirements/recommendations for international students: Required—TOEFL (minimum score 550 paper-based). *Application deadline:* For fall admission, 7/1 priority date for domestic and international students; for spring admission, 11/1 priority date for domestic and international students. Applications are processed on a rolling basis. *Expenses:* Contact institution. *Financial support:* Fellowships, Federal Work-Study, and institutionally sponsored loans available. Support available to part-time students. Financial award applicants required to submit FAFSA. *Faculty research:* Financial accounting, consumer research, capital budgeting research, business strategy research. *Unit head:* Robert H. Ducoffe, Dean, 574-520-4228, Fax: 574-520-4866. *Application contact:* Tracy White, Assistant Director of Graduate Business Program, 574-520-4138, E-mail: whitet@iusb.edu.
Website: https://www.iusb.edu/buse/graduate_programs/.

Indiana Wesleyan University, College of Adult and Professional Studies, Graduate Studies in Business, Marion, IN 46953. Offers accounting (MBA, Graduate Certificate); applied management (MBA); business administration (MBA); health care (MBA, Graduate Certificate); human resources (MBA, Graduate Certificate); management (MS); organizational leadership (MA). Part-time and evening/weekend programs available. Postbaccalaureate distance learning degree programs offered (no on-campus study). *Degree requirements:* For master's, applied business or management project. *Entrance requirements:* For master's, minimum GPA of 2.5, 2 years of related work experience. Additional exam requirements/recommendations for international students: Required—TOEFL (minimum score 550 paper-based). Electronic applications accepted. *Expenses: Tuition:* Full-time $8712; part-time $484 per credit hour. *Required fees:* $1673; $105 per credit hour. Tuition and fees vary according to course load, degree level, campus/location and program.

Instituto Tecnologico de Santo Domingo, Graduate School, Area of Humanities and Social Sciences, Santo Domingo, Dominican Republic. Offers accounting (Certificate); adult education (Certificate); applied linguistics (MA); economics (MA); education (M Ed); educational psychology (MA, Certificate); gender and development (MA, Certificate); humanistic studies (MA); international marketing management (Certificate); international relations in the Caribbean basin (Certificate); intervention systems in family therapy (MA); linguistic and literary communication (Certificate); pedagogical support (MA); social science education (M Ed); sustainable human development (MA); terminal illness and death psychology (Certificate); youth and adult education (M Ed).

Inter American University of Puerto Rico, Aguadilla Campus, Graduate School, Aguadilla, PR 00605. Offers accounting (MBA); counseling psychology specializing in family (MS); criminal justice (MA); educative management and leadership (MA); elementary education (M Ed); finance (MBA); human resources (MBA); industrial management (MBA); management information systems (MBA); marketing (MBA). Part-time and evening/weekend programs available. *Degree requirements:* For master's, comprehensive exam. *Entrance requirements:* For master's, EXADEP, 2 letters of recommendation, minimum GPA of 2.5. Electronic applications accepted.

Inter American University of Puerto Rico, Arecibo Campus, Program in Business Administration, Arecibo, PR 00614-4050. Offers accounting (MBA); finance (MBA); human resources (MBA).

Inter American University of Puerto Rico, Barranquitas Campus, Program in Business Administration, Barranquitas, PR 00794. Offers accounting (IMBA); finance (IMBA).

Inter American University of Puerto Rico, Metropolitan Campus, Graduate Programs, Program in Accounting, San Juan, PR 00919-1293. Offers MBA. *Degree requirements:* For master's, comprehensive exam. *Entrance requirements:* For master's, GRE or EXADEP, interview. Electronic applications accepted.

Inter American University of Puerto Rico, Ponce Campus, Graduate School, Mercedita, PR 00715-1602. Offers accounting (MBA); biology (M Ed); chemistry (M Ed); criminal justice (MA); elementary education (M Ed); English as a Second Language (M Ed); finance (MBA); history (M Ed); human resources (MBA); marketing (MBA); mathematics (M Ed); Spanish (M Ed). *Entrance requirements:* For master's, minimum GPA of 2.5.

Inter American University of Puerto Rico, San Germán Campus, Graduate Studies Center, Program in Business Administration, San Germán, PR 00683-5008. Offers accounting (MBA); finance (MBA); general business administration (MBA); human resources (MBA, PhD); industrial relations (MBA); information systems (MBA); international and interregional business (PhD); management (MBA); marketing (MBA). Part-time and evening/weekend programs available. *Faculty:* 8 full-time (2 women), 4 part-time/adjunct (3 women). *Students:* 138 full-time (80 women), 35 part-time (21 women); includes 172 minority (all Hispanic/Latino). 60 applicants, 65% accepted, 38 enrolled. In 2013, 38 master's, 3 doctorates awarded. *Degree requirements:* For master's, comprehensive exam. *Entrance requirements:* For master's, GRE General Test or EXADEP, minimum GPA of 3.0. *Application deadline:* For fall admission, 4/30 priority date for domestic students; for spring admission, 11/15 for domestic students. Applications are processed on a rolling basis. Application fee: $31. *Expenses: Tuition:* Full-time $2424; part-time $202 per credit hour. *Required fees:* $260 per semester. Tuition and fees vary according to course level, course load, degree level and program. *Financial support:* Teaching assistantships, Federal Work-Study, and unspecified assistantships available. *Unit head:* Dr. Elba T. Irizarry, Director of Graduate Studies Center, 787-264-1912 Ext. 7357, Fax: 787-892-6350, E-mail: elbat@sg.inter.edu. *Application contact:* Dr. Ailin Padilla, Coordinator, 787-264-1912 Ext. 7355, E-mail: ailin_padilla@intersg.edu.

Iona College, Hagan School of Business, Department of Accounting, New Rochelle, NY 10801-1890. Offers general accounting (MBA, AC); public accounting (MBA, MS, AC). Part-time and evening/weekend programs available. *Faculty:* 6 full-time (1 woman). *Students:* 28 full-time (10 women), 50 part-time (20 women); includes 12 minority (4 Black or African American, non-Hispanic/Latino; 2 Asian, non-Hispanic/Latino; 6 Hispanic/Latino), 3 international. Average age 29. 24 applicants, 100% accepted, 16 enrolled. In 2013, 41 master's, 9 other advanced degrees awarded. *Entrance requirements:* For master's, GMAT, two letters of recommendation, minimum GPA of 3.0; for AC, GMAT, minimum GPA of 3.0. Additional exam requirements/recommendations for international students: Required—TOEFL (minimum score 550 paper-based; 80 iBT), IELTS (minimum score 6.5). *Application deadline:* For fall admission, 8/15 priority date for domestic students, 8/1 priority date for international students; for winter admission, 11/15 priority date for domestic students, 11/1 priority date for international students; for spring admission, 2/15 priority date for domestic students, 2/1 priority date for international students; for summer admission, 5/15 priority date for domestic students, 5/1 priority date for international students. Applications are processed on a rolling basis. Application fee: $50. Electronic applications accepted. *Expenses: Tuition:* Part-time $948 per credit. *Required fees:* $235 per term. *Financial support:* In 2013–14, 40 students received support. Scholarships/grants, tuition waivers (partial), and unspecified assistantships available. Support available to part-time students. Financial award application deadline: 4/15; financial award applicants required to submit FAFSA. *Faculty research:* Tax policy, investment returns, international accounting standards. *Unit head:* Dr. Huldah Ryan, Chair, 914-633-2527, E-mail: hryan@iona.edu. *Application contact:* Cameron Hudson, Director of MBA Admissions, 914-633-2288, Fax: 914-637-2708, E-mail: chudson@iona.edu.
Website: http://www.iona.edu/Academics/Hagan-School-of-Business/Departments/Accounting/Graduate-Programs.aspx.

Iowa State University of Science and Technology, Department of Accounting, Ames, IA 50011. Offers M Acc. *Accreditation:* AACSB. *Degree requirements:* For master's, thesis or alternative. *Entrance requirements:* For master's, GMAT, resume. Additional exam requirements/recommendations for international students: Recommended—TOEFL (minimum score 600 paper-based; 100 iBT), IELTS (minimum score 7). Electronic applications accepted.

Ithaca College, School of Business, Program in Professional Accountancy, Ithaca, NY 14850. Offers MBA. Part-time programs available. *Faculty:* 5 full-time (2 women), 1 part-time/adjunct (0 women). *Students:* 19 full-time (8 women), 3 part-time (2 women); includes 2 minority (1 Hispanic/Latino; 1 Two or more races, non-Hispanic/Latino), 2 international. Average age 23. 28 applicants, 82% accepted, 18 enrolled. In 2013, 20 master's awarded. *Degree requirements:* For master's, thesis optional. *Entrance requirements:* For master's, GMAT, minimum GPA of 3.0. Additional exam requirements/recommendations for international students: Required—TOEFL (minimum score 550 paper-based; 80 iBT). *Application deadline:* For fall admission, 3/1 for domestic and international students; for spring admission, 11/1 for domestic and international students. Applications are processed on a rolling basis. Application fee: $40. Electronic applications accepted. *Expenses:* Contact institution. *Financial support:* In 2013–14, 16 students received support, including 16 fellowships (averaging $13,479 per year); career-related internships or fieldwork, Federal Work-Study, and scholarships/grants also available. Support available to part-time students. Financial award application deadline: 3/1; financial award applicants required to submit CSS PROFILE or FAFSA. *Unit head:* Dr. Barbara Howard, MBA Program Director, 607-274-1762, Fax: 607-274-1263, E-mail: bhoward@ithaca.edu. *Application contact:* Gerard Turbide,

Director, Office of Admission, 607-274-3143, Fax: 607-274-1263, E-mail: gps@ithaca.edu.
Website: http://www.ithaca.edu/business/mba.

Jackson State University, Graduate School, College of Business, Department of Accounting, Jackson, MS 39217. Offers MPA. *Accreditation:* AACSB. Part-time and evening/weekend programs available. *Degree requirements:* For master's, comprehensive exam. *Entrance requirements:* For master's, GRE General Test, GMAT. Additional exam requirements/recommendations for international students: Required—TOEFL (minimum score 520 paper-based; 67 iBT).

Jacksonville University, Davis College of Business, Accelerated Day-time MBA Program, Jacksonville, FL 32211. Offers accounting and finance (MBA); management (MBA); management accounting (MBA). *Faculty:* 12 full-time (1 woman). *Students:* 35 full-time (19 women), 2 part-time (0 women); includes 6 minority (2 Black or African American, non-Hispanic/Latino; 1 Asian, non-Hispanic/Latino; 3 Hispanic/Latino), 21 international. Average age 26. 47 applicants, 66% accepted, 22 enrolled. In 2013, 59 master's awarded. *Entrance requirements:* For master's, GRE or GMAT (may be waived for 3.3 undergraduate GPA or higher from AACSB-accredited institution). Additional exam requirements/recommendations for international students: Required—TOEFL, IELTS. *Application deadline:* For fall admission, 8/1 priority date for domestic students, 7/15 priority date for international students; for spring admission, 12/1 priority date for domestic students, 11/15 priority date for international students. Application fee: $50. Electronic applications accepted. *Expenses:* Contact institution. *Financial support:* In 2013–14, 4 students received support. Scholarships/grants and unspecified assistantships available. Financial award applicants required to submit FAFSA. *Faculty research:* Behavioral finance, game theory, regional economic integration, information sabotage, public choice and public finance. *Unit head:* Dr. Mohamad Sepehri, Associate Dean and Graduate Programs Director, 904-256-7435, Fax: 904-256-7168, E-mail: msepehr@ju.edu. *Application contact:* AnnaMaria Murphy, Admissions Counselor, 904-256-7426, Fax: 904-256-7168, E-mail: mba@ju.edu.
Website: http://www.ju.edu/dcob/AcademicPrograms/Pages/Accelerated-MBA.aspx.

Jacksonville University, Davis College of Business, FLEX Master of Business Administration Program, Jacksonville, FL 32211. Offers accounting and finance (MBA); management (MBA); management accounting (MBA). *Accreditation:* AACSB. Part-time and evening/weekend programs available. *Faculty:* 19 full-time (3 women). *Students:* 77 full-time (32 women), 35 part-time (16 women); includes 40 minority (23 Black or African American, non-Hispanic/Latino; 1 American Indian or Alaska Native, non-Hispanic/Latino; 7 Asian, non-Hispanic/Latino; 8 Hispanic/Latino; 1 Native Hawaiian or other Pacific Islander, non-Hispanic/Latino), 4 international. Average age 31. 77 applicants, 38% accepted, 24 enrolled. In 2013, 54 master's awarded. *Entrance requirements:* For master's, GMAT or GRE (may be waived for 3.3 or higher undergraduate GPA from AACSB-accredited institution). Additional exam requirements/recommendations for international students: Required—TOEFL, IELTS. *Application deadline:* For fall admission, 8/1 priority date for domestic students, 7/15 priority date for international students; for spring admission, 12/1 priority date for domestic students, 11/15 priority date for international students; for summer admission, 4/1 priority date for domestic students, 3/15 priority date for international students. Applications are processed on a rolling basis. Application fee: $50. Electronic applications accepted. *Expenses:* Contact institution. *Financial support:* Application deadline: 3/15; applicants required to submit FAFSA. *Faculty research:* Downsizing with integrity; impact of YouTube videos; game theory; analysis of effective tax rates; creativity innovation and change. *Unit head:* Dr. Mohamad Sepehri, Associate Dean and Director of Graduate Studies, 904-256-7435, Fax: 904-256-7168, E-mail: mba@ju.edu. *Application contact:* AnnaMaria Murphy, Admissions Counselor, 904-256-7426, Fax: 904-256-7168, E-mail: mba@ju.edu.

James Madison University, The Graduate School, College of Business, Program in Accounting, Harrisonburg, VA 22807. Offers MS. *Accreditation:* AACSB. Part-time and evening/weekend programs available. *Students:* 74 full-time (22 women), 6 part-time (3 women); includes 11 minority (1 Black or African American, non-Hispanic/Latino; 4 Asian, non-Hispanic/Latino; 3 Hispanic/Latino; 3 Two or more races, non-Hispanic/Latino), 3 international. Average age 27. In 2013, 61 master's awarded. *Entrance requirements:* For master's, GMAT or CPA exam. Additional exam requirements/recommendations for international students: Required—TOEFL. *Application deadline:* For fall admission, 5/1 priority date for domestic students, 5/1 for international students; for spring admission, 9/1 priority date for domestic students, 9/1 for international students. Applications are processed on a rolling basis. Application fee: $55. Electronic applications accepted. *Financial support:* In 2013–14, 25 students received support. Federal Work-Study and 25 graduate assistantships (averaging $7530) available. Financial award application deadline: 3/1; financial award applicants required to submit FAFSA. *Faculty research:* Controllership, government accounting. *Unit head:* Dr. Paul A. Copley, Academic Unit Head, 540-568-3081. *Application contact:* Dr. Nancy Nichols, Program Director, 540-568-3081.

John Carroll University, Graduate School, John M. and Mary Jo Boler School of Business, University Heights, OH 44118-4581. Offers accountancy (MS); business (MBA). *Accreditation:* AACSB. Part-time and evening/weekend programs available. *Entrance requirements:* For master's, GMAT, minimum GPA of 2.5. Additional exam requirements/recommendations for international students: Required—TOEFL (minimum score 550 paper-based). Electronic applications accepted. *Expenses:* Contact institution. *Faculty research:* Accounting, economics and finance, management, marketing and logistics.

John Hancock University, MBA Program, Oakbrook Terrace, IL 60181. Offers e-commerce (MBA); finance (MBA); general business (MBA); global management (MBA); health care administration (MBA); leadership (MBA); management of information systems (MBA); marketing (MBA); professional accounting (MBA); project management (MBA); public accounting (MBA); risk management (MBA).

Jones International University, School of Business, Centennial, CO 80112. Offers accounting (MBA); business communication (MABC); entrepreneurship (MABC, MBA); finance (MBA); global enterprise management (MBA); health care management (MBA); information security management (MBA); information technology management (MBA); leadership and influence (MABC); leading the customer-driven organization (MABC); negotiation and conflict management (MBA); project management (MABC, MBA). Program only offered online. Part-time and evening/weekend programs available. Postbaccalaureate distance learning degree programs offered (no on-campus study). *Degree requirements:* For master's, capstone project. *Entrance requirements:* For master's, minimum cumulative GPA of 2.5. Additional exam requirements/recommendations for international students: Recommended—TOEFL (minimum score 550 paper-based). Electronic applications accepted.

Juniata College, Department of Accounting, Business, and Economics, Huntingdon, PA 16652-2119. Offers accounting (M Acc).

Kansas State University, Graduate School, College of Business Administration, Department of Accounting, Manhattan, KS 66506. Offers M Acc. *Accreditation:* AACSB. Part-time programs available. *Faculty:* 11 full-time (4 women). *Students:* 35 full-time (21 women), 9 part-time (4 women); includes 2 minority (1 Black or African American, non-Hispanic/Latino; 1 Hispanic/Latino), 11 international. Average age 23. 50 applicants, 52% accepted, 18 enrolled. In 2013, 44 master's awarded. *Entrance requirements:* For master's, GMAT (minimum score of 500), minimum undergraduate GPA of 3.0. Additional exam requirements/recommendations for international students: Required—TOEFL (minimum score 550 paper-based; 79 iBT); Recommended—IELTS (minimum score 7). *Application deadline:* For fall admission, 2/1 priority date for domestic and international students; for spring admission, 10/1 priority date for domestic students, 8/1 priority date for international students. Applications are processed on a rolling basis. Application fee: $70 ($80 for international students). Electronic applications accepted. *Financial support:* In 2013–14, 6 students received support, including 6 teaching assistantships with full tuition reimbursements available (averaging $9,472 per year); institutionally sponsored loans and scholarships/grants also available. Financial award application deadline: 3/1; financial award applicants required to submit FAFSA. *Faculty research:* Accounting education, accounting ethics, capital markets (empirical/archival), research in tax and financial reporting, behavioral research in accounting. *Total annual research expenditures:* $10,347. *Unit head:* Dr. Dan S. Deines, Head, 785-532-6184, Fax: 785-532-5959. *Application contact:* Lynn Waugh, Graduate Program Specialist, 785-532-7190, Fax: 785-532-7809, E-mail: lwaugh@ksu.edu.
Website: http://cba.k-state.edu/about/departments-initiatives/accounting/index.html.

Kean University, College of Business and Public Management, Program in Accounting, Union, NJ 07083. Offers MS. Part-time programs available. *Faculty:* 14 full-time (4 women). *Students:* 19 full-time (10 women), 21 part-time (9 women); includes 14 minority (6 Black or African American, non-Hispanic/Latino; 4 Asian, non-Hispanic/Latino; 4 Hispanic/Latino), 5 international. Average age 30. 33 applicants, 94% accepted, 21 enrolled. In 2013, 20 master's awarded. *Entrance requirements:* For master's, GMAT, two letters of recommendation; professional resume/curriculum vitae; personal statement. Additional exam requirements/recommendations for international students: Required—TOEFL (minimum score 550 paper-based; 79 iBT). *Application deadline:* For fall admission, 6/1 for domestic and international students; for spring admission, 12/1 for domestic and international students. Applications are processed on a rolling basis. Application fee: $75 ($150 for international students). Electronic applications accepted. *Expenses:* Tuition, state resident: full-time $12,099; part-time $589 per credit. Tuition, nonresident: full-time $16,399; part-time $722 per credit. *Required fees:* $3050; $139 per credit. Part-time tuition and fees vary according to course level, course load, degree level and program. *Financial support:* In 2013–14, 1 research assistantship with full tuition reimbursement (averaging $3,713 per year) was awarded; unspecified assistantships also available. Financial award applicants required to submit FAFSA. *Unit head:* Dr. Peter Lohrey, Program Coordinator, 908-737-4170, E-mail: lohreyp@kean.edu. *Application contact:* Reenat Hasan, Admissions Counselor, 908-737-5923, Fax: 908-737-5925, E-mail: rhasan@exchange.kean.edu.
Website: http://grad.kean.edu/masters-programs/accounting.

Keiser University, Master of Accountancy Program, Ft. Lauderdale, FL 33309. Offers forensic accounting (M Acc); general accounting (M Acc). *Entrance requirements:* For master's, baccalaureate degree from accredited institution in accounting, business or a related discipline.

Keiser University, Master of Business Administration Program, Ft. Lauderdale, FL 33309. Offers accounting (MBA); health services management (MBA); information security management (MBA); international business (MBA); leadership for managers (MBA); marketing (MBA). All concentrations except information security management also offered in Mandarin; leadership for managers and international business also offered in Spanish. Part-time programs available. Postbaccalaureate distance learning degree programs offered (minimal on-campus study).

Kennesaw State University, Michael J. Coles College of Business, Program in Accounting, Kennesaw, GA 30144-5591. Offers M Acc. *Accreditation:* AACSB. Part-time and evening/weekend programs available. *Students:* 66 full-time (31 women), 4 part-time (1 woman); includes 24 minority (14 Black or African American, non-Hispanic/Latino; 4 Asian, non-Hispanic/Latino; 5 Hispanic/Latino; 1 Two or more races, non-Hispanic/Latino), 3 international. Average age 28. 159 applicants, 53% accepted, 58 enrolled. In 2013, 66 master's awarded. *Entrance requirements:* For master's, GMAT, minimum GPA of 2.8. Additional exam requirements/recommendations for international students: Required—TOEFL (minimum score 550 paper-based; 80 iBT), IELTS (minimum score 6.5). *Application deadline:* For fall admission, 4/1 for domestic and international students. Applications are processed on a rolling basis. Application fee: $60. Electronic applications accepted. *Expenses:* Tuition, state resident: full-time $4806; part-time $267 per semester hour. Tuition, nonresident: full-time $17,298; part-time $961 per semester hour. *Required fees:* $1834; $784.50 per semester. *Financial support:* In 2013–14, 4 research assistantships with tuition reimbursements (averaging $8,000 per year) were awarded; career-related internships or fieldwork, scholarships/grants, and unspecified assistantships also available. Financial award application deadline: 4/1; financial award applicants required to submit FAFSA. *Unit head:* Dr. Kathyrn Epps, Director, 770-423-6085, E-mail: kepps@kennesaw.edu. *Application contact:* Lauren Smith, Admissions Counselor, 678-797-2240, Fax: 770-423-6885, E-mail: ksugrad@kennesaw.edu.
Website: http://www.kennesaw.edu.

Kent State University, College of Business Administration, Doctoral Program in Accounting, Kent, OH 44242. Offers PhD. *Faculty:* 8 full-time (3 women). *Students:* 8 full-time (4 women), 4 international. Average age 31. 21 applicants, 14% accepted, 3 enrolled. *Degree requirements:* For doctorate, comprehensive exam, thesis/dissertation, oral defense. *Entrance requirements:* For doctorate, GMAT. Additional exam requirements/recommendations for international students: Required—TOEFL (minimum score 600 paper-based; 100 iBT). *Application deadline:* For fall admission, 2/1 for domestic students, 1/1 for international students. Application fee: $30 ($70 for international students). Electronic applications accepted. *Financial support:* In 2013–14, 7 students received support, including 7 teaching assistantships with full tuition reimbursements available (averaging $29,500 per year); Federal Work-Study also available. Financial award application deadline: 2/1; financial award applicants required to submit FAFSA. *Faculty research:* Information economics, capital management, use of accounting information, curriculum design. *Unit head:* Dr. Linda Zucca, Chair and Associate Professor, 330-672-2545, Fax: 330-672-2548, E-mail: lzucca@kent.edu. *Application contact:* Felecia A. Urbanek, Coordinator, Graduate Programs, 330-672-2282, Fax: 330-672-7303, E-mail: gradbus@kent.edu.
Website: http://www.kent.edu/business/Grad/phd/index.cfm.

Kent State University, College of Business Administration, Master's Program in Accounting, Kent, OH 44242. Offers MS. Part-time programs available. *Faculty:* 12 full-time (4 women). *Students:* 28 full-time (18 women), 9 part-time (3 women); includes 3 minority (1 Asian, non-Hispanic/Latino; 1 Hispanic/Latino; 1 Two or more races, non-Hispanic/Latino), 18 international. Average age 24. 43 applicants, 72% accepted, 14 enrolled. In 2013, 28 master's awarded. *Degree requirements:* For master's, internship. *Entrance requirements:* For master's, GMAT, minimum GPA of 2.75. Additional exam requirements/recommendations for international students: Required—TOEFL (minimum score 550 paper-based; 79 iBT). *Application deadline:* For fall admission, 3/1 priority date for domestic students, 4/1 for international students; for spring admission, 12/1 for domestic students. Applications are processed on a rolling basis. Application fee: $30 ($70 for international students). Electronic applications accepted. *Financial support:* In

2013–14, 6 students received support, including 6 research assistantships with full tuition reimbursements available (averaging $14,500 per year); Federal Work-Study also available. Financial award application deadline: 3/1; financial award applicants required to submit FAFSA. *Faculty research:* Financial accounting, managerial accounting, auditing, systems, nonprofit. *Unit head:* Dr. Linda Zucca, Chair and Associate Professor, 330-672-2545, Fax: 330-672-2548, E-mail: lzucca@kent.edu. *Application contact:* Louise M. Ditchey, Administrative Director, 330-672-2282, Fax: 330-672-7303, E-mail: gradbus@kent.edu.
Website: http://www.kent.edu/business/Grad/msa/index.cfm.

Lakeland College, Graduate Studies Division, Program in Business Administration, Sheboygan, WI 53082-0359. Offers accounting (MBA); finance (MBA); healthcare management (MBA); project management (MBA). *Entrance requirements:* For master's, GMAT. *Expenses:* Contact institution.

Lamar University, College of Graduate Studies, College of Business, Beaumont, TX 77710. Offers accounting (MBA); experiential business and entrepreneurship (MBA); financial management (MBA); healthcare administration (MBA); information systems (MBA); management (MBA). *Accreditation:* AACSB. Part-time and evening/weekend programs available. *Degree requirements:* For master's, comprehensive exam (for some programs), thesis optional. *Entrance requirements:* For master's, GMAT. Additional exam requirements/recommendations for international students: Required—TOEFL (minimum score 525 paper-based). *Faculty research:* Marketing, finance, quantitative methods, management information systems, legal, environmental.

La Roche College, School of Graduate Studies and Adult Education, Program in Accounting, Pittsburgh, PA 15237-5898. Offers MS. Part-time and evening/weekend programs available. *Faculty:* 1 full-time (0 women), 2 part-time/adjunct (both women). *Students:* 1 full-time (0 women), 9 part-time (3 women); includes 1 minority (Black or African American, non-Hispanic/Latino), 2 international. Average age 31. 5 applicants, 80% accepted, 4 enrolled. *Entrance requirements:* For master's, baccalaureate degree in business, accounting or finance from accredited college or university; two letters of recommendation; resume; personal essay. *Application deadline:* For fall admission, 8/15 for domestic and international students; for spring admission, 12/15 for domestic and international students. Applications are processed on a rolling basis. Application fee: $50. Electronic applications accepted. *Expenses: Tuition:* Full-time $15,360. *Unit head:* Mark Dawson, CPA, MBA, Professor/Department Chair of Accounting and Finance, 412-536-1190, Fax: 412-536-1179, E-mail: mark.dawson@laroche.edu. *Application contact:* Hope Schiffgens, Director of Graduate Studies and Adult Education, 412-536-1266, Fax: 412-536-1283, E-mail: schombh1@laroche.edu.

La Salle University, School of Business, Philadelphia, PA 19141-1199. Offers accounting (MBA, Post-MBA Certificate); business systems and analytics (MBA, Post-MBA Certificate); finance (MBA, Post-MBA Certificate); general business administration (MBA); human resource management (MBA, Post-MBA Certificate); international business (Post-MBA Certificate); management (MBA, Post-MBA Certificate); marketing (MBA, Post-MBA Certificate); MSN/MBA. *Accreditation:* AACSB. Part-time and evening/weekend programs available. Postbaccalaureate distance learning degree programs offered (minimal on-campus study). *Faculty:* 27 full-time (13 women), 15 part-time/adjunct (4 women). *Students:* 81 full-time (30 women), 428 part-time (211 women); includes 109 minority (47 Black or African American, non-Hispanic/Latino; 39 Asian, non-Hispanic/Latino; 18 Hispanic/Latino; 5 Two or more races, non-Hispanic/Latino), 6 international. Average age 30. 215 applicants, 90% accepted, 120 enrolled. In 2013, 182 master's, 1 other advanced degree awarded. *Entrance requirements:* For master's, GMAT or GRE, two letters of reference; resume; for Post-MBA Certificate, MBA with minimum GPA of 3.0. Additional exam requirements/recommendations for international students: Required—TOEFL. *Application deadline:* For fall admission, 8/15 priority date for domestic students, 7/15 for international students; for spring admission, 12/15 priority date for domestic students, 11/15 for international students; for summer admission, 4/15 priority date for domestic students, 3/15 for international students. Applications are processed on a rolling basis. Application fee: $35. Electronic applications accepted. Application fee is waived when completed online. *Expenses:* Contact institution. *Financial support:* In 2013–14, 88 students received support. Career-related internships or fieldwork, Federal Work-Study, scholarships/grants, and unspecified assistantships available. Support available to part-time students. Financial award application deadline: 8/31; financial award applicants required to submit FAFSA. *Unit head:* Dr. Gary Giamartino, Dean, 215-951-1040, Fax: 215-951-1886, E-mail: giamartino@lasalle.edu. *Application contact:* Paul J. Reilly, Assistant Vice President, Enrollment Services, 215-951-1946, Fax: 215-951-1462, E-mail: reilly@lasalle.edu.
Website: http://www.lasalle.edu/grad/index.php?section-mba&page-index.

La Sierra University, School of Business and Management, Riverside, CA 92515. Offers accounting (MBA); finance (MBA); general management (MBA); human resources management (MBA); leadership, values, and ethics for business and management (Certificate); marketing (MBA). *Degree requirements:* For master's, research project. *Entrance requirements:* For master's, GMAT, minimum GPA of 3.0. Additional exam requirements/recommendations for international students: Required—TOEFL. *Faculty research:* Financial econometrics, institutional assessment and strategic planning, legal issues in management, behavioral finance, content of financial reports.

Lehigh University, College of Business and Economics, Department of Accounting, Bethlehem, PA 18015. Offers accounting and information analysis (MS). *Accreditation:* AACSB. *Faculty:* 8 full-time (3 women), 2 part-time/adjunct (0 women). *Students:* 105 full-time (81 women), 2 part-time (both women); includes 2 minority (1 Asian, non-Hispanic/Latino; 1 Hispanic/Latino), 98 international. Average age 23. 191 applicants, 66% accepted, 46 enrolled. In 2013, 33 master's awarded. *Entrance requirements:* For master's, GMAT. Additional exam requirements/recommendations for international students: Required—TOEFL (minimum score 105 iBT). *Application deadline:* For fall admission, 2/28 for domestic and international students. Applications are processed on a rolling basis. Application fee: $100. Electronic applications accepted. *Financial support:* In 2013–14, 6 research assistantships with partial tuition reimbursements (averaging $2,500 per year) were awarded; scholarships/grants and tuition waivers (partial) also available. Financial award application deadline: 1/15. *Faculty research:* Behavioral accounting, internal control, information systems, supply chain management, financial accounting. *Unit head:* Dr. Parveen Gupta, Chairman, 610-758-3443, Fax: 610-758-6429, E-mail: ppg0@lehigh.edu. *Application contact:* Jen Giordano, Director of Recruitment and Admissions, 610-758-3418, Fax: 610-758-5283, E-mail: dlg210@lehigh.edu.
Website: http://www4.lehigh.edu/business/academics/depts/accounting.

Lehman College of the City University of New York, School of Natural and Social Sciences, Department of Economics and Accounting, Bronx, NY 10468-1589. Offers accounting (MS). *Entrance requirements:* For master's, GMAT.

Lenoir-Rhyne University, Graduate Programs, Charles M. Snipes School of Business, Hickory, NC 28601. Offers accounting (MBA); entrepreneurship (MBA); global leadership (MBA); leadership development (MBA). *Accreditation:* ACBSP. Part-time and evening/weekend programs available. *Degree requirements:* For master's, capstone course. *Entrance requirements:* For master's, GMAT, minimum undergraduate GPA of 2.7, graduate 3.0. Additional exam requirements/recommendations for international students: Required—TOEFL (minimum score 600 paper-based). Electronic applications accepted. *Expenses:* Contact institution.

Lewis University, College of Business, Graduate School of Management, Program in Business Administration, Romeoville, IL 60446. Offers accounting (MBA); custom elective option (MBA); e-business (MBA); finance (MBA); healthcare management (MBA); human resources management (MBA); international business (MBA); management information systems (MBA); marketing (MBA); project management (MBA); technology and operations management (MBA). Part-time and evening/weekend programs available. *Students:* 115 full-time (55 women), 227 part-time (129 women); includes 128 minority (74 Black or African American, non-Hispanic/Latino; 1 American Indian or Alaska Native, non-Hispanic/Latino; 9 Asian, non-Hispanic/Latino; 40 Hispanic/Latino; 4 Two or more races, non-Hispanic/Latino), 10 international. Average age 31. In 2013, 99 master's awarded. *Entrance requirements:* For master's, interview, bachelor's degree, resume, 2 recommendations. Additional exam requirements/recommendations for international students: Required—TOEFL (minimum score 550 paper-based). *Application deadline:* For fall admission, 8/15 priority date for domestic students, 5/1 priority date for international students; for spring admission, 11/15 priority date for international students. Applications are processed on a rolling basis. Application fee: $40. Electronic applications accepted. *Financial support:* Career-related internships or fieldwork, Federal Work-Study, scholarships/grants, and unspecified assistantships available. Financial award application deadline: 5/1; financial award applicants required to submit FAFSA. *Unit head:* Dr. Maureen Culleeney, Academic Program Director, 815-838-0500 Ext. 5631, E-mail: culleema@lewisu.edu. *Application contact:* Michele Ryan, Director of Admission, 815-838-0500 Ext. 5384, E-mail: gsm@lewisu.edu.

Liberty University, School of Business, Lynchburg, VA 24515. Offers accounting (MBA, MS, DBA); business administration (MBA); criminal justice (MBA); cyber security (MS); executive leadership (MA); healthcare (MBA); human resources (DBA); information systems (MS), including information assurance, technology management; international business (MBA, DBA); leadership (MBA, DBA); management and leadership (MA); marketing (MBA, MS, DBA), including digital marketing and advertising (MS), project management (MS), public relations (MS), sports marketing and media (MS); project management (MBA, DBA); public administration (MBA); public relations (MBA). Part-time programs available. Postbaccalaureate distance learning degree programs offered (minimal on-campus study). *Students:* 1,342 full-time (749 women), 3,704 part-time (1,820 women); includes 1,657 minority (1,221 Black or African American, non-Hispanic/Latino; 11 American Indian or Alaska Native, non-Hispanic/Latino; 74 Asian, non-Hispanic/Latino; 209 Hispanic/Latino; 13 Native Hawaiian or other Pacific Islander, non-Hispanic/Latino; 129 Two or more races, non-Hispanic/Latino), 40 international. Average age 35. 5,899 applicants, 48% accepted, 1716 enrolled. In 2013, 1,535 master's awarded. *Entrance requirements:* For master's, minimum undergraduate GPA of 3.0, 15 hours of upper-level business courses. Additional exam requirements/recommendations for international students: Required—TOEFL (minimum score 600 paper-based; 100 iBT). *Application deadline:* Applications are processed on a rolling basis. Application fee: $50. Electronic applications accepted. *Expenses:* Contact institution. *Unit head:* Dr. Scott Hicks, Dean, 434-592-4808, Fax: 434-582-2366, E-mail: smhicks@liberty.edu. *Application contact:* Jay Bridge, Director of Graduate Admissions, 800-424-9595, Fax: 800-628-7977, E-mail: gradadmissions@liberty.edu.
Website: http://www.liberty.edu/academics/business/index.cfm?PID-149.

Lincoln University, Graduate Studies, Jefferson City, MO 65101. Offers business administration (MBA), including accounting, entrepreneurship, management, public administration and policy; educational leadership (Ed S), including elementary leadership, secondary leadership, superintendency; guidance and counseling (M Ed), including community/agency counseling, elementary school, secondary school; history (MA); school administration and supervision (M Ed), including elementary school administration, secondary school administration, special education administration; school teaching (M Ed), including elementary school teaching, secondary school teaching; sociology (MA); sociology/criminal justice (MA). Part-time and evening/weekend programs available. Postbaccalaureate distance learning degree programs offered (minimal on-campus study). *Students:* 42 full-time (29 women), 109 part-time (66 women); includes 51 minority (37 Black or African American, non-Hispanic/Latino; 10 American Indian or Alaska Native, non-Hispanic/Latino; 1 Asian, non-Hispanic/Latino; 2 Hispanic/Latino; 1 Two or more races, non-Hispanic/Latino), 10 international. Average age 33. 84 applicants, 76% accepted, 51 enrolled. In 2013, 73 master's, 6 other advanced degrees awarded. *Degree requirements:* For master's and Ed S, comprehensive exam, thesis optional. *Entrance requirements:* For master's and Ed S, GRE, MAT or GMAT, minimum GPA of 2.75 in major, 2.5 overall; 3 letters of recommendation; minimum C average in English composition; personal statement of purpose. Additional exam requirements/recommendations for international students: Required—TOEFL (minimum score 500 paper-based; 61 iBT). *Application deadline:* For fall admission, 8/1 priority date for domestic and international students; for spring admission, 12/1 priority date for domestic and international students; for summer admission, 5/1 priority date for domestic and international students. Applications are processed on a rolling basis. Application fee: $30. *Expenses:* Tuition, state resident: full-time $6840; part-time $285 per credit hour. Tuition, nonresident: full-time $12,720; part-time $530 per credit hour. *Required fees:* $587; $587 per year. Tuition and fees vary according to course load. *Financial support:* Federal Work-Study and scholarships/grants available. Support available to part-time students. Financial award application deadline: 3/1; financial award applicants required to submit FAFSA. *Unit head:* Dr. Linda S. Bickel, Dean, 573-681-5247, Fax: 573-681-5106, E-mail: gradschool@lincolnu.edu. *Application contact:* Irasema Steck, Administrative Assistant, 573-681-5247, Fax: 573-681-5106, E-mail: gradschool@lincolnu.edu.
Website: http://www.lincolnu.edu/web/graduate-studies/graduate-studies.

Lindenwood University, Graduate Programs, School of Business and Entrepreneurship, St. Charles, MO 63301-1695. Offers accountancy (MA); accounting (MBA); business administration (MBA); entrepreneurial studies (MBA); finance (MBA, MS); human resource management (MBA); international business (MBA); leadership (MA); management (MBA); marketing (MBA, MS); public management (MBA); sport management (MA); supply chain management (MBA). *Accreditation:* ACBSP. Part-time and evening/weekend programs available. Postbaccalaureate distance learning degree programs offered (no on-campus study). *Faculty:* 18 full-time (8 women), 33 part-time/adjunct (8 women). *Students:* 292 full-time (130 women), 111 part-time (46 women); includes 59 minority (42 Black or African American, non-Hispanic/Latino; 5 American Indian or Alaska Native, non-Hispanic/Latino; 1 Asian, non-Hispanic/Latino; 5 Hispanic/Latino; 6 Two or more races, non-Hispanic/Latino), 112 international. Average age 29. 212 applicants, 51% accepted, 102 enrolled. In 2013, 221 master's awarded. *Degree requirements:* For master's, comprehensive exam (for some programs), thesis (for some programs), minimum GPA of 3.0. *Entrance requirements:* For master's, interview, minimum GPA of 3.0, letter of recommendation. Additional exam requirements/recommendations for international students: Required—TOEFL (minimum score 550 paper-based; 80 iBT). *Application deadline:* For fall admission, 8/12 priority date for domestic and international students; for winter admission, 1/6 priority date for domestic and international students; for spring admission, 3/10 priority date for domestic and international students; for summer admission, 5/27 priority date for domestic and

international students. Applications are processed on a rolling basis. Application fee: $30 ($100 for international students). Electronic applications accepted. *Expenses: Tuition:* Full-time $14,800; part-time $428 per credit hour. *Required fees:* $350. Tuition and fees vary according to course level and course load. *Financial support:* In 2013–14, 268 students received support. Career-related internships or fieldwork, Federal Work-Study, institutionally sponsored loans, scholarships/grants, tuition waivers (partial), and unspecified assistantships available. Financial award application deadline: 6/30; financial award applicants required to submit FAFSA. *Unit head:* Roger Ellis, Dean, 636-949-4839, E-mail: rellis@lindenwood.edu. *Application contact:* Brett Barger, Dean of Evening Admissions and Extension Campuses, 636-949-4934, Fax: 636-949-4109, E-mail: adultadmissions@lindenwood.edu.
Website: http://www.lindenwood.edu.

Lipscomb University, Graduate School of Business, Nashville, TN 37204-3951. Offers accountancy (M Acc); accounting (MBA); conflict management (MBA); distributive (general) (MBA); financial services (MBA); health care informatics (MBA); healthcare management (MBA); human resources (MHR); information security (MBA); leadership (MBA); nonprofit management (MBA); professional accountancy (Certificate); sports management (MBA); strategic human resources (MBA); sustainability (MBA); MBA/MS. *Accreditation:* ACBSP. Part-time and evening/weekend programs available. *Faculty:* 12 full-time (1 woman), 12 part-time/adjunct (2 women). *Students:* 90 full-time (44 women), 104 part-time (51 women); includes 28 minority (24 Black or African American, non-Hispanic/Latino; 3 Hispanic/Latino; 1 Two or more races, non-Hispanic/Latino), 6 international. Average age 33. 145 applicants, 79% accepted, 69 enrolled. In 2013, 98 master's, 1 other advanced degree awarded. *Entrance requirements:* For master's, GMAT, transcripts, interview, 2 references, resume. Additional exam requirements/recommendations for international students: Required—TOEFL (minimum score 570 paper-based). *Application deadline:* For fall admission, 6/15 for domestic students, 2/1 for international students; for winter admission, 6/1 for international students; for spring admission, 11/15 for domestic students. Applications are processed on a rolling basis. Application fee: $50 ($75 for international students). Electronic applications accepted. *Expenses:* Contact institution. *Financial support:* Career-related internships or fieldwork, scholarships/grants, tuition waivers (partial), and unspecified assistantships available. Support available to part-time students. Financial award application deadline: 7/1; financial award applicants required to submit FAFSA. *Faculty research:* Impact of spirituality on organization commitment, women in corporate leadership, psychological empowerment, training. *Unit head:* Joe Ivey, Associate Dean of Graduate Business Programs, 615-966-6229, Fax: 615-966-1818, E-mail: joe.ivey@lipscomb.edu. *Application contact:* Lisa Shacklett, Assistant Dean of Enrollment and Marketing, 615-966-5968, E-mail: lisa.shacklett@lipscomb.edu.
Website: http://www.lipscomb.edu/business/Graduate-Programs.

Long Island University–LIU Brooklyn, School of Business, Public Administration and Information Sciences, Program in Accountancy, Taxation and Law, Brooklyn, NY 11201-8423. Offers accounting (MS); taxation (MS). Part-time and evening/weekend programs available. *Entrance requirements:* For master's, GMAT or GRE General Test, 2 letters of recommendation. Additional exam requirements/recommendations for international students: Required—TOEFL (minimum score 500 paper-based). Electronic applications accepted.

Long Island University–LIU Post, College of Management, School of Business, Brookville, NY 11548-1300. Offers accounting and taxation (Certificate); business administration (Certificate); finance (MBA, Certificate); general business administration (MBA); international business (MBA, Certificate); management (MBA, Certificate); management information systems (MBA, Certificate); marketing (MBA, Certificate). *Accreditation:* AACSB. Part-time and evening/weekend programs available. *Entrance requirements:* For master's, GMAT, resume, minimum GPA of 3.0, 2 letters of recommendation. Additional exam requirements/recommendations for international students: Required—TOEFL (minimum score 527 paper-based). Electronic applications accepted. *Faculty research:* Financial markets, consumer behavior.

Long Island University–LIU Post, College of Management, School of Professional Accountancy, Brookville, NY 11548-1300. Offers accounting (MS); taxation (MS). Part-time and evening/weekend programs available. *Entrance requirements:* For master's, GMAT, minimum GPA of 2.5, BS in accounting from accredited college or university. Electronic applications accepted. *Faculty research:* International taxation.

Louisiana State University and Agricultural & Mechanical College, Graduate School, E. J. Ourso College of Business, Department of Accounting, Baton Rouge, LA 70803. Offers MS, PhD. *Faculty:* 11 full-time (3 women). *Students:* 87 full-time (54 women), 6 part-time (4 women); includes 12 minority (3 Black or African American, non-Hispanic/Latino; 7 Asian, non-Hispanic/Latino; 1 Hispanic/Latino; 1 Two or more races, non-Hispanic/Latino), 13 international. Average age 25. 105 applicants, 30% accepted, 29 enrolled. In 2013, 66 master's, 3 doctorates awarded. *Degree requirements:* For doctorate, thesis/dissertation. *Entrance requirements:* For master's, GMAT, minimum GPA of 3.2; for doctorate, GMAT, minimum GPA of 3.4. Additional exam requirements/recommendations for international students: Required—TOEFL (minimum score 550 paper-based; 79 IBT), IELTS (minimum score 6.5), or PTE (minimum score 59). *Application deadline:* For fall admission, 1/25 priority date for domestic students, 5/15 for international students; for spring admission, 10/15 for international students. Applications are processed on a rolling basis. Application fee: $50 ($70 for international students). Electronic applications accepted. *Financial support:* In 2013–14, 47 students received support, including 6 research assistantships with full and partial tuition reimbursements available (averaging $13,667 per year), 19 teaching assistantships with full and partial tuition reimbursements available (averaging $14,066 per year); fellowships, Federal Work-Study, scholarships/grants, health care benefits, tuition waivers (full and partial), and unspecified assistantships also available. Support available to part-time students. Financial award application deadline: 4/15; financial award applicants required to submit FAFSA. *Faculty research:* Financial accounting, auditing fraud. *Total annual research expenditures:* $14,929. *Unit head:* Dr. Tommy Phillips, Chair, 225-578-6202, Fax: 225-578-6201, E-mail: tphillips@lsu.edu. *Application contact:* Dr. Jacquelyn Moffit, MS Program Advisor, 225-578-6219, Fax: 225-578-6201, E-mail: jsmoff22@lsu.edu.
Website: http://business.lsu.edu/Accounting/Pages/About-Us.aspx.

Louisiana Tech University, Graduate School, College of Business, School of Accounting and Information Systems, Ruston, LA 71272. Offers accounting (MBA, MPA); accounting and information systems (DBA). *Accreditation:* AACSB. Part-time programs available. *Degree requirements:* For doctorate, thesis/dissertation. *Entrance requirements:* For master's and doctorate, GMAT. *Application deadline:* For fall admission, 7/29 for domestic students; for spring admission, 2/3 for domestic students. Application fee: $20 ($30 for international students). *Financial support:* Fellowships, research assistantships, and teaching assistantships available. Financial award application deadline: 2/1. *Unit head:* Dr. Andrea Drake, Interim Director, 318-257-2822, Fax: 318-257-4253, E-mail: adrake@latech.edu. *Application contact:* Marilyn J. Robinson, Assistant to the Dean, 318-257-2924, Fax: 318-257-4487.
Website: http://www.business.latech.edu/accounting/.

Loyola Marymount University, College of Business Administration, Master of Science in Accounting Program, Los Angeles, CA 90045-2659. Offers MS. Part-time programs available. *Faculty:* 15 full-time (7 women). *Students:* 4 full-time (3 women); includes 1 minority (Asian, non-Hispanic/Latino), 1 international. Average age 26. 25 applicants, 52% accepted, 4 enrolled. *Entrance requirements:* For master's, GMAT/GRE, minimum of 24 units (semester hours) of accounting subjects, including intermediate accounting, advanced accounting, auditing, accounting information systems, cost accounting and taxation; minimum of 24 units in business-related subjects, including 6 units of business law. Additional exam requirements/recommendations for international students: Required—TOEFL (minimum score 600 paper-based; 100 iBT). *Application deadline:* Applications are processed on a rolling basis. Application fee: $50. *Financial support:* In 2013–14, 3 students received support. Application deadline: 6/30; applicants required to submit FAFSA. *Unit head:* Dr. Michael Moore, Director, 310-568-6266. *Application contact:* Chake H Kouyoumjian, Associate Dean of Graduate Studies, 310-338-2721, E-mail: ckouyoum@lmu.edu.
Website: http://cba.lmu.edu/academicprogramscenters/masterofscienceinaccounting/.

Loyola University Chicago, Quinlan School of Business, Accountancy Department, Chicago, IL 60610. Offers MSA, MSA/MBA. *Accreditation:* AACSB. Part-time and evening/weekend programs available. *Faculty:* 11 full-time (3 women), 9 part-time/adjunct (3 women). *Students:* 84 full-time (61 women), 65 part-time (42 women); includes 12 minority (4 Black or African American, non-Hispanic/Latino; 5 Asian, non-Hispanic/Latino; 3 Hispanic/Latino), 103 international. Average age 24. 349 applicants, 44% accepted, 56 enrolled. In 2013, 81 master's awarded. *Entrance requirements:* For master's, GMAT or GRE, official transcripts, letters of recommendation, statement of purpose, resume. Additional exam requirements/recommendations for international students: Required—TOEFL (minimum score 90 iBT) or IELTS (minimum score 6.5). *Application deadline:* For fall admission, 7/15 for domestic and international students; for winter admission, 10/1 for domestic and international students; for spring admission, 1/15 for domestic and international students; for summer admission, 4/1 for domestic and international students. Applications are processed on a rolling basis. Application fee: $50. Electronic applications accepted. Application fee is waived when completed online. *Expenses: Tuition:* Full-time $16,740; part-time $930 per credit. *Required fees:* $135 per semester. *Financial support:* Scholarships/grants and unspecified assistantships available. Financial award application deadline: 3/15. *Faculty research:* Financial disclosure, Web-based accounting issues, activities-based costing. *Unit head:* Dr. Brian Stanko, Chair, 312-915-7106, Fax: 312-915-7224, E-mail: bstanko@luc.edu. *Application contact:* Jessica Gagle, Enrollment Advisor, Quinlan School of Business Graduate Programs, 312-915-8908, Fax: 312-915-7207, E-mail: jgagle@luc.edu.
Website: http://www.luc.edu/quinlan/mba/masters-in-accounting/index.shtml.

Loyola University Chicago, Quinlan School of Business, MBA Programs, Chicago, IL 60610. Offers accounting (MBA); business ethics (MBA); derivative markets (MBA); economics (MBA); entrepreneurship (MBA); executive (MBA); finance (MBA); healthcare management (MBA); human resources management (MBA); information systems management (MBA); intercontinental (MBA); international business (MBA); marketing (MBA); operations management (MBA); risk management (MBA); JD/MBA. Part-time and evening/weekend programs available. *Faculty:* 76 full-time (20 women), 10 part-time/adjunct (4 women). *Students:* 73 full-time (34 women), 294 part-time (129 women); includes 60 minority (18 Black or African American, non-Hispanic/Latino; 28 Asian, non-Hispanic/Latino; 14 Hispanic/Latino), 19 international. Average age 31. 529 applicants, 51% accepted, 153 enrolled. In 2013, 229 master's awarded. *Entrance requirements:* For master's, GMAT or GRE, official transcripts, two letters of recommendation, statement of purpose, resume. Additional exam requirements/recommendations for international students: Required—TOEFL (minimum score 90 iBT) or IELTS (minimum score 6.5). *Application deadline:* For fall admission, 7/15 for domestic and international students; for winter admission, 10/1 for domestic and international students; for spring admission, 1/15 for domestic and international students; for summer admission, 4/1 for domestic and international students. Applications are processed on a rolling basis. Application fee: $50. Electronic applications accepted. Application fee is waived when completed online. *Expenses: Tuition:* Full-time $16,740; part-time $930 per credit. *Required fees:* $135 per semester. *Financial support:* Scholarships/grants and unspecified assistantships available. *Faculty research:* Social enterprise and responsibility, emerging markets, supply chain management, risk management. *Unit head:* Jennifer Huntley, Assistant Dean for Graduate Programs, 312-915-6124, Fax: 312-915-7207, E-mail: jhuntle@luc.edu. *Application contact:* Jessica Gagle, Enrollment Advisor, Quinlan School of Business Graduate Programs, 312-915-8908, Fax: 312-915-7207, E-mail: jgagle@luc.edu.

Loyola University Maryland, Graduate Programs, Sellinger School of Business and Management, Certificate Program in Accounting, Baltimore, MD 21210-2699. Offers Certificate. *Entrance requirements:* Additional exam requirements/recommendations for international students: Required—TOEFL.

Loyola University Maryland, Graduate Programs, Sellinger School of Business and Management, Program in Business Administration, Baltimore, MD 21210-2699. Offers accounting (MBA); finance (MBA); general business (MBA); information systems operations management (MBA); international business (MBA); management (MBA); marketing (MBA). *Accreditation:* AACSB. Part-time and evening/weekend programs available. *Entrance requirements:* For master's, GMAT, letter of recommendation, resume, essay. Additional exam requirements/recommendations for international students: Required—TOEFL (minimum score 550 paper-based).

Maharishi University of Management, Graduate Studies, Program in Business Administration, Fairfield, IA 52557. Offers accounting (MBA); business administration (PhD); sustainability (MBA). Evening/weekend programs available. Postbaccalaureate distance learning degree programs offered (minimal on-campus study). *Degree requirements:* For doctorate, thesis/dissertation. *Entrance requirements:* For master's, GMAT, minimum GPA of 3.0; for doctorate, minimum GPA of 3.0. Additional exam requirements/recommendations for international students: Required—TOEFL. *Faculty research:* Leadership, effects of the group dynamics of consciousness on the economy, innovation, employee development, cooperative strategy.

Marquette University, Graduate School of Management, Program in Accounting, Milwaukee, WI 53201-1881. Offers MSA. *Accreditation:* AACSB. Part-time and evening/weekend programs available. *Faculty:* 12 full-time (5 women), 1 part-time/adjunct (0 women). *Students:* 57 full-time (42 women), 10 part-time (9 women), 51 international. Average age 23. 294 applicants, 38% accepted, 28 enrolled. In 2013, 48 master's awarded. *Entrance requirements:* For master's, GMAT or GRE, letters of recommendation (if applying for financial aid). Additional exam requirements/recommendations for international students: Required—TOEFL (minimum score 550 paper-based; 88 iBT), IELTS (minimum score 6.5), PTE. *Application deadline:* For fall admission, 2/15 for domestic and international students. Applications are processed on a rolling basis. Application fee: $50. Electronic applications accepted. *Financial support:* In 2013–14, 2 teaching assistantships were awarded; fellowships and research assistantships also available. Financial award application deadline: 2/15. *Faculty research:* Financial (accounting) literacy, international perception of corruption, effect of carbon credits on accounting and tax transactions, targeted tax breaks. *Unit head:* Dr. Mark Eppli, Dean, 414-288-5724. *Application contact:* Dr. Jeanne Simmons, Associate Dean, 414-288-7145.
Website: http://www.busadm.mu.edu/graduate/.

Accounting

Marshall University, Academic Affairs Division, College of Business, Program in Accountancy, Huntington, WV 25755. Offers MS. *Students:* 13 full-time (7 women), 10 part-time (7 women); includes 3 minority (1 Asian, non-Hispanic/Latino; 2 Hispanic/Latino), 7 international. Average age 28. In 2013, 18 master's awarded. *Entrance requirements:* For master's, undergraduate degree in accounting with minimum GPA of 3.0 or GMAT. *Unit head:* Dr. Jeffrey Archambault, Director, 304-696-2655. *Application contact:* Wesley Spradlin, Information Contact, 304-746-8964, Fax: 304-746-1902, E-mail: spradlin2@marshall.edu.
Website: http://www.marshall.edu/wpmu/cob/graduate/m-s-in-accounting/.

Maryville University of Saint Louis, The John E. Simon School of Business, St. Louis, MO 63141-7299. Offers accounting (MBA, PGC); management (MBA, PGC); marketing (MBA, PGC); process and project management (MBA, PGC); sport and entertainment management (MBA, PGC). *Accreditation:* ACBSP. Part-time and evening/weekend programs available. *Faculty:* 5 full-time (3 women), 14 part-time/adjunct (4 women). *Students:* 21 full-time (12 women), 85 part-time (41 women); includes 22 minority (8 Black or African American, non-Hispanic/Latino; 2 Asian, non-Hispanic/Latino; 7 Hispanic/Latino; 5 Two or more races, non-Hispanic/Latino), 3 international. Average age 31. In 2013, 39 master's awarded. *Entrance requirements:* For master's, GMAT (unless applicant possesses undergraduate business degree with minimum cumulative GPA of 3.0, or has completed master's degree from accredited university or one early access course prior to undergraduate degree). Additional exam requirements/recommendations for international students: Required—TOEFL (minimum score 85 iBT). *Application deadline:* Applications are processed on a rolling basis. Application fee: $40 ($60 for international students). Electronic applications accepted. Application fee is waived when completed online. *Expenses: Tuition:* Full-time $23,812; part-time $728 per credit hour. *Required fees:* $395 per year. Tuition and fees vary according to course load, degree level and program. *Financial support:* Career-related internships or fieldwork, Federal Work-Study, tuition waivers (partial), and campus employment available. Financial award application deadline: 3/1; financial award applicants required to submit FAFSA. *Faculty research:* International business, e-marketing, strategic planning, interpersonal management skills, financial analysis. *Unit head:* Dr. Pamela Horwitz, Dean, 314-529-9418, Fax: 314-529-9975, E-mail: horwitz@maryville.edu. *Application contact:* Kathy Dougherty, Director of MBA Programs, 314-529-9382, Fax: 314-529-9975, E-mail: business@maryville.edu.
Website: http://www.maryville.edu/bu/business-administration-masters/.

McGill University, Faculty of Graduate and Postdoctoral Studies, Desautels Faculty of Management, Montréal, QC H3A 2T5, Canada. Offers administration (PhD); entrepreneurial studies (MBA); finance (MBA); general management (Post Master's Certificate); information systems (MBA); international business (MBA); international practicing management (MM); management (MBA); management for development (MBA); manufacturing management (MMM); marketing (MBA); operations management (MBA); public accountancy (Diploma); strategic management (MBA); MBA/LL B; MD/MBA. MMM offered jointly with Faculty of Engineering; PhD with Concordia University, HEC Montreal, Université de Montréal, Université du Québec à Montréal.

Mercer University, Graduate Studies, Cecil B. Day Campus, Eugene W. Stetson School of Business and Economics (Atlanta), Atlanta, GA 30341. Offers accounting (M Acc); business administration (EMBA, PMBA); international business (MBA); MBA/M Acc; Pharm D/MBA. *Accreditation:* AACSB. Part-time and evening/weekend programs available. Postbaccalaureate distance learning degree programs offered (no on-campus study). *Faculty:* 20 full-time (9 women), 7 part-time/adjunct (2 women). *Students:* 207 full-time (112 women), 103 part-time (62 women); includes 143 minority (116 Black or African American, non-Hispanic/Latino; 2 American Indian or Alaska Native, non-Hispanic/Latino; 18 Asian, non-Hispanic/Latino; 6 Hispanic/Latino; 1 Native Hawaiian or other Pacific Islander, non-Hispanic/Latino), 43 international. Average age 32. 117 applicants, 97% accepted, 94 enrolled. In 2013, 150 master's awarded. *Entrance requirements:* For master's, GMAT or GRE. Additional exam requirements/recommendations for international students: Required—TOEFL (minimum score 550 paper-based; 80 iBT). *Application deadline:* For fall admission, 7/1 priority date for domestic students, 7/1 for international students; for spring admission, 11/1 priority date for domestic students, 11/1 for international students. Applications are processed on a rolling basis. Application fee: $50 ($100 for international students). Electronic applications accepted. *Financial support:* Federal Work-Study available. Financial award application deadline: 5/1; financial award applicants required to submit FAFSA. *Faculty research:* Entrepreneurship, market studies, international business strategy, financial analysis. *Unit head:* Dr. Michael Weber, Associate Dean, 678-547-6056, Fax: 678-547-6337, E-mail: weber_jm@mercer.edu. *Application contact:* Lael Whiteside, Admissions Counselor, 678-547-6147, Fax: 678-547-6160, E-mail: graduatessbe@mercer.edu.
Website: http://business.mercer.edu.

Mercy College, School of Business, Program in Public Accounting, Dobbs Ferry, NY 10522-1189. Offers MS. Part-time and evening/weekend programs available. *Students:* 20 full-time (9 women), 1 part-time (0 women); includes 13 minority (5 Black or African American, non-Hispanic/Latino; 3 Asian, non-Hispanic/Latino; 5 Hispanic/Latino). Average age 32. 28 applicants, 18% accepted, 4 enrolled. In 2013, 22 master's awarded. *Entrance requirements:* For master's, interview, essay, two letters of reference, undergraduate transcripts. Additional exam requirements/recommendations for international students: Required—TOEFL (minimum score 600 paper-based; 100 iBT), IELTS (minimum score 8). *Application deadline:* For fall admission, 8/1 for international students. Applications are processed on a rolling basis. Application fee: $40. Electronic applications accepted. *Expenses: Tuition:* Full-time $19,344; part-time $806 per credit. *Required fees:* $580; $806 per credit. $145 per term. Tuition and fees vary according to course load, degree level and program. *Financial support:* Career-related internships or fieldwork, Federal Work-Study, scholarships/grants, and unspecified assistantships available. Support available to part-time students. Financial award applicants required to submit FAFSA. *Unit head:* Ed Weis, Dean, School of Business, 914-674-7490, E-mail: eweis@mercy.edu. *Application contact:* Allison Gurdineer, Senior Director of Admissions, 877-637-2946, Fax: 914-674-7382, E-mail: admissions@mercy.edu.
Website: https://www.mercy.edu/academics/school-of-business/department-of-accounting/ms-in-public-accounting/.

Mercyhurst University, Graduate Studies, Program in Organizational Leadership, Erie, PA 16546. Offers accounting (MS); entrepreneurship (MS); higher education administration (MS); human resources (MS); nonprofit management (MS); organizational leadership (Certificate); sports leadership (MS). Part-time and evening/weekend programs available. *Degree requirements:* For master's, thesis. *Entrance requirements:* For master's, GRE General Test or MAT, interview, resume, essay, three professional references, transcripts. Additional exam requirements/recommendations for international students: Required—TOEFL. Electronic applications accepted. *Faculty research:* Leadership training, organizational communication, leadership pedagogy.

Metropolitan State University of Denver, School of Business, Denver, CO 80217-3362. Offers accounting (MP Acc). *Entrance requirements:* For master's, GMAT.

Miami University, Farmer School of Business, Department of Accountancy, Oxford, OH 45056. Offers M Acc. *Accreditation:* AACSB. *Students:* 22 full-time (8 women); includes 4 minority (1 Black or African American, non-Hispanic/Latino; 2 Asian, non-Hispanic/Latino; 1 Hispanic/Latino), 1 international. Average age 24. In 2013, 23 master's awarded. *Entrance requirements:* For master's, GMAT, minimum cumulative undergraduate GPA of 3.0. Additional exam requirements/recommendations for international students: Recommended—TOEFL (minimum score 95 iBT). *Application deadline:* For fall admission, 1/1 priority date for domestic students, 11/15 for international students. Application fee: $50. Electronic applications accepted. *Expenses:* Tuition, state resident: full-time $12,634; part-time $526 per credit hour. Tuition, nonresident: full-time $27,892; part-time $1162 per credit hour. Part-time tuition and fees vary according to course load, campus/location and program. *Financial support:* Fellowships with full and partial tuition reimbursements, research assistantships with full and partial tuition reimbursements, Federal Work-Study, scholarships/grants, health care benefits, tuition waivers (full), and unspecified assistantships available. Financial award application deadline: 1/1; financial award applicants required to submit FAFSA. *Unit head:* Marc Rubin, Chair, 513-529-6200, Fax: 513-529-4740, E-mail: miamiacc@miamioh.edu. *Application contact:* Gretchen Radler, Academic Program Coordinator, 513-529-3372, E-mail: miamiacc@miamioh.edu.
Website: http://www.MiamiOH.edu/accountancy.

Michigan State University, The Graduate School, Eli Broad College of Business, Department of Accounting and Information Systems, East Lansing, MI 48824. Offers accounting (MS, PhD), including information systems (MS), public and corporate accounting (MS), taxation (MS); business information systems (PhD). *Accreditation:* AACSB. *Faculty:* 36. *Students:* 193. 500 applicants, 34% accepted. In 2013, 123 master's awarded. *Degree requirements:* For doctorate, comprehensive exam, thesis/dissertation. *Entrance requirements:* For master's, GMAT (minimum score 550), bachelor's degree in accounting; minimum cumulative GPA of 3.0 at any institution attended and in any junior-/senior-level accounting courses taken; 3 letters of recommendation (at least 1 from faculty); working knowledge of computers including word processing, spreadsheets, networking, and database management system; for doctorate, GMAT (minimum score 600), bachelor's degree; transcripts; 3 letters of recommendation; statement of purpose; resume; on-campus interview; personal qualifications of sound character, perseverance, intellectual curiosity, and interest in scholarly research. Additional exam requirements/recommendations for international students: Required—TOEFL (minimum score 600 paper-based; 100 iBT), IELTS (minimum score 7) accepted for MS only. *Application deadline:* For fall admission, 1/1 for domestic and international students; for spring admission, 10/1 for domestic and international students; for summer admission, 1/1 for domestic and international students. Applications are processed on a rolling basis. Electronic applications accepted. *Financial support:* Research assistantships with tuition reimbursements, teaching assistantships with tuition reimbursements, scholarships/grants, and unspecified assistantships available. Financial award application deadline: 1/1. *Unit head:* Dr. Sanjay Gupta, Associate Dean for MBA and Professional Master's Programs, 517-432-6488, Fax: 517-432-1101, E-mail: gupta@broad.msu.edu. *Application contact:* Program Information Contact, 517-355-7486, Fax: 517-432-1101, E-mail: acct@broad.msu.edu.
Website: http://accounting.broad.msu.edu.

Middle Tennessee State University, College of Graduate Studies, Jennings A. Jones College of Business, Department of Accounting, Murfreesboro, TN 37132. Offers M Acc. *Accreditation:* AACSB. Part-time and evening/weekend programs available. Postbaccalaureate distance learning degree programs offered. *Faculty:* 9 full-time (5 women), 1 part-time/adjunct (0 women). *Students:* 45 full-time (26 women), 57 part-time (30 women); includes 28 minority (12 Black or African American, non-Hispanic/Latino; 13 Asian, non-Hispanic/Latino; 3 Hispanic/Latino). 107 applicants, 57% accepted. In 2013, 29 master's awarded. *Entrance requirements:* Additional exam requirements/recommendations for international students: Required—TOEFL (minimum score 525 paper-based; 71 iBT) or IELTS (minimum score 6). *Application deadline:* For fall admission, 6/1 for domestic and international students. Applications are processed on a rolling basis. Application fee: $25 ($30 for international students). Electronic applications accepted. *Financial support:* In 2013–14, 10 students received support. Tuition waivers available. Support available to part-time students. Financial award application deadline: 5/1; financial award applicants required to submit FAFSA. *Faculty research:* Forensic accounting, healthcare applications. *Unit head:* Dr. G. Robert Smith, Jr., Interim Chair, 615-898-2558, Fax: 615-898-5839, E-mail: smitty.smith@mtsu.edu. *Application contact:* Dr. Michael D. Allen, Vice Provost for Research and Dean, 615-898-2840, Fax: 615-904-8020, E-mail: michael.allen@mtsu.edu.

Millennia Atlantic University, Graduate Programs, Doral, FL 33178. Offers accounting (MBA); business administration (MBA); health information management (MS); human resource management (MA). Postbaccalaureate distance learning degree programs offered (no on-campus study).

Millsaps College, Else School of Management, Jackson, MS 39210-0001. Offers accounting (M Acc); business administration (MBA). *Accreditation:* AACSB. Part-time programs available. *Entrance requirements:* For master's, GMAT. Additional exam requirements/recommendations for international students: Required—TOEFL. Electronic applications accepted. *Faculty research:* Ethics, audit independence, satisfaction with assurance services, political business cycles, economic development, commercialization of new products.

Misericordia University, College of Professional Studies and Social Sciences, Master of Business Administration Program, Dallas, PA 18612-1098. Offers accounting (MBA); human resources (MBA); management (MBA); sport management (MBA). Part-time and evening/weekend programs available. Postbaccalaureate distance learning degree programs offered (no on-campus study). *Faculty:* 4 full-time (2 women), 5 part-time/adjunct (2 women). *Students:* 100 part-time (53 women); includes 1 minority (Black or African American, non-Hispanic/Latino), 1 international. Average age 33. In 2013, 32 master's awarded. *Entrance requirements:* For master's, GMAT, MAT, GRE (50th percentile or higher), or minimum undergraduate GPA of 3.0, interview. Additional exam requirements/recommendations for international students: Required—TOEFL. *Application deadline:* Applications are processed on a rolling basis. Application fee: $35. Electronic applications accepted. Application fee is waived when completed online. *Expenses: Tuition:* Full-time $14,450; part-time $680 per credit. Tuition and fees vary according to degree level. *Financial support:* In 2013–14, 68 students received support. Scholarships/grants and unspecified assistantships available. Support available to part-time students. Financial award applicants required to submit FAFSA. *Unit head:* Dr. Timothy Kearney, Chair of Business Department, 570-674-1487, E-mail: tkearney@misericordia.edu. *Application contact:* David Pasquini, Assistant Director of Admissions, 570-674-8183, Fax: 570-674-6232, E-mail: dpasquin@misericordia.edu.
Website: http://www.misericordia.edu/mba.

Mississippi College, Graduate School, School of Business, Clinton, MS 39058. Offers accounting (Certificate); business administration (MBA), including accounting; business education (M Ed); finance (MBA, Certificate); JD/MBA. Part-time and evening/weekend programs available. *Degree requirements:* For master's, comprehensive exam, thesis optional. *Entrance requirements:* For master's, GMAT, minimum GPA of 2.5, 24 hours of undergraduate course work in business. Additional exam requirements/

recommendations for international students: Recommended—TOEFL, IELTS. Electronic applications accepted.

Mississippi State University, College of Business, Adkerson School of Accountancy, Mississippi State, MS 39762. Offers accounting (MPA); systems (MPA); taxation (MTX). *Accreditation:* AACSB. *Faculty:* 8 full-time (3 women), 2 part-time/adjunct (0 women). *Students:* 35 full-time (17 women), 8 part-time (5 women); includes 4 minority (3 Asian, non-Hispanic/Latino; 1 Two or more races, non-Hispanic/Latino), 4 international. Average age 26. 60 applicants, 32% accepted, 13 enrolled. In 2013, 40 master's awarded. *Degree requirements:* For master's, comprehensive exam. *Entrance requirements:* For master's, GMAT (minimum score of 510), minimum GPA of 3.0 over last 60 hours of undergraduate course work. Additional exam requirements/recommendations for international students: Required—TOEFL (minimum score 575 paper-based; 84 iBT); Recommended—IELTS (minimum score 7). *Application deadline:* For fall admission, 7/1 for domestic students, 5/1 for international students; for spring admission, 11/1 for domestic students, 9/1 for international students. Applications are processed on a rolling basis. Application fee: $60. Electronic applications accepted. *Financial support:* Career-related internships or fieldwork, Federal Work-Study, institutionally sponsored loans, scholarships/grants, and unspecified assistantships available. Support available to part-time students. Financial award application deadline: 4/1; financial award applicants required to submit FAFSA. *Faculty research:* Income tax, financial accounting system, managerial accounting, auditing. *Unit head:* Dr. Jim Scheiner, Director and Graduate Coordinator, 662-325-3710, Fax: 662-325-1646, E-mail: sac@cobilan.msstate.edu. *Application contact:* Dr. Marcia Watson, Graduate Coordinator, 662-325-3710, Fax: 662-325-1646, E-mail: sac@business.msstate.edu. Website: http://www.business.msstate.edu/programs/adkerson.

Mississippi State University, College of Business, Department of Management and Information Systems, Mississippi State, MS 39762. Offers business administration (MBA, PhD), including accounting, business administration (MBA), business information systems (PhD), finance (PhD), management (PhD), marketing (PhD); information systems (MSIS); project management (MBA). Part-time programs available. *Faculty:* 12 full-time (4 women). *Students:* 69 full-time (20 women), 245 part-time (69 women); includes 34 minority (9 Black or African American, non-Hispanic/Latino; 12 Asian, non-Hispanic/Latino; 7 Hispanic/Latino; 1 Native Hawaiian or other Pacific Islander, non-Hispanic/Latino; 5 Two or more races, non-Hispanic/Latino), 20 international. Average age 31. 367 applicants, 29% accepted, 73 enrolled. In 2013, 127 master's, 2 doctorates awarded. *Degree requirements:* For master's, comprehensive exam; for doctorate, comprehensive exam, thesis/dissertation. *Entrance requirements:* For master's, GMAT, minimum GPA of 3.0 in last 60 hours of undergraduate course work; for doctorate, GMAT (minimum score of 550), minimum GPA of 3.25 on all graduate work; BS with minimum GPA of 3.0 cumulative and last 60 hours. Additional exam requirements/recommendations for international students: Required—TOEFL (minimum score 575 paper-based; 84 iBT); Recommended—IELTS (minimum score 7). *Application deadline:* For fall admission, 7/1 for domestic students, 5/1 for international students; for spring admission, 11/1 for domestic students, 9/1 for international students. Applications are processed on a rolling basis. Application fee: $60. Electronic applications accepted. *Financial support:* In 2013–14, 1 teaching assistantship (averaging $13,497 per year) was awarded; career-related internships or fieldwork, Federal Work-Study, institutionally sponsored loans, scholarships/grants, and unspecified assistantships also available. Financial award applicants required to submit FAFSA. *Faculty research:* Electronic commerce, management of information technology. *Unit head:* Dr. Tim Barnett, Department Chairperson and Professor of Management, 662-325-3928, Fax: 662-325-8651, E-mail: tim.barnett@msstate.edu. *Application contact:* Dr. Rebecca Long, Graduate Coordinator, 662-325-3928, E-mail: gsb@cobian.msstate.edu. Website: http://www.business.msstate.edu/programs/mis/index.php.

Missouri State University, Graduate College, College of Business Administration, School of Accountancy, Springfield, MO 65897. Offers M Acc. *Accreditation:* AACSB. Part-time and evening/weekend programs available. *Faculty:* 15 full-time (3 women). *Students:* 86 full-time (57 women), 41 part-time (30 women); includes 2 minority (1 Asian, non-Hispanic/Latino; 1 Hispanic/Latino), 69 international. Average age 28. 58 applicants, 78% accepted, 32 enrolled. In 2013, 51 master's awarded. *Entrance requirements:* For master's, GMAT, minimum GPA of 2.75. Additional exam requirements/recommendations for international students: Required—TOEFL (minimum score 550 paper-based; 79 iBT). *Application deadline:* For fall admission, 7/20 priority date for domestic students, 5/1 for international students; for spring admission, 12/20 priority date for domestic students, 9/1 for international students. Applications are processed on a rolling basis. Application fee: $35 ($50 for international students). Electronic applications accepted. *Expenses:* Tuition, state resident: full-time $4500; part-time $250 per credit hour. Tuition, nonresident: full-time $9018; part-time $501 per credit hour. *Required fees:* $361 per semester. Tuition and fees vary according to course level, course load and program. *Financial support:* In 2013–14, 2 teaching assistantships with full tuition reimbursements (averaging $8,324 per year) were awarded; career-related internships or fieldwork, Federal Work-Study, institutionally sponsored loans, scholarships/grants, tuition waivers (partial), and unspecified assistantships also available. Support available to part-time students. Financial award application deadline: 3/31; financial award applicants required to submit FAFSA. *Faculty research:* Forensic accounting, international accounting standards, accounting education, tax compliance. *Unit head:* Dr. John R. Williams, Director, 417-836-5414, Fax: 417-836-6337, E-mail: accountancy@missouristate.edu. *Application contact:* Misty Stewart, Coordinator for Graduate Admissions and Recruitment, 417-836-6079, Fax: 417-836-6200, E-mail: mistystewart@missouristate.edu. Website: http://www.missouristate.edu/soa/.

Molloy College, Graduate Business Program, Rockville Centre, NY 11571-5002. Offers accounting (MBA); accounting and finance (MBA); accounting and management (MBA); finance (MBA); finance and management (MBA); finance and personal financial planning (MBA); healthcare administration (MBA); management (MBA); management and personal financial planning (MBA); marketing (MBA); personal financial planning (MBA). Part-time programs available. *Faculty:* 8 full-time (3 women), 7 part-time/adjunct (1 woman). *Students:* 41 full-time (19 women), 104 part-time (36 women); includes 45 minority (21 Black or African American, non-Hispanic/Latino; 8 Asian, non-Hispanic/Latino; 14 Hispanic/Latino; 1 Native Hawaiian or other Pacific Islander, non-Hispanic/Latino; 1 Two or more races, non-Hispanic/Latino), 4 international. Average age 29. 48 applicants, 71% accepted, 27 enrolled. In 2013, 33 master's awarded. *Application deadline:* Applications are processed on a rolling basis. Application fee: $60. *Expenses: Tuition:* Full-time $16,920; part-time $940 per credit. *Required fees:* $880. *Faculty research:* Leadership, marketing, accounting, finance, international. *Unit head:* Dr. Daniel Cillis, Associate Dean and Director, MBA Program, 516-323-3080, E-mail: dcillis@molloy.edu. *Application contact:* Alina Haitz, Assistant Director of Graduate Admissions, 516-323-4008, E-mail: ahaitz@molloy.edu.

Monmouth University, The Graduate School, Leon Hess Business School, West Long Branch, NJ 07764-1898. Offers accounting (MBA, Post-Master's Certificate); business (MBA); finance (MBA); real estate (MBA). *Accreditation:* AACSB. Part-time and evening/weekend programs available. *Faculty:* 32 full-time (10 women), 5 part-time/adjunct (0 women). *Students:* 92 full-time (35 women), 98 part-time (45 women); includes 30 minority (9 Black or African American, non-Hispanic/Latino; 12 Asian, non-Hispanic/Latino; 6 Hispanic/Latino; 3 Two or more races, non-Hispanic/Latino), 9 international. Average age 27. 157 applicants, 82% accepted, 84 enrolled. In 2013, 134 master's awarded. *Degree requirements:* For master's, capstone course. *Entrance requirements:* For master's, GMAT, minimum GPA of 3.0 in major, 2.75 overall. Additional exam requirements/recommendations for international students: Required—TOEFL (minimum score 550 paper-based; 79 iBT), IELTS (minimum score 6), Michigan English Language Assessment Battery (minimum score 77). *Application deadline:* For fall admission, 7/15 priority date for domestic students, 6/1 for international students; for spring admission, 11/15 priority date for domestic students, 11/1 for international students. Applications are processed on a rolling basis. Application fee: $50. Electronic applications accepted. *Expenses: Tuition:* Part-time $1004 per credit hour. *Required fees:* $157 per semester. *Financial support:* In 2013–14, 119 students received support, including 281 fellowships (averaging $1,244 per year), 27 research assistantships (averaging $6,273 per year); career-related internships or fieldwork, scholarships/grants, and unspecified assistantships also available. Support available to part-time students. Financial award applicants required to submit FAFSA. *Faculty research:* Information technology and marketing, behavioral research in accounting, human resources, management of technology. *Unit head:* Dr. Susan Gupta, MBA Program Director, 732-571-3639, Fax: 732-263-5517, E-mail: sgupta@monmouth.edu. *Application contact:* Lauren Vento-Cifelli, Associate Vice President of Undergraduate and Graduate Admission, 732-571-3452, Fax: 732-263-5123, E-mail: gradadm@monmouth.edu. Website: http://www.monmouth.edu/mba.

See Display on page 116 and Close-Up on page 187.

Montana State University, College of Graduate Studies, College of Business, Bozeman, MT 59717. Offers professional accountancy (MP Ac). *Accreditation:* AACSB. Part-time programs available. *Degree requirements:* For master's, comprehensive exam. *Entrance requirements:* For master's, GRE General Test, GMAT, minimum undergraduate GPA of 3.1 (preferred). Additional exam requirements/recommendations for international students: Required—TOEFL (minimum score 550 paper-based). Electronic applications accepted. *Faculty research:* Tax research, accounting education, fraud issues, CPA exams.

Montclair State University, The Graduate School, School of Business, Department of Accounting, Law and Taxation, Post Master's Certificate Program in Accounting, Montclair, NJ 07043-1624. Offers Post Master's Certificate. Part-time and evening/weekend programs available. *Entrance requirements:* For degree, 2 letters of recommendation, essay. Additional exam requirements/recommendations for international students: Required—TOEFL (minimum score 83 iBT), IELTS (minimum score 6.5). Electronic applications accepted. *Faculty research:* Costs and benefits (to the economy) of tax incentive programs, sustainability and financial accounting, auditors' (expanded) role post-Great Recession, revising rules for restructuring charges, aggressive accounting and ethical behavior.

Montclair State University, The Graduate School, School of Business, Department of Accounting, Law and Taxation, Program in Accounting, Montclair, NJ 07043-1624. Offers MS. Part-time and evening/weekend programs available. *Degree requirements:* For master's, culminating experience. *Entrance requirements:* For master's, GMAT, 2 letters of recommendation, resume, essay. Additional exam requirements/recommendations for international students: Required—TOEFL (minimum score 83 iBT), IELTS (minimum score 6.5). Electronic applications accepted. *Faculty research:* Costs and benefits (to the economy) of tax incentive programs, sustainability and financial accounting, auditors' (expanded) role post-Great Recession, revising rules for restructuring charges, aggressive accounting and ethical behavior.

Moravian College, Moravian College Comenius Center, Business and Management Programs, Bethlehem, PA 18018-6650. Offers accounting (MBA); business analytics (MBA); general management (MBA); health administration (MHA); healthcare management (MBA); human resource management (MBA); leadership (MSHRM); learning and performance management (MSHRM); supply chain management (MBA). Part-time and evening/weekend programs available. *Entrance requirements:* For master's, GMAT. Additional exam requirements/recommendations for international students: Required—TOEFL (minimum score 550 paper-based; 90 iBT). Application fee is waived when completed online. *Expenses:* Contact institution. *Faculty research:* Leadership, change management, human resources.

Murray State University, College of Business and Public Affairs, Master of Professional Accountancy (MPAC) Program, Murray, KY 42071. Offers MPAC. Part-time programs available. *Degree requirements:* For master's, thesis. *Entrance requirements:* For master's, GMAT or GRE. Additional exam requirements/recommendations for international students: Required—TOEFL (minimum score 525 paper-based). *Faculty research:* Corporate governance, information systems innovations, public finances, accounting education.

National University, Academic Affairs, School of Business and Management, La Jolla, CA 92037-1011. Offers accountancy (Certificate); business administration (GMBA, MBA), including financial management (MBA), human resource management (MBA), integrated marketing communications (MBA), international business (MBA), management accounting (MBA), marketing (MBA), mobile marketing and social media (MBA), organizational leadership (MA, MBA), professional golf management (MBA); global management (MGM); human resource management (MA), including organizational development and change, organizational leadership (MA, MBA); international business (Certificate); management information systems (MS); organizational leadership (MS), including community development; sustainability management (MS). Part-time and evening/weekend programs available. Postbaccalaureate distance learning degree programs offered (no on-campus study). *Faculty:* 30 full-time (8 women), 88 part-time/adjunct (25 women). *Students:* 688 full-time (357 women), 331 part-time (161 women); includes 453 minority (105 Black or African American, non-Hispanic/Latino; 2 American Indian or Alaska Native, non-Hispanic/Latino; 143 Asian, non-Hispanic/Latino; 162 Hispanic/Latino; 13 Native Hawaiian or other Pacific Islander, non-Hispanic/Latino; 28 Two or more races, non-Hispanic/Latino), 165 international. Average age 33. 286 applicants, 100% accepted, 217 enrolled. In 2013, 641 master's awarded. *Degree requirements:* For master's, thesis (for some programs). *Entrance requirements:* For master's, interview, minimum GPA of 2.5. Additional exam requirements/recommendations for international students: Required—TOEFL (minimum score 550 paper-based; 79 iBT), IELTS (minimum score 6). *Application deadline:* Applications are processed on a rolling basis. Application fee: $60 ($65 for international students). Electronic applications accepted. *Expenses: Tuition:* Full-time $13,824; part-time $1728 per course. One-time fee: $160. *Financial support:* Career-related internships or fieldwork, scholarships/grants, and tuition waivers (partial) available. Support available to part-time students. Financial award application deadline: 6/30; financial award applicants required to submit FAFSA. *Unit head:* School of Business and Management, 800-628-8648, Fax: 858-642-8719, E-mail: sobm@nu.edu. *Application contact:* Louis Cruz, Interim Vice President for Enrollment Services, 800-628-8648, E-mail: advisor@nu.edu. Website: http://www.nu.edu/OurPrograms/SchoolOfBusinessAndManagement.html.

Accounting

New England College, Program in Management, Henniker, NH 03242-3293. Offers accounting (MSA); healthcare administration (MS); international relations (MA); marketing management (MS); nonprofit leadership (MS); project management (MS); strategic leadership (MS). Part-time and evening/weekend programs available. *Degree requirements:* For master's, independent research project. Electronic applications accepted.

New Jersey City University, Graduate Studies and Continuing Education, College of Professional Studies, Department of Business Administration, Program in Accounting, Jersey City, NJ 07305-1597. Offers MS. Part-time and evening/weekend programs available. *Students:* 25 full-time (15 women), 64 part-time (35 women); includes 50 minority (13 Black or African American, non-Hispanic/Latino; 15 Asian, non-Hispanic/Latino; 22 Hispanic/Latino), 10 international. Average age 33. In 2013, 17 master's awarded. *Entrance requirements:* Additional exam requirements/recommendations for international students: Required—TOEFL (minimum score 61 iBT). *Expenses: Tuition, area resident:* Part-time $527.90 per credit. Tuition, nonresident: part-time $947.75 per credit. *Unit head:* Robert J. Matthews, Graduate Coordinator, 201-200-3353, E-mail: rmatthews@njcu.edu. *Application contact:* Dr. William Bajor, Dean of Graduate Studies, 201-200-3409, Fax: 201-200-3411, E-mail: wbajor@njcu.edu.

New Mexico State University, Graduate School, College of Business, Department of Accounting and Information Systems, Las Cruces, NM 88003. Offers M Acct. *Accreditation:* AACSB. Part-time programs available. *Faculty:* 11 full-time (4 women). *Students:* 35 full-time (17 women), 10 part-time (5 women); includes 19 minority (2 American Indian or Alaska Native, non-Hispanic/Latino; 1 Asian, non-Hispanic/Latino; 15 Hispanic/Latino; 1 Two or more races, non-Hispanic/Latino), 3 international. Average age 28. 33 applicants, 67% accepted, 17 enrolled. In 2013, 19 master's awarded. *Degree requirements:* For master's, comprehensive exam, thesis optional. *Entrance requirements:* For master's, GMAT, minimum undergraduate accounting GPA of 3.0 (upper-division). Additional exam requirements/recommendations for international students: Required—TOEFL (minimum score 530 paper-based; 79 iBT), IELTS (minimum score 6.5). *Application deadline:* For fall admission, 7/1 priority date for domestic students, 3/1 priority date for international students; for spring admission, 11/1 priority date for domestic students. Applications are processed on a rolling basis. Application fee: $40 ($50 for international students). Electronic applications accepted. *Expenses:* Tuition, state resident: full-time $5398; part-time $224.90 per credit. Tuition, nonresident: full-time $18,821; part-time $784.20 per credit. *Required fees:* $1310; $54.60 per credit. *Financial support:* In 2013–14, 29 students received support, including 17 teaching assistantships (averaging $9,087 per year); career-related internships or fieldwork, Federal Work-Study, scholarships/grants, traineeships, health care benefits, and unspecified assistantships also available. Support available to part-time students. Financial award application deadline: 3/1. *Faculty research:* Taxation, financial accounting, managerial accounting, accounting systems, accounting education. *Total annual research expenditures:* $643. *Unit head:* Dr. Kevin Melendrez, Department Head, 575-646-4901, Fax: 575-646-1552, E-mail: kdm@nmsu.edu. *Application contact:* Dr. Cindy L. Seipel, Master of Accountancy Director, 575-646-5206, Fax: 575-646-1552, E-mail: cseipel@nmsu.edu.
Website: http://business.nmsu.edu/academics/accounting-is/.

New York Institute of Technology, School of Management, Department of Business Administration, Old Westbury, NY 11568-8000. Offers management (MBA), including decision science, finance, management, marketing; professional accounting (MBA). Part-time and evening/weekend programs available. *Faculty:* 22 full-time (6 women), 17 part-time/adjunct (3 women). *Students:* 151 full-time (74 women), 120 part-time (47 women); includes 44 minority (13 Black or African American, non-Hispanic/Latino; 23 Asian, non-Hispanic/Latino; 4 Hispanic/Latino; 4 Two or more races, non-Hispanic/Latino), 177 international. Average age 27. 355 applicants, 66% accepted, 110 enrolled. In 2013, 151 master's awarded. *Degree requirements:* For master's, thesis (for some programs). *Entrance requirements:* For master's, minimum QPA of 2.85. Additional exam requirements/recommendations for international students: Required—TOEFL (minimum score 550 paper-based; 79 iBT), IELTS (minimum score 6). *Application deadline:* For fall admission, 7/1 priority date for domestic students, 6/1 for international students; for spring admission, 12/1 priority date for domestic students, 12/1 for international students. Applications are processed on a rolling basis. Application fee: $50. Electronic applications accepted. *Expenses: Tuition:* Full-time $18,900; part-time $1050 per credit. *Financial support:* Research assistantships with partial tuition reimbursements, career-related internships or fieldwork, scholarships/grants, health care benefits, tuition waivers (full and partial), and unspecified assistantships available. Support available to part-time students. Financial award applicants required to submit FAFSA. *Faculty research:* Accounting, economics, finance, management, marketing. *Unit head:* Dr. Diamando Afxentiou, Director, 212-261-1602, E-mail: dafxenti@nyit.edu. *Application contact:* Alice Dolitsky, Director, Graduate Admissions, 516-686-7520, Fax: 516-686-1116, E-mail: nyitgrad@nyit.edu.
Website: http://www.nyit.edu/management/mba.

New York University, Leonard N. Stern School of Business, Department of Accounting, New York, NY 10012-1019. Offers MBA, PhD. *Expenses: Tuition:* Full-time $35,856; part-time $1494 per unit. *Required fees:* $1408; $64 per unit. $473 per term. Tuition and fees vary according to course load and program. *Faculty research:* Earnings management and financial analysis effectiveness and accounting policy, value-relevance of financial reporting, intangibles-related reporting and analysis, equity.

North Carolina Agricultural and Technical State University, School of Graduate Studies, School of Business and Economics, Greensboro, NC 27411. Offers accounting (MSM); business education (MAT); human resources management (MSM); supply chain systems (MSM).

North Carolina State University, Graduate School, Poole College of Management, Program in Accounting, Raleigh, NC 27695. Offers MAC. Part-time programs available. *Degree requirements:* For master's, thesis optional. *Entrance requirements:* For master's, GMAT, interview. Additional exam requirements/recommendations for international students: Required—TOEFL. Electronic applications accepted. *Faculty research:* Financial reporting issues using positive economic models and empirical studies of human behavior related to accounting decisions.

Northeastern Illinois University, College of Graduate Studies and Research, College of Business and Management, Master of Science in Accounting Program, Chicago, IL 60625-4699. Offers MSA.

Northeastern State University, College of Business and Technology, Program in Accounting and Financial Analysis, Tahlequah, OK 74464-2399. Offers MS. Part-time and evening/weekend programs available. *Faculty:* 7 full-time (0 women). *Students:* 11 full-time (3 women), 49 part-time (34 women); includes 18 minority (6 Black or African American, non-Hispanic/Latino; 5 American Indian or Alaska Native, non-Hispanic/Latino; 2 Asian, non-Hispanic/Latino; 3 Hispanic/Latino; 2 Two or more races, non-Hispanic/Latino), 4 international. Average age 33. In 2013, 13 master's awarded. *Entrance requirements:* For master's, GMAT. Additional exam requirements/recommendations for international students: Required—TOEFL. *Application deadline:* For fall admission, 6/1 priority date for domestic students. Applications are processed on a rolling basis. Application fee: $25. Electronic applications accepted. *Expenses:* Tuition, state resident: full-time $3029; part-time $168.25 per credit hour. Tuition, nonresident: full-time $7709; part-time $428.25 per credit hour. *Required fees:* $35.90 per credit hour. *Faculty research:* Information systems and organizational performance, capital markets, sustainability. *Unit head:* Dr. Gary Freeman, Coordinator, 918-449-6524, E-mail: freemandg@nsuok.edu. *Application contact:* Margie Railey, Administrative Assistant, 918-456-5511 Ext. 2093, Fax: 918-458-2061, E-mail: railey@nsouk.edu.
Website: http://academics.nsuok.edu/businesstechnology/Graduate/MAFA.aspx.

Northeastern University, D'Amore-McKim School of Business, Boston, MA 02115-5096. Offers accounting (MS); business administration (EMBA, MBA); finance (MS); international business (MS); taxation (MS); technological entrepreneurship (MS); JD/MBA; MBA/MSN; MS/MBA. Part-time and evening/weekend programs available. Postbaccalaureate distance learning degree programs offered (no on-campus study). *Entrance requirements:* For master's, GMAT or GRE, interview. Additional exam requirements/recommendations for international students: Required—TOEFL (minimum score 600 paper-based; 100 iBT). Electronic applications accepted. *Expenses:* Contact institution.

Northern Illinois University, Graduate School, College of Business, Department of Accountancy, De Kalb, IL 60115-2854. Offers MAS, MST. *Accreditation:* AACSB. Part-time and evening/weekend programs available. *Faculty:* 14 full-time (4 women). *Students:* 133 full-time (57 women), 61 part-time (31 women); includes 41 minority (8 Black or African American, non-Hispanic/Latino; 18 Asian, non-Hispanic/Latino; 11 Hispanic/Latino; 4 Two or more races, non-Hispanic/Latino), 24 international. Average age 28. 135 applicants, 58% accepted, 45 enrolled. In 2013, 129 master's awarded. *Degree requirements:* For master's, thesis optional. *Entrance requirements:* For master's, GMAT, minimum GPA of 2.75. Additional exam requirements/recommendations for international students: Required—TOEFL (minimum score 550 paper-based). *Application deadline:* For fall admission, 4/1 priority date for domestic students, 5/1 for international students; for spring admission, 9/15 priority date for domestic students, 10/1 for international students. Applications are processed on a rolling basis. Application fee: $40. Electronic applications accepted. *Financial support:* In 2013–14, 27 research assistantships with full tuition reimbursements, 16 teaching assistantships with full tuition reimbursements were awarded; fellowships with full tuition reimbursements, career-related internships or fieldwork, Federal Work-Study, scholarships/grants, tuition waivers (full), and unspecified assistantships also available. Support available to part-time students. Financial award applicants required to submit FAFSA. *Faculty research:* Accounting fraud, governmental accounting, corporate income tax planning, auditing, ethics. *Unit head:* Dr. James C. Young, Chair, 815-753-1250, Fax: 815-753-8515. *Application contact:* Dr. Rowene Linden, Graduate Adviser, 815-753-6200.
Website: http://www.cob.niu.edu/accy/.

Northern Kentucky University, Office of Graduate Programs, College of Business, Program in Accountancy, Highland Heights, KY 41099. Offers accountancy (M Acc); advanced taxation (Certificate). Part-time and evening/weekend programs available. *Faculty:* 6 full-time (1 woman), 2 part-time/adjunct (both women). *Students:* 16 full-time (5 women), 51 part-time (20 women); includes 7 minority (6 Black or African American, non-Hispanic/Latino; 1 Asian, non-Hispanic/Latino). Average age 31. 81 applicants, 52% accepted, 32 enrolled. In 2013, 21 master's awarded. *Degree requirements:* For master's, capstone course. *Entrance requirements:* For master's, GMAT (minimum score 450), minimum GPA of 2.5, resume, statement of purpose. Additional exam requirements/recommendations for international students: Required—TOEFL (minimum score 550 paper-based; 79 iBT); Recommended—IELTS (minimum score 6.5). *Application deadline:* For fall admission, 7/1 priority date for domestic students, 6/1 for international students; for spring admission, 12/1 priority date for domestic students, 10/1 for international students; for summer admission, 5/1 priority date for domestic students, 3/1 for international students. Applications are processed on a rolling basis. Application fee: $40. Electronic applications accepted. *Expenses:* Tuition, state resident: full-time $4446; part-time $494 per credit hour. Tuition, nonresident: full-time $6885; part-time $765 per credit hour. *Required fees:* $72 per semester. One-time fee: $125.50. Part-time tuition and fees vary according to course load, degree level, program and reciprocity agreements. *Financial support:* In 2013–14, 24 students received support. Unspecified assistantships available. Financial award applicants required to submit FAFSA. *Faculty research:* Behavioral influences on accounting decisions, historical development of accounting, auditing and accounting failures. *Unit head:* Robert Salyer, Director, 859-572-7695, Fax: 859-572-7694, E-mail: salyerb@nku.edu. *Application contact:* Dr. Christian Gamm, Director of Graduate Programs, 859-572-6364, Fax: 859-572-6670, E-mail: gammc1@nku.edu.
Website: http://cob.nku.edu/graduatedegrees/accountancy.html.

Northwestern University, The Graduate School, Kellogg School of Management, Department of Accounting Information and Management, Evanston, IL 60208. Offers PhD. Admissions and degree offered through The Graduate School. *Degree requirements:* For doctorate, comprehensive exam, thesis/dissertation. *Entrance requirements:* For doctorate, GMAT or GRE General Test. Additional exam requirements/recommendations for international students: Required—TOEFL. Electronic applications accepted. *Faculty research:* Managerial and financial accounting theory, financial accounting/theory, managerial accounting and performance measurement, international accounting, joint cost allocation.

Northwestern University, The Graduate School, Kellogg School of Management, Management Programs, Evanston, IL 60208. Offers accounting information and management (MBA, PhD); analytical finance (MBA); business administration (MBA); decision sciences (MBA); entrepreneurship and innovation (MBA); finance (MBA, PhD); health enterprise management (MBA); human resources management (MBA); international business (MBA); management and organizations (MBA, PhD); management and organizations and sociology (PhD); management and strategy (MBA); management studies (MS); managerial analytics (MBA); managerial economics (MBA); managerial economics and strategy (PhD); marketing (MBA, PhD); marketing management (MBA); media management (MBA); operations management (MBA, PhD); real estate (MBA); social enterprise at Kellogg (MBA); JD/MBA. Part-time and evening/weekend programs available. Terminal master's awarded for partial completion of doctoral program. *Degree requirements:* For doctorate, thesis/dissertation, 2 years of coursework, qualifying (field) exam and candidacy, summer research papers and presentations to faculty, proposal defense, final exam/defense. *Entrance requirements:* For master's, GMAT, GRE, interview, 2 letters of recommendation, college transcripts, resume, essays, Kellogg honor code; for doctorate, GMAT, GRE, statement of purpose, transcripts, 2 letters of recommendation, resume, interview. Additional exam requirements/recommendations for international students: Required—TOEFL, IELTS. Electronic applications accepted. *Expenses:* Contact institution. *Faculty research:* Business cycles and international finance, health policy, networks, non-market strategy, consumer psychology.

Nova Southeastern University, H. Wayne Huizenga School of Business and Entrepreneurship, Fort Lauderdale, FL 33314-7796. Offers accounting (M Acc); business administration (MBA, DBA); human resource management (MSHRM); international business administration (MIBA); leadership (MS); public administration (MPA, DPA); real estate development (MS); taxation (M Tax); JD/MBA; Pharm D/MBA.

Part-time and evening/weekend programs available. Postbaccalaureate distance learning degree programs offered (minimal on-campus study). *Faculty:* 67 full-time (24 women), 135 part-time/adjunct (37 women). *Students:* 207 full-time (110 women), 3,069 part-time (1,888 women); includes 2,213 minority (1,077 Black or African American, non-Hispanic/Latino; 2 American Indian or Alaska Native, non-Hispanic/Latino; 108 Asian, non-Hispanic/Latino; 975 Hispanic/Latino; 2 Native Hawaiian or other Pacific Islander, non-Hispanic/Latino; 49 Two or more races, non-Hispanic/Latino), 190 international. Average age 33. 1,291 applicants, 68% accepted, 636 enrolled. In 2013, 1,146 master's, 17 doctorates awarded. *Degree requirements:* For master's, thesis optional; for doctorate, comprehensive exam, thesis/dissertation. *Entrance requirements:* For doctorate, GMAT. Additional exam requirements/recommendations for international students: Required—TOEFL (minimum score 550 paper-based; 79 iBT), IELTS (minimum score 6). *Application deadline:* Applications are processed on a rolling basis. Application fee: $50. Electronic applications accepted. *Financial support:* In 2013–14, 2 students received support. Federal Work-Study and scholarships/grants available. Support available to part-time students. Financial award applicants required to submit FAFSA. *Faculty research:* Reputation management, call centers, international social capital, corporate earnings guidance, corporate governance. *Unit head:* Dr. J. Preston Jones, Dean, 954-262-5127, E-mail: fieldsm@nova.edu. *Application contact:* Karen Goldberg, Associate Director of Recruitment and Special Events, 954-262-5039, Fax: 954-262-3822, E-mail: karen@nova.edu.
Website: http://www.huizenga.nova.edu.

Oakland University, Graduate Study and Lifelong Learning, School of Business Administration, Department of Accounting and Finance, Rochester, MI 48309-4401. Offers accounting (M Acc, Certificate); finance (Certificate). *Faculty:* 13 full-time (6 women), 2 part-time/adjunct (0 women). *Students:* 41 full-time (22 women), 28 part-time (19 women); includes 8 minority (2 Black or African American, non-Hispanic/Latino; 4 Asian, non-Hispanic/Latino; 1 Hispanic/Latino; 1 Two or more races, non-Hispanic/Latino), 9 international. Average age 40. 50 applicants, 52% accepted, 26 enrolled. In 2013, 37 master's, 2 Certificates awarded. Application fee: $0. *Unit head:* Mohinder Parkash, Interim Chair, 248-370-4288, Fax: 248-370-4604. *Application contact:* Donna Free, Coordinator, 248-370-3281.

Ohio Dominican University, Graduate Programs, Division of Business, Columbus, OH 43219-2099. Offers accounting (MBA); business administration (MBA); finance (MBA); leadership (MBA); public administration (MBA). *Accreditation:* ACBSP. Part-time and evening/weekend programs available. Postbaccalaureate distance learning degree programs offered (no on-campus study). *Degree requirements:* For master's, thesis or alternative. *Entrance requirements:* For master's, minimum GPA of 3.0, 3 letters of recommendation. Additional exam requirements/recommendations for international students: Required—TOEFL (minimum score 550 paper-based), IELTS (minimum score 6.5).

The Ohio State University, Graduate School, Max M. Fisher College of Business, Department of Accounting and Management Information Systems, Columbus, OH 43210. Offers M Acc, PhD. *Accreditation:* AACSB. *Faculty:* 23. *Students:* 89 full-time (44 women), 2 part-time (1 woman); includes 10 minority (1 Black or African American, non-Hispanic/Latino; 4 Asian, non-Hispanic/Latino; 2 Hispanic/Latino; 1 Native Hawaiian or other Pacific Islander, non-Hispanic/Latino; 2 Two or more races, non-Hispanic/Latino), 35 international. Average age 24. In 2013, 85 master's, 2 doctorates awarded. Terminal master's awarded for partial completion of doctoral program. *Degree requirements:* For doctorate, thesis/dissertation. *Entrance requirements:* For master's and doctorate, GMAT (preferred) or GRE. Additional exam requirements/recommendations for international students: Required—TOEFL (minimum score 600 paper-based; 100 iBT), Michigan English Language Assessment Battery (minimum score 86); Recommended—IELTS (minimum score 7.5). *Application deadline:* For fall admission, 11/15 priority date for domestic students, 11/1 priority date for international students; for winter admission, 12/1 for domestic students, 11/1 for international students; for spring admission, 3/1 for domestic students, 2/1 for international students. Applications are processed on a rolling basis. Application fee: $60 ($70 for international students). Electronic applications accepted. *Financial support:* Fellowships with tuition reimbursements, research assistantships with tuition reimbursements, teaching assistantships with tuition reimbursements, career-related internships or fieldwork, Federal Work-Study, and institutionally sponsored loans available. Support available to part-time students. *Faculty research:* Artificial intelligence, protocol analysis, database design in decision-supporting systems. *Unit head:* Waleed Muhanna, Chair, 614-292-2082, Fax: 614-292-2118, E-mail: muhanna.1@osu.edu. *Application contact:* Graduate Admissions, 614-292-6031, Fax: 614-292-3656, E-mail: gradadmissions@osu.edu.
Website: http://fisher.osu.edu/departments/accounting-and-mis/.

The Ohio State University, Graduate School, Max M. Fisher College of Business, Program in Accounting, Columbus, OH 43210. Offers M Acc. *Faculty:* 23. *Students:* 79 full-time (40 women), 1 (woman) part-time; includes 8 minority (1 Black or African American, non-Hispanic/Latino; 3 Asian, non-Hispanic/Latino; 2 Hispanic/Latino; 1 Native Hawaiian or other Pacific Islander, non-Hispanic/Latino; 1 Two or more races, non-Hispanic/Latino), 30 international. Average age 23. In 2013, 85 master's awarded. *Entrance requirements:* For master's, GMAT. Additional exam requirements/recommendations for international students: Required—TOEFL (minimum score 600 paper-based; 100 iBT), Michigan English Language Assessment Battery (minimum score 86); Recommended—IELTS (minimum score 7). *Application deadline:* For fall admission, 11/15 priority date for domestic students, 11/1 priority date for international students. Applications are processed on a rolling basis. Application fee: $60 ($70 for international students). Electronic applications accepted. *Financial support:* Fellowships with tuition reimbursements available. *Unit head:* Waleed Muhanna, Chair, 614-292-2082, Fax: 614-292-2118, E-mail: muhanna.1@osu.edu. *Application contact:* Graduate Admissions, 614-292-6031, Fax: 614-292-3656, E-mail: gradadmissions@osu.edu.
Website: http://fisher.osu.edu/macc.

Oklahoma Christian University, Graduate School of Business, Oklahoma City, OK 73136-1100. Offers accounting (MBA); electronic business (MBA); financial services (MBA); health services management (MBA); human resources (MBA); international business (MBA); leadership and organizational development (MBA); marketing (MBA); project management (MBA). Postbaccalaureate distance learning degree programs offered (no on-campus study). *Entrance requirements:* For master's, bachelor's degree. Electronic applications accepted.

Oklahoma City University, Meinders School of Business, Program in Accounting, Oklahoma City, OK 73106-1402. Offers financial leadership (MSA); general (MSA); taxation (MSA). Part-time and evening/weekend programs available. *Students:* 11 full-time (8 women), 2 part-time (0 women); includes 5 minority (all Asian, non-Hispanic/Latino), 8 international. Average age 29. 28 applicants, 79% accepted, 8 enrolled. In 2013, 15 master's awarded. *Entrance requirements:* For master's, bachelor's degree from accredited institution, minimum GPA of 3.0, essay, recommendation letters. Additional exam requirements/recommendations for international students: Required—TOEFL (minimum score 570 paper-based; 80 iBT). *Application deadline:* Applications are processed on a rolling basis. Application fee: $50. Electronic applications accepted. *Expenses: Tuition:* Full-time $16,848; part-time $936 per credit hour. Tuition and fees vary according to course load, degree level and program. *Financial support:* Career-related internships or fieldwork, Federal Work-Study, institutionally sponsored loans, scholarships/grants, and tuition waivers available. Support available to part-time students. Financial award application deadline: 8/1; financial award applicants required to submit FAFSA. *Faculty research:* Financial accounting, auditing, tax. *Unit head:* Dr. Steve Agee, Dean, 405-208-5130 Ext. `, Fax: 405-208-5098, E-mail: sagee@okcu.edu. *Application contact:* Heidi Puckett, Director, Admissions, 800-633-7242, Fax: 405-208-5916, E-mail: gadmissions@okcu.edu.
Website: http://www.okcu.edu/msa/.

Oklahoma City University, Meinders School of Business, Program in Business Administration, Oklahoma City, OK 73106-1402. Offers accounting (MBA); finance (MBA); general (MBA); marketing (MBA); JD/MBA; MSN/MBA. *Accreditation:* ACBSP. Part-time and evening/weekend programs available. *Students:* 82 full-time (39 women), 101 part-time (41 women); includes 18 minority (7 Black or African American, non-Hispanic/Latino; 6 American Indian or Alaska Native, non-Hispanic/Latino; 3 Asian, non-Hispanic/Latino; 2 Two or more races, non-Hispanic/Latino), 50 international. Average age 31. 109 applicants, 61% accepted, 19 enrolled. In 2013, 114 master's awarded. *Degree requirements:* For master's, comprehensive exam. *Entrance requirements:* For master's, GRE or GMAT, bachelor's degree from accredited institution, minimum GPA of 3.0, essay, recommendation letters. Additional exam requirements/recommendations for international students: Required—TOEFL (minimum score 550 paper-based; 80 iBT). *Application deadline:* Applications are processed on a rolling basis. Application fee: $50. Electronic applications accepted. *Expenses: Tuition:* Full-time $16,848; part-time $936 per credit hour. Tuition and fees vary according to course load, degree level and program. *Financial support:* Career-related internships or fieldwork, Federal Work-Study, institutionally sponsored loans, scholarships/grants, and tuition waivers (partial) available. Support available to part-time students. Financial award application deadline: 6/1; financial award applicants required to submit FAFSA. *Faculty research:* Management information systems, international business strategies. *Unit head:* Dr. Steve Agee, Dean, 405-208-5130, Fax: 405-208-5098, E-mail: sagee@okcu.edu. *Application contact:* Heidi Puckett, Director of Graduate Admissions, 800-633-7242, Fax: 405-208-5916, E-mail: gadmissions@okcu.edu.
Website: http://msb.okcu.edu/graduate/.

Oklahoma State University, Spears School of Business, School of Accounting, Stillwater, OK 74078. Offers MS, PhD. *Accreditation:* AACSB. Part-time programs available. *Faculty:* 15 full-time (7 women), 4 part-time/adjunct (2 women). *Students:* 66 full-time (30 women), 33 part-time (11 women); includes 10 minority (4 American Indian or Alaska Native, non-Hispanic/Latino; 2 Asian, non-Hispanic/Latino; 3 Hispanic/Latino; 1 Two or more races, non-Hispanic/Latino), 6 international. Average age 24. 104 applicants, 38% accepted, 34 enrolled. In 2013, 59 master's, 4 doctorates awarded. *Degree requirements:* For master's, thesis or alternative; for doctorate, comprehensive exam, thesis/dissertation. *Entrance requirements:* For master's and doctorate, GRE or GMAT. Additional exam requirements/recommendations for international students: Required—TOEFL (minimum score 550 paper-based; 79 iBT). *Application deadline:* For fall admission, 3/1 priority date for international students; for spring admission, 8/1 priority date for international students. Applications are processed on a rolling basis. Application fee: $40 ($75 for international students). Electronic applications accepted. *Expenses:* Tuition, state resident: full-time $4272; part-time $178 per credit hour. Tuition, nonresident: full-time $17,472; part-time $709 per credit hour. *Required fees:* $2413.20; $100.55 per credit hour. One-time fee: $50 full-time. Part-time tuition and fees vary according to course load and campus/location. *Financial support:* In 2013–14, 11 research assistantships (averaging $14,661 per year), 24 teaching assistantships (averaging $7,275 per year) were awarded; career-related internships or fieldwork, Federal Work-Study, scholarships/grants, health care benefits, tuition waivers (partial), and unspecified assistantships also available. Support available to part-time students. Financial award application deadline: 3/1; financial award applicants required to submit FAFSA. *Faculty research:* International accounting, accounting education, cost-management, taxation, oil and gas. *Unit head:* Dr. Robert Cornell, Department Head, 405-744-5123, Fax: 405-744-1680, E-mail: robert.cornell@okstate.edu. *Application contact:* Dr. Alyssa Vowell, Graduate Coordinator, 405-744-6635, Fax: 405-744-1680, E-mail: alyssa.vowell@okstate.edu.
Website: http://spears.okstate.edu/accounting.

Old Dominion University, College of Business and Public Administration, Program in Accounting, Norfolk, VA 23529. Offers MS. *Accreditation:* AACSB. Part-time and evening/weekend programs available. *Faculty:* 7 full-time (3 women), 4 part-time/adjunct (2 women). *Students:* 20 full-time (12 women), 25 part-time (16 women); includes 12 minority (7 Black or African American, non-Hispanic/Latino; 2 Asian, non-Hispanic/Latino; 1 Hispanic/Latino; 1 Native Hawaiian or other Pacific Islander, non-Hispanic/Latino; 1 Two or more races, non-Hispanic/Latino), 8 international. Average age 29. 38 applicants, 68% accepted, 19 enrolled. In 2013, 17 master's awarded. *Degree requirements:* For master's, comprehensive exam. *Entrance requirements:* For master's, GMAT, minimum GPA of 3.0. Additional exam requirements/recommendations for international students: Required—TOEFL (minimum score 550 paper-based). *Application deadline:* For fall admission, 7/1 priority date for domestic students, 4/15 priority date for international students; for spring admission, 11/1 priority date for domestic students, 10/1 priority date for international students. Applications are processed on a rolling basis. Application fee: $50. *Expenses:* Tuition, state resident: full-time $9888; part-time $412 per credit. Tuition, nonresident: full-time $25,152; part-time $1048 per credit. *Required fees:* $59 per semester. One-time fee: $50. *Financial support:* In 2013–14, 4 students received support, including 8 research assistantships with partial tuition reimbursements available (averaging $6,400 per year); career-related internships or fieldwork and unspecified assistantships also available. Financial award application deadline: 2/15; financial award applicants required to submit FAFSA. *Faculty research:* Assurance services, international accounting, strategic costing, business valuation. *Unit head:* Dr. Yin Xu, Graduate Program Director, 757-683-3554, Fax: 757-683-5639, E-mail: yxu@odu.edu. *Application contact:* Dr. Yin Xu, Graduate Program Director, 757-683-3554, Fax: 757-683-5639, E-mail: yxu@odu.edu.
Website: http://bpa.odu.edu/bpa/academics/msa.shtml.

Oral Roberts University, School of Business, Tulsa, OK 74171. Offers accounting (MBA); entrepreneurship (MBA); finance (MBA); international business (MBA); management (MBA); marketing (MBA); non-profit management (MBA); not for profit management (MNM). *Accreditation:* ACBSP. Part-time programs available. Postbaccalaureate distance learning degree programs offered (minimal on-campus study). *Degree requirements:* For master's, thesis optional. *Entrance requirements:* For master's, minimum cumulative GPA of 3.0. Additional exam requirements/recommendations for international students: Required—TOEFL (minimum score 550 paper-based; 79 iBT). Electronic applications accepted. *Faculty research:* Social media, international business and marketing.

Oregon State University, College of Business, Program in Business Administration and Accounting, Corvallis, OR 97331. Offers MBA. Part-time programs available. *Faculty:* 34 full-time (13 women), 2 part-time/adjunct (1 woman). *Students:* 14 full-time (7 women), 3 part-time (2 women); includes 3 minority (2 Asian, non-Hispanic/Latino; 1 Two or more races, non-Hispanic/Latino), 8 international. Average age 30. 7 applicants, 100% accepted, 6 enrolled. In 2013, 10 master's awarded. *Entrance requirements:* For

master's, GMAT. Additional exam requirements/recommendations for international students: Required—TOEFL (minimum score 91 iBT), IELTS (minimum score 7). *Application deadline:* Applications are processed on a rolling basis. Application fee: $60. *Expenses:* Contact institution. *Unit head:* Dr. David Baldridge, Director for Business Master's Programs, 541-737-6062.
Website: http://business.oregonstate.edu/mba/degrees/accountancy.

Our Lady of the Lake University of San Antonio, School of Business and Leadership, Program in Accounting/Finance, San Antonio, TX 78207-4689. Offers accounting (MS); finance (MBA). Part-time and evening/weekend programs available. *Faculty:* 2 full-time (both women), 1 part-time/adjunct (0 women). *Students:* 25 full-time (17 women), 8 part-time (6 women); includes 25 minority (3 Black or African American, non-Hispanic/Latino; 1 Asian, non-Hispanic/Latino; 21 Hispanic/Latino). Average age 33. 280 applicants, 84% accepted, 14 enrolled. In 2013, 11 master's awarded. *Entrance requirements:* For master's, GMAT, GRE General Test, or MAT. Additional exam requirements/recommendations for international students: Required—TOEFL. *Application deadline:* Applications are processed on a rolling basis. Application fee: $25 ($50 for international students). Electronic applications accepted. *Expenses: Tuition:* Full-time $9120; part-time $760 per credit. *Required fees:* $698; $334 per trimester. Tuition and fees vary according to course load, degree level, campus/location and program. *Financial support:* Fellowships, career-related internships or fieldwork, Federal Work-Study, institutionally sponsored loans, scholarships/grants, and tuition waivers (partial) available. Support available to part-time students. Financial award application deadline: 4/15. *Faculty research:* Decision-making, problem-solving, administration, leadership, management. *Unit head:* Dr. Kathryn Winney, Chair of the Business Department, 210-434-6711 Ext. 2297, Fax: 210-434-0821, E-mail: kmwinney@lake.ollusa.edu. *Application contact:* Graduate Admission, 210-431-3961, Fax: 210-431-4013, E-mail: gradadm@ollusa.edu.
Website: http://www.ollusa.edu/s/1190/ollu-3-column-noads.aspx?sid=1190&gid=1&pgid=6390.

Pace University, Lubin School of Business, Accounting Program, New York, NY 10038. Offers managerial accounting (MBA); public accounting (MBA, MS). *Accreditation:* AACSB. Part-time and evening/weekend programs available. *Students:* 76 full-time (41 women), 328 part-time (215 women); includes 66 minority (11 Black or African American, non-Hispanic/Latino; 1 American Indian or Alaska Native, non-Hispanic/Latino; 46 Asian, non-Hispanic/Latino; 7 Hispanic/Latino; 1 Two or more races, non-Hispanic/Latino), 236 international. Average age 26. 421 applicants, 46% accepted, 139 enrolled. In 2013, 141 master's awarded. *Entrance requirements:* For master's, GMAT, GRE. Additional exam requirements/recommendations for international students: Required—TOEFL. *Application deadline:* For fall admission, 8/1 priority date for domestic students, 6/1 for international students; for spring admission, 12/1 priority date for domestic students, 10/1 for international students. Applications are processed on a rolling basis. Application fee: $70. Electronic applications accepted. *Expenses: Tuition:* Part-time $1075 per credit. *Required fees:* $192 per semester. Tuition and fees vary according to course load, degree level and program. *Financial support:* Research assistantships, career-related internships or fieldwork, and Federal Work-Study available. Support available to part-time students. Financial award applicants required to submit FAFSA. *Unit head:* Dr. Kaustav Sen, Chairperson, 212-618-6413, E-mail: ksen@pace.edu. *Application contact:* Susan Ford-Goldschein, Director of Graduate Admissions, 212-346-1531, Fax: 212-346-1585, E-mail: gradnyc@pace.edu.
Website: http://www.pace.edu/lubin.

Pacific States University, College of Business, Los Angeles, CA 90006. Offers accounting (MBA); finance (MBA); international business (MBA, DBA); management of information technology (MBA); real estate management (MBA). Part-time and evening/weekend programs available. Postbaccalaureate distance learning degree programs offered (no on-campus study). *Degree requirements:* For doctorate, comprehensive exam, thesis/dissertation. *Entrance requirements:* For master's, minimum undergraduate GPA of 2.5 during last 90 hours of course work. Additional exam requirements/recommendations for international students: Required—TOEFL (minimum score 500 paper-based; 61 iBT), IELTS (minimum score 5.5).

Penn State University Park, Graduate School, The Mary Jean and Frank P. Smeal College of Business Administration, State College, PA 16802. Offers accounting (M Acc); business administration (MBA, MS, PhD); supply chain management (MPS). *Accreditation:* AACSB. Part-time and evening/weekend programs available. *Students:* 297 full-time (94 women), 4 part-time (1 woman); includes 58 minority (19 Black or African American, non-Hispanic/Latino; 30 Asian, non-Hispanic/Latino; 9 Hispanic/Latino), 96 international. Average age 30. 1,153 applicants, 20% accepted, 141 enrolled. In 2013, 245 master's, 20 doctorates awarded. *Entrance requirements:* Additional exam requirements/recommendations for international students: Required—TOEFL (minimum score 550 paper-based; 80 iBT). *Application deadline:* Applications are processed on a rolling basis. Application fee: $65. Electronic applications accepted. *Financial support:* Fellowships, research assistantships, teaching assistantships, career-related internships or fieldwork, Federal Work-Study, and unspecified assistantships available. Support available to part-time students. Financial award application deadline: 2/15; financial award applicants required to submit FAFSA. *Unit head:* Dr. Charles H. Whiteman, Dean, 814-863-0448, Fax: 814-865-7064, E-mail: chw17@psu.edu. *Application contact:* Cynthia E. Nicosia, Director, Graduate Enrollment Services, 814-865-1834, Fax: 814-863-4627, E-mail: cey1@psu.edu.
Website: http://www.smeal.psu.edu/.

Pittsburg State University, Graduate School, Kelce College of Business, Department of Accounting, Pittsburg, KS 66762. Offers MBA. *Degree requirements:* For master's, thesis or alternative. *Entrance requirements:* For master's, GMAT. *Faculty research:* Accountant's legal liability, computer audit.

Polytechnic University of Puerto Rico, Miami Campus, Graduate School, Miami, FL 33166. Offers accounting (MBA); business administration (MBA); construction management (MEM); environmental management (MEM); finance (MBA); human resources management (MBA); logistics and supply chain management (MBA); management of international enterprises (MBA); manufacturing management (MEM); marketing management (MBA); project management (MBA). Part-time and evening/weekend programs available. Postbaccalaureate distance learning degree programs offered (no on-campus study). *Entrance requirements:* For master's, minimum GPA of 3.0. Electronic applications accepted.

Polytechnic University of Puerto Rico, Orlando Campus, Graduate School, Winter Park, FL 32792. Offers accounting (MBA); business administration (MBA); construction management (MEM); engineering management (MEM); environmental management (MEM); finance (MBA); human resources management (MBA); management of international enterprises (MBA); management of technology (MBA); manufacturing management (MEM). Part-time and evening/weekend programs available. Postbaccalaureate distance learning degree programs offered (no on-campus study). *Entrance requirements:* For master's, minimum GPA of 3.0. Additional exam requirements/recommendations for international students: Recommended—TOEFL. Electronic applications accepted.

Pontifical Catholic University of Puerto Rico, College of Business Administration, Program in Accounting, Ponce, PR 00717-0777. Offers MBA. Part-time and evening/weekend programs available. *Degree requirements:* For master's, thesis. *Entrance requirements:* For master's, GRE, interview, minimum GPA of 2.75.

Pontifical Catholic University of Puerto Rico, College of Business Administration, Program in Management and Accounting, Ponce, PR 00717-0777. Offers Professional Certificate.

Post University, Program in Business Administration, Waterbury, CT 06723-2540. Offers accounting (MSA); business administration (MBA); corporate innovation (MBA); entrepreneurship (MBA); finance (MBA); healthcare (MBA); leadership (MBA); marketing (MBA); project management (MBA). *Accreditation:* ACBSP. Postbaccalaureate distance learning degree programs offered.

Prairie View A&M University, College of Business, Prairie View, TX 77446-0519. Offers accounting (MS); general business administration (MBA). *Accreditation:* AACSB. Part-time and evening/weekend programs available. *Faculty:* 7 full-time (0 women), 10 part-time/adjunct (3 women). *Students:* 61 full-time (38 women), 169 part-time (103 women); includes 207 minority (186 Black or African American, non-Hispanic/Latino; 13 Asian, non-Hispanic/Latino; 7 Hispanic/Latino; 1 Two or more races, non-Hispanic/Latino), 16 international. Average age 31. 268 applicants, 53% accepted, 105 enrolled. In 2013, 37 master's awarded. *Entrance requirements:* For master's, GMAT, minimum GPA of 2.45. Additional exam requirements/recommendations for international students: Required—TOEFL. *Application deadline:* For fall admission, 7/1 for domestic students, 7/1 priority date for international students; for spring admission, 11/1 for domestic students, 11/1 priority date for international students. Applications are processed on a rolling basis. Application fee: $50. Electronic applications accepted. *Expenses:* Tuition, state resident: full-time $3776; part-time $209.77 per credit hour. Tuition, nonresident: full-time $10,183; part-time $565.77 per credit hour. *Required fees:* $2037; $446.50 per credit hour. *Financial support:* In 2013–14, 9 research assistantships (averaging $6,240 per year), 7 teaching assistantships (averaging $6,240 per year) were awarded; career-related internships or fieldwork, Federal Work-Study, institutionally sponsored loans, and tuition waivers (partial) also available. Support available to part-time students. Financial award application deadline: 4/1; financial award applicants required to submit FAFSA. *Faculty research:* Operations, finance, marketing. *Total annual research expenditures:* $30,000. *Unit head:* Dr. Munir Quddus, Dean, 936-261-9200, Fax: 936-261-9241, E-mail: cob@pvamu.edu. *Application contact:* Dr. John Dyck, Director, Graduate Programs in Business, 936-261-9217, Fax: 936-261-9232, E-mail: cob@pvamu.edu.
Website: http://www.pvamu.edu.

Providence College, School of Business, Providence, RI 02918. Offers accounting (MBA); finance (MBA); international business (MBA); management (MBA); marketing (MBA); not-for-profit organizations (MBA). Part-time and evening/weekend programs available. *Faculty:* 14 full-time (5 women), 3 part-time/adjunct (1 woman). *Students:* 68 full-time (25 women), 54 part-time (25 women); includes 12 minority (3 Black or African American, non-Hispanic/Latino; 1 Asian, non-Hispanic/Latino; 6 Hispanic/Latino; 2 Two or more races, non-Hispanic/Latino), 7 international. Average age 25. 43 applicants, 95% accepted, 36 enrolled. In 2013, 38 master's awarded. *Degree requirements:* For master's, thesis optional. *Entrance requirements:* For master's, GMAT. Additional exam requirements/recommendations for international students: Required—TOEFL (minimum score 550 paper-based; 80 iBT). *Application deadline:* For fall admission, 7/15 priority date for domestic and international students; for spring admission, 11/15 priority date for domestic and international students; for summer admission, 4/15 priority date for domestic students. Applications are processed on a rolling basis. Application fee: $55. *Expenses:* Contact institution. *Financial support:* Federal Work-Study, institutionally sponsored loans, and unspecified assistantships available. Support available to part-time students. Financial award application deadline: 8/1; financial award applicants required to submit FAFSA. *Unit head:* Jacqueline Elcik, Director, 401-865-2131, E-mail: jelcik@providence.edu. *Application contact:* MBA Program, 401-865-2294, E-mail: mba@providence.edu.
Website: http://www.providence.edu/business/Pages/default.aspx.

Purdue University Calumet, Graduate Studies Office, School of Management, Hammond, IN 46323-2094. Offers accountancy (M Acc); business administration (MBA); business administration for executives (EMBA). Part-time and evening/weekend programs available. *Entrance requirements:* For master's, GMAT. Additional exam requirements/recommendations for international students: Required—TOEFL. Electronic applications accepted.

Queens College of the City University of New York, Division of Graduate Studies, Social Science Division, Department of Accounting, Flushing, NY 11367-1597. Offers MS.

Regis University, College for Professional Studies, School of Management, MBA Program, Denver, CO 80221-1099. Offers finance and accounting (MBA); general business (MBA); health industry leadership (MBA); marketing (MBA); operations management (MBA); organizational performance management (MBA); strategic management (MBA). Part-time and evening/weekend programs available. Postbaccalaureate distance learning degree programs offered (no on-campus study). *Faculty:* 10 full-time (3 women), 74 part-time/adjunct (17 women). *Students:* 386 full-time (183 women), 269 part-time (134 women); includes 190 minority (38 Black or African American, non-Hispanic/Latino; 2 American Indian or Alaska Native, non-Hispanic/Latino; 30 Asian, non-Hispanic/Latino; 109 Hispanic/Latino; 1 Native Hawaiian or other Pacific Islander, non-Hispanic/Latino; 10 Two or more races, non-Hispanic/Latino), 11 international. Average age 42. 152 applicants, 91% accepted, 112 enrolled. In 2013, 318 master's awarded. *Degree requirements:* For master's, thesis (for some programs), final research project. *Entrance requirements:* For master's, official transcript reflecting baccalaureate degree awarded from regionally-accredited college or university, work experience, resume, letters of recommendation. Additional exam requirements/recommendations for international students: Required—TOEFL (minimum score 550 paper-based; 82 iBT). *Application deadline:* Applications are processed on a rolling basis. Application fee: $75. Electronic applications accepted. *Expenses:* Contact institution. *Financial support:* In 2013–14, 22 students received support. Federal Work-Study and scholarships/grants available. Financial award application deadline: 4/15; financial award applicants required to submit FAFSA. *Unit head:* Dr. Anthony Vrba, Interim Dean, 303-964-5384, Fax: 303-964-5538, E-mail: avrba@regis.edu. *Application contact:* Sarah Engel, Director of Admissions, 303-458-4900, Fax: 303-964-5534, E-mail: regisadm@regis.edu.
Website: http://www.regis.edu/CPS/Academics/Degrees-and-Programs/Graduate-Programs/MBA-College-for-Professional-Studies.aspx.

Regis University, College for Professional Studies, School of Management, MS in Accounting Program, Denver, CO 80221-1099. Offers MS. Part-time and evening/weekend programs available. Postbaccalaureate distance learning degree programs offered (no on-campus study). *Faculty:* 3 full-time (1 woman), 16 part-time/adjunct (4 women). *Students:* 64 full-time (38 women), 47 part-time (25 women); includes 33 minority (9 Black or African American, non-Hispanic/Latino; 8 Asian, non-Hispanic/Latino; 12 Hispanic/Latino; 1 Native Hawaiian or other Pacific Islander, non-Hispanic/Latino; 3 Two or more races, non-Hispanic/Latino), 2 international. Average age 39. 21 applicants, 90% accepted, 14 enrolled. In 2013, 41 master's awarded. *Degree*

requirements: For master's, thesis (for some programs), capstone and final research project. *Entrance requirements:* For master's, official transcript reflecting baccalaureate degree awarded from regionally-accredited college or university, work experience, resume, letters of recommendation. Additional exam requirements/recommendations for international students: Required—TOEFL (minimum score 550 paper-based; 82 iBT). *Application deadline:* Applications are processed on a rolling basis. Application fee: $75. Electronic applications accepted. *Expenses:* Contact institution. *Financial support:* Federal Work-Study and scholarships/grants available. Financial award application deadline: 4/15; financial award applicants required to submit FAFSA. *Unit head:* Dr. Anthony Vrba, Interim Dean, 303-964-5384, Fax: 303-964-5538. *Application contact:* Sarah Engel, Director of Admissions, 303-458-4900, Fax: 303-964-5534, E-mail: regisadm@regis.edu.
Website: http://www.regis.edu/CPS/Academics/Degrees-and-Programs/Graduate-Programs/MS-Accounting.aspx.

Rhode Island College, School of Graduate Studies, School of Management, Department of Accounting and Computer Information Systems, Providence, RI 02908-1991. Offers accounting (MP Ac); financial planning (CGS). *Accreditation:* AACSB. Part-time and evening/weekend programs available. *Faculty:* 1 (woman) full-time, 2 part-time/adjunct (1 woman). *Students:* 7 full-time (4 women), 21 part-time (9 women); includes 4 minority (2 Asian, non-Hispanic/Latino; 2 Hispanic/Latino). Average age 26. In 2013, 13 master's awarded. *Entrance requirements:* For master's, GMAT (unless applicant is a CPA or has passed a state bar exam); for CGS, GMAT, bachelor's degree from an accredited college or university, official transcripts of all undergraduate and graduate records. Additional exam requirements/recommendations for international students: Recommended—TOEFL (minimum score 550 paper-based; 79 iBT). *Application deadline:* For fall admission, 3/1 for domestic students. Applications are processed on a rolling basis. Application fee: $50. *Expenses:* Tuition, state resident: full-time $8928; part-time $372 per credit hour. Tuition, nonresident: full-time $17,376; part-time $724 per credit hour. *Required fees:* $602; $22 per credit. $72 per term. *Financial support:* Federal Work-Study, scholarships/grants, and health care benefits available. Support available to part-time students. Financial award application deadline: 5/15; financial award applicants required to submit FAFSA. *Unit head:* Prof. Jane Przybyla, Chair, 401-456-8036. *Application contact:* Graduate Studies, 401-456-8700.
Website: http://www.ric.edu/accountingComputerInformationSystems/.

Rhodes College, Department of Commerce and Business, Memphis, TN 38112-1690. Offers accounting (MS). Part-time programs available. *Entrance requirements:* For master's, GMAT. Additional exam requirements/recommendations for international students: Required—TOEFL (minimum score 550 paper-based).

Rider University, College of Business Administration, Program in Accountancy, Lawrenceville, NJ 08648-3001. Offers M Acc. *Accreditation:* AACSB. *Entrance requirements:* For master's, GMAT, resume. Additional exam requirements/recommendations for international students: Required—TOEFL (minimum score 550 paper-based). Electronic applications accepted. *Faculty research:* Financial reporting, corporate governance, information technology, ethics, pedagogy.

Robert Morris University Illinois, Morris Graduate School of Management, Chicago, IL 60605. Offers accounting (MBA); accounting/finance (MBA); business analytics (MIS); design and media (MM); educational technology (MM); health care administration (MM); higher education administration (MM); human resource management (MBA); information security (MIS); information systems (MIS); law enforcement administration (MM); management (MBA); management/finance (MBA); management/human resource management (MBA); mobile computing (MIS); sports administration (MM). Part-time and evening/weekend programs available. *Faculty:* 12 full-time (5 women), 18 part-time/adjunct (4 women). *Students:* 240 full-time (128 women), 195 part-time (127 women); includes 242 minority (147 Black or African American, non-Hispanic/Latino; 2 American Indian or Alaska Native, non-Hispanic/Latino; 24 Asian, non-Hispanic/Latino; 63 Hispanic/Latino; 1 Native Hawaiian or other Pacific Islander, non-Hispanic/Latino; 5 Two or more races, non-Hispanic/Latino), 26 international. Average age 33. 210 applicants, 63% accepted, 116 enrolled. In 2013, 278 master's awarded. *Entrance requirements:* For master's, official transcripts, two letters of recommendation. Additional exam requirements/recommendations for international students: Required—TOEFL (minimum score 550 paper-based). *Application deadline:* Applications are processed on a rolling basis. Application fee: $20 ($100 for international students). Electronic applications accepted. *Expenses: Tuition:* Full-time $14,400; part-time $2400 per course. *Financial support:* In 2013–14, 488 students received support. Federal Work-Study and scholarships/grants available. Support available to part-time students. Financial award applicants required to submit FAFSA. *Unit head:* Kayed Akkawi, Dean for Morris Graduate School of Management, 312-935-6050, Fax: 312-935-6020, E-mail: kakkawi@robertmorris.edu. *Application contact:* Fernando Villeda, Dean of Graduate Enrollment, 312-935-6050, Fax: 312-935-6020, E-mail: fvilleda@robertmorris.edu.

Rochester Institute of Technology, Graduate Enrollment Services, Saunders College of Business, Program in Accounting, Rochester, NY 14623-5603. Offers MBA. Part-time programs available. *Students:* 22 full-time (14 women), 4 part-time (1 woman); includes 2 minority (1 Black or African American, non-Hispanic/Latino; 1 Asian, non-Hispanic/Latino), 7 international. Average age 27. 60 applicants, 47% accepted, 16 enrolled. In 2013, 16 master's awarded. *Entrance requirements:* For master's, GMAT or GRE. Additional exam requirements/recommendations for international students: Required—PTE (minimum score 63), TOEFL (minimum score 580 paper-based; 92 iBT) or IELTS (minimum score 7). *Application deadline:* For fall admission, 2/15 for domestic and international students; for winter admission, 11/1 for domestic students; for spring admission, 2/1 for domestic students. Applications are processed on a rolling basis. Application fee: $60. Electronic applications accepted. *Expenses: Tuition:* Full-time $37,236; part-time $1552 per credit hour. *Required fees:* $250. *Financial support:* Research assistantships with partial tuition reimbursements, teaching assistantships with partial tuition reimbursements, career-related internships or fieldwork, scholarships/grants, and unspecified assistantships available. Support available to part-time students. Financial award applicants required to submit FAFSA. *Faculty research:* Formation and taxation of business entities, auditor independence: the conundrum of tax services, ethics in accounting and business or the lack thereof, accounting crisis: a curricular response. *Unit head:* Charles Ackley, Graduate Program Director, 585-475-6916, E-mail: cackley@saunders.rit.edu. *Application contact:* Diane Ellison, Assistant Vice President, Graduate Enrollment Services, 585-475-2229, Fax: 585-475-7164, E-mail: gradinfo@rit.edu.
Website: http://saunders.rit.edu/graduate/index.php.

Rocky Mountain College, Program in Accountancy, Billings, MT 59102-1796. Offers M Acc. Part-time programs available. *Entrance requirements:* Additional exam requirements/recommendations for international students: Required—TOEFL (minimum score 570 paper-based; 88 iBT), IELTS (minimum score 6.5). Electronic applications accepted.

Roosevelt University, Graduate Division, Walter E. Heller College of Business Administration, Program in Accounting, Chicago, IL 60605. Offers MSA. Part-time and evening/weekend programs available. *Entrance requirements:* For master's, GMAT.

Rowan University, Graduate School, William G. Rohrer College of Business, Program in Accounting, Glassboro, NJ 08028-1701. Offers CAGS. Part-time and evening/weekend programs available. *Students:* 5 full-time (1 woman), 12 part-time (6 women); includes 2 minority (1 Black or African American, non-Hispanic/Latino; 1 Hispanic/Latino). Average age 30. 9 applicants, 78% accepted, 6 enrolled. *Entrance requirements:* Additional exam requirements/recommendations for international students: Required—TOEFL. *Application deadline:* Applications are processed on a rolling basis. Application fee: $65 ($200 for international students). Electronic applications accepted. *Expenses: Tuition, area resident:* Part-time $638 per credit. Tuition, state resident: full-time $5742. *Required fees:* $142 per credit. Tuition and fees vary according to course level and program. *Financial support:* Career-related internships or fieldwork, Federal Work-Study, and unspecified assistantships available. Support available to part-time students. *Unit head:* Dr. Horacio Sosa, Dean, College of Graduate and Continuing Education, 856-256-4747, Fax: 856-256-5638, E-mail: sosa@rowan.edu. *Application contact:* Karen Haynes, Graduate Coordinator, 856-256-4052, E-mail: haynes@rowan.edu.

Rutgers, The State University of New Jersey, Newark, Graduate School, Program in Management, Newark, NJ 07102. Offers accounting (PhD); accounting information systems (PhD); computer information systems (PhD); finance (PhD); information technology (PhD); international business (PhD); management science (PhD); marketing (PhD); organization management (PhD). Program offered jointly with New Jersey Institute of Technology. *Accreditation:* AACSB. *Degree requirements:* For doctorate, thesis/dissertation, cumulative exams. *Entrance requirements:* For doctorate, GMAT or GRE General Test, minimum undergraduate B average. Additional exam requirements/recommendations for international students: Required—TOEFL. Electronic applications accepted. *Faculty research:* Technology management, leadership and teams, consumer behavior, financial and markets, logistics.

Rutgers, The State University of New Jersey, Newark, Rutgers Business School–Newark and New Brunswick, Doctoral Programs in Management, Newark, NJ 07102. Offers accounting (PhD); accounting information systems (PhD); economics (PhD); finance (PhD); individualized study (PhD); information technology (PhD); international business (PhD); management science (PhD); marketing science (PhD); organizational management (PhD); science, technology and management (PhD); supply chain management (PhD). *Degree requirements:* For doctorate, comprehensive exam, thesis/dissertation. *Entrance requirements:* For doctorate, GRE or GMAT. Additional exam requirements/recommendations for international students: Required—TOEFL (minimum score 550 paper-based; 79 iBT). Electronic applications accepted.

Sacred Heart University, Graduate Programs, John F. Welch College of Business, Department of Management, Fairfield, CT 06825-1000. Offers accounting (Certificate); business (MBA); human resource management (MS); international business (Certificate); leadership (Certificate); marketing (Certificate). *Faculty:* 6 full-time (3 women), 2 part-time/adjunct (both women). *Students:* 24 full-time (9 women), 141 part-time (81 women); includes 29 minority (11 Black or African American, non-Hispanic/Latino; 5 Asian, non-Hispanic/Latino; 13 Hispanic/Latino), 4 international. Average age 32. 14 applicants, 79% accepted, 9 enrolled. In 2013, 81 master's awarded. *Entrance requirements:* For master's, GMAT (minimum score of 400), bachelor's degree in related field of business, microeconomics, macroeconomics or statistics; minimum GPA of 3.0. Additional exam requirements/recommendations for international students: Required—PTE; Recommended—TOEFL (minimum score 570 paper-based; 80 iBT), IELTS (minimum score 6.5). *Application deadline:* Applications are processed on a rolling basis. Application fee: $60. Electronic applications accepted. *Expenses: Tuition:* Full-time $22,775; part-time $617 per credit. *Financial support:* Applicants required to submit FAFSA. *Unit head:* Dr. John Chalykoff, Dean, 203-396-8084, E-mail: chalykoffj@sacredheart.edu. *Application contact:* Kathy Dilks, Executive Director of Graduate Admissions, 203-365-7619, Fax: 203-365-4732, E-mail: dilksk@sacredheart.edu.
Website: http://www.sacredheart.edu/academics/johnfwelchcollegeofbusiness/.

St. Ambrose University, College of Business, Program in Accounting, Davenport, IA 52803-2898. Offers MAC. Part-time and evening/weekend programs available. *Degree requirements:* For master's, comprehensive exam (for some programs), thesis or alternative, capstone seminar. *Entrance requirements:* For master's, GMAT. Electronic applications accepted.

St. Edward's University, School of Management and Business, Area of Business Administration, Austin, TX 78704. Offers accounting (MBA); business management (MBA); finance (Certificate); global entrepreneurship (MBA); marketing (MBA). Part-time and evening/weekend programs available. *Students:* 29 full-time (12 women), 181 part-time (85 women); includes 88 minority (15 Black or African American, non-Hispanic/Latino; 1 American Indian or Alaska Native, non-Hispanic/Latino; 4 Asian, non-Hispanic/Latino; 61 Hispanic/Latino; 7 Two or more races, non-Hispanic/Latino), 10 international. Average age 33. 85 applicants, 79% accepted, 38 enrolled. In 2013, 79 master's awarded. *Degree requirements:* For master's, minimum of 24 resident hours. *Entrance requirements:* For master's, GMAT or GRE General Test, minimum GPA of 2.75 in last 60 hours of course work. Additional exam requirements/recommendations for international students: Required—TOEFL (minimum score 79 iBT) or IELTS (minimum score 6). *Application deadline:* For fall admission, 6/1 priority date for domestic and international students; for spring admission, 10/1 priority date for domestic and international students; for summer admission, 3/1 priority date for domestic and international students. Applications are processed on a rolling basis. Application fee: $50. Electronic applications accepted. *Expenses: Tuition:* Full-time $20,664; part-time $1148 per credit hour. *Required fees:* $50 per trimester. Full-time tuition and fees vary according to course load and program. *Unit head:* Dr. Stan Horner, Director, 512-428-1279, Fax: 512-448-8492, E-mail: stanleyh@stedwards.edu. *Application contact:* Office of Admission, 512-448-8500, Fax: 512-464-8877, E-mail: seu.admit@stedwards.edu.
Website: http://www.stedwards.edu.

St. Edward's University, School of Management and Business, Program in Accounting, Austin, TX 78704. Offers M Ac. Part-time and evening/weekend programs available. *Students:* 10 full-time (5 women), 37 part-time (22 women); includes 10 minority (1 Black or African American, non-Hispanic/Latino; 1 Asian, non-Hispanic/Latino; 8 Hispanic/Latino), 3 international. Average age 31. 26 applicants, 65% accepted, 10 enrolled. In 2013, 14 master's awarded. *Degree requirements:* For master's, minimum of 24 resident hours. *Entrance requirements:* For master's, GMAT or GRE General Test, minimum GPA of 2.75 in last 60 hours of course work and in accounting. Additional exam requirements/recommendations for international students: Required—TOEFL (minimum score 79 iBT) or IELTS (minimum score 6). *Application deadline:* For fall admission, 6/1 priority date for domestic and international students; for spring admission, 10/1 priority date for domestic and international students; for summer admission, 3/1 priority date for domestic and international students. Applications are processed on a rolling basis. Application fee: $50. Electronic applications accepted. *Expenses: Tuition:* Full-time $20,664; part-time $1148 per credit hour. *Required fees:* $50 per trimester. Full-time tuition and fees vary according to course load and program. *Unit head:* Dr. Louise E. Single, Director, 512-492-3114, Fax: 512-448-8492, E-mail: louises@stedwards.edu. *Application contact:* Office of Admission, 512-448-8500, Fax: 512-464-8877, E-mail: seu.admit@stedwards.edu.
Website: http://www.stedwards.edu.

Accounting

St. Francis College, Program in Professional Accountancy, Brooklyn Heights, NY 11201-4398. Offers MS.

St. John's University, The Peter J. Tobin College of Business, Department of Accounting and Taxation, Program in Accounting, Queens, NY 11439. Offers accounting (MBA, MS); controllership (MBA, Adv C). *Accreditation:* AACSB. Part-time and evening/weekend programs available. Postbaccalaureate distance learning degree programs offered (no on-campus study). *Students:* 208 full-time (134 women), 69 part-time (32 women); includes 69 minority (12 Black or African American, non-Hispanic/Latino; 40 Asian, non-Hispanic/Latino; 15 Hispanic/Latino; 1 Native Hawaiian or other Pacific Islander, non-Hispanic/Latino; 1 Two or more races, non-Hispanic/Latino), 134 international. Average age 25. 305 applicants, 77% accepted, 122 enrolled. In 2013, 151 master's awarded. *Degree requirements:* For master's, comprehensive exam (for some programs), thesis optional. *Entrance requirements:* For master's, GMAT, 2 letters of recommendation, resume, transcripts, statement of goals, bachelor's degree in business; for Adv C, GMAT, 2 letters of recommendation, resume, undergraduate and graduate transcript, essay, MBA. Additional exam requirements/recommendations for international students: Required—TOEFL (minimum score 600 paper-based; 100 iBT), IELTS (minimum score 7). *Application deadline:* For fall admission, 5/1 priority date for domestic and international students; for spring admission, 11/1 priority date for domestic and international students. Applications are processed on a rolling basis. Application fee: $50. Electronic applications accepted. *Expenses:* Contact institution. *Financial support:* Research assistantships, scholarships/grants, and unspecified assistantships available. Support available to part-time students. Financial award application deadline: 3/1; financial award applicants required to submit FAFSA. *Unit head:* Dr. Adrian Fitzsimons, Chair, 718-990-7306, E-mail: fitzsima@stjohns.edu. *Application contact:* Carol J. Swanberg, Assistant Dean/Director of Graduate Admissions, 718-990-1345, Fax: 718-990-5242, E-mail: tobingradnyc@stjohns.edu.

St. Joseph's College, Long Island Campus, Program in Accounting, Patchogue, NY 11772-2399. Offers MBA.

St. Joseph's College, New York, Graduate Programs, Programs in Business, Field of Accounting, Brooklyn, NY 11205-3688. Offers MBA.

Saint Joseph's College of Maine, Master of Accountancy Program, Standish, ME 04084. Offers M Acc. Part-time programs available. Postbaccalaureate distance learning degree programs offered (no on-campus study). *Entrance requirements:* For master's, baccalaureate degree with minimum cumulative GPA of 2.5; successful completion of each of the following prior to program enrollment: financial accounting, managerial accounting, introduction of finance/business finance and macroeconomics. Electronic applications accepted.

Saint Joseph's University, Erivan K. Haub School of Business, Professional MBA Program, Philadelphia, PA 19131-1395. Offers accounting (MBA, Postbaccalaureate Certificate); business intelligence (MBA); finance (MBA); general business (MBA); health and medical services administration (MBA); international business (MBA); international marketing (MBA); managing human capital (MBA); marketing (MBA); DO/MBA. DO/MBA offered jointly with Philadelphia College of Osteopathic Medicine. Part-time and evening/weekend programs available. *Students:* 81 full-time (37 women), 478 part-time (195 women); includes 85 minority (35 Black or African American, non-Hispanic/Latino; 1 American Indian or Alaska Native, non-Hispanic/Latino; 23 Asian, non-Hispanic/Latino; 13 Hispanic/Latino; 1 Native Hawaiian or other Pacific Islander, non-Hispanic/Latino; 12 Two or more races, non-Hispanic/Latino), 44 international. Average age 30. In 2013, 195 master's awarded. *Degree requirements:* For master's and Postbaccalaureate Certificate, minimum GPA of 3.0. *Entrance requirements:* For master's, GMAT or GRE, 2 letters of recommendation, resume, personal statement, official undergraduate and graduate transcripts; for Postbaccalaureate Certificate, official master's-level transcripts. Additional exam requirements/recommendations for international students: Required—TOEFL (minimum score 550 paper-based, 80 iBT), IELTS (minimum score 6.5), or PTE (minimum score 60). *Application deadline:* For fall admission, 7/15 priority date for domestic students, 5/15 priority date for international students; for spring admission, 11/15 priority date for domestic students, 10/15 priority date for international students; for summer admission, 4/15 priority date for domestic students, 2/15 priority date for international students. Applications are processed on a rolling basis. Application fee: $35. Electronic applications accepted. *Expenses:* Tuition: Part-time $786 per credit hour. Tuition and fees vary according to degree level and program. *Financial support:* In 2013–14, 2 research assistantships with partial tuition reimbursements (averaging $4,000 per year) were awarded; scholarships/grants and unspecified assistantships also available. Support available to part-time students. Financial award application deadline: 5/1; financial award applicants required to submit FAFSA. *Unit head:* Christine Hartmann, Director, MBA Program, 610-660-1659, Fax: 610-660-1599, E-mail: chartman@sju.edu. *Application contact:* Jeannine Lajeunesse, Assistant Director, MBA Program, 610-660-1695, Fax: 610-660-1599, E-mail: jlajeune@sju.edu.
Website: http://www.sju.edu/haubmba.

Saint Leo University, Graduate Business Studies, Saint Leo, FL 33574-6665. Offers accounting (M Acc, MBA); business (MBA); health care management (MBA); human resource management (MBA); information security management (MBA); marketing (MBA); marketing research and social media analytics (MBA); project management (MBA); sport business (MBA). Part-time and evening/weekend programs available. Postbaccalaureate distance learning degree programs offered (no on-campus study). *Faculty:* 48 full-time (12 women), 61 part-time/adjunct (21 women). *Students:* 1,855 full-time (1,020 women); includes 810 minority (587 Black or African American, non-Hispanic/Latino; 7 American Indian or Alaska Native, non-Hispanic/Latino; 36 Asian, non-Hispanic/Latino; 161 Hispanic/Latino; 3 Native Hawaiian or other Pacific Islander, non-Hispanic/Latino; 16 Two or more races, non-Hispanic/Latino), 33 international. Average age 38. In 2013, 905 master's awarded. *Entrance requirements:* For master's, GMAT (minimum score 500 if applicant has less than 3.0 in the last two years of undergraduate study), bachelor's degree with minimum GPA of 3.0 in the last 60 hours of coursework from regionally-accredited college or university; 2 years of professional work experience; resume; 2 letters of recommendation. Additional exam requirements/recommendations for international students: Required—TOEFL (minimum score 550 paper-based; 80 iBT). *Application deadline:* For fall admission, 7/1 priority date for domestic and international students; for spring admission, 11/12 priority date for domestic students, 11/1 for international students. Applications are processed on a rolling basis. Application fee: $80. Electronic applications accepted. *Expenses:* Tuition: Full-time $12,114; part-time $673 per semester hour. Tuition and fees vary according to degree level, campus/location and program. *Financial support:* In 2013–14, 116 students received support. Career-related internships or fieldwork, Federal Work-Study, scholarships/grants, and health care benefits available. Financial award application deadline: 3/1; financial award applicants required to submit FAFSA. *Unit head:* Dr. Lorrie McGovern, Assistant Dean, Graduate Studies in Business, 352-588-7390, Fax: 352-588-8585, E-mail: mbaslu@saintleo.edu. *Application contact:* Joshua Stagner, Director of Graduate Admission, 800-707-8846, Fax: 352-588-7873, E-mail: grad.admissions@saintleo.edu.
Website: http://www.saintleo.edu/academics/graduate.aspx.

Saint Louis University, Graduate Education, John Cook School of Business, Department of Accounting, St. Louis, MO 63103-2097. Offers M Acct, MBA. Part-time and evening/weekend programs available. *Entrance requirements:* For master's, GMAT. Additional exam requirements/recommendations for international students: Required—TOEFL (minimum score 570 paper-based; 88 iBT). Electronic applications accepted. *Expenses:* Contact institution. *Faculty research:* Tax policy, market valuation/corporate governance, foreign currency translation, accounting for income taxes, earnings quality.

St. Mary's University, Graduate School, Bill Greehey School of Business, Program in Accounting, San Antonio, TX 78228-8507. Offers MBA. Part-time programs available. Postbaccalaureate distance learning degree programs offered (minimal on-campus study). *Degree requirements:* For master's, comprehensive exam. *Entrance requirements:* For master's, GMAT. Additional exam requirements/recommendations for international students: Required—TOEFL (minimum score 550 paper-based; 80 iBT). Electronic applications accepted.

Saint Mary's University of Minnesota, Schools of Graduate and Professional Programs, Graduate School of Business and Technology, Accountancy Program, Winona, MN 55987-1399. Offers MS. Postbaccalaureate distance learning degree programs offered. *Unit head:* Melanie Torborg, Program Director, 612-238-4525, E-mail: mtorborg@smumn.edu. *Application contact:* Russell Kreager, Director of Admissions for Graduate and Professional Programs, 612-728-5207, Fax: 612-728-5121, E-mail: rkreager@smumn.edu.
Website: http://www.smumn.edu/graduate-home/areas-of-study/graduate-school-of-business-technology/ms-in-accountancy.

Saint Peter's University, Graduate Business Programs, Program in Accountancy, Jersey City, NJ 07306-5997. Offers MS, MBA/MS. Part-time and evening/weekend programs available. *Entrance requirements:* Additional exam requirements/recommendations for international students: Required—TOEFL. Electronic applications accepted.

St. Thomas University, School of Business, Department of Management, Miami Gardens, FL 33054-6459. Offers accounting (MBA); general management (MSM, Certificate); health management (MBA, MSM, Certificate); human resource management (MBA, MSM, Certificate); international business (MBA, MIB, MSM, Certificate); justice administration (MSM, Certificate); management accounting (MSM, Certificate); public management (MSM, Certificate); sports administration (MS). Part-time and evening/weekend programs available. *Degree requirements:* For master's, comprehensive exam. *Entrance requirements:* For master's, interview, minimum GPA of 3.0 or GMAT. Additional exam requirements/recommendations for international students: Required—TOEFL (minimum score 550 paper-based; 79 iBT). Electronic applications accepted.

Salisbury University, Program in Business Administration, Salisbury, MD 21801. Offers accounting (MBA); business administration (MBA). *Accreditation:* AACSB. Part-time and evening/weekend programs available. *Faculty:* 5 full-time (1 woman). *Students:* 18 full-time (10 women), 6 part-time (0 women); includes 1 minority (Black or African American, non-Hispanic/Latino), 2 international. Average age 26. 49 applicants, 37% accepted, 18 enrolled. In 2013, 26 master's awarded. *Entrance requirements:* For master's, GMAT, resume, 2 recommendations, essay, foundation course completions with minimum C grade. Additional exam requirements/recommendations for international students: Required—TOEFL (minimum score 550 paper-based; 79 iBT), IELTS (minimum score 6.5). *Application deadline:* For fall admission, 3/1 priority date for domestic and international students; for spring admission, 10/15 for domestic students. Application fee: $50. Electronic applications accepted. *Expenses:* Tuition, area resident: Part-time $342 per credit hour. Tuition, state resident: part-time $342 per credit hour. Tuition, nonresident: part-time $631 per credit hour. *Required fees:* $76 per credit hour. Tuition and fees vary according to program. *Financial support:* In 2013–14, 1 teaching assistantship with full tuition reimbursement (averaging $5,000 per year) was awarded; institutionally sponsored loans, scholarships/grants, and unspecified assistantships also available. Support available to part-time students. Financial award application deadline: 3/1; financial award applicants required to submit FAFSA. *Faculty research:* Supply chain management, accounting. *Unit head:* Yvonne Downie, Director of MBA Program, 410-548-3983, E-mail: yxdownie@salisbury.edu. *Application contact:* Kristi Horner, Administrative Assistant, MBA Program Office and Global Programs, 410-548-3377, E-mail: kmhorner@salisbury.edu.
Website: http://mba.salisbury.edu.

Sam Houston State University, College of Business Administration, Department of Accounting, Huntsville, TX 77341. Offers MS. Part-time programs available. *Faculty:* 13 full-time (6 women), 1 (woman) part-time/adjunct. *Students:* 21 full-time (8 women), 10 part-time (8 women); includes 4 minority (1 Asian, non-Hispanic/Latino; 3 Hispanic/Latino), 6 international. Average age 26. 23 applicants, 91% accepted, 12 enrolled. In 2013, 30 master's awarded. *Degree requirements:* For master's, comprehensive exam. *Entrance requirements:* For master's, GMAT. Additional exam requirements/recommendations for international students: Required—TOEFL (minimum score 550 paper-based; 79 iBT), IELTS (minimum score 6.5). *Application deadline:* For fall admission, 8/1 for domestic students, 6/25 for international students; for spring admission, 12/1 for domestic students, 11/12 for international students. Applications are processed on a rolling basis. Application fee: $45 ($75 for international students). Electronic applications accepted. *Financial support:* Career-related internships or fieldwork, Federal Work-Study, institutionally sponsored loans, scholarships/grants, tuition waivers (partial), and unspecified assistantships available. Support available to part-time students. Financial award application deadline: 5/31; financial award applicants required to submit FAFSA. *Unit head:* Dr. Philip Morris, Chair, 936-294-1259, E-mail: morris@shsu.edu. *Application contact:* Rick Thaler, Associate Director, Graduate Studies and Distance Learning, 936-294-1239, Fax: 936-294-3612, E-mail: busgrad@shsu.edu.

San Diego State University, Graduate and Research Affairs, College of Business Administration, Charles W. Lamden School of Accountancy, San Diego, CA 92182. Offers MS. *Accreditation:* AACSB. *Degree requirements:* For master's, thesis or alternative. *Entrance requirements:* For master's, GMAT, resume, letters of reference. Additional exam requirements/recommendations for international students: Required—TOEFL. Electronic applications accepted.

San Francisco State University, Division of Graduate Studies, College of Business, Department of Accounting, San Francisco, CA 94132-1722. Offers accounting (MBA, MSA). Part-time programs available. *Entrance requirements:* For master's, GMAT, copy of transcripts, written statement of purpose, resume, two letters of reference. Additional exam requirements/recommendations for international students: Required—TOEFL or IELTS. Electronic applications accepted. *Unit head:* Dr. Joanne Duke, Director, 415-817-4300, E-mail: mba@sfsu.edu. *Application contact:* Armaan Moattari, Assistant Director, Graduate Programs, 415-817-4314, Fax: 817-4340, E-mail: amoatt@sfsu.edu. Website: http://cob.sfsu.edu/cob/graduate-programs/msa.cfm.

San Jose State University, Graduate Studies and Research, Lucas Graduate School of Business, Program in Accounting, San Jose, CA 95192-0001. Offers MS. *Degree requirements:* For master's, comprehensive exam, thesis or alternative. *Entrance*

requirements: For master's, GMAT, minimum GPA of 3.0. Electronic applications accepted.

Seattle University, Albers School of Business and Economics, Master of Professional Accounting Program, Seattle, WA 98122-1090. Offers MPAC. Part-time and evening/weekend programs available. *Faculty:* 24 full-time (7 women), 4 part-time/adjunct (3 women). *Students:* 63 full-time (49 women), 30 part-time (18 women); includes 23 minority (1 Black or African American, non-Hispanic/Latino; 2 American Indian or Alaska Native, non-Hispanic/Latino; 15 Asian, non-Hispanic/Latino; 2 Hispanic/Latino; 3 Two or more races, non-Hispanic/Latino), 49 international. Average age 26. 122 applicants, 57% accepted, 29 enrolled. In 2013, 30 master's awarded. *Entrance requirements:* For master's, GMAT, minimum GPA of 3.0. Additional exam requirements/recommendations for international students: Required—TOEFL (minimum score 580 paper-based; 92 iBT). *Application deadline:* For fall admission, 5/1 priority date for domestic students, 4/1 priority date for international students; for winter admission, 11/20 priority date for domestic students, 9/1 priority date for international students; for spring admission, 2/20 priority date for domestic students, 12/1 priority date for international students. Applications are processed on a rolling basis. Application fee: $55. Electronic applications accepted. *Financial support:* In 2013–14, 23 students received support. Career-related internships or fieldwork and Federal Work-Study available. Support available to part-time students. Financial award applicants required to submit FAFSA. *Unit head:* Dr. Bruce Koch, Program Director, 206-296-5700, Fax: 206-296-5795, E-mail: kochb@seattleu.edu. *Application contact:* Janet Shandley, Director of Graduate Admissions, 206-296-5900, Fax: 206-298-5656, E-mail: grad_admissions@seattleu.edu.
Website: http://www.seattleu.edu/albers/mpac/.

Seton Hall University, Stillman School of Business, Department of Accounting, South Orange, NJ 07079-2697. Offers accounting (MS, Certificate); professional accounting (MS); taxation (Certificate). Part-time and evening/weekend programs available. *Faculty:* 7 full-time (0 women), 1 part-time/adjunct (0 women). *Students:* 43 full-time (23 women), 109 part-time (45 women); includes 7 minority (1 Black or African American, non-Hispanic/Latino; 3 Asian, non-Hispanic/Latino; 2 Hispanic/Latino; 1 Native Hawaiian or other Pacific Islander, non-Hispanic/Latino). Average age 30. 106 applicants, 85% accepted, 67 enrolled. In 2013, 63 master's awarded. *Entrance requirements:* For master's, GMAT, GRE or CPA, advanced degree from AACSB institution, MS in a business discipline, professional degree (MD, JD, PhD, DVM, DDS, etc.), minimum undergraduate GPA of 3.0. Additional exam requirements/recommendations for international students: Required—TOEFL (minimum score 102 iBT), IELTS or PTE. *Application deadline:* For fall admission, 5/31 priority date for domestic students, 3/31 for international students; for spring admission, 10/31 for domestic students, 9/30 for international students. Applications are processed on a rolling basis. Application fee: $75. Electronic applications accepted. *Financial support:* In 2013–14, 2 students received support, including research assistantships with full tuition reimbursements available (averaging $23,956 per year); career-related internships or fieldwork, scholarships/grants, and unspecified assistantships also available. Support available to part-time students. Financial award application deadline: 6/30; financial award applicants required to submit FAFSA. *Faculty research:* Voluntary disclosure, international accounting, pension and retirement accounting, ethics in financial reporting, executive compensation. *Total annual research expenditures:* $20,000. *Unit head:* Dr. Mark Holtzman, Chair, 973-761-9133, Fax: 973-761-9217, E-mail: mark.holtzman@shu.edu. *Application contact:* Catherine Bianchi, Director of Graduate Admissions, 973-761-9262, Fax: 973-761-9208, E-mail: catherine.bianchi@shu.edu.
Website: http://www.shu.edu/academics/business/ms-programs.cfm.

Seton Hall University, Stillman School of Business, Programs in Business Administration, South Orange, NJ 07079-2697. Offers accounting (MBA); finance (MBA); information technology management (MBA); international business (MBA); management (MBA); marketing (MBA); sport management (MBA); supply chain management (MBA). Part-time and evening/weekend programs available. *Faculty:* 32 full-time (6 women), 20 part-time/adjunct (3 women). *Students:* 67 full-time (23 women), 162 part-time (66 women); includes 28 minority (7 Black or African American, non-Hispanic/Latino; 7 Asian, non-Hispanic/Latino; 6 Hispanic/Latino; 8 Native Hawaiian or other Pacific Islander, non-Hispanic/Latino). Average age 31. 216 applicants, 28% accepted, 39 enrolled. In 2013, 139 master's awarded. *Degree requirements:* For master's, 20 hours of community service (Social Responsibility Project). *Entrance requirements:* For master's, GMAT, GRE or CPA, advanced degree from AACSB institution, MS in a business discipline, professional degree (MD, JD, PhD, DVM, DDS, etc.), minimum undergraduate GPA of 3.0. Additional exam requirements/recommendations for international students: Required—TOEFL (minimum score 102 iBT), IELTS or PTE. *Application deadline:* For fall admission, 5/31 priority date for domestic students, 3/31 priority date for international students; for spring admission, 10/31 priority date for domestic students, 9/30 priority date for international students. Applications are processed on a rolling basis. Application fee: $75. Electronic applications accepted. *Financial support:* In 2013–14, research assistantships with full tuition reimbursements (averaging $23,956 per year) were awarded; career-related internships or fieldwork, Federal Work-Study, scholarships/grants, and unspecified assistantships also available. Support available to part-time students. Financial award application deadline: 6/30; financial award applicants required to submit FAFSA. *Faculty research:* Sport, hedge funds, international business, legal issues, disclosure and branding. *Total annual research expenditures:* $68,000. *Unit head:* Dr. Joyce Strawser, Dean, 973-761-9013, Fax: 973-761-9217, E-mail: joyce.strawser@shu.edu. *Application contact:* Catherine Bianchi, Director of Graduate Admissions, 973-761-9262, Fax: 973-761-9208, E-mail: catherine.bianchi@shu.edu.
Website: http://www.shu.edu/academics/business.

Seton Hill University, Program in Business Administration, Greensburg, PA 15601. Offers accounting (MBA); entrepreneurship (MBA, Certificate); management (MBA); sports management (MBA). Part-time and evening/weekend programs available. *Faculty:* 9 full-time (3 women), 6 part-time/adjunct (1 woman). *Students:* 37 full-time (15 women), 52 part-time (34 women); includes 4 minority (3 Black or African American, non-Hispanic/Latino; 1 Hispanic/Latino), 8 international. Average age 30. 93 applicants, 47% accepted, 28 enrolled. In 2013, 15 master's awarded. *Entrance requirements:* For master's, resume, 3 letters of recommendation, personal statement, transcripts. Additional exam requirements/recommendations for international students: Required—TOEFL (minimum score 600 paper-based; 100 iBT), IELTS (minimum score 6.5). *Application deadline:* Applications are processed on a rolling basis. Application fee: $0. Electronic applications accepted. *Expenses: Tuition:* Full-time $14,220; part-time $790 per credit. *Required fees:* $700; $34 per credit. $50 per semester. *Financial support:* Federal Work-Study, scholarships/grants, and tuition discounts available. Financial award application deadline: 8/15. *Faculty research:* Entrepreneurship, leadership and strategy, knowledge management, sports management, human resources. *Unit head:* Dr. Douglas Nelson, Director, 724-830-4738, E-mail: dnelson@setonhill.edu. *Application contact:* Laurel Komarny, Program Counselor, 724-838-4209, E-mail: lkomarny@setonhill.edu.
Website: http://www.setonhill.edu/academics/graduate_programs/mba.

Shorter University, Professional Studies, Rome, GA 30165. Offers accountancy (MAC); business administration (MBA); curriculum and instruction (M Ed); leadership (MA). Evening/weekend programs available. *Degree requirements:* For master's, project. *Entrance requirements:* For master's, minimum undergraduate GPA of 2.75 in last 60 hours, 3 years of work experience. Additional exam requirements/recommendations for international students: Required—TOEFL (minimum score 550 paper-based; 79 iBT). *Faculty research:* Systems design, leadership, pedagogy using technology.

Southeastern Louisiana University, College of Business, Hammond, LA 70402. Offers accounting (MBA); general (MBA). *Accreditation:* AACSB. *Faculty:* 12 full-time (1 woman). *Students:* 66 full-time (37 women), 20 part-time (12 women); includes 13 minority (8 Black or African American, non-Hispanic/Latino; 2 Asian, non-Hispanic/Latino; 3 Hispanic/Latino), 6 international. Average age 27. 37 applicants, 100% accepted, 23 enrolled. In 2013, 73 master's awarded. *Entrance requirements:* For master's, GMAT (minimum score 450), minimum cumulative GPA of 2.75 for all undergraduate work attempted or 3.0 all upper-division. Additional exam requirements/recommendations for international students: Required—TOEFL (minimum score 525 paper-based; 61 iBT), IELTS (minimum score 6). *Application deadline:* For fall admission, 7/15 priority date for domestic students, 6/1 priority date for international students; for spring admission, 12/1 priority date for domestic students, 10/1 priority date for international students. Applications are processed on a rolling basis. Application fee: $20 ($30 for international students). Electronic applications accepted. *Expenses:* Tuition, state resident: full-time $5047. Tuition, nonresident: full-time $17,066. *Required fees:* $1213. Tuition and fees vary according to degree level. *Financial support:* Career-related internships or fieldwork, Federal Work-Study, institutionally sponsored loans, and scholarships/grants available. Support available to part-time students. Financial award application deadline: 5/1; financial award applicants required to submit FAFSA. *Faculty research:* Ethical decision-making in accounting, entrepreneurship and emerging information, leadership and organizational performance. *Total annual research expenditures:* $18,824. *Unit head:* Dr. Antoinette Phillips, Interim Dean, 985-549-2258, Fax: 985-549-5038, E-mail: business@selu.edu. *Application contact:* Sandra Meyers, Graduate Admissions Analyst, 985-549-5620, Fax: 985-549-5882, E-mail: admissions@selu.edu.
Website: http://www.selu.edu/acad_research/colleges/bus/index.html.

Southeast Missouri State University, School of Graduate Studies, Harrison College of Business, Cape Girardeau, MO 63701-4799. Offers accounting (MBA); entrepreneurship (MBA); environmental management (MBA); financial management (MBA); general management (MBA); health administration (MBA); industrial management (MBA); international business (MBA); organizational management (MS); sport management (MBA). *Accreditation:* AACSB. Part-time and evening/weekend programs available. Postbaccalaureate distance learning degree programs offered (no on-campus study). *Faculty:* 27 full-time (7 women), 1 (woman) part-time/adjunct. *Students:* 59 full-time (27 women), 83 part-time (28 women); includes 10 minority (5 Black or African American, non-Hispanic/Latino; 3 Asian, non-Hispanic/Latino; 1 Hispanic/Latino; 1 Two or more races, non-Hispanic/Latino), 40 international. Average age 28. 77 applicants, 79% accepted, 48 enrolled. In 2013, 50 master's awarded. *Degree requirements:* For master's, variable foreign language requirement, comprehensive exam (for some programs), thesis or alternative, applied research project. *Entrance requirements:* For master's, GMAT or GRE, minimum undergraduate GPA of 2.5, C or better in prerequisite courses. Additional exam requirements/recommendations for international students: Required—TOEFL (minimum score 550 paper-based; 79 iBT), IELTS (minimum score 6), PTE (minimum score 53). *Application deadline:* For fall admission, 8/1 for domestic students, 6/1 for international students; for spring admission, 11/21 for domestic students, 10/1 for international students; for summer admission, 5/15 for domestic students. Applications are processed on a rolling basis. Application fee: $30 ($40 for international students). Electronic applications accepted. *Expenses:* Tuition, state resident: full-time $5139; part-time $285.50 per credit hour. Tuition, nonresident: full-time $9099; part-time $505.50 per credit hour. *Financial support:* In 2013–14, 52 students received support, including 12 teaching assistantships with full tuition reimbursements available (averaging $8,144 per year); career-related internships or fieldwork, Federal Work-Study, scholarships/grants, traineeships, tuition waivers (full), and unspecified assistantships also available. Financial award application deadline: 6/30; financial award applicants required to submit FAFSA. *Faculty research:* Ethics, corporate finance, generational difference, leadership, organizational justice. *Unit head:* Dr. Kenneth A. Heischmidt, Director, Graduate Business Studies, 573-651-2912, Fax: 573-651-5032, E-mail: kheischmidt@semo.edu. *Application contact:* Gail Amick, Admissions Specialist, 573-651-2590, Fax: 573-651-5936, E-mail: gamick@semo.edu.
Website: http://www.semo.edu/mba.

Southern Adventist University, School of Business and Management, Collegedale, TN 37315-0370. Offers accounting (MBA); church administration (MSA); church and nonprofit leadership (MBA); financial management (MFM); healthcare administration (MBA); management (MBA); marketing management (MBA); outdoor education (MSA). Part-time and evening/weekend programs available. Postbaccalaureate distance learning degree programs offered (no on-campus study). *Entrance requirements:* For master's, GMAT. Additional exam requirements/recommendations for international students: Required—TOEFL (minimum score 600 paper-based; 100 iBT). Electronic applications accepted.

Southern Illinois University Carbondale, Graduate School, College of Business and Administration, School of Accountancy, Carbondale, IL 62901-4701. Offers M Acc, PhD, JD/M Acc. *Accreditation:* AACSB. Part-time programs available. *Faculty:* 10 full-time (1 woman), 2 part-time/adjunct (both women). *Students:* 62 full-time (31 women), 13 part-time (7 women); includes 14 minority (11 Black or African American, non-Hispanic/Latino; 1 American Indian or Alaska Native, non-Hispanic/Latino; 1 Asian, non-Hispanic/Latino; 1 Hispanic/Latino), 21 international. 54 applicants, 63% accepted, 20 enrolled. In 2013, 47 master's awarded. *Degree requirements:* For doctorate, thesis/dissertation. *Entrance requirements:* For master's, GMAT, minimum GPA of 2.7; for doctorate, GMAT, minimum graduate GPA of 3.25. Additional exam requirements/recommendations for international students: Required—TOEFL. *Application deadline:* For fall admission, 6/15 priority date for domestic students. Applications are processed on a rolling basis. Application fee: $50. *Financial support:* In 2013–14, 15 students received support, including 6 research assistantships with full tuition reimbursements available, 6 teaching assistantships with full tuition reimbursements available; fellowships with full tuition reimbursements available, Federal Work-Study, and institutionally sponsored loans also available. Support available to part-time students. Financial award application deadline: 4/1. *Faculty research:* Not-for-profit accounting, SEC regulations, computers and accounting education, taxation. *Unit head:* Dr. Marcus Odom, Director, 618-453-2289, E-mail: modom@business.siu.edu. *Application contact:* Leslee Hammers, Administrative Clerk, 618-453-1400, E-mail: lhammers@business.siu.edu.

Southern Illinois University Edwardsville, Graduate School, School of Business, Department of Accounting, Edwardsville, IL 62026. Offers accountancy (MSA); taxation (MSA). *Accreditation:* AACSB. Part-time and evening/weekend programs available.

Faculty: 8 full-time (3 women). *Students:* 20 full-time (12 women), 14 part-time (11 women), 1 international. 23 applicants, 48% accepted. In 2013, 24 master's awarded. *Degree requirements:* For master's, thesis or alternative, final exam. *Entrance requirements:* For master's, GMAT. Additional exam requirements/recommendations for international students: Required—TOEFL (minimum score 550 paper-based, 79 iBT), IELTS (minimum score 6.5), Michigan Test of English Language Proficiency or PTE. *Application deadline:* For fall admission, 7/18 for domestic students, 6/1 for international students; for spring admission, 12/12 for domestic students, 10/1 for international students; for summer admission, 4/24 for domestic students, 3/1 for international students. Applications are processed on a rolling basis. Application fee: $30. Electronic applications accepted. *Expenses:* Tuition, state resident: full-time $3551. Tuition, nonresident: full-time $8378. *Financial support:* In 2013–14, 9 students received support, including 2 fellowships with full tuition reimbursements available (averaging $8,370 per year), 1 research assistantship with full tuition reimbursement available (averaging $9,585 per year), 6 teaching assistantships with full tuition reimbursements available (averaging $9,585 per year); institutionally sponsored loans, scholarships/grants, and unspecified assistantships also available. Financial award application deadline: 3/1; financial award applicants required to submit FAFSA. *Unit head:* Dr. Michael Costigan, Chair, 618-650-2633, E-mail: mcostig@siue.edu. *Application contact:* Melissa K. Mace, Assistant Director of Graduate and International Recruitment, 618-650-2756, Fax: 618-650-3618, E-mail: mmace@siue.edu.
Website: http://www.siue.edu/business/accounting/.

Southern Methodist University, Cox School of Business, MBA Program, Dallas, TX 75275. Offers accounting (MBA, PMBA); business administration (EMBA); finance (MBA); financial statement analysis (PMBA); general business (MBA); information technology and operations management (MBA); management (MBA); marketing (MBA); real estate (MBA); strategy (MBA); strategy and entrepreneurship (MBA); JD/MBA; MA/MBA. Part-time and evening/weekend programs available. *Entrance requirements:* For master's, GMAT. Additional exam requirements/recommendations for international students: Required—TOEFL. Electronic applications accepted. *Expenses:* Contact institution. *Faculty research:* Corporate finance, financial reporting, modeling consumer decision-making, competition between national brands and store brands, institutional determinants of firms' strategy.

Southern Methodist University, Cox School of Business, Program in Accounting, Dallas, TX 75275. Offers MSA. Part-time and evening/weekend programs available. *Entrance requirements:* For master's, GMAT. Additional exam requirements/recommendations for international students: Required—TOEFL. *Expenses:* Contact institution. *Faculty research:* Capital markets, taxation, business combinations, intangibles accounting, accounting history.

Southern New Hampshire University, School of Business, Manchester, NH 03106-1045. Offers accounting (MBA, MS, Graduate Certificate); accounting finance (MS); accounting/auditing (MS); accounting/forensic accounting (MS); accounting/taxation (MS); athletic administration (MBA, Graduate Certificate); business administration (IMBA, MBA, Certificate, Graduate Certificate), including accounting (Certificate), business administration (MBA), business information systems (Graduate Certificate), human resource management (Certificate); corporate social responsibility (MBA); entrepreneurship (MBA); finance (MBA, MS, Graduate Certificate); finance/corporate finance (MS); finance/investments and securities (MS); forensic accounting (MBA); healthcare informatics (MBA); healthcare management (MBA); human resource management (Graduate Certificate); information technology (MS, Graduate Certificate); information technology management (MBA); international business (Graduate Certificate); international business and information technology (Graduate Certificate); international finance (Graduate Certificate); international sport management (Graduate Certificate); justice studies (MBA); leadership of nonprofit organizations (Graduate Certificate); marketing (MBA, MS, Graduate Certificate); operations and project management (MS); operations and supply chain management (MBA, Graduate Certificate); organizational leadership (MS); project management (MBA, Graduate Certificate); Six Sigma (MBA); Six Sigma quality (Graduate Certificate); social media marketing (MBA); sport management (MBA, MS, Graduate Certificate); sustainability and environmental compliance (MBA); workplace conflict management (MBA); MBA/Certificate. *Accreditation:* ACBSP. Part-time and evening/weekend programs available. Postbaccalaureate distance learning degree programs offered (no on-campus study). Terminal master's awarded for partial completion of doctoral program. *Degree requirements:* For master's, one foreign language, comprehensive exam (for some programs), thesis or alternative. *Entrance requirements:* For master's, minimum GPA of 2.5. Additional exam requirements/recommendations for international students: Required—TOEFL (minimum score 500 paper-based). Electronic applications accepted.

Southern Oregon University, Graduate Studies, School of Business, Ashland, OR 97520. Offers accounting (Postbaccalaureate Certificate); business administration (MBA); international management (MIM). *Accreditation:* ACBSP. Part-time and evening/weekend programs available. Postbaccalaureate distance learning degree programs offered (minimal on-campus study). *Faculty:* 19 full-time (5 women), 7 part-time/adjunct (2 women). *Students:* 37 full-time (16 women), 75 part-time (31 women); includes 11 minority (2 Black or African American, non-Hispanic/Latino; 2 American Indian or Alaska Native, non-Hispanic/Latino; 2 Hispanic/Latino; 5 Two or more races, non-Hispanic/Latino), 26 international. Average age 35. 83 applicants, 71% accepted, 34 enrolled. *Degree requirements:* For master's, comprehensive exam. *Entrance requirements:* For master's, GMAT, minimum cumulative GPA of 3.0 in the last 90 quarter credits (60 semester credits) of undergraduate coursework. Additional exam requirements/recommendations for international students: Required—TOEFL (minimum score 540 paper-based; 76 iBT), IELTS (minimum score 6), ELPT (minimum score 964) or ELS (minimum score 112). *Application deadline:* For fall admission, 7/31 priority date for domestic and international students; for winter admission, 11/15 priority date for domestic students, 11/14 priority date for international students; for spring admission, 1/7 priority date for domestic and international students. Applications are processed on a rolling basis. Application fee: $50. Electronic applications accepted. *Expenses:* Tuition, state resident: full-time $13,635; part-time $378.72 per credit hour. Tuition, nonresident: full-time $17,042; part-time $473.40 per credit hour. *Required fees:* $408 per quarter. *Financial support:* In 2013–14, 7 students received support, including 7 research assistantships with partial tuition reimbursements available; career-related internships or fieldwork, institutionally sponsored loans, scholarships/grants, and unspecified assistantships also available. *Unit head:* Dr. Mark Siders, Graduate Program Coordinator, 541-552-6709, E-mail: sidersm@sou.edu. *Application contact:* Kelly Moutsatson, Director of Admissions, 541-552-6411, Fax: 541-552-8403, E-mail: admissions@sou.edu.
Website: http://www.sou.edu/business/graduate-programs.html.

Southern Polytechnic State University, School of Engineering Technology and Management, Department of Business Administration, Marietta, GA 30060-2896. Offers accounting (MBA, MSA); business administration (Graduate Transition Certificate); finance (MBA); general (MBA); management (MBA); management information systems (MBA); marketing (MBA); operations and technology management (MBA). *Accreditation:* ACBSP. Part-time and evening/weekend programs available. Postbaccalaureate distance learning degree programs offered (no on-campus study). *Degree requirements:* For master's, comprehensive exam (for some programs), capstone course and major field exam (for MBA); 30 semester hours of course work (for MSA). *Entrance requirements:* For master's, GMAT or GRE, letters of recommendation, statement of purpose, resume, minimum GPA of 2.75 or undergraduate degree in business with up to 6 transition courses; undergraduate degree in accounting from regionally-accredited school (for MSA). Additional exam requirements/recommendations for international students: Required—TOEFL (minimum score 550 paper-based; 79 iBT), IELTS (minimum score 6.5). Electronic applications accepted. *Faculty research:* Ethics, virtual reality, sustainability, management of technology, quality management, capacity planning, human-computer interaction/interface, enterprise integration planning, economic impact of educational institutions, behavioral accounting, accounting ethics, taxation, information security, visualization simulation, human-computer interaction, supply chain, logistics, economics.

Southern Utah University, Master of Accountancy/MBA Dual Degree Program, Cedar City, UT 84720-2498. Offers MBA/M Acc. Part-time programs available. Postbaccalaureate distance learning degree programs offered. *Students:* 2 full-time (0 women). Average age 30. 7 applicants, 43% accepted, 4 enrolled. *Entrance requirements:* Additional exam requirements/recommendations for international students: Required—TOEFL (minimum score 550 paper-based, 79 iBT) or IELTS (minimum score 6). *Application deadline:* For fall admission, 3/1 for domestic and international students; for spring admission, 10/1 for domestic and international students; for summer admission, 3/1 for domestic and international students. Applications are processed on a rolling basis. Application fee: $60 ($65 for international students). Electronic applications accepted. *Expenses:* Contact institution. *Financial support:* Unspecified assistantships available. *Application contact:* Paula Alger, Advisor/Curriculum Coordinator, 435-865-8157, Fax: 435-586-5493, E-mail: alger@suu.edu.
Website: http://www.suu.edu/business/grad.html.

Southern Utah University, Program in Accounting, Cedar City, UT 84720-2498. Offers M Acc. Part-time programs available. Postbaccalaureate distance learning degree programs offered. *Students:* 43 full-time (10 women), 24 part-time (14 women); includes 5 minority (3 Hispanic/Latino; 2 Native Hawaiian or other Pacific Islander, non-Hispanic/Latino), 1 international. Average age 29. 47 applicants, 79% accepted, 10 enrolled. In 2013, 39 master's awarded. *Entrance requirements:* For master's, GMAT or GRE, official transcripts of all academic work prior to admission with transcripts verifying minimum GPA of 3.0 for all work completed; three letters of recommendation from former/current college professors, assigned mentors, supervisors or associates (for non-SUU business majors). Additional exam requirements/recommendations for international students: Required—TOEFL (minimum score 550 paper-based, 79 iBT) or IELTS (minimum score 6). *Application deadline:* For fall admission, 3/1 for domestic and international students; for spring admission, 10/1 for domestic and international students; for summer admission, 3/1 for domestic and international students. Applications are processed on a rolling basis. Application fee: $60 ($65 for international students). Electronic applications accepted. *Expenses:* Contact institution. *Financial support:* Unspecified assistantships available. *Faculty research:* Cost accounting, intermediate accounting text, GAAP policy, statements on Standards for Accounting and Review Services (SSARS). *Unit head:* Dr. David Christensen, Chair, Accounting Department, 435-865-8058, Fax: 435-586-5493, E-mail: christensen@suu.edu. *Application contact:* Paula Alger, Advisor/Curriculum Coordinator, 435-865-8157, Fax: 435-586-5493, E-mail: alger@suu.edu.
Website: http://www.suu.edu/business/acct/macc.html.

Southwestern Adventist University, Business Administration Department, Keene, TX 76059. Offers accounting (MBA); finance (MBA); management/leadership (MBA). Part-time and evening/weekend programs available. *Degree requirements:* For master's, capstone course. *Entrance requirements:* For master's, GMAT, GRE General Test.

Southwestern College, Professional Studies Programs, Wichita, KS 67207. Offers accountancy (MA); business administration (MBA); leadership (MS); management (MS); security administration (MS); specialized ministries (MA); theological studies (MA). Part-time and evening/weekend programs available. Postbaccalaureate distance learning degree programs offered (minimal on-campus study). *Faculty:* 33 part-time/adjunct (6 women). *Students:* 125 part-time (48 women); includes 28 minority (12 Black or African American, non-Hispanic/Latino; 1 American Indian or Alaska Native, non-Hispanic/Latino; 2 Asian, non-Hispanic/Latino; 7 Hispanic/Latino; 6 Two or more races, non-Hispanic/Latino). Average age 37. 95 applicants, 57% accepted, 29 enrolled. In 2013, 85 master's awarded. *Degree requirements:* For master's, practicum/capstone project. *Entrance requirements:* For master's, baccalaureate degree; minimum GPA of 2.5 (for MA and MS), 3.0 (for MBA). Additional exam requirements/recommendations for international students: Required—TOEFL (minimum score 550 paper-based). *Application deadline:* For fall admission, 8/1 for domestic students; for spring admission, 12/1 for domestic students. Applications are processed on a rolling basis. Application fee: $0. Electronic applications accepted. *Expenses: Tuition:* Full-time $8968; part-time $498 per credit hour. Tuition and fees vary according to course level and program. *Financial support:* In 2013–14, 8 students received support. Federal Work-Study, tuition waivers (partial), and unspecified assistantships available. Financial award application deadline: 4/1; financial award applicants required to submit FAFSA. *Unit head:* Susan Backofen, Vice President for Enrollment Management, 888-684-5335 Ext. 214, Fax: 316-688-5218, E-mail: susan.backofen@sckans.edu. *Application contact:* Elmer Patterson, Enrollment Manager, 888-684-5335 Ext. 131, Fax: 316-688-5218, E-mail: elmer.patterson@sckans.edu.
Website: http://www.southwesterncollege.org.

State University of New York at New Paltz, Graduate School, School of Business, New Paltz, NY 12561. Offers business administration (MBA); public accountancy (MBA). Part-time and evening/weekend programs available. *Faculty:* 20 full-time (7 women), 2 part-time/adjunct (1 woman). *Students:* 54 full-time (29 women), 18 part-time (13 women); includes 15 minority (2 Black or African American, non-Hispanic/Latino; 8 Asian, non-Hispanic/Latino; 4 Hispanic/Latino; 1 Two or more races, non-Hispanic/Latino), 22 international. Average age 27. 48 applicants, 90% accepted, 30 enrolled. In 2013, 45 master's awarded. *Degree requirements:* For master's, internship. *Entrance requirements:* For master's, GMAT or GRE, minimum GPA of 3.0. Additional exam requirements/recommendations for international students: Required—TOEFL (minimum score 550 paper-based; 80 iBT), IELTS (minimum score 6.5). *Application deadline:* For fall admission, 5/15 priority date for domestic students, 5/15 for international students; for spring admission, 11/15 for domestic and international students. Applications are processed on a rolling basis. Application fee: $50. Electronic applications accepted. *Expenses:* Contact institution. *Financial support:* In 2013–14, 6 research assistantships with partial tuition reimbursements (averaging $5,000 per year), 1 teaching assistantship with partial tuition reimbursement (averaging $5,000 per year) were awarded; scholarships/grants, traineeships, and unspecified assistantships also available. Financial award application deadline: 8/1. *Faculty research:* Cognitive styles in management education, supporting SME e-commerce migration through e-learning, earnings management and board activity, trading future spread portfolio, global equity market correlation and volatility. *Unit head:* Dr. Chih-Yang Tsai, Interim Dean, 845-257-

2930, E-mail: mba@newpaltz.edu. *Application contact:* Aaron Hines, Director of MBA Program, 845-257-2968, E-mail: mba@newpaltz.edu. Website: http://mba.newpaltz.edu.

State University of New York College at Geneseo, Graduate Studies, School of Business, Geneseo, NY 14454. Offers accounting (MS). *Accreditation:* AACSB. *Faculty:* 4 full-time (1 woman), 1 part-time/adjunct (0 women). *Students:* 13 full-time (4 women); includes 1 minority (Asian, non-Hispanic/Latino), 1 international. Average age 25. 21 applicants, 100% accepted, 14 enrolled. In 2013, 13 master's awarded. *Entrance requirements:* For master's, GMAT, bachelor's degree in accounting. *Application deadline:* For fall admission, 2/1 priority date for domestic students; for spring admission, 9/1 for domestic students. Application fee: $50. *Expenses:* Tuition, state resident: full-time $8790; part-time $411 per credit hour. Tuition, nonresident: full-time $18,350; part-time $765 per credit hour. *Required fees:* $795; $32.90 per credit hour. *Financial support:* Application deadline: 4/1; applicants required to submit FAFSA. *Unit head:* Dr. Michael D. Schinski, Associate Professor, 585-245-5367, Fax: 585-245-5467, E-mail: schinski@geneseo.edu. *Application contact:* Dr. Harry Howe, Professor/Coordinator, 585-245-5465, Fax: 585-245-5467, E-mail: howeh@geneseo.edu.

State University of New York College at Old Westbury, School of Business, Old Westbury, NY 11568-0210. Offers accounting (MS); taxation (MS). Part-time and evening/weekend programs available. *Faculty:* 8 full-time (1 woman), 2 part-time/adjunct (0 women). *Students:* 39 full-time (19 women), 66 part-time (32 women); includes 31 minority (6 Black or African American, non-Hispanic/Latino; 12 Asian, non-Hispanic/Latino; 13 Hispanic/Latino). Average age 33. 65 applicants, 83% accepted, 36 enrolled. In 2013, 36 master's awarded. *Entrance requirements:* For master's, GMAT, 2 letters of recommendation. Additional exam requirements/recommendations for international students: Required—TOEFL (minimum score 550 paper-based). *Application deadline:* For fall admission, 6/15 priority date for domestic students; for spring admission, 11/15 priority date for domestic students. Applications are processed on a rolling basis. Application fee: $50. Electronic applications accepted. *Expenses:* Tuition, state resident: full-time $9370; part-time $390 per credit. Tuition, nonresident: full-time $16,680; part-time $695 per credit. *Required fees:* $45.85 per credit. $47 per term. *Faculty research:* Corporate governance, asset pricing, corporate finance, hedge funds, taxation. *Unit head:* Rita Buttermilch, Director of Graduate Business Programs, 516-876-3900, E-mail: buttermilchr@oldwestbury.edu. *Application contact:* Philip D'Angelo, Graduate Admissions Office, 516-876-3073, E-mail: enroll@oldwestbury.edu.

State University of New York Institute of Technology, Program in Accountancy, Utica, NY 13504-3050. Offers MS. *Accreditation:* AACSB. Part-time programs available. Postbaccalaureate distance learning degree programs offered (no on-campus study). *Faculty:* 6 full-time (1 woman). *Students:* 23 full-time (14 women), 54 part-time (38 women); includes 15 minority (8 Black or African American, non-Hispanic/Latino; 3 Asian, non-Hispanic/Latino; 3 Hispanic/Latino; 1 Two or more races, non-Hispanic/Latino), 1 international. Average age 34. 76 applicants, 51% accepted, 28 enrolled. In 2013, 21 master's awarded. *Degree requirements:* For master's, capstone courses. *Entrance requirements:* For master's, GMAT, one letter of reference, resume. Additional exam requirements/recommendations for international students: Required—TOEFL (minimum score 550 paper-based; 79 iBT), IELTS (minimum score 6.5). *Application deadline:* For fall admission, 8/1 priority date for domestic students, 7/1 for international students; for spring admission, 12/1 for domestic students, 11/1 for international students. Applications are processed on a rolling basis. Application fee: $60. Electronic applications accepted. *Expenses:* Tuition, state resident: full-time $9870; part-time $411 per credit hour. Tuition, nonresident: full-time $20,150; part-time $765 per credit hour. *Required fees:* $1180; $50.73 per credit hour. *Financial support:* In 2013–14, 4 students received support, including 2 fellowships with full tuition reimbursements available (averaging $7,266 per year), 2 research assistantships with full tuition reimbursements available (averaging $4,699 per year); unspecified assistantships also available. Financial award application deadline: 6/1; financial award applicants required to submit FAFSA. *Faculty research:* Cash flows, accounting earnings, stock price analysis. *Unit head:* Dr. Hoseoup Lee, Program Coordinator/Associate Professor, 315-792-7337, Fax: 315-792-7138, E-mail: hoseoup.lee@sunyit.edu. *Application contact:* Maryrose Raab, Coordinator of Graduate Center, 315-792-7347, Fax: 315-792-7221, E-mail: maryrose.raab@sunyit.edu. Website: http://www.sunyit.edu/programs/graduate/msacc/.

State University of New York Institute of Technology, Program in Business Administration in Technology Management, Utica, NY 13504-3050. Offers accounting and finance (MBA); business management (MBA); health services management (MBA); human resource management (MBA); marketing management (MBA). Part-time programs available. Postbaccalaureate distance learning degree programs offered (no on-campus study). *Faculty:* 10 full-time (2 women), 2 part-time/adjunct (1 woman). *Students:* 29 full-time (13 women), 89 part-time (26 women); includes 17 minority (5 Black or African American, non-Hispanic/Latino; 8 Asian, non-Hispanic/Latino; 3 Hispanic/Latino; 1 Two or more races, non-Hispanic/Latino), 1 international. Average age 33. 78 applicants, 54% accepted, 29 enrolled. In 2013, 57 master's awarded. *Degree requirements:* For master's, capstone course. *Entrance requirements:* For master's, GMAT, resume, one letter of reference. Additional exam requirements/recommendations for international students: Required—TOEFL (minimum score 550 paper-based; 79 iBT), IELTS (minimum score 6.5). *Application deadline:* For fall admission, 8/1 priority date for domestic students, 7/1 for international students; for spring admission, 12/1 for domestic students, 11/1 for international students. Applications are processed on a rolling basis. Application fee: $60. Electronic applications accepted. *Expenses:* Tuition, state resident: full-time $9870; part-time $411 per credit hour. Tuition, nonresident: full-time $20,150; part-time $765 per credit hour. *Required fees:* $1180; $50.73 per credit hour. *Financial support:* In 2013–14, 3 students received support, including 1 fellowship with full tuition reimbursement available (averaging $5,545 per year), 2 research assistantships with partial tuition reimbursements available (averaging $4,000 per year); unspecified assistantships also available. Financial award application deadline: 6/1; financial award applicants required to submit FAFSA. *Faculty research:* Technology management, writing schools, leadership, new products. *Unit head:* Dr. Rafael Romero, Program Coordinator and Associate Professor, 315-792-7337, Fax: 315-792-7138, E-mail: rafael.romero@sunyit.edu. *Application contact:* Maryrose Raab, Coordinator of Graduate Center, 315-792-7347, Fax: 315-792-7221, E-mail: maryrose.raab@sunyit.edu. Website: http://www.sunyit.edu/programs/graduate/mbatm/.

Stephen F. Austin State University, Graduate School, College of Business, Program in Professional Accountancy, Nacogdoches, TX 75962. Offers MPAC. Students admitted at the undergraduate level. *Degree requirements:* For master's, comprehensive exam. *Entrance requirements:* For master's, GMAT. Additional exam requirements/recommendations for international students: Required—TOEFL.

Stetson University, School of Business Administration, Program in Accounting, DeLand, FL 32723. Offers M Acc. *Accreditation:* AACSB. Part-time programs available. *Faculty:* 13 full-time (3 women), 6 part-time/adjunct (2 women). *Students:* 28 full-time (12 women), 5 part-time (4 women); includes 1 minority (Asian, non-Hispanic/Latino), 2 international. Average age 32. 44 applicants, 66% accepted, 21 enrolled. In 2013, 32 master's awarded. *Entrance requirements:* For master's, GMAT, GRE. Additional exam

requirements/recommendations for international students: Required—TOEFL (minimum score 90 iBT), IELTS (minimum score 7.5). *Application deadline:* For fall admission, 7/21 for domestic students; for spring admission, 12/20 for domestic students; for summer admission, 4/14 for domestic students. Applications are processed on a rolling basis. Application fee: $50. Electronic applications accepted. *Financial support:* In 2013–14, 3 research assistantships were awarded; Federal Work-Study and institutionally sponsored loans also available. Support available to part-time students. Financial award application deadline: 3/15. *Unit head:* Dr. Michael E. Bitter, Director, 386-822-7410. *Application contact:* John F Moore, Jr., Assistant Director of Graduate Admissions, 386-822-7100, Fax: 386-822-7112, E-mail: jfmoore@stetson.edu.

Stratford University, School of Graduate Studies, Falls Church, VA 22043. Offers accounting (MS); business administration (IMBA, MBA); enterprise business management (MS); entrepreneurial management (MS); information assurance (MS); information systems (MS); software engineering (MS); telecommunications (MS). Part-time and evening/weekend programs available. Postbaccalaureate distance learning degree programs offered (no on-campus study). *Degree requirements:* For master's, comprehensive exam, capstone project. *Entrance requirements:* For master's, GRE or GMAT, baccalaureate degree. Additional exam requirements/recommendations for international students: Required—TOEFL (minimum score 79 iBT) or IELTS (6.5). Electronic applications accepted.

Strayer University, Graduate Studies, Washington, DC 20005-2603. Offers accounting (MS); acquisition (MBA); business administration (MBA); communications technology (MS); educational management (M Ed); finance (MBA); health services administration (MHSA); hospitality and tourism management (MBA); human resource management (MBA); information systems (MS), including computer security management, decision support system management, enterprise resource management, network management, software engineering management, systems development management; management (MBA); management information systems (MS); marketing (MBA); professional accounting (MS), including accounting information systems, controllership, taxation; public administration (MPA); supply chain management (MBA); technology in education (M Ed). Programs also offered at campus locations in Birmingham, AL; Chamblee, GA; Cobb County, GA; Morrow, GA; White Marsh, MD; Charleston, SC; Columbia, SC; Greensboro, NC; Greenville, SC; Lexington, KY; Louisville, KY; Nashville, TN; North Raleigh, NC; Washington, DC. Part-time and evening/weekend programs available. Postbaccalaureate distance learning degree programs offered (minimal on-campus study). *Degree requirements:* For master's, thesis. *Entrance requirements:* For master's, GMAT, GRE General Test, bachelor's degree from an accredited college or university, minimum undergraduate GPA of 2.75. Electronic applications accepted.

Suffolk University, Sawyer Business School, Department of Accounting, Boston, MA 02108-2770. Offers accounting (MSA, GDPA); taxation (MST); GDPA/MST; MBA/GDPA; MBA/MSA; MBA/MST. *Accreditation:* AACSB. Part-time and evening/weekend programs available. *Faculty:* 12 full-time (3 women), 8 part-time/adjunct (2 women). *Students:* 106 full-time (77 women), 139 part-time (72 women); includes 47 minority (16 Black or African American, non-Hispanic/Latino; 19 Asian, non-Hispanic/Latino; 11 Hispanic/Latino; 1 Two or more races, non-Hispanic/Latino), 78 international. Average age 28. 418 applicants, 70% accepted, 110 enrolled. In 2013, 116 master's, 4 GDPAs awarded. *Entrance requirements:* For master's, GMAT. Additional exam requirements/recommendations for international students: Required—TOEFL (minimum score 550 paper-based; 80 iBT). *Application deadline:* For fall admission, 6/15 priority date for domestic students, 6/15 for international students; for spring admission, 11/1 priority date for domestic students, 11/1 for international students. Applications are processed on a rolling basis. Application fee: $50. Electronic applications accepted. *Expenses:* Tuition: Full-time $38,374; part-time $1279 per credit. *Required fees:* $40; $20 per semester. Tuition and fees vary according to program. *Financial support:* In 2013–14, 80 students received support, including 79 fellowships (averaging $19,005 per year); career-related internships or fieldwork, Federal Work-Study, and institutionally sponsored loans also available. Support available to part-time students. Financial award application deadline: 4/1; financial award applicants required to submit FAFSA. *Faculty research:* Tax policy, tax research, decision-making in accounting, accounting information systems, capital markets and strategic planning. *Unit head:* Lewis Shaw, Chair, 617-573-8615, Fax: 617-994-4260, E-mail: lshaw@suffolk.edu. *Application contact:* Cory Meyers, Director of Graduate Admissions, 617-573-8302, Fax: 617-305-1733, E-mail: grad.admission@suffolk.edu. Website: http://www.suffolk.edu/msa.

Suffolk University, Sawyer Business School, Master of Business Administration Program, Boston, MA 02108-2770. Offers accounting (MBA); business administration (APC); entrepreneurship (MBA); executive business administration (EMBA); finance (MBA); global business administration (GMBA); health administration (MBA); international business (MBA); marketing (MBA); nonprofit management (MBA); organizational behavior (MBA); strategic management (MBA); supply chain management (MBA); taxation (MBA); JD/MBA; MBA/GDPA; MBA/MHA; MBA/MSA; MBA/MSF; MBA/MST. *Accreditation:* AACSB. Part-time and evening/weekend programs available. Postbaccalaureate distance learning degree programs offered (no on-campus study). *Faculty:* 29 full-time (9 women), 12 part-time/adjunct (2 women). *Students:* 106 full-time (44 women), 334 part-time (184 women); includes 57 minority (20 Black or African American, non-Hispanic/Latino; 1 American Indian or Alaska Native, non-Hispanic/Latino; 18 Asian, non-Hispanic/Latino; 14 Hispanic/Latino; 4 Two or more races, non-Hispanic/Latino), 61 international. Average age 30. 448 applicants, 61% accepted, 135 enrolled. In 2013, 217 master's awarded. *Entrance requirements:* For master's, GMAT, minimum undergraduate GPA of 2.75 (MBA), 5 years of managerial experience (EMBA). Additional exam requirements/recommendations for international students: Required—TOEFL (minimum score 550 paper-based; 80 iBT). *Application deadline:* For fall admission, 6/15 priority date for domestic students, 6/15 for international students; for spring admission, 11/1 priority date for domestic students, 11/1 for international students. Applications are processed on a rolling basis. Application fee: $50. Electronic applications accepted. *Expenses:* Tuition: Full-time $38,374; part-time $1279 per credit. *Required fees:* $40; $20 per semester. Tuition and fees vary according to program. *Financial support:* In 2013–14, 107 students received support, including 91 fellowships with full and partial tuition reimbursements available (averaging $12,428 per year); career-related internships or fieldwork, Federal Work-Study, and institutionally sponsored loans also available. Support available to part-time students. Financial award application deadline: 4/1; financial award applicants required to submit FAFSA. *Faculty research:* Foreign investments; career strategies and boundaryless careers; corporate ethics codes; interest rates, inflation, and growth options; innovation and product development performance. *Unit head:* Heather Hewitt, Assistant Dean of Graduate Programs/Director of MBA Programs, 617-573-8306, E-mail: hhewitt@suffolk.edu. *Application contact:* Cory Meyers, Director of Graduate Admissions, 617-573-8302, Fax: 617-305-1733, E-mail: grad.admission@suffolk.edu. Website: http://www.suffolk.edu/mba.

Syracuse University, Martin J. Whitman School of Management, PhD Program in Business Administration, Syracuse, NY 13244. Offers accounting (PhD); finance (PhD); management information systems (PhD); managerial statistics (PhD); marketing (PhD); operations management (PhD); organizational behavior (PhD); strategy and human

resources (PhD); supply chain management (PhD). *Faculty:* 79 full-time (20 women), 25 part-time/adjunct (6 women). *Students:* 26 full-time (8 women), 1 part-time (0 women); includes 2 minority (1 Black or African American, non-Hispanic/Latino; 1 Asian, non-Hispanic/Latino), 20 international. Average age 30. 130 applicants, 9% accepted, 7 enrolled. In 2013, 15 doctorates awarded. *Degree requirements:* For doctorate, comprehensive exam, thesis/dissertation, summer research paper. *Entrance requirements:* For doctorate, GMAT or GRE General Test, 3 recommendations. Additional exam requirements/recommendations for international students: Required—TOEFL (minimum score 600 paper-based; 100 iBT). *Application deadline:* For fall admission, 1/15 priority date for domestic and international students. Applications are processed on a rolling basis. Application fee: $75. Electronic applications accepted. *Financial support:* In 2013–14, 1 fellowship with full tuition reimbursement (averaging $19,570 per year), 30 teaching assistantships with full tuition reimbursements (averaging $17,000 per year) were awarded; research assistantships with full tuition reimbursements also available. Financial award application deadline: 1/15. *Faculty research:* Marketing models, market microstructure, supply chain, auditing, corporate governance. *Unit head:* Dr. Michel Benarock, Director of the PhD Program, 315-443-3429, E-mail: mbeanaroc@syr.edu. *Application contact:* Carol Hilleges, Administrative Specialist, 315-443-9601, Fax: 315-443-3671, E-mail: clhilleg@syr.edu.
Website: http://whitman.syr.edu/phd/.

Syracuse University, Martin J. Whitman School of Management, Program in Accounting, Syracuse, NY 13244. Offers MS Acct, JD/MS Acct. *Faculty:* 79 full-time (20 women), 25 part-time/adjunct (6 women). *Students:* 91 full-time (55 women), 9 part-time (5 women); includes 18 minority (2 Black or African American, non-Hispanic/Latino; 13 Asian, non-Hispanic/Latino; 1 Hispanic/Latino; 2 Two or more races, non-Hispanic/Latino), 53 international. Average age 24. 341 applicants, 38% accepted, 61 enrolled. In 2013, 52 master's awarded. *Entrance requirements:* For master's, GMAT, 2 letters of recommendation, bachelor's degree in accounting. Additional exam requirements/recommendations for international students: Required—TOEFL (minimum score 600 paper-based; 100 iBT). *Application deadline:* For fall admission, 11/30 priority date for domestic and international students; for winter admission, 11/1 for domestic and international students. Applications are processed on a rolling basis. Application fee: $75. Electronic applications accepted. *Financial support:* In 2013–14, 5 students received support. Fellowships with full tuition reimbursements available, teaching assistantships with partial tuition reimbursements available, career-related internships or fieldwork, scholarships/grants, and tuition waivers (partial) available. Financial award application deadline: 1/1. *Unit head:* Dr. William Walsh, Director, Joseph I. Lubin School of Accounting, 315-443-3589, Fax: 315-443-9517, E-mail: wiwalsh@syr.edu. *Application contact:* Danielle Goodroe, Director of Graduate Enrollment, 315-443-3006, Fax: 315-443-9517, E-mail: mbainfo@syr.edu.
Website: http://whitman.syr.edu/msacc/.

Syracuse University, Martin J. Whitman School of Management, Program in Business Administration, Syracuse, NY 13244. Offers accounting (MBA); entrepreneurship (MBA); finance (MBA); marketing (MBA); supply chain management (MBA). Postbaccalaureate distance learning degree programs offered (minimal on-campus study). *Faculty:* 79 full-time (20 women), 25 part-time/adjunct (6 women). *Students:* 112 full-time (41 women), 181 part-time (49 women); includes 52 minority (19 Black or African American, non-Hispanic/Latino; 18 Asian, non-Hispanic/Latino; 11 Hispanic/Latino; 4 Two or more races, non-Hispanic/Latino), 56 international. Average age 33. 179 applicants, 50% accepted, 36 enrolled. In 2013, 115 master's awarded. *Entrance requirements:* For master's, GMAT, 2 letters of recommendation. Additional exam requirements/recommendations for international students: Required—TOEFL (minimum score 600 paper-based; 100 iBT). *Application deadline:* For fall admission, 11/30 priority date for domestic and international students. Applications are processed on a rolling basis. Application fee: $75. Electronic applications accepted. *Financial support:* In 2013–14, 17 students received support. Fellowships with full and partial tuition reimbursements available, teaching assistantships with partial tuition reimbursements available, career-related internships or fieldwork, scholarships/grants, tuition waivers (partial), and unspecified assistantships available. Support available to part-time students. Financial award application deadline: 3/1. *Unit head:* Dr. Don Harter, Associate Dean for Master's Programs, 315-443-3502, Fax: 315-443-9517, E-mail: dharter@syr.edu. *Application contact:* Danielle Goodroe, Director, Graduate Enrollment, 315-443-3006, Fax: 315-443-9517, E-mail: mbainfo@syr.edu.
Website: http://whitman.syr.edu/ftmba/.

Syracuse University, Martin J. Whitman School of Management, Program in Professional Accounting, Syracuse, NY 13244. Offers MS. Part-time programs available. Postbaccalaureate distance learning degree programs offered (minimal on-campus study). *Students:* 2 part-time (both women). Average age 24. In 2013, 1 master's awarded. *Entrance requirements:* For master's, GMAT. Additional exam requirements/recommendations for international students: Required—TOEFL (minimum score 100 iBT). *Application deadline:* For fall admission, 11/30 priority date for domestic and international students. Application fee: $75. Electronic applications accepted. *Unit head:* Dr. William Walsh, Director, Joseph I. Lubin School of Accounting, 315-443-3589, E-mail: wiwalsh@syr.edu. *Application contact:* Danielle Goodroe, Director of Graduate Admissions, 315-443-3006, Fax: 315-443-9517, E-mail: mbainfo@syr.edu.
Website: http://whitman.syr.edu/.

Tabor College, Graduate Program, Hillsboro, KS 67063. Offers accounting (MBA). Program offered at the Wichita campus only.

Temple University, Fox School of Business, Doctoral Programs in Business, Philadelphia, PA 19122-6096. Offers accounting (PhD); entrepreneurship (PhD); finance (PhD); international business (PhD); management information systems (PhD); marketing (PhD); risk management and insurance (PhD); statistics (PhD); strategic management (PhD); tourism and sport (PhD). *Accreditation:* AACSB. *Degree requirements:* For doctorate, thesis/dissertation. *Entrance requirements:* For doctorate, GRE General Test, GMAT, minimum GPA of 3.0, master's degree. Additional exam requirements/recommendations for international students: Required—TOEFL (minimum score 600 paper-based; 100 iBT), IELTS (minimum score 7.5). Electronic applications accepted.

Temple University, Fox School of Business, MBA Programs, Philadelphia, PA 19122-6096. Offers accounting (MBA); business management (MBA); financial management (MBA); healthcare and life sciences innovation (MBA); human resource management (MBA); international business (IMBA); IT management (MBA); marketing management (MBA); pharmaceutical management (MBA); strategic management (EMBA, MBA). EMBA offered in Philadelphia, PA and Tokyo, Japan. *Accreditation:* AACSB. Part-time and evening/weekend programs available. Postbaccalaureate distance learning degree programs offered (minimal on-campus study). *Entrance requirements:* For master's, GMAT, minimum undergraduate GPA of 3.0. Additional exam requirements/recommendations for international students: Required—TOEFL (minimum score 600 paper-based; 100 iBT), IELTS (minimum score 7.5).

Temple University, Fox School of Business, Specialized Master's Programs, Philadelphia, PA 19122-6096. Offers accountancy (MS); actuarial science (MS); finance (MS); financial engineering (MS); human resource management (MS); innovation management and entrepreneurship (MS); marketing (MS); statistics (MS). MS in innovation management and entrepreneurship delivered jointly with College of Engineering. *Accreditation:* AACSB. Part-time programs available. *Entrance requirements:* For master's, GRE General Test or GMAT, minimum undergraduate GPA of 3.0. Additional exam requirements/recommendations for international students: Required—TOEFL (minimum score 600 paper-based; 100 iBT), IELTS (minimum score 7.5).

Tennessee Technological University, College of Graduate Studies, College of Business, Cookeville, TN 38505. Offers accounting (MBA); finance (MBA); human resource management (MBA); international business (MBA); management information systems (MBA). *Accreditation:* AACSB. Part-time and evening/weekend programs available. Postbaccalaureate distance learning degree programs offered (no on-campus study). *Faculty:* 28 full-time (5 women). *Students:* 54 full-time (22 women), 115 part-time (44 women); includes 11 minority (5 Black or African American, non-Hispanic/Latino; 1 Asian, non-Hispanic/Latino; 1 Hispanic/Latino; 4 Two or more races, non-Hispanic/Latino), 8 international. Average age 25. 171 applicants, 47% accepted, 50 enrolled. In 2013, 87 master's awarded. *Entrance requirements:* For master's, GMAT, GRE. Additional exam requirements/recommendations for international students: Required—TOEFL (minimum score 550 paper-based; 79 iBT), IELTS (minimum score 5.5), PTE (minimum score 53), or TOEIC (Test of English as an International Communication). *Application deadline:* For fall admission, 8/1 for domestic students, 5/1 for international students; for spring admission, 12/1 for domestic students, 10/1 for international students. Applications are processed on a rolling basis. Application fee: $35 ($40 for international students). Electronic applications accepted. *Expenses:* Tuition, state resident: full-time $9347; part-time $465 per credit hour. Tuition, nonresident: full-time $23,635; part-time $1152 per credit hour. *Financial support:* In 2013–14, 5 fellowships (averaging $10,000 per year), 18 research assistantships (averaging $4,000 per year), teaching assistantships (averaging $4,000 per year) were awarded. Support available to part-time students. Financial award application deadline: 4/1. *Unit head:* Amanda L. Brown, Interim Director, 931-372-3600, Fax: 931-372-6249, E-mail: albrown@tntech.edu. *Application contact:* Shelia K. Kendrick, Coordinator of Graduate Studies, 931-372-3808, Fax: 931-372-3497, E-mail: skendrick@tntech.edu.
Website: http://www.tntech.edu/mba.

Texas A&M International University, Office of Graduate Studies and Research, A.R. Sanchez School of Business, Division of International Banking and Finance Studies, Laredo, TX 78041-1900. Offers accounting (MP Acc); international banking and finance (MBA). *Faculty:* 12 full-time (2 women). *Students:* 13 full-time (6 women), 36 part-time (18 women); includes 48 minority (1 Black or African American, non-Hispanic/Latino; 2 Asian, non-Hispanic/Latino; 45 Hispanic/Latino). Average age 31. 13 applicants, 85% accepted, 13 enrolled. In 2013, 30 master's awarded. *Entrance requirements:* For master's, GMAT or GRE General Test. Additional exam requirements/recommendations for international students: Required—TOEFL (minimum score 550 paper-based; 79 iBT). *Application deadline:* For fall admission, 4/30 priority date for domestic students, 4/30 for international students; for spring admission, 11/30 for domestic students, 10/1 for international students. Applications are processed on a rolling basis. Application fee: $35 ($50 for international students). *Expenses:* Tuition, state resident: full-time $5184. *International tuition:* $11,556 full-time. *Financial support:* In 2013–14, 3 students received support, including 1 research assistantship. *Unit head:* Dr. Antonio Rodriguez, Chair, 956-326-2517, Fax: 956-326-2481, E-mail: rodriguez@tamiu.edu. *Application contact:* Imelda Lopez, Graduate Admissions Counselor, 956-326-2485, Fax: 956-326-2459, E-mail: lopez@tamiu.edu.
Website: http://www.tamiu.edu/arssb/ibfs.shtml.

Texas A&M University, Mays Business School, Department of Accounting, College Station, TX 77843. Offers MS, PhD. *Accreditation:* AACSB. *Faculty:* 16. *Students:* 150 full-time (70 women), 14 part-time (4 women); includes 24 minority (5 Black or African American, non-Hispanic/Latino; 7 Asian, non-Hispanic/Latino; 11 Hispanic/Latino; 1 Two or more races, non-Hispanic/Latino), 8 international. Average age 24. 279 applicants, 15% accepted, 19 enrolled. In 2013, 114 master's, 4 doctorates awarded. Terminal master's awarded for partial completion of doctoral program. *Degree requirements:* For master's, comprehensive exam; for doctorate, thesis/dissertation. *Entrance requirements:* For master's, GMAT; for doctorate, GMAT or GRE General Test. Additional exam requirements/recommendations for international students: Required—TOEFL. *Application deadline:* For fall admission, 3/1 priority date for domestic students; for spring admission, 8/1 for domestic students. Applications are processed on a rolling basis. Application fee: $50 ($75 for international students). *Expenses:* Tuition, state resident: full-time $4078; part-time $226.55 per credit hour. Tuition, nonresident: full-time $10,450; part-time $580.55 per credit hour. *Required fees:* $2328; $278.50 per credit hour. $642.45 per semester. *Financial support:* Fellowships, research assistantships, teaching assistantships, career-related internships or fieldwork, and institutionally sponsored loans available. Financial award application deadline: 2/1. *Faculty research:* Financial reporting, taxation management, decision-making, accounting information systems, government accounting. *Unit head:* Dr. James J. Benjamin, Head, 979-845-0356, Fax: 979-845-0028, E-mail: jbenjamin@mays.tamu.edu. *Application contact:* Dr. Mary Lea McAnally, Associate Dean for Graduate Programs, 979-845-4714, Fax: 979-845-0028, E-mail: mmcanally@mays.tamu.edu.
Website: http://mays.tamu.edu/acct/.

Texas A&M University–Commerce, Graduate School, College of Business, MS Programs, Commerce, TX 75429-3011. Offers accounting (MS); economics (MA); finance (MS); management (MS); marketing (MS). Part-time programs available. *Degree requirements:* For master's, comprehensive exam, thesis (for some programs). *Entrance requirements:* For master's, GMAT or GRE General Test. Electronic applications accepted. *Expenses:* Tuition, state resident: full-time $3630; part-time $2420 per year. Tuition, nonresident: full-time $9948; part-time $6632.16 per year. *Required fees:* $1006 per year. Tuition and fees vary according to course load. *Faculty research:* Economic activity, forensic economics, volatility and finance, international economics.

Texas A&M University–Corpus Christi, Graduate Studies and Research, College of Business, Corpus Christi, TX 78412-5503. Offers accounting (M Acc); health care administration (MBA); international business (MBA). *Accreditation:* AACSB. Part-time and evening/weekend programs available. *Degree requirements:* For master's, comprehensive exam, thesis (for some programs). *Entrance requirements:* For master's, GMAT. Additional exam requirements/recommendations for international students: Required—TOEFL. Electronic applications accepted.

Texas A&M University–San Antonio, School of Business, San Antonio, TX 78224. Offers business administration (MBA); enterprise resource planning systems (MBA); finance (MBA); healthcare management (MBA); human resources management (MBA); information assurance and security (MBA); international business (MBA); professional accounting (MPA); project management (MBA); supply chain management (MBA). Part-time and evening/weekend programs available. *Entrance requirements:* For master's, GMAT. Additional exam requirements/recommendations for international students: Required—TOEFL (minimum score 550 paper-based; 80 iBT), IELTS (minimum score 6). Electronic applications accepted.

Texas A&M University–Texarkana, Graduate Studies and Research, College of Business, Texarkana, TX 75505-5518. Offers accounting (MSA); business

administration (MBA, MS). Part-time and evening/weekend programs available. *Degree requirements:* For master's, thesis or alternative. *Entrance requirements:* For master's, minimum GPA of 2.5 in last 60 hours of bachelor's degree. Additional exam requirements/recommendations for international students: Required—TOEFL. Electronic applications accepted.

Texas Christian University, Neeley School of Business at TCU, Master of Accounting Program, Fort Worth, TX 76129-0002. Offers M Ac. *Accreditation:* AACSB. *Faculty:* 10 full-time (3 women), 1 part-time/adjunct (0 women). *Students:* 40 full-time (17 women); includes 2 minority (1 Black or African American, non-Hispanic/Latino; 1 Asian, non-Hispanic/Latino), 5 international. Average age 23. 34 applicants, 100% accepted, 30 enrolled. In 2013, 54 master's awarded. *Entrance requirements:* For master's, GMAT, undergraduate degree in accounting from U.S.-accredited university. Additional exam requirements/recommendations for international students: Required—TOEFL (minimum score 600 paper-based; 100 iBT). *Application deadline:* For fall admission, 2/15 priority date for domestic students, 2/15 for international students; for spring admission, 9/15 priority date for domestic students, 9/15 for international students. Applications are processed on a rolling basis. Electronic applications accepted. *Expenses: Tuition:* Part-time $1270 per credit hour. Tuition and fees vary according to course load and program. *Financial support:* Tuition waivers (partial) and unspecified assistantships available. Financial award application deadline: 2/15; financial award applicants required to submit FAFSA. *Unit head:* Emily Beaver, Assistant Director, Professional Program in Accounting, 817-257-5112, E-mail: e.beaver@tcu.edu. *Application contact:* Emily Beaver, Assistant Director, Professional Program in Accounting, 817-257-5112, Fax: 817-257-7227, E-mail: e.beaver@tcu.edu.
Website: http://www.neeley.tcu.edu/Academics/Master_of_Accounting/MAc.aspx.

Texas State University, Graduate School, Emmett and Miriam McCoy College of Business Administration, Program in Accounting, San Marcos, TX 78666. Offers M Acy. Part-time programs available. *Faculty:* 12 full-time (6 women), 1 part-time/adjunct (0 women). *Students:* 55 full-time (31 women), 24 part-time (11 women); includes 19 minority (2 Black or African American, non-Hispanic/Latino; 7 Asian, non-Hispanic/Latino; 10 Hispanic/Latino), 4 international. Average age 28. 70 applicants, 47% accepted, 21 enrolled. In 2013, 56 master's awarded. *Degree requirements:* For master's, comprehensive exam. *Entrance requirements:* For master's, GMAT (minimum preferred score of 450 prior to admission decision), minimum GPA of 2.0 in last 60 hours of undergraduate work. Additional exam requirements/recommendations for international students: Required—TOEFL (minimum score 550 paper-based; 78 iBT). *Application deadline:* For fall admission, 6/1 for domestic and international students; for spring admission, 10/1 for domestic and international students. Applications are processed on a rolling basis. Application fee: $40 ($90 for international students). Electronic applications accepted. *Expenses:* Tuition, state resident: full-time $6663; part-time $278 per credit hour. Tuition, nonresident: full-time $15,159; part-time $632 per credit hour. *Required fees:* $1872; $54 per credit hour. $306 per term. Tuition and fees vary according to course load. *Financial support:* In 2013–14, 51 students received support, including 2 research assistantships (averaging $11,090 per year), 5 teaching assistantships (averaging $11,280 per year); Federal Work-Study, institutionally sponsored loans, scholarships/grants, health care benefits, and unspecified assistantships also available. Support available to part-time students. Financial award application deadline: 4/1; financial award applicants required to submit FAFSA. *Unit head:* Dr. William Chittenden, Graduate Advisor, 512-245-3591, E-mail: wc10@txstate.edu. *Application contact:* Dr. Andrea Golato, Dean of Graduate School, 512-245-2581, Fax: 512-245-8365, E-mail: gradcollege@txstate.edu.
Website: http://accounting.mccoy.txstate.edu/degrees-programs/MAcy.html.

Texas State University, Graduate School, Emmett and Miriam McCoy College of Business Administration, Program in Accounting and Information Technology, San Marcos, TX 78666. Offers MS. *Faculty:* 8 full-time (1 woman), 1 part-time/adjunct (0 women). *Students:* 6 full-time (2 women), 10 part-time (4 women); includes 3 minority (2 Asian, non-Hispanic/Latino; 1 Hispanic/Latino), 1 international. Average age 32. 14 applicants, 36% accepted, 2 enrolled. In 2013, 7 master's awarded. *Degree requirements:* For master's, comprehensive exam. *Entrance requirements:* For master's, GMAT, official transcript from each college or university attended, 2 letters of recommendation, resume. Additional exam requirements/recommendations for international students: Required—TOEFL (minimum score 550 paper-based; 78 iBT). *Application deadline:* For fall admission, 6/1 for domestic and international students; for spring admission, 10/1 for domestic and international students. Application fee: $40 ($90 for international students). *Expenses:* Tuition, state resident: full-time $6663; part-time $278 per credit hour. Tuition, nonresident: full-time $15,159; part-time $632 per credit hour. *Required fees:* $1872; $54 per credit hour. $306 per term. Tuition and fees vary according to course load. *Financial support:* In 2013–14, 5 students received support, including 1 research assistantship (averaging $10,950 per year), 3 teaching assistantships (averaging $11,280 per year); Federal Work-Study, institutionally sponsored loans, scholarships/grants, health care benefits, and unspecified assistantships also available. Support available to part-time students. *Unit head:* Dr. William Chittenden, Graduate Advisor, 512-245-3591, Fax: 512-245-7973, E-mail: wc10@txstate.edu. *Application contact:* Dr. Andrea Golato, Dean of Graduate School, 512-245-2581, Fax: 512-245-8365, E-mail: gradcollege@txstate.edu.

Texas Tech University, Graduate School, Rawls College of Business Administration, Area of Accounting, Lubbock, TX 79409. Offers accounting (PhD); audit/financial reporting (MSA); taxation (MSA); JD/MSA. *Accreditation:* AACSB. Part-time programs available. *Faculty:* 10 full-time (2 women), 1 part-time/adjunct (0 women). *Students:* 202 full-time (104 women); includes 10 minority (3 Black or African American, non-Hispanic/Latino; 1 American Indian or Alaska Native, non-Hispanic/Latino; 2 Asian, non-Hispanic/Latino; 4 Hispanic/Latino), 6 international. Average age 24. 122 applicants, 70% accepted, 79 enrolled. In 2013, 133 master's, 1 doctorate awarded. Terminal master's awarded for partial completion of doctoral program. *Degree requirements:* For master's, capstone course; for doctorate, comprehensive exam, thesis/dissertation, qualifying exams. *Entrance requirements:* For master's and doctorate, GMAT, holistic profile of academic credentials. Additional exam requirements/recommendations for international students: Required—TOEFL (minimum score 550 paper-based; 79 iBT). *Application deadline:* For fall admission, 2/1 for domestic students, 1/15 for international students; for spring admission, 12/1 for domestic students. Applications are processed on a rolling basis. Application fee: $60. Electronic applications accepted. *Expenses:* Tuition, state resident: full-time $6062; part-time $252.57 per credit hour. Tuition, nonresident: full-time $14,558; part-time $606.57 per credit hour. *Required fees:* $2655; $35 per credit hour. $907.50 per semester. Tuition and fees vary according to course load. *Financial support:* In 2013–14, 7 research assistantships (averaging $14,933 per year), 1 teaching assistantship (averaging $18,000 per year) were awarded; fellowships, career-related internships or fieldwork, Federal Work-Study, scholarships/grants, health care benefits, and unspecified assistantships also available. Financial award applicants required to submit FAFSA. *Faculty research:* Governmental and nonprofit accounting, managerial and financial accounting. *Unit head:* Dr. Robert Ricketts, Area Coordinator, 806-742-3180, Fax: 806-742-3182, E-mail: robert.ricketts@ttu.edu. *Application contact:* Terri Boston, Applications Manager, Graduate and Professional Programs, 806-742-3184, Fax: 806-742-3958, E-mail: rawlsgrad@ttu.edu.
Website: http://accounting.ba.ttu.edu.

Towson University, Joint Program in Accounting and Business Advisory Services, Towson, MD 21252-0001. Offers MS. Program offered jointly with University of Baltimore. *Accreditation:* AACSB. Part-time and evening/weekend programs available. *Students:* 31 full-time (18 women), 20 part-time (12 women); includes 15 minority (8 Black or African American, non-Hispanic/Latino; 7 Asian, non-Hispanic/Latino), 12 international. *Entrance requirements:* For master's, GMAT, GRE General Test, minimum GPA of 3.0; prerequisite courses in accounting, economics, communications, math, marketing, finance, business law, and business ethics. *Application deadline:* Applications are processed on a rolling basis. Application fee: $45. Electronic applications accepted. *Unit head:* Dr. Martin Freedman, Graduate Program Director, 410-704-4143, E-mail: mfreedman@towson.edu. *Application contact:* Alicia Arkell-Kleis, Information Contact, 410-704-6004, E-mail: grads@towson.edu.
Website: http://grad.towson.edu/program/master/acbs-ms/.

Trinity University, Department of Business Administration, San Antonio, TX 78212-7200. Offers accounting (MS). *Accreditation:* AACSB. Part-time programs available. *Entrance requirements:* For master's, GMAT, minimum GPA of 3.0, course work in accounting and business law.

Troy University, Graduate School, College of Business, Program in Accountancy, Troy, AL 36082. Offers M Acc. Part-time and evening/weekend programs available. *Faculty:* 6 full-time (3 women). *Students:* 19 full-time (12 women), 8 part-time (5 women); includes 3 minority (1 Black or African American, non-Hispanic/Latino; 1 American Indian or Alaska Native, non-Hispanic/Latino; 1 Asian, non-Hispanic/Latino). 15 applicants, 93% accepted, 8 enrolled. *Degree requirements:* For master's, minimum GPA of 3.0, research course. *Entrance requirements:* For master's, GMAT (minimum score of 500), bachelor's degree; minimum undergraduate GPA of 2.5 or 3.0 on last 30 semester hours, letter of recommendation. Additional exam requirements/recommendations for international students: Required—TOEFL (minimum score 523 paper-based; 70 iBT), IELTS (minimum score 6). *Expenses:* Tuition, state resident: full-time $6084; part-time $338 per credit hour. Tuition, nonresident: full-time $12,168; part-time $676 per credit hour. *Required fees:* $630; $35 per credit hour. $50 per semester. *Unit head:* Dr. Kay Sheridan, Director, 334-670-3154, Fax: 334-670-3599, E-mail: ksheridan@troy.edu. *Application contact:* Brenda K. Campbell, Director of Graduate Admissions, 334-670-3178, Fax: 334-670-3733, E-mail: bcamp@troy.edu.

Troy University, Graduate School, College of Business, Program in Business Administration, Troy, AL 36082. Offers accounting (EMBA, MBA); criminal justice (EMBA); finance (MBA); general management (EMBA, MBA); healthcare management (EMBA); information systems (EMBA, MBA); international economic development (MBA). *Accreditation:* ACBSP. Part-time and evening/weekend programs available. *Faculty:* 56 full-time (20 women), 3 part-time/adjunct (0 women). *Students:* 142 full-time (89 women), 310 part-time (192 women); includes 265 minority (185 Black or African American, non-Hispanic/Latino; 3 American Indian or Alaska Native, non-Hispanic/Latino; 62 Asian, non-Hispanic/Latino; 8 Hispanic/Latino; 1 Native Hawaiian or other Pacific Islander, non-Hispanic/Latino; 6 Two or more races, non-Hispanic/Latino). Average age 29. 472 applicants, 68% accepted, 51 enrolled. In 2013, 293 master's awarded. *Degree requirements:* For master's, minimum GPA of 3.0, capstone course, research course. *Entrance requirements:* For master's, GMAT (minimum score 500) or GRE General Test (minimum score 900 on old exam or 294 on new exam), bachelor's degree; minimum undergraduate GPA of 2.5 or 3.0 on last 30 semester hours, letter of recommendation. Additional exam requirements/recommendations for international students: Required—TOEFL (minimum score 523 paper-based; 70 iBT), IELTS (minimum score 6). *Application deadline:* Applications are processed on a rolling basis. Application fee: $50. *Expenses:* Tuition, state resident: full-time $6084; part-time $338 per credit hour. Tuition, nonresident: full-time $12,168; part-time $676 per credit hour. *Required fees:* $630; $35 per credit hour. $50 per semester. *Unit head:* Dr. Bob Wheatley, Director, Graduate Business Programs, 334-670-3194, Fax: 334-670-3599, E-mail: rwheat@troy.edu. *Application contact:* Brenda K. Campbell, Director of Graduate Admissions, 334-670-3178, Fax: 334-670-3733, E-mail: bcamp@troy.edu.

Truman State University, Graduate School, School of Business, Program in Accounting, Kirksville, MO 63501-4221. Offers M Ac. *Accreditation:* AACSB. *Degree requirements:* For master's, comprehensive exam. *Entrance requirements:* For master's, GMAT, minimum GPA of 3.0. Additional exam requirements/recommendations for international students: Required—TOEFL (minimum score 550 paper-based). Electronic applications accepted.

Universidad del Este, Graduate School, Carolina, PR 00984. Offers accounting (MBA); adult education (M Ed); agribusiness (MBA); criminal justice and criminology (MA); curriculum and instruction - early education (M Ed); curriculum and instruction - elementary (M Ed); curriculum and instruction - English (M Ed); curriculum and instruction - Spanish (M Ed); human resources (MBA); information security management (MBA); information technology and Web business development (MBA); management (MBA); public policy (MPA); social work (MA), including clinical social work; special education (M Ed); strategic leadership (MBA). *Students:* 464 full-time (322 women), 669 part-time (499 women); all minorities (all Hispanic/Latino). Average age 35. 693 applicants, 61% accepted, 332 enrolled. In 2013, 228 master's awarded. *Unit head:* Jose R. Clintron, Dean, 787-257-7373 Ext. 3007, E-mail: ue_jcintron@suagm.edu. *Application contact:* Clotilde Santiago, Director of Admissions, 787-257-7373 Ext. 3400, E-mail: ue_csantiago@suagm.edu.

Universidad del Turabo, Graduate Programs, School in Business Administration, Program in Accounting, Gurabo, PR 00778-3030. Offers MBA. Part-time and evening/weekend programs available. *Entrance requirements:* For master's, GRE, EXADEP, interview.

Universidad Metropolitana, School of Business Administration, Program in Accounting, San Juan, PR 00928-1150. Offers MBA. Part-time programs available. *Degree requirements:* For master's, thesis or alternative. *Entrance requirements:* For master's, GMAT, PAEG, interview. Electronic applications accepted.

Université de Sherbrooke, Faculty of Administration, Program in Accounting, Sherbrooke, QC J1K 2R1, Canada. Offers M Sc. *Degree requirements:* For master's, one foreign language, thesis. *Entrance requirements:* For master's, bachelor's degree in related field, minimum GPA of 3.0 (on 4.3 scale). Electronic applications accepted. *Faculty research:* Financial analysis, management accounting, certification, system and control.

Université du Québec à Montréal, Graduate Programs, Program in Accounting, Montréal, QC H3C 3P8, Canada. Offers M Sc, MPA, Diploma. Part-time programs available. *Degree requirements:* For master's, thesis (for some programs). *Entrance requirements:* For master's, appropriate bachelor's degree or equivalent and proficiency in French.

Université du Québec à Trois-Rivières, Graduate Programs, Program in Accounting Science, Trois-Rivières, QC G9A 5H7, Canada. Offers MBA.

Université du Québec en Outaouais, Graduate Programs, Program in Accounting, Gatineau, QC J8X 3X7, Canada. Offers MA, DESS, Diploma. Part-time and evening/weekend programs available.

Accounting

Université du Québec en Outaouais, Graduate Programs, Program in Executive Certified Management Accounting, Gatineau, QC J8X 3X7, Canada. Offers MA, MBA, DESS. Part-time and evening/weekend programs available. *Degree requirements:* For master's, thesis (for some programs).

Université Laval, Faculty of Administrative Sciences, Programs in Business Administration, Québec, QC G1K 7P4, Canada. Offers accounting (MBA); agri-food management (MBA); electronic business (MBA, Diploma); factory management and logistics (MBA); finance (MBA); firm management (MBA); geomatic management (MBA); information technology management (MBA); international management (MBA); management (MBA); management accounting (MBA, Diploma); marketing (MBA); modeling and organizational decision (MBA); occupational health and safety management (MBA); pharmacy management (MBA); social and environmental responsibility (MBA); technological entrepreneurship (Diploma). *Accreditation:* AACSB. Part-time and evening/weekend programs available. Postbaccalaureate distance learning degree programs offered (no on-campus study). *Entrance requirements:* For master's and Diploma, knowledge of French and English. Electronic applications accepted.

Université Laval, Faculty of Administrative Sciences, Programs in Public Accountancy, Québec, QC G1K 7P4, Canada. Offers MBA, Diploma. Part-time programs available. *Entrance requirements:* For master's and Diploma, knowledge of French and English. Electronic applications accepted.

University at Albany, State University of New York, School of Business, Department of Accounting and Law, Albany, NY 12222-0001. Offers accounting (MS); taxation (MS). *Accreditation:* AACSB. *Degree requirements:* For master's, research project. *Entrance requirements:* For master's, GMAT. Additional exam requirements/recommendations for international students: Required—TOEFL (minimum score 550 paper-based). Electronic applications accepted. *Faculty research:* Professional ethics, statistical analysis, cost management systems, accounting theory.

University at Buffalo, the State University of New York, Graduate School, School of Management, Buffalo, NY 14260. Offers accounting (MS); business administration (EMBA, MBA, PMBA); finance (MS), including financial management, quantitative finance; management (PhD); management information systems (MS); supply chains and operations management (MS); Au D/MBA; DDS/MBA; JD/MBA; M Arch/MBA; MA/MBA; MD/MBA; MPH/MBA; MSW/MBA; Pharm D/MBA. *Accreditation:* AACSB. Part-time and evening/weekend programs available. *Faculty:* 72 full-time (23 women), 51 part-time/adjunct (13 women). *Students:* 627 full-time (266 women), 181 part-time (65 women); includes 50 minority (16 Black or African American, non-Hispanic/Latino; 5 American Indian or Alaska Native, non-Hispanic/Latino; 5 Asian, non-Hispanic/Latino; 3 Hispanic/Latino; 21 Native Hawaiian or other Pacific Islander, non-Hispanic/Latino), 332 international. Average age 28. 2,083 applicants, 52% accepted, 432 enrolled. In 2013, 476 master's, 10 doctorates awarded. *Degree requirements:* For master's, thesis (for some programs); for doctorate, comprehensive exam, thesis/dissertation. *Entrance requirements:* For master's, GMAT (for MS in accounting); GRE or GMAT (for MBA and all other MS concentrations), essays, letters of recommendation; for doctorate, GMAT or GRE, essays, writing sample, letters of recommendation. Additional exam requirements/recommendations for international students: Required—IELTS or PTE; Recommended—TOEFL (minimum score 95 iBT). *Application deadline:* For fall admission, 5/2 priority date for domestic students, 2/1 priority date for international students. Applications are processed on a rolling basis. Application fee: $100. Electronic applications accepted. *Expenses:* Contact institution. *Financial support:* In 2013–14, 115 students received support, including 40 fellowships (averaging $5,250 per year), 33 research assistantships with full and partial tuition reimbursements available (averaging $18,000 per year), 42 teaching assistantships with partial tuition reimbursements available (averaging $10,255 per year); career-related internships or fieldwork, Federal Work-Study, institutionally sponsored loans, scholarships/grants, health care benefits, and unspecified assistantships also available. Financial award application deadline: 2/15; financial award applicants required to submit FAFSA. *Faculty research:* Earnings management and electronic information assurance, supply chain and operations management, corporate financing and asset pricing, consumer behavior and quantitative modeling of marketing behavior, leadership and politics in organizations. *Total annual research expenditures:* $155,000. *Unit head:* Erin K. O'Brien, Assistant Dean and Director of Graduate Programs, 716-645-3204, Fax: 716-645-2341, E-mail: ekobrien@buffalo.edu. *Application contact:* Meghan Felser, Associate Director of Admissions and Recruiting, 716-645-3204, Fax: 716-645-2341, E-mail: mpwood@buffalo.edu.
Website: http://mgt.buffalo.edu/.

The University of Akron, Graduate School, College of Business Administration, School of Accountancy, Akron, OH 44325. Offers accounting information systems (MS); professional accountancy (MS); taxation (MT); JD/MT. *Accreditation:* AACSB. Part-time and evening/weekend programs available. *Faculty:* 10 full-time (1 woman), 15 part-time/adjunct (2 women). *Students:* 74 full-time (34 women), 50 part-time (17 women); includes 8 minority (4 Black or African American, non-Hispanic/Latino; 4 Asian, non-Hispanic/Latino), 18 international. Average age 29. 53 applicants, 85% accepted, 38 enrolled. In 2013, 58 master's awarded. *Entrance requirements:* For master's, GMAT, minimum GPA of 2.75, two letters of recommendation, resume, statement of purpose. Additional exam requirements/recommendations for international students: Required—TOEFL (minimum score 550 paper-based; 79 iBT). *Application deadline:* For fall admission, 7/15 for domestic and international students; for spring admission, 11/15 for domestic and international students. Applications are processed on a rolling basis. Application fee: $40 ($60 for international students). Electronic applications accepted. *Expenses:* Tuition, state resident: full-time $7430; part-time $412.80 per credit hour. Tuition, nonresident: full-time $12,722; part-time $706.80 per credit hour. *Required fees:* $53 per credit hour. $12 per semester. Tuition and fees vary according to course load and program. *Financial support:* In 2013–14, 31 teaching assistantships with full tuition reimbursements were awarded. *Faculty research:* Financial reporting and management accounting auditing and assurance of financial information, business and information systems risk and security management, corporate governance and ethics, accounting education. *Total annual research expenditures:* $51,195. *Unit head:* Dr. Thomas Calderon, Chair, 330-972-6099, E-mail: tcalderon@uakron.edu. *Application contact:* Dr. William Hauser, Director of Graduate Business Programs, 330-972-7043, Fax: 330-972-6588, E-mail: whauser@uakron.edu.
Website: http://www.uakron.edu/cba/departments/accountancy/.

The University of Alabama, Graduate School, Manderson Graduate School of Business, Culverhouse School of Accountancy, Tuscaloosa, AL 35487. Offers accounting (M Acc, PhD); tax accounting (MTA). *Accreditation:* AACSB. *Faculty:* 17 full-time (4 women). *Students:* 126 full-time (58 women), 4 part-time (2 women); includes 15 minority (10 Black or African American, non-Hispanic/Latino; 2 Asian, non-Hispanic/Latino; 3 Hispanic/Latino), 4 international. Average age 24. 251 applicants, 51% accepted, 104 enrolled. In 2013, 97 master's, 4 doctorates awarded. *Degree requirements:* For doctorate, thesis/dissertation. *Entrance requirements:* For master's, GMAT, minimum GPA of 3.0 overall or on last 60 hours; for doctorate, GMAT, minimum GPA of 3.0. Additional exam requirements/recommendations for international students: Required—TOEFL. *Application deadline:* For fall admission, 7/1 priority date for

domestic students, 6/1 priority date for international students; for spring admission, 11/1 priority date for domestic students, 9/1 priority date for international students. Applications are processed on a rolling basis. Application fee: $50 ($60 for international students). Electronic applications accepted. *Expenses:* Tuition, state resident: full-time $9450. Tuition, nonresident: full-time $23,950. *Financial support:* In 2013–14, 79 students received support, including 4 fellowships with full tuition reimbursements available (averaging $15,000 per year), 23 research assistantships with full and partial tuition reimbursements available (averaging $9,765 per year), 19 teaching assistantships with full and partial tuition reimbursements available (averaging $13,352 per year); career-related internships or fieldwork, Federal Work-Study, institutionally sponsored loans, scholarships/grants, health care benefits, and unspecified assistantships also available. Financial award application deadline: 3/31. *Faculty research:* Corporate governance, audit decision-making, earning management, valuation, executive compensation, not-for-profit. *Unit head:* Dr. Mary S. Stone, Director, 205-348-2915, Fax: 205-348-8453, E-mail: mstone@cba.ua.edu. *Application contact:* Sandy D. Davidson, Advisor, 205-348-6131, Fax: 205-348-8453, E-mail: sdavidso@cba.ua.edu.
Website: http://www.cba.ua.edu/accounting/.

The University of Alabama at Birmingham, School of Business, Program in Accounting, Birmingham, AL 35294-4460. Offers accounting (M Acct), including internal auditing. *Accreditation:* AACSB. Part-time and evening/weekend programs available. Postbaccalaureate distance learning degree programs offered (no on-campus study). *Students:* 43 full-time (22 women), 47 part-time (32 women); includes 15 minority (9 Black or African American, non-Hispanic/Latino; 2 Asian, non-Hispanic/Latino; 4 Hispanic/Latino), 7 international. Average age 30. In 2013, 39 master's awarded. *Entrance requirements:* For master's, GMAT (minimum score of 500). Additional exam requirements/recommendations for international students: Required—TOEFL (minimum score 80 iBT). *Application deadline:* For fall admission, 7/1 for domestic and international students; for spring admission, 11/1 for domestic students, 10/1 for international students; for summer admission, 4/1 for domestic and international students. Application fee: $60 ($75 for international students). Electronic applications accepted. *Unit head:* Dr. Arline Savage, Director, Master of Accounting Program, 205-934-8825, Fax: 205-975-4429, E-mail: arlsav@uab.edu. *Application contact:* Christy Manning, Admissions Counselor, 205-934-8815, Fax: 205-975-5933, E-mail: cmanning@uab.edu.
Website: http://www.uab.edu/business/degrees-certificates/master-of-accounting.

The University of Alabama in Huntsville, School of Graduate Studies, College of Business Administration, Program in Accounting, Huntsville, AL 35899. Offers accounting (M Acc), including CPA preparatory with an emphasis in taxation, CPA preparatory with emphasis in assurance and financial reporting, general accounting, information systems audit and control (ISAC). *Accreditation:* AACSB. Part-time and evening/weekend programs available. *Faculty:* 9 full-time (3 women). *Students:* 14 full-time (6 women), 27 part-time (16 women); includes 8 minority (6 Black or African American, non-Hispanic/Latino; 2 Asian, non-Hispanic/Latino), 6 international. Average age 30. 24 applicants, 63% accepted, 8 enrolled. In 2013, 29 master's awarded. *Degree requirements:* For master's, comprehensive exam, thesis or alternative. *Entrance requirements:* For master's, GMAT (minimum score 500), minimum AACSB index of 1080. Additional exam requirements/recommendations for international students: Required—TOEFL (minimum score 550 paper-based; 80 iBT), IELTS (minimum score 6.5). *Application deadline:* For fall admission, 7/15 priority date for domestic students, 4/1 priority date for international students; for spring admission, 11/30 priority date for domestic students, 9/1 priority date for international students. Applications are processed on a rolling basis. Application fee: $50. Electronic applications accepted. *Expenses:* Tuition, state resident: full-time $8912; part-time $540 per credit hour. Tuition, nonresident: full-time $20,774; part-time $1252 per credit hour. *Required fees:* $148 per semester. One-time fee: $150. *Financial support:* Teaching assistantships, career-related internships or fieldwork, Federal Work-Study, institutionally sponsored loans, scholarships/grants, health care benefits, and unspecified assistantships available. Support available to part-time students. Financial award application deadline: 4/1; financial award applicants required to submit FAFSA. *Faculty research:* Accounting information systems, managerial accounting, behavioral accounting, state and local taxation, financial accounting. *Unit head:* Dr. Allen Wilhite, Interim Chair, 256-824-6591, Fax: 256-824-2929, E-mail: allen.wilhite@uah.edu. *Application contact:* Jennifer Pettitt, Director of Graduate Programs, 256-824-6681, Fax: 256-824-7571, E-mail: jennifer.pettitt@uah.edu.

The University of Alabama in Huntsville, School of Graduate Studies, College of Business Administration, Programs in Business and Management, Huntsville, AL 35899. Offers federal contracting and procurement management (Certificate); management (MBA), including acquisition management, entrepreneurship, federal contract accounting, finance, human resource management, logistics and supply chain management, marketing, project management; supply chain management (Certificate); technology and innovation management (Certificate). *Accreditation:* AACSB. Part-time and evening/weekend programs available. *Faculty:* 13 full-time (3 women), 5 part-time/adjunct (0 women). *Students:* 41 full-time (19 women), 144 part-time (59 women); includes 35 minority (13 Black or African American, non-Hispanic/Latino; 1 American Indian or Alaska Native, non-Hispanic/Latino; 9 Asian, non-Hispanic/Latino; 11 Hispanic/Latino; 1 Two or more races, non-Hispanic/Latino), 13 international. Average age 33. 131 applicants, 78% accepted, 67 enrolled. In 2013, 83 master's, 5 other advanced degrees awarded. *Degree requirements:* For master's, comprehensive exam, thesis or alternative. *Entrance requirements:* For master's, GMAT (minimum score 500), minimum AACSB index of 1080. Additional exam requirements/recommendations for international students: Required—TOEFL (minimum score 550 paper-based; 80 iBT), IELTS (minimum score 6.5). *Application deadline:* For fall admission, 7/15 priority date for domestic students, 4/1 priority date for international students; for spring admission, 11/30 priority date for domestic students, 9/1 priority date for international students. Applications are processed on a rolling basis. Application fee: $50. Electronic applications accepted. *Expenses:* Tuition, state resident: full-time $8912; part-time $540 per credit hour. Tuition, nonresident: full-time $20,774; part-time $1252 per credit hour. *Required fees:* $148 per semester. One-time fee: $150. *Financial support:* In 2013–14, 10 students received support, including 4 research assistantships with full and partial tuition reimbursements available (averaging $7,750 per year), 5 teaching assistantships with full and partial tuition reimbursements available (averaging $9,000 per year); career-related internships or fieldwork, Federal Work-Study, institutionally sponsored loans, scholarships/grants, health care benefits, tuition waivers (full and partial), and unspecified assistantships also available. Support available to part-time students. Financial award application deadline: 4/1; financial award applicants required to submit FAFSA. *Faculty research:* Supply chain management, management of research and development, international marketing and branding, organizational behavior and human resource management, social networks and computational economics. *Total annual research expenditures:* $2.1 million. *Unit head:* Dr. Cynthia Gramm, Chair, 256-824-6913, Fax: 256-824-6328, E-mail: cynthia.gramm@uah.edu. *Application contact:* Jennifer Pettitt, Director of Graduate Programs, 256-824-6681, Fax: 256-824-7571, E-mail: jennifer.pettitt@uah.edu.

University of Alberta, Faculty of Graduate Studies and Research, Doctoral Program in Business, Edmonton, AB T6G 2E1, Canada. Offers accounting (PhD); finance (PhD); human resources/industrial relations (PhD); management science (PhD); marketing (PhD); organizational analysis (PhD); MBA/PhD. *Accreditation:* AACSB. Part-time programs available. *Degree requirements:* For doctorate, comprehensive exam, thesis/dissertation. *Entrance requirements:* For doctorate, GMAT. Additional exam requirements/recommendations for international students: Required—TOEFL (minimum score 550 paper-based). Electronic applications accepted. *Faculty research:* Accounting, capital markets and corporate finance, organizational change and human resource management, marketing, strategic management.

The University of Arizona, Eller College of Management, Department of Accounting, Tucson, AZ 85721. Offers M Ac, MS, PhD. *Accreditation:* AACSB. Part-time programs available. *Faculty:* 9 full-time (4 women), 1 (woman) part-time/adjunct. *Students:* 81 full-time (39 women), 9 part-time (3 women); includes 19 minority (7 Asian, non-Hispanic/Latino; 4 Hispanic/Latino; 8 Two or more races, non-Hispanic/Latino), 11 international. Average age 28. 138 applicants, 52% accepted, 50 enrolled. In 2013, 70 master's awarded. *Degree requirements:* For master's, comprehensive exam, 1-year residency. *Entrance requirements:* For master's, GMAT (minimum score 550), 2 letters of recommendation, 3 writing samples, resume. Additional exam requirements/recommendations for international students: Required—TOEFL (minimum score 600 paper-based; 100 iBT). *Application deadline:* For fall admission, 3/1 priority date for domestic and international students; for spring admission, 10/1 priority date for domestic and international students. Applications are processed on a rolling basis. Application fee: $75. Electronic applications accepted. *Expenses:* Contact institution. *Financial support:* In 2013–14, 44 teaching assistantships with full tuition reimbursements (averaging $26,000 per year) were awarded; career-related internships or fieldwork, Federal Work-Study, scholarships/grants, health care benefits, tuition waivers (partial), and unspecified assistantships also available. Financial award application deadline: 3/15. *Faculty research:* Auditing, financial reporting and financial markets, taxation policy and markets, behavioral research in accounting. *Unit head:* Dr. Dan S. Dhaliwal, Head, 520-621-2146, Fax: 520-621-3742, E-mail: dhaliwal@eller.arizona.edu. *Application contact:* Leslie Cohen, Programs Coordinator, 520-621-2910, Fax: 520-621-3742, E-mail: accounting@eller.arizona.edu.
Website: http://accounting.eller.arizona.edu/.

University of Arkansas, Graduate School, Sam M. Walton College of Business Administration, Department of Accounting, Fayetteville, AR 72701-1201. Offers M Acc. *Accreditation:* AACSB. *Entrance requirements:* For master's, GMAT.

University of Arkansas at Little Rock, Graduate School, College of Business Administration, Little Rock, AR 72204-1099. Offers accountancy (M Acc, Graduate Certificate); business administration (MBA); construction management (Graduate Certificate); management (Graduate Certificate); management information system (MIS); management information systems (Graduate Certificate); management information systems leadership (Graduate Certificate); taxation (MS, Graduate Certificate). *Accreditation:* AACSB. Part-time and evening/weekend programs available. *Entrance requirements:* For master's, GMAT, minimum undergraduate GPA of 2.7. Additional exam requirements/recommendations for international students: Required—TOEFL (minimum score 525 paper-based). *Expenses:* Tuition, state resident: full-time $5690; part-time $284.50 per credit hour. Tuition, nonresident: full-time $13,030; part-time $651.50 per credit hour. *Required fees:* $1121; $672 per term. One-time fee: $40 full-time.

University of Baltimore, Graduate School, Merrick School of Business, Department of Accounting and Management Information Systems, Baltimore, MD 21201-5779. Offers accounting and business advisory services (MS); accounting fundamentals (Graduate Certificate); forensic accounting (Graduate Certificate). Part-time and evening/weekend programs available. *Entrance requirements:* For master's, GMAT. Additional exam requirements/recommendations for international students: Required—TOEFL (minimum score 550 paper-based). Electronic applications accepted. *Faculty research:* Health care, accounting and administration, managerial accounting, financial accounting theory, accounting information.

University of Bridgeport, School of Business, Bridgeport, CT 06604. Offers accounting (MBA); finance (MBA); general business (MBA); global financial services (MBA); human resource management (MBA); information systems and knowledge management (MBA); international business (MBA); management (MBA); marketing (MBA); operations management (MBA); small business and entrepreneurship (MBA); specialized business (MBA). *Accreditation:* ACBSP. Part-time and evening/weekend programs available. *Faculty:* 11 full-time (2 women), 39 part-time/adjunct (8 women). *Students:* 162 full-time (90 women), 69 part-time (45 women); includes 44 minority (20 Black or African American, non-Hispanic/Latino; 7 Asian, non-Hispanic/Latino; 15 Hispanic/Latino; 2 Two or more races, non-Hispanic/Latino), 163 international. Average age 28. 492 applicants, 48% accepted, 55 enrolled. In 2013, 144 master's awarded. *Degree requirements:* For master's, thesis optional. *Entrance requirements:* For master's, GMAT. Additional exam requirements/recommendations for international students: Recommended—TOEFL (minimum score 550 paper-based; 80 iBT), IELTS (minimum score 6.5). *Application deadline:* For fall admission, 8/1 priority date for domestic and international students; for spring admission, 12/1 priority date for domestic and international students. Applications are processed on a rolling basis. Application fee: $50. Electronic applications accepted. *Expenses:* Contact institution. *Financial support:* In 2013–14, 69 students received support. Fellowships, research assistantships, teaching assistantships, career-related internships or fieldwork, Federal Work-Study, institutionally sponsored loans, and tuition waivers (partial) available. Support available to part-time students. Financial award application deadline: 6/1; financial award applicants required to submit FAFSA. *Unit head:* Dr. Lloyd G. Gibson, Dean, 203-576-4384, Fax: 203-576-4388, E-mail: llgibson@bridgeport.edu. *Application contact:* Leanne Proctor, Director of Graduate Admissions, 203-576-4552, Fax: 203-576-4941, E-mail: mba@bridgeport.edu.
Website: http://www.bridgeport.edu.

The University of British Columbia, Sauder School of Business, Doctoral Program in Commerce and Business Administration, Vancouver, BC V6T 1Z1, Canada. Offers accounting (PhD); finance (PhD); management information systems (PhD); management science (PhD); marketing (PhD); organizational behavior (PhD); strategy and business economics (PhD); transportation and logistics (PhD); urban land economics (PhD). *Faculty:* 91 full-time (22 women). *Students:* 66 full-time (24 women). Average age 30. 418 applicants, 2% accepted, 8 enrolled. In 2013, 7 doctorates awarded. *Degree requirements:* For doctorate, comprehensive exam, thesis/dissertation. *Entrance requirements:* For doctorate, GMAT or GRE. Additional exam requirements/recommendations for international students: Required—TOEFL (minimum score 600 paper-based; 100 iBT). *Application deadline:* For fall admission, 1/31 for domestic students, 12/31 for international students. Applications are processed on a rolling basis. Application fee: $95 Canadian dollars ($153 Canadian dollars for international students). Electronic applications accepted. *Expenses: Tuition, area resident:* Full-time $8000 Canadian dollars. *Financial support:* In 2013–14, fellowships with full tuition reimbursements (averaging $17,500 per year), research assistantships with full tuition reimbursements (averaging $8,500 per year), teaching assistantships with full tuition reimbursements (averaging $17,500 per year) were awarded. Financial award application deadline: 12/31. *Unit head:* Dr. Ralph Winter, Director, 604-822-8366, Fax: 604-822-8755. *Application contact:* Elaine Cho, Administrator, PhD and M Sc Programs, 604-822-8366, Fax: 604-822-8755, E-mail: phd.program@sauder.ubc.ca.
Website: http://www.sauder.ubc.ca/.

University of California, Berkeley, Graduate Division, Haas School of Business, PhD in Business Administration Program, Berkeley, CA 94720-1500. Offers accounting (PhD); business and public policy (PhD); finance (PhD); management of organizations (PhD); marketing (PhD); operations management (PhD); real estate (PhD). *Accreditation:* AACSB. *Students:* 74 full-time (28 women); includes 11 minority (9 Asian, non-Hispanic/Latino; 2 Hispanic/Latino), 38 international. Average age 27. 490 applicants, 6% accepted, 14 enrolled. In 2013, 14 doctorates awarded. *Degree requirements:* For doctorate, comprehensive exam, thesis/dissertation, written preliminary exams, oral qualifying exam. *Entrance requirements:* For doctorate, GMAT or GRE, minimum GPA of 3.0 in undergraduate and graduate coursework. Additional exam requirements/recommendations for international students: Required—TOEFL (minimum score 570 paper-based; 70 iBT), IELTS (minimum score 7). *Application deadline:* For fall admission, 12/10 for domestic and international students. Application fee: $80 ($100 for international students). Electronic applications accepted. *Financial support:* In 2013–14, 74 students received support, including 62 fellowships with full and partial tuition reimbursements available (averaging $30,000 per year), research assistantships with full and partial tuition reimbursements available (averaging $12,000 per year), teaching assistantships with full and partial tuition reimbursements available (averaging $13,000 per year); scholarships/grants, health care benefits, tuition waivers (full), unspecified assistantships, and transit passes, travel grants also available. Financial award application deadline: 12/10; financial award applicants required to submit FAFSA. *Faculty research:* Accounting, business and public policy, entrepreneurship, finance, management of organizations, marketing, operations and information technology management, real estate. *Unit head:* Dr. Martin Lettau, Director, 510-643-6349, Fax: 510-643-4255, E-mail: kimg@haas.berkeley.edu. *Application contact:* Kim Guilfoyle, Director, Student Affairs, 510-642-3944, Fax: 510-643-4255, E-mail: kimg@haas.berkeley.edu.
Website: http://www.haas.berkeley.edu/Phd/.

University of California, Berkeley, UC Berkeley Extension, Certificate Programs in Business, Berkeley, CA 94720-1500. Offers accounting (Certificate); business administration (Certificate); finance (Certificate); human resource management (Certificate); management (Certificate); marketing (Certificate); project management (Certificate). *Accreditation:* AACSB. Postbaccalaureate distance learning degree programs offered.

University of California, Davis, Graduate School of Management, Master of Professional Accountancy Program, Davis, CA 95616. Offers MP Ac. *Faculty:* 32 full-time (13 women), 25 part-time/adjunct (0 women). *Students:* 39 full-time (21 women); includes 8 minority (4 Asian, non-Hispanic/Latino; 2 Hispanic/Latino; 2 Two or more races, non-Hispanic/Latino), 16 international. Average age 25. 471 applicants, 19% accepted, 39 enrolled. In 2013, 29 master's awarded. *Degree requirements:* For master's, comprehensive exam. *Entrance requirements:* For master's, GMAT or GRE, letters of recommendation, resume, essays, equivalent of a 4-year U.S. undergraduate degree. Additional exam requirements/recommendations for international students: Required—TOEFL (minimum score 600 paper-based; 100 iBT), IELTS (minimum score 7), PTE (minimum score 68). *Application deadline:* For fall admission, 11/13 priority date for domestic and international students. Applications are processed on a rolling basis. Application fee: $125. Electronic applications accepted. *Financial support:* In 2013–14, 3 students received support. Fellowships and scholarships/grants available. Financial award applicants required to submit FAFSA. *Unit head:* James R. Stevens, Senior Assistant Dean of Student Affairs, 530-752-7658, Fax: 530-754-9355, E-mail: admissions@gsm.ucdavis.edu. *Application contact:* Kathy Gleed, Senior Director of Admission, 530-752-7658, Fax: 530-754-9355, E-mail: admissions@gsm.ucdavis.edu.
Website: http://gsm.ucdavis.edu/master-professional-accountancy.

University of California, Los Angeles, Graduate Division, UCLA Anderson School of Management, Los Angeles, CA 90095-1481. Offers accounting (PhD); Americas (EMBA); Asia Pacific (EMBA); business administration (EMBA, MBA); decisions, operations and technology management (PhD); finance (PhD); financial engineering (MFE); global economics and management (PhD); management and organizations (PhD); marketing (PhD); strategy and policy (PhD); DDS/MBA; MBA/JD; MBA/MD; MBA/MLAS; MBA/MLIS; MBA/MPH; MBA/MPP; MBA/MSCS; MBA/MSN; MBA/MUP. *Accreditation:* AACSB. Part-time programs available. *Faculty:* 104 full-time (20 women), 28 part-time/adjunct (4 women). *Students:* 1,069 full-time (324 women), 879 part-time (251 women); includes 664 minority (37 Black or African American, non-Hispanic/Latino; 1 American Indian or Alaska Native, non-Hispanic/Latino; 470 Asian, non-Hispanic/Latino; 34 Hispanic/Latino; 2 Native Hawaiian or other Pacific Islander, non-Hispanic/Latino; 120 Two or more races, non-Hispanic/Latino), 444 international. Average age 30. 5,084 applicants, 27% accepted, 845 enrolled. In 2013, 801 master's, 14 doctorates awarded. *Degree requirements:* For master's, comprehensive exam, field study consulting project (for MBA); thesis (for MFE); for doctorate, comprehensive exam, thesis/dissertation, oral and written qualifying exams. *Entrance requirements:* For master's, GMAT (for MBA); GMAT or GRE General Test (for MFE), 4-year bachelor's degree or equivalent; recommendation letters (1 for MBA, 2 for MFE); two essays; interview (by invitation only for MBA); for doctorate, GMAT or GRE General Test, bachelor's degree from college or university of fully-recognized standing; minimum B average in undergraduate coursework or B+ average in prior graduate work; statement of purpose; three recommendation letters. Additional exam requirements/recommendations for international students: Required—TOEFL (minimum score 560 paper-based; 87 iBT). *Application deadline:* For fall admission, 10/22 priority date for domestic and international students; for winter admission, 1/7 for domestic and international students; for spring admission, 4/15 for domestic and international students. Applications are processed on a rolling basis. Application fee: $200. Electronic applications accepted. *Expenses:* Contact institution. *Financial support:* In 2013–14, 522 students received support. Fellowships, research assistantships with partial tuition reimbursements available, teaching assistantships with partial tuition reimbursements available, career-related internships or fieldwork, institutionally sponsored loans, scholarships/grants, health care benefits, and tuition waivers (partial) available. Financial award application deadline: 4/15; financial award applicants required to submit FAFSA. *Faculty research:* Asset pricing, decision-making, behavioral finance, international finance and economics, global macroeconomics. *Total annual research expenditures:* $368,086. *Unit head:* Dr. Judy D. Olian, Dean/Chair in Management, 310-825-7982, Fax: 310-206-2073, E-mail: judy.olian@anderson.ucla.edu. *Application contact:* Alex Lawrence, Assistant Dean, MBA Admissions and Financial Aid, 310-825-6944, Fax: 310-825-8582, E-mail: mba.admissions@anderson.ucla.edu.
Website: http://www.anderson.ucla.edu/.

See Display on page 145 and Close-Up on page 191.

University of California, Riverside, Graduate Division, A. Gary Anderson Graduate School of Management, Riverside, CA 92521-0102. Offers accountancy (MPAC); business administration (MBA, PhD); finance (M Fin). *Accreditation:* AACSB. Part-time and evening/weekend programs available. *Faculty:* 24 full-time (6 women), 11 part-time/

adjunct (3 women). *Students:* 295 full-time (161 women), 1 part-time (0 women); includes 38 minority (2 Black or African American, non-Hispanic/Latino; 31 Asian, non-Hispanic/Latino; 5 Hispanic/Latino), 237 international. Average age 24. 565 applicants, 82% accepted, 186 enrolled. In 2013, 89 master's awarded. Terminal master's awarded for partial completion of doctoral program. *Degree requirements:* For master's, thesis optional; for doctorate, comprehensive exam, thesis/dissertation. *Entrance requirements:* For master's, GMAT or GRE, minimum GPA of 3.2; for doctorate, GMAT or GRE. Additional exam requirements/recommendations for international students: Required—TOEFL (minimum score 550 paper-based; 80 iBT), IELTS. *Application deadline:* For fall admission, 9/1 for domestic students, 5/1 for international students; for winter admission, 12/1 for domestic students, 9/1 for international students; for spring admission, 3/1 for domestic students, 10/1 for international students. Applications are processed on a rolling basis. Application fee: $100 ($125 for international students). *Expenses:* Contact institution. *Financial support:* In 2013–14, 58 fellowships with partial tuition reimbursements (averaging $22,848 per year), 46 teaching assistantships with partial tuition reimbursements (averaging $20,000 per year) were awarded; research assistantships with full tuition reimbursements, career-related internships or fieldwork, institutionally sponsored loans, scholarships/grants, and tuition waivers (full) also available. Financial award application deadline: 5/1; financial award applicants required to submit FAFSA. *Faculty research:* Option pricing, marketing, decision modeling, new technologies in cost accounting, supply chain management, operations, production and inventory systems, entrepreneurial finance, e-commerce. *Unit head:* Dr. Yunzeng Wang, Dean, 951-827-6329, Fax: 951-827-3970, E-mail: mba@ucr.edu. *Application contact:* Dr. Rami Zwick, Associate Dean/Graduate Adviser, 951-827-7766, Fax: 951-827-3970, E-mail: mba@ucr.edu.
Website: http://agsm.ucr.edu/.

University of Central Arkansas, Graduate School, College of Business Administration, Program in Accounting, Conway, AR 72035-0001. Offers M Acc. Part-time programs available. *Degree requirements:* For master's, capstone course. *Entrance requirements:* For master's, GMAT or GRE, minimum GPA of 2.7. Additional exam requirements/recommendations for international students: Required—TOEFL (minimum score 550 paper-based; 80 iBT).

University of Central Florida, College of Business Administration, Kenneth G. Dixon School of Accounting, Orlando, FL 32816. Offers MSA, MST. *Accreditation:* AACSB. Part-time and evening/weekend programs available. *Faculty:* 21 full-time (9 women), 2 part-time/adjunct (1 woman). *Students:* 99 full-time (49 women), 110 part-time (58 women); includes 53 minority (8 Black or African American, non-Hispanic/Latino; 21 Asian, non-Hispanic/Latino; 22 Hispanic/Latino; 2 Two or more races, non-Hispanic/Latino), 5 international. Average age 28. 119 applicants, 61% accepted, 55 enrolled. In 2013, 92 master's awarded. *Degree requirements:* For master's, comprehensive exam. *Entrance requirements:* For master's, GMAT, minimum GPA of 3.0 in last 60 hours. Additional exam requirements/recommendations for international students: Required—TOEFL. *Application deadline:* For fall admission, 6/15 priority date for domestic students; for spring admission, 11/1 priority date for domestic students. Electronic applications accepted. *Financial support:* In 2013–14, 11 students received support, including 11 teaching assistantships with partial tuition reimbursements available (averaging $7,000 per year); career-related internships or fieldwork, Federal Work-Study, institutionally sponsored loans, tuition waivers (partial), and unspecified assistantships also available. Financial award application deadline: 3/1; financial award applicants required to submit FAFSA. *Unit head:* Dr. Sean Robb, Director, 407-823-2871, Fax: 407-823-3881, E-mail: srobb@bus.ucf.edu. *Application contact:* Judy Ryder, Director, Graduate Admissions, 407-235-3916, Fax: 407-823-0219, E-mail: jryder@ucf.edu.
Website: http://web.bus.ucf.edu/accounting/.

University of Central Missouri, The Graduate School, Warrensburg, MO 6409. Offers accountancy (MA); accounting (MBA); applied mathematics (MS); aviation safety (MA); biology (MS); business administration (MBA); career and technical education leadership (MS); college student personnel administration (MS); communication (MA); computer science (MS); counseling (MS); criminal justice (MS); educational leadership (Ed D); educational technology (MS); elementary and early childhood education (MSE); English (MA); environmental studies (MA); finance (MBA); history (MA); human services/educational technology (Ed S); human services/learning resources (Ed S); human services/professional counseling (Ed S); industrial hygiene (MS); industrial management (MS); information systems (MBA); information technology (MS); kinesiology (MS); library science and information services (MS); literacy education (MSE); marketing (MBA); mathematics (MS); music (MA); occupational safety management (MS); psychology (MS); rural family nursing (MS); school administration (MSE); social gerontology (MS); sociology (MA); special education (MSE); speech language pathology (MS); superintendency (Ed S); teaching (MAT); teaching English as a second language (MA); technology (MS); technology management (PhD); theatre (MA). Part-time programs available. *Faculty:* 233. *Students:* 890 full-time (396 women), 1,486 part-time (1,001 women); includes 192 minority (97 Black or African American, non-Hispanic/Latino; 9 American Indian or Alaska Native, non-Hispanic/Latino; 32 Asian, non-Hispanic/Latino; 40 Hispanic/Latino; 3 Native Hawaiian or other Pacific Islander, non-Hispanic/Latino; 11 Two or more races, non-Hispanic/Latino), 539 international. Average age 31. 1,953 applicants, 75% accepted. In 2013, 719 master's, 58 other advanced degrees awarded. *Degree requirements:* For master's and Ed S, comprehensive exam (for some programs), thesis (for some programs). *Entrance requirements:* Additional exam requirements/recommendations for international students: Required—TOEFL (minimum score 550 paper-based; 79 iBT). *Application deadline:* For fall admission, 6/1 for domestic students; for spring admission, 10/1 for domestic and international students. Applications are processed on a rolling basis. Application fee: $30 ($75 for international students). Electronic applications accepted. *Expenses:* Tuition, state resident: full-time $7326; part-time $276.25 per credit hour. Tuition, nonresident: full-time $13,956; part-time $552.50 per credit hour. *Required fees:* $29 per credit hour. *Financial support:* In 2013–14, 118 students received support, including 271 research assistantships with full and partial tuition reimbursements available (averaging $7,500 per year), 109 teaching assistantships with full and partial tuition reimbursements available (averaging $7,500 per year); career-related internships or fieldwork, Federal Work-Study, scholarships/grants, and administrative and laboratory assistantships also available. Support available to part-time students. Financial award application deadline: 3/1; financial award applicants required to submit FAFSA. *Unit head:* Dr. Joseph Vaughn, Assistant Provost for Research/Dean, 660-543-4092, Fax: 660-543-4778, E-mail: vaughn@ucmo.edu. *Application contact:* Brittany Lawrence, Graduate Student Services Coordinator, 660-543-4621, Fax: 660-543-4778, E-mail: gradinfo@ucmo.edu.
Website: http://www.ucmo.edu/graduate/.

University of Central Oklahoma, The Jackson College of Graduate Studies, College of Business, Edmond, OK 73034-5209. Offers accounting (MBA); management (MBA). Part-time programs available. *Faculty:* 12 full-time (3 women). *Students:* 68 full-time (38 women), 111 part-time (40 women); includes 32 minority (7 Black or African American, non-Hispanic/Latino; 4 American Indian or Alaska Native, non-Hispanic/Latino; 6 Asian, non-Hispanic/Latino; 10 Hispanic/Latino; 5 Two or more races, non-Hispanic/Latino), 23 international. Average age 29. 153 applicants, 73% accepted, 53 enrolled. In 2013, 89 master's awarded. *Degree requirements:* For master's, comprehensive exam (for some programs), thesis optional. *Entrance requirements:* For master's, GMAT, GRE. Additional exam requirements/recommendations for international students: Required—TOEFL (minimum score 550 paper-based; 79 iBT), IELTS (minimum score 6.5). *Application deadline:* For fall admission, 7/15 for domestic students, 7/1 for international students; for spring admission, 11/15 for domestic students, 11/1 for international students. Applications are processed on a rolling basis. Application fee: $50. Electronic applications accepted. *Expenses:* Contact institution. *Financial support:* In 2013–14, 32 students received support, including 3 research assistantships (averaging $6,901 per year), 2 teaching assistantships (averaging $11,825 per year); career-related internships or fieldwork, Federal Work-Study, scholarships/grants, tuition waivers (partial), and unspecified assistantships also available. Financial award application deadline: 3/31; financial award applicants required to submit FAFSA. *Unit head:* Dr. Mickey Hepner, Dean, 405-974-2809, E-mail: mhepner@uco.edu. *Application contact:* Dr. Richard Bernard, Dean, Graduate College, 405-974-3493, Fax: 405-974-3852, E-mail: gradcoll@uco.edu.

University of Charleston, Executive Master of Forensic Accounting Program, Charleston, WV 25304-1099. Offers EMFA. Part-time programs available. Postbaccalaureate distance learning degree programs offered (minimal on-campus study). *Students:* 4 full-time (2 women). Average age 45. In 2013, 8 master's awarded. *Degree requirements:* For master's, capstone project with mock trial testimony. *Entrance requirements:* Additional exam requirements/recommendations for international students: Required—TOEFL. *Application deadline:* Applications are processed on a rolling basis. Application fee: $50. Electronic applications accepted. *Financial support:* In 2013–14, 1 student received support. Applicants required to submit FAFSA. *Unit head:* Dr. Scott Bellamy, Dean of the School of Business, 304-357-4373, E-mail: scottbellamy@ucwv.edu. *Application contact:* Robert Rufus, Program Coordinator, 304-522-8770, E-mail: mfa@ucwv.edu.
Website: http://www.ucwv.edu/Forensic-Accounting/.

University of Chicago, Booth School of Business, Full-Time MBA Program, Chicago, IL 60637. Offers accounting (MBA); analytic finance (MBA); analytic management (MBA); econometrics and statistics (MBA); economics (MBA); entrepreneurship (MBA); finance (MBA); general management (MBA); health administration and policy (Certificate); human resource management (MBA); international business (MBA); managerial and organizational behavior (MBA); marketing management (MBA); operations management (MBA); strategic management (MBA); MBA/AM; MBA/JD; MBA/MA; MBA/MD; MBA/MPP. *Accreditation:* AACSB. Part-time and evening/weekend programs available. Terminal master's awarded for partial completion of doctoral program. *Entrance requirements:* For master's, GMAT, 2 letters of recommendation, 3 essays, resume, interview. Additional exam requirements/recommendations for international students: Required—TOEFL (minimum score 600 paper-based; 104 iBT), IELTS. Electronic applications accepted. *Expenses:* Contact institution. *Faculty research:* Finance, marketing, economics, entrepreneurship, strategy, management.

University of Cincinnati, Graduate School, Carl H. Lindner College of Business, MS Program, Cincinnati, OH 45221. Offers accounting (MS); business analytics (MS); finance (MS); information systems (MS); marketing (MS); taxation (MS). Part-time and evening/weekend programs available. *Faculty:* 39 full-time (11 women), 11 part-time/adjunct (3 women). *Students:* 275 full-time (105 women), 165 part-time (69 women); includes 29 minority (14 Black or African American, non-Hispanic/Latino; 9 Asian, non-Hispanic/Latino; 1 Native Hawaiian or other Pacific Islander, non-Hispanic/Latino; 5 Two or more races, non-Hispanic/Latino), 273 international. 953 applicants, 37% accepted, 258 enrolled. In 2013, 144 master's awarded. *Degree requirements:* For master's, thesis (for some programs). *Entrance requirements:* For master's, GMAT, GRE, resume, transcripts, essays, letters of recommendation. Additional exam requirements/recommendations for international students: Required—TOEFL (minimum score 600 paper-based; 100 iBT), IELTS (minimum score 6.5). *Application deadline:* For fall admission, 3/15 priority date for domestic students, 4/1 for international students. Applications are processed on a rolling basis. Application fee: $65 ($70 for international students). Electronic applications accepted. *Expenses:* Contact institution. *Financial support:* In 2013–14, 124 students received support, including 12 teaching assistantships with full and partial tuition reimbursements available (averaging $3,500 per year); scholarships/grants, tuition waivers (full and partial), and unspecified assistantships also available. Financial award application deadline: 2/1; financial award applicants required to submit FAFSA. *Faculty research:* Real estate, empirical pricing, organization information pricing, strategic management, portfolio choice in institutional investment. *Unit head:* Dr. David Szymanski, Dean, 513-556-7001, Fax: 513-556-4891, E-mail: david.szymanski@uc.edu. *Application contact:* Dona Clary, Director, Graduate Programs, 513-556-3546, Fax: 513-558-7006, E-mail: dona.clary@uc.edu.

University of Cincinnati, Graduate School, Carl H. Lindner College of Business, PhD Programs, Cincinnati, OH 45221. Offers accounting (PhD); economics (PhD); finance (PhD); information systems (PhD); management (PhD); marketing (PhD); operations and business analytics (PhD). *Faculty:* 62 full-time (13 women). *Students:* 27 full-time (15 women), 9 part-time (1 woman); includes 2 minority (1 Asian, non-Hispanic/Latino; 1 Hispanic/Latino), 16 international. Average age 29. 86 applicants, 13% accepted, 6 enrolled. In 2013, 8 doctorates awarded. *Degree requirements:* For doctorate, comprehensive exam, thesis/dissertation. *Entrance requirements:* For doctorate, GMAT, GRE, transcripts, essays, resume, letters of recommendation. Additional exam requirements/recommendations for international students: Required—TOEFL (minimum score 600 paper-based; 100 iBT), IELTS (minimum score 6.5). *Application deadline:* For fall admission, 1/15 for domestic and international students. Application fee: $65 ($70 for international students). Electronic applications accepted. *Expenses:* Contact institution. *Financial support:* In 2013–14, 33 students received support, including 25 research assistantships with full and partial tuition reimbursements available (averaging $23,250 per year); scholarships/grants, tuition waivers (full and partial), and unspecified assistantships also available. Financial award application deadline: 1/15; financial award applicants required to submit FAFSA. *Unit head:* Dr. Suzanne Masterson, Director, 513-556-7125, Fax: 513-556-5499, E-mail: suzanne.masterson@uc.edu. *Application contact:* Angel Elvin, Assistant Director, 513-556-7190, Fax: 513-558-7006, E-mail: angel.elvin@uc.edu.
Website: http://www.business.uc.edu/phd.

University of Colorado Boulder, Leeds School of Business, Division of Business Administration, Boulder, CO 80309. Offers accounting (MS, PhD); finance (PhD); information systems (PhD); marketing (PhD); operations (PhD); strategic, organizational, and entrepreneurial studies (PhD). *Students:* 143 full-time (72 women), 2 part-time (1 woman); includes 15 minority (1 Black or African American, non-Hispanic/Latino; 2 American Indian or Alaska Native, non-Hispanic/Latino; 5 Asian, non-Hispanic/Latino; 6 Hispanic/Latino; 1 Two or more races, non-Hispanic/Latino), 37 international. Average age 25. 281 applicants, 12% accepted, 19 enrolled. In 2013, 50 master's, 8 doctorates awarded. *Entrance requirements:* For master's, GMAT, minimum undergraduate GPA of 3.0. *Application deadline:* For fall admission, 3/31 for domestic students, 3/1 for international students; for spring admission, 10/31 for domestic and international students. Application fee: $50 ($60 for international students). Electronic applications accepted. *Financial support:* In 2013–14, 145 students received support, including 37 fellowships (averaging $3,977 per year), 27 research assistantships with full

and partial tuition reimbursements available (averaging $40,893 per year), 12 teaching assistantships with full and partial tuition reimbursements available (averaging $38,197 per year); institutionally sponsored loans, scholarships/grants, health care benefits, and unspecified assistantships also available. Financial award applicants required to submit FAFSA.

University of Colorado Denver, Business School, Program in Accounting, Denver, CO 80217. Offers auditing and forensic accounting (MS); controllership/financial officer (MS); information systems audit control (MS); taxation (MS). *Accreditation:* AACSB. Part-time and evening/weekend programs available. *Students:* 122 full-time (62 women), 36 part-time (19 women); includes 32 minority (3 Black or African American, non-Hispanic/Latino; 14 Asian, non-Hispanic/Latino; 13 Hispanic/Latino; 2 Two or more races, non-Hispanic/Latino), 22 international. Average age 31. 95 applicants, 64% accepted, 32 enrolled. In 2013, 67 master's awarded. *Degree requirements:* For master's, 30 semester hours. *Entrance requirements:* For master's, GMAT (waived for students who already hold a graduate degree, or an undergraduate degree from CU Denver), essay, resume, two letters of recommendation; financial statements (for international students). Additional exam requirements/recommendations for international students: Required—TOEFL (minimum score 537 paper-based; 75 iBT); Recommended—IELTS (minimum score 6.5). *Application deadline:* For fall admission, 4/15 priority date for domestic students, 3/15 priority date for international students; for spring admission, 10/15 for domestic students, 9/15 priority date for international students. Applications are processed on a rolling basis. Application fee: $50 ($75 for international students). Electronic applications accepted. *Expenses:* Contact institution. *Financial support:* In 2013–14, 15 students received support. Fellowships, research assistantships, teaching assistantships, Federal Work-Study, institutionally sponsored loans, scholarships/grants, and traineeships available. Financial award application deadline: 4/1; financial award applicants required to submit FAFSA. *Faculty research:* Transfer pricing, behavioral accounting, environmental accounting, health services, international auditing. *Unit head:* Bruce Neumann, Professor, 303-315-8473, E-mail: bruce.neumann@ucdenver.edu. *Application contact:* Shelly Townley, Admissions Director, Graduate Programs, 303-315-8202, E-mail: shelly.townley@ucdenver.edu. Website: http://www.ucdenver.edu/academics/colleges/business/degrees/ms/accounting/Pages/Accounting.aspx.

University of Colorado Denver, Business School, Program in Information Systems, Denver, CO 80217. Offers accounting and information systems audit and control (MS); business intelligence systems (MS); ehealth and healthcare service entrepreneurship (MS); enterprise risk management (MS); enterprise technology management (MS); geographic information systems (MS); health information technology (MS); technology innovation and entrepreneurship (MS); Web and mobile computing (MS). Part-time and evening/weekend programs available. Postbaccalaureate distance learning degree programs offered (no on-campus study). *Students:* 55 full-time (14 women), 23 part-time (8 women); includes 10 minority (2 Black or African American, non-Hispanic/Latino; 7 Asian, non-Hispanic/Latino; 1 Hispanic/Latino), 15 international. Average age 33. 54 applicants, 78% accepted, 14 enrolled. In 2013, 27 master's awarded. *Degree requirements:* For master's, 30 credit hours. *Entrance requirements:* For master's, GMAT, resume, essay, two letters of recommendation, financial statements (for international applicants). Additional exam requirements/recommendations for international students: Required—TOEFL (minimum score 537 paper-based; 75 iBT); Recommended—IELTS (minimum score 6.5). *Application deadline:* For fall admission, 4/15 for domestic students, 3/15 for international students; for spring admission, 10/15 for domestic students, 9/15 for international students. Applications are processed on a rolling basis. Application fee: $50 ($75 for international students). Electronic applications accepted. *Expenses:* Contact institution. *Financial support:* In 2013–14, 18 students received support. Fellowships, research assistantships, teaching assistantships, Federal Work-Study, institutionally sponsored loans, scholarships/grants, and traineeships available. Financial award application deadline: 4/1; financial award applicants required to submit FAFSA. *Faculty research:* Human-computer interaction, expert systems, database management, electronic commerce, object-oriented software development. *Unit head:* Dr. Jahangir Karimi, Director of Information Systems Programs, 303-315-8430, E-mail: jahangir.karimi@ucdenver.edu. *Application contact:* Shelly Townley, Admissions Director, Graduate Programs, 303-315-8202, E-mail: shelly.townley@ucdenver.edu. Website: http://www.ucdenver.edu/academics/colleges/business/degrees/ms/IS/Pages/Information-Systems.aspx.

University of Connecticut, Graduate School, School of Business, Field of Accounting, Storrs, CT 06269. Offers MS, PhD. *Accreditation:* AACSB. *Entrance requirements:* Additional exam requirements/recommendations for international students: Required—TOEFL (minimum score 550 paper-based). Electronic applications accepted.

University of Dallas, Graduate School of Management, Irving, TX 75062-4736. Offers accounting (MBA, MM, MS); business management (MBA, MM); corporate finance (MBA, MM); financial services (MBA); global business (MBA, MM); health services management (MBA, MM); human resource management (MBA, MM); information assurance (MBA, MM, MS); information technology (MBA, MM, MS); information technology service management (MBA, MM, MS); marketing management (MBA, MM); organization development (MBA, MM); project management (MBA, MM); sports and entertainment management (MBA, MM); strategic leadership (MBA, MM); supply chain management (MBA); supply chain management and market logistics (MM). *Accreditation:* ACBSP. Part-time and evening/weekend programs available. Postbaccalaureate distance learning degree programs offered (no on-campus study). *Entrance requirements:* Additional exam requirements/recommendations for international students: Required—TOEFL. Electronic applications accepted. *Expenses:* Contact institution.

University of Dayton, School of Business Administration, Dayton, OH 45469-1300. Offers accounting (MBA); cyber security (MBA); finance (MBA); marketing (MBA); JD/MBA. *Accreditation:* AACSB. Part-time and evening/weekend programs available. *Faculty:* 20 full-time (7 women), 8 part-time/adjunct (1 woman). *Students:* 166 full-time (76 women), 85 part-time (43 women); includes 10 minority (4 Black or African American, non-Hispanic/Latino; 4 Asian, non-Hispanic/Latino; 2 Hispanic/Latino), 96 international. Average age 27. 437 applicants, 44% accepted, 53 enrolled. In 2013, 119 master's awarded. *Entrance requirements:* For master's, GMAT or GRE. Additional exam requirements/recommendations for international students: Required—TOEFL (minimum score 550 paper-based; 80 iBT); Recommended—IELTS (minimum score 6.5). *Application deadline:* For fall admission, 5/1 priority date for international students; for winter admission, 7/1 for international students; for spring admission, 11/1 priority date for international students. Applications are processed on a rolling basis. Application fee: $0 ($50 for international students). Electronic applications accepted. *Expenses:* Contact institution. *Financial support:* In 2013–14, 10 research assistantships with partial tuition reimbursements (averaging $7,020 per year) were awarded; institutionally sponsored loans, health care benefits, and unspecified assistantships also available. Financial award application deadline: 3/1; financial award applicants required to submit FAFSA. *Faculty research:* Management information systems, economics, finance, entrepreneurship, marketing, accounting and cyber security. *Unit head:* John M. Gentner, Director, MBA Program, 937-229-3733, Fax: 937-229-3882, E-mail: jgentner1@udayton.edu. *Application contact:* Mandy Schrank, Assistant Director, MBA Program, 937-229-3733, Fax: 937-229-3882, E-mail: mschrank2@udayton.edu. Website: http://business.udayton.edu/mba/.

University of Delaware, Alfred Lerner College of Business and Economics, Department of Accounting and Management Information Systems, Newark, DE 19716. Offers accounting (MS); information systems and technology management (MS). *Accreditation:* AACSB. Part-time and evening/weekend programs available. *Degree requirements:* For master's, thesis optional. *Entrance requirements:* For master's, GMAT. Additional exam requirements/recommendations for international students: Required—TOEFL (minimum score 550 paper-based). Electronic applications accepted. *Faculty research:* External reporting, managerial accounting, auditing information systems, taxation.

University of Denver, Daniels College of Business, School of Accountancy, Denver, CO 80208. Offers accountancy (M Acc); accounting (MBA). *Accreditation:* AACSB. Part-time and evening/weekend programs available. *Faculty:* 19 full-time (6 women), 6 part-time/adjunct (2 women). *Students:* 60 full-time (38 women), 69 part-time (52 women); includes 3 minority (all Asian, non-Hispanic/Latino), 99 international. Average age 24. 490 applicants, 62% accepted, 95 enrolled. In 2013, 87 master's awarded. *Entrance requirements:* For master's, GRE General Test or GMAT, bachelor's degree, transcripts, resume, two letters of recommendation, essays, interview. Additional exam requirements/recommendations for international students: Required—TOEFL (minimum score 570 paper-based; 88 iBT). *Application deadline:* For fall admission, 11/15 priority date for domestic and international students; for spring admission, 10/15 priority date for domestic and international students. Applications are processed on a rolling basis. Application fee: $100. Electronic applications accepted. *Financial support:* In 2013–14, 50 students received support, including 8 teaching assistantships with full and partial tuition reimbursements available (averaging $7,038 per year); career-related internships or fieldwork, Federal Work-Study, institutionally sponsored loans, scholarships/grants, and unspecified assistantships also available. Support available to part-time students. Financial award application deadline: 2/15; financial award applicants required to submit FAFSA. *Faculty research:* Management accounting, activity-based management, benchmarking, financial management and human services, derivatives. *Unit head:* Dr. Sharon Lassar, Director, 303-871-2032, E-mail: slassar@du.edu. *Application contact:* Lynn Noel, Graduate Admissions Manager, 303-871-7895, E-mail: lynn.noel@du.edu. Website: http://daniels.du.edu/masters-degrees/accountancy/.

University of Florida, Graduate School, Warrington College of Business Administration, Fisher School of Accounting, Gainesville, FL 32611. Offers M Acc, PhD, JD/M Acc. *Accreditation:* AACSB. Part-time programs available. *Faculty:* 10 full-time (2 women), 7 part-time/adjunct (2 women). *Students:* 179 full-time (77 women), 11 part-time (5 women); includes 40 minority (1 Black or African American, non-Hispanic/Latino; 17 Asian, non-Hispanic/Latino; 22 Hispanic/Latino), 18 international. Average age 23. 281 applicants, 35% accepted, 69 enrolled. In 2013, 122 master's, 1 doctorate awarded. *Degree requirements:* For master's, comprehensive exam, thesis optional; for doctorate, comprehensive exam, thesis/dissertation. *Entrance requirements:* For master's, GMAT (minimum score of 465) or GRE General Test, minimum GPA of 3.0; for doctorate, GRE General Test, GMAT (minimum score 465), minimum GPA of 3.0, BS. Additional exam requirements/recommendations for international students: Required—TOEFL (minimum score 550 paper-based; 80 iBT), IELTS (minimum score 6). *Application deadline:* Applications are processed on a rolling basis. Application fee: $30. Electronic applications accepted. *Expenses:* Tuition, state resident: full-time $12,640. Tuition, nonresident: full-time $30,000. *Financial support:* In 2013–14, 9 students received support, including 1 fellowship (averaging $4,599 per year), 9 research assistantships (averaging $33,840 per year); Federal Work-Study and unspecified assistantships also available. Support available to part-time students. Financial award application deadline: 1/15; financial award applicants required to submit FAFSA. *Faculty research:* Financial reporting, managerial accounting, auditing, taxation. *Unit head:* Gary McGill, PhD, Director and Associate Dean, 352-273-0219, Fax: 352-392-7962, E-mail: mcgill@ufl.edu. *Application contact:* Dominique A. DeSantiago, Lecturer and Associate Director, 352-273-0200, Fax: 352-392-7962, E-mail: dom.desantiago@cba.ufl.edu. Website: http://www.cba.ufl.edu/fsoa/.

University of Georgia, Terry College of Business, J.M. Tull School of Accounting, Athens, GA 30602. Offers M Acc, JD/M Acc. *Accreditation:* AACSB. *Entrance requirements:* For master's, GMAT. Electronic applications accepted.

University of Hartford, Barney School of Business, Department of Accounting and Taxation, West Hartford, CT 06117-1599. Offers professional accounting (Certificate); taxation (MSAT). Part-time and evening/weekend programs available. *Entrance requirements:* For master's, GMAT, 2 letters of recommendation, resume. Additional exam requirements/recommendations for international students: Required—TOEFL (minimum score 550 paper-based). Electronic applications accepted.

University of Hawaii at Manoa, Graduate Division, Shidler College of Business, Program in Accounting, Honolulu, HI 96822. Offers accounting (M Acc); accounting law (M Acc); information systems (M Acc); taxation (M Acc). Part-time programs available. *Entrance requirements:* For master's, GMAT, bachelor's degree in accounting, minimum GPA of 3.0. Additional exam requirements/recommendations for international students: Required—TOEFL (minimum score 550 paper-based; 79 iBT), IELTS (minimum score 5). *Faculty research:* International accounting, current tax topics, insurance industry financial reporting, behavioral accounting, auditing.

University of Hawaii at Manoa, Graduate Division, Shidler College of Business, Program in International Management, Honolulu, HI 96822. Offers Asian finance (PhD); global information technology management (PhD); international accounting (PhD); international marketing (PhD); international organization and strategy (PhD). Part-time programs available. *Degree requirements:* For doctorate, comprehensive exam, thesis/dissertation. *Entrance requirements:* For doctorate, GMAT or GRE General Test, minimum GPA of 3.0. Additional exam requirements/recommendations for international students: Required—TOEFL (minimum score 600 paper-based; 100 iBT), IELTS (minimum score 7). *Expenses:* Contact institution.

University of Houston, Bauer College of Business, Accountancy and Taxation Program, Houston, TX 77204. Offers accountancy (MS Accy); accountancy and taxation (PhD). *Accreditation:* AACSB. Part-time and evening/weekend programs available. *Degree requirements:* For master's, 30 hours completed in residence, minimum cumulative GPA of 3.0 at UH, no more than 11 semester hours of 'C' grades or below in graduate courses taken at UH; for doctorate, continuous full time enrollment, dissertation defense within 6 years of entering the program. *Entrance requirements:* For master's, GMAT, official transcripts from all higher education institutions attended, letters of recommendation, resume, goals statement; for doctorate, GMAT or GRE, letter of financial backing, statement of understanding, reference letters, statement of academic and research interests. Additional exam requirements/recommendations for international students: Required—TOEFL (minimum score 550 paper-based; 79 iBT), IELTS (minimum score 6.5), PTE (minimum score 70). Electronic applications accepted. *Faculty research:* Accountancy and taxation, finance, international business, management.

University of Houston–Clear Lake, School of Business, Program in Accounting, Houston, TX 77058-1002. Offers accounting (MS); professional accounting (MS).

Accounting

Accreditation: AACSB. Part-time and evening/weekend programs available. *Degree requirements:* For master's, thesis optional. *Entrance requirements:* For master's, GMAT. Additional exam requirements/recommendations for international students: Required—TOEFL (minimum score 550 paper-based). Electronic applications accepted.

University of Houston–Victoria, School of Business Administration, Victoria, TX 77901-4450. Offers accounting (MBA); economic development and entrepreneurship (MS); finance (GMBA, MBA); general business (MBA); international business (MBA); management (GMBA, MBA); marketing (MBA). *Accreditation:* AACSB. Part-time and evening/weekend programs available. Postbaccalaureate distance learning degree programs offered (minimal on-campus study). *Faculty:* 45 full-time (15 women). *Students:* 193 full-time (93 women), 673 part-time (325 women); includes 489 minority (185 Black or African American, non-Hispanic/Latino; 169 Asian, non-Hispanic/Latino; 114 Hispanic/Latino; 1 Native Hawaiian or other Pacific Islander, non-Hispanic/Latino; 20 Two or more races, non-Hispanic/Latino), 94 international. *Entrance requirements:* For master's, GMAT. Additional exam requirements/recommendations for international students: Required—TOEFL (minimum score 550 paper-based). *Application deadline:* For fall admission, 6/1 for international students; for spring admission, 10/1 for international students. Applications are processed on a rolling basis. Application fee: $0. Electronic applications accepted. *Expenses:* Tuition, state resident: full-time $4534; part-time $251 per credit hour. Tuition, nonresident: full-time $10,906; part-time $606 per contact hour. *Required fees:* $68 per semester hour. Tuition and fees vary according to course load. *Financial support:* In 2013–14, research assistantships with partial tuition reimbursements (averaging $2,000 per year), teaching assistantships with partial tuition reimbursements (averaging $2,000 per year) were awarded; Federal Work-Study, scholarships/grants, and unspecified assistantships also available. Support available to part-time students. Financial award application deadline: 4/15; financial award applicants required to submit FAFSA. *Faculty research:* Economic development, marketing, finance. *Unit head:* Dr. Farhang Niroomand, Dean, 361-570-4230, Fax: 361-580-5599, E-mail: niroomandf@uhv.edu. *Application contact:* Admissions and Records, 361-570-4359, Fax: 361-580-5500, E-mail: admissions@uhv.edu.
Website: http://www.uhv.edu/bus/.

University of Idaho, College of Graduate Studies, College of Business and Economics, Department of Accounting, Moscow, ID 83844-3161. Offers accountancy (M Acct). *Accreditation:* AACSB. *Faculty:* 5 full-time. *Students:* 28 full-time, 4 part-time. Average age 28. In 2013, 29 master's awarded. *Degree requirements:* For master's, comprehensive exam. *Entrance requirements:* For master's, minimum GPA of 3.0. *Application deadline:* For fall admission, 8/1 for domestic students; for spring admission, 12/15 for domestic students. Applications are processed on a rolling basis. Application fee: $60. Electronic applications accepted. *Expenses:* Tuition, state resident: full-time $5596; part-time $363 per credit hour. Tuition, nonresident: full-time $18,672; part-time $1089 per credit hour. *Financial support:* Research assistantships and teaching assistantships available. Financial award applicants required to submit FAFSA. *Unit head:* Dr. Marla Kraut, Head, 208-885-6453, Fax: 208-885-6296, E-mail: amberg@uidaho.edu. *Application contact:* Stephanie Thomas, Graduate Recruitment Coordinator, 208-885-4001, Fax: 208-885-4406, E-mail: gadms@uidaho.edu.
Website: http://www.uidaho.edu/cbe/accounting/.

University of Illinois at Chicago, Graduate College, Liautaud Graduate School of Business, Department of Accounting, Chicago, IL 60607-7128. Offers MS, MBA/MS. *Accreditation:* AACSB. Part-time programs available. *Faculty:* 10 full-time (2 women), 7 part-time/adjunct (3 women). *Students:* 173 full-time (116 women), 35 part-time (14 women); includes 40 minority (4 Black or African American, non-Hispanic/Latino; 29 Asian, non-Hispanic/Latino; 7 Hispanic/Latino), 101 international. Average age 26. 384 applicants, 62% accepted, 92 enrolled. In 2013, 80 master's awarded. *Entrance requirements:* For master's, GMAT, minimum GPA of 2.75. Additional exam requirements/recommendations for international students: Required—TOEFL. *Application deadline:* For fall admission, 5/15 for domestic students, 2/15 for international students; for spring admission, 11/1 for domestic students, 7/1 for international students. Applications are processed on a rolling basis. Application fee: $40 ($50 for international students). Electronic applications accepted. *Expenses:* Tuition, state resident: full-time $11,066; part-time $3689 per term. Tuition, nonresident: full-time $23,064; part-time $7688 per term. *Required fees:* $3004; $1190 per term. Tuition and fees vary according to course level and program. *Financial support:* In 2013–14, 25 students received support. Fellowships with full tuition reimbursements available, research assistantships with full tuition reimbursements available, teaching assistantships with full tuition reimbursements available, career-related internships or fieldwork, Federal Work-Study, institutionally sponsored loans, traineeships, tuition waivers (full), and unspecified assistantships available. Support available to part-time students. Financial award application deadline: 2/15. *Faculty research:* Governmental accounting, managerial accounting, auditing. *Unit head:* Prof. Somnath Das, Department Head, 312-996-4482, E-mail: sdas@uic.edu.
Website: http://business.uic.edu/academic-departments-and-faculty/academic-departments/department-of-accounting.

University of Illinois at Springfield, Graduate Programs, College of Business and Management, Program in Accountancy, Springfield, IL 62703-5407. Offers MA. Part-time and evening/weekend programs available. *Faculty:* 7 full-time (1 woman), 1 part-time/adjunct (0 women). *Students:* 53 full-time (28 women), 55 part-time (37 women); includes 17 minority (9 Black or African American, non-Hispanic/Latino; 3 Asian, non-Hispanic/Latino; 4 Hispanic/Latino; 1 Two or more races, non-Hispanic/Latino), 14 international. Average age 29. 69 applicants, 65% accepted, 35 enrolled. In 2013, 25 master's awarded. *Degree requirements:* For master's, capstone course. *Entrance requirements:* For master's, minimum undergraduate GPA of 2.5 in prerequisite coursework, introductory course in financial and managerial accounting, college math through business calculus, principles of economics (micro and macro), statistics, computer applications. Additional exam requirements/recommendations for international students: Required—TOEFL (minimum score 550 paper-based). *Application deadline:* Applications are processed on a rolling basis. Application fee: $60 ($75 for international students). Electronic applications accepted. *Expenses:* Tuition, state resident: full-time $7440. Tuition, nonresident: full-time $15,744. *Required fees:* $2985.60. *Financial support:* In 2013–14, fellowships with full tuition reimbursements (averaging $9,900 per year), research assistantships with full tuition reimbursements (averaging $9,550 per year), teaching assistantships with full tuition reimbursements (averaging $9,700 per year) were awarded; career-related internships or fieldwork, Federal Work-Study, scholarships/grants, health care benefits, and unspecified assistantships also available. Support available to part-time students. Financial award application deadline: 11/15; financial award applicants required to submit FAFSA. *Unit head:* Dr. Leonard Branson, Program Administrator, 217-206-6299, Fax: 217-206-7541, E-mail: lbran1@uis.edu. *Application contact:* Dr. Lynn Pardie, Office of Graduate Studies, 800-252-8533, Fax: 217-206-7623, E-mail: lpard1@uis.edu.
Website: http://www.uis.edu/accountancy.

University of Illinois at Urbana–Champaign, Graduate College, College of Business, Department of Accountancy, Champaign, IL 61820. Offers accountancy (MAS, MS, PhD); taxation (MS). *Accreditation:* AACSB. *Students:* 459 (272 women). Application fee: $75 ($90 for international students). *Unit head:* Jon S. Davis, Head, 217-333-0857, Fax: 217-244-0902, E-mail: jondavis@illinois.edu. *Application contact:* Cindy K. Wood, Administrative Aide, 217-333-4572, Fax: 217-244-0902, E-mail: ckwood@illinois.edu.
Website: http://www1.business.illinois.edu/accountancy.

The University of Iowa, Henry B. Tippie College of Business, M Ac Program in Accounting, Iowa City, IA 52242-1316. Offers M Ac, JD/M Ac. Part-time programs available. *Faculty:* 16 full-time (3 women), 5 part-time/adjunct (1 woman). *Students:* 41 full-time (21 women); includes 11 minority (1 Black or African American, non-Hispanic/Latino; 10 Two or more races, non-Hispanic/Latino). Average age 26. 185 applicants, 18% accepted, 18 enrolled. In 2013, 39 master's awarded. *Entrance requirements:* For master's, GMAT (minimum score 550 with at least 50% verbal). Additional exam requirements/recommendations for international students: Required—TOEFL (minimum score 600 paper-based; 100 iBT), IELTS (minimum score 7). *Application deadline:* For fall admission, 7/15 for domestic students, 4/15 for international students; for spring admission, 12/1 for domestic students, 10/1 for international students. Applications are processed on a rolling basis. Application fee: $60 ($100 for international students). Electronic applications accepted. *Financial support:* In 2013–14, 33 students received support, including 1 research assistantship (averaging $17,330 per year), 16 teaching assistantships (averaging $17,330 per year); fellowships, career-related internships or fieldwork, Federal Work-Study, institutionally sponsored loans, scholarships/grants, health care benefits, and unspecified assistantships also available. Financial award application deadline: 4/15; financial award applicants required to submit FAFSA. *Unit head:* Prof. Douglas V. DeJong, Dean, 319-335-0910, Fax: 319-335-1956, E-mail: douglas-dejong@uiowa.edu. *Application contact:* Prof. Thomas J. Carroll, Director, Admissions and Financial Aid, 319-335-2727, Fax: 319-335-3604, E-mail: thomas-carroll@uiowa.edu.
Website: http://tippie.uiowa.edu/accounting/mac/.

The University of Iowa, Henry B. Tippie College of Business, PhD Program in Accounting, Iowa City, IA 52242-1316. Offers PhD. *Accreditation:* AACSB. *Faculty:* 16 full-time (3 women), 5 part-time/adjunct (1 woman). *Students:* 14 full-time (5 women); includes 2 minority (1 Black or African American, non-Hispanic/Latino; 1 Asian, non-Hispanic/Latino), 4 international. Average age 30. 53 applicants, 8% accepted, 2 enrolled. In 2013, 1 doctorate awarded. *Degree requirements:* For doctorate, comprehensive exam, thesis/dissertation, thesis defense. *Entrance requirements:* For doctorate, GMAT. Additional exam requirements/recommendations for international students: Recommended—TOEFL (minimum score 100 iBT), IELTS (minimum score 7). *Application deadline:* For fall admission, 1/15 priority date for domestic students, 1/15 for international students. Applications are processed on a rolling basis. Application fee: $60 ($100 for international students). Electronic applications accepted. *Financial support:* In 2013–14, 11 students received support, including 11 fellowships with full tuition reimbursements available (averaging $10,820 per year), 1 research assistantship with full tuition reimbursement available (averaging $17,680 per year), 10 teaching assistantships with full tuition reimbursements available (averaging $17,680 per year); institutionally sponsored loans, scholarships/grants, health care benefits, and unspecified assistantships also available. Financial award application deadline: 1/15. *Faculty research:* Corporate financial reporting issues; financial statement information and capital markets; cost structure: analysis, estimation, and management; experimental and prediction economics; income taxes and interaction of financial and tax reporting systems. *Unit head:* Prof. Douglas V. DeJong, Department Executive Officer, 319-335-0910, Fax: 319-335-1956, E-mail: douglas-dejong@uiowa.edu. *Application contact:* Renea L. Jay, PhD Coordinator, 319-335-0830, Fax: 319-335-1956, E-mail: renea-jay@uiowa.edu.
Website: http://tippie.uiowa.edu/accounting/.

The University of Kansas, Graduate Studies, School of Business, Master of Accounting (MAcc) Program, Lawrence, KS 66045. Offers M Acc. *Accreditation:* AACSB. Part-time programs available. *Faculty:* 8. *Students:* 102 full-time (51 women), 8 part-time (3 women); includes 11 minority (4 Black or African American, non-Hispanic/Latino; 4 Asian, non-Hispanic/Latino; 3 Hispanic/Latino), 7 international. Average age 24. 103 applicants, 78% accepted, 64 enrolled. In 2013, 112 master's awarded. *Degree requirements:* For master's, 30 credits. *Entrance requirements:* For master's, GMAT. Additional exam requirements/recommendations for international students: Required—TOEFL (minimum score 53 paper-based); Recommended—IELTS (minimum score 6). *Application deadline:* For fall admission, 3/1 priority date for domestic students, 2/15 priority date for international students; for spring admission, 11/1 for domestic students, 10/1 priority date for international students. Applications are processed on a rolling basis. Application fee: $65. Electronic applications accepted. *Financial support:* Fellowships, research assistantships, teaching assistantships, career-related internships or fieldwork, Federal Work-Study, institutionally sponsored loans, and scholarships/grants available. Financial award application deadline: 6/1; financial award applicants required to submit FAFSA. *Faculty research:* Earnings quality, financial reporting conservatism, internal control systems, auditing and corporate governance, financial reporting restatements. *Unit head:* Dr. John T. Sweeney, Director, 785-864-4500, Fax: 785-864-5328, E-mail: jtsweeney@ku.edu. *Application contact:* Karen Heintzen, Assistant Director, 785-864-7558, Fax: 785-864-5376, E-mail: heintzen@ku.edu.
Website: http://www.business.ku.edu/.

University of Kentucky, Graduate School, Gatton College of Business and Economics, Program in Accounting, Lexington, KY 40506-0032. Offers MSACC. *Accreditation:* AACSB. *Degree requirements:* For master's, comprehensive exam. *Entrance requirements:* For master's, GRE General Test, minimum undergraduate GPA of 2.75. Additional exam requirements/recommendations for international students: Required—TOEFL (minimum score 550 paper-based). Electronic applications accepted. *Faculty research:* Taxation, financial accounting and auditing, managerial accounting, not-for-profit accounting.

University of La Verne, College of Business and Public Management, Graduate Programs in Business Administration, La Verne, CA 91750-4443. Offers accounting (MBA); executive management (MBA-EP); finance (MBA, MBA-EP); health services management (MBA); information technology (MBA, MBA-EP); international business (MBA, MBA-EP); leadership (MBA-EP); managed care (MBA); management (MBA, MBA-EP); marketing (MBA, MBA-EP). Part-time and evening/weekend programs available. *Faculty:* 22 full-time (9 women), 37 part-time/adjunct (10 women). *Students:* 793 full-time (356 women), 164 part-time (80 women); includes 153 minority (17 Black or African American, non-Hispanic/Latino; 21 Asian, non-Hispanic/Latino; 110 Hispanic/Latino; 5 Two or more races, non-Hispanic/Latino), 691 international. Average age 27. In 2013, 514 master's awarded. *Entrance requirements:* For master's, GMAT, MAT, or GRE, minimum undergraduate GPA of 3.0, 2 letters of recommendation, resume, statement of purpose. Additional exam requirements/recommendations for international students: Required—TOEFL (minimum score 550 paper-based; 85 iBT). *Application deadline:* Applications are processed on a rolling basis. Application fee: $50. *Expenses:* Contact institution. *Financial support:* Career-related internships or fieldwork, institutionally sponsored loans, and scholarships/grants available. Financial award application deadline: 3/2; financial award applicants required to submit FAFSA. *Unit head:* Dr. Abe Helou, Chairperson, 909-593-3511 Ext. 4211, Fax: 909-392-2704, E-mail: ihelou@laverne.edu. *Application contact:* Rina Lazarian-Chehab, Senior Associate

Director of Graduate Admissions, 909-593-3511 Ext. 4317, Fax: 909-392-2704, E-mail: rlazarian@laverne.edu.

University of La Verne, Regional and Online Campuses, Graduate Programs, Inland Empire Campus, Ontario, CA 91761. Offers business administration (MBA, MBA-EP), including accounting (MBA), finance (MBA), health services management (MBA-EP), information technology (MBA-EP), international business (MBA), managed care (MBA), management and leadership (MBA-EP), marketing (MBA-EP), supply chain management (MBA); leadership and management (MS), including human resource management, nonprofit management, organizational development. Part-time and evening/weekend programs available. *Faculty:* 1 full-time (0 women), 14 part-time/adjunct (6 women). *Students:* 26 full-time (15 women), 106 part-time (65 women); includes 92 minority (15 Black or African American, non-Hispanic/Latino; 29 Asian, non-Hispanic/Latino; 43 Hispanic/Latino; 1 Native Hawaiian or other Pacific Islander, non-Hispanic/Latino; 4 Two or more races, non-Hispanic/Latino). Average age 37. In 2013, 49 master's awarded. *Application deadline:* Applications are processed on a rolling basis. Application fee: $50. *Expenses:* Contact institution. *Financial support:* Institutionally sponsored loans available. Financial award application deadline: 3/2; financial award applicants required to submit FAFSA. *Unit head:* Allen Stout, Campus Director, Inland Empire Regional Campus in Ontario, 909-937-6987, E-mail: astout@laverne.edu. *Application contact:* Karen Schumann, Senior Associate Director of Admissions, Inland Empire Regional Campus in Ontario, 909-937-6991, E-mail: kschumann@laverne.edu.
Website: http://laverne.edu/locations/inland-empire/.

University of Lethbridge, School of Graduate Studies, Lethbridge, AB T1K 3M4, Canada. Offers accounting (MScM); addictions counseling (M Sc); agricultural biotechnology (M Sc); agricultural studies (M Sc, MA); anthropology (MA); archaeology (M Sc, MA); art (MA, MFA); biochemistry (M Sc); biological sciences (M Sc); biomolecular science (PhD); biosystems and biodiversity (PhD); Canadian studies (MA); chemistry (M Sc); computer science (M Sc); computer science and geographical information science (M Sc); counseling (MC); counseling psychology (M Ed); dramatic arts (MA); earth, space, and physical science (PhD); economics (MA); education (MA); educational leadership (M Ed); English (MA); environmental science (M Sc); evolution and behavior (PhD); exercise science (M Sc); finance (MScM); French (MA); French/German (MA); French/Spanish (MA); general education (M Ed); general management (MScM); geography (M Sc, MA); German (MA); health sciences (M Sc); human resource management and labour relations (MScM); individualized multidisciplinary (M Sc, MA); information systems (MScM); international management (MScM); kinesiology (M Sc, MA); marketing (MScM); mathematics (M Sc); modern languages (MA); music (M Mus, MA); Native American studies (MA); neuroscience (M Sc, PhD); new media (MA, MFA); nursing (M Sc); philosophy (MA); physics (M Sc); policy and strategy (MScM); political science (MA); psychology (M Sc, MA); religious studies (MA); sociology (MA); theatre and dramatic arts (MFA); theoretical and computational science (PhD); urban and regional studies (MA); women and gender studies (MA). Part-time and evening/weekend programs available. *Degree requirements:* For doctorate, comprehensive exam, thesis/dissertation. *Entrance requirements:* For master's, GMAT (for M Sc in management), bachelor's degree in related field, minimum GPA of 3.0 during previous 20 graded semester courses, 2 years teaching or related experience (M Ed); for doctorate, master's degree, minimum graduate GPA of 3.5. Additional exam requirements/recommendations for international students: Required—TOEFL. Application fee: $60 Canadian dollars. *Financial support:* Fellowships, research assistantships, teaching assistantships, scholarships/grants, health care benefits, and unspecified assistantships available. *Faculty research:* Movement and brain plasticity, gibberellin physiology, photosynthesis, carbon cycling, molecular properties of main-group ring components. *Application contact:* School of Graduate Studies, 403-329-2793, Fax: 403-332-5239, E-mail: sgsinquiries@uleth.ca.
Website: http://www.uleth.ca/graduatestudies//.

University of Louisville, Graduate School, College of Business, School of Accountancy, Louisville, KY 40292-0001. Offers MAC, MBA/MAC. *Accreditation:* AACSB. Part-time and evening/weekend programs available. *Students:* 1 full-time (0 women), 24 part-time (13 women); includes 4 minority (2 Black or African American, non-Hispanic/Latino; 1 Asian, non-Hispanic/Latino; 1 Hispanic/Latino). Average age 35. 3 applicants. In 2013, 4 master's awarded. *Entrance requirements:* For master's, GMAT, 2 letters of reference, resume, personal statement, personal interview, transcript. Additional exam requirements/recommendations for international students: Required—TOEFL (minimum score 83 iBT). *Application deadline:* For fall admission, 5/15 priority date for domestic students. Applications are processed on a rolling basis. Application fee: $60. *Expenses:* Tuition, state resident: full-time $10,788; part-time $599 per credit hour. Tuition, nonresident: full-time $22,446; part-time $1247 per credit hour. *Required fees:* $196. Tuition and fees vary according to program and reciprocity agreements. *Financial support:* In 2013–14, research assistantships with full tuition reimbursements (averaging $1,200 per year) were awarded; health care benefits and unspecified assistantships also available. Financial award application deadline: 3/15; financial award applicants required to submit FAFSA. *Faculty research:* Audit judgment and decision-making, information systems, taxation, cost and managerial accounting. *Unit head:* Dr. Susan M. Callahan, Dean, 502-852-6440, Fax: 502-852-7557, E-mail: cmcall04@louisville.edu. *Application contact:* Susan E. Hildebrand, Director of IT and Master's Programs Admissions/Recruiting Manager, 502-852-7257, Fax: 502-852-4901, E-mail: s.hildebrand@louisville.edu.
Website: http://business.louisville.edu/graduate-programs/.

University of Maine, Graduate School, The Maine Business School, Orono, ME 04469. Offers accounting (MBA); business administration (CGS); business and sustainability (MBA); finance (MBA); international business (MBA); management (MBA). *Accreditation:* AACSB. Part-time and evening/weekend programs available. Postbaccalaureate distance learning degree programs offered. *Faculty:* 23 full-time (7 women). *Students:* 31 full-time (12 women), 12 part-time (9 women); includes 5 minority (1 Black or African American, non-Hispanic/Latino; 3 Asian, non-Hispanic/Latino; 1 Hispanic/Latino), 4 international. Average age 29. 41 applicants, 71% accepted, 24 enrolled. In 2013, 28 master's awarded. *Entrance requirements:* For master's, GMAT. Additional exam requirements/recommendations for international students: Required—TOEFL (minimum score 550 paper-based). *Application deadline:* For fall admission, 6/1 priority date for domestic and international students; for spring admission, 11/15 priority date for domestic and international students. Applications are processed on a rolling basis. Application fee: $65. Electronic applications accepted. *Expenses:* Contact institution. *Financial support:* In 2013–14, 14 students received support, including 3 teaching assistantships with full tuition reimbursements available (averaging $14,100 per year); career-related internships or fieldwork, Federal Work-Study, institutionally sponsored loans, scholarships/grants, tuition waivers (full and partial), and unspecified assistantships also available. Financial award application deadline: 3/1. *Faculty research:* Entrepreneurship, investment management, international markets, decision support systems, strategic planning. *Total annual research expenditures:* $5,089. *Unit head:* Carol Mandzik, Manager of MBA Programs, Executive Education and Internships, 207-581-1971, Fax: 207-581-1930, E-mail: carol.mandzik@maine.edu. *Application*

contact: Scott G. Delcourt, Associate Dean of the Graduate School, 207-581-3291, Fax: 207-581-3232, E-mail: graduate@maine.edu.
Website: http://www.umaine.edu/business/.

The University of Manchester, Manchester Business School, Manchester, United Kingdom. Offers accounting (M Phil, PhD); business (M Ent, D Ent); business and management (M Phil); business management (PhD).

University of Mary, Gary Tharaldson School of Business, Bismarck, ND 58504-9652. Offers accountancy (MBA); business administration (MBA); health care (MBA); human resource management (MBA); management (MBA); project management (MPM); strategic leadership (MSSL). Part-time and evening/weekend programs available. *Degree requirements:* For master's, strategic planning seminar. *Entrance requirements:* For master's, minimum GPA of 2.5. Additional exam requirements/recommendations for international students: Required—TOEFL (minimum score 500 paper-based; 71 iBT).

University of Mary Hardin-Baylor, Graduate Studies in Business Administration, Belton, TX 76513. Offers accounting (MBA); information systems management (MBA); international business (MBA); management (MBA). Part-time and evening/weekend programs available. *Faculty:* 10 full-time (4 women), 2 part-time/adjunct (1 woman). *Students:* 26 full-time (11 women), 52 part-time (19 women); includes 20 minority (7 Black or African American, non-Hispanic/Latino; 3 Asian, non-Hispanic/Latino; 9 Hispanic/Latino; 1 Two or more races, non-Hispanic/Latino), 21 international. Average age 30. 55 applicants, 75% accepted, 27 enrolled. In 2013, 23 master's awarded. *Degree requirements:* For master's, comprehensive exam. *Entrance requirements:* For master's, minimum GPA of 3.0, interview. Additional exam requirements/recommendations for international students: Required—TOEFL (minimum score 550 paper-based; 80 iBT), IELTS (minimum score 6). *Application deadline:* For fall admission, 6/1 for domestic students, 6/15 priority date for international students; for spring admission, 11/1 for domestic students, 10/15 priority date for international students. Applications are processed on a rolling basis. Application fee: $35 ($135 for international students). Electronic applications accepted. *Expenses:* Tuition: Full-time $14,130; part-time $785 per credit hour. *Required fees:* $1350; $75 per credit hour. $50 per term. *Financial support:* Federal Work-Study, unspecified assistantships, and scholarships (for some active duty military personnel only) available. Financial award applicants required to submit FAFSA. *Unit head:* Dr. Nancy Bonner, Assistant Professor/Program Director, 254-295-5405, E-mail: nbonner@umhb.edu. *Application contact:* Melissa Ford, Director of Graduate Admissions, 254-295-4020, Fax: 254-295-5038, E-mail: mford@umhb.edu.
Website: http://www.graduate.umhb.edu/mba.

University of Maryland University College, Graduate School of Management and Technology, Program in Accounting and Financial Management, Adelphi, MD 20783. Offers MS, Certificate. *Accreditation:* AACSB. Part-time and evening/weekend programs available. Postbaccalaureate distance learning degree programs offered (no on-campus study). *Students:* 11 full-time (7 women), 422 part-time (268 women); includes 232 minority (160 Black or African American, non-Hispanic/Latino; 33 Asian, non-Hispanic/Latino; 29 Hispanic/Latino; 2 Native Hawaiian or other Pacific Islander, non-Hispanic/Latino; 8 Two or more races, non-Hispanic/Latino), 14 international. Average age 36. 131 applicants, 100% accepted, 83 enrolled. In 2013, 110 master's awarded. *Degree requirements:* For master's, thesis or alternative, capstone course. *Application deadline:* Applications are processed on a rolling basis. Application fee: $50. Electronic applications accepted. *Financial support:* Federal Work-Study and scholarships/grants available. Support available to part-time students. Financial award application deadline: 6/1; financial award applicants required to submit FAFSA. *Unit head:* Dr. James Howard, Director, 240-684-2400, Fax: 240-684-2401, E-mail: james.howard@umuc.edu. *Application contact:* Coordinator, Graduate Admissions, 800-888-8682, Fax: 240-684-2151, E-mail: newgrad@umuc.edu.
Website: http://www.umuc.edu/grad/msaf.html.

University of Maryland University College, Graduate School of Management and Technology, Program in Accounting and Information Systems, Adelphi, MD 20783. Offers MS, Certificate. *Accreditation:* AACSB. Part-time and evening/weekend programs available. Postbaccalaureate distance learning degree programs offered (no on-campus study). *Students:* 2 full-time (1 woman), 145 part-time (89 women); includes 99 minority (79 Black or African American, non-Hispanic/Latino; 9 Asian, non-Hispanic/Latino; 10 Hispanic/Latino; 1 Native Hawaiian or other Pacific Islander, non-Hispanic/Latino), 4 international. Average age 36. 64 applicants, 100% accepted, 35 enrolled. In 2013, 40 master's, 3 other advanced degrees awarded. *Degree requirements:* For master's, thesis or alternative, capstone course. *Application deadline:* Applications are processed on a rolling basis. Application fee: $50. Electronic applications accepted. *Financial support:* Federal Work-Study and scholarships/grants available. Support available to part-time students. Financial award application deadline: 6/1; financial award applicants required to submit FAFSA. *Unit head:* Dr. Kathryn Klose, Director, 240-684-2400, Fax: 240-684-2401, E-mail: kathryn.klose@umuc.edu. *Application contact:* Coordinator, Graduate Admissions, 800-888-8682, Fax: 240-684-2151, E-mail: newgrad@umuc.edu.

University of Massachusetts Amherst, Graduate School, Isenberg School of Management, Department of Accounting, Amherst, MA 01003. Offers MSA. *Accreditation:* AACSB. Part-time programs available. *Students:* 23 full-time (13 women), 7 part-time (0 women); includes 9 minority (5 Asian, non-Hispanic/Latino; 4 Two or more races, non-Hispanic/Latino), 1 international. Average age 24. 46 applicants, 83% accepted, 24 enrolled. In 2013, 27 master's awarded. *Entrance requirements:* For master's, GMAT. Additional exam requirements/recommendations for international students: Required—TOEFL (minimum score 550 paper-based; 80 iBT), IELTS (minimum score 6.5). *Application deadline:* For fall admission, 2/1 for domestic and international students. Applications are processed on a rolling basis. Application fee: $75. Electronic applications accepted. *Unit head:* Dr. James F. Smith, Graduate Program Director, 413-545-5645, Fax: 413-545-3858. *Application contact:* Lindsay DeSantis, Supervisor of Admissions, 413-545-0722, Fax: 413-577-0010, E-mail: gradadm@grad.umass.edu.
Website: http://www.isenberg.umass.edu/accounting/Graduate/MSA/.

University of Massachusetts Amherst, Graduate School, Isenberg School of Management, Program in Management, Amherst, MA 01003. Offers accounting (PhD); business administration (MBA); entrepreneurship (MBA); finance (MBA, PhD); healthcare administration (MBA); hospitality and tourism management (PhD); management science (PhD); marketing (MBA, PhD); organization studies (PhD); sport management (PhD); strategic management (PhD); MBA/MS. *Accreditation:* AACSB. Part-time and evening/weekend programs available. Postbaccalaureate distance learning degree programs offered. *Faculty:* 68 full-time (14 women). *Students:* 140 full-time (59 women), 1,127 part-time (319 women); includes 229 minority (24 Black or African American, non-Hispanic/Latino; 2 American Indian or Alaska Native, non-Hispanic/Latino; 135 Asian, non-Hispanic/Latino; 51 Hispanic/Latino; 6 Native Hawaiian or other Pacific Islander, non-Hispanic/Latino; 11 Two or more races, non-Hispanic/Latino), 131 international. Average age 36. 828 applicants, 56% accepted, 351 enrolled. In 2013, 361 master's, 12 doctorates awarded. Terminal master's awarded for partial completion of doctoral program. *Degree requirements:* For doctorate, comprehensive exam, thesis/dissertation. *Entrance requirements:* For master's and doctorate, GMAT or GRE General Test. Additional exam requirements/recommendations for international

students: Required—TOEFL (minimum score 550 paper-based; 80 iBT), IELTS (minimum score 6.5). *Application deadline:* For fall admission, 1/20 for domestic and international students. Applications are processed on a rolling basis. Application fee: $75. Electronic applications accepted. *Financial support:* Fellowships with full and partial tuition reimbursements, research assistantships with full and partial tuition reimbursements, teaching assistantships with full and partial tuition reimbursements, career-related internships or fieldwork, Federal Work-Study, scholarships/grants, traineeships, health care benefits, tuition waivers (full and partial), and unspecified assistantships available. Support available to part-time students. Financial award application deadline: 1/20; financial award applicants required to submit FAFSA. *Unit head:* Dr. John Wells, Chair, 413-545-7609, Fax: 413-577-2234. *Application contact:* Lindsay DeSantis, Supervisor of Admissions, 413-545-0722, Fax: 413-577-0010, E-mail: gradadm@grad.umass.edu.
Website: http://www.isenberg.umass.edu/.

University of Massachusetts Dartmouth, Graduate School, Charlton College of Business, Program in Business Administration, North Dartmouth, MA 02747-2300. Offers accounting (Postbaccalaureate Certificate); business administration (MBA); business foundations (Graduate Certificate); finance (Postbaccalaureate Certificate); international business (Graduate Certificate); management (Postbaccalaureate Certificate); marketing (Postbaccalaureate Certificate); organizational leadership (Graduate Certificate); supply chain management (Postbaccalaureate Certificate). *Accreditation:* AACSB. Part-time programs available. Postbaccalaureate distance learning degree programs offered (no on-campus study). *Faculty:* 36 full-time (12 women), 27 part-time/adjunct (10 women). *Students:* 154 full-time (73 women), 120 part-time (55 women); includes 28 minority (2 Black or African American, non-Hispanic/Latino; 1 American Indian or Alaska Native, non-Hispanic/Latino; 6 Asian, non-Hispanic/Latino; 11 Hispanic/Latino; 8 Two or more races, non-Hispanic/Latino), 129 international. Average age 29. 204 applicants, 82% accepted, 112 enrolled. In 2013, 71 master's, 15 other advanced degrees awarded. *Degree requirements:* For master's, portfolio of MBA course work. *Entrance requirements:* For master's, GMAT, statement of purpose (minimum of 300 words), resume, 2 letters of recommendation, official transcripts; for other advanced degree, statement of purpose (minimum of 300 words), resume, official transcripts. Additional exam requirements/recommendations for international students: Required—TOEFL (minimum score 500 paper-based; 72 iBT), IELTS (minimum score 6). *Application deadline:* For fall admission, 8/1 priority date for domestic students, 5/1 priority date for international students; for spring admission, 1/1 priority date for domestic students, 10/1 priority date for international students. Applications are processed on a rolling basis. Application fee: $60. Electronic applications accepted. *Expenses:* Tuition, state resident: full-time $2071; part-time $86.29 per credit. Tuition, nonresident: full-time $8099; part-time $337.46 per credit. Tuition and fees vary according to course load and reciprocity agreements. *Financial support:* Federal Work-Study and unspecified assistantships available. Support available to part-time students. Financial award application deadline: 3/1; financial award applicants required to submit FAFSA. *Faculty research:* E-commerce, managing diversity, agile manufacturing, green business, activity-based management, build-to-order supply chain management. *Total annual research expenditures:* $330,000. *Unit head:* Toby Stapleton, Assistant Dean for Graduate Studies, 508-999-8543, Fax: 508-999-8646, E-mail: tstapleton@umassd.edu. *Application contact:* Steven Briggs, Director of Marketing and Recruitment for Graduate Studies, 508-999-8604, Fax: 508-999-8183, E-mail: graduate@umassd.edu.
Website: http://www.umassd.edu/charlton/.

University of Massachusetts Lowell, Manning School of Business, Lowell, MA 01854-2881. Offers accounting (MSA); business administration (MBA, PhD); financial management (Graduate Certificate); foundations of business (Graduate Certificate); healthcare innovation and entrepreneurship (MS); innovation and technological entrepreneurship (MS); new venture creation (Graduate Certificate); supply chain and operations management (Graduate Certificate). *Accreditation:* AACSB. Part-time and evening/weekend programs available. *Entrance requirements:* For master's, GMAT.

University of Memphis, Graduate School, Fogelman College of Business and Economics, Program in Business Administration, Memphis, TN 38152. Offers accounting (MBA, PhD); economics (MBA, PhD); executive business administration (MBA); finance (PhD); finance, insurance, and real estate (MBA, MS); international business administration (IMBA); management (MBA, MS, PhD); management information systems (MBA, MS, PhD); management science (MBA); marketing (MBA, MS); marketing and supply chain management (PhD); real estate development (MS); JD/MBA. *Accreditation:* AACSB. *Faculty:* 44 full-time (9 women), 5 part-time/adjunct (0 women). *Students:* 238 full-time (101 women), 315 part-time (113 women); includes 146 minority (80 Black or African American, non-Hispanic/Latino; 1 American Indian or Alaska Native, non-Hispanic/Latino; 46 Asian, non-Hispanic/Latino; 13 Hispanic/Latino; 2 Native Hawaiian or other Pacific Islander, non-Hispanic/Latino; 4 Two or more races, non-Hispanic/Latino), 104 international. Average age 32. 343 applicants, 62% accepted, 102 enrolled. In 2013, 140 master's, 17 doctorates awarded. *Degree requirements:* For master's, comprehensive exam; for doctorate, comprehensive exam, thesis/dissertation. *Entrance requirements:* For master's, GMAT, resume; for doctorate, GMAT, interview, minimum GPA of 3.4, resume, letter of recommendation. Additional exam requirements/recommendations for international students: Required—TOEFL (minimum score 550 paper-based). *Application deadline:* For fall admission, 8/1 for domestic students; for spring admission, 12/1 for domestic students. Application fee: $35 ($60 for international students). *Financial support:* In 2013–14, 164 students received support. Research assistantships with full tuition reimbursements available, teaching assistantships with full tuition reimbursements available, career-related internships or fieldwork, Federal Work-Study, scholarships/grants, and unspecified assistantships available. Financial award application deadline: 2/15; financial award applicants required to submit FAFSA. *Faculty research:* Competitive business strategy, finance microstructures, supply chain management innovations, health care economics, litigation risks and corporate audits. *Unit head:* Rajiv Grover, Dean, 901-678-3759, E-mail: rgrover@memphis.edu. *Application contact:* Dr. Carol V. Danehower, Associate Dean, 901-678-5402, Fax: 901-678-3579, E-mail: fcbegp@memphis.edu.
Website: http://www.memphis.edu/fcbe/grad_programs.php.

University of Memphis, Graduate School, Fogelman College of Business and Economics, School of Accountancy, Memphis, TN 38152. Offers accounting (MS); accounting systems (MS); taxation (MS). *Accreditation:* AACSB. *Faculty:* 9 full-time (2 women), 1 (woman) part-time/adjunct. *Students:* 35 full-time (19 women), 44 part-time (27 women); includes 28 minority (19 Black or African American, non-Hispanic/Latino; 8 Asian, non-Hispanic/Latino; 1 Two or more races, non-Hispanic/Latino), 1 international. Average age 29. 54 applicants, 76% accepted, 6 enrolled. In 2013, 27 master's awarded. *Degree requirements:* For master's, comprehensive exam. *Entrance requirements:* For master's, GMAT. *Application deadline:* For fall admission, 8/1 for domestic students; for spring admission, 12/1 for domestic students. Application fee: $35 ($60 for international students). *Financial support:* In 2013–14, 32 students received support. Research assistantships with full tuition reimbursements available, teaching assistantships with full tuition reimbursements available, Federal Work-Study, scholarships/grants, and unspecified assistantships available. Financial award application deadline: 2/15; financial award applicants required to submit FAFSA. *Faculty research:* Financial accounting, corporate governance, EDP auditing, evolution of system analysis, investor behavior and investment decisions. *Unit head:* Dr. Carolyn Callahan, Director, 901-678-4022, E-mail: cmcllhan@memphis.edu. *Application contact:* Dr. Craig Langstraat, Program Coordinator, 901-678-4577, E-mail: cjlngstr@memphis.edu.
Website: http://www.memphis.edu/accountancy/.

University of Miami, Graduate School, School of Business Administration, Department of Accounting, Coral Gables, FL 33124. Offers professional accounting (MP Acc); taxation (MS Tax). *Accreditation:* AACSB. Part-time and evening/weekend programs available. *Entrance requirements:* For master's, GMAT or CPA exam. Additional exam requirements/recommendations for international students: Required—TOEFL. Electronic applications accepted. *Faculty research:* Financial reporting, audit risk, public policy and taxation issues, government accounting and public choice, corporate governance.

University of Miami, Graduate School, School of Business Administration, Program in Business Administration, Coral Gables, FL 33124. Offers accounting (MBA); computer information systems (MBA); executive and professional (MBA), including international business, management; finance (MBA); international business (MBA); management (MBA); management science (MBA); marketing (MBA); professional management (MSPM); JD/MBA; MBA/MSIE. *Accreditation:* AACSB. Evening/weekend programs available. *Degree requirements:* For master's, comprehensive exam. *Entrance requirements:* For master's, GMAT. Additional exam requirements/recommendations for international students: Required—TOEFL (minimum score 550 paper-based; 59 iBT). Electronic applications accepted. *Faculty research:* Leadership, e-commerce, supply chain management.

University of Michigan, Ross School of Business, Ann Arbor, MI 48109-1234. Offers accounting (M Acc); business (MBA); business administration (PhD); supply chain management (MSCM); JD/MBA; MBA/M Arch; MBA/M Eng; MBA/MA; MBA/MEM; MBA/MHSA; MBA/MM; MBA/MPP; MBA/MS; MBA/MSE; MBA/MSI; MBA/MSW; MBA/MUP; MD/MBA; MHSA/MBA. Part-time and evening/weekend programs available. *Degree requirements:* For doctorate, comprehensive exam, thesis/dissertation, oral defense of dissertation, preliminary exam. *Entrance requirements:* For master's, GMAT or GRE, completion of equivalent of four-year U.S. bachelor's degree, two letters of recommendation, essays, resume; for doctorate, GMAT or GRE. Additional exam requirements/recommendations for international students: Required—TOEFL (minimum score 600 paper-based; 100 iBT). Electronic applications accepted. Tuition and fees vary according to course level, course load, degree level, program and student level. *Faculty research:* Finance and accounting, marketing, technology and operations management, corporate strategy, management and organizations.

University of Michigan–Dearborn, College of Business, Dearborn, MI 48128-1491. Offers accounting (MBA, MS); business analytics (MS); finance (MBA, MS); human resource management (MBA); information systems (MS); international business (MBA); investment (MBA); management (MBA); management information systems (MBA); marketing (MBA); supply chain management (MBA, MS); taxation (MBA); MBA/MHSA; MBA/MSE; MBA/MSF; MBA/MSIS; MBA/MSSCM; MSF/MSA. *Accreditation:* AACSB. Part-time and evening/weekend programs available. Postbaccalaureate distance learning degree programs offered (no on-campus study). *Faculty:* 24 full-time (8 women), 5 part-time/adjunct (2 women). *Students:* 82 full-time (31 women), 323 part-time (116 women); includes 72 minority (17 Black or African American, non-Hispanic/Latino; 2 American Indian or Alaska Native, non-Hispanic/Latino; 30 Asian, non-Hispanic/Latino; 15 Hispanic/Latino; 8 Two or more races, non-Hispanic/Latino), 65 international. Average age 32. 290 applicants, 44% accepted, 99 enrolled. In 2013, 143 master's awarded. *Entrance requirements:* For master's, GMAT or GRE, pre-calculus or finite mathematics; 18 credits of accounting course work beyond introductory courses (MS in accounting). Additional exam requirements/recommendations for international students: Required—TOEFL (minimum score 560 paper-based; 84 iBT), IELTS. *Application deadline:* For fall admission, 8/1 priority date for domestic students, 5/1 priority date for international students; for winter admission, 12/1 priority date for domestic students, 9/1 priority date for international students; for spring admission, 4/1 priority date for domestic students, 1/1 priority date for international students. Applications are processed on a rolling basis. Application fee: $60. Electronic applications accepted. *Expenses:* Contact institution. *Financial support:* Career-related internships or fieldwork, Federal Work-Study, and scholarships/grants available. Support available to part-time students. Financial award application deadline: 9/1; financial award applicants required to submit FAFSA. *Faculty research:* Cultural diversity, buyer-supplier relations, error detection in data, economic evolution. *Unit head:* Dr. Raju Balakrishnan, Dean, 313-593-5248, Fax: 313-271-9835, E-mail: rajub@umich.edu. *Application contact:* Joan Doherty, Academic Advisor/Counselor, 313-593-5460, Fax: 313-271-9838, E-mail: umd-gradbusiness@umich.edu.
Website: http://www.cob.umd.umich.edu.

University of Michigan–Flint, School of Management, Flint, MI 48502-1950. Offers accounting (MBA, MSA); business (Graduate Certificate); computer information systems (MBA); finance (MBA); health care management (MBA); international business (MBA); lean manufacturing (MBA); marketing (MBA); organizational leadership (MBA). *Accreditation:* AACSB. Part-time and evening/weekend programs available. Postbaccalaureate distance learning degree programs offered (minimal on-campus study). *Faculty:* 13 full-time (3 women), 4 part-time/adjunct (0 women). *Students:* 19 full-time (6 women), 234 part-time (72 women); includes 50 minority (21 Black or African American, non-Hispanic/Latino; 5 American Indian or Alaska Native, non-Hispanic/Latino; 12 Asian, non-Hispanic/Latino; 5 Hispanic/Latino; 7 Two or more races, non-Hispanic/Latino), 30 international. Average age 32. 195 applicants, 56% accepted, 88 enrolled. In 2013, 73 master's awarded. *Degree requirements:* For master's, thesis or alternative. *Entrance requirements:* For master's, GMAT or GRE, minimum GPA of 3.0. Additional exam requirements/recommendations for international students: Required—TOEFL (minimum score 560 paper-based; 84 iBT), IELTS (minimum score 6.5). *Application deadline:* For fall admission, 8/1 for domestic students, 5/1 for international students; for winter admission, 11/1 for domestic students, 9/1 for international students; for spring admission, 2/15 for domestic students, 1/15 for international students. Applications are processed on a rolling basis. Application fee: $55. Electronic applications accepted. *Financial support:* Federal Work-Study, scholarships/grants, and unspecified assistantships available. Support available to part-time students. Financial award application deadline: 3/1; financial award applicants required to submit FAFSA. *Unit head:* Dr. Scott Johnson, Dean, School of Management, 810-762-3164, Fax: 810-237-6685, E-mail: scotjohn@umflint.edu. *Application contact:* Jeremiah Cook, Marketing Communications Specialist, 810-424-5583, Fax: 810-766-6789, E-mail: jecook@umflint.edu.
Website: http://www.umflint.edu/som/.

University of Minnesota, Twin Cities Campus, Carlson School of Management, Doctoral Program in Business Administration, Minneapolis, MN 55455-0213. Offers accounting (PhD); finance (PhD); information and decision sciences (PhD); marketing (PhD); operations and management science (PhD); strategic management and entrepreneurship (PhD). *Faculty:* 102 full-time (31 women). *Students:* 74 full-time (25 women); includes 8 minority (1 Black or African American, non-Hispanic/Latino; 5 Asian,

non-Hispanic/Latino; 2 Hispanic/Latino), 46 international. Average age 30. 274 applicants, 8% accepted, 15 enrolled. In 2013, 10 doctorates awarded. *Degree requirements:* For doctorate, comprehensive exam, thesis/dissertation, written and oral preliminary exams, proposal defense, final defense. *Entrance requirements:* For doctorate, GMAT, GRE General Test. Additional exam requirements/recommendations for international students: Required—TOEFL (minimum score 600 paper-based; 100 iBT); Recommended—IELTS (minimum score 7.5). *Application deadline:* For fall admission, 12/31 for domestic students, 12/31 priority date for international students. Applications are processed on a rolling basis. Application fee: $75 ($95 for international students). Electronic applications accepted. *Expenses:* Contact institution. *Financial support:* In 2013–14, 68 students received support, including 96 fellowships with full tuition reimbursements available (averaging $6,300 per year), 65 research assistantships with full tuition reimbursements available (averaging $12,500 per year), 64 teaching assistantships with full tuition reimbursements available (averaging $12,500 per year); institutionally sponsored loans, scholarships/grants, health care benefits, unspecified assistantships, and full student fee waivers also available. Financial award application deadline: 12/31. *Faculty research:* Corporate strategy, finance, entrepreneurship, marketing, information and decision science, operations, accounting, supply chain. *Unit head:* Dr. Shawn P. Curley, Director, 612-624-6546, Fax: 612-624-8221, E-mail: curley@umn.edu. *Application contact:* Earlene K. Bronson, Assistant Director, 612-624-0875, Fax: 612-624-8221, E-mail: brons003@umn.edu.
Website: http://www.csom.umn.edu/phd-BA/.

University of Minnesota, Twin Cities Campus, Carlson School of Management, Master's Program in Accountancy, Minneapolis, MN 55455-0213. Offers M Acc. *Accreditation:* AACSB. Part-time and evening/weekend programs available. *Faculty:* 23 full-time (5 women), 1 part-time/adjunct (0 women). *Students:* 70 full-time (33 women), 7 part-time (4 women); includes 7 minority (2 Black or African American, non-Hispanic/Latino; 4 Asian, non-Hispanic/Latino; 1 Hispanic/Latino), 29 international. Average age 23. 403 applicants, 22% accepted, 70 enrolled. In 2013, 34 master's awarded. *Entrance requirements:* For master's, GMAT, letters of recommendation. Additional exam requirements/recommendations for international students: Required—TOEFL (minimum score 550 paper-based; 79 iBT), IELTS (minimum score 6.5). *Application deadline:* For fall admission, 3/31 priority date for domestic students, 2/28 priority date for international students; for spring admission, 10/15 priority date for domestic and international students. Applications are processed on a rolling basis. Application fee: $75 ($95 for international students). Electronic applications accepted. *Expenses:* Contact institution. *Financial support:* In 2013–14, 52 students received support, including 5 fellowships (averaging $2,500 per year), 7 teaching assistantships with partial tuition reimbursements available (averaging $9,000 per year); institutionally sponsored loans also available. Financial award application deadline: 7/15. *Faculty research:* Capitol market-based accounting, cognitive skill acquisition in auditing, incentives and control in organizations, economic consequences of securities regulation, earnings management. *Unit head:* Larry Kallio, Director of Graduate Studies, 612-624-9818, Fax: 612-626-7795, E-mail: kalli008@umn.edu. *Application contact:* Information Contact, 612-625-3014, Fax: 612-625-6002, E-mail: gsquest@umn.edu.
Website: http://www.carlsonschool.umn.edu/macc.

University of Mississippi, Graduate School, School of Accountancy, Oxford, MS 38677. Offers accountancy (M Acc, PhD); taxation accounting (M Tax). *Accreditation:* AACSB. *Faculty:* 14 full-time (4 women), 4 part-time/adjunct (2 women). *Students:* 131 full-time (60 women), 13 part-time (6 women); includes 14 minority (6 Black or African American, non-Hispanic/Latino; 4 Asian, non-Hispanic/Latino; 1 Hispanic/Latino; 3 Two or more races, non-Hispanic/Latino), 6 international. In 2013, 90 master's, 3 doctorates awarded. *Degree requirements:* For doctorate, thesis/dissertation. *Entrance requirements:* For master's, GMAT, minimum GPA of 3.0; for doctorate, GMAT. Additional exam requirements/recommendations for international students: Required—TOEFL. *Application deadline:* For fall admission, 4/1 for domestic students; for spring admission, 10/1 for domestic students. Applications are processed on a rolling basis. Application fee: $40. *Financial support:* Scholarships/grants available. Financial award application deadline: 3/1; financial award applicants required to submit FAFSA. *Unit head:* Dr. Mark Wilder, Interim Dean, 662-915-7468, Fax: 662-915-7483, E-mail: umaccy@olemiss.edu. *Application contact:* Dr. Christy M. Wyandt, Associate Dean, 662-915-7474, Fax: 662-915-7577, E-mail: cwyandt@olemiss.edu.

University of Missouri, Graduate School, Robert J. Trulaske, Sr. College of Business, School of Accountancy, Columbia, MO 65211. Offers accountancy (M Acc, PhD); taxation (Certificate). *Accreditation:* AACSB. Part-time programs available. *Faculty:* 15 full-time (7 women). *Students:* 141 full-time (59 women), 8 part-time (2 women); includes 8 minority (5 Black or African American, non-Hispanic/Latino; 2 Asian, non-Hispanic/Latino; 1 Hispanic/Latino), 14 international. Average age 23. 119 applicants, 47% accepted, 55 enrolled. In 2013, 130 master's, 2 doctorates, 27 other advanced degrees awarded. *Degree requirements:* For master's, thesis or alternative; for doctorate, thesis/dissertation. *Entrance requirements:* For master's and doctorate, GMAT, minimum GPA of 3.0. Additional exam requirements/recommendations for international students: Required—TOEFL (minimum score 600 paper-based; 100 iBT). *Application deadline:* For fall admission, 2/1 priority date for domestic and international students. Applications are processed on a rolling basis. Application fee: $55 ($75 for international students). Electronic applications accepted. *Financial support:* Fellowships with full and partial tuition reimbursements, research assistantships with full and partial tuition reimbursements, teaching assistantships with full and partial tuition reimbursements, institutionally sponsored loans, scholarships/grants, health care benefits, and unspecified assistantships available. Support available to part-time students. *Unit head:* Dr. Vairam Arunachalam, Director, 573-882-4463, E-mail: arunachalam@missouri.edu. *Application contact:* Karen L. Brammer, Administrative Assistant, 573-882-4463, E-mail: brammerk@missouri.edu.
Website: http://business.missouri.edu/43/default.aspx.

University of Missouri–Kansas City, Henry W. Bloch School of Management, Kansas City, MO 64110-2499. Offers accounting (MS); business administration (MBA); entrepreneurial real estate (MERE); entrepreneurship and innovation (PhD); finance (MS); public affairs (MPA, PhD); JD/MBA; LL M/MPA. PhD (interdisciplinary) offered through the School of Graduate Studies. *Accreditation:* AACSB; NASPAA. Part-time and evening/weekend programs available. *Faculty:* 57 full-time (15 women), 32 part-time/adjunct (10 women). *Students:* 309 full-time (151 women), 377 part-time (163 women); includes 100 minority (39 Black or African American, non-Hispanic/Latino; 2 American Indian or Alaska Native, non-Hispanic/Latino; 27 Asian, non-Hispanic/Latino; 24 Hispanic/Latino; 1 Native Hawaiian or other Pacific Islander, non-Hispanic/Latino; 7 Two or more races, non-Hispanic/Latino), 93 international. Average age 30. 489 applicants, 54% accepted, 252 enrolled. In 2013, 252 master's, 1 doctorate awarded. Terminal master's awarded for partial completion of doctoral program. *Entrance requirements:* For master's, GMAT, GRE, 2 essays, 2 references, support of employer; for doctorate, GRE, minimum GPA of 3.0. Additional exam requirements/recommendations for international students: Required—TOEFL (minimum score 550 paper-based; 80 iBT). *Application deadline:* For fall admission, 5/1 priority date for domestic and international students; for spring admission, 10/1 priority date for domestic and international students. Applications are processed on a rolling basis. Application fee: $45 ($50 for international students). Electronic applications accepted. *Expenses:* Tuition, state resident: full-time $6073; part-time $337.40 per credit hour. Tuition, nonresident: full-time $15,680; part-time $871.10 per credit hour. *Required fees:* $97.59 per credit hour. Full-time tuition and fees vary according to program. *Financial support:* In 2013–14, 38 research assistantships with partial tuition reimbursements (averaging $10,499 per year), 6 teaching assistantships with partial tuition reimbursements (averaging $13,380 per year) were awarded; career-related internships or fieldwork, Federal Work-Study, institutionally sponsored loans, scholarships/grants, tuition waivers (full and partial), and unspecified assistantships also available. Support available to part-time students. Financial award application deadline: 3/1; financial award applicants required to submit FAFSA. *Faculty research:* Entrepreneurship, finance, non-profit, risk management. *Unit head:* Dr. David Donnelly, Dean, 816-235-1333, Fax: 816-235-2206, E-mail: donnellyd@umkc.edu. *Application contact:* 816-235-1111, E-mail: admit@umkc.edu.
Website: http://www.bloch.umkc.edu.

University of Missouri–St. Louis, College of Business Administration, Program in Accounting, St. Louis, MO 63121. Offers M Acc. *Accreditation:* AACSB. Part-time and evening/weekend programs available. *Faculty:* 7 full-time (4 women), 5 part-time/adjunct (3 women). *Students:* 31 full-time (12 women), 34 part-time (19 women); includes 5 minority (4 Asian, non-Hispanic/Latino; 1 Hispanic/Latino), 3 international. Average age 28. 34 applicants, 65% accepted, 18 enrolled. In 2013, 43 master's awarded. *Entrance requirements:* For master's, GMAT, 2 letters of recommendation. Additional exam requirements/recommendations for international students: Recommended—TOEFL (minimum score 550 paper-based; 79 iBT), IELTS (minimum score 6.5). *Application deadline:* For fall admission, 3/15 for domestic and international students; for spring admission, 10/15 for domestic and international students. Application fee: $50 ($40 for international students). Electronic applications accepted. *Expenses:* Tuition, state resident: full-time $7364; part-time $409.10 per credit hour. Tuition, nonresident: full-time $19,162; part-time $1008.50 per credit hour. *Financial support:* In 2013–14, 1 research assistantship with full and partial tuition reimbursement (averaging $5,625 per year) was awarded; career-related internships or fieldwork, Federal Work-Study, and institutionally sponsored loans also available. Support available to part-time students. Financial award application deadline: 4/1; financial award applicants required to submit FAFSA. *Faculty research:* Accounting information in contracts, financial reporting issues, empirical valuation issues. *Unit head:* Francesca Ferrari, Assistant Director, 314-516-5885, Fax: 314-516-6420, E-mail: mba@umsl.edu. *Application contact:* 314-516-5458, Fax: 314-516-6996, E-mail: gradadm@umsl.edu.
Website: http://www.umsl.edu/academics/PDFS/program_guide_business.pdf.

University of Missouri–St. Louis, College of Business Administration, Program in Business Administration, St. Louis, MO 63121. Offers accounting (MBA); business administration (Certificate); business intelligence (Certificate); finance (MBA); human resource management (Certificate); information systems (MBA); logistics and supply chain management (MBA, PhD, Certificate); marketing (MBA); marketing management (Certificate); operations management (MBA). *Accreditation:* AACSB. Part-time and evening/weekend programs available. *Faculty:* 30 full-time (5 women), 20 part-time/adjunct (8 women). *Students:* 114 full-time (51 women), 269 part-time (100 women); includes 43 minority (16 Black or African American, non-Hispanic/Latino; 14 Asian, non-Hispanic/Latino; 11 Hispanic/Latino; 1 Native Hawaiian or other Pacific Islander, non-Hispanic/Latino; 1 Two or more races, non-Hispanic/Latino), 56 international. Average age 31. 153 applicants, 91% accepted, 110 enrolled. In 2013, 136 master's, 7 other advanced degrees awarded. *Degree requirements:* For doctorate, thesis/dissertation. *Entrance requirements:* For master's, GMAT, 2 letters of recommendation. Additional exam requirements/recommendations for international students: Recommended—TOEFL (minimum score 550 paper-based; 79 iBT), IELTS (minimum score 6.5). *Application deadline:* For fall admission, 7/1 for domestic and international students; for spring admission, 12/1 for domestic and international students. Applications are processed on a rolling basis. Application fee: $50 ($40 for international students). Electronic applications accepted. *Expenses:* Tuition, state resident: full-time $7364; part-time $409.10 per credit hour. Tuition, nonresident: full-time $19,162; part-time $1008.50 per credit hour. *Financial support:* In 2013–14, 14 research assistantships with full and partial tuition reimbursements (averaging $5,625 per year), 6 teaching assistantships with full and partial tuition reimbursements (averaging $9,403 per year) were awarded; career-related internships or fieldwork, Federal Work-Study, and institutionally sponsored loans also available. Support available to part-time students. Financial award application deadline: 4/1; financial award applicants required to submit FAFSA. *Faculty research:* Human resources, strategic management, marketing strategy, consumer behavior product development, advertising. *Unit head:* Francesca Ferrari, Assistant Director, 314-516-5885, Fax: 314-516-6420, E-mail: mba@umsl.edu. *Application contact:* 314-516-5458, Fax: 314-516-6996, E-mail: gradadm@umsl.edu.
Website: http://mba.umsl.edu/Degree%20Programs/index.html.

The University of Montana, Graduate School, School of Business Administration, Department of Accounting and Finance, Missoula, MT 59812-0002. Offers accounting (M Acct). *Accreditation:* AACSB. *Degree requirements:* For master's, thesis optional. *Entrance requirements:* For master's, GMAT. Additional exam requirements/recommendations for international students: Required—TOEFL (minimum score 580 paper-based). *Faculty research:* Income tax, financial markets, nonprofit accounting, accounting information systems, auditing.

University of Nebraska at Kearney, Graduate Programs, College of Business and Technology, Department of Business, Kearney, NE 68849-0001. Offers accounting (MBA); generalist (MBA); human resources (MBA); human services (MBA); marketing (MBA). *Accreditation:* AACSB. Part-time and evening/weekend programs available. *Degree requirements:* For master's, thesis optional. *Entrance requirements:* For master's, GMAT or GRE, letters of recommendation, work history, letter of interest, resume. Additional exam requirements/recommendations for international students: Required—TOEFL (minimum score 550 paper-based; 79 iBT). Electronic applications accepted. *Faculty research:* Small business financial management, employment law, expert systems, international trade and marketing, environmental economics.

University of Nebraska at Omaha, Graduate Studies, College of Business Administration, Department of Accounting, Omaha, NE 68182. Offers M Acc. Part-time and evening/weekend programs available. *Faculty:* 9 full-time (4 women). *Students:* 11 full-time (6 women), 33 part-time (19 women); includes 7 minority (1 Black or African American, non-Hispanic/Latino; 4 Asian, non-Hispanic/Latino; 1 Hispanic/Latino; 1 Two or more races, non-Hispanic/Latino). Average age 29. 38 applicants, 47% accepted, 16 enrolled. In 2013, 16 master's awarded. *Degree requirements:* For master's, comprehensive exam (for some programs), thesis (for some programs). *Entrance requirements:* For master's, GMAT, minimum GPA of 3.0 in undergraduate courses related to accounting, official transcript. Additional exam requirements/recommendations for international students: Required—TOEFL, IELTS, PTE. *Application deadline:* For fall admission, 8/1 priority date for domestic students; for spring admission, 12/1 priority date for domestic students. Applications are processed on a rolling basis. Application fee: $45. Electronic applications accepted. *Financial support:* In 2013–14, 2 students received support, including 2 research assistantships with tuition reimbursements available; Federal Work-Study, institutionally sponsored loans, scholarships/grants, tuition waivers (partial), and unspecified assistantships also available. Support available to part-time students. Financial award application deadline:

3/1; financial award applicants required to submit FAFSA. *Unit head:* Dr. Susan Eldridge, Chairperson, 402-554-3650. *Application contact:* Dr. Jennifer Riley, Graduate Program Chair, 402-554-3984, E-mail: graduate@unomaha.edu.

University of Nebraska–Lincoln, Graduate College, College of Business Administration, Interdepartmental Area of Business, Lincoln, NE 68588. Offers accountancy (PhD); business (MBA); finance (MA, PhD), including business; management (MA, PhD), including business; marketing (MA, PhD), including business; JD/MBA; M Arch/MBA. *Accreditation:* AACSB. Part-time programs available. Postbaccalaureate distance learning degree programs offered. *Degree requirements:* For doctorate, comprehensive exam, thesis/dissertation. *Entrance requirements:* For master's and doctorate, GMAT. Additional exam requirements/recommendations for international students: Required—TOEFL (minimum score 550 paper-based). Electronic applications accepted.

University of Nebraska–Lincoln, Graduate College, College of Business Administration, School of Accountancy, Lincoln, NE 68588. Offers MPA, PhD, JD/MPA. *Accreditation:* AACSB. *Entrance requirements:* For master's, GMAT. Additional exam requirements/recommendations for international students: Required—TOEFL (minimum score 550 paper-based). Electronic applications accepted. *Faculty research:* Auditing, financial accounting, managerial accounting, capital markets, tax accounting.

University of Nevada, Las Vegas, Graduate College, College of Business, Department of Accounting, Las Vegas, NV 89154-6003. Offers MS, Advanced Certificate, Certificate. *Accreditation:* AACSB. Part-time and evening/weekend programs available. *Faculty:* 9 full-time (5 women), 5 part-time/adjunct (1 woman). *Students:* 54 full-time (25 women), 63 part-time (34 women); includes 41 minority (2 Black or African American, non-Hispanic/Latino; 22 Asian, non-Hispanic/Latino; 10 Hispanic/Latino; 7 Two or more races, non-Hispanic/Latino), 9 international. Average age 30. 59 applicants, 71% accepted, 32 enrolled. In 2013, 59 master's awarded. *Entrance requirements:* For master's, GMAT. Additional exam requirements/recommendations for international students: Required—TOEFL (minimum score 550 paper-based; 80 iBT), IELTS (minimum score 7). *Application deadline:* For fall admission, 8/1 for domestic students, 5/1 for international students; for spring admission, 12/1 for domestic students, 10/1 for international students; for summer admission, 5/15 for domestic students, 4/15 for international students. Application fee: $60 ($95 for international students). Electronic applications accepted. *Expenses:* Tuition, state resident: full-time $4752; part-time $264 per credit. Tuition, nonresident: full-time $18,662; part-time $554.50 per credit. *International tuition:* $18,952 full-time. *Required fees:* $532; $12 per credit. $266 per semester. One-time fee: $35. Tuition and fees vary according to course load and program. *Financial support:* In 2013–14, 16 students received support, including 2 research assistantships with partial tuition reimbursements available (averaging $10,000 per year), 14 teaching assistantships with partial tuition reimbursements available (averaging $7,857 per year); institutionally sponsored loans, scholarships/grants, health care benefits, and unspecified assistantships also available. Financial award application deadline: 3/1. *Faculty research:* Audit judgments and decision-making, fraud, corporate governance, professional skepticism, internal audit. *Total annual research expenditures:* $3,629. *Unit head:* Dr. Paulette Tandy, Chair/Associate Professor, 702-895-1559, Fax: 702-895-4306, E-mail: paulette.tandy@unlv.edu. *Application contact:* Graduate College Admissions Evaluator, 702-895-3320, Fax: 702-895-4180, E-mail: gradcollege@unlv.edu.
Website: http://business.unlv.edu/accounting/.

University of Nevada, Reno, Graduate School, College of Business Administration, Department of Accounting and Information Systems, Reno, NV 89557. Offers M Acc. *Accreditation:* AACSB. *Entrance requirements:* For master's, GMAT or GRE (if undergraduate degree is not from an AACSB-accredited business school with minimum GPA of 3.5), minimum GPA of 2.75. Additional exam requirements/recommendations for international students: Required—TOEFL (minimum score 500 paper-based; 61 iBT), IELTS (minimum score 6). Electronic applications accepted. *Faculty research:* Financial reporting/auditing, taxation.

University of New Hampshire, Graduate School, Peter T. Paul College of Business and Economics, Department of Accounting and Finance, Durham, NH 03824. Offers accounting (MS). Part-time programs available. *Faculty:* 11 full-time (2 women). *Students:* 32 full-time (17 women); includes 1 minority (Asian, non-Hispanic/Latino). Average age 23. 88 applicants, 42% accepted, 30 enrolled. In 2013, 21 master's awarded. *Entrance requirements:* For master's, GMAT. Additional exam requirements/recommendations for international students: Required—TOEFL (minimum score 550 paper-based; 80 iBT). *Application deadline:* For fall admission, 5/1 priority date for domestic students, 4/1 for international students; for spring admission, 12/1 for domestic students. Applications are processed on a rolling basis. Application fee: $65. Electronic applications accepted. *Expenses:* Tuition, state resident: full-time $13,500; part-time $750 per credit hour. Tuition, nonresident: full-time $26,200; part-time $1100 per credit hour. *Required fees:* $1741; $435.25 per term. Tuition and fees vary according to course level, course load, campus/location and program. *Financial support:* In 2013–14, 17 students received support. Fellowships, research assistantships, and teaching assistantships available. Financial award application deadline: 2/15. *Unit head:* Stephen Ciccone, Chairperson, 603-862-3343, E-mail: ahmad.etebari@unh.edu. *Application contact:* Wendy Harris, Administrative Assistant, 603-862-3326, E-mail: wsbe.grad@unh.edu.
Website: http://paulcollege.unh.edu/academics/graduate-programs/ms-accounting.

University of New Haven, Graduate School, College of Business, Program in Accounting, West Haven, CT 06516-1916. Offers MBA, Certificate. *Students:* 14 full-time (11 women), 22 part-time (12 women); includes 6 minority (3 Black or African American, non-Hispanic/Latino; 1 Asian, non-Hispanic/Latino; 2 Hispanic/Latino), 13 international. 14 applicants, 100% accepted, 4 enrolled. In 2013, 26 master's, 1 other advanced degree awarded. *Degree requirements:* For master's, thesis. *Application deadline:* Applications are processed on a rolling basis. Application fee: $75. *Expenses: Tuition:* Full-time $21,600; part-time $800 per credit hour. *Required fees:* $45 per trimester. *Financial support:* Research assistantships with partial tuition reimbursements, teaching assistantships with partial tuition reimbursements, and Federal Work-Study available. Support available to part-time students. Financial award application deadline: 5/1; financial award applicants required to submit FAFSA. *Unit head:* Robert E. Wnek, Chairman of Accounting, 203-932-7111, E-mail: rwnek@newhaven.edu. *Application contact:* Eloise Gormley, Director of Graduate Admissions, 203-932-7440, E-mail: gradinfo@newhaven.edu.

University of New Haven, Graduate School, College of Business, Program in Business Administration, West Haven, CT 06516-1916. Offers accounting (MBA, Certificate), including CPA (MBA); business administration (MBA); business management (Certificate); business policy and strategic leadership (MBA); finance (MBA), including CFA; global marketing (MBA); human resource management (Certificate); human resources management (MBA); international business (Certificate); marketing (MBA, Certificate); sports management (MBA). Part-time and evening/weekend programs available. *Students:* 125 full-time (55 women), 88 part-time (30 women); includes 31 minority (16 Black or African American, non-Hispanic/Latino; 1 American Indian or Alaska Native, non-Hispanic/Latino; 8 Asian, non-Hispanic/Latino; 5 Hispanic/Latino; 1 Native Hawaiian or other Pacific Islander, non-Hispanic/Latino), 72 international. 196 applicants, 89% accepted, 72 enrolled. In 2013, 143 master's, 24 other advanced degrees awarded. *Degree requirements:* For master's, thesis optional. *Entrance requirements:* For master's, GMAT. Additional exam requirements/recommendations for international students: Required—TOEFL (minimum score 80 iBT), IELTS, PTE (minimum score 53). *Application deadline:* For fall admission, 5/31 for international students; for winter admission, 10/15 for international students; for spring admission, 1/15 for international students. Applications are processed on a rolling basis. Application fee: $75. Electronic applications accepted. Application fee is waived when completed online. *Expenses: Tuition:* Full-time $21,600; part-time $800 per credit hour. *Required fees:* $45 per trimester. *Financial support:* Research assistantships with partial tuition reimbursements, teaching assistantships with partial tuition reimbursements, career-related internships or fieldwork, Federal Work-Study, scholarships/grants, and unspecified assistantships available. Support available to part-time students. Financial award applicants required to submit FAFSA. *Unit head:* Dr. Armando Rodriguez, Director, 203-932-7372, E-mail: arodriguez@newhaven.edu. *Application contact:* Eloise Gormley, Director of Graduate Admissions, 203-932-7440, E-mail: gradinfo@newhaven.edu.
Website: http://www.newhaven.edu/7433/.

University of New Mexico, Anderson Graduate School of Management, Department of Accounting, Albuquerque, NM 87131. Offers accounting (MBA); advanced accounting (M Acct); information assurance (M Acct); professional accounting (M Acct); tax accounting (M Acct); JD/M Acct. *Accreditation:* AACSB. Part-time and evening/weekend programs available. *Faculty:* 11 full-time (4 women), 4 part-time/adjunct (3 women). In 2013, 75 master's awarded. *Entrance requirements:* For master's, GMAT or GRE, minimum GPA of 3.0 on last 60 hours of coursework. Additional exam requirements/recommendations for international students: Required—TOEFL (minimum score 550 paper-based; 79 iBT). *Application deadline:* For fall admission, 4/1 priority date for domestic and international students; for spring admission, 10/1 priority date for domestic and international students. Applications are processed on a rolling basis. Application fee: $50. Electronic applications accepted. *Expenses:* Contact institution. *Financial support:* Fellowships, research assistantships, career-related internships or fieldwork, Federal Work-Study, scholarships/grants, and unspecified assistantships available. Support available to part-time students. Financial award application deadline: 6/1; financial award applicants required to submit FAFSA. *Faculty research:* Critical accounting, accounting pedagogy, theory, taxation, information fraud. *Unit head:* Dr. Craig White, Chair, 505-277-6471, Fax: 505-277-7108, E-mail: cwhite@unm.edu. *Application contact:* Tina Armijo, Office Administrator, 505-277-6471, Fax: 505-277-7108, E-mail: tmarmijo@unm.edu.
Website: http://mba.mgt.unm.edu/default.asp.

University of New Orleans, Graduate School, College of Business Administration, Department of Accounting, Program in Accounting, New Orleans, LA 70148. Offers MS. *Accreditation:* AACSB. Part-time and evening/weekend programs available. *Degree requirements:* For master's, thesis optional. *Entrance requirements:* For master's, GMAT. Additional exam requirements/recommendations for international students: Required—TOEFL (minimum score 550 paper-based; 79 iBT). Electronic applications accepted.

University of North Alabama, College of Business, Florence, AL 35632-0001. Offers accounting (MBA); enterprise resource planning systems (MBA); finance (MBA); health care management (MBA); information systems (MBA); professional (MBA); project management (MBA). *Accreditation:* ACBSP. Part-time and evening/weekend programs available. *Faculty:* 20 full-time (2 women). *Students:* 118 full-time (50 women), 273 part-time (130 women); includes 115 minority (37 Black or African American, non-Hispanic/Latino; 4 American Indian or Alaska Native, non-Hispanic/Latino; 68 Asian, non-Hispanic/Latino; 4 Hispanic/Latino; 2 Two or more races, non-Hispanic/Latino), 36 international. Average age 34. 296 applicants, 82% accepted, 149 enrolled. In 2013, 179 master's awarded. *Entrance requirements:* For master's, GMAT, GRE, minimum GPA of 2.75 in last 60 hours, 2.5 overall on a 3.0 scale; 27 hours of course work in business and economics. Additional exam requirements/recommendations for international students: Required—TOEFL (minimum score 500 paper-based; 79 iBT), IELTS (minimum score 6). *Application deadline:* For fall admission, 7/1 priority date for domestic students, 7/1 for international students; for spring admission, 12/1 for domestic and international students. Applications are processed on a rolling basis. Application fee: $25 ($50 for international students). Electronic applications accepted. *Expenses:* Tuition, state resident: full-time $4968; part-time $3312 per year. Tuition, nonresident: full-time $9936; part-time $6624 per year. *Required fees:* $970; $60.33 per credit. $362 per semester. *Financial support:* Federal Work-Study available. Support available to part-time students. Financial award application deadline: 4/1; financial award applicants required to submit FAFSA. *Unit head:* Dr. Kerry Gatlin, Dean, 256-765-4261, Fax: 256-765-4170, E-mail: kpgatlin@una.edu. *Application contact:* Russ Darracott, Graduate Admissions Counselor, 256-765-4447, E-mail: erdarracott@una.edu.
Website: http://www.una.edu/business/.

The University of North Carolina at Chapel Hill, Kenan-Flagler Business School, Accounting Program, Chapel Hill, NC 27599. Offers MAC. *Entrance requirements:* For master's, GMAT. Additional exam requirements/recommendations for international students: Required—TOEFL. *Expenses:* Contact institution. *Faculty research:* Corporate taxation, international taxation, financial accounting, corporate governance, strategy.

The University of North Carolina at Chapel Hill, Kenan-Flagler Business School, Doctoral Program in Business Administration, Chapel Hill, NC 27599. Offers accounting (PhD); finance (PhD); marketing (PhD); operations management (PhD); organizational behavior (PhD); strategy (PhD). *Accreditation:* AACSB. *Degree requirements:* For doctorate, thesis/dissertation. *Entrance requirements:* For doctorate, GMAT or GRE General Test. Electronic applications accepted. *Expenses:* Contact institution.

The University of North Carolina at Charlotte, The Graduate School, Belk College of Business, Department of Accounting, Charlotte, NC 28223-0001. Offers M Acc. *Accreditation:* AACSB. Part-time and evening/weekend programs available. *Faculty:* 10 full-time (3 women). *Students:* 45 full-time (21 women), 58 part-time (34 women); includes 21 minority (8 Black or African American, non-Hispanic/Latino; 8 Asian, non-Hispanic/Latino; 3 Hispanic/Latino; 2 Two or more races, non-Hispanic/Latino), 9 international. Average age 29. 132 applicants, 58% accepted, 56 enrolled. In 2013, 83 master's awarded. *Degree requirements:* For master's, thesis or alternative. *Entrance requirements:* For master's, GMAT or GRE, minimum GPA of 3.0 in undergraduate major, 2.8 overall, three letters of recommendation, essay. Additional exam requirements/recommendations for international students: Required—TOEFL (minimum score 557 paper-based; 83 iBT). *Application deadline:* For fall admission, 5/1 priority date for domestic and international students; for spring admission, 10/1 priority date for domestic and international students. Applications are processed on a rolling basis. Application fee: $75. Electronic applications accepted. *Expenses:* Tuition, state resident: full-time $3522. Tuition, nonresident: full-time $16,051. *Required fees:* $2585. Tuition and fees vary according to course load and program. *Financial support:* Career-related internships or fieldwork, institutionally sponsored loans, scholarships/grants, and unspecified assistantships available. Support available to part-time students. Financial award application deadline: 4/1; financial award applicants required to submit FAFSA. *Faculty research:* Corporate financial reporting trends, use of latest software for

accounting and business applications, latest developments in federal and international taxation. *Unit head:* Dr. Hughlene Burton, Chair, 704-687-7696, Fax: 704-687-6938, E-mail: haburton@uncc.edu. *Application contact:* Kathy B. Giddings, Director of Graduate Admissions, 704-687-5503, Fax: 704-687-1668, E-mail: gradadm@uncc.edu.
Website: http://belkcollege.uncc.edu/about-college/departments/accounting.

The University of North Carolina at Greensboro, Graduate School, Bryan School of Business and Economics, Department of Accounting and Finance, Greensboro, NC 27412-5001. Offers accounting (MS); financial analysis (PMC). *Accreditation:* AACSB. *Entrance requirements:* For master's, GMAT, GRE General Test, previous course work in accounting and business. Additional exam requirements/recommendations for international students: Required—TOEFL. Electronic applications accepted.

The University of North Carolina Wilmington, School of Business, Accountancy and Business Law Program, Wilmington, NC 28403-3297. Offers MSA. *Faculty:* 9 full-time (3 women), 3 part-time/adjunct (1 woman). *Students:* 67 full-time (32 women); includes 6 minority (2 Asian, non-Hispanic/Latino; 4 Hispanic/Latino). Average age 24. 113 applicants, 86% accepted, 67 enrolled. In 2013, 63 master's awarded. *Degree requirements:* For master's, thesis or alternative, portfolio project. *Entrance requirements:* For master's, GMAT. Additional exam requirements/recommendations for international students: Required—TOEFL (minimum score 550 paper-based; 79 iBT), IELTS (minimum score 6.5). *Application deadline:* For fall admission, 5/1 for domestic students. Applications are processed on a rolling basis. Application fee: $60. *Expenses:* Tuition, state resident: full-time $4163. Tuition, nonresident: full-time $16,098. *Financial support:* In 2013–14, 12 teaching assistantships with full and partial tuition reimbursements (averaging $9,000 per year) were awarded; career-related internships or fieldwork and Federal Work-Study also available. Support available to part-time students. Financial award application deadline: 3/15. *Unit head:* Dr. Daniel Ivancevich, Department Chair, 910-962-7681, Fax: 910-962-3663, E-mail: ivancevichd@uncw.edu. *Application contact:* Karen Barnhill, Graduate Program Coordinator, 910-962-3903, E-mail: barnhillk@uncw.edu.
Website: http://www.csb.uncw.edu/msa/.

University of North Dakota, Graduate School, College of Business and Public Administration, Department of Accountancy, Grand Forks, ND 58202. Offers M Acc. Part-time programs available. *Degree requirements:* For master's, comprehensive exam, thesis or alternative, final exam. *Entrance requirements:* For master's, GMAT, minimum GPA of 3.0. Additional exam requirements/recommendations for international students: Required—TOEFL (minimum score 550 paper-based; 79 iBT), IELTS (minimum score 6.5). Electronic applications accepted.

University of Northern Colorado, Graduate School, Monfort College of Business, Greeley, CO 80639. Offers accounting (MA). *Accreditation:* AACSB.

University of Northern Iowa, Graduate College, College of Business Administration, M Acc Program in Accounting, Cedar Falls, IA 50614. Offers M Acc. *Students:* 18 full-time (6 women); includes 1 minority (Native Hawaiian or other Pacific Islander, non-Hispanic/Latino), 2 international. 33 applicants, 58% accepted, 15 enrolled. In 2013, 20 master's awarded. *Degree requirements:* For master's, thesis or alternative. *Entrance requirements:* For master's, GMAT. Additional exam requirements/recommendations for international students: Required—TOEFL (minimum score 575 paper-based; 89 iBT). *Application deadline:* For fall admission, 8/1 priority date for domestic students. Applications are processed on a rolling basis. Application fee: $50 ($70 for international students). *Financial support:* Application deadline: 2/1. *Unit head:* Dr. Mary Christ, Acting Head, 319-273-2394, Fax: 319-273-2922, E-mail: mary.christ.@uni.edu. *Application contact:* Laurie S. Russell, Record Analyst, 319-273-2623, Fax: 319-273-2885, E-mail: laurie.russell@uni.edu.
Website: http://business.uni.edu/web/pages/academics/masteraccounting.cfm.

University of North Florida, Coggin College of Business, M Acc Program, Jacksonville, FL 32224. Offers M Acc. *Accreditation:* AACSB. Part-time and evening/weekend programs available. *Faculty:* 15 full-time (2 women), 1 part-time/adjunct (0 women). *Students:* 25 full-time (17 women), 30 part-time (15 women); includes 7 minority (4 Black or African American, non-Hispanic/Latino; 3 Asian, non-Hispanic/Latino), 2 international. Average age 28. 42 applicants, 60% accepted, 16 enrolled. In 2013, 14 master's awarded. *Entrance requirements:* For master's, GMAT or GRE, U.S. bachelor's degree from regionally-accredited university or equivalent foreign degree. Additional exam requirements/recommendations for international students: Required—TOEFL (minimum score 550 paper-based; 79 iBT). *Application deadline:* For fall admission, 8/1 priority date for domestic students, 5/1 for international students; for spring admission, 12/1 priority date for domestic students, 10/1 for international students; for summer admission, 3/15 priority date for domestic students. Applications are processed on a rolling basis. Application fee: $30. Electronic applications accepted. *Expenses:* Tuition, state resident: full-time $9794; part-time $408.10 per credit hour. Tuition, nonresident: full-time $22,383; part-time $932.61 per credit hour. *Required fees:* $2020; $84.20 per credit hour. Tuition and fees vary according to course load and program. *Financial support:* In 2013–14, 10 students received support. Teaching assistantships, career-related internships or fieldwork, Federal Work-Study, and tuition waivers (partial) available. Financial award application deadline: 4/1; financial award applicants required to submit FAFSA. *Faculty research:* Enterprise-wide risk management, accounting input in the strategic planning process, accounting information systems, taxation issues in lawsuits and damage awards, database design. *Total annual research expenditures:* $39,091. *Unit head:* Dr. David Jaeger, Chair, 904-620-1671, E-mail: djaeger@unf.edu. *Application contact:* Dr. Amanda Pascale, Director, The Graduate School, 904-620-1360, Fax: 904-620-1362, E-mail: graduateschool@unf.edu.
Website: http://www.unf.edu/coggin/academics/graduate/macc.aspx.

University of North Florida, Coggin College of Business, MBA Program, Jacksonville, FL 32224. Offers accounting (MBA); construction management (MBA); e-commerce (MBA); economics (MBA); finance (MBA); human resource management (MBA); international business (MBA); logistics (MBA); management applications (MBA). *Accreditation:* AACSB. Part-time and evening/weekend programs available. *Faculty:* 14 full-time (6 women), 1 part-time/adjunct (0 women). *Students:* 90 full-time (41 women), 231 part-time (84 women); includes 47 minority (18 Black or African American, non-Hispanic/Latino; 8 Asian, non-Hispanic/Latino; 16 Hispanic/Latino; 5 Two or more races, non-Hispanic/Latino), 29 international. Average age 29. 222 applicants, 47% accepted, 80 enrolled. In 2013, 152 master's awarded. *Entrance requirements:* For master's, GMAT or GRE, U.S. bachelor's degree from regionally-accredited university or equivalent foreign degree. Additional exam requirements/recommendations for international students: Required—TOEFL (minimum score 550 paper-based; 79 iBT). *Application deadline:* For fall admission, 7/1 priority date for domestic students, 5/1 for international students; for spring admission, 11/1 priority date for domestic students, 10/1 for international students. Application fee: $30. *Expenses:* Tuition, state resident: full-time $9794; part-time $408.10 per credit hour. Tuition, nonresident: full-time $22,383; part-time $932.61 per credit hour. *Required fees:* $2020; $84.20 per credit hour. Tuition and fees vary according to course load and program. *Financial support:* In 2013–14, 35 students received support, including 1 research assistantship (averaging $2,700 per year); teaching assistantships, Federal Work-Study, and tuition waivers (partial) also available. Support available to part-time students. Financial award application deadline: 4/1; financial award applicants required to submit FAFSA. *Faculty research:* Performance measures, costing, and inventory issues in logistics and supply chain management; inter-organizational systems; international management and marketing practices; e-commerce; organizational learning and socialization processes. *Total annual research expenditures:* $12,025. *Application contact:* Cheryl Campbell, Graduate Advisor, 904-620-2575, Fax: 904-620-2832, E-mail: ccampbell@unf.edu.
Website: http://www.unf.edu/coggin/academics/graduate/mba.aspx.

University of North Texas, Robert B. Toulouse School of Graduate Studies, Denton, TN 76203-5017. Offers accounting (MS, PhD); applied anthropology (MA, MS); applied behavior analysis (Certificate); applied technology and performance improvement (M Ed, MS, PhD); art education (MA, PhD); art history (MA); art museum education (Certificate); arts leadership (Certificate); audiology (Au D); behavior analysis (MS); biochemistry and molecular biology (MS, PhD); biology (MA, MS, PhD); business (PhD); business computer information systems (PhD); chemistry (MS, PhD); clinical psychology (PhD); communication studies (MA, MS); computer engineering (MS); computer science (MS); computer science and engineering (PhD); counseling (M Ed, MS, PhD), including clinical mental health counseling (MS), college and university counseling (M Ed, MS), elementary school counseling (M Ed, MS), secondary school counseling (M Ed, MS); counseling psychology (PhD); creative writing (MA); criminal justice (MS); curriculum and instruction (M Ed, PhD), including curriculum studies (PhD), early childhood studies (PhD), language and literacy studies (PhD); decision sciences (MBA); design (MA, MFA), including fashion design (MFA), innovation studies, interior design (MFA); early childhood studies (MS); economics (MS); educational leadership (M Ed, Ed D, PhD); educational psychology (MS), including family studies, gifted and talented (MS, PhD), human development, learning and cognition, research, measurement and evaluation; educational research (PhD), including gifted and talented (MS, PhD), human development and family studies, psychological aspects of sports and exercise, research, measurement and statistics; electrical engineering (MS); emergency management (MPA); engineering systems (MS); English (MA, PhD); environmental science (MS, PhD); experimental psychology (PhD); finance (MBA, MS, PhD); financial management (MPA); French (MA); health psychology and behavioral medicine (PhD); health services management (MBA); higher education (M Ed, Ed D, PhD); history (MA, MS, PhD), including European history (PhD), military history (PhD), United States history (PhD); hospitality management (MS); human resources management (MPA); information science (MS, PhD); information technologies (MBA); information technology and decision sciences (MS); interdisciplinary studies (MA, MS); international sustainable tourism (MS); jazz studies (MM); journalism (MA, MJ, Graduate Certificate), including interactive and virtual digital communication (Graduate Certificate), narrative journalism (Graduate Certificate), public relations (Graduate Certificate); kinesiology (MS); learning technologies (MS, PhD); library science (MS); local government management (MPA); logistics and supply chain management (MBA, PhD); long-term care, senior housing, and aging services (MA, MS); management science (PhD); marketing (MBA, PhD); materials science and engineering (MS, PhD); mathematics (MA, PhD); merchandising (MS); music (MA, MM Ed, PhD), including ethnomusicology (MA), music education (MM Ed, PhD), music theory (MA, PhD), musicology (MA, PhD), performance (MA); nonprofit management (MPA); operations and supply chain management (MBA); performance (MM, DMA); philosophy (MA, PhD); physics (MS, PhD); political science (MA, MS, PhD); public administration and management (PhD), including emergency management, nonprofit management, public financial management, urban management; radio, television and film (MA, MFA); recreation, event and sport management (MS); rehabilitation counseling (MS, Certificate); sociology (MA, MS, PhD); Spanish (MA); special education (M Ed, PhD), including autism intervention (PhD), emotional/behavioral disorders (PhD), mild/moderate disabilities (PhD); speech-language pathology (MA, MS); strategic management (MBA); studio art (MFA); taxation (MS); teaching (M Ed); MBA/MS; MS/MPH; MSES/MBA. Part-time and evening/weekend programs available. Postbaccalaureate distance learning degree programs offered. *Faculty:* 661 full-time (213 women), 240 part-time/adjunct (144 women). *Students:* 3,106 full-time (1,620 women), 3,543 part-time (2,221 women); includes 1,740 minority (533 Black or African American, non-Hispanic/Latino; 15 American Indian or Alaska Native, non-Hispanic/Latino; 286 Asian, non-Hispanic/Latino; 746 Hispanic/Latino; 3 Native Hawaiian or other Pacific Islander, non-Hispanic/Latino; 157 Two or more races, non-Hispanic/Latino), 1,145 international. Average age 32. 6,289 applicants, 43% accepted, 1751 enrolled. In 2013, 1,778 master's, 239 doctorates, 10 other advanced degrees awarded. Terminal master's awarded for partial completion of doctoral program. *Degree requirements:* For master's, variable foreign language requirement, comprehensive exam (for some programs), thesis (for some programs); for doctorate, variable foreign language requirement, comprehensive exam (for some programs), thesis/dissertation; for other advanced degree, variable foreign language requirement, comprehensive exam (for some programs). *Entrance requirements:* For master's and doctorate, GRE, GMAT. Additional exam requirements/recommendations for international students: Required—TOEFL (minimum score 550 paper-based; 79 iBT). *Application deadline:* For fall admission, 7/15 for domestic students, 3/15 for international students; for spring admission, 11/15 for domestic students, 9/15 for international students; for summer admission, 5/1 for domestic students. Applications are processed on a rolling basis. Application fee: $60. Electronic applications accepted. *Financial support:* Fellowships with partial tuition reimbursements, research assistantships with partial tuition reimbursements, teaching assistantships, career-related internships or fieldwork, Federal Work-Study, institutionally sponsored loans, scholarships/grants, health care benefits, and library assistantships available. Support available to part-time students. Financial award applicants required to submit FAFSA. *Unit head:* Mark Wardell, Dean, 940-565-2383, E-mail: mark.wardell@unt.edu. *Application contact:* Toulouse School of Graduate Studies, 940-565-2383, Fax: 940-565-2141, E-mail: gradsch@unt.edu.
Website: http://tsgs.unt.edu/.

University of Notre Dame, Mendoza College of Business, Program in Accountancy, Notre Dame, IN 46556. Offers financial reporting and assurance services (MS); tax services (MS). *Accreditation:* AACSB. *Faculty:* 35 full-time (5 women), 21 part-time/adjunct (2 women). *Students:* 100 full-time (35 women); includes 19 minority (3 Black or African American, non-Hispanic/Latino; 4 Asian, non-Hispanic/Latino; 4 Hispanic/Latino; 8 Two or more races, non-Hispanic/Latino), 17 international. Average age 22. 413 applicants, 31% accepted, 100 enrolled. In 2013, 110 master's awarded. *Entrance requirements:* For master's, GMAT. Additional exam requirements/recommendations for international students: Required—TOEFL (minimum score 630 paper-based; 109 iBT). *Application deadline:* For fall admission, 10/31 for domestic and international students; for spring admission, 5/1 for domestic and international students. Applications are processed on a rolling basis. Application fee: $50 ($100 for international students). Electronic applications accepted. *Financial support:* In 2013–14, 98 students received support, including 98 fellowships (averaging $17,076 per year); scholarships/grants and unspecified assistantships also available. Financial award application deadline: 2/28; financial award applicants required to submit FAFSA. *Faculty research:* Stock valuation, accounting information in decision-making, choice of accounting method, taxes cost on capital. *Unit head:* Dr. Michael H. Morris, Director, 574-631-9732, Fax: 574-631-5300, E-mail: msacct.1@nd.edu. *Application contact:* Helen High, Assistant Director of

Admissions and Student Services, 574-631-6499, Fax: 574-631-5300, E-mail: msacct.1@nd.edu.
Website: http://business.nd.edu/msa.

University of Oklahoma, Michael F. Price College of Business, School of Accounting, Norman, OK 73019. Offers M Acc, PhD. *Accreditation:* AACSB. Part-time programs available. *Faculty:* 11 full-time (4 women), 1 part-time/adjunct (0 women). *Students:* 29 full-time (12 women), 11 part-time (5 women); includes 5 minority (2 Asian, non-Hispanic/Latino; 1 Hispanic/Latino; 2 Two or more races, non-Hispanic/Latino), 11 international. Average age 26. 49 applicants, 22% accepted, 9 enrolled. In 2013, 41 master's awarded. Terminal master's awarded for partial completion of doctoral program. *Degree requirements:* For master's, comprehensive exam; for doctorate, comprehensive exam, thesis/dissertation. *Entrance requirements:* For master's and doctorate, GMAT. Additional exam requirements/recommendations for international students: Required—TOEFL (minimum score 100 iBT). *Application deadline:* For fall admission, 6/15 for domestic students, 3/1 for international students; for spring admission, 11/15 for domestic students, 8/1 for international students; for summer admission, 3/15 for domestic students, 1/1 for international students. Application fee: $50 ($100 for international students). Electronic applications accepted. *Expenses:* Tuition, state resident: full-time $4205; part-time $175.20 per credit hour. Tuition, nonresident: full-time $16,205; part-time $675.20 per credit hour. *Required fees:* $2745; $103.85 per credit hour. $126.50 per semester. *Financial support:* In 2013–14, 40 students received support, including 4 research assistantships with partial tuition reimbursements available (averaging $16,718 per year), 5 teaching assistantships with partial tuition reimbursements available (averaging $13,831 per year); career-related internships or fieldwork, scholarships/grants, and unspecified assistantships also available. Support available to part-time students. Financial award application deadline: 6/1; financial award applicants required to submit FAFSA. *Faculty research:* Tax professional judgment and taxpayer compliance, financial disclosure and reporting decisions, regulation of auditing profession, behavioral issues of auditor-client dyad, market based accounting research. *Unit head:* Terry Craine, Director of the School of Accounting/Chair of Accounting, 405-325-5768, Fax: 405-325-7348, E-mail: tcrain@ou.edu. *Application contact:* Callen Brehm, Academic Counselor, 405-325-2074, Fax: 405-325-7753, E-mail: cbrehm@ou.edu.
Website: http://www.ou.edu/content/price/accounting.html.

See Display on page 158 and Close-Up on page 193.

University of Oregon, Graduate School, Charles H. Lundquist College of Business, Department of Accounting, Eugene, OR 97403. Offers M Actg, PhD. *Accreditation:* AACSB. Part-time programs available. *Degree requirements:* For doctorate, thesis/dissertation, 2 comprehensive exams. *Entrance requirements:* For master's, GMAT, minimum GPA of 3.0, bachelor's degree in accounting or equivalent; for doctorate, GMAT. Additional exam requirements/recommendations for international students: Required—TOEFL. *Faculty research:* Empirical financial accounting, effects of regulation on accounting standards, use of protocol analysis as a research methodology in accounting.

University of Pennsylvania, Wharton School, Accounting Department, Philadelphia, PA 19104. Offers MBA, PhD. *Accreditation:* AACSB. Terminal master's awarded for partial completion of doctoral program. *Degree requirements:* For doctorate, thesis/dissertation. *Entrance requirements:* For master's, GMAT; for doctorate, GMAT or GRE. *Faculty research:* Financial reporting, information disclosure, performance measurement, executive compensation, corporate governance.

University of Phoenix–Atlanta Campus, School of Business, Sandy Springs, GA 30350-4153. Offers accounting (MBA); business administration (MBA); global management (MBA); human resources management (MBA, MM); management (MM); marketing (MBA); public administration (MM). Evening/weekend programs available. Postbaccalaureate distance learning degree programs offered. *Degree requirements:* For master's, thesis (for some programs). *Entrance requirements:* For master's, minimum undergraduate GPA of 3.0, 3 years of work experience. Additional exam requirements/recommendations for international students: Required—TOEFL (minimum score 550 paper-based; 79 iBT).

University of Phoenix–Augusta Campus, School of Business, Augusta, GA 30909-4583. Offers accounting (MBA); business administration (MBA); business and management (MBA, MM); global management (MBA); human resources management (MBA, MM); management (MM); marketing (MBA); public administration (MBA, MM). Postbaccalaureate distance learning degree programs offered.

University of Phoenix–Austin Campus, School of Business, Austin, TX 78759. Offers accounting (MBA); business administration (MBA); business and management (MBA); e-business (MBA); global management (MBA); human resources management (MBA, MM); management (MM); marketing (MBA); public administration (MBA). Postbaccalaureate distance learning degree programs offered.

University of Phoenix–Bay Area Campus, School of Business, San Jose, CA 95134-1805. Offers accountancy (MS); accounting (MBA); business administration (MBA, DBA); energy management (MBA); global management (MBA); health care management (MBA); human resource management (MBA); human resources management (MM); management (MM); marketing (MBA); organizational leadership (DM); project management (MBA); public administration (MPA); technology management (MBA). Evening/weekend programs available. Postbaccalaureate distance learning degree programs offered (no on-campus study). *Degree requirements:* For master's, thesis (for some programs). *Entrance requirements:* For master's, minimum undergraduate GPA of 3.0, 3 years of work experience. Additional exam requirements/recommendations for international students: Required—TOEFL (minimum score 550 paper-based; 79 iBT). Electronic applications accepted.

University of Phoenix–Birmingham Campus, College of Graduate Business and Management, Birmingham, AL 35242. Offers accounting (MBA); business administration (MBA); global management (MBA); human resources management (MBA, MM); management (MM); marketing (MBA); public administration (MM).

University of Phoenix–Central Valley Campus, School of Business, Fresno, CA 93720-1562. Offers accounting (MBA); business administration (MBA); global management (MBA); human resources management (MBA, MM); management (MM); marketing (MBA); public administration (MBA, MM).

University of Phoenix–Charlotte Campus, School of Business, Charlotte, NC 28273-3409. Offers accounting (MBA); business administration (MBA); global management (MBA). Evening/weekend programs available. *Degree requirements:* For master's, thesis (for some programs). *Entrance requirements:* For master's, minimum undergraduate GPA of 3.0, 3 years work experience. Additional exam requirements/recommendations for international students: Required—TOEFL (minimum score 550 paper-based; 79 iBT). Electronic applications accepted.

University of Phoenix–Chattanooga Campus, School of Business, Chattanooga, TN 37421-3707. Offers accounting (MBA); business administration (MBA); business and management (MBA); global management (MBA); human resources management (MBA, MM); management (MM); marketing (MBA); public administration (MBA, MM). Postbaccalaureate distance learning degree programs offered.

University of Phoenix–Cincinnati Campus, School of Business, West Chester, OH 45069-4875. Offers accounting (MBA); business administration (MBA); global management (MBA); human resources management (MBA, MM); management (MM); marketing (MBA); public administration (MM). Evening/weekend programs available. *Degree requirements:* For master's, thesis (for some programs). *Entrance requirements:* For master's, minimum undergraduate GPA of 3.0, 3 years of work experience. Additional exam requirements/recommendations for international students: Required—TOEFL (minimum score 550 paper-based; 79 iBT). Electronic applications accepted.

University of Phoenix–Cleveland Campus, School of Business, Independence, OH 44131-2194. Offers accounting (MBA); business administration (MBA); global management (MBA); human resources management (MBA, MM); management (MM); marketing (MBA); public administration (MBA, MM). Evening/weekend programs available. Postbaccalaureate distance learning degree programs offered (no on-campus study). *Degree requirements:* For master's, thesis (for some programs). *Entrance requirements:* For master's, minimum undergraduate GPA of 3.0, 3 years of work experience. Additional exam requirements/recommendations for international students: Required—TOEFL (minimum score 550 paper-based; 79 iBT). Electronic applications accepted.

University of Phoenix–Columbus Georgia Campus, School of Business, Columbus, GA 31909. Offers accounting (MBA); business administration (MBA); global management (MBA); human resources management (MBA, MM); management (MM); marketing (MBA); public administration (MBA). Evening/weekend programs available. *Degree requirements:* For master's, thesis (for some programs). *Entrance requirements:* For master's, minimum undergraduate GPA of 3.0, 3 years of work experience. Additional exam requirements/recommendations for international students: Required—TOEFL (minimum score 550 paper-based; 79 iBT). Electronic applications accepted.

University of Phoenix–Columbus Ohio Campus, School of Business, Columbus, OH 43240-4032. Offers accounting (MBA); business administration (MBA); global management (MBA); human resources management (MBA, MM); management (MM); marketing (MBA); public administration (MM). Evening/weekend programs available. Postbaccalaureate distance learning degree programs offered. *Degree requirements:* For master's, thesis (for some programs). *Entrance requirements:* For master's, minimum undergraduate GPA of 3.0, 3 years of work experience. Additional exam requirements/recommendations for international students: Required—TOEFL (minimum score 550 paper-based; 79 iBT). Electronic applications accepted.

University of Phoenix–Dallas Campus, School of Business, Dallas, TX 75251. Offers accounting (MBA); business administration (MBA); global management (MBA); human resources management (MBA, MM); management (MM); marketing (MBA); public administration (MBA, MM). Evening/weekend programs available. Postbaccalaureate distance learning degree programs offered. *Degree requirements:* For master's, thesis (for some programs). *Entrance requirements:* For master's, 3 years of work experience, minimum undergraduate GPA of 3.0. Additional exam requirements/recommendations for international students: Required—TOEFL (minimum score 550 paper-based; 79 iBT). Electronic applications accepted.

University of Phoenix–Denver Campus, School of Business, Lone Tree, CO 80124-5453. Offers accountancy (MSA); accounting (MBA); business administration (MBA); e-business (MBA); global management (MBA); human resources management (MBA, MM); management (MM); marketing (MBA); public administration (MBA, MM). Evening/weekend programs available. Postbaccalaureate distance learning degree programs offered. *Degree requirements:* For master's, thesis (for some programs). *Entrance requirements:* For master's, minimum undergraduate GPA of 3.0, 3 years work experience. Additional exam requirements/recommendations for international students: Required—TOEFL (minimum score 550 paper-based; 79 iBT). Electronic applications accepted.

University of Phoenix–Des Moines Campus, School of Business, Des Moines, IA 50309. Offers accounting (MBA); business administration (MBA); global management (MBA); human resources management (MBA, MM); management (MM); marketing (MBA); public administration (MBA, MM). Postbaccalaureate distance learning degree programs offered.

University of Phoenix–Eastern Washington Campus, School of Business, Spokane, WA 99212-2531. Offers accounting (MBA); business administration (MBA); human resources management (MBA); marketing (MBA); public administration (MBA). Evening/weekend programs available. *Degree requirements:* For master's, thesis (for some programs). *Entrance requirements:* For master's, minimum undergraduate GPA of 3.0, 3 years of work experience. Additional exam requirements/recommendations for international students: Required—TOEFL (minimum score 550 paper-based; 79 iBT). Electronic applications accepted.

University of Phoenix–Hawaii Campus, School of Business, Honolulu, HI 96813-4317. Offers accounting (MBA); business administration (MBA); global management (MBA); human resources management (MBA, MM); management (MM); marketing (MBA); public administration (MBA, MM). Evening/weekend programs available. *Degree requirements:* For master's, thesis (for some programs). *Entrance requirements:* For master's, minimum undergraduate GPA of 3.0, 3 years of work experience. Additional exam requirements/recommendations for international students: Required—TOEFL (minimum score 550 paper-based; 79 iBT). Electronic applications accepted.

University of Phoenix–Houston Campus, School of Business, Houston, TX 77079-2004. Offers accounting (MBA); business administration (MBA); global management (MBA); human resources management (MBA, MM); management (MM); marketing (MBA); public administration (MBA, MM). Evening/weekend programs available. Postbaccalaureate distance learning degree programs offered. *Degree requirements:* For master's, thesis (for some programs). *Entrance requirements:* For master's, 3 years of work experience, minimum undergraduate GPA of 3.0. Additional exam requirements/recommendations for international students: Required—TOEFL (minimum score 550 paper-based; 79 iBT). Electronic applications accepted.

University of Phoenix–Idaho Campus, School of Business, Meridian, ID 83642-5114. Offers accounting (MBA); administration (MBA); global management (MBA); human resources management (MBA, MM); management (MM); marketing (MBA); public administration (MM). Evening/weekend programs available. Postbaccalaureate distance learning degree programs offered. *Degree requirements:* For master's, thesis (for some programs). *Entrance requirements:* For master's, 3 years of work experience, minimum undergraduate GPA of 3.0. Additional exam requirements/recommendations for international students: Required—TOEFL (minimum score 550 paper-based). Electronic applications accepted.

University of Phoenix–Indianapolis Campus, School of Business, Indianapolis, IN 46250-932. Offers accounting (MBA); business administration (MBA); global management (MBA); human resources management (MBA, MM); management (MM); marketing (MBA); public administration (MM). Evening/weekend programs available. *Degree requirements:* For master's, thesis (for some programs). *Entrance requirements:* For master's, minimum undergraduate GPA of 3.0, 3 years of work experience. Additional exam requirements/recommendations for international students: Required—TOEFL (minimum score 550 paper-based). Electronic applications accepted.

University of Phoenix–Jersey City Campus, School of Business, Jersey City, NJ 07310. Offers accounting (MBA); business administration (MBA); global management (MBA); human resources management (MBA, MM); management (MM); marketing (MBA); public administration (MBA, MM).

University of Phoenix–Kansas City Campus, School of Business, Kansas City, MO 64131. Offers accounting (MBA); business administration (MBA); global management (MBA); human resources management (MBA, MM); management (MM); marketing (MBA); public administration (MBA). Evening/weekend programs available. *Degree requirements:* For master's, thesis (for some programs). *Entrance requirements:* For master's, minimum undergraduate GPA of 3.0, 3 years of work experience. Additional exam requirements/recommendations for international students: Required—TOEFL (minimum score 550 paper-based). Electronic applications accepted.

University of Phoenix–Las Vegas Campus, School of Business, Las Vegas, NV 89135. Offers accounting (MBA); business administration (MBA); global management (MBA); human resources management (MBA, MM); management (MM); marketing (MBA); public administration (MM). Evening/weekend programs available. Postbaccalaureate distance learning degree programs offered (no on-campus study). *Degree requirements:* For master's, thesis (for some programs). *Entrance requirements:* For master's, minimum undergraduate GPA of 3.0, 3 years of work experience. Additional exam requirements/recommendations for international students: Required—TOEFL (minimum score 550 paper-based; 79 iBT). Electronic applications accepted.

University of Phoenix–Louisiana Campus, School of Business, Metairie, LA 70001-2082. Offers accounting (MBA); business administration (MBA); global management (MBA); human resources management (MBA, MM); management (MM); marketing (MBA); public administration (MBA). Evening/weekend programs available. *Degree requirements:* For master's, thesis (for some programs). *Entrance requirements:* For master's, minimum undergraduate GPA of 3.0, 3 years work experience. Additional exam requirements/recommendations for international students: Required—TOEFL (minimum score 550 paper-based; 79 iBT). Electronic applications accepted.

University of Phoenix–Madison Campus, School of Business, Madison, WI 53718-2416. Offers accounting (MBA); business and management (MBA); e-business (MBA); global management (MBA); human resources management (MBA, MM); management (MM); marketing (MBA); public administration (MBA).

University of Phoenix–Memphis Campus, School of Business, Cordova, TN 38018. Offers accounting (MBA); business and management (MBA); e-business (MBA); global management (MBA); human resources management (MBA, MM); management (MM); marketing (MBA); public administration (MBA, MM).

University of Phoenix–Milwaukee Campus, School of Business, Milwaukee, WI 53224. Offers accounting (MBA); business administration (MBA); energy management (MBA); global management (MBA); health care management (MBA); human resource management (MBA); management (MM); marketing (MBA); project management (MBA); technology management (MBA). Evening/weekend programs available. Postbaccalaureate distance learning degree programs offered. *Entrance requirements:* Additional exam requirements/recommendations for international students: Required—TOEFL, TOEIC (Test of English as an International Communication), Berlitz Online English Proficiency Exam, PTE, or IELTS. Electronic applications accepted. *Expenses:* Contact institution.

University of Phoenix–Minneapolis/St. Louis Park Campus, School of Business, St. Louis Park, MN 55426. Offers accounting (MBA); business administration (MBA); global management (MBA); human resources management (MBA); management (MM); marketing (MBA); public administration (MBA).

University of Phoenix–New Mexico Campus, School of Business, Albuquerque, NM 87113-1570. Offers accounting (MBA); business administration (MBA); global management (MBA); human resources management (MBA, MM); management (MM); marketing (MBA). Evening/weekend programs available. *Degree requirements:* For master's, thesis (for some programs). *Entrance requirements:* For master's, 3 years of work experience, minimum undergraduate GPA of 3.0. Additional exam requirements/recommendations for international students: Required—TOEFL (minimum score 550 paper-based; 79 iBT). Electronic applications accepted.

University of Phoenix–North Florida Campus, School of Business, Jacksonville, FL 32216-0959. Offers accounting (MBA); business administration (MBA); global management (MBA); human resources management (MBA, MM); management (MM); marketing (MBA); public administration (MBA, MM). Evening/weekend programs available. *Degree requirements:* For master's, thesis (for some programs). *Entrance requirements:* For master's, minimum undergraduate GPA of 3.0, 3 years work experience. Additional exam requirements/recommendations for international students: Required—TOEFL (minimum score 550 paper-based; 79 iBT). Electronic applications accepted.

University of Phoenix–Northwest Arkansas Campus, School of Business, Rogers, AR 72756-9615. Offers accounting (MBA); business and management (MBA); global management (MBA); human resources management (MBA, MM); management (MM); marketing (MBA); public administration (MBA, MM).

University of Phoenix–Oklahoma City Campus, School of Business, Oklahoma City, OK 73116-8244. Offers accounting (MBA); business administration (MBA); global management (MBA); human resource management (MBA); management (MM); marketing (MBA). Evening/weekend programs available. *Degree requirements:* For master's, thesis (for some programs). *Entrance requirements:* For master's, minimum undergraduate GPA of 3.0, 3 years of work experience. Additional exam requirements/recommendations for international students: Required—TOEFL (minimum score 550 paper-based; 79 iBT). Electronic applications accepted.

University of Phoenix–Omaha Campus, School of Business, Omaha, NE 68154-5240. Offers accounting (MBA); business and management (MBA); global management (MBA); human resources management (MBA, MM); management (MM); marketing (MBA); public administration (MBA, MM).

University of Phoenix–Online Campus, School of Business, Phoenix, AZ 85034-7209. Offers accountancy (MS); accounting (MBA, Certificate); business administration (MBA); energy management (MBA); global management (MBA); health care management (MBA); human resource management (MBA, Certificate); human resources management (MM); management (MM); marketing (MBA, Certificate); project management (MBA, Certificate); public administration (MBA, MM); technology management (MBA). Evening/weekend programs available. Postbaccalaureate distance learning degree programs offered. *Entrance requirements:* Additional exam requirements/recommendations for international students: Required—TOEFL, TOEIC (Test of English as an International Communication), Berlitz Online English Proficiency Exam, PTE, or IELTS. Electronic applications accepted. *Expenses:* Contact institution.

University of Phoenix–Oregon Campus, School of Business, Tigard, OR 97223. Offers accounting (MBA); business administration (MBA); global management (MBA); human resource management (MM); human resources management (MBA); management (MM); marketing (MBA); public administration (MM). Evening/weekend programs available. *Degree requirements:* For master's, thesis (for some programs). *Entrance requirements:* For master's, minimum undergraduate GPA of 3.0, 3 years of work experience. Additional exam requirements/recommendations for international students: Required—TOEFL (minimum score 550 paper-based; 79 iBT). Electronic applications accepted.

University of Phoenix–Philadelphia Campus, School of Business, Wayne, PA 19087-2121. Offers accounting (MBA); business administration (MBA); global management (MBA); human resources management (MBA, MM); management (MM); marketing (MBA); public administration (MM). Evening/weekend programs available. *Degree requirements:* For master's, thesis (for some programs). *Entrance requirements:* For master's, minimum undergraduate GPA of 3.0, 3 years work experience. Additional exam requirements/recommendations for international students: Required—TOEFL (minimum score 550 paper-based; 79 iBT). Electronic applications accepted.

University of Phoenix–Phoenix Campus, School of Business, Tempe, AZ 85282-2371. Offers accounting (MBA, MS, Certificate); business administration (MBA); energy management (MBA); global management (MBA); health care management (MBA); human resource management (MBA, Certificate); management (MM); marketing (MBA); project management (MBA); technology management (MBA). Evening/weekend programs available. Postbaccalaureate distance learning degree programs offered. *Entrance requirements:* Additional exam requirements/recommendations for international students: Required—TOEFL, TOEIC (Test of English as an International Communication), Berlitz Online English Proficiency Exam, PTE, or IELTS. Electronic applications accepted. *Expenses:* Contact institution.

University of Phoenix–Pittsburgh Campus, School of Business, Pittsburgh, PA 15276. Offers accounting (MBA); business administration (MBA); global management (MBA); human resources management (MBA, MM); management (MM); marketing (MBA); public administration (MBA, MM). Evening/weekend programs available. *Degree requirements:* For master's, thesis (for some programs). *Entrance requirements:* For master's, minimum undergraduate GPA of 3.0, 3 years work experience. Additional exam requirements/recommendations for international students: Required—TOEFL (minimum score 550 paper-based; 79 iBT). Electronic applications accepted.

University of Phoenix–Puerto Rico Campus, School of Business, Guaynabo, PR 00968. Offers accounting (MBA); energy management (MBA); global management (MBA); human resource management (MBA); marketing (MBA); project management (MBA); small business administration (MBA). Evening/weekend programs available. *Degree requirements:* For master's, thesis (for some programs). *Entrance requirements:* For master's, minimum undergraduate GPA of 3.0, 3 years work experience. Additional exam requirements/recommendations for international students: Required—TOEFL (minimum score 550 paper-based; 79 iBT). Electronic applications accepted.

University of Phoenix–Richmond-Virginia Beach Campus, School of Business, Glen Allen, VA 23060. Offers accounting (MBA); business administration (MBA); global management (MBA); human resources management (MBA, MM); management (MM); marketing (MBA); public administration (MBA, MM). Evening/weekend programs available. *Degree requirements:* For master's, thesis (for some programs). *Entrance requirements:* For master's, minimum undergraduate GPA of 3.0, 3 years work experience. Additional exam requirements/recommendations for international students: Required—TOEFL (minimum score 550 paper-based; 79 iBT). Electronic applications accepted.

University of Phoenix–Sacramento Valley Campus, School of Business, Sacramento, CA 95833-3632. Offers accounting (MBA); business administration (MBA); global management (MBA); human resources management (MBA, MM); management (MM); marketing (MBA); public administration (MBA, MM). Evening/weekend programs available. *Degree requirements:* For master's, thesis (for some programs). *Entrance requirements:* For master's, minimum undergraduate GPA of 3.0, 3 years work experience. Additional exam requirements/recommendations for international students: Required—TOEFL (minimum score 550 paper-based; 79 iBT). Electronic applications accepted.

University of Phoenix–St. Louis Campus, School of Business, St. Louis, MO 63043. Offers accounting (MBA); business administration (MBA); global management (MBA); human resources management (MBA, MM); management (MM); marketing (MBA); public administration (MM). Evening/weekend programs available. *Degree requirements:* For master's, thesis (for some programs). *Entrance requirements:* For master's, 3 years of work experience, minimum undergraduate GPA of 3.0. Additional exam requirements/recommendations for international students: Required—TOEFL (minimum score 550 paper-based; 79 iBT). Electronic applications accepted.

University of Phoenix–San Antonio Campus, School of Business, San Antonio, TX 78230. Offers accounting (MBA); business administration (MBA); e-business (MBA); global management (MBA); human resources management (MBA, MM); management (MM); marketing (MBA); public administration (MBA, MM).

University of Phoenix–San Diego Campus, School of Business, San Diego, CA 92123. Offers accounting (MBA); business administration (MBA); global management (MBA); human resources management (MBA, MM); management (MM); marketing (MBA); public administration (MBA). Evening/weekend programs available. *Degree requirements:* For master's, thesis (for some programs). *Entrance requirements:* For master's, 3 years of work experience, minimum undergraduate GPA of 3.0. Additional exam requirements/recommendations for international students: Required—TOEFL (minimum score 550 paper-based; 79 iBT). Electronic applications accepted.

University of Phoenix–Savannah Campus, School of Business, Savannah, GA 31405-7400. Offers accounting (MBA); business administration (MBA); global management (MBA); human resources management (MBA, MM); management (MM); marketing (MBA); public administration (MBA, MM).

University of Phoenix–Southern Arizona Campus, School of Business, Tucson, AZ 85711. Offers accountancy (MS); accounting (MBA); business administration (MBA); global management (MBA); human resources management (MBA); management (MM); marketing (MBA). Evening/weekend programs available. *Degree requirements:* For master's, thesis (for some programs). *Entrance requirements:* For master's, minimum undergraduate GPA of 3.0, 3 years of work experience. Additional exam requirements/recommendations for international students: Required—TOEFL (minimum score 550 paper-based; 79 iBT). Electronic applications accepted.

University of Phoenix–Southern California Campus, School of Business, Costa Mesa, CA 92626. Offers accounting (MBA); business administration (MBA); energy management (MBA); global management (MBA); health care management (MBA); human resource management (MBA); management (MM); marketing (MBA); project management (MBA); technology management (MBA). Evening/weekend programs available. Postbaccalaureate distance learning degree programs offered. *Entrance requirements:* Additional exam requirements/recommendations for international students: Required—TOEFL, TOEIC (Test of English as an International Communication), Berlitz Online English Proficiency Exam, PTE, or IELTS. Electronic applications accepted. *Expenses:* Contact institution.

University of Phoenix–Southern Colorado Campus, School of Business, Colorado Springs, CO 80903. Offers accounting (MBA); business administration (MBA); global management (MBA); human resources management (MBA, MM); management (MM);

marketing (MBA); public administration (MM). Evening/weekend programs available. *Degree requirements:* For master's, thesis (for some programs). *Entrance requirements:* For master's, minimum undergraduate GPA of 3.0, 3 years of work experience. Additional exam requirements/recommendations for international students: Required—TOEFL (minimum score 550 paper-based; 79 iBT). Electronic applications accepted.

University of Phoenix–South Florida Campus, School of Business, Miramar, FL 33030. Offers accounting (MBA); business administration (MBA); global management (MBA); human resource management (MBA); human resources management (MM); management (MM); marketing (MBA); public administration (MBA, MM). Evening/weekend programs available. *Degree requirements:* For master's, thesis (for some programs). *Entrance requirements:* For master's, minimum undergraduate GPA of 3.0, 3 years work experience. Additional exam requirements/recommendations for international students: Required—TOEFL (minimum score 550 paper-based; 79 iBT). Electronic applications accepted.

University of Phoenix–Springfield Campus, School of Business, Springfield, MO 65804-7211. Offers accounting (MBA); business administration (MBA); global management (MBA); human resources management (MBA, MM); management (MM); marketing (MBA); public administration (MBA, MM).

University of Phoenix–Tulsa Campus, School of Business, Tulsa, OK 74134-1412. Offers accounting (MBA); business (MM); business administration (MBA); global management (MBA); human resources management (MBA); marketing (MBA). Evening/weekend programs available. *Degree requirements:* For master's, thesis (for some programs). *Entrance requirements:* For master's, minimum undergraduate GPA of 3.0, 3 years work experience. Additional exam requirements/recommendations for international students: Required—TOEFL (minimum score 550 paper-based; 79 iBT).

University of Phoenix–Utah Campus, School of Business, Salt Lake City, UT 84123-4617. Offers accounting (MBA); business administration (MBA); global management (MBA); human resource management (MBA, MM); management (MM); marketing (MBA); technology management (MBA). Evening/weekend programs available. *Degree requirements:* For master's, thesis (for some programs). *Entrance requirements:* For master's, minimum undergraduate GPA of 3.0, 3 years of work experience. Additional exam requirements/recommendations for international students: Required—TOEFL (minimum score 550 paper-based; 79 iBT). Electronic applications accepted.

University of Phoenix–Washington D.C. Campus, School of Business, Washington, DC 20001. Offers accountancy (MS); business administration (MBA, DBA); human resources management (MM); management (MM); organizational leadership (DM); public administration (MPA).

University of Phoenix–West Florida Campus, School of Business, Temple Terrace, FL 33637. Offers accounting (MBA); business administration (MBA); global management (MBA); human resources management (MBA, MM); management (MM); marketing (MBA); public administration (MBA, MM). Evening/weekend programs available. *Degree requirements:* For master's, thesis (for some programs). *Entrance requirements:* For master's, 3 years of work experience, minimum undergraduate GPA of 3.0. Additional exam requirements/recommendations for international students: Required—TOEFL (minimum score 550 paper-based; 79 iBT). Electronic applications accepted.

University of Pittsburgh, Katz Graduate School of Business, Doctoral Program in Business Administration, Pittsburgh, PA 15260. Offers accounting (PhD); finance (PhD); information systems (PhD); marketing (PhD); operations/decision sciences/artificial intelligence (PhD); organizational behavior and human resource management (PhD); strategic planning (PhD). *Accreditation:* AACSB. *Faculty:* 60 full-time (17 women). *Students:* 50 full-time (22 women); includes 4 minority (2 Black or African American, non-Hispanic/Latino; 2 Asian, non-Hispanic/Latino), 27 international. 321 applicants, 7% accepted, 14 enrolled. In 2013, 10 doctorates awarded. *Degree requirements:* For doctorate, comprehensive exam, thesis/dissertation. *Entrance requirements:* For doctorate, GMAT or GRE, 3 recommendations, statement of purpose, transcripts of all previous course work and degrees. Additional exam requirements/recommendations for international students: Required—TOEFL. *Application deadline:* For fall admission, 1/1 priority date for domestic and international students. Applications are processed on a rolling basis. Application fee: $50. Electronic applications accepted. *Expenses:* Tuition, state resident: full-time $19,964; part-time $807 per credit. Tuition, nonresident: full-time $32,686; part-time $1337 per credit. *Required fees:* $740; $200. Tuition and fees vary according to program. *Financial support:* In 2013–14, 40 students received support, including 30 research assistantships with full tuition reimbursements available (averaging $23,045 per year), 10 teaching assistantships with full tuition reimbursements available (averaging $26,055 per year); fellowships, Federal Work-Study, scholarships/grants, health care benefits, and unspecified assistantships also available. Financial award application deadline: 1/1. *Faculty research:* Accounting systems/financial reporting, corporate finance, shopper marketing/consumer behavior, management information systems, organizational behavior and entrepreneurship. *Unit head:* Dr. Dennis Galletta, Director, 412-648-1699, Fax: 412-624-3633, E-mail: galletta@katz.pitt.edu. *Application contact:* Carrie Woods, Assistant Director, 412-648-1525, Fax: 412-624-3633, E-mail: cawoods@katz.pitt.edu.
Website: http://www.business.pitt.edu/katz/phd/.

University of Pittsburgh, Katz Graduate School of Business, Master of Science in Accounting Program, Pittsburgh, PA 15260. Offers MS. Part-time programs available. *Faculty:* 8 full-time (4 women), 6 part-time/adjunct (2 women). *Students:* 81 full-time (31 women), 7 part-time (4 women); includes 5 minority (all Black or African American, non-Hispanic/Latino), 43 international. Average age 26. 479 applicants, 25% accepted, 57 enrolled. In 2013, 53 master's awarded. *Degree requirements:* For master's, minimum GPA of 3.0. *Entrance requirements:* For master's, GMAT, GRE, references, work experience relevant for program, interview, essays, resume, transcripts. Additional exam requirements/recommendations for international students: Required—TOEFL or IELTS. *Application deadline:* For fall admission, 4/1 priority date for domestic students, 2/1 priority date for international students. Applications are processed on a rolling basis. Application fee: $50. Electronic applications accepted. *Expenses:* Contact institution. *Financial support:* In 2013–14, 33 students received support. Scholarships/grants available. Financial award application deadline: 2/1; financial award applicants required to submit FAFSA. *Faculty research:* Accounting systems/financial reporting, corporate finance, shopper marketing/consumer behavior, management information systems, organizational behavior and entrepreneurship. *Unit head:* Dr. Karen Shastri, Director, 412-648-1533, Fax: 412-624-5198, E-mail: kshastri@katz.pitt.edu. *Application contact:* Jessica Quarterman, Administrative Assistant, 412-624-0147, Fax: 412-624-5198, E-mail: macc@katz.pitt.edu.
Website: http://www.business.pitt.edu/katz/macc/.

University of Puerto Rico, Río Piedras Campus, College of Business Administration, San Juan, PR 00931-3300. Offers accounting (MBA); finance (MBA, PhD); general business (MBA); human resources management (MBA); international trade and business (MBA, PhD); marketing (MBA); operations management (MBA); quantitative methods (MBA). Part-time programs available. *Degree requirements:* For master's, comprehensive exam, thesis or alternative, research project. *Entrance requirements:* For master's, GMAT or PAEG, minimum GPA of 3.0, letter of recommendation; for doctorate, GMAT, PAEG, minimum GPA of 3.0, master degree. *Faculty research:* Management.

University of Rhode Island, Graduate School, College of Business Administration, Kingston, RI 02881. Offers accounting (MS); business administration (MBA, PhD), including finance and insurance (PhD), management (PhD), marketing (PhD), operations and supply chain management (MBA); finance (MBA); general business (MBA); management (MBA); marketing (MBA); supply chain management (MBA). *Accreditation:* AACSB. Part-time and evening/weekend programs available. *Faculty:* 43 full-time (16 women). *Students:* 103 full-time (37 women), 196 part-time (82 women); includes 42 minority (6 Black or African American, non-Hispanic/Latino; 1 American Indian or Alaska Native, non-Hispanic/Latino; 16 Asian, non-Hispanic/Latino; 13 Hispanic/Latino; 6 Two or more races, non-Hispanic/Latino), 29 international. In 2013, 119 master's, 3 doctorates awarded. *Degree requirements:* For master's, comprehensive exam (for some programs), thesis optional; for doctorate, comprehensive exam, thesis/dissertation. *Entrance requirements:* For master's, GMAT or GRE, 2 letters of recommendation, resume; for doctorate, GMAT or GRE, 3 letters of recommendation, resume. Additional exam requirements/recommendations for international students: Required—TOEFL (minimum score 575 paper-based; 91 iBT). *Application deadline:* For fall admission, 4/15 for domestic students, 2/15 for international students. Application fee: $65. Electronic applications accepted. *Expenses:* Tuition, state resident: full-time $11,532; part-time $641 per credit. Tuition, nonresident: full-time $23,606; part-time $1311 per credit. *Required fees:* $1388; $36 per credit. $35 per semester. One-time fee: $130. *Financial support:* In 2013–14, 14 teaching assistantships with full and partial tuition reimbursements (averaging $15,220 per year) were awarded. Financial award application deadline: 4/15; financial award applicants required to submit FAFSA. *Total annual research expenditures:* $66,948. *Unit head:* Dr. Mark Higgins, Dean, 401-874-4244, Fax: 401-874-4312, E-mail: markhiggins@uri.edu. *Application contact:* Lisa Lancellotta, Coordinator, MBA Programs, 401-874-4241, Fax: 401-874-4312, E-mail: mba@uri.edu.
Website: http://www.cba.uri.edu/.

University of Rochester, Simon Business School, Full-Time Master's Program in Business Administration, Rochester, NY 14627. Offers accounting and information systems (MBA); business environment and public policy (MBA); business systems consulting (MBA); competitive and organizational strategy - pricing (MBA); computers and information systems (MBA); corporate accounting (MBA); electronic commerce (MBA); entrepreneurship (MBA); finance (MBA); health sciences management (MBA); international management (MBA); marketing - brand management and pricing (MBA); operations management - manufacturing (MBA); operations management - services (MBA); public accounting (MBA). *Accreditation:* AACSB. Part-time and evening/weekend programs available. *Faculty:* 60 full-time (11 women), 23 part-time/adjunct (3 women). *Students:* 282 full-time (74 women); includes 55 minority (29 Black or African American, non-Hispanic/Latino; 1 American Indian or Alaska Native, non-Hispanic/Latino; 11 Asian, non-Hispanic/Latino; 12 Hispanic/Latino; 2 Two or more races, non-Hispanic/Latino), 144 international. 673 applicants, 33% accepted, 65 enrolled. In 2013, 176 master's awarded. *Entrance requirements:* For master's, GMAT/GRE, previous course work in calculus. Additional exam requirements/recommendations for international students: Required—TOEFL. *Application deadline:* For fall admission, 10/15 for domestic and international students; for winter admission, 1/5 for domestic and international students; for spring admission, 3/15 for domestic and international students; for summer admission, 5/15 for domestic students. Applications are processed on a rolling basis. Application fee: $150. Electronic applications accepted. *Expenses: Tuition:* Full-time $44,580; part-time $1394 per credit hour. *Required fees:* $492. *Financial support:* In 2013–14, 72 students received support. Fellowships, research assistantships, teaching assistantships, institutionally sponsored loans, scholarships/grants, and tuition waivers (partial) available. Financial award application deadline: 3/1; financial award applicants required to submit CSS PROFILE or FAFSA. *Unit head:* Mark Zupan, Dean, 585-275-3316. *Application contact:* Rebekah S. Lewin, Assistant Dean of Admissions and Student Engagement, 585-275-3533, E-mail: admissions@simon.rochester.edu.

University of Rochester, Simon Business School, Master of Science Program in Accountancy, Rochester, NY 14627. Offers MS. Part-time and evening/weekend programs available. *Faculty:* 60 full-time (11 women), 23 part-time/adjunct (3 women). *Students:* 54 full-time (44 women), 5 part-time (4 women); includes 3 minority (1 Black or African American, non-Hispanic/Latino; 2 Asian, non-Hispanic/Latino), 46 international. 534 applicants, 17% accepted, 54 enrolled. In 2013, 37 master's awarded. *Entrance requirements:* For master's, GMAT/GRE, bachelor's degree. Additional exam requirements/recommendations for international students: Required—TOEFL. *Application deadline:* For fall admission, 10/15 for domestic and international students; for winter admission, 1/5 for domestic and international students; for spring admission, 3/15 for domestic and international students; for summer admission, 5/15 for domestic students. Applications are processed on a rolling basis. Application fee: $150. Electronic applications accepted. *Expenses: Tuition:* Full-time $44,580; part-time $1394 per credit hour. *Required fees:* $492. *Financial support:* In 2013–14, 31 students received support. Institutionally sponsored loans, scholarships/grants, and tuition waivers available. Financial award application deadline: 5/15; financial award applicants required to submit CSS PROFILE or FAFSA. *Unit head:* Mark Zupan, Dean, 585-275-3316. *Application contact:* Rebekah S. Lewin, Assistant Dean of Admissions and Student Engagement, 585-275-3533, Fax: 585-271-3907, E-mail: admissions@simon.rochester.edu.

University of Rochester, Simon Business School, Part-Time MBA Program, Rochester, NY 14627. Offers accounting and information systems (MBA); business environment and public policy (MBA); business systems consulting (MBA); competitive and organizational strategy (MBA); computers and information systems (MBA); corporate accounting (MBA); electronic commerce (MBA); entrepreneurship (MBA); finance (MBA); health sciences management (MBA); international management (MBA); manufacturing management (MBA); marketing (MBA); operations management - services (MBA); public accounting (MBA). Part-time and evening/weekend programs available. *Faculty:* 59 full-time (10 women), 23 part-time/adjunct (3 women). *Students:* 270 part-time (75 women); includes 38 minority (5 Black or African American, non-Hispanic/Latino; 1 American Indian or Alaska Native, non-Hispanic/Latino; 24 Asian, non-Hispanic/Latino; 5 Hispanic/Latino; 3 Two or more races, non-Hispanic/Latino). Average age 32. 56 applicants, 98% accepted, 51 enrolled. In 2013, 77 master's awarded. *Entrance requirements:* For master's, GRE or GMAT, resume, recommendation letters, essays, transcipts. *Application deadline:* For fall admission, 8/15 for domestic students; for winter admission, 11/15 for domestic students; for spring admission, 2/15 for domestic students; for summer admission, 5/15 for domestic students. Applications are processed on a rolling basis. Application fee: $150. Electronic applications accepted. *Expenses: Tuition:* Full-time $44,580; part-time $1394 per credit hour. *Required fees:* $492. *Financial support:* Scholarships/grants and tuition waivers available. Financial award applicants required to submit CSS PROFILE. *Unit head:* Mark Zupan, Dean, 585-275-3316, E-mail: mark.zupan@simon.rochester.edu. *Application*

contact: Jennifer Mossotti, Associate Director of Part-Time Programs, 585-275-3803, E-mail: jennifer.mossotti@simon.rochester.edu. Website: http://www.simon.rochester.edu/programs/part-time-mba-programs/index.aspx.

University of St. Thomas, Graduate Studies, Opus College of Business, Master of Science in Accountancy Program, Minneapolis, MN 55403. Offers MS. *Students:* 16 full-time (8 women); includes 1 minority (Black or African American, non-Hispanic/Latino), 1 international. Average age 23. 33 applicants, 76% accepted, 16 enrolled. In 2013, 23 master's awarded. *Entrance requirements:* For master's, GMAT. Additional exam requirements/recommendations for international students: Required—TOEFL (minimum score 94 iBT), IELTS (minimum score 7). *Application deadline:* For spring admission, 5/4 for domestic students, 1/13 for international students. Applications are processed on a rolling basis. Application fee: $60. Electronic applications accepted. *Financial support:* Career-related internships or fieldwork and scholarships/grants available. *Unit head:* Kristine Sharockman, Program Director, 651-962-4110, Fax: 651-962-4141, E-mail: msacct@stthomas.edu. *Application contact:* Cathy Davis, Program Manager, 651-962-4110, Fax: 651-962-4141, E-mail: msacct@stthomas.edu. Website: http://www.stthomas.edu/accountancy.

University of San Diego, School of Business Administration, Programs in Accountancy and Taxation, San Diego, CA 92110-2492. Offers accountancy (MS); taxation (MS). Part-time and evening/weekend programs available. *Students:* 23 full-time (15 women), 5 part-time (4 women); includes 8 minority (5 Asian, non-Hispanic/Latino; 2 Hispanic/Latino; 1 Two or more races, non-Hispanic/Latino), 11 international. Average age 24. In 2013, 33 master's awarded. *Entrance requirements:* For master's, GMAT (minimum score of 550), minimum GPA of 3.0. Additional exam requirements/recommendations for international students: Required—TOEFL (minimum score 580 paper-based; 92 iBT), TWE. *Application deadline:* For fall admission, 4/1 for domestic students; for spring admission, 10/1 for domestic students. Application fee: $80. *Expenses: Tuition:* Full-time $23,580; part-time $1310 per credit. *Required fees:* $350. *Financial support:* In 2013–14, 11 students received support. Career-related internships or fieldwork, Federal Work-Study, institutionally sponsored loans, scholarships/grants, and unspecified assistantships available. Support available to part-time students. Financial award application deadline: 4/1; financial award applicants required to submit FAFSA. *Faculty research:* Accounting, financial report, taxation, Sarbanes-Oxley. *Unit head:* Dr. Diane Pattison, Academic Director, Accountancy Programs, 619-260-4850, E-mail: pattison@sandiego.edu. *Application contact:* Monica Mahon, Associate Director of Graduate Admissions, 619-260-4524, Fax: 619-260-4158, E-mail: grads@sandiego.edu. Website: http://www.sandiego.edu/business/programs/accounting-tax/.

University of Saskatchewan, College of Graduate Studies and Research, Edwards School of Business, Department of Accounting, Saskatoon, SK S7N 5A2, Canada. Offers M Sc, MP Acc. Part-time programs available. *Degree requirements:* For master's, thesis (for some programs). *Entrance requirements:* For master's, GMAT. Additional exam requirements/recommendations for international students: Required—TOEFL. *Expenses: Tuition, area resident:* Full-time $3585 Canadian dollars; part-time $585 Canadian dollars per course. *Tuition, nonresident:* part-time $877 Canadian dollars per course. *International tuition:* $5377 Canadian dollars full-time. *Required fees:* $889.51 Canadian dollars.

The University of Scranton, College of Graduate and Continuing Education, Program in Business Administration, Scranton, PA 18510. Offers accounting (MBA); finance (MBA); general business administration (MBA); health care management (MBA); international business (MBA); management information systems (MBA); marketing (MBA); operations management (MBA). *Accreditation:* AACSB. Part-time and evening/weekend programs available. Postbaccalaureate distance learning degree programs offered (no on-campus study). *Faculty:* 34 full-time (8 women). *Students:* 316 full-time (134 women), 241 part-time (94 women); includes 104 minority (43 Black or African American, non-Hispanic/Latino; 3 American Indian or Alaska Native, non-Hispanic/Latino; 29 Asian, non-Hispanic/Latino; 27 Hispanic/Latino; 2 Two or more races, non-Hispanic/Latino), 47 international. Average age 34. 249 applicants, 85% accepted. In 2013, 200 master's awarded. *Degree requirements:* For master's, capstone experience. *Entrance requirements:* For master's, GMAT, minimum GPA of 3.0. Additional exam requirements/recommendations for international students: Required—TOEFL (minimum score 500 paper-based), IELTS (minimum score 6). *Application deadline:* Applications are processed on a rolling basis. Application fee: $0. *Financial support:* In 2013–14, 13 students received support, including 13 teaching assistantships with full and partial tuition reimbursements available (averaging $8,800 per year); fellowships, career-related internships or fieldwork, Federal Work-Study, and unspecified assistantships also available. Support available to part-time students. Financial award application deadline: 3/1. *Faculty research:* Financial markets, strategic impact of total quality management, internal accounting controls, consumer preference, information systems and the Internet. *Unit head:* Dr. Murli Rajan, Director, 570-941-4043, Fax: 570-941-4342. *Application contact:* Joseph M. Roback, Director of Admissions, 570-941-4385, Fax: 570-941-5928, E-mail: robackj2@scranton.edu. Website: http://www.scranton.edu/academics/cgce/busad.shtml.

University of South Africa, College of Economic and Management Sciences, Pretoria, South Africa. Offers accounting (D Admin, D Com); accounting science (DA); auditing (D Admin, D Com); business administration (M Tech); business economics (D Admin); business leadership (DBL); business management (D Admin, D Com); economic management analysis (M Tech); economics (D Admin, D Com, PhD); human resource development (M Tech); industrial psychology (D Admin, D Com, PhD); logistics (D Com); marketing (M Tech); public administration (D Admin, D Com, DPA, PhD); public management (M Tech); quantitative management (D Admin, D Com); real estate (M Tech); statistics (D Admin, PhD); tourism management (D Admin, D Com); transport economics (D Admin, D Com).

University of South Alabama, Graduate School, Mitchell College of Business, Program in Accounting, Mobile, AL 36688-0002. Offers M Acc. Part-time and evening/weekend programs available. *Faculty:* 4 full-time (1 woman). *Students:* 20 full-time (15 women), 2 part-time (1 woman); includes 2 minority (1 Black or African American, non-Hispanic/Latino; 1 Asian, non-Hispanic/Latino). 34 applicants, 56% accepted, 12 enrolled. In 2013, 15 master's awarded. *Degree requirements:* For master's, comprehensive exam. *Entrance requirements:* For master's, GMAT, minimum undergraduate GPA of 3.0. *Application deadline:* For fall admission, 7/15 priority date for domestic students, 6/15 priority date for international students; for spring admission, 12/1 priority date for domestic students, 11/1 priority date for international students. Applications are processed on a rolling basis. Application fee: $35. *Expenses: Tuition,* state resident: full-time $8976; part-time $374 per credit hour. Tuition, nonresident: full-time $17,952; part-time $748 per credit hour. *Financial support:* Available to part-time students. Application deadline: 4/1. *Unit head:* Dr. Carl Moore, Dean, Mitchell College of Business, 251-460-6419. *Application contact:* Dr. John Gamble, Director of Graduate Studies, 251-460-6418. Website: http://www.southalabama.edu/mcob/accounting.html.

University of South Carolina, The Graduate School, Darla Moore School of Business, Master of Accountancy Program, Columbia, SC 29208. Offers business measurement and assurance (M Acc); JD/M Acc. *Accreditation:* AACSB. Part-time programs available.

Degree requirements: For master's, comprehensive exam. *Entrance requirements:* For master's, GMAT. Additional exam requirements/recommendations for international students: Required—TOEFL (minimum score 100 iBT); Recommended—IELTS. Electronic applications accepted. *Faculty research:* Judgment modeling, international accounting, accounting information systems, behavioral accounting, cost/management accounting.

The University of South Dakota, Graduate School, School of Business, Department of Accounting, Vermillion, SD 57069-2390. Offers professional accountancy (MP Acc); JD/MP Acc. Part-time programs available. Postbaccalaureate distance learning degree programs offered. *Degree requirements:* For master's, comprehensive exam. *Entrance requirements:* For master's, GMAT, minimum GPA of 2.7, resume. Additional exam requirements/recommendations for international students: Required—TOEFL (minimum score 550 paper-based; 79 iBT). Electronic applications accepted.

University of Southern California, Graduate School, Marshall School of Business, Leventhal School of Accounting, Los Angeles, CA 90089. Offers accounting (M Acc); business taxation (MBT); JD/MBT. Part-time programs available. *Degree requirements:* For master's, 30-48 units of study. *Entrance requirements:* For master's, GMAT, undergraduate degree, communication skills. Additional exam requirements/recommendations for international students: Required—TOEFL. Electronic applications accepted. *Faculty research:* State and local taxation, Securities and Exchange Commission, governance, auditing fees, financial accounting, enterprise zones, women in business.

University of Southern Maine, College of Management and Human Service, School of Business, Portland, ME 04104-9300. Offers accounting (MBA); business administration (MBA); finance (MBA); health management and policy (MBA); sustainability (MBA); JD/MBA; MBA/MSA; MBA/MSN; MS/MBA. *Accreditation:* AACSB. Part-time and evening/weekend programs available. *Faculty:* 10 part-time/adjunct (2 women). *Students:* 89 part-time (37 women); includes 4 minority (3 American Indian or Alaska Native, non-Hispanic/Latino; 1 Asian, non-Hispanic/Latino), 2 international. Average age 31. 36 applicants, 56% accepted, 16 enrolled. In 2013, 34 master's awarded. *Entrance requirements:* For master's, GMAT or GRE, minimum AACSB index of 1100. Additional exam requirements/recommendations for international students: Required—TOEFL (minimum score 550 paper-based; 79 iBT). *Application deadline:* For fall admission, 8/1 priority date for domestic students, 5/1 priority date for international students; for spring admission, 12/1 priority date for domestic students, 9/1 priority date for international students. Applications are processed on a rolling basis. Application fee: $65. Electronic applications accepted. *Expenses: Tuition,* state resident: part-time $380 per credit. Tuition, nonresident: part-time $1026 per credit. Part-time tuition and fees vary according to program. *Financial support:* In 2013–14, 3 research assistantships with partial tuition reimbursements (averaging $9,000 per year), 3 teaching assistantships with partial tuition reimbursements (averaging $9,000 per year) were awarded; career-related internships or fieldwork, Federal Work-Study, scholarships/grants, tuition waivers (full and partial), and unspecified assistantships also available. Support available to part-time students. Financial award application deadline: 2/15; financial award applicants required to submit FAFSA. *Faculty research:* Economic development, management information systems, real options, system dynamics, simulation. *Unit head:* Joseph W. McDonnell, Dean, 207-228-8002, Fax: 207-780-4060, E-mail: jmcdonnell@usm.maine.edu. *Application contact:* Alice B. Cash, Assistant Director for Student Affairs, 207-780-4184, Fax: 207-780-4662, E-mail: acash@usm.maine.edu. Website: http://www.usm.maine.edu/sb.

University of Southern Mississippi, Graduate School, College of Business, School of Accountancy and Information Systems, Hattiesburg, MS 39406-0001. Offers accountancy (MPA). *Accreditation:* AACSB. Part-time and evening/weekend programs available. *Faculty:* 7 full-time (4 women), 2 part-time/adjunct (both women). *Students:* 14 full-time (8 women), 5 part-time (2 women); includes 2 minority (both Black or African American, non-Hispanic/Latino). Average age 30. 17 applicants, 94% accepted, 14 enrolled. In 2013, 20 master's awarded. *Degree requirements:* For master's, comprehensive exam. *Entrance requirements:* For master's, GMAT, minimum GPA of 2.75 on last 60 hours. Additional exam requirements/recommendations for international students: Required—TOEFL, IELTS. *Application deadline:* For fall admission, 7/15 priority date for domestic students, 7/15 for international students; for spring admission, 11/15 priority date for domestic students, 11/15 for international students. Applications are processed on a rolling basis. Application fee: $50. Electronic applications accepted. *Financial support:* In 2013–14, 7 research assistantships with full tuition reimbursements (averaging $7,200 per year) were awarded; Federal Work-Study, institutionally sponsored loans, scholarships/grants, health care benefits, and unspecified assistantships also available. Support available to part-time students. Financial award application deadline: 3/15; financial award applicants required to submit FAFSA. *Faculty research:* Bank liquidity, subchapter S corporations, internal auditing, governmental accounting, inflation accounting. *Unit head:* Dr. Skip Hughes, Director, 601-266-4322, Fax: 601-266-4639. *Application contact:* Dr. Michael Dugan, Director of Graduate Studies, 601-266-4641, Fax: 601-266-5814. Website: http://www.usm.edu/graduateschool/table.php.

University of South Florida, College of Business, School of Accountancy, Tampa, FL 33620-9951. Offers audit/systems (M Acc); business administration (PhD), including accounting; generalist (M Acc); tax (M Acc). *Accreditation:* AACSB. Part-time and evening/weekend programs available. *Faculty:* 10 full-time (5 women), 2 part-time/adjunct (1 woman). *Students:* 50 full-time (22 women), 42 part-time (25 women); includes 20 minority (2 Black or African American, non-Hispanic/Latino; 5 Asian, non-Hispanic/Latino; 11 Hispanic/Latino; 2 Two or more races, non-Hispanic/Latino), 1 international. Average age 28. 92 applicants, 60% accepted, 37 enrolled. In 2013, 54 master's, 2 doctorates awarded. Terminal master's awarded for partial completion of doctoral program. *Degree requirements:* For master's, thesis or alternative; for doctorate, comprehensive exam, thesis/dissertation. *Entrance requirements:* For master's, GMAT (preferred minimum score of 500), minimum overall GPA of 3.0 in general upper-level coursework and in upper-level accounting coursework (minimum of 21 hours at a U.S. accredited program within past 5 years); for doctorate, GMAT or GRE, personal statement, recommendations, interview. Additional exam requirements/recommendations for international students: Required—TOEFL (minimum score 550 paper-based; 79 iBT) or IELTS (minimum score 6.5). *Application deadline:* For fall admission, 6/1 for domestic students, 1/2 for international students; for spring admission, 10/15 for domestic students, 6/1 for international students. Application fee: $30. Electronic applications accepted. *Financial support:* In 2013–14, 18 students received support, including 18 teaching assistantships with tuition reimbursements available (averaging $12,273 per year); scholarships/grants, health care benefits, and unspecified assistantships also available. Financial award applicants required to submit FAFSA. *Faculty research:* Auditing, auditor independence, audit committee decisions, fraud detection and reporting, disclosure effects, effects of information technology on accounting, governmental accounting/auditing, accounting information systems, data modeling and design methodologies for accounting systems, auditing computer-based systems, expert systems, group support systems in accounting, fair value accounting issues, corporate governance, financial accounting, financial reporting quality. *Total annual research expenditures:* $236,586. *Unit head:* Dr. Uday Murthy, Interim Director,

Accounting

School of Accountancy, 813-974-6516, Fax: 813-974-6528, E-mail: umurthy@usf.edu. *Application contact:* Christy Ward, Advisor and Graduation Specialist, 813-974-4290, Fax: 813-974-2797, E-mail: cward@usf.edu.
Website: http://business.usf.edu/departments/accountancy/.

The University of Tampa, John H. Sykes College of Business, Tampa, FL 33606-1490. Offers accounting (MS); entrepreneurship (MBA); finance (MBA, MS); information systems management (MBA); innovation management (MBA); international business (MBA); marketing (MBA, MS); nonprofit management (MBA). *Accreditation:* AACSB. Part-time and evening/weekend programs available. *Faculty:* 41 full-time (15 women), 5 part-time/adjunct (1 woman). *Students:* 406 full-time (171 women), 152 part-time (61 women); includes 104 minority (18 Black or African American, non-Hispanic/Latino; 1 American Indian or Alaska Native, non-Hispanic/Latino; 20 Asian, non-Hispanic/Latino; 59 Hispanic/Latino; 6 Two or more races, non-Hispanic/Latino), 154 international. Average age 33. 1,341 applicants, 37% accepted, 256 enrolled. In 2013, 218 master's awarded. *Degree requirements:* For master's, capstone. *Entrance requirements:* For master's, GMAT or GRE, 4-year undergraduate degree, minimum GPA of 3.0, professional experience (for Executive MBA). Additional exam requirements/ recommendations for international students: Required—TOEFL (minimum score 577 paper-based; 90 iBT); Recommended—IELTS (minimum score 7.5). *Application deadline:* Applications are processed on a rolling basis. Application fee: $40. Electronic applications accepted. *Expenses: Tuition:* Full-time $8928; part-time $558 per credit hour. *Required fees:* $80; $80 $40 per term. Tuition and fees vary according to program. *Financial support:* In 2013–14, 110 students received support. Career-related internships or fieldwork, scholarships/grants, and unspecified assistantships available. Financial award applicants required to submit FAFSA. *Faculty research:* Job market signaling, on-line shopping behaviors and social media, the Tampa Bay economy, digital literacy, entrepreneurship in small businesses. *Unit head:* Dr. Stephanie Thomason, Associate Dean, 813-253-6289, E-mail: sthomason@ut.edu. *Application contact:* Charlene Tobie, Associate Director of Admissions, 813-257-3566, E-mail: ctobie@ut.edu.
Website: http://www.ut.edu/business/.

The University of Tennessee, Graduate School, College of Business Administration, Department of Accounting, Knoxville, TN 37996. Offers accounting (M Acc), including assurance; systems (M Acc); taxation (M Acc). *Accreditation:* AACSB. *Degree requirements:* For master's, thesis or alternative. *Entrance requirements:* For master's, GMAT, minimum GPA of 2.7. Additional exam requirements/recommendations for international students: Required—TOEFL. Electronic applications accepted. *Expenses:* Tuition, state resident: full-time $9540; part-time $531 per credit hour. Tuition, nonresident: full-time $27,728; part-time $1542 per credit hour. *Required fees:* $1404; $67 per credit hour.

The University of Tennessee, Graduate School, College of Business Administration, Program in Business Administration, Knoxville, TN 37996. Offers accounting (PhD); finance (MBA, PhD); logistics and transportation (MBA, PhD); management (PhD); marketing (MBA, PhD); operations management (MBA); professional business administration (MBA); statistics (PhD); JD/MBA; MS/MBA; Pharm D/MBA. Pharm D/MBA offered jointly with The University of Tennessee Health Science Center. *Accreditation:* AACSB. Postbaccalaureate distance learning degree programs offered. *Degree requirements:* For master's, thesis or alternative; for doctorate, thesis/ dissertation. *Entrance requirements:* For master's and doctorate, GMAT, minimum GPA of 2.7. Additional exam requirements/recommendations for international students: Required—TOEFL. Electronic applications accepted. *Expenses:* Tuition, state resident: full-time $9540; part-time $531 per credit hour. Tuition, nonresident: full-time $27,728; part-time $1542 per credit hour. *Required fees:* $1404; $67 per credit hour.

The University of Tennessee at Chattanooga, Graduate School, College of Business, Program in Accountancy, Chattanooga, TN 37403. Offers M Acc. *Accreditation:* AACSB. Part-time and evening/weekend programs available. *Faculty:* 5 full-time (2 women). *Students:* 22 full-time (9 women), 20 part-time (10 women); includes 12 minority (5 Black or African American, non-Hispanic/Latino; 2 Asian, non-Hispanic/Latino; 2 Hispanic/Latino; 3 Two or more races, non-Hispanic/Latino). Average age 27. 26 applicants, 69% accepted, 13 enrolled. In 2013, 17 master's awarded. *Entrance requirements:* For master's, GMAT (minimum score 450). Additional exam requirements/recommendations for international students: Required—TOEFL (minimum score 550 paper-based; 79 iBT), IELTS (minimum score 6). *Application deadline:* For fall admission, 6/13 priority date for domestic students, 6/1 for international students; for spring admission, 10/15 priority date for domestic students, 10/1 for international students. Applications are processed on a rolling basis. Application fee: $30 ($35 for international students). Electronic applications accepted. *Financial support:* In 2013–14, 1 research assistantship with tuition reimbursement (averaging $6,860 per year), 1 teaching assistantship with tuition reimbursement (averaging $6,860 per year) were awarded; career-related internships or fieldwork, scholarships/grants, and unspecified assistantships also available. Support available to part-time students. Financial award applicants required to submit FAFSA. *Faculty research:* Performance measurement, auditing, income taxation, corporate efficiency, portfolio management and performance. *Unit head:* Dr. Dan Hollingsworth, Department Head, 423-425-4664, Fax: 423-425-5255, E-mail: dan-hollingsworth@utc.edu. *Application contact:* Dr. J. Randy Walker, Interim Dean of Graduate Studies, 423-425-4478, Fax: 423-425-5223, E-mail: randy-walker@utc.edu.
Website: http://www.utc.edu/Academic/BusinessGraduatePrograms/MAcc.php.

The University of Texas at Arlington, Graduate School, College of Business, Accounting Department, Arlington, TX 76019. Offers accounting (MP Acc, MS, PhD); taxation (MS). *Accreditation:* AACSB. Part-time and evening/weekend programs available. *Degree requirements:* For master's, thesis optional; for doctorate, comprehensive exam, thesis/dissertation. *Entrance requirements:* For master's and doctorate, GMAT. Additional exam requirements/recommendations for international students: Required—TOEFL (minimum score 550 paper-based; 79 iBT).

The University of Texas at Arlington, Graduate School, College of Business, Program in Business Administration, Arlington, TX 76019. Offers accounting (PhD); business statistics (PhD); finance (MBA, PhD); information systems (MBA, PhD); management (MBA, PhD); marketing (MBA, PhD); operations management (MBA, PhD); real estate (MBA). *Accreditation:* AACSB. Part-time and evening/weekend programs available. *Degree requirements:* For master's, thesis optional; for doctorate, comprehensive exam, thesis/dissertation. *Entrance requirements:* For master's, GMAT or GRE; for doctorate, GMAT, minimum GPA of 3.0 (undergraduate), 3.4 (graduate); 30 hours of graduate course work. Additional exam requirements/recommendations for international students: Required—TOEFL (minimum score 550 paper-based; 79 iBT). Electronic applications accepted.

The University of Texas at Austin, Graduate School, McCombs School of Business, Department of Accounting, Austin, TX 78712-1111. Offers MPA, PhD. *Accreditation:* AACSB. *Degree requirements:* For doctorate, comprehensive exam, thesis/dissertation. *Entrance requirements:* For master's and doctorate, GMAT. Additional exam requirements/recommendations for international students: Required—TOEFL. Electronic applications accepted.

The University of Texas at Dallas, Naveen Jindal School of Management, Program in Accounting, Richardson, TX 75080. Offers MS. *Accreditation:* AACSB. *Faculty:* 19 full-time (6 women), 12 part-time/adjunct (5 women). *Students:* 477 full-time (302 women), 260 part-time (155 women); includes 117 minority (9 Black or African American, non-Hispanic/Latino; 2 American Indian or Alaska Native, non-Hispanic/Latino; 73 Asian, non-Hispanic/Latino; 24 Hispanic/Latino; 9 Two or more races, non-Hispanic/Latino), 459 international. Average age 27. 998 applicants, 50% accepted, 263 enrolled. In 2013, 426 master's awarded. *Entrance requirements:* For master's, GMAT, minimum GPA of 3.0 in upper-level course work in field. Additional exam requirements/recommendations for international students: Required—TOEFL (minimum score 550 paper-based). *Application deadline:* For fall admission, 7/15 for domestic students, 5/1 priority date for international students; for spring admission, 11/15 for domestic students, 9/1 priority date for international students. Applications are processed on a rolling basis. Application fee: $50 ($100 for international students). Electronic applications accepted. *Expenses:* Tuition, state resident: full-time $11,940; part-time $663.33 per credit hour. Tuition, nonresident: full-time $21,606; part-time $1200.33 per credit hour. *Financial support:* In 2013–14, 181 students received support. Research assistantships with partial tuition reimbursements available, teaching assistantships with partial tuition reimbursements available, career-related internships or fieldwork, Federal Work-Study, institutionally sponsored loans, scholarships/grants, and unspecified assistantships available. Support available to part-time students. Financial award application deadline: 4/30; financial award applicants required to submit FAFSA. *Faculty research:* Privatization and accounting/auditing, corporate performance and executive compensation, risk management, information technology in accounting. *Unit head:* Dr. William Cready, Area Coordinator, 972-883-4185, Fax: 972-883-6823, E-mail: cready@utdallas.edu. *Application contact:* Melissa Palmer, Program Coordinator, 972-883-5851, E-mail: mrp110130@utdallas.edu.
Website: http://jindal.utdallas.edu/academic-areas/accounting/.

The University of Texas at Dallas, Naveen Jindal School of Management, Programs in Management Science, Richardson, TX 75080. Offers accounting (PhD); finance (PhD); information systems (PhD); marketing (PhD); operations management (PhD). *Accreditation:* AACSB. Part-time and evening/weekend programs available. *Faculty:* 13 full-time (3 women), 7 part-time/adjunct (2 women). *Students:* 78 full-time (27 women), 9 part-time (3 women); includes 6 minority (all Asian, non-Hispanic/Latino), 73 international. Average age 30. 258 applicants, 9% accepted, 16 enrolled. In 2013, 14 doctorates awarded. *Degree requirements:* For doctorate, thesis/dissertation. *Entrance requirements:* For doctorate, GMAT, minimum GPA of 3.0. Additional exam requirements/recommendations for international students: Required—TOEFL (minimum score 550 paper-based). *Application deadline:* For fall admission, 7/15 for domestic students, 5/1 priority date for international students; for spring admission, 11/15 for domestic students, 9/1 priority date for international students. Applications are processed on a rolling basis. Application fee: $50 ($100 for international students). Electronic applications accepted. *Expenses:* Tuition, state resident: full-time $11,940; part-time $663.33 per credit hour. Tuition, nonresident: full-time $21,606; part-time $1200.33 per credit hour. *Financial support:* In 2013–14, 81 students received support. Research assistantships with partial tuition reimbursements available, teaching assistantships with partial tuition reimbursements available, career-related internships or fieldwork, Federal Work-Study, institutionally sponsored loans, scholarships/grants, and unspecified assistantships available. Support available to part-time students. Financial award application deadline: 4/30; financial award applicants required to submit FAFSA. *Faculty research:* Empirical generalizations in marketing, diffusion of generations of technology, stochastic brand-choice theory, acceptance of trade deals by supermarkets, nonparametric estimations of market share response. *Unit head:* Dr. Sumit Sarkar, Program Director, 972-883-2745, Fax: 972-883-5977, E-mail: som_phd.@utdallas.edu. *Application contact:* Ashley J. Desouza, Program Administrator, 972-883-2745, Fax: 972-883-5977, E-mail: ashley.desouza@utdallas.edu.
Website: http://jindal.utdallas.edu/academic-programs/phd-programs/management-science/.

The University of Texas at El Paso, Graduate School, College of Business Administration, Department of Accounting, El Paso, TX 79968-0001. Offers M Acc. *Accreditation:* AACSB. Part-time and evening/weekend programs available. *Entrance requirements:* For master's, GMAT, minimum GPA of 3.0. Additional exam requirements/recommendations for international students: Required—TOEFL; Recommended—IELTS. Electronic applications accepted. *Faculty research:* Financial and managerial accounting, auditing and accounting information systems.

The University of Texas at San Antonio, College of Business, Department of Accounting, San Antonio, TX 78249-0617. Offers M Acy, PhD. *Accreditation:* AACSB. Part-time and evening/weekend programs available. *Faculty:* 12 full-time (3 women), 2 part-time/adjunct (1 woman). *Students:* 54 full-time (27 women), 50 part-time (26 women); includes 36 minority (2 Black or African American, non-Hispanic/Latino; 3 Asian, non-Hispanic/Latino; 30 Hispanic/Latino; 1 Two or more races, non-Hispanic/Latino), 7 international. Average age 28. 80 applicants, 51% accepted, 28 enrolled. In 2013, 49 master's awarded. *Degree requirements:* For master's, thesis or alternative. *Entrance requirements:* For master's, GMAT, bachelor's degree, transcripts, statement of purpose. Additional exam requirements/recommendations for international students: Required—TOEFL (minimum score 550 paper-based; 79 iBT), IELTS (minimum score 6.5). *Application deadline:* For fall admission, 7/1 for domestic students, 4/1 for international students; for spring admission, 11/1 for domestic students, 9/1 for international students. Application fee: $45 ($80 for international students). Electronic applications accepted. *Expenses:* Tuition, state resident: full-time $4671. Tuition, nonresident: full-time $8708. *International tuition:* $17,415 full-time. *Required fees:* $1924.60. Tuition and fees vary according to course load and degree level. *Financial support:* In 2013–14, 9 teaching assistantships (averaging $44,000 per year) were awarded; Federal Work-Study and scholarships/grants also available. *Faculty research:* Capital markets, corporate governance, auditing, health care accounting, fraud. *Unit head:* Dr. James E. Groff, Chair, 210-458-5239, Fax: 210-458-4322, E-mail: james.groff@utsa.edu. *Application contact:* Dr. Jeff Boone, Advisor of Record for Accounting Doctoral Programs, 210-458-7091, E-mail: jeff.boone@utsa.edu.
Website: http://business.utsa.edu/accounting/.

The University of Texas of the Permian Basin, Office of Graduate Studies, School of Business, Program in Accountancy, Odessa, TX 79762-0001. Offers MPA. *Entrance requirements:* For master's, GMAT. Additional exam requirements/recommendations for international students: Required—TOEFL (minimum score 550 paper-based).

The University of Texas–Pan American, College of Business Administration, Program in Accounting, Edinburg, TX 78539. Offers M Acc, MS. Part-time and evening/weekend programs available. *Entrance requirements:* For master's, GMAT. Additional exam requirements/recommendations for international students: Required—TOEFL (minimum score 500 paper-based). Electronic applications accepted. *Expenses:* Tuition, state resident: full-time $5986; part-time $333 per credit hour. Tuition, nonresident: full-time $12,358; part-time $687 per credit hour. *Required fees:* $782. Tuition and fees vary according to program. *Faculty research:* Financial and managerial accounting, international accounting, taxation, ethics.

University of the Cumberlands, Hutton School of Business, Williamsburg, KY 40769-1372. Offers accounting (MBA); business (MBA). Part-time programs available. Postbaccalaureate distance learning degree programs offered (no on-campus study). *Entrance requirements:* For master's, GMAT, GRE. Additional exam requirements/recommendations for international students: Required—TOEFL. Electronic applications accepted.

University of the Incarnate Word, School of Graduate Studies and Research, H-E-B School of Business and Administration, Programs in Accounting, San Antonio, TX 78209-6397. Offers MS. Part-time and evening/weekend programs available. *Faculty:* 4 full-time (3 women), 5 part-time/adjunct (3 women). *Students:* 38 full-time (19 women), 26 part-time (16 women); includes 29 minority (2 Black or African American, non-Hispanic/Latino; 2 Asian, non-Hispanic/Latino; 24 Hispanic/Latino; 1 Two or more races, non-Hispanic/Latino), 15 international. Average age 29. 56 applicants, 61% accepted, 22 enrolled. In 2013, 40 master's awarded. *Entrance requirements:* For master's, GMAT. Additional exam requirements/recommendations for international students: Required—TOEFL (minimum score 560 paper-based; 83 iBT). *Application deadline:* Applications are processed on a rolling basis. Application fee: $20. Electronic applications accepted. *Expenses: Tuition:* Part-time $815 per credit hour. *Required fees:* $86 per credit hour. One-time fee: $40 part-time. Tuition and fees vary according to degree level and program. *Financial support:* Federal Work-Study and scholarships/grants available. Financial award applicants required to submit FAFSA. *Unit head:* Dr. Henry Elrod, Associate Professor, 210-829-3184, Fax: 210-805-3564, E-mail: elrod@uiwtx.edu. *Application contact:* Andrea Cyterski-Acosta, Dean of Enrollment, 210-829-6005, Fax: 210-829-3921, E-mail: admis@uiwtx.edu.
Website: http://www.uiw.edu/gradstudies/documents/msaccounting.pdf.

University of the Sacred Heart, Graduate Programs, Department of Business Administration, San Juan, PR 00914-0383. Offers human resource management (MBA); information systems auditing (MS); information technology (Certificate); international marketing (MBA); management information systems (MBA); production and marketing of special events (Certificate); taxation (MBA). Part-time and evening/weekend programs available. *Degree requirements:* For master's, thesis. *Entrance requirements:* For master's, EXADEP, minimum undergraduate GPA of 2.75, interview.

The University of Toledo, College of Graduate Studies, College of Business and Innovation, Department of Accounting, Toledo, OH 43606-3390. Offers MBA, MSA. Part-time and evening/weekend programs available. *Faculty:* 8. *Students:* 19 full-time (9 women), 35 part-time (25 women); includes 5 minority (1 Black or African American, non-Hispanic/Latino; 1 Asian, non-Hispanic/Latino; 3 Hispanic/Latino), 31 international. Average age 25. 37 applicants, 68% accepted, 18 enrolled. In 2013, 21 master's awarded. *Entrance requirements:* For master's, GMAT, GRE, or LSAT, minimum GPA of 2.7 for all prior academic work, three letters of recommendation, statement of purpose, transcripts from all prior institutions attended. Additional exam requirements/recommendations for international students: Required—TOEFL (minimum score 550 paper-based; 80 iBT). *Application deadline:* For fall admission, 8/1 for domestic students, 5/1 for international students; for spring admission, 11/15 for domestic students, 10/1 for international students; for summer admission, 4/1 for domestic students, 3/1 for international students. Applications are processed on a rolling basis. Application fee: $45 ($75 for international students). Electronic applications accepted. *Financial support:* In 2013–14, 8 research assistantships with full and partial tuition reimbursements (averaging $5,804 per year) were awarded; career-related internships or fieldwork, Federal Work-Study, institutionally sponsored loans, scholarships/grants, tuition waivers (full and partial), unspecified assistantships, and administrative assistantships also available. Support available to part-time students. Financial award applicants required to submit FAFSA. *Faculty research:* Estate gift tax, audit and legal liability, corporate tax, accounting information systems. *Unit head:* Dr. Hassan HassabElnaby, Chair, 419-530-2780, E-mail: hassan.hassabelnaby@utoledo.edu. *Application contact:* Graduate School Office, 419-530-4723, Fax: 419-530-4724, E-mail: grdsch@utnet.utoledo.edu.

The University of Tulsa, Graduate School, Collins College of Business, Master of Business Administration Program, Tulsa, OK 74104-3189. Offers accounting (MBA); business administration (MBA); energy management (MBA); finance (MBA); international business (MBA); management information systems (MBA); taxation (MBA); JD/MBA; MBA/MSCS; MBA/MSF. *Accreditation:* AACSB. Part-time and evening/weekend programs available. *Faculty:* 32 full-time (6 women). *Students:* 59 full-time (28 women), 29 part-time (9 women); includes 11 minority (1 Black or African American, non-Hispanic/Latino; 5 American Indian or Alaska Native, non-Hispanic/Latino; 3 Asian, non-Hispanic/Latino; 1 Hispanic/Latino; 1 Two or more races, non-Hispanic/Latino), 16 international. Average age 27. 53 applicants, 81% accepted, 28 enrolled. In 2013, 39 master's awarded. *Entrance requirements:* For master's, GMAT. Additional exam requirements/recommendations for international students: Required—TOEFL (minimum score 577 paper-based; 91 iBT), IELTS (minimum score 6.5). *Application deadline:* Applications are processed on a rolling basis. Application fee: $40. Electronic applications accepted. *Expenses: Tuition:* Full-time $19,566; part-time $1087 per credit hour. *Required fees:* $1690; $5 per credit hour. $160 per semester. Tuition and fees vary according to course load. *Financial support:* In 2013–14, 31 students received support, including 1 research assistantship (averaging $1,500 per year), 30 teaching assistantships (averaging $10,112 per year); fellowships, career-related internships or fieldwork, institutionally sponsored loans, scholarships/grants, health care benefits, tuition waivers (full and partial), and unspecified assistantships also available. Support available to part-time students. Financial award application deadline: 2/1; financial award applicants required to submit FAFSA. *Faculty research:* Accounting, energy management, finance, international business, management information systems, taxation. *Unit head:* Dr. Linda Nichols, Associate Dean of the Collins College of Business, 918-631-2142, Fax: 918-631-2142, E-mail: linda-nichols@utulsa.edu. *Application contact:* Information Contact, 918-631-2242, E-mail: graduate-business@utulsa.edu.
Website: http://www.utulsa.edu/academics/colleges/collins-college-of-business/bus-dept-schools/graduate-business-programs/degree-programs/MBA-Programs.aspx.

The University of Tulsa, Graduate School, Collins College of Business, Program in Accounting, Tulsa, OK 74104-3189. Offers M Acc. Part-time programs available. *Faculty:* 8 full-time (2 women). *Students:* 18 full-time (6 women), 3 part-time (1 woman); includes 2 minority (1 American Indian or Alaska Native, non-Hispanic/Latino; 1 Asian, non-Hispanic/Latino), 4 international. Average age 26. 51 applicants, 24% accepted, 5 enrolled. In 2013, 8 master's awarded. *Entrance requirements:* For master's, GMAT. Additional exam requirements/recommendations for international students: Required—TOEFL (minimum score 577 paper-based; 91 iBT). *Application deadline:* Applications are processed on a rolling basis. Application fee: $0. Electronic applications accepted. *Expenses: Tuition:* Full-time $19,566; part-time $1087 per credit hour. *Required fees:* $1690; $5 per credit hour. $160 per semester. Tuition and fees vary according to course load. *Financial support:* In 2013–14, 9 students received support, including 9 teaching assistantships (averaging $9,741 per year); fellowships, research assistantships, career-related internships or fieldwork, Federal Work-Study, scholarships/grants, health care benefits, tuition waivers (full and partial), and unspecified assistantships also available. Support available to part-time students. Financial award application deadline: 2/1; financial award applicants required to submit FAFSA. *Faculty research:* Capital markets, financial reporting, innovation in accounting. *Unit head:* Dr. Linda Nichols, Associate Dean, 918-631-2242, Fax: 918-631-2142, E-mail: linda-nichols@utulsa.edu. *Application contact:* Information Contact, 918-631-2242, E-mail: graduate-business@utulsa.edu.
Website: http://www.utulsa.edu/academics/colleges/collins-college-of-business/bus-dept-schools/graduate-business-programs/degree-programs/Master-of-Accountancy.

University of Utah, Graduate School, David Eccles School of Business, Business Administration Program, Salt Lake City, UT 84112. Offers accounting (PhD); business administration (EMBA, MBA, PMBA); finance (PhD); information systems (PhD); marketing (PhD); operations management (PhD); organizational behavior (PhD); strategic management (PhD); MBA/JD; MBA/MHA; MBA/MS. Part-time and evening/weekend programs available. *Faculty:* 58 full-time (21 women), 37 part-time/adjunct (7 women). *Students:* 481 full-time (108 women), 109 part-time (19 women); includes 39 minority (2 Black or African American, non-Hispanic/Latino; 13 Asian, non-Hispanic/Latino; 18 Hispanic/Latino; 1 Native Hawaiian or other Pacific Islander, non-Hispanic/Latino; 5 Two or more races, non-Hispanic/Latino), 39 international. Average age 32. 486 applicants, 56% accepted, 215 enrolled. In 2013, 326 master's, 10 doctorates awarded. *Degree requirements:* For doctorate, comprehensive exam, thesis/dissertation. *Entrance requirements:* For master's, GMAT or GRE; for doctorate, GMAT. Additional exam requirements/recommendations for international students: Required—TOEFL (minimum score 600 paper-based; 100 iBT), IELTS (minimum score 7). *Application deadline:* For fall admission, 11/1 priority date for domestic students, 3/1 priority date for international students; for spring admission, 11/1 for domestic and international students. Applications are processed on a rolling basis. Application fee: $55 ($65 for international students). Electronic applications accepted. *Expenses:* Contact institution. *Financial support:* In 2013–14, 48 students received support, including 41 fellowships with partial tuition reimbursements available (averaging $8,600 per year), 35 research assistantships with partial tuition reimbursements available (averaging $6,378 per year), 57 teaching assistantships with full tuition reimbursements available (averaging $17,000 per year); scholarships/grants and unspecified assistantships also available. Financial award application deadline: 2/1; financial award applicants required to submit FAFSA. *Faculty research:* Corporate finance, strategy services, consumer behavior, financial disclosures, operations. *Unit head:* Dr. William Hesterly, Associate Dean, PhD Program, 801-581-7676, Fax: 801-581-3380, E-mail: mastersinfo@business.utah.edu. *Application contact:* Andrea Miller, Coordinator, 801-581-7785, Fax: 801-581-3666, E-mail: mastersinfo@business.utah.edu.
Website: http://business.utah.edu/full-time-mba.

University of Utah, Graduate School, David Eccles School of Business, School of Accounting, Salt Lake City, UT 84112. Offers M Acc, PhD. *Accreditation:* AACSB. Part-time and evening/weekend programs available. *Faculty:* 13 full-time (6 women), 7 part-time/adjunct (2 women). *Students:* 104 full-time (29 women), 40 part-time (13 women); includes 15 minority (1 Black or African American, non-Hispanic/Latino; 8 Asian, non-Hispanic/Latino; 6 Hispanic/Latino), 16 international. Average age 28. 138 applicants, 83% accepted, 95 enrolled. In 2013, 109 master's awarded. *Degree requirements:* For doctorate, comprehensive exam, thesis/dissertation, oral qualifying exams, written qualifying exams. *Entrance requirements:* For master's, GMAT, minimum undergraduate GPA of 3.0; for doctorate, GMAT. Additional exam requirements/recommendations for international students: Required—TOEFL (minimum score 600 paper-based; 100 iBT), IELTS (minimum score 7). *Application deadline:* For fall admission, 3/1 priority date for domestic and international students; for spring admission, 10/15 priority date for domestic students, 8/1 priority date for international students. Applications are processed on a rolling basis. Application fee: $55 ($65 for international students). Electronic applications accepted. *Expenses:* Contact institution. *Financial support:* In 2013–14, 32 students received support, including 13 research assistantships with partial tuition reimbursements available (averaging $6,250 per year), 2 teaching assistantships with full and partial tuition reimbursements available (averaging $12,500 per year); scholarships/grants, tuition waivers (partial), and unspecified assistantships also available. Financial award application deadline: 2/1; financial award applicants required to submit FAFSA. *Faculty research:* Auditing, taxation, information systems, financial accounting, accounting theory, international accounting. *Total annual research expenditures:* $86,000. *Unit head:* Dr. Martha Eining, Chair, 801-581-7673, Fax: 801-581-3581, E-mail: martha.eining@utah.edu. *Application contact:* Olivia Hansen, M Acc Admissions Coordinator, 801-587-3282, Fax: 801-581-3581, E-mail: olivia.hansen@business.utah.edu.
Website: http://www.business.utah.edu/accounting/.

University of Vermont, Graduate College, School of Business Administration, Program in Accounting, Burlington, VT 05405. Offers M Acc. *Students:* 33 (22 women), 22 international. 114 applicants, 45% accepted, 17 enrolled. In 2013, 15 master's awarded. *Entrance requirements:* For master's, GMAT, GRE, resume. Additional exam requirements/recommendations for international students: Required—TOEFL (minimum score 550 paper-based; 80 iBT). *Application deadline:* For fall admission, 4/1 for domestic and international students; for spring admission, 11/15 for domestic and international students. Applications are processed on a rolling basis. Application fee: $65. Electronic applications accepted. *Unit head:* Dr. Sanjay Sharma, Dean, 802-656-4119. *Application contact:* Prof. Susan Hughes, Coordinator, 802-656-4119.

University of Virginia, McIntire School of Commerce, Program in Accounting, Charlottesville, VA 22903. Offers MS, JD/MS. *Accreditation:* AACSB. *Students:* 57 full-time (37 women); includes 11 minority (3 Black or African American, non-Hispanic/Latino; 4 Asian, non-Hispanic/Latino; 3 Hispanic/Latino; 1 Two or more races, non-Hispanic/Latino), 19 international. Average age 23. 239 applicants, 48% accepted, 59 enrolled. In 2013, 56 master's awarded. *Entrance requirements:* For master's, GMAT, 2 letters of recommendation, 12 hours of accounting courses. Additional exam requirements/recommendations for international students: Required—TOEFL (minimum score 600 paper-based; 100 iBT), IELTS (minimum score 7). *Application deadline:* For fall admission, 9/1 priority date for domestic students, 12/1 for international students. Applications are processed on a rolling basis. Application fee: $75. Electronic applications accepted. *Expenses:* Contact institution. *Financial support:* Fellowships and Federal Work-Study available. Financial award applicants required to submit FAFSA. *Unit head:* Roger Martin, Director, 434-982-2182, Fax: 434-924-4511, E-mail: rdm3h@virginia.edu. *Application contact:* Emma Candalier, Associate Director of Graduate Recruiting, 434-243-4992, Fax: 434-924-4511, E-mail: ecandalier@virginia.edu.
Website: http://www.commerce.virginia.edu/msaccounting/Pages/default.aspx.

University of Washington, Graduate School, Michael G. Foster School of Business, Seattle, WA 98195-3200. Offers auditing and assurance (MP Acc); business administration (MBA, PhD); executive business administration (MBA); global executive business administration (MBA); taxation (MP Acc); technology management (MBA); JD/MBA; MBA/MAIS; MBA/MHA. *Accreditation:* AACSB. Part-time and evening/weekend programs available. *Faculty:* 100 full-time (28 women), 55 part-time/adjunct (22 women). *Students:* 407 full-time (130 women), 369 part-time (110 women); includes 199 minority (16 Black or African American, non-Hispanic/Latino; 5 American Indian or Alaska Native, non-Hispanic/Latino; 139 Asian, non-Hispanic/Latino; 25 Hispanic/Latino; 7 Native

Hawaiian or other Pacific Islander, non-Hispanic/Latino; 7 Two or more races, non-Hispanic/Latino), 178 international. Average age 32. 2,474 applicants, 40% accepted, 776 enrolled. In 2013, 468 master's, 8 doctorates awarded. Terminal master's awarded for partial completion of doctoral program. *Degree requirements:* For doctorate, comprehensive exam, thesis/dissertation. *Entrance requirements:* For master's, GMAT; for doctorate, GMAT, GRE. Additional exam requirements/recommendations for international students: Required—TOEFL (minimum score 600 paper-based; 100 iBT). *Application deadline:* For fall admission, 3/15 for domestic students, 1/20 for international students. Application fee: $85. Electronic applications accepted. *Expenses:* Contact institution. *Financial support:* Fellowships with partial tuition reimbursements, research assistantships with partial tuition reimbursements, teaching assistantships with partial tuition reimbursements, Federal Work-Study, institutionally sponsored loans, and scholarships/grants available. Financial award application deadline: 2/28; financial award applicants required to submit FAFSA. *Faculty research:* Finance, marketing, organizational behavior, information technology, strategy. *Unit head:* Dr. James Jiambalvo, Dean, 206-543-4750. *Application contact:* Erin Town, Director of Admissions, 206-543-4661, Fax: 206-616-7351, E-mail: mba@uw.edu.
Website: http://www.foster.washington.edu/.

University of Washington, Tacoma, Graduate Programs, MBA Programs, Tacoma, WA 98402-3100. Offers accounting (MBA); business administration (MBA); certified financial analyst (MBA). *Accreditation:* AACSB. Part-time and evening/weekend programs available. *Entrance requirements:* For master's, GMAT, minimum GPA of 3.0 in final graded 90 quarter credits or 60 graded semester credits; at least 2 years of professional/management work experience. Additional exam requirements/recommendations for international students: Required—TOEFL (minimum score 580 paper-based; 92 iBT). Electronic applications accepted. *Expenses:* Contact institution. *Faculty research:* International accounting, marketing, change management, investments, corporate social responsibility.

University of Waterloo, Graduate Studies, Faculty of Arts, School of Accounting and Finance, Waterloo, ON N2L 3G1, Canada. Offers accounting (M Acc, PhD); finance (M Acc); taxation (M Tax). *Degree requirements:* For master's, thesis or alternative; for doctorate, thesis/dissertation. *Entrance requirements:* For master's, honors degree, minimum B average, resumé; for doctorate, GMAT, master's degree, minimum A-average, resume. Additional exam requirements/recommendations for international students: Required—TOEFL, TWE. Electronic applications accepted. *Expenses:* Contact institution. *Faculty research:* Auditing, management accounting.

University of West Florida, College of Business, Department of Accounting, Pensacola, FL 32514-5750. Offers M Acc. Part-time and evening/weekend programs available. *Entrance requirements:* For master's, GMAT (minimum score 450) or equivalent GRE score, official transcripts; bachelor's degree; two letters of recommendation; letter of intent. Additional exam requirements/recommendations for international students: Required—TOEFL (minimum score 550 paper-based). *Faculty research:* Audit risk, tax legislation, product costing, bank core deposit intangibles, financial reporting.

University of West Georgia, Richards College of Business, Department of Accounting and Finance, Carrollton, GA 30118. Offers MP Acc. *Accreditation:* AACSB. Part-time and evening/weekend programs available. *Faculty:* 10 full-time (4 women). *Students:* 15 full-time (9 women), 15 part-time (11 women); includes 6 minority (5 Black or African American, non-Hispanic/Latino; 1 Asian, non-Hispanic/Latino), 4 international. Average age 29. 19 applicants, 84% accepted, 11 enrolled. In 2013, 13 master's awarded. *Degree requirements:* For master's, comprehensive exam. *Entrance requirements:* For master's, GMAT, minimum GPA of 2.5. Additional exam requirements/recommendations for international students: Required—TOEFL (minimum score 550 paper-based; 79 iBT); Recommended—IELTS (minimum score 6.5). *Application deadline:* For fall admission, 7/15 for domestic students, 6/1 for international students; for spring admission, 11/15 for domestic students, 10/15 for international students. Applications are processed on a rolling basis. Application fee: $40. Electronic applications accepted. *Expenses:* Contact institution. *Financial support:* In 2013–14, 5 students received support, including 6 research assistantships with full tuition reimbursements available (averaging $3,500 per year); tuition waivers (partial) also available. Financial award application deadline: 4/1; financial award applicants required to submit FAFSA. *Faculty research:* Taxpayer insolvency, non-gap financial measures, deferred taxes, financial accounting issues. *Unit head:* Dr. James R. Colley, Chair, 678-839-4811, Fax: 678-839-5040, E-mail: rcolley@westga.edu. *Application contact:* Dr. Hope Udombon, Administrative Director of Graduate Business Programs, 678-839-5355, Fax: 678-839-5040, E-mail: hudombon@westga.edu.
Website: http://www.westga.edu/accfin/.

University of Wisconsin–Madison, Graduate School, Wisconsin School of Business, Doctoral Program in Accounting and Information Systems, Madison, WI 53706-1380. Offers PhD. *Accreditation:* AACSB. *Faculty:* 11 full-time (3 women). *Students:* 14 full-time (7 women); includes 1 minority (American Indian or Alaska Native, non-Hispanic/Latino), 1 international. Average age 31. 43 applicants, 12% accepted, 3 enrolled. In 2013, 1 doctorate awarded. *Degree requirements:* For doctorate, comprehensive exam, thesis/dissertation. *Entrance requirements:* For doctorate, GMAT or GRE. Additional exam requirements/recommendations for international students: Recommended—TOEFL (minimum score 623 paper-based; 106 iBT), IELTS (minimum score 7.5). *Application deadline:* For fall admission, 12/15 priority date for domestic and international students. Application fee: $56. Electronic applications accepted. *Expenses:* Contact institution. *Financial support:* In 2013–14, 14 students received support, including 1 fellowship with full tuition reimbursement available (averaging $19,125 per year), 4 research assistantships with full tuition reimbursements available (averaging $14,746 per year), 9 teaching assistantships with full tuition reimbursements available (averaging $14,746 per year); Federal Work-Study, institutionally sponsored loans, scholarships/grants, health care benefits, and unspecified assistantships also available. Financial award application deadline: 12/15. *Faculty research:* Auditing, financial reporting, economic theory, strategy, computer models. *Unit head:* Prof. Terry Warfield, Chair, 608-262-1028, E-mail: twarfield@bus.wisc.edu. *Application contact:* Belle Heberling, Assistant Director for Research Programs, 608-262-3749, Fax: 608-890-0180, E-mail: phd@bus.wisc.edu.
Website: http://www.bus.wisc.edu/phd.

University of Wisconsin–Madison, Graduate School, Wisconsin School of Business, Master of Accountancy Program, Madison, WI 53706-1380. Offers accountancy (M Acc); tax (M Acc). *Faculty:* 11 full-time (3 women), 8 part-time/adjunct (3 women). *Students:* 113 full-time (59 women); includes 8 minority (6 Asian, non-Hispanic/Latino; 2 Hispanic/Latino), 23 international. Average age 23. 233 applicants, 46% accepted, 103 enrolled. In 2013, 100 master's awarded. *Degree requirements:* For master's, minimum GPA of 3.0. *Entrance requirements:* For master's, GMAT, essays. Additional exam requirements/recommendations for international students: Required—TOEFL, PTE. *Application deadline:* For fall admission, 9/30 for domestic and international students; for winter admission, 1/7 for domestic and international students; for spring admission, 2/28 for domestic and international students. Application fee: $56. Electronic applications accepted. *Expenses:* Tuition, state resident: full-time $10,728; part-time $790 per credit. Tuition, nonresident: full-time $24,054; part-time $1623 per credit. *Required fees:* $1130; $119 per credit. *Financial support:* In 2013–14, 96 students received support, including 5 research assistantships with full tuition reimbursements available (averaging $4,915 per year), 44 teaching assistantships with full tuition reimbursements available (averaging $7,373 per year); career-related internships or fieldwork, scholarships/grants, health care benefits, and unspecified assistantships also available. Financial award application deadline: 5/1. *Faculty research:* Internal control deficiencies, impairment recognition, accounting misstatements, earnings restatements, voluntary disclosure. *Unit head:* Prof. Terry Warfield, Professor/Chair of Accounting and Information Systems, 608-262-1028, E-mail: twarfield@bus.wisc.edu. *Application contact:* Kristen Ann Fuhremann, Director, 608-262-0316, Fax: 608-263-0477, E-mail: kfuhremann@bus.wisc.edu.
Website: http://bus.wisc.edu/degrees-programs/msmacc.

University of Wisconsin–Whitewater, School of Graduate Studies, College of Business and Economics, Department of Accounting, Whitewater, WI 53190-1790. Offers MPA. Part-time and evening/weekend programs available. Postbaccalaureate distance learning degree programs offered (no on-campus study). *Degree requirements:* For master's, thesis or alternative. *Entrance requirements:* For master's, GMAT or GRE, minimum AACSB index of 1000, minimum GPA of 2.75. Additional exam requirements/recommendations for international students: Required—TOEFL (minimum score 550 paper-based; 80 iBT), IELTS (minimum score 6). Electronic applications accepted. *Faculty research:* Laws/economy/quality of life; tax, accounting and public policy.

University of Wyoming, College of Business, Program in Accounting, Laramie, WY 82071. Offers MS. *Degree requirements:* For master's, thesis optional. *Entrance requirements:* For master's, GMAT or GRE, minimum GPA of 3.0. Additional exam requirements/recommendations for international students: Required—TOEFL (minimum score 540 paper-based; 76 iBT). Electronic applications accepted. *Faculty research:* Taxation, accounting education, assessment, not-for-profit accounting, fraud examination, ethics, management accounting.

Upper Iowa University, Online Master's Programs, Fayette, IA 52142-1857. Offers accounting (MBA); corporate financial management (MBA); global business (MBA); health and human services (MPA); higher education administration (MHEA); homeland security (MPA); human resources management (MBA); justice administration (MPA); organizational development (MBA); public personnel management (MPA); quality management (MBA). MBA also available at Madison, WI campus. Part-time programs available. Postbaccalaureate distance learning degree programs offered (no on-campus study). *Degree requirements:* For master's, research project. *Entrance requirements:* For master's, GMAT, GRE, or minimum GPA of 2.7 during last 60 hours. Additional exam requirements/recommendations for international students: Required—TOEFL (minimum score 570 paper-based). Electronic applications accepted. *Faculty research:* Total quality management, CQI, teams, organization culture and climate, management.

Utah State University, School of Graduate Studies, College of Business, School of Accountancy, Logan, UT 84322. Offers M Acc. *Accreditation:* AACSB. Part-time programs available. *Entrance requirements:* For master's, GMAT, minimum GPA of 3.0, 3 recommendation letters. Additional exam requirements/recommendations for international students: Required—TOEFL. *Faculty research:* Relationship theory, enterprise systems, just in time/loan, reported earnings measures, accounting education.

Utah Valley University, MBA Program, Orem, UT 84058-5999. Offers accounting (MBA); management (MBA). *Accreditation:* AACSB. Part-time and evening/weekend programs available. *Students:* 79 part-time (16 women). *Entrance requirements:* For master's, GMAT, official transcripts, current resume, three letters of recommendation. Additional exam requirements/recommendations for international students: Required—TOEFL (minimum score 79 iBT). *Application deadline:* For fall admission, 2/1 priority date for domestic students. Applications are processed on a rolling basis. Application fee: $45. Electronic applications accepted. *Expenses:* Tuition, state resident: full-time $8520; part-time $355 per credit. Tuition, nonresident: full-time $21,232; part-time $885 per credit. *Required fees:* $700; $350 per semester. Tuition and fees vary according to program. *Unit head:* Trisha Alexander, Director, 801-863-5504, E-mail: trishan@uvu.edu.
Website: http://www.uvu.edu/mba/.

Utica College, Program in Accountancy, Utica, NY 13502-4892. Offers MBA. Part-time and evening/weekend programs available. *Faculty:* 3 full-time (1 woman). *Students:* 4 full-time (3 women), 6 part-time (5 women); includes 2 minority (1 Black or African American, non-Hispanic/Latino; 1 Hispanic/Latino). Average age 36. In 2013, 5 master's awarded. *Entrance requirements:* For master's, BS, minimum GPA of 3.0. Additional exam requirements/recommendations for international students: Required—TOEFL (minimum score 525 paper-based). *Application deadline:* Applications are processed on a rolling basis. Application fee: $50. Electronic applications accepted. *Expenses:* Contact institution. *Financial support:* Career-related internships or fieldwork, scholarships/grants, tuition waivers (partial), and unspecified assistantships available. Support available to part-time students. Financial award application deadline: 3/15; financial award applicants required to submit FAFSA. *Unit head:* Dr. Zhaodan Huang, MBA Director, 315-792-3247, E-mail: zhuang@utica.edu. *Application contact:* John D. Rowe, Director of Graduate Admissions, 315-792-3824, Fax: 315-792-3003, E-mail: jrowe@utica.edu.
Website: http://onlineuticacollege.com/programs/mba-in-accountancy.asp.

Vanderbilt University, Vanderbilt Graduate School of Management and Graduate School, Vanderbilt Master of Accountancy Program, Nashville, TN 37240-1001. Offers traditional (M Acc); valuation (M Acc). *Accreditation:* AACSB. *Students:* 44 full-time (18 women); includes 8 minority (2 Black or African American, non-Hispanic/Latino; 4 Asian, non-Hispanic/Latino; 2 Hispanic/Latino). Average age 23. 246 applicants, 24% accepted, 44 enrolled. In 2013, 38 master's awarded. *Entrance requirements:* For master's, GMAT or GRE. Additional exam requirements/recommendations for international students: Required—TOEFL, IELTS. *Application deadline:* For fall admission, 9/3 priority date for domestic students, 10/10 for international students; for winter admission, 1/20 for domestic students, 1/9 for international students; for spring admission, 3/17 for domestic students. Application fee: $50. Electronic applications accepted. *Expenses:* Contact institution. *Financial support:* In 2013–14, 37 students received support. Scholarships/grants and tuition waivers available. Financial award application deadline: 6/1; financial award applicants required to submit FAFSA. *Unit head:* Lindsay Donald, Director, MAcc Programs, 615-322-2215, E-mail: linday.donald@owen.vanderbilt.edu. *Application contact:* Emily Cochran, Associate Director, MAcc Programs, 615-322-6509, Fax: 615-343-1175, E-mail: emily.cochran@owen.vanderbilt.edu.
Website: http://www.owen.vanderbilt.edu.

Vanderbilt University, Vanderbilt Graduate School of Management, Vanderbilt MBA Program (Full-time), Nashville, TN 37203. Offers accounting (MBA); finance (MBA); general management (MBA); human and organizational performance (MBA); marketing (MBA); operations (MBA); strategy (MBA); MBA/JD; MBA/M Div; MBA/MD; MBA/MTS; MBA/PhD. *Accreditation:* AACSB. *Students:* 341 full-time (119 women); includes 42 minority (20 Black or African American, non-Hispanic/Latino; 12 Asian, non-Hispanic/Latino; 5 Hispanic/Latino; 5 Two or more races, non-Hispanic/Latino), 73 international.

Average age 28. 1,059 applicants, 38% accepted, 166 enrolled. In 2013, 161 master's awarded. *Entrance requirements:* For master's, GMAT (preferred) or GRE, 2 years of work experience (recommended). Additional exam requirements/recommendations for international students: Required—TOEFL. *Application deadline:* For fall admission, 10/1 priority date for domestic and international students; for winter admission, 1/6 priority date for domestic and international students; for spring admission, 3/3 priority date for domestic students, 3/5 priority date for international students; for summer admission, 4/5 for domestic students, 5/5 for international students. Applications are processed on a rolling basis. Application fee: $75 ($175 for international students). Electronic applications accepted. *Financial support:* In 2013–14, 237 students received support. Scholarships/grants and tuition waivers (full and partial) available. Financial award application deadline: 5/15; financial award applicants required to submit FAFSA. *Unit head:* Nancy Lea Hyer, Associate Dean, 615-322-2530, Fax: 615-343-7110, E-mail: nancy.lea.hyer@owen.vanderbilt.edu. *Application contact:* Dinah Webster, Administrative Assistant, 615-322-6469, Fax: 615-343-1175, E-mail: mba@owen.vanderbilt.edu.
Website: http://www.owen.vanderbilt.edu.

Villanova University, Villanova School of Business, Master of Accountancy Program, Villanova, PA 19085. Offers MAC. *Accreditation:* AACSB. *Faculty:* 101 full-time (33 women), 36 part-time/adjunct (3 women). *Students:* 47 part-time (15 women); includes 8 minority (1 Black or African American, non-Hispanic/Latino; 5 Asian, non-Hispanic/Latino; 2 Two or more races, non-Hispanic/Latino). Average age 24. 98 applicants, 43% accepted, 34 enrolled. In 2013, 26 master's awarded. *Degree requirements:* For master's, minimum cumulative GPA of 3.0. *Entrance requirements:* For master's, undergraduate accounting major or the following pre-requisite courses: intermediate accounting I and II, federal income tax and auditing. Additional exam requirements/recommendations for international students: Required—TOEFL (minimum score 550 paper-based; 90 iBT). *Application deadline:* For fall admission, 6/30 for domestic and international students; for winter admission, 11/15 for domestic and international students; for spring admission, 11/15 for domestic and international students; for summer admission, 3/31 for domestic and international students. Applications are processed on a rolling basis. Application fee: $50. Electronic applications accepted. *Financial support:* Scholarships/grants available. Financial award application deadline: 6/30; financial award applicants required to submit FAFSA. *Faculty research:* Business analytics; creativity, innovation and entrepreneurship; global leadership; real estate; church management; business ethics. *Unit head:* Zelon Crawford, Director of Graduate Business Programs, 610-519-6283, Fax: 610-519-6273, E-mail: zelon.crawford@villanova.edu. *Application contact:* Meredith L. Lockyer, Manager of Recruiting, 610-519-7016, Fax: 610-519-6273, E-mail: meredith.lockyer@villanova.edu.
Website: http://www1.villanova.edu/villanova/business/graduate/specializedprograms/mac.html.

Virginia Commonwealth University, Graduate School, School of Business, Program in Accounting, Richmond, VA 23284-9005. Offers M Acc, MBA, PhD. *Accreditation:* AACSB. *Degree requirements:* For doctorate, thesis/dissertation. *Entrance requirements:* For master's, GMAT; for doctorate, GMAT, relevant work experience. Additional exam requirements/recommendations for international students: Required—TOEFL (minimum score 600 paper-based; 100 iBT). Electronic applications accepted.

Virginia International University, School of Business, Fairfax, VA 22030. Offers accounting (MBA); executive management (Graduate Certificate); global logistics (MBA); health care management (MBA); human resources management (MBA); international business management (MBA); international finance (MBA); marketing management (MBA). Part-time programs available. *Entrance requirements:* For master's and Graduate Certificate, bachelor's degree. Additional exam requirements/recommendations for international students: Required—TOEFL (minimum score 550 paper-based; 80 iBT), IELTS (minimum score 6). Electronic applications accepted.

Virginia Polytechnic Institute and State University, Graduate School, Pamplin College of Business, Blacksburg, VA 24061. Offers accounting and information systems (MACIS); business (PhD); business administration (MBA, MS); hospitality and tourism management (MS, PhD). *Faculty:* 118 full-time (35 women), 1 part-time/adjunct (0 women). *Students:* 333 full-time (149 women), 129 part-time (47 women); includes 75 minority (14 Black or African American, non-Hispanic/Latino; 42 Asian, non-Hispanic/Latino; 12 Hispanic/Latino; 7 Two or more races, non-Hispanic/Latino), 115 international. Average age 30. 520 applicants, 38% accepted, 157 enrolled. In 2013, 199 master's, 12 doctorates awarded. *Degree requirements:* For master's, comprehensive exam (for some programs), thesis (for some programs); for doctorate, comprehensive exam (for some programs), thesis/dissertation (for some programs). *Entrance requirements:* For master's and doctorate, GRE/GMAT (may vary by department). Additional exam requirements/recommendations for international students: Required—TOEFL (minimum score 550 paper-based). *Application deadline:* For fall admission, 8/1 for domestic students, 4/1 for international students; for spring admission, 1/1 for domestic students, 9/1 for international students. Applications are processed on a rolling basis. Application fee: $75. Electronic applications accepted. *Expenses:* Tuition, state resident: full-time $11,185; part-time $621.50 per credit hour. Tuition, nonresident: full-time $22,146; part-time $1230.25 per credit hour. *Required fees:* $2442; $449.25 per semester. Tuition and fees vary according to course load, campus/location and program. *Financial support:* In 2013–14, 5 fellowships with full tuition reimbursements (averaging $19,435 per year), 61 teaching assistantships with full tuition reimbursements (averaging $15,805 per year) were awarded. Financial award application deadline: 3/1; financial award applicants required to submit FAFSA. *Total annual research expenditures:* $2.5 million. *Unit head:* Dr. Robert T. Sumichrast, Dean, 540-231-6601, Fax: 540-231-4487, E-mail: busdean@vt.edu. *Application contact:* Martha Hilton, Executive Assistant to the Dean, 540-231-9647, Fax: 540-231-4487, E-mail: cartermc@vt.edu.
Website: http://www.pamplin.vt.edu/.

Wagner College, Division of Graduate Studies, Department of Business Administration, Program in Accounting, Staten Island, NY 10301-4495. Offers MS. Part-time programs available. *Faculty:* 3 full-time (all women), 1 part-time/adjunct (0 women). *Students:* 9 full-time (7 women), 4 part-time (3 women), 1 international. Average age 23. 14 applicants, 93% accepted, 8 enrolled. In 2013, 20 master's awarded. *Degree requirements:* For master's, thesis. *Entrance requirements:* For master's, bachelor's degree in accounting or business with a concentration in accounting. Additional exam requirements/recommendations for international students: Required—TOEFL (minimum score 550 paper-based; 79 iBT). *Application deadline:* For fall admission, 5/1 priority date for domestic students, 3/1 priority date for international students; for spring admission, 12/1 priority date for domestic students, 10/1 for international students. Applications are processed on a rolling basis. Application fee: $50. *Expenses: Tuition:* Full-time $17,496; part-time $972 per credit. Tuition and fees vary according to course load. *Financial support:* In 2013–14, 11 students received support. Career-related internships or fieldwork, unspecified assistantships, and alumni fellowship grants available. Financial award applicants required to submit FAFSA. *Unit head:* Prof. Margaret Horan, Director, 718-390-3437, E-mail: phoran@wagner.edu. *Application contact:* Patricia Clancy, Administrative Assistant, Admissions, 718-420-4464, Fax: 718-390-3105, E-mail: patricia.clancy@wagner.edu.

Wake Forest University, Graduate School of Arts and Sciences, Department of Accountancy, Winston-Salem, NC 27109. Offers MSA. *Accreditation:* AACSB. *Entrance requirements:* For master's, GMAT. Additional exam requirements/recommendations for international students: Required—TOEFL. Electronic applications accepted.

Wake Forest University, School of Business, MS in Accountancy Program, Winston-Salem, NC 27106. Offers assurance services (MSA); tax consulting (MSA); transaction services (MSA). *Faculty:* 77 full-time (21 women), 32 part-time/adjunct (8 women). *Students:* 210 full-time (82 women); includes 32 minority (11 Black or African American, non-Hispanic/Latino; 1 American Indian or Alaska Native, non-Hispanic/Latino; 4 Asian, non-Hispanic/Latino; 15 Hispanic/Latino; 1 Native Hawaiian or other Pacific Islander, non-Hispanic/Latino), 40 international. Average age 25. In 2013, 115 master's awarded. *Degree requirements:* For master's, 30 credit hours. *Entrance requirements:* For master's, GMAT, letters of recommendation, official transcripts, current resume or curriculum vitae. Additional exam requirements/recommendations for international students: Required—TOEFL (minimum score 600 paper-based; 100 iBT), PTE. *Application deadline:* For fall admission, 6/1 for domestic and international students. Applications are processed on a rolling basis. Application fee: $100. Electronic applications accepted. *Financial support:* In 2013–14, 135 students received support. Career-related internships or fieldwork and scholarships/grants available. Financial award application deadline: 2/15; financial award applicants required to submit FAFSA. *Faculty research:* The influence of personal relationships on business decision-making and management of change; drivers of perceived value and consumer behavior; impact of accounting on auditing, financial, managerial, systems and taxation stakeholders; corporate governance and executive compensation; impact of operations strategies on competitiveness. *Unit head:* Jack Wilkerson, Senior Associate Dean of Accounting Programs, 336-758-5422, Fax: 336-758-5830, E-mail: busadmissions@wfu.edu. *Application contact:* Tamara Paquee, Administrative Assistant, 336-758-5422, Fax: 336-758-5830, E-mail: busadmissions@wfu.edu.
Website: http://www.business.wfu.edu/.

Walden University, Graduate Programs, School of Management, Minneapolis, MN 55401. Offers accounting (MBA, MS, DBA), including accounting for the professional (MS); accounting with CPA emphasis (MS), self-designed (MS, PhD); accounting and management (MS), including accountants as strategic managers, self-designed (MS, PhD); advanced project management (Graduate Certificate); applied project management (Graduate Certificate); bridge to business administration (Post-Doctoral Certificate); bridge to management (Post-Doctoral Certificate); business administration (EMBA); business management (Graduate Certificate); communication (MS, Graduate Certificate); corporate finance (MBA); entrepreneurship (DBA); entrepreneurship and small business (MBA); finance (DBA); global supply chain management (DBA); healthcare management (MBA, DBA); human resource management (MBA, MS, Graduate Certificate), including functional human resource management (MS), general program (MS), integrating functional and strategic human resource management (MS), organizational strategy (MS); human resources management (DBA); information systems management (DBA); international business (MBA, DBA); leadership (MBA, MS, DBA), including general program (MS), human resources leadership (MS), leader development (MS), self-designed (MS, PhD); management (MS, PhD), including accounting (PhD), engineering management (PhD), finance (PhD), general program (MS), healthcare management (MS), human resource management (MS), human resources management (PhD), information systems management (PhD), leadership (MS), leadership and organizational change (PhD), marketing (MS), operations research (PhD), project management (MS), self-designed, strategy and operations (MS); marketing (MBA, DBA); project management (MBA, MS, DBA); self-designed (MBA, DBA); social impact management (DBA); technology entrepreneurship (DBA). Part-time and evening/weekend programs available. Postbaccalaureate distance learning degree programs offered (minimal on-campus study). *Faculty:* 24 full-time (9 women), 337 part-time/adjunct (127 women). *Students:* 4,369 full-time (2,379 women), 2,181 part-time (1,304 women); includes 3,669 minority (3,020 Black or African American, non-Hispanic/Latino; 22 American Indian or Alaska Native, non-Hispanic/Latino; 156 Asian, non-Hispanic/Latino; 331 Hispanic/Latino; 11 Native Hawaiian or other Pacific Islander, non-Hispanic/Latino; 129 Two or more races, non-Hispanic/Latino), 107 international. Average age 41. 2,030 applicants, 94% accepted, 1436 enrolled. In 2013, 757 master's, 128 doctorates, 32 other advanced degrees awarded. *Degree requirements:* For master's, residency (for some programs); for doctorate, thesis/dissertation (for some programs), residency. *Entrance requirements:* For master's, bachelor's degree or higher; minimum GPA of 2.5; official transcripts; goal statement (for some programs); access to computer and Internet; for doctorate, master's degree or higher; three years of related professional or academic experience (preferred); minimum GPA of 3.0; goal statement and current resume (select programs); official transcripts; access to computer and Internet; for other advanced degree, relevant work experience; access to computer and Internet. Additional exam requirements/recommendations for international students: Required—TOEFL (minimum score 550 paper-based; 79 iBT), IELTS (minimum score 6.5), Michigan English Language Assessment Battery (minimum score 82), or PTE. *Application deadline:* Applications are processed on a rolling basis. Application fee: $0. Electronic applications accepted. *Expenses: Tuition:* Full-time $11,813.55; part-time $500 per credit. *Required fees:* $618.76. *Financial support:* Fellowships, Federal Work-Study, scholarships/grants, unspecified assistantships, and family tuition reduction, active duty/veteran tuition reduction, group tuition reduction, interest-free payment plans, employee tuition reduction available. Support available to part-time students. Financial award applicants required to submit FAFSA. *Unit head:* Dr. Ward Ulmer, III, Associate Dean, 800-925-3368. *Application contact:* Jennifer Hall, Vice President of Enrollment Management, 866-4-WALDEN, E-mail: info@waldenu.edu.
Website: http://www.waldenu.edu/programs/colleges-schools/management.

Walsh College of Accountancy and Business Administration, Graduate Programs, Program in Accountancy, Troy, MI 48007-7006. Offers MSPA. Part-time and evening/weekend programs available. *Degree requirements:* For master's, thesis optional. *Entrance requirements:* For master's, minimum GPA of 2.75, previous course work in business. Additional exam requirements/recommendations for international students: Required—TOEFL. Electronic applications accepted.

Washburn University, School of Business, Topeka, KS 66621. Offers accountancy (M Acc). *Accreditation:* AACSB. Part-time and evening/weekend programs available. *Entrance requirements:* For master's, GMAT, minimum GPA of 2.75. Additional exam requirements/recommendations for international students: Required—TOEFL (minimum score 550 paper-based; 80 iBT); Recommended—IELTS (minimum score 6.5). *Application deadline:* For fall admission, 7/1 priority date for domestic and international students; for spring admission, 11/15 priority date for domestic and international students. Applications are processed on a rolling basis. Application fee: $40 ($70 for international students). Electronic applications accepted. *Expenses:* Tuition, state resident: full-time $5850; part-time $325 per credit hour. Tuition, nonresident: full-time $11,916; part-time $662 per credit hour. *Required fees:* $86; $43 per semester. Tuition and fees vary according to program. *Financial support:* Available to part-time students. Application deadline: 2/15; applicants required to submit FAFSA. *Faculty research:* Ethics in information technology, forecasting for shareholder value creation, model for measuring expected losses from litigation contingencies, business vs. family commitment in family businesses, calculated intangible value and brand recognition.

Accounting

Unit head: Dr. David L. Sollars, Dean, 785-670-2045, Fax: 785-670-1063, E-mail: david.sollars@washburn.edu. Application contact: Dr. Robert J. Boncella, MBA Director, 785-670-1308, Fax: 785-670-1063, E-mail: bob.boncella@washburn.edu.

Washington State University, Graduate School, College of Business, Department of Accounting, Pullman, WA 99164-4729. Offers accounting (PhD); accounting and assurance or audit (M Acc); accounting and taxation (M Acc). Accreditation: AACSB. Part-time programs available. Degree requirements: For master's, comprehensive exam, thesis or alternative; for doctorate, comprehensive exam, thesis/dissertation, oral and written exams. Entrance requirements: For master's, GMAT (minimum score of 500), minimum GPA of 3.0, statement of purpose; for doctorate, GMAT (minimum score of 600), resume; statement of purpose identifying area of interest, experiences, and intended research focus; minimum GPA 3.25. Additional exam requirements/recommendations for international students: Required—TOEFL (minimum score 580 paper-based; 93 iBT), IELTS (minimum score 7.5). Electronic applications accepted. Faculty research: Ethics, taxation, auditing, finance.

Washington State University Vancouver, Graduate Programs, Program in Accounting, Vancouver, WA 98686-9600. Offers taxation (M Acc).

Washington University in St. Louis, Olin Business School, Program in Accounting, St. Louis, MO 63130-4899. Offers MS. Part-time programs available. Faculty: 82 full-time (18 women), 38 part-time/adjunct (8 women). Students: 97 full-time (77 women); includes 14 minority (2 Black or African American, non-Hispanic/Latino; 10 Asian, non-Hispanic/Latino; 2 Hispanic/Latino), 68 international. Average age 24. 494 applicants, 23% accepted, 53 enrolled. In 2013, 54 master's awarded. Entrance requirements: For master's, GMAT or GRE. Additional exam requirements/recommendations for international students: Required—TOEFL, IELTS. Application deadline: For fall admission, 10/1 for domestic and international students; for winter admission, 10/15 for domestic students, 11/15 for international students; for spring admission, 4/1 for domestic and international students. Application fee: $100. Electronic applications accepted. Financial support: Applicants required to submit FAFSA. Unit head: Greg Hutchings, Associate Dean/Director of Specialized Master's Programs, 314-935-6380, Fax: 314-935-4464, E-mail: hutchings@wustl.edu. Application contact: Nikki Lemley, Associate Director, Specialized Master's Programs Admissions, 314-935-8469, Fax: 314-935-4464, E-mail: nlemley@wustl.edu.

Wayland Baptist University, Graduate Programs, Programs in Business Administration/Management, Plainview, TX 79072-6998. Offers accounting (MBA); general business (MBA); health care administration (MAM, MBA); healthcare administration (MBA); human resource management (MAM, MBA); international management (MBA); management (MBA); management information systems (MBA); organization management (MAM); project management (MBA). Part-time and evening/weekend programs available. Postbaccalaureate distance learning degree programs offered (no on-campus study). Faculty: 30 full-time (5 women), 38 part-time/adjunct (9 women). Students: 44 full-time (20 women), 702 part-time (315 women); includes 348 minority (149 Black or African American, non-Hispanic/Latino; 4 American Indian or Alaska Native, non-Hispanic/Latino; 23 Asian, non-Hispanic/Latino; 139 Hispanic/Latino; 9 Native Hawaiian or other Pacific Islander, non-Hispanic/Latino; 24 Two or more races, non-Hispanic/Latino), 5 international. Average age 40. 147 applicants, 94% accepted, 73 enrolled. In 2013, 296 master's awarded. Degree requirements: For master's, capstone course. Entrance requirements: For master's, GMAT, GRE or MAT. Additional exam requirements/recommendations for international students: Required—TOEFL (minimum score 500 paper-based; 61 iBT). Application deadline: Applications are processed on a rolling basis. Application fee: $50. Electronic applications accepted. Expenses: Tuition: Full-time $8190; part-time $455 per credit hour. Required fees: $970; $455 per credit hour. $485 per semester. Financial support: Federal Work-Study, institutionally sponsored loans, and scholarships/grants available. Support available to part-time students. Financial award application deadline: 5/1; financial award applicants required to submit FAFSA. Unit head: Dr. Otto Schacht, Chairman, 806-291-1020, Fax: 806-291-1957, E-mail: schachto@wbu.edu. Application contact: Amanda Stanton, Graduate Studies, 806-291-3423, Fax: 806-291-1950, E-mail: stanton@wbu.edu.

Wayne State University, School of Business Administration, Detroit, MI 48202. Offers accounting (MS, Postbaccalaureate Certificate); business (Graduate Certificate); business administration (MBA, PhD); taxation (MST); JD/MBA. Accreditation: AACSB. Part-time and evening/weekend programs available. Postbaccalaureate distance learning degree programs offered (no on-campus study). Students: 143 full-time (67 women), 539 part-time (211 women); includes 179 minority (80 Black or African American, non-Hispanic/Latino; 2 American Indian or Alaska Native, non-Hispanic/Latino; 67 Asian, non-Hispanic/Latino; 22 Hispanic/Latino; 8 Two or more races, non-Hispanic/Latino), 71 international. Average age 31. 648 applicants, 26% accepted, 107 enrolled. In 2013, 281 master's, 3 doctorates, 1 other advanced degree awarded. Degree requirements: For doctorate, thesis/dissertation. Entrance requirements: For master's, GMAT; for doctorate, GMAT (minimum score of 600), minimum undergraduate GPA of 3.0, 3.5 upper-division or graduate; three letters of recommendation; brief essay. Additional exam requirements/recommendations for international students: Required—TOEFL (minimum score 550 paper-based; 79 iBT), Michigan English Language Assessment Battery (minimum score 85); Recommended—IELTS (minimum score 6.5), TWE (minimum score 5.5). Application deadline: For fall admission, 6/1 priority date for domestic students, 5/1 priority date for international students; for winter admission, 10/1 priority date for domestic students, 9/1 priority date for international students; for spring admission, 2/1 priority date for domestic students, 1/1 priority date for international students. Applications are processed on a rolling basis. Application fee: $0. Electronic applications accepted. Expenses: Contact institution. Financial support: In 2013–14, 105 students received support, including 2 fellowships with tuition reimbursements available (averaging $18,000 per year), 2 teaching assistantships with tuition reimbursements available (averaging $9,000 per year); scholarships/grants, health care benefits, and unspecified assistantships also available. Support available to part-time students. Financial award application deadline: 3/31; financial award applicants required to submit FAFSA. Faculty research: Executive compensation and stock performance, consumer reactions to pricing strategies, communication across the automotive supply chain, performance of firms in sub-Saharan Africa, implementation issues with ERP software. Unit head: Margaret Williams, Interim Dean, School of Business Administration, 313-577-4501, Fax: 313-577-4557, E-mail: margaret.l.williams@wayne.edu. Application contact: Amber Conway, Director, Graduate Programs Office, 313-577-4511, Fax: 313-577-9442, E-mail: ck8173@wayne.edu.
Website: http://business.wayne.edu/.

Webber International University, Graduate School of Business, Babson Park, FL 33827-0096. Offers accounting (MBA); management (MBA); security management (MBA); sports management (MBA). Part-time and evening/weekend programs available. Degree requirements: For master's, thesis or alternative. Entrance requirements: For master's, previous course work in financial and managerial accounting. Additional exam requirements/recommendations for international students: Required—TOEFL. Faculty research: Finance strategy, market research, investments, intranet.

Weber State University, John B. Goddard School of Business and Economics, School of Accountancy, Ogden, UT 84408-1001. Offers accounting (M Acc); taxation (M Tax). Accreditation: AACSB. Part-time programs available. Faculty: 8 full-time (0 women), 2 part-time/adjunct (0 women). Students: 31 full-time (15 women), 30 part-time (13 women); includes 4 minority (1 Black or African American, non-Hispanic/Latino; 2 Asian, non-Hispanic/Latino; 1 Hispanic/Latino), 3 international. Average age 31. 64 applicants, 61% accepted, 28 enrolled. In 2013, 44 master's awarded. Entrance requirements: For master's, GMAT. Additional exam requirements/recommendations for international students: Required—TOEFL (minimum score 80 iBT). Application deadline: For fall admission, 8/1 priority date for domestic students; for spring admission, 12/1 priority date for domestic students; for summer admission, 4/1 for domestic students. Applications are processed on a rolling basis. Application fee: $60 ($90 for international students). Expenses: Tuition, state resident: full-time $7118; part-time $253 per credit hour. Tuition, nonresident: full-time $12,480; part-time $634 per credit hour. Required fees: $34.33; $34.33 per credit hour. $257 per semester. Full-time tuition and fees vary according to course load. Financial support: In 2013–14, 11 students received support. Federal Work-Study, institutionally sponsored loans, scholarships/grants, and tuition waivers (full and partial) available. Financial award application deadline: 4/1; financial award applicants required to submit FAFSA. Faculty research: Taxation, financial accounting, auditing, managerial accounting, accounting education. Unit head: Dr. Matt Mouritsen, Chair, 801-626-8151, Fax: 801-626-7423, E-mail: mmouritsen@weber.edu. Application contact: Dr. Larry A. Deppe, Graduate Coordinator, 801-626-7838, Fax: 801-626-7423, E-mail: ldeppe1@weber.edu.
Website: http://www.weber.edu/SBE/masters_of_accounting.html.

Webster University, George Herbert Walker School of Business and Technology, Department of Business, St. Louis, MO 63119-3194. Offers business and organizational security management (MBA); decision support systems (MBA); environmental management (MBA); finance (MBA, MS); forensic accounting (MS); gerontology (MBA); human resources development (MBA); human resources management (MBA); information technology management (MBA); international business (MA, MBA); international relations (MBA); management and leadership (MBA); marketing (MBA); media communications (MBA); procurement and acquisitions management (MBA); Web services (MBA). Accreditation: ACBSP. Part-time and evening/weekend programs available. Postbaccalaureate distance learning degree programs offered (no on-campus study). Degree requirements: For master's, comprehensive exam (for some programs), thesis (for some programs). Entrance requirements: Additional exam requirements/recommendations for international students: Required—TOEFL. Expenses: Tuition: Full-time $11,610; part-time $645 per credit hour. Tuition and fees vary according to campus/location and program.

Western Carolina University, Graduate School, College of Business, Program in Accountancy, Cullowhee, NC 28723. Offers M Ac. Part-time and evening/weekend programs available. Entrance requirements: For master's, GMAT, appropriate undergraduate degree, 3 letters of recommendation. Additional exam requirements/recommendations for international students: Required—TOEFL (minimum score 550 paper-based; 79 iBT).

Western Connecticut State University, Division of Graduate Studies, Ancell School of Business, Program in Business Administration, Danbury, CT 06810-6885. Offers accounting (MBA); business administration (MBA). Part-time programs available. Degree requirements: For master's, comprehensive exam, completion of program within 8 years. Entrance requirements: For master's, GMAT. Additional exam requirements/recommendations for international students: Recommended—TOEFL (minimum score 550 paper-based; 79 iBT), IELTS (minimum score 6). Faculty research: Global strategic marketing planning, project management and team coordination; email, discussion boards that act as blogs and videoconferencing.

Western Illinois University, School of Graduate Studies, College of Business and Technology, Department of Accountancy, Macomb, IL 61455-1390. Offers M Acct. Accreditation: AACSB. Part-time programs available. Students: 20 full-time (13 women), 2 part-time (both women); includes 3 minority (1 Black or African American, non-Hispanic/Latino; 1 Asian, non-Hispanic/Latino; 1 Hispanic/Latino), 1 international. Average age 24. 12 applicants, 67% accepted. In 2013, 10 master's awarded. Degree requirements: For master's, thesis or alternative. Entrance requirements: For master's, GMAT. Additional exam requirements/recommendations for international students: Required—TOEFL (minimum score 550 paper-based; 80 iBT). Application deadline: Applications are processed on a rolling basis. Application fee: $30. Electronic applications accepted. Financial support: In 2013–14, 10 students received support, including 1 research assistantship with full tuition reimbursement available (averaging $7,544 per year), 9 teaching assistantships with full tuition reimbursements available (averaging $8,688 per year). Financial award applicants required to submit FAFSA. Unit head: Dr. Gregg Woodruff, Chairperson, 309-298-1152. Application contact: Dr. Nancy Parsons, Assistant Director of Graduate Studies, 309-298-1806, Fax: 309-298-2345, E-mail: grad-office@wiu.edu.
Website: http://wiu.edu/accountancy.

Western Michigan University, Graduate College, Haworth College of Business, Department of Accountancy, Kalamazoo, MI 49008. Offers MSA. Accreditation: AACSB. Entrance requirements: For master's, GMAT.

Western New England University, College of Business, Program in Accounting, Springfield, MA 01119. Offers MSA, JD/MSA. Part-time and evening/weekend programs available. Faculty: 10 full-time (2 women). Students: 33 part-time (14 women); includes 2 minority (1 Asian, non-Hispanic/Latino; 1 Hispanic/Latino). Average age 29. 160 applicants. In 2013, 23 master's awarded. Entrance requirements: For master's, GMAT, official transcript, two letters of recommendation, essay, resume. Additional exam requirements/recommendations for international students: Required—TOEFL. Application deadline: Applications are processed on a rolling basis. Application fee: $30. Electronic applications accepted. Tuition and fees vary according to program. Financial support: Application deadline: 4/15; applicants required to submit FAFSA. Unit head: Dr. William Bosworth, Chair, Accounting and Finance, 413-782-1738, E-mail: william.bosworth@wne.edu. Application contact: Matthew Fox, Director of Recruiting and Marketing for Adult Learners, 413-782-1517, Fax: 413-782-1779, E-mail: study@wne.edu.
Website: http://www1.wne.edu/adultlearning/index.cfm?selection-doc.6279.

Westminster College, The Bill and Vieve Gore School of Business, Salt Lake City, UT 84105-3697. Offers accountancy (M Acc); business administration (MBA, Certificate); technology management (MBATM). Accreditation: ACBSP. Part-time and evening/weekend programs available. Postbaccalaureate distance learning degree programs offered (minimal on-campus study). Faculty: 24 full-time (5 women), 12 part-time/adjunct (6 women). Students: 245 full-time (83 women), 156 part-time (57 women); includes 60 minority (3 Black or African American, non-Hispanic/Latino; 3 American Indian or Alaska Native, non-Hispanic/Latino; 21 Asian, non-Hispanic/Latino; 28 Hispanic/Latino; 1 Native Hawaiian or other Pacific Islander, non-Hispanic/Latino; 4 Two or more races, non-Hispanic/Latino), 17 international. Average age 33. 256 applicants, 59% accepted, 77 enrolled. In 2013, 201 master's, 46 other advanced degrees awarded. Degree requirements: For master's, international trip, minimum grade of C in all classes. Entrance requirements: For master's, GMAT, 2 professional recommendations, employer letter of support, personal resume, essay, official transcripts. Additional exam requirements/recommendations for international students: Required—TOEFL (minimum score 600 paper-based; 100 iBT), IELTS (minimum score 7.5). Application deadline: For

fall admission, 8/31 for domestic students, 5/31 for international students; for spring admission, 1/1 for domestic students; for summer admission, 5/1 for domestic students. Applications are processed on a rolling basis. Application fee: $50. Electronic applications accepted. *Expenses:* Contact institution. *Financial support:* In 2013–14, 46 students received support. Career-related internships or fieldwork, unspecified assistantships, and tuition reimbursements, tuition remission available. Support available to part-time students. Financial award applicants required to submit FAFSA. *Faculty research:* Innovation and entrepreneurship, business strategy and change, financial analysis and capital budgeting, leadership development, knowledge management. *Unit head:* Dr. Jin Wang, Dean, Gore School of Business, 801-832-2600, Fax: 801-832-3106, E-mail: jwang@westminstercollege.edu. *Application contact:* Dr. John Baworowsky, Vice President of Enrollment Management, 801-832-2200, Fax: 801-832-3101, E-mail: admission@westminstercollege.edu.
Website: http://www.westminstercollege.edu/mba/.

West Texas A&M University, College of Business, Department of Accounting, Economics, and Finance, Program in Professional Accounting, Canyon, TX 79016-0001. Offers MPA. Integrated accounting program that allows students to enter program as undergraduates after bachelor's degree in business administration is earned. Part-time programs available. Postbaccalaureate distance learning degree programs offered (minimal on-campus study). *Entrance requirements:* For master's, GMAT. Additional exam requirements/recommendations for international students: Required—TOEFL (minimum score 550 paper-based). Electronic applications accepted.

West Virginia University, College of Business and Economics, Division of Accounting, Morgantown, WV 26506. Offers MPA. *Accreditation:* AACSB. Part-time and evening/weekend programs available. *Entrance requirements:* For master's, GMAT (minimum 50th percentile), BS in accounting or equivalent, minimum GPA of 3.0. Additional exam requirements/recommendations for international students: Required—TOEFL. Electronic applications accepted. *Faculty research:* Financial reporting, government/not-for-profit accounting, information systems/technology, forensic accounting, internal control.

Wheeling Jesuit University, Department of Business, Wheeling, WV 26003-6295. Offers accounting (MSA); business administration (MBA). *Accreditation:* ACBSP. Part-time and evening/weekend programs available. *Entrance requirements:* For master's, minimum undergraduate GPA of 2.8. Additional exam requirements/recommendations for international students: Required—TOEFL (minimum score 600 paper-based; 100 iBT). Electronic applications accepted. *Faculty research:* Forensic economics, consumer behavior, economic development, capitalism, leadership.

Wichita State University, Graduate School, W. Frank Barton School of Business, School of Accountancy, Wichita, KS 67260. Offers M Acc. *Accreditation:* AACSB. Part-time and evening/weekend programs available. *Unit head:* Dr. Paul D. Harrison, Director, 316-978-3215, Fax: 316-978-3660, E-mail: paul.harrison@wichita.edu. *Application contact:* Jordan Oleson, Admissions Coordinator, 316-978-3095, Fax: 316-978-3253, E-mail: jordan.oleson@wichita.edu.
Website: http://www.wichita.edu/.

Widener University, School of Business Administration, Program in Accounting Information Systems, Chester, PA 19013-5792. Offers MS. Part-time and evening/weekend programs available. *Faculty:* 6 full-time (2 women), 3 part-time/adjunct (0 women). *Students:* 9 applicants, 100% accepted. In 2013, 5 master's awarded. *Entrance requirements:* For master's, Certified Management Accountant Exam, Certified Public Accountant Exam, or GMAT, minimum GPA of 2.5. *Application deadline:* For fall admission, 8/1 priority date for domestic students; for spring admission, 12/1 for domestic students. Applications are processed on a rolling basis. Application fee: $25 ($300 for international students). Electronic applications accepted. *Expenses: Tuition:* Full-time $30,000; part-time $950 per credit. *Financial support:* Application deadline: 5/1. *Unit head:* Frank C. Lordi, Head, 610-499-4308, E-mail: frank.c.lordi@widener.edu. *Application contact:* Ann Seltzer, Graduate Enrollment Administrator, 610-499-4305, E-mail: apseltzer@widener.edu.

Wilfrid Laurier University, Faculty of Graduate and Postdoctoral Studies, School of Business and Economics, Department of Business, Waterloo, ON N2L 3C5, Canada. Offers accounting (PhD); finance (M Fin); financial economics (PhD); marketing (PhD); operations and supply chain management (PhD); organizational behavior and human resource management (M Sc); organizational behaviour and human resource management (PhD); supply chain management (M Sc); technology management (EMTM). *Accreditation:* AACSB. Part-time and evening/weekend programs available. *Degree requirements:* For master's, thesis optional; for doctorate, comprehensive exam, thesis/dissertation. *Entrance requirements:* For master's, GMAT, 4-year honors degree with minimum B+ average; for doctorate, GMAT, master's degree, minimum B+ average. Additional exam requirements/recommendations for international students: Required—TOEFL (minimum score 89 iBT). Electronic applications accepted. *Faculty research:* Financial economics, management and organizational behavior, operations and supply chain management.

Wilkes University, College of Graduate and Professional Studies, Jay S. Sidhu School of Business and Leadership, Wilkes-Barre, PA 18766-0002. Offers accounting (MBA); entrepreneurship (MBA); finance (MBA); health care administration (MBA); human resource management (MBA); international business (MBA); marketing (MBA); operations management (MBA); organizational leadership and development (MBA). *Accreditation:* ACBSP. Part-time and evening/weekend programs available. *Students:* 41 full-time (20 women), 119 part-time (48 women); includes 20 minority (5 Black or African American, non-Hispanic/Latino; 3 Asian, non-Hispanic/Latino; 7 Hispanic/Latino; 5 Two or more races, non-Hispanic/Latino), 7 international. Average age 31. In 2013, 55 master's awarded. *Entrance requirements:* For master's, GMAT. Additional exam requirements/recommendations for international students: Required—TOEFL (minimum score 550 paper-based; 79 iBT). *Application deadline:* Applications are processed on a rolling basis. Application fee: $45 ($65 for international students). Electronic applications accepted. *Expenses:* Contact institution. *Financial support:* Federal Work-Study and unspecified assistantships available. Financial award application deadline: 3/1; financial award applicants required to submit FAFSA. *Unit head:* Dr. Jeffrey Alves, Dean, 570-408-4702, Fax: 570-408-7846, E-mail: jeffrey.alves@wilkes.edu. *Application contact:* Joanne Thomas, Interim Director of Graduate Enrollment, 570-408-4234, Fax: 570-408-7846, E-mail: joanne.thomas1@wilkes.edu.
Website: http://www.wilkes.edu/pages/457.asp.

Wilmington University, College of Business, New Castle, DE 19720-6491. Offers accounting (MBA, MS); business administration (MBA, DBA); environmental stewardship (MBA); finance (MBA); health care administration (MBA, MSM); homeland security (MBA, MSM); human resource management (MSM); management information systems (MBA, MSN); marketing (MSM); marketing management (MBA); military leadership (MSM); organizational leadership (MBA, MSM); public administration (MSM). Part-time and evening/weekend programs available. *Entrance requirements:* Additional exam requirements/recommendations for international students: Required—TOEFL (minimum score 500 paper-based). Electronic applications accepted.

Worcester State University, Graduate Studies, Program in Management, Worcester, MA 01602-2597. Offers accounting (MS); managerial leadership (MS). Part-time and evening/weekend programs available. *Faculty:* 4 full-time (3 women), 3 part-time/adjunct (0 women). *Students:* 6 full-time (4 women), 29 part-time (15 women); includes 12 minority (4 Black or African American, non-Hispanic/Latino; 3 Asian, non-Hispanic/Latino; 4 Hispanic/Latino; 1 Two or more races, non-Hispanic/Latino), 4 international. Average age 31. 30 applicants, 60% accepted, 7 enrolled. In 2013, 6 master's awarded. *Degree requirements:* For master's, comprehensive exam (for some programs), thesis optional. *Entrance requirements:* For master's, GMAT. Additional exam requirements/recommendations for international students: Required—TOEFL (minimum score 500 paper-based; 61 iBT). *Application deadline:* For fall admission, 6/15 for domestic and international students; for spring admission, 4/1 for domestic and international students. Applications are processed on a rolling basis. Application fee: $40. Electronic applications accepted. *Expenses: Tuition, area resident:* Part-time $150 per credit. Tuition, state resident: part-time $150 per credit. Tuition, nonresident: part-time $150 per credit. *Required fees:* $114.50 per credit. *Financial support:* In 2013–14, 2 students received support, including 2 research assistantships with full tuition reimbursements available (averaging $4,800 per year); career-related internships or fieldwork, scholarships/grants, and unspecified assistantships also available. Financial award application deadline: 3/1; financial award applicants required to submit FAFSA. *Unit head:* Dr. Rodney Oudan, Coordinator, 508-929-8751, Fax: 508-929-8048, E-mail: roudan@worcester.edu. *Application contact:* Sara Grady, Assistant Dean of Continuing Education, 508-929-8787, Fax: 508-929-8100, E-mail: sara.grady@worcester.edu.

Wright State University, School of Graduate Studies, Raj Soin College of Business, Department of Accountancy, Accountancy Program, Dayton, OH 45435. Offers M Acc.

Yale University, Yale School of Management and Graduate School of Arts and Sciences, Doctoral Program in Management, New Haven, CT 06520. Offers accounting (PhD); financial economics (PhD); marketing (PhD); organizations and management (PhD). *Accreditation:* AACSB. *Degree requirements:* For doctorate, comprehensive exam, thesis/dissertation. *Entrance requirements:* For doctorate, GMAT or GRE General Test. Additional exam requirements/recommendations for international students: Required—TOEFL or IELTS. Electronic applications accepted. *Expenses:* Contact institution. *Faculty research:* Pricing of options and futures, term structure of interest rates, use of accounting numbers in debt contracts, product differentiation, e-commerce and marketing, behavioral finance.

Yeshiva University, Sy Syms School of Business, New York, NY 10016. Offers accounting (MS). Part-time programs available. *Entrance requirements:* For master's, minimum GPA of 3.5 or GMAT.

York University, Faculty of Graduate Studies, Schulich School of Business, Toronto, ON M3J 1P3, Canada. Offers accounting (M Acc); administration (PhD); business (MBA); business analytics (MBA); finance (MF); international business (IMBA); MBA/JD; MBA/MA; MBA/MFA. Part-time and evening/weekend programs available. *Students:* 683 full-time (255 women), 407 part-time (125 women). Average age 29. 1,498 applicants, 30% accepted, 409 enrolled. In 2013, 587 master's, 96 doctorates awarded. *Median time to degree:* Of those who began their doctoral program in fall 2005, 55% received their degree in 8 years or less. *Degree requirements:* For master's, advanced proficiency in a second language, work term (IMBA); for doctorate, comprehensive exam, thesis/dissertation. *Entrance requirements:* For master's, GMAT or GRE, minimum GPA of 3.0 (3.3 for MF, MBA in business analytics, and IMBA); for doctorate, GMAT or GRE, minimum GPA of 3.3. Additional exam requirements/recommendations for international students: Required—TOEFL (minimum score 600 paper-based; 100 iBT), IELTS (minimum score 7), York English Language Test (minimum score 1); PearsonVUE (minimum score 64). *Application deadline:* For fall admission, 4/30 for domestic students, 2/28 for international students; for winter admission, 9/1 for domestic and international students. Applications are processed on a rolling basis. Application fee: $150. Electronic applications accepted. *Financial support:* In 2013–14, 800 students received support, including fellowships (averaging $5,000 per year), research assistantships (averaging $3,000 per year), teaching assistantships (averaging $7,000 per year); career-related internships or fieldwork, scholarships/grants, and bursaries (for part-time students) also available. Financial award application deadline: 2/1. *Faculty research:* Accounting, finance, marketing, operations management and information systems, organizational studies, strategic management. *Unit head:* Dezso Horvath, Dean, 416-736-5070, E-mail: dhorvath@schulich.yorku.ca. *Application contact:* Graduate Admissions, 416-736-5060, Fax: 416-650-8174, E-mail: admissions@schulich.yorku.ca.
Website: http://www.schulich.yorku.ca.

Youngstown State University, Graduate School, Williamson College of Business Administration, Department of Accounting and Finance, Youngstown, OH 44555-0001. Offers accounting (MBA). *Accreditation:* AACSB. Part-time and evening/weekend programs available. *Degree requirements:* For master's, thesis optional. *Entrance requirements:* For master's, GMAT, minimum GPA of 2.7. Additional exam requirements/recommendations for international students: Required—TOEFL. *Faculty research:* Taxation and compliance, capital markets, accounting information systems, accounting theory, tax and government accounting.

Finance and Banking

Adelphi University, Robert B. Willumstad School of Business, MBA Program, Garden City, NY 11530-0701. Offers finance (MBA); management information systems (MBA); management/human resource management (MBA); marketing/e-commerce (MBA). *Accreditation:* AACSB. Part-time and evening/weekend programs available. *Students:* 254 full-time (129 women), 118 part-time (63 women); includes 60 minority (13 Black or African American, non-Hispanic/Latino; 18 Asian, non-Hispanic/Latino; 28 Hispanic/Latino; 1 Native Hawaiian or other Pacific Islander, non-Hispanic/Latino), 200 international. Average age 28. In 2013, 182 master's awarded. *Degree requirements:* For master's, capstone course. *Entrance requirements:* For master's, GMAT, 2 letters of recommendation. Additional exam requirements/recommendations for international

students: Required—TOEFL (minimum score 550 paper-based; 80 iBT). *Application deadline:* For fall admission, 4/1 for international students; for spring admission, 11/1 for international students. Applications are processed on a rolling basis. Application fee: $50. Electronic applications accepted. *Expenses: Tuition:* Full-time $32,530; part-time $1010 per credit. *Required fees:* $1150. Tuition and fees vary according to degree level and program. *Financial support:* Research assistantships with partial tuition reimbursements, career-related internships or fieldwork, Federal Work-Study, institutionally sponsored loans, scholarships/grants, tuition waivers (partial), and unspecified assistantships available. Financial award application deadline: 3/1; financial award applicants required to submit FAFSA. *Faculty research:* Supply chain management, distribution channels, productivity benchmark analysis, data envelopment analysis, financial portfolio analysis. *Unit head:* Dr. Rakesh Gupta, Associate Dean, 516-877-4629. *Application contact:* Christine Murphy, Director of Admissions, 516-877-3050, Fax: 516-877-3039, E-mail: graduateadmissions@adelphi.edu.
Website: http://business.adelphi.edu/degree-programs/graduate-degree-programs/m-b-a/.

See Display on page 70 and Close-Up on page 181.

The American College, Graduate Programs, Bryn Mawr, PA 19010-2105. Offers financial services (MSFS); leadership (MSM). Part-time and evening/weekend programs available. Postbaccalaureate distance learning degree programs offered (minimal on-campus study). Electronic applications accepted. *Faculty research:* Retirement counseling, social security, aging, family composition, inflation.

American College of Thessaloniki, Department of Business Administration, Pylea-Thessaloniki, Greece. Offers banking and finance (MBA); entrepreneurship (MBA, Certificate); finance (Certificate); management (MBA, Certificate); marketing (MBA, Certificate). Part-time and evening/weekend programs available. *Degree requirements:* For master's, thesis. *Entrance requirements:* For master's, bachelor's degree. Additional exam requirements/recommendations for international students: Recommended—TOEFL. Electronic applications accepted.

American InterContinental University Online, Program in Business Administration, Schaumburg, IL 60173. Offers accounting and finance (MBA); finance (MBA); healthcare management (MBA); human resource management (MBA); international business (MBA); management (MBA); marketing (MBA); operations management (MBA); organizational psychology and development (MBA); project management (MBA). *Accreditation:* ACBSP. Evening/weekend programs available. Postbaccalaureate distance learning degree programs offered (no on-campus study). *Entrance requirements:* Additional exam requirements/recommendations for international students: Required—TOEFL (minimum score 550 paper-based). Electronic applications accepted.

American InterContinental University South Florida, Program in International Business, Weston, FL 33326. Offers accounting and finance (MBA); human resource management (MBA); management (MBA); marketing (MBA). Part-time and evening/weekend programs available. Postbaccalaureate distance learning degree programs offered. Electronic applications accepted.

American Public University System, AMU/APU Graduate Programs, Charles Town, WV 25414. Offers accounting (MBA, MS); criminal justice (MA), including business administration, emergency and disaster management, general (MA, MS); educational leadership (M Ed); emergency and disaster management (MA); entrepreneurship (MBA); environmental policy and management (MS), including environmental planning, environmental sustainability, fish and wildlife management, general (MA, MS), global environmental management; finance (MBA); general (MBA); global business management (MBA); history (MA), including American history, ancient and classical history, European history, global history, public history; homeland security (MA), including business administration, counter-terrorism studies, criminal justice, cyber, emergency management and public health, intelligence studies, transportation security; homeland security resource allocation (MBA); humanities (MA); information technology (MS), including digital forensics, enterprise software development, information assurance and security, IT project management; information technology management (MBA); intelligence studies (MA), including criminal intelligence, cyber, general (MA, MS), homeland security, intelligence analysis, intelligence collection, intelligence management, intelligence operations, terrorism studies; international relations and conflict resolution (MA), including comparative and security issues, conflict resolution, international and transnational security issues, peacekeeping; legal studies (MA); management (MA), including defense management, general (MA, MS), human resource management, organizational leadership, public administration; marketing (MBA); military history (MA), including American military history, American Revolution, civil war, war since 1945, World War II; military studies (MA), including joint warfare, strategic leadership; national security studies (MA), including general (MA, MS), homeland security, regional security studies, security and intelligence analysis, terrorism studies; nonprofit management (MBA); political science (MA), including American politics and government, comparative government and development, general (MA, MS), international relations, public policy; psychology (MA), including general (MA, MS), maritime engineering management, reverse logistics management; public administration (MPA), including disaster management, environmental policy, health policy, human resources, national security, organizational management, security management; public health (MPH); reverse logistics management (MA); school counseling (M Ed); security management (MA); space studies (MS), including aerospace science, general (MA, MS), planetary science; sports and health sciences (MS); teaching (M Ed), including curriculum and instruction for elementary teachers, elementary reading, English language learners, instructional leadership, online learning, special education; transportation and logistics management (MA), including general (MA, MS), maritime engineering management, reverse logistics management. Programs offered via distance learning only. Part-time and evening/weekend programs available. Postbaccalaureate distance learning degree programs offered (no on-campus study). *Faculty:* 432 full-time (242 women), 1,722 part-time/adjunct (829 women). *Students:* 511 full-time (241 women), 10,947 part-time (4,294 women); includes 3,760 minority (2,058 Black or African American, non-Hispanic/Latino; 88 American Indian or Alaska Native, non-Hispanic/Latino; 293 Asian, non-Hispanic/Latino; 876 Hispanic/Latino; 91 Native Hawaiian or other Pacific Islander, non-Hispanic/Latino; 354 Two or more races, non-Hispanic/Latino), 134 international. Average age 36. In 2013, 3,323 master's awarded. *Degree requirements:* For master's, comprehensive exam or practicum. *Entrance requirements:* For master's, official transcript showing earned bachelor's degree from institution accredited by recognized accrediting body. Additional exam requirements/recommendations for international students: Required—TOEFL (minimum score 550 paper-based), IELTS (minimum score 6.5). *Application deadline:* Applications are processed on a rolling basis. Application fee: $0. Electronic applications accepted. *Expenses: Tuition:* Part-time $325 per semester hour. *Financial support:* Applicants required to submit FAFSA. *Faculty research:* Military history, criminal justice, management performance, national security. *Unit head:* Dr. Karan Powell, Executive Vice President and Provost, 877-468-6268, Fax: 304-724-3780. *Application contact:* Terry Grant, Vice President of Enrollment Management, 877-468-6268, Fax: 304-724-3780, E-mail: info@apus.edu.
Website: http://www.apus.edu.

American University, Kogod School of Business, Washington, DC 20016-8044. Offers accounting (MS); business administration (MBA); business fundamentals (Certificate); entrepreneurship (Certificate); finance (MS); forensic accounting (Certificate); management (MS); marketing (MS); real estate (MS, Certificate); sustainability management (MS); tax (Certificate); taxation (MS). *Accreditation:* AACSB. Part-time and evening/weekend programs available. Postbaccalaureate distance learning degree programs offered. *Faculty:* 75 full-time (24 women), 36 part-time/adjunct (7 women). *Students:* 194 full-time (95 women), 370 part-time (184 women); includes 168 minority (69 Black or African American, non-Hispanic/Latino; 60 Asian, non-Hispanic/Latino; 33 Hispanic/Latino; 2 Native Hawaiian or other Pacific Islander, non-Hispanic/Latino; 4 Two or more races, non-Hispanic/Latino), 108 international. Average age 30. 940 applicants, 46% accepted, 193 enrolled. In 2013, 221 master's, 4 other advanced degrees awarded. *Entrance requirements:* For master's, GMAT, resume, personal statement, interview, 2 letters of recommendation, transcripts. Additional exam requirements/recommendations for international students: Required—TOEFL (minimum score 100 iBT). *Application deadline:* Applications are processed on a rolling basis. Application fee: $100. Electronic applications accepted. *Expenses:* Contact institution. *Financial support:* Fellowships, career-related internships or fieldwork, Federal Work-Study, institutionally sponsored loans, and tuition waivers (partial) available. Support available to part-time students. Financial award application deadline: 2/1. *Unit head:* Dr. Michael Ginzberg, Dean, 202-885-1985, E-mail: ginzberg@american.edu. *Application contact:* Jason Kennedy, Associate Director of Graduate Admissions, 202-885-1968, E-mail: jkennedy@american.edu.
Website: http://www.kogod.american.edu/.

American University, School of Public Affairs, Washington, DC 20016-8022. Offers justice, law and criminology (MS, PhD); leadership for organizational change (Certificate); nonprofit management (Certificate); organization development (MS); political communication (MA); political science (MA, PhD); public administration (MPA, PhD); public administration: key executive leadership (MPA); public financial management (Certificate); public management (Certificate); public policy (MPP); public policy analysis (Certificate); terrorism and homeland security policy (MS); women, policy and political leadership (Certificate). Part-time and evening/weekend programs available. *Faculty:* 82 full-time (36 women), 56 part-time/adjunct (16 women). *Students:* 364 full-time (220 women), 238 part-time (146 women); includes 158 minority (76 Black or African American, non-Hispanic/Latino; 7 American Indian or Alaska Native, non-Hispanic/Latino; 26 Asian, non-Hispanic/Latino; 40 Hispanic/Latino; 2 Native Hawaiian or other Pacific Islander, non-Hispanic/Latino; 7 Two or more races, non-Hispanic/Latino), 39 international. Average age 28. In 2013, 239 master's, 10 doctorates, 7 other advanced degrees awarded. Terminal master's awarded for partial completion of doctoral program. *Degree requirements:* For master's, comprehensive exam; for doctorate, comprehensive exam, thesis/dissertation. *Entrance requirements:* For master's, GRE, statement of purpose; 2 recommendations, resume, transcript; for doctorate, GRE, 3 recommendations, statement of purpose, resume, writing sample, transcript. Additional exam requirements/recommendations for international students: Required—TOEFL (minimum score 100 iBT). *Application deadline:* For fall admission, 2/1 for domestic and international students. Application fee: $55. Electronic applications accepted. *Expenses: Tuition:* Full-time $25,920; part-time $1482 per credit hour. *Required fees:* $430. Tuition and fees vary according to course load and program. *Financial support:* Fellowships with tuition reimbursements, research assistantships with tuition reimbursements, teaching assistantships with tuition reimbursements, career-related internships or fieldwork, Federal Work-Study, institutionally sponsored loans, scholarships/grants, and tuition waivers (full and partial) available. Financial award application deadline: 2/1. *Unit head:* Dr. Barbara Romzek, Dean, 202-885-2940, E-mail: bromzek@american.edu. *Application contact:* Brenda Manley, Director of Graduate Admissions, 202-885-6202, E-mail: bmanley@american.edu.
Website: http://www.american.edu/spa/.

The American University in Dubai, Graduate Programs, Dubai, United Arab Emirates. Offers construction management (MS); education (M Ed); finance (MBA); generalist (MBA); marketing (MBA). Part-time and evening/weekend programs available. *Degree requirements:* For master's, thesis optional. *Entrance requirements:* For master's, GMAT (for MBA); GRE (for M Ed and MS), minimum undergraduate GPA of 3.0, official transcripts, two reference forms, curriculum vitae/resume, statement of career objectives, work experience. Additional exam requirements/recommendations for international students: Required—TOEFL (minimum score 550 paper-based; 79 iBT). Electronic applications accepted.

American University of Beirut, Graduate Programs, Faculty of Arts and Sciences, Beirut, Lebanon. Offers anthropology (MA); Arab and Middle Eastern history (PhD); Arabic language and literature (MA, PhD); archaeology (MA); biology (MS); cell and molecular biology (PhD); chemistry (MS); clinical psychology (MA); computational sciences (MS); computer science (MS); economics (MA); education (MA); English language (MA); English literature (MA); environmental policy planning (MS); financial economics (MA); geology (MS); history (MA); mathematics (MA, MS); media studies (MA); Middle Eastern studies (MA); philosophy (MA); physics (MS); political studies (MA); psychology (MA); public administration (MA); sociology (MA); statistics (MA, MS); theoretical physics (PhD); transnational American studies (MA). Part-time programs available. *Faculty:* 88 full-time (22 women). *Students:* Average age 25. In 2013, 112 master's, 87 doctorates awarded. *Degree requirements:* For master's, one foreign language, comprehensive exam, thesis (for some programs); for doctorate, one foreign language, comprehensive exam, thesis/dissertation. *Entrance requirements:* For master's, GRE, letter of recommendation; for doctorate, GRE, letters of recommendation. Additional exam requirements/recommendations for international students: Required—TOEFL (minimum score 600 paper-based; 97 iBT), IELTS (minimum score 7). *Application deadline:* For fall admission, 4/30 for domestic students, 4/18 for international students; for spring admission, 11/1 for domestic and international students. Application fee: $50. *Expenses: Tuition:* Full-time $14,724; part-time $818 per credit. *Required fees:* $692; $692. Tuition and fees vary according to course load and program. *Financial support:* Research assistantships, career-related internships or fieldwork, institutionally sponsored loans, scholarships/grants, health care benefits, and unspecified assistantships available. Financial award application deadline: 2/4; financial award applicants required to submit FAFSA. *Faculty research:* Modern Middle East history; Near Eastern archaeology; Islamic history; European history; software engineering; scientific computing; data mining; the applications of cooperative learning in language teaching and teacher education; world/comparative literature; rhetoric and composition; creative writing; public management; public policy and international affairs; hydrogeology; mineralogy, petrology, and geochemistry; tectonics and structural geology; cell and molecular biology; ecology. *Unit head:* Dr. Patrick McGreevy, Dean, 961-1374374 Ext. 3800, Fax: 961-1744461, E-mail: pm07@aub.edu.lb. *Application contact:* Dr. Salim Kanaan, Director, Admissions Office, 961-1-350000 Ext. 2590, Fax: 96-1-1750775, E-mail: sk00@aub.edu.lb.
Website: http://www.aub.edu.lb/fas/.

American University of Beirut, Graduate Programs, Suliman S. Olayan School of Business, Master's in Finance Program, Beirut, Lebanon. Offers M Fin. Part-time programs available. *Faculty:* 4 full-time (0 women), 1 (woman) part-time/adjunct. *Students:* 42 full-time (25 women), 5 part-time (4 women). Average age 23. 111

applicants, 73% accepted, 42 enrolled. In 2013, 17 master's awarded. *Entrance requirements:* For master's, minimum undergraduate average of 80. Additional exam requirements/recommendations for international students: Required—TOEFL (minimum score 600 paper-based; 97 iBT), IELTS (minimum score 7). *Application deadline:* For fall admission, 4/1 for domestic and international students. Application fee: $50. Electronic applications accepted. *Expenses: Tuition:* Full-time $14,724; part-time $818 per credit. *Required fees:* $692; $692. Tuition and fees vary according to course load and program. *Financial support:* In 2013–14, 11 students received support, including 13 teaching assistantships with partial tuition reimbursements available (averaging $16,000 per year); unspecified assistantships also available. Support available to part-time students. Financial award application deadline: 2/20. *Faculty research:* Risk management, capital acquisition, money management, corporate finance, executive and director compensation. *Unit head:* Dr. Wassim Dbouk, Master's in Finance Coordinator, 961-1374374 Ext. 3762, E-mail: wd08@aub.edu.lb. *Application contact:* Dr. Rabih Talhouk, Graduate Council Chair, 961-1-350000 Ext. 3895, E-mail: rtalhouk@aub.edu.lb. Website: http://www.aub.edu.lb/osb/osb_home/program/MFIN/Pages/index.aspx.

Andrews University, School of Graduate Studies, School of Business, Graduate Programs in Business, Berrien Springs, MI 49104. Offers MBA, MSA. *Faculty:* 10 full-time (4 women). *Students:* 21 full-time (16 women), 39 part-time (22 women); includes 25 minority (10 Black or African American, non-Hispanic/Latino; 4 Asian, non-Hispanic/Latino; 10 Hispanic/Latino; 1 Native Hawaiian or other Pacific Islander, non-Hispanic/Latino), 20 international. Average age 32. 90 applicants, 44% accepted, 24 enrolled. In 2013, 13 master's awarded. *Entrance requirements:* For master's, GMAT. Additional exam requirements/recommendations for international students: Required—TOEFL (minimum score 550 paper-based). Application fee: $40. *Unit head:* Dr. Leonard K. Gashugi, Chair, 769-471-3429, E-mail: gashugi@andrews.edu. *Application contact:* Monica Wringer, Supervisor of Graduate Admission, 800-253-2874, Fax: 269-471-6321, E-mail: graduate@andrews.edu.

Argosy University, Atlanta, College of Business, Atlanta, GA 30328. Offers accounting (DBA); corporate compliance (MBA); customized professional concentration (MBA, DBA); finance (MBA); healthcare administration (MBA); information systems (DBA); information systems management (MBA); international business (MBA, DBA); management (MBA, MSM, DBA); marketing (MBA, DBA).

Argosy University, Chicago, College of Business, Chicago, IL 60601. Offers accounting (DBA); customized professional concentration (MBA, DBA); finance (MBA); fraud examination (MBA); global business sustainability (DBA); healthcare administration (MBA); information systems (DBA); information systems management (MBA); international business (MBA, DBA); management (MBA, MSM, DBA); marketing (MBA, DBA); organizational leadership (Ed D); public administration (MBA); sustainable management (MBA). Postbaccalaureate distance learning degree programs offered (minimal on-campus study).

Argosy University, Dallas, College of Business, Farmers Branch, TX 75244. Offers accounting (DBA, AGC); corporate compliance (MBA, Graduate Certificate); customized professional concentration (MBA); finance (MBA, Graduate Certificate); fraud examination (MBA, Graduate Certificate); global business sustainability (DBA, AGC); healthcare administration (Graduate Certificate); healthcare management (MBA); information systems (MBA, DBA, AGC); information systems management (Graduate Certificate); international business (MBA, DBA, AGC, Graduate Certificate); management (MBA, DBA, AGC, Graduate Certificate); marketing (MBA, DBA, AGC, Graduate Certificate); public administration (MBA, Graduate Certificate); sustainable management (MBA, Graduate Certificate).

Argosy University, Denver, College of Business, Denver, CO 80231. Offers accounting (DBA); corporate compliance (MBA); customized professional concentration (MBA, DBA); finance (MBA); fraud examination (MBA); global business sustainability (DBA); healthcare administration (MBA); information systems (DBA); information systems management (MBA); international business (MBA, DBA); management (MBA, MSM, DBA); marketing (MBA, DBA); organizational leadership (Ed D); public administration (MBA); sustainable management (MBA).

Argosy University, Hawai`i, College of Business, Honolulu, HI 96813. Offers accounting (DBA); corporate compliance (MBA); customized professional concentration (MBA, DBA); finance (MBA, Certificate); fraud examination (MBA); global business sustainability (DBA); healthcare administration (MBA, Certificate); information systems (DBA); information systems management (MBA, Certificate); international business (MBA, DBA, Certificate); management (MBA, MSM, DBA); marketing (MBA, DBA, Certificate); organizational leadership (Ed D); public administration (MBA); sustainable management (MBA).

Argosy University, Inland Empire, College of Business, Ontario, CA 91761. Offers accounting (DBA); corporate compliance (MBA); customized professional concentration (MBA, DBA); finance (MBA); fraud examination (MBA); global business sustainability (DBA); healthcare administration (MBA); information systems (DBA); information systems management (MBA); international business (MBA, DBA); management (MBA, MSM, DBA); marketing (MBA, DBA); organizational leadership (Ed D); public administration (MBA); sustainable management (MBA).

Argosy University, Los Angeles, College of Business, Santa Monica, CA 90045. Offers accounting (DBA); corporate compliance (MBA); customized professional concentration (MBA, DBA); finance (MBA); fraud examination (MBA); global business sustainability (DBA); healthcare administration (MBA); information systems (DBA); information systems management (MBA); international business (MBA, DBA); management (MBA, MSM, DBA); marketing (MBA, DBA); organizational leadership (Ed D); public administration (MBA); sustainable management (MBA).

Argosy University, Nashville, College of Business, Nashville, TN 37214. Offers accounting (DBA); customized professional concentration (MBA, DBA); finance (MBA); healthcare administration (MBA); information systems (MBA, DBA); international business (MBA, DBA); management (MBA, MSM, DBA); marketing (MBA, DBA).

Argosy University, Orange County, College of Business, Orange, CA 92868. Offers accounting (DBA, Adv C); corporate compliance (MBA); customized professional concentration (MBA, DBA); finance (MBA, Certificate); fraud examination (MBA); global business sustainability (DBA); healthcare administration (MBA, Certificate); information systems (DBA, Adv C, Certificate); information systems management (MBA); international business (MBA, DBA, Adv C, Certificate); management (MBA, MSM, DBA, Adv C); marketing (MBA, DBA, Adv C, Certificate); organizational leadership (Ed D); public administration (MBA, Certificate); sustainable management (MBA).

Argosy University, Phoenix, College of Business, Phoenix, AZ 85021. Offers accounting (DBA); corporate compliance (MBA); customized professional concentration (MBA, DBA); finance (MBA); fraud examination (MBA); global business sustainability (DBA); healthcare administration (MBA); information systems (DBA); information systems management (MBA); international business (MBA, DBA); management (MBA, DBA); marketing (MBA, DBA); public administration (MBA); sustainable management (MBA).

Argosy University, Salt Lake City, College of Business, Draper, UT 84020. Offers accounting (DBA); corporate compliance (MBA); customized professional concentration (MBA, DBA); finance (MBA); fraud examination (MBA); global business sustainability (DBA); healthcare administration (MBA); information systems (DBA); information systems management (MBA); international business (MBA, DBA); management (MBA, DBA); marketing (MBA, DBA); public administration (MBA); sustainable management (MBA).

Argosy University, San Diego, College of Business, San Diego, CA 92108. Offers accounting (DBA); corporate compliance (MBA); customized professional concentration (MBA, DBA); finance (MBA); fraud examination (MBA); global business sustainability (DBA); information systems (DBA); information systems management (MBA); international business (MBA, DBA); management (MBA, MSM, DBA); marketing (MBA, DBA); organizational leadership (Ed D); public administration (MBA).

Argosy University, San Francisco Bay Area, College of Business, Alameda, CA 94501. Offers accounting (DBA); corporate compliance (MBA); customized professional concentration (MBA, DBA); finance (MBA); fraud examination (MBA); global business sustainability (DBA); healthcare administration (MBA); information systems (DBA); information systems management (MBA); international business (MBA, DBA); management (MBA, MSM, DBA); marketing (MBA, DBA); organizational leadership (Ed D); public administration (MBA); sustainable management (MBA).

Argosy University, Sarasota, College of Business, Sarasota, FL 34235. Offers accounting (DBA, Adv C); corporate compliance (MBA, DBA, Certificate); customized professional concentration (MBA, DBA); finance (MBA, Certificate); fraud examination (MBA, Certificate); global business sustainability (DBA, Adv C); healthcare administration (MBA, Certificate); information systems (DBA, Adv C, Certificate); information systems management (MBA); international business (MBA, DBA, Adv C, Certificate); management (MBA, MSM, DBA, Adv C, Certificate); marketing (MBA, DBA, Adv C, Certificate); organizational leadership (Ed D); public administration (MBA, Certificate); sustainable management (MBA, Certificate).

Argosy University, Schaumburg, College of Business, Schaumburg, IL 60173-5403. Offers accounting (DBA, Adv C); customized professional concentration (MBA, DBA); finance (MBA, Certificate); fraud examination (MBA); global business sustainability (DBA); healthcare administration (MBA, Certificate); information systems (DBA, Adv C, Certificate); information systems management (MBA); international business (MBA, DBA, Adv C, Certificate); management (MBA, MSM, DBA, Adv C, Certificate); marketing (MBA, DBA, Adv C, Certificate); organizational leadership (Ed D); public administration (MBA); sustainable management (MBA).

Argosy University, Seattle, College of Business, Seattle, WA 98121. Offers accounting (DBA); corporate compliance (MBA); customized professional concentration (MBA, DBA); finance (MBA); fraud examination (MBA); global business sustainability (DBA); healthcare administration (MBA); information systems (DBA); information systems management (MBA); international business (MBA, DBA); management (MBA, MSM, DBA); marketing (MBA, DBA); organizational leadership (Ed D); public administration (MBA); sustainable management (MBA).

Argosy University, Tampa, College of Business, Tampa, FL 33607. Offers accounting (DBA); corporate compliance (MBA); customized professional concentration (MBA, DBA); finance (MBA); fraud examination (MBA); global business sustainability (DBA); healthcare administration (MBA); information systems (DBA); information systems management (MBA); international business (MBA, DBA); management (MBA, MSM, DBA); marketing (MBA, DBA); organizational leadership (Ed D); public administration (MBA); sustainable management (MBA).

Argosy University, Twin Cities, College of Business, Eagan, MN 55121. Offers accounting (DBA); customized professional concentration (MBA, DBA); finance (MBA); fraud examination (MBA); global business sustainability (DBA); healthcare administration (MBA); information systems (DBA); information systems management (MBA); international business (MBA, DBA); management (MBA, MSM, DBA); marketing (MBA, DBA); organizational leadership (Ed D); public administration (MBA); sustainable management (MBA).

Argosy University, Washington DC, College of Business, Arlington, VA 22209. Offers accounting (DBA); customized professional concentration (MBA, DBA); finance (MBA); fraud examination (MBA); global business sustainability (DBA); healthcare administration (MBA); information systems (DBA); information systems management (MBA); international business (MBA, DBA, Certificate); management (MBA, MSM, DBA); marketing (MBA, DBA, Certificate); organizational leadership (Ed D); public administration (MBA); sustainable management (MBA).

Arizona State University at the Tempe campus, W. P. Carey School of Business, Program in Business Administration, Tempe, AZ 85287-4906. Offers accountancy (PhD); agribusiness (PhD); business administration (MBA); finance (PhD); financial management and markets (MBA); information management (MBA); information systems (PhD); management (PhD); marketing (PhD); strategic marketing and services leadership (MBA); supply chain financial management (MBA); supply chain management (MBA, PhD); JD/MBA; MBA/M Acc; MBA/M Arch. *Accreditation:* AACSB. Part-time and evening/weekend programs available. Postbaccalaureate distance learning degree programs offered (minimal on-campus study). Terminal master's awarded for partial completion of doctoral program. *Degree requirements:* For master's, thesis or alternative, internship, interactive Program of Study (iPOS) submitted before completing 50 percent of required credit hours; for doctorate, comprehensive exam, thesis/dissertation, interactive Program of Study (iPOS) submitted before completing 50 percent of required credit hours. *Entrance requirements:* For master's, GMAT, minimum GPA of 3.0 in last 2 years of work leading to bachelor's degree, 2 letters of recommendation, professional resume, official transcripts, 3 essays; for doctorate, GMAT or GRE, minimum GPA of 3.0 in last 2 years of work leading to bachelor's degree, 3 letters of recommendation, resume, personal statement/essay. Additional exam requirements/recommendations for international students: Required—TOEFL (minimum score 550 paper-based; 80 iBT), IELTS (minimum score 6.5). Electronic applications accepted. *Expenses:* Contact institution.

Aspen University, Program in Business Administration, Denver, CO 80246-1930. Offers business administration (MBA); finance (MBA); information management (MBA); project management (MBA, Certificate). Part-time and evening/weekend programs available. Postbaccalaureate distance learning degree programs offered (no on-campus study). *Entrance requirements:* Additional exam requirements/recommendations for international students: Required—TOEFL (minimum score 530 paper-based). Electronic applications accepted.

Assumption College, Graduate Studies, Department of Business Studies, Worcester, MA 01609-1296. Offers accounting (MBA); business administration (CAGS); finance/economics (MBA); frontline management (CGS); general business (MBA); human resources (MBA); international business (MBA); management (MBA); marketing (MBA); nonprofit leadership (MBA, CGS); organizational communication (CGS). Part-time and evening/weekend programs available. *Faculty:* 5 full-time (0 women), 20 part-time/adjunct (7 women). *Students:* 20 full-time (7 women), 130 part-time (68 women); includes 20 minority (8 Black or African American, non-Hispanic/Latino; 2 Asian, non-Hispanic/Latino; 8 Hispanic/Latino; 1 Native Hawaiian or other Pacific Islander, non-Hispanic/Latino; 1 Two or more races, non-Hispanic/Latino), 2 international. Average

age 31. 63 applicants, 62% accepted, 22 enrolled. In 2013, 58 master's, 1 other advanced degree awarded. *Degree requirements:* For master's, thesis, capstone. *Entrance requirements:* For master's and other advanced degree, 3 letters of recommendation, resume, essay. Additional exam requirements/recommendations for international students: Required—TOEFL (minimum score 540 paper-based; 76 iBT), IELTS (minimum score 6). *Application deadline:* For fall admission, 10/1 for domestic and international students; for winter admission, 2/1 for domestic and international students; for spring admission, 4/1 for domestic and international students. Applications are processed on a rolling basis. Application fee: $30. Electronic applications accepted. *Expenses: Tuition:* Full-time $10,098; part-time $561 per credit. *Required fees:* $20 per term. Full-time tuition and fees vary according to course load and program. *Financial support:* In 2013–14, 15 students received support. Tuition waivers (full and partial), unspecified assistantships, and institutional discounts available. Financial award application deadline: 5/1; financial award applicants required to submit FAFSA. *Faculty research:* Workplace diversity, dynamics of team interaction, utilization of leased employees, experiential learning project on due diligence market for prostheses. *Unit head:* Dr. J. Bart Morrison, Director, 508-767-7458, Fax: 508-767-7252, E-mail: jmorrison@assumption.edu. *Application contact:* Laura Lawrence, Graduate Programs Operations Manager, 508-767-7387, Fax: 508-767-7030, E-mail: graduate@assumption.edu.
Website: http://graduate.assumption.edu/mba/assumption-mba.

Auburn University, Graduate School, College of Business, Department of Finance, Auburn University, AL 36849. Offers MS. *Faculty:* 14 full-time (3 women), 4 part-time/adjunct (3 women). *Students:* 16 full-time (5 women), 1 (woman) part-time; includes 1 minority (Black or African American, non-Hispanic/Latino), 6 international. Average age 25. 163 applicants, 13% accepted, 5 enrolled. In 2013, 15 master's awarded. Application fee: $50 ($60 for international students). *Expenses:* Tuition, state resident: full-time $8262; part-time $459 per credit hour. Tuition, nonresident: full-time $24,786; part-time $1377 per credit hour. Tuition and fees vary according to degree level and program. *Financial support:* Applicants required to submit FAFSA. *Unit head:* Dr. Larry L. Colquitt, Jr., Chair, 334-844-3000. *Application contact:* Dr. George Flowers, Dean of the Graduate School, 334-844-2125.

Avila University, School of Business, Kansas City, MO 64145-1698. Offers accounting (MBA); finance (MBA); health care administration (MBA); international business (MBA); management (MBA); management information systems (MBA); marketing (MBA). Part-time and evening/weekend programs available. *Faculty:* 9 full-time (4 women), 12 part-time/adjunct (3 women). *Students:* 66 full-time (32 women), 46 part-time (27 women); includes 34 minority (22 Black or African American, non-Hispanic/Latino; 1 American Indian or Alaska Native, non-Hispanic/Latino; 4 Asian, non-Hispanic/Latino; 7 Hispanic/Latino), 27 international. Average age 32. 30 applicants, 80% accepted, 24 enrolled. In 2013, 61 master's awarded. *Degree requirements:* For master's, comprehensive exam, capstone course. *Entrance requirements:* For master's, GMAT (minimum score 420), minimum GPA of 3.0, interview. Additional exam requirements/recommendations for international students: Required—TOEFL (minimum score 550 paper-based). *Application deadline:* For fall admission, 7/30 priority date for domestic and international students; for winter admission, 11/30 priority date for domestic and international students; for spring admission, 2/28 priority date for domestic and international students; for summer admission, 6/1 priority date for domestic and international students. Applications are processed on a rolling basis. Application fee: $0. Electronic applications accepted. *Expenses:* Contact institution. *Financial support:* In 2013–14, 11 students received support. Career-related internships or fieldwork and scholarships/grants available. Support available to part-time students. Financial award applicants required to submit FAFSA. *Faculty research:* Leadership characteristics, financial hedging, group dynamics. *Unit head:* Dr. Richard Woodall, Dean, 816-501-3720, Fax: 816-501-2463, E-mail: richard.woodall@avila.edu. *Application contact:* Sarah Belanus, MBA Admissions Director, 816-501-3601, Fax: 816-501-2463, E-mail: sarah.belanus@avila.edu.
Website: http://www.avila.edu/mba.

Azusa Pacific University, School of Business and Management, Azusa, CA 91702-7000. Offers business administration (MBA); diversity for strategic advantage (MA); entrepreneurship (MBA); finance (MBA); human and organizational development (MA); human resources and organizational development (MBA); human resources management (MA); international business (MBA); marketing (MBA); non-profit management (MA); organizational development and change (MA); performance improvement (MA); public administration (MA); strategic management (MBA). Part-time and evening/weekend programs available. *Degree requirements:* For master's, thesis (for some programs), final project. *Entrance requirements:* For master's, GMAT, minimum GPA of 3.0. Additional exam requirements/recommendations for international students: Required—TOEFL (minimum score 600 paper-based). *Expenses:* Contact institution. *Faculty research:* Gender issues, financial risk, leadership and ethics, marketing strategy.

Baker College Center for Graduate Studies - Online, Graduate Programs, Flint, MI 48507-9843. Offers accounting (MBA); business administration (DBA); finance (MBA); general business (MBA); health care management (MBA); human resources management (MBA); information management (MBA); leadership studies (MBA); management information systems (MSIS); marketing (MBA). Part-time and evening/weekend programs available. Postbaccalaureate distance learning degree programs offered. *Degree requirements:* For master's, portfolio. *Entrance requirements:* For master's, 3 years of work experience, minimum undergraduate GPA of 2.5, writing sample, 3 letters of recommendation; for doctorate, MBA or acceptable related master's degree from accredited association, 5 years work experience, minimum graduate GPA of 3.25, writing sample, 3 professional references. Additional exam requirements/recommendations for international students: Required—TOEFL (minimum score 550 paper-based). Electronic applications accepted.

Barry University, Andreas School of Business, Graduate Certificate Programs, Miami Shores, FL 33161-6695. Offers finance (Certificate); health services administration (Certificate); international business (Certificate); management (Certificate); management information systems (Certificate); marketing (Certificate).

Baruch College of the City University of New York, Zicklin School of Business, Department of Economics and Finance, Program in Finance, New York, NY 10010-5585. Offers MBA, MS, PhD. PhD offered jointly with Graduate School and University Center of the City University of New York. Part-time and evening/weekend programs available. *Degree requirements:* For doctorate, comprehensive exam, thesis/dissertation. *Entrance requirements:* For master's, GMAT, 2 letters of recommendation, resume, 2 years of work experience; for doctorate, GMAT. Additional exam requirements/recommendations for international students: Required—TOEFL (minimum score 590 paper-based), TWE (minimum score 5).

Baruch College of the City University of New York, Zicklin School of Business, Zicklin Executive Programs, Executive Program in Finance, New York, NY 10010-5585. Offers MS. Evening/weekend programs available. *Entrance requirements:* For master's, personal interview, work experience. *Expenses:* Contact institution. *Faculty research:* Corporate finance, investments, options, securities, system risk.

Bayamón Central University, Graduate Programs, Program in Business Administration, Bayamón, PR 00960-1725. Offers accounting (MBA); finance (MBA); general business (MBA); management (MBA); marketing (MBA). Part-time and evening/weekend programs available. *Degree requirements:* For master's, comprehensive exam (for some programs). *Entrance requirements:* For master's, EXADEP, bachelor's degree in business or related field.

Bellevue University, Graduate School, College of Business, Bellevue, NE 68005-3098. Offers acquisition and contract management (MS); business administration (MBA); finance (MS); human capital management (PhD); management (MSM).

Benedictine University, Graduate Programs, Program in Business Administration, Lisle, IL 60532-0900. Offers accounting (MBA); entrepreneurship and managing innovation (MBA); financial management (MBA); health administration (MBA); human resource management (MBA); information systems security (MBA); international business (MBA); management consulting (MBA); management information systems (MBA); marketing management (MBA); operations management and logistics (MBA); organizational leadership (MBA). Part-time and evening/weekend programs available. Postbaccalaureate distance learning degree programs offered (minimal on-campus study). *Faculty:* 4 full-time (2 women), 24 part-time/adjunct (3 women). *Students:* 144 full-time (83 women), 599 part-time (328 women); includes 189 minority (115 Black or African American, non-Hispanic/Latino; 5 American Indian or Alaska Native, non-Hispanic/Latino; 43 Asian, non-Hispanic/Latino; 24 Hispanic/Latino; 2 Native Hawaiian or other Pacific Islander, non-Hispanic/Latino), 14 international. Average age 34. 211 applicants, 89% accepted, 155 enrolled. In 2013, 376 master's awarded. *Entrance requirements:* For master's, GMAT. Additional exam requirements/recommendations for international students: Required—TOEFL (minimum score 550 paper-based). *Application deadline:* For fall admission, 9/1 for domestic students; for winter admission, 12/1 for domestic students; for spring admission, 2/15 for domestic students. Applications are processed on a rolling basis. Application fee: $40. Electronic applications accepted. *Expenses: Tuition:* Part-time $590 per credit hour. *Financial support:* Career-related internships or fieldwork and health care benefits available. Support available to part-time students. *Faculty research:* Strategic leadership in professional organizations, sociology of professions, organizational change, social identity theory, applications to change management. *Unit head:* Dr. Sharon Borowicz, Director, 630-829-6219, E-mail: sborowicz@ben.edu. *Application contact:* Kari Gibbons, Director, Admissions, 630-829-6200, Fax: 630-829-6584, E-mail: kgibbons@ben.edu.

Bentley University, McCallum Graduate School of Business, Master's Program in Financial Planning, Waltham, MA 02452-4705. Offers MSFP. Part-time and evening/weekend programs available. Postbaccalaureate distance learning degree programs offered (no on-campus study). *Faculty:* 91 full-time (29 women), 22 part-time/adjunct (4 women). *Students:* 9 full-time (6 women), 23 part-time (7 women); includes 6 minority (2 Black or African American, non-Hispanic/Latino; 1 American Indian or Alaska Native, non-Hispanic/Latino; 1 Asian, non-Hispanic/Latino; 1 Hispanic/Latino; 1 Two or more races, non-Hispanic/Latino), 7 international. Average age 34. 26 applicants, 73% accepted, 9 enrolled. In 2013, 18 master's awarded. *Entrance requirements:* For master's, GMAT or GRE General Test. Additional exam requirements/recommendations for international students: Required—TOEFL (minimum score 600 paper-based; 100 iBT) or IELTS (minimum score 7). *Application deadline:* For fall admission, 12/1 priority date for domestic and international students; for spring admission, 10/1 priority date for domestic and international students. Application fee: $50. Electronic applications accepted. *Expenses: Tuition:* Full-time $30,400; part-time $1267 per credit. *Required fees:* $404. Tuition and fees vary according to course load and program. *Financial support:* In 2013–14, 2 students received support. Scholarships/grants and tuition waivers available. Financial award application deadline: 6/1; financial award applicants required to submit CSS PROFILE or FAFSA. *Faculty research:* International financial planning, compensation and benefits, retirement planning. *Unit head:* John Lynch, Jr., Director, 781-891-2624, E-mail: jlynch@bentley.edu. *Application contact:* Sharon Hill, Director of Graduate Admissions, 781-891-2108, Fax: 781-891-2464, E-mail: bentleygraduateadmissions@bentley.edu.
Website: http://www.bentley.edu/graduate/degree-programs/ms-programs/financial-planning.

Bentley University, McCallum Graduate School of Business, Program in Finance, Waltham, MA 02452-4705. Offers MSF. Part-time and evening/weekend programs available. *Faculty:* 91 full-time (29 women), 22 part-time/adjunct (4 women). *Students:* 107 full-time (48 women), 28 part-time (7 women); includes 10 minority (2 Black or African American, non-Hispanic/Latino; 4 Asian, non-Hispanic/Latino; 4 Hispanic/Latino), 97 international. Average age 25. 376 applicants, 55% accepted, 59 enrolled. In 2013, 90 master's awarded. *Entrance requirements:* For master's, GMAT or GRE General Test. Additional exam requirements/recommendations for international students: Required—TOEFL (minimum score 600 paper-based; 100 iBT) or IELTS (minimum score 7). *Application deadline:* For fall admission, 12/1 priority date for domestic and international students; for spring admission, 10/1 priority date for domestic students, 10/1 for international students. Application fee: $50. Electronic applications accepted. *Expenses: Tuition:* Full-time $30,400; part-time $1267 per credit. *Required fees:* $404. Tuition and fees vary according to course load and program. *Financial support:* In 2013–14, 14 students received support. Scholarships/grants and unspecified assistantships available. Financial award application deadline: 6/1; financial award applicants required to submit CSS PROFILE or FAFSA. *Faculty research:* Management of financial institutions; corporate governance and executive compensation; asset valuation; international mergers and acquisitions; hedging, risk management and derivatives. *Unit head:* Charles Hadlock, Director, 781-891-2178, E-mail: chadlock@bentley.edu. *Application contact:* Sharon Hill, Director of Graduate Admissions, 781-891-2108, Fax: 781-891-2464, E-mail: bentleygraduateadmissions@bentley.edu.
Website: http://www.bentley.edu/graduate/degree-programs/ms-programs/finance.

Binghamton University, State University of New York, Graduate School, School of Arts and Sciences, Department of Economics, Vestal, NY 13850. Offers economics (MA, PhD); economics and finance (MA, PhD). *Faculty:* 20 full-time (6 women), 6 part-time/adjunct (2 women). *Students:* 31 full-time (13 women), 22 part-time (10 women); includes 2 minority (1 Black or African American, non-Hispanic/Latino; 1 Hispanic/Latino), 43 international. Average age 28. 121 applicants, 66% accepted, 16 enrolled. In 2013, 13 master's, 13 doctorates awarded. Terminal master's awarded for partial completion of doctoral program. *Degree requirements:* For doctorate, thesis/dissertation. *Entrance requirements:* For master's and doctorate, GRE General Test. Additional exam requirements/recommendations for international students: Required—TOEFL (minimum score 550 paper-based; 80 iBT). *Application deadline:* For fall admission, 8/1 priority date for domestic and international students. Applications are processed on a rolling basis. Application fee: $75. Electronic applications accepted. *Financial support:* In 2013–14, 32 students received support, including 29 teaching assistantships with full tuition reimbursements available (averaging $15,000 per year); career-related internships or fieldwork, Federal Work-Study, institutionally sponsored loans, scholarships/grants, health care benefits, tuition waivers (full and partial), and unspecified assistantships also available. Financial award application deadline: 2/15; financial award applicants required to submit FAFSA. *Unit head:* Dr. Florenz Plassmann,

Chairperson, 607-777-4304, E-mail: fplass@binghamton.edu. *Application contact:* Kishan Zuber, Recruiting and Admissions Coordinator, 607-777-2151, Fax: 607-777-2501, E-mail: kzuber@binghamton.edu.

Boston College, Carroll School of Management, Graduate Finance Programs, Chestnut Hill, MA 02467-3800. Offers MSF, PhD, MBA/MSF. Part-time programs available. *Faculty:* 16 full-time (2 women), 2 part-time/adjunct (0 women). *Students:* 68 full-time (20 women), 30 part-time (8 women); includes 11 minority (2 Black or African American, non-Hispanic/Latino; 6 Asian, non-Hispanic/Latino; 2 Hispanic/Latino; 1 Two or more races, non-Hispanic/Latino), 50 international. Average age 27. 1,060 applicants, 11% accepted, 57 enrolled. In 2013, 74 master's, 2 doctorates awarded. *Degree requirements:* For doctorate, thesis/dissertation. *Entrance requirements:* For master's, GMAT or GRE, resume, recommendations; for doctorate, GMAT or GRE, curriculum vitae, recommendations. Additional exam requirements/recommendations for international students: Required—TOEFL (minimum score 600 paper-based, 100 iBT), IELTS (minimum score 7.5), or PTE (minimum score 68). *Application deadline:* For fall admission, 1/5 for domestic and international students; for winter admission, 2/15 for domestic and international students; for spring admission, 4/1 for domestic and international students; for summer admission, 5/1 for domestic and international students. Applications are processed on a rolling basis. Application fee: $100. Electronic applications accepted. *Financial support:* In 2013–14, 35 students received support, including 35 fellowships with full and partial tuition reimbursements available (averaging $10,050 per year), 31 research assistantships with full and partial tuition reimbursements available (averaging $20,088 per year); Federal Work-Study, scholarships/grants, and unspecified assistantships also available. Financial award application deadline: 3/1. *Faculty research:* Security and derivative markets, financial institutions, corporate finance and capital markets, market macrostructure, investments, portfolio analysis. *Unit head:* Dr. Jeffrey L. Ringuest, Associate Dean for Graduate Programs, 617-552-9100, Fax: 617-552-0541, E-mail: gsomdean@bc.edu. *Application contact:* Shelley A. Burt, Director of Graduate Enrollment, 617-552-3920, Fax: 617-552-8078, E-mail: bcmba@bc.edu.
Website: http://www.bc.edu/content/bc/schools/csom/graduate/msf.html.

Boston University, Metropolitan College, Department of Administrative Sciences, Boston, MA 02215. Offers banking and financial management (MSM); business continuity in emergency management (MSM); economics development and tourism management (MSAS); electronic commerce, systems, and technology (MSAS); financial economics (MSAS); innovation and technology (MSAS); insurance management (MSM); international market management (MSM); multinational commerce (MSAS); project management (MS). *Accreditation:* AACSB. Part-time and evening/weekend programs available. Postbaccalaureate distance learning degree programs offered (no on-campus study). *Faculty:* 15 full-time (3 women), 22 part-time/adjunct (3 women). *Students:* 177 full-time (85 women), 560 part-time (293 women); includes 89 minority (31 Black or African American, non-Hispanic/Latino; 31 Asian, non-Hispanic/Latino; 25 Hispanic/Latino; 2 Two or more races, non-Hispanic/Latino), 242 international. Average age 31. 509 applicants, 71% accepted, 222 enrolled. In 2013, 158 master's awarded. *Degree requirements:* For master's, thesis optional. *Entrance requirements:* For master's, 1 year of work experience, minimum GPA of 3.0. Additional exam requirements/recommendations for international students: Required—TOEFL (minimum score 84 iBT). *Application deadline:* Applications are processed on a rolling basis. Application fee: $80. Electronic applications accepted. *Expenses: Tuition:* Full-time $43,970; part-time $1374 per credit hour. *Required fees:* $60 per semester. Tuition and fees vary according to class time, course level and program. *Financial support:* In 2013–14, 15 students received support, including 7 research assistantships (averaging $8,400 per year); career-related internships or fieldwork, Federal Work-Study, and unspecified assistantships also available. *Faculty research:* International business, innovative process. *Unit head:* Dr. Kip Becker, Chairman, 617-353-3016, E-mail: adminsc@bu.edu. *Application contact:* Fiona Niven, Administrative Sciences Department, 617-353-3016, E-mail: adminsc@bu.edu.
Website: http://www.bu.edu/met/academic-community/departments/administrative-sciences/.

Boston University, School of Law, Boston, MA 02215. Offers American law (LL M); banking (LL M); intellectual property law (LL M); international business law (LL M); law (JD); taxation (LL M); JD/LL M; JD/MA; JD/MBA; JD/MPH; JD/MS; JD/MSW. *Accreditation:* ABA. *Faculty:* 48 full-time (19 women), 91 part-time/adjunct (26 women). *Students:* 842 full-time (462 women), 118 part-time (54 women); includes 206 minority (19 Black or African American, non-Hispanic/Latino; 1 American Indian or Alaska Native, non-Hispanic/Latino; 83 Asian, non-Hispanic/Latino; 77 Hispanic/Latino; 26 Two or more races, non-Hispanic/Latino), 157 international. Average age 27. 4,584 applicants, 35% accepted, 220 enrolled. In 2013, 183 master's, 272 doctorates awarded. *Degree requirements:* For master's, thesis (for some programs); for doctorate, thesis/dissertation, research project resulting in a paper. *Entrance requirements:* For master's, JD; for doctorate, LSAT. Additional exam requirements/recommendations for international students: Required—TOEFL (minimum score 600 paper-based; 100 iBT). *Application deadline:* For fall admission, 4/1 for domestic and international students. Applications are processed on a rolling basis. Application fee: $80. Electronic applications accepted. *Expenses: Tuition:* Full-time $43,970; part-time $1374 per credit hour. *Required fees:* $60 per semester. Tuition and fees vary according to class time, course level and program. *Financial support:* In 2013–14, 600 students received support. Career-related internships or fieldwork, Federal Work-Study, institutionally sponsored loans, and scholarships/grants available. Financial award application deadline: 3/1; financial award applicants required to submit FAFSA. *Faculty research:* Health law, tax, intellectual property, Constitutional law, corporate law, business organizations and financial law, international law, and family law. *Unit head:* Maureen A. O'Rourke, Dean, 617-353-3112, Fax: 617-353-7400, E-mail: lawdean@bu.edu. *Application contact:* Alissa Leonard, Director of Admissions and Financial Aid, 617-353-3100, Fax: 617-353-0578, E-mail: bulawadm@bu.edu.
Website: http://www.bu.edu/law/.

Brandeis University, International Business School, Master of Arts Program in International Economics and Finance, Waltham, MA 02454-9110. Offers MA. *Entrance requirements:* For master's, GRE or GMAT. Additional exam requirements/recommendations for international students: Required—TOEFL (minimum score 600 paper-based; 100 iBT), IELTS (minimum score 7). Electronic applications accepted. *Faculty research:* International economic policy analysis, U.S. economic policy analysis, real estate, municipal finance and macroeconomics.

Bridgewater State University, School of Graduate Studies, School of Business, Department of Accounting and Finance, Bridgewater, MA 02325-0001. Offers MSM. Part-time and evening/weekend programs available. *Entrance requirements:* For master's, GMAT.

Brigham Young University, Graduate Studies, Marriott School of Management, Master of Public Administration Program, Provo, UT 84602. Offers finance (MPA); human resources (MPA); local government (MPA); nonprofit management (MPA); JD/MPA. *Entrance requirements:* For master's, GRE or GMAT, minimum GPA of 3.0. Additional exam requirements/recommendations for international students: Required—TOEFL (minimum score 580 paper-based; 85 iBT), IELTS (minimum score 7). Electronic applications accepted. *Expenses: Tuition:* Full-time $6130; part-time $340 per credit hour. Tuition and fees vary according to program and student's religious affiliation. *Faculty research:* Taxes, budgeting, nonprofit, ethics, decision modeling, work balance, organizational behavior.

Brooklyn College of the City University of New York, Division of Graduate Studies, Department of Economics, Brooklyn, NY 11210-2889. Offers accounting (MS); business economics (MS), including economic analysis, global business and finance; economics (MA). Part-time and evening/weekend programs available. *Degree requirements:* For master's, comprehensive exam, thesis or alternative. *Entrance requirements:* For master's, GMAT (for MS), 2 letters of recommendation. Additional exam requirements/recommendations for international students: Required—TOEFL (minimum score 550 paper-based; 79 iBT). Electronic applications accepted. *Faculty research:* Econometrics, environmental economics, microeconomics, macroeconomics, taxation.

Bryant University, Graduate School of Business, Master of Business Administration Program, Smithfield, RI 02917. Offers general business (MBA); global finance (MBA); global supply chain management (MBA); international business (MBA). *Accreditation:* AACSB. Part-time and evening/weekend programs available. *Entrance requirements:* For master's, GMAT, transcripts, recommendation, resume, statement of objectives. Additional exam requirements/recommendations for international students: Required—TOEFL (minimum score 580 paper-based; 90 iBT). *Application deadline:* For fall admission, 7/15 for domestic and international students; for spring admission, 11/15 for domestic and international students. Applications are processed on a rolling basis. Application fee: $80. Electronic applications accepted. *Expenses: Tuition:* Full-time $26,832; part-time $1118 per credit hour. *Financial support:* In 2013–14, 11 research assistantships (averaging $6,708 per year) were awarded; unspecified assistantships also available. Financial award application deadline: 7/15; financial award applicants required to submit FAFSA. *Faculty research:* International business, information systems security, leadership, financial markets microstructure, commercial lending practice. *Unit head:* Richard S. Cheney, Director of Operations for Graduate Programs, School of Business, 401-232-6707, Fax: 401-232-6494, E-mail: rcheney@bryant.edu. *Application contact:* Linda Denzer, Assistant Director of Graduate Admission, 401-232-6529, Fax: 401-232-6494, E-mail: ldenzer@bryant.edu.

California College of the Arts, Graduate Programs, MBA in Design Strategy Program, San Francisco, CA 94107. Offers MBA. *Accreditation:* NASAD. *Faculty:* 4 full-time (1 woman), 30 part-time/adjunct (11 women). *Students:* 113 full-time (69 women); includes 32 minority (5 Black or African American, non-Hispanic/Latino; 21 Asian, non-Hispanic/Latino; 6 Hispanic/Latino), 22 international. Average age 32. 150 applicants, 79% accepted, 59 enrolled. In 2013, 53 master's awarded. *Degree requirements:* For master's, thesis. *Entrance requirements:* Additional exam requirements/recommendations for international students: Required—TOEFL (minimum score 600 paper-based; 100 iBT). *Application deadline:* For fall admission, 1/5 for domestic and international students. Application fee: $70. *Expenses: Tuition:* Full-time $60,350; part-time $1445 per credit. *Required fees:* $350; $350 $175. Full-time tuition and fees vary according to class time, course level, course load, degree level, campus/location and student level. *Financial support:* In 2013–14, 3 fellowships (averaging $20,000 per year) were awarded. *Unit head:* Nathan Shedroff, Program Chair, 800-447-1ART, E-mail: nshedroff@cca.edu. *Application contact:* Heidi Geis, Assistant Director of Graduate Admissions, 415-703-9533, Fax: 415-703-9539, E-mail: hgeis@cca.edu.

California Intercontinental University, School of Business, Diamond Bar, CA 91765. Offers banking and finance (MBA); entrepreneurship and business management (DBA); global business leadership (DBA); international management and marketing (MBA); organizational management and human resource management (MBA).

California Lutheran University, Graduate Studies, School of Management, Thousand Oaks, CA 91360-2787. Offers business (IMBA); computer science (MS); econometrics (MBA); economics (MS); entrepreneurship (MBA, Certificate); finance (MBA, Certificate); financial planning (MBA, Certificate); information systems and technology (MS); information technology management (MBA, Certificate); international business (MBA, Certificate); management and organization behavior (MBA); management and organizational behavior (Certificate); marketing (MBA, Certificate); microeconomics (MBA); nonprofit and social enterprise (MBA). Part-time and evening/weekend programs available. Postbaccalaureate distance learning degree programs offered (no on-campus study). *Faculty:* 26 full-time (9 women), 50 part-time/adjunct (11 women). *Students:* 426 full-time (175 women), 220 part-time (91 women); includes 114 minority (14 Black or African American, non-Hispanic/Latino; 30 Asian, non-Hispanic/Latino; 57 Hispanic/Latino; 13 Two or more races, non-Hispanic/Latino), 321 international. Average age 31. 495 applicants, 76% accepted, 119 enrolled. In 2013, 297 master's awarded. *Entrance requirements:* For master's, GMAT, interview, minimum GPA of 3.0. *Application deadline:* Applications are processed on a rolling basis. Application fee: $50. *Expenses:* Contact institution. *Unit head:* Dr. Gerhard Apfelthaler, Dean, 805-493-3360. *Application contact:* 805-493-3325, Fax: 805-493-3861, E-mail: clugrad@callutheran.edu.
Website: http://www.callutheran.edu/business/.

California State University, East Bay, Office of Academic Programs and Graduate Studies, College of Business and Economics, Department of Accounting and Finance, Option in Accounting/Finance, Hayward, CA 94542-3000. Offers MBA. *Degree requirements:* For master's, comprehensive exam or thesis. *Entrance requirements:* For master's, GMAT, minimum GPA of 2.75. Additional exam requirements/recommendations for international students: Required—TOEFL (minimum score 550 paper-based). Electronic applications accepted.

California State University, East Bay, Office of Academic Programs and Graduate Studies, College of Business and Economics, MBA Program, Hayward, CA 94542-3000. Offers entrepreneurship (MBA); finance (MBA); global innovators (MBA); human resources and organizational behavior (MBA); information technology management (MBA); marketing management (MBA); operations and supply chain management (MBA); strategy and international business (MBA). Part-time and evening/weekend programs available. *Degree requirements:* For master's, comprehensive exam or thesis. *Entrance requirements:* For master's, GMAT (minimum 20th percentile verbal and quantitative section), bachelor's degree, minimum GPA of 2.75. Additional exam requirements/recommendations for international students: Required—TOEFL (minimum score 550 paper-based; 79 iBT). Electronic applications accepted. *Expenses:* Contact institution.

California State University, Fullerton, Graduate Studies, College of Business and Economics, Department of Finance, Fullerton, CA 92834-9480. Offers MBA. Part-time programs available. *Students:* 29 full-time (8 women), 26 part-time (5 women); includes 21 minority (15 Asian, non-Hispanic/Latino; 5 Hispanic/Latino; 1 Two or more races, non-Hispanic/Latino), 13 international. Average age 29. In 2013, 44 master's awarded. *Degree requirements:* For master's, project or thesis. *Entrance requirements:* For master's, GMAT, minimum AACSB index of 950. Application fee: $55. *Financial support:* Career-related internships or fieldwork, Federal Work-Study, institutionally sponsored loans, and scholarships/grants available. Support available to part-time students. Financial award application deadline: 3/1; financial award applicants required to submit FAFSA. *Unit head:* Mark Hoven Stohs, Chair, 657-278-2217. *Application contact:* Admissions/Applications, 657-278-2371.

Finance and Banking

California State University, Los Angeles, Graduate Studies, College of Business and Economics, Department of Finance and Law, Los Angeles, CA 90032-8530. Offers finance and banking (MBA, MS). Part-time and evening/weekend programs available. *Faculty:* 1 (woman) full-time, 1 part-time/adjunct (0 women). *Students:* 4 full-time (2 women), 5 part-time (4 women); includes 3 minority (2 Asian, non-Hispanic/Latino; 1 Hispanic/Latino), 6 international. Average age 28. In 2013, 19 master's awarded. *Degree requirements:* For master's, comprehensive exam (MBA), thesis (MS). *Entrance requirements:* For master's, GMAT, minimum GPA of 2.5 during previous 2 years of course work. Additional exam requirements/recommendations for international students: Required—TOEFL (minimum score 550 paper-based). *Application deadline:* For fall admission, 5/1 for domestic and international students. Applications are processed on a rolling basis. Application fee: $55. Electronic applications accepted. *Financial support:* Career-related internships or fieldwork and Federal Work-Study available. Support available to part-time students. Financial award application deadline: 3/1. *Unit head:* Dr. Hsing Fang, Chair, 323-343-2870, Fax: 323-343-2885, E-mail: hfang@calstatela.edu. *Application contact:* Dr. Larry Fritz, Dean of Graduate Studies, 323-343-3820, Fax: 323-343-5653, E-mail: lfritz@calstatela.edu.
Website: http://cbe.calstatela.edu/fin/.

California State University, San Bernardino, Graduate Studies, College of Business and Public Administration, Master in Business Administration Program, San Bernardino, CA 92407. Offers accounting (MBA); cyber security (MBA); entrepreneurship (MBA); finance (MBA); information systems and technology (MBA); management (MBA); marketing management (MBA); supply chain management (MBA). MBA is also offered online. *Accreditation:* AACSB. Part-time and evening/weekend programs available. Postbaccalaureate distance learning degree programs offered (no on-campus study). *Faculty:* 27 full-time (6 women), 8 part-time/adjunct (1 woman). *Students:* 161 full-time (59 women), 47 part-time (18 women); includes 74 minority (12 Black or African American, non-Hispanic/Latino; 19 Asian, non-Hispanic/Latino; 42 Hispanic/Latino; 1 Two or more races, non-Hispanic/Latino), 74 international. Average age 29. 281 applicants, 38% accepted, 67 enrolled. In 2013, 79 master's awarded. *Degree requirements:* For master's, comprehensive exam, thesis, portfolio, 60 units, minimum GPA of 3.0. *Entrance requirements:* For master's, GMAT or GRE, minimum GPA of 2.5. Additional exam requirements/recommendations for international students: Required—TOEFL (minimum score 550 paper-based; 79 iBT). *Application deadline:* For fall admission, 7/20 for domestic and international students; for winter admission, 10/20 for domestic and international students; for spring admission, 1/20 for domestic and international students. Applications are processed on a rolling basis. Application fee: $55. Electronic applications accepted. *Expenses:* Contact institution. *Financial support:* In 2013–14, 79 students received support, including 21 fellowships (averaging $4,867 per year), 29 research assistantships (averaging $2,748 per year), 6 teaching assistantships (averaging $5,162 per year); career-related internships or fieldwork, Federal Work-Study, institutionally sponsored loans, scholarships/grants, and unspecified assistantships also available. Support available to part-time students. Financial award application deadline: 3/1; financial award applicants required to submit FAFSA. *Faculty research:* Market reaction to Form 20-F, tax Constitutional questions in Obamacare, the performance of the faith and ethical investment products prior to and following the 2008 meltdown, capital appreciation bonds: a ruinous decision for an unborn generation, the effects of calorie count display on consumer eating behavior, local government bankruptcy. *Total annual research expenditures:* $2.3 million. *Unit head:* Dr. Lawrence C. Rose, Dean, 909-537-3703, Fax: 909-537-7026, E-mail: lrose@csusb.edu. *Application contact:* Dr. Vipin Gupta, Associate Dean/MBA Director, 909-537-7380, Fax: 909-537-7026, E-mail: vgupta@csusb.edu.
Website: http://mba.csusb.edu/.

Capella University, School of Business and Technology, Doctoral Programs in Business, Minneapolis, MN 55402. Offers accounting (DBA, PhD); business intelligence (DBA); finance (DBA, PhD); general business management (PhD); human resource management (DBA, PhD); leadership (DBA, PhD); management education (PhD); marketing (DBA, PhD); project management (DBA, PhD); strategy and innovation (DBA, PhD).

Capella University, School of Business and Technology, Master's Programs in Business, Minneapolis, MN 55402. Offers accounting (MBA); business analysis (MS); business intelligence (MBA); entrepreneurship (MBA); finance (MBA); general business administration (MBA); general human resource management (MS); general leadership (MS); health care management (MBA); human resource management (MBA); marketing (MBA); project management (MBA, MS).

Capital University, School of Management, Columbus, OH 43209-2394. Offers entrepreneurship (MBA); finance (MBA); leadership (MBA); marketing (MBA); MBA/JD; MBA/LL M; MBA/MSN; MBA/MT. *Accreditation:* ACBSP. Part-time and evening/weekend programs available. *Faculty:* 17 full-time (7 women), 23 part-time/adjunct (1 woman). *Students:* 192 (77 women). Average age 31. 34 applicants, 74% accepted, 20 enrolled. In 2013, 1 master's awarded. *Entrance requirements:* For master's, GMAT, 2 years of work experience. Additional exam requirements/recommendations for international students: Required—TOEFL (minimum score 550 paper-based); Recommended—IELTS (minimum score 6.5). *Application deadline:* For fall admission, 7/1 priority date for domestic students; for winter admission, 11/1 for domestic students; for spring admission, 11/1 priority date for domestic students; for summer admission, 4/1 priority date for domestic students. Applications are processed on a rolling basis. Electronic applications accepted. *Financial support:* Application deadline: 8/1; applicants required to submit FAFSA. *Faculty research:* Taxation, public policy, health care, management of non-profits. *Unit head:* Dr. David Schwantes, MBA Director, 614-236-6984, Fax: 614-236-6923, E-mail: dschwant@capital.edu. *Application contact:* Carli Isgrigg, Assistant Director of Adult and Graduate Education Recruitment, 614-236-6546, Fax: 614-236-6923, E-mail: cisgrigg@capital.edu.
Website: http://www.capital.edu/capital-mba/.

Carnegie Mellon University, Tepper School of Business, Program in Financial Economics, Pittsburgh, PA 15213-3891. Offers PhD. *Degree requirements:* For doctorate, thesis/dissertation. *Entrance requirements:* For doctorate, GRE General Test.

Case Western Reserve University, Weatherhead School of Management, Department of Banking and Finance, Cleveland, OH 44106. Offers MBA. *Entrance requirements:* For master's, GMAT. *Faculty research:* Monetary and fiscal policy, corporate finance, future markets, derivative pricing, capital market efficiency.

Case Western Reserve University, Weatherhead School of Management, Department of Operations, Cleveland, OH 44106. Offers management (MS, MSM), including finance (MS), information systems (MS), marketing (MS), operations research, quality management (MS), supply chain (MSM); management for liberal arts graduates (MSM); operations research (PhD); MBA/MSM. Part-time programs available. *Degree requirements:* For doctorate, thesis/dissertation. *Entrance requirements:* For master's, GRE General Test; for doctorate, GMAT, GRE General Test. *Faculty research:* Mathematical finance, mathematical programming, scheduling, stochastic optimization, environmental/energy models.

Central European University, CEU Business School, Budapest, Hungary. Offers executive business administration (EMBA); finance (MBA); general management (MBA);

information technology management (M Sc); marketing (MBA). Part-time and evening/weekend programs available. *Faculty:* 18 full-time (5 women), 6 part-time/adjunct (1 woman). *Students:* 37 full-time (16 women), 82 part-time (20 women). Average age 32. 219 applicants, 34% accepted, 35 enrolled. In 2013, 69 master's awarded. *Degree requirements:* For master's, one foreign language. *Entrance requirements:* For master's, GMAT. Additional exam requirements/recommendations for international students: Required—TOEFL (minimum score 570 paper-based); Recommended—IELTS (minimum score 6.5). *Application deadline:* For fall admission, 5/15 for domestic students, 5/22 for international students; for winter admission, 11/15 for domestic students, 11/10 for international students. Applications are processed on a rolling basis. Application fee: $40. Electronic applications accepted. *Expenses: Tuition:* Full-time 62,700 Hungarian forints. *Financial support:* Tuition waivers (partial) available. *Faculty research:* Social and ethical business, marketing, international business, international trade and investment, management development in Central and East Europe, non-market strategies of emerging-market multinationals, macro and micro analysis of the business environment, international competitive analysis, the transition process from emerging economies to established market economies and its social impact, the regulation of natural monopolies. *Unit head:* Dr. Mel Horwitch, Dean and Managing Director, 361-887-5050, E-mail: mhorwitch@ceubusiness.com. *Application contact:* Miao Tan, Recruitment Coordinator, 361-887-5061, Fax: 361-887-5133, E-mail: tanm@ceubusiness.org.
Website: http://business.ceu.hu/.

Central Michigan University, College of Graduate Studies, College of Business Administration, MBA Program, Mount Pleasant, MI 48859. Offers accounting (MBA); business economics (MBA); consulting (MBA); finance (MBA); general business (MBA); human resource management (MBA); information systems (MBA); international business (MBA); logistics management (MBA); marketing (MBA); value-driven organization (MBA). Part-time and evening/weekend programs available. Postbaccalaureate distance learning degree programs offered (no on-campus study). Electronic applications accepted. *Faculty research:* Accounting, consulting, international business, marketing, information systems.

Charleston Southern University, School of Business, Charleston, SC 29423-8087. Offers accounting (MBA); finance (MBA); general management (MBA); leadership (MBA); management information systems (MBA). Part-time and evening/weekend programs available. *Degree requirements:* For master's, thesis optional. *Entrance requirements:* For master's, GMAT. Additional exam requirements/recommendations for international students: Required—TOEFL (minimum score 550 paper-based; 79 iBT).

City University of Seattle, Graduate Division, School of Management, Bellevue, WA 98005. Offers accounting (Certificate); change leadership (MBA, Certificate); computer systems (MS); finance (Certificate); financial management (MBA); general management (MBA); general management-Europe (MBA); global marketing (MBA); human resources management (Certificate); individualized study (MBA); information security (MS); information systems (MBA); leadership (MA); marketing (MBA, Certificate); project management (MBA, MS, Certificate); sustainable business (Certificate); technology management (MBA, Certificate). Part-time and evening/weekend programs available. Postbaccalaureate distance learning degree programs offered (no on-campus study). *Degree requirements:* For master's, comprehensive exam (for some programs), thesis (for some programs). *Entrance requirements:* Additional exam requirements/recommendations for international students: Required—TOEFL (minimum score 567 paper-based; 87 iBT); Recommended—IELTS. Electronic applications accepted.

Claremont McKenna College, Robert Day School of Economics and Finance, Claremont, CA 91711. Offers finance (MA). *Entrance requirements:* For master's, GMAT or GRE, 2 letters of recommendation, resume, interview. Additional exam requirements/recommendations for international students: Required—TOEFL. Electronic applications accepted.

Clark University, Graduate School, Graduate School of Management, Business Administration Program, Worcester, MA 01610-1477. Offers accounting (MBA); finance (MBA); global business (MBA); information systems (MBA); management (MBA); marketing (MBA); social change (MBA); sustainability (MBA). *Accreditation:* AACSB. Part-time and evening/weekend programs available. *Students:* 109 full-time (50 women), 151 part-time (67 women); includes 16 minority (9 Black or African American, non-Hispanic/Latino; 3 Asian, non-Hispanic/Latino; 4 Hispanic/Latino), 74 international. Average age 30. 359 applicants, 50% accepted, 81 enrolled. In 2013, 125 master's awarded. *Degree requirements:* For master's, thesis optional. *Application deadline:* For fall admission, 6/1 priority date for domestic students; for spring admission, 12/1 priority date for domestic students. Applications are processed on a rolling basis. Application fee: $50. Electronic applications accepted. *Expenses: Tuition:* Full-time $39,200; part-time $1225 per credit hour. *Financial support:* In 2013–14, research assistantships with partial tuition reimbursements (averaging $4,800 per year), teaching assistantships with partial tuition reimbursements (averaging $4,800 per year) were awarded; fellowships, career-related internships or fieldwork, Federal Work-Study, institutionally sponsored loans, and tuition waivers (partial) also available. Support available to part-time students. Financial award application deadline: 5/31. *Faculty research:* Marketing, accounting, human resource management, management information systems, business finance. *Unit head:* Dr. Catherine Usoff, Dean, 508-793-8822, Fax: 508-793-8822, E-mail: clarkmba@clarku.edu. *Application contact:* Patrick Oroszko, Enrollment and Marketing Director, 508-793-8822, Fax: 508-793-8822, E-mail: clarkmba@clarku.edu.
Website: http://www.clarku.edu/gsom/graduate/fulltime/.

Clark University, Graduate School, Graduate School of Management, Program in Finance, Worcester, MA 01610-1477. Offers MSF. *Students:* 181 full-time (101 women), 179 international. Average age 23. 1,008 applicants, 62% accepted, 90 enrolled. In 2013, 118 master's awarded. *Degree requirements:* For master's, thesis optional. *Application deadline:* For fall admission, 6/1 priority date for domestic students; for spring admission, 12/1 priority date for domestic students. Applications are processed on a rolling basis. Application fee: $50. Electronic applications accepted. *Expenses: Tuition:* Full-time $39,200; part-time $1225 per credit hour. *Financial support:* In 2013–14, research assistantships with partial tuition reimbursements (averaging $4,800 per year), teaching assistantships with partial tuition reimbursements (averaging $4,800 per year) were awarded; fellowships and tuition waivers (partial) also available. Financial award application deadline: 5/31. *Faculty research:* Marketing, accounting, human resource management, management information systems, business finance. *Unit head:* Dr. Catherine Usoff, Dean, 508-793-8822, Fax: 508-793-8822, E-mail: clarkmba@clarku.edu. *Application contact:* Patrick Oroszko, Enrollment and Marketing Director, 508-793-8822, Fax: 508-793-8822, E-mail: clarkmba@clarku.edu.
Website: http://www.clarku.edu/gsom/graduate/msf/.

Cleary University, Online Program in Business Administration, Ann Arbor, MI 48105-2659. Offers accounting (MBA); financial planning (MBA); financial planning (Graduate Certificate); green business strategy (MBA, Graduate Certificate); health care leadership (MBA); management (MBA); nonprofit management (MBA, Graduate Certificate); organizational leadership (MBA). Part-time and evening/weekend programs available. Postbaccalaureate distance learning degree programs offered (no on-campus study). *Degree requirements:* For master's, thesis. *Entrance requirements:* For master's, bachelor's degree; minimum GPA of 2.5; professional resume indicating minimum of 2

years of management or related experience; undergraduate degree from accredited college or university with at least 18 quarter hours (or 12 semester hours) of accounting study (for MBA in accounting). Additional exam requirements/recommendations for international students: Required—TOEFL (minimum score 550 paper-based; 79 iBT), Michigan English Language Assessment Battery (minimum score 75). Electronic applications accepted.

Cleveland State University, College of Graduate Studies, Maxine Goodman Levin College of Urban Affairs, Program in Environmental Studies, Cleveland, OH 44115. Offers environmental nonprofit management (MAES); environmental planning (MAES); geographic information systems (Certificate); policy and administration (MAES); sustainable economic development (MAES); urban economic development (Certificate); urban real estate development and finance (Certificate); JD/MAES. Part-time and evening/weekend programs available. *Faculty:* 21 full-time (10 women), 11 part-time/adjunct (3 women). *Students:* 2 full-time (both women), 5 part-time (3 women); includes 1 minority (Hispanic/Latino). Average age 34. 4 applicants, 25% accepted. In 2013, 11 master's awarded. *Degree requirements:* For master's, thesis or alternative, exit project. *Entrance requirements:* For master's, GRE General Test (minimum score: verbal and quantitative combined 40th percentile, analytical writing 4.0), minimum GPA of 3.0. Additional exam requirements/recommendations for international students: Required—TOEFL (minimum score 525 paper-based; 65 iBT), IELTS or ITEP. *Application deadline:* For fall admission, 7/15 priority date for domestic students, 5/15 for international students; for spring admission, 11/1 for international students. Applications are processed on a rolling basis. Application fee: $30. Electronic applications accepted. *Expenses:* Tuition, state resident: full-time $8335; part-time $521 per credit hour. Tuition, nonresident: full-time $15,670; part-time $979 per credit hour. *Required fees:* $50; $25 per semester. *Financial support:* In 2013–14, 4 students received support, including 4 research assistantships with full and partial tuition reimbursements available (averaging $3,625 per year); career-related internships or fieldwork, scholarships/grants, traineeships, and unspecified assistantships also available. Support available to part-time students. Financial award application deadline: 3/1; financial award applicants required to submit FAFSA. *Faculty research:* Environmental policy and administration, environmental planning, geographic information systems (GIS), urban sustainability planning and management, energy policy, land re-use. *Unit head:* Dr. Sanda Kaufman, Director, 216-687-2367, Fax: 216-687-9342, E-mail: s.kaufman@csuohio.edu. *Application contact:* David Arrighi, Graduate Academic Advisor, 216-523-7522, Fax: 216-687-5398, E-mail: urbanprograms@csuohio.edu.
Website: http://urban.csuohio.edu/academics/graduate/maes/.

Cleveland State University, College of Graduate Studies, Maxine Goodman Levin College of Urban Affairs, Program in Public Administration, Cleveland, OH 44115. Offers city management (MPA); economic development (MPA); healthcare administration (MPA); local and urban management (Certificate); non-profit management (MPA, Certificate); public financial management (MPA); public management (MPA); urban economic development (Certificate); JD/MPA. *Accreditation:* NASPAA. Part-time and evening/weekend programs available. *Faculty:* 21 full-time (10 women), 11 part-time/adjunct (3 women). *Students:* 16 full-time (11 women), 64 part-time (40 women); includes 23 minority (19 Black or African American, non-Hispanic/Latino; 3 Hispanic/Latino; 1 Two or more races, non-Hispanic/Latino), 3 international. Average age 36. 67 applicants, 51% accepted, 13 enrolled. In 2013, 56 master's awarded. *Degree requirements:* For master's, thesis or alternative, capstone course. *Entrance requirements:* For master's, GRE General Test (minimum scores in 40th percentile verbal and quantitative, 4.0 writing), minimum GPA of 3.0. Additional exam requirements/recommendations for international students: Required—TOEFL (minimum score 525 paper-based; 65 iBT), IELTS or ITEP. *Application deadline:* For fall admission, 7/15 priority date for domestic students, 5/15 for international students; for spring admission, 11/1 for international students. Applications are processed on a rolling basis. Application fee: $30. Electronic applications accepted. *Expenses:* Tuition, state resident: full-time $8335; part-time $521 per credit hour. Tuition, nonresident: full-time $15,670; part-time $979 per credit hour. *Required fees:* $50; $25 per semester. *Financial support:* In 2013–14, 16 students received support, including 12 research assistantships with full and partial tuition reimbursements available (averaging $4,800 per year), 4 teaching assistantships with full and partial tuition reimbursements available (averaging $3,300 per year); career-related internships or fieldwork, scholarships/grants, traineeships, and unspecified assistantships also available. Support available to part-time students. Financial award application deadline: 3/1; financial award applicants required to submit FAFSA. *Faculty research:* City management, nonprofit management, health care administration, public management, economic development. *Unit head:* Dr. Nicholas Zingale, Director, 216-802-3398, Fax: 216-687-9342, E-mail: n.zingale@csuohio.edu. *Application contact:* David Arrighi, Graduate Academic Advisor, 216-523-7522, Fax: 216-687-5398, E-mail: urbanprograms@csuohio.edu.
Website: http://urban.csuohio.edu/academics/graduate/mpa/.

Cleveland State University, College of Graduate Studies, Maxine Goodman Levin College of Urban Affairs, Program in Urban Planning, Design, and Development, Cleveland, OH 44115. Offers economic development (MUPDD); environmental sustainability (MUPDD); geographic information systems (MUPDD, Certificate); historic preservation (MUPDD); housing and neighborhood development (MUPDD); urban economic development (Certificate); urban real estate development and finance (MUPDD, Certificate); JD/MUPDD. *Accreditation:* ACSP. Part-time and evening/weekend programs available. *Faculty:* 21 full-time (10 women), 11 part-time/adjunct (3 women). *Students:* 11 full-time (5 women), 25 part-time (10 women); includes 8 minority (2 Black or African American, non-Hispanic/Latino; 1 Asian, non-Hispanic/Latino; 2 Hispanic/Latino; 3 Two or more races, non-Hispanic/Latino), 3 international. Average age 38. 48 applicants, 56% accepted, 5 enrolled. In 2013, 23 master's awarded. *Degree requirements:* For master's, thesis or alternative, planning studio. *Entrance requirements:* For master's, GRE General Test (minimum score: 50th percentile combined verbal and quantitative, 4.0 analytical writing), minimum GPA of 3.0. Additional exam requirements/recommendations for international students: Required—TOEFL (minimum score 525 paper-based; 65 iBT), IELTS or ITEP. *Application deadline:* For fall admission, 7/15 priority date for domestic students, 5/15 for international students; for spring admission, 11/1 for international students. Applications are processed on a rolling basis. Application fee: $30. Electronic applications accepted. *Expenses:* Tuition, state resident: full-time $8335; part-time $521 per credit hour. Tuition, nonresident: full-time $15,670; part-time $979 per credit hour. *Required fees:* $50; $25 per semester. *Financial support:* In 2013–14, 10 students received support, including 7 research assistantships with full and partial tuition reimbursements available (averaging $7,200 per year), 3 teaching assistantships with full and partial tuition reimbursements available (averaging $4,000 per year); career-related internships or fieldwork, Federal Work-Study, scholarships/grants, tuition waivers, and unspecified assistantships also available. Support available to part-time students. Financial award application deadline: 3/1; financial award applicants required to submit FAFSA. *Faculty research:* Housing and neighborhood development, urban housing policy, environmental sustainability, economic development, GIS and planning decision support. *Unit head:* Dr. Dennis Keating, Director, 216-687-2298, Fax: 216-687-2013, E-mail: w.keating@csuohio.edu. *Application contact:* David Arrighi, Graduate Academic Advisor, 216-523-7522, Fax: 216-687-5398, E-mail: urbanprograms@csuohio.edu.
Website: http://urban.csuohio.edu/academics/graduate/mupdd/.

Cleveland State University, College of Graduate Studies, Maxine Goodman Levin College of Urban Affairs, Program in Urban Studies, Cleveland, OH 44115. Offers community and neighborhood development (MS); economic development (MS); law and public policy (MS); public finance (MS); urban economic development (Certificate); urban policy analysis (MS); urban real estate development (MS); urban real estate development and finance (Certificate). Part-time and evening/weekend programs available. *Faculty:* 21 full-time (10 women), 11 part-time/adjunct (3 women). *Students:* 5 full-time (1 woman), 8 part-time (2 women); includes 1 minority (Black or African American, non-Hispanic/Latino). Average age 34. 21 applicants, 29% accepted, 4 enrolled. In 2013, 8 master's awarded. *Degree requirements:* For master's, thesis or alternative, exit project. *Entrance requirements:* For master's, GRE General Test (minimum score: verbal and quantitative combined 40th percentile, analytical writing 4.0), minimum GPA of 3.0. Additional exam requirements/recommendations for international students: Required—TOEFL (minimum score 525 paper-based; 65 iBT), IELTS or ITEP. *Application deadline:* For fall admission, 1/15 priority date for domestic students, 1/15 for international students. Applications are processed on a rolling basis. Application fee: $30. Electronic applications accepted. *Expenses:* Tuition, state resident: full-time $8335; part-time $521 per credit hour. Tuition, nonresident: full-time $15,670; part-time $979 per credit hour. *Required fees:* $50; $25 per semester. *Financial support:* In 2013–14, 4 students received support, including 3 research assistantships with full and partial tuition reimbursements available (averaging $7,200 per year), 1 teaching assistantship with full and partial tuition reimbursement available (averaging $7,200 per year); career-related internships or fieldwork, scholarships/grants, traineeships, and unspecified assistantships also available. Support available to part-time students. Financial award application deadline: 3/1; financial award applicants required to submit FAFSA. *Faculty research:* Environmental issues, economic development, urban and public policy, public management. *Unit head:* Dr. Brian Mikelbank, Director, 216-875-9980, Fax: 216-687-9342, E-mail: b.mikelbank@csuohio.edu. *Application contact:* David Arrighi, Graduate Academic Advisor, 216-523-7522, Fax: 216-687-5398, E-mail: urbanprograms@csuohio.edu.
Website: http://urban.csuohio.edu/academics/graduate/msus/.

Cleveland State University, College of Graduate Studies, Monte Ahuja College of Business, Doctor of Business Administration Program, Cleveland, OH 44115. Offers finance (DBA); global business (DBA); information systems (DBA); marketing (DBA); operations management (DBA). *Accreditation:* AACSB. Part-time and evening/weekend programs available. *Faculty:* 50 full-time (11 women). *Students:* 36 part-time (18 women); includes 6 minority (2 Black or African American, non-Hispanic/Latino; 4 Asian, non-Hispanic/Latino), 8 international. Average age 39. 96 applicants, 27% accepted, 6 enrolled. In 2013, 1 doctorate awarded. *Degree requirements:* For doctorate, comprehensive exam, thesis/dissertation, oral dissertation defense. *Entrance requirements:* For doctorate, GMAT, MBA or equivalent. Additional exam requirements/recommendations for international students: Required—TOEFL (minimum score 550 paper-based; 79 iBT). *Application deadline:* For spring admission, 2/28 priority date for domestic and international students. Application fee: $30. Electronic applications accepted. *Expenses:* Tuition, state resident: full-time $8335; part-time $521 per credit hour. Tuition, nonresident: full-time $15,670; part-time $979 per credit hour. *Required fees:* $50; $25 per semester. *Financial support:* In 2013–14, 5 research assistantships with full tuition reimbursements (averaging $12,700 per year), 4 teaching assistantships with full tuition reimbursements (averaging $12,700 per year) were awarded; tuition waivers (full) and unspecified assistantships also available. *Faculty research:* Supply chain management, international business, strategic management, risk analysis, consumer behavior. *Unit head:* Dr. Raj Shekhar G. Javalgi, Director, 216-687-3786, Fax: 216-687-9354, E-mail: r.javalgi@csuohio.edu. *Application contact:* Melinda J. Arnold, Administrative Secretary, 216-687-6952, Fax: 216-687-9257, E-mail: m.arnold@csuohio.edu.
Website: http://www.csuohio.edu/business/academics/doctoral.html.

College for Financial Planning, Graduate Programs, Centennial, CO 80112. Offers finance (MSF); financial analysis (MSF); personal financial planning (MS). Part-time and evening/weekend programs available. Postbaccalaureate distance learning degree programs offered (no on-campus study). *Degree requirements:* For master's, capstone course or thesis. *Entrance requirements:* Additional exam requirements/recommendations for international students: Required—TOEFL (minimum score 550 paper-based). Electronic applications accepted.

Colorado State University, Graduate School, College of Business, Program in Financial Risk Management, Fort Collins, CO 80523-1201. Offers MSBA. *Students:* 16 full-time (8 women), 1 part-time (0 women), 10 international. Average age 24. 46 applicants, 83% accepted, 12 enrolled. In 2013, 15 master's awarded. *Entrance requirements:* For master's, GMAT or GRE, undergraduate degree with minimum GPA of 3.0; coursework in business finance, probability and statistics, and differential equations; academic experience with computer programming; current resume; 3 letters of recommendation, English proficiency. Additional exam requirements/recommendations for international students: Required—TOEFL (minimum score 565 paper-based; 86 iBT) or IELTS (minimum score 6.5). *Application deadline:* For fall admission, 7/1 for domestic students, 6/1 for international students. Application fee: $50. Electronic applications accepted. *Expenses:* Tuition, state resident: full-time $9075.40; part-time $504 per credit. Tuition, nonresident: full-time $22,248; part-time $1236 per credit. *Required fees:* $1819; $60 per credit. *Faculty research:* Changes in risk landscape, safety of market mechanisms. *Unit head:* Dr. Ajay Menon, Dean, 970-491-2398, Fax: 970-491-0596, E-mail: ajay.menon@colostate.edu. *Application contact:* Janet Estes, Graduate Programs Advisor, 970-491-4612, Fax: 970-491-3949, E-mail: janet.estes@colostate.edu.
Website: http://biz.colostate.edu/FRM/pages/default.aspx.

Colorado Technical University Colorado Springs, Graduate Studies, Program in Management, Colorado Springs, CO 80907-3896. Offers accounting (MBA, MSA); business administration (MBA); finance (MBA); human resources management (MBA); logistics/supply chain management (MBA); management (DM); marketing (MBA); mediation and dispute resolution (MBA); operations management (MBA); project management (MBA); technology management (MBA). Part-time and evening/weekend programs available. Postbaccalaureate distance learning degree programs offered. *Degree requirements:* For master's, thesis or alternative; for doctorate, thesis/dissertation. *Entrance requirements:* For doctorate, minimum graduate GPA of 3.0, 5 years of related work experience. *Faculty research:* Sexual harassment, performance evaluation, critical thinking.

Colorado Technical University Denver South, Programs in Business Administration and Management, Aurora, CO 80014. Offers accounting (MBA); business administration (MBA); business administration and management (EMBA); finance (MBA); human resource management (MBA); marketing (MBA); mediation and dispute resolution (MBA); operations management (MBA); project management (MBA); technology management (MBA). Part-time and evening/weekend programs available. *Degree*

requirements: For master's, thesis or alternative. *Entrance requirements:* For master's, minimum undergraduate GPA of 3.0, resume.

Columbia Southern University, MBA Program, Orange Beach, AL 36561. Offers finance (MBA); health care management (MBA); human resource management (MBA); marketing (MBA); project management (MBA); public administration (MBA). Part-time and evening/weekend programs available. Postbaccalaureate distance learning degree programs offered (no on-campus study). *Entrance requirements:* For master's, bachelor's degree from accredited/approved institution. Additional exam requirements/recommendations for international students: Required—TOEFL. Electronic applications accepted.

Columbia University, Graduate School of Arts and Sciences, New York, NY 10027. Offers African-American studies (MA); American studies (MA); anthropology (MA, PhD); art history and archaeology (MA, PhD); astronomy (PhD); biological sciences (PhD); biotechnology (MA); chemical physics (PhD); chemistry (PhD); classical studies (MA, PhD); classics (MA, PhD); climate and society (MA); earth and environmental sciences (PhD); East Asia: regional studies (MA); East Asian languages and cultures (MA, PhD); ecology, evolution and environmental biology (MA), including conservation biology; ecology, evolution, and environmental biology (PhD), including ecology and evolutionary biology, evolutionary primatology; economics (PhD); English and comparative literature (MA, PhD); French and Romance philology (MA, PhD); Germanic languages (MA, PhD); global French studies (MA); Hispanic cultural studies (MA); history (PhD); history and literature (MA); human rights studies (MA); Islamic studies (MA); Italian (MA, PhD); Japanese pedagogy (MA); Jewish studies (MA); Latin America and the Caribbean: regional studies (MA); Latin American and Iberian cultures (PhD); mathematics (MA, PhD), including finance (MA); medieval and Renaissance studies (MA); Middle Eastern, South Asian, and African studies (MA, PhD); modern art: critical and curatorial studies (MA); modern European studies (MA); museum anthropology (MA); music (DMA, PhD); oral history (MA); philosophical foundations of physics (MA); philosophy (MA, PhD); physics (PhD); political science (MA, PhD); psychology (PhD); quantitative methods in the social sciences (MA); religion (MA, PhD); Russia, Eurasia and East Europe: regional studies (MA); Russian translation (MA); Slavic cultures (MA); Slavic languages (MA, PhD); sociology (MA, PhD); South Asian studies (MA); statistics (MA, PhD); theatre (PhD); JD/PhD; MA/MS; MD/PhD; MPA/MA. Dual-degree programs require admission to both Graduate School of Arts and Sciences and another Columbia school. Part-time and evening/weekend programs available. *Faculty:* 808 full-time (310 women). *Students:* 2,755 full-time, 354 part-time; includes 493 minority (80 Black or African American, non-Hispanic/Latino; 6 American Indian or Alaska Native, non-Hispanic/Latino; 215 Asian, non-Hispanic/Latino; 135 Hispanic/Latino; 3 Native Hawaiian or other Pacific Islander, non-Hispanic/Latino; 54 Two or more races, non-Hispanic/Latino), 1,433 international. 12,949 applicants, 19% accepted, 998 enrolled. In 2013, 969 master's, 461 doctorates awarded. Terminal master's awarded for partial completion of doctoral program. *Degree requirements:* For master's, thesis (for some programs); for doctorate, comprehensive exam, thesis/dissertation. *Entrance requirements:* For master's and doctorate, GRE General Test, GRE Subject Test (for some programs). Application fee: $105. Electronic applications accepted. *Financial support:* Application deadline: 12/15. *Faculty research:* Humanities, natural sciences, social sciences. *Unit head:* Carlos J. Alonso, Dean of the Graduate School of Arts and Sciences, 212-854-5177. *Application contact:* GSAS Office of Admissions, 212-854-8903, E-mail: gsas-admissions@columbia.edu.
Website: http://gsas.columbia.edu/.

Columbia University, Graduate School of Business, Doctoral Program in Business, New York, NY 10027. Offers business (PhD), including accounting, decision, risk, and operations, finance and economics, management, marketing. *Accreditation:* AACSB. *Degree requirements:* For doctorate, comprehensive exam, thesis/dissertation, major field exam, research paper, thesis proposal. *Entrance requirements:* For doctorate, GMAT or GRE (finance), 2 letters of reference, resume. Additional exam requirements/recommendations for international students: Required—TOEFL. Electronic applications accepted. *Expenses:* Contact institution. *Faculty research:* Human decision making and behavioral research; real estate market and mortgage defaults; financial crisis and corporate governance; international business; security analysis and accounting.

Columbia University, Graduate School of Business, MBA Program, New York, NY 10027. Offers accounting (MBA); decision, risk, and operations (MBA); entrepreneurship (MBA); finance and economics (MBA); healthcare and pharmaceutical management (MBA); human resource management (MBA); international business (MBA); leadership and ethics (MBA); management (MBA); marketing (MBA); media (MBA); private equity (MBA); real estate (MBA); social enterprise (MBA); value investing (MBA); DDS/MBA; JD/MBA; MBA/MIA; MBA/MPH; MBA/MS; MD/MBA. *Entrance requirements:* For master's, GMAT, 2 letters of recommendation. Additional exam requirements/recommendations for international students: Required—TOEFL. Electronic applications accepted. *Expenses:* Contact institution. *Faculty research:* Human decision making and behavioral research; real estate market and mortgage defaults; financial crisis and corporate governance; international business; security analysis and accounting.

Concordia University, School of Graduate Studies, John Molson School of Business, Montreal, QC H3G 1M8, Canada. Offers administration (M Sc), including finance, management, marketing; business administration (MBA, PhD, Certificate, Diploma); executive business administration (EMBA); investment management (MBA). PhD program offered jointly with HEC Montreal, McGill University, and Université du Québec à Montréal. *Accreditation:* AACSB. Part-time and evening/weekend programs available. *Degree requirements:* For master's, one foreign language, thesis (for some programs), research project; for doctorate, one foreign language, thesis/dissertation; for other advanced degree, one foreign language. *Entrance requirements:* For master's, GMAT, minimum 2 years of work experience (for MBA); letters of recommendation, bachelor's degree from recognized university with minimum GPA of 3.0, curriculum vitae; for doctorate, GMAT (minimum score of 600), official transcripts, curriculum vitae, 3 letters of reference, statement of purpose; for other advanced degree, minimum GPA of 2.7, 2 letters of reference, statement of purpose, resume. Additional exam requirements/recommendations for international students: Required—TOEFL (minimum score 90 iBT), IELTS (minimum score 7). Electronic applications accepted. *Expenses:* Contact institution. *Faculty research:* General business, capital markets, international business.

Concordia University Wisconsin, Graduate Programs, School of Business and Legal Studies, MBA Program, Mequon, WI 53097-2402. Offers finance (MBA); health care administration (MBA); human resource management (MBA); international business (MBA); international business-bilingual English/Chinese (MBA); management (MBA); management information systems (MBA); managerial communications (MBA); marketing (MBA); public administration (MBA); risk management (MBA). Postbaccalaureate distance learning degree programs offered (minimal on-campus study). *Degree requirements:* For master's, comprehensive exam, thesis or alternative. *Entrance requirements:* Additional exam requirements/recommendations for international students: Required—TOEFL. *Expenses:* Contact institution.

Cornell University, Graduate School, Graduate Field of Management, Ithaca, NY 14853. Offers accounting (PhD); finance (PhD); marketing (PhD); organizational behavior (PhD); production and operations management (PhD). *Accreditation:* AACSB. *Faculty:* 54 full-time (7 women). *Students:* 37 full-time (13 women); includes 5 minority (4 Asian, non-Hispanic/Latino; 1 Two or more races, non-Hispanic/Latino), 24 international. Average age 29. 486 applicants, 4% accepted, 11 enrolled. In 2013, 8 doctorates awarded. *Degree requirements:* For doctorate, comprehensive exam, thesis/dissertation. *Entrance requirements:* For doctorate, GMAT or GRE General Test. Additional exam requirements/recommendations for international students: Required—TOEFL (minimum score 600 paper-based; 77 iBT). *Application deadline:* For fall admission, 1/3 for domestic students. Application fee: $95. Electronic applications accepted. *Expenses:* Contact institution. *Financial support:* In 2013–14, 33 students received support, including 31 research assistantships with full tuition reimbursements available, 2 teaching assistantships with full tuition reimbursements available; fellowships with full tuition reimbursements available, institutionally sponsored loans, scholarships/grants, health care benefits, tuition waivers (full and partial), and unspecified assistantships also available. Financial award applicants required to submit FAFSA. *Faculty research:* Operations and manufacturing. *Unit head:* Director of Graduate Studies, 607-255-3669. *Application contact:* Graduate Field Assistant, 607-255-9431, E-mail: js_phd@cornell.edu.
Website: http://www.gradschool.cornell.edu/fields.php?id-91&a-2.

Cornell University, Graduate School, Graduate Fields of Arts and Sciences, Field of Economics, Ithaca, NY 14853-0001. Offers applied economics (PhD); basic analytical economics (PhD); econometrics and economic statistics (PhD); economic development and planning (PhD); economic theory (PhD); industrial organization and control (PhD); international economics (PhD); labor economics (PhD); monetary and macro economics (PhD); public finance (PhD). *Faculty:* 94 full-time (12 women). *Students:* 98 full-time (30 women); includes 12 minority (1 American Indian or Alaska Native, non-Hispanic/Latino; 8 Asian, non-Hispanic/Latino; 3 Hispanic/Latino), 51 international. Average age 27. 661 applicants, 10% accepted, 18 enrolled. In 2013, 24 doctorates awarded. *Degree requirements:* For doctorate, comprehensive exam, thesis/dissertation. *Entrance requirements:* For doctorate, GRE General Test, 3 letters of recommendation. Additional exam requirements/recommendations for international students: Required—TOEFL (minimum score 550 paper-based; 77 iBT). *Application deadline:* For fall admission, 1/15 priority date for domestic students. Application fee: $95. Electronic applications accepted. *Financial support:* In 2013–14, 86 students received support, including 22 fellowships with full tuition reimbursements available, 23 research assistantships with full tuition reimbursements available, 41 teaching assistantships with full tuition reimbursements available; institutionally sponsored loans, scholarships/grants, health care benefits, tuition waivers (full and partial), and unspecified assistantships also available. Financial award applicants required to submit FAFSA. *Faculty research:* Learning and games, economics of education, political economy, transfer payments, time series and nonparametrics. *Unit head:* Director of Graduate Studies, 607-255-4893, Fax: 607-255-2818. *Application contact:* Graduate Field Assistant, 607-255-4893, Fax: 607-255-2818, E-mail: econ_phd@cornell.edu.
Website: http://www.gradschool.cornell.edu/fields.php?id-79&a-2.

Curry College, Graduate Studies, Program in Business Administration, Milton, MA 02186-9984. Offers business administration (MBA); finance (Certificate). Part-time and evening/weekend programs available. *Degree requirements:* For master's, capstone applied project. *Entrance requirements:* For master's, resume, recommendations, interview, written statement. Additional exam requirements/recommendations for international students: Required—TOEFL (minimum score 550 paper-based; 80 iBT). *Expenses:* Contact institution.

Dalhousie University, Faculty of Management, Centre for Advanced Management Education, Halifax, NS B3H 3J5, Canada. Offers financial services (MBA); information management (MIM); management (MPA); natural resources (MBA). Part-time programs available. Postbaccalaureate distance learning degree programs offered. *Entrance requirements:* For master's, GMAT, minimum GPA of 3.0, resume. Additional exam requirements/recommendations for international students: Required—TOEFL, IELTS, CANTEST, CAEL, or Michigan English Language Assessment Battery. Electronic applications accepted.

Dalhousie University, Faculty of Management, School of Business Administration, Halifax, NS B3H 3J5, Canada. Offers business administration (MBA); financial services (MBA); LL B/MBA; MBA/MLIS. Part-time programs available. *Entrance requirements:* For master's, GMAT, letter of non-financial guarantee for non-Canadian students, resume, Corporate Residency Preference Form. Additional exam requirements/recommendations for international students: Required—TOEFL, IELTS, CANTEST, CAEL, or Michigan English Language Assessment Battery. Electronic applications accepted. *Faculty research:* International business, quantitative methods, operations research, MIS, marketing, finance.

Dallas Baptist University, College of Business, Business Administration Program, Dallas, TX 75211-9299. Offers accounting (MBA); business communication (MBA); conflict resolution management (MBA); entrepreneurship (MBA); finance (MBA); health care management (MBA); international business (MBA); leading the non-profit organization (MBA); management (MBA); management information systems (MBA); marketing (MBA); project management (MBA); technology and engineering (MBA). *Accreditation:* ACBSP. Part-time and evening/weekend programs available. *Entrance requirements:* For master's, GMAT, minimum GPA of 3.0. Additional exam requirements/recommendations for international students: Required—TOEFL, IELTS. *Application deadline:* Applications are processed on a rolling basis. Application fee: $25. Electronic applications accepted. *Expenses: Tuition:* Full-time $13,410; part-time $745 per credit hour. *Required fees:* $300; $150 per semester. Tuition and fees vary according to degree level. *Financial support:* Federal Work-Study, institutionally sponsored loans, scholarships/grants, and tuition waivers (full and partial) available. Support available to part-time students. Financial award applicants required to submit FAFSA. *Faculty research:* Sports management, services marketing, retailing, strategic management, financial planning/investments. *Unit head:* Dr. Sandra S. Reid, Chair, 214-333-5280, Fax: 214-333-5293, E-mail: graduate@dbu.edu. *Application contact:* Kit P. Montgomery, Director of Graduate Programs, 214-333-5242, Fax: 214-333-5579, E-mail: graduate@dbu.edu.
Website: http://www3.dbu.edu/graduate/mba.asp.

Davenport University, Sneden Graduate School, Grand Rapids, MI 49512. Offers accounting (MBA); business administration (EMBA); finance (MBA); health care management (MBA); human resources (MBA); information assurance (MS); public health (MPH); strategic management (MBA). Evening/weekend programs available. *Entrance requirements:* For master's, GMAT, minimum undergraduate GPA of 2.75. Additional exam requirements/recommendations for international students: Required—TOEFL. Electronic applications accepted. *Faculty research:* Leadership, management, marketing, organizational culture.

Delaware Valley College, MBA Program, Doylestown, PA 18901-2697. Offers accounting (MBA); entrepreneurship (MBA); finance (MBA); food and agribusiness (MBA); general business (MBA); global executive leadership (MBA); human resource management (MBA); supply chain management (MBA). Part-time and evening/weekend programs available. Postbaccalaureate distance learning degree programs offered (no on-campus study). *Students:* 32 full-time (17 women), 183 part-time (99 women). Average age 34. 97 applicants, 78% accepted, 74 enrolled. *Entrance requirements:* For master's, minimum undergraduate GPA of 3.0. *Application deadline:* Applications are

processed on a rolling basis. Application fee: $50. Electronic applications accepted. *Expenses:* Contact institution. *Financial support:* Applicants required to submit FAFSA. *Unit head:* Mike Prushan, Director of MBA Program, 215-489-2322, E-mail: michael.prushan@delval.edu. *Application contact:* Robin Mathews, Graduate and Continuing Studies Enrollment Manager, 215-489-2955, Fax: 215-489-4832, E-mail: robin.mathews@delval.edu.
Website: http://www.delval.edu/academics/graduate/master-of-business-administration.

DePaul University, Charles H. Kellstadt Graduate School of Business, Chicago, IL 60604. Offers accountancy (M Acc, MS, MSA); applied economics (MBA); banking (MBA); behavioral finance (MBA); brand and product management (MBA); business development (MBA); business information technology (MS); business strategy and decision-making (MBA); computational finance (MS); consumer insights (MBA); corporate finance (MBA); economic policy analysis (MS); entrepreneurship (MBA, MS); finance (MBA, MS); financial analysis (MBA); general business (MBA); health sector management (MBA); hospitality leadership (MBA); hospitality leadership and operational performance (MS); human resource management (MBA); human resources (MS); investment management (MBA); leadership and change management (MBA); management accounting (MBA); marketing (MBA, MS); marketing analysis (MS); marketing strategy and planning (MBA); operations management (MBA); organizational diversity (MBA); real estate (MS); real estate finance and investment (MBA); revenue management (MBA); sports management (MBA); strategic global marketing (MBA); strategy, execution and valuation (MBA); sustainable management (MBA, MS); taxation (MS); wealth management (MS); JD/MBA. *Accreditation:* AACSB. Part-time and evening/weekend programs available. Postbaccalaureate distance learning degree programs offered (no on-campus study). *Faculty:* 81 full-time (20 women), 45 part-time/adjunct (8 women). *Students:* 1,238 full-time (605 women), 617 part-time (223 women); includes 295 minority (71 Black or African American, non-Hispanic/Latino; 129 Asian, non-Hispanic/Latino; 74 Hispanic/Latino; 4 Native Hawaiian or other Pacific Islander, non-Hispanic/Latino; 17 Two or more races, non-Hispanic/Latino), 462 international. Average age 29. In 2013, 911 master's awarded. *Entrance requirements:* For master's, GMAT, 2 letters of recommendation, resume, essay, official transcripts. Additional exam requirements/recommendations for international students: Required—TOEFL (minimum score 550 paper-based; 80 iBT). *Application deadline:* For fall admission, 7/1 for domestic students, 6/1 for international students; for winter admission, 10/1 for domestic students, 9/1 for international students; for spring admission, 2/1 for domestic students, 1/1 for international students. Applications are processed on a rolling basis. Application fee: $60. Electronic applications accepted. *Expenses:* Contact institution. *Financial support:* Application deadline: 4/1; applicants required to submit FAFSA. *Unit head:* Robert T. Ryan, Assistant Dean and Director, 312-362-8810, Fax: 312-362-6677, E-mail: rryan1@depaul.edu. *Application contact:* James Parker, Director of Recruitment and Admission, 312-362-8810, Fax: 312-362-6677, E-mail: kgsb@depaul.edu.
Website: http://kellstadt.depaul.edu.

DeSales University, Graduate Division, Division of Business, Center Valley, PA 18034-9568. Offers accounting (MBA); computer information systems (MBA); finance (MBA); health care systems management (MBA); human resources management (MBA); management (MBA); marketing (MBA); project management (MBA); self-design (MBA). *Accreditation:* ACBSP. Part-time and evening/weekend programs available. Postbaccalaureate distance learning degree programs offered (no on-campus study). *Students:* 444 part-time. Average age 37. In 2013, 1 master's awarded. *Entrance requirements:* For master's, GMAT, minimum GPA of 3.0, 2 years of work experience. Additional exam requirements/recommendations for international students: Required—TOEFL. *Application deadline:* Applications are processed on a rolling basis. Application fee: $50. Electronic applications accepted. *Expenses: Tuition:* Part-time $790 per credit. *Financial support:* Applicants required to submit FAFSA. *Faculty research:* Quality improvement, executive development, productivity, cross-cultural managerial differences, leadership. *Unit head:* Dr. David Gilfoil, Director, 610-282-1100 Ext. 1828, Fax: 610-282-2869, E-mail: david.gilfoil@desales.edu. *Application contact:* Abigail Wernicki, Director of Graduate Admissions, 610-282-1100 Ext. 1768, E-mail: gradadmissions@desales.edu.

DeVry University, Graduate Programs, Downers Grove, IL 60515. Offers accounting and financial management (MAFM); business administration (MBA); education (MS); educational technology (MS); electrical engineering (MS); human resources management (MHRM); information systems management (MISM); network and communications management (MNCM); project management (MPM); public administration (MPA).

Dowling College, School of Business, Oakdale, NY 11769. Offers aviation management (MBA, Certificate); corporate finance (MBA, Certificate); health care management (MBA); human resource management (Certificate); information systems management (MBA); management and leadership (MBA); marketing (Certificate); project management (Certificate); public management (MBA); school district business leader (MBA); sport, event and entertainment management (Certificate); JD/MBA. Part-time and evening/weekend programs available. Postbaccalaureate distance learning degree programs offered (minimal on-campus study). *Faculty:* 7 full-time (2 women), 43 part-time/adjunct (7 women). *Students:* 183 full-time (79 women), 299 part-time (142 women); includes 137 minority (84 Black or African American, non-Hispanic/Latino; 14 Asian, non-Hispanic/Latino; 20 Hispanic/Latino; 19 Native Hawaiian or other Pacific Islander, non-Hispanic/Latino). Average age 32. 360 applicants, 58% accepted, 127 enrolled. In 2013, 235 master's, 15 other advanced degrees awarded. *Degree requirements:* For master's, comprehensive exam, thesis optional. *Entrance requirements:* For master's, minimum GPA of 2.8, 2 letters of recommendation, courses or seminar in accounting and finance, resume. Additional exam requirements/recommendations for international students: Required—TOEFL (minimum score 550 paper-based). *Application deadline:* For fall admission, 9/1 priority date for domestic students; for winter admission, 1/1 priority date for domestic students; for spring admission, 2/1 priority date for domestic students. Applications are processed on a rolling basis. Application fee: $50. Electronic applications accepted. *Expenses: Tuition:* Full-time $22,731; part-time $1029 per credit. *Required fees:* $956; $956. *Financial support:* Career-related internships or fieldwork and Federal Work-Study available. Support available to part-time students. Financial award application deadline: 6/30; financial award applicants required to submit FAFSA. *Faculty research:* International finance, computer applications, labor relations, executive development. *Unit head:* Dr. Elana Zolfo, Dean, 631-244-3266, Fax: 631-244-1018, E-mail: zolfoe@dowling.edu. *Application contact:* Mary Boullianne, Dean of Admissions, 631-244-3274, Fax: 631-244-1059, E-mail: boulliam@dowling.edu.

Drexel University, LeBow College of Business, Department of Finance, Philadelphia, PA 19104-2875. Offers MS. *Degree requirements:* For master's, seminar paper. *Entrance requirements:* For master's, GMAT, minimum GPA of 2.75. Additional exam requirements/recommendations for international students: Required—TOEFL. Electronic applications accepted. *Faculty research:* Investment analysis, portfolio mix, capital budgeting, banking and financial institutions, international finance.

Drexel University, LeBow College of Business, Program in Business Administration, Philadelphia, PA 19104-2875. Offers business administration (MBA, PhD, APC), including accounting (MBA, PhD), decision sciences (PhD), economics (MBA, PhD), finance (MBA, PhD), legal studies (MBA), management (MBA), marketing (MBA, PhD), organizational sciences (PhD), quantitative methods (MBA), strategic management (PhD). *Accreditation:* AACSB. Part-time and evening/weekend programs available. Postbaccalaureate distance learning degree programs offered (minimal on-campus study). Terminal master's awarded for partial completion of doctoral program. *Entrance requirements:* For master's, GMAT, minimum GPA of 2.75; for doctorate, GMAT. Additional exam requirements/recommendations for international students: Required—TOEFL. Electronic applications accepted. *Faculty research:* Decision support systems, individual and group behavior, operations research, techniques and strategy.

Duke University, The Fuqua School of Business, Cross Continent Executive MBA Program, Durham, NC 27708-0586. Offers business administration (MBA); energy and the environment (MBA); entrepreneurship and innovation (MBA); finance (MBA); health sector management (Certificate); marketing (MBA); strategy (MBA). *Faculty:* 91 full-time (15 women), 53 part-time/adjunct (9 women). *Students:* 121 full-time (34 women); includes 23 minority (3 Black or African American, non-Hispanic/Latino; 15 Asian, non-Hispanic/Latino; 4 Hispanic/Latino; 1 Native Hawaiian or other Pacific Islander, non-Hispanic/Latino), 31 international. Average age 30. In 2013, 147 master's awarded. *Degree requirements:* For master's, one foreign language. *Entrance requirements:* For master's, GMAT or GRE, transcripts, essays, resume, recommendation letters, interview. Additional exam requirements/recommendations for international students: Required—TOEFL, IELTS, PTE. *Application deadline:* For fall admission, 10/16 for domestic students, 10/6 for international students; for winter admission, 2/12 for domestic and international students; for spring admission, 5/6 for domestic and international students; for summer admission, 6/4 for domestic students. Application fee: $225. Electronic applications accepted. *Financial support:* In 2013–14, 16 students received support. Institutionally sponsored loans and scholarships/grants available. Financial award applicants required to submit FAFSA. *Unit head:* John Gallagher, Associate Dean for Executive MBA Programs, 919-660-7641, E-mail: johng@duke.edu. *Application contact:* Liz Riley Hargrove, Associate Dean for Admissions, 919-660-1956, Fax: 919-681-8026, E-mail: admissions-info@fuqua.duke.edu.
Website: http://www.fuqua.duke.edu/programs/duke_mba/cross_continent/.

Duke University, The Fuqua School of Business, Daytime MBA Program, Durham, NC 27708-0586. Offers academic excellence in finance (Certificate); business administration (MBA); decision sciences (MBA); energy and environment (MBA); energy finance (MBA); entrepreneurship and innovation (MBA); finance (MBA); financial analysis (MBA); health sector management (Certificate); leadership and ethics (MBA); management (MBA); marketing (MBA); operations management (MBA); social entrepreneurship (MBA); strategy (MBA). *Faculty:* 91 full-time (15 women), 53 part-time/adjunct (9 women). *Students:* 862 full-time (283 women); includes 179 minority (34 Black or African American, non-Hispanic/Latino; 1 American Indian or Alaska Native, non-Hispanic/Latino; 92 Asian, non-Hispanic/Latino; 42 Hispanic/Latino; 2 Native Hawaiian or other Pacific Islander, non-Hispanic/Latino; 8 Two or more races, non-Hispanic/Latino), 342 international. Average age 29. In 2013, 437 master's awarded. *Entrance requirements:* For master's, GMAT or GRE, transcripts, essays, resume, recommendation letters, interview. Additional exam requirements/recommendations for international students: Required—TOEFL, IELTS, PTE. *Application deadline:* For fall admission, 9/18 for domestic and international students; for winter admission, 10/21 for domestic and international students; for spring admission, 1/6 for domestic and international students; for summer admission, 3/20 for domestic and international students. Application fee: $225. Electronic applications accepted. *Financial support:* In 2013–14, 331 students received support. Institutionally sponsored loans and scholarships/grants available. Financial award applicants required to submit FAFSA. *Unit head:* Russ Morgan, Associate Dean for the Daytime MBA Program, 919-660-2931, Fax: 919-684-8742, E-mail: ruskin.morgan@duke.edu. *Application contact:* Liz Riley Hargrove, Associate Dean of Admissions, 919-660-7705, Fax: 919-681-8026, E-mail: liz.riley@duke.edu.
Website: http://www.fuqua.duke.edu/daytime-mba/.

Duke University, The Fuqua School of Business, Global Executive MBA Program, Durham, NC 27708-0586. Offers business administration (MBA); energy and the environment (MBA); entrepreneurship and innovation (MBA); finance (MBA); health sector management (Certificate); marketing (MBA); strategy (MBA). *Faculty:* 91 full-time (15 women), 53 part-time/adjunct (9 women). *Students:* 49 full-time (7 women); includes 7 minority (1 Black or African American, non-Hispanic/Latino; 3 Asian, non-Hispanic/Latino; 3 Hispanic/Latino), 17 international. Average age 39. In 2013, 51 master's awarded. *Entrance requirements:* For master's, transcripts, essays, resume, recommendation letters, interview. Additional exam requirements/recommendations for international students: Required—TOEFL, IELTS, PTE. *Application deadline:* For fall admission, 9/4 for domestic and international students; for winter admission, 10/16 for domestic and international students; for spring admission, 12/5 for domestic and international students; for summer admission, 1/13 for domestic and international students. Application fee: $225. *Financial support:* In 2013–14, 8 students received support. Institutionally sponsored loans and scholarships/grants available. Financial award applicants required to submit FAFSA. *Unit head:* John Gallagher, Associate Dean for Executive MBA Programs, 919-660-7728, E-mail: johng@duke.edu. *Application contact:* Liz Riley Hargrove, Director of EMBA Admissions, 919-660-7705, Fax: 919-681-8026, E-mail: admissions-info@fuqua.duke.edu.
Website: http://www.fuqua.duke.edu/programs/duke_mba/global-executive/.

Duke University, The Fuqua School of Business, PhD Program, Durham, NC 27708-0586. Offers accounting (PhD); decision sciences (PhD); finance (PhD); management and organizations (PhD); marketing (PhD); operations management (PhD); strategy (PhD). *Faculty:* 91 full-time (15 women). *Students:* 78 full-time (27 women); includes 4 minority (1 Black or African American, non-Hispanic/Latino; 3 Asian, non-Hispanic/Latino), 49 international. 589 applicants, 5% accepted, 16 enrolled. In 2013, 26 doctorates awarded. *Degree requirements:* For doctorate, thesis/dissertation, major field requirement (exam or major paper, depending upon the area). *Entrance requirements:* For doctorate, GMAT or GRE, transcripts, essays, recommendation letters, statement of purpose. Additional exam requirements/recommendations for international students: Required—TOEFL (minimum score 577 paper-based; 90 iBT), IELTS (minimum score 7). *Application deadline:* For fall admission, 12/8 priority date for domestic and international students. Application fee: $80. Electronic applications accepted. *Financial support:* In 2013–14, 70 fellowships with full tuition reimbursements (averaging $25,300 per year), 56 research assistantships with full tuition reimbursements (averaging $7,000 per year) were awarded; institutionally sponsored loans, scholarships/grants, and tuition waivers (full) also available. Financial award applicants required to submit FAFSA. *Unit head:* William Boulding, Dean, 919-660-7822, Fax: 919-684-8742, E-mail: bb1@duke.edu. *Application contact:* Dr. James R. Bettman, Director of Graduate Studies, 919-660-7851, Fax: 919-681-6245, E-mail: jrb12@mail.duke.edu.

Duke University, The Fuqua School of Business, Weekend Executive MBA Program, Durham, NC 27708-0586. Offers business administration (MBA); energy and environment (MBA); entrepreneurship and innovation (MBA); finance (MBA); health sector management (Certificate); marketing (MBA); strategy (MBA). *Faculty:* 91 full-time (15 women), 53 part-time/adjunct (9 women). *Students:* 93 full-time (14 women); includes 33 minority (5 Black or African American, non-Hispanic/Latino; 24 Asian, non-

Hispanic/Latino; 3 Hispanic/Latino; 1 Two or more races, non-Hispanic/Latino), 15 international. Average age 36. In 2013, 103 master's awarded. *Degree requirements:* For master's, one foreign language. *Entrance requirements:* For master's, GMAT (preferred) or GRE, transcripts, essays, resume, recommendation letters, interview. Additional exam requirements/recommendations for international students: Required—TOEFL, IELTS, PTE. *Application deadline:* For fall admission, 9/4 for domestic and international students; for winter admission, 10/16 for domestic and international students; for spring admission, 2/12 for domestic and international students; for summer admission, 4/2 for domestic and international students. Application fee: $225. Electronic applications accepted. *Financial support:* In 2013–14, 14 students received support. Institutionally sponsored loans and scholarships/grants available. Financial award applicants required to submit FAFSA. *Unit head:* John Gallagher, Associate Dean for Executive MBA Programs, 919-660-7728, E-mail: johng@duke.edu. *Application contact:* Liz Riley Hargrove, Director of EMBA Admissions, 919-660-7705, Fax: 919-681-8026, E-mail: admissions-info@fuqua.duke.edu.
Website: http://www.fuqua.duke.edu/programs/duke_mba/weekend_executive/.

Duquesne University, John F. Donahue Graduate School of Business, Pittsburgh, PA 15282-0001. Offers accounting (M Acc); finance (MBA); information systems management (MBA, MSISM); management (MBA); marketing (MBA); supply chain management (MBA); sustainability (MBA); JD/MBA; MBA/M Acc; MBA/MA; MBA/MES; MBA/MHMS; MBA/MSN; MSISM/MBA; Pharm D/MBA. *Accreditation:* AACSB. Part-time and evening/weekend programs available. *Faculty:* 58 full-time (17 women), 40 part-time/adjunct (8 women). *Students:* 117 full-time (59 women), 147 part-time (54 women); includes 14 minority (7 Black or African American, non-Hispanic/Latino; 1 Asian, non-Hispanic/Latino; 6 Hispanic/Latino), 53 international. Average age 27. 418 applicants, 46% accepted, 109 enrolled. In 2013, 133 master's awarded. *Entrance requirements:* For master's, GMAT, undergraduate transcripts, 2 letters of recommendation, current resume, personal statement. Additional exam requirements/recommendations for international students: Required—TOEFL (minimum score 577 paper-based; 90 iBT), IELTS (minimum score 7). *Application deadline:* For fall admission, 7/1 priority date for domestic students, 6/1 for international students; for spring admission, 11/1 for domestic and international students. Applications are processed on a rolling basis. Application fee: $0. Electronic applications accepted. *Expenses: Tuition:* Full-time $18,162; part-time $1009 per credit. *Required fees:* $1728; $96 per credit. Tuition and fees vary according to program. *Financial support:* In 2013–14, 39 students received support, including 6 fellowships with partial tuition reimbursements available (averaging $4,541 per year), 33 research assistantships with partial tuition reimbursements available (averaging $9,081 per year); career-related internships or fieldwork, scholarships/grants, and unspecified assistantships also available. Support available to part-time students. Financial award application deadline: 7/1; financial award applicants required to submit FAFSA. *Faculty research:* International business, investment management, business ethics, technology management, supply chain management, business strategy, finance. *Unit head:* Thomas J. Nist, Director of Graduate Programs, 412-396-6276, Fax: 412-396-1726, E-mail: nist@duq.edu. *Application contact:* Maria W. DeCrosta, Enrollment Manager, 412-396-5529, Fax: 412-396-1726, E-mail: decrostam@duq.edu.
Website: http://www.duq.edu/business/grad.

Eastern Michigan University, Graduate School, College of Business, Programs in Business Administration, Ypsilanti, MI 48197. Offers business administration (MBA, Graduate Certificate); computer information systems (Graduate Certificate); e-business (MBA, Graduate Certificate); enterprise business intelligence (MBA); entrepreneurship (MBA, Graduate Certificate); finance (MBA, Graduate Certificate); human resources (MBA); human resources management (Graduate Certificate); information systems (MBA); internal auditing (MBA); international business (MBA, Graduate Certificate); marketing management (Graduate Certificate); nonprofit management (MBA); organizational development (Graduate Certificate); supply chain management (MBA, Graduate Certificate). *Accreditation:* AACSB. Part-time programs available. Postbaccalaureate distance learning degree programs offered (no on-campus study). *Students:* 74 full-time (28 women), 342 part-time (183 women); includes 122 minority (84 Black or African American, non-Hispanic/Latino; 2 American Indian or Alaska Native, non-Hispanic/Latino; 19 Asian, non-Hispanic/Latino; 7 Hispanic/Latino; 10 Two or more races, non-Hispanic/Latino), 38 international. Average age 33. 305 applicants, 72% accepted, 131 enrolled. In 2013, 69 master's, 57 other advanced degrees awarded. *Entrance requirements:* For master's, GMAT (minimum score 450), minimum cumulative undergraduate GPA of 2.75. Additional exam requirements/recommendations for international students: Required—TOEFL. *Application deadline:* For fall admission, 5/15 for domestic students, 5/1 for international students; for winter admission, 10/15 for domestic students, 10/1 for international students; for spring admission, 3/15 for domestic students, 3/1 for international students. Applications are processed on a rolling basis. Application fee: $35. *Expenses:* Tuition, state resident: full-time $12,300; part-time $466 per credit hour. Tuition, nonresident: full-time $23,159; part-time $918 per credit hour. *Required fees:* $71 per credit hour. $46 per semester. One-time fee: $100. Tuition and fees vary according to course level and degree level. *Financial support:* Fellowships, research assistantships with full tuition reimbursements, teaching assistantships with full tuition reimbursements, career-related internships or fieldwork, Federal Work-Study, institutionally sponsored loans, scholarships/grants, tuition waivers (partial), and unspecified assistantships available. Support available to part-time students. Financial award applicants required to submit FAFSA. *Unit head:* K. Michelle Henry, Director, Academic Services, 734-487-4444, Fax: 734-483-1316, E-mail: mhenry1@emich.edu. *Application contact:* Beste Windes, Advisor, 734-487-4444, Fax: 734-483-1316, E-mail: bwindes@emich.edu.
Website: http://www.emich.edu/public/cob/gr/grad.html.

East Tennessee State University, School of Graduate Studies, College of Arts and Sciences, Department of Political Science, International Affairs and Public Administration, Johnson City, TN 37614. Offers economic development (Postbaccalaureate Certificate); not-for-profit administration (MPA); planning and development (MPA); public financial management (MPA); urban planning (Postbaccalaureate Certificate). Part-time programs available. *Faculty:* 6 full-time (2 women), 3 part-time/adjunct (2 women). *Students:* 17 full-time (4 women), 8 part-time (2 women); includes 2 minority (both Black or African American, non-Hispanic/Latino), 4 international. Average age 29. 32 applicants, 50% accepted, 13 enrolled. In 2013, 11 master's awarded. *Degree requirements:* For master's, internship. *Entrance requirements:* For master's, GRE General Test, three letters of recommendation; for Postbaccalaureate Certificate, GRE General Test. Additional exam requirements/recommendations for international students: Required—TOEFL (minimum score 550 paper-based; 79 iBT). *Application deadline:* For fall admission, 6/1 for domestic students, 4/29 for international students; for spring admission, 11/1 for domestic students, 9/30 for international students. Application fee: $35 ($45 for international students). Electronic applications accepted. *Expenses:* Tuition, state resident: full-time $7900; part-time $395 per credit hour. Tuition, nonresident: full-time $21,960; part-time $1098 per credit hour. *Required fees:* $1345; $84 per credit hour. *Financial support:* In 2013–14, 16 students received support, including 7 research assistantships with full tuition reimbursements available (averaging $6,000 per year), 1 teaching assistantship with full tuition reimbursement available (averaging $6,000 per year); career-related internships or fieldwork, institutionally sponsored loans, scholarships/grants, and unspecified assistantships also available. Financial award application deadline: 7/1; financial award applicants required to submit FAFSA. *Faculty research:* Labor issues, presidency, public law in American politics, East Asian politics, European politics, Middle Eastern politics, development in comparative politics, international political economy, international relations, world politics in international affairs. *Unit head:* Dr. Weixing Chen, Chair, 423-439-4217, Fax: 423-439-4348, E-mail: chen@etsu.edu. *Application contact:* Gail Powers, Graduate Specialist, 423-439-4703, Fax: 423-439-5624, E-mail: pwersg@etsu.edu.
Website: http://www.etsu.edu/cas/PoliSci/.

Edgewood College, Program in Business, Madison, WI 53711-1997. Offers accountancy (MS); accounting (MBA); business administration (MBA); finance (MBA); management (MBA); marketing (MBA); organization development (MS); sustainability leadership (MBA). *Accreditation:* ACBSP. Part-time and evening/weekend programs available. *Students:* 24 full-time (8 women), 136 part-time (82 women); includes 18 minority (5 Black or African American, non-Hispanic/Latino; 1 American Indian or Alaska Native, non-Hispanic/Latino; 4 Asian, non-Hispanic/Latino; 4 Hispanic/Latino; 4 Two or more races, non-Hispanic/Latino), 10 international. Average age 33. In 2013, 55 master's awarded. *Entrance requirements:* For master's, GMAT (minimum score 430), minimum GPA of 2.75, 2 letters of recommendation. Additional exam requirements/recommendations for international students: Required—TOEFL. *Application deadline:* For fall admission, 8/15 for domestic students, 5/1 for international students; for spring admission, 1/8 for domestic students, 11/1 for international students. Applications are processed on a rolling basis. Application fee: $30. Electronic applications accepted. *Financial support:* Career-related internships or fieldwork and scholarships/grants available. *Unit head:* Martin Preizler, Dean, 608-663-2898, Fax: 608-663-3291, E-mail: martinpreizler@edgewood.edu. *Application contact:* Joann Eastman, Admissions Counselor, 608-663-3250, Fax: 608-663-2214, E-mail: gps@edgewood.edu.
Website: http://www.edgewood.edu/Academics/School-of-Business.

Embry-Riddle Aeronautical University–Daytona, Daytona Beach Campus Graduate Program, Department of Business Administration, Daytona Beach, FL 32114-3900. Offers MBA, MBA-AM, MSAF. *Accreditation:* ACBSP. Part-time programs available. *Degree requirements:* For master's, thesis or alternative. *Entrance requirements:* For master's, GMAT, minimum GPA of 2.5. Additional exam requirements/recommendations for international students: Required—TOEFL (minimum score 550 paper-based; 79 iBT). Electronic applications accepted. *Faculty research:* Aircraft safety operations analysis, energy consumption analysis, statistical analysis of general aviation accidents, airport funding strategies, industry assessment and marketing analysis for ENAER aerospace.
See Display on page 616 and Close-Up on page 635.

Emory University, Goizueta Business School, Doctoral Program in Business, Atlanta, GA 30322-1100. Offers accounting (PhD); finance (PhD); information systems (PhD); marketing (PhD); organization and management (PhD). *Faculty:* 53 full-time (12 women). *Students:* 41 full-time (15 women); includes 28 minority (all Asian, non-Hispanic/Latino). Average age 29. 195 applicants, 9% accepted, 9 enrolled. In 2013, 1 doctorate awarded. *Degree requirements:* For doctorate, comprehensive exam, thesis/dissertation. *Entrance requirements:* For doctorate, GMAT (strongly preferred) or GRE. Additional exam requirements/recommendations for international students: Required—TOEFL. *Application deadline:* For fall admission, 1/3 priority date for domestic and international students. Application fee: $75. Electronic applications accepted. *Financial support:* In 2013–14, 35 students received support, including 3 fellowships (averaging $1,166 per year). *Unit head:* Dr. Anand Swaminathan, Associate Dean, Doctoral Program, 404-727-2306, Fax: 404-727-5337, E-mail: anand.swaminathan@emory.edu. *Application contact:* Allison Gilmore, Director of Admissions and Student Services, 404-727-6353, Fax: 404-727-5337, E-mail: phd@bus.emory.edu.

Fairfield University, Charles F. Dolan School of Business, Fairfield, CT 06824-5195. Offers accounting (MBA, MS, CAS); accounting information systems (MBA, CAS); entrepreneurship (MBA, CAS); finance (MBA, MS, CAS); general management (MBA, CAS); human resource management (MBA, CAS); information systems and operations (MBA); information systems and operations management (CAS); marketing (MBA, CAS); taxation (MBA, CAS). *Accreditation:* AACSB. Part-time and evening/weekend programs available. *Faculty:* 18 full-time (9 women), 15 part-time/adjunct (4 women). *Students:* 94 full-time (45 women), 72 part-time (26 women); includes 49 minority (7 Black or African American, non-Hispanic/Latino; 33 Asian, non-Hispanic/Latino; 8 Hispanic/Latino; 1 Two or more races, non-Hispanic/Latino), 9 international. Average age 29. 116 applicants, 43% accepted, 26 enrolled. In 2013, 100 master's awarded. *Degree requirements:* For master's, capstone course. *Entrance requirements:* For master's, GMAT (minimum score 500), 2 letters of reference, resume, minimum GPA of 3.0. Additional exam requirements/recommendations for international students: Required—TOEFL (minimum score 550 paper-based; 80 iBT) or IELTS (minimum score 6.5). *Application deadline:* For fall admission, 5/15 for international students; for spring admission, 10/15 for international students. Applications are processed on a rolling basis. Application fee: $60. Electronic applications accepted. *Expenses:* Contact institution. *Financial support:* In 2013–14, 28 students received support. Scholarships/grants, unspecified assistantships, and merit-based one-time entrance scholarships available. Financial award applicants required to submit FAFSA. *Faculty research:* International finance, leadership and careers, ethics in accounting, emotions in consumer behavior, supply chain analysis, organizational leadership attributes, emotions in the workplace, real estate finance, effect of social media on stock prices. *Unit head:* Dr. Donald Gibson, Dean, 203-254-4070, Fax: 203-254-4105, E-mail: dgibson@fairfield.edu. *Application contact:* Marianne Gumpper, Director of Graduate and Continuing Studies Admission, 203-254-4184, Fax: 203-254-4073, E-mail: gradadmis@fairfield.edu.
Website: http://fairfield.edu/mba.

Fairleigh Dickinson University, College at Florham, Silberman College of Business, Department of Economics, Finance, and International Business, Program in Finance, Madison, NJ 07940-1099. Offers MBA, Certificate.

Fairleigh Dickinson University, Metropolitan Campus, Silberman College of Business, Department of Economics, Finance and International Business, Program in Finance, Teaneck, NJ 07666-1914. Offers MBA, Certificate.

Florida Agricultural and Mechanical University, Division of Graduate Studies, Research, and Continuing Education, School of Business and Industry, Tallahassee, FL 32307-3200. Offers accounting (MBA); finance (MBA); management information systems (MBA); marketing (MBA). *Accreditation:* ACBSP. *Degree requirements:* For master's, residency. *Entrance requirements:* For master's, GMAT, minimum GPA of 3.0.

Florida Atlantic University, College of Business, Department of Finance, Boca Raton, FL 33431-0991. Offers PhD. *Expenses:* Tuition, state resident: full-time $6660; part-time $370 per credit hour. Tuition, nonresident: full-time $18,450; part-time $1025 per credit hour. Tuition and fees vary according to course load. *Unit head:* Dr. Daniel Gropper, Dean, 561-297-3629, Fax: 561-297-3686, E-mail: vhale4@fau.edu. *Application contact:* Dr. Marcy Krugel, Graduate Adviser, 561-297-3940, Fax: 561-297-0801, E-mail: krugel@fau.edu.

Florida Institute of Technology, Graduate Programs, Nathan M. Bisk College of Business, Online Programs, Melbourne, FL 32901-6975. Offers accounting (MBA); accounting and finance (MBA); business administration (MBA); finance (MBA); healthcare management (MBA); information assurance and cybersecurity (MS); information technology (MS); information technology cybersecurity (MS); information technology management (MBA); international business (MBA); Internet marketing (MBA); management (MBA); marketing (MBA); project management (MBA); supply chain management (MS). Part-time and evening/weekend programs available. Postbaccalaureate distance learning degree programs offered (no on-campus study). *Faculty:* 3 full-time (1 woman), 41 part-time/adjunct (13 women). *Students:* 6 full-time (1 woman), 1,121 part-time (530 women); includes 424 minority (276 Black or African American, non-Hispanic/Latino; 10 American Indian or Alaska Native, non-Hispanic/Latino; 45 Asian, non-Hispanic/Latino; 88 Hispanic/Latino; 5 Native Hawaiian or other Pacific Islander, non-Hispanic/Latino), 32 international. Average age 36. 348 applicants, 42% accepted, 146 enrolled. In 2013, 475 master's awarded. *Entrance requirements:* For master's, GMAT or resume showing 8 years of supervised experience, 2 letters of recommendation, resume, competency in math past college algebra. Additional exam requirements/recommendations for international students: Required—TOEFL (minimum score 550 paper-based; 79 iBT). *Application deadline:* For fall admission, 4/1 for international students; for spring admission, 9/30 for international students. Applications are processed on a rolling basis. Electronic applications accepted. *Expenses:* Contact institution. *Financial support:* Available to part-time students. Application deadline: 3/1; applicants required to submit FAFSA. *Unit head:* Brian Ehrlich, Associate Vice President/Director of Online Learning, 321-674-8202, E-mail: behrlich@fit.edu. *Application contact:* Carolyn Farrior, Director of Graduate Admissions, Online Learning and Off-Campus Programs, 321-674-7118.
Website: http://online.fit.edu.

Florida International University, Alvah H. Chapman, Jr. Graduate School of Business, Department of Finance, Miami, FL 33199. Offers MSF. Part-time and evening/weekend programs available. *Entrance requirements:* For master's, GMAT or GRE, minimum GPA of 3.0 (upper-level coursework); letter of intent; resume. Additional exam requirements/recommendations for international students: Required—TOEFL (minimum score 550 paper-based; 80 iBT) or IELTS (minimum score 6.5). Electronic applications accepted. *Expenses:* Contact institution. *Faculty research:* Investment, corporate and international finance, commercial real estate.

Florida National University, Program in Business Administration, Hialeah, FL 33012. Offers finance (MBA); general management (MBA); marketing (MBA). Postbaccalaureate distance learning degree programs offered (no on-campus study). *Degree requirements:* For master's, capstone.

Florida State University, The Graduate School, College of Business, Tallahassee, FL 32306-1110. Offers accounting (M Acc), including accounting information services, assurance services, corporate accounting, taxation; business administration (MBA, PhD), including accounting (PhD), finance (PhD), management information systems (PhD), marketing (PhD), organizational behavior and human resources (PhD), risk management and insurance (PhD), strategic management (PhD); finance (MS); insurance (MSM); management information systems (MS); marketing (MS); JD/MBA; MSW/MBA. *Accreditation:* AACSB. Part-time programs available. Postbaccalaureate distance learning degree programs offered (no on-campus study). *Faculty:* 102 full-time (31 women), 5 part-time/adjunct (0 women). *Students:* 280 full-time (117 women), 278 part-time (88 women); includes 127 minority (26 Black or African American, non-Hispanic/Latino; 7 American Indian or Alaska Native, non-Hispanic/Latino; 44 Asian, non-Hispanic/Latino; 50 Hispanic/Latino). Average age 30. 630 applicants, 28% accepted, 103 enrolled. In 2013, 265 master's, 11 doctorates awarded. Terminal master's awarded for partial completion of doctoral program. *Degree requirements:* For doctorate, comprehensive exam, thesis/dissertation. *Entrance requirements:* For master's, GMAT, work experience (MBA, MS), minimum GPA of 3.0, letters of recommendation; for doctorate, GMAT, minimum graduate GPA of 3.5, letters of recommendation. Additional exam requirements/recommendations for international students: Required—TOEFL (minimum score 600 paper-based; 100 iBT); Recommended—IELTS (minimum score 6.5). *Application deadline:* For fall admission, 6/1 for domestic students, 5/1 for international students; for spring admission, 10/1 for domestic students, 9/1 for international students. Applications are processed on a rolling basis. Application fee: $30. Electronic applications accepted. *Expenses:* Tuition, state resident: part-time $403.51 per credit hour. Tuition, nonresident: part-time $1004.85 per credit hour. *Required fees:* $75.81 per credit hour. One-time fee: $20 part-time. Tuition and fees vary according to course load, campus/location and student level. *Financial support:* In 2013–14, 92 students received support, including 10 fellowships with full tuition reimbursements available (averaging $1,500 per year), 20 research assistantships with full tuition reimbursements available (averaging $20,000 per year), 35 teaching assistantships with full tuition reimbursements available (averaging $20,000 per year); career-related internships or fieldwork, scholarships/grants, health care benefits, and unspecified assistantships also available. Financial award application deadline: 1/1. *Unit head:* Dr. Caryn Beck-Dudley, Dean, 850-644-3090, Fax: 850-644-0915. *Application contact:* Lisa Beverly, Director, Graduate Programs Admissions, 850-644-6458, Fax: 850-644-0588, E-mail: lbeverly@cob.fsu.edu.
Website: http://www.cob.fsu.edu/.

Fordham University, Graduate School of Business, New York, NY 10023. Offers accounting (MBA); communications and media management (MBA); executive business administration (EMBA); finance (MBA, MS); information systems (MBA, MS); management systems (MBA); marketing (MBA); media management (MS); taxation (MS); taxation and accounting (MTA); JD/MBA; MBA/MIM; MS/MBA. MBA/MIM offered jointly with Thunderbird School of Global Management. *Accreditation:* AACSB. Part-time and evening/weekend programs available. *Entrance requirements:* For master's, GMAT, 2 letters of recommendation, resume. Additional exam requirements/recommendations for international students: Required—TOEFL (minimum score 600 paper-based; 100 iBT). Electronic applications accepted. *Expenses:* Contact institution.

Gannon University, School of Graduate Studies, College of Engineering and Business, Dahlkemper School of Business, Program in Business Administration, Erie, PA 16541-0001. Offers business administration (MBA); finance (MBA); human resources management (MBA); marketing (MBA). *Accreditation:* ACBSP. Part-time and evening/weekend programs available. Postbaccalaureate distance learning degree programs offered (no on-campus study). *Students:* 44 full-time (20 women), 87 part-time (30 women); includes 7 minority (4 Black or African American, non-Hispanic/Latino; 1 Asian, non-Hispanic/Latino; 2 Hispanic/Latino), 22 international. Average age 28. 279 applicants, 84% accepted, 59 enrolled. In 2013, 40 master's awarded. *Degree requirements:* For master's, comprehensive exam, thesis. *Entrance requirements:* For master's, GMAT, resume, transcripts, 3 letters of recommendation. Additional exam requirements/recommendations for international students: Required—TOEFL (minimum score 79 iBT). *Application deadline:* Applications are processed on a rolling basis. Application fee: $25. Electronic applications accepted. *Expenses: Tuition:* Full-time $15,930; part-time $885 per credit. *Required fees:* $430; $18 per credit. Tuition and fees vary according to course load, degree level and program. *Financial support:* Administrative assistantships available. Financial award application deadline: 7/1; financial award applicants required to submit FAFSA. *Unit head:* Dr. Donna Mottilla, Director, 814-871-7780, E-mail: mottilla001@gannon.edu. *Application contact:* Kara Morgan, Director of Graduate Admissions, 814-871-5831, Fax: 814-871-5827, E-mail: graduate@gannon.edu.

Geneva College, Program in Business Administration, Beaver Falls, PA 15010-3599. Offers business administration (MBA); finance (MBA); marketing (MBA); operations (MBA). *Accreditation:* ACBSP. Part-time and evening/weekend programs available. *Faculty:* 5 full-time (1 woman), 1 part-time/adjunct (0 women). *Students:* 1 (woman) full-time, 19 part-time (8 women); includes 3 minority (1 Black or African American, non-Hispanic/Latino; 2 Asian, non-Hispanic/Latino). Average age 33. 9 applicants, 100% accepted, 6 enrolled. In 2013, 9 master's awarded. *Degree requirements:* For master's, 36 credit hours of course work (30 of which are required of all students). *Entrance requirements:* For master's, GMAT (if college GPA less than 2.5), undergraduate transcript, 2 letters of recommendation, resume, goals statement. Additional exam requirements/recommendations for international students: Required—TOEFL. *Application deadline:* For fall admission, 3/1 priority date for domestic students; for spring admission, 11/1 priority date for domestic students. Applications are processed on a rolling basis. Electronic applications accepted. *Expenses:* Contact institution. *Financial support:* In 2013–14, 1 student received support. Scholarships/grants available. Financial award application deadline: 8/1; financial award applicants required to submit FAFSA. *Unit head:* Dr. Gary Vander Plaats, Director of the MBA Program, 724-847-6619, E-mail: gpvander@geneva.edu. *Application contact:* Marina Frazier, Director of Graduate Enrollment, 724-847-6697, E-mail: mba@geneva.edu.
Website: http://www.geneva.edu/page/masters_business.

George Fox University, College of Business, Newberg, OR 97132-2697. Offers finance (MBA); management (DBA); management and leadership (MBA); marketing (DBA); organizational strategy (MBA); strategic human resource management (MBA). MBA offered in Newberg, OR and in Portland, OR. *Accreditation:* ACBSP. Part-time and evening/weekend programs available. Postbaccalaureate distance learning degree programs offered (minimal on-campus study). *Faculty:* 8 full-time (2 women), 5 part-time/adjunct (2 women). *Students:* 31 full-time (15 women), 194 part-time (76 women); includes 21 minority (6 Black or African American, non-Hispanic/Latino; 4 American Indian or Alaska Native, non-Hispanic/Latino; 6 Asian, non-Hispanic/Latino; 3 Hispanic/Latino; 2 Two or more races, non-Hispanic/Latino), 15 international. Average age 39. 98 applicants, 79% accepted, 62 enrolled. In 2013, 98 master's, 2 doctorates awarded. *Degree requirements:* For master's, capstone project; for doctorate, credit-applied research project. *Entrance requirements:* For master's, resume (5 years of professional experience); 3 professional references; interview; financial e-learning course, official transcripts; for doctorate, GRE or GMAT, resume; personal mission statement; academic research writing sample; official transcript from each college/university attended; three professional references. Additional exam requirements/recommendations for international students: Required—TOEFL (minimum score 577 paper-based; 90 iBT) or IELTS (minimum score 7). *Application deadline:* For fall admission, 8/1 for domestic and international students; for spring admission, 12/1 for domestic and international students. Applications are processed on a rolling basis. Application fee: $40. Electronic applications accepted. *Expenses:* Contact institution. *Financial support:* Applicants required to submit FAFSA. *Unit head:* Dr. Chris Meade, Professor/Dean, 800-631-0921. *Application contact:* Ty Sohlman, Admissions Counselor, 800-493-4937, Fax: 503-554-6111, E-mail: business@georgefox.edu.
Website: http://www.georgefox.edu/business/index.html.

Georgetown University, Graduate School of Arts and Sciences, Department of Economics, Washington, DC 20057. Offers econometrics (PhD); economic development (PhD); economic theory (PhD); industrial organization (PhD); international macro and finance (PhD); international trade (PhD); labor economics (PhD); macroeconomics (PhD); public economics and political economics (PhD); MA/PhD; MS/MA. *Degree requirements:* For doctorate, comprehensive exam, thesis/dissertation. *Entrance requirements:* For doctorate, GRE General Test. Additional exam requirements/recommendations for international students: Required—TOEFL. *Faculty research:* International economics, economic development.

The George Washington University, School of Business, Department of Finance, Washington, DC 20052. Offers finance (MSF, PhD); finance and investments (MBA); real estate and urban development (MBA). Part-time and evening/weekend programs available. *Faculty:* 18 full-time (4 women). *Students:* 207 full-time (83 women), 11 part-time (3 women); includes 21 minority (9 Black or African American, non-Hispanic/Latino; 4 Asian, non-Hispanic/Latino; 7 Hispanic/Latino; 1 Two or more races, non-Hispanic/Latino), 164 international. Average age 28. 780 applicants, 25% accepted, 91 enrolled. In 2013, 115 master's awarded. *Degree requirements:* For doctorate, thesis/dissertation. *Entrance requirements:* For master's, GMAT; for doctorate, GMAT or GRE. Additional exam requirements/recommendations for international students: Required—TOEFL. *Application deadline:* For fall admission, 4/1 priority date for domestic students; for spring admission, 10/1 for domestic students. Applications are processed on a rolling basis. Application fee: $75. *Financial support:* In 2013–14, 38 students received support. Fellowships, teaching assistantships, career-related internships or fieldwork, Federal Work-Study, and institutionally sponsored loans available. Financial award application deadline: 4/1. *Unit head:* Robert Van Order, Chair, 202-994-2559, E-mail: rvo@gwu.edu. *Application contact:* Kristin Williams, Assistant Vice President for Graduate and Special Enrollment Management, 202-994-0467, Fax: 202-994-0371, E-mail: ksw@gwu.edu.

Georgia Institute of Technology, Graduate Studies and Research, College of Management, Program in Business Administration, Atlanta, GA 30332-0001. Offers accounting (MBA); e-commerce (Certificate); engineering entrepreneurship (MBA); entrepreneurship (Certificate); finance (MBA); information technology management (MBA); international business (MBA, Certificate); management of technology (Certificate); marketing (MBA); operations management (MBA); organizational behavior (MBA); strategic management (MBA). *Accreditation:* AACSB.

Georgia Institute of Technology, Graduate Studies and Research, College of Management, Program in Management, Atlanta, GA 30332-0001. Offers accounting (PhD); finance (PhD); information technology management (PhD); marketing (PhD); operations management (PhD); organizational behavior (PhD); quantitative and computational finance (MS); strategic management (PhD). *Accreditation:* AACSB. *Degree requirements:* For doctorate, comprehensive exam, thesis/dissertation, oral exams. *Entrance requirements:* For master's and doctorate, GMAT. Additional exam requirements/recommendations for international students: Required—TOEFL. *Faculty research:* Management information systems, management of technology, international business, entrepreneurship, operations management.

Georgia State University, Andrew Young School of Policy Studies, Department of Economics, Atlanta, GA 30302-3083. Offers economics (MA); environmental economics (PhD); experimental economics (PhD); labor economics (PhD); policy (MA); public finance (PhD); urban and regional economics (PhD). MA offered through the College of Arts and Sciences. Part-time programs available. *Faculty:* 27 full-time (6 women), 2 part-time/adjunct (0 women). *Students:* 128 full-time (46 women), 16 part-time (3 women); includes 15 minority (7 Black or African American, non-Hispanic/Latino; 2 Asian, non-Hispanic/Latino; 5 Hispanic/Latino; 1 Two or more races, non-Hispanic/Latino), 77

international. Average age 29. 165 applicants, 50% accepted, 36 enrolled. In 2013, 41 master's, 8 doctorates awarded. Terminal master's awarded for partial completion of doctoral program. *Degree requirements:* For master's, thesis optional; for doctorate, comprehensive exam, thesis/dissertation. *Entrance requirements:* For master's, GRE; for doctorate, GRE. Additional exam requirements/recommendations for international students: Required—TOEFL (minimum score 603 paper-based; 100 iBT) or IELTS (minimum score 7). *Application deadline:* For fall admission, 2/15 for domestic and international students; for spring admission, 10/1 for domestic and international students. Application fee: $50. Electronic applications accepted. *Expenses: Tuition, area resident:* Full-time $4176; part-time $348 per credit hour. Tuition, state resident: full-time $14,544; part-time $1212 per credit hour. Tuition, nonresident: full-time $14,544; part-time $1212 per credit hour. Tuition and fees vary according to course load and program. *Financial support:* In 2013–14, fellowships with full tuition reimbursements (averaging $11,333 per year), research assistantships with full tuition reimbursements (averaging $9,788 per year), teaching assistantships with full tuition reimbursements (averaging $3,000 per year) were awarded; career-related internships or fieldwork also available. Financial award application deadline: 2/15. *Faculty research:* Public, experimental, urban/environmental, labor, and health economics. *Unit head:* Dr. Sally Wallace, Department Chair, 404-413-0046, Fax: 404-413-0145, E-mail: swallace@gsu.edu. *Application contact:* Charisma Parker, Admissions Coordinator, 404-413-0030, Fax: 404-413-0023, E-mail: cparker28@gsu.edu.
Website: http://aysps.gsu.edu/econ.

Georgia State University, Andrew Young School of Policy Studies, Department of Public Management and Policy, Atlanta, GA 30303. Offers criminal justice (MPA); disaster management (Certificate); disaster policy (MPA); environmental policy (PhD); health policy (PhD); management and finance (MPA); nonprofit management (MPA, Certificate); nonprofit policy (MPA); planning and economic development (MPP, Certificate); policy analysis and evaluation (MPA), including planning and economic development; public and nonprofit management (PhD); public finance and budgeting (PhD), including science and technology policy, urban and regional economic development; public finance policy (MPA), including social policy; public health (MPA). *Accreditation:* NASPAA (one or more programs are accredited). Part-time programs available. *Faculty:* 17 full-time (8 women), 3 part-time/adjunct (0 women). *Students:* 139 full-time (76 women), 95 part-time (59 women); includes 98 minority (69 Black or African American, non-Hispanic/Latino; 9 Asian, non-Hispanic/Latino; 11 Hispanic/Latino; 9 Two or more races, non-Hispanic/Latino), 19 international. Average age 29. 310 applicants, 55% accepted, 68 enrolled. In 2013, 68 master's, 9 other advanced degrees awarded. Terminal master's awarded for partial completion of doctoral program. *Degree requirements:* For master's, thesis optional; for doctorate, comprehensive exam, thesis/dissertation. *Entrance requirements:* For master's and doctorate, GRE. Additional exam requirements/recommendations for international students: Required—TOEFL (minimum score 603 paper-based; 100 iBT) or IELTS (minimum score 7). *Application deadline:* For fall admission, 2/15 for domestic and international students; for spring admission, 10/1 for domestic and international students. Application fee: $50. Electronic applications accepted. *Expenses: Tuition, area resident:* Full-time $4176; part-time $348 per credit hour. Tuition, state resident: full-time $14,544; part-time $1212 per credit hour. Tuition, nonresident: full-time $14,544; part-time $1212 per credit hour. Tuition and fees vary according to course load and program. *Financial support:* In 2013–14, fellowships (averaging $8,194 per year), research assistantships (averaging $8,068 per year), teaching assistantships (averaging $3,600 per year) were awarded; institutionally sponsored loans, scholarships/grants, health care benefits, and unspecified assistantships also available. Financial award application deadline: 2/1. *Faculty research:* Public budgeting and finance, public management, nonprofit management, performance measurement and management, urban development. *Unit head:* Dr. Gregory Burr Lewis, Chair and Professor, 404-413-0114, Fax: 404-413-0104, E-mail: glewis@gsu.edu. *Application contact:* Charisma Parker, Admissions Coordinator, 404-413-0030, Fax: 404-413-0023, E-mail: cparker28@gsu.edu.
Website: http://aysps.gsu.edu/pmap/.

Georgia State University, J. Mack Robinson College of Business, Department of Finance, Atlanta, GA 30302-3083. Offers MBA, MS, PhD. Part-time and evening/weekend programs available. *Faculty:* 11 full-time (2 women). *Students:* 47 full-time (15 women), 20 part-time (2 women); includes 22 minority (12 Black or African American, non-Hispanic/Latino; 5 Asian, non-Hispanic/Latino; 4 Hispanic/Latino; 1 Two or more races, non-Hispanic/Latino), 16 international. Average age 31. 94 applicants, 7% accepted, 5 enrolled. In 2013, 60 master's, 2 doctorates awarded. *Degree requirements:* For doctorate, comprehensive exam, thesis/dissertation. *Entrance requirements:* For master's, GRE or GMAT, transcripts from all institutions attended, resume, essays; for doctorate, GRE or GMAT, three letters of recommendation, personal statement, transcripts from all institutions attended, resume. Additional exam requirements/recommendations for international students: Required—TOEFL (minimum score 610 paper-based; 101 iBT), IELTS (minimum score 7). *Application deadline:* For fall admission, 5/1 priority date for domestic students, 2/1 priority date for international students; for spring admission, 9/15 priority date for domestic students, 4/1 priority date for international students. Applications are processed on a rolling basis. Application fee: $50. Electronic applications accepted. *Expenses: Tuition, area resident:* Full-time $4176; part-time $348 per credit hour. Tuition, state resident: full-time $14,544; part-time $1212 per credit hour. Tuition, nonresident: full-time $14,544; part-time $1212 per credit hour. Tuition and fees vary according to course load and program. *Financial support:* Research assistantships, teaching assistantships, scholarships/grants, tuition waivers, and unspecified assistantships available. *Faculty research:* Mergers and acquisitions, asset pricing, mutual and hedge funds, derivatives, corporate governance. *Unit head:* Dr. Gerald D. Gay, Professor of Finance and Chair of the Department of Finance, 404-413-7310, Fax: 404-413-7312. *Application contact:* Toby McChesney, Assistant Dean for Graduate Recruiting and Student Services, 404-413-7167, Fax: 404-413-7162, E-mail: rcbgradadmissions@gsu.edu.
Website: http://www.robinson.gsu.edu/finance/.

Georgia State University, J. Mack Robinson College of Business, Department of Risk Management and Insurance, Program in Risk Management and Insurance, Atlanta, GA 30302-3083. Offers enterprise risk management (MBA, Certificate); financial risk management (MBA); mathematical risk management (MS); risk and insurance (MS); risk management and insurance (MBA, PhD); MAS/MRM. Part-time and evening/weekend programs available. *Students:* Average age 0. *Degree requirements:* For doctorate, comprehensive exam, thesis/dissertation. *Entrance requirements:* For master's, GRE or GMAT, transcripts from all institutions attended, resume, essays. Additional exam requirements/recommendations for international students: Required—TOEFL (minimum score 610 paper-based; 101 iBT), IELTS (minimum score 7). *Application deadline:* For fall admission, 5/1 priority date for domestic students, 2/1 priority date for international students; for spring admission, 9/15 priority date for domestic students, 4/1 priority date for international students. Applications are processed on a rolling basis. Application fee: $50. Electronic applications accepted. *Expenses: Tuition, area resident:* Full-time $4176; part-time $348 per credit hour. Tuition, state resident: full-time $14,544; part-time $1212 per credit hour. Tuition, nonresident: full-time $14,544; part-time $1212 per credit hour. Tuition and fees vary according to course load and program. *Financial support:* Research assistantships, scholarships/grants, tuition waivers, and unspecified assistantships available. *Faculty research:* Insurance economics, structure and performance of insurance markets, regulation and policy in insurance markets, asset pricing theory, financial econometrics. *Unit head:* Dr. Martin Grace, Professor of Risk Management and Legal Studies/Chair of the Department of Risk Management and Insurance, 404-413-7500, Fax: 404-413-7499. *Application contact:* Toby McChesney, Graduate Recruiting Contact, 404-413-7167, Fax: 404-413-7162, E-mail: rcbgradadmissions@gsu.edu.
Website: http://www.rmi.gsu.edu/graduate/grad_rmi.shtml.

Golden Gate University, Ageno School of Business, San Francisco, CA 94105-2968. Offers accounting (MBA); business administration (EMBA, MBA, PMBA, DBA); finance (MBA, MS, Certificate); financial planning (MS, Certificate); healthcare information systems (Certificate); human resource management (MBA, MS); human resources management (Certificate); information systems (MS); information technology (MBA); information technology management (Certificate); integrated marketing and communications (MS, Certificate); international business (MBA); management (MBA); marketing (MBA, MS, Certificate); operations supply chain management (Certificate); psychology (MA, Certificate); public administration (EMPA); public relations (MS, Certificate); technical market analysis (Certificate); JD/MBA. Part-time and evening/weekend programs available. *Degree requirements:* For doctorate, thesis/dissertation, qualifying examination. *Entrance requirements:* For master's, GMAT (MBA), minimum GPA of 2.5 (MS). Additional exam requirements/recommendations for international students: Required—TOEFL (minimum score 550 paper-based; 79 iBT). Electronic applications accepted. *Expenses:* Contact institution.

Goldey-Beacom College, Graduate Program, Wilmington, DE 19808-1999. Offers business administration (MBA); finance (MS); financial management (MBA); health care management (MBA); human resource management (MBA); information technology (MBA); international business management (MBA); major finance (MBA); major taxation (MBA); management (MM); marketing management (MBA); taxation (MBA, MS). *Accreditation:* ACBSP. Part-time and evening/weekend programs available. *Entrance requirements:* For master's, GMAT, MAT, GRE, minimum GPA of 3.0. Additional exam requirements/recommendations for international students: Required—TOEFL (minimum score 65 iBT); Recommended—IELTS (minimum score 6). Electronic applications accepted.

The Graduate Center, City University of New York, Graduate Studies, Program in Business, New York, NY 10016-4039. Offers accounting (PhD); behavioral science (PhD); finance (PhD); management planning systems (PhD). *Degree requirements:* For doctorate, thesis/dissertation. *Entrance requirements:* For doctorate, GMAT, writing sample (15 pages). Additional exam requirements/recommendations for international students: Required—TOEFL. Electronic applications accepted.

Grand Canyon University, College of Business, Phoenix, AZ 85017-1097. Offers accounting (MBA); corporate business administration (MBA); disaster preparedness and crisis management (MBA); executive fire service leadership (MS); finance (MBA); general management (MBA); government and policy (MPA); health care management (MPA); health systems management (MBA); human resource management (MBA); innovation (MBA); leadership (MBA, MS); management of information system (MBA); marketing (MBA); project-based (MBA); six sigma (MBA); strategic human resource management (MBA). *Accreditation:* ACBSP. Part-time and evening/weekend programs available. Postbaccalaureate distance learning degree programs offered (no on-campus study). *Entrance requirements:* For master's, equivalent of two years full-time professional work experience. Additional exam requirements/recommendations for international students: Required—TOEFL (minimum score 575 paper-based; 90 iBT), IELTS (minimum score 7). Electronic applications accepted.

Hawai`i Pacific University, College of Business Administration, Honolulu, HI 96813. Offers accounting/CPA (MBA); e-business (MBA); economics (MBA); finance (MBA); healthcare management (MBA); human resource management (MA, MBA); information systems (MBA, MSIS); international business (MBA); management (MBA); marketing (MBA); organizational change (MA, MBA); travel industry management (MBA). Part-time and evening/weekend programs available. *Faculty:* 22 full-time (9 women), 6 part-time/adjunct (0 women). *Students:* 232 full-time (100 women), 174 part-time (84 women); includes 241 minority (18 Black or African American, non-Hispanic/Latino; 112 Asian, non-Hispanic/Latino; 33 Hispanic/Latino; 11 Native Hawaiian or other Pacific Islander, non-Hispanic/Latino; 67 Two or more races, non-Hispanic/Latino). Average age 31. 240 applicants, 81% accepted, 102 enrolled. In 2013, 206 master's awarded. *Degree requirements:* For master's, thesis. *Entrance requirements:* For master's, GMAT. Additional exam requirements/recommendations for international students: Recommended—TOEFL (minimum score 550 paper-based; 80 iBT), TWE (minimum score 5). *Application deadline:* For fall admission, 2/15 priority date for domestic students; for spring admission, 10/15 priority date for domestic students. Applications are processed on a rolling basis. Application fee: $50. Electronic applications accepted. *Financial support:* In 2013–14, 90 students received support. Research assistantships, career-related internships or fieldwork, Federal Work-Study, scholarships/grants, tuition waivers, and unspecified assistantships available. Financial award application deadline: 3/1; financial award applicants required to submit FAFSA. *Faculty research:* Statistical control process as used by management, studies in comparative cross-cultural management styles, not-for-profit management. *Unit head:* Dr. Deborah Crown, Dean, 808-544-0275, Fax: 808-544-0283, E-mail: dcrown@hpu.edu. *Application contact:* Rumi Yoshida, Associate Director of Graduate Admissions, 808-543-8034, Fax: 808-544-0280, E-mail: grad@hpu.edu.
Website: http://www.hpu.edu/CBA/Graduate/index.html.

HEC Montreal, School of Business Administration, Graduate Diplomas Programs in Administration, Program in Financial Professions, Montréal, QC H3T 2A7, Canada. Offers Graduate Diploma. All courses are given in French. *Students:* 37 full-time (12 women), 2 part-time (1 woman). 93 applicants, 61% accepted, 37 enrolled. In 2013, 14 Graduate Diplomas awarded. *Entrance requirements:* For degree, bachelor's degree in administration (for finance option). *Application deadline:* For fall admission, 4/15 for domestic and international students. Application fee: $83. Electronic applications accepted. *Expenses: Tuition, area resident:* Part-time $74.14 per credit. Tuition, state resident: full-time $2669.04; part-time $201.83 per credit. Tuition, nonresident: full-time $7266; part-time $500.59 per credit. *International tuition:* $18,021.24 full-time. *Required fees:* $1529.70; $36.20 per credit. $65.50 per term. Tuition and fees vary according to degree level and program. *Financial support:* In 2013–14, 1,007 students received support. Research assistantships, teaching assistantships, and scholarships/grants available. Financial award application deadline: 9/2. *Unit head:* Silvia Ponce, Academic Supervisor, 514-340-6393, Fax: 514-340-6915, E-mail: silvia.ponce@hec.ca. *Application contact:* Jo Anne Audet, Administrative Director, 514-340-1315, Fax: 514-340-6411, E-mail: joanne.audet@hec.ca.
Website: http://www.hec.ca/programmes_formations/des/dess/dess_professions_financieres/index.html.

HEC Montreal, School of Business Administration, Master of Science Programs in Administration, Program in Applied Financial Economics, Montréal, QC H3T 2A7, Canada. Offers M Sc. All courses are given in French. *Students:* 22 full-time (8 women), 5 part-time (0 women). 23 applicants, 48% accepted, 6 enrolled. In 2013, 8 master's awarded. *Degree requirements:* For master's, one foreign language, thesis. *Entrance*

requirements: For master's, Test de francais international (TFI) with minimum score of 850 (for those who have never studied in French), BBA, undergraduate degree in another field, degree deemed equivalent by program director and minimum GPA of 3.0 on 4.3 scale. *Application deadline:* For fall admission, 3/15 for domestic and international students; for winter admission, 9/15 for domestic and international students. Application fee: $83 Canadian dollars. Electronic applications accepted. *Expenses: Tuition, area resident:* Part-time $74.14 per credit. Tuition, state resident: full-time $2669.04; part-time $201.83 per credit. Tuition, nonresident: full-time $7266; part-time $500.59 per credit. *International tuition:* $18,021.24 full-time. *Required fees:* $1529.70; $36.20 per credit. $65.50 per term. Tuition and fees vary according to degree level and program. *Financial support:* In 2013–14, 1,007 students received support. Research assistantships, teaching assistantships, and scholarships/grants available. Financial award application deadline: 9/2. *Unit head:* Dr. Anne Bourhis, Director, 514-340-6873, Fax: 514-340-6880, E-mail: anne.bourhis@hec.ca. *Application contact:* Marianne de Moura, Administrative Director, 514-340-7106, Fax: 514-340-6411, E-mail: marianne.de-moura@hec.ca.
Website: http://www.hec.ca/programmes_formations/msc/options/finance/economie_fin_appliquee/index.html.

HEC Montreal, School of Business Administration, Master of Science Programs in Administration, Program in Finance, Montréal, QC H3T 2A7, Canada. Offers M Sc. All courses are given in French. *Students:* 103 full-time (23 women), 15 part-time (3 women). 108 applicants, 53% accepted, 40 enrolled. In 2013, 31 master's awarded. *Degree requirements:* For master's, one foreign language. *Entrance requirements:* For master's, Test de francais international (TFI) with minimum score of 850 (for those who have never studied in French), BBA, undergraduate degree in another field, degree deemed equivalent by program director and minimum GPA of 3.0 on 4.3 scale. *Application deadline:* For fall admission, 3/15 for domestic and international students; for winter admission, 9/15 for domestic and international students. Application fee: $83 Canadian dollars. Electronic applications accepted. *Expenses: Tuition, area resident:* Part-time $74.14 per credit. Tuition, state resident: full-time $2669.04; part-time $201.83 per credit. Tuition, nonresident: full-time $7266; part-time $500.59 per credit. *International tuition:* $18,021.24 full-time. *Required fees:* $1529.70; $36.20 per credit. $65.50 per term. Tuition and fees vary according to degree level and program. *Financial support:* In 2013–14, 1,007 students received support. Research assistantships, teaching assistantships, and scholarships/grants available. Financial award application deadline: 9/2. *Unit head:* Dr. Anne Bourhis, Director, 514-340-6873, Fax: 514-340-6880, E-mail: anne.bourhis@hec.ca. *Application contact:* Marianne de Moura, Administrative Director, 514-340-7106, Fax: 514-340-6411, E-mail: marianne.de-moura@hec.ca.
Website: http://www.hec.ca/programmes_formations/msc/options/finance/finance/index.html.

Hofstra University, Frank G. Zarb School of Business, Programs in Finance, Hempstead, NY 11549. Offers business administration (MBA), including finance, real estate management; corporate finance (Advanced Certificate); finance (MS); investment management (Advanced Certificate); quantitative finance (MS).

Holy Family University, Division of Extended Learning, Bensalem, PA 19020. Offers business administration (MBA); finance (MBA); health care administration (MBA); human resources management (MBA). *Accreditation:* ACBSP. Part-time and evening/weekend programs available. *Faculty:* 13 part-time/adjunct (3 women). *Students:* 116 part-time (59 women); includes 4 minority (2 Black or African American, non-Hispanic/Latino; 1 Asian, non-Hispanic/Latino; 1 Hispanic/Latino). Average age 34. 25 applicants, 96% accepted, 6 enrolled. In 2013, 52 master's awarded. *Entrance requirements:* For master's, minimum GPA of 3.0, interview, essay/professional statement, 2 recommendations, current resume, official transcripts of college or university work. Additional exam requirements/recommendations for international students: Required—TOEFL (minimum score 550 paper-based; 79 iBT). *Application deadline:* For fall admission, 7/1 priority date for domestic and international students; for spring admission, 11/1 priority date for domestic and international students; for summer admission, 4/1 priority date for domestic and international students. Applications are processed on a rolling basis. Application fee: $50. Electronic applications accepted. *Expenses: Tuition:* Full-time $12,060. *Required fees:* $250. Tuition and fees vary according to degree level. *Financial support:* In 2013–14, 3 students received support. Available to part-time students. Applicants required to submit FAFSA. *Unit head:* Chris Quinn, Director of Academic Services, 267-341-5006, Fax: 215-633-0558, E-mail: cquinn1@holyfamily.edu. *Application contact:* Don Reinmold, Director of Admissions, 267-341-5001 Ext. 3230, Fax: 215-633-0558, E-mail: dreinmold@holyfamily.edu.

Holy Names University, Graduate Division, Department of Business, Oakland, CA 94619-1699. Offers energy and environment management (MBA); finance (MBA); management and leadership (MBA); marketing (MBA); sports management (MBA). Part-time and evening/weekend programs available. *Faculty:* 4 full-time, 12 part-time/adjunct. *Students:* 23 full-time (14 women), 20 part-time (12 women); includes 30 minority (19 Black or African American, non-Hispanic/Latino; 4 Asian, non-Hispanic/Latino; 7 Hispanic/Latino), 4 international. Average age 32. 35 applicants, 31% accepted, 7 enrolled. In 2013, 30 master's awarded. *Entrance requirements:* For master's, minimum undergraduate GPA of 2.6 overall, 3.0 in major; two recommendations (letter or form) from previous professors or current or previous work supervisors, 1-3 page personal statement, resume. Additional exam requirements/recommendations for international students: Required—TOEFL (minimum score 550 paper-based; 79 iBT). *Application deadline:* For fall admission, 8/1 priority date for domestic students, 7/15 for international students; for spring admission, 12/1 priority date for domestic students, 12/1 for international students; for summer admission, 5/1 priority date for domestic students, 5/1 for international students. Applications are processed on a rolling basis. Application fee: $65. Electronic applications accepted. Application fee is waived when completed online. *Expenses: Tuition:* Part-time $866 per unit. *Financial support:* Career-related internships or fieldwork, Federal Work-Study, scholarships/grants, and unspecified assistantships available. Support available to part-time students. Financial award application deadline: 3/2; financial award applicants required to submit FAFSA. *Faculty research:* Business ethics, sustainable economics, accounting models, cross-cultural management, diversity in organizations. *Unit head:* Dr. Hector Saez, MBA Program Director, 510-436-1622, E-mail: saez@hnu.edu. *Application contact:* 800-430-1321, Fax: 510-436-1325, E-mail: graduateadmissions@hnu.edu.
Website: http://www.hnu.edu.

Hood College, Graduate School, Department of Economics and Business Administration, Frederick, MD 21701-8575. Offers accounting (MBA); administration and management (MBA); finance (MBA); human resource management (MBA); information systems (MBA); marketing (MBA); public management (MBA). *Accreditation:* ACBSP. Part-time and evening/weekend programs available. *Faculty:* 6 full-time (2 women), 7 part-time/adjunct (1 woman). *Students:* 31 full-time (21 women), 131 part-time (66 women); includes 36 minority (18 Black or African American, non-Hispanic/Latino; 7 Asian, non-Hispanic/Latino; 8 Hispanic/Latino; 3 Two or more races, non-Hispanic/Latino), 12 international. Average age 31. 78 applicants, 56% accepted, 33 enrolled. In 2013, 35 master's awarded. *Degree requirements:* For master's, capstone/final research project. *Entrance requirements:* For master's, minimum GPA of 2.75, resume, letters of recommendation. Additional exam requirements/recommendations for international students: Required—TOEFL (minimum score 575 paper-based; 89 iBT), IELTS (minimum score 6.5). *Application deadline:* For fall admission, 7/15 priority date for domestic students, 7/15 for international students; for spring admission, 12/1 priority date for domestic students, 12/1 for international students. Applications are processed on a rolling basis. Application fee: $35. Electronic applications accepted. Application fee is waived when completed online. *Expenses: Tuition:* Part-time $405 per credit. *Required fees:* $100 per semester. *Financial support:* In 2013–14, 11 students received support. Tuition waivers (partial) and unspecified assistantships available. Financial award applicants required to submit FAFSA. *Faculty research:* Corporate strategy and sustainable competitive advantages, business ethics, entrepreneurship, investments management, economic development. *Unit head:* Dr. Anita Jose, Program Director, 301-696-3691, Fax: 301-696-3597, E-mail: jose@hood.edu. *Application contact:* Dr. Maria Green Cowles, Dean of Graduate School, 301-696-3811, Fax: 301-696-3597, E-mail: gofurther@hood.edu.

Howard University, School of Business, Graduate Programs in Business, Washington, DC 20059-0002. Offers accounting (MBA); entrepreneurship (MBA); finance (MBA); general management (MBA); human resources management (MBA); information systems (MBA); international business (MBA); marketing (MBA); supply chain management (MBA); JD/MBA. *Accreditation:* AACSB. Part-time and evening/weekend programs available. Postbaccalaureate distance learning degree programs offered (no on-campus study). *Entrance requirements:* For master's, GMAT, minimum 1 year post undergraduate work experience, resume, 3 letters of recommendation, advanced college algebra. Additional exam requirements/recommendations for international students: Required—TOEFL. *Faculty research:* Marketing research in multi-ethnic populations, U.S. trade policies and international relations, risk management (finance).

Hult International Business School, Program in Business Administration - Hult London Campus, London WC 1B 4JP, United Kingdom. Offers entrepreneurship (MBA); international business (MBA); international finance (MBA); marketing (MBA). Part-time programs available. *Degree requirements:* For master's, comprehensive exam, thesis, internship. *Entrance requirements:* Additional exam requirements/recommendations for international students: Required—TOEFL (minimum score 580 paper-based), TWE (minimum score 5). Electronic applications accepted.

Hult International Business School, Program in Finance, Cambridge, MA 02141. Offers MF.

Hult International Business School, Program in Finance - Hult Dubai Campus, Dubai, MA 02141, United Arab Emirates. Offers MF.

Hult International Business School, Program in Finance - Hult London Campus, London WC 1B 4JP, United Kingdom. Offers MF. *Entrance requirements:* Additional exam requirements/recommendations for international students: Required—TOEFL (minimum score 580 paper-based), TWE (minimum score 5). Electronic applications accepted.

Illinois Institute of Technology, Chicago-Kent College of Law, Chicago, IL 60661-3691. Offers family law (LL M); financial services (LL M); international intellectual property (LL M); law (JD); taxation (LL M); U.S., international, and transnational law (LL M); JD/LL M; JD/MBA; JD/MPA; JD/MPH; JD/MS. *Accreditation:* ABA. Part-time and evening/weekend programs available. *Faculty:* 71 full-time (27 women), 154 part-time/adjunct (40 women). *Students:* 856 full-time (403 women), 137 part-time (63 women); includes 230 minority (44 Black or African American, non-Hispanic/Latino; 56 Asian, non-Hispanic/Latino; 108 Hispanic/Latino; 2 Native Hawaiian or other Pacific Islander, non-Hispanic/Latino; 20 Two or more races, non-Hispanic/Latino), 115 international. Average age 27. 2,676 applicants, 55% accepted, 282 enrolled. In 2013, 106 master's, 286 doctorates awarded. Terminal master's awarded for partial completion of doctoral program. *Entrance requirements:* For master's, 1st degree in law or certified license to practice law; for doctorate, LSAT. Additional exam requirements/recommendations for international students: Required—TOEFL (minimum score 600 paper-based; 100 iBT); Recommended—IELTS (minimum score 7). *Application deadline:* For fall admission, 3/15 priority date for domestic students, 2/1 priority date for international students. Applications are processed on a rolling basis. Application fee: $0 ($75 for international students). Electronic applications accepted. *Expenses:* Contact institution. *Financial support:* In 2013–14, 742 students received support. Career-related internships or fieldwork, Federal Work-Study, institutionally sponsored loans, scholarships/grants, and tuition waivers (full) available. Support available to part-time students. Financial award application deadline: 3/15; financial award applicants required to submit FAFSA. *Faculty research:* Constitutional law, bioethics, environmental law, intellectual property. *Total annual research expenditures:* $217,995. *Unit head:* Harold J. Krent, Dean, 312-906-5010, Fax: 312-906-5335, E-mail: hkrent@kentlaw.iit.edu. *Application contact:* Nicole Vilches, Assistant Dean, 312-906-5020, Fax: 312-906-5274, E-mail: admissions@kentlaw.iit.edu.
Website: http://www.kentlaw.iit.edu/.

Illinois Institute of Technology, Graduate College, College of Science and Letters, Department of Computer Science, Chicago, IL 60616. Offers business (MCS); computational intelligence (MCS); computer networking and telecommunications (MCS); computer science (MCS, MS, PhD); cyber-physical systems (MCS); data analytics (MCS); distributed and cloud computing (MCS); education (MCS); finance (MCS); information security and assurance (MCS); information systems (MCS); software engineering (MCS); teaching (MST). Part-time and evening/weekend programs available. Postbaccalaureate distance learning degree programs offered (no on-campus study). Terminal master's awarded for partial completion of doctoral program. *Degree requirements:* For master's, thesis optional; for doctorate, comprehensive exam, thesis/dissertation. *Entrance requirements:* For master's, GRE General Test (minimum scores: 1000 Quantitative and Verbal, 3.0 Analytical Writing), minimum undergraduate GPA of 3.0; for doctorate, GRE General Test (minimum scores: 1100 Quantitative and Verbal, 3.5 Analytical Writing), minimum undergraduate GPA of 3.0. Additional exam requirements/recommendations for international students: Required—TOEFL (minimum score 523 paper-based; 70 iBT). Electronic applications accepted. *Faculty research:* Algorithms, data structures, artificial intelligence, computer architecture, computer graphics, computer networking and telecommunications, computer vision, database systems, distributed and parallel processing, I/O systems, image processing, information retrieval, natural language processing, software engineering and system software, machine learning, cloud computing.

Illinois Institute of Technology, Stuart School of Business, Program in Business Administration, Chicago, IL 60661. Offers financial management (MBA); innovation and emerging enterprises (MBA); management science (MBA); marketing (MBA); sustainability (MBA); JD/MBA; M Des/MBA; MBA/MS. *Accreditation:* AACSB. Part-time and evening/weekend programs available. *Entrance requirements:* For master's, GRE (minimum score 1000) or GMAT (500). Additional exam requirements/recommendations for international students: Required—TOEFL (minimum score 600 paper-based; 85 iBT); Recommended—IELTS (minimum score 7). Electronic applications accepted. *Expenses:* Contact institution. *Faculty research:* Global management and marketing strategy, technological innovation, management science, financial management, knowledge management.

Illinois Institute of Technology, Stuart School of Business, Program in Finance, Chicago, IL 60661. Offers MS, JD/MS, MBA/MS. Part-time and evening/weekend programs available. *Entrance requirements:* For master's, GRE (minimum score 1200) or GMAT (600). Additional exam requirements/recommendations for international students: Required—TOEFL (minimum score 600 paper-based; 85 iBT); Recommended—IELTS (minimum score 7). Electronic applications accepted. *Expenses:* Contact institution. *Faculty research:* Factor models for investment management, credit rating and credit risk management, hedge fund performance analysis, option trading and risk management, global asset allocation strategies.

Indiana University Bloomington, School of Public and Environmental Affairs, Public Affairs Programs, Bloomington, IN 47405. Offers economic development (MPA); energy (MPA); environmental policy (PhD); environmental policy and natural resource management (MPA); information systems (MPA); international development (MPA); local government management (MPA); nonprofit management (MPA, Certificate); policy analysis (MPA); public budgeting and financial management (Certificate); public finance (PhD); public financial administration (MPA); public management (MPA, PhD, Certificate); public policy analysis (PhD); social entrepreneurship (Certificate); specialized public affairs (MPA); sustainability and sustainable development (MPA); JD/MPA; MPA/MA; MPA/MIS; MPA/MLS; MSES/MPA. *Accreditation:* NASPAA (one or more programs are accredited). Part-time programs available. *Faculty:* 79 full-time (32 women), 8 part-time/adjunct (3 women). *Students:* 433 full-time (232 women), 75 part-time (39 women); includes 90 minority (19 Black or African American, non-Hispanic/Latino; 1 American Indian or Alaska Native, non-Hispanic/Latino; 49 Asian, non-Hispanic/Latino; 14 Hispanic/Latino; 2 Native Hawaiian or other Pacific Islander, non-Hispanic/Latino; 5 Two or more races, non-Hispanic/Latino), 70 international. Average age 27. 714 applicants, 73% accepted, 253 enrolled. In 2013, 171 master's, 3 doctorates, 4 other advanced degrees awarded. *Degree requirements:* For master's, capstone, internship; for doctorate, comprehensive exam, thesis/dissertation. *Entrance requirements:* For master's, GRE General Test or GMAT, official transcripts, 3 letters of recommendation, resume, personal statement; for doctorate, GRE General Test, official transcripts, 3 letters of recommendation, statement of purpose. Additional exam requirements/recommendations for international students: Required—TOEFL (minimum score 600 paper-based; 96 iBT); Recommended—IELTS (minimum score 7). *Application deadline:* For fall admission, 2/1 priority date for domestic students, 12/1 priority date for international students; for spring admission, 11/15 for domestic students, 9/1 for international students. Applications are processed on a rolling basis. Application fee: $55 ($65 for international students). Electronic applications accepted. *Financial support:* Fellowships with partial tuition reimbursements, research assistantships with full and partial tuition reimbursements, teaching assistantships with full and partial tuition reimbursements, career-related internships or fieldwork, Federal Work-Study, scholarships/grants, health care benefits, unspecified assistantships, and Service Corps Program; Educational Opportunity Fellowships available. Financial award application deadline: 2/1; financial award applicants required to submit FAFSA. *Faculty research:* International development, environmental policy and resource management, policy analysis, public finance, public management, urban management, nonprofit management, energy policy, social policy, public finance. *Unit head:* Megan Siehl, Assistant Director, Admissions and Financial Aid, 812-855-9485, Fax: 812-856-3665, E-mail: speampo@indiana.edu. *Application contact:* Lane Bowman, Admissions Services Coordinator, 812-855-2840, Fax: 812-856-3665, E-mail: speaapps@indiana.edu.
Website: http://www.indiana.edu/~spea/prospective_students/masters/.

Indiana University Southeast, School of Business, New Albany, IN 47150-6405. Offers business administration (MBA); strategic finance (MS). *Accreditation:* AACSB. *Faculty:* 11 full-time (2 women). *Students:* 7 full-time (0 women), 187 part-time (78 women); includes 17 minority (5 Black or African American, non-Hispanic/Latino; 7 Asian, non-Hispanic/Latino; 1 Hispanic/Latino; 2 Native Hawaiian or other Pacific Islander, non-Hispanic/Latino; 2 Two or more races, non-Hispanic/Latino), 6 international. Average age 31. 60 applicants, 75% accepted, 36 enrolled. In 2013, 76 master's awarded. *Degree requirements:* For master's, community service. *Entrance requirements:* For master's, GMAT, work experience. Additional exam requirements/recommendations for international students: Required—TOEFL. *Expenses:* Contact institution. *Financial support:* In 2013–14, 2 teaching assistantships (averaging $4,500 per year) were awarded. *Unit head:* Dr. Jay White, Dean, 812-941-2362, Fax: 812-941-2672. *Application contact:* Admissions Counselor, 812-941-2212, Fax: 812-941-2595, E-mail: admissions@ius.edu.
Website: http://www.ius.edu/mba.

Instituto Centroamericano de Administración de Empresas, Graduate Programs, La Garita, Costa Rica. Offers agribusiness management (MIAM); business administration (EMBA); finance (MBA); real estate management (MGREM); sustainable development (MBA); technology (MBA). *Degree requirements:* For master's, comprehensive exam, essay. *Entrance requirements:* For master's, GMAT or GRE General Test, fluency in Spanish, interview, letters of recommendation, minimum 1 year of work experience. Additional exam requirements/recommendations for international students: Recommended—TOEFL. Electronic applications accepted. *Faculty research:* Competitiveness, production.

Instituto Tecnologico de Santo Domingo, Graduate School, Area of Business, Santo Domingo, Dominican Republic. Offers banking and securities markets (M Mgmt); corporate finance (M Mgmt); human resources management (M Mgmt, Certificate); international trade management (M Mgmt); marketing (M Mgmt); organizational development (M Mgmt); quality and productivity management (Certificate); tax management and planning (M Mgmt); upper management (M Mgmt).

Instituto Tecnológico y de Estudios Superiores de Monterrey, Campus Central de Veracruz, Graduate Programs, Córdoba, Mexico. Offers administration (MA); administration of information technologies (MTI); computer sciences (MCC); education (MEE); educational institution administration (MAD); educational technology (MTE); electronic commerce (MCE); finance (MAF); humanistic studies (MEH); international business for Latin America (MNL); marketing (MMT); science (MCP). Part-time and evening/weekend programs available. Postbaccalaureate distance learning degree programs offered (minimal on-campus study). *Degree requirements:* For master's, thesis (for some programs). *Entrance requirements:* For master's, PAEP College Board. Electronic applications accepted.

Instituto Tecnológico y de Estudios Superiores de Monterrey, Campus Ciudad de México, School of Business Administration, Ciudad de Mexico, Mexico. Offers business administration (EMBA, MBA, PhD); economy (MBA); finance (MBA). EMBA program offered jointly with The University of Texas at Austin. Part-time and evening/weekend programs available. Postbaccalaureate distance learning degree programs offered (minimal on-campus study). *Entrance requirements:* For master's and doctorate, Instituto entrance exam. Additional exam requirements/recommendations for international students: Required—TOEFL.

Instituto Tecnológico y de Estudios Superiores de Monterrey, Campus Ciudad Obregón, Program in Finance, Ciudad Obregón, Mexico. Offers MF.

Instituto Tecnológico y de Estudios Superiores de Monterrey, Campus Cuernavaca, Programs in Business Administration, Temixco, Mexico. Offers finance (MA); human resources management (MA); international business (MA); marketing (MA).

Instituto Tecnológico y de Estudios Superiores de Monterrey, Campus Estado de México, Professional and Graduate Division, Estado de Mexico, Mexico. Offers administration of information technologies (MITA); architecture (M Arch); business administration (GMBA, MBA); computer sciences (MCS, PhD); education (M Ed); educational institution administration (MAD); educational technology and innovation (PhD); electronic commerce (MEC); environmental systems (MS); finance (MAF); humanistic studies (MHS); information sciences and knowledge management (MISKM); information systems (MS); manufacturing systems (MS); marketing (MEM); quality systems and productivity (MS); science and materials engineering (PhD); telecommunications management (MTM). Part-time programs available. Postbaccalaureate distance learning degree programs offered (minimal on-campus study). *Degree requirements:* For master's, one foreign language, thesis (for some programs); for doctorate, one foreign language, thesis/dissertation. *Entrance requirements:* For master's, E-PAEP 500, interview; for doctorate, E-PAEP 500, research proposal. Additional exam requirements/recommendations for international students: Required—TOEFL (minimum score 550 paper-based). *Faculty research:* Surface treatments by plasmas, mechanical properties, robotics, graphical computing, mechatronics security protocols.

Instituto Tecnológico y de Estudios Superiores de Monterrey, Campus Guadalajara, Program in Finance, Zapopan, Mexico. Offers MF. *Degree requirements:* For master's, one foreign language, thesis. *Entrance requirements:* For master's, ITESM admission test.

Instituto Tecnológico y de Estudios Superiores de Monterrey, Campus Irapuato, Graduate Programs, Irapuato, Mexico. Offers administration (MBA); administration of information technology (MAIT); administration of telecommunications (MAT); architecture (M Arch); computer science (MCS); education (M Ed); educational administration (MEA); educational innovation and technology (DEIT); educational technology (MET); electronic commerce (MBA); environmental administration and planning (MEAP); environmental systems (MES); finances (MBA); humanistic studies (MHS); international management for Latin American executives (MIMLAE); library and information science (MLIS); manufacturing quality management (MMQM); marketing research (MBA).

Instituto Tecnológico y de Estudios Superiores de Monterrey, Campus Monterrey, Graduate School of Business Administration and Leadership, Program in Business Administration, Monterrey, Mexico. Offers business administration (MA, MBA); finance (M Sc); international business (M Sc); marketing (M Sc). *Accreditation:* AACSB. Part-time programs available. *Degree requirements:* For master's, one foreign language, thesis. *Entrance requirements:* For master's, GMAT. Additional exam requirements/recommendations for international students: Required—TOEFL. *Faculty research:* Technology management, quality management, organizational theory and behavior.

Inter American University of Puerto Rico, Aguadilla Campus, Graduate School, Aguadilla, PR 00605. Offers accounting (MBA); counseling psychology specializing in family (MS); criminal justice (MA); educative management and leadership (MA); elementary education (M Ed); finance (MBA); human resources (MBA); industrial management (MBA); management information systems (MBA); marketing (MBA). Part-time and evening/weekend programs available. *Degree requirements:* For master's, comprehensive exam. *Entrance requirements:* For master's, EXADEP, 2 letters of recommendation, minimum GPA of 2.5. Electronic applications accepted.

Inter American University of Puerto Rico, Arecibo Campus, Program in Business Administration, Arecibo, PR 00614-4050. Offers accounting (MBA); finance (MBA); human resources (MBA).

Inter American University of Puerto Rico, Barranquitas Campus, Program in Business Administration, Barranquitas, PR 00794. Offers accounting (IMBA); finance (IMBA).

Inter American University of Puerto Rico, Metropolitan Campus, Graduate Programs, Program in Finance, San Juan, PR 00919-1293. Offers MBA. *Degree requirements:* For master's, comprehensive exam. *Entrance requirements:* For master's, GRE or EXADEP, interview. Electronic applications accepted.

Inter American University of Puerto Rico, Ponce Campus, Graduate School, Mercedita, PR 00715-1602. Offers accounting (MBA); biology (M Ed); chemistry (M Ed); criminal justice (MA); elementary education (M Ed); English as a Second Language (M Ed); finance (MBA); history (M Ed); human resources (MBA); marketing (MBA); mathematics (M Ed); Spanish (M Ed). *Entrance requirements:* For master's, minimum GPA of 2.5.

Inter American University of Puerto Rico, San Germán Campus, Graduate Studies Center, Program in Business Administration, San Germán, PR 00683-5008. Offers accounting (MBA); finance (MBA); general business administration (MBA); human resources (MBA, PhD); industrial relations (MBA); information systems (MBA); international and interregional business (PhD); management (MBA); marketing (MBA). Part-time and evening/weekend programs available. *Faculty:* 8 full-time (2 women), 4 part-time/adjunct (3 women). *Students:* 138 full-time (80 women), 35 part-time (21 women); includes 172 minority (all Hispanic/Latino). 60 applicants, 65% accepted, 38 enrolled. In 2013, 38 master's, 3 doctorates awarded. *Degree requirements:* For master's, comprehensive exam. *Entrance requirements:* For master's, GRE General Test or EXADEP, minimum GPA of 3.0. *Application deadline:* For fall admission, 4/30 priority date for domestic students; for spring admission, 11/15 for domestic students. Applications are processed on a rolling basis. Application fee: $31. *Expenses: Tuition:* Full-time $2424; part-time $202 per credit hour. *Required fees:* $260 per semester. Tuition and fees vary according to course level, course load, degree level and program. *Financial support:* Teaching assistantships, Federal Work-Study, and unspecified assistantships available. *Unit head:* Dr. Elba T. Irizarry, Director of Graduate Studies Center, 787-264-1912 Ext. 7357, Fax: 787-892-6350, E-mail: elbat@sg.inter.edu. *Application contact:* Dr. Ailin Padilla, Coordinator, 787-264-1912 Ext. 7355, E-mail: ailin_padilla@intersg.edu.

The International University of Monaco, Graduate Programs, Monte Carlo, Monaco. Offers entrepreneurship (EMBA, MBA); financial engineering (M Sc); hedge fund and private equity (M Sc); international marketing (EMBA, MBA); international wealth management (M Sc); luxury goods and services (EMBA, M Sc, MBA); wealth and asset management (EMBA, MBA). Part-time programs available. *Degree requirements:* For master's, comprehensive exam (for some programs), applied research project. *Entrance requirements:* Additional exam requirements/recommendations for international students: Required—TOEFL (minimum score 550 paper-based), IELTS. Electronic applications accepted. *Faculty research:* Gaming, leadership, disintermediation.

Iona College, Hagan School of Business, Department of Finance, Business Economics and Legal Studies, New Rochelle, NY 10801-1890. Offers finance (MS); financial management (MBA, PMC); financial services (MS); international finance (MS). Part-time and evening/weekend programs available. *Faculty:* 8 full-time (2 women), 7 part-time/

adjunct (1 woman). *Students:* 41 full-time (16 women), 62 part-time (23 women); includes 10 minority (2 Black or African American, non-Hispanic/Latino; 4 Asian, non-Hispanic/Latino; 4 Hispanic/Latino), 11 international. Average age 27. 30 applicants, 90% accepted, 19 enrolled. In 2013, 71 master's awarded. *Entrance requirements:* For master's, GMAT, 2 letters of recommendation, minimum GPA of 3.0; for PMC, minimum GPA of 3.0. Additional exam requirements/recommendations for international students: Required—TOEFL (minimum score 550 paper-based; 80 iBT), IELTS (minimum score 6.5). *Application deadline:* For fall admission, 8/15 priority date for domestic students, 8/1 priority date for international students; for winter admission, 11/15 priority date for domestic students, 11/1 priority date for international students; for spring admission, 2/15 priority date for domestic students, 2/1 priority date for international students; for summer admission, 5/15 priority date for domestic students, 5/1 priority date for international students. Applications are processed on a rolling basis. Application fee: $50. Electronic applications accepted. *Expenses:* Contact institution. *Financial support:* In 2013–14, 41 students received support. Scholarships/grants, tuition waivers (partial), and unspecified assistantships available. Support available to part-time students. Financial award application deadline: 4/15; financial award applicants required to submit FAFSA. *Faculty research:* Options, insurance financing, asset depreciation ranges, international finance, emerging markets. *Unit head:* Dr. Anand Shetty, Chairman, 914-633-2284, E-mail: ashetty@iona.edu. *Application contact:* Cameron Hudson, Director of MBA Admissions, 914-633-2288, Fax: 914-637-2708, E-mail: chudson@iona.edu. Website: http://www.iona.edu/Academics/Hagan-School-of-Business/Departments/Finance-Business-Economics-Legal-Studies/Graduate-Programs.aspx.

Iowa State University of Science and Technology, Program in Finance, Ames, IA 50011. Offers M Fin. *Entrance requirements:* For master's, GMAT, GRE Writing Test, minimum undergraduate GPA of 3.25, resume, three letters of recommendation, personal essay. Additional exam requirements/recommendations for international students: Required—TOEFL (minimum score 600 paper-based; 100 iBT), IELTS (minimum score 7).

Jacksonville University, Davis College of Business, Accelerated Day-time MBA Program, Jacksonville, FL 32211. Offers accounting and finance (MBA); management (MBA); management accounting (MBA). *Faculty:* 12 full-time (1 woman). *Students:* 35 full-time (19 women), 2 part-time (0 women); includes 6 minority (2 Black or African American, non-Hispanic/Latino; 1 Asian, non-Hispanic/Latino; 3 Hispanic/Latino), 21 international. Average age 26. 47 applicants, 66% accepted, 22 enrolled. In 2013, 59 master's awarded. *Entrance requirements:* For master's, GRE or GMAT (may be waived for 3.3 undergraduate GPA or higher from AACSB-accredited institution). Additional exam requirements/recommendations for international students: Required—TOEFL, IELTS. *Application deadline:* For fall admission, 8/1 priority date for domestic students, 7/15 priority date for international students; for spring admission, 12/1 priority date for domestic students, 11/15 priority date for international students. Application fee: $50. Electronic applications accepted. *Expenses:* Contact institution. *Financial support:* In 2013–14, 4 students received support. Scholarships/grants and unspecified assistantships available. Financial award applicants required to submit FAFSA. *Faculty research:* Behavioral finance, game theory, regional economic integration, information sabotage, public choice and public finance. *Unit head:* Dr. Mohamad Sepehri, Associate Dean and Graduate Programs Director, 904-256-7435, Fax: 904-256-7168, E-mail: msepehr@ju.edu. *Application contact:* AnnaMaria Murphy, Admissions Counselor, 904-256-7426, Fax: 904-256-7168, E-mail: mba@ju.edu. Website: http://www.ju.edu/dcob/AcademicPrograms/Pages/Accelerated-MBA.aspx.

Jacksonville University, Davis College of Business, FLEX Master of Business Administration Program, Jacksonville, FL 32211. Offers accounting and finance (MBA); management (MBA); management accounting (MBA). *Accreditation:* AACSB. Part-time and evening/weekend programs available. *Faculty:* 19 full-time (3 women). *Students:* 77 full-time (32 women), 35 part-time (16 women); includes 40 minority (23 Black or African American, non-Hispanic/Latino; 1 American Indian or Alaska Native, non-Hispanic/Latino; 7 Asian, non-Hispanic/Latino; 8 Hispanic/Latino; 1 Native Hawaiian or other Pacific Islander, non-Hispanic/Latino), 4 international. Average age 31. 77 applicants, 38% accepted, 24 enrolled. In 2013, 54 master's awarded. *Entrance requirements:* For master's, GMAT or GRE (may be waived for 3.3 or higher undergraduate GPA from AACSB-accredited institution). Additional exam requirements/recommendations for international students: Required—TOEFL, IELTS. *Application deadline:* For fall admission, 8/1 priority date for domestic students, 7/15 priority date for international students; for spring admission, 12/1 priority date for domestic students, 11/15 priority date for international students; for summer admission, 4/1 priority date for domestic students, 3/15 priority date for international students. Applications are processed on a rolling basis. Application fee: $50. Electronic applications accepted. *Expenses:* Contact institution. *Financial support:* Application deadline: 3/15; applicants required to submit FAFSA. *Faculty research:* Downsizing with integrity; impact of YouTube videos; game theory; analysis of effective tax rates; creativity innovation and change. *Unit head:* Dr. Mohamad Sepehri, Associate Dean and Director of Graduate Studies, 904-256-7435, Fax: 904-256-7168, E-mail: mba@ju.edu. *Application contact:* AnnaMaria Murphy, Admissions Counselor, 904-256-7426, Fax: 904-256-7168, E-mail: mba@ju.edu.

John Hancock University, MBA Program, Oakbrook Terrace, IL 60181. Offers e-commerce (MBA); finance (MBA); general business (MBA); global management (MBA); health care administration (MBA); leadership (MBA); management of information systems (MBA); marketing (MBA); professional accounting (MBA); project management (MBA); public accounting (MBA); risk management (MBA).

Johns Hopkins University, Carey Business School, Finance Programs, Baltimore, MD 21218-2699. Offers finance (MS); financial management (Certificate); investments (Certificate). Part-time and evening/weekend programs available. *Faculty:* 29 full-time (6 women), 135 part-time/adjunct (29 women). *Students:* 331 full-time (187 women), 125 part-time (52 women); includes 45 minority (10 Black or African American, non-Hispanic/Latino; 1 American Indian or Alaska Native, non-Hispanic/Latino; 28 Asian, non-Hispanic/Latino; 3 Hispanic/Latino; 3 Two or more races, non-Hispanic/Latino), 347 international. Average age 30. 823 applicants, 65% accepted, 307 enrolled. In 2013, 123 master's, 15 other advanced degrees awarded. *Degree requirements:* For master's, 36 credits including final project. *Entrance requirements:* For master's, GMAT or GRE (recommended), minimum GPA of 3.0, resume, work experience, two letters of recommendation; for Certificate, minimum GPA of 3.0, resume, work experience, two letters of recommendation. Additional exam requirements/recommendations for international students: Required—TOEFL (minimum score 600 paper-based; 100 iBT). *Application deadline:* For fall admission, 4/1 for international students; for spring admission, 9/15 for international students. Applications are processed on a rolling basis. Application fee: $100. Electronic applications accepted. *Financial support:* In 2013–14, 9 students received support. Scholarships/grants available. Support available to part-time students. Financial award application deadline: 4/15; financial award applicants required to submit FAFSA. *Faculty research:* Financial econometrics, high frequency data modeling, corporate finance. *Unit head:* Dr. Dipankar Chakravarti, Vice Dean of Programs, 410-234-9311, E-mail: dipankar.chakravarti@jhu.edu. *Application contact:* Robin Greenberg, Admissions Coordinator, 410-234-9227, Fax: 443-529-1554, E-mail: carey.admissions@jhu.edu.

Johns Hopkins University, Paul H. Nitze School of Advanced International Studies, Washington, DC 20036. Offers international development (MA, Certificate), including international economics (MA); international economics and finance (MA); international public policy (MIPP); international relations (PhD); international studies (Certificate); Japan studies (MA), including international economics; Korea studies (MA), including international economics; South Asia studies (MA), including international economics; Southeast Asia studies (MA), including international economics; JD/MA; MBA/MA; MHS/MA. *Faculty:* 79 full-time (24 women), 5 part-time/adjunct (1 woman). *Students:* 694 full-time (327 women), 38 part-time (21 women); includes 146 minority (14 Black or African American, non-Hispanic/Latino; 1 American Indian or Alaska Native, non-Hispanic/Latino; 65 Asian, non-Hispanic/Latino; 45 Hispanic/Latino; 1 Native Hawaiian or other Pacific Islander, non-Hispanic/Latino; 20 Two or more races, non-Hispanic/Latino), 213 international. Average age 27. 1,878 applicants, 64% accepted, 214 enrolled. In 2013, 434 master's, 9 doctorates, 7 other advanced degrees awarded. Terminal master's awarded for partial completion of doctoral program. *Degree requirements:* For master's, 4-6 international economics courses, 5-6 functional or regional concentration courses, 2 core examinations, proficiency in language other than native language, capstone project; for doctorate, 2 foreign languages, thesis/dissertation, 3 comprehensive exams, economics, quantitative and qualitative course, dissertation prospectus and defense. *Entrance requirements:* For master's, GMAT or GRE General Test, previous course work in economics, foreign language, undergraduate degree; for doctorate, GRE General Test, master's degree. Additional exam requirements/recommendations for international students: Required—TOEFL (minimum score 600 paper-based; 100 iBT) or IELTS (minimum score 7). *Application deadline:* For fall admission, 1/7 for domestic and international students. Application fee: $85. Electronic applications accepted. *Expenses:* Contact institution. *Financial support:* In 2013–14, 450 students received support, including 450 fellowships (averaging $12,000 per year), 32 teaching assistantships (averaging $3,906 per year); career-related internships or fieldwork, Federal Work-Study, and scholarships/grants also available. Financial award application deadline: 2/15; financial award applicants required to submit FAFSA. *Faculty research:* Regional studies, international relations, international economics, energy and environment, international development. *Total annual research expenditures:* $8.1 million. *Unit head:* Sidney Jackson, Director of Admissions, 202-663-5700, Fax: 202-663-7788. *Application contact:* Admissions, 202-663-5700, Fax: 202-663-7788, E-mail: admissions.sais@jhu.edu. Website: http://www.sais-jhu.edu/.

Jones International University, School of Business, Centennial, CO 80112. Offers accounting (MBA); business communication (MABC); entrepreneurship (MABC, MBA); finance (MBA); global enterprise management (MBA); health care management (MBA); information security management (MBA); information technology management (MBA); leadership and influence (MABC); leading the customer-driven organization (MABC); negotiation and conflict management (MBA); project management (MABC, MBA). Program only offered online. Part-time and evening/weekend programs available. Postbaccalaureate distance learning degree programs offered (no on-campus study). *Degree requirements:* For master's, capstone project. *Entrance requirements:* For master's, minimum cumulative GPA of 2.5. Additional exam requirements/recommendations for international students: Recommended—TOEFL (minimum score 550 paper-based). Electronic applications accepted.

Kansas State University, Graduate School, College of Business Administration, Program in Business Administration, Manhattan, KS 66506. Offers enterprise information systems (MBA); entrepreneurial technology (MBA); finance (MBA); management (MBA); supply chain management (MBA). *Accreditation:* AACSB. Part-time programs available. *Faculty:* 1 full-time (0 women), 2 part-time/adjunct (0 women). *Students:* 54 full-time (25 women), 24 part-time (14 women); includes 9 minority (3 Black or African American, non-Hispanic/Latino; 2 Asian, non-Hispanic/Latino; 2 Hispanic/Latino; 2 Two or more races, non-Hispanic/Latino), 22 international. Average age 26. 121 applicants, 69% accepted, 23 enrolled. In 2013, 28 master's awarded. *Entrance requirements:* For master's, GMAT (minimum score of 500), minimum undergraduate GPA of 3.0. Additional exam requirements/recommendations for international students: Required—TOEFL (minimum score 550 paper-based; 79 iBT); Recommended—IELTS (minimum score 7). *Application deadline:* For fall admission, 2/1 priority date for domestic and international students; for spring admission, 10/1 priority date for domestic students, 8/1 priority date for international students. Applications are processed on a rolling basis. Application fee: $70 ($80 for international students). Electronic applications accepted. *Financial support:* In 2013–14, 1 research assistantship with partial tuition reimbursement (averaging $8,320 per year) was awarded; institutionally sponsored loans and scholarships/grants also available. Financial award application deadline: 3/1; financial award applicants required to submit FAFSA. *Faculty research:* Organizational citizenship behavior, service marketing, impression management, human resources management, lean manufacturing and supply chain management, financial market behavior and investment management. *Total annual research expenditures:* $11,288. *Unit head:* Dr. Ali Malekzadeh, Dean, 785-532-7227, Fax: 785-532-7216. *Application contact:* Dr. Stacy Kovar, Associate Dean for Academic Programs, 785-532-7190, Fax: 785-532-7809, E-mail: gradbusiness@ksu.edu. Website: http://www.cba.k-state.edu/.

Kansas State University, Graduate School, College of Human Ecology, School of Family Studies and Human Services, Manhattan, KS 66506. Offers communication sciences and disorders (MS); conflict resolution (Graduate Certificate); early childhood education (MS); family and community services (MS); family studies (MS, PhD); life span human development (MS, PhD); marriage and family therapy (MS, PhD); personal financial planning (MS, PhD, Graduate Certificate); youth development (MS, Graduate Certificate). *Accreditation:* AAMFT/COAMFTE; ASHA. Part-time programs available. Postbaccalaureate distance learning degree programs offered (no on-campus study). *Faculty:* 34 full-time (22 women), 11 part-time/adjunct (8 women). *Students:* 68 full-time (56 women), 131 part-time (86 women); includes 42 minority (19 Black or African American, non-Hispanic/Latino; 2 American Indian or Alaska Native, non-Hispanic/Latino; 4 Asian, non-Hispanic/Latino; 14 Hispanic/Latino; 1 Native Hawaiian or other Pacific Islander, non-Hispanic/Latino; 2 Two or more races, non-Hispanic/Latino), 3 international. Average age 31. 248 applicants, 29% accepted, 48 enrolled. In 2013, 35 master's, 7 doctorates awarded. *Degree requirements:* For master's, thesis or alternative. *Entrance requirements:* For master's, GRE, minimum GPA of 3.0 in last 2 years of undergraduate study; for doctorate, GRE. Additional exam requirements/recommendations for international students: Required—TOEFL (minimum score 600 paper-based). *Application deadline:* For fall admission, 2/1 priority date for domestic students, 1/1 priority date for international students; for spring admission, 10/1 priority date for domestic students, 8/1 priority date for international students; for summer admission, 2/1 priority date for domestic students, 12/1 priority date for international students. Applications are processed on a rolling basis. Application fee: $50 ($75 for international students). Electronic applications accepted. *Financial support:* In 2013–14, 63 students received support, including 45 research assistantships (averaging $13,500 per year), 18 teaching assistantships with full tuition reimbursements available (averaging $11,000 per year). Financial award application deadline: 3/1. *Faculty research:* Health and security of military families, personal and family risk assessment and evaluation, disorders of communication and swallowing, families and health. *Total*

annual research expenditures: $14.9 million. *Unit head:* Dr. Maurice MacDonald, Director, 785-532-5510, Fax: 785-532-5505, E-mail: morey@ksu.edu. *Application contact:* Connie Fechter, Administrative Specialist, 785-532-5510, Fax: 785-532-5505, E-mail: fechter@ksu.edu.
Website: http://www.he.k-state.edu/fshs/.

Kaplan University, Davenport Campus, School of Business, Davenport, IA 52807-2095. Offers business administration (MBA); change leadership (MS); entrepreneurship (MBA); finance (MBA); health care management (MBA, MS); human resource (MBA); international business (MBA); management (MS); marketing (MBA); project management (MBA, MS); supply chain management and logistics (MBA, MS). *Accreditation:* ACBSP. Part-time and evening/weekend programs available. Postbaccalaureate distance learning degree programs offered (no on-campus study). *Entrance requirements:* Additional exam requirements/recommendations for international students: Required—TOEFL (minimum score 550 paper-based; 80 iBT). Electronic applications accepted.

Kent State University, College of Business Administration, Doctoral Program in Finance, Kent, OH 44242-0001. Offers PhD. *Faculty:* 6 full-time (3 women). *Students:* 15 full-time (6 women), 7 international. Average age 36. 35 applicants, 9% accepted, 3 enrolled. In 2013, 5 doctorates awarded. *Degree requirements:* For doctorate, comprehensive exam, thesis/dissertation, oral defense. *Entrance requirements:* For doctorate, GMAT or GRE. Additional exam requirements/recommendations for international students: Required—TOEFL (minimum score 600 paper-based; 100 iBT). *Application deadline:* For fall admission, 2/1 for domestic students, 1/1 for international students. Application fee: $30 ($70 for international students). Electronic applications accepted. *Financial support:* In 2013–14, 11 students received support, including 11 teaching assistantships with full tuition reimbursements available (averaging $29,500 per year); Federal Work-Study also available. Financial award application deadline: 2/1; financial award applicants required to submit FAFSA. *Faculty research:* Corporate finance, investments, international finance, futures and options, risk and insurance. *Unit head:* Dr. John Thornton, Chair and Associate Professor, 330-672-2426, Fax: 330-672-9806, E-mail: jthornt5@kent.edu. *Application contact:* Felecia A. Urbanek, Coordinator, Graduate Programs, 330-672-2282, Fax: 330-672-7303, E-mail: gradbus@kent.edu.
Website: http://www.kent.edu/business/finance/index.cfm.

Lake Forest Graduate School of Management, The Leadership MBA Program, Lake Forest, IL 60045. Offers finance (MBA); global business (MBA); healthcare management (MBA); management (MBA); marketing (MBA); organizational behavior (MBA). Part-time and evening/weekend programs available. *Entrance requirements:* For master's, 4 years of work experience in field, interview, 2 letters of recommendation. Electronic applications accepted.

Lakeland College, Graduate Studies Division, Program in Business Administration, Sheboygan, WI 53082-0359. Offers accounting (MBA); finance (MBA); healthcare management (MBA); project management (MBA). *Entrance requirements:* For master's, GMAT. *Expenses:* Contact institution.

Lamar University, College of Graduate Studies, College of Business, Beaumont, TX 77710. Offers accounting (MBA); experiential business and entrepreneurship (MBA); financial management (MBA); healthcare administration (MBA); information systems (MBA); management (MBA). *Accreditation:* AACSB. Part-time and evening/weekend programs available. *Degree requirements:* For master's, comprehensive exam (for some programs), thesis optional. *Entrance requirements:* For master's, GMAT. Additional exam requirements/recommendations for international students: Required—TOEFL (minimum score 525 paper-based). *Faculty research:* Marketing, finance, quantitative methods, management information systems, legal, environmental.

La Salle University, School of Business, Philadelphia, PA 19141-1199. Offers accounting (MBA, Post-MBA Certificate); business systems and analytics (MBA, Post-MBA Certificate); finance (MBA, Post-MBA Certificate); general business administration (MBA); human resource management (MBA, Post-MBA Certificate); international business (Post-MBA Certificate); management (MBA, Post-MBA Certificate); marketing (MBA, Post-MBA Certificate); MSN/MBA. *Accreditation:* AACSB. Part-time and evening/weekend programs available. Postbaccalaureate distance learning degree programs offered (minimal on-campus study). *Faculty:* 27 full-time (13 women), 15 part-time/adjunct (4 women). *Students:* 81 full-time (30 women), 428 part-time (211 women); includes 109 minority (47 Black or African American, non-Hispanic/Latino; 39 Asian, non-Hispanic/Latino; 18 Hispanic/Latino; 5 Two or more races, non-Hispanic/Latino), 6 international. Average age 30. 215 applicants, 90% accepted, 120 enrolled. In 2013, 182 master's, 1 other advanced degree awarded. *Entrance requirements:* For master's, GMAT or GRE, two letters of reference; resume; for Post-MBA Certificate, MBA with minimum GPA of 3.0. Additional exam requirements/recommendations for international students: Required—TOEFL. *Application deadline:* For fall admission, 8/15 priority date for domestic students, 7/15 for international students; for spring admission, 12/15 priority date for domestic students, 11/15 for international students; for summer admission, 4/15 priority date for domestic students, 3/15 for international students. Applications are processed on a rolling basis. Application fee: $35. Electronic applications accepted. Application fee is waived when completed online. *Expenses:* Contact institution. *Financial support:* In 2013–14, 88 students received support. Career-related internships or fieldwork, Federal Work-Study, scholarships/grants, and unspecified assistantships available. Support available to part-time students. Financial award application deadline: 8/31; financial award applicants required to submit FAFSA. *Unit head:* Dr. Gary Giamartino, Dean, 215-951-1040, Fax: 215-951-1886, E-mail: giamartino@lasalle.edu. *Application contact:* Paul J. Reilly, Assistant Vice President, Enrollment Services, 215-951-1946, Fax: 215-951-1462, E-mail: reilly@lasalle.edu.
Website: http://www.lasalle.edu/grad/index.php?section-mba&page-index.

La Sierra University, School of Business and Management, Riverside, CA 92515. Offers accounting (MBA); finance (MBA); general management (MBA); human resources management (MBA); leadership, values, and ethics for business and management (Certificate); marketing (MBA). *Degree requirements:* For master's, research project. *Entrance requirements:* For master's, GMAT, minimum GPA of 3.0. Additional exam requirements/recommendations for international students: Required—TOEFL. *Faculty research:* Financial econometrics, institutional assessment and strategic planning, legal issues in management, behavioral finance, content of financial reports.

Lehigh University, College of Business and Economics, Department of Finance, Bethlehem, PA 18015. Offers analytical finance (MS). *Faculty:* 7 full-time (0 women), 1 part-time/adjunct (0 women). *Students:* 60 full-time (37 women), 7 part-time (4 women); includes 1 minority (Asian, non-Hispanic/Latino), 66 international. Average age 23. 510 applicants, 23% accepted, 35 enrolled. In 2013, 24 master's awarded. *Degree requirements:* For master's, capstone project. *Entrance requirements:* For master's, GMAT or GRE, bachelor's degree from a mathematically rigorous program, minimum GPA of 3.0. Additional exam requirements/recommendations for international students: Required—TOEFL (minimum score 600 paper-based; 94 iBT). *Application deadline:* For fall admission, 7/15 for domestic students, 2/15 for international students. Applications are processed on a rolling basis. Application fee: $100. Electronic applications accepted. *Financial support:* Application deadline: 1/15. *Unit head:* Richard Kish, Department Chair, 610-758-4205, E-mail: rjk7@lehigh.edu. *Application contact:* Jen Giordano, Director of Recruitment and Admissions, 610-758-3418, Fax: 610-758-5283, E-mail: jlg210@lehigh.edu.
Website: http://www4.lehigh.edu/business/academics/depts/finance.

Lewis University, College of Business, Graduate School of Management, Program in Business Administration, Romeoville, IL 60446. Offers accounting (MBA); custom elective option (MBA); e-business (MBA); finance (MBA); healthcare management (MBA); human resources management (MBA); international business (MBA); management information systems (MBA); marketing (MBA); project management (MBA); technology and operations management (MBA). Part-time and evening/weekend programs available. *Students:* 115 full-time (55 women), 227 part-time (129 women); includes 128 minority (74 Black or African American, non-Hispanic/Latino; 1 American Indian or Alaska Native, non-Hispanic/Latino; 9 Asian, non-Hispanic/Latino; 40 Hispanic/Latino; 4 Two or more races, non-Hispanic/Latino), 10 international. Average age 31. In 2013, 99 master's awarded. *Entrance requirements:* For master's, interview, bachelor's degree, resume, 2 recommendations. Additional exam requirements/recommendations for international students: Required—TOEFL (minimum score 550 paper-based). *Application deadline:* For fall admission, 8/15 priority date for domestic students, 5/1 priority date for international students; for spring admission, 11/15 priority date for international students. Applications are processed on a rolling basis. Application fee: $40. Electronic applications accepted. *Financial support:* Career-related internships or fieldwork, Federal Work-Study, scholarships/grants, and unspecified assistantships available. Financial award application deadline: 5/1; financial award applicants required to submit FAFSA. *Unit head:* Dr. Maureen Culleeney, Academic Program Director, 815-838-0500 Ext. 5631, E-mail: culleema@lewisu.edu. *Application contact:* Michele Ryan, Director of Admission, 815-838-0500 Ext. 5384, E-mail: gsm@lewisu.edu.

Lewis University, College of Business, Graduate School of Management, Program in Finance, Romeoville, IL 60446. Offers MS. Part-time and evening/weekend programs available. *Students:* 50 full-time (3 women), 22 part-time (6 women); includes 8 minority (5 Black or African American, non-Hispanic/Latino; 3 Hispanic/Latino), 2 international. Average age 28. *Entrance requirements:* For master's, bachelor's degree, interview, resume, 2 recommendations, minimum GPA of 2.75. Additional exam requirements/recommendations for international students: Required—TOEFL (minimum score 550 paper-based; 80 iBT). *Application deadline:* For fall admission, 5/1 priority date for international students; for spring admission, 11/15 priority date for international students. Applications are processed on a rolling basis. Application fee: $40. Electronic applications accepted. *Financial support:* Career-related internships or fieldwork, Federal Work-Study, scholarships/grants, and unspecified assistantships available. Support available to part-time students. Financial award application deadline: 5/1; financial award applicants required to submit FAFSA. *Unit head:* Dr. Robert Atra, Academic Program Director, 815-838-0500 Ext. 5804, E-mail: atraro@lewisu.edu. *Application contact:* Michele Ryan, Director of Admission, 815-838-0500 Ext. 5384, E-mail: gsm@lewisu.edu.

Lincoln University, Graduate Programs, Philadelphia, PA 19104. Offers early childhood education (M Ed); educational leadership (M Ed); human resources (MSA), including finance, human resources management; human services (MHS); reading (MSR). Evening/weekend programs available. *Faculty:* 10 full-time (4 women), 34 part-time/adjunct (19 women). *Students:* 224 full-time (145 women), 115 part-time (74 women); includes 328 minority (311 Black or African American, non-Hispanic/Latino; 17 Hispanic/Latino). Average age 40. 237 applicants, 65% accepted, 64 enrolled. In 2013, 155 master's awarded. *Degree requirements:* For master's, thesis. *Entrance requirements:* For master's, working as full-time, paid staff member in the human services field, at least one year of paid experience in this field, and undergraduate degree in human services or a related field from an accredited institution (for MHS). *Application deadline:* For fall admission, 6/1 priority date for domestic and international students. Applications are processed on a rolling basis. Application fee: $50. *Expenses:* Tuition, state resident: full-time $10,106; part-time $567 per hour. Tuition, nonresident: full-time $17,636; part-time $949 per hour. *Financial support:* Application deadline: 8/1. *Unit head:* Dr. Cheryl Gooch, Dean, School of Humanities and Graduate Studies, 484-365-7664, E-mail: cgooch@lincoln.edu. *Application contact:* Jernice Lea, Director of Graduate Admissions, 215-590-8233, Fax: 215-387-3859, E-mail: jlea@lincoln.edu.
Website: http://www.lincoln.edu/academicaffairs/uc.html.

Lincoln University, Graduate Studies, Oakland, CA 94612. Offers finance and investments (DBA); finance management and investment banking (MBA); general business (MBA); human resource management (MBA, DBA); international business (MBA); management information systems (MBA). Part-time and evening/weekend programs available. *Faculty:* 8 full-time (2 women), 22 part-time/adjunct (7 women). *Students:* 372 full-time (171 women), 4 part-time (1 woman); includes 8 minority (2 Black or African American, non-Hispanic/Latino; 6 Asian, non-Hispanic/Latino), 363 international. Average age 26. 421 applicants, 71% accepted, 133 enrolled. *Degree requirements:* For master's, research project (thesis), internship report, or comprehensive exam; for doctorate, comprehensive exam, thesis/dissertation. *Entrance requirements:* For master's, minimum GPA of 2.7; for doctorate, GMAT (minimum score: 550), GRE (minimum score: 1000), or equivalent test results (waived for master's degree with minimum cumulative GPA of 3.3). Additional exam requirements/recommendations for international students: Required—TOEFL (minimum score 525 paper-based; 71 iBT) or IELTS (minimum score 5.5) for MBA; TOEFL (minimum score 550 paper-based; 79 iBT) or IELTS (minimum score 6) for DBA. *Application deadline:* For fall admission, 7/1 priority date for domestic and international students; for spring admission, 11/1 priority date for domestic and international students; for summer admission, 5/1 for domestic and international students. Applications are processed on a rolling basis. Application fee: $75. Electronic applications accepted. *Expenses: Tuition:* Full-time $7290; part-time $405 per unit. *Required fees:* $375; $405 per unit. $375 per year. Tuition and fees vary according to course level and degree level. *Financial support:* Teaching assistantships with tuition reimbursements, career-related internships or fieldwork, and scholarships/grants available. Financial award application deadline: 7/31; financial award applicants required to submit FAFSA. *Unit head:* Dr. Marshall Burak, Director of Graduate Programs, 510-628-8016, Fax: 510-628-8012, E-mail: mburak@lincolnuca.edu. *Application contact:* Reenu Shrestha, Admissions Officer, 510-628-8010 Ext. 8030, Fax: 510-628-8012, E-mail: admissions@lincolnuca.edu.
Website: http://www.lincolnuca.edu/.

Lindenwood University, Graduate Programs, School of Business and Entrepreneurship, St. Charles, MO 63301-1695. Offers accountancy (MA); accounting (MBA); business administration (MBA); entrepreneurial studies (MBA); finance (MBA, MS); human resource management (MBA); international business (MBA); leadership (MA); management (MBA); marketing (MBA, MS); public management (MBA); sport management (MA); supply chain management (MBA). *Accreditation:* ACBSP. Part-time and evening/weekend programs available. Postbaccalaureate distance learning degree programs offered (no on-campus study). *Faculty:* 18 full-time (8 women), 33 part-time/adjunct (8 women). *Students:* 292 full-time (130 women), 111 part-time (46 women); includes 59 minority (42 Black or African American, non-Hispanic/Latino; 5 American Indian or Alaska Native, non-Hispanic/Latino; 1 Asian, non-Hispanic/Latino; 5 Hispanic/

Latino; 6 Two or more races, non-Hispanic/Latino), 112 international. Average age 29. 212 applicants, 51% accepted, 102 enrolled. In 2013, 221 master's awarded. *Degree requirements:* For master's, comprehensive exam (for some programs), thesis (for some programs), minimum GPA of 3.0. *Entrance requirements:* For master's, interview, minimum GPA of 3.0, letter of recommendation. Additional exam requirements/recommendations for international students: Required—TOEFL (minimum score 550 paper-based; 80 iBT). *Application deadline:* For fall admission, 8/12 priority date for domestic and international students; for winter admission, 1/6 priority date for domestic and international students; for spring admission, 3/10 priority date for domestic and international students; for summer admission, 5/27 priority date for domestic and international students. Applications are processed on a rolling basis. Application fee: $30 ($100 for international students). Electronic applications accepted. *Expenses: Tuition:* Full-time $14,800; part-time $428 per credit hour. *Required fees:* $350. Tuition and fees vary according to course level and course load. *Financial support:* In 2013–14, 268 students received support. Career-related internships or fieldwork, Federal Work-Study, institutionally sponsored loans, scholarships/grants, tuition waivers (partial), and unspecified assistantships available. Financial award application deadline: 6/30; financial award applicants required to submit FAFSA. *Unit head:* Roger Ellis, Dean, 636-949-4839, E-mail: rellis@lindenwood.edu. *Application contact:* Brett Barger, Dean of Evening Admissions and Extension Campuses, 636-949-4934, Fax: 636-949-4109, E-mail: adultadmissions@lindenwood.edu.
Website: http://www.lindenwood.edu.

Lipscomb University, Graduate School of Business, Nashville, TN 37204-3951. Offers accountancy (M Acc); accounting (MBA); conflict management (MBA); distributive (general) (MBA); financial services (MBA); health care informatics (MBA); healthcare management (MBA); human resources (MHR); information security (MBA); leadership (MBA); nonprofit management (MBA); professional accountancy (Certificate); sports management (MBA); strategic human resources (MBA); sustainability (MBA); MBA/MS. *Accreditation:* ACBSP. Part-time and evening/weekend programs available. *Faculty:* 12 full-time (1 woman), 12 part-time/adjunct (2 women). *Students:* 90 full-time (44 women), 104 part-time (51 women); includes 28 minority (24 Black or African American, non-Hispanic/Latino; 3 Hispanic/Latino; 1 Two or more races, non-Hispanic/Latino), 6 international. Average age 33. 145 applicants, 79% accepted, 69 enrolled. In 2013, 98 master's, 1 other advanced degree awarded. *Entrance requirements:* For master's, GMAT, transcripts, interview, 2 references, resume. Additional exam requirements/recommendations for international students: Required—TOEFL (minimum score 570 paper-based). *Application deadline:* For fall admission, 6/15 for domestic students, 2/1 for international students; for winter admission, 6/1 for international students; for spring admission, 11/15 for domestic students. Applications are processed on a rolling basis. Application fee: $50 ($75 for international students). Electronic applications accepted. *Expenses:* Contact institution. *Financial support:* Career-related internships or fieldwork, scholarships/grants, tuition waivers (partial), and unspecified assistantships available. Support available to part-time students. Financial award application deadline: 7/1; financial award applicants required to submit FAFSA. *Faculty research:* Impact of spirituality on organization commitment, women in corporate leadership, psychological empowerment, training. *Unit head:* Joe Ivey, Associate Dean of Graduate Business Programs, 615-966-6229, Fax: 615-966-1818, E-mail: joe.ivey@lipscomb.edu. *Application contact:* Lisa Shacklett, Assistant Dean of Enrollment and Marketing, 615-966-5968, E-mail: lisa.shacklett@lipscomb.edu.
Website: http://www.lipscomb.edu/business/Graduate-Programs.

Long Island University–Hudson at Rockland, Graduate School, Master of Business Administration Program, Orangeburg, NY 10962. Offers business administration (Post Master's Certificate); entrepreneurship (MBA); finance (MBA); healthcare sector management (MBA); management (MBA). Part-time and evening/weekend programs available. *Entrance requirements:* For master's, GMAT, college transcripts, two letters of recommendation, personal statement, resume.

Long Island University–LIU Post, College of Management, School of Business, Brookville, NY 11548-1300. Offers accounting and taxation (Certificate); business administration (Certificate); finance (MBA, Certificate); general business administration (MBA); international business (MBA, Certificate); management (MBA, Certificate); management information systems (MBA, Certificate); marketing (MBA, Certificate). *Accreditation:* AACSB. Part-time and evening/weekend programs available. *Entrance requirements:* For master's, GMAT, resume, minimum GPA of 3.0, 2 letters of recommendation. Additional exam requirements/recommendations for international students: Required—TOEFL (minimum score 527 paper-based). Electronic applications accepted. *Faculty research:* Financial markets, consumer behavior.

Louisiana State University and Agricultural & Mechanical College, Graduate School, E. J. Ourso College of Business, Department of Finance, Baton Rouge, LA 70803. Offers business administration (PhD), including finance; finance (MS). *Faculty:* 13 full-time (4 women). *Students:* 24 full-time (9 women), 6 part-time (1 woman); includes 2 minority (1 Black or African American, non-Hispanic/Latino; 1 Asian, non-Hispanic/Latino), 11 international. Average age 25. 70 applicants, 21% accepted, 8 enrolled. In 2013, 21 master's, 2 doctorates awarded. *Degree requirements:* For master's, thesis or alternative; for doctorate, thesis/dissertation. *Entrance requirements:* For master's and doctorate, GMAT. Additional exam requirements/recommendations for international students: Required—TOEFL (minimum score 550 paper-based; 79 iBT), IELTS (minimum score 6.5), or PTE (minimum score 59). *Application deadline:* For fall admission, 1/25 priority date for domestic students, 5/15 for international students; for spring admission, 10/15 for international students. Applications are processed on a rolling basis. Application fee: $50 ($70 for international students). *Financial support:* In 2013–14, 19 students received support, including 5 research assistantships with full and partial tuition reimbursements available (averaging $19,000 per year), 5 teaching assistantships with full and partial tuition reimbursements available (averaging $9,600 per year); fellowships, career-related internships or fieldwork, Federal Work-Study, scholarships/grants, health care benefits, and unspecified assistantships also available. Support available to part-time students. Financial award application deadline: 4/1; financial award applicants required to submit FAFSA. *Faculty research:* Derivatives and risk management, capital structure, asset pricing, spatial statistics, financial institutions and underwriting. *Total annual research expenditures:* $56,155. *Unit head:* Dr. Vestor Carlos Slawson, Jr., Interim Chair, 225-578-6291, Fax: 225-578-6366, E-mail: cslawson@lsu.edu. *Application contact:* Dr. Rajesh Narayanan, Graduate Adviser, 225-578-6236, Fax: 225-578-6366, E-mail: rnarayan@lsu.edu.
Website: http://business.lsu.edu/finance.

Louisiana Tech University, Graduate School, College of Business, Department of Economics and Finance, Ruston, LA 71272. Offers finance (MBA, DBA); finance and economics (DBA). Part-time programs available. *Degree requirements:* For doctorate, thesis/dissertation. *Entrance requirements:* For master's and doctorate, GMAT. *Application deadline:* For fall admission, 7/29 for domestic students; for spring admission, 2/3 for domestic students. Application fee: $20 ($30 for international students). *Financial support:* Fellowships, research assistantships, and teaching assistantships available. Financial award application deadline: 2/1. *Unit head:* Dr. Otis Gilley, Director, 318-257-4140, Fax: 318-257-4253, E-mail: gilley@latech.edu.

Application contact: Marilyn J. Robinson, Assistant to the Dean, 318-257-2924, Fax: 318-257-4487.
Website: http://www.business.latech.edu/econ_fin/.

Loyola University Chicago, Quinlan School of Business, Finance Department, Chicago, IL 60610. Offers asset management (MSF); corporate finance (MSF); risk management (MSF); MBA/MSF. Part-time and evening/weekend programs available. *Faculty:* 11 full-time (3 women), 6 part-time/adjunct (0 women). *Students:* 11 full-time (7 women), 31 part-time (17 women); includes 1 minority (Asian, non-Hispanic/Latino), 30 international. Average age 25. 226 applicants, 27% accepted, 11 enrolled. In 2013, 24 master's awarded. *Entrance requirements:* For master's, GMAT or GRE, official transcripts, letters of recommendation, statement of purpose, resume. Additional exam requirements/recommendations for international students: Required—TOEFL (minimum score 90 iBT) or IELTS (minimum score 6.5). *Application deadline:* For fall admission, 7/15 for domestic and international students; for winter admission, 10/1 for domestic and international students; for spring admission, 1/15 for domestic and international students; for summer admission, 4/1 for domestic and international students. Applications are processed on a rolling basis. Application fee: $50. Electronic applications accepted. Application fee is waived when completed online. *Expenses: Tuition:* Full-time $16,740; part-time $930 per credit. *Required fees:* $135 per semester. *Financial support:* Scholarships/grants and unspecified assistantships available. *Faculty research:* Corporate governance, financial markets, international finance, risk management, monetary policy. *Unit head:* Dr. Steven Todd, Chair, Department of Finance, 312-915-7218, Fax: 312-915-8508, E-mail: stodd@luc.edu. *Application contact:* Jessica Gagle, Enrollment Advisor, Quinlan School of Business Graduate Programs, 312-915-8908, Fax: 312-915-7207, E-mail: jgagle@luc.edu.
Website: http://www.luc.edu/quinlan/mba/masters/masters-in-finance/index.shtml.

Loyola University Chicago, Quinlan School of Business, MBA Programs, Chicago, IL 60610. Offers accounting (MBA); business ethics (MBA); derivative markets (MBA); economics (MBA); entrepreneurship (MBA); executive (MBA); finance (MBA); healthcare management (MBA); human resources management (MBA); information systems management (MBA); intercontinental (MBA); international business (MBA); marketing (MBA); operations management (MBA); risk management (MBA); JD/MBA. Part-time and evening/weekend programs available. *Faculty:* 76 full-time (20 women), 10 part-time/adjunct (4 women). *Students:* 73 full-time (34 women), 294 part-time (129 women); includes 60 minority (18 Black or African American, non-Hispanic/Latino; 28 Asian, non-Hispanic/Latino; 14 Hispanic/Latino), 19 international. Average age 31. 529 applicants, 51% accepted, 153 enrolled. In 2013, 229 master's awarded. *Entrance requirements:* For master's, GMAT or GRE, official transcripts, two letters of recommendation, statement of purpose, resume. Additional exam requirements/recommendations for international students: Required—TOEFL (minimum score 90 iBT) or IELTS (minimum score 6.5). *Application deadline:* For fall admission, 7/15 for domestic and international students; for winter admission, 10/1 for domestic and international students; for spring admission, 1/15 for domestic and international students; for summer admission, 4/1 for domestic and international students. Applications are processed on a rolling basis. Application fee: $50. Electronic applications accepted. Application fee is waived when completed online. *Expenses: Tuition:* Full-time $16,740; part-time $930 per credit. *Required fees:* $135 per semester. *Financial support:* Scholarships/grants and unspecified assistantships available. *Faculty research:* Social enterprise and responsibility, emerging markets, supply chain management, risk management. *Unit head:* Jennifer Huntley, Assistant Dean for Graduate Programs, 312-915-6124, Fax: 312-915-7207, E-mail: jhuntle@luc.edu. *Application contact:* Jessica Gagle, Enrollment Advisor, Quinlan School of Business Graduate Programs, 312-915-8908, Fax: 312-915-7207, E-mail: jgagle@luc.edu.

Loyola University Maryland, Graduate Programs, Sellinger School of Business and Management, Program in Business Administration, Baltimore, MD 21210-2699. Offers accounting (MBA); finance (MBA); general business (MBA); information systems operations management (MBA); international business (MBA); management (MBA); marketing (MBA). *Accreditation:* AACSB. Part-time and evening/weekend programs available. *Entrance requirements:* For master's, GMAT, letter of recommendation, resume, essay. Additional exam requirements/recommendations for international students: Required—TOEFL (minimum score 550 paper-based).

Loyola University Maryland, Graduate Programs, Sellinger School of Business and Management, Program in Finance, Baltimore, MD 21210-2699. Offers MSF. Part-time programs available. *Entrance requirements:* For master's, GMAT, letter of recommendation, resume, essay. Additional exam requirements/recommendations for international students: Required—TOEFL (minimum score 550 paper-based). Electronic applications accepted.

Manhattanville College, School of Business, Program in Finance, Purchase, NY 10577-2132. Offers MS. Part-time and evening/weekend programs available. *Degree requirements:* For master's, final project. *Entrance requirements:* Additional exam requirements/recommendations for international students: Required—TOEFL. Electronic applications accepted.

Marquette University, Graduate School of Management, Executive MBA Program, Milwaukee, WI 53201-1881. Offers economics (MBA); finance (MBA); human resources (MBA); international business (MBA); management information systems (MBA); marketing (MBA); operations and supply chain management (MBA); sports business (MBA). *Accreditation:* AACSB. *Students:* 38 full-time (12 women), 1 international. Average age 36. 36 applicants. In 2013, 21 master's awarded. *Degree requirements:* For master's, international trip. *Entrance requirements:* For master's, GMAT or GRE, two letters of recommendation, official transcripts from current and previous colleges/universities. Additional exam requirements/recommendations for international students: Required—TOEFL (minimum score 550 paper-based; 88 iBT), IELTS (minimum score 6.5), PTE. *Application deadline:* For fall admission, 2/15 for domestic and international students. Application fee: $50. Electronic applications accepted. *Expenses:* Contact institution. *Financial support:* Application deadline: 2/15. *Faculty research:* International trade and finance, customer relationship management, consumer satisfaction, customer service. *Unit head:* Dr. Mark Eppli, Dean, 414-288-5724. *Application contact:* Dr. Jeanne Simmons, Associate Dean, 414-288-7145.
Website: http://www.busadm.mu.edu/emba/.

Marquette University, Graduate School of Management, Program in Business Administration, Milwaukee, WI 53201-1881. Offers business administration (MBA); economics (MBA); entrepreneurship (Certificate); finance (MBA); human resources (MBA); international business (MBA); management information systems (MBA); marketing (MBA); operations and supply chain management (MBA); sports business (MBA); JD/MBA; MBA/MA; MBA/MSN. *Accreditation:* AACSB. Part-time and evening/weekend programs available. *Students:* 28 full-time (13 women), 265 part-time (66 women); includes 20 minority (7 Black or African American, non-Hispanic/Latino; 8 Asian, non-Hispanic/Latino; 5 Hispanic/Latino), 11 international. Average age 31. 185 applicants. In 2013, 129 master's, 2 other advanced degrees awarded. *Degree requirements:* For Certificate, business plan. *Entrance requirements:* For master's, GMAT or GRE, letters of recommendation. Additional exam requirements/recommendations for international students: Required—TOEFL (minimum score 550 paper-based; 88 iBT), IELTS (minimum score 6.5), PTE. *Application deadline:* For fall

admission, 2/15 for domestic and international students. Applications are processed on a rolling basis. Application fee: $50. Electronic applications accepted. *Financial support:* In 2013–14, 4 fellowships, 11 teaching assistantships were awarded; research assistantships, Federal Work-Study, institutionally sponsored loans, scholarships/grants, and tuition waivers (full and partial) also available. Support available to part-time students. Financial award application deadline: 2/15. *Faculty research:* Ethics in the professions, services marketing, technology impact on decision-making, mentoring. *Unit head:* Dr. Mark Eppli, Dean, 414-288-5724. *Application contact:* Dr. Jeanne Simmons, Associate Dean, 414-288-7145.
Website: http://business.marquette.edu/academics/mba.

Marylhurst University, Department of Business Administration, Marylhurst, OR 97036-0261. Offers finance (MBA); general management (MBA); government policy and administration (MBA); green development (MBA); health care management (MBA); marketing (MBA); natural and organic resources (MBA); nonprofit management (MBA); organizational behavior (MBA); real estate (MBA); renewable energy (MBA); sustainable business (MBA). Part-time and evening/weekend programs available. Postbaccalaureate distance learning degree programs offered (no on-campus study). *Degree requirements:* For master's, comprehensive exam, capstone course. *Entrance requirements:* For master's, GMAT (if GPA less than 3.0 and fewer than 5 years of work experience), interview, resume, 2 letters of recommendation. Additional exam requirements/recommendations for international students: Recommended—TOEFL (minimum score 550 paper-based; 80 iBT). Electronic applications accepted.

Marywood University, Academic Affairs, College of Liberal Arts and Sciences, School of Business and Global Innovation, Emphasis in Financial Information Systems, Scranton, PA 18509-1598. Offers MBA, MS. *Entrance requirements:* For master's, GMAT. Additional exam requirements/recommendations for international students: Required—TOEFL (minimum score 550 paper-based; 79 iBT). *Application deadline:* For fall admission, 4/1 priority date for domestic students, 3/31 priority date for international students; for spring admission, 11/1 priority date for domestic students, 8/31 priority date for international students. Applications are processed on a rolling basis. Application fee: $35. Electronic applications accepted. *Expenses: Tuition:* Part-time $775 per credit. Tuition and fees vary according to degree level. *Financial support:* Career-related internships or fieldwork, scholarships/grants, and unspecified assistantships available. Support available to part-time students. Financial award application deadline: 6/30; financial award applicants required to submit FAFSA. *Faculty research:* Accountant/auditor liability, corporate finance acquisitions and mergers, corporate bankruptcy. *Unit head:* Dr. Arthur Comstock, Chairman, 570-348-6211 Ext. 2449, E-mail: comstock@marywood.edu. *Application contact:* Tammy Manka, Assistant Director of Graduate Admissions, 570-348-6211 Ext. 2322, E-mail: tmanka@marywood.edu.
Website: http://www.marywood.edu/academics/gradcatalog/.

McGill University, Faculty of Graduate and Postdoctoral Studies, Desautels Faculty of Management, Montréal, QC H3A 2T5, Canada. Offers administration (PhD); entrepreneurial studies (MBA); finance (MBA); general management (Post Master's Certificate); information systems (MBA); international business (MBA); international practicing management (MM); management (MBA); management for development (MBA); manufacturing management (MMM); marketing (MBA); operations management (MBA); public accountancy (Diploma); strategic management (MBA); MBA/LL B; MD/MBA. MMM offered jointly with Faculty of Engineering; PhD with Concordia University, HEC Montreal, Université de Montréal, Université du Québec à Montréal.

Michigan State University, The Graduate School, Eli Broad College of Business, Department of Finance, East Lansing, MI 48824. Offers MS, PhD. PhD program admits students only in odd-numbered years. *Faculty:* 33. *Students:* 31. In 2013, 13 master's awarded. *Degree requirements:* For doctorate, comprehensive exam, thesis/dissertation. *Entrance requirements:* For master's, GMAT (minimum score 550) or GRE (minimum score 1050 verbal and quantitative taken within 5 years), 4-year bachelor's degree or equivalent with minimum cumulative GPA of 3.0, transcripts, at least 2 years' work experience, 2 letters of recommendation, working knowledge of computers, laptop computer; for doctorate, GMAT or GRE, transcripts from all colleges/universities attended, 3 letters of recommendation, statement of purpose. Additional exam requirements/recommendations for international students: Required—TOEFL (minimum score 600 paper-based; 100 iBT), IELTS (minimum score 7) accepted for MS only. Application fee: $85. Electronic applications accepted. *Financial support:* Research assistantships with tuition reimbursements, teaching assistantships with tuition reimbursements, and unspecified assistantships available. Financial award applicants required to submit FAFSA. *Unit head:* Dr. Naveen Khanna, Chairperson, 517-353-1853, Fax: 517-432-1080, E-mail: khanna@broad.msu.edu. *Application contact:* Celeste Shoulders, Program Information Contact, 517-353-1745, Fax: 517-432-1080, E-mail: fin@broad.msu.edu.
Website: http://finance.broad.msu.edu/.

Michigan State University, The Graduate School, Eli Broad College of Business, Program in Business Administration, East Lansing, MI 48824. Offers finance (MBA); human resource management (MBA); integrative management (MBA); marketing (MBA); supply chain management (MBA). MBA in integrative management is through Weekend MBA Program; other 4 concentrations are through Full-Time MBA Program. Evening/weekend programs available. *Students:* 432. In 2013, 241 degrees awarded. *Degree requirements:* For master's, enrichment experience. *Entrance requirements:* For master's, GMAT or GRE, 4-year bachelor's degree; resume; work experience (minimum of 5 years for Weekend MBA); 2-3 personal essays; 2 letters of recommendation; personal interview. Additional exam requirements/recommendations for international students: Required—PTE (minimum score 70), TOEFL (minimum score 100 iBT) or IELTS (minimum score 7) for Full-Time MBA applicants. *Application deadline:* Applications are processed on a rolling basis. Application fee: $50. Electronic applications accepted. *Expenses:* Contact institution. *Financial support:* Fellowships with tuition reimbursements, research assistantships with tuition reimbursements, teaching assistantships with tuition reimbursements, scholarships/grants, unspecified assistantships, and non-resident tuition waivers (for all military veterans and their dependents in the Full-Time MBA Program) available. Financial award applicants required to submit FAFSA. *Unit head:* Dr. Sanjay Gupta, Associate Dean for MBA and Professional Master's Programs, 517-432-6488, Fax: 517-353-6395, E-mail: gupta@broad.msu.edu. *Application contact:* Program Information Contact, 517-355-7604, Fax: 517-353-1649, E-mail: mba@msu.edu.
Website: http://mba.broad.msu.edu.

MidAmerica Nazarene University, Graduate Studies in Management, Olathe, KS 66062-1899. Offers management (MBA); organizational administration (MA), including finance, international business, leadership, non-profit. Evening/weekend programs available. *Entrance requirements:* For master's, mathematical assessment, minimum undergraduate GPA of 3.0, letters of recommendation. Additional exam requirements/recommendations for international students: Required—TOEFL. Electronic applications accepted. *Faculty research:* Economic development, international finance, business development, employee evaluation.

Mississippi College, Graduate School, School of Business, Clinton, MS 39058. Offers accounting (Certificate); business administration (MBA), including accounting; business education (M Ed); finance (MBA, Certificate); JD/MBA. Part-time and evening/weekend programs available. *Degree requirements:* For master's, comprehensive exam, thesis optional. *Entrance requirements:* For master's, GMAT, minimum GPA of 2.5, 24 hours of undergraduate course work in business. Additional exam requirements/recommendations for international students: Recommended—TOEFL, IELTS. Electronic applications accepted.

Mississippi State University, College of Business, Department of Finance and Economics, Mississippi State, MS 39762. Offers applied economics (PhD); economics (MA); finance (PhD). PhD in applied economics offered jointly with Department of Agricultural Economics. Part-time programs available. *Faculty:* 6 full-time (2 women). *Students:* 8 full-time (3 women), 2 part-time (0 women), all international. Average age 34. 49 applicants, 12% accepted, 4 enrolled. In 2013, 1 master's, 1 doctorate awarded. Terminal master's awarded for partial completion of doctoral program. *Degree requirements:* For master's, comprehensive exam, thesis optional; for doctorate, comprehensive exam, thesis/dissertation, written and oral exams. *Entrance requirements:* For master's, GRE, previously completed intermediate microeconomics and macroeconomics; for doctorate, GRE, BS with minimum GPA of 3.0 cumulative and over last 60 hours of undergraduate work and 3.25 on all graduate work. Additional exam requirements/recommendations for international students: Required—TOEFL (minimum score 575 paper-based; 84 iBT); Recommended—IELTS (minimum score 6.5). *Application deadline:* For fall admission, 7/1 for domestic students, 5/1 for international students; for spring admission, 11/1 for domestic students, 10/1 for international students. Applications are processed on a rolling basis. Application fee: $60. Electronic applications accepted. *Financial support:* In 2013–14, 4 teaching assistantships with tuition reimbursements (averaging $13,804 per year) were awarded; Federal Work-Study, scholarships/grants, health care benefits, and unspecified assistantships also available. Financial award application deadline: 4/1; financial award applicants required to submit FAFSA. *Faculty research:* Economics development, mergers, event studies, economic education, bank performance. *Total annual research expenditures:* $1.4 million. *Unit head:* Dr. Mike Highfield, Department Head, 662-325-3928, Fax: 662-325-1977, E-mail: mhighfield@msstate.edu. *Application contact:* Dr. Randy Campbell, Associate Professor/Graduate Coordinator, Economics, 662-325-1516, Fax: 662-325-1977, E-mail: mhighfield@msstate.edu.
Website: http://www.business.msstate.edu/programs/fe/index.php.

Mississippi State University, College of Business, Department of Management and Information Systems, Mississippi State, MS 39762. Offers business administration (MBA, PhD), including accounting, business administration (MBA), business information systems (PhD), finance (PhD), management (PhD), marketing (PhD); information systems (MSIS); project management (MBA). Part-time programs available. *Faculty:* 12 full-time (4 women). *Students:* 69 full-time (20 women), 245 part-time (69 women); includes 34 minority (9 Black or African American, non-Hispanic/Latino; 12 Asian, non-Hispanic/Latino; 7 Hispanic/Latino; 1 Native Hawaiian or other Pacific Islander, non-Hispanic/Latino; 5 Two or more races, non-Hispanic/Latino), 20 international. Average age 31. 367 applicants, 29% accepted, 73 enrolled. In 2013, 127 master's, 2 doctorates awarded. *Degree requirements:* For master's, comprehensive exam; for doctorate, comprehensive exam, thesis/dissertation. *Entrance requirements:* For master's, GMAT, minimum GPA of 3.0 in last 60 hours of undergraduate course work; for doctorate, GMAT (minimum score of 550), minimum GPA of 3.25 on all graduate work; BS with minimum GPA of 3.0 cumulative and last 60 hours. Additional exam requirements/recommendations for international students: Required—TOEFL (minimum score 575 paper-based; 84 iBT); Recommended—IELTS (minimum score 7). *Application deadline:* For fall admission, 7/1 for domestic students, 5/1 for international students; for spring admission, 11/1 for domestic students, 9/1 for international students. Applications are processed on a rolling basis. Application fee: $60. Electronic applications accepted. *Financial support:* In 2013–14, 1 teaching assistantship (averaging $13,497 per year) was awarded; career-related internships or fieldwork, Federal Work-Study, institutionally sponsored loans, scholarships/grants, and unspecified assistantships also available. Financial award applicants required to submit FAFSA. *Faculty research:* Electronic commerce, management of information technology. *Unit head:* Dr. Tim Barnett, Department Chairperson and Professor of Management, 662-325-3928, Fax: 662-325-8651, E-mail: tim.barnett@msstate.edu. *Application contact:* Dr. Rebecca Long, Graduate Coordinator, 662-325-3928, E-mail: gsb@cobian.msstate.edu.
Website: http://www.business.msstate.edu/programs/mis/index.php.

Molloy College, Graduate Business Program, Rockville Centre, NY 11571-5002. Offers accounting (MBA); accounting and finance (MBA); accounting and management (MBA); finance (MBA); finance and management (MBA); finance and personal financial planning (MBA); healthcare administration (MBA); management (MBA); management and personal financial planning (MBA); marketing (MBA); personal financial planning (MBA). Part-time programs available. *Faculty:* 8 full-time (3 women), 7 part-time/adjunct (1 woman). *Students:* 41 full-time (19 women), 104 part-time (36 women); includes 45 minority (21 Black or African American, non-Hispanic/Latino; 8 Asian, non-Hispanic/Latino; 14 Hispanic/Latino; 1 Native Hawaiian or other Pacific Islander, non-Hispanic/Latino; 1 Two or more races, non-Hispanic/Latino), 4 international. Average age 29. 48 applicants, 71% accepted, 27 enrolled. In 2013, 33 master's awarded. *Application deadline:* Applications are processed on a rolling basis. Application fee: $60. *Expenses: Tuition:* Full-time $16,920; part-time $940 per credit. *Required fees:* $880. *Faculty research:* Leadership, marketing, accounting, finance, international. *Unit head:* Dr. Daniel Cillis, Associate Dean and Director, MBA Program, 516-323-3080, E-mail: dcillis@molloy.edu. *Application contact:* Alina Haitz, Assistant Director of Graduate Admissions, 516-323-4008, E-mail: ahaitz@molloy.edu.

Monmouth University, The Graduate School, Leon Hess Business School, West Long Branch, NJ 07764-1898. Offers accounting (MBA, Post-Master's Certificate); business (MBA); finance (MBA); real estate (MBA). *Accreditation:* AACSB. Part-time and evening/weekend programs available. *Faculty:* 32 full-time (10 women), 5 part-time/adjunct (0 women). *Students:* 92 full-time (35 women), 98 part-time (45 women); includes 30 minority (9 Black or African American, non-Hispanic/Latino; 12 Asian, non-Hispanic/Latino; 6 Hispanic/Latino; 3 Two or more races, non-Hispanic/Latino), 9 international. Average age 27. 157 applicants, 82% accepted, 84 enrolled. In 2013, 134 master's awarded. *Degree requirements:* For master's, capstone course. *Entrance requirements:* For master's, GMAT, minimum GPA of 3.0 in major, 2.75 overall. Additional exam requirements/recommendations for international students: Required—TOEFL (minimum score 550 paper-based; 79 iBT), IELTS (minimum score 6), Michigan English Language Assessment Battery (minimum score 77). *Application deadline:* For fall admission, 7/15 priority date for domestic students, 6/1 for international students; for spring admission, 11/15 priority date for domestic students, 11/1 for international students. Applications are processed on a rolling basis. Application fee: $50. Electronic applications accepted. *Expenses: Tuition:* Part-time $1004 per credit hour. *Required fees:* $157 per semester. *Financial support:* In 2013–14, 119 students received support, including 281 fellowships (averaging $1,244 per year), 27 research assistantships (averaging $6,273 per year); career-related internships or fieldwork, scholarships/grants, and unspecified assistantships also available. Support available to part-time students. Financial award applicants required to submit FAFSA. *Faculty research:* Information technology and marketing, behavioral research in accounting, human resources, management of technology. *Unit head:* Dr. Susan Gupta, MBA Program Director, 732-571-3639, Fax: 732-263-5517, E-mail: sgupta@monmouth.edu. *Application contact:* Lauren Vento-

Cifelli, Associate Vice President of Undergraduate and Graduate Admission, 732-571-3452, Fax: 732-263-5123, E-mail: gradadm@monmouth.edu.
Website: http://www.monmouth.edu/mba.

See Display on page 116 and Close-Up on page 187.

Montclair State University, The Graduate School, School of Business, Post Master's Certificate Program in Finance, Montclair, NJ 07043-1624. Offers Post Master's Certificate. Part-time and evening/weekend programs available. *Entrance requirements:* For degree, essay. Additional exam requirements/recommendations for international students: Required—TOEFL (minimum score 83 iBT) or IELTS (minimum score 6.5). Electronic applications accepted. *Faculty research:* Foreign direct investment, central banking and inflation, African economic development, intraday trade, working capital management.

Mount Saint Mary College, Division of Business, Newburgh, NY 12550-3494. Offers business (MBA); financial planning (MBA). Part-time and evening/weekend programs available. *Faculty:* 7 full-time (2 women), 3 part-time/adjunct (1 woman). *Students:* 40 full-time (18 women), 51 part-time (22 women); includes 18 minority (6 Black or African American, non-Hispanic/Latino; 1 Asian, non-Hispanic/Latino; 11 Hispanic/Latino). Average age 30. 42 applicants, 69% accepted, 22 enrolled. In 2013, 25 master's awarded. *Degree requirements:* For master's, thesis or alternative. *Entrance requirements:* For master's, GMAT or minimum undergraduate GPA of 2.7. *Application deadline:* Applications are processed on a rolling basis. Application fee: $45. Application fee is waived when completed online. *Expenses: Tuition:* Full-time $13,356; part-time $742 per credit. *Required fees:* $70 per semester. *Financial support:* In 2013–14, 31 students received support. Unspecified assistantships available. Financial award application deadline: 4/15; financial award applicants required to submit FAFSA. *Faculty research:* Financial reform, entrepreneurship and small business development, global business relations, technology's impact on business decision-making, college-assisted business education. *Unit head:* Dr. Andrew Weiss, Graduate Coordinator, 845-569-3121, Fax: 845-562-6762, E-mail: andrew.weiss@msmc.edu. *Application contact:* Lisa Gallina, Director of Admissions for Graduate Programs and Adult Degree Completion, 845-569-3166, Fax: 845-569-3450, E-mail: lisa.gallina@msmc.edu.
Website: http://www.msmc.edu/Academics/Graduate_Programs/master_of_business_administration.be.

National University, Academic Affairs, School of Business and Management, La Jolla, CA 92037-1011. Offers accountancy (Certificate); business administration (GMBA, MBA), including financial management (MBA), human resource management (MBA), integrated marketing communications (MBA), international business (MBA), management accounting (MBA), marketing (MBA), mobile marketing and social media (MBA), organizational leadership (MA, MBA), professional golf management (MBA); global management (MGM); human resource management (MA), including organizational development and change, organizational leadership (MA, MBA); international business (Certificate); management information systems (MS); organizational leadership (MS), including community development; sustainability management (MS). Part-time and evening/weekend programs available. Postbaccalaureate distance learning degree programs offered (no on-campus study). *Faculty:* 30 full-time (8 women), 88 part-time/adjunct (25 women). *Students:* 688 full-time (357 women), 331 part-time (161 women); includes 453 minority (105 Black or African American, non-Hispanic/Latino; 2 American Indian or Alaska Native, non-Hispanic/Latino; 143 Asian, non-Hispanic/Latino; 162 Hispanic/Latino; 13 Native Hawaiian or other Pacific Islander, non-Hispanic/Latino; 28 Two or more races, non-Hispanic/Latino), 165 international. Average age 33. 286 applicants, 100% accepted, 217 enrolled. In 2013, 641 master's awarded. *Degree requirements:* For master's, thesis (for some programs). *Entrance requirements:* For master's, interview, minimum GPA of 2.5. Additional exam requirements/recommendations for international students: Required—TOEFL (minimum score 550 paper-based; 79 iBT), IELTS (minimum score 6). *Application deadline:* Applications are processed on a rolling basis. Application fee: $60 ($65 for international students). Electronic applications accepted. *Expenses: Tuition:* Full-time $13,824; part-time $1728 per course. One-time fee: $160. *Financial support:* Career-related internships or fieldwork, scholarships/grants, and tuition waivers (partial) available. Support available to part-time students. Financial award application deadline: 6/30; financial award applicants required to submit FAFSA. *Unit head:* School of Business and Management, 800-628-8648, Fax: 858-642-8719, E-mail: sobm@nu.edu. *Application contact:* Louis Cruz, Interim Vice President for Enrollment Services, 800-628-8648, E-mail: advisor@nu.edu.
Website: http://www.nu.edu/OurPrograms/SchoolOfBusinessAndManagement.html.

National University, Academic Affairs, School of Professional Studies, La Jolla, CA 92037-1011. Offers criminal justice (MCJ); digital cinema (MFA); digital journalism (MA); juvenile justice (MS); professional screen writing (MFA); public administration (MPA), including human resource management, organizational leadership, public finance. Part-time and evening/weekend programs available. Postbaccalaureate distance learning degree programs offered (no on-campus study). *Faculty:* 14 full-time (6 women), 28 part-time/adjunct (8 women). *Students:* 265 full-time (140 women), 130 part-time (69 women); includes 233 minority (90 Black or African American, non-Hispanic/Latino; 3 American Indian or Alaska Native, non-Hispanic/Latino; 23 Asian, non-Hispanic/Latino; 92 Hispanic/Latino; 8 Native Hawaiian or other Pacific Islander, non-Hispanic/Latino; 17 Two or more races, non-Hispanic/Latino), 4 international. Average age 37. 89 applicants, 100% accepted, 70 enrolled. *Degree requirements:* For master's, thesis (for some programs). *Entrance requirements:* For master's, interview, minimum GPA of 2.5. Additional exam requirements/recommendations for international students: Required—TOEFL (minimum score 550 paper-based; 79 iBT), IELTS (minimum score 6). *Application deadline:* Applications are processed on a rolling basis. Application fee: $60 ($65 for international students). Electronic applications accepted. *Expenses: Tuition:* Full-time $13,824; part-time $1728 per course. One-time fee: $160. *Financial support:* Career-related internships or fieldwork, institutionally sponsored loans, scholarships/grants, and tuition waivers (partial) available. Support available to part-time students. Financial award application deadline: 6/30; financial award applicants required to submit FAFSA. *Unit head:* School of Professional Studies, 800-628-8648, E-mail: sops@nu.edu. *Application contact:* Louis Cruz, Interim Vice President for Enrollment Services, 800-628-8648, E-mail: advisor@nu.edu.
Website: http://www.nu.edu/OurPrograms/School-of-Professional-Studies.html.

Naval Postgraduate School, Departments and Academic Groups, Department of Defense Analysis, Monterey, CA 93943. Offers command and control (MS); communications (MS); defense analysis (MS), including astronautics; financial management (MS); information operations (MS); irregular warfare (MS); national security affairs (MS); operations analysis (MS); special operations (MA, MS), including command and control (MS), communications (MS), financial management (MS), information operations (MS), irregular warfare (MS), national security affairs, operations analysis (MS), tactile missiles (MS), terrorist operations and financing (MS); tactile missiles (MS); terrorist operations and financing (MS). Program only open to commissioned officers of the United States and friendly nations and selected United States federal civilian employees. Part-time programs available. *Degree requirements:* For master's, thesis. *Faculty research:* CTF Global Ecco Project, Afghanistan endgames, core lab Philippines project, Defense Manpower Data Center (DMDC) data vulnerability.

Naval Postgraduate School, Departments and Academic Groups, Graduate School of Business and Public Policy, Monterey, CA 93943. Offers acquisition and contract management (MBA); business administration (EMBA, MBA); contract management (MS); defense business management (MBA); defense systems analysis (MS), including management; defense systems management (international) (MBA); financial management (MBA); information management (MBA); manpower systems analysis (MS); material logistics support management (MBA); program management (MS); resource planning and management for international defense (MBA); supply chain management (MBA); systems acquisition management (MBA); transportation management (MBA). Program only open to commissioned officers of the United States and friendly nations and selected United States federal civilian employees. *Accreditation:* AACSB; NASPAA. Part-time programs available. Postbaccalaureate distance learning degree programs offered (minimal on-campus study). *Degree requirements:* For master's, thesis (for some programs), terminal project/capstone (for some programs). *Faculty research:* U.S. and European public procurement policies for small and medium-sized enterprises, examining external validity criticisms in the choice of students as subjects in accounting experiment studies, assurance of learning in contract management education, contracting for cloud computing: opportunities and risks, NPS, Apple App Store as a business model supporting U. S. Navy requirements.

New Charter University, College of Business, San Francisco, CA 94105. Offers finance (MBA); health care management (MBA); management (MBA). Part-time and evening/weekend programs available. Postbaccalaureate distance learning degree programs offered (no on-campus study). *Entrance requirements:* For master's, course work in calculus, statistics, macroeconomics. Additional exam requirements/recommendations for international students: Required—TOEFL (minimum score 550 paper-based). Electronic applications accepted.

New England College of Business and Finance, Program in Finance, Boston, MA 02111-2645. Offers MSF. Postbaccalaureate distance learning degree programs offered (no on-campus study).

New Jersey City University, Graduate Studies and Continuing Education, College of Professional Studies, Department of Business Administration, Program in Finance, Jersey City, NJ 07305-1597. Offers MS. Part-time and evening/weekend programs available. *Students:* 20 full-time (7 women), 27 part-time (15 women); includes 21 minority (11 Black or African American, non-Hispanic/Latino; 3 Asian, non-Hispanic/Latino; 7 Hispanic/Latino), 19 international. Average age 31. In 2013, 13 master's awarded. *Degree requirements:* For master's, thesis. *Entrance requirements:* Additional exam requirements/recommendations for international students: Required—TOEFL (minimum score 61 iBT). *Expenses: Tuition, area resident:* Part-time $527.90 per credit. Tuition, nonresident: part-time $947.75 per credit. *Unit head:* Rosilyn Overton, Graduate Coordinator, 201-200-3353, E-mail: roverton@njcu.edu. *Application contact:* Dr. William Bajor, Dean of Graduate Studies, 201-200-3409, Fax: 201-200-3411, E-mail: wbajor@njcu.edu.

Newman University, MBA Program, Wichita, KS 67213-2097. Offers finance (MBA); international business (MBA); leadership (MBA); management (MBA); management information technology (MBA). Part-time programs available. *Faculty:* 7 full-time (1 woman), 7 part-time/adjunct (4 women). *Students:* 31 full-time (19 women), 56 part-time (24 women); includes 24 minority (6 Black or African American, non-Hispanic/Latino; 1 American Indian or Alaska Native, non-Hispanic/Latino; 9 Asian, non-Hispanic/Latino; 5 Hispanic/Latino; 3 Two or more races, non-Hispanic/Latino), 9 international. Average age 31. 83 applicants, 63% accepted, 32 enrolled. In 2013, 47 master's awarded. *Degree requirements:* For master's, thesis optional. *Entrance requirements:* For master's, minimum GPA of 3.0; 2 letters of recommendation; course work in algebra, statistics, macroeconomics, and financial accounting. Additional exam requirements/recommendations for international students: Required—TOEFL (minimum score 600 paper-based; 100 iBT). *Application deadline:* For fall admission, 8/1 priority date for domestic students, 7/15 priority date for international students; for winter admission, 1/1 priority date for domestic students; for spring admission, 1/1 priority date for domestic students, 11/15 priority date for international students. Applications are processed on a rolling basis. Application fee: $25 ($40 for international students). Electronic applications accepted. *Expenses:* Contact institution. *Financial support:* In 2013–14, 8 students received support. Scholarships/grants available. Financial award application deadline: 8/15; financial award applicants required to submit FAFSA. *Unit head:* Dr. Wendy Munday, Director of MBA Program, 316-942-4291 Ext. 2296, Fax: 316-942-4483, E-mail: mundayw@newmanu.edu. *Application contact:* Linda Kay Sabala, Director of Graduate Admissions, 316-942-4291 Ext. 2230, Fax: 316-942-4483, E-mail: sabalal@newmanu.edu.
Website: http://www.newmanu.edu.

New Mexico State University, Graduate School, College of Business, Department of Finance, Las Cruces, NM 88003-8001. Offers Graduate Certificate. *Faculty:* 11 full-time (4 women), 1 (woman) part-time/adjunct. *Students:* 1 full-time (0 women), all international. Average age 35. 1 applicant, 100% accepted, 1 enrolled. In 2013, 1 Graduate Certificate awarded. *Entrance requirements:* Additional exam requirements/recommendations for international students: Required—TOEFL (minimum score 550 paper-based; 79 iBT), IELTS (minimum score 6.5). *Application deadline:* Applications are processed on a rolling basis. Application fee: $40 ($50 for international students). *Expenses:* Tuition, state resident: full-time $5398; part-time $224.90 per credit. Tuition, nonresident: full-time $18,821; part-time $784.20 per credit. *Required fees:* $1310; $54.60 per credit. *Financial support:* Health care benefits and unspecified assistantships available. Support available to part-time students. *Unit head:* Dr. Lizbeth Ellis, Head, 575-646-3201, Fax: 575-646-2820, E-mail: lellis@nmsu.edu. *Application contact:* Coordinator, 575-646-2736, Fax: 575-646-7721, E-mail: gradinfo@nmsu.edu.
Website: http://business.nmsu.edu/academics/finance/.

The New School, The New School for Social Research, Department of Economics, New York, NY 10003. Offers economics (M Phil, MA, MS, DS Sc, PhD); global finance (MS); global political economy and finance (MA). Part-time and evening/weekend programs available. Terminal master's awarded for partial completion of doctoral program. *Degree requirements:* For master's, exam; for doctorate, one foreign language, thesis/dissertation, qualifying exam. *Entrance requirements:* For master's, GRE General Test; for doctorate, GRE General Test, MA. Additional exam requirements/recommendations for international students: Required—TOEFL (minimum score 600 paper-based; 100 iBT). Electronic applications accepted. *Faculty research:* Heterodox, history of economic thought, post-Keynesian, global political economy and finance.

New York Institute of Technology, School of Management, Department of Business Administration, Old Westbury, NY 11568-8000. Offers management (MBA), including decision science, finance, management, marketing; professional accounting (MBA). Part-time and evening/weekend programs available. *Faculty:* 22 full-time (6 women), 17 part-time/adjunct (3 women). *Students:* 151 full-time (74 women), 120 part-time (47 women); includes 44 minority (13 Black or African American, non-Hispanic/Latino; 23 Asian, non-Hispanic/Latino; 4 Hispanic/Latino; 4 Two or more races, non-Hispanic/

Latino), 177 international. Average age 27. 355 applicants, 66% accepted, 110 enrolled. In 2013, 151 master's awarded. *Degree requirements:* For master's, thesis (for some programs). *Entrance requirements:* For master's, minimum QPA of 2.85. Additional exam requirements/recommendations for international students: Required—TOEFL (minimum score 550 paper-based; 79 iBT), IELTS (minimum score 6). *Application deadline:* For fall admission, 7/1 priority date for domestic students, 6/1 for international students; for spring admission, 12/1 priority date for domestic students, 12/1 for international students. Applications are processed on a rolling basis. Application fee: $50. Electronic applications accepted. *Expenses: Tuition:* Full-time $18,900; part-time $1050 per credit. *Financial support:* Research assistantships with partial tuition reimbursements, career-related internships or fieldwork, scholarships/grants, health care benefits, tuition waivers (full and partial), and unspecified assistantships available. Support available to part-time students. Financial award applicants required to submit FAFSA. *Faculty research:* Accounting, economics, finance, management, marketing. *Unit head:* Dr. Diamando Afxentiou, Director, 212-261-1602, E-mail: dafxenti@nyit.edu. *Application contact:* Alice Dolitsky, Director, Graduate Admissions, 516-686-7520, Fax: 516-686-1116, E-mail: nyitgrad@nyit.edu.
Website: http://www.nyit.edu/management/mba.

New York Law School, Graduate Programs, New York, NY 10013. Offers American business law (LL M); financial services (LL M); law (JD); mental disability law (MA); real estate (LL M); taxation (LL M); JD/MA; JD/MBA. JD/MBA offered jointly with Bernard M. Baruch College of the City University of New York; JD/MA in forensic psychology offered jointly with John Jay College of Criminal Justice of the City University of New York. *Accreditation:* ABA. Part-time and evening/weekend programs available. *Faculty:* 79 full-time (31 women), 103 part-time/adjunct (44 women). *Students:* 891 full-time (453 women), 415 part-time (212 women); includes 411 minority (95 Black or African American, non-Hispanic/Latino; 1 American Indian or Alaska Native, non-Hispanic/Latino; 96 Asian, non-Hispanic/Latino; 194 Hispanic/Latino; 3 Native Hawaiian or other Pacific Islander, non-Hispanic/Latino; 22 Two or more races, non-Hispanic/Latino), 42 international. Average age 27. 3,484 applicants, 59% accepted, 341 enrolled. In 2013, 33 master's, 562 doctorates awarded. *Entrance requirements:* For master's, JD (for LL M); for doctorate, LSAT, undergraduate degree, letter of recommendation, resume, essay/personal statement. Additional exam requirements/recommendations for international students: Required—TOEFL (minimum score 600 paper-based; 100 iBT). *Application deadline:* For fall admission, 7/1 priority date for domestic and international students. Applications are processed on a rolling basis. Application fee: $0. Electronic applications accepted. *Expenses: Tuition:* Full-time $47,600; part-time $36,680 per year. *Required fees:* $1640; $1200. Part-time tuition and fees vary according to course load, degree level and student level. *Financial support:* In 2013–14, 495 students received support, including 142 fellowships (averaging $3,000 per year), 46 research assistantships (averaging $4,615 per year), 29 teaching assistantships (averaging $4,379 per year); career-related internships or fieldwork, Federal Work-Study, institutionally sponsored loans, and scholarships/grants also available. Support available to part-time students. Financial award application deadline: 7/1; financial award applicants required to submit FAFSA. *Faculty research:* Immigration law, corporate law, civil rights, family law, international law. *Unit head:* Anthony W. Crowell, Dean and President, 212-431-2840, Fax: 212-219-3752, E-mail: acrowell@nyls.edu. *Application contact:* Adam Barrett, Associate Dean of Admissions and Financial Aid, 212-431-2888, Fax: 212-966-1522, E-mail: admissions@nyls.edu.
Website: http://www.nyls.edu.

New York University, Leonard N. Stern School of Business, Department of Finance, New York, NY 10012-1019. Offers MBA, PhD. *Expenses: Tuition:* Full-time $35,856; part-time $1494 per unit. *Required fees:* $1408; $64 per unit. $473 per term. Tuition and fees vary according to course load and program. *Faculty research:* Derivative securities, pricing of assets, credit risk, portfolio management, international finance.

New York University, Polytechnic School of Engineering, Department of Finance and Risk Engineering, New York, NY 10012-1019. Offers financial engineering (MS, Advanced Certificate), including capital markets (MS), computational finance (MS), financial technology (MS); financial technology management (Advanced Certificate); organizational behavior (Advanced Certificate); risk management (Advanced Certificate); technology management (Advanced Certificate). MS program also offered in Manhattan. Part-time and evening/weekend programs available. *Faculty:* 8 full-time (3 women), 26 part-time/adjunct (5 women). *Students:* 232 full-time (76 women), 30 part-time (5 women); includes 19 minority (2 Black or African American, non-Hispanic/Latino; 15 Asian, non-Hispanic/Latino; 2 Hispanic/Latino), 221 international. Average age 25. 634 applicants, 57% accepted, 124 enrolled. In 2013, 111 master's awarded. *Degree requirements:* For master's, comprehensive exam (for some programs), thesis (for some programs). *Entrance requirements:* For master's, GMAT, minimum B average in undergraduate course work. Additional exam requirements/recommendations for international students: Required—TOEFL (minimum score 550 paper-based; 80 iBT); Recommended—IELTS (minimum score 6.5). *Application deadline:* For fall admission, 7/31 priority date for domestic students, 4/30 priority date for international students; for spring admission, 12/31 priority date for domestic students, 11/30 priority date for international students. Applications are processed on a rolling basis. Application fee: $75. Electronic applications accepted. *Expenses: Tuition:* Full-time $35,856; part-time $1494 per unit. *Required fees:* $1408; $64 per unit. $473 per term. Tuition and fees vary according to course load and program. *Financial support:* Institutionally sponsored loans, scholarships/grants, and unspecified assistantships available. Support available to part-time students. Financial award applicants required to submit FAFSA. *Faculty research:* Optimal control theory, general modeling and analysis, risk parity optimality, a new algorithmic approach to entangled political economy. *Total annual research expenditures:* $176,428. *Unit head:* Prof. Charles S. Tapiero, Academic Director, 718-260-3653, Fax: 718-260-3874, E-mail: ctapiero@poly.edu. *Application contact:* Raymond Lutzky, Director, Graduate Enrollment Management, 718-637-5984, Fax: 718-260-3624, E-mail: rlutzky@poly.edu.

New York University, Robert F. Wagner Graduate School of Public Service, Program in Public Administration, New York, NY 10012. Offers public administration (PhD); public and nonprofit management and policy (MPA, Advanced Certificate), including developmental administration (Advanced Certificate), financial management and public finance, human resources management (Advanced Certificate), international administration (Advanced Certificate), management (MPA), management for public and nonprofit organizations (Advanced Certificate), public policy analysis, quantitative analysis and computer applications (Advanced Certificate), urban public policy (Advanced Certificate); JD/MPA; MBA/MPA; MPA/MA. *Accreditation:* NASPAA (one or more programs are accredited). Part-time programs available. *Faculty:* 29 full-time (13 women), 41 part-time/adjunct (21 women). *Students:* 373 full-time (275 women), 245 part-time (176 women); includes 207 minority (56 Black or African American, non-Hispanic/Latino; 2 American Indian or Alaska Native, non-Hispanic/Latino; 70 Asian, non-Hispanic/Latino; 64 Hispanic/Latino; 2 Native Hawaiian or other Pacific Islander, non-Hispanic/Latino; 13 Two or more races, non-Hispanic/Latino), 122 international. Average age 28. 1,163 applicants, 61% accepted, 250 enrolled. In 2013, 233 master's, 6 doctorates, 1 other advanced degree awarded. *Degree requirements:* For master's, thesis or alternative, capstone end event; for doctorate, one foreign language, comprehensive exam, thesis/dissertation, preliminary qualifying examination. *Entrance requirements:* Additional exam requirements/recommendations for international students: Required—TOEFL (minimum score 100 iBT), IELTS (minimum score 7.5), TWE. *Application deadline:* For fall admission, 1/6 for domestic and international students; for spring admission, 10/1 for domestic and international students. Application fee: $85. Electronic applications accepted. *Expenses:* Contact institution. *Financial support:* In 2013–14, 152 students received support, including 141 fellowships with full and partial tuition reimbursements available (averaging $10,100 per year), 5 research assistantships with full tuition reimbursements available (averaging $39,643 per year); career-related internships or fieldwork, Federal Work-Study, scholarships/grants, health care benefits, and unspecified assistantships also available. Support available to part-time students. Financial award application deadline: 1/5; financial award applicants required to submit FAFSA. *Unit head:* Prof. Katherine O'Regan, Associate Professor of Public Policy, 212-998-7498, E-mail: katherine.oregan@nyu.edu. *Application contact:* Janet Barzilay, Admissions Officer, 212-998-7414, Fax: 212-995-4611, E-mail: wagner.admissions@nyu.edu.
Website: http://wagner.nyu.edu/.

New York University, School of Continuing and Professional Studies, The Preston Robert Tisch Center for Hospitality, Tourism, and Sports Management, Program in Hospitality Industry Studies, New York, NY 10012-1019. Offers brand strategy (MS); hospitality industry studies (Advanced Certificate); hotel finance (MS); lodging operations (MS); revenue management (MS). Part-time and evening/weekend programs available. *Faculty:* 5 full-time (2 women), 12 part-time/adjunct (2 women). *Students:* 70 full-time (58 women), 38 part-time (21 women); includes 14 minority (2 Black or African American, non-Hispanic/Latino; 9 Asian, non-Hispanic/Latino; 2 Hispanic/Latino; 1 Two or more races, non-Hispanic/Latino), 59 international. Average age 26. 98 applicants, 69% accepted, 42 enrolled. In 2013, 31 master's awarded. *Degree requirements:* For master's, thesis. *Entrance requirements:* For master's, bachelor's degree, resume with relevant professional work, internship or volunteer experience, two letters of recommendation, statement of purpose. Additional exam requirements/recommendations for international students: Required—TOEFL (minimum score 600 paper-based; 100 iBT), IELTS (minimum score 7). *Application deadline:* For fall admission, 2/1 priority date for domestic and international students; for spring admission, 10/15 priority date for domestic students, 8/15 priority date for international students. Applications are processed on a rolling basis. Application fee: $150. Electronic applications accepted. *Expenses: Tuition:* Full-time $35,856; part-time $1494 per unit. *Required fees:* $1408; $64 per unit. $473 per term. Tuition and fees vary according to course load and program. *Financial support:* In 2013–14, 25 students received support, including 24 fellowships (averaging $2,697 per year); scholarships/grants also available. Support available to part-time students. Financial award application deadline: 2/15; financial award applicants required to submit FAFSA. *Unit head:* Bjorn Hanson, Division Dean and Clinical Professor, 212-998-7100. *Application contact:* Admissions Office, 212-998-7100, E-mail: scps.gradadmissions@nyu.edu.
Website: http://www.scps.nyu.edu/areas-of-study/tisch/graduate-programs/ms-hospitality-industry-studies/.

New York University, School of Continuing and Professional Studies, Schack Institute of Real Estate, New York, NY 10012-1019. Offers construction management (MS, Advanced Certificate); real estate (MS, Advanced Certificate), including finance and investment (MS), real estate (Advanced Certificate), strategic real estate management (MS); real estate development (MS), including business of development, global real estate, sustainable development. Part-time and evening/weekend programs available. *Faculty:* 13 full-time (5 women), 72 part-time/adjunct (8 women). *Students:* 173 full-time (60 women), 393 part-time (89 women); includes 68 minority (18 Black or African American, non-Hispanic/Latino; 1 American Indian or Alaska Native, non-Hispanic/Latino; 34 Asian, non-Hispanic/Latino; 12 Hispanic/Latino; 3 Two or more races, non-Hispanic/Latino), 124 international. Average age 30. 400 applicants, 75% accepted, 165 enrolled. In 2013, 205 master's, 18 other advanced degrees awarded. *Degree requirements:* For master's, thesis. *Entrance requirements:* For master's, bachelor's degree, resume with relevant professional work, internship or volunteer experience, two letters of recommendation, statement of purpose. Additional exam requirements/recommendations for international students: Required—TOEFL (minimum score 600 paper-based; 100 iBT), IELTS (minimum score 7). *Application deadline:* For fall admission, 2/1 priority date for domestic and international students; for spring admission, 10/15 priority date for domestic students, 8/15 priority date for international students. Applications are processed on a rolling basis. Application fee: $150. Electronic applications accepted. *Expenses: Tuition:* Full-time $35,856; part-time $1494 per unit. *Required fees:* $1408; $64 per unit. $473 per term. Tuition and fees vary according to course load and program. *Financial support:* In 2013–14, 153 students received support, including 153 fellowships (averaging $2,056 per year); scholarships/grants also available. Support available to part-time students. Financial award application deadline: 3/1; financial award applicants required to submit FAFSA. *Faculty research:* Project financial management, sustainable design, impact of large-scale development projects, economics and market cycles, international property rights, comparative metropolitan economies, current market trends. *Unit head:* Rosemary Scanlon, Division Dean, 212-992-3250. *Application contact:* Office of Admissions, 212-998-7100, E-mail: scps.gradadmissions@nyu.edu.
Website: http://www.scps.nyu.edu/areas-of-study/real-estate/.

Niagara University, Graduate Division of Business Administration, Niagara Falls, NY 14109. Offers business (MBA); commerce (MBA); finance (MS). *Accreditation:* AACSB. Part-time and evening/weekend programs available. *Faculty:* 24 full-time (6 women), 17 part-time/adjunct (4 women). *Students:* 149 full-time (54 women), 92 part-time (46 women); includes 20 minority (6 Black or African American, non-Hispanic/Latino; 1 American Indian or Alaska Native, non-Hispanic/Latino; 4 Asian, non-Hispanic/Latino; 5 Hispanic/Latino; 4 Two or more races, non-Hispanic/Latino), 70 international. Average age 28. In 2013, 132 master's awarded. *Entrance requirements:* For master's, GMAT. Additional exam requirements/recommendations for international students: Required—TOEFL (minimum score 550 paper-based, 79 iBT) or IELTS (minimum score 6). *Application deadline:* For fall admission, 8/1 for domestic students; for spring admission, 11/1 for domestic students. Applications are processed on a rolling basis. Application fee: $30. Electronic applications accepted. Tuition and fees vary according to program. *Financial support:* Fellowships, research assistantships, career-related internships or fieldwork, and Federal Work-Study available. Support available to part-time students. Financial award application deadline: 4/15; financial award applicants required to submit FAFSA. *Faculty research:* Capital flows, Federal Reserve policy, human resource management, public policy, issues in marketing, auctions, economics of information, risk and capital markets, management strategy, consumer behavior, Internet and social media marketing. *Unit head:* Dr. Paul Richardson, Director, 716-286-8169, Fax: 716-286-8206, E-mail: psr@niagara.edu. *Application contact:* Evan Pierce, Associate Director for Graduate Recruitment, 716-286-8769, Fax: 716-286-8170, E-mail: epierce@niagara.edu.
Website: http://mba.niagara.edu.

North Central College, Graduate and Continuing Studies Programs, Department of Business, Program in Business Administration, Naperville, IL 60566-7063. Offers change management (MBA); finance (MBA); human resource management (MBA); international business administration (MIBA); management (MBA); marketing (MBA).

Part-time and evening/weekend programs available. *Faculty:* 13 full-time (4 women), 8 part-time/adjunct (0 women). *Students:* 31 full-time (8 women), 67 part-time (32 women); includes 16 minority (6 Black or African American, non-Hispanic/Latino; 5 Asian, non-Hispanic/Latino; 5 Hispanic/Latino), 3 international. Average age 30. 99 applicants, 54% accepted, 29 enrolled. In 2013, 51 master's awarded. *Degree requirements:* For master's, thesis optional, project. *Entrance requirements:* For master's, interview. Additional exam requirements/recommendations for international students: Required—TOEFL (minimum score 577 paper-based; 90 iBT). *Application deadline:* For fall admission, 8/15 for domestic students; for winter admission, 12/1 for domestic students; for spring admission, 2/1 for domestic students. Application fee: $25. *Expenses: Tuition:* Full-time $4716; part-time $786 per credit hour. *Financial support:* Scholarships/grants available. Support available to part-time students. *Unit head:* Dr. Robert Moussetis, Program Coordinator, 630-637-5475, E-mail: rcmoussetis@noctrl.edu. *Application contact:* Wendy Kulpinski, Director of Graduate and Continuing Education Admission, 630-637-5808, Fax: 630-637-5844, E-mail: wekulpinski@noctrl.edu.

Northeastern Illinois University, College of Graduate Studies and Research, College of Business and Management, Chicago, IL 60625-4699. Offers accounting (MSA); business administration (MBA); finance (MBA); management (MBA); marketing (MBA). Part-time and evening/weekend programs available. *Degree requirements:* For master's, thesis optional. *Entrance requirements:* For master's, GMAT, minimum GPA of 2.75. Additional exam requirements/recommendations for international students: Required—TOEFL (minimum score 550 paper-based; 79 iBT). Electronic applications accepted. *Faculty research:* Perception of accountants and non-accountants toward the future of the accounting industry, asynchronous learning outcomes, cost and efficiency of financial markets, impact of deregulation on airline industry, analysis of derivational instruments.

Northeastern State University, College of Business and Technology, Program in Accounting and Financial Analysis, Tahlequah, OK 74464-2399. Offers MS. Part-time and evening/weekend programs available. *Faculty:* 7 full-time (0 women). *Students:* 11 full-time (3 women), 49 part-time (34 women); includes 18 minority (6 Black or African American, non-Hispanic/Latino; 5 American Indian or Alaska Native, non-Hispanic/Latino; 2 Asian, non-Hispanic/Latino; 3 Hispanic/Latino; 2 Two or more races, non-Hispanic/Latino), 4 international. Average age 33. In 2013, 13 master's awarded. *Entrance requirements:* For master's, GMAT. Additional exam requirements/recommendations for international students: Required—TOEFL. *Application deadline:* For fall admission, 6/1 priority date for domestic students. Applications are processed on a rolling basis. Application fee: $25. Electronic applications accepted. *Expenses:* Tuition, state resident: full-time $3029; part-time $168.25 per credit hour. Tuition, nonresident: full-time $7709; part-time $428.25 per credit hour. *Required fees:* $35.90 per credit hour. *Faculty research:* Information systems and organizational performance, capital markets, sustainability. *Unit head:* Dr. Gary Freeman, Coordinator, 918-449-6524, E-mail: freemandg@nsuok.edu. *Application contact:* Margie Railey, Administrative Assistant, 918-456-5511 Ext. 2093, Fax: 918-458-2061, E-mail: railey@nsouk.edu. Website: http://academics.nsuok.edu/businesstechnology/Graduate/MAFA.aspx.

Northeastern University, D'Amore-McKim School of Business, Boston, MA 02115-5096. Offers accounting (MS); business administration (EMBA, MBA); finance (MS); international business (MS); taxation (MS); technological entrepreneurship (MS); JD/MBA; MBA/MSN; MS/MBA. Part-time and evening/weekend programs available. Postbaccalaureate distance learning degree programs offered (no on-campus study). *Entrance requirements:* For master's, GMAT or GRE, interview. Additional exam requirements/recommendations for international students: Required—TOEFL (minimum score 600 paper-based; 100 iBT). Electronic applications accepted. *Expenses:* Contact institution.

Northern State University, MS Program in Banking and Financial Services, Aberdeen, SD 57401-7198. Offers MS. Part-time programs available. Postbaccalaureate distance learning degree programs offered (minimal on-campus study). *Faculty:* 6 full-time (1 woman), 1 (woman) part-time/adjunct. *Students:* 18 part-time (8 women); includes 1 minority (Black or African American, non-Hispanic/Latino). Average age 25. 12 applicants, 83% accepted, 10 enrolled. *Degree requirements:* For master's, capstone course. *Entrance requirements:* For master's, GMAT or GRE, minimum GPA of 2.75. Additional exam requirements/recommendations for international students: Required—TOEFL (minimum score 550 paper-based; 78 iBT), IELTS (minimum score 6). *Application deadline:* Applications are processed on a rolling basis. Application fee: $35. Electronic applications accepted. *Expenses:* Tuition, state resident: full-time $3634. Tuition, nonresident: full-time $7690. One-time fee: $35 full-time. Part-time tuition and fees vary according to course load, degree level, campus/location and reciprocity agreements. *Financial support:* In 2013–14, 2 students received support. Federal Work-Study and institutionally sponsored loans available. Support available to part-time students. Financial award application deadline: 3/1; financial award applicants required to submit FAFSA. *Unit head:* Dr. Willard Broucek, Dean of Business, 605-626-2400, Fax: 605-626-2980, E-mail: willard.broucek@northern.edu. *Application contact:* Tammy K. Griffith, Program Assistant, 605-626-2558, E-mail: gradoff@northern.edu. Website: http://www.northern.edu/business/.

North Greenville University, T. Walter Brashier Graduate School, Greer, SC 29651. Offers Christian ministry (MCM, D Min); education (M Ed, MAT); financial planning (MBA); human resources (MBA). Part-time and evening/weekend programs available. Postbaccalaureate distance learning degree programs offered (no on-campus study). *Faculty:* 10 full-time (2 women), 8 part-time/adjunct (1 woman). *Students:* 164 full-time (52 women), 186 part-time (52 women); includes 45 minority (35 Black or African American, non-Hispanic/Latino; 2 American Indian or Alaska Native, non-Hispanic/Latino; 8 Hispanic/Latino). Average age 38. 200 applicants, 90% accepted, 130 enrolled. In 2013, 71 master's, 3 doctorates awarded. *Degree requirements:* For master's, comprehensive exam (for some programs), thesis or alternative, capstone course. *Entrance requirements:* For master's, minimum GPA of 2.25 overall, 2.5 in major; for doctorate, MAT. Additional exam requirements/recommendations for international students: Required—TOEFL (minimum score 550 paper-based). *Application deadline:* For fall admission, 8/1 for domestic students, 6/1 for international students; for winter admission, 1/1 for domestic students, 10/1 for international students; for spring admission, 3/1 for domestic students, 1/1 for international students. Applications are processed on a rolling basis. Application fee: $30. Electronic applications accepted. *Expenses: Tuition:* Part-time $425 per hour. *Financial support:* In 2013–14, 112 students received support, including 1 research assistantship (averaging $2,000 per year); Federal Work-Study, institutionally sponsored loans, scholarships/grants, tuition waivers (partial), and unspecified assistantships also available. Support available to part-time students. Financial award applicants required to submit FAFSA. *Faculty research:* Organizational behavior, church growth, homiletics, human resources, business strategy. *Unit head:* Dr. Joseph Samuel Isgett, Jr., Vice President for Graduate Studies, 864-877-3052, Fax: 864-877-1653, E-mail: sisgett@ngu.edu. *Application contact:* Tawana P. Scott, Dean of Graduate Academic Services, 864-877-1598, Fax: 864-877-1653, E-mail: tscott@ngu.edu. Website: http://www.ngu.edu/gradschool.php.

Northwestern University, The Graduate School, Kellogg School of Management, Department of Finance, Evanston, IL 60208. Offers PhD. Admissions and degree offered through The Graduate School. *Degree requirements:* For doctorate, comprehensive exam, thesis/dissertation. *Entrance requirements:* For doctorate, GMAT or GRE General Test, 2 years of undergraduate course work in mathematics. Additional exam requirements/recommendations for international students: Required—TOEFL. Electronic applications accepted. *Faculty research:* Corporate finance, asset pricing, international finance, micro-structure, empirical finance.

Northwestern University, The Graduate School, Kellogg School of Management, Management Programs, Evanston, IL 60208. Offers accounting information and management (MBA, PhD); analytical finance (MBA); business administration (MBA); decision sciences (MBA); entrepreneurship and innovation (MBA); finance (MBA, PhD); health enterprise management (MBA); human resources management (MBA); international business (MBA); management and organizations (MBA, PhD); management and organizations and sociology (PhD); management and strategy (MBA); management studies (MS); managerial analytics (MBA); managerial economics (MBA); managerial economics and strategy (PhD); marketing (MBA, PhD); marketing management (MBA); media management (MBA); operations management (MBA, PhD); real estate (MBA); social enterprise at Kellogg (MBA); JD/MBA. Part-time and evening/weekend programs available. Terminal master's awarded for partial completion of doctoral program. *Degree requirements:* For doctorate, thesis/dissertation, 2 years of coursework, qualifying (field) exam and candidacy, summer research papers and presentations to faculty, proposal defense, final exam/defense. *Entrance requirements:* For master's, GMAT, GRE, interview, 2 letters of recommendation, college transcripts, resume, essays, Kellogg honor code; for doctorate, GMAT, GRE, statement of purpose, transcripts, 2 letters of recommendation, resume, interview. Additional exam requirements/recommendations for international students: Required—TOEFL, IELTS. Electronic applications accepted. *Expenses:* Contact institution. *Faculty research:* Business cycles and international finance, health policy, networks, non-market strategy, consumer psychology.

Norwich University, College of Graduate and Continuing Studies, Master of Business Administration Program, Northfield, VT 05663. Offers finance (MBA); organizational leadership (MBA); project management (MBA). *Accreditation:* ACBSP. Evening/weekend programs available. Postbaccalaureate distance learning degree programs offered (minimal on-campus study). *Faculty:* 16 part-time/adjunct (6 women). *Students:* 198 full-time (57 women); includes 33 minority (18 Black or African American, non-Hispanic/Latino; 9 Asian, non-Hispanic/Latino; 3 Hispanic/Latino; 3 Two or more races, non-Hispanic/Latino). Average age 36. 200 applicants, 41% accepted, 82 enrolled. In 2013, 89 master's awarded. *Degree requirements:* For master's, comprehensive exam, thesis optional. *Entrance requirements:* For master's, minimum undergraduate GPA of 2.75. Additional exam requirements/recommendations for international students: Required—TOEFL (minimum score 600 paper-based; 94 iBT). *Application deadline:* For fall admission, 8/1 for domestic and international students; for winter admission, 11/1 for domestic and international students; for spring admission, 2/1 for domestic and international students; for summer admission, 5/1 for domestic and international students. Applications are processed on a rolling basis. Application fee: $50. Electronic applications accepted. *Expenses:* Contact institution. *Financial support:* In 2013–14, 65 students received support. Scholarships/grants available. Financial award applicants required to submit FAFSA. *Unit head:* Dr. Jose Cordova, Program Director, 802-485-2567, Fax: 802-485-2533, E-mail: jcordova@norwich.edu. *Application contact:* Ashley Farren, Associate Program Director, 802-485-2748, Fax: 802-485-2533, E-mail: afarren@norwich.edu. Website: http://online.norwich.edu/degree-programs/masters/master-business-administration/overview.

Notre Dame de Namur University, Division of Academic Affairs, School of Business and Management, Program in Business Administration, Belmont, CA 94002-1908. Offers business administration (MBA); entrepreneurship (MBA); finance (MBA); human resource management (MBA); marketing (MBA); media and promotion (MBA); technology and operations management (MBA). *Accreditation:* ACBSP. Part-time and evening/weekend programs available. *Entrance requirements:* For master's, minimum GPA of 2.5. Additional exam requirements/recommendations for international students: Required—TOEFL (minimum score 550 paper-based; 79 iBT). Electronic applications accepted.

Oakland University, Graduate Study and Lifelong Learning, School of Business Administration, Department of Accounting and Finance, Rochester, MI 48309-4401. Offers accounting (M Acc, Certificate); finance (Certificate). *Faculty:* 13 full-time (6 women), 2 part-time/adjunct (0 women). *Students:* 41 full-time (22 women), 28 part-time (19 women); includes 8 minority (2 Black or African American, non-Hispanic/Latino; 4 Asian, non-Hispanic/Latino; 1 Hispanic/Latino; 1 Two or more races, non-Hispanic/Latino), 9 international. Average age 40. 50 applicants, 52% accepted, 26 enrolled. In 2013, 37 master's, 2 Certificates awarded. Application fee: $0. *Unit head:* Mohinder Parkash, Interim Chair, 248-370-4288, Fax: 248-370-4604. *Application contact:* Donna Free, Coordinator, 248-370-3281.

Ohio Dominican University, Graduate Programs, Division of Business, Columbus, OH 43219-2099. Offers accounting (MBA); business administration (MBA); finance (MBA); leadership (MBA); public administration (MBA). *Accreditation:* ACBSP. Part-time and evening/weekend programs available. Postbaccalaureate distance learning degree programs offered (no on-campus study). *Degree requirements:* For master's, thesis or alternative. *Entrance requirements:* For master's, minimum GPA of 3.0, 3 letters of recommendation. Additional exam requirements/recommendations for international students: Required—TOEFL (minimum score 550 paper-based), IELTS (minimum score 6.5).

Ohio University, Graduate College, College of Arts and Sciences, Department of Economics, Athens, OH 45701-2979. Offers applied economics (MA); financial economics (MFE). Part-time and evening/weekend programs available. *Degree requirements:* For master's, thesis or alternative. *Entrance requirements:* For master's, GRE or GMAT (recommended), minimum GPA of 3.0. Additional exam requirements/recommendations for international students: Required—TOEFL (minimum score 550 paper-based; 80 iBT) or IELTS (minimum score 6.5). Electronic applications accepted. *Faculty research:* Macroeconomics, public finance, international economics and finance, monetary theory, healthcare economics.

Ohio University, Graduate College, College of Business, Program in Business Administration, Athens, OH 45701-2979. Offers executive management (MBA); finance (MBA); healthcare (MBA). *Accreditation:* AACSB. Part-time and evening/weekend programs available. Postbaccalaureate distance learning degree programs offered (minimal on-campus study). *Entrance requirements:* For master's, minimum GPA of 3.0. Additional exam requirements/recommendations for international students: Required—TOEFL (minimum score 600 paper-based). Electronic applications accepted. *Expenses:* Contact institution.

Oklahoma Christian University, Graduate School of Business, Oklahoma City, OK 73136-1100. Offers accounting (MBA); electronic business (MBA); financial services (MBA); health services management (MBA); human resources (MBA); international business (MBA); leadership and organizational development (MBA); marketing (MBA); project management (MBA). Postbaccalaureate distance learning degree programs

offered (no on-campus study). *Entrance requirements:* For master's, bachelor's degree. Electronic applications accepted.

Oklahoma City University, Meinders School of Business, Program in Business Administration, Oklahoma City, OK 73106-1402. Offers accounting (MBA); finance (MBA); general (MBA); marketing (MBA); JD/MBA; MSN/MBA. *Accreditation:* ACBSP. Part-time and evening/weekend programs available. *Students:* 82 full-time (39 women), 101 part-time (41 women); includes 18 minority (7 Black or African American, non-Hispanic/Latino; 6 American Indian or Alaska Native, non-Hispanic/Latino; 3 Asian, non-Hispanic/Latino; 2 Two or more races, non-Hispanic/Latino), 50 international. Average age 31. 109 applicants, 61% accepted, 19 enrolled. In 2013, 114 master's awarded. *Degree requirements:* For master's, comprehensive exam. *Entrance requirements:* For master's, GRE or GMAT, bachelor's degree from accredited institution, minimum GPA of 3.0, essay, recommendation letters. Additional exam requirements/recommendations for international students: Required—TOEFL (minimum score 550 paper-based; 80 iBT). *Application deadline:* Applications are processed on a rolling basis. Application fee: $50. Electronic applications accepted. *Expenses: Tuition:* Full-time $16,848; part-time $936 per credit hour. Tuition and fees vary according to course load, degree level and program. *Financial support:* Career-related internships or fieldwork, Federal Work-Study, institutionally sponsored loans, scholarships/grants, and tuition waivers (partial) available. Support available to part-time students. Financial award application deadline: 6/1; financial award applicants required to submit FAFSA. *Faculty research:* Management information systems, international business strategies. *Unit head:* Dr. Steve Agee, Dean, 405-208-5130, Fax: 405-208-5098, E-mail: sagee@okcu.edu. *Application contact:* Heidi Puckett, Director of Graduate Admissions, 800-633-7242, Fax: 405-208-5916, E-mail: gadmissions@okcu.edu.
Website: http://msb.okcu.edu/graduate/.

Oklahoma State University, Spears School of Business, Department of Finance, Stillwater, OK 74078. Offers finance (PhD); quantitative financial economics (MS). Part-time programs available. *Faculty:* 13 full-time (1 woman), 2 part-time/adjunct (0 women). *Students:* 15 full-time (5 women), 11 part-time (4 women); includes 3 minority (2 Black or African American, non-Hispanic/Latino; 1 Hispanic/Latino), 13 international. Average age 29. 47 applicants, 32% accepted, 8 enrolled. In 2013, 5 master's awarded. *Degree requirements:* For master's, thesis or alternative; for doctorate, comprehensive exam, thesis/dissertation. *Entrance requirements:* For master's and doctorate, GRE or GMAT. Additional exam requirements/recommendations for international students: Required—TOEFL (minimum score 550 paper-based; 79 iBT). *Application deadline:* For fall admission, 3/1 priority date for international students; for spring admission, 8/1 priority date for international students. Applications are processed on a rolling basis. Application fee: $40 ($75 for international students). Electronic applications accepted. *Expenses:* Tuition, state resident: full-time $4272; part-time $178 per credit hour. Tuition, nonresident: full-time $17,472; part-time $709 per credit hour. *Required fees:* $2413.20; $100.55 per credit hour. One-time fee: $50 full-time. Part-time tuition and fees vary according to course load and campus/location. *Financial support:* In 2013–14, 18 research assistantships (averaging $11,565 per year), 2 teaching assistantships (averaging $22,304 per year) were awarded; career-related internships or fieldwork, Federal Work-Study, scholarships/grants, health care benefits, tuition waivers (partial), and unspecified assistantships also available. Support available to part-time students. Financial award application deadline: 3/1; financial award applicants required to submit FAFSA. *Faculty research:* Corporate risk management, derivatives banking, investments and securities issuance, corporate governance, banking. *Unit head:* Dr. John Polonchek, Department Head, 405-744-5199, Fax: 405-744-5180, E-mail: john.polonchek@okstate.edu.
Website: http://spears.okstate.edu/finance/.

Old Dominion University, College of Business and Public Administration, Doctoral Program in Business Administration, Norfolk, VA 23529. Offers finance (PhD); information technology (PhD); marketing (PhD); strategic management (PhD). *Accreditation:* AACSB. *Faculty:* 29 full-time (6 women). *Students:* 29 full-time (8 women), 29 part-time (13 women); includes 3 minority (1 Black or African American, non-Hispanic/Latino; 1 Asian, non-Hispanic/Latino; 1 Native Hawaiian or other Pacific Islander, non-Hispanic/Latino), 41 international. Average age 33. 77 applicants, 35% accepted, 12 enrolled. In 2013, 8 doctorates awarded. *Degree requirements:* For doctorate, comprehensive exam, thesis/dissertation. *Entrance requirements:* For doctorate, GMAT. Additional exam requirements/recommendations for international students: Required—TOEFL (minimum score 550 paper-based; 79 iBT). *Application deadline:* For fall admission, 3/1 priority date for domestic and international students. Application fee: $50. Electronic applications accepted. *Expenses:* Tuition, state resident: full-time $9888; part-time $412 per credit. Tuition, nonresident: full-time $25,152; part-time $1048 per credit. *Required fees:* $59 per semester. One-time fee: $50. *Financial support:* In 2013–14, 27 students received support, including 14 fellowships with full tuition reimbursements available (averaging $7,500 per year), 24 research assistantships with full tuition reimbursements available (averaging $7,500 per year), 16 teaching assistantships with full tuition reimbursements available (averaging $7,500 per year); scholarships/grants and unspecified assistantships also available. Financial award application deadline: 3/1; financial award applicants required to submit FAFSA. *Faculty research:* International business, buyer behavior, financial markets, strategy, operations research. *Unit head:* Dr. John B. Ford, Graduate Program Director, 757-683-3587, Fax: 757-683-4076, E-mail: jbford@odu.edu. *Application contact:* Katrina Davenport, Program Coordinator, 757-683-5138, Fax: 757-683-4076, E-mail: kdavenpo@odu.edu.
Website: http://bpa.odu.edu/bpa/academics/baphd.shtml.

Old Dominion University, College of Business and Public Administration, MBA Program, Norfolk, VA 23529. Offers business and economic forecasting (MBA); financial analysis and valuation (MBA); health sciences administration (MBA); information technology and enterprise integration (MBA); international business (MBA); maritime and port management (MBA); public administration (MBA). *Accreditation:* AACSB. Part-time and evening/weekend programs available. Postbaccalaureate distance learning degree programs offered (no on-campus study). *Faculty:* 83 full-time (19 women), 5 part-time/adjunct (2 women). *Students:* 42 full-time (20 women), 103 part-time (42 women); includes 18 minority (8 Black or African American, non-Hispanic/Latino; 4 Asian, non-Hispanic/Latino; 1 Hispanic/Latino; 1 Native Hawaiian or other Pacific Islander, non-Hispanic/Latino; 4 Two or more races, non-Hispanic/Latino), 16 international. Average age 30. 161 applicants, 71% accepted, 75 enrolled. In 2013, 61 master's awarded. *Entrance requirements:* For master's, GMAT, GRE, letter of reference, resume, essay. Additional exam requirements/recommendations for international students: Required—TOEFL (minimum score 550 paper-based; 80 iBT). *Application deadline:* For fall admission, 6/1 priority date for domestic students, 4/15 priority date for international students; for spring admission, 11/1 priority date for domestic students, 10/1 priority date for international students. Applications are processed on a rolling basis. Application fee: $50. Electronic applications accepted. *Expenses:* Tuition, state resident: full-time $9888; part-time $412 per credit. Tuition, nonresident: full-time $25,152; part-time $1048 per credit. *Required fees:* $59 per semester. One-time fee: $50. *Financial support:* In 2013–14, 47 students received support, including 94 research assistantships with partial tuition reimbursements available (averaging $8,900 per year); career-related internships or fieldwork, scholarships/grants, and unspecified assistantships also available. Support available to part-time students. Financial award application deadline: 2/15; financial award applicants required to submit FAFSA. *Faculty research:* International business, buyer behavior, financial markets, strategy, operations research, maritime and transportation economics. *Unit head:* Dr. Kiran Karaude, Graduate Program Director, 757-683-3585, Fax: 757-683-5750, E-mail: mbainfo@odu.edu. *Application contact:* Sandi Phillips, MBA Program Assistant, 757-683-3585, Fax: 757-683-5750, E-mail: mbainfo@odu.edu.
Website: http://www.odu.edu/mba/.

Oral Roberts University, School of Business, Tulsa, OK 74171. Offers accounting (MBA); entrepreneurship (MBA); finance (MBA); international business (MBA); management (MBA); marketing (MBA); non-profit management (MBA); not for profit management (MNM). *Accreditation:* ACBSP. Part-time programs available. Postbaccalaureate distance learning degree programs offered (minimal on-campus study). *Degree requirements:* For master's, thesis optional. *Entrance requirements:* For master's, minimum cumulative GPA of 3.0. Additional exam requirements/recommendations for international students: Required—TOEFL (minimum score 550 paper-based; 79 iBT). Electronic applications accepted. *Faculty research:* Social media, international business and marketing.

Oregon State University, College of Business, Program in Business Administration, Corvallis, OR 97331. Offers clean technology (MBA); commercialization (MBA); executive leadership (MBA); global operations (MBA); marketing (MBA); research thesis (MBA); wealth management (MBA). Part-time programs available. *Faculty:* 34 full-time (13 women), 2 part-time/adjunct (1 woman). *Students:* 153 full-time (67 women), 44 part-time (18 women); includes 20 minority (1 Black or African American, non-Hispanic/Latino; 12 Asian, non-Hispanic/Latino; 3 Hispanic/Latino; 1 Native Hawaiian or other Pacific Islander, non-Hispanic/Latino; 3 Two or more races, non-Hispanic/Latino), 97 international. Average age 29. 194 applicants, 64% accepted, 106 enrolled. In 2013, 61 degrees awarded. *Degree requirements:* For master's, thesis optional. *Entrance requirements:* For master's, GMAT. Additional exam requirements/recommendations for international students: Required—TOEFL (minimum score 91 iBT), IELTS (minimum score 7). *Application deadline:* Applications are processed on a rolling basis. Application fee: $60. *Expenses:* Contact institution. *Unit head:* Dr. David Baldridge, Director for Business Master's Program, 541-737-6062, E-mail: david.baldridge@bus.oregonstate.edu.
Website: http://business.oregonstate.edu/mba/degrees.

Ottawa University, Graduate Studies-Arizona, Programs in Business, Ottawa, KS 66067-3399. Offers business administration (MBA); finance (MBA); human resources (MA, MBA); leadership (MBA); marketing (MBA). Programs offered in Mesa, Phoenix, Tempe and West Valley, AZ. Part-time and evening/weekend programs available. Postbaccalaureate distance learning degree programs offered. *Degree requirements:* For master's, thesis or alternative. *Entrance requirements:* For master's, minimum undergraduate GPA of 3.0. Additional exam requirements/recommendations for international students: Required—TOEFL (minimum score 550 paper-based). Electronic applications accepted.

Our Lady of the Lake University of San Antonio, School of Business and Leadership, Program in Accounting/Finance, San Antonio, TX 78207-4689. Offers accounting (MS); finance (MBA). Part-time and evening/weekend programs available. *Faculty:* 2 full-time (both women), 1 part-time/adjunct (0 women). *Students:* 25 full-time (17 women), 8 part-time (6 women); includes 25 minority (3 Black or African American, non-Hispanic/Latino; 1 Asian, non-Hispanic/Latino; 21 Hispanic/Latino). Average age 33. 280 applicants, 84% accepted, 14 enrolled. In 2013, 11 master's awarded. *Entrance requirements:* For master's, GMAT, GRE General Test, or MAT. Additional exam requirements/recommendations for international students: Required—TOEFL. *Application deadline:* Applications are processed on a rolling basis. Application fee: $25 ($50 for international students). Electronic applications accepted. *Expenses: Tuition:* Full-time $9120; part-time $760 per credit. *Required fees:* $698; $334 per trimester. Tuition and fees vary according to course load, degree level, campus/location and program. *Financial support:* Fellowships, career-related internships or fieldwork, Federal Work-Study, institutionally sponsored loans, scholarships/grants, and tuition waivers (partial) available. Support available to part-time students. Financial award application deadline: 4/15. *Faculty research:* Decision-making, problem-solving, administration, leadership, management. *Unit head:* Dr. Kathryn Winney, Chair of the Business Department, 210-434-6711 Ext. 2297, Fax: 210-434-0821, E-mail: kmwinney@lake.ollusa.edu. *Application contact:* Graduate Admission, 210-431-3961, Fax: 210-431-4013, E-mail: gradadm@ollusa.edu.
Website: http://www.ollusa.edu/s/1190/ollu-3-column-noads.aspx?sid=1190&gid=1&pgid=6390.

Pace University, Lubin School of Business, Financial Management Program, New York, NY 10038. Offers banking and finance (MBA); corporate financial management (MBA); financial management (MBA); investment management (MBA, MS). Part-time and evening/weekend programs available. *Students:* 93 full-time (43 women), 315 part-time (141 women); includes 54 minority (16 Black or African American, non-Hispanic/Latino; 28 Asian, non-Hispanic/Latino; 8 Hispanic/Latino; 2 Two or more races, non-Hispanic/Latino), 268 international. Average age 26. 505 applicants, 33% accepted, 119 enrolled. In 2013, 193 master's awarded. *Entrance requirements:* For master's, GMAT, GRE. Additional exam requirements/recommendations for international students: Required—TOEFL. *Application deadline:* For fall admission, 8/1 priority date for domestic students, 6/1 for international students; for spring admission, 12/1 for domestic students, 10/1 for international students. Applications are processed on a rolling basis. Application fee: $70. Electronic applications accepted. *Expenses: Tuition:* Part-time $1075 per credit. *Required fees:* $192 per semester. Tuition and fees vary according to course load, degree level and program. *Financial support:* Research assistantships, career-related internships or fieldwork, Federal Work-Study, and tuition waivers (full and partial) available. Support available to part-time students. Financial award application deadline: 8/15; financial award applicants required to submit FAFSA. *Unit head:* Dr. P. V. Viswanath, Chairperson, 212-618-6518, E-mail: pviswanath@pace.edu. *Application contact:* Susan Ford-Goldschein, Director of Graduate Admissions, 212-346-1531, Fax: 212-346-1585, E-mail: gradnyc@pace.edu.
Website: http://www.pace.edu/.

Pacific Lutheran University, Graduate Programs and Continuing Education, School of Business, Master of Science in Finance Program, Tacoma, WA 98447. Offers MSF. *Faculty:* 13 full-time (6 women), 1 part-time/adjunct (0 women). *Students:* 19 full-time (5 women); includes 3 minority (all Asian, non-Hispanic/Latino), 6 international. Average age 24. 31 applicants, 71% accepted, 19 enrolled. *Entrance requirements:* Additional exam requirements/recommendations for international students: Required—TOEFL (minimum score 550 paper-based; 88 iBT). *Application deadline:* For fall admission, 3/1 priority date for domestic students. Applications are processed on a rolling basis. Application fee: $40. Electronic applications accepted. *Expenses: Tuition:* Full-time $18,560; part-time $1160. Tuition and fees vary according to program and student level. *Financial support:* In 2013–14, 10 students received support. Fellowships, career-related internships or fieldwork, Federal Work-Study, institutionally sponsored loans, and scholarships/grants available. Financial award application deadline: 3/1; financial award applicants required to submit FAFSA. *Unit head:* Dr. Nancy Albers-Miller, Dean, School of Business, 253-535-7224, Fax: 253-535-8723, E-mail: renfromm@plu.edu.

Application contact: Michael Renfrow, Associate Director of the MSF Program for the School of Business, 253-535-7224, Fax: 253-535-8723, E-mail: renfromm@plu.edu.
Website: http://www.plu.edu/msf/.

Pacific States University, College of Business, Los Angeles, CA 90006. Offers accounting (MBA); finance (MBA); international business (MBA, DBA); management of information technology (MBA); real estate management (MBA). Part-time and evening/weekend programs available. Postbaccalaureate distance learning degree programs offered (no on-campus study). *Degree requirements:* For doctorate, comprehensive exam, thesis/dissertation. *Entrance requirements:* For master's, minimum undergraduate GPA of 2.5 during last 90 hours of course work. Additional exam requirements/recommendations for international students: Required—TOEFL (minimum score 500 paper-based; 61 iBT), IELTS (minimum score 5.5).

Park University, School of Graduate and Professional Studies, Kansas City, MO 54105. Offers adult education (M Ed); business and government leadership (Graduate Certificate); business, government, and global society (MPA); communication and leadership (MA); creative and life writing (Graduate Certificate); disaster and emergency management (MPA, Graduate Certificate); educational leadership (M Ed); finance (MBA, Graduate Certificate); general business (MBA); global business (Graduate Certificate); healthcare administration (MHA); healthcare services management and leadership (Graduate Certificate); international business (MBA); language and literacy (M Ed), including English for speakers of other languages, special reading teacher/literacy coach; leadership of international healthcare organizations (Graduate Certificate); management information systems (MBA, Graduate Certificate); music performance (ADP, Graduate Certificate), including cello (MM, ADP), piano (MM, ADP), viola (MM, ADP), violin (MM, ADP); nonprofit and community services management (MPA); nonprofit leadership (Graduate Certificate); performance (MM), including cello (MM, ADP), piano (MM, ADP), viola (MM, ADP), violin (MM, ADP); public management (MPA); social work (MSW); teacher leadership (M Ed), including curriculum and assessment, instructional leader. Part-time and evening/weekend programs available. Postbaccalaureate distance learning degree programs offered (no on-campus study). *Students:* 862 full-time (482 women); includes 55 minority (30 Black or African American, non-Hispanic/Latino; 2 American Indian or Alaska Native, non-Hispanic/Latino; 4 Asian, non-Hispanic/Latino; 14 Hispanic/Latino; 5 Two or more races, non-Hispanic/Latino), 141 international. Average age 34. 497 applicants, 62% accepted, 119 enrolled. In 2013, 281 master's, 14 other advanced degrees awarded. *Degree requirements:* For master's, comprehensive exam (for some programs), thesis (for some programs), internship (for some programs); exam (for some programs). *Entrance requirements:* For master's, GRE or GMAT (for some programs), teacher certification (for some M Ed programs), letters of recommendation, essay, resume (for some programs). Additional exam requirements/recommendations for international students: Required—TOEFL (minimum score 550 paper-based; 79 iBT), IELTS (minimum score 6). *Application deadline:* For fall admission, 8/1 priority date for domestic students, 7/15 priority date for international students; for spring admission, 1/1 priority date for domestic students, 11/1 priority date for international students. Applications are processed on a rolling basis. Application fee: $50 ($100 for international students). Electronic applications accepted. *Financial support:* In 2013–14, 2 research assistantships with full tuition reimbursements (averaging $15,760 per year) were awarded. Financial award applicants required to submit FAFSA. *Unit head:* Dr. Laurie Dipadova-Stocks, Dean of Graduate and Professional Studies, 816-559-5624, Fax: 816-472-1173, E-mail: ldipadovastocks@park.edu. *Application contact:* Judith Appollis, Director of Graduate Admissions and Internationalization, School of Graduate and Professional Studies, 816-559-5627, Fax: 816-472-1173, E-mail: gradschool@park.edu.
Website: http://www.park.edu/grad.

Penn State Great Valley, Graduate Studies, Management Division, Malvern, PA 19355-1488. Offers business administration (MBA); finance (M Fin); leadership development (MLD). *Accreditation:* AACSB. *Unit head:* Dr. Craig S. Edelbrock, Chancellor, 610-648-3202, Fax: 610-889-1334, E-mail: cse1@psu.edu. *Application contact:* JoAnn Kelly, Director of Admissions, 610-648-3315, Fax: 610-725-5296, E-mail: jek2@psu.edu.
Website: http://www.sgps.psu.edu/Academics/Degrees/31885.htm.

Pepperdine University, Graziadio School of Business and Management, MS in Applied Finance Program, Malibu, CA 90263. Offers MS. *Students:* 99 full-time (65 women), 1 (woman) part-time; includes 2 minority (1 Black or African American, non-Hispanic/Latino; 1 Asian, non-Hispanic/Latino), 97 international. 456 applicants, 68% accepted, 82 enrolled. In 2013, 70 master's awarded. *Entrance requirements:* For master's, GMAT or GRE, two letters of recommendation. Additional exam requirements/recommendations for international students: Required—TOEFL. *Application deadline:* For fall admission, 1/10 for domestic students. Application fee: $75. Tuition and fees vary according to program. *Financial support:* Scholarships/grants available. Financial award applicants required to submit FAFSA. *Unit head:* Dr. Michael L. Williams, Associate Dean for Full-Time Programs, Graziadio School of Business and Management, 310-506-4100, E-mail: michael.williams@pepperdine.edu.
Website: http://bschool.pepperdine.edu/programs/masters-finance/.

Polytechnic University of Puerto Rico, Miami Campus, Graduate School, Miami, FL 33166. Offers accounting (MBA); business administration (MBA); construction management (MEM); environmental management (MEM); finance (MBA); human resources management (MBA); logistics and supply chain management (MBA); management of international enterprises (MBA); manufacturing management (MEM); marketing management (MBA); project management (MBA). Part-time and evening/weekend programs available. Postbaccalaureate distance learning degree programs offered (no on-campus study). *Entrance requirements:* For master's, minimum GPA of 3.0. Electronic applications accepted.

Polytechnic University of Puerto Rico, Orlando Campus, Graduate School, Winter Park, FL 32792. Offers accounting (MBA); business administration (MBA); construction management (MEM); engineering management (MEM); environmental management (MEM); finance (MBA); human resources management (MBA); management of international enterprises (MBA); management of technology (MBA); manufacturing management (MEM). Part-time and evening/weekend programs available. Postbaccalaureate distance learning degree programs offered (no on-campus study). *Entrance requirements:* For master's, minimum GPA of 3.0. Additional exam requirements/recommendations for international students: Recommended—TOEFL. Electronic applications accepted.

Pontifical Catholic University of Puerto Rico, College of Business Administration, Program in Finance, Ponce, PR 00717-0777. Offers MBA. Part-time and evening/weekend programs available. *Degree requirements:* For master's, thesis. *Entrance requirements:* For master's, GRE, interview, minimum GPA of 2.75.

Pontificia Universidad Catolica Madre y Maestra, Graduate School, Faculty of Social and Administrative Sciences, Santiago, Dominican Republic. Offers business administration (MBA), including business development, finance, international business, management skills (M Mgmt, MBA), marketing, operations, strategic cost management, strategy, tourist destination planning and management; law (LL M), including civil law, corporate business law, criminal law, international relations, real estate law; management (M Mgmt), including higher financial management, insurance program administration, management skills (M Mgmt, MBA); psychology (MA), including clinical child and adolescent psychology, forensic psychology; strategic human resources (EMBA).

Portland State University, Graduate Studies, School of Business Administration, Master of Science in Financial Analysis Program, Portland, OR 97207-0751. Offers MSFA. Part-time and evening/weekend programs available. *Students:* 26 full-time (16 women), 30 part-time (16 women); includes 8 minority (5 Asian, non-Hispanic/Latino; 2 Hispanic/Latino; 1 Two or more races, non-Hispanic/Latino), 22 international. Average age 28. 91 applicants, 53% accepted, 31 enrolled. In 2013, 29 master's awarded. *Entrance requirements:* For master's, GMAT, minimum GPA of 2.75, 2 recommendations, resume, interview. Additional exam requirements/recommendations for international students: Required—TOEFL (minimum score 550 paper-based). *Application deadline:* For fall admission, 4/1 priority date for domestic students, 3/1 priority date for international students. Applications are processed on a rolling basis. Application fee: $50. *Expenses:* Tuition, state resident: full-time $9207; part-time $341 per credit. Tuition, nonresident: full-time $14,391; part-time $533 per credit. *Required fees:* $1263; $22 per credit. $98 per quarter. One-time fee: $150. Tuition and fees vary according to program. *Financial support:* Research assistantships with partial tuition reimbursements, career-related internships or fieldwork, Federal Work-Study, and scholarships/grants available. Financial award application deadline: 3/1; financial award applicants required to submit FAFSA. *Unit head:* Dr. Berrin Erdogan, Coordinator, 503-725-3798, Fax: 503-725-5850, E-mail: berrine@sba.pdx.edu. *Application contact:* Pam Mitchell, Administrator, 503-725-3730, Fax: 503-725-5850, E-mail: pamm@sba.pdx.edu.
Website: http://www.pdx.edu/gradbusiness/master-of-science-in-financial-analysis.

Post University, Program in Business Administration, Waterbury, CT 06723-2540. Offers accounting (MSA); business administration (MBA); corporate innovation (MBA); entrepreneurship (MBA); finance (MBA); healthcare (MBA); leadership (MBA); marketing (MBA); project management (MBA). *Accreditation:* ACBSP. Postbaccalaureate distance learning degree programs offered.

Princeton University, Graduate School, Bendheim Center for Finance, Princeton, NJ 08544-1019. Offers M Fin. *Entrance requirements:* For master's, GRE General Test. Additional exam requirements/recommendations for international students: Required—TOEFL (minimum score 600 paper-based). Electronic applications accepted.

Providence College, School of Business, Providence, RI 02918. Offers accounting (MBA); finance (MBA); international business (MBA); management (MBA); marketing (MBA); not-for-profit organizations (MBA). Part-time and evening/weekend programs available. *Faculty:* 14 full-time (5 women), 3 part-time/adjunct (1 woman). *Students:* 68 full-time (25 women), 54 part-time (25 women); includes 12 minority (3 Black or African American, non-Hispanic/Latino; 1 Asian, non-Hispanic/Latino; 6 Hispanic/Latino; 2 Two or more races, non-Hispanic/Latino), 7 international. Average age 25. 43 applicants, 95% accepted, 36 enrolled. In 2013, 38 master's awarded. *Degree requirements:* For master's, thesis optional. *Entrance requirements:* For master's, GMAT. Additional exam requirements/recommendations for international students: Required—TOEFL (minimum score 550 paper-based; 80 iBT). *Application deadline:* For fall admission, 7/15 priority date for domestic and international students; for spring admission, 11/15 priority date for domestic and international students; for summer admission, 4/15 priority date for domestic students. Applications are processed on a rolling basis. Application fee: $55. *Expenses:* Contact institution. *Financial support:* Federal Work-Study, institutionally sponsored loans, and unspecified assistantships available. Support available to part-time students. Financial award application deadline: 8/1; financial award applicants required to submit FAFSA. *Unit head:* Jacqueline Elcik, Director, 401-865-2131, E-mail: jelcik@providence.edu. *Application contact:* MBA Program, 401-865-2294, E-mail: mba@providence.edu.
Website: http://www.providence.edu/business/Pages/default.aspx.

Purdue University, Graduate School, Krannert School of Management, Master of Science in Finance Program, West Lafayette, IN 47907. Offers MSF. *Entrance requirements:* For master's, GMAT or GRE, minimum GPA of 3.0, four-year baccalaureate degree, essays, letters of recommendation. Additional exam requirements/recommendations for international students: Required—TOEFL (minimum score 550 paper-based; 77 iBT). Electronic applications accepted. *Expenses:* Contact institution.

Queen's University at Kingston, Queens School of Business, Program in Business Administration, Kingston, ON K7L 3N6, Canada. Offers consulting and project management (MBA); finance (MBA); innovation and entrepreneurship (MBA); marketing (MBA). *Accreditation:* AACSB. *Degree requirements:* For master's, thesis optional, research project. *Entrance requirements:* For master's, GMAT, minimum B+ average. Additional exam requirements/recommendations for international students: Required—TOEFL. Electronic applications accepted. *Faculty research:* Management fundamentals, strategic thinking, global business, innovation and change, leadership.

Quinnipiac University, School of Business and Engineering, Program in Business Administration, Hamden, CT 06518-1940. Offers chartered financial analyst (MBA); finance (MBA); healthcare management (MBA); information systems management (MBA); marketing (MBA); supply chain management (MBA); JD/MBA. *Accreditation:* AACSB. Part-time and evening/weekend programs available. Postbaccalaureate distance learning degree programs offered (no on-campus study). *Faculty:* 33 full-time (10 women), 7 part-time/adjunct (3 women). *Students:* 109 full-time (48 women), 225 part-time (101 women); includes 44 minority (14 Black or African American, non-Hispanic/Latino; 2 American Indian or Alaska Native, non-Hispanic/Latino; 12 Asian, non-Hispanic/Latino; 15 Hispanic/Latino; 1 Two or more races, non-Hispanic/Latino), 17 international. 230 applicants, 80% accepted, 154 enrolled. In 2013, 124 master's awarded. *Entrance requirements:* For master's, GMAT or GRE, minimum GPA of 3.0. Additional exam requirements/recommendations for international students: Required—TOEFL (minimum score 575 paper-based; 90 iBT), IELTS (minimum score 6.5). *Application deadline:* For fall admission, 7/30 priority date for domestic students, 4/30 priority date for international students; for spring admission, 12/15 priority date for domestic students, 9/15 priority date for international students. Applications are processed on a rolling basis. Application fee: $45. Electronic applications accepted. *Expenses: Tuition:* Part-time $920 per credit. *Required fees:* $37 per credit. *Financial support:* In 2013–14, 41 students received support. Career-related internships or fieldwork, Federal Work-Study, scholarships/grants, and unspecified assistantships available. Support available to part-time students. Financial award application deadline: 6/1; financial award applicants required to submit FAFSA. *Faculty research:* Financial markets and investments, international business, supply chain management, health care management, corporate governance. *Unit head:* Lisa Braiewa, MBA Program Director, E-mail: lisa.braiewa@quinnipiac.edu. *Application contact:* Office of Graduate Admissions, 800-462-1944, Fax: 203-582-3443, E-mail: graduate@quinnipiac.edu.
Website: http://www.quinnipiac.edu/mba.

Regent's University London, Webster Graduate School, London, United Kingdom. Offers business (MBA); finance (MS); human resources (MA); information technology management (MA); international business (MA); international non-governmental

organizations (MA); international relations (MA); management and leadership (MA); marketing (MA). Part-time programs available.

Regis University, College for Professional Studies, School of Management, MBA Program, Denver, CO 80221-1099. Offers finance and accounting (MBA); general business (MBA); health industry leadership (MBA); marketing (MBA); operations management (MBA); organizational performance management (MBA); strategic management (MBA). Part-time and evening/weekend programs available. Postbaccalaureate distance learning degree programs offered (no on-campus study). *Faculty:* 10 full-time (3 women), 74 part-time/adjunct (17 women). *Students:* 386 full-time (183 women), 269 part-time (134 women); includes 190 minority (38 Black or African American, non-Hispanic/Latino; 2 American Indian or Alaska Native, non-Hispanic/Latino; 30 Asian, non-Hispanic/Latino; 109 Hispanic/Latino; 1 Native Hawaiian or other Pacific Islander, non-Hispanic/Latino; 10 Two or more races, non-Hispanic/Latino), 11 international. Average age 42. 152 applicants, 91% accepted, 112 enrolled. In 2013, 318 master's awarded. *Degree requirements:* For master's, thesis (for some programs), final research project. *Entrance requirements:* For master's, official transcript reflecting baccalaureate degree awarded from regionally-accredited college or university, work experience, resume, letters of recommendation. Additional exam requirements/recommendations for international students: Required—TOEFL (minimum score 550 paper-based; 82 iBT). *Application deadline:* Applications are processed on a rolling basis. Application fee: $75. Electronic applications accepted. *Expenses:* Contact institution. *Financial support:* In 2013–14, 22 students received support. Federal Work-Study and scholarships/grants available. Financial award application deadline: 4/15; financial award applicants required to submit FAFSA. *Unit head:* Dr. Anthony Vrba, Interim Dean, 303-964-5384, Fax: 303-964-5538, E-mail: avrba@regis.edu. *Application contact:* Sarah Engel, Director of Admissions, 303-458-4900, Fax: 303-964-5534, E-mail: regisadm@regis.edu.
Website: http://www.regis.edu/CPS/Academics/Degrees-and-Programs/Graduate-Programs/MBA-College-for-Professional-Studies.aspx.

Rhode Island College, School of Graduate Studies, School of Management, Department of Accounting and Computer Information Systems, Providence, RI 02908-1991. Offers accounting (MP Ac); financial planning (CGS). *Accreditation:* AACSB. Part-time and evening/weekend programs available. *Faculty:* 1 (woman) full-time, 2 part-time/adjunct (1 woman). *Students:* 7 full-time (4 women), 21 part-time (9 women); includes 4 minority (2 Asian, non-Hispanic/Latino; 2 Hispanic/Latino). Average age 26. In 2013, 13 master's awarded. *Entrance requirements:* For master's, GMAT (unless applicant is a CPA or has passed a state bar exam); for CGS, GMAT, bachelor's degree from an accredited college or university, official transcripts of all undergraduate and graduate records. Additional exam requirements/recommendations for international students: Recommended—TOEFL (minimum score 550 paper-based; 79 iBT). *Application deadline:* For fall admission, 3/1 for domestic students. Applications are processed on a rolling basis. Application fee: $50. *Expenses:* Tuition, state resident: full-time $8928; part-time $372 per credit hour. Tuition, nonresident: full-time $17,376; part-time $724 per credit hour. *Required fees:* $602; $22 per credit. $72 per term. *Financial support:* Federal Work-Study, scholarships/grants, and health care benefits available. Support available to part-time students. Financial award application deadline: 5/15; financial award applicants required to submit FAFSA. *Unit head:* Prof. Jane Przybyla, Chair, 401-456-8036. *Application contact:* Graduate Studies, 401-456-8700.
Website: http://www.ric.edu/accountingComputerInformationSystems/.

Robert Morris University Illinois, Morris Graduate School of Management, Chicago, IL 60605. Offers accounting (MBA); accounting/finance (MBA); business analytics (MIS); design and media (MM); educational technology (MM); health care administration (MM); higher education administration (MM); human resource management (MBA); information security (MIS); information systems (MIS); law enforcement administration (MM); management (MBA); management/finance (MBA); management/human resource management (MBA); mobile computing (MIS); sports administration (MM). Part-time and evening/weekend programs available. *Faculty:* 12 full-time (5 women), 18 part-time/adjunct (4 women). *Students:* 240 full-time (128 women), 195 part-time (127 women); includes 242 minority (147 Black or African American, non-Hispanic/Latino; 2 American Indian or Alaska Native, non-Hispanic/Latino; 24 Asian, non-Hispanic/Latino; 63 Hispanic/Latino; 1 Native Hawaiian or other Pacific Islander, non-Hispanic/Latino; 5 Two or more races, non-Hispanic/Latino), 26 international. Average age 33. 210 applicants, 63% accepted, 116 enrolled. In 2013, 278 master's awarded. *Entrance requirements:* For master's, official transcripts, two letters of recommendation. Additional exam requirements/recommendations for international students: Required—TOEFL (minimum score 550 paper-based). *Application deadline:* Applications are processed on a rolling basis. Application fee: $20 ($100 for international students). Electronic applications accepted. *Expenses: Tuition:* Full-time $14,400; part-time $2400 per course. *Financial support:* In 2013–14, 488 students received support. Federal Work-Study and scholarships/grants available. Support available to part-time students. Financial award applicants required to submit FAFSA. *Unit head:* Kayed Akkawi, Dean for Morris Graduate School of Management, 312-935-6050, Fax: 312-935-6020, E-mail: kakkawi@robertmorris.edu. *Application contact:* Fernando Villeda, Dean of Graduate Enrollment, 312-935-6050, Fax: 312-935-6020, E-mail: fvilleda@robertmorris.edu.

Rochester Institute of Technology, Graduate Enrollment Services, Saunders College of Business, Program in Finance, Rochester, NY 14623-5603. Offers MS. Part-time programs available. *Students:* 28 full-time (11 women), 12 part-time (4 women), 39 international. Average age 24. 182 applicants, 41% accepted, 16 enrolled. In 2013, 23 master's awarded. *Degree requirements:* For master's, comprehensive exam (for some programs), thesis (for some programs). *Entrance requirements:* For master's, GMAT or GRE. Additional exam requirements/recommendations for international students: Required—PTE (minimum score 63), TOEFL (minimum score 580 paper-based; 92 iBT) or IELTS (minimum score 7). *Application deadline:* For fall admission, 2/15 for domestic and international students; for winter admission, 11/1 for domestic students; for spring admission, 2/1 for domestic students. Applications are processed on a rolling basis. Application fee: $60. Electronic applications accepted. *Expenses: Tuition:* Full-time $37,236; part-time $1552 per credit hour. *Required fees:* $250. *Financial support:* Research assistantships with partial tuition reimbursements, teaching assistantships with partial tuition reimbursements, career-related internships or fieldwork, scholarships/grants, and unspecified assistantships available. Support available to part-time students. Financial award applicants required to submit FAFSA. *Faculty research:* Formation and taxation of business entities, modeling demand, production and cost functions in computerized business and economic simulations, economic games and educational software. *Unit head:* Charles Ackley, Graduate Program Director, 585-475-6916, E-mail: cackley@saunders.rit.edu. *Application contact:* Diane Ellison, Assistant Vice President, Graduate Enrollment Services, 585-475-2229, Fax: 585-475-7164, E-mail: gradinfo@rit.edu.
Website: http://saunders.rit.edu/graduate/index.php.

Rollins College, Crummer Graduate School of Business, Winter Park, FL 32789-4499. Offers business administration (EDBA); entrepreneurship (MBA); finance (MBA); international business (MBA); management (MBA); marketing (MBA); operations and technology management (MBA). *Accreditation:* AACSB. Part-time and evening/weekend programs available. Postbaccalaureate distance learning degree programs offered (minimal on-campus study). *Faculty:* 21 full-time (3 women), 2 part-time/adjunct (1 woman). *Students:* 157 full-time (86 women), 135 part-time (83 women); includes 60 minority (12 Black or African American, non-Hispanic/Latino; 1 American Indian or Alaska Native, non-Hispanic/Latino; 17 Asian, non-Hispanic/Latino; 23 Hispanic/Latino; 1 Native Hawaiian or other Pacific Islander, non-Hispanic/Latino; 6 Two or more races, non-Hispanic/Latino), 19 international. Average age 37. 264 applicants, 53% accepted, 105 enrolled. In 2013, 169 master's awarded. *Degree requirements:* For master's, minimum GPA of 2.85; for doctorate, thesis/dissertation, minimum GPA of 3.0. *Entrance requirements:* For master's, GMAT or GRE, official transcripts, two letters of recommendation, essay, current resume/curriculum vitae, interview; for doctorate, official transcripts, two letters of recommendation, essays, current resume/curriculum vitae, interview with EDBA academic committee. Additional exam requirements/recommendations for international students: Required—TOEFL (minimum score 100 iBT) or IELTS (minimum score 7). *Application deadline:* Applications are processed on a rolling basis. Application fee: $50. Electronic applications accepted. *Expenses:* Contact institution. *Financial support:* In 2013–14, 87 students received support. Federal Work-Study and scholarships/grants available. Support available to part-time students. Financial award applicants required to submit FAFSA. *Faculty research:* Sustainability, world financial markets, international business, market research, strategic marketing. *Unit head:* Dr. Craig M. McAllaster, Dean, 407-646-2249, Fax: 407-646-1550, E-mail: cmcallaster@rollins.edu. *Application contact:* Eva Gauthier Oleksiw, Admissions Coordinator, 407-646-2405, Fax: 407-646-1550, E-mail: mbaadmissions@rollins.edu.
Website: http://www.rollins.edu/mba/.

Rutgers, The State University of New Jersey, Newark, Graduate School, Program in Management, Newark, NJ 07102. Offers accounting (PhD); accounting information systems (PhD); computer information systems (PhD); finance (PhD); information technology (PhD); international business (PhD); management science (PhD); marketing (PhD); organization management (PhD). Program offered jointly with New Jersey Institute of Technology. *Accreditation:* AACSB. *Degree requirements:* For doctorate, thesis/dissertation, cumulative exams. *Entrance requirements:* For doctorate, GMAT or GRE General Test, minimum undergraduate B average. Additional exam requirements/recommendations for international students: Required—TOEFL. Electronic applications accepted. *Faculty research:* Technology management, leadership and teams, consumer behavior, financial and markets, logistics.

Rutgers, The State University of New Jersey, Newark, Rutgers Business School–Newark and New Brunswick, Doctoral Programs in Management, Newark, NJ 07102. Offers accounting (PhD); accounting information systems (PhD); economics (PhD); finance (PhD); individualized study (PhD); information technology (PhD); international business (PhD); management science (PhD); marketing science (PhD); organizational management (PhD); science, technology and management (PhD); supply chain management (PhD). *Degree requirements:* For doctorate, comprehensive exam, thesis/dissertation. *Entrance requirements:* For doctorate, GRE or GMAT. Additional exam requirements/recommendations for international students: Required—TOEFL (minimum score 550 paper-based; 79 iBT). Electronic applications accepted.

Sacred Heart University, Graduate Programs, John F. Welch College of Business, Department of Finance, Fairfield, CT 06825-1000. Offers corporate finance (Certificate); finance (DBA); financial management (Certificate); global investments (Certificate). *Faculty:* 3 full-time (1 woman), 1 part-time/adjunct (0 women). *Students:* 4 full-time (1 woman), 14 part-time (9 women); includes 6 minority (1 Black or African American, non-Hispanic/Latino; 5 Hispanic/Latino). Average age 30. 111 applicants, 81% accepted, 70 enrolled. *Entrance requirements:* Additional exam requirements/recommendations for international students: Required—PTE; Recommended—TOEFL (minimum score 570 paper-based; 80 iBT), IELTS (minimum score 6.5). *Application deadline:* Applications are processed on a rolling basis. Application fee: $60. Electronic applications accepted. *Expenses: Tuition:* Full-time $22,775; part-time $617 per credit. *Unit head:* Dr. John Chalykoff, Dean, 203-396-8084, E-mail: chalykoffj@sacredheart.edu. *Application contact:* Kathy Dilks, Executive Director of Graduate Admissions, 203-365-7619, Fax: 203-365-4732, E-mail: dilksk@sacredheart.edu.
Website: http://www.sacredheart.edu/academics/johnfwelchcollegeofbusiness/aboutthecollege/.

Sage Graduate School, School of Management, Program in Business Administration, Troy, NY 12180-4115. Offers business strategy (MBA); finance (MBA); human resources (MBA); marketing (MBA); JD/MBA. Part-time and evening/weekend programs available. *Faculty:* 2 full-time (both women), 9 part-time/adjunct (2 women). *Students:* 10 full-time (5 women), 53 part-time (33 women); includes 14 minority (5 Black or African American, non-Hispanic/Latino; 6 Asian, non-Hispanic/Latino; 2 Hispanic/Latino; 1 Two or more races, non-Hispanic/Latino). Average age 30. 52 applicants, 54% accepted, 16 enrolled. In 2013, 22 master's awarded. *Entrance requirements:* For master's, minimum GPA of 2.75, resume, 2 letters of recommendation. Additional exam requirements/recommendations for international students: Required—TOEFL (minimum score 550 paper-based). *Application deadline:* Applications are processed on a rolling basis. Application fee: $40. *Expenses: Tuition:* Full-time $11,880; part-time $660 per credit hour. *Financial support:* Fellowships, research assistantships, Federal Work-Study, scholarships/grants, and unspecified assistantships available. Support available to part-time students. Financial award application deadline: 3/1; financial award applicants required to submit FAFSA. *Unit head:* Dr. Daniel Robeson, Dean, School of Management, 518-292-8657, Fax: 518-292-1964, E-mail: robesd@sage.edu. *Application contact:* Wendy D. Diefendorf, Director of Graduate and Adult Admission, 518-244-2443, Fax: 518-244-6880, E-mail: diefew@sage.edu.

St. Edward's University, School of Management and Business, Area of Business Administration, Austin, TX 78704. Offers accounting (MBA); business management (MBA); finance (Certificate); global entrepreneurship (MBA); marketing (MBA). Part-time and evening/weekend programs available. *Students:* 29 full-time (12 women), 181 part-time (85 women); includes 88 minority (15 Black or African American, non-Hispanic/Latino; 1 American Indian or Alaska Native, non-Hispanic/Latino; 4 Asian, non-Hispanic/Latino; 61 Hispanic/Latino; 7 Two or more races, non-Hispanic/Latino), 10 international. Average age 33. 85 applicants, 79% accepted, 38 enrolled. In 2013, 79 master's awarded. *Degree requirements:* For master's, minimum of 24 resident hours. *Entrance requirements:* For master's, GMAT or GRE General Test, minimum GPA of 2.75 in last 60 hours of course work. Additional exam requirements/recommendations for international students: Required—TOEFL (minimum score 79 iBT) or IELTS (minimum score 6). *Application deadline:* For fall admission, 6/1 priority date for domestic and international students; for spring admission, 10/1 priority date for domestic and international students; for summer admission, 3/1 priority date for domestic and international students. Applications are processed on a rolling basis. Application fee: $50. Electronic applications accepted. *Expenses: Tuition:* Full-time $20,664; part-time $1148 per credit hour. *Required fees:* $50 per trimester. Full-time tuition and fees vary according to course load and program. *Unit head:* Dr. Stan Horner, Director, 512-428-1279, Fax: 512-448-8492, E-mail: stanleyh@stedwards.edu. *Application contact:* Office of Admission, 512-448-8500, Fax: 512-464-8877, E-mail: seu.admit@stedwards.edu.
Website: http://www.stedwards.edu.

St. John's University, The Peter J. Tobin College of Business, Department of Economics and Finance, Program in Finance, Queens, NY 11439. Offers finance (MBA,

Adv C); investment management (MS). Part-time and evening/weekend programs available. *Students:* 132 full-time (68 women), 44 part-time (18 women); includes 24 minority (7 Black or African American, non-Hispanic/Latino; 9 Asian, non-Hispanic/Latino; 8 Hispanic/Latino), 116 international. Average age 26. 148 applicants, 77% accepted, 59 enrolled. In 2013, 66 master's, 1 other advanced degree awarded. *Degree requirements:* For master's, comprehensive exam (for some programs), thesis optional. *Entrance requirements:* For master's, GMAT, 2 letters of recommendation, resume, transcripts, essay; for Adv C, GMAT, 2 letters of recommendation, resume, undergraduate and graduate transcripts, essay, MBA. Additional exam requirements/recommendations for international students: Required—TOEFL (minimum score 600 paper-based; 100 iBT), IELTS (minimum score 7). *Application deadline:* For fall admission, 5/1 priority date for domestic and international students; for spring admission, 11/1 priority date for domestic and international students. Applications are processed on a rolling basis. Application fee: $50. Electronic applications accepted. *Expenses:* Contact institution. *Financial support:* Research assistantships, scholarships/grants, and unspecified assistantships available. Support available to part-time students. Financial award application deadline: 3/1; financial award applicants required to submit FAFSA. *Unit head:* Dr. Vipul K. Bansal, Chair, 718-990-2113, E-mail: bansalv@stjohns.edu. *Application contact:* Carol J. Swanberg, Assistant Dean/Director of Graduate Admissions, 718-990-1345, Fax: 718-990-5242, E-mail: tobingradnyc@stjohns.edu.

Saint Joseph's University, Erivan K. Haub School of Business, MS in Financial Services Program, Philadelphia, PA 19131-1395. Offers MS. Part-time and evening/weekend programs available. *Students:* 101 full-time (60 women), 37 part-time (11 women); includes 7 minority (5 Black or African American, non-Hispanic/Latino; 2 Hispanic/Latino), 105 international. Average age 25. In 2013, 46 master's awarded. *Degree requirements:* For master's, minimum GPA of 3.0. *Entrance requirements:* For master's, GMAT or GRE, 2 letters of recommendation, resume, personal statement, official undergraduate and graduate transcripts. Additional exam requirements/recommendations for international students: Required—TOEFL (minimum score 550 paper-based, 80 iBT), IELTS (minimum score 6.5), or PTE (minimum score 60). *Application deadline:* For fall admission, 7/15 priority date for domestic students, 5/15 priority date for international students; for spring admission, 11/15 priority date for domestic students, 10/15 priority date for international students; for summer admission, 4/15 priority date for domestic students. Applications are processed on a rolling basis. Application fee: $35. Electronic applications accepted. *Expenses: Tuition:* Part-time $786 per credit hour. Tuition and fees vary according to degree level and program. *Financial support:* Scholarships/grants available. Support available to part-time students. Financial award application deadline: 5/1; financial award applicants required to submit FAFSA. *Unit head:* David Benglian, Director, 610-660-1626, Fax: 610-660-1599, E-mail: david.benglian@sju.edu. *Application contact:* Karena Whitmore, Administrative Assistant, MS Programs, 610-660-3211, Fax: 610-660-1599, E-mail: kwhitmor@sju.edu.
Website: http://www.sju.edu/msfs.

Saint Joseph's University, Erivan K. Haub School of Business, Professional MBA Program, Philadelphia, PA 19131-1395. Offers accounting (MBA, Postbaccalaureate Certificate); business intelligence (MBA); finance (MBA); general business (MBA); health and medical services administration (MBA); international business (MBA); international marketing (MBA); managing human capital (MBA); marketing (MBA); DO/MBA. DO/MBA offered jointly with Philadelphia College of Osteopathic Medicine. Part-time and evening/weekend programs available. *Students:* 81 full-time (37 women), 478 part-time (195 women); includes 85 minority (35 Black or African American, non-Hispanic/Latino; 1 American Indian or Alaska Native, non-Hispanic/Latino; 23 Asian, non-Hispanic/Latino; 13 Hispanic/Latino; 1 Native Hawaiian or other Pacific Islander, non-Hispanic/Latino; 12 Two or more races, non-Hispanic/Latino), 44 international. Average age 30. In 2013, 195 master's awarded. *Degree requirements:* For master's and Postbaccalaureate Certificate, minimum GPA of 3.0. *Entrance requirements:* For master's, GMAT or GRE, 2 letters of recommendation, resume, personal statement, official undergraduate and graduate transcripts; for Postbaccalaureate Certificate, official master's-level transcripts. Additional exam requirements/recommendations for international students: Required—TOEFL (minimum score 550 paper-based, 80 iBT), IELTS (minimum score 6.5), or PTE (minimum score 60). *Application deadline:* For fall admission, 7/15 priority date for domestic students, 5/15 priority date for international students; for spring admission, 11/15 priority date for domestic students, 10/15 priority date for international students; for summer admission, 4/15 priority date for domestic students, 2/15 priority date for international students. Applications are processed on a rolling basis. Application fee: $35. Electronic applications accepted. *Expenses: Tuition:* Part-time $786 per credit hour. Tuition and fees vary according to degree level and program. *Financial support:* In 2013–14, 2 research assistantships with partial tuition reimbursements (averaging $4,000 per year) were awarded; scholarships/grants and unspecified assistantships also available. Support available to part-time students. Financial award application deadline: 5/1; financial award applicants required to submit FAFSA. *Unit head:* Christine Hartmann, Director, MBA Program, 610-660-1659, Fax: 610-660-1599, E-mail: chartman@sju.edu. *Application contact:* Jeannine Lajeunesse, Assistant Director, MBA Program, 610-660-1695, Fax: 610-660-1599, E-mail: jlajeune@sju.edu.
Website: http://www.sju.edu/haubmba.

Saint Louis University, Graduate Education, John Cook School of Business, Department of Finance, St. Louis, MO 63103-2097. Offers MBA, MSF. Part-time and evening/weekend programs available. *Degree requirements:* For master's, thesis. *Entrance requirements:* For master's, GMAT or GRE General Test, letters of recommendation, resume. Additional exam requirements/recommendations for international students: Required—TOEFL (minimum score 570 paper-based; 88 iBT). Electronic applications accepted. *Expenses:* Contact institution. *Faculty research:* Market microstructure, corporate governance, banking, portfolio performance and asset allocation.

Saint Mary's College of California, School of Economics and Business Administration, MS in Financial Analysis and Investment Management Program, Moraga, CA 94556. Offers MS.

St. Mary's University, Graduate School, Bill Greehey School of Business, MBA Program, San Antonio, TX 78228-8507. Offers finance (MBA); international business (MBA); management (MBA). Part-time and evening/weekend programs available. Postbaccalaureate distance learning degree programs offered (minimal on-campus study). *Degree requirements:* For master's, comprehensive exam. *Entrance requirements:* For master's, GMAT. Additional exam requirements/recommendations for international students: Required—TOEFL (minimum score 570 paper-based; 80 iBT).

Saint Peter's University, Graduate Business Programs, MBA Program, Jersey City, NJ 07306-5997. Offers finance (MBA); health care administration (MBA); human resource management (MBA); international business (MBA); management (MBA); management information systems (MBA); marketing (MBA); risk management (MBA); MBA/MS. Part-time and evening/weekend programs available. *Entrance requirements:* Additional exam requirements/recommendations for international students: Required—TOEFL. Electronic applications accepted. *Faculty research:* Finance, health care management, human resource management, international business, management, management information systems, marketing, risk management.

St. Thomas Aquinas College, Division of Business Administration, Sparkill, NY 10976. Offers business administration (MBA); finance (MBA); management (MBA); marketing (MBA). Part-time and evening/weekend programs available. *Entrance requirements:* For master's, GMAT. Additional exam requirements/recommendations for international students: Required—TOEFL. Electronic applications accepted.

Saint Xavier University, Graduate Studies, Graham School of Management, Chicago, IL 60655-3105. Offers employee health benefits (Certificate); finance (MBA); financial fraud examination and management (MBA, Certificate); financial planning (MBA, Certificate); generalist/individualized (MBA); health administration (MBA); managed care (Certificate); management (MBA); marketing (MBA); project management (MBA, Certificate); MBA/MS. *Accreditation:* ACBSP. Part-time and evening/weekend programs available. *Entrance requirements:* For master's, GMAT, minimum GPA of 3.0, 2 years of work experience. Electronic applications accepted. *Expenses:* Contact institution.

Sam Houston State University, College of Business Administration, Department of General Business and Finance, Huntsville, TX 77341. Offers banking and financial institutions (EMBA); business administration (MBA); project management (MS). Part-time and evening/weekend programs available. Postbaccalaureate distance learning degree programs offered (minimal on-campus study). *Faculty:* 22 full-time (7 women). *Students:* 94 full-time (47 women), 283 part-time (122 women); includes 109 minority (39 Black or African American, non-Hispanic/Latino; 1 American Indian or Alaska Native, non-Hispanic/Latino; 17 Asian, non-Hispanic/Latino; 40 Hispanic/Latino; 2 Native Hawaiian or other Pacific Islander, non-Hispanic/Latino; 10 Two or more races, non-Hispanic/Latino), 29 international. Average age 35. 279 applicants, 89% accepted, 89 enrolled. In 2013, 92 master's awarded. *Degree requirements:* For master's, comprehensive exam. *Entrance requirements:* For master's, GMAT. Additional exam requirements/recommendations for international students: Required—TOEFL (minimum score 550 paper-based; 79 iBT), IELTS (minimum score 6.5). *Application deadline:* For fall admission, 8/1 for domestic students, 6/25 for international students; for spring admission, 12/1 for domestic students, 11/12 for international students. Applications are processed on a rolling basis. Application fee: $45 ($75 for international students). Electronic applications accepted. *Financial support:* Career-related internships or fieldwork, Federal Work-Study, institutionally sponsored loans, scholarships/grants, tuition waivers, and unspecified assistantships available. Support available to part-time students. Financial award application deadline: 5/31; financial award applicants required to submit FAFSA. *Unit head:* Dr. Kurt Jesswein, Chair, 936-294-4582, E-mail: kurt.jesswein@shsu.edu. *Application contact:* Rick Thaler, Associate Director, 936-294-1239, Fax: 936-294-3612, E-mail: busgrad@shsu.edu.
Website: http://www.shsu.edu/~gba_www/.

San Diego State University, Graduate and Research Affairs, College of Business Administration, Department of Finance, San Diego, CA 92182. Offers MS. Part-time and evening/weekend programs available. *Degree requirements:* For master's, thesis or alternative. *Entrance requirements:* For master's, GMAT, resume, letters of reference. Additional exam requirements/recommendations for international students: Required—TOEFL. Electronic applications accepted.

San Francisco State University, Division of Graduate Studies, College of Business, Program in Business Administration, San Francisco, CA 94132-1722. Offers decision sciences/operations research (MBA); finance (MBA); information systems (MBA); leadership (MBA); management (MBA); marketing (MBA); sustainable business (MBA). *Accreditation:* AACSB. Part-time and evening/weekend programs available. *Faculty:* 100. *Students:* 850 (408 women). 839 applicants, 56% accepted, 241 enrolled. *Degree requirements:* For master's, thesis, essay test. *Entrance requirements:* For master's, GMAT, minimum GPA of 2.7 in last 60 units. Additional exam requirements/recommendations for international students: Required—TOEFL (minimum score 550 paper-based). *Application deadline:* For fall admission, 5/1 priority date for domestic students, 4/1 for international students; for spring admission, 11/1 for domestic students, 10/15 for international students. Applications are processed on a rolling basis. Application fee: $55. *Financial support:* Application deadline: 3/1. *Unit head:* Linda Oubre, Dean, 415-817-4300, E-mail: loubre@sfsu.edu. *Application contact:* Armaan Moattari, Assistant Director, Graduate Programs, 415-817-4314, Fax: 817-4340, E-mail: amoatt@sfsu.edu.
Website: http://cob.sfsu.edu/.

Santa Clara University, Leavey School of Business, Santa Clara, CA 95053. Offers accelerated business administration (MBA); business administration (MBA); emerging professional business administration (MBA); entrepreneurship (MS); executive business administration (MBA); finance (MSF); information systems (MSIS); JD/MBA; MSIS/JD. *Accreditation:* AACSB. Part-time and evening/weekend programs available. *Faculty:* 85 full-time (21 women), 64 part-time/adjunct (20 women). *Students:* 292 full-time (154 women), 543 part-time (196 women); includes 262 minority (9 Black or African American, non-Hispanic/Latino; 203 Asian, non-Hispanic/Latino; 43 Hispanic/Latino; 2 Native Hawaiian or other Pacific Islander, non-Hispanic/Latino; 5 Two or more races, non-Hispanic/Latino), 260 international. Average age 30. 428 applicants, 77% accepted, 212 enrolled. In 2013, 345 master's awarded. *Degree requirements:* For master's, thesis or alternative. *Entrance requirements:* For master's, GMAT, GRE. Additional exam requirements/recommendations for international students: Required—TOEFL (minimum score 600 paper-based; 100 iBT). *Application deadline:* For fall admission, 6/1 for domestic and international students; for spring admission, 1/19 for domestic and international students. Applications are processed on a rolling basis. Application fee: $100 ($150 for international students). Electronic applications accepted. *Expenses:* Contact institution. *Financial support:* In 2013–14, 348 students received support. Career-related internships or fieldwork, Federal Work-Study, institutionally sponsored loans, and scholarships/grants available. Support available to part-time students. Financial award applicants required to submit FAFSA. *Faculty research:* Sovereign debt default, empire, and trade during the gold standard; CISE pathways to revitalized undergraduate computing education. *Unit head:* Elizabeth B. Ford, Senior Assistant Dean, 408-554-2752, Fax: 408-554-4571, E-mail: eford@scu.edu. *Application contact:* Tammy Fox, Director, Graduate Admissions and Financial Aid, 408-554-7858, E-mail: mbaadmissions@scu.edu.
Website: http://www.scu.edu/business/graduates.

Schiller International University, MBA Programs, Florida, Largo, FL 33771. Offers financial planning (MBA); information technology (MBA); international business (MBA); international hotel and tourism management (MBA). Part-time and evening/weekend programs available. Postbaccalaureate distance learning degree programs offered (no on-campus study). *Degree requirements:* For master's, thesis optional. *Entrance requirements:* Additional exam requirements/recommendations for international students: Required—TOEFL (minimum score 550 paper-based).

Seattle University, Albers School of Business and Economics, Master of Science in Finance Program, Seattle, WA 98122-1090. Offers MSF, Certificate, JD/MSF. Part-time and evening/weekend programs available. *Faculty:* 13 full-time (5 women), 1 part-time/adjunct (0 women). *Students:* 18 full-time (6 women), 33 part-time (6 women); includes 13 minority (3 Black or African American, non-Hispanic/Latino; 5 Asian, non-Hispanic/

Latino; 4 Hispanic/Latino; 1 Native Hawaiian or other Pacific Islander, non-Hispanic/ Latino), 8 international. Average age 31. 54 applicants, 30% accepted, 9 enrolled. In 2013, 17 master's awarded. *Entrance requirements:* For master's, GMAT, minimum GPA of 3.0, 2 years of related work experience. Additional exam requirements/ recommendations for international students: Required—TOEFL (minimum score 580 paper-based; 92 iBT). *Application deadline:* For fall admission, 8/20 priority date for domestic students, 4/1 priority date for international students; for winter admission, 11/ 20 priority date for domestic students, 9/1 priority date for international students; for spring admission, 2/20 priority date for domestic students, 12/1 priority date for international students. Applications are processed on a rolling basis. Application fee: $55. Electronic applications accepted. *Financial support:* In 2013–14, 12 students received support. Career-related internships or fieldwork and Federal Work-Study available. Support available to part-time students. Financial award applicants required to submit FAFSA. *Unit head:* Dr. Fiona Robertson, Chair, 206-296-5791, Fax: 206-296-5795, E-mail: robertsf@seattleu.edu. *Application contact:* Janet Shandley, Director of Graduate Admissions, 206-296-5900, Fax: 206-298-5656, E-mail: grad_admissions@ seattleu.edu.
Website: http://www.seattleu.edu/albers/msf/.

Seton Hall University, Stillman School of Business, Programs in Business Administration, South Orange, NJ 07079-2697. Offers accounting (MBA); finance (MBA); information technology management (MBA); international business (MBA); management (MBA); marketing (MBA); sport management (MBA); supply chain management (MBA). Part-time and evening/weekend programs available. *Faculty:* 32 full-time (6 women), 20 part-time/adjunct (3 women). *Students:* 67 full-time (23 women), 162 part-time (66 women); includes 28 minority (7 Black or African American, non-Hispanic/Latino; 7 Asian, non-Hispanic/Latino; 6 Hispanic/Latino; 8 Native Hawaiian or other Pacific Islander, non-Hispanic/Latino). Average age 31. 216 applicants, 28% accepted, 39 enrolled. In 2013, 139 master's awarded. *Degree requirements:* For master's, 20 hours of community service (Social Responsibility Project). *Entrance requirements:* For master's, GMAT, GRE or CPA, advanced degree from AACSB institution, MS in a business discipline, professional degree (MD, JD, PhD, DVM, DDS, etc.), minimum undergraduate GPA of 3.0. Additional exam requirements/ recommendations for international students: Required—TOEFL (minimum score 102 iBT), IELTS or PTE. *Application deadline:* For fall admission, 5/31 priority date for domestic students, 3/31 priority date for international students; for spring admission, 10/ 31 priority date for domestic students, 9/30 priority date for international students. Applications are processed on a rolling basis. Application fee: $75. Electronic applications accepted. *Financial support:* In 2013–14, research assistantships with full tuition reimbursements (averaging $23,956 per year) were awarded; career-related internships or fieldwork, Federal Work-Study, scholarships/grants, and unspecified assistantships also available. Support available to part-time students. Financial award application deadline: 6/30; financial award applicants required to submit FAFSA. *Faculty research:* Sport, hedge funds, international business, legal issues, disclosure and branding. *Total annual research expenditures:* $68,000. *Unit head:* Dr. Joyce Strawser, Dean, 973-761-9013, Fax: 973-761-9217, E-mail: joyce.strawser@shu.edu. *Application contact:* Catherine Bianchi, Director of Graduate Admissions, 973-761-9262, Fax: 973-761-9208, E-mail: catherine.bianchi@shu.edu.
Website: http://www.shu.edu/academics/business.

Simon Fraser University, Office of Graduate Studies, Faculty of Business Administration, Vancouver, BC V5A 1S6, Canada. Offers business administration (EMBA, PhD, Graduate Diploma); finance (M Sc); management of technology (MBA); management of technology/biotechnology (MBA). *Accreditation:* AACSB. Postbaccalaureate distance learning degree programs offered. *Students:* 422 full-time (177 women), 120 part-time (48 women). 767 applicants, 43% accepted, 231 enrolled. In 2013, 219 master's, 9 doctorates, 65 other advanced degrees awarded. *Degree requirements:* For master's, thesis (for some programs); for doctorate, comprehensive exam, thesis/dissertation. *Entrance requirements:* For master's, GMAT, minimum GPA of 3.0 (on scale of 4.33), or 3.33 based on last 60 credits of undergraduate courses; for doctorate, minimum GPA of 3.5 (on scale of 4.33); for Graduate Diploma, minimum GPA of 2.5 (on scale of 4.33), or 2.67 based on the last 60 credits of undergraduate courses. Additional exam requirements/recommendations for international students: Recommended—TOEFL (minimum score 580 paper-based; 93 iBT), IELTS (minimum score 7), TWE (minimum score 5). *Application deadline:* For fall admission, 4/2 for domestic students; for winter admission, 10/1 for domestic students; for spring admission, 2/2 for domestic students. Application fee: $90 ($125 for international students). *Expenses:* Contact institution. *Financial support:* In 2013–14, 20 students received support, including 27 fellowships (averaging $6,250 per year), teaching assistantships (averaging $5,608 per year); research assistantships, career-related internships or fieldwork, and scholarships/grants also available. *Faculty research:* Accounting, management and organizational studies, technology and operations management, finance, international business. *Unit head:* Dr. Colleen Collins, Associate Dean, Graduate Programs, 778-782-5195, Fax: 778-782-4920, E-mail: grad-business@ sfu.ca. *Application contact:* Graduate Secretary, 778-782-5013, Fax: 778-782-5122, E-mail: grad-business@sfu.ca.
Website: http://beedie.sfu.ca/segal/.

Southeast Missouri State University, School of Graduate Studies, Harrison College of Business, Cape Girardeau, MO 63701-4799. Offers accounting (MBA); entrepreneurship (MBA); environmental management (MBA); financial management (MBA); general management (MBA); health administration (MBA); industrial management (MBA); international business (MBA); organizational management (MS); sport management (MBA). *Accreditation:* AACSB. Part-time and evening/weekend programs available. Postbaccalaureate distance learning degree programs offered (no on-campus study). *Faculty:* 27 full-time (7 women), 1 (woman) part-time/adjunct. *Students:* 59 full-time (27 women), 83 part-time (28 women); includes 10 minority (5 Black or African American, non-Hispanic/Latino; 3 Asian, non-Hispanic/Latino; 1 Hispanic/Latino; 1 Two or more races, non-Hispanic/Latino), 40 international. Average age 28. 77 applicants, 79% accepted, 48 enrolled. In 2013, 50 master's awarded. *Degree requirements:* For master's, variable foreign language requirement, comprehensive exam (for some programs), thesis or alternative, applied research project. *Entrance requirements:* For master's, GMAT or GRE, minimum undergraduate GPA of 2.5, C or better in prerequisite courses. Additional exam requirements/ recommendations for international students: Required—TOEFL (minimum score 550 paper-based; 79 iBT), IELTS (minimum score 6), PTE (minimum score 53). *Application deadline:* For fall admission, 8/1 for domestic students, 6/1 for international students; for spring admission, 11/21 for domestic students, 10/1 for international students; for summer admission, 5/15 for domestic students. Applications are processed on a rolling basis. Application fee: $30 ($40 for international students). Electronic applications accepted. *Expenses:* Tuition, state resident: full-time $5139; part-time $285.50 per credit hour. Tuition, nonresident: full-time $9099; part-time $505.50 per credit hour. *Financial support:* In 2013–14, 52 students received support, including 12 teaching assistantships with full tuition reimbursements available (averaging $8,144 per year); career-related internships or fieldwork, Federal Work-Study, scholarships/grants, traineeships, tuition waivers (full), and unspecified assistantships also available. Financial award application deadline: 6/30; financial award applicants required to submit FAFSA. *Faculty research:* Ethics, corporate finance, generational difference, leadership, organizational justice. *Unit head:* Dr. Kenneth A. Heischmidt, Director, Graduate Business Studies, 573-651-2912, Fax: 573-651-5032, E-mail: kheischmidt@semo.edu. *Application contact:* Gail Amick, Admissions Specialist, 573-651-2590, Fax: 573-651-5936, E-mail: gamick@semo.edu.
Website: http://www.semo.edu/mba.

Southern Adventist University, School of Business and Management, Collegedale, TN 37315-0370. Offers accounting (MBA); church administration (MSA); church and nonprofit leadership (MBA); financial management (MFM); healthcare administration (MBA); management (MBA); marketing management (MBA); outdoor education (MSA). Part-time and evening/weekend programs available. Postbaccalaureate distance learning degree programs offered (no on-campus study). *Entrance requirements:* For master's, GMAT. Additional exam requirements/recommendations for international students: Required—TOEFL (minimum score 600 paper-based; 100 iBT). Electronic applications accepted.

Southern Illinois University Edwardsville, Graduate School, School of Business, Department of Economics and Finance, Edwardsville, IL 62026. Offers MA, MS. Part-time and evening/weekend programs available. *Faculty:* 11 full-time (2 women). *Students:* 11 full-time (6 women), 15 part-time (2 women); includes 4 minority (1 Black or African American, non-Hispanic/Latino; 2 Asian, non-Hispanic/Latino; 1 Hispanic/ Latino), 5 international. 30 applicants, 43% accepted. In 2013, 7 master's awarded. *Degree requirements:* For master's, thesis or alternative, final exam, portfolio. *Entrance requirements:* For master's, GMAT or GRE. Additional exam requirements/ recommendations for international students: Required—TOEFL (minimum score 550 paper-based, 79 iBT), IELTS (minimum score 6.5), Michigan Test of English Language Proficiency or PTE. *Application deadline:* For fall admission, 7/18 for domestic students, 6/1 for international students; for spring admission, 12/12 for domestic students, 10/1 for international students; for summer admission, 4/24 for domestic students, 3/1 for international students. Applications are processed on a rolling basis. Application fee: $30. Electronic applications accepted. *Expenses:* Tuition, state resident: full-time $3551. Tuition, nonresident: full-time $8378. *Financial support:* In 2013–14, 13 students received support, including 1 fellowship with full tuition reimbursement available (averaging $8,370 per year), 8 research assistantships with full tuition reimbursements available (averaging $9,585 per year), 4 teaching assistantships with full tuition reimbursements available (averaging $9,585 per year); institutionally sponsored loans, scholarships/grants, and unspecified assistantships also available. Financial award application deadline: 3/1; financial award applicants required to submit FAFSA. *Unit head:* Dr. Ayse Evrensel, Chair, 618-650-2542, E-mail: aevrens@siue.edu. *Application contact:* Dr. Riza Demirer, Program Director, 618-650-2939, E-mail: rdemire@siue.edu.
Website: http://www.siue.edu/business/economicsandfinance/.

Southern Methodist University, Cox School of Business, MBA Program, Dallas, TX 75275. Offers accounting (MBA, PMBA); business administration (EMBA); finance (MBA); financial statement analysis (PMBA); general business (MBA); information technology and operations management (MBA); management (MBA); marketing (MBA); real estate (MBA); strategy (MBA); strategy and entrepreneurship (MBA); JD/MBA; MA/ MBA. Part-time and evening/weekend programs available. *Entrance requirements:* For master's, GMAT. Additional exam requirements/recommendations for international students: Required—TOEFL. Electronic applications accepted. *Expenses:* Contact institution. *Faculty research:* Corporate finance, financial reporting, modeling consumer decision-making, competition between national brands and store brands, institutional determinants of firms' strategy.

Southern New Hampshire University, School of Business, Manchester, NH 03106-1045. Offers accounting (MBA, MS, Graduate Certificate); accounting finance (MS); accounting/auditing (MS); accounting/forensic accounting (MS); accounting/taxation (MS); athletic administration (MBA, Graduate Certificate); business administration (IMBA, MBA, Certificate, Graduate Certificate), including accounting (Certificate), business administration (MBA), business information systems (Graduate Certificate), human resource management (Certificate); corporate social responsibility (MBA); entrepreneurship (MBA); finance (MBA, MS, Graduate Certificate); finance/corporate finance (MS); finance/investments and securities (MS); forensic accounting (MBA); healthcare informatics (MBA); healthcare management (MBA); human resource management (Graduate Certificate); information technology (MS, Graduate Certificate); information technology management (MBA); international business (Graduate Certificate); international business and information technology (Graduate Certificate); international finance (Graduate Certificate); international sport management (Graduate Certificate); justice studies (MBA); leadership of nonprofit organizations (Graduate Certificate); marketing (MBA, MS, Graduate Certificate); operations and project management (MS); operations and supply chain management (MBA, Graduate Certificate); organizational leadership (MS); project management (MBA, Graduate Certificate); Six Sigma (MBA); Six Sigma quality (Graduate Certificate); social media marketing (MBA); sport management (MBA, MS, Graduate Certificate); sustainability and environmental compliance (MBA); workplace conflict management (MBA); MBA/ Certificate. *Accreditation:* ACBSP. Part-time and evening/weekend programs available. Postbaccalaureate distance learning degree programs offered (no on-campus study). Terminal master's awarded for partial completion of doctoral program. *Degree requirements:* For master's, one foreign language, comprehensive exam (for some programs), thesis or alternative. *Entrance requirements:* For master's, minimum GPA of 2.5. Additional exam requirements/recommendations for international students: Required—TOEFL (minimum score 500 paper-based). Electronic applications accepted.

Southern Polytechnic State University, School of Engineering Technology and Management, Department of Business Administration, Marietta, GA 30060-2896. Offers accounting (MBA, MSA); business administration (Graduate Transition Certificate); finance (MBA); general (MBA); management (MBA); management information systems (MBA); marketing (MBA); operations and technology management (MBA). *Accreditation:* ACBSP. Part-time and evening/weekend programs available. Postbaccalaureate distance learning degree programs offered (no on-campus study). *Degree requirements:* For master's, comprehensive exam (for some programs), capstone course and major field exam (for MBA); 30 semester hours of course work (for MSA). *Entrance requirements:* For master's, GMAT or GRE, letters of recommendation, statement of purpose, resume, minimum GPA of 2.75 or undergraduate degree in business with up to 6 transition courses; undergraduate degree in accounting from regionally-accredited school (for MSA). Additional exam requirements/recommendations for international students: Required—TOEFL (minimum score 550 paper-based; 79 iBT), IELTS (minimum score 6.5). Electronic applications accepted. *Faculty research:* Ethics, virtual reality, sustainability, management of technology, quality management, capacity planning, human-computer interaction/interface, enterprise integration planning, economic impact of educational institutions, behavioral accounting, accounting ethics, taxation, information security, visualization simulation, human-computer interaction, supply chain, logistics, economics.

Southwestern Adventist University, Business Administration Department, Keene, TX 76059. Offers accounting (MBA); finance (MBA); management/leadership (MBA). Part-

time and evening/weekend programs available. *Degree requirements:* For master's, capstone course. *Entrance requirements:* For master's, GMAT, GRE General Test.

State University of New York Institute of Technology, Program in Business Administration in Technology Management, Utica, NY 13504-3050. Offers accounting and finance (MBA); business management (MBA); health services management (MBA); human resource management (MBA); marketing management (MBA). Part-time programs available. Postbaccalaureate distance learning degree programs offered (no on-campus study). *Faculty:* 10 full-time (2 women), 2 part-time/adjunct (1 woman). *Students:* 29 full-time (13 women), 89 part-time (26 women); includes 17 minority (5 Black or African American, non-Hispanic/Latino; 8 Asian, non-Hispanic/Latino; 3 Hispanic/Latino; 1 Two or more races, non-Hispanic/Latino), 1 international. Average age 33. 78 applicants, 54% accepted, 29 enrolled. In 2013, 57 master's awarded. *Degree requirements:* For master's, capstone course. *Entrance requirements:* For master's, GMAT, resume, one letter of reference. Additional exam requirements/recommendations for international students: Required—TOEFL (minimum score 550 paper-based; 79 iBT), IELTS (minimum score 6.5). *Application deadline:* For fall admission, 8/1 priority date for domestic students, 7/1 for international students; for spring admission, 12/1 for domestic students, 11/1 for international students. Applications are processed on a rolling basis. Application fee: $60. Electronic applications accepted. *Expenses:* Tuition, state resident: full-time $9870; part-time $411 per credit hour. Tuition, nonresident: full-time $20,150; part-time $765 per credit hour. *Required fees:* $1180; $50.73 per credit hour. *Financial support:* In 2013–14, 3 students received support, including 1 fellowship with full tuition reimbursement available (averaging $5,545 per year), 2 research assistantships with partial tuition reimbursements available (averaging $4,000 per year); unspecified assistantships also available. Financial award application deadline: 6/1; financial award applicants required to submit FAFSA. *Faculty research:* Technology management, writing schools, leadership, new products. *Unit head:* Dr. Rafael Romero, Program Coordinator and Associate Professor, 315-792-7337, Fax: 315-792-7138, E-mail: rafael.romero@sunyit.edu. *Application contact:* Maryrose Raab, Coordinator of Graduate Center, 315-792-7347, Fax: 315-792-7221, E-mail: maryrose.raab@sunyit.edu.
Website: http://www.sunyit.edu/programs/graduate/mbatm/.

Stevens Institute of Technology, Graduate School, Wesley J. Howe School of Technology Management, Program in Business Administration, Hoboken, NJ 07030. Offers engineering management (MBA); financial engineering (MBA); information management (MBA); information technology in financial services (MBA); information technology in the pharmaceutical industry (MBA); information technology outsourcing (MBA); pharmaceutical management (MBA); project management (MBA); technology management (MBA); telecommunications management (MBA).

Stony Brook University, State University of New York, Graduate School, College of Business, Program in Business Administration, Stony Brook, NY 11794. Offers finance (MBA, Certificate); health care management (MBA, Certificate); human resource management (Certificate); human resources (MBA); information systems management (MBA, Certificate); management (MBA); marketing (MBA). *Faculty:* 32 full-time (7 women), 29 part-time/adjunct (8 women). *Students:* 189 full-time (102 women), 111 part-time (40 women); includes 50 minority (10 Black or African American, non-Hispanic/Latino; 1 American Indian or Alaska Native, non-Hispanic/Latino; 25 Asian, non-Hispanic/Latino; 14 Hispanic/Latino), 114 international. 255 applicants, 53% accepted, 70 enrolled. In 2013, 157 master's, 1 other advanced degree awarded. *Entrance requirements:* For master's, GMAT, 3 letters of recommendation from current or former employers or professors, transcripts, personal statement, resume. Additional exam requirements/recommendations for international students: Required—TOEFL (minimum score 550 paper-based; 90 iBT), IELTS (minimum score 6.5). *Application deadline:* For fall admission, 6/1 for domestic students, 3/15 for international students; for spring admission, 12/1 for domestic students, 11/1 for international students. Application fee: $100. *Expenses:* Tuition, state resident: full-time $9870; part-time $411 per credit. Tuition, nonresident: full-time $18,350; part-time $765 per credit. *Financial support:* Teaching assistantships available. *Total annual research expenditures:* $53,718. *Unit head:* Dr. Manuel London, Dean and Director, Center for Human Resource Management, 631-632-7159, Fax: 631-632-8181, E-mail: manuel.london@stonybrook.edu. *Application contact:* Dr. Dmytro Holod, Interim Associate Dean/Graduate Program Director, 631-632-7183, Fax: 631-632-8181, E-mail: dmytro.holod@stonybrook.edu.

Strayer University, Graduate Studies, Washington, DC 20005-2603. Offers accounting (MS); acquisition (MBA); business administration (MBA); communications technology (MS); educational management (M Ed); finance (MBA); health services administration (MHSA); hospitality and tourism management (MBA); human resource management (MBA); information systems (MS), including computer security management, decision support system management, enterprise resource management, network management, software engineering management, systems development management; management (MBA); management information systems (MS); marketing (MBA); professional accounting (MS), including accounting information systems, controllership, taxation; public administration (MPA); supply chain management (MBA); technology in education (M Ed). Programs also offered at campus locations in Birmingham, AL; Chamblee, GA; Cobb County, GA; Morrow, GA; White Marsh, MD; Charleston, SC; Columbia, SC; Greensboro, NC; Greenville, SC; Lexington, KY; Louisville, KY; Nashville, TN; North Raleigh, NC; Washington, DC. Part-time and evening/weekend programs available. Postbaccalaureate distance learning degree programs offered (minimal on-campus study). *Degree requirements:* For master's, thesis. *Entrance requirements:* For master's, GMAT, GRE General Test, bachelor's degree from an accredited college or university, minimum undergraduate GPA of 2.75. Electronic applications accepted.

Suffolk University, Sawyer Business School, Master of Business Administration Program, Boston, MA 02108-2770. Offers accounting (MBA); business administration (APC); entrepreneurship (MBA); executive business administration (EMBA); finance (MBA); global business administration (GMBA); health administration (MBA); international business (MBA); marketing (MBA); nonprofit management (MBA); organizational behavior (MBA); strategic management (MBA); supply chain management (MBA); taxation (MBA); JD/MBA; MBA/GDPA; MBA/MHA; MBA/MSA; MBA/MSF; MBA/MST. *Accreditation:* AACSB. Part-time and evening/weekend programs available. Postbaccalaureate distance learning degree programs offered (no on-campus study). *Faculty:* 29 full-time (9 women), 12 part-time/adjunct (2 women). *Students:* 106 full-time (44 women), 334 part-time (184 women); includes 57 minority (20 Black or African American, non-Hispanic/Latino; 1 American Indian or Alaska Native, non-Hispanic/Latino; 18 Asian, non-Hispanic/Latino; 14 Hispanic/Latino; 4 Two or more races, non-Hispanic/Latino), 61 international. Average age 30. 448 applicants, 61% accepted, 135 enrolled. In 2013, 217 master's awarded. *Entrance requirements:* For master's, GMAT, minimum undergraduate GPA of 2.75 (MBA), 5 years of managerial experience (EMBA). Additional exam requirements/recommendations for international students: Required—TOEFL (minimum score 550 paper-based; 80 iBT). *Application deadline:* For fall admission, 6/15 priority date for domestic students, 6/15 for international students; for spring admission, 11/1 priority date for domestic students, 11/1 for international students. Applications are processed on a rolling basis. Application fee: $50. Electronic applications accepted. *Expenses: Tuition:* Full-time $38,374; part-time $1279 per credit. *Required fees:* $40; $20 per semester. Tuition and fees vary according to program. *Financial support:* In 2013–14, 107 students received support, including 91 fellowships with full and partial tuition reimbursements available (averaging $12,428 per year); career-related internships or fieldwork, Federal Work-Study, and institutionally sponsored loans also available. Support available to part-time students. Financial award application deadline: 4/1; financial award applicants required to submit FAFSA. *Faculty research:* Foreign investments; career strategies and boundaryless careers; corporate ethics codes; interest rates, inflation, and growth options; innovation and product development performance. *Unit head:* Heather Hewitt, Assistant Dean of Graduate Programs/Director of MBA Programs, 617-573-8306, E-mail: hhewitt@suffolk.edu. *Application contact:* Cory Meyers, Director of Graduate Admissions, 617-573-8302, Fax: 617-305-1733, E-mail: grad.admission@suffolk.edu.
Website: http://www.suffolk.edu/mba.

Suffolk University, Sawyer Business School, Programs in Finance, Boston, MA 02108-2770. Offers MSF, MSFSB, CPASF, JD/MSF. *Accreditation:* AACSB. Part-time and evening/weekend programs available. *Faculty:* 11 full-time (3 women), 7 part-time/adjunct (1 woman). *Students:* 23 full-time (10 women), 45 part-time (17 women); includes 4 minority (3 Asian, non-Hispanic/Latino; 1 Hispanic/Latino), 29 international. Average age 30. 226 applicants, 48% accepted, 28 enrolled. In 2013, 38 master's awarded. *Entrance requirements:* For master's, GMAT, interview. Additional exam requirements/recommendations for international students: Required—TOEFL (minimum score 550 paper-based; 80 iBT). *Application deadline:* For fall admission, 6/15 priority date for domestic students, 6/15 for international students; for spring admission, 11/1 priority date for domestic students, 11/1 for international students. Applications are processed on a rolling basis. Application fee: $50. Electronic applications accepted. *Expenses:* Contact institution. *Financial support:* In 2013–14, 15 students received support, including 15 fellowships (averaging $13,801 per year); career-related internships or fieldwork, Federal Work-Study, and institutionally sponsored loans also available. Support available to part-time students. Financial award application deadline: 4/1; financial award applicants required to submit FAFSA. *Faculty research:* Financial institutions, corporate finance, ownership structure, dividend policy, corporate restructuring. *Unit head:* Dr. Shahriar Khaksari, Chairperson/Professor of Finance, 617-573-8366, E-mail: skhaksari@suffolk.edu. *Application contact:* Cory Meyers, Director of Graduate Admissions, 617-573-8302, Fax: 617-305-1733, E-mail: grad.admission@suffolk.edu.
Website: http://www.suffolk.edu/msf.

Syracuse University, Martin J. Whitman School of Management, PhD Program in Business Administration, Syracuse, NY 13244. Offers accounting (PhD); finance (PhD); management information systems (PhD); managerial statistics (PhD); marketing (PhD); operations management (PhD); organizational behavior (PhD); strategy and human resources (PhD); supply chain management (PhD). *Faculty:* 79 full-time (20 women), 25 part-time/adjunct (6 women). *Students:* 26 full-time (8 women), 1 part-time (0 women); includes 2 minority (1 Black or African American, non-Hispanic/Latino; 1 Asian, non-Hispanic/Latino), 20 international. Average age 30. 130 applicants, 9% accepted, 7 enrolled. In 2013, 15 doctorates awarded. *Degree requirements:* For doctorate, comprehensive exam, thesis/dissertation, summer research paper. *Entrance requirements:* For doctorate, GMAT or GRE General Test, 3 recommendations. Additional exam requirements/recommendations for international students: Required—TOEFL (minimum score 600 paper-based; 100 iBT). *Application deadline:* For fall admission, 1/15 priority date for domestic and international students. Applications are processed on a rolling basis. Application fee: $75. Electronic applications accepted. *Financial support:* In 2013–14, 1 fellowship with full tuition reimbursement (averaging $19,570 per year), 30 teaching assistantships with full tuition reimbursements (averaging $17,000 per year) were awarded; research assistantships with full tuition reimbursements also available. Financial award application deadline: 1/15. *Faculty research:* Marketing models, market microstructure, supply chain, auditing, corporate governance. *Unit head:* Dr. Michel Benarock, Director of the PhD Program, 315-443-3429, E-mail: mbeanaroc@syr.edu. *Application contact:* Carol Hilleges, Administrative Specialist, 315-443-9601, Fax: 315-443-3671, E-mail: clhilleg@syr.edu.
Website: http://whitman.syr.edu/phd/.

Syracuse University, Martin J. Whitman School of Management, Program in Business Administration, Syracuse, NY 13244. Offers accounting (MBA); entrepreneurship (MBA); finance (MBA); marketing (MBA); supply chain management (MBA). Postbaccalaureate distance learning degree programs offered (minimal on-campus study). *Faculty:* 79 full-time (20 women), 25 part-time/adjunct (6 women). *Students:* 112 full-time (41 women), 181 part-time (49 women); includes 52 minority (19 Black or African American, non-Hispanic/Latino; 18 Asian, non-Hispanic/Latino; 11 Hispanic/Latino; 4 Two or more races, non-Hispanic/Latino), 56 international. Average age 33. 179 applicants, 50% accepted, 36 enrolled. In 2013, 115 master's awarded. *Entrance requirements:* For master's, GMAT, 2 letters of recommendation. Additional exam requirements/recommendations for international students: Required—TOEFL (minimum score 600 paper-based; 100 iBT). *Application deadline:* For fall admission, 11/30 priority date for domestic and international students. Applications are processed on a rolling basis. Application fee: $75. Electronic applications accepted. *Financial support:* In 2013–14, 17 students received support. Fellowships with full and partial tuition reimbursements available, teaching assistantships with partial tuition reimbursements available, career-related internships or fieldwork, scholarships/grants, tuition waivers (partial), and unspecified assistantships available. Support available to part-time students. Financial award application deadline: 3/1. *Unit head:* Dr. Don Harter, Associate Dean for Master's Programs, 315-443-3502, Fax: 315-443-9517, E-mail: dharter@syr.edu. *Application contact:* Danielle Goodroe, Director, Graduate Enrollment, 315-443-3006, Fax: 315-443-9517, E-mail: mbainfo@syr.edu.
Website: http://whitman.syr.edu/ftmba/.

Syracuse University, Martin J. Whitman School of Management, Program in Finance, Syracuse, NY 13244. Offers MS, JD/MSF. *Faculty:* 79 full-time (20 women), 25 part-time/adjunct (6 women). *Students:* 85 full-time (58 women), 13 part-time (9 women), 97 international. Average age 23. 654 applicants, 41% accepted, 56 enrolled. In 2013, 45 master's awarded. *Entrance requirements:* For master's, GMAT, 2 letters of recommendation, bachelor's degree in finance or economics. Additional exam requirements/recommendations for international students: Required—TOEFL (minimum score 600 paper-based; 100 iBT). *Application deadline:* For fall admission, 11/30 priority date for domestic and international students; for winter admission, 11/1 for domestic and international students. Applications are processed on a rolling basis. Application fee: $75. Electronic applications accepted. *Financial support:* Fellowships with full tuition reimbursements and career-related internships or fieldwork available. Financial award application deadline: 3/1. *Unit head:* Dr. Don Harter, Associate Dean of Graduate Programs, 315-443-3963, Fax: 315-443-9517, E-mail: dharter@syr.edu. *Application contact:* Danielle Goodroe, Director of Graduate Enrollment, 315-443-3006, Fax: 315-443-9517, E-mail: mbainfo@syr.edu.
Website: http://whitman.syr.edu/msfin/.

Télé-université, Graduate Programs, Québec, QC G1K 9H5, Canada. Offers computer science (PhD); corporate finance (MS); distance learning (MS). Part-time programs available.

Finance and Banking

Temple University, Fox School of Business, Doctoral Programs in Business, Philadelphia, PA 19122-6096. Offers accounting (PhD); entrepreneurship (PhD); finance (PhD); international business (PhD); management information systems (PhD); marketing (PhD); risk management and insurance (PhD); statistics (PhD); strategic management (PhD); tourism and sport (PhD). *Accreditation:* AACSB. *Degree requirements:* For doctorate, thesis/dissertation. *Entrance requirements:* For doctorate, GRE General Test, GMAT, minimum GPA of 3.0, master's degree. Additional exam requirements/recommendations for international students: Required—TOEFL (minimum score 600 paper-based; 100 iBT), IELTS (minimum score 7.5). Electronic applications accepted.

Temple University, Fox School of Business, Specialized Master's Programs, Philadelphia, PA 19122-6096. Offers accountancy (MS); actuarial science (MS); finance (MS); financial engineering (MS); human resource management (MS); innovation management and entrepreneurship (MS); marketing (MS); statistics (MS). MS in innovation management and entrepreneurship delivered jointly with College of Engineering. *Accreditation:* AACSB. Part-time programs available. *Entrance requirements:* For master's, GRE General Test or GMAT, minimum undergraduate GPA of 3.0. Additional exam requirements/recommendations for international students: Required—TOEFL (minimum score 600 paper-based; 100 iBT), IELTS (minimum score 7.5).

Tennessee Technological University, College of Graduate Studies, College of Business, Cookeville, TN 38505. Offers accounting (MBA); finance (MBA); human resource management (MBA); international business (MBA); management information systems (MBA). *Accreditation:* AACSB. Part-time and evening/weekend programs available. Postbaccalaureate distance learning degree programs offered (no on-campus study). *Faculty:* 28 full-time (5 women). *Students:* 54 full-time (22 women), 115 part-time (44 women); includes 11 minority (5 Black or African American, non-Hispanic/Latino; 1 Asian, non-Hispanic/Latino; 1 Hispanic/Latino; 4 Two or more races, non-Hispanic/Latino), 8 international. Average age 25. 171 applicants, 47% accepted, 50 enrolled. In 2013, 87 master's awarded. *Entrance requirements:* For master's, GMAT, GRE. Additional exam requirements/recommendations for international students: Required—TOEFL (minimum score 550 paper-based; 79 iBT), IELTS (minimum score 5.5), PTE (minimum score 53), or TOEIC (Test of English as an International Communication). *Application deadline:* For fall admission, 8/1 for domestic students, 5/1 for international students; for spring admission, 12/1 for domestic students, 10/1 for international students. Applications are processed on a rolling basis. Application fee: $35 ($40 for international students). Electronic applications accepted. *Expenses:* Tuition, state resident: full-time $9347; part-time $465 per credit hour. Tuition, nonresident: full-time $23,635; part-time $1152 per credit hour. *Financial support:* In 2013–14, 5 fellowships (averaging $10,000 per year), 18 research assistantships (averaging $4,000 per year), teaching assistantships (averaging $4,000 per year) were awarded. Support available to part-time students. Financial award application deadline: 4/1. *Unit head:* Amanda L. Brown, Interim Director, 931-372-3600, Fax: 931-372-6249, E-mail: albrown@tntech.edu. *Application contact:* Shelia K. Kendrick, Coordinator of Graduate Studies, 931-372-3808, Fax: 931-372-3497, E-mail: skendrick@tntech.edu.
Website: http://www.tntech.edu/mba.

Texas A&M International University, Office of Graduate Studies and Research, A.R. Sanchez School of Business, Division of International Banking and Finance Studies, Laredo, TX 78041-1900. Offers accounting (MP Acc); international banking and finance (MBA). *Faculty:* 12 full-time (2 women). *Students:* 13 full-time (6 women), 36 part-time (18 women); includes 48 minority (1 Black or African American, non-Hispanic/Latino; 2 Asian, non-Hispanic/Latino; 45 Hispanic/Latino). Average age 31. 13 applicants, 85% accepted, 13 enrolled. In 2013, 30 master's awarded. *Entrance requirements:* For master's, GMAT or GRE General Test. Additional exam requirements/recommendations for international students: Required—TOEFL (minimum score 550 paper-based; 79 iBT). *Application deadline:* For fall admission, 4/30 priority date for domestic students, 4/30 for international students; for spring admission, 11/30 for domestic students, 10/1 for international students. Applications are processed on a rolling basis. Application fee: $35 ($50 for international students). *Expenses:* Tuition, state resident: full-time $5184. *International tuition:* $11,556 full-time. *Financial support:* In 2013–14, 3 students received support, including 1 research assistantship. *Unit head:* Dr. Antonio Rodriguez, Chair, 956-326-2517, Fax: 956-326-2481, E-mail: rodriguez@tamiu.edu. *Application contact:* Imelda Lopez, Graduate Admissions Counselor, 956-326-2485, Fax: 956-326-2459, E-mail: lopez@tamiu.edu.
Website: http://www.tamiu.edu/arssb/ibfs.shtml.

Texas A&M University, Mays Business School, Department of Finance, College Station, TX 77843. Offers finance (MS, PhD); land economics and real estate (MRE). *Faculty:* 16. *Students:* 159 full-time (61 women), 1 part-time (0 women); includes 16 minority (7 Asian, non-Hispanic/Latino; 7 Hispanic/Latino; 2 Two or more races, non-Hispanic/Latino), 14 international. Average age 24. 127 applicants, 35% accepted, 36 enrolled. In 2013, 120 master's, 2 doctorates awarded. Terminal master's awarded for partial completion of doctoral program. *Degree requirements:* For master's, comprehensive exam; for doctorate, thesis/dissertation. *Entrance requirements:* For master's, GMAT; for doctorate, GMAT or GRE General Test. Additional exam requirements/recommendations for international students: Required—TOEFL. *Application deadline:* For fall admission, 3/1 priority date for domestic students; for spring admission, 8/1 for domestic students. Applications are processed on a rolling basis. Application fee: $50 ($75 for international students). *Expenses:* Tuition, state resident: full-time $4078; part-time $226.55 per credit hour. Tuition, nonresident: full-time $10,450; part-time $580.55 per credit hour. *Required fees:* $2328; $278.50 per credit hour. $642.45 per semester. *Financial support:* In 2013–14, 30 students received support. Fellowships, research assistantships, teaching assistantships, career-related internships or fieldwork, and institutionally sponsored loans available. Financial award application deadline: 2/1. *Unit head:* Dr. Sorin Sorescu, Head, 979-458-0380, Fax: 979-845-3884, E-mail: smsorescu@mays.tamu.edu. *Application contact:* Angela G. Degelman, Program Coordinator/Graduate Academic Advisor, 979-845-4858, Fax: 979-845-3884, E-mail: adegelman@mays.tamu.edu.
Website: http://mays.tamu.edu/finc/.

Texas A&M University–Commerce, Graduate School, College of Business, MS Programs, Commerce, TX 75429-3011. Offers accounting (MS); economics (MA); finance (MS); management (MS); marketing (MS). Part-time programs available. *Degree requirements:* For master's, comprehensive exam, thesis (for some programs). *Entrance requirements:* For master's, GMAT or GRE General Test. Electronic applications accepted. *Expenses:* Tuition, state resident: full-time $3630; part-time $2420 per year. Tuition, nonresident: full-time $9948; part-time $6632.16 per year. *Required fees:* $1006 per year. Tuition and fees vary according to course load. *Faculty research:* Economic activity, forensic economics, volatility and finance, international economics.

Texas A&M University–San Antonio, School of Business, San Antonio, TX 78224. Offers business administration (MBA); enterprise resource planning systems (MBA); finance (MBA); healthcare management (MBA); human resources management (MBA); information assurance and security (MBA); international business (MBA); professional accounting (MPA); project management (MBA); supply chain management (MBA). Part-time and evening/weekend programs available. *Entrance requirements:* For master's, GMAT. Additional exam requirements/recommendations for international students: Required—TOEFL (minimum score 550 paper-based; 80 iBT), IELTS (minimum score 6). Electronic applications accepted.

Texas Tech University, Graduate School, Rawls College of Business Administration, Area of Finance, Lubbock, TX 79409. Offers MS, PhD. Part-time programs available. *Faculty:* 11 full-time (2 women). *Students:* 25 full-time (3 women); includes 6 minority (1 Black or African American, non-Hispanic/Latino; 5 Asian, non-Hispanic/Latino), 7 international. Average age 29. 13 applicants, 77% accepted, 6 enrolled. In 2013, 11 master's, 1 doctorate awarded. Terminal master's awarded for partial completion of doctoral program. *Degree requirements:* For master's, capstone course; for doctorate, comprehensive exam, thesis/dissertation, qualifying exams. *Entrance requirements:* For master's and doctorate, GMAT, holistic review of academic credentials. Additional exam requirements/recommendations for international students: Required—TOEFL (minimum score 550 paper-based; 79 iBT). *Application deadline:* For fall admission, 7/1 priority date for domestic students, 1/15 for international students; for spring admission, 11/1 priority date for domestic students, 6/15 for international students. Applications are processed on a rolling basis. Application fee: $60. Electronic applications accepted. *Expenses:* Tuition, state resident: full-time $6062; part-time $252.57 per credit hour. Tuition, nonresident: full-time $14,558; part-time $606.57 per credit hour. *Required fees:* $2655; $35 per credit hour. $907.50 per semester. Tuition and fees vary according to course load. *Financial support:* In 2013–14, 8 research assistantships (averaging $15,700 per year), 3 teaching assistantships (averaging $18,000 per year) were awarded; Federal Work-Study and scholarships/grants also available. Support available to part-time students. Financial award applicants required to submit FAFSA. *Faculty research:* Portfolio theory, banking and financial institutions, corporate finance, securities and options futures. *Unit head:* Dr. Jeff Mercer, Area Coordinator, 806-742-3350, Fax: 806-742-2099, E-mail: jeffrey.mercer@ttu.edu. *Application contact:* Terri Boston, Applications Manager, Graduate and Professional Programs, 806-742-3184, Fax: 806-742-3958, E-mail: rawlsrad@ttu.edu.
Website: http://finance.ba.ttu.edu.

Thomas M. Cooley Law School, JD and LL M Programs, Lansing, MI 48901-3038. Offers administrative law (public law) (JD); business transactions (JD); Canadian law practice (JD); Constitutional law and civil rights (public law) (JD); corporate law and finance (LL M); environmental law (public law) (JD); general practice (JD), including solo and small firm; homeland and national security law (LL M); insurance law (LL M); intellectual property (JD); intellectual property law (LL M); international law (JD); litigation (JD); self-directed (LL M, JD); tax law (LL M); taxation (JD); U.S. legal studies for foreign attorneys (LL M); JD/MBA; JD/MPA; JD/MSW. *Accreditation:* ABA. Part-time and evening/weekend programs available. Postbaccalaureate distance learning degree programs offered (no on-campus study). *Degree requirements:* For master's, thesis optional; for doctorate, minimum of 3 credits of clinical experience. *Entrance requirements:* For master's, JD or LL B; for doctorate, LSAT. Additional exam requirements/recommendations for international students: Required—TOEFL (for U.S. legal studies for foreign attorneys LL M program). Electronic applications accepted. *Faculty research:* Wrongful convictions, civil rights, environmental law, litigation techniques, data mining, intellectual property, practical and skills-based legal education.

Tiffin University, Program in Business Administration, Tiffin, OH 44883-2161. Offers finance (MBA); general management (MBA); healthcare administration (MBA); human resources (MBA); international business (MBA); leadership (MBA); marketing (MBA); sports management (MBA). *Accreditation:* ACBSP. Part-time and evening/weekend programs available. Postbaccalaureate distance learning degree programs offered (no on-campus study). *Entrance requirements:* For master's, minimum undergraduate GPA of 2.5, work experience. Additional exam requirements/recommendations for international students: Required—TOEFL (minimum score 550 paper-based; 79 iBT). Electronic applications accepted. *Faculty research:* Small business, executive development operations, research and statistical analysis, market research, management information systems.

Trident University International, College of Business Administration, Program in Business Administration, Cypress, CA 90630. Offers business administration (PhD); conflict and negotiation management (MBA); criminal justice administration (MBA); entrepreneurship (MBA); finance (MBA); general management (MBA); government accounting (MBA); human resource management (MBA); information security and digital assurance management (MBA); information technology management (MBA); international business (MBA); logistics management (MBA); marketing (MBA); project management (MBA); public management (MBA); quality management (MBA); strategic leadership (MBA). Part-time and evening/weekend programs available. Postbaccalaureate distance learning degree programs offered (no on-campus study). *Degree requirements:* For doctorate, comprehensive exam, thesis/dissertation, defense of dissertation. *Entrance requirements:* For master's, minimum GPA of 2.5 (students with GPA 3.0 or greater may transfer up to 30% of graduate level credits); for doctorate, minimum GPA of 3.4, curriculum vitae, course work in research methods or statistics. Additional exam requirements/recommendations for international students: Required—TOEFL. Electronic applications accepted.

Troy University, Graduate School, College of Business, Program in Business Administration, Troy, AL 36082. Offers accounting (EMBA, MBA); criminal justice (EMBA); finance (MBA); general management (EMBA, MBA); healthcare management (EMBA); information systems (EMBA, MBA); international economic development (MBA). *Accreditation:* ACBSP. Part-time and evening/weekend programs available. *Faculty:* 56 full-time (20 women), 3 part-time/adjunct (0 women). *Students:* 142 full-time (89 women), 310 part-time (192 women); includes 265 minority (185 Black or African American, non-Hispanic/Latino; 3 American Indian or Alaska Native, non-Hispanic/Latino; 62 Asian, non-Hispanic/Latino; 8 Hispanic/Latino; 1 Native Hawaiian or other Pacific Islander, non-Hispanic/Latino; 6 Two or more races, non-Hispanic/Latino). Average age 29. 472 applicants, 68% accepted, 51 enrolled. In 2013, 293 master's awarded. *Degree requirements:* For master's, minimum GPA of 3.0, capstone course, research course. *Entrance requirements:* For master's, GMAT (minimum score 500) or GRE General Test (minimum score 900 on old exam or 294 on new exam), bachelor's degree; minimum undergraduate GPA of 2.5 or 3.0 on last 30 semester hours, letter of recommendation. Additional exam requirements/recommendations for international students: Required—TOEFL (minimum score 523 paper-based; 70 iBT), IELTS (minimum score 6). *Application deadline:* Applications are processed on a rolling basis. Application fee: $50. *Expenses:* Tuition, state resident: full-time $6084; part-time $338 per credit hour. Tuition, nonresident: full-time $12,168; part-time $676 per credit hour. *Required fees:* $630; $35 per credit hour. $50 per semester. *Unit head:* Dr. Bob Wheatley, Director, Graduate Business Programs, 334-670-3194, Fax: 334-670-3599, E-mail: rwheat@troy.edu. *Application contact:* Brenda K. Campbell, Director of Graduate Admissions, 334-670-3178, Fax: 334-670-3733, E-mail: bcamp@troy.edu.

United States International University, School of Business Administration, Nairobi, Kenya. Offers business administration (GEMBA); entrepreneurship (MBA); finance (MBA); human resource management (MBA); information technology management (MBA); integrated studies (MBA); international business administration (MBA); management and organizational development (MS); marketing (MBA); organizational development (EMS); strategic management (MBA). Part-time and evening/weekend

programs available. *Degree requirements:* For master's, thesis. *Entrance requirements:* For master's, GMAT, 2 letters of reference, resume. Additional exam requirements/recommendations for international students: Required—TOEFL (minimum score 550 paper-based). *Faculty research:* Marketing in small business enterprises, total quality management in Kenya.

Universidad Central del Este, Graduate School, San Pedro de Macoris, Dominican Republic. Offers environmental engineering (ME); financial management (M Ad); higher education (M Ed), including higher education management, higher education pedagogy; human resources (M Ad). *Entrance requirements:* For master's, letters of recommendation.

Universidad de las Americas, A.C., Program in Business Administration, Mexico City, Mexico. Offers finance (MBA); marketing research (MBA); production and quality (MBA).

Universidad de las Américas Puebla, Division of Graduate Studies, School of Business and Economics, Puebla, Mexico. Offers business administration (MBA); finance (M Adm). Part-time and evening/weekend programs available. *Degree requirements:* For master's, one foreign language, thesis. *Entrance requirements:* Additional exam requirements/recommendations for international students: Required—TOEFL. *Faculty research:* System dynamics, information technology, marketing, international business, strategic planning, quality.

Universidad de las Américas Puebla, Division of Graduate Studies, School of Social Sciences, Program in Economics, Puebla, Mexico. Offers economics (MA); finance (M Adm). Part-time and evening/weekend programs available. *Degree requirements:* For master's, one foreign language, thesis. *Faculty research:* Economic models (mathematics), industrial organization, assets and values market.

Universidad Metropolitana, School of Business Administration, Program in Finance, San Juan, PR 00928-1150. Offers MBA.

Université de Sherbrooke, Faculty of Administration, Program in Finance, Sherbrooke, QC J1K 2R1, Canada. Offers M Sc. *Degree requirements:* For master's, one foreign language, thesis. *Entrance requirements:* For master's, bachelor's degree in related field, minimum GPA of 3.0 (on 4.3 scale). Electronic applications accepted. *Faculty research:* Public projects analysis, financial econometrics, risk management, portfolio management.

Université du Québec à Montréal, Graduate Programs, Program in Finance, Montréal, QC H3C 3P8, Canada. Offers Diploma. Part-time programs available. *Entrance requirements:* For degree, appropriate bachelor's degree or equivalent, proficiency in French.

Université du Québec à Trois-Rivières, Graduate Programs, Program in Finance, Trois-Rivières, QC G9A 5H7, Canada. Offers DESS.

Université du Québec en Outaouais, Graduate Programs, Program in Financial Services, Gatineau, QC J8X 3X7, Canada. Offers MBA, DESS, Diploma. Part-time and evening/weekend programs available. *Degree requirements:* For master's, thesis (for some programs).

Université Laval, Faculty of Administrative Sciences, Programs in Business Administration, Québec, QC G1K 7P4, Canada. Offers accounting (MBA); agri-food management (MBA); electronic business (MBA, Diploma); factory management and logistics (MBA); finance (MBA); firm management (MBA); geomatic management (MBA); information technology management (MBA); international management (MBA); management (MBA); management accounting (MBA, Diploma); marketing (MBA); modeling and organizational decision (MBA); occupational health and safety management (MBA); pharmacy management (MBA); social and environmental responsibility (MBA); technological entrepreneurship (Diploma). *Accreditation:* AACSB. Part-time and evening/weekend programs available. Postbaccalaureate distance learning degree programs offered (no on-campus study). *Entrance requirements:* For master's and Diploma, knowledge of French and English. Electronic applications accepted.

University at Buffalo, the State University of New York, Graduate School, School of Management, Buffalo, NY 14260. Offers accounting (MS); business administration (EMBA, MBA, PMBA); finance (MS), including financial management, quantitative finance; management (PhD); management information systems (MS); supply chains and operations management (MS); Au D/MBA; DDS/MBA; JD/MBA; M Arch/MBA; MA/MBA; MD/MBA; MPH/MBA; MSW/MBA; Pharm D/MBA. *Accreditation:* AACSB. Part-time and evening/weekend programs available. *Faculty:* 72 full-time (23 women), 51 part-time/adjunct (13 women). *Students:* 627 full-time (266 women), 181 part-time (65 women); includes 50 minority (16 Black or African American, non-Hispanic/Latino; 5 American Indian or Alaska Native, non-Hispanic/Latino; 5 Asian, non-Hispanic/Latino; 3 Hispanic/Latino; 21 Native Hawaiian or other Pacific Islander, non-Hispanic/Latino), 332 international. Average age 28. 2,083 applicants, 52% accepted, 432 enrolled. In 2013, 476 master's, 10 doctorates awarded. *Degree requirements:* For master's, thesis (for some programs); for doctorate, comprehensive exam, thesis/dissertation. *Entrance requirements:* For master's, GMAT (for MS in accounting); GRE or GMAT (for MBA and all other MS concentrations), essays, letters of recommendation; for doctorate, GMAT or GRE, essays, writing sample, letters of recommendation. Additional exam requirements/recommendations for international students: Required—IELTS or PTE; Recommended—TOEFL (minimum score 95 iBT). *Application deadline:* For fall admission, 5/2 priority date for domestic students, 2/1 priority date for international students. Applications are processed on a rolling basis. Application fee: $100. Electronic applications accepted. *Expenses:* Contact institution. *Financial support:* In 2013–14, 115 students received support, including 40 fellowships (averaging $5,250 per year), 33 research assistantships with full and partial tuition reimbursements available (averaging $18,000 per year), 42 teaching assistantships with partial tuition reimbursements available (averaging $10,255 per year); career-related internships or fieldwork, Federal Work-Study, institutionally sponsored loans, scholarships/grants, health care benefits, and unspecified assistantships also available. Financial award application deadline: 2/15; financial award applicants required to submit FAFSA. *Faculty research:* Earnings management and electronic information assurance, supply chain and operations management, corporate financing and asset pricing, consumer behavior and quantitative modeling of marketing behavior, leadership and politics in organizations. *Total annual research expenditures:* $155,000. *Unit head:* Erin K. O'Brien, Assistant Dean and Director of Graduate Programs, 716-645-3204, Fax: 716-645-2341, E-mail: ekobrien@buffalo.edu. *Application contact:* Meghan Felser, Associate Director of Admissions and Recruiting, 716-645-3204, Fax: 716-645-2341, E-mail: mpwood@buffalo.edu.
Website: http://mgt.buffalo.edu/.

The University of Akron, Graduate School, College of Business Administration, Department of Finance, Akron, OH 44325. Offers MBA. Part-time and evening/weekend programs available. *Faculty:* 11 full-time (3 women), 6 part-time/adjunct (0 women). *Students:* 20 full-time (6 women), 29 part-time (4 women); includes 1 minority (Black or African American, non-Hispanic/Latino), 14 international. Average age 28. 24 applicants, 71% accepted, 11 enrolled. In 2013, 28 master's awarded. *Entrance requirements:* For master's, GMAT, minimum GPA of 2.75, two letters of recommendation, statement of purpose, resume. Additional exam requirements/recommendations for international

students: Required—TOEFL (minimum score 550 paper-based; 79 iBT). *Application deadline:* For fall admission, 7/15 for domestic and international students; for spring admission, 11/15 for domestic and international students. Application fee: $40 ($60 for international students). Electronic applications accepted. *Expenses:* Tuition, state resident: full-time $7430; part-time $412.80 per credit hour. Tuition, nonresident: full-time $12,722; part-time $706.80 per credit hour. *Required fees:* $53 per credit hour. $12 per semester. Tuition and fees vary according to course load and program. *Financial support:* In 2013–14, 10 teaching assistantships with full tuition reimbursements were awarded. *Faculty research:* Corporate finance, financial markets and institutions, investment and equity market analysis, personal financial planning, real estate. *Unit head:* Dr. James Thomson, Chair, 330-972-6329, E-mail: thomson1@uakron.edu. *Application contact:* Dr. William Hauser, Director of Graduate Business Programs, 330-972-7043, Fax: 330-972-6588, E-mail: whauser@uakron.edu.
Website: http://www.uakron.edu/cba/departments/finance/.

The University of Alabama, Graduate School, College of Human Environmental Sciences, Program in Human Environmental Science, Tuscaloosa, AL 35487. Offers family financial planning and counseling (MS); interactive technology (MS); quality management (MS); restaurant and meeting management (MS); rural community health (MS); sport management (MS). *Faculty:* 1 full-time (0 women). *Students:* 55 full-time (34 women), 98 part-time (48 women); includes 41 minority (30 Black or African American, non-Hispanic/Latino; 2 American Indian or Alaska Native, non-Hispanic/Latino; 2 Asian, non-Hispanic/Latino; 2 Hispanic/Latino; 5 Two or more races, non-Hispanic/Latino), 1 international. Average age 34. 102 applicants, 69% accepted, 60 enrolled. In 2013, 88 master's awarded. *Degree requirements:* For master's, comprehensive exam. *Entrance requirements:* For master's, GRE (for some specializations), minimum GPA of 3.0. Additional exam requirements/recommendations for international students: Required—TOEFL. *Application deadline:* Applications are processed on a rolling basis. Application fee: $50 ($60 for international students). Electronic applications accepted. *Expenses:* Tuition, state resident: full-time $9450. Tuition, nonresident: full-time $23,950. *Faculty research:* Hospitality management, sports medicine education, technology and education. *Unit head:* Dr. Milla D. Boschung, Dean, 205-348-6250, Fax: 205-348-1786, E-mail: mboschun@ches.ua.edu. *Application contact:* Dr. Stuart Usdan, Associate Dean, 205-348-6150, Fax: 205-348-3789, E-mail: susdan@ches.ua.edu.

The University of Alabama, Graduate School, Manderson Graduate School of Business, Economics, Finance and Legal Studies Department, Tuscaloosa, AL 35487. Offers economics (MA, PhD); finance (MS, PhD). *Faculty:* 30 full-time (2 women). *Students:* 68 full-time (20 women), 11 part-time (4 women); includes 10 minority (7 Black or African American, non-Hispanic/Latino; 2 Asian, non-Hispanic/Latino; 1 Hispanic/Latino), 25 international. Average age 29. 253 applicants, 31% accepted, 22 enrolled. In 2013, 37 master's, 5 doctorates awarded. Terminal master's awarded for partial completion of doctoral program. *Degree requirements:* For master's, comprehensive exam (MA), thesis (MS); for doctorate, comprehensive exam, thesis/dissertation. *Entrance requirements:* For master's, GMAT, GRE; for doctorate, GRE or GMAT. Additional exam requirements/recommendations for international students: Required—TOEFL (minimum score 550 paper-based; 79 iBT). *Application deadline:* For fall admission, 7/1 priority date for domestic students, 1/15 for international students; for spring admission, 11/1 priority date for domestic students, 6/1 for international students. Applications are processed on a rolling basis. Application fee: $50 ($60 for international students). Electronic applications accepted. *Expenses:* Tuition, state resident: full-time $9450. Tuition, nonresident: full-time $23,950. *Financial support:* In 2013–14, 43 students received support, including 24 research assistantships with full and partial tuition reimbursements available (averaging $15,000 per year), 19 teaching assistantships with full and partial tuition reimbursements available (averaging $15,000 per year); fellowships, Federal Work-Study, institutionally sponsored loans, and unspecified assistantships also available. Financial award application deadline: 1/15. *Faculty research:* Taxation, futures market, monetary theory and policy, income distribution. *Unit head:* Prof. Matthew T. Holt, Department Head, 205-348-8980, E-mail: mtholt@cba.ua.edu. *Application contact:* Debra F. Wheatley, Graduate Programs Secretary, 205-348-6683, Fax: 205-348-0590, E-mail: dwheatle@cba.ua.edu.
Website: http://www.cba.ua.edu/.

The University of Alabama at Birmingham, School of Business, Program in Business Administration, Birmingham, AL 35294-4460. Offers business administration (MBA), including finance, health care management, information technology management, marketing. Part-time and evening/weekend programs available. *Students:* 59 full-time (25 women), 249 part-time (93 women); includes 74 minority (53 Black or African American, non-Hispanic/Latino; 13 Asian, non-Hispanic/Latino; 7 Hispanic/Latino; 1 Two or more races, non-Hispanic/Latino), 16 international. Average age 32. In 2013, 128 master's awarded. *Entrance requirements:* For master's, GMAT. Additional exam requirements/recommendations for international students: Required—TOEFL. *Application deadline:* For fall admission, 7/1 for domestic and international students; for spring admission, 11/1 for domestic and international students; for summer admission, 4/1 for domestic and international students. Application fee: $60 ($75 for international students). *Unit head:* Dr. Ken Miller, Executive Director, MBA Programs, 205-934-8855, E-mail: klmiller@uab.edu. *Application contact:* Christy Manning, Coordinator of Graduate Programs in Business, 205-934-8817, E-mail: cmanning@uab.edu.
Website: http://www.uab.edu/business/degrees-certificates/MBA.

The University of Alabama in Huntsville, School of Graduate Studies, College of Business Administration, Program in Accounting, Huntsville, AL 35899. Offers accounting (M Acc), including CPA preparatory with an emphasis in taxation, CPA preparatory with emphasis in assurance and financial reporting, general accounting, information systems audit and control (ISAC). *Accreditation:* AACSB. Part-time and evening/weekend programs available. *Faculty:* 9 full-time (3 women). *Students:* 14 full-time (6 women), 27 part-time (16 women); includes 8 minority (6 Black or African American, non-Hispanic/Latino; 2 Asian, non-Hispanic/Latino), 6 international. Average age 30. 24 applicants, 63% accepted, 8 enrolled. In 2013, 29 master's awarded. *Degree requirements:* For master's, comprehensive exam, thesis or alternative. *Entrance requirements:* For master's, GMAT (minimum score 500), minimum AACSB index of 1080. Additional exam requirements/recommendations for international students: Required—TOEFL (minimum score 550 paper-based; 80 iBT), IELTS (minimum score 6.5). *Application deadline:* For fall admission, 7/15 priority date for domestic students, 4/1 priority date for international students; for spring admission, 11/30 priority date for domestic students, 9/1 priority date for international students. Applications are processed on a rolling basis. Application fee: $50. Electronic applications accepted. *Expenses:* Tuition, state resident: full-time $8912; part-time $540 per credit hour. Tuition, nonresident: full-time $20,774; part-time $1252 per credit hour. *Required fees:* $148 per semester. One-time fee: $150. *Financial support:* Teaching assistantships, career-related internships or fieldwork, Federal Work-Study, institutionally sponsored loans, scholarships/grants, health care benefits, and unspecified assistantships available. Support available to part-time students. Financial award application deadline: 4/1; financial award applicants required to submit FAFSA. *Faculty research:* Accounting information systems, managerial accounting, behavioral accounting, state and local taxation, financial accounting. *Unit head:* Dr. Allen Wilhite, Interim Chair, 256-824-6591, Fax: 256-824-2929, E-mail: allen.wilhite@uah.edu. *Application contact:* Jennifer Pettitt,

Director of Graduate Programs, 256-824-6681, Fax: 256-824-7571, E-mail: jennifer.pettitt@uah.edu.

The University of Alabama in Huntsville, School of Graduate Studies, College of Business Administration, Programs in Business and Management, Huntsville, AL 35899. Offers federal contracting and procurement management (Certificate); management (MBA), including acquisition management, entrepreneurship, federal contract accounting, finance, human resource management, logistics and supply chain management, marketing, project management; supply chain management (Certificate); technology and innovation management (Certificate). *Accreditation:* AACSB. Part-time and evening/weekend programs available. *Faculty:* 13 full-time (3 women), 5 part-time/adjunct (0 women). *Students:* 41 full-time (19 women), 144 part-time (59 women); includes 35 minority (13 Black or African American, non-Hispanic/Latino; 1 American Indian or Alaska Native, non-Hispanic/Latino; 9 Asian, non-Hispanic/Latino; 11 Hispanic/Latino; 1 Two or more races, non-Hispanic/Latino), 13 international. Average age 33. 131 applicants, 78% accepted, 67 enrolled. In 2013, 83 master's, 5 other advanced degrees awarded. *Degree requirements:* For master's, comprehensive exam, thesis or alternative. *Entrance requirements:* For master's, GMAT (minimum score 500), minimum AACSB index of 1080. Additional exam requirements/recommendations for international students: Required—TOEFL (minimum score 550 paper-based; 80 iBT), IELTS (minimum score 6.5). *Application deadline:* For fall admission, 7/15 priority date for domestic students, 4/1 priority date for international students; for spring admission, 11/30 priority date for domestic students, 9/1 priority date for international students. Applications are processed on a rolling basis. Application fee: $50. Electronic applications accepted. *Expenses:* Tuition, state resident: full-time $8912; part-time $540 per credit hour. Tuition, nonresident: full-time $20,774; part-time $1252 per credit hour. *Required fees:* $148 per semester. One-time fee: $150. *Financial support:* In 2013–14, 10 students received support, including 4 research assistantships with full and partial tuition reimbursements available (averaging $7,750 per year), 5 teaching assistantships with full and partial tuition reimbursements available (averaging $9,000 per year); career-related internships or fieldwork, Federal Work-Study, institutionally sponsored loans, scholarships/grants, health care benefits, tuition waivers (full and partial), and unspecified assistantships also available. Support available to part-time students. Financial award application deadline: 4/1; financial award applicants required to submit FAFSA. *Faculty research:* Supply chain management, management of research and development, international marketing and branding, organizational behavior and human resource management, social networks and computational economics. *Total annual research expenditures:* $2.1 million. *Unit head:* Dr. Cynthia Gramm, Chair, 256-824-6913, Fax: 256-824-6328, E-mail: cynthia.gramm@uah.edu. *Application contact:* Jennifer Pettitt, Director of Graduate Programs, 256-824-6681, Fax: 256-824-7571, E-mail: jennifer.pettitt@uah.edu.

University of Alaska Fairbanks, School of Management, Department of Business Administration, Fairbanks, AK 99775-6080. Offers capital markets (MBA); general management (MBA). *Accreditation:* AACSB. Part-time programs available. *Faculty:* 10 full-time (4 women). *Students:* 29 full-time (18 women), 41 part-time (20 women); includes 13 minority (2 American Indian or Alaska Native, non-Hispanic/Latino; 2 Asian, non-Hispanic/Latino; 2 Hispanic/Latino; 7 Two or more races, non-Hispanic/Latino), 4 international. Average age 34. 36 applicants, 56% accepted, 19 enrolled. In 2013, 28 master's awarded. *Degree requirements:* For master's, comprehensive exam, thesis or alternative. *Entrance requirements:* For master's, GMAT. Additional exam requirements/recommendations for international students: Required—TOEFL (minimum score 550 paper-based; 80 iBT). *Application deadline:* For fall admission, 6/1 priority date for domestic students, 2/1 for international students; for spring admission, 10/15 priority date for domestic students, 9/1 for international students. Applications are processed on a rolling basis. Application fee: $60. Electronic applications accepted. *Expenses:* Tuition, state resident: full-time $7254; part-time $403 per credit. Tuition, nonresident: full-time $14,814; part-time $823 per credit. Tuition and fees vary according to course level, course load and reciprocity agreements. *Financial support:* In 2013–14, 6 teaching assistantships with tuition reimbursements (averaging $11,115 per year) were awarded; fellowships with tuition reimbursements, research assistantships with tuition reimbursements, career-related internships or fieldwork, Federal Work-Study, scholarships/grants, health care benefits, and unspecified assistantships also available. Support available to part-time students. Financial award application deadline: 2/15; financial award applicants required to submit FAFSA. *Faculty research:* Consumer behavior, marketing, international finance and business, strategic risk, organization theory. *Total annual research expenditures:* $116,000. *Unit head:* Dr. Liz Ross, Director, MBA Program, 907-474-7793, Fax: 907-474-5219, E-mail: bmross@alaska.edu. *Application contact:* Libby Eddy, Registrar and Director of Admissions, 907-474-7500, Fax: 907-474-7097, E-mail: admissions@uaf.edu.
Website: http://www.uaf.edu/som/degrees/graduate/.

University of Alberta, Faculty of Graduate Studies and Research, Department of Economics, Edmonton, AB T6G 2E1, Canada. Offers economics (MA, PhD); economics and finance (MA); environmental and natural resource economics (PhD). Part-time programs available. *Degree requirements:* For doctorate, thesis/dissertation. *Entrance requirements:* For master's and doctorate, GRE. Additional exam requirements/recommendations for international students: Required—TOEFL. *Faculty research:* Public finance, international trade, industrial organization, Pacific Rim economics, monetary economics.

University of Alberta, Faculty of Graduate Studies and Research, Doctoral Program in Business, Edmonton, AB T6G 2E1, Canada. Offers accounting (PhD); finance (PhD); human resources/industrial relations (PhD); management science (PhD); marketing (PhD); organizational analysis (PhD); MBA/PhD. *Accreditation:* AACSB. Part-time programs available. *Degree requirements:* For doctorate, comprehensive exam, thesis/dissertation. *Entrance requirements:* For doctorate, GMAT. Additional exam requirements/recommendations for international students: Required—TOEFL (minimum score 550 paper-based). Electronic applications accepted. *Faculty research:* Accounting, capital markets and corporate finance, organizational change and human resource management, marketing, strategic management.

The University of Arizona, Eller College of Management, Department of Finance, Tucson, AZ 85721. Offers MS, PhD. Part-time programs available. *Faculty:* 8 full-time (2 women). *Students:* 20 full-time (9 women), 3 part-time (0 women); includes 2 minority (1 Asian, non-Hispanic/Latino; 1 Hispanic/Latino), 15 international. Average age 24. Terminal master's awarded for partial completion of doctoral program. *Degree requirements:* For master's, project; for doctorate, comprehensive exam, thesis/dissertation. *Entrance requirements:* Additional exam requirements/recommendations for international students: Required—TOEFL (minimum score 550 paper-based; 79 iBT). *Application deadline:* For fall admission, 2/15 for domestic and international students. Applications are processed on a rolling basis. Application fee: $75. Electronic applications accepted. *Expenses:* Contact institution. *Financial support:* In 2013–14, 1 research assistantship with full tuition reimbursement (averaging $26,000 per year), 10 teaching assistantships with full tuition reimbursements (averaging $27,000 per year) were awarded; health care benefits, tuition waivers (partial), and unspecified assistantships also available. Financial award application deadline: 3/15. *Faculty research:* Corporate finance, banking, investments, stock market. *Total annual research expenditures:* $57,000. *Unit head:* Dr. Richard Sias, Head, 520-621-7554, Fax: 520-621-1261, E-mail: sias@email.arizona.edu. *Application contact:* Kay Ross, Program Coordinator, 520-621-1520, Fax: 520-621-1261, E-mail: kross@eller.arizona.edu.
Website: http://finance.eller.arizona.edu/.

University of Baltimore, Graduate School, Merrick School of Business, Department of Economics, Finance, and Management Science, Baltimore, MD 21201-5779. Offers business/finance (MS). Part-time and evening/weekend programs available. *Entrance requirements:* For master's, GMAT. Additional exam requirements/recommendations for international students: Required—TOEFL (minimum score 550 paper-based). Electronic applications accepted. *Faculty research:* International finance, corporate finance, health care, regional economics, small business.

University of Bridgeport, School of Business, Bridgeport, CT 06604. Offers accounting (MBA); finance (MBA); general business (MBA); global financial services (MBA); human resource management (MBA); information systems and knowledge management (MBA); international business (MBA); management (MBA); marketing (MBA); operations management (MBA); small business and entrepreneurship (MBA); specialized business (MBA). *Accreditation:* ACBSP. Part-time and evening/weekend programs available. *Faculty:* 11 full-time (2 women), 39 part-time/adjunct (8 women). *Students:* 162 full-time (90 women), 69 part-time (45 women); includes 44 minority (20 Black or African American, non-Hispanic/Latino; 7 Asian, non-Hispanic/Latino; 15 Hispanic/Latino; 2 Two or more races, non-Hispanic/Latino), 163 international. Average age 28. 492 applicants, 48% accepted, 55 enrolled. In 2013, 144 master's awarded. *Degree requirements:* For master's, thesis optional. *Entrance requirements:* For master's, GMAT. Additional exam requirements/recommendations for international students: Recommended—TOEFL (minimum score 550 paper-based; 80 iBT), IELTS (minimum score 6.5). *Application deadline:* For fall admission, 8/1 priority date for domestic and international students; for spring admission, 12/1 priority date for domestic and international students. Applications are processed on a rolling basis. Application fee: $50. Electronic applications accepted. *Expenses:* Contact institution. *Financial support:* In 2013–14, 69 students received support. Fellowships, research assistantships, teaching assistantships, career-related internships or fieldwork, Federal Work-Study, institutionally sponsored loans, and tuition waivers (partial) available. Support available to part-time students. Financial award application deadline: 6/1; financial award applicants required to submit FAFSA. *Unit head:* Dr. Lloyd G. Gibson, Dean, 203-576-4384, Fax: 203-576-4388, E-mail: llgibson@bridgeport.edu. *Application contact:* Leanne Proctor, Director of Graduate Admissions, 203-576-4552, Fax: 203-576-4941, E-mail: mba@bridgeport.edu.
Website: http://www.bridgeport.edu.

The University of British Columbia, Sauder School of Business, Doctoral Program in Commerce and Business Administration, Vancouver, BC V6T 1Z1, Canada. Offers accounting (PhD); finance (PhD); management information systems (PhD); management science (PhD); marketing (PhD); organizational behavior (PhD); strategy and business economics (PhD); transportation and logistics (PhD); urban land economics (PhD). *Faculty:* 91 full-time (22 women). *Students:* 66 full-time (24 women). Average age 30. 418 applicants, 2% accepted, 8 enrolled. In 2013, 7 doctorates awarded. *Degree requirements:* For doctorate, comprehensive exam, thesis/dissertation. *Entrance requirements:* For doctorate, GMAT or GRE. Additional exam requirements/recommendations for international students: Required—TOEFL (minimum score 600 paper-based; 100 iBT). *Application deadline:* For fall admission, 1/31 for domestic students, 12/31 for international students. Applications are processed on a rolling basis. Application fee: $95 Canadian dollars ($153 Canadian dollars for international students). Electronic applications accepted. *Expenses: Tuition, area resident:* Full-time $8000 Canadian dollars. *Financial support:* In 2013–14, fellowships with full tuition reimbursements (averaging $17,500 per year), research assistantships with full tuition reimbursements (averaging $8,500 per year), teaching assistantships with full tuition reimbursements (averaging $17,500 per year) were awarded. Financial award application deadline: 12/31. *Unit head:* Dr. Ralph Winter, Director, 604-822-8366, Fax: 604-822-8755. *Application contact:* Elaine Cho, Administrator, PhD and M Sc Programs, 604-822-8366, Fax: 604-822-8755, E-mail: phd.program@sauder.ubc.ca.
Website: http://www.sauder.ubc.ca/.

University of California, Berkeley, Graduate Division, Haas School of Business, PhD in Business Administration Program, Berkeley, CA 94720-1500. Offers accounting (PhD); business and public policy (PhD); finance (PhD); management of organizations (PhD); marketing (PhD); operations management (PhD); real estate (PhD). *Accreditation:* AACSB. *Students:* 74 full-time (28 women); includes 11 minority (9 Asian, non-Hispanic/Latino; 2 Hispanic/Latino), 38 international. Average age 27. 490 applicants, 6% accepted, 14 enrolled. In 2013, 14 doctorates awarded. *Degree requirements:* For doctorate, comprehensive exam, thesis/dissertation, written preliminary exams, oral qualifying exam. *Entrance requirements:* For doctorate, GMAT or GRE, minimum GPA of 3.0 in undergraduate and graduate coursework. Additional exam requirements/recommendations for international students: Required—TOEFL (minimum score 570 paper-based; 70 iBT), IELTS (minimum score 7). *Application deadline:* For fall admission, 12/10 for domestic and international students. Application fee: $80 ($100 for international students). Electronic applications accepted. *Financial support:* In 2013–14, 74 students received support, including 62 fellowships with full and partial tuition reimbursements available (averaging $30,000 per year), research assistantships with full and partial tuition reimbursements available (averaging $12,000 per year), teaching assistantships with full and partial tuition reimbursements available (averaging $13,000 per year); scholarships/grants, health care benefits, tuition waivers (full), unspecified assistantships, and transit passes, travel grants also available. Financial award application deadline: 12/10; financial award applicants required to submit FAFSA. *Faculty research:* Accounting, business and public policy, entrepreneurship, finance, management of organizations, marketing, operations and information technology management, real estate. *Unit head:* Dr. Martin Lettau, Director, 510-643-6349, Fax: 510-643-4255, E-mail: kimg@haas.berkeley.edu. *Application contact:* Kim Guilfoyle, Director, Student Affairs, 510-642-3944, Fax: 510-643-4255, E-mail: kimg@haas.berkeley.edu.
Website: http://www.haas.berkeley.edu/Phd/.

University of California, Berkeley, UC Berkeley Extension, Certificate Programs in Business, Berkeley, CA 94720-1500. Offers accounting (Certificate); business administration (Certificate); finance (Certificate); human resource management (Certificate); management (Certificate); marketing (Certificate); project management (Certificate). *Accreditation:* AACSB. Postbaccalaureate distance learning degree programs offered.

University of California, Berkeley, UC Berkeley Extension, International Diploma Programs, Berkeley, CA 94720-1500. Offers business administration (Certificate); finance (Certificate); global business management (Certificate); marketing (Certificate); project management (Certificate). *Accreditation:* AACSB.

University of California, Los Angeles, Graduate Division, UCLA Anderson School of Management, Los Angeles, CA 90095-1481. Offers accounting (PhD); Americas (EMBA); Asia Pacific (EMBA); business administration (EMBA, MBA); decisions, operations and technology management (PhD); finance (PhD); financial engineering (MFE); global economics and management (PhD); management and organizations (PhD); marketing (PhD); strategy and policy (PhD); DDS/MBA; MBA/JD; MBA/MD;

MBA/MLAS; MBA/MLIS; MBA/MPH; MBA/MPP; MBA/MSCS; MBA/MSN; MBA/MUP. *Accreditation:* AACSB. Part-time programs available. *Faculty:* 104 full-time (20 women), 28 part-time/adjunct (4 women). *Students:* 1,069 full-time (324 women), 879 part-time (251 women); includes 664 minority (37 Black or African American, non-Hispanic/Latino; 1 American Indian or Alaska Native, non-Hispanic/Latino; 470 Asian, non-Hispanic/Latino; 34 Hispanic/Latino; 2 Native Hawaiian or other Pacific Islander, non-Hispanic/Latino; 120 Two or more races, non-Hispanic/Latino), 444 international. Average age 30. 5,084 applicants, 27% accepted, 845 enrolled. In 2013, 801 master's, 14 doctorates awarded. *Degree requirements:* For master's, comprehensive exam, field study consulting project (for MBA); thesis (for MFE); for doctorate, comprehensive exam, thesis/dissertation, oral and written qualifying exams. *Entrance requirements:* For master's, GMAT (for MBA); GMAT or GRE General Test (for MFE), 4-year bachelor's degree or equivalent; recommendation letters (1 for MBA, 2 for MFE); two essays; interview (by invitation only for MBA); for doctorate, GMAT or GRE General Test, bachelor's degree from college or university of fully-recognized standing; minimum B average in undergraduate coursework or B+ average in prior graduate work; statement of purpose; three recommendation letters. Additional exam requirements/recommendations for international students: Required—TOEFL (minimum score 560 paper-based; 87 iBT). *Application deadline:* For fall admission, 10/22 priority date for domestic and international students; for winter admission, 1/7 for domestic and international students; for spring admission, 4/15 for domestic and international students. Applications are processed on a rolling basis. Application fee: $200. Electronic applications accepted. *Expenses:* Contact institution. *Financial support:* In 2013–14, 522 students received support. Fellowships, research assistantships with partial tuition reimbursements available, teaching assistantships with partial tuition reimbursements available, career-related internships or fieldwork, institutionally sponsored loans, scholarships/grants, health care benefits, and tuition waivers (partial) available. Financial award application deadline: 4/15; financial award applicants required to submit FAFSA. *Faculty research:* Asset pricing, decision-making, behavioral finance, international finance and economics, global macroeconomics. *Total annual research expenditures:* $368,086. *Unit head:* Dr. Judy D. Olian, Dean/Chair in Management, 310-825-7982, Fax: 310-206-2073, E-mail: judy.olian@anderson.ucla.edu. *Application contact:* Alex Lawrence, Assistant Dean, MBA Admissions and Financial Aid, 310-825-6944, Fax: 310-825-8582, E-mail: mba.admissions@anderson.ucla.edu.
Website: http://www.anderson.ucla.edu/.

See Display on page 145 and Close-Up on page 191.

University of California, Riverside, Graduate Division, A. Gary Anderson Graduate School of Management, Riverside, CA 92521-0102. Offers accountancy (MPAC); business administration (MBA, PhD); finance (M Fin). *Accreditation:* AACSB. Part-time and evening/weekend programs available. *Faculty:* 24 full-time (6 women), 11 part-time/adjunct (3 women). *Students:* 295 full-time (161 women), 1 part-time (0 women); includes 38 minority (2 Black or African American, non-Hispanic/Latino; 31 Asian, non-Hispanic/Latino; 5 Hispanic/Latino), 237 international. Average age 24. 565 applicants, 82% accepted, 186 enrolled. In 2013, 89 master's awarded. Terminal master's awarded for partial completion of doctoral program. *Degree requirements:* For master's, thesis optional; for doctorate, comprehensive exam, thesis/dissertation. *Entrance requirements:* For master's, GMAT or GRE, minimum GPA of 3.2; for doctorate, GMAT or GRE. Additional exam requirements/recommendations for international students: Required—TOEFL (minimum score 550 paper-based; 80 iBT), IELTS. *Application deadline:* For fall admission, 9/1 for domestic students, 5/1 for international students; for winter admission, 12/1 for domestic students, 9/1 for international students; for spring admission, 3/1 for domestic students, 10/1 for international students. Applications are processed on a rolling basis. Application fee: $100 ($125 for international students). *Expenses:* Contact institution. *Financial support:* In 2013–14, 58 fellowships with partial tuition reimbursements (averaging $22,848 per year), 46 teaching assistantships with partial tuition reimbursements (averaging $20,000 per year) were awarded; research assistantships with full tuition reimbursements, career-related internships or fieldwork, institutionally sponsored loans, scholarships/grants, and tuition waivers (full) also available. Financial award application deadline: 5/1; financial award applicants required to submit FAFSA. *Faculty research:* Option pricing, marketing, decision modeling, new technologies in cost accounting, supply chain management, operations, production and inventory systems, entrepreneurial finance, e-commerce. *Unit head:* Dr. Yunzeng Wang, Dean, 951-827-6329, Fax: 951-827-3970, E-mail: mba@ucr.edu. *Application contact:* Dr. Rami Zwick, Associate Dean/Graduate Adviser, 951-827-7766, Fax: 951-827-3970, E-mail: mba@ucr.edu.
Website: http://agsm.ucr.edu/.

University of California, San Diego, Office of Graduate Studies, Rady School of Management, La Jolla, CA 92093. Offers business administration (MBA); finance (MF); management (PhD). Part-time and evening/weekend programs available. *Students:* 218 full-time (152 women), 51 part-time (35 women); includes 78 minority (5 Black or African American, non-Hispanic/Latino; 53 Asian, non-Hispanic/Latino; 20 Hispanic/Latino), 63 international. 532 applicants, 31% accepted, 99 enrolled. In 2013, 112 master's awarded. *Degree requirements:* For doctorate, thesis/dissertation. *Entrance requirements:* For master's, GMAT (for MBA); GMAT or GRE General Test (for MF); for doctorate, GMAT or GRE General Test. Additional exam requirements/recommendations for international students: Required—TOEFL, IELTS. Application fee: $80 ($100 for international students). Electronic applications accepted. *Expenses:* Tuition, state resident: full-time $11,220; part-time $1870 per quarter. Tuition, nonresident: full-time $26,322; part-time $4387 per quarter. *Required fees:* $519.50 per quarter. Part-time tuition and fees vary according to course load and program. *Financial support:* Fellowships, teaching assistantships, and scholarships/grants available. Financial award applicants required to submit FAFSA. *Unit head:* Robert Sullivan, Dean, 858-822-0830, E-mail: rss@ucsd.edu. *Application contact:* Laurel Nelson, Graduate Coordinator, 858-822-4279, E-mail: lrnelson@ucsd.edu.
Website: http://rady.ucsd.edu/.

University of California, Santa Barbara, Graduate Division, College of Letters and Sciences, Division of Social Sciences, Department of Economics, Santa Barbara, CA 93106-9210. Offers econometrics (PhD); economics (MA, PhD); environmental and natural resources (PhD); experimental and behavioral economics (PhD); labor economics (PhD); macroeconomic theory and policy (PhD); mathematical economics (PhD); public finance (PhD); MA/PhD. *Faculty:* 27 full-time (4 women), 21 part-time/adjunct (7 women). *Students:* 88 full-time (29 women); includes 13 minority (9 Asian, non-Hispanic/Latino; 4 Hispanic/Latino), 22 international. Average age 28. 412 applicants, 38% accepted, 29 enrolled. In 2013, 48 master's, 6 doctorates awarded. Terminal master's awarded for partial completion of doctoral program. *Degree requirements:* For master's, comprehensive exam; for doctorate, comprehensive exam, thesis/dissertation. *Entrance requirements:* For master's and doctorate, GRE General Test, 3 letters of recommendation, statement of purpose, personal achievements/contributions statement, resume/curriculum vitae, transcripts for post-secondary institutions attended. Additional exam requirements/recommendations for international students: Required—TOEFL (minimum score 550 paper-based; 80 iBT), IELTS (minimum score 7). *Application deadline:* For fall admission, 12/1 priority date for domestic and international students. Application fee: $80 ($100 for international students). Electronic applications accepted. *Expenses:* Tuition, state resident: part-time $5148.26 per quarter. Tuition, nonresident: part-time $10,182.26 per quarter. *Financial support:* In 2013–14, 65 students received support, including 17 fellowships with full and partial tuition reimbursements available (averaging $19,000 per year), 7 research assistantships with full and partial tuition reimbursements available (averaging $19,000 per year), 106 teaching assistantships with partial tuition reimbursements available (averaging $17,000 per year); Federal Work-Study, institutionally sponsored loans, scholarships/grants, health care benefits, tuition waivers (full and partial), and unspecified assistantships also available. Support available to part-time students. Financial award application deadline: 12/1; financial award applicants required to submit FAFSA. *Faculty research:* Labor economics, econometrics, macroeconomic theory and policy, environmental and natural resources economics, experimental and behavioral economics. *Unit head:* Prof. Javier Birchenall, Director of Graduate Studies, 805-893-5275, Fax: 805-893-8830, E-mail: jabirche@econ.ucsb.edu. *Application contact:* Mark Patterson, Graduate Advisor, 805-893-2205, Fax: 805-893-8830, E-mail: mark.patterson@.ucsb.edu.
Website: http://www.econ.ucsb.edu/.

University of California, Santa Cruz, Division of Graduate Studies, Division of Social Sciences, Program in Applied Economics and Finance, Santa Cruz, CA 95064. Offers MS. *Degree requirements:* For master's, thesis or alternative, project. *Entrance requirements:* For master's, GRE General Test, GRE Subject Test. Additional exam requirements/recommendations for international students: Required—TOEFL (minimum score 550 paper-based; 83 iBT); Recommended—IELTS (minimum score 8). Electronic applications accepted. *Faculty research:* Economic decision-making skills for the design and operation of complex institutional systems.

University of Central Missouri, The Graduate School, Warrensburg, MO 6409. Offers accountancy (MA); accounting (MBA); applied mathematics (MS); aviation safety (MA); biology (MS); business administration (MBA); career and technical education leadership (MS); college student personnel administration (MS); communication (MA); computer science (MS); counseling (MS); criminal justice (MS); educational leadership (Ed D); educational technology (MS); elementary and early childhood education (MSE); English (MA); environmental studies (MA); finance (MBA); history (MA); human services/educational technology (Ed S); human services/learning resources (Ed S); human services/professional counseling (Ed S); industrial hygiene (MS); industrial management (MS); information systems (MBA); information technology (MS); kinesiology (MS); library science and information services (MS); literacy education (MSE); marketing (MBA); mathematics (MS); music (MA); occupational safety management (MS); psychology (MS); rural family nursing (MS); school administration (MSE); social gerontology (MS); sociology (MA); special education (MSE); speech language pathology (MS); superintendency (Ed S); teaching (MAT); teaching English as a second language (MA); technology (MS); technology management (PhD); theatre (MA). Part-time programs available. *Faculty:* 233. *Students:* 890 full-time (396 women), 1,486 part-time (1,001 women); includes 192 minority (97 Black or African American, non-Hispanic/Latino; 9 American Indian or Alaska Native, non-Hispanic/Latino; 32 Asian, non-Hispanic/Latino; 40 Hispanic/Latino; 3 Native Hawaiian or other Pacific Islander, non-Hispanic/Latino; 11 Two or more races, non-Hispanic/Latino), 539 international. Average age 31. 1,953 applicants, 75% accepted. In 2013, 719 master's, 58 other advanced degrees awarded. *Degree requirements:* For master's and Ed S, comprehensive exam (for some programs), thesis (for some programs). *Entrance requirements:* Additional exam requirements/recommendations for international students: Required—TOEFL (minimum score 550 paper-based; 79 iBT). *Application deadline:* For fall admission, 6/1 for domestic students; for spring admission, 10/1 for domestic and international students. Applications are processed on a rolling basis. Application fee: $30 ($75 for international students). Electronic applications accepted. *Expenses:* Tuition, state resident: full-time $7326; part-time $276.25 per credit hour. Tuition, nonresident: full-time $13,956; part-time $552.50 per credit hour. *Required fees:* $29 per credit hour. *Financial support:* In 2013–14, 118 students received support, including 271 research assistantships with full and partial tuition reimbursements available (averaging $7,500 per year), 109 teaching assistantships with full and partial tuition reimbursements available (averaging $7,500 per year); career-related internships or fieldwork, Federal Work-Study, scholarships/grants, and administrative and laboratory assistantships also available. Support available to part-time students. Financial award application deadline: 3/1; financial award applicants required to submit FAFSA. *Unit head:* Dr. Joseph Vaughn, Assistant Provost for Research/Dean, 660-543-4092, Fax: 660-543-4778, E-mail: vaughn@ucmo.edu. *Application contact:* Brittany Lawrence, Graduate Student Services Coordinator, 660-543-4621, Fax: 660-543-4778, E-mail: gradinfo@ucmo.edu.
Website: http://www.ucmo.edu/graduate/.

University of Chicago, Booth School of Business, Full-Time MBA Program, Chicago, IL 60637. Offers accounting (MBA); analytic finance (MBA); analytic management (MBA); econometrics and statistics (MBA); economics (MBA); entrepreneurship (MBA); finance (MBA); general management (MBA); health administration and policy (Certificate); human resource management (MBA); international business (MBA); managerial and organizational behavior (MBA); marketing management (MBA); operations management (MBA); strategic management (MBA); MBA/AM; MBA/JD; MBA/MA; MBA/MD; MBA/MPP. *Accreditation:* AACSB. Part-time and evening/weekend programs available. Terminal master's awarded for partial completion of doctoral program. *Entrance requirements:* For master's, GMAT, 2 letters of recommendation, 3 essays, resume, interview. Additional exam requirements/recommendations for international students: Required—TOEFL (minimum score 600 paper-based; 104 iBT), IELTS. Electronic applications accepted. *Expenses:* Contact institution. *Faculty research:* Finance, marketing, economics, entrepreneurship, strategy, management.

University of Cincinnati, Graduate School, Carl H. Lindner College of Business, MS Program, Cincinnati, OH 45221. Offers accounting (MS); business analytics (MS); finance (MS); information systems (MS); marketing (MS); taxation (MS). Part-time and evening/weekend programs available. *Faculty:* 39 full-time (11 women), 11 part-time/adjunct (3 women). *Students:* 275 full-time (105 women), 165 part-time (69 women); includes 29 minority (14 Black or African American, non-Hispanic/Latino; 9 Asian, non-Hispanic/Latino; 1 Native Hawaiian or other Pacific Islander, non-Hispanic/Latino; 5 Two or more races, non-Hispanic/Latino), 273 international. 953 applicants, 37% accepted, 258 enrolled. In 2013, 144 master's awarded. *Degree requirements:* For master's, thesis (for some programs). *Entrance requirements:* For master's, GMAT, GRE, resume, transcripts, essays, letters of recommendation. Additional exam requirements/recommendations for international students: Required—TOEFL (minimum score 600 paper-based; 100 iBT), IELTS (minimum score 6.5). *Application deadline:* For fall admission, 3/15 priority date for domestic students, 4/1 for international students. Applications are processed on a rolling basis. Application fee: $65 ($70 for international students). Electronic applications accepted. *Expenses:* Contact institution. *Financial support:* In 2013–14, 124 students received support, including 12 teaching assistantships with full and partial tuition reimbursements available (averaging $3,500 per year); scholarships/grants, tuition waivers (full and partial), and unspecified assistantships also available. Financial award application deadline: 2/1; financial award applicants required to submit FAFSA. *Faculty research:* Real estate, empirical pricing, organization information pricing, strategic management, portfolio choice in institutional investment. *Unit head:* Dr. David Szymanski, Dean, 513-556-7001, Fax: 513-556-4891,

E-mail: david.szymanski@uc.edu. *Application contact:* Dona Clary, Director, Graduate Programs, 513-556-3546, Fax: 513-558-7006, E-mail: dona.clary@uc.edu.

University of Cincinnati, Graduate School, Carl H. Lindner College of Business, PhD Programs, Cincinnati, OH 45221. Offers accounting (PhD); economics (PhD); finance (PhD); information systems (PhD); management (PhD); marketing (PhD); operations and business analytics (PhD). *Faculty:* 62 full-time (13 women). *Students:* 27 full-time (15 women), 9 part-time (1 woman); includes 2 minority (1 Asian, non-Hispanic/Latino; 1 Hispanic/Latino), 16 international. Average age 29. 86 applicants, 13% accepted, 6 enrolled. In 2013, 8 doctorates awarded. *Degree requirements:* For doctorate, comprehensive exam, thesis/dissertation. *Entrance requirements:* For doctorate, GMAT, GRE, transcripts, essays, resume, letters of recommendation. Additional exam requirements/recommendations for international students: Required—TOEFL (minimum score 600 paper-based; 100 iBT), IELTS (minimum score 6.5). *Application deadline:* For fall admission, 1/15 for domestic and international students. Application fee: $65 ($70 for international students). Electronic applications accepted. *Expenses:* Contact institution. *Financial support:* In 2013–14, 33 students received support, including 25 research assistantships with full and partial tuition reimbursements available (averaging $23,250 per year); scholarships/grants, tuition waivers (full and partial), and unspecified assistantships also available. Financial award application deadline: 1/15; financial award applicants required to submit FAFSA. *Unit head:* Dr. Suzanne Masterson, Director, 513-556-7125, Fax: 513-556-5499, E-mail: suzanne.masterson@uc.edu. *Application contact:* Angel Elvin, Assistant Director, 513-556-7190, Fax: 513-558-7006, E-mail: angel.elvin@uc.edu.
Website: http://www.business.uc.edu/phd.

University of Colorado Boulder, Leeds School of Business, Division of Business Administration, Boulder, CO 80309. Offers accounting (MS, PhD); finance (PhD); information systems (PhD); marketing (PhD); operations (PhD); strategic, organizational, and entrepreneurial studies (PhD). *Students:* 143 full-time (72 women), 2 part-time (1 woman); includes 15 minority (1 Black or African American, non-Hispanic/Latino; 2 American Indian or Alaska Native, non-Hispanic/Latino; 5 Asian, non-Hispanic/Latino; 6 Hispanic/Latino; 1 Two or more races, non-Hispanic/Latino), 37 international. Average age 25. 281 applicants, 12% accepted, 19 enrolled. In 2013, 50 master's, 8 doctorates awarded. *Entrance requirements:* For master's, GMAT, minimum undergraduate GPA of 3.0. *Application deadline:* For fall admission, 3/31 for domestic students, 3/1 for international students; for spring admission, 10/31 for domestic and international students. Application fee: $50 ($60 for international students). Electronic applications accepted. *Financial support:* In 2013–14, 145 students received support, including 37 fellowships (averaging $3,977 per year), 27 research assistantships with full and partial tuition reimbursements available (averaging $40,893 per year), 12 teaching assistantships with full and partial tuition reimbursements available (averaging $38,197 per year); institutionally sponsored loans, scholarships/grants, health care benefits, and unspecified assistantships also available. Financial award applicants required to submit FAFSA.

University of Colorado Denver, Business School, Master of Business Administration Program, Denver, CO 80217. Offers bioinnovation and entrepreneurship (MBA); business intelligence (MBA); business strategy (MBA); business to business marketing (MBA); business to consumer marketing (MBA); change management (MBA); corporate financial management (MBA); enterprise technology management (MBA); entrepreneurship (MBA); health administration (MBA), including financial management, health administration, health information technologies, international health management and policy; human resources management (MBA); international business (MBA); investment management (MBA); managing for sustainability (MBA); sports and entertainment management (MBA). *Accreditation:* AACSB. Part-time and evening/weekend programs available. Postbaccalaureate distance learning degree programs offered (no on-campus study). *Students:* 611 full-time (246 women), 144 part-time (58 women); includes 102 minority (14 Black or African American, non-Hispanic/Latino; 2 American Indian or Alaska Native, non-Hispanic/Latino; 38 Asian, non-Hispanic/Latino; 42 Hispanic/Latino; 6 Two or more races, non-Hispanic/Latino), 26 international. Average age 32. 330 applicants, 64% accepted, 125 enrolled. In 2013, 398 master's awarded. *Degree requirements:* For master's, 48 semester hours, including 30 of core courses, 3 in international business, and 15 in electives from over 50 other graduate business courses. *Entrance requirements:* For master's, GMAT, resume, official transcripts, essay, two letters of recommendation, financial statements (for international applicants). Additional exam requirements/recommendations for international students: Required—TOEFL (minimum score 560 paper-based; 83 iBT); Recommended—IELTS (minimum score 6.5). *Application deadline:* For fall admission, 4/15 priority date for domestic students, 3/15 priority date for international students; for spring admission, 10/15 priority date for domestic students, 9/15 priority date for international students. Applications are processed on a rolling basis. Application fee: $50 ($75 for international students). Electronic applications accepted. *Expenses:* Contact institution. *Financial support:* In 2013–14, 62 students received support. Fellowships, research assistantships, teaching assistantships, Federal Work-Study, institutionally sponsored loans, scholarships/grants, traineeships, and unspecified assistantships available. Financial award application deadline: 4/1; financial award applicants required to submit FAFSA. *Faculty research:* Marketing, management, entrepreneurship, finance, health administration. *Unit head:* Elizabeth Cooperman, Professor of Finance and Managing for Sustainability/MBA Program Director, 303-315-8422, E-mail: elizabeth.cooperman@ucdenver.edu. *Application contact:* Shelly Townley, Admissions Director, Graduate Programs, 303-315-8202, E-mail: shelly.townley@ucdenver.edu.
Website: http://www.ucdenver.edu/academics/colleges/business/degrees/mba/Pages/MBA.aspx.

University of Colorado Denver, Business School, Program in Finance, Denver, CO 80217. Offers economics (MS); finance (MS); financial analysis and management (MS); financial and commodities risk management (MS); risk management and insurance (MS); MS/MA; MS/MBA. Part-time and evening/weekend programs available. *Students:* 84 full-time (22 women), 29 part-time (6 women); includes 16 minority (2 Black or African American, non-Hispanic/Latino; 6 Asian, non-Hispanic/Latino; 6 Hispanic/Latino; 2 Two or more races, non-Hispanic/Latino), 36 international. Average age 28. 119 applicants, 68% accepted, 38 enrolled. In 2013, 36 master's awarded. *Degree requirements:* For master's, 30 semester hours (18 of required core courses, 9 of finance electives, and 3 of free elective). *Entrance requirements:* For master's, GMAT, essay, resume, two letters of recommendation, financial statements (for international students). Additional exam requirements/recommendations for international students: Required—TOEFL (minimum score 537 paper-based; 75 iBT); Recommended—IELTS (minimum score 6.5). *Application deadline:* For fall admission, 4/15 for domestic students, 3/15 for international students; for spring admission, 10/15 for domestic students, 9/15 for international students. Applications are processed on a rolling basis. Application fee: $50 ($75 for international students). Electronic applications accepted. *Expenses:* Contact institution. *Financial support:* In 2013–14, 20 students received support. Teaching assistantships, Federal Work-Study, institutionally sponsored loans, scholarships/grants, and traineeships available. Financial award application deadline: 4/1; financial award applicants required to submit FAFSA. *Faculty research:* Corporate governance, debt maturity policies, regulation and financial markets, option management strategies. *Unit head:* Dr. Ajeyo Banerjee, Associate Professor/Director of MS in Finance Program, 303-315-8456, E-mail: ajeyo.banerjee@ucdenver.edu. *Application contact:* Shelly Townley, Director of Graduate Admissions, 303-315-8202, E-mail: shelly.townley@ucdenver.edu.
Website: http://www.ucdenver.edu/academics/colleges/business/degrees/ms/finance/Pages/Finance.aspx.

University of Connecticut, Graduate School, College of Liberal Arts and Sciences, Department of Public Policy, Field of Public Administration, Storrs, CT 06269. Offers nonprofit management (Graduate Certificate); public administration (MPA); public financial management (Graduate Certificate); JD/MPA; MPA/MSW. *Accreditation:* NASPAA. *Degree requirements:* For master's, comprehensive exam, internship. *Entrance requirements:* For master's, GRE General Test. Additional exam requirements/recommendations for international students: Required—TOEFL (minimum score 550 paper-based). Electronic applications accepted.

University of Connecticut, Graduate School, School of Business, Storrs, CT 06269. Offers accounting (MS, PhD); business administration (Exec MBA, MBA, PhD); finance (PhD); health care management and insurance studies (MBA); management (PhD); management consulting (MBA); marketing (PhD); marketing intelligence (MBA); MA/MBA; MBA/MSW. *Accreditation:* AACSB. *Degree requirements:* For master's, comprehensive exam; for doctorate, thesis/dissertation. *Entrance requirements:* For master's and doctorate, GMAT. Additional exam requirements/recommendations for international students: Required—TOEFL (minimum score 550 paper-based). Electronic applications accepted.

University of Dallas, Graduate School of Management, Irving, TX 75062-4736. Offers accounting (MBA, MM, MS); business management (MBA, MM); corporate finance (MBA, MM); financial services (MBA); global business (MBA, MM); health services management (MBA, MM); human resource management (MBA, MM); information assurance (MBA, MM, MS); information technology (MBA, MM, MS); information technology service management (MBA, MM, MS); marketing management (MBA, MM); organization development (MBA, MM); project management (MBA, MM); sports and entertainment management (MBA, MM); strategic leadership (MBA, MM); supply chain management (MBA); supply chain management and market logistics (MM). *Accreditation:* ACBSP. Part-time and evening/weekend programs available. Postbaccalaureate distance learning degree programs offered (no on-campus study). *Entrance requirements:* Additional exam requirements/recommendations for international students: Required—TOEFL. Electronic applications accepted. *Expenses:* Contact institution.

University of Dayton, School of Business Administration, Dayton, OH 45469-1300. Offers accounting (MBA); cyber security (MBA); finance (MBA); marketing (MBA); JD/MBA. *Accreditation:* AACSB. Part-time and evening/weekend programs available. *Faculty:* 20 full-time (7 women), 8 part-time/adjunct (1 woman). *Students:* 166 full-time (76 women), 85 part-time (43 women); includes 10 minority (4 Black or African American, non-Hispanic/Latino; 4 Asian, non-Hispanic/Latino; 2 Hispanic/Latino), 96 international. Average age 27. 437 applicants, 44% accepted, 53 enrolled. In 2013, 119 master's awarded. *Entrance requirements:* For master's, GMAT or GRE. Additional exam requirements/recommendations for international students: Required—TOEFL (minimum score 550 paper-based; 80 iBT); Recommended—IELTS (minimum score 6.5). *Application deadline:* For fall admission, 5/1 priority date for international students; for winter admission, 7/1 for international students; for spring admission, 11/1 priority date for international students. Applications are processed on a rolling basis. Application fee: $0 ($50 for international students). Electronic applications accepted. *Expenses:* Contact institution. *Financial support:* In 2013–14, 10 research assistantships with partial tuition reimbursements (averaging $7,020 per year) were awarded; institutionally sponsored loans, health care benefits, and unspecified assistantships also available. Financial award application deadline: 3/1; financial award applicants required to submit FAFSA. *Faculty research:* Management information systems, economics, finance, entrepreneurship, marketing, accounting and cyber security. *Unit head:* John M. Gentner, Director, MBA Program, 937-229-3733, Fax: 937-229-3882, E-mail: jgentner1@udayton.edu. *Application contact:* Mandy Schrank, Assistant Director, MBA Program, 937-229-3733, Fax: 937-229-3882, E-mail: mschrank2@udayton.edu.
Website: http://business.udayton.edu/mba/.

University of Delaware, Alfred Lerner College of Business and Economics, Department of Finance, Newark, DE 19716. Offers MS.

University of Denver, Daniels College of Business, Reiman School of Finance, Denver, CO 80208. Offers IMBA, MBA, MS. Part-time and evening/weekend programs available. *Faculty:* 18 full-time (4 women), 5 part-time/adjunct (0 women). *Students:* 88 full-time (47 women), 38 part-time (20 women); includes 1 minority (Asian, non-Hispanic/Latino), 111 international. Average age 25. 647 applicants, 53% accepted, 61 enrolled. In 2013, 74 master's awarded. *Entrance requirements:* For master's, GRE General Test or GMAT, bachelor's degree, transcripts, resume, two letters of recommendation, essays, interview. Additional exam requirements/recommendations for international students: Required—TOEFL (minimum score 570 paper-based; 88 iBT). *Application deadline:* For fall admission, 11/15 priority date for domestic and international students; for spring admission, 10/15 priority date for domestic and international students. Applications are processed on a rolling basis. Application fee: $100. Electronic applications accepted. *Financial support:* In 2013–14, 31 students received support, including 8 teaching assistantships with full and partial tuition reimbursements available (averaging $7,728 per year); career-related internships or fieldwork, Federal Work-Study, institutionally sponsored loans, scholarships/grants, and unspecified assistantships also available. Support available to part-time students. Financial award application deadline: 2/15; financial award applicants required to submit FAFSA. *Unit head:* Dr. Thomajean (Tommi) Johnsen, Associate Professor and Director, 303-871-2282, E-mail: thomajean_johnsen@du.edu. *Application contact:* Lynn Noel, Graduate Admissions Manager, 303-871-7895, E-mail: lynn.noel@du.edu.
Website: http://daniels.du.edu/masters-degrees/finance/.

University of Florida, Graduate School, Warrington College of Business Administration, Hough Graduate School of Business, Department of Finance, Insurance and Real Estate, Gainesville, FL 32611. Offers entrepreneurship (MS); finance (MS, PhD); financial services (Certificate); insurance (PhD); quantitative finance (PhD); real estate (MS); real estate and urban analysis (PhD); JD/MBA; JD/MS. *Faculty:* 17 full-time (0 women), 6 part-time/adjunct (0 women). *Students:* 77 full-time (20 women), 4 part-time (2 women); includes 11 minority (3 Black or African American, non-Hispanic/Latino; 1 American Indian or Alaska Native, non-Hispanic/Latino; 2 Asian, non-Hispanic/Latino; 5 Hispanic/Latino), 23 international. Average age 27. 226 applicants, 4% accepted, 8 enrolled. In 2013, 92 master's, 5 doctorates awarded. Terminal master's awarded for partial completion of doctoral program. *Degree requirements:* For master's, comprehensive exam, thesis; for doctorate, comprehensive exam, thesis/dissertation. *Entrance requirements:* For master's, GMAT (minimum score of 465) or GRE General Test, minimum GPA of 3.0 for last 60 hours of undergraduate degree, work experience (preferred); for doctorate, GMAT (minimum score of 465) or GRE General Test, minimum GPA of 3.0. Additional exam requirements/recommendations for international students: Required—TOEFL (minimum score 550 paper-based; 80 iBT), IELTS (minimum score 6). *Application deadline:* For fall admission, 1/15 priority date for domestic students, 1/15 for international students. Applications are processed on a

rolling basis. Application fee: $30. Electronic applications accepted. *Expenses:* Tuition, state resident: full-time $12,640. Tuition, nonresident: full-time $30,000. *Financial support:* In 2013–14, 19 students received support, including 13 research assistantships (averaging $18,787 per year), 6 teaching assistantships (averaging $14,970 per year); career-related internships or fieldwork, scholarships/grants, and unspecified assistantships also available. Financial award application deadline: 1/15; financial award applicants required to submit FAFSA. *Faculty research:* Banking, empirical corporate finance, hedge funds. *Unit head:* Mahendrarajah Nimalendran, PhD, Chair, 352-392-9526, Fax: 352-392-0301, E-mail: nimal@ufl.edu. *Application contact:* Office of Admissions, 352-392-1365, E-mail: webrequests@admissions.ufl.edu.
Website: http://www.cba.ufl.edu/fire/.

University of Florida, Graduate School, Warrington College of Business Administration, Hough Graduate School of Business, Programs in Business Administration, Gainesville, FL 32611. Offers business administration (MBA); competitive strategy (MBA); entrepreneurship (MBA); finance (MBA); global management (MBA); Graham-Buffett security analysis (MBA); human resource management (MBA); information systems and operations management (MBA); international studies (MBA); Latin American business (MBA); management (MBA); marketing (MBA); real estate (MBA); sports administration (MBA); JD/MBA; MBA/MS; MBA/PhD; MBA/Pharm D; MD/MBA. *Accreditation:* AACSB. Part-time and evening/weekend programs available. Postbaccalaureate distance learning degree programs offered. *Faculty:* 72 full-time (10 women), 29 part-time/adjunct (7 women). *Students:* 440 full-time (122 women), 472 part-time (159 women); includes 203 minority (43 Black or African American, non-Hispanic/Latino; 3 American Indian or Alaska Native, non-Hispanic/Latino; 64 Asian, non-Hispanic/Latino; 92 Hispanic/Latino; 1 Native Hawaiian or other Pacific Islander, non-Hispanic/Latino), 39 international. Average age 32. 568 applicants, 58% accepted, 261 enrolled. In 2013, 405 master's awarded. *Degree requirements:* For master's, capstone course. *Entrance requirements:* For master's, GMAT (minimum score 465), minimum GPA of 3.0, interview. Additional exam requirements/recommendations for international students: Required—TOEFL (minimum score 550 paper-based; 80 iBT), IELTS (minimum score 6). *Application deadline:* For fall admission, 7/1 for domestic students, 1/1 for international students; for spring admission, 12/1 for domestic and international students. Applications are processed on a rolling basis. Application fee: $30. Electronic applications accepted. *Expenses:* Tuition, state resident: full-time $12,640. Tuition, nonresident: full-time $30,000. *Financial support:* In 2013–14, 24 students received support, including 24 teaching assistantships (averaging $6,143 per year); career-related internships or fieldwork, scholarships/grants, and unspecified assistantships also available. Support available to part-time students. Financial award applicants required to submit FAFSA. *Faculty research:* Accounting, finance, insurance, management, real estate, urban analysis marketing. *Unit head:* Alexander D. Sevilla, Assistant Dean/Director of MBA Program, 352-273-3252, Fax: 352-392-8791, E-mail: alex.sevilla@warrington.ufl.edu. *Application contact:* Andrew S. Lord, Senior Director of Admissions, 352-273-3241, Fax: 352-392-8791, E-mail: andrew.lord@warrington.ufl.edu.
Website: http://www.floridamba.ufl.edu/.

University of Hawaii at Manoa, Graduate Division, Shidler College of Business, Program in Business Administration, Honolulu, HI 96822. Offers Asian business studies (MBA); Chinese business studies (MBA); decision sciences (MBA); entrepreneurship (MBA); finance (MBA); finance and banking (MBA); human resources management (MBA); information management (MBA); information technology (MBA); international business (MBA); Japanese business studies (MBA); marketing (MBA); organizational behavior (MBA); organizational management (MBA); real estate (MBA); student-designed track (MBA). *Accreditation:* AACSB. Part-time and evening/weekend programs available. *Degree requirements:* For master's, thesis optional. *Entrance requirements:* For master's, GMAT, minimum GPA of 3.0. Additional exam requirements/recommendations for international students: Required—TOEFL (minimum score 600 paper-based; 100 iBT), IELTS (minimum score 7). *Expenses:* Contact institution.

University of Hawaii at Manoa, Graduate Division, Shidler College of Business, Program in International Management, Honolulu, HI 96822. Offers Asian finance (PhD); global information technology management (PhD); international accounting (PhD); international marketing (PhD); international organization and strategy (PhD). Part-time programs available. *Degree requirements:* For doctorate, comprehensive exam, thesis/dissertation. *Entrance requirements:* For doctorate, GMAT or GRE General Test, minimum GPA of 3.0. Additional exam requirements/recommendations for international students: Required—TOEFL (minimum score 600 paper-based; 100 iBT), IELTS (minimum score 7). *Expenses:* Contact institution.

University of Houston, Bauer College of Business, Finance Program, Houston, TX 77204. Offers MS. Part-time and evening/weekend programs available. *Degree requirements:* For master's, 30 hours completed in residence, minimum cumulative GPA of 3.0 at UH, no more than 11 semester hours of 'C' grades or below in graduate courses taken at UH. *Entrance requirements:* For master's, GMAT or GRE, official transcripts from all higher education institutions attended, resume, goal statement, letters of recommendation. Additional exam requirements/recommendations for international students: Required—TOEFL (minimum score 620 paper-based; 105 iBT), IELTS (minimum score 7.5). Electronic applications accepted. *Faculty research:* Accountancy and taxation, finance, international business, management.

University of Houston–Clear Lake, School of Business, Program in Finance, Houston, TX 77058-1002. Offers MS. Part-time and evening/weekend programs available. *Degree requirements:* For master's, thesis optional. *Entrance requirements:* For master's, GMAT. Additional exam requirements/recommendations for international students: Required—TOEFL (minimum score 550 paper-based). Electronic applications accepted.

University of Houston–Downtown, College of Business, Houston, TX 77002. Offers finance (MBA); general management (MBA); human resource management (MBA); leadership (MBA); sales management and business development (MBA); supply chain management (MBA). Evening/weekend programs available. *Faculty:* 18 full-time (7 women). *Students:* 1 (woman) full-time, 88 part-time (32 women); includes 60 minority (18 Black or African American, non-Hispanic/Latino; 10 Asian, non-Hispanic/Latino; 30 Hispanic/Latino; 1 Native Hawaiian or other Pacific Islander, non-Hispanic/Latino; 1 Two or more races, non-Hispanic/Latino), 2 international. Average age 33. 41 applicants, 63% accepted, 24 enrolled. *Entrance requirements:* For master's, GMAT, official transcripts, bachelor's degree or equivalent, resume, 2 professional references. Additional exam requirements/recommendations for international students: Required—TOEFL (minimum score 81 iBT). *Application deadline:* For fall admission, 7/15 for domestic and international students. Applications are processed on a rolling basis. Application fee: $35 ($60 for international students). Electronic applications accepted. *Expenses:* Contact institution. *Financial support:* In 2013–14, 2 fellowships (averaging $6,000 per year) were awarded. Financial award application deadline: 4/1; financial award applicants required to submit FAFSA. *Faculty research:* Corporate finance, sustainability, recruitment and selection, international strategic management, gender and race discrimination. *Unit head:* Dr. D. Michael Fields, Dean, College of Business, 713-221-8179, Fax: 713-221-8675, E-mail: fieldsd@uhd.edu. *Application contact:* Ceshia Love, Assistant Director of Graduate Admissions, 713-221-8093, Fax: 713-223-7408, E-mail: gradadmissions@uhd.edu.
Website: http://mba.uhd.edu/.

University of Houston–Victoria, School of Business Administration, Victoria, TX 77901-4450. Offers accounting (MBA); economic development and entrepreneurship (MS); finance (GMBA, MBA); general business (MBA); international business (MBA); management (GMBA, MBA); marketing (MBA). *Accreditation:* AACSB. Part-time and evening/weekend programs available. Postbaccalaureate distance learning degree programs offered (minimal on-campus study). *Faculty:* 45 full-time (15 women). *Students:* 193 full-time (93 women), 673 part-time (325 women); includes 489 minority (185 Black or African American, non-Hispanic/Latino; 169 Asian, non-Hispanic/Latino; 114 Hispanic/Latino; 1 Native Hawaiian or other Pacific Islander, non-Hispanic/Latino; 20 Two or more races, non-Hispanic/Latino), 94 international. *Entrance requirements:* For master's, GMAT. Additional exam requirements/recommendations for international students: Required—TOEFL (minimum score 550 paper-based). *Application deadline:* For fall admission, 6/1 for international students; for spring admission, 10/1 for international students. Applications are processed on a rolling basis. Application fee: $0. Electronic applications accepted. *Expenses:* Tuition, state resident: full-time $4534; part-time $251 per credit hour. Tuition, nonresident: full-time $10,906; part-time $606 per contact hour. *Required fees:* $68 per semester hour. Tuition and fees vary according to course load. *Financial support:* In 2013–14, research assistantships with partial tuition reimbursements (averaging $2,000 per year), teaching assistantships with partial tuition reimbursements (averaging $2,000 per year) were awarded; Federal Work-Study, scholarships/grants, and unspecified assistantships also available. Support available to part-time students. Financial award application deadline: 4/15; financial award applicants required to submit FAFSA. *Faculty research:* Economic development, marketing, finance. *Unit head:* Dr. Farhang Niroomand, Dean, 361-570-4230, Fax: 361-580-5599, E-mail: niroomandf@uhv.edu. *Application contact:* Admissions and Records, 361-570-4359, Fax: 361-580-5500, E-mail: admissions@uhv.edu.
Website: http://www.uhv.edu/bus/.

University of Illinois at Urbana–Champaign, Graduate College, College of Business, Department of Finance, Champaign, IL 61820. Offers MS, PhD. *Students:* 138 (65 women). Application fee: $75 ($90 for international students). *Unit head:* Louis K. Chan, Chair, 217-333-6391, Fax: 217-244-3102, E-mail: l-chan2@illinois.edu. *Application contact:* Denise Madden, Office Support Associate, 217-244-2371, Fax: 217-244-9867, E-mail: djmadden@illinois.edu.
Website: http://www.business.illinois.edu/finance.

The University of Iowa, Henry B. Tippie College of Business, Department of Finance, Iowa City, IA 52242-1316. Offers PhD. *Faculty:* 22 full-time (4 women), 11 part-time/adjunct (2 women). *Students:* 15 full-time (5 women), 1 part-time (0 women); includes 2 minority (both Asian, non-Hispanic/Latino), 9 international. Average age 32. 74 applicants, 7% accepted, 4 enrolled. *Degree requirements:* For doctorate, comprehensive exam, thesis/dissertation, thesis defense. *Entrance requirements:* For doctorate, GMAT or GRE. Additional exam requirements/recommendations for international students: Recommended—TOEFL (minimum score 100 iBT), IELTS (minimum score 7). *Application deadline:* For fall admission, 1/15 for domestic and international students. Applications are processed on a rolling basis. Application fee: $60 ($100 for international students). Electronic applications accepted. *Financial support:* In 2013–14, 15 students received support, including 2 fellowships with full tuition reimbursements available (averaging $17,680 per year), 13 teaching assistantships with full tuition reimbursements available (averaging $17,680 per year); institutionally sponsored loans, scholarships/grants, health care benefits, and unspecified assistantships also available. Financial award application deadline: 1/15. *Faculty research:* International finance, real estate finance, theoretical and empirical corporate finance, theoretical and empirical asset pricing bond pricing and derivatives. *Unit head:* Prof. Erik Lie, Department Executive Officer, 319-335-0929, Fax: 319-335-3690, E-mail: erik-lie@uiowa.edu. *Application contact:* Renea L. Jay, PhD Program Coordinator, 319-335-0830, Fax: 319-335-1956, E-mail: renea-jay@uiowa.edu.
Website: http://tippie.uiowa.edu/finance/.

The University of Iowa, Henry B. Tippie College of Business, Henry B. Tippie School of Management, Iowa City, IA 52242-1316. Offers corporate finance (MBA); investment management (MBA); marketing (MBA); strategic management and innovation (MBA); supply chain and analytics (MBA); JD/MBA; MBA/MA; MBA/MD; MBA/MHA; MBA/MSN. *Accreditation:* AACSB. Part-time and evening/weekend programs available. *Faculty:* 113 full-time (27 women), 89 part-time/adjunct (23 women). *Students:* 110 full-time (28 women), 786 part-time (236 women); includes 51 minority (13 Black or African American, non-Hispanic/Latino; 3 American Indian or Alaska Native, non-Hispanic/Latino; 23 Asian, non-Hispanic/Latino; 12 Hispanic/Latino), 162 international. Average age 33. 622 applicants, 73% accepted, 383 enrolled. In 2013, 333 master's awarded. *Degree requirements:* For master's, minimum GPA of 2.75. *Entrance requirements:* For master's, GMAT, GRE, quality work experience and leadership as shown through resume, references, and essays. Additional exam requirements/recommendations for international students: Required—TOEFL (minimum score 600 paper-based; 100 iBT), IELTS (minimum score 7). *Application deadline:* For fall admission, 7/30 for domestic students, 4/1 for international students; for spring admission, 12/30 for domestic and international students. Applications are processed on a rolling basis. Application fee: $60 ($100 for international students). Electronic applications accepted. *Expenses:* Contact institution. *Financial support:* In 2013–14, 96 students received support, including 102 fellowships (averaging $9,519 per year), 83 research assistantships with partial tuition reimbursements available (averaging $8,893 per year), 14 teaching assistantships with partial tuition reimbursements available (averaging $17,049 per year); career-related internships or fieldwork, scholarships/grants, health care benefits, and unspecified assistantships also available. Financial award application deadline: 7/30; financial award applicants required to submit FAFSA. *Faculty research:* Capital markets, econometrics, optimization, investments and empirical corporate finance, Iowa electronic markets. *Unit head:* Prof. David W. Frasier, Associate Dean, Tippie School of Management, 800-622-4692, Fax: 319-335-3604, E-mail: david-frasier@uiowa.edu. *Application contact:* Jodi Schafer, Director, MBA Admissions and Financial Aid, 319-335-0864, Fax: 319-335-3604, E-mail: jodi-schafer@uiowa.edu.
Website: http://tippie.uiowa.edu/mba.

University of La Verne, College of Business and Public Management, Graduate Programs in Business Administration, La Verne, CA 91750-4443. Offers accounting (MBA); executive management (MBA-EP); finance (MBA, MBA-EP); health services management (MBA); information technology (MBA, MBA-EP); international business (MBA, MBA-EP); leadership (MBA-EP); managed care (MBA); management (MBA, MBA-EP); marketing (MBA, MBA-EP). Part-time and evening/weekend programs available. *Faculty:* 22 full-time (9 women), 37 part-time/adjunct (10 women). *Students:* 793 full-time (356 women), 164 part-time (80 women); includes 153 minority (17 Black or African American, non-Hispanic/Latino; 21 Asian, non-Hispanic/Latino; 110 Hispanic/Latino; 5 Two or more races, non-Hispanic/Latino), 691 international. Average age 27. In 2013, 514 master's awarded. *Entrance requirements:* For master's, GMAT, MAT, or GRE, minimum undergraduate GPA of 3.0, 2 letters of recommendation, resume, statement of purpose. Additional exam requirements/recommendations for international

students: Required—TOEFL (minimum score 550 paper-based; 85 iBT). *Application deadline:* Applications are processed on a rolling basis. Application fee: $50. *Expenses:* Contact institution. *Financial support:* Career-related internships or fieldwork, institutionally sponsored loans, and scholarships/grants available. Financial award application deadline: 3/2; financial award applicants required to submit FAFSA. *Unit head:* Dr. Abe Helou, Chairperson, 909-593-3511 Ext. 4211, Fax: 909-392-2704, E-mail: ihelou@laverne.edu. *Application contact:* Rina Lazarian-Chehab, Senior Associate Director of Graduate Admissions, 909-593-3511 Ext. 4317, Fax: 909-392-2704, E-mail: rlazarian@laverne.edu.

University of La Verne, Regional and Online Campuses, Graduate Programs, Inland Empire Campus, Ontario, CA 91761. Offers business administration (MBA, MBA-EP), including accounting (MBA), finance (MBA), health services management (MBA-EP), information technology (MBA-EP), international business (MBA), managed care (MBA), management and leadership (MBA-EP), marketing (MBA-EP), supply chain management (MBA); leadership and management (MS), including human resource management, nonprofit management, organizational development. Part-time and evening/weekend programs available. *Faculty:* 1 full-time (0 women), 14 part-time/adjunct (6 women). *Students:* 26 full-time (15 women), 106 part-time (65 women); includes 92 minority (15 Black or African American, non-Hispanic/Latino; 29 Asian, non-Hispanic/Latino; 43 Hispanic/Latino; 1 Native Hawaiian or other Pacific Islander, non-Hispanic/Latino; 4 Two or more races, non-Hispanic/Latino). Average age 37. In 2013, 49 master's awarded. *Application deadline:* Applications are processed on a rolling basis. Application fee: $50. *Expenses:* Contact institution. *Financial support:* Institutionally sponsored loans available. Financial award application deadline: 3/2; financial award applicants required to submit FAFSA. *Unit head:* Allen Stout, Campus Director, Inland Empire Regional Campus in Ontario, 909-937-6987, E-mail: astout@laverne.edu. *Application contact:* Karen Schumann, Senior Associate Director of Admissions, Inland Empire Regional Campus in Ontario, 909-937-6991, E-mail: kschumann@laverne.edu.
Website: http://laverne.edu/locations/inland-empire/.

University of Lethbridge, School of Graduate Studies, Lethbridge, AB T1K 3M4, Canada. Offers accounting (MScM); addictions counseling (M Sc); agricultural biotechnology (M Sc); agricultural studies (M Sc, MA); anthropology (MA); archaeology (M Sc, MA); art (MA, MFA); biochemistry (M Sc); biological sciences (M Sc); biomolecular science (PhD); biosystems and biodiversity (PhD); Canadian studies (MA); chemistry (M Sc); computer science (M Sc); computer science and geographical information science (M Sc); counseling (MC); counseling psychology (M Ed); dramatic arts (MA); earth, space, and physical science (PhD); economics (MA); education (MA); educational leadership (M Ed); English (MA); environmental science (M Sc); evolution and behavior (PhD); exercise science (M Sc); finance (MScM); French (MA); French/German (MA); French/Spanish (MA); general education (M Ed); general management (MScM); geography (M Sc, MA); German (MA); health sciences (M Sc); human resource management and labour relations (MScM); individualized multidisciplinary (M Sc, MA); information systems (MScM); international management (MScM); kinesiology (M Sc, MA); marketing (MScM); mathematics (M Sc); modern languages (MA); music (M Mus, MA); Native American studies (MA); neuroscience (M Sc, PhD); new media (MA, MFA); nursing (M Sc); philosophy (MA); physics (M Sc); policy and strategy (MScM); political science (MA); psychology (M Sc, MA); religious studies (MA); sociology (MA); theatre and dramatic arts (MFA); theoretical and computational science (PhD); urban and regional studies (MA); women and gender studies (MA). Part-time and evening/weekend programs available. *Degree requirements:* For doctorate, comprehensive exam, thesis/dissertation. *Entrance requirements:* For master's, GMAT (for M Sc in management), bachelor's degree in related field, minimum GPA of 3.0 during previous 20 graded semester courses, 2 years teaching or related experience (M Ed); for doctorate, master's degree, minimum graduate GPA of 3.5. Additional exam requirements/recommendations for international students: Required—TOEFL. Application fee: $60 Canadian dollars. *Financial support:* Fellowships, research assistantships, teaching assistantships, scholarships/grants, health care benefits, and unspecified assistantships available. *Faculty research:* Movement and brain plasticity, gibberellin physiology, photosynthesis, carbon cycling, molecular properties of main-group ring components. *Application contact:* School of Graduate Studies, 403-329-2793, Fax: 403-332-5239, E-mail: sgsinquiries@uleth.ca.
Website: http://www.uleth.ca/graduatestudies/.

University of Maine, Graduate School, College of Natural Sciences, Forestry, and Agriculture, School of Economics, Orono, ME 04469. Offers economics (MA); financial economics (MA); resource economics and policy (MS). Part-time programs available. *Faculty:* 17 full-time (4 women), 3 part-time/adjunct (0 women). *Students:* 19 full-time (8 women), 5 international. Average age 26. 21 applicants, 62% accepted, 5 enrolled. In 2013, 7 master's awarded. *Degree requirements:* For master's, thesis (for some programs). *Entrance requirements:* For master's, GRE General Test. Additional exam requirements/recommendations for international students: Required—TOEFL. *Application deadline:* For fall admission, 2/1 priority date for domestic students. Applications are processed on a rolling basis. Application fee: $65. Electronic applications accepted. *Expenses:* Tuition, state resident: full-time $7524. Tuition, nonresident: full-time $23,112. *Required fees:* $1970. *Financial support:* In 2013–14, 9 students received support, including 5 research assistantships (averaging $14,600 per year), 3 teaching assistantships with full tuition reimbursements available (averaging $14,600 per year); career-related internships or fieldwork, Federal Work-Study, institutionally sponsored loans, scholarships/grants, and tuition waivers (full and partial) also available. Support available to part-time students. Financial award application deadline: 3/1. *Faculty research:* Energy, food safety, transportation, education, economic development. *Total annual research expenditures:* $463,200. *Unit head:* Dr. Mario Teisl, Director, 207-581-3151, Fax: 207-581-4278. *Application contact:* Scott G. Delcourt, Associate Dean of the Graduate School, 207-581-3291, Fax: 207-581-3232, E-mail: graduate@maine.edu.
Website: http://umaine.edu/soe/.

University of Maine, Graduate School, The Maine Business School, Orono, ME 04469. Offers accounting (MBA); business administration (CGS); business and sustainability (MBA); finance (MBA); international business (MBA); management (MBA). *Accreditation:* AACSB. Part-time and evening/weekend programs available. Postbaccalaureate distance learning degree programs offered. *Faculty:* 23 full-time (7 women). *Students:* 31 full-time (12 women), 12 part-time (9 women); includes 5 minority (1 Black or African American, non-Hispanic/Latino; 3 Asian, non-Hispanic/Latino; 1 Hispanic/Latino), 4 international. Average age 29. 41 applicants, 71% accepted, 24 enrolled. In 2013, 28 master's awarded. *Entrance requirements:* For master's, GMAT. Additional exam requirements/recommendations for international students: Required—TOEFL (minimum score 550 paper-based). *Application deadline:* For fall admission, 6/1 priority date for domestic and international students; for spring admission, 11/15 priority date for domestic and international students. Applications are processed on a rolling basis. Application fee: $65. Electronic applications accepted. *Expenses:* Contact institution. *Financial support:* In 2013–14, 14 students received support, including 3 teaching assistantships with full tuition reimbursements available (averaging $14,100 per year); career-related internships or fieldwork, Federal Work-Study, institutionally sponsored loans, scholarships/grants, tuition waivers (full and partial), and unspecified assistantships also available. Financial award application deadline: 3/1. *Faculty research:* Entrepreneurship, investment management, international markets, decision support systems, strategic planning. *Total annual research expenditures:* $5,089. *Unit head:* Carol Mandzik, Manager of MBA Programs, Executive Education and Internships, 207-581-1971, Fax: 207-581-1930, E-mail: carol.mandzik@maine.edu. *Application contact:* Scott G. Delcourt, Associate Dean of the Graduate School, 207-581-3291, Fax: 207-581-3232, E-mail: graduate@maine.edu.
Website: http://www.umaine.edu/business/.

University of Maryland University College, Graduate School of Management and Technology, Program in Accounting and Financial Management, Adelphi, MD 20783. Offers MS, Certificate. *Accreditation:* AACSB. Part-time and evening/weekend programs available. Postbaccalaureate distance learning degree programs offered (no on-campus study). *Students:* 11 full-time (7 women), 422 part-time (268 women); includes 232 minority (160 Black or African American, non-Hispanic/Latino; 33 Asian, non-Hispanic/Latino; 29 Hispanic/Latino; 2 Native Hawaiian or other Pacific Islander, non-Hispanic/Latino; 8 Two or more races, non-Hispanic/Latino), 14 international. Average age 36. 131 applicants, 100% accepted, 83 enrolled. In 2013, 110 master's awarded. *Degree requirements:* For master's, thesis or alternative, capstone course. *Application deadline:* Applications are processed on a rolling basis. Application fee: $50. Electronic applications accepted. *Financial support:* Federal Work-Study and scholarships/grants available. Support available to part-time students. Financial award application deadline: 6/1; financial award applicants required to submit FAFSA. *Unit head:* Dr. James Howard, Director, 240-684-2400, Fax: 240-684-2401, E-mail: james.howard@umuc.edu. *Application contact:* Coordinator, Graduate Admissions, 800-888-8682, Fax: 240-684-2151, E-mail: newgrad@umuc.edu.
Website: http://www.umuc.edu/grad/msaf.html.

University of Maryland University College, Graduate School of Management and Technology, Program in Financial Management and Information Systems, Adelphi, MD 20783. Offers MS, Certificate. Part-time and evening/weekend programs available. Postbaccalaureate distance learning degree programs offered (no on-campus study). *Students:* 135 part-time (60 women); includes 91 minority (67 Black or African American, non-Hispanic/Latino; 14 Asian, non-Hispanic/Latino; 5 Hispanic/Latino; 5 Two or more races, non-Hispanic/Latino), 5 international. Average age 34. 43 applicants, 100% accepted, 22 enrolled. In 2013, 44 master's awarded. *Degree requirements:* For master's, thesis or alternative. *Application deadline:* Applications are processed on a rolling basis. Application fee: $50. Electronic applications accepted. *Financial support:* Federal Work-Study and scholarships/grants available. Support available to part-time students. Financial award application deadline: 6/1; financial award applicants required to submit FAFSA. *Unit head:* Dr. Jayanta Sen, Director, 240-684-2400, Fax: 240-684-2401, E-mail: jayanta.sen@umuc.edu. *Application contact:* Coordinator, Graduate Admissions, 800-888-8682, Fax: 240-684-2151, E-mail: newgrad@umuc.edu.
Website: http://www.umuc.edu/programs/grad/fmis/.

University of Massachusetts Amherst, Graduate School, Isenberg School of Management, Program in Management, Amherst, MA 01003. Offers accounting (PhD); business administration (MBA); entrepreneurship (MBA); finance (MBA, PhD); healthcare administration (MBA); hospitality and tourism management (PhD); management science (PhD); marketing (MBA, PhD); organization studies (PhD); sport management (PhD); strategic management (PhD); MBA/MS. *Accreditation:* AACSB. Part-time and evening/weekend programs available. Postbaccalaureate distance learning degree programs offered. *Faculty:* 68 full-time (14 women). *Students:* 140 full-time (59 women), 1,127 part-time (319 women); includes 229 minority (24 Black or African American, non-Hispanic/Latino; 2 American Indian or Alaska Native, non-Hispanic/Latino; 135 Asian, non-Hispanic/Latino; 51 Hispanic/Latino; 6 Native Hawaiian or other Pacific Islander, non-Hispanic/Latino; 11 Two or more races, non-Hispanic/Latino), 131 international. Average age 36. 828 applicants, 56% accepted, 351 enrolled. In 2013, 361 master's, 12 doctorates awarded. Terminal master's awarded for partial completion of doctoral program. *Degree requirements:* For doctorate, comprehensive exam, thesis/dissertation. *Entrance requirements:* For master's and doctorate, GMAT or GRE General Test. Additional exam requirements/recommendations for international students: Required—TOEFL (minimum score 550 paper-based; 80 iBT), IELTS (minimum score 6.5). *Application deadline:* For fall admission, 1/20 for domestic and international students. Applications are processed on a rolling basis. Application fee: $75. Electronic applications accepted. *Financial support:* Fellowships with full and partial tuition reimbursements, research assistantships with full and partial tuition reimbursements, teaching assistantships with full and partial tuition reimbursements, career-related internships or fieldwork, Federal Work-Study, scholarships/grants, traineeships, health care benefits, tuition waivers (full and partial), and unspecified assistantships available. Support available to part-time students. Financial award application deadline: 1/20; financial award applicants required to submit FAFSA. *Unit head:* Dr. John Wells, Chair, 413-545-7609, Fax: 413-577-2234. *Application contact:* Lindsay DeSantis, Supervisor of Admissions, 413-545-0722, Fax: 413-577-0010, E-mail: gradadm@grad.umass.edu.
Website: http://www.isenberg.umass.edu/.

University of Massachusetts Dartmouth, Graduate School, Charlton College of Business, Program in Business Administration, North Dartmouth, MA 02747-2300. Offers accounting (Postbaccalaureate Certificate); business administration (MBA); business foundations (Graduate Certificate); finance (Postbaccalaureate Certificate); international business (Graduate Certificate); management (Postbaccalaureate Certificate); marketing (Postbaccalaureate Certificate); organizational leadership (Graduate Certificate); supply chain management (Postbaccalaureate Certificate). *Accreditation:* AACSB. Part-time programs available. Postbaccalaureate distance learning degree programs offered (no on-campus study). *Faculty:* 36 full-time (12 women), 27 part-time/adjunct (10 women). *Students:* 154 full-time (73 women), 120 part-time (55 women); includes 28 minority (2 Black or African American, non-Hispanic/Latino; 1 American Indian or Alaska Native, non-Hispanic/Latino; 6 Asian, non-Hispanic/Latino; 11 Hispanic/Latino; 8 Two or more races, non-Hispanic/Latino), 129 international. Average age 29. 204 applicants, 82% accepted, 112 enrolled. In 2013, 71 master's, 15 other advanced degrees awarded. *Degree requirements:* For master's, portfolio of MBA course work. *Entrance requirements:* For master's, GMAT, statement of purpose (minimum of 300 words), resume, 2 letters of recommendation, official transcripts; for other advanced degree, statement of purpose (minimum of 300 words), resume, official transcripts. Additional exam requirements/recommendations for international students: Required—TOEFL (minimum score 500 paper-based; 72 iBT), IELTS (minimum score 6). *Application deadline:* For fall admission, 8/1 priority date for domestic students, 5/1 priority date for international students; for spring admission, 1/1 priority date for domestic students, 10/1 priority date for international students. Applications are processed on a rolling basis. Application fee: $60. Electronic applications accepted. *Expenses:* Tuition, state resident: full-time $2071; part-time $86.29 per credit. Tuition, nonresident: full-time $8099; part-time $337.46 per credit. Tuition and fees vary according to course load and reciprocity agreements. *Financial support:* Federal Work-Study and unspecified assistantships available. Support available to part-time students. Financial award application deadline: 3/1; financial award applicants required to submit FAFSA. *Faculty research:* E-commerce, managing diversity, agile manufacturing, green business, activity-based management, build-to-

order supply chain management. *Total annual research expenditures:* $330,000. *Unit head:* Toby Stapleton, Assistant Dean for Graduate Studies, 508-999-8543, Fax: 508-999-8646, E-mail: tstapleton@umassd.edu. *Application contact:* Steven Briggs, Director of Marketing and Recruitment for Graduate Studies, 508-999-8604, Fax: 508-999-8183, E-mail: graduate@umassd.edu.
Website: http://www.umassd.edu/charlton/.

University of Massachusetts Lowell, Manning School of Business, Lowell, MA 01854-2881. Offers accounting (MSA); business administration (MBA, PhD); financial management (Graduate Certificate); foundations of business (Graduate Certificate); healthcare innovation and entrepreneurship (MS); innovation and technological entrepreneurship (MS); new venture creation (Graduate Certificate); supply chain and operations management (Graduate Certificate). *Accreditation:* AACSB. Part-time and evening/weekend programs available. *Entrance requirements:* For master's, GMAT.

University of Memphis, Graduate School, Fogelman College of Business and Economics, Program in Business Administration, Memphis, TN 38152. Offers accounting (MBA, PhD); economics (MBA, PhD); executive business administration (MBA); finance (PhD); finance, insurance, and real estate (MBA, MS); international business administration (IMBA); management (MBA, MS, PhD); management information systems (MBA, MS, PhD); management science (MBA); marketing (MBA, MS); marketing and supply chain management (PhD); real estate development (MS); JD/MBA. *Accreditation:* AACSB. *Faculty:* 44 full-time (9 women), 5 part-time/adjunct (0 women). *Students:* 238 full-time (101 women), 315 part-time (113 women); includes 146 minority (80 Black or African American, non-Hispanic/Latino; 1 American Indian or Alaska Native, non-Hispanic/Latino; 46 Asian, non-Hispanic/Latino; 13 Hispanic/Latino; 2 Native Hawaiian or other Pacific Islander, non-Hispanic/Latino; 4 Two or more races, non-Hispanic/Latino), 104 international. Average age 32. 343 applicants, 62% accepted, 102 enrolled. In 2013, 140 master's, 17 doctorates awarded. *Degree requirements:* For master's, comprehensive exam; for doctorate, comprehensive exam, thesis/dissertation. *Entrance requirements:* For master's, GMAT, resume; for doctorate, GMAT, interview, minimum GPA of 3.4, resume, letter of recommendation. Additional exam requirements/recommendations for international students: Required—TOEFL (minimum score 550 paper-based). *Application deadline:* For fall admission, 8/1 for domestic students; for spring admission, 12/1 for domestic students. Application fee: $35 ($60 for international students). *Financial support:* In 2013–14, 164 students received support. Research assistantships with full tuition reimbursements available, teaching assistantships with full tuition reimbursements available, career-related internships or fieldwork, Federal Work-Study, scholarships/grants, and unspecified assistantships available. Financial award application deadline: 2/15; financial award applicants required to submit FAFSA. *Faculty research:* Competitive business strategy, finance microstructures, supply chain management innovations, health care economics, litigation risks and corporate audits. *Unit head:* Rajiv Grover, Dean, 901-678-3759, E-mail: rgrover@memphis.edu. *Application contact:* Dr. Carol V. Danehower, Associate Dean, 901-678-5402, Fax: 901-678-3579, E-mail: fcbegp@memphis.edu.
Website: http://www.memphis.edu/fcbe/grad_programs.php.

University of Miami, Graduate School, School of Business Administration, Program in Business Administration, Coral Gables, FL 33124. Offers accounting (MBA); computer information systems (MBA); executive and professional (MBA), including international business, management; finance (MBA); international business (MBA); management (MBA); management science (MBA); marketing (MBA); professional management (MSPM); JD/MBA; MBA/MSIE. *Accreditation:* AACSB. Evening/weekend programs available. *Degree requirements:* For master's, comprehensive exam. *Entrance requirements:* For master's, GMAT. Additional exam requirements/recommendations for international students: Required—TOEFL (minimum score 550 paper-based; 59 iBT). Electronic applications accepted. *Faculty research:* Leadership, e-commerce, supply chain management.

University of Michigan–Dearborn, College of Business, Dearborn, MI 48128-1491. Offers accounting (MBA, MS); business analytics (MS); finance (MBA, MS); human resource management (MBA); information systems (MS); international business (MBA); investment (MBA); management (MBA); management information systems (MBA); marketing (MBA); supply chain management (MBA, MS); taxation (MBA); MBA/MHSA; MBA/MSE; MBA/MSF; MBA/MSIS; MBA/MSSCM; MSF/MSA. *Accreditation:* AACSB. Part-time and evening/weekend programs available. Postbaccalaureate distance learning degree programs offered (no on-campus study). *Faculty:* 24 full-time (8 women), 5 part-time/adjunct (2 women). *Students:* 82 full-time (31 women), 323 part-time (116 women); includes 72 minority (17 Black or African American, non-Hispanic/Latino; 2 American Indian or Alaska Native, non-Hispanic/Latino; 30 Asian, non-Hispanic/Latino; 15 Hispanic/Latino; 8 Two or more races, non-Hispanic/Latino), 65 international. Average age 32. 290 applicants, 44% accepted, 99 enrolled. In 2013, 143 master's awarded. *Entrance requirements:* For master's, GMAT or GRE, pre-calculus or finite mathematics; 18 credits of accounting course work beyond introductory courses (MS in accounting). Additional exam requirements/recommendations for international students: Required—TOEFL (minimum score 560 paper-based; 84 iBT), IELTS. *Application deadline:* For fall admission, 8/1 priority date for domestic students, 5/1 priority date for international students; for winter admission, 12/1 priority date for domestic students, 9/1 priority date for international students; for spring admission, 4/1 priority date for domestic students, 1/1 priority date for international students. Applications are processed on a rolling basis. Application fee: $60. Electronic applications accepted. *Expenses:* Contact institution. *Financial support:* Career-related internships or fieldwork, Federal Work-Study, and scholarships/grants available. Support available to part-time students. Financial award application deadline: 9/1; financial award applicants required to submit FAFSA. *Faculty research:* Cultural diversity, buyer-supplier relations, error detection in data, economic evolution. *Unit head:* Dr. Raju Balakrishnan, Dean, 313-593-5248, Fax: 313-271-9835, E-mail: rajub@umich.edu. *Application contact:* Joan Doherty, Academic Advisor/Counselor, 313-593-5460, Fax: 313-271-9838, E-mail: umd-gradbusiness@umich.edu.
Website: http://www.cob.umd.umich.edu.

University of Michigan–Flint, School of Management, Flint, MI 48502-1950. Offers accounting (MBA, MSA); business (Graduate Certificate); computer information systems (MBA); finance (MBA); health care management (MBA); international business (MBA); lean manufacturing (MBA); marketing (MBA); organizational leadership (MBA). *Accreditation:* AACSB. Part-time and evening/weekend programs available. Postbaccalaureate distance learning degree programs offered (minimal on-campus study). *Faculty:* 13 full-time (3 women), 4 part-time/adjunct (0 women). *Students:* 19 full-time (6 women), 234 part-time (72 women); includes 50 minority (21 Black or African American, non-Hispanic/Latino; 5 American Indian or Alaska Native, non-Hispanic/Latino; 12 Asian, non-Hispanic/Latino; 5 Hispanic/Latino; 7 Two or more races, non-Hispanic/Latino), 30 international. Average age 32. 195 applicants, 56% accepted, 88 enrolled. In 2013, 73 master's awarded. *Degree requirements:* For master's, thesis or alternative. *Entrance requirements:* For master's, GMAT or GRE, minimum GPA of 3.0. Additional exam requirements/recommendations for international students: Required—TOEFL (minimum score 560 paper-based; 84 iBT), IELTS (minimum score 6.5). *Application deadline:* For fall admission, 8/1 for domestic students, 5/1 for international students; for winter admission, 11/1 for domestic students, 9/1 for international students;

for spring admission, 2/15 for domestic students, 1/15 for international students. Applications are processed on a rolling basis. Application fee: $55. Electronic applications accepted. *Financial support:* Federal Work-Study, scholarships/grants, and unspecified assistantships available. Support available to part-time students. Financial award application deadline: 3/1; financial award applicants required to submit FAFSA. *Unit head:* Dr. Scott Johnson, Dean, School of Management, 810-762-3164, Fax: 810-237-6685, E-mail: scotjohn@umflint.edu. *Application contact:* Jeremiah Cook, Marketing Communications Specialist, 810-424-5583, Fax: 810-766-6789, E-mail: jecook@umflint.edu.
Website: http://www.umflint.edu/som/.

University of Minnesota, Twin Cities Campus, Carlson School of Management, Carlson Full-Time MBA Program, Minneapolis, MN 55455. Offers finance (MBA); information technology (MBA); management (MBA); marketing (MBA); medical industry orientation (MBA); supply chain and operations (MBA); JD/MBA; MBA/MPP; MD/MBA; MHA/MBA; Pharm D/MBA. *Accreditation:* AACSB. *Faculty:* 137 full-time (42 women), 16 part-time/adjunct (5 women). *Students:* 222 full-time (62 women); includes 30 minority (2 Black or African American, non-Hispanic/Latino; 17 Asian, non-Hispanic/Latino; 5 Hispanic/Latino; 6 Two or more races, non-Hispanic/Latino), 60 international. Average age 28. 565 applicants, 44% accepted, 113 enrolled. In 2013, 96 master's awarded. *Entrance requirements:* For master's, GMAT or GRE. Additional exam requirements/recommendations for international students: Required—TOEFL (minimum score 580 paper-based; 84 iBT), IELTS (minimum score 7), PTE. *Application deadline:* For fall admission, 4/1 for domestic students, 2/1 for international students. Application fee: $60 ($90 for international students). Electronic applications accepted. *Expenses:* Contact institution. *Financial support:* In 2013–14, 133 students received support, including 133 fellowships with full and partial tuition reimbursements available (averaging $29,445 per year); research assistantships with partial tuition reimbursements available, teaching assistantships with partial tuition reimbursements available, career-related internships or fieldwork, Federal Work-Study, institutionally sponsored loans, scholarships/grants, health care benefits, and unspecified assistantships also available. Financial award application deadline: 4/1; financial award applicants required to submit FAFSA. *Faculty research:* Finance and accounting: financial reporting, asset pricing models and corporate finance; information and decision sciences: on-line auctions, information transparency and recommender systems; marketing: psychological influences on consumer behavior, brand equity, pricing and marketing channels; operations: lean manufacturing, quality management and global supply chains; strategic management and organization: global strategy, networks, entrepreneurship and innovation, sustainability. *Unit head:* Philip J. Miller, Assistant Dean, MBA Programs and Graduate Business Career Center, 612-625-5555, Fax: 612-625-1012, E-mail: mba@umn.edu. *Application contact:* Linh Gilles, Director of Admissions and Recruiting, 612-625-5555, Fax: 612-625-1012, E-mail: ftmba@umn.edu.
Website: http://www.csom.umn.edu/MBA/full-time/.

University of Minnesota, Twin Cities Campus, Carlson School of Management, Carlson Part-Time MBA Program, Minneapolis, MN 55455. Offers finance (MBA); information technology (MBA); management (MBA); marketing (MBA); medical industry orientation (MBA); supply chain and operations (MBA). Part-time and evening/weekend programs available. *Faculty:* 137 full-time (42 women), 15 part-time/adjunct (3 women). *Students:* 1,207 part-time (393 women); includes 108 minority (21 Black or African American, non-Hispanic/Latino; 4 American Indian or Alaska Native, non-Hispanic/Latino; 72 Asian, non-Hispanic/Latino; 5 Hispanic/Latino; 1 Native Hawaiian or other Pacific Islander, non-Hispanic/Latino; 5 Two or more races, non-Hispanic/Latino), 66 international. Average age 28. 291 applicants, 86% accepted, 205 enrolled. In 2013, 372 master's awarded. *Entrance requirements:* For master's, GMAT or GRE. Additional exam requirements/recommendations for international students: Required—TOEFL (minimum score 580 paper-based; 84 iBT), IELTS (minimum score 7), PTE. *Application deadline:* For fall admission, 5/1 priority date for domestic and international students; for spring admission, 10/1 priority date for domestic and international students. Applications are processed on a rolling basis. Application fee: $60 ($90 for international students). Electronic applications accepted. *Expenses:* Contact institution. *Financial support:* Applicants required to submit FAFSA. *Faculty research:* Finance and accounting: financial reporting, asset pricing models and corporate finance; information and decision sciences: on-line auctions, information transparency and recommender systems; marketing: psychological influences on consumer behavior, brand equity, pricing and marketing channels; operations: lean manufacturing, quality management and global supply chains; strategic management and organization: global strategy, networks, entrepreneurship and innovation, sustainability. *Unit head:* Philip J. Miller, Assistant Dean, MBA Programs and Graduate Business Career Center, 612-624-2039, Fax: 612-625-1012, E-mail: mba@umn.edu. *Application contact:* Linh Gilles, Director of Admissions and Recruiting, 612-625-5555, Fax: 612-625-1012, E-mail: ptmba@umn.edu.
Website: http://www.carlsonschool.umn.edu/ptmba.

University of Minnesota, Twin Cities Campus, Carlson School of Management, Doctoral Program in Business Administration, Minneapolis, MN 55455-0213. Offers accounting (PhD); finance (PhD); information and decision sciences (PhD); marketing (PhD); operations and management science (PhD); strategic management and entrepreneurship (PhD). *Faculty:* 102 full-time (31 women). *Students:* 74 full-time (25 women); includes 8 minority (1 Black or African American, non-Hispanic/Latino; 5 Asian, non-Hispanic/Latino; 2 Hispanic/Latino), 46 international. Average age 30. 274 applicants, 8% accepted, 15 enrolled. In 2013, 10 doctorates awarded. *Degree requirements:* For doctorate, comprehensive exam, thesis/dissertation, written and oral preliminary exams, proposal defense, final defense. *Entrance requirements:* For doctorate, GMAT, GRE General Test. Additional exam requirements/recommendations for international students: Required—TOEFL (minimum score 600 paper-based; 100 iBT); Recommended—IELTS (minimum score 7.5). *Application deadline:* For fall admission, 12/31 for domestic students, 12/31 priority date for international students. Applications are processed on a rolling basis. Application fee: $75 ($95 for international students). Electronic applications accepted. *Expenses:* Contact institution. *Financial support:* In 2013–14, 68 students received support, including 96 fellowships with full tuition reimbursements available (averaging $6,300 per year), 65 research assistantships with full tuition reimbursements available (averaging $12,500 per year), 64 teaching assistantships with full tuition reimbursements available (averaging $12,500 per year); institutionally sponsored loans, scholarships/grants, health care benefits, unspecified assistantships, and full student fee waivers also available. Financial award application deadline: 12/31. *Faculty research:* Corporate strategy, finance, entrepreneurship, marketing, information and decision science, operations, accounting, supply chain. *Unit head:* Dr. Shawn P. Curley, Director, 612-624-6546, Fax: 612-624-8221, E-mail: curley@umn.edu. *Application contact:* Earlene K. Bronson, Assistant Director, 612-624-0875, Fax: 612-624-8221, E-mail: brons003@umn.edu.
Website: http://www.csom.umn.edu/phd-bA/.

University of Missouri, Graduate School, Robert J. Trulaske, Sr. College of Business, Program in Business Administration, Columbia, MO 65211. Offers business administration (MBA); executive (MBA); finance (PhD); management (PhD); marketing (PhD); MBA/JD; MBA/MHA; MBA/MSIE. *Accreditation:* AACSB. *Faculty:* 42 full-time (9 women), 4 part-time/adjunct (2 women). *Students:* 208 full-time (69 women), 16 part-

time (6 women); includes 9 minority (2 Black or African American, non-Hispanic/Latino; 1 Asian, non-Hispanic/Latino; 4 Hispanic/Latino; 2 Two or more races, non-Hispanic/Latino), 63 international. Average age 29. 435 applicants, 30% accepted, 86 enrolled. In 2013, 101 master's, 6 doctorates awarded. *Degree requirements:* For doctorate, thesis/dissertation. *Entrance requirements:* For master's and doctorate, GMAT, minimum GPA of 3.0. Additional exam requirements/recommendations for international students: Required—TOEFL (minimum score 500 paper-based; 61 iBT). *Application deadline:* For fall admission, 2/1 priority date for domestic and international students. Applications are processed on a rolling basis. Application fee: $55 ($75 for international students). Electronic applications accepted. *Financial support:* Fellowships with full and partial tuition reimbursements, research assistantships with full and partial tuition reimbursements, teaching assistantships with full and partial tuition reimbursements, institutionally sponsored loans, scholarships/grants, health care benefits, and unspecified assistantships available. Support available to part-time students. *Faculty research:* International relations, management, finance, marketing, entrepreneurship, organization and process theory, mentoring and networking processes, capital market regulation, corporate governance, bankruptcy. *Unit head:* Joan T.A. Gabel, Dean, 573-882-6688, E-mail: gabelj@missouri.edu. *Application contact:* Jan Curry, Administrative Assistant, 573-882-2750, E-mail: curryja@missouri.edu. Website: http://business.missouri.edu/.

University of Missouri–Kansas City, Henry W. Bloch School of Management, Kansas City, MO 64110-2499. Offers accounting (MS); business administration (MBA); entrepreneurial real estate (MERE); entrepreneurship and innovation (PhD); finance (MS); public affairs (MPA, PhD); JD/MBA; LL M/MPA. PhD (interdisciplinary) offered through the School of Graduate Studies. *Accreditation:* AACSB; NASPAA. Part-time and evening/weekend programs available. *Faculty:* 57 full-time (15 women), 32 part-time/adjunct (10 women). *Students:* 309 full-time (151 women), 377 part-time (163 women); includes 100 minority (39 Black or African American, non-Hispanic/Latino; 2 American Indian or Alaska Native, non-Hispanic/Latino; 27 Asian, non-Hispanic/Latino; 24 Hispanic/Latino; 1 Native Hawaiian or other Pacific Islander, non-Hispanic/Latino; 7 Two or more races, non-Hispanic/Latino), 93 international. Average age 30. 489 applicants, 54% accepted, 252 enrolled. In 2013, 252 master's, 1 doctorate awarded. Terminal master's awarded for partial completion of doctoral program. *Entrance requirements:* For master's, GMAT, GRE, 2 essays, 2 references, support of employer; for doctorate, GRE, minimum GPA of 3.0. Additional exam requirements/recommendations for international students: Required—TOEFL (minimum score 550 paper-based; 80 iBT). *Application deadline:* For fall admission, 5/1 priority date for domestic and international students; for spring admission, 10/1 priority date for domestic and international students. Applications are processed on a rolling basis. Application fee: $45 ($50 for international students). Electronic applications accepted. *Expenses:* Tuition, state resident: full-time $6073; part-time $337.40 per credit hour. Tuition, nonresident: full-time $15,680; part-time $871.10 per credit hour. *Required fees:* $97.59 per credit hour. Full-time tuition and fees vary according to program. *Financial support:* In 2013–14, 38 research assistantships with partial tuition reimbursements (averaging $10,499 per year), 6 teaching assistantships with partial tuition reimbursements (averaging $13,380 per year) were awarded; career-related internships or fieldwork, Federal Work-Study, institutionally sponsored loans, scholarships/grants, tuition waivers (full and partial), and unspecified assistantships also available. Support available to part-time students. Financial award application deadline: 3/1; financial award applicants required to submit FAFSA. *Faculty research:* Entrepreneurship, finance, non-profit, risk management. *Unit head:* Dr. David Donnelly, Dean, 816-235-1333, Fax: 816-235-2206, E-mail: donnellyd@umkc.edu. *Application contact:* 816-235-1111, E-mail: admit@umkc.edu. Website: http://www.bloch.umkc.edu.

University of Missouri–St. Louis, College of Business Administration, Program in Business Administration, St. Louis, MO 63121. Offers accounting (MBA); business administration (Certificate); business intelligence (Certificate); finance (MBA); human resource management (Certificate); information systems (MBA); logistics and supply chain management (MBA, PhD, Certificate); marketing (MBA); marketing management (Certificate); operations management (MBA). *Accreditation:* AACSB. Part-time and evening/weekend programs available. *Faculty:* 30 full-time (5 women), 20 part-time/adjunct (8 women). *Students:* 114 full-time (51 women), 269 part-time (100 women); includes 43 minority (16 Black or African American, non-Hispanic/Latino; 14 Asian, non-Hispanic/Latino; 11 Hispanic/Latino; 1 Native Hawaiian or other Pacific Islander, non-Hispanic/Latino; 1 Two or more races, non-Hispanic/Latino), 56 international. Average age 31. 153 applicants, 91% accepted, 110 enrolled. In 2013, 136 master's, 7 other advanced degrees awarded. *Degree requirements:* For doctorate, thesis/dissertation. *Entrance requirements:* For master's, GMAT, 2 letters of recommendation. Additional exam requirements/recommendations for international students: Recommended—TOEFL (minimum score 550 paper-based; 79 iBT), IELTS (minimum score 6.5). *Application deadline:* For fall admission, 7/1 for domestic and international students; for spring admission, 12/1 for domestic and international students. Applications are processed on a rolling basis. Application fee: $50 ($40 for international students). Electronic applications accepted. *Expenses:* Tuition, state resident: full-time $7364; part-time $409.10 per credit hour. Tuition, nonresident: full-time $19,162; part-time $1008.50 per credit hour. *Financial support:* In 2013–14, 14 research assistantships with full and partial tuition reimbursements (averaging $5,625 per year), 6 teaching assistantships with full and partial tuition reimbursements (averaging $9,403 per year) were awarded; career-related internships or fieldwork, Federal Work-Study, and institutionally sponsored loans also available. Support available to part-time students. Financial award application deadline: 4/1; financial award applicants required to submit FAFSA. *Faculty research:* Human resources, strategic management, marketing strategy, consumer behavior product development, advertising. *Unit head:* Francesca Ferrari, Assistant Director, 314-516-5885, Fax: 314-516-6420, E-mail: mba@umsl.edu. *Application contact:* 314-516-5458, Fax: 314-516-6996, E-mail: gradadm@umsl.edu. Website: http://mba.umsl.edu/Degree%20Programs/index.html.

University of Nebraska–Lincoln, Graduate College, College of Business Administration, Interdepartmental Area of Business, Department of Finance, Lincoln, NE 68588. Offers business (MA, PhD). *Degree requirements:* For doctorate, comprehensive exam, thesis/dissertation. *Entrance requirements:* For master's and doctorate, GMAT. Additional exam requirements/recommendations for international students: Required—TOEFL (minimum score 100 iBT). Electronic applications accepted. *Faculty research:* Banking, investments, international finance, insurance, corporate finance.

University of Nevada, Reno, Graduate School, College of Business Administration, Department of Finance, Reno, NV 89557. Offers MS. Part-time programs available. *Degree requirements:* For master's, thesis optional. *Entrance requirements:* For master's, GMAT or GRE, minimum GPA of 2.75. Additional exam requirements/recommendations for international students: Required—TOEFL (minimum score 500 paper-based; 61 iBT), IELTS (minimum score 6). Electronic applications accepted. *Faculty research:* Financial business problems, economic theory, financial concepts theory.

University of New Haven, Graduate School, College of Business, Program in Business Administration, West Haven, CT 06516-1916. Offers accounting (MBA, Certificate), including CPA (MBA); business administration (MBA); business management

(Certificate); business policy and strategic leadership (MBA); finance (MBA), including CFA; global marketing (MBA); human resource management (Certificate); human resources management (MBA); international business (Certificate); marketing (MBA, Certificate); sports management (MBA). Part-time and evening/weekend programs available. *Students:* 125 full-time (55 women), 88 part-time (30 women); includes 31 minority (16 Black or African American, non-Hispanic/Latino; 1 American Indian or Alaska Native, non-Hispanic/Latino; 8 Asian, non-Hispanic/Latino; 5 Hispanic/Latino; 1 Native Hawaiian or other Pacific Islander, non-Hispanic/Latino), 72 international. 196 applicants, 89% accepted, 72 enrolled. In 2013, 143 master's, 24 other advanced degrees awarded. *Degree requirements:* For master's, thesis optional. *Entrance requirements:* For master's, GMAT. Additional exam requirements/recommendations for international students: Required—TOEFL (minimum score 80 iBT), IELTS, PTE (minimum score 53). *Application deadline:* For fall admission, 5/31 for international students; for winter admission, 10/15 for international students; for spring admission, 1/15 for international students. Applications are processed on a rolling basis. Application fee: $75. Electronic applications accepted. Application fee is waived when completed online. *Expenses: Tuition:* Full-time $21,600; part-time $800 per credit hour. *Required fees:* $45 per trimester. *Financial support:* Research assistantships with partial tuition reimbursements, teaching assistantships with partial tuition reimbursements, career-related internships or fieldwork, Federal Work-Study, scholarships/grants, and unspecified assistantships available. Support available to part-time students. Financial award applicants required to submit FAFSA. *Unit head:* Dr. Armando Rodriguez, Director, 203-932-7372, E-mail: arodriguez@newhaven.edu. *Application contact:* Eloise Gormley, Director of Graduate Admissions, 203-932-7440, E-mail: gradinfo@newhaven.edu. Website: http://www.newhaven.edu/7433/.

University of New Haven, Graduate School, College of Business, Program in Finance and Financial Services, West Haven, CT 06516-1916. Offers finance (MBA, Certificate). *Students:* 7 full-time (4 women), 14 part-time (5 women); includes 2 minority (both Hispanic/Latino), 11 international. 23 applicants, 91% accepted, 4 enrolled. In 2013, 18 master's, 1 other advanced degree awarded. *Application deadline:* Applications are processed on a rolling basis. Application fee: $75. *Expenses: Tuition:* Full-time $21,600; part-time $800 per credit hour. *Required fees:* $45 per trimester. *Financial support:* Research assistantships with partial tuition reimbursements, teaching assistantships with partial tuition reimbursements, career-related internships or fieldwork, and Federal Work-Study available. Financial award application deadline: 5/1; financial award applicants required to submit FAFSA. *Unit head:* Dr. Charlie Boynton, Chair, 203-932-7356, E-mail: cboynton@newhaven.edu. *Application contact:* Eloise Gormley, Director of Graduate Admissions, 203-932-7440, E-mail: gradinfo@newhaven.edu.

University of New Mexico, Anderson Graduate School of Management, Department of Finance, International, Technology and Entrepreneurship, Albuquerque, NM 87131-1221. Offers entrepreneurship (MBA); finance (MBA); international management (MBA); international management in Latin America (MBA); management of technology (MBA). Part-time and evening/weekend programs available. *Faculty:* 16 full-time (2 women), 5 part-time/adjunct (1 woman). In 2013, 72 master's awarded. *Entrance requirements:* For master's, GMAT or GRE, minimum GPA of 3.0 on last 60 hours of coursework. Additional exam requirements/recommendations for international students: Required—TOEFL (minimum score 550 paper-based; 79 iBT). *Application deadline:* For fall admission, 4/1 priority date for domestic and international students; for spring admission, 10/1 priority date for domestic and international students. Applications are processed on a rolling basis. Application fee: $50. Electronic applications accepted. *Expenses:* Contact institution. *Financial support:* Fellowships, research assistantships, career-related internships or fieldwork, Federal Work-Study, scholarships/grants, and unspecified assistantships available. Support available to part-time students. Financial award application deadline: 6/1; financial award applicants required to submit FAFSA. *Faculty research:* Corporate finance, investments, management in Latin America, management of technology, entrepreneurship. *Unit head:* Dr. Leslie Boni, Chair, 505-277-6471, Fax: 505-277-7108, E-mail: boni01@unm.edu. *Application contact:* Tracy Wilkey, Manager, Academic Advisement, 505-277-3290, Fax: 505-277-8436, E-mail: andersonadvising@unm.edu. Website: http://mba.mgt.unm.edu/default.asp.

University of New Orleans, Graduate School, College of Business Administration, Department of Economics and Finance, New Orleans, LA 70148. Offers economics and finance (MS); financial economics (PhD). *Accreditation:* AACSB. Terminal master's awarded for partial completion of doctoral program. *Degree requirements:* For master's, thesis optional; for doctorate, one foreign language, comprehensive exam, thesis/dissertation, general exams. *Entrance requirements:* For doctorate, GRE General Test, minimum GPA of 3.0. Additional exam requirements/recommendations for international students: Required—TOEFL (minimum score 550 paper-based; 79 iBT). *Faculty research:* Monetary economics, international economics, urban economics, real estate.

University of North Alabama, College of Business, Florence, AL 35632-0001. Offers accounting (MBA); enterprise resource planning systems (MBA); finance (MBA); health care management (MBA); information systems (MBA); professional (MBA); project management (MBA). *Accreditation:* ACBSP. Part-time and evening/weekend programs available. *Faculty:* 20 full-time (2 women). *Students:* 118 full-time (50 women), 273 part-time (130 women); includes 115 minority (37 Black or African American, non-Hispanic/Latino; 4 American Indian or Alaska Native, non-Hispanic/Latino; 68 Asian, non-Hispanic/Latino; 4 Hispanic/Latino; 2 Two or more races, non-Hispanic/Latino), 36 international. Average age 34. 296 applicants, 82% accepted, 149 enrolled. In 2013, 179 master's awarded. *Entrance requirements:* For master's, GMAT, GRE, minimum GPA of 2.75 in last 60 hours, 2.5 overall on a 3.0 scale; 27 hours of course work in business and economics. Additional exam requirements/recommendations for international students: Required—TOEFL (minimum score 500 paper-based; 79 iBT), IELTS (minimum score 6). *Application deadline:* For fall admission, 7/1 priority date for domestic students, 7/1 for international students; for spring admission, 12/1 for domestic and international students. Applications are processed on a rolling basis. Application fee: $25 ($50 for international students). Electronic applications accepted. *Expenses:* Tuition, state resident: full-time $4968; part-time $3312 per year. Tuition, nonresident: full-time $9936; part-time $6624 per year. *Required fees:* $970; $60.33 per credit. $362 per semester. *Financial support:* Federal Work-Study available. Support available to part-time students. Financial award application deadline: 4/1; financial award applicants required to submit FAFSA. *Unit head:* Dr. Kerry Gatlin, Dean, 256-765-4261, Fax: 256-765-4170, E-mail: kpgatlin@una.edu. *Application contact:* Russ Darracott, Graduate Admissions Counselor, 256-765-4447, E-mail: erdarracott@una.edu. Website: http://www.una.edu/business/.

The University of North Carolina at Chapel Hill, Kenan-Flagler Business School, Doctoral Program in Business Administration, Chapel Hill, NC 27599. Offers accounting (PhD); finance (PhD); marketing (PhD); operations management (PhD); organizational behavior (PhD); strategy (PhD). *Accreditation:* AACSB. *Degree requirements:* For doctorate, thesis/dissertation. *Entrance requirements:* For doctorate, GMAT or GRE General Test. Electronic applications accepted. *Expenses:* Contact institution.

The University of North Carolina at Charlotte, The Graduate School, College of Liberal Arts and Sciences, Department of Political Science and Public Administration,

Charlotte, NC 28223-0001. Offers emergency management (Graduate Certificate); non-profit management (Graduate Certificate); public administration (MPA), including arts administration, emergency management, non-profit management, public finance; public finance (Graduate Certificate); urban management and policy (Graduate Certificate). *Accreditation:* NASPAA. Part-time and evening/weekend programs available. *Faculty:* 16 full-time (8 women), 4 part-time/adjunct (0 women). *Students:* 24 full-time (14 women), 80 part-time (47 women); includes 37 minority (27 Black or African American, non-Hispanic/Latino; 1 American Indian or Alaska Native, non-Hispanic/Latino; 1 Asian, non-Hispanic/Latino; 6 Hispanic/Latino; 2 Two or more races, non-Hispanic/Latino), 1 international. Average age 29. 68 applicants, 72% accepted, 35 enrolled. In 2013, 24 master's, 9 other advanced degrees awarded. Terminal master's awarded for partial completion of doctoral program. *Degree requirements:* For master's, thesis or alternative. *Entrance requirements:* For master's, GRE General Test or MAT, minimum GPA of 3.0 in undergraduate major, 2.75 overall. Additional exam requirements/recommendations for international students: Required—TOEFL (minimum score 557 paper-based; 83 iBT). *Application deadline:* For fall admission, 5/1 priority date for domestic students, 5/1 for international students; for spring admission, 10/1 priority date for domestic students, 10/1 for international students. Applications are processed on a rolling basis. Application fee: $75. Electronic applications accepted. *Expenses:* Tuition, state resident: full-time $3522. Tuition, nonresident: full-time $16,051. *Required fees:* $2585. Tuition and fees vary according to course load and program. *Financial support:* In 2013–14, 9 students received support, including 9 research assistantships (averaging $9,444 per year); career-related internships or fieldwork, Federal Work-Study, institutionally sponsored loans, scholarships/grants, and unspecified assistantships also available. Support available to part-time students. Financial award application deadline: 4/1; financial award applicants required to submit FAFSA. *Faculty research:* Health policy and politics, managed care, issues of ethnic and racial disparities in health, aging policies, Central Asia. *Total annual research expenditures:* $276,620. *Unit head:* Dr. Greg Weeks, Chair, 704-687-7574, Fax: 704-687-1400, E-mail: gbweeks@uncc.edu. *Application contact:* Kathy B. Giddings, Director of Graduate Admissions, 704-687-5503, Fax: 704-687-1668, E-mail: gradadm@uncc.edu.
Website: https://politicalscience.uncc.edu/graduate.

The University of North Carolina at Greensboro, Graduate School, Bryan School of Business and Economics, Department of Accounting and Finance, Greensboro, NC 27412-5001. Offers accounting (MS); financial analysis (PMC). *Accreditation:* AACSB. *Entrance requirements:* For master's, GMAT, GRE General Test, previous course work in accounting and business. Additional exam requirements/recommendations for international students: Required—TOEFL. Electronic applications accepted.

University of North Florida, Coggin College of Business, MBA Program, Jacksonville, FL 32224. Offers accounting (MBA); construction management (MBA); e-commerce (MBA); economics (MBA); finance (MBA); human resource management (MBA); international business (MBA); logistics (MBA); management applications (MBA). *Accreditation:* AACSB. Part-time and evening/weekend programs available. *Faculty:* 14 full-time (6 women), 1 part-time/adjunct (0 women). *Students:* 90 full-time (41 women), 231 part-time (84 women); includes 47 minority (18 Black or African American, non-Hispanic/Latino; 8 Asian, non-Hispanic/Latino; 16 Hispanic/Latino; 5 Two or more races, non-Hispanic/Latino), 29 international. Average age 29. 222 applicants, 47% accepted, 80 enrolled. In 2013, 152 master's awarded. *Entrance requirements:* For master's, GMAT or GRE, U.S. bachelor's degree from regionally-accredited university or equivalent foreign degree. Additional exam requirements/recommendations for international students: Required—TOEFL (minimum score 550 paper-based; 79 iBT). *Application deadline:* For fall admission, 7/1 priority date for domestic students, 5/1 for international students; for spring admission, 11/1 priority date for domestic students, 10/1 for international students. Application fee: $30. *Expenses:* Tuition, state resident: full-time $9794; part-time $408.10 per credit hour. Tuition, nonresident: full-time $22,383; part-time $932.61 per credit hour. *Required fees:* $2020; $84.20 per credit hour. Tuition and fees vary according to course load and program. *Financial support:* In 2013–14, 35 students received support, including 1 research assistantship (averaging $2,700 per year); teaching assistantships, Federal Work-Study, and tuition waivers (partial) also available. Support available to part-time students. Financial award application deadline: 4/1; financial award applicants required to submit FAFSA. *Faculty research:* Performance measures, costing, and inventory issues in logistics and supply chain management; inter-organizational systems; international management and marketing practices; e-commerce; organizational learning and socialization processes. *Total annual research expenditures:* $12,025. *Application contact:* Cheryl Campbell, Graduate Advisor, 904-620-2575, Fax: 904-620-2832, E-mail: ccampbell@unf.edu.
Website: http://www.unf.edu/coggin/academics/graduate/mba.aspx.

University of North Texas, Robert B. Toulouse School of Graduate Studies, Denton, TN 76203-5017. Offers accounting (MS, PhD); applied anthropology (MA, MS); applied behavior analysis (Certificate); applied technology and performance improvement (M Ed, MS, PhD); art education (MA, PhD); art history (MA); art museum education (Certificate); arts leadership (Certificate); audiology (Au D); behavior analysis (MS); biochemistry and molecular biology (MS, PhD); biology (MA, MS, PhD); business (PhD); business computer information systems (PhD); chemistry (MS, PhD); clinical psychology (PhD); communication studies (MA, MS); computer engineering (MS); computer science (MS); computer science and engineering (PhD); counseling (M Ed, MS, PhD), including clinical mental health counseling (MS), college and university counseling (M Ed, MS), elementary school counseling (M Ed, MS), secondary school counseling (M Ed, MS); counseling psychology (PhD); creative writing (MA); criminal justice (MS); curriculum and instruction (M Ed, PhD), including curriculum studies (PhD), early childhood studies (PhD), language and literacy studies (PhD); decision sciences (MBA); design (MA, MFA), including fashion design (MFA), innovation studies, interior design (MFA); early childhood studies (MS); economics (MS); educational leadership (M Ed, Ed D, PhD); educational psychology (MS), including family studies, gifted and talented (MS, PhD), human development, learning and cognition, research, measurement and evaluation; educational research (PhD), including gifted and talented (MS, PhD), human development and family studies, psychological aspects of sports and exercise, research, measurement and statistics; electrical engineering (MS); emergency management (MPA); engineering systems (MS); English (MA, PhD); environmental science (MS, PhD); experimental psychology (PhD); finance (MBA, MS, PhD); financial management (MPA); French (MA); health psychology and behavioral medicine (PhD); health services management (MBA); higher education (M Ed, Ed D, PhD); history (MA, MS, PhD), including European history (PhD), military history (PhD), United States history (PhD); hospitality management (MS); human resources management (MPA); information science (MS, PhD); information technologies (MBA); information technology and decision sciences (MS); interdisciplinary studies (MA, MS); international sustainable tourism (MS); jazz studies (MM); journalism (MA, MJ, Graduate Certificate), including interactive and virtual digital communication (Graduate Certificate), narrative journalism (Graduate Certificate), public relations (Graduate Certificate); kinesiology (MS); learning technologies (MS, PhD); library science (MS); local government management (MPA); logistics and supply chain management (MBA, PhD); long-term care, senior housing, and aging services (MA, MS); management science (PhD); marketing (MBA, PhD); materials science and engineering (MS, PhD); mathematics (MA, PhD); merchandising (MS); music (MA, MM Ed, PhD), including ethnomusicology (MA), music education (MM Ed, PhD), music theory (MA, PhD), musicology (MA, PhD), performance (MA); nonprofit management (MPA); operations and supply chain management (MBA); performance (MM, DMA); philosophy (MA, PhD); physics (MS, PhD); political science (MA, MS, PhD); public administration and management (PhD), including emergency management, nonprofit management, public financial management, urban management; radio, television and film (MA, MFA); recreation, event and sport management (MS); rehabilitation counseling (MS, Certificate); sociology (MA, MS, PhD); Spanish (MA); special education (M Ed, PhD), including autism intervention (PhD), emotional/behavioral disorders (PhD), mild/moderate disabilities (PhD); speech-language pathology (MA, MS); strategic management (MBA); studio art (MFA); taxation (MS); teaching (M Ed); MBA/MS; MS/MPH; MSES/MBA. Part-time and evening/weekend programs available. Postbaccalaureate distance learning degree programs offered. *Faculty:* 661 full-time (213 women), 240 part-time/adjunct (144 women). *Students:* 3,106 full-time (1,620 women), 3,543 part-time (2,221 women); includes 1,740 minority (533 Black or African American, non-Hispanic/Latino; 15 American Indian or Alaska Native, non-Hispanic/Latino; 286 Asian, non-Hispanic/Latino; 746 Hispanic/Latino; 3 Native Hawaiian or other Pacific Islander, non-Hispanic/Latino; 157 Two or more races, non-Hispanic/Latino), 1,145 international. Average age 32. 6,289 applicants, 43% accepted, 1751 enrolled. In 2013, 1,778 master's, 239 doctorates, 10 other advanced degrees awarded. Terminal master's awarded for partial completion of doctoral program. *Degree requirements:* For master's, variable foreign language requirement, comprehensive exam (for some programs), thesis (for some programs); for doctorate, variable foreign language requirement, comprehensive exam (for some programs), thesis/dissertation; for other advanced degree, variable foreign language requirement, comprehensive exam (for some programs). *Entrance requirements:* For master's and doctorate, GRE, GMAT. Additional exam requirements/recommendations for international students: Required—TOEFL (minimum score 550 paper-based; 79 iBT). *Application deadline:* For fall admission, 7/15 for domestic students, 3/15 for international students; for spring admission, 11/15 for domestic students, 9/15 for international students; for summer admission, 5/1 for domestic students. Applications are processed on a rolling basis. Application fee: $60. Electronic applications accepted. *Financial support:* Fellowships with partial tuition reimbursements, research assistantships with partial tuition reimbursements, teaching assistantships, career-related internships or fieldwork, Federal Work-Study, institutionally sponsored loans, scholarships/grants, health care benefits, and library assistantships available. Support available to part-time students. Financial award applicants required to submit FAFSA. *Unit head:* Mark Wardell, Dean, 940-565-2383, E-mail: mark.wardell@unt.edu. *Application contact:* Toulouse School of Graduate Studies, 940-565-2383, Fax: 940-565-2141, E-mail: gradsch@unt.edu.
Website: http://tsgs.unt.edu/.

University of Oregon, Graduate School, Charles H. Lundquist College of Business, Department of Finance, Eugene, OR 97403. Offers PhD. Part-time programs available. Terminal master's awarded for partial completion of doctoral program. *Degree requirements:* For doctorate, thesis/dissertation, 2 comprehensive exams. *Entrance requirements:* For doctorate, GMAT. Additional exam requirements/recommendations for international students: Required—TOEFL. *Faculty research:* Changes in firm value in response to corporate takeovers and defenses, capital structure, regulatory changes, financial intermediaries.

University of Ottawa, Faculty of Graduate and Postdoctoral Studies, Interdisciplinary Programs, Ottawa, ON K1N 6N5, Canada. Offers e-business (Certificate); e-commerce (Certificate); finance (Certificate); health services and policies research (Diploma); population health (PhD); population health risk assessment and management (Certificate); public management and governance (Certificate); systems science (Certificate).

University of Pennsylvania, Wharton School, Finance Department, Philadelphia, PA 19104. Offers MBA, PhD. *Degree requirements:* For doctorate, thesis/dissertation. *Entrance requirements:* For doctorate, GMAT or GRE. *Faculty research:* Corporate finance, investments, macroeconomics, international finance.

University of Pittsburgh, Katz Graduate School of Business, Doctoral Program in Business Administration, Pittsburgh, PA 15260. Offers accounting (PhD); finance (PhD); information systems (PhD); marketing (PhD); operations/decision sciences/artificial intelligence (PhD); organizational behavior and human resource management (PhD); strategic planning (PhD). *Accreditation:* AACSB. *Faculty:* 60 full-time (17 women). *Students:* 50 full-time (22 women); includes 4 minority (2 Black or African American, non-Hispanic/Latino; 2 Asian, non-Hispanic/Latino), 27 international. 321 applicants, 7% accepted, 14 enrolled. In 2013, 10 doctorates awarded. *Degree requirements:* For doctorate, comprehensive exam, thesis/dissertation. *Entrance requirements:* For doctorate, GMAT or GRE, 3 recommendations, statement of purpose, transcripts of all previous course work and degrees. Additional exam requirements/recommendations for international students: Required—TOEFL. *Application deadline:* For fall admission, 1/1 priority date for domestic and international students. Applications are processed on a rolling basis. Application fee: $50. Electronic applications accepted. *Expenses:* Tuition, state resident: full-time $19,964; part-time $807 per credit. Tuition, nonresident: full-time $32,686; part-time $1337 per credit. *Required fees:* $740; $200. Tuition and fees vary according to program. *Financial support:* In 2013–14, 40 students received support, including 30 research assistantships with full tuition reimbursements available (averaging $23,045 per year), 10 teaching assistantships with full tuition reimbursements available (averaging $26,055 per year); fellowships, Federal Work-Study, scholarships/grants, health care benefits, and unspecified assistantships also available. Financial award application deadline: 1/1. *Faculty research:* Accounting systems/financial reporting, corporate finance, shopper marketing/consumer behavior, management information systems, organizational behavior and entrepreneurship. *Unit head:* Dr. Dennis Galletta, Director, 412-648-1699, Fax: 412-624-3633, E-mail: galletta@katz.pitt.edu. *Application contact:* Carrie Woods, Assistant Director, 412-648-1525, Fax: 412-624-3633, E-mail: cawoods@katz.pitt.edu.
Website: http://www.business.pitt.edu/katz/phd/.

University of Pittsburgh, Katz Graduate School of Business, Master of Business Administration Programs, Pittsburgh, PA 15260. Offers finance (MBA); information systems (MBA); marketing (MBA); operations management (MBA); organizational behavior and human resource management (MBA); strategy, environment and organizations (MBA); MBA/JD; MBA/MIB; MBA/MPIA; MBA/MSE; MBA/MSIS; MID/MBA. *Accreditation:* AACSB. Part-time and evening/weekend programs available. *Faculty:* 60 full-time (14 women), 21 part-time/adjunct (5 women). *Students:* 107 full-time (31 women), 428 part-time (155 women); includes 55 minority (15 Black or African American, non-Hispanic/Latino; 26 Asian, non-Hispanic/Latino; 10 Hispanic/Latino; 4 Two or more races, non-Hispanic/Latino), 83 international. Average age 30. 449 applicants, 23% accepted, 63 enrolled. In 2013, 279 master's awarded. *Degree requirements:* For master's, minimum GPA of 3.0. *Entrance requirements:* For master's, GMAT, recommendations, undergraduate transcripts, essay, resume, interview, bachelor's degree. Additional exam requirements/recommendations for international students: Required—TOEFL (minimum score 600 paper-based; 100 iBT) or IELTS. *Application deadline:* For fall admission, 4/1 priority date for domestic students, 2/1 priority date for international students. Application fee: $50. Electronic applications

accepted. *Expenses:* Tuition, state resident: full-time $19,964; part-time $807 per credit. Tuition, nonresident: full-time $32,686; part-time $1337 per credit. *Required fees:* $740; $200. Tuition and fees vary according to program. *Financial support:* In 2013–14, 60 students received support. Career-related internships or fieldwork and scholarships/grants available. Financial award application deadline: 2/1. *Faculty research:* Accounting systems/financial reporting, corporate finance, shopper marketing/consumer behavior, management information systems, organizational behavior and entrepreneurship. *Unit head:* Tim Robison, Assistant Dean, 412-648-1700, Fax: 412-648-1659, E-mail: trobison@katz.pitt.edu. *Application contact:* Thomas Keller, Director of MBA Admissions, 412-648-1700, Fax: 412-648-1659, E-mail: mba@katz.pitt.edu.
Website: http://www.business.pitt.edu/katz/mba/.

University of Portland, Dr. Robert B. Pamplin, Jr. School of Business, Portland, OR 97203-5798. Offers entrepreneurship (MBA); finance (MBA, MS); health care management (MBA); marketing (MBA); nonprofit management (EMBA); operations and technology management (MBA, MS); sustainability (MBA). *Accreditation:* AACSB. Part-time and evening/weekend programs available. *Faculty:* 26 full-time (5 women), 8 part-time/adjunct (1 woman). *Students:* 37 full-time (11 women), 93 part-time (44 women); includes 15 minority (1 Black or African American, non-Hispanic/Latino; 7 Asian, non-Hispanic/Latino; 5 Hispanic/Latino; 2 Two or more races, non-Hispanic/Latino), 21 international. Average age 32. In 2013, 68 master's awarded. *Entrance requirements:* For master's, GMAT, minimum GPA of 3.0, resume, 2 letters of recommendation. Additional exam requirements/recommendations for international students: Required—TOEFL (minimum score 570 paper-based; 89 iBT), IELTS (minimum score 7). *Application deadline:* For fall admission, 7/15 priority date for domestic and international students; for spring admission, 12/15 priority date for domestic and international students. Applications are processed on a rolling basis. Application fee: $50. *Expenses:* Contact institution. *Financial support:* Federal Work-Study, scholarships/grants, and tuition waivers (partial) available. Support available to part-time students. Financial award application deadline: 3/1; financial award applicants required to submit FAFSA. *Unit head:* Melissa McCarthy, Director, 503-943-7224, E-mail: mba-up@up.edu.
Website: http://business.up.edu/mba/default.aspx?cid-1179&pid-6450.

University of Puerto Rico, Mayagüez Campus, Graduate Studies, College of Business Administration, Mayagüez, PR 00681-9000. Offers business administration (MBA); finance (MBA); human resources (MBA); industrial management (MBA). Part-time and evening/weekend programs available. *Faculty:* 42 full-time (26 women), 1 part-time/adjunct (0 women). *Students:* 36 full-time (18 women), 15 part-time (11 women). 26 applicants, 50% accepted, 10 enrolled. In 2013, 7 master's awarded. *Degree requirements:* For master's, comprehensive exam. *Entrance requirements:* For master's, GMAT or EXADEP, bachelor's degree with courses in calculus, microeconomics, accounting and statistics. Additional exam requirements/recommendations for international students: Required—TOEFL (minimum score 500 paper-based). *Application deadline:* For fall admission, 2/15 for domestic and international students; for spring admission, 9/15 for domestic and international students. Applications are processed on a rolling basis. Application fee: $25. *Expenses: Tuition, area resident:* Full-time $2466; part-time $822 per year. *International tuition:* $6371 full-time. *Required fees:* $1095; $1095. Tuition and fees vary according to course level, course load and reciprocity agreements. *Financial support:* In 2013–14, 7 students received support, including 2 research assistantships (averaging $8,725 per year), 5 teaching assistantships (averaging $4,106 per year); fellowships with full tuition reimbursements available, Federal Work-Study, institutionally sponsored loans, and unspecified assistantships also available. *Faculty research:* Organizational studies, management, accounting. *Total annual research expenditures:* $20,000. *Unit head:* Dr. Ana Martin, Graduate Student Coordinator, 787-832-4040 Ext. 3800, Fax: 787-832-5320, E-mail: ana.martin@upr.edu. *Application contact:* Milagros Soto, Student Administrator, 787-265-3887, Fax: 787-832-5320, E-mail: milagros.soto1@upr.edu.
Website: http://enterprise.uprm.edu/.

University of Puerto Rico, Río Piedras Campus, College of Business Administration, San Juan, PR 00931-3300. Offers accounting (MBA); finance (MBA, PhD); general business (MBA); human resources management (MBA); international trade and business (MBA, PhD); marketing (MBA); operations management (MBA); quantitative methods (MBA). Part-time programs available. *Degree requirements:* For master's, comprehensive exam, thesis or alternative, research project. *Entrance requirements:* For master's, GMAT or PAEG, minimum GPA of 3.0, letter of recommendation; for doctorate, GMAT, PAEG, minimum GPA of 3.0, master degree. *Faculty research:* Management.

University of Rhode Island, Graduate School, College of Business Administration, Kingston, RI 02881. Offers accounting (MS); business administration (MBA, PhD), including finance and insurance (PhD), management (PhD), marketing (PhD), operations and supply chain management (MBA); finance (MBA); general business (MBA); management (MBA); marketing (MBA); supply chain management (MBA). *Accreditation:* AACSB. Part-time and evening/weekend programs available. *Faculty:* 43 full-time (16 women). *Students:* 103 full-time (37 women), 196 part-time (82 women); includes 42 minority (6 Black or African American, non-Hispanic/Latino; 1 American Indian or Alaska Native, non-Hispanic/Latino; 16 Asian, non-Hispanic/Latino; 13 Hispanic/Latino; 6 Two or more races, non-Hispanic/Latino), 29 international. In 2013, 119 master's, 3 doctorates awarded. *Degree requirements:* For master's, comprehensive exam (for some programs), thesis optional; for doctorate, comprehensive exam, thesis/dissertation. *Entrance requirements:* For master's, GMAT or GRE, 2 letters of recommendation, resume; for doctorate, GMAT or GRE, 3 letters of recommendation, resume. Additional exam requirements/recommendations for international students: Required—TOEFL (minimum score 575 paper-based; 91 iBT). *Application deadline:* For fall admission, 4/15 for domestic students, 2/15 for international students. Application fee: $65. Electronic applications accepted. *Expenses:* Tuition, state resident: full-time $11,532; part-time $641 per credit. Tuition, nonresident: full-time $23,606; part-time $1311 per credit. *Required fees:* $1388; $36 per credit. $35 per semester. One-time fee: $130. *Financial support:* In 2013–14, 14 teaching assistantships with full and partial tuition reimbursements (averaging $15,220 per year) were awarded. Financial award application deadline: 4/15; financial award applicants required to submit FAFSA. *Total annual research expenditures:* $66,948. *Unit head:* Dr. Mark Higgins, Dean, 401-874-4244, Fax: 401-874-4312, E-mail: markhiggins@uri.edu. *Application contact:* Lisa Lancellotta, Coordinator, MBA Programs, 401-874-4241, Fax: 401-874-4312, E-mail: mba@uri.edu.
Website: http://www.cba.uri.edu/.

University of Rochester, Simon Business School, Full-Time Master's Program in Business Administration, Rochester, NY 14627. Offers accounting and information systems (MBA); business environment and public policy (MBA); business systems consulting (MBA); competitive and organizational strategy - pricing (MBA); computers and information systems (MBA); corporate accounting (MBA); electronic commerce (MBA); entrepreneurship (MBA); finance (MBA); health sciences management (MBA); international management (MBA); marketing - brand management and pricing (MBA); operations management - manufacturing (MBA); operations management - services (MBA); public accounting (MBA). *Accreditation:* AACSB. Part-time and evening/weekend programs available. *Faculty:* 60 full-time (11 women), 23 part-time/adjunct (3 women). *Students:* 282 full-time (74 women); includes 55 minority (29 Black or African American, non-Hispanic/Latino; 1 American Indian or Alaska Native, non-Hispanic/Latino; 11 Asian, non-Hispanic/Latino; 12 Hispanic/Latino; 2 Two or more races, non-Hispanic/Latino), 144 international. 673 applicants, 33% accepted, 65 enrolled. In 2013, 176 master's awarded. *Entrance requirements:* For master's, GMAT/GRE, previous course work in calculus. Additional exam requirements/recommendations for international students: Required—TOEFL. *Application deadline:* For fall admission, 10/15 for domestic and international students; for winter admission, 1/5 for domestic and international students; for spring admission, 3/15 for domestic and international students; for summer admission, 5/15 for domestic students. Applications are processed on a rolling basis. Application fee: $150. Electronic applications accepted. *Expenses: Tuition:* Full-time $44,580; part-time $1394 per credit hour. *Required fees:* $492. *Financial support:* In 2013–14, 72 students received support. Fellowships, research assistantships, teaching assistantships, institutionally sponsored loans, scholarships/grants, and tuition waivers (partial) available. Financial award application deadline: 3/1; financial award applicants required to submit CSS PROFILE or FAFSA. *Unit head:* Mark Zupan, Dean, 585-275-3316. *Application contact:* Rebekah S. Lewin, Assistant Dean of Admissions and Student Engagement, 585-275-3533, E-mail: admissions@simon.rochester.edu.

University of Rochester, Simon Business School, Master's Program in Finance, Rochester, NY 14627. Offers MS. Part-time and evening/weekend programs available. *Faculty:* 60 full-time (11 women), 23 part-time/adjunct (3 women). *Students:* 142 full-time (73 women); includes 6 minority (4 Asian, non-Hispanic/Latino; 2 Hispanic/Latino), 124 international. Average age 24. 1,769 applicants, 17% accepted, 145 enrolled. In 2013, 103 master's awarded. *Entrance requirements:* For master's, GRE/GMAT, bachelor's degree. Additional exam requirements/recommendations for international students: Required—TOEFL. *Application deadline:* For fall admission, 10/15 for domestic and international students; for winter admission, 1/5 for domestic and international students; for spring admission, 3/15 for domestic and international students; for summer admission, 5/15 for domestic students. Applications are processed on a rolling basis. Application fee: $150. Electronic applications accepted. *Expenses: Tuition:* Full-time $44,580; part-time $1394 per credit hour. *Required fees:* $492. *Financial support:* In 2013–14, 91 students received support. Institutionally sponsored loans, scholarships/grants, and tuition waivers available. Support available to part-time students. Financial award application deadline: 5/15. *Unit head:* Mark Zupan, Dean, 585-275-3316. *Application contact:* Rebekah S. Lewin, Assistant Dean of Admissions and Student Engagement, 585-275-3533, E-mail: admissions@simon.rochester.edu.

University of Rochester, Simon Business School, MS Program in Finance, New York City, Rochester, NY 14627. Offers MS. Part-time and evening/weekend programs available. *Faculty:* 60 full-time (11 women), 23 part-time/adjunct (3 women). *Students:* 26 part-time (5 women); includes 4 minority (2 Black or African American, non-Hispanic/Latino; 2 Asian, non-Hispanic/Latino), 4 international. Average age 29. 34 applicants, 100% accepted, 26 enrolled. In 2013, 24 master's awarded. *Entrance requirements:* For master's, GRE or GMAT. *Application deadline:* For winter admission, 1/31 for domestic and international students. Applications are processed on a rolling basis. Application fee: $150. Electronic applications accepted. *Expenses: Tuition:* Full-time $44,580; part-time $1394 per credit hour. *Required fees:* $492. *Financial support:* In 2013–14, 20 students received support. Scholarships/grants available. Financial award application deadline: 1/31. *Unit head:* Janet Anderson, Executive Director of NYC-Based Programs, 585-275-3439, Fax: 585-244-3612.
Website: http://www.simon.rochester.edu/programs/ms-finance-new-york-city/index.aspx.

University of Rochester, Simon Business School, Part-Time MBA Program, Rochester, NY 14627. Offers accounting and information systems (MBA); business environment and public policy (MBA); business systems consulting (MBA); competitive and organizational strategy (MBA); computers and information systems (MBA); corporate accounting (MBA); electronic commerce (MBA); entrepreneurship (MBA); finance (MBA); health sciences management (MBA); international management (MBA); manufacturing management (MBA); marketing (MBA); operations management - services (MBA); public accounting (MBA). Part-time and evening/weekend programs available. *Faculty:* 59 full-time (10 women), 23 part-time/adjunct (3 women). *Students:* 270 part-time (75 women); includes 38 minority (5 Black or African American, non-Hispanic/Latino; 1 American Indian or Alaska Native, non-Hispanic/Latino; 24 Asian, non-Hispanic/Latino; 5 Hispanic/Latino; 3 Two or more races, non-Hispanic/Latino). Average age 32. 56 applicants, 98% accepted, 51 enrolled. In 2013, 77 master's awarded. *Entrance requirements:* For master's, GRE or GMAT, resume, recommendation letters, essays, transcipts. *Application deadline:* For fall admission, 8/15 for domestic students; for winter admission, 11/15 for domestic students; for spring admission, 2/15 for domestic students; for summer admission, 5/15 for domestic students. Applications are processed on a rolling basis. Application fee: $150. Electronic applications accepted. *Expenses: Tuition:* Full-time $44,580; part-time $1394 per credit hour. *Required fees:* $492. *Financial support:* Scholarships/grants and tuition waivers available. Financial award applicants required to submit CSS PROFILE. *Unit head:* Mark Zupan, Dean, 585-275-3316, E-mail: mark.zupan@simon.rochester.edu. *Application contact:* Jennifer Mossotti, Associate Director of Part-Time Programs, 585-275-3803, E-mail: jennifer.mossotti@simon.rochester.edu.
Website: http://www.simon.rochester.edu/programs/part-time-mba-programs/index.aspx.

University of Saint Mary, Graduate Programs, Program in Business Administration, Leavenworth, KS 66048-5082. Offers enterprise risk management (MBA); finance (MBA); general management (MBA); health care management (MBA); human resource management (MBA); marketing and advertising management (MBA). Part-time and evening/weekend programs available. Postbaccalaureate distance learning degree programs offered (no on-campus study). *Students:* 151 full-time (87 women), 61 part-time (39 women); includes 60 minority (38 Black or African American, non-Hispanic/Latino; 1 American Indian or Alaska Native, non-Hispanic/Latino; 10 Asian, non-Hispanic/Latino; 11 Hispanic/Latino). *Degree requirements:* For master's, thesis. *Entrance requirements:* For master's, minimum undergraduate GPA of 2.75, official transcripts, two letters of recommendation. *Application deadline:* Applications are processed on a rolling basis. Application fee: $25. *Expenses: Tuition:* Part-time $550 per credit hour. *Unit head:* Rick Gunter, Director, 913-319-3007. *Application contact:* Patrick Smith, Coordinator of Business Programs, 913-319-3007, E-mail: smithp@stmary.edu.

University of San Francisco, School of Management, Master of Business Administration Program, San Francisco, CA 94105. Offers entrepreneurship and innovation (MBA); finance (MBA); international business (MBA); marketing (MBA); organization development (MBA); DDS/MBA; JD/MBA; MBA/MAPS. *Accreditation:* AACSB. Part-time and evening/weekend programs available. *Faculty:* 18 full-time (4 women), 20 part-time/adjunct (10 women). *Students:* 157 full-time (69 women), 14 part-time (7 women); includes 57 minority (7 Black or African American, non-Hispanic/Latino; 31 Asian, non-Hispanic/Latino; 14 Hispanic/Latino; 5 Two or more races, non-Hispanic/Latino), 30 international. Average age 29. 345 applicants, 68% accepted, 79 enrolled. In 2013, 131 master's awarded. *Entrance requirements:* For master's, GMAT or GRE, resume (two years of professional work experience required for Part-Time MBA,

preferred for Full-Time MBA), transcripts from each college or university attended, two letters of recommendation, a personal statement and an interview. Additional exam requirements/recommendations for international students: Required—TOEFL (minimum score 600 paper-based, 100 iBT), IELTS (minimum score 7) or PTE (minimum score 68). *Application deadline:* For fall admission, 6/5 for domestic students, 5/15 for international students; for spring admission, 11/30 for domestic students. Application fee: $55. Electronic applications accepted. *Expenses: Tuition:* Full-time $21,150; part-time $1175 per unit. Tuition and fees vary according to course load, campus/location and program. *Financial support:* In 2013–14, 42 students received support. Fellowships and scholarships/grants available. Financial award application deadline: 3/2; financial award applicants required to submit FAFSA. *Faculty research:* International financial markets, technology transfer licensing, international marketing, strategic planning. *Total annual research expenditures:* $50,000. *Unit head:* Dr. John Veitch, Associate Dean and Program Director, 415-422-2221, Fax: 415-422-6315, E-mail: management@usfca.edu. *Application contact:* Office of Graduate Recruiting and Admissions, 415-422-2221, Fax: 415-422-6315, E-mail: management@usfca.edu.
Website: http://www.usfca.edu/mba.

University of San Francisco, School of Management, Master of Science in Financial Analysis Program, San Francisco, CA 94105. Offers MSFA, MS/MBA. Part-time and evening/weekend programs available. *Faculty:* 5 full-time (0 women), 8 part-time/adjunct (0 women). *Students:* 103 full-time (57 women), 7 part-time (3 women); includes 25 minority (1 Black or African American, non-Hispanic/Latino; 13 Asian, non-Hispanic/Latino; 8 Hispanic/Latino; 1 Native Hawaiian or other Pacific Islander, non-Hispanic/Latino; 2 Two or more races, non-Hispanic/Latino), 68 international. Average age 26. 401 applicants, 59% accepted, 68 enrolled. In 2013, 87 master's awarded. *Entrance requirements:* For master's, GMAT or GRE, resume (a minimum of two years of professional work experience is required for the Professional MSFA), transcripts from each college or university attended showing completion of required foundation courses, two letters of recommendation, personal statement. Additional exam requirements/recommendations for international students: Required—TOEFL (minimum score 600 paper-based, 100 iBT), IELTS (minimum score 7) or PTE (minimum score 68). *Application deadline:* For fall admission, 6/15 for domestic students, 5/15 for international students; for spring admission, 11/15 for domestic students, 10/15 for international students. Application fee: $55. Electronic applications accepted. *Expenses: Tuition:* Full-time $21,150; part-time $1175 per unit. Tuition and fees vary according to course load, campus/location and program. *Financial support:* In 2013–14, 41 students received support. Scholarships/grants available. Financial award applicants required to submit FAFSA. *Unit head:* Dr. John Veitch, Program Director, 415-422-2221, E-mail: management@usfca.edu. *Application contact:* Office of Graduate Recruiting and Admission, 415-422-2221, Fax: 415-422-6315, E-mail: management@usfca.edu.
Website: http://www.usfca.edu/msfa.

University of Saskatchewan, College of Graduate Studies and Research, Edwards School of Business, Department of Finance and Management Science, Saskatoon, SK S7N 5A2, Canada. Offers finance (M Sc). Part-time programs available. *Degree requirements:* For master's, thesis. *Entrance requirements:* For master's, GMAT. Additional exam requirements/recommendations for international students: Required—TOEFL. *Expenses: Tuition, area resident:* Full-time $3585 Canadian dollars; part-time $585 Canadian dollars per course. Tuition, nonresident: part-time $877 Canadian dollars per course. *International tuition:* $5377 Canadian dollars full-time. *Required fees:* $889.51 Canadian dollars.

The University of Scranton, College of Graduate and Continuing Education, Program in Business Administration, Scranton, PA 18510. Offers accounting (MBA); finance (MBA); general business administration (MBA); health care management (MBA); international business (MBA); management information systems (MBA); marketing (MBA); operations management (MBA). *Accreditation:* AACSB. Part-time and evening/weekend programs available. Postbaccalaureate distance learning degree programs offered (no on-campus study). *Faculty:* 34 full-time (8 women). *Students:* 316 full-time (134 women), 241 part-time (94 women); includes 104 minority (43 Black or African American, non-Hispanic/Latino; 3 American Indian or Alaska Native, non-Hispanic/Latino; 29 Asian, non-Hispanic/Latino; 27 Hispanic/Latino; 2 Two or more races, non-Hispanic/Latino), 47 international. Average age 34. 249 applicants, 85% accepted. In 2013, 200 master's awarded. *Degree requirements:* For master's, capstone experience. *Entrance requirements:* For master's, GMAT, minimum GPA of 3.0. Additional exam requirements/recommendations for international students: Required—TOEFL (minimum score 500 paper-based), IELTS (minimum score 6). *Application deadline:* Applications are processed on a rolling basis. Application fee: $0. *Financial support:* In 2013–14, 13 students received support, including 13 teaching assistantships with full and partial tuition reimbursements available (averaging $8,800 per year); fellowships, career-related internships or fieldwork, Federal Work-Study, and unspecified assistantships also available. Support available to part-time students. Financial award application deadline: 3/1. *Faculty research:* Financial markets, strategic impact of total quality management, internal accounting controls, consumer preference, information systems and the Internet. *Unit head:* Dr. Murli Rajan, Director, 570-941-4043, Fax: 570-941-4342. *Application contact:* Joseph M. Roback, Director of Admissions, 570-941-4385, Fax: 570-941-5928, E-mail: robackj2@scranton.edu.
Website: http://www.scranton.edu/academics/cgce/busad.shtml.

University of Southern Maine, College of Management and Human Service, School of Business, Portland, ME 04104-9300. Offers accounting (MBA); business administration (MBA); finance (MBA); health management and policy (MBA); sustainability (MBA); JD/MBA; MBA/MSA; MBA/MSN; MS/MBA. *Accreditation:* AACSB. Part-time and evening/weekend programs available. *Faculty:* 10 part-time/adjunct (2 women). *Students:* 89 part-time (37 women); includes 4 minority (3 American Indian or Alaska Native, non-Hispanic/Latino; 1 Asian, non-Hispanic/Latino), 2 international. Average age 31. 36 applicants, 56% accepted, 16 enrolled. In 2013, 34 master's awarded. *Entrance requirements:* For master's, GMAT or GRE, minimum AACSB index of 1100. Additional exam requirements/recommendations for international students: Required—TOEFL (minimum score 550 paper-based; 79 iBT). *Application deadline:* For fall admission, 8/1 priority date for domestic students, 5/1 priority date for international students; for spring admission, 12/1 priority date for domestic students, 9/1 priority date for international students. Applications are processed on a rolling basis. Application fee: $65. Electronic applications accepted. *Expenses:* Tuition, state resident: part-time $380 per credit. Tuition, nonresident: part-time $1026 per credit. Part-time tuition and fees vary according to program. *Financial support:* In 2013–14, 3 research assistantships with partial tuition reimbursements (averaging $9,000 per year), 3 teaching assistantships with partial tuition reimbursements (averaging $9,000 per year) were awarded; career-related internships or fieldwork, Federal Work-Study, scholarships/grants, tuition waivers (full and partial), and unspecified assistantships also available. Support available to part-time students. Financial award application deadline: 2/15; financial award applicants required to submit FAFSA. *Faculty research:* Economic development, management information systems, real options, system dynamics, simulation. *Unit head:* Joseph W. McDonnell, Dean, 207-228-8002, Fax: 207-780-4060, E-mail: jmcdonnell@usm.maine.edu. *Application contact:* Alice B. Cash, Assistant Director for Student Affairs, 207-780-4184, Fax: 207-780-4662, E-mail: acash@usm.maine.edu.
Website: http://www.usm.maine.edu/sb.

University of South Florida, College of Business, Department of Finance, Tampa, FL 33620-9951. Offers business administration (PhD), including finance; finance (MS); real estate (MSRE). Part-time and evening/weekend programs available. *Faculty:* 14 full-time (2 women), 1 part-time/adjunct (0 women). *Students:* 90 full-time (37 women), 10 part-time (7 women); includes 1 minority (Two or more races, non-Hispanic/Latino), 80 international. Average age 26. 149 applicants, 57% accepted, 38 enrolled. In 2013, 37 master's, 3 doctorates awarded. Terminal master's awarded for partial completion of doctoral program. *Degree requirements:* For master's, thesis or alternative; for doctorate, comprehensive exam, thesis/dissertation. *Entrance requirements:* For master's, GMAT (minimum score of 550), minimum undergraduate GPA of 3.0 in upper-division coursework; for doctorate, GMAT or GRE, minimum undergraduate GPA of 3.0 in upper-division coursework, personal statement, recommendations, interview. Additional exam requirements/recommendations for international students: Required—TOEFL (minimum score 550 paper-based; 79 iBT) or IELTS (minimum score 6.5). *Application deadline:* For fall admission, 6/1 for domestic students, 1/2 for international students; for spring admission, 10/15 for domestic students, 6/1 for international students. Application fee: $30. Electronic applications accepted. *Financial support:* In 2013–14, 17 students received support, including 8 research assistantships (averaging $14,357 per year), 9 teaching assistantships with tuition reimbursements available (averaging $11,972 per year); scholarships/grants, health care benefits, and unspecified assistantships also available. Financial award application deadline: 6/30. *Faculty research:* International corporate finance, corporate finance, market efficiency, mergers and acquisitions, agency theory, corporate governance, investments, mutual fund industry, mergers and acquisitions, corporate creditworthiness, credit risk issues, empirical asset pricing, financial intermediation, corporate finance theory, public offerings, business strategy. *Total annual research expenditures:* $361,660. *Unit head:* Dr. Scott Besley, Chairperson and Associate Professor, 813-974-6341, Fax: 813-974-3084, E-mail: sbesley@usf.edu. *Application contact:* Amy Dunkel, Office Manager, Finance Department, 813-974-6294, Fax: 813-974-3084, E-mail: adunkel@usf.edu.
Website: http://business.usf.edu/departments/finance/.

The University of Tampa, John H. Sykes College of Business, Tampa, FL 33606-1490. Offers accounting (MS); entrepreneurship (MBA); finance (MBA, MS); information systems management (MBA); innovation management (MBA); international business (MBA); marketing (MBA, MS); nonprofit management (MBA). *Accreditation:* AACSB. Part-time and evening/weekend programs available. *Faculty:* 41 full-time (15 women), 5 part-time/adjunct (1 woman). *Students:* 406 full-time (171 women), 152 part-time (61 women); includes 104 minority (18 Black or African American, non-Hispanic/Latino; 1 American Indian or Alaska Native, non-Hispanic/Latino; 20 Asian, non-Hispanic/Latino; 59 Hispanic/Latino; 6 Two or more races, non-Hispanic/Latino), 154 international. Average age 33. 1,341 applicants, 37% accepted, 256 enrolled. In 2013, 218 master's awarded. *Degree requirements:* For master's, capstone. *Entrance requirements:* For master's, GMAT or GRE, 4-year undergraduate degree, minimum GPA of 3.0, professional experience (for Executive MBA). Additional exam requirements/recommendations for international students: Required—TOEFL (minimum score 577 paper-based; 90 iBT); Recommended—IELTS (minimum score 7.5). *Application deadline:* Applications are processed on a rolling basis. Application fee: $40. Electronic applications accepted. *Expenses: Tuition:* Full-time $8928; part-time $558 per credit hour. *Required fees:* $80; $80 $40 per term. Tuition and fees vary according to program. *Financial support:* In 2013–14, 110 students received support. Career-related internships or fieldwork, scholarships/grants, and unspecified assistantships available. Financial award applicants required to submit FAFSA. *Faculty research:* Job market signaling, on-line shopping behaviors and social media, the Tampa Bay economy, digital literacy, entrepreneurship in small businesses. *Unit head:* Dr. Stephanie Thomason, Associate Dean, 813-253-6289, E-mail: sthomason@ut.edu. *Application contact:* Charlene Tobie, Associate Director of Admissions, 813-257-3566, E-mail: ctobie@ut.edu.
Website: http://www.ut.edu/business/.

The University of Tennessee, Graduate School, College of Business Administration, Program in Business Administration, Knoxville, TN 37996. Offers accounting (PhD); finance (MBA, PhD); logistics and transportation (MBA, PhD); management (PhD); marketing (MBA, PhD); operations management (MBA); professional business administration (MBA); statistics (PhD); JD/MBA; MS/MBA; Pharm D/MBA. Pharm D/MBA offered jointly with The University of Tennessee Health Science Center. *Accreditation:* AACSB. Postbaccalaureate distance learning degree programs offered. *Degree requirements:* For master's, thesis or alternative; for doctorate, thesis/dissertation. *Entrance requirements:* For master's and doctorate, GMAT, minimum GPA of 2.7. Additional exam requirements/recommendations for international students: Required—TOEFL. Electronic applications accepted. *Expenses:* Tuition, state resident: full-time $9540; part-time $531 per credit hour. Tuition, nonresident: full-time $27,728; part-time $1542 per credit hour. *Required fees:* $1404; $67 per credit hour.

The University of Texas at Arlington, Graduate School, College of Business, Department of Finance and Real Estate, Arlington, TX 76019. Offers finance (PhD); quantitative finance (MS); real estate (MS). Part-time and evening/weekend programs available. *Degree requirements:* For master's, thesis optional; for doctorate, comprehensive exam, thesis/dissertation. *Entrance requirements:* For master's, GMAT/GRE, minimum GPA of 3.0; for doctorate, GMAT/GRE. Additional exam requirements/recommendations for international students: Required—TOEFL (minimum score 550 paper-based; 79 iBT).

The University of Texas at Arlington, Graduate School, College of Business, Program in Business Administration, Arlington, TX 76019. Offers accounting (PhD); business statistics (PhD); finance (MBA, PhD); information systems (MBA, PhD); management (MBA, PhD); marketing (MBA, PhD); operations management (MBA, PhD); real estate (MBA). *Accreditation:* AACSB. Part-time and evening/weekend programs available. *Degree requirements:* For master's, thesis optional; for doctorate, comprehensive exam, thesis/dissertation. *Entrance requirements:* For master's, GMAT or GRE; for doctorate, GMAT, minimum GPA of 3.0 (undergraduate), 3.4 (graduate); 30 hours of graduate course work. Additional exam requirements/recommendations for international students: Required—TOEFL (minimum score 550 paper-based; 79 iBT). Electronic applications accepted.

The University of Texas at Austin, Graduate School, McCombs School of Business, Department of Finance, Austin, TX 78712-1111. Offers MSF, PhD. *Entrance requirements:* For doctorate, GMAT or GRE. Electronic applications accepted.

The University of Texas at Dallas, Naveen Jindal School of Management, Program in Finance and Managerial Economics, Richardson, TX 75080. Offers finance (MS); financial analysis (MS); financial risk management (MS); investment management (MS). Part-time and evening/weekend programs available. *Faculty:* 21 full-time (3 women), 10 part-time/adjunct (5 women). *Students:* 368 full-time (192 women), 69 part-time (23 women); includes 31 minority (2 Black or African American, non-Hispanic/Latino; 19 Asian, non-Hispanic/Latino; 10 Hispanic/Latino), 364 international. Average age 25. 1,060 applicants, 54% accepted, 189 enrolled. In 2013, 256 master's awarded. *Entrance requirements:* For master's, GMAT or GRE. Additional exam requirements/recommendations for international students: Required—TOEFL (minimum score 550 paper-based). *Application deadline:* For fall admission, 7/15 for domestic students, 5/1

priority date for international students; for spring admission, 11/15 for domestic students, 9/1 priority date for international students. Applications are processed on a rolling basis. Application fee: $50 ($100 for international students). Electronic applications accepted. *Expenses:* Tuition, state resident: full-time $11,940; part-time $663.33 per credit hour. Tuition, nonresident: full-time $21,606; part-time $1200.33 per credit hour. *Financial support:* In 2013–14, 57 students received support. Research assistantships with partial tuition reimbursements available, teaching assistantships with partial tuition reimbursements available, career-related internships or fieldwork, Federal Work-Study, institutionally sponsored loans, scholarships/grants, and unspecified assistantships available. Support available to part-time students. Financial award application deadline: 4/30; financial award applicants required to submit FAFSA. *Faculty research:* Econometrics, industrial organization, auction theory, file-sharing copyrights and bundling, international financial management, entrepreneurial finance. *Unit head:* Dr. Robert Kieschnick, Area Coordinator, 972-883-6273, E-mail: rkiesch@utdallas.edu. *Application contact:* Carolyn Reichert, Graduate Program Director, 972-883-5854, E-mail: carolyn@utdallas.edu.
Website: http://jindal.utdallas.edu/academic-areas/finance-and-managerial-economics/.

The University of Texas at Dallas, Naveen Jindal School of Management, Programs in Management Science, Richardson, TX 75080. Offers accounting (PhD); finance (PhD); information systems (PhD); marketing (PhD); operations management (PhD). *Accreditation:* AACSB. Part-time and evening/weekend programs available. *Faculty:* 13 full-time (3 women), 7 part-time/adjunct (2 women). *Students:* 78 full-time (27 women), 9 part-time (3 women); includes 6 minority (all Asian, non-Hispanic/Latino), 73 international. Average age 30. 258 applicants, 9% accepted, 16 enrolled. In 2013, 14 doctorates awarded. *Degree requirements:* For doctorate, thesis/dissertation. *Entrance requirements:* For doctorate, GMAT, minimum GPA of 3.0. Additional exam requirements/recommendations for international students: Required—TOEFL (minimum score 550 paper-based). *Application deadline:* For fall admission, 7/15 for domestic students, 5/1 priority date for international students; for spring admission, 11/15 for domestic students, 9/1 priority date for international students. Applications are processed on a rolling basis. Application fee: $50 ($100 for international students). Electronic applications accepted. *Expenses:* Tuition, state resident: full-time $11,940; part-time $663.33 per credit hour. Tuition, nonresident: full-time $21,606; part-time $1200.33 per credit hour. *Financial support:* In 2013–14, 81 students received support. Research assistantships with partial tuition reimbursements available, teaching assistantships with partial tuition reimbursements available, career-related internships or fieldwork, Federal Work-Study, institutionally sponsored loans, scholarships/grants, and unspecified assistantships available. Support available to part-time students. Financial award application deadline: 4/30; financial award applicants required to submit FAFSA. *Faculty research:* Empirical generalizations in marketing, diffusion of generations of technology, stochastic brand-choice theory, acceptance of trade deals by supermarkets, nonparametric estimations of market share response. *Unit head:* Dr. Sumit Sarkar, Program Director, 972-883-2745, Fax: 972-883-5977, E-mail: som_phd.@utdallas.edu. *Application contact:* Ashley J. Desouza, Program Administrator, 972-883-2745, Fax: 972-883-5977, E-mail: ashley.desouza@utdallas.edu.
Website: http://jindal.utdallas.edu/academic-programs/phd-programs/management-science/.

The University of Texas at San Antonio, College of Business, Department of Finance, San Antonio, TX 78249. Offers business (MBA), including finance; construction science and management (MS); finance (MS, PhD). Part-time and evening/weekend programs available. *Faculty:* 11 full-time (1 woman), 2 part-time/adjunct (0 women). *Students:* 27 full-time (13 women), 56 part-time (10 women); includes 27 minority (3 Black or African American, non-Hispanic/Latino; 1 Asian, non-Hispanic/Latino; 22 Hispanic/Latino; 1 Native Hawaiian or other Pacific Islander, non-Hispanic/Latino), 12 international. Average age 30. 73 applicants, 56% accepted, 22 enrolled. In 2013, 36 master's awarded. *Degree requirements:* For master's, comprehensive exam, thesis or alternative, 33 semester credit hours; for doctorate, comprehensive exam, thesis/dissertation, 87 semester hours. *Entrance requirements:* For master's and doctorate, GMAT or GRE, statement of purpose; 3 letters of recommendation. Additional exam requirements/recommendations for international students: Required—TOEFL (minimum score 500 paper-based; 61 iBT), IELTS (minimum score 5). *Application deadline:* For fall admission, 7/1 for domestic students, 4/1 for international students; for spring admission, 11/1 for domestic students, 9/1 for international students. Applications are processed on a rolling basis. Application fee: $45 ($80 for international students). Electronic applications accepted. *Expenses:* Tuition, state resident: full-time $4671. Tuition, nonresident: full-time $8708. *International tuition:* $17,415 full-time. *Required fees:* $1924.60. Tuition and fees vary according to course load and degree level. *Financial support:* In 2013–14, 12 students received support, including 1 research assistantship (averaging $10,000 per year), 10 teaching assistantships (averaging $10,000 per year). *Faculty research:* Corporate finance: governance, capital structure, compensations, venture capital, restructuring, bankruptcy; international finance: market interrelationships, pricing; options and futures; market micro-structure: interest rate, instruments and strategies. *Total annual research expenditures:* $5,000. *Unit head:* Dr. Lalatendu Misra, Chair, 210-458-6315, Fax: 210-458-6320, E-mail: lalatendu.misra@utsa.edu. *Application contact:* Katherine Pope, Graduate Advisor of Record, 210-458-7316, Fax: 210-458-7316, E-mail: katherine.pope@utsa.edu.

The University of Texas–Pan American, College of Business Administration, Program in Business Administration, Edinburg, TX 78539. Offers business administration (MBA); finance (PhD); management (PhD); marketing (PhD). Part-time and evening/weekend programs available. Postbaccalaureate distance learning degree programs offered (no on-campus study). *Degree requirements:* For master's, thesis optional. *Entrance requirements:* For master's, GMAT, minimum GPA of 3.0. Additional exam requirements/recommendations for international students: Required—TOEFL (minimum score 500 paper-based). Electronic applications accepted. *Expenses:* Tuition, state resident: full-time $5986; part-time $333 per credit hour. Tuition, nonresident: full-time $12,358; part-time $687 per credit hour. *Required fees:* $782. Tuition and fees vary according to program. *Faculty research:* Human resources, border region, entrepreneurship, marketing.

University of the West, Department of Business Administration, Rosemead, CA 91770. Offers business administration (EMBA); computer information systems (MBA); finance (MBA); international business (MBA); nonprofit organization management (MBA). Part-time and evening/weekend programs available. *Entrance requirements:* Additional exam requirements/recommendations for international students: Required—TOEFL. *Application deadline:* For fall admission, 6/15 for domestic and international students; for winter admission, 4/1 for domestic and international students; for spring admission, 11/15 for domestic and international students. Applications are processed on a rolling basis. Application fee: $50 ($100 for international students). *Expenses: Tuition:* Full-time $7200; part-time $400 per credit hour. *Required fees:* $750; $400 per credit hour. $275 per semester. One-time fee: $75. Tuition and fees vary according to course level and program. *Financial support:* Career-related internships or fieldwork, Federal Work-Study, scholarships/grants, and tuition waivers (partial) available. Financial award applicants required to submit FAFSA. *Unit head:* Dr. Bill Y. Chen, Chair, 626-656-2125, Fax: 626-571-1413, E-mail: billchen@uwest.edu. *Application contact:* Jason Kosareff, Enrollment Counselor, 626-571-8811 Ext. 311, Fax: 626-571-1413, E-mail: jasonk@uwest.edu.

The University of Toledo, College of Graduate Studies, College of Business and Innovation, Department of Finance, Toledo, OH 43606-3390. Offers MBA. Part-time and evening/weekend programs available. *Faculty:* 7. *Students:* 11 full-time (4 women), 41 part-time (12 women); includes 4 minority (3 Black or African American, non-Hispanic/Latino; 1 Asian, non-Hispanic/Latino), 14 international. Average age 28. 22 applicants, 91% accepted, 10 enrolled. In 2013, 52 master's awarded. *Entrance requirements:* For master's, GMAT, GRE, or LSAT, minimum GPA of 2.7 for all prior academic work, three letters of recommendation, statement of purpose, transcripts from all prior institutions attended. Additional exam requirements/recommendations for international students: Required—TOEFL (minimum score 550 paper-based; 80 iBT). *Application deadline:* For fall admission, 8/1 for domestic students, 5/1 for international students; for spring admission, 11/15 for domestic students, 10/1 for international students; for summer admission, 4/15 for domestic students, 3/1 for international students. Applications are processed on a rolling basis. Application fee: $45 ($75 for international students). Electronic applications accepted. *Financial support:* In 2013–14, 5 research assistantships with full and partial tuition reimbursements (averaging $3,000 per year) were awarded; career-related internships or fieldwork, Federal Work-Study, institutionally sponsored loans, scholarships/grants, tuition waivers (full and partial), unspecified assistantships, and administrative assistantships also available. Support available to part-time students. *Faculty research:* Financial management, banking, international finance, investments. *Unit head:* Dr. Ozcan Sezer, Chair, 419-530-2367, E-mail: ozcan.sezer@utoledo.edu. *Application contact:* Graduate School Office, 419-530-4723, Fax: 419-530-4724, E-mail: grdsch@utnet.utoledo.edu.
Website: http://www.utoledo.edu/business/index.html.

University of Toronto, School of Graduate Studies, Faculty of Arts and Science, Department of Economics, Program in Financial Economics, Toronto, ON M5S 1A1, Canada. Offers MFE. *Entrance requirements:* Additional exam requirements/recommendations for international students: Required—TOEFL (minimum score 102 iBT), TWE. Electronic applications accepted.

The University of Tulsa, Graduate School, Collins College of Business, Finance/Applied Mathematics Program, Tulsa, OK 74104-3189. Offers MS/MS. Part-time and evening/weekend programs available. *Students:* 3 full-time (1 woman), 1 part-time (0 women), 2 international. Average age 24. 5 applicants, 80% accepted, 2 enrolled. *Entrance requirements:* Additional exam requirements/recommendations for international students: Required—TOEFL (minimum score 577 paper-based; 91 iBT), IELTS (minimum score 6.5). *Application deadline:* Applications are processed on a rolling basis. Application fee: $40. Electronic applications accepted. *Expenses: Tuition:* Full-time $19,566; part-time $1087 per credit hour. *Required fees:* $1690; $5 per credit hour. $160 per semester. Tuition and fees vary according to course load. *Financial support:* In 2013–14, 2 students received support, including 2 teaching assistantships (averaging $9,963 per year); fellowships, career-related internships or fieldwork, Federal Work-Study, institutionally sponsored loans, scholarships/grants, health care benefits, tuition waivers (full and partial), and unspecified assistantships also available. Support available to part-time students. Financial award application deadline: 2/1; financial award applicants required to submit FAFSA. *Unit head:* Dr. Linda Nichols, Associate Dean, 918-631-2242, Fax: 918-631-2142, E-mail: linda-nichols@utulsa.edu. *Application contact:* Information Contact, 918-631-2242, E-mail: graduate-business@utulsa.edu.

The University of Tulsa, Graduate School, Collins College of Business, Master of Business Administration Program, Tulsa, OK 74104-3189. Offers accounting (MBA); business administration (MBA); energy management (MBA); finance (MBA); international business (MBA); management information systems (MBA); taxation (MBA); JD/MBA; MBA/MSCS; MBA/MSF. *Accreditation:* AACSB. Part-time and evening/weekend programs available. *Faculty:* 32 full-time (6 women). *Students:* 59 full-time (28 women), 29 part-time (9 women); includes 11 minority (1 Black or African American, non-Hispanic/Latino; 5 American Indian or Alaska Native, non-Hispanic/Latino; 3 Asian, non-Hispanic/Latino; 1 Hispanic/Latino; 1 Two or more races, non-Hispanic/Latino), 16 international. Average age 27. 53 applicants, 81% accepted, 28 enrolled. In 2013, 39 master's awarded. *Entrance requirements:* For master's, GMAT. Additional exam requirements/recommendations for international students: Required—TOEFL (minimum score 577 paper-based; 91 iBT), IELTS (minimum score 6.5). *Application deadline:* Applications are processed on a rolling basis. Application fee: $40. Electronic applications accepted. *Expenses: Tuition:* Full-time $19,566; part-time $1087 per credit hour. *Required fees:* $1690; $5 per credit hour. $160 per semester. Tuition and fees vary according to course load. *Financial support:* In 2013–14, 31 students received support, including 1 research assistantship (averaging $1,500 per year), 30 teaching assistantships (averaging $10,112 per year); fellowships, career-related internships or fieldwork, institutionally sponsored loans, scholarships/grants, health care benefits, tuition waivers (full and partial), and unspecified assistantships also available. Support available to part-time students. Financial award application deadline: 2/1; financial award applicants required to submit FAFSA. *Faculty research:* Accounting, energy management, finance, international business, management information systems, taxation. *Unit head:* Dr. Linda Nichols, Associate Dean of the Collins College of Business, 918-631-2242, Fax: 918-631-2142, E-mail: linda-nichols@utulsa.edu. *Application contact:* Information Contact, 918-631-2242, E-mail: graduate-business@utulsa.edu.
Website: http://www.utulsa.edu/academics/colleges/collins-college-of-business/bus-dept-schools/graduate-business-programs/degree-programs/MBA-Programs.aspx.

The University of Tulsa, Graduate School, Collins College of Business, MBA/MS Program in Finance, Tulsa, OK 74104-3189. Offers MBA/MS. Part-time and evening/weekend programs available. *Students:* 3 full-time (0 women), 7 part-time (0 women); includes 1 minority (American Indian or Alaska Native, non-Hispanic/Latino), 1 international. Average age 30. 5 applicants, 80% accepted, 3 enrolled. *Entrance requirements:* Additional exam requirements/recommendations for international students: Required—TOEFL (minimum score 577 paper-based; 91 iBT), IELTS (minimum score 6.5). *Application deadline:* Applications are processed on a rolling basis. Application fee: $40. Electronic applications accepted. *Expenses: Tuition:* Full-time $19,566; part-time $1087 per credit hour. *Required fees:* $1690; $5 per credit hour. $160 per semester. Tuition and fees vary according to course load. *Financial support:* In 2013–14, 1 student received support, including 1 teaching assistantship (averaging $13,543 per year); fellowships, career-related internships or fieldwork, Federal Work-Study, institutionally sponsored loans, scholarships/grants, health care benefits, tuition waivers, and unspecified assistantships also available. Support available to part-time students. Financial award application deadline: 2/1. *Unit head:* Dr. Linda Nichols, Associate Dean, 918-631-2242, Fax: 918-631-2142, E-mail: linda-nichols@utulsa.edu. *Application contact:* Information Contact, 918-631-2242, E-mail: graduate-business@utulsa.edu.
Website: http://www.utulsa.edu/academics/colleges/collins-college-of-business/bus-dept-schools/graduate-business-programs/degree-programs/Dual-Degrees.aspx#MBA.

The University of Tulsa, Graduate School, Collins College of Business, Program in Finance, Tulsa, OK 74104-3189. Offers corporate finance (MS); investments and portfolio management (MS); risk management (MS); JD/MSF; MBA/MSF; MSF/MSAM.

Part-time and evening/weekend programs available. *Faculty:* 10 full-time (1 woman). *Students:* 27 full-time (10 women), 4 part-time (1 woman); includes 1 minority (Hispanic/Latino), 23 international. Average age 24. 129 applicants, 50% accepted, 4 enrolled. In 2013, 11 master's awarded. *Degree requirements:* For master's, thesis optional. *Entrance requirements:* For master's, GMAT. Additional exam requirements/recommendations for international students: Required—TOEFL (minimum score 577 paper-based; 91 iBT), IELTS (minimum score 6.5). *Application deadline:* Applications are processed on a rolling basis. Application fee: $40. Electronic applications accepted. *Expenses: Tuition:* Full-time $19,566; part-time $1087 per credit hour. *Required fees:* $1690; $5 per credit hour. $160 per semester. Tuition and fees vary according to course load. *Financial support:* In 2013–14, 4 students received support, including 4 teaching assistantships with full and partial tuition reimbursements available (averaging $8,367 per year); fellowships with full and partial tuition reimbursements available, research assistantships with full and partial tuition reimbursements available, career-related internships or fieldwork, Federal Work-Study, institutionally sponsored loans, scholarships/grants, health care benefits, tuition waivers (full and partial), and unspecified assistantships also available. Support available to part-time students. Financial award application deadline: 2/1; financial award applicants required to submit FAFSA. *Unit head:* Dr. Linda Nichols, Associate Dean, 918-631-2242, Fax: 918-631-2142, E-mail: linda-nichols@utulsa.edu. *Application contact:* Information Contact, 918-631-2242, E-mail: graduate-business@utulsa.edu.

University of Utah, Graduate School, David Eccles School of Business, Business Administration Program, Salt Lake City, UT 84112. Offers accounting (PhD); business administration (EMBA, MBA, PMBA); finance (PhD); information systems (PhD); marketing (PhD); operations management (PhD); organizational behavior (PhD); strategic management (PhD); MBA/JD; MBA/MHA; MBA/MS. Part-time and evening/weekend programs available. *Faculty:* 58 full-time (21 women), 37 part-time/adjunct (7 women). *Students:* 481 full-time (108 women), 109 part-time (19 women); includes 39 minority (2 Black or African American, non-Hispanic/Latino; 13 Asian, non-Hispanic/Latino; 18 Hispanic/Latino; 1 Native Hawaiian or other Pacific Islander, non-Hispanic/Latino; 5 Two or more races, non-Hispanic/Latino), 39 international. Average age 32. 486 applicants, 56% accepted, 215 enrolled. In 2013, 326 master's, 10 doctorates awarded. *Degree requirements:* For doctorate, comprehensive exam, thesis/dissertation. *Entrance requirements:* For master's, GMAT or GRE; for doctorate, GMAT. Additional exam requirements/recommendations for international students: Required—TOEFL (minimum score 600 paper-based; 100 iBT), IELTS (minimum score 7). *Application deadline:* For fall admission, 11/1 priority date for domestic students, 3/1 priority date for international students; for spring admission, 11/1 for domestic and international students. Applications are processed on a rolling basis. Application fee: $55 ($65 for international students). Electronic applications accepted. *Expenses:* Contact institution. *Financial support:* In 2013–14, 48 students received support, including 41 fellowships with partial tuition reimbursements available (averaging $8,600 per year), 35 research assistantships with partial tuition reimbursements available (averaging $6,378 per year), 57 teaching assistantships with full tuition reimbursements available (averaging $17,000 per year); scholarships/grants and unspecified assistantships also available. Financial award application deadline: 2/1; financial award applicants required to submit FAFSA. *Faculty research:* Corporate finance, strategy services, consumer behavior, financial disclosures, operations. *Unit head:* Dr. William Hesterly, Associate Dean, PhD Program, 801-581-7676, Fax: 801-581-3380, E-mail: mastersinfo@business.utah.edu. *Application contact:* Andrea Miller, Coordinator, 801-581-7785, Fax: 801-581-3666, E-mail: mastersinfo@business.utah.edu.
Website: http://business.utah.edu/full-time-mba.

University of Utah, Graduate School, David Eccles School of Business, Master of Science in Finance Program, Salt Lake City, UT 84112. Offers MS, PhD. Part-time programs available. *Faculty:* 15 full-time (4 women), 8 part-time/adjunct (0 women). *Students:* 61 full-time (20 women), 41 part-time (11 women); includes 6 minority (3 Asian, non-Hispanic/Latino; 2 Hispanic/Latino; 1 Two or more races, non-Hispanic/Latino), 51 international. Average age 27. 110 applicants, 70% accepted, 42 enrolled. In 2013, 39 master's awarded. Terminal master's awarded for partial completion of doctoral program. *Degree requirements:* For master's, comprehensive exam; for doctorate, thesis/dissertation, oral qualifying exams, written qualifying exams, research paper. *Entrance requirements:* For master's, GMAT or GRE, minimum undergraduate GPA of 3.0; for doctorate, GMAT/GRE. Additional exam requirements/recommendations for international students: Required—TOEFL (minimum score 600 paper-based; 100 iBT), IELTS (minimum score 7). *Application deadline:* For fall admission, 3/1 priority date for domestic and international students. Applications are processed on a rolling basis. Application fee: $55 ($65 for international students). Electronic applications accepted. *Expenses:* Tuition, state resident: full-time $5259. Tuition, nonresident: full-time $18,569. *Required fees:* $841. Tuition and fees vary according to course load. *Financial support:* In 2013–14, 22 students received support, including 9 fellowships with partial tuition reimbursements available (averaging $3,472 per year); tuition waivers (full and partial) and unspecified assistantships also available. Financial award application deadline: 2/1; financial award applicants required to submit FAFSA. *Faculty research:* Investment, managerial finance, corporate finance, capital budgeting, risk management. *Total annual research expenditures:* $43,423. *Unit head:* Dr. Uri Loewenstein, Chair, 801-581-4419, Fax: 801-581-3956, E-mail: uri.lowenstein@business.utah.edu. *Application contact:* Mallorie Mecham, Program Coordinator, 801-585-1719, Fax: 801-581-3666, E-mail: mallorie.mecham@business.utah.edu.
Website: http://msf.business.utah.edu/.

University of Virginia, McIntire School of Commerce, Program in Commerce, Charlottesville, VA 22903. Offers financial services (MSC); marketing and management (MSC). *Students:* 103 full-time (44 women), 1 part-time (0 women); includes 19 minority (2 Black or African American, non-Hispanic/Latino; 11 Asian, non-Hispanic/Latino; 3 Hispanic/Latino; 3 Two or more races, non-Hispanic/Latino), 18 international. Average age 22. 317 applicants, 47% accepted, 105 enrolled. In 2013, 92 master's awarded. *Entrance requirements:* For master's, GMAT, 2 letters of recommendation; prerequisite course work in financial accounting, microeconomics, and introduction to business. Additional exam requirements/recommendations for international students: Required—TOEFL (minimum score 600 paper-based; 100 iBT), IELTS (minimum score 7). *Application deadline:* For fall admission, 9/15 priority date for domestic students, 1/15 priority date for international students. Applications are processed on a rolling basis. Application fee: $75. Electronic applications accepted. *Expenses:* Contact institution. *Financial support:* Scholarships/grants available. Financial award application deadline: 3/1; financial award applicants required to submit CSS PROFILE or FAFSA. *Unit head:* Ira C. Harris, Head, 434-924-8816, Fax: 434-924-7074, E-mail: ich3x@comm.virginia.edu. *Application contact:* Emma Candalier, Associate Director of Graduate Recruiting, 434-243-4992, Fax: 434-924-4511, E-mail: ecandalier@virginia.edu.
Website: http://www.commerce.virginia.edu/academic_programs/MSCommerce/Pages/index.aspx.

University of Washington, Tacoma, Graduate Programs, MBA Programs, Tacoma, WA 98402-3100. Offers accounting (MBA); business administration (MBA); certified financial analyst (MBA). *Accreditation:* AACSB. Part-time and evening/weekend programs available. *Entrance requirements:* For master's, GMAT, minimum GPA of 3.0 in final graded 90 quarter credits or 60 graded semester credits; at least 2 years of professional/management work experience. Additional exam requirements/recommendations for international students: Required—TOEFL (minimum score 580 paper-based; 92 iBT). Electronic applications accepted. *Expenses:* Contact institution. *Faculty research:* International accounting, marketing, change management, investments, corporate social responsibility.

University of Waterloo, Graduate Studies, Faculty of Arts, School of Accounting and Finance, Waterloo, ON N2L 3G1, Canada. Offers accounting (M Acc, PhD); finance (M Acc); taxation (M Tax). *Degree requirements:* For master's, thesis or alternative; for doctorate, thesis/dissertation. *Entrance requirements:* For master's, honors degree, minimum B average, resumé; for doctorate, GMAT, master's degree, minimum A-average, resume. Additional exam requirements/recommendations for international students: Required—TOEFL, TWE. Electronic applications accepted. *Expenses:* Contact institution. *Faculty research:* Auditing, management accounting.

The University of Western Ontario, Richard Ivey School of Business, London, ON N6A 3K7, Canada. Offers business (EMBA, PhD); corporate strategy and leadership elective (MBA); entrepreneurship elective (MBA); finance elective (MBA); health sector stream (MBA); international management elective (MBA); marketing elective (MBA); JD/MBA. *Degree requirements:* For master's, thesis (for some programs); for doctorate, thesis/dissertation. *Entrance requirements:* For master's, GMAT, 2 years of full-time work experience, interview. Additional exam requirements/recommendations for international students: Required—TOEFL (minimum score 100 iBT) or IELTS (minimium score 6). Electronic applications accepted. *Faculty research:* Strategy, organizational behavior, international business, finance, operations management.

University of Wisconsin–Madison, Graduate School, Wisconsin School of Business, Doctoral Program in Finance, Investment and Banking, Madison, WI 53706-1380. Offers PhD. *Faculty:* 15 full-time (2 women), 7 part-time/adjunct (3 women). *Students:* 9 full-time (2 women), 7 international. Average age 28. 66 applicants, 9% accepted, 3 enrolled. *Degree requirements:* For doctorate, comprehensive exam, thesis/dissertation. *Entrance requirements:* For doctorate, GMAT or GRE. Additional exam requirements/recommendations for international students: Recommended—TOEFL (minimum score 623 paper-based; 106 iBT), IELTS (minimum score 7.5), TSE (minimum score 73). *Application deadline:* For fall admission, 12/15 priority date for domestic and international students. Application fee: $56. Electronic applications accepted. *Expenses:* Contact institution. *Financial support:* In 2013–14, 9 students received support, including 2 fellowships with full tuition reimbursements available (averaging $19,125 per year), research assistantships with full tuition reimbursements available (averaging $14,746 per year), 7 teaching assistantships with full tuition reimbursements available (averaging $14,746 per year); Federal Work-Study, institutionally sponsored loans, scholarships/grants, health care benefits, and unspecified assistantships also available. Financial award application deadline: 12/15; financial award applicants required to submit FAFSA. *Faculty research:* Banking and financial institutions, business cycles, investments, derivatives, corporate finance. *Unit head:* Prof. Mark Ready, Chair, 608-262-5226, Fax: 608-265-4195, E-mail: mready@bus.wisc.edu. *Application contact:* Belle Heberling, Assistant Director for Research Programs, 608-262-3749, Fax: 608-890-0180, E-mail: phd@bus.wisc.edu.
Website: http://www.bus.wisc.edu/phd.

University of Wisconsin–Madison, Graduate School, Wisconsin School of Business, MS Program in Quantitative Finance, Madison, WI 53706-1380. Offers MS. *Faculty:* 1 full-time (0 women). In 2013, 3 master's awarded. *Entrance requirements:* For master's, GMAT or GRE. Additional exam requirements/recommendations for international students: Required—PTE (minimum score 73; written 80); Recommended—TOEFL, IELTS. *Application deadline:* For fall admission, 3/15 for domestic and international students. Application fee: $56. Electronic applications accepted. *Expenses:* Contact institution. *Financial support:* In 2013–14, teaching assistantships with full tuition reimbursements (averaging $9,831 per year) were awarded; career-related internships or fieldwork, Federal Work-Study, institutionally sponsored loans, scholarships/grants, health care benefits, and unspecified assistantships also available. Financial award application deadline: 3/15; financial award applicants required to submit FAFSA. *Faculty research:* Capital markets, derivatives, financial markets, liquidity constraints. *Unit head:* Prof. David Brown, Director, 608-265-5281, Fax: 608-265-4195, E-mail: dbrown@bus.wisc.edu. *Application contact:* Belle Heberling, Assistant Director for Research Programs, 608-262-3749, Fax: 608-890-0180, E-mail: ms@bus.wisc.edu.
Website: http://www.bus.wisc.edu/.

University of Wisconsin–Madison, Graduate School, Wisconsin School of Business, Wisconsin Full-Time MBA Program, Madison, WI 53706. Offers applied security analysis (MBA); arts administration (MBA); brand and product management (MBA); corporate finance and investment banking (MBA); marketing research (MBA); operations and technology management (MBA); real estate (MBA); risk management and insurance (MBA); strategic human resource management (MBA); supply chain management (MBA). *Faculty:* 34 full-time (5 women), 30 part-time/adjunct (15 women). *Students:* 193 full-time (61 women); includes 37 minority (10 Black or African American, non-Hispanic/Latino; 14 Asian, non-Hispanic/Latino; 12 Hispanic/Latino; 1 Native Hawaiian or other Pacific Islander, non-Hispanic/Latino), 37 international. Average age 28. 460 applicants, 33% accepted, 101 enrolled. In 2013, 110 master's awarded. *Degree requirements:* For master's, thesis (for arts administration specialization). *Entrance requirements:* For master's, GMAT or GRE, bachelor's or equivalent degree, 2 years of work experience, letters of recommendation, resume. Additional exam requirements/recommendations for international students: Required—TOEFL (minimum score 600 paper-based; 100 iBT), IELTS. *Application deadline:* For fall admission, 11/5 for domestic and international students; for winter admission, 2/4 for domestic and international students; for spring admission, 4/28 for domestic students, 4/2 for international students. Applications are processed on a rolling basis. Application fee: $56. Electronic applications accepted. *Expenses:* Contact institution. *Financial support:* In 2013–14, 176 students received support, including 12 fellowships with full tuition reimbursements available (averaging $37,956 per year), 42 research assistantships with full tuition reimbursements available (averaging $28,175 per year), 43 teaching assistantships with full tuition reimbursements available (averaging $28,175 per year); scholarships/grants, health care benefits, and unspecified assistantships also available. Financial award application deadline: 4/26; financial award applicants required to submit FAFSA. *Faculty research:* Market consequences of International Financial Reporting Standards (IFRS), inter-firm relationships and strategic partnerships, application of Bayesian statistical methods and applied probability models to understanding individuals' behaviors in the context of customer relationship management (CRM) applications, liquidity provision and the structure of financial markets, strategic management of global startups. *Unit head:* Prof. Larry W. Hunter, Associate Dean of Master's Programs, 608-265-3494, Fax: 608-265-4192, E-mail: lhunter@bus.wisc.edu. *Application contact:* William H. Wait, Assistant Director of MBA Marketing and Recruiting, 608-262-4000, Fax: 608-265-4192, E-mail: wwait@bus.wisc.edu.
Website: http://www.bus.wisc.edu/mba.

University of Wisconsin–Whitewater, School of Graduate Studies, College of Business and Economics, Program in Business Administration, Whitewater, WI 53190-1790. Offers finance (MBA); human resource management (MBA); information

technology management (MBA); international business (MBA); management (MBA); marketing (MBA); operations and supply chain management (MBA). *Accreditation:* AACSB. Part-time and evening/weekend programs available. Postbaccalaureate distance learning degree programs offered (no on-campus study). *Entrance requirements:* For master's, GMAT or GRE, minimum AACSB index of 1000, minimum GPA of 2.75. Additional exam requirements/recommendations for international students: Required—TOEFL (minimum score 550 paper-based; 80 iBT), IELTS (minimum score 6). Electronic applications accepted. *Faculty research:* Interface between social institutions and individual behavior, technology and innovation management, occupational mental health, workplace deviance and workplace romance.

University of Wyoming, College of Business, Department of Economics and Finance, Program in Economics and Finance, Laramie, WY 82071. Offers MS. *Degree requirements:* For master's, thesis. *Entrance requirements:* For master's, GRE, minimum GPA of 3.0. Additional exam requirements/recommendations for international students: Required—TOEFL (minimum score 540 paper-based; 76 iBT). *Faculty research:* Financial economics.

University of Wyoming, College of Business, Department of Economics and Finance, Program in Finance, Laramie, WY 82071. Offers MS. Part-time programs available. *Degree requirements:* For master's, thesis. *Entrance requirements:* For master's, GMAT, GRE, minimum GPA of 3.0. Additional exam requirements/recommendations for international students: Required—TOEFL (minimum score 540 paper-based; 76 iBT). *Faculty research:* Banking.

Upper Iowa University, Online Master's Programs, Fayette, IA 52142-1857. Offers accounting (MBA); corporate financial management (MBA); global business (MBA); health and human services (MPA); higher education administration (MHEA); homeland security (MPA); human resources management (MBA); justice administration (MPA); organizational development (MBA); public personnel management (MPA); quality management (MBA). MBA also available at Madison, WI campus. Part-time programs available. Postbaccalaureate distance learning degree programs offered (no on-campus study). *Degree requirements:* For master's, research project. *Entrance requirements:* For master's, GMAT, GRE, or minimum GPA of 2.7 during last 60 hours. Additional exam requirements/recommendations for international students: Required—TOEFL (minimum score 570 paper-based). Electronic applications accepted. *Faculty research:* Total quality management, CQI, teams, organization culture and climate, management.

Valparaiso University, Graduate School, College of Business, Valparaiso, IN 46383. Offers business administration (MBA); business intelligence (Certificate); engineering management (Certificate); entrepreneurship (Certificate); finance (Certificate); general business (Certificate); management (Certificate); marketing (Certificate); sustainability (Certificate); JD/MBA; MSN/MBA. *Accreditation:* AACSB. Part-time and evening/weekend programs available. Postbaccalaureate distance learning degree programs offered (minimal on-campus study). *Faculty:* 11 part-time/adjunct (2 women). *Students:* 13 full-time (3 women), 48 part-time (21 women); includes 6 minority (3 Black or African American, non-Hispanic/Latino; 2 Hispanic/Latino; 1 Two or more races, non-Hispanic/Latino), 5 international. Average age 33. In 2013, 19 master's, 3 other advanced degrees awarded. *Entrance requirements:* For master's, GMAT, GRE, minimum GPA of 3.0. Additional exam requirements/recommendations for international students: Required—TOEFL (minimum score 550 paper-based; 80 iBT), IELTS (minimum score 6). *Application deadline:* Applications are processed on a rolling basis. Application fee: $30 ($50 for international students). Electronic applications accepted. *Expenses:* Contact institution. *Financial support:* Available to part-time students. Applicants required to submit FAFSA. *Unit head:* Bruce MacLean, Director of Graduate Programs in Management, 219-465-7952, Fax: 219-464-5789, E-mail: bruce.maclean@valpo.edu. *Application contact:* Cindy Scanlan, Assistant Director of Graduate Programs in Management, 219-465-7952, Fax: 219-464-5789, E-mail: cindy.scanlan@valpo.edu. Website: http://www.valpo.edu/mba/.

Valparaiso University, Graduate School, Program in International Economics and Finance, Valparaiso, IN 46383. Offers MS. Part-time and evening/weekend programs available. *Students:* 36 full-time (16 women), 21 part-time (7 women); includes 1 minority (Black or African American, non-Hispanic/Latino), 51 international. Average age 24. In 2013, 20 master's awarded. *Entrance requirements:* For master's, 1 semester of college-level calculus; 1 statistics or quantitative methods class; 2 semesters of introductory economics (course content in introductory economics must include both introductory microeconomics and macroeconomics); 1 introductory accounting course; minimum undergraduate GPA of 3.0; 2 letters of recommendation. Additional exam requirements/recommendations for international students: Required—TOEFL (minimum score 550 paper-based; 80 iBT), IELTS (minimum score 6). Application fee: $30 ($50 for international students). *Expenses: Tuition:* Full-time $10,350; part-time $575 per credit hour. *Required fees:* $378; $101 per term. Tuition and fees vary according to course load and program. *Financial support:* Available to part-time students. Applicants required to submit FAFSA. *Unit head:* Dr. Jennifer A. Ziegler, Dean, Graduate School and Continuing Education, 219-464-5313, Fax: 219-464-5381, E-mail: jennifer.ziegler@valpo.edu. *Application contact:* Jessica Choquette, Graduate Admissions Specialist, 219-464-5313, Fax: 219-464-5381, E-mail: jessica.ziegler@valpo.edu. Website: http://www.valpo.edu/grad/ief/.

Vancouver Island University, Master of Business Administration Program, Nanaimo, BC V9R 5S5, Canada. Offers international business (MBA), including finance, marketing. Program offered jointly with University of Hertfordshire. *Accreditation:* ACBSP. Part-time programs available. *Degree requirements:* For master's, thesis. *Entrance requirements:* Additional exam requirements/recommendations for international students: Required—TOEFL (minimum score 550 paper-based). Electronic applications accepted. *Faculty research:* Tourism development, entrepreneurship, organizational development, strategic planning, international business strategy, intercultural team work.

Vanderbilt University, Vanderbilt Graduate School of Management, Vanderbilt MBA Program (Full-time), Nashville, TN 37203. Offers accounting (MBA); finance (MBA); general management (MBA); human and organizational performance (MBA); marketing (MBA); operations (MBA); strategy (MBA); MBA/JD; MBA/M Div; MBA/MD; MBA/MTS; MBA/PhD. *Accreditation:* AACSB. *Students:* 341 full-time (119 women); includes 42 minority (20 Black or African American, non-Hispanic/Latino; 12 Asian, non-Hispanic/Latino; 5 Hispanic/Latino; 5 Two or more races, non-Hispanic/Latino), 73 international. Average age 28. 1,059 applicants, 38% accepted, 166 enrolled. In 2013, 161 master's awarded. *Entrance requirements:* For master's, GMAT (preferred) or GRE, 2 years of work experience (recommended). Additional exam requirements/recommendations for international students: Required—TOEFL. *Application deadline:* For fall admission, 10/1 priority date for domestic and international students; for winter admission, 1/6 priority date for domestic and international students; for spring admission, 3/3 priority date for domestic students, 3/5 priority date for international students; for summer admission, 4/5 for domestic students, 5/5 for international students. Applications are processed on a rolling basis. Application fee: $75 ($175 for international students). Electronic applications accepted. *Financial support:* In 2013–14, 237 students received support. Scholarships/grants and tuition waivers (full and partial) available. Financial award application deadline: 5/15; financial award applicants required to submit FAFSA. *Unit head:* Nancy Lea Hyer, Associate Dean, 615-322-2530, Fax: 615-343-7110, E-mail:

nancy.lea.hyer@owen.vanderbilt.edu. *Application contact:* Dinah Webster, Administrative Assistant, 615-322-6469, Fax: 615-343-1175, E-mail: mba@owen.vanderbilt.edu. Website: http://www.owen.vanderbilt.edu.

Vanderbilt University, Vanderbilt Graduate School of Management, Vanderbilt MS Finance Program, Nashville, TN 37203. Offers MS. *Students:* 43 full-time (10 women); includes 4 minority (2 Black or African American, non-Hispanic/Latino; 1 Asian, non-Hispanic/Latino; 1 Hispanic/Latino), 10 international. Average age 26. 899 applicants, 9% accepted, 44 enrolled. In 2013, 34 master's awarded. *Entrance requirements:* For master's, GMAT and/or GRE. Additional exam requirements/recommendations for international students: Required—TOEFL (minimum score 105 iBT). *Application deadline:* For fall admission, 10/31 priority date for domestic and international students; for winter admission, 12/10 priority date for domestic and international students; for spring admission, 3/11 priority date for domestic students, 3/11 for international students; for summer admission, 5/15 for domestic students, 4/15 for international students. Applications are processed on a rolling basis. Application fee: $90. Electronic applications accepted. *Financial support:* In 2013–14, 29 students received support. Scholarships/grants and tuition waivers (partial) available. Financial award application deadline: 5/15; financial award applicants required to submit FAFSA. *Unit head:* Kate Barraclough, PhD, Faculty Program Director, 615-343-8108, E-mail: kate.barraclough@owen.vanderbilt.edu. *Application contact:* Dinah Webster, Administrative Assistant, 615-322-6469, Fax: 615-343-1175, E-mail: msfinance@owen.vanderbilt.edu. Website: http://www.owen.vanderbilt.edu.

Villanova University, Villanova School of Business, Master of Science in Finance Program, Villanova, PA 19085. Offers MSF. *Faculty:* 101 full-time (33 women), 36 part-time/adjunct (3 women). *Students:* 24 full-time (4 women); includes 4 minority (2 American Indian or Alaska Native, non-Hispanic/Latino; 2 Asian, non-Hispanic/Latino), 5 international. Average age 24. 133 applicants, 41% accepted, 26 enrolled. In 2013, 22 master's awarded. *Degree requirements:* For master's, minimum cumulative GPA of 3.0. *Entrance requirements:* For master's, GMAT, prerequisite course in principles of finance. Additional exam requirements/recommendations for international students: Required—TOEFL (minimum score 550 paper-based; 90 iBT). *Application deadline:* For spring admission, 3/15 for domestic and international students. Application fee: $50. Electronic applications accepted. *Financial support:* In 2013–14, 4 research assistantships (averaging $6,550 per year) were awarded; scholarships/grants and unspecified assistantships also available. Financial award application deadline: 6/30; financial award applicants required to submit FAFSA. *Faculty research:* Business analytics; creativity, innovation and entrepreneurship; global leadership; real estate; church management; business ethics. *Unit head:* Zelon Crawford, Director of Graduate Business Programs, 610-519-6283, Fax: 610-519-6273, E-mail: zelon.crawford@villanova.edu. *Application contact:* Meredith L. Lockyer, Manager of Recruiting, 610-519-7016, Fax: 610-519-6273, E-mail: meredith.lockyer@villanova.edu. Website: http://www1.villanova.edu/villanova/business/graduate/specializedprograms/msf.html.

Villanova University, Villanova School of Business, MBA - The Fast Track Program, Villanova, PA 19085. Offers finance (MBA); health care management (MBA); international business (MBA); management information systems (MBA); marketing (MBA); real estate (MBA); strategic management (MBA). *Accreditation:* AACSB. Part-time and evening/weekend programs available. *Faculty:* 101 full-time (33 women), 36 part-time/adjunct (3 women). *Students:* 140 part-time (44 women); includes 22 minority (1 Black or African American, non-Hispanic/Latino; 17 Asian, non-Hispanic/Latino; 3 Hispanic/Latino; 1 Two or more races, non-Hispanic/Latino), 3 international. Average age 29. 127 applicants, 72% accepted, 75 enrolled. In 2013, 61 master's awarded. *Degree requirements:* For master's, minimum GPA of 3.0. *Entrance requirements:* For master's, GMAT or GRE, work experience. Additional exam requirements/recommendations for international students: Required—TOEFL (minimum score 550 paper-based; 90 iBT). *Application deadline:* For fall admission, 6/30 for domestic and international students. Application fee: $50. Electronic applications accepted. *Financial support:* Scholarships/grants available. Financial award application deadline: 6/30; financial award applicants required to submit FAFSA. *Faculty research:* Business analytics; creativity, innovation and entrepreneurship; global leadership; real estate; church management; business ethics. *Unit head:* Zelon Crawford, Director of Graduate Business Programs, 610-519-6283, Fax: 610-519-6273, E-mail: zelon.crawford@villanova.edu. *Application contact:* Meredith L. Lockyer, Manager of Recruiting, 610-519-7016, Fax: 610-519-6273, E-mail: meredith.lockyer@villanova.edu. Website: http://www1.villanova.edu/villanova/business/graduate/mba/fasttrack.html.

Villanova University, Villanova School of Business, MBA - The Flex Track Program, Villanova, PA 19085. Offers finance (MBA); health care management (MBA); international business (MBA); management information systems (MBA); marketing (MBA); real estate (MBA); strategic management (MBA); JD/MBA. *Accreditation:* AACSB. Part-time and evening/weekend programs available. Postbaccalaureate distance learning degree programs offered (minimal on-campus study). *Faculty:* 101 full-time (33 women), 36 part-time/adjunct (3 women). *Students:* 13 full-time (5 women), 413 part-time (127 women); includes 63 minority (13 Black or African American, non-Hispanic/Latino; 1 American Indian or Alaska Native, non-Hispanic/Latino; 29 Asian, non-Hispanic/Latino; 14 Hispanic/Latino; 1 Native Hawaiian or other Pacific Islander, non-Hispanic/Latino; 5 Two or more races, non-Hispanic/Latino), 9 international. Average age 29. 84 applicants, 83% accepted, 66 enrolled. In 2013, 133 master's awarded. *Degree requirements:* For master's, minimum GPA of 3.0. *Entrance requirements:* For master's, GMAT or GRE, work experience. Additional exam requirements/recommendations for international students: Required—TOEFL (minimum score 550 paper-based; 90 iBT). *Application deadline:* For fall admission, 6/30 for domestic and international students; for winter admission, 11/15 for domestic and international students; for spring admission, 11/15 for domestic and international students; for summer admission, 3/31 for domestic and international students. Applications are processed on a rolling basis. Application fee: $50. Electronic applications accepted. *Financial support:* In 2013–14, 13 research assistantships with full tuition reimbursements (averaging $13,100 per year) were awarded; scholarships/grants and unspecified assistantships also available. Financial award application deadline: 6/30; financial award applicants required to submit FAFSA. *Faculty research:* Business analytics; creativity, innovation and entrepreneurship; global leadership; real estate; church management; business ethics. *Unit head:* Zelon Crawford, Director of Graduate Business Programs, 610-610-6283, Fax: 610-519-6273, E-mail: zelon.crawford@villanova.edu. *Application contact:* Meredith L. Lockyer, Manager of Recruiting, 610-519-7016, Fax: 610-519-6273, E-mail: meredith.lockyer@villanova.edu. Website: http://www1.villanova.edu/villanova/business/graduate/mba/flextrack.html.

Virginia Commonwealth University, Graduate School, School of Business, Program in Finance, Insurance, and Real Estate, Richmond, VA 23284-9005. Offers MS. *Entrance requirements:* For master's, GMAT. Additional exam requirements/recommendations for international students: Required—TOEFL (minimum score 600 paper-based; 100 iBT); Recommended—IELTS (minimum score 6.5). Electronic applications accepted.

Virginia International University, School of Business, Fairfax, VA 22030. Offers accounting (MBA); executive management (Graduate Certificate); global logistics

(MBA); health care management (MBA); human resources management (MBA); international business management (MBA); international finance (MBA); marketing management (MBA). Part-time programs available. *Entrance requirements:* For master's and Graduate Certificate, bachelor's degree. Additional exam requirements/recommendations for international students: Required—TOEFL (minimum score 550 paper-based; 80 iBT), IELTS (minimum score 6). Electronic applications accepted.

Wagner College, Division of Graduate Studies, Department of Business Administration, Program in Finance, Staten Island, NY 10301-4495. Offers MBA. Part-time and evening/weekend programs available. *Faculty:* 1 (woman) full-time, 2 part-time/adjunct (0 women). *Students:* 12 full-time (3 women), 5 part-time (1 woman); includes 2 minority (both Black or African American, non-Hispanic/Latino), 1 international. Average age 25. 7 applicants, 100% accepted, 4 enrolled. In 2013, 7 master's awarded. *Degree requirements:* For master's, thesis optional. *Entrance requirements:* For master's, GMAT, minimum GPA of 2.6, computer and math proficiency. Additional exam requirements/recommendations for international students: Required—TOEFL (minimum score 550 paper-based; 79 iBT). *Application deadline:* For fall admission, 4/1 priority date for domestic students, 3/1 priority date for international students; for spring admission, 12/1 priority date for domestic students, 10/1 priority date for international students. Applications are processed on a rolling basis. Application fee: $50. *Expenses: Tuition:* Full-time $17,496; part-time $972 per credit. Tuition and fees vary according to course load. *Financial support:* In 2013–14, 15 students received support. Career-related internships or fieldwork, unspecified assistantships, and alumni fellowship grants available. Financial award applicants required to submit FAFSA. *Unit head:* Dr. John J. Moran, Director, 718-390-3255, Fax: 718-390-3255, E-mail: jmoran@wagner.edu. *Application contact:* Patricia Clancy, Administrative Assistant, Admissions, 718-420-4464, Fax: 718-390-3105, E-mail: patricia.clancy@wagner.edu.

Wake Forest University, School of Business, Full-time MBA Program, Winston-Salem, NC 27106. Offers finance (MBA); marketing (MBA); operations management (MBA); JD/MBA; MD/MBA; MSA/MBA. *Accreditation:* AACSB. *Faculty:* 77 full-time (21 women), 32 part-time/adjunct (8 women). *Students:* 107 full-time (33 women); includes 22 minority (11 Black or African American, non-Hispanic/Latino; 4 Asian, non-Hispanic/Latino; 3 Hispanic/Latino; 4 Two or more races, non-Hispanic/Latino), 21 international. Average age 30. In 2013, 66 master's awarded. *Degree requirements:* For master's, 65.5 credit hours. *Entrance requirements:* For master's, GMAT or GRE, letters of recommendation, official transcripts, current resume or curriculum vitae, 2 years of work experience. Additional exam requirements/recommendations for international students: Required—TOEFL (minimum score 600 paper-based; 100 iBT), PTE. *Application deadline:* For fall admission, 4/15 for domestic and international students. Applications are processed on a rolling basis. Application fee: $100. Electronic applications accepted. *Expenses:* Contact institution. *Financial support:* In 2013–14, 90 students received support. Career-related internships or fieldwork, scholarships/grants, and unspecified assistantships available. Financial award application deadline: 2/15; financial award applicants required to submit FAFSA. *Faculty research:* The influence of personal relationships on business decision-making and management of change; drivers of perceived value and consumer behavior; impact of accounting on auditing, financial, managerial, systems and taxation stakeholders; corporate governance and executive compensation; impact of operations strategies on competitiveness. *Unit head:* Scott Schaffer, Associate Dean, 336-758-5422, Fax: 336-758-5830, E-mail: busadmissions@wfu.edu. *Application contact:* Tamara Paquee, Administrative Assistant, 336-758-5422, Fax: 336-758-5830, E-mail: busadmissions@wfu.edu.
Website: http://www.business.wfu.edu/.

Walden University, Graduate Programs, School of Management, Minneapolis, MN 55401. Offers accounting (MBA, MS, DBA), including accounting for the professional (MS), accounting with CPA emphasis (MS), self-designed (MS, PhD); accounting and management (MS), including accountants as strategic managers, self-designed (MS, PhD); advanced project management (Graduate Certificate); applied project management (Graduate Certificate); bridge to business administration (Post-Doctoral Certificate); bridge to management (Post-Doctoral Certificate); business administration (EMBA); business management (Graduate Certificate); communication (MS, Graduate Certificate); corporate finance (MBA); entrepreneurship (DBA); entrepreneurship and small business (MBA); finance (DBA); global supply chain management (DBA); healthcare management (MBA, DBA); human resource management (MBA, MS, Graduate Certificate), including functional human resource management (MS), general program (MS), integrating functional and strategic human resource management (MS), organizational strategy (MS); human resources management (DBA); information systems management (DBA); international business (MBA, DBA); leadership (MBA, MS, DBA), including general program (MS), human resources leadership (MS), leader development (MS), self-designed (MS, PhD); management (MS, PhD), including accounting (PhD), engineering management (PhD), finance (PhD), general program (MS), healthcare management (MS), human resource management (MS), human resources management (PhD), information systems management (PhD), leadership (MS), leadership and organizational change (PhD), marketing (MS), operations research (PhD), project management (MS), self-designed, strategy and operations (MS); marketing (MBA, DBA); project management (MBA, MS, DBA); self-designed (MBA, DBA); social impact management (DBA); technology entrepreneurship (DBA). Part-time and evening/weekend programs available. Postbaccalaureate distance learning degree programs offered (minimal on-campus study). *Faculty:* 24 full-time (9 women), 337 part-time/adjunct (127 women). *Students:* 4,369 full-time (2,379 women), 2,181 part-time (1,304 women); includes 3,669 minority (3,020 Black or African American, non-Hispanic/Latino; 22 American Indian or Alaska Native, non-Hispanic/Latino; 156 Asian, non-Hispanic/Latino; 331 Hispanic/Latino; 11 Native Hawaiian or other Pacific Islander, non-Hispanic/Latino; 129 Two or more races, non-Hispanic/Latino), 107 international. Average age 41. 2,030 applicants, 94% accepted, 1436 enrolled. In 2013, 757 master's, 128 doctorates, 32 other advanced degrees awarded. *Degree requirements:* For master's, residency (for some programs); for doctorate, thesis/dissertation (for some programs), residency. *Entrance requirements:* For master's, bachelor's degree or higher; minimum GPA of 2.5; official transcripts; goal statement (for some programs); access to computer and Internet; for doctorate, master's degree or higher; three years of related professional or academic experience (preferred); minimum GPA of 3.0; goal statement and current resume (select programs); official transcripts; access to computer and Internet; for other advanced degree, relevant work experience; access to computer and Internet. Additional exam requirements/recommendations for international students: Required—TOEFL (minimum score 550 paper-based; 79 iBT), IELTS (minimum score 6.5), Michigan English Language Assessment Battery (minimum score 82), or PTE. *Application deadline:* Applications are processed on a rolling basis. Application fee: $0. Electronic applications accepted. *Expenses: Tuition:* Full-time $11,813.55; part-time $500 per credit. *Required fees:* $618.76. *Financial support:* Fellowships, Federal Work-Study, scholarships/grants, unspecified assistantships, and family tuition reduction, active duty/veteran tuition reduction, group tuition reduction, interest-free payment plans, employee tuition reduction available. Support available to part-time students. Financial award applicants required to submit FAFSA. *Unit head:* Dr. Ward Ulmer, III, Associate Dean, 800-925-3368. *Application contact:* Jennifer Hall, Vice President of Enrollment Management, 866-4-WALDEN, E-mail: info@waldenu.edu.
Website: http://www.waldenu.edu/programs/colleges-schools/management.

Walsh College of Accountancy and Business Administration, Graduate Programs, Program in Finance, Troy, MI 48007-7006. Offers MSF. Part-time and evening/weekend programs available. *Entrance requirements:* For master's, minimum GPA of 2.75, previous course work in business. Additional exam requirements/recommendations for international students: Required—TOEFL. Electronic applications accepted.

Washington State University, Graduate School, College of Business, Online MBA Program, Pullman, WA 99164. Offers finance (MBA); general business (MBA); international business (MBA); marketing (MBA). Postbaccalaureate distance learning degree programs offered (no on-campus study).

Washington State University, Graduate School, College of Business, PhD Program in Finance, Pullman, WA 99164. Offers PhD. *Degree requirements:* For doctorate, thesis/dissertation, qualifying exam, written field examination.

Washington University in St. Louis, Olin Business School, Program in Finance, St. Louis, MO 63130-4899. Offers MS. Part-time programs available. *Faculty:* 82 full-time (18 women), 38 part-time/adjunct (8 women). *Students:* 75 full-time (20 women), 9 part-time (1 woman); includes 14 minority (8 Asian, non-Hispanic/Latino; 3 Hispanic/Latino; 3 Two or more races, non-Hispanic/Latino), 45 international. Average age 24. 1,485 applicants, 16% accepted, 75 enrolled. In 2013, 52 master's awarded. *Entrance requirements:* For master's, GMAT or GRE. Additional exam requirements/recommendations for international students: Required—TOEFL, IELTS. *Application deadline:* For fall admission, 10/1 for domestic and international students; for winter admission, 11/15 for domestic and international students; for spring admission, 4/1 for domestic and international students. Application fee: $100. Electronic applications accepted. *Expenses:* Contact institution. *Financial support:* Applicants required to submit FAFSA. *Unit head:* Greg Hutchings, Associate Dean/Director of Specialized Master's Programs, 314-935-6380, Fax: 314-935-4464, E-mail: hutchings@wustl.edu. *Application contact:* Nikki Lemley, Associate Director, Specialized Master's Programs Admissions, 314-935-8469, Fax: 314-935-4464, E-mail: nlemley@wustl.edu.
Website: http://www.olin.wustl.edu/prospective/.

Waynesburg University, Graduate and Professional Studies, Canonsburg, PA 15370. Offers business (MBA), including energy management, finance, health systems, human resources, leadership, market development; counseling (MA), including addictions counseling, clinical mental health; education (M Ed, MAT), including autism (M Ed), curriculum and instruction (M Ed), educational leadership (M Ed), online teaching (M Ed); nursing (MSN), including administration, education, informatics; nursing practice (DNP); special education (M Ed); technology (M Ed); MSN/MBA. *Accreditation:* AACN. Part-time and evening/weekend programs available. *Faculty:* 11 full-time (5 women), 136 part-time/adjunct (80 women). *Students:* 146 full-time (99 women), 419 part-time (268 women). In 2013, 290 master's, 7 doctorates awarded. *Degree requirements:* For doctorate, thesis/dissertation. *Entrance requirements:* Additional exam requirements/recommendations for international students: Required—TOEFL. *Application deadline:* For fall admission, 8/1 priority date for domestic students. Applications are processed on a rolling basis. Electronic applications accepted. *Financial support:* Available to part-time students. Application deadline: 5/1. *Unit head:* David Mariner, Dean, 724-743-4420, Fax: 724-743-4425, E-mail: dmariner@waynesburg.edu. *Application contact:* Dr. Michael Bednarski, Director of Enrollment, 724-743-4420, Fax: 724-743-4425, E-mail: mbednars@waynesburg.edu.
Website: http://www.waynesburg.edu/.

Wayne State University, College of Liberal Arts and Sciences, Department of Political Science, Program in Public Administration, Detroit, MI 48202. Offers aging policy and management (MPA); criminal justice policy and management (MPA); economic development policy and management (MPA); health and human services policy and management (MPA); human and fiscal resource management (MPA); information technology management (MPA); nonprofit policy and management (MPA); organizational behavior and management (MPA); public budgeting and financial management (MPA); public policy analysis and program evaluation (MPA); social welfare policy and management (MPA); urban and metropolitan policy and management (MPA). *Accreditation:* NASPAA. Evening/weekend programs available. *Students:* 11 full-time (5 women), 55 part-time (43 women); includes 20 minority (14 Black or African American, non-Hispanic/Latino; 2 Asian, non-Hispanic/Latino; 2 Hispanic/Latino; 2 Two or more races, non-Hispanic/Latino), 1 international. Average age 33. 83 applicants, 34% accepted, 17 enrolled. In 2013, 19 master's awarded. *Degree requirements:* For master's, comprehensive exam. *Entrance requirements:* For master's, GRE General Test, minimum undergraduate upper-division GPA of 3.0 or master's degree. Additional exam requirements/recommendations for international students: Required—TOEFL (minimum score 550 paper-based; 79 iBT), TWE (minimum score 5.5), Michigan English Language Assessment Battery (minimum score 85); Recommended—IELTS (minimum score 6.5). *Application deadline:* For fall admission, 6/1 priority date for domestic students, 5/1 priority date for international students; for winter admission, 10/1 priority date for domestic students, 9/1 priority date for international students; for spring admission, 2/1 priority date for domestic students, 1/1 priority date for international students. Applications are processed on a rolling basis. Application fee: $0. Electronic applications accepted. *Expenses:* Tuition, state resident: part-time $554.15 per credit. Tuition, nonresident: part-time $1200.35 per credit. *Required fees:* $42.15 per credit. $268.30 per semester. Tuition and fees vary according to course load and program. *Financial support:* In 2013–14, 21 students received support. Fellowships, teaching assistantships, scholarships/grants, and unspecified assistantships available. Financial award application deadline: 3/31; financial award applicants required to submit FAFSA. *Faculty research:* Urban politics, urban education, state administration. *Unit head:* Dr. Daniel Geller, Department Chair, 313-577-6328, E-mail: dgeller@wayne.edu. *Application contact:* Dr. Brady Baybeck, Associate Professor/Director, Graduate Program in Public Administration, E-mail: mpa@wayne.edu.
Website: http://clasweb.clas.wayne.edu/mpa.

Wayne State University, Law School, Detroit, MI 48202. Offers corporate and finance law (LL M); labor and employment law (LL M); law (JD); taxation (LL M); United States law (LL M); JD/MA; JD/MADR; JD/MBA. *Accreditation:* ABA. Part-time and evening/weekend programs available. *Faculty:* 35 full-time (16 women), 21 part-time/adjunct (7 women). *Students:* 418 full-time (178 women), 82 part-time (48 women); includes 75 minority (40 Black or African American, non-Hispanic/Latino; 3 American Indian or Alaska Native, non-Hispanic/Latino; 18 Asian, non-Hispanic/Latino; 11 Hispanic/Latino; 3 Two or more races, non-Hispanic/Latino), 13 international. Average age 27. 807 applicants, 48% accepted, 139 enrolled. In 2013, 2 master's, 172 doctorates awarded. *Degree requirements:* For master's, essay. *Entrance requirements:* For master's, admission to the Graduate School, JD from ABA-accredited institution and member institution of the AALS; for doctorate, LSAT, LDAS report, bachelor's degree from accredited institution, personal statement, transcripts from all U.S. undergraduate schools attended and an analysis and summary of the transcripts; letter of recommendation (up to two are accepted). Additional exam requirements/recommendations for international students: Required—TOEFL (minimum score 600 paper-based), Michigan English Language Assessment Battery (minimum score 85); Recommended—IELTS (minimum score 6.5). *Application deadline:* For fall admission, 5/15 for domestic and international students. Application fee: $0. Electronic applications accepted. *Expenses:* Contact institution. *Financial support:* Scholarships/grants

Finance and Banking

available. Support available to part-time students. Financial award application deadline: 3/31; financial award applicants required to submit FAFSA. *Faculty research:* Public interest law, tax law, international law, environmental law, health law. *Unit head:* Jocelyn Benson, Dean, 313-577-3933. *Application contact:* Marcia McDonald, Director of Admissions, 313-577-3937, Fax: 313-993-8129, E-mail: marcia.mcdonald2@wayne.edu.
Website: http://law.wayne.edu/.

Webster University, George Herbert Walker School of Business and Technology, Department of Business, St. Louis, MO 63119-3194. Offers business and organizational security management (MBA); decision support systems (MBA); environmental management (MBA); finance (MBA, MS); forensic accounting (MS); gerontology (MBA); human resources development (MBA); human resources management (MBA); information technology management (MBA); international business (MA, MBA); international relations (MBA); management and leadership (MBA); marketing (MBA); media communications (MBA); procurement and acquisitions management (MBA); Web services (MBA). *Accreditation:* ACBSP. Part-time and evening/weekend programs available. Postbaccalaureate distance learning degree programs offered (no on-campus study). *Degree requirements:* For master's, comprehensive exam (for some programs), thesis (for some programs). *Entrance requirements:* Additional exam requirements/recommendations for international students: Required—TOEFL. *Expenses: Tuition:* Full-time $11,610; part-time $645 per credit hour. Tuition and fees vary according to campus/location and program.

Western International University, Graduate Programs in Business, Master of Business Administration Program in Finance, Phoenix, AZ 85021-2718. Offers MBA. Part-time and evening/weekend programs available. Postbaccalaureate distance learning degree programs offered (no on-campus study). *Entrance requirements:* For master's, minimum GPA of 2.75. Additional exam requirements/recommendations for international students: Required—TOEFL (minimum score 550 paper-based; 79 iBT), TWE (minimum score 5), or IELTS (minimum score 6.5). Electronic applications accepted.

Western Michigan University, Graduate College, Haworth College of Business, Department of Finance and Commercial Law, Kalamazoo, MI 49008. Offers finance (MBA). *Accreditation:* AACSB. *Entrance requirements:* For master's, GMAT.

West Texas A&M University, College of Business, Department of Accounting, Economics, and Finance, Program in Finance and Economics, Canyon, TX 79016-0001. Offers MS. Part-time and evening/weekend programs available. Postbaccalaureate distance learning degree programs offered (minimal on-campus study). *Degree requirements:* For master's, comprehensive exam, thesis optional. *Entrance requirements:* For master's, GMAT. Additional exam requirements/recommendations for international students: Required—TOEFL (minimum score 550 paper-based). Electronic applications accepted. *Faculty research:* International trade composition, cycle of poverty, trade effects in Asian countries, structural problems in Japanese economy, reform and the US sugar program-Nebraska.

Wilfrid Laurier University, Faculty of Graduate and Postdoctoral Studies, School of Business and Economics, Department of Business, Waterloo, ON N2L 3C5, Canada. Offers accounting (PhD); finance (M Fin); financial economics (PhD); marketing (PhD); operations and supply chain management (PhD); organizational behavior and human resource management (M Sc); organizational behaviour and human resource management (PhD); supply chain management (M Sc); technology management (EMTM). *Accreditation:* AACSB. Part-time and evening/weekend programs available. *Degree requirements:* For master's, thesis optional; for doctorate, comprehensive exam, thesis/dissertation. *Entrance requirements:* For master's, GMAT, 4-year honors degree with minimum B+ average; for doctorate, GMAT, master's degree, minimum B+ average. Additional exam requirements/recommendations for international students: Required—TOEFL (minimum score 89 iBT). Electronic applications accepted. *Faculty research:* Financial economics, management and organizational behavior, operations and supply chain management.

Wilkes University, College of Graduate and Professional Studies, Jay S. Sidhu School of Business and Leadership, Wilkes-Barre, PA 18766-0002. Offers accounting (MBA); entrepreneurship (MBA); finance (MBA); health care administration (MBA); human resource management (MBA); international business (MBA); marketing (MBA); operations management (MBA); organizational leadership and development (MBA). *Accreditation:* ACBSP. Part-time and evening/weekend programs available. *Students:* 41 full-time (20 women), 119 part-time (48 women); includes 20 minority (5 Black or African American, non-Hispanic/Latino; 3 Asian, non-Hispanic/Latino; 7 Hispanic/Latino; 5 Two or more races, non-Hispanic/Latino), 7 international. Average age 31. In 2013, 55 master's awarded. *Entrance requirements:* For master's, GMAT. Additional exam requirements/recommendations for international students: Required—TOEFL (minimum score 550 paper-based; 79 iBT). *Application deadline:* Applications are processed on a rolling basis. Application fee: $45 ($65 for international students). Electronic applications accepted. *Expenses:* Contact institution. *Financial support:* Federal Work-Study and unspecified assistantships available. Financial award application deadline: 3/1; financial award applicants required to submit FAFSA. *Unit head:* Dr. Jeffrey Alves, Dean, 570-408-4702, Fax: 570-408-7846, E-mail: jeffrey.alves@wilkes.edu. *Application contact:* Joanne Thomas, Interim Director of Graduate Enrollment, 570-408-4234, Fax: 570-408-7846, E-mail: joanne.thomas1@wilkes.edu.
Website: http://www.wilkes.edu/pages/457.asp.

Wilmington University, College of Business, New Castle, DE 19720-6491. Offers accounting (MBA, MS); business administration (MBA, DBA); environmental stewardship (MBA); finance (MBA); health care administration (MBA, MSM); homeland security (MBA, MSM); human resource management (MSM); management information systems (MBA, MSN); marketing (MSM); marketing management (MBA); military leadership (MSM); organizational leadership (MBA, MSM); public administration (MSM). Part-time and evening/weekend programs available. *Entrance requirements:* Additional exam requirements/recommendations for international students: Required—TOEFL (minimum score 500 paper-based). Electronic applications accepted.

Wright State University, School of Graduate Studies, Raj Soin College of Business, Department of Finance and Financial Services, Dayton, OH 45435. Offers finance (MBA); MBA/MS. *Entrance requirements:* For master's, GMAT, minimum AACSB index of 1000. Additional exam requirements/recommendations for international students: Required—TOEFL.

Xavier University, Williams College of Business, Master of Business Administration Program, Cincinnati, OH 45207-3221. Offers business administration (Exec MBA, MBA); business intelligence (MBA); finance (MBA); health industry (MBA); international business (MBA); marketing (MBA); values-based leadership (MBA); MBA/MHSA; MSN/MBA. *Accreditation:* AACSB. Part-time and evening/weekend programs available.

Faculty: 39 full-time (17 women), 12 part-time/adjunct (2 women). *Students:* 163 full-time (47 women), 483 part-time (162 women); includes 91 minority (28 Black or African American, non-Hispanic/Latino; 3 American Indian or Alaska Native, non-Hispanic/Latino; 42 Asian, non-Hispanic/Latino; 14 Hispanic/Latino; 4 Two or more races, non-Hispanic/Latino), 33 international. Average age 30. 190 applicants, 86% accepted, 110 enrolled. In 2013, 319 master's awarded. *Degree requirements:* For master's, capstone course. *Entrance requirements:* For master's, GMAT or GRE. Additional exam requirements/recommendations for international students: Required—TOEFL (minimum score 550 paper-based; 79 iBT). *Application deadline:* For fall admission, 8/1 priority date for domestic students, 5/1 for international students; for spring admission, 12/1 priority date for domestic students, 9/1 for international students. Applications are processed on a rolling basis. Application fee: $0. Electronic applications accepted. *Expenses:* Contact institution. *Financial support:* In 2013–14, 115 students received support. Scholarships/grants, tuition waivers (partial), and unspecified assistantships available. Financial award application deadline: 3/1; financial award applicants required to submit FAFSA. *Unit head:* Jennifer Bush, Assistant Dean of Graduate Programs, Williams College of Business, 513-745-3527, Fax: 513-745-2929, E-mail: bush@xavier.edu. *Application contact:* Lauren Parcell, MBA Advisor, 513-745-1014, Fax: 513-745-2929, E-mail: parcell@xavier.edu.
Website: http://www.xavier.edu/williams/mba/.

Yale University, Yale School of Management and Graduate School of Arts and Sciences, Doctoral Program in Management, New Haven, CT 06520. Offers accounting (PhD); financial economics (PhD); marketing (PhD); organizations and management (PhD). *Accreditation:* AACSB. *Degree requirements:* For doctorate, comprehensive exam, thesis/dissertation. *Entrance requirements:* For doctorate, GMAT or GRE General Test. Additional exam requirements/recommendations for international students: Required—TOEFL or IELTS. Electronic applications accepted. *Expenses:* Contact institution. *Faculty research:* Pricing of options and futures, term structure of interest rates, use of accounting numbers in debt contracts, product differentiation, e-commerce and marketing, behavioral finance.

York College of Pennsylvania, Graham School of Business, York, PA 17405-7199. Offers continuous improvement (MBA); financial management (MBA); health care management (MBA); management (MBA); marketing (MBA); self-designed focus (MBA). *Accreditation:* ACBSP. Part-time and evening/weekend programs available. *Faculty:* 13 full-time (3 women), 2 part-time/adjunct (0 women). *Students:* 6 full-time (all women), 109 part-time (40 women); includes 8 minority (2 Black or African American, non-Hispanic/Latino; 1 Asian, non-Hispanic/Latino; 1 Hispanic/Latino; 4 Two or more races, non-Hispanic/Latino), 3 international. Average age 30. 62 applicants, 63% accepted, 23 enrolled. In 2013, 24 master's awarded. *Entrance requirements:* For master's, GMAT. Additional exam requirements/recommendations for international students: Required—TOEFL (minimum score 530 paper-based; 72 iBT). *Application deadline:* For fall admission, 7/15 priority date for domestic students; for spring admission, 12/15 priority date for domestic students. Applications are processed on a rolling basis. Application fee: $50. Electronic applications accepted. *Expenses: Tuition:* Full-time $12,870; part-time $715 per credit. *Required fees:* $1660; $360 per semester. Tuition and fees vary according to degree level. *Financial support:* In 2013–14, 4 students received support. Scholarships/grants available. Financial award application deadline: 4/15; financial award applicants required to submit FAFSA. *Unit head:* Dr. David Greisler, MBA Director, 717-815-6410, Fax: 717-600-3999, E-mail: dgreisle@ycp.edu. *Application contact:* Brenda Adams, Assistant Director, MBA Program, 717-815-1749, Fax: 717-600-3999, E-mail: badams@ycp.edu.
Website: http://www.ycp.edu/mba.

York University, Faculty of Graduate Studies, Schulich School of Business, Toronto, ON M3J 1P3, Canada. Offers accounting (M Acc); administration (PhD); business (MBA); business analytics (MBA); finance (MF); international business (IMBA); MBA/JD; MBA/MA; MBA/MFA. Part-time and evening/weekend programs available. *Students:* 683 full-time (255 women), 407 part-time (125 women). Average age 29. 1,498 applicants, 30% accepted, 409 enrolled. In 2013, 587 master's, 96 doctorates awarded. *Median time to degree:* Of those who began their doctoral program in fall 2005, 55% received their degree in 8 years or less. *Degree requirements:* For master's, advanced proficiency in a second language, work term (IMBA); for doctorate, comprehensive exam, thesis/dissertation. *Entrance requirements:* For master's, GMAT or GRE, minimum GPA of 3.0 (3.3 for MF, MBA in business analytics, and IMBA); for doctorate, GMAT or GRE, minimum GPA of 3.3. Additional exam requirements/recommendations for international students: Required—TOEFL (minimum score 600 paper-based; 100 iBT), IELTS (minimum score 7), York English Language Test (minimum score 1); PearsonVUE (minimum score 64). *Application deadline:* For fall admission, 4/30 for domestic students, 2/28 for international students; for winter admission, 9/1 for domestic and international students. Applications are processed on a rolling basis. Application fee: $150. Electronic applications accepted. *Financial support:* In 2013–14, 800 students received support, including fellowships (averaging $5,000 per year), research assistantships (averaging $3,000 per year), teaching assistantships (averaging $7,000 per year); career-related internships or fieldwork, scholarships/grants, and bursaries (for part-time students) also available. Financial award application deadline: 2/1. *Faculty research:* Accounting, finance, marketing, operations management and information systems, organizational studies, strategic management. *Unit head:* Dezso Horvath, Dean, 416-736-5070, E-mail: dhorvath@schulich.yorku.ca. *Application contact:* Graduate Admissions, 416-736-5060, Fax: 416-650-8174, E-mail: admissions@schulich.yorku.ca.
Website: http://www.schulich.yorku.ca.

Youngstown State University, Graduate School, College of Liberal Arts and Social Sciences, Department of Economics, Youngstown, OH 44555-0001. Offers economics (MA); financial economics (MA). Part-time programs available. *Degree requirements:* For master's, comprehensive exam, thesis optional. *Entrance requirements:* For master's, minimum GPA of 2.7, 21 hours in economics. Additional exam requirements/recommendations for international students: Required—TOEFL. *Faculty research:* Forecasting, applied econometrics, labor economics, applied macroeconomics, industrial organization.

Youngstown State University, Graduate School, Williamson College of Business Administration, Department of Accounting and Finance, Youngstown, OH 44555-0001. Offers accounting (MBA). *Accreditation:* AACSB. Part-time and evening/weekend programs available. *Degree requirements:* For master's, thesis optional. *Entrance requirements:* For master's, GMAT, minimum GPA of 2.7. Additional exam requirements/recommendations for international students: Required—TOEFL. *Faculty research:* Taxation and compliance, capital markets, accounting information systems, accounting theory, tax and government accounting.

Investment Management

Alaska Pacific University, Graduate Programs, Business Administration Department, Anchorage, AK 99508-4672. Offers business administration (MBA), including business administration, health services administration; information and communication technology (MBAICT); investment (CGS). Part-time and evening/weekend programs available. *Degree requirements:* For master's, capstone course. *Entrance requirements:* For master's, GMAT or GRE General Test, minimum GPA of 3.0. Additional exam requirements/recommendations for international students: Required—TOEFL (minimum score 550 paper-based).

Boston University, School of Management, Boston, MA 02215. Offers business administration (MBA); executive business administration (EMBA); investment management (MS); management (PhD); mathematical finance (MS, PhD); JD/MBA; MBA/MA; MBA/MPH; MBA/MS; MBA/MSIS; MD/MBA; MS/MBA. *Accreditation:* AACSB. Part-time and evening/weekend programs available. *Faculty:* 185 full-time (49 women), 60 part-time/adjunct (15 women). *Students:* 497 full-time (171 women), 723 part-time (269 women); includes 162 minority (16 Black or African American, non-Hispanic/Latino; 108 Asian, non-Hispanic/Latino; 29 Hispanic/Latino; 9 Two or more races, non-Hispanic/Latino), 278 international. Average age 29. 1,387 applicants, 28% accepted, 160 enrolled. In 2013, 486 master's, 2 doctorates awarded. *Degree requirements:* For doctorate, comprehensive exam, thesis/dissertation. *Entrance requirements:* For master's, GMAT (for MBA and MS in investment management); GMAT or GRE General Test (for MS in mathematical finance), resume, 2 letters of recommendation; for doctorate, GMAT or GRE General Test, resume, personal statement, 3 letters of recommendation, 3 essays, official transcripts. *Application deadline:* For fall admission, 1/5 for domestic and international students; for spring admission, 11/1 for domestic students. Application fee: $125. Electronic applications accepted. *Expenses: Tuition:* Full-time $43,970; part-time $1374 per credit hour. *Required fees:* $60 per semester. Tuition and fees vary according to class time, course level and program. *Financial support:* Career-related internships or fieldwork, Federal Work-Study, institutionally sponsored loans, scholarships/grants, and tuition waivers (partial) available. Financial award applicants required to submit FAFSA. *Faculty research:* Innovation policy and productivity, corporate social responsibility, risk management, information systems, entrepreneurship, clean energy, sustainability. *Unit head:* Kenneth W. Freeman, Professor/Dean, 617-353-9720, Fax: 617-353-5581, E-mail: kfreeman@bu.edu. *Application contact:* Patti Cudney, Assistant Dean, Graduate Admissions, 617-353-2670, Fax: 617-353-7368, E-mail: mba@bu.edu.
Website: http://management.bu.edu/.

Concordia University, School of Graduate Studies, John Molson School of Business, Montreal, QC H3G 1M8, Canada. Offers administration (M Sc), including finance, management, marketing; business administration (MBA, PhD, Certificate, Diploma); executive business administration (EMBA); investment management (MBA). PhD program offered jointly with HEC Montreal, McGill University, and Université du Québec à Montréal. *Accreditation:* AACSB. Part-time and evening/weekend programs available. *Degree requirements:* For master's, one foreign language, thesis (for some programs), research project; for doctorate, one foreign language, thesis/dissertation; for other advanced degree, one foreign language. *Entrance requirements:* For master's, GMAT, minimum 2 years of work experience (for MBA); letters of recommendation, bachelor's degree from recognized university with minimum GPA of 3.0, curriculum vitae; for doctorate, GMAT (minimum score of 600), official transcripts, curriculum vitae, 3 letters of reference, statement of purpose; for other advanced degree, minimum GPA of 2.7, 2 letters of reference, statement of purpose, resume. Additional exam requirements/recommendations for international students: Required—TOEFL (minimum score 90 iBT), IELTS (minimum score 7). Electronic applications accepted. *Expenses:* Contact institution. *Faculty research:* General business, capital markets, international business.

DePaul University, Charles H. Kellstadt Graduate School of Business, Chicago, IL 60604. Offers accountancy (M Acc, MS, MSA); applied economics (MBA); banking (MBA); behavioral finance (MBA); brand and product management (MBA); business development (MBA); business information technology (MS); business strategy and decision-making (MBA); computational finance (MS); consumer insights (MBA); corporate finance (MBA); economic policy analysis (MS); entrepreneurship (MBA, MS); finance (MBA, MS); financial analysis (MBA); general business (MBA); health sector management (MBA); hospitality leadership (MBA); hospitality leadership and operational performance (MS); human resource management (MBA); human resources (MS); investment management (MBA); leadership and change management (MBA); management accounting (MBA); marketing (MBA, MS); marketing analysis (MS); marketing strategy and planning (MBA); operations management (MBA); organizational diversity (MBA); real estate (MS); real estate finance and investment (MBA); revenue management (MBA); sports management (MBA); strategic global marketing (MBA); strategy, execution and valuation (MBA); sustainable management (MBA, MS); taxation (MS); wealth management (MS); JD/MBA. *Accreditation:* AACSB. Part-time and evening/weekend programs available. Postbaccalaureate distance learning degree programs offered (no on-campus study). *Faculty:* 81 full-time (20 women), 45 part-time/adjunct (8 women). *Students:* 1,238 full-time (605 women), 617 part-time (223 women); includes 295 minority (71 Black or African American, non-Hispanic/Latino; 129 Asian, non-Hispanic/Latino; 74 Hispanic/Latino; 4 Native Hawaiian or other Pacific Islander, non-Hispanic/Latino; 17 Two or more races, non-Hispanic/Latino), 462 international. Average age 29. In 2013, 911 master's awarded. *Entrance requirements:* For master's, GMAT, 2 letters of recommendation, resume, essay, official transcripts. Additional exam requirements/recommendations for international students: Required—TOEFL (minimum score 550 paper-based; 80 iBT). *Application deadline:* For fall admission, 7/1 for domestic students, 6/1 for international students; for winter admission, 10/1 for domestic students, 9/1 for international students; for spring admission, 2/1 for domestic students, 1/1 for international students. Applications are processed on a rolling basis. Application fee: $60. Electronic applications accepted. *Expenses:* Contact institution. *Financial support:* Application deadline: 4/1; applicants required to submit FAFSA. *Unit head:* Robert T. Ryan, Assistant Dean and Director, 312-362-8810, Fax: 312-362-6677, E-mail: rryan1@depaul.edu. *Application contact:* James Parker, Director of Recruitment and Admission, 312-362-8810, Fax: 312-362-6677, E-mail: kgsb@depaul.edu.
Website: http://kellstadt.depaul.edu.

The George Washington University, School of Business, Department of Finance, Washington, DC 20052. Offers finance (MSF, PhD); finance and investments (MBA); real estate and urban development (MBA). Part-time and evening/weekend programs available. *Faculty:* 18 full-time (4 women). *Students:* 207 full-time (83 women), 11 part-time (3 women); includes 21 minority (9 Black or African American, non-Hispanic/Latino; 4 Asian, non-Hispanic/Latino; 7 Hispanic/Latino; 1 Two or more races, non-Hispanic/Latino), 164 international. Average age 28. 780 applicants, 25% accepted, 91 enrolled. In 2013, 115 master's awarded. *Degree requirements:* For doctorate, thesis/dissertation. *Entrance requirements:* For master's, GMAT; for doctorate, GMAT or GRE. Additional

exam requirements/recommendations for international students: Required—TOEFL. *Application deadline:* For fall admission, 4/1 priority date for domestic students; for spring admission, 10/1 for domestic students. Applications are processed on a rolling basis. Application fee: $75. *Financial support:* In 2013–14, 38 students received support. Fellowships, teaching assistantships, career-related internships or fieldwork, Federal Work-Study, and institutionally sponsored loans available. Financial award application deadline: 4/1. *Unit head:* Robert Van Order, Chair, 202-994-2559, E-mail: rvo@gwu.edu. *Application contact:* Kristin Williams, Assistant Vice President for Graduate and Special Enrollment Management, 202-994-0467, Fax: 202-994-0371, E-mail: ksw@gwu.edu.

Hofstra University, Frank G. Zarb School of Business, Programs in Finance, Hempstead, NY 11549. Offers business administration (MBA), including finance, real estate management; corporate finance (Advanced Certificate); finance (MS); investment management (Advanced Certificate); quantitative finance (MS).

Johns Hopkins University, Carey Business School, Finance Programs, Baltimore, MD 21218-2699. Offers finance (MS); financial management (Certificate); investments (Certificate). Part-time and evening/weekend programs available. *Faculty:* 29 full-time (6 women), 135 part-time/adjunct (29 women). *Students:* 331 full-time (187 women), 125 part-time (52 women); includes 45 minority (10 Black or African American, non-Hispanic/Latino; 1 American Indian or Alaska Native, non-Hispanic/Latino; 28 Asian, non-Hispanic/Latino; 3 Hispanic/Latino; 3 Two or more races, non-Hispanic/Latino), 347 international. Average age 30. 823 applicants, 65% accepted, 307 enrolled. In 2013, 123 master's, 15 other advanced degrees awarded. *Degree requirements:* For master's, 36 credits including final project. *Entrance requirements:* For master's, GMAT or GRE (recommended), minimum GPA of 3.0, resume, work experience, two letters of recommendation; for Certificate, minimum GPA of 3.0, resume, work experience, two letters of recommendation. Additional exam requirements/recommendations for international students: Required—TOEFL (minimum score 600 paper-based; 100 iBT). *Application deadline:* For fall admission, 4/1 for international students; for spring admission, 9/15 for international students. Applications are processed on a rolling basis. Application fee: $100. Electronic applications accepted. *Financial support:* In 2013–14, 9 students received support. Scholarships/grants available. Support available to part-time students. Financial award application deadline: 4/15; financial award applicants required to submit FAFSA. *Faculty research:* Financial econometrics, high frequency data modeling, corporate finance. *Unit head:* Dr. Dipankar Chakravarti, Vice Dean of Programs, 410-234-9311, E-mail: dipankar.chakravarti@jhu.edu. *Application contact:* Robin Greenberg, Admissions Coordinator, 410-234-9227, Fax: 443-529-1554, E-mail: carey.admissions@jhu.edu.

Lincoln University, Graduate Studies, Oakland, CA 94612. Offers finance and investments (DBA); finance management and investment banking (MBA); general business (MBA); human resource management (MBA, DBA); international business (MBA); management information systems (MBA). Part-time and evening/weekend programs available. *Faculty:* 8 full-time (2 women), 22 part-time/adjunct (7 women). *Students:* 372 full-time (171 women), 4 part-time (1 woman); includes 8 minority (2 Black or African American, non-Hispanic/Latino; 6 Asian, non-Hispanic/Latino), 363 international. Average age 26. 421 applicants, 71% accepted, 133 enrolled. *Degree requirements:* For master's, research project (thesis), internship report, or comprehensive exam; for doctorate, comprehensive exam, thesis/dissertation. *Entrance requirements:* For master's, minimum GPA of 2.7; for doctorate, GMAT (minimum score: 550), GRE (minimum score: 1000), or equivalent test results (waived for master's degree with minimum cumulative GPA of 3.3). Additional exam requirements/recommendations for international students: Required—TOEFL (minimum score 525 paper-based; 71 iBT) or IELTS (minimum score 5.5) for MBA; TOEFL (minimum score 550 paper-based; 79 iBT) or IELTS (minimum score 6) for DBA. *Application deadline:* For fall admission, 7/1 priority date for domestic and international students; for spring admission, 11/1 priority date for domestic and international students; for summer admission, 5/1 for domestic and international students. Applications are processed on a rolling basis. Application fee: $75. Electronic applications accepted. *Expenses: Tuition:* Full-time $7290; part-time $405 per unit. *Required fees:* $375; $405 per unit. $375 per year. Tuition and fees vary according to course level and degree level. *Financial support:* Teaching assistantships with tuition reimbursements, career-related internships or fieldwork, and scholarships/grants available. Financial award application deadline: 7/31; financial award applicants required to submit FAFSA. *Unit head:* Dr. Marshall Burak, Director of Graduate Programs, 510-628-8016, Fax: 510-628-8012, E-mail: mburak@lincolnuca.edu. *Application contact:* Reenu Shrestha, Admissions Officer, 510-628-8010 Ext. 8030, Fax: 510-628-8012, E-mail: admissions@lincolnuca.edu.
Website: http://www.lincolnuca.edu/.

Lynn University, College of Business and Management, Boca Raton, FL 33431-5598. Offers aviation management (MBA); financial valuation and investment management (MBA); hospitality management (MBA); international business (MBA); marketing (MBA); mass communication and media management (MBA); sports and athletics administration (MBA). Part-time and evening/weekend programs available. Postbaccalaureate distance learning degree programs offered. *Faculty:* 16 full-time (6 women), 8 part-time/adjunct (3 women). *Students:* 181 full-time (95 women), 83 part-time (37 women); includes 41 minority (22 Black or African American, non-Hispanic/Latino; 1 Asian, non-Hispanic/Latino; 17 Hispanic/Latino; 1 Two or more races, non-Hispanic/Latino), 77 international. Average age 28. 137 applicants, 100% accepted, 107 enrolled. In 2013, 149 master's awarded. *Degree requirements:* For master's, projects. *Entrance requirements:* For master's, GMAT or GRE, bachelor's degree from accredited institution, minimum undergraduate GPA of 2.5, resume, 2 letters of recommendation. Additional exam requirements/recommendations for international students: Required—TOEFL (minimum score 550 paper-based). *Application deadline:* Applications are processed on a rolling basis. Application fee: $45. Electronic applications accepted. *Expenses: Tuition:* Full-time $23,760; part-time $660 per credit. *Required fees:* $300; $50 per term. Tuition and fees vary according to degree level and program. *Financial support:* Career-related internships or fieldwork, Federal Work-Study, institutionally sponsored loans, scholarships/grants, tuition waivers (full and partial), and unspecified assistantships available. Support available to part-time students. Financial award application deadline: 8/1; financial award applicants required to submit FAFSA. *Faculty research:* Labor relations, dynamic balance in leisure-time skills, ethics in athletics, hotel development. *Unit head:* Dr. Ralph Norcio, Senior Associate Dean, 561-237-7010, Fax: 561-237-7014, E-mail: rnorcio@lynn.edu. *Application contact:* Steven Pruitt, Director of Graduate and Undergraduate Evening Admission, 561-237-7834, Fax: 561-237-7100, E-mail: spruitt@lynn.edu.
Website: http://www.lynn.edu/academics/colleges/business-and-management.

Investment Management

Marywood University, Academic Affairs, College of Liberal Arts and Sciences, School of Business and Global Innovation, Emphasis in Financial Information Systems, Scranton, PA 18509-1598. Offers MBA, MS. *Entrance requirements:* For master's, GMAT. Additional exam requirements/recommendations for international students: Required—TOEFL (minimum score 550 paper-based; 79 iBT). *Application deadline:* For fall admission, 4/1 priority date for domestic students, 3/31 priority date for international students; for spring admission, 11/1 priority date for domestic students, 8/31 priority date for international students. Applications are processed on a rolling basis. Application fee: $35. Electronic applications accepted. *Expenses: Tuition:* Part-time $775 per credit. Tuition and fees vary according to degree level. *Financial support:* Career-related internships or fieldwork, scholarships/grants, and unspecified assistantships available. Support available to part-time students. Financial award application deadline: 6/30; financial award applicants required to submit FAFSA. *Faculty research:* Accountant/auditor liability, corporate finance acquisitions and mergers, corporate bankruptcy. *Unit head:* Dr. Arthur Comstock, Chairman, 570-348-6211 Ext. 2449, E-mail: comstock@marywood.edu. *Application contact:* Tammy Manka, Assistant Director of Graduate Admissions, 570-348-6211 Ext. 2322, E-mail: tmanka@marywood.edu.
Website: http://www.marywood.edu/academics/gradcatalog/.

Oregon State University, College of Business, Program in Business Administration, Corvallis, OR 97331. Offers clean technology (MBA); commercialization (MBA); executive leadership (MBA); global operations (MBA); marketing (MBA); research thesis (MBA); wealth management (MBA). Part-time programs available. *Faculty:* 34 full-time (13 women), 2 part-time/adjunct (1 woman). *Students:* 153 full-time (67 women), 44 part-time (18 women); includes 20 minority (1 Black or African American, non-Hispanic/Latino; 12 Asian, non-Hispanic/Latino; 3 Hispanic/Latino; 1 Native Hawaiian or other Pacific Islander, non-Hispanic/Latino; 3 Two or more races, non-Hispanic/Latino), 97 international. Average age 29. 194 applicants, 64% accepted, 106 enrolled. In 2013, 61 degrees awarded. *Degree requirements:* For master's, thesis optional. *Entrance requirements:* For master's, GMAT. Additional exam requirements/recommendations for international students: Required—TOEFL (minimum score 91 iBT), IELTS (minimum score 7). *Application deadline:* Applications are processed on a rolling basis. Application fee: $60. *Expenses:* Contact institution. *Unit head:* Dr. David Baldridge, Director for Business Master's Program, 541-737-6062, E-mail: david.baldridge@bus.oregonstate.edu.
Website: http://business.oregonstate.edu/mba/degrees.

Pace University, Lubin School of Business, Financial Management Program, New York, NY 10038. Offers banking and finance (MBA); corporate financial management (MBA); financial management (MBA); investment management (MBA, MS). Part-time and evening/weekend programs available. *Students:* 93 full-time (43 women), 315 part-time (141 women); includes 54 minority (16 Black or African American, non-Hispanic/Latino; 28 Asian, non-Hispanic/Latino; 8 Hispanic/Latino; 2 Two or more races, non-Hispanic/Latino), 268 international. Average age 26. 505 applicants, 33% accepted, 119 enrolled. In 2013, 193 master's awarded. *Entrance requirements:* For master's, GMAT, GRE. Additional exam requirements/recommendations for international students: Required—TOEFL. *Application deadline:* For fall admission, 8/1 priority date for domestic students, 6/1 for international students; for spring admission, 12/1 for domestic students, 10/1 for international students. Applications are processed on a rolling basis. Application fee: $70. Electronic applications accepted. *Expenses: Tuition:* Part-time $1075 per credit. *Required fees:* $192 per semester. Tuition and fees vary according to course load, degree level and program. *Financial support:* Research assistantships, career-related internships or fieldwork, Federal Work-Study, and tuition waivers (full and partial) available. Support available to part-time students. Financial award application deadline: 8/15; financial award applicants required to submit FAFSA. *Unit head:* Dr. P. V. Viswanath, Chairperson, 212-618-6518, E-mail: pviswanath@pace.edu. *Application contact:* Susan Ford-Goldschein, Director of Graduate Admissions, 212-346-1531, Fax: 212-346-1585, E-mail: gradnyc@pace.edu.
Website: http://www.pace.edu/.

Quinnipiac University, School of Business and Engineering, Program in Business Administration, Hamden, CT 06518-1940. Offers chartered financial analyst (MBA); finance (MBA); healthcare management (MBA); information systems management (MBA); marketing (MBA); supply chain management (MBA); JD/MBA. *Accreditation:* AACSB. Part-time and evening/weekend programs available. Postbaccalaureate distance learning degree programs offered (no on-campus study). *Faculty:* 33 full-time (10 women), 7 part-time/adjunct (3 women). *Students:* 109 full-time (48 women), 225 part-time (101 women); includes 44 minority (14 Black or African American, non-Hispanic/Latino; 2 American Indian or Alaska Native, non-Hispanic/Latino; 12 Asian, non-Hispanic/Latino; 15 Hispanic/Latino; 1 Two or more races, non-Hispanic/Latino), 17 international. 230 applicants, 80% accepted, 154 enrolled. In 2013, 124 master's awarded. *Entrance requirements:* For master's, GMAT or GRE, minimum GPA of 3.0. Additional exam requirements/recommendations for international students: Required—TOEFL (minimum score 575 paper-based; 90 iBT), IELTS (minimum score 6.5). *Application deadline:* For fall admission, 7/30 priority date for domestic students, 4/30 priority date for international students; for spring admission, 12/15 priority date for domestic students, 9/15 priority date for international students. Applications are processed on a rolling basis. Application fee: $45. Electronic applications accepted. *Expenses: Tuition:* Part-time $920 per credit. *Required fees:* $37 per credit. *Financial support:* In 2013–14, 41 students received support. Career-related internships or fieldwork, Federal Work-Study, scholarships/grants, and unspecified assistantships available. Support available to part-time students. Financial award application deadline: 6/1; financial award applicants required to submit FAFSA. *Faculty research:* Financial markets and investments, international business, supply chain management, health care management, corporate governance. *Unit head:* Lisa Braiewa, MBA Program Director, E-mail: lisa.braiewa@quinnipiac.edu. *Application contact:* Office of Graduate Admissions, 800-462-1944, Fax: 203-582-3443, E-mail: graduate@quinnipiac.edu.
Website: http://www.quinnipiac.edu/mba.

St. John's University, The Peter J. Tobin College of Business, Department of Economics and Finance, Program in Finance, Queens, NY 11439. Offers finance (MBA, Adv C); investment management (MS). Part-time and evening/weekend programs available. *Students:* 132 full-time (68 women), 44 part-time (18 women); includes 24 minority (7 Black or African American, non-Hispanic/Latino; 9 Asian, non-Hispanic/Latino; 8 Hispanic/Latino), 116 international. Average age 26. 148 applicants, 77% accepted, 59 enrolled. In 2013, 66 master's, 1 other advanced degree awarded. *Degree requirements:* For master's, comprehensive exam (for some programs), thesis optional. *Entrance requirements:* For master's, GMAT, 2 letters of recommendation, resume, transcripts, essay; for Adv C, GMAT, 2 letters of recommendation, resume, undergraduate and graduate transcripts, essay, MBA. Additional exam requirements/recommendations for international students: Required—TOEFL (minimum score 600 paper-based; 100 iBT), IELTS (minimum score 7). *Application deadline:* For fall admission, 5/1 priority date for domestic and international students; for spring admission, 11/1 priority date for domestic and international students. Applications are processed on a rolling basis. Application fee: $50. Electronic applications accepted. *Expenses:* Contact institution. *Financial support:* Research assistantships, scholarships/grants, and unspecified assistantships available. Support available to part-time students. Financial award application deadline: 3/1; financial award applicants required to submit FAFSA. *Unit head:* Dr. Vipul K. Bansal, Chair, 718-990-2113, E-mail: bansalv@stjohns.edu. *Application contact:* Carol J. Swanberg, Assistant Dean/Director of Graduate Admissions, 718-990-1345, Fax: 718-990-5242, E-mail: tobingradnyc@stjohns.edu.

Saint Mary's College of California, School of Economics and Business Administration, MS in Financial Analysis and Investment Management Program, Moraga, CA 94556. Offers MS.

Southern New Hampshire University, School of Business, Manchester, NH 03106-1045. Offers accounting (MBA, MS, Graduate Certificate); accounting finance (MS); accounting/auditing (MS); accounting/forensic accounting (MS); accounting/taxation (MS); athletic administration (MBA, Graduate Certificate); business administration (IMBA, MBA, Certificate, Graduate Certificate), including accounting (Certificate), business administration (MBA), business information systems (Graduate Certificate), human resource management (Certificate); corporate social responsibility (MBA); entrepreneurship (MBA); finance (MBA, MS, Graduate Certificate); finance/corporate finance (MS); finance/investments and securities (MS); forensic accounting (MBA); healthcare informatics (MBA); healthcare management (MBA); human resource management (Graduate Certificate); information technology (MS, Graduate Certificate); information technology management (MBA); international business (Graduate Certificate); international business and information technology (Graduate Certificate); international finance (Graduate Certificate); international sport management (Graduate Certificate); justice studies (MBA); leadership of nonprofit organizations (Graduate Certificate); marketing (MBA, MS, Graduate Certificate); operations and project management (MS); operations and supply chain management (MBA, Graduate Certificate); organizational leadership (MS); project management (MBA, Graduate Certificate); Six Sigma (MBA); Six Sigma quality (Graduate Certificate); social media marketing (MBA); sport management (MBA, MS, Graduate Certificate); sustainability and environmental compliance (MBA); workplace conflict management (MBA); MBA/Certificate. *Accreditation:* ACBSP. Part-time and evening/weekend programs available. Postbaccalaureate distance learning degree programs offered (no on-campus study). Terminal master's awarded for partial completion of doctoral program. *Degree requirements:* For master's, one foreign language, comprehensive exam (for some programs), thesis or alternative. *Entrance requirements:* For master's, minimum GPA of 2.5. Additional exam requirements/recommendations for international students: Required—TOEFL (minimum score 500 paper-based). Electronic applications accepted.

University of Colorado Denver, Business School, Master of Business Administration Program, Denver, CO 80217. Offers bioinnovation and entrepreneurship (MBA); business intelligence (MBA); business strategy (MBA); business to business marketing (MBA); business to consumer marketing (MBA); change management (MBA); corporate financial management (MBA); enterprise technology management (MBA); entrepreneurship (MBA); health administration (MBA), including financial management, health administration, health information technologies, international health management and policy; human resources management (MBA); international business (MBA); investment management (MBA); managing for sustainability (MBA); sports and entertainment management (MBA). *Accreditation:* AACSB. Part-time and evening/weekend programs available. Postbaccalaureate distance learning degree programs offered (no on-campus study). *Students:* 611 full-time (246 women), 144 part-time (58 women); includes 102 minority (14 Black or African American, non-Hispanic/Latino; 2 American Indian or Alaska Native, non-Hispanic/Latino; 38 Asian, non-Hispanic/Latino; 42 Hispanic/Latino; 6 Two or more races, non-Hispanic/Latino), 26 international. Average age 32. 330 applicants, 64% accepted, 125 enrolled. In 2013, 398 master's awarded. *Degree requirements:* For master's, 48 semester hours, including 30 of core courses, 3 in international business, and 15 in electives from over 50 other graduate business courses. *Entrance requirements:* For master's, GMAT, resume, official transcripts, essay, two letters of recommendation, financial statements (for international applicants). Additional exam requirements/recommendations for international students: Required—TOEFL (minimum score 560 paper-based; 83 iBT); Recommended—IELTS (minimum score 6.5). *Application deadline:* For fall admission, 4/15 priority date for domestic students, 3/15 priority date for international students; for spring admission, 10/15 priority date for domestic students, 9/15 priority date for international students. Applications are processed on a rolling basis. Application fee: $50 ($75 for international students). Electronic applications accepted. *Expenses:* Contact institution. *Financial support:* In 2013–14, 62 students received support. Fellowships, research assistantships, teaching assistantships, Federal Work-Study, institutionally sponsored loans, scholarships/grants, traineeships, and unspecified assistantships available. Financial award application deadline: 4/1; financial award applicants required to submit FAFSA. *Faculty research:* Marketing, management, entrepreneurship, finance, health administration. *Unit head:* Elizabeth Cooperman, Professor of Finance and Managing for Sustainability/MBA Program Director, 303-315-8422, E-mail: elizabeth.cooperman@ucdenver.edu. *Application contact:* Shelly Townley, Admissions Director, Graduate Programs, 303-315-8202, E-mail: shelly.townley@ucdenver.edu.
Website: http://www.ucdenver.edu/academics/colleges/business/degrees/mba/Pages/MBA.aspx.

The University of Iowa, Henry B. Tippie College of Business, Henry B. Tippie School of Management, Iowa City, IA 52242-1316. Offers corporate finance (MBA); investment management (MBA); marketing (MBA); strategic management and innovation (MBA); supply chain and analytics (MBA); JD/MBA; MBA/MA; MBA/MD; MBA/MHA; MBA/MSN. *Accreditation:* AACSB. Part-time and evening/weekend programs available. *Faculty:* 113 full-time (27 women), 89 part-time/adjunct (23 women). *Students:* 110 full-time (28 women), 786 part-time (236 women); includes 51 minority (13 Black or African American, non-Hispanic/Latino; 3 American Indian or Alaska Native, non-Hispanic/Latino; 23 Asian, non-Hispanic/Latino; 12 Hispanic/Latino), 162 international. Average age 33. 622 applicants, 73% accepted, 383 enrolled. In 2013, 333 master's awarded. *Degree requirements:* For master's, minimum GPA of 2.75. *Entrance requirements:* For master's, GMAT, GRE, quality work experience and leadership as shown through resume, references, and essays. Additional exam requirements/recommendations for international students: Required—TOEFL (minimum score 600 paper-based; 100 iBT), IELTS (minimum score 7). *Application deadline:* For fall admission, 7/30 for domestic students, 4/1 for international students; for spring admission, 12/30 for domestic and international students. Applications are processed on a rolling basis. Application fee: $60 ($100 for international students). Electronic applications accepted. *Expenses:* Contact institution. *Financial support:* In 2013–14, 96 students received support, including 102 fellowships (averaging $9,519 per year), 83 research assistantships with partial tuition reimbursements available (averaging $8,893 per year), 14 teaching assistantships with partial tuition reimbursements available (averaging $17,049 per year); career-related internships or fieldwork, scholarships/grants, health care benefits, and unspecified assistantships also available. Financial award application deadline: 7/30; financial award applicants required to submit FAFSA. *Faculty research:* Capital markets, econometrics, optimization, investments and empirical corporate finance, Iowa electronic markets. *Unit head:* Prof. David W. Frasier, Associate Dean, Tippie School of Management, 800-622-4692, Fax: 319-335-3604, E-mail: david-frasier@uiowa.edu. *Application contact:* Jodi Schafer, Director, MBA Admissions and Financial Aid, 319-335-0864, Fax: 319-335-3604, E-mail: jodi-schafer@uiowa.edu.
Website: http://tippie.uiowa.edu/mba.

University of Michigan–Dearborn, College of Business, Dearborn, MI 48128-1491. Offers accounting (MBA, MS); business analytics (MS); finance (MBA, MS); human resource management (MBA); information systems (MS); international business (MBA); investment (MBA); management (MBA); management information systems (MBA); marketing (MBA); supply chain management (MBA, MS); taxation (MBA); MBA/MHSA; MBA/MSE; MBA/MSF; MBA/MSIS; MBA/MSSCM; MSF/MSA. *Accreditation:* AACSB. Part-time and evening/weekend programs available. Postbaccalaureate distance learning degree programs offered (no on-campus study). *Faculty:* 24 full-time (8 women), 5 part-time/adjunct (2 women). *Students:* 82 full-time (31 women), 323 part-time (116 women); includes 72 minority (17 Black or African American, non-Hispanic/Latino; 2 American Indian or Alaska Native, non-Hispanic/Latino; 30 Asian, non-Hispanic/Latino; 15 Hispanic/Latino; 8 Two or more races, non-Hispanic/Latino), 65 international. Average age 32. 290 applicants, 44% accepted, 99 enrolled. In 2013, 143 master's awarded. *Entrance requirements:* For master's, GMAT or GRE, pre-calculus or finite mathematics; 18 credits of accounting course work beyond introductory courses (MS in accounting). Additional exam requirements/recommendations for international students: Required—TOEFL (minimum score 560 paper-based; 84 iBT), IELTS. *Application deadline:* For fall admission, 8/1 priority date for domestic students, 5/1 priority date for international students; for winter admission, 12/1 priority date for domestic students, 9/1 priority date for international students; for spring admission, 4/1 priority date for domestic students, 1/1 priority date for international students. Applications are processed on a rolling basis. Application fee: $60. Electronic applications accepted. *Expenses:* Contact institution. *Financial support:* Career-related internships or fieldwork, Federal Work-Study, and scholarships/grants available. Support available to part-time students. Financial award application deadline: 9/1; financial award applicants required to submit FAFSA. *Faculty research:* Cultural diversity, buyer-supplier relations, error detection in data, economic evolution. *Unit head:* Dr. Raju Balakrishnan, Dean, 313-593-5248, Fax: 313-271-9835, E-mail: rajub@umich.edu. *Application contact:* Joan Doherty, Academic Advisor/Counselor, 313-593-5460, Fax: 313-271-9838, E-mail: umd-gradbusiness@umich.edu.
Website: http://www.cob.umd.umich.edu.

University of San Francisco, School of Management, Master of Science in Risk Management Program, San Francisco, CA 94105. Offers MSRM. Part-time and evening/weekend programs available. *Entrance requirements:* For master's, GMAT or GRE, resume (one year of professional work experience preferred), transcripts from each college or university attended showing completion of required foundation courses, two letters of recommendation, personal statement. Additional exam requirements/recommendations for international students: Required—TOEFL (minimum score 600 paper-based, 100 iBT), IELTS (minimum score 7) or PTE (minimum score 68). *Application deadline:* For fall admission, 6/15 for domestic students, 5/14 for international students. Application fee: $55. Electronic applications accepted. *Expenses: Tuition:* Full-time $21,150; part-time $1175 per unit. Tuition and fees vary according to course load, campus/location and program. *Financial support:* Scholarships/grants available. Financial award applicants required to submit FAFSA. *Unit head:* Dr. John Veitch, Program Director, 415-422-2221, E-mail: management@usfca.edu. *Application contact:* Office of Graduate Recruiting and Admissions, 415-422-2221, Fax: 415-422-6315, E-mail: management@usfca.edu.
Website: https://www.usfca.edu/catalog/Management/Graduate/Master_of_Science_in_Risk_Management/.

The University of Texas at Dallas, Naveen Jindal School of Management, Program in Finance and Managerial Economics, Richardson, TX 75080. Offers finance (MS); financial analysis (MS); financial risk management (MS); investment management (MS). Part-time and evening/weekend programs available. *Faculty:* 21 full-time (3 women), 10 part-time/adjunct (5 women). *Students:* 368 full-time (192 women), 69 part-time (23 women); includes 31 minority (2 Black or African American, non-Hispanic/Latino; 19 Asian, non-Hispanic/Latino; 10 Hispanic/Latino), 364 international. Average age 25. 1,060 applicants, 54% accepted, 189 enrolled. In 2013, 256 master's awarded. *Entrance requirements:* For master's, GMAT or GRE. Additional exam requirements/recommendations for international students: Required—TOEFL (minimum score 550 paper-based). *Application deadline:* For fall admission, 7/15 for domestic students, 5/1 priority date for international students; for spring admission, 11/15 for domestic students, 9/1 priority date for international students. Applications are processed on a rolling basis. Application fee: $50 ($100 for international students). Electronic applications accepted. *Expenses:* Tuition, state resident: full-time $11,940; part-time $663.33 per credit hour. Tuition, nonresident: full-time $21,606; part-time $1200.33 per credit hour. *Financial support:* In 2013–14, 57 students received support. Research assistantships with partial tuition reimbursements available, teaching assistantships with partial tuition reimbursements available, career-related internships or fieldwork, Federal Work-Study, institutionally sponsored loans, scholarships/grants, and unspecified assistantships available. Support available to part-time students. Financial award application deadline: 4/30; financial award applicants required to submit FAFSA. *Faculty research:* Econometrics, industrial organization, auction theory, file-sharing copyrights and bundling, international financial management, entrepreneurial finance. *Unit head:* Dr. Robert Kieschnick, Area Coordinator, 972-883-6273, E-mail: rkiesch@utdallas.edu. *Application contact:* Carolyn Reichert, Graduate Program Director, 972-883-5854, E-mail: carolyn@utdallas.edu.
Website: http://jindal.utdallas.edu/academic-areas/finance-and-managerial-economics/.

The University of Tulsa, Graduate School, Collins College of Business, Program in Finance, Tulsa, OK 74104-3189. Offers corporate finance (MS); investments and portfolio management (MS); risk management (MS); JD/MSF; MBA/MSF; MSF/MSAM. Part-time and evening/weekend programs available. *Faculty:* 10 full-time (1 woman). *Students:* 27 full-time (10 women), 4 part-time (1 woman); includes 1 minority (Hispanic/Latino), 23 international. Average age 24. 129 applicants, 50% accepted, 4 enrolled. In 2013, 11 master's awarded. *Degree requirements:* For master's, thesis optional. *Entrance requirements:* For master's, GMAT. Additional exam requirements/recommendations for international students: Required—TOEFL (minimum score 577 paper-based; 91 iBT), IELTS (minimum score 6.5). *Application deadline:* Applications are processed on a rolling basis. Application fee: $40. Electronic applications accepted. *Expenses: Tuition:* Full-time $19,566; part-time $1087 per credit hour. *Required fees:* $1690; $5 per credit hour. $160 per semester. Tuition and fees vary according to course load. *Financial support:* In 2013–14, 4 students received support, including 4 teaching assistantships with full and partial tuition reimbursements available (averaging $8,367 per year); fellowships with full and partial tuition reimbursements available, research assistantships with full and partial tuition reimbursements available, career-related internships or fieldwork, Federal Work-Study, institutionally sponsored loans, scholarships/grants, health care benefits, tuition waivers (full and partial), and unspecified assistantships also available. Support available to part-time students. Financial award application deadline: 2/1; financial award applicants required to submit FAFSA. *Unit head:* Dr. Linda Nichols, Associate Dean, 918-631-2242, Fax: 918-631-2142, E-mail: linda-nichols@utulsa.edu. *Application contact:* Information Contact, 918-631-2242, E-mail: graduate-business@utulsa.edu.

University of Wisconsin–Madison, Graduate School, Wisconsin School of Business, Doctoral Program in Finance, Investment and Banking, Madison, WI 53706-1380. Offers PhD. *Faculty:* 15 full-time (2 women), 7 part-time/adjunct (3 women). *Students:* 9 full-time (2 women), 7 international. Average age 28. 66 applicants, 9% accepted, 3 enrolled. *Degree requirements:* For doctorate, comprehensive exam, thesis/dissertation. *Entrance requirements:* For doctorate, GMAT or GRE. Additional exam requirements/recommendations for international students: Recommended—TOEFL (minimum score 623 paper-based; 106 iBT), IELTS (minimum score 7.5), TSE (minimum score 73). *Application deadline:* For fall admission, 12/15 priority date for domestic and international students. Application fee: $56. Electronic applications accepted. *Expenses:* Contact institution. *Financial support:* In 2013–14, 9 students received support, including 2 fellowships with full tuition reimbursements available (averaging $19,125 per year), research assistantships with full tuition reimbursements available (averaging $14,746 per year), 7 teaching assistantships with full tuition reimbursements available (averaging $14,746 per year); Federal Work-Study, institutionally sponsored loans, scholarships/grants, health care benefits, and unspecified assistantships also available. Financial award application deadline: 12/15; financial award applicants required to submit FAFSA. *Faculty research:* Banking and financial institutions, business cycles, investments, derivatives, corporate finance. *Unit head:* Prof. Mark Ready, Chair, 608-262-5226, Fax: 608-265-4195, E-mail: mready@bus.wisc.edu. *Application contact:* Belle Heberling, Assistant Director for Research Programs, 608-262-3749, Fax: 608-890-0180, E-mail: phd@bus.wisc.edu.
Website: http://www.bus.wisc.edu/phd.

University of Wisconsin–Milwaukee, Graduate School, Sheldon B. Lubar School of Business, Milwaukee, WI 53201. Offers business administration (MBA); enterprise resource planning (Certificate); investment management (Certificate); management science (MS, PhD); nonprofit management and leadership (MS, Certificate); state and local taxation (Certificate); MS/MBA. *Accreditation:* AACSB. Part-time and evening/weekend programs available. *Faculty:* 50 full-time (11 women), 4 part-time/adjunct (2 women). *Students:* 282 full-time (123 women), 322 part-time (126 women); includes 87 minority (30 Black or African American, non-Hispanic/Latino; 2 American Indian or Alaska Native, non-Hispanic/Latino; 28 Asian, non-Hispanic/Latino; 3 Hispanic/Latino; 24 Two or more races, non-Hispanic/Latino), 93 international. Average age 32. 517 applicants, 54% accepted, 154 enrolled. In 2013, 245 master's, 10 doctorates awarded. *Degree requirements:* For master's, comprehensive exam (for some programs); for doctorate, comprehensive exam, thesis/dissertation. *Entrance requirements:* For master's and doctorate, GMAT or GRE General Test. Additional exam requirements/recommendations for international students: Required—TOEFL (minimum score 550 paper-based; 79 iBT), IELTS (minimum score 6.5). *Application deadline:* For fall admission, 1/1 priority date for domestic students; for spring admission, 9/1 for domestic students. Applications are processed on a rolling basis. Application fee: $56 ($96 for international students). Electronic applications accepted. *Expenses:* Contact institution. *Financial support:* In 2013–14, 5 fellowships with full tuition reimbursements, 2 research assistantships with full tuition reimbursements, 41 teaching assistantships with full tuition reimbursements were awarded; career-related internships or fieldwork, Federal Work-Study, health care benefits, unspecified assistantships, and project assistantships also available. Support available to part-time students. Financial award application deadline: 4/15; financial award applicants required to submit FAFSA. *Faculty research:* Applied management research in finance, management information systems, marketing, operations research, organizational sciences. *Total annual research expenditures:* $616,761. *Unit head:* Timothy L. Smunt, Dean, 414-229-6256, Fax: 414-229-2372, E-mail: tsmunt@uwm.edu. *Application contact:* Matthew Jensen, Administrative Program Manager III, 414-229-5403, E-mail: mba-ms@uwm.edu.
Website: http://www4.uwm.edu/business.

Taxation

American International College, Graduate Business Programs, Master of Science in Accounting and Taxation Program, Springfield, MA 01109-3189. Offers MSAT. Part-time and evening/weekend programs available. *Faculty:* 4 part-time/adjunct (0 women). *Students:* 1 full-time (0 women), 18 part-time (5 women); includes 5 minority (3 Black or African American, non-Hispanic/Latino; 1 Asian, non-Hispanic/Latino; 1 Hispanic/Latino). Average age 30. 9 applicants, 89% accepted, 5 enrolled. In 2013, 6 master's awarded. *Entrance requirements:* For master's, bachelor's degree, minimum GPA of 2.75. Additional exam requirements/recommendations for international students: Required—TOEFL or IELTS. *Application deadline:* Applications are processed on a rolling basis. Application fee: $50. Electronic applications accepted. *Expenses: Tuition:* Full-time $14,040; part-time $780 per credit. Tuition and fees vary according to course load, degree level and program. *Financial support:* Career-related internships or fieldwork available. Financial award applicants required to submit FAFSA. *Unit head:* Thomas Barron, Director, 413-205-3305, Fax: 413-205-3943, E-mail: thomas.barron@aic.edu. *Application contact:* Kerry Barnes, Director of Graduate Admissions, 413-205-3703, Fax: 413-205-3051, E-mail: kerry.barnes@aic.edu.

American University, Kogod School of Business, Washington, DC 20016-8044. Offers accounting (MS); business administration (MBA); business fundamentals (Certificate); entrepreneurship (Certificate); finance (MS); forensic accounting (Certificate); management (MS); marketing (MS); real estate (MS, Certificate); sustainability management (MS); tax (Certificate); taxation (MS). *Accreditation:* AACSB. Part-time and evening/weekend programs available. Postbaccalaureate distance learning degree programs offered. *Faculty:* 75 full-time (24 women), 36 part-time/adjunct (7 women). *Students:* 194 full-time (95 women), 370 part-time (184 women); includes 168 minority (69 Black or African American, non-Hispanic/Latino; 60 Asian, non-Hispanic/Latino; 33 Hispanic/Latino; 2 Native Hawaiian or other Pacific Islander, non-Hispanic/Latino; 4 Two or more races, non-Hispanic/Latino), 108 international. Average age 30. 940 applicants, 46% accepted, 193 enrolled. In 2013, 221 master's, 4 other advanced degrees awarded. *Entrance requirements:* For master's, GMAT, resume, personal statement, interview, 2 letters of recommendation, transcripts. Additional exam requirements/recommendations for international students: Required—TOEFL (minimum score 100 iBT). *Application deadline:* Applications are processed on a rolling basis. Application fee: $100. Electronic

applications accepted. *Expenses:* Contact institution. *Financial support:* Fellowships, career-related internships or fieldwork, Federal Work-Study, institutionally sponsored loans, and tuition waivers (partial) available. Support available to part-time students. Financial award application deadline: 2/1. *Unit head:* Dr. Michael Ginzberg, Dean, 202-885-1985, E-mail: ginzberg@american.edu. *Application contact:* Jason Kennedy, Associate Director of Graduate Admissions, 202-885-1968, E-mail: jkennedy@american.edu.
Website: http://www.kogod.american.edu/.

Appalachian State University, Cratis D. Williams Graduate School, Department of Accounting, Boone, NC 28608. Offers taxation (MS). Part-time programs available. *Degree requirements:* For master's, comprehensive exam, thesis optional. *Entrance requirements:* For master's, GMAT, 3 letters of recommendation. Additional exam requirements/recommendations for international students: Required—TOEFL (minimum score 550 paper-based; 79 iBT), IELTS (minimum score 6.5). Electronic applications accepted. *Faculty research:* Audit assurance risk, state taxation, financial accounting inconsistencies, management information systems, charitable contribution taxation.

Baruch College of the City University of New York, Zicklin School of Business, Department of Accounting, Program in Taxation, New York, NY 10010-5585. Offers MBA, MS. Part-time and evening/weekend programs available. *Entrance requirements:* For master's, GMAT, 2 letters of recommendation, resume, 2 years of work experience. Additional exam requirements/recommendations for international students: Required—TOEFL (minimum score 590 paper-based), TWE.

Bentley University, McCallum Graduate School of Business, Master's Program in Taxation, Waltham, MA 02452-4705. Offers MST. Part-time and evening/weekend programs available. Postbaccalaureate distance learning degree programs offered (no on-campus study). *Faculty:* 91 full-time (29 women), 22 part-time/adjunct (4 women). *Students:* 35 full-time (16 women), 139 part-time (54 women); includes 28 minority (6 Black or African American, non-Hispanic/Latino; 15 Asian, non-Hispanic/Latino; 5 Hispanic/Latino; 2 Two or more races, non-Hispanic/Latino), 10 international. Average age 30. 93 applicants, 90% accepted, 70 enrolled. In 2013, 82 master's awarded. *Entrance requirements:* For master's, GMAT or GRE General Test. Additional exam requirements/recommendations for international students: Required—TOEFL (minimum score 600 paper-based; 100 iBT) or IELTS (minimum score 7). *Application deadline:* For fall admission, 12/1 priority date for domestic and international students; for spring admission, 10/1 priority date for domestic and international students. Application fee: $50. Electronic applications accepted. *Expenses: Tuition:* Full-time $30,400; part-time $1267 per credit. *Required fees:* $404. Tuition and fees vary according to course load and program. *Financial support:* In 2013–14, 17 students received support. Scholarships/grants available. Financial award application deadline: 6/1; financial award applicants required to submit CSS PROFILE or FAFSA. *Faculty research:* Taxation of intellectual property, tax dispute resolution, corporate tax planning and advocacy, estate and financial planning. *Unit head:* John Lynch, Jr., Director, 781-891-2624, E-mail: jlynch@bentley.edu. *Application contact:* Sharon Hill, Director of Graduate Admissions, 781-891-2108, Fax: 781-891-2464, E-mail: bentleygraduateadmissions@bentley.edu.
Website: http://www.bentley.edu/graduate/degree-programs/ms-programs/taxation.

Boise State University, College of Business and Economics, Program in Accountancy, Boise, ID 83725-0399. Offers accountancy (MSA); taxation (MSA). *Accreditation:* AACSB. Part-time programs available. *Entrance requirements:* For master's, GMAT, minimum GPA of 3.0. Additional exam requirements/recommendations for international students: Required—TOEFL. Electronic applications accepted.

Boston University, School of Law, Boston, MA 02215. Offers American law (LL M); banking (LL M); intellectual property law (LL M); international business law (LL M); law (JD); taxation (LL M); JD/LL M; JD/MA; JD/MBA; JD/MPH; JD/MS; JD/MSW. *Accreditation:* ABA. *Faculty:* 48 full-time (19 women), 91 part-time/adjunct (26 women). *Students:* 842 full-time (462 women), 118 part-time (54 women); includes 206 minority (19 Black or African American, non-Hispanic/Latino; 1 American Indian or Alaska Native, non-Hispanic/Latino; 83 Asian, non-Hispanic/Latino; 77 Hispanic/Latino; 26 Two or more races, non-Hispanic/Latino), 157 international. Average age 27. 4,584 applicants, 35% accepted, 220 enrolled. In 2013, 183 master's, 272 doctorates awarded. *Degree requirements:* For master's, thesis (for some programs); for doctorate, thesis/dissertation, research project resulting in a paper. *Entrance requirements:* For master's, JD; for doctorate, LSAT. Additional exam requirements/recommendations for international students: Required—TOEFL (minimum score 600 paper-based; 100 iBT). *Application deadline:* For fall admission, 4/1 for domestic and international students. Applications are processed on a rolling basis. Application fee: $80. Electronic applications accepted. *Expenses: Tuition:* Full-time $43,970; part-time $1374 per credit hour. *Required fees:* $60 per semester. Tuition and fees vary according to class time, course level and program. *Financial support:* In 2013–14, 600 students received support. Career-related internships or fieldwork, Federal Work-Study, institutionally sponsored loans, and scholarships/grants available. Financial award application deadline: 3/1; financial award applicants required to submit FAFSA. *Faculty research:* Health law, tax, intellectual property, Constitutional law, corporate law, business organizations and financial law, international law, and family law. *Unit head:* Maureen A. O'Rourke, Dean, 617-353-3112, Fax: 617-353-7400, E-mail: lawdean@bu.edu. *Application contact:* Alissa Leonard, Director of Admissions and Financial Aid, 617-353-3100, Fax: 617-353-0578, E-mail: bulawadm@bu.edu.
Website: http://www.bu.edu/law/.

Bryant University, Graduate School of Business, Master of Professional Accountancy Program, Smithfield, RI 02917. Offers accounting (MPAC); tax (MPAC). *Entrance requirements:* For master's, GMAT (waived for students with a minimum cumulative GPA of 3.5 from an AACSB-accredited institution), transcripts, resume, recommendation, statement of objectives. Additional exam requirements/recommendations for international students: Required—TOEFL (minimum score 580 paper-based; 90 iBT). *Application deadline:* For fall admission, 7/15 for domestic and international students; for spring admission, 11/15 for domestic and international students; for summer admission, 4/1 for domestic and international students. Applications are processed on a rolling basis. Application fee: $80. Electronic applications accepted. *Expenses: Tuition:* Full-time $26,832; part-time $1118 per credit hour. *Financial support:* In 2013–14, 10 students received support, including 10 fellowships with partial tuition reimbursements available (averaging $11,289 per year); scholarships/grants also available. Financial award application deadline: 2/15; financial award applicants required to submit FAFSA. *Faculty research:* Director compensation, public sector auditing, employee stock options, financial disclosure. *Unit head:* Richard S. Cheney, Director of Operations for Graduate Programs, School of Business, 401-232-6707, Fax: 401-232-6494, E-mail: rcheney@bryant.edu. *Application contact:* Nancy Terry, Assistant Director of Graduate Admission, 401-232-6205, Fax: 401-232-6494, E-mail: nterry@bryant.edu.
Website: http://gradschool.bryant.edu/business/mpac.htm.

Bryant University, Graduate School of Business, Master of Science in Taxation Program, Smithfield, RI 02917. Offers MST. Part-time and evening/weekend programs available. *Entrance requirements:* For master's, GMAT (waived for applicants with a terminal degree, CPA, or enrolled agent), recommendation, resume, statement of objectives, official transcripts from all schools attended. Additional exam requirements/recommendations for international students: Required—TOEFL (minimum score 580 paper-based; 90 iBT). *Application deadline:* For fall admission, 7/15 for domestic and international students; for spring admission, 11/15 for domestic and international students; for summer admission, 4/15 for domestic students. Applications are processed on a rolling basis. Application fee: $80. Electronic applications accepted. *Expenses:* Contact institution. *Financial support:* Application deadline: 2/15; applicants required to submit FAFSA. *Faculty research:* Tax efficiencies of mutual funds, cost segregation studies, taxation of partnerships, property transactions. *Unit head:* Richard S. Cheney, Director of Operations for Graduate Programs, School of Business, 401-232-6707, Fax: 401-232-6494, E-mail: rcheney@bryant.edu. *Application contact:* Nancy Terry, Assistant Director of Graduate Admission, 401-232-6205, Fax: 401-232-6494, E-mail: nterry@bryant.edu.
Website: http://gradschool.bryant.edu/business/mst.htm.

California Miramar University, Program in Taxation and Trade for Executives, San Diego, CA 92126. Offers MT.

California Polytechnic State University, San Luis Obispo, Orfalea College of Business, Graduate Programs in Business, San Luis Obispo, CA 93407. Offers business (MBA); taxation (MSA). *Faculty:* 1 full-time (0 women), 5 part-time/adjunct (all women). *Students:* 33 full-time (14 women), 9 part-time (6 women); includes 8 minority (3 Asian, non-Hispanic/Latino; 5 Hispanic/Latino), 3 international. Average age 25. 75 applicants, 59% accepted, 30 enrolled. In 2013, 58 master's awarded. *Degree requirements:* For master's, comprehensive exam (for some programs), thesis or alternative. *Entrance requirements:* For master's, GMAT. Additional exam requirements/recommendations for international students: Required—TOEFL (minimum score 550 paper-based) or IELTS (minimum score 6). *Application deadline:* For fall admission, 7/1 for domestic students, 11/30 for international students. Applications are processed on a rolling basis. Application fee: $55. Electronic applications accepted. *Financial support:* Fellowships, career-related internships or fieldwork, Federal Work-Study, institutionally sponsored loans, scholarships/grants, and unspecified assistantships available. Support available to part-time students. Financial award application deadline: 3/2; financial award applicants required to submit FAFSA. *Faculty research:* International business, organizational behavior, graphic communication document systems management, commercial development of innovative technologies, effective communication skills for managers. *Unit head:* Vicki Walls, Graduate Coordinator, 805-756-2637, Fax: 805-756-0110, E-mail: vwalls@calpoly.edu. *Application contact:* Vicki Walls, Graduate Coordinator, 805-756-5637, Fax: 805-756-0110, E-mail: vwalls@calpoly.edu.
Website: http://mba.calpoly.edu/.

California State University, East Bay, Office of Academic Programs and Graduate Studies, College of Business and Economics, Department of Accounting and Finance, Taxation Program, Hayward, CA 94542-3000. Offers MS. Part-time and evening/weekend programs available. Postbaccalaureate distance learning degree programs offered. *Degree requirements:* For master's, final project. *Entrance requirements:* For master's, GMAT, U.S. CPA exam or Enrolled Agents Exam, minimum GPA of 2.75. Additional exam requirements/recommendations for international students: Required—TOEFL (minimum score 550 paper-based). Electronic applications accepted.

California State University, Fullerton, Graduate Studies, College of Business and Economics, Department of Accounting, Fullerton, CA 92834-9480. Offers accounting (MBA, MS); taxation (MS). *Accreditation:* AACSB. Part-time programs available. *Students:* 138 full-time (85 women), 75 part-time (43 women); includes 104 minority (3 Black or African American, non-Hispanic/Latino; 79 Asian, non-Hispanic/Latino; 20 Hispanic/Latino; 2 Two or more races, non-Hispanic/Latino), 71 international. Average age 27. 275 applicants, 60% accepted, 75 enrolled. In 2013, 74 master's awarded. *Degree requirements:* For master's, thesis or alternative, project. *Entrance requirements:* For master's, GMAT, minimum AACSB index of 950. *Application deadline:* Applications are processed on a rolling basis. Application fee: $55. Electronic applications accepted. *Financial support:* Career-related internships or fieldwork, Federal Work-Study, institutionally sponsored loans, and scholarships/grants available. Support available to part-time students. Financial award application deadline: 3/1; financial award applicants required to submit FAFSA. *Unit head:* Dr. Betty Chavis, Chair, 657-278-2225. *Application contact:* Admissions/Applications, 657-278-2371.

California State University, Los Angeles, Graduate Studies, College of Business and Economics, Department of Accounting, Los Angeles, CA 90032-8530. Offers accountancy (MS), including business taxation, financial accounting, information systems, management accounting; accounting (MBA). Part-time and evening/weekend programs available. *Faculty:* 4 full-time (0 women), 4 part-time/adjunct (2 women). *Students:* 35 full-time (23 women), 48 part-time (23 women); includes 38 minority (5 Black or African American, non-Hispanic/Latino; 26 Asian, non-Hispanic/Latino; 7 Hispanic/Latino), 33 international. Average age 31. 155 applicants, 48% accepted, 37 enrolled. In 2013, 36 master's awarded. *Degree requirements:* For master's, comprehensive exam (MBA), thesis (MS). *Entrance requirements:* For master's, GMAT, minimum GPA of 2.5 during previous 2 years of course work. Additional exam requirements/recommendations for international students: Required—TOEFL (minimum score 550 paper-based). *Application deadline:* For fall admission, 5/1 for domestic and international students. Applications are processed on a rolling basis. Application fee: $55. Electronic applications accepted. *Financial support:* Career-related internships or fieldwork and Federal Work-Study available. Support available to part-time students. Financial award application deadline: 3/1. *Unit head:* Dr. Kathryn Hansen, Chair, 323-343-2830, Fax: 323-343-6439, E-mail: khansen3@calstatela.edu. *Application contact:* Dr. Larry Fritz, Dean of Graduate Studies, 323-343-3820, Fax: 323-343-5653, E-mail: lfritz@calstatela.edu.
Website: http://cbe.calstatela.edu/acct/.

California State University, Northridge, Graduate Studies, The Tseng College of Extended Learning, Northridge, CA 91330. Offers business administration (Graduate Certificate); health administration (MPA); health education (MPH); knowledge management (MKM); music industry administration (MA); nonprofit-sector management (Graduate Certificate); public administration (MPA); public sector management and leadership (MPA); social work (MSW); taxation (MS); tourism, hospitality and recreation management (MS). *Entrance requirements:* For master's, GRE (if cumulative undergraduate GPA less than 3.0).

Capital University, Law School, Program in Business Law and Taxation, Columbus, OH 43209-2394. Offers business (LL M); business and taxation (LL M); taxation (LL M); JD/LL M. Part-time and evening/weekend programs available. *Degree requirements:* For master's, thesis or alternative. *Entrance requirements:* For master's, previous course work in accounting, business law, and taxation. Additional exam requirements/recommendations for international students: Required—TOEFL (minimum score 600 paper-based). Electronic applications accepted.

Capital University, Law School, Program in Taxation, Columbus, OH 43209-2394. Offers taxation (MT). Part-time and evening/weekend programs available. *Degree requirements:* For master's, thesis or alternative. *Entrance requirements:* For master's, previous course work in accounting, business law, and taxation. Additional exam requirements/recommendations for international students: Required—TOEFL (minimum

score 600 paper-based). Electronic applications accepted. *Expenses:* Contact institution.

Chapman University, School of Law, Orange, CA 92866. Offers advocacy and dispute resolution (JD); entertainment and media law (LL M); entertainment law (JD); environmental, land use, and real estate (JD); international law (JD); law (JD); prosecutorial science (LL M); tax law (JD); taxation (LL M); trial advocacy (LL M); JD/MBA; JD/MFA. *Accreditation:* ABA. Part-time and evening/weekend programs available. *Faculty:* 47 full-time (19 women), 35 part-time/adjunct (4 women). *Students:* 483 full-time (241 women), 71 part-time (28 women); includes 164 minority (5 Black or African American, non-Hispanic/Latino; 1 American Indian or Alaska Native, non-Hispanic/Latino; 84 Asian, non-Hispanic/Latino; 47 Hispanic/Latino; 1 Native Hawaiian or other Pacific Islander, non-Hispanic/Latino; 26 Two or more races, non-Hispanic/Latino), 76 international. Average age 26. 1,691 applicants, 51% accepted, 157 enrolled. In 2013, 36 master's, 187 doctorates awarded. *Entrance requirements:* For doctorate, LSAT, minimum undergraduate GPA of 2.75. Additional exam requirements/recommendations for international students: Required—TOEFL (minimum score 600 paper-based; 80 iBT). *Application deadline:* For fall admission, 4/15 priority date for domestic students. Applications are processed on a rolling basis. Application fee: $65. Electronic applications accepted. *Expenses:* Contact institution. *Financial support:* Fellowships, Federal Work-Study, and scholarships/grants available. Financial award applicants required to submit FAFSA. *Unit head:* Dr. Tom Campbell, Dean, 714-628-2500. *Application contact:* Karman Hsu, Assistant Dean of Admissions and Diversity Initiatives, 877-CHAPLAW, E-mail: mvargas@chapman.edu.
Website: http://www.chapman.edu/law/.

Cleveland State University, College of Graduate Studies, Monte Ahuja College of Business, Department of Accounting, Cleveland, OH 44115. Offers financial accounting/audit (M Acc); taxation (M Acc). *Accreditation:* AACSB. Part-time and evening/weekend programs available. *Faculty:* 13 full-time (3 women), 11 part-time/adjunct (3 women). *Students:* 118 full-time (63 women), 166 part-time (77 women); includes 42 minority (17 Black or African American, non-Hispanic/Latino; 18 Asian, non-Hispanic/Latino; 5 Hispanic/Latino; 2 Two or more races, non-Hispanic/Latino), 111 international. Average age 29. 182 applicants, 63% accepted, 54 enrolled. In 2013, 91 master's awarded. *Entrance requirements:* For master's, GMAT, minimum GPA of 2.75. Additional exam requirements/recommendations for international students: Required—TOEFL (minimum score 525 paper-based). *Application deadline:* For fall admission, 7/15 priority date for domestic students; for spring admission, 12/15 priority date for domestic students. Applications are processed on a rolling basis. Application fee: $30. *Expenses:* Tuition, state resident: full-time $8335; part-time $521 per credit hour. Tuition, nonresident: full-time $15,670; part-time $979 per credit hour. *Required fees:* $50; $25 per semester. *Financial support:* In 2013–14, 3 research assistantships with full and partial tuition reimbursements (averaging $6,960 per year) were awarded; career-related internships or fieldwork, Federal Work-Study, scholarships/grants, and unspecified assistantships also available. Financial award applicants required to submit FAFSA. *Faculty research:* Internal auditing, computer auditing, accounting education, managerial accounting. *Unit head:* Bruce W. McClain, Chair, 216-687-3652, Fax: 216-687-9212, E-mail: b.mcclain@csuohio.edu. *Application contact:* Bruce Gottschalk, MBA Programs Administrator, 216-687-3730, Fax: 216-687-5311, E-mail: cbacsu@csuohio.edu.
Website: http://www.csuohio.edu/business/academics/act/macc.html.

DePaul University, Charles H. Kellstadt Graduate School of Business, Chicago, IL 60604. Offers accountancy (M Acc, MS, MSA); applied economics (MBA); banking (MBA); behavioral finance (MBA); brand and product management (MBA); business development (MBA); business information technology (MS); business strategy and decision-making (MBA); computational finance (MS); consumer insights (MBA); corporate finance (MBA); economic policy analysis (MS); entrepreneurship (MBA, MS); finance (MBA, MS); financial analysis (MBA); general business (MBA); health sector management (MBA); hospitality leadership (MBA); hospitality leadership and operational performance (MS); human resource management (MBA); human resources (MS); investment management (MBA); leadership and change management (MBA); management accounting (MBA); marketing (MBA, MS); marketing analysis (MS); marketing strategy and planning (MBA); operations management (MBA); organizational diversity (MBA); real estate (MS); real estate finance and investment (MBA); revenue management (MBA); sports management (MBA); strategic global marketing (MBA); strategy, execution and valuation (MBA); sustainable management (MBA, MS); taxation (MS); wealth management (MS); JD/MBA. *Accreditation:* AACSB. Part-time and evening/weekend programs available. Postbaccalaureate distance learning degree programs offered (no on-campus study). *Faculty:* 81 full-time (20 women), 45 part-time/adjunct (8 women). *Students:* 1,238 full-time (605 women), 617 part-time (223 women); includes 295 minority (71 Black or African American, non-Hispanic/Latino; 129 Asian, non-Hispanic/Latino; 74 Hispanic/Latino; 4 Native Hawaiian or other Pacific Islander, non-Hispanic/Latino; 17 Two or more races, non-Hispanic/Latino), 462 international. Average age 29. In 2013, 911 master's awarded. *Entrance requirements:* For master's, GMAT, 2 letters of recommendation, resume, essay, official transcripts. Additional exam requirements/recommendations for international students: Required—TOEFL (minimum score 550 paper-based; 80 iBT). *Application deadline:* For fall admission, 7/1 for domestic students, 6/1 for international students; for winter admission, 10/1 for domestic students, 9/1 for international students; for spring admission, 2/1 for domestic students, 1/1 for international students. Applications are processed on a rolling basis. Application fee: $60. Electronic applications accepted. *Expenses:* Contact institution. *Financial support:* Application deadline: 4/1; applicants required to submit FAFSA. *Unit head:* Robert T. Ryan, Assistant Dean and Director, 312-362-8810, Fax: 312-362-6677, E-mail: rryan1@depaul.edu. *Application contact:* James Parker, Director of Recruitment and Admission, 312-362-8810, Fax: 312-362-6677, E-mail: kgsb@depaul.edu.
Website: http://kellstadt.depaul.edu.

DePaul University, College of Law, Chicago, IL 60604-2287. Offers health law (LL M); intellectual property law (LL M); international law (LL M); law (JD); taxation (LL M); JD/MA; JD/MBA; JD/MPS; JD/MS. *Accreditation:* ABA. Part-time and evening/weekend programs available. *Faculty:* 52 full-time (23 women), 53 part-time/adjunct (23 women). In 2013, 25 master's, 287 doctorates awarded. *Entrance requirements:* For doctorate, LSAT, LSAC applicant evaluation/letter of recommendation, personal statement, resume. Additional exam requirements/recommendations for international students: Required—TOEFL (minimum score 577 paper-based; 90 iBT), IELTS (minimum score 6.5). *Application deadline:* For fall admission, 3/1 for domestic and international students. Applications are processed on a rolling basis. Electronic applications accepted. *Expenses:* Contact institution. *Financial support:* Application deadline: 3/1; applicants required to submit FAFSA. *Unit head:* Gregory Mark, Dean, 312-362-5595, E-mail: gmark@depaul.edu. *Application contact:* Michael S. Burns, Director of Law Admission/Associate Dean, 312-362-6831, Fax: 312-362-5280, E-mail: lawinfo@depaul.edu.
Website: http://www.law.depaul.edu.

Fairfield University, Charles F. Dolan School of Business, Fairfield, CT 06824-5195. Offers accounting (MBA, MS, CAS); accounting information systems (MBA, CAS); entrepreneurship (MBA, CAS); finance (MBA, MS, CAS); general management (MBA, CAS); human resource management (MBA, CAS); information systems and operations

(MBA); information systems and operations management (CAS); marketing (MBA, CAS); taxation (MBA, CAS). *Accreditation:* AACSB. Part-time and evening/weekend programs available. *Faculty:* 18 full-time (9 women), 15 part-time/adjunct (4 women). *Students:* 94 full-time (45 women), 72 part-time (26 women); includes 49 minority (7 Black or African American, non-Hispanic/Latino; 33 Asian, non-Hispanic/Latino; 8 Hispanic/Latino; 1 Two or more races, non-Hispanic/Latino), 9 international. Average age 29. 116 applicants, 43% accepted, 26 enrolled. In 2013, 100 master's awarded. *Degree requirements:* For master's, capstone course. *Entrance requirements:* For master's, GMAT (minimum score 500), 2 letters of reference, resume, minimum GPA of 3.0. Additional exam requirements/recommendations for international students: Required—TOEFL (minimum score 550 paper-based; 80 iBT) or IELTS (minimum score 6.5). *Application deadline:* For fall admission, 5/15 for international students; for spring admission, 10/15 for international students. Applications are processed on a rolling basis. Application fee: $60. Electronic applications accepted. *Expenses:* Contact institution. *Financial support:* In 2013–14, 28 students received support. Scholarships/grants, unspecified assistantships, and merit-based one-time entrance scholarships available. Financial award applicants required to submit FAFSA. *Faculty research:* International finance, leadership and careers, ethics in accounting, emotions in consumer behavior, supply chain analysis, organizational leadership attributes, emotions in the workplace, real estate finance, effect of social media on stock prices. *Unit head:* Dr. Donald Gibson, Dean, 203-254-4070, Fax: 203-254-4105, E-mail: dgibson@fairfield.edu. *Application contact:* Marianne Gumpper, Director of Graduate and Continuing Studies Admission, 203-254-4184, Fax: 203-254-4073, E-mail: gradadmis@fairfield.edu.
Website: http://fairfield.edu/mba.

Fairleigh Dickinson University, College at Florham, Silberman College of Business, Department of Accounting, Law, and Tax, Program in Taxation, Madison, NJ 07940-1099. Offers MS, Certificate.

Fairleigh Dickinson University, Metropolitan Campus, Silberman College of Business, Department of Accounting, Law, and Tax, Program in Taxation, Teaneck, NJ 07666-1914. Offers MS.

Florida Atlantic University, College of Business, School of Accounting, Boca Raton, FL 33431-0991. Offers accounting (MAC, MBA, PhD); accounting information systems (MAC); business valuation (Exec MAC); forensic accounting (Exec MAC); taxation (MAC). *Accreditation:* AACSB. Part-time and evening/weekend programs available. Postbaccalaureate distance learning degree programs offered (minimal on-campus study). *Faculty:* 18 full-time (8 women), 10 part-time/adjunct (4 women). *Students:* 105 full-time (35 women), 365 part-time (200 women); includes 154 minority (50 Black or African American, non-Hispanic/Latino; 30 Asian, non-Hispanic/Latino; 68 Hispanic/Latino; 6 Two or more races, non-Hispanic/Latino), 9 international. Average age 33. 284 applicants, 42% accepted, 92 enrolled. In 2013, 201 master's awarded. *Degree requirements:* For master's, comprehensive exam, thesis optional. *Entrance requirements:* For master's, GMAT with minimum score 500 (preferred) or GRE (minimum score 1000 old test, 153 Verbal, 144 Quantitative, 4 Writing) taken within last 5 years, BS in accounting or equivalent, minimum GPA of 3.0 in last 60 hours of undergraduate study. Additional exam requirements/recommendations for international students: Required—TOEFL (minimum score 600 paper-based; 61 iBT), IELTS (minimum score 6). *Application deadline:* For fall admission, 7/1 priority date for domestic students, 2/15 priority date for international students; for spring admission, 11/1 priority date for domestic students, 7/15 priority date for international students. Applications are processed on a rolling basis. Application fee: $30. *Expenses:* Tuition, state resident: full-time $6660; part-time $370 per credit hour. Tuition, nonresident: full-time $18,450; part-time $1025 per credit hour. Tuition and fees vary according to course load. *Financial support:* Fellowships, research assistantships with partial tuition reimbursements, teaching assistantships, career-related internships or fieldwork, Federal Work-Study, institutionally sponsored loans, scholarships/grants, and tuition waivers (partial) available. Support available to part-time students. Financial award application deadline: 3/1. *Faculty research:* Systems and computer applications, accounting theory, information systems. *Unit head:* Dr. Kimberly Dunn, Director, 561-297-3638, Fax: 561-297-7023, E-mail: kdunn@fau.edu. *Application contact:* Dr. Marcy Krugel, Graduate Adviser, 561-297-3940, Fax: 561-297-1315, E-mail: krugel@fau.edu.
Website: http://business.fau.edu/departments/accounting/index.aspx.

Florida Gulf Coast University, Lutgert College of Business, Program in Accounting and Taxation, Fort Myers, FL 33965-6565. Offers MS. Part-time and evening/weekend programs available. *Degree requirements:* For master's, thesis or alternative. *Entrance requirements:* For master's, GMAT, minimum GPA of 3.0. Additional exam requirements/recommendations for international students: Required—TOEFL (minimum score 550 paper-based). Electronic applications accepted. *Faculty research:* Stock petitions, mergers and acquisitions, deferred taxes, fraud and accounting regulations, graphical reporting practices.

Florida International University, Alvah H. Chapman, Jr. Graduate School of Business, School of Accounting, Program in Taxation, Miami, FL 33199. Offers MST. Part-time and evening/weekend programs available. *Entrance requirements:* For master's, GMAT or GRE, minimum GPA of 3.0; resume. Additional exam requirements/recommendations for international students: Required—TOEFL (minimum score 550 paper-based; 80 iBT) or IELTS (minimum score 6.5). Electronic applications accepted. *Expenses:* Contact institution. *Faculty research:* Corporate taxation, small business taxation.

Florida State University, The Graduate School, College of Business, Tallahassee, FL 32306-1110. Offers accounting (M Acc), including accounting information services, assurance services, corporate accounting, taxation; business administration (MBA, PhD), including accounting (PhD), finance (PhD), management information systems (PhD), marketing (PhD), organizational behavior and human resources (PhD), risk management and insurance (PhD), strategic management (PhD); finance (MS); insurance (MSM); management information systems (MS); marketing (MS); JD/MBA; MSW/MBA. *Accreditation:* AACSB. Part-time programs available. Postbaccalaureate distance learning degree programs offered (no on-campus study). *Faculty:* 102 full-time (31 women), 5 part-time/adjunct (0 women). *Students:* 280 full-time (117 women), 278 part-time (88 women); includes 127 minority (26 Black or African American, non-Hispanic/Latino; 7 American Indian or Alaska Native, non-Hispanic/Latino; 44 Asian, non-Hispanic/Latino; 50 Hispanic/Latino). Average age 30. 630 applicants, 28% accepted, 103 enrolled. In 2013, 265 master's, 11 doctorates awarded. Terminal master's awarded for partial completion of doctoral program. *Degree requirements:* For doctorate, comprehensive exam, thesis/dissertation. *Entrance requirements:* For master's, GMAT, work experience (MBA, MS), minimum GPA of 3.0, letters of recommendation; for doctorate, GMAT, minimum graduate GPA of 3.5, letters of recommendation. Additional exam requirements/recommendations for international students: Required—TOEFL (minimum score 600 paper-based; 100 iBT); Recommended—IELTS (minimum score 6.5). *Application deadline:* For fall admission, 6/1 for domestic students, 5/1 for international students; for spring admission, 10/1 for domestic students, 9/1 for international students. Applications are processed on a rolling basis. Application fee: $30. Electronic applications accepted. *Expenses:* Tuition, state resident: part-time $403.51 per credit hour. Tuition, nonresident: part-time $1004.85 per credit hour. *Required fees:* $75.81 per credit hour. One-time fee: $20 part-time. Tuition

and fees vary according to course load, campus/location and student level. *Financial support:* In 2013–14, 92 students received support, including 10 fellowships with full tuition reimbursements available (averaging $1,500 per year), 20 research assistantships with full tuition reimbursements available (averaging $20,000 per year), 35 teaching assistantships with full tuition reimbursements available (averaging $20,000 per year); career-related internships or fieldwork, scholarships/grants, health care benefits, and unspecified assistantships also available. Financial award application deadline: 1/1. *Unit head:* Dr. Caryn Beck-Dudley, Dean, 850-644-3090, Fax: 850-644-0915. *Application contact:* Lisa Beverly, Director, Graduate Programs Admissions, 850-644-6458, Fax: 850-644-0588, E-mail: lbeverly@cob.fsu.edu.
Website: http://www.cob.fsu.edu/.

Fordham University, Graduate School of Business, New York, NY 10023. Offers accounting (MBA); communications and media management (MBA); executive business administration (EMBA); finance (MBA, MS); information systems (MBA, MS); management systems (MBA); marketing (MBA); media management (MS); taxation (MS); taxation and accounting (MTA); JD/MBA; MBA/MIM; MS/MBA. MBA/MIM offered jointly with Thunderbird School of Global Management. *Accreditation:* AACSB. Part-time and evening/weekend programs available. *Entrance requirements:* For master's, GMAT, 2 letters of recommendation, resume. Additional exam requirements/recommendations for international students: Required—TOEFL (minimum score 600 paper-based; 100 iBT). Electronic applications accepted. *Expenses:* Contact institution.

Georgetown University, Law Center, Washington, DC 20001. Offers global health law (LL M); individualized study (LL M); international business and economic law (LL M); law (JD, SJD); national security law (LL M); securities and financial regulation (LL M); taxation (LL M); JD/LL M; JD/MA; JD/MBA; JD/MPH; JD/PhD. *Accreditation:* ABA. Part-time and evening/weekend programs available. *Degree requirements:* For master's, thesis; for doctorate, thesis/dissertation (for some programs). *Entrance requirements:* For master's, JD, LL B, or first law degree earned in country of origin; for doctorate, LSAT (for JD). Additional exam requirements/recommendations for international students: Required—TOEFL. *Expenses:* Contact institution. *Faculty research:* Constitutional law, legal history, jurisprudence.

Georgia State University, J. Mack Robinson College of Business, School of Accountancy, Program in Taxation, Atlanta, GA 30303. Offers M Tax, JD/M Tax. Part-time and evening/weekend programs available. *Students:* Average age 0. *Entrance requirements:* For master's, GRE or GMAT, transcripts from all institutions attended, resume, essays. Additional exam requirements/recommendations for international students: Required—TOEFL (minimum score 610 paper-based; 101 iBT), IELTS (minimum score 7). *Application deadline:* For fall admission, 5/1 priority date for domestic students, 2/1 priority date for international students; for spring admission, 9/1 priority date for domestic students, 4/1 priority date for international students. Applications are processed on a rolling basis. Application fee: $50. Electronic applications accepted. *Expenses: Tuition, area resident:* Full-time $4176; part-time $348 per credit hour. Tuition, state resident: full-time $14,544; part-time $1212 per credit hour. Tuition, nonresident: full-time $14,544; part-time $1212 per credit hour. Tuition and fees vary according to course load and program. *Financial support:* Research assistantships, career-related internships or fieldwork, scholarships/grants, tuition waivers, and unspecified assistantships available. Financial award application deadline: 5/1. *Unit head:* Dr. Tad Ransopher, Director, 404-413-7229, Fax: 404-651-1033. *Application contact:* Toby McChesney, Assistant Dean for Graduate Recruiting and Student Services, 404-413-7167, Fax: 404-413-7162, E-mail: rcbgradadmissions@gsu.edu.
Website: http://robinson.gsu.edu/accountancy/mtx.html.

Golden Gate University, School of Accounting, San Francisco, CA 94105-2968. Offers accounting (M Ac, MSA, Graduate Certificate); forensic accounting (M Ac, MSA, Graduate Certificate); taxation (M Ac). Part-time and evening/weekend programs available. *Entrance requirements:* For master's, minimum GPA of 3.0. Additional exam requirements/recommendations for international students: Required—TOEFL. Electronic applications accepted. *Faculty research:* Forensic accounting, audit, tax, CPA exam.

Golden Gate University, School of Law, San Francisco, CA 94105-2968. Offers environmental law (LL M); intellectual property law (LL M); international legal studies (LL M, SJD); law (JD); taxation (LL M); U. S. legal studies (LL M); JD/MBA; JD/PhD. *Accreditation:* ABA. Part-time and evening/weekend programs available. *Degree requirements:* For doctorate, thesis/dissertation (for some programs). *Entrance requirements:* For doctorate, LSAT (for JD). Additional exam requirements/recommendations for international students: Required—TOEFL (minimum score 600 paper-based). Electronic applications accepted. *Expenses:* Contact institution. *Faculty research:* International law, intellectual property law, environmental law, real estate, civil rights.

Golden Gate University, School of Taxation, San Francisco, CA 94105-2968. Offers advanced studies in taxation (Certificate); estate planning (Certificate); international tax (Certificate); tax (Certificate); taxation (MS). Part-time and evening/weekend programs available. *Entrance requirements:* For master's, minimum GPA of 3.0. Additional exam requirements/recommendations for international students: Required—TOEFL. Electronic applications accepted. *Expenses:* Contact institution.

Goldey-Beacom College, Graduate Program, Wilmington, DE 19808-1999. Offers business administration (MBA); finance (MS); financial management (MBA); health care management (MBA); human resource management (MBA); information technology (MBA); international business management (MBA); major finance (MBA); major taxation (MBA); management (MM); marketing management (MBA); taxation (MBA, MS). *Accreditation:* ACBSP. Part-time and evening/weekend programs available. *Entrance requirements:* For master's, GMAT, MAT, GRE, minimum GPA of 3.0. Additional exam requirements/recommendations for international students: Required—TOEFL (minimum score 65 iBT); Recommended—IELTS (minimum score 6). Electronic applications accepted.

Grand Valley State University, Seidman College of Business, Program in Taxation, Allendale, MI 49401-9403. Offers MST. Part-time and evening/weekend programs available. *Entrance requirements:* For master's, GMAT. Additional exam requirements/recommendations for international students: Required—TOEFL. Electronic applications accepted. *Faculty research:* Individual income taxation, state taxation, pass-through entities, estate and gift taxation, sale-leasebacks.

HEC Montreal, School of Business Administration, Graduate Diplomas Programs in Administration, Program in Taxation, Montréal, QC H3T 2A7, Canada. Offers Graduate Diploma. All courses are given in French. *Students:* 35 full-time (20 women), 67 part-time (33 women). 92 applicants, 53% accepted, 30 enrolled. In 2013, 14 Graduate Diplomas awarded. *Degree requirements:* For Graduate Diploma, one foreign language. *Entrance requirements:* For degree, bachelor diploma in law, accounting, or economics. *Application deadline:* For fall admission, 4/1 for domestic and international students; for winter admission, 9/15 for domestic and international students. Application fee: $83 Canadian dollars. Electronic applications accepted. *Expenses: Tuition, area resident:* Part-time $74.14 per credit. Tuition, state resident: full-time $2669.04; part-time $201.83 per credit. Tuition, nonresident: full-time $7266; part-time $500.59 per credit. *International tuition:* $18,021.24 full-time. *Required fees:* $1529.70; $36.20 per credit. $65.50 per term. Tuition and fees vary according to degree level and program. *Financial support:* In 2013–14, 1,007 students received support. Research assistantships, teaching assistantships, and scholarships/grants available. Financial award application deadline: 9/2. *Unit head:* Silvia Ponce, Director, 514-340-6393, Fax: 514-340-6915, E-mail: silvia.ponce@hec.ca. *Application contact:* Jo Anne Audet, Administrative Director, 514-340-1315, Fax: 514-340-6411, E-mail: joanne.audet@hec.ca.
Website: http://www.hec.ca/programmes_formations/des/dess/dess_fiscalite/index.html.

HEC Montreal, School of Business Administration, Master of Science Programs in Administration, LL M Program in Taxation, Montréal, QC H3T 2A7, Canada. Offers LL M. Program offered in French only. *Students:* 7 full-time (4 women), 27 part-time (13 women). In 2013, 41 master's awarded. *Degree requirements:* For master's, one foreign language. *Entrance requirements:* For master's, bachelor's degree in taxation. *Application deadline:* For fall admission, 4/1 for domestic and international students. Application fee: $83. Electronic applications accepted. *Expenses: Tuition, area resident:* Part-time $74.14 per credit. Tuition, state resident: full-time $2669.04; part-time $201.83 per credit. Tuition, nonresident: full-time $7266; part-time $500.59 per credit. *International tuition:* $18,021.24 full-time. *Required fees:* $1529.70; $36.20 per credit. $65.50 per term. Tuition and fees vary according to degree level and program. *Financial support:* In 2013–14, 1,007 students received support. Research assistantships, teaching assistantships, and scholarships/grants available. Financial award application deadline: 9/2. *Unit head:* Silvia Ponce, Director, 514-340-6393, Fax: 514-340-6915, E-mail: silvia.ponce@hec.ca. *Application contact:* Jo Anne Audet, Administrative Director, 514-340-1315, Fax: 514-340-6411, E-mail: joanne.audet@hec.ca.
Website: http://www.hec.ca/programmes_formations/des/maitrises_professionnelles/llm/index.html.

Hofstra University, Frank G. Zarb School of Business, Programs in Accounting and Taxation, Hempstead, NY 11549. Offers accounting (MS, Advanced Certificate); business administration (MBA), including accounting, professional accountancy, taxation; taxation (MS, Advanced Certificate).

Illinois Institute of Technology, Chicago-Kent College of Law, Chicago, IL 60661-3691. Offers family law (LL M); financial services (LL M); international intellectual property (LL M); law (JD); taxation (LL M); U.S., international, and transnational law (LL M); JD/LL M; JD/MBA; JD/MPA; JD/MPH; JD/MS. *Accreditation:* ABA. Part-time and evening/weekend programs available. *Faculty:* 71 full-time (27 women), 154 part-time/adjunct (40 women). *Students:* 856 full-time (403 women), 137 part-time (63 women); includes 230 minority (44 Black or African American, non-Hispanic/Latino; 56 Asian, non-Hispanic/Latino; 108 Hispanic/Latino; 2 Native Hawaiian or other Pacific Islander, non-Hispanic/Latino; 20 Two or more races, non-Hispanic/Latino), 115 international. Average age 27. 2,676 applicants, 55% accepted, 282 enrolled. In 2013, 106 master's, 286 doctorates awarded. Terminal master's awarded for partial completion of doctoral program. *Entrance requirements:* For master's, 1st degree in law or certified license to practice law; for doctorate, LSAT. Additional exam requirements/recommendations for international students: Required—TOEFL (minimum score 600 paper-based; 100 iBT); Recommended—IELTS (minimum score 7). *Application deadline:* For fall admission, 3/15 priority date for domestic students, 2/1 priority date for international students. Applications are processed on a rolling basis. Application fee: $0 ($75 for international students). Electronic applications accepted. *Expenses:* Contact institution. *Financial support:* In 2013–14, 742 students received support. Career-related internships or fieldwork, Federal Work-Study, institutionally sponsored loans, scholarships/grants, and tuition waivers (full) available. Support available to part-time students. Financial award application deadline: 3/15; financial award applicants required to submit FAFSA. *Faculty research:* Constitutional law, bioethics, environmental law, intellectual property. *Total annual research expenditures:* $217,995. *Unit head:* Harold J. Krent, Dean, 312-906-5010, Fax: 312-906-5335, E-mail: hkrent@kentlaw.iit.edu. *Application contact:* Nicole Vilches, Assistant Dean, 312-906-5020, Fax: 312-906-5274, E-mail: admissions@kentlaw.iit.edu.
Website: http://www.kentlaw.iit.edu/.

Instituto Tecnologico de Santo Domingo, Graduate School, Area of Business, Santo Domingo, Dominican Republic. Offers banking and securities markets (M Mgmt); corporate finance (M Mgmt); human resources management (M Mgmt, Certificate); international trade management (M Mgmt); marketing (M Mgmt); organizational development (M Mgmt); quality and productivity management (Certificate); tax management and planning (M Mgmt); upper management (M Mgmt).

John Marshall Law School, Graduate and Professional Programs, Chicago, IL 60604-3968. Offers employee benefits (LL M, MS); estate planning (LL M); global legal studies (LL M); information technology (MS); information technology and privacy law (LL M); intellectual property (LL M, MS); international business and trade (LL M); law (JD); real estate (LL M, MS); taxation (LL M, MS); trial advocacy (LL M); JD/LL M; JD/MA; JD/MBA; JD/MPA. JD/MBA offered jointly with Dominican University; JD/MA and JD/MPA with Roosevelt University. *Accreditation:* ABA. Part-time and evening/weekend programs available. *Faculty:* 71 full-time (26 women), 132 part-time/adjunct (49 women). *Students:* 1,045 full-time (512 women), 421 part-time (211 women); includes 403 minority (152 Black or African American, non-Hispanic/Latino; 8 American Indian or Alaska Native, non-Hispanic/Latino; 89 Asian, non-Hispanic/Latino; 138 Hispanic/Latino; 3 Native Hawaiian or other Pacific Islander, non-Hispanic/Latino; 13 Two or more races, non-Hispanic/Latino), 57 international. Average age 27. 2,694 applicants, 73% accepted, 419 enrolled. In 2013, 81 master's, 445 doctorates awarded. *Degree requirements:* For master's, 24 credits; for doctorate, 90 credits. *Entrance requirements:* For master's, JD; for doctorate, LSAT. Additional exam requirements/recommendations for international students: Required—TOEFL. *Application deadline:* For fall admission, 3/1 priority date for domestic and international students; for spring admission, 10/15 priority date for domestic and international students. Applications are processed on a rolling basis. Application fee: $0. Electronic applications accepted. *Expenses:* Contact institution. *Financial support:* In 2013–14, 1,275 students received support. Scholarships/grants and tuition waivers (full and partial) available. Support available to part-time students. Financial award application deadline: 4/1; financial award applicants required to submit FAFSA. *Unit head:* John Corkery, Dean, 312-427-2737. *Application contact:* William B. Powers, Associate Dean of Admission and Student Affairs, 800-537-4280, Fax: 312-427-5136, E-mail: admission@jmls.edu.

Long Island University–LIU Brooklyn, School of Business, Public Administration and Information Sciences, Program in Accountancy, Taxation and Law, Brooklyn, NY 11201-8423. Offers accounting (MS); taxation (MS). Part-time and evening/weekend programs available. *Entrance requirements:* For master's, GMAT or GRE General Test, 2 letters of recommendation. Additional exam requirements/recommendations for international students: Required—TOEFL (minimum score 500 paper-based). Electronic applications accepted.

Long Island University–LIU Post, College of Management, School of Business, Brookville, NY 11548-1300. Offers accounting and taxation (Certificate); business administration (Certificate); finance (MBA, Certificate); general business administration (MBA); international business (MBA, Certificate); management (MBA, Certificate); management information systems (MBA, Certificate); marketing (MBA, Certificate). *Accreditation:* AACSB. Part-time and evening/weekend programs available. *Entrance*

requirements: For master's, GMAT, resume, minimum GPA of 3.0, 2 letters of recommendation. Additional exam requirements/recommendations for international students: Required—TOEFL (minimum score 527 paper-based). Electronic applications accepted. *Faculty research:* Financial markets, consumer behavior.

Long Island University–LIU Post, College of Management, School of Professional Accountancy, Brookville, NY 11548-1300. Offers accounting (MS); taxation (MS). Part-time and evening/weekend programs available. *Entrance requirements:* For master's, GMAT, minimum GPA of 2.5, BS in accounting from accredited college or university. Electronic applications accepted. *Faculty research:* International taxation.

Loyola Marymount University, Loyola Law School Los Angeles, Los Angeles, CA 90015. Offers foreign-trained attorneys (LL M); law (JD); taxation (LL M); JD/LL M; JD/MBA. *Accreditation:* ABA. Part-time and evening/weekend programs available. *Degree requirements:* For master's and doctorate, comprehensive exam. *Entrance requirements:* For master's, JD; for doctorate, LSAT. Electronic applications accepted.

Loyola University Chicago, School of Law, Chicago, IL 60611. Offers advocacy (LL M); business law (LL M, MJ); child and family law (LL M); children's law and policy (MJ); health law (LL M, MJ); health law and policy (D Law, SJD); international law (LL M); law (JD); rule of law development (LL M); tax law (LL M); JD/MA; JD/MBA; JD/MSW; MJ/MSW. MJ in business law offered in partnership with Concord Law School. *Accreditation:* ABA. Part-time and evening/weekend programs available. Postbaccalaureate distance learning degree programs offered (minimal on-campus study). *Faculty:* 48 full-time (16 women), 174 part-time/adjunct (98 women). *Students:* 851 full-time (461 women), 271 part-time (206 women); includes 333 minority (142 Black or African American, non-Hispanic/Latino; 3 American Indian or Alaska Native, non-Hispanic/Latino; 55 Asian, non-Hispanic/Latino; 98 Hispanic/Latino; 2 Native Hawaiian or other Pacific Islander, non-Hispanic/Latino; 33 Two or more races, non-Hispanic/Latino), 33 international. Average age 31. 3,333 applicants, 51% accepted, 213 enrolled. In 2013, 144 master's, 282 doctorates awarded. *Entrance requirements:* For doctorate, LSAT. Additional exam requirements/recommendations for international students: Required—TOEFL (minimum score 550 paper-based; 79 iBT), IELTS (minimum score 6.5). *Application deadline:* For fall admission, 3/1 for domestic and international students. Applications are processed on a rolling basis. Application fee: $0. Electronic applications accepted. *Expenses:* Contact institution. *Financial support:* In 2013–14, 676 students received support, including 72 fellowships; Federal Work-Study and scholarships/grants also available. Financial award application deadline: 3/1; financial award applicants required to submit FAFSA. *Unit head:* Pamela Bloomquist, Assistant Dean for Admission and Financial Assistance, Law School, 312-915-7170, Fax: 312-915-7906, E-mail: ploom@luc.edu. *Application contact:* Ron Martin, Associate Director, Graduate and Professional Enrollment Management Operations, 312-915-8951, E-mail: rmarti7@luc.edu.
Website: http://www.luc.edu/law/.

Michigan State University, The Graduate School, Eli Broad College of Business, Department of Accounting and Information Systems, East Lansing, MI 48824. Offers accounting (MS, PhD), including information systems (MS), public and corporate accounting (MS), taxation (MS); business information systems (PhD). *Accreditation:* AACSB. *Faculty:* 36. *Students:* 193. 500 applicants, 34% accepted. In 2013, 123 master's awarded. *Degree requirements:* For doctorate, comprehensive exam, thesis/dissertation. *Entrance requirements:* For master's, GMAT (minimum score 550), bachelor's degree in accounting; minimum cumulative GPA of 3.0 at any institution attended and in any junior-/senior-level accounting courses taken; 3 letters of recommendation (at least 1 from faculty); working knowledge of computers including word processing, spreadsheets, networking, and database management system; for doctorate, GMAT (minimum score 600), bachelor's degree; transcripts; 3 letters of recommendation; statement of purpose; resume; on-campus interview; personal qualifications of sound character, perseverance, intellectual curiosity, and interest in scholarly research. Additional exam requirements/recommendations for international students: Required—TOEFL (minimum score 600 paper-based; 100 iBT), IELTS (minimum score 7) accepted for MS only. *Application deadline:* For fall admission, 1/1 for domestic and international students; for spring admission, 10/1 for domestic and international students; for summer admission, 1/1 for domestic and international students. Applications are processed on a rolling basis. Electronic applications accepted. *Financial support:* Research assistantships with tuition reimbursements, teaching assistantships with tuition reimbursements, scholarships/grants, and unspecified assistantships available. Financial award application deadline: 1/1. *Unit head:* Dr. Sanjay Gupta, Associate Dean for MBA and Professional Master's Programs, 517-432-6488, Fax: 517-432-1101, E-mail: gupta@broad.msu.edu. *Application contact:* Program Information Contact, 517-355-7486, Fax: 517-432-1101, E-mail: acct@broad.msu.edu.
Website: http://accounting.broad.msu.edu.

Mississippi State University, College of Business, Adkerson School of Accountancy, Mississippi State, MS 39762. Offers accounting (MPA); systems (MPA); taxation (MTX). *Accreditation:* AACSB. *Faculty:* 8 full-time (3 women), 2 part-time/adjunct (0 women). *Students:* 35 full-time (17 women), 8 part-time (5 women); includes 4 minority (3 Asian, non-Hispanic/Latino; 1 Two or more races, non-Hispanic/Latino), 4 international. Average age 26. 60 applicants, 32% accepted, 13 enrolled. In 2013, 40 master's awarded. *Degree requirements:* For master's, comprehensive exam. *Entrance requirements:* For master's, GMAT (minimum score of 510), minimum GPA of 3.0 over last 60 hours of undergraduate course work. Additional exam requirements/recommendations for international students: Required—TOEFL (minimum score 575 paper-based; 84 iBT); Recommended—IELTS (minimum score 7). *Application deadline:* For fall admission, 7/1 for domestic students, 5/1 for international students; for spring admission, 11/1 for domestic students, 9/1 for international students. Applications are processed on a rolling basis. Application fee: $60. Electronic applications accepted. *Financial support:* Career-related internships or fieldwork, Federal Work-Study, institutionally sponsored loans, scholarships/grants, and unspecified assistantships available. Support available to part-time students. Financial award application deadline: 4/1; financial award applicants required to submit FAFSA. *Faculty research:* Income tax, financial accounting system, managerial accounting, auditing. *Unit head:* Dr. Jim Scheiner, Director and Graduate Coordinator, 662-325-3710, Fax: 662-325-1646, E-mail: sac@cobilan.msstate.edu. *Application contact:* Dr. Marcia Watson, Graduate Coordinator, 662-325-3710, Fax: 662-325-1646, E-mail: sac@business.msstate.edu.
Website: http://www.business.msstate.edu/programs/adkerson.

New York Law School, Graduate Programs, New York, NY 10013. Offers American business law (LL M); financial services (LL M); law (JD); mental disability law (MA); real estate (LL M); taxation (LL M); JD/MA; JD/MBA. JD/MBA offered jointly with Bernard M. Baruch College of the City University of New York; JD/MA in forensic psychology offered jointly with John Jay College of Criminal Justice of the City University of New York. *Accreditation:* ABA. Part-time and evening/weekend programs available. *Faculty:* 79 full-time (31 women), 103 part-time/adjunct (44 women). *Students:* 891 full-time (453 women), 415 part-time (212 women); includes 411 minority (95 Black or African American, non-Hispanic/Latino; 1 American Indian or Alaska Native, non-Hispanic/Latino; 96 Asian, non-Hispanic/Latino; 194 Hispanic/Latino; 3 Native Hawaiian or other Pacific Islander, non-Hispanic/Latino; 22 Two or more races, non-Hispanic/Latino), 42 international. Average age 27. 3,484 applicants, 59% accepted, 341 enrolled. In 2013, 33 master's, 562 doctorates awarded. *Entrance requirements:* For master's, JD (for LL M); for doctorate, LSAT, undergraduate degree, letter of recommendation, resume, essay/personal statement. Additional exam requirements/recommendations for international students: Required—TOEFL (minimum score 600 paper-based; 100 iBT). *Application deadline:* For fall admission, 7/1 priority date for domestic and international students. Applications are processed on a rolling basis. Application fee: $0. Electronic applications accepted. *Expenses: Tuition:* Full-time $47,600; part-time $36,680 per year. *Required fees:* $1640; $1200. Part-time tuition and fees vary according to course load, degree level and student level. *Financial support:* In 2013–14, 495 students received support, including 142 fellowships (averaging $3,000 per year), 46 research assistantships (averaging $4,615 per year), 29 teaching assistantships (averaging $4,379 per year); career-related internships or fieldwork, Federal Work-Study, institutionally sponsored loans, and scholarships/grants also available. Support available to part-time students. Financial award application deadline: 7/1; financial award applicants required to submit FAFSA. *Faculty research:* Immigration law, corporate law, civil rights, family law, international law. *Unit head:* Anthony W. Crowell, Dean and President, 212-431-2840, Fax: 212-219-3752, E-mail: acrowell@nyls.edu. *Application contact:* Adam Barrett, Associate Dean of Admissions and Financial Aid, 212-431-2888, Fax: 212-966-1522, E-mail: admissions@nyls.edu.
Website: http://www.nyls.edu.

New York University, School of Law, New York, NY 10012-1019. Offers law (LL M, JD, JSD); law and business (Advanced Certificate); taxation (MSL, Advanced Certificate); JD/JD; JD/LL B; JD/MA; JD/MBA; JD/MPA; JD/MPP; JD/MSW; JD/MUP; JD/PhD. *Accreditation:* ABA. Part-time programs available. Postbaccalaureate distance learning degree programs offered. *Faculty:* 137 full-time (44 women), 68 part-time/adjunct (18 women). *Students:* 1,418 full-time (619 women); includes 394 minority (80 Black or African American, non-Hispanic/Latino; 1 American Indian or Alaska Native, non-Hispanic/Latino; 165 Asian, non-Hispanic/Latino; 120 Hispanic/Latino; 28 Two or more races, non-Hispanic/Latino), 69 international. 5,730 applicants, 437 enrolled. In 2013, 532 master's, 537 doctorates awarded. *Entrance requirements:* For doctorate, LSAT (for JD). *Application deadline:* For fall admission, 2/15 for domestic students. Application fee: $85. Electronic applications accepted. *Expenses:* Contact institution. *Financial support:* Fellowships, research assistantships, teaching assistantships, career-related internships or fieldwork, Federal Work-Study, scholarships/grants, and loan repayment assistance available. Financial award application deadline: 4/15; financial award applicants required to submit FAFSA. *Faculty research:* International law, environmental law, corporate law, globalization of law, philosophy of law. *Unit head:* Trevor Morrison, Dean, 212-998-6000, Fax: 212-995-3150. *Application contact:* Kenneth J. Kleinrock, Assistant Dean for Admissions, 212-998-6060, Fax: 212-995-4527.
Website: http://www.law.nyu.edu/.

Northeastern University, D'Amore-McKim School of Business, Boston, MA 02115-5096. Offers accounting (MS); business administration (EMBA, MBA); finance (MS); international business (MS); taxation (MS); technological entrepreneurship (MS); JD/MBA; MBA/MSN; MS/MBA. Part-time and evening/weekend programs available. Postbaccalaureate distance learning degree programs offered (no on-campus study). *Entrance requirements:* For master's, GMAT or GRE, interview. Additional exam requirements/recommendations for international students: Required—TOEFL (minimum score 600 paper-based; 100 iBT). Electronic applications accepted. *Expenses:* Contact institution.

Northern Illinois University, Graduate School, College of Business, Department of Accountancy, De Kalb, IL 60115-2854. Offers MAS, MST. *Accreditation:* AACSB. Part-time and evening/weekend programs available. *Faculty:* 14 full-time (4 women). *Students:* 133 full-time (57 women), 61 part-time (31 women); includes 41 minority (8 Black or African American, non-Hispanic/Latino; 18 Asian, non-Hispanic/Latino; 11 Hispanic/Latino; 4 Two or more races, non-Hispanic/Latino), 24 international. Average age 28. 135 applicants, 58% accepted, 45 enrolled. In 2013, 129 master's awarded. *Degree requirements:* For master's, thesis optional. *Entrance requirements:* For master's, GMAT, minimum GPA of 2.75. Additional exam requirements/recommendations for international students: Required—TOEFL (minimum score 550 paper-based). *Application deadline:* For fall admission, 4/1 priority date for domestic students, 5/1 for international students; for spring admission, 9/15 priority date for domestic students, 10/1 for international students. Applications are processed on a rolling basis. Application fee: $40. Electronic applications accepted. *Financial support:* In 2013–14, 27 research assistantships with full tuition reimbursements, 16 teaching assistantships with full tuition reimbursements were awarded; fellowships with full tuition reimbursements, career-related internships or fieldwork, Federal Work-Study, scholarships/grants, tuition waivers (full), and unspecified assistantships also available. Support available to part-time students. Financial award applicants required to submit FAFSA. *Faculty research:* Accounting fraud, governmental accounting, corporate income tax planning, auditing, ethics. *Unit head:* Dr. James C. Young, Chair, 815-753-1250, Fax: 815-753-8515. *Application contact:* Dr. Rowene Linden, Graduate Adviser, 815-753-6200.
Website: http://www.cob.niu.edu/accy/.

Northern Kentucky University, Office of Graduate Programs, College of Business, Program in Accountancy, Highland Heights, KY 41099. Offers accountancy (M Acc); advanced taxation (Certificate). Part-time and evening/weekend programs available. *Faculty:* 6 full-time (1 woman), 2 part-time/adjunct (both women). *Students:* 16 full-time (5 women), 51 part-time (20 women); includes 7 minority (6 Black or African American, non-Hispanic/Latino; 1 Asian, non-Hispanic/Latino). Average age 31. 81 applicants, 52% accepted, 32 enrolled. In 2013, 21 master's awarded. *Degree requirements:* For master's, capstone course. *Entrance requirements:* For master's, GMAT (minimum score 450), minimum GPA of 2.5, resume, statement of purpose. Additional exam requirements/recommendations for international students: Required—TOEFL (minimum score 550 paper-based; 79 iBT); Recommended—IELTS (minimum score 6.5). *Application deadline:* For fall admission, 7/1 priority date for domestic students, 6/1 for international students; for spring admission, 12/1 priority date for domestic students, 10/1 for international students; for summer admission, 5/1 priority date for domestic students, 3/1 for international students. Applications are processed on a rolling basis. Application fee: $40. Electronic applications accepted. *Expenses:* Tuition, state resident: full-time $4446; part-time $494 per credit hour. Tuition, nonresident: full-time $6885; part-time $765 per credit hour. *Required fees:* $72 per semester. One-time fee: $125.50. Part-time tuition and fees vary according to course load, degree level, program and reciprocity agreements. *Financial support:* In 2013–14, 24 students received support. Unspecified assistantships available. Financial award applicants required to submit FAFSA. *Faculty research:* Behavioral influences on accounting decisions, historical development of accounting, auditing and accounting failures. *Unit head:* Robert Salyer, Director, 859-572-7695, Fax: 859-572-7694, E-mail: salyerb@nku.edu. *Application contact:* Dr. Christian Gamm, Director of Graduate Programs, 859-572-6364, Fax: 859-572-6670, E-mail: gammc1@nku.edu.
Website: http://cob.nku.edu/graduatedegrees/accountancy.html.

Northwestern University, Law School, Chicago, IL 60611-3069. Offers international human rights (LL M); law (JD); law and business (LL M); tax (LL M in Tax); JD/LL M; JD/

MBA; JD/PhD; LL M/Certificate. Executive LL M programs offered in Madrid (Spain), Seoul (South Korea), and Tel Aviv (Israel). *Accreditation:* ABA. *Entrance requirements:* For master's, law degree or equivalent, letter of recommendation, resume; for doctorate, LSAT, 1 letter of recommendation, resume. Additional exam requirements/recommendations for international students: Required—TOEFL. Electronic applications accepted. *Expenses:* Contact institution. *Faculty research:* Constitutional law, corporate law, international law, law and social policy, ethical studies.

Nova Southeastern University, H. Wayne Huizenga School of Business and Entrepreneurship, Fort Lauderdale, FL 33314-7796. Offers accounting (M Acc); business administration (MBA, DBA); human resource management (MSHRM); international business administration (MIBA); leadership (MS); public administration (MPA, DPA); real estate development (MS); taxation (M Tax); JD/MBA; Pharm D/MBA. Part-time and evening/weekend programs available. Postbaccalaureate distance learning degree programs offered (minimal on-campus study). *Faculty:* 67 full-time (24 women), 135 part-time/adjunct (37 women). *Students:* 207 full-time (110 women), 3,069 part-time (1,888 women); includes 2,213 minority (1,077 Black or African American, non-Hispanic/Latino; 2 American Indian or Alaska Native, non-Hispanic/Latino; 108 Asian, non-Hispanic/Latino; 975 Hispanic/Latino; 2 Native Hawaiian or other Pacific Islander, non-Hispanic/Latino; 49 Two or more races, non-Hispanic/Latino), 190 international. Average age 33. 1,291 applicants, 68% accepted, 636 enrolled. In 2013, 1,146 master's, 17 doctorates awarded. *Degree requirements:* For master's, thesis optional; for doctorate, comprehensive exam, thesis/dissertation. *Entrance requirements:* For doctorate, GMAT. Additional exam requirements/recommendations for international students: Required—TOEFL (minimum score 550 paper-based; 79 iBT), IELTS (minimum score 6). *Application deadline:* Applications are processed on a rolling basis. Application fee: $50. Electronic applications accepted. *Financial support:* In 2013–14, 2 students received support. Federal Work-Study and scholarships/grants available. Support available to part-time students. Financial award applicants required to submit FAFSA. *Faculty research:* Reputation management, call centers, international social capital, corporate earnings guidance, corporate governance. *Unit head:* Dr. J. Preston Jones, Dean, 954-262-5127, E-mail: fieldsm@nova.edu. *Application contact:* Karen Goldberg, Associate Director of Recruitment and Special Events, 954-262-5039, Fax: 954-262-3822, E-mail: karen@nova.edu.
Website: http://www.huizenga.nova.edu.

Oklahoma City University, Meinders School of Business, Program in Accounting, Oklahoma City, OK 73106-1402. Offers financial leadership (MSA); general (MSA); taxation (MSA). Part-time and evening/weekend programs available. *Students:* 11 full-time (8 women), 2 part-time (0 women); includes 5 minority (all Asian, non-Hispanic/Latino), 8 international. Average age 29. 28 applicants, 79% accepted, 8 enrolled. In 2013, 15 master's awarded. *Entrance requirements:* For master's, bachelor's degree from accredited institution, minimum GPA of 3.0, essay, recommendation letters. Additional exam requirements/recommendations for international students: Required—TOEFL (minimum score 570 paper-based; 80 iBT). *Application deadline:* Applications are processed on a rolling basis. Application fee: $50. Electronic applications accepted. *Expenses: Tuition:* Full-time $16,848; part-time $936 per credit hour. Tuition and fees vary according to course load, degree level and program. *Financial support:* Career-related internships or fieldwork, Federal Work-Study, institutionally sponsored loans, scholarships/grants, and tuition waivers available. Support available to part-time students. Financial award application deadline: 8/1; financial award applicants required to submit FAFSA. *Faculty research:* Financial accounting, auditing, tax. *Unit head:* Dr. Steve Agee, Dean, 405-208-5130 Ext. ', Fax: 405-208-5098, E-mail: sagee@okcu.edu. *Application contact:* Heidi Puckett, Director, Admissions, 800-633-7242, Fax: 405-208-5916, E-mail: gadmissions@okcu.edu.
Website: http://www.okcu.edu/msa/.

Pace University, Lubin School of Business, Taxation Program, New York, NY 10038. Offers MBA, MS. Part-time and evening/weekend programs available. *Students:* 7 full-time (5 women), 64 part-time (31 women); includes 28 minority (7 Black or African American, non-Hispanic/Latino; 19 Asian, non-Hispanic/Latino; 2 Hispanic/Latino), 12 international. Average age 30. 63 applicants, 56% accepted, 20 enrolled. In 2013, 16 master's awarded. *Entrance requirements:* For master's, GMAT or GRE. Additional exam requirements/recommendations for international students: Required—TOEFL. *Application deadline:* For fall admission, 8/1 priority date for domestic students, 6/1 for international students; for spring admission, 12/1 priority date for domestic students, 10/1 for international students. Applications are processed on a rolling basis. Application fee: $70. Electronic applications accepted. *Expenses: Tuition:* Part-time $1075 per credit. *Required fees:* $192 per semester. Tuition and fees vary according to course load, degree level and program. *Financial support:* Research assistantships, career-related internships or fieldwork, and Federal Work-Study available. Support available to part-time students. Financial award applicants required to submit FAFSA. *Unit head:* Dr. Richard Kraus, Chairperson, Legal Studies and Taxation Department, 212-618-6476, E-mail: rkraus@pace.edu. *Application contact:* Susan Ford-Goldschein, Director of Graduate Admissions, 212-346-1531, Fax: 212-346-1585, E-mail: gradnyc@pace.edu.
Website: http://www.pace.edu/lubin.

Philadelphia University, School of Business Administration, Program in Taxation, Philadelphia, PA 19144. Offers MS. Part-time and evening/weekend programs available. *Entrance requirements:* For master's, GMAT. Additional exam requirements/recommendations for international students: Required—TOEFL (minimum score 550 paper-based; 79 iBT). Electronic applications accepted.

Robert Morris University, Graduate Studies, School of Business, Moon Township, PA 15108-1189. Offers business administration (MBA); human resource management (MS); nonprofit management (MS); taxation (MS). *Accreditation:* AACSB. Part-time and evening/weekend programs available. Postbaccalaureate distance learning degree programs offered (no on-campus study). *Faculty:* 25 full-time (10 women), 8 part-time/adjunct (2 women). *Students:* 247 part-time (99 women); includes 10 minority (1 Black or African American, non-Hispanic/Latino; 2 Asian, non-Hispanic/Latino; 7 Two or more races, non-Hispanic/Latino), 5 international. Average age 26. 214 applicants, 40% accepted, 62 enrolled. In 2013, 187 master's awarded. *Entrance requirements:* For master's, GMAT, letters of recommendation. Additional exam requirements/recommendations for international students: Required—TOEFL (minimum score 550 paper-based; 79 iBT). *Application deadline:* For fall admission, 7/1 priority date for domestic and international students; for spring admission, 11/1 priority date for domestic and international students. Applications are processed on a rolling basis. Application fee: $35. Electronic applications accepted. *Expenses: Tuition:* Part-time $825 per credit. Part-time tuition and fees vary according to degree level and program. *Financial support:* Research assistantships with partial tuition reimbursements, Federal Work-Study, institutionally sponsored loans, and unspecified assistantships available. Support available to part-time students. Financial award application deadline: 5/1; financial award applicants required to submit FAFSA. *Unit head:* Dr. John M. Beehler, Dean, 412-397-5445, Fax: 412-397-2172, E-mail: beehler@rmu.edu. *Application contact:* 412-397-5200, Fax: 412-397-5915, E-mail: graduateadmissions@rmu.edu.
Website: http://www.rmu.edu/web/cms/schools/sbus/Pages/default.aspx.

St. John's University, The Peter J. Tobin College of Business, Department of Accounting and Taxation, Program in Taxation, Queens, NY 11439. Offers MBA, MS, Adv C. Part-time and evening/weekend programs available. Postbaccalaureate distance learning degree programs offered (no on-campus study). *Students:* 38 full-time (13 women), 33 part-time (13 women); includes 34 minority (4 Black or African American, non-Hispanic/Latino; 22 Asian, non-Hispanic/Latino; 5 Hispanic/Latino; 1 Native Hawaiian or other Pacific Islander, non-Hispanic/Latino; 2 Two or more races, non-Hispanic/Latino), 9 international. Average age 28. 82 applicants, 78% accepted, 33 enrolled. In 2013, 47 master's awarded. *Degree requirements:* For master's, comprehensive exam (for some programs), thesis optional. *Entrance requirements:* For master's, GMAT (waived for MS applicants who have successfully completed the CPA exam), 2 letters of recommendation, resume, transcripts, statement of goals, bachelor's degree in accounting; for Adv C, GMAT, 2 letters of recommendation, resume, undergraduate and graduate transcripts, essay, MBA in accounting. Additional exam requirements/recommendations for international students: Required—TOEFL (minimum score 600 paper-based; 100 iBT), IELTS (minimum score 7). *Application deadline:* For fall admission, 5/1 priority date for domestic and international students; for spring admission, 11/1 priority date for domestic and international students. Applications are processed on a rolling basis. Application fee: $50. Electronic applications accepted. *Expenses:* Contact institution. *Financial support:* Research assistantships, scholarships/grants, and unspecified assistantships available. Support available to part-time students. Financial award application deadline: 3/1; financial award applicants required to submit FAFSA. *Unit head:* Dr. Adrian Fitzsimons, Chair, 718-990-7306, E-mail: fitzsima@stjohns.edu. *Application contact:* Carol J. Swanberg, Assistant Dean/Director of Graduate Admissions, 718-990-1345, Fax: 718-990-5242, E-mail: tobingradnyc@stjohns.edu.

St. Thomas University, School of Law, Miami Gardens, FL 33054-6459. Offers international human rights (LL M); international taxation (LL M); law (JD); JD/MBA; JD/MS. *Accreditation:* ABA. Postbaccalaureate distance learning degree programs offered (no on-campus study). *Degree requirements:* For master's, thesis (international taxation). *Entrance requirements:* For doctorate, LSAT. Electronic applications accepted. *Expenses:* Contact institution.

San Jose State University, Graduate Studies and Research, Lucas Graduate School of Business, Program in Taxation, San Jose, CA 95192-0001. Offers MS. *Degree requirements:* For master's, comprehensive exam, thesis or alternative. *Entrance requirements:* For master's, GMAT, minimum GPA of 3.0. Electronic applications accepted.

Seton Hall University, Stillman School of Business, Department of Accounting, South Orange, NJ 07079-2697. Offers accounting (MS, Certificate); professional accounting (MS); taxation (Certificate). Part-time and evening/weekend programs available. *Faculty:* 7 full-time (0 women), 1 part-time/adjunct (0 women). *Students:* 43 full-time (23 women), 109 part-time (45 women); includes 7 minority (1 Black or African American, non-Hispanic/Latino; 3 Asian, non-Hispanic/Latino; 2 Hispanic/Latino; 1 Native Hawaiian or other Pacific Islander, non-Hispanic/Latino). Average age 30. 106 applicants, 85% accepted, 67 enrolled. In 2013, 63 master's awarded. *Entrance requirements:* For master's, GMAT, GRE or CPA, advanced degree from AACSB institution, MS in a business discipline, professional degree (MD, JD, PhD, DVM, DDS, etc.), minimum undergraduate GPA of 3.0. Additional exam requirements/recommendations for international students: Required—TOEFL (minimum score 102 iBT), IELTS or PTE. *Application deadline:* For fall admission, 5/31 priority date for domestic students, 3/31 for international students; for spring admission, 10/31 for domestic students, 9/30 for international students. Applications are processed on a rolling basis. Application fee: $75. Electronic applications accepted. *Financial support:* In 2013–14, 2 students received support, including research assistantships with full tuition reimbursements available (averaging $23,956 per year); career-related internships or fieldwork, scholarships/grants, and unspecified assistantships also available. Support available to part-time students. Financial award application deadline: 6/30; financial award applicants required to submit FAFSA. *Faculty research:* Voluntary disclosure, international accounting, pension and retirement accounting, ethics in financial reporting, executive compensation. *Total annual research expenditures:* $20,000. *Unit head:* Dr. Mark Holtzman, Chair, 973-761-9133, Fax: 973-761-9217, E-mail: mark.holtzman@shu.edu. *Application contact:* Catherine Bianchi, Director of Graduate Admissions, 973-761-9262, Fax: 973-761-9208, E-mail: catherine.bianchi@shu.edu.
Website: http://www.shu.edu/academics/business/ms-programs.cfm.

Seton Hall University, Stillman School of Business, Department of Taxation, South Orange, NJ 07079-2697. Offers MS, Certificate. Part-time and evening/weekend programs available. *Faculty:* 1 full-time (0 women), 2 part-time/adjunct (0 women). *Students:* 4 part-time (1 woman). Average age 48. 3 applicants, 100% accepted, 3 enrolled. In 2013, 1 master's awarded. *Entrance requirements:* For master's, GMAT, GRE or CPA, advanced degree from AACSB institution, MS in a business discipline, professional degree (MD, JD, PhD, DVM, DDS, etc.), minimum undergraduate GPA of 3.0. Additional exam requirements/recommendations for international students: Required—TOEFL (minimum score 102 iBT), IELTS or PTE. *Application deadline:* For fall admission, 6/1 priority date for domestic students, 4/11 for international students; for spring admission, 11/1 priority date for domestic students, 10/1 for international students. Application fee: $75. Electronic applications accepted. *Expenses:* Contact institution. *Financial support:* In 2013–14, research assistantships with full tuition reimbursements (averaging $35,610 per year) were awarded; career-related internships or fieldwork, scholarships/grants, and unspecified assistantships also available. Support available to part-time students. Financial award application deadline: 6/1; financial award applicants required to submit FAFSA. *Faculty research:* Issues affecting cost capitalization, estate valuation discounts, qualified terminable interest property elections, eastern European tax initiatives, realigning the capital structure of closely-held business enterprises. *Total annual research expenditures:* $1,000. *Unit head:* Dr. Mark Holtzman, Department Chair, 973-761-9133, Fax: 973-761-9217, E-mail: eastonre@shu.edu. *Application contact:* Catherine Bianchi, Director of Graduate Admissions, 973-761-9220, Fax: 973-761-9208, E-mail: catherine.bianchi@shu.edu.
Website: http://www.shu.edu/academics/business/mba/.

Southern Illinois University Edwardsville, Graduate School, School of Business, Department of Accounting, Edwardsville, IL 62026. Offers accountancy (MSA); taxation (MSA). *Accreditation:* AACSB. Part-time and evening/weekend programs available. *Faculty:* 8 full-time (3 women). *Students:* 20 full-time (12 women), 14 part-time (11 women), 1 international. 23 applicants, 48% accepted. In 2013, 24 master's awarded. *Degree requirements:* For master's, thesis or alternative, final exam. *Entrance requirements:* For master's, GMAT. Additional exam requirements/recommendations for international students: Required—TOEFL (minimum score 550 paper-based, 79 iBT), IELTS (minimum score 6.5), Michigan Test of English Language Proficiency or PTE. *Application deadline:* For fall admission, 7/18 for domestic students, 6/1 for international students; for spring admission, 12/12 for domestic students, 10/1 for international students; for summer admission, 4/24 for domestic students, 3/1 for international students. Applications are processed on a rolling basis. Application fee: $30. Electronic applications accepted. *Expenses:* Tuition, state resident: full-time $3551. Tuition, nonresident: full-time $8378. *Financial support:* In 2013–14, 9 students received support, including 2 fellowships with full tuition reimbursements available (averaging $8,370 per year), 1 research assistantship with full tuition reimbursement available

(averaging $9,585 per year), 6 teaching assistantships with full tuition reimbursements available (averaging $9,585 per year); institutionally sponsored loans, scholarships/grants, and unspecified assistantships also available. Financial award application deadline: 3/1; financial award applicants required to submit FAFSA. *Unit head:* Dr. Michael Costigan, Chair, 618-650-2633, E-mail: mcostig@siue.edu. *Application contact:* Melissa K. Mace, Assistant Director of Graduate and International Recruitment, 618-650-2756, Fax: 618-650-3618, E-mail: mmace@siue.edu.
Website: http://www.siue.edu/business/accounting/.

Southern Methodist University, Dedman School of Law, Dallas, TX 75275-0110. Offers law (JD, SJD); law (for foreign law school graduates) (LL M); law (general) (LL M); taxation (LL M); JD/MA; JD/MBA. *Accreditation:* ABA. Part-time and evening/weekend programs available. *Degree requirements:* For master's, thesis optional; for doctorate, thesis/dissertation (for some programs), 30 hours of public service (for JD). *Entrance requirements:* For master's, JD; for doctorate, LSAT (for JD). Additional exam requirements/recommendations for international students: Required—TOEFL (minimum score 575 paper-based; 91 iBT). Electronic applications accepted. *Expenses:* Contact institution. *Faculty research:* Corporate law, intellectual property, international law, commercial law, dispute resolution.

Southern New Hampshire University, School of Business, Manchester, NH 03106-1045. Offers accounting (MBA, MS, Graduate Certificate); accounting finance (MS); accounting/auditing (MS); accounting/forensic accounting (MS); accounting/taxation (MS); athletic administration (MBA, Graduate Certificate); business administration (IMBA, MBA, Certificate, Graduate Certificate, including accounting (Certificate), business administration (MBA), business information systems (Graduate Certificate), human resource management (Certificate); corporate social responsibility (MBA); entrepreneurship (MBA); finance (MBA, MS, Graduate Certificate); finance/corporate finance (MS); finance/investments and securities (MS); forensic accounting (MBA); healthcare informatics (MBA); healthcare management (MBA); human resource management (Graduate Certificate); information technology (MS, Graduate Certificate); information technology management (MBA); international business (Graduate Certificate); international business and information technology (Graduate Certificate); international finance (Graduate Certificate); international sport management (Graduate Certificate); justice studies (MBA); leadership of nonprofit organizations (Graduate Certificate); marketing (MBA, MS, Graduate Certificate); operations and project management (MS); operations and supply chain management (MBA, Graduate Certificate); organizational leadership (MS); project management (MBA, Graduate Certificate); Six Sigma (MBA); Six Sigma quality (Graduate Certificate); social media marketing (MBA); sport management (MBA, MS, Graduate Certificate); sustainability and environmental compliance (MBA); workplace conflict management (MBA); MBA/Certificate. *Accreditation:* ACBSP. Part-time and evening/weekend programs available. Postbaccalaureate distance learning degree programs offered (no on-campus study). Terminal master's awarded for partial completion of doctoral program. *Degree requirements:* For master's, one foreign language, comprehensive exam (for some programs), thesis or alternative. *Entrance requirements:* For master's, minimum GPA of 2.5. Additional exam requirements/recommendations for international students: Required—TOEFL (minimum score 500 paper-based). Electronic applications accepted.

State University of New York College at Old Westbury, School of Business, Old Westbury, NY 11568-0210. Offers accounting (MS); taxation (MS). Part-time and evening/weekend programs available. *Faculty:* 8 full-time (1 woman), 2 part-time/adjunct (0 women). *Students:* 39 full-time (19 women), 66 part-time (32 women); includes 31 minority (6 Black or African American, non-Hispanic/Latino; 12 Asian, non-Hispanic/Latino; 13 Hispanic/Latino). Average age 33. 65 applicants, 83% accepted, 36 enrolled. In 2013, 36 master's awarded. *Entrance requirements:* For master's, GMAT, 2 letters of recommendation. Additional exam requirements/recommendations for international students: Required—TOEFL (minimum score 550 paper-based). *Application deadline:* For fall admission, 6/15 priority date for domestic students; for spring admission, 11/15 priority date for domestic students. Applications are processed on a rolling basis. Application fee: $50. Electronic applications accepted. *Expenses:* Tuition, state resident: full-time $9370; part-time $390 per credit. Tuition, nonresident: full-time $16,680; part-time $695 per credit. *Required fees:* $45.85 per credit. $47 per term. *Faculty research:* Corporate governance, asset pricing, corporate finance, hedge funds, taxation. *Unit head:* Rita Buttermilch, Director of Graduate Business Programs, 516-876-3900, E-mail: buttermilchr@oldwestbury.edu. *Application contact:* Philip D'Angelo, Graduate Admissions Office, 516-876-3073, E-mail: enroll@oldwestbury.edu.

Strayer University, Graduate Studies, Washington, DC 20005-2603. Offers accounting (MS); acquisition (MBA); business administration (MBA); communications technology (MS); educational management (M Ed); finance (MBA); health services administration (MHSA); hospitality and tourism management (MBA); human resource management (MBA); information systems (MS), including computer security management, decision support system management, enterprise resource management, network management, software engineering management, systems development management; management (MBA); management information systems (MS); marketing (MBA); professional accounting (MS), including accounting information systems, controllership, taxation; public administration (MPA); supply chain management (MBA); technology in education (M Ed). Programs also offered at campus locations in Birmingham, AL; Chamblee, GA; Cobb County, GA; Morrow, GA; White Marsh, MD; Charleston, SC; Columbia, SC; Greensboro, NC; Greenville, SC; Lexington, KY; Louisville, KY; Nashville, TN; North Raleigh, NC; Washington, DC. Part-time and evening/weekend programs available. Postbaccalaureate distance learning degree programs offered (minimal on-campus study). *Degree requirements:* For master's, thesis. *Entrance requirements:* For master's, GMAT, GRE General Test, bachelor's degree from an accredited college or university, minimum undergraduate GPA of 2.75. Electronic applications accepted.

Suffolk University, Sawyer Business School, Department of Accounting, Boston, MA 02108-2770. Offers accounting (MSA, GDPA); taxation (MST); GDPA/MST; MBA/GDPA; MBA/MSA; MBA/MST. *Accreditation:* AACSB. Part-time and evening/weekend programs available. *Faculty:* 12 full-time (3 women), 8 part-time/adjunct (2 women). *Students:* 106 full-time (77 women), 139 part-time (72 women); includes 47 minority (16 Black or African American, non-Hispanic/Latino; 19 Asian, non-Hispanic/Latino; 11 Hispanic/Latino; 1 Two or more races, non-Hispanic/Latino), 78 international. Average age 28. 418 applicants, 70% accepted, 110 enrolled. In 2013, 116 master's, 4 GDPAs awarded. *Entrance requirements:* For master's, GMAT. Additional exam requirements/recommendations for international students: Required—TOEFL (minimum score 550 paper-based; 80 iBT). *Application deadline:* For fall admission, 6/15 priority date for domestic students, 6/15 for international students; for spring admission, 11/1 priority date for domestic students, 11/1 for international students. Applications are processed on a rolling basis. Application fee: $50. Electronic applications accepted. *Expenses:* Tuition: Full-time $38,374; part-time $1279 per credit. *Required fees:* $40; $20 per semester. Tuition and fees vary according to program. *Financial support:* In 2013–14, 80 students received support, including 79 fellowships (averaging $19,005 per year); career-related internships or fieldwork, Federal Work-Study, and institutionally sponsored loans also available. Support available to part-time students. Financial award application deadline: 4/1; financial award applicants required to submit FAFSA. *Faculty research:* Tax policy, tax research, decision-making in accounting, accounting

information systems, capital markets and strategic planning. *Unit head:* Lewis Shaw, Chair, 617-573-8615, Fax: 617-994-4260, E-mail: lshaw@suffolk.edu. *Application contact:* Cory Meyers, Director of Graduate Admissions, 617-573-8302, Fax: 617-305-1733, E-mail: grad.admission@suffolk.edu.
Website: http://www.suffolk.edu/msa.

Suffolk University, Sawyer Business School, Master of Business Administration Program, Boston, MA 02108-2770. Offers accounting (MBA); business administration (APC); entrepreneurship (MBA); executive business administration (EMBA); finance (MBA); global business administration (GMBA); health administration (MBA); international business (MBA); marketing (MBA); nonprofit management (MBA); organizational behavior (MBA); strategic management (MBA); supply chain management (MBA); taxation (MBA); JD/MBA; MBA/GDPA; MBA/MHA; MBA/MSA; MBA/MSF; MBA/MST. *Accreditation:* AACSB. Part-time and evening/weekend programs available. Postbaccalaureate distance learning degree programs offered (no on-campus study). *Faculty:* 29 full-time (9 women), 12 part-time/adjunct (2 women). *Students:* 106 full-time (44 women), 334 part-time (184 women); includes 57 minority (20 Black or African American, non-Hispanic/Latino; 1 American Indian or Alaska Native, non-Hispanic/Latino; 18 Asian, non-Hispanic/Latino; 14 Hispanic/Latino; 4 Two or more races, non-Hispanic/Latino), 61 international. Average age 30. 448 applicants, 61% accepted, 135 enrolled. In 2013, 217 master's awarded. *Entrance requirements:* For master's, GMAT, minimum undergraduate GPA of 2.75 (MBA), 5 years of managerial experience (EMBA). Additional exam requirements/recommendations for international students: Required—TOEFL (minimum score 550 paper-based; 80 iBT). *Application deadline:* For fall admission, 6/15 priority date for domestic students, 6/15 for international students; for spring admission, 11/1 priority date for domestic students, 11/1 for international students. Applications are processed on a rolling basis. Application fee: $50. Electronic applications accepted. *Expenses:* Tuition: Full-time $38,374; part-time $1279 per credit. *Required fees:* $40; $20 per semester. Tuition and fees vary according to program. *Financial support:* In 2013–14, 107 students received support, including 91 fellowships with full and partial tuition reimbursements available (averaging $12,428 per year); career-related internships or fieldwork, Federal Work-Study, and institutionally sponsored loans also available. Support available to part-time students. Financial award application deadline: 4/1; financial award applicants required to submit FAFSA. *Faculty research:* Foreign investments; career strategies and boundaryless careers; corporate ethics codes; interest rates, inflation, and growth options; innovation and product development performance. *Unit head:* Heather Hewitt, Assistant Dean of Graduate Programs/Director of MBA Programs, 617-573-8306, E-mail: hhewitt@suffolk.edu. *Application contact:* Cory Meyers, Director of Graduate Admissions, 617-573-8302, Fax: 617-305-1733, E-mail: grad.admission@suffolk.edu.
Website: http://www.suffolk.edu/mba.

Taft Law School, Graduate Programs, Santa Ana, CA 92704-6954. Offers American jurisprudence (LL M); law (JD); taxation (LL M).

Temple University, James E. Beasley School of Law, Philadelphia, PA 19122. Offers law (JD); legal education (SJD); taxation (LL M); transnational law (LL M); trial advocacy (LL M); JD/LL M; JD/MBA. *Accreditation:* ABA. Part-time and evening/weekend programs available. *Entrance requirements:* For doctorate, LSAT (for JD). Additional exam requirements/recommendations for international students: Recommended—TOEFL. Electronic applications accepted. *Expenses:* Contact institution. *Faculty research:* Evidence, gender issues, health care law, immigration law, and intellectual property law.

Texas Tech University, Graduate School, Rawls College of Business Administration, Area of Accounting, Lubbock, TX 79409. Offers accounting (PhD); audit/financial reporting (MSA); taxation (MSA); JD/MSA. *Accreditation:* AACSB. Part-time programs available. *Faculty:* 10 full-time (2 women), 1 part-time/adjunct (0 women). *Students:* 202 full-time (104 women); includes 10 minority (3 Black or African American, non-Hispanic/Latino; 1 American Indian or Alaska Native, non-Hispanic/Latino; 2 Asian, non-Hispanic/Latino; 4 Hispanic/Latino), 6 international. Average age 24. 122 applicants, 70% accepted, 79 enrolled. In 2013, 133 master's, 1 doctorate awarded. Terminal master's awarded for partial completion of doctoral program. *Degree requirements:* For master's, capstone course; for doctorate, comprehensive exam, thesis/dissertation, qualifying exams. *Entrance requirements:* For master's and doctorate, GMAT, holistic profile of academic credentials. Additional exam requirements/recommendations for international students: Required—TOEFL (minimum score 550 paper-based; 79 iBT). *Application deadline:* For fall admission, 2/1 for domestic students, 1/15 for international students; for spring admission, 12/1 for domestic students. Applications are processed on a rolling basis. Application fee: $60. Electronic applications accepted. *Expenses:* Tuition, state resident: full-time $6062; part-time $252.57 per credit hour. Tuition, nonresident: full-time $14,558; part-time $606.57 per credit hour. *Required fees:* $2655; $35 per credit hour. $907.50 per semester. Tuition and fees vary according to course load. *Financial support:* In 2013–14, 7 research assistantships (averaging $14,933 per year), 1 teaching assistantship (averaging $18,000 per year) were awarded; fellowships, career-related internships or fieldwork, Federal Work-Study, scholarships/grants, health care benefits, and unspecified assistantships also available. Financial award applicants required to submit FAFSA. *Faculty research:* Governmental and nonprofit accounting, managerial and financial accounting. *Unit head:* Dr. Robert Ricketts, Area Coordinator, 806-742-3180, Fax: 806-742-3182, E-mail: robert.ricketts@ttu.edu. *Application contact:* Terri Boston, Applications Manager, Graduate and Professional Programs, 806-742-3184, Fax: 806-742-3958, E-mail: rawlsgrad@ttu.edu.
Website: http://accounting.ba.ttu.edu.

Thomas M. Cooley Law School, JD and LL M Programs, Lansing, MI 48901-3038. Offers administrative law (public law) (JD); business transactions (JD); Canadian law practice (JD); Constitutional law and civil rights (public law) (JD); corporate law and finance (LL M); environmental law (public law) (JD); general practice (JD), including solo and small firm; homeland and national security law (LL M); insurance law (LL M); intellectual property (JD); intellectual property law (LL M); international law (JD); litigation (JD); self-directed (LL M, JD); tax law (LL M); taxation (JD); U.S. legal studies for foreign attorneys (LL M); JD/MBA; JD/MPA; JD/MSW. *Accreditation:* ABA. Part-time and evening/weekend programs available. Postbaccalaureate distance learning degree programs offered (no on-campus study). *Degree requirements:* For master's, thesis optional; for doctorate, minimum of 3 credits of clinical experience. *Entrance requirements:* For master's, JD or LL B; for doctorate, LSAT. Additional exam requirements/recommendations for international students: Required—TOEFL (for U.S. legal studies for foreign attorneys LL M program). Electronic applications accepted. *Faculty research:* Wrongful convictions, civil rights, environmental law, litigation techniques, data mining, intellectual property, practical and skills-based legal education.

Troy University, Graduate School, College of Business, Program in Taxation, Troy, AL 36082. Offers MTX, Certificate. Part-time and evening/weekend programs available. *Faculty:* 3 full-time (1 woman). *Students:* 16 part-time (8 women); includes 11 minority (all Black or African American, non-Hispanic/Latino). Average age 31. 16 applicants, 75% accepted, 3 enrolled. In 2013, 4 master's awarded. *Degree requirements:* For master's, minimum GPA of 3.0, research paper, capstone course. *Entrance requirements:* For master's, GMAT (minimum score of 500), bachelor's degree; minimum undergraduate GPA of 2.5 or 3.0 on last 30 semester hours, letter of

recommendation. Additional exam requirements/recommendations for international students: Required—TOEFL (minimum score 523 paper-based; 70 iBT), IELTS (minimum score 6). *Application deadline:* Applications are processed on a rolling basis. Application fee: $50. Electronic applications accepted. *Expenses:* Tuition, state resident: full-time $6084; part-time $338 per credit hour. Tuition, nonresident: full-time $12,168; part-time $676 per credit hour. *Required fees:* $630; $35 per credit hour. $50 per semester. *Unit head:* Dr. Kay Sheridan, Director, 334-670-3154, Fax: 334-670-3599, E-mail: ksheridan@troy.edu. *Application contact:* Brenda K. Campbell, Director of Graduate Admissions, 334-670-3178, Fax: 334-670-3733, E-mail: bcamp@troy.edu.

Université de Montréal, Faculty of Law, Montréal, QC H3C 3J7, Canada. Offers business law (DESS); common law (North America) (JD); international law (DESS); law (LL M, LL D, DDN, DESS, LL B); tax law (LL M). Part-time programs available. *Degree requirements:* For master's, thesis; for doctorate, thesis/dissertation, project; for other advanced degree, thesis (for some programs). Electronic applications accepted. *Faculty research:* Legal theory; constitutional, private, and public law.

Université de Sherbrooke, Faculty of Administration, Program in Taxation, Sherbrooke, QC J1K 2R1, Canada. Offers M Tax, Diploma. Part-time and evening/weekend programs available. *Degree requirements:* For master's, one foreign language, thesis. *Entrance requirements:* For master's, bachelor's degree in business, law or economics; basic knowledge of Canadian taxation (2 courses). Electronic applications accepted. *Faculty research:* Taxation research, public finances.

University at Albany, State University of New York, School of Business, Department of Accounting and Law, Albany, NY 12222-0001. Offers accounting (MS); taxation (MS). *Accreditation:* AACSB. *Degree requirements:* For master's, research project. *Entrance requirements:* For master's, GMAT. Additional exam requirements/recommendations for international students: Required—TOEFL (minimum score 550 paper-based). Electronic applications accepted. *Faculty research:* Professional ethics, statistical analysis, cost management systems, accounting theory.

The University of Akron, Graduate School, College of Business Administration, School of Accountancy, Program in Taxation, Akron, OH 44325. Offers MT, JD/MT. *Students:* 20 full-time (10 women), 25 part-time (7 women); includes 6 minority (3 Black or African American, non-Hispanic/Latino; 3 Asian, non-Hispanic/Latino), 2 international. Average age 31. 19 applicants, 89% accepted, 16 enrolled. In 2013, 21 master's awarded. *Entrance requirements:* For master's, GMAT, minimum GPA of 2.75, two letters of recommendation, resume, statement of purpose. Additional exam requirements/recommendations for international students: Required—TOEFL (minimum score 550 paper-based; 79 iBT). *Application deadline:* For fall admission, 7/15 for domestic and international students; for spring admission, 11/15 for domestic and international students. Application fee: $40 ($60 for international students). Electronic applications accepted. *Expenses:* Tuition, state resident: full-time $7430; part-time $412.80 per credit hour. Tuition, nonresident: full-time $12,722; part-time $706.80 per credit hour. *Required fees:* $53 per credit hour. $12 per semester. Tuition and fees vary according to course load and program. *Unit head:* Dr. Thomas Calderon, Department Chair, 330-972-6228, E-mail: tcalderon@uakron.edu. *Application contact:* Dr. Wiliam Hauser, Director of Graduate Business Programs, 330-972-7043, Fax: 330-972-6588, E-mail: whauser@uakron.edu.

The University of Alabama, Graduate School, Manderson Graduate School of Business, Culverhouse School of Accountancy, Tuscaloosa, AL 35487. Offers accounting (M Acc, PhD); tax accounting (MTA). *Accreditation:* AACSB. *Faculty:* 17 full-time (4 women). *Students:* 126 full-time (58 women), 4 part-time (2 women); includes 15 minority (10 Black or African American, non-Hispanic/Latino; 2 Asian, non-Hispanic/Latino; 3 Hispanic/Latino), 4 international. Average age 24. 251 applicants, 51% accepted, 104 enrolled. In 2013, 97 master's, 4 doctorates awarded. *Degree requirements:* For doctorate, thesis/dissertation. *Entrance requirements:* For master's, GMAT, minimum GPA of 3.0 overall or on last 60 hours; for doctorate, GMAT, minimum GPA of 3.0. Additional exam requirements/recommendations for international students: Required—TOEFL. *Application deadline:* For fall admission, 7/1 priority date for domestic students, 6/1 priority date for international students; for spring admission, 11/1 priority date for domestic students, 9/1 priority date for international students. Applications are processed on a rolling basis. Application fee: $50 ($60 for international students). Electronic applications accepted. *Expenses:* Tuition, state resident: full-time $9450. Tuition, nonresident: full-time $23,950. *Financial support:* In 2013–14, 79 students received support, including 4 fellowships with full tuition reimbursements available (averaging $15,000 per year), 23 research assistantships with full and partial tuition reimbursements available (averaging $9,765 per year), 19 teaching assistantships with full and partial tuition reimbursements available (averaging $13,352 per year); career-related internships or fieldwork, Federal Work-Study, institutionally sponsored loans, scholarships/grants, health care benefits, and unspecified assistantships also available. Financial award application deadline: 3/31. *Faculty research:* Corporate governance, audit decision-making, earning management, valuation, executive compensation, not-for-profit. *Unit head:* Dr. Mary S. Stone, Director, 205-348-2915, Fax: 205-348-8453, E-mail: mstone@cba.ua.edu. *Application contact:* Sandy D. Davidson, Advisor, 205-348-6131, Fax: 205-348-8453, E-mail: sdavidso@cba.ua.edu.
Website: http://www.cba.ua.edu/accounting/.

The University of Alabama, School of Law, Tuscaloosa, AL 35487. Offers business transactions (LL M); comparative law (LL M, JSD); law (JD, JSD); taxation (LL M in Tax); JD/MBA. *Accreditation:* ABA. *Faculty:* 56 full-time (24 women), 51 part-time/adjunct (13 women). *Students:* 466 full-time (192 women), 148 part-time (57 women); includes 93 minority (60 Black or African American, non-Hispanic/Latino; 2 American Indian or Alaska Native, non-Hispanic/Latino; 9 Asian, non-Hispanic/Latino; 13 Hispanic/Latino; 9 Two or more races, non-Hispanic/Latino), 1 international. 2,038 applicants, 29% accepted, 217 enrolled. In 2013, 167 doctorates awarded. *Degree requirements:* For master's, 24 hours, exams; for doctorate, 90 hours, including 3 hours of professional skills, 1 seminar, and 36 required hours. *Entrance requirements:* For master's, LSAT, undergraduate degree in law, letters of recommendation; for doctorate, LSAT, undergraduate degree, letter of recommendation, resume. Additional exam requirements/recommendations for international students: Required—TOEFL, IELTS. *Application deadline:* Applications are processed on a rolling basis. Application fee: $40. Electronic applications accepted. *Expenses:* Contact institution. *Financial support:* Applicants required to submit FAFSA. *Faculty research:* Public interest law, Constitutional law, civil rights, international law, tax law. *Unit head:* Claude R. Arrington, Associate Dean for Academic Affairs, 205-348-6557, Fax: 205-348-3077, E-mail: carrington@law.ua.edu. *Application contact:* Martha Griffith, Assistant Director for Admissions, 205-348-7945, Fax: 205-348-3917, E-mail: mgriffith@law.ua.edu.
Website: http://www.law.ua.edu/.

The University of Alabama in Huntsville, School of Graduate Studies, College of Business Administration, Program in Accounting, Huntsville, AL 35899. Offers accounting (M Acc), including CPA preparatory with an emphasis in taxation, CPA preparatory with emphasis in assurance and financial reporting, general accounting, information systems audit and control (ISAC). *Accreditation:* AACSB. Part-time and evening/weekend programs available. *Faculty:* 9 full-time (3 women). *Students:* 14 full-time (6 women), 27 part-time (16 women); includes 8 minority (6 Black or African American, non-Hispanic/Latino; 2 Asian, non-Hispanic/Latino), 6 international. Average age 30. 24 applicants, 63% accepted, 8 enrolled. In 2013, 29 master's awarded. *Degree requirements:* For master's, comprehensive exam, thesis or alternative. *Entrance requirements:* For master's, GMAT (minimum score 500), minimum AACSB index of 1080. Additional exam requirements/recommendations for international students: Required—TOEFL (minimum score 550 paper-based; 80 iBT), IELTS (minimum score 6.5). *Application deadline:* For fall admission, 7/15 priority date for domestic students, 4/1 priority date for international students; for spring admission, 11/30 priority date for domestic students, 9/1 priority date for international students. Applications are processed on a rolling basis. Application fee: $50. Electronic applications accepted. *Expenses:* Tuition, state resident: full-time $8912; part-time $540 per credit hour. Tuition, nonresident: full-time $20,774; part-time $1252 per credit hour. *Required fees:* $148 per semester. One-time fee: $150. *Financial support:* Teaching assistantships, career-related internships or fieldwork, Federal Work-Study, institutionally sponsored loans, scholarships/grants, health care benefits, and unspecified assistantships available. Support available to part-time students. Financial award application deadline: 4/1; financial award applicants required to submit FAFSA. *Faculty research:* Accounting information systems, managerial accounting, behavioral accounting, state and local taxation, financial accounting. *Unit head:* Dr. Allen Wilhite, Interim Chair, 256-824-6591, Fax: 256-824-2929, E-mail: allen.wilhite@uah.edu. *Application contact:* Jennifer Pettitt, Director of Graduate Programs, 256-824-6681, Fax: 256-824-7571, E-mail: jennifer.pettitt@uah.edu.

University of Arkansas at Little Rock, Graduate School, College of Business Administration, Little Rock, AR 72204-1099. Offers accountancy (M Acc, Graduate Certificate); business administration (MBA); construction management (Graduate Certificate); management (Graduate Certificate); management information system (MIS); management information systems (Graduate Certificate); management information systems leadership (Graduate Certificate); taxation (MS, Graduate Certificate). *Accreditation:* AACSB. Part-time and evening/weekend programs available. *Entrance requirements:* For master's, GMAT, minimum undergraduate GPA of 2.7. Additional exam requirements/recommendations for international students: Required—TOEFL (minimum score 525 paper-based). *Expenses:* Tuition, state resident: full-time $5690; part-time $284.50 per credit hour. Tuition, nonresident: full-time $13,030; part-time $651.50 per credit hour. *Required fees:* $1121; $672 per term. One-time fee: $40 full-time.

University of Baltimore, Graduate School, Merrick School of Business, Program in Taxation, Baltimore, MD 21201-5779. Offers MS. Part-time and evening/weekend programs available. *Entrance requirements:* For master's, GMAT, minimum GPA of 3.0. Additional exam requirements/recommendations for international students: Required—TOEFL (minimum score 550 paper-based). *Expenses:* Contact institution. *Faculty research:* Taxation of not-for-profit entities.

University of Baltimore, School of Law, Baltimore, MD 21201. Offers law (JD); law of the United States (LL M); taxation (LL M); JD/LL M; JD/MBA; JD/MPA; JD/MS; JD/PhD. JD/MS offered jointly with Division of Criminology, Criminal Justice, and Social Policy; JD/PhD with University of Maryland, Baltimore. *Accreditation:* ABA. Part-time and evening/weekend programs available. *Faculty:* 54 full-time (18 women), 45 part-time/adjunct (12 women). *Students:* 654 full-time (325 women), 325 part-time (150 women); includes 254 minority (121 Black or African American, non-Hispanic/Latino; 1 American Indian or Alaska Native, non-Hispanic/Latino; 51 Asian, non-Hispanic/Latino; 53 Hispanic/Latino; 1 Native Hawaiian or other Pacific Islander, non-Hispanic/Latino; 27 Two or more races, non-Hispanic/Latino), 4 international. Average age 27. 1,352 applicants, 63% accepted, 287 enrolled. In 2013, 310 doctorates awarded. *Entrance requirements:* For doctorate, LSAT. *Application deadline:* For fall admission, 4/1 priority date for domestic and international students. Applications are processed on a rolling basis. Application fee: $60. Electronic applications accepted. *Expenses:* Contact institution. *Financial support:* In 2013–14, 257 students received support. Research assistantships, teaching assistantships, career-related internships or fieldwork, Federal Work-Study, institutionally sponsored loans, and scholarships/grants available. Support available to part-time students. Financial award application deadline: 4/1; financial award applicants required to submit FAFSA. *Faculty research:* Plain view doctrine, statute of limitations, bankruptcy, family law, international and comparative law, Constitutional law. *Unit head:* Ronald Weich, Dean, 410-837-4458. *Application contact:* Jeffrey L. Zavrotny, Assistant Dean for Admissions, 410-837-5809, Fax: 410-837-4188, E-mail: jzavrotny@ubalt.edu.
Website: http://law.ubalt.edu/.

University of Central Florida, College of Business Administration, Kenneth G. Dixon School of Accounting, Program in Taxation, Orlando, FL 32816. Offers MST. Part-time and evening/weekend programs available. *Students:* 15 full-time (11 women), 24 part-time (12 women); includes 3 minority (1 Asian, non-Hispanic/Latino; 2 Hispanic/Latino). Average age 27. 21 applicants, 52% accepted, 7 enrolled. In 2013, 22 master's awarded. *Degree requirements:* For master's, comprehensive exam. *Entrance requirements:* For master's, GMAT, minimum GPA of 3.0 in last 60 hours of course work. Additional exam requirements/recommendations for international students: Required—TOEFL. *Application deadline:* For fall admission, 2/1 priority date for domestic students; for spring admission, 11/1 priority date for domestic students. Application fee: $30. Electronic applications accepted. *Financial support:* Career-related internships or fieldwork, Federal Work-Study, institutionally sponsored loans, tuition waivers (partial), and unspecified assistantships available. Financial award application deadline: 3/1; financial award applicants required to submit FAFSA. *Unit head:* Dr. Sean Robb, Director, 407-823-2876. *Application contact:* Judy Ryder, Director, Graduate Admissions, 407-235-3916, Fax: 407-823-0219, E-mail: jryder@ucf.edu.
Website: http://web.bus.ucf.edu/accounting/?page-1265.

University of Cincinnati, Graduate School, Carl H. Lindner College of Business, MS Program, Cincinnati, OH 45221. Offers accounting (MS); business analytics (MS); finance (MS); information systems (MS); marketing (MS); taxation (MS). Part-time and evening/weekend programs available. *Faculty:* 39 full-time (11 women), 11 part-time/adjunct (3 women). *Students:* 275 full-time (105 women), 165 part-time (69 women); includes 29 minority (14 Black or African American, non-Hispanic/Latino; 9 Asian, non-Hispanic/Latino; 1 Native Hawaiian or other Pacific Islander, non-Hispanic/Latino; 5 Two or more races, non-Hispanic/Latino), 273 international. 953 applicants, 37% accepted, 258 enrolled. In 2013, 144 master's awarded. *Degree requirements:* For master's, thesis (for some programs). *Entrance requirements:* For master's, GMAT, GRE, resume, transcripts, essays, letters of recommendation. Additional exam requirements/recommendations for international students: Required—TOEFL (minimum score 600 paper-based; 100 iBT), IELTS (minimum score 6.5). *Application deadline:* For fall admission, 3/15 priority date for domestic students, 4/1 for international students. Applications are processed on a rolling basis. Application fee: $65 ($70 for international students). Electronic applications accepted. *Expenses:* Contact institution. *Financial support:* In 2013–14, 124 students received support, including 12 teaching assistantships with full and partial tuition reimbursements available (averaging $3,500 per year); scholarships/grants, tuition waivers (full and partial), and unspecified assistantships also available. Financial award application deadline: 2/1; financial award applicants required to submit FAFSA. *Faculty research:* Real estate, empirical pricing,

organization information pricing, strategic management, portfolio choice in institutional investment. *Unit head:* Dr. David Szymanski, Dean, 513-556-7001, Fax: 513-556-4891, E-mail: david.szymanski@uc.edu. *Application contact:* Dona Clary, Director, Graduate Programs, 513-556-3546, Fax: 513-558-7006, E-mail: dona.clary@uc.edu.

University of Denver, Sturm College of Law, Graduate Tax Program, Denver, CO 80208. Offers LL M, MT. Part-time and evening/weekend programs available. *Faculty:* 5 full-time (2 women), 4 part-time/adjunct (1 woman). *Students:* 47 full-time (18 women), 107 part-time (48 women); includes 30 minority (4 Black or African American, non-Hispanic/Latino; 14 Asian, non-Hispanic/Latino; 8 Hispanic/Latino; 4 Two or more races, non-Hispanic/Latino), 13 international. Average age 32. 97 applicants, 97% accepted, 57 enrolled. In 2013, 72 master's awarded. *Entrance requirements:* For master's, LSAT (for LL M), GMAT (for MT), transcripts, JD from ABA-approved institution (for LL M). Additional exam requirements/recommendations for international students: Required—TOEFL (minimum score 550 paper-based; 80 iBT). *Application deadline:* Applications are processed on a rolling basis. Application fee: $30. *Expenses:* Contact institution. *Financial support:* In 2013–14, 55 students received support. Federal Work-Study, institutionally sponsored loans, scholarships/grants, and tuition waivers (full and partial) available. Support available to part-time students. Financial award application deadline: 6/30; financial award applicants required to submit FAFSA. *Faculty research:* All areas of tax including individual, estate and gift, state and local, qualified plans, partnerships, C corporations and S corporations, procedural and ethical aspects of the practice of tax. *Unit head:* Stacy Anderson, Registrar/Program Coordinator, 303-871-6209, Fax: 303-871-6358, E-mail: stacy.r.anderson@du.edu. *Application contact:* Information Contact, 303-871-6239, Fax: 303-871-6358, E-mail: gtp@du.edu.
Website: http://www.du.edu/tax/.

University of Florida, Levin College of Law, Gainesville, FL 32611. Offers comparative law (LL M); environmental law (LL M); international taxation (LL M); law (JD); taxation (LL M, SJD). *Accreditation:* ABA. *Faculty:* 77 full-time (37 women), 36 part-time/adjunct (10 women). *Students:* 1,072 full-time (452 women); includes 283 minority (69 Black or African American, non-Hispanic/Latino; 13 American Indian or Alaska Native, non-Hispanic/Latino; 45 Asian, non-Hispanic/Latino; 115 Hispanic/Latino; 41 Two or more races, non-Hispanic/Latino), 37 international. Average age 24. 2,686 applicants, 33% accepted, 284 enrolled. In 2013, 356 doctorates awarded. *Entrance requirements:* For doctorate, LSAT (for JD). *Application deadline:* For fall admission, 3/15 for domestic and international students. Applications are processed on a rolling basis. Application fee: $30. Electronic applications accepted. *Expenses:* Tuition, state resident: full-time $12,640. Tuition, nonresident: full-time $30,000. *Financial support:* In 2013–14, 446 students received support, including 42 research assistantships (averaging $9,261 per year); Federal Work-Study, institutionally sponsored loans, scholarships/grants, health care benefits, and unspecified assistantships also available. Financial award application deadline: 3/15; financial award applicants required to submit FAFSA. *Faculty research:* Environmental and land use law, taxation, dispute resolution, family law, Constitutional law. *Unit head:* Robert Jerry, Dean, 352-273-0600, Fax: 352-392-8727, E-mail: jerryr@law.ufl.edu. *Application contact:* Michelle Adorno, Assistant Dean for Admissions, 352-273-0890, Fax: 352-392-4087, E-mail: madorno@law.ufl.edu.
Website: http://www.law.ufl.edu/.

University of Hartford, Barney School of Business, Department of Accounting and Taxation, West Hartford, CT 06117-1599. Offers professional accounting (Certificate); taxation (MSAT). Part-time and evening/weekend programs available. *Entrance requirements:* For master's, GMAT, 2 letters of recommendation, resume. Additional exam requirements/recommendations for international students: Required—TOEFL (minimum score 550 paper-based). Electronic applications accepted.

University of Hawaii at Manoa, Graduate Division, Shidler College of Business, Program in Accounting, Honolulu, HI 96822. Offers accounting (M Acc); accounting law (M Acc); information systems (M Acc); taxation (M Acc). Part-time programs available. *Entrance requirements:* For master's, GMAT, bachelor's degree in accounting, minimum GPA of 3.0. Additional exam requirements/recommendations for international students: Required—TOEFL (minimum score 550 paper-based; 79 iBT), IELTS (minimum score 5). *Faculty research:* International accounting, current tax topics, insurance industry financial reporting, behavioral accounting, auditing.

University of Houston, Law Center, Houston, TX 77204-6060. Offers energy, environment, and natural resources (LL M); health law (LL M); intellectual property and information law (LL M); international law (LL M); law (LL M, JD); tax law (LL M). *Accreditation:* ABA. Part-time and evening/weekend programs available. *Entrance requirements:* For doctorate, LSAT. Additional exam requirements/recommendations for international students: Required—TOEFL (minimum score 600 paper-based; 100 iBT). Electronic applications accepted. *Expenses:* Contact institution. *Faculty research:* Health law, international, tax, environmental/energy, information law/intellectual property.

University of Illinois at Urbana–Champaign, Graduate College, College of Business, Department of Accountancy, Champaign, IL 61820. Offers accountancy (MAS, MS, PhD); taxation (MS). *Accreditation:* AACSB. *Students:* 459 (272 women). Application fee: $75 ($90 for international students). *Unit head:* Jon S. Davis, Head, 217-333-0857, Fax: 217-244-0902, E-mail: jondavis@illinois.edu. *Application contact:* Cindy K. Wood, Administrative Aide, 217-333-4572, Fax: 217-244-0902, E-mail: ckwood@illinois.edu.
Website: http://www1.business.illinois.edu/accountancy.

University of Memphis, Graduate School, Fogelman College of Business and Economics, School of Accountancy, Memphis, TN 38152. Offers accounting (MS); accounting systems (MS); taxation (MS). *Accreditation:* AACSB. *Faculty:* 9 full-time (2 women), 1 (woman) part-time/adjunct. *Students:* 35 full-time (19 women), 44 part-time (27 women); includes 28 minority (19 Black or African American, non-Hispanic/Latino; 8 Asian, non-Hispanic/Latino; 1 Two or more races, non-Hispanic/Latino), 1 international. Average age 29. 54 applicants, 76% accepted, 6 enrolled. In 2013, 27 master's awarded. *Degree requirements:* For master's, comprehensive exam. *Entrance requirements:* For master's, GMAT. *Application deadline:* For fall admission, 8/1 for domestic students; for spring admission, 12/1 for domestic students. Application fee: $35 ($60 for international students). *Financial support:* In 2013–14, 32 students received support. Research assistantships with full tuition reimbursements available, teaching assistantships with full tuition reimbursements available, Federal Work-Study, scholarships/grants, and unspecified assistantships available. Financial award application deadline: 2/15; financial award applicants required to submit FAFSA. *Faculty research:* Financial accounting, corporate governance, EDP auditing, evolution of system analysis, investor behavior and investment decisions. *Unit head:* Dr. Carolyn Callahan, Director, 901-678-4022, E-mail: cmcllhan@memphis.edu. *Application contact:* Dr. Craig Langstraat, Program Coordinator, 901-678-4577, E-mail: cjlngstr@memphis.edu.
Website: http://www.memphis.edu/accountancy/.

University of Miami, Graduate School, School of Business Administration, Department of Accounting, Coral Gables, FL 33124. Offers professional accounting (MP Acc); taxation (MS Tax). *Accreditation:* AACSB. Part-time and evening/weekend programs available. *Entrance requirements:* For master's, GMAT or CPA exam. Additional exam requirements/recommendations for international students: Required—TOEFL.

Electronic applications accepted. *Faculty research:* Financial reporting, audit risk, public policy and taxation issues, government accounting and public choice, corporate governance.

University of Miami, Graduate School, School of Law, Coral Gables, FL 33124-8087. Offers business and financial, international, employment, labor and immigration law, litigation specialization (Certificate); employment, labor and immigration law (JD); estate planning (LL M); international law (LL M), including general international law, inter-American law, international arbitration, U.S. transnational law for foreign lawyers; law (JD); ocean and coastal law (LL M); real property development (real estate) (LL M); taxation (LL M); JD/LL M; JD/LL M/MBA; JD/MA; JD/MBA; JD/MD; JD/MM; JD/MPH; JD/MPS; JD/MS Ed; JD/PhD. *Accreditation:* ABA. *Faculty:* 82 full-time (42 women), 108 part-time/adjunct (36 women). *Students:* 1,176 full-time (521 women); includes 402 minority (79 Black or African American, non-Hispanic/Latino; 7 American Indian or Alaska Native, non-Hispanic/Latino; 31 Asian, non-Hispanic/Latino; 266 Hispanic/Latino; 1 Native Hawaiian or other Pacific Islander, non-Hispanic/Latino; 18 Two or more races, non-Hispanic/Latino), 38 international. Average age 24. 3,300 applicants, 53% accepted, 308 enrolled. In 2013, 430 doctorates awarded. *Entrance requirements:* For doctorate, LSAT, 2 letters of recommendation. Additional exam requirements/recommendations for international students: Required—TOEFL (minimum score 580 paper-based; 92 iBT). *Application deadline:* For fall admission, 1/6 priority date for domestic and international students. Applications are processed on a rolling basis. Application fee: $60. Electronic applications accepted. *Expenses:* Contact institution. *Financial support:* Fellowships, research assistantships, career-related internships or fieldwork, Federal Work-Study, institutionally sponsored loans, scholarships/grants, and unspecified assistantships available. Financial award application deadline: 3/1; financial award applicants required to submit FAFSA. *Faculty research:* National security law, international finance, Internet law/law of electronic commerce, law of the seas, art law/cultural heritage law. *Unit head:* Michael Goodnight, Associate Dean of Admissions and Enrollment Management, 305-284-2527, Fax: 305-284-3084, E-mail: mgoodnig@law.miami.edu. *Application contact:* Therese Lambert, Director of Student Recruitment, 305-284-6746, Fax: 305-284-3084, E-mail: tlambert@law.miami.edu.
Website: http://www.law.miami.edu/.

University of Michigan, Law School, Ann Arbor, MI 48109-1215. Offers comparative law (MCL); international tax (LL M); law (LL M, JD, SJD); JD/MA; JD/MBA; JD/MHSA; JD/MPH; JD/MPP; JD/MS; JD/MSI; JD/MSW; JD/MUP; JD/PhD. *Accreditation:* ABA. *Faculty:* 94 full-time (33 women), 52 part-time/adjunct (12 women). *Students:* 1,055 full-time (479 women); includes 236 minority (36 Black or African American, non-Hispanic/Latino; 3 American Indian or Alaska Native, non-Hispanic/Latino; 101 Asian, non-Hispanic/Latino; 56 Hispanic/Latino; 40 Two or more races, non-Hispanic/Latino), 33 international. 4,875 applicants, 27% accepted, 315 enrolled. In 2013, 34 master's, 399 doctorates awarded. *Entrance requirements:* For doctorate, LSAT. Additional exam requirements/recommendations for international students: Required—TOEFL. *Application deadline:* For fall admission, 2/15 for domestic students. Applications are processed on a rolling basis. Application fee: $75. Electronic applications accepted. *Expenses:* Contact institution. *Financial support:* In 2013–14, 759 students received support. Career-related internships or fieldwork, Federal Work-Study, institutionally sponsored loans, and scholarships/grants available. Financial award applicants required to submit FAFSA. *Unit head:* Mark D. West, Dean, 734-764-1358. *Application contact:* Sarah C. Zearfoss, Assistant Dean and Director of Admissions, 734-764-0537, Fax: 734-647-3218, E-mail: law.jd.admissions@umich.edu.
Website: http://www.law.umich.edu/.

University of Michigan–Dearborn, College of Business, Dearborn, MI 48128-1491. Offers accounting (MBA, MS); business analytics (MS); finance (MBA, MS); human resource management (MBA); information systems (MS); international business (MBA); investment (MBA); management (MBA); management information systems (MBA); marketing (MBA); supply chain management (MBA, MS); taxation (MBA); MBA/MHSA; MBA/MSE; MBA/MSF; MBA/MSIS; MBA/MSSCM; MSF/MSA. *Accreditation:* AACSB. Part-time and evening/weekend programs available. Postbaccalaureate distance learning degree programs offered (no on-campus study). *Faculty:* 24 full-time (8 women), 5 part-time/adjunct (2 women). *Students:* 82 full-time (31 women), 323 part-time (116 women); includes 72 minority (17 Black or African American, non-Hispanic/Latino; 2 American Indian or Alaska Native, non-Hispanic/Latino; 30 Asian, non-Hispanic/Latino; 15 Hispanic/Latino; 8 Two or more races, non-Hispanic/Latino), 65 international. Average age 32. 290 applicants, 44% accepted, 99 enrolled. In 2013, 143 master's awarded. *Entrance requirements:* For master's, GMAT or GRE, pre-calculus or finite mathematics; 18 credits of accounting course work beyond introductory courses (MS in accounting). Additional exam requirements/recommendations for international students: Required—TOEFL (minimum score 560 paper-based; 84 iBT), IELTS. *Application deadline:* For fall admission, 8/1 priority date for domestic students, 5/1 priority date for international students; for winter admission, 12/1 priority date for domestic students, 9/1 priority date for international students; for spring admission, 4/1 priority date for domestic students, 1/1 priority date for international students. Applications are processed on a rolling basis. Application fee: $60. Electronic applications accepted. *Expenses:* Contact institution. *Financial support:* Career-related internships or fieldwork, Federal Work-Study, and scholarships/grants available. Support available to part-time students. Financial award application deadline: 9/1; financial award applicants required to submit FAFSA. *Faculty research:* Cultural diversity, buyer-supplier relations, error detection in data, economic evolution. *Unit head:* Dr. Raju Balakrishnan, Dean, 313-593-5248, Fax: 313-271-9835, E-mail: rajub@umich.edu. *Application contact:* Joan Doherty, Academic Advisor/Counselor, 313-593-5460, Fax: 313-271-9838, E-mail: umd-gradbusiness@umich.edu.
Website: http://www.cob.umd.umich.edu.

University of Minnesota, Twin Cities Campus, Carlson School of Management, Master's Program in Business Taxation, Minneapolis, MN 55455-0213. Offers MBT. Part-time and evening/weekend programs available. *Faculty:* 23 full-time (5 women), 14 part-time/adjunct (3 women). *Students:* 28 full-time (15 women), 67 part-time (36 women); includes 9 minority (8 Asian, non-Hispanic/Latino; 1 Hispanic/Latino), 18 international. Average age 32. 65 applicants, 82% accepted, 42 enrolled. In 2013, 29 master's awarded. *Entrance requirements:* For master's, GMAT or LSAT. Additional exam requirements/recommendations for international students: Required—TOEFL (minimum score 550 paper-based; 79 iBT), IELTS (minimum score 6.5). *Application deadline:* For fall admission, 6/15 priority date for domestic and international students; for spring admission, 10/15 priority date for domestic and international students. Applications are processed on a rolling basis. Application fee: $75 ($95 for international students). Electronic applications accepted. *Expenses:* Contact institution. *Financial support:* In 2013–14, 14 students received support, including 14 fellowships (averaging $2,200 per year), 5 teaching assistantships with partial tuition reimbursements available (averaging $7,500 per year); career-related internships or fieldwork and institutionally sponsored loans also available. Financial award application deadline: 8/1; financial award applicants required to submit FAFSA. *Faculty research:* Partnership taxation, tax theory, corporate taxation. *Unit head:* Paul Gutterman, Director of Graduate Studies, 612-624-8515, Fax: 612-626-7795, E-mail: pgutterm@umn.edu. *Application contact:* Information Contact, 612-626-7511, E-mail: gsguest@umn.edu.
Website: http://www.carlson.umn.edu/master-business-taxation/.

Taxation

University of Mississippi, Graduate School, School of Accountancy, Oxford, MS 38677. Offers accountancy (M Acc, PhD); taxation accounting (M Tax). *Accreditation:* AACSB. *Faculty:* 14 full-time (4 women), 4 part-time/adjunct (2 women). *Students:* 131 full-time (60 women), 13 part-time (6 women); includes 14 minority (6 Black or African American, non-Hispanic/Latino; 4 Asian, non-Hispanic/Latino; 1 Hispanic/Latino; 3 Two or more races, non-Hispanic/Latino), 6 international. In 2013, 90 master's, 3 doctorates awarded. *Degree requirements:* For doctorate, thesis/dissertation. *Entrance requirements:* For master's, GMAT, minimum GPA of 3.0; for doctorate, GMAT. Additional exam requirements/recommendations for international students: Required—TOEFL. *Application deadline:* For fall admission, 4/1 for domestic students; for spring admission, 10/1 for domestic students. Applications are processed on a rolling basis. Application fee: $40. *Financial support:* Scholarships/grants available. Financial award application deadline: 3/1; financial award applicants required to submit FAFSA. *Unit head:* Dr. Mark Wilder, Interim Dean, 662-915-7468, Fax: 662-915-7483, E-mail: umaccy@olemiss.edu. *Application contact:* Dr. Christy M. Wyandt, Associate Dean, 662-915-7474, Fax: 662-915-7577, E-mail: cwyandt@olemiss.edu.

University of Missouri, Graduate School, Robert J. Trulaske, Sr. College of Business, School of Accountancy, Columbia, MO 65211. Offers accountancy (M Acc, PhD); taxation (Certificate). *Accreditation:* AACSB. Part-time programs available. *Faculty:* 15 full-time (7 women). *Students:* 141 full-time (59 women), 8 part-time (2 women); includes 8 minority (5 Black or African American, non-Hispanic/Latino; 2 Asian, non-Hispanic/Latino; 1 Hispanic/Latino), 14 international. Average age 23. 119 applicants, 47% accepted, 55 enrolled. In 2013, 130 master's, 2 doctorates, 27 other advanced degrees awarded. *Degree requirements:* For master's, thesis or alternative; for doctorate, thesis/dissertation. *Entrance requirements:* For master's and doctorate, GMAT, minimum GPA of 3.0. Additional exam requirements/recommendations for international students: Required—TOEFL (minimum score 600 paper-based; 100 iBT). *Application deadline:* For fall admission, 2/1 priority date for domestic and international students. Applications are processed on a rolling basis. Application fee: $55 ($75 for international students). Electronic applications accepted. *Financial support:* Fellowships with full and partial tuition reimbursements, research assistantships with full and partial tuition reimbursements, teaching assistantships with full and partial tuition reimbursements, institutionally sponsored loans, scholarships/grants, health care benefits, and unspecified assistantships available. Support available to part-time students. *Unit head:* Dr. Vairam Arunachalam, Director, 573-882-4463, E-mail: arunachalam@missouri.edu. *Application contact:* Karen L. Brammer, Administrative Assistant, 573-882-4463, E-mail: brammerk@missouri.edu.
Website: http://business.missouri.edu/43/default.aspx.

University of Missouri–Kansas City, School of Law, Kansas City, MO 64110-2499. Offers law (LL M, JD), including general (LL M), taxation (LL M); JD/LL M; JD/MBA; JD/MPA; LL M/MPA. *Accreditation:* ABA. Part-time programs available. *Faculty:* 36 full-time (15 women), 9 part-time/adjunct (5 women). *Students:* 458 full-time (186 women), 51 part-time (18 women); includes 66 minority (24 Black or African American, non-Hispanic/Latino; 2 American Indian or Alaska Native, non-Hispanic/Latino; 10 Asian, non-Hispanic/Latino; 25 Hispanic/Latino; 5 Two or more races, non-Hispanic/Latino), 17 international. Average age 28. 665 applicants, 57% accepted, 203 enrolled. In 2013, 33 master's, 159 doctorates awarded. *Degree requirements:* For master's, thesis (for general). *Entrance requirements:* For master's, LSAT, minimum GPA of 3.0 (for general), 2.7 (for taxation); for doctorate, LSAT. Additional exam requirements/recommendations for international students: Required—TOEFL (minimum score 550 paper-based; 80 iBT). *Application deadline:* For fall admission, 3/1 priority date for domestic and international students. Applications are processed on a rolling basis. Application fee: $50. Electronic applications accepted. *Expenses:* Contact institution. *Financial support:* In 2013–14, 21 teaching assistantships with partial tuition reimbursements (averaging $2,570 per year) were awarded; career-related internships or fieldwork, Federal Work-Study, institutionally sponsored loans, scholarships/grants, and tuition waivers (full and partial) also available. Support available to part-time students. Financial award application deadline: 3/1; financial award applicants required to submit FAFSA. *Faculty research:* Family and children's issues, litigation, estate planning, urban law, business, tax entrepreneurial law. *Unit head:* Ellen Y. Suni, Dean, 816-235-1007, Fax: 816-235-5276, E-mail: sunie@umkc.edu. *Application contact:* Lydia Dagenais, Director of Law School Admissions, 816-235-1677, Fax: 816-235-5276, E-mail: dagenaisl@umkc.edu.
Website: http://www.law.umkc.edu/.

University of New Haven, Graduate School, College of Business, Program in Taxation, West Haven, CT 06516-1916. Offers MS, Certificate. Part-time and evening/weekend programs available. *Students:* 1 (woman) full-time, 49 part-time (32 women); includes 11 minority (7 Black or African American, non-Hispanic/Latino; 1 Asian, non-Hispanic/Latino; 2 Hispanic/Latino; 1 Two or more races, non-Hispanic/Latino), 1 international. 9 applicants, 100% accepted, 8 enrolled. In 2013, 5 master's awarded. *Degree requirements:* For master's, thesis or alternative. *Entrance requirements:* For master's, GMAT. Additional exam requirements/recommendations for international students: Required—TOEFL (minimum score 80 iBT), IELTS, PTE (minimum score 53). *Application deadline:* For fall admission, 5/31 for international students; for winter admission, 10/15 for international students; for spring admission, 1/15 for international students. Applications are processed on a rolling basis. Application fee: $75. Electronic applications accepted. Application fee is waived when completed online. *Expenses:* Contact institution. *Financial support:* Research assistantships with partial tuition reimbursements, teaching assistantships with partial tuition reimbursements, career-related internships or fieldwork, Federal Work-Study, scholarships/grants, and unspecified assistantships available. Support available to part-time students. Financial award application deadline: 5/1; financial award applicants required to submit FAFSA. *Unit head:* Robert E. Wnek, Chair, 203-932-7111, E-mail: rwnek@newhaven.edu. *Application contact:* Eloise Gormley, Director of Graduate Admissions, 203-932-7440, E-mail: gradinfo@newhaven.edu.
Website: http://www.newhaven.edu/6856/.

University of New Mexico, Anderson Graduate School of Management, Department of Accounting, Albuquerque, NM 87131. Offers accounting (MBA); advanced accounting (M Acct); information assurance (M Acct); professional accounting (M Acct); tax accounting (M Acct); JD/M Acct. *Accreditation:* AACSB. Part-time and evening/weekend programs available. *Faculty:* 11 full-time (4 women), 4 part-time/adjunct (3 women). In 2013, 75 master's awarded. *Entrance requirements:* For master's, GMAT or GRE, minimum GPA of 3.0 on last 60 hours of coursework. Additional exam requirements/recommendations for international students: Required—TOEFL (minimum score 550 paper-based; 79 iBT). *Application deadline:* For fall admission, 4/1 priority date for domestic and international students; for spring admission, 10/1 priority date for domestic and international students. Applications are processed on a rolling basis. Application fee: $50. Electronic applications accepted. *Expenses:* Contact institution. *Financial support:* Fellowships, research assistantships, career-related internships or fieldwork, Federal Work-Study, scholarships/grants, and unspecified assistantships available. Support available to part-time students. Financial award application deadline: 6/1; financial award applicants required to submit FAFSA. *Faculty research:* Critical accounting, accounting pedagogy, theory, taxation, information fraud. *Unit head:* Dr. Craig White, Chair, 505-277-6471, Fax: 505-277-7108, E-mail: cwhite@unm.edu.

Application contact: Tina Armijo, Office Administrator, 505-277-6471, Fax: 505-277-7108, E-mail: tmarmijo@unm.edu.
Website: http://mba.mgt.unm.edu/default.asp.

University of New Orleans, Graduate School, College of Business Administration, Department of Accounting, Program in Taxation, New Orleans, LA 70148. Offers MS. Part-time and evening/weekend programs available. *Degree requirements:* For master's, thesis optional. *Entrance requirements:* For master's, GMAT. Additional exam requirements/recommendations for international students: Required—TOEFL (minimum score 550 paper-based; 79 iBT). Electronic applications accepted.

University of North Texas, Robert B. Toulouse School of Graduate Studies, Denton, TN 76203-5017. Offers accounting (MS, PhD); applied anthropology (MA, MS); applied behavior analysis (Certificate); applied technology and performance improvement (M Ed, MS, PhD); art education (MA, PhD); art history (MA); art museum education (Certificate); arts leadership (Certificate); audiology (Au D); behavior analysis (MS); biochemistry and molecular biology (MS, PhD); biology (MA, MS, PhD); business (PhD); business computer information systems (PhD); chemistry (MS, PhD); clinical psychology (PhD); communication studies (MA, MS); computer engineering (MS); computer science (MS); computer science and engineering (PhD); counseling (M Ed, MS, PhD), including clinical mental health counseling (MS), college and university counseling (M Ed, MS), elementary school counseling (M Ed, MS), secondary school counseling (M Ed, MS); counseling psychology (PhD); creative writing (MA); criminal justice (MS); curriculum and instruction (M Ed, PhD), including curriculum studies (PhD), early childhood studies (PhD), language and literacy studies (PhD); decision sciences (MBA); design (MA, MFA), including fashion design (MFA), innovation studies, interior design (MFA); early childhood studies (MS); economics (MS); educational leadership (M Ed, Ed D, PhD); educational psychology (MS), including family studies, gifted and talented (MS, PhD); human development, learning and cognition, research, measurement and evaluation; educational research (PhD), including gifted and talented (MS, PhD), human development and family studies, psychological aspects of sports and exercise, research, measurement and statistics; electrical engineering (MS); emergency management (MPA); engineering systems (MS); English (MA, PhD); environmental science (MS, PhD); experimental psychology (PhD); finance (MBA, MS, PhD); financial management (MPA); French (MA); health psychology and behavioral medicine (PhD); health services management (MBA); higher education (M Ed, Ed D, PhD); history (MA, MS, PhD), including European history (PhD), military history (PhD), United States history (PhD); hospitality management (MS); human resources management (MPA); information science (MS, PhD); information technologies (MBA); information technology and decision sciences (MS); interdisciplinary studies (MA, MS); international sustainable tourism (MS); jazz studies (MM); journalism (MA, MJ, Graduate Certificate), including interactive and virtual digital communication (Graduate Certificate), narrative journalism (Graduate Certificate), public relations (Graduate Certificate); kinesiology (MS); learning technologies (MS, PhD); library science (MS); local government management (MPA); logistics and supply chain management (MBA, PhD); long-term care, senior housing, and aging services (MA, MS); management science (PhD); marketing (MBA, PhD); materials science and engineering (MS, PhD); mathematics (MA, PhD); merchandising (MS); music (MA, MM Ed, PhD), including ethnomusicology (MA), music education (MM Ed, PhD), music theory (MA, PhD), musicology (MA, PhD), performance (MA); nonprofit management (MPA); operations and supply chain management (MBA); performance (MM, DMA); philosophy (MA, PhD); physics (MS, PhD); political science (MA, MS, PhD); public administration and management (PhD), including emergency management, nonprofit management, public financial management, urban management; radio, television and film (MA, MFA); recreation, event and sport management (MS); rehabilitation counseling (MS, Certificate); sociology (MA, MS, PhD); Spanish (MA); special education (M Ed, PhD), including autism intervention (PhD), emotional/behavioral disorders (PhD), mild/moderate disabilities (PhD); speech-language pathology (MA, MS); strategic management (MBA); studio art (MFA); taxation (MS); teaching (M Ed); MBA/MS; MS/MPH; MSES/MBA. Part-time and evening/weekend programs available. Postbaccalaureate distance learning degree programs offered. *Faculty:* 661 full-time (213 women), 240 part-time/adjunct (144 women). *Students:* 3,106 full-time (1,620 women), 3,543 part-time (2,221 women); includes 1,740 minority (533 Black or African American, non-Hispanic/Latino; 15 American Indian or Alaska Native, non-Hispanic/Latino; 286 Asian, non-Hispanic/Latino; 746 Hispanic/Latino; 3 Native Hawaiian or other Pacific Islander, non-Hispanic/Latino; 157 Two or more races, non-Hispanic/Latino), 1,145 international. Average age 32. 6,289 applicants, 43% accepted, 1751 enrolled. In 2013, 1,778 master's, 239 doctorates, 10 other advanced degrees awarded. Terminal master's awarded for partial completion of doctoral program. *Degree requirements:* For master's, variable foreign language requirement, comprehensive exam (for some programs), thesis (for some programs); for doctorate, variable foreign language requirement, comprehensive exam (for some programs), thesis/dissertation; for other advanced degree, variable foreign language requirement, comprehensive exam (for some programs). *Entrance requirements:* For master's and doctorate, GRE, GMAT. Additional exam requirements/recommendations for international students: Required—TOEFL (minimum score 550 paper-based; 79 iBT). *Application deadline:* For fall admission, 7/15 for domestic students, 3/15 for international students; for spring admission, 11/15 for domestic students, 9/15 for international students; for summer admission, 5/1 for domestic students. Applications are processed on a rolling basis. Application fee: $60. Electronic applications accepted. *Financial support:* Fellowships with partial tuition reimbursements, research assistantships with partial tuition reimbursements, teaching assistantships, career-related internships or fieldwork, Federal Work-Study, institutionally sponsored loans, scholarships/grants, health care benefits, and library assistantships available. Support available to part-time students. Financial award applicants required to submit FAFSA. *Unit head:* Mark Wardell, Dean, 940-565-2383, E-mail: mark.wardell@unt.edu. *Application contact:* Toulouse School of Graduate Studies, 940-565-2383, Fax: 940-565-2141, E-mail: gradsch@unt.edu.
Website: http://tsgs.unt.edu.

University of Notre Dame, Mendoza College of Business, Program in Accountancy, Notre Dame, IN 46556. Offers financial reporting and assurance services (MS); tax services (MS). *Accreditation:* AACSB. *Faculty:* 35 full-time (5 women), 21 part-time/adjunct (2 women). *Students:* 100 full-time (35 women); includes 19 minority (3 Black or African American, non-Hispanic/Latino; 4 Asian, non-Hispanic/Latino; 4 Hispanic/Latino; 8 Two or more races, non-Hispanic/Latino), 17 international. Average age 22. 413 applicants, 31% accepted, 100 enrolled. In 2013, 110 master's awarded. *Entrance requirements:* For master's, GMAT. Additional exam requirements/recommendations for international students: Required—TOEFL (minimum score 630 paper-based; 109 iBT). *Application deadline:* For fall admission, 10/31 for domestic and international students; for spring admission, 5/1 for domestic and international students. Applications are processed on a rolling basis. Application fee: $50 ($100 for international students). Electronic applications accepted. *Financial support:* In 2013–14, 98 students received support, including 98 fellowships (averaging $17,076 per year); scholarships/grants and unspecified assistantships also available. Financial award application deadline: 2/28; financial award applicants required to submit FAFSA. *Faculty research:* Stock valuation, accounting information in decision-making, choice of accounting method, taxes cost on capital. *Unit head:* Dr. Michael H. Morris, Director, 574-631-9732, Fax: 574-631-5300,

E-mail: msacct.1@nd.edu. *Application contact:* Helen High, Assistant Director of Admissions and Student Services, 574-631-6499, Fax: 574-631-5300, E-mail: msacct.1@nd.edu.
Website: http://business.nd.edu/msa.

University of San Diego, School of Business Administration, Programs in Accountancy and Taxation, San Diego, CA 92110-2492. Offers accountancy (MS); taxation (MS). Part-time and evening/weekend programs available. *Students:* 23 full-time (15 women), 5 part-time (4 women); includes 8 minority (5 Asian, non-Hispanic/Latino; 2 Hispanic/Latino; 1 Two or more races, non-Hispanic/Latino), 11 international. Average age 24. In 2013, 33 master's awarded. *Entrance requirements:* For master's, GMAT (minimum score of 550), minimum GPA of 3.0. Additional exam requirements/recommendations for international students: Required—TOEFL (minimum score 580 paper-based; 92 iBT), TWE. *Application deadline:* For fall admission, 4/1 for domestic students; for spring admission, 10/1 for domestic students. Application fee: $80. *Expenses: Tuition:* Full-time $23,580; part-time $1310 per credit. *Required fees:* $350. *Financial support:* In 2013–14, 11 students received support. Career-related internships or fieldwork, Federal Work-Study, institutionally sponsored loans, scholarships/grants, and unspecified assistantships available. Support available to part-time students. Financial award application deadline: 4/1; financial award applicants required to submit FAFSA. *Faculty research:* Accounting, financial report, taxation, Sarbanes-Oxley. *Unit head:* Dr. Diane Pattison, Academic Director, Accountancy Programs, 619-260-4850, E-mail: pattison@sandiego.edu. *Application contact:* Monica Mahon, Associate Director of Graduate Admissions, 619-260-4524, Fax: 619-260-4158, E-mail: grads@sandiego.edu.
Website: http://www.sandiego.edu/business/programs/accounting-tax/.

University of San Diego, School of Law, San Diego, CA 92110. Offers business and corporate law (LL M); comparative law (LL M); general studies (LL M); international law (LL M); law (JD); taxation (LL M, Diploma); JD/IMBA; JD/MA; JD/MBA. *Accreditation:* ABA. Part-time and evening/weekend programs available. *Faculty:* 48 full-time (16 women), 67 part-time/adjunct (24 women). *Students:* 708 full-time (357 women), 155 part-time (73 women); includes 269 minority (18 Black or African American, non-Hispanic/Latino; 4 American Indian or Alaska Native, non-Hispanic/Latino; 127 Asian, non-Hispanic/Latino; 98 Hispanic/Latino; 3 Native Hawaiian or other Pacific Islander, non-Hispanic/Latino; 19 Two or more races, non-Hispanic/Latino), 33 international. Average age 27. 2,844 applicants, 48% accepted, 243 enrolled. In 2013, 63 master's, 316 doctorates awarded. *Entrance requirements:* For master's, JD, LL B or equivalent from an ABA-accredited law school; for doctorate, LSAT, bachelor's degree, registration with the Credential Assemble Service (CAS). Additional exam requirements/recommendations for international students: Required—TOEFL (minimum score 600 paper-based; 100 iBT). *Application deadline:* For fall admission, 2/1 priority date for domestic students. Applications are processed on a rolling basis. Application fee: $50. Electronic applications accepted. *Expenses:* Contact institution. *Financial support:* In 2013–14, 610 students received support. Career-related internships or fieldwork, Federal Work-Study, institutionally sponsored loans, and scholarships/grants available. Support available to part-time students. Financial award application deadline: 3/1; financial award applicants required to submit FAFSA. *Faculty research:* Corporate law, children's advocacy, Constitutional and criminal law, international and comparative law, public interest law, intellectual property and tax law. *Unit head:* Dr. Stephen C. Ferruolo, Dean, 619-260-4527, E-mail: lawdean@sandiego.edu. *Application contact:* Jorge Garcia, Assistant Dean, JD Admissions, 619-260-4528, Fax: 619-260-2218, E-mail: jdinfo@sandiego.edu.
Website: http://www.sandiego.edu/law/.

University of San Francisco, School of Law, San Francisco, CA 94117-1080. Offers law (LL M, JD), including intellectual property and technology law (LL M), international transactions and comparative law (LL M), taxation (LL M); JD/MBA. *Accreditation:* ABA. Part-time and evening/weekend programs available. *Faculty:* 15 full-time (8 women), 61 part-time/adjunct (22 women). *Students:* 473 full-time (256 women), 103 part-time (52 women); includes 251 minority (39 Black or African American, non-Hispanic/Latino; 3 American Indian or Alaska Native, non-Hispanic/Latino; 74 Asian, non-Hispanic/Latino; 88 Hispanic/Latino; 1 Native Hawaiian or other Pacific Islander, non-Hispanic/Latino; 46 Two or more races, non-Hispanic/Latino), 16 international. Average age 26. 2,961 applicants, 50% accepted, 178 enrolled. In 2013, 12 master's, 204 doctorates awarded. *Entrance requirements:* For doctorate, LSAT, minimum undergraduate GPA of 3.2. *Application deadline:* For fall admission, 4/1 for domestic students. Applications are processed on a rolling basis. *Expenses:* Contact institution. *Financial support:* In 2013–14, 246 students received support. Career-related internships or fieldwork, Federal Work-Study, and institutionally sponsored loans available. Support available to part-time students. Financial award application deadline: 3/2; financial award applicants required to submit FAFSA. *Unit head:* John Trasvia, Dean, 415-422-6304. *Application contact:* Alan P. Guerrero, Director of Admissions, 415-422-2975, E-mail: lawadmissions@usfca.edu.
Website: http://www.law.usfca.edu/.

University of Southern California, Graduate School, Marshall School of Business, Leventhal School of Accounting, Los Angeles, CA 90089. Offers accounting (M Acc); business taxation (MBT); JD/MBT. Part-time programs available. *Degree requirements:* For master's, 30-48 units of study. *Entrance requirements:* For master's, GMAT, undergraduate degree, communication skills. Additional exam requirements/recommendations for international students: Required—TOEFL. Electronic applications accepted. *Faculty research:* State and local taxation, Securities and Exchange Commission, governance, auditing fees, financial accounting, enterprise zones, women in business.

University of South Florida, College of Business, School of Accountancy, Tampa, FL 33620-9951. Offers audit/systems (M Acc); business administration (PhD), including accounting; generalist (M Acc); tax (M Acc). *Accreditation:* AACSB. Part-time and evening/weekend programs available. *Faculty:* 10 full-time (5 women), 2 part-time/adjunct (1 woman). *Students:* 50 full-time (22 women), 42 part-time (25 women); includes 20 minority (2 Black or African American, non-Hispanic/Latino; 5 Asian, non-Hispanic/Latino; 11 Hispanic/Latino; 2 Two or more races, non-Hispanic/Latino), 1 international. Average age 28. 92 applicants, 60% accepted, 37 enrolled. In 2013, 54 master's, 2 doctorates awarded. Terminal master's awarded for partial completion of doctoral program. *Degree requirements:* For master's, thesis or alternative; for doctorate, comprehensive exam, thesis/dissertation. *Entrance requirements:* For master's, GMAT (preferred minimum score of 500), minimum overall GPA of 3.0 in general upper-level coursework and in upper-level accounting coursework (minimum of 21 hours at a U.S. accredited program within past 5 years); for doctorate, GMAT or GRE, personal statement, recommendations, interview. Additional exam requirements/recommendations for international students: Required—TOEFL (minimum score 550 paper-based; 79 iBT) or IELTS (minimum score 6.5). *Application deadline:* For fall admission, 6/1 for domestic students, 1/2 for international students; for spring admission, 10/15 for domestic students, 6/1 for international students. Application fee: $30. Electronic applications accepted. *Financial support:* In 2013–14, 18 students received support, including 18 teaching assistantships with tuition reimbursements available (averaging $12,273 per year); scholarships/grants, health care benefits, and unspecified assistantships also available. Financial award applicants required to submit FAFSA. *Faculty research:* Auditing, auditor independence, audit committee decisions, fraud detection and reporting, disclosure effects, effects of information technology on accounting, governmental accounting/auditing, accounting information systems, data modeling and design methodologies for accounting systems, auditing computer-based systems, expert systems, group support systems in accounting, fair value accounting issues, corporate governance, financial accounting, financial reporting quality. *Total annual research expenditures:* $236,586. *Unit head:* Dr. Uday Murthy, Interim Director, School of Accountancy, 813-974-6516, Fax: 813-974-6528, E-mail: umurthy@usf.edu. *Application contact:* Christy Ward, Advisor and Graduation Specialist, 813-974-4290, Fax: 813-974-2797, E-mail: cward@usf.edu.
Website: http://business.usf.edu/departments/accountancy/.

The University of Texas at Arlington, Graduate School, College of Business, Accounting Department, Arlington, TX 76019. Offers accounting (MP Acc, MS, PhD); taxation (MS). *Accreditation:* AACSB. Part-time and evening/weekend programs available. *Degree requirements:* For master's, thesis optional; for doctorate, comprehensive exam, thesis/dissertation. *Entrance requirements:* For master's and doctorate, GMAT. Additional exam requirements/recommendations for international students: Required—TOEFL (minimum score 550 paper-based; 79 iBT).

University of the Pacific, McGeorge School of Law, Sacramento, CA 95817. Offers advocacy (JD); criminal justice (JD); experiential law teaching (LL M); intellectual property (JD); international legal studies (JD); international water resources law (LL M, JSD); law (JD); public law and policy (JD); public policy and law (LL M); tax (JD); transnational business practice (LL M); U.S. law and policy (LL M), including public law and policy, U.S. law; water resources law (LL M), including international law, U.S. law; JD/MBA; JD/MPPA. *Accreditation:* ABA. Part-time and evening/weekend programs available. *Faculty:* 38 full-time (16 women), 32 part-time/adjunct (8 women). *Students:* 486 full-time (242 women), 179 part-time (79 women); includes 215 minority (17 Black or African American, non-Hispanic/Latino; 14 American Indian or Alaska Native, non-Hispanic/Latino; 108 Asian, non-Hispanic/Latino; 75 Hispanic/Latino; 1 Two or more races, non-Hispanic/Latino), 17 international. Average age 28. 1,558 applicants, 65% accepted, 162 enrolled. In 2013, 37 master's, 308 doctorates awarded. *Degree requirements:* For master's, thesis (for some programs); for doctorate, thesis/dissertation (for some programs). *Entrance requirements:* For master's, JD; for doctorate, LSAT (for JD), LL M (for JSD). Additional exam requirements/recommendations for international students: Required—TOEFL (minimum score 600 paper-based; 100 iBT). *Application deadline:* For fall admission, 3/15 priority date for domestic students. Applications are processed on a rolling basis. Application fee: $50. Electronic applications accepted. *Expenses:* Contact institution. *Financial support:* Fellowships, research assistantships, teaching assistantships, career-related internships or fieldwork, Federal Work-Study, institutionally sponsored loans, and scholarships/grants available. Support available to part-time students. Financial award applicants required to submit FAFSA. *Faculty research:* International legal studies, public policy and law, advocacy, intellectual property law, taxation, criminal law. *Unit head:* Francis Jay Mootz, III, Dean, 916-739-7151, E-mail: jmootz@pacific.edu. *Application contact:* 916-739-7105, Fax: 916-739-7301, E-mail: mcgeorge@pacific.edu.
Website: http://www.mcgeorge.edu/.

University of the Sacred Heart, Graduate Programs, Department of Business Administration, Program in Taxation, San Juan, PR 00914-0383. Offers MBA. Part-time and evening/weekend programs available. *Degree requirements:* For master's, thesis. *Entrance requirements:* For master's, EXADEP, minimum undergraduate GPA of 2.75, interview.

The University of Tulsa, Graduate School, Collins College of Business, Master of Business Administration Program, Tulsa, OK 74104-3189. Offers accounting (MBA); business administration (MBA); energy management (MBA); finance (MBA); international business (MBA); management information systems (MBA); taxation (MBA); JD/MBA; MBA/MSCS; MBA/MSF. *Accreditation:* AACSB. Part-time and evening/weekend programs available. *Faculty:* 32 full-time (6 women). *Students:* 59 full-time (28 women), 29 part-time (9 women); includes 11 minority (1 Black or African American, non-Hispanic/Latino; 5 American Indian or Alaska Native, non-Hispanic/Latino; 3 Asian, non-Hispanic/Latino; 1 Hispanic/Latino; 1 Two or more races, non-Hispanic/Latino), 16 international. Average age 27. 53 applicants, 81% accepted, 28 enrolled. In 2013, 39 master's awarded. *Entrance requirements:* For master's, GMAT. Additional exam requirements/recommendations for international students: Required—TOEFL (minimum score 577 paper-based; 91 iBT), IELTS (minimum score 6.5). *Application deadline:* Applications are processed on a rolling basis. Application fee: $40. Electronic applications accepted. *Expenses: Tuition:* Full-time $19,566; part-time $1087 per credit hour. *Required fees:* $1690; $5 per credit hour. $160 per semester. Tuition and fees vary according to course load. *Financial support:* In 2013–14, 31 students received support, including 1 research assistantship (averaging $1,500 per year), 30 teaching assistantships (averaging $10,112 per year); fellowships, career-related internships or fieldwork, institutionally sponsored loans, scholarships/grants, health care benefits, tuition waivers (full and partial), and unspecified assistantships also available. Support available to part-time students. Financial award application deadline: 2/1; financial award applicants required to submit FAFSA. *Faculty research:* Accounting, energy management, finance, international business, management information systems, taxation. *Unit head:* Dr. Linda Nichols, Associate Dean of the Collins College of Business, 918-631-2242, Fax: 918-631-2142, E-mail: linda-nichols@utulsa.edu. *Application contact:* Information Contact, 918-631-2242, E-mail: graduate-business@utulsa.edu.
Website: http://www.utulsa.edu/academics/colleges/collins-college-of-business/bus-dept-schools/graduate-business-programs/degree-programs/MBA-Programs.aspx.

The University of Tulsa, Graduate School, Collins College of Business, Online Program in Taxation, Tulsa, OK 74104-3189. Offers M Tax, JD/M Tax. Part-time and evening/weekend programs available. Postbaccalaureate distance learning degree programs offered (no on-campus study). *Faculty:* 4 full-time (2 women), 1 part-time/adjunct (0 women). *Students:* 8 part-time (6 women); includes 1 minority (Hispanic/Latino). Average age 37. In 2013, 16 master's awarded. *Entrance requirements:* For master's, GMAT or LSAT. Additional exam requirements/recommendations for international students: Required—TOEFL (minimum score 577 paper-based; 91 iBT), IELTS (minimum score 6.5). *Application deadline:* Applications are processed on a rolling basis. Application fee: $40. Electronic applications accepted. *Expenses: Tuition:* Full-time $19,566; part-time $1087 per credit hour. *Required fees:* $1690; $5 per credit hour. $160 per semester. Tuition and fees vary according to course load. *Financial support:* Fellowships, research assistantships, teaching assistantships with partial tuition reimbursements, career-related internships or fieldwork, Federal Work-Study, institutionally sponsored loans, scholarships/grants, health care benefits, tuition waivers (full and partial), and unspecified assistantships available. Support available to part-time students. Financial award application deadline: 2/1; financial award applicants required to submit FAFSA. *Unit head:* Dr. Linda Nichols, Associate Dean of the Collins College of Business, 918-631-2242, Fax: 918-631-2142, E-mail: linda-nichols@utulsa.edu. *Application contact:* Information Contact, 918-631-2242, E-mail: graduate-business@utulsa.edu.

Taxation

University of Washington, Graduate School, Michael G. Foster School of Business, Seattle, WA 98195-3200. Offers auditing and assurance (MP Acc); business administration (MBA, PhD); executive business administration (MBA); global executive business administration (MBA); taxation (MP Acc); technology management (MBA); JD/MBA; MBA/MAIS; MBA/MHA. *Accreditation:* AACSB. Part-time and evening/weekend programs available. *Faculty:* 100 full-time (28 women), 55 part-time/adjunct (22 women). *Students:* 407 full-time (130 women), 369 part-time (110 women); includes 199 minority (16 Black or African American, non-Hispanic/Latino; 5 American Indian or Alaska Native, non-Hispanic/Latino; 139 Asian, non-Hispanic/Latino; 25 Hispanic/Latino; 7 Native Hawaiian or other Pacific Islander, non-Hispanic/Latino; 7 Two or more races, non-Hispanic/Latino), 178 international. Average age 32. 2,474 applicants, 40% accepted, 776 enrolled. In 2013, 468 master's, 8 doctorates awarded. Terminal master's awarded for partial completion of doctoral program. *Degree requirements:* For doctorate, comprehensive exam, thesis/dissertation. *Entrance requirements:* For master's, GMAT; for doctorate, GMAT, GRE. Additional exam requirements/recommendations for international students: Required—TOEFL (minimum score 600 paper-based; 100 iBT). *Application deadline:* For fall admission, 3/15 for domestic students, 1/20 for international students. Application fee: $85. Electronic applications accepted. *Expenses:* Contact institution. *Financial support:* Fellowships with partial tuition reimbursements, research assistantships with partial tuition reimbursements, teaching assistantships with partial tuition reimbursements, Federal Work-Study, institutionally sponsored loans, and scholarships/grants available. Financial award application deadline: 2/28; financial award applicants required to submit FAFSA. *Faculty research:* Finance, marketing, organizational behavior, information technology, strategy. *Unit head:* Dr. James Jiambalvo, Dean, 206-543-4750. *Application contact:* Erin Town, Director of Admissions, 206-543-4661, Fax: 206-616-7351, E-mail: mba@uw.edu.
Website: http://www.foster.washington.edu/.

University of Washington, Graduate School, School of Law, Seattle, WA 98195-3020. Offers Asian law (LL M, PhD); intellectual property law and policy (LL M); law (JD); law of sustainable international development (LL M); taxation (LL M); JD/LL M; JD/MA; JD/MAIS; JD/MBA; JD/MPA; JD/MS; JD/PhD. *Accreditation:* ABA. *Degree requirements:* For master's, thesis; for doctorate, thesis/dissertation (for some programs). *Entrance requirements:* For master's, language proficiency (LL M in Asian law); for doctorate, LSAT (for JD). Additional exam requirements/recommendations for international students: Required—TOEFL. *Expenses:* Contact institution. *Faculty research:* Asian, international and comparative law, intellectual property law, health law, environmental law, taxation.

University of Waterloo, Graduate Studies, Faculty of Arts, School of Accounting and Finance, Waterloo, ON N2L 3G1, Canada. Offers accounting (M Acc, PhD); finance (M Acc); taxation (M Tax). *Degree requirements:* For master's, thesis or alternative; for doctorate, thesis/dissertation. *Entrance requirements:* For master's, honors degree, minimum B average, resumé; for doctorate, GMAT, master's degree, minimum A-average, resume. Additional exam requirements/recommendations for international students: Required—TOEFL, TWE. Electronic applications accepted. *Expenses:* Contact institution. *Faculty research:* Auditing, management accounting.

University of Wisconsin–Madison, Graduate School, Wisconsin School of Business, Master of Accountancy Program, Madison, WI 53706-1380. Offers accountancy (M Acc); tax (M Acc). *Faculty:* 11 full-time (3 women), 8 part-time/adjunct (3 women). *Students:* 113 full-time (59 women); includes 8 minority (6 Asian, non-Hispanic/Latino; 2 Hispanic/Latino), 23 international. Average age 23. 233 applicants, 46% accepted, 103 enrolled. In 2013, 100 master's awarded. *Degree requirements:* For master's, minimum GPA of 3.0. *Entrance requirements:* For master's, GMAT, essays. Additional exam requirements/recommendations for international students: Required—TOEFL, PTE. *Application deadline:* For fall admission, 9/30 for domestic and international students; for winter admission, 1/7 for domestic and international students; for spring admission, 2/28 for domestic and international students. Application fee: $56. Electronic applications accepted. *Expenses:* Tuition, state resident: full-time $10,728; part-time $790 per credit. Tuition, nonresident: full-time $24,054; part-time $1623 per credit. *Required fees:* $1130; $119 per credit. *Financial support:* In 2013–14, 96 students received support, including 5 research assistantships with full tuition reimbursements available (averaging $4,915 per year), 44 teaching assistantships with full tuition reimbursements available (averaging $7,373 per year); career-related internships or fieldwork, scholarships/grants, health care benefits, and unspecified assistantships also available. Financial award application deadline: 5/1. *Faculty research:* Internal control deficiencies, impairment recognition, accounting misstatements, earnings restatements, voluntary disclosure. *Unit head:* Prof. Terry Warfield, Professor/Chair of Accounting and Information Systems, 608-262-1028, E-mail: twarfield@bus.wisc.edu. *Application contact:* Kristen Ann Fuhremann, Director, 608-262-0316, Fax: 608-263-0477, E-mail: kfuhremann@bus.wisc.edu.
Website: http://bus.wisc.edu/degrees-programs/msmacc.

University of Wisconsin–Milwaukee, Graduate School, Sheldon B. Lubar School of Business, Milwaukee, WI 53201. Offers business administration (MBA); enterprise resource planning (Certificate); investment management (Certificate); management science (MS, PhD); nonprofit management and leadership (MS, Certificate); state and local taxation (Certificate); MS/MBA. *Accreditation:* AACSB. Part-time and evening/weekend programs available. *Faculty:* 50 full-time (11 women), 4 part-time/adjunct (2 women). *Students:* 282 full-time (123 women), 322 part-time (126 women); includes 87 minority (30 Black or African American, non-Hispanic/Latino; 2 American Indian or Alaska Native, non-Hispanic/Latino; 28 Asian, non-Hispanic/Latino; 3 Hispanic/Latino; 24 Two or more races, non-Hispanic/Latino), 93 international. Average age 32. 517 applicants, 54% accepted, 154 enrolled. In 2013, 245 master's, 10 doctorates awarded. *Degree requirements:* For master's, comprehensive exam (for some programs); for doctorate, comprehensive exam, thesis/dissertation. *Entrance requirements:* For master's and doctorate, GMAT or GRE General Test. Additional exam requirements/recommendations for international students: Required—TOEFL (minimum score 550 paper-based; 79 iBT), IELTS (minimum score 6.5). *Application deadline:* For fall admission, 1/1 priority date for domestic students; for spring admission, 9/1 for domestic students. Applications are processed on a rolling basis. Application fee: $56 ($96 for international students). Electronic applications accepted. *Expenses:* Contact institution. *Financial support:* In 2013–14, 5 fellowships with full tuition reimbursements, 2 research assistantships with full tuition reimbursements, 41 teaching assistantships with full tuition reimbursements were awarded; career-related internships or fieldwork, Federal Work-Study, health care benefits, unspecified assistantships, and project assistantships also available. Support available to part-time students. Financial award application deadline: 4/15; financial award applicants required to submit FAFSA. *Faculty research:* Applied management research in finance, management information systems, marketing, operations research, organizational sciences. *Total annual research expenditures:* $616,761. *Unit head:* Timothy L. Smunt, Dean, 414-229-6256, Fax: 414-229-2372, E-mail: tsmunt@uwm.edu. *Application contact:* Matthew Jensen, Administrative Program Manager III, 414-229-5403, E-mail: mba-ms@uwm.edu.
Website: http://www4.uwm.edu/business.

Villanova University, School of Law and Villanova School of Business, Tax Program, Villanova, PA 19085-1699. Offers LL M, JD/LL M. Part-time and evening/weekend programs available. *Faculty:* 5 full-time (2 women), 34 part-time/adjunct (4 women). *Students:* 3 full-time (1 woman), 56 part-time (28 women); includes 8 minority (4 Black or African American, non-Hispanic/Latino; 1 Asian, non-Hispanic/Latino; 3 Hispanic/Latino), 3 international. Average age 34. 31 applicants, 87% accepted, 14 enrolled. In 2013, 27 master's awarded. *Entrance requirements:* For master's, LSAT, JD (for LL M). Additional exam requirements/recommendations for international students: Required—TOEFL (minimum score 600 paper-based). *Application deadline:* For fall admission, 7/31 for domestic and international students; for spring admission, 11/30 for domestic students, 10/30 for international students. Applications are processed on a rolling basis. Application fee: $50. Electronic applications accepted. *Expenses:* Contact institution. *Financial support:* In 2013–14, 18 students received support, including 3 research assistantships; career-related internships or fieldwork and unspecified assistantships also available. Support available to part-time students. Financial award application deadline: 3/15; financial award applicants required to submit FAFSA. *Faculty research:* Taxation and estate planning, corporate tax planning, international taxation, state taxation. *Unit head:* Linda Love Vines, Interim Director, Graduate Tax Program/Visiting Assistant Professor of Law, 610-519-4533, Fax: 610-519-8018, E-mail: vines@law.villanova.edu.

Wake Forest University, School of Business, MS in Accountancy Program, Winston-Salem, NC 27106. Offers assurance services (MSA); tax consulting (MSA); transaction services (MSA). *Faculty:* 77 full-time (21 women), 32 part-time/adjunct (8 women). *Students:* 210 full-time (82 women); includes 32 minority (11 Black or African American, non-Hispanic/Latino; 1 American Indian or Alaska Native, non-Hispanic/Latino; 4 Asian, non-Hispanic/Latino; 15 Hispanic/Latino; 1 Native Hawaiian or other Pacific Islander, non-Hispanic/Latino), 40 international. Average age 25. In 2013, 115 master's awarded. *Degree requirements:* For master's, 30 credit hours. *Entrance requirements:* For master's, GMAT, letters of recommendation, official transcripts, current resume or curriculum vitae. Additional exam requirements/recommendations for international students: Required—TOEFL (minimum score 600 paper-based; 100 iBT), PTE. *Application deadline:* For fall admission, 6/1 for domestic and international students. Applications are processed on a rolling basis. Application fee: $100. Electronic applications accepted. *Financial support:* In 2013–14, 135 students received support. Career-related internships or fieldwork and scholarships/grants available. Financial award application deadline: 2/15; financial award applicants required to submit FAFSA. *Faculty research:* The influence of personal relationships on business decision-making and management of change; drivers of perceived value and consumer behavior; impact of accounting on auditing, financial, managerial, systems and taxation stakeholders; corporate governance and executive compensation; impact of operations strategies on competitiveness. *Unit head:* Jack Wilkerson, Senior Associate Dean of Accounting Programs, 336-758-5422, Fax: 336-758-5830, E-mail: busadmissions@wfu.edu. *Application contact:* Tamara Paquee, Administrative Assistant, 336-758-5422, Fax: 336-758-5830, E-mail: busadmissions@wfu.edu.
Website: http://www.business.wfu.edu/.

Walsh College of Accountancy and Business Administration, Graduate Programs, Program in Taxation, Troy, MI 48007-7006. Offers MST. Part-time and evening/weekend programs available. *Entrance requirements:* For master's, minimum GPA of 2.75, previous course work in individual income taxation and business. Additional exam requirements/recommendations for international students: Required—TOEFL. Electronic applications accepted.

Washington State University, Graduate School, College of Business, Department of Accounting, Pullman, WA 99164-4729. Offers accounting (PhD); accounting and assurance or audit (M Acc); accounting and taxation (M Acc). *Accreditation:* AACSB. Part-time programs available. *Degree requirements:* For master's, comprehensive exam, thesis or alternative; for doctorate, comprehensive exam, thesis/dissertation, oral and written exams. *Entrance requirements:* For master's, GMAT (minimum score of 500), minimum GPA of 3.0, statement of purpose; for doctorate, GMAT (minimum score of 600), resume; statement of purpose identifying area of interest, experiences, and intended research focus; minimum GPA 3.25. Additional exam requirements/recommendations for international students: Required—TOEFL (minimum score 580 paper-based; 93 iBT), IELTS (minimum score 7.5). Electronic applications accepted. *Faculty research:* Ethics, taxation, auditing, finance.

Washington State University Vancouver, Graduate Programs, Program in Accounting, Vancouver, WA 98686-9600. Offers taxation (M Acc).

Wayne State University, Law School, Detroit, MI 48202. Offers corporate and finance law (LL M); labor and employment law (LL M); law (JD); taxation (LL M); United States law (LL M); JD/MA; JD/MADR; JD/MBA. *Accreditation:* ABA. Part-time and evening/weekend programs available. *Faculty:* 35 full-time (16 women), 21 part-time/adjunct (7 women). *Students:* 418 full-time (178 women), 82 part-time (48 women); includes 75 minority (40 Black or African American, non-Hispanic/Latino; 3 American Indian or Alaska Native, non-Hispanic/Latino; 18 Asian, non-Hispanic/Latino; 11 Hispanic/Latino; 3 Two or more races, non-Hispanic/Latino), 13 international. Average age 27. 807 applicants, 48% accepted, 139 enrolled. In 2013, 2 master's, 172 doctorates awarded. *Degree requirements:* For master's, essay. *Entrance requirements:* For master's, admission to the Graduate School, JD from ABA-accredited institution and member institution of the AALS; for doctorate, LSAT, LDAS report, bachelor's degree from accredited institution, personal statement, transcripts from all U.S. undergraduate schools attended and an analysis and summary of the transcripts; letter of recommendation (up to two are accepted). Additional exam requirements/recommendations for international students: Required—TOEFL (minimum score 600 paper-based), Michigan English Language Assessment Battery (minimum score 85); Recommended—IELTS (minimum score 6.5). *Application deadline:* For fall admission, 5/15 for domestic and international students. Application fee: $0. Electronic applications accepted. *Expenses:* Contact institution. *Financial support:* Scholarships/grants available. Support available to part-time students. Financial award application deadline: 3/31; financial award applicants required to submit FAFSA. *Faculty research:* Public interest law, tax law, international law, environmental law, health law. *Unit head:* Jocelyn Benson, Dean, 313-577-3933. *Application contact:* Marcia McDonald, Director of Admissions, 313-577-3937, Fax: 313-993-8129, E-mail: marcia.mcdonald2@wayne.edu.
Website: http://law.wayne.edu/.

Wayne State University, School of Business Administration, Detroit, MI 48202. Offers accounting (MS, Postbaccalaureate Certificate); business (Graduate Certificate); business administration (MBA, PhD); taxation (MST); JD/MBA. *Accreditation:* AACSB. Part-time and evening/weekend programs available. Postbaccalaureate distance learning degree programs offered (no on-campus study). *Students:* 143 full-time (67 women), 539 part-time (211 women); includes 179 minority (80 Black or African American, non-Hispanic/Latino; 2 American Indian or Alaska Native, non-Hispanic/Latino; 67 Asian, non-Hispanic/Latino; 22 Hispanic/Latino; 8 Two or more races, non-Hispanic/Latino), 71 international. Average age 31. 648 applicants, 26% accepted, 107 enrolled. In 2013, 281 master's, 3 doctorates, 1 other advanced degree awarded. *Degree requirements:* For doctorate, thesis/dissertation. *Entrance requirements:* For master's, GMAT; for doctorate, GMAT (minimum score of 600), minimum undergraduate GPA of 3.0, 3.5 upper-division or graduate; three letters of recommendation; brief essay.

Additional exam requirements/recommendations for international students: Required—TOEFL (minimum score 550 paper-based; 79 iBT), Michigan English Language Assessment Battery (minimum score 85); Recommended—IELTS (minimum score 6.5), TWE (minimum score 5.5). *Application deadline:* For fall admission, 6/1 priority date for domestic students, 5/1 priority date for international students; for winter admission, 10/1 priority date for domestic students, 9/1 priority date for international students; for spring admission, 2/1 priority date for domestic students, 1/1 priority date for international students. Applications are processed on a rolling basis. Application fee: $0. Electronic applications accepted. *Expenses:* Contact institution. *Financial support:* In 2013–14, 105 students received support, including 2 fellowships with tuition reimbursements available (averaging $18,000 per year), 2 teaching assistantships with tuition reimbursements available (averaging $9,000 per year); scholarships/grants, health care benefits, and unspecified assistantships also available. Support available to part-time students. Financial award application deadline: 3/31; financial award applicants required to submit FAFSA. *Faculty research:* Executive compensation and stock performance, consumer reactions to pricing strategies, communication across the automotive supply chain, performance of firms in sub-Saharan Africa, implementation issues with ERP software. *Unit head:* Margaret Williams, Interim Dean, School of Business Administration, 313-577-4501, Fax: 313-577-4557, E-mail: margaret.l.williams@wayne.edu. *Application contact:* Amber Conway, Director, Graduate Programs Office, 313-577-4511, Fax: 313-577-9442, E-mail: ck8173@wayne.edu.
Website: http://business.wayne.edu/.

Weber State University, John B. Goddard School of Business and Economics, School of Accountancy, Ogden, UT 84408-1001. Offers accounting (M Acc); taxation (M Tax). *Accreditation:* AACSB. Part-time programs available. *Faculty:* 8 full-time (0 women), 2 part-time/adjunct (0 women). *Students:* 31 full-time (15 women), 30 part-time (13 women); includes 4 minority (1 Black or African American, non-Hispanic/Latino; 2 Asian, non-Hispanic/Latino; 1 Hispanic/Latino), 3 international. Average age 31. 64 applicants, 61% accepted, 28 enrolled. In 2013, 44 master's awarded. *Entrance requirements:* For master's, GMAT. Additional exam requirements/recommendations for international students: Required—TOEFL (minimum score 80 iBT). *Application deadline:* For fall admission, 8/1 priority date for domestic students; for spring admission, 12/1 priority date for domestic students; for summer admission, 4/1 for domestic students. Applications are processed on a rolling basis. Application fee: $60 ($90 for international students). *Expenses:* Tuition, state resident: full-time $7118; part-time $253 per credit hour. Tuition, nonresident: full-time $12,480; part-time $634 per credit hour. *Required fees:* $34.33; $34.33 per credit hour. $257 per semester. Full-time tuition and fees vary according to course load. *Financial support:* In 2013–14, 11 students received support. Federal Work-Study, institutionally sponsored loans, scholarships/grants, and tuition waivers (full and partial) available. Financial award application deadline: 4/1; financial award applicants required to submit FAFSA. *Faculty research:* Taxation, financial accounting, auditing, managerial accounting, accounting education. *Unit head:* Dr. Matt Mouritsen, Chair, 801-626-8151, Fax: 801-626-7423, E-mail: mmouritsen@weber.edu. *Application contact:* Dr. Larry A. Deppe, Graduate Coordinator, 801-626-7838, Fax: 801-626-7423, E-mail: ldeppe1@weber.edu.
Website: http://www.weber.edu/SBE/masters_of_accounting.html.

Widener University, School of Business Administration, Program in Taxation, Chester, PA 19013-5792. Offers MS. Part-time and evening/weekend programs available. *Faculty:* 2 full-time (1 woman), 2 part-time/adjunct (1 woman). *Students:* 5 full-time (1 woman), 30 part-time (13 women); includes 10 minority (7 Black or African American, non-Hispanic/Latino; 1 American Indian or Alaska Native, non-Hispanic/Latino; 2 Asian, non-Hispanic/Latino), 3 international. Average age 35. 34 applicants, 94% accepted. In 2013, 11 master's awarded. *Entrance requirements:* For master's, Certified Public Accountant Exam or GMAT. *Application deadline:* For fall admission, 8/1 priority date for domestic students; for spring admission, 12/1 for domestic students. Applications are processed on a rolling basis. Application fee: $25 ($300 for international students). Electronic applications accepted. *Expenses: Tuition:* Full-time $30,000; part-time $950 per credit. *Financial support:* Available to part-time students. Application deadline: 5/1. *Faculty research:* Financial planning, taxation fraud. *Unit head:* Frank C. Lordi, Head, 610-499-4308, E-mail: frank.c.lordi@widener.edu. *Application contact:* Ann Seltzer, Graduate Enrollment Administrator, 610-499-4305, E-mail: apseltzer@widener.edu.

William Howard Taft University, Graduate Programs, W. Edwards Deming School of Business, Santa Ana, CA 92704. Offers taxation (MS).

Section 3
Advertising and Public Relations

This section contains a directory of institutions offering graduate work in advertising and public relations. Additional information about programs listed in the directory may be obtained by writing directly to the dean of a graduate school or chair of a department at the address given in the directory.

For programs offering related work, see also in this book *Business Administration* and *Management and Marketing*. In another guide in this series:

Graduate Programs in the Humanities, Arts & Social Sciences
See *Communication and Media*

CONTENTS

Program Directory
Advertising and Public Relations   308

Advertising and Public Relations

Academy of Art University, Graduate Program, School of Advertising, San Francisco, CA 94105-3410. Offers MFA. Part-time programs available. Postbaccalaureate distance learning degree programs offered (no on-campus study). *Faculty:* 8 full-time (2 women), 45 part-time/adjunct (12 women). *Students:* 177 full-time (102 women), 61 part-time (47 women); includes 28 minority (10 Black or African American, non-Hispanic/Latino; 8 Asian, non-Hispanic/Latino; 7 Hispanic/Latino; 3 Two or more races, non-Hispanic/ Latino), 147 international. Average age 28. 55 applicants, 100% accepted, 28 enrolled. In 2013, 55 degrees awarded. *Degree requirements:* For master's, final review. *Entrance requirements:* For master's, statement of intent; resume; portfolio/reel; official college transcripts. *Application deadline:* Applications are processed on a rolling basis. Application fee: $100. Electronic applications accepted. *Expenses: Tuition:* Part-time $885 per unit. *Financial support:* Career-related internships or fieldwork and Federal Work-Study available. Support available to part-time students. Financial award application deadline: 8/10; financial award applicants required to submit FAFSA. *Unit head:* 800-544-ARTS, E-mail: info@academyart.edu. *Application contact:* 800-544-ARTS, Fax: 415-263-4130, E-mail: info@academyart.edu.
Website: http://www.academyart.edu/advertising-school/index.html.

Ball State University, Graduate School, College of Communication, Information, and Media, Department of Journalism, Muncie, IN 47306-1099. Offers journalism (MA); public relations (MA). *Faculty:* 9 full-time (4 women), 1 part-time/adjunct (0 women). *Students:* 23 full-time (10 women), 28 part-time (21 women); includes 3 minority (1 Black or African American, non-Hispanic/Latino; 2 Hispanic/Latino), 14 international. Average age 26. 8 applicants, 63% accepted. In 2013, 18 master's awarded. *Entrance requirements:* For master's, resume. Application fee: $50. *Financial support:* In 2013–14, 16 students received support, including 8 teaching assistantships with full and partial tuition reimbursements available (averaging $8,505 per year); career-related internships or fieldwork also available. Financial award application deadline: 3/1. *Faculty research:* Image studies, readership surveys, audience perception studies. *Unit head:* Dr. William J. Willis, Chairperson, 765-285-8201, Fax: 765-285-7997, E-mail: jwillis@bsu.edu. *Application contact:* Dan Waechter, Information Contact, 765-285-8221, Fax: 765-285-7997, E-mail: dwaechter@bsu.edu.
Website: http://www.bsu.edu/jounalism/.

Boston University, College of Communication, Department of Mass Communication, Advertising, and Public Relations, Boston, MA 02215. Offers advertising (MS); communication research (MS); communication studies (MS); public relations (MS); JD/ MS. Part-time programs available. *Faculty:* 26 full-time, 33 part-time/adjunct. *Students:* 113 full-time (87 women), 57 part-time (45 women); includes 19 minority (5 Black or African American, non-Hispanic/Latino; 4 Asian, non-Hispanic/Latino; 6 Hispanic/Latino; 4 Two or more races, non-Hispanic/Latino), 68 international. Average age 25. 444 applicants, 45% accepted, 86 enrolled. In 2013, 45 master's awarded. *Degree requirements:* For master's, comprehensive exam (for some programs), thesis (for some programs). *Entrance requirements:* For master's, GRE General Test, samples of written work. Additional exam requirements/recommendations for international students: Required—TOEFL (minimum score 600 paper-based; 100 iBT). *Application deadline:* For fall admission, 2/1 for domestic and international students. Application fee: $80. Electronic applications accepted. *Expenses: Tuition:* Full-time $43,970; part-time $1374 per credit hour. *Required fees:* $60 per semester. Tuition and fees vary according to class time, course level and program. *Financial support:* Research assistantships, teaching assistantships with partial tuition reimbursements, career-related internships or fieldwork, Federal Work-Study, institutionally sponsored loans, scholarships/grants, and unspecified assistantships available. Support available to part-time students. Financial award application deadline: 2/1; financial award applicants required to submit FAFSA. *Unit head:* T. Barton Carter, Chairman, 617-353-3482, E-mail: comlaw@bu.edu. *Application contact:* Manny Dotel, Administrator of Graduate Services, 617-353-3481, E-mail: comgrad@bu.edu.
Website: http://www.bu.edu/com/academics/masscomm-ad-pr/.

Boston University, Metropolitan College, Program in Advertising, Boston, MA 02215. Offers MS. Part-time and evening/weekend programs available. *Faculty:* 12 part-time/ adjunct (4 women). *Students:* 35 part-time (24 women); includes 2 minority (both Two or more races, non-Hispanic/Latino). Average age 31. 16 applicants, 88% accepted, 14 enrolled. In 2013, 53 master's awarded. *Entrance requirements:* For master's, undergraduate degree in appropriate field of study. *Application deadline:* Applications are processed on a rolling basis. Application fee: $80. Electronic applications accepted. *Expenses: Tuition:* Full-time $43,970; part-time $1374 per credit hour. *Required fees:* $60 per semester. Tuition and fees vary according to class time, course level and program. *Financial support:* Unspecified assistantships available. Support available to part-time students. Financial award applicants required to submit FAFSA. *Faculty research:* Communication and advertising. *Unit head:* Dr. Christopher Cakebread, Associate Professor, 617-353-3476, E-mail: ccakebr@bu.edu. *Application contact:* Sonia M. Parker, Assistant Dean, 617-353-2975, Fax: 617-353-2686, E-mail: soparker@ bu.edu.
Website: http://www.bu.edu/met/advertising.

California Baptist University, Program in Public Relations, Riverside, CA 92503. Offers MA. Part-time and evening/weekend programs available. Postbaccalaureate distance learning degree programs offered (no on-campus study). *Faculty:* 2 full-time (both women). *Students:* 16 full-time (13 women), 3 part-time (2 women); includes 9 minority (5 Black or African American, non-Hispanic/Latino; 4 Hispanic/Latino). Average age 32. 18 applicants, 50% accepted, 8 enrolled. In 2013, 6 master's awarded. *Degree requirements:* For master's, comprehensive capstone. *Entrance requirements:* For master's, minimum undergraduate GPA of 2.75, bachelor's degree, official transcripts, 2 recommendations, current resume, 500-word essay. Additional exam requirements/ recommendations for international students: Required—TOEFL (minimum score 80 iBT). *Application deadline:* For fall admission, 8/1 priority date for domestic students, 7/1 for international students; for spring admission, 12/1 priority date for domestic students, 11/1 priority date for international students. Applications are processed on a rolling basis. Application fee: $45. Electronic applications accepted. *Expenses:* Contact institution. *Financial support:* Applicants required to submit CSS PROFILE or FAFSA. *Unit head:* Dr. David Poole, Vice President of Online and Professional Studies, 951-343-3902, E-mail: dpoole@calbaptist.edu. *Application contact:* Dr. Maryann Pearson, Program Director, MA in Public Relations, 951-343-3967, E-mail: mpearson@ calbaptist.edu.
Website: http://www.cbuonline.edu/programs/program/master-of-arts-in-public-relations.

California State University, Fullerton, Graduate Studies, College of Communications, Department of Communications, Fullerton, CA 92834-9480. Offers advertising (MA); mass communications research and theory (MA); professional communications (MA); tourism and entertainment (MA). Part-time programs available. *Students:* 22 full-time (17 women), 21 part-time (14 women); includes 19 minority (4 Black or African American, non-Hispanic/Latino; 6 Asian, non-Hispanic/Latino; 8 Hispanic/Latino; 1 Two or more races, non-Hispanic/Latino), 4 international. Average age 28. 69 applicants, 42% accepted, 18 enrolled. In 2013, 36 master's awarded. *Degree requirements:* For master's, project or thesis. *Entrance requirements:* For master's, GRE General Test. Application fee: $55. *Financial support:* Teaching assistantships, career-related internships or fieldwork, Federal Work-Study, institutionally sponsored loans, and scholarships/grants available. Support available to part-time students. Financial award application deadline: 3/1; financial award applicants required to submit FAFSA. *Unit head:* Dr. Diane F. Witmer, Chair, 657-278-7008. *Application contact:* Coordinator, 657-278-3832.

Central Connecticut State University, School of Graduate Studies, School of Arts and Sciences, Department of Communication, New Britain, CT 06050-4010. Offers organizational communication (MS); public relations/promotions (Certificate). Part-time and evening/weekend programs available. *Faculty:* 7 full-time (2 women). *Students:* 8 full-time (4 women), 30 part-time (22 women); includes 6 minority (3 Black or African American, non-Hispanic/Latino; 1 Asian, non-Hispanic/Latino; 1 Hispanic/Latino; 1 Two or more races, non-Hispanic/Latino), 3 international. Average age 37. 25 applicants, 60% accepted, 11 enrolled. In 2013, 4 master's awarded. *Degree requirements:* For master's, comprehensive exam, thesis or alternative; for Certificate, qualifying exam. *Entrance requirements:* For master's, minimum undergraduate GPA of 3.0, resume, references, essay. Additional exam requirements/recommendations for international students: Required—TOEFL (minimum score 550 paper-based; 79 iBT). *Application deadline:* For fall admission, 6/1 for domestic students, 5/1 for international students; for spring admission, 11/1 for domestic and international students. Applications are processed on a rolling basis. Application fee: $50. Electronic applications accepted. Part-time tuition and fees vary according to degree level. *Financial support:* In 2013–14, 4 students received support, including 1 research assistantship; career-related internships or fieldwork, Federal Work-Study, scholarships/grants, and unspecified assistantships also available. Support available to part-time students. Financial award application deadline: 3/1; financial award applicants required to submit FAFSA. *Faculty research:* Organizational communication, mass communication, intercultural communication, political communication, information management. *Unit head:* Dr. Christopher Pudlinski, Chair, 860-832-2690, E-mail: pudlinskic@ccsu.edu. *Application contact:* Patricia Gardner, Associate Director of Graduate Studies, 860-832-2350, Fax: 860-832-2362, E-mail: graduateadmissions@ccsu.edu.
Website: http://web.ccsu.edu/communication/.

Clarion University of Pennsylvania, Office of Transfer, Adult and Graduate Admissions, Online Certificate Programs, Clarion, PA 16214. Offers family nurse practitioner (Post-Master's Certificate); library science (CAS); nurse educator (Post-Master's Certificate); public relations (Certificate). *Accreditation:* ALA (one or more programs are accredited at the [master's] level). Part-time programs available. Postbaccalaureate distance learning degree programs offered (no on-campus study). *Faculty:* 34 full-time (20 women). *Students:* 15 part-time (12 women); includes 1 minority (Black or African American, non-Hispanic/Latino). Average age 35. 16 applicants, 100% accepted, 7 enrolled. In 2013, 12 CASs awarded. *Entrance requirements:* Additional exam requirements/recommendations for international students: Required—TOEFL (minimum score 550 paper-based; 80 iBT), IELTS (minimum score 7). *Application deadline:* For fall admission, 8/1 priority date for domestic students, 4/15 priority date for international students; for spring admission, 12/1 priority date for domestic students, 9/ 15 priority date for international students. Applications are processed on a rolling basis. Application fee: $40. Electronic applications accepted. *Expenses:* Tuition, state resident: part-time $442 per credit. Tuition, nonresident: part-time $451 per credit. *Required fees:* $142.40 per semester. One-time fee: $150 part-time. *Financial support:* Research assistantships available. Financial award application deadline: 3/1. *Unit head:* Dr. William Buchanan, Chair, Library Science, 814-393-2271, Fax: 814-393-2150. *Application contact:* Michelle Ritzler, Assistant Director, Graduate Programs, 814-393-2337, Fax: 814-393-2722, E-mail: gradstudies@clarion.edu.
Website: http://www.clarion.edu/991/.

Colorado State University, Graduate School, College of Liberal Arts, Department of Journalism and Technical Communication, Fort Collins, CO 80523-1785. Offers public communication and technology (MS, PhD); technical communication (MS). Part-time programs available. *Faculty:* 15 full-time (6 women). *Students:* 33 full-time (17 women), 38 part-time (29 women); includes 4 minority (1 American Indian or Alaska Native, non-Hispanic/Latino; 2 Hispanic/Latino; 1 Two or more races, non-Hispanic/Latino), 6 international. Average age 33. 41 applicants, 51% accepted, 17 enrolled. In 2013, 11 master's, 2 doctorates awarded. *Degree requirements:* For master's, variable foreign language requirement, comprehensive exam (for some programs), thesis (for some programs); for doctorate, variable foreign language requirement, comprehensive exam (for some programs), thesis/dissertation (for some programs). *Entrance requirements:* For master's, GRE General Test, samples of written work, letters of recommendation, resume or curriculum vitae, 3 writing/communication projects, statement of purpose, transcripts; for doctorate, GRE General Test, master's degree, minimum GPA of 3.0, scholarly/professional work, letters of recommendation, statement of career plans, resume, transcripts. Additional exam requirements/recommendations for international students: Required—TOEFL (minimum score 550 paper-based; 80 iBT). *Application deadline:* For fall admission, 2/15 priority date for domestic students, 12/15 priority date for international students; for spring admission, 6/15 priority date for domestic students. Applications are processed on a rolling basis. Application fee: $50. Electronic applications accepted. *Expenses:* Tuition, state resident: full-time $9075.40; part-time $504 per credit. Tuition, nonresident: full-time $22,248; part-time $1236 per credit. *Required fees:* $1819; $60 per credit. *Financial support:* In 2013–14, 30 students received support, including 3 research assistantships with full and partial tuition reimbursements available (averaging $13,128 per year), 27 teaching assistantships with partial tuition reimbursements available (averaging $14,656 per year); career-related internships or fieldwork, Federal Work-Study, institutionally sponsored loans, scholarships/grants, traineeships, and unspecified assistantships also available. Support available to part-time students. Financial award application deadline: 3/1; financial award applicants required to submit FAFSA. *Faculty research:* Technical/ science communication, public relations, health/risk communication, Web/new media technologies, environmental communication. *Total annual research expenditures:* $714,047. *Unit head:* Dr. Greg Luft, Chair, 970-491-1979, Fax: 970-491-2908, E-mail: greg.luft@colostate.edu. *Application contact:* Dr. Linda Kidder, Graduate Program Coordinator, 970-491-5132, Fax: 970-491-2908, E-mail: linda.kidder@colostate.edu.
Website: http://journalism.colostate.edu/.

DePaul University, College of Communication, Chicago, IL 60614. Offers digital communication and media arts (MA); health communication (MA); journalism (MA); media and cinema studies (MA); organizational and multicultural communication (MA);

public relations and advertising (MA); relational communication (MA). Part-time and evening/weekend programs available. *Faculty:* 17 full-time (8 women), 9 part-time/adjunct (8 women). *Students:* 175 full-time (137 women), 55 part-time (42 women); includes 91 minority (47 Black or African American, non-Hispanic/Latino; 7 Asian, non-Hispanic/Latino; 23 Hispanic/Latino; 14 Two or more races, non-Hispanic/Latino), 11 international. Average age 27. In 2013, 112 master's awarded. *Entrance requirements:* Additional exam requirements/recommendations for international students: Required—TOEFL (minimum score 590 paper-based; 96 iBT), IELTS (minimum score 7.5) or PTE. *Application deadline:* For fall admission, 6/1 priority date for domestic students; for winter admission, 10/1 priority date for domestic students; for spring admission, 2/15 priority date for domestic students. Applications are processed on a rolling basis. Application fee: $40. Electronic applications accepted. Tuition and fees vary according to course level, course load and degree level. *Financial support:* Applicants required to submit FAFSA. *Unit head:* Jean-Claude Teboul, Interim Dean, 312-362-8600, Fax: 312-362-8620. *Application contact:* Ann Spittle, Director of Graduate Admission, 773-325-7315, Fax: 312-362-8620, E-mail: graddepaul@depaul.edu.
Website: http://communication.depaul.edu/.

Emerson College, Graduate Studies, School of Communication, Department of Marketing Communication, Boston, MA 02116-4624. Offers global marketing communication and advertising (MA); integrated marketing communication (MA). *Faculty:* 16 full-time (7 women), 7 part-time/adjunct (6 women). *Students:* 160 full-time (119 women), 24 part-time (19 women); includes 15 minority (4 Black or African American, non-Hispanic/Latino; 4 Asian, non-Hispanic/Latino; 5 Hispanic/Latino; 1 Native Hawaiian or other Pacific Islander, non-Hispanic/Latino; 1 Two or more races, non-Hispanic/Latino), 103 international. Average age 24. 341 applicants, 72% accepted, 82 enrolled. In 2013, 102 master's awarded. *Entrance requirements:* For master's, GMAT or GRE General Test. Additional exam requirements/recommendations for international students: Required—TOEFL (minimum score 550 paper-based; 80 iBT), IELTS (minimum score 6.5). *Application deadline:* For fall admission, 6/1 priority date for domestic students, 5/1 priority date for international students; for spring admission, 11/1 priority date for domestic and international students. Applications are processed on a rolling basis. Application fee: $60 ($75 for international students). Electronic applications accepted. *Expenses: Tuition:* Part-time $1145 per credit. *Financial support:* In 2013–14, 27 students received support, including 27 fellowships with partial tuition reimbursements available (averaging $9,500 per year), 21 research assistantships with partial tuition reimbursements available (averaging $10,000 per year); Federal Work-Study, scholarships/grants, and unspecified assistantships also available. Financial award application deadline: 3/1; financial award applicants required to submit FAFSA. *Unit head:* John Davis, Chair, E-mail: john_davis@emerson.edu. *Application contact:* Sean Ganas, Office of Graduate Admission, 617-824-8610, Fax: 617-824-8614.
Website: http://www.emerson.edu/graduate_admission.

George Mason University, College of Visual and Performing Arts, Program in Arts Management, Fairfax, VA 22030. Offers arts management (MA); entrepreneurship in the arts (Certificate); fund-raising and development in the arts (Certificate); marketing and public relations in the arts (Certificate); programming and project management (Certificate). *Accreditation:* NASAD. *Faculty:* 2 full-time (both women), 6 part-time/adjunct (5 women). *Students:* 38 full-time (36 women), 41 part-time (35 women); includes 15 minority (7 Black or African American, non-Hispanic/Latino; 3 Asian, non-Hispanic/Latino; 3 Hispanic/Latino; 2 Two or more races, non-Hispanic/Latino), 12 international. Average age 29. 106 applicants, 52% accepted, 22 enrolled. In 2013, 37 master's awarded. *Degree requirements:* For master's, internship. *Entrance requirements:* For master's and Certificate, GRE (recommended), undergraduate degree with minimum GPA of 3.0, official transcripts, 2 letters of recommendation, statement of purpose, resume. Additional exam requirements/recommendations for international students: Required—TOEFL (minimum score 570 paper-based; 88 iBT), IELTS (minimum score 6.5), PTE. *Application deadline:* For fall admission, 3/1 for domestic students, 2/15 for international students; for spring admission, 10/1 for domestic students, 9/15 for international students. Application fee: $65 ($80 for international students). Electronic applications accepted. *Expenses:* Tuition, state resident: full-time $9350; part-time $390 per credit. Tuition, nonresident: full-time $25,754; part-time $1073 per credit. *Required fees:* $2688; $112 per credit. *Financial support:* In 2013–14, 1 student received support, including 1 teaching assistantship with full and partial tuition reimbursement available (averaging $10,920 per year); career-related internships or fieldwork, Federal Work-Study, scholarships/grants, unspecified assistantships, and health care benefits (for full-time research or teaching assistantship recipients) also available. Support available to part-time students. Financial award application deadline: 3/1; financial award applicants required to submit FAFSA. *Faculty research:* Information technology for arts managers, special topics in arts management, directions in gallery management, arts in society, public relations/marketing strategies for art organizations. *Unit head:* Claire Huschle, Interim Program Director, 703-993-8719, Fax: 703-993-9829, E-mail: chuschle@gmu.edu. *Application contact:* Allison Byers, Administrative Assistant, 703-993-8926, Fax: 703-993-9829, E-mail: abyers3@gmu.edu.
Website: http://artsmanagement.gmu.edu/arts-management-ma/.

Georgetown University, Graduate School of Arts and Sciences, School of Continuing Studies, Program in Public Relations and Corporate Communications, Washington, DC 20057. Offers MPS. *Degree requirements:* For master's, capstone course.

Golden Gate University, Ageno School of Business, San Francisco, CA 94105-2968. Offers accounting (MBA); business administration (EMBA, MBA, PMBA, DBA); finance (MBA, MS, Certificate); financial planning (MS, Certificate); healthcare information systems (Certificate); human resource management (MBA, MS); human resources management (Certificate); information systems (MS); information technology (MBA); information technology management (Certificate); integrated marketing and communications (MS, Certificate); international business (MBA); management (MBA); marketing (MBA, MS, Certificate); operations supply chain management (Certificate); psychology (MA, Certificate); public administration (EMPA); public relations (MS, Certificate); technical market analysis (Certificate); JD/MBA. Part-time and evening/weekend programs available. *Degree requirements:* For doctorate, thesis/dissertation, qualifying examination. *Entrance requirements:* For master's, GMAT (MBA), minimum GPA of 2.5 (MS). Additional exam requirements/recommendations for international students: Required—TOEFL (minimum score 550 paper-based; 79 iBT). Electronic applications accepted. *Expenses:* Contact institution.

Hofstra University, School of Communication, Hempstead, NY 11549. Offers documentary studies and production (MFA); journalism (MA); public relations (MA); rhetorical studies (MA).

Iona College, School of Arts and Science, Department of Mass Communication, New Rochelle, NY 10801-1890. Offers non-profit public relations (Certificate); public relations (MA). *Accreditation:* ACEJMC (one or more programs are accredited). Part-time and evening/weekend programs available. *Faculty:* 3 full-time (0 women), 2 part-time/adjunct (both women). *Students:* 12 full-time (8 women), 24 part-time (19 women); includes 8 minority (5 Black or African American, non-Hispanic/Latino; 3 Hispanic/Latino), 9 international. Average age 27. 29 applicants, 86% accepted, 17 enrolled. In 2013, 16 master's, 6 other advanced degrees awarded. *Degree requirements:* For master's, comprehensive exam (for some programs), thesis or alternative. *Entrance requirements:* For master's, GRE General Test, Required if undergraduate GPA is below 3.0. Additional exam requirements/recommendations for international students: Required—TOEFL (minimum score 550 paper-based; 80 iBT), IELTS (minimum score 6). *Application deadline:* For fall admission, 8/1 for domestic students, 5/1 for international students; for spring admission, 1/1 for domestic students, 9/1 for international students. Applications are processed on a rolling basis. Application fee: $50. Electronic applications accepted. *Expenses:* Contact institution. *Financial support:* In 2013–14, 13 students received support. Scholarships/grants, tuition waivers (partial), and unspecified assistantships available. Support available to part-time students. Financial award application deadline: 4/15; financial award applicants required to submit FAFSA. *Faculty research:* Media ecology, new media, corporate communication, media images, organizational learning in public relations. *Unit head:* Robert Petrausch, PhD, Chair, 914-633-2354, E-mail: rpetausch@iona.edu. *Application contact:* Veronica Jarek-Prinz, Director, Graduate Admissions, 914-633-2420, Fax: 914-633-2277, E-mail: vjarekprinz@iona.edu.
Website: http://www.iona.edu/Academics/School-of-Arts-Science/Departments/Mass-Communication/Graduate-Programs.aspx.

Kansas State University, Graduate School, College of Arts and Sciences, A.Q. Miller School of Journalism and Mass Communications, Manhattan, KS 66506. Offers advertising (MS); community journalism (MS); global communication (MS); health communication (MS); media management (MS); public relations (MS); risk communication (MS); strategic communications (MS). Part-time and evening/weekend programs available. *Faculty:* 15 full-time (7 women), 1 (woman) part-time/adjunct. *Students:* 27 full-time (14 women), 4 part-time (2 women); includes 5 minority (1 Black or African American, non-Hispanic/Latino; 4 Asian, non-Hispanic/Latino), 6 international. Average age 26. 14 applicants, 93% accepted, 12 enrolled. In 2013, 2 master's awarded. *Degree requirements:* For master's, comprehensive exam, thesis. *Entrance requirements:* For master's, GRE General Test, minimum GPA of 3.0. Additional exam requirements/recommendations for international students: Required—TOEFL (minimum score 79 iBT). *Application deadline:* For fall admission, 2/1 priority date for domestic and international students; for spring admission, 8/1 priority date for domestic and international students. Applications are processed on a rolling basis. Application fee: $50 ($75 for international students). Electronic applications accepted. *Financial support:* In 2013–14, 10 students received support, including 2 research assistantships with full tuition reimbursements available (averaging $7,500 per year), 7 teaching assistantships with full tuition reimbursements available (averaging $7,500 per year); scholarships/grants, health care benefits, and unspecified assistantships also available. Financial award application deadline: 2/1; financial award applicants required to submit FAFSA. *Faculty research:* Health communication, risk communication, strategic communications, community journalism, global communication. *Total annual research expenditures:* $293,982. *Unit head:* Dr. Birgit Wassmuth, Director, 785-532-6890, Fax: 785-532-5484, E-mail: wassmuth@ksu.edu. *Application contact:* Dr. Nancy Muturi, Associate Director of Graduate Studies, 785-532-3890, Fax: 785-532-5484, E-mail: nmuturi@ksu.edu.
Website: http://jmc.ksu.edu/.

La Salle University, School of Arts and Sciences, Program in Professional and Business Communication, Philadelphia, PA 19141-1199. Offers communication consulting and development (MA); communication management (MA); general professional communication (MA); professional and business communication (Certificate); public relations (MA); social and new media (Certificate). Part-time and evening/weekend programs available. Postbaccalaureate distance learning degree programs offered (minimal on-campus study). *Faculty:* 5 full-time (4 women), 6 part-time/adjunct (3 women). *Students:* 28 full-time (16 women), 51 part-time (38 women); includes 25 minority (22 Black or African American, non-Hispanic/Latino; 1 Asian, non-Hispanic/Latino; 2 Hispanic/Latino), 23 international. Average age 28. 34 applicants, 97% accepted, 25 enrolled. In 2013, 51 master's, 4 other advanced degrees awarded. *Degree requirements:* For master's, practicum. *Entrance requirements:* For master's, writing assessment, professional resume; minimum overall B average; two letters of recommendation (if GPA below 3.25); brief personal statement (about 500 words); interview; for Certificate, writing assessment, minimum GPA of 2.75 in undergraduate studies; brief personal statement (about 500 words); interview. Additional exam requirements/recommendations for international students: Required—TOEFL. *Application deadline:* For fall admission, 8/15 priority date for domestic students, 7/15 for international students; for spring admission, 12/15 priority date for domestic students, 11/15 for international students; for summer admission, 4/15 priority date for domestic students, 3/15 for international students. Applications are processed on a rolling basis. Application fee: $35. Electronic applications accepted. Application fee is waived when completed online. *Expenses:* Contact institution. *Financial support:* In 2013–14, 27 students received support. Career-related internships or fieldwork and scholarships/grants available. Support available to part-time students. Financial award application deadline: 8/31; financial award applicants required to submit FAFSA. *Unit head:* Dr. Pamela Lannutti, Director, 215-951-1935, Fax: 215-951-5043, E-mail: annutti95@lasalle.edu. *Application contact:* Paul J. Reilly, Assistant Vice President, Enrollment Services, 215-951-1946, Fax: 214-951-1462, E-mail: reilly@lasalle.edu.
Website: http://www.lasalle.edu/grad/index.php?section-comm&page-index.

Lasell College, Graduate and Professional Studies in Communication, Newton, MA 02466-2709. Offers health communication (MSC, Graduate Certificate); integrated marketing communication (MSC, Graduate Certificate); public relations (MSC, Graduate Certificate). Part-time and evening/weekend programs available. Postbaccalaureate distance learning degree programs offered (minimal on-campus study). *Faculty:* 5 full-time (3 women), 10 part-time/adjunct (5 women). *Students:* 48 full-time (35 women), 92 part-time (72 women); includes 40 minority (25 Black or African American, non-Hispanic/Latino; 2 American Indian or Alaska Native, non-Hispanic/Latino; 4 Asian, non-Hispanic/Latino; 8 Hispanic/Latino; 1 Two or more races, non-Hispanic/Latino), 19 international. Average age 30. 124 applicants, 66% accepted, 43 enrolled. In 2013, 22 master's awarded. *Entrance requirements:* For master's and Graduate Certificate, bachelor's degree from an accredited institution. Additional exam requirements/recommendations for international students: Required—TOEFL (minimum score 550 paper-based; 79 iBT), IELTS. *Application deadline:* For fall admission, 8/31 priority date for domestic students, 6/30 priority date for international students; for spring admission, 12/31 priority date for domestic students, 10/31 priority date for international students. Applications are processed on a rolling basis. Electronic applications accepted. *Expenses: Tuition:* Part-time $575 per credit. *Required fees:* $80 per semester. *Financial support:* Available to part-time students. Application deadline: 8/31; applicants required to submit FAFSA. *Unit head:* Dr. Joan Dolamore, Dean of Graduate and Professional Studies, 617-243-2485, Fax: 617-243-2450, E-mail: gradinfo@lasell.edu. *Application contact:* Adrienne Franciosi, Director of Graduate Admission, 617-243-2214, Fax: 617-243-2450, E-mail: gradinfo@lasell.edu.
Website: http://www.lasell.edu/Academics/Graduate-and-Professional-Studies/MS-in-Communication.html.

Lasell College, Graduate and Professional Studies in Management, Newton, MA 02466-2709. Offers business administration (PMBA); elder care management (MSM, Graduate Certificate); elder care marketing (MSM); human resource management

(Graduate Certificate); human resources management (MSM); integrated marketing communication (Graduate Certificate); management (MSM, Graduate Certificate); marketing (MSM, Graduate Certificate); non-profit management (MSM, Graduate Certificate); project management (MSM, Graduate Certificate); public relations (Graduate Certificate). Part-time and evening/weekend programs available. Postbaccalaureate distance learning degree programs offered (no on-campus study). *Faculty:* 3 full-time (1 woman), 16 part-time/adjunct (9 women). *Students:* 46 full-time (33 women), 105 part-time (73 women); includes 35 minority (24 Black or African American, non-Hispanic/Latino; 1 American Indian or Alaska Native, non-Hispanic/Latino; 3 Asian, non-Hispanic/Latino; 7 Hispanic/Latino), 22 international. Average age 32. 88 applicants, 55% accepted, 29 enrolled. In 2013, 61 master's awarded. *Entrance requirements:* For master's and Graduate Certificate, bachelor's degree from an accredited institution. Additional exam requirements/recommendations for international students: Required—TOEFL (minimum score 550 paper-based; 79 iBT). *Application deadline:* For fall admission, 8/31 priority date for domestic students, 6/30 priority date for international students; for spring admission, 12/31 priority date for domestic students, 10/31 priority date for international students. Applications are processed on a rolling basis. Electronic applications accepted. *Expenses: Tuition:* Part-time $575 per credit. *Required fees:* $80 per semester. *Financial support:* Available to part-time students. Application deadline: 8/31; applicants required to submit FAFSA. *Unit head:* Dr. Joan Dolamore, Dean of Graduate and Professional Studies, 617-243-2485, Fax: 617-243-2450, E-mail: gradinfo@lasell.edu. *Application contact:* Adrienne Franciosi, Director of Graduate Admission, 617-243-2214, Fax: 617-243-2450, E-mail: gradinfo@lasell.edu.
Website: http://www.lasell.edu/Academics/Graduate-and-Professional-Studies/MS-in-Management.html.

La Sierra University, College of Arts and Sciences, Department of English and Communication, Riverside, CA 92515. Offers communication (MA), including public relations/advertising, theory emphasis; English (MA), including literary emphasis, writing emphasis. Part-time programs available. *Degree requirements:* For master's, one foreign language. *Entrance requirements:* For master's, GRE General Test.

Liberty University, School of Business, Lynchburg, VA 24515. Offers accounting (MBA, MS, DBA); business administration (MBA); criminal justice (MBA); cyber security (MS); executive leadership (MA); healthcare (MBA); human resources (DBA); information systems (MS), including information assurance, technology management; international business (MBA, DBA); leadership (MBA, DBA); management and leadership (MA); marketing (MBA, MS, DBA), including digital marketing and advertising (MS), project management (MS), public relations (MS), sports marketing and media (MS); project management (MBA, DBA); public administration (MBA); public relations (MBA). Part-time programs available. Postbaccalaureate distance learning degree programs offered (minimal on-campus study). *Students:* 1,342 full-time (749 women), 3,704 part-time (1,820 women); includes 1,657 minority (1,221 Black or African American, non-Hispanic/Latino; 11 American Indian or Alaska Native, non-Hispanic/Latino; 74 Asian, non-Hispanic/Latino; 209 Hispanic/Latino; 13 Native Hawaiian or other Pacific Islander, non-Hispanic/Latino; 129 Two or more races, non-Hispanic/Latino), 40 international. Average age 35. 5,899 applicants, 48% accepted, 1716 enrolled. In 2013, 1,535 master's awarded. *Entrance requirements:* For master's, minimum undergraduate GPA of 3.0, 15 hours of upper-level business courses. Additional exam requirements/recommendations for international students: Required—TOEFL (minimum score 600 paper-based; 100 iBT). *Application deadline:* Applications are processed on a rolling basis. Application fee: $50. Electronic applications accepted. *Expenses:* Contact institution. *Unit head:* Dr. Scott Hicks, Dean, 434-592-4808, Fax: 434-582-2366, E-mail: smhicks@liberty.edu. *Application contact:* Jay Bridge, Director of Graduate Admissions, 800-424-9595, Fax: 800-628-7977, E-mail: gradadmissions@liberty.edu.
Website: http://www.liberty.edu/academics/business/index.cfm?PID-149.

Marquette University, Graduate School, College of Communication, Milwaukee, WI 53201-1881. Offers advertising and public relations (MA); broadcasting and electronic communications (MA); communications studies (MA); digital storytelling (Certificate); health, environment, science and sustainability (MA); journalism (MA); mass communications (MA). *Accreditation:* ACEJMC (one or more programs are accredited). Part-time and evening/weekend programs available. *Faculty:* 36 full-time (18 women), 41 part-time/adjunct (17 women). *Students:* 25 full-time (14 women), 21 part-time (15 women); includes 3 minority (1 Black or African American, non-Hispanic/Latino; 2 Hispanic/Latino), 6 international. Average age 29. 112 applicants, 53% accepted, 21 enrolled. In 2013, 15 master's, 7 other advanced degrees awarded. *Degree requirements:* For master's, comprehensive exam, thesis or alternative. *Entrance requirements:* For master's, GRE, official transcripts from all current and previous colleges/universities except Marquette, three letters of recommendation, statement of academic and professional goals. Additional exam requirements/recommendations for international students: Required—TOEFL (minimum score 530 paper-based). *Application deadline:* Applications are processed on a rolling basis. Application fee: $50. Electronic applications accepted. *Financial support:* In 2013–14, 41 students received support, including 2 fellowships with partial tuition reimbursements available (averaging $10,385 per year), 6 research assistantships with full tuition reimbursements available (averaging $13,285 per year), 12 teaching assistantships with full tuition reimbursements available (averaging $13,285 per year); career-related internships or fieldwork, scholarships/grants, health care benefits, tuition waivers (full and partial), and unspecified assistantships also available. Support available to part-time students. Financial award application deadline: 2/15. *Faculty research:* Urban journalism, gender and communication, intercultural communication, religious communication. *Total annual research expenditures:* $58,350. *Unit head:* Dr. Lori Bergen, Dean, 414-288-7133, Fax: 414-288-1578. *Application contact:* Dr. Steven Goldzwig, Professor and Associate Dean, 414-288-3497.
Website: http://www.marquette.edu/comm/grad/index.shtml.

Michigan State University, The Graduate School, College of Communication Arts and Sciences, Department of Advertising, Public Relations and Retailing, East Lansing, MI 48824. Offers advertising (MA); public relations (MA); retailing (MS, PhD). *Entrance requirements:* Additional exam requirements/recommendations for international students: Required—TOEFL. Electronic applications accepted.

Mississippi College, Graduate School, College of Arts and Sciences, School of Christian Studies and the Arts, Department of Communication, Clinton, MS 39058. Offers applied communication (MSC); public relations and corporate communication (MSC). Part-time programs available. *Degree requirements:* For master's, comprehensive exam, thesis optional. *Entrance requirements:* For master's, GRE or NTE, minimum GPA of 2.5. Additional exam requirements/recommendations for international students: Recommended—TOEFL, IELTS. Electronic applications accepted.

Monmouth University, The Graduate School, Department of Corporate and Public Communication, West Long Branch, NJ 07764-1898. Offers corporate and public communication (MA); human resources management and communication (Certificate); public service communication (Certificate); strategic public relations and new media (Certificate). Part-time and evening/weekend programs available. *Faculty:* 9 full-time (6 women). *Students:* 5 full-time (4 women), 20 part-time (14 women); includes 2 minority (1 Hispanic/Latino; 1 Two or more races, non-Hispanic/Latino), 2 international. Average age 29. 17 applicants, 88% accepted, 12 enrolled. In 2013, 10 master's awarded. *Degree requirements:* For master's, comprehensive exam, project. *Entrance requirements:* For master's, GRE, baccalaureate degree with minimum GPA of 3.0 in major, 2.75 overall; two letters of recommendation, personal essay, resume. Additional exam requirements/recommendations for international students: Required—TOEFL (minimum score 550 paper-based; 79 iBT), IELTS (minimum score 6), Michigan English Language Assessment Battery (minimum score 77). *Application deadline:* For fall admission, 7/15 priority date for domestic students, 6/1 for international students; for spring admission, 11/15 priority date for domestic students, 11/1 for international students. Applications are processed on a rolling basis. Application fee: $50. Electronic applications accepted. *Expenses: Tuition:* Part-time $1004 per credit hour. *Required fees:* $157 per semester. *Financial support:* In 2013–14, 10 students received support, including 8 fellowships (averaging $3,037 per year), 1 research assistantship (averaging $3,321 per year); scholarships/grants and unspecified assistantships also available. Support available to part-time students. Financial award applicants required to submit FAFSA. *Faculty research:* Service-learning, history of television, feminism and the media, executive communication, public relations pedagogy. *Unit head:* Dr. Deanna Shoemaker, Program Director, 732-263-5449, Fax: 732-571-3609, E-mail: dshoemak@monmouth.edu. *Application contact:* Lauren Vento-Cifelli, Associate Vice President of Undergraduate and Graduate Admission, 732-571-3452, Fax: 732-263-5123, E-mail: gradadm@monmouth.edu.
Website: http://www.monmouth.edu/cpc.

Montana State University Billings, College of Arts and Sciences, Department of Communication and Theater, Billings, MT 59101-0298. Offers public relations (MS). Part-time programs available. Postbaccalaureate distance learning degree programs offered. *Degree requirements:* For master's, thesis optional. *Entrance requirements:* For master's, GRE General Test, minimum undergraduate GPA of 3.0, 3 letters of recommendation. *Application deadline:* For fall admission, 3/15 for domestic students, 7/15 for international students; for spring admission, 10/15 for domestic students, 12/1 for international students. Applications are processed on a rolling basis. Application fee: $40. *Expenses:* Tuition, state resident: full-time $2653.75; part-time $1718 per semester. Tuition, nonresident: full-time $7015; part-time $4640 per semester. *Required fees:* $2445; $444 per credit. *Financial support:* Teaching assistantships, career-related internships or fieldwork, Federal Work-Study, institutionally sponsored loans, and scholarships/grants available. Support available to part-time students. Financial award application deadline: 5/1; financial award applicants required to submit FAFSA. *Unit head:* Dr. Sarah Keller, Chair, 406-896-5824, E-mail: skeller@msubillings.edu. *Application contact:* David M. Sullivan, Graduate Studies Counselor, 406-657-2053, Fax: 406-657-2299, E-mail: dsullivan@msubillings.edu.

Montclair State University, The Graduate School, College of the Arts, School of Communication and Media, Montclair, NJ 07043-1624. Offers public and organizational relations (MA). Part-time and evening/weekend programs available. *Degree requirements:* For master's, comprehensive exam. *Entrance requirements:* For master's, GRE General Test, 2 letters of recommendation. Additional exam requirements/recommendations for international students: Required—TOEFL (minimum score 83 iBT) or IELTS (minimum score 6.5). Electronic applications accepted. *Faculty research:* Organizational problem solving/innovation, social media, health communication, globalization, organizational change management.

New York University, School of Continuing and Professional Studies, Division of Programs in Business, Program in Public Relations and Corporate Communication, New York, NY 10012-1019. Offers corporate and organizational communication (MS); public relations management (MS). Part-time and evening/weekend programs available. *Faculty:* 2 full-time (0 women), 46 part-time/adjunct (18 women). *Students:* 240 full-time (198 women), 144 part-time (114 women); includes 63 minority (28 Black or African American, non-Hispanic/Latino; 16 Asian, non-Hispanic/Latino; 17 Hispanic/Latino; 2 Two or more races, non-Hispanic/Latino), 198 international. Average age 26. 372 applicants, 74% accepted, 128 enrolled. In 2013, 96 master's awarded. *Degree requirements:* For master's, thesis. *Entrance requirements:* For master's, bachelor's degree, resume with relevant professional work, internship or volunteer experience, two letters of recommendation, statement of purpose. Additional exam requirements/recommendations for international students: Required—TOEFL (minimum score 600 paper-based; 100 iBT), IELTS (minimum score 7). *Application deadline:* For fall admission, 2/1 priority date for domestic and international students; for spring admission, 10/15 priority date for domestic students, 8/15 priority date for international students. Applications are processed on a rolling basis. Application fee: $150. Electronic applications accepted. *Expenses: Tuition:* Full-time $35,856; part-time $1494 per unit. *Required fees:* $1408; $64 per unit. $473 per term. Tuition and fees vary according to course load and program. *Financial support:* In 2013–14, 124 students received support, including 124 fellowships (averaging $2,653 per year). Financial award application deadline: 3/1; financial award applicants required to submit FAFSA. *Unit head:* Paula Payton, Academic Director, 212-998-3228, E-mail: pp64@nyu.edu. *Application contact:* Admissions Office, 212-998-7100, E-mail: scps.gradadmissions@nyu.edu.
Website: http://www.scps.nyu.edu/academics/departments/marketing-and-pr.html.

Northern Kentucky University, Office of Graduate Programs, College of Informatics, Program in Communication, Highland Heights, KY 41099. Offers communication (MA); communication teaching (Certificate); documentary studies (Certificate); public relations (Certificate); relationships (Certificate). Part-time and evening/weekend programs available. *Faculty:* 8 full-time (3 women). *Students:* 9 full-time (2 women), 25 part-time (15 women); includes 1 minority (Black or African American, non-Hispanic/Latino), 2 international. Average age 33. 28 applicants, 71% accepted, 10 enrolled. In 2013, 11 master's, 5 other advanced degrees awarded. *Degree requirements:* For master's, thesis (for some programs), capstone experience, internship. *Entrance requirements:* For master's, GRE, minimum GPA of 3.0, 3 letters of recommendation, letter of intent. Additional exam requirements/recommendations for international students: Required—TOEFL (minimum score 550 paper-based; 79 iBT); Recommended—IELTS (minimum score 6.5). *Application deadline:* For fall admission, 8/1 for domestic students, 6/1 for international students; for spring admission, 12/1 for domestic students, 10/1 for international students. Applications are processed on a rolling basis. Application fee: $40. Electronic applications accepted. *Expenses:* Tuition, state resident: full-time $4446; part-time $494 per credit hour. Tuition, nonresident: full-time $6885; part-time $765 per credit hour. *Required fees:* $72 per semester. One-time fee: $125.50. Part-time tuition and fees vary according to course load, degree level, program and reciprocity agreements. *Financial support:* In 2013–14, 11 students received support. Unspecified assistantships available. Financial award applicants required to submit FAFSA. *Faculty research:* Mediating effect of Latino cultural values (familialism, social support) on poor health behaviors, end of life planning communication within families, parental sense-making of prenatal genetic disorder diagnoses, employee organizational exit storytelling, co-management of meaning between game developers and end users. *Total annual research expenditures:* $20,000. *Unit head:* Dr. Zachary Hart, Department of Communication Chair, 859-572-5573, E-mail: hartz@nku.edu. *Application contact:*

Dr. Christian Gamm, Director of Graduate Programs, 859-572-6364, Fax: 859-572-6670, E-mail: gammc1@nku.edu.
Website: http://informatics.nku.edu/content/informatics/departments/communication/programs/communication—m-a—.html.

Quinnipiac University, School of Communications, Program in Public Relations, Hamden, CT 06518-1940. Offers MS. Part-time and evening/weekend programs available. *Faculty:* 3 full-time (2 women), 2 part-time/adjunct (1 woman). *Students:* 11 full-time (8 women), 9 part-time (8 women); includes 2 minority (both Black or African American, non-Hispanic/Latino), 2 international. 15 applicants, 73% accepted, 5 enrolled. In 2013, 5 master's awarded. *Entrance requirements:* For master's, GRE. Additional exam requirements/recommendations for international students: Required—TOEFL (minimum score 575 paper-based; 90 iBT), IELTS (minimum score 6.5). *Application deadline:* For fall admission, 7/31 priority date for domestic students, 4/30 for international students; for spring admission, 12/15 for domestic students. Applications are processed on a rolling basis. Application fee: $45. Electronic applications accepted. *Expenses: Tuition:* Part-time $920 per credit. *Required fees:* $37 per credit. *Financial support:* In 2013–14, 8 students received support. Career-related internships or fieldwork, Federal Work-Study, scholarships/grants, and unspecified assistantships available. Support available to part-time students. Financial award application deadline: 6/1; financial award applicants required to submit FAFSA. *Faculty research:* Social media, corporate social responsibility, ethics, international communications and international public relations, public diplomacy, non-profit management, crisis management, investor relations. *Unit head:* Alexander Laskin, Program Director, E-mail: alexander.laskin@quinnipiac.edu. *Application contact:* Office of Graduate Admissions, 203-582-8672, Fax: 203-582-3443, E-mail: graduate@quinnipiac.edu.
Website: http://www.quinnipiac.edu/gradpr.

Rowan University, Graduate School, College of Communication and Creative Arts, Program in Public Relations/Advertising, Glassboro, NJ 08028-1701. Offers MA. Part-time and evening/weekend programs available. *Faculty:* 6 full-time (1 woman). *Students:* 12 full-time (7 women), 9 part-time (4 women); includes 7 minority (5 Black or African American, non-Hispanic/Latino; 2 Hispanic/Latino), 1 international. Average age 28. 10 applicants, 100% accepted, 5 enrolled. In 2013, 6 master's awarded. *Degree requirements:* For master's, thesis. *Entrance requirements:* For master's, GRE General Test. Additional exam requirements/recommendations for international students: Required—TOEFL. *Application deadline:* Applications are processed on a rolling basis. Application fee: $65. Electronic applications accepted. *Expenses: Tuition, area resident:* Part-time $638 per credit. Tuition, state resident: full-time $5742. *Required fees:* $142 per credit. Tuition and fees vary according to course level and program. *Financial support:* Career-related internships or fieldwork available. Support available to part-time students. *Unit head:* Dr. Horacio Sosa, Dean, College of Graduate and Continuing Education, 856-256-5435, Fax: 856-256-5638, E-mail: sosa@rowan.edu. *Application contact:* Admissions and Enrollment Services, 856-256-5145, Fax: 856-256-5637, E-mail: cgceadmissions@rowan.edu.

Royal Roads University, Graduate Studies, Applied Leadership and Management Program, Victoria, BC V9B 5Y2, Canada. Offers executive coaching (Graduate Certificate); health systems leadership (Graduate Certificate); project management (Graduate Certificate); public relations management (Graduate Certificate); strategic human resources management (Graduate Certificate).

Sacred Heart University, Graduate Programs, College of Arts and Sciences, Department of Communication, Fairfield, CT 06825-1000. Offers corporate communication and public relations (MA Comm); digital/multimedia journalism (MA Comm); digital/multimedia production (MA Comm). Part-time and evening/weekend programs available. *Faculty:* 4 full-time (1 woman), 3 part-time/adjunct (0 women). *Students:* 54 full-time (33 women), 27 part-time (14 women); includes 31 minority (19 Black or African American, non-Hispanic/Latino; 1 Asian, non-Hispanic/Latino; 9 Hispanic/Latino; 1 Native Hawaiian or other Pacific Islander, non-Hispanic/Latino; 1 Two or more races, non-Hispanic/Latino), 3 international. Average age 27. 80 applicants, 95% accepted, 50 enrolled. In 2013, 25 master's awarded. *Entrance requirements:* For master's, bachelor's degree. Additional exam requirements/recommendations for international students: Required—PTE; Recommended—TOEFL (minimum score 570 paper-based; 80 iBT), IELTS (minimum score 6.5). *Application deadline:* Applications are processed on a rolling basis. Application fee: $60. Electronic applications accepted. *Expenses: Tuition:* Full-time $22,775; part-time $617 per credit. *Financial support:* Career-related internships or fieldwork, institutionally sponsored loans, scholarships/grants, and unspecified assistantships available. Support available to part-time students. *Unit head:* Dr. James Castonguay, Chair, 203-371-7710, E-mail: castonguayj@sacredheart.edu. *Application contact:* Brendan Hummel, Assistant Director of Graduate Admissions, 203-365-4748, Fax: 203-365-4732, E-mail: hummelb@sacredheart.edu.

San Diego State University, Graduate and Research Affairs, College of Professional Studies and Fine Arts, School of Communication, San Diego, CA 92182. Offers advertising and public relations (MA); critical-cultural studies (MA); interaction studies (MA); intercultural and international studies (MA); new media studies (MA); news and information studies (MA); telecommunications and media management (MA). *Degree requirements:* For master's, thesis. *Entrance requirements:* For master's, GRE General Test, 3 letters of recommendation. Additional exam requirements/recommendations for international students: Required—TOEFL. Electronic applications accepted.

Savannah College of Art and Design, Graduate School, Program in Advertising, Savannah, GA 31402-3146. Offers MA, MFA. Part-time programs available. *Faculty:* 12 full-time (4 women), 4 part-time/adjunct (1 woman). *Students:* 35 full-time (19 women), 8 part-time (5 women); includes 11 minority (7 Black or African American, non-Hispanic/Latino; 3 Hispanic/Latino; 1 Native Hawaiian or other Pacific Islander, non-Hispanic/Latino), 15 international. Average age 27. 60 applicants, 38% accepted, 16 enrolled. In 2013, 19 master's awarded. *Degree requirements:* For master's, final project (for MA); thesis (for MFA). *Entrance requirements:* For master's, portfolio. Additional exam requirements/recommendations for international students: Required—TOEFL (minimum score 550 paper-based, 85 iBT), IELTS (minimum score 6.5), or ACTFL. *Application deadline:* For fall admission, 4/1 for domestic and international students. Applications are processed on a rolling basis. Application fee: $35. Electronic applications accepted. *Expenses: Tuition:* Full-time $33,750; part-time $3750 per course. One-time fee: $500. Tuition and fees vary according to course load. *Financial support:* Fellowships, career-related internships or fieldwork, Federal Work-Study, and scholarships/grants available. Financial award application deadline: 4/1; financial award applicants required to submit FAFSA. *Unit head:* Luke Longstreet Sullivan, Chair. *Application contact:* Jenny Jaquillard, Executive Director of Admissions, Recruitment and Events, 912-525-5100, Fax: 912-525-5985, E-mail: admission@scad.edu.
Website: http://www.scad.edu/academics/programs/advertising.

Southern Illinois University Edwardsville, Graduate School, College of Arts and Sciences, Department of Speech Communication, Program in Public Relations, Edwardsville, IL 62026. Offers MA. Part-time and evening/weekend programs available. *Degree requirements:* For master's, comprehensive exam (for some programs), thesis (for some programs). *Entrance requirements:* Additional exam requirements/recommendations for international students: Required—TOEFL (minimum score 550 paper-based, 79 iBT), IELTS (minimum score 6.5), Michigan Test of English Language Proficiency or PTE. *Expenses:* Tuition, state resident: full-time $3551. Tuition, nonresident: full-time $8378. *Financial support:* Application deadline: 3/1; applicants required to submit FAFSA. *Unit head:* Dr. Jocelyn DeGroot Brown, Program Director, 618-650-5828, E-mail: jocbrow@siue.edu. *Application contact:* Melissa K. Mace, Assistant Director of Graduate and International Recruitment, 618-650-2756, Fax: 618-650-3618, E-mail: mmace@siue.edu.
Website: http://www.siue.edu/artsandsciences/spc/.

Southern Methodist University, Meadows School of the Arts, Temerlin Advertising Institute, Dallas, TX 75275. Offers MA. *Entrance requirements:* For master's, GRE, GMAT. Additional exam requirements/recommendations for international students: Required—TOEFL (minimum score 550 paper-based; 80 iBT). Electronic applications accepted.

Suffolk University, College of Arts and Sciences, Department of Communication and Journalism, Boston, MA 02108-2770. Offers communication studies (MAC); integrated marketing communication (MAC); public relations and advertising (MAC). Part-time and evening/weekend programs available. *Faculty:* 9 full-time (6 women). *Students:* 27 full-time (21 women), 19 part-time (15 women); includes 5 minority (1 Black or African American, non-Hispanic/Latino; 1 Asian, non-Hispanic/Latino; 3 Hispanic/Latino), 18 international. Average age 24. 98 applicants, 66% accepted, 19 enrolled. In 2013, 23 master's awarded. *Degree requirements:* For master's, thesis optional. *Entrance requirements:* For master's, GRE General Test, MAT, or GMAT, 2 letters of recommendation, resume. Additional exam requirements/recommendations for international students: Required—TOEFL (minimum score 550 paper-based; 80 iBT). *Application deadline:* For fall admission, 6/15 priority date for domestic students, 6/15 for international students; for spring admission, 11/1 priority date for domestic students, 11/1 for international students. Applications are processed on a rolling basis. Application fee: $50. Electronic applications accepted. *Expenses:* Contact institution. *Financial support:* In 2013–14, 38 students received support, including 36 fellowships (averaging $7,982 per year); career-related internships or fieldwork, Federal Work-Study, and institutionally sponsored loans also available. Support available to part-time students. Financial award application deadline: 4/1; financial award applicants required to submit FAFSA. *Faculty research:* Branding law and management, health care communication, gender roles and violence in video games, new media, political communication. *Unit head:* Dr. Robert Rosenthal, Chair, 617-573-8502, Fax: 617-742-6982, E-mail: rrosenth@suffolk.edu. *Application contact:* Cory Meyers, Director of Graduate Admissions, 617-573-8302, Fax: 617-305-1733, E-mail: grad.admission@suffolk.edu.
Website: http://www.suffolk.edu/college/departments/10483.php.

Syracuse University, S. I. Newhouse School of Public Communications, Program in Advertising, Syracuse, NY 13244. Offers MA. *Students:* 17 full-time (11 women); includes 5 minority (3 Black or African American, non-Hispanic/Latino; 1 Asian, non-Hispanic/Latino; 1 Hispanic/Latino), 6 international. Average age 23. 86 applicants, 37% accepted, 16 enrolled. In 2013, 20 master's awarded. *Degree requirements:* For master's, capstone course. *Entrance requirements:* For master's, GRE General Test. Additional exam requirements/recommendations for international students: Required—TOEFL (minimum score 600 paper-based; 100 iBT). *Application deadline:* For fall admission, 2/1 priority date for domestic and international students; for summer admission, 1/15 priority date for domestic and international students. Application fee: $45. Electronic applications accepted. *Financial support:* Fellowships with full tuition reimbursements, research assistantships with partial tuition reimbursements, and teaching assistantships with full tuition reimbursements available. Financial award application deadline: 1/1. *Unit head:* Prof. James Tsao, Chair, 315-443-7401, Fax: 315-443-3946, E-mail: pcgrad@syr.edu. *Application contact:* Graduate Records Office, 315-443-4039, Fax: 315-443-1834, E-mail: pcgrad@syr.edu.
Website: http://newhouse.syr.edu/.

Syracuse University, S. I. Newhouse School of Public Communications, Program in Public Relations, Syracuse, NY 13244. Offers MS. *Students:* 29 full-time (23 women), 3 part-time (2 women); includes 4 minority (3 Black or African American, non-Hispanic/Latino; 1 Hispanic/Latino), 14 international. Average age 24. 207 applicants, 44% accepted, 21 enrolled. In 2013, 32 master's awarded. *Degree requirements:* For master's, thesis (for some programs). *Entrance requirements:* For master's, GRE General Test. Additional exam requirements/recommendations for international students: Required—TOEFL (minimum score 600 paper-based; 100 iBT). *Application deadline:* For fall admission, 2/1 for domestic and international students; for summer admission, 1/15 priority date for domestic and international students. Application fee: $45. Electronic applications accepted. *Financial support:* Fellowships with full tuition reimbursements, research assistantships with partial tuition reimbursements, and teaching assistantships with partial tuition reimbursements available. Financial award application deadline: 2/1. *Unit head:* Prof. Rochelle Ford, Chair, 315-443-7401, E-mail: pcgrad@syr.edu. *Application contact:* Graduate Records Office, 315-443-4039, Fax: 315-443-1834, E-mail: pcgrad@syr.edu.
Website: http://newhouse.syr.edu/.

Universidad Autonoma de Guadalajara, Graduate Programs, Guadalajara, Mexico. Offers administrative law and justice (LL M); advertising and corporate communications (MA); architecture (M Arch); business (MBA); computational science (MCC); education (Ed M, Ed D); English-Spanish translation (MA); entrepreneurship and management (MBA); integrated management of digital animation (MA); international business (MIB); international corporate law (LL M); internet technologies (MS); manufacturing systems (MMS); occupational health (MS); philosophy (MA, PhD); power electronics (MS); quality systems (MQS); renewable energy (MS); social evaluation of projects (MBA); strategic market research (MBA); tax law (MA); teaching mathematics (MA).

Université Laval, Faculty of Letters, Program in Public Relations, Québec, QC G1K 7P4, Canada. Offers Diploma. Part-time and evening/weekend programs available. *Entrance requirements:* For degree, knowledge of French, comprehension of written English. Electronic applications accepted.

The University of Alabama, Graduate School, College of Communication and Information Sciences, Department of Advertising and Public Relations, Tuscaloosa, AL 35487-0172. Offers MA. Part-time programs available. *Faculty:* 14 full-time (7 women). *Students:* 22 full-time (18 women); includes 3 minority (2 Black or African American, non-Hispanic/Latino; 1 Native Hawaiian or other Pacific Islander, non-Hispanic/Latino), 2 international. Average age 24. 104 applicants, 46% accepted, 19 enrolled. In 2013, 13 master's awarded. *Degree requirements:* For master's, comprehensive exam, thesis or alternative. *Entrance requirements:* For master's, GRE (minimum score: 300 verbal plus quantitative, 145 in each; 4.0 in writing), minimum undergraduate GPA of 3.0 for last 60 hours. Additional exam requirements/recommendations for international students: Required—TOEFL (minimum score 600 paper-based; 100 iBT). *Application deadline:* For fall admission, 3/1 priority date for domestic and international students. Applications are processed on a rolling basis. Application fee: $50 ($60 for international students). Electronic applications accepted. *Expenses:* Tuition, state resident: full-time $9450. Tuition, nonresident: full-time $23,950. *Financial support:* In 2013–14, 7 students received support, including 2 fellowships, 4 research assistantships with partial tuition reimbursements available, 3 teaching assistantships with full tuition reimbursements available; career-related internships or fieldwork, scholarships/grants, health care benefits, and unspecified assistantships also available. Financial award application

deadline: 3/1. *Faculty research:* Advertising and public relations management, leadership, ethics, public opinion, political communication, advertising media, social and digital media, international communication, creativity, consumer privacy, crisis communication, disaster communication, sports communication, advertising and public relations history. *Unit head:* Dr. Joseph Edward Phelps, Professor and Chairman, 205-348-8646, E-mail: phelps@apr.ua.edu. *Application contact:* Dr. Lance Kinney, Associate Professor, 205-348-7706, E-mail: kinney@apr.ua.edu.
Website: http://www.apr.ua.edu.

University of Denver, University College, Denver, CO 80208. Offers arts and culture (MLS, Certificate), including art, literature, and culture, arts development and program management (Certificate), creative writing; environmental policy and management (MAS, Certificate), including energy and sustainability (Certificate), environmental assessment of nuclear power (Certificate), environmental health and safety (Certificate), environmental management, natural resource management (Certificate); geographic information systems (MAS, Certificate); global affairs (MLS, Certificate), including translation studies, world history and culture; healthcare leadership (MPH, Certificate), including healthcare policy, law, and ethics, medical and healthcare information technologies, strategic management of healthcare; information and communications technology (MCIS, Certificate), including database design and administration (Certificate), geographic information systems (MCIS), information security systems security (Certificate), information systems security (MCIS), project management (MCIS, MPS, Certificate), software design and administration (Certificate), software design and programming (MCIS), technology management, telecommunications technology (MCIS), Web design and development; leadership and organizations (MPS, Certificate), including human capital in organizations, philanthropic leadership, project management (MCIS, MPS, Certificate), strategic innovation and change; organizational and professional communication (MPS, Certificate), including alternative dispute resolution, organizational communication, organizational development and training, public relations and marketing; security management (MAS, Certificate), including emergency planning and response, information security (MAS), organizational security; strategic human resource management (MPS, Certificate), including global human resources (MPS), human resource management and development (MPS). Part-time and evening/weekend programs available. Postbaccalaureate distance learning degree programs offered (no on-campus study). *Faculty:* 139 part-time/adjunct (61 women). *Students:* 49 full-time (16 women), 1,297 part-time (732 women); includes 272 minority (92 Black or African American, non-Hispanic/Latino; 5 American Indian or Alaska Native, non-Hispanic/Latino; 30 Asian, non-Hispanic/Latino; 114 Hispanic/Latino; 3 Native Hawaiian or other Pacific Islander, non-Hispanic/Latino; 28 Two or more races, non-Hispanic/Latino), 92 international. Average age 35. 542 applicants, 95% accepted, 362 enrolled. In 2013, 374 master's, 128 other advanced degrees awarded. *Degree requirements:* For master's, capstone project. *Entrance requirements:* For master's, transcripts, two letters of recommendation, personal statement, resume. Additional exam requirements/recommendations for international students: Required—TOEFL (minimum score 550 paper-based; 80 iBT). *Application deadline:* For fall admission, 7/18 priority date for domestic students, 5/2 priority date for international students; for winter admission, 10/24 priority date for domestic students, 9/19 priority date for international students; for spring admission, 2/1 for domestic students, 12/14 for international students; for summer admission, 4/18 priority date for domestic students, 3/7 priority date for international students. Applications are processed on a rolling basis. Application fee: $75. Electronic applications accepted. *Expenses:* Contact institution. *Financial support:* In 2013–14, 28 students received support. Applicants required to submit FAFSA. *Unit head:* Dr. Michael McGuire, Interim Dean, 303-871-3518, E-mail: mmcguire@du.edu. *Application contact:* Information Contact, 303-871-2291, E-mail: ucoladm@du.edu.
Website: http://www.universitycollege.du.edu/.

University of Florida, Graduate School, College of Journalism and Communications, Department of Advertising, Gainesville, FL 32611. Offers M Adv. *Faculty:* 6 full-time (4 women). *Students:* 8 full-time (4 women), 4 part-time (2 women); includes 15 minority (1 Black or African American, non-Hispanic/Latino; 12 American Indian or Alaska Native, non-Hispanic/Latino; 1 Asian, non-Hispanic/Latino; 1 Hispanic/Latino). Average age 26. 90 applicants, 32% accepted, 5 enrolled. In 2013, 7 master's awarded. *Degree requirements:* For master's, thesis or terminal project. *Entrance requirements:* For master's, GRE General Test, minimum GPA of 3.0. Additional exam requirements/recommendations for international students: Required—TOEFL (minimum score 550 paper-based; 80 iBT), IELTS (minimum score 6). *Application deadline:* For fall admission, 4/1 for domestic students, 1/30 for international students. Applications are processed on a rolling basis. Application fee: $30. Electronic applications accepted. *Expenses:* Tuition, state resident: full-time $12,640. Tuition, nonresident: full-time $30,000. *Financial support:* In 2013–14, 1 student received support, including 1 teaching assistantship (averaging $5,742 per year). Financial award applicants required to submit FAFSA. *Faculty research:* Branding, information flow between clients and suppliers, message and media strategies, emotional response. *Unit head:* Dr. Joseph R. Pisani, Professor and Interim Chair, 352-392-4046, E-mail: jpisani@jou.ufl.edu.
Website: http://www.jou.ufl.edu/academic/adv/.

University of Florida, Graduate School, College of Journalism and Communications, Department of Public Relations, Gainesville, FL 32611. Offers MAMC. *Entrance requirements:* For master's, GRE General Test, minimum GPA of 3.0. Additional exam requirements/recommendations for international students: Required—TOEFL (minimum score 550 paper-based; 80 iBT), IELTS (minimum score 6). *Application deadline:* For fall admission, 4/1 for domestic students, 1/30 for international students. Applications are processed on a rolling basis. Application fee: $30. *Expenses:* Tuition, state resident: full-time $12,640. Tuition, nonresident: full-time $30,000. *Financial support:* Applicants required to submit FAFSA. *Faculty research:* Social media/interactive media adoption and communication strategy; health and science communication, nonprofits, social marketing, public communications, and philanthropy; public relationships, partnerships and coalitions; strategic communication. *Unit head:* Juan C. Molleda, Chair, 352-273-1220, Fax: 352-392-1227, E-mail: jmolleda@jou.ufl.edu.
Website: http://www.jou.ufl.edu/academics/bachelors/public-relations/.

University of Houston, College of Liberal Arts and Social Sciences, School of Communication, Houston, TX 77204. Offers health communication (MA); mass communication studies (MA); public relations studies (MA); speech communication (MA). Part-time programs available. *Degree requirements:* For master's, comprehensive exam (for some programs), thesis (for some programs), 30-33 hours. *Entrance requirements:* For master's, GRE. Additional exam requirements/recommendations for international students: Required—TOEFL. Electronic applications accepted.

University of Illinois at Urbana–Champaign, Graduate College, College of Media, Department of Advertising, Champaign, IL 61820. Offers MS. *Students:* 19 (13 women). Application fee: $75 ($90 for international students). *Unit head:* Kevin R. Wise, Acting Head, 217-333-1602, Fax: 217-244-3348, E-mail: krwise@illinois.edu. *Application contact:* Janette Bradley Wright, Office Administrator, 217-333-1602, Fax: 217-244-3348, E-mail: wjbradle@illinois.edu.
Website: http://www.media.illinois.edu/advertising/.

University of Maryland, College Park, Academic Affairs, College of Arts and Humanities, Department of Communication, College Park, MD 20742. Offers MA, PhD. *Faculty:* 40 full-time (26 women), 5 part-time/adjunct (3 women). *Students:* 77 full-time (60 women), 4 part-time (3 women); includes 17 minority (5 Black or African American, non-Hispanic/Latino; 7 Asian, non-Hispanic/Latino; 5 Hispanic/Latino), 22 international. 135 applicants, 35% accepted, 41 enrolled. In 2013, 13 doctorates awarded. *Degree requirements:* For master's, thesis optional; for doctorate, comprehensive exam, thesis/dissertation. *Entrance requirements:* For master's, GRE General Test, minimum GPA of 3.0, sample of scholarly writing, 3 letters of recommendation, statement of goals and experiences; for doctorate, GRE General Test. Additional exam requirements/recommendations for international students: Required—TOEFL. *Application deadline:* For fall admission, 12/1 for domestic and international students. Applications are processed on a rolling basis. Application fee: $75. Electronic applications accepted. *Expenses:* Tuition, state resident: full-time $10,314; part-time $573 per credit hour. Tuition, nonresident: full-time $22,248; part-time $1236 per credit. *Required fees:* $1446; $403.15 per semester. Tuition and fees vary according to program. *Financial support:* In 2013–14, 9 fellowships with full tuition reimbursements (averaging $16,058 per year), 34 teaching assistantships (averaging $16,848 per year) were awarded; Federal Work-Study, scholarships/grants, and unspecified assistantships also available. Support available to part-time students. Financial award applicants required to submit FAFSA. *Faculty research:* Health communication, interpersonal communication, persuasion, intercultural communication, contemporary rhetoric theory. *Total annual research expenditures:* $62,616. *Unit head:* Dr. Elizabeth L. Toth, Chair, 301-405-0870, Fax: 301-314-9471, E-mail: eltoth@umd.edu. *Application contact:* Dr. Charles A. Caramello, Dean of Graduate School, 301-405-0358, Fax: 301-314-9305.
Website: http://www.comm.umd.edu/.

University of Miami, Graduate School, School of Communication, Coral Gables, FL 33124. Offers communication (PhD); communication studies (MA); film studies (MA, PhD); motion pictures (MFA), including production, producing, and screenwriting; print journalism (MA); public relations (MA); Spanish language journalism (MA); television broadcast journalism (MA). Part-time programs available. *Degree requirements:* For master's, comprehensive exam (for some programs), thesis (for some programs); for doctorate, comprehensive exam, thesis/dissertation. *Entrance requirements:* For master's, GRE General Test; for doctorate, GRE General Test, master's thesis or scholarly research. Additional exam requirements/recommendations for international students: Required—TOEFL (minimum score 600 paper-based; 100 iBT). Electronic applications accepted. *Faculty research:* Communication studies, mass communication, international/interpersonal communication, film studies, journalism.

University of Nebraska–Lincoln, Graduate College, College of Arts and Sciences, Department of Communication Studies, Lincoln, NE 68588. Offers instructional communication (MA, PhD); interpersonal communication (MA, PhD); marketing, communication studies, and advertising (MA, PhD); organizational communication (MA, PhD); rhetoric and culture (MA, PhD). *Degree requirements:* For master's, thesis optional; for doctorate, comprehensive exam, thesis/dissertation. *Entrance requirements:* For master's and doctorate, GRE General Test, writing sample. Additional exam requirements/recommendations for international students: Required—TOEFL (minimum score 600 paper-based). Electronic applications accepted. *Faculty research:* Message strategies, gender communication, political communication, organizational communication, instructional communication.

University of Nebraska–Lincoln, Graduate College, College of Journalism and Mass Communications, Lincoln, NE 68588. Offers marketing, communication and advertising (MA); professional journalism (MA). Postbaccalaureate distance learning degree programs offered (no on-campus study). *Degree requirements:* For master's, thesis. *Entrance requirements:* For master's, samples of work. Additional exam requirements/recommendations for international students: Required—TOEFL (minimum score 600 paper-based). Electronic applications accepted. *Faculty research:* Interactive media and the Internet, community newspapers, children's radio, advertising involvement, telecommunications policy.

The University of North Carolina at Charlotte, The Graduate School, College of Liberal Arts and Sciences, Department of Communication Studies, Charlotte, NC 28223-0001. Offers communication studies (Graduate Certificate); health communication (MA); organizational communication (MA); public relations and international public relations (MA); rhetoric, media studies, and popular culture (MA). Part-time and evening/weekend programs available. *Faculty:* 11 full-time (5 women). *Students:* 6 full-time (5 women), 18 part-time (15 women); includes 3 minority (2 Black or African American, non-Hispanic/Latino; 1 Hispanic/Latino), 3 international. Average age 29. 39 applicants, 62% accepted, 10 enrolled. In 2013, 15 master's awarded. Terminal master's awarded for partial completion of doctoral program. *Degree requirements:* For master's, project, thesis, or comprehensive exam. *Entrance requirements:* For master's, GRE General Test, minimum GPA of 2.75 overall. Additional exam requirements/recommendations for international students: Required—TOEFL (minimum score 557 paper-based; 83 iBT). *Application deadline:* For fall admission, 3/1 for domestic and international students; for spring admission, 11/15 for domestic students, 10/1 for international students. Application fee: $75. Electronic applications accepted. *Expenses:* Tuition, state resident: full-time $3522. Tuition, nonresident: full-time $16,051. *Required fees:* $2585. Tuition and fees vary according to course load and program. *Financial support:* In 2013–14, 9 students received support, including 9 teaching assistantships (averaging $15,446 per year); career-related internships or fieldwork, institutionally sponsored loans, scholarships/grants, and unspecified assistantships also available. Support available to part-time students. Financial award application deadline: 4/1; financial award applicants required to submit FAFSA. *Faculty research:* Rhetorical approaches to analyzing public relations controversies, participant empowerment and engagement in Community-Based Participatory Action Research, human factors constraining the management of knowledge in a large financial services organization, models of Internet governance, race and class politics of mediated sports. *Unit head:* Dr. Shawn Long, Chair, 704-687-0783, Fax: 704-687-6900, E-mail: shawn.long@uncc.edu. *Application contact:* Kathy B. Giddings, Director of Graduate Admissions, 704-687-5503, Fax: 704-687-1668, E-mail: gradadm@uncc.edu.
Website: http://gradcomm.uncc.edu/.

University of North Texas, Robert B. Toulouse School of Graduate Studies, Denton, TN 76203-5017. Offers accounting (MS, PhD); applied anthropology (MA, MS); applied behavior analysis (Certificate); applied technology and performance improvement (M Ed, MS, PhD); art education (MA, PhD); art history (MA); art museum education (Certificate); arts leadership (Certificate); audiology (Au D); behavior analysis (MS); biochemistry and molecular biology (MS, PhD); biology (MA, MS, PhD); business (PhD); business computer information systems (PhD); chemistry (MS, PhD); clinical psychology (PhD); communication studies (MA, MS); computer engineering (MS); computer science (MS); computer science and engineering (PhD); counseling (M Ed, MS, PhD), including clinical mental health counseling (MS), college and university counseling (M Ed, MS), elementary school counseling (M Ed, MS), secondary school counseling (M Ed, MS); counseling psychology (PhD); creative writing (MA); criminal justice (MS); curriculum and instruction (M Ed, PhD), including curriculum studies (PhD), early childhood studies (PhD), language and literacy studies (PhD); decision sciences (MBA); design (MA, MFA), including fashion design (MFA), innovation studies, interior design (MFA); early childhood studies (MS); economics (MS); educational leadership (M Ed, Ed D, PhD);

educational psychology (MS), including family studies, gifted and talented (MS, PhD), human development, learning and cognition, research, measurement and evaluation; educational research (PhD), including gifted and talented (MS, PhD), human development and family studies, psychological aspects of sports and exercise, research, measurement and statistics; electrical engineering (MS); emergency management (MPA); engineering systems (MS); English (MA, PhD); environmental science (MS, PhD); experimental psychology (PhD); finance (MBA, MS, PhD); financial management (MPA); French (MA); health psychology and behavioral medicine (PhD); health services management (MBA); higher education (M Ed, Ed D, PhD); history (MA, MS, PhD), including European history (PhD), military history (PhD), United States history (PhD); hospitality management (MS); human resources management (MPA); information science (MS, PhD); information technologies (MBA); information technology and decision sciences (MS); interdisciplinary studies (MA, MS); international sustainable tourism (MS); jazz studies (MM); journalism (MA, MJ, Graduate Certificate), including interactive and virtual digital communication (Graduate Certificate), narrative journalism (Graduate Certificate), public relations (Graduate Certificate); kinesiology (MS); learning technologies (MS, PhD); library science (MS); local government management (MPA); logistics and supply chain management (MBA, PhD); long-term care, senior housing, and aging services (MA, MS); management science (PhD); marketing (MBA, PhD); materials science and engineering (MS, PhD); mathematics (MA, PhD); merchandising (MS); music (MA, MM Ed, PhD), including ethnomusicology (MA), music education (MM Ed, PhD), music theory (MA, PhD), musicology (MA, PhD), performance (MA); nonprofit management (MPA); operations and supply chain management (MBA); performance (MM, DMA); philosophy (MA, PhD); physics (MS, PhD); political science (MA, MS, PhD); public administration and management (PhD), including emergency management, nonprofit management, public financial management, urban management; radio, television and film (MA, MFA); recreation, event and sport management (MS); rehabilitation counseling (MS, Certificate); sociology (MA, MS, PhD); Spanish (MA); special education (M Ed, PhD), including autism intervention (PhD), emotional/behavioral disorders (PhD), mild/moderate disabilities (PhD); speech-language pathology (MA, MS); strategic management (MBA); studio art (MFA); taxation (MS); teaching (M Ed); MBA/MS; MS/MPH; MSES/MBA. Part-time and evening/weekend programs available. Postbaccalaureate distance learning degree programs offered. *Faculty:* 661 full-time (213 women), 240 part-time/adjunct (144 women). *Students:* 3,106 full-time (1,620 women), 3,543 part-time (2,221 women); includes 1,740 minority (533 Black or African American, non-Hispanic/Latino; 15 American Indian or Alaska Native, non-Hispanic/Latino; 286 Asian, non-Hispanic/Latino; 746 Hispanic/Latino; 3 Native Hawaiian or other Pacific Islander, non-Hispanic/Latino; 157 Two or more races, non-Hispanic/Latino), 1,145 international. Average age 32. 6,289 applicants, 43% accepted, 1751 enrolled. In 2013, 1,778 master's, 239 doctorates, 10 other advanced degrees awarded. Terminal master's awarded for partial completion of doctoral program. *Degree requirements:* For master's, variable foreign language requirement, comprehensive exam (for some programs), thesis (for some programs); for doctorate, variable foreign language requirement, comprehensive exam (for some programs), thesis/dissertation; for other advanced degree, variable foreign language requirement, comprehensive exam (for some programs). *Entrance requirements:* For master's and doctorate, GRE, GMAT. Additional exam requirements/recommendations for international students: Required—TOEFL (minimum score 550 paper-based; 79 iBT). *Application deadline:* For fall admission, 7/15 for domestic students, 3/15 for international students; for spring admission, 11/15 for domestic students, 9/15 for international students; for summer admission, 5/1 for domestic students. Applications are processed on a rolling basis. Application fee: $60. Electronic applications accepted. *Financial support:* Fellowships with partial tuition reimbursements, research assistantships with partial tuition reimbursements, teaching assistantships, career-related internships or fieldwork, Federal Work-Study, institutionally sponsored loans, scholarships/grants, health care benefits, and library assistantships available. Support available to part-time students. Financial award applicants required to submit FAFSA. *Unit head:* Mark Wardell, Dean, 940-565-2383, E-mail: mark.wardell@unt.edu. *Application contact:* Toulouse School of Graduate Studies, 940-565-2383, Fax: 940-565-2141, E-mail: gradsch@unt.edu.
Website: http://tsgs.unt.edu/.

University of Saint Mary, Graduate Programs, Program in Business Administration, Leavenworth, KS 66048-5082. Offers enterprise risk management (MBA); finance (MBA); general management (MBA); health care management (MBA); human resource management (MBA); marketing and advertising management (MBA). Part-time and evening/weekend programs available. Postbaccalaureate distance learning degree programs offered (no on-campus study). *Students:* 151 full-time (87 women), 61 part-time (39 women); includes 60 minority (38 Black or African American, non-Hispanic/Latino; 1 American Indian or Alaska Native, non-Hispanic/Latino; 10 Asian, non-Hispanic/Latino; 11 Hispanic/Latino). *Degree requirements:* For master's, thesis. *Entrance requirements:* For master's, minimum undergraduate GPA of 2.75, official transcripts, two letters of recommendation. *Application deadline:* Applications are processed on a rolling basis. Application fee: $25. *Expenses: Tuition:* Part-time $550 per credit hour. *Unit head:* Rick Gunter, Director, 913-319-3007. *Application contact:* Patrick Smith, Coordinator of Business Programs, 913-319-3007, E-mail: smithp@stmary.edu.

University of Southern California, Graduate School, Annenberg School for Communication and Journalism, School of Journalism, Program in Strategic Public Relations, Los Angeles, CA 90089. Offers MA. Part-time and evening/weekend programs available. *Students:* 132 full-time, 7 part-time; includes 37 minority (7 Black or African American, non-Hispanic/Latino; 2 American Indian or Alaska Native, non-Hispanic/Latino; 9 Asian, non-Hispanic/Latino; 13 Hispanic/Latino; 6 Two or more races, non-Hispanic/Latino), 52 international. Average age 24. 196 applicants, 59% accepted, 58 enrolled. In 2013, 66 master's awarded. *Degree requirements:* For master's, comprehensive exam, thesis optional. *Entrance requirements:* For master's, GRE General Test, resume, writing samples, letters of recommendation, statement of purpose. Additional exam requirements/recommendations for international students: Required—TOEFL (minimum score 114 iBT) or IELTS (minimum score 8). *Application deadline:* For fall admission, 1/2 priority date for domestic students, 12/1 priority date for international students. Application fee: $85. Electronic applications accepted. *Financial support:* In 2013–14, 2 fellowships with full tuition reimbursements (averaging $74,208 per year), 2 teaching assistantships with tuition reimbursements (averaging $74,208 per year) were awarded; career-related internships or fieldwork, Federal Work-Study, scholarships/grants, and health care benefits also available. Support available to part-time students. Financial award application deadline: 1/2; financial award applicants required to submit FAFSA. *Unit head:* Jerry Swerling, Director, 213-821-1275, E-mail: swerling@usc.edu. *Application contact:* Allyson Hill, Associate Dean for Admissions, 213-821-0770, Fax: 213-740-1933, E-mail: ascadm@usc.edu.
Website: http://www.annenberg.usc.edu/.

University of Southern Mississippi, Graduate School, College of Arts and Letters, School of Mass Communication and Journalism, Hattiesburg, MS 39406-0001. Offers mass communication (MA, MS, PhD); public relations (MS). Part-time programs available. *Faculty:* 10 full-time (3 women), 1 part-time/adjunct (0 women). *Students:* 32 full-time (16 women), 26 part-time (16 women); includes 9 minority (6 Black or African American, non-Hispanic/Latino; 1 Hispanic/Latino; 2 Two or more races, non-Hispanic/Latino), 7 international. Average age 35. 33 applicants, 70% accepted, 11 enrolled. In 2013, 17 master's, 10 doctorates awarded. *Degree requirements:* For master's, comprehensive exam, thesis optional; for doctorate, comprehensive exam, thesis/dissertation. *Entrance requirements:* For master's, GRE General Test, minimum GPA of 3.0 in field of study, 2.75 in last 2 years; for doctorate, GRE General Test, minimum GPA of 3.5. Additional exam requirements/recommendations for international students: Required—TOEFL, IELTS. *Application deadline:* For fall admission, 3/1 priority date for domestic students, 3/1 for international students; for spring admission, 1/10 priority date for domestic and international students. Applications are processed on a rolling basis. Application fee: $50. *Financial support:* In 2013–14, 18 students received support, including 12 teaching assistantships with full tuition reimbursements available (averaging $8,000 per year); fellowships with full tuition reimbursements available, research assistantships with full tuition reimbursements available, career-related internships or fieldwork, Federal Work-Study, institutionally sponsored loans, scholarships/grants, health care benefits, and unspecified assistantships also available. Financial award application deadline: 3/15; financial award applicants required to submit FAFSA. *Unit head:* Dr. Christopher Campbell, Director, 601-266-5650, Fax: 601-266-4263. *Application contact:* Dr. Fei Xue, Graduate Coordinator, 601-266-5652, Fax: 601-266-6473, E-mail: fei.xue@usm.edu.
Website: http://www.usm.edu/mcj.

The University of Tennessee, Graduate School, College of Communication and Information, Knoxville, TN 37996. Offers advertising (MS, PhD); broadcasting (MS, PhD); communications (MS, PhD); information sciences (MS, PhD); journalism (MS, PhD); public relations (MS, PhD); speech communication (MS, PhD). Part-time and evening/weekend programs available. Postbaccalaureate distance learning degree programs offered (no on-campus study). *Degree requirements:* For master's, thesis or alternative; for doctorate, thesis/dissertation. *Entrance requirements:* For master's and doctorate, GRE General Test, minimum GPA of 2.7. Additional exam requirements/recommendations for international students: Required—TOEFL. Electronic applications accepted. *Expenses:* Tuition, state resident: full-time $9540; part-time $531 per credit hour. Tuition, nonresident: full-time $27,728; part-time $1542 per credit hour. *Required fees:* $1404; $67 per credit hour.

The University of Texas at Austin, Graduate School, College of Communication, Department of Advertising, Austin, TX 78712-1111. Offers MA, PhD. *Entrance requirements:* For master's and doctorate, GRE General Test. Electronic applications accepted. *Faculty research:* Interactive advertising, advertising laws and ethics, advertising creativity, media planning and modeling, international advertising.

The University of Texas–Pan American, College of Arts and Humanities, Department of Communication, Edinburg, TX 78539. Offers communication (MA); communication training and consulting (Graduate Certificate); strategic communication and media relations (Graduate Certificate); theatre (MA). *Accreditation:* NAST. Part-time and evening/weekend programs available. *Degree requirements:* For master's, comprehensive exam, thesis or alternative. *Entrance requirements:* For master's, minimum GPA of 3.0. Additional exam requirements/recommendations for international students: Required—TOEFL. *Expenses:* Tuition, state resident: full-time $5986; part-time $333 per credit hour. Tuition, nonresident: full-time $12,358; part-time $687 per credit hour. *Required fees:* $782. Tuition and fees vary according to program. *Faculty research:* Rhetorical theory, intercultural and mass communication, American theatre, multicultural theatre and drama, television and film.

University of the Sacred Heart, Graduate Programs, Department of Communication, Program in Public Relations, San Juan, PR 00914-0383. Offers MA. Part-time and evening/weekend programs available. *Degree requirements:* For master's, thesis. *Entrance requirements:* For master's, EXADEP, minimum undergraduate GPA of 2.75, interview.

University of Wisconsin–Stevens Point, College of Fine Arts and Communication, Division of Communication, Stevens Point, WI 54481-3897. Offers interpersonal communication (MA); media studies (MA); organizational communication (MA); public relations (MA). Part-time programs available. *Degree requirements:* For master's, thesis or alternative. *Entrance requirements:* For master's, GRE. Additional exam requirements/recommendations for international students: Required—TOEFL (minimum score 575 paper-based). *Faculty research:* Communication theory and research, film history.

Virginia Commonwealth University, Graduate School, College of Humanities and Sciences, School of Mass Communications, Brandcenter, Richmond, VA 23284-9005. Offers art direction (MS); communication strategy (MS); copywriting (MS); creative brand management (MS); creative media planning (MS). *Degree requirements:* For master's, comprehensive exam, thesis optional. *Entrance requirements:* For master's, GRE or GMAT, interview, portfolio. Additional exam requirements/recommendations for international students: Required—TOEFL (minimum score 600 paper-based; 100 iBT); Recommended—IELTS (minimum score 6.5). Electronic applications accepted. *Faculty research:* Art direction, copywriting, communications strategy, creative brand management, creative technology.

Virginia Commonwealth University, Graduate School, College of Humanities and Sciences, School of Mass Communications, Program in Mass Communications, Richmond, VA 23284-9005. Offers multimedia journalism (MS); strategic public relations (MS). *Degree requirements:* For master's, comprehensive exam, thesis optional. *Entrance requirements:* For master's, GRE General Test. Additional exam requirements/recommendations for international students: Required—TOEFL (minimum score 600 paper-based; 100 iBT); Recommended—IELTS (minimum score 6.5). Electronic applications accepted. *Faculty research:* Multimedia journalism, strategic public relations.

Wayne State University, College of Fine, Performing and Communication Arts, Department of Communication, Detroit, MI 48202. Offers communication (PhD); communication and new media (Graduate Certificate); communication studies (MA); dispute resolution (MADR, Graduate Certificate); health communication (Graduate Certificate); journalism (MA); media arts (MA); media studies (MA); public relations and organizational communication (MA); JD/MADR. PhD program admits students for fall session only (application deadline 1/15). *Students:* 62 full-time (39 women), 84 part-time (57 women); includes 40 minority (27 Black or African American, non-Hispanic/Latino; 4 Asian, non-Hispanic/Latino; 7 Hispanic/Latino; 2 Two or more races, non-Hispanic/Latino), 14 international. Average age 34. 144 applicants, 31% accepted, 34 enrolled. In 2013, 39 master's, 6 doctorates, 14 other advanced degrees awarded. *Degree requirements:* For master's, thesis or essay; for doctorate, thesis/dissertation. *Entrance requirements:* For master's, GRE (for MA applicants with undergraduate GPA less than 3.2), BA or BS in communication or related field with minimum upper-division GPA of 3.2, sample of academic writing, and personal statement (for MA); admittance to Graduate School, minimum upper-division undergraduate GPA of 3.0, personal statement, and 3 letters of recommendation (for MADR); for doctorate, GRE, MA in communication or related field with minimum GPA of 3.5, three letters of recommendation; personal statement; sample of written scholarship. Additional exam requirements/recommendations for international students: Required—TOEFL (minimum score 600 paper-based; 100 iBT), IELTS (minimum score 6.5), TWE (minimum score 6).

Advertising and Public Relations

Application deadline: For fall admission, 8/1 for domestic and international students; for winter admission, 11/1 for domestic and international students; for spring admission, 4/1 for domestic and international students. Application fee: $0. Electronic applications accepted. *Expenses:* Contact institution. *Financial support:* In 2013–14, 40 students received support, including 6 fellowships with tuition reimbursements available (averaging $14,660 per year), 21 teaching assistantships with tuition reimbursements available (averaging $15,506 per year); research assistantships with tuition reimbursements available, career-related internships or fieldwork, scholarships/grants, and unspecified assistantships also available. Financial award application deadline: 3/31; financial award applicants required to submit FAFSA. *Faculty research:* Rhetorical theory and criticism; mass media theory and research; argumentation; organizational communication; risk and crisis communication; interpersonal, family, and health communication. *Total annual research expenditures:* $30,725. *Unit head:* Dr. Lee Wilikins, Chair, 313-577-2943, E-mail: eh8899@wayne.edu. Website: http://comm.wayne.edu/.

Webster University, School of Communications, Program in Advertising and Marketing Communications, St. Louis, MO 63119-3194. Offers MA. *Expenses: Tuition:* Full-time $11,610; part-time $645 per credit hour. Tuition and fees vary according to campus/location and program.

Webster University, School of Communications, Program in Public Relations, St. Louis, MO 63119-3194. Offers MA. *Expenses: Tuition:* Full-time $11,610; part-time $645 per credit hour. Tuition and fees vary according to campus/location and program.

Western New England University, College of Arts and Sciences, Program in Communication, Springfield, MA 01119. Offers public relations (MA). Part-time and evening/weekend programs available. *Faculty:* 5 full-time (4 women), 8 part-time/adjunct (5 women). *Students:* 10 part-time (9 women). Average age 36. 19 applicants. *Degree requirements:* For master's, independent study or thesis. *Entrance requirements:* For master's, official transcript, personal statement, resume, three letters of recommendation. Additional exam requirements/recommendations for international students: Required—TOEFL. *Application deadline:* Applications are processed on a rolling basis. Application fee: $30. Electronic applications accepted. Tuition and fees vary according to program. *Financial support:* Application deadline: 4/15; applicants required to submit FAFSA. *Unit head:* Dr. Saeed Ghahramani, Dean, 413-782-1218, Fax: 413-796-2118, E-mail: sghahram@wne.edu. *Application contact:* Matthew Fox, Director of Recruiting and Marketing for Adult Learners, 413-782-1517, Fax: 413-782-1777, E-mail: study@wne.edu.

William Woods University, Graduate and Adult Studies, Fulton, MO 65251-1098. Offers administration (M Ed, Ed S); athletic/activities administration (M Ed); curriculum and instruction (M Ed, Ed S); educational leadership (Ed D); equestrian education (M Ed); health management (MBA); human resources (MBA); leadership (MBA); marketing, advertising, and public relations (MBA); teaching and technology (M Ed). Part-time and evening/weekend programs available. *Faculty:* 231 part-time/adjunct (87 women). *Students:* 418 full-time (276 women), 716 part-time (433 women); includes 51 minority (34 Black or African American, non-Hispanic/Latino; 4 American Indian or Alaska Native, non-Hispanic/Latino; 5 Asian, non-Hispanic/Latino; 3 Hispanic/Latino; 5 Two or more races, non-Hispanic/Latino), 4 international. Average age 35. In 2013, 507 master's, 8 doctorates, 143 other advanced degrees awarded. *Degree requirements:* For master's, capstone course (MBA), action research (M Ed); for Ed S, field experience. *Entrance requirements:* Additional exam requirements/recommendations for international students: Required—TOEFL (minimum score 550 paper-based). *Application deadline:* Applications are processed on a rolling basis. Application fee: $0. Electronic applications accepted. *Expenses:* Contact institution. *Financial support:* Institutionally sponsored loans available. Financial award applicants required to submit FAFSA. *Unit head:* Dr. Michael Westerfield, Vice President and Dean of the Graduate College, 573-592-4383, Fax: 573-592-1164. *Application contact:* Jessica Brush, Director of Operations, 573-592-4227, Fax: 573-592-1164, E-mail: jessica.brush@williamwoods.ede.
Website: http://www.williamwoods.edu/evening_programs/index.asp.

Section 4
Electronic Commerce

This section contains a directory of institutions offering graduate work in electronic commerce. Additional information about programs listed in the directory but not augmented by an in-depth entry may be obtained by writing directly to the dean of a graduate school or chair of a department at the address given in the directory.

CONTENTS

Program Directory
Electronic Commerce   316

Display and Close-Up

See:

Adelphi University—Business Administration and
   Management   70, 181

Electronic Commerce

Adelphi University, Robert B. Willumstad School of Business, MBA Program, Garden City, NY 11530-0701. Offers finance (MBA); management information systems (MBA); management/human resource management (MBA); marketing/e-commerce (MBA). *Accreditation:* AACSB. Part-time and evening/weekend programs available. *Students:* 254 full-time (129 women), 118 part-time (63 women); includes 60 minority (13 Black or African American, non-Hispanic/Latino; 18 Asian, non-Hispanic/Latino; 28 Hispanic/Latino; 1 Native Hawaiian or other Pacific Islander, non-Hispanic/Latino; 200 international. Average age 28. In 2013, 182 master's awarded. *Degree requirements:* For master's, capstone course. *Entrance requirements:* For master's, GMAT, 2 letters of recommendation. Additional exam requirements/recommendations for international students: Required—TOEFL (minimum score 550 paper-based; 80 iBT). *Application deadline:* For fall admission, 4/1 for international students; for spring admission, 11/1 for international students. Applications are processed on a rolling basis. Application fee: $50. Electronic applications accepted. *Expenses: Tuition:* Full-time $32,530; part-time $1010 per credit. *Required fees:* $1150. Tuition and fees vary according to degree level and program. *Financial support:* Research assistantships with partial tuition reimbursements, career-related internships or fieldwork, Federal Work-Study, institutionally sponsored loans, scholarships/grants, tuition waivers (partial), and unspecified assistantships available. Financial award application deadline: 3/1; financial award applicants required to submit FAFSA. *Faculty research:* Supply chain management, distribution channels, productivity benchmark analysis, data envelopment analysis, financial portfolio analysis. *Unit head:* Dr. Rakesh Gupta, Associate Dean, 516-877-4629. *Application contact:* Christine Murphy, Director of Admissions, 516-877-3050, Fax: 516-877-3039, E-mail: graduateadmissions@adelphi.edu. Website: http://business.adelphi.edu/degree-programs/graduate-degree-programs/m-b-a/.

See Display on page 70 and Close-Up on page 181.

Boston University, Metropolitan College, Department of Administrative Sciences, Boston, MA 02215. Offers banking and financial management (MSM); business continuity in emergency management (MSM); economics development and tourism management (MSAS); electronic commerce, systems, and technology (MSAS); financial economics (MSAS); innovation and technology (MSAS); insurance management (MSM); international market management (MSM); multinational commerce (MSAS); project management (MS). *Accreditation:* AACSB. Part-time and evening/weekend programs available. Postbaccalaureate distance learning degree programs offered (no on-campus study). *Faculty:* 15 full-time (3 women), 22 part-time/adjunct (3 women). *Students:* 177 full-time (85 women), 560 part-time (293 women); includes 89 minority (31 Black or African American, non-Hispanic/Latino; 31 Asian, non-Hispanic/Latino; 25 Hispanic/Latino; 2 Two or more races, non-Hispanic/Latino), 242 international. Average age 31. 509 applicants, 71% accepted, 222 enrolled. In 2013, 158 master's awarded. *Degree requirements:* For master's, thesis optional. *Entrance requirements:* For master's, 1 year of work experience, minimum GPA of 3.0. Additional exam requirements/recommendations for international students: Required—TOEFL (minimum score 84 iBT). *Application deadline:* Applications are processed on a rolling basis. Application fee: $80. Electronic applications accepted. *Expenses: Tuition:* Full-time $43,970; part-time $1374 per credit hour. *Required fees:* $60 per semester. Tuition and fees vary according to class time, course level and program. *Financial support:* In 2013–14, 15 students received support, including 7 research assistantships (averaging $8,400 per year); career-related internships or fieldwork, Federal Work-Study, and unspecified assistantships also available. *Faculty research:* International business, innovative process. *Unit head:* Dr. Kip Becker, Chairman, 617-353-3016, E-mail: adminsc@bu.edu. *Application contact:* Fiona Niven, Administrative Sciences Department, 617-353-3016, E-mail: adminsc@bu.edu. Website: http://www.bu.edu/met/academic-community/departments/administrative-sciences/.

California State University, Fullerton, Graduate Studies, College of Business and Economics, Department of Information Systems and Decision Sciences, Fullerton, CA 92834-9480. Offers decision science (MBA); information systems (MBA, MS); information systems and decision sciences (MS); information systems and e-commerce (MS); information technology (MS). Part-time programs available. *Students:* 28 full-time (12 women), 74 part-time (17 women); includes 50 minority (4 Black or African American, non-Hispanic/Latino; 27 Asian, non-Hispanic/Latino; 15 Hispanic/Latino; 4 Two or more races, non-Hispanic/Latino), 22 international. Average age 31. 146 applicants, 55% accepted, 42 enrolled. In 2013, 26 master's awarded. *Degree requirements:* For master's, project or thesis. *Entrance requirements:* For master's, GMAT, minimum AACSB index of 950. Application fee: $55. *Financial support:* Career-related internships or fieldwork, Federal Work-Study, institutionally sponsored loans, and scholarships/grants available. Support available to part-time students. Financial award application deadline: 3/1; financial award applicants required to submit FAFSA. *Unit head:* Dr. Bhushan Kapoor, Chair, 657-278-2221. *Application contact:* Admissions/Applications, 657-278-2371. Website: http://business.fullerton.edu/isds/.

Carnegie Mellon University, Tepper School of Business and School of Computer Science, Program in Electronic Commerce, Pittsburgh, PA 15213-3891. Offers MS. *Entrance requirements:* For master's, GRE General Test or GMAT. Additional exam requirements/recommendations for international students: Required—TOEFL.

Claremont Graduate University, Graduate Programs, Center for Information Systems and Technology, Claremont, CA 91711-6160. Offers electronic commerce (MS, PhD); health information management (MS); information systems (Certificate); knowledge management (MS, PhD); systems development (MS, PhD); telecommunications and networking (MS, PhD); MBA/MS. Part-time programs available. *Faculty:* 6 full-time (1 woman). *Students:* 52 full-time (21 women), 62 part-time (18 women); includes 27 minority (9 Black or African American, non-Hispanic/Latino; 14 Asian, non-Hispanic/Latino; 4 Hispanic/Latino), 49 international. Average age 38. In 2013, 14 master's, 1 doctorate awarded. *Degree requirements:* For doctorate, comprehensive exam, thesis/dissertation, portfolio. *Entrance requirements:* For master's and doctorate, GMAT, GRE General Test. Additional exam requirements/recommendations for international students: Required—TOEFL (minimum score 550 paper-based; 80 iBT). *Application deadline:* For fall admission, 2/1 priority date for domestic and international students. Applications are processed on a rolling basis. Application fee: $80. Electronic applications accepted. *Expenses: Tuition:* Full-time $40,560; part-time $1690 per credit. *Required fees:* $275 per semester. Tuition and fees vary according to program. *Financial support:* Fellowships, research assistantships, teaching assistantships, Federal Work-Study, institutionally sponsored loans, and scholarships/grants available. Support available to part-time students. Financial award application deadline: 2/15; financial award applicants required to submit FAFSA. *Faculty research:* Man-machine

interaction, organizational aspects of computing, implementation of information systems, information systems practice. *Unit head:* Tom Horan, Dean, 909-607-9302, Fax: 909-621-8564, E-mail: tom.horan@cgu.edu. *Application contact:* Leah Litwack, CISAT/Kay Center Administrative Assistant, 909-621-8209, E-mail: leah.litwack@cgu.edu. Website: http://www.cgu.edu/pages/153.asp.

Dalhousie University, Faculty of Computer Science, Halifax, NS B3H 1W5, Canada. Offers computational biology and bioinformatics (M Sc); computer science (MA Sc, MC Sc, PhD); electronic commerce (MEC); health informatics (MHI). *Degree requirements:* For master's, thesis (for some programs); for doctorate, thesis/dissertation. *Entrance requirements:* Additional exam requirements/recommendations for international students: Required—1 of 5 approved tests: TOEFL, IELTS, CANTEST, CAEL, Michigan English Language Assessment Battery. Electronic applications accepted.

DePaul University, College of Computing and Digital Media, Chicago, IL 60604. Offers animation (MA, MFA); business information technology (MS); cinema (MFA); cinema production (MS); computational finance (MS); computer and information sciences (PhD); computer game development (MS); computer information and network security (MS); computer science (MS); e-commerce technology (MS); health informatics (MS); human-computer interaction (MS); information systems (MS); information technology project management (MS); network engineering and management (MS); predictive analytics (MS); screenwriting (MFA); software engineering (MS); JD/MS. Part-time and evening/weekend programs available. Postbaccalaureate distance learning degree programs offered (no on-campus study). *Faculty:* 77 full-time (28 women), 44 part-time/adjunct (7 women). *Students:* 1,063 full-time (329 women), 877 part-time (248 women); includes 631 minority (240 Black or African American, non-Hispanic/Latino; 2 American Indian or Alaska Native, non-Hispanic/Latino; 186 Asian, non-Hispanic/Latino; 143 Hispanic/Latino; 9 Native Hawaiian or other Pacific Islander, non-Hispanic/Latino; 51 Two or more races, non-Hispanic/Latino), 288 international. Average age 32. In 2013, 511 master's, 3 doctorates awarded. *Degree requirements:* For master's, thesis (for some programs); for doctorate, comprehensive exam, thesis/dissertation. *Entrance requirements:* For master's, GRE or GMAT (for MS in computational finance only), bachelor's degree, resume (MS in predictive analytics only), IT experience (MS in information technology project management only), portfolio review (all MFA programs and MA in animation); for doctorate, GRE, master's degree in computer science. Additional exam requirements/recommendations for international students: Required—TOEFL (minimum score 590 paper-based; 80 iBT), IELTS (minimum score 6.5), PTE (minimum score 53). *Application deadline:* For fall admission, 8/1 priority date for domestic students, 6/15 priority date for international students; for winter admission, 12/1 priority date for domestic students, 10/15 priority date for international students; for spring admission, 3/1 priority date for domestic students, 1/15 priority date for international students; for summer admission, 5/1 for domestic students, 4/15 for international students. Applications are processed on a rolling basis. Application fee: $25. Electronic applications accepted. *Expenses:* Contact institution. *Financial support:* In 2013–14, 102 students received support, including 3 fellowships with full tuition reimbursements available (averaging $30,000 per year), 5 research assistantships with full and partial tuition reimbursements available (averaging $20,400 per year), 94 teaching assistantships with full and partial tuition reimbursements available (averaging $4,334 per year); Federal Work-Study, scholarships/grants, tuition waivers (full and partial), and unspecified assistantships also available. Support available to part-time students. Financial award application deadline: 4/20; financial award applicants required to submit FAFSA. *Faculty research:* Data mining, computer science, human-computer interaction, security, animation and film. *Total annual research expenditures:* $3.6 million. *Unit head:* Elly Kafritsas-Wessels, Senior Administrative Assistant, 312-362-5816, Fax: 312-362-5185, E-mail: ekafrits@cdm.depaul.edu. *Application contact:* Office of Admission, 312-362-8714, E-mail: admission@cdm.depaul.edu. Website: http://cdm.depaul.edu.

Eastern Michigan University, Graduate School, College of Business, Department of Marketing, Ypsilanti, MI 48197. Offers e-business (MBA); integrated marketing communications (MS); international business (MBA); marketing management (MBA); supply chain management (MBA). Part-time and evening/weekend programs available. Postbaccalaureate distance learning degree programs offered (minimal on-campus study). *Faculty:* 15 full-time (8 women). *Students:* 25 full-time (20 women), 41 part-time (34 women); includes 16 minority (9 Black or African American, non-Hispanic/Latino; 1 Asian, non-Hispanic/Latino; 1 Hispanic/Latino; 5 Two or more races, non-Hispanic/Latino), 1 international. Average age 34. 41 applicants, 71% accepted, 16 enrolled. In 2013, 28 master's awarded. *Entrance requirements:* For master's, GMAT. Additional exam requirements/recommendations for international students: Required—TOEFL. *Application deadline:* For fall admission, 5/15 priority date for domestic and international students; for winter admission, 10/15 priority date for domestic and international students; for spring admission, 3/15 priority date for domestic and international students. Applications are processed on a rolling basis. Application fee: $35. *Expenses:* Tuition, state resident: full-time $12,300; part-time $466 per credit hour. Tuition, nonresident: full-time $23,159; part-time $918 per credit hour. *Required fees:* $71 per credit hour. $46 per semester. One-time fee: $100. Tuition and fees vary according to course level and degree level. *Financial support:* Fellowships, research assistantships with full tuition reimbursements, teaching assistantships with full tuition reimbursements, career-related internships or fieldwork, Federal Work-Study, institutionally sponsored loans, scholarships/grants, tuition waivers (partial), and unspecified assistantships available. Support available to part-time students. Financial award applicants required to submit FAFSA. *Unit head:* Dr. Paul Chao, Department Head, 734-487-3323, Fax: 734-487-7099, E-mail: pchao@emich.edu. *Application contact:* K. Michelle Henry, Director, Academic Services, 734-487-4444, Fax: 734-483-1316, E-mail: mhenry1@emich.edu. Website: http://www.mkt.emich.edu/index.html.

Eastern Michigan University, Graduate School, College of Business, Programs in Business Administration, Ypsilanti, MI 48197. Offers business administration (MBA, Graduate Certificate); computer information systems (Graduate Certificate); e-business (MBA, Graduate Certificate); enterprise business intelligence (MBA); entrepreneurship (MBA, Graduate Certificate); finance (MBA, Graduate Certificate); human resources (MBA); human resources management (Graduate Certificate); information systems (MBA); internal auditing (MBA); international business (MBA, Graduate Certificate); marketing management (Graduate Certificate); nonprofit management (MBA); organizational development (Graduate Certificate); supply chain management (MBA, Graduate Certificate). *Accreditation:* AACSB. Part-time programs available. Postbaccalaureate distance learning degree programs offered (no on-campus study). *Students:* 74 full-time (28 women), 342 part-time (183 women); includes 122 minority (84 Black or African American, non-Hispanic/Latino; 2 American Indian or Alaska Native, non-Hispanic/Latino; 19 Asian, non-Hispanic/Latino; 7 Hispanic/Latino; 10 Two or more

races, non-Hispanic/Latino), 38 international. Average age 33. 305 applicants, 72% accepted, 131 enrolled. In 2013, 69 master's, 57 other advanced degrees awarded. *Entrance requirements:* For master's, GMAT (minimum score 450), minimum cumulative undergraduate GPA of 2.75. Additional exam requirements/recommendations for international students: Required—TOEFL. *Application deadline:* For fall admission, 5/15 for domestic students, 5/1 for international students; for winter admission, 10/15 for domestic students, 10/1 for international students; for spring admission, 3/15 for domestic students, 3/1 for international students. Applications are processed on a rolling basis. Application fee: $35. *Expenses:* Tuition, state resident: full-time $12,300; part-time $466 per credit hour. Tuition, nonresident: full-time $23,159; part-time $918 per credit hour. *Required fees:* $71 per credit hour. $46 per semester. One-time fee: $100. Tuition and fees vary according to course level and degree level. *Financial support:* Fellowships, research assistantships with full tuition reimbursements, teaching assistantships with full tuition reimbursements, career-related internships or fieldwork, Federal Work-Study, institutionally sponsored loans, scholarships/grants, tuition waivers (partial), and unspecified assistantships available. Support available to part-time students. Financial award applicants required to submit FAFSA. *Unit head:* K. Michelle Henry, Director, Academic Services, 734-487-4444, Fax: 734-483-1316, E-mail: mhenry1@emich.edu. *Application contact:* Beste Windes, Advisor, 734-487-4444, Fax: 734-483-1316, E-mail: bwindes@emich.edu.
Website: http://www.emich.edu/public/cob/gr/grad.html.

Fairleigh Dickinson University, Metropolitan Campus, University College: Arts, Sciences, and Professional Studies, School of Computer Sciences and Engineering, Program in E-Commerce, Teaneck, NJ 07666-1914. Offers MS.

Florida Institute of Technology, Graduate Programs, Extended Studies Division, Melbourne, FL 32901-6975. Offers acquisition and contract management (MS); aerospace engineering (MS); business administration (MBA, DBA); computer information systems (MS); computer science (MS); electrical engineering (MS); engineering management (MS); human resources management (MS); logistics management (MS), including humanitarian and disaster relief logistics; management (MS), including acquisition and contract management, e-business, human resources management, information systems, logistics management, management, transportation management; material acquisition management (MS); mechanical engineering (MS); operations research (MS); project management (MS), including information systems, operations research; public administration (MPA); quality management (MS); software engineering (MS); space systems (MS); space systems management (MS); supply chain management (MS); systems management (MS), including information systems, operations research; technology management (MS). Part-time and evening/weekend programs available. Postbaccalaureate distance learning degree programs offered (no on-campus study). *Faculty:* 8 full-time (1 woman), 96 part-time/adjunct (25 women). *Students:* 94 full-time (46 women), 912 part-time (397 women); includes 436 minority (290 Black or African American, non-Hispanic/Latino; 18 American Indian or Alaska Native, non-Hispanic/Latino; 38 Asian, non-Hispanic/Latino; 62 Hispanic/Latino; 2 Native Hawaiian or other Pacific Islander, non-Hispanic/Latino; 26 Two or more races, non-Hispanic/Latino), 9 international. Average age 37. 591 applicants, 44% accepted, 220 enrolled. In 2013, 522 master's awarded. *Degree requirements:* For master's, comprehensive exam (for some programs), capstone course. *Entrance requirements:* For master's, GMAT or resume showing 8 years of supervised experience, minimum GPA of 3.0, 2 letters of recommendation, resume. Additional exam requirements/recommendations for international students: Required—TOEFL (minimum score 550 paper-based; 79 iBT). *Application deadline:* For fall admission, 4/1 for international students; for spring admission, 9/30 for international students. Applications are processed on a rolling basis. Electronic applications accepted. *Expenses:* Contact institution. *Financial support:* Application deadline: 3/1; applicants required to submit FAFSA. *Unit head:* Dr. Theodore R. Richardson, III, Senior Associate Dean, 321-674-8123, Fax: 321-674-7597, E-mail: trichardson@fit.edu. *Application contact:* Carolyn Farrior, Director of Graduate Admissions, Online Learning and Off-Campus Programs, 321-674-7118, Fax: 321-674-8216, E-mail: cfarrior@fit.edu.
Website: http://es.fit.edu.

Florida Institute of Technology, Graduate Programs, Nathan M. Bisk College of Business, Online Programs, Melbourne, FL 32901-6975. Offers accounting (MBA); accounting and finance (MBA); business administration (MBA); finance (MBA); healthcare management (MBA); information assurance and cybersecurity (MS); information technology (MS); information technology cybersecurity (MS); information technology management (MBA); international business (MBA); Internet marketing (MBA); management (MBA); marketing (MBA); project management (MBA); supply chain management (MS). Part-time and evening/weekend programs available. Postbaccalaureate distance learning degree programs offered (no on-campus study). *Faculty:* 3 full-time (1 woman), 41 part-time/adjunct (13 women). *Students:* 6 full-time (1 woman), 1,121 part-time (530 women); includes 424 minority (276 Black or African American, non-Hispanic/Latino; 10 American Indian or Alaska Native, non-Hispanic/Latino; 45 Asian, non-Hispanic/Latino; 88 Hispanic/Latino; 5 Native Hawaiian or other Pacific Islander, non-Hispanic/Latino), 32 international. Average age 36. 348 applicants, 42% accepted, 146 enrolled. In 2013, 475 master's awarded. *Entrance requirements:* For master's, GMAT or resume showing 8 years of supervised experience, 2 letters of recommendation, resume, competency in math past college algebra. Additional exam requirements/recommendations for international students: Required—TOEFL (minimum score 550 paper-based; 79 iBT). *Application deadline:* For fall admission, 4/1 for international students; for spring admission, 9/30 for international students. Applications are processed on a rolling basis. Electronic applications accepted. *Expenses:* Contact institution. *Financial support:* Available to part-time students. Application deadline: 3/1; applicants required to submit FAFSA. *Unit head:* Brian Ehrlich, Associate Vice President/Director of Online Learning, 321-674-8202, E-mail: behrlich@fit.edu. *Application contact:* Carolyn Farrior, Director of Graduate Admissions, Online Learning and Off-Campus Programs, 321-674-7118.
Website: http://online.fit.edu.

George Mason University, Volgenau School of Engineering, Department of Computer Science, Fairfax, VA 22030. Offers computer networking (Certificate); computer science (MS, PhD); e-commerce (Certificate); foundations of information systems (Certificate); information engineering (Certificate); information security and assurance (MS, Certificate); information systems (MS); software architecture (Certificate); software engineering (MS, Certificate); software engineering for C41 (Certificate); Web-based software engineering (Certificate). MS program offered jointly with Old Dominion University, University of Virginia, Virginia Commonwealth University, and Virginia Polytechnic Institute and State University. *Faculty:* 46 full-time (10 women), 13 part-time/adjunct (0 women). *Students:* 230 full-time (63 women), 303 part-time (57 women); includes 100 minority (15 Black or African American, non-Hispanic/Latino; 66 Asian, non-Hispanic/Latino; 14 Hispanic/Latino; 5 Two or more races, non-Hispanic/Latino), 215 international. Average age 30. 977 applicants, 49% accepted, 152 enrolled. In 2013, 183 master's, 8 doctorates, 26 other advanced degrees awarded. *Degree requirements:* For master's, thesis optional; for doctorate, comprehensive exam, thesis/dissertation. *Entrance requirements:* For master's, GRE, proof of financial support; 2 official college transcripts; resume; self-evaluation form; official bank statement; photocopy of passport; 3 letters of recommendation; baccalaureate degree related to computer science; minimum GPA of 3.0 in last 2 years of undergraduate work; 1 year beyond 1st-year calculus; personal goals statement; for doctorate, GRE, personal goals statement; 2 official copies of transcripts; self-evaluation form; 3 letters of recommendation; photocopy of passport; proof of financial support; official bank statement; resume; 4-year baccalaureate degree with strong background in computer science. Additional exam requirements/recommendations for international students: Required—TOEFL (minimum score 575 paper-based; 88 iBT), IELTS (minimum score 6.5), PTE. *Application deadline:* For fall admission, 1/15 priority date for domestic students; for spring admission, 8/15 priority date for domestic students. Application fee: $65 ($80 for international students). Electronic applications accepted. *Expenses:* Contact institution. *Financial support:* In 2013–14, 109 students received support, including 3 fellowships (averaging $5,267 per year), 53 research assistantships (averaging $16,866 per year), 56 teaching assistantships (averaging $13,625 per year); career-related internships or fieldwork, Federal Work-Study, scholarships/grants, unspecified assistantships, and health care benefits (for full-time research or teaching assistantship recipients) also available. Support available to part-time students. Financial award application deadline: 3/1; financial award applicants required to submit FAFSA. *Faculty research:* Artificial intelligence, image processing/graphics, parallel/distributed systems, software engineering systems. *Total annual research expenditures:* $2.8 million. *Unit head:* Sanjeev Setia, Chair, 703-993-4098, Fax: 703-993-1710, E-mail: setia@gmu.edu. *Application contact:* Michele Pieper, Office Manager, 703-993-9483, Fax: 703-993-1710, E-mail: mpieper@gmu.edu.
Website: http://cs.gmu.edu/.

Georgia Institute of Technology, Graduate Studies and Research, College of Management, Program in Business Administration, Atlanta, GA 30332-0001. Offers accounting (MBA); e-commerce (Certificate); engineering entrepreneurship (MBA); entrepreneurship (Certificate); finance (MBA); information technology management (MBA); international business (MBA, Certificate); management of technology (Certificate); marketing (MBA); operations management (MBA); organizational behavior (MBA); strategic management (MBA). *Accreditation:* AACSB.

Hawai`i Pacific University, College of Business Administration, Honolulu, HI 96813. Offers accounting/CPA (MBA); e-business (MBA); economics (MBA); finance (MBA); healthcare management (MBA); human resource management (MA, MBA); information systems (MBA, MSIS); international business (MBA); management (MBA); marketing (MBA); organizational change (MA, MBA); travel industry management (MBA). Part-time and evening/weekend programs available. *Faculty:* 22 full-time (9 women), 6 part-time/adjunct (0 women). *Students:* 232 full-time (100 women), 174 part-time (84 women); includes 241 minority (18 Black or African American, non-Hispanic/Latino; 112 Asian, non-Hispanic/Latino; 33 Hispanic/Latino; 11 Native Hawaiian or other Pacific Islander, non-Hispanic/Latino; 67 Two or more races, non-Hispanic/Latino). Average age 31. 240 applicants, 81% accepted, 102 enrolled. In 2013, 206 master's awarded. *Degree requirements:* For master's, thesis. *Entrance requirements:* For master's, GMAT. Additional exam requirements/recommendations for international students: Recommended—TOEFL (minimum score 550 paper-based; 80 iBT), TWE (minimum score 5). *Application deadline:* For fall admission, 2/15 priority date for domestic students; for spring admission, 10/15 priority date for domestic students. Applications are processed on a rolling basis. Application fee: $50. Electronic applications accepted. *Financial support:* In 2013–14, 90 students received support. Research assistantships, career-related internships or fieldwork, Federal Work-Study, scholarships/grants, tuition waivers, and unspecified assistantships available. Financial award application deadline: 3/1; financial award applicants required to submit FAFSA. *Faculty research:* Statistical control process as used by management, studies in comparative cross-cultural management styles, not-for-profit management. *Unit head:* Dr. Deborah Crown, Dean, 808-544-0275, Fax: 808-544-0283, E-mail: dcrown@hpu.edu. *Application contact:* Rumi Yoshida, Associate Director of Graduate Admissions, 808-543-8034, Fax: 808-544-0280, E-mail: grad@hpu.edu.
Website: http://www.hpu.edu/CBA/Graduate/index.html.

HEC Montreal, School of Business Administration, Graduate Diplomas Programs in Administration, Program in E-Business, Montréal, QC H3T 2A7, Canada. Offers Graduate Diploma. All courses are given in French. *Students:* 17 full-time (8 women), 44 part-time (22 women). 43 applicants, 60% accepted, 18 enrolled. In 2013, 13 Graduate Diplomas awarded. *Degree requirements:* For Graduate Diploma, one foreign language. *Entrance requirements:* For degree, bachelor's degree in administration or equivalent. *Application deadline:* For fall admission, 4/15 for domestic and international students; for winter admission, 9/15 for domestic and international students. Application fee: $83 Canadian dollars. Electronic applications accepted. *Expenses: Tuition, area resident:* Part-time $74.14 per credit. Tuition, state resident: full-time $2669.04; part-time $201.83 per credit. Tuition, nonresident: full-time $7266; part-time $500.59 per credit. *International tuition:* $18,021.24 full-time. *Required fees:* $1529.70; $36.20 per credit. $65.50 per term. Tuition and fees vary according to degree level and program. *Financial support:* In 2013–14, 1,007 students received support. Research assistantships, teaching assistantships, and scholarships/grants available. Financial award application deadline: 9/2. *Unit head:* Silvia Ponce, Director, 514-340-6393, Fax: 514-340-6915, E-mail: silvia.ponce@hec.ca. *Application contact:* Jo Anne Audet, Administrative Director, 514-340-1315, Fax: 514-340-6411, E-mail: joanne.audet@hec.ca.
Website: http://www.hec.ca/programmes_formations/des/dess/dess_affaires_electroniques/index.html.

HEC Montreal, School of Business Administration, Master of Science Programs in Administration, Program in Electronic Commerce, Montréal, QC H3T 2A7, Canada. Offers M Sc. Program offered jointly with University of Montreal. *Students:* 22 full-time (14 women), 24 part-time (14 women). 32 applicants, 63% accepted, 16 enrolled. In 2013, 25 master's awarded. *Degree requirements:* For master's, one foreign language. *Entrance requirements:* For master's, bachelor's degree in law, management, information systems or related field. *Application deadline:* For fall admission, 4/1 for domestic and international students. Application fee: $83 Canadian dollars. Electronic applications accepted. *Expenses: Tuition, area resident:* Part-time $74.14 per credit. Tuition, state resident: full-time $2669.04; part-time $201.83 per credit. Tuition, nonresident: full-time $7266; part-time $500.59 per credit. *International tuition:* $18,021.24 full-time. *Required fees:* $1529.70; $36.20 per credit. $65.50 per term. Tuition and fees vary according to degree level and program. *Financial support:* In 2013–14, 1,007 students received support. Research assistantships, teaching assistantships, and scholarships/grants available. Financial award application deadline: 9/2. *Unit head:* Silvia Ponce, Co-Director, 514-340-6393, Fax: 514-340-6915, E-mail: silvia.ponce@hec.ca. *Application contact:* Jo Anne Audet, Administrative Director, 514-340-1315, Fax: 514-340-6411, E-mail: joanne.audet@hec.ca.
Website: http://www.hec.ca/programmes_formations/des/maitrises_professionnelles/maitrise_commerce_electronique/index.html.

Instituto Tecnológico y de Estudios Superiores de Monterrey, Campus Central de Veracruz, Graduate Programs, Córdoba, Mexico. Offers administration (MA); administration of information technologies (MTI); computer sciences (MCC); education (MEE); educational institution administration (MAD); educational technology (MTE); electronic commerce (MCE); finance (MAF); humanistic studies (MEH); international business for Latin America (MNL); marketing (MMT); science (MCP). Part-time and

evening/weekend programs available. Postbaccalaureate distance learning degree programs offered (minimal on-campus study). *Degree requirements:* For master's, thesis (for some programs). *Entrance requirements:* For master's, PAEP College Board. Electronic applications accepted.

Instituto Tecnológico y de Estudios Superiores de Monterrey, Campus Ciudad Juárez, Program in Electronic Commerce, Ciudad Juárez, Mexico. Offers MEC.

Instituto Tecnológico y de Estudios Superiores de Monterrey, Campus Estado de México, Professional and Graduate Division, Estado de Mexico, Mexico. Offers administration of information technologies (MITA); architecture (M Arch); business administration (GMBA, MBA); computer sciences (MCS, PhD); education (M Ed); educational institution administration (MAD); educational technology and innovation (PhD); electronic commerce (MEC); environmental systems (MS); finance (MAF); humanistic studies (MHS); information sciences and knowledge management (MISKM); information systems (MS); manufacturing systems (MS); marketing (MEM); quality systems and productivity (MS); science and materials engineering (PhD); telecommunications management (MTM). Part-time programs available. Postbaccalaureate distance learning degree programs offered (minimal on-campus study). *Degree requirements:* For master's, one foreign language, thesis (for some programs); for doctorate, one foreign language, thesis/dissertation. *Entrance requirements:* For master's, E-PAEP 500, interview; for doctorate, E-PAEP 500, research proposal. Additional exam requirements/recommendations for international students: Required—TOEFL (minimum score 550 paper-based). *Faculty research:* Surface treatments by plasmas, mechanical properties, robotics, graphical computing, mechatronics security protocols.

Instituto Tecnológico y de Estudios Superiores de Monterrey, Campus Irapuato, Graduate Programs, Irapuato, Mexico. Offers administration (MBA); administration of information technology (MAIT); administration of telecommunications (MAT); architecture (M Arch); computer science (MCS); education (M Ed); educational administration (MEA); educational innovation and technology (DEIT); educational technology (MET); electronic commerce (MBA); environmental administration and planning (MEAP); environmental systems (MES); finances (MBA); humanistic studies (MHS); international management for Latin American executives (MIMLAE); library and information science (MLIS); manufacturing quality management (MMQM); marketing research (MBA).

John Hancock University, MBA Program, Oakbrook Terrace, IL 60181. Offers e-commerce (MBA); finance (MBA); general business (MBA); global management (MBA); health care administration (MBA); leadership (MBA); management of information systems (MBA); marketing (MBA); professional accounting (MBA); project management (MBA); public accounting (MBA); risk management (MBA).

Lewis University, College of Business, Graduate School of Management, Program in Business Administration, Romeoville, IL 60446. Offers accounting (MBA); custom elective option (MBA); e-business (MBA); finance (MBA); healthcare management (MBA); human resources management (MBA); international business (MBA); management information systems (MBA); marketing (MBA); project management (MBA); technology and operations management (MBA). Part-time and evening/weekend programs available. *Students:* 115 full-time (55 women), 227 part-time (129 women); includes 128 minority (74 Black or African American, non-Hispanic/Latino; 1 American Indian or Alaska Native, non-Hispanic/Latino; 9 Asian, non-Hispanic/Latino; 40 Hispanic/Latino; 4 Two or more races, non-Hispanic/Latino), 10 international. Average age 31. In 2013, 99 master's awarded. *Entrance requirements:* For master's, interview, bachelor's degree, resume, 2 recommendations. Additional exam requirements/recommendations for international students: Required—TOEFL (minimum score 550 paper-based). *Application deadline:* For fall admission, 8/15 priority date for domestic students, 5/1 priority date for international students; for spring admission, 11/15 priority date for international students. Applications are processed on a rolling basis. Application fee: $40. Electronic applications accepted. *Financial support:* Career-related internships or fieldwork, Federal Work-Study, scholarships/grants, and unspecified assistantships available. Financial award application deadline: 5/1; financial award applicants required to submit FAFSA. *Unit head:* Dr. Maureen Culleeney, Academic Program Director, 815-838-0500 Ext. 5631, E-mail: culleema@lewisu.edu. *Application contact:* Michele Ryan, Director of Admission, 815-838-0500 Ext. 5384, E-mail: gsm@lewisu.edu.

New York University, Polytechnic School of Engineering, Department of Technology Management, New York, NY 10012-1019. Offers construction management (Advanced Certificate); electronic business management (Advanced Certificate); entrepreneurship (Advanced Certificate); human resources management (Advanced Certificate); industrial engineering (MS); information management (Advanced Certificate); management (MS); management of technology (MS); manufacturing engineering (MS); organizational behavior (MS, Advanced Certificate); project management (Advanced Certificate); technology management (MBA, PhD, Advanced Certificate); telecommunications management (Advanced Certificate). Part-time and evening/weekend programs available. *Faculty:* 7 full-time (1 woman), 41 part-time/adjunct (2 women). *Students:* 285 full-time (132 women), 116 part-time (45 women); includes 50 minority (10 Black or African American, non-Hispanic/Latino; 29 Asian, non-Hispanic/Latino; 11 Hispanic/Latino), 284 international. Average age 30. 726 applicants, 60% accepted, 140 enrolled. In 2013, 137 master's awarded. *Degree requirements:* For master's, comprehensive exam (for some programs), thesis (for some programs); for doctorate, comprehensive exam, thesis/dissertation. *Entrance requirements:* For master's, GMAT, minimum B average in undergraduate course work. Additional exam requirements/recommendations for international students: Required—TOEFL (minimum score 550 paper-based; 80 iBT); Recommended—IELTS (minimum score 6.5). *Application deadline:* For fall admission, 7/31 priority date for domestic students, 4/30 priority date for international students; for spring admission, 12/31 priority date for domestic students, 11/30 priority date for international students. Applications are processed on a rolling basis. Application fee: $75. Electronic applications accepted. *Expenses: Tuition:* Full-time $35,856; part-time $1494 per unit. *Required fees:* $1408; $64 per unit. $473 per term. Tuition and fees vary according to course load and program. *Financial support:* In 2013–14, 1 fellowship (averaging $26,400 per year) was awarded; research assistantships, teaching assistantships, institutionally sponsored loans, scholarships/grants, and unspecified assistantships also available. Support available to part-time students. *Faculty research:* Global innovation and research and development strategy, managing emerging technologies, technology and development, service design and innovation, tech entrepreneurship and commercialization, sustainable and clean-tech innovation, impacts of information technology upon individuals, organizations and society. *Total annual research expenditures:* $692,936. *Unit head:* Prof. Bharadwaj Rao, Head, 718-260-3617, Fax: 718-260-3874, E-mail: brao@poly.edu. *Application contact:* Raymond Lutzky, Director of Graduate Enrollment Management, 718-637-5984, Fax: 718-260-3624, E-mail: rlutzky@poly.edu.
Website: http://www.poly.edu/academics/departments/technology/.

North Dakota State University, College of Graduate and Interdisciplinary Studies, College of Science and Mathematics, Department of Computer Science, Fargo, ND 58108. Offers computer science (MS, PhD); digital enterprise (Certificate); operations research (MS); software engineering (MS, PhD, Certificate). Part-time programs available. *Faculty:* 15 full-time (5 women), 2 part-time/adjunct (1 woman). *Students:* 87 full-time (24 women), 114 part-time (31 women); includes 16 minority (3 Black or African American, non-Hispanic/Latino; 1 American Indian or Alaska Native, non-Hispanic/Latino; 6 Asian, non-Hispanic/Latino; 6 Two or more races, non-Hispanic/Latino), 152 international. Average age 31. 125 applicants, 70% accepted, 53 enrolled. In 2013, 66 master's, 8 doctorates awarded. *Degree requirements:* For master's, comprehensive exam, thesis optional; for doctorate, thesis/dissertation, qualifying exam. *Entrance requirements:* For master's, minimum GPA of 3.0, BS in computer science or related field; for doctorate, minimum GPA of 3.25, MS in computer science or related field. Additional exam requirements/recommendations for international students: Required—TOEFL (minimum score 550 paper-based; 79 iBT). *Application deadline:* For fall admission, 3/31 priority date for domestic students. Applications are processed on a rolling basis. Application fee: $35. Electronic applications accepted. *Financial support:* In 2013–14, 37 research assistantships with full tuition reimbursements (averaging $10,000 per year), 17 teaching assistantships with full tuition reimbursements (averaging $4,500 per year) were awarded; career-related internships or fieldwork, Federal Work-Study, institutionally sponsored loans, and tuition waivers (full) also available. Financial award application deadline: 4/15. *Faculty research:* Networking, software engineering, artificial intelligence, database, programming languages. *Unit head:* Dr. Brian Slator, Head, 701-231-8562, Fax: 701-231-8255. *Application contact:* Dr. Ken R. Nygard, Graduate Coordinator, 701-231-9460, Fax: 701-231-8255, E-mail: kendall.nygard@ndsu.edu.
Website: http://www.cs.ndsu.nodak.edu/.

Northwestern University, Medill School of Journalism, Media, and Integrated Marketing Communications, Integrated Marketing Communications Program, Evanston, IL 60208. Offers brand strategy (MSIMC); content marketing (MSIMC); direct and interactive marketing (MSIMC); marketing analytics (MSIMC); strategic communications (MSIMC). Part-time programs available. *Entrance requirements:* For master's, GRE General Test or GMAT, full-time work experience (preferred). Additional exam requirements/recommendations for international students: Required—TOEFL. Electronic applications accepted. *Faculty research:* Data mining, business to business marketing, values in advertising, political advertising.

Northwestern University, School of Professional Studies, Program in Predictive Analytics, Evanston, IL 60208. Offers computer-based data mining (MS); marketing analytics (MS); predictive modeling (MS); risk analytics (MS); Web analytics (MS). Postbaccalaureate distance learning degree programs offered. *Entrance requirements:* For master's, official transcripts, two letters of recommendation, statement of purpose, current resume or curriculum vitae. Additional exam requirements/recommendations for international students: Required—TOEFL (minimum score 600 paper-based; 100 iBT) or IELTS (minimum score 7).

Oklahoma Christian University, Graduate School of Business, Oklahoma City, OK 73136-1100. Offers accounting (MBA); electronic business (MBA); financial services (MBA); health services management (MBA); human resources (MBA); international business (MBA); leadership and organizational development (MBA); marketing (MBA); project management (MBA). Postbaccalaureate distance learning degree programs offered (no on-campus study). *Entrance requirements:* For master's, bachelor's degree. Electronic applications accepted.

Stevens Institute of Technology, Graduate School, Wesley J. Howe School of Technology Management, Program in Information Systems, Hoboken, NJ 07030. Offers computer science (MS); e-commerce (MS); enterprise systems (MS); entrepreneurial information technology (MS); information architecture (MS); information management (MS, Certificate); information security (MS); information technology in financial services industry (MS); information technology in the pharmaceutical industry (MS); information technology outsourcing management (MS); project management (MS, Certificate); software engineering (MS); telecommunications (MS). *Degree requirements:* For master's, thesis optional. *Entrance requirements:* For master's, GMAT, GRE General Test. Additional exam requirements/recommendations for international students: Required—TOEFL. Electronic applications accepted.

Towson University, Program in e-Business and Technology Management, Towson, MD 21252-0001. Offers project, program and portfolio management (Postbaccalaureate Certificate); supply chain management (MS, Postbaccalaureate Certificate). *Students:* 5 full-time (1 woman), 68 part-time (33 women); includes 16 minority (12 Black or African American, non-Hispanic/Latino; 2 Asian, non-Hispanic/Latino; 2 Hispanic/Latino), 6 international. *Entrance requirements:* For master's and Postbaccalaureate Certificate, GRE or GMAT, bachelor's degree in relevant field and/or three years of post-bachelor's experience working in supply chain related areas; minimum cumulative GPA of 3.0; resume; 1-2 page statement; 2 reference letters. Additional exam requirements/recommendations for international students: Required—TOEFL (minimum score 550 paper-based). *Application deadline:* Applications are processed on a rolling basis. Application fee: $45. Electronic applications accepted. *Unit head:* Dr. Tobin Porterfield, Director, 410-704-3265, E-mail: tporterfield@towson.edu. *Application contact:* Jennifer Bethke, Information Contact, 410-704-6004, E-mail: grads@towson.edu.

Universidad del Este, Graduate School, Carolina, PR 00984. Offers accounting (MBA); adult education (M Ed); agribusiness (MBA); criminal justice and criminology (MA); curriculum and instruction - early education (M Ed); curriculum and instruction - elementary (M Ed); curriculum and instruction - English (M Ed); curriculum and instruction - Spanish (M Ed); human resources (MBA); information security management (MBA); information technology and Web business development (MBA); management (MBA); public policy (MPA); social work (MA), including clinical social work; special education (M Ed); strategic leadership (MBA). *Students:* 464 full-time (322 women), 669 part-time (499 women); all minorities (all Hispanic/Latino). Average age 35. 693 applicants, 61% accepted, 332 enrolled. In 2013, 228 master's awarded. *Unit head:* Jose R. Clintron, Dean, 787-257-7373 Ext. 3007, E-mail: ue_jcintron@suagm.edu. *Application contact:* Clotilde Santiago, Director of Admissions, 787-257-7373 Ext. 3400, E-mail: ue_csantiago@suagm.edu.

Université de Montréal, Faculty of Arts and Sciences, Department of Computer Science and Operational Research, Montréal, QC H3C 3J7, Canada. Offers computer systems (M Sc, PhD); electronic commerce (M Sc). Part-time programs available. Terminal master's awarded for partial completion of doctoral program. *Degree requirements:* For master's, one foreign language, thesis; for doctorate, one foreign language, thesis/dissertation, general exam. *Entrance requirements:* For master's, B Sc in related field; for doctorate, MA or M Sc in related field. Electronic applications accepted. *Faculty research:* Optimization statistics, programming languages, telecommunications, theoretical computer science, artificial intelligence.

Université de Sherbrooke, Faculty of Administration, Program in E-Commerce, Sherbrooke, QC J1K 2R1, Canada. Offers M Sc. *Degree requirements:* For master's, one foreign language, thesis. *Entrance requirements:* For master's, bachelor's degree in related field, minimum GPA of 3.0 (on 4.3 scale), letters of reference, fluency in French. Electronic applications accepted. *Faculty research:* Radio frequency identification (RFID), Web value concept.

Université Laval, Faculty of Administrative Sciences, Programs in Business Administration, Québec, QC G1K 7P4, Canada. Offers accounting (MBA); agri-food management (MBA); electronic business (MBA, Diploma); factory management and

logistics (MBA); finance (MBA); firm management (MBA); geomatic management (MBA); information technology management (MBA); international management (MBA); management (MBA); management accounting (MBA, Diploma); marketing (MBA); modeling and organizational decision (MBA); occupational health and safety management (MBA); pharmacy management (MBA); social and environmental responsibility (MBA); technological entrepreneurship (Diploma). *Accreditation:* AACSB. Part-time and evening/weekend programs available. Postbaccalaureate distance learning degree programs offered (no on-campus study). *Entrance requirements:* For master's and Diploma, knowledge of French and English. Electronic applications accepted.

University at Buffalo, the State University of New York, Graduate School, College of Arts and Sciences, Department of Economics, Buffalo, NY 14260. Offers economics (MA, MS, PhD); financial economics (Certificate); health services (Certificate); information and Internet economics (Certificate); international economics (Certificate); law and regulation (Certificate); urban and regional economics (Certificate). Part-time programs available. Terminal master's awarded for partial completion of doctoral program. *Degree requirements:* For master's, comprehensive exam; for doctorate, comprehensive exam, thesis/dissertation, field and theory exams. *Entrance requirements:* For master's, GRE General Test or GMAT; for doctorate, GRE General Test. Additional exam requirements/recommendations for international students: Required—TOEFL (minimum score 550 paper-based; 79 iBT), TWE. Electronic applications accepted. *Faculty research:* Human capital, international economics, econometrics, applied economics, urban economics, economic growth and development.

The University of Akron, Graduate School, College of Business Administration, Department of Management, Akron, OH 44325. Offers global technological innovation (MBA); healthcare management (MBA); information systems management (MSM); leadership and organizational change (MBA); management (MBA); supply chain management (MBA); technological innovation (MSM); JD/MSM. *Accreditation:* AACSB. Part-time and evening/weekend programs available. *Faculty:* 19 full-time (4 women), 14 part-time/adjunct (3 women). *Students:* 55 full-time (23 women), 102 part-time (34 women); includes 13 minority (3 Black or African American, non-Hispanic/Latino; 7 Asian, non-Hispanic/Latino; 2 Hispanic/Latino; 1 Two or more races, non-Hispanic/Latino), 40 international. Average age 30. 102 applicants, 66% accepted, 41 enrolled. In 2013, 52 master's awarded. *Entrance requirements:* For master's, GMAT, minimum GPA of 2.75, two letters of recommendation, statement of purpose, resume. Additional exam requirements/recommendations for international students: Required—TOEFL (minimum score 550 paper-based; 79 iBT). *Application deadline:* For fall admission, 7/15 for domestic and international students; for spring admission, 11/15 for domestic and international students. Application fee: $40 ($60 for international students). Electronic applications accepted. *Expenses:* Tuition, state resident: full-time $7430; part-time $412.80 per credit hour. Tuition, nonresident: full-time $12,722; part-time $706.80 per credit hour. *Required fees:* $53 per credit hour. $12 per semester. Tuition and fees vary according to course load and program. *Financial support:* In 2013–14, 32 teaching assistantships with full tuition reimbursements were awarded; career-related internships or fieldwork and Federal Work-Study also available. *Faculty research:* Human resource management, innovation, entrepreneurship, technology management and technology transfer, artificial intelligence and belief functions. *Total annual research expenditures:* $48,868. *Unit head:* Dr. Steve Ash, Interim Chair, 330-972-6086, E-mail: ash@uakron.edu. *Application contact:* Dr. William Hauser, Director of Graduate Business Programs, 330-972-7043, Fax: 330-972-6588, E-mail: whauser@uakron.edu. Website: http://www.uakron.edu/cba/departments/management/.

University of Colorado Denver, Business School, Program in Marketing, Denver, CO 80217. Offers brand management and marketing communication (MS); global marketing (MS); high-tech and entrepreneurial marketing (MS); Internet marketing (MS); marketing for sustainability (MS); marketing research (MS); sports and entertainment marketing (MS). Part-time and evening/weekend programs available. *Students:* 36 full-time (15 women), 12 part-time (4 women); includes 3 minority (1 Asian, non-Hispanic/Latino; 1 Hispanic/Latino; 1 Two or more races, non-Hispanic/Latino), 11 international. Average age 29. 47 applicants, 55% accepted, 11 enrolled. In 2013, 20 master's awarded. *Degree requirements:* For master's, 30 semester hours (21 of marketing core courses, 9 of marketing electives). *Entrance requirements:* For master's, GMAT, resume, essay, two letters of recommendation, financial statements (for international applicants). Additional exam requirements/recommendations for international students: Required—TOEFL (minimum score 537 paper-based; 75 iBT); Recommended—IELTS (minimum score 6.5). *Application deadline:* For fall admission, 4/15 for domestic students, 3/15 for international students; for spring admission, 10/15 for domestic students, 9/15 for international students. Applications are processed on a rolling basis. Application fee: $50 ($75 for international students). Electronic applications accepted. *Expenses:* Contact institution. *Financial support:* In 2013–14, 7 students received support. Fellowships, research assistantships, teaching assistantships, Federal Work-Study, institutionally sponsored loans, scholarships/grants, and traineeships available. Financial award application deadline: 4/1; financial award applicants required to submit FAFSA. *Faculty research:* Marketing issues in the Chinese environment, impact of individual difference and contextual factors on the risk-taking behaviors of managers making new-business creation decisions, attribution theory perspective of conflict between marketers and engineers, organizational identity and identification, international market entry strategies. *Unit head:* Dr. David Forlani, Associate Professor/Director of Marketing Programs, 303-315-8420, E-mail: david.forlani@ucdenver.edu. *Application contact:* Shelly Townley, Admissions Director, Graduate Programs, 303-315-8202, E-mail: shelly.townley@ucdenver.edu. Website: http://www.ucdenver.edu/academics/colleges/business/degrees/ms/marketing/Pages/Marketing.aspx.

University of New Brunswick Saint John, Faculty of Business, Saint John, NB E2L 4L5, Canada. Offers administration (MBA); electronic commerce (MBA); international business (MBA); natural resource management (MBA). Part-time programs available. *Faculty:* 7 full-time (3 women), 2 part-time/adjunct (1 woman). *Students:* 72 full-time (28 women), 100 part-time (47 women). In 2013, 102 master's awarded. *Entrance requirements:* For master's, GMAT (minimum score of 550) or GRE (minimum 54th percentile), minimum GPA of 3.0. Additional exam requirements/recommendations for international students: Required—TOEFL (minimum score 580 paper-based; 93 iBT), TWE (minimum score 4.5). *Application deadline:* For fall admission, 5/31 for domestic students, 7/15 for international students. Application fee: $100. Electronic applications accepted. *Expenses:* Contact institution. *Financial support:* In 2013–14, 4 students received support. Career-related internships or fieldwork and scholarships/grants available. *Faculty research:* International business, project management, innovation and technology management; business use of Weblogs and podcasts to communicate; corporate governance; high-involvement work systems; international competitiveness; supply chain management and logistics. *Unit head:* Dr. Shelley Rinehart, Director of Graduate Studies, 506-648-5902, Fax: 506-648-5574, E-mail: rinehart@unb.ca. *Application contact:* Tammy Morin, Secretary, 506-648-5746, Fax: 506-648-5574, E-mail: tmorin@unbsj.ca. Website: http://go.unb.ca/gradprograms.

University of North Florida, Coggin College of Business, MBA Program, Jacksonville, FL 32224. Offers accounting (MBA); construction management (MBA); e-commerce (MBA); economics (MBA); finance (MBA); human resource management (MBA); international business (MBA); logistics (MBA); management applications (MBA). *Accreditation:* AACSB. Part-time and evening/weekend programs available. *Faculty:* 14 full-time (6 women), 1 part-time/adjunct (0 women). *Students:* 90 full-time (41 women), 231 part-time (84 women); includes 47 minority (18 Black or African American, non-Hispanic/Latino; 8 Asian, non-Hispanic/Latino; 16 Hispanic/Latino; 5 Two or more races, non-Hispanic/Latino), 29 international. Average age 29. 222 applicants, 47% accepted, 80 enrolled. In 2013, 152 master's awarded. *Entrance requirements:* For master's, GMAT or GRE, U.S. bachelor's degree from regionally-accredited university or equivalent foreign degree. Additional exam requirements/recommendations for international students: Required—TOEFL (minimum score 550 paper-based; 79 iBT). *Application deadline:* For fall admission, 7/1 priority date for domestic students, 5/1 for international students; for spring admission, 11/1 priority date for domestic students, 10/1 for international students. Application fee: $30. *Expenses:* Tuition, state resident: full-time $9794; part-time $408.10 per credit hour. Tuition, nonresident: full-time $22,383; part-time $932.61 per credit hour. *Required fees:* $2020; $84.20 per credit hour. Tuition and fees vary according to course load and program. *Financial support:* In 2013–14, 35 students received support, including 1 research assistantship (averaging $2,700 per year); teaching assistantships, Federal Work-Study, and tuition waivers (partial) also available. Support available to part-time students. Financial award application deadline: 4/1; financial award applicants required to submit FAFSA. *Faculty research:* Performance measures, costing, and inventory issues in logistics and supply chain management; inter-organizational systems; international management and marketing practices; e-commerce; organizational learning and socialization processes. *Total annual research expenditures:* $12,025. *Application contact:* Cheryl Campbell, Graduate Advisor, 904-620-2575, Fax: 904-620-2832, E-mail: ccampbell@unf.edu. Website: http://www.unf.edu/coggin/academics/graduate/mba.aspx.

University of Ottawa, Faculty of Graduate and Postdoctoral Studies, Interdisciplinary Programs, Ottawa, ON K1N 6N5, Canada. Offers e-business (Certificate); e-commerce (Certificate); finance (Certificate); health services and policies research (Diploma); population health (PhD); population health risk assessment and management (Certificate); public management and governance (Certificate); systems science (Certificate).

University of Ottawa, Faculty of Graduate and Postdoctoral Studies, Program in E-Business Technologies, Ottawa, ON K1N 6N5, Canada. Offers M Sc, MEBT. *Degree requirements:* For master's, thesis or alternative, project. *Entrance requirements:* For master's, honours degree or equivalent, minimum B average.

University of Phoenix–Austin Campus, School of Business, Austin, TX 78759. Offers accounting (MBA); business administration (MBA); business and management (MBA); e-business (MBA); global management (MBA); human resources management (MBA, MM); management (MM); marketing (MBA); public administration (MBA). Postbaccalaureate distance learning degree programs offered.

University of Phoenix–Chicago Campus, College of Information Systems and Technology, Schaumburg, IL 60173-4399. Offers e-business (MBA); information systems (MIS); management (MM); technology management (MBA). Evening/weekend programs available. *Degree requirements:* For master's, thesis (for some programs). *Entrance requirements:* For master's, 3 years of work experience, minimum undergraduate GPA of 3.0. Additional exam requirements/recommendations for international students: Required—TOEFL (minimum score 550 paper-based; 79 iBT). Electronic applications accepted.

University of Phoenix–Cincinnati Campus, College of Information Systems and Technology, West Chester, OH 45069-4875. Offers electronic business (MBA); information systems (MIS); technology management (MBA). Evening/weekend programs available. Postbaccalaureate distance learning degree programs offered. *Degree requirements:* For master's, thesis (for some programs). *Entrance requirements:* For master's, minimum undergraduate GPA of 2.5, 3 years of work experience. Additional exam requirements/recommendations for international students: Required—TOEFL (minimum score 550 paper-based; 79 iBT). Electronic applications accepted.

University of Phoenix–Columbus Georgia Campus, College of Information Systems and Technology, Columbus, GA 31909. Offers e-business (MBA); information systems (MIS); technology management (MBA). Evening/weekend programs available. Postbaccalaureate distance learning degree programs offered. *Degree requirements:* For master's, thesis (for some programs). *Entrance requirements:* For master's, minimum undergraduate GPA of 3.0, 3 years of work experience. Additional exam requirements/recommendations for international students: Required—TOEFL (minimum score 550 paper-based; 79 iBT). Electronic applications accepted.

University of Phoenix–Dallas Campus, College of Information Systems and Technology, Dallas, TX 75251. Offers e-business (MBA); information systems (MIS); technology management (MBA). Evening/weekend programs available. *Degree requirements:* For master's, thesis (for some programs). *Entrance requirements:* For master's, minimum undergraduate GPA of 3.0, 3 years of work experience. Additional exam requirements/recommendations for international students: Required—TOEFL (minimum score 550 paper-based; 79 iBT). Electronic applications accepted.

University of Phoenix–Denver Campus, College of Information Systems and Technology, Lone Tree, CO 80124-5453. Offers e-business (MBA); management (MIS); technology management (MBA). Evening/weekend programs available. Postbaccalaureate distance learning degree programs offered. *Degree requirements:* For master's, thesis (for some programs). *Entrance requirements:* For master's, minimum undergraduate GPA of 3.0, 3 years of work experience. Additional exam requirements/recommendations for international students: Required—TOEFL (minimum score 550 paper-based; 79 iBT). Electronic applications accepted.

University of Phoenix–Denver Campus, School of Business, Lone Tree, CO 80124-5453. Offers accountancy (MSA); accounting (MBA); business administration (MBA); e-business (MBA); global management (MBA); human resources management (MBA, MM); management (MM); marketing (MBA); public administration (MBA, MM). Evening/weekend programs available. Postbaccalaureate distance learning degree programs offered. *Degree requirements:* For master's, thesis (for some programs). *Entrance requirements:* For master's, minimum undergraduate GPA of 3.0, 3 years work experience. Additional exam requirements/recommendations for international students: Required—TOEFL (minimum score 550 paper-based; 79 iBT). Electronic applications accepted.

University of Phoenix–Houston Campus, College of Information Systems and Technology, Houston, TX 77079-2004. Offers e-business (MBA); information systems (MIS); technology management (MBA). Evening/weekend programs available. Postbaccalaureate distance learning degree programs offered. *Degree requirements:* For master's, comprehensive exam (for some programs), thesis. *Entrance requirements:* For master's, minimum undergraduate GPA of 3.0, 3 years of work experience. Additional exam requirements/recommendations for international students: Required—TOEFL (minimum score 550 paper-based; 79 iBT). Electronic applications accepted.

Electronic Commerce

University of Phoenix–Madison Campus, School of Business, Madison, WI 53718-2416. Offers accounting (MBA); business and management (MBA); e-business (MBA); global management (MBA); human resources management (MBA, MM); management (MM); marketing (MBA); public administration (MBA).

University of Phoenix–Memphis Campus, School of Business, Cordova, TN 38018. Offers accounting (MBA); business and management (MBA); e-business (MBA); global management (MBA); human resources management (MBA, MM); management (MM); marketing (MBA); public administration (MBA, MM).

University of Phoenix–New Mexico Campus, College of Information Systems and Technology, Albuquerque, NM 87113-1570. Offers e-business (MBA); information systems (MS); technology management (MBA). Evening/weekend programs available. *Degree requirements:* For master's, thesis (for some programs). *Entrance requirements:* For master's, minimum undergraduate GPA of 3.0, 3 years of work experience. Additional exam requirements/recommendations for international students: Required—TOEFL (minimum score 550 paper-based; 79 iBT). Electronic applications accepted.

University of Phoenix–Oklahoma City Campus, College of Information Systems and Technology, Oklahoma City, OK 73116-8244. Offers e-business (MBA); technology management (MBA). Evening/weekend programs available. *Degree requirements:* For master's, thesis (for some programs). *Entrance requirements:* For master's, minimum undergraduate GPA of 3.0, 3 years of work experience. Additional exam requirements/recommendations for international students: Required—TOEFL (minimum score 550 paper-based; 79 iBT). Electronic applications accepted.

University of Phoenix–Pittsburgh Campus, College of Information Systems and Technology, Pittsburgh, PA 15276. Offers e-business (MBA); information systems (MIS); technology management (MBA). Evening/weekend programs available. *Degree requirements:* For master's, thesis (for some programs). *Entrance requirements:* For master's, minimum undergraduate GPA of 3.0, 3 years work experience. Additional exam requirements/recommendations for international students: Required—TOEFL (minimum score 550 paper-based; 79 iBT). Electronic applications accepted.

University of Phoenix–San Antonio Campus, School of Business, San Antonio, TX 78230. Offers accounting (MBA); business administration (MBA); e-business (MBA); global management (MBA); human resources management (MBA, MM); management (MM); marketing (MBA); public administration (MBA, MM).

University of Rochester, Simon Business School, Full-Time Master's Program in Business Administration, Rochester, NY 14627. Offers accounting and information systems (MBA); business environment and public policy (MBA); business systems consulting (MBA); competitive and organizational strategy - pricing (MBA); computers and information systems (MBA); corporate accounting (MBA); electronic commerce (MBA); entrepreneurship (MBA); finance (MBA); health sciences management (MBA); international management (MBA); marketing - brand management and pricing (MBA); operations management - manufacturing (MBA); operations management - services (MBA); public accounting (MBA). *Accreditation:* AACSB. Part-time and evening/weekend programs available. *Faculty:* 60 full-time (11 women), 23 part-time/adjunct (3 women). *Students:* 282 full-time (74 women); includes 55 minority (29 Black or African American, non-Hispanic/Latino; 1 American Indian or Alaska Native, non-Hispanic/Latino; 11 Asian, non-Hispanic/Latino; 12 Hispanic/Latino; 2 Two or more races, non-Hispanic/Latino), 144 international. 673 applicants, 33% accepted, 65 enrolled. In 2013, 176 master's awarded. *Entrance requirements:* For master's, GMAT/GRE, previous course work in calculus. Additional exam requirements/recommendations for international students: Required—TOEFL. *Application deadline:* For fall admission, 10/15 for domestic and international students; for winter admission, 1/5 for domestic and international students; for spring admission, 3/15 for domestic and international students; for summer admission, 5/15 for domestic students. Applications are processed on a rolling basis. Application fee: $150. Electronic applications accepted. *Expenses: Tuition:* Full-time $44,580; part-time $1394 per credit hour. *Required fees:* $492. *Financial support:* In 2013–14, 72 students received support. Fellowships, research assistantships, teaching assistantships, institutionally sponsored loans, scholarships/grants, and tuition waivers (partial) available. Financial award application deadline: 3/1; financial award applicants required to submit CSS PROFILE or FAFSA. *Unit head:* Mark Zupan, Dean, 585-275-3316. *Application contact:* Rebekah S. Lewin, Assistant Dean of Admissions and Student Engagement, 585-275-3533, E-mail: admissions@simon.rochester.edu.

University of Rochester, Simon Business School, Part-Time MBA Program, Rochester, NY 14627. Offers accounting and information systems (MBA); business environment and public policy (MBA); business systems consulting (MBA); competitive and organizational strategy (MBA); computers and information systems (MBA); corporate accounting (MBA); electronic commerce (MBA); entrepreneurship (MBA); finance (MBA); health sciences management (MBA); international management (MBA); manufacturing management (MBA); marketing (MBA); operations management - services (MBA); public accounting (MBA). Part-time and evening/weekend programs available. *Faculty:* 59 full-time (10 women), 23 part-time/adjunct (3 women). *Students:* 270 part-time (75 women); includes 38 minority (5 Black or African American, non-Hispanic/Latino; 1 American Indian or Alaska Native, non-Hispanic/Latino; 24 Asian, non-Hispanic/Latino; 5 Hispanic/Latino; 3 Two or more races, non-Hispanic/Latino). Average age 32. 56 applicants, 98% accepted, 51 enrolled. In 2013, 77 master's awarded. *Entrance requirements:* For master's, GRE or GMAT, resume, recommendation letters, essays, transcipts. *Application deadline:* For fall admission, 8/15 for domestic students; for winter admission, 11/15 for domestic students; for spring admission, 2/15 for domestic students; for summer admission, 5/15 for domestic students. Applications are processed on a rolling basis. Application fee: $150. Electronic applications accepted. *Expenses: Tuition:* Full-time $44,580; part-time $1394 per credit hour. *Required fees:* $492. *Financial support:* Scholarships/grants and tuition waivers available. Financial award applicants required to submit CSS PROFILE. *Unit head:* Mark Zupan, Dean, 585-275-3316, E-mail: mark.zupan@simon.rochester.edu. *Application contact:* Jennifer Mossotti, Associate Director of Part-Time Programs, 585-275-3803, E-mail: jennifer.mossotti@simon.rochester.edu.
Website: http://www.simon.rochester.edu/programs/part-time-mba-programs/index.aspx.

Section 5
Entrepreneurship

This section contains a directory of institutions offering graduate work in entrepreneurship. Additional information about programs listed in the directory but not augmented by an in-depth entry may be obtained by writing directly to the dean of a graduate school or chair of a department at the address given in the directory.

For programs offering related work, see also in this book *Business Administration and Management, International Business,* and *Education (Business Education)*

CONTENTS

Program Directory

Entrepreneurship   322

Display and Close-Up

See:

North Carolina State University—Business Administration   120, 189

Entrepreneurship

American College of Thessaloniki, Department of Business Administration, Pylea-Thessaloniki, Greece. Offers banking and finance (MBA); entrepreneurship (MBA, Certificate); finance (Certificate); management (MBA, Certificate); marketing (MBA, Certificate). Part-time and evening/weekend programs available. *Degree requirements:* For master's, thesis. *Entrance requirements:* For master's, bachelor's degree. Additional exam requirements/recommendations for international students: Recommended—TOEFL. Electronic applications accepted.

American Public University System, AMU/APU Graduate Programs, Charles Town, WV 25414. Offers accounting (MBA, MS); criminal justice (MA), including business administration, emergency and disaster management, general (MA, MS); educational leadership (M Ed); emergency and disaster management (MA); entrepreneurship (MBA); environmental policy and management (MS), including environmental planning, environmental sustainability, fish and wildlife management, general (MA, MS), global environmental management; finance (MBA); general (MBA); global business management (MBA); history (MA), including American history, ancient and classical history, European history, global history, public history; homeland security (MA), including business administration, counter-terrorism studies, criminal justice, cyber, emergency management and public health, intelligence studies, transportation security; homeland security resource allocation (MBA); humanities (MA); information technology (MS), including digital forensics, enterprise software development, information assurance and security, IT project management; information technology management (MBA); intelligence studies (MA), including criminal intelligence, cyber, general (MA, MS), homeland security, intelligence analysis, intelligence collection, intelligence management, intelligence operations, terrorism studies; international relations and conflict resolution (MA), including comparative and security issues, conflict resolution, international and transnational security issues, peacekeeping; legal studies (MA); management (MA), including defense management, general (MA, MS), human resource management, organizational leadership, public administration; marketing (MBA); military history (MA), including American military history, American Revolution, civil war, war since 1945, World War II; military studies (MA), including joint warfare, strategic leadership; national security studies (MA), including general (MA, MS), homeland security, regional security studies, security and intelligence analysis, terrorism studies; nonprofit management (MBA); political science (MA), including American politics and government, comparative government and development, general (MA, MS), international relations, public policy; psychology (MA), including general (MA, MS); maritime engineering management, reverse logistics management; public administration (MPA), including disaster management, environmental policy, health policy, human resources, national security, organizational management, security management; public health (MPH); reverse logistics management (MA); school counseling (M Ed); security management (MA); space studies (MS), including aerospace science, general (MA, MS), planetary science; sports and health sciences (MS); teaching (M Ed), including curriculum and instruction for elementary teachers, elementary reading, English language learners, instructional leadership, online learning, special education; transportation and logistics management (MA), including general (MA, MS), maritime engineering management, reverse logistics management. Programs offered via distance learning only. Part-time and evening/weekend programs available. Postbaccalaureate distance learning degree programs offered (no on-campus study). *Faculty:* 432 full-time (242 women), 1,722 part-time/adjunct (829 women). *Students:* 511 full-time (241 women), 10,947 part-time (4,294 women); includes 3,760 minority (2,058 Black or African American, non-Hispanic/Latino; 88 American Indian or Alaska Native, non-Hispanic/Latino; 293 Asian, non-Hispanic/Latino; 876 Hispanic/Latino; 91 Native Hawaiian or other Pacific Islander, non-Hispanic/Latino; 354 Two or more races, non-Hispanic/Latino), 134 international. Average age 36. In 2013, 3,323 master's awarded. *Degree requirements:* For master's, comprehensive exam or practicum. *Entrance requirements:* For master's, official transcript showing earned bachelor's degree from institution accredited by recognized accrediting body. Additional exam requirements/recommendations for international students: Required—TOEFL (minimum score 550 paper-based), IELTS (minimum score 6.5). *Application deadline:* Applications are processed on a rolling basis. Application fee: $0. Electronic applications accepted. *Expenses: Tuition:* Part-time $325 per semester hour. *Financial support:* Applicants required to submit FAFSA. *Faculty research:* Military history, criminal justice, management performance, national security. *Unit head:* Dr. Karan Powell, Executive Vice President and Provost, 877-468-6268, Fax: 304-724-3780. *Application contact:* Terry Grant, Vice President of Enrollment Management, 877-468-6268, Fax: 304-724-3780, E-mail: info@apus.edu. Website: http://www.apus.edu.

American University, Kogod School of Business, Washington, DC 20016-8044. Offers accounting (MS); business administration (MBA); business fundamentals (Certificate); entrepreneurship (Certificate); finance (MS); forensic accounting (Certificate); management (MS); marketing (MS); real estate (MS, Certificate); sustainability management (MS); tax (Certificate); taxation (MS). *Accreditation:* AACSB. Part-time and evening/weekend programs available. Postbaccalaureate distance learning degree programs offered. *Faculty:* 75 full-time (24 women), 36 part-time/adjunct (7 women). *Students:* 194 full-time (95 women), 370 part-time (184 women); includes 168 minority (69 Black or African American, non-Hispanic/Latino; 60 Asian, non-Hispanic/Latino; 33 Hispanic/Latino; 2 Native Hawaiian or other Pacific Islander, non-Hispanic/Latino; 4 Two or more races, non-Hispanic/Latino), 108 international. Average age 30. 940 applicants, 46% accepted, 193 enrolled. In 2013, 221 master's, 4 other advanced degrees awarded. *Entrance requirements:* For master's, GMAT, resume, personal statement, interview, 2 letters of recommendation, transcripts. Additional exam requirements/recommendations for international students: Required—TOEFL (minimum score 100 iBT). *Application deadline:* Applications are processed on a rolling basis. Application fee: $100. Electronic applications accepted. *Expenses:* Contact institution. *Financial support:* Fellowships, career-related internships or fieldwork, Federal Work-Study, institutionally sponsored loans, and tuition waivers (partial) available. Support available to part-time students. Financial award application deadline: 2/1. *Unit head:* Dr. Michael Ginzberg, Dean, 202-885-1985, E-mail: ginzberg@american.edu. *Application contact:* Jason Kennedy, Associate Director of Graduate Admissions, 202-885-1968, E-mail: jkennedy@american.edu. Website: http://www.kogod.american.edu/.

American University, School of International Service, Washington, DC 20016-8071. Offers comparative and international disability policy (MA); comparative and regional studies (Certificate); cross-cultural communication (Certificate); development management (MS); ethics, peace, and global affairs (MA); European studies (Certificate); global environmental policy (MA, Certificate); global information technology (Certificate); international affairs (MA), including comparative and international disability policy, comparative and regional studies, international economic relations, international politics, natural resources and sustainable development, U.S. foreign policy; international communication (MA, Certificate); international development (MA, Certificate); international economic policy (Certificate); international economic relations (Certificate); international media (MA); international peace and conflict resolution (MA, Certificate); international politics (Certificate); international relations (PhD); international service (MIS); peacebuilding (Certificate); social enterprise (MA); the Americas (Certificate); United States foreign policy (Certificate); JD/MA. Part-time and evening/weekend programs available. Postbaccalaureate distance learning degree programs offered (no on-campus study). *Faculty:* 116 full-time (43 women), 49 part-time/adjunct (19 women). *Students:* 598 full-time (362 women), 382 part-time (233 women); includes 239 minority (85 Black or African American, non-Hispanic/Latino; 8 American Indian or Alaska Native, non-Hispanic/Latino; 54 Asian, non-Hispanic/Latino; 77 Hispanic/Latino; 1 Native Hawaiian or other Pacific Islander, non-Hispanic/Latino; 14 Two or more races, non-Hispanic/Latino), 125 international. Average age 27. In 2013, 443 master's, 7 doctorates, 14 other advanced degrees awarded. Terminal master's awarded for partial completion of doctoral program. *Degree requirements:* For master's, one foreign language, comprehensive exam, thesis or alternative; for doctorate, one foreign language, comprehensive exam, thesis/dissertation. *Entrance requirements:* For master's, GRE, transcripts, resume, 2 letters of recommendation, statement of purpose; for doctorate, GRE, transcripts, resume, 3 letters of recommendation, statement of purpose. Additional exam requirements/recommendations for international students: Required—TOEFL (minimum score 600 paper-based; 100 iBT). *Application deadline:* For fall admission, 1/15 for domestic students; for spring admission, 10/1 for domestic students. Electronic applications accepted. *Expenses: Tuition:* Full-time $25,920; part-time $1482 per credit hour. *Required fees:* $430. Tuition and fees vary according to course load and program. *Financial support:* Fellowships with partial tuition reimbursements, research assistantships with partial tuition reimbursements, career-related internships or fieldwork, Federal Work-Study, institutionally sponsored loans, and scholarships/grants available. Financial award application deadline: 1/15. *Unit head:* Dr. James Goldgeier, Dean, 202-885-1603, E-mail: jgoldgei@american.edu. *Application contact:* Jia Jiang, Associate Director, Graduate Education Enrollment, 202-885-1689, E-mail: jiang@american.edu. Website: http://www.american.edu/sis/.

Anaheim University, Programs in Business Administration, Anaheim, CA 92806-5150. Offers entrepreneurship (ME, DBA); global sustainable management (MBA); international business (MBA, DBA, Certificate, Diploma); management (DBA); sustainable management (DBA, Certificate, Diploma). Postbaccalaureate distance learning degree programs offered.

Arizona State University at the Tempe campus, College of Technology and Innovation, Department of Technology Management, Mesa, AZ 85212. Offers technology (aviation management and human factors) (MS); technology (environmental technology management) (MS); technology (global technology and development) (MS); technology (graphic information technology) (MS); technology (management of technology) (MS). Part-time and evening/weekend programs available. Postbaccalaureate distance learning degree programs offered (minimal on-campus study). *Degree requirements:* For master's, thesis or applied project and oral defense; interactive Program of Study (iPOS) submitted before completing 50 percent of required credit hours. *Entrance requirements:* For master's, GRE, minimum GPA of 3.0 or equivalent in last 2 years of work leading to bachelor's degree. Additional exam requirements/recommendations for international students: Required—TOEFL (minimum score 83 iBT), TOEFL, IELTS, or PTE. Electronic applications accepted. *Faculty research:* Digital imaging, digital publishing, Internet development/e-commerce, information aviation human factors, pilot selection, databases, multimedia, commercial digital photography, digital workflow, computer graphics modeling and animation, information design, sociotechnology, visual and technical literacy, environmental management, quality management, project management, industrial ethics, hazardous materials, environmental chemistry.

Azusa Pacific University, School of Business and Management, Azusa, CA 91702-7000. Offers business administration (MBA); diversity for strategic advantage (MA); entrepreneurship (MBA); finance (MBA); human and organizational development (MA); human resources and organizational development (MBA); human resources management (MA); international business (MBA); marketing (MBA); non-profit management (MA); organizational development and change (MA); performance improvement (MA); public administration (MA); strategic management (MBA). Part-time and evening/weekend programs available. *Degree requirements:* For master's, thesis (for some programs), final project. *Entrance requirements:* For master's, GMAT, minimum GPA of 3.0. Additional exam requirements/recommendations for international students: Required—TOEFL (minimum score 600 paper-based). *Expenses:* Contact institution. *Faculty research:* Gender issues, financial risk, leadership and ethics, marketing strategy.

Babson College, F. W. Olin Graduate School of Business, Wellesley, MA 02457-0310. Offers accounting (MSA); advanced management (Certificate); business administration (MBA); global entrepreneurship (MS); technological entrepreneurship (MS). *Accreditation:* AACSB. Part-time and evening/weekend programs available. Postbaccalaureate distance learning degree programs offered (minimal on-campus study). *Entrance requirements:* For master's, GMAT, 2 years of work experience, resume, letters of recommendation. Additional exam requirements/recommendations for international students: Required—TOEFL (minimum score 100 iBT), IELTS (minimum score 6.5). Electronic applications accepted. *Faculty research:* Entrepreneurship, sustainability, global markets, process of innovation, social media and advertising.

Bakke Graduate University, Programs in Pastoral Ministry and Business, Seattle, WA 98104. Offers business administration (MBA); church and ministry multiplication (D Min); global urban leadership (MA); leadership (D Min); ministry in complex contexts (D Min); social and civic entrepreneurship (MA); theology of work (D Min); theology reflection (D Min); transformational leadership (DTL); urban youth ministry (D Min). Part-time programs available. Postbaccalaureate distance learning degree programs offered (minimal on-campus study). *Faculty:* 5 full-time (3 women), 19 part-time/adjunct (7 women). *Students:* 72 full-time (36 women), 129 part-time (51 women). *Degree requirements:* For master's, thesis; for doctorate, thesis/dissertation. *Entrance requirements:* For master's, 2 years of ministry experience, BA in Biblical studies or theology; for doctorate, 3 years of ministry experience, M Div. Additional exam requirements/recommendations for international students: Required—TOEFL. *Application deadline:* For fall admission, 7/1 priority date for domestic students; for winter admission, 12/1 for domestic students; for spring admission, 3/15 for domestic students. Applications are processed on a rolling basis. Application fee: $75. Electronic applications accepted. *Financial support:* Scholarships/grants and tuition waivers (partial) available. Financial award applicants required to submit FAFSA. *Faculty*

research: Theological systems, church management, worship. *Unit head:* Dr. Gwen Dewey, Academic Dean, 206-264-9119, Fax: 206-264-8828, E-mail: gwend@bgu.edu. *Application contact:* Dr. Judith A. Melton, Registrar, 206-246-9114, Fax: 206-264-8828. Website: http://www.bgu.edu/.

Baldwin Wallace University, Graduate Programs, Division of Business, Program in Entrepreneurship, Berea, OH 44017-2088. Offers MBA. Part-time and evening/weekend programs available. *Students:* 12 full-time (7 women), 13 part-time (4 women); includes 3 minority (all Black or African American, non-Hispanic/Latino). Average age 31. 2 applicants, 100% accepted, 2 enrolled. In 2013, 11 master's awarded. *Degree requirements:* For master's, minimum overall GPA of 3.0, completion of all required courses. *Entrance requirements:* For master's, GMAT or minimum GPA of 3.0, bachelor's degree in any field, work experience. Additional exam requirements/recommendations for international students: Required—TOEFL (minimum score 523 paper-based; 70 iBT). *Application deadline:* For fall admission, 7/25 priority date for domestic students, 4/30 priority date for international students; for spring admission, 12/15 priority date for domestic students, 9/30 priority date for international students. Applications are processed on a rolling basis. Application fee: $25. Electronic applications accepted. Application fee is waived when completed online. *Expenses:* Contact institution. *Financial support:* Application deadline: 5/1; applicants required to submit FAFSA. *Unit head:* Ven Ochaya, Director, 440-826-2391, Fax: 440-826-3868, E-mail: vochaya@bw.edu. *Application contact:* Laura Spencer, Graduate Application Specialist, 440-826-2191, Fax: 440-826-3868, E-mail: lspencer@bw.edu. Website: http://www.bw.edu/academics/bus/programs/entre/.

Baruch College of the City University of New York, Zicklin School of Business, Department of Management, New York, NY 10010-5585. Offers entrepreneurship (MBA); management (PhD); operations management (MBA); organizational behavior/human resources management (MBA); sustainable business (MBA). PhD offered jointly with Graduate School and University Center of the City University of New York. Part-time and evening/weekend programs available. *Degree requirements:* For doctorate, comprehensive exam, thesis/dissertation. *Entrance requirements:* For master's, GMAT, 2 letters of recommendation, resume, 2 years of work experience; for doctorate, GMAT. Additional exam requirements/recommendations for international students: Required—TOEFL (minimum score 590 paper-based), TWE.

Baruch College of the City University of New York, Zicklin School of Business, International Executive MS Programs, New York, NY 10010-5585. Offers entrepreneurship (MS). Part-time and evening/weekend programs available. *Entrance requirements:* For master's, GMAT, 2 letters of recommendation, resume, 2 years of work experience. Additional exam requirements/recommendations for international students: Required—TOEFL (minimum score 590 paper-based), TWE (minimum score 5).

Bay Path College, Program in Entrepreneurial Thinking and Innovative Practices, Longmeadow, MA 01106-2292. Offers MBA. Part-time and evening/weekend programs available. Postbaccalaureate distance learning degree programs offered (no on-campus study). *Students:* 19 full-time (18 women), 45 part-time (42 women); includes 21 minority (11 Black or African American, non-Hispanic/Latino; 1 Asian, non-Hispanic/Latino; 9 Hispanic/Latino). Average age 35. 16 applicants, 88% accepted, 7 enrolled. In 2013, 40 master's awarded. *Degree requirements:* For master's, 12 courses - eight core courses and four electives (each course is eight weeks long). *Entrance requirements:* For master's, GMAT (waived if candidate has taken the GRE, holds another graduate degree or professional licensure such as a CPA or CMA, has five years of professional work history, or has significant analytical background). *Application deadline:* Applications are processed on a rolling basis. Application fee: $45. Electronic applications accepted. Application fee is waived when completed online. *Financial support:* In 2013–14, 15 students received support. Scholarships/grants available. Financial award applicants required to submit FAFSA. *Unit head:* Mo Sattar, Program Director, 413-565-1228. *Application contact:* Lisa Adams, Director of Graduate Admissions, 413-565-1317, Fax: 413-565-1250, E-mail: ladams@baypath.edu. Website: http://graduate.baypath.edu/Graduate-Programs/Programs-On-Campus/MBA-Program/Entrepreneurial-Thinking-and-Innovative-Practices.

Benedictine University, Graduate Programs, Program in Business Administration, Lisle, IL 60532-0900. Offers accounting (MBA); entrepreneurship and managing innovation (MBA); financial management (MBA); health administration (MBA); human resource management (MBA); information systems security (MBA); international business (MBA); management consulting (MBA); management information systems (MBA); marketing management (MBA); operations management and logistics (MBA); organizational leadership (MBA). Part-time and evening/weekend programs available. Postbaccalaureate distance learning degree programs offered (minimal on-campus study). *Faculty:* 4 full-time (2 women), 24 part-time/adjunct (3 women). *Students:* 144 full-time (83 women), 599 part-time (328 women); includes 189 minority (115 Black or African American, non-Hispanic/Latino; 5 American Indian or Alaska Native, non-Hispanic/Latino; 43 Asian, non-Hispanic/Latino; 24 Hispanic/Latino; 2 Native Hawaiian or other Pacific Islander, non-Hispanic/Latino), 14 international. Average age 34. 211 applicants, 89% accepted, 155 enrolled. In 2013, 376 master's awarded. *Entrance requirements:* For master's, GMAT. Additional exam requirements/recommendations for international students: Required—TOEFL (minimum score 550 paper-based). *Application deadline:* For fall admission, 9/1 for domestic students; for winter admission, 12/1 for domestic students; for spring admission, 2/15 for domestic students. Applications are processed on a rolling basis. Application fee: $40. Electronic applications accepted. *Expenses:* Tuition: Part-time $590 per credit hour. *Financial support:* Career-related internships or fieldwork and health care benefits available. Support available to part-time students. *Faculty research:* Strategic leadership in professional organizations, sociology of professions, organizational change, social identity theory, applications to change management. *Unit head:* Dr. Sharon Borowicz, Director, 630-829-6219, E-mail: sborowicz@ben.edu. *Application contact:* Kari Gibbons, Director, Admissions, 630-829-6200, Fax: 630-829-6584, E-mail: kgibbons@ben.edu.

California Baptist University, Program in Public Administration, Riverside, CA 92504-3206. Offers public administration (MPA); strategic innovation (MPA). Part-time and evening/weekend programs available. Postbaccalaureate distance learning degree programs offered (minimal on-campus study). *Faculty:* 4 full-time (3 women), 2 part-time/adjunct (1 woman). *Students:* 142 full-time (99 women), 22 part-time (13 women); includes 92 minority (21 Black or African American, non-Hispanic/Latino; 14 Asian, non-Hispanic/Latino; 55 Hispanic/Latino; 2 Native Hawaiian or other Pacific Islander, non-Hispanic/Latino), 1 international. Average age 37. 90 applicants, 66% accepted, 36 enrolled. In 2013, 39 master's awarded. *Degree requirements:* For master's, comprehensive exam or thesis. *Entrance requirements:* For master's, minimum GPA of 3.0; bachelor's degree in applicable field or any field with five years of managerial experience; three recommendations; resume; 500-word essay. Additional exam requirements/recommendations for international students: Required—TOEFL (minimum score 80 iBT). *Application deadline:* For fall admission, 8/1 priority date for domestic students, 7/1 for international students; for spring admission, 12/1 priority date for domestic students, 11/1 for international students. Applications are processed on a rolling basis. Application fee: $45. Electronic applications accepted. *Expenses:* Contact institution. *Financial support:* Applicants required to submit CSS PROFILE or FAFSA.

Faculty research: Policy networks, water policy, democratic theory, international relations, political theory and philosophy. *Unit head:* Dr. David Poole, Vice President, Online and Professional Studies, 951-343-3902, E-mail: dpoole@calbaptist.edu. *Application contact:* Dr. Elaine Ahumada, Director, MPA Program, 951-343-3929, Fax: 951-343-4661, E-mail: eahumada@calbaptist.edu. Website: http://www.cbuonline.edu/programs/program/master-of-public-administration.

California Intercontinental University, School of Business, Diamond Bar, CA 91765. Offers banking and finance (MBA); entrepreneurship and business management (DBA); global business leadership (DBA); international management and marketing (MBA); organizational management and human resource management (MBA).

California Lutheran University, Graduate Studies, School of Management, Thousand Oaks, CA 91360-2787. Offers business (IMBA); computer science (MS); econometrics (MBA); economics (MS); entrepreneurship (MBA, Certificate); finance (MBA, Certificate); financial planning (MBA, Certificate); information systems and technology (MS); information technology management (MBA, Certificate); international business (MBA, Certificate); management and organization behavior (MBA); management and organizational behavior (Certificate); marketing (MBA, Certificate); microeconomics (MBA); nonprofit and social enterprise (MBA). Part-time and evening/weekend programs available. Postbaccalaureate distance learning degree programs offered (no on-campus study). *Faculty:* 26 full-time (9 women), 50 part-time/adjunct (11 women). *Students:* 426 full-time (175 women), 220 part-time (91 women); includes 114 minority (14 Black or African American, non-Hispanic/Latino; 30 Asian, non-Hispanic/Latino; 57 Hispanic/Latino; 13 Two or more races, non-Hispanic/Latino), 321 international. Average age 31. 495 applicants, 76% accepted, 119 enrolled. In 2013, 297 master's awarded. *Entrance requirements:* For master's, GMAT, interview, minimum GPA of 3.0. *Application deadline:* Applications are processed on a rolling basis. Application fee: $50. *Expenses:* Contact institution. *Unit head:* Dr. Gerhard Apfelthaler, Dean, 805-493-3360. *Application contact:* 805-493-3325, Fax: 805-493-3861, E-mail: clugrad@callutheran.edu. Website: http://www.callutheran.edu/business/.

California State University, East Bay, Office of Academic Programs and Graduate Studies, College of Business and Economics, Department of Marketing, Option in Entrepreneurship, Hayward, CA 94542-3000. Offers MBA. *Entrance requirements:* Additional exam requirements/recommendations for international students: Required—TOEFL (minimum score 550 paper-based).

California State University, East Bay, Office of Academic Programs and Graduate Studies, College of Business and Economics, MBA Program, Hayward, CA 94542-3000. Offers entrepreneurship (MBA); finance (MBA); global innovators (MBA); human resources and organizational behavior (MBA); information technology management (MBA); marketing management (MBA); operations and supply chain management (MBA); strategy and international business (MBA). Part-time and evening/weekend programs available. *Degree requirements:* For master's, comprehensive exam or thesis. *Entrance requirements:* For master's, GMAT (minimum 20th percentile verbal and quantitative section), bachelor's degree, minimum GPA of 2.75. Additional exam requirements/recommendations for international students: Required—TOEFL (minimum score 550 paper-based; 79 iBT). Electronic applications accepted. *Expenses:* Contact institution.

California State University, Fullerton, Graduate Studies, College of Business and Economics, Department of Management, Fullerton, CA 92834-9480. Offers entrepreneurship (MBA); management (MBA). *Accreditation:* AACSB. Part-time programs available. *Students:* 17 full-time (8 women), 32 part-time (14 women); includes 19 minority (1 Black or African American, non-Hispanic/Latino; 11 Asian, non-Hispanic/Latino; 7 Hispanic/Latino), 5 international. Average age 28. In 2013, 32 master's awarded. *Degree requirements:* For master's, project or thesis. *Entrance requirements:* For master's, GMAT, minimum AACSB index of 950. Application fee: $55. *Financial support:* Career-related internships or fieldwork, Federal Work-Study, institutionally sponsored loans, and scholarships/grants available. Support available to part-time students. Financial award application deadline: 3/1; financial award applicants required to submit FAFSA. *Unit head:* Dr. Gus Manoochehri, Chair, 657-278-3071. *Application contact:* Admissions/Applications, 657-278-2371.

California State University, San Bernardino, Graduate Studies, College of Business and Public Administration, Master in Business Administration Program, San Bernardino, CA 92407. Offers accounting (MBA); cyber security (MBA); entrepreneurship (MBA); finance (MBA); information systems and technology (MBA); management (MBA); marketing management (MBA); supply chain management (MBA). MBA is also offered online. *Accreditation:* AACSB. Part-time and evening/weekend programs available. Postbaccalaureate distance learning degree programs offered (no on-campus study). *Faculty:* 27 full-time (6 women), 8 part-time/adjunct (1 woman). *Students:* 161 full-time (59 women), 47 part-time (18 women); includes 74 minority (12 Black or African American, non-Hispanic/Latino; 19 Asian, non-Hispanic/Latino; 42 Hispanic/Latino; 1 Two or more races, non-Hispanic/Latino), 74 international. Average age 29. 281 applicants, 38% accepted, 67 enrolled. In 2013, 79 master's awarded. *Degree requirements:* For master's, comprehensive exam, thesis, portfolio, 60 units, minimum GPA of 3.0. *Entrance requirements:* For master's, GMAT or GRE, minimum GPA of 2.5. Additional exam requirements/recommendations for international students: Required—TOEFL (minimum score 550 paper-based; 79 iBT). *Application deadline:* For fall admission, 7/20 for domestic and international students; for winter admission, 10/20 for domestic and international students; for spring admission, 1/20 for domestic and international students. Applications are processed on a rolling basis. Application fee: $55. Electronic applications accepted. *Expenses:* Contact institution. *Financial support:* In 2013–14, 79 students received support, including 21 fellowships (averaging $4,867 per year), 29 research assistantships (averaging $2,748 per year), 6 teaching assistantships (averaging $5,162 per year); career-related internships or fieldwork, Federal Work-Study, institutionally sponsored loans, scholarships/grants, and unspecified assistantships also available. Support available to part-time students. Financial award application deadline: 3/1; financial award applicants required to submit FAFSA. *Faculty research:* Market reaction to Form 20-F, tax Constitutional questions in Obamacare, the performance of the faith and ethical investment products prior to and following the 2008 meltdown, capital appreciation bonds: a ruinous decision for an unborn generation, the effects of calorie count display on consumer eating behavior, local government bankruptcy. *Total annual research expenditures:* $2.3 million. *Unit head:* Dr. Lawrence C. Rose, Dean, 909-537-3703, Fax: 909-537-7026, E-mail: lrose@csusb.edu. *Application contact:* Dr. Vipin Gupta, Associate Dean/MBA Director, 909-537-7380, Fax: 909-537-7026, E-mail: vgupta@csusb.edu. Website: http://mba.csusb.edu/.

Cambridge College, School of Management, Cambridge, MA 02138-5304. Offers business negotiation and conflict resolution (M Mgt); general business (M Mgt); health care informatics (M Mgt); health care management (M Mgt); leadership in human and organizational dynamics (M Mgt); non-profit and public organization management (M Mgt); small business development (M Mgt); technology management (M Mgt). Part-time and evening/weekend programs available. *Degree requirements:* For master's, thesis, seminars. *Entrance requirements:* For master's, resume, 2 professional references. Additional exam requirements/recommendations for international students: Required—TOEFL (minimum score 550 paper-based; 79 iBT), Michigan English

Language Assessment Battery (minimum score 85); Recommended—IELTS (minimum score 6). Electronic applications accepted. *Expenses:* Contact institution. *Faculty research:* Negotiation, mediation and conflict resolution; leadership; management of diverse organizations; case studies and simulation methodologies for management education, digital as a second language: social networking for digital immigrants, non-profit and public management.

Cameron University, Office of Graduate Studies, Program in Entrepreneurial Studies, Lawton, OK 73505-6377. Offers MS. Part-time and evening/weekend programs available. Postbaccalaureate distance learning degree programs offered (no on-campus study). *Degree requirements:* For master's, comprehensive exam. *Entrance requirements:* Additional exam requirements/recommendations for international students: Required—TOEFL (minimum score 550 paper-based). Electronic applications accepted. *Faculty research:* Entrepreneurial competition, new venture creation, legal issues, electronic commerce.

Capella University, School of Business and Technology, Doctoral Programs in Business, Minneapolis, MN 55402. Offers accounting (DBA, PhD); business intelligence (DBA); finance (DBA, PhD); general business management (PhD); human resource management (DBA, PhD); leadership (DBA, PhD); management education (PhD); marketing (DBA, PhD); project management (DBA, PhD); strategy and innovation (DBA, PhD).

Capella University, School of Business and Technology, Master's Programs in Business, Minneapolis, MN 55402. Offers accounting (MBA); business analysis (MS); business intelligence (MBA); entrepreneurship (MBA); finance (MBA); general business administration (MBA); general human resource management (MS); general leadership (MS); health care management (MBA); human resource management (MBA); marketing (MBA); project management (MBA, MS).

Capital University, School of Management, Columbus, OH 43209-2394. Offers entrepreneurship (MBA); finance (MBA); leadership (MBA); marketing (MBA); MBA/JD; MBA/LL M; MBA/MSN; MBA/MT. *Accreditation:* ACBSP. Part-time and evening/weekend programs available. *Faculty:* 17 full-time (7 women), 23 part-time/adjunct (1 woman). *Students:* 192 (77 women). Average age 31. 34 applicants, 74% accepted, 20 enrolled. In 2013, 1 master's awarded. *Entrance requirements:* For master's, GMAT, 2 years of work experience. Additional exam requirements/recommendations for international students: Required—TOEFL (minimum score 550 paper-based); Recommended—IELTS (minimum score 6.5). *Application deadline:* For fall admission, 7/1 priority date for domestic students; for winter admission, 11/1 for domestic students; for spring admission, 11/1 priority date for domestic students; for summer admission, 4/1 priority date for domestic students. Applications are processed on a rolling basis. Electronic applications accepted. *Financial support:* Application deadline: 8/1; applicants required to submit FAFSA. *Faculty research:* Taxation, public policy, health care, management of non-profits. *Unit head:* Dr. David Schwantes, MBA Director, 614-236-6984, Fax: 614-236-6923, E-mail: dschwant@capital.edu. *Application contact:* Carli Isgrigg, Assistant Director of Adult and Graduate Education Recruitment, 614-236-6546, Fax: 614-236-6923, E-mail: cisgrigg@capital.edu.
Website: http://www.capital.edu/capital-mba/.

Carlos Albizu University, Miami Campus, Graduate Programs, Miami, FL 33172-2209. Offers clinical psychology (Psy D); entrepreneurship (MBA); exceptional student education (MS); human services (PhD); industrial/organizational psychology (MS); marriage and family therapy (MS); mental health counseling (MS); nonprofit management (MBA); organizational management (MBA); psychology (MS); school counseling (MS); teaching English as a second language (MS). *Accreditation:* APA. Part-time and evening/weekend programs available. *Faculty:* 26 full-time (20 women), 34 part-time/adjunct (16 women). *Students:* 416 full-time (335 women), 281 part-time (237 women); includes 604 minority (57 Black or African American, non-Hispanic/Latino; 1 American Indian or Alaska Native, non-Hispanic/Latino; 13 Asian, non-Hispanic/Latino; 533 Hispanic/Latino), 14 international. Average age 36. 176 applicants, 59% accepted, 96 enrolled. In 2013, 176 master's, 37 doctorates awarded. Terminal master's awarded for partial completion of doctoral program. *Degree requirements:* For master's, one foreign language, comprehensive exam, integrative project (MBA), research project (exceptional student education, teaching English as a second language); for doctorate, one foreign language, comprehensive exam, internship, project. *Entrance requirements:* For master's, 3 letters of recommendation, interview, minimum GPA of 3.0, resume, statement of purpose, official transcripts; for doctorate, 3 letters of recommendation, minimum GPA of 3.0, resume, interview, statement of purpose, official transcripts. Additional exam requirements/recommendations for international students: Required—Michigan Test of English Language Proficiency. *Application deadline:* For fall admission, 4/1 priority date for domestic students, 5/1 priority date for international students; for spring admission, 11/1 priority date for domestic students, 9/1 priority date for international students. Applications are processed on a rolling basis. Application fee: $50. Electronic applications accepted. *Expenses: Tuition:* Full-time $9360; part-time $520 per credit. *Required fees:* $298 per term. Tuition and fees vary according to course load, degree level and program. *Financial support:* In 2013–14, 62 students received support. Federal Work-Study, scholarships/grants, and tuition discounts available. Financial award application deadline: 6/1; financial award applicants required to submit FAFSA. *Faculty research:* Psychotherapy, forensic psychology, neuropsychology, marketing strategy, entrepreneurship, special education. *Unit head:* Peter M. Rubio, Interim Chancellor, 305-593-1223 Ext. 3120, Fax: 305-592-7930, E-mail: prubio@albizu.edu. *Application contact:* Vanessa Almendarez, Administrative Assistant, 305-593-1223 Ext. 3137, Fax: 305-593-1854, E-mail: valmendarez@albizu.edu.

Carnegie Mellon University, College of Humanities and Social Sciences, Department of Social and Decision Sciences, Pittsburgh, PA 15213-3891. Offers behavioral decision research (PhD); behavioral decision research and psychology (PhD); social and decision science (PhD); strategy, entrepeneurship, and technological change (PhD). Terminal master's awarded for partial completion of doctoral program. *Degree requirements:* For doctorate, comprehensive exam, thesis/dissertation, research paper. *Entrance requirements:* For doctorate, GRE General Test. Additional exam requirements/recommendations for international students: Required—TOEFL. Electronic applications accepted. *Faculty research:* Organization theory, political science, sociology, technology studies.

Clemson University, Graduate School, College of Business and Behavioral Science, Program in Business Administration, Clemson, SC 29634. Offers entrepreneurship and innovation (MBA). *Accreditation:* AACSB. Part-time and evening/weekend programs available. *Faculty:* 30 full-time (5 women). *Students:* 101 full-time (40 women), 214 part-time (74 women); includes 34 minority (16 Black or African American, non-Hispanic/Latino; 3 Asian, non-Hispanic/Latino; 14 Hispanic/Latino; 1 Two or more races, non-Hispanic/Latino), 31 international. Average age 31. 223 applicants, 70% accepted, 109 enrolled. In 2013, 120 master's awarded. *Entrance requirements:* For master's, GMAT. Additional exam requirements/recommendations for international students: Required—TOEFL. *Application deadline:* For fall admission, 6/1 priority date for domestic students, 4/15 for international students; for spring admission, 11/1 for domestic and international students. Applications are processed on a rolling basis. Application fee: $70 ($80 for international students). Electronic applications accepted. *Financial support:* In 2013–14, 5 students received support, including 3 fellowships with full and partial tuition reimbursements available (averaging $1,333 per year), 2 research assistantships with partial tuition reimbursements available (averaging $8,080 per year); teaching assistantships with partial tuition reimbursements available, institutionally sponsored loans, and scholarships/grants also available. Financial award application deadline: 5/1; financial award applicants required to submit FAFSA. *Unit head:* Dr. Gregory Pickett, Director, 864-656-3975, Fax: 864-656-0947. *Application contact:* Deanna Burns, Director of Admissions, 864-656-8173, E-mail: dchambe@clemson.edu.
Website: http://www.clemson.edu/cbbs/departments/mba/.

Cogswell Polytechnical College, Program in Entrepreneurship and Innovation, Sunnyvale, CA 94089-1299. Offers MA.

Columbia University, Graduate School of Business, MBA Program, New York, NY 10027. Offers accounting (MBA); decision, risk, and operations (MBA); entrepreneurship (MBA); finance and economics (MBA); healthcare and pharmaceutical management (MBA); human resource management (MBA); international business (MBA); leadership and ethics (MBA); management (MBA); marketing (MBA); media (MBA); private equity (MBA); real estate (MBA); social enterprise (MBA); value investing (MBA); DDS/MBA; JD/MBA; MBA/MIA; MBA/MPH; MBA/MS; MD/MBA. *Entrance requirements:* For master's, GMAT, 2 letters of recommendation. Additional exam requirements/recommendations for international students: Required—TOEFL. Electronic applications accepted. *Expenses:* Contact institution. *Faculty research:* Human decision making and behavioral research; real estate market and mortgage defaults; financial crisis and corporate governance; international business; security analysis and accounting.

Dallas Baptist University, College of Business, Business Administration Program, Dallas, TX 75211-9299. Offers accounting (MBA); business communication (MBA); conflict resolution management (MBA); entrepreneurship (MBA); finance (MBA); health care management (MBA); international business (MBA); leading the non-profit organization (MBA); management (MBA); management information systems (MBA); marketing (MBA); project management (MBA); technology and engineering (MBA). *Accreditation:* ACBSP. Part-time and evening/weekend programs available. *Entrance requirements:* For master's, GMAT, minimum GPA of 3.0. Additional exam requirements/recommendations for international students: Required—TOEFL, IELTS. *Application deadline:* Applications are processed on a rolling basis. Application fee: $25. Electronic applications accepted. *Expenses: Tuition:* Full-time $13,410; part-time $745 per credit hour. *Required fees:* $300; $150 per semester. Tuition and fees vary according to degree level. *Financial support:* Federal Work-Study, institutionally sponsored loans, scholarships/grants, and tuition waivers (full and partial) available. Support available to part-time students. Financial award applicants required to submit FAFSA. *Faculty research:* Sports management, services marketing, retailing, strategic management, financial planning/investments. *Unit head:* Dr. Sandra S. Reid, Chair, 214-333-5280, Fax: 214-333-5293, E-mail: graduate@dbu.edu. *Application contact:* Kit P. Montgomery, Director of Graduate Programs, 214-333-5242, Fax: 214-333-5579, E-mail: graduate@dbu.edu.
Website: http://www3.dbu.edu/graduate/mba.asp.

Dallas Baptist University, College of Business, Management Program, Dallas, TX 75211-9299. Offers conflict resolution management (MA); general management (MA); health care management (MA); human resource management (MA); organizational management (MA); performance management (MA); professional sales and management optimization (MA). Part-time and evening/weekend programs available. *Entrance requirements:* For master's, GRE General Test, minimum GPA of 3.0. Additional exam requirements/recommendations for international students: Required—TOEFL, IELTS. *Application deadline:* Applications are processed on a rolling basis. Application fee: $25. Electronic applications accepted. *Expenses: Tuition:* Full-time $13,410; part-time $745 per credit hour. *Required fees:* $300; $150 per semester. Tuition and fees vary according to degree level. *Financial support:* Federal Work-Study, institutionally sponsored loans, scholarships/grants, and tuition waivers (full and partial) available. Support available to part-time students. Financial award applicants required to submit FAFSA. *Faculty research:* Organizational behavior, conflict personalities. *Unit head:* Joanne Hix, Director, 214-333-5280, Fax: 214-333-5293, E-mail: graduate@dbu.edu. *Application contact:* Kit P. Montgomery, Director of Graduate Programs, 214-333-5242, Fax: 214-333-5579, E-mail: graduate@dbu.edu.
Website: http://www3.dbu.edu/graduate/maom.asp.

Delaware Valley College, MBA Program, Doylestown, PA 18901-2697. Offers accounting (MBA); entrepreneurship (MBA); finance (MBA); food and agribusiness (MBA); general business (MBA); global executive leadership (MBA); human resource management (MBA); supply chain management (MBA). Part-time and evening/weekend programs available. Postbaccalaureate distance learning degree programs offered (no on-campus study). *Students:* 32 full-time (17 women), 183 part-time (99 women). Average age 34. 97 applicants, 78% accepted, 74 enrolled. *Entrance requirements:* For master's, minimum undergraduate GPA of 3.0. *Application deadline:* Applications are processed on a rolling basis. Application fee: $50. Electronic applications accepted. *Expenses:* Contact institution. *Financial support:* Applicants required to submit FAFSA. *Unit head:* Mike Prushan, Director of MBA Program, 215-489-2322, E-mail: michael.prushan@delval.edu. *Application contact:* Robin Mathews, Graduate and Continuing Studies Enrollment Manager, 215-489-2955, Fax: 215-489-4832, E-mail: robin.mathews@delval.edu.
Website: http://www.delval.edu/academics/graduate/master-of-business-administration.

DePaul University, Charles H. Kellstadt Graduate School of Business, Chicago, IL 60604. Offers accountancy (M Acc, MS, MSA); applied economics (MBA); banking (MBA); behavioral finance (MBA); brand and product management (MBA); business development (MBA); business information technology (MS); business strategy and decision-making (MBA); computational finance (MS); consumer insights (MBA); corporate finance (MBA); economic policy analysis (MS); entrepreneurship (MBA, MS); finance (MBA, MS); financial analysis (MBA); general business (MBA); health sector management (MBA); hospitality leadership (MBA); hospitality leadership and operational performance (MS); human resource management (MBA); human resources (MS); investment management (MBA); leadership and change management (MBA); management accounting (MBA); marketing (MBA, MS); marketing analysis (MS); marketing strategy and planning (MBA); operations management (MBA); organizational diversity (MBA); real estate (MS); real estate finance and investment (MBA); revenue management (MBA); sports management (MBA); strategic global marketing (MBA); strategy, execution and valuation (MBA); sustainable management (MBA, MS); taxation (MS); wealth management (MS); JD/MBA. *Accreditation:* AACSB. Part-time and evening/weekend programs available. Postbaccalaureate distance learning degree programs offered (no on-campus study). *Faculty:* 81 full-time (20 women), 45 part-time/adjunct (8 women). *Students:* 1,238 full-time (605 women), 617 part-time (223 women); includes 295 minority (71 Black or African American, non-Hispanic/Latino; 129 Asian, non-Hispanic/Latino; 74 Hispanic/Latino; 4 Native Hawaiian or other Pacific Islander, non-Hispanic/Latino; 17 Two or more races, non-Hispanic/Latino), 462 international. Average age 29. In 2013, 911 master's awarded. *Entrance requirements:* For master's, GMAT, 2 letters of recommendation, resume, essay, official transcripts. Additional exam requirements/recommendations for international students: Required—TOEFL (minimum score 550 paper-based; 80 iBT). *Application deadline:* For fall admission, 7/1 for domestic students, 6/1 for international students; for winter admission, 10/1 for domestic

students, 9/1 for international students; for spring admission, 2/1 for domestic students, 1/1 for international students. Applications are processed on a rolling basis. Application fee: $60. Electronic applications accepted. *Expenses:* Contact institution. *Financial support:* Application deadline: 4/1; applicants required to submit FAFSA. *Unit head:* Robert T. Ryan, Assistant Dean and Director, 312-362-8810, Fax: 312-362-6677, E-mail: rryan1@depaul.edu. *Application contact:* James Parker, Director of Recruitment and Admission, 312-362-8810, Fax: 312-362-6677, E-mail: kgsb@depaul.edu.
Website: http://kellstadt.depaul.edu.

Drexel University, Goodwin College of Professional Studies, School of Technology and Professional Studies, Philadelphia, PA 19104-2875. Offers construction management (MS); creativity and innovation (MS); engineering technology (MS); food science (MS); hospitality management (MS); professional studies: creativity studies (MS); professional studies: e-learning leadership (MS); professional studies: homeland security management (MS); project management (MS); property management (MS); sport management (MS). Part-time and evening/weekend programs available. *Entrance requirements:* Additional exam requirements/recommendations for international students: Required—TOEFL, IELTS. Electronic applications accepted. Application fee is waived when completed online.

Duke University, The Fuqua School of Business, Cross Continent Executive MBA Program, Durham, NC 27708-0586. Offers business administration (MBA); energy and the environment (MBA); entrepreneurship and innovation (MBA); finance (MBA); health sector management (Certificate); marketing (MBA); strategy (MBA). *Faculty:* 91 full-time (15 women), 53 part-time/adjunct (9 women). *Students:* 121 full-time (34 women); includes 23 minority (3 Black or African American, non-Hispanic/Latino; 15 Asian, non-Hispanic/Latino; 4 Hispanic/Latino; 1 Native Hawaiian or other Pacific Islander, non-Hispanic/Latino), 31 international. Average age 30. In 2013, 147 master's awarded. *Degree requirements:* For master's, one foreign language. *Entrance requirements:* For master's, GMAT or GRE, transcripts, essays, resume, recommendation letters, interview. Additional exam requirements/recommendations for international students: Required—TOEFL, IELTS, PTE. *Application deadline:* For fall admission, 10/16 for domestic students, 10/6 for international students; for winter admission, 2/12 for domestic and international students; for spring admission, 5/6 for domestic and international students; for summer admission, 6/4 for domestic students. Application fee: $225. Electronic applications accepted. *Financial support:* In 2013–14, 16 students received support. Institutionally sponsored loans and scholarships/grants available. Financial award applicants required to submit FAFSA. *Unit head:* John Gallagher, Associate Dean for Executive MBA Programs, 919-660-7641, E-mail: johng@duke.edu. *Application contact:* Liz Riley Hargrove, Associate Dean for Admissions, 919-660-1956, Fax: 919-681-8026, E-mail: admissions-info@fuqua.duke.edu.
Website: http://www.fuqua.duke.edu/programs/duke_mba/cross_continent/.

Duke University, The Fuqua School of Business, Daytime MBA Program, Durham, NC 27708-0586. Offers academic excellence in finance (Certificate); business administration (MBA); decision sciences (MBA); energy and environment (MBA); energy finance (MBA); entrepreneurship and innovation (MBA); finance (MBA); financial analysis (MBA); health sector management (Certificate); leadership and ethics (MBA); management (MBA); marketing (MBA); operations management (MBA); social entrepreneurship (MBA); strategy (MBA). *Faculty:* 91 full-time (15 women), 53 part-time/adjunct (9 women). *Students:* 862 full-time (283 women); includes 179 minority (34 Black or African American, non-Hispanic/Latino; 1 American Indian or Alaska Native, non-Hispanic/Latino; 92 Asian, non-Hispanic/Latino; 42 Hispanic/Latino; 2 Native Hawaiian or other Pacific Islander, non-Hispanic/Latino; 8 Two or more races, non-Hispanic/Latino), 342 international. Average age 29. In 2013, 437 master's awarded. *Entrance requirements:* For master's, GMAT or GRE, transcripts, essays, resume, recommendation letters, interview. Additional exam requirements/recommendations for international students: Required—TOEFL, IELTS, PTE. *Application deadline:* For fall admission, 9/18 for domestic and international students; for winter admission, 10/21 for domestic and international students; for spring admission, 1/6 for domestic and international students; for summer admission, 3/20 for domestic and international students. Application fee: $225. Electronic applications accepted. *Financial support:* In 2013–14, 331 students received support. Institutionally sponsored loans and scholarships/grants available. Financial award applicants required to submit FAFSA. *Unit head:* Russ Morgan, Associate Dean for the Daytime MBA Program, 919-660-2931, Fax: 919-684-8742, E-mail: ruskin.morgan@duke.edu. *Application contact:* Liz Riley Hargrove, Associate Dean of Admissions, 919-660-7705, Fax: 919-681-8026, E-mail: liz.riley@duke.edu.
Website: http://www.fuqua.duke.edu/daytime-mba/.

Duke University, The Fuqua School of Business, Global Executive MBA Program, Durham, NC 27708-0586. Offers business administration (MBA); energy and the environment (MBA); entrepreneurship and innovation (MBA); finance (MBA); health sector management (Certificate); marketing (MBA); strategy (MBA). *Faculty:* 91 full-time (15 women), 53 part-time/adjunct (9 women). *Students:* 49 full-time (7 women); includes 7 minority (1 Black or African American, non-Hispanic/Latino; 3 Asian, non-Hispanic/Latino; 3 Hispanic/Latino), 17 international. Average age 39. In 2013, 51 master's awarded. *Entrance requirements:* For master's, transcripts, essays, resume, recommendation letters, interview. Additional exam requirements/recommendations for international students: Required—TOEFL, IELTS, PTE. *Application deadline:* For fall admission, 9/4 for domestic and international students; for winter admission, 10/16 for domestic and international students; for spring admission, 12/5 for domestic and international students; for summer admission, 1/13 for domestic and international students. Application fee: $225. *Financial support:* In 2013–14, 8 students received support. Institutionally sponsored loans and scholarships/grants available. Financial award applicants required to submit FAFSA. *Unit head:* John Gallagher, Associate Dean for Executive MBA Programs, 919-660-7728, E-mail: johng@duke.edu. *Application contact:* Liz Riley Hargrove, Director of EMBA Admissions, 919-660-7705, Fax: 919-681-8026, E-mail: admissions-info@fuqua.duke.edu.
Website: http://www.fuqua.duke.edu/programs/duke_mba/global-executive/.

Duke University, The Fuqua School of Business, Weekend Executive MBA Program, Durham, NC 27708-0586. Offers business administration (MBA); energy and environment (MBA); entrepreneurship and innovation (MBA); finance (MBA); health sector management (Certificate); marketing (MBA); strategy (MBA). *Faculty:* 91 full-time (15 women), 53 part-time/adjunct (9 women). *Students:* 93 full-time (14 women); includes 33 minority (5 Black or African American, non-Hispanic/Latino; 24 Asian, non-Hispanic/Latino; 3 Hispanic/Latino; 1 Two or more races, non-Hispanic/Latino), 15 international. Average age 36. In 2013, 103 master's awarded. *Degree requirements:* For master's, one foreign language. *Entrance requirements:* For master's, GMAT (preferred) or GRE, transcripts, essays, resume, recommendation letters, interview. Additional exam requirements/recommendations for international students: Required—TOEFL, IELTS, PTE. *Application deadline:* For fall admission, 9/4 for domestic and international students; for winter admission, 10/16 for domestic and international students; for spring admission, 2/12 for domestic and international students; for summer admission, 4/2 for domestic and international students. Application fee: $225. Electronic applications accepted. *Financial support:* In 2013–14, 14 students received support. Institutionally sponsored loans and scholarships/grants available. Financial award applicants required to submit FAFSA. *Unit head:* John Gallagher, Associate Dean for Executive MBA Programs, 919-660-7728, E-mail: johng@duke.edu. *Application contact:* Liz Riley Hargrove, Director of EMBA Admissions, 919-660-7705, Fax: 919-681-8026, E-mail: admissions-info@fuqua.duke.edu.
Website: http://www.fuqua.duke.edu/programs/duke_mba/weekend_executive/.

Eastern Michigan University, Graduate School, College of Business, Programs in Business Administration, Ypsilanti, MI 48197. Offers business administration (MBA, Graduate Certificate); computer information systems (Graduate Certificate); e-business (MBA, Graduate Certificate); enterprise business intelligence (MBA); entrepreneurship (MBA, Graduate Certificate); finance (MBA, Graduate Certificate); human resources (MBA); human resources management (Graduate Certificate); information systems (MBA); internal auditing (MBA); international business (MBA, Graduate Certificate); marketing management (Graduate Certificate); nonprofit management (MBA); organizational development (Graduate Certificate); supply chain management (MBA, Graduate Certificate). *Accreditation:* AACSB. Part-time programs available. Postbaccalaureate distance learning degree programs offered (no on-campus study). *Students:* 74 full-time (28 women), 342 part-time (183 women); includes 122 minority (84 Black or African American, non-Hispanic/Latino; 2 American Indian or Alaska Native, non-Hispanic/Latino; 19 Asian, non-Hispanic/Latino; 7 Hispanic/Latino; 10 Two or more races, non-Hispanic/Latino), 38 international. Average age 33. 305 applicants, 72% accepted, 131 enrolled. In 2013, 69 master's, 57 other advanced degrees awarded. *Entrance requirements:* For master's, GMAT (minimum score 450), minimum cumulative undergraduate GPA of 2.75. Additional exam requirements/recommendations for international students: Required—TOEFL. *Application deadline:* For fall admission, 5/15 for domestic students, 5/1 for international students; for winter admission, 10/15 for domestic students, 10/1 for international students; for spring admission, 3/15 for domestic students, 3/1 for international students. Applications are processed on a rolling basis. Application fee: $35. *Expenses:* Tuition, state resident: full-time $12,300; part-time $466 per credit hour. Tuition, nonresident: full-time $23,159; part-time $918 per credit hour. *Required fees:* $71 per credit hour. $46 per semester. One-time fee: $100. Tuition and fees vary according to course level and degree level. *Financial support:* Fellowships, research assistantships with full tuition reimbursements, teaching assistantships with full tuition reimbursements, career-related internships or fieldwork, Federal Work-Study, institutionally sponsored loans, scholarships/grants, tuition waivers (partial), and unspecified assistantships available. Support available to part-time students. Financial award applicants required to submit FAFSA. *Unit head:* K. Michelle Henry, Director, Academic Services, 734-487-4444, Fax: 734-483-1316, E-mail: mhenry1@emich.edu. *Application contact:* Beste Windes, Advisor, 734-487-4444, Fax: 734-483-1316, E-mail: bwindes@emich.edu.
Website: http://www.emich.edu/public/cob/gr/grad.html.

East Tennessee State University, School of Graduate Studies, College of Business and Technology, Department of Engineering Technology, Surveying and Digital Media, Johnson City, TN 37614. Offers entrepreneurial leadership (Postbaccalaureate Certificate); technology (MS), including digital media, engineering technology, entrepreneurial leadership. Part-time programs available. *Faculty:* 22 full-time (3 women), 4 part-time/adjunct (0 women). *Students:* 15 full-time (5 women), 13 part-time (3 women); includes 7 minority (6 Black or African American, non-Hispanic/Latino; 1 Asian, non-Hispanic/Latino), 6 international. Average age 32. 21 applicants, 57% accepted, 8 enrolled. In 2013, 16 master's awarded. *Degree requirements:* For master's, comprehensive exam, thesis optional, strategic experience, capstone; for Postbaccalaureate Certificate, strategic experience. *Entrance requirements:* For master's, bachelor's degree in technical or related area, minimum GPA of 3.0; for Postbaccalaureate Certificate, minimum GPA of 2.5, three letters of recommendation. Additional exam requirements/recommendations for international students: Required—TOEFL (minimum score 550 paper-based; 79 iBT). *Application deadline:* For fall admission, 6/1 for domestic students, 4/30 for international students; for spring admission, 11/1 for domestic students, 9/30 for international students. Application fee: $35 ($45 for international students). Electronic applications accepted. *Expenses:* Tuition, state resident: full-time $7900; part-time $395 per credit hour. Tuition, nonresident: full-time $21,960; part-time $1098 per credit hour. *Required fees:* $1345; $84 per credit hour. *Financial support:* In 2013–14, 16 students received support, including 8 research assistantships with full tuition reimbursements available (averaging $6,000 per year), 1 teaching assistantship with full tuition reimbursement available (averaging $6,000 per year); career-related internships or fieldwork, institutionally sponsored loans, scholarships/grants, and unspecified assistantships also available. Financial award application deadline: 7/1; financial award applicants required to submit FAFSA. *Faculty research:* Computer-integrated manufacturing, alternative energy, sustainability, CAD/CAM, organizational change. *Unit head:* Dr. Keith V. Johnson, Chair, 423-439-7822, Fax: 423-439-7750, E-mail: johnsonk@etsu.edu. *Application contact:* Kimberly Brockman, Graduate Specialist, 423-439-6165, Fax: 423-439-5624, E-mail: brockmank@etsu.edu.
Website: http://applieddesign.etsu.edu/.

Fairfield University, Charles F. Dolan School of Business, Fairfield, CT 06824-5195. Offers accounting (MBA, MS, CAS); accounting information systems (MBA, CAS); entrepreneurship (MBA, CAS); finance (MBA, MS, CAS); general management (MBA, CAS); human resource management (MBA, CAS); information systems and operations (MBA); information systems and operations management (CAS); marketing (MBA, CAS); taxation (MBA, CAS). *Accreditation:* AACSB. Part-time and evening/weekend programs available. *Faculty:* 18 full-time (9 women), 15 part-time/adjunct (4 women). *Students:* 94 full-time (45 women), 72 part-time (26 women); includes 49 minority (7 Black or African American, non-Hispanic/Latino; 33 Asian, non-Hispanic/Latino; 8 Hispanic/Latino; 1 Two or more races, non-Hispanic/Latino), 9 international. Average age 29. 116 applicants, 43% accepted, 26 enrolled. In 2013, 100 master's awarded. *Degree requirements:* For master's, capstone course. *Entrance requirements:* For master's, GMAT (minimum score 500), 2 letters of reference, resume, minimum GPA of 3.0. Additional exam requirements/recommendations for international students: Required—TOEFL (minimum score 550 paper-based; 80 iBT) or IELTS (minimum score 6.5). *Application deadline:* For fall admission, 5/15 for international students; for spring admission, 10/15 for international students. Applications are processed on a rolling basis. Application fee: $60. Electronic applications accepted. *Expenses:* Contact institution. *Financial support:* In 2013–14, 28 students received support. Scholarships/grants, unspecified assistantships, and merit-based one-time entrance scholarships available. Financial award applicants required to submit FAFSA. *Faculty research:* International finance, leadership and careers, ethics in accounting, emotions in consumer behavior, supply chain analysis, organizational leadership attributes, emotions in the workplace, real estate finance, effect of social media on stock prices. *Unit head:* Dr. Donald Gibson, Dean, 203-254-4070, Fax: 203-254-4105, E-mail: dgibson@fairfield.edu. *Application contact:* Marianne Gumpper, Director of Graduate and Continuing Studies Admission, 203-254-4184, Fax: 203-254-4073, E-mail: gradadmis@fairfield.edu.
Website: http://fairfield.edu/mba.

Fairleigh Dickinson University, College at Florham, Silberman College of Business, Departments of Management, Marketing, and Entrepreneurial Studies, Program in Entrepreneurial Studies, Madison, NJ 07940-1099. Offers MBA, Certificate.

Entrepreneurship

Fairleigh Dickinson University, Metropolitan Campus, Silberman College of Business, Departments of Management, Marketing, and Entrepreneurial Studies, Program in Entrepreneurial Studies, Teaneck, NJ 07666-1914. Offers MBA, Certificate.

Felician College, Program in Business, Lodi, NJ 07644-2117. Offers innovation and entrepreneurship (MBA). Part-time and evening/weekend programs available. *Students:* 30 part-time (12 women); includes 9 minority (3 Black or African American, non-Hispanic/Latino; 2 Asian, non-Hispanic/Latino; 4 Hispanic/Latino). *Entrance requirements:* For master's, GMAT. *Application deadline:* Applications are processed on a rolling basis. *Expenses: Tuition:* Part-time $945 per credit. *Required fees:* $317.50 per semester. *Unit head:* Dr. Beth Castiglia, Dean, Division of Business and Management Services, 201-559-6140, E-mail: mctaggartp@felician.edu. *Application contact:* Nicole Vitale, Assistant Director of Graduate Admissions, 201-559-6077, Fax: 201-559-6138, E-mail: graduate@felician.edu.
Website: http://www2.felician.edu/school-of-business/business-management-sciences/graduate/mba-innovation-entrepreneurial-leadership.

Florida Atlantic University, College of Business, Department of Management, Boca Raton, FL 33431-0991. Offers business administration (Exec MBA, MBA); entrepreneurship (MBA); health administration (MBA, MHA, MS); international business (MBA); management (PhD); sports management (MBA). *Faculty:* 22 full-time (10 women), 11 part-time/adjunct (6 women). *Students:* 267 full-time (120 women), 397 part-time (194 women); includes 279 minority (92 Black or African American, non-Hispanic/Latino; 31 Asian, non-Hispanic/Latino; 147 Hispanic/Latino; 9 Two or more races, non-Hispanic/Latino), 37 international. Average age 32. 551 applicants, 50% accepted, 216 enrolled. In 2013, 255 master's, 7 doctorates awarded. *Entrance requirements:* For master's, GMAT or GRE General Test, minimum GPA of 3.0 in last 60 hours of course work. Additional exam requirements/recommendations for international students: Required—TOEFL (minimum score 600 paper-based; 61 iBT), IELTS (minimum score 6). *Application deadline:* For fall admission, 7/25 for domestic students, 2/15 for international students; for spring admission, 12/10 for domestic students, 7/15 for international students. Applications are processed on a rolling basis. Application fee: $30. Electronic applications accepted. *Expenses:* Tuition, state resident: full-time $6660; part-time $370 per credit hour. Tuition, nonresident: full-time $18,450; part-time $1025 per credit hour. Tuition and fees vary according to course load. *Financial support:* Research assistantships with full tuition reimbursements, career-related internships or fieldwork, tuition waivers (partial), and unspecified assistantships available. *Faculty research:* Sports administration, healthcare, policy, finance, real estate, senior living. *Unit head:* Dr. Peggy Golden, Chair, 561-297-2675, E-mail: golden@fau.edu. *Application contact:* Dr. Marcy Krugel, Graduate Adviser, 561-297-3633, Fax: 561-297-1315, E-mail: krugel@fau.edu.
Website: http://business.fau.edu/departments/management/index.aspx.

Florida Institute of Technology, Graduate Programs, Nathan M. Bisk College of Business, Program in Innovation and Entrepreneurship, Melbourne, FL 32901-6975. Offers MS. Part-time and evening/weekend programs available. *Faculty:* 8 full-time (3 women). *Students:* 3 full-time (1 woman), 1 part-time (0 women); includes 1 minority (Hispanic/Latino). Average age 36. 16 applicants, 69% accepted, 4 enrolled. *Entrance requirements:* For master's, GMAT or GRE, bachelor's degree from regionally-accredited institution with minimum GPA of 3.0. *Application deadline:* For fall admission, 4/1 for international students; for spring admission, 9/1 for international students. *Expenses: Tuition:* Full-time $20,214; part-time $1123 per credit. Tuition and fees vary according to campus/location. *Financial support:* Application deadline: 3/1. *Unit head:* Dr. S Ann Becker, Dean, 321-674-7327, Fax: 321-674-8896, E-mail: abecker@fit.edu. *Application contact:* Cheryl A. Brown, Associate Director of Graduate Admissions, 321-674-7581, Fax: 321-723-9468, E-mail: cbrown@fit.edu.
Website: http://www.fit.edu/programs/grad/ms_innovation_entrepreneurship.

George Mason University, College of Visual and Performing Arts, Program in Arts Management, Fairfax, VA 22030. Offers arts management (MA); entrepreneurship in the arts (Certificate); fund-raising and development in the arts (Certificate); marketing and public relations in the arts (Certificate); programming and project management (Certificate). *Accreditation:* NASAD. *Faculty:* 2 full-time (both women), 6 part-time/adjunct (5 women). *Students:* 38 full-time (36 women), 41 part-time (35 women); includes 15 minority (7 Black or African American, non-Hispanic/Latino; 3 Asian, non-Hispanic/Latino; 3 Hispanic/Latino; 2 Two or more races, non-Hispanic/Latino), 12 international. Average age 29. 106 applicants, 52% accepted, 22 enrolled. In 2013, 37 master's awarded. *Degree requirements:* For master's, internship. *Entrance requirements:* For master's and Certificate, GRE (recommended), undergraduate degree with minimum GPA of 3.0, official transcripts, 2 letters of recommendation, statement of purpose, resume. Additional exam requirements/recommendations for international students: Required—TOEFL (minimum score 570 paper-based; 88 iBT), IELTS (minimum score 6.5), PTE. *Application deadline:* For fall admission, 3/1 for domestic students, 2/15 for international students; for spring admission, 10/1 for domestic students, 9/15 for international students. Application fee: $65 ($80 for international students). Electronic applications accepted. *Expenses:* Tuition, state resident: full-time $9350; part-time $390 per credit. Tuition, nonresident: full-time $25,754; part-time $1073 per credit. *Required fees:* $2688; $112 per credit. *Financial support:* In 2013–14, 1 student received support, including 1 teaching assistantship with full and partial tuition reimbursement available (averaging $10,920 per year); career-related internships or fieldwork, Federal Work-Study, scholarships/grants, unspecified assistantships, and health care benefits (for full-time research or teaching assistantship recipients) also available. Support available to part-time students. Financial award application deadline: 3/1; financial award applicants required to submit FAFSA. *Faculty research:* Information technology for arts managers, special topics in arts management, directions in gallery management, arts in society, public relations/marketing strategies for art organizations. *Unit head:* Claire Huschle, Interim Program Director, 703-993-8719, Fax: 703-993-9829, E-mail: chuschle@gmu.edu. *Application contact:* Allison Byers, Administrative Assistant, 703-993-8926, Fax: 703-993-9829, E-mail: abyers3@gmu.edu.
Website: http://artsmanagement.gmu.edu/arts-management-ma/.

Georgia Institute of Technology, Graduate Studies and Research, College of Management, Program in Business Administration, Atlanta, GA 30332-0001. Offers accounting (MBA); e-commerce (Certificate); engineering entrepreneurship (MBA); entrepreneurship (Certificate); finance (MBA); information technology management (MBA); international business (MBA, Certificate); management of technology (Certificate); marketing (MBA); operations management (MBA); organizational behavior (MBA); strategic management (MBA). *Accreditation:* AACSB.

Georgia State University, J. Mack Robinson College of Business, Department of Managerial Sciences, Atlanta, GA 30302-3083. Offers business analysis (MBA, MS); entrepreneurship (MBA); human resources management (MBA, MS); operations management (MBA, MS); organization behavior/human resource management (PhD); organization management (MBA); organizational change (MS); strategic management (PhD). *Accreditation:* AACSB. Part-time and evening/weekend programs available. *Faculty:* 18 full-time (6 women). *Students:* 31 full-time (15 women), 22 part-time (14 women); includes 20 minority (11 Black or African American, non-Hispanic/Latino; 1 American Indian or Alaska Native, non-Hispanic/Latino; 2 Asian, non-Hispanic/Latino; 2

Hispanic/Latino; 4 Two or more races, non-Hispanic/Latino), 16 international. Average age 31. 92 applicants, 20% accepted, 13 enrolled. In 2013, 45 master's, 2 doctorates awarded. *Degree requirements:* For doctorate, comprehensive exam, thesis/dissertation. *Entrance requirements:* For master's, GRE or GMAT, transcripts from all institutions attended, resume, essays; for doctorate, GMAT, three letters of recommendation, personal statement, transcripts from all institutions attended, resume. Additional exam requirements/recommendations for international students: Required—TOEFL (minimum score 610 paper-based; 101 iBT), IELTS (minimum score 7). *Application deadline:* For fall admission, 5/1 priority date for domestic students, 2/1 priority date for international students; for spring admission, 9/15 priority date for domestic students, 4/1 priority date for international students. Applications are processed on a rolling basis. Application fee: $50. Electronic applications accepted. *Expenses: Tuition, area resident:* Full-time $4176; part-time $348 per credit hour. Tuition, state resident: full-time $14,544; part-time $1212 per credit hour. Tuition, nonresident: full-time $14,544; part-time $1212 per credit hour. Tuition and fees vary according to course load and program. *Financial support:* Research assistantships, teaching assistantships, scholarships/grants, tuition waivers, and unspecified assistantships available. *Faculty research:* Entrepreneurship and Innovation; strategy process; workplace interactions, relationships, and processes; leadership and culture; supply chain management. *Unit head:* Dr. Pamela S. Barr, Interim Chair, 404-413-7525, Fax: 404-413-7571. *Application contact:* Toby McChesney, Assistant Dean for Graduate Recruiting and Student Services, 404-413-7167, Fax: 404-413-7162, E-mail: rcbgradadmissions@gsu.edu.
Website: http://mgmt.robinson.gsu.edu/.

Georgia State University, J. Mack Robinson College of Business, Institute of International Business, Atlanta, GA 30303. Offers international business (GMBA, MBA, MIB); international business and information technology (MBA); international entrepreneurship (MBA); MIB/MIA. Part-time and evening/weekend programs available. *Faculty:* 7 full-time (3 women). *Students:* 41 full-time (29 women), 22 part-time (13 women); includes 26 minority (14 Black or African American, non-Hispanic/Latino; 1 Asian, non-Hispanic/Latino; 11 Hispanic/Latino), 15 international. Average age 32. 60 applicants, 52% accepted, 21 enrolled. In 2013, 25 master's awarded. *Entrance requirements:* For master's, GRE or GMAT, transcripts from all institutions attended, resume, essays. Additional exam requirements/recommendations for international students: Required—TOEFL (minimum score 610 paper-based; 101 iBT), IELTS (minimum score 7). *Application deadline:* For fall admission, 5/1 priority date for domestic students, 2/1 priority date for international students; for spring admission, 9/15 priority date for domestic students, 5/1 priority date for international students. Applications are processed on a rolling basis. Application fee: $50. Electronic applications accepted. *Expenses: Tuition, area resident:* Full-time $4176; part-time $348 per credit hour. Tuition, state resident: full-time $14,544; part-time $1212 per credit hour. Tuition, nonresident: full-time $14,544; part-time $1212 per credit hour. Tuition and fees vary according to course load and program. *Financial support:* Research assistantships, teaching assistantships, scholarships/grants, tuition waivers (partial), and unspecified assistantships available. Financial award application deadline: 5/1. *Faculty research:* Business challenges in emerging markets (especially in India and China); interorganizational relationships in an international context, such as strategic alliances and global supply chain relations; globalization and entry mode strategy or new (or emerging) multinationals; emerging market development and business environments; cross-cultural effects on business processes and performance. *Unit head:* Dr. Daniel Bello, Professor/Director of the Institute of International Business, 404-413-7275, Fax: 404-413-7276. *Application contact:* Toby McChesney, Assistant Dean for Graduate Recruiting and Student Services, 404-413-7167, Fax: 404-413-7162, E-mail: rcbgradadmissions@gsu.edu.
Website: http://iib.gsu.edu/.

Grand Canyon University, College of Business, Phoenix, AZ 85017-1097. Offers accounting (MBA); corporate business administration (MBA); disaster preparedness and crisis management (MBA); executive fire service leadership (MS); finance (MBA); general management (MBA); government and policy (MPA); health care management (MPA); health systems management (MBA); human resource management (MBA); innovation (MBA); leadership (MBA, MS); management of information system (MBA); marketing (MBA); project-based (MBA); six sigma (MBA); strategic human resource management (MBA). *Accreditation:* ACBSP. Part-time and evening/weekend programs available. Postbaccalaureate distance learning degree programs offered (no on-campus study). *Entrance requirements:* For master's, equivalent of two years full-time professional work experience. Additional exam requirements/recommendations for international students: Required—TOEFL (minimum score 575 paper-based; 90 iBT), IELTS (minimum score 7). Electronic applications accepted.

Harrisburg University of Science and Technology, Program in Information Systems Engineering and Management, Harrisburg, PA 17101. Offers digital government (MS); digital health (MS); entrepreneurship (MS). Part-time programs available. *Degree requirements:* For master's, comprehensive exam, thesis optional. *Entrance requirements:* For master's, baccalaureate degree. Additional exam requirements/recommendations for international students: Required—TOEFL (minimum score 520 paper-based; 80 iBT). Electronic applications accepted.

Hult International Business School, Program in Business Administration - Hult London Campus, London WC 1B 4JP, United Kingdom. Offers entrepreneurship (MBA); international business (MBA); international finance (MBA); marketing (MBA). Part-time programs available. *Degree requirements:* For master's, comprehensive exam, thesis, internship. *Entrance requirements:* Additional exam requirements/recommendations for international students: Required—TOEFL (minimum score 580 paper-based), TWE (minimum score 5). Electronic applications accepted.

The International University of Monaco, Graduate Programs, Monte Carlo, Monaco. Offers entrepreneurship (EMBA, MBA); financial engineering (M Sc); hedge fund and private equity (M Sc); international marketing (EMBA, MBA); international wealth management (M Sc); luxury goods and services (EMBA, M Sc, MBA); wealth and asset management (EMBA, MBA). Part-time programs available. *Degree requirements:* For master's, comprehensive exam (for some programs), applied research project. *Entrance requirements:* Additional exam requirements/recommendations for international students: Required—TOEFL (minimum score 550 paper-based), IELTS. Electronic applications accepted. *Faculty research:* Gaming, leadership, disintermediation.

Jones International University, School of Business, Centennial, CO 80112. Offers accounting (MBA); business communication (MABC); entrepreneurship (MABC, MBA); finance (MBA); global enterprise management (MBA); health care management (MBA); information security management (MBA); information technology management (MBA); leadership and influence (MABC); leading the customer-driven organization (MABC); negotiation and conflict management (MBA); project management (MABC, MBA). Program only offered online. Part-time and evening/weekend programs available. Postbaccalaureate distance learning degree programs offered (no on-campus study). *Degree requirements:* For master's, capstone project. *Entrance requirements:* For master's, minimum cumulative GPA of 2.5. Additional exam requirements/recommendations for international students: Recommended—TOEFL (minimum score 550 paper-based). Electronic applications accepted.

Kaplan University, Davenport Campus, School of Business, Davenport, IA 52807-2095. Offers business administration (MBA); change leadership (MS); entrepreneurship (MBA); finance (MBA); health care management (MBA, MS); human resource (MBA); international business (MBA); management (MS); marketing (MBA); project management (MBA, MS); supply chain management and logistics (MBA, MS). *Accreditation:* ACBSP. Part-time and evening/weekend programs available. Postbaccalaureate distance learning degree programs offered (no on-campus study). *Entrance requirements:* Additional exam requirements/recommendations for international students: Required—TOEFL (minimum score 550 paper-based; 80 iBT). Electronic applications accepted.

Lamar University, College of Graduate Studies, College of Business, Beaumont, TX 77710. Offers accounting (MBA); experiential business and entrepreneurship (MBA); financial management (MBA); healthcare administration (MBA); information systems (MBA); management (MBA). *Accreditation:* AACSB. Part-time and evening/weekend programs available. *Degree requirements:* For master's, comprehensive exam (for some programs), thesis optional. *Entrance requirements:* For master's, GMAT. Additional exam requirements/recommendations for international students: Required—TOEFL (minimum score 525 paper-based). *Faculty research:* Marketing, finance, quantitative methods, management information systems, legal, environmental.

Lehigh University, College of Business and Economics, Department of Management, Bethlehem, PA 18015. Offers business administration (MBA); corporate entrepreneurship (MBA); international business (MBA); marketing (MBA); project management (MBA); supply chain management (MBA); MBA/E; MBA/M Ed. *Accreditation:* AACSB. Part-time and evening/weekend programs available. Postbaccalaureate distance learning degree programs offered (minimal on-campus study). *Faculty:* 11 full-time (4 women), 13 part-time/adjunct (4 women). *Students:* 28 full-time (10 women), 171 part-time (54 women); includes 32 minority (2 Black or African American, non-Hispanic/Latino; 21 Asian, non-Hispanic/Latino; 6 Hispanic/Latino; 3 Two or more races, non-Hispanic/Latino), 21 international. Average age 33. 108 applicants, 63% accepted, 25 enrolled. In 2013, 79 master's awarded. *Entrance requirements:* For master's, GMAT or GRE. Additional exam requirements/recommendations for international students: Required—TOEFL (minimum score 600 paper-based; 94 iBT). *Application deadline:* For fall admission, 7/15 for domestic students, 5/1 for international students; for spring admission, 12/1 for domestic students. Applications are processed on a rolling basis. Application fee: $100. Electronic applications accepted. *Financial support:* In 2013–14, 33 students received support, including 10 teaching assistantships with full and partial tuition reimbursements available (averaging $14,200 per year); career-related internships or fieldwork, scholarships/grants, health care benefits, tuition waivers (full and partial), and unspecified assistantships also available. Support available to part-time students. Financial award application deadline: 1/15. *Faculty research:* Information systems, organizational behavior, supply chain management, strategic management, entrepreneurship. *Total annual research expenditures:* $77,886. *Unit head:* Dr. Robert J. Trent, Department Chair, 610-758-4952, Fax: 610-758-6941, E-mail: rjt2@lehigh.edu. *Application contact:* Jen Giordano, Director of Recruitment and Admissions, 610-758-3418, Fax: 610-758-5283, E-mail: jlg210@lehigh.edu. Website: http://www4.lehigh.edu/business/academics/depts/management.

Lehigh University, P.C. Rossin College of Engineering and Applied Science, Technical Entrepreneurship Program, Bethlehem, PA 18015. Offers M Eng. *Faculty:* 3 full-time (0 women). *Students:* 28 full-time (10 women); includes 12 minority (2 Black or African American, non-Hispanic/Latino; 3 Asian, non-Hispanic/Latino; 4 Hispanic/Latino; 3 Two or more races, non-Hispanic/Latino), 2 international. Average age 24. 61 applicants, 46% accepted, 27 enrolled. In 2013, 14 master's awarded. *Entrance requirements:* For master's, bachelor's degree. *Application deadline:* For fall admission, 1/15 priority date for domestic students. Application fee: $75. Electronic applications accepted. *Unit head:* Dr. John Ochs, Director, 610-758-4593, Fax: 610-758-6131, E-mail: jbo0@lehigh.edu. *Application contact:* Jodie L. Johnson, Coordinator, 610-758-4789, Fax: 610-758-6131, E-mail: jlk4@lehigh.edu. Website: http://www.lehigh.edu/~innovate/.

Lenoir-Rhyne University, Graduate Programs, Charles M. Snipes School of Business, Hickory, NC 28601. Offers accounting (MBA); entrepreneurship (MBA); global leadership (MBA); leadership development (MBA). *Accreditation:* ACBSP. Part-time and evening/weekend programs available. *Degree requirements:* For master's, capstone course. *Entrance requirements:* For master's, GMAT, minimum undergraduate GPA of 2.7, graduate 3.0. Additional exam requirements/recommendations for international students: Required—TOEFL (minimum score 600 paper-based). Electronic applications accepted. *Expenses:* Contact institution.

LIM College, MBA Program, New York, NY 10022-5268. Offers entrepreneurship (MBA); fashion management (MBA). *Accreditation:* ACBSP. *Faculty:* 4 full-time (1 woman), 9 part-time/adjunct (4 women). *Students:* 44 full-time (43 women), 26 part-time (20 women). 46 applicants, 61% accepted, 21 enrolled. *Entrance requirements:* For master's, interview. Additional exam requirements/recommendations for international students: Required—TOEFL (minimum score 550 paper-based; 80 iBT), IELTS (minimum score 6.5). *Application deadline:* For fall admission, 7/1 for domestic students, 7/15 for international students; for spring admission, 1/15 for domestic and international students. *Expenses:* Tuition: Full-time $25,050; part-time $835 per credit hour. Tuition and fees vary according to course load. *Financial support:* Institutionally sponsored loans and scholarships/grants available. *Unit head:* Jacqueline Jenkins, Graduate Studies Director, 212-752-1530 Ext. 416, Fax: 212-750-3779, E-mail: mba@limcollege.edu. *Application contact:* Paul Mucciarone, Graduate Admission Coordinator, 646-218-4124, Fax: 212-750-3779, E-mail: paul.mucciarone@limcollege.edu. Website: http://graduate.limcollege.edu/mba.

Lincoln University, Graduate Studies, Jefferson City, MO 65101. Offers business administration (MBA), including accounting, entrepreneurship, management, public administration and policy; educational leadership (Ed S), including elementary leadership, secondary leadership, superintendency; guidance and counseling (M Ed), including community/agency counseling, elementary school, secondary school; history (MA); school administration and supervision (M Ed), including elementary school administration, secondary school administration, special education administration; school teaching (M Ed), including elementary school teaching, secondary school teaching; sociology (MA); sociology/criminal justice (MA). Part-time and evening/weekend programs available. Postbaccalaureate distance learning degree programs offered (minimal on-campus study). *Students:* 42 full-time (29 women), 109 part-time (66 women); includes 51 minority (37 Black or African American, non-Hispanic/Latino; 10 American Indian or Alaska Native, non-Hispanic/Latino; 1 Asian, non-Hispanic/Latino; 2 Hispanic/Latino; 1 Two or more races, non-Hispanic/Latino), 10 international. Average age 33. 84 applicants, 76% accepted, 51 enrolled. In 2013, 73 master's, 6 other advanced degrees awarded. *Degree requirements:* For master's and Ed S, comprehensive exam, thesis optional. *Entrance requirements:* For master's and Ed S, GRE, MAT or GMAT, minimum GPA of 2.75 in major, 2.5 overall; 3 letters of recommendation; minimum C average in English composition; personal statement of purpose. Additional exam requirements/recommendations for international students: Required—TOEFL (minimum score 500 paper-based; 61 iBT). *Application deadline:* For fall admission, 8/1 priority date for domestic and international students; for spring

admission, 12/1 priority date for domestic and international students; for summer admission, 5/1 priority date for domestic and international students. Applications are processed on a rolling basis. Application fee: $30. *Expenses:* Tuition, state resident: full-time $6840; part-time $285 per credit hour. Tuition, nonresident: full-time $12,720; part-time $530 per credit hour. *Required fees:* $587; $587 per year. Tuition and fees vary according to course load. *Financial support:* Federal Work-Study and scholarships/grants available. Support available to part-time students. Financial award application deadline: 3/1; financial award applicants required to submit FAFSA. *Unit head:* Dr. Linda S. Bickel, Dean, 573-681-5247, Fax: 573-681-5106, E-mail: gradschool@lincolnu.edu. *Application contact:* Irasema Steck, Administrative Assistant, 573-681-5247, Fax: 573-681-5106, E-mail: gradschool@lincolnu.edu. Website: http://www.lincolnu.edu/web/graduate-studies/graduate-studies.

Lindenwood University, Graduate Programs, School of Business and Entrepreneurship, St. Charles, MO 63301-1695. Offers accountancy (MA); accounting (MBA); business administration (MBA); entrepreneurial studies (MBA); finance (MBA, MS); human resource management (MBA); international business (MBA); leadership (MA); management (MBA); marketing (MBA, MS); public management (MBA); sport management (MA); supply chain management (MBA). *Accreditation:* ACBSP. Part-time and evening/weekend programs available. Postbaccalaureate distance learning degree programs offered (no on-campus study). *Faculty:* 18 full-time (8 women), 33 part-time/adjunct (8 women). *Students:* 292 full-time (130 women), 111 part-time (46 women); includes 59 minority (42 Black or African American, non-Hispanic/Latino; 5 American Indian or Alaska Native, non-Hispanic/Latino; 1 Asian, non-Hispanic/Latino; 5 Hispanic/Latino; 6 Two or more races, non-Hispanic/Latino), 112 international. Average age 29. 212 applicants, 51% accepted, 102 enrolled. In 2013, 221 master's awarded. *Degree requirements:* For master's, comprehensive exam (for some programs), thesis (for some programs), minimum GPA of 3.0. *Entrance requirements:* For master's, interview, minimum GPA of 3.0, letter of recommendation. Additional exam requirements/recommendations for international students: Required—TOEFL (minimum score 550 paper-based; 80 iBT). *Application deadline:* For fall admission, 8/12 priority date for domestic and international students; for winter admission, 1/6 priority date for domestic and international students; for spring admission, 3/10 priority date for domestic and international students; for summer admission, 5/27 priority date for domestic and international students. Applications are processed on a rolling basis. Application fee: $30 ($100 for international students). Electronic applications accepted. *Expenses:* Tuition: Full-time $14,800; part-time $428 per credit hour. *Required fees:* $350. Tuition and fees vary according to course level and course load. *Financial support:* In 2013–14, 268 students received support. Career-related internships or fieldwork, Federal Work-Study, institutionally sponsored loans, scholarships/grants, tuition waivers (partial), and unspecified assistantships available. Financial award application deadline: 6/30; financial award applicants required to submit FAFSA. *Unit head:* Roger Ellis, Dean, 636-949-4839, E-mail: rellis@lindenwood.edu. *Application contact:* Brett Barger, Dean of Evening Admissions and Extension Campuses, 636-949-4934, Fax: 636-949-4109, E-mail: adultadmissions@lindenwood.edu. Website: http://www.lindenwood.edu.

Long Island University–Hudson at Rockland, Graduate School, Master of Business Administration Program, Orangeburg, NY 10962. Offers business administration (Post Master's Certificate); entrepreneurship (MBA); finance (MBA); healthcare sector management (MBA); management (MBA). Part-time and evening/weekend programs available. *Entrance requirements:* For master's, GMAT, college transcripts, two letters of recommendation, personal statement, resume.

Loyola University Chicago, Quinlan School of Business, MBA Programs, Chicago, IL 60610. Offers accounting (MBA); business ethics (MBA); derivative markets (MBA); economics (MBA); entrepreneurship (MBA); executive (MBA); finance (MBA); healthcare management (MBA); human resources management (MBA); information systems management (MBA); intercontinental (MBA); international business (MBA); marketing (MBA); operations management (MBA); risk management (MBA); JD/MBA. Part-time and evening/weekend programs available. *Faculty:* 76 full-time (20 women), 10 part-time/adjunct (4 women). *Students:* 73 full-time (34 women), 294 part-time (129 women); includes 60 minority (18 Black or African American, non-Hispanic/Latino; 28 Asian, non-Hispanic/Latino; 14 Hispanic/Latino), 19 international. Average age 31. 529 applicants, 51% accepted, 153 enrolled. In 2013, 229 master's awarded. *Entrance requirements:* For master's, GMAT or GRE, official transcripts, two letters of recommendation, statement of purpose, resume. Additional exam requirements/recommendations for international students: Required—TOEFL (minimum score 90 iBT) or IELTS (minimum score 6.5). *Application deadline:* For fall admission, 7/15 for domestic and international students; for winter admission, 10/1 for domestic and international students; for spring admission, 1/15 for domestic and international students; for summer admission, 4/1 for domestic and international students. Applications are processed on a rolling basis. Application fee: $50. Electronic applications accepted. Application fee is waived when completed online. *Expenses:* Tuition: Full-time $16,740; part-time $930 per credit. *Required fees:* $135 per semester. *Financial support:* Scholarships/grants and unspecified assistantships available. *Faculty research:* Social enterprise and responsibility, emerging markets, supply chain management, risk management. *Unit head:* Jennifer Huntley, Assistant Dean for Graduate Programs, 312-915-6124, Fax: 312-915-7207, E-mail: jhuntle@luc.edu. *Application contact:* Jessica Gagle, Enrollment Advisor, Quinlan School of Business Graduate Programs, 312-915-8908, Fax: 312-915-7207, E-mail: jgagle@luc.edu.

Marquette University, Graduate School of Management, Program in Business Administration, Milwaukee, WI 53201-1881. Offers business administration (MBA); economics (MBA); entrepreneurship (Certificate); finance (MBA); human resources (MBA); international business (MBA); management information systems (MBA); marketing (MBA); operations and supply chain management (MBA); sports business (MBA); JD/MBA; MBA/MA; MBA/MSN. *Accreditation:* AACSB. Part-time and evening/weekend programs available. *Students:* 28 full-time (13 women), 265 part-time (66 women); includes 20 minority (7 Black or African American, non-Hispanic/Latino; 8 Asian, non-Hispanic/Latino; 5 Hispanic/Latino), 11 international. Average age 31. 185 applicants. In 2013, 129 master's, 2 other advanced degrees awarded. *Degree requirements:* For Certificate, business plan. *Entrance requirements:* For master's, GMAT or GRE, letters of recommendation. Additional exam requirements/recommendations for international students: Required—TOEFL (minimum score 550 paper-based; 88 iBT), IELTS (minimum score 6.5), PTE. *Application deadline:* For fall admission, 2/15 for domestic and international students. Applications are processed on a rolling basis. Application fee: $50. Electronic applications accepted. *Financial support:* In 2013–14, 4 fellowships, 11 teaching assistantships were awarded; research assistantships, Federal Work-Study, institutionally sponsored loans, scholarships/grants, and tuition waivers (full and partial) also available. Support available to part-time students. Financial award application deadline: 2/15. *Faculty research:* Ethics in the professions, services marketing, technology impact on decision-making, mentoring. *Unit head:* Dr. Mark Eppli, Dean, 414-288-5724. *Application contact:* Dr. Jeanne Simmons, Associate Dean, 414-288-7145. Website: http://business.marquette.edu/academics/mba.

Entrepreneurship

McGill University, Faculty of Graduate and Postdoctoral Studies, Desautels Faculty of Management, Montréal, QC H3A 2T5, Canada. Offers administration (PhD); entrepreneurial studies (MBA); finance (MBA); general management (Post Master's Certificate); information systems (MBA); international business (MBA); international practicing management (MM); management (MBA); management for development (MBA); manufacturing management (MMM); marketing (MBA); operations management (MBA); public accountancy (Diploma); strategic management (MBA); MBA/LL B; MD/MBA. MMM offered jointly with Faculty of Engineering; PhD with Concordia University, HEC Montreal, Université de Montréal, Université du Québec à Montréal.

Mercyhurst University, Graduate Studies, Program in Organizational Leadership, Erie, PA 16546. Offers accounting (MS); entrepreneurship (MS); higher education administration (MS); human resources (MS); nonprofit management (MS); organizational leadership (Certificate); sports leadership (MS). Part-time and evening/weekend programs available. *Degree requirements:* For master's, thesis. *Entrance requirements:* For master's, GRE General Test or MAT, interview, resume, essay, three professional references, transcripts. Additional exam requirements/recommendations for international students: Required—TOEFL. Electronic applications accepted. *Faculty research:* Leadership training, organizational communication, leadership pedagogy.

Michigan Technological University, Graduate School, Institute for Leadership and Innovation, Houghton, MI 49931. Offers Graduate Certificate.

New York University, Polytechnic School of Engineering, Department of Chemical and Biomolecular Engineering, Major in Biotechnology and Entrepreneurship, New York, NY 10012-1019. Offers MS. *Students:* 19 full-time (12 women), 5 part-time (3 women); includes 3 minority (2 Asian, non-Hispanic/Latino; 1 Hispanic/Latino), 17 international. Average age 24. 58 applicants, 60% accepted, 13 enrolled. In 2013, 11 master's awarded. *Entrance requirements:* Additional exam requirements/recommendations for international students: Required—TOEFL (minimum score 550 paper-based; 80 iBT); Recommended—IELTS (minimum score 6.5). *Application deadline:* For fall admission, 7/31 priority date for domestic students, 4/30 priority date for international students; for spring admission, 12/31 priority date for domestic students, 10/30 priority date for international students. Applications are processed on a rolling basis. Application fee: $75. Electronic applications accepted. *Expenses: Tuition:* Full-time $35,856; part-time $1494 per unit. *Required fees:* $1408; $64 per unit. $473 per term. Tuition and fees vary according to course load and program. *Financial support:* Institutionally sponsored loans, scholarships/grants, and unspecified assistantships available. Support available to part-time students. *Unit head:* Dr. Bruce Garetz, Department Head, 718-260-3287, E-mail: bgaretz@poly.edu. *Application contact:* Raymond Lutzky, Director, Graduate Enrollment Management, 718-637-5984, Fax: 718-260-3624, E-mail: rlutzky@poly.edu.

New York University, Polytechnic School of Engineering, Department of Technology Management, New York, NY 10012-1019. Offers construction management (Advanced Certificate); electronic business management (Advanced Certificate); entrepreneurship (Advanced Certificate); human resources management (Advanced Certificate); industrial engineering (MS); information management (Advanced Certificate); management (MS); management of technology (MS); manufacturing engineering (MS); organizational behavior (MS, Advanced Certificate); project management (Advanced Certificate); technology management (MBA, PhD, Advanced Certificate); telecommunications management (Advanced Certificate). Part-time and evening/weekend programs available. *Faculty:* 7 full-time (1 woman), 41 part-time/adjunct (2 women). *Students:* 285 full-time (132 women), 116 part-time (45 women); includes 50 minority (10 Black or African American, non-Hispanic/Latino; 29 Asian, non-Hispanic/Latino; 11 Hispanic/Latino), 284 international. Average age 30. 726 applicants, 60% accepted, 140 enrolled. In 2013, 137 master's awarded. *Degree requirements:* For master's, comprehensive exam (for some programs), thesis (for some programs); for doctorate, comprehensive exam, thesis/dissertation. *Entrance requirements:* For master's, GMAT, minimum B average in undergraduate course work. Additional exam requirements/recommendations for international students: Required—TOEFL (minimum score 550 paper-based; 80 iBT); Recommended—IELTS (minimum score 6.5). *Application deadline:* For fall admission, 7/31 priority date for domestic students, 4/30 priority date for international students; for spring admission, 12/31 priority date for domestic students, 11/30 priority date for international students. Applications are processed on a rolling basis. Application fee: $75. Electronic applications accepted. *Expenses: Tuition:* Full-time $35,856; part-time $1494 per unit. *Required fees:* $1408; $64 per unit. $473 per term. Tuition and fees vary according to course load and program. *Financial support:* In 2013–14, 1 fellowship (averaging $26,400 per year) was awarded; research assistantships, teaching assistantships, institutionally sponsored loans, scholarships/grants, and unspecified assistantships also available. Support available to part-time students. *Faculty research:* Global innovation and research and development strategy, managing emerging technologies, technology and development, service design and innovation, tech entrepreneurship and commercialization, sustainable and clean-tech innovation, impacts of information technology upon individuals, organizations and society. *Total annual research expenditures:* $692,936. *Unit head:* Prof. Bharadwaj Rao, Head, 718-260-3617, Fax: 718-260-3874, E-mail: brao@poly.edu. *Application contact:* Raymond Lutzky, Director of Graduate Enrollment Management, 718-637-5984, Fax: 718-260-3624, E-mail: rlutzky@poly.edu.
Website: http://www.poly.edu/academics/departments/technology/.

North Carolina State University, Graduate School, Poole College of Management, Program in Business Administration, Raleigh, NC 27695. Offers biosciences management (MBA); entrepreneurship and technology commercialization (MBA); financial management (MBA); innovation management (MBA); marketing management (MBA); services management (MBA); supply chain management (MBA). *Accreditation:* AACSB. Part-time programs available. *Degree requirements:* For master's, thesis optional. *Entrance requirements:* For master's, GMAT, interview, 3 letters of recommendation. Additional exam requirements/recommendations for international students: Required—TOEFL (minimum score 600 paper-based; 100 iBT). Electronic applications accepted. *Faculty research:* Manufacturing strategy, information systems, technology commercialization, managing research and development, historical stock returns.

See Display on page 120 and Close-Up on page 189.

Northwestern University, The Graduate School, Kellogg School of Management, Management Programs, Evanston, IL 60208. Offers accounting information and management (MBA, PhD); analytical finance (MBA); business administration (MBA); decision sciences (MBA); entrepreneurship and innovation (MBA); finance (MBA, PhD); health enterprise management (MBA); human resources management (MBA); international business (MBA); management and organizations (MBA, PhD); management and organizations and sociology (PhD); management and strategy (MBA); management studies (MS); managerial analytics (MBA); managerial economics (MBA); managerial economics and strategy (PhD); marketing (MBA, PhD); marketing management (MBA); media management (MBA); operations management (MBA, PhD); real estate (MBA); social enterprise at Kellogg (MBA); JD/MBA. Part-time and evening/weekend programs available. Terminal master's awarded for partial completion of doctoral program. *Degree requirements:* For doctorate, thesis/dissertation, 2 years of coursework, qualifying (field) exam and candidacy, summer research papers and presentations to faculty, proposal defense, final exam/defense. *Entrance requirements:* For master's, GMAT, GRE, interview, 2 letters of recommendation, college transcripts, resume, essays, Kellogg honor code; for doctorate, GMAT, GRE, statement of purpose, transcripts, 2 letters of recommendation, resume, interview. Additional exam requirements/recommendations for international students: Required—TOEFL, IELTS. Electronic applications accepted. *Expenses:* Contact institution. *Faculty research:* Business cycles and international finance, health policy, networks, non-market strategy, consumer psychology.

Notre Dame de Namur University, Division of Academic Affairs, School of Business and Management, Program in Business Administration, Belmont, CA 94002-1908. Offers business administration (MBA); entrepreneurship (MBA); finance (MBA); human resource management (MBA); marketing (MBA); media and promotion (MBA); technology and operations management (MBA). *Accreditation:* ACBSP. Part-time and evening/weekend programs available. *Entrance requirements:* For master's, minimum GPA of 2.5. Additional exam requirements/recommendations for international students: Required—TOEFL (minimum score 550 paper-based; 79 iBT). Electronic applications accepted.

Notre Dame de Namur University, Division of Academic Affairs, School of Business and Management, Program in Public Administration, Belmont, CA 94002-1908. Offers human resource management (MPA); public administration (MPA); public affairs administration (MPA); social enterprise (MPA). Part-time and evening/weekend programs available. Postbaccalaureate distance learning degree programs offered (no on-campus study). *Entrance requirements:* For master's, interview, minimum GPA of 2.5. Additional exam requirements/recommendations for international students: Required—TOEFL (minimum score 550 paper-based; 79 iBT). Electronic applications accepted.

Oakland University, Graduate Study and Lifelong Learning, School of Business Administration, Department of Management and Marketing, Rochester, MI 48309-4401. Offers business administration (MBA); entrepreneurship (Certificate); general management (Certificate); human resource management (Certificate); international business (Certificate); marketing (Certificate). *Faculty:* 11 full-time (4 women), 2 part-time/adjunct (both women). *Students:* 72 full-time (28 women), 232 part-time (63 women); includes 51 minority (17 Black or African American, non-Hispanic/Latino; 2 American Indian or Alaska Native, non-Hispanic/Latino; 25 Asian, non-Hispanic/Latino; 7 Hispanic/Latino), 25 international. Average age 32. 238 applicants, 43% accepted, 88 enrolled. In 2013, 144 master's, 4 other advanced degrees awarded. Application fee: $0. *Unit head:* Ravi Parameswaran, Chair, 238-370-3279, Fax: 249-370-4275. *Application contact:* Donna Free, Coordinator, 248-370-3281.

Oklahoma State University, Graduate College, Stillwater, OK 74078. Offers aerospace security (Graduate Certificate); bioenergy and sustainable technology (Graduate Certificate); bioinformatics (Graduate Certificate); business data mining (Graduate Certificate); business sustainability (Graduate Certificate); engineering and technology management (Graduate Certificate); entrepreneurship (Graduate Certificate); environmental science (MS); global issues (Graduate Certificate); grassland management (Graduate Certificate); information assurance (Graduate Certificate); interdisciplinary sciences (MS); interdisciplinary toxicology (Graduate Certificate); international studies (MS); non-profit management (Graduate Certificate); online teaching (Graduate Certificate); photonics (PhD); plant science (PhD); teaching English to speakers of other languages (Graduate Certificate); telecommunications management (MS). Programs are interdisciplinary. *Faculty:* 4 full-time (2 women), 2 part-time/adjunct (1 woman). *Students:* 74 full-time (58 women), 147 part-time (74 women); includes 44 minority (12 Black or African American, non-Hispanic/Latino; 8 American Indian or Alaska Native, non-Hispanic/Latino; 10 Asian, non-Hispanic/Latino; 6 Hispanic/Latino; 8 Two or more races, non-Hispanic/Latino), 43 international. Average age 32. 495 applicants, 70% accepted, 75 enrolled. In 2013, 55 master's, 11 doctorates awarded. *Degree requirements:* For master's, thesis (for some programs); for doctorate, comprehensive exam, thesis/dissertation. *Entrance requirements:* For master's and doctorate, GRE or GMAT. Additional exam requirements/recommendations for international students: Required—TOEFL (minimum score 550 paper-based; 79 iBT). *Application deadline:* For fall admission, 3/1 priority date for international students; for spring admission, 8/1 priority date for international students. Applications are processed on a rolling basis. Application fee: $40 ($75 for international students). Electronic applications accepted. *Expenses:* Tuition, state resident: full-time $4272; part-time $178 per credit hour. Tuition, nonresident: full-time $17,472; part-time $709 per credit hour. *Required fees:* $2413.20; $100.55 per credit hour. One-time fee: $50 full-time. Part-time tuition and fees vary according to course load and campus/location. *Financial support:* Career-related internships or fieldwork, Federal Work-Study, scholarships/grants, health care benefits, tuition waivers (partial), and unspecified assistantships available. Support available to part-time students. Financial award application deadline: 3/1; financial award applicants required to submit FAFSA. *Unit head:* Dr. Sheryl Tucker, Dean, 405-744-7099, Fax: 405-744-0355, E-mail: grad-i@okstate.edu. *Application contact:* Dr. Susan Mathew, Coordinator of Admissions, 405-744-6368, Fax: 405-744-0355, E-mail: grad-i@okstate.edu.
Website: http://gradcollege.okstate.edu/.

Oklahoma State University, Spears School of Business, School of Entrepreneurship, Stillwater, OK 74078. Offers MBA, MS, PhD. Part-time programs available. *Faculty:* 12 full-time (1 woman), 2 part-time/adjunct (1 woman). *Students:* 39 full-time (12 women), 94 part-time (18 women); includes 35 minority (11 Black or African American, non-Hispanic/Latino; 2 American Indian or Alaska Native, non-Hispanic/Latino; 7 Asian, non-Hispanic/Latino; 12 Hispanic/Latino; 1 Native Hawaiian or other Pacific Islander, non-Hispanic/Latino; 2 Two or more races, non-Hispanic/Latino), 15 international. 135 applicants, 29% accepted, 29 enrolled. In 2013, 34 master's, 1 doctorate awarded. *Degree requirements:* For master's, thesis or alternative; for doctorate, comprehensive exam, thesis/dissertation. *Entrance requirements:* For master's and doctorate, GMAT. Additional exam requirements/recommendations for international students: Required—TOEFL (minimum score 550 paper-based; 89 iBT). *Application deadline:* For fall admission, 3/1 priority date for international students; for spring admission, 8/1 priority date for international students. Applications are processed on a rolling basis. Application fee: $40 ($75 for international students). Electronic applications accepted. *Expenses:* Tuition, state resident: full-time $4272; part-time $178 per credit hour. Tuition, nonresident: full-time $17,472; part-time $709 per credit hour. *Required fees:* $2413.20; $100.55 per credit hour. One-time fee: $50 full-time. Part-time tuition and fees vary according to course load and campus/location. *Financial support:* In 2013–14, 11 research assistantships (averaging $17,212 per year), 15 teaching assistantships (averaging $10,770 per year) were awarded; career-related internships or fieldwork, Federal Work-Study, scholarships/grants, health care benefits, tuition waivers (partial), and unspecified assistantships also available. Support available to part-time students. Financial award application deadline: 3/1; financial award applicants required to submit FAFSA. *Unit head:* Dr. Bruce Barringer, Department Head, 405-744-9702, E-mail: bruce.barringer@okstate.edu.
Website: http://entrepreneurship.okstate.edu/.

Oral Roberts University, School of Business, Tulsa, OK 74171. Offers accounting (MBA); entrepreneurship (MBA); finance (MBA); international business (MBA);

management (MBA); marketing (MBA); non-profit management (MBA); not for profit management (MNM). *Accreditation:* ACBSP. Part-time programs available. Postbaccalaureate distance learning degree programs offered (minimal on-campus study). *Degree requirements:* For master's, thesis optional. *Entrance requirements:* For master's, minimum cumulative GPA of 3.0. Additional exam requirements/recommendations for international students: Required—TOEFL (minimum score 550 paper-based; 79 iBT). Electronic applications accepted. *Faculty research:* Social media, international business and marketing.

Pace University, Lubin School of Business, Program in Management, New York, NY 10038. Offers entrepreneurial studies (MBA); executive management (MBA); human resource management (MBA, MS); management (MBA); strategic management (MBA). Part-time and evening/weekend programs available. *Students:* 20 full-time (9 women), 141 part-time (78 women); includes 40 minority (19 Black or African American, non-Hispanic/Latino; 15 Asian, non-Hispanic/Latino; 6 Hispanic/Latino), 44 international. Average age 29. 343 applicants, 39% accepted, 69 enrolled. In 2013, 44 master's awarded. *Entrance requirements:* For master's, GMAT, GRE. Additional exam requirements/recommendations for international students: Required—TOEFL. *Application deadline:* For fall admission, 8/1 priority date for domestic students, 6/1 for international students; for spring admission, 12/1 for domestic students, 10/1 for international students. Applications are processed on a rolling basis. Application fee: $70. Electronic applications accepted. *Expenses: Tuition:* Part-time $1075 per credit. *Required fees:* $192 per semester. Tuition and fees vary according to course load, degree level and program. *Financial support:* Research assistantships, career-related internships or fieldwork, and Federal Work-Study available. Support available to part-time students. Financial award applicants required to submit FAFSA. *Unit head:* Dr. John C. Byrne, Chairperson, 212-618-6581, E-mail: jbyrne@pace.edu. *Application contact:* Susan Ford-Goldschein, Director of Graduate Admissions, 212-346-1531, Fax: 212-346-1585, E-mail: gradnyc@pace.edu.
Website: http://www.pace.edu/lubin.

Peru State College, Graduate Programs, Program in Organizational Management, Peru, NE 68421. Offers MS. Program offered online only. Part-time programs available. Postbaccalaureate distance learning degree programs offered (no on-campus study). *Faculty:* 6. *Students:* 48 part-time (22 women); includes 1 minority (Black or African American, non-Hispanic/Latino). Average age 34. 38 applicants, 95% accepted, 25 enrolled. *Degree requirements:* For master's, thesis (for some programs). *Application deadline:* For fall admission, 8/6 priority date for domestic students; for spring admission, 1/5 priority date for domestic students. Application fee: $0. *Expenses:* Contact institution. *Faculty research:* Emotional intelligence. *Unit head:* Dr. Greg Seay, Dean of Graduate Programs, 402-872-2283, Fax: 402-872-2413, E-mail: gseay@peru.edu. *Application contact:* Emily Volker, Program Coordinator, 402-872-2282, Fax: 402-872-2413, E-mail: evolker@peru.edu.

Pontificia Universidad Catolica Madre y Maestra, Graduate School, Faculty of Social and Administrative Sciences, Santiago, Dominican Republic. Offers business administration (MBA), including business development, finance, international business, management skills (M Mgmt, MBA), marketing, operations, strategic cost management, strategy, tourist destination planning and management; law (LL M), including civil law, corporate business law, criminal law, international relations, real estate law; management (M Mgmt), including higher financial management, insurance program administration, management skills (M Mgmt, MBA); psychology (MA), including clinical child and adolescent psychology, forensic psychology; strategic human resources (EMBA).

Post University, Program in Business Administration, Waterbury, CT 06723-2540. Offers accounting (MSA); business administration (MBA); corporate innovation (MBA); entrepreneurship (MBA); finance (MBA); healthcare (MBA); leadership (MBA); marketing (MBA); project management (MBA). *Accreditation:* ACBSP. Postbaccalaureate distance learning degree programs offered.

Queen's University at Kingston, Queens School of Business, Program in Business Administration, Kingston, ON K7L 3N6, Canada. Offers consulting and project management (MBA); finance (MBA); innovation and entrepreneurship (MBA); marketing (MBA). *Accreditation:* AACSB. *Degree requirements:* For master's, thesis optional, research project. *Entrance requirements:* For master's, GMAT, minimum B+ average. Additional exam requirements/recommendations for international students: Required—TOEFL. Electronic applications accepted. *Faculty research:* Management fundamentals, strategic thinking, global business, innovation and change, leadership.

Regent University, Graduate School, School of Business and Leadership, Virginia Beach, VA 23464-9800. Offers business administration (MBA); leadership (Certificate); organizational leadership (MA, PhD), including ecclesial leadership (PhD), entrepreneurial leadership (PhD), human resource development (PhD); strategic foresight (MA); strategic leadership (DSL), including global consulting, leadership coaching, strategic foresight. Part-time and evening/weekend programs available. Postbaccalaureate distance learning degree programs offered (minimal on-campus study). *Faculty:* 11 full-time (4 women), 6 part-time/adjunct (3 women). *Students:* 34 full-time (19 women), 655 part-time (276 women); includes 222 minority (175 Black or African American, non-Hispanic/Latino; 2 American Indian or Alaska Native, non-Hispanic/Latino; 16 Asian, non-Hispanic/Latino; 29 Hispanic/Latino), 117 international. Average age 42. 384 applicants, 53% accepted, 120 enrolled. In 2013, 74 master's, 72 doctorates awarded. *Degree requirements:* For master's, thesis or alternative, 3 credit hour culminating experience; for doctorate, thesis/dissertation. *Entrance requirements:* For master's, GRE, GMAT, minimum undergraduate GPA of 2.75, computer literacy survey, 2 recommendations, resume, transcripts, essay; for doctorate, GRE, GMAT, sample of writing, minimum 3 years of relevant experience, computer literacy survey, 2 recommendations, resume, essay, transcripts; for Certificate, writing sample, resume, transcripts. Additional exam requirements/recommendations for international students: Required—TOEFL (minimum score 577 paper-based). *Application deadline:* For fall admission, 5/1 priority date for domestic students; for spring admission, 10/1 priority date for domestic students. Applications are processed on a rolling basis. Application fee: $50. Electronic applications accepted. *Expenses:* Contact institution. *Financial support:* Career-related internships or fieldwork, scholarships/grants, and tuition waivers (full and partial) available. Support available to part-time students. Financial award application deadline: 9/1. *Faculty research:* Servant leadership, ethics and values, telecommuting and family values, organizational communications, distance education. *Unit head:* Dr. Doris Gomez, Interim Dean, 757-352-4686, Fax: 757-352-4634, E-mail: dorigom@regent.edu. *Application contact:* Matthew Chadwick, Director of Enrollment Support Services, 800-373-5504, Fax: 757-352-4381, E-mail: admissions@regent.edu.
Website: http://www.regent.edu/acad/global/.

Rensselaer Polytechnic Institute, Graduate School, Lally School of Management, Program in Technology Commercialization and Entrepreneurship, Troy, NY 12180-3590. Offers MS. Program is an interdisciplinary collaboration with 11 other RPI departments and Albany Law School. Part-time programs available. *Faculty:* 21 full-time (5 women), 2 part-time/adjunct (0 women). *Students:* 4 full-time (1 woman), 3 international. Average age 24. 16 applicants, 69% accepted, 5 enrolled. In 2013, 5 master's awarded. *Entrance requirements:* For master's, GMAT or GRE. Additional

exam requirements/recommendations for international students: Required—TOEFL (minimum score 570 paper-based; 88 iBT), IELTS (minimum score 6.5), PTE (minimum score 60). *Application deadline:* For fall admission, 1/1 for domestic and international students. Application fee: $75. *Expenses: Tuition:* Full-time $45,100; part-time $1879 per credit hour. *Required fees:* $1983. *Financial support:* In 2013–14, 4 students received support. Scholarships/grants available. Financial award application deadline: 1/1. *Unit head:* Dr. Gina O'Connor, Graduate Program Director, 518-276-6842, E-mail: oconng@rpi.edu. *Application contact:* Office of Graduate Admissions, 518-276-6216, E-mail: gradadmissions@rpi.edu.
Website: http://lallyschool.rpi.edu/academics/ms_tce.html.

Rochester Institute of Technology, Graduate Enrollment Services, Saunders College of Business, Program in Entrepreneurship and Innovative Ventures, Rochester, NY 14623-5603. Offers MS. Part-time programs available. *Students:* 4 full-time (all women), 1 part-time (0 women). Average age 22. 22 applicants, 27% accepted, 4 enrolled. In 2013, 5 master's awarded. *Degree requirements:* For master's, project or research paper. *Entrance requirements:* For master's, GMAT or GRE. Additional exam requirements/recommendations for international students: Required—PTE (minimum score 63), TOEFL (minimum score 580 paper-based; 92 iBT) or IELTS (minimum score 7). Application fee: $60. Electronic applications accepted. *Expenses: Tuition:* Full-time $37,236; part-time $1552 per credit hour. *Required fees:* $250. *Unit head:* Charles Ackley, Graduate Program Director, 585-475-6916, E-mail: cackley@saunders.rit.edu. *Application contact:* Diane Ellison, Assistant Vice President and Director, Graduate Enrollment Services, 585-475-2229, Fax: 585-475-7164, E-mail: gradinfo@rit.edu.
Website: http://saunders.rit.edu/programs/graduate/innovation_management/.

Rollins College, Crummer Graduate School of Business, Winter Park, FL 32789-4499. Offers business administration (EDBA); entrepreneurship (MBA); finance (MBA); international business (MBA); management (MBA); marketing (MBA); operations and technology management (MBA). *Accreditation:* AACSB. Part-time and evening/weekend programs available. Postbaccalaureate distance learning degree programs offered (minimal on-campus study). *Faculty:* 21 full-time (3 women), 2 part-time/adjunct (1 woman). *Students:* 157 full-time (86 women), 135 part-time (83 women); includes 60 minority (12 Black or African American, non-Hispanic/Latino; 1 American Indian or Alaska Native, non-Hispanic/Latino; 17 Asian, non-Hispanic/Latino; 23 Hispanic/Latino; 1 Native Hawaiian or other Pacific Islander, non-Hispanic/Latino; 6 Two or more races, non-Hispanic/Latino), 19 international. Average age 37. 264 applicants, 53% accepted, 105 enrolled. In 2013, 169 master's awarded. *Degree requirements:* For master's, minimum GPA of 2.85; for doctorate, thesis/dissertation, minimum GPA of 3.0. *Entrance requirements:* For master's, GMAT or GRE, official transcripts, two letters of recommendation, essay, current resume/curriculum vitae, interview; for doctorate, official transcripts, two letters of recommendation, essays, current resume/curriculum vitae, interview with EDBA academic committee. Additional exam requirements/recommendations for international students: Required—TOEFL (minimum score 100 iBT) or IELTS (minimum score 7). *Application deadline:* Applications are processed on a rolling basis. Application fee: $50. Electronic applications accepted. *Expenses:* Contact institution. *Financial support:* In 2013–14, 87 students received support. Federal Work-Study and scholarships/grants available. Support available to part-time students. Financial award applicants required to submit FAFSA. *Faculty research:* Sustainability, world financial markets, international business, market research, strategic marketing. *Unit head:* Dr. Craig M. McAllaster, Dean, 407-646-2249, Fax: 407-646-1550, E-mail: cmcallaster@rollins.edu. *Application contact:* Eva Gauthier Oleksiw, Admissions Coordinator, 407-646-2405, Fax: 407-646-1550, E-mail: mbaadmissions@rollins.edu.
Website: http://www.rollins.edu/mba/.

Salve Regina University, Program in Business Administration, Newport, RI 02840-4192. Offers cybersecurity issues in business (MBA); entrepreneurial enterprise (MBA); health care administration and management (MBA); social ventures (MBA). Part-time and evening/weekend programs available. Postbaccalaureate distance learning degree programs offered (no on-campus study). *Faculty:* 3 full-time (2 women), 12 part-time/adjunct (5 women). *Students:* 32 full-time (15 women), 67 part-time (31 women); includes 8 minority (4 Black or African American, non-Hispanic/Latino; 1 American Indian or Alaska Native, non-Hispanic/Latino; 2 Hispanic/Latino; 1 Two or more races, non-Hispanic/Latino), 2 international. Average age 29. 49 applicants, 82% accepted, 20 enrolled. In 2013, 68 master's awarded. *Entrance requirements:* For master's, GMAT, GRE General Test, or MAT, 6 undergraduate credits each in accounting, economics, quantitative analysis and calculus or statistics. Additional exam requirements/recommendations for international students: Required—TOEFL (minimum score 600 paper-based; 100 iBT) or IELTS. *Application deadline:* For fall admission, 3/15 priority date for domestic and international students; for spring admission, 9/15 priority date for domestic and international students. Applications are processed on a rolling basis. Application fee: $60. Electronic applications accepted. *Expenses: Tuition:* Full-time $8280; part-time $460 per credit. *Required fees:* $40 per term. Tuition and fees vary according to course level, course load, degree level and program. *Financial support:* Career-related internships or fieldwork and Federal Work-Study available. Support available to part-time students. Financial award application deadline: 3/1; financial award applicants required to submit FAFSA. *Unit head:* Dr. Arlene Nicholas, Director, 401-341-3280, E-mail: arlene.nicholas@salve.edu. *Application contact:* Kelly Alverson, Director of Graduate Admissions, 401-341-2153, Fax: 401-341-2973, E-mail: kelly.alverson@salve.edu.
Website: http://salve.edu/graduate-studies/business-administration-and-management.

San Diego State University, Graduate and Research Affairs, College of Business Administration, Department of Management, San Diego, CA 92182. Offers entrepreneurship (MS); human resources management (MS); management science (MS). Part-time and evening/weekend programs available. *Degree requirements:* For master's, thesis or alternative. *Entrance requirements:* For master's, GMAT, resume, letters of reference. Additional exam requirements/recommendations for international students: Required—TOEFL. Electronic applications accepted.

Santa Clara University, Leavey School of Business, Santa Clara, CA 95053. Offers accelerated business administration (MBA); business administration (MBA); emerging professional business administration (MBA); entrepreneurship (MS); executive business administration (MBA); finance (MSF); information systems (MSIS); JD/MBA; MSIS/JD. *Accreditation:* AACSB. Part-time and evening/weekend programs available. *Faculty:* 85 full-time (21 women), 64 part-time/adjunct (20 women). *Students:* 292 full-time (154 women), 543 part-time (196 women); includes 262 minority (9 Black or African American, non-Hispanic/Latino; 203 Asian, non-Hispanic/Latino; 43 Hispanic/Latino; 2 Native Hawaiian or other Pacific Islander, non-Hispanic/Latino; 5 Two or more races, non-Hispanic/Latino), 260 international. Average age 30. 428 applicants, 77% accepted, 212 enrolled. In 2013, 345 master's awarded. *Degree requirements:* For master's, thesis or alternative. *Entrance requirements:* For master's, GMAT, GRE. Additional exam requirements/recommendations for international students: Required—TOEFL (minimum score 600 paper-based; 100 iBT). *Application deadline:* For fall admission, 6/1 for domestic and international students; for spring admission, 1/19 for domestic and international students. Applications are processed on a rolling basis. Application fee: $100 ($150 for international students). Electronic applications accepted. *Expenses:* Contact institution. *Financial support:* In 2013–14, 348 students received support.

Entrepreneurship

Career-related internships or fieldwork, Federal Work-Study, institutionally sponsored loans, and scholarships/grants available. Support available to part-time students. Financial award applicants required to submit FAFSA. *Faculty research:* Sovereign debt default, empire, and trade during the gold standard; CISE pathways to revitalized undergraduate computing education. *Unit head:* Elizabeth B. Ford, Senior Assistant Dean, 408-554-2752, Fax: 408-554-4571, E-mail: eford@scu.edu. *Application contact:* Tammy Fox, Director, Graduate Admissions and Financial Aid, 408-554-7858, E-mail: mbaadmissions@scu.edu.
Website: http://www.scu.edu/business/graduates.

Seton Hill University, Program in Business Administration, Greensburg, PA 15601. Offers accounting (MBA); entrepreneurship (MBA, Certificate); management (MBA); sports management (MBA). Part-time and evening/weekend programs available. *Faculty:* 9 full-time (3 women), 6 part-time/adjunct (1 woman). *Students:* 37 full-time (15 women), 52 part-time (34 women); includes 4 minority (3 Black or African American, non-Hispanic/Latino; 1 Hispanic/Latino), 8 international. Average age 30. 93 applicants, 47% accepted, 28 enrolled. In 2013, 15 master's awarded. *Entrance requirements:* For master's, resume, 3 letters of recommendation, personal statement, transcripts. Additional exam requirements/recommendations for international students: Required—TOEFL (minimum score 600 paper-based; 100 iBT), IELTS (minimum score 6.5). *Application deadline:* Applications are processed on a rolling basis. Application fee: $0. Electronic applications accepted. *Expenses:* Tuition: Full-time $14,220; part-time $790 per credit. *Required fees:* $700; $34 per credit. $50 per semester. *Financial support:* Federal Work-Study, scholarships/grants, and tuition discounts available. Financial award application deadline: 8/15. *Faculty research:* Entrepreneurship, leadership and strategy, knowledge management, sports management, human resources. *Unit head:* Dr. Douglas Nelson, Director, 724-830-4738, E-mail: dnelson@setonhill.edu. *Application contact:* Laurel Komarny, Program Counselor, 724-838-4209, E-mail: lkomarny@setonhill.edu.
Website: http://www.setonhill.edu/academics/graduate_programs/mba.

Simmons College, School of Management, Boston, MA 02115. Offers business administration (MBA); business and financial analytics (MBA); corporate social responsibility and sustainability (MBA); entrepreneurship (MBA); healthcare management (MBA); management (MS), including communications management, non-profit management; marketing (MBA); nonprofit management (MBA); organizational leadership (MBA); MBA/MSW; MS/MA. *Accreditation:* AACSB. Part-time and evening/weekend programs available. *Students:* 34 full-time (33 women), 233 part-time (214 women); includes 67 minority (41 Black or African American, non-Hispanic/Latino; 1 American Indian or Alaska Native, non-Hispanic/Latino; 9 Asian, non-Hispanic/Latino; 10 Hispanic/Latino; 2 Native Hawaiian or other Pacific Islander, non-Hispanic/Latino; 4 Two or more races, non-Hispanic/Latino), 7 international. In 2013, 133 master's awarded. *Entrance requirements:* For master's, GMAT or GRE. Additional exam requirements/recommendations for international students: Required—TOEFL. *Application deadline:* Applications are processed on a rolling basis. Application fee: $75. Electronic applications accepted. *Financial support:* Scholarships/grants and unspecified assistantships available. Financial award applicants required to submit FAFSA. *Faculty research:* Gender and organizations, leadership, health care management. *Unit head:* Cathy Minehan, Dean, 617-521-2846. *Application contact:* Melissa Terrio, Director of Graduate Admissions, 617-521-3840, Fax: 617-521-3880, E-mail: somadm@simmons.edu.
Website: http://www.simmons.edu/som.

South Carolina State University, School of Graduate and Professional Studies, Department of Business Administration, Orangeburg, SC 29117-0001. Offers agribusiness (MBA); entrepreneurship (MBA). Part-time and evening/weekend programs available. *Faculty:* 3 full-time (1 woman). *Students:* 7 full-time (2 women), 2 part-time (1 woman); all minorities (all Black or African American, non-Hispanic/Latino). Average age 26. 4 applicants, 100% accepted, 4 enrolled. In 2013, 7 master's awarded. *Degree requirements:* For master's, comprehensive exam, business plan. *Entrance requirements:* For master's, GMAT, minimum GPA of 2.8. Additional exam requirements/recommendations for international students: Required—TOEFL. *Application deadline:* For fall admission, 6/15 for domestic and international students; for spring admission, 11/1 for domestic and international students. Applications are processed on a rolling basis. Application fee: $25. Electronic applications accepted. *Expenses:* Tuition, state resident: full-time $8906; part-time $543 per credit hour. Tuition, nonresident: full-time $18,040; part-time $1051 per credit hour. *Financial support:* Fellowships, research assistantships, career-related internships or fieldwork, Federal Work-Study, institutionally sponsored loans, and unspecified assistantships available. Financial award application deadline: 6/1. *Faculty research:* Small farm income and profitability, agricultural credit, aquaculture, low-input sustainable agriculture, rural development. *Unit head:* Dr. Renu Singh, Chair, 803-536-7138, Fax: 803-536-8078, E-mail: rsingh2@scsu.edu. *Application contact:* Dr. Stacey Settle, MBA Director, 803-536-8300, Fax: 803-516-4651, E-mail: ssettle@scsu.edu.

Southeast Missouri State University, School of Graduate Studies, Harrison College of Business, Cape Girardeau, MO 63701-4799. Offers accounting (MBA); entrepreneurship (MBA); environmental management (MBA); financial management (MBA); general management (MBA); health administration (MBA); industrial management (MBA); international business (MBA); organizational management (MS); sport management (MBA). *Accreditation:* AACSB. Part-time and evening/weekend programs available. Postbaccalaureate distance learning degree programs offered (no on-campus study). *Faculty:* 27 full-time (7 women), 1 (woman) part-time/adjunct. *Students:* 59 full-time (27 women), 83 part-time (28 women); includes 10 minority (5 Black or African American, non-Hispanic/Latino; 3 Asian, non-Hispanic/Latino; 1 Hispanic/Latino; 1 Two or more races, non-Hispanic/Latino), 40 international. Average age 28. 77 applicants, 79% accepted, 48 enrolled. In 2013, 50 master's awarded. *Degree requirements:* For master's, variable foreign language requirement, comprehensive exam (for some programs), thesis or alternative, applied research project. *Entrance requirements:* For master's, GMAT or GRE, minimum undergraduate GPA of 2.5, C or better in prerequisite courses. Additional exam requirements/recommendations for international students: Required—TOEFL (minimum score 550 paper-based; 79 iBT), IELTS (minimum score 6), PTE (minimum score 53). *Application deadline:* For fall admission, 8/1 for domestic students, 6/1 for international students; for spring admission, 11/21 for domestic students, 10/1 for international students; for summer admission, 5/15 for domestic students. Applications are processed on a rolling basis. Application fee: $30 ($40 for international students). Electronic applications accepted. *Expenses:* Tuition, state resident: full-time $5139; part-time $285.50 per credit hour. Tuition, nonresident: full-time $9099; part-time $505.50 per credit hour. *Financial support:* In 2013–14, 52 students received support, including 12 teaching assistantships with full tuition reimbursements available (averaging $8,144 per year); career-related internships or fieldwork, Federal Work-Study, scholarships/grants, traineeships, tuition waivers (full), and unspecified assistantships also available. Financial award application deadline: 6/30; financial award applicants required to submit FAFSA. *Faculty research:* Ethics, corporate finance, generational difference, leadership, organizational justice. *Unit head:* Dr. Kenneth A. Heischmidt, Director, Graduate Business Studies, 573-651-2912, Fax: 573-651-5032, E-mail: kheischmidt@semo.edu.

Application contact: Gail Amick, Admissions Specialist, 573-651-2590, Fax: 573-651-5936, E-mail: gamick@semo.edu. Website: http://www.semo.edu/mba.

Southern Methodist University, Cox School of Business, MBA Program, Dallas, TX 75275. Offers accounting (MBA, PMBA); business administration (EMBA); finance (MBA); financial statement analysis (PMBA); general business (MBA); information technology and operations management (MBA); management (MBA); marketing (MBA); real estate (MBA); strategy (MBA); strategy and entrepreneurship (MBA); JD/MBA; MA/MBA. Part-time and evening/weekend programs available. *Entrance requirements:* For master's, GMAT. Additional exam requirements/recommendations for international students: Required—TOEFL. Electronic applications accepted. *Expenses:* Contact institution. *Faculty research:* Corporate finance, financial reporting, modeling consumer decision-making, competition between national brands and store brands, institutional determinants of firms' strategy.

Southern Methodist University, Cox School of Business, Program in Entrepreneurship, Dallas, TX 75275. Offers MS.

Southern New Hampshire University, School of Business, Manchester, NH 03106-1045. Offers accounting (MBA, MS, Graduate Certificate); accounting finance (MS); accounting/auditing (MS); accounting/forensic accounting (MS); accounting/taxation (MS); athletic administration (MBA, Graduate Certificate); business administration (IMBA, MBA, Certificate, Graduate Certificate), including accounting (Certificate), business administration (MBA), business information systems (Graduate Certificate), human resource management (Certificate); corporate social responsibility (MBA); entrepreneurship (MBA); finance (MBA, MS, Graduate Certificate); finance/corporate finance (MS); finance/investments and securities (MS); forensic accounting (MBA); healthcare informatics (MBA); healthcare management (MBA); human resource management (Graduate Certificate); information technology (MS, Graduate Certificate); information technology management (MBA); international business (Graduate Certificate); international business and information technology (Graduate Certificate); international finance (Graduate Certificate); international sport management (Graduate Certificate); justice studies (MBA); leadership of nonprofit organizations (Graduate Certificate); marketing (MBA, MS, Graduate Certificate); operations and project management (MS); operations and supply chain management (MBA, Graduate Certificate); organizational leadership (MS); project management (MBA, Graduate Certificate); Six Sigma (MBA); Six Sigma quality (Graduate Certificate); social media marketing (MBA); sport management (MBA, MS, Graduate Certificate); sustainability and environmental compliance (MBA); workplace conflict management (MBA); MBA/Certificate. *Accreditation:* ACBSP. Part-time and evening/weekend programs available. Postbaccalaureate distance learning degree programs offered (no on-campus study). Terminal master's awarded for partial completion of doctoral program. *Degree requirements:* For master's, one foreign language, comprehensive exam (for some programs), thesis or alternative. *Entrance requirements:* For master's, minimum GPA of 2.5. Additional exam requirements/recommendations for international students: Required—TOEFL (minimum score 500 paper-based). Electronic applications accepted.

South University, Graduate Programs, College of Business, Savannah, GA 31406. Offers corrections (MBA); entrepreneurship and small business (MBA); healthcare administration (MBA); hospitality management (MBA); leadership (MS); public administration (MPA); sustainability (MBA).

Stevens Institute of Technology, Graduate School, Wesley J. Howe School of Technology Management, Program in Information Systems, Hoboken, NJ 07030. Offers computer science (MS); e-commerce (MS); enterprise systems (MS); entrepreneurial information technology (MS); information architecture (MS); information management (MS, Certificate); information security (MS); information technology in financial services industry (MS); information technology in the pharmaceutical industry (MS); information technology outsourcing management (MS); project management (MS, Certificate); software engineering (MS); telecommunications (MS). *Degree requirements:* For master's, thesis optional. *Entrance requirements:* For master's, GMAT, GRE General Test. Additional exam requirements/recommendations for international students: Required—TOEFL. Electronic applications accepted.

Stratford University, School of Graduate Studies, Falls Church, VA 22043. Offers accounting (MS); business administration (IMBA, MBA); enterprise business management (MS); entrepreneurial management (MS); information assurance (MS); information systems (MS); software engineering (MS); telecommunications (MS). Part-time and evening/weekend programs available. Postbaccalaureate distance learning degree programs offered (no on-campus study). *Degree requirements:* For master's, comprehensive exam, capstone project. *Entrance requirements:* For master's, GRE or GMAT, baccalaureate degree. Additional exam requirements/recommendations for international students: Required—TOEFL (minimum score 79 iBT) or IELTS (6.5). Electronic applications accepted.

Suffolk University, Sawyer Business School, Master of Business Administration Program, Boston, MA 02108-2770. Offers accounting (MBA); business administration (APC); entrepreneurship (MBA); executive business administration (EMBA); finance (MBA); global business administration (GMBA); health administration (MBA); international business (MBA); marketing (MBA); nonprofit management (MBA); organizational behavior (MBA); strategic management (MBA); supply chain management (MBA); taxation (MBA); JD/MBA; MBA/GDPA; MBA/MHA; MBA/MSA; MBA/MSF; MBA/MST. *Accreditation:* AACSB. Part-time and evening/weekend programs available. Postbaccalaureate distance learning degree programs offered (no on-campus study). *Faculty:* 29 full-time (9 women), 12 part-time/adjunct (2 women). *Students:* 106 full-time (44 women), 334 part-time (184 women); includes 57 minority (20 Black or African American, non-Hispanic/Latino; 1 American Indian or Alaska Native, non-Hispanic/Latino; 18 Asian, non-Hispanic/Latino; 14 Hispanic/Latino; 4 Two or more races, non-Hispanic/Latino), 61 international. Average age 30. 448 applicants, 61% accepted, 135 enrolled. In 2013, 217 master's awarded. *Entrance requirements:* For master's, GMAT, minimum undergraduate GPA of 2.75 (MBA), 5 years of managerial experience (EMBA). Additional exam requirements/recommendations for international students: Required—TOEFL (minimum score 550 paper-based; 80 iBT). *Application deadline:* For fall admission, 6/15 priority date for domestic students, 6/15 for international students; for spring admission, 11/1 priority date for domestic students, 11/1 for international students. Applications are processed on a rolling basis. Application fee: $50. Electronic applications accepted. *Expenses:* Tuition: Full-time $38,374; part-time $1279 per credit. *Required fees:* $40; $20 per semester. Tuition and fees vary according to program. *Financial support:* In 2013–14, 107 students received support, including 91 fellowships with full and partial tuition reimbursements available (averaging $12,428 per year); career-related internships or fieldwork, Federal Work-Study, and institutionally sponsored loans also available. Support available to part-time students. Financial award application deadline: 4/1; financial award applicants required to submit FAFSA. *Faculty research:* Foreign investments; career strategies and boundaryless careers; corporate ethics codes; interest rates, inflation, and growth options; innovation and product development performance. *Unit head:* Heather Hewitt, Assistant Dean of Graduate Programs/Director of MBA Programs, 617-573-8306, E-mail: hhewitt@

suffolk.edu. *Application contact:* Cory Meyers, Director of Graduate Admissions, 617-573-8302, Fax: 617-305-1733, E-mail: grad.admission@suffolk.edu. Website: http://www.suffolk.edu/mba.

Syracuse University, Martin J. Whitman School of Management, Program in Business Administration, Syracuse, NY 13244. Offers accounting (MBA); entrepreneurship (MBA); finance (MBA); marketing (MBA); supply chain management (MBA). Postbaccalaureate distance learning degree programs offered (minimal on-campus study). *Faculty:* 79 full-time (20 women), 25 part-time/adjunct (6 women). *Students:* 112 full-time (41 women), 181 part-time (49 women); includes 52 minority (19 Black or African American, non-Hispanic/Latino; 18 Asian, non-Hispanic/Latino; 11 Hispanic/Latino; 4 Two or more races, non-Hispanic/Latino), 56 international. Average age 33. 179 applicants, 50% accepted, 36 enrolled. In 2013, 115 master's awarded. *Entrance requirements:* For master's, GMAT, 2 letters of recommendation. Additional exam requirements/recommendations for international students: Required—TOEFL (minimum score 600 paper-based; 100 iBT). *Application deadline:* For fall admission, 11/30 priority date for domestic and international students. Applications are processed on a rolling basis. Application fee: $75. Electronic applications accepted. *Financial support:* In 2013–14, 17 students received support. Fellowships with full and partial tuition reimbursements available, teaching assistantships with partial tuition reimbursements available, career-related internships or fieldwork, scholarships/grants, tuition waivers (partial), and unspecified assistantships available. Support available to part-time students. Financial award application deadline: 3/1. *Unit head:* Dr. Don Harter, Associate Dean for Master's Programs, 315-443-3502, Fax: 315-443-9517, E-mail: dharter@syr.edu. *Application contact:* Danielle Goodroe, Director, Graduate Enrollment, 315-443-3006, Fax: 315-443-9517, E-mail: mbainfo@syr.edu. Website: http://whitman.syr.edu/ftmba/.

Syracuse University, Martin J. Whitman School of Management, Program in Entrepreneurship and Emerging Enterprises, Syracuse, NY 13244. Offers MS. *Students:* 6 full-time (1 woman), 1 part-time (0 women), 4 international. Average age 23. 24 applicants, 54% accepted, 6 enrolled. In 2013, 6 master's awarded. *Entrance requirements:* For master's, GMAT. Additional exam requirements/recommendations for international students: Required—TOEFL. *Application deadline:* For fall admission, 11/30 priority date for domestic and international students. Application fee: $75. Electronic applications accepted. *Financial support:* Fellowships with full tuition reimbursements and research assistantships with full and partial tuition reimbursements available. *Unit head:* Prof. Alexander McKelvie, Associate Professor, 315-443-7252, E-mail: mckelvie@syr.edu. *Application contact:* Danielle Goodroe, Director of Graduate Enrollment, 315-443-3006, Fax: 315-443-9517, E-mail: mbainfo@syr.edu. Website: http://whitman.syr.edu/programs-and-academics/academics/eee/index.aspx.

Temple University, Fox School of Business, Doctoral Programs in Business, Philadelphia, PA 19122-6096. Offers accounting (PhD); entrepreneurship (PhD); finance (PhD); international business (PhD); management information systems (PhD); marketing (PhD); risk management and insurance (PhD); statistics (PhD); strategic management (PhD); tourism and sport (PhD). *Accreditation:* AACSB. *Degree requirements:* For doctorate, thesis/dissertation. *Entrance requirements:* For doctorate, GRE General Test, GMAT, minimum GPA of 3.0, master's degree. Additional exam requirements/recommendations for international students: Required—TOEFL (minimum score 600 paper-based; 100 iBT), IELTS (minimum score 7.5). Electronic applications accepted.

Temple University, Fox School of Business, Specialized Master's Programs, Philadelphia, PA 19122-6096. Offers accountancy (MS); actuarial science (MS); finance (MS); financial engineering (MS); human resource management (MS); innovation management and entrepreneurship (MS); marketing (MS); statistics (MS). MS in innovation management and entrepreneurship delivered jointly with College of Engineering. *Accreditation:* AACSB. Part-time programs available. *Entrance requirements:* For master's, GRE General Test or GMAT, minimum undergraduate GPA of 3.0. Additional exam requirements/recommendations for international students: Required—TOEFL (minimum score 600 paper-based; 100 iBT), IELTS (minimum score 7.5).

United States International University, School of Business Administration, Nairobi, Kenya. Offers business administration (GEMBA); entrepreneurship (MBA); finance (MBA); human resource management (MBA); information technology management (MBA); integrated studies (MBA); international business administration (MBA); management and organizational development (MS); marketing (MBA); organizational development (EMS); strategic management (MBA). Part-time and evening/weekend programs available. *Degree requirements:* For master's, thesis. *Entrance requirements:* For master's, GMAT, 2 letters of reference, resume. Additional exam requirements/recommendations for international students: Required—TOEFL (minimum score 550 paper-based). *Faculty research:* Marketing in small business enterprises, total quality management in Kenya.

Université Laval, Faculty of Administrative Sciences, Programs in Business Administration, Québec, QC G1K 7P4, Canada. Offers accounting (MBA); agri-food management (MBA); electronic business (MBA, Diploma); factory management and logistics (MBA); finance (MBA); firm management (MBA); geomatic management (MBA); information technology management (MBA); international management (MBA); management (MBA); management accounting (MBA, Diploma); marketing (MBA); modeling and organizational decision (MBA); occupational health and safety management (MBA); pharmacy management (MBA); social and environmental responsibility (MBA); technological entrepreneurship (Diploma). *Accreditation:* AACSB. Part-time and evening/weekend programs available. Postbaccalaureate distance learning degree programs offered (no on-campus study). *Entrance requirements:* For master's and Diploma, knowledge of French and English. Electronic applications accepted.

The University of Alabama in Huntsville, School of Graduate Studies, College of Business Administration, Programs in Business and Management, Huntsville, AL 35899. Offers federal contracting and procurement management (Certificate); management (MBA), including acquisition management, entrepreneurship, federal contract accounting, finance, human resource management, logistics and supply chain management, marketing, project management; supply chain management (Certificate); technology and innovation management (Certificate). *Accreditation:* AACSB. Part-time and evening/weekend programs available. *Faculty:* 13 full-time (3 women), 5 part-time/adjunct (0 women). *Students:* 41 full-time (19 women), 144 part-time (59 women); includes 35 minority (13 Black or African American, non-Hispanic/Latino; 1 American Indian or Alaska Native, non-Hispanic/Latino; 9 Asian, non-Hispanic/Latino; 11 Hispanic/Latino; 1 Two or more races, non-Hispanic/Latino), 13 international. Average age 33. 131 applicants, 78% accepted, 67 enrolled. In 2013, 83 master's, 5 other advanced degrees awarded. *Degree requirements:* For master's, comprehensive exam, thesis or alternative. *Entrance requirements:* For master's, GMAT (minimum score 500), minimum AACSB index of 1080. Additional exam requirements/recommendations for international students: Required—TOEFL (minimum score 550 paper-based; 80 iBT), IELTS (minimum score 6.5). *Application deadline:* For fall admission, 7/15 priority date for domestic students, 4/1 priority date for international students; for spring admission, 11/30 priority date for domestic students, 9/1 priority date for international students.

Applications are processed on a rolling basis. Application fee: $50. Electronic applications accepted. *Expenses:* Tuition, state resident: full-time $8912; part-time $540 per credit hour. Tuition, nonresident: full-time $20,774; part-time $1252 per credit hour. *Required fees:* $148 per semester. One-time fee: $150. *Financial support:* In 2013–14, 10 students received support, including 4 research assistantships with full and partial tuition reimbursements available (averaging $7,750 per year), 5 teaching assistantships with full and partial tuition reimbursements available (averaging $9,000 per year); career-related internships or fieldwork, Federal Work-Study, institutionally sponsored loans, scholarships/grants, health care benefits, tuition waivers (full and partial), and unspecified assistantships also available. Support available to part-time students. Financial award application deadline: 4/1; financial award applicants required to submit FAFSA. *Faculty research:* Supply chain management, management of research and development, international marketing and branding, organizational behavior and human resource management, social networks and computational economics. *Total annual research expenditures:* $2.1 million. *Unit head:* Dr. Cynthia Gramm, Chair, 256-824-6913, Fax: 256-824-6328, E-mail: cynthia.gramm@uah.edu. *Application contact:* Jennifer Pettitt, Director of Graduate Programs, 256-824-6681, Fax: 256-824-7571, E-mail: jennifer.pettitt@uah.edu.

University of Arkansas at Little Rock, Graduate School, George W. Donaghey College of Engineering and Information Technology, Graduate Certificate in Technology Innovation Program, Little Rock, AR 72204-1099. Offers Graduate Certificate. Part-time and evening/weekend programs available. *Faculty:* 6 full-time (0 women). *Students:* 8 full-time (3 women), 5 international. Average age 24. In 2013, 1 Graduate Certificate awarded. *Degree requirements:* For Graduate Certificate, 1 year of full-time study. *Entrance requirements:* For degree, minimum GPA of 3.0 in the last 60 hours of undergraduate credit. Additional exam requirements/recommendations for international students: Required—TOEFL (minimum score 525 paper-based). *Application deadline:* For fall admission, 8/1 for domestic students; for spring admission, 12/15 for domestic students; for summer admission, 5/1 for domestic students. Applications are processed on a rolling basis. Application fee: $40. Electronic applications accepted. *Expenses:* Tuition, state resident: full-time $5690; part-time $284.50 per credit hour. Tuition, nonresident: full-time $13,030; part-time $651.50 per credit hour. *Required fees:* $1121; $672 per term. One-time fee: $40 full-time. *Financial support:* Scholarships/grants available. Financial award applicants required to submit FAFSA. *Faculty research:* Web computing, robotics, text mining, technology foresight, biotechnology. *Unit head:* Dr. Gary Anderson, Chair, 501-569-8021, E-mail: gtanderson@ualr.edu. Website: http://ualr.edu/technologyinnovation/.

University of Bridgeport, School of Business, Bridgeport, CT 06604. Offers accounting (MBA); finance (MBA); general business (MBA); global financial services (MBA); human resource management (MBA); information systems and knowledge management (MBA); international business (MBA); management (MBA); marketing (MBA); operations management (MBA); small business and entrepreneurship (MBA); specialized business (MBA). *Accreditation:* ACBSP. Part-time and evening/weekend programs available. *Faculty:* 11 full-time (2 women), 39 part-time/adjunct (8 women). *Students:* 162 full-time (90 women), 69 part-time (45 women); includes 44 minority (20 Black or African American, non-Hispanic/Latino; 7 Asian, non-Hispanic/Latino; 15 Hispanic/Latino; 2 Two or more races, non-Hispanic/Latino), 163 international. Average age 28. 492 applicants, 48% accepted, 55 enrolled. In 2013, 144 master's awarded. *Degree requirements:* For master's, thesis optional. *Entrance requirements:* For master's, GMAT. Additional exam requirements/recommendations for international students: Recommended—TOEFL (minimum score 550 paper-based; 80 iBT), IELTS (minimum score 6.5). *Application deadline:* For fall admission, 8/1 priority date for domestic and international students; for spring admission, 12/1 priority date for domestic and international students. Applications are processed on a rolling basis. Application fee: $50. Electronic applications accepted. *Expenses:* Contact institution. *Financial support:* In 2013–14, 69 students received support. Fellowships, research assistantships, teaching assistantships, career-related internships or fieldwork, Federal Work-Study, institutionally sponsored loans, and tuition waivers (partial) available. Support available to part-time students. Financial award application deadline: 6/1; financial award applicants required to submit FAFSA. *Unit head:* Dr. Lloyd G. Gibson, Dean, 203-576-4384, Fax: 203-576-4388, E-mail: llgibson@bridgeport.edu. *Application contact:* Leanne Proctor, Director of Graduate Admissions, 203-576-4552, Fax: 203-576-4941, E-mail: mba@bridgeport.edu. Website: http://www.bridgeport.edu.

University of Central Florida, College of Arts and Humanities, School of Visual Arts and Design, Orlando, FL 32816. Offers digital media (MA); emerging media (MFA), including digital media, entrepreneurial digital cinema, studio art and the computer. *Faculty:* 52 full-time (15 women), 16 part-time/adjunct (10 women). *Students:* 40 full-time (18 women), 9 part-time (1 woman); includes 8 minority (1 Black or African American, non-Hispanic/Latino; 1 American Indian or Alaska Native, non-Hispanic/Latino; 1 Asian, non-Hispanic/Latino; 5 Hispanic/Latino), 7 international. Average age 32. 43 applicants, 56% accepted, 14 enrolled. In 2013, 12 master's awarded. Application fee: $30. Electronic applications accepted. *Financial support:* In 2013–14, 25 students received support, including 11 fellowships (averaging $8,500 per year), 16 teaching assistantships (averaging $6,300 per year); scholarships/grants and unspecified assistantships also available. *Unit head:* Byron Clercx, Director, 407-823-3145, E-mail: byron.clercx@ucf.edu. *Application contact:* Barbara Rodriguez Lamas, Director, Admissions and Student Services, 407-823-2766, Fax: 407-823-6442, E-mail: gradadmissions@ucf.edu. Website: http://svad.cah.ucf.edu/.

University of Central Florida, College of Business Administration, Department of Management, Orlando, FL 32816. Offers entrepreneurship (Graduate Certificate); management (MSM); technology ventures (Graduate Certificate). *Accreditation:* AACSB. *Faculty:* 27 full-time (10 women), 6 part-time/adjunct (2 women). *Students:* 36 part-time (30 women); includes 15 minority (7 Black or African American, non-Hispanic/Latino; 2 Asian, non-Hispanic/Latino; 6 Hispanic/Latino). Average age 33. 19 applicants, 84% accepted, 12 enrolled. In 2013, 14 other advanced degrees awarded. *Entrance requirements:* For master's, GMAT, minimum GPA of 3.0 in last 60 hours. *Application deadline:* For fall admission, 2/1 priority date for domestic students; for spring admission, 11/1 priority date for domestic students. Application fee: $30. Electronic applications accepted. *Financial support:* Fellowships, research assistantships, and teaching assistantships available. *Unit head:* Dr. Stephen Goodman, Chair, 407-823-2675, Fax: 407-823-3725, E-mail: sgoodman@bus.ucf.edu. *Application contact:* Judy Ryder, Director, Graduate Admissions, 407-823-2364, Fax: 407-823-0219, E-mail: jryder@bus.ucf.edu. Website: http://www.graduatecatalog.ucf.edu/programs/program.aspx?id-1080&program-Management MS.

University of Chicago, Booth School of Business, Full-Time MBA Program, Chicago, IL 60637. Offers accounting (MBA); analytic finance (MBA); analytic management (MBA); econometrics and statistics (MBA); economics (MBA); entrepreneurship (MBA); finance (MBA); general management (MBA); health administration and policy (Certificate); human resource management (MBA); international business (MBA); managerial and organizational behavior (MBA); marketing management (MBA); operations management (MBA); strategic management (MBA); MBA/AM; MBA/JD; MBA/MA; MBA/MD; MBA/

MPP. *Accreditation:* AACSB. Part-time and evening/weekend programs available. Terminal master's awarded for partial completion of doctoral program. *Entrance requirements:* For master's, GMAT, 2 letters of recommendation, 3 essays, resume, interview. Additional exam requirements/recommendations for international students: Required—TOEFL (minimum score 600 paper-based; 104 iBT), IELTS. Electronic applications accepted. *Expenses:* Contact institution. *Faculty research:* Finance, marketing, economics, entrepreneurship, strategy, management.

University of Colorado Boulder, Leeds School of Business, Division of Business Administration, Boulder, CO 80309. Offers accounting (MS, PhD); finance (PhD); information systems (PhD); marketing (PhD); operations (PhD); strategic, organizational, and entrepreneurial studies (PhD). *Students:* 143 full-time (72 women), 2 part-time (1 woman); includes 15 minority (1 Black or African American, non-Hispanic/Latino; 2 American Indian or Alaska Native, non-Hispanic/Latino; 5 Asian, non-Hispanic/Latino; 6 Hispanic/Latino; 1 Two or more races, non-Hispanic/Latino), 37 international. Average age 25. 281 applicants, 12% accepted, 19 enrolled. In 2013, 50 master's, 8 doctorates awarded. *Entrance requirements:* For master's, GMAT, minimum undergraduate GPA of 3.0. *Application deadline:* For fall admission, 3/31 for domestic students, 3/1 for international students; for spring admission, 10/31 for domestic and international students. Application fee: $50 ($60 for international students). Electronic applications accepted. *Financial support:* In 2013–14, 145 students received support, including 37 fellowships (averaging $3,977 per year), 27 research assistantships with full and partial tuition reimbursements available (averaging $40,893 per year), 12 teaching assistantships with full and partial tuition reimbursements available (averaging $38,197 per year); institutionally sponsored loans, scholarships/grants, health care benefits, and unspecified assistantships also available. Financial award applicants required to submit FAFSA.

University of Colorado Denver, Business School, Master of Business Administration Program, Denver, CO 80217. Offers bioinnovation and entrepreneurship (MBA); business intelligence (MBA); business strategy (MBA); business to business marketing (MBA); business to consumer marketing (MBA); change management (MBA); corporate financial management (MBA); enterprise technology management (MBA); entrepreneurship (MBA); health administration (MBA), including financial management, health administration, health information technologies, international health management and policy; human resources management (MBA); international business (MBA); investment management (MBA); managing for sustainability (MBA); sports and entertainment management (MBA). *Accreditation:* AACSB. Part-time and evening/weekend programs available. Postbaccalaureate distance learning degree programs offered (no on-campus study). *Students:* 611 full-time (246 women), 144 part-time (58 women); includes 102 minority (14 Black or African American, non-Hispanic/Latino; 2 American Indian or Alaska Native, non-Hispanic/Latino; 38 Asian, non-Hispanic/Latino; 42 Hispanic/Latino; 6 Two or more races, non-Hispanic/Latino), 26 international. Average age 32. 330 applicants, 64% accepted, 125 enrolled. In 2013, 398 master's awarded. *Degree requirements:* For master's, 48 semester hours, including 30 of core courses, 3 in international business, and 15 in electives from over 50 other graduate business courses. *Entrance requirements:* For master's, GMAT, resume, official transcripts, essay, two letters of recommendation, financial statements (for international applicants). Additional exam requirements/recommendations for international students: Required—TOEFL (minimum score 560 paper-based; 83 iBT); Recommended—IELTS (minimum score 6.5). *Application deadline:* For fall admission, 4/15 priority date for domestic students, 3/15 priority date for international students; for spring admission, 10/15 priority date for domestic students, 9/15 priority date for international students. Applications are processed on a rolling basis. Application fee: $50 ($75 for international students). Electronic applications accepted. *Expenses:* Contact institution. *Financial support:* In 2013–14, 62 students received support. Fellowships, research assistantships, teaching assistantships, Federal Work-Study, institutionally sponsored loans, scholarships/grants, traineeships, and unspecified assistantships available. Financial award application deadline: 4/1; financial award applicants required to submit FAFSA. *Faculty research:* Marketing, management, entrepreneurship, finance, health administration. *Unit head:* Elizabeth Cooperman, Professor of Finance and Managing for Sustainability/MBA Program Director, 303-315-8422, E-mail: elizabeth.cooperman@ucdenver.edu. *Application contact:* Shelly Townley, Admissions Director, Graduate Programs, 303-315-8202, E-mail: shelly.townley@ucdenver.edu.
Website: http://www.ucdenver.edu/academics/colleges/business/degrees/mba/Pages/MBA.aspx.

University of Colorado Denver, Business School, Program in Information Systems, Denver, CO 80217. Offers accounting and information systems audit and control (MS); business intelligence systems (MS); ehealth and healthcare service entrepreneurship (MS); enterprise risk management (MS); enterprise technology management (MS); geographic information systems (MS); health information technology (MS); technology innovation and entrepreneurship (MS); Web and mobile computing (MS). Part-time and evening/weekend programs available. Postbaccalaureate distance learning degree programs offered (no on-campus study). *Students:* 55 full-time (14 women), 23 part-time (8 women); includes 10 minority (2 Black or African American, non-Hispanic/Latino; 7 Asian, non-Hispanic/Latino; 1 Hispanic/Latino), 15 international. Average age 33. 54 applicants, 78% accepted, 14 enrolled. In 2013, 27 master's awarded. *Degree requirements:* For master's, 30 credit hours. *Entrance requirements:* For master's, GMAT, resume, essay, two letters of recommendation, financial statements (for international applicants). Additional exam requirements/recommendations for international students: Required—TOEFL (minimum score 537 paper-based; 75 iBT); Recommended—IELTS (minimum score 6.5). *Application deadline:* For fall admission, 4/15 for domestic students, 3/15 for international students; for spring admission, 10/15 for domestic students, 9/15 for international students. Applications are processed on a rolling basis. Application fee: $50 ($75 for international students). Electronic applications accepted. *Expenses:* Contact institution. *Financial support:* In 2013–14, 18 students received support. Fellowships, research assistantships, teaching assistantships, Federal Work-Study, institutionally sponsored loans, scholarships/grants, and traineeships available. Financial award application deadline: 4/1; financial award applicants required to submit FAFSA. *Faculty research:* Human-computer interaction, expert systems, database management, electronic commerce, object-oriented software development. *Unit head:* Dr. Jahangir Karimi, Director of Information Systems Programs, 303-315-8430, E-mail: jahangir.karimi@ucdenver.edu. *Application contact:* Shelly Townley, Admissions Director, Graduate Programs, 303-315-8202, E-mail: shelly.townley@ucdenver.edu.
Website: http://www.ucdenver.edu/academics/colleges/business/degrees/ms/IS/Pages/Information-Systems.aspx.

University of Colorado Denver, Business School, Program in Management and Organization, Denver, CO 80217. Offers business strategy (MS); change and innovation (MS); enterprise technology management (MS); entrepreneurship and innovation (MS); global management (MS); human resources management (MS); leadership and management (MS); quantitative decision methods (MS); sports and entertainment management (MS); sustainability management (MS). *Accreditation:* AACSB. Part-time and evening/weekend programs available. Postbaccalaureate distance learning degree programs offered (no on-campus study). *Students:* 27 full-time (19 women), 14 part-time (7 women); includes 4 minority (1 Black or African American, non-Hispanic/Latino; 2 Hispanic/Latino; 1 Two or more races, non-Hispanic/Latino), 6 international. Average age 29. 38 applicants, 45% accepted, 8 enrolled. In 2013, 28 master's awarded. *Degree requirements:* For master's, 30 semester hours (12 of required courses, 12 of management electives, and 6 of free electives). *Entrance requirements:* For master's, GMAT, resume, two letters of recommendation, essay, financial statements (for international applicants). Additional exam requirements/recommendations for international students: Required—TOEFL (minimum score 537 paper-based; 75 iBT); Recommended—IELTS (minimum score 6.5). *Application deadline:* For fall admission, 4/15 for domestic students, 3/15 for international students; for spring admission, 10/15 for domestic students, 9/15 for international students. Applications are processed on a rolling basis. Application fee: $50 ($75 for international students). Electronic applications accepted. *Expenses:* Contact institution. *Financial support:* In 2013–14, 5 students received support. Fellowships, research assistantships, teaching assistantships, Federal Work-Study, institutionally sponsored loans, scholarships/grants, and traineeships available. Financial award application deadline: 4/1; financial award applicants required to submit FAFSA. *Faculty research:* Human resource management, management of catastrophe, turnaround strategies. *Unit head:* Dr. Kenneth Bettenhausen, Associate Professor/Director of MS in Management, 303-315-8425, E-mail: kenneth.bettenhausen@ucdenver.edu. *Application contact:* Shelly Townley, Admissions Director, Graduate Programs, 303-315-8202, E-mail: shelly.townley@ucdenver.edu.
Website: http://www.ucdenver.edu/academics/colleges/business/degrees/ms/management/Pages/Management.aspx.

University of Colorado Denver, College of Engineering and Applied Science, Department of Bioengineering, Aurora, CO 80045-2560. Offers assistive technology and rehabilitation engineering (MS, PhD); device design and entrepreneurship (MS, PhD); research (MS, PhD); translational bioengineering (MS, PhD). Part-time programs available. *Faculty:* 9 full-time (3 women), 5 part-time/adjunct (2 women). *Students:* 43 full-time (17 women), 14 part-time (7 women); includes 12 minority (4 Black or African American, non-Hispanic/Latino; 4 Asian, non-Hispanic/Latino; 1 Hispanic/Latino; 3 Two or more races, non-Hispanic/Latino), 4 international. Average age 27. 56 applicants, 43% accepted, 13 enrolled. In 2013, 6 master's awarded. Terminal master's awarded for partial completion of doctoral program. *Degree requirements:* For master's, thesis or alternative, 30 credit hours; for doctorate, comprehensive exam, 36 credit hours of classwork (18 core, 18 elective), additional 30 hours of thesis work, three formal examinations, approval of dissertations. *Entrance requirements:* For master's and doctorate, GRE, transcripts, three letters of recommendation, resume, statement of purpose. Additional exam requirements/recommendations for international students: Required—TOEFL (minimum score 550 paper-based; 79 iBT), TOEFL (minimum score 600 paper-based; 100 iBT) for PhD. *Application deadline:* For fall admission, 1/15 priority date for domestic students, 1/1 priority date for international students. Application fee: $50 ($75 for international students). Electronic applications accepted. *Expenses:* Contact institution. *Financial support:* In 2013–14, 28 students received support. Fellowships, research assistantships, teaching assistantships, Federal Work-Study, institutionally sponsored loans, scholarships/grants, and traineeships available. Financial award application deadline: 4/1; financial award applicants required to submit FAFSA. *Faculty research:* Imaging and biophotonics, cardiovascular biomechanics and hemodynamics, orthopedic biomechanics, ophthalmology, neuroscience engineering, diabetes, surgery and urological sciences. *Unit head:* Dr. Robin Shandas, Chair, 303-724-4196, E-mail: robin.shandas@ucdenver.edu. *Application contact:* Graduate School Admissions, 303-556-2704, E-mail: admissions@ucdenver.edu.
Website: http://www.ucdenver.edu/academics/colleges/Engineering/Programs/bioengineering/Pages/Bioengineering.aspx.

University of Delaware, Alfred Lerner College of Business and Economics, Department of Economics, Newark, DE 19716. Offers economic education (PhD); economics (MA, MS, PhD); economics for entrepreneurship and educators (MA); MA/MBA. Part-time programs available. *Degree requirements:* For master's, comprehensive exam, thesis (for some programs), mathematics review exam, research project; for doctorate, comprehensive exam, thesis/dissertation, field exam. *Entrance requirements:* For master's, GMAT or GRE General Test, minimum GPA of 2.5; for doctorate, GRE General Test, minimum GPA of 3.5 in graduate economics course work. Additional exam requirements/recommendations for international students: Required—TOEFL (minimum score 550 paper-based). Electronic applications accepted. *Faculty research:* Applied quantitative economics, industrial organization, resource economics, monetary economics, labor economics.

University of Florida, Graduate School, Warrington College of Business Administration, Hough Graduate School of Business, Department of Finance, Insurance and Real Estate, Gainesville, FL 32611. Offers entrepreneurship (MS); finance (MS, PhD); financial services (Certificate); insurance (PhD); quantitative finance (PhD); real estate (MS); real estate and urban analysis (PhD); JD/MBA; JD/MS. *Faculty:* 17 full-time (0 women), 6 part-time/adjunct (0 women). *Students:* 77 full-time (20 women), 4 part-time (2 women); includes 11 minority (3 Black or African American, non-Hispanic/Latino; 1 American Indian or Alaska Native, non-Hispanic/Latino; 2 Asian, non-Hispanic/Latino; 5 Hispanic/Latino), 23 international. Average age 27. 226 applicants, 4% accepted, 8 enrolled. In 2013, 92 master's, 5 doctorates awarded. Terminal master's awarded for partial completion of doctoral program. *Degree requirements:* For master's, comprehensive exam, thesis; for doctorate, comprehensive exam, thesis/dissertation. *Entrance requirements:* For master's, GMAT (minimum score of 465) or GRE General Test, minimum GPA of 3.0 for last 60 hours of undergraduate degree, work experience (preferred); for doctorate, GMAT (minimum score of 465) or GRE General Test, minimum GPA of 3.0. Additional exam requirements/recommendations for international students: Required—TOEFL (minimum score 550 paper-based; 80 iBT), IELTS (minimum score 6). *Application deadline:* For fall admission, 1/15 priority date for domestic students, 1/15 for international students. Applications are processed on a rolling basis. Application fee: $30. Electronic applications accepted. *Expenses:* Tuition, state resident: full-time $12,640. Tuition, nonresident: full-time $30,000. *Financial support:* In 2013–14, 19 students received support, including 13 research assistantships (averaging $18,787 per year), 6 teaching assistantships (averaging $14,970 per year); career-related internships or fieldwork, scholarships/grants, and unspecified assistantships also available. Financial award application deadline: 1/15; financial award applicants required to submit FAFSA. *Faculty research:* Banking, empirical corporate finance, hedge funds. *Unit head:* Mahendrarajah Nimalendran, PhD, Chair, 352-392-9526, Fax: 352-392-0301, E-mail: nimal@ufl.edu. *Application contact:* Office of Admissions, 352-392-1365, E-mail: webrequests@admissions.ufl.edu.
Website: http://www.cba.ufl.edu/fire/.

University of Florida, Graduate School, Warrington College of Business Administration, Hough Graduate School of Business, Programs in Business Administration, Gainesville, FL 32611. Offers business administration (MBA); competitive strategy (MBA); entrepreneurship (MBA); finance (MBA); global management (MBA); Graham-Buffett security analysis (MBA); human resource management (MBA); information systems and operations management (MBA); international studies (MBA); Latin American business (MBA); management (MBA); marketing (MBA); real estate (MBA); sports administration (MBA); JD/MBA; MBA/MS; MBA/PhD; MBA/Pharm D; MD/MBA. *Accreditation:* AACSB. Part-time and evening/weekend programs available. Postbaccalaureate distance learning degree programs

offered. *Faculty:* 72 full-time (10 women), 29 part-time/adjunct (7 women). *Students:* 440 full-time (122 women), 472 part-time (159 women); includes 203 minority (43 Black or African American, non-Hispanic/Latino; 3 American Indian or Alaska Native, non-Hispanic/Latino; 64 Asian, non-Hispanic/Latino; 92 Hispanic/Latino; 1 Native Hawaiian or other Pacific Islander, non-Hispanic/Latino), 39 international. Average age 32. 568 applicants, 58% accepted, 261 enrolled. In 2013, 405 master's awarded. *Degree requirements:* For master's, capstone course. *Entrance requirements:* For master's, GMAT (minimum score 465), minimum GPA of 3.0, interview. Additional exam requirements/recommendations for international students: Required—TOEFL (minimum score 550 paper-based; 80 iBT), IELTS (minimum score 6). *Application deadline:* For fall admission, 7/1 for domestic students, 1/1 for international students; for spring admission, 12/1 for domestic and international students. Applications are processed on a rolling basis. Application fee: $30. Electronic applications accepted. *Expenses:* Tuition, state resident: full-time $12,640. Tuition, nonresident: full-time $30,000. *Financial support:* In 2013–14, 24 students received support, including 24 teaching assistantships (averaging $6,143 per year); career-related internships or fieldwork, scholarships/grants, and unspecified assistantships also available. Support available to part-time students. Financial award applicants required to submit FAFSA. *Faculty research:* Accounting, finance, insurance, management, real estate, urban analysis marketing. *Unit head:* Alexander D. Sevilla, Assistant Dean/Director of MBA Program, 352-273-3252, Fax: 352-392-8791, E-mail: alex.sevilla@warrington.ufl.edu. *Application contact:* Andrew S. Lord, Senior Director of Admissions, 352-273-3241, Fax: 352-392-8791, E-mail: andrew.lord@warrington.ufl.edu.
Website: http://www.floridamba.ufl.edu/.

University of Hawaii at Manoa, Graduate Division, Shidler College of Business, The Pacific Asian Center for Entrepreneurship and E-Business (PACE), Honolulu, HI 96822. Offers entrepreneurship (Graduate Certificate). Part-time programs available. *Entrance requirements:* Additional exam requirements/recommendations for international students: Required—TOEFL (minimum score 500 paper-based; 61 iBT).

University of Hawaii at Manoa, Graduate Division, Shidler College of Business, Program in Business Administration, Honolulu, HI 96822. Offers Asian business studies (MBA); Chinese business studies (MBA); decision sciences (MBA); entrepreneurship (MBA); finance (MBA); finance and banking (MBA); human resources management (MBA); information management (MBA); information technology (MBA); international business (MBA); Japanese business studies (MBA); marketing (MBA); organizational behavior (MBA); organizational management (MBA); real estate (MBA); student-designed track (MBA). *Accreditation:* AACSB. Part-time and evening/weekend programs available. *Degree requirements:* For master's, thesis optional. *Entrance requirements:* For master's, GMAT, minimum GPA of 3.0. Additional exam requirements/recommendations for international students: Required—TOEFL (minimum score 600 paper-based; 100 iBT), IELTS (minimum score 7). *Expenses:* Contact institution.

University of Houston–Downtown, College of Business, Houston, TX 77002. Offers finance (MBA); general management (MBA); human resource management (MBA); leadership (MBA); sales management and business development (MBA); supply chain management (MBA). Evening/weekend programs available. *Faculty:* 18 full-time (7 women). *Students:* 1 (woman) full-time, 88 part-time (32 women); includes 60 minority (18 Black or African American, non-Hispanic/Latino; 10 Asian, non-Hispanic/Latino; 30 Hispanic/Latino; 1 Native Hawaiian or other Pacific Islander, non-Hispanic/Latino; 1 Two or more races, non-Hispanic/Latino), 2 international. Average age 33. 41 applicants, 63% accepted, 24 enrolled. *Entrance requirements:* For master's, GMAT, official transcripts, bachelor's degree or equivalent, resume, 2 professional references. Additional exam requirements/recommendations for international students: Required—TOEFL (minimum score 81 iBT). *Application deadline:* For fall admission, 7/15 for domestic and international students. Applications are processed on a rolling basis. Application fee: $35 ($60 for international students). Electronic applications accepted. *Expenses:* Contact institution. *Financial support:* In 2013–14, 2 fellowships (averaging $6,000 per year) were awarded. Financial award application deadline: 4/1; financial award applicants required to submit FAFSA. *Faculty research:* Corporate finance, sustainability, recruitment and selection, international strategic management, gender and race discrimination. *Unit head:* Dr. D. Michael Fields, Dean, College of Business, 713-221-8179, Fax: 713-221-8675, E-mail: fieldsd@uhd.edu. *Application contact:* Ceshia Love, Assistant Director of Graduate Admissions, 713-221-8093, Fax: 713-223-7408, E-mail: gradadmissions@uhd.edu.
Website: http://mba.uhd.edu/.

University of Houston–Victoria, School of Business Administration, Victoria, TX 77901-4450. Offers accounting (MBA); economic development and entrepreneurship (MS); finance (GMBA, MBA); general business (MBA); international business (MBA); management (GMBA, MBA); marketing (MBA). *Accreditation:* AACSB. Part-time and evening/weekend programs available. Postbaccalaureate distance learning degree programs offered (minimal on-campus study). *Faculty:* 45 full-time (15 women). *Students:* 193 full-time (93 women), 673 part-time (325 women); includes 489 minority (185 Black or African American, non-Hispanic/Latino; 169 Asian, non-Hispanic/Latino; 114 Hispanic/Latino; 1 Native Hawaiian or other Pacific Islander, non-Hispanic/Latino; 20 Two or more races, non-Hispanic/Latino), 94 international. *Entrance requirements:* For master's, GMAT. Additional exam requirements/recommendations for international students: Required—TOEFL (minimum score 550 paper-based). *Application deadline:* For fall admission, 6/1 for international students; for spring admission, 10/1 for international students. Applications are processed on a rolling basis. Application fee: $0. Electronic applications accepted. *Expenses:* Tuition, state resident: full-time $4534; part-time $251 per credit hour. Tuition, nonresident: full-time $10,906; part-time $606 per contact hour. *Required fees:* $68 per semester hour. Tuition and fees vary according to course load. *Financial support:* In 2013–14, research assistantships with partial tuition reimbursements (averaging $2,000 per year), teaching assistantships with partial tuition reimbursements (averaging $2,000 per year) were awarded; Federal Work-Study, scholarships/grants, and unspecified assistantships also available. Support available to part-time students. Financial award application deadline: 4/15; financial award applicants required to submit FAFSA. *Faculty research:* Economic development, marketing, finance. *Unit head:* Dr. Farhang Niroomand, Dean, 361-570-4230, Fax: 361-580-5599, E-mail: niroomandf@uhv.edu. *Application contact:* Admissions and Records, 361-570-4359, Fax: 361-580-5500, E-mail: admissions@uhv.edu.
Website: http://www.uhv.edu/bus/.

University of Idaho, College of Law, Moscow, ID 83844-2321. Offers business law and entrepreneurship (JD); law (JD); litigation and alternative dispute resolution (JD); Native American law (JD); natural resources and environmental law (JD). *Accreditation:* ABA. *Faculty:* 31 full-time, 7 part-time/adjunct. *Students:* 314 full-time, 8 part-time. Average age 29. *Entrance requirements:* For doctorate, LSAT, Law School Admission Council Credential Assembly Service (CAS) Report. Additional exam requirements/recommendations for international students: Required—TOEFL. *Application deadline:* For fall admission, 2/15 for domestic students. Applications are processed on a rolling basis. Application fee: $50 ($60 for international students). Electronic applications accepted. *Expenses:* Tuition, state resident: full-time $5596; part-time $363 per credit hour. Tuition, nonresident: full-time $18,672; part-time $1089 per credit hour. *Financial support:* Career-related internships or fieldwork, Federal Work-Study, and institutionally

sponsored loans available. Financial award applicants required to submit FAFSA. *Faculty research:* Transboundary river governance, tribal protection and stewardship, regional water issues, environmental law. *Unit head:* Michael Satz, Jr., Dean, 208-885-4977, E-mail: uilaw@uidaho.edu. *Application contact:* Carole Wells, Interim Director of Admissions, 208-885-2300, Fax: 208-885-2252, E-mail: lawadmit@uidaho.edu.
Website: http://www.uidaho.edu/law/.

University of Louisville, Graduate School, College of Business, MBA Programs, Louisville, KY 40292-0001. Offers entrepreneurship (MBA); global business (MBA); health sector management (MBA). *Accreditation:* AACSB. Part-time and evening/weekend programs available. *Students:* 202 full-time (65 women), 42 part-time (15 women); includes 21 minority (9 Black or African American, non-Hispanic/Latino; 1 American Indian or Alaska Native, non-Hispanic/Latino; 7 Asian, non-Hispanic/Latino; 3 Hispanic/Latino; 1 Two or more races, non-Hispanic/Latino), 38 international. Average age 29. 314 applicants, 42% accepted, 116 enrolled. In 2013, 61 master's awarded. *Degree requirements:* For master's, international learning experience. *Entrance requirements:* For master's, GMAT, 2 letters of reference, personal interview, resume, personal statement, college transcript(s). Additional exam requirements/recommendations for international students: Required—TOEFL (minimum score 83 iBT). *Application deadline:* For fall admission, 7/1 for domestic students; for spring admission, 12/1 for domestic students. Applications are processed on a rolling basis. Application fee: $60. *Expenses:* Tuition, state resident: full-time $10,788; part-time $599 per credit hour. Tuition, nonresident: full-time $22,446; part-time $1247 per credit hour. *Required fees:* $196. Tuition and fees vary according to program and reciprocity agreements. *Financial support:* Fellowships with full tuition reimbursements, research assistantships with full tuition reimbursements, health care benefits, and unspecified assistantships available. Financial award application deadline: 3/31; financial award applicants required to submit FAFSA. *Faculty research:* Entrepreneurship, venture capital, retailing/franchising, corporate governance and leadership, supply chain management. *Unit head:* Dr. Carolyn M. Callahan, Dean, 502-852-6440, Fax: 502-852-7557, E-mail: cmcall04@louisville.edu. *Application contact:* Susan E. Hildebrand, Program Director, 502-852-7257, Fax: 502-852-4901, E-mail: s.hildebrand@louisville.edu.
Website: http://business.louisville.edu/mba.

University of Louisville, Graduate School, College of Business, PhD Program in Entrepreneurship, Louisville, KY 40292-0001. Offers PhD. *Students:* 12 full-time (4 women); includes 1 minority (Asian, non-Hispanic/Latino), 9 international. Average age 33. 33 applicants, 27% accepted, 5 enrolled. In 2013, 4 doctorates awarded. *Degree requirements:* For doctorate, comprehensive exam, thesis/dissertation, paper of sufficient quality for journal publication. *Entrance requirements:* For doctorate, GMAT, 3 letters of recommendation, curriculum vitae, personal interview. Additional exam requirements/recommendations for international students: Required—TOEFL (minimum score 83 iBT). *Application deadline:* For fall admission, 12/31 priority date for domestic students, 3/31 for international students. Applications are processed on a rolling basis. Application fee: $60. Electronic applications accepted. *Expenses:* Tuition, state resident: full-time $10,788; part-time $599 per credit hour. Tuition, nonresident: full-time $22,446; part-time $1247 per credit hour. *Required fees:* $196. Tuition and fees vary according to program and reciprocity agreements. *Financial support:* Fellowships with full tuition reimbursements, research assistantships with full tuition reimbursements, teaching assistantships with full tuition reimbursements, scholarships/grants, health care benefits, and unspecified assistantships available. Financial award application deadline: 3/15; financial award applicants required to submit FAFSA. *Faculty research:* Entrepreneurship, supply chain management, venture capital, retailing/franchising, corporate governance. *Total annual research expenditures:* $146,460. *Unit head:* Dr. Carolyn M. Callahan, Dean, 502-852-6440, Fax: 502-852-7557, E-mail: cmcall04@louisville.edu. *Application contact:* Susan E. Hildebrand, Program Director, 502-852-7257, Fax: 502-852-4901, E-mail: s.hildebrand@louisville.edu.
Website: http://business.louisville.edu/entrepreneurshipphd.

University of Massachusetts Amherst, Graduate School, Isenberg School of Management, Program in Management, Amherst, MA 01003. Offers accounting (PhD); business administration (MBA); entrepreneurship (MBA); finance (MBA, PhD); healthcare administration (MBA); hospitality and tourism management (PhD); management science (PhD); marketing (MBA, PhD); organization studies (PhD); sport management (PhD); strategic management (PhD); MBA/MS. *Accreditation:* AACSB. Part-time and evening/weekend programs available. Postbaccalaureate distance learning degree programs offered. *Faculty:* 68 full-time (14 women). *Students:* 140 full-time (59 women), 1,127 part-time (319 women); includes 229 minority (24 Black or African American, non-Hispanic/Latino; 2 American Indian or Alaska Native, non-Hispanic/Latino; 135 Asian, non-Hispanic/Latino; 51 Hispanic/Latino; 6 Native Hawaiian or other Pacific Islander, non-Hispanic/Latino; 11 Two or more races, non-Hispanic/Latino), 131 international. Average age 36. 828 applicants, 56% accepted, 351 enrolled. In 2013, 361 master's, 12 doctorates awarded. Terminal master's awarded for partial completion of doctoral program. *Degree requirements:* For doctorate, comprehensive exam, thesis/dissertation. *Entrance requirements:* For master's and doctorate, GMAT or GRE General Test. Additional exam requirements/recommendations for international students: Required—TOEFL (minimum score 550 paper-based; 80 iBT), IELTS (minimum score 6.5). *Application deadline:* For fall admission, 1/20 for domestic and international students. Applications are processed on a rolling basis. Application fee: $75. Electronic applications accepted. *Financial support:* Fellowships with full and partial tuition reimbursements, research assistantships with full and partial tuition reimbursements, teaching assistantships with full and partial tuition reimbursements, career-related internships or fieldwork, Federal Work-Study, scholarships/grants, traineeships, health care benefits, tuition waivers (full and partial), and unspecified assistantships available. Support available to part-time students. Financial award application deadline: 1/20; financial award applicants required to submit FAFSA. *Unit head:* Dr. John Wells, Chair, 413-545-7609, Fax: 413-577-2234. *Application contact:* Lindsay DeSantis, Supervisor of Admissions, 413-545-0722, Fax: 413-577-0010, E-mail: gradadm@grad.umass.edu.
Website: http://www.isenberg.umass.edu/.

University of Massachusetts Lowell, Manning School of Business, Lowell, MA 01854-2881. Offers accounting (MSA); business administration (MBA, PhD); financial management (Graduate Certificate); foundations of business (Graduate Certificate); healthcare innovation and entrepreneurship (MS); innovation and technological entrepreneurship (MS); new venture creation (Graduate Certificate); supply chain and operations management (Graduate Certificate). *Accreditation:* AACSB. Part-time and evening/weekend programs available. *Entrance requirements:* For master's, GMAT.

University of Minnesota, Twin Cities Campus, Carlson School of Management, Doctoral Program in Business Administration, Minneapolis, MN 55455-0213. Offers accounting (PhD); finance (PhD); information and decision sciences (PhD); marketing (PhD); operations and management science (PhD); strategic management and entrepreneurship (PhD). *Faculty:* 102 full-time (31 women). *Students:* 74 full-time (25 women); includes 8 minority (1 Black or African American, non-Hispanic/Latino; 5 Asian, non-Hispanic/Latino; 2 Hispanic/Latino), 46 international. Average age 30. 274 applicants, 8% accepted, 15 enrolled. In 2013, 10 doctorates awarded. *Degree*

requirements: For doctorate, comprehensive exam, thesis/dissertation, written and oral preliminary exams, proposal defense, final defense. *Entrance requirements:* For doctorate, GMAT, GRE General Test. Additional exam requirements/recommendations for international students: Required—TOEFL (minimum score 600 paper-based; 100 iBT); Recommended—IELTS (minimum score 7.5). *Application deadline:* For fall admission, 12/31 for domestic students, 12/31 priority date for international students. Applications are processed on a rolling basis. Application fee: $75 ($95 for international students). Electronic applications accepted. *Expenses:* Contact institution. *Financial support:* In 2013–14, 68 students received support, including 96 fellowships with full tuition reimbursements available (averaging $6,300 per year), 65 research assistantships with full tuition reimbursements available (averaging $12,500 per year), 64 teaching assistantships with full tuition reimbursements available (averaging $12,500 per year); institutionally sponsored loans, scholarships/grants, health care benefits, unspecified assistantships, and full student fee waivers also available. Financial award application deadline: 12/31. *Faculty research:* Corporate strategy, finance, entrepreneurship, marketing, information and decision science, operations, accounting, supply chain. *Unit head:* Dr. Shawn P. Curley, Director, 612-624-6546, Fax: 612-624-8221, E-mail: curley@umn.edu. *Application contact:* Earlene K. Bronson, Assistant Director, 612-624-0875, Fax: 612-624-8221, E-mail: brons003@umn.edu.
Website: http://www.csom.umn.edu/phd-BA/.

University of Missouri–Kansas City, Henry W. Bloch School of Management, Kansas City, MO 64110-2499. Offers accounting (MS); business administration (MBA); entrepreneurial real estate (MERE); entrepreneurship and innovation (PhD); finance (MS); public affairs (MPA, PhD); JD/MBA; LL M/MPA. PhD (interdisciplinary) offered through the School of Graduate Studies. *Accreditation:* AACSB; NASPAA. Part-time and evening/weekend programs available. *Faculty:* 57 full-time (15 women), 32 part-time/adjunct (10 women). *Students:* 309 full-time (151 women), 377 part-time (163 women); includes 100 minority (39 Black or African American, non-Hispanic/Latino; 2 American Indian or Alaska Native, non-Hispanic/Latino; 27 Asian, non-Hispanic/Latino; 24 Hispanic/Latino; 1 Native Hawaiian or other Pacific Islander, non-Hispanic/Latino; 7 Two or more races, non-Hispanic/Latino), 93 international. Average age 30. 489 applicants, 54% accepted, 252 enrolled. In 2013, 252 master's, 1 doctorate awarded. Terminal master's awarded for partial completion of doctoral program. *Entrance requirements:* For master's, GMAT, GRE, 2 essays, 2 references, support of employer; for doctorate, GRE, minimum GPA of 3.0. Additional exam requirements/recommendations for international students: Required—TOEFL (minimum score 550 paper-based; 80 iBT). *Application deadline:* For fall admission, 5/1 priority date for domestic and international students; for spring admission, 10/1 priority date for domestic and international students. Applications are processed on a rolling basis. Application fee: $45 ($50 for international students). Electronic applications accepted. *Expenses:* Tuition, state resident: full-time $6073; part-time $337.40 per credit hour. Tuition, nonresident: full-time $15,680; part-time $871.10 per credit hour. *Required fees:* $97.59 per credit hour. Full-time tuition and fees vary according to program. *Financial support:* In 2013–14, 38 research assistantships with partial tuition reimbursements (averaging $10,499 per year), 6 teaching assistantships with partial tuition reimbursements (averaging $13,380 per year) were awarded; career-related internships or fieldwork, Federal Work-Study, institutionally sponsored loans, scholarships/grants, tuition waivers (full and partial), and unspecified assistantships also available. Support available to part-time students. Financial award application deadline: 3/1; financial award applicants required to submit FAFSA. *Faculty research:* Entrepreneurship, finance, non-profit, risk management. *Unit head:* Dr. David Donnelly, Dean, 816-235-1333, Fax: 816-235-2206, E-mail: donnellyd@umkc.edu. *Application contact:* 816-235-1111, E-mail: admit@umkc.edu.
Website: http://www.bloch.umkc.edu.

University of Nevada, Las Vegas, Graduate College, College of Business, Department of Management, Entrepreneurship and Technology, Las Vegas, NV 89154-6034. Offers management (Certificate); management information systems (MS, Certificate); new venture management (Certificate); MS/MS. Part-time and evening/weekend programs available. *Faculty:* 9 full-time (1 woman), 1 (woman) part-time/adjunct. *Students:* 30 full-time (8 women), 19 part-time (6 women); includes 11 minority (2 Black or African American, non-Hispanic/Latino; 3 Asian, non-Hispanic/Latino; 4 Hispanic/Latino; 1 Native Hawaiian or other Pacific Islander, non-Hispanic/Latino; 1 Two or more races, non-Hispanic/Latino), 18 international. Average age 31. 55 applicants, 82% accepted, 19 enrolled. In 2013, 21 master's, 1 other advanced degree awarded. *Entrance requirements:* For master's and Certificate, GMAT or GRE. Additional exam requirements/recommendations for international students: Required—TOEFL (minimum score 550 paper-based; 80 iBT), IELTS (minimum score 7). *Application deadline:* For fall admission, 8/1 for domestic students, 5/1 for international students; for spring admission, 11/15 for domestic students, 10/1 for international students. Application fee: $60 ($95 for international students). Electronic applications accepted. *Expenses:* Tuition, state resident: full-time $4752; part-time $264 per credit. Tuition, nonresident: full-time $18,662; part-time $554.50 per credit. *International tuition:* $18,952 full-time. *Required fees:* $532; $12 per credit. $266 per semester. One-time fee: $35. Tuition and fees vary according to course load and program. *Financial support:* In 2013–14, 8 students received support, including 5 research assistantships with partial tuition reimbursements available (averaging $8,000 per year), 3 teaching assistantships with partial tuition reimbursements available (averaging $8,333 per year); institutionally sponsored loans, scholarships/grants, health care benefits, and unspecified assistantships also available. Financial award application deadline: 3/1. *Faculty research:* Decision-making, publish or perish, ethical issues in information systems, IT-enabled decision making, business ethics. *Unit head:* Alan Miller, Chair/Associate Professor, 702-895-1724, E-mail: alan.miller@unlv.edu. *Application contact:* Graduate College Admissions Evaluator, 702-895-3320, Fax: 702-895-4180, E-mail: gradcollege@unlv.edu.
Website: http://business.unlv.edu/met/.

University of New Brunswick Fredericton, School of Graduate Studies, Faculty of Business Administration, Fredericton, NB E3B 5A3, Canada. Offers business administration (MBA); engineering management (MBA); entrepreneurship (MBA); sports and recreation management (MBA); MBA/LL B. Part-time programs available. *Faculty:* 23 full-time (3 women), 5 part-time/adjunct (2 women). *Students:* 48 full-time (15 women), 31 part-time (12 women), 1 international. In 2013, 30 master's awarded. *Degree requirements:* For master's, thesis optional. *Entrance requirements:* For master's, GMAT (minimum score 550), minimum GPA of 3.0; 3-5 years of work experience; 3 letters of reference with at least one academic reference. Additional exam requirements/recommendations for international students: Required—TOEFL (minimum score 580 paper-based; 92 iBT) or IELTS (minimum score 7). *Application deadline:* For fall admission, 10/31 priority date for domestic and international students; for spring admission, 3/31 priority date for domestic and international students. Application fee: $50 Canadian dollars. Electronic applications accepted. *Financial support:* In 2013–14, 6 fellowships, 3 research assistantships (averaging $4,500 per year), 22 teaching assistantships (averaging $2,250 per year) were awarded. *Faculty research:* Entrepreneurship, finance, law, sport and recreation management, and engineering management. *Unit head:* Judy Roy, Director of Graduate Studies, 506-458-7307, Fax: 506-453-3561, E-mail: jroy@unb.ca. *Application contact:* Marilyn Davis, Acting Graduate Secretary, 506-453-4766, Fax: 506-453-3561, E-mail: mbacontact@unb.ca.
Website: http://go.unb.ca/gradprograms.

University of New Mexico, Anderson Graduate School of Management, Department of Finance, International, Technology and Entrepreneurship, Albuquerque, NM 87131-1221. Offers entrepreneurship (MBA); finance (MBA); international management (MBA); international management in Latin America (MBA); management of technology (MBA). Part-time and evening/weekend programs available. *Faculty:* 16 full-time (2 women), 5 part-time/adjunct (1 woman). In 2013, 72 master's awarded. *Entrance requirements:* For master's, GMAT or GRE, minimum GPA of 3.0 on last 60 hours of coursework. Additional exam requirements/recommendations for international students: Required—TOEFL (minimum score 550 paper-based; 79 iBT). *Application deadline:* For fall admission, 4/1 priority date for domestic and international students; for spring admission, 10/1 priority date for domestic and international students. Applications are processed on a rolling basis. Application fee: $50. Electronic applications accepted. *Expenses:* Contact institution. *Financial support:* Fellowships, research assistantships, career-related internships or fieldwork, Federal Work-Study, scholarships/grants, and unspecified assistantships available. Support available to part-time students. Financial award application deadline: 6/1; financial award applicants required to submit FAFSA. *Faculty research:* Corporate finance, investments, management in Latin America, management of technology, entrepreneurship. *Unit head:* Dr. Leslie Boni, Chair, 505-277-6471, Fax: 505-277-7108, E-mail: boni01@unm.edu. *Application contact:* Tracy Wilkey, Manager, Academic Advisement, 505-277-3290, Fax: 505-277-8436, E-mail: andersonadvising@unm.edu.
Website: http://mba.mgt.unm.edu/default.asp.

University of Pennsylvania, School of Engineering and Applied Science, Integrated Product Design Program, Philadelphia, PA 19104. Offers ME, MIPD. Program offered jointly with the Wharton School and the School of Design. *Students:* 11 full-time (8 women), 3 part-time (all women); includes 1 minority (Two or more races, non-Hispanic/Latino), 7 international. 77 applicants, 32% accepted, 14 enrolled. In 2013, 2 master's awarded. *Unit head:* Eduardo D. Glandt, Dean, 215-898-7244, E-mail: seasdean@seas.upenn.edu. *Application contact:* School of Engineering and Applied Science Graduate Admissions, 215-898-4542, E-mail: gradstudies@seas.upenn.edu.
Website: http://www.me.upenn.edu/ipd.

University of Phoenix–Puerto Rico Campus, School of Business, Guaynabo, PR 00968. Offers accounting (MBA); energy management (MBA); global management (MBA); human resource management (MBA); marketing (MBA); project management (MBA); small business administration (MBA). Evening/weekend programs available. *Degree requirements:* For master's, thesis (for some programs). *Entrance requirements:* For master's, minimum undergraduate GPA of 3.0, 3 years work experience. Additional exam requirements/recommendations for international students: Required—TOEFL (minimum score 550 paper-based; 79 iBT). Electronic applications accepted.

University of Portland, Dr. Robert B. Pamplin, Jr. School of Business, Portland, OR 97203-5798. Offers entrepreneurship (MBA); finance (MBA, MS); health care management (MBA); marketing (MBA); nonprofit management (EMBA); operations and technology management (MBA, MS); sustainability (MBA). *Accreditation:* AACSB. Part-time and evening/weekend programs available. *Faculty:* 26 full-time (5 women), 8 part-time/adjunct (1 woman). *Students:* 37 full-time (11 women), 93 part-time (44 women); includes 15 minority (1 Black or African American, non-Hispanic/Latino; 7 Asian, non-Hispanic/Latino; 5 Hispanic/Latino; 2 Two or more races, non-Hispanic/Latino), 21 international. Average age 32. In 2013, 68 master's awarded. *Entrance requirements:* For master's, GMAT, minimum GPA of 3.0, resume, 2 letters of recommendation. Additional exam requirements/recommendations for international students: Required—TOEFL (minimum score 570 paper-based; 89 iBT), IELTS (minimum score 7). *Application deadline:* For fall admission, 7/15 priority date for domestic and international students; for spring admission, 12/15 priority date for domestic and international students. Applications are processed on a rolling basis. Application fee: $50. *Expenses:* Contact institution. *Financial support:* Federal Work-Study, scholarships/grants, and tuition waivers (partial) available. Support available to part-time students. Financial award application deadline: 3/1; financial award applicants required to submit FAFSA. *Unit head:* Melissa McCarthy, Director, 503-943-7224, E-mail: mba-up@up.edu.
Website: http://business.up.edu/mba/default.aspx?cid-1179&pid-6450.

University of Rochester, Hajim School of Engineering and Applied Sciences, Master of Science in Technical Entrepreneurship and Management Program, Rochester, NY 14642. Offers biomedical engineering (MS); chemical engineering (MS); computer science (MS); electrical and computer engineering (MS); energy and the environment (MS); materials science (MS); mechanical engineering (MS); optics (MS). Program offered in collaboration with the Simon School of Business. Part-time programs available. *Faculty:* 621 full-time, 21 part-time/adjunct. *Students:* 35 full-time (7 women), 4 part-time (0 women); includes 5 minority (2 Black or African American, non-Hispanic/Latino; 1 Asian, non-Hispanic/Latino; 2 Hispanic/Latino), 28 international. Average age 24. 154 applicants, 57% accepted, 22 enrolled. In 2013, 22 master's awarded. *Degree requirements:* For master's, comprehensive exam. *Entrance requirements:* For master's, GRE or GMAT, 3 letters of recommendation; personal statement; official transcript; bachelor's degree (or equivalent for international students) in engineering, science, or mathematics. Additional exam requirements/recommendations for international students: Required—TOEFL or IELTS. *Application deadline:* For fall admission, 2/1 for domestic and international students. Applications are processed on a rolling basis. Application fee: $60. Electronic applications accepted. *Expenses: Tuition:* Full-time $44,580; part-time $1394 per credit hour. *Required fees:* $492. *Financial support:* In 2013–14, 23 students received support. Career-related internships or fieldwork and scholarships/grants available. Financial award application deadline: 2/1. *Faculty research:* High efficiency solar cells, macromolecular self-assembly, digital signal processing, memory hierarchy management, molecular and physical mechanisms in cell migration, optical imaging systems. *Unit head:* Duncan T. Moore, Vice Provost for Entrepreneurship, 585-275-5248, Fax: 585-473-6745, E-mail: moore@optics.rochester.edu. *Application contact:* Andrea M. Galati, Executive Director, 585-276-3407, Fax: 585-276-2357, E-mail: andrea.galati@rochester.edu.
Website: http://www.rochester.edu/team.

University of Rochester, Simon Business School, Full-Time Master's Program in Business Administration, Rochester, NY 14627. Offers accounting and information systems (MBA); business environment and public policy (MBA); business systems consulting (MBA); competitive and organizational strategy - pricing (MBA); computers and information systems (MBA); corporate accounting (MBA); electronic commerce (MBA); entrepreneurship (MBA); finance (MBA); health sciences management (MBA); international management (MBA); marketing - brand management and pricing (MBA); operations management - manufacturing (MBA); operations management - services (MBA); public accounting (MBA). *Accreditation:* AACSB. Part-time and evening/weekend programs available. *Faculty:* 60 full-time (11 women), 23 part-time/adjunct (3 women). *Students:* 282 full-time (74 women); includes 55 minority (29 Black or African American, non-Hispanic/Latino; 1 American Indian or Alaska Native, non-Hispanic/Latino; 11 Asian, non-Hispanic/Latino; 12 Hispanic/Latino; 2 Two or more races, non-Hispanic/Latino), 144 international. 673 applicants, 33% accepted, 65 enrolled. In 2013,

176 master's awarded. *Entrance requirements:* For master's, GMAT/GRE, previous course work in calculus. Additional exam requirements/recommendations for international students: Required—TOEFL. *Application deadline:* For fall admission, 10/15 for domestic and international students; for winter admission, 1/5 for domestic and international students; for spring admission, 3/15 for domestic and international students; for summer admission, 5/15 for domestic students. Applications are processed on a rolling basis. Application fee: $150. Electronic applications accepted. *Expenses: Tuition:* Full-time $44,580; part-time $1394 per credit hour. *Required fees:* $492. *Financial support:* In 2013–14, 72 students received support. Fellowships, research assistantships, teaching assistantships, institutionally sponsored loans, scholarships/grants, and tuition waivers (partial) available. Financial award application deadline: 3/1; financial award applicants required to submit CSS PROFILE or FAFSA. *Unit head:* Mark Zupan, Dean, 585-275-3316. *Application contact:* Rebekah S. Lewin, Assistant Dean of Admissions and Student Engagement, 585-275-3533, E-mail: admissions@simon.rochester.edu.

University of Rochester, Simon Business School, Part-Time MBA Program, Rochester, NY 14627. Offers accounting and information systems (MBA); business environment and public policy (MBA); business systems consulting (MBA); competitive and organizational strategy (MBA); computers and information systems (MBA); corporate accounting (MBA); electronic commerce (MBA); entrepreneurship (MBA); finance (MBA); health sciences management (MBA); international management (MBA); manufacturing management (MBA); marketing (MBA); operations management - services (MBA); public accounting (MBA). Part-time and evening/weekend programs available. *Faculty:* 59 full-time (10 women), 23 part-time/adjunct (3 women). *Students:* 270 part-time (75 women); includes 38 minority (5 Black or African American, non-Hispanic/Latino; 1 American Indian or Alaska Native, non-Hispanic/Latino; 24 Asian, non-Hispanic/Latino; 5 Hispanic/Latino; 3 Two or more races, non-Hispanic/Latino). Average age 32. 56 applicants, 98% accepted, 51 enrolled. In 2013, 77 master's awarded. *Entrance requirements:* For master's, GRE or GMAT, resume, recommendation letters, essays, transcipts. *Application deadline:* For fall admission, 8/15 for domestic students; for winter admission, 11/15 for domestic students; for spring admission, 2/15 for domestic students; for summer admission, 5/15 for domestic students. Applications are processed on a rolling basis. Application fee: $150. Electronic applications accepted. *Expenses: Tuition:* Full-time $44,580; part-time $1394 per credit hour. *Required fees:* $492. *Financial support:* Scholarships/grants and tuition waivers available. Financial award applicants required to submit CSS PROFILE. *Unit head:* Mark Zupan, Dean, 585-275-3316, E-mail: mark.zupan@simon.rochester.edu. *Application contact:* Jennifer Mossotti, Associate Director of Part-Time Programs, 585-275-3803, E-mail: jennifer.mossotti@simon.rochester.edu.
Website: http://www.simon.rochester.edu/programs/part-time-mba-programs/index.aspx.

University of San Francisco, College of Arts and Sciences, Web Science Program, San Francisco, CA 94117-1080. Offers MS. *Faculty:* 7 full-time (5 women). *Students:* 12 full-time (3 women), 3 part-time (0 women); includes 2 minority (1 Asian, non-Hispanic/Latino; 1 Two or more races, non-Hispanic/Latino), 6 international. Average age 28. 13 applicants, 77% accepted, 6 enrolled. In 2013, 5 master's awarded. *Application deadline:* For fall admission, 3/1 for domestic students; for spring admission, 10/15 for domestic students. *Expenses: Tuition:* Full-time $21,150; part-time $1175 per unit. Tuition and fees vary according to course load, campus/location and program. *Financial support:* In 2013–14, 6 students received support. *Unit head:* Dr. Sophie Engle, Graduate Director, 415-422-6530, Fax: 415-422-5800. *Application contact:* Mark Landerghini, Graduate Adviser, 415-422-5101, E-mail: asgraduate@usfca.edu.
Website: http://www1.cs.usfca.edu/grad/msws/.

University of San Francisco, School of Management, Master in Global Entrepreneurial Management Program, San Francisco, CA 94105. Offers MGEM. Program offered jointly with IQS in Barcelona, Spain and Fu Jen Catholic University in Taipei, Taiwan. *Faculty:* 2 full-time (both women), 2 part-time/adjunct (0 women). *Students:* 40 full-time (19 women); includes 6 minority (3 Asian, non-Hispanic/Latino; 2 Hispanic/Latino; 1 Two or more races, non-Hispanic/Latino), 27 international. Average age 24. 73 applicants, 66% accepted, 35 enrolled. In 2013, 34 master's awarded. *Entrance requirements:* For master's, resume, transcripts from each college or university attended, two letters of recommendation, personal statement. Additional exam requirements/recommendations for international students: Required—TOEFL (minimum score 550 paper-based, 79 iBT), IELTS (minimum score 6), or PTE (minimum score 53). *Application deadline:* For fall admission, 5/15 for domestic students. Application fee: $55. Electronic applications accepted. *Expenses: Tuition:* Full-time $21,150; part-time $1175 per unit. Tuition and fees vary according to course load, campus/location and program. *Financial support:* In 2013–14, 3 students received support. Application deadline: 3/2; applicants required to submit FAFSA. *Unit head:* Dr. Jennifer Walske, Director, 415-422-2221, E-mail: management@usfca.edu. *Application contact:* Office of Graduate Recruiting and Admissions, 415-422-2221, Fax: 415-422-6315, E-mail: management@usfca.edu.
Website: http://www.usfca.edu/mgem.

University of San Francisco, School of Management, Master of Business Administration Program, San Francisco, CA 94105. Offers entrepreneurship and innovation (MBA); finance (MBA); international business (MBA); marketing (MBA); organization development (MBA); DDS/MBA; JD/MBA; MBA/MAPS. *Accreditation:* AACSB. Part-time and evening/weekend programs available. *Faculty:* 18 full-time (4 women), 20 part-time/adjunct (10 women). *Students:* 157 full-time (69 women), 14 part-time (7 women); includes 57 minority (7 Black or African American, non-Hispanic/Latino; 31 Asian, non-Hispanic/Latino; 14 Hispanic/Latino; 5 Two or more races, non-Hispanic/Latino), 30 international. Average age 29. 345 applicants, 68% accepted, 79 enrolled. In 2013, 131 master's awarded. *Entrance requirements:* For master's, GMAT or GRE, resume (two years of professional work experience required for Part-Time MBA, preferred for Full-Time MBA), transcripts from each college or university attended, two letters of recommendation, a personal statement and an interview. Additional exam requirements/recommendations for international students: Required—TOEFL (minimum score 600 paper-based, 100 iBT), IELTS (minimum score 7) or PTE (minimum score 68). *Application deadline:* For fall admission, 6/5 for domestic students, 5/15 for international students; for spring admission, 11/30 for domestic students. Application fee: $55. Electronic applications accepted. *Expenses: Tuition:* Full-time $21,150; part-time $1175 per unit. Tuition and fees vary according to course load, campus/location and program. *Financial support:* In 2013–14, 42 students received support. Fellowships and scholarships/grants available. Financial award application deadline: 3/2; financial award applicants required to submit FAFSA. *Faculty research:* International financial markets, technology transfer licensing, international marketing, strategic planning. *Total annual research expenditures:* $50,000. *Unit head:* Dr. John Veitch, Associate Dean and Program Director, 415-422-2221, Fax: 415-422-6315, E-mail: management@usfca.edu. *Application contact:* Office of Graduate Recruiting and Admissions, 415-422-2221, Fax: 415-422-6315, E-mail: management@usfca.edu.
Website: http://www.usfca.edu/mba.

University of Sioux Falls, Vucurevich School of Business, Sioux Falls, SD 57105-1699. Offers entrepreneurial leadership (MBA); general management (MBA); health care management (MBA); marketing (MBA). Part-time and evening/weekend programs available. *Degree requirements:* For master's, project. *Entrance requirements:* For master's, minimum GPA of 3.0. Additional exam requirements/recommendations for international students: Required—TOEFL. *Expenses:* Contact institution.

University of South Florida, College of Business, Center for Entrepreneurship, Tampa, FL 33620-9951. Offers applied technologies (MS); MS/MS; MSBE/MS. Part-time and evening/weekend programs available. *Faculty:* 4 full-time (2 women), 1 part-time/adjunct (0 women). *Students:* 40 full-time (12 women), 22 part-time (7 women); includes 11 minority (5 Black or African American, non-Hispanic/Latino; 2 Asian, non-Hispanic/Latino; 4 Hispanic/Latino), 19 international. Average age 31. 54 applicants, 74% accepted, 25 enrolled. In 2013, 44 master's awarded. *Degree requirements:* For master's, thesis optional. *Entrance requirements:* For master's, GMAT or GRE (preferred), MCAT or LSAT, minimum undergraduate GPA of 3.0 in upper-division course work, two letters of recommendation, letter of interest, statement of purpose, personal interview. Additional exam requirements/recommendations for international students: Required—TOEFL (minimum score 550 paper-based; 79 iBT) or IELTS (minimum score 6.5). *Application deadline:* For fall admission, 2/15 for domestic students, 1/2 for international students; for spring admission, 10/15 for domestic students, 6/1 for international students. Applications are processed on a rolling basis. Application fee: $30. Electronic applications accepted. *Faculty research:* The underlying success factors which drive the creation, growth and failures of businesses and technologies in the life sciences industry; the influences of individual company geographic location, financial parameters, intellectual property, FDA and regulatory compliance, and press coverage on stock performance of over 1000 publicly traded life sciences companies. *Total annual research expenditures:* $87,527. *Unit head:* Dr. Michael W. Fountain, Director, Center for Entrepreneurship, 813-974-7825, Fax: 813-974-6175, E-mail: fountain@usf.edu. *Application contact:* Dr. Tapas Das, Assistant Director/Professor, 813-974-5585, Fax: 813-974-5953, E-mail: das@usf.edu.
Website: http://www.ce.usf.edu/.

University of South Florida, College of Global Sustainability, Tampa, FL 33620-9951. Offers entrepreneurship (MA); sustainable energy (MA); sustainable tourism (MA); water (MA); MA/MS. *Faculty:* 7 full-time (2 women), 1 (woman) part-time/adjunct. *Students:* 39 full-time (27 women), 26 part-time (15 women); includes 15 minority (3 Black or African American, non-Hispanic/Latino; 1 American Indian or Alaska Native, non-Hispanic/Latino; 8 Hispanic/Latino; 3 Two or more races, non-Hispanic/Latino), 13 international. Average age 39. 58 applicants, 59% accepted, 8 enrolled. In 2013, 10 master's awarded. *Degree requirements:* For master's, comprehensive exam (for some programs), thesis or alternative, internship. *Entrance requirements:* For master's, minimum GPA of 3.0 in undergraduate coursework; at least two letters of recommendation (one must be academic); 200-250-word essay on student's background, professional goals, and reasons for seeking degree. Additional exam requirements/recommendations for international students: Required—TOEFL (minimum score 550 paper-based; 79 iBT). *Faculty research:* Global sustainability, integrated resource management, systems thinking, green communities, entrepreneurship, ecotourism. *Total annual research expenditures:* $564,596. *Unit head:* Dr. Kalanithy Vairavamoorthy, Dean, 813-974-9694, E-mail: vairavk@grad.usf.edu. *Application contact:* Dr. Carl Herndl, Associate Dean, 813-974-5397, E-mail: cgh@usf.edu.
Website: http://psgs.usf.edu/.

University of South Florida, University College/Distance Education, Tampa, FL 33620-9951. *Unit head:* Kathy Barnes, Interdisciplinary Programs Coordinator, 813-974-8031, Fax: 813-974-7061, E-mail: barnesk@usf.edu. *Application contact:* Karen Tylinski, Metro Initiatives, 813-974-9943, Fax: 813-974-7061, E-mail: ktylinsk@usf.edu.
Website: http://uc.usf.edu/.

The University of Tampa, John H. Sykes College of Business, Tampa, FL 33606-1490. Offers accounting (MS); entrepreneurship (MBA); finance (MBA, MS); information systems management (MBA); innovation management (MBA); international business (MBA); marketing (MBA, MS); nonprofit management (MBA). *Accreditation:* AACSB. Part-time and evening/weekend programs available. *Faculty:* 41 full-time (15 women), 5 part-time/adjunct (1 woman). *Students:* 406 full-time (171 women), 152 part-time (61 women); includes 104 minority (18 Black or African American, non-Hispanic/Latino; 1 American Indian or Alaska Native, non-Hispanic/Latino; 20 Asian, non-Hispanic/Latino; 59 Hispanic/Latino; 6 Two or more races, non-Hispanic/Latino), 154 international. Average age 33. 1,341 applicants, 37% accepted, 256 enrolled. In 2013, 218 master's awarded. *Degree requirements:* For master's, capstone. *Entrance requirements:* For master's, GMAT or GRE, 4-year undergraduate degree, minimum GPA of 3.0, professional experience (for Executive MBA). Additional exam requirements/recommendations for international students: Required—TOEFL (minimum score 577 paper-based; 90 iBT); Recommended—IELTS (minimum score 7.5). *Application deadline:* Applications are processed on a rolling basis. Application fee: $40. Electronic applications accepted. *Expenses: Tuition:* Full-time $8928; part-time $558 per credit hour. *Required fees:* $80; $80 $40 per term. Tuition and fees vary according to program. *Financial support:* In 2013–14, 110 students received support. Career-related internships or fieldwork, scholarships/grants, and unspecified assistantships available. Financial award applicants required to submit FAFSA. *Faculty research:* Job market signaling, on-line shopping behaviors and social media, the Tampa Bay economy, digital literacy, entrepreneurship in small businesses. *Unit head:* Dr. Stephanie Thomason, Associate Dean, 813-253-6289, E-mail: sthomason@ut.edu. *Application contact:* Charlene Tobie, Associate Director of Admissions, 813-257-3566, E-mail: ctobie@ut.edu.
Website: http://www.ut.edu/business/.

The University of Texas at Austin, Graduate School, McCombs School of Business, Program in Technology Commercialization, Austin, TX 78712-1111. Offers MS. Twelve-month program, beginning in May, with classes held every other Friday and Saturday. Evening/weekend programs available. Postbaccalaureate distance learning degree programs offered (no on-campus study). *Degree requirements:* For master's, year-long global teaming project. *Entrance requirements:* For master's, GRE General Test or GMAT. Additional exam requirements/recommendations for international students: Required—TOEFL (minimum score 550 paper-based; 79 iBT). Electronic applications accepted. *Expenses:* Contact institution. *Faculty research:* Technology transfer; entrepreneurship; commercialization; research, development and innovation.

The University of Texas at Dallas, Naveen Jindal School of Management, Program in Innovation and Entrepreneurship, Richardson, TX 75080. Offers innovation within the corporation (MS); new venture (MS). Part-time and evening/weekend programs available. *Faculty:* 4 part-time/adjunct (0 women). *Students:* 11 full-time (2 women), 10 part-time (2 women); includes 6 minority (1 American Indian or Alaska Native, non-Hispanic/Latino; 5 Asian, non-Hispanic/Latino), 6 international. Average age 30. 25 applicants, 56% accepted, 7 enrolled. In 2013, 10 master's awarded. *Degree requirements:* For master's, thesis optional. *Entrance requirements:* For master's, GMAT or GRE, minimum GPA of 3.0 in upper-level course work in field. Additional exam requirements/recommendations for international students: Required—TOEFL (minimum score 550 paper-based). *Application deadline:* For fall admission, 7/15 for domestic students, 5/1 priority date for international students; for spring admission, 11/15 for domestic students, 9/1 priority date for international students. Applications are processed on a rolling basis. Application fee: $50 ($100 for international students).

Entrepreneurship

Electronic applications accepted. *Expenses:* Tuition, state resident: full-time $11,940; part-time $663.33 per credit hour. Tuition, nonresident: full-time $21,606; part-time $1200.33 per credit hour. *Financial support:* In 2013–14, 4 students received support. Research assistantships with partial tuition reimbursements available, teaching assistantships with partial tuition reimbursements available, career-related internships or fieldwork, Federal Work-Study, institutionally sponsored loans, scholarships/grants, and unspecified assistantships available. Support available to part-time students. Financial award application deadline: 4/30; financial award applicants required to submit FAFSA. *Unit head:* Dr. Joseph C. Picken, Program Director, 972-883-4986, E-mail: jpicken@utdallas.edu. *Application contact:* Madison F. Pedigo, Associate Director, 972-883-4481, E-mail: mpedigo@utdallas.edu.
Website: http://jindal.utdallas.edu/academic-programs/masters-programs/master-of-science-in-innovation-and-entrepreneurship/.

University of the Incarnate Word, School of Graduate Studies and Research, Dreeben School of Education, Programs in Education, San Antonio, TX 78209-6397. Offers adult education (M Ed, MA); cross-cultural education (M Ed, MA); early childhood literacy (M Ed, MA); general education (M Ed, MA); higher education (PhD); instructional technology (M Ed, MA); international education and entrepreneurship (PhD); kinesiology (M Ed, MA); literacy (M Ed, MA); organizational leadership (PhD); organizational learning and learning (M Ed, MA); reading (M Ed, MA); special education (M Ed, MA); teacher leadership (M Ed, MA). Part-time and evening/weekend programs available. *Faculty:* 17 full-time (9 women), 6 part-time/adjunct (all women). *Students:* 23 full-time (13 women), 187 part-time (122 women); includes 114 minority (24 Black or African American, non-Hispanic/Latino; 1 American Indian or Alaska Native, non-Hispanic/Latino; 3 Asian, non-Hispanic/Latino; 85 Hispanic/Latino; 1 Two or more races, non-Hispanic/Latino), 30 international. Average age 41. 52 applicants, 67% accepted, 25 enrolled. In 2013, 12 master's, 14 doctorates awarded. *Degree requirements:* For master's, capstone; for doctorate, thesis/dissertation, qualifying exam. *Entrance requirements:* For master's, baccalaureate degree; minimum foundation GPA of 2.5; interview; for doctorate, master's degree; interview; supervised writing sample. Additional exam requirements/recommendations for international students: Required—TOEFL (minimum score 560 paper-based; 83 iBT). *Application deadline:* Applications are processed on a rolling basis. Application fee: $20. Electronic applications accepted. *Expenses: Tuition:* Part-time $815 per credit hour. *Required fees:* $86 per credit hour. One-time fee: $40 part-time. Tuition and fees vary according to degree level and program. *Financial support:* In 2013–14, 5 research assistantships were awarded; Federal Work-Study and scholarships/grants also available. Financial award applicants required to submit FAFSA. *Unit head:* Dr. Denise Staudt, Dean, Dreeben School of Education, 210-829-2762, E-mail: staudt@uiwtx.edu. *Application contact:* Andrea Cyterski-Acosta, Dean of Enrollment, 210-829-6005, Fax: 210-829-3921, E-mail: admis@uiwtx.edu.
Website: http://www.uiw.edu/education/index.htm.

University of Waterloo, Graduate Studies, Centre for Business, Entrepreneurship and Technology, Waterloo, ON N2L 3G1, Canada. Offers MBET. *Entrance requirements:* For master's, honors degree. Additional exam requirements/recommendations for international students: Required—TOEFL (minimum score 550 paper-based), TWE. Electronic applications accepted.

The University of Western Ontario, Richard Ivey School of Business, London, ON N6A 3K7, Canada. Offers business (EMBA, PhD); corporate strategy and leadership elective (MBA); entrepreneurship elective (MBA); finance elective (MBA); health sector stream (MBA); international management elective (MBA); marketing elective (MBA); JD/MBA. *Degree requirements:* For master's, thesis (for some programs); for doctorate, thesis/dissertation. *Entrance requirements:* For master's, GMAT, 2 years of full-time work experience, interview. Additional exam requirements/recommendations for international students: Required—TOEFL (minimum score 100 iBT) or IELTS (minimum score 6). Electronic applications accepted. *Faculty research:* Strategy, organizational behavior, international business, finance, operations management.

Valparaiso University, Graduate School, College of Business, Valparaiso, IN 46383. Offers business administration (MBA); business intelligence (Certificate); engineering management (Certificate); entrepreneurship (Certificate); finance (Certificate); general business (Certificate); management (Certificate); marketing (Certificate); sustainability (Certificate); JD/MBA; MSN/MBA. *Accreditation:* AACSB. Part-time and evening/weekend programs available. Postbaccalaureate distance learning degree programs offered (minimal on-campus study). *Faculty:* 11 part-time/adjunct (2 women). *Students:* 13 full-time (3 women), 48 part-time (21 women); includes 6 minority (3 Black or African American, non-Hispanic/Latino; 2 Hispanic/Latino; 1 Two or more races, non-Hispanic/Latino), 5 international. Average age 33. In 2013, 19 master's, 3 other advanced degrees awarded. *Entrance requirements:* For master's, GMAT, GRE, minimum GPA of 3.0. Additional exam requirements/recommendations for international students: Required—TOEFL (minimum score 550 paper-based; 80 iBT), IELTS (minimum score 6). *Application deadline:* Applications are processed on a rolling basis. Application fee: $30 ($50 for international students). Electronic applications accepted. *Expenses:* Contact institution. *Financial support:* Available to part-time students. Applicants required to submit FAFSA. *Unit head:* Bruce MacLean, Director of Graduate Programs in Management, 219-465-7952, Fax: 219-464-5789, E-mail: bruce.maclean@valpo.edu. *Application contact:* Cindy Scanlan, Assistant Director of Graduate Programs in Management, 219-465-7952, Fax: 219-464-5789, E-mail: cindy.scanlan@valpo.edu.
Website: http://www.valpo.edu/mba/.

Walden University, Graduate Programs, School of Management, Minneapolis, MN 55401. Offers accounting (MBA, MS, DBA), including accounting for the professional (MS), accounting with CPA emphasis (MS), self-designed (MS, PhD); accounting and management (MS), including accountants as strategic managers, self-designed (MS, PhD); advanced project management (Graduate Certificate); applied project management (Graduate Certificate); bridge to business administration (Post-Doctoral Certificate); bridge to management (Post-Doctoral Certificate); business administration (EMBA); business management (Graduate Certificate); communication (MS, Graduate Certificate); corporate finance (MBA); entrepreneurship (DBA); entrepreneurship and small business (MBA); finance (DBA); global supply chain management (DBA); healthcare management (MBA, DBA); human resource management (MBA, MS, Graduate Certificate), including functional human resource management (MS), general program (MS), integrating functional and strategic human resource management (MS), organizational strategy (MS); human resources management (DBA); information systems management (DBA); international business (MBA, DBA); leadership (MBA, MS, DBA), including general program (MS), human resources leadership (MS), leader development (MS), self-designed (MS, PhD); management (MS, PhD), including accounting (PhD), engineering management (PhD), finance (PhD), general program (MS), healthcare management (MS), human resource management (MS), human resources management (PhD), information systems management (PhD), leadership (MS), leadership and organizational change (PhD), marketing (MS), operations research (PhD), project management (MS), self-designed, strategy and operations (MS); marketing (MBA, DBA); project management (MBA, MS, DBA); self-designed (MBA, DBA); social impact management (DBA); technology entrepreneurship (DBA). Part-time and evening/weekend programs available. Postbaccalaureate distance learning degree programs offered (minimal on-campus study). *Faculty:* 24 full-time (9 women), 337 part-time/adjunct (127 women). *Students:* 4,369 full-time (2,379 women), 2,181 part-time (1,304 women); includes 3,669 minority (3,020 Black or African American, non-Hispanic/Latino; 22 American Indian or Alaska Native, non-Hispanic/Latino; 156 Asian, non-Hispanic/Latino; 331 Hispanic/Latino; 11 Native Hawaiian or other Pacific Islander, non-Hispanic/Latino; 129 Two or more races, non-Hispanic/Latino), 107 international. Average age 41. 2,030 applicants, 94% accepted, 1436 enrolled. In 2013, 757 master's, 128 doctorates, 32 other advanced degrees awarded. *Degree requirements:* For master's, residency (for some programs); for doctorate, thesis/dissertation (for some programs), residency. *Entrance requirements:* For master's, bachelor's degree or higher; minimum GPA of 2.5; official transcripts; goal statement (for some programs); access to computer and Internet; for doctorate, master's degree or higher; three years of related professional or academic experience (preferred); minimum GPA of 3.0; goal statement and current resume (select programs); official transcripts; access to computer and Internet; for other advanced degree, relevant work experience; access to computer and Internet. Additional exam requirements/recommendations for international students: Required—TOEFL (minimum score 550 paper-based; 79 iBT), IELTS (minimum score 6.5), Michigan English Language Assessment Battery (minimum score 82), or PTE. *Application deadline:* Applications are processed on a rolling basis. Application fee: $0. Electronic applications accepted. *Expenses: Tuition:* Full-time $11,813.55; part-time $500 per credit. *Required fees:* $618.76. *Financial support:* Fellowships, Federal Work-Study, scholarships/grants, unspecified assistantships, and family tuition reduction, active duty/veteran tuition reduction, group tuition reduction, interest-free payment plans, employee tuition reduction available. Support available to part-time students. Financial award applicants required to submit FAFSA. *Unit head:* Dr. Ward Ulmer, III, Associate Dean, 800-925-3368. *Application contact:* Jennifer Hall, Vice President of Enrollment Management, 866-4-WALDEN, E-mail: info@waldenu.edu.
Website: http://www.waldenu.edu/programs/colleges-schools/management.

Walsh University, Graduate Studies, MBA Program, North Canton, OH 44720-3396. Offers entrepreneurship (MBA); healthcare management (MBA); management (MBA); marketing (MBA). Part-time and evening/weekend programs available. Postbaccalaureate distance learning degree programs offered (no on-campus study). *Faculty:* 5 full-time (1 woman), 16 part-time/adjunct (4 women). *Students:* 29 full-time (15 women), 147 part-time (77 women); includes 6 minority (5 Black or African American, non-Hispanic/Latino; 1 American Indian or Alaska Native, non-Hispanic/Latino), 2 international. Average age 34. 69 applicants, 94% accepted, 31 enrolled. In 2013, 63 master's awarded. *Degree requirements:* For master's, capstone course in strategic management. *Entrance requirements:* For master's, GMAT (minimum score of 490), minimum GPA of 3.0. Additional exam requirements/recommendations for international students: Required—TOEFL (minimum score 500 paper-based; 61 iBT). *Application deadline:* For fall admission, 7/15 priority date for domestic students. Applications are processed on a rolling basis. Application fee: $25. Electronic applications accepted. *Expenses: Tuition:* Full-time $10,890; part-time $605 per credit hour. *Required fees:* $100; $100. *Financial support:* In 2013–14, 91 students received support, including 4 research assistantships with partial tuition reimbursements available (averaging $8,088 per year), 4 teaching assistantships (averaging $6,806 per year); scholarships/grants, tuition waivers (partial), unspecified assistantships, and tuition discounts also available. Support available to part-time students. Financial award application deadline: 12/31; financial award applicants required to submit FAFSA. *Faculty research:* Patient and physician satisfaction, advancing and improving learning with information technology, consumer-driven healthcare, branding and the service industry, service provider training and customer satisfaction, entrepreneurship, business strategy, social media, curriculum redesign, leadership, educational funding. *Total annual research expenditures:* $3,100. *Unit head:* Dr. Michael A. Petrochuk, Director of the MBA Program/Assistant Professor, 330-244-4764, Fax: 330-490-7359, E-mail: mpetrochuk@walsh.edu. *Application contact:* Audra Dice, Graduate and Transfer Admissions Counselor, 330-490-7181, Fax: 330-244-4925, E-mail: adice@walsh.edu.
Website: http://www.walsh.edu/mba-program.

West Chester University of Pennsylvania, College of Education, Department of Professional and Secondary Education, West Chester, PA 19383. Offers education for sustainability (Certificate); educational technology (Certificate); entrepreneurial education (Certificate); secondary education (M Ed). Part-time programs available. *Faculty:* 9 full-time (4 women). *Students:* 1 (woman) full-time, 20 part-time (14 women); includes 2 minority (1 Black or African American, non-Hispanic/Latino; 1 Two or more races, non-Hispanic/Latino). Average age 29. 19 applicants, 89% accepted, 12 enrolled. In 2013, 15 master's, 3 Certificates awarded. *Degree requirements:* For master's, comprehensive exam, thesis (for some programs), 36 credits. *Entrance requirements:* For master's, GRE or MAT, teaching certification (strongly recommended); for Certificate, minimum GPA of 3.0. Additional exam requirements/recommendations for international students: Required—TOEFL (minimum score 550 paper-based; 80 iBT). *Application deadline:* For fall admission, 4/15 priority date for domestic students, 3/15 for international students; for spring admission, 10/15 priority date for domestic students, 9/1 for international students. Applications are processed on a rolling basis. Application fee: $45. Electronic applications accepted. *Expenses:* Tuition, state resident: full-time $7956; part-time $442 per credit. Tuition, nonresident: full-time $11,934; part-time $663 per credit. *Required fees:* $2134.20; $106.24 per credit. Tuition and fees vary according to campus/location and program. *Financial support:* Unspecified assistantships available. Support available to part-time students. Financial award application deadline: 2/15; financial award applicants required to submit FAFSA. *Faculty research:* Technology integration: preparing our teachers for the twenty-first century, critical pedagogy. *Unit head:* Dr. John Elmore, Chair, 610-436-6934, Fax: 610-436-3102, E-mail: jelmore@wcupa.edu. *Application contact:* Dr. Rob Haworth, Graduate Coordinator, 610-436-2246, Fax: 610-436-3102, E-mail: rhaworth@wcupa.edu.
Website: http://www.wcupa.edu/_academics/sch_sed.prof&seced/.

Western Carolina University, Graduate School, College of Business, Program in Entrepreneurship, Cullowhee, NC 28723. Offers ME. Part-time and evening/weekend programs available. Postbaccalaureate distance learning degree programs offered (no on-campus study). *Entrance requirements:* For master's, GMAT or GRE General Test. Additional exam requirements/recommendations for international students: Required—TOEFL (minimum score 550 paper-based; 79 iBT).

Wilkes University, College of Graduate and Professional Studies, Jay S. Sidhu School of Business and Leadership, Wilkes-Barre, PA 18766-0002. Offers accounting (MBA); entrepreneurship (MBA); finance (MBA); health care administration (MBA); human resource management (MBA); international business (MBA); marketing (MBA); operations management (MBA); organizational leadership and development (MBA). *Accreditation:* ACBSP. Part-time and evening/weekend programs available. *Students:* 41 full-time (20 women), 119 part-time (48 women); includes 20 minority (5 Black or African American, non-Hispanic/Latino; 3 Asian, non-Hispanic/Latino; 7 Hispanic/Latino; 5 Two or more races, non-Hispanic/Latino), 7 international. Average age 31. In 2013, 55 master's awarded. *Entrance requirements:* For master's, GMAT. Additional exam requirements/recommendations for international students: Required—TOEFL (minimum score 550 paper-based; 79 iBT). *Application deadline:* Applications are processed on a rolling basis. Application fee: $45 ($65 for international students). Electronic applications accepted. *Expenses:* Contact institution. *Financial support:* Federal Work-Study and

unspecified assistantships available. Financial award application deadline: 3/1; financial award applicants required to submit FAFSA. *Unit head:* Dr. Jeffrey Alves, Dean, 570-408-4702, Fax: 570-408-7846, E-mail: jeffrey.alves@wilkes.edu. *Application contact:* Joanne Thomas, Interim Director of Graduate Enrollment, 570-408-4234, Fax: 570-408-7846, E-mail: joanne.thomas1@wilkes.edu. Website: http://www.wilkes.edu/pages/457.asp.

Section 6
Facilities and Entertainment Management

This section contains a directory of institutions offering graduate work in facilities and entertainment management. Additional information about programs listed in the directory may be obtained by writing directly to the dean of a graduate school or chair of a department at the address given in the directory.

For programs offering related work, see also in this book *Business Administration and Management.*

CONTENTS

Program Directories

Entertainment Management 340
Facilities Management 341

Entertainment Management

Berklee College of Music, Master's Programs, 46013 Valencia, Spain. Offers contemporary performance careers (MM); global entertainment and music business (MA); music technology innovation (MM); scoring for film, television, and video games (MM). Programs offered at Valencia, Spain campus.

California Intercontinental University, Hollywood College of the Entertainment Industry, Diamond Bar, CA 91765. Offers Hollywood and entertainment management (MBA).

California State University, Fullerton, Graduate Studies, College of Communications, Department of Communications, Fullerton, CA 92834-9480. Offers advertising (MA); mass communications research and theory (MA); professional communications (MA); tourism and entertainment (MA). Part-time programs available. *Students:* 22 full-time (17 women), 21 part-time (14 women); includes 19 minority (4 Black or African American, non-Hispanic/Latino; 6 Asian, non-Hispanic/Latino; 8 Hispanic/Latino; 1 Two or more races, non-Hispanic/Latino), 4 international. Average age 28. 69 applicants, 42% accepted, 18 enrolled. In 2013, 36 master's awarded. *Degree requirements:* For master's, project or thesis. *Entrance requirements:* For master's, GRE General Test. Application fee: $55. *Financial support:* Teaching assistantships, career-related internships or fieldwork, Federal Work-Study, institutionally sponsored loans, and scholarships/grants available. Support available to part-time students. Financial award application deadline: 3/1; financial award applicants required to submit FAFSA. *Unit head:* Dr. Diane F. Witmer, Chair, 657-278-7008. *Application contact:* Coordinator, 657-278-3832.

California State University, Northridge, Graduate Studies, The Tseng College of Extended Learning, Northridge, CA 91330. Offers business administration (Graduate Certificate); health administration (MPA); health education (MPH); knowledge management (MKM); music industry administration (MA); nonprofit-sector management (Graduate Certificate); public administration (MPA); public sector management and leadership (MPA); social work (MSW); taxation (MS); tourism, hospitality and recreation management (MS). *Entrance requirements:* For master's, GRE (if cumulative undergraduate GPA less than 3.0).

Carnegie Mellon University, Heinz College, School of Public Policy and Management, Master of Entertainment Industry Management Program, Pittsburgh, PA 15213-3891. Offers MEIM. *Accreditation:* AACSB. *Entrance requirements:* For master's, GRE or GMAT, college-level course in advanced algebra/pre-calculus; college-level courses in economics and statistics (recommended). Additional exam requirements/recommendations for international students: Required—TOEFL or IELTS.

Columbia College Chicago, Graduate School, Department of Business and Entrepreneurship, Chicago, IL 60605-1996. Offers arts, entertainment and media management (MA), including visual arts management. Part-time programs available. *Degree requirements:* For master's, thesis, internship. *Entrance requirements:* For master's, self-assessment essay. Additional exam requirements/recommendations for international students: Required—TOEFL (minimum score 550 paper-based). *Application deadline:* For fall admission, 1/15 for domestic and international students. Application fee: $55. Electronic applications accepted. *Financial support:* Fellowships, career-related internships or fieldwork, Federal Work-Study, scholarships/grants, and unspecified assistantships available. Support available to part-time students. Financial award application deadline: 8/13; financial award applicants required to submit FAFSA. *Unit head:* Prof. Dawn Larsen, Director of Graduate Studies, 312-369-7639, E-mail: dlarsen@colum.edu. *Application contact:* Kara Leffler, Associate Director of Graduate Admissions, 312-369-7262, Fax: 312-369-8024, E-mail: kleffler@colum.edu.
Website: http://www.colum.edu/Admissions/Graduate/programs/business-and-entrepreneurship/index.php.

Dowling College, School of Business, Oakdale, NY 11769. Offers aviation management (MBA, Certificate); corporate finance (MBA, Certificate); health care management (MBA); human resource management (Certificate); information systems management (MBA); management and leadership (MBA); marketing (Certificate); project management (Certificate); public management (MBA); school district business leader (MBA); sport, event and entertainment management (Certificate); JD/MBA. Part-time and evening/weekend programs available. Postbaccalaureate distance learning degree programs offered (minimal on-campus study). *Faculty:* 7 full-time (2 women), 43 part-time/adjunct (7 women). *Students:* 183 full-time (79 women), 299 part-time (142 women); includes 137 minority (84 Black or African American, non-Hispanic/Latino; 14 Asian, non-Hispanic/Latino; 20 Hispanic/Latino; 19 Native Hawaiian or other Pacific Islander, non-Hispanic/Latino). Average age 32. 360 applicants, 58% accepted, 127 enrolled. In 2013, 235 master's, 15 other advanced degrees awarded. *Degree requirements:* For master's, comprehensive exam, thesis optional. *Entrance requirements:* For master's, minimum GPA of 2.8, 2 letters of recommendation, courses or seminar in accounting and finance, resume. Additional exam requirements/recommendations for international students: Required—TOEFL (minimum score 550 paper-based). *Application deadline:* For fall admission, 9/1 priority date for domestic students; for winter admission, 1/1 priority date for domestic students; for spring admission, 2/1 priority date for domestic students. Applications are processed on a rolling basis. Application fee: $50. Electronic applications accepted. *Expenses: Tuition:* Full-time $22,731; part-time $1029 per credit. *Required fees:* $956; $956. *Financial support:* Career-related internships or fieldwork and Federal Work-Study available. Support available to part-time students. Financial award application deadline: 6/30; financial award applicants required to submit FAFSA. *Faculty research:* International finance, computer applications, labor relations, executive development. *Unit head:* Dr. Elana Zolfo, Dean, 631-244-3266, Fax: 631-244-1018, E-mail: zolfoe@dowling.edu. *Application contact:* Mary Boullianne, Dean of Admissions, 631-244-3274, Fax: 631-244-1059, E-mail: boulliam@dowling.edu.

Full Sail University, Entertainment Business Master of Science Program - Campus, Winter Park, FL 32792-7437. Offers MS.

Full Sail University, Entertainment Business Master of Science Program - Online, Winter Park, FL 32792-7437. Offers MS. Postbaccalaureate distance learning degree programs offered. *Entrance requirements:* Additional exam requirements/recommendations for international students: Required—TOEFL (minimum score 550 paper-based; 79 iBT).

Hofstra University, Frank G. Zarb School of Business, Programs in Management and General Business, Hempstead, NY 11549. Offers business administration (MBA), including health services management, management, sports and entertainment management; general management (Advanced Certificate); human resource management (MS, Advanced Certificate).

Maryville University of Saint Louis, The John E. Simon School of Business, St. Louis, MO 63141-7299. Offers accounting (MBA, PGC); management (MBA, PGC); marketing (MBA, PGC); process and project management (MBA, PGC); sport and entertainment management (MBA, PGC). *Accreditation:* ACBSP. Part-time and evening/weekend programs available. *Faculty:* 5 full-time (3 women), 14 part-time/adjunct (4 women). *Students:* 21 full-time (12 women), 85 part-time (41 women); includes 22 minority (8 Black or African American, non-Hispanic/Latino; 2 Asian, non-Hispanic/Latino; 7 Hispanic/Latino; 5 Two or more races, non-Hispanic/Latino), 3 international. Average age 31. In 2013, 39 master's awarded. *Entrance requirements:* For master's, GMAT (unless applicant possesses undergraduate business degree with minimum cumulative GPA of 3.0, or has completed master's degree from accredited university or one early access course prior to undergraduate degree). Additional exam requirements/recommendations for international students: Required—TOEFL (minimum score 85 iBT). *Application deadline:* Applications are processed on a rolling basis. Application fee: $40 ($60 for international students). Electronic applications accepted. Application fee is waived when completed online. *Expenses: Tuition:* Full-time $23,812; part-time $728 per credit hour. *Required fees:* $395 per year. Tuition and fees vary according to course load, degree level and program. *Financial support:* Career-related internships or fieldwork, Federal Work-Study, tuition waivers (partial), and campus employment available. Financial award application deadline: 3/1; financial award applicants required to submit FAFSA. *Faculty research:* International business, e-marketing, strategic planning, interpersonal management skills, financial analysis. *Unit head:* Dr. Pamela Horwitz, Dean, 314-529-9418, Fax: 314-529-9975, E-mail: horwitz@maryville.edu. *Application contact:* Kathy Dougherty, Director of MBA Programs, 314-529-9382, Fax: 314-529-9975, E-mail: business@maryville.edu.
Website: http://www.maryville.edu/bu/business-administration-masters/.

Syracuse University, College of Visual and Performing Arts, Program in Audio Arts, Syracuse, NY 13244. Offers MA. Program taught in conjunction with the S.I. Newhouse School of Public Communications. *Entrance requirements:* For master's, resume, sample of work or writing sample. Additional exam requirements/recommendations for international students: Required—TOEFL (minimum score 100 iBT). *Application deadline:* For summer admission, 2/1 priority date for domestic and international students. Application fee: $75. Electronic applications accepted. *Financial support:* Application deadline: 1/1. *Unit head:* Prof. Douglas Quin, Co-Director, 315-443-7398, E-mail: dhquin@syr.edu. *Application contact:* Information Contact, 315-443-0137, E-mail: admissg@syr.edu.
Website: http://vpa.syr.edu/prospective-students/graduate/audio-arts.

Universidad Autonoma de Guadalajara, Graduate Programs, Guadalajara, Mexico. Offers administrative law and justice (LL M); advertising and corporate communications (MA); architecture (M Arch); business (MBA); computational science (MCC); education (Ed M, Ed D); English-Spanish translation (MA); entrepreneurship and management (MBA); integrated management of digital animation (MA); international business (MIB); international corporate law (LL M); internet technologies (MS); manufacturing systems (MMS); occupational health (MS); philosophy (MA, PhD); power electronics (MS); quality systems (MQS); renewable energy (MS); social evaluation of projects (MBA); strategic market research (MBA); tax law (MA); teaching mathematics (MA).

University of Colorado Denver, Business School, Master of Business Administration Program, Denver, CO 80217. Offers bioinnovation and entrepreneurship (MBA); business intelligence (MBA); business strategy (MBA); business to business marketing (MBA); business to consumer marketing (MBA); change management (MBA); corporate financial management (MBA); enterprise technology management (MBA); entrepreneurship (MBA); health administration (MBA), including financial management, health administration, health information technologies, international health management and policy; human resources management (MBA); international business (MBA); investment management (MBA); managing for sustainability (MBA); sports and entertainment management (MBA). *Accreditation:* AACSB. Part-time and evening/weekend programs available. Postbaccalaureate distance learning degree programs offered (no on-campus study). *Students:* 611 full-time (246 women), 144 part-time (58 women); includes 102 minority (14 Black or African American, non-Hispanic/Latino; 2 American Indian or Alaska Native, non-Hispanic/Latino; 38 Asian, non-Hispanic/Latino; 42 Hispanic/Latino; 6 Two or more races, non-Hispanic/Latino), 26 international. Average age 32. 330 applicants, 64% accepted, 125 enrolled. In 2013, 398 master's awarded. *Degree requirements:* For master's, 48 semester hours, including 30 of core courses, 3 in international business, and 15 in electives from over 50 other graduate business courses. *Entrance requirements:* For master's, GMAT, resume, official transcripts, essay, two letters of recommendation, financial statements (for international applicants). Additional exam requirements/recommendations for international students: Required—TOEFL (minimum score 560 paper-based; 83 iBT); Recommended—IELTS (minimum score 6.5). *Application deadline:* For fall admission, 4/15 priority date for domestic students, 3/15 priority date for international students; for spring admission, 10/15 priority date for domestic students, 9/15 priority date for international students. Applications are processed on a rolling basis. Application fee: $50 ($75 for international students). Electronic applications accepted. *Expenses:* Contact institution. *Financial support:* In 2013–14, 62 students received support. Fellowships, research assistantships, teaching assistantships, Federal Work-Study, institutionally sponsored loans, scholarships/grants, traineeships, and unspecified assistantships available. Financial award application deadline: 4/1; financial award applicants required to submit FAFSA. *Faculty research:* Marketing, management, entrepreneurship, finance, health administration. *Unit head:* Elizabeth Cooperman, Professor of Finance and Managing for Sustainability/MBA Program Director, 303-315-8422, E-mail: elizabeth.cooperman@ucdenver.edu. *Application contact:* Shelly Townley, Admissions Director, Graduate Programs, 303-315-8202, E-mail: shelly.townley@ucdenver.edu.
Website: http://www.ucdenver.edu/academics/colleges/business/degrees/mba/Pages/MBA.aspx.

University of Colorado Denver, Business School, Program in Management and Organization, Denver, CO 80217. Offers business strategy (MS); change and innovation (MS); enterprise technology management (MS); entrepreneurship and innovation (MS); global management (MS); human resources management (MS); leadership and management (MS); quantitative decision methods (MS); sports and entertainment management (MS); sustainability management (MS). *Accreditation:* AACSB. Part-time and evening/weekend programs available. Postbaccalaureate distance learning degree programs offered (no on-campus study). *Students:* 27 full-time (19 women), 14 part-time (7 women); includes 4 minority (1 Black or African American, non-Hispanic/Latino; 2 Hispanic/Latino; 1 Two or more races, non-Hispanic/Latino), 6 international. Average age 29. 38 applicants, 45% accepted, 8 enrolled. In 2013, 28 master's awarded. *Degree requirements:* For master's, 30 semester hours (12 of required courses, 12 of management electives, and 6 of free electives). *Entrance requirements:* For master's, GMAT, resume, two letters of recommendation, essay, financial statements (for international applicants). Additional exam requirements/recommendations for

international students: Required—TOEFL (minimum score 537 paper-based; 75 iBT); Recommended—IELTS (minimum score 6.5). *Application deadline:* For fall admission, 4/15 for domestic students, 3/15 for international students; for spring admission, 10/15 for domestic students, 9/15 for international students. Applications are processed on a rolling basis. Application fee: $50 ($75 for international students). Electronic applications accepted. *Expenses:* Contact institution. *Financial support:* In 2013–14, 5 students received support. Fellowships, research assistantships, teaching assistantships, Federal Work-Study, institutionally sponsored loans, scholarships/grants, and traineeships available. Financial award application deadline: 4/1; financial award applicants required to submit FAFSA. *Faculty research:* Human resource management, management of catastrophe, turnaround strategies. *Unit head:* Dr. Kenneth Bettenhausen, Associate Professor/Director of MS in Management, 303-315-8425, E-mail: kenneth.bettenhausen@ucdenver.edu. *Application contact:* Shelly Townley, Admissions Director, Graduate Programs, 303-315-8202, E-mail: shelly.townley@ucdenver.edu.
Website: http://www.ucdenver.edu/academics/colleges/business/degrees/ms/management/Pages/Management.aspx.

University of Colorado Denver, Business School, Program in Marketing, Denver, CO 80217. Offers brand management and marketing communication (MS); global marketing (MS); high-tech and entrepreneurial marketing (MS); Internet marketing (MS); marketing for sustainability (MS); marketing research (MS); sports and entertainment marketing (MS). Part-time and evening/weekend programs available. *Students:* 36 full-time (15 women), 12 part-time (4 women); includes 3 minority (1 Asian, non-Hispanic/Latino; 1 Hispanic/Latino; 1 Two or more races, non-Hispanic/Latino), 11 international. Average age 29. 47 applicants, 55% accepted, 11 enrolled. In 2013, 20 master's awarded. *Degree requirements:* For master's, 30 semester hours (21 of marketing core courses, 9 of marketing electives). *Entrance requirements:* For master's, GMAT, resume, essay, two letters of recommendation, financial statements (for international applicants). Additional exam requirements/recommendations for international students: Required—TOEFL (minimum score 537 paper-based; 75 iBT); Recommended—IELTS (minimum score 6.5). *Application deadline:* For fall admission, 4/15 for domestic students, 3/15 for international students; for spring admission, 10/15 for domestic students, 9/15 for international students. Applications are processed on a rolling basis. Application fee: $50 ($75 for international students). Electronic applications accepted. *Expenses:* Contact institution. *Financial support:* In 2013–14, 7 students received support. Fellowships, research assistantships, teaching assistantships, Federal Work-Study, institutionally sponsored loans, scholarships/grants, and traineeships available. Financial award application deadline: 4/1; financial award applicants required to submit FAFSA. *Faculty research:* Marketing issues in the Chinese environment, impact of individual difference and contextual factors on the risk-taking behaviors of managers making new-business creation decisions, attribution theory perspective of conflict between marketers and engineers, organizational identity and identification, international market entry strategies. *Unit head:* Dr. David Forlani, Associate Professor/Director of Marketing Programs, 303-315-8420, E-mail: david.forlani@ucdenver.edu. *Application contact:* Shelly Townley, Admissions Director, Graduate Programs, 303-315-8202, E-mail: shelly.townley@ucdenver.edu.
Website: http://www.ucdenver.edu/academics/colleges/business/degrees/ms/marketing/Pages/Marketing.aspx.

University of Dallas, Graduate School of Management, Irving, TX 75062-4736. Offers accounting (MBA, MM, MS); business management (MBA, MM); corporate finance (MBA, MM); financial services (MBA); global business (MBA, MM); health services management (MBA, MM); human resource management (MBA, MM); information assurance (MBA, MM, MS); information technology (MBA, MM, MS); information technology service management (MBA, MM, MS); marketing management (MBA, MM); organization development (MBA, MM); project management (MBA, MM); sports and entertainment management (MBA, MM); strategic leadership (MBA, MM); supply chain management (MBA); supply chain management and market logistics (MM). *Accreditation:* ACBSP. Part-time and evening/weekend programs available. Postbaccalaureate distance learning degree programs offered (no on-campus study). *Entrance requirements:* Additional exam requirements/recommendations for international students: Required—TOEFL. Electronic applications accepted. *Expenses:* Contact institution.

University of Massachusetts Amherst, Graduate School, Interdisciplinary Programs, Dual Degree Program in Business Administration and Civil Engineering, Amherst, MA 01003. Offers MSCE/MBA. Part-time programs available. *Entrance requirements:* Additional exam requirements/recommendations for international students: Required—TOEFL (minimum score 600 paper-based; 100 iBT), IELTS (minimum score 7). *Application deadline:* For fall admission, 1/2 for domestic and international students. Applications are processed on a rolling basis. Application fee: $75. Electronic applications accepted. *Financial support:* Career-related internships or fieldwork, Federal Work-Study, scholarships/grants, traineeships, health care benefits, tuition waivers (full), and unspecified assistantships available. Support available to part-time students. Financial award application deadline: 1/2. *Unit head:* Dr. Sanjay Arwade, Graduate Program Director, 413-545-0686, Fax: 413-545-2840, E-mail: muriel@ecs.umass.edu. *Application contact:* Lindsay DeSantis, Supervisor of Admissions, 413-545-0722, Fax: 413-577-0010, E-mail: gradadm@grad.umass.edu.
Website: http://www-new.ecs.umass.edu/dual-degrees.

University of South Carolina, The Graduate School, College of Hospitality, Retail, and Sport Management, Department of Sport and Entertainment Management, Columbia, SC 29208. Offers live sport and entertainment events (MS); public assembly facilities management (MS). Part-time programs available. *Degree requirements:* For master's, comprehensive exam, thesis optional. *Entrance requirements:* For master's, GRE General Test or GMAT (preferred), minimum GPA of 3.0. Additional exam requirements/recommendations for international students: Required—TOEFL (minimum score 570 paper-based; 70 iBT). Electronic applications accepted. *Expenses:* Contact institution. *Faculty research:* Public assembly marketing, operations, box office, booking and scheduling, law/economic impacts.

Valparaiso University, Graduate School, Program in Arts and Entertainment Administration, Valparaiso, IN 46383. Offers MA. Part-time and evening/weekend programs available. *Students:* 16 full-time (11 women), 4 part-time (all women); includes 1 minority (Hispanic/Latino), 17 international. Average age 25. In 2013, 1 master's awarded. *Degree requirements:* For master's, internship or research project. *Entrance requirements:* Additional exam requirements/recommendations for international students: Required—TOEFL (minimum score 550 paper-based; 80 iBT), IELTS (minimum score 6). *Application deadline:* Applications are processed on a rolling basis. Application fee: $30 ($50 for international students). Electronic applications accepted. *Expenses: Tuition:* Full-time $10,350; part-time $575 per credit hour. *Required fees:* $378; $101 per term. Tuition and fees vary according to course load and program. *Financial support:* Available to part-time students. Applicants required to submit FAFSA. *Unit head:* Dr. Jennifer A. Ziegler, Dean, Graduate School and Continuing Education, 219-464-5313, Fax: 219-464-5381, E-mail: jennifer.ziegler@valpo.edu. *Application contact:* Jessica Choquette, Graduate Admissions Specialist, 219-464-5313, Fax: 219-464-5381, E-mail: jessica.choquette@valpo.edu.
Website: http://www.valpo.edu/grad/aea/.

Facilities Management

Cornell University, Graduate School, Graduate Fields of Human Ecology, Field of Design and Environmental Analysis, Ithaca, NY 14853. Offers applied research in human-environment relations (MS); facilities planning and management (MS); housing and design (MS); human factors and ergonomics (MS); human-environment relations (MS); interior design (MA, MPS). *Faculty:* 15 full-time (7 women). *Students:* 26 full-time (23 women); includes 4 minority (2 Black or African American, non-Hispanic/Latino; 2 Asian, non-Hispanic/Latino), 9 international. Average age 27. 76 applicants, 25% accepted, 13 enrolled. In 2013, 13 master's awarded. *Degree requirements:* For master's, thesis. *Entrance requirements:* For master's, GRE General Test, portfolio or slides of recent work; bachelor's degree in interior design, architecture or related design discipline; 2 letters of recommendation. Additional exam requirements/recommendations for international students: Required—TOEFL (minimum score 600 paper-based; 105 iBT). *Application deadline:* For fall admission, 2/1 priority date for domestic students. Application fee: $95. Electronic applications accepted. *Financial support:* In 2013–14, 15 students received support, including 4 fellowships with full tuition reimbursements available, 2 research assistantships with full tuition reimbursements available, 9 teaching assistantships with full tuition reimbursements available; institutionally sponsored loans, scholarships/grants, health care benefits, tuition waivers (full and partial), and unspecified assistantships also available. Financial award applicants required to submit FAFSA. *Faculty research:* Facility planning and management, environmental psychology, housing, interior design, ergonomics and human factors. *Unit head:* Director of Graduate Studies, 607-255-2168, Fax: 607-255-0305. *Application contact:* Graduate Field Assistant, 607-255-2168, Fax: 607-255-0305, E-mail: deagrad@cornell.edu.
Website: http://www.gradschool.cornell.edu/fields.php?id-77&a-2.

Maastricht School of Management, Graduate Programs, Maastricht, Netherlands. Offers business administration (MBA, DBA, PhD); facility management (Exec MBA); management (M Sc); sustainability (Exec MBA).

Massachusetts Maritime Academy, Program in Facilities Management, Buzzards Bay, MA 02532-1803. Offers MS. Part-time and evening/weekend programs available. *Entrance requirements:* For master's, GRE or GMAT, interview.

Pratt Institute, School of Architecture, Program in Facilities Management, New York, NY 10011. Offers MS. Part-time programs available. *Faculty:* 1 (woman) full-time, 5 part-time/adjunct (0 women). *Students:* 20 full-time (11 women), 1 part-time (0 women); includes 5 minority (3 Black or African American, non-Hispanic/Latino; 2 Hispanic/Latino), 7 international. Average age 30. 23 applicants, 91% accepted, 8 enrolled. In 2013, 11 master's awarded. *Degree requirements:* For master's, thesis. *Entrance requirements:* For master's, writing sample, bachelor's degree, transcripts, letters of recommendation, portfolio. Additional exam requirements/recommendations for international students: Required—TOEFL (minimum score 550 paper-based; 79 iBT). *Application deadline:* For fall admission, 1/5 for domestic and international students; for spring admission, 10/1 for domestic and international students. Applications are processed on a rolling basis. Application fee: $50 ($90 for international students). Electronic applications accepted. *Expenses: Tuition:* Full-time $26,478; part-time $1471 per credit. *Required fees:* $1830; $1050 per year. *Financial support:* Career-related internships or fieldwork, Federal Work-Study, institutionally sponsored loans, scholarships/grants, health care benefits, and unspecified assistantships available. Support available to part-time students. Financial award application deadline: 2/1; financial award applicants required to submit FAFSA. *Faculty research:* Benchmarking, organizational studies, resource planning and management, computer-aided facilities management, value analysis. *Unit head:* Harriet Markis, Chairperson, 212-647-7524, Fax: 212-367-2497, E-mail: hmarkis@pratt.edu. *Application contact:* Young Hah, Director of Graduate Admissions, 718-636-3683, Fax: 718-399-4242, E-mail: yhah@pratt.edu.
Website: https://www.pratt.edu/academics/architecture/facilities-management/.

Université Laval, Faculty of Administrative Sciences, Programs in Business Administration, Québec, QC G1K 7P4, Canada. Offers accounting (MBA); agri-food management (MBA); electronic business (MBA, Diploma); factory management and logistics (MBA); finance (MBA); firm management (MBA); geomatic management (MBA); information technology management (MBA); international management (MBA); management (MBA); management accounting (MBA, Diploma); marketing (MBA); modeling and organizational decision (MBA); occupational health and safety management (MBA); pharmacy management (MBA); social and environmental responsibility (MBA); technological entrepreneurship (Diploma). *Accreditation:* AACSB. Part-time and evening/weekend programs available. Postbaccalaureate distance learning degree programs offered (no on-campus study). *Entrance requirements:* For master's and Diploma, knowledge of French and English. Electronic applications accepted.

University of California, Berkeley, UC Berkeley Extension, Certificate Programs in Engineering, Construction and Facilities Management, Berkeley, CA 94720-1500. Offers construction management (Certificate); HVAC (Certificate); integrated circuit design and techniques (online) (Certificate). Postbaccalaureate distance learning degree programs offered.

The University of Kansas, Graduate Studies, School of Architecture, Design, and Planning, Department of Architecture, Lawrence, KS 66045. Offers architecture (M Arch, MA, PhD); facility management (Certificate); M Arch/MBA; M Arch/MUP. *Faculty:* 43. *Students:* 121 full-time (47 women), 27 part-time (17 women); includes 15 minority (4 Black or African American, non-Hispanic/Latino; 6 Asian, non-Hispanic/Latino; 3 Hispanic/Latino; 2 Two or more races, non-Hispanic/Latino), 29 international. Average age 27. 140 applicants, 67% accepted, 54 enrolled. In 2013, 101 master's awarded. Terminal master's awarded for partial completion of doctoral program. *Degree requirements:* For master's, thesis or alternative, 1 summer abroad; for doctorate,

Facilities Management

comprehensive exam, thesis/dissertation. *Entrance requirements:* For master's, portfolio, minimum GPA of 3.0, letters of recommendation; for doctorate, GRE, portfolio, master's degree, letters of recommendation. Additional exam requirements/recommendations for international students: Required—TOEFL, IELTS. *Application deadline:* For fall admission, 3/1 for domestic and international students; for spring admission, 11/1 for domestic and international students. Applications are processed on a rolling basis. Application fee: $55 ($75 for international students). Electronic applications accepted. *Financial support:* Fellowships, research assistantships with partial tuition reimbursements, teaching assistantships with full and partial tuition reimbursements, scholarships/grants, health care benefits, and unspecified assistantships available. Financial award application deadline: 2/1; financial award applicants required to submit FAFSA. *Faculty research:* Design build, sustainability, emergent technology, healthy places, urban design. *Unit head:* Prof. Paola Sanguinetti, Chair, 785-864-1577, Fax: 785-864-5185, E-mail: paolas@ku.edu. *Application contact:* Gera Elliott, Admissions Coordinator, 785-864-3167, Fax: 785-864-5185, E-mail: archku@ku.edu.
Website: http://architecture.ku.edu/.

University of New Haven, Graduate School, College of Business, Program in Sports Management, West Haven, CT 06516-1916. Offers collegiate athletic administration (MS); facility management (MS); management of sports industries (Certificate); sports management (MS). Part-time and evening/weekend programs available. *Students:* 18 full-time (8 women), 8 part-time (0 women); includes 2 minority (1 Black or African American, non-Hispanic/Latino; 1 Asian, non-Hispanic/Latino), 8 international. 24 applicants, 83% accepted, 10 enrolled. In 2013, 11 master's awarded. *Entrance requirements:* For master's, GMAT. Additional exam requirements/recommendations for international students: Required—TOEFL (minimum score 80 iBT), IELTS, PTE (minimum score 53). *Application deadline:* For fall admission, 5/31 for international students; for winter admission, 10/15 for international students; for spring admission, 1/15 for international students. Applications are processed on a rolling basis. Application fee: $75. Electronic applications accepted. Application fee is waived when completed online. *Expenses: Tuition:* Full-time $21,600; part-time $800 per credit hour. *Required fees:* $45 per trimester. *Financial support:* Research assistantships with partial tuition reimbursements, teaching assistantships with partial tuition reimbursements, career-related internships or fieldwork, Federal Work-Study, scholarships/grants, and unspecified assistantships available. Support available to part-time students. Financial award applicants required to submit FAFSA. *Unit head:* Prof. Gil B. Fried, Chair, 203-932-7081, E-mail: gfried@newhaven.edu. *Application contact:* Eloise Gormley, Director of Graduate Admissions, 203-932-7440, E-mail: gradinfo@newhaven.edu.
Website: http://www.newhaven.edu/6851/.

The University of North Carolina at Charlotte, The Graduate School, The William States Lee College of Engineering, Department of Engineering Technology and Construction Management, Charlotte, NC 28223-0001. Offers applied energy and electromechanical systems (MS); construction and facilities management (MS); fire protection and administration (MS). *Faculty:* 28 full-time (6 women). *Students:* 22 full-time (3 women), 9 part-time (0 women); includes 4 minority (2 Black or African American, non-Hispanic/Latino; 1 Hispanic/Latino; 1 Two or more races, non-Hispanic/Latino), 5 international. Average age 28. 32 applicants, 97% accepted, 17 enrolled. In 2013, 11 master's awarded. *Degree requirements:* For master's, comprehensive exam, thesis optional. *Entrance requirements:* Additional exam requirements/recommendations for international students: Required—TOEFL (minimum score 553 paper-based; 83 iBT). *Application deadline:* For fall admission, 5/1 for domestic and international students; for spring admission, 10/1 for domestic and international students. Application fee: $75. Electronic applications accepted. *Expenses:* Tuition, state resident: full-time $3522. Tuition, nonresident: full-time $16,051. *Required fees:* $2585. Tuition and fees vary according to course load and program. *Financial support:* In 2013–14, 19 students received support, including 17 research assistantships (averaging $6,250 per year), 2 teaching assistantships (averaging $4,000 per year). *Total annual research expenditures:* $1.3 million. *Unit head:* Dr. Cheng Liu, Chair Emeritus, 704-687-2474, E-mail: liu@uncc.edu. *Application contact:* Kathy B. Giddings, Director of Graduate Admissions, 704-687-5503, Fax: 704-687-1668, E-mail: gradadm@uncc.edu.
Website: http://et.uncc.edu/.

Washington State University Spokane, Graduate Programs, Program in Engineering and Technology Management, Pullman, WA 99164-2785. Offers constraints management (Graduate Certificate); construction project management (Graduate Certificate); engineering and technology management (METM); facilities management (Graduate Certificate); logistics and supply chain management (Graduate Certificate); manufacturing leadership (Graduate Certificate); project management (Graduate Certificate); Six Sigma quality management (Graduate Certificate); systems engineering management (Graduate Certificate). *Degree requirements:* For master's, comprehensive exam (for some programs), thesis (for some programs), comprehensive exam or project. *Entrance requirements:* For master's, GMAT (for applicants with less than 3.0 GPA), minimum GPA of 3.0, 3 letters of reference, resume, personal statement, math through college algebra (prefer math through calculus I), experience in the engineering/technology area. Additional exam requirements/recommendations for international students: Required—TOEFL. *Expenses:* Contact institution. *Faculty research:* Operations research for decision analysis quality control and liability, analytical techniques to formulating decisions.

Wentworth Institute of Technology, Program in Facility Management, Boston, MA 02115-5998. Offers MS. Part-time and evening/weekend programs available. *Degree requirements:* For master's, thesis optional. *Entrance requirements:* For master's, current resume, two recommendation forms from current or former employer, undergraduate degree in one of the following: architecture, facility management, engineering, construction management, business or interior design. Additional exam requirements/recommendations for international students: Required—TOEFL (minimum score 525 paper-based). Electronic applications accepted. *Expenses:* Contact institution.

Section 7
Hospitality Management

This section contains a directory of institutions offering graduate work in hospitality management. Additional information about programs listed in the directory may be obtained by writing directly to the dean of a graduate school or chair of a department at the address given in the directory.

For programs offering related work, see also in this book *Business Administration and Management* and *Advertising and Public Relations*.

In the other guides in this series:

Graduate Programs in the Biological/Biomedical Sciences & Health-Related Medical Professions
See *Health Services*

Graduate Programs in the Physical Sciences, Mathematics, Agricultural Sciences, the Environment & Natural Resources
See *Agricultural and Food Sciences (Food Science and Technology)*

CONTENTS

Program Directories

Hospitality Management   344
Travel and Tourism   349

Hospitality Management

Auburn University, Graduate School, College of Human Sciences, Department of Nutrition and Food Science, Auburn University, AL 36849. Offers global hospitality and retailing (Graduate Certificate); nutrition (MS, PhD). Part-time programs available. *Faculty:* 13 full-time (5 women). *Students:* 28 full-time (18 women), 18 part-time (10 women); includes 9 minority (6 Black or African American, non-Hispanic/Latino; 3 Asian, non-Hispanic/Latino), 17 international. Average age 30. 55 applicants, 44% accepted, 10 enrolled. In 2013, 16 master's, 2 doctorates awarded. *Degree requirements:* For master's, thesis (for some programs); for doctorate, thesis/dissertation. *Entrance requirements:* For master's and doctorate, GRE General Test. *Application deadline:* For fall admission, 7/7 for domestic students; for spring admission, 11/24 for domestic students. Applications are processed on a rolling basis. Application fee: $50 ($60 for international students). Electronic applications accepted. *Expenses:* Tuition, state resident: full-time $8262; part-time $459 per credit hour. Tuition, nonresident: full-time $24,786; part-time $1377 per credit hour. Tuition and fees vary according to degree level and program. *Financial support:* Research assistantships, teaching assistantships, career-related internships or fieldwork, and Federal Work-Study available. Support available to part-time students. Financial award application deadline: 3/15; financial award applicants required to submit FAFSA. *Faculty research:* Food quality and safety, diet, food supply, physical activity in maintenance of health, prevention of selected chronic disease states. *Unit head:* Dr. Martin O'Neill, Head, 334-844-3266. *Application contact:* Dr. George Flowers, Dean of the Graduate School, 334-844-2125. Website: http://www.humsci.auburn.edu/nufs/.

California State Polytechnic University, Pomona, Academic Affairs, College of the Extended University, Program in Hospitality Management, Pomona, CA 91768-2557. Offers MS. *Students:* 13 full-time (9 women), 29 part-time (21 women); includes 6 minority (4 Asian, non-Hispanic/Latino; 2 Hispanic/Latino), 30 international. Average age 26. 48 applicants, 58% accepted, 15 enrolled. In 2013, 5 master's awarded. *Degree requirements:* For master's, thesis or professional paper. *Expenses:* Tuition, state resident: full-time $6738. Tuition, nonresident: full-time $12,690. *Required fees:* $878; $248 per credit hour. *Unit head:* Laura L. Smith, Program Development Manager, 909-869-3996, E-mail: laualsmith@csupomona.edu. *Application contact:* Deborah L. Brandon, Executive Director, Admissions and Outreach, 909-869-3427, Fax: 909-869-5315, E-mail: dlbrandon@csupomona.edu. Website: http://www.ceu.csupomona.edu/specialsessions/degree_programs/hm.html.

California State University, Long Beach, Graduate Studies, College of Health and Human Services, Department of Family and Consumer Sciences, Master of Science in Nutritional Science Program, Long Beach, CA 90840. Offers food science (MS); hospitality foodservice and hotel management (MS); nutritional science (MS). Part-time programs available. *Degree requirements:* For master's, thesis, oral presentation of thesis or directed project. *Entrance requirements:* For master's, GRE, minimum GPA of 2.5 in last 60 units. Electronic applications accepted. *Faculty research:* Protein and water-soluble vitamins, sensory evaluation of foods, mineral deficiencies in humans, child nutrition, minerals and blood pressure.

California State University, Northridge, Graduate Studies, College of Health and Human Development, Department of Recreation and Tourism Management, Northridge, CA 91330. Offers hospitality and tourism (MS); recreational sport management/campus recreation (MS). *Degree requirements:* For master's, thesis (for some programs). *Entrance requirements:* For master's, GRE (if cumulative undergraduate GPA less than 3.0). Additional exam requirements/recommendations for international students: Required—TOEFL.

California State University, Northridge, Graduate Studies, The Tseng College of Extended Learning, Northridge, CA 91330. Offers business administration (Graduate Certificate); health administration (MPA); health education (MPH); knowledge management (MKM); music industry administration (MA); nonprofit-sector management (Graduate Certificate); public administration (MPA); public sector management and leadership (MPA); social work (MSW); taxation (MS); tourism, hospitality and recreation management (MS). *Entrance requirements:* For master's, GRE (if cumulative undergraduate GPA less than 3.0).

Cornell University, Graduate School, Field of Hotel Administration, Ithaca, NY 14853. Offers hospitality management (MMH); hotel administration (MS, PhD). *Faculty:* 41 full-time (11 women). *Students:* 64 full-time (29 women); includes 11 minority (1 Black or African American, non-Hispanic/Latino; 7 Asian, non-Hispanic/Latino; 2 Hispanic/Latino; 1 Two or more races, non-Hispanic/Latino), 38 international. Average age 28. 174 applicants, 39% accepted, 63 enrolled. In 2013, 54 master's, 5 doctorates awarded. Terminal master's awarded for partial completion of doctoral program. *Degree requirements:* For master's, thesis (MS); for doctorate, comprehensive exam, thesis/dissertation. *Entrance requirements:* For master's and doctorate, GMAT, 1 academic and 1 employer letter of recommendation, 2 interviews. Additional exam requirements/recommendations for international students: Required—TOEFL (minimum score 600 paper-based). *Application deadline:* For fall admission, 2/1 for domestic students. Application fee: $95. Electronic applications accepted. *Financial support:* In 2013–14, 5 students received support, including 5 teaching assistantships with full tuition reimbursements available; fellowships with full tuition reimbursements available, research assistantships with full tuition reimbursements available, institutionally sponsored loans, scholarships/grants, health care benefits, tuition waivers (full and partial), and unspecified assistantships also available. Financial award applicants required to submit FAFSA. *Faculty research:* Hospitality finance; property-asset management; real estate; management, strategy, and human resources; organizational communication. *Unit head:* Director of Graduate Studies, 607-255-7245. *Application contact:* Graduate Field Assistant, 607-255-6376, E-mail: mmh@cornell.edu. Website: http://www.gradschool.cornell.edu/fields.php?id=82&a-2.

Cornell University, Graduate School, Graduate Fields of Agriculture and Life Sciences, Field of Applied Economics and Management, Ithaca, NY 14853-0001. Offers agricultural finance (MS, PhD); applied econometrics and qualitative analysis (MS, PhD); economics of development (MS, PhD); environmental economics (MS, PhD); environmental management (MPS); farm management and production economics (MS, PhD); marketing and food distribution (MS, PhD); public policy analysis (MS, PhD); resource economics (PhD). *Faculty:* 50 full-time (9 women). *Students:* 85 full-time (45 women); includes 6 minority (3 Black or African American, non-Hispanic/Latino; 3 Asian, non-Hispanic/Latino), 55 international. Average age 28. 321 applicants, 12% accepted, 16 enrolled. In 2013, 12 master's, 8 doctorates awarded. *Entrance requirements:* For master's and doctorate, GRE. Additional exam requirements/recommendations for international students: Required—TOEFL. Application fee: $95. *Financial support:* In 2013–14, 52 students received support, including 5 fellowships, 27 research

assistantships, 20 teaching assistantships. *Unit head:* Dr. Barbara Knuth, Dean, 607-255-5417. *Application contact:* Graduate School Application Requests, 607-255-5820. Website: http://www.gradschool.cornell.edu/fields.php?id-71&-a-2.

DePaul University, Charles H. Kellstadt Graduate School of Business, Chicago, IL 60604. Offers accountancy (M Acc, MS, MSA); applied economics (MBA); banking (MBA); behavioral finance (MBA); brand and product management (MBA); business development (MBA); business information technology (MS); business strategy and decision-making (MBA); computational finance (MS); consumer insights (MBA); corporate finance (MBA); economic policy analysis (MS); entrepreneurship (MBA, MS); finance (MBA, MS); financial analysis (MBA); general business (MBA); health sector management (MBA); hospitality leadership (MBA); hospitality leadership and operational performance (MS); human resource management (MBA); human resources (MS); investment management (MBA); leadership and change management (MBA); management accounting (MBA); marketing (MBA, MS); marketing analysis (MS); marketing strategy and planning (MBA); operations management (MBA); organizational diversity (MBA); real estate (MS); real estate finance and investment (MBA); revenue management (MBA); sports management (MBA); strategic global marketing (MBA); strategy, execution and valuation (MBA); sustainable management (MBA, MS); taxation (MS); wealth management (MS); JD/MBA. *Accreditation:* AACSB. Part-time and evening/weekend programs available. Postbaccalaureate distance learning degree programs offered (no on-campus study). *Faculty:* 81 full-time (20 women), 45 part-time/adjunct (8 women). *Students:* 1,238 full-time (605 women), 617 part-time (223 women); includes 295 minority (71 Black or African American, non-Hispanic/Latino; 129 Asian, non-Hispanic/Latino; 74 Hispanic/Latino; 4 Native Hawaiian or other Pacific Islander, non-Hispanic/Latino; 17 Two or more races, non-Hispanic/Latino), 462 international. Average age 29. In 2013, 911 master's awarded. *Entrance requirements:* For master's, GMAT, 2 letters of recommendation, resume, essay, official transcripts. Additional exam requirements/recommendations for international students: Required—TOEFL (minimum score 550 paper-based; 80 iBT). *Application deadline:* For fall admission, 7/1 for domestic students, 6/1 for international students; for winter admission, 10/1 for domestic students, 9/1 for international students; for spring admission, 2/1 for domestic students, 1/1 for international students. Applications are processed on a rolling basis. Application fee: $60. Electronic applications accepted. *Expenses:* Contact institution. *Financial support:* Application deadline: 4/1; applicants required to submit FAFSA. *Unit head:* Robert T. Ryan, Assistant Dean and Director, 312-362-8810, Fax: 312-362-6677, E-mail: rryan1@depaul.edu. *Application contact:* James Parker, Director of Recruitment and Admission, 312-362-8810, Fax: 312-362-6677, E-mail: kgsb@depaul.edu. Website: http://kellstadt.depaul.edu.

Drexel University, Goodwin College of Professional Studies, School of Technology and Professional Studies, Philadelphia, PA 19104-2875. Offers construction management (MS); creativity and innovation (MS); engineering technology (MS); food science (MS); hospitality management (MS); professional studies: creativity studies (MS); professional studies: e-learning leadership (MS); professional studies: homeland security management (MS); project management (MS); property management (MS); sport management (MS). Part-time and evening/weekend programs available. *Entrance requirements:* Additional exam requirements/recommendations for international students: Required—TOEFL, IELTS. Electronic applications accepted. Application fee is waived when completed online.

East Carolina University, Graduate School, College of Human Ecology, School of Hospitality Leadership, Greenville, NC 27858-4353. Offers hospitality management (MBA). *Expenses:* Tuition, state resident: full-time $4223. Tuition, nonresident: full-time $16,540. *Required fees:* $2184.

Eastern Michigan University, Graduate School, College of Technology, School of Technology Studies, Program in Hotel and Restaurant Management, Ypsilanti, MI 48197. Offers MS, Graduate Certificate. Part-time and evening/weekend programs available. Postbaccalaureate distance learning degree programs offered (minimal on-campus study). *Students:* 3 full-time (2 women), 4 part-time (1 woman); includes 1 minority (Black or African American, non-Hispanic/Latino), 3 international. Average age 26. 6 applicants, 50% accepted, 3 enrolled. In 2013, 2 master's awarded. *Entrance requirements:* Additional exam requirements/recommendations for international students: Required—TOEFL. *Application deadline:* Applications are processed on a rolling basis. Application fee: $35. *Expenses:* Tuition, state resident: full-time $12,300; part-time $466 per credit hour. Tuition, nonresident: full-time $23,159; part-time $918 per credit hour. *Required fees:* $71 per credit hour. $46 per semester. One-time fee: $100. Tuition and fees vary according to course level and degree level. *Financial support:* Fellowships, research assistantships with full tuition reimbursements, teaching assistantships with full tuition reimbursements, career-related internships or fieldwork, Federal Work-Study, institutionally sponsored loans, scholarships/grants, tuition waivers (partial), and unspecified assistantships available. Support available to part-time students. Financial award applicants required to submit FAFSA. *Unit head:* Dr. Matt Evett, Interim Director, 734-487-1161, Fax: 734-487-7690, E-mail: mevett@emich.edu. *Application contact:* Dr. Susan Gregory, Program Coordinator, 734-487-0845, Fax: 734-487-7690, E-mail: sgregory5@emich.edu.

Ecole Hôtelière de Lausanne, Program in Hospitality Administration, Lausanne, Switzerland. Offers MHA. *Degree requirements:* For master's, project.

Endicott College, Apicius International School of Hospitality, Florence, 50122, Italy. Offers international tourism (MOM). Program held entirely in Florence, Italy. *Degree requirements:* For master's, thesis. *Entrance requirements:* For master's, MAT or GRE, 250-500 word essay explaining professional goals, official transcripts of all academic work, bachelor's degree, two letters of recommendation, personal interview. *Application deadline:* For fall admission, 6/30 for domestic and international students. Application fee: $50. *Financial support:* Applicants required to submit FAFSA. *Application contact:* E-mail: admissions@fua.it. Website: http://www.apicius.it.

ESSEC Business School, Graduate Programs, Paris, France. Offers business administration (PhD); executive business administration (MBA); global business administration (MBA); hospitality management (MBA); international luxury brand management (MBA); management (MSM).

Fairleigh Dickinson University, College at Florham, Anthony J. Petrocelli College of Continuing Studies, International School of Hospitality and Tourism Management, Madison, NJ 07940-1099. Offers hospitality management studies (MS).

Fairleigh Dickinson University, Metropolitan Campus, Anthony J. Petrocelli College of Continuing Studies, International School of Hospitality and Tourism Management, Teaneck, NJ 07666-1914. Offers hospitality management (MS).

Florida International University, School of Hospitality and Tourism Management, Hospitality Management Program, Miami, FL 33199. Offers MS. Part-time and evening/weekend programs available. Postbaccalaureate distance learning degree programs offered. *Entrance requirements:* For master's, minimum GPA of 3.0, letters of recommendation, 5 years of management experience (for executive track). Additional exam requirements/recommendations for international students: Required—TOEFL (minimum score 550 paper-based). Electronic applications accepted.

The George Washington University, School of Business, Department of Tourism and Hospitality Management, Washington, DC 20052. Offers event and meeting management (MTA); event management (Professional Certificate); hospitality management (MTA, Professional Certificate); sport management (MTA); sports business management (Professional Certificate); sustainable tourism destination management (MTA); tourism administration (MTA); tourism and hospitality management (MBA); tourism destination management (Professional Certificate). Part-time programs available. Postbaccalaureate distance learning degree programs offered. *Faculty:* 2 full-time (1 woman). *Students:* 99 full-time (79 women), 58 part-time (45 women); includes 32 minority (24 Black or African American, non-Hispanic/Latino; 4 Asian, non-Hispanic/Latino; 3 Hispanic/Latino; 1 Two or more races, non-Hispanic/Latino), 63 international. Average age 28. 124 applicants, 71% accepted, 52 enrolled. In 2013, 68 master's awarded. *Degree requirements:* For master's, comprehensive exam, thesis. *Entrance requirements:* For master's, GRE General Test. Additional exam requirements/recommendations for international students: Required—TOEFL. *Application deadline:* For fall admission, 4/1 priority date for domestic students; for spring admission, 10/1 for domestic students. Applications are processed on a rolling basis. Application fee: $75. *Financial support:* In 2013–14, 32 students received support. Fellowships, teaching assistantships, career-related internships or fieldwork, Federal Work-Study, institutionally sponsored loans, and tuition waivers (partial) available. Financial award application deadline: 4/1. *Faculty research:* Tourism policy, tourism impact forecasting, geotourism. *Unit head:* Larry Yu, Director, 202-994-6380, E-mail: lyu@gwu.edu. *Application contact:* Kristin Williams, Assistant Vice President for Graduate and Special Enrollment Management, 202-994-0467, Fax: 202-994-0371, E-mail: ksw@gwu.edu.
Website: http://business.gwu.edu/tourism/.

Glion Institute of Higher Education, Graduate Programs, Glion-sur-Montreux, Switzerland. Offers hospitality organizational training (M Ed); hotel management with leadership (MBA); hotel management with marketing (MBA); international hospitality management (MBA). Evening/weekend programs available.

Husson University, Master of Business Administration Program, Bangor, ME 04401-2999. Offers general business administration (MBA); healthcare management (MBA); hospitality and tourism management (MBA); non-profit management (MBA). Part-time and evening/weekend programs available. *Faculty:* 7 full-time (4 women), 16 part-time/adjunct (3 women). *Students:* 91 full-time (55 women), 87 part-time (47 women); includes 21 minority (7 Black or African American, non-Hispanic/Latino; 11 Asian, non-Hispanic/Latino; 3 Two or more races, non-Hispanic/Latino), 4 international. 112 applicants, 88% accepted, 86 enrolled. In 2013, 163 master's awarded. *Degree requirements:* For master's, comprehensive exam (for some programs), thesis optional. *Entrance requirements:* For master's, GMAT or GRE, minimum GPA of 3.0. Additional exam requirements/recommendations for international students: Required—TOEFL (minimum score 550 paper-based). *Application deadline:* Applications are processed on a rolling basis. Application fee: $40. Electronic applications accepted. *Expenses:* Contact institution. *Financial support:* In 2013–14, 6 students received support. Career-related internships or fieldwork, Federal Work-Study, scholarships/grants, and unspecified assistantships available. Financial award application deadline: 4/15; financial award applicants required to submit FAFSA. *Unit head:* Prof. Stephanie Shayne, Director, Graduate and Online Programs, 207-404-5632, Fax: 207-992-4987, E-mail: shaynes@husson.edu. *Application contact:* Kristen Card, Director of Graduate Admissions, 207-404-5660, Fax: 207-941-7935, E-mail: cardk@husson.edu.
Website: http://www.husson.edu/mba.

Iowa State University of Science and Technology, Department of Apparel, Education Studies, and Hospitality Management, Ames, IA 50011. Offers family and consumer sciences education and studies (M Ed, MS, PhD); foodservice and lodging management (MFCS, MS, PhD); textiles and clothing (MFCS, MS, PhD). *Degree requirements:* For doctorate, thesis/dissertation. *Entrance requirements:* For master's and doctorate, GRE General Test. Additional exam requirements/recommendations for international students: Required—TOEFL (minimum score 550 paper-based; 79 iBT), IELTS (minimum score 6.5). Electronic applications accepted.

Johnson & Wales University, MAT Program in Teacher Education, Providence, RI 02903-3703. Offers business education and secondary special education (MAT); elementary education and elementary special education (MAT); elementary education and elementary/secondary special education (MAT); elementary education and secondary special education (MAT); food service education (MAT). Part-time and evening/weekend programs available. *Entrance requirements:* For master's, MAT, minimum GPA of 2.75. Additional exam requirements/recommendations for international students: Required—TOEFL (minimum score 550 paper-based) or IELTS (recommended). *Faculty research:* Secondary education, student teaching, educational reform, evaluation procedures.

Kansas State University, Graduate School, College of Human Ecology, Department of Hospitality Management and Dietetics, Manhattan, KS 66506. Offers dietetics (MS); hospitality and dietetics administration (MS). Part-time programs available. *Faculty:* 8 full-time (4 women). *Students:* 16 full-time (14 women), 38 part-time (33 women); includes 10 minority (all Asian, non-Hispanic/Latino), 10 international. Average age 29. 16 applicants, 63% accepted, 10 enrolled. In 2013, 10 master's awarded. *Degree requirements:* For master's, thesis or alternative, residency. *Entrance requirements:* Additional exam requirements/recommendations for international students: Required—TOEFL. *Application deadline:* For fall admission, 2/1 priority date for domestic and international students; for spring admission, 8/1 priority date for domestic and international students. Applications are processed on a rolling basis. Application fee: $50 ($75 for international students). Electronic applications accepted. *Financial support:* In 2013–14, 1 fellowship with full tuition reimbursement (averaging $5,000 per year), 3 research assistantships (averaging $16,000 per year), 3 teaching assistantships with full tuition reimbursements (averaging $13,000 per year) were awarded; Federal Work-Study, institutionally sponsored loans, scholarships/grants, and unspecified assistantships also available. Support available to part-time students. Financial award application deadline: 3/1; financial award applicants required to submit FAFSA. *Faculty research:* Customer satisfaction, brand loyalty, food safety and biosecurity issues in foodservice operations; gerontology and the hospitality industry; education, training, and career development in dietetics and hospitality. *Total annual research expenditures:* $900,000. *Unit head:* Jeannie Sneed, Head, 785-532-5507, Fax: 785-532-5522, E-mail: jsneed@ksu.edu. *Application contact:* Jayme Reid, Administrative Specialist, 785-532-5521, Fax: 785-532-5522, E-mail: jayme2@k-state.edu.
Website: http://www.he.k-state.edu/hmd/.

Kansas State University, Graduate School, College of Human Ecology, Program in Human Ecology, Manhattan, KS 66506. Offers apparel and textiles (PhD); family life education and consultation (PhD); food service and hospitality management (PhD); lifespan and human development (PhD); marriage and family therapy (PhD); personal financial planning (PhD). *Students:* 47 full-time (28 women), 51 part-time (29 women); includes 20 minority (11 Black or African American, non-Hispanic/Latino; 2 Asian, non-Hispanic/Latino; 3 Hispanic/Latino; 1 Native Hawaiian or other Pacific Islander, non-Hispanic/Latino; 3 Two or more races, non-Hispanic/Latino), 13 international. Average age 39. 60 applicants, 33% accepted, 17 enrolled. In 2013, 11 doctorates awarded. *Degree requirements:* For doctorate, thesis/dissertation. *Application deadline:* For fall admission, 2/1 priority date for domestic and international students; for spring admission, 8/1 priority date for domestic and international students. Applications are processed on a rolling basis. Application fee: $50 ($75 for international students). Electronic applications accepted. *Financial support:* Application deadline: 3/1. *Total annual research expenditures:* $3.3 million. *Unit head:* Dr. John Buckwalter, Dean, 785-532-5500, Fax: 785-532-5504, E-mail: jbb3@ksu.edu. *Application contact:* Connie Fechter, Application Contact, 785-532-1473, Fax: 785-532-3796, E-mail: fechter@ksu.edu.

Kent State University, Graduate School of Education, Health, and Human Services, School of Foundations, Leadership and Administration, Program in Hospitality and Tourism Management, Kent, OH 44242-0001. Offers MS. Part-time programs available. *Faculty:* 6 full-time (3 women), 6 part-time/adjunct (2 women). *Students:* 13 full-time (11 women), 13 part-time (8 women); includes 2 minority (1 Asian, non-Hispanic/Latino; 1 Hispanic/Latino), 14 international. 30 applicants, 53% accepted. In 2013, 8 master's awarded. *Degree requirements:* For master's, thesis optional. *Entrance requirements:* For master's, minimum GPA of 3.0, 3 letters of recommendation, resume, goals statement. Additional exam requirements/recommendations for international students: Required—TOEFL (minimum score 550 paper-based; 80 iBT). *Application deadline:* Applications are processed on a rolling basis. Application fee: $30 ($60 for international students). Electronic applications accepted. *Financial support:* In 2013–14, 4 students received support, including 5 research assistantships with full tuition reimbursements available (averaging $8,500 per year); teaching assistantships, Federal Work-Study, scholarships/grants, and unspecified assistantships also available. Financial award application deadline: 2/1; financial award applicants required to submit FAFSA. *Faculty research:* Training human service workers, health care services for older adults, early adolescent development, care-giving arrangements with aging families, peace and war. *Unit head:* Barb Scheule, Coordinator, 330-672-3796, E-mail: bscheule@kent.edu. *Application contact:* Nancy Miller, Academic Program Director, Office of Graduate Student Services, 330-672-2576, Fax: 330-672-9162, E-mail: ogs@kent.edu.

Lasell College, Graduate and Professional Studies in Sport Management, Newton, MA 02466-2709. Offers sport hospitality management (MS, Graduate Certificate); sport leadership (MS, Graduate Certificate); sport non-profit management (MS, Graduate Certificate). Part-time programs available. Postbaccalaureate distance learning degree programs offered (no on-campus study). *Faculty:* 2 full-time (0 women), 6 part-time/adjunct (5 women). *Students:* 13 full-time (4 women), 42 part-time (16 women); includes 17 minority (11 Black or African American, non-Hispanic/Latino; 3 American Indian or Alaska Native, non-Hispanic/Latino; 2 Hispanic/Latino; 1 Two or more races, non-Hispanic/Latino). Average age 30. 34 applicants, 62% accepted, 11 enrolled. In 2013, 11 master's awarded. *Entrance requirements:* For master's and Graduate Certificate, bachelor's degree from an accredited institution. Additional exam requirements/recommendations for international students: Required—TOEFL (minimum score 550 paper-based; 79 iBT), IELTS. *Application deadline:* For fall admission, 8/31 priority date for domestic students, 6/30 priority date for international students; for spring admission, 12/31 priority date for domestic students, 10/31 priority date for international students. Applications are processed on a rolling basis. Electronic applications accepted. *Expenses: Tuition:* Part-time $575 per credit. *Required fees:* $80 per semester. *Financial support:* Available to part-time students. Application deadline: 8/31; applicants required to submit FAFSA. *Unit head:* Dr. Joan Dolamore, Dean of Graduate and Professional Studies, 617-243-2485, Fax: 617-243-2450, E-mail: gradinfo@lasell.edu. *Application contact:* Adrienne Franciosi, Director of Graduate Admission, 617-243-2214, Fax: 617-243-2450, E-mail: gradinfo@lasell.edu.
Website: http://www.lasell.edu/Academics/Graduate-and-Professional-Studies/MS-in-Sport-Management-.html.

Les Roches International School of Hotel Management, Program in Hospitality Management, Bluche, Switzerland. Offers MBA. Available only at Switzerland campus.

Lynn University, College of Business and Management, Boca Raton, FL 33431-5598. Offers aviation management (MBA); financial valuation and investment management (MBA); hospitality management (MBA); international business (MBA); marketing (MBA); mass communication and media management (MBA); sports and athletics administration (MBA). Part-time and evening/weekend programs available. Postbaccalaureate distance learning degree programs offered. *Faculty:* 16 full-time (6 women), 8 part-time/adjunct (3 women). *Students:* 181 full-time (95 women), 83 part-time (37 women); includes 41 minority (22 Black or African American, non-Hispanic/Latino; 1 Asian, non-Hispanic/Latino; 17 Hispanic/Latino; 1 Two or more races, non-Hispanic/Latino), 77 international. Average age 28. 137 applicants, 100% accepted, 107 enrolled. In 2013, 149 master's awarded. *Degree requirements:* For master's, projects. *Entrance requirements:* For master's, GMAT or GRE, bachelor's degree from accredited institution, minimum undergraduate GPA of 2.5, resume, 2 letters of recommendation. Additional exam requirements/recommendations for international students: Required—TOEFL (minimum score 550 paper-based). *Application deadline:* Applications are processed on a rolling basis. Application fee: $45. Electronic applications accepted. *Expenses: Tuition:* Full-time $23,760; part-time $660 per credit. *Required fees:* $300; $50 per term. Tuition and fees vary according to degree level and program. *Financial support:* Career-related internships or fieldwork, Federal Work-Study, institutionally sponsored loans, scholarships/grants, tuition waivers (full and partial), and unspecified assistantships available. Support available to part-time students. Financial award application deadline: 8/1; financial award applicants required to submit FAFSA. *Faculty research:* Labor relations, dynamic balance in leisure-time skills, ethics in athletics, hotel development. *Unit head:* Dr. Ralph Norcio, Senior Associate Dean, 561-237-7010, Fax: 561-237-7014, E-mail: rnorcio@lynn.edu. *Application contact:* Steven Pruitt, Director of Graduate and Undergraduate Evening Admission, 561-237-7834, Fax: 561-237-7100, E-mail: spruitt@lynn.edu.
Website: http://www.lynn.edu/academics/colleges/business-and-management.

Michigan State University, The Graduate School, Eli Broad College of Business, The School of Hospitality Business, East Lansing, MI 48824. Offers foodservice business management (MS); hospitality business management (MS). *Faculty:* 14 full-time. *Students:* 53. In 2013, 20 master's awarded. *Degree requirements:* For master's, comprehensive exam, research project. *Entrance requirements:* For master's, GMAT or GRE, minimum GPA of 3.0 in last 2 years of undergraduate course work, resume, 3 letters of recommendation, 2 official transcripts, at least 1 year of professional work experience. Additional exam requirements/recommendations for international students: Required—TOEFL (minimum score 580 paper-based; 87 iBT). *Application deadline:* For fall admission, 12/27 for domestic students. Application fee: $50. Electronic applications accepted. *Faculty research:* Corporate food service management, entrepreneurial and food service management, hospitality business. *Unit head:* Dr. Ronald F. Cichy, Director, 517-355-5080, Fax: 517-432-1170, E-mail: cichy@broad.msu.edu. *Application*

Hospitality Management

contact: Melissa Bankroff, Graduate Programs Coordinator, 517-353-9211, Fax: 517-432-1170, E-mail: mshb@broad.msu.edu. Website: http://hospitalitybusiness.broad.msu.edu/.

Monroe College, King Graduate School, Bronx, NY 10468-5407. Offers business management (MBA); criminal justice (MS); executive leadership in hospitality management (MS); public health (MPH). Program also offered in New Rochelle, NY. Postbaccalaureate distance learning degree programs offered.

New York University, School of Continuing and Professional Studies, The Preston Robert Tisch Center for Hospitality, Tourism, and Sports Management, Program in Hospitality Industry Studies, New York, NY 10012-1019. Offers brand strategy (MS); hospitality industry studies (Advanced Certificate); hotel finance (MS); lodging operations (MS); revenue management (MS). Part-time and evening/weekend programs available. *Faculty:* 5 full-time (2 women), 12 part-time/adjunct (2 women). *Students:* 70 full-time (58 women), 38 part-time (21 women); includes 14 minority (2 Black or African American, non-Hispanic/Latino; 9 Asian, non-Hispanic/Latino; 2 Hispanic/Latino; 1 Two or more races, non-Hispanic/Latino), 59 international. Average age 26. 98 applicants, 69% accepted, 42 enrolled. In 2013, 31 master's awarded. *Degree requirements:* For master's, thesis. *Entrance requirements:* For master's, bachelor's degree, resume with relevant professional work, internship or volunteer experience, two letters of recommendation, statement of purpose. Additional exam requirements/recommendations for international students: Required—TOEFL (minimum score 600 paper-based; 100 iBT), IELTS (minimum score 7). *Application deadline:* For fall admission, 2/1 priority date for domestic and international students; for spring admission, 10/15 priority date for domestic students, 8/15 priority date for international students. Applications are processed on a rolling basis. Application fee: $150. Electronic applications accepted. *Expenses: Tuition:* Full-time $35,856; part-time $1494 per unit. *Required fees:* $1408; $64 per unit. $473 per term. Tuition and fees vary according to course load and program. *Financial support:* In 2013–14, 25 students received support, including 24 fellowships (averaging $2,697 per year); scholarships/grants also available. Support available to part-time students. Financial award application deadline: 2/15; financial award applicants required to submit FAFSA. *Unit head:* Bjorn Hanson, Division Dean and Clinical Professor, 212-998-7100. *Application contact:* Admissions Office, 212-998-7100, E-mail: scps.gradadmissions@nyu.edu. Website: http://www.scps.nyu.edu/areas-of-study/tisch/graduate-programs/ms-hospitality-industry-studies/.

New York University, Steinhardt School of Culture, Education, and Human Development, Department of Nutrition, Food Studies, and Public Health, Program in Food Studies and Food Management, New York, NY 10003. Offers food studies (MA), including food culture, food systems; food studies and food management (PhD). Part-time programs available. *Faculty:* 7 full-time (6 women). *Students:* 36 full-time (34 women), 126 part-time (115 women); includes 39 minority (4 Black or African American, non-Hispanic/Latino; 2 American Indian or Alaska Native, non-Hispanic/Latino; 9 Asian, non-Hispanic/Latino; 18 Hispanic/Latino; 2 Native Hawaiian or other Pacific Islander, non-Hispanic/Latino; 4 Two or more races, non-Hispanic/Latino), 12 international. Average age 30. 166 applicants, 66% accepted, 61 enrolled. In 2013, 40 master's awarded. *Degree requirements:* For master's, thesis (for some programs); for doctorate, thesis/dissertation. *Entrance requirements:* For doctorate, GRE General Test, interview. Additional exam requirements/recommendations for international students: Required—TOEFL (minimum score 100 iBT). *Application deadline:* For fall admission, 12/1 priority date for domestic students, 12/1 for international students; for spring admission, 10/1 for domestic and international students. Applications are processed on a rolling basis. Application fee: $75. Electronic applications accepted. *Expenses: Tuition:* Full-time $35,856; part-time $1494 per unit. *Required fees:* $1408; $64 per unit. $473 per term. Tuition and fees vary according to course load and program. *Financial support:* Fellowships with full and partial tuition reimbursements, career-related internships or fieldwork, Federal Work-Study, institutionally sponsored loans, scholarships/grants, tuition waivers (partial), and unspecified assistantships available. Financial award application deadline: 2/1; financial award applicants required to submit FAFSA. *Faculty research:* Cultural and social history of food, food systems and agriculture, food and aesthetics, political economy of food. *Unit head:* Prof. Jennifer Berg, Director, 212-998-5580, Fax: 212-995-4194, E-mail: jennifer.berg@nyu.edu. *Application contact:* 212-998-5030, Fax: 212-995-4328, E-mail: steinhardt.gradadmissions@nyu.edu. Website: http://steinhardt.nyu.edu/nutrition/food.

Northeastern University, College of Professional Studies, Boston, MA 02115-5096. Offers applied nutrition (MS); commerce and economic development (MS); corporate and organizational communication (MS); digital media (MPS); geographic information technology (MPS); global studies and international affairs (MS); homeland security (MA); human services (MS); informatics (MPS); leadership (MS); nonprofit management (MS); project management (MS); regulatory affairs for drugs, biologics, and medical devices (MS); regulatory affairs of food and food industries (MS); respiratory care leadership (MS); technical communication (MS). Postbaccalaureate distance learning degree programs offered (no on-campus study).

Oklahoma State University, College of Human Sciences, School of Hotel and Restaurant Administration, Stillwater, OK 74078. Offers MS, PhD. *Faculty:* 17 full-time (7 women), 3 part-time/adjunct (2 women). *Students:* 14 full-time (11 women), 21 part-time (11 women); includes 4 minority (1 Black or African American, non-Hispanic/Latino; 3 Hispanic/Latino), 24 international. Average age 33. 36 applicants, 31% accepted, 5 enrolled. In 2013, 4 master's, 7 doctorates awarded. *Degree requirements:* For master's, thesis (for some programs); for doctorate, comprehensive exam, thesis/dissertation. *Entrance requirements:* For master's and doctorate, GRE or GMAT. Additional exam requirements/recommendations for international students: Required—TOEFL (minimum score 550 paper-based; 79 iBT). *Application deadline:* For fall admission, 3/1 priority date for international students; for spring admission, 8/1 priority date for international students. Applications are processed on a rolling basis. Application fee: $40 ($75 for international students). Electronic applications accepted. *Expenses:* Tuition, state resident: full-time $4272; part-time $178 per credit hour. Tuition, nonresident: full-time $17,472; part-time $709 per credit hour. *Required fees:* $2413.20; $100.55 per credit hour. One-time fee: $50 full-time. Part-time tuition and fees vary according to course load and campus/location. *Financial support:* In 2013–14, 7 research assistantships (averaging $9,375 per year), 7 teaching assistantships (averaging $11,839 per year) were awarded; career-related internships or fieldwork, Federal Work-Study, scholarships/grants, health care benefits, tuition waivers (partial), and unspecified assistantships also available. Support available to part-time students. Financial award application deadline: 3/1; financial award applicants required to submit FAFSA. *Faculty research:* Hotel operations and management, restaurant/food service management, hospitality education, hospitality human resources management, tourism. *Unit head:* Dr. Sue Williams, Department Head, 405-744-6713, Fax: 405-744-6299, E-mail: sue.williams@okstate.edu. *Application contact:* Dr. Hancer Murat, Graduate Coordinator, 405-744-8645, Fax: 405-744-6299, E-mail: murat.hancer@okstate.edu. Website: http://humansciences.okstate.edu/hrad/.

Penn State University Park, Graduate School, College of Health and Human Development, School of Hospitality Management, State College, PA 16802. Offers MS, PhD. *Unit head:* Dr. Ann C. Crouter, Dean, 814-865-1420, Fax: 814-865-3282, E-mail:

ac1@psu.edu. *Application contact:* Cynthia E. Nicosia, Director, Graduate Enrollment Services, 814-865-1834, Fax: 814-863-4627, E-mail: cey1@psu.edu. Website: http://www.hhdev.psu.edu/shm.

Pontificia Universidad Catolica Madre y Maestra, Graduate School, Faculty of Social and Administrative Sciences, Santiago, Dominican Republic. Offers business administration (MBA), including business development, finance, international business, management skills (M Mgmt, MBA), marketing, operations, strategic cost management, strategy, tourist destination planning and management; law (LL M), including civil law, corporate business law, criminal law, international relations, real estate law; management (M Mgmt), including higher financial management, insurance program administration, management skills (M Mgmt, MBA); psychology (MA), including clinical child and adolescent psychology, forensic psychology; strategic human resources (EMBA).

Purdue University, Graduate School, College of Health and Human Sciences, Department of Hospitality and Tourism Management, West Lafayette, IN 47907. Offers MS, PhD. *Faculty:* 15 full-time (5 women), 3 part-time/adjunct (1 woman). *Students:* 58 full-time (39 women), 28 part-time (21 women); includes 4 minority (3 Asian, non-Hispanic/Latino; 1 Hispanic/Latino), 71 international. Average age 27. 187 applicants, 24% accepted, 18 enrolled. In 2013, 17 master's, 8 doctorates awarded. *Degree requirements:* For master's, thesis; for doctorate, thesis/dissertation. *Entrance requirements:* For master's, GMAT (minimum score of 550) or GRE General Test (minimum combined verbal and quantitative score of 290 new scoring, minimum of 145 each section, or 1000 with 500 each section, old scoring), minimum GPA of 3.0; for doctorate, GMAT (minimum score of 550) or GRE General Test (minimum combined verbal and quantitative score of 290 new scoring, minimum of 145 each section, or 1000 with 500 each section, old scoring), minimum undergraduate GPA of 3.0; master's degree with minimum GPA of 3.0 or equivalent. Additional exam requirements/recommendations for international students: Required—TOEFL (minimum score 77 iBT), TWE. *Application deadline:* For fall admission, 3/5 priority date for domestic and international students; for spring admission, 9/20 for domestic and international students. Applications are processed on a rolling basis. Application fee: $60 ($75 for international students). Electronic applications accepted. *Financial support:* Research assistantships, teaching assistantships, and career-related internships or fieldwork available. Support available to part-time students. Financial award applicants required to submit FAFSA. *Faculty research:* Human resources, marketing, hotel and restaurant operations, food product and equipment development, tourism development. *Unit head:* Dr. Richard F. Ghiselli, Head, 765-494-2636, E-mail: ghiselli@purdue.edu. *Application contact:* Maria D. Campos, Graduate Contact, 765-494-9811, E-mail: camposm@purdue.edu. Website: http://www.purdue.edu/hhs/htm/.

Rochester Institute of Technology, Graduate Enrollment Services, College of Applied Science and Technology, School of International Hospitality and Service Innovation, Department of Hospitality and Service Management, Program in Hospitality and Tourism Management, Rochester, NY 14623-5603. Offers MS. Part-time programs available. *Students:* 18 full-time (10 women), 10 part-time (4 women), 21 international. Average age 25. 44 applicants, 64% accepted, 8 enrolled. In 2013, 5 master's awarded. *Degree requirements:* For master's, thesis or project. *Entrance requirements:* For master's, minimum GPA of 3.0. Additional exam requirements/recommendations for international students: Required—TOEFL (minimum score 550 paper-based; 79 iBT) or IELTS (minimum score 6.5). *Application deadline:* For fall admission, 2/15 priority date for domestic and international students; for winter admission, 11/1 for domestic students, 10/1 for international students; for spring admission, 2/1 priority date for domestic students, 1/1 priority date for international students. Applications are processed on a rolling basis. Application fee: $60. Electronic applications accepted. *Expenses: Tuition:* Full-time $37,236; part-time $1552 per credit hour. *Required fees:* $250. *Financial support:* Research assistantships with partial tuition reimbursements, teaching assistantships with partial tuition reimbursements, career-related internships or fieldwork, scholarships/grants, and unspecified assistantships available. Support available to part-time students. Financial award application deadline: 2/15; financial award applicants required to submit FAFSA. *Unit head:* Dr. Carol Whitlock, E-mail: cbwism@rit.edu. *Application contact:* Diane Ellison, Assistant Vice President, Graduate Enrollment Services, 585-475-2229, Fax: 585-475-7164, E-mail: gradinfo@rit.edu. Website: http://www.rit.edu/cast/htm/graduate/.

Rochester Institute of Technology, Graduate Enrollment Services, College of Applied Science and Technology, School of International Hospitality and Service Innovation, Department of Service Systems, Program in Service Leadership and Innovation, Rochester, NY 14623-5603. Offers MS. Part-time and evening/weekend programs available. Postbaccalaureate distance learning degree programs offered (no on-campus study). *Students:* 24 full-time (12 women), 26 part-time (13 women); includes 3 minority (2 Black or African American, non-Hispanic/Latino; 1 Hispanic/Latino), 3 international. Average age 31. 90 applicants, 37% accepted, 22 enrolled. In 2013, 35 master's awarded. *Degree requirements:* For master's, thesis or alternative. *Entrance requirements:* For master's, minimum GPA of 3.0. Additional exam requirements/recommendations for international students: Required—TOEFL (minimum score 550 paper-based; 79 iBT) or IELTS (minimum score 6.5). *Application deadline:* For fall admission, 2/15 priority date for domestic and international students; for winter admission, 11/1 for domestic and international students; for spring admission, 2/1 for domestic and international students. Applications are processed on a rolling basis. Application fee: $60. Electronic applications accepted. *Expenses: Tuition:* Full-time $37,236; part-time $1552 per credit hour. *Required fees:* $250. *Financial support:* Research assistantships with partial tuition reimbursements, teaching assistantships with partial tuition reimbursements, career-related internships or fieldwork, institutionally sponsored loans, scholarships/grants, and unspecified assistantships available. Support available to part-time students. Financial award application deadline: 2/15; financial award applicants required to submit FAFSA. *Faculty research:* Global resource development, service/product innovation and implementation. *Unit head:* Dr. Linda Underhill, Department Chair, 585-475-7359, E-mail: lmuism@rit.edu. *Application contact:* Diane Ellison, Assistant Vice President, Graduate Enrollment Services, 585-475-2229, Fax: 585-475-7164, E-mail: gradinfo@rit.edu. Website: http://www.rit.edu/cast/servicesystems/service-leadership-and-innovation.php.

Roosevelt University, Graduate Division, College of Professional Studies, Program in Hospitality Management, Chicago, IL 60605. Offers MS. *Degree requirements:* For master's, thesis. *Entrance requirements:* For master's, minimum GPA of 2.75, work experience.

Royal Roads University, Graduate Studies, Tourism and Hotel Management Program, Victoria, BC V9B 5Y2, Canada. Offers destination development (Graduate Certificate); international hotel management (MA); sustainable tourism (Graduate Certificate); tourism leadership (Graduate Certificate); tourism management (MA).

Schiller International University, MBA Programs, Florida, Program in International Hotel and Tourism Management, Largo, FL 33771. Offers MBA. *Degree requirements:* For master's, thesis optional. *Entrance requirements:* Additional exam requirements/recommendations for international students: Required—TOEFL (minimum score 550 paper-based).

South Dakota State University, Graduate School, College of Education and Human Sciences, Department of Nutrition, Food Science and Hospitality, Brookings, SD 57007. Offers dietetics (MS); nutrition, food science and hospitality (MFCS); nutritional sciences (MS, PhD). Part-time programs available. *Degree requirements:* For master's, comprehensive exam (for some programs), thesis (for some programs), oral exam. *Entrance requirements:* Additional exam requirements/recommendations for international students: Required—TOEFL (minimum score 525 paper-based). *Faculty research:* Food chemistry, bone density, functional food, nutrition education, nutrition biochemistry.

South University, Graduate Programs, College of Business, Savannah, GA 31406. Offers corrections (MBA); entrepreneurship and small business (MBA); healthcare administration (MBA); hospitality management (MBA); leadership (MS); public administration (MPA); sustainability (MBA).

Stratford University, Program in International Hospitality Management, Baltimore, MD 21202-3230. Offers MS. Part-time and evening/weekend programs available. Postbaccalaureate distance learning degree programs offered.

Strayer University, Graduate Studies, Washington, DC 20005-2603. Offers accounting (MS); acquisition (MBA); business administration (MBA); communications technology (MS); educational management (M Ed); finance (MBA); health services administration (MHSA); hospitality and tourism management (MBA); human resource management (MBA); information systems (MS), including computer security management, decision support system management, enterprise resource management, network management, software engineering management, systems development management; management (MBA); management information systems (MS); marketing (MBA); professional accounting (MS), including accounting information systems, controllership, taxation; public administration (MPA); supply chain management (MBA); technology in education (M Ed). Programs also offered at campus locations in Birmingham, AL; Chamblee, GA; Cobb County, GA; Morrow, GA; White Marsh, MD; Charleston, SC; Columbia, SC; Greensboro, NC; Greenville, SC; Lexington, KY; Louisville, KY; Nashville, TN; North Raleigh, NC; Washington, DC. Part-time and evening/weekend programs available. Postbaccalaureate distance learning degree programs offered (minimal on-campus study). *Degree requirements:* For master's, thesis. *Entrance requirements:* For master's, GMAT, GRE General Test, bachelor's degree from an accredited college or university, minimum undergraduate GPA of 2.75. Electronic applications accepted.

Temple University, Fox School of Business, Doctoral Programs in Business, Philadelphia, PA 19122-6096. Offers accounting (PhD); entrepreneurship (PhD); finance (PhD); international business (PhD); management information systems (PhD); marketing (PhD); risk management and insurance (PhD); statistics (PhD); strategic management (PhD); tourism and sport (PhD). *Accreditation:* AACSB. *Degree requirements:* For doctorate, thesis/dissertation. *Entrance requirements:* For doctorate, GRE General Test, GMAT, minimum GPA of 3.0, master's degree. Additional exam requirements/recommendations for international students: Required—TOEFL (minimum score 600 paper-based; 100 iBT), IELTS (minimum score 7.5). Electronic applications accepted.

Temple University, School of Tourism and Hospitality Management, Program in Tourism and Hospitality Management, Philadelphia, PA 19122-6096. Offers hospitality operations (MTHM); tourism and hospitality marketing (MTHM). Part-time and evening/weekend programs available. *Faculty:* 10 full-time (3 women), 3 part-time/adjunct (0 women). *Students:* 23 full-time (21 women), 4 part-time (2 women); includes 2 minority (1 Asian, non-Hispanic/Latino; 1 Two or more races, non-Hispanic/Latino), 22 international. 57 applicants, 58% accepted, 8 enrolled. In 2013, 11 master's awarded. *Degree requirements:* For master's, thesis optional, internship or project. *Entrance requirements:* For master's, GRE General Test, GMAT, or MAT, bachelor's degree or equivalent with minimum GPA of 3.0, 500-word essay, 2 letters of recommendation, resume. Additional exam requirements/recommendations for international students: Required—TOEFL (minimum score 550 paper-based; 79 iBT), IELTS (minimum score 6.5). *Application deadline:* For fall admission, 3/1 priority date for domestic students, 1/15 priority date for international students; for spring admission, 8/15 priority date for domestic students, 6/30 priority date for international students. Applications are processed on a rolling basis. Application fee: $60. Electronic applications accepted. *Expenses:* Contact institution. *Financial support:* In 2013–14, 1 research assistantship with full tuition reimbursement (averaging $18,000 per year) was awarded. Financial award application deadline: 3/1; financial award applicants required to submit FAFSA. *Faculty research:* Consumer behavior, revenue management, tourism marketing, advertising evaluation and information technology, brand management, service management, customer relationship management, emotional labor and emotional intelligence, employee knowledge sharing, event management, destination marketing evaluation. *Unit head:* Dr. Ceridwyn King, Assistant Professor/Director of Programs in Tourism and Hospitality Management, 215-204-8701, Fax: 215-204-8705, E-mail: ceridwyn.king@temple.edu. *Application contact:* Michael J. Usino, Senior Associate Director of Recruitment, 215-204-3103, Fax: 215-204-8705, E-mail: musino@temple.edu.
Website: http://sthm.temple.edu/cms/main/graduate-programs/.

Texas Tech University, Graduate School, College of Human Sciences, Department of Nutrition, Hospitality, and Retailing, Lubbock, TX 79409-1240. Offers hospitality administration (PhD); hospitality and retail management (MS); nutritional sciences (MS, PhD). Part-time and evening/weekend programs available. *Faculty:* 24 full-time (14 women). *Students:* 90 full-time (66 women), 16 part-time (10 women); includes 11 minority (1 Black or African American, non-Hispanic/Latino; 4 Asian, non-Hispanic/Latino; 6 Hispanic/Latino), 41 international. Average age 29. 74 applicants, 64% accepted, 33 enrolled. In 2013, 23 master's, 17 doctorates awarded. Terminal master's awarded for partial completion of doctoral program. *Degree requirements:* For master's, thesis or alternative; for doctorate, thesis/dissertation. *Entrance requirements:* For master's, GRE, professional experience (restaurant, hotel, and institutional management); for doctorate, GRE General Test. Additional exam requirements/recommendations for international students: Required—TOEFL (minimum score 550 paper-based; 79 iBT). *Application deadline:* For fall admission, 6/1 priority date for domestic students, 1/15 priority date for international students; for spring admission, 9/1 priority date for domestic students, 6/15 priority date for international students. Applications are processed on a rolling basis. Application fee: $60. Electronic applications accepted. *Expenses:* Tuition, state resident: full-time $6062; part-time $252.57 per credit hour. Tuition, nonresident: full-time $14,558; part-time $606.57 per credit hour. *Required fees:* $2655; $35 per credit hour. $907.50 per semester. Tuition and fees vary according to course load. *Financial support:* In 2013–14, 80 students received support, including 61 fellowships (averaging $2,868 per year), 11 research assistantships (averaging $5,042 per year), 43 teaching assistantships (averaging $5,073 per year). Financial award application deadline: 4/15; financial award applicants required to submit FAFSA. *Faculty research:* Selenium, obesity prevention, wine marketing, food safety, cross-border retailing. *Total annual research expenditures:* $305,963. *Unit head:* Dr. Shane Blum, Chair, 806-742-3068 Ext. 253, Fax: 806-742-3042, E-mail: shane.blum@ttu.edu. *Application contact:* Dr. Debra Reed, Graduate Advisor, Nutritional Sciences, 806-742-3068 Ext. 251, Fax: 806-742-3042, E-mail: debra.reed@ttu.edu.
Website: http://www.depts.ttu.edu/hs/nhr.

Troy University, Graduate School, College of Business, Program in Management, Troy, AL 36082. Offers applied management (MSM); healthcare management (MSM); human resources management (MSM); information systems (MSM); international hospitality management (MSM); international management (MSM); leadership and organizational effectiveness (MSM); public management (MS, MSM). *Accreditation:* ACBSP. Part-time and evening/weekend programs available. *Faculty:* 15 full-time (8 women), 3 part-time/adjunct (0 women). *Students:* 18 full-time (14 women), 148 part-time (86 women); includes 95 minority (75 Black or African American, non-Hispanic/Latino; 1 American Indian or Alaska Native, non-Hispanic/Latino; 4 Asian, non-Hispanic/Latino; 8 Hispanic/Latino; 7 Two or more races, non-Hispanic/Latino). Average age 35. 124 applicants, 79% accepted, 30 enrolled. In 2013, 75 master's awarded. *Degree requirements:* For master's, Graduate Educational Testing Service Major Field Test, capstone exam, minimum GPA of 3.0. *Entrance requirements:* For master's, GRE (minimum score of 900 on old exam or 294 on new exam) or GMAT (minimum score of 500), bachelor's degree; minimum undergraduate GPA of 2.5 or 3.0 on last 30 semester hours, letter of recommendation. Additional exam requirements/recommendations for international students: Required—TOEFL (minimum score 523 paper-based; 70 iBT), IELTS (minimum score 6). *Application deadline:* Applications are processed on a rolling basis. Application fee: $50. Electronic applications accepted. *Expenses:* Contact institution. *Unit head:* Dr. Bob Wheatley, Director, Graduate Business Programs, 334-670-3143, Fax: 334-670-3599, E-mail: rwheat@troy.edu. *Application contact:* Brenda K. Campbell, Director of Graduate Admissions, 334-670-3178, Fax: 334-670-3733, E-mail: bcamp@troy.edu.

The University of Alabama, Graduate School, College of Human Environmental Sciences, Department of Human Nutrition and Hospitality Management, Tuscaloosa, AL 35487. Offers MSHES. Part-time programs available. Postbaccalaureate distance learning degree programs offered (no on-campus study). *Faculty:* 11 full-time (10 women). *Students:* 14 full-time (all women), 70 part-time (68 women); includes 8 minority (2 Black or African American, non-Hispanic/Latino; 1 Asian, non-Hispanic/Latino; 5 Hispanic/Latino), 1 international. Average age 31. 68 applicants, 54% accepted, 28 enrolled. In 2013, 36 master's awarded. *Degree requirements:* For master's, comprehensive exam, thesis optional. *Entrance requirements:* For master's, minimum GPA of 3.0. Additional exam requirements/recommendations for international students: Required—TOEFL, IELTS. *Application deadline:* For fall admission, 7/1 for domestic students; for spring admission, 11/1 for domestic students. Applications are processed on a rolling basis. Application fee: $50 ($60 for international students). Electronic applications accepted. *Expenses:* Tuition, state resident: full-time $9450. Tuition, nonresident: full-time $23,950. *Financial support:* In 2013–14, 4 students received support, including 2 research assistantships (averaging $8,100 per year), 4 teaching assistantships (averaging $8,100 per year); career-related internships or fieldwork also available. Financial award application deadline: 3/15. *Faculty research:* Maternal and child nutrition, childhood obesity, community nutrition interventions, geriatric nutrition, family eating patterns, food chemistry, phytochemicals, dietary antioxidants. *Unit head:* Dr. Mary K. Meyer, Chair/Professor, 205-348-6150, Fax: 205-348-3789, E-mail: mkmeyer@ches.ua.edu. *Application contact:* Patrick D. Fuller, Admissions Officer, 205-348-5923, Fax: 205-348-0400, E-mail: patrick.d.fuller@ua.edu.
Website: http://www.ches.ua.edu/.

The University of Alabama, Graduate School, College of Human Environmental Sciences, Program in Human Environmental Science, Tuscaloosa, AL 35487. Offers family financial planning and counseling (MS); interactive technology (MS); quality management (MS); restaurant and meeting management (MS); rural community health (MS); sport management (MS). *Faculty:* 1 full-time (0 women). *Students:* 55 full-time (34 women), 98 part-time (48 women); includes 41 minority (30 Black or African American, non-Hispanic/Latino; 2 American Indian or Alaska Native, non-Hispanic/Latino; 2 Asian, non-Hispanic/Latino; 2 Hispanic/Latino; 5 Two or more races, non-Hispanic/Latino), 1 international. Average age 34. 102 applicants, 69% accepted, 60 enrolled. In 2013, 88 master's awarded. *Degree requirements:* For master's, comprehensive exam. *Entrance requirements:* For master's, GRE (for some specializations), minimum GPA of 3.0. Additional exam requirements/recommendations for international students: Required—TOEFL. *Application deadline:* Applications are processed on a rolling basis. Application fee: $50 ($60 for international students). Electronic applications accepted. *Expenses:* Tuition, state resident: full-time $9450. Tuition, nonresident: full-time $23,950. *Faculty research:* Hospitality management, sports medicine education, technology and education. *Unit head:* Dr. Milla D. Boschung, Dean, 205-348-6250, Fax: 205-348-1786, E-mail: mboschun@ches.ua.edu. *Application contact:* Dr. Stuart Usdan, Associate Dean, 205-348-6150, Fax: 205-348-3789, E-mail: susdan@ches.ua.edu.

University of Central Florida, Rosen College of Hospitality Management, Orlando, FL 32816. Offers hospitality and tourism management (MS); hospitality management (PhD, Certificate). *Faculty:* 47 full-time (18 women), 24 part-time/adjunct (8 women). *Students:* 52 full-time (33 women), 30 part-time (21 women); includes 14 minority (4 Black or African American, non-Hispanic/Latino; 5 Asian, non-Hispanic/Latino; 3 Hispanic/Latino; 2 Two or more races, non-Hispanic/Latino), 11 international. Average age 29. 83 applicants, 41% accepted, 18 enrolled. In 2013, 43 master's, 23 other advanced degrees awarded. *Degree requirements:* For master's, thesis or alternative. *Entrance requirements:* For master's, GMAT or GRE, minimum GPA of 3.0 in last 60 hours. Additional exam requirements/recommendations for international students: Required—TOEFL. *Application deadline:* For fall admission, 2/1 for domestic students. Application fee: $30. Electronic applications accepted. *Financial support:* In 2013–14, 11 students received support, including 3 fellowships with partial tuition reimbursements available (averaging $1,900 per year), 2 research assistantships with partial tuition reimbursements available (averaging $7,700 per year), 10 teaching assistantships with partial tuition reimbursements available (averaging $9,600 per year). *Unit head:* Dr. Abraham C. Pizam, Dean, 407-903-8010, E-mail: abraham.pizam@ucf.edu. *Application contact:* Barbara Rodriguez Lamas, Director, Admissions and Student Services, 407-823-2766, Fax: 407-823-6442, E-mail: gradadmissions@ucf.edu.
Website: http://www.hospitality.ucf.edu/.

University of Delaware, Alfred Lerner College of Business and Economics, Program in Hospitality Information Management, Newark, DE 19716. Offers MS. *Entrance requirements:* Additional exam requirements/recommendations for international students: Required—TOEFL (minimum score 550 paper-based). Electronic applications accepted. *Faculty research:* Foodservice, lodging and tourism management.

The University of Findlay, Office of Graduate Admissions, Findlay, OH 45840-3653. Offers athletic training (MAT); business (MBA), including health care management, hospitality management, organizational leadership, public management; education (MA Ed), including administration, children's literature, early childhood, human resource development, reading, science, special education, technology; environmental, safety and health management (MSEM); health informatics (MS); occupational therapy (MOT); pharmacy (Pharm D); physical therapy (DPT); physician assistant (MPA); rhetoric and writing (MA); teaching English to speakers of other languages (TESOL) and bilingual education (MA). Part-time and evening/weekend programs available. Postbaccalaureate

distance learning degree programs offered (no on-campus study). *Faculty:* 209 full-time (98 women), 69 part-time/adjunct (38 women). *Students:* 551 full-time (332 women), 457 part-time (276 women); includes 77 minority (37 Black or African American, non-Hispanic/Latino; 1 American Indian or Alaska Native, non-Hispanic/Latino; 15 Asian, non-Hispanic/Latino; 23 Hispanic/Latino; 1 Native Hawaiian or other Pacific Islander, non-Hispanic/Latino), 135 international. Average age 28. 637 applicants, 66% accepted, 241 enrolled. In 2013, 267 master's, 91 doctorates awarded. *Degree requirements:* For master's, thesis, cumulative project, capstone project. *Entrance requirements:* For master's, GRE/GMAT, bachelor's degree from accredited institution, minimum undergraduate GPA of 2.5 in last 64 hours of course work; for doctorate, GRE, minimum cumulative GPA of 3.0. Additional exam requirements/recommendations for international students: Required—TOEFL (minimum score 80 iBT). *Application deadline:* Applications are processed on a rolling basis. Application fee: $25. Electronic applications accepted. *Expenses: Required fees:* $146 per semester. Tuition and fees vary according to degree level and program. *Financial support:* In 2013–14, 11 research assistantships with full and partial tuition reimbursements (averaging $4,000 per year), 10 teaching assistantships with full and partial tuition reimbursements (averaging $3,600 per year) were awarded; career-related internships or fieldwork, Federal Work-Study, health care benefits, and unspecified assistantships also available. Financial award application deadline: 4/1; financial award applicants required to submit FAFSA. *Unit head:* Christopher M. Harris, Director of Admissions, 419-434-4347, E-mail: harrisc1@findlay.edu. *Application contact:* Emily Ickes, Graduate Admissions Counselor, 419-434-6933, Fax: 419-434-4898, E-mail: ickese@findlay.edu.
Website: http://www.findlay.edu/admissions/graduate/Pages/default.aspx.

University of Guelph, Graduate Studies, College of Management and Economics, MBA Program, Guelph, ON N1G 2W1, Canada. Offers food and agribusiness management (MBA); hospitality and tourism management (MBA). Part-time and evening/weekend programs available. Postbaccalaureate distance learning degree programs offered (minimal on-campus study). *Entrance requirements:* For master's, minimum B-average, minimum of 3 years of relevant work experience. Additional exam requirements/recommendations for international students: Required—TOEFL (minimum score 550 paper-based). Electronic applications accepted. *Faculty research:* Marketing, operations management, business policy, financial management, organizational behavior.

University of Houston, Conrad N. Hilton College of Hotel and Restaurant Management, Houston, TX 77204. Offers hospitality management (MS). Part-time programs available. *Degree requirements:* For master's, practicum or thesis. *Entrance requirements:* For master's, GMAT or GRE General Test. Additional exam requirements/recommendations for international students: Required—TOEFL (minimum score 100 iBT) or IELTS (minimum score 7). Electronic applications accepted. *Faculty research:* Catering, tourism, hospitality marketing, security and risk management, purchasing and financial information usage.

University of Kentucky, Graduate School, College of Agriculture, Food and Environment, Program in Hospitality and Dietetics Administration, Lexington, KY 40506-0032. Offers MS. *Degree requirements:* For master's, comprehensive exam, thesis optional. *Entrance requirements:* For master's, GRE General Test, minimum undergraduate GPA of 2.75. Additional exam requirements/recommendations for international students: Required—TOEFL (minimum score 550 paper-based). Electronic applications accepted.

University of Massachusetts Amherst, Graduate School, Isenberg School of Management, Program in Management, Amherst, MA 01003. Offers accounting (PhD); business administration (MBA); entrepreneurship (MBA); finance (MBA, PhD); healthcare administration (MBA); hospitality and tourism management (PhD); management science (PhD); marketing (MBA, PhD); organization studies (PhD); sport management (PhD); strategic management (PhD); MBA/MS. *Accreditation:* AACSB. Part-time and evening/weekend programs available. Postbaccalaureate distance learning degree programs offered. *Faculty:* 68 full-time (14 women). *Students:* 140 full-time (59 women), 1,127 part-time (319 women); includes 229 minority (24 Black or African American, non-Hispanic/Latino; 2 American Indian or Alaska Native, non-Hispanic/Latino; 135 Asian, non-Hispanic/Latino; 51 Hispanic/Latino; 6 Native Hawaiian or other Pacific Islander, non-Hispanic/Latino; 11 Two or more races, non-Hispanic/Latino), 131 international. Average age 36. 828 applicants, 56% accepted, 351 enrolled. In 2013, 361 master's, 12 doctorates awarded. Terminal master's awarded for partial completion of doctoral program. *Degree requirements:* For doctorate, comprehensive exam, thesis/dissertation. *Entrance requirements:* For master's and doctorate, GMAT or GRE General Test. Additional exam requirements/recommendations for international students: Required—TOEFL (minimum score 550 paper-based; 80 iBT), IELTS (minimum score 6.5). *Application deadline:* For fall admission, 1/20 for domestic and international students. Applications are processed on a rolling basis. Application fee: $75. Electronic applications accepted. *Financial support:* Fellowships with full and partial tuition reimbursements, research assistantships with full and partial tuition reimbursements, teaching assistantships with full and partial tuition reimbursements, career-related internships or fieldwork, Federal Work-Study, scholarships/grants, traineeships, health care benefits, tuition waivers (full and partial), and unspecified assistantships available. Support available to part-time students. Financial award application deadline: 1/20; financial award applicants required to submit FAFSA. *Unit head:* Dr. John Wells, Chair, 413-545-7609, Fax: 413-577-2234. *Application contact:* Lindsay DeSantis, Supervisor of Admissions, 413-545-0722, Fax: 413-577-0010, E-mail: gradadm@grad.umass.edu.
Website: http://www.isenberg.umass.edu/.

University of Missouri, Graduate School, College of Agriculture, Food and Natural Resources, Department of Food Science, Columbia, MO 65211. Offers food science (MS, PhD); foods and food systems management (MS); human nutrition (MS). *Faculty:* 12 full-time (4 women), 2 part-time/adjunct (0 women). *Students:* 24 full-time (14 women), 25 part-time (14 women); includes 2 minority (1 Hispanic/Latino; 1 Two or more races, non-Hispanic/Latino), 33 international. Average age 28. 79 applicants, 15% accepted, 10 enrolled. In 2013, 5 master's, 3 doctorates awarded. Terminal master's awarded for partial completion of doctoral program. *Degree requirements:* For doctorate, comprehensive exam, thesis/dissertation. *Entrance requirements:* For master's, GRE General Test (minimum score: Verbal and Quantitative 1000 with neither section below 400, 297 combined under new scoring; Analytical 3.5), minimum GPA of 3.0; BS in food science from accredited university; for doctorate, GRE General Test (minimum score: Verbal and Quantitative 1000 with neither section below 400, Analytical 3.5), minimum GPA of 3.0; BS and MS in food science from accredited university. Additional exam requirements/recommendations for international students: Required—TOEFL (minimum score 550 paper-based; 79 iBT). *Application deadline:* For fall admission, 4/1 priority date for domestic students; for winter admission, 10/31 priority date for domestic students. Application fee: $55 ($75 for international students). Electronic applications accepted. *Financial support:* Fellowships, research assistantships with tuition reimbursements, teaching assistantships with tuition reimbursements, institutionally sponsored loans, scholarships/grants, health care benefits, and unspecified assistantships available. Support available to part-time students. *Faculty research:* Food chemistry, food analysis, food microbiology, food engineering and process control, functional foods, meat science and processing technology. *Unit head:* Dr. Jinglu Tan, Department Chair, 573-882-2369, E-mail: tanj@missouri.edu. *Application contact:* Starsha Ferguson, Office Support Assistant IV, 573-882-4113, E-mail: fergusonsd@missouri.edu.
Website: http://foodscience.missouri.edu/graduate/.

University of Nevada, Las Vegas, Graduate College, William F. Harrah College of Hotel Administration, Program in Hotel Administration, Las Vegas, NV 89154-6013. Offers MHA, MS, PhD. MHA program also offered in Singapore. Part-time programs available. Postbaccalaureate distance learning degree programs offered (no on-campus study). *Faculty:* 20 full-time (7 women). *Students:* 52 full-time (26 women), 65 part-time (28 women); includes 24 minority (5 Black or African American, non-Hispanic/Latino; 3 American Indian or Alaska Native, non-Hispanic/Latino; 5 Asian, non-Hispanic/Latino; 6 Hispanic/Latino; 1 Native Hawaiian or other Pacific Islander, non-Hispanic/Latino; 4 Two or more races, non-Hispanic/Latino), 28 international. Average age 34. 172 applicants, 30% accepted, 41 enrolled. In 2013, 62 master's, 10 doctorates awarded. *Degree requirements:* For master's, comprehensive exam, thesis (for some programs), professional paper; for doctorate, comprehensive exam, thesis/dissertation, dissertation defense, seminar. *Entrance requirements:* Additional exam requirements/recommendations for international students: Required—TOEFL (minimum score 550 paper-based; 80 iBT), IELTS (minimum score 7). *Application deadline:* For fall admission, 2/1 for domestic students, 5/1 for international students; for spring admission, 11/15 for domestic students, 10/1 for international students; for summer admission, 3/1 for domestic students. Application fee: $60 ($95 for international students). Electronic applications accepted. *Expenses:* Tuition, state resident: full-time $4752; part-time $264 per credit. Tuition, nonresident: full-time $18,662; part-time $554.50 per credit. *International tuition:* $18,952 full-time. *Required fees:* $532; $12 per credit. $266 per semester. One-time fee: $35. Tuition and fees vary according to course load and program. *Financial support:* In 2013–14, 27 students received support, including 13 research assistantships with partial tuition reimbursements available (averaging $8,615 per year), 14 teaching assistantships with partial tuition reimbursements available (averaging $11,857 per year); institutionally sponsored loans, scholarships/grants, health care benefits, and unspecified assistantships also available. Financial award application deadline: 3/1. *Faculty research:* Marketing, human resources, financial analysis, tourism, gaming. *Total annual research expenditures:* $430,819. *Unit head:* Dr. Pat Moreo, Chair/Professor, 702-895-1052, E-mail: pat.moreo@unlv.edu. *Application contact:* Graduate College Admissions Evaluator, 702-895-3320, Fax: 702-895-4180, E-mail: gradcollege@unlv.edu.
Website: http://hotel.unlv.edu.

University of New Orleans, Graduate School, College of Business Administration, School of Hotel, Restaurant, and Tourism Administration, Program in Hospitality and Tourism Management, New Orleans, LA 70148. Offers MS. *Entrance requirements:* Additional exam requirements/recommendations for international students: Required—TOEFL (minimum score 550 paper-based; 79 iBT).

University of North Texas, Robert B. Toulouse School of Graduate Studies, Denton, TN 76203-5017. Offers accounting (MS, PhD); applied anthropology (MA, MS); applied behavior analysis (Certificate); applied technology and performance improvement (M Ed, MS, PhD); art education (MA, PhD); art history (MA); art museum education (Certificate); arts leadership (Certificate); audiology (Au D); behavior analysis (MS); biochemistry and molecular biology (MS, PhD); biology (MA, MS, PhD); business (PhD); business computer information systems (PhD); chemistry (MS, PhD); clinical psychology (PhD); communication studies (MA, MS); computer engineering (MS); computer science (MS); computer science and engineering (PhD); counseling (M Ed, MS, PhD), including clinical mental health counseling (MS), college and university counseling (M Ed, MS), elementary school counseling (M Ed, MS), secondary school counseling (M Ed, MS); counseling psychology (PhD); creative writing (MA); criminal justice (MS); curriculum and instruction (M Ed, PhD), including curriculum studies (PhD), early childhood studies (PhD), language and literacy studies (PhD); decision sciences (MBA); design (MA, MFA), including fashion design (MFA), innovation studies, interior design (MFA); early childhood studies (MS); economics (MS); educational leadership (M Ed, Ed D, PhD); educational psychology (MS), including family studies, gifted and talented (MS, PhD), human development, learning and cognition, research, measurement and evaluation; educational research (PhD), including gifted and talented (MS, PhD), human development and family studies, psychological aspects of sports and exercise, research, measurement and statistics; electrical engineering (MS); emergency management (MPA); engineering systems (MS); English (MA, PhD); environmental science (MS, PhD); experimental psychology (PhD); finance (MBA, MS, PhD); financial management (MPA); French (MA); health psychology and behavioral medicine (PhD); health services management (MBA); higher education (M Ed, Ed D, PhD); history (MA, MS, PhD), including European history (PhD), military history (PhD), United States history (PhD); hospitality management (MS); human resources management (MPA); information science (MS, PhD); information technologies (MBA); information technology and decision sciences (MS); interdisciplinary studies (MA, MS); international sustainable tourism (MS); jazz studies (MM); journalism (MA, MJ, Graduate Certificate), including interactive and virtual digital communication (Graduate Certificate), narrative journalism (Graduate Certificate), public relations (Graduate Certificate); kinesiology (MS); learning technologies (MS, PhD); library science (MS); local government management (MPA); logistics and supply chain management (MBA, PhD); long-term care, senior housing, and aging services (MA, MS); management science (PhD); marketing (MBA, PhD); materials science and engineering (MS, PhD); mathematics (MA, PhD); merchandising (MS); music (MA, MM Ed, PhD), including ethnomusicology (MA), music education (MM Ed, PhD), music theory (MA, PhD), musicology (MA, PhD), performance (MA); nonprofit management (MPA); operations and supply chain management (MBA); performance (MM, DMA); philosophy (MA, PhD); physics (MS, PhD); political science (MA, MS, PhD); public administration and management (PhD), including emergency management, nonprofit management, public financial management, urban management; radio, television and film (MA, MFA); recreation, event and sport management (MS); rehabilitation counseling (MS, Certificate); sociology (MA, MS, PhD); Spanish (MA); special education (M Ed, PhD), including autism intervention (PhD), emotional/behavioral disorders (PhD), mild/moderate disabilities (PhD); speech-language pathology (MA, MS); strategic management (MBA); studio art (MFA); taxation (MS); teaching (M Ed); MBA/MS; MS/MPH; MSES/MBA. Part-time and evening/weekend programs available. Postbaccalaureate distance learning degree programs offered. *Faculty:* 661 full-time (213 women), 240 part-time/adjunct (144 women). *Students:* 3,106 full-time (1,620 women), 3,543 part-time (2,221 women); includes 1,740 minority (533 Black or African American, non-Hispanic/Latino; 15 American Indian or Alaska Native, non-Hispanic/Latino; 286 Asian, non-Hispanic/Latino; 746 Hispanic/Latino; 3 Native Hawaiian or other Pacific Islander, non-Hispanic/Latino; 157 Two or more races, non-Hispanic/Latino), 1,145 international. Average age 32. 6,289 applicants, 43% accepted, 1751 enrolled. In 2013, 1,778 master's, 239 doctorates, 10 other advanced degrees awarded. Terminal master's awarded for partial completion of doctoral program. *Degree requirements:* For master's, variable foreign language requirement, comprehensive exam (for some programs), thesis (for some programs); for doctorate, variable foreign language requirement, comprehensive exam (for some programs), thesis/dissertation; for other advanced degree, variable foreign language

requirement, comprehensive exam (for some programs). *Entrance requirements:* For master's and doctorate, GRE, GMAT. Additional exam requirements/recommendations for international students: Required—TOEFL (minimum score 550 paper-based; 79 iBT). *Application deadline:* For fall admission, 7/15 for domestic students, 3/15 for international students; for spring admission, 11/15 for domestic students, 9/15 for international students; for summer admission, 5/1 for domestic students. Applications are processed on a rolling basis. Application fee: $60. Electronic applications accepted. *Financial support:* Fellowships with partial tuition reimbursements, research assistantships with partial tuition reimbursements, teaching assistantships, career-related internships or fieldwork, Federal Work-Study, institutionally sponsored loans, scholarships/grants, health care benefits, and library assistantships available. Support available to part-time students. Financial award applicants required to submit FAFSA. *Unit head:* Mark Wardell, Dean, 940-565-2383, E-mail: mark.wardell@unt.edu. *Application contact:* Toulouse School of Graduate Studies, 940-565-2383, Fax: 940-565-2141, E-mail: gradsch@unt.edu.
Website: http://tsgs.unt.edu/.

University of South Carolina, The Graduate School, College of Hospitality, Retail, and Sport Management, School of Hotel, Restaurant and Tourism Management, Columbia, SC 29208. Offers MIHTM. *Entrance requirements:* For master's, GMAT or GRE General Test, minimum GPA of 3.0, 2 letters of recommendation. Electronic applications accepted. *Faculty research:* Corporate strategy and management practices, sustainable tourism, club management, tourism technology, revenue management.

University of South Florida Sarasota-Manatee, College of Hospitality and Technology Leadership, Sarasota, FL 34243. Offers hospitality management (MS). Part-time programs available. *Faculty:* 3 full-time (2 women). *Students:* 14 full-time (6 women), 9 part-time (6 women); includes 7 minority (1 Asian, non-Hispanic/Latino; 6 Hispanic/Latino), 4 international. Average age 32. 26 applicants, 54% accepted, 9 enrolled. In 2013, 2 master's awarded. *Degree requirements:* For master's, thesis or professional project. *Entrance requirements:* For master's, GRE/GMAT if upper level GPA is less than 3.0, essay; letters of recommendation. Additional exam requirements/recommendations for international students: Required—TOEFL (minimum score 550 paper-based; 79 iBT), IELTS (minimum score 6.5). *Application deadline:* For fall admission, 3/1 priority date for domestic students, 3/1 for international students; for spring admission, 10/1 priority date for domestic students, 10/1 for international students. Applications are processed on a rolling basis. Application fee: $30. Electronic applications accepted. *Expenses:* Tuition, state resident: full-time $10,029; part-time $418 per credit. Tuition, nonresident: full-time $20,727; part-time $863 per credit. *Required fees:* $10; $5. Tuition and fees vary according to program. *Financial support:* In 2013–14, 4 students received support, including 4 research assistantships (averaging $8,032 per year); career-related internships or fieldwork, institutionally sponsored loans, scholarships/grants, health care benefits, and unspecified assistantships also available. Support available to part-time students. Financial award application deadline: 3/1; financial award applicants required to submit FAFSA. *Faculty research:* Technology's impact on hospitality industry, hospitality accounting and cost control, international tourism development, service quality. *Unit head:* Dr. Cihan Cobanoglu, Dean, 941-359-4244, E-mail: cihan@sar.usf.edu. *Application contact:* Andy Telatovich, Director, Admissions, 941-359-4330, E-mail: atelatovich@sar.usf.edu.
Website: http://www.usfsm.edu/chtl/.

The University of Tennessee, Graduate School, College of Education, Health and Human Sciences, Department of Consumer and Industry Services Management, Program in Hotel, Restaurant, and Tourism Management, Knoxville, TN 37996. Offers hospitality management (MS); tourism (MS). Part-time programs available. *Degree requirements:* For master's, thesis or alternative. *Entrance requirements:* For master's, GRE General Test, minimum GPA of 2.7. Additional exam requirements/recommendations for international students: Required—TOEFL. Electronic applications accepted. *Expenses:* Tuition, state resident: full-time $9540; part-time $531 per credit hour. Tuition, nonresident: full-time $27,728; part-time $1542 per credit hour. *Required fees:* $1404; $67 per credit hour.

Virginia Polytechnic Institute and State University, Graduate School, Pamplin College of Business, Blacksburg, VA 24061. Offers accounting and information systems (MACIS); business (PhD); business administration (MBA, MS); hospitality and tourism management (MS, PhD). *Faculty:* 118 full-time (35 women), 1 part-time/adjunct (0 women). *Students:* 333 full-time (149 women), 129 part-time (47 women); includes 75 minority (14 Black or African American, non-Hispanic/Latino; 42 Asian, non-Hispanic/Latino; 12 Hispanic/Latino; 7 Two or more races, non-Hispanic/Latino), 115 international. Average age 30. 520 applicants, 38% accepted, 157 enrolled. In 2013, 199 master's, 12 doctorates awarded. *Degree requirements:* For master's, comprehensive exam (for some programs), thesis (for some programs); for doctorate, comprehensive exam (for some programs), thesis/dissertation (for some programs). *Entrance requirements:* For master's and doctorate, GRE/GMAT (may vary by department). Additional exam requirements/recommendations for international students: Required—TOEFL (minimum score 550 paper-based). *Application deadline:* For fall admission, 8/1 for domestic students, 4/1 for international students; for spring admission, 1/1 for domestic students, 9/1 for international students. Applications are processed on a rolling basis. Application fee: $75. Electronic applications accepted. *Expenses:* Tuition, state resident: full-time $11,185; part-time $621.50 per credit hour. Tuition, nonresident: full-time $22,146; part-time $1230.25 per credit hour. *Required fees:* $2442; $449.25 per semester. Tuition and fees vary according to course load, campus/location and program. *Financial support:* In 2013–14, 5 fellowships with full tuition reimbursements (averaging $19,435 per year), 61 teaching assistantships with full tuition reimbursements (averaging $15,805 per year) were awarded. Financial award application deadline: 3/1; financial award applicants required to submit FAFSA. *Total annual research expenditures:* $2.5 million. *Unit head:* Dr. Robert T. Sumichrast, Dean, 540-231-6601, Fax: 540-231-4487, E-mail: busdean@vt.edu. *Application contact:* Martha Hilton, Executive Assistant to the Dean, 540-231-9647, Fax: 540-231-4487, E-mail: cartermc@vt.edu.
Website: http://www.pamplin.vt.edu/.

Washington State University, Graduate School, College of Business, PhD Program in Hospitality and Tourism, Pullman, WA 99164. Offers PhD. *Entrance requirements:* For doctorate, GMAT (minimum recommended score of 600), master's degree (MS or MA in a related discipline or an MBA); minimum GPA of 3.25; letters of recommendation; work experience. Additional exam requirements/recommendations for international students: Required—TOEFL (minimum score 580 paper-based).

Travel and Tourism

Arizona State University at the Tempe campus, College of Public Programs, School of Community Resources and Development, Phoenix, AZ 85004-0685. Offers community resources and development (PhD); nonprofit leadership and management (Graduate Certificate); nonprofit studies (MNpS); recreation and tourism studies (MS). *Accreditation:* ACSP. Part-time and evening/weekend programs available. Terminal master's awarded for partial completion of doctoral program. *Degree requirements:* For master's, thesis or alternative, interactive Program of Study (iPOS) submitted before completing 50 percent of required credit hours; for doctorate, comprehensive exam, thesis/dissertation, interactive Program of Study (iPOS) submitted before completing 50 percent of required credit hours. *Entrance requirements:* For master's and doctorate, GRE, minimum GPA of 3.0 or equivalent in last 2 years of work leading to bachelor's degree. Additional exam requirements/recommendations for international students: Required—TOEFL (minimum score 80 iBT), TOEFL, IELTS, or PTE. Electronic applications accepted. *Expenses:* Contact institution.

Boston University, Metropolitan College, Department of Administrative Sciences, Boston, MA 02215. Offers banking and financial management (MSM); business continuity in emergency management (MSM); economics development and tourism management (MSAS); electronic commerce, systems, and technology (MSAS); financial economics (MSAS); innovation and technology (MSAS); insurance management (MSM); international market management (MSM); multinational commerce (MSAS); project management (MS). *Accreditation:* AACSB. Part-time and evening/weekend programs available. Postbaccalaureate distance learning degree programs offered (no on-campus study). *Faculty:* 15 full-time (3 women), 22 part-time/adjunct (3 women). *Students:* 177 full-time (85 women), 560 part-time (293 women); includes 89 minority (31 Black or African American, non-Hispanic/Latino; 31 Asian, non-Hispanic/Latino; 25 Hispanic/Latino; 2 Two or more races, non-Hispanic/Latino), 242 international. Average age 31. 509 applicants, 71% accepted, 222 enrolled. In 2013, 158 master's awarded. *Degree requirements:* For master's, thesis optional. *Entrance requirements:* For master's, 1 year of work experience, minimum GPA of 3.0. Additional exam requirements/recommendations for international students: Required—TOEFL (minimum score 84 iBT). *Application deadline:* Applications are processed on a rolling basis. Application fee: $80. Electronic applications accepted. *Expenses: Tuition:* Full-time $43,970; part-time $1374 per credit hour. *Required fees:* $60 per semester. Tuition and fees vary according to class time, course level and program. *Financial support:* In 2013–14, 15 students received support, including 7 research assistantships (averaging $8,400 per year); career-related internships or fieldwork, Federal Work-Study, and unspecified assistantships also available. *Faculty research:* International business, innovative process. *Unit head:* Dr. Kip Becker, Chairman, 617-353-3016, E-mail: adminsc@bu.edu. *Application contact:* Fiona Niven, Administrative Sciences Department, 617-353-3016, E-mail: adminsc@bu.edu.
Website: http://www.bu.edu/met/academic-community/departments/administrative-sciences/.

California State University, East Bay, Office of Academic Programs and Graduate Studies, College of Education and Allied Studies, Department of Hospitality, Recreation and Tourism, Hayward, CA 94542-3000. Offers recreation and tourism (MS). Part-time and evening/weekend programs available. Postbaccalaureate distance learning degree programs offered (no on-campus study). *Degree requirements:* For master's, thesis optional. *Entrance requirements:* For master's, minimum GPA of 2.75; 2 years' related work experience; 3 letters of recommendation; resume; baccalaureate degree. Additional exam requirements/recommendations for international students: Required—TOEFL (minimum score 550 paper-based). Electronic applications accepted. *Faculty research:* Leisure, online vs. face-to-face (F2F) learning, risk management, leadership, tourism consumer behavior.

California State University, Fullerton, Graduate Studies, College of Communications, Department of Communications, Fullerton, CA 92834-9480. Offers advertising (MA); mass communications research and theory (MA); professional communications (MA); tourism and entertainment (MA). Part-time programs available. *Students:* 22 full-time (17 women), 21 part-time (14 women); includes 19 minority (4 Black or African American, non-Hispanic/Latino; 6 Asian, non-Hispanic/Latino; 8 Hispanic/Latino; 1 Two or more races, non-Hispanic/Latino), 4 international. Average age 28. 69 applicants, 42% accepted, 18 enrolled. In 2013, 36 master's awarded. *Degree requirements:* For master's, project or thesis. *Entrance requirements:* For master's, GRE General Test. Application fee: $55. *Financial support:* Teaching assistantships, career-related internships or fieldwork, Federal Work-Study, institutionally sponsored loans, and scholarships/grants available. Support available to part-time students. Financial award application deadline: 3/1; financial award applicants required to submit FAFSA. *Unit head:* Dr. Diane F. Witmer, Chair, 657-278-7008. *Application contact:* Coordinator, 657-278-3832.

California State University, Northridge, Graduate Studies, College of Health and Human Development, Department of Recreation and Tourism Management, Northridge, CA 91330. Offers hospitality and tourism (MS); recreational sport management/campus recreation (MS). *Degree requirements:* For master's, thesis (for some programs). *Entrance requirements:* For master's, GRE (if cumulative undergraduate GPA less than 3.0). Additional exam requirements/recommendations for international students: Required—TOEFL.

Clemson University, Graduate School, College of Health, Education, and Human Development, Department of Parks, Recreation, and Tourism Management, Clemson, SC 29634. Offers MS, PhD. Part-time programs available. Postbaccalaureate distance learning degree programs offered (no on-campus study). *Faculty:* 19 full-time (8 women), 1 (woman) part-time/adjunct. *Students:* 49 full-time (27 women), 44 part-time (26 women); includes 10 minority (4 Black or African American, non-Hispanic/Latino; 2 Hispanic/Latino; 4 Two or more races, non-Hispanic/Latino), 20 international. Average age 28. 69 applicants, 67% accepted, 35 enrolled. In 2013, 11 master's, 8 doctorates awarded. *Median time to degree:* Of those who began their doctoral program in fall 2005, 100% received their degree in 8 years or less. *Degree requirements:* For master's, thesis (for some programs); for doctorate, thesis/dissertation. *Entrance requirements:* For master's, GRE (for on-campus thesis MS), minimum undergraduate GPA of 3.0; for doctorate, GRE General Test, minimum graduate GPA of 3.0. Additional exam requirements/recommendations for international students: Required—TOEFL. *Application deadline:* For fall admission, 5/1 priority date for domestic students; for

spring admission, 10/1 for domestic students. Applications are processed on a rolling basis. Application fee: $70 ($80 for international students). Electronic applications accepted. *Financial support:* In 2013–14, 48 students received support, including 1 fellowship with full and partial tuition reimbursement available (averaging $3,000 per year), 2 research assistantships with partial tuition reimbursements available (averaging $11,752 per year), 32 teaching assistantships with partial tuition reimbursements available (averaging $17,275 per year); career-related internships or fieldwork, scholarships/grants, health care benefits, tuition waivers (partial), and unspecified assistantships also available. Support available to part-time students. Financial award application deadline: 1/15; financial award applicants required to submit FAFSA. *Faculty research:* Recreation resource management, leisure behavior, therapeutic recreation, community leisure. *Total annual research expenditures:* $422,028. *Unit head:* Dr. Brett A. Wright, Chair, 864-656-3036, Fax: 864-656-2226, E-mail: wright@clemson.edu. *Application contact:* Dr. Denise M. Anderson, Graduate Coordinator, 864-656-5679, Fax: 864-656-2226, E-mail: dander2@clemson.edu.
Website: http://www.hehd.clemson.edu/prtm/.

Eastern Michigan University, Graduate School, College of Arts and Sciences, Department of Geography and Geology, Programs in Historic Preservation, Ypsilanti, MI 48197. Offers heritage interpretation and tourism (MS); historic preservation (MS, Graduate Certificate). Part-time and evening/weekend programs available. Postbaccalaureate distance learning degree programs offered (minimal on-campus study). *Students:* 20 full-time (17 women), 48 part-time (35 women); includes 2 minority (1 American Indian or Alaska Native, non-Hispanic/Latino; 1 Two or more races, non-Hispanic/Latino). Average age 33. 41 applicants, 76% accepted, 16 enrolled. In 2013, 21 master's, 1 other advanced degree awarded. *Entrance requirements:* Additional exam requirements/recommendations for international students: Required—TOEFL. *Application deadline:* Applications are processed on a rolling basis. Application fee: $35. *Expenses:* Tuition, state resident: full-time $12,300; part-time $466 per credit hour. Tuition, nonresident: full-time $23,159; part-time $918 per credit hour. *Required fees:* $71 per credit hour. $46 per semester. One-time fee: $100. Tuition and fees vary according to course level and degree level. *Financial support:* Fellowships, research assistantships with full tuition reimbursements, teaching assistantships with full tuition reimbursements, career-related internships or fieldwork, Federal Work-Study, institutionally sponsored loans, scholarships/grants, tuition waivers (partial), and unspecified assistantships available. Support available to part-time students. Financial award applicants required to submit FAFSA. *Unit head:* Dr. Richard Sambrook, Department Head, 734-487-0218, Fax: 734-487-6979, E-mail: rsambroo@emich.edu. *Application contact:* Dr. Ted Ligibel, Program Director, 734-487-0232, Fax: 734-487-6979, E-mail: tligibel@emich.edu.

Endicott College, Apicius International School of Hospitality, Florence, 50122, Italy. Offers international tourism (MOM). Program held entirely in Florence, Italy. *Degree requirements:* For master's, thesis. *Entrance requirements:* For master's, MAT or GRE, 250-500 word essay explaining professional goals, official transcripts of all academic work, bachelor's degree, two letters of recommendation, personal interview. *Application deadline:* For fall admission, 6/30 for domestic and international students. Application fee: $50. *Financial support:* Applicants required to submit FAFSA. *Application contact:* E-mail: admissions@fua.it.
Website: http://www.apicius.it.

Florida Atlantic University, College of Design and Social Inquiry, School of Urban and Regional Planning, Boca Raton, FL 33431-0991. Offers economic development and tourism (Certificate); environmental planning (Certificate); sustainable community planning (Certificate); urban and regional planning (MURP); visual planning technology (Certificate). *Accreditation:* ACSP. Part-time and evening/weekend programs available. *Faculty:* 5 full-time (3 women). *Students:* 20 full-time (16 women), 14 part-time (8 women); includes 16 minority (7 Black or African American, non-Hispanic/Latino; 8 Hispanic/Latino; 1 Two or more races, non-Hispanic/Latino), 1 international. Average age 28. 38 applicants, 53% accepted, 13 enrolled. In 2013, 15 master's awarded. *Entrance requirements:* For master's, GRE General Test, minimum GPA of 3.0. Additional exam requirements/recommendations for international students: Required—TOEFL (minimum score 500 paper-based; 61 iBT), IELTS (minimum score 6). *Application deadline:* For fall admission, 5/1 priority date for domestic students, 2/15 for international students; for spring admission, 11/1 priority date for domestic students, 7/15 for international students. Applications are processed on a rolling basis. Application fee: $30. *Expenses:* Tuition, state resident: full-time $6660; part-time $370 per credit hour. Tuition, nonresident: full-time $18,450; part-time $1025 per credit hour. Tuition and fees vary according to course load. *Financial support:* Fellowships with full tuition reimbursements, research assistantships, career-related internships or fieldwork, Federal Work-Study, institutionally sponsored loans, and tuition waivers (partial) available. Financial award application deadline: 4/1. *Faculty research:* Growth management, urban design, computer applications/geographical information systems, environmental planning. *Unit head:* Dr. Eric Dumbaugh, Chair, 954-762-5030, Fax: 954-762-5673, E-mail: dumbaugh@fau.edu. *Application contact:* Joanna Arlington, Manager, Graduate Admissions, 561-297-2428, Fax: 561-297-2117, E-mail: arlingto@fau.edu.
Website: http://www.fau.edu/durp/.

The George Washington University, School of Business, Department of Tourism and Hospitality Management, Washington, DC 20052. Offers event and meeting management (MTA); event management (Professional Certificate); hospitality management (MTA, Professional Certificate); sport management (MTA); sports business management (Professional Certificate); sustainable tourism destination management (MTA); tourism administration (MTA); tourism and hospitality management (MBA); tourism destination management (Professional Certificate). Part-time programs available. Postbaccalaureate distance learning degree programs offered. *Faculty:* 2 full-time (1 woman). *Students:* 99 full-time (79 women), 58 part-time (45 women); includes 32 minority (24 Black or African American, non-Hispanic/Latino; 4 Asian, non-Hispanic/Latino; 3 Hispanic/Latino; 1 Two or more races, non-Hispanic/Latino), 63 international. Average age 28. 124 applicants, 71% accepted, 52 enrolled. In 2013, 68 master's awarded. *Degree requirements:* For master's, comprehensive exam, thesis. *Entrance requirements:* For master's, GRE General Test. Additional exam requirements/recommendations for international students: Required—TOEFL. *Application deadline:* For fall admission, 4/1 priority date for domestic students; for spring admission, 10/1 for domestic students. Applications are processed on a rolling basis. Application fee: $75. *Financial support:* In 2013–14, 32 students received support. Fellowships, teaching assistantships, career-related internships or fieldwork, Federal Work-Study, institutionally sponsored loans, and tuition waivers (partial) available. Financial award application deadline: 4/1. *Faculty research:* Tourism policy, tourism impact forecasting, geotourism. *Unit head:* Larry Yu, Director, 202-994-6380, E-mail: lyu@gwu.edu. *Application contact:* Kristin Williams, Assistant Vice President for Graduate and Special Enrollment Management, 202-994-0467, Fax: 202-994-0371, E-mail: ksw@gwu.edu.
Website: http://business.gwu.edu/tourism/.

Hawai`i Pacific University, College of Business Administration, Honolulu, HI 96813. Offers accounting/CPA (MBA); e-business (MBA); economics (MBA); finance (MBA); healthcare management (MBA); human resource management (MA, MBA); information systems (MBA, MSIS); international business (MBA); management (MBA); marketing (MBA); organizational change (MA, MBA); travel industry management (MBA). Part-time and evening/weekend programs available. *Faculty:* 22 full-time (9 women), 6 part-time/adjunct (0 women). *Students:* 232 full-time (100 women), 174 part-time (84 women); includes 241 minority (18 Black or African American, non-Hispanic/Latino; 112 Asian, non-Hispanic/Latino; 33 Hispanic/Latino; 11 Native Hawaiian or other Pacific Islander, non-Hispanic/Latino; 67 Two or more races, non-Hispanic/Latino). Average age 31. 240 applicants, 81% accepted, 102 enrolled. In 2013, 206 master's awarded. *Degree requirements:* For master's, thesis. *Entrance requirements:* For master's, GMAT. Additional exam requirements/recommendations for international students: Recommended—TOEFL (minimum score 550 paper-based; 80 iBT), TWE (minimum score 5). *Application deadline:* For fall admission, 2/15 priority date for domestic students; for spring admission, 10/15 priority date for domestic students. Applications are processed on a rolling basis. Application fee: $50. Electronic applications accepted. *Financial support:* In 2013–14, 90 students received support. Research assistantships, career-related internships or fieldwork, Federal Work-Study, scholarships/grants, tuition waivers, and unspecified assistantships available. Financial award application deadline: 3/1; financial award applicants required to submit FAFSA. *Faculty research:* Statistical control process as used by management, studies in comparative cross-cultural management styles, not-for-profit management. *Unit head:* Dr. Deborah Crown, Dean, 808-544-0275, Fax: 808-544-0283, E-mail: dcrown@hpu.edu. *Application contact:* Rumi Yoshida, Associate Director of Graduate Admissions, 808-543-8034, Fax: 808-544-0280, E-mail: grad@hpu.edu.
Website: http://www.hpu.edu/CBA/Graduate/index.html.

Indiana University Bloomington, School of Public Health, Department of Recreation, Park, and Tourism Studies, Bloomington, IN 47405-7000. Offers leisure behavior (PhD); outdoor recreation (MS); park and public lands management (MS); recreation administration (MS); recreational sports administration (MS); recreational therapy (MS); tourism management (MS). *Faculty:* 16 full-time (5 women), 1 (woman) part-time/adjunct. *Students:* 43 full-time (21 women), 9 part-time (6 women); includes 6 minority (2 Black or African American, non-Hispanic/Latino; 2 Hispanic/Latino; 2 Two or more races, non-Hispanic/Latino), 17 international. Average age 31. 47 applicants, 81% accepted, 18 enrolled. In 2013, 21 master's, 4 doctorates awarded. Terminal master's awarded for partial completion of doctoral program. *Degree requirements:* For master's, thesis optional; for doctorate, comprehensive exam, thesis/dissertation. *Entrance requirements:* For master's, GRE General Test, minimum GPA of 2.8; for doctorate, GRE General Test, minimum GPA of 3.0 (undergraduate), 3.5 (graduate). Additional exam requirements/recommendations for international students: Required—TOEFL (minimum score 550 paper-based; 80 iBT). *Application deadline:* For fall admission, 1/1 priority date for international students; for spring admission, 9/1 priority date for international students. Applications are processed on a rolling basis. Application fee: $55 ($65 for international students). Electronic applications accepted. *Financial support:* In 2013–14, 19 students received support. Fellowships, research assistantships, teaching assistantships with partial tuition reimbursements available, career-related internships or fieldwork, Federal Work-Study, institutionally sponsored loans, scholarships/grants, health care benefits, tuition waivers (partial), unspecified assistantships, and fee remissions available. Support available to part-time students. Financial award application deadline: 3/1; financial award applicants required to submit FAFSA. *Faculty research:* Leisure counseling, gerontology, special populations, planning and development. *Unit head:* Dr. Bryan McCormick, Chair, 812-855-3482, E-mail: bmccormi@indiana.edu. *Application contact:* Program Office, 812-855-4711, Fax: 812-855-3998, E-mail: recpark@indiana.edu.
Website: http://www.publichealth.indiana.edu/departments/recreation-park-tourism-studies/index.shtml.

Kent State University, Graduate School of Education, Health, and Human Services, School of Foundations, Leadership and Administration, Program in Hospitality and Tourism Management, Kent, OH 44242-0001. Offers MS. Part-time programs available. *Faculty:* 6 full-time (3 women), 6 part-time/adjunct (2 women). *Students:* 13 full-time (11 women), 13 part-time (8 women); includes 2 minority (1 Asian, non-Hispanic/Latino; 1 Hispanic/Latino), 14 international. 30 applicants, 53% accepted. In 2013, 8 master's awarded. *Degree requirements:* For master's, thesis optional. *Entrance requirements:* For master's, minimum GPA of 3.0, 3 letters of recommendation, resume, goals statement. Additional exam requirements/recommendations for international students: Required—TOEFL (minimum score 550 paper-based; 80 iBT). *Application deadline:* Applications are processed on a rolling basis. Application fee: $30 ($60 for international students). Electronic applications accepted. *Financial support:* In 2013–14, 4 students received support, including 5 research assistantships with full tuition reimbursements available (averaging $8,500 per year); teaching assistantships, Federal Work-Study, scholarships/grants, and unspecified assistantships also available. Financial award application deadline: 2/1; financial award applicants required to submit FAFSA. *Faculty research:* Training human service workers, health care services for older adults, early adolescent development, care-giving arrangements with aging families, peace and war. *Unit head:* Barb Scheule, Coordinator, 330-672-3796, E-mail: bscheule@kent.edu. *Application contact:* Nancy Miller, Academic Program Director, Office of Graduate Student Services, 330-672-2576, Fax: 330-672-9162, E-mail: ogs@kent.edu.

Liberty University, School of Education, Lynchburg, VA 24515. Offers administration and supervision (M Ed); curriculum and instruction (Ed D, Ed S); early childhood education (M Ed); educational leadership (Ed D, Ed S); educational technology and online instruction (M Ed); elementary education (M Ed, MAT); English (M Ed); gifted education (M Ed); history (M Ed); leadership (M Ed); math specialist (M Ed); middle grades (M Ed, MAT); outdoor adventure sport (MS); reading specialist (M Ed); school counseling (M Ed); secondary education (MAT); special education (M Ed, MAT); sport management (MS), including administration, outdoor recreation, sport management, tourism; sports administration (MS); student service (M Ed); teaching and learning (M Ed); tourism (MS). *Accreditation:* NCATE. Part-time programs available. Postbaccalaureate distance learning degree programs offered (minimal on-campus study). *Students:* 2,241 full-time (1,639 women), 4,413 part-time (3,240 women); includes 2,052 minority (1,588 Black or African American, non-Hispanic/Latino; 37 American Indian or Alaska Native, non-Hispanic/Latino; 67 Asian, non-Hispanic/Latino; 173 Hispanic/Latino; 37 Native Hawaiian or other Pacific Islander, non-Hispanic/Latino; 150 Two or more races, non-Hispanic/Latino), 15 international. Average age 37. 6,185 applicants, 43% accepted, 1603 enrolled. In 2013, 1,256 master's, 117 doctorates, 470 other advanced degrees awarded. *Degree requirements:* For doctorate, comprehensive exam, thesis/dissertation. *Entrance requirements:* For master's, GRE General Test or MAT (if taken in or before 1999), 2 letters of recommendation, minimum undergraduate GPA of 3.0, curriculum vitae; for doctorate and Ed S, GRE General Test or MAT (if taken before 1999), minimum master's GPA of 3.0, 3 years of teaching experience. Additional exam requirements/recommendations for international students: Required—TOEFL (minimum score 600 paper-based; 100 iBT). *Application deadline:* For fall admission, 6/1 for domestic students; for spring admission, 11/1 for domestic students. Applications are processed on a rolling basis. Application fee: $50. Electronic applications accepted. *Expenses:* Contact institution. *Financial support:* Federal Work-Study and tuition waivers (partial) available. *Faculty research:* Self-determination, character education, bibliotherapy, learning styles, distance education. *Unit head:* Dr. Karen L. Parker, Dean, 434-582-2195, Fax: 434-582-2468, E-mail: kparker@liberty.edu. *Application contact:*

Jay Bridge, Director of Graduate Admissions, 800-424-9595, Fax: 800-628-7977, E-mail: gradadmissions@liberty.edu.
Website: http://www.liberty.edu/academics/education/graduate/.

New York University, School of Continuing and Professional Studies, The Preston Robert Tisch Center for Hospitality, Tourism, and Sports Management, Program in Tourism Management, New York, NY 10012-1019. Offers MS, Advanced Certificate. Part-time and evening/weekend programs available. *Faculty:* 2 full-time (both women), 5 part-time/adjunct (3 women). *Students:* 20 full-time (16 women), 19 part-time (15 women); includes 9 minority (4 Black or African American, non-Hispanic/Latino; 1 Asian, non-Hispanic/Latino; 4 Hispanic/Latino), 18 international. Average age 28. 31 applicants, 71% accepted, 16 enrolled. In 2013, 22 master's, 3 other advanced degrees awarded. *Degree requirements:* For master's, thesis. *Entrance requirements:* For master's, bachelor's degree, resume with relevant professional work, internship or volunteer experience, two letters of recommendation, statement of purpose. Additional exam requirements/recommendations for international students: Required—TOEFL (minimum score 600 paper-based; 100 iBT), IELTS (minimum score 7). *Application deadline:* For fall admission, 2/1 priority date for domestic and international students; for spring admission, 10/15 priority date for domestic students, 8/15 priority date for international students. Applications are processed on a rolling basis. Application fee: $150. Electronic applications accepted. *Expenses: Tuition:* Full-time $35,856; part-time $1494 per unit. *Required fees:* $1408; $64 per unit. $473 per term. Tuition and fees vary according to course load and program. *Financial support:* In 2013–14, 15 students received support, including 14 fellowships (averaging $2,727 per year); career-related internships or fieldwork, Federal Work-Study, and scholarships/grants also available. Financial award application deadline: 2/15; financial award applicants required to submit FAFSA. *Faculty research:* Tourism planning for national parks and protected areas, leadership and organizational behavior issues. *Unit head:* Bjorn Hanson, Division Dean and Clinical Professor, 212-998-7100. *Application contact:* Office of Admissions, 212-998-7100, E-mail: scps.gradadmissions@nyu.edu.
Website: http://www.scps.nyu.edu/academics/departments/tisch.html.

North Carolina State University, Graduate School, College of Natural Resources, Department of Parks, Recreation and Tourism Management, Raleigh, NC 27695. Offers natural resource management (MPRTM, MS); park and recreation management (MPRTM, MS); parks, recreation and tourism management (PhD); recreational sport management (MPRTM, MS); spatial information science (MPRTM, MS); tourism policy and development (MPRTM, MS). *Degree requirements:* For master's, thesis (for some programs); for doctorate, thesis/dissertation. *Entrance requirements:* For master's and doctorate, GRE General Test. Additional exam requirements/recommendations for international students: Required—TOEFL. Electronic applications accepted. *Faculty research:* Tourism policy and development, spatial information systems, natural resource management, recreational sports management, park and recreation management.

Penn State University Park, Graduate School, College of Health and Human Development, Department of Recreation, Park and Tourism Management, State College, PA 16802. Offers M Ed, MS, PhD. *Unit head:* Dr. Ann C. Crouter, Dean, 814-865-1420, Fax: 814-865-3282, E-mail: ac1@psu.edu. *Application contact:* Cynthia E. Nicosia, Director, Graduate Enrollment Services, 814-865-1834, Fax: 814-863-4627, E-mail: cey1@psu.edu.
Website: http://www.hhdev.psu.edu/rptm.

Pontificia Universidad Catolica Madre y Maestra, Graduate School, Faculty of Social and Administrative Sciences, Santiago, Dominican Republic. Offers business administration (MBA), including business development, finance, international business, management skills (M Mgmt, MBA), marketing, operations, strategic cost management, strategy, tourist destination planning and management; law (LL M), including civil law, corporate business law, criminal law, international relations, real estate law; management (M Mgmt), including higher financial management, insurance program administration, management skills (M Mgmt, MBA); psychology (MA), including clinical child and adolescent psychology, forensic psychology; strategic human resources (EMBA).

Purdue University, Graduate School, College of Health and Human Sciences, Department of Hospitality and Tourism Management, West Lafayette, IN 47907. Offers MS, PhD. *Faculty:* 15 full-time (5 women), 3 part-time/adjunct (1 woman). *Students:* 58 full-time (39 women), 28 part-time (21 women); includes 4 minority (3 Asian, non-Hispanic/Latino; 1 Hispanic/Latino), 71 international. Average age 27. 187 applicants, 24% accepted, 18 enrolled. In 2013, 17 master's, 8 doctorates awarded. *Degree requirements:* For master's, thesis; for doctorate, thesis/dissertation. *Entrance requirements:* For master's, GMAT (minimum score of 550) or GRE General Test (minimum combined verbal and quantitative score of 290 new scoring, minimum of 145 each section, or 1000 with 500 each section, old scoring), minimum GPA of 3.0; for doctorate, GMAT (minimum score of 550) or GRE General Test (minimum combined verbal and quantitative score of 290 new scoring, minimum of 145 each section, or 1000 with 500 each section, old scoring), minimum undergraduate GPA of 3.0; master's degree with minimum GPA of 3.0 or equivalent. Additional exam requirements/recommendations for international students: Required—TOEFL (minimum score 77 iBT), TWE. *Application deadline:* For fall admission, 3/5 priority date for domestic and international students; for spring admission, 9/20 for domestic and international students. Applications are processed on a rolling basis. Application fee: $60 ($75 for international students). Electronic applications accepted. *Financial support:* Research assistantships, teaching assistantships, and career-related internships or fieldwork available. Support available to part-time students. Financial award applicants required to submit FAFSA. *Faculty research:* Human resources, marketing, hotel and restaurant operations, food product and equipment development, tourism development. *Unit head:* Dr. Richard F. Ghiselli, Head, 765-494-2636, E-mail: ghiselli@purdue.edu. *Application contact:* Maria D. Campos, Graduate Contact, 765-494-9811, E-mail: camposm@purdue.edu.
Website: http://www.purdue.edu/hhs/htm/.

Rochester Institute of Technology, Graduate Enrollment Services, College of Applied Science and Technology, School of International Hospitality and Service Innovation, Department of Hospitality and Service Management, Program in Hospitality and Tourism Management, Rochester, NY 14623-5603. Offers MS. Part-time programs available. *Students:* 18 full-time (10 women), 10 part-time (4 women), 21 international. Average age 25. 44 applicants, 64% accepted, 8 enrolled. In 2013, 5 master's awarded. *Degree requirements:* For master's, thesis or project. *Entrance requirements:* For master's, minimum GPA of 3.0. Additional exam requirements/recommendations for international students: Required—TOEFL (minimum score 550 paper-based; 79 iBT) or IELTS (minimum score 6.5). *Application deadline:* For fall admission, 2/15 priority date for domestic and international students; for winter admission, 11/1 for domestic students, 10/1 for international students; for spring admission, 2/1 priority date for domestic students, 1/1 priority date for international students. Applications are processed on a rolling basis. Application fee: $60. Electronic applications accepted. *Expenses: Tuition:* Full-time $37,236; part-time $1552 per credit hour. *Required fees:* $250. *Financial support:* Research assistantships with partial tuition reimbursements, teaching assistantships with partial tuition reimbursements, career-related internships or fieldwork, scholarships/grants, and unspecified assistantships available. Support available to part-time students. Financial award application deadline: 2/15; financial award applicants required to submit FAFSA. *Unit head:* Dr. Carol Whitlock, E-mail: cbwism@rit.edu. *Application contact:* Diane Ellison, Assistant Vice President, Graduate Enrollment Services, 585-475-2229, Fax: 585-475-7164, E-mail: gradinfo@rit.edu.
Website: http://www.rit.edu/cast/htm/graduate/.

Rochester Institute of Technology, Graduate Enrollment Services, College of Applied Science and Technology, School of International Hospitality and Service Innovation, Department of Service Systems, Program in Service Leadership and Innovation, Rochester, NY 14623-5603. Offers MS. Part-time and evening/weekend programs available. Postbaccalaureate distance learning degree programs offered (no on-campus study). *Students:* 24 full-time (12 women), 26 part-time (13 women); includes 3 minority (2 Black or African American, non-Hispanic/Latino; 1 Hispanic/Latino), 3 international. Average age 31. 90 applicants, 37% accepted, 22 enrolled. In 2013, 35 master's awarded. *Degree requirements:* For master's, thesis or alternative. *Entrance requirements:* For master's, minimum GPA of 3.0. Additional exam requirements/recommendations for international students: Required—TOEFL (minimum score 550 paper-based; 79 iBT) or IELTS (minimum score 6.5). *Application deadline:* For fall admission, 2/15 priority date for domestic and international students; for winter admission, 11/1 for domestic and international students; for spring admission, 2/1 for domestic and international students. Applications are processed on a rolling basis. Application fee: $60. Electronic applications accepted. *Expenses: Tuition:* Full-time $37,236; part-time $1552 per credit hour. *Required fees:* $250. *Financial support:* Research assistantships with partial tuition reimbursements, teaching assistantships with partial tuition reimbursements, career-related internships or fieldwork, institutionally sponsored loans, scholarships/grants, and unspecified assistantships available. Support available to part-time students. Financial award application deadline: 2/15; financial award applicants required to submit FAFSA. *Faculty research:* Global resource development, service/product innovation and implementation. *Unit head:* Dr. Linda Underhill, Department Chair, 585-475-7359, E-mail: lmuism@rit.edu. *Application contact:* Diane Ellison, Assistant Vice President, Graduate Enrollment Services, 585-475-2229, Fax: 585-475-7164, E-mail: gradinfo@rit.edu.
Website: http://www.rit.edu/cast/servicesystems/service-leadership-and-innovation.php.

Royal Roads University, Graduate Studies, Tourism and Hotel Management Program, Victoria, BC V9B 5Y2, Canada. Offers destination development (Graduate Certificate); international hotel management (MA); sustainable tourism (Graduate Certificate); tourism leadership (Graduate Certificate); tourism management (MA).

San Francisco State University, Division of Graduate Studies, College of Health and Social Sciences, Department of Recreation, Parks, and Tourism, San Francisco, CA 94132-1722. Offers MS. Part-time programs available. *Application deadline:* Applications are processed on a rolling basis. *Financial support:* Career-related internships or fieldwork available. *Unit head:* Dr. Patrick Tierney, Chair, 415-338-2030, E-mail: ptierney@sfsu.edu. *Application contact:* Prof. Jackson Wilson, Graduate Coordinator, 415-338-1487, E-mail: wilsonj@sfsu.edu.
Website: http://recdept.sfsu.edu/.

Savannah College of Art and Design, Graduate School, Program in Themed Entertainment Design, Savannah, GA 31402-3146. Offers MFA. Part-time programs available. *Students:* 20 full-time (13 women); includes 2 minority (1 Black or African American, non-Hispanic/Latino; 1 Hispanic/Latino), 8 international. Average age 26. 24 applicants, 46% accepted, 10 enrolled. *Degree requirements:* For master's, thesis. *Entrance requirements:* For master's, portfolio. Additional exam requirements/recommendations for international students: Required—TOEFL (minimum score 550 paper-based, 85 iBT), IELTS (minimum score 6.5), or ACTFL. *Application deadline:* Applications are processed on a rolling basis. Application fee: $35. Electronic applications accepted. *Expenses: Tuition:* Full-time $33,750; part-time $3750 per course. One-time fee: $500. Tuition and fees vary according to course load. *Financial support:* Fellowships, career-related internships or fieldwork, Federal Work-Study, and scholarships/grants available. Financial award applicants required to submit FAFSA. *Unit head:* Gregory Beck, Dean of the School of Entertainment Arts. *Application contact:* Jenny Jaquillard, Executive Director of Admissions, Recruitment and Events, 912-525-5100, Fax: 912-525-5985, E-mail: admission@scad.edu.
Website: http://www.scad.edu/academics/programs/themed-entertainment-design.

Schiller International University, MBA Programs, Florida, Program in International Hotel and Tourism Management, Largo, FL 33771. Offers MBA. *Degree requirements:* For master's, thesis optional. *Entrance requirements:* Additional exam requirements/recommendations for international students: Required—TOEFL (minimum score 550 paper-based).

Strayer University, Graduate Studies, Washington, DC 20005-2603. Offers accounting (MS); acquisition (MBA); business administration (MBA); communications technology (MS); educational management (M Ed); finance (MBA); health services administration (MHSA); hospitality and tourism management (MBA); human resource management (MBA); information systems (MS), including computer security management, decision support system management, enterprise resource management, network management, software engineering management, systems development management; management (MBA); management information systems (MS); marketing (MBA); professional accounting (MS), including accounting information systems, controllership, taxation; public administration (MPA); supply chain management (MBA); technology in education (M Ed). Programs also offered at campus locations in Birmingham, AL; Chamblee, GA; Cobb County, GA; Morrow, GA; White Marsh, MD; Charleston, SC; Columbia, SC; Greensboro, NC; Greenville, SC; Lexington, KY; Louisville, KY; Nashville, TN; North Raleigh, NC; Washington, DC. Part-time and evening/weekend programs available. Postbaccalaureate distance learning degree programs offered (minimal on-campus study). *Degree requirements:* For master's, thesis. *Entrance requirements:* For master's, GMAT, GRE General Test, bachelor's degree from an accredited college or university, minimum undergraduate GPA of 2.75. Electronic applications accepted.

Syracuse University, Falk College of Sport and Human Dynamics, Program in Sport Venue and Event Management, Syracuse, NY 13244. Offers MS. *Students:* 17 full-time (10 women), 4 part-time (3 women); includes 4 minority (2 Black or African American, non-Hispanic/Latino; 1 Asian, non-Hispanic/Latino; 1 Two or more races, non-Hispanic/Latino), 6 international. Average age 25. 38 applicants, 47% accepted, 12 enrolled. *Entrance requirements:* For master's, GRE, undergraduate transcripts, three recommendations, resume, personal statement. Additional exam requirements/recommendations for international students: Required—TOEFL (minimum score 100 iBT). *Application deadline:* For fall admission, 3/15 for domestic students; for summer admission, 3/15 priority date for domestic and international students. Application fee: $75. Electronic applications accepted. *Financial support:* Application deadline: 1/1; applicants required to submit FAFSA. *Unit head:* Chad McEvoy, Graduate Program Director, 315-443-2630, Fax: 315-443-2562, E-mail: falk@syr.edu. *Application contact:* Felicia Otero, Director of Admissions, 315-443-5555, Fax: 315-443-1018, E-mail: falk@syr.edu.
Website: http://falk.syr.edu/SportManagement/Default.aspx.

Travel and Tourism

Temple University, School of Tourism and Hospitality Management, Program in Tourism and Hospitality Management, Philadelphia, PA 19122-6096. Offers hospitality operations (MTHM); tourism and hospitality marketing (MTHM). Part-time and evening/weekend programs available. *Faculty:* 10 full-time (3 women), 3 part-time/adjunct (0 women). *Students:* 23 full-time (21 women), 4 part-time (2 women); includes 2 minority (1 Asian, non-Hispanic/Latino; 1 Two or more races, non-Hispanic/Latino), 22 international. 57 applicants, 58% accepted, 8 enrolled. In 2013, 11 master's awarded. *Degree requirements:* For master's, thesis optional, internship or project. *Entrance requirements:* For master's, GRE General Test, GMAT, or MAT, bachelor's degree or equivalent with minimum GPA of 3.0, 500-word essay, 2 letters of recommendation, resume. Additional exam requirements/recommendations for international students: Required—TOEFL (minimum score 550 paper-based; 79 iBT), IELTS (minimum score 6.5). *Application deadline:* For fall admission, 3/1 priority date for domestic students, 1/15 priority date for international students; for spring admission, 8/15 priority date for domestic students, 6/30 priority date for international students. Applications are processed on a rolling basis. Application fee: $60. Electronic applications accepted. *Expenses:* Contact institution. *Financial support:* In 2013–14, 1 research assistantship with full tuition reimbursement (averaging $18,000 per year) was awarded. Financial award application deadline: 3/1; financial award applicants required to submit FAFSA. *Faculty research:* Consumer behavior, revenue management, tourism marketing, advertising evaluation and information technology, brand management, service management, customer relationship management, emotional labor and emotional intelligence, employee knowledge sharing, event management, destination marketing evaluation. *Unit head:* Dr. Ceridwyn King, Assistant Professor/Director of Programs in Tourism and Hospitality Management, 215-204-8701, Fax: 215-204-8705, E-mail: ceridwyn.king@temple.edu. *Application contact:* Michael J. Usino, Senior Associate Director of Recruitment, 215-204-3103, Fax: 215-204-8705, E-mail: musino@temple.edu.
Website: http://sthm.temple.edu/cms/main/graduate-programs/.

Tropical Agriculture Research and Higher Education Center, Graduate School, Turrialba, Costa Rica. Offers agribusiness management (MS); agroforestry systems (PhD); development practices (MS); ecological agriculture (MS); environmental socioeconomics (MS); forestry in tropical and subtropical zones (PhD); integrated watershed management (MS); international sustainable tourism (MS); management and conservation of tropical rainforests and biodiversity (MS); tropical agriculture (PhD); tropical agroforestry (MS). *Entrance requirements:* For master's, GRE, 2 years of related professional experience, letters of recommendation; for doctorate, GRE, 4 letters of recommendation, letter of support from employing organization, master's degree in agronomy, biological sciences, forestry, natural resources or related field. Additional exam requirements/recommendations for international students: Required—TOEFL (minimum score 550 paper-based). Electronic applications accepted. *Faculty research:* Biodiversity in fragmented landscapes, ecosystem management, integrated pest management, environmental livestock production, biotechnology carbon balances in diverse land uses.

Université du Québec à Trois-Rivières, Graduate Programs, Program in Leisure, Culture and Tourism Sciences, Trois-Rivières, QC G9A 5H7, Canada. Offers MA, DESS. Part-time programs available. *Degree requirements:* For master's, thesis optional. *Entrance requirements:* For master's, appropriate bachelor's degree, proficiency in French.

University of Central Florida, Rosen College of Hospitality Management, Orlando, FL 32816. Offers hospitality and tourism management (MS); hospitality management (PhD, Certificate). *Faculty:* 47 full-time (18 women), 24 part-time/adjunct (8 women). *Students:* 52 full-time (33 women), 30 part-time (21 women); includes 14 minority (4 Black or African American, non-Hispanic/Latino; 5 Asian, non-Hispanic/Latino; 3 Hispanic/Latino; 2 Two or more races, non-Hispanic/Latino), 11 international. Average age 29. 83 applicants, 41% accepted, 18 enrolled. In 2013, 43 master's, 23 other advanced degrees awarded. *Degree requirements:* For master's, thesis or alternative. *Entrance requirements:* For master's, GMAT or GRE, minimum GPA of 3.0 in last 60 hours. Additional exam requirements/recommendations for international students: Required—TOEFL. *Application deadline:* For fall admission, 2/1 for domestic students. Application fee: $30. Electronic applications accepted. *Financial support:* In 2013–14, 11 students received support, including 3 fellowships with partial tuition reimbursements available (averaging $1,900 per year), 2 research assistantships with partial tuition reimbursements available (averaging $7,700 per year), 10 teaching assistantships with partial tuition reimbursements available (averaging $9,600 per year). *Unit head:* Dr. Abraham C. Pizam, Dean, 407-903-8010, E-mail: abraham.pizam@ucf.edu. *Application contact:* Barbara Rodriguez Lamas, Director, Admissions and Student Services, 407-823-2766, Fax: 407-823-6442, E-mail: gradadmissions@ucf.edu.
Website: http://www.hospitality.ucf.edu/.

University of Florida, Graduate School, College of Health and Human Performance, Department of Tourism, Recreation and Sport Management, Gainesville, FL 32611. Offers health and human performance (PhD), including recreation, parks and tourism (MS, PhD), sport management; recreation, parks and tourism (MS), including natural resource recreation, recreation, parks and tourism (MS, PhD), therapeutic recreation, tourism; sport management (MS); JD/MS; MSM/MS. *Faculty:* 7 full-time (5 women). *Students:* 64 full-time (27 women), 13 part-time (4 women); includes 11 minority (7 Black or African American, non-Hispanic/Latino; 1 Asian, non-Hispanic/Latino; 3 Hispanic/Latino), 27 international. Average age 27. 15 applicants, 40% accepted, 1 enrolled. In 2013, 51 master's, 4 doctorates awarded. *Degree requirements:* For master's, comprehensive exam (for some programs), thesis (for some programs); for doctorate, comprehensive exam, thesis/dissertation. *Entrance requirements:* For master's and doctorate, GRE General Test, minimum GPA of 3.0. Additional exam requirements/recommendations for international students: Required—TOEFL (minimum score 550 paper-based; 80 iBT), IELTS (minimum score 6). *Application deadline:* For fall admission, 3/1 for domestic students, 12/1 for international students; for spring admission, 10/15 for domestic students, 5/1 for international students. Applications are processed on a rolling basis. Application fee: $30. Electronic applications accepted. *Expenses:* Tuition, state resident: full-time $12,640. Tuition, nonresident: full-time $30,000. *Financial support:* In 2013–14, 27 students received support, including 10 research assistantships (averaging $15,850 per year), 20 teaching assistantships (averaging $11,840 per year); career-related internships or fieldwork, Federal Work-Study, and unspecified assistantships also available. Financial award application deadline: 2/1; financial award applicants required to submit FAFSA. *Faculty research:* Hospitality, natural resource management, sport management, tourism. *Unit head:* Michael Sagas, PhD, Department Chair and Professor, 352-294-1640, Fax: 352-392-7588, E-mail: msagas@hhp.ufl.edu. *Application contact:* Stephen M. Holland, PhD, Professor/Graduate Coordinator, 352-294-1669, Fax: 352-392-7588, E-mail: sholland@hhp.ufl.edu.
Website: http://www.hhp.ufl.edu/trsm/.

University of Hawaii at Manoa, Graduate Division, School of Travel Industry Management, Honolulu, HI 96822. Offers MS. Part-time programs available. *Degree requirements:* For master's, thesis optional. *Entrance requirements:* For master's, GRE General Test, minimum GPA of 3.0. Additional exam requirements/recommendations for international students: Required—TOEFL (minimum score 560 paper-based; 83 iBT), IELTS (minimum score 5). Electronic applications accepted. *Faculty research:* Travel information technology, tourism development and policy, transportation management and policy, hospitality management, sustainable tourism development.

University of Massachusetts Amherst, Graduate School, Isenberg School of Management, Program in Management, Amherst, MA 01003. Offers accounting (PhD); business administration (MBA); entrepreneurship (MBA); finance (MBA, PhD); healthcare administration (MBA); hospitality and tourism management (PhD); management science (PhD); marketing (MBA, PhD); organization studies (PhD); sport management (PhD); strategic management (PhD); MBA/MS. *Accreditation:* AACSB. Part-time and evening/weekend programs available. Postbaccalaureate distance learning degree programs offered. *Faculty:* 68 full-time (14 women). *Students:* 140 full-time (59 women), 1,127 part-time (319 women); includes 229 minority (24 Black or African American, non-Hispanic/Latino; 2 American Indian or Alaska Native, non-Hispanic/Latino; 135 Asian, non-Hispanic/Latino; 51 Hispanic/Latino; 6 Native Hawaiian or other Pacific Islander, non-Hispanic/Latino; 11 Two or more races, non-Hispanic/Latino), 131 international. Average age 36. 828 applicants, 56% accepted, 351 enrolled. In 2013, 361 master's, 12 doctorates awarded. Terminal master's awarded for partial completion of doctoral program. *Degree requirements:* For doctorate, comprehensive exam, thesis/dissertation. *Entrance requirements:* For master's and doctorate, GMAT or GRE General Test. Additional exam requirements/recommendations for international students: Required—TOEFL (minimum score 550 paper-based; 80 iBT), IELTS (minimum score 6.5). *Application deadline:* For fall admission, 1/20 for domestic and international students. Applications are processed on a rolling basis. Application fee: $75. Electronic applications accepted. *Financial support:* Fellowships with full and partial tuition reimbursements, research assistantships with full and partial tuition reimbursements, teaching assistantships with full and partial tuition reimbursements, career-related internships or fieldwork, Federal Work-Study, scholarships/grants, traineeships, health care benefits, tuition waivers (full and partial), and unspecified assistantships available. Support available to part-time students. Financial award application deadline: 1/20; financial award applicants required to submit FAFSA. *Unit head:* Dr. John Wells, Chair, 413-545-7609, Fax: 413-577-2234. *Application contact:* Lindsay DeSantis, Supervisor of Admissions, 413-545-0722, Fax: 413-577-0010, E-mail: gradadm@grad.umass.edu.
Website: http://www.isenberg.umass.edu/.

University of Minnesota, Twin Cities Campus, Graduate School, College of Food, Agricultural and Natural Resource Sciences, Program in Natural Resources Science and Management, St. Paul, MN 55108. Offers assessment, monitoring, and geospatial analysis (MS, PhD); economics, policy, management, and society (MS, PhD); forest hydrology and watershed management (MS, PhD); forest products (MS, PhD); forests: biology, ecology, conservation, and management (MS, PhD); natural resources science and management (MS, PhD); paper science and engineering (MS, PhD); recreation resources, tourism, and environmental education (MS, PhD); wildlife ecology and management (MS, PhD). Part-time programs available. *Faculty:* 65 full-time, 55 part-time/adjunct. *Students:* 73 full-time (38 women), 38 part-time (12 women); includes 16 minority (3 Black or African American, non-Hispanic/Latino; 1 American Indian or Alaska Native, non-Hispanic/Latino; 9 Asian, non-Hispanic/Latino; 3 Hispanic/Latino), 10 international. 90 applicants, 44% accepted, 26 enrolled. In 2013, 17 master's, 5 doctorates awarded. Terminal master's awarded for partial completion of doctoral program. *Degree requirements:* For master's, comprehensive exam, thesis; for doctorate, comprehensive exam, thesis/dissertation. *Entrance requirements:* For master's and doctorate, GRE General Test. Additional exam requirements/recommendations for international students: Required—TOEFL (minimum score 550 paper-based; 79 iBT), IELTS (minimum score 6.5). *Application deadline:* For fall admission, 12/16 priority date for domestic and international students; for spring admission, 10/15 for domestic and international students. Applications are processed on a rolling basis. Application fee: $75 ($95 for international students). Electronic applications accepted. *Financial support:* In 2013–14, fellowships with full tuition reimbursements (averaging $40,000 per year), research assistantships with full tuition reimbursements (averaging $40,000 per year), teaching assistantships with full tuition reimbursements (averaging $40,000 per year) were awarded; scholarships/grants, health care benefits, tuition waivers (full and partial), and unspecified assistantships also available. *Faculty research:* Paper science, forestry, recreation resource management, wildlife ecology, environmental education, hydrology, conservation, tourism, economics, policy, watershed management, GIS, forest products. *Unit head:* Dr. Michael Kilgore, Director of Graduate Studies, 612-624-6298, E-mail: mkilgore@umn.edu. *Application contact:* Jennifer Welsh, Program Coordinator, 612-624-7683, Fax: 612-625-5212, E-mail: jwelsh@umn.edu.
Website: http://www.nrsm.umn.edu.

University of New Orleans, Graduate School, College of Business Administration, School of Hotel, Restaurant, and Tourism Administration, Program in Hospitality and Tourism Management, New Orleans, LA 70148. Offers MS. *Entrance requirements:* Additional exam requirements/recommendations for international students: Required—TOEFL (minimum score 550 paper-based; 79 iBT).

University of North Texas, Robert B. Toulouse School of Graduate Studies, Denton, TN 76203-5017. Offers accounting (MS, PhD); applied anthropology (MA, MS); applied behavior analysis (Certificate); applied technology and performance improvement (M Ed, MS, PhD); art education (MA, PhD); art history (MA); art museum education (Certificate); arts leadership (Certificate); audiology (Au D); behavior analysis (MS); biochemistry and molecular biology (MS, PhD); biology (MA, MS, PhD); business (PhD); business computer information systems (PhD); chemistry (MS, PhD); clinical psychology (PhD); communication studies (MA, MS); computer engineering (MS); computer science (MS); computer science and engineering (PhD); counseling (M Ed, MS, PhD), including clinical mental health counseling (MS), college and university counseling (M Ed, MS), elementary school counseling (M Ed, MS), secondary school counseling (M Ed, MS); counseling psychology (PhD); creative writing (MA); criminal justice (MS); curriculum and instruction (M Ed, PhD), including curriculum studies (PhD), early childhood studies (PhD), language and literacy studies (PhD); decision sciences (MBA); design (MA, MFA), including fashion design (MFA), innovation studies, interior design (MFA); early childhood studies (MS); economics (MS); educational leadership (M Ed, Ed D, PhD); educational psychology (MS), including family studies, gifted and talented (MS, PhD), human development, learning and cognition, research, measurement and evaluation; educational research (PhD), including gifted and talented (MS, PhD), human development and family studies, psychological aspects of sports and exercise, research, measurement and statistics; electrical engineering (MS); emergency management (MPA); engineering systems (MS); English (MA, PhD); environmental science (MS, PhD); experimental psychology (PhD); finance (MBA, MS, PhD); financial management (MPA); French (MA); health psychology and behavioral medicine (PhD); health services management (MBA); higher education (M Ed, Ed D, PhD); history (MA, MS, PhD), including European history (PhD), military history (PhD), United States history (PhD); hospitality management (MS); human resources management (MPA); information science (MS, PhD); information technologies (MBA); information technology and decision sciences (MS); interdisciplinary studies (MA, MS); international sustainable tourism (MS); jazz studies (MM); journalism (MA, MJ, Graduate Certificate), including

interactive and virtual digital communication (Graduate Certificate), narrative journalism (Graduate Certificate), public relations (Graduate Certificate); kinesiology (MS); learning technologies (MS, PhD); library science (MS); local government management (MPA); logistics and supply chain management (MBA, PhD); long-term care, senior housing, and aging services (MA, MS); management science (PhD); marketing (MBA, PhD); materials science and engineering (MS, PhD); mathematics (MA, PhD); merchandising (MS); music (MA, MM Ed, PhD), including ethnomusicology (MA), music education (MM Ed, PhD), music theory (MA, PhD), musicology (MA, PhD), performance (MA); nonprofit management (MPA); operations and supply chain management (MBA); performance (MM, DMA); philosophy (MA, PhD); physics (MS, PhD); political science (MA, MS, PhD); public administration and management (PhD), including emergency management, nonprofit management, public financial management, urban management; radio, television and film (MA, MFA); recreation, event and sport management (MS); rehabilitation counseling (MS, Certificate); sociology (MA, MS, PhD); Spanish (MA); special education (M Ed, PhD), including autism intervention (PhD), emotional/behavioral disorders (PhD), mild/moderate disabilities (PhD); speech-language pathology (MA, MS); strategic management (MBA); studio art (MFA); taxation (MS); teaching (M Ed); MBA/MS; MS/MPH; MSES/MBA. Part-time and evening/weekend programs available. Postbaccalaureate distance learning degree programs offered. *Faculty:* 661 full-time (213 women), 240 part-time/adjunct (144 women). *Students:* 3,106 full-time (1,620 women), 3,543 part-time (2,221 women); includes 1,740 minority (533 Black or African American, non-Hispanic/Latino; 15 American Indian or Alaska Native, non-Hispanic/Latino; 286 Asian, non-Hispanic/Latino; 746 Hispanic/Latino; 3 Native Hawaiian or other Pacific Islander, non-Hispanic/Latino; 157 Two or more races, non-Hispanic/Latino), 1,145 international. Average age 32. 6,289 applicants, 43% accepted, 1751 enrolled. In 2013, 1,778 master's, 239 doctorates, 10 other advanced degrees awarded. Terminal master's awarded for partial completion of doctoral program. *Degree requirements:* For master's, variable foreign language requirement, comprehensive exam (for some programs), thesis (for some programs); for doctorate, variable foreign language requirement, comprehensive exam (for some programs), thesis/dissertation; for other advanced degree, variable foreign language requirement, comprehensive exam (for some programs). *Entrance requirements:* For master's and doctorate, GRE, GMAT. Additional exam requirements/recommendations for international students: Required—TOEFL (minimum score 550 paper-based; 79 iBT). *Application deadline:* For fall admission, 7/15 for domestic students, 3/15 for international students; for spring admission, 11/15 for domestic students, 9/15 for international students; for summer admission, 5/1 for domestic students. Applications are processed on a rolling basis. Application fee: $60. Electronic applications accepted. *Financial support:* Fellowships with partial tuition reimbursements, research assistantships with partial tuition reimbursements, teaching assistantships, career-related internships or fieldwork, Federal Work-Study, institutionally sponsored loans, scholarships/grants, health care benefits, and library assistantships available. Support available to part-time students. Financial award applicants required to submit FAFSA. *Unit head:* Mark Wardell, Dean, 940-565-2383, E-mail: mark.wardell@unt.edu. *Application contact:* Toulouse School of Graduate Studies, 940-565-2383, Fax: 940-565-2141, E-mail: gradsch@unt.edu.
Website: http://tsgs.unt.edu/.

University of South Africa, College of Economic and Management Sciences, Pretoria, South Africa. Offers accounting (D Admin, D Com); accounting science (DA); auditing (D Admin, D Com); business administration (M Tech); business economics (D Admin); business leadership (DBL); business management (D Admin, D Com); economic management analysis (M Tech); economics (D Admin, D Com, PhD); human resource development (M Tech); industrial psychology (D Admin, D Com, PhD); logistics (D Com); marketing (M Tech); public administration (D Admin, D Com, DPA, PhD); public management (M Tech); quantitative management (D Admin, D Com); real estate (M Tech); statistics (D Admin, PhD); tourism management (D Admin, D Com); transport economics (D Admin, D Com).

University of South Carolina, The Graduate School, College of Hospitality, Retail, and Sport Management, School of Hotel, Restaurant and Tourism Management, Columbia, SC 29208. Offers MIHTM. *Entrance requirements:* For master's, GMAT or GRE General Test, minimum GPA of 3.0, 2 letters of recommendation. Electronic applications accepted. *Faculty research:* Corporate strategy and management practices, sustainable tourism, club management, tourism technology, revenue management.

University of South Florida, College of Global Sustainability, Tampa, FL 33620-9951. Offers entrepreneurship (MA); sustainable energy (MA); sustainable tourism (MA); water (MA); MA/MS. *Faculty:* 7 full-time (2 women), 1 (woman) part-time/adjunct. *Students:* 39 full-time (27 women), 26 part-time (15 women); includes 15 minority (3 Black or African American, non-Hispanic/Latino; 1 American Indian or Alaska Native, non-Hispanic/Latino; 8 Hispanic/Latino; 3 Two or more races, non-Hispanic/Latino), 13 international. Average age 39. 58 applicants, 59% accepted, 8 enrolled. In 2013, 10 master's awarded. *Degree requirements:* For master's, comprehensive exam (for some programs), thesis or alternative, internship. *Entrance requirements:* For master's, minimum GPA of 3.0 in undergraduate coursework; at least two letters of recommendation (one must be academic); 200-250-word essay on student's background, professional goals, and reasons for seeking degree. Additional exam requirements/recommendations for international students: Required—TOEFL (minimum score 550 paper-based; 79 iBT). *Faculty research:* Global sustainability, integrated resource management, systems thinking, green communities, entrepreneurship, ecotourism. *Total annual research expenditures:* $564,596. *Unit head:* Dr. Kalanithy Vairavamoorthy, Dean, 813-974-9694, E-mail: vairavk@grad.usf.edu. *Application contact:* Dr. Carl Herndl, Associate Dean, 813-974-5397, E-mail: cgh@usf.edu.
Website: http://psgs.usf.edu/.

The University of Tennessee, Graduate School, College of Education, Health and Human Sciences, Department of Consumer and Industry Services Management, Program in Hotel, Restaurant, and Tourism Management, Knoxville, TN 37996. Offers hospitality management (MS); tourism (MS). Part-time programs available. *Degree requirements:* For master's, thesis or alternative. *Entrance requirements:* For master's, GRE General Test, minimum GPA of 2.7. Additional exam requirements/recommendations for international students: Required—TOEFL. Electronic applications accepted. *Expenses:* Tuition, state resident: full-time $9540; part-time $531 per credit hour. Tuition, nonresident: full-time $27,728; part-time $1542 per credit hour. *Required fees:* $1404; $67 per credit hour.

University of Waterloo, Graduate Studies, Faculty of Environment, Program in Tourism Policy and Planning, Waterloo, ON N2L 3G1, Canada. Offers MAES. Part-time programs available. *Degree requirements:* For master's, research paper. *Entrance requirements:* For master's, honors degree in related field, minimum B average. Additional exam requirements/recommendations for international students: Required—TOEFL, TWE. Electronic applications accepted. *Faculty research:* Urban and regional economics, regional economic development, strategic planning, environmental economics, economic geography.

Virginia Polytechnic Institute and State University, Graduate School, Pamplin College of Business, Blacksburg, VA 24061. Offers accounting and information systems (MACIS); business (PhD); business administration (MBA, MS); hospitality and tourism management (MS, PhD). *Faculty:* 118 full-time (35 women), 1 part-time/adjunct (0 women). *Students:* 333 full-time (149 women), 129 part-time (47 women); includes 75 minority (14 Black or African American, non-Hispanic/Latino; 42 Asian, non-Hispanic/Latino; 12 Hispanic/Latino; 7 Two or more races, non-Hispanic/Latino), 115 international. Average age 30. 520 applicants, 38% accepted, 157 enrolled. In 2013, 199 master's, 12 doctorates awarded. *Degree requirements:* For master's, comprehensive exam (for some programs), thesis (for some programs); for doctorate, comprehensive exam (for some programs), thesis/dissertation (for some programs). *Entrance requirements:* For master's and doctorate, GRE/GMAT (may vary by department). Additional exam requirements/recommendations for international students: Required—TOEFL (minimum score 550 paper-based). *Application deadline:* For fall admission, 8/1 for domestic students, 4/1 for international students; for spring admission, 1/1 for domestic students, 9/1 for international students. Applications are processed on a rolling basis. Application fee: $75. Electronic applications accepted. *Expenses:* Tuition, state resident: full-time $11,185; part-time $621.50 per credit hour. Tuition, nonresident: full-time $22,146; part-time $1230.25 per credit hour. *Required fees:* $2442; $449.25 per semester. Tuition and fees vary according to course load, campus/location and program. *Financial support:* In 2013–14, 5 fellowships with full tuition reimbursements (averaging $19,435 per year), 61 teaching assistantships with full tuition reimbursements (averaging $15,805 per year) were awarded. Financial award application deadline: 3/1; financial award applicants required to submit FAFSA. *Total annual research expenditures:* $2.5 million. *Unit head:* Dr. Robert T. Sumichrast, Dean, 540-231-6601, Fax: 540-231-4487, E-mail: busdean@vt.edu. *Application contact:* Martha Hilton, Executive Assistant to the Dean, 540-231-9647, Fax: 540-231-4487, E-mail: cartermc@vt.edu.
Website: http://www.pamplin.vt.edu/.

Washington State University, Graduate School, College of Business, PhD Program in Hospitality and Tourism, Pullman, WA 99164. Offers PhD. *Entrance requirements:* For doctorate, GMAT (minimum recommended score of 600), master's degree (MS or MA in a related discipline or an MBA); minimum GPA of 3.25; letters of recommendation; work experience. Additional exam requirements/recommendations for international students: Required—TOEFL (minimum score 580 paper-based).

Western Illinois University, School of Graduate Studies, College of Education and Human Services, Department of Recreation, Park, and Tourism Administration, Macomb, IL 61455-1390. Offers MS. Part-time programs available. *Students:* 22 full-time (10 women), 11 part-time (5 women); includes 3 minority (1 Black or African American, non-Hispanic/Latino; 1 Asian, non-Hispanic/Latino; 1 Hispanic/Latino), 4 international. Average age 31. In 2013, 24 master's awarded. *Degree requirements:* For master's, thesis or alternative. *Entrance requirements:* Additional exam requirements/recommendations for international students: Required—TOEFL (minimum score 550 paper-based; 80 iBT). *Application deadline:* Applications are processed on a rolling basis. Application fee: $30. Electronic applications accepted. *Financial support:* In 2013–14, 17 students received support, including 15 research assistantships with full tuition reimbursements available (averaging $7,544 per year), 2 teaching assistantships with tuition reimbursements available (averaging $8,688 per year). Financial award applicants required to submit FAFSA. *Unit head:* Dr. Dan Yoder, Interim Chairperson, 309-298-1967. *Application contact:* Dr. Nancy Parsons, Assistant Director of Graduate Studies, 309-298-1806, Fax: 309-298-2345, E-mail: grad-office@wiu.edu.
Website: http://www.wiu.edu/rpta.

Section 8
Human Resources

This section contains a directory of institutions offering graduate work in human resources. Additional information about programs listed in the directory but not augmented by an in-depth entry may be obtained by writing directly to the dean of a graduate school or chair of a department at the address given in the directory.

For programs offering related work, see also in this book *Business Administration and Management, Advertising and Public Relations, Hospitality Management, Industrial and Manufacturing Management,* and *Organizational Behavior.* In another guide in this series:

Graduate Programs in the Humanities, Arts & Social Sciences
See *Public, Regional, and Industrial Affairs (Industrial and Labor Relations)*

CONTENTS

Program Directories

Human Resources Development 356
Human Resources Management 362

Displays and Close-Ups

See:

Adelphi University—Business Administration and
    Management 70, 181
University of California, Los Angeles—Business
    Administration and Management 145, 191

Human Resources Development

Abilene Christian University, Graduate School, College of Arts and Sciences, Department of Communication, Program in Organizational Development, Abilene, TX 79699-9100. Offers MS. Part-time and evening/weekend programs available. Postbaccalaureate distance learning degree programs offered (no on-campus study). *Students:* 91 full-time (61 women), 25 part-time (20 women); includes 37 minority (21 Black or African American, non-Hispanic/Latino; 2 American Indian or Alaska Native, non-Hispanic/Latino; 4 Asian, non-Hispanic/Latino; 8 Hispanic/Latino; 2 Two or more races, non-Hispanic/Latino), 1 international. 48 applicants, 94% accepted, 45 enrolled. In 2013, 34 master's awarded. *Degree requirements:* For master's, thesis. *Entrance requirements:* Additional exam requirements/recommendations for international students: Required—TOEFL (minimum score 550 paper-based; 90 iBT), IELTS (minimum score 6.5), PTE. *Application deadline:* For fall admission, 8/15 priority date for domestic students; for winter admission, 10/1 priority date for domestic students; for spring admission, 12/15 priority date for domestic students; for summer admission, 4/5 priority date for domestic students. Applications are processed on a rolling basis. Application fee: $100. Electronic applications accepted. *Expenses:* Contact institution. *Financial support:* In 2013–14, 5 students received support. Available to part-time students. Application deadline: 4/1; applicants required to submit FAFSA. *Unit head:* Dr. Jonathan Camp, Graduate Director, 325-674-2136, E-mail: jwc03b@acu.edu. *Application contact:* Corey Patterson, Director of Graduate Admission and Recruiting, 325-674-6566, Fax: 325-674-6717, E-mail: gradinfo@acu.edu.
Website: http://acuonline.acu.edu/.

Adler Graduate School, Program in Adlerian Counseling and Psychotherapy, Richfield, MN 55423. Offers art therapy (MA); career development (MA); clinical counseling (MA); co-occurring disorders (MA); marriage and family therapy (MA); non-licensing Adlerian studies (MA); online Adlerian studies (MA); school counseling (MA). Part-time and evening/weekend programs available. *Faculty:* 10 full-time (5 women), 47 part-time/adjunct (33 women). *Students:* 380 part-time (300 women); includes 61 minority (35 Black or African American, non-Hispanic/Latino; 4 American Indian or Alaska Native, non-Hispanic/Latino; 14 Asian, non-Hispanic/Latino; 8 Hispanic/Latino). Average age 40. In 2013, 90 master's awarded. *Degree requirements:* For master's, thesis or alternative, 500-700 hour internship (depending on license choice). *Entrance requirements:* For master's, personal goal statement, three letters of reference, resume or work history, official transcripts. *Application deadline:* Applications are processed on a rolling basis. Application fee: $50. Electronic applications accepted. *Financial support:* Career-related internships or fieldwork and tuition waivers available. Support available to part-time students. Financial award applicants required to submit FAFSA. *Unit head:* Dr. Dan Haugen, President, 612-767-7048, Fax: 612-861-7559, E-mail: haugen@alfredadler.edu. *Application contact:* Evelyn B. Haas, Director of Student Services and Admissions, 612-767-7044, Fax: 612-861-7559, E-mail: ev@alfredadler.edu.
Website: http://www.alfredadler.edu/academics/index.htm.

Amberton University, Graduate School, Program in Human Relations and Business, Garland, TX 75041-5595. Offers MA, MS. Part-time and evening/weekend programs available. *Entrance requirements:* For master's, minimum GPA of 3.0. *Expenses: Tuition:* Full-time $5808; part-time $242 per credit hour.

Antioch University Los Angeles, Graduate Programs, Program in Organizational Management, Culver City, CA 90230. Offers human resource development (MA); leadership (MA); organizational development (MA). Part-time and evening/weekend programs available. *Entrance requirements:* For master's, interview. Additional exam requirements/recommendations for international students: Required—TOEFL. *Faculty research:* Systems thinking and chaos theory, technology and organizational structure, nonprofit management, power and empowerment.

Azusa Pacific University, School of Business and Management, Program in Human and Organizational Development, Azusa, CA 91702-7000. Offers MA. Part-time and evening/weekend programs available. *Degree requirements:* For master's, comprehensive exam, final project. *Entrance requirements:* For master's, minimum GPA of 3.0.

Barry University, School of Education, Program in Human Resource Development and Administration, Miami Shores, FL 33161-6695. Offers MS. Part-time and evening/weekend programs available. *Degree requirements:* For master's, comprehensive exam, practicum. *Entrance requirements:* For master's, GRE General Test or MAT, minimum GPA of 3.0. Electronic applications accepted.

Barry University, School of Education, Program in Leadership and Education, Miami Shores, FL 33161-6695. Offers educational technology (PhD); exceptional student education (PhD); higher education administration (PhD); human resource development (PhD); leadership (PhD). Part-time and evening/weekend programs available. *Degree requirements:* For doctorate, thesis/dissertation. *Entrance requirements:* For doctorate, GRE General Test, minimum GPA of 3.25. Electronic applications accepted.

Bowie State University, Graduate Programs, Program in Human Resource Development, Bowie, MD 20715-9465. Offers MA. Part-time and evening/weekend programs available. *Degree requirements:* For master's, comprehensive exam, thesis optional, research paper. *Entrance requirements:* For master's, minimum GPA of 2.5. Electronic applications accepted. *Expenses:* Tuition, state resident: full-time $8665. Tuition, nonresident: full-time $16,007. *Required fees:* $1927.

California State University, Sacramento, Office of Graduate Studies, College of Business Administration, Sacramento, CA 95819. Offers accountancy (MS); business administration (IMBA, MBA); human resources (MBA); urban land development (MBA). *Accreditation:* AACSB. Part-time and evening/weekend programs available. *Degree requirements:* For master's, thesis or alternative, writing proficiency exam. *Entrance requirements:* For master's, GMAT. Additional exam requirements/recommendations for international students: Required—TOEFL. *Application deadline:* For fall admission, 2/1 for domestic students, 3/1 for international students; for spring admission, 9/15 for domestic students, 9/30 for international students. Applications are processed on a rolling basis. Application fee: $55. Electronic applications accepted. *Financial support:* Research assistantships, teaching assistantships, career-related internships or fieldwork, and Federal Work-Study available. Support available to part-time students. Financial award applicants required to submit FAFSA. *Unit head:* Dr. Sanjay Varshney, Dean, 916-278-6942, Fax: 916-278-5793, E-mail: cba@csus.edu. *Application contact:* Jose Martinez, Graduate Admissions Supervisor, 916-278-7871, E-mail: martinj@skymail.csus.edu.
Website: http://www.cba.csus.edu.

Claremont Graduate University, Graduate Programs, School of Social Science, Policy and Evaluation, Department of Psychology, Claremont, CA 91711-6160. Offers advanced study in evaluation (Certificate); cognitive psychology (MA, PhD); developmental psychology (MA, PhD); evaluation and applied research methods (MA, PhD); health behavior research and evaluation (MA, PhD); human resource development and evaluation (MA); industrial/organizational psychology (MA, PhD); organizational behavior (MA, PhD); organizational psychology (MA, PhD); social psychology (MA, PhD); MBA/PhD. Part-time programs available. *Faculty:* 17 full-time (7 women), 2 part-time/adjunct (0 women). *Students:* 242 full-time (152 women), 74 part-time (47 women); includes 83 minority (14 Black or African American, non-Hispanic/Latino; 2 American Indian or Alaska Native, non-Hispanic/Latino; 24 Asian, non-Hispanic/Latino; 26 Hispanic/Latino; 17 Two or more races, non-Hispanic/Latino), 36 international. Average age 30. In 2013, 45 master's, 12 doctorates, 7 other advanced degrees awarded. Terminal master's awarded for partial completion of doctoral program. *Entrance requirements:* For master's and doctorate, GRE General Test. Additional exam requirements/recommendations for international students: Required—TOEFL (minimum score 550 paper-based; 80 iBT). *Application deadline:* For fall admission, 1/15 priority date for domestic and international students. Applications are processed on a rolling basis. Application fee: $80. Electronic applications accepted. *Expenses: Tuition:* Full-time $40,560; part-time $1690 per credit. *Required fees:* $275 per semester. Tuition and fees vary according to program. *Financial support:* Fellowships, research assistantships, teaching assistantships, Federal Work-Study, institutionally sponsored loans, scholarships/grants, and tuition waivers (full and partial) available. Support available to part-time students. Financial award application deadline: 2/15; financial award applicants required to submit FAFSA. *Faculty research:* Social intervention, diversity in organizations, eyewitness memory, aging and cognition, drug policy. *Unit head:* William Crano, Chair, 909-621-8084, E-mail: william.crano@cgu.edu. *Application contact:* Annekah Hall, Assistant Director of Admissions, 909-607-3371, E-mail: annekah.hall@cgu.edu.
Website: http://www.cgu.edu/pages/502.asp.

Clemson University, Graduate School, College of Health, Education, and Human Development, Eugene T. Moore School of Education, Program in Human Resource Development, Clemson, SC 29634. Offers MHRD. Part-time and evening/weekend programs available. Postbaccalaureate distance learning degree programs offered (no on-campus study). *Students:* 6 full-time (3 women), 130 part-time (68 women); includes 39 minority (32 Black or African American, non-Hispanic/Latino; 5 Hispanic/Latino; 2 Two or more races, non-Hispanic/Latino). Average age 34. 91 applicants, 93% accepted, 75 enrolled. In 2013, 31 master's awarded. *Degree requirements:* For master's, comprehensive exam. *Entrance requirements:* For master's, GRE General Test. Additional exam requirements/recommendations for international students: Required—TOEFL; Recommended—IELTS. *Application deadline:* For fall admission, 7/1 for domestic students. Application fee: $70 ($80 for international students). Electronic applications accepted. *Expenses:* Contact institution. *Financial support:* In 2013–14, 1 student received support. Application deadline: 6/1; applicants required to submit FAFSA. *Faculty research:* Organizational development, human performance improvement, attachment theory, social constructivism, technology-mediated teaching and learning, corporate universities. *Unit head:* Dr. Michael J. Padilla, Director/Associate Dean, 864-656-4444, Fax: 864-656-0311, E-mail: pmcgee@clemson.edu. *Application contact:* Dr. David Fleming, Coordinator, 864-656-1881, Fax: 864-656-0311, E-mail: dflemin@clemson.edu.
Website: http://www.hehd.clemson.edu/MHRD/SoE_Webpage/MHRD.html.

The College of New Rochelle, Graduate School, Division of Human Services, Program in Career Development, New Rochelle, NY 10805-2308. Offers MS. Part-time programs available. *Degree requirements:* For master's, fieldwork, internship. *Entrance requirements:* For master's, interview, minimum GPA of 3.0, writing sample. *Expenses: Tuition:* Part-time $894 per credit. *Required fees:* $300 per semester. One-time fee: $200. Tuition and fees vary according to course load. *Faculty research:* Technology.

Drexel University, Goodwin College of Professional Studies, School of Education, Philadelphia, PA 19104-2875. Offers educational administration (MS); educational improvement and transformation (MS); educational leadership and management (Ed D); educational leadership development and learning technologies (PhD); global and international education (MS); higher education (MS); human resources development (MS); learning technologies (MS); mathematics, learning and teaching (MS); special education (MS); teaching, learning and curriculum (MS). Part-time and evening/weekend programs available. Postbaccalaureate distance learning degree programs offered (no on-campus study). *Degree requirements:* For doctorate, thesis/dissertation. *Entrance requirements:* For doctorate, GRE or GMAT. Additional exam requirements/recommendations for international students: Required—TOEFL, IELTS. Electronic applications accepted. Application fee is waived when completed online. *Expenses:* Contact institution. *Faculty research:* Leadership development, mathematics education, literacy, autism, educational technology.

Florida International University, College of Education, Department of Leadership and Professional Studies, Miami, FL 33199. Offers adult education and human resource development (MS, Ed D); counseling (MS), including rehabilitation counseling, school counseling; counselor education (MS), including clinical mental health counseling; educational administration and supervision (Ed D); educational leadership (MS, Certificate, Ed S); higher education (Ed D); higher education administration (MS); recreation and sport management (MS), including recreation and sport management, recreational therapy; school psychology (Ed S); urban education (MS), including instruction in urban settings, learning technologies, multicultural/bilingual, multicultural/TESOL, urban education. Part-time and evening/weekend programs available. *Degree requirements:* For doctorate, thesis/dissertation. *Entrance requirements:* For master's, minimum GPA of 3.0; for doctorate and other advanced degree, GRE General Test. Additional exam requirements/recommendations for international students: Required—TOEFL (minimum score 550 paper-based; 80 iBT), IELTS (minimum score 6.3). Electronic applications accepted.

The George Washington University, Graduate School of Education and Human Development, Department of Human and Organizational Learning, Program in Essentials of Human Resource Development, Washington, DC 20052. Offers Graduate Certificate. *Students:* 1 (woman) full-time, 1 (woman) part-time; both minorities (both Black or African American, non-Hispanic/Latino). Average age 26. 2 applicants, 100% accepted, 1 enrolled. In 2013, 1 Graduate Certificate awarded. *Entrance requirements:* For degree, two letters of recommendation, resume, statement of purpose. Electronic applications accepted. *Unit head:* Dr. Mary Hatwood Futrell, Dean, 202-994-6161, Fax: 202-994-7207, E-mail: mfutrell@gwu.edu. *Application contact:* Sarah Lang, Director of Graduate Admissions, 202-994-1447, Fax: 202-994-7207, E-mail: slang@gwu.edu.
Website: http://gsehd.gwu.edu/essentials-human-resource-development-certificate-0.

The George Washington University, Graduate School of Education and Human Development, Department of Human and Organizational Learning, Program in Human Resource Development, Washington, DC 20052. Offers MA. Part-time and evening/

weekend programs available. *Students:* 20 full-time (17 women), 50 part-time (36 women); includes 23 minority (19 Black or African American, non-Hispanic/Latino; 2 Asian, non-Hispanic/Latino; 1 Hispanic/Latino; 1 Two or more races, non-Hispanic/Latino), 20 international. Average age 36. 68 applicants, 56% accepted, 23 enrolled. In 2013, 44 master's awarded. *Entrance requirements:* For master's, GRE, MAT, or GMAT, two letters of recommendtion, statement of purpose, official transcripts, resume. Additional exam requirements/recommendations for international students: Required—TOEFL or IELTS. Electronic applications accepted. *Financial support:* Fellowships available. *Unit head:* Kristin Furio, Program Manager, 202-994-1040, Fax: 202-994-4928, E-mail: hrd@gwu.edu. *Application contact:* Sarah Lang, Director of Graduate Admissions, 202-994-1447, Fax: 202-994-7207, E-mail: slang@gwu.edu. Website: http://gsehd.gwu.edu/human-resource-development-masters.

The George Washington University, Graduate School of Education and Human Development, Department of Human and Organizational Learning, Program in Leadership Development, Washington, DC 20052. Offers Graduate Certificate. *Students:* 3 full-time (1 woman), 15 part-time (13 women); includes 10 minority (4 Black or African American, non-Hispanic/Latino; 3 Asian, non-Hispanic/Latino; 2 Hispanic/Latino; 1 Two or more races, non-Hispanic/Latino), 2 international. Average age 37. 21 applicants, 100% accepted, 16 enrolled. In 2013, 16 Graduate Certificates awarded. *Degree requirements:* For Graduate Certificate, practicum. *Entrance requirements:* For degree, two letters of recommendation, resume, statement of purpose. Electronic applications accepted. *Unit head:* Dr. Mary Hatwood Futrell, Dean, 202-994-6161, Fax: 202-994-7207, E-mail: mfutrell@gwu.edu. *Application contact:* Sarah Lang, Director of Graduate Admissions, 202-994-1447, Fax: 202-994-7207, E-mail: slang@gwu.edu. Website: http://gsehd.gwu.edu/academics/programs/certificates/leadership-development/overview.

The George Washington University, Graduate School of Education and Human Development, Department of Human and Organizational Learning, Programs in Human and Organizational Learning, Washington, DC 20052. Offers Ed D. *Students:* 51 full-time (22 women), 113 part-time (66 women); includes 42 minority (33 Black or African American, non-Hispanic/Latino; 1 American Indian or Alaska Native, non-Hispanic/Latino; 7 Hispanic/Latino; 1 Two or more races, non-Hispanic/Latino), 6 international. Average age 46. 57 applicants, 93% accepted, 32 enrolled. In 2013, 19 doctorates awarded. *Degree requirements:* For doctorate, comprehensive exam, thesis/dissertation. *Entrance requirements:* For doctorate, GRE General Test or MAT, interview, minimum GPA of 3.3. *Application deadline:* For fall admission, 1/15 priority date for domestic students; for spring admission, 10/1 for domestic students. Applications are processed on a rolling basis. Application fee: $75. *Financial support:* Fellowships, research assistantships, teaching assistantships, career-related internships or fieldwork, Federal Work-Study, and tuition waivers (partial) available. Financial award application deadline: 1/15; financial award applicants required to submit FAFSA. *Faculty research:* Organizational learning, program evaluation. *Unit head:* David Schwandt, Program Manager, 703-726-8396, E-mail: chwandt@gwu.edu. *Application contact:* Sarah Lang, Director of Graduate Admissions, 202-994-1447, E-mail: slang@gwu.edu. Website: http://gsehd.gwu.edu/human-and-organizational-learning-doctoral.

Grantham University, Mark Skousen School of Business, Lenexa, KS 66219. Offers business administration (MBA); business intelligence (MS); information management (MBA); information management technology (MS); information technology (MS); performance improvement (MS); project management (MBA, MS). Part-time and evening/weekend programs available. Postbaccalaureate distance learning degree programs offered (no on-campus study). *Faculty:* 3 full-time (2 women), 35 part-time/adjunct (11 women). *Students:* 233 full-time (75 women), 559 part-time (207 women); includes 399 minority (296 Black or African American, non-Hispanic/Latino; 6 American Indian or Alaska Native, non-Hispanic/Latino; 14 Asian, non-Hispanic/Latino; 58 Hispanic/Latino; 1 Native Hawaiian or other Pacific Islander, non-Hispanic/Latino; 24 Two or more races, non-Hispanic/Latino). Average age 40. 792 applicants, 100% accepted, 792 enrolled. In 2013, 404 master's awarded. *Degree requirements:* For master's, thesis, capstone project, simulation game. *Entrance requirements:* For master's, bachelor's degree from accredited degree-granting institution with minimum GPA of 2.5. Additional exam requirements/recommendations for international students: Required—TOEFL (minimum score 530 paper-based; 71 iBT). *Application deadline:* Applications are processed on a rolling basis. Application fee: $30. Electronic applications accepted. *Expenses: Tuition:* Full-time $3900; part-time $325 per credit hour. *Required fees:* $35 per term. One-time fee: $100. *Financial support:* In 2013–14, 792 students received support. Scholarships/grants available. *Faculty research:* Relationship between media choices and teaching experience in online courses, online best teaching practices, strategy for co-creation of value with consumers, political identity and party polarization in the American Electorate, political participation and Web 2.0. *Unit head:* Dr. Niccole Buckley, Dean, Mark Skousen School of Business, 800-955-2527, E-mail: admissions@grantham.edu. *Application contact:* Jared Parlette, Vice President of Admissions, 800-955-2527, E-mail: admissions@grantham.edu. Website: http://www.grantham.edu/colleges-and-schools/school-of-business/.

Illinois Institute of Technology, Graduate College, College of Psychology, Chicago, IL 60616. Offers clinical psychology (PhD); industrial/organizational psychology (PhD); personnel/human resource development (MS); rehabilitation (PhD); rehabilitation counseling (MS). *Accreditation:* APA (one or more programs are accredited); CORE. Part-time and evening/weekend programs available. Terminal master's awarded for partial completion of doctoral program. *Degree requirements:* For master's, thesis (for some programs); for doctorate, comprehensive exam, thesis/dissertation, 96-108 credit hours, internship (for clinical and industrial/organizational specializations). *Entrance requirements:* For master's, GRE General Test (minimum score 1000 Quantitative and Verbal, 3.0 Analytical Writing), minimum high school GPA of 3.0; at least 18 credit hours of undergraduate study in psychology with at least one course each in experimental psychology and statistics; official transcripts; 3 letters of recommendation; personal statement; for doctorate, GRE General Test (minimum score 1000 Quantitative and Verbal, 3.0 Analytical Writing), minimum undergraduate GPA of 3.0, graduate 3.5; at least 18 credit hours of undergraduate study in psychology with at least one course each in experimental psychology and statistics; official transcripts; 3 letters of recommendation; personal statement. Additional exam requirements/recommendations for international students: Required—TOEFL (minimum score 550 paper-based; 80 iBT); Recommended—IELTS (minimum score 5.5). Electronic applications accepted. *Faculty research:* Health psychology, attachment, child social and emotional development, educational assessment, eating disorders, mood disorders.

Indiana State University, College of Graduate and Professional Studies, College of Technology, Department of Industrial Technology Education, Terre Haute, IN 47809. Offers career and technical education (MS); human resource development (MS); technology education (MS); MA/MS. *Accreditation:* NCATE (one or more programs are accredited). *Entrance requirements:* For master's, bachelor's degree in industrial technology or related field. Additional exam requirements/recommendations for international students: Required—TOEFL. Electronic applications accepted.

Indiana Tech, Program in Business Administration, Fort Wayne, IN 46803-1297. Offers accounting (MBA); health care administration (MBA); human resources (MBA); management (MBA); marketing (MBA). Part-time and evening/weekend programs available. Postbaccalaureate distance learning degree programs offered (no on-campus study). *Students:* 160 full-time (94 women), 97 part-time (53 women); includes 69 minority (58 Black or African American, non-Hispanic/Latino; 1 Asian, non-Hispanic/Latino; 8 Hispanic/Latino; 2 Two or more races, non-Hispanic/Latino), 11 international. Average age 36. *Entrance requirements:* For master's, GMAT, bachelor's degree from regionally-accredited university; minimum undergraduate GPA of 2.5; 2 years of significant work experience; 3 letters of recommendation. *Application deadline:* Applications are processed on a rolling basis. Application fee: $25. Electronic applications accepted. *Expenses: Tuition:* Full-time $8910; part-time $495 per credit. Tuition and fees vary according to course load, degree level and program. *Financial support:* Applicants required to submit FAFSA. *Unit head:* Dr. Andrew I. Nwanne, Associate Dean of Business/Academic Coordinator, 260-422-5561 Ext. 2214, E-mail: ainwanne@indianatech.edu. Website: http://www.indianatech.edu/.

Indiana University of Pennsylvania, School of Graduate Studies and Research, Eberly College of Business and Information Technology, Department of Technology Support and Training, Program in Business/Workforce Development, Indiana, PA 15705-1087. Offers M Ed. Part-time programs available. *Faculty:* 2 full-time (both women). *Students:* 1 full-time (0 women), all international. Average age 25. 2 applicants, 50% accepted, 1 enrolled. In 2013, 2 master's awarded. *Degree requirements:* For master's, thesis optional. *Entrance requirements:* For master's, GMAT or GRE. Additional exam requirements/recommendations for international students: Required—TOEFL (minimum score 540 paper-based). *Application deadline:* Applications are processed on a rolling basis. Application fee: $50. Electronic applications accepted. *Expenses:* Tuition, state resident: full-time $3978; part-time $442 per credit. Tuition, nonresident: full-time $5967; part-time $663 per credit. *Required fees:* $2080; $115.55 per credit. $93 per semester. Tuition and fees vary according to degree level and program. *Financial support:* In 2013–14, 1 research assistantship with full and partial tuition reimbursement (averaging $5,940 per year) was awarded; career-related internships or fieldwork and Federal Work-Study also available. Support available to part-time students. Financial award application deadline: 4/15; financial award applicants required to submit FAFSA. *Unit head:* Dr. Lucinda Willis, Graduate Coordinator, 724-357-2061, E-mail: willisl@iup.edu. Website: http://www.iup.edu/upper.aspx?id-89005.

Inter American University of Puerto Rico, Metropolitan Campus, Graduate Programs, Program in Human Resources, San Juan, PR 00919-1293. Offers MBA. *Degree requirements:* For master's, comprehensive exam. *Entrance requirements:* For master's, GRE or EXADEP, interview. Electronic applications accepted.

Inter American University of Puerto Rico, San Germán Campus, Graduate Studies Center, Program in Business Administration, San Germán, PR 00683-5008. Offers accounting (MBA); finance (MBA); general business administration (MBA); human resources (MBA, PhD); industrial relations (MBA); information systems (MBA); international and interregional business (PhD); management (MBA); marketing (MBA). Part-time and evening/weekend programs available. *Faculty:* 8 full-time (2 women), 4 part-time/adjunct (3 women). *Students:* 138 full-time (80 women), 35 part-time (21 women); includes 172 minority (all Hispanic/Latino). 60 applicants, 65% accepted, 38 enrolled. In 2013, 38 master's, 3 doctorates awarded. *Degree requirements:* For master's, comprehensive exam. *Entrance requirements:* For master's, GRE General Test or EXADEP, minimum GPA of 3.0. *Application deadline:* For fall admission, 4/30 priority date for domestic students; for spring admission, 11/15 for domestic students. Applications are processed on a rolling basis. Application fee: $31. *Expenses: Tuition:* Full-time $2424; part-time $202 per credit hour. *Required fees:* $260 per semester. Tuition and fees vary according to course level, course load, degree level and program. *Financial support:* Teaching assistantships, Federal Work-Study, and unspecified assistantships available. *Unit head:* Dr. Elba T. Irizarry, Director of Graduate Studies Center, 787-264-1912 Ext. 7357, Fax: 787-892-6350, E-mail: elbat@sg.inter.edu. *Application contact:* Dr. Ailin Padilla, Coordinator, 787-264-1912 Ext. 7355, E-mail: ailin_padilla@intersg.edu.

Iowa State University of Science and Technology, Department of Educational Leadership and Policy Studies, Ames, IA 50011. Offers counselor education (M Ed, MS); educational administration (M Ed, MS); educational leadership (PhD); higher education (M Ed, MS); organizational learning and human resource development (M Ed, MS); research and evaluation (MS); student affairs (MS). *Degree requirements:* For master's, thesis or alternative; for doctorate, thesis/dissertation. *Entrance requirements:* For master's and doctorate, GRE General Test. Additional exam requirements/recommendations for international students: Required—TOEFL (minimum score 560 paper-based; 83 iBT), IELTS (minimum score 6.5). Electronic applications accepted.

John F. Kennedy University, School of Management, Program in Career Development, Pleasant Hill, CA 94523-4817. Offers career coaching (Certificate); career development (MA, Certificate). Part-time and evening/weekend programs available. *Degree requirements:* For master's, thesis or alternative. *Entrance requirements:* For master's, interview. Additional exam requirements/recommendations for international students: Required—TOEFL.

Kentucky State University, College of Professional Studies, Frankfort, KY 40601. Offers public administration (MPA), including human resource management, international development, management information systems, nonprofit management, special education (MA). Part-time and evening/weekend programs available. Postbaccalaureate distance learning degree programs offered (minimal on-campus study). *Degree requirements:* For master's, comprehensive exam, thesis optional. *Entrance requirements:* For master's, GMAT, GRE. Additional exam requirements/recommendations for international students: Required—TOEFL (minimum score 525 paper-based). Electronic applications accepted.

La Salle University, College of Professional and Continuing Studies, Program in Human Capital Development, Philadelphia, PA 19141-1199. Offers MS, Certificate. Part-time and evening/weekend programs available. Postbaccalaureate distance learning degree programs offered (no on-campus study). *Faculty:* 5. *Students:* 42 part-time (33 women); includes 26 minority (20 Black or African American, non-Hispanic/Latino; 4 Hispanic/Latino; 1 Native Hawaiian or other Pacific Islander, non-Hispanic/Latino; 1 Two or more races, non-Hispanic/Latino). Average age 37. 4 applicants, 100% accepted, 3 enrolled. *Entrance requirements:* For master's and Certificate, professional resume; 2 letters of recommendation; 500-word essay stating interest in program and goals. Additional exam requirements/recommendations for international students: Required—TOEFL. *Application deadline:* For fall admission, 8/15 priority date for domestic students, 7/15 for international students; for spring admission, 12/15 for domestic students, 11/15 for international students; for summer admission, 4/14 for domestic students, 3/15 for international students. Applications are processed on a rolling basis. Application fee: $35. Electronic applications accepted. Application fee is waived when completed online. *Expenses: Tuition:* Full-time $20,750; part-time $695 per credit hour. *Required fees:* $300; $200 per year. Tuition and fees vary according to program. *Financial support:* In 2013–14, 6 students received support. Federal Work-Study and scholarships/grants available. Support available to part-time students. Financial award application deadline: 8/31; financial award applicants required to submit

FAFSA. *Unit head:* Kathy Finnegan, 215-951-3682, E-mail: finnegan@lasalle.edu. *Application contact:* Paul J. Reilly, Director of Marketing and Graduate Enrollment, 215-951-1946, Fax: 215-951-1462, E-mail: reilly@lasalle.edu.
Website: http://www.lasalle.edu/grad/index.php?section=hcd&page=index.

Lincoln Memorial University, Carter and Moyers School of Education, Harrogate, TN 37752-1901. Offers administration and supervision (M Ed, Ed S); counseling and guidance (M Ed); curriculum and instruction (M Ed, Ed D, Ed S); English (M Ed); executive leadership (Ed D); higher education administration (Ed D); human resource development (Ed D); leadership and administration (Ed D). Part-time and evening/weekend programs available. Postbaccalaureate distance learning degree programs offered. *Degree requirements:* For master's, comprehensive exam, thesis optional; for Ed S, comprehensive exam. *Entrance requirements:* For master's, PRAXIS, NTE, GRE, MAT, letters of recommendation; for Ed S, graduate transcripts. Additional exam requirements/recommendations for international students: Recommended—TOEFL. *Faculty research:* Brain compatible teaching and learning; poverty in Appalachia; leadership for change; ethics, moral responsibility and social justice; human and organizational learning.

Louisiana State University and Agricultural & Mechanical College, Graduate School, College of Human Sciences and Education, School of Human Resource Education and Workforce Development, Baton Rouge, LA 70803. Offers agriculture and extension education and youth development (MS, PhD); career and technical education (MS, PhD); comprehensive vocational education (MS, PhD); extension and international education (MS, PhD); human resource and leadership development (MS, PhD); industrial education (MS); vocational agriculture education (MS, PhD); vocational business education (MS); vocational home economics education (MS). *Accreditation:* NCATE. Part-time programs available. *Faculty:* 10 full-time (5 women). *Students:* 46 full-time (28 women), 138 part-time (96 women); includes 65 minority (52 Black or African American, non-Hispanic/Latino; 2 American Indian or Alaska Native, non-Hispanic/Latino; 2 Asian, non-Hispanic/Latino; 6 Hispanic/Latino; 3 Two or more races, non-Hispanic/Latino), 6 international. Average age 35. 120 applicants, 62% accepted, 49 enrolled. In 2013, 23 master's, 14 doctorates awarded. Terminal master's awarded for partial completion of doctoral program. *Degree requirements:* For master's, thesis (for some programs); for doctorate, thesis/dissertation. *Entrance requirements:* For master's and doctorate, GRE General Test, minimum GPA of 3.0. Additional exam requirements/recommendations for international students: Required—TOEFL (minimum score 550 paper-based; 79 IBT), IELTS (minimum score 6.5), or PTE (minimum score 59). *Application deadline:* For fall admission, 1/25 priority date for domestic students, 5/15 for international students; for spring admission, 10/15 for international students. Applications are processed on a rolling basis. Application fee: $50 ($70 for international students). Electronic applications accepted. *Financial support:* In 2013–14, 85 students received support, including 4 fellowships with full and partial tuition reimbursements available (averaging $31,175 per year), 9 research assistantships with full and partial tuition reimbursements available (averaging $15,422 per year), 14 teaching assistantships with partial tuition reimbursements available (averaging $14,289 per year); career-related internships or fieldwork, Federal Work-Study, institutionally sponsored loans, health care benefits, tuition waivers (full and partial), and unspecified assistantships also available. Financial award application deadline: 3/1; financial award applicants required to submit FAFSA. *Faculty research:* Adult education, history and philosophy of vocational education, curriculum and instruction, career decision-making. *Total annual research expenditures:* $4,454. *Unit head:* Dr. Ed Holton, Director, 225-578-5748, Fax: 225-578-5755, E-mail: eholton@lsu.edu.
Website: http://www.lsu.edu/hrleader/.

Marquette University, Graduate School of Management, Program in Human Resources, Milwaukee, WI 53201-1881. Offers MSHR. Part-time and evening/weekend programs available. *Students:* 23 full-time (21 women), 21 part-time (16 women), 25 international. Average age 26. 172 applicants, 27% accepted, 15 enrolled. In 2013, 15 master's awarded. *Entrance requirements:* For master's, GMAT or GRE General Test, letters of recommendation. Additional exam requirements/recommendations for international students: Required—TOEFL (minimum score 550 paper-based; 88 iBT), IELTS (minimum score 6.5), PTE. *Application deadline:* For fall admission, 2/15 for domestic and international students. Applications are processed on a rolling basis. Electronic applications accepted. *Financial support:* In 2013–14, 3 teaching assistantships were awarded; fellowships, research assistantships, Federal Work-Study, institutionally sponsored loans, and tuition waivers (full and partial) also available. Support available to part-time students. Financial award application deadline: 2/15. *Faculty research:* Diversity, mentoring, executive compensation. *Unit head:* Dr. Mark Eppli, Dean, 414-288-5724. *Application contact:* Dr. Connie O'Neill, Associate Professor, 414-288-1458.
Website: http://business.marquette.edu/academics/mshr.

McDaniel College, Graduate and Professional Studies, Program in Human Resources Development, Westminster, MD 21157-4390. Offers MS. Part-time and evening/weekend programs available. *Degree requirements:* For master's, portfolio, internship. *Entrance requirements:* For master's, 3 letters of reference. Additional exam requirements/recommendations for international students: Required—TOEFL.

Midwestern State University, Graduate School, West College of Education, Program in Counseling, Wichita Falls, TX 76308. Offers counseling (MA); human resource development (MA); school counseling (M Ed); training and development (MA). Part-time and evening/weekend programs available. *Degree requirements:* For master's, comprehensive exam, thesis (for some programs). *Entrance requirements:* For master's, GRE General Test, MAT, or GMAT, valid teaching certificate (M Ed). Additional exam requirements/recommendations for international students: Required—TOEFL (minimum score 550 paper-based). *Application deadline:* For fall admission, 7/1 priority date for domestic students, 4/1 for international students; for spring admission, 11/1 priority date for domestic students, 8/1 for international students. Applications are processed on a rolling basis. Application fee: $35 ($50 for international students). Electronic applications accepted. *Expenses:* Tuition, state resident: full-time $3627; part-time $201.50 per credit hour. Tuition, nonresident: full-time $10,899; part-time $605.50 per credit hour. *Required fees:* $1357. *Financial support:* Teaching assistantships with partial tuition reimbursements, career-related internships or fieldwork, Federal Work-Study, institutionally sponsored loans, scholarships/grants, tuition waivers (partial), and unspecified assistantships available. Support available to part-time students. Financial award application deadline: 3/1; financial award applicants required to submit FAFSA. *Faculty research:* Social development of students with disabilities, autism, criminal justice counseling, conflict resolution issues, leadership. *Unit head:* Dr. Michaelle Kitchen, Chair, 940-397-4141, Fax: 940-397-4694, E-mail: michaelle.kitchen@mwsu.edu.
Website: http://www.mwsu.edu/academics/education/.

Mississippi State University, College of Education, Department of Instructional Systems and Workforce Development, Mississippi State, MS 39762. Offers education (Ed S), including technology; instructional systems and workforce development (PhD); instructional technology (MSIT); technology (MS). *Faculty:* 8 full-time (5 women). *Students:* 20 full-time (9 women), 68 part-time (56 women); includes 59 minority (57 Black or African American, non-Hispanic/Latino; 2 Two or more races, non-Hispanic/Latino), 1 international. Average age 36. 54 applicants, 37% accepted, 19 enrolled. In 2013, 7 master's, 6 doctorates awarded. *Degree requirements:* For master's, thesis optional, comprehensive oral or written exam; for doctorate, thesis/dissertation, comprehensive oral and written exam; for Ed S, thesis, comprehensive written exam. *Entrance requirements:* For master's, GRE, minimum GPA of 2.75 on undergraduate work, 3.0 on graduate work; for doctorate, GRE, minimum GPA of 3.4 on graduate work; for Ed S, GRE, minimum GPA of 3.2, master's degree. Additional exam requirements/recommendations for international students: Required—TOEFL (minimum score 550 paper-based; 79 iBT); Recommended—IELTS (minimum score 6.5). *Application deadline:* For fall admission, 7/1 for domestic students, 5/1 for international students; for spring admission, 11/1 for domestic students, 9/1 for international students. Applications are processed on a rolling basis. Application fee: $60. Electronic applications accepted. *Financial support:* In 2013–14, 3 teaching assistantships with full tuition reimbursements (averaging $10,800 per year) were awarded; Federal Work-Study, institutionally sponsored loans, scholarships/grants, and unspecified assistantships also available. Financial award application deadline: 4/1; financial award applicants required to submit FAFSA. *Faculty research:* Computer technology, nontraditional students, interactive video, instructional technology, educational leadership. *Unit head:* Dr. Connie Forde, Professor and Department Head, 662-325-2281, Fax: 662-325-7599, E-mail: cforde@colled.msstate.edu. *Application contact:* Dr. James Adams, Associate Professor and Graduate Coordinator, 662-325-7563, Fax: 662-325-7258, E-mail: jadams@colled.msstate.edu.
Website: http://www.iswd.msstate.edu.

Moravian College, Moravian College Comenius Center, Business and Management Programs, Bethlehem, PA 18018-6650. Offers accounting (MBA); business analytics (MBA); general management (MBA); health administration (MHA); healthcare management (MBA); human resource management (MBA); leadership (MSHRM); learning and performance management (MSHRM); supply chain management (MBA). Part-time and evening/weekend programs available. *Entrance requirements:* For master's, GMAT. Additional exam requirements/recommendations for international students: Required—TOEFL (minimum score 550 paper-based; 90 iBT). Application fee is waived when completed online. *Expenses:* Contact institution. *Faculty research:* Leadership, change management, human resources.

National Louis University, College of Management and Business, Chicago, IL 60603. Offers business administration (MBA); human resource management and development (MS); management (MS). Part-time and evening/weekend programs available. *Entrance requirements:* For master's, college-administered critical thinking and writing skills test, minimum GPA of 3.0, resume, 3 references. Additional exam requirements/recommendations for international students: Required—TOEFL (minimum score 550 paper-based; 79 iBT).

New York University, School of Continuing and Professional Studies, Division of Programs in Business, Program in Leadership and Human Capital Management, New York, NY 10012-1019. Offers benefits and compensation (Advanced Certificate); human resource management (Advanced Certificate); human resource management and development (MS), including human resource development, human resource management, organizational effectiveness; organizational and executive coaching (Advanced Certificate). Part-time and evening/weekend programs available. Postbaccalaureate distance learning degree programs offered (no on-campus study). *Faculty:* 1 (woman) full-time, 49 part-time/adjunct (25 women). *Students:* 73 full-time (54 women), 161 part-time (140 women); includes 66 minority (25 Black or African American, non-Hispanic/Latino; 22 Asian, non-Hispanic/Latino; 14 Hispanic/Latino; 1 Native Hawaiian or other Pacific Islander, non-Hispanic/Latino; 4 Two or more races, non-Hispanic/Latino), 61 international. Average age 29. 239 applicants, 62% accepted, 72 enrolled. In 2013, 77 master's, 11 other advanced degrees awarded. *Degree requirements:* For master's, thesis. *Entrance requirements:* For master's, bachelor's degree, resume with relevant professional work, internship or volunteer experience, two letters of recommendation, statement of purpose. Additional exam requirements/recommendations for international students: Required—TOEFL (minimum score 600 paper-based; 100 iBT), IELTS (minimum score 7). *Application deadline:* For fall admission, 2/1 priority date for domestic and international students; for spring admission, 10/15 priority date for domestic students, 8/15 priority date for international students. Applications are processed on a rolling basis. Application fee: $150. Electronic applications accepted. *Expenses: Tuition:* Full-time $35,856; part-time $1494 per unit. *Required fees:* $1408; $64 per unit. $473 per term. Tuition and fees vary according to course load and program. *Financial support:* In 2013–14, 98 students received support, including 98 fellowships (averaging $1,944 per year). *Unit head:* Vish Ganpati, Academic Director, 212-998-7112, E-mail: vg36@nyu.edu. *Application contact:* Admissions Office, 212-998-7100, E-mail: scps.gradadmissions@nyu.edu.
Website: http://www.scps.nyu.edu/areas-of-study/leadership/.

North Carolina State University, Graduate School, College of Education, Department of Adult and Higher Education, Program in Human Resource Development, Raleigh, NC 27695. Offers MS. *Degree requirements:* For master's, thesis. *Entrance requirements:* For master's, GRE, 3 letters of recommendation, resume.

Northeastern Illinois University, College of Graduate Studies and Research, College of Education, Program in Human Resource Development, Chicago, IL 60625-4699. Offers educational leadership (MA); human resource development (MA). Part-time and evening/weekend programs available. *Degree requirements:* For master's, comprehensive papers. *Entrance requirements:* For master's, minimum GPA of 2.75, BA in human resource development. Additional exam requirements/recommendations for international students: Required—TOEFL (minimum score 550 paper-based; 79 iBT). Electronic applications accepted. *Faculty research:* Analogics, development of expertise, case-based instruction, action science organizational development, theoretical model building.

Oakland University, Graduate Study and Lifelong Learning, School of Education and Human Services, Department of Human Resource Development, Rochester, MI 48309-4401. Offers MTD. *Faculty:* 3 full-time (1 woman), 2 part-time/adjunct (both women). *Students:* 27 full-time (20 women), 17 part-time (16 women); includes 13 minority (10 Black or African American, non-Hispanic/Latino; 1 Hispanic/Latino; 2 Two or more races, non-Hispanic/Latino). Average age 32. 29 applicants, 66% accepted, 18 enrolled. In 2013, 15 master's awarded. *Entrance requirements:* For master's, minimum GPA of 3.0 for unconditional admission. Additional exam requirements/recommendations for international students: Required—TOEFL (minimum score 550 paper-based). *Application deadline:* For fall admission, 8/1 priority date for domestic students, 5/1 priority date for international students; for winter admission, 12/1 priority date for domestic students, 9/1 priority date for international students; for spring admission, 4/1 priority date for domestic students. Applications are processed on a rolling basis. Application fee: $35. Electronic applications accepted. *Financial support:* Application deadline: 3/1. *Unit head:* Dr. Michael P. Long, Chair, 248-370-4109, Fax: 248-370-4095, E-mail: mlong@oakland.edu. *Application contact:* Christina J. Grabowski, Associate Director of Graduate Study and Lifelong Learning, 248-370-3167, Fax: 248-370-4114, E-mail: grabowsk@oakland.edu.

Ottawa University, Graduate Studies-Kansas City, Overland Park, KS 66211. Offers business administration (MBA); human resources (MA). Part-time and evening/weekend

programs available. Postbaccalaureate distance learning degree programs offered (minimal on-campus study). *Degree requirements:* For master's, thesis or alternative. *Entrance requirements:* For master's, resume, 3 letters of recommendation. Additional exam requirements/recommendations for international students: Required—TOEFL (minimum score 550 paper-based). Electronic applications accepted. *Expenses:* Contact institution.

Penn State Great Valley, Graduate Studies, Management Division, Malvern, PA 19355-1488. Offers business administration (MBA); finance (M Fin); leadership development (MLD). *Accreditation:* AACSB. *Unit head:* Dr. Craig S. Edelbrock, Chancellor, 610-648-3202, Fax: 610-889-1334, E-mail: cse1@psu.edu. *Application contact:* JoAnn Kelly, Director of Admissions, 610-648-3315, Fax: 610-725-5296, E-mail: jek2@psu.edu.
Website: http://www.sgps.psu.edu/Academics/Degrees/31885.htm.

Penn State University Park, Graduate School, College of Education, Department of Learning and Performance Systems, State College, PA 16802. Offers adult education (M Ed, D Ed, PhD, Certificate); instructional systems (Certificate); learning, design, and technology (M Ed, MS, D Ed, PhD, Certificate); organization development and change (MPS); workforce education and development (M Ed, MS, PhD). *Unit head:* Dr. David H. Monk, Dean, 814-865-2523, Fax: 814-865-0555, E-mail: dhm6@psu.edu. *Application contact:* Cynthia E. Nicosia, Director, Graduate Enrollment Services, 814-865-1834, Fax: 814-863-4627, E-mail: cey1@psu.edu.
Website: http://www.ed.psu.edu/educ/lps/dept-lps.

Penn State University Park, Graduate School, College of the Liberal Arts, School of Labor and Employment Relations, State College, PA 16802. Offers human resources and employee relations (MPS, MS). Postbaccalaureate distance learning degree programs offered. *Unit head:* Dr. Susan Welch, Dean, 814-865-7691, Fax: 814-863-2085, E-mail: swelch@psu.edu. *Application contact:* Cynthia E. Nicosia, Director, Graduate Enrollment Services, 814-865-1834, Fax: 814-863-4627, E-mail: cey1@psu.edu.
Website: http://lser.la.psu.edu/.

Pittsburg State University, Graduate School, College of Technology, Department of Technology and Workforce Learning, Program in Human Resource Development, Pittsburg, KS 66762. Offers MS. *Degree requirements:* For master's, thesis or alternative.

Regent University, Graduate School, School of Business and Leadership, Virginia Beach, VA 23464-9800. Offers business administration (MBA); leadership (Certificate); organizational leadership (MA, PhD), including ecclesial leadership (PhD), entrepreneurial leadership (PhD), human resource development (PhD); strategic foresight (MA); strategic leadership (DSL), including global consulting, leadership coaching, strategic foresight. Part-time and evening/weekend programs available. Postbaccalaureate distance learning degree programs offered (minimal on-campus study). *Faculty:* 11 full-time (4 women), 6 part-time/adjunct (3 women). *Students:* 34 full-time (19 women), 655 part-time (276 women); includes 222 minority (175 Black or African American, non-Hispanic/Latino; 2 American Indian or Alaska Native, non-Hispanic/Latino; 16 Asian, non-Hispanic/Latino; 29 Hispanic/Latino), 117 international. Average age 42. 384 applicants, 53% accepted, 120 enrolled. In 2013, 74 master's, 72 doctorates awarded. *Degree requirements:* For master's, thesis or alternative, 3 credit hour culminating experience; for doctorate, thesis/dissertation. *Entrance requirements:* For master's, GRE, GMAT, minimum undergraduate GPA of 2.75, computer literacy survey, 2 recommendations, resume, transcripts, essay; for doctorate, GRE, GMAT, sample of writing, minimum 3 years of relevant experience, computer literacy survey, 2 recommendations, resume, essay, transcripts; for Certificate, writing sample, resume, transcripts. Additional exam requirements/recommendations for international students: Required—TOEFL (minimum score 577 paper-based). *Application deadline:* For fall admission, 5/1 priority date for domestic students; for spring admission, 10/1 priority date for domestic students. Applications are processed on a rolling basis. Application fee: $50. Electronic applications accepted. *Expenses:* Contact institution. *Financial support:* Career-related internships or fieldwork, scholarships/grants, and tuition waivers (full and partial) available. Support available to part-time students. Financial award application deadline: 9/1. *Faculty research:* Servant leadership, ethics and values, telecommuting and family values, organizational communications, distance education. *Unit head:* Dr. Doris Gomez, Interim Dean, 757-352-4686, Fax: 757-352-4634, E-mail: dorigom@regent.edu. *Application contact:* Matthew Chadwick, Director of Enrollment Support Services, 800-373-5504, Fax: 757-352-4381, E-mail: admissions@regent.edu.
Website: http://www.regent.edu/acad/global/.

Rochester Institute of Technology, Graduate Enrollment Services, College of Applied Science and Technology, School of International Hospitality and Service Innovation, Department of Service Systems, Program in Human Resources Development, Rochester, NY 14623-5603. Offers MS. Part-time and evening/weekend programs available. *Students:* 19 full-time (13 women), 16 part-time (10 women); includes 5 minority (3 Black or African American, non-Hispanic/Latino; 2 Hispanic/Latino), 18 international. Average age 32. 97 applicants, 34% accepted, 14 enrolled. In 2013, 27 master's awarded. *Degree requirements:* For master's, thesis or alternative. *Entrance requirements:* For master's, minimum GPA of 3.0. Additional exam requirements/recommendations for international students: Required—TOEFL (minimum score 570 paper-based; 88 iBT) or IELTS (minimum score 6.5). *Application deadline:* For fall admission, 2/15 priority date for domestic and international students; for winter admission, 11/1 for domestic and international students; for spring admission, 2/1 for domestic and international students. Applications are processed on a rolling basis. Application fee: $60. Electronic applications accepted. *Expenses: Tuition:* Full-time $37,236; part-time $1552 per credit hour. *Required fees:* $250. *Financial support:* Research assistantships with partial tuition reimbursements, teaching assistantships with partial tuition reimbursements, career-related internships or fieldwork, scholarships/grants, and unspecified assistantships available. Support available to part-time students. Financial award application deadline: 2/15; financial award applicants required to submit FAFSA. *Faculty research:* Global resource development, service/product innovation and implementation. *Unit head:* Dr. Linda Underhill, Director, 585-475-7359, Fax: 585-475-5099, E-mail: lmuism@rit.edu. *Application contact:* Diane Ellison, Assistant Vice President, Graduate Enrollment Services, 585-475-2229, Fax: 585-475-7164, E-mail: gradinfo@rit.edu.
Website: http://www.rit.edu/cast/servicesystems/human-resources-development.php.

Rollins College, Hamilton Holt School, Master of Human Resources Program, Winter Park, FL 32789. Offers MHR. Part-time and evening/weekend programs available. *Faculty:* 4 full-time (0 women), 4 part-time/adjunct (1 woman). *Students:* 8 full-time (6 women), 49 part-time (41 women); includes 21 minority (7 Black or African American, non-Hispanic/Latino; 4 Asian, non-Hispanic/Latino; 10 Hispanic/Latino), 2 international. Average age 33. 35 applicants, 94% accepted, 29 enrolled. In 2013, 20 master's awarded. *Degree requirements:* For master's, thesis optional. *Entrance requirements:* For master's, GMAT or GRE, official transcripts, two letters of recommendation, essay, current resume. Additional exam requirements/recommendations for international students: Required—TOEFL (minimum score 550 paper-based; 80 iBT). *Application deadline:* For fall admission, 4/1 for domestic students; for spring admission, 12/1 for

domestic students. Application fee: $50. *Expenses:* Contact institution. *Financial support:* In 2013–14, 18 students received support. Federal Work-Study, scholarships/grants, and unspecified assistantships available. Support available to part-time students. Financial award applicants required to submit FAFSA. *Unit head:* Dr. Donald Rogers, Faculty Director, 407-646-2348, E-mail: drogers@rollins.edu. *Application contact:* Tonya Parker, Coordinator of Records and Registration, 407-646-2653, Fax: 407-646-1551, E-mail: tparker@rollins.edu.
Website: http://www.rollins.edu/holt/graduate/mhr.html.

Roosevelt University, Graduate Division, College of Professional Studies, Program in Training and Development, Chicago, IL 60605. Offers MA. *Degree requirements:* For master's, thesis. *Entrance requirements:* For master's, minimum GPA of 2.75, relevant work experience.

Syracuse University, Martin J. Whitman School of Management, PhD Program in Business Administration, Syracuse, NY 13244. Offers accounting (PhD); finance (PhD); management information systems (PhD); managerial statistics (PhD); marketing (PhD); operations management (PhD); organizational behavior (PhD); strategy and human resources (PhD); supply chain management (PhD). *Faculty:* 79 full-time (20 women), 25 part-time/adjunct (6 women). *Students:* 26 full-time (8 women), 1 part-time (0 women); includes 2 minority (1 Black or African American, non-Hispanic/Latino; 1 Asian, non-Hispanic/Latino), 20 international. Average age 30. 130 applicants, 9% accepted, 7 enrolled. In 2013, 15 doctorates awarded. *Degree requirements:* For doctorate, comprehensive exam, thesis/dissertation, summer research paper. *Entrance requirements:* For doctorate, GMAT or GRE General Test, 3 recommendations. Additional exam requirements/recommendations for international students: Required—TOEFL (minimum score 600 paper-based; 100 iBT). *Application deadline:* For fall admission, 1/15 priority date for domestic and international students. Applications are processed on a rolling basis. Application fee: $75. Electronic applications accepted. *Financial support:* In 2013–14, 1 fellowship with full tuition reimbursement (averaging $19,570 per year), 30 teaching assistantships with full tuition reimbursements (averaging $17,000 per year) were awarded; research assistantships with full tuition reimbursements also available. Financial award application deadline: 1/15. *Faculty research:* Marketing models, market microstructure, supply chain, auditing, corporate governance. *Unit head:* Dr. Michel Benarock, Director of the PhD Program, 315-443-3429, E-mail: mbeanaroc@syr.edu. *Application contact:* Carol Hilleges, Administrative Specialist, 315-443-9601, Fax: 315-443-3671, E-mail: clhilleg@syr.edu.
Website: http://whitman.syr.edu/phd/.

Texas A&M University, College of Education and Human Development, Department of Educational Administration and Human Resource Development, College Station, TX 77843. Offers educational administration (M Ed, MS, Ed D, PhD); educational human resource development (MS, PhD). Part-time programs available. *Faculty:* 33. *Students:* 109 full-time (77 women), 247 part-time (155 women); includes 139 minority (55 Black or African American, non-Hispanic/Latino; 11 Asian, non-Hispanic/Latino; 71 Hispanic/Latino; 2 Two or more races, non-Hispanic/Latino), 39 international. Average age 38. 139 applicants, 55% accepted, 63 enrolled. In 2013, 88 master's, 33 doctorates awarded. *Degree requirements:* For master's, thesis optional; for doctorate, thesis/dissertation. *Entrance requirements:* For master's, GRE General Test, writing exam, interview, professional experience; for doctorate, GRE General Test, writing exam, interview/presentation, professional experience. Additional exam requirements/recommendations for international students: Required—TOEFL. *Application deadline:* For fall admission, 12/1 for domestic and international students; for spring admission, 8/15 for domestic and international students. Application fee: $50 ($75 for international students). Electronic applications accepted. *Expenses: Tuition, state resident:* full-time $4078; part-time $226.55 per credit hour. Tuition, nonresident: full-time $10,450; part-time $580.55 per credit hour. *Required fees:* $2328; $278.50 per credit hour. $642.45 per semester. *Financial support:* In 2013–14, fellowships (averaging $20,000 per year), research assistantships (averaging $12,000 per year) were awarded; career-related internships or fieldwork and institutionally sponsored loans also available. Support available to part-time students. Financial award application deadline: 3/1; financial award applicants required to submit FAFSA. *Faculty research:* Higher education administration, public school administration, student affairs. *Unit head:* Dr. Fred M. Nafukho, Head, 979-862-3395, Fax: 979-862-4347, E-mail: fnafukho@tamu.edu. *Application contact:* Joyce Nelson, Director of Academic Advising, 979-847-9098, Fax: 979-862-4347, E-mail: jnelson@tamu.edu.
Website: http://eahr.tamu.edu.

Towson University, Program in Human Resource Development, Towson, MD 21252-0001. Offers MS. Part-time and evening/weekend programs available. *Students:* 26 full-time (18 women), 198 part-time (145 women); includes 49 minority (31 Black or African American, non-Hispanic/Latino; 1 American Indian or Alaska Native, non-Hispanic/Latino; 4 Asian, non-Hispanic/Latino; 8 Hispanic/Latino; 5 Two or more races, non-Hispanic/Latino), 3 international. *Degree requirements:* For master's, comprehensive exam. *Entrance requirements:* For master's, bachelor's degree, 2 letters of recommendation, minimum GPA of 3.0, essay, resume. Additional exam requirements/recommendations for international students: Required—TOEFL. *Application deadline:* Applications are processed on a rolling basis. Application fee: $45. Electronic applications accepted. *Financial support:* Application deadline: 4/1. *Unit head:* Dr. Alan Clardy, Graduate Program Director, 410-704-3069, E-mail: aclardy@towson.edu. *Application contact:* Alicia Arkell-Kleis, Information Contact, 410-704-6004, E-mail: grads@towson.edu.

Universidad Central del Este, Graduate School, San Pedro de Macoris, Dominican Republic. Offers environmental engineering (ME); financial management (M Ad); higher education (M Ed), including higher education management, higher education pedagogy; human resources (M Ad). *Entrance requirements:* For master's, letters of recommendation.

Universidad Iberoamericana, Graduate School, Santo Domingo D.N., Dominican Republic. Offers business administration (MBA, PMBA); constitutional law (LL M); dentistry (DMD); educational management (MA); integrated marketing communication (MA); psychopedagogical intervention (M Ed); real estate law (LL M); strategic management of human talent (MM).

University of Arkansas, Graduate School, College of Education and Health Professions, Department of Rehabilitation, Human Resources and Communication Disorders, Program in Human Resource and Workforce Development Education, Fayetteville, AR 72701-1201. Offers M Ed, Ed D. Part-time and evening/weekend programs available. Postbaccalaureate distance learning degree programs offered. Electronic applications accepted.

University of Bridgeport, School of Arts and Sciences, Department of Counseling, Bridgeport, CT 06604. Offers clinical mental health counseling (MS); college student personnel (MS); community counseling (MS); human resource development (MS); human service (MS). Part-time and evening/weekend programs available. *Faculty:* 7 full-time (4 women), 13 part-time/adjunct (7 women). *Students:* 28 full-time (22 women), 79 part-time (61 women); includes 60 minority (45 Black or African American, non-Hispanic/Latino; 11 Hispanic/Latino; 4 Two or more races, non-Hispanic/Latino), 3 international. Average age 34. 124 applicants, 46% accepted, 29 enrolled. In 2013, 26 master's

awarded. *Degree requirements:* For master's, thesis, project. *Entrance requirements:* Additional exam requirements/recommendations for international students: Recommended—TOEFL (minimum score 550 paper-based; 80 iBT), IELTS (minimum score 6.5). *Application deadline:* For fall admission, 8/1 priority date for domestic and international students; for spring admission, 12/1 priority date for domestic and international students. Applications are processed on a rolling basis. Application fee: $50. Electronic applications accepted. *Expenses:* Contact institution. *Financial support:* In 2013–14, 27 students received support. Fellowships, research assistantships, teaching assistantships, career-related internships or fieldwork, Federal Work-Study, and institutionally sponsored loans available. Support available to part-time students. Financial award application deadline: 6/1; financial award applicants required to submit FAFSA. *Faculty research:* Corporate elder care programs. *Unit head:* Dr. Sara L. Connolly, Director, Division of Counseling and Human Resources, 203-576-4183, Fax: 203-576-4219, E-mail: sconnoll@bridgeport.edu. *Application contact:* Leanne Proctor, Director of Graduate Admissions, 203-576-4552, Fax: 203-576-4941, E-mail: admit@bridgeport.edu.

University of California, Los Angeles, Graduate Division, UCLA Anderson School of Management, Los Angeles, CA 90095-1481. Offers accounting (PhD); Americas (EMBA); Asia Pacific (EMBA); business administration (EMBA, MBA); decisions, operations and technology management (PhD); finance (PhD); financial engineering (MFE); global economics and management (PhD); management and organizations (PhD); marketing (PhD); strategy and policy (PhD); DDS/MBA; MBA/JD; MBA/MD; MBA/MLAS; MBA/MLIS; MBA/MPH; MBA/MPP; MBA/MSCS; MBA/MSN; MBA/MUP. *Accreditation:* AACSB. Part-time programs available. *Faculty:* 104 full-time (20 women), 28 part-time/adjunct (4 women). *Students:* 1,069 full-time (324 women), 879 part-time (251 women); includes 664 minority (37 Black or African American, non-Hispanic/Latino; 1 American Indian or Alaska Native, non-Hispanic/Latino; 470 Asian, non-Hispanic/Latino; 34 Hispanic/Latino; 2 Native Hawaiian or other Pacific Islander, non-Hispanic/Latino; 120 Two or more races, non-Hispanic/Latino), 444 international. Average age 30. 5,084 applicants, 27% accepted, 845 enrolled. In 2013, 801 master's, 14 doctorates awarded. *Degree requirements:* For master's, comprehensive exam, field study consulting project (for MBA); thesis (for MFE); for doctorate, comprehensive exam, thesis/dissertation, oral and written qualifying exams. *Entrance requirements:* For master's, GMAT (for MBA); GMAT or GRE General Test (for MFE), 4-year bachelor's degree or equivalent; recommendation letters (1 for MBA, 2 for MFE); two essays; interview (by invitation only for MBA); for doctorate, GMAT or GRE General Test, bachelor's degree from college or university of fully-recognized standing; minimum B average in undergraduate coursework or B+ average in prior graduate work; statement of purpose; three recommendation letters. Additional exam requirements/recommendations for international students: Required—TOEFL (minimum score 560 paper-based; 87 iBT). *Application deadline:* For fall admission, 10/22 priority date for domestic and international students; for winter admission, 1/7 for domestic and international students; for spring admission, 4/15 for domestic and international students. Applications are processed on a rolling basis. Application fee: $200. Electronic applications accepted. *Expenses:* Contact institution. *Financial support:* In 2013–14, 522 students received support. Fellowships, research assistantships with partial tuition reimbursements available, teaching assistantships with partial tuition reimbursements available, career-related internships or fieldwork, institutionally sponsored loans, scholarships/grants, health care benefits, and tuition waivers (partial) available. Financial award application deadline: 4/15; financial award applicants required to submit FAFSA. *Faculty research:* Asset pricing, decision-making, behavioral finance, international finance and economics, global macroeconomics. *Total annual research expenditures:* $368,086. *Unit head:* Dr. Judy D. Olian, Dean/Chair in Management, 310-825-7982, Fax: 310-206-2073, E-mail: judy.olian@anderson.ucla.edu. *Application contact:* Alex Lawrence, Assistant Dean, MBA Admissions and Financial Aid, 310-825-6944, Fax: 310-825-8582, E-mail: mba.admissions@anderson.ucla.edu.
Website: http://www.anderson.ucla.edu/.

See Display on page 145 and Close-Up on page 191.

University of Connecticut, Graduate School, Center for Continuing Studies, Program in Human Resource Management, Storrs, CT 06269. Offers labor relations (MPS); personnel (MPS).

University of Denver, University College, Denver, CO 80208. Offers arts and culture (MLS, Certificate), including art, literature, and culture, arts development and program management (Certificate), creative writing; environmental policy and management (MAS, Certificate), including energy and sustainability (Certificate), environmental assessment of nuclear power (Certificate), environmental health and safety (Certificate), environmental management, natural resource management (Certificate); geographic information systems (MAS, Certificate); global affairs (MLS, Certificate), including translation studies, world history and culture; healthcare leadership (MPH, Certificate), including healthcare policy, law, and ethics, medical and healthcare information technologies, strategic management of healthcare; information and communications technology (MCIS, Certificate), including database design and administration (Certificate), geographic information systems (MCIS), information security systems security (Certificate), information systems security (MCIS), project management (MCIS, MPS, Certificate), software design and administration (Certificate), software design and programming (MCIS), technology management, telecommunications technology (MCIS), Web design and development; leadership and organizations (MPS, Certificate), including human capital in organizations, philanthropic leadership, project management (MCIS, MPS, Certificate), strategic innovation and change; organizational and professional communication (MPS, Certificate), including alternative dispute resolution, organizational communication, organizational development and training, public relations and marketing; security management (MAS, Certificate), including emergency planning and response, information security (MAS), organizational security; strategic human resource management (MPS, Certificate), including global human resources (MPS), human resource management and development (MPS). Part-time and evening/weekend programs available. Postbaccalaureate distance learning degree programs offered (no on-campus study). *Faculty:* 139 part-time/adjunct (61 women). *Students:* 49 full-time (16 women), 1,297 part-time (732 women); includes 272 minority (92 Black or African American, non-Hispanic/Latino; 5 American Indian or Alaska Native, non-Hispanic/Latino; 30 Asian, non-Hispanic/Latino; 114 Hispanic/Latino; 3 Native Hawaiian or other Pacific Islander, non-Hispanic/Latino; 28 Two or more races, non-Hispanic/Latino), 92 international. Average age 35. 542 applicants, 95% accepted, 362 enrolled. In 2013, 374 master's, 128 other advanced degrees awarded. *Degree requirements:* For master's, capstone project. *Entrance requirements:* For master's, transcripts, two letters of recommendation, personal statement, resume. Additional exam requirements/recommendations for international students: Required—TOEFL (minimum score 550 paper-based; 80 iBT). *Application deadline:* For fall admission, 7/18 priority date for domestic students, 5/2 priority date for international students; for winter admission, 10/24 priority date for domestic students, 9/19 priority date for international students; for spring admission, 2/1 for domestic students, 12/14 for international students; for summer admission, 4/18 priority date for domestic students, 3/7 priority date for international students. Applications are processed on a rolling basis. Application fee: $75. Electronic applications accepted. *Expenses:* Contact institution. *Financial support:* In 2013–14, 28 students received support. Applicants required to submit FAFSA. *Unit head:* Dr. Michael McGuire, Interim Dean, 303-871-3518, E-mail: mmcguire@du.edu. *Application contact:* Information Contact, 303-871-2291, E-mail: ucoladm@du.edu.
Website: http://www.universitycollege.du.edu/.

University of Houston, College of Technology, Department of Human Development and Consumer Science, Houston, TX 77204. Offers future studies in commerce (MS); human resources development (MS). Part-time programs available. *Degree requirements:* For master's, project or thesis. *Entrance requirements:* For master's, GMAT, MAT. Additional exam requirements/recommendations for international students: Required—TOEFL (minimum score 550 paper-based; 79 iBT). Electronic applications accepted.

University of Illinois at Urbana–Champaign, Graduate College, College of Education, Department of Human Resource Education, Champaign, IL 61820. Offers Ed M, MS, Ed D, PhD, CAS, MBA/M Ed. Part-time and evening/weekend programs available. Postbaccalaureate distance learning degree programs offered. *Students:* 48 full-time (21 women), 118 part-time (81 women); includes 30 minority (19 Black or African American, non-Hispanic/Latino; 6 Asian, non-Hispanic/Latino; 5 Hispanic/Latino), 38 international. Application fee: $75 ($90 for international students). *Unit head:* James D. Anderson, Head, 217-333-7404, Fax: 217-244-5632, E-mail: janders@illinois.edu. *Application contact:* Laura Ketchum, Business Manager, 217-333-2155, Fax: 217-244-5632, E-mail: ketchum@illinois.edu.
Website: http://education.illinois.edu/hre/index.html.

University of Louisville, Graduate School, College of Education and Human Development, Department of Leadership, Foundations and Human Resource Education, Louisville, KY 40292-0001. Offers educational leadership and organizational development (Ed D, PhD); higher education (MA); human resource education (MS); P-12 educational administration (M Ed, Ed S). *Accreditation:* NCATE. Part-time and evening/weekend programs available. Postbaccalaureate distance learning degree programs offered. *Students:* 68 full-time (44 women), 319 part-time (227 women); includes 80 minority (61 Black or African American, non-Hispanic/Latino; 5 Asian, non-Hispanic/Latino; 9 Hispanic/Latino; 1 Native Hawaiian or other Pacific Islander, non-Hispanic/Latino; 4 Two or more races, non-Hispanic/Latino), 27 international. Average age 36. 219 applicants, 76% accepted, 136 enrolled. In 2013, 19 master's, 5 doctorates, 4 other advanced degrees awarded. *Degree requirements:* For doctorate, comprehensive exam, thesis/dissertation. *Entrance requirements:* For master's, doctorate, and Ed S, GRE General Test. Additional exam requirements/recommendations for international students: Required—TOEFL (minimum score 560 paper-based; 83 iBT). *Application deadline:* For fall admission, 5/1 priority date for international students; for winter admission, 11/1 priority date for international students; for summer admission, 1/1 priority date for international students. Applications are processed on a rolling basis. Application fee: $60. Electronic applications accepted. *Expenses:* Tuition, state resident: full-time $10,788; part-time $599 per credit hour. Tuition, nonresident: full-time $22,446; part-time $1247 per credit hour. *Required fees:* $196. Tuition and fees vary according to program and reciprocity agreements. *Financial support:* Fellowships, research assistantships, teaching assistantships, career-related internships or fieldwork, Federal Work-Study, scholarships/grants, health care benefits, and unspecified assistantships available. Financial award application deadline: 6/1; financial award applicants required to submit FAFSA. *Faculty research:* Evaluation of methods and programs to improve elementary and secondary education; research on organizational and human resource development; student access, retention and success in post-secondary education; educational policy analysis; multivariate quantitative research methods. *Unit head:* Dr. Gaetane Jean-Marie, Chair, 502-852-0634, Fax: 502-852-1164, E-mail: g0jean01@louisville.edu. *Application contact:* Libby Leggett, Director, Graduate Admissions, 502-852-3101, Fax: 502-852-6536, E-mail: gradadm@louisville.edu.
Website: http://www.louisville.edu/education/departments/elfh.

University of Minnesota, Twin Cities Campus, Graduate School, College of Education and Human Development, Department of Organizational Leadership, Policy and Development, Program in Human Resource Development, Minneapolis, MN 55455-0213. Offers M Ed, MA, Ed D, PhD, Certificate. *Students:* 39 full-time (28 women), 34 part-time (20 women); includes 22 minority (8 Black or African American, non-Hispanic/Latino; 2 American Indian or Alaska Native, non-Hispanic/Latino; 7 Asian, non-Hispanic/Latino; 5 Hispanic/Latino), 16 international. Average age 38. 69 applicants, 42% accepted, 27 enrolled. In 2013, 23 master's, 85 other advanced degrees awarded. Application fee: $75 ($95 for international students). *Unit head:* Dr. Rebecca Ropers-Huilman, Chair, 612-624-1006, Fax: 612-624-3377, E-mail: ropers@umn.edu. *Application contact:* Dr. Jennifer Engler, Assistant Dean, 612-626-2887, Fax: 612-626-7496, E-mail: engle009@umn.edu.
Website: http://cehd.umn.edu/WHRE//HRD.

University of Missouri–St. Louis, Graduate School, Program in Public Policy Administration, St. Louis, MO 63121. Offers local government management (MPPA, Certificate); managing human resources and organization (MPPA); nonprofit organization management (MPPA); nonprofit organization management and leadership (Certificate); policy research and analysis (MPPA). *Accreditation:* NASPAA. Part-time and evening/weekend programs available. *Faculty:* 9 full-time (4 women), 13 part-time/adjunct (9 women). *Students:* 19 full-time (12 women), 59 part-time (36 women); includes 20 minority (17 Black or African American, non-Hispanic/Latino; 1 Asian, non-Hispanic/Latino; 1 Hispanic/Latino; 1 Two or more races, non-Hispanic/Latino), 4 international. Average age 33. 39 applicants, 74% accepted, 16 enrolled. In 2013, 25 master's, 27 Certificates awarded. *Degree requirements:* For master's, exit project. *Entrance requirements:* For master's, 3 letters of recommendation. Additional exam requirements/recommendations for international students: Recommended—TOEFL (minimum score 550 paper-based), IELTS (minimum score 6.5). *Application deadline:* For fall admission, 7/1 priority date for domestic and international students; for spring admission, 12/1 priority date for domestic and international students. Applications are processed on a rolling basis. Application fee: $50 ($40 for international students). Electronic applications accepted. *Expenses:* Tuition, state resident: full-time $7364; part-time $409.10 per credit hour. Tuition, nonresident: full-time $19,162; part-time $1008.50 per credit hour. *Financial support:* In 2013–14, 2 research assistantships with full and partial tuition reimbursements (averaging $12,000 per year) were awarded; career-related internships or fieldwork also available. Financial award application deadline: 4/1; financial award applicants required to submit FAFSA. *Faculty research:* Urban policy, public finance, evaluation. *Unit head:* Dr. Deborah Balser, Director, 314-516-5145, Fax: 314-516-5210, E-mail: balserd@msx.umsl.edu. *Application contact:* 314-516-5458, Fax: 314-516-6996, E-mail: gradadm@umsl.edu.
Website: http://www.umsl.edu/divisions/graduate/mppa/.

University of Nebraska at Omaha, Graduate Studies, College of Communication, Fine Arts and Media, School of Communication, Omaha, NE 68182. Offers communication (MA); human resources and training (Certificate); technical communication (Certificate). Part-time and evening/weekend programs available. *Faculty:* 23 full-time (12 women). *Students:* 7 full-time (3 women), 41 part-time (28 women); includes 9 minority (4 Black or African American, non-Hispanic/Latino; 1 Asian, non-Hispanic/Latino; 2 Hispanic/Latino; 2 Two or more races, non-Hispanic/Latino), 3 international. Average age 32. 47

applicants, 57% accepted, 19 enrolled. In 2013, 20 master's, 10 other advanced degrees awarded. *Degree requirements:* For master's, comprehensive exam, thesis (for some programs). *Entrance requirements:* For master's, minimum GPA of 3.0, 15 undergraduate communication courses, resume, statement of purpose, 3 letters of recommendation. Additional exam requirements/recommendations for international students: Required—TOEFL, IELTS, PTE. *Application deadline:* For fall admission, 3/1 priority date for domestic students; for spring admission, 10/1 priority date for domestic students. Applications are processed on a rolling basis. Application fee: $45. Electronic applications accepted. *Financial support:* In 2013–14, 13 students received support, including 1 research assistantship with tuition reimbursement available, 12 teaching assistantships with tuition reimbursements available; fellowships, Federal Work-Study, institutionally sponsored loans, scholarships/grants, tuition waivers (partial), and unspecified assistantships also available. Support available to part-time students. Financial award application deadline: 3/1; financial award applicants required to submit FAFSA. *Unit head:* Dr. Hugh Reilly, Interim Director, 402-554-2600. *Application contact:* Dr. Barbara Pickering, Graduate Program Chair, 402-554-2204, E-mail: graduate@unomaha.edu.

University of Nevada, Las Vegas, Graduate College, Greenspun College of Urban Affairs, School of Environmental and Public Affairs, Las Vegas, NV 89154-4030. Offers environmental science (MS, PhD); non-profit management (Certificate); public administration (MPA, MS), including crisis and emergency management (MS); public affairs (PhD); public management (Certificate); solar and renewable energy (Certificate); urban leadership (MA); workforce development and organizational leadership (PhD). Part-time programs available. *Faculty:* 8 full-time (6 women), 6 part-time/adjunct (5 women). *Students:* 73 full-time (35 women), 133 part-time (63 women); includes 81 minority (29 Black or African American, non-Hispanic/Latino; 2 American Indian or Alaska Native, non-Hispanic/Latino; 5 Asian, non-Hispanic/Latino; 29 Hispanic/Latino; 2 Native Hawaiian or other Pacific Islander, non-Hispanic/Latino; 14 Two or more races, non-Hispanic/Latino), 7 international. Average age 37. 86 applicants, 71% accepted, 53 enrolled. In 2013, 60 master's, 6 doctorates, 17 other advanced degrees awarded. *Degree requirements:* For master's, comprehensive exam (for some programs), thesis; for doctorate, comprehensive exam (for some programs), thesis/dissertation. *Entrance requirements:* Additional exam requirements/recommendations for international students: Required—TOEFL (minimum score 550 paper-based; 80 iBT), IELTS (minimum score 7). *Application deadline:* For fall admission, 2/15 for domestic students, 5/1 for international students; for spring admission, 11/1 for domestic students, 10/1 for international students. Application fee: $60 ($95 for international students). Electronic applications accepted. *Expenses:* Tuition, state resident: full-time $4752; part-time $264 per credit. Tuition, nonresident: full-time $18,662; part-time $554.50 per credit. *International tuition:* $18,952 full-time. *Required fees:* $532; $12 per credit. $266 per semester. One-time fee: $35. Tuition and fees vary according to course load and program. *Financial support:* In 2013–14, 28 students received support, including 19 research assistantships with partial tuition reimbursements available (averaging $11,301 per year), 9 teaching assistantships with partial tuition reimbursements available (averaging $12,028 per year); institutionally sponsored loans, scholarships/grants, health care benefits, and unspecified assistantships also available. Financial award application deadline: 3/1. *Faculty research:* Community and organizational resilience; environmental decision-making and management; budgeting and human resource/workforce management; urban design, sustainability and governance; public and non-profit management. *Total annual research expenditures:* $333,798. *Unit head:* Dr. Christopher Stream, Chair/Associate Professor, 702-895-5120, Fax: 702-895-4436, E-mail: chris.stream@unlv.edu. *Application contact:* Graduate College Admissions Evaluator, 702-895-3320, Fax: 702-895-4180, E-mail: gradcollege@unlv.edu. Website: http://sepa.unlv.edu/.

University of Regina, Faculty of Graduate Studies and Research, Faculty of Education, Department of Human Resource Development, Regina, SK S4S 0A2, Canada. Offers MHRD. Part-time programs available. *Faculty:* 42 full-time (23 women), 18 part-time/adjunct (10 women). *Students:* 7 full-time (4 women), 4 part-time (2 women). 11 applicants, 64% accepted. In 2013, 9 master's awarded. *Degree requirements:* For master's, thesis (for some programs), practicum, project, or thesis. *Entrance requirements:* For master's, 4-year B Ed, two years of teaching or other relevant professional experience. Additional exam requirements/recommendations for international students: Required—TOEFL (minimum score 580 paper-based; 80 iBT), IELTS (minimum score 6.5). *Application deadline:* For fall admission, 2/15 for domestic and international students; for winter admission, 10/15 for domestic and international students; for spring admission, 2/15 for domestic and international students. Application fee: $100. Electronic applications accepted. *Expenses: Tuition, area resident:* Full-time $4338 Canadian dollars. *International tuition:* $7338 Canadian dollars full-time. *Required fees:* $449.25 Canadian dollars. *Financial support:* In 2013–14, 1 fellowship (averaging $6,000 per year), 1 research assistantship (averaging $5,500 per year), 1 teaching assistantship (averaging $2,356 per year) were awarded; scholarships/grants also available. Financial award application deadline: 6/15. *Faculty research:* Foundations of adult development, theory and practice of adult education and human resource development, design and assessment of curriculum and instruction, planning and curriculum development, learning and the workplace. *Unit head:* Dr. Ken Montgomery, Associate Dean, Research and Graduate Programs in Education, 306-585-5031, Fax: 306-585-5387, E-mail: ken.montgomery@uregina.ca. *Application contact:* Tania Gates, Graduate Program Coordinator, 306-585-4506, Fax: 306-585-5387, E-mail: edgrad@uregina.ca.

University of St. Thomas, Graduate Studies, School of Education, Department of Organization Learning and Development, St. Paul, MN 55105-1096. Offers human resources and change leadership (MA); learning, performance and technology (MA); organization development (Ed D). Part-time and evening/weekend programs available. Postbaccalaureate distance learning degree programs offered (minimal on-campus study). *Degree requirements:* For master's, practicum; for doctorate, comprehensive exam, thesis/dissertation. *Entrance requirements:* For master's, minimum GPA of 3.0, 2 letters of reference, personal statement, 2-5 years of organization experience; for doctorate, minimum GPA of 3.5, interview, 5-7 years of OD or leadership experience. Additional exam requirements/recommendations for international students: Required—TOEFL (minimum score 550 paper-based). *Application deadline:* For fall admission, 8/1 priority date for domestic and international students; for winter admission, 12/1 priority date for domestic students, 12/1 for international students; for spring admission, 12/1 priority date for domestic and international students. Applications are processed on a rolling basis. Application fee: $50. Electronic applications accepted. *Expenses:* Contact institution. *Financial support:* Fellowships, research assistantships, institutionally sponsored loans, and scholarships/grants available. Support available to part-time students. Financial award applicants required to submit FAFSA. *Faculty research:* Workplace conflict, physician leaders, virtual teams, technology use in schools/workplace, developing masterful practitioners. *Unit head:* Dr. David W. Jamieson, Chair, 651-962-4387, Fax: 651-962-4169, E-mail: djamieson@stthomas.edu. *Application contact:* Liz G. Knight, Program Manager, 651-962-4459, Fax: 651-962-4169, E-mail: egknight@stthomas.edu.

The University of Scranton, College of Graduate and Continuing Education, Department of Health Administration and Human Resources, Program in Human Resources, Scranton, PA 18510. Offers MS. Part-time and evening/weekend programs available. *Students:* 101 full-time (73 women), 51 part-time (40 women); includes 41 minority (22 Black or African American, non-Hispanic/Latino; 4 Asian, non-Hispanic/Latino; 15 Hispanic/Latino), 2 international. Average age 32. 28 applicants, 96% accepted. In 2013, 42 master's awarded. *Degree requirements:* For master's, capstone experience. *Entrance requirements:* Additional exam requirements/recommendations for international students: Required—TOEFL (minimum score 550 paper-based), IELTS (minimum score 5.5). Application fee: $0. *Financial support:* Fellowships, teaching assistantships, and career-related internships or fieldwork available. Financial award application deadline: 3/1. *Unit head:* Dr. Daniel J. West, Chair, 570-941-4126, Fax: 570-941-4201, E-mail: westd1@scranton.edu. *Application contact:* Joseph M. Roback, Director of Admissions, 570-941-4385, Fax: 570-941-5928, E-mail: robackj2@scranton.edu. Website: http://elearning.scranton.edu/mshr/masters-human-resources.

The University of Scranton, College of Graduate and Continuing Education, Department of Health Administration and Human Resources, Program in Human Resources Administration, Scranton, PA 18510. Offers human resources (MS); human resources development (MS); organizational leadership (MS). Part-time and evening/weekend programs available. *Students:* 1 (woman) part-time. Average age 39. *Degree requirements:* For master's, capstone experience. *Entrance requirements:* For master's, minimum GPA of 2.75. Additional exam requirements/recommendations for international students: Required—TOEFL (minimum score 500 paper-based), IELTS (minimum score 5.5). *Application deadline:* Applications are processed on a rolling basis. Application fee: $0. *Financial support:* Fellowships, teaching assistantships, career-related internships or fieldwork, Federal Work-Study, and unspecified assistantships available. Support available to part-time students. Financial award application deadline: 3/1. *Unit head:* Dr. Daniel J. West, Director, 570-941-6218, E-mail: westd1@scranton.edu. *Application contact:* Joseph M. Roback, Director of Admissions, 570-941-4385, Fax: 570-941-5928, E-mail: robackj2@scranton.edu.

University of South Africa, College of Economic and Management Sciences, Pretoria, South Africa. Offers accounting (D Admin, D Com); accounting science (DA); auditing (D Admin, D Com); business administration (M Tech); business economics (D Admin); business leadership (DBL); business management (D Admin, D Com); economic management analysis (M Tech); economics (D Admin, D Com, PhD); human resource development (M Tech); industrial psychology (D Admin, D Com, PhD); logistics (D Com); marketing (M Tech); public administration (D Admin, D Com, DPA, PhD); public management (M Tech); quantitative management (D Admin, D Com); real estate (M Tech); statistics (D Admin, PhD); tourism management (D Admin, D Com); transport economics (D Admin, D Com).

University of South Florida, University College/Distance Education, Tampa, FL 33620-9951. *Unit head:* Kathy Barnes, Interdisciplinary Programs Coordinator, 813-974-8031, Fax: 813-974-7061, E-mail: barnesk@usf.edu. *Application contact:* Karen Tylinski, Metro Initiatives, 813-974-9943, Fax: 813-974-7061, E-mail: ktylinsk@usf.edu. Website: http://uc.usf.edu/.

The University of Tennessee, Graduate School, College of Business Administration, Program in Human Resource Development, Knoxville, TN 37996. Offers teacher licensure (MS); training and development (MS). Part-time programs available. *Degree requirements:* For master's, thesis. *Entrance requirements:* For master's, GRE General Test, minimum GPA of 2.7. Electronic applications accepted. *Expenses:* Tuition, state resident: full-time $9540; part-time $531 per credit hour. Tuition, nonresident: full-time $27,728; part-time $1542 per credit hour. *Required fees:* $1404; $67 per credit hour.

The University of Texas at Tyler, College of Business and Technology, School of Human Resource Development and Technology, Tyler, TX 75799-0001. Offers human resource development (MS, PhD); industrial management (MS). Part-time and evening/weekend programs available. Postbaccalaureate distance learning degree programs offered (no on-campus study). *Degree requirements:* For master's, comprehensive exam. *Entrance requirements:* For master's, GRE General Test or MAT. Additional exam requirements/recommendations for international students: Required—TOEFL. Electronic applications accepted. *Faculty research:* Human resource development.

University of Wisconsin–Milwaukee, Graduate School, College of Letters and Sciences, Interdepartmental Program in Human Resources and Labor Relations, Milwaukee, WI 53201-0413. Offers human resources and labor relations (MHRLR); international human resources and labor relations (Certificate); mediation and negotiation (Certificate). Part-time programs available. *Faculty:* 2 full-time (0 women). *Students:* 16 full-time (10 women), 28 part-time (23 women); includes 11 minority (5 Black or African American, non-Hispanic/Latino; 3 Asian, non-Hispanic/Latino; 2 Hispanic/Latino; 1 Two or more races, non-Hispanic/Latino), 5 international. Average age 32. 31 applicants, 45% accepted, 7 enrolled. In 2013, 20 master's awarded. *Entrance requirements:* For master's, GMAT or GRE General Test. Additional exam requirements/recommendations for international students: Required—TOEFL (minimum score 550 paper-based; 79 iBT), IELTS (minimum score 6.5). *Application deadline:* For fall admission, 1/1 priority date for domestic students; for spring admission, 9/1 for domestic students. Applications are processed on a rolling basis. Application fee: $56 ($96 for international students). Electronic applications accepted. *Financial support:* Career-related internships or fieldwork available. Support available to part-time students. Financial award application deadline: 4/15; financial award applicants required to submit FAFSA. *Unit head:* Susan M. Donohue-Davies, Representative, 414-299-4009, Fax: 414-229-5915, E-mail: suedono@uwm.edu. *Application contact:* General Information Contact, 414-229-4982, Fax: 414-229-6967, E-mail: gradschool@uwm.edu. Website: http://www.uwm.edu/dept/MHRLR/.

University of Wisconsin–Stout, Graduate School, College of Technology, Engineering, and Management, Program in Training and Development, Menomonie, WI 54751. Offers MS. Part-time programs available. *Degree requirements:* For master's, thesis. *Entrance requirements:* For master's, minimum GPA of 2.75. Additional exam requirements/recommendations for international students: Required—TOEFL (minimum score 500 paper-based; 61 iBT). Electronic applications accepted. *Faculty research:* Organizational behavior, performance, learning and performance, strategic planning.

Villanova University, Graduate School of Liberal Arts and Sciences, Department of Human Resource Development, Villanova, PA 19085-1699. Offers MS. Part-time and evening/weekend programs available. Postbaccalaureate distance learning degree programs offered (no on-campus study). *Faculty:* 23. *Students:* 294 full-time (231 women), 213 part-time (161 women); includes 139 minority (68 Black or African American, non-Hispanic/Latino; 1 American Indian or Alaska Native, non-Hispanic/Latino; 14 Asian, non-Hispanic/Latino; 49 Hispanic/Latino; 2 Native Hawaiian or other Pacific Islander, non-Hispanic/Latino; 5 Two or more races, non-Hispanic/Latino), 7 international. Average age 38. 169 applicants, 92% accepted, 103 enrolled. In 2013, 196 master's awarded. *Degree requirements:* For master's, comprehensive exam. *Entrance requirements:* For master's, GRE General Test, minimum GPA of 3.0, statement of goals, resume, 3 letters of recommendation. Additional exam requirements/recommendations for international students: Required—TOEFL. *Application deadline:* For fall admission, 5/1 priority date for international students; for spring admission, 10/15 priority date for international students. Applications are processed on a rolling basis.

Application fee: $50. Electronic applications accepted. *Financial support:* Research assistantships, scholarships/grants, and unspecified assistantships available. Financial award applicants required to submit FAFSA. *Unit head:* Dr. David F. Bush, Director, 610-519-4746, E-mail: david.bush@villanova.edu.
Website: http://www.villanova.edu/artsci/hrd/.

Virginia Commonwealth University, Graduate School, School of Education, Program in Adult Learning, Richmond, VA 23284-9005. Offers adult literacy (M Ed); human resource development (M Ed); teaching and learning with technology (M Ed). *Accreditation:* NCATE. Part-time programs available. *Entrance requirements:* For master's, GRE General Test or MAT. Additional exam requirements/recommendations for international students: Required—TOEFL (minimum score 600 paper-based; 100 iBT). Electronic applications accepted. *Faculty research:* Adult development and learning, program planning and evaluation.

Webster University, George Herbert Walker School of Business and Technology, Department of Business, St. Louis, MO 63119-3194. Offers business and organizational security management (MBA); decision support systems (MBA); environmental management (MBA); finance (MBA, MS); forensic accounting (MS); gerontology (MBA); human resources development (MBA); human resources management (MBA); information technology management (MBA); international business (MA, MBA); international relations (MBA); management and leadership (MBA); marketing (MBA); media communications (MBA); procurement and acquisitions management (MBA); Web services (MBA). *Accreditation:* ACBSP. Part-time and evening/weekend programs available. Postbaccalaureate distance learning degree programs offered (no on-campus study). *Degree requirements:* For master's, comprehensive exam (for some programs), thesis (for some programs). *Entrance requirements:* Additional exam requirements/recommendations for international students: Required—TOEFL. *Expenses: Tuition:* Full-time $11,610; part-time $645 per credit hour. Tuition and fees vary according to campus/location and program.

Webster University, George Herbert Walker School of Business and Technology, Department of Management, St. Louis, MO 63119-3194. Offers business and organizational security management (MA); health administration (MHA); health care management (MA); health services management (MA); human resources development (MA); human resources management (MA); information technology management (MS); management and leadership (MA); marketing (MA); nonprofit leadership (MA); procurement and acquisitions management (MA); public administration (MPA); space systems operations management (MS). Part-time and evening/weekend programs available. Postbaccalaureate distance learning degree programs offered (no on-campus study). *Degree requirements:* For master's, thesis (for some programs). *Entrance requirements:* Additional exam requirements/recommendations for international students: Required—TOEFL. *Expenses: Tuition:* Full-time $11,610; part-time $645 per credit hour. Tuition and fees vary according to campus/location and program.

Western Carolina University, Graduate School, College of Education and Allied Professions, Department of Human Services, Cullowhee, NC 28723. Offers counseling (M Ed, MA Ed, MS), including community counseling (M Ed, MS), school counseling (MA Ed); human resources (MS). *Accreditation:* ACA (one or more programs are accredited). Part-time and evening/weekend programs available. Postbaccalaureate distance learning degree programs offered. *Degree requirements:* For master's, comprehensive exam, thesis or alternative. *Entrance requirements:* For master's, GRE General Test, appropriate undergraduate degree with minimum GPA of 3.0, 3 recommendations, writing sample, resume. Additional exam requirements/recommendations for international students: Required—TOEFL (minimum score 550 paper-based; 79 iBT). *Faculty research:* Marital and family development, spirituality in counseling, home school law, sexuality education, employee recruitment/retention.

Western Michigan University, Graduate College, College of Education and Human Development, Department of Counselor Education and Counseling Psychology, Kalamazoo, MI 49008. Offers counseling psychology (MA, PhD); counselor education (MA, PhD); human resources development (MA). *Accreditation:* ACA (one or more programs are accredited); APA (one or more programs are accredited); CORE; NCATE. *Degree requirements:* For doctorate, thesis/dissertation, oral exams. *Entrance requirements:* For doctorate, GRE General Test.

Western Seminary, Graduate Programs, Program in Ministry and Leadership, Portland, OR 97215-3367. Offers chaplaincy (MA); coaching (MA); Jewish ministry (MA); pastoral care to women (MA); youth ministry (MA). *Degree requirements:* For master's, practicum. *Entrance requirements:* Additional exam requirements/recommendations for international students: Required—TOEFL.

William Woods University, Graduate and Adult Studies, Fulton, MO 65251-1098. Offers administration (M Ed, Ed S); athletic/activities administration (M Ed); curriculum and instruction (M Ed, Ed S); educational leadership (Ed D); equestrian education (M Ed); health management (MBA); human resources (MBA); leadership (MBA); marketing, advertising, and public relations (MBA); teaching and technology (M Ed). Part-time and evening/weekend programs available. *Faculty:* 231 part-time/adjunct (87 women). *Students:* 418 full-time (276 women), 716 part-time (433 women); includes 51 minority (34 Black or African American, non-Hispanic/Latino; 4 American Indian or Alaska Native, non-Hispanic/Latino; 5 Asian, non-Hispanic/Latino; 3 Hispanic/Latino; 5 Two or more races, non-Hispanic/Latino), 4 international. Average age 35. In 2013, 507 master's, 8 doctorates, 143 other advanced degrees awarded. *Degree requirements:* For master's, capstone course (MBA), action research (M Ed); for Ed S, field experience. *Entrance requirements:* Additional exam requirements/recommendations for international students: Required—TOEFL (minimum score 550 paper-based). *Application deadline:* Applications are processed on a rolling basis. Application fee: $0. Electronic applications accepted. *Expenses:* Contact institution. *Financial support:* Institutionally sponsored loans available. Financial award applicants required to submit FAFSA. *Unit head:* Dr. Michael Westerfield, Vice President and Dean of the Graduate College, 573-592-4383, Fax: 573-592-1164. *Application contact:* Jessica Brush, Director of Operations, 573-592-4227, Fax: 573-592-1164, E-mail: jessica.brush@williamwoods.ede.
Website: http://www.williamwoods.edu/evening_programs/index.asp.

Xavier University, College of Social Sciences, Health and Education, School of Education, Department of Educational Leadership and Human Resource Development, Program in Human Resource Development, Cincinnati, OH 45207. Offers MS. Part-time and evening/weekend programs available. *Faculty:* 2 full-time (both women), 3 part-time/adjunct (1 woman). *Students:* 1 full-time (0 women), 55 part-time (41 women); includes 20 minority (16 Black or African American, non-Hispanic/Latino; 1 Asian, non-Hispanic/Latino; 2 Hispanic/Latino; 1 Two or more races, non-Hispanic/Latino), 2 international. Average age 34. 33 applicants, 100% accepted, 27 enrolled. In 2013, 33 master's awarded. *Entrance requirements:* For master's, MAT, GRE, GMAT, and LSAT, resume, goal statement, two references. Additional exam requirements/recommendations for international students: Required—TOEFL (minimum score 550 paper-based; 79 iBT). *Application deadline:* For fall admission, 8/1 priority date for domestic and international students. Applications are processed on a rolling basis. Application fee: $35. Electronic applications accepted. *Expenses:* Contact institution. *Financial support:* In 2013–14, 15 students received support. Unspecified assistantships available. Financial award applicants required to submit FAFSA. *Faculty research:* Graduate education, group dynamics, organizational behavior, reflection-in-action. *Unit head:* Dr. Brenda Levya-Gardner, Associate Professor/Director, 513-745-4287, Fax: 513-745-1052, E-mail: gardner@xavier.edu. *Application contact:* Roger Bosse, Graduate Services Director, 513-745-3357, Fax: 513-745-1048, E-mail: bosse@xavier.edu.
Website: http://www.xavier.edu/hrd/.

Human Resources Management

Adelphi University, Robert B. Willumstad School of Business, Certificate Program in Human Resource Management, Garden City, NY 11530-0701. Offers Certificate. Part-time and evening/weekend programs available. *Students:* 3 part-time (all women). Average age 34. In 2013, 11 Certificates awarded. *Entrance requirements:* For degree, GMAT or master's degree. Additional exam requirements/recommendations for international students: Required—TOEFL (minimum score 550 paper-based; 80 iBT). *Application deadline:* For fall admission, 4/1 for international students; for spring admission, 11/1 for international students. Applications are processed on a rolling basis. Application fee: $50. Electronic applications accepted. *Expenses: Tuition:* Full-time $32,530; part-time $1010 per credit. *Required fees:* $1150. Tuition and fees vary according to degree level and program. *Financial support:* Career-related internships or fieldwork, Federal Work-Study, tuition waivers, and unspecified assistantships available. Financial award application deadline: 3/1; financial award applicants required to submit FAFSA. *Unit head:* Brian Rothschild, Assistant Dean, 516-877-4670, Fax: 516-877-4607, E-mail: gradbusinquiries@adelphi.edu. *Application contact:* Christine Murphy, Director of Admissions, 516-877-3050, Fax: 516-877-3039, E-mail: graduateadmissions@adelphi.edu.
Website: http://business.adelphi.edu/academics/certificate-programs/advanced-certificate-in-human-resource-management/.

Adelphi University, Robert B. Willumstad School of Business, MBA Program, Garden City, NY 11530-0701. Offers finance (MBA); management information systems (MBA); management/human resource management (MBA); marketing/e-commerce (MBA). *Accreditation:* AACSB. Part-time and evening/weekend programs available. *Students:* 254 full-time (129 women), 118 part-time (63 women); includes 60 minority (13 Black or African American, non-Hispanic/Latino; 18 Asian, non-Hispanic/Latino; 28 Hispanic/Latino; 1 Native Hawaiian or other Pacific Islander, non-Hispanic/Latino), 200 international. Average age 28. In 2013, 182 master's awarded. *Degree requirements:* For master's, capstone course. *Entrance requirements:* For master's, GMAT, 2 letters of recommendation. Additional exam requirements/recommendations for international students: Required—TOEFL (minimum score 550 paper-based; 80 iBT). *Application deadline:* For fall admission, 4/1 for international students; for spring admission, 11/1 for international students. Applications are processed on a rolling basis. Application fee: $50. Electronic applications accepted. *Expenses: Tuition:* Full-time $32,530; part-time $1010 per credit. *Required fees:* $1150. Tuition and fees vary according to degree level and program. *Financial support:* Research assistantships with partial tuition reimbursements, career-related internships or fieldwork, Federal Work-Study, institutionally sponsored loans, scholarships/grants, tuition waivers (partial), and unspecified assistantships available. Financial award application deadline: 3/1; financial award applicants required to submit FAFSA. *Faculty research:* Supply chain management, distribution channels, productivity benchmark analysis, data envelopment analysis, financial portfolio analysis. *Unit head:* Dr. Rakesh Gupta, Associate Dean, 516-877-4629. *Application contact:* Christine Murphy, Director of Admissions, 516-877-3050, Fax: 516-877-3039, E-mail: graduateadmissions@adelphi.edu.
Website: http://business.adelphi.edu/degree-programs/graduate-degree-programs/m-b-a/.

See Display on page 70 and Close-Up on page 181.

Alabama Agricultural and Mechanical University, School of Graduate Studies, School of Education, Department of Counseling and Special Education, Huntsville, AL 35811. Offers communicative disorders (M Ed, MS); psychology and counseling (MS, Ed S), including clinical psychology (MS), counseling and guidance, counseling psychology (MS), personnel management (MS), psychometry (MS), school psychology (MS); special education (M Ed, MS). *Accreditation:* CORE; NCATE. Part-time and evening/weekend programs available. *Degree requirements:* For master's, comprehensive exam. *Entrance requirements:* For master's, GRE General Test. Additional exam requirements/recommendations for international students: Required—TOEFL (minimum score 500 paper-based; 61 iBT). *Faculty research:* Increasing numbers of minorities in special education and speech-language pathology.

Albany State University, College of Arts and Humanities, Albany, GA 31705-2717. Offers English education (M Ed); public administration (MPA), including community and economic development administration, criminal justice administration, general administration, health administration and policy, human resources management, public policy, water resources management; social work (MSW). Part-time programs available. *Degree requirements:* For master's, comprehensive exam, professional portfolio (for MPA), internship, capstone report. *Entrance requirements:* For master's, GRE, MAT, minimum GPA of 3.0, official transcript, pre-medical record/certificate of immunization, letters of reference. Electronic applications accepted. *Faculty research:* HIV prevention for minority students.

Amberton University, Graduate School, Program in Human Relations and Business, Garland, TX 75041-5595. Offers MA, MS. Part-time and evening/weekend programs available. *Entrance requirements:* For master's, minimum GPA of 3.0. *Expenses: Tuition:* Full-time $5808; part-time $242 per credit hour.

American InterContinental University Online, Program in Business Administration, Schaumburg, IL 60173. Offers accounting and finance (MBA); finance (MBA); healthcare management (MBA); human resource management (MBA); international

business (MBA); management (MBA); marketing (MBA); operations management (MBA); organizational psychology and development (MBA); project management (MBA). *Accreditation:* ACBSP. Evening/weekend programs available. Postbaccalaureate distance learning degree programs offered (no on-campus study). *Entrance requirements:* Additional exam requirements/recommendations for international students: Required—TOEFL (minimum score 550 paper-based). Electronic applications accepted.

American InterContinental University South Florida, Program in International Business, Weston, FL 33326. Offers accounting and finance (MBA); human resource management (MBA); management (MBA); marketing (MBA). Part-time and evening/weekend programs available. Postbaccalaureate distance learning degree programs offered. Electronic applications accepted.

American Public University System, AMU/APU Graduate Programs, Charles Town, WV 25414. Offers accounting (MBA, MS); criminal justice (MA), including business administration, emergency and disaster management, general (MA, MS); educational leadership (M Ed); emergency and disaster management (MA); entrepreneurship (MBA); environmental policy and management (MS), including environmental planning, environmental sustainability, fish and wildlife management, general (MA, MS), global environmental management; finance (MBA); general (MBA); global business management (MBA); history (MA), including American history, ancient and classical history, European history, global history, public history; homeland security (MA), including business administration, counter-terrorism studies, criminal justice, cyber, emergency management and public health, intelligence studies, transportation security; homeland security resource allocation (MBA); humanities (MA); information technology (MS), including digital forensics, enterprise software development, information assurance and security, IT project management; information technology management (MBA); intelligence studies (MA), including criminal intelligence, cyber, general (MA, MS), homeland security, intelligence analysis, intelligence collection, intelligence management, intelligence operations, terrorism studies; international relations and conflict resolution (MA), including comparative and security issues, conflict resolution, international and transnational security issues, peacekeeping; legal studies (MA); management (MA), including defense management, general (MA, MS), human resource management, organizational leadership, public administration; marketing (MBA); military history (MA), including American military history, American Revolution, civil war, war since 1945, World War II; military studies (MA), including joint warfare, strategic leadership; national security studies (MA), including general (MA, MS), homeland security, regional security studies, security and intelligence analysis, terrorism studies; nonprofit management (MBA); political science (MA), including American politics and government, comparative government and development, general (MA, MS), international relations, public policy; psychology (MA), including general (MA, MS), maritime engineering management, reverse logistics management; public administration (MPA), including disaster management, environmental policy, health policy, human resources, national security, organizational management, security management; public health (MPH); reverse logistics management (MA); school counseling (M Ed); security management (MA); space studies (MS), including aerospace science, general (MA, MS), planetary science; sports and health sciences (MS); teaching (M Ed), including curriculum and instruction for elementary teachers, elementary reading, English language learners, instructional leadership, online learning, special education; transportation and logistics management (MA), including general (MA, MS), maritime engineering management, reverse logistics management. Programs offered via distance learning only. Part-time and evening/weekend programs available. Postbaccalaureate distance learning degree programs offered (no on-campus study). *Faculty:* 432 full-time (242 women), 1,722 part-time/adjunct (829 women). *Students:* 511 full-time (241 women), 10,947 part-time (4,294 women); includes 3,760 minority (2,058 Black or African American, non-Hispanic/Latino; 88 American Indian or Alaska Native, non-Hispanic/Latino; 293 Asian, non-Hispanic/Latino; 876 Hispanic/Latino; 91 Native Hawaiian or other Pacific Islander, non-Hispanic/Latino; 354 Two or more races, non-Hispanic/Latino), 134 international. Average age 36. In 2013, 3,323 master's awarded. *Degree requirements:* For master's, comprehensive exam or practicum. *Entrance requirements:* For master's, official transcript showing earned bachelor's degree from institution accredited by recognized accrediting body. Additional exam requirements/recommendations for international students: Required—TOEFL (minimum score 550 paper-based), IELTS (minimum score 6.5). *Application deadline:* Applications are processed on a rolling basis. Application fee: $0. Electronic applications accepted. *Expenses: Tuition:* Part-time $325 per semester hour. *Financial support:* Applicants required to submit FAFSA. *Faculty research:* Military history, criminal justice, management performance, national security. *Unit head:* Dr. Karan Powell, Executive Vice President and Provost, 877-468-6268, Fax: 304-724-3780. *Application contact:* Terry Grant, Vice President of Enrollment Management, 877-468-6268, Fax: 304-724-3780, E-mail: info@apus.edu.
Website: http://www.apus.edu.

American University of Beirut, Graduate Programs, Suliman S. Olayan School of Business, Master in Human Resource Management Program, Beirut, Lebanon. Offers MHRM. Evening/weekend programs available. *Faculty:* 2 full-time (both women). *Students:* 31 full-time (25 women). Average age 27. 60 applicants, 38% accepted, 16 enrolled. *Degree requirements:* For master's, thesis, project. *Entrance requirements:* For master's, at least 2 years of relevant work experience preferably in the field of human resources, minimum undergraduate average of 80 or equivalent in any major, undergraduate degree from recognized university. Additional exam requirements/recommendations for international students: Required—TOEFL (minimum score 600 paper-based; 97 iBT), IELTS (minimum score 7). *Application deadline:* For fall admission, 4/1 for domestic and international students. Application fee: $50. Electronic applications accepted. *Expenses: Tuition:* Full-time $14,724; part-time $818 per credit. *Required fees:* $692; $692. Tuition and fees vary according to course load and program. *Financial support:* In 2013–14, 3 students received support, including 4 teaching assistantships with partial tuition reimbursements available (averaging $16,000 per year); unspecified assistantships also available. Support available to part-time students. Financial award application deadline: 2/20. *Faculty research:* Corporate governance, organizational behavior, corporate social responsibility, business ethics, women at work in the Arab MENA. *Unit head:* Dr. Fida Afiouni, Program Coordinator, 961-1374374 Ext. 3725, E-mail: fa16@aub.edu.lb. *Application contact:* Dr. Rabih Talhouk, Graduate Council Chair, 961-1-350000 Ext. 3895, E-mail: rtalhouk@aub.edu.lb.
Website: http://www.aub.edu.lb/osb/osb_home/program/MHRM/Pages/index.aspx.

Ashworth College, Graduate Programs, Norcross, GA 30092. Offers business administration (MBA); criminal justice (MS); health care administration (MBA, MS); human resource management (MBA, MS); international business (MBA); management (MS); marketing (MBA, MS).

Assumption College, Graduate Studies, Department of Business Studies, Worcester, MA 01609-1296. Offers accounting (MBA); business administration (CAGS); finance/economics (MBA); frontline management (CGS); general business (MBA); human resources (MBA); international business (MBA); management (MBA); marketing (MBA); nonprofit leadership (MBA, CGS); organizational communication (CGS). Part-time and evening/weekend programs available. *Faculty:* 5 full-time (0 women), 20 part-time/adjunct (7 women). *Students:* 20 full-time (7 women), 130 part-time (68 women); includes 20 minority (8 Black or African American, non-Hispanic/Latino; 2 Asian, non-Hispanic/Latino; 8 Hispanic/Latino; 1 Native Hawaiian or other Pacific Islander, non-Hispanic/Latino; 1 Two or more races, non-Hispanic/Latino), 2 international. Average age 31. 63 applicants, 62% accepted, 22 enrolled. In 2013, 58 master's, 1 other advanced degree awarded. *Degree requirements:* For master's, thesis, capstone. *Entrance requirements:* For master's and other advanced degree, 3 letters of recommendation, resume, essay. Additional exam requirements/recommendations for international students: Required—TOEFL (minimum score 540 paper-based; 76 iBT), IELTS (minimum score 6). *Application deadline:* For fall admission, 10/1 for domestic and international students; for winter admission, 2/1 for domestic and international students; for spring admission, 4/1 for domestic and international students. Applications are processed on a rolling basis. Application fee: $30. Electronic applications accepted. *Expenses: Tuition:* Full-time $10,098; part-time $561 per credit. *Required fees:* $20 per term. Full-time tuition and fees vary according to course load and program. *Financial support:* In 2013–14, 15 students received support. Tuition waivers (full and partial), unspecified assistantships, and institutional discounts available. Financial award application deadline: 5/1; financial award applicants required to submit FAFSA. *Faculty research:* Workplace diversity, dynamics of team interaction, utilization of leased employees, experiential learning project on due diligence market for prostheses. *Unit head:* Dr. J. Bart Morrison, Director, 508-767-7458, Fax: 508-767-7252, E-mail: jmorrison@assumption.edu. *Application contact:* Laura Lawrence, Graduate Programs Operations Manager, 508-767-7387, Fax: 508-767-7030, E-mail: graduate@assumption.edu.
Website: http://graduate.assumption.edu/mba/assumption-mba.

Auburn University, Graduate School, College of Business, Department of Management, Auburn University, AL 36849. Offers human resource management (PhD); management (MS, PhD); management information systems (MS, PhD). *Accreditation:* AACSB. Part-time programs available. *Faculty:* 42 full-time (9 women), 10 part-time/adjunct (2 women). *Students:* 94 full-time (43 women), 329 part-time (61 women); includes 77 minority (40 Black or African American, non-Hispanic/Latino; 2 American Indian or Alaska Native, non-Hispanic/Latino; 22 Asian, non-Hispanic/Latino; 13 Hispanic/Latino), 46 international. Average age 34. 408 applicants, 55% accepted, 126 enrolled. In 2013, 173 master's, 6 doctorates awarded. *Degree requirements:* For master's, thesis (for some programs); for doctorate, thesis/dissertation. *Entrance requirements:* For master's, GMAT, GRE General Test (MS); for doctorate, GMAT, GRE General Test. Additional exam requirements/recommendations for international students: Required—TOEFL. *Application deadline:* For fall admission, 7/7 for domestic students; for spring admission, 11/24 for domestic students. Applications are processed on a rolling basis. Application fee: $50 ($60 for international students). Electronic applications accepted. *Expenses:* Tuition, state resident: full-time $8262; part-time $459 per credit hour. Tuition, nonresident: full-time $24,786; part-time $1377 per credit hour. Tuition and fees vary according to degree level and program. *Financial support:* Teaching assistantships and Federal Work-Study available. Support available to part-time students. Financial award application deadline: 3/15; financial award applicants required to submit FAFSA. *Unit head:* Dr. Christopher Shook, Head, 334-844-9565. *Application contact:* Dr. George Flowers, Dean of the Graduate School, 334-844-2125.
Website: http://business.auburn.edu/academics/departments/department-of-management/.

Avila University, School of Professional Studies, Kansas City, MO 64145-1698. Offers executive leadership development (MS); fundraising (MA); instructional design and technology (MA); leadership coaching (MS); organizational development (MS); project management (MA); strategic human resources (MS). Part-time and evening/weekend programs available. Postbaccalaureate distance learning degree programs offered (no on-campus study). *Faculty:* 2 full-time (1 woman), 10 part-time/adjunct (7 women). *Students:* 73 full-time (50 women), 68 part-time (54 women); includes 46 minority (33 Black or African American, non-Hispanic/Latino; 1 Asian, non-Hispanic/Latino; 11 Hispanic/Latino; 1 Two or more races, non-Hispanic/Latino), 11 international. Average age 38. 47 applicants, 64% accepted, 27 enrolled. In 2013, 42 master's awarded. *Degree requirements:* For master's, thesis optional. *Entrance requirements:* For master's, 2 letters of recommendation, minimum GPA of 3.0 during last 60 hours, resume, statement of intent. Additional exam requirements/recommendations for international students: Required—TOEFL. *Application deadline:* Applications are processed on a rolling basis. Application fee: $0. Electronic applications accepted. *Expenses: Tuition:* Full-time $8430; part-time $468 per credit hour. *Required fees:* $648; $36 per credit hour. Tuition and fees vary according to program. *Financial support:* In 2013–14, 20 students received support. Unspecified assistantships available. Support available to part-time students. Financial award applicants required to submit FAFSA. *Unit head:* Dr. Steve Iliff, Dean, 816-501-3737, Fax: 816-941-4650, E-mail: advantage@avila.edu. *Application contact:* Linda Dubar, School of Professional Studies, 816-501-3737, Fax: 816-941-4650, E-mail: advantage@avila.edu.
Website: http://www.avila.edu/advantage.

Azusa Pacific University, School of Business and Management, Azusa, CA 91702-7000. Offers business administration (MBA); diversity for strategic advantage (MA); entrepreneurship (MBA); finance (MBA); human and organizational development (MA); human resources and organizational development (MBA); human resources management (MA); international business (MBA); marketing (MBA); non-profit management (MA); organizational development and change (MA); performance improvement (MA); public administration (MA); strategic management (MBA). Part-time and evening/weekend programs available. *Degree requirements:* For master's, thesis (for some programs), final project. *Entrance requirements:* For master's, GMAT, minimum GPA of 3.0. Additional exam requirements/recommendations for international students: Required—TOEFL (minimum score 600 paper-based). *Expenses:* Contact institution. *Faculty research:* Gender issues, financial risk, leadership and ethics, marketing strategy.

Baker College Center for Graduate Studies - Online, Graduate Programs, Flint, MI 48507-9843. Offers accounting (MBA); business administration (DBA); finance (MBA); general business (MBA); health care management (MBA); human resources management (MBA); information management (MBA); leadership studies (MBA); management information systems (MSIS); marketing (MBA). Part-time and evening/weekend programs available. Postbaccalaureate distance learning degree programs offered. *Degree requirements:* For master's, portfolio. *Entrance requirements:* For master's, 3 years of work experience, minimum undergraduate GPA of 2.5, writing sample, 3 letters of recommendation; for doctorate, MBA or acceptable related master's degree from accredited association, 5 years work experience, minimum graduate GPA of 3.25, writing sample, 3 professional references. Additional exam requirements/recommendations for international students: Required—TOEFL (minimum score 550 paper-based). Electronic applications accepted.

Baldwin Wallace University, Graduate Programs, Division of Business, Program in Human Resources, Berea, OH 44017-2088. Offers MBA. Part-time and evening/weekend programs available. *Students:* 12 full-time (9 women), 14 part-time (12 women); includes 5 minority (2 Black or African American, non-Hispanic/Latino; 1 Asian, non-Hispanic/Latino; 1 Hispanic/Latino; 1 Two or more races, non-Hispanic/Latino).

Human Resources Management

Average age 33. 11 applicants, 73% accepted, 5 enrolled. In 2013, 5 master's awarded. *Degree requirements:* For master's, minimum overall GPA of 3.0, completion of all required courses. *Entrance requirements:* For master's, GMAT or minimum GPA of 3.0, bachelor's degree in any field, work experience. Additional exam requirements/recommendations for international students: Required—TOEFL (minimum score 523 paper-based; 70 iBT). *Application deadline:* For fall admission, 7/25 priority date for domestic students, 4/30 priority date for international students; for spring admission, 12/15 priority date for domestic students, 9/30 priority date for international students. Applications are processed on a rolling basis. Application fee: $25. Electronic applications accepted. Application fee is waived when completed online. *Expenses:* Contact institution. *Financial support:* Application deadline: 5/1; applicants required to submit FAFSA. *Unit head:* Dale Kramer, Director, 440-826-3331, Fax: 440-826-3868, E-mail: dkramer@bw.edu. *Application contact:* Laura Spencer, Graduate Application Specialist, 440-826-2191, Fax: 440-826-3868, E-mail: lspencer@bw.edu. Website: http://www.bw.edu/academics/bus/programs/humres.

Barry University, School of Education, Graduate Certificate Programs, Miami Shores, FL 33161-6695. Offers advanced teaching and learning with technology (Certificate); distance education (Certificate); higher education technology integration (Certificate); human resources: not for profit and religious organizations (Certificate); K-12 technology integration (Certificate).

Baruch College of the City University of New York, Zicklin School of Business, Department of Management, New York, NY 10010-5585. Offers entrepreneurship (MBA); management (PhD); operations management (MBA); organizational behavior/human resources management (MBA); sustainable business (MBA). PhD offered jointly with Graduate School and University Center of the City University of New York. Part-time and evening/weekend programs available. *Degree requirements:* For doctorate, comprehensive exam, thesis/dissertation. *Entrance requirements:* For master's, GMAT, 2 letters of recommendation, resume, 2 years of work experience; for doctorate, GMAT. Additional exam requirements/recommendations for international students: Required—TOEFL (minimum score 590 paper-based), TWE.

Belhaven University, School of Business, Jackson, MS 39202-1789. Offers business administration (MBA); health administration (MBA); human resources (MBA, MSL); leadership (MBA); public administration (MPA); sports administration (MBA). MBA program also offered in Houston, TX, Memphis, TN and Orlando, FL. Part-time and evening/weekend programs available. Postbaccalaureate distance learning degree programs offered. *Faculty:* 21 full-time (4 women), 34 part-time/adjunct (12 women). *Students:* 166 full-time (112 women), 688 part-time (460 women); includes 576 minority (540 Black or African American, non-Hispanic/Latino; 2 American Indian or Alaska Native, non-Hispanic/Latino; 2 Asian, non-Hispanic/Latino; 26 Hispanic/Latino; 6 Two or more races, non-Hispanic/Latino). Average age 36. 325 applicants, 72% accepted, 185 enrolled. In 2013, 189 master's awarded. *Degree requirements:* For master's, comprehensive exam (for some programs), thesis (for some programs). *Entrance requirements:* For master's, GMAT, GRE General Test or MAT, minimum GPA of 2.8. *Application deadline:* Applications are processed on a rolling basis. Application fee: $25. Electronic applications accepted. *Financial support:* Applicants required to submit FAFSA. *Unit head:* Dr. Ralph Mason, Dean, 601-968-8949, Fax: 601-968-8951, E-mail: cmason@belhaven.edu. *Application contact:* Dr. Audrey Kelleher, Vice President of Adult and Graduate Marketing and Development, 407-804-1424, Fax: 407-620-5210, E-mail: akelleher@belhaven.edu. Website: http://www.belhaven.edu/campuses/index.htm.

Bellevue University, Graduate School, College of Business, Bellevue, NE 68005-3098. Offers acquisition and contract management (MS); business administration (MBA); finance (MS); human capital management (PhD); management (MSM).

Benedictine University, Graduate Programs, Program in Business Administration, Lisle, IL 60532-0900. Offers accounting (MBA); entrepreneurship and managing innovation (MBA); financial management (MBA); health administration (MBA); human resource management (MBA); information systems security (MBA); international business (MBA); management consulting (MBA); management information systems (MBA); marketing management (MBA); operations management and logistics (MBA); organizational leadership (MBA). Part-time and evening/weekend programs available. Postbaccalaureate distance learning degree programs offered (minimal on-campus study). *Faculty:* 4 full-time (2 women), 24 part-time/adjunct (3 women). *Students:* 144 full-time (83 women), 599 part-time (328 women); includes 189 minority (115 Black or African American, non-Hispanic/Latino; 5 American Indian or Alaska Native, non-Hispanic/Latino; 43 Asian, non-Hispanic/Latino; 24 Hispanic/Latino; 2 Native Hawaiian or other Pacific Islander, non-Hispanic/Latino), 14 international. Average age 34. 211 applicants, 89% accepted, 155 enrolled. In 2013, 376 master's awarded. *Entrance requirements:* For master's, GMAT. Additional exam requirements/recommendations for international students: Required—TOEFL (minimum score 550 paper-based). *Application deadline:* For fall admission, 9/1 for domestic students; for winter admission, 12/1 for domestic students; for spring admission, 2/15 for domestic students. Applications are processed on a rolling basis. Application fee: $40. Electronic applications accepted. *Expenses: Tuition:* Part-time $590 per credit hour. *Financial support:* Career-related internships or fieldwork and health care benefits available. Support available to part-time students. *Faculty research:* Strategic leadership in professional organizations, sociology of professions, organizational change, social identity theory, applications to change management. *Unit head:* Dr. Sharon Borowicz, Director, 630-829-6219, E-mail: sborowicz@ben.edu. *Application contact:* Kari Gibbons, Director, Admissions, 630-829-6200, Fax: 630-829-6584, E-mail: kgibbons@ben.edu.

Brandman University, School of Business and Professional Studies, Irvine, CA 92618. Offers business administration (MBA); human resources (MS); organizational leadership (MA); public administration (MPA).

Briar Cliff University, Program in Human Resource Management, Sioux City, IA 51104-0100. Offers MA. Part-time and evening/weekend programs available. *Degree requirements:* For master's, thesis optional. *Entrance requirements:* For master's, minimum undergraduate GPA of 2.77. Electronic applications accepted. *Faculty research:* Diversity in the workplace.

Brigham Young University, Graduate Studies, Marriott School of Management, Master of Public Administration Program, Provo, UT 84602. Offers finance (MPA); human resources (MPA); local government (MPA); nonprofit management (MPA); JD/MPA. *Entrance requirements:* For master's, GRE or GMAT, minimum GPA of 3.0. Additional exam requirements/recommendations for international students: Required—TOEFL (minimum score 580 paper-based; 85 iBT), IELTS (minimum score 7). Electronic applications accepted. *Expenses: Tuition:* Full-time $6130; part-time $340 per credit hour. Tuition and fees vary according to program and student's religious affiliation. *Faculty research:* Taxes, budgeting, nonprofit, ethics, decision modeling, work balance, organizational behavior.

Buffalo State College, State University of New York, The Graduate School, Faculty of Applied Science and Education, Department of Educational Foundations, Program in Adult Education, Buffalo, NY 14222-1095. Offers adult education (MS, Certificate); human resources development (Certificate). Part-time and evening/weekend programs available. Postbaccalaureate distance learning degree programs offered (no on-campus study). *Degree requirements:* For master's, comprehensive exam. *Entrance requirements:* Additional exam requirements/recommendations for international students: Required—TOEFL (minimum score 550 paper-based).

California Coast University, School of Administration and Management, Santa Ana, CA 92701. Offers business marketing (MBA); health care management (MBA); human resource management (MBA); management (MBA, MS). Postbaccalaureate distance learning degree programs offered (no on-campus study). Electronic applications accepted.

California Intercontinental University, School of Business, Diamond Bar, CA 91765. Offers banking and finance (MBA); entrepreneurship and business management (DBA); global business leadership (DBA); international management and marketing (MBA); organizational management and human resource management (MBA).

California State University, East Bay, Office of Academic Programs and Graduate Studies, College of Business and Economics, MBA Program, Hayward, CA 94542-3000. Offers entrepreneurship (MBA); finance (MBA); global innovators (MBA); human resources and organizational behavior (MBA); information technology management (MBA); marketing management (MBA); operations and supply chain management (MBA); strategy and international business (MBA). Part-time and evening/weekend programs available. *Degree requirements:* For master's, comprehensive exam or thesis. *Entrance requirements:* For master's, GMAT (minimum 20th percentile verbal and quantitative section), bachelor's degree, minimum GPA of 2.75. Additional exam requirements/recommendations for international students: Required—TOEFL (minimum score 550 paper-based; 79 iBT). Electronic applications accepted. *Expenses:* Contact institution.

California State University, East Bay, Office of Academic Programs and Graduate Studies, College of Business and Economics, Option in Human Resources and Organizational Behavior, Hayward, CA 94542-3000. Offers MBA. Part-time and evening/weekend programs available. *Degree requirements:* For master's, comprehensive exam or thesis. *Entrance requirements:* For master's, GMAT, minimum GPA of 2.75. Additional exam requirements/recommendations for international students: Required—TOEFL (minimum score 550 paper-based). Electronic applications accepted.

California State University, East Bay, Office of Academic Programs and Graduate Studies, College of Letters, Arts, and Social Sciences, Department of Public Affairs and Administration, Program in Public Administration, Hayward, CA 94542-3000. Offers health care administration (MPA); management of human resources and change (MPA); public management and policy analysis (MPA). Part-time and evening/weekend programs available. *Degree requirements:* For master's, comprehensive exam (for some programs), comprehensive exam or thesis. *Entrance requirements:* For master's, minimum GPA of 2.5; statement of purpose; 2 letters of recommendation; professional resume/curriculum vitae. Additional exam requirements/recommendations for international students: Required—TOEFL (minimum score 550 paper-based; 79 iBT). Electronic applications accepted.

California State University, Sacramento, Office of Graduate Studies, College of Business Administration, Sacramento, CA 95819. Offers accountancy (MS); business administration (IMBA, MBA); human resources (MBA); urban land development (MBA). *Accreditation:* AACSB. Part-time and evening/weekend programs available. *Degree requirements:* For master's, thesis or alternative, writing proficiency exam. *Entrance requirements:* For master's, GMAT. Additional exam requirements/recommendations for international students: Required—TOEFL. *Application deadline:* For fall admission, 2/1 for domestic students, 3/1 for international students; for spring admission, 9/15 for domestic students, 9/30 for international students. Applications are processed on a rolling basis. Application fee: $55. Electronic applications accepted. *Financial support:* Research assistantships, teaching assistantships, career-related internships or fieldwork, and Federal Work-Study available. Support available to part-time students. Financial award applicants required to submit FAFSA. *Unit head:* Dr. Sanjay Varshney, Dean, 916-278-6942, Fax: 916-278-5793, E-mail: cba@csus.edu. *Application contact:* Jose Martinez, Graduate Admissions Supervisor, 916-278-7871, E-mail: martinj@skymail.csus.edu. Website: http://www.cba.csus.edu.

Capella University, School of Business and Technology, Doctoral Programs in Business, Minneapolis, MN 55402. Offers accounting (DBA, PhD); business intelligence (DBA); finance (DBA, PhD); general business management (PhD); human resource management (DBA, PhD); leadership (DBA, PhD); management education (PhD); marketing (DBA, PhD); project management (DBA, PhD); strategy and innovation (DBA, PhD).

Capella University, School of Business and Technology, Master's Programs in Business, Minneapolis, MN 55402. Offers accounting (MBA); business analysis (MS); business intelligence (MBA); entrepreneurship (MBA); finance (MBA); general business administration (MBA); general human resource management (MS); general leadership (MS); health care management (MBA); human resource management (MBA); marketing (MBA); project management (MBA, MS).

Caribbean University, Graduate School, Bayamón, PR 00960-0493. Offers administration and supervision (MA Ed); criminal justice (MA); curriculum and instruction (MA Ed, PhD), including elementary education (MA Ed), English education (MA Ed), history education (MA Ed), mathematics education (MA Ed), primary education (MA Ed), science education (MA Ed), Spanish education (MA Ed), educational technology in instructional systems (MA Ed); gerontology (MSN); human resources (MBA); museology, archiving and art history (MA Ed); neonatal pediatrics (MSN); physical education (MA Ed); special education (MA Ed). *Entrance requirements:* For master's, interview, minimum GPA of 2.5.

Case Western Reserve University, Weatherhead School of Management, Department of Marketing and Policy Studies, Division of Labor and Human Resource Policy, Cleveland, OH 44106. Offers MBA. Part-time and evening/weekend programs available. *Entrance requirements:* For master's, GMAT. *Faculty research:* Strategic human resource management, negotiations and conflict management, human resources in high performance organizations, international human resources management, union management relations and collective bargaining.

The Catholic University of America, Metropolitan School of Professional Studies, Washington, DC 20064. Offers human resource management (MA); management (MSM). Part-time and evening/weekend programs available. *Faculty:* 54 part-time/adjunct (22 women). *Students:* 44 full-time (25 women), 206 part-time (141 women); includes 133 minority (92 Black or African American, non-Hispanic/Latino; 1 American Indian or Alaska Native, non-Hispanic/Latino; 8 Asian, non-Hispanic/Latino; 24 Hispanic/Latino; 1 Native Hawaiian or other Pacific Islander, non-Hispanic/Latino; 7 Two or more races, non-Hispanic/Latino), 13 international. Average age 37. 152 applicants, 77% accepted, 81 enrolled. In 2013, 67 master's awarded. *Degree requirements:* For master's, minimum GPA of 3.0, capstone course. *Entrance requirements:* For master's, statement of purpose, official copies of academic transcripts, three letters of recommendation, resume. Additional exam requirements/recommendations for international students: Required—TOEFL (minimum score 93 iBT). *Application deadline:* For fall admission, 8/1 priority date for domestic students, 7/15 for international students;

for spring admission, 12/1 priority date for domestic students, 10/15 for international students. Application fee: $55. *Expenses: Tuition:* Full-time $38,500; part-time $1490 per credit hour. *Required fees:* $400; $1525 per credit hour. One-time fee: $425. Tuition and fees vary according to program. *Total annual research expenditures:* $183,115. *Unit head:* Dr. Sara Thompson, Dean, 202-319-5256, Fax: 202-319-6032, E-mail: thompsons@cua.edu. *Application contact:* Andrew Woodall, Director of Graduate Admissions, 202-319-5057, Fax: 202-319-6533, E-mail: cua-admissions@cua.edu. Website: http://metro.cua.edu/.

Central Michigan University, Central Michigan University Global Campus, Program in Administration, Mount Pleasant, MI 48859. Offers acquisitions administration (MSA, Certificate); engineering management administration (MSA, Certificate); general administration (MSA, Certificate); health services administration (MSA, Certificate); human resources administration (MSA, Certificate); information resource management (MSA); information resource management administration (Certificate); international administration (MSA, Certificate); leadership (MSA, Certificate); philanthropy and fundraising administration (MSA, Certificate); public administration (MSA, Certificate); recreation and park administration (MSA); research administration (MSA, Certificate). Part-time and evening/weekend programs available. Postbaccalaureate distance learning degree programs offered (no on-campus study). *Students:* Average age 38. *Entrance requirements:* For master's, minimum GPA of 2.7 in major. *Application deadline:* Applications are processed on a rolling basis. Application fee: $50. Electronic applications accepted. *Financial support:* Scholarships/grants available. Support available to part-time students. Financial award applicants required to submit FAFSA. *Unit head:* Dr. Patricia Chase, Director, 989-774-1845, E-mail: chase1pb@cmich.edu. *Application contact:* 877-268-4636, E-mail: cmuglobal@cmich.edu.

Central Michigan University, Central Michigan University Global Campus, Program in Business Administration, Mount Pleasant, MI 48859. Offers enterprise resource planning (MBA, Certificate); human resource management (MBA); logistics management (MBA, Certificate); marketing (MBA); value-driven organization (MBA). Part-time and evening/weekend programs available. *Entrance requirements:* For master's, GMAT. *Financial support:* Scholarships/grants available. Support available to part-time students. *Unit head:* Dr. Debasish Chakraborty, 989-774-3678, E-mail: chakt1d@cmich.edu. *Application contact:* Global Campus Student Services Call Center, 877-268-4636, E-mail: cmuglobal@cmich.edu.

Central Michigan University, College of Graduate Studies, College of Business Administration, MBA Program, Mount Pleasant, MI 48859. Offers accounting (MBA); business economics (MBA); consulting (MBA); finance (MBA); general business (MBA); human resource management (MBA); information systems (MBA); international business (MBA); logistics management (MBA); marketing (MBA); value-driven organization (MBA). Part-time and evening/weekend programs available. Postbaccalaureate distance learning degree programs offered (no on-campus study). Electronic applications accepted. *Faculty research:* Accounting, consulting, international business, marketing, information systems.

Central Michigan University, College of Graduate Studies, Interdisciplinary Administration Programs, Mount Pleasant, MI 48859. Offers acquisitions administration (MSA, Graduate Certificate); general administration (MSA, Graduate Certificate); health services administration (MSA, Graduate Certificate); human resource administration (Graduate Certificate); human resources administration (MSA); information resource management (MSA, Graduate Certificate); international administration (MSA, Graduate Certificate); leadership (MSA, Graduate Certificate); public administration (MSA, Graduate Certificate); research administration (Graduate Certificate); sport administration (MSA). *Accreditation:* AACSB. Part-time and evening/weekend programs available. Postbaccalaureate distance learning degree programs offered (no on-campus study). *Degree requirements:* For master's, thesis or alternative. *Entrance requirements:* For master's, bachelor's degree with minimum GPA of 2.7. Electronic applications accepted. *Faculty research:* Interdisciplinary studies in acquisitions administration, health services administration, sport administration, recreation and park administration, and international administration.

City University of Seattle, Graduate Division, School of Management, Bellevue, WA 98005. Offers accounting (Certificate); change leadership (MBA, Certificate); computer systems (MS); finance (Certificate); financial management (MBA); general management (MBA); general management-Europe (MBA); global marketing (MBA); human resources management (Certificate); individualized study (MBA); information security (MS); information systems (MBA); leadership (MA); marketing (MBA, Certificate); project management (MBA, MS, Certificate); sustainable business (Certificate); technology management (MBA, Certificate). Part-time and evening/weekend programs available. Postbaccalaureate distance learning degree programs offered (no on-campus study). *Degree requirements:* For master's, comprehensive exam (for some programs), thesis (for some programs). *Entrance requirements:* Additional exam requirements/recommendations for international students: Required—TOEFL (minimum score 567 paper-based; 87 iBT); Recommended—IELTS. Electronic applications accepted.

Claremont Graduate University, Graduate Programs, School of Social Science, Policy and Evaluation, Program in Human Resources Design, Claremont, CA 91711-6160. Offers MS. Part-time and evening/weekend programs available. *Students:* 9 full-time (5 women), 5 part-time (3 women); includes 4 minority (2 Asian, non-Hispanic/Latino; 1 Hispanic/Latino; 1 Two or more races, non-Hispanic/Latino), 6 international. Average age 27. In 2013, 12 master's awarded. *Entrance requirements:* For master's, GMAT or GRE General Test. Additional exam requirements/recommendations for international students: Required—TOEFL (minimum score 550 paper-based; 80 iBT). *Application deadline:* For fall admission, 1/15 priority date for domestic and international students. Applications are processed on a rolling basis. Application fee: $80. Electronic applications accepted. *Expenses: Tuition:* Full-time $40,560; part-time $1690 per credit. *Required fees:* $275 per semester. Tuition and fees vary according to program. *Financial support:* Fellowships, Federal Work-Study, institutionally sponsored loans, and scholarships/grants available. Support available to part-time students. Financial award application deadline: 2/15; financial award applicants required to submit FAFSA. *Unit head:* Stewart Donaldson, Dean. *Application contact:* Annekah Hall, Assistant Director of Admissions, 909-607-3371, E-mail: annekah.hall@cgu.edu. Website: http://www.cgu.edu/pages/672.asp.

Clemson University, Graduate School, College of Health, Education, and Human Development, Eugene T. Moore School of Education, Program in Human Resource Development, Clemson, SC 29634. Offers MHRD. Part-time and evening/weekend programs available. Postbaccalaureate distance learning degree programs offered (no on-campus study). *Students:* 6 full-time (3 women), 130 part-time (68 women); includes 39 minority (32 Black or African American, non-Hispanic/Latino; 5 Hispanic/Latino; 2 Two or more races, non-Hispanic/Latino). Average age 34. 91 applicants, 93% accepted, 75 enrolled. In 2013, 31 master's awarded. *Degree requirements:* For master's, comprehensive exam. *Entrance requirements:* For master's, GRE General Test. Additional exam requirements/recommendations for international students: Required—TOEFL; Recommended—IELTS. *Application deadline:* For fall admission, 7/1 for domestic students. Application fee: $70 ($80 for international students). Electronic applications accepted. *Expenses:* Contact institution. *Financial support:* In 2013–14, 1 student received support. Application deadline: 6/1; applicants required to submit FAFSA. *Faculty research:* Organizational development, human performance improvement, attachment theory, social constructivism, technology-mediated teaching and learning, corporate universities. *Unit head:* Dr. Michael J. Padilla, Director/Associate Dean, 864-656-4444, Fax: 864-656-0311, E-mail: pmcgee@clemson.edu. *Application contact:* Dr. David Fleming, Coordinator, 864-656-1881, Fax: 864-656-0311, E-mail: dflemin@clemson.edu. Website: http://www.hehd.clemson.edu/MHRD/SoE_Webpage/MHRD.html.

Cleveland State University, College of Graduate Studies, Monte Ahuja College of Business, Department of Management, Cleveland, OH 44115. Offers labor relations and human resources (MLRHR). Part-time and evening/weekend programs available. *Faculty:* 10 full-time (6 women), 8 part-time/adjunct (2 women). *Students:* 33 full-time (27 women), 40 part-time (31 women); includes 14 minority (9 Black or African American, non-Hispanic/Latino; 1 Asian, non-Hispanic/Latino; 2 Hispanic/Latino; 2 Two or more races, non-Hispanic/Latino), 17 international. Average age 29. 98 applicants, 44% accepted, 12 enrolled. In 2013, 29 master's awarded. *Entrance requirements:* For master's, GMAT or GRE, minimum GPA of 3.0. Additional exam requirements/recommendations for international students: Required—TOEFL (minimum score 525 paper-based). *Application deadline:* For fall admission, 7/15 for domestic students; for spring admission, 12/15 for domestic students. Applications are processed on a rolling basis. Application fee: $30. Electronic applications accepted. *Expenses:* Tuition, state resident: full-time $8335; part-time $521 per credit hour. Tuition, nonresident: full-time $15,670; part-time $979 per credit hour. *Required fees:* $50; $25 per semester. *Financial support:* In 2013–14, 3 students received support, including 3 research assistantships with full and partial tuition reimbursements available (averaging $6,960 per year); tuition waivers (full) and unspecified assistantships also available. Financial award application deadline: 5/1; financial award applicants required to submit FAFSA. *Faculty research:* Human resource management, strategic management, organizational behavior, health care management. *Unit head:* Dr. Timothy G. DeGroot, Chairperson, 216-687-4747, Fax: 216-687-4708, E-mail: t.degroot@csuohio.edu. *Application contact:* Lisa Sample, Administrative Secretary, 216-687-4726, E-mail: l.m.sample@csuohio.edu. Website: http://www.csuohio.edu/business/academics/mlr/.

College of Saint Elizabeth, Department of Business Administration and Management, Morristown, NJ 07960-6989. Offers human resource management (MS); organizational change (MS). Part-time programs available. *Faculty:* 1 full-time (0 women), 2 part-time/adjunct (1 woman). *Students:* 6 full-time (5 women), 33 part-time (25 women); includes 14 minority (8 Black or African American, non-Hispanic/Latino; 1 Asian, non-Hispanic/Latino; 5 Hispanic/Latino), 1 international. Average age 34. In 2013, 17 master's awarded. *Entrance requirements:* For master's, minimum GPA of 3.0, personal statement/self-assessment. Additional exam requirements/recommendations for international students: Required—TOEFL. *Application deadline:* Applications are processed on a rolling basis. Application fee: $35. Electronic applications accepted. *Expenses: Tuition:* Full-time $19,152; part-time $1064 per credit. *Financial support:* Career-related internships or fieldwork, tuition waivers (partial), and unspecified assistantships available. Support available to part-time students. Financial award application deadline: 3/15; financial award applicants required to submit FAFSA. *Unit head:* Dr. Jonathan H. Silver, Professor, Graduate Program in Management, 973-290-4113, E-mail: jsilver@cse.edu. *Application contact:* Deborah S. Cobo, Associate Director of Graduate Admission, 973-290-4194, Fax: 973-290-4710, E-mail: dscobo@cse.edu. Website: http://www.cse.edu/academics/catalog/academic-programs/business-administration.dot.

Colorado Technical University Colorado Springs, Graduate Studies, Program in Management, Colorado Springs, CO 80907-3896. Offers accounting (MBA, MSA); business administration (MBA); finance (MBA); human resources management (MBA); logistics/supply chain management (MBA); management (DM); marketing (MBA); mediation and dispute resolution (MBA); operations management (MBA); project management (MBA); technology management (MBA). Part-time and evening/weekend programs available. Postbaccalaureate distance learning degree programs offered. *Degree requirements:* For master's, thesis or alternative; for doctorate, thesis/dissertation. *Entrance requirements:* For doctorate, minimum graduate GPA of 3.0, 5 years of related work experience. *Faculty research:* Sexual harassment, performance evaluation, critical thinking.

Colorado Technical University Denver South, Programs in Business Administration and Management, Aurora, CO 80014. Offers accounting (MBA); business administration (MBA); business administration and management (EMBA); finance (MBA); human resource management (MBA); marketing (MBA); mediation and dispute resolution (MBA); operations management (MBA); project management (MBA); technology management (MBA). Part-time and evening/weekend programs available. *Degree requirements:* For master's, thesis or alternative. *Entrance requirements:* For master's, minimum undergraduate GPA of 3.0, resume.

Columbia Southern University, MBA Program, Orange Beach, AL 36561. Offers finance (MBA); health care management (MBA); human resource management (MBA); marketing (MBA); project management (MBA); public administration (MBA). Part-time and evening/weekend programs available. Postbaccalaureate distance learning degree programs offered (no on-campus study). *Entrance requirements:* For master's, bachelor's degree from accredited/approved institution. Additional exam requirements/recommendations for international students: Required—TOEFL. Electronic applications accepted.

Columbia University, Graduate School of Business, MBA Program, New York, NY 10027. Offers accounting (MBA); decision, risk, and operations (MBA); entrepreneurship (MBA); finance and economics (MBA); healthcare and pharmaceutical management (MBA); human resource management (MBA); international business (MBA); leadership and ethics (MBA); management (MBA); marketing (MBA); media (MBA); private equity (MBA); real estate (MBA); social enterprise (MBA); value investing (MBA); DDS/MBA; JD/MBA; MBA/MIA; MBA/MPH; MBA/MS; MD/MBA. *Entrance requirements:* For master's, GMAT, 2 letters of recommendation. Additional exam requirements/recommendations for international students: Required—TOEFL. Electronic applications accepted. *Expenses:* Contact institution. *Faculty research:* Human decision making and behavioral research; real estate market and mortgage defaults; financial crisis and corporate governance; international business; security analysis and accounting.

Concordia University, St. Paul, College of Business and Organizational Leadership, St. Paul, MN 55104-5494. Offers business and organizational leadership (MBA); criminal justice leadership (MA); forensic mental health (MA); health care management (MBA); human resource management (MA); leadership and management (MA). *Accreditation:* ACBSP. Evening/weekend programs available. Postbaccalaureate distance learning degree programs offered (minimal on-campus study). *Faculty:* 10 full-time (3 women), 20 part-time/adjunct (9 women). *Students:* 336 full-time (222 women), 84 part-time (44 women); includes 82 minority (46 Black or African American, non-Hispanic/Latino; 1 American Indian or Alaska Native, non-Hispanic/Latino; 17 Asian, non-Hispanic/Latino; 9 Hispanic/Latino; 1 Native Hawaiian or other Pacific Islander, non-Hispanic/Latino; 8 Two or more races, non-Hispanic/Latino), 1 international. Average age 34. 405 applicants, 50% accepted, 187 enrolled. In 2013, 253 master's awarded.

Human Resources Management

Degree requirements: For master's, thesis (for some programs). *Entrance requirements:* For master's, official transcripts from regionally-accredited institution stating the conferral of a bachelor's degree with minimum cumulative GPA of 3.0; personal statement; professional resume. Additional exam requirements/recommendations for international students: Recommended—TOEFL (minimum score 547 paper-based; 78 iBT), IELTS (minimum score 6). *Application deadline:* For fall admission, 8/1 for domestic and international students; for spring admission, 12/1 for domestic and international students; for summer admission, 5/1 for domestic and international students. Applications are processed on a rolling basis. Application fee: $50. Electronic applications accepted. *Expenses: Tuition:* Full-time $6200; part-time $425 per credit. Tuition and fees vary according to degree level and program. *Financial support:* Applicants required to submit FAFSA. *Unit head:* Lonn Maly, Dean, 651-641-8203, Fax: 651-641-8807, E-mail: maly@csp.edu. *Application contact:* Kimberly Craig, Director of Graduate and Cohort Admission, 651-603-6223, Fax: 651-603-6320, E-mail: craig@csp.edu.

Concordia University Wisconsin, Graduate Programs, School of Business and Legal Studies, MBA Program, Mequon, WI 53097-2402. Offers finance (MBA); health care administration (MBA); human resource management (MBA); international business (MBA); international business-bilingual English/Chinese (MBA); management (MBA); management information systems (MBA); managerial communications (MBA); marketing (MBA); public administration (MBA); risk management (MBA). Postbaccalaureate distance learning degree programs offered (minimal on-campus study). *Degree requirements:* For master's, comprehensive exam, thesis or alternative. *Entrance requirements:* Additional exam requirements/recommendations for international students: Required—TOEFL. *Expenses:* Contact institution.

Cornell University, Graduate School, Graduate Fields of Industrial and Labor Relations, Ithaca, NY 14853. Offers collective bargaining, labor law and labor history (MILR, MPS, MS, PhD); economic and social statistics (MILR); human resource studies (MILR, MPS, MS, PhD); industrial and labor relations problems (MILR, MPS, MS, PhD); international and comparative labor (MILR, MPS, MS, PhD); labor economics (MILR, MPS, MS, PhD); organizational behavior (MILR, MPS, MS, PhD). *Faculty:* 55 full-time (15 women). *Students:* 174 full-time (102 women); includes 30 minority (10 Black or African American, non-Hispanic/Latino; 11 Asian, non-Hispanic/Latino; 5 Hispanic/Latino; 4 Two or more races, non-Hispanic/Latino), 60 international. Average age 29. 353 applicants, 25% accepted, 77 enrolled. In 2013, 69 master's, 4 doctorates awarded. *Degree requirements:* For master's, thesis (MS); for doctorate, comprehensive exam, thesis/dissertation, teaching experience. *Entrance requirements:* For master's and doctorate, GMAT or GRE General Test, 2 academic recommendations. Additional exam requirements/recommendations for international students: Required—TOEFL (minimum score 550 paper-based; 77 iBT). Application fee: $95. Electronic applications accepted. *Expenses:* Contact institution. *Financial support:* In 2013–14, 64 students received support, including 9 fellowships with full tuition reimbursements available, 24 research assistantships with full tuition reimbursements available, 31 teaching assistantships with full tuition reimbursements available; institutionally sponsored loans, scholarships/grants, health care benefits, tuition waivers (full and partial), and unspecified assistantships also available. Financial award applicants required to submit FAFSA. *Unit head:* Director of Graduate Studies, 607-255-1522. *Application contact:* Graduate Field Assistant, 607-255-1522, E-mail: ilrgradapplicant@cornell.edu.
Website: http://www.gradschool.cornell.edu/fields.php?id-85&a-2.

Dallas Baptist University, College of Business, Management Program, Dallas, TX 75211-9299. Offers conflict resolution management (MA); general management (MA); health care management (MA); human resource management (MA); organizational management (MA); performance management (MA); professional sales and management optimization (MA). Part-time and evening/weekend programs available. *Entrance requirements:* For master's, GRE General Test, minimum GPA of 3.0. Additional exam requirements/recommendations for international students: Required—TOEFL, IELTS. *Application deadline:* Applications are processed on a rolling basis. Application fee: $25. Electronic applications accepted. *Expenses: Tuition:* Full-time $13,410; part-time $745 per credit hour. *Required fees:* $300; $150 per semester. Tuition and fees vary according to degree level. *Financial support:* Federal Work-Study, institutionally sponsored loans, scholarships/grants, and tuition waivers (full and partial) available. Support available to part-time students. Financial award applicants required to submit FAFSA. *Faculty research:* Organizational behavior, conflict personalities. *Unit head:* Joanne Hix, Director, 214-333-5280, Fax: 214-333-5293, E-mail: graduate@dbu.edu. *Application contact:* Kit P. Montgomery, Director of Graduate Programs, 214-333-5242, Fax: 214-333-5579, E-mail: graduate@dbu.edu.
Website: http://www3.dbu.edu/graduate/maom.asp.

Davenport University, Sneden Graduate School, Grand Rapids, MI 49512. Offers accounting (MBA); business administration (EMBA); finance (MBA); health care management (MBA); human resources (MBA); information assurance (MS); public health (MPH); strategic management (MBA). Evening/weekend programs available. *Entrance requirements:* For master's, GMAT, minimum undergraduate GPA of 2.75. Additional exam requirements/recommendations for international students: Required—TOEFL. Electronic applications accepted. *Faculty research:* Leadership, management, marketing, organizational culture.

Delaware Valley College, MBA Program, Doylestown, PA 18901-2697. Offers accounting (MBA); entrepreneurship (MBA); finance (MBA); food and agribusiness (MBA); general business (MBA); global executive leadership (MBA); human resource management (MBA); supply chain management (MBA). Part-time and evening/weekend programs available. Postbaccalaureate distance learning degree programs offered (no on-campus study). *Students:* 32 full-time (17 women), 183 part-time (99 women). Average age 34. 97 applicants, 78% accepted, 74 enrolled. *Entrance requirements:* For master's, minimum undergraduate GPA of 3.0. *Application deadline:* Applications are processed on a rolling basis. Application fee: $50. Electronic applications accepted. *Expenses:* Contact institution. *Financial support:* Applicants required to submit FAFSA. *Unit head:* Mike Prushan, Director of MBA Program, 215-489-2322, E-mail: michael.prushan@delval.edu. *Application contact:* Robin Mathews, Graduate and Continuing Studies Enrollment Manager, 215-489-2955, Fax: 215-489-4832, E-mail: robin.mathews@delval.edu.
Website: http://www.delval.edu/academics/graduate/master-of-business-administration.

DePaul University, Charles H. Kellstadt Graduate School of Business, Chicago, IL 60604. Offers accountancy (M Acc, MS, MSA); applied economics (MBA); banking (MBA); behavioral finance (MBA); brand and product management (MBA); business development (MBA); business information technology (MS); business strategy and decision-making (MBA); computational finance (MS); consumer insights (MBA); corporate finance (MBA); economic policy analysis (MS); entrepreneurship (MBA, MS); finance (MBA, MS); financial analysis (MBA); general business (MBA); health sector management (MBA); hospitality leadership (MBA); hospitality leadership and operational performance (MS); human resource management (MBA); human resources (MS); investment management (MBA); leadership and change management (MBA); management accounting (MBA); marketing (MBA, MS); marketing analysis (MS); marketing strategy and planning (MBA); operations management (MBA); organizational diversity (MBA); real estate (MS); real estate finance and investment (MBA); revenue management (MBA); sports management (MBA); strategic global marketing (MBA); strategy, execution and valuation (MBA); sustainable management (MBA, MS); taxation (MS); wealth management (MS); JD/MBA. *Accreditation:* AACSB. Part-time and evening/weekend programs available. Postbaccalaureate distance learning degree programs offered (no on-campus study). *Faculty:* 81 full-time (20 women), 45 part-time/adjunct (8 women). *Students:* 1,238 full-time (605 women), 617 part-time (223 women); includes 295 minority (71 Black or African American, non-Hispanic/Latino; 129 Asian, non-Hispanic/Latino; 74 Hispanic/Latino; 4 Native Hawaiian or other Pacific Islander, non-Hispanic/Latino; 17 Two or more races, non-Hispanic/Latino), 462 international. Average age 29. In 2013, 911 master's awarded. *Entrance requirements:* For master's, GMAT, 2 letters of recommendation, resume, essay, official transcripts. Additional exam requirements/recommendations for international students: Required—TOEFL (minimum score 550 paper-based; 80 iBT). *Application deadline:* For fall admission, 7/1 for domestic students, 6/1 for international students; for winter admission, 10/1 for domestic students, 9/1 for international students; for spring admission, 2/1 for domestic students, 1/1 for international students. Applications are processed on a rolling basis. Application fee: $60. Electronic applications accepted. *Expenses:* Contact institution. *Financial support:* Application deadline: 4/1; applicants required to submit FAFSA. *Unit head:* Robert T. Ryan, Assistant Dean and Director, 312-362-8810, Fax: 312-362-6677, E-mail: rryan1@depaul.edu. *Application contact:* James Parker, Director of Recruitment and Admission, 312-362-8810, Fax: 312-362-6677, E-mail: kgsb@depaul.edu.
Website: http://kellstadt.depaul.edu.

DeSales University, Graduate Division, Division of Business, Center Valley, PA 18034-9568. Offers accounting (MBA); computer information systems (MBA); finance (MBA); health care systems management (MBA); human resources management (MBA); management (MBA); marketing (MBA); project management (MBA); self-design (MBA). *Accreditation:* ACBSP. Part-time and evening/weekend programs available. Postbaccalaureate distance learning degree programs offered (no on-campus study). *Students:* 444 part-time. Average age 37. In 2013, 1 master's awarded. *Entrance requirements:* For master's, GMAT, minimum GPA of 3.0, 2 years of work experience. Additional exam requirements/recommendations for international students: Required—TOEFL. *Application deadline:* Applications are processed on a rolling basis. Application fee: $50. Electronic applications accepted. *Expenses: Tuition:* Part-time $790 per credit. *Financial support:* Applicants required to submit FAFSA. *Faculty research:* Quality improvement, executive development, productivity, cross-cultural managerial differences, leadership. *Unit head:* Dr. David Gilfoil, Director, 610-282-1100 Ext. 1828, Fax: 610-282-2869, E-mail: david.gilfoil@desales.edu. *Application contact:* Abigail Wernicki, Director of Graduate Admissions, 610-282-1100 Ext. 1768, E-mail: gradadmissions@desales.edu.

DeVry University, Graduate Programs, Downers Grove, IL 60515. Offers accounting and financial management (MAFM); business administration (MBA); education (MS); educational technology (MS); electrical engineering (MS); human resources management (MHRM); information systems management (MISM); network and communications management (MNCM); project management (MPM); public administration (MPA).

Dowling College, School of Business, Oakdale, NY 11769. Offers aviation management (MBA, Certificate); corporate finance (MBA, Certificate); health care management (MBA); human resource management (Certificate); information systems management (MBA); management and leadership (MBA); marketing (Certificate); project management (Certificate); public management (MBA); school district business leader (MBA); sport, event and entertainment management (Certificate); JD/MBA. Part-time and evening/weekend programs available. Postbaccalaureate distance learning degree programs offered (minimal on-campus study). *Faculty:* 7 full-time (2 women), 43 part-time/adjunct (7 women). *Students:* 183 full-time (79 women), 299 part-time (142 women); includes 137 minority (84 Black or African American, non-Hispanic/Latino; 14 Asian, non-Hispanic/Latino; 20 Hispanic/Latino; 19 Native Hawaiian or other Pacific Islander, non-Hispanic/Latino). Average age 32. 360 applicants, 58% accepted, 127 enrolled. In 2013, 235 master's, 15 other advanced degrees awarded. *Degree requirements:* For master's, comprehensive exam, thesis optional. *Entrance requirements:* For master's, minimum GPA of 2.8, 2 letters of recommendation, courses or seminar in accounting and finance, resume. Additional exam requirements/recommendations for international students: Required—TOEFL (minimum score 550 paper-based). *Application deadline:* For fall admission, 9/1 priority date for domestic students; for winter admission, 1/1 priority date for domestic students; for spring admission, 2/1 priority date for domestic students. Applications are processed on a rolling basis. Application fee: $50. Electronic applications accepted. *Expenses: Tuition:* Full-time $22,731; part-time $1029 per credit. *Required fees:* $956; $956. *Financial support:* Career-related internships or fieldwork and Federal Work-Study available. Support available to part-time students. Financial award application deadline: 6/30; financial award applicants required to submit FAFSA. *Faculty research:* International finance, computer applications, labor relations, executive development. *Unit head:* Dr. Elana Zolfo, Dean, 631-244-3266, Fax: 631-244-1018, E-mail: zolfoe@dowling.edu. *Application contact:* Mary Boullianne, Dean of Admissions, 631-244-3274, Fax: 631-244-1059, E-mail: boulliam@dowling.edu.

East Central University, School of Graduate Studies, Department of Human Resources, Ada, OK 74820-6899. Offers administration (MSHR); counseling (MSHR); criminal justice (MSHR); human services (MSHR); rehabilitation counseling (MSHR). *Accreditation:* CORE. Part-time and evening/weekend programs available. *Degree requirements:* For master's, thesis optional. *Entrance requirements:* For master's, GRE General Test, MAT, minimum GPA of 2.5. Electronic applications accepted.

Eastern Michigan University, Graduate School, College of Arts and Sciences, Department of Political Science, Programs in Public Administration, Ypsilanti, MI 48197. Offers local government management (Graduate Certificate); management of public healthcare services (Graduate Certificate); public administration (MPA, Graduate Certificate); public budget management (Graduate Certificate); public land planning (Graduate Certificate); public management (Graduate Certificate); public personnel management (Graduate Certificate); public policy analysis (Graduate Certificate). *Accreditation:* NASPAA. *Students:* 8 full-time (5 women), 59 part-time (30 women); includes 14 minority (10 Black or African American, non-Hispanic/Latino; 2 Asian, non-Hispanic/Latino; 2 Hispanic/Latino), 1 international. Average age 36. 43 applicants, 63% accepted, 13 enrolled. In 2013, 25 master's, 6 other advanced degrees awarded. Application fee: $35. *Expenses:* Tuition, state resident: full-time $12,300; part-time $466 per credit hour. Tuition, nonresident: full-time $23,159; part-time $918 per credit hour. *Required fees:* $71 per credit hour. $46 per semester. One-time fee: $100. Tuition and fees vary according to course level and degree level. *Unit head:* Dr. Arnold Fleischmann, Department Head, 734-487-3113, Fax: 734-487-3340, E-mail: afleisch@emich.edu. *Application contact:* Dr. Gregory Plagens, Program Director, 734-487-2522, Fax: 734-487-3340, E-mail: gregory.plagens@emich.edu.

Eastern Michigan University, Graduate School, College of Business, Department of Management, Program in Human Resources Management and Organizational Development, Ypsilanti, MI 48197. Offers MSHROD. Part-time and evening/weekend programs available. Postbaccalaureate distance learning degree programs offered (minimal on-campus study). *Students:* 10 full-time (7 women), 60 part-time (46 women);

includes 18 minority (13 Black or African American, non-Hispanic/Latino; 2 Asian, non-Hispanic/Latino; 2 Hispanic/Latino; 1 Two or more races, non-Hispanic/Latino), 9 international. Average age 30. 39 applicants, 59% accepted, 9 enrolled. In 2013, 83 master's awarded. *Degree requirements:* For master's, thesis optional. *Entrance requirements:* For master's, GMAT. Additional exam requirements/recommendations for international students: Required—TOEFL. *Application deadline:* Applications are processed on a rolling basis. Application fee: $35. *Expenses:* Tuition, state resident: full-time $12,300; part-time $466 per credit hour. Tuition, nonresident: full-time $23,159; part-time $918 per credit hour. *Required fees:* $71 per credit hour. $46 per semester. One-time fee: $100. Tuition and fees vary according to course level and degree level. *Financial support:* Fellowships, research assistantships with full tuition reimbursements, teaching assistantships with full tuition reimbursements, career-related internships or fieldwork, Federal Work-Study, institutionally sponsored loans, scholarships/grants, tuition waivers (partial), and unspecified assistantships available. Support available to part-time students. Financial award applicants required to submit FAFSA. *Unit head:* Dr. Fraya Wagner-Marsh, Department Head, 734-487-3240, Fax: 734-487-4100, E-mail: fraya.wagner@emich.edu. *Application contact:* Dr. Fraya Wagner-Marsh, Department Head/Advisor, 734-487-3240, Fax: 734-483-4100, E-mail: fray.wagner@emich.edu. Website: http://www.emich.edu/public/cob/management/mshrod.

Eastern Michigan University, Graduate School, College of Business, Programs in Business Administration, Ypsilanti, MI 48197. Offers business administration (MBA, Graduate Certificate); computer information systems (Graduate Certificate); e-business (MBA, Graduate Certificate); enterprise business intelligence (MBA); entrepreneurship (MBA, Graduate Certificate); finance (MBA, Graduate Certificate); human resources (MBA); human resources management (Graduate Certificate); information systems (MBA); internal auditing (MBA); international business (MBA, Graduate Certificate); marketing management (Graduate Certificate); nonprofit management (MBA); organizational development (Graduate Certificate); supply chain management (MBA, Graduate Certificate). *Accreditation:* AACSB. Part-time programs available. Postbaccalaureate distance learning degree programs offered (no on-campus study). *Students:* 74 full-time (28 women), 342 part-time (183 women); includes 122 minority (84 Black or African American, non-Hispanic/Latino; 2 American Indian or Alaska Native, non-Hispanic/Latino; 19 Asian, non-Hispanic/Latino; 7 Hispanic/Latino; 10 Two or more races, non-Hispanic/Latino), 38 international. Average age 33. 305 applicants, 72% accepted, 131 enrolled. In 2013, 69 master's, 57 other advanced degrees awarded. *Entrance requirements:* For master's, GMAT (minimum score 450), minimum cumulative undergraduate GPA of 2.75. Additional exam requirements/recommendations for international students: Required—TOEFL. *Application deadline:* For fall admission, 5/15 for domestic students, 5/1 for international students; for winter admission, 10/15 for domestic students, 10/1 for international students; for spring admission, 3/15 for domestic students, 3/1 for international students. Applications are processed on a rolling basis. Application fee: $35. *Expenses:* Tuition, state resident: full-time $12,300; part-time $466 per credit hour. Tuition, nonresident: full-time $23,159; part-time $918 per credit hour. *Required fees:* $71 per credit hour. $46 per semester. One-time fee: $100. Tuition and fees vary according to course level and degree level. *Financial support:* Fellowships, research assistantships with full tuition reimbursements, teaching assistantships with full tuition reimbursements, career-related internships or fieldwork, Federal Work-Study, institutionally sponsored loans, scholarships/grants, tuition waivers (partial), and unspecified assistantships available. Support available to part-time students. Financial award applicants required to submit FAFSA. *Unit head:* K. Michelle Henry, Director, Academic Services, 734-487-4444, Fax: 734-483-1316, E-mail: mhenry1@emich.edu. *Application contact:* Beste Windes, Advisor, 734-487-4444, Fax: 734-483-1316, E-mail: bwindes@emich.edu. Website: http://www.emich.edu/public/cob/gr/grad.html.

Emmanuel College, Graduate Studies, Graduate Programs in Management, Boston, MA 02115. Offers biopharmaceutical leadership (MSM, Graduate Certificate); human resource management (MSM, Graduate Certificate); management (MSM); management and leadership (Graduate Certificate); research administration (MSM, Graduate Certificate). Part-time and evening/weekend programs available. Postbaccalaureate distance learning degree programs offered (no on-campus study). *Faculty:* 1 (woman) full-time, 41 part-time/adjunct (15 women). *Students:* 5 full-time (4 women), 152 part-time (123 women); includes 49 minority (31 Black or African American, non-Hispanic/Latino; 1 American Indian or Alaska Native, non-Hispanic/Latino; 4 Asian, non-Hispanic/Latino; 13 Hispanic/Latino). Average age 36. In 2013, 82 master's, 4 other advanced degrees awarded. *Degree requirements:* For master's, thesis or alternative, 36 credits, including 6-credit capstone project. *Entrance requirements:* For master's and Graduate Certificate, transcripts from all regionally-accredited institutions attended (showing proof of bachelor's degree completion), 2 letters of recommendation, essay, resume, interview. Additional exam requirements/recommendations for international students: Required—TOEFL (minimum score 600 paper-based; 106 iBT) or IELTS (minimum score 6.5). *Application deadline:* For fall admission, 7/31 priority date for domestic students; for spring admission, 11/30 priority date for domestic students. Applications are processed on a rolling basis. Application fee: $0. Electronic applications accepted. *Financial support:* Applicants required to submit FAFSA. *Unit head:* Sandy Robbins, Dean of Enrollment, 617-735-9700, Fax: 617-507-0434, E-mail: graduatestudies@emmanuel.edu. *Application contact:* Enrollment Counselor, 617-735-9700, Fax: 617-507-0434, E-mail: graduatestudies@emmanuel.edu. Website: http://www.emmanuel.edu/graduate-studies-nursing/academics/management.html.

Emmanuel College, Graduate Studies, Program in Human Resource Management, Boston, MA 02115. Offers MS, Graduate Certificate. Part-time and evening/weekend programs available. *Faculty:* 1 (woman) full-time, 27 part-time/adjunct (8 women). *Students:* 1 full-time (0 women), 62 part-time (47 women); includes 17 minority (13 Black or African American, non-Hispanic/Latino; 1 American Indian or Alaska Native, non-Hispanic/Latino; 3 Hispanic/Latino). Average age 32. In 2013, 19 master's awarded. *Entrance requirements:* For master's, interview, resume, 2 letters of recommendation, essay, bachelor's degree; for Graduate Certificate, interview, resume, letter of recommendation. Additional exam requirements/recommendations for international students: Required—TOEFL (minimum score 600 paper-based). *Application deadline:* For fall admission, 8/15 priority date for domestic students; for spring admission, 12/8 priority date for domestic students. Applications are processed on a rolling basis. Application fee: $50. Electronic applications accepted. *Unit head:* Sandy Robbins, Dean of Enrollment, 617-735-9700, Fax: 617-507-0434, E-mail: graduatestudies@emmanuel.edu. *Application contact:* Enrollment Counselor, 617-735-9700, Fax: 617-507-0434, E-mail: graduatestudies@emmanuel.edu. Website: http://www.emmanuel.edu/graduate-studies-nursing/academics/management/human-resource-management.html.

Everest University, Department of Business Administration, Tampa, FL 33614-5899. Offers accounting (MBA); human resources (MBA); international business (MBA). Part-time and evening/weekend programs available. *Degree requirements:* For master's, thesis optional. *Entrance requirements:* For master's, GMAT or GRE General Test, minimum GPA of 3.0.

Everest University, Program in Business Administration, Largo, FL 33770. Offers accounting (MBA); human resources management (MBA); international business (MBA). *Faculty research:* Management fads, learning styles, effective use of technology.

Everest University, Program in Business Administration, Orlando, FL 32819. Offers accounting (MBA); general management (MBA); human resources (MBA); international management (MBA).

Fairfield University, Charles F. Dolan School of Business, Fairfield, CT 06824-5195. Offers accounting (MBA, MS, CAS); accounting information systems (MBA, CAS); entrepreneurship (MBA, CAS); finance (MBA, MS, CAS); general management (MBA, CAS); human resource management (MBA, CAS); information systems and operations (MBA); information systems and operations management (CAS); marketing (MBA, CAS); taxation (MBA, CAS). *Accreditation:* AACSB. Part-time and evening/weekend programs available. *Faculty:* 18 full-time (9 women), 15 part-time/adjunct (4 women). *Students:* 94 full-time (45 women), 72 part-time (26 women); includes 49 minority (7 Black or African American, non-Hispanic/Latino; 33 Asian, non-Hispanic/Latino; 8 Hispanic/Latino; 1 Two or more races, non-Hispanic/Latino), 9 international. Average age 29. 116 applicants, 43% accepted, 26 enrolled. In 2013, 100 master's awarded. *Degree requirements:* For master's, capstone course. *Entrance requirements:* For master's, GMAT (minimum score 500), 2 letters of reference, resume, minimum GPA of 3.0. Additional exam requirements/recommendations for international students: Required—TOEFL (minimum score 550 paper-based; 80 iBT) or IELTS (minimum score 6.5). *Application deadline:* For fall admission, 5/15 for international students; for spring admission, 10/15 for international students. Applications are processed on a rolling basis. Application fee: $60. Electronic applications accepted. *Expenses:* Contact institution. *Financial support:* In 2013–14, 28 students received support. Scholarships/grants, unspecified assistantships, and merit-based one-time entrance scholarships available. Financial award applicants required to submit FAFSA. *Faculty research:* International finance, leadership and careers, ethics in accounting, emotions in consumer behavior, supply chain analysis, organizational leadership attributes, emotions in the workplace, real estate finance, effect of social media on stock prices. *Unit head:* Dr. Donald Gibson, Dean, 203-254-4070, Fax: 203-254-4105, E-mail: dgibson@fairfield.edu. *Application contact:* Marianne Gumpper, Director of Graduate and Continuing Studies Admission, 203-254-4184, Fax: 203-254-4073, E-mail: gradadmis@fairfield.edu. Website: http://fairfield.edu/mba.

Fairleigh Dickinson University, College at Florham, Silberman College of Business, Center for Human Resource Management Studies, Program in Human Resource Management, Madison, NJ 07940-1099. Offers MBA, MA/MBA.

Fairleigh Dickinson University, Metropolitan Campus, Silberman College of Business, Center for Human Resources Management Studies, Program in Human Resource Management, Teaneck, NJ 07666-1914. Offers MBA, Certificate.

Fitchburg State University, Division of Graduate and Continuing Education, Program in Business Administration, Fitchburg, MA 01420-2697. Offers accounting (MBA); human resource management (MBA); management (MBA). Part-time and evening/weekend programs available. Postbaccalaureate distance learning degree programs offered (no on-campus study). *Entrance requirements:* Additional exam requirements/recommendations for international students: Required—TOEFL (minimum score 550 paper-based; 79 iBT). Electronic applications accepted.

Florida Institute of Technology, Graduate Programs, Extended Studies Division, Melbourne, FL 32901-6975. Offers acquisition and contract management (MS); aerospace engineering (MS); business administration (MBA, DBA); computer information systems (MS); computer science (MS); electrical engineering (MS); engineering management (MS); human resources management (MS); logistics management (MS), including humanitarian and disaster relief logistics; management (MS), including acquisition and contract management, e-business, human resources management, information systems, logistics management, management, transportation management; material acquisition management (MS); mechanical engineering (MS); operations research (MS); project management (MS), including information systems, operations research; public administration (MPA); quality management (MS); software engineering (MS); space systems (MS); space systems management (MS); supply chain management (MS); systems management (MS), including information systems, operations research; technology management (MS). Part-time and evening/weekend programs available. Postbaccalaureate distance learning degree programs offered (no on-campus study). *Faculty:* 8 full-time (1 woman), 96 part-time/adjunct (25 women). *Students:* 94 full-time (46 women), 912 part-time (397 women); includes 436 minority (290 Black or African American, non-Hispanic/Latino; 18 American Indian or Alaska Native, non-Hispanic/Latino; 38 Asian, non-Hispanic/Latino; 62 Hispanic/Latino; 2 Native Hawaiian or other Pacific Islander, non-Hispanic/Latino; 26 Two or more races, non-Hispanic/Latino), 9 international. Average age 37. 591 applicants, 44% accepted, 220 enrolled. In 2013, 522 master's awarded. *Degree requirements:* For master's, comprehensive exam (for some programs), capstone course. *Entrance requirements:* For master's, GMAT or resume showing 8 years of supervised experience, minimum GPA of 3.0, 2 letters of recommendation, resume. Additional exam requirements/recommendations for international students: Required—TOEFL (minimum score 550 paper-based; 79 iBT). *Application deadline:* For fall admission, 4/1 for international students; for spring admission, 9/30 for international students. Applications are processed on a rolling basis. Electronic applications accepted. *Expenses:* Contact institution. *Financial support:* Application deadline: 3/1; applicants required to submit FAFSA. *Unit head:* Dr. Theodore R. Richardson, III, Senior Associate Dean, 321-674-8123, Fax: 321-674-7597, E-mail: trichardson@fit.edu. *Application contact:* Carolyn Farrior, Director of Graduate Admissions, Online Learning and Off-Campus Programs, 321-674-7118, Fax: 321-674-8216, E-mail: cfarrior@fit.edu. Website: http://es.fit.edu.

Florida International University, Alvah H. Chapman, Jr. Graduate School of Business, Department of Management and International Business, Human Resources Management Program, Miami, FL 33199. Offers MSHRM. Part-time and evening/weekend programs available. *Entrance requirements:* For master's, GRE (minimum score of 1000) or GMAT (minimum score of 500), minimum GPA of 3.0 (upper-level coursework); two letters of recommendation; letter of intent; minimum of five years of professional (exempt) experience, of which at least two years are in HR field. Additional exam requirements/recommendations for international students: Required—TOEFL (minimum score 550 paper-based; 80 iBT) or IELTS (minimum score 6.5). Electronic applications accepted. *Expenses:* Contact institution. *Faculty research:* Compensation, labor issues, labor law, human resource strategy.

Florida State University, The Graduate School, College of Business, Tallahassee, FL 32306-1110. Offers accounting (M Acc), including accounting information services, assurance services, corporate accounting, taxation; business administration (MBA, PhD), including accounting (PhD), finance (PhD), management information systems (PhD), marketing (PhD), organizational behavior and human resources (PhD), risk management and insurance (PhD), strategic management (PhD); finance (MS); insurance (MSM); management information systems (MS); marketing (MS); JD/MBA; MSW/MBA. *Accreditation:* AACSB. Part-time programs available. Postbaccalaureate

distance learning degree programs offered (no on-campus study). *Faculty:* 102 full-time (31 women), 5 part-time/adjunct (0 women). *Students:* 280 full-time (117 women), 278 part-time (88 women); includes 127 minority (26 Black or African American, non-Hispanic/Latino; 7 American Indian or Alaska Native, non-Hispanic/Latino; 44 Asian, non-Hispanic/Latino; 50 Hispanic/Latino). Average age 30. 630 applicants, 28% accepted, 103 enrolled. In 2013, 265 master's, 11 doctorates awarded. Terminal master's awarded for partial completion of doctoral program. *Degree requirements:* For doctorate, comprehensive exam, thesis/dissertation. *Entrance requirements:* For master's, GMAT, work experience (MBA, MS), minimum GPA of 3.0, letters of recommendation; for doctorate, GMAT, minimum graduate GPA of 3.5, letters of recommendation. Additional exam requirements/recommendations for international students: Required—TOEFL (minimum score 600 paper-based; 100 iBT); Recommended—IELTS (minimum score 6.5). *Application deadline:* For fall admission, 6/1 for domestic students, 5/1 for international students; for spring admission, 10/1 for domestic students, 9/1 for international students. Applications are processed on a rolling basis. Application fee: $30. Electronic applications accepted. *Expenses:* Tuition, state resident: part-time $403.51 per credit hour. Tuition, nonresident: part-time $1004.85 per credit hour. *Required fees:* $75.81 per credit hour. One-time fee: $20 part-time. Tuition and fees vary according to course load, campus/location and student level. *Financial support:* In 2013–14, 92 students received support, including 10 fellowships with full tuition reimbursements available (averaging $1,500 per year), 20 research assistantships with full tuition reimbursements available (averaging $20,000 per year), 35 teaching assistantships with full tuition reimbursements available (averaging $20,000 per year); career-related internships or fieldwork, scholarships/grants, health care benefits, and unspecified assistantships also available. Financial award application deadline: 1/1. *Unit head:* Dr. Caryn Beck-Dudley, Dean, 850-644-3090, Fax: 850-644-0915. *Application contact:* Lisa Beverly, Director, Graduate Programs Admissions, 850-644-6458, Fax: 850-644-0588, E-mail: lbeverly@cob.fsu.edu.
Website: http://www.cob.fsu.edu/.

Fordham University, Graduate School of Education, Division of Educational Leadership, Administration and Policy, New York, NY 10023. Offers administration and supervision (MSE, Adv C); administration and supervision for church leaders (PhD); educational administration and supervision (Ed D, PhD); human resource program administration (MS). *Accreditation:* NCATE. *Degree requirements:* For doctorate, thesis/dissertation. *Entrance requirements:* For doctorate, MAT, GRE General Test.

Framingham State University, Continuing Education, Program in Human Resource Management, Framingham, MA 01701-9101. Offers MA. Part-time and evening/weekend programs available.

Franklin Pierce University, Graduate Studies, Rindge, NH 03461-0060. Offers curriculum and instruction (M Ed); emerging network technologies (Graduate Certificate); energy and sustainability studies (MBA); health administration (MBA, Graduate Certificate); human resource management (MBA, Graduate Certificate); information technology (MBA); information technology management (MS); leadership (MBA, DA); nursing (MS); physical therapy (DPT); physician assistant studies (MPAS); special education (M Ed); sports management (MBA). *Accreditation:* APTA. Part-time programs available. Postbaccalaureate distance learning degree programs offered (no on-campus study). *Degree requirements:* For master's, concentrated original research projects; student teaching; fieldwork and/or internship; leadership project; PRAXIS I and II (for M Ed); for doctorate, concentrated original research projects, clinical fieldwork and/or internship, leadership project. *Entrance requirements:* For master's, minimum GPA of 2.5, 3 letters of recommendation; competencies in accounting, economics, statistics, and computer skills through life experience or undergraduate coursework (for MBA); certification/e-portfolio, minimum C grade in all education courses (for M Ed); license to practice as RN (for MS in nursing); for doctorate, GRE, BA/BS, 3 letters of recommendation, personal mission statement, interview, writing sample, minimum cumulative GPA of 2.8, master's degree (for DA); 80 hours of observation/work in PT settings, completion of anatomy, chemistry, physics, and statistics, minimum GPA of 3.0 (for DPT). Additional exam requirements/recommendations for international students: Required—TOEFL (minimum score 550 paper-based; 61 iBT). Electronic applications accepted. *Faculty research:* Evidence-based practice in sports physical therapy, human resource management in economic crisis, leadership in nursing, innovation in sports facility management, differentiated learning and understanding by design.

Gannon University, School of Graduate Studies, College of Engineering and Business, Dahlkemper School of Business, Program in Business Administration, Erie, PA 16541-0001. Offers business administration (MBA); finance (MBA); human resources management (MBA); marketing (MBA). *Accreditation:* ACBSP. Part-time and evening/weekend programs available. Postbaccalaureate distance learning degree programs offered (no on-campus study). *Students:* 44 full-time (20 women), 87 part-time (30 women); includes 7 minority (4 Black or African American, non-Hispanic/Latino; 1 Asian, non-Hispanic/Latino; 2 Hispanic/Latino), 22 international. Average age 28. 279 applicants, 84% accepted, 59 enrolled. In 2013, 40 master's awarded. *Degree requirements:* For master's, comprehensive exam, thesis. *Entrance requirements:* For master's, GMAT, resume, transcripts, 3 letters of recommendation. Additional exam requirements/recommendations for international students: Required—TOEFL (minimum score 79 iBT). *Application deadline:* Applications are processed on a rolling basis. Application fee: $25. Electronic applications accepted. *Expenses: Tuition:* Full-time $15,930; part-time $885 per credit. *Required fees:* $430; $18 per credit. Tuition and fees vary according to course load, degree level and program. *Financial support:* Administrative assistantships available. Financial award application deadline: 7/1; financial award applicants required to submit FAFSA. *Unit head:* Dr. Donna Mottilla, Director, 814-871-7780, E-mail: mottilla001@gannon.edu. *Application contact:* Kara Morgan, Director of Graduate Admissions, 814-871-5831, Fax: 814-871-5827, E-mail: graduate@gannon.edu.

George Fox University, College of Business, Newberg, OR 97132-2697. Offers finance (MBA); management (DBA); management and leadership (MBA); marketing (DBA); organizational strategy (MBA); strategic human resource management (MBA). MBA offered in Newberg, OR and in Portland, OR. *Accreditation:* ACBSP. Part-time and evening/weekend programs available. Postbaccalaureate distance learning degree programs offered (minimal on-campus study). *Faculty:* 8 full-time (2 women), 5 part-time/adjunct (2 women). *Students:* 31 full-time (15 women), 194 part-time (76 women); includes 21 minority (6 Black or African American, non-Hispanic/Latino; 4 American Indian or Alaska Native, non-Hispanic/Latino; 6 Asian, non-Hispanic/Latino; 3 Hispanic/Latino; 2 Two or more races, non-Hispanic/Latino), 15 international. Average age 39. 98 applicants, 79% accepted, 62 enrolled. In 2013, 98 master's, 2 doctorates awarded. *Degree requirements:* For master's, capstone project; for doctorate, credit-applied research project. *Entrance requirements:* For master's, resume (5 years of professional experience); 3 professional references; interview; financial e-learning course, official transcripts; for doctorate, GRE or GMAT, resume; personal mission statement; academic research writing sample; official transcript from each college/university attended; three professional references. Additional exam requirements/recommendations for international students: Required—TOEFL (minimum score 577 paper-based; 90 iBT) or IELTS (minimum score 7). *Application deadline:* For fall admission, 8/1 for domestic and international students; for spring admission, 12/1 for domestic and international students. Applications are processed on a rolling basis. Application fee: $40. Electronic applications accepted. *Expenses:* Contact institution. *Financial support:* Applicants required to submit FAFSA. *Unit head:* Dr. Chris Meade, Professor/Dean, 800-631-0921. *Application contact:* Ty Sohlman, Admissions Counselor, 800-493-4937, Fax: 503-554-6111, E-mail: business@georgefox.edu.
Website: http://www.georgefox.edu/business/index.html.

George Mason University, School of Policy, Government, and International Affairs, Program in Organization Development and Knowledge Management, Arlington, VA 22201. Offers MS. *Faculty:* 5 full-time (3 women), 4 part-time/adjunct (0 women). *Students:* 4 full-time (all women), 55 part-time (43 women); includes 20 minority (12 Black or African American, non-Hispanic/Latino; 4 Asian, non-Hispanic/Latino; 3 Hispanic/Latino; 1 Two or more races, non-Hispanic/Latino), 1 international. Average age 33. 64 applicants, 59% accepted, 27 enrolled. In 2013, 40 master's awarded. *Degree requirements:* For master's, thesis or alternative, internship. *Entrance requirements:* For master's, GRE (for students seeking merit-based scholarships), bachelor's degree with minimum GPA of 3.0, current resume, 2 letters of recommendation, expanded goals statement, 2 copies of official transcripts. Additional exam requirements/recommendations for international students: Required—TOEFL (minimum score 575 paper-based; 88 iBT), IELTS (minimum score 6.5), PTE. *Application deadline:* For fall admission, 6/1 priority date for domestic students, 5/1 priority date for international students; for spring admission, 12/1 priority date for domestic students, 11/1 priority date for international students. Applications are processed on a rolling basis. Application fee: $65 ($80 for international students). Electronic applications accepted. *Expenses:* Contact institution. *Financial support:* Career-related internships or fieldwork, Federal Work-Study, scholarships/grants, unspecified assistantships, and health care benefits (for full-time research or teaching assistantship recipients) available. Financial award application deadline: 3/1; financial award applicants required to submit FAFSA. *Unit head:* Tojo Joseph Thatchenkery, Director, 703-993-3808, Fax: 703-993-8215, E-mail: thatchen@gmu.edu. *Application contact:* Travis Major, Director of Graduate Admissions, 703-993-1383, E-mail: tmajor@gmu.edu.
Website: http://policy.gmu.edu/academic-professional-programs/masters-programs/organization-development-knowledge-management-odkm/.

Georgetown University, Graduate School of Arts and Sciences, School of Continuing Studies, Washington, DC 20057. Offers American studies (MALS); Catholic studies (MALS); classical civilizations (MALS); emergency and disaster management (MPS); ethics and the professions (MALS); human resources management (MPS); humanities (MALS); individualized study (MALS); international affairs (MALS); Islam and Muslim-Christian relations (MALS); journalism (MPS); liberal studies (DLS); literature and society (MALS); medieval and early modern European studies (MALS); public relations and corporate communications (MPS); real estate (MPS); religious studies (MALS); social and public policy (MALS); sports industry management (MPS); systems engineering management (MPS); technology management (MPS); the theory and practice of American democracy (MALS); urban and regional planning (MPS); visual culture (MALS). MPS in systems engineering management offered in conjunction with Stevens Institute of Technology. *Entrance requirements:* Additional exam requirements/recommendations for international students: Required—TOEFL.

The George Washington University, Columbian College of Arts and Sciences, Department of Organizational Sciences and Communication, Washington, DC 20052. Offers human resources management (MA); industrial/organizational psychology (PhD); organizational management (MA). Part-time and evening/weekend programs available. *Faculty:* 11 full-time (6 women). *Students:* 26 full-time (20 women), 41 part-time (30 women); includes 21 minority (9 Black or African American, non-Hispanic/Latino; 2 Asian, non-Hispanic/Latino; 5 Hispanic/Latino; 1 Native Hawaiian or other Pacific Islander, non-Hispanic/Latino; 4 Two or more races, non-Hispanic/Latino), 10 international. Average age 28. 78 applicants, 95% accepted, 24 enrolled. In 2013, 24 master's awarded. *Degree requirements:* For master's, comprehensive exam. *Entrance requirements:* For master's, GRE General Test, minimum GPA of 3.0. Additional exam requirements/recommendations for international students: Required—TOEFL (minimum score 500 paper-based; 80 iBT). *Application deadline:* For fall admission, 1/15 priority date for domestic and international students; for spring admission, 10/1 priority date for domestic students, 9/1 priority date for international students. Applications are processed on a rolling basis. Application fee: $75. Electronic applications accepted. *Financial support:* Federal Work-Study and institutionally sponsored loans available. *Unit head:* Dr. Clay Warren, Chair, 202-994-1870, Fax: 202-994-1881, E-mail: claywar@gwu.edu. *Application contact:* Information Contact, 202-994-1880, Fax: 202-994-1881.
Website: http://www.gwu.edu/~orgsci/.

Georgia State University, J. Mack Robinson College of Business, Department of Managerial Sciences, Atlanta, GA 30302-3083. Offers business analysis (MBA, MS); entrepreneurship (MBA); human resources management (MBA, MS); operations management (MBA, MS); organization behavior/human resource management (PhD); organization management (MBA); organizational change (MS); strategic management (PhD). *Accreditation:* AACSB. Part-time and evening/weekend programs available. *Faculty:* 18 full-time (6 women). *Students:* 31 full-time (15 women), 22 part-time (14 women); includes 20 minority (11 Black or African American, non-Hispanic/Latino; 1 American Indian or Alaska Native, non-Hispanic/Latino; 2 Asian, non-Hispanic/Latino; 2 Hispanic/Latino; 4 Two or more races, non-Hispanic/Latino), 16 international. Average age 31. 92 applicants, 20% accepted, 13 enrolled. In 2013, 45 master's, 2 doctorates awarded. *Degree requirements:* For doctorate, comprehensive exam, thesis/dissertation. *Entrance requirements:* For master's, GRE or GMAT, transcripts from all institutions attended, resume, essays; for doctorate, GMAT, three letters of recommendation, personal statement, transcripts from all institutions attended, resume. Additional exam requirements/recommendations for international students: Required—TOEFL (minimum score 610 paper-based; 101 iBT), IELTS (minimum score 7). *Application deadline:* For fall admission, 5/1 priority date for domestic students, 2/1 priority date for international students; for spring admission, 9/15 priority date for domestic students, 4/1 priority date for international students. Applications are processed on a rolling basis. Application fee: $50. Electronic applications accepted. *Expenses: Tuition, area resident:* Full-time $4176; part-time $348 per credit hour. Tuition, state resident: full-time $14,544; part-time $1212 per credit hour. Tuition, nonresident: full-time $14,544; part-time $1212 per credit hour. Tuition and fees vary according to course load and program. *Financial support:* Research assistantships, teaching assistantships, scholarships/grants, tuition waivers, and unspecified assistantships available. *Faculty research:* Entrepreneurship and Innovation; strategy process; workplace interactions, relationships, and processes; leadership and culture; supply chain management. *Unit head:* Dr. Pamela S. Barr, Interim Chair, 404-413-7525, Fax: 404-413-7571. *Application contact:* Toby McChesney, Assistant Dean for Graduate Recruiting and Student Services, 404-413-7167, Fax: 404-413-7162, E-mail: rcbgradadmissions@gsu.edu.
Website: http://mgmt.robinson.gsu.edu/.

Golden Gate University, Ageno School of Business, San Francisco, CA 94105-2968. Offers accounting (MBA); business administration (EMBA, MBA, PMBA, DBA); finance (MBA, MS, Certificate); financial planning (MS, Certificate); healthcare information

systems (Certificate); human resource management (MBA, MS); human resources management (Certificate); information systems (MS); information technology (MBA); information technology management (Certificate); integrated marketing and communications (MS, Certificate); international business (MBA); management (MBA); marketing (MBA, MS, Certificate); operations supply chain management (Certificate); psychology (MA, Certificate); public administration (EMPA); public relations (MS, Certificate); technical market analysis (Certificate); JD/MBA. Part-time and evening/weekend programs available. *Degree requirements:* For doctorate, thesis/dissertation, qualifying examination. *Entrance requirements:* For master's, GMAT (MBA), minimum GPA of 2.5 (MS). Additional exam requirements/recommendations for international students: Required—TOEFL (minimum score 550 paper-based; 79 iBT). Electronic applications accepted. *Expenses:* Contact institution.

Goldey-Beacom College, Graduate Program, Wilmington, DE 19808-1999. Offers business administration (MBA); finance (MS); financial management (MBA); health care management (MBA); human resource management (MBA); information technology (MBA); international business management (MBA); major finance (MBA); major taxation (MBA); management (MM); marketing management (MBA); taxation (MBA, MS). *Accreditation:* ACBSP. Part-time and evening/weekend programs available. *Entrance requirements:* For master's, GMAT, MAT, GRE, minimum GPA of 3.0. Additional exam requirements/recommendations for international students: Required—TOEFL (minimum score 65 iBT); Recommended—IELTS (minimum score 6). Electronic applications accepted.

Grambling State University, School of Graduate Studies and Research, College of Arts and Sciences, Department of Political Science and Public Administration, Grambling, LA 71270. Offers health services administration (MPA); human resource management (MPA); public management (MPA); state and local government (MPA). *Accreditation:* NASPAA. Part-time programs available. *Faculty:* 5 full-time (1 woman). *Students:* 47 full-time (33 women), 28 part-time (23 women); includes 62 minority (61 Black or African American, non-Hispanic/Latino; 1 Asian, non-Hispanic/Latino), 13 international. Average age 29. In 2013, 11 master's awarded. *Degree requirements:* For master's, comprehensive exam (for some programs), thesis optional. *Entrance requirements:* For master's, GRE, minimum GPA of 2.75 on last degree. Additional exam requirements/recommendations for international students: Required—TOEFL (minimum score 500 paper-based; 62 iBT). *Application deadline:* For fall admission, 7/1 for domestic and international students; for spring admission, 12/1 for domestic and international students; for summer admission, 5/1 for domestic and international students. Applications are processed on a rolling basis. Application fee: $20 ($30 for international students). Electronic applications accepted. *Financial support:* Research assistantships, health care benefits, tuition waivers (full), and unspecified assistantships available. Financial award application deadline: 5/31. *Unit head:* Dr. Rose M. Harris, Department Head, 318-274-2310, Fax: 318-274-3427, E-mail: harrisr@gram.edu. *Application contact:* Katina S. Crowe-Fields, Special Assistant to Associate Vice President/Dean, 318-274-2158, Fax: 318-274-7373, E-mail: croweks@gram.edu. Website: http://www.gram.edu/academics/majors/arts%20and%20sciences/departments/poli-science/mpa/.

Grand Canyon University, College of Business, Phoenix, AZ 85017-1097. Offers accounting (MBA); corporate business administration (MBA); disaster preparedness and crisis management (MBA); executive fire service leadership (MS); finance (MBA); general management (MBA); government and policy (MPA); health care management (MPA); health systems management (MBA); human resource management (MBA); innovation (MBA); leadership (MBA, MS); management of information system (MBA); marketing (MBA); project-based (MBA); six sigma (MBA); strategic human resource management (MBA). *Accreditation:* ACBSP. Part-time and evening/weekend programs available. Postbaccalaureate distance learning degree programs offered (no on-campus study). *Entrance requirements:* For master's, equivalent of two years full-time professional work experience. Additional exam requirements/recommendations for international students: Required—TOEFL (minimum score 575 paper-based; 90 iBT), IELTS (minimum score 7). Electronic applications accepted.

Hawai`i Pacific University, College of Business Administration, Program in Human Resource Management, Honolulu, HI 96813. Offers MA. Part-time and evening/weekend programs available. *Faculty:* 9 full-time (2 women), 4 part-time/adjunct (0 women). *Students:* 31 full-time (22 women), 16 part-time (15 women); includes 24 minority (2 Black or African American, non-Hispanic/Latino; 11 Asian, non-Hispanic/Latino; 3 Hispanic/Latino; 1 Native Hawaiian or other Pacific Islander, non-Hispanic/Latino; 7 Two or more races, non-Hispanic/Latino). Average age 30. 34 applicants, 85% accepted, 17 enrolled. *Entrance requirements:* Additional exam requirements/recommendations for international students: Required—TOEFL (minimum score 550 paper-based; 80 iBT), IELTS (minimum score 6), TWE (minimum score 5). *Application deadline:* Applications are processed on a rolling basis. Application fee: $50. Electronic applications accepted. *Financial support:* In 2013–14, 2 students received support. Career-related internships or fieldwork, Federal Work-Study, scholarships/grants, tuition waivers, and unspecified assistantships available. *Unit head:* Dr. Deborah Crown, Program Chair, 808-544-0275, E-mail: dcrown@hpu.edu. *Application contact:* Rumi Yoshida, Director of Graduate Admissions, 808-543-8034, Fax: 808-544-0280, E-mail: grad@hpu.edu.
Website: http://www.hpu.edu/CBA/Graduate/MAHRM.html.

HEC Montreal, School of Business Administration, Master of Science Programs in Administration, Program in Human Resources Management, Montréal, QC H3T 2A7, Canada. Offers M Sc. All courses are given in French. *Students:* 39 full-time (35 women), 10 part-time (8 women). 53 applicants, 66% accepted, 17 enrolled. In 2013, 14 master's awarded. *Degree requirements:* For master's, one foreign language, thesis. *Entrance requirements:* For master's, Test de francais international (TFI) with minimum score of 850 (for those who have never studied in French), BBA, undergraduate degree in another field, degree deemed equivalent by program director and minimum GPA of 3.0 on 4.3 scale. *Application deadline:* For fall admission, 3/15 for domestic and international students; for winter admission, 9/15 for domestic and international students. Application fee: $83 Canadian dollars. Electronic applications accepted. *Expenses: Tuition, area resident:* Part-time $74.14 per credit. Tuition, state resident: full-time $2669.04; part-time $201.83 per credit. Tuition, nonresident: full-time $7266; part-time $500.59 per credit. *International tuition:* $18,021.24 full-time. *Required fees:* $1529.70; $36.20 per credit. $65.50 per term. Tuition and fees vary according to degree level and program. *Financial support:* In 2013–14, 1,007 students received support. Research assistantships, teaching assistantships, and scholarships/grants available. Financial award application deadline: 9/2. *Unit head:* Dr. Anne Bourhis, Director, 514-340-6873, Fax: 514-340-6880, E-mail: anne.bourhis@hec.ca. *Application contact:* Marianne de Moura, Administrative Director, 514-340-7106, Fax: 514-340-6411, E-mail: marianne.de-moura@hec.ca.
Website: http://www.hec.ca/programmes_formations/msc/options/gestion_rh/index.html.

Herzing University Online, Program in Business Administration, Milwaukee, WI 53203. Offers accounting (MBA); business administration (MBA); business management (MBA); healthcare management (MBA); human resources (MBA); marketing (MBA); project management (MBA); technology management (MBA). Postbaccalaureate distance learning degree programs offered (no on-campus study).

Hofstra University, Frank G. Zarb School of Business, Programs in Management and General Business, Hempstead, NY 11549. Offers business administration (MBA), including health services management, management, sports and entertainment management; general management (Advanced Certificate); human resource management (MS, Advanced Certificate).

Holy Family University, Division of Extended Learning, Bensalem, PA 19020. Offers business administration (MBA); finance (MBA); health care administration (MBA); human resources management (MBA). *Accreditation:* ACBSP. Part-time and evening/weekend programs available. *Faculty:* 13 part-time/adjunct (3 women). *Students:* 116 part-time (59 women); includes 4 minority (2 Black or African American, non-Hispanic/Latino; 1 Asian, non-Hispanic/Latino; 1 Hispanic/Latino). Average age 34. 25 applicants, 96% accepted, 6 enrolled. In 2013, 52 master's awarded. *Entrance requirements:* For master's, minimum GPA of 3.0, interview, essay/professional statement, 2 recommendations, current resume, official transcripts of college or university work. Additional exam requirements/recommendations for international students: Required—TOEFL (minimum score 550 paper-based; 79 iBT). *Application deadline:* For fall admission, 7/1 priority date for domestic and international students; for spring admission, 11/1 priority date for domestic and international students; for summer admission, 4/1 priority date for domestic and international students. Applications are processed on a rolling basis. Application fee: $50. Electronic applications accepted. *Expenses: Tuition:* Full-time $12,060. *Required fees:* $250. Tuition and fees vary according to degree level. *Financial support:* In 2013–14, 3 students received support. Available to part-time students. Applicants required to submit FAFSA. *Unit head:* Chris Quinn, Director of Academic Services, 267-341-5006, Fax: 215-633-0558, E-mail: cquinn1@holyfamily.edu. *Application contact:* Don Reinmold, Director of Admissions, 267-341-5001 Ext. 3230, Fax: 215-633-0558, E-mail: dreinmold@holyfamily.edu.

Holy Family University, Graduate School, School of Business Administration, Program in Human Resources Management, Philadelphia, PA 19114. Offers MS. Part-time and evening/weekend programs available. *Faculty:* 1 (woman) full-time, 5 part-time/adjunct (4 women). *Students:* 4 full-time (2 women), 31 part-time (25 women); includes 15 minority (12 Black or African American, non-Hispanic/Latino; 1 Asian, non-Hispanic/Latino; 2 Hispanic/Latino). Average age 33. 8 applicants, 63% accepted, 3 enrolled. In 2013, 15 master's awarded. *Degree requirements:* For master's, thesis optional. *Entrance requirements:* For master's, minimum GPA of 3.0, interview, essay/personal statement, current resume, official transcript of all college or university work. Additional exam requirements/recommendations for international students: Required—TOEFL (minimum score 550 paper-based; 79 iBT), IELTS (minimum score 6), PTE (minimum score 54). *Application deadline:* For fall admission, 7/1 priority date for domestic and international students; for winter admission, 1/1 for domestic students; for spring admission, 11/1 priority date for domestic and international students; for summer admission, 4/1 priority date for domestic and international students. Applications are processed on a rolling basis. Application fee: $25. Electronic applications accepted. *Expenses: Tuition:* Full-time $12,060. *Required fees:* $250. Tuition and fees vary according to degree level. *Financial support:* In 2013–14, 2 students received support. Available to part-time students. Application deadline: 5/1; applicants required to submit FAFSA. *Unit head:* Dr. Barry Dickinson, Dean of the School of Business, 267-341-3440, Fax: 215-637-5937, E-mail: jdickinson@holyfamily.edu. *Application contact:* Gidget Marie Montelibano, Associate Director of Graduate Admissions, 267-341-3558, Fax: 215-637-1478, E-mail: gmontelibano@holyfamily.edu.
Website: http://www.holyfamily.edu/choosing-holy-family-u/academics/schools-of-study/school-of-business-administration/graduate-programs/163-human-resources.

Hood College, Graduate School, Department of Economics and Business Administration, Frederick, MD 21701-8575. Offers accounting (MBA); administration and management (MBA); finance (MBA); human resource management (MBA); information systems (MBA); marketing (MBA); public management (MBA). *Accreditation:* ACBSP. Part-time and evening/weekend programs available. *Faculty:* 6 full-time (2 women), 7 part-time/adjunct (1 woman). *Students:* 31 full-time (21 women), 131 part-time (66 women); includes 36 minority (18 Black or African American, non-Hispanic/Latino; 7 Asian, non-Hispanic/Latino; 8 Hispanic/Latino; 3 Two or more races, non-Hispanic/Latino), 12 international. Average age 31. 78 applicants, 56% accepted, 33 enrolled. In 2013, 35 master's awarded. *Degree requirements:* For master's, capstone/final research project. *Entrance requirements:* For master's, minimum GPA of 2.75, resume, letters of recommendation. Additional exam requirements/recommendations for international students: Required—TOEFL (minimum score 575 paper-based; 89 iBT), IELTS (minimum score 6.5). *Application deadline:* For fall admission, 7/15 priority date for domestic students, 7/15 for international students; for spring admission, 12/1 priority date for domestic students, 12/1 for international students. Applications are processed on a rolling basis. Application fee: $35. Electronic applications accepted. Application fee is waived when completed online. *Expenses: Tuition:* Part-time $405 per credit. *Required fees:* $100 per semester. *Financial support:* In 2013–14, 11 students received support. Tuition waivers (partial) and unspecified assistantships available. Financial award applicants required to submit FAFSA. *Faculty research:* Corporate strategy and sustainable competitive advantages, business ethics, entrepreneurship, investments management, economic development. *Unit head:* Dr. Anita Jose, Program Director, 301-696-3691, Fax: 301-696-3597, E-mail: jose@hood.edu. *Application contact:* Dr. Maria Green Cowles, Dean of Graduate School, 301-696-3811, Fax: 301-696-3597, E-mail: gofurther@hood.edu.

Houston Baptist University, School of Business, Program in Human Resources Management, Houston, TX 77074-3298. Offers MSHRM. Part-time and evening/weekend programs available. *Entrance requirements:* For master's, GMAT, minimum GPA of 2.5. Additional exam requirements/recommendations for international students: Required—TOEFL (minimum score 550 paper-based). *Expenses:* Contact institution.

Howard University, School of Business, Graduate Programs in Business, Washington, DC 20059-0002. Offers accounting (MBA); entrepreneurship (MBA); finance (MBA); general management (MBA); human resources management (MBA); information systems (MBA); international business (MBA); marketing (MBA); supply chain management (MBA); JD/MBA. *Accreditation:* AACSB. Part-time and evening/weekend programs available. Postbaccalaureate distance learning degree programs offered (no on-campus study). *Entrance requirements:* For master's, GMAT, minimum 1 year post undergraduate work experience, resume, 3 letters of recommendation, advanced college algebra. Additional exam requirements/recommendations for international students: Required—TOEFL. *Faculty research:* Marketing research in multi-ethnic populations, U.S. trade policies and international relations, risk management (finance).

Indiana Tech, Program in Business Administration, Fort Wayne, IN 46803-1297. Offers accounting (MBA); health care administration (MBA); human resources (MBA); management (MBA); marketing (MBA). Part-time and evening/weekend programs available. Postbaccalaureate distance learning degree programs offered (no on-campus study). *Students:* 160 full-time (94 women), 97 part-time (53 women); includes 69 minority (58 Black or African American, non-Hispanic/Latino; 1 Asian, non-Hispanic/Latino; 8 Hispanic/Latino; 2 Two or more races, non-Hispanic/Latino), 11 international. Average age 36. *Entrance requirements:* For master's, GMAT, bachelor's degree from regionally-accredited university; minimum undergraduate GPA of 2.5; 2 years of significant work experience; 3 letters of recommendation. *Application deadline:*

Human Resources Management

Applications are processed on a rolling basis. Application fee: $25. Electronic applications accepted. *Expenses: Tuition:* Full-time $8910; part-time $495 per credit. Tuition and fees vary according to course load, degree level and program. *Financial support:* Applicants required to submit FAFSA. *Unit head:* Dr. Andrew I. Nwanne, Associate Dean of Business/Academic Coordinator, 260-422-5561 Ext. 2214, E-mail: ainwanne@indianatech.edu. Website: http://www.indianatech.edu/.

Indiana Wesleyan University, College of Adult and Professional Studies, Graduate Studies in Business, Marion, IN 46953. Offers accounting (MBA, Graduate Certificate); applied management (MBA); business administration (MBA); health care (MBA, Graduate Certificate); human resources (MBA, Graduate Certificate); management (MS); organizational leadership (MA). Part-time and evening/weekend programs available. Postbaccalaureate distance learning degree programs offered (no on-campus study). *Degree requirements:* For master's, applied business or management project. *Entrance requirements:* For master's, minimum GPA of 2.5, 2 years of related work experience. Additional exam requirements/recommendations for international students: Required—TOEFL (minimum score 550 paper-based). Electronic applications accepted. *Expenses: Tuition:* Full-time $8712; part-time $484 per credit hour. *Required fees:* $1673; $105 per credit hour. Tuition and fees vary according to course load, degree level, campus/location and program.

Instituto Tecnologico de Santo Domingo, Graduate School, Area of Business, Santo Domingo, Dominican Republic. Offers banking and securities markets (M Mgmt); corporate finance (M Mgmt); human resources management (M Mgmt, Certificate); international trade management (M Mgmt); marketing (M Mgmt); organizational development (M Mgmt); quality and productivity management (Certificate); tax management and planning (M Mgmt); upper management (M Mgmt).

Instituto Tecnologico de Santo Domingo, Graduate School, Area of Engineering, Santo Domingo, Dominican Republic. Offers construction administration (MS, Certificate); data telecommunications (M Eng, MS, Certificate); industrial engineering (M Eng, Certificate); industrial management (M Mgmt); information technology (Certificate); maintenance engineering (M Eng); occupational hazard prevention (M Mgmt); production management (Certificate); quantitative methods (Certificate); sanitary and environmental engineering (M Eng); structural engineering (M Eng); systems engineering and electronic data processing (Certificate); transportation (Certificate).

Instituto Tecnológico y de Estudios Superiores de Monterrey, Campus Cuernavaca, Programs in Business Administration, Temixco, Mexico. Offers finance (MA); human resources management (MA); international business (MA); marketing (MA).

Inter American University of Puerto Rico, Aguadilla Campus, Graduate School, Aguadilla, PR 00605. Offers accounting (MBA); counseling psychology specializing in family (MS); criminal justice (MA); educative management and leadership (MA); elementary education (M Ed); finance (MBA); human resources (MBA); industrial management (MBA); management information systems (MBA); marketing (MBA). Part-time and evening/weekend programs available. *Degree requirements:* For master's, comprehensive exam. *Entrance requirements:* For master's, EXADEP, 2 letters of recommendation, minimum GPA of 2.5. Electronic applications accepted.

Inter American University of Puerto Rico, Arecibo Campus, Program in Business Administration, Arecibo, PR 00614-4050. Offers accounting (MBA); finance (MBA); human resources (MBA).

Inter American University of Puerto Rico, Bayamón Campus, Graduate School, Bayamón, PR 00957. Offers biology (MS), including environmental sciences and ecology, molecular biotechnology; human resources (MBA). Part-time and evening/weekend programs available. *Degree requirements:* For master's, comprehensive exam, research project. *Entrance requirements:* For master's, EXADEP, GRE General Test, letters of recommendation.

Inter American University of Puerto Rico, Metropolitan Campus, Graduate Programs, Program in Human Resources, San Juan, PR 00919-1293. Offers MBA. *Degree requirements:* For master's, comprehensive exam. *Entrance requirements:* For master's, GRE or EXADEP, interview. Electronic applications accepted.

Inter American University of Puerto Rico, Ponce Campus, Graduate School, Mercedita, PR 00715-1602. Offers accounting (MBA); biology (M Ed); chemistry (M Ed); criminal justice (MA); elementary education (M Ed); English as a Second Language (M Ed); finance (MBA); history (M Ed); human resources (MBA); marketing (MBA); mathematics (M Ed); Spanish (M Ed). *Entrance requirements:* For master's, minimum GPA of 2.5.

Inter American University of Puerto Rico, San Germán Campus, Graduate Studies Center, Program in Business Administration, San Germán, PR 00683-5008. Offers accounting (MBA); finance (MBA); general business administration (MBA); human resources (MBA, PhD); industrial relations (MBA); information systems (MBA); international and interregional business (PhD); management (MBA); marketing (MBA). Part-time and evening/weekend programs available. *Faculty:* 8 full-time (2 women), 4 part-time/adjunct (3 women). *Students:* 138 full-time (80 women), 35 part-time (21 women); includes 172 minority (all Hispanic/Latino). 60 applicants, 65% accepted, 38 enrolled. In 2013, 38 master's, 3 doctorates awarded. *Degree requirements:* For master's, comprehensive exam. *Entrance requirements:* For master's, GRE General Test or EXADEP, minimum GPA of 3.0. *Application deadline:* For fall admission, 4/30 priority date for domestic students; for spring admission, 11/15 for domestic students. Applications are processed on a rolling basis. Application fee: $31. *Expenses: Tuition:* Full-time $2424; part-time $202 per credit hour. *Required fees:* $260 per semester. Tuition and fees vary according to course level, course load, degree level and program. *Financial support:* Teaching assistantships, Federal Work-Study, and unspecified assistantships available. *Unit head:* Dr. Elba T. Irizarry, Director of Graduate Studies Center, 787-264-1912 Ext. 7357, Fax: 787-892-6350, E-mail: elbat@sg.inter.edu. *Application contact:* Dr. Ailin Padilla, Coordinator, 787-264-1912 Ext. 7355, E-mail: ailin_padilla@intersg.edu.

International College of the Cayman Islands, Graduate Program in Management, Newlands, Cayman Islands. Offers business administration (MBA); management (MS), including education, human resources. Part-time and evening/weekend programs available. *Degree requirements:* For master's, comprehensive exam. *Entrance requirements:* Additional exam requirements/recommendations for international students: Recommended—TOEFL. *Faculty research:* International human resources administration.

Iona College, Hagan School of Business, Department of Management, Business Administration and Health Care Management, New Rochelle, NY 10801-1890. Offers business administration (MBA); health care management (MBA, AC); human resource management (MBA, PMC); long term care services management (AC); management (MBA, PMC). Part-time and evening/weekend programs available. *Faculty:* 7 full-time (1 woman), 4 part-time/adjunct (1 woman). *Students:* 31 full-time (20 women), 78 part-time (46 women); includes 20 minority (6 Black or African American, non-Hispanic/Latino; 1 Asian, non-Hispanic/Latino; 13 Hispanic/Latino), 7 international. Average age 30. 28

applicants, 96% accepted, 24 enrolled. In 2013, 62 master's, 60 other advanced degrees awarded. *Entrance requirements:* For master's, GMAT, 2 letters of recommendation, minimum GPA of 3.0; for other advanced degree, GMAT, minimum GPA of 3.0. Additional exam requirements/recommendations for international students: Required—TOEFL (minimum score 550 paper-based; 80 iBT), IELTS (minimum score 6.5). *Application deadline:* For fall admission, 8/15 priority date for domestic students, 8/1 priority date for international students; for winter admission, 11/15 priority date for domestic students, 11/1 priority date for international students; for spring admission, 2/15 priority date for domestic students, 2/1 priority date for international students; for summer admission, 5/15 priority date for domestic students, 5/1 priority date for international students. Applications are processed on a rolling basis. Application fee: $50. Electronic applications accepted. *Expenses:* Contact institution. *Financial support:* In 2013–14, 39 students received support. Scholarships/grants, tuition waivers (partial), and unspecified assistantships available. Support available to part-time students. Financial award application deadline: 4/15; financial award applicants required to submit FAFSA. *Faculty research:* Information systems, strategic management, corporate values and ethics. *Unit head:* Prof. Hugh McCabe, Acting Chair, 914-633-2631, E-mail: hmccabe@iona.edu. *Application contact:* Cameron Hudson, Director of MBA Admissions, 914-633-2288, Fax: 914-637-2708, E-mail: chudson@iona.edu. Website: http://www.iona.edu/Academics/Hagan-School-of-Business/Departments/Management-Business-Administration-Health-Car/Graduate-Programs.aspx.

Iona College, School of Arts and Science, Department of Psychology, New Rochelle, NY 10801-1890. Offers general-experimental (MA); human resources (Certificate); industrial-organizational (MA); mental health counseling (MA); organizational behavior (Certificate); psychology (MA); school psychology (MA). Part-time programs available. *Faculty:* 9 full-time (6 women), 3 part-time/adjunct (1 woman). *Students:* 54 full-time (41 women), 35 part-time (31 women); includes 28 minority (10 Black or African American, non-Hispanic/Latino; 2 Asian, non-Hispanic/Latino; 15 Hispanic/Latino; 1 Two or more races, non-Hispanic/Latino), 1 international. Average age 25. 88 applicants, 90% accepted, 34 enrolled. In 2013, 45 master's awarded. *Degree requirements:* For master's, thesis (for some programs), literature review (for some programs). *Entrance requirements:* For master's, BA in psychology or 9 credits in psychology including 3 credits in psychology statistics; 3 credits in psychology research methods. Additional exam requirements/recommendations for international students: Required—TOEFL (minimum score 550 paper-based), IELTS (minimum score 6.5). *Application deadline:* For fall admission, 8/1 for domestic students, 5/1 for international students; for spring admission, 1/1 for domestic students, 9/1 for international students. Applications are processed on a rolling basis. Application fee: $50. Electronic applications accepted. *Expenses: Tuition:* Part-time $948 per credit. *Required fees:* $235 per term. *Financial support:* In 2013–14, 42 students received support, including 1 research assistantship with partial tuition reimbursement available (averaging $8,000 per year); tuition waivers (partial) and unspecified assistantships also available. Support available to part-time students. Financial award application deadline: 4/15; financial award applicants required to submit FAFSA. *Faculty research:* Non-suicidal self-injury, trauma response, performance appraisal and evaluation, self-promotion and immigrant status in hiring decisions, assessment of student learning outcomes. *Unit head:* Patricia Oswald, PhD, Chair, 914-633-7788, E-mail: poswald@iona.edu. *Application contact:* Veronica Jarek-Prinz, Director, Graduate Admissions, 914-633-2420, Fax: 914-633-2277, E-mail: vjarekprinz@iona.edu. Website: http://www.iona.edu/Academics/School-of-Arts-Science/Departments/Psychology/Graduate-Programs.aspx.

Kaplan University, Davenport Campus, School of Business, Davenport, IA 52807-2095. Offers business administration (MBA); change leadership (MS); entrepreneurship (MBA); finance (MBA); health care management (MBA, MS); human resource (MBA); international business (MBA); management (MS); marketing (MBA); project management (MBA, MS); supply chain management and logistics (MBA, MS). *Accreditation:* ACBSP. Part-time and evening/weekend programs available. Postbaccalaureate distance learning degree programs offered (no on-campus study). *Entrance requirements:* Additional exam requirements/recommendations for international students: Required—TOEFL (minimum score 550 paper-based; 80 iBT). Electronic applications accepted.

La Roche College, School of Graduate Studies and Adult Education, Program in Human Resources Management, Pittsburgh, PA 15237-5898. Offers MS, Certificate. *Accreditation:* ACBSP. Part-time and evening/weekend programs available. *Faculty:* 2 full-time (both women), 8 part-time/adjunct (3 women). *Students:* 9 full-time (5 women), 48 part-time (38 women); includes 2 minority (both Black or African American, non-Hispanic/Latino), 1 international. Average age 34. 36 applicants, 83% accepted, 25 enrolled. In 2013, 20 master's awarded. *Entrance requirements:* For master's, GMAT, GRE or MAT, minimum GPA of 3.0 during previous 2 years. Additional exam requirements/recommendations for international students: Recommended—TOEFL (minimum score 550 paper-based). *Application deadline:* For fall admission, 8/15 priority date for domestic students, 8/15 for international students; for spring admission, 12/15 priority date for domestic students, 12/15 for international students. Applications are processed on a rolling basis. Application fee: $50. Electronic applications accepted. *Expenses: Tuition:* Full-time $15,360. *Financial support:* Unspecified assistantships available. Financial award application deadline: 3/31; financial award applicants required to submit FAFSA. *Faculty research:* Personnel administration, human resources development. *Unit head:* Dr. Jean Forti, Coordinator, 412-536-1193, Fax: 412-536-1179, E-mail: fortij1@laroche.edu. *Application contact:* Hope Schiffgens, Director of Graduate Studies and Adult Education, 412-536-1266, Fax: 412-536-1283, E-mail: schombh1@laroche.edu.

La Salle University, School of Arts and Sciences, Program in Counseling and Family Therapy, Philadelphia, PA 19141-1199. Offers industrial/organizational management and human resources (MA); marriage and family therapy (MA); pastoral counseling (MA); professional clinical counseling (MA). *Accreditation:* APA. Part-time and evening/weekend programs available. *Faculty:* 9 full-time (5 women), 30 part-time/adjunct (21 women). *Students:* 121 full-time (101 women), 243 part-time (184 women); includes 92 minority (66 Black or African American, non-Hispanic/Latino; 7 Asian, non-Hispanic/Latino; 15 Hispanic/Latino; 4 Two or more races, non-Hispanic/Latino), 14 international. Average age 31. 176 applicants, 93% accepted, 73 enrolled. In 2013, 114 master's awarded. *Degree requirements:* For master's, comprehensive exam. *Entrance requirements:* For master's, GRE or MAT (waived for applicants that already possess a master's degree in any field or for applicants that have a cumulative GPA of 3.5 or higher), minimum of 15 hours in psychology, counseling, or marriage and family studies; minimum GPA of 3.0; three letters of recommendation; personal statement; work experience (paid or volunteer). Additional exam requirements/recommendations for international students: Required—TOEFL. *Application deadline:* For fall admission, 8/15 priority date for domestic students, 7/15 for international students; for spring admission, 12/15 priority date for domestic students, 11/15 for international students; for summer admission, 4/15 priority date for domestic students, 3/15 for international students. Applications are processed on a rolling basis. Application fee: $35. Electronic applications accepted. Application fee is waived when completed online. *Expenses:* Contact institution. *Financial support:* In 2013–14, 42 students received support, including 2 research assistantships (averaging $3,000 per year); career-related

internships or fieldwork, scholarships/grants, and unspecified assistantships also available. Support available to part-time students. Financial award application deadline: 8/31; financial award applicants required to submit FAFSA. *Faculty research:* Cognitive therapy, attribution theory, work habits, single parent families, treatment of addictions. *Unit head:* Dr. Donna A. Tonrey, Director, 215-951-1767, Fax: 215-951-1843, E-mail: psyma@lasalle.edu. *Application contact:* Paul J. Reilly, Assistant Vice President, Enrollment Services, 215-951-1946, Fax: 215-951-1462, E-mail: reilly@lasalle.edu. *Website:* http://www.lasalle.edu/grad/index.php?section-clinical&page-index.

La Salle University, School of Business, Philadelphia, PA 19141-1199. Offers accounting (MBA, Post-MBA Certificate); business systems and analytics (MBA, Post-MBA Certificate); finance (MBA, Post-MBA Certificate); general business administration (MBA); human resource management (MBA, Post-MBA Certificate); international business (Post-MBA Certificate); management (MBA, Post-MBA Certificate); marketing (MBA, Post-MBA Certificate); MSN/MBA. *Accreditation:* AACSB. Part-time and evening/weekend programs available. Postbaccalaureate distance learning degree programs offered (minimal on-campus study). *Faculty:* 27 full-time (13 women), 15 part-time/adjunct (4 women). *Students:* 81 full-time (30 women), 428 part-time (211 women); includes 109 minority (47 Black or African American, non-Hispanic/Latino; 39 Asian, non-Hispanic/Latino; 18 Hispanic/Latino; 5 Two or more races, non-Hispanic/Latino), 6 international. Average age 30. 215 applicants, 90% accepted, 120 enrolled. In 2013, 182 master's, 1 other advanced degree awarded. *Entrance requirements:* For master's, GMAT or GRE, two letters of reference; resume; for Post-MBA Certificate, MBA with minimum GPA of 3.0. Additional exam requirements/recommendations for international students: Required—TOEFL. *Application deadline:* For fall admission, 8/15 priority date for domestic students, 7/15 for international students; for spring admission, 12/15 priority date for domestic students, 11/15 for international students; for summer admission, 4/15 priority date for domestic students, 3/15 for international students. Applications are processed on a rolling basis. Application fee: $35. Electronic applications accepted. Application fee is waived when completed online. *Expenses:* Contact institution. *Financial support:* In 2013–14, 88 students received support. Career-related internships or fieldwork, Federal Work-Study, scholarships/grants, and unspecified assistantships available. Support available to part-time students. Financial award application deadline: 8/31; financial award applicants required to submit FAFSA. *Unit head:* Dr. Gary Giamartino, Dean, 215-951-1040, Fax: 215-951-1886, E-mail: giamartino@lasalle.edu. *Application contact:* Paul J. Reilly, Assistant Vice President, Enrollment Services, 215-951-1946, Fax: 215-951-1462, E-mail: reilly@lasalle.edu. *Website:* http://www.lasalle.edu/grad/index.php?section-mba&page-index.

Lasell College, Graduate and Professional Studies in Management, Newton, MA 02466-2709. Offers business administration (PMBA); elder care management (MSM, Graduate Certificate); elder care marketing (MSM); human resource management (Graduate Certificate); human resources management (MSM); integrated marketing communication (Graduate Certificate); management (MSM, Graduate Certificate); marketing (MSM, Graduate Certificate); non-profit management (MSM, Graduate Certificate); project management (MSM, Graduate Certificate); public relations (Graduate Certificate). Part-time and evening/weekend programs available. Postbaccalaureate distance learning degree programs offered (no on-campus study). *Faculty:* 3 full-time (1 woman), 16 part-time/adjunct (9 women). *Students:* 46 full-time (33 women), 105 part-time (73 women); includes 35 minority (24 Black or African American, non-Hispanic/Latino; 1 American Indian or Alaska Native, non-Hispanic/Latino; 3 Asian, non-Hispanic/Latino; 7 Hispanic/Latino), 22 international. Average age 32. 88 applicants, 55% accepted, 29 enrolled. In 2013, 61 master's awarded. *Entrance requirements:* For master's and Graduate Certificate, bachelor's degree from an accredited institution. Additional exam requirements/recommendations for international students: Required—TOEFL (minimum score 550 paper-based; 79 iBT). *Application deadline:* For fall admission, 8/31 priority date for domestic students, 6/30 priority date for international students; for spring admission, 12/31 priority date for domestic students, 10/31 priority date for international students. Applications are processed on a rolling basis. Electronic applications accepted. *Expenses:* Tuition: Part-time $575 per credit. *Required fees:* $80 per semester. *Financial support:* Available to part-time students. Application deadline: 8/31; applicants required to submit FAFSA. *Unit head:* Dr. Joan Dolamore, Dean of Graduate and Professional Studies, 617-243-2485, Fax: 617-243-2450, E-mail: gradinfo@lasell.edu. *Application contact:* Adrienne Franciosi, Director of Graduate Admission, 617-243-2214, Fax: 617-243-2450, E-mail: gradinfo@lasell.edu. *Website:* http://www.lasell.edu/Academics/Graduate-and-Professional-Studies/MS-in-Management.html.

La Sierra University, School of Business and Management, Riverside, CA 92515. Offers accounting (MBA); finance (MBA); general management (MBA); human resources management (MBA); leadership, values, and ethics for business and management (Certificate); marketing (MBA). *Degree requirements:* For master's, research project. *Entrance requirements:* For master's, GMAT, minimum GPA of 3.0. Additional exam requirements/recommendations for international students: Required—TOEFL. *Faculty research:* Financial econometrics, institutional assessment and strategic planning, legal issues in management, behavioral finance, content of financial reports.

Lewis University, College of Business, Graduate School of Management, Program in Business Administration, Romeoville, IL 60446. Offers accounting (MBA); custom elective option (MBA); e-business (MBA); finance (MBA); healthcare management (MBA); human resources management (MBA); international business (MBA); management information systems (MBA); marketing (MBA); project management (MBA); technology and operations management (MBA). Part-time and evening/weekend programs available. *Students:* 115 full-time (55 women), 227 part-time (129 women); includes 128 minority (74 Black or African American, non-Hispanic/Latino; 1 American Indian or Alaska Native, non-Hispanic/Latino; 9 Asian, non-Hispanic/Latino; 40 Hispanic/Latino; 4 Two or more races, non-Hispanic/Latino), 10 international. Average age 31. In 2013, 99 master's awarded. *Entrance requirements:* For master's, interview, bachelor's degree, resume, 2 recommendations. Additional exam requirements/recommendations for international students: Required—TOEFL (minimum score 550 paper-based). *Application deadline:* For fall admission, 8/15 priority date for domestic students, 5/1 priority date for international students; for spring admission, 11/15 priority date for international students. Applications are processed on a rolling basis. Application fee: $40. Electronic applications accepted. *Financial support:* Career-related internships or fieldwork, Federal Work-Study, scholarships/grants, and unspecified assistantships available. Financial award application deadline: 5/1; financial award applicants required to submit FAFSA. *Unit head:* Dr. Maureen Culleeney, Academic Program Director, 815-838-0500 Ext. 5631, E-mail: culleema@lewisu.edu. *Application contact:* Michele Ryan, Director of Admission, 815-838-0500 Ext. 5384, E-mail: gsm@lewisu.edu.

Liberty University, School of Business, Lynchburg, VA 24515. Offers accounting (MBA, MS, DBA); business administration (MBA); criminal justice (MBA); cyber security (MS); executive leadership (MA); healthcare (MBA); human resources (DBA); information systems (MS), including information assurance, technology management; international business (MBA, DBA); leadership (MBA, DBA); management and leadership (MA); marketing (MBA, MS, DBA), including digital marketing and advertising (MS), project management (MS), public relations (MS), sports marketing and media

(MS); project management (MBA, DBA); public administration (MBA); public relations (MBA). Part-time programs available. Postbaccalaureate distance learning degree programs offered (minimal on-campus study). *Students:* 1,342 full-time (749 women), 3,704 part-time (1,820 women); includes 1,657 minority (1,221 Black or African American, non-Hispanic/Latino; 11 American Indian or Alaska Native, non-Hispanic/Latino; 74 Asian, non-Hispanic/Latino; 209 Hispanic/Latino; 13 Native Hawaiian or other Pacific Islander, non-Hispanic/Latino; 129 Two or more races, non-Hispanic/Latino), 40 international. Average age 35. 5,899 applicants, 48% accepted, 1716 enrolled. In 2013, 1,535 master's awarded. *Entrance requirements:* For master's, minimum undergraduate GPA of 3.0, 15 hours of upper-level business courses. Additional exam requirements/recommendations for international students: Required—TOEFL (minimum score 600 paper-based; 100 iBT). *Application deadline:* Applications are processed on a rolling basis. Application fee: $50. Electronic applications accepted. *Expenses:* Contact institution. *Unit head:* Dr. Scott Hicks, Dean, 434-592-4808, Fax: 434-582-2366, E-mail: smhicks@liberty.edu. *Application contact:* Jay Bridge, Director of Graduate Admissions, 800-424-9595, Fax: 800-628-7977, E-mail: gradadmissions@liberty.edu. *Website:* http://www.liberty.edu/academics/business/index.cfm?PID-149.

Lincoln University, Graduate Programs, Philadelphia, PA 19104. Offers early childhood education (M Ed); educational leadership (M Ed); human resources (MSA), including finance, human resources management; human services (MHS); reading (MSR). Evening/weekend programs available. *Faculty:* 10 full-time (4 women), 34 part-time/adjunct (19 women). *Students:* 224 full-time (145 women), 115 part-time (74 women); includes 328 minority (311 Black or African American, non-Hispanic/Latino; 17 Hispanic/Latino). Average age 40. 237 applicants, 65% accepted, 64 enrolled. In 2013, 155 master's awarded. *Degree requirements:* For master's, thesis. *Entrance requirements:* For master's, working as full-time, paid staff member in the human services field, at least one year of paid experience in this field, and undergraduate degree in human services or a related field from an accredited institution (for MHS). *Application deadline:* For fall admission, 6/1 priority date for domestic and international students. Applications are processed on a rolling basis. Application fee: $50. *Expenses:* Tuition, state resident: full-time $10,106; part-time $567 per hour. Tuition, nonresident: full-time $17,636; part-time $949 per hour. *Financial support:* Application deadline: 8/1. *Unit head:* Dr. Cheryl Gooch, Dean, School of Humanities and Graduate Studies, 484-365-7664, E-mail: cgooch@lincoln.edu. *Application contact:* Jernice Lea, Director of Graduate Admissions, 215-590-8233, Fax: 215-387-3859, E-mail: jlea@lincoln.edu. *Website:* http://www.lincoln.edu/academicaffairs/uc.html.

Lincoln University, Graduate Studies, Oakland, CA 94612. Offers finance and investments (DBA); finance management and investment banking (MBA); general business (MBA); human resource management (MBA, DBA); international business (MBA); management information systems (MBA). Part-time and evening/weekend programs available. *Faculty:* 8 full-time (2 women), 22 part-time/adjunct (7 women). *Students:* 372 full-time (171 women), 4 part-time (1 woman); includes 8 minority (2 Black or African American, non-Hispanic/Latino; 6 Asian, non-Hispanic/Latino), 363 international. Average age 26. 421 applicants, 71% accepted, 133 enrolled. *Degree requirements:* For master's, research project (thesis), internship report, or comprehensive exam; for doctorate, comprehensive exam, thesis/dissertation. *Entrance requirements:* For master's, minimum GPA of 2.7; for doctorate, GMAT (minimum score: 550), GRE (minimum score: 1000), or equivalent test results (waived for master's degree with minimum cumulative GPA of 3.3). Additional exam requirements/recommendations for international students: Required—TOEFL (minimum score 525 paper-based; 71 iBT) or IELTS (minimum score 5.5) for MBA; TOEFL (minimum score 550 paper-based; 79 iBT) or IELTS (minimum score 6) for DBA. *Application deadline:* For fall admission, 7/1 priority date for domestic and international students; for spring admission, 11/1 priority date for domestic and international students; for summer admission, 5/1 for domestic and international students. Applications are processed on a rolling basis. Application fee: $75. Electronic applications accepted. *Expenses: Tuition:* Full-time $7290; part-time $405 per unit. *Required fees:* $375; $405 per unit. $375 per year. Tuition and fees vary according to course level and degree level. *Financial support:* Teaching assistantships with tuition reimbursements, career-related internships or fieldwork, and scholarships/grants available. Financial award application deadline: 7/31; financial award applicants required to submit FAFSA. *Unit head:* Dr. Marshall Burak, Director of Graduate Programs, 510-628-8016, Fax: 510-628-8012, E-mail: mburak@lincolnuca.edu. *Application contact:* Reenu Shrestha, Admissions Officer, 510-628-8010 Ext. 8030, Fax: 510-628-8012, E-mail: admissions@lincolnuca.edu. *Website:* http://www.lincolnuca.edu/.

Lindenwood University, Graduate Programs, College of Individualized Education, St. Charles, MO 63301-1695. Offers administration (MSA); business administration (MBA); communications (MA); criminal justice and administration (MS); gerontology (MA); healthcare administration (MS); human resource management (MS); information technology (MBA, Certificate); managing information technology (MS); writing (MFA). Part-time and evening/weekend programs available. *Faculty:* 20 full-time (7 women), 96 part-time/adjunct (36 women). *Students:* 928 full-time (587 women), 85 part-time (53 women); includes 394 minority (336 Black or African American, non-Hispanic/Latino; 2 American Indian or Alaska Native, non-Hispanic/Latino; 7 Asian, non-Hispanic/Latino; 24 Hispanic/Latino; 2 Native Hawaiian or other Pacific Islander, non-Hispanic/Latino; 23 Two or more races, non-Hispanic/Latino), 33 international. Average age 34. 569 applicants, 62% accepted, 331 enrolled. In 2013, 487 master's awarded. *Degree requirements:* For master's, thesis (for some programs). *Entrance requirements:* For master's, interview, minimum GPA of 3.0. Additional exam requirements/recommendations for international students: Required—TOEFL (minimum score 550 paper-based; 80 iBT). *Application deadline:* For fall admission, 10/5 priority date for domestic and international students; for winter admission, 1/6 priority date for domestic and international students; for spring admission, 4/7 priority date for domestic and international students. Applications are processed on a rolling basis. Application fee: $30 ($100 for international students). Electronic applications accepted. *Expenses: Tuition:* Full-time $14,800; part-time $428 per credit hour. *Required fees:* $350. Tuition and fees vary according to course level and course load. *Financial support:* In 2013–14, 654 students received support. Career-related internships or fieldwork, institutionally sponsored loans, scholarships/grants, tuition waivers (partial), and unspecified assistantships available. Financial award application deadline: 6/30; financial award applicants required to submit FAFSA. *Unit head:* Dan Kemper, Dean, 636-949-4501, Fax: 636-949-4505, E-mail: dkemper@lindenwood.edu. *Application contact:* Brett Barger, Dean of Evening Admissions and Extension Campuses, 636-949-4934, Fax: 636-949-4109, E-mail: adultadmissions@lindenwood.edu.

Lindenwood University, Graduate Programs, School of Business and Entrepreneurship, St. Charles, MO 63301-1695. Offers accountancy (MA); accounting (MBA); business administration (MBA); entrepreneurial studies (MBA); finance (MBA, MS); human resource management (MBA); international business (MBA); leadership (MA); management (MBA); marketing (MBA, MS); public management (MBA); sport management (MA); supply chain management (MBA). *Accreditation:* ACBSP. Part-time and evening/weekend programs available. Postbaccalaureate distance learning degree programs offered (no on-campus study). *Faculty:* 18 full-time (8 women), 33 part-time/adjunct (8 women). *Students:* 292 full-time (130 women), 111 part-time (46 women);

includes 59 minority (42 Black or African American, non-Hispanic/Latino; 5 American Indian or Alaska Native, non-Hispanic/Latino; 1 Asian, non-Hispanic/Latino; 5 Hispanic/Latino; 6 Two or more races, non-Hispanic/Latino), 112 international. Average age 29. 212 applicants, 51% accepted, 102 enrolled. In 2013, 221 master's awarded. *Degree requirements:* For master's, comprehensive exam (for some programs), thesis (for some programs), minimum GPA of 3.0. *Entrance requirements:* For master's, interview, minimum GPA of 3.0, letter of recommendation. Additional exam requirements/recommendations for international students: Required—TOEFL (minimum score 550 paper-based; 80 iBT). *Application deadline:* For fall admission, 8/12 priority date for domestic and international students; for winter admission, 1/6 priority date for domestic and international students; for spring admission, 3/10 priority date for domestic and international students; for summer admission, 5/27 priority date for domestic and international students. Applications are processed on a rolling basis. Application fee: $30 ($100 for international students). Electronic applications accepted. *Expenses: Tuition:* Full-time $14,800; part-time $428 per credit hour. *Required fees:* $350. Tuition and fees vary according to course level and course load. *Financial support:* In 2013–14, 268 students received support. Career-related internships or fieldwork, Federal Work-Study, institutionally sponsored loans, scholarships/grants, tuition waivers (partial), and unspecified assistantships available. Financial award application deadline: 6/30; financial award applicants required to submit FAFSA. *Unit head:* Roger Ellis, Dean, 636-949-4839, E-mail: rellis@lindenwood.edu. *Application contact:* Brett Barger, Dean of Evening Admissions and Extension Campuses, 636-949-4934, Fax: 636-949-4109, E-mail: adultadmissions@lindenwood.edu.
Website: http://www.lindenwood.edu.

Lindenwood University–Belleville, Graduate Programs, Belleville, IL 62226. Offers business administration (MBA); communications (MA), including digital and multimedia, media management, promotions, training and development; counseling (MA); criminal justice administration (MS); education (MA); healthcare administration (MS); human resource management (MS); school administration (MA); teaching (MAT).

Lipscomb University, Graduate School of Business, Nashville, TN 37204-3951. Offers accountancy (M Acc); accounting (MBA); conflict management (MBA); distributive (general) (MBA); financial services (MBA); health care informatics (MBA); healthcare management (MBA); human resources (MHR); information security (MBA); leadership (MBA); nonprofit management (MBA); professional accountancy (Certificate); sports management (MBA); strategic human resources (MBA); sustainability (MBA); MBA/MS. *Accreditation:* ACBSP. Part-time and evening/weekend programs available. *Faculty:* 12 full-time (1 woman), 12 part-time/adjunct (2 women). *Students:* 90 full-time (44 women), 104 part-time (51 women); includes 28 minority (24 Black or African American, non-Hispanic/Latino; 3 Hispanic/Latino; 1 Two or more races, non-Hispanic/Latino), 6 international. Average age 33. 145 applicants, 79% accepted, 69 enrolled. In 2013, 98 master's, 1 other advanced degree awarded. *Entrance requirements:* For master's, GMAT, transcripts, interview, 2 references, resume. Additional exam requirements/recommendations for international students: Required—TOEFL (minimum score 570 paper-based). *Application deadline:* For fall admission, 6/15 for domestic students, 2/1 for international students; for winter admission, 6/1 for international students; for spring admission, 11/15 for domestic students. Applications are processed on a rolling basis. Application fee: $50 ($75 for international students). Electronic applications accepted. *Expenses:* Contact institution. *Financial support:* Career-related internships or fieldwork, scholarships/grants, tuition waivers (partial), and unspecified assistantships available. Support available to part-time students. Financial award application deadline: 7/1; financial award applicants required to submit FAFSA. *Faculty research:* Impact of spirituality on organization commitment, women in corporate leadership, psychological empowerment, training. *Unit head:* Joe Ivey, Associate Dean of Graduate Business Programs, 615-966-6229, Fax: 615-966-1818, E-mail: joe.ivey@lipscomb.edu. *Application contact:* Lisa Shacklett, Assistant Dean of Enrollment and Marketing, 615-966-5968, E-mail: lisa.shacklett@lipscomb.edu.
Website: http://www.lipscomb.edu/business/Graduate-Programs.

Long Island University–LIU Brooklyn, School of Business, Public Administration and Information Sciences, Program in Human Resources Management, Brooklyn, NY 11201-8423. Offers MS. *Entrance requirements:* For master's, GMAT or GRE, 2 letters of recommendation. Additional exam requirements/recommendations for international students: Required—TOEFL (minimum score 500 paper-based).

Loyola University Chicago, Quinlan School of Business, Institute of Human Resources and Employee Relations, Chicago, IL 60610. Offers MSHR, MBA/MSHR. Part-time and evening/weekend programs available. *Faculty:* 5 full-time (1 woman), 4 part-time/adjunct (2 women). *Students:* 8 full-time (6 women), 26 part-time (21 women); includes 8 minority (5 Black or African American, non-Hispanic/Latino; 1 American Indian or Alaska Native, non-Hispanic/Latino; 1 Asian, non-Hispanic/Latino; 1 Hispanic/Latino), 8 international. Average age 29. 85 applicants, 44% accepted, 12 enrolled. In 2013, 22 master's awarded. *Entrance requirements:* For master's, GMAT or GRE, official transcripts, letters of recommendation, statement of purpose, resume. Additional exam requirements/recommendations for international students: Required—TOEFL (minimum score 90 iBT) or IELTS (minimum score 6.5). *Application deadline:* For fall admission, 7/15 for domestic and international students; for winter admission, 10/1 for domestic and international students; for spring admission, 1/15 for domestic and international students; for summer admission, 4/1 for domestic and international students. Applications are processed on a rolling basis. Application fee: $50. Electronic applications accepted. Application fee is waived when completed online. *Expenses:* Contact institution. *Financial support:* Scholarships/grants and unspecified assistantships available. *Faculty research:* Human resource management, labor relations, global human resource management, organizational development, compensation. *Unit head:* Dr. Al Gini, Chair, 312-915-6093, E-mail: agini@luc.edu. *Application contact:* Jessica Gagle, Enrollment Advisor, Quinlan School of Business Graduate Programs, 312-915-8908, Fax: 312-915-7207, E-mail: jgagle@luc.edu.
Website: http://www.luc.edu/quinlan/mba/masters-degree-in-human-resources/index.shtml.

Loyola University Chicago, Quinlan School of Business, MBA Programs, Chicago, IL 60610. Offers accounting (MBA); business ethics (MBA); derivative markets (MBA); economics (MBA); entrepreneurship (MBA); executive (MBA); finance (MBA); healthcare management (MBA); human resources management (MBA); information systems management (MBA); intercontinental (MBA); international business (MBA); marketing (MBA); operations management (MBA); risk management (MBA); JD/MBA. Part-time and evening/weekend programs available. *Faculty:* 76 full-time (20 women), 10 part-time/adjunct (4 women). *Students:* 73 full-time (34 women), 294 part-time (129 women); includes 60 minority (18 Black or African American, non-Hispanic/Latino; 28 Asian, non-Hispanic/Latino; 14 Hispanic/Latino), 19 international. Average age 31. 529 applicants, 51% accepted, 153 enrolled. In 2013, 229 master's awarded. *Entrance requirements:* For master's, GMAT or GRE, official transcripts, two letters of recommendation, statement of purpose, resume. Additional exam requirements/recommendations for international students: Required—TOEFL (minimum score 90 iBT) or IELTS (minimum score 6.5). *Application deadline:* For fall admission, 7/15 for domestic and international students; for winter admission, 10/1 for domestic and international students; for spring admission, 1/15 for domestic and international students; for summer admission, 4/1 for domestic and international students. Applications are processed on a rolling basis. Application fee: $50. Electronic applications accepted. Application fee is waived when completed online. *Expenses: Tuition:* Full-time $16,740; part-time $930 per credit. *Required fees:* $135 per semester. *Financial support:* Scholarships/grants and unspecified assistantships available. *Faculty research:* Social enterprise and responsibility, emerging markets, supply chain management, risk management. *Unit head:* Jennifer Huntley, Assistant Dean for Graduate Programs, 312-915-6124, Fax: 312-915-7207, E-mail: jhuntle@luc.edu. *Application contact:* Jessica Gagle, Enrollment Advisor, Quinlan School of Business Graduate Programs, 312-915-8908, Fax: 312-915-7207, E-mail: jgagle@luc.edu.

Manhattanville College, School of Business, Program in Human Resource Management and Organizational Effectiveness, Purchase, NY 10577-2132. Offers MS. Part-time and evening/weekend programs available. *Degree requirements:* For master's, thesis, final project. *Entrance requirements:* For master's, interview, 2 letters of recommendation. Additional exam requirements/recommendations for international students: Required—TOEFL.

Marquette University, Graduate School of Management, Executive MBA Program, Milwaukee, WI 53201-1881. Offers economics (MBA); finance (MBA); human resources (MBA); international business (MBA); management information systems (MBA); marketing (MBA); operations and supply chain management (MBA); sports business (MBA). *Accreditation:* AACSB. *Students:* 38 full-time (12 women), 1 international. Average age 36. 36 applicants. In 2013, 21 master's awarded. *Degree requirements:* For master's, international trip. *Entrance requirements:* For master's, GMAT or GRE, two letters of recommendation, official transcripts from current and previous colleges/universities. Additional exam requirements/recommendations for international students: Required—TOEFL (minimum score 550 paper-based; 88 iBT), IELTS (minimum score 6.5), PTE. *Application deadline:* For fall admission, 2/15 for domestic and international students. Application fee: $50. Electronic applications accepted. *Expenses:* Contact institution. *Financial support:* Application deadline: 2/15. *Faculty research:* International trade and finance, customer relationship management, consumer satisfaction, customer service. *Unit head:* Dr. Mark Eppli, Dean, 414-288-5724. *Application contact:* Dr. Jeanne Simmons, Associate Dean, 414-288-7145.
Website: http://www.busadm.mu.edu/emba/.

Marquette University, Graduate School of Management, Program in Business Administration, Milwaukee, WI 53201-1881. Offers business administration (MBA); economics (MBA); entrepreneurship (Certificate); finance (MBA); human resources (MBA); international business (MBA); management information systems (MBA); marketing (MBA); operations and supply chain management (MBA); sports business (MBA); JD/MBA; MBA/MA; MBA/MSN. *Accreditation:* AACSB. Part-time and evening/weekend programs available. *Students:* 28 full-time (13 women), 265 part-time (66 women); includes 20 minority (7 Black or African American, non-Hispanic/Latino; 8 Asian, non-Hispanic/Latino; 5 Hispanic/Latino), 11 international. Average age 31. 185 applicants. In 2013, 129 master's, 2 other advanced degrees awarded. *Degree requirements:* For Certificate, business plan. *Entrance requirements:* For master's, GMAT or GRE, letters of recommendation. Additional exam requirements/recommendations for international students: Required—TOEFL (minimum score 550 paper-based; 88 iBT), IELTS (minimum score 6.5), PTE. *Application deadline:* For fall admission, 2/15 for domestic and international students. Applications are processed on a rolling basis. Application fee: $50. Electronic applications accepted. *Financial support:* In 2013–14, 4 fellowships, 11 teaching assistantships were awarded; research assistantships, Federal Work-Study, institutionally sponsored loans, scholarships/grants, and tuition waivers (full and partial) also available. Support available to part-time students. Financial award application deadline: 2/15. *Faculty research:* Ethics in the professions, services marketing, technology impact on decision-making, mentoring. *Unit head:* Dr. Mark Eppli, Dean, 414-288-5724. *Application contact:* Dr. Jeanne Simmons, Associate Dean, 414-288-7145.
Website: http://business.marquette.edu/academics/mba.

Marquette University, Graduate School of Management, Program in Human Resources, Milwaukee, WI 53201-1881. Offers MSHR. Part-time and evening/weekend programs available. *Students:* 23 full-time (21 women), 21 part-time (16 women), 25 international. Average age 26. 172 applicants, 27% accepted, 15 enrolled. In 2013, 15 master's awarded. *Entrance requirements:* For master's, GMAT or GRE General Test, letters of recommendation. Additional exam requirements/recommendations for international students: Required—TOEFL (minimum score 550 paper-based; 88 iBT), IELTS (minimum score 6.5), PTE. *Application deadline:* For fall admission, 2/15 for domestic and international students. Applications are processed on a rolling basis. Electronic applications accepted. *Financial support:* In 2013–14, 3 teaching assistantships were awarded; fellowships, research assistantships, Federal Work-Study, institutionally sponsored loans, and tuition waivers (full and partial) also available. Support available to part-time students. Financial award application deadline: 2/15. *Faculty research:* Diversity, mentoring, executive compensation. *Unit head:* Dr. Mark Eppli, Dean, 414-288-5724. *Application contact:* Dr. Connie O'Neill, Associate Professor, 414-288-1458.
Website: http://business.marquette.edu/academics/mshr.

Marshall University, Academic Affairs Division, College of Business, Program in Human Resource Management, Huntington, WV 25755. Offers MS. Part-time and evening/weekend programs available. *Students:* 39 full-time (28 women), 21 part-time (11 women); includes 12 minority (6 Black or African American, non-Hispanic/Latino; 1 Asian, non-Hispanic/Latino; 3 Hispanic/Latino; 2 Two or more races, non-Hispanic/Latino), 14 international. Average age 30. In 2013, 30 master's awarded. *Degree requirements:* For master's, comprehensive assessment. *Entrance requirements:* For master's, GMAT or GRE General Test. *Application deadline:* Applications are processed on a rolling basis. Application fee: $40. *Financial support:* Tuition waivers (full) available. Support available to part-time students. Financial award applicants required to submit FAFSA. *Unit head:* Dr. Margie McInerney, Associate Dean, 304-696-2675, E-mail: mcinerney@marshall.edu. *Application contact:* Wesley Spradlin, Information Contact, 304-746-8964, Fax: 304-746-1902, E-mail: spradlin2@marshall.edu.

Marygrove College, Graduate Division, Program in Human Resource Management, Detroit, MI 48221-2599. Offers MA. *Entrance requirements:* For master's, interview, writing sample.

Marymount University, School of Business Administration, Program in Human Resource Management, Arlington, VA 22207-4299. Offers human resource management (MA, Certificate); organization development (Certificate). Part-time and evening/weekend programs available. *Faculty:* 5 full-time (3 women). *Students:* 12 full-time (all women), 51 part-time (39 women); includes 23 minority (8 Black or African American, non-Hispanic/Latino; 6 Asian, non-Hispanic/Latino; 5 Hispanic/Latino; 4 Two or more races, non-Hispanic/Latino), 6 international. Average age 35. 39 applicants, 97% accepted, 24 enrolled. In 2013, 16 master's, 12 other advanced degrees awarded. *Degree requirements:* For master's, thesis or alternative. *Entrance requirements:* For master's, GMAT or GRE General Test, resume; for Certificate, resume. Additional exam requirements/recommendations for international students: Required—TOEFL (minimum score 600 paper-based; 96 iBT), IELTS (minimum score 6.5). *Application deadline:* For fall admission, 7/15 priority date for domestic students, 7/1 for international students; for

spring admission, 11/15 priority date for domestic students, 11/15 for international students. Applications are processed on a rolling basis. Application fee: $40. Electronic applications accepted. *Expenses: Tuition:* Part-time $850 per credit. *Required fees:* $10 per credit. One-time fee: $200 part-time. Tuition and fees vary according to program. *Financial support:* In 2013–14, 2 students received support, including 1 teaching assistantship; research assistantships with full and partial tuition reimbursements available, career-related internships or fieldwork, Federal Work-Study, scholarships/grants, and unspecified assistantships also available. Support available to part-time students. Financial award applicants required to submit FAFSA. *Unit head:* Dr. Virginia Bianco-Mathis, Chair/Director, 703-284-5957, Fax: 703-527-3830, E-mail: virginia.bianco-mathis@marymount.edu. *Application contact:* Francesca Reed, Director, Graduate Admissions, 703-284-5901, Fax: 703-527-3815, E-mail: grad.admissions@marymount.edu.
Website: http://www.marymount.edu/academics/programs/hrMgt.

McKendree University, Graduate Programs, Master of Business Administration Program, Lebanon, IL 62254-1299. Offers business administration (MBA); human resource management (MBA); international business (MBA). Part-time and evening/weekend programs available. Postbaccalaureate distance learning degree programs offered (no on-campus study). *Entrance requirements:* For master's, official transcripts from all institutions attended, essay, minimum GPA of 3.0, three references, resume. Additional exam requirements/recommendations for international students: Required—TOEFL. Electronic applications accepted.

McMaster University, School of Graduate Studies, Faculty of Business, Program in Human Resources and Management, Hamilton, ON L8S 4M2, Canada. Offers MBA, PhD. Part-time programs available. *Degree requirements:* For doctorate, comprehensive exam, thesis/dissertation. *Entrance requirements:* For master's, GMAT; for doctorate, GMAT or GRE, master's degree, minimum B+ average. Additional exam requirements/recommendations for international students: Required—TOEFL (minimum score 580 paper-based). *Faculty research:* Leadership, occupational mental health, work attitudes, human resources recruitment, change and stress management strategies.

Mercy College, School of Business, Program in Human Resource Management, Dobbs Ferry, NY 10522-1189. Offers MS. Part-time and evening/weekend programs available. Postbaccalaureate distance learning degree programs offered (no on-campus study). *Students:* 48 full-time (39 women), 56 part-time (44 women); includes 69 minority (39 Black or African American, non-Hispanic/Latino; 5 Asian, non-Hispanic/Latino; 24 Hispanic/Latino; 1 Two or more races, non-Hispanic/Latino), 3 international. Average age 32. 84 applicants, 71% accepted, 34 enrolled. In 2013, 27 master's awarded. *Entrance requirements:* For master's, interview, two letters of reference, undergraduate transcripts. Additional exam requirements/recommendations for international students: Required—TOEFL (minimum score 600 paper-based; 100 iBT), IELTS (minimum score 8). *Application deadline:* For fall admission, 8/1 for international students. Applications are processed on a rolling basis. Application fee: $40. Electronic applications accepted. *Expenses: Tuition:* Full-time $19,344; part-time $806 per credit. *Required fees:* $580; $806 per credit. $145 per term. Tuition and fees vary according to course load, degree level and program. *Financial support:* Career-related internships or fieldwork, Federal Work-Study, scholarships/grants, and unspecified assistantships available. Support available to part-time students. Financial award applicants required to submit FAFSA. *Unit head:* Ed Weis, Dean, School of Business, 914-674-7490, E-mail: eweis@mercy.edu. *Application contact:* Allison Gurdineer, Senior Director of Admissions, 877-637-2946, Fax: 914-674-7382, E-mail: admissions@mercy.edu.
Website: https://www.mercy.edu/academics/school-of-business/department-of-business-administration/ms-in-human-resource-management/.

Mercyhurst University, Graduate Studies, Program in Organizational Leadership, Erie, PA 16546. Offers accounting (MS); entrepreneurship (MS); higher education administration (MS); human resources (MS); nonprofit management (MS); organizational leadership (Certificate); sports leadership (MS). Part-time and evening/weekend programs available. *Degree requirements:* For master's, thesis. *Entrance requirements:* For master's, GRE General Test or MAT, interview, resume, essay, three professional references, transcripts. Additional exam requirements/recommendations for international students: Required—TOEFL. Electronic applications accepted. *Faculty research:* Leadership training, organizational communication, leadership pedagogy.

Michigan State University, The Graduate School, College of Social Science, School of Labor and Industrial Relations, East Lansing, MI 48824. Offers human resources and labor relations (MLRHR); industrial relations and human resources (PhD). *Entrance requirements:* Additional exam requirements/recommendations for international students: Required—TOEFL.

Michigan State University, The Graduate School, Eli Broad College of Business, Program in Business Administration, East Lansing, MI 48824. Offers finance (MBA); human resource management (MBA); integrative management (MBA); marketing (MBA); supply chain management (MBA). MBA in integrative management is through Weekend MBA Program; other 4 concentrations are through Full-Time MBA Program. Evening/weekend programs available. *Students:* 432. In 2013, 241 degrees awarded. *Degree requirements:* For master's, enrichment experience. *Entrance requirements:* For master's, GMAT or GRE, 4-year bachelor's degree; resume; work experience (minimum of 5 years for Weekend MBA); 2-3 personal essays; 2 letters of recommendation; personal interview. Additional exam requirements/recommendations for international students: Required—PTE (minimum score 70), TOEFL (minimum score 100 iBT) or IELTS (minimum score 7) for Full-Time MBA applicants. *Application deadline:* Applications are processed on a rolling basis. Application fee: $50. Electronic applications accepted. *Expenses:* Contact institution. *Financial support:* Fellowships with tuition reimbursements, research assistantships with tuition reimbursements, teaching assistantships with tuition reimbursements, scholarships/grants, unspecified assistantships, and non-resident tuition waivers (for all military veterans and their dependents in the Full-Time MBA Program) available. Financial award applicants required to submit FAFSA. *Unit head:* Dr. Sanjay Gupta, Associate Dean for MBA and Professional Master's Programs, 517-432-6488, Fax: 517-353-6395, E-mail: gupta@broad.msu.edu. *Application contact:* Program Information Contact, 517-355-7604, Fax: 517-353-1649, E-mail: mba@msu.edu.
Website: http://mba.broad.msu.edu.

Millennia Atlantic University, Graduate Programs, Doral, FL 33178. Offers accounting (MBA); business administration (MBA); health information management (MS); human resource management (MA). Postbaccalaureate distance learning degree programs offered (no on-campus study).

Misericordia University, College of Professional Studies and Social Sciences, Master of Business Administration Program, Dallas, PA 18612-1098. Offers accounting (MBA); human resources (MBA); management (MBA); sport management (MBA). Part-time and evening/weekend programs available. Postbaccalaureate distance learning degree programs offered (no on-campus study). *Faculty:* 4 full-time (2 women), 5 part-time/adjunct (2 women). *Students:* 100 part-time (53 women); includes 1 minority (Black or African American, non-Hispanic/Latino), 1 international. Average age 33. In 2013, 32 master's awarded. *Entrance requirements:* For master's, GMAT, MAT, GRE (50th

percentile or higher), or minimum undergraduate GPA of 3.0, interview. Additional exam requirements/recommendations for international students: Required—TOEFL. *Application deadline:* Applications are processed on a rolling basis. Application fee: $35. Electronic applications accepted. Application fee is waived when completed online. *Expenses: Tuition:* Full-time $14,450; part-time $680 per credit. Tuition and fees vary according to degree level. *Financial support:* In 2013–14, 68 students received support. Scholarships/grants and unspecified assistantships available. Support available to part-time students. Financial award applicants required to submit FAFSA. *Unit head:* Dr. Timothy Kearney, Chair of Business Department, 570-674-1487, E-mail: tkearney@misericordia.edu. *Application contact:* David Pasquini, Assistant Director of Admissions, 570-674-8183, Fax: 570-674-6232, E-mail: dpasquin@misericordia.edu.
Website: http://www.misericordia.edu/mba.

Misericordia University, College of Professional Studies and Social Sciences, Program in Organizational Management, Dallas, PA 18612-1098. Offers human resource management (MS); information technology management (MS); management (MS); not-for-profit management (MS). Part-time and evening/weekend programs available. Postbaccalaureate distance learning degree programs offered (no on-campus study). *Faculty:* 3 full-time (0 women), 6 part-time/adjunct (0 women). *Students:* 82 part-time (53 women); includes 2 minority (1 Hispanic/Latino; 1 Native Hawaiian or other Pacific Islander, non-Hispanic/Latino). Average age 33. In 2013, 25 master's awarded. *Entrance requirements:* For master's, GRE General Test, MAT (35th percentile or higher), or minimum undergraduate GPA of 3.0. Additional exam requirements/recommendations for international students: Required—TOEFL. *Application deadline:* Applications are processed on a rolling basis. Application fee: $35. Electronic applications accepted. Application fee is waived when completed online. *Expenses:* Contact institution. *Financial support:* In 2013–14, 55 students received support. Scholarships/grants available. Support available to part-time students. Financial award application deadline: 6/30; financial award applicants required to submit FAFSA. *Unit head:* Dr. Timothy Kearney, Chair of Business Department, 570-674-1487, E-mail: tkearney@misericordia.edu. *Application contact:* David Pasquini, Assistant Director of Admissions, 570-674-8183, Fax: 570-674-6232, E-mail: dpasquin@misericordia.edu.
Website: http://www.misericordia.edu/om.

Monmouth University, The Graduate School, Department of Corporate and Public Communication, West Long Branch, NJ 07764-1898. Offers corporate and public communication (MA); human resources management and communication (Certificate); public service communication (Certificate); strategic public relations and new media (Certificate). Part-time and evening/weekend programs available. *Faculty:* 9 full-time (6 women). *Students:* 5 full-time (4 women), 20 part-time (14 women); includes 2 minority (1 Hispanic/Latino; 1 Two or more races, non-Hispanic/Latino), 2 international. Average age 29. 17 applicants, 88% accepted, 12 enrolled. In 2013, 10 master's awarded. *Degree requirements:* For master's, comprehensive exam, project. *Entrance requirements:* For master's, GRE, baccalaureate degree with minimum GPA of 3.0 in major, 2.75 overall; two letters of recommendation, personal essay, resume. Additional exam requirements/recommendations for international students: Required—TOEFL (minimum score 550 paper-based; 79 iBT), IELTS (minimum score 6), Michigan English Language Assessment Battery (minimum score 77). *Application deadline:* For fall admission, 7/15 priority date for domestic students, 6/1 for international students; for spring admission, 11/15 priority date for domestic students, 11/1 for international students. Applications are processed on a rolling basis. Application fee: $50. Electronic applications accepted. *Expenses: Tuition:* Part-time $1004 per credit hour. *Required fees:* $157 per semester. *Financial support:* In 2013–14, 10 students received support, including 8 fellowships (averaging $3,037 per year), 1 research assistantship (averaging $3,321 per year); scholarships/grants and unspecified assistantships also available. Support available to part-time students. Financial award applicants required to submit FAFSA. *Faculty research:* Service-learning, history of television, feminism and the media, executive communication, public relations pedagogy. *Unit head:* Dr. Deanna Shoemaker, Program Director, 732-263-5449, Fax: 732-571-3609, E-mail: dshoemak@monmouth.edu. *Application contact:* Lauren Vento-Cifelli, Associate Vice President of Undergraduate and Graduate Admission, 732-571-3452, Fax: 732-263-5123, E-mail: gradadm@monmouth.edu.
Website: http://www.monmouth.edu/cpc.

Moravian College, Moravian College Comenius Center, Business and Management Programs, Bethlehem, PA 18018-6650. Offers accounting (MBA); business analytics (MBA); general management (MBA); health administration (MHA); healthcare management (MBA); human resource management (MBA); leadership (MSHRM); learning and performance management (MSHRM); supply chain management (MBA). Part-time and evening/weekend programs available. *Entrance requirements:* For master's, GMAT. Additional exam requirements/recommendations for international students: Required—TOEFL (minimum score 550 paper-based; 90 iBT). Application fee is waived when completed online. *Expenses:* Contact institution. *Faculty research:* Leadership, change management, human resources.

National Louis University, College of Management and Business, Chicago, IL 60603. Offers business administration (MBA); human resource management and development (MS); management (MS). Part-time and evening/weekend programs available. *Entrance requirements:* For master's, college-administered critical thinking and writing skills test, minimum GPA of 3.0, resume, 3 references. Additional exam requirements/recommendations for international students: Required—TOEFL (minimum score 550 paper-based; 79 iBT).

National University, Academic Affairs, School of Business and Management, La Jolla, CA 92037-1011. Offers accountancy (Certificate); business administration (GMBA, MBA), including financial management (MBA), human resource management (MBA), integrated marketing communications (MBA), international business (MBA), management accounting (MBA), marketing (MBA), mobile marketing and social media (MBA), organizational leadership (MA, MBA), professional golf management (MBA); global management (MGM); human resource management (MA), including organizational development and change, organizational leadership (MA, MBA); international business (Certificate); management information systems (MS); organizational leadership (MS), including community development; sustainability management (MS). Part-time and evening/weekend programs available. Postbaccalaureate distance learning degree programs offered (no on-campus study). *Faculty:* 30 full-time (8 women), 88 part-time/adjunct (25 women). *Students:* 688 full-time (357 women), 331 part-time (161 women); includes 453 minority (105 Black or African American, non-Hispanic/Latino; 2 American Indian or Alaska Native, non-Hispanic/Latino; 143 Asian, non-Hispanic/Latino; 162 Hispanic/Latino; 13 Native Hawaiian or other Pacific Islander, non-Hispanic/Latino; 28 Two or more races, non-Hispanic/Latino), 165 international. Average age 33. 286 applicants, 100% accepted, 217 enrolled. In 2013, 641 master's awarded. *Degree requirements:* For master's, thesis (for some programs). *Entrance requirements:* For master's, interview, minimum GPA of 2.5. Additional exam requirements/recommendations for international students: Required—TOEFL (minimum score 550 paper-based; 79 iBT), IELTS (minimum score 6). *Application deadline:* Applications are processed on a rolling basis. Application fee: $60 ($65 for international students). Electronic applications accepted. *Expenses: Tuition:* Full-time $13,824; part-time $1728 per course. One-time fee: $160. *Financial support:*

Career-related internships or fieldwork, scholarships/grants, and tuition waivers (partial) available. Support available to part-time students. Financial award application deadline: 6/30; financial award applicants required to submit FAFSA. *Unit head:* School of Business and Management, 800-628-8648, Fax: 858-642-8719, E-mail: sobm@nu.edu. *Application contact:* Louis Cruz, Interim Vice President for Enrollment Services, 800-628-8648, E-mail: advisor@nu.edu.
Website: http://www.nu.edu/OurPrograms/SchoolOfBusinessAndManagement.html.

National University, Academic Affairs, School of Professional Studies, La Jolla, CA 92037-1011. Offers criminal justice (MCJ); digital cinema (MFA); digital journalism (MA); juvenile justice (MS); professional screen writing (MFA); public administration (MPA), including human resource management, organizational leadership, public finance. Part-time and evening/weekend programs available. Postbaccalaureate distance learning degree programs offered (no on-campus study). *Faculty:* 14 full-time (6 women), 28 part-time/adjunct (8 women). *Students:* 265 full-time (140 women), 130 part-time (69 women); includes 233 minority (90 Black or African American, non-Hispanic/Latino; 3 American Indian or Alaska Native, non-Hispanic/Latino; 23 Asian, non-Hispanic/Latino; 92 Hispanic/Latino; 8 Native Hawaiian or other Pacific Islander, non-Hispanic/Latino; 17 Two or more races, non-Hispanic/Latino), 4 international. Average age 37. 89 applicants, 100% accepted, 70 enrolled. *Degree requirements:* For master's, thesis (for some programs). *Entrance requirements:* For master's, interview, minimum GPA of 2.5. Additional exam requirements/recommendations for international students: Required—TOEFL (minimum score 550 paper-based; 79 iBT), IELTS (minimum score 6). *Application deadline:* Applications are processed on a rolling basis. Application fee: $60 ($65 for international students). Electronic applications accepted. *Expenses: Tuition:* Full-time $13,824; part-time $1728 per course. One-time fee: $160. *Financial support:* Career-related internships or fieldwork, institutionally sponsored loans, scholarships/grants, and tuition waivers (partial) available. Support available to part-time students. Financial award application deadline: 6/30; financial award applicants required to submit FAFSA. *Unit head:* School of Professional Studies, 800-628-8648, E-mail: sops@nu.edu. *Application contact:* Louis Cruz, Interim Vice President for Enrollment Services, 800-628-8648, E-mail: advisor@nu.edu.
Website: http://www.nu.edu/OurPrograms/School-of-Professional-Studies.html.

Nazareth College of Rochester, Graduate Studies, Department of Business, Program in Human Resource Management, Rochester, NY 14618-3790. Offers MS. *Entrance requirements:* For master's, minimum GPA of 3.0.

New Mexico Highlands University, Graduate Studies, School of Business, Media and Technology, Las Vegas, NM 87701. Offers business administration (MBA), including government nonprofit management, human resource management, international business, management, management information systems; media arts and technology (MA), including media arts and computer science. *Accreditation:* ACBSP. *Faculty:* 13 full-time (5 women). *Students:* 65 full-time (34 women), 146 part-time (89 women); includes 137 minority (3 Black or African American, non-Hispanic/Latino; 9 American Indian or Alaska Native, non-Hispanic/Latino; 1 Asian, non-Hispanic/Latino; 120 Hispanic/Latino; 2 Native Hawaiian or other Pacific Islander, non-Hispanic/Latino; 2 Two or more races, non-Hispanic/Latino), 23 international. Average age 34. In 2013, 56 master's awarded. *Degree requirements:* For master's, comprehensive exam, thesis or alternative. *Entrance requirements:* For master's, minimum undergraduate GPA of 3.0. Additional exam requirements/recommendations for international students: Required—TOEFL (minimum score 540 paper-based). *Application deadline:* For fall admission, 8/1 priority date for domestic students. Applications are processed on a rolling basis. Application fee: $15. *Expenses:* Tuition, state resident: full-time $4278; part-time $178 per credit hour. Tuition, nonresident: full-time $6716; part-time $281 per credit hour. One-time fee: $15. *Financial support:* Career-related internships or fieldwork, Federal Work-Study, institutionally sponsored loans, scholarships/grants, tuition waivers (full and partial), and unspecified assistantships available. Support available to part-time students. Financial award application deadline: 3/1; financial award applicants required to submit FAFSA. *Faculty research:* Real estate valuation, studying expert judgments in complex accounting, decision environments, green marketing, environmentalism, marketing research methodology. *Unit head:* Dr. Margaret Young, Dean, 505-454-3522, Fax: 505-454-3354, E-mail: young_m@nmhu.edu. *Application contact:* Diane Trujillo, Administrative Assistant, Graduate Studies, 505-454-3266, Fax: 505-426-2117, E-mail: dtrujillo@nmhu.edu.

New York Institute of Technology, School of Management, Department of Human Resource Management Studies, Old Westbury, NY 11568-8000. Offers human resource management (Advanced Certificate); human resource management and labor relations (MS). Part-time and evening/weekend programs available. *Faculty:* 4 full-time (1 woman), 7 part-time/adjunct (4 women). *Students:* 31 full-time (19 women), 45 part-time (32 women); includes 34 minority (14 Black or African American, non-Hispanic/Latino; 1 American Indian or Alaska Native, non-Hispanic/Latino; 5 Asian, non-Hispanic/Latino; 12 Hispanic/Latino; 2 Two or more races, non-Hispanic/Latino), 29 international. Average age 29. 59 applicants, 73% accepted, 21 enrolled. In 2013, 26 master's awarded. *Degree requirements:* For master's, comprehensive exam, thesis optional. *Entrance requirements:* For master's, GRE, minimum QPA of 2.85, interview, 2 letters of recommendation. Additional exam requirements/recommendations for international students: Required—TOEFL (minimum score 550 paper-based; 79 iBT), IELTS (minimum score 6). *Application deadline:* For fall admission, 7/1 priority date for domestic students, 6/1 for international students; for spring admission, 12/1 priority date for domestic students, 12/1 for international students. Applications are processed on a rolling basis. Application fee: $50. Electronic applications accepted. *Expenses: Tuition:* Full-time $18,900; part-time $1050 per credit. *Financial support:* Research assistantships, career-related internships or fieldwork, scholarships/grants, health care benefits, tuition waivers (full and partial), and unspecified assistantships available. Support available to part-time students. Financial award applicants required to submit FAFSA. *Faculty research:* Compensation and benefits, organizational management, industrial relations, disabilities. *Unit head:* Maya Kroumova, Chairperson, 212-261-1667, Fax: 516-686-7425, E-mail: mkroumov@nyit.edu. *Application contact:* Alice Dolitsky, Director, Graduate Admissions, 516-686-7520, Fax: 516-686-1116, E-mail: nyitgrad@nyit.edu.
Website: http://www.nyit.edu/management/ms_programs.

New York University, Polytechnic School of Engineering, Department of Technology Management, New York, NY 10012-1019. Offers construction management (Advanced Certificate); electronic business management (Advanced Certificate); entrepreneurship (Advanced Certificate); human resources management (Advanced Certificate); industrial engineering (MS); information management (Advanced Certificate); management (MS); management of technology (MS); manufacturing engineering (MS); organizational behavior (MS, Advanced Certificate); project management (Advanced Certificate); technology management (MBA, PhD, Advanced Certificate); telecommunications management (Advanced Certificate). Part-time and evening/weekend programs available. *Faculty:* 7 full-time (1 woman), 41 part-time/adjunct (2 women). *Students:* 285 full-time (132 women), 116 part-time (45 women); includes 50 minority (10 Black or African American, non-Hispanic/Latino; 29 Asian, non-Hispanic/Latino; 11 Hispanic/Latino), 284 international. Average age 30. 726 applicants, 60% accepted, 140 enrolled. In 2013, 137 master's awarded. *Degree requirements:* For master's, comprehensive exam (for some programs), thesis (for some programs); for doctorate, comprehensive exam, thesis/dissertation. *Entrance requirements:* For master's, GMAT, minimum B average in undergraduate course work. Additional exam requirements/recommendations for international students: Required—TOEFL (minimum score 550 paper-based; 80 iBT); Recommended—IELTS (minimum score 6.5). *Application deadline:* For fall admission, 7/31 priority date for domestic students, 4/30 priority date for international students; for spring admission, 12/31 priority date for domestic students, 11/30 priority date for international students. Applications are processed on a rolling basis. Application fee: $75. Electronic applications accepted. *Expenses: Tuition:* Full-time $35,856; part-time $1494 per unit. *Required fees:* $1408; $64 per unit. $473 per term. Tuition and fees vary according to course load and program. *Financial support:* In 2013–14, 1 fellowship (averaging $26,400 per year) was awarded; research assistantships, teaching assistantships, institutionally sponsored loans, scholarships/grants, and unspecified assistantships also available. Support available to part-time students. *Faculty research:* Global innovation and research and development strategy, managing emerging technologies, technology and development, service design and innovation, tech entrepreneurship and commercialization, sustainable and clean-tech innovation, impacts of information technology upon individuals, organizations and society. *Total annual research expenditures:* $692,936. *Unit head:* Prof. Bharadwaj Rao, Head, 718-260-3617, Fax: 718-260-3874, E-mail: brao@poly.edu. *Application contact:* Raymond Lutzky, Director of Graduate Enrollment Management, 718-637-5984, Fax: 718-260-3624, E-mail: rlutzky@poly.edu.
Website: http://www.poly.edu/academics/departments/technology/.

New York University, Robert F. Wagner Graduate School of Public Service, Program in Public Administration, New York, NY 10012. Offers public administration (PhD); public and nonprofit management and policy (MPA, Advanced Certificate), including developmental administration (Advanced Certificate), financial management and public finance, human resources management (Advanced Certificate), international administration (Advanced Certificate), management (MPA), management for public and nonprofit organizations (Advanced Certificate), public policy analysis, quantitative analysis and computer applications (Advanced Certificate), urban public policy (Advanced Certificate); JD/MPA; MBA/MPA; MPA/MA. *Accreditation:* NASPAA (one or more programs are accredited). Part-time programs available. *Faculty:* 29 full-time (13 women), 41 part-time/adjunct (21 women). *Students:* 373 full-time (275 women), 245 part-time (176 women); includes 207 minority (56 Black or African American, non-Hispanic/Latino; 2 American Indian or Alaska Native, non-Hispanic/Latino; 70 Asian, non-Hispanic/Latino; 64 Hispanic/Latino; 2 Native Hawaiian or other Pacific Islander, non-Hispanic/Latino; 13 Two or more races, non-Hispanic/Latino), 122 international. Average age 28. 1,163 applicants, 61% accepted, 250 enrolled. In 2013, 233 master's, 6 doctorates, 1 other advanced degree awarded. *Degree requirements:* For master's, thesis or alternative, capstone end event; for doctorate, one foreign language, comprehensive exam, thesis/dissertation, preliminary qualifying examination. *Entrance requirements:* Additional exam requirements/recommendations for international students: Required—TOEFL (minimum score 100 iBT), IELTS (minimum score 7.5), TWE. *Application deadline:* For fall admission, 1/6 for domestic and international students; for spring admission, 10/1 for domestic and international students. Application fee: $85. Electronic applications accepted. *Expenses:* Contact institution. *Financial support:* In 2013–14, 152 students received support, including 141 fellowships with full and partial tuition reimbursements available (averaging $10,100 per year), 5 research assistantships with full tuition reimbursements available (averaging $39,643 per year); career-related internships or fieldwork, Federal Work-Study, scholarships/grants, health care benefits, and unspecified assistantships also available. Support available to part-time students. Financial award application deadline: 1/5; financial award applicants required to submit FAFSA. *Unit head:* Prof. Katherine O'Regan, Associate Professor of Public Policy, 212-998-7498, E-mail: katherine.oregan@nyu.edu. *Application contact:* Janet Barzilay, Admissions Officer, 212-998-7414, Fax: 212-995-4611, E-mail: wagner.admissions@nyu.edu.
Website: http://wagner.nyu.edu/.

New York University, School of Continuing and Professional Studies, Division of Programs in Business, Program in Leadership and Human Capital Management, New York, NY 10012-1019. Offers benefits and compensation (Advanced Certificate); human resource management (Advanced Certificate); human resource management and development (MS), including human resource development, human resource management, organizational effectiveness; organizational and executive coaching (Advanced Certificate). Part-time and evening/weekend programs available. Postbaccalaureate distance learning degree programs offered (no on-campus study). *Faculty:* 1 (woman) full-time, 49 part-time/adjunct (25 women). *Students:* 73 full-time (54 women), 161 part-time (140 women); includes 66 minority (25 Black or African American, non-Hispanic/Latino; 22 Asian, non-Hispanic/Latino; 14 Hispanic/Latino; 1 Native Hawaiian or other Pacific Islander, non-Hispanic/Latino; 4 Two or more races, non-Hispanic/Latino), 61 international. Average age 29. 239 applicants, 62% accepted, 72 enrolled. In 2013, 77 master's, 11 other advanced degrees awarded. *Degree requirements:* For master's, thesis. *Entrance requirements:* For master's, bachelor's degree, resume with relevant professional work, internship or volunteer experience, two letters of recommendation, statement of purpose. Additional exam requirements/recommendations for international students: Required—TOEFL (minimum score 600 paper-based; 100 iBT), IELTS (minimum score 7). *Application deadline:* For fall admission, 2/1 priority date for domestic and international students; for spring admission, 10/15 priority date for domestic students, 8/15 priority date for international students. Applications are processed on a rolling basis. Application fee: $150. Electronic applications accepted. *Expenses: Tuition:* Full-time $35,856; part-time $1494 per unit. *Required fees:* $1408; $64 per unit. $473 per term. Tuition and fees vary according to course load and program. *Financial support:* In 2013–14, 98 students received support, including 98 fellowships (averaging $1,944 per year). *Unit head:* Vish Ganpati, Academic Director, 212-998-7112, E-mail: vg36@nyu.edu. *Application contact:* Admissions Office, 212-998-7100, E-mail: scps.gradadmissions@nyu.edu.
Website: http://www.scps.nyu.edu/areas-of-study/leadership/.

North Carolina Agricultural and Technical State University, School of Graduate Studies, School of Business and Economics, Greensboro, NC 27411. Offers accounting (MSM); business education (MAT); human resources management (MSM); supply chain systems (MSM).

North Central College, Graduate and Continuing Studies Programs, Department of Business, Program in Business Administration, Naperville, IL 60566-7063. Offers change management (MBA); finance (MBA); human resource management (MBA); international business administration (MIBA); management (MBA); marketing (MBA). Part-time and evening/weekend programs available. *Faculty:* 13 full-time (4 women), 8 part-time/adjunct (0 women). *Students:* 31 full-time (8 women), 67 part-time (32 women); includes 16 minority (6 Black or African American, non-Hispanic/Latino; 5 Asian, non-Hispanic/Latino; 5 Hispanic/Latino), 3 international. Average age 30. 99 applicants, 54% accepted, 29 enrolled. In 2013, 51 master's awarded. *Degree requirements:* For master's, thesis optional, project. *Entrance requirements:* For master's, interview. Additional exam requirements/recommendations for international students: Required—TOEFL (minimum score 577 paper-based; 90 iBT). *Application deadline:* For fall admission, 8/15 for domestic students; for winter admission, 12/1 for domestic students;

for spring admission, 2/1 for domestic students. Application fee: $25. *Expenses: Tuition:* Full-time $4716; part-time $786 per credit hour. *Financial support:* Scholarships/grants available. Support available to part-time students. *Unit head:* Dr. Robert Moussetis, Program Coordinator, 630-637-5475, E-mail: rcmoussetis@noctrl.edu. *Application contact:* Wendy Kulpinski, Director of Graduate and Continuing Education Admission, 630-637-5808, Fax: 630-637-5844, E-mail: wekulpinski@noctrl.edu.

Northern Michigan University, College of Graduate Studies, College of Health Sciences and Professional Studies, School of Education, Leadership and Public Service, Program in Public Administration, Marquette, MI 49855-5301. Offers criminal justice administration (MPA); healthcare administration (MPA); human resource administration (MPA); public management (MPA); state and local government (MPA). Part-time and evening/weekend programs available. Postbaccalaureate distance learning degree programs offered (no on-campus study). *Faculty:* 1 (woman) full-time, 4 part-time/adjunct (1 woman). *Students:* 18 full-time (14 women), 12 part-time (4 women). In 2013, 11 master's awarded. *Degree requirements:* For master's, thesis or alternative. *Entrance requirements:* For master's, minimum GPA of 3.0, resume, personal interview. Additional exam requirements/recommendations for international students: Required—TOEFL (minimum score 550 paper-based; 70 iBT), IELTS (minimum score 6.5). *Application deadline:* For fall admission, 7/1 for domestic students; for winter admission, 11/15 for domestic students; for spring admission, 3/17 for domestic students. Applications are processed on a rolling basis. Application fee: $50. Electronic applications accepted. *Expenses:* Tuition, state resident: part-time $427 per credit. Tuition, nonresident: part-time $614.50 per credit. *Required fees:* $325 per semester. Tuition and fees vary according to course load and program. *Financial support:* Fellowships, research assistantships with full and partial tuition reimbursements, teaching assistantships with full and partial tuition reimbursements, career-related internships or fieldwork, Federal Work-Study, institutionally sponsored loans, tuition waivers (full and partial), and unspecified assistantships available. Support available to part-time students. Financial award application deadline: 3/1; financial award applicants required to submit FAFSA. *Unit head:* Dr. Joseph Lubig, Department Head, 906-227-1880, E-mail: jlubig@nmu.edu. *Application contact:* Dr. Jennifer James-Mesloh, MPA Program Coordinator/Assistant Professor, 906-227-1858, Fax: 906-227-2315, E-mail: jjamesme@nmu.edu.
Website: http://www.nmu.edu/education/MPA-online.

North Greenville University, T. Walter Brashier Graduate School, Greer, SC 29651. Offers Christian ministry (MCM, D Min); education (M Ed, MAT); financial planning (MBA); human resources (MBA). Part-time and evening/weekend programs available. Postbaccalaureate distance learning degree programs offered (no on-campus study). *Faculty:* 10 full-time (2 women), 8 part-time/adjunct (1 woman). *Students:* 164 full-time (52 women), 186 part-time (52 women); includes 45 minority (35 Black or African American, non-Hispanic/Latino; 2 American Indian or Alaska Native, non-Hispanic/Latino; 8 Hispanic/Latino). Average age 38. 200 applicants, 90% accepted, 130 enrolled. In 2013, 71 master's, 3 doctorates awarded. *Degree requirements:* For master's, comprehensive exam (for some programs), thesis or alternative, capstone course. *Entrance requirements:* For master's, minimum GPA of 2.25 overall, 2.5 in major; for doctorate, MAT. Additional exam requirements/recommendations for international students: Required—TOEFL (minimum score 550 paper-based). *Application deadline:* For fall admission, 8/1 for domestic students, 6/1 for international students; for winter admission, 1/1 for domestic students, 10/1 for international students; for spring admission, 3/1 for domestic students, 1/1 for international students. Applications are processed on a rolling basis. Application fee: $30. Electronic applications accepted. *Expenses: Tuition:* Part-time $425 per hour. *Financial support:* In 2013–14, 112 students received support, including 1 research assistantship (averaging $2,000 per year); Federal Work-Study, institutionally sponsored loans, scholarships/grants, tuition waivers (partial), and unspecified assistantships also available. Support available to part-time students. Financial award applicants required to submit FAFSA. *Faculty research:* Organizational behavior, church growth, homiletics, human resources, business strategy. *Unit head:* Dr. Joseph Samuel Isgett, Jr., Vice President for Graduate Studies, 864-877-3052, Fax: 864-877-1653, E-mail: sisgett@ngu.edu. *Application contact:* Tawana P. Scott, Dean of Graduate Academic Services, 864-877-1598, Fax: 864-877-1653, E-mail: tscott@ngu.edu.
Website: http://www.ngu.edu/gradschool.php.

Northwestern University, The Graduate School, Kellogg School of Management, Management Programs, Evanston, IL 60208. Offers accounting information and management (MBA, PhD); analytical finance (MBA); business administration (MBA); decision sciences (MBA); entrepreneurship and innovation (MBA); finance (MBA, PhD); health enterprise management (MBA); human resources management (MBA); international business (MBA); management and organizations (MBA, PhD); management and organizations and sociology (PhD); management and strategy (MBA); management studies (MS); managerial analytics (MBA); managerial economics (MBA); managerial economics and strategy (PhD); marketing (MBA, PhD); marketing management (MBA); media management (MBA); operations management (MBA, PhD); real estate (MBA); social enterprise at Kellogg (MBA); JD/MBA. Part-time and evening/weekend programs available. Terminal master's awarded for partial completion of doctoral program. *Degree requirements:* For doctorate, thesis/dissertation, 2 years of coursework, qualifying (field) exam and candidacy, summer research papers and presentations to faculty, proposal defense, final exam/defense. *Entrance requirements:* For master's, GMAT, GRE, interview, 2 letters of recommendation, college transcripts, resume, essays, Kellogg honor code; for doctorate, GMAT, GRE, statement of purpose, transcripts, 2 letters of recommendation, resume, interview. Additional exam requirements/recommendations for international students: Required—TOEFL, IELTS. Electronic applications accepted. *Expenses:* Contact institution. *Faculty research:* Business cycles and international finance, health policy, networks, non-market strategy, consumer psychology.

Notre Dame de Namur University, Division of Academic Affairs, School of Business and Management, Program in Business Administration, Belmont, CA 94002-1908. Offers business administration (MBA); entrepreneurship (MBA); finance (MBA); human resource management (MBA); marketing (MBA); media and promotion (MBA); technology and operations management (MBA). *Accreditation:* ACBSP. Part-time and evening/weekend programs available. *Entrance requirements:* For master's, minimum GPA of 2.5. Additional exam requirements/recommendations for international students: Required—TOEFL (minimum score 550 paper-based; 79 iBT). Electronic applications accepted.

Notre Dame de Namur University, Division of Academic Affairs, School of Business and Management, Program in Public Administration, Belmont, CA 94002-1908. Offers human resource management (MPA); public administration (MPA); public affairs administration (MPA); social enterprise (MPA). Part-time and evening/weekend programs available. Postbaccalaureate distance learning degree programs offered (no on-campus study). *Entrance requirements:* For master's, interview, minimum GPA of 2.5. Additional exam requirements/recommendations for international students: Required—TOEFL (minimum score 550 paper-based; 79 iBT). Electronic applications accepted.

Nova Southeastern University, H. Wayne Huizenga School of Business and Entrepreneurship, Fort Lauderdale, FL 33314-7796. Offers accounting (M Acc); business administration (MBA, DBA); human resource management (MSHRM); international business administration (MIBA); leadership (MS); public administration (MPA, DPA); real estate development (MS); taxation (M Tax); JD/MBA; Pharm D/MBA. Part-time and evening/weekend programs available. Postbaccalaureate distance learning degree programs offered (minimal on-campus study). *Faculty:* 67 full-time (24 women), 135 part-time/adjunct (37 women). *Students:* 207 full-time (110 women), 3,069 part-time (1,888 women); includes 2,213 minority (1,077 Black or African American, non-Hispanic/Latino; 2 American Indian or Alaska Native, non-Hispanic/Latino; 108 Asian, non-Hispanic/Latino; 975 Hispanic/Latino; 2 Native Hawaiian or other Pacific Islander, non-Hispanic/Latino; 49 Two or more races, non-Hispanic/Latino), 190 international. Average age 33. 1,291 applicants, 68% accepted, 636 enrolled. In 2013, 1,146 master's, 17 doctorates awarded. *Degree requirements:* For master's, thesis optional; for doctorate, comprehensive exam, thesis/dissertation. *Entrance requirements:* For doctorate, GMAT. Additional exam requirements/recommendations for international students: Required—TOEFL (minimum score 550 paper-based; 79 iBT), IELTS (minimum score 6). *Application deadline:* Applications are processed on a rolling basis. Application fee: $50. Electronic applications accepted. *Financial support:* In 2013–14, 2 students received support. Federal Work-Study and scholarships/grants available. Support available to part-time students. Financial award applicants required to submit FAFSA. *Faculty research:* Reputation management, call centers, international social capital, corporate earnings guidance, corporate governance. *Unit head:* Dr. J. Preston Jones, Dean, 954-262-5127, E-mail: fieldsm@nova.edu. *Application contact:* Karen Goldberg, Associate Director of Recruitment and Special Events, 954-262-5039, Fax: 954-262-3822, E-mail: karen@nova.edu.
Website: http://www.huizenga.nova.edu.

Oakland University, Graduate Study and Lifelong Learning, School of Business Administration, Department of Management and Marketing, Rochester, MI 48309-4401. Offers business administration (MBA); entrepreneurship (Certificate); general management (Certificate); human resource management (Certificate); international business (Certificate); marketing (Certificate). *Faculty:* 11 full-time (4 women), 2 part-time/adjunct (both women). *Students:* 72 full-time (28 women), 232 part-time (63 women); includes 51 minority (17 Black or African American, non-Hispanic/Latino; 2 American Indian or Alaska Native, non-Hispanic/Latino; 25 Asian, non-Hispanic/Latino; 7 Hispanic/Latino), 25 international. Average age 32. 238 applicants, 43% accepted, 88 enrolled. In 2013, 144 master's, 4 other advanced degrees awarded. Application fee: $0. *Unit head:* Ravi Parameswaran, Chair, 238-370-3279, Fax: 249-370-4275. *Application contact:* Donna Free, Coordinator, 248-370-3281.

The Ohio State University, Graduate School, Max M. Fisher College of Business, Program in Human Resource Management, Columbus, OH 43210. Offers human resource management (MHRM, PhD); labor and human resources (MLHR, PhD). Part-time programs available. *Faculty:* 27. *Students:* 90 full-time (61 women), 18 part-time (11 women); includes 13 minority (7 Black or African American, non-Hispanic/Latino; 1 Asian, non-Hispanic/Latino; 2 Hispanic/Latino; 3 Two or more races, non-Hispanic/Latino), 33 international. Average age 26. In 2013, 55 master's, 2 doctorates awarded. *Degree requirements:* For doctorate, thesis/dissertation. *Entrance requirements:* For master's and doctorate, GRE General Test or GMAT. Additional exam requirements/recommendations for international students: Required—Michigan English Language Assessment Battery (minimum score 86); Recommended—TOEFL (minimum score 600 paper-based; 100 iBT), IELTS (minimum score 7). *Application deadline:* For fall admission, 12/6 priority date for domestic students, 11/15 priority date for international students. Applications are processed on a rolling basis. Application fee: $60 ($70 for international students). Electronic applications accepted. *Financial support:* Fellowships with tuition reimbursements, research assistantships with tuition reimbursements, and teaching assistantships with tuition reimbursements available. *Unit head:* David Greenberger, Chair, 614-292-5291, E-mail: greenberger.1@osu.edu. *Application contact:* Graduate Admissions, 614-292-6031, Fax: 614-292-3656, E-mail: gradadmissions@osu.edu.
Website: http://fisher.osu.edu/departments/management-and-hr/.

Oklahoma Christian University, Graduate School of Business, Oklahoma City, OK 73136-1100. Offers accounting (MBA); electronic business (MBA); financial services (MBA); health services management (MBA); human resources (MBA); international business (MBA); leadership and organizational development (MBA); marketing (MBA); project management (MBA). Postbaccalaureate distance learning degree programs offered (no on-campus study). *Entrance requirements:* For master's, bachelor's degree. Electronic applications accepted.

Ottawa University, Graduate Studies-Arizona, Programs in Business, Ottawa, KS 66067-3399. Offers business administration (MBA); finance (MBA); human resources (MA, MBA); leadership (MBA); marketing (MBA). Programs offered in Mesa, Phoenix, Tempe and West Valley, AZ. Part-time and evening/weekend programs available. Postbaccalaureate distance learning degree programs offered. *Degree requirements:* For master's, thesis or alternative. *Entrance requirements:* For master's, minimum undergraduate GPA of 3.0. Additional exam requirements/recommendations for international students: Required—TOEFL (minimum score 550 paper-based). Electronic applications accepted.

Pace University, Lubin School of Business, Program in Management, New York, NY 10038. Offers entrepreneurial studies (MBA); executive management (MBA); human resource management (MBA, MS); management (MBA); strategic management (MBA). Part-time and evening/weekend programs available. *Students:* 20 full-time (9 women), 141 part-time (78 women); includes 40 minority (19 Black or African American, non-Hispanic/Latino; 15 Asian, non-Hispanic/Latino; 6 Hispanic/Latino), 44 international. Average age 29. 343 applicants, 39% accepted, 69 enrolled. In 2013, 44 master's awarded. *Entrance requirements:* For master's, GMAT, GRE. Additional exam requirements/recommendations for international students: Required—TOEFL. *Application deadline:* For fall admission, 8/1 priority date for domestic students, 6/1 for international students; for spring admission, 12/1 for domestic students, 10/1 for international students. Applications are processed on a rolling basis. Application fee: $70. Electronic applications accepted. *Expenses: Tuition:* Part-time $1075 per credit. *Required fees:* $192 per semester. Tuition and fees vary according to course load, degree level and program. *Financial support:* Research assistantships, career-related internships or fieldwork, and Federal Work-Study available. Support available to part-time students. Financial award applicants required to submit FAFSA. *Unit head:* Dr. John C. Byrne, Chairperson, 212-618-6581, E-mail: jbyrne@pace.edu. *Application contact:* Susan Ford-Goldschein, Director of Graduate Admissions, 212-346-1531, Fax: 212-346-1585, E-mail: gradnyc@pace.edu.
Website: http://www.pace.edu/lubin.

Penn State University Park, Graduate School, College of the Liberal Arts, School of Labor and Employment Relations, State College, PA 16802. Offers human resources and employee relations (MPS, MS). Postbaccalaureate distance learning degree programs offered. *Unit head:* Dr. Susan Welch, Dean, 814-865-7691, Fax: 814-863-2085, E-mail: swelch@psu.edu. *Application contact:* Cynthia E. Nicosia, Director,

Human Resources Management

Graduate Enrollment Services, 814-865-1834, Fax: 814-863-4627, E-mail: cey1@psu.edu. Website: http://lser.la.psu.edu/.

Polytechnic University of Puerto Rico, Miami Campus, Graduate School, Miami, FL 33166. Offers accounting (MBA); business administration (MBA); construction management (MEM); environmental management (MEM); finance (MBA); human resources management (MBA); logistics and supply chain management (MBA); management of international enterprises (MBA); manufacturing management (MEM); marketing management (MBA); project management (MBA). Part-time and evening/weekend programs available. Postbaccalaureate distance learning degree programs offered (no on-campus study). *Entrance requirements:* For master's, minimum GPA of 3.0. Electronic applications accepted.

Polytechnic University of Puerto Rico, Orlando Campus, Graduate School, Winter Park, FL 32792. Offers accounting (MBA); business administration (MBA); construction management (MEM); engineering management (MEM); environmental management (MEM); finance (MBA); human resources management (MBA); management of international enterprises (MBA); management of technology (MBA); manufacturing management (MEM). Part-time and evening/weekend programs available. Postbaccalaureate distance learning degree programs offered (no on-campus study). *Entrance requirements:* For master's, minimum GPA of 3.0. Additional exam requirements/recommendations for international students: Recommended—TOEFL. Electronic applications accepted.

Pontifical Catholic University of Puerto Rico, College of Business Administration, Program in Human Resources, Ponce, PR 00717-0777. Offers MBA, Professional Certificate. Part-time and evening/weekend programs available. *Degree requirements:* For master's, thesis. *Entrance requirements:* For master's, GRE, interview, minimum GPA of 2.75.

Pontificia Universidad Catolica Madre y Maestra, Graduate School, Faculty of Social and Administrative Sciences, Santiago, Dominican Republic. Offers business administration (MBA), including business development, finance, international business, management skills (M Mgmt, MBA), marketing, operations, strategic cost management, strategy, tourist destination planning and management; law (LL M), including civil law, corporate business law, criminal law, international relations, real estate law; management (M Mgmt), including higher financial management, insurance program administration, management skills (M Mgmt, MBA); psychology (MA), including clinical child and adolescent psychology, forensic psychology; strategic human resources (EMBA).

Purdue University, Graduate School, Krannert School of Management, Doctoral Program in Organizational Behavior and Human Resource Management, West Lafayette, IN 47907-2056. Offers PhD. *Degree requirements:* For doctorate, comprehensive exam, thesis/dissertation, dissertation proposal, dissertation defense. *Entrance requirements:* For doctorate, GMAT or GRE, bachelor's degree, two semesters of calculus, one semester each of linear algebra and statistics. Additional exam requirements/recommendations for international students: Required—TOEFL (minimum score 575 paper-based); Recommended—TWE. Electronic applications accepted. *Faculty research:* Human resource management, organizational behavior.

Purdue University, Graduate School, Krannert School of Management, Master of Science in Human Resource Management Program, West Lafayette, IN 47907. Offers MSHRM. *Entrance requirements:* For master's, GMAT or GRE, essays, recommendation letters, work experience/internship, minimum GPA of 3.0, four-year baccalaureate degree. Additional exam requirements/recommendations for international students: Required—TOEFL (minimum score 550 paper-based, 77 iBT), IELTS (minimum score 6.5), or PTE. Electronic applications accepted. *Faculty research:* Performance periods and the dynamics of the performance-risk relationship, reactions to unfair events in computer-mediated groups: a test of uncertainty management theory, influences on job search self-efficacy of spouses of military personnel, Cross-Cultural Social Intelligence: An Assessment for Employees Working in Cross-National Contexts, Will You Trust Your New Boss? The Role of Affective Reactions to Leadership Succession.

Regent's University London, Webster Graduate School, London, United Kingdom. Offers business (MBA); finance (MS); human resources (MA); information technology management (MA); international business (MA); international non-governmental organizations (MA); international relations (MA); management and leadership (MA); marketing (MA). Part-time programs available.

Regis University, College for Professional Studies, School of Management, Denver, CO 80221-1099. Offers accounting (MS); business administration (MBA), including finance and accounting, general business, health industry leadership, marketing, operations management, organizational performance management, strategic management; emerging markets (MBA); enterprise resource leadership and planning (MSOL); human resource management and leadership (MSOL); organizational leadership (MSOL, Certificate), including executive project management (Certificate), organizational leadership and management (MSOL), strategic human resource integration (Certificate); organizational management (Certificate), including executive leadership; project leadership and management (MSOL). Offered at Colorado Springs Campus, Northwest Denver Campus, Southeast Denver Campus, Fort Collins Campus, Broomfield Campus, Henderson (Nevada) Campus, Summerlin (Nevada) Campus and online. Part-time and evening/weekend programs available. Postbaccalaureate distance learning degree programs offered (no on-campus study). *Faculty:* 14 full-time (5 women), 94 part-time/adjunct (30 women). *Students:* 594 full-time (313 women), 439 part-time (235 women); includes 307 minority (71 Black or African American, non-Hispanic/Latino; 3 American Indian or Alaska Native, non-Hispanic/Latino; 50 Asian, non-Hispanic/Latino; 162 Hispanic/Latino; 2 Native Hawaiian or other Pacific Islander, non-Hispanic/Latino; 19 Two or more races, non-Hispanic/Latino), 17 international. Average age 42. 502 applicants, 89% accepted, 330 enrolled. In 2013, 464 master's awarded. *Degree requirements:* For master's, thesis (for some programs), capstone or final research project. *Entrance requirements:* For master's, official transcript reflecting baccalaureate degree awarded from regionally-accredited college or university, interview, 2 years of full-time related work experience, resume, letters of recommendation. Additional exam requirements/recommendations for international students: Required—TOEFL (minimum score 550 paper-based, 82 iBT), TWE (minimum score 5) or university-based test. *Application deadline:* For fall admission, 8/13 for domestic and international students; for winter admission, 10/8 for domestic students, 9/8 for international students; for spring admission, 12/17 for domestic students, 11/17 for international students. Applications are processed on a rolling basis. Application fee: $75. Electronic applications accepted. *Expenses:* Contact institution. *Financial support:* In 2013–14, 45 students received support. Federal Work-Study and scholarships/grants available. Financial award application deadline: 4/15; financial award applicants required to submit FAFSA. *Faculty research:* Impact of information technology on small business regulation of accounting, international project financing, mineral development, delivery of healthcare to rural indigenous communities. *Unit head:* Dr. Peter Bemski, Chair, 303-

458-1805, E-mail: pbemski@regis.edu. *Application contact:* Sarah Engel, Information Contact, 303-458-4900, Fax: 303-964-5534, E-mail: regisadm@regis.edu. Website: http://www.regis.edu/CPS/Schools/School-of-Management.aspx.

Robert Morris University, Graduate Studies, School of Business, Moon Township, PA 15108-1189. Offers business administration (MBA); human resource management (MS); nonprofit management (MS); taxation (MS). *Accreditation:* AACSB. Part-time and evening/weekend programs available. Postbaccalaureate distance learning degree programs offered (no on-campus study). *Faculty:* 25 full-time (10 women), 8 part-time/adjunct (2 women). *Students:* 247 part-time (99 women); includes 10 minority (1 Black or African American, non-Hispanic/Latino; 2 Asian, non-Hispanic/Latino; 7 Two or more races, non-Hispanic/Latino), 5 international. Average age 26. 214 applicants, 40% accepted, 62 enrolled. In 2013, 187 master's awarded. *Entrance requirements:* For master's, GMAT, letters of recommendation. Additional exam requirements/recommendations for international students: Required—TOEFL (minimum score 550 paper-based; 79 iBT). *Application deadline:* For fall admission, 7/1 priority date for domestic and international students; for spring admission, 11/1 priority date for domestic and international students. Applications are processed on a rolling basis. Application fee: $35. Electronic applications accepted. *Expenses: Tuition:* Part-time $825 per credit. Part-time tuition and fees vary according to degree level and program. *Financial support:* Research assistantships with partial tuition reimbursements, Federal Work-Study, institutionally sponsored loans, and unspecified assistantships available. Support available to part-time students. Financial award application deadline: 5/1; financial award applicants required to submit FAFSA. *Unit head:* Dr. John M. Beehler, Dean, 412-397-5445, Fax: 412-397-2172, E-mail: beehler@rmu.edu. *Application contact:* 412-397-5200, Fax: 412-397-5915, E-mail: graduateadmissions@rmu.edu. Website: http://www.rmu.edu/web/cms/schools/sbus/Pages/default.aspx.

Robert Morris University Illinois, Morris Graduate School of Management, Chicago, IL 60605. Offers accounting (MBA); accounting/finance (MBA); business analytics (MIS); design and media (MM); educational technology (MM); health care administration (MM); higher education administration (MM); human resource management (MBA); information security (MIS); information systems (MIS); law enforcement administration (MM); management (MBA); management/finance (MBA); management/human resource management (MBA); mobile computing (MIS); sports administration (MM). Part-time and evening/weekend programs available. *Faculty:* 12 full-time (5 women), 18 part-time/adjunct (4 women). *Students:* 240 full-time (128 women), 195 part-time (127 women); includes 242 minority (147 Black or African American, non-Hispanic/Latino; 2 American Indian or Alaska Native, non-Hispanic/Latino; 24 Asian, non-Hispanic/Latino; 63 Hispanic/Latino; 1 Native Hawaiian or other Pacific Islander, non-Hispanic/Latino; 5 Two or more races, non-Hispanic/Latino), 26 international. Average age 33. 210 applicants, 63% accepted, 116 enrolled. In 2013, 278 master's awarded. *Entrance requirements:* For master's, official transcripts, two letters of recommendation. Additional exam requirements/recommendations for international students: Required—TOEFL (minimum score 550 paper-based). *Application deadline:* Applications are processed on a rolling basis. Application fee: $20 ($100 for international students). Electronic applications accepted. *Expenses: Tuition:* Full-time $14,400; part-time $2400 per course. *Financial support:* In 2013–14, 488 students received support. Federal Work-Study and scholarships/grants available. Support available to part-time students. Financial award applicants required to submit FAFSA. *Unit head:* Kayed Akkawi, Dean for Morris Graduate School of Management, 312-935-6050, Fax: 312-935-6020, E-mail: kakkawi@robertmorris.edu. *Application contact:* Fernando Villeda, Dean of Graduate Enrollment, 312-935-6050, Fax: 312-935-6020, E-mail: fvilleda@robertmorris.edu.

Rollins College, Hamilton Holt School, Master of Human Resources Program, Winter Park, FL 32789. Offers MHR. Part-time and evening/weekend programs available. *Faculty:* 4 full-time (0 women), 4 part-time/adjunct (1 woman). *Students:* 8 full-time (6 women), 49 part-time (41 women); includes 21 minority (7 Black or African American, non-Hispanic/Latino; 4 Asian, non-Hispanic/Latino; 10 Hispanic/Latino), 2 international. Average age 33. 35 applicants, 94% accepted, 29 enrolled. In 2013, 20 master's awarded. *Degree requirements:* For master's, thesis optional. *Entrance requirements:* For master's, GMAT or GRE, official transcripts, two letters of recommendation, essay, current resume. Additional exam requirements/recommendations for international students: Required—TOEFL (minimum score 550 paper-based; 80 iBT). *Application deadline:* For fall admission, 4/1 for domestic students; for spring admission, 12/1 for domestic students. Application fee: $50. *Expenses:* Contact institution. *Financial support:* In 2013–14, 18 students received support. Federal Work-Study, scholarships/grants, and unspecified assistantships available. Support available to part-time students. Financial award applicants required to submit FAFSA. *Unit head:* Dr. Donald Rogers, Faculty Director, 407-646-2348, E-mail: drogers@rollins.edu. *Application contact:* Tonya Parker, Coordinator of Records and Registration, 407-646-2653, Fax: 407-646-1551, E-mail: tparker@rollins.edu. Website: http://www.rollins.edu/holt/graduate/mhr.html.

Roosevelt University, Graduate Division, Walter E. Heller College of Business Administration, Program in Human Resource Management, Chicago, IL 60605. Offers MSHRM.

Royal Roads University, Graduate Studies, Applied Leadership and Management Program, Victoria, BC V9B 5Y2, Canada. Offers executive coaching (Graduate Certificate); health systems leadership (Graduate Certificate); project management (Graduate Certificate); public relations management (Graduate Certificate); strategic human resources management (Graduate Certificate).

Royal Roads University, Graduate Studies, Faculty of Management, Victoria, BC V9B 5Y2, Canada. Offers digital technologies management (MBA); executive management (MBA), including global aviation management, knowledge management, leadership; human resources management (MBA). Postbaccalaureate distance learning degree programs offered (minimal on-campus study). *Degree requirements:* For master's, thesis. *Entrance requirements:* For master's, 5-7 years of related work experience. Additional exam requirements/recommendations for international students: Required—TOEFL (paper-based 570) or IELTS (7) recommended. Electronic applications accepted. *Expenses:* Contact institution. *Faculty research:* Global venture analysis standards; computer assisted venture opportunity screening; teaching philosophies, instructions and methods.

Rutgers, The State University of New Jersey, Newark, Graduate School, Program in Public Administration, Newark, NJ 07102. Offers health care administration (MPA); human resources administration (MPA); public administration (PhD); public management (MPA); public policy analysis (MPA); urban systems and issues (MPA). *Accreditation:* NASPAA (one or more programs are accredited). Part-time and evening/weekend programs available. *Degree requirements:* For master's, comprehensive exam, thesis or alternative; for doctorate, thesis/dissertation. *Entrance requirements:* For master's, GRE, minimum undergraduate B average; for doctorate, GRE, MPA, minimum B average. Electronic applications accepted. *Faculty research:* Government finance, municipal and state government, public productivity.

Rutgers, The State University of New Jersey, New Brunswick, School of Management and Labor Relations, Program in Human Resource Management, Piscataway, NJ 08854-8097. Offers MHRM. Part-time and evening/weekend programs

available. *Entrance requirements:* For master's, GMAT or GRE General Test, 3 letters of recommendation. Additional exam requirements/recommendations for international students: Required—TOEFL (minimum score 575 paper-based). Electronic applications accepted. *Expenses:* Contact institution. *Faculty research:* Human resource policy and planning, employee ownership and profit sharing, compensation and appraisal of performance, law and public policy, computers and decision making.

Rutgers, The State University of New Jersey, New Brunswick, School of Management and Labor Relations, Program in Industrial Relations and Human Resources, Piscataway, NJ 08854-8097. Offers PhD. Part-time programs available. *Degree requirements:* For doctorate, comprehensive exam, thesis/dissertation. *Entrance requirements:* For doctorate, GRE or GMAT, 3 letters of recommendation. Additional exam requirements/recommendations for international students: Required—TOEFL (minimum score 575 paper-based; 91 iBT). Electronic applications accepted. *Faculty research:* Strategic human resources, labor relations, organizational change, worker representation.

Sacred Heart University, Graduate Programs, John F. Welch College of Business, Department of Management, Fairfield, CT 06825-1000. Offers accounting (Certificate); business (MBA); human resource management (MS); international business (Certificate); leadership (Certificate); marketing (Certificate). *Faculty:* 6 full-time (3 women), 2 part-time/adjunct (both women). *Students:* 24 full-time (9 women), 141 part-time (81 women); includes 29 minority (11 Black or African American, non-Hispanic/Latino; 5 Asian, non-Hispanic/Latino; 13 Hispanic/Latino), 4 international. Average age 32. 14 applicants, 79% accepted, 9 enrolled. In 2013, 81 master's awarded. *Entrance requirements:* For master's, GMAT (minimum score of 400), bachelor's degree in related field of business, microeconomics, macroeconomics or statistics; minimum GPA of 3.0. Additional exam requirements/recommendations for international students: Required—PTE; Recommended—TOEFL (minimum score 570 paper-based; 80 iBT), IELTS (minimum score 6.5). *Application deadline:* Applications are processed on a rolling basis. Application fee: $60. Electronic applications accepted. *Expenses: Tuition:* Full-time $22,775; part-time $617 per credit. *Financial support:* Applicants required to submit FAFSA. *Unit head:* Dr. John Chalykoff, Dean, 203-396-8084, E-mail: chalykoffj@sacredheart.edu. *Application contact:* Kathy Dilks, Executive Director of Graduate Admissions, 203-365-7619, Fax: 203-365-4732, E-mail: dilksk@sacredheart.edu.
Website: http://www.sacredheart.edu/academics/johnfwelchcollegeofbusiness/.

Sage Graduate School, School of Management, Program in Business Administration, Troy, NY 12180-4115. Offers business strategy (MBA); finance (MBA); human resources (MBA); marketing (MBA); JD/MBA. Part-time and evening/weekend programs available. *Faculty:* 2 full-time (both women), 9 part-time/adjunct (2 women). *Students:* 10 full-time (5 women), 53 part-time (33 women); includes 14 minority (5 Black or African American, non-Hispanic/Latino; 6 Asian, non-Hispanic/Latino; 2 Hispanic/Latino; 1 Two or more races, non-Hispanic/Latino). Average age 30. 52 applicants, 54% accepted, 16 enrolled. In 2013, 22 master's awarded. *Entrance requirements:* For master's, minimum GPA of 2.75, resume, 2 letters of recommendation. Additional exam requirements/recommendations for international students: Required—TOEFL (minimum score 550 paper-based). *Application deadline:* Applications are processed on a rolling basis. Application fee: $40. *Expenses: Tuition:* Full-time $11,880; part-time $660 per credit hour. *Financial support:* Fellowships, research assistantships, Federal Work-Study, scholarships/grants, and unspecified assistantships available. Support available to part-time students. Financial award application deadline: 3/1; financial award applicants required to submit FAFSA. *Unit head:* Dr. Daniel Robeson, Dean, School of Management, 518-292-8657, Fax: 518-292-1964, E-mail: robesd@sage.edu. *Application contact:* Wendy D. Diefendorf, Director of Graduate and Adult Admission, 518-244-2443, Fax: 518-244-6880, E-mail: diefew@sage.edu.

St. Ambrose University, College of Business, Program in Business Administration, Davenport, IA 52803-2898. Offers business administration (DBA); health care (MBA); human resources (MBA). *Accreditation:* ACBSP. Part-time and evening/weekend programs available. *Degree requirements:* For master's, comprehensive exam (for some programs), thesis or alternative, capstone seminar; for doctorate, comprehensive exam, thesis/dissertation, oral and written exams. *Entrance requirements:* For master's, GMAT; for doctorate, GMAT, master's degree. Additional exam requirements/recommendations for international students: Required—TOEFL. Electronic applications accepted. *Expenses:* Contact institution.

Saint Francis University, School of Business, Loretto, PA 15640. Offers business administration (MBA); human resource management (MHRM). Part-time and evening/weekend programs available. *Faculty:* 8 full-time (2 women), 25 part-time/adjunct (12 women). *Students:* 25 full-time (10 women), 122 part-time (68 women); includes 11 minority (8 Black or African American, non-Hispanic/Latino; 2 Asian, non-Hispanic/Latino; 1 Hispanic/Latino). Average age 30. 25 applicants, 96% accepted, 20 enrolled. In 2013, 60 master's awarded. *Degree requirements:* For master's, comprehensive exam (for some programs), thesis (for some programs). *Entrance requirements:* For master's, GMAT (waived if undergraduate QPA is 3.3 or above), 2 letters of recommendation, minimum GPA of 2.75, two essays. Additional exam requirements/recommendations for international students: Required—TOEFL (minimum score 550 paper-based; 57 iBT). *Application deadline:* For fall admission, 8/15 priority date for domestic and international students; for spring admission, 12/1 priority date for domestic students, 12/1 for international students. Applications are processed on a rolling basis. Application fee: $30. *Expenses:* Contact institution. *Financial support:* Fellowships with partial tuition reimbursements, career-related internships or fieldwork, and unspecified assistantships available. Financial award application deadline: 8/15. *Unit head:* Dr. Randy L. Frye, Director, Graduate Business Programs, 814-472-3041, Fax: 814-472-3174, E-mail: rfrye@francis.edu. *Application contact:* Nicole Marie Bauman, Coordinator, Graduate Business Programs, 814-472-3026, Fax: 814-472-3369, E-mail: nbauman@francis.edu.
Website: http://francis.edu/school-of-business/.

St. Joseph's College, Long Island Campus, Program in Management, Patchogue, NY 11772-2399. Offers health care (AC); health care management (MS); human resource management (AC); human resources management (MS); organizational management (MS).

Saint Joseph's University, Erivan K. Haub School of Business, Professional MBA Program, Philadelphia, PA 19131-1395. Offers accounting (MBA, Postbaccalaureate Certificate); business intelligence (MBA); finance (MBA); general business (MBA); health and medical services administration (MBA); international business (MBA); international marketing (MBA); managing human capital (MBA); marketing (MBA); DO/MBA. DO/MBA offered jointly with Philadelphia College of Osteopathic Medicine. Part-time and evening/weekend programs available. *Students:* 81 full-time (37 women), 478 part-time (195 women); includes 85 minority (35 Black or African American, non-Hispanic/Latino; 1 American Indian or Alaska Native, non-Hispanic/Latino; 23 Asian, non-Hispanic/Latino; 13 Hispanic/Latino; 1 Native Hawaiian or other Pacific Islander, non-Hispanic/Latino; 12 Two or more races, non-Hispanic/Latino), 44 international. Average age 30. In 2013, 195 master's awarded. *Degree requirements:* For master's and Postbaccalaureate Certificate, minimum GPA of 3.0. *Entrance requirements:* For master's, GMAT or GRE, 2 letters of recommendation, resume, personal statement, official undergraduate and graduate transcripts; for Postbaccalaureate Certificate, official master's-level transcripts. Additional exam requirements/recommendations for international students: Required—TOEFL (minimum score 550 paper-based, 80 iBT), IELTS (minimum score 6.5), or PTE (minimum score 60). *Application deadline:* For fall admission, 7/15 priority date for domestic students, 5/15 priority date for international students; for spring admission, 11/15 priority date for domestic students, 10/15 priority date for international students; for summer admission, 4/15 priority date for domestic students, 2/15 priority date for international students. Applications are processed on a rolling basis. Application fee: $35. Electronic applications accepted. *Expenses: Tuition:* Part-time $786 per credit hour. Tuition and fees vary according to degree level and program. *Financial support:* In 2013–14, 2 research assistantships with partial tuition reimbursements (averaging $4,000 per year) were awarded; scholarships/grants and unspecified assistantships also available. Support available to part-time students. Financial award application deadline: 5/1; financial award applicants required to submit FAFSA. *Unit head:* Christine Hartmann, Director, MBA Program, 610-660-1659, Fax: 610-660-1599, E-mail: chartman@sju.edu. *Application contact:* Jeannine Lajeunesse, Assistant Director, MBA Program, 610-660-1695, Fax: 610-660-1599, E-mail: jlajeune@sju.edu.
Website: http://www.sju.edu/haubmba.

Saint Leo University, Graduate Business Studies, Saint Leo, FL 33574-6665. Offers accounting (M Acc, MBA); business (MBA); health care management (MBA); human resource management (MBA); information security management (MBA); marketing (MBA); marketing research and social media analytics (MBA); project management (MBA); sport business (MBA). Part-time and evening/weekend programs available. Postbaccalaureate distance learning degree programs offered (no on-campus study). *Faculty:* 48 full-time (12 women), 61 part-time/adjunct (21 women). *Students:* 1,855 full-time (1,020 women); includes 810 minority (587 Black or African American, non-Hispanic/Latino; 7 American Indian or Alaska Native, non-Hispanic/Latino; 36 Asian, non-Hispanic/Latino; 161 Hispanic/Latino; 3 Native Hawaiian or other Pacific Islander, non-Hispanic/Latino; 16 Two or more races, non-Hispanic/Latino), 33 international. Average age 38. In 2013, 905 master's awarded. *Entrance requirements:* For master's, GMAT (minimum score 500 if applicant has less than 3.0 in the last two years of undergraduate study), bachelor's degree with minimum GPA of 3.0 in the last 60 hours of coursework from regionally-accredited college or university; 2 years of professional work experience; resume; 2 letters of recommendation. Additional exam requirements/recommendations for international students: Required—TOEFL (minimum score 550 paper-based; 80 iBT). *Application deadline:* For fall admission, 7/1 priority date for domestic and international students; for spring admission, 11/12 priority date for domestic students, 11/1 for international students. Applications are processed on a rolling basis. Application fee: $80. Electronic applications accepted. *Expenses: Tuition:* Full-time $12,114; part-time $673 per semester hour. Tuition and fees vary according to degree level, campus/location and program. *Financial support:* In 2013–14, 116 students received support. Career-related internships or fieldwork, Federal Work-Study, scholarships/grants, and health care benefits available. Financial award application deadline: 3/1; financial award applicants required to submit FAFSA. *Unit head:* Dr. Lorrie McGovern, Assistant Dean, Graduate Studies in Business, 352-588-7390, Fax: 352-588-8585, E-mail: mbaslu@saintleo.edu. *Application contact:* Joshua Stagner, Director of Graduate Admission, 800-707-8846, Fax: 352-588-7873, E-mail: grad.admissions@saintleo.edu.
Website: http://www.saintleo.edu/academics/graduate.aspx.

Saint Mary's University of Minnesota, Schools of Graduate and Professional Programs, Graduate School of Business and Technology, Human Resource Management Program, Winona, MN 55987-1399. Offers MA. *Unit head:* Holly Tapper, Director, 612-238-4547, E-mail: htapper@smumn.edu. *Application contact:* Russell Kreager, Director of Admissions for Graduate and Professional Programs, 612-728-5207, Fax: 612-728-5121, E-mail: rkreager@smumn.edu.
Website: http://www.smumn.edu/graduate-home/areas-of-study/graduate-school-of-business-technology/ma-in-human-resource-management.

Saint Peter's University, Graduate Business Programs, MBA Program, Jersey City, NJ 07306-5997. Offers finance (MBA); health care administration (MBA); human resource management (MBA); international business (MBA); management (MBA); management information systems (MBA); marketing (MBA); risk management (MBA); MBA/MS. Part-time and evening/weekend programs available. *Entrance requirements:* Additional exam requirements/recommendations for international students: Required—TOEFL. Electronic applications accepted. *Faculty research:* Finance, health care management, human resource management, international business, management, management information systems, marketing, risk management.

St. Thomas University, School of Business, Department of Management, Miami Gardens, FL 33054-6459. Offers accounting (MBA); general management (MSM, Certificate); health management (MBA, MSM, Certificate); human resource management (MBA, MSM, Certificate); international business (MBA, MIB, MSM, Certificate); justice administration (MSM, Certificate); management accounting (MSM, Certificate); public management (MSM, Certificate); sports administration (MS). Part-time and evening/weekend programs available. *Degree requirements:* For master's, comprehensive exam. *Entrance requirements:* For master's, interview, minimum GPA of 3.0 or GMAT. Additional exam requirements/recommendations for international students: Required—TOEFL (minimum score 550 paper-based; 79 iBT). Electronic applications accepted.

San Diego State University, Graduate and Research Affairs, College of Business Administration, Department of Management, San Diego, CA 92182. Offers entrepreneurship (MS); human resources management (MS); management science (MS). Part-time and evening/weekend programs available. *Degree requirements:* For master's, thesis or alternative. *Entrance requirements:* For master's, GMAT, resume, letters of reference. Additional exam requirements/recommendations for international students: Required—TOEFL. Electronic applications accepted.

Savannah State University, Master of Public Administration Program, Savannah, GA 31404. Offers city management (MPA); general public administration (MPA); human resources (MPA); non-profit management (MPA). *Accreditation:* NASPAA. Part-time programs available. *Faculty:* 4 full-time (1 woman). *Students:* 8 full-time (6 women), 11 part-time (7 women); includes 14 minority (13 Black or African American, non-Hispanic/Latino; 1 Hispanic/Latino), 1 international. Average age 34. 7 applicants, 57% accepted, 3 enrolled. In 2013, 22 master's awarded. *Degree requirements:* For master's, comprehensive exam, thesis, public service internship, capstone seminar. *Entrance requirements:* For master's, GRE General Test, GMAT, or MAT, minimum cumulative GPA of 2.5, 3 letters of recommendation, essay, official transcripts, resume, essay of 500-1000 words detailing reasons for pursuing degree. Additional exam requirements/recommendations for international students: Required—TOEFL. *Application deadline:* For fall admission, 5/23 for domestic students, 5/15 for international students; for spring admission, 10/31 for domestic students, 10/1 for international students. Applications are processed on a rolling basis. Application fee: $25. *Expenses:* Tuition, state resident: full-time $4482; part-time $187 per credit hour. Tuition, nonresident: full-time $16,660; part-time $694 per credit hour. *Required fees:* $1716; $858 per term. *Financial support:* Career-related internships or fieldwork, Federal Work-Study, institutionally sponsored loans, scholarships/grants, health care benefits, and unspecified assistantships available. Financial award applicants required to submit FAFSA. *Faculty research:*

Human Resources Management

Community development, human resources, leadership, conflict resolution, city management, non-profit management. *Unit head:* Dr. David Bell, MPA Program Coordinator, 912-358-3211, E-mail: mpa@savannahstate.edu. *Application contact:* Dr. Nat Hardy, Director of Graduate Studies, 912-358-4195, E-mail: grad@savannahstate.edu.
Website: http://www.savannahstate.edu/prospective-student/degrees-grad-pa.shtml.

Seattle Pacific University, Master of Arts in Management Program, Seattle, WA 98119-1997. Offers faith and business (MA); human resources (MA); social and sustainable management (MA). *Entrance requirements:* For master's, GMAT or GRE (waived with cumulative GPA of 3.3 or above), bachelor's degree from accredited college or university, resume, essay, official transcript. *Application deadline:* For fall admission, 6/15 for domestic students. Application fee: $50. *Unit head:* Vicki Eveland, Program Director, 206-281-2088, E-mail: evelav@spu.edu. *Application contact:* John Glancy, Director, Graduate Admissions and Marketing, 206-281-2325, Fax: 206-281-2877, E-mail: jglancy@spu.edu.
Website: http://spu.edu/academics/school-of-business-and-economics/graduate-programs/ma-management/massm.

Southern New Hampshire University, School of Business, Manchester, NH 03106-1045. Offers accounting (MBA, MS, Graduate Certificate); accounting finance (MS); accounting/auditing (MS); accounting/forensic accounting (MS); accounting/taxation (MS); athletic administration (MBA, Graduate Certificate); business administration (IMBA, MBA, Certificate, Graduate Certificate), including accounting (Certificate), business administration (MBA), business information systems (Graduate Certificate), human resource management (Certificate); corporate social responsibility (MBA); entrepreneurship (MBA); finance (MBA, MS, Graduate Certificate); finance/corporate finance (MS); finance/investments and securities (MS); forensic accounting (MBA); healthcare informatics (MBA); healthcare management (MBA); human resource management (Graduate Certificate); information technology (MS, Graduate Certificate); information technology management (MBA); international business (Graduate Certificate); international business and information technology (Graduate Certificate); international finance (Graduate Certificate); international sport management (Graduate Certificate); justice studies (MBA); leadership of nonprofit organizations (Graduate Certificate); marketing (MBA, MS, Graduate Certificate); operations and project management (MS); operations and supply chain management (MBA, Graduate Certificate); organizational leadership (MS); project management (MBA, Graduate Certificate); Six Sigma (MBA); Six Sigma quality (Graduate Certificate); social media marketing (MBA); sport management (MBA, MS, Graduate Certificate); sustainability and environmental compliance (MBA); workplace conflict management (MBA); MBA/Certificate. *Accreditation:* ACBSP. Part-time and evening/weekend programs available. Postbaccalaureate distance learning degree programs offered (no on-campus study). Terminal master's awarded for partial completion of doctoral program. *Degree requirements:* For master's, one foreign language, comprehensive exam (for some programs), thesis or alternative. *Entrance requirements:* For master's, minimum GPA of 2.5. Additional exam requirements/recommendations for international students: Required—TOEFL (minimum score 500 paper-based). Electronic applications accepted.

State University of New York Institute of Technology, Program in Business Administration in Technology Management, Utica, NY 13504-3050. Offers accounting and finance (MBA); business management (MBA); health services management (MBA); human resource management (MBA); marketing management (MBA). Part-time programs available. Postbaccalaureate distance learning degree programs offered (no on-campus study). *Faculty:* 10 full-time (2 women), 2 part-time/adjunct (1 woman). *Students:* 29 full-time (13 women), 89 part-time (26 women); includes 17 minority (5 Black or African American, non-Hispanic/Latino; 8 Asian, non-Hispanic/Latino; 3 Hispanic/Latino; 1 Two or more races, non-Hispanic/Latino), 1 international. Average age 33. 78 applicants, 54% accepted, 29 enrolled. In 2013, 57 master's awarded. *Degree requirements:* For master's, capstone course. *Entrance requirements:* For master's, GMAT, resume, one letter of reference. Additional exam requirements/recommendations for international students: Required—TOEFL (minimum score 550 paper-based; 79 iBT), IELTS (minimum score 6.5). *Application deadline:* For fall admission, 8/1 priority date for domestic students, 7/1 for international students; for spring admission, 12/1 for domestic students, 11/1 for international students. Applications are processed on a rolling basis. Application fee: $60. Electronic applications accepted. *Expenses:* Tuition, state resident: full-time $9870; part-time $411 per credit hour. Tuition, nonresident: full-time $20,150; part-time $765 per credit hour. *Required fees:* $1180; $50.73 per credit hour. *Financial support:* In 2013–14, 3 students received support, including 1 fellowship with full tuition reimbursement available (averaging $5,545 per year), 2 research assistantships with partial tuition reimbursements available (averaging $4,000 per year); unspecified assistantships also available. Financial award application deadline: 6/1; financial award applicants required to submit FAFSA. *Faculty research:* Technology management, writing schools, leadership, new products. *Unit head:* Dr. Rafael Romero, Program Coordinator and Associate Professor, 315-792-7337, Fax: 315-792-7138, E-mail: rafael.romero@sunyit.edu. *Application contact:* Maryrose Raab, Coordinator of Graduate Center, 315-792-7347, Fax: 315-792-7221, E-mail: maryrose.raab@sunyit.edu.
Website: http://www.sunyit.edu/programs/graduate/mbatm/.

Stevens Institute of Technology, Graduate School, Wesley J. Howe School of Technology Management, Program in Management, Hoboken, NJ 07030. Offers general management (MS); global innovation management (MS); human resource management (MS); information management (MS); project management (MS); technology commercialization (MS); technology management (MS). Part-time programs available. *Degree requirements:* For master's, thesis optional. *Entrance requirements:* For master's, GMAT, GRE General Test. Additional exam requirements/recommendations for international students: Required—TOEFL. Electronic applications accepted. *Faculty research:* Industrial economics.

Stony Brook University, State University of New York, Graduate School, College of Business, Program in Business Administration, Stony Brook, NY 11794. Offers finance (MBA, Certificate); health care management (MBA, Certificate); human resource management (Certificate); human resources (MBA); information systems management (MBA, Certificate); management (MBA); marketing (MBA). *Faculty:* 32 full-time (7 women), 29 part-time/adjunct (8 women). *Students:* 189 full-time (102 women), 111 part-time (40 women); includes 50 minority (10 Black or African American, non-Hispanic/Latino; 1 American Indian or Alaska Native, non-Hispanic/Latino; 25 Asian, non-Hispanic/Latino; 14 Hispanic/Latino), 114 international. 255 applicants, 53% accepted, 70 enrolled. In 2013, 157 master's, 1 other advanced degree awarded. *Entrance requirements:* For master's, GMAT, 3 letters of recommendation from current or former employers or professors, transcripts, personal statement, resume. Additional exam requirements/recommendations for international students: Required—TOEFL (minimum score 550 paper-based; 90 iBT), IELTS (minimum score 6.5). *Application deadline:* For fall admission, 6/1 for domestic students, 3/15 for international students; for spring admission, 12/1 for domestic students, 11/1 for international students. Application fee: $100. *Expenses:* Tuition, state resident: full-time $9870; part-time $411 per credit. Tuition, nonresident: full-time $18,350; part-time $765 per credit. *Financial support:* Teaching assistantships available. *Total annual research expenditures:* $53,718. *Unit head:* Dr. Manuel London, Dean and Director, Center for Human Resource Management, 631-632-7159, Fax: 631-632-8181, E-mail: manuel.london@stonybrook.edu. *Application contact:* Dr. Dmytro Holod, Interim Associate Dean/Graduate Program Director, 631-632-7183, Fax: 631-632-8181, E-mail: dmytro.holod@stonybrook.edu.

Stony Brook University, State University of New York, School of Professional Development, Stony Brook, NY 11794. Offers biology (MAT); chemistry (MAT); coaching (Graduate Certificate); earth science (MAT); educational computing (Graduate Certificate); educational leadership (Advanced Certificate); English (MAT); environmental management (Graduate Certificate); French (MAT); German (MAT); higher education administration (MA, Certificate); human resource management (MS, Graduate Certificate); industrial management (Graduate Certificate); information systems management (Graduate Certificate); Italian (MAT); liberal studies (MA); mathematics (MAT); operations research (Graduate Certificate); physics (MAT); school district business leadership (Advanced Certificate); social science and the professions (MPS), including environmental management, human resource management; social studies (MAT); Spanish (MAT). Part-time and evening/weekend programs available. Postbaccalaureate distance learning degree programs offered. *Faculty:* 2 full-time (1 woman), 70 part-time/adjunct (30 women). *Students:* 241 full-time (135 women), 954 part-time (673 women); includes 209 minority (65 Black or African American, non-Hispanic/Latino; 2 American Indian or Alaska Native, non-Hispanic/Latino; 32 Asian, non-Hispanic/Latino; 104 Hispanic/Latino; 6 Two or more races, non-Hispanic/Latino), 7 international. Average age 28. 353 applicants, 92% accepted, 248 enrolled. In 2013, 312 master's, 131 other advanced degrees awarded. *Degree requirements:* For master's, one foreign language, thesis or alternative. *Application deadline:* For fall admission, 1/15 for domestic students; for spring admission, 10/1 for domestic students. Applications are processed on a rolling basis. Application fee: $100. *Expenses:* Tuition, state resident: full-time $9870; part-time $411 per credit. Tuition, nonresident: full-time $18,350; part-time $765 per credit. *Financial support:* Fellowships, research assistantships, teaching assistantships, and career-related internships or fieldwork available. Support available to part-time students. *Unit head:* Dr. Thomas Sexton, Interim Dean, 631-632-7181, Fax: 631-632-9046, E-mail: thomas.sexton@stonybrook.edu. *Application contact:* 631-632-7050 Ext. 1, E-mail: spd@stonybrook.edu.
Website: http://www.stonybrook.edu/spd/.

Strayer University, Graduate Studies, Washington, DC 20005-2603. Offers accounting (MS); acquisition (MBA); business administration (MBA); communications technology (MS); educational management (M Ed); finance (MBA); health services administration (MHSA); hospitality and tourism management (MBA); human resource management (MBA); information systems (MS), including computer security management, decision support system management, enterprise resource management, network management, software engineering management, systems development management; management (MBA); management information systems (MS); marketing (MBA); professional accounting (MS), including accounting information systems, controllership, taxation; public administration (MPA); supply chain management (MBA); technology in education (M Ed). Programs also offered at campus locations in Birmingham, AL; Chamblee, GA; Cobb County, GA; Morrow, GA; White Marsh, MD; Charleston, SC; Columbia, SC; Greensboro, NC; Greenville, SC; Lexington, KY; Louisville, KY; Nashville, TN; North Raleigh, NC; Washington, DC. Part-time and evening/weekend programs available. Postbaccalaureate distance learning degree programs offered (minimal on-campus study). *Degree requirements:* For master's, thesis. *Entrance requirements:* For master's, GMAT, GRE General Test, bachelor's degree from an accredited college or university, minimum undergraduate GPA of 2.75. Electronic applications accepted.

Tarleton State University, College of Graduate Studies, College of Business Administration, Department of Management, Marketing, and Administrative Systems, Stephenville, TX 76402. Offers business administration (MBA); human resource management (MS); management and leadership (MS). Part-time and evening/weekend programs available. Postbaccalaureate distance learning degree programs offered. *Faculty:* 8 full-time (0 women), 9 part-time/adjunct (4 women). *Students:* 53 full-time (32 women), 333 part-time (192 women); includes 106 minority (51 Black or African American, non-Hispanic/Latino; 8 Asian, non-Hispanic/Latino; 44 Hispanic/Latino; 3 Two or more races, non-Hispanic/Latino), 6 international. Average age 32. 214 applicants, 79% accepted, 148 enrolled. In 2013, 112 master's awarded. *Degree requirements:* For master's, comprehensive exam. *Entrance requirements:* For master's, GRE, GMAT, minimum GPA of 3.0. Additional exam requirements/recommendations for international students: Required—TOEFL (minimum score 550 paper-based; 80 iBT). *Application deadline:* For fall admission, 8/15 priority date for domestic students; for spring admission, 1/7 for domestic students. Applications are processed on a rolling basis. Application fee: $30 ($130 for international students). Electronic applications accepted. *Expenses:* Tuition, state resident: full-time $3312; part-time $184 per credit hour. Tuition, nonresident: full-time $9144; part-time $508 per credit hour. *Required fees:* $1916. Tuition and fees vary according to course load and campus/location. *Financial support:* Research assistantships, teaching assistantships, Federal Work-Study, scholarships/grants, and unspecified assistantships available. Financial award application deadline: 5/1; financial award applicants required to submit FAFSA. *Unit head:* Dr. Thomas Bradley, Head, 254-968-9785, E-mail: tbradley@tarleton.edu. *Application contact:* Information Contact, 254-968-9104, Fax: 254-968-9670, E-mail: gradoffice@tarleton.edu.
Website: http://www.tarleton.edu/COBAWEB/mmas.

Temple University, Fox School of Business, MBA Programs, Philadelphia, PA 19122-6096. Offers accounting (MBA); business management (MBA); financial management (MBA); healthcare and life sciences innovation (MBA); human resource management (MBA); international business (IMBA); IT management (MBA); marketing management (MBA); pharmaceutical management (MBA); strategic management (EMBA, MBA). EMBA offered in Philadelphia, PA and Tokyo, Japan. *Accreditation:* AACSB. Part-time and evening/weekend programs available. Postbaccalaureate distance learning degree programs offered (minimal on-campus study). *Entrance requirements:* For master's, GMAT, minimum undergraduate GPA of 3.0. Additional exam requirements/recommendations for international students: Required—TOEFL (minimum score 600 paper-based; 100 iBT), IELTS (minimum score 7.5).

Temple University, Fox School of Business, Specialized Master's Programs, Philadelphia, PA 19122-6096. Offers accountancy (MS); actuarial science (MS); finance (MS); financial engineering (MS); human resource management (MS); innovation management and entrepreneurship (MS); marketing (MS); statistics (MS). MS in innovation management and entrepreneurship delivered jointly with College of Engineering. *Accreditation:* AACSB. Part-time programs available. *Entrance requirements:* For master's, GRE General Test or GMAT, minimum undergraduate GPA of 3.0. Additional exam requirements/recommendations for international students: Required—TOEFL (minimum score 600 paper-based; 100 iBT), IELTS (minimum score 7.5).

Tennessee State University, The School of Graduate Studies and Research, College of Public Service and Urban Affairs, Nashville, TN 37209-1561. Offers human resource management (MPS); public administration (MPA, PhD); social work (MSW); strategic leadership (MPS); training and development (MPS). *Accreditation:* NASPAA (one or

more programs are accredited). Part-time and evening/weekend programs available. *Students:* 49 full-time (28 women), 108 part-time (67 women); includes 90 minority (86 Black or African American, non-Hispanic/Latino; 2 American Indian or Alaska Native, non-Hispanic/Latino; 1 Asian, non-Hispanic/Latino; 1 Hispanic/Latino). Average age 35. *Degree requirements:* For master's, comprehensive exam, thesis optional; for doctorate, comprehensive exam, thesis/dissertation. *Entrance requirements:* For master's, GRE General Test, minimum GPA of 2.5, writing sample; for doctorate, GRE General Test, minimum GPA of 3.25, writing sample. *Application deadline:* For fall admission, 3/1 priority date for domestic students. Application fee: $25. *Financial support:* Research assistantships and teaching assistantships available. Support available to part-time students. *Faculty research:* Total quality management and process improvement, national health care policy and administration, starting non-profit ventures, public service ethics, state education financing across the U.S. public. *Unit head:* Dr. Michael Harris, Dean, 615-963-7201, Fax: 615-963-7275, E-mail: mharris50@tnstate.edu. *Application contact:* Deborah Chisom, Director of Graduate Admissions, 615-963-5962, Fax: 615-963-5963, E-mail: dchiscom@tnstate.edu.
Website: http://www.tnstate.edu/cpsua/.

Tennessee Technological University, College of Graduate Studies, College of Business, Cookeville, TN 38505. Offers accounting (MBA); finance (MBA); human resource management (MBA); international business (MBA); management information systems (MBA). *Accreditation:* AACSB. Part-time and evening/weekend programs available. Postbaccalaureate distance learning degree programs offered (no on-campus study). *Faculty:* 28 full-time (5 women). *Students:* 54 full-time (22 women), 115 part-time (44 women); includes 11 minority (5 Black or African American, non-Hispanic/Latino; 1 Asian, non-Hispanic/Latino; 1 Hispanic/Latino; 4 Two or more races, non-Hispanic/Latino), 8 international. Average age 25. 171 applicants, 47% accepted, 50 enrolled. In 2013, 87 master's awarded. *Entrance requirements:* For master's, GMAT, GRE. Additional exam requirements/recommendations for international students: Required—TOEFL (minimum score 550 paper-based; 79 iBT), IELTS (minimum score 5.5), PTE (minimum score 53), or TOEIC (Test of English as an International Communication). *Application deadline:* For fall admission, 8/1 for domestic students, 5/1 for international students; for spring admission, 12/1 for domestic students, 10/1 for international students. Applications are processed on a rolling basis. Application fee: $35 ($40 for international students). Electronic applications accepted. *Expenses:* Tuition, state resident: full-time $9347; part-time $465 per credit hour. Tuition, nonresident: full-time $23,635; part-time $1152 per credit hour. *Financial support:* In 2013–14, 5 fellowships (averaging $10,000 per year), 18 research assistantships (averaging $4,000 per year), teaching assistantships (averaging $4,000 per year) were awarded. Support available to part-time students. Financial award application deadline: 4/1. *Unit head:* Amanda L. Brown, Interim Director, 931-372-3600, Fax: 931-372-6249, E-mail: albrown@tntech.edu. *Application contact:* Shelia K. Kendrick, Coordinator of Graduate Studies, 931-372-3808, Fax: 931-372-3497, E-mail: skendrick@tntech.edu.
Website: http://www.tntech.edu/mba.

Tennessee Technological University, College of Graduate Studies, School of Professional Studies, Cookeville, TN 38505. Offers human resources leadership (MPS); strategic leadership (MPS); training and development (MPS). Part-time and evening/weekend programs available. Postbaccalaureate distance learning degree programs offered (no on-campus study). *Students:* 4 full-time (1 woman), 31 part-time (18 women); includes 4 minority (all Black or African American, non-Hispanic/Latino). 21 applicants, 71% accepted, 8 enrolled. In 2013, 8 master's awarded. *Degree requirements:* For master's, comprehensive exam, thesis or alternative. *Entrance requirements:* For master's, GRE. Additional exam requirements/recommendations for international students: Required—TOEFL (minimum score 527 paper-based; 71 iBT), IELTS (minimum score 5.5), PTE (minimum score 48), or TOEIC (Test of English as an International Communication). *Application deadline:* For fall admission, 8/1 for domestic students, 5/1 for international students; for spring admission, 12/1 for domestic students, 10/1 for international students. Applications are processed on a rolling basis. Application fee: $35 ($40 for international students). Electronic applications accepted. *Expenses:* Tuition, state resident: full-time $9347; part-time $465 per credit hour. Tuition, nonresident: full-time $23,635; part-time $1152 per credit hour. *Financial support:* Application deadline: 4/1. *Unit head:* Dr. Melissa J. Geist, Interim Dean, College of Interdisciplinary Studies, 931-372-3394, Fax: 372-372-3499, E-mail: mgeist@tntech.edu. *Application contact:* Shelia K. Kendrick, Coordinator of Graduate Studies, 931-372-3808, Fax: 931-372-3497, E-mail: skendrick@tntech.edu.
Website: https://www.tntech.edu/is/sps/.

Texas A&M University–San Antonio, School of Business, San Antonio, TX 78224. Offers business administration (MBA); enterprise resource planning systems (MBA); finance (MBA); healthcare management (MBA); human resources management (MBA); information assurance and security (MBA); international business (MBA); professional accounting (MPA); project management (MBA); supply chain management (MBA). Part-time and evening/weekend programs available. *Entrance requirements:* For master's, GMAT. Additional exam requirements/recommendations for international students: Required—TOEFL (minimum score 550 paper-based; 80 iBT), IELTS (minimum score 6). Electronic applications accepted.

Texas State University, Graduate School, Emmett and Miriam McCoy College of Business Administration, Program in Human Resource Management, San Marcos, TX 78666. Offers MS. *Students:* 2 full-time (1 woman), 6 part-time (all women); includes 2 minority (1 Asian, non-Hispanic/Latino; 1 Hispanic/Latino), 1 international. Average age 31. 14 applicants, 29% accepted, 3 enrolled. *Degree requirements:* For master's, comprehensive exam, thesis optional. *Entrance requirements:* For master's, GRE (minimum score 1000 verbal and quantitative preferred), bachelor's degree in biology or related field, minimum GPA of 3.0 in last 60 hours of undergraduate work. Additional exam requirements/recommendations for international students: Required—TOEFL (minimum score 550 paper-based; 78 iBT). *Application deadline:* For fall admission, 6/15 priority date for domestic students, 6/1 for international students; for spring admission, 10/15 priority date for domestic students, 10/1 for international students. Applications are processed on a rolling basis. Application fee: $40 ($90 for international students). *Expenses:* Tuition, state resident: full-time $6663; part-time $278 per credit hour. Tuition, nonresident: full-time $15,159; part-time $632 per credit hour. *Required fees:* $1872; $54 per credit hour. $306 per term. Tuition and fees vary according to course load. *Financial support:* In 2013–14, 2 students received support. Research assistantships, teaching assistantships, Federal Work-Study, institutionally sponsored loans, scholarships/grants, health care benefits, and unspecified assistantships available. Support available to part-time students. Financial award application deadline: 4/1; financial award applicants required to submit FAFSA. *Unit head:* Dr. William Chittenden, Graduate Advisor, 512-245-3591, E-mail: wc10@txstate.edu. *Application contact:* Dr. Andrea Golato, Dean of Graduate School, 512-245-2581, Fax: 512-245-8365, E-mail: gradcollege@txstate.edu.
Website: http://www.gradcollege.txstate.edu/bhrm.html.

Thomas College, Graduate School, Programs in Business, Waterville, ME 04901-5097. Offers business (MBA); computer technology education (MS); education (MS); human resource management (MBA). Part-time and evening/weekend programs available. *Entrance requirements:* For master's, GMAT, GRE, MAT or minimum GPA of 3.3 in first 3 graduate-level courses. Additional exam requirements/recommendations for international students: Recommended—TOEFL.

Thomas Edison State College, School of Business and Management, Program in Human Resources Management, Trenton, NJ 08608-1176. Offers MSHRM, Graduate Certificate. Part-time programs available. Postbaccalaureate distance learning degree programs offered (no on-campus study). *Degree requirements:* For master's, final/capstone project. *Entrance requirements:* For master's, bachelor's degree from a regionally-accredited college or university; minimum 2 letters of recommendation; 3-5 years of related working experience; current resume. Additional exam requirements/recommendations for international students: Required—TOEFL (minimum score 550 paper-based; 79 iBT). Electronic applications accepted.

Tiffin University, Program in Business Administration, Tiffin, OH 44883-2161. Offers finance (MBA); general management (MBA); healthcare administration (MBA); human resources (MBA); international business (MBA); leadership (MBA); marketing (MBA); sports management (MBA). *Accreditation:* ACBSP. Part-time and evening/weekend programs available. Postbaccalaureate distance learning degree programs offered (no on-campus study). *Entrance requirements:* For master's, minimum undergraduate GPA of 2.5, work experience. Additional exam requirements/recommendations for international students: Required—TOEFL (minimum score 550 paper-based; 79 iBT). Electronic applications accepted. *Faculty research:* Small business, executive development operations, research and statistical analysis, market research, management information systems.

Trident University International, College of Business Administration, Program in Business Administration, Cypress, CA 90630. Offers business administration (PhD); conflict and negotiation management (MBA); criminal justice administration (MBA); entrepreneurship (MBA); finance (MBA); general management (MBA); government accounting (MBA); human resource management (MBA); information security and digital assurance management (MBA); information technology management (MBA); international business (MBA); logistics management (MBA); marketing (MBA); project management (MBA); public management (MBA); quality management (MBA); strategic leadership (MBA). Part-time and evening/weekend programs available. Postbaccalaureate distance learning degree programs offered (no on-campus study). *Degree requirements:* For doctorate, comprehensive exam, thesis/dissertation, defense of dissertation. *Entrance requirements:* For master's, minimum GPA of 2.5 (students with GPA 3.0 or greater may transfer up to 30% of graduate level credits); for doctorate, minimum GPA of 3.4, curriculum vitae, course work in research methods or statistics. Additional exam requirements/recommendations for international students: Required—TOEFL. Electronic applications accepted.

Trinity Washington University, School of Business and Graduate Studies, Washington, DC 20017-1094. Offers business administration (MBA); communication (MA); international security studies (MA); organizational management (MSA), including federal program management, human resource management, nonprofit management, organizational development, public and community health. Part-time and evening/weekend programs available. *Degree requirements:* For master's, thesis (for some programs), capstone project (MSA). *Entrance requirements:* For master's, minimum GPA of 2.5. Additional exam requirements/recommendations for international students: Required—TOEFL (minimum score 550 paper-based). *Application deadline:* For fall admission, 4/1 priority date for domestic students; for winter admission, 11/1 priority date for domestic students; for spring admission, 11/1 priority date for domestic students. Applications are processed on a rolling basis. Application fee: $40. *Expenses: Tuition:* Part-time $715 per credit. *Financial support:* Career-related internships or fieldwork and unspecified assistantships available. Support available to part-time students. Financial award application deadline: 4/1; financial award applicants required to submit FAFSA. *Unit head:* Dr. Peggy Lewis, Associate Dean, 202-884-9204, E-mail: lewisp@trinitydc.edu. *Application contact:* Alesha Tyson, Director of Admissions for School of Business and Graduate Studies, 202-884-9400, Fax: 202-884-9229, E-mail: tysona@trinitydc.edu.
Website: http://www.trinitydc.edu/bgs/.

Troy University, Graduate School, College of Arts and Sciences, Program in Public Administration, Troy, AL 36082. Offers education (MPA); environmental management (MPA); government contracting (MPA); health care administration (MPA); justice administration (MPA); national security affairs (MPA); nonprofit management (MPA); public human resources management (MPA); public management (MPA). *Accreditation:* NASPAA. Part-time and evening/weekend programs available. Postbaccalaureate distance learning degree programs offered (no on-campus study). *Faculty:* 15 full-time (9 women), 7 part-time/adjunct (4 women). *Students:* 95 full-time (62 women), 307 part-time (204 women); includes 231 minority (195 Black or African American, non-Hispanic/Latino; 3 American Indian or Alaska Native, non-Hispanic/Latino; 5 Asian, non-Hispanic/Latino; 15 Hispanic/Latino; 13 Two or more races, non-Hispanic/Latino). Average age 32. 172 applicants, 87% accepted, 107 enrolled. In 2013, 159 master's awarded. *Degree requirements:* For master's, capstone course with minimum B grade, minimum GPA of 3.0, admission to candidacy. *Entrance requirements:* For master's, GRE (minimum score of 850 on old exam or 294 on new exam), MAT (minimum score of 400) or GMAT (minimum score of 490), bachelor's degree; minimum undergraduate GPA of 2.5 or 3.0 on last 30 semester hours, letter of recommendation; essay. Additional exam requirements/recommendations for international students: Required—TOEFL (minimum score 523 paper-based; 70 iBT), IELTS (minimum score 6). *Application deadline:* Applications are processed on a rolling basis. Application fee: $50. Electronic applications accepted. *Expenses:* Tuition, state resident: full-time $6084; part-time $338 per credit hour. Tuition, nonresident: full-time $12,168; part-time $676 per credit hour. *Required fees:* $630; $35 per credit hour. $50 per semester. *Financial support:* Available to part-time students. Applicants required to submit FAFSA. *Unit head:* Dr. Sam Shelton, Chairman, 334-670-3754, Fax: 334-670-5647, E-mail: sshelton1@troy.edu. *Application contact:* Brenda K. Campbell, Director of Graduate Admissions, 334-670-3178, Fax: 334-670-3733, E-mail: bcamp@troy.edu.

Troy University, Graduate School, College of Business, Program in Human Resources Management, Troy, AL 36082. Offers MS. Part-time and evening/weekend programs available. *Faculty:* 10 full-time (2 women), 3 part-time/adjunct (2 women). *Students:* 42 full-time (30 women), 148 part-time (116 women); includes 142 minority (124 Black or African American, non-Hispanic/Latino; 1 American Indian or Alaska Native, non-Hispanic/Latino; 4 Asian, non-Hispanic/Latino; 10 Hispanic/Latino; 3 Two or more races, non-Hispanic/Latino). Average age 34. 123 applicants, 86% accepted, 88 enrolled. In 2013, 108 master's awarded. *Degree requirements:* For master's, minimum GPA of 3.0; admission to candidacy. *Entrance requirements:* For master's, GRE (minimum score of 900 on old exam or 294 on new exam) or GMAT (minimum score of 500), bachelor's degree; minimum undergraduate GPA of 2.5 or 3.0 on last 30 semester hours, letter of recommendation. Additional exam requirements/recommendations for international students: Required—TOEFL (minimum score 523 paper-based; 70 iBT), IELTS (minimum score 6). *Application deadline:* Applications are processed on a rolling basis. Application fee: $50. *Expenses:* Tuition, state resident: full-time $6084; part-time $338 per credit hour. Tuition, nonresident: full-time $12,168; part-time $676 per credit hour. *Required fees:* $630; $35 per credit hour. $50 per semester. *Unit head:* Dr. Bob Wheatley, Director, Graduate Business Programs, 334-241-3194 Ext. 334, Fax: 241-

241-3599, E-mail: rwheat@troy.edu. *Application contact:* Brenda K. Campbell, Director of Graduate Admissions, 334-670-3178, Fax: 334-670-3733, E-mail: bcamp@troy.edu.

Troy University, Graduate School, College of Business, Program in Management, Troy, AL 36082. Offers applied management (MSM); healthcare management (MSM); human resources management (MSM); information systems (MSM); international hospitality management (MSM); international management (MSM); leadership and organizational effectiveness (MSM); public management (MS, MSM). *Accreditation:* ACBSP. Part-time and evening/weekend programs available. *Faculty:* 15 full-time (8 women), 3 part-time/adjunct (0 women). *Students:* 18 full-time (14 women), 148 part-time (86 women); includes 95 minority (75 Black or African American, non-Hispanic/Latino; 1 American Indian or Alaska Native, non-Hispanic/Latino; 4 Asian, non-Hispanic/Latino; 8 Hispanic/Latino; 7 Two or more races, non-Hispanic/Latino). Average age 35. 124 applicants, 79% accepted, 30 enrolled. In 2013, 75 master's awarded. *Degree requirements:* For master's, Graduate Educational Testing Service Major Field Test, capstone exam, minimum GPA of 3.0. *Entrance requirements:* For master's, GRE (minimum score of 900 on old exam or 294 on new exam) or GMAT (minimum score of 500), bachelor's degree; minimum undergraduate GPA of 2.5 or 3.0 on last 30 semester hours, letter of recommendation. Additional exam requirements/recommendations for international students: Required—TOEFL (minimum score 523 paper-based; 70 iBT), IELTS (minimum score 6). *Application deadline:* Applications are processed on a rolling basis. Application fee: $50. Electronic applications accepted. *Expenses:* Contact institution. *Unit head:* Dr. Bob Wheatley, Director, Graduate Business Programs, 334-670-3143, Fax: 334-670-3599, E-mail: rwheat@troy.edu. *Application contact:* Brenda K. Campbell, Director of Graduate Admissions, 334-670-3178, Fax: 334-670-3733, E-mail: bcamp@troy.edu.

Union Graduate College, School of Management, Schenectady, NY 12308-3107. Offers business administration (MBA); general management (Certificate); health systems administration (MBA, Certificate); human resources (Certificate). *Accreditation:* AACSB. Part-time and evening/weekend programs available. Postbaccalaureate distance learning degree programs offered (minimal on-campus study). *Faculty:* 16 full-time (3 women), 9 part-time/adjunct (4 women). *Students:* 77 full-time (31 women), 70 part-time (31 women); includes 23 minority (2 Black or African American, non-Hispanic/Latino; 19 Asian, non-Hispanic/Latino; 2 Two or more races, non-Hispanic/Latino), 5 international. Average age 27. In 2013, 94 master's, 11 other advanced degrees awarded. *Degree requirements:* For master's, internship, capstone course. *Entrance requirements:* For master's, GMAT, GRE, minimum GPA of 3.0, 3 letters of recommendation. Additional exam requirements/recommendations for international students: Required—TOEFL (minimum score 550 paper-based). *Application deadline:* Applications are processed on a rolling basis. Application fee: $60. *Financial support:* Research assistantships, career-related internships or fieldwork, Federal Work-Study, scholarships/grants, health care benefits, and tuition waivers (partial) available. Support available to part-time students. Financial award applicants required to submit FAFSA. *Unit head:* Bela Musits, Dean, 518-631-9890, Fax: 518-631-9902, E-mail: musitsb@uniongraduatecollege.edu. *Application contact:* Diane Trzaskos, Admissions Coordinator, 518-631-9837, Fax: 518-631-9901, E-mail: trzaskod@uniongraduatecollege.edu.
Website: http://www.uniongraduatecollege.edu.

United States International University, School of Business Administration, Nairobi, Kenya. Offers business administration (GEMBA); entrepreneurship (MBA); finance (MBA); human resource management (MBA); information technology management (MBA); integrated studies (MBA); international business administration (MBA); management and organizational development (MS); marketing (MBA); organizational development (EMS); strategic management (MBA). Part-time and evening/weekend programs available. *Degree requirements:* For master's, thesis. *Entrance requirements:* For master's, GMAT, 2 letters of reference, resume. Additional exam requirements/recommendations for international students: Required—TOEFL (minimum score 550 paper-based). *Faculty research:* Marketing in small business enterprises, total quality management in Kenya.

Universidad del Este, Graduate School, Carolina, PR 00984. Offers accounting (MBA); adult education (M Ed); agribusiness (MBA); criminal justice and criminology (MA); curriculum and instruction - early education (M Ed); curriculum and instruction - elementary (M Ed); curriculum and instruction - English (M Ed); curriculum and instruction - Spanish (M Ed); human resources (MBA); information security management (MBA); information technology and Web business development (MBA); management (MBA); public policy (MPA); social work (MA), including clinical social work; special education (M Ed); strategic leadership (MBA). *Students:* 464 full-time (322 women), 669 part-time (499 women); all minorities (all Hispanic/Latino). Average age 35. 693 applicants, 61% accepted, 332 enrolled. In 2013, 228 master's awarded. *Unit head:* Jose R. Clintron, Dean, 787-257-7373 Ext. 3007, E-mail: ue_jcintron@suagm.edu. *Application contact:* Clotilde Santiago, Director of Admissions, 787-257-7373 Ext. 3400, E-mail: ue_csantiago@suagm.edu.

Universidad del Turabo, Graduate Programs, School in Business Administration, Program in Human Resources, Gurabo, PR 00778-3030. Offers MBA.

Universidad Metropolitana, School of Business Administration, Program in Human Resources Management, San Juan, PR 00928-1150. Offers MBA. Part-time programs available.

University at Albany, State University of New York, School of Business, MBA Programs, Albany, NY 12222. Offers business administration (MBA); human resource information systems (MBA); information technology management (MBA); JD/MBA. Part-time and evening/weekend programs available. *Faculty:* 21 full-time (5 women), 15 part-time/adjunct (5 women). *Students:* 77 full-time (36 women), 225 part-time (78 women); includes 48 minority (11 Black or African American, non-Hispanic/Latino; 24 Asian, non-Hispanic/Latino; 13 Hispanic/Latino), 24 international. Average age 25. 226 applicants, 71% accepted, 125 enrolled. In 2013, 88 master's awarded. *Degree requirements:* For master's, thesis (for some programs), field project. *Entrance requirements:* For master's, GMAT. Additional exam requirements/recommendations for international students: Required—TOEFL (minimum score 600 paper-based; 100 iBT); Recommended—IELTS. *Application deadline:* For fall admission, 3/1 priority date for domestic students, 2/1 for international students. Applications are processed on a rolling basis. Application fee: $75. Electronic applications accepted. *Financial support:* Unspecified assistantships available. Financial award application deadline: 3/1. *Faculty research:* Cyber security, entrepreneurship, human resource information systems, information technology management, finance, marketing. *Unit head:* Donald S. Siegel, Dean, 518-956-8370, E-mail: dsiegel@albany.edu. *Application contact:* Zina Mega Lawrence, Director, Graduate Student Services, 518-956-8320, Fax: 518-442-4042, E-mail: zlawrence@albany.edu.
Website: http://www.albany.edu/business.

University at Buffalo, the State University of New York, Graduate School, Graduate School of Education, Department of Educational Leadership and Policy, Buffalo, NY 14260. Offers education studies (Ed M); educational administration (Ed M, Ed D, PhD); educational culture, policy and society (PhD); higher education administration (Ed M, PhD); school building leadership (Certificate); school business and human resource administration (Certificate); school district business leadership (Certificate); school district leadership (Certificate). Part-time and evening/weekend programs available. *Faculty:* 13 full-time (7 women), 8 part-time/adjunct (all women). *Students:* 65 full-time (40 women), 139 part-time (83 women); includes 40 minority (24 Black or African American, non-Hispanic/Latino; 6 Asian, non-Hispanic/Latino; 10 Hispanic/Latino), 15 international. Average age 35. 159 applicants, 71% accepted, 65 enrolled. In 2013, 44 master's, 14 doctorates, 19 other advanced degrees awarded. *Degree requirements:* For master's, comprehensive exam (for some programs), thesis optional; for doctorate, comprehensive exam, thesis/dissertation. *Entrance requirements:* For master's, interview, letters of reference; for doctorate, GRE General Test or MAT, writing sample, letters of reference. Additional exam requirements/recommendations for international students: Required—TOEFL (minimum score 550 paper-based; 79 iBT). *Application deadline:* For fall admission, 2/1 priority date for domestic students, 2/1 for international students; for spring admission, 11/15 priority date for domestic students, 10/1 for international students. Applications are processed on a rolling basis. Application fee: $50. Electronic applications accepted. *Financial support:* In 2013–14, 20 fellowships (averaging $6,639 per year), 6 research assistantships with tuition reimbursements (averaging $10,500 per year) were awarded; career-related internships or fieldwork, Federal Work-Study, institutionally sponsored loans, scholarships/grants, health care benefits, tuition waivers, and unspecified assistantships also available. Financial award application deadline: 3/15; financial award applicants required to submit FAFSA. *Faculty research:* College access and choice, school leadership preparation and practice, public policy, curriculum and pedagogy, comparative and international education. *Total annual research expenditures:* $455,347. *Unit head:* Dr. Janina C. Brutt-Griffler, Chair, 716-645-2471, Fax: 716-645-2481, E-mail: bruttg@buffalo.edu. *Application contact:* Ryan Taugrin, Admission and Student Services Coordinator, 716-645-2110, Fax: 716-645-7937, E-mail: ryantaug@buffalo.edu.
Website: http://gse.buffalo.edu/elp.

The University of Akron, Graduate School, College of Business Administration, Department of Management, Akron, OH 44325. Offers global technological innovation (MBA); healthcare management (MBA); information systems management (MSM); leadership and organizational change (MBA); management (MBA); supply chain management (MBA); technological innovation (MSM); JD/MSM. *Accreditation:* AACSB. Part-time and evening/weekend programs available. *Faculty:* 19 full-time (4 women), 14 part-time/adjunct (3 women). *Students:* 55 full-time (23 women), 102 part-time (34 women); includes 13 minority (3 Black or African American, non-Hispanic/Latino; 7 Asian, non-Hispanic/Latino; 2 Hispanic/Latino; 1 Two or more races, non-Hispanic/Latino), 40 international. Average age 30. 102 applicants, 66% accepted, 41 enrolled. In 2013, 52 master's awarded. *Entrance requirements:* For master's, GMAT, minimum GPA of 2.75, two letters of recommendation, statement of purpose, resume. Additional exam requirements/recommendations for international students: Required—TOEFL (minimum score 550 paper-based; 79 iBT). *Application deadline:* For fall admission, 7/15 for domestic and international students; for spring admission, 11/15 for domestic and international students. Application fee: $40 ($60 for international students). Electronic applications accepted. *Expenses:* Tuition, state resident: full-time $7430; part-time $412.80 per credit hour. Tuition, nonresident: full-time $12,722; part-time $706.80 per credit hour. *Required fees:* $53 per credit hour. $12 per semester. Tuition and fees vary according to course load and program. *Financial support:* In 2013–14, 32 teaching assistantships with full tuition reimbursements were awarded; career-related internships or fieldwork and Federal Work-Study also available. *Faculty research:* Human resource management, innovation, entrepreneurship, technology management and technology transfer, artificial intelligence and belief functions. *Total annual research expenditures:* $48,868. *Unit head:* Dr. Steve Ash, Interim Chair, 330-972-6086, E-mail: ash@uakron.edu. *Application contact:* Dr. William Hauser, Director of Graduate Business Programs, 330-972-7043, Fax: 330-972-6588, E-mail: whauser@uakron.edu.
Website: http://www.uakron.edu/cba/departments/management/.

The University of Alabama in Huntsville, School of Graduate Studies, College of Business Administration, Programs in Business and Management, Huntsville, AL 35899. Offers federal contracting and procurement management (Certificate); management (MBA), including acquisition management, entrepreneurship, federal contract accounting, finance, human resource management, logistics and supply chain management, marketing, project management; supply chain management (Certificate); technology and innovation management (Certificate). *Accreditation:* AACSB. Part-time and evening/weekend programs available. *Faculty:* 13 full-time (3 women), 5 part-time/adjunct (0 women). *Students:* 41 full-time (19 women), 144 part-time (59 women); includes 35 minority (13 Black or African American, non-Hispanic/Latino; 1 American Indian or Alaska Native, non-Hispanic/Latino; 9 Asian, non-Hispanic/Latino; 11 Hispanic/Latino; 1 Two or more races, non-Hispanic/Latino), 13 international. Average age 33. 131 applicants, 78% accepted, 67 enrolled. In 2013, 83 master's, 5 other advanced degrees awarded. *Degree requirements:* For master's, comprehensive exam, thesis or alternative. *Entrance requirements:* For master's, GMAT (minimum score 500), minimum AACSB index of 1080. Additional exam requirements/recommendations for international students: Required—TOEFL (minimum score 550 paper-based; 80 iBT), IELTS (minimum score 6.5). *Application deadline:* For fall admission, 7/15 priority date for domestic students, 4/1 priority date for international students; for spring admission, 11/30 priority date for domestic students, 9/1 priority date for international students. Applications are processed on a rolling basis. Application fee: $50. Electronic applications accepted. *Expenses:* Tuition, state resident: full-time $8912; part-time $540 per credit hour. Tuition, nonresident: full-time $20,774; part-time $1252 per credit hour. *Required fees:* $148 per semester. One-time fee: $150. *Financial support:* In 2013–14, 10 students received support, including 4 research assistantships with full and partial tuition reimbursements available (averaging $7,750 per year), 5 teaching assistantships with full and partial tuition reimbursements available (averaging $9,000 per year); career-related internships or fieldwork, Federal Work-Study, institutionally sponsored loans, scholarships/grants, health care benefits, tuition waivers (full and partial), and unspecified assistantships also available. Support available to part-time students. Financial award application deadline: 4/1; financial award applicants required to submit FAFSA. *Faculty research:* Supply chain management, management of research and development, international marketing and branding, organizational behavior and human resource management, social networks and computational economics. *Total annual research expenditures:* $2.1 million. *Unit head:* Dr. Cynthia Gramm, Chair, 256-824-6913, Fax: 256-824-6328, E-mail: cynthia.gramm@uah.edu. *Application contact:* Jennifer Pettitt, Director of Graduate Programs, 256-824-6681, Fax: 256-824-7571, E-mail: jennifer.pettitt@uah.edu.

University of Bridgeport, School of Business, Bridgeport, CT 06604. Offers accounting (MBA); finance (MBA); general business (MBA); global financial services (MBA); human resource management (MBA); information systems and knowledge management (MBA); international business (MBA); management (MBA); marketing (MBA); operations management (MBA); small business and entrepreneurship (MBA); specialized business (MBA). *Accreditation:* ACBSP. Part-time and evening/weekend programs available. *Faculty:* 11 full-time (2 women), 39 part-time/adjunct (8 women). *Students:* 162 full-time (90 women), 69 part-time (45 women); includes 44 minority (20 Black or African American, non-Hispanic/Latino; 7 Asian, non-Hispanic/Latino; 15 Hispanic/Latino; 2 Two or more races, non-Hispanic/Latino), 163 international. Average age 28. 492 applicants,

48% accepted, 55 enrolled. In 2013, 144 master's awarded. *Degree requirements:* For master's, thesis optional. *Entrance requirements:* For master's, GMAT. Additional exam requirements/recommendations for international students: Recommended—TOEFL (minimum score 550 paper-based; 80 iBT), IELTS (minimum score 6.5). *Application deadline:* For fall admission, 8/1 priority date for domestic and international students; for spring admission, 12/1 priority date for domestic and international students. Applications are processed on a rolling basis. Application fee: $50. Electronic applications accepted. *Expenses:* Contact institution. *Financial support:* In 2013–14, 69 students received support. Fellowships, research assistantships, teaching assistantships, career-related internships or fieldwork, Federal Work-Study, institutionally sponsored loans, and tuition waivers (partial) available. Support available to part-time students. Financial award application deadline: 6/1; financial award applicants required to submit FAFSA. *Unit head:* Dr. Lloyd G. Gibson, Dean, 203-576-4384, Fax: 203-576-4388, E-mail: llgibson@bridgeport.edu. *Application contact:* Leanne Proctor, Director of Graduate Admissions, 203-576-4552, Fax: 203-576-4941, E-mail: mba@bridgeport.edu.
Website: http://www.bridgeport.edu.

University of California, Berkeley, UC Berkeley Extension, Certificate Programs in Business, Berkeley, CA 94720-1500. Offers accounting (Certificate); business administration (Certificate); finance (Certificate); human resource management (Certificate); management (Certificate); marketing (Certificate); project management (Certificate). *Accreditation:* AACSB. Postbaccalaureate distance learning degree programs offered.

University of Chicago, Booth School of Business, Full-Time MBA Program, Chicago, IL 60637. Offers accounting (MBA); analytic finance (MBA); analytic management (MBA); econometrics and statistics (MBA); economics (MBA); entrepreneurship (MBA); finance (MBA); general management (MBA); health administration and policy (Certificate); human resource management (MBA); international business (MBA); managerial and organizational behavior (MBA); marketing management (MBA); operations management (MBA); strategic management (MBA); MBA/AM; MBA/JD; MBA/MA; MBA/MD; MBA/MPP. *Accreditation:* AACSB. Part-time and evening/weekend programs available. Terminal master's awarded for partial completion of doctoral program. *Entrance requirements:* For master's, GMAT, 2 letters of recommendation, 3 essays, resume, interview. Additional exam requirements/recommendations for international students: Required—TOEFL (minimum score 600 paper-based; 104 iBT), IELTS. Electronic applications accepted. *Expenses:* Contact institution. *Faculty research:* Finance, marketing, economics, entrepreneurship, strategy, management.

University of Colorado Denver, Business School, Master of Business Administration Program, Denver, CO 80217. Offers bioinnovation and entrepreneurship (MBA); business intelligence (MBA); business strategy (MBA); business to business marketing (MBA); business to consumer marketing (MBA); change management (MBA); corporate financial management (MBA); enterprise technology management (MBA); entrepreneurship (MBA); health administration (MBA), including financial management, health administration, health information technologies, international health management and policy; human resources management (MBA); international business (MBA); investment management (MBA); managing for sustainability (MBA); sports and entertainment management (MBA). *Accreditation:* AACSB. Part-time and evening/weekend programs available. Postbaccalaureate distance learning degree programs offered (no on-campus study). *Students:* 611 full-time (246 women), 144 part-time (58 women); includes 102 minority (14 Black or African American, non-Hispanic/Latino; 2 American Indian or Alaska Native, non-Hispanic/Latino; 38 Asian, non-Hispanic/Latino; 42 Hispanic/Latino; 6 Two or more races, non-Hispanic/Latino), 26 international. Average age 32. 330 applicants, 64% accepted, 125 enrolled. In 2013, 398 master's awarded. *Degree requirements:* For master's, 48 semester hours, including 30 of core courses, 3 in international business, and 15 in electives from over 50 other graduate business courses. *Entrance requirements:* For master's, GMAT, resume, official transcripts, essay, two letters of recommendation, financial statements (for international applicants). Additional exam requirements/recommendations for international students: Required—TOEFL (minimum score 560 paper-based; 83 iBT); Recommended—IELTS (minimum score 6.5). *Application deadline:* For fall admission, 4/15 priority date for domestic students, 3/15 priority date for international students; for spring admission, 10/15 priority date for domestic students, 9/15 priority date for international students. Applications are processed on a rolling basis. Application fee: $50 ($75 for international students). Electronic applications accepted. *Expenses:* Contact institution. *Financial support:* In 2013–14, 62 students received support. Fellowships, research assistantships, teaching assistantships, Federal Work-Study, institutionally sponsored loans, scholarships/grants, traineeships, and unspecified assistantships available. Financial award application deadline: 4/1; financial award applicants required to submit FAFSA. *Faculty research:* Marketing, management, entrepreneurship, finance, health administration. *Unit head:* Elizabeth Cooperman, Professor of Finance and Managing for Sustainability/MBA Program Director, 303-315-8422, E-mail: elizabeth.cooperman@ucdenver.edu. *Application contact:* Shelly Townley, Admissions Director, Graduate Programs, 303-315-8202, E-mail: shelly.townley@ucdenver.edu.
Website: http://www.ucdenver.edu/academics/colleges/business/degrees/mba/Pages/MBA.aspx.

University of Colorado Denver, Business School, Program in Management and Organization, Denver, CO 80217. Offers business strategy (MS); change and innovation (MS); enterprise technology management (MS); entrepreneurship and innovation (MS); global management (MS); human resources management (MS); leadership and management (MS); quantitative decision methods (MS); sports and entertainment management (MS); sustainability management (MS). *Accreditation:* AACSB. Part-time and evening/weekend programs available. Postbaccalaureate distance learning degree programs offered (no on-campus study). *Students:* 27 full-time (19 women), 14 part-time (7 women); includes 4 minority (1 Black or African American, non-Hispanic/Latino; 2 Hispanic/Latino; 1 Two or more races, non-Hispanic/Latino), 6 international. Average age 29. 38 applicants, 45% accepted, 8 enrolled. In 2013, 28 master's awarded. *Degree requirements:* For master's, 30 semester hours (12 of required courses, 12 of management electives, and 6 of free electives). *Entrance requirements:* For master's, GMAT, resume, two letters of recommendation, essay, financial statements (for international applicants). Additional exam requirements/recommendations for international students: Required—TOEFL (minimum score 537 paper-based; 75 iBT); Recommended—IELTS (minimum score 6.5). *Application deadline:* For fall admission, 4/15 for domestic students, 3/15 for international students; for spring admission, 10/15 for domestic students, 9/15 for international students. Applications are processed on a rolling basis. Application fee: $50 ($75 for international students). Electronic applications accepted. *Expenses:* Contact institution. *Financial support:* In 2013–14, 5 students received support. Fellowships, research assistantships, teaching assistantships, Federal Work-Study, institutionally sponsored loans, scholarships/grants, and traineeships available. Financial award application deadline: 4/1; financial award applicants required to submit FAFSA. *Faculty research:* Human resource management, management of catastrophe, turnaround strategies. *Unit head:* Dr. Kenneth Bettenhausen, Associate Professor/Director of MS in Management, 303-315-8425, E-mail: kenneth.bettenhausen@ucdenver.edu. *Application contact:* Shelly Townley, Admissions Director, Graduate Programs, 303-315-8202, E-mail: shelly.townley@ucdenver.edu.
Website: http://www.ucdenver.edu/academics/colleges/business/degrees/ms/management/Pages/Management.aspx.

University of Connecticut, Graduate School, Center for Continuing Studies, Program in Human Resource Management, Storrs, CT 06269. Offers labor relations (MPS); personnel (MPS).

University of Dallas, Graduate School of Management, Irving, TX 75062-4736. Offers accounting (MBA, MM, MS); business management (MBA, MM); corporate finance (MBA, MM); financial services (MBA); global business (MBA, MM); health services management (MBA, MM); human resource management (MBA, MM); information assurance (MBA, MM, MS); information technology (MBA, MM, MS); information technology service management (MBA, MM, MS); marketing management (MBA, MM); organization development (MBA, MM); project management (MBA, MM); sports and entertainment management (MBA, MM); strategic leadership (MBA, MM); supply chain management (MBA); supply chain management and market logistics (MM). *Accreditation:* ACBSP. Part-time and evening/weekend programs available. Postbaccalaureate distance learning degree programs offered (no on-campus study). *Entrance requirements:* Additional exam requirements/recommendations for international students: Required—TOEFL. Electronic applications accepted. *Expenses:* Contact institution.

University of Denver, University College, Denver, CO 80208. Offers arts and culture (MLS, Certificate), including art, literature, and culture, arts development and program management (Certificate), creative writing; environmental policy and management (MAS, Certificate), including energy and sustainability (Certificate), environmental assessment of nuclear power (Certificate), environmental health and safety (Certificate), environmental management, natural resource management (Certificate); geographic information systems (MAS, Certificate); global affairs (MLS, Certificate), including translation studies, world history and culture; healthcare leadership (MPH, Certificate), including healthcare policy, law, and ethics, medical and healthcare information technologies, strategic management of healthcare; information and communications technology (MCIS, Certificate), including database design and administration (Certificate), geographic information systems (MCIS), information security systems security (Certificate), information systems security (MCIS), project management (MCIS, MPS, Certificate), software design and administration (Certificate), software design and programming (MCIS), technology management, telecommunications technology (MCIS), Web design and development; leadership and organizations (MPS, Certificate), including human capital in organizations, philanthropic leadership, project management (MCIS, MPS, Certificate), strategic innovation and change; organizational and professional communication (MPS, Certificate), including alternative dispute resolution, organizational communication, organizational development and training, public relations and marketing; security management (MAS, Certificate), including emergency planning and response, information security (MAS), organizational security; strategic human resource management (MPS, Certificate), including global human resources (MPS), human resource management and development (MPS). Part-time and evening/weekend programs available. Postbaccalaureate distance learning degree programs offered (no on-campus study). *Faculty:* 139 part-time/adjunct (61 women). *Students:* 49 full-time (16 women), 1,297 part-time (732 women); includes 272 minority (92 Black or African American, non-Hispanic/Latino; 5 American Indian or Alaska Native, non-Hispanic/Latino; 30 Asian, non-Hispanic/Latino; 114 Hispanic/Latino; 3 Native Hawaiian or other Pacific Islander, non-Hispanic/Latino; 28 Two or more races, non-Hispanic/Latino), 92 international. Average age 35. 542 applicants, 95% accepted, 362 enrolled. In 2013, 374 master's, 128 other advanced degrees awarded. *Degree requirements:* For master's, capstone project. *Entrance requirements:* For master's, transcripts, two letters of recommendation, personal statement, resume. Additional exam requirements/recommendations for international students: Required—TOEFL (minimum score 550 paper-based; 80 iBT). *Application deadline:* For fall admission, 7/18 priority date for domestic students, 5/2 priority date for international students; for winter admission, 10/24 priority date for domestic students, 9/19 priority date for international students; for spring admission, 2/1 for domestic students, 12/14 for international students; for summer admission, 4/18 priority date for domestic students, 3/7 priority date for international students. Applications are processed on a rolling basis. Application fee: $75. Electronic applications accepted. *Expenses:* Contact institution. *Financial support:* In 2013–14, 28 students received support. Applicants required to submit FAFSA. *Unit head:* Dr. Michael McGuire, Interim Dean, 303-871-3518, E-mail: mmcguire@du.edu. *Application contact:* Information Contact, 303-871-2291, E-mail: ucoladm@du.edu.
Website: http://www.universitycollege.du.edu/.

University of Florida, Graduate School, Warrington College of Business Administration, Hough Graduate School of Business, Programs in Business Administration, Gainesville, FL 32611. Offers business administration (MBA); competitive strategy (MBA); entrepreneurship (MBA); finance (MBA); global management (MBA); Graham-Buffett security analysis (MBA); human resource management (MBA); information systems and operations management (MBA); international studies (MBA); Latin American business (MBA); management (MBA); marketing (MBA); real estate (MBA); sports administration (MBA); JD/MBA; MBA/MS; MBA/PhD; MBA/Pharm D; MD/MBA. *Accreditation:* AACSB. Part-time and evening/weekend programs available. Postbaccalaureate distance learning degree programs offered. *Faculty:* 72 full-time (10 women), 29 part-time/adjunct (7 women). *Students:* 440 full-time (122 women), 472 part-time (159 women); includes 203 minority (43 Black or African American, non-Hispanic/Latino; 3 American Indian or Alaska Native, non-Hispanic/Latino; 64 Asian, non-Hispanic/Latino; 92 Hispanic/Latino; 1 Native Hawaiian or other Pacific Islander, non-Hispanic/Latino), 39 international. Average age 32. 568 applicants, 58% accepted, 261 enrolled. In 2013, 405 master's awarded. *Degree requirements:* For master's, capstone course. *Entrance requirements:* For master's, GMAT (minimum score 465), minimum GPA of 3.0, interview. Additional exam requirements/recommendations for international students: Required—TOEFL (minimum score 550 paper-based; 80 iBT), IELTS (minimum score 6). *Application deadline:* For fall admission, 7/1 for domestic students, 1/1 for international students; for spring admission, 12/1 for domestic and international students. Applications are processed on a rolling basis. Application fee: $30. Electronic applications accepted. *Expenses:* Tuition, state resident: full-time $12,640. Tuition, nonresident: full-time $30,000. *Financial support:* In 2013–14, 24 students received support, including 24 teaching assistantships (averaging $6,143 per year); career-related internships or fieldwork, scholarships/grants, and unspecified assistantships also available. Support available to part-time students. Financial award applicants required to submit FAFSA. *Faculty research:* Accounting, finance, insurance, management, real estate, urban analysis marketing. *Unit head:* Alexander D. Sevilla, Assistant Dean/Director of MBA Program, 352-273-3252, Fax: 352-392-8791, E-mail: alex.sevilla@warrington.ufl.edu. *Application contact:* Andrew S. Lord, Senior Director of Admissions, 352-273-3241, Fax: 352-392-8791, E-mail: andrew.lord@warrington.ufl.edu.
Website: http://www.floridamba.ufl.edu/.

University of Georgia, College of Education, Department of Lifelong Education, Administration and Policy, Athens, GA 30602. Offers adult education (M Ed, Ed D, PhD,

Ed S); educational administration and policy (M Ed, PhD, Ed S); educational leadership (Ed D); human resource and organizational design (M Ed). *Accreditation:* NCATE. *Entrance requirements:* For master's and Ed S, GRE General Test or MAT; for doctorate, GRE General Test. Electronic applications accepted.

University of Hawaii at Manoa, Graduate Division, Shidler College of Business, Program in Business Administration, Honolulu, HI 96822. Offers Asian business studies (MBA); Chinese business studies (MBA); decision sciences (MBA); entrepreneurship (MBA); finance (MBA); finance and banking (MBA); human resources management (MBA); information management (MBA); information technology (MBA); international business (MBA); Japanese business studies (MBA); marketing (MBA); organizational behavior (MBA); organizational management (MBA); real estate (MBA); student-designed track (MBA). *Accreditation:* AACSB. Part-time and evening/weekend programs available. *Degree requirements:* For master's, thesis optional. *Entrance requirements:* For master's, GMAT, minimum GPA of 3.0. Additional exam requirements/recommendations for international students: Required—TOEFL (minimum score 600 paper-based; 100 iBT), IELTS (minimum score 7). *Expenses:* Contact institution.

University of Hawaii at Manoa, Graduate Division, Shidler College of Business, Program in Human Resources Management, Honolulu, HI 96822. Offers MHRM. Part-time programs available. *Entrance requirements:* Additional exam requirements/recommendations for international students: Required—TOEFL (minimum score 600 paper-based; 100 iBT), IELTS (minimum score 7). *Expenses:* Contact institution.

University of Houston–Clear Lake, School of Business, Program in Administrative Science, Houston, TX 77058-1002. Offers environmental management (MS); human resource management (MA). Part-time and evening/weekend programs available. *Degree requirements:* For master's, thesis optional. *Entrance requirements:* For master's, GMAT. Additional exam requirements/recommendations for international students: Required—TOEFL (minimum score 550 paper-based). Electronic applications accepted.

University of Houston–Downtown, College of Business, Houston, TX 77002. Offers finance (MBA); general management (MBA); human resource management (MBA); leadership (MBA); sales management and business development (MBA); supply chain management (MBA). Evening/weekend programs available. *Faculty:* 18 full-time (7 women). *Students:* 1 (woman) full-time, 88 part-time (32 women); includes 60 minority (18 Black or African American, non-Hispanic/Latino; 10 Asian, non-Hispanic/Latino; 30 Hispanic/Latino; 1 Native Hawaiian or other Pacific Islander, non-Hispanic/Latino; 1 Two or more races, non-Hispanic/Latino), 2 international. Average age 33. 41 applicants, 63% accepted, 24 enrolled. *Entrance requirements:* For master's, GMAT, official transcripts, bachelor's degree or equivalent, resume, 2 professional references. Additional exam requirements/recommendations for international students: Required—TOEFL (minimum score 81 iBT). *Application deadline:* For fall admission, 7/15 for domestic and international students. Applications are processed on a rolling basis. Application fee: $35 ($60 for international students). Electronic applications accepted. *Expenses:* Contact institution. *Financial support:* In 2013–14, 2 fellowships (averaging $6,000 per year) were awarded. Financial award application deadline: 4/1; financial award applicants required to submit FAFSA. *Faculty research:* Corporate finance, sustainability, recruitment and selection, international strategic management, gender and race discrimination. *Unit head:* Dr. D. Michael Fields, Dean, College of Business, 713-221-8179, Fax: 713-221-8675, E-mail: fieldsd@uhd.edu. *Application contact:* Ceshia Love, Assistant Director of Graduate Admissions, 713-221-8093, Fax: 713-223-7408, E-mail: gradadmissions@uhd.edu.
Website: http://mba.uhd.edu/.

University of Illinois at Urbana–Champaign, Graduate College, College of Education, Department of Education Policy, Organization, and Leadership, Champaign, IL 61820. Offers educational organization and leadership (Ed M, MS, Ed D, PhD, CAS); educational policy studies (Ed M, MA, PhD); human resource education (Ed M, MS, Ed D, PhD, CAS). Part-time programs available. Postbaccalaureate distance learning degree programs offered (no on-campus study). *Students:* 518 (342 women). Application fee: $75 ($90 for international students). *Unit head:* James Anderson, Head, 217-333-2446, Fax: 217-244-5632, E-mail: janders@illinois.edu. *Application contact:* Rebecca Grady, Office Support Specialist, 217-265-5404, Fax: 217-244-5632, E-mail: rgrady@illinois.edu.
Website: http://education.illinois.edu/epol.

University of Illinois at Urbana–Champaign, Graduate College, School of Labor and Employment Relations, Champaign, IL 61820. Offers human resources and industrial relations (MHRIR, PhD); MHRIR/JD; MHRIR/MBA. *Students:* 170 (117 women). Terminal master's awarded for partial completion of doctoral program. Application fee: $75 ($90 for international students). *Unit head:* Dr. Fritz Drasgow, Interim Dean, 217-333-1482, Fax: 217-244-9290, E-mail: fdrasgow@illinois.edu. *Application contact:* Elizabeth Barker, Assistant Dean, 217-333-2381, Fax: 217-244-9290, E-mail: ebarker@illinois.edu.
Website: http://www.ler.illinois.edu.

University of La Verne, College of Business and Public Management, Program in Health Administration, La Verne, CA 91750-4443. Offers financial management (MHA); health information systems (MHA); human resource management (MHA); managed care (MHA); management and leadership (MHA); marketing and business development (MHA). Part-time programs available. *Faculty:* 3 full-time (1 woman), 5 part-time/adjunct (1 woman). *Students:* 43 full-time (31 women), 35 part-time (20 women); includes 29 minority (9 Black or African American, non-Hispanic/Latino; 9 Asian, non-Hispanic/Latino; 11 Hispanic/Latino), 13 international. Average age 31. In 2013, 31 master's awarded. *Entrance requirements:* For master's, minimum undergraduate GPA of 2.5, 3 letters of reference, curriculum vitae or resume, writing sample. Additional exam requirements/recommendations for international students: Required—TOEFL (minimum score 550 paper-based). *Application deadline:* Applications are processed on a rolling basis. Application fee: $50. *Expenses:* Contact institution. *Financial support:* Application deadline: 3/2; applicants required to submit FAFSA. *Unit head:* Dr. Kathy Duncan, Program Chairperson, 909-593-3511 Ext. 4415, E-mail: kduncan2@laverne.edu. *Application contact:* Barbara Cox, Program and Admissions Specialist, 909-593-3511 Ext. 4004, Fax: 909-392-2761, E-mail: bcox@laverne.edu.
Website: http://www.laverne.edu/business-and-public-administration/healthadmin-gerontology/.

University of La Verne, College of Business and Public Management, Program in Organizational Management and Leadership, La Verne, CA 91750-4443. Offers leadership and management (MS), including human resource management, nonprofit management, organizational development; nonprofit management (Certificate); organizational leadership (Certificate). Part-time programs available. *Faculty:* 2 full-time (1 woman), 8 part-time/adjunct (6 women). *Students:* 77 full-time (39 women), 67 part-time (47 women); includes 69 minority (7 Black or African American, non-Hispanic/Latino; 3 Asian, non-Hispanic/Latino; 55 Hispanic/Latino; 2 Native Hawaiian or other Pacific Islander, non-Hispanic/Latino; 2 Two or more races, non-Hispanic/Latino), 38 international. Average age 32. In 2013, 183 master's awarded. *Degree requirements:* For master's, thesis or research project. *Entrance requirements:* For master's, minimum undergraduate GPA of 2.75, 2 letters of recommendation, interview, resume. Additional

exam requirements/recommendations for international students: Required—TOEFL (minimum score 550 paper-based). *Application deadline:* Applications are processed on a rolling basis. Application fee: $50. *Expenses:* Contact institution. *Financial support:* Institutionally sponsored loans available. Financial award application deadline: 3/2; financial award applicants required to submit FAFSA. *Unit head:* Dr. Kathy Duncan, Program Director, 909-593-3511 Ext. 4415, E-mail: kduncan2@laverne.edu. *Application contact:* Rina Lazarian-Chehab, Senior Associate Director of Graduate Admissions, 909-593-3511 Ext. 4317, Fax: 909-392-2761, E-mail: rlazarian@laverne.edu.
Website: http://www.laverne.edu/business-and-public-administration/org-mgmt/.

University of La Verne, Regional and Online Campuses, Graduate Programs, Inland Empire Campus, Ontario, CA 91761. Offers business administration (MBA, MBA-EP), including accounting (MBA), finance (MBA), health services management (MBA-EP), information technology (MBA-EP), international business (MBA), managed care (MBA), management and leadership (MBA-EP), marketing (MBA-EP), supply chain management (MBA); leadership and management (MS), including human resource management, nonprofit management, organizational development. Part-time and evening/weekend programs available. *Faculty:* 1 full-time (0 women), 14 part-time/adjunct (6 women). *Students:* 26 full-time (15 women), 106 part-time (65 women); includes 92 minority (15 Black or African American, non-Hispanic/Latino; 29 Asian, non-Hispanic/Latino; 43 Hispanic/Latino; 1 Native Hawaiian or other Pacific Islander, non-Hispanic/Latino; 4 Two or more races, non-Hispanic/Latino). Average age 37. In 2013, 49 master's awarded. *Application deadline:* Applications are processed on a rolling basis. Application fee: $50. *Expenses:* Contact institution. *Financial support:* Institutionally sponsored loans available. Financial award application deadline: 3/2; financial award applicants required to submit FAFSA. *Unit head:* Allen Stout, Campus Director, Inland Empire Regional Campus in Ontario, 909-937-6987, E-mail: astout@laverne.edu. *Application contact:* Karen Schumann, Senior Associate Director of Admissions, Inland Empire Regional Campus in Ontario, 909-937-6991, E-mail: kschumann@laverne.edu.
Website: http://laverne.edu/locations/inland-empire/.

University of Lethbridge, School of Graduate Studies, Lethbridge, AB T1K 3M4, Canada. Offers accounting (MScM); addictions counseling (M Sc); agricultural biotechnology (M Sc); agricultural studies (M Sc, MA); anthropology (MA); archaeology (M Sc, MA); art (MA, MFA); biochemistry (M Sc); biological sciences (M Sc); biomolecular science (PhD); biosystems and biodiversity (PhD); Canadian studies (MA); chemistry (M Sc); computer science (M Sc); computer science and geographical information science (M Sc); counseling (MC); counseling psychology (M Ed); dramatic arts (MA); earth, space, and physical science (PhD); economics (MA); education (MA); educational leadership (M Ed); English (MA); environmental science (M Sc); evolution and behavior (PhD); exercise science (M Sc); finance (MScM); French (MA); French/German (MA); French/Spanish (MA); general education (M Ed); general management (MScM); geography (M Sc, MA); German (MA); health sciences (M Sc); human resource management and labour relations (MScM); individualized multidisciplinary (M Sc, MA); information systems (MScM); international management (MScM); kinesiology (M Sc, MA); marketing (MScM); mathematics (M Sc); modern languages (MA); music (M Mus, MA); Native American studies (MA); neuroscience (M Sc, PhD); new media (MA, MFA); nursing (M Sc); philosophy (MA); physics (M Sc); policy and strategy (MScM); political science (MA); psychology (M Sc, MA); religious studies (MA); sociology (MA); theatre and dramatic arts (MFA); theoretical and computational science (PhD); urban and regional studies (MA); women and gender studies (MA). Part-time and evening/weekend programs available. *Degree requirements:* For doctorate, comprehensive exam, thesis/dissertation. *Entrance requirements:* For master's, GMAT (for M Sc in management), bachelor's degree in related field, minimum GPA of 3.0 during previous 20 graded semester courses, 2 years teaching or related experience (M Ed); for doctorate, master's degree, minimum graduate GPA of 3.5. Additional exam requirements/recommendations for international students: Required—TOEFL. Application fee: $60 Canadian dollars. *Financial support:* Fellowships, research assistantships, teaching assistantships, scholarships/grants, health care benefits, and unspecified assistantships available. *Faculty research:* Movement and brain plasticity, gibberellin physiology, photosynthesis, carbon cycling, molecular properties of main-group ring components. *Application contact:* School of Graduate Studies, 403-329-2793, Fax: 403-332-5239, E-mail: sgsinquiries@uleth.ca.
Website: http://www.uleth.ca/graduatestudies/.

University of Louisville, Graduate School, College of Arts and Sciences, Department of Urban and Public Affairs, Louisville, KY 40208. Offers public administration (MPA), including human resources management, non-profit management, public policy and administration; urban and public affairs (PhD), including urban planning and development, urban policy and administration; urban planning (MUP), including administration of planning organizations, housing and community development, land use and environmental planning, spatial analysis. Part-time and evening/weekend programs available. *Students:* 65 full-time (31 women), 27 part-time (16 women); includes 10 minority (5 Black or African American, non-Hispanic/Latino; 2 Asian, non-Hispanic/Latino; 2 Hispanic/Latino; 1 Two or more races, non-Hispanic/Latino), 7 international. Average age 31. 93 applicants, 62% accepted, 30 enrolled. In 2013, 17 master's, 3 doctorates awarded. Terminal master's awarded for partial completion of doctoral program. *Degree requirements:* For master's, internship; for doctorate, comprehensive exam, thesis/dissertation. *Entrance requirements:* For master's, GRE General Test, minimum GPA of 3.0; for doctorate, GRE General Test, master's degree in appropriate field. Additional exam requirements/recommendations for international students: Required—TOEFL (minimum score 550 paper-based; 79 iBT). *Application deadline:* For fall admission, 7/15 for domestic students, 5/1 priority date for international students; for spring admission, 11/15 for domestic students, 11/1 priority date for international students; for summer admission, 4/1 priority date for international students. Applications are processed on a rolling basis. Application fee: $60. Electronic applications accepted. *Expenses:* Tuition, state resident: full-time $10,788; part-time $599 per credit hour. Tuition, nonresident: full-time $22,446; part-time $1247 per credit hour. *Required fees:* $196. Tuition and fees vary according to program and reciprocity agreements. *Financial support:* Fellowships, research assistantships, and health care benefits available. Financial award application deadline: 3/1. *Faculty research:* Housing and community development, performance-based budgeting, environmental policy and natural hazards, sustainability, real estate development, comparative urban development. *Unit head:* Dr. David Simpson, Chair, 502-852-8019, Fax: 502-852-4558, E-mail: dave.simpson@louisville.edu. *Application contact:* Libby Leggett, Director, Graduate Admissions, 502-852-3101, Fax: 502-852-4558, E-mail: gradadm@louisville.edu.
Website: http://supa.louisville.edu.

University of Mary, Gary Tharaldson School of Business, Bismarck, ND 58504-9652. Offers accountancy (MBA); business administration (MBA); health care (MBA); human resource management (MBA); management (MBA); project management (MPM); strategic leadership (MSSL). Part-time and evening/weekend programs available. *Degree requirements:* For master's, strategic planning seminar. *Entrance requirements:* For master's, minimum GPA of 2.5. Additional exam requirements/recommendations for international students: Required—TOEFL (minimum score 500 paper-based; 71 iBT).

University of Michigan–Dearborn, College of Business, Dearborn, MI 48128-1491. Offers accounting (MBA, MS); business analytics (MS); finance (MBA, MS); human resource management (MBA); information systems (MS); international business (MBA); investment (MBA); management (MBA); management information systems (MBA); marketing (MBA); supply chain management (MBA, MS); taxation (MBA); MBA/MHSA; MBA/MSE; MBA/MSF; MBA/MSIS; MBA/MSSCM; MSF/MSA. *Accreditation:* AACSB. Part-time and evening/weekend programs available. Postbaccalaureate distance learning degree programs offered (no on-campus study). *Faculty:* 24 full-time (8 women), 5 part-time/adjunct (2 women). *Students:* 82 full-time (31 women), 323 part-time (116 women); includes 72 minority (17 Black or African American, non-Hispanic/Latino; 2 American Indian or Alaska Native, non-Hispanic/Latino; 30 Asian, non-Hispanic/Latino; 15 Hispanic/Latino; 8 Two or more races, non-Hispanic/Latino), 65 international. Average age 32. 290 applicants, 44% accepted, 99 enrolled. In 2013, 143 master's awarded. *Entrance requirements:* For master's, GMAT or GRE, pre-calculus or finite mathematics; 18 credits of accounting course work beyond introductory courses (MS in accounting). Additional exam requirements/recommendations for international students: Required—TOEFL (minimum score 560 paper-based; 84 iBT), IELTS. *Application deadline:* For fall admission, 8/1 priority date for domestic students, 5/1 priority date for international students; for winter admission, 12/1 priority date for domestic students, 9/1 priority date for international students; for spring admission, 4/1 priority date for domestic students, 1/1 priority date for international students. Applications are processed on a rolling basis. Application fee: $60. Electronic applications accepted. *Expenses:* Contact institution. *Financial support:* Career-related internships or fieldwork, Federal Work-Study, and scholarships/grants available. Support available to part-time students. Financial award application deadline: 9/1; financial award applicants required to submit FAFSA. *Faculty research:* Cultural diversity, buyer-supplier relations, error detection in data, economic evolution. *Unit head:* Dr. Raju Balakrishnan, Dean, 313-593-5248, Fax: 313-271-9835, E-mail: rajub@umich.edu. *Application contact:* Joan Doherty, Academic Advisor/Counselor, 313-593-5460, Fax: 313-271-9838, E-mail: umd-gradbusiness@umich.edu.
Website: http://www.cob.umd.umich.edu.

University of Minnesota, Twin Cities Campus, Carlson School of Management, Program in Human Resources and Industrial Relations, Minneapolis, MN 55455-0213. Offers MA, PhD. *Accreditation:* AACSB. Part-time and evening/weekend programs available. *Faculty:* 16 full-time (9 women), 12 part-time/adjunct (5 women). *Students:* 139 full-time (85 women), 46 part-time (34 women); includes 25 minority (6 Black or African American, non-Hispanic/Latino; 1 American Indian or Alaska Native, non-Hispanic/Latino; 15 Asian, non-Hispanic/Latino; 3 Hispanic/Latino), 53 international. Average age 26. 433 applicants, 19% accepted, 66 enrolled. In 2013, 103 master's, 2 doctorates awarded. *Degree requirements:* For master's, thesis or alternative, 48 course credits; for doctorate, comprehensive exam, thesis/dissertation. *Entrance requirements:* For master's, GMAT or GRE General Test, undergraduate degree from accredited institution, course in microeconomics. Additional exam requirements/recommendations for international students: Required—TOEFL (minimum score 550 paper-based; 79 iBT), IELTS (minimum score 6.5). *Application deadline:* For fall admission, 6/15 for domestic and international students; for spring admission, 10/15 for domestic and international students. Applications are processed on a rolling basis. Application fee: $75 ($95 for international students). *Expenses:* Contact institution. *Financial support:* In 2013–14, 53 students received support, including 43 fellowships with full tuition reimbursements available (averaging $7,500 per year), 15 research assistantships with full and partial tuition reimbursements available (averaging $13,700 per year), 23 teaching assistantships with full and partial tuition reimbursements available (averaging $14,500 per year); career-related internships or fieldwork, Federal Work-Study, institutionally sponsored loans, scholarships/grants, health care benefits, tuition waivers (full and partial), and unspecified assistantships also available. Financial award application deadline: 2/1; financial award applicants required to submit FAFSA. *Faculty research:* Staffing, training, and development; compensation and benefits; organization theory; collective bargaining. *Total annual research expenditures:* $13,660. *Unit head:* Stacy Doepner-Hove, Director, 612-625-8732, Fax: 612-624-8360, E-mail: doepn002@umn.edu. *Application contact:* Patti Blair, Admissions Coordinator, 612-624-5704, Fax: 612-624-8360, E-mail: hrirgrad@umn.edu.
Website: http://www.csom.umn.edu/chrls/.

University of Missouri–St. Louis, College of Business Administration, Program in Business Administration, St. Louis, MO 63121. Offers accounting (MBA); business administration (Certificate); business intelligence (Certificate); finance (MBA); human resource management (Certificate); information systems (MBA); logistics and supply chain management (MBA, PhD, Certificate); marketing (MBA); marketing management (Certificate); operations management (MBA). *Accreditation:* AACSB. Part-time and evening/weekend programs available. *Faculty:* 30 full-time (5 women), 20 part-time/adjunct (8 women). *Students:* 114 full-time (51 women), 269 part-time (100 women); includes 43 minority (16 Black or African American, non-Hispanic/Latino; 14 Asian, non-Hispanic/Latino; 11 Hispanic/Latino; 1 Native Hawaiian or other Pacific Islander, non-Hispanic/Latino; 1 Two or more races, non-Hispanic/Latino), 56 international. Average age 31. 153 applicants, 91% accepted, 110 enrolled. In 2013, 136 master's, 7 other advanced degrees awarded. *Degree requirements:* For doctorate, thesis/dissertation. *Entrance requirements:* For master's, GMAT, 2 letters of recommendation. Additional exam requirements/recommendations for international students: Recommended—TOEFL (minimum score 550 paper-based; 79 iBT), IELTS (minimum score 6.5). *Application deadline:* For fall admission, 7/1 for domestic and international students; for spring admission, 12/1 for domestic and international students. Applications are processed on a rolling basis. Application fee: $50 ($40 for international students). Electronic applications accepted. *Expenses:* Tuition, state resident: full-time $7364; part-time $409.10 per credit hour. Tuition, nonresident: full-time $19,162; part-time $1008.50 per credit hour. *Financial support:* In 2013–14, 14 research assistantships with full and partial tuition reimbursements (averaging $5,625 per year), 6 teaching assistantships with full and partial tuition reimbursements (averaging $9,403 per year) were awarded; career-related internships or fieldwork, Federal Work-Study, and institutionally sponsored loans also available. Support available to part-time students. Financial award application deadline: 4/1; financial award applicants required to submit FAFSA. *Faculty research:* Human resources, strategic management, marketing strategy, consumer behavior product development, advertising. *Unit head:* Francesca Ferrari, Assistant Director, 314-516-5885, Fax: 314-516-6420, E-mail: mba@umsl.edu. *Application contact:* 314-516-5458, Fax: 314-516-6996, E-mail: gradadm@umsl.edu.
Website: http://mba.umsl.edu/Degree%20Programs/index.html.

University of Nebraska at Kearney, Graduate Programs, College of Business and Technology, Department of Business, Kearney, NE 68849-0001. Offers accounting (MBA); generalist (MBA); human resources (MBA); human services (MBA); marketing (MBA). *Accreditation:* AACSB. Part-time and evening/weekend programs available. *Degree requirements:* For master's, thesis optional. *Entrance requirements:* For master's, GMAT or GRE, letters of recommendation, work history, letter of interest, resume. Additional exam requirements/recommendations for international students: Required—TOEFL (minimum score 550 paper-based; 79 iBT). Electronic applications accepted. *Faculty research:* Small business financial management, employment law, expert systems, international trade and marketing, environmental economics.

University of New Haven, Graduate School, College of Arts and Sciences, Program in Industrial and Organizational Psychology, West Haven, CT 06516-1916. Offers conflict management (MA); human resource management (MA); industrial organizational psychology (MA); organizational development (MA); psychology of conflict management (Certificate). Part-time and evening/weekend programs available. *Students:* 73 full-time (49 women), 20 part-time (15 women); includes 24 minority (11 Black or African American, non-Hispanic/Latino; 4 Asian, non-Hispanic/Latino; 6 Hispanic/Latino; 3 Two or more races, non-Hispanic/Latino), 10 international. 125 applicants, 95% accepted, 51 enrolled. In 2013, 49 master's, 1 other advanced degree awarded. *Degree requirements:* For master's, thesis or alternative, internship or practicum. *Entrance requirements:* Additional exam requirements/recommendations for international students: Required—TOEFL (minimum score 80 iBT), IELTS, PTE (minimum score 53). *Application deadline:* For fall admission, 5/31 for international students; for winter admission, 10/15 for international students; for spring admission, 1/15 for international students. Applications are processed on a rolling basis. Application fee: $75. Electronic applications accepted. Application fee is waived when completed online. *Expenses:* Contact institution. *Financial support:* Research assistantships with partial tuition reimbursements, teaching assistantships with partial tuition reimbursements, career-related internships or fieldwork, Federal Work-Study, scholarships/grants, and unspecified assistantships available. Support available to part-time students. Financial award applicants required to submit FAFSA. *Unit head:* Dr. Dennis McGough, Coordinator, 203-479-4986, E-mail: dmcgough@newhaven.edu. *Application contact:* Eloise Gormley, Information Contact, 203-932-7440.
Website: http://www.newhaven.edu/4730/.

University of New Haven, Graduate School, College of Business, Program in Business Administration, West Haven, CT 06516-1916. Offers accounting (MBA, Certificate), including CPA (MBA); business administration (MBA); business management (Certificate); business policy and strategic leadership (MBA); finance (MBA), including CFA; global marketing (MBA); human resource management (Certificate); human resources management (MBA); international business (Certificate); marketing (MBA, Certificate); sports management (MBA). Part-time and evening/weekend programs available. *Students:* 125 full-time (55 women), 88 part-time (30 women); includes 31 minority (16 Black or African American, non-Hispanic/Latino; 1 American Indian or Alaska Native, non-Hispanic/Latino; 8 Asian, non-Hispanic/Latino; 5 Hispanic/Latino; 1 Native Hawaiian or other Pacific Islander, non-Hispanic/Latino), 72 international. 196 applicants, 89% accepted, 72 enrolled. In 2013, 143 master's, 24 other advanced degrees awarded. *Degree requirements:* For master's, thesis optional. *Entrance requirements:* For master's, GMAT. Additional exam requirements/recommendations for international students: Required—TOEFL (minimum score 80 iBT), IELTS, PTE (minimum score 53). *Application deadline:* For fall admission, 5/31 for international students; for winter admission, 10/15 for international students; for spring admission, 1/15 for international students. Applications are processed on a rolling basis. Application fee: $75. Electronic applications accepted. Application fee is waived when completed online. *Expenses: Tuition:* Full-time $21,600; part-time $800 per credit hour. *Required fees:* $45 per trimester. *Financial support:* Research assistantships with partial tuition reimbursements, teaching assistantships with partial tuition reimbursements, career-related internships or fieldwork, Federal Work-Study, scholarships/grants, and unspecified assistantships available. Support available to part-time students. Financial award applicants required to submit FAFSA. *Unit head:* Dr. Armando Rodriguez, Director, 203-932-7372, E-mail: arodriguez@newhaven.edu. *Application contact:* Eloise Gormley, Director of Graduate Admissions, 203-932-7440, E-mail: gradinfo@newhaven.edu.
Website: http://www.newhaven.edu/7433/.

University of New Haven, Graduate School, College of Business, Program in Public Administration, West Haven, CT 06516-1916. Offers city management (MPA); community-clinical services (MPA); health care management (MPA); long-term health care (MPA); personnel and labor relations (MPA); public administration (MPA, Certificate); public management (Certificate); MBA/MPA. Part-time and evening/weekend programs available. *Students:* 39 full-time (21 women), 20 part-time (9 women); includes 16 minority (12 Black or African American, non-Hispanic/Latino; 2 Asian, non-Hispanic/Latino; 1 Hispanic/Latino; 1 Native Hawaiian or other Pacific Islander, non-Hispanic/Latino), 11 international. 44 applicants, 84% accepted, 13 enrolled. In 2013, 15 master's, 12 other advanced degrees awarded. *Degree requirements:* For master's, thesis or alternative. *Entrance requirements:* Additional exam requirements/recommendations for international students: Required—TOEFL (minimum score 80 iBT), IELTS, PTE (minimum score 53). *Application deadline:* For fall admission, 5/31 for international students; for winter admission, 10/15 for international students; for spring admission, 1/15 for international students. Applications are processed on a rolling basis. Application fee: $75. Electronic applications accepted. Application fee is waived when completed online. *Expenses:* Contact institution. *Financial support:* Research assistantships with partial tuition reimbursements, teaching assistantships with partial tuition reimbursements, career-related internships or fieldwork, Federal Work-Study, scholarships/grants, and unspecified assistantships available. Support available to part-time students. Financial award application deadline: 5/1; financial award applicants required to submit FAFSA. *Unit head:* Cynthia Conrad, Chair, 203-932-7486, E-mail: cconrad@newhaven.edu. *Application contact:* Eloise Gormley, Director of Graduate Admissions, 203-932-7440, E-mail: gradinfo@newhaven.edu.
Website: http://www.newhaven.edu/6854/.

University of New Mexico, Anderson Graduate School of Management, Department of Organizational Studies, Albuquerque, NM 87131. Offers human resources management (MBA); policy and planning (MBA). Part-time and evening/weekend programs available. *Faculty:* 11 full-time (5 women), 11 part-time/adjunct (5 women). In 2013, 56 master's awarded. *Entrance requirements:* For master's, GMAT or GRE, minimum GPA of 3.0 on last 60 hours of coursework. Additional exam requirements/recommendations for international students: Required—TOEFL (minimum score 550 paper-based; 79 iBT). *Application deadline:* For fall admission, 4/1 priority date for domestic and international students; for spring admission, 10/1 priority date for domestic and international students. Applications are processed on a rolling basis. Application fee: $50. Electronic applications accepted. *Expenses:* Contact institution. *Financial support:* Fellowships, research assistantships, career-related internships or fieldwork, Federal Work-Study, scholarships/grants, and unspecified assistantships available. Support available to part-time students. Financial award application deadline: 6/1; financial award applicants required to submit FAFSA. *Faculty research:* Business ethics and social corporate responsibility, diversity, human resources, organizational strategy, organizational behavior. *Unit head:* Dr. Jacqueline Hood, Chair, 505-277-6471, Fax: 505-277-7108, E-mail: jnhood@unm.edu. *Application contact:* Tracy Wilkey, Manager, Academic Advisement, 505-277-3290, Fax: 505-277-8436, E-mail: andersonadvising@unm.edu.
Website: http://mba.mgt.unm.edu/default.asp.

University of North Florida, Coggin College of Business, MBA Program, Jacksonville, FL 32224. Offers accounting (MBA); construction management (MBA); e-commerce (MBA); economics (MBA); finance (MBA); human resource management (MBA); international business (MBA); logistics (MBA); management applications (MBA). *Accreditation:* AACSB. Part-time and evening/weekend programs available. *Faculty:* 14

full-time (6 women), 1 part-time/adjunct (0 women). *Students:* 90 full-time (41 women), 231 part-time (84 women); includes 47 minority (18 Black or African American, non-Hispanic/Latino; 8 Asian, non-Hispanic/Latino; 16 Hispanic/Latino; 5 Two or more races, non-Hispanic/Latino), 29 international. Average age 29. 222 applicants, 47% accepted, 80 enrolled. In 2013, 152 master's awarded. *Entrance requirements:* For master's, GMAT or GRE, U.S. bachelor's degree from regionally-accredited university or equivalent foreign degree. Additional exam requirements/recommendations for international students: Required—TOEFL (minimum score 550 paper-based; 79 iBT). *Application deadline:* For fall admission, 7/1 priority date for domestic students, 5/1 for international students; for spring admission, 11/1 priority date for domestic students, 10/1 for international students. Application fee: $30. *Expenses:* Tuition, state resident: full-time $9794; part-time $408.10 per credit hour. Tuition, nonresident: full-time $22,383; part-time $932.61 per credit hour. *Required fees:* $2020; $84.20 per credit hour. Tuition and fees vary according to course load and program. *Financial support:* In 2013–14, 35 students received support, including 1 research assistantship (averaging $2,700 per year); teaching assistantships, Federal Work-Study, and tuition waivers (partial) also available. Support available to part-time students. Financial award application deadline: 4/1; financial award applicants required to submit FAFSA. *Faculty research:* Performance measures, costing, and inventory issues in logistics and supply chain management; inter-organizational systems; international management and marketing practices; e-commerce; organizational learning and socialization processes. *Total annual research expenditures:* $12,025. *Application contact:* Cheryl Campbell, Graduate Advisor, 904-620-2575, Fax: 904-620-2832, E-mail: ccampbell@unf.edu.
Website: http://www.unf.edu/coggin/academics/graduate/mba.aspx.

University of North Texas, Robert B. Toulouse School of Graduate Studies, Denton, TN 76203-5017. Offers accounting (MS, PhD); applied anthropology (MA, MS); applied behavior analysis (Certificate); applied technology and performance improvement (M Ed, MS, PhD); art education (MA, PhD); art history (MA); art museum education (Certificate); arts leadership (Certificate); audiology (Au D); behavior analysis (MS); biochemistry and molecular biology (MS, PhD); biology (MA, MS, PhD); business (PhD); business computer information systems (PhD); chemistry (MS, PhD); clinical psychology (PhD); communication studies (MA, MS); computer engineering (MS); computer science (MS); computer science and engineering (PhD); counseling (M Ed, MS, PhD), including clinical mental health counseling (MS), college and university counseling (M Ed, MS), elementary school counseling (M Ed, MS), secondary school counseling (M Ed, MS); counseling psychology (PhD); creative writing (MA); criminal justice (MS); curriculum and instruction (M Ed, PhD), including curriculum studies (PhD), early childhood studies (PhD), language and literacy studies (PhD); decision sciences (MBA); design (MA, MFA), including fashion design (MFA), innovation studies, interior design (MFA); early childhood studies (MS); economics (MS); educational leadership (M Ed, Ed D, PhD); educational psychology (MS), including family studies, gifted and talented (MS, PhD), human development, learning and cognition, research, measurement and evaluation; educational research (PhD), including gifted and talented (MS, PhD), human development and family studies, psychological aspects of sports and exercise, research, measurement and statistics; electrical engineering (MS); emergency management (MPA); engineering systems (MS); English (MA, PhD); environmental science (MS, PhD); experimental psychology (PhD); finance (MBA, MS, PhD); financial management (MPA); French (MA); health psychology and behavioral medicine (PhD); health services management (MBA); higher education (M Ed, Ed D, PhD); history (MA, MS, PhD), including European history (PhD), military history (PhD), United States history (PhD); hospitality management (MS); human resources management (MPA); information science (MS, PhD); information technologies (MBA); information technology and decision sciences (MS); interdisciplinary studies (MA, MS); international sustainable tourism (MS); jazz studies (MM); journalism (MA, MJ, Graduate Certificate), including interactive and virtual digital communication (Graduate Certificate), narrative journalism (Graduate Certificate), public relations (Graduate Certificate); kinesiology (MS); learning technologies (MS, PhD); library science (MS); local government management (MPA); logistics and supply chain management (MBA, PhD); long-term care, senior housing, and aging services (MA, MS); management science (PhD); marketing (MBA, PhD); materials science and engineering (MS, PhD); mathematics (MA, PhD); merchandising (MS); music (MA, MM Ed, PhD), including ethnomusicology (MA), music education (MM Ed, PhD), music theory (MA, PhD), musicology (MA, PhD), performance (MA); nonprofit management (MPA); operations and supply chain management (MBA); performance (MM, DMA); philosophy (MA, PhD); physics (MS, PhD); political science (MA, MS, PhD); public administration and management (PhD), including emergency management, nonprofit management, public financial management, urban management; radio, television and film (MA, MFA); recreation, event and sport management (MS); rehabilitation counseling (MS, Certificate); sociology (MA, MS, PhD); Spanish (MA); special education (M Ed, PhD), including autism intervention (PhD), emotional/behavioral disorders (PhD), mild/moderate disabilities (PhD); speech-language pathology (MA, MS); strategic management (MBA); studio art (MFA); taxation (MS); teaching (M Ed); MBA/MS; MS/MPH; MSES/MBA. Part-time and evening/weekend programs available. Postbaccalaureate distance learning degree programs offered. *Faculty:* 661 full-time (213 women), 240 part-time/adjunct (144 women). *Students:* 3,106 full-time (1,620 women), 3,543 part-time (2,221 women); includes 1,740 minority (533 Black or African American, non-Hispanic/Latino; 15 American Indian or Alaska Native, non-Hispanic/Latino; 286 Asian, non-Hispanic/Latino; 746 Hispanic/Latino; 3 Native Hawaiian or other Pacific Islander, non-Hispanic/Latino; 157 Two or more races, non-Hispanic/Latino), 1,145 international. Average age 32. 6,289 applicants, 43% accepted, 1751 enrolled. In 2013, 1,778 master's, 239 doctorates, 10 other advanced degrees awarded. Terminal master's awarded for partial completion of doctoral program. *Degree requirements:* For master's, variable foreign language requirement, comprehensive exam (for some programs), thesis (for some programs); for doctorate, variable foreign language requirement, comprehensive exam (for some programs), thesis/dissertation; for other advanced degree, variable foreign language requirement, comprehensive exam (for some programs). *Entrance requirements:* For master's and doctorate, GRE, GMAT. Additional exam requirements/recommendations for international students: Required—TOEFL (minimum score 550 paper-based; 79 iBT). *Application deadline:* For fall admission, 7/15 for domestic students, 3/15 for international students; for spring admission, 11/15 for domestic students, 9/15 for international students; for summer admission, 5/1 for domestic students. Applications are processed on a rolling basis. Application fee: $60. Electronic applications accepted. *Financial support:* Fellowships with partial tuition reimbursements, research assistantships with partial tuition reimbursements, teaching assistantships, career-related internships or fieldwork, Federal Work-Study, institutionally sponsored loans, scholarships/grants, health care benefits, and library assistantships available. Support available to part-time students. Financial award applicants required to submit FAFSA. *Unit head:* Mark Wardell, Dean, 940-565-2383, E-mail: mark.wardell@unt.edu. *Application contact:* Toulouse School of Graduate Studies, 940-565-2383, Fax: 940-565-2141, E-mail: gradsch@unt.edu.
Website: http://tsgs.unt.edu/.

University of Oklahoma, College of Architecture, Division of Architecture, Norman, OK 73019. Offers architectural urban studies (MS), including architectural urban studies, environmental technology, human resources; architecture (M Arch). *Faculty:* 29 full-time (7 women). *Students:* 13 full-time (6 women), 12 part-time (9 women); includes 9 minority (1 American Indian or Alaska Native, non-Hispanic/Latino; 1 Asian, non-Hispanic/Latino; 3 Hispanic/Latino; 4 Two or more races, non-Hispanic/Latino), 3 international. Average age 33. 33 applicants, 64% accepted, 7 enrolled. In 2013, 6 master's awarded. *Degree requirements:* For master's, thesis or alternative, portfolio, project. *Entrance requirements:* For master's, GRE General Test, portfolio. Additional exam requirements/recommendations for international students: Required—TOEFL (minimum score 79 iBT). *Application deadline:* For fall admission, 4/1 for domestic and international students. Application fee: $50 ($100 for international students). Electronic applications accepted. *Expenses:* Tuition, state resident: full-time $4205; part-time $175.20 per credit hour. Tuition, nonresident: full-time $16,205; part-time $675.20 per credit hour. *Required fees:* $2745; $103.85 per credit hour. $126.50 per semester. *Financial support:* In 2013–14, 19 students received support, including 1 research assistantship with partial tuition reimbursement available (averaging $10,168 per year), 3 teaching assistantships with partial tuition reimbursements available (averaging $10,168 per year); scholarships/grants and unspecified assistantships also available. Financial award application deadline: 6/1; financial award applicants required to submit FAFSA. *Faculty research:* Rammed earth bricks, energy sustainability, acoustics, Italian architecture, architectural design. *Total annual research expenditures:* $352,588. *Unit head:* Dr. Hans Butzer, Director, 405-325-2444, Fax: 405-325-7558, E-mail: butzer@ou.edu. *Application contact:* Joel Dietrich, 405-325-2444, Fax: 405-325-7558, E-mail: dietrich@ou.edu.
Website: http://arch.ou.edu.

University of Oklahoma, College of Arts and Sciences, Department of Psychology, Norman, OK 73019. Offers organizational dynamics (MA), including human resource management, technical project management; psychology (MS, PhD), including industrial and organizational psychology, psychology. Part-time and evening/weekend programs available. *Faculty:* 25 full-time (12 women). *Students:* 65 full-time (36 women), 32 part-time (15 women); includes 22 minority (4 Black or African American, non-Hispanic/Latino; 3 American Indian or Alaska Native, non-Hispanic/Latino; 6 Asian, non-Hispanic/Latino; 4 Hispanic/Latino; 1 Native Hawaiian or other Pacific Islander, non-Hispanic/Latino; 4 Two or more races, non-Hispanic/Latino), 4 international. Average age 30. 102 applicants, 20% accepted, 19 enrolled. In 2013, 34 master's, 8 doctorates awarded. Terminal master's awarded for partial completion of doctoral program. *Degree requirements:* For master's, thesis (for some programs); for doctorate, thesis/dissertation (for some programs). *Entrance requirements:* Additional exam requirements/recommendations for international students: Required—TOEFL (minimum score 79 iBT). *Application deadline:* For fall admission, 1/1 for domestic and international students; for spring admission, 11/1 for domestic and international students. Application fee: $50 ($100 for international students). Electronic applications accepted. *Expenses:* Tuition, state resident: full-time $4205; part-time $175.20 per credit hour. Tuition, nonresident: full-time $16,205; part-time $675.20 per credit hour. *Required fees:* $2745; $103.85 per credit hour. $126.50 per semester. *Financial support:* In 2013–14, 66 students received support, including 10 fellowships with full tuition reimbursements available (averaging $3,300 per year), 13 research assistantships with partial tuition reimbursements available (averaging $16,594 per year), 39 teaching assistantships with partial tuition reimbursements available (averaging $14,807 per year); scholarships/grants, health care benefits, and unspecified assistantships also available. Financial award application deadline: 6/1; financial award applicants required to submit FAFSA. *Faculty research:* Industrial organizational psychology including leadership and creativity; cognitive psychology with an emphasis in modeling, memory, and decision science; quantitative methods (measurement, modeling, and statistics); social psychology (self and stereotype thinking); personality and animal behavior. *Total annual research expenditures:* $1.2 million. *Unit head:* Dr. Jorge Mendoza, Chair, 405-325-4511, Fax: 405-325-4737, E-mail: jmendoza@ou.edu. *Application contact:* Kathryn Paine, Graduate Admissions Coordinator, 405-325-4512, Fax: 405-325-4737, E-mail: kpaine@ou.edu.
Website: http://www.ou.edu/cas/psychology.

University of Phoenix–Atlanta Campus, School of Business, Sandy Springs, GA 30350-4153. Offers accounting (MBA); business administration (MBA); global management (MBA); human resources management (MBA, MM); management (MM); marketing (MBA); public administration (MM). Evening/weekend programs available. Postbaccalaureate distance learning degree programs offered. *Degree requirements:* For master's, thesis (for some programs). *Entrance requirements:* For master's, minimum undergraduate GPA of 3.0, 3 years of work experience. Additional exam requirements/recommendations for international students: Required—TOEFL (minimum score 550 paper-based; 79 iBT).

University of Phoenix–Augusta Campus, School of Business, Augusta, GA 30909-4583. Offers accounting (MBA); business administration (MBA); business and management (MBA, MM); global management (MBA); human resources management (MBA, MM); management (MM); marketing (MBA); public administration (MBA, MM). Postbaccalaureate distance learning degree programs offered.

University of Phoenix–Austin Campus, School of Business, Austin, TX 78759. Offers accounting (MBA); business administration (MBA); business and management (MBA); e-business (MBA); global management (MBA); human resources management (MBA, MM); management (MM); marketing (MBA); public administration (MBA). Postbaccalaureate distance learning degree programs offered.

University of Phoenix–Bay Area Campus, School of Business, San Jose, CA 95134-1805. Offers accountancy (MS); accounting (MBA); business administration (MBA, DBA); energy management (MBA); global management (MBA); health care management (MBA); human resource management (MBA); human resources management (MM); management (MM); marketing (MBA); organizational leadership (DM); project management (MBA); public administration (MPA); technology management (MBA). Evening/weekend programs available. Postbaccalaureate distance learning degree programs offered (no on-campus study). *Degree requirements:* For master's, thesis (for some programs). *Entrance requirements:* For master's, minimum undergraduate GPA of 3.0, 3 years of work experience. Additional exam requirements/recommendations for international students: Required—TOEFL (minimum score 550 paper-based; 79 iBT). Electronic applications accepted.

University of Phoenix–Birmingham Campus, College of Graduate Business and Management, Birmingham, AL 35242. Offers accounting (MBA); business administration (MBA); global management (MBA); human resources management (MBA, MM); management (MM); marketing (MBA); public administration (MM).

University of Phoenix–Central Valley Campus, School of Business, Fresno, CA 93720-1562. Offers accounting (MBA); business administration (MBA); global management (MBA); human resources management (MBA, MM); management (MM); marketing (MBA); public administration (MBA, MM).

University of Phoenix–Chattanooga Campus, School of Business, Chattanooga, TN 37421-3707. Offers accounting (MBA); business administration (MBA); business and management (MBA); global management (MBA); human resources management (MBA, MM); management (MM); marketing (MBA); public administration (MBA, MM). Postbaccalaureate distance learning degree programs offered.

University of Phoenix–Cheyenne Campus, School of Business, Cheyenne, WY 82009. Offers global management (MBA); human resources management (MBA, MM); management (MM); marketing (MBA); public administration (MBA, MM). Postbaccalaureate distance learning degree programs offered.

University of Phoenix–Chicago Campus, School of Business, Schaumburg, IL 60173-4399. Offers business administration (MBA); global management (MBA); human resources management (MBA); information systems (MIS); management (MM). Evening/weekend programs available. *Degree requirements:* For master's, thesis (for some programs). *Entrance requirements:* For master's, minimum undergraduate GPA of 3.0, 3 years of work experience. Additional exam requirements/recommendations for international students: Required—TOEFL (minimum score 550 paper-based; 79 iBT). Electronic applications accepted.

University of Phoenix–Cincinnati Campus, School of Business, West Chester, OH 45069-4875. Offers accounting (MBA); business administration (MBA); global management (MBA); human resources management (MBA, MM); management (MM); marketing (MBA); public administration (MM). Evening/weekend programs available. *Degree requirements:* For master's, thesis (for some programs). *Entrance requirements:* For master's, minimum undergraduate GPA of 3.0, 3 years of work experience. Additional exam requirements/recommendations for international students: Required—TOEFL (minimum score 550 paper-based; 79 iBT). Electronic applications accepted.

University of Phoenix–Cleveland Campus, School of Business, Independence, OH 44131-2194. Offers accounting (MBA); business administration (MBA); global management (MBA); human resources management (MBA, MM); management (MM); marketing (MBA); public administration (MBA, MM). Evening/weekend programs available. Postbaccalaureate distance learning degree programs offered (no on-campus study). *Degree requirements:* For master's, thesis (for some programs). *Entrance requirements:* For master's, minimum undergraduate GPA of 3.0, 3 years of work experience. Additional exam requirements/recommendations for international students: Required—TOEFL (minimum score 550 paper-based; 79 iBT). Electronic applications accepted.

University of Phoenix–Columbus Georgia Campus, School of Business, Columbus, GA 31909. Offers accounting (MBA); business administration (MBA); global management (MBA); human resources management (MBA, MM); management (MM); marketing (MBA); public administration (MBA). Evening/weekend programs available. *Degree requirements:* For master's, thesis (for some programs). *Entrance requirements:* For master's, minimum undergraduate GPA of 3.0, 3 years of work experience. Additional exam requirements/recommendations for international students: Required—TOEFL (minimum score 550 paper-based; 79 iBT). Electronic applications accepted.

University of Phoenix–Columbus Ohio Campus, School of Business, Columbus, OH 43240-4032. Offers accounting (MBA); business administration (MBA); global management (MBA); human resources management (MBA, MM); management (MM); marketing (MBA); public administration (MM). Evening/weekend programs available. Postbaccalaureate distance learning degree programs offered. *Degree requirements:* For master's, thesis (for some programs). *Entrance requirements:* For master's, minimum undergraduate GPA of 3.0, 3 years of work experience. Additional exam requirements/recommendations for international students: Required—TOEFL (minimum score 550 paper-based; 79 iBT). Electronic applications accepted.

University of Phoenix–Dallas Campus, School of Business, Dallas, TX 75251. Offers accounting (MBA); business administration (MBA); global management (MBA); human resources management (MBA, MM); management (MM); marketing (MBA); public administration (MBA, MM). Evening/weekend programs available. Postbaccalaureate distance learning degree programs offered. *Degree requirements:* For master's, thesis (for some programs). *Entrance requirements:* For master's, 3 years of work experience, minimum undergraduate GPA of 3.0. Additional exam requirements/recommendations for international students: Required—TOEFL (minimum score 550 paper-based; 79 iBT). Electronic applications accepted.

University of Phoenix–Denver Campus, School of Business, Lone Tree, CO 80124-5453. Offers accountancy (MSA); accounting (MBA); business administration (MBA); e-business (MBA); global management (MBA); human resources management (MBA, MM); management (MM); marketing (MBA); public administration (MBA, MM). Evening/weekend programs available. Postbaccalaureate distance learning degree programs offered. *Degree requirements:* For master's, thesis (for some programs). *Entrance requirements:* For master's, minimum undergraduate GPA of 3.0, 3 years of work experience. Additional exam requirements/recommendations for international students: Required—TOEFL (minimum score 550 paper-based; 79 iBT). Electronic applications accepted.

University of Phoenix–Des Moines Campus, School of Business, Des Moines, IA 50309. Offers accounting (MBA); business administration (MBA); global management (MBA); human resources management (MBA, MM); management (MM); marketing (MBA); public administration (MBA, MM). Postbaccalaureate distance learning degree programs offered.

University of Phoenix–Eastern Washington Campus, School of Business, Spokane, WA 99212-2531. Offers accounting (MBA); business administration (MBA); human resources management (MBA); marketing (MBA); public administration (MBA). Evening/weekend programs available. *Degree requirements:* For master's, thesis (for some programs). *Entrance requirements:* For master's, minimum undergraduate GPA of 3.0, 3 years of work experience. Additional exam requirements/recommendations for international students: Required—TOEFL (minimum score 550 paper-based; 79 iBT). Electronic applications accepted.

University of Phoenix–Hawaii Campus, School of Business, Honolulu, HI 96813-4317. Offers accounting (MBA); business administration (MBA); global management (MBA); human resources management (MBA, MM); management (MM); marketing (MBA); public administration (MBA, MM). Evening/weekend programs available. *Degree requirements:* For master's, thesis (for some programs). *Entrance requirements:* For master's, minimum undergraduate GPA of 3.0, 3 years of work experience. Additional exam requirements/recommendations for international students: Required—TOEFL (minimum score 550 paper-based; 79 iBT). Electronic applications accepted.

University of Phoenix–Houston Campus, School of Business, Houston, TX 77079-2004. Offers accounting (MBA); business administration (MBA); global management (MBA); human resources management (MBA, MM); management (MM); marketing (MBA); public administration (MBA, MM). Evening/weekend programs available. Postbaccalaureate distance learning degree programs offered. *Degree requirements:* For master's, thesis (for some programs). *Entrance requirements:* For master's, 3 years of work experience, minimum undergraduate GPA of 3.0. Additional exam requirements/recommendations for international students: Required—TOEFL (minimum score 550 paper-based; 79 iBT). Electronic applications accepted.

University of Phoenix–Idaho Campus, School of Business, Meridian, ID 83642-5114. Offers accounting (MBA); administration (MBA); global management (MBA); human resources management (MBA, MM); management (MM); marketing (MBA); public administration (MM). Evening/weekend programs available. Postbaccalaureate distance learning degree programs offered. *Degree requirements:* For master's, thesis (for some programs). *Entrance requirements:* For master's, 3 years of work experience, minimum undergraduate GPA of 3.0. Additional exam requirements/recommendations for international students: Required—TOEFL (minimum score 550 paper-based). Electronic applications accepted.

University of Phoenix–Indianapolis Campus, School of Business, Indianapolis, IN 46250-932. Offers accounting (MBA); business administration (MBA); global management (MBA); human resources management (MBA, MM); management (MM); marketing (MBA); public administration (MM). Evening/weekend programs available. *Degree requirements:* For master's, thesis (for some programs). *Entrance requirements:* For master's, minimum undergraduate GPA of 3.0, 3 years of work experience. Additional exam requirements/recommendations for international students: Required—TOEFL (minimum score 550 paper-based). Electronic applications accepted.

University of Phoenix–Jersey City Campus, School of Business, Jersey City, NJ 07310. Offers accounting (MBA); business administration (MBA); global management (MBA); human resources management (MBA, MM); management (MM); marketing (MBA); public administration (MBA, MM).

University of Phoenix–Kansas City Campus, School of Business, Kansas City, MO 64131. Offers accounting (MBA); business administration (MBA); global management (MBA); human resources management (MBA, MM); management (MM); marketing (MBA); public administration (MBA). Evening/weekend programs available. *Degree requirements:* For master's, thesis (for some programs). *Entrance requirements:* For master's, minimum undergraduate GPA of 3.0, 3 years of work experience. Additional exam requirements/recommendations for international students: Required—TOEFL (minimum score 550 paper-based). Electronic applications accepted.

University of Phoenix–Las Vegas Campus, School of Business, Las Vegas, NV 89135. Offers accounting (MBA); business administration (MBA); global management (MBA); human resources management (MBA, MM); management (MM); marketing (MBA); public administration (MM). Evening/weekend programs available. Postbaccalaureate distance learning degree programs offered (no on-campus study). *Degree requirements:* For master's, thesis (for some programs). *Entrance requirements:* For master's, minimum undergraduate GPA of 3.0, 3 years of work experience. Additional exam requirements/recommendations for international students: Required—TOEFL (minimum score 550 paper-based; 79 iBT). Electronic applications accepted.

University of Phoenix–Louisiana Campus, School of Business, Metairie, LA 70001-2082. Offers accounting (MBA); business administration (MBA); global management (MBA); human resources management (MBA, MM); management (MM); marketing (MBA); public administration (MBA). Evening/weekend programs available. *Degree requirements:* For master's, thesis (for some programs). *Entrance requirements:* For master's, minimum undergraduate GPA of 3.0, 3 years work experience. Additional exam requirements/recommendations for international students: Required—TOEFL (minimum score 550 paper-based; 79 iBT). Electronic applications accepted.

University of Phoenix–Madison Campus, School of Business, Madison, WI 53718-2416. Offers accounting (MBA); business and management (MBA); e-business (MBA); global management (MBA); human resources management (MBA, MM); management (MM); marketing (MBA); public administration (MBA).

University of Phoenix–Memphis Campus, School of Business, Cordova, TN 38018. Offers accounting (MBA); business and management (MBA); e-business (MBA); global management (MBA); human resources management (MBA, MM); management (MM); marketing (MBA); public administration (MBA, MM).

University of Phoenix–Milwaukee Campus, School of Business, Milwaukee, WI 53224. Offers accounting (MBA); business administration (MBA); energy management (MBA); global management (MBA); health care management (MBA); human resource management (MBA); management (MM); marketing (MBA); project management (MBA); technology management (MBA). Evening/weekend programs available. Postbaccalaureate distance learning degree programs offered. *Entrance requirements:* Additional exam requirements/recommendations for international students: Required—TOEFL, TOEIC (Test of English as an International Communication), Berlitz Online English Proficiency Exam, PTE, or IELTS. Electronic applications accepted. *Expenses:* Contact institution.

University of Phoenix–Minneapolis/St. Louis Park Campus, School of Business, St. Louis Park, MN 55426. Offers accounting (MBA); business administration (MBA); global management (MBA); human resources management (MBA); management (MM); marketing (MBA); public administration (MBA).

University of Phoenix–Nashville Campus, School of Business, Nashville, TN 37214-5048. Offers business administration (MBA); human resources management (MBA); management (MM). Evening/weekend programs available. *Degree requirements:* For master's, thesis (for some programs). *Entrance requirements:* For master's, minimum undergraduate GPA of 3.0, 3 years of work experience. Additional exam requirements/recommendations for international students: Required—TOEFL (minimum score 550 paper-based; 79 iBT). Electronic applications accepted.

University of Phoenix–New Mexico Campus, School of Business, Albuquerque, NM 87113-1570. Offers accounting (MBA); business administration (MBA); global management (MBA); human resources management (MBA, MM); management (MM); marketing (MBA). Evening/weekend programs available. *Degree requirements:* For master's, thesis (for some programs). *Entrance requirements:* For master's, 3 years of work experience, minimum undergraduate GPA of 3.0. Additional exam requirements/recommendations for international students: Required—TOEFL (minimum score 550 paper-based; 79 iBT). Electronic applications accepted.

University of Phoenix–North Florida Campus, School of Business, Jacksonville, FL 32216-0959. Offers accounting (MBA); business administration (MBA); global management (MBA); human resources management (MBA, MM); management (MM); marketing (MBA); public administration (MBA, MM). Evening/weekend programs available. *Degree requirements:* For master's, thesis (for some programs). *Entrance requirements:* For master's, minimum undergraduate GPA of 3.0, 3 years work experience. Additional exam requirements/recommendations for international students: Required—TOEFL (minimum score 550 paper-based; 79 iBT). Electronic applications accepted.

University of Phoenix–Northwest Arkansas Campus, School of Business, Rogers, AR 72756-9615. Offers accounting (MBA); business and management (MBA); global management (MBA); human resources management (MBA, MM); management (MM); marketing (MBA); public administration (MBA, MM).

University of Phoenix–Oklahoma City Campus, School of Business, Oklahoma City, OK 73116-8244. Offers accounting (MBA); business administration (MBA); global management (MBA); human resource management (MBA); management (MM); marketing (MBA). Evening/weekend programs available. *Degree requirements:* For master's, thesis (for some programs). *Entrance requirements:* For master's, minimum undergraduate GPA of 3.0, 3 years of work experience. Additional exam requirements/recommendations for international students: Required—TOEFL (minimum score 550 paper-based; 79 iBT). Electronic applications accepted.

Human Resources Management

University of Phoenix–Omaha Campus, School of Business, Omaha, NE 68154-5240. Offers accounting (MBA); business and management (MBA); global management (MBA); human resources management (MBA, MM); management (MM); marketing (MBA); public administration (MBA, MM).

University of Phoenix–Online Campus, School of Business, Phoenix, AZ 85034-7209. Offers accountancy (MS); accounting (MBA, Certificate); business administration (MBA); energy management (MBA); global management (MBA); health care management (MBA); human resource management (MBA, Certificate); human resources management (MM); management (MM); marketing (MBA, Certificate); project management (MBA, Certificate); public administration (MBA, MM); technology management (MBA). Evening/weekend programs available. Postbaccalaureate distance learning degree programs offered. *Entrance requirements:* Additional exam requirements/recommendations for international students: Required—TOEFL, TOEIC (Test of English as an International Communication), Berlitz Online English Proficiency Exam, PTE, or IELTS. Electronic applications accepted. *Expenses:* Contact institution.

University of Phoenix–Oregon Campus, School of Business, Tigard, OR 97223. Offers accounting (MBA); business administration (MBA); global management (MBA); human resource management (MM); human resources management (MBA); management (MM); marketing (MBA); public administration (MM). Evening/weekend programs available. *Degree requirements:* For master's, thesis (for some programs). *Entrance requirements:* For master's, minimum undergraduate GPA of 3.0, 3 years of work experience. Additional exam requirements/recommendations for international students: Required—TOEFL (minimum score 550 paper-based; 79 iBT). Electronic applications accepted.

University of Phoenix–Philadelphia Campus, School of Business, Wayne, PA 19087-2121. Offers accounting (MBA); business administration (MBA); global management (MBA); human resources management (MBA, MM); management (MM); marketing (MBA); public administration (MM). Evening/weekend programs available. *Degree requirements:* For master's, thesis (for some programs). *Entrance requirements:* For master's, minimum undergraduate GPA of 3.0, 3 years work experience. Additional exam requirements/recommendations for international students: Required—TOEFL (minimum score 550 paper-based; 79 iBT). Electronic applications accepted.

University of Phoenix–Phoenix Campus, School of Business, Tempe, AZ 85282-2371. Offers accounting (MBA, MS, Certificate); business administration (MBA); energy management (MBA); global management (MBA); health care management (MBA); human resource management (MBA, Certificate); management (MM); marketing (MBA); project management (MBA); technology management (MBA). Evening/weekend programs available. Postbaccalaureate distance learning degree programs offered. *Entrance requirements:* Additional exam requirements/recommendations for international students: Required—TOEFL, TOEIC (Test of English as an International Communication), Berlitz Online English Proficiency Exam, PTE, or IELTS. Electronic applications accepted. *Expenses:* Contact institution.

University of Phoenix–Pittsburgh Campus, School of Business, Pittsburgh, PA 15276. Offers accounting (MBA); business administration (MBA); global management (MBA); human resources management (MBA, MM); management (MM); marketing (MBA); public administration (MBA, MM). Evening/weekend programs available. *Degree requirements:* For master's, thesis (for some programs). *Entrance requirements:* For master's, minimum undergraduate GPA of 3.0, 3 years work experience. Additional exam requirements/recommendations for international students: Required—TOEFL (minimum score 550 paper-based; 79 iBT). Electronic applications accepted.

University of Phoenix–Puerto Rico Campus, School of Business, Guaynabo, PR 00968. Offers accounting (MBA); energy management (MBA); global management (MBA); human resource management (MBA); marketing (MBA); project management (MBA); small business administration (MBA). Evening/weekend programs available. *Degree requirements:* For master's, thesis (for some programs). *Entrance requirements:* For master's, minimum undergraduate GPA of 3.0, 3 years work experience. Additional exam requirements/recommendations for international students: Required—TOEFL (minimum score 550 paper-based; 79 iBT). Electronic applications accepted.

University of Phoenix–Richmond-Virginia Beach Campus, School of Business, Glen Allen, VA 23060. Offers accounting (MBA); business administration (MBA); global management (MBA); human resources management (MBA, MM); management (MM); marketing (MBA); public administration (MBA, MM). Evening/weekend programs available. *Degree requirements:* For master's, thesis (for some programs). *Entrance requirements:* For master's, minimum undergraduate GPA of 3.0, 3 years work experience. Additional exam requirements/recommendations for international students: Required—TOEFL (minimum score 550 paper-based; 79 iBT). Electronic applications accepted.

University of Phoenix–Sacramento Valley Campus, School of Business, Sacramento, CA 95833-3632. Offers accounting (MBA); business administration (MBA); global management (MBA); human resources management (MBA, MM); management (MM); marketing (MBA); public administration (MBA, MM). Evening/weekend programs available. *Degree requirements:* For master's, thesis (for some programs). *Entrance requirements:* For master's, minimum undergraduate GPA of 3.0, 3 years work experience. Additional exam requirements/recommendations for international students: Required—TOEFL (minimum score 550 paper-based; 79 iBT). Electronic applications accepted.

University of Phoenix–St. Louis Campus, School of Business, St. Louis, MO 63043. Offers accounting (MBA); business administration (MBA); global management (MBA); human resources management (MBA, MM); management (MM); marketing (MBA); public administration (MM). Evening/weekend programs available. *Degree requirements:* For master's, thesis (for some programs). *Entrance requirements:* For master's, 3 years of work experience, minimum undergraduate GPA of 3.0. Additional exam requirements/recommendations for international students: Required—TOEFL (minimum score 550 paper-based; 79 iBT). Electronic applications accepted.

University of Phoenix–San Antonio Campus, School of Business, San Antonio, TX 78230. Offers accounting (MBA); business administration (MBA); e-business (MBA); global management (MBA); human resources management (MBA, MM); management (MM); marketing (MBA); public administration (MBA, MM).

University of Phoenix–San Diego Campus, School of Business, San Diego, CA 92123. Offers accounting (MBA); business administration (MBA); global management (MBA); human resources management (MBA, MM); management (MM); marketing (MBA); public administration (MBA). Evening/weekend programs available. *Degree requirements:* For master's, thesis (for some programs). *Entrance requirements:* For master's, 3 years of work experience, minimum undergraduate GPA of 3.0. Additional exam requirements/recommendations for international students: Required—TOEFL (minimum score 550 paper-based; 79 iBT). Electronic applications accepted.

University of Phoenix–Savannah Campus, School of Business, Savannah, GA 31405-7400. Offers accounting (MBA); business administration (MBA); global management (MBA); human resources management (MBA, MM); management (MM); marketing (MBA); public administration (MBA, MM).

University of Phoenix–Southern Arizona Campus, School of Business, Tucson, AZ 85711. Offers accountancy (MS); accounting (MBA); business administration (MBA); global management (MBA); human resources management (MBA); management (MM); marketing (MBA). Evening/weekend programs available. *Degree requirements:* For master's, thesis (for some programs). *Entrance requirements:* For master's, minimum undergraduate GPA of 3.0, 3 years of work experience. Additional exam requirements/recommendations for international students: Required—TOEFL (minimum score 550 paper-based; 79 iBT). Electronic applications accepted.

University of Phoenix–Southern California Campus, School of Business, Costa Mesa, CA 92626. Offers accounting (MBA); business administration (MBA); energy management (MBA); global management (MBA); health care management (MBA); human resource management (MBA); management (MM); marketing (MBA); project management (MBA); technology management (MBA). Evening/weekend programs available. Postbaccalaureate distance learning degree programs offered. *Entrance requirements:* Additional exam requirements/recommendations for international students: Required—TOEFL, TOEIC (Test of English as an International Communication), Berlitz Online English Proficiency Exam, PTE, or IELTS. Electronic applications accepted. *Expenses:* Contact institution.

University of Phoenix–Southern Colorado Campus, School of Business, Colorado Springs, CO 80903. Offers accounting (MBA); business administration (MBA); global management (MBA); human resources management (MBA, MM); management (MM); marketing (MBA); public administration (MM). Evening/weekend programs available. *Degree requirements:* For master's, thesis (for some programs). *Entrance requirements:* For master's, minimum undergraduate GPA of 3.0, 3 years of work experience. Additional exam requirements/recommendations for international students: Required—TOEFL (minimum score 550 paper-based; 79 iBT). Electronic applications accepted.

University of Phoenix–South Florida Campus, School of Business, Miramar, FL 33030. Offers accounting (MBA); business administration (MBA); global management (MBA); human resource management (MBA); human resources management (MM); management (MM); marketing (MBA); public administration (MBA, MM). Evening/weekend programs available. *Degree requirements:* For master's, thesis (for some programs). *Entrance requirements:* For master's, minimum undergraduate GPA of 3.0, 3 years work experience. Additional exam requirements/recommendations for international students: Required—TOEFL (minimum score 550 paper-based; 79 iBT). Electronic applications accepted.

University of Phoenix–Springfield Campus, School of Business, Springfield, MO 65804-7211. Offers accounting (MBA); business administration (MBA); global management (MBA); human resources management (MBA, MM); management (MM); marketing (MBA); public administration (MBA, MM).

University of Phoenix–Tulsa Campus, School of Business, Tulsa, OK 74134-1412. Offers accounting (MBA); business (MM); business administration (MBA); global management (MBA); human resources management (MBA); marketing (MBA). Evening/weekend programs available. *Degree requirements:* For master's, thesis (for some programs). *Entrance requirements:* For master's, minimum undergraduate GPA of 3.0, 3 years work experience. Additional exam requirements/recommendations for international students: Required—TOEFL (minimum score 550 paper-based; 79 iBT).

University of Phoenix–Utah Campus, School of Business, Salt Lake City, UT 84123-4617. Offers accounting (MBA); business administration (MBA); global management (MBA); human resource management (MBA, MM); management (MM); marketing (MBA); technology management (MBA). Evening/weekend programs available. *Degree requirements:* For master's, thesis (for some programs). *Entrance requirements:* For master's, minimum undergraduate GPA of 3.0, 3 years of work experience. Additional exam requirements/recommendations for international students: Required—TOEFL (minimum score 550 paper-based; 79 iBT). Electronic applications accepted.

University of Phoenix–Washington D.C. Campus, School of Business, Washington, DC 20001. Offers accountancy (MS); business administration (MBA, DBA); human resources management (MM); management (MM); organizational leadership (DM); public administration (MPA).

University of Phoenix–West Florida Campus, School of Business, Temple Terrace, FL 33637. Offers accounting (MBA); business administration (MBA); global management (MBA); human resources management (MBA, MM); management (MM); marketing (MBA); public administration (MBA, MM). Evening/weekend programs available. *Degree requirements:* For master's, thesis (for some programs). *Entrance requirements:* For master's, 3 years of work experience, minimum undergraduate GPA of 3.0. Additional exam requirements/recommendations for international students: Required—TOEFL (minimum score 550 paper-based; 79 iBT). Electronic applications accepted.

University of Pittsburgh, Katz Graduate School of Business, Doctoral Program in Business Administration, Pittsburgh, PA 15260. Offers accounting (PhD); finance (PhD); information systems (PhD); marketing (PhD); operations/decision sciences/artificial intelligence (PhD); organizational behavior and human resource management (PhD); strategic planning (PhD). *Accreditation:* AACSB. *Faculty:* 60 full-time (17 women). *Students:* 50 full-time (22 women); includes 4 minority (2 Black or African American, non-Hispanic/Latino; 2 Asian, non-Hispanic/Latino), 27 international. 321 applicants, 7% accepted, 14 enrolled. In 2013, 10 doctorates awarded. *Degree requirements:* For doctorate, comprehensive exam, thesis/dissertation. *Entrance requirements:* For doctorate, GMAT or GRE, 3 recommendations, statement of purpose, transcripts of all previous course work and degrees. Additional exam requirements/recommendations for international students: Required—TOEFL. *Application deadline:* For fall admission, 1/1 priority date for domestic and international students. Applications are processed on a rolling basis. Application fee: $50. Electronic applications accepted. *Expenses:* Tuition, state resident: full-time $19,964; part-time $807 per credit. Tuition, nonresident: full-time $32,686; part-time $1337 per credit. *Required fees:* $740; $200. Tuition and fees vary according to program. *Financial support:* In 2013–14, 40 students received support, including 30 research assistantships with full tuition reimbursements available (averaging $23,045 per year), 10 teaching assistantships with full tuition reimbursements available (averaging $26,055 per year); fellowships, Federal Work-Study, scholarships/grants, health care benefits, and unspecified assistantships also available. Financial award application deadline: 1/1. *Faculty research:* Accounting systems/financial reporting, corporate finance, shopper marketing/consumer behavior, management information systems, organizational behavior and entrepreneurship. *Unit head:* Dr. Dennis Galletta, Director, 412-648-1699, Fax: 412-624-3633, E-mail: galletta@katz.pitt.edu. *Application contact:* Carrie Woods, Assistant Director, 412-648-1525, Fax: 412-624-3633, E-mail: cawoods@katz.pitt.edu. Website: http://www.business.pitt.edu/katz/phd/.

University of Pittsburgh, Katz Graduate School of Business, Master of Business Administration Programs, Pittsburgh, PA 15260. Offers finance (MBA); information systems (MBA); marketing (MBA); operations management (MBA); organizational behavior and human resource management (MBA); strategy, environment and organizations (MBA); MBA/JD; MBA/MIB; MBA/MPIA; MBA/MSE; MBA/MSIS; MID/MBA. *Accreditation:* AACSB. Part-time and evening/weekend programs available. *Faculty:* 60 full-time (14 women), 21 part-time/adjunct (5 women). *Students:* 107 full-time

(31 women), 428 part-time (155 women); includes 55 minority (15 Black or African American, non-Hispanic/Latino; 26 Asian, non-Hispanic/Latino; 10 Hispanic/Latino; 4 Two or more races, non-Hispanic/Latino), 83 international. Average age 30. 449 applicants, 23% accepted, 63 enrolled. In 2013, 279 master's awarded. *Degree requirements:* For master's, minimum GPA of 3.0. *Entrance requirements:* For master's, GMAT, recommendations, undergraduate transcripts, essay, resume, interview, bachelor's degree. Additional exam requirements/recommendations for international students: Required—TOEFL (minimum score 600 paper-based; 100 iBT) or IELTS. *Application deadline:* For fall admission, 4/1 priority date for domestic students, 2/1 priority date for international students. Application fee: $50. Electronic applications accepted. *Expenses:* Tuition, state resident: full-time $19,964; part-time $807 per credit. Tuition, nonresident: full-time $32,686; part-time $1337 per credit. *Required fees:* $740; $200. Tuition and fees vary according to program. *Financial support:* In 2013–14, 60 students received support. Career-related internships or fieldwork and scholarships/grants available. Financial award application deadline: 2/1. *Faculty research:* Accounting systems/financial reporting, corporate finance, shopper marketing/consumer behavior, management information systems, organizational behavior and entrepreneurship. *Unit head:* Tim Robison, Assistant Dean, 412-648-1700, Fax: 412-648-1659, E-mail: trobison@katz.pitt.edu. *Application contact:* Thomas Keller, Director of MBA Admissions, 412-648-1700, Fax: 412-648-1659, E-mail: mba@katz.pitt.edu. Website: http://www.business.pitt.edu/katz/mba/.

University of Puerto Rico, Mayagüez Campus, Graduate Studies, College of Business Administration, Mayagüez, PR 00681-9000. Offers business administration (MBA); finance (MBA); human resources (MBA); industrial management (MBA). Part-time and evening/weekend programs available. *Faculty:* 42 full-time (26 women), 1 part-time/adjunct (0 women). *Students:* 36 full-time (18 women), 15 part-time (11 women). 26 applicants, 50% accepted, 10 enrolled. In 2013, 7 master's awarded. *Degree requirements:* For master's, comprehensive exam. *Entrance requirements:* For master's, GMAT or EXADEP, bachelor's degree with courses in calculus, microeconomics, accounting and statistics. Additional exam requirements/recommendations for international students: Required—TOEFL (minimum score 500 paper-based). *Application deadline:* For fall admission, 2/15 for domestic and international students; for spring admission, 9/15 for domestic and international students. Applications are processed on a rolling basis. Application fee: $25. *Expenses: Tuition, area resident:* Full-time $2466; part-time $822 per year. *International tuition:* $6371 full-time. *Required fees:* $1095; $1095. Tuition and fees vary according to course level, course load and reciprocity agreements. *Financial support:* In 2013–14, 7 students received support, including 2 research assistantships (averaging $8,725 per year), 5 teaching assistantships (averaging $4,106 per year); fellowships with full tuition reimbursements available, Federal Work-Study, institutionally sponsored loans, and unspecified assistantships also available. *Faculty research:* Organizational studies, management, accounting. *Total annual research expenditures:* $20,000. *Unit head:* Dr. Ana Martin, Graduate Student Coordinator, 787-832-4040 Ext. 3800, Fax: 787-832-5320, E-mail: ana.martin@upr.edu. *Application contact:* Milagros Soto, Student Administrator, 787-265-3887, Fax: 787-832-5320, E-mail: milagros.soto1@upr.edu. Website: http://enterprise.uprm.edu/.

University of Puerto Rico, Río Piedras Campus, College of Business Administration, San Juan, PR 00931-3300. Offers accounting (MBA); finance (MBA, PhD); general business (MBA); human resources management (MBA); international trade and business (MBA, PhD); marketing (MBA); operations management (MBA); quantitative methods (MBA). Part-time programs available. *Degree requirements:* For master's, comprehensive exam, thesis or alternative, research project. *Entrance requirements:* For master's, GMAT or PAEG, minimum GPA of 3.0, letter of recommendation; for doctorate, GMAT, PAEG, minimum GPA of 3.0, master degree. *Faculty research:* Management.

University of Regina, Faculty of Graduate Studies and Research, Kenneth Levene Graduate School of Business, Program in Human Resources Management, Regina, SK S4S 0A2, Canada. Offers MHRM, Master's Certificate. Part-time programs available. *Faculty:* 39 full-time (14 women), 7 part-time/adjunct (0 women). *Students:* 21 full-time (9 women), 14 part-time (11 women). 60 applicants, 15% accepted. In 2013, 11 master's, 3 other advanced degrees awarded. *Degree requirements:* For master's, project. *Entrance requirements:* For master's, two years of relevant work experience. Additional exam requirements/recommendations for international students: Required—TOEFL (minimum score 580 paper-based; 80 iBT), IELTS (minimum score 6.5). *Application deadline:* Applications are processed on a rolling basis. Application fee: $100. Electronic applications accepted. *Expenses:* Contact institution. *Financial support:* In 2013–14, 1 fellowship (averaging $6,000 per year), 1 teaching assistantship (averaging $2,356 per year) were awarded; research assistantships and scholarships/grants also available. Financial award application deadline: 6/15. *Faculty research:* Human behavior in organizations, labor relations and collective bargaining, organization theory, staffing organizations, human resources systems analysis. *Unit head:* Dr. Andrew Gaudes, Dean, 306-585-4162, Fax: 306-585-5361, E-mail: andrew.gaudes@uregina.ca. *Application contact:* Steve Wield, Manager, Graduate Programs, 306-337-8463, Fax: 306-585-5361, E-mail: steve.wield@uregina.ca. Website: http://www.uregina.ca/business/levene/.

University of Rhode Island, Graduate School, Labor Research Center, Kingston, RI 02881. Offers labor relations and human resources (MS); MS/JD. Part-time and evening/weekend programs available. *Faculty:* 1 full-time (0 women), 3 part-time/adjunct (2 women). *Students:* 9 full-time (6 women), 26 part-time (21 women); includes 7 minority (3 Black or African American, non-Hispanic/Latino; 1 American Indian or Alaska Native, non-Hispanic/Latino; 2 Asian, non-Hispanic/Latino; 1 Two or more races, non-Hispanic/Latino), 1 international. In 2013, 9 master's awarded. *Entrance requirements:* For master's, GRE, MAT, GMAT, or LSAT, 2 letters of recommendation. Additional exam requirements/recommendations for international students: Required—TOEFL (minimum score 550 paper-based). *Application deadline:* For fall admission, 7/15 for domestic students, 2/1 for international students; for spring admission, 11/15 for domestic students, 7/15 for international students. Application fee: $65. Electronic applications accepted. *Expenses:* Tuition, state resident: full-time $11,532; part-time $641 per credit. Tuition, nonresident: full-time $23,606; part-time $1311 per credit. *Required fees:* $1388; $36 per credit. $35 per semester. One-time fee: $130. *Financial support:* Institutionally sponsored loans available. Financial award application deadline: 2/1; financial award applicants required to submit FAFSA. *Unit head:* Dr. Richard Scholl, Director, 401-874-4347, Fax: 401-874-2954, E-mail: rscholl@uri.edu. *Application contact:* Graduate Admission, 401-874-2872, E-mail: gradadm@etal.uri.edu. Website: http://www.uri.edu/research/lrc/.

University of Saint Mary, Graduate Programs, Program in Business Administration, Leavenworth, KS 66048-5082. Offers enterprise risk management (MBA); finance (MBA); general management (MBA); health care management (MBA); human resource management (MBA); marketing and advertising management (MBA). Part-time and evening/weekend programs available. Postbaccalaureate distance learning degree programs offered (no on-campus study). *Students:* 151 full-time (87 women), 61 part-time (39 women); includes 60 minority (38 Black or African American, non-Hispanic/Latino; 1 American Indian or Alaska Native, non-Hispanic/Latino; 10 Asian, non-

Hispanic/Latino; 11 Hispanic/Latino). *Degree requirements:* For master's, thesis. *Entrance requirements:* For master's, minimum undergraduate GPA of 2.75, official transcripts, two letters of recommendation. *Application deadline:* Applications are processed on a rolling basis. Application fee: $25. *Expenses:* Tuition: Part-time $550 per credit hour. *Unit head:* Rick Gunter, Director, 913-319-3007. *Application contact:* Patrick Smith, Coordinator of Business Programs, 913-319-3007, E-mail: smithp@stmary.edu.

The University of Scranton, College of Graduate and Continuing Education, Department of Health Administration and Human Resources, Program in Human Resources Administration, Scranton, PA 18510. Offers human resources (MS); human resources development (MS); organizational leadership (MS). Part-time and evening/weekend programs available. *Students:* 1 (woman) part-time. Average age 39. *Degree requirements:* For master's, capstone experience. *Entrance requirements:* For master's, minimum GPA of 2.75. Additional exam requirements/recommendations for international students: Required—TOEFL (minimum score 500 paper-based), IELTS (minimum score 5.5). *Application deadline:* Applications are processed on a rolling basis. Application fee: $0. *Financial support:* Fellowships, teaching assistantships, career-related internships or fieldwork, Federal Work-Study, and unspecified assistantships available. Support available to part-time students. Financial award application deadline: 3/1. *Unit head:* Dr. Daniel J. West, Director, 570-941-6218, E-mail: westd1@scranton.edu. *Application contact:* Joseph M. Roback, Director of Admissions, 570-941-4385, Fax: 570-941-5928, E-mail: robackj2@scranton.edu.

University of South Carolina, The Graduate School, Darla Moore School of Business, Human Resources Program, Columbia, SC 29208. Offers MHR, JD/MHR. Part-time programs available. *Degree requirements:* For master's, internship. *Entrance requirements:* For master's, GMAT or GRE, minimum GPA of 3.0. Additional exam requirements/recommendations for international students: Required—TOEFL (minimum score 100 iBT); Recommended—IELTS. Electronic applications accepted. *Expenses:* Contact institution. *Faculty research:* Management and compensation, performance appraisal, work values, grievance systems, union formation, group behavior.

The University of South Dakota, Graduate School, College of Arts and Sciences, Program in Administrative Studies, Vermillion, SD 57069-2390. Offers alcohol and drug studies (MSA); criminal justice (MSA); health services administration (MSA); human resource management (MSA); interdisciplinary (MSA); long term care administration (MSA); organizational leadership (MSA). Part-time and evening/weekend programs available. Postbaccalaureate distance learning degree programs offered (no on-campus study). *Degree requirements:* For master's, thesis or alternative. *Entrance requirements:* For master's, 3 years of work or experience, minimum GPA of 2.7, resume. Additional exam requirements/recommendations for international students: Required—TOEFL (minimum score 550 paper-based; 79 iBT). Electronic applications accepted.

The University of Texas at Arlington, Graduate School, College of Business, Department of Management, Arlington, TX 76019. Offers human resources (MSHRM). Part-time and evening/weekend programs available. *Degree requirements:* For master's, thesis optional. *Entrance requirements:* For master's, GMAT/GRE. Additional exam requirements/recommendations for international students: Required—TOEFL (minimum score 550 paper-based; 79 iBT). *Faculty research:* Compensations, training, diversity, strategic human resources.

University of the Sacred Heart, Graduate Programs, Department of Business Administration, Program in Human Resource Management, San Juan, PR 00914-0383. Offers MBA. Part-time and evening/weekend programs available. *Degree requirements:* For master's, thesis. *Entrance requirements:* For master's, EXADEP, minimum undergraduate GPA of 2.75, interview.

University of Toronto, School of Graduate Studies, Faculty of Arts and Science, Centre for Industrial Relations and Human Resources, Toronto, ON M5S 1A1, Canada. Offers MIRHR, PhD. Part-time programs available. *Degree requirements:* For doctorate, thesis/dissertation. *Entrance requirements:* For master's, GRE or GMAT (for applicants who completed degree outside of Canada), minimum B+ in final 2 years of bachelor's degree completion, 2 letters of reference, resume; for doctorate, GRE or GMAT, MIR or equivalent, minimum B+ average, 3 letters of reference, resume. Additional exam requirements/recommendations for international students: Required—TOEFL (minimum score 600 paper-based; 100 iBT), IELTS, TWE (minimum score 5), Michigan English Language Assessment Battery, or COPE. Electronic applications accepted. *Expenses:* Contact institution.

University of Wisconsin–Madison, Graduate School, Wisconsin School of Business, Doctoral Program in Management and Human Resources, Madison, WI 53706-1380. Offers PhD. *Faculty:* 13 full-time (2 women). *Students:* 8 full-time (5 women), 3 international. Average age 31. 38 applicants, 21% accepted, 1 enrolled. In 2013, 2 doctorates awarded. *Degree requirements:* For doctorate, comprehensive exam, thesis/dissertation. *Entrance requirements:* For doctorate, GMAT or GRE. Additional exam requirements/recommendations for international students: Recommended—TOEFL (minimum score 623 paper-based; 106 iBT), IELTS (minimum score 7.5), TSE. *Application deadline:* For fall admission, 12/15 priority date for domestic and international students. Application fee: $56. Electronic applications accepted. *Expenses:* Contact institution. *Financial support:* In 2013–14, 8 students received support, including 1 fellowship with tuition reimbursement available (averaging $19,125 per year), 1 research assistantship with full tuition reimbursement available (averaging $14,746 per year), 6 teaching assistantships with full tuition reimbursements available (averaging $14,088 per year); Federal Work-Study, institutionally sponsored loans, scholarships/grants, health care benefits, and unspecified assistantships also available. Financial award application deadline: 12/15; financial award applicants required to submit FAFSA. *Faculty research:* Employee compensation, performance for work groups, small business management, venture financing, arts industry. *Unit head:* Prof. Randy Dunham, Chair, 608-263-2120, E-mail: rdunham@bus.wisc.edu. *Application contact:* Belle Heberling, Assistant Director for Research Programs, 608-262-3749, Fax: 608-890-0180, E-mail: phd@bus.wisc.edu. Website: http://www.bus.wisc.edu/phd/.

University of Wisconsin–Madison, Graduate School, Wisconsin School of Business, Wisconsin Full-Time MBA Program, Madison, WI 53706. Offers applied security analysis (MBA); arts administration (MBA); brand and product management (MBA); corporate finance and investment banking (MBA); marketing research (MBA); operations and technology management (MBA); real estate (MBA); risk management and insurance (MBA); strategic human resource management (MBA); supply chain management (MBA). *Faculty:* 34 full-time (5 women), 30 part-time/adjunct (15 women). *Students:* 193 full-time (61 women); includes 37 minority (10 Black or African American, non-Hispanic/Latino; 14 Asian, non-Hispanic/Latino; 12 Hispanic/Latino; 1 Native Hawaiian or other Pacific Islander, non-Hispanic/Latino), 37 international. Average age 28. 460 applicants, 33% accepted, 101 enrolled. In 2013, 110 master's awarded. *Degree requirements:* For master's, thesis (for arts administration specialization). *Entrance requirements:* For master's, GMAT or GRE, bachelor's or equivalent degree, 2 years of work experience, letters of recommendation, resume. Additional exam requirements/recommendations for international students: Required—TOEFL (minimum score 600 paper-based; 100 iBT), IELTS. *Application deadline:* For fall admission, 11/5 for domestic and international students; for winter admission, 2/4 for domestic and

international students; for spring admission, 4/28 for domestic students, 4/2 for international students. Applications are processed on a rolling basis. Application fee: $56. Electronic applications accepted. *Expenses:* Contact institution. *Financial support:* In 2013–14, 176 students received support, including 12 fellowships with full tuition reimbursements available (averaging $37,956 per year), 42 research assistantships with full tuition reimbursements available (averaging $28,175 per year), 43 teaching assistantships with full tuition reimbursements available (averaging $28,175 per year); scholarships/grants, health care benefits, and unspecified assistantships also available. Financial award application deadline: 4/26; financial award applicants required to submit FAFSA. *Faculty research:* Market consequences of International Financial Reporting Standards (IFRS), inter-firm relationships and strategic partnerships, application of Bayesian statistical methods and applied probability models to understanding individuals' behaviors in the context of customer relationship management (CRM) applications, liquidity provision and the structure of financial markets, strategic management of global startups. *Unit head:* Prof. Larry W. Hunter, Associate Dean of Master's Programs, 608-265-3494, Fax: 608-265-4192, E-mail: lhunter@bus.wisc.edu. *Application contact:* William H. Wait, Assistant Director of MBA Marketing and Recruiting, 608-262-4000, Fax: 608-265-4192, E-mail: wwait@bus.wisc.edu.
Website: http://www.bus.wisc.edu/mba.

University of Wisconsin–Whitewater, School of Graduate Studies, College of Business and Economics, Program in Business Administration, Whitewater, WI 53190-1790. Offers finance (MBA); human resource management (MBA); information technology management (MBA); international business (MBA); management (MBA); marketing (MBA); operations and supply chain management (MBA). *Accreditation:* AACSB. Part-time and evening/weekend programs available. Postbaccalaureate distance learning degree programs offered (no on-campus study). *Entrance requirements:* For master's, GMAT or GRE, minimum AACSB index of 1000, minimum GPA of 2.75. Additional exam requirements/recommendations for international students: Required—TOEFL (minimum score 550 paper-based; 80 iBT), IELTS (minimum score 6). Electronic applications accepted. *Faculty research:* Interface between social institutions and individual behavior, technology and innovation management, occupational mental health, workplace deviance and workplace romance.

Upper Iowa University, Online Master's Programs, Fayette, IA 52142-1857. Offers accounting (MBA); corporate financial management (MBA); global business (MBA); health and human services (MPA); higher education administration (MHEA); homeland security (MPA); human resources management (MBA); justice administration (MPA); organizational development (MBA); public personnel management (MPA); quality management (MBA). MBA also available at Madison, WI campus. Part-time programs available. Postbaccalaureate distance learning degree programs offered (no on-campus study). *Degree requirements:* For master's, research project. *Entrance requirements:* For master's, GMAT, GRE, or minimum GPA of 2.7 during last 60 hours. Additional exam requirements/recommendations for international students: Required—TOEFL (minimum score 570 paper-based). Electronic applications accepted. *Faculty research:* Total quality management, CQI, teams, organization culture and climate, management.

Utah State University, School of Graduate Studies, College of Business, Program in Human Resource Management, Logan, UT 84322. Offers MS. Part-time and evening/weekend programs available. Postbaccalaureate distance learning degree programs offered. *Entrance requirements:* For master's, GMAT or GRE, minimum GPA of 3.0. Additional exam requirements/recommendations for international students: Required—TOEFL. Electronic applications accepted. *Expenses:* Contact institution. *Faculty research:* International human resources, aging workforce.

Virginia International University, School of Business, Fairfax, VA 22030. Offers accounting (MBA); executive management (Graduate Certificate); global logistics (MBA); health care management (MBA); human resources management (MBA); international business management (MBA); international finance (MBA); marketing management (MBA). Part-time programs available. *Entrance requirements:* For master's and Graduate Certificate, bachelor's degree. Additional exam requirements/recommendations for international students: Required—TOEFL (minimum score 550 paper-based; 80 iBT), IELTS (minimum score 6). Electronic applications accepted.

Walden University, Graduate Programs, School of Management, Minneapolis, MN 55401. Offers accounting (MBA, MS, DBA), including accounting for the professional (MS), accounting with CPA emphasis (MS), self-designed (MS, PhD); accounting and management (MS), including accountants as strategic managers, self-designed (MS, PhD); advanced project management (Graduate Certificate); applied project management (Graduate Certificate); bridge to business administration (Post-Doctoral Certificate); bridge to management (Post-Doctoral Certificate); business administration (EMBA); business management (Graduate Certificate); communication (MS, Graduate Certificate); corporate finance (MBA); entrepreneurship (DBA); entrepreneurship and small business (MBA); finance (DBA); global supply chain management (DBA); healthcare management (MBA, DBA); human resource management (MBA, MS, Graduate Certificate), including functional human resource management (MS), general program (MS), integrating functional and strategic human resource management (MS), organizational strategy (MS); human resources management (DBA); information systems management (DBA); international business (MBA, DBA); leadership (MBA, MS, DBA), including general program (MS), human resources leadership (MS), leader development (MS), self-designed (MS, PhD); management (MS, PhD), including accounting (PhD), engineering management (PhD), finance (PhD), general program (MS), healthcare management (MS), human resource management (MS), human resources management (PhD), information systems management (PhD), leadership (MS), leadership and organizational change (PhD), marketing (MS), operations research (PhD), project management (MS), self-designed, strategy and operations (MS); marketing (MBA, DBA); project management (MBA, MS, DBA); self-designed (MBA, DBA); social impact management (DBA); technology entrepreneurship (DBA). Part-time and evening/weekend programs available. Postbaccalaureate distance learning degree programs offered (minimal on-campus study). *Faculty:* 24 full-time (9 women), 337 part-time/adjunct (127 women). *Students:* 4,369 full-time (2,379 women), 2,181 part-time (1,304 women); includes 3,669 minority (3,020 Black or African American, non-Hispanic/Latino; 22 American Indian or Alaska Native, non-Hispanic/Latino; 156 Asian, non-Hispanic/Latino; 331 Hispanic/Latino; 11 Native Hawaiian or other Pacific Islander, non-Hispanic/Latino; 129 Two or more races, non-Hispanic/Latino), 107 international. Average age 41. 2,030 applicants, 94% accepted, 1436 enrolled. In 2013, 757 master's, 128 doctorates, 32 other advanced degrees awarded. *Degree requirements:* For master's, residency (for some programs); for doctorate, thesis/dissertation (for some programs), residency. *Entrance requirements:* For master's, bachelor's degree or higher; minimum GPA of 2.5; official transcripts; goal statement (for some programs); access to computer and Internet; for doctorate, master's degree or higher; three years of related professional or academic experience (preferred); minimum GPA of 3.0; goal statement and current resume (select programs); official transcripts; access to computer and Internet; for other advanced degree, relevant work experience; access to computer and Internet. Additional exam requirements/recommendations for international students: Required—TOEFL (minimum score 550 paper-based; 79 iBT), IELTS (minimum score 6.5), Michigan English Language Assessment Battery (minimum score 82), or PTE. *Application deadline:* Applications are processed on a rolling basis. Application fee: $0. Electronic applications accepted. *Expenses: Tuition:* Full-time $11,813.55; part-time $500 per credit. *Required fees:* $618.76. *Financial support:* Fellowships, Federal Work-Study, scholarships/grants, unspecified assistantships, and family tuition reduction, active duty/veteran tuition reduction, group tuition reduction, interest-free payment plans, employee tuition reduction available. Support available to part-time students. Financial award applicants required to submit FAFSA. *Unit head:* Dr. Ward Ulmer, III, Associate Dean, 800-925-3368. *Application contact:* Jennifer Hall, Vice President of Enrollment Management, 866-4-WALDEN, E-mail: info@waldenu.edu.
Website: http://www.waldenu.edu/programs/colleges-schools/management.

Wayland Baptist University, Graduate Programs, Program in Education, Plainview, TX 79072-6998. Offers education administration (M Ed); education diagnostics (M Ed); education literacy (M Ed); elementary certification (M Ed); English (M Ed); English as a second language (M Ed); higher education administration (M Ed); human resources (M Ed); instructional leadership (M Ed); instructional technology (M Ed); science education (M Ed); secondary certification (M Ed); social studies (M Ed); special education (M Ed). Part-time and evening/weekend programs available. Postbaccalaureate distance learning degree programs offered (no on-campus study). *Faculty:* 33 full-time (17 women), 28 part-time/adjunct (17 women). *Students:* 22 full-time (15 women), 316 part-time (189 women); includes 130 minority (48 Black or African American, non-Hispanic/Latino; 3 American Indian or Alaska Native, non-Hispanic/Latino; 71 Hispanic/Latino; 1 Native Hawaiian or other Pacific Islander, non-Hispanic/Latino; 7 Two or more races, non-Hispanic/Latino). Average age 39. 80 applicants, 96% accepted, 44 enrolled. In 2013, 170 master's awarded. *Degree requirements:* For master's, comprehensive exam, capstone course. *Entrance requirements:* For master's, GRE, GMAT or MAT. Additional exam requirements/recommendations for international students: Required—TOEFL (minimum score 500 paper-based; 61 iBT). *Application deadline:* Applications are processed on a rolling basis. Application fee: $50. Electronic applications accepted. *Expenses: Tuition:* Full-time $8190; part-time $455 per credit hour. *Required fees:* $970; $455 per credit hour. $485 per semester. *Financial support:* Federal Work-Study, institutionally sponsored loans, and scholarships/grants available. Support available to part-time students. Financial award application deadline: 5/1; financial award applicants required to submit FAFSA. *Unit head:* Dr. Jim Todd, Chairman, 806-291-1045, Fax: 806-291-1951. *Application contact:* Amanda Stanton, Coordinator of Graduate Studies, 806-291-3423, Fax: 806-291-1950, E-mail: stanton@wbu.edu.

Wayland Baptist University, Graduate Programs, Programs in Business Administration/Management, Plainview, TX 79072-6998. Offers accounting (MBA); general business (MBA); health care administration (MAM, MBA); healthcare administration (MBA); human resource management (MAM, MBA); international management (MBA); management (MBA); management information systems (MBA); organization management (MAM); project management (MBA). Part-time and evening/weekend programs available. Postbaccalaureate distance learning degree programs offered (no on-campus study). *Faculty:* 30 full-time (5 women), 38 part-time/adjunct (9 women). *Students:* 44 full-time (20 women), 702 part-time (315 women); includes 348 minority (149 Black or African American, non-Hispanic/Latino; 4 American Indian or Alaska Native, non-Hispanic/Latino; 23 Asian, non-Hispanic/Latino; 139 Hispanic/Latino; 9 Native Hawaiian or other Pacific Islander, non-Hispanic/Latino; 24 Two or more races, non-Hispanic/Latino), 5 international. Average age 40. 147 applicants, 94% accepted, 73 enrolled. In 2013, 296 master's awarded. *Degree requirements:* For master's, capstone course. *Entrance requirements:* For master's, GMAT, GRE or MAT. Additional exam requirements/recommendations for international students: Required—TOEFL (minimum score 500 paper-based; 61 iBT). *Application deadline:* Applications are processed on a rolling basis. Application fee: $50. Electronic applications accepted. *Expenses: Tuition:* Full-time $8190; part-time $455 per credit hour. *Required fees:* $970; $455 per credit hour. $485 per semester. *Financial support:* Federal Work-Study, institutionally sponsored loans, and scholarships/grants available. Support available to part-time students. Financial award application deadline: 5/1; financial award applicants required to submit FAFSA. *Unit head:* Dr. Otto Schacht, Chairman, 806-291-1020, Fax: 806-291-1957, E-mail: schachto@wbu.edu. *Application contact:* Amanda Stanton, Graduate Studies, 806-291-3423, Fax: 806-291-1950, E-mail: stanton@wbu.edu.

Waynesburg University, Graduate and Professional Studies, Canonsburg, PA 15370. Offers business (MBA), including energy management, finance, health systems, human resources, leadership, market development; counseling (MA), including addictions counseling, clinical mental health; education (M Ed, MAT), including autism (M Ed), curriculum and instruction (M Ed), educational leadership (M Ed), online teaching (M Ed); nursing (MSN), including administration, education, informatics; nursing practice (DNP); special education (M Ed); technology (M Ed); MSN/MBA. *Accreditation:* AACN. Part-time and evening/weekend programs available. *Faculty:* 11 full-time (5 women), 136 part-time/adjunct (80 women). *Students:* 146 full-time (99 women), 419 part-time (268 women). In 2013, 290 master's, 7 doctorates awarded. *Degree requirements:* For doctorate, thesis/dissertation. *Entrance requirements:* Additional exam requirements/recommendations for international students: Required—TOEFL. *Application deadline:* For fall admission, 8/1 priority date for domestic students. Applications are processed on a rolling basis. Electronic applications accepted. *Financial support:* Available to part-time students. Application deadline: 5/1. *Unit head:* David Mariner, Dean, 724-743-4420, Fax: 724-743-4425, E-mail: dmariner@waynesburg.edu. *Application contact:* Dr. Michael Bednarski, Director of Enrollment, 724-743-4420, Fax: 724-743-4425, E-mail: mbednars@waynesburg.edu.
Website: http://www.waynesburg.edu/.

Wayne State University, College of Liberal Arts and Sciences, Department of Economics, Detroit, MI 48202. Offers health economics (MA, PhD); industrial organization (MA, PhD); international economics (MA, PhD); labor and human resources (MA, PhD); JD/MA. *Faculty:* 13 full-time (3 women). *Students:* 49 full-time (20 women), 11 part-time (3 women); includes 13 minority (7 Black or African American, non-Hispanic/Latino; 5 Asian, non-Hispanic/Latino; 1 Hispanic/Latino), 26 international. Average age 32. 80 applicants, 44% accepted, 14 enrolled. In 2013, 14 master's, 6 doctorates awarded. *Degree requirements:* For master's, comprehensive exam, thesis optional; for doctorate, thesis/dissertation, oral examination on research, completion of course work in quantitative methods. *Entrance requirements:* For master's, minimum upper-division GPA of 3.0, prior coursework in intermediate microeconomic and macroeconomic theory, statistics, and elementary calculus; for doctorate, GRE, minimum upper-division GPA of 3.0, prior coursework in intermediate microeconomic and macroeconomic theory, statistics, two courses in calculus, three letters of recommendation from officials or teaching staff at institution(s) most recently attended. Additional exam requirements/recommendations for international students: Required—TOEFL (minimum score 550 paper-based; 79 iBT), TWE (minimum score 5.5), Michigan English Language Assessment Battery (minimum score 85); Recommended—IELTS (minimum score 6.5). *Application deadline:* For fall admission, 6/1 priority date for domestic students, 5/1 priority date for international students; for winter admission, 10/1 priority date for domestic students, 9/1 priority date for international students; for spring admission, 2/1 priority date for domestic students, 1/1 priority date for international students. Applications are processed on a rolling basis. Application fee: $0. Electronic applications accepted. *Expenses:* Tuition, state resident: part-time $554.15 per credit. Tuition, nonresident: part-time $1200.35 per credit. *Required fees:* $42.15 per credit.

$268.30 per semester. Tuition and fees vary according to course load and program. *Financial support:* In 2013–14, 22 students received support, including 2 fellowships with tuition reimbursements available (averaging $16,842 per year), 17 teaching assistantships with tuition reimbursements available (averaging $16,508 per year); research assistantships with tuition reimbursements available, scholarships/grants, health care benefits, and unspecified assistantships also available. Support available to part-time students. Financial award application deadline: 3/31; financial award applicants required to submit FAFSA. *Faculty research:* Health economics, international economics, macro economics, urban and labor economics, econometrics. *Unit head:* Dr. Stephen J. Spurr, Interim Chair, 313-577-3345, Fax: 313-577-9564, E-mail: sspurr@wayne.edu. *Application contact:* Dr. Allen Charles Goodman, Graduate Director, 313-577-3235, Fax: 313-577-9564, E-mail: allen.goodman@wayne.edu.
Website: http://clasweb.clas.wayne.edu/economics.

Wayne State University, College of Liberal Arts and Sciences, Department of Political Science, Program in Public Administration, Detroit, MI 48202. Offers aging policy and management (MPA); criminal justice policy and management (MPA); economic development policy and management (MPA); health and human services policy and management (MPA); human and fiscal resource management (MPA); information technology management (MPA); nonprofit policy and management (MPA); organizational behavior and management (MPA); public budgeting and financial management (MPA); public policy analysis and program evaluation (MPA); social welfare policy and management (MPA); urban and metropolitan policy and management (MPA). *Accreditation:* NASPAA. Evening/weekend programs available. *Students:* 11 full-time (5 women), 55 part-time (43 women); includes 20 minority (14 Black or African American, non-Hispanic/Latino; 2 Asian, non-Hispanic/Latino; 2 Hispanic/Latino; 2 Two or more races, non-Hispanic/Latino), 1 international. Average age 33. 83 applicants, 34% accepted, 17 enrolled. In 2013, 19 master's awarded. *Degree requirements:* For master's, comprehensive exam. *Entrance requirements:* For master's, GRE General Test, minimum undergraduate upper-division GPA of 3.0 or master's degree. Additional exam requirements/recommendations for international students: Required—TOEFL (minimum score 550 paper-based; 79 iBT), TWE (minimum score 5.5), Michigan English Language Assessment Battery (minimum score 85); Recommended—IELTS (minimum score 6.5). *Application deadline:* For fall admission, 6/1 priority date for domestic students, 5/1 priority date for international students; for winter admission, 10/1 priority date for domestic students, 9/1 priority date for international students; for spring admission, 2/1 priority date for domestic students, 1/1 priority date for international students. Applications are processed on a rolling basis. Application fee: $0. Electronic applications accepted. *Expenses:* Tuition, state resident: part-time $554.15 per credit. Tuition, nonresident: part-time $1200.35 per credit. *Required fees:* $42.15 per credit. $268.30 per semester. Tuition and fees vary according to course load and program. *Financial support:* In 2013–14, 21 students received support. Fellowships, teaching assistantships, scholarships/grants, and unspecified assistantships available. Financial award application deadline: 3/31; financial award applicants required to submit FAFSA. *Faculty research:* Urban politics, urban education, state administration. *Unit head:* Dr. Daniel Geller, Department Chair, 313-577-6328, E-mail: dgeller@wayne.edu. *Application contact:* Dr. Brady Baybeck, Associate Professor/Director, Graduate Program in Public Administration, E-mail: mpa@wayne.edu.
Website: http://clasweb.clas.wayne.edu/mpa.

Wayne State University, College of Liberal Arts and Sciences, Program in Employment and Labor Relations, Detroit, MI 48202. Offers MA. *Students:* 6 full-time (4 women), 27 part-time (17 women); includes 18 minority (14 Black or African American, non-Hispanic/Latino; 2 Asian, non-Hispanic/Latino; 1 Hispanic/Latino; 1 Two or more races, non-Hispanic/Latino), 1 international. Average age 38. 20 applicants, 60% accepted, 7 enrolled. In 2013, 11 master's awarded. *Entrance requirements:* For master's, GRE or GMAT, three letters of recommendation written by former college or university professors and/or current employers, baccalaureate degree from accredited institution. Additional exam requirements/recommendations for international students: Required—TOEFL (minimum score 550 paper-based; 79 iBT), IELTS (minimum score 6.5), Michigan English Language Assessment Battery (minimum score 85). *Application deadline:* For fall admission, 6/1 priority date for domestic students, 5/1 priority date for international students; for winter admission, 10/1 priority date for domestic students, 9/1 priority date for international students; for spring admission, 2/1 priority date for domestic students, 1/1 priority date for international students. Applications are processed on a rolling basis. Application fee: $0. Electronic applications accepted. *Expenses:* Tuition, state resident: part-time $554.15 per credit. Tuition, nonresident: part-time $1200.35 per credit. *Required fees:* $42.15 per credit. $268.30 per semester. Tuition and fees vary according to course load and program. *Financial support:* In 2013–14, 3 students received support. Scholarships/grants available. Financial award application deadline: 3/31; financial award applicants required to submit FAFSA. *Total annual research expenditures:* $76,303. *Unit head:* Marick Masters, Director, 313-577-5358, E-mail: marickm@wayne.edu. *Application contact:* Linda Johnson, Academic Services Officer, 313-577-0175, E-mail: ab1232@wayne.edu.
Website: http://www.clas.wayne.edu/maelr/.

Webster University, George Herbert Walker School of Business and Technology, Department of Business, St. Louis, MO 63119-3194. Offers business and organizational security management (MBA); decision support systems (MBA); environmental management (MBA); finance (MBA, MS); forensic accounting (MS); gerontology (MBA); human resources development (MBA); human resources management (MBA); information technology management (MBA); international business (MA, MBA); international relations (MBA); management and leadership (MBA); marketing (MBA); media communications (MBA); procurement and acquisitions management (MBA); Web services (MBA). *Accreditation:* ACBSP. Part-time and evening/weekend programs available. Postbaccalaureate distance learning degree programs offered (no on-campus study). *Degree requirements:* For master's, comprehensive exam (for some programs), thesis (for some programs). *Entrance requirements:* Additional exam requirements/recommendations for international students: Required—TOEFL. *Expenses: Tuition:* Full-time $11,610; part-time $645 per credit hour. Tuition and fees vary according to campus/location and program.

Webster University, George Herbert Walker School of Business and Technology, Department of Management, St. Louis, MO 63119-3194. Offers business and organizational security management (MA); health administration (MHA); health care management (MA); health services management (MA); human resources development (MA); human resources management (MA); information technology management (MS); management and leadership (MA); marketing (MA); nonprofit leadership (MA); procurement and acquisitions management (MA); public administration (MPA); space systems operations management (MS). Part-time and evening/weekend programs available. Postbaccalaureate distance learning degree programs offered (no on-campus study). *Degree requirements:* For master's, thesis (for some programs). *Entrance requirements:* Additional exam requirements/recommendations for international students: Required—TOEFL. *Expenses: Tuition:* Full-time $11,610; part-time $645 per credit hour. Tuition and fees vary according to campus/location and program.

West Chester University of Pennsylvania, College of Business and Public Affairs, Department of Public Policy and Administration, West Chester, PA 19383. Offers general public administration (MPA); human resource management (MPA, Certificate); non profit administration (Certificate); nonprofit administration (MPA); public administration (Certificate). Part-time and evening/weekend programs available. *Faculty:* 6 full-time (3 women), 3 part-time/adjunct (0 women). *Students:* 58 full-time (37 women), 94 part-time (54 women); includes 55 minority (44 Black or African American, non-Hispanic/Latino; 3 Asian, non-Hispanic/Latino; 8 Hispanic/Latino), 3 international. Average age 29. 84 applicants, 88% accepted, 52 enrolled. In 2013, 54 master's, 8 other advanced degrees awarded. *Degree requirements:* For master's, capstone project. *Entrance requirements:* For master's and Certificate, statement of professional goals, resume, two letters of reference, academic transcripts. Additional exam requirements/recommendations for international students: Required—TOEFL (minimum score 550 paper-based; 80 iBT). *Application deadline:* For fall admission, 4/15 priority date for domestic students, 3/15 for international students; for spring admission, 10/15 priority date for domestic students, 9/1 for international students. Applications are processed on a rolling basis. Application fee: $45. Electronic applications accepted. *Expenses:* Tuition, state resident: full-time $7956; part-time $442 per credit. Tuition, nonresident: full-time $11,934; part-time $663 per credit. *Required fees:* $2134.20; $106.24 per credit. Tuition and fees vary according to campus/location and program. *Financial support:* Unspecified assistantships available. Support available to part-time students. Financial award application deadline: 2/15; financial award applicants required to submit FAFSA. *Faculty research:* Public policy, economic development, research methodology, urban politics, public administration. *Unit head:* Dr. Jeffery Osgoods, Department Chair and Graduate Coordinator, 610-436-2286, E-mail: josgood@wcupa.edu.
Website: http://www.wcupa.edu/_ACADEMICS/sch_sba/g-mpa.html.

Widener University, School of Business Administration, Program in Human Resource Management, Chester, PA 19013-5792. Offers MHR, MS, Psy D/MHR. Part-time and evening/weekend programs available. *Faculty:* 5 full-time (1 woman), 5 part-time/adjunct (3 women). *Students:* 38 applicants, 87% accepted. In 2013, 3 master's awarded. *Entrance requirements:* For master's, GMAT, GRE, or MAT, minimum GPA of 2.5. *Application deadline:* For fall admission, 8/1 priority date for domestic students; for spring admission, 12/1 for domestic students. Applications are processed on a rolling basis. Application fee: $25 ($300 for international students). Electronic applications accepted. *Expenses: Tuition:* Full-time $30,000; part-time $950 per credit. *Financial support:* Research assistantships and Federal Work-Study available. Support available to part-time students. Financial award application deadline: 5/1. *Faculty research:* Training and development, collective bargaining and arbitration, business communication. *Unit head:* Dr. Caryl Carpenter, Director, 610-499-4109. *Application contact:* Ann Seltzer, Graduate Enrollment Administrator, 610-499-4305, E-mail: apseltzer@widener.edu.

Wilfrid Laurier University, Faculty of Graduate and Postdoctoral Studies, School of Business and Economics, Department of Business, Waterloo, ON N2L 3C5, Canada. Offers accounting (PhD); finance (M Fin); financial economics (PhD); marketing (PhD); operations and supply chain management (PhD); organizational behavior and human resource management (M Sc); organizational behaviour and human resource management (PhD); supply chain management (M Sc); technology management (EMTM). *Accreditation:* AACSB. Part-time and evening/weekend programs available. *Degree requirements:* For master's, thesis optional; for doctorate, comprehensive exam, thesis/dissertation. *Entrance requirements:* For master's, GMAT, 4-year honors degree with minimum B+ average; for doctorate, GMAT, master's degree, minimum B+ average. Additional exam requirements/recommendations for international students: Required—TOEFL (minimum score 89 iBT). Electronic applications accepted. *Faculty research:* Financial economics, management and organizational behavior, operations and supply chain management.

Wilkes University, College of Graduate and Professional Studies, Jay S. Sidhu School of Business and Leadership, Wilkes-Barre, PA 18766-0002. Offers accounting (MBA); entrepreneurship (MBA); finance (MBA); health care administration (MBA); human resource management (MBA); international business (MBA); marketing (MBA); operations management (MBA); organizational leadership and development (MBA). *Accreditation:* ACBSP. Part-time and evening/weekend programs available. *Students:* 41 full-time (20 women), 119 part-time (48 women); includes 20 minority (5 Black or African American, non-Hispanic/Latino; 3 Asian, non-Hispanic/Latino; 7 Hispanic/Latino; 5 Two or more races, non-Hispanic/Latino), 7 international. Average age 31. In 2013, 55 master's awarded. *Entrance requirements:* For master's, GMAT. Additional exam requirements/recommendations for international students: Required—TOEFL (minimum score 550 paper-based; 79 iBT). *Application deadline:* Applications are processed on a rolling basis. Application fee: $45 ($65 for international students). Electronic applications accepted. *Expenses:* Contact institution. *Financial support:* Federal Work-Study and unspecified assistantships available. Financial award application deadline: 3/1; financial award applicants required to submit FAFSA. *Unit head:* Dr. Jeffrey Alves, Dean, 570-408-4702, Fax: 570-408-7846, E-mail: jeffrey.alves@wilkes.edu. *Application contact:* Joanne Thomas, Interim Director of Graduate Enrollment, 570-408-4234, Fax: 570-408-7846, E-mail: joanne.thomas1@wilkes.edu.
Website: http://www.wilkes.edu/pages/457.asp.

Wilmington University, College of Business, New Castle, DE 19720-6491. Offers accounting (MBA, MS); business administration (MBA, DBA); environmental stewardship (MBA); finance (MBA); health care administration (MBA, MSM); homeland security (MBA, MSM); human resource management (MSM); management information systems (MBA, MSN); marketing (MSM); marketing management (MBA); military leadership (MSM); organizational leadership (MBA, MSM); public administration (MSM). Part-time and evening/weekend programs available. *Entrance requirements:* Additional exam requirements/recommendations for international students: Required—TOEFL (minimum score 500 paper-based). Electronic applications accepted.

York University, Faculty of Graduate Studies, Atkinson Faculty of Liberal and Professional Studies, Program in Human Resources Management, Toronto, ON M3J 1P3, Canada. Offers MHRM, PhD. Part-time programs available. *Degree requirements:* For master's, thesis or alternative. *Entrance requirements:* Additional exam requirements/recommendations for international students: Required—TOEFL (minimum score 600 paper-based). Electronic applications accepted.

Section 9
Industrial and Manufacturing Management

This section contains a directory of institutions offering graduate work in industrial and manufacturing management. Additional information about programs listed in the directory but not augmented by an in-depth entry may be obtained by writing directly to the dean of a graduate school or chair of a department at the address given in the directory.

For programs offering related work, see also in this book *Business Administration and Management* and *Human Resources.* In another guide in this series:

Graduate Programs in the Humanities, Arts & Social Sciences
See *Public, Regional, and Industrial Affairs (Industrial* and *Labor Relations)*

CONTENTS

Program Directory

Industrial and Manufacturing Management   392

Display and Close-Up

See:

University of California, Los Angeles—Business
   Administration and Management   145, 191

Industrial and Manufacturing Management

American InterContinental University Online, Program in Business Administration, Schaumburg, IL 60173. Offers accounting and finance (MBA); finance (MBA); healthcare management (MBA); human resource management (MBA); international business (MBA); management (MBA); marketing (MBA); operations management (MBA); organizational psychology and development (MBA); project management (MBA). *Accreditation:* ACBSP. Evening/weekend programs available. Postbaccalaureate distance learning degree programs offered (no on-campus study). *Entrance requirements:* Additional exam requirements/recommendations for international students: Required—TOEFL (minimum score 550 paper-based). Electronic applications accepted.

The American University in Cairo, School of Sciences and Engineering, Department of Mechanical Engineering, Cairo, Egypt. Offers mechanical engineering (MS); product development and systems management (M Eng). Tuition and fees vary according to course level, course load and program.

Baruch College of the City University of New York, Zicklin School of Business, Department of Management, New York, NY 10010-5585. Offers entrepreneurship (MBA); management (PhD); operations management (MBA); organizational behavior/human resources management (MBA); sustainable business (MBA). PhD offered jointly with Graduate School and University Center of the City University of New York. Part-time and evening/weekend programs available. *Degree requirements:* For doctorate, comprehensive exam, thesis/dissertation. *Entrance requirements:* For master's, GMAT, 2 letters of recommendation, resume, 2 years of work experience; for doctorate, GMAT. Additional exam requirements/recommendations for international students: Required—TOEFL (minimum score 590 paper-based), TWE.

California Polytechnic State University, San Luis Obispo, Orfalea College of Business, Department of Business and Technology, San Luis Obispo, CA 93407. Offers MS. Part-time programs available. *Faculty:* 2 full-time (0 women). *Students:* 1 (woman) full-time, 1 part-time (0 women); includes 1 minority (Two or more races, non-Hispanic/Latino). Average age 23. *Degree requirements:* For master's, thesis or alternative. *Entrance requirements:* For master's, GRE General Test or GMAT, minimum GPA of 2.8 in last 90 quarter units of course work, 2 letters of recommendation. Additional exam requirements/recommendations for international students: Required—TOEFL (minimum score 550 paper-based) or IELTS (minimum score 6). *Application deadline:* For fall admission, 7/1 for domestic students, 11/30 for international students. Applications are processed on a rolling basis. Application fee: $55. Electronic applications accepted. *Financial support:* Career-related internships or fieldwork, Federal Work-Study, institutionally sponsored loans, and scholarships/grants available. Support available to part-time students. Financial award application deadline: 3/2; financial award applicants required to submit FAFSA. *Faculty research:* Valve chain management, packing science and technology, technology entrepreneurship and innovation, industrial processes and systems. *Unit head:* Dr. Bradford Anderson, Graduate Coordinator, 805-756-5210, Fax: 805-756-6111, E-mail: bpanders@calpoly.edu. *Application contact:* Dr. Bradford Anderson, Graduate Coordinator, 805-756-5219, Fax: 805-756-0110, E-mail: bpanders@calpoly.edu.

California State University, East Bay, Office of Academic Programs and Graduate Studies, College of Business and Economics, Program in Information Technology Management, Option in Operations and Supply Chain Management, Hayward, CA 94542-3000. Offers MBA. *Degree requirements:* For master's, comprehensive exam or thesis. *Entrance requirements:* For master's, GMAT, minimum GPA of 2.75. Additional exam requirements/recommendations for international students: Required—TOEFL (minimum score 550 paper-based). Electronic applications accepted.

Carnegie Mellon University, Carnegie Institute of Technology and School of Design, Program in Product Development, Pittsburgh, PA 15213-3891. Offers MPD. *Entrance requirements:* For master's, GRE General Test, undergraduate degree in engineering, industrial design, or related fields, 3 letters of reference, 2 years of professional experience. Additional exam requirements/recommendations for international students: Required—TOEFL or TSE.

Carnegie Mellon University, College of Fine Arts, School of Design, Pittsburgh, PA 15213-3891. Offers communication planning and information design (M Des); design (PhD); design theory (PhD); interaction design (M Des, PhD); new product development (PhD); product development (MPD); typography and information design (PhD). *Accreditation:* NASAD.

Carnegie Mellon University, Tepper School of Business, Program in Management of Manufacturing and Automation, Pittsburgh, PA 15213-3891. Offers PhD. *Degree requirements:* For doctorate, thesis/dissertation.

Case Western Reserve University, Weatherhead School of Management, Department of Operations, Cleveland, OH 44106. Offers management (MS, MSM), including finance (MS), information systems (MS), marketing (MS), operations research, quality management (MS), supply chain (MSM); management for liberal arts graduates (MSM); operations research (PhD); MBA/MSM. Part-time programs available. *Degree requirements:* For doctorate, thesis/dissertation. *Entrance requirements:* For master's, GRE General Test; for doctorate, GMAT, GRE General Test. *Faculty research:* Mathematical finance, mathematical programming, scheduling, stochastic optimization, environmental/energy models.

Central Connecticut State University, School of Graduate Studies, School of Technology, Department of Manufacturing and Construction Management, New Britain, CT 06050-4010. Offers construction management (MS, Certificate); lean manufacturing and Six Sigma (Certificate); supply chain and logistics (Certificate); technology management (MS). Part-time and evening/weekend programs available. *Faculty:* 7 full-time (1 woman), 5 part-time/adjunct (0 women). *Students:* 23 full-time (5 women), 88 part-time (21 women); includes 24 minority (12 Black or African American, non-Hispanic/Latino; 8 Asian, non-Hispanic/Latino; 3 Hispanic/Latino; 1 Two or more races, non-Hispanic/Latino), 8 international. Average age 34. 63 applicants, 67% accepted, 28 enrolled. In 2013, 39 master's awarded. *Degree requirements:* For master's, comprehensive exam, thesis or alternative; for Certificate, qualifying exam. *Entrance requirements:* For master's, minimum undergraduate GPA of 2.7. Additional exam requirements/recommendations for international students: Required—TOEFL (minimum score 550 paper-based; 79 iBT). *Application deadline:* For fall admission, 6/1 for domestic students, 5/1 for international students; for spring admission, 11/1 for domestic and international students. Applications are processed on a rolling basis. Application fee: $50. Electronic applications accepted. Part-time tuition and fees vary according to degree level. *Financial support:* In 2013–14, 4 students received support, including 4 research assistantships; career-related internships or fieldwork, Federal Work-Study, scholarships/grants, and unspecified assistantships also available. Support available to part-time students. Financial award application deadline: 3/1; financial award applicants

required to submit FAFSA. *Faculty research:* All aspects of middle management, technical supervision in the workplace. *Unit head:* Dr. Jacob Kovel, Chair, 860-832-1830, E-mail: kovelj@ccsu.edu. *Application contact:* Patricia Gardner, Associate Director of Graduate Studies, 860-832-2350, Fax: 860-832-2362, E-mail: graduateadmissions@ccsu.edu.
Website: http://www.ccsu.edu/page.cfm?p=6497.

Central Michigan University, College of Graduate Studies, College of Science and Technology, School of Engineering and Technology, Mount Pleasant, MI 48859. Offers industrial management and technology (MA). Part-time programs available. *Degree requirements:* For master's, thesis or alternative. Electronic applications accepted. *Faculty research:* Computer applications, manufacturing process control, mechanical engineering automation, industrial technology.

Cleveland State University, College of Graduate Studies, Monte Ahuja College of Business, Doctor of Business Administration Program, Cleveland, OH 44115. Offers finance (DBA); global business (DBA); information systems (DBA); marketing (DBA); operations management (DBA). *Accreditation:* AACSB. Part-time and evening/weekend programs available. *Faculty:* 50 full-time (11 women). *Students:* 36 part-time (18 women); includes 6 minority (2 Black or African American, non-Hispanic/Latino; 4 Asian, non-Hispanic/Latino), 8 international. Average age 39. 96 applicants, 27% accepted, 6 enrolled. In 2013, 1 doctorate awarded. *Degree requirements:* For doctorate, comprehensive exam, thesis/dissertation, oral dissertation defense. *Entrance requirements:* For doctorate, GMAT, MBA or equivalent. Additional exam requirements/recommendations for international students: Required—TOEFL (minimum score 550 paper-based; 79 iBT). *Application deadline:* For spring admission, 2/28 priority date for domestic and international students. Application fee: $30. Electronic applications accepted. *Expenses:* Tuition, state resident: full-time $8335; part-time $521 per credit hour. Tuition, nonresident: full-time $15,670; part-time $979 per credit hour. *Required fees:* $50; $25 per semester. *Financial support:* In 2013–14, 5 research assistantships with full tuition reimbursements (averaging $12,700 per year), 4 teaching assistantships with full tuition reimbursements (averaging $12,700 per year) were awarded; tuition waivers (full) and unspecified assistantships also available. *Faculty research:* Supply chain management, international business, strategic management, risk analysis, consumer behavior. *Unit head:* Dr. Raj Shekhar G. Javalgi, Director, 216-687-3786, Fax: 216-687-9354, E-mail: r.javalgi@csuohio.edu. *Application contact:* Melinda J. Arnold, Administrative Secretary, 216-687-6952, Fax: 216-687-9257, E-mail: m.arnold@csuohio.edu.
Website: http://www.csuohio.edu/business/academics/doctoral.html.

Colorado Technical University Colorado Springs, Graduate Studies, Program in Management, Colorado Springs, CO 80907-3896. Offers accounting (MBA, MSA); business administration (MBA); finance (MBA); human resources management (MBA); logistics/supply chain management (MBA); management (DM); marketing (MBA); mediation and dispute resolution (MBA); operations management (MBA); project management (MBA); technology management (MBA). Part-time and evening/weekend programs available. Postbaccalaureate distance learning degree programs offered. *Degree requirements:* For master's, thesis or alternative; for doctorate, thesis/dissertation. *Entrance requirements:* For doctorate, minimum graduate GPA of 3.0, 5 years of related work experience. *Faculty research:* Sexual harassment, performance evaluation, critical thinking.

Colorado Technical University Denver South, Programs in Business Administration and Management, Aurora, CO 80014. Offers accounting (MBA); business administration (MBA); business administration and management (EMBA); finance (MBA); human resource management (MBA); marketing (MBA); mediation and dispute resolution (MBA); operations management (MBA); project management (MBA); technology management (MBA). Part-time and evening/weekend programs available. *Degree requirements:* For master's, thesis or alternative. *Entrance requirements:* For master's, minimum undergraduate GPA of 3.0, resume.

DePaul University, Charles H. Kellstadt Graduate School of Business, Chicago, IL 60604. Offers accountancy (M Acc, MS, MSA); applied economics (MBA); banking (MBA); behavioral finance (MBA); brand and product management (MBA); business development (MBA); business information technology (MS); business strategy and decision-making (MBA); computational finance (MS); consumer insights (MBA); corporate finance (MBA); economic policy analysis (MS); entrepreneurship (MBA, MS); finance (MBA, MS); financial analysis (MBA); general business (MBA); health sector management (MBA); hospitality leadership (MBA); hospitality leadership and operational performance (MS); human resource management (MBA); human resources (MS); investment management (MBA); leadership and change management (MBA); management accounting (MBA); marketing (MBA, MS); marketing analysis (MS); marketing strategy and planning (MBA); operations management (MBA); organizational diversity (MBA); real estate (MS); real estate finance and investment (MBA); revenue management (MBA); sports management (MBA); strategic global marketing (MBA); strategy, execution and valuation (MBA); sustainable management (MBA, MS); taxation (MS); wealth management (MS); JD/MBA. *Accreditation:* AACSB. Part-time and evening/weekend programs available. Postbaccalaureate distance learning degree programs offered (no on-campus study). *Faculty:* 81 full-time (20 women), 45 part-time/adjunct (8 women). *Students:* 1,238 full-time (605 women), 617 part-time (223 women); includes 295 minority (71 Black or African American, non-Hispanic/Latino; 129 Asian, non-Hispanic/Latino; 74 Hispanic/Latino; 4 Native Hawaiian or other Pacific Islander, non-Hispanic/Latino; 17 Two or more races, non-Hispanic/Latino), 462 international. Average age 29. In 2013, 911 master's awarded. *Entrance requirements:* For master's, GMAT, 2 letters of recommendation, resume, essay, official transcripts. Additional exam requirements/recommendations for international students: Required—TOEFL (minimum score 550 paper-based; 80 iBT). *Application deadline:* For fall admission, 7/1 for domestic students, 6/1 for international students; for winter admission, 10/1 for domestic students, 9/1 for international students; for spring admission, 2/1 for domestic students, 1/1 for international students. Applications are processed on a rolling basis. Application fee: $60. Electronic applications accepted. *Expenses:* Contact institution. *Financial support:* Application deadline: 4/1; applicants required to submit FAFSA. *Unit head:* Robert T. Ryan, Assistant Dean and Director, 312-362-8810, Fax: 312-362-6677, E-mail: rryan1@depaul.edu. *Application contact:* James Parker, Director of Recruitment and Admission, 312-362-8810, Fax: 312-362-6677, E-mail: kgsb@depaul.edu.
Website: http://kellstadt.depaul.edu.

Duke University, The Fuqua School of Business, Daytime MBA Program, Durham, NC 27708-0586. Offers academic excellence in finance (Certificate); business administration (MBA); decision sciences (MBA); energy and environment (MBA); energy finance (MBA); entrepreneurship and innovation (MBA); finance (MBA); financial analysis (MBA); health sector management (Certificate); leadership and ethics (MBA);

management (MBA); marketing (MBA); operations management (MBA); social entrepreneurship (MBA); strategy (MBA). *Faculty:* 91 full-time (15 women), 53 part-time/adjunct (9 women). *Students:* 862 full-time (283 women); includes 179 minority (34 Black or African American, non-Hispanic/Latino; 1 American Indian or Alaska Native, non-Hispanic/Latino; 92 Asian, non-Hispanic/Latino; 42 Hispanic/Latino; 2 Native Hawaiian or other Pacific Islander, non-Hispanic/Latino; 8 Two or more races, non-Hispanic/Latino), 342 international. Average age 29. In 2013, 437 master's awarded. *Entrance requirements:* For master's, GMAT or GRE, transcripts, essays, resume, recommendation letters, interview. Additional exam requirements/recommendations for international students: Required—TOEFL, IELTS, PTE. *Application deadline:* For fall admission, 9/18 for domestic and international students; for winter admission, 10/21 for domestic and international students; for spring admission, 1/6 for domestic and international students; for summer admission, 3/20 for domestic and international students. Application fee: $225. Electronic applications accepted. *Financial support:* In 2013–14, 331 students received support. Institutionally sponsored loans and scholarships/grants available. Financial award applicants required to submit FAFSA. *Unit head:* Russ Morgan, Associate Dean for the Daytime MBA Program, 919-660-2931, Fax: 919-684-8742, E-mail: ruskin.morgan@duke.edu. *Application contact:* Liz Riley Hargrove, Associate Dean of Admissions, 919-660-7705, Fax: 919-681-8026, E-mail: liz.riley@duke.edu.
Website: http://www.fuqua.duke.edu/daytime-mba/.

Duke University, The Fuqua School of Business, PhD Program, Durham, NC 27708-0586. Offers accounting (PhD); decision sciences (PhD); finance (PhD); management and organizations (PhD); marketing (PhD); operations management (PhD); strategy (PhD). *Faculty:* 91 full-time (15 women). *Students:* 78 full-time (27 women); includes 4 minority (1 Black or African American, non-Hispanic/Latino; 3 Asian, non-Hispanic/Latino), 49 international. 589 applicants, 5% accepted, 16 enrolled. In 2013, 26 doctorates awarded. *Degree requirements:* For doctorate, thesis/dissertation, major field requirement (exam or major paper, depending upon the area). *Entrance requirements:* For doctorate, GMAT or GRE, transcripts, essays, recommendation letters, statement of purpose. Additional exam requirements/recommendations for international students: Required—TOEFL (minimum score 577 paper-based; 90 iBT), IELTS (minimum score 7). *Application deadline:* For fall admission, 12/8 priority date for domestic and international students. Application fee: $80. Electronic applications accepted. *Financial support:* In 2013–14, 70 fellowships with full tuition reimbursements (averaging $25,300 per year), 56 research assistantships with full tuition reimbursements (averaging $7,000 per year) were awarded; institutionally sponsored loans, scholarships/grants, and tuition waivers (full) also available. Financial award applicants required to submit FAFSA. *Unit head:* William Boulding, Dean, 919-660-7822, Fax: 919-684-8742, E-mail: bb1@duke.edu. *Application contact:* Dr. James R. Bettman, Director of Graduate Studies, 919-660-7851, Fax: 919-681-6245, E-mail: jrb12@mail.duke.edu.

East Carolina University, Graduate School, College of Technology and Computer Science, Department of Technology Systems, Greenville, NC 27858-4353. Offers computer network professional (Certificate); industrial technology (MS), including computer networking management, digital communications, industrial distribution and logistics, information security, manufacturing, performance improvement, quality systems; information assurance (Certificate); Lean Six Sigma Black Belt (Certificate); occupational safety (MS); technology management (PhD); Website developer (Certificate). *Entrance requirements:* For master's and Certificate, GRE General Test or MAT, minimum GPA of 2.5; for doctorate, GRE General Test, related work experience. *Expenses:* Tuition, state resident: full-time $4223. Tuition, nonresident: full-time $16,540. *Required fees:* $2184.

Embry-Riddle Aeronautical University–Worldwide, Worldwide Headquarters - Graduate Programs, Program in Business Administration and Management, Daytona Beach, FL 32114-3900. Offers air transportation management (Graduate Certificate); airport planning design and development (Graduate Certificate); aviation (MBAA); aviation enterprises in the global environment (Graduate Certificate); aviation-aerospace industrial management (Graduate Certificate); engineering management (MSEM); integrated logistics management (Graduate Certificate); leadership (MSL); logistics and supply chain management (MSLSCM); management (MSM); modeling and simulation management (Graduate Certificate); occupational safety management (MSOSM); project management (MSPM, Graduate Certificate). Part-time and evening/weekend programs available. Postbaccalaureate distance learning degree programs offered (no on-campus study). *Degree requirements:* For master's, comprehensive exam (for some programs), thesis (for some programs). *Entrance requirements:* Additional exam requirements/recommendations for international students: Recommended—TOEFL (minimum score 550 paper-based; 79 iBT). Electronic applications accepted. *Faculty research:* Healthcare operations management, humanitarian logistics, supply chain risk management, collaborative supply chain management, intersection of collaborative supply chain management and the learning organization, development of assessment tool measuring supply chain collaborative capacity, teaching effectiveness, teaching quality, management style effectiveness, aeronautics, small/medium-sized business leadership study, leadership factors, critical thinking, efficacy of ePortfolio.

Friends University, Graduate School, Wichita, KS 67213. Offers business law (MBL); Christian ministry (MACM); family therapy (MSFT); global (MBA), including accounting, business law, change management, health care leadership, management information systems, supply chain management and logistics; health care leadership (MHCL); management information systems (MMIS); operations management (MSOM); professional (MBA), including accounting, business law, change management, health care leadership, management information systems, supply chain management and logistics; teaching (MAT). Part-time and evening/weekend programs available. Postbaccalaureate distance learning degree programs offered (no on-campus study). *Faculty:* 18 full-time (8 women), 62 part-time/adjunct (28 women). *Students:* 161 full-time (111 women), 408 part-time (258 women); includes 157 minority (68 Black or African American, non-Hispanic/Latino; 7 American Indian or Alaska Native, non-Hispanic/Latino; 28 Asian, non-Hispanic/Latino; 18 Hispanic/Latino; 1 Native Hawaiian or other Pacific Islander, non-Hispanic/Latino; 35 Two or more races, non-Hispanic/Latino). Average age 36. 371 applicants, 90% accepted, 178 enrolled. In 2013, 432 master's awarded. *Degree requirements:* For master's, research project. *Entrance requirements:* For master's, bachelor's degree from accredited institution, official transcripts, interview with program director, letter(s) of recommendation. Additional exam requirements/recommendations for international students: Required—TOEFL (minimum score 560 paper-based). *Application deadline:* Applications are processed on a rolling basis. Application fee: $35 ($50 for international students). Electronic applications accepted. *Expenses: Tuition:* Part-time $631 per credit hour. Tuition and fees vary according to program. *Financial support:* In 2013–14, 30 students received support. Applicants required to submit FAFSA. *Unit head:* Dr. David Hofmeister, Dean of the Graduate School, 800-794-6945 Ext. 5858, Fax: 316-295-5040, E-mail: david_hofmeister@friends.edu. *Application contact:* Rachel Steiner, Manager, Graduate Recruiting Services, 800-794-6945, Fax: 316-295-5872, E-mail: rachel_steiner@friends.edu.
Website: http://www.friends.edu/.

Georgetown University, Graduate School of Arts and Sciences, Department of Economics, Washington, DC 20057. Offers econometrics (PhD); economic development (PhD); economic theory (PhD); industrial organization (PhD); international macro and finance (PhD); international trade (PhD); labor economics (PhD); macroeconomics (PhD); public economics and political economics (PhD); MA/PhD; MS/MA. *Degree requirements:* For doctorate, comprehensive exam, thesis/dissertation. *Entrance requirements:* For doctorate, GRE General Test. Additional exam requirements/recommendations for international students: Required—TOEFL. *Faculty research:* International economics, economic development.

Harvard University, Harvard Business School, Doctoral Programs in Management, Boston, MA 02163. Offers accounting and management (DBA); business economics (PhD); health policy management (PhD); management (DBA); marketing (DBA); organizational behavior (PhD); science, technology and management (PhD); strategy (DBA); technology and operations management (DBA). *Degree requirements:* For doctorate, comprehensive exam (for some programs), thesis/dissertation. *Entrance requirements:* For doctorate, GRE General Test or GMAT. Additional exam requirements/recommendations for international students: Required—TOEFL. *Expenses: Tuition:* Full-time $38,888. *Required fees:* $958. Tuition and fees vary according to campus/location, program and student level.

HEC Montreal, School of Business Administration, Master of Science Programs in Administration, Program in Operations Management, Montréal, QC H3T 2A7, Canada. Offers M Sc. All courses are given in French. *Students:* 10 full-time (7 women), 4 part-time (2 women). 10 applicants, 90% accepted, 6 enrolled. In 2013, 15 master's awarded. *Degree requirements:* For master's, one foreign language, thesis. *Entrance requirements:* For master's, Test de francais international (TFI) with minimum score of 850 (for those who have never studied in French), BBA, undergraduate degree in another field, degree deemed equivalent by program director and minimum GPA of 3.0 on 4.3 scale. *Application deadline:* For fall admission, 3/15 for domestic and international students; for winter admission, 9/15 for domestic and international students. Application fee: $83 Canadian dollars. Electronic applications accepted. *Expenses: Tuition, area resident:* Part-time $74.14 per credit. Tuition, state resident: full-time $2669.04; part-time $201.83 per credit. Tuition, nonresident: full-time $7266; part-time $500.59 per credit. International tuition: $18,021.24 full-time. *Required fees:* $1529.70; $36.20 per credit. $65.50 per term. Tuition and fees vary according to degree level and program. *Financial support:* In 2013–14, 1,007 students received support. Research assistantships, teaching assistantships, and scholarships/grants available. Financial award application deadline: 9/2. *Unit head:* Dr. Anne Bourhis, Director, 514-340-6873, Fax: 514-340-6880, E-mail: anne.bourhis@hec.ca. *Application contact:* Marianne de Moura, Administrative Director, 514-340-7106, Fax: 514-340-6411, E-mail: marianne.de-moura@hec.ca.
Website: http://www.hec.ca/programmes_formations/msc/options/gestion_operations/index.html.

Illinois Institute of Technology, Graduate College, School of Applied Technology, Program in Industrial Technology and Management, Wheaton, IL 60189. Offers MITO. Part-time and evening/weekend programs available. Postbaccalaureate distance learning degree programs offered (no on-campus study). *Entrance requirements:* For master's, GRE (minimum score 900 Quantitative and Verbal, 2.5 Analytical Writing), bachelor's degree with minimum cumulative undergraduate GPA of 3.0 (or its equivalent) from accredited institution. Additional exam requirements/recommendations for international students: Required—TOEFL (minimum score 523 paper-based; 70 iBT); Recommended—IELTS (minimum score 5.5). Electronic applications accepted. *Faculty research:* Industrial logistics, industrial facilities, manufacturing technology, entrepreneurship, energy options.

Instituto Tecnologico de Santo Domingo, Graduate School, Area of Engineering, Santo Domingo, Dominican Republic. Offers construction administration (MS, Certificate); data telecommunications (M Eng, MS, Certificate); industrial engineering (M Eng, Certificate); industrial management (M Mgmt); information technology (Certificate); maintenance engineering (M Eng); occupational hazard prevention (M Mgmt); production management (Certificate); quantitative methods (Certificate); sanitary and environmental engineering (M Eng); structural engineering (M Eng); systems engineering and electronic data processing (Certificate); transportation (Certificate).

Instituto Tecnológico y de Estudios Superiores de Monterrey, Campus Estado de México, Professional and Graduate Division, Estado de Mexico, Mexico. Offers administration of information technologies (MITA); architecture (M Arch); business administration (GMBA, MBA); computer sciences (MCS, PhD); education (M Ed); educational institution administration (MAD); educational technology and innovation (PhD); electronic commerce (MEC); environmental systems (MS); finance (MAF); humanistic studies (MHS); information sciences and knowledge management (MISKM); information systems (MS); manufacturing systems (MS); marketing (MEM); quality systems and productivity (MS); science and materials engineering (PhD); telecommunications management (MTM). Part-time programs available. Postbaccalaureate distance learning degree programs offered (minimal on-campus study). *Degree requirements:* For master's, one foreign language, thesis (for some programs); for doctorate, one foreign language, thesis/dissertation. *Entrance requirements:* For master's, E-PAEP 500, interview; for doctorate, E-PAEP 500, research proposal. Additional exam requirements/recommendations for international students: Required—TOEFL (minimum score 550 paper-based). *Faculty research:* Surface treatments by plasmas, mechanical properties, robotics, graphical computing, mechatronics security protocols.

Instituto Tecnológico y de Estudios Superiores de Monterrey, Campus Irapuato, Graduate Programs, Irapuato, Mexico. Offers administration (MBA); administration of information technology (MAIT); administration of telecommunications (MAT); architecture (M Arch); computer science (MCS); education (M Ed); educational administration (MEA); educational innovation and technology (DEIT); educational technology (MET); electronic commerce (MBA); environmental administration and planning (MEAP); environmental systems (MES); finances (MBA); humanistic studies (MHS); international management for Latin American executives (MIMLAE); library and information science (MLIS); manufacturing quality management (MMQM); marketing research (MBA).

Inter American University of Puerto Rico, Metropolitan Campus, Graduate Programs, Program in Industrial Management, San Juan, PR 00919-1293. Offers MBA. *Degree requirements:* For master's, comprehensive exam. *Entrance requirements:* For master's, GRE or EXADEP, interview. Electronic applications accepted.

Inter American University of Puerto Rico, San Germán Campus, Graduate Studies Center, Program in Business Administration, San Germán, PR 00683-5008. Offers accounting (MBA); finance (MBA); general business administration (MBA); human resources (MBA, PhD); industrial relations (MBA); information systems (MBA); international and interregional business (PhD); management (MBA); marketing (MBA). Part-time and evening/weekend programs available. *Faculty:* 8 full-time (2 women), 4 part-time/adjunct (3 women). *Students:* 138 full-time (80 women), 35 part-time (21 women); includes 172 minority (all Hispanic/Latino). 60 applicants, 65% accepted, 38 enrolled. In 2013, 38 master's, 3 doctorates awarded. *Degree requirements:* For master's, comprehensive exam. *Entrance requirements:* For master's, GRE General

Industrial and Manufacturing Management

Test or EXADEP, minimum GPA of 3.0. *Application deadline:* For fall admission, 4/30 priority date for domestic students; for spring admission, 11/15 for domestic students. Applications are processed on a rolling basis. Application fee: $31. *Expenses: Tuition:* Full-time $2424; part-time $202 per credit hour. *Required fees:* $260 per semester. Tuition and fees vary according to course level, course load, degree level and program. *Financial support:* Teaching assistantships, Federal Work-Study, and unspecified assistantships available. *Unit head:* Dr. Elba T. Irizarry, Director of Graduate Studies Center, 787-264-1912 Ext. 7357, Fax: 787-892-6350, E-mail: elbat@sg.inter.edu. *Application contact:* Dr. Ailin Padilla, Coordinator, 787-264-1912 Ext. 7355, E-mail: ailin_padilla@intersg.edu.

International Technological University, Program in Industrial Management, San Jose, CA 95113. Offers MIM.

Kansas State University, Graduate School, College of Human Ecology, Department of Apparel, Textiles, and Interior Design, Manhattan, KS 66506. Offers apparel and textiles (MS), including design, general apparel and textiles, marketing, merchandising, product development. Postbaccalaureate distance learning degree programs offered (no on-campus study). *Faculty:* 11 full-time (9 women). *Students:* 7 full-time (6 women), 19 part-time (18 women); includes 7 minority (3 Black or African American, non-Hispanic/Latino; 2 Asian, non-Hispanic/Latino; 2 Hispanic/Latino), 6 international. Average age 28. 12 applicants, 75% accepted, 5 enrolled. In 2013, 9 master's awarded. *Degree requirements:* For master's, comprehensive exam (for some programs), thesis (for some programs). *Entrance requirements:* For master's, GRE General Test (except for merchandising applicants), minimum undergraduate GPA of 3.0. Additional exam requirements/recommendations for international students: Required—TOEFL (minimum score 550 paper-based; 79 iBT), IELTS (minimum score 6.1). *Application deadline:* For fall admission, 1/1 priority date for domestic and international students; for spring admission, 8/1 priority date for domestic and international students; for summer admission, 12/1 priority date for domestic and international students. Applications are processed on a rolling basis. Application fee: $50 ($75 for international students). Electronic applications accepted. *Financial support:* In 2013–14, 6 students received support, including 1 fellowship (averaging $8,652 per year), 2 research assistantships (averaging $17,674 per year), 3 teaching assistantships with full tuition reimbursements available (averaging $11,760 per year); career-related internships or fieldwork, Federal Work-Study, institutionally sponsored loans, scholarships/grants, and unspecified assistantships also available. Support available to part-time students. Financial award application deadline: 2/1; financial award applicants required to submit FAFSA. *Faculty research:* Apparel marketing and consumer behavior, social and environmental responsibility, apparel design, new product development. *Total annual research expenditures:* $76,055. *Unit head:* Prof. Barbara G. Anderson, Head, 785-532-6993, Fax: 785-532-3796, E-mail: barbara@ksu.edu. *Application contact:* Gina Jackson, Application Contact, 785-532-6693, Fax: 785-532-3796, E-mail: gjackson@ksu.edu. Website: http://www.he.k-state.edu/atid/.

Marquette University, Graduate School of Management, Executive MBA Program, Milwaukee, WI 53201-1881. Offers economics (MBA); finance (MBA); human resources (MBA); international business (MBA); management information systems (MBA); marketing (MBA); operations and supply chain management (MBA); sports business (MBA). *Accreditation:* AACSB. *Students:* 38 full-time (12 women), 1 international. Average age 36. 36 applicants. In 2013, 21 master's awarded. *Degree requirements:* For master's, international trip. *Entrance requirements:* For master's, GMAT or GRE, two letters of recommendation, official transcripts from current and previous colleges/universities. Additional exam requirements/recommendations for international students: Required—TOEFL (minimum score 550 paper-based; 88 iBT), IELTS (minimum score 6.5), PTE. *Application deadline:* For fall admission, 2/15 for domestic and international students. Application fee: $50. Electronic applications accepted. *Expenses:* Contact institution. *Financial support:* Application deadline: 2/15. *Faculty research:* International trade and finance, customer relationship management, consumer satisfaction, customer service. *Unit head:* Dr. Mark Eppli, Dean, 414-288-5724. *Application contact:* Dr. Jeanne Simmons, Associate Dean, 414-288-7145. Website: http://www.busadm.mu.edu/emba/.

Marquette University, Graduate School of Management, Program in Business Administration, Milwaukee, WI 53201-1881. Offers business administration (MBA); economics (MBA); entrepreneurship (Certificate); finance (MBA); human resources (MBA); international business (MBA); management information systems (MBA); marketing (MBA); operations and supply chain management (MBA); sports business (MBA); JD/MBA; MBA/MA; MBA/MSN. *Accreditation:* AACSB. Part-time and evening/weekend programs available. *Students:* 28 full-time (13 women), 265 part-time (66 women); includes 20 minority (7 Black or African American, non-Hispanic/Latino; 8 Asian, non-Hispanic/Latino; 5 Hispanic/Latino), 11 international. Average age 31. 185 applicants. In 2013, 129 master's, 2 other advanced degrees awarded. *Degree requirements:* For Certificate, business plan. *Entrance requirements:* For master's, GMAT or GRE, letters of recommendation. Additional exam requirements/recommendations for international students: Required—TOEFL (minimum score 550 paper-based; 88 iBT), IELTS (minimum score 6.5), PTE. *Application deadline:* For fall admission, 2/15 for domestic and international students. Applications are processed on a rolling basis. Application fee: $50. Electronic applications accepted. *Financial support:* In 2013–14, 4 fellowships, 11 teaching assistantships were awarded; research assistantships, Federal Work-Study, institutionally sponsored loans, scholarships/grants, and tuition waivers (full and partial) also available. Support available to part-time students. Financial award application deadline: 2/15. *Faculty research:* Ethics in the professions, services marketing, technology impact on decision-making, mentoring. *Unit head:* Dr. Mark Eppli, Dean, 414-288-5724. *Application contact:* Dr. Jeanne Simmons, Associate Dean, 414-288-7145. Website: http://business.marquette.edu/academics/mba.

McGill University, Faculty of Graduate and Postdoctoral Studies, Desautels Faculty of Management, Montréal, QC H3A 2T5, Canada. Offers administration (PhD); entrepreneurial studies (MBA); finance (MBA); general management (Post Master's Certificate); information systems (MBA); international business (MBA); international practicing management (MM); management (MBA); management for development (MBA); manufacturing management (MMM); marketing (MBA); operations management (MBA); public accountancy (Diploma); strategic management (MBA); MBA/LL B; MD/MBA. MMM offered jointly with Faculty of Engineering; PhD with Concordia University, HEC Montreal, Université de Montréal, Université du Québec à Montréal.

McGill University, Faculty of Graduate and Postdoctoral Studies, Faculty of Engineering, Department of Mechanical Engineering and Desautels Faculty of Management, Master in Manufacturing Management, Montréal, QC H3A 2T5, Canada. Offers MMM.

Milwaukee School of Engineering, Rader School of Business, Program in New Product Management, Milwaukee, WI 53202-3109. Offers MS. Part-time and evening/weekend programs available. *Faculty:* 1 full-time (0 women), 2 part-time/adjunct (1 woman). *Students:* 1 (woman) full-time, 11 part-time (2 women); includes 2 minority (1 Black or African American, non-Hispanic/Latino; 1 Hispanic/Latino), 1 international. Average age 30. 5 applicants, 60% accepted, 3 enrolled. In 2013, 2 master's awarded. *Degree requirements:* For master's, thesis, thesis defense or capstone project. Entrance

requirements: For master's, GRE General Test or GMAT if undergraduate GPA less than 2.8, 2 letters of recommendation. Additional exam requirements/recommendations for international students: Required—TOEFL (minimum score 79 iBT), IELTS (minimum score 6.5). *Application deadline:* Applications are processed on a rolling basis. Application fee: $0. Electronic applications accepted. Application fee is waived when completed online. *Expenses: Tuition:* Full-time $6939; part-time $771 per credit. *Financial support:* Career-related internships or fieldwork, institutionally sponsored loans, and scholarships/grants available. Financial award application deadline: 3/15; financial award applicants required to submit FAFSA. *Faculty research:* New product development, product research and design, product development. *Unit head:* David Schmitz, Director, 414-277-2487, Fax: 414-277-2487, E-mail: schmitz@msoe.edu. *Application contact:* Katie Weinschenk, Graduate Program Associate, 800-321-6763, Fax: 414-277-7208, E-mail: weinschenk@msoe.edu.

Northern Illinois University, Graduate School, College of Engineering and Engineering Technology, Department of Technology, De Kalb, IL 60115-2854. Offers industrial management (MS). Part-time and evening/weekend programs available. *Faculty:* 14 full-time (1 woman), 1 part-time/adjunct (0 women). *Students:* 7 full-time (1 woman), 21 part-time (4 women); includes 7 minority (3 Black or African American, non-Hispanic/Latino; 3 Asian, non-Hispanic/Latino; 1 Hispanic/Latino), 7 international. Average age 33. 27 applicants, 37% accepted, 5 enrolled. In 2013, 14 master's awarded. *Degree requirements:* For master's, thesis optional. *Entrance requirements:* For master's, GRE General Test, minimum GPA of 2.75. Additional exam requirements/recommendations for international students: Required—TOEFL (minimum score 550 paper-based). *Application deadline:* For fall admission, 6/1 for domestic students, 5/1 for international students; for spring admission, 11/1 for domestic students, 10/1 for international students. Applications are processed on a rolling basis. Application fee: $40. Electronic applications accepted. *Financial support:* In 2013–14, 1 research assistantship with full tuition reimbursement, 7 teaching assistantships with full tuition reimbursements were awarded; fellowships with full tuition reimbursements, career-related internships or fieldwork, Federal Work-Study, scholarships/grants, tuition waivers (full), and unspecified assistantships also available. Support available to part-time students. Financial award applicants required to submit FAFSA. *Faculty research:* Digital control, intelligent systems, engineering graphic design, occupational safety, ergonomics. *Unit head:* Dr. Clifford Mirman, Chair, 815-753-1349, Fax: 815-753-3702, E-mail: mirman@ceet.niu.edu. *Application contact:* Graduate School Office, 815-753-0395, E-mail: gradsch@niu.edu. Website: http://www.niu.edu/tech/.

Northwestern University, The Graduate School, Kellogg School of Management, Management Programs, Evanston, IL 60208. Offers accounting information and management (MBA, PhD); analytical finance (MBA); business administration (MBA); decision sciences (MBA); entrepreneurship and innovation (MBA); finance (MBA, PhD); health enterprise management (MBA); human resources management (MBA); international business (MBA); management and organizations (MBA, PhD); management and organizations and sociology (PhD); management and strategy (MBA); management studies (MS); managerial analytics (MBA); managerial economics (MBA); managerial economics and strategy (PhD); marketing (MBA, PhD); marketing management (MBA); media management (MBA); operations management (MBA, PhD); real estate (MBA); social enterprise at Kellogg (MBA); JD/MBA. Part-time and evening/weekend programs available. Terminal master's awarded for partial completion of doctoral program. *Degree requirements:* For doctorate, thesis/dissertation, 2 years of coursework, qualifying (field) exam and candidacy, summer research papers and presentations to faculty, proposal defense, final exam/defense. *Entrance requirements:* For master's, GMAT, GRE, interview, 2 letters of recommendation, college transcripts, resume, essays, Kellogg honor code; for doctorate, GMAT, GRE, statement of purpose, transcripts, 2 letters of recommendation, resume, interview. Additional exam requirements/recommendations for international students: Required—TOEFL, IELTS. Electronic applications accepted. *Expenses:* Contact institution. *Faculty research:* Business cycles and international finance, health policy, networks, non-market strategy, consumer psychology.

Notre Dame de Namur University, Division of Academic Affairs, School of Business and Management, Program in Business Administration, Belmont, CA 94002-1908. Offers business administration (MBA); entrepreneurship (MBA); finance (MBA); human resource management (MBA); marketing (MBA); media and promotion (MBA); technology and operations management (MBA). *Accreditation:* ACBSP. Part-time and evening/weekend programs available. *Entrance requirements:* For master's, minimum GPA of 2.5. Additional exam requirements/recommendations for international students: Required—TOEFL (minimum score 550 paper-based; 79 iBT). Electronic applications accepted.

Oakland University, Graduate Study and Lifelong Learning, School of Business Administration, Department of Decision and Information Sciences, Rochester, MI 48309-4401. Offers information technology management (MS); management information systems (Certificate); production and operations management (Certificate). *Faculty:* 8 full-time (1 woman), 1 part-time/adjunct (0 women). *Students:* 17 full-time (6 women), 25 part-time (9 women); includes 9 minority (2 Black or African American, non-Hispanic/Latino; 7 Asian, non-Hispanic/Latino), 11 international. Average age 32. 78 applicants, 31% accepted, 24 enrolled. In 2013, 6 master's, 2 other advanced degrees awarded. Application fee: $0. *Unit head:* Dr. Thomas Lauer, Chair, 248-370-3283, Fax: 248-370-4604. *Application contact:* Donna Free, Coordinator, 248-370-3281.

Penn State Erie, The Behrend College, Graduate School, Erie, PA 16563-0001. Offers business administration (MBA); project management (MPM); quality and manufacturing management (MMM). *Accreditation:* AACSB. Part-time programs available. *Students:* 31 full-time (10 women), 83 part-time (23 women); includes 8 minority (2 Black or African American, non-Hispanic/Latino; 3 Asian, non-Hispanic/Latino; 3 Hispanic/Latino), 3 international. Average age 29. 71 applicants, 79% accepted, 45 enrolled. In 2013, 52 master's awarded. *Entrance requirements:* Additional exam requirements/recommendations for international students: Required—TOEFL (minimum score 550 paper-based; 80 iBT). *Application deadline:* Applications are processed on a rolling basis. Application fee: $65. Electronic applications accepted. *Financial support:* Federal Work-Study available. Financial award application deadline: 2/15; financial award applicants required to submit FAFSA. *Unit head:* Dr. Donald L. Birx, Chancellor, 814-898-6160, Fax: 814-898-6461, E-mail: dlb69@psu.edu. *Application contact:* Ann M. Burbules, Assistant Director, Graduate Admissions, 866-374-3378, Fax: 814-898-6053, E-mail: psbehrendmba@psu.edu. Website: http://psbehrend.psu.edu/.

Polytechnic University of Puerto Rico, Graduate School, Hato Rey, PR 00919. Offers business administration (MBA), including computer information systems, general management, management of information systems, management of international enterprises; civil engineering (ME, MS); computer engineering (ME, MS); computer science (MCS, MS); electrical engineering (ME, MS); engineering management (MEM); environmental management (MEM); landscape architecture (M Land Arch); manufacturing competitiveness (MMC, MS); manufacturing engineering (ME, MS); mechanical engineering (M Mech E). Part-time and evening/weekend programs available. *Entrance requirements:* For master's, 3 letters of recommendation.

Polytechnic University of Puerto Rico, Miami Campus, Graduate School, Miami, FL 33166. Offers accounting (MBA); business administration (MBA); construction management (MEM); environmental management (MEM); finance (MBA); human resources management (MBA); logistics and supply chain management (MBA); management of international enterprises (MBA); manufacturing management (MEM); marketing management (MBA); project management (MBA). Part-time and evening/weekend programs available. Postbaccalaureate distance learning degree programs offered (no on-campus study). *Entrance requirements:* For master's, minimum GPA of 3.0. Electronic applications accepted.

Polytechnic University of Puerto Rico, Orlando Campus, Graduate School, Winter Park, FL 32792. Offers accounting (MBA); business administration (MBA); construction management (MEM); engineering management (MEM); environmental management (MEM); finance (MBA); human resources management (MBA); management of international enterprises (MBA); management of technology (MBA); manufacturing management (MEM). Part-time and evening/weekend programs available. Postbaccalaureate distance learning degree programs offered (no on-campus study). *Entrance requirements:* For master's, minimum GPA of 3.0. Additional exam requirements/recommendations for international students: Recommended—TOEFL. Electronic applications accepted.

Portland State University, Graduate Studies, Maseeh College of Engineering and Computer Science, Department of Engineering and Technology Management, Portland, OR 97207-0751. Offers engineering and technology management (M Eng); engineering management (MS); manufacturing engineering (ME); manufacturing management (M Eng); systems science/engineering management (PhD); MS/MBA; MS/MS. Part-time and evening/weekend programs available. *Faculty:* 7 full-time (2 women), 3 part-time/adjunct (0 women). *Students:* 53 full-time (23 women), 56 part-time (13 women); includes 19 minority (3 Black or African American, non-Hispanic/Latino; 1 American Indian or Alaska Native, non-Hispanic/Latino; 8 Asian, non-Hispanic/Latino; 5 Hispanic/Latino; 2 Two or more races, non-Hispanic/Latino), 52 international. Average age 35. 133 applicants, 44% accepted, 37 enrolled. In 2013, 34 master's, 9 doctorates awarded. *Degree requirements:* For master's, thesis optional; for doctorate, one foreign language, thesis/dissertation, oral and written exams. *Entrance requirements:* For master's, minimum GPA of 3.0 in upper-division course work, BS in civil engineering; for doctorate, GRE General Test, GRE Subject Test, minimum GPA of 3.0 in upper-division course work. Additional exam requirements/recommendations for international students: Required—TOEFL (minimum score 550 paper-based). *Application deadline:* For fall admission, 4/1 for domestic students, 3/1 for international students; for winter admission, 9/1 for domestic students, 7/1 for international students; for spring admission, 11/1 for domestic students, 9/1 for international students. Applications are processed on a rolling basis. Application fee: $50. *Expenses:* Tuition, state resident: full-time $9207; part-time $341 per credit. Tuition, nonresident: full-time $14,391; part-time $533 per credit. *Required fees:* $1263; $22 per credit. $98 per quarter. One-time fee: $150. Tuition and fees vary according to program. *Financial support:* In 2013–14, 5 research assistantships with full and partial tuition reimbursements (averaging $10,612 per year), 11 teaching assistantships with full and partial tuition reimbursements (averaging $5,334 per year) were awarded; career-related internships or fieldwork, Federal Work-Study, scholarships/grants, and unspecified assistantships also available. Support available to part-time students. Financial award application deadline: 3/1; financial award applicants required to submit FAFSA. *Faculty research:* Scheduling, hierarchical decision modeling, operations research, knowledge-based information systems. *Total annual research expenditures:* $123,524. *Unit head:* Dr. Dundar F. Kocaoglu, Chair, 503-725-4660, Fax: 503-725-4667, E-mail: kocaoglu@etm.pdx.edu. *Application contact:* Shawn Wall, 503-725-4660, Fax: 503-547-8887, E-mail: info@etm.pdx.edu.
Website: http://www.emp.pdx.edu/.

Purdue University, Graduate School, Krannert School of Management, Master of Science in Industrial Administration Program, West Lafayette, IN 47907. Offers MSIA. *Entrance requirements:* For master's, GMAT or GRE, work experience, essays, minimum GPA of 3.0, four-year baccalaureate degree, letters of recommendation. Additional exam requirements/recommendations for international students: Required—TOEFL (minimum score 550 paper-based, 77 iBT), IELTS (minimum score 6.5), or PTE. Electronic applications accepted.

Quincy University, Program in Business Administration, Quincy, IL 62301-2699. Offers general business administration (MBA); operations management (MBA); organizational leadership (MBA). Part-time and evening/weekend programs available. Postbaccalaureate distance learning degree programs offered (no on-campus study). *Faculty:* 5 full-time (3 women). *Students:* 5 full-time (0 women), 18 part-time (5 women), 1 international. In 2013, 20 master's awarded. *Entrance requirements:* For master's, GMAT, previous course work in accounting, economics, finance, management or marketing, and statistics. Additional exam requirements/recommendations for international students: Required—TOEFL (minimum score 550 paper-based; 79 iBT). *Application deadline:* Applications are processed on a rolling basis. Application fee: $25. Electronic applications accepted. *Expenses:* Contact institution. *Financial support:* Applicants required to submit FAFSA. *Faculty research:* Macroeconomic forecasting. *Unit head:* Dr. Cynthia Haliemun, Director, 217-228-5432 Ext. 3067, E-mail: haliecy@quincy.edu. *Application contact:* Office of Admissions, 217-228-5210, Fax: 217-228-5479, E-mail: admissions@quincy.edu.
Website: http://www.quincy.edu/academics/graduate-programs/business-administration.

Rochester Institute of Technology, Graduate Enrollment Services, College of Applied Science and Technology, School of Engineering Technology, Department of Civil Engineering Technology, Environmental Management and Safety, Program in Facility Management, Rochester, NY 14623-5603. Offers MS. Part-time programs available. Postbaccalaureate distance learning degree programs offered (no on-campus study). *Students:* 3 full-time (0 women), 16 part-time (2 women); includes 3 minority (2 Black or African American, non-Hispanic/Latino; 1 Asian, non-Hispanic/Latino), 2 international. Average age 37. 33 applicants, 33% accepted, 6 enrolled. In 2013, 9 master's awarded. *Degree requirements:* For master's, thesis or alternative, project. *Entrance requirements:* For master's, minimum GPA of 3.0. Additional exam requirements/recommendations for international students: Required—TOEFL (minimum score 550 paper-based; 79 iBT) or IELTS (minimum score 6.5). *Application deadline:* For fall admission, 2/15 priority date for domestic and international students; for winter admission, 11/1 for domestic students, 10/1 for international students; for spring admission, 2/1 priority date for domestic students, 1/1 priority date for international students. Applications are processed on a rolling basis. Application fee: $60. Electronic applications accepted. *Expenses: Tuition:* Full-time $37,236; part-time $1552 per credit hour. *Required fees:* $250. *Financial support:* Career-related internships or fieldwork and scholarships/grants available. Support available to part-time students. Financial award applicants required to submit FAFSA. *Faculty research:* Sustainability. *Unit head:* Dr. Jeff Rogers, Graduate Program Director, 585-475-4185, E-mail: jwrite@rit.edu. *Application contact:* Diane Ellison, Assistant Vice President, Graduate Enrollment Services, 585-475-2229, Fax: 585-475-7164, E-mail: gradinfo@rit.edu.
Website: http://www.rit.edu/cast/cetems/ms-in-facility-management.php.

Rochester Institute of Technology, Graduate Enrollment Services, College of Applied Science and Technology, School of Engineering Technology, Department of Electrical, Computer and Telecommunications Engineering Technology, Rochester, NY 14623-5603. Offers facility management (MS); manufacturing and mechanical systems integration (MS); telecommunications engineering technology (MS). Part-time and evening/weekend programs available. Postbaccalaureate distance learning degree programs offered (no on-campus study). *Students:* 50 full-time (12 women), 34 part-time (10 women); includes 5 minority (1 Asian, non-Hispanic/Latino; 2 Hispanic/Latino; 2 Two or more races, non-Hispanic/Latino), 73 international. Average age 25. 230 applicants, 53% accepted, 34 enrolled. In 2013, 31 master's awarded. *Degree requirements:* For master's, thesis. *Entrance requirements:* For master's, GRE, minimum GPA of 3.0. Additional exam requirements/recommendations for international students: Required—TOEFL (minimum score 550 paper-based; 79 iBT) or IELTS (minimum score 6.5). *Application deadline:* For fall admission, 2/15 priority date for domestic and international students; for winter admission, 11/1 for domestic and international students; for spring admission, 2/1 for domestic and international students. Applications are processed on a rolling basis. Application fee: $60. Electronic applications accepted. *Expenses: Tuition:* Full-time $37,236; part-time $1552 per credit hour. *Required fees:* $250. *Financial support:* Research assistantships with partial tuition reimbursements, teaching assistantships with partial tuition reimbursements, career-related internships or fieldwork, and unspecified assistantships available. Support available to part-time students. Financial award application deadline: 2/15; financial award applicants required to submit FAFSA. *Faculty research:* Fiber optic networks, next generation networks, project management. *Unit head:* Michael Eastman, Department Chair, 585-475-7787, Fax: 585-475-2178, E-mail: mgeiee@rit.edu. *Application contact:* Diane Ellison, Assistant Vice President, Graduate Enrollment Services, 585-475-2229, Fax: 585-475-7164, E-mail: gradinfo@rit.edu.
Website: http://www.rit.edu/cast/ectet/.

Rochester Institute of Technology, Graduate Enrollment Services, Kate Gleason College of Engineering, Program in Manufacturing Leadership, Rochester, NY 14623-5603. Offers MS. Part-time and evening/weekend programs available. Postbaccalaureate distance learning degree programs offered (minimal on-campus study). *Students:* 2 full-time (1 woman), 27 part-time (9 women); includes 2 minority (1 Black or African American, non-Hispanic/Latino; 1 Asian, non-Hispanic/Latino), 5 international. Average age 35. 17 applicants, 53% accepted, 8 enrolled. In 2013, 18 master's awarded. *Degree requirements:* For master's, capstone. *Entrance requirements:* For master's, GMAT. Additional exam requirements/recommendations for international students: Required—TOEFL (minimum score 570 paper-based; 88 iBT) or IELTS (minimum score 6.5). *Application deadline:* For fall admission, 2/15 for domestic and international students. Applications are processed on a rolling basis. Application fee: $60. Electronic applications accepted. *Expenses: Tuition:* Full-time $37,236; part-time $1552 per credit hour. *Required fees:* $250. *Financial support:* Institutionally sponsored loans and scholarships/grants available. Support available to part-time students. Financial award applicants required to submit FAFSA. *Faculty research:* Supply chain management, global manufacturing and operations, lean thinking, leadership. *Unit head:* Mark Smith, Graduate Program Director, 585-475-7971, Fax: 585-475-7955, E-mail: mmlmail@rit.edu. *Application contact:* Diane Ellison, Assistant Vice President, Graduate Enrollment Services, 585-475-2229, Fax: 585-475-7164, E-mail: gradinfo@rit.edu.
Website: http://www.rit.edu/kgcoe/program/manufacturing-leadership.

San Francisco State University, Division of Graduate Studies, College of Business, Program in Business Administration, San Francisco, CA 94132-1722. Offers decision sciences/operations research (MBA); finance (MBA); information systems (MBA); leadership (MBA); management (MBA); marketing (MBA); sustainable business (MBA). *Accreditation:* AACSB. Part-time and evening/weekend programs available. *Faculty:* 100. *Students:* 850 (408 women). 839 applicants, 56% accepted, 241 enrolled. *Degree requirements:* For master's, thesis, essay test. *Entrance requirements:* For master's, GMAT, minimum GPA of 2.7 in last 60 units. Additional exam requirements/recommendations for international students: Required—TOEFL (minimum score 550 paper-based). *Application deadline:* For fall admission, 5/1 priority date for domestic students, 4/1 for international students; for spring admission, 11/1 for domestic students, 10/15 for international students. Applications are processed on a rolling basis. Application fee: $55. *Financial support:* Application deadline: 3/1. *Unit head:* Linda Oubre, Dean, 415-817-4300, E-mail: loubre@sfsu.edu. *Application contact:* Armaan Moattari, Assistant Director, Graduate Programs, 415-817-4314, Fax: 817-4340, E-mail: amoatt@sfsu.edu.
Website: http://cob.sfsu.edu/.

San Jose State University, Graduate Studies and Research, Lucas Graduate School of Business, Programs in Business Administration, San Jose, CA 95192-0001. Offers MBA. *Accreditation:* AACSB. *Degree requirements:* For master's, comprehensive exam, thesis or alternative. *Entrance requirements:* For master's, GMAT, minimum GPA of 3.0. Electronic applications accepted.

Southeast Missouri State University, School of Graduate Studies, Harrison College of Business, Cape Girardeau, MO 63701-4799. Offers accounting (MBA); entrepreneurship (MBA); environmental management (MBA); financial management (MBA); general management (MBA); health administration (MBA); industrial management (MBA); international business (MBA); organizational management (MS); sport management (MBA). *Accreditation:* AACSB. Part-time and evening/weekend programs available. Postbaccalaureate distance learning degree programs offered (no on-campus study). *Faculty:* 27 full-time (7 women), 1 (woman) part-time/adjunct. *Students:* 59 full-time (27 women), 83 part-time (28 women); includes 10 minority (5 Black or African American, non-Hispanic/Latino; 3 Asian, non-Hispanic/Latino; 1 Hispanic/Latino; 1 Two or more races, non-Hispanic/Latino), 40 international. Average age 28. 77 applicants, 79% accepted, 48 enrolled. In 2013, 50 master's awarded. *Degree requirements:* For master's, variable foreign language requirement, comprehensive exam (for some programs), thesis or alternative, applied research project. *Entrance requirements:* For master's, GMAT or GRE, minimum undergraduate GPA of 2.5, C or better in prerequisite courses. Additional exam requirements/recommendations for international students: Required—TOEFL (minimum score 550 paper-based; 79 iBT), IELTS (minimum score 6), PTE (minimum score 53). *Application deadline:* For fall admission, 8/1 for domestic students, 6/1 for international students; for spring admission, 11/21 for domestic students, 10/1 for international students; for summer admission, 5/15 for domestic students. Applications are processed on a rolling basis. Application fee: $30 ($40 for international students). Electronic applications accepted. *Expenses:* Tuition, state resident: full-time $5139; part-time $285.50 per credit hour. Tuition, nonresident: full-time $9099; part-time $505.50 per credit hour. *Financial support:* In 2013–14, 52 students received support, including 12 teaching assistantships with full tuition reimbursements available (averaging $8,144 per year); career-related internships or fieldwork, Federal Work-Study, scholarships/grants, traineeships, tuition waivers (full), and unspecified assistantships also available. Financial award application deadline: 6/30; financial award applicants required to submit FAFSA. *Faculty research:* Ethics, corporate finance, generational difference, leadership, organizational justice. *Unit head:* Dr. Kenneth A. Heischmidt, Director, Graduate Business Studies, 573-651-2912, Fax: 573-651-5032, E-mail: kheischmidt@semo.edu.

Application contact: Gail Amick, Admissions Specialist, 573-651-2590, Fax: 573-651-5936, E-mail: gamick@semo.edu.
Website: http://www.semo.edu/mba.

Southern New Hampshire University, School of Business, Manchester, NH 03106-1045. Offers accounting (MBA, MS, Graduate Certificate); accounting finance (MS); accounting/auditing (MS); accounting/forensic accounting (MS); accounting/taxation (MS); athletic administration (MBA, Graduate Certificate); business administration (IMBA, MBA, Certificate, Graduate Certificate), including accounting (Certificate), business administration (MBA), business information systems (Graduate Certificate), human resource management (Certificate); corporate social responsibility (MBA); entrepreneurship (MBA); finance (MBA, MS, Graduate Certificate); finance/corporate finance (MS); finance/investments and securities (MS); forensic accounting (MBA); healthcare informatics (MBA); healthcare management (MBA); human resource management (Graduate Certificate); information technology (MS, Graduate Certificate); information technology management (MBA); international business (Graduate Certificate); international business and information technology (Graduate Certificate); international finance (Graduate Certificate); international sport management (Graduate Certificate); justice studies (MBA); leadership of nonprofit organizations (Graduate Certificate); marketing (MBA, MS, Graduate Certificate); operations and project management (MS); operations and supply chain management (MBA, Graduate Certificate); organizational leadership (MS); project management (MBA, Graduate Certificate); Six Sigma (MBA); Six Sigma quality (Graduate Certificate); social media marketing (MBA); sport management (MBA, MS, Graduate Certificate); sustainability and environmental compliance (MBA); workplace conflict management (MBA); MBA/Certificate. *Accreditation:* ACBSP. Part-time and evening/weekend programs available. Postbaccalaureate distance learning degree programs offered (no on-campus study). Terminal master's awarded for partial completion of doctoral program. *Degree requirements:* For master's, one foreign language, comprehensive exam (for some programs), thesis or alternative. *Entrance requirements:* For master's, minimum GPA of 2.5. Additional exam requirements/recommendations for international students: Required—TOEFL (minimum score 500 paper-based). Electronic applications accepted.

Southern Polytechnic State University, School of Engineering Technology and Management, Department of Business Administration, Marietta, GA 30060-2896. Offers accounting (MBA, MSA); business administration (Graduate Transition Certificate); finance (MBA); general (MBA); management (MBA); management information systems (MBA); marketing (MBA); operations and technology management (MBA). *Accreditation:* ACBSP. Part-time and evening/weekend programs available. Postbaccalaureate distance learning degree programs offered (no on-campus study). *Degree requirements:* For master's, comprehensive exam (for some programs), capstone course and major field exam (for MBA); 30 semester hours of course work (for MSA). *Entrance requirements:* For master's, GMAT or GRE, letters of recommendation, statement of purpose, resume, minimum GPA of 2.75 or undergraduate degree in business with up to 6 transition courses; undergraduate degree in accounting from regionally-accredited school (for MSA). Additional exam requirements/recommendations for international students: Required—TOEFL (minimum score 550 paper-based; 79 iBT), IELTS (minimum score 6.5). Electronic applications accepted. *Faculty research:* Ethics, virtual reality, sustainability, management of technology, quality management, capacity planning, human-computer interaction/interface, enterprise integration planning, economic impact of educational institutions, behavioral accounting, accounting ethics, taxation, information security, visualization simulation, human-computer interaction, supply chain, logistics, economics.

Stevens Institute of Technology, Graduate School, Charles V. Schaefer Jr. School of Engineering, Department of Mechanical Engineering, Program in Integrated Product Development, Hoboken, NJ 07030. Offers armament engineering (M Eng); computer and electrical engineering (M Eng); manufacturing technologies (M Eng); systems reliability and design (M Eng).

Syracuse University, Martin J. Whitman School of Management, PhD Program in Business Administration, Syracuse, NY 13244. Offers accounting (PhD); finance (PhD); management information systems (PhD); managerial statistics (PhD); marketing (PhD); operations management (PhD); organizational behavior (PhD); strategy and human resources (PhD); supply chain management (PhD). *Faculty:* 79 full-time (20 women), 25 part-time/adjunct (6 women). *Students:* 26 full-time (8 women), 1 part-time (0 women); includes 2 minority (1 Black or African American, non-Hispanic/Latino; 1 Asian, non-Hispanic/Latino), 20 international. Average age 30. 130 applicants, 9% accepted, 7 enrolled. In 2013, 15 doctorates awarded. *Degree requirements:* For doctorate, comprehensive exam, thesis/dissertation, summer research paper. *Entrance requirements:* For doctorate, GMAT or GRE General Test, 3 recommendations. Additional exam requirements/recommendations for international students: Required—TOEFL (minimum score 600 paper-based; 100 iBT). *Application deadline:* For fall admission, 1/15 priority date for domestic and international students. Applications are processed on a rolling basis. Application fee: $75. Electronic applications accepted. *Financial support:* In 2013–14, 1 fellowship with full tuition reimbursement (averaging $19,570 per year), 30 teaching assistantships with full tuition reimbursements (averaging $17,000 per year) were awarded; research assistantships with full tuition reimbursements also available. Financial award application deadline: 1/15. *Faculty research:* Marketing models, market microstructure, supply chain, auditing, corporate governance. *Unit head:* Dr. Michel Benarock, Director of the PhD Program, 315-443-3429, E-mail: mbeanaroc@syr.edu. *Application contact:* Carol Hilleges, Administrative Specialist, 315-443-9601, Fax: 315-443-3671, E-mail: clhilleg@syr.edu.
Website: http://whitman.syr.edu/phd/.

Texas Tech University, Graduate School, Rawls College of Business Administration, Area of Information Systems and Quantitative Sciences, Lubbock, TX 79409. Offers business statistics (MS, PhD); healthcare management (MS); management information systems (MS, PhD); production and operations management (PhD). Part-time programs available. *Faculty:* 13 full-time (0 women). *Students:* 107 full-time (24 women); includes 3 minority (1 Black or African American, non-Hispanic/Latino; 1 American Indian or Alaska Native, non-Hispanic/Latino; 1 Asian, non-Hispanic/Latino), 79 international. Average age 27. 125 applicants, 55% accepted, 40 enrolled. In 2013, 17 master's, 5 doctorates awarded. Terminal master's awarded for partial completion of doctoral program. *Degree requirements:* For master's, comprehensive exam or capstone course; for doctorate, thesis/dissertation, qualifying exams. *Entrance requirements:* For master's and doctorate, GMAT, holistic profile of academic credentials. Additional exam requirements/recommendations for international students: Required—TOEFL (minimum score 550 paper-based; 79 iBT). *Application deadline:* For fall admission, 7/1 priority date for domestic students, 1/15 for international students; for spring admission, 11/1 priority date for domestic students, 6/15 priority date for international students. Applications are processed on a rolling basis. Application fee: $60. Electronic applications accepted. *Expenses:* Tuition, state resident: full-time $6062; part-time $252.57 per credit hour. Tuition, nonresident: full-time $14,558; part-time $606.57 per credit hour. *Required fees:* $2655; $35 per credit hour. $907.50 per semester. Tuition and fees vary according to course load. *Financial support:* In 2013–14, 5 research assistantships (averaging $16,160 per year), 5 teaching assistantships (averaging $18,000 per year) were awarded; Federal Work-Study, scholarships/grants, and unspecified assistantships also available. Financial award applicants required to submit FAFSA. *Faculty research:* Database management systems, systems management and engineering, expert systems and adaptive knowledge-based sciences, statistical analysis and design. *Unit head:* Dr. Glenn Browne, Area Coordinator, 806-834-0969, Fax: 806-742-3193, E-mail: glenn.browne@ttu.edu. *Application contact:* Terri Boston, Applications Manager, Graduate and Professional Programs, 806-742-3184, Fax: 806-742-3958, E-mail: rawlsgrad@ttu.edu.
Website: http://is.ba.ttu.edu.

Universidad de las Américas Puebla, Division of Graduate Studies, School of Engineering, Program in Industrial Engineering, Puebla, Mexico. Offers industrial engineering (MS); production management (M Adm). Part-time and evening/weekend programs available. *Degree requirements:* For master's, one foreign language, thesis. *Faculty research:* Textile industry, quality control.

Universidad de las Américas Puebla, Division of Graduate Studies, School of Engineering, Program in Manufacturing Administration, Puebla, Mexico. Offers MS. *Faculty research:* Operations research, construction.

The University of Alabama, Graduate School, Manderson Graduate School of Business, Department of Information Systems, Statistics, and Management Science, Program in Operations Management, Tuscaloosa, AL 35487. Offers MS, PhD. *Accreditation:* AACSB. Part-time programs available. Postbaccalaureate distance learning degree programs offered (no on-campus study). *Faculty:* 9 full-time (1 woman). *Students:* 17 full-time (5 women), 42 part-time (7 women); includes 9 minority (2 Black or African American, non-Hispanic/Latino; 4 Hispanic/Latino; 1 Native Hawaiian or other Pacific Islander, non-Hispanic/Latino; 2 Two or more races, non-Hispanic/Latino), 11 international. Average age 31. 87 applicants, 40% accepted, 19 enrolled. In 2013, 34 master's, 4 doctorates awarded. Terminal master's awarded for partial completion of doctoral program. *Degree requirements:* For master's, comprehensive exam, business calculus; for doctorate, comprehensive exam, thesis/dissertation. *Entrance requirements:* For master's, GMAT or GRE; for doctorate, GRE or GMAT. Additional exam requirements/recommendations for international students: Required—TOEFL (minimum score 550 paper-based), IELTS (minimum score 6.5). *Application deadline:* For spring admission, 3/1 priority date for domestic and international students. Applications are processed on a rolling basis. Application fee: $50 ($60 for international students). Electronic applications accepted. *Expenses:* Tuition, state resident: full-time $9450. Tuition, nonresident: full-time $23,950. *Financial support:* In 2013–14, 11 students received support, including 7 teaching assistantships with full tuition reimbursements available (averaging $13,500 per year); scholarships/grants and health care benefits also available. Financial award application deadline: 3/1. *Faculty research:* Supply chain management, inventory, simulation, logistics. *Unit head:* Dr. Charles R. Sox, Head, 205-348-8992, Fax: 205-348-0560, E-mail: csox@cba.ua.edu. *Application contact:* Dana Merchant, Administrative Secretary, 205-348-8904, E-mail: dmerchan@cba.ua.edu.

University of Arkansas, Graduate School, College of Engineering, Department of Industrial Engineering, Operations Management Program, Fayetteville, AR 72701-1201. Offers MS. Part-time and evening/weekend programs available. Postbaccalaureate distance learning degree programs offered. *Degree requirements:* For master's, thesis optional. Electronic applications accepted.

University of Bridgeport, School of Business, Bridgeport, CT 06604. Offers accounting (MBA); finance (MBA); general business (MBA); global financial services (MBA); human resource management (MBA); information systems and knowledge management (MBA); international business (MBA); management (MBA); marketing (MBA); operations management (MBA); small business and entrepreneurship (MBA); specialized business (MBA). *Accreditation:* ACBSP. Part-time and evening/weekend programs available. *Faculty:* 11 full-time (2 women), 39 part-time/adjunct (8 women). *Students:* 162 full-time (90 women), 69 part-time (45 women); includes 44 minority (20 Black or African American, non-Hispanic/Latino; 7 Asian, non-Hispanic/Latino; 15 Hispanic/Latino; 2 Two or more races, non-Hispanic/Latino), 163 international. Average age 28. 492 applicants, 48% accepted, 55 enrolled. In 2013, 144 master's awarded. *Degree requirements:* For master's, thesis optional. *Entrance requirements:* For master's, GMAT. Additional exam requirements/recommendations for international students: Recommended—TOEFL (minimum score 550 paper-based; 80 iBT), IELTS (minimum score 6.5). *Application deadline:* For fall admission, 8/1 priority date for domestic and international students; for spring admission, 12/1 priority date for domestic and international students. Applications are processed on a rolling basis. Application fee: $50. Electronic applications accepted. *Expenses:* Contact institution. *Financial support:* In 2013–14, 69 students received support. Fellowships, research assistantships, teaching assistantships, career-related internships or fieldwork, Federal Work-Study, institutionally sponsored loans, and tuition waivers (partial) available. Support available to part-time students. Financial award application deadline: 6/1; financial award applicants required to submit FAFSA. *Unit head:* Dr. Lloyd G. Gibson, Dean, 203-576-4384, Fax: 203-576-4388, E-mail: llgibson@bridgeport.edu. *Application contact:* Leanne Proctor, Director of Graduate Admissions, 203-576-4552, Fax: 203-576-4941, E-mail: mba@bridgeport.edu.
Website: http://www.bridgeport.edu.

University of California, Berkeley, Graduate Division, Haas School of Business, PhD in Business Administration Program, Berkeley, CA 94720-1500. Offers accounting (PhD); business and public policy (PhD); finance (PhD); management of organizations (PhD); marketing (PhD); operations management (PhD); real estate (PhD). *Accreditation:* AACSB. *Students:* 74 full-time (28 women); includes 11 minority (9 Asian, non-Hispanic/Latino; 2 Hispanic/Latino), 38 international. Average age 27. 490 applicants, 6% accepted, 14 enrolled. In 2013, 14 doctorates awarded. *Degree requirements:* For doctorate, comprehensive exam, thesis/dissertation, written preliminary exams, oral qualifying exam. *Entrance requirements:* For doctorate, GMAT or GRE, minimum GPA of 3.0 in undergraduate and graduate coursework. Additional exam requirements/recommendations for international students: Required—TOEFL (minimum score 570 paper-based; 70 iBT), IELTS (minimum score 7). *Application deadline:* For fall admission, 12/10 for domestic and international students. Application fee: $80 ($100 for international students). Electronic applications accepted. *Financial support:* In 2013–14, 74 students received support, including 62 fellowships with full and partial tuition reimbursements available (averaging $30,000 per year), research assistantships with full and partial tuition reimbursements available (averaging $12,000 per year), teaching assistantships with full and partial tuition reimbursements available (averaging $13,000 per year); scholarships/grants, health care benefits, tuition waivers (full), unspecified assistantships, and transit passes, travel grants also available. Financial award application deadline: 12/10; financial award applicants required to submit FAFSA. *Faculty research:* Accounting, business and public policy, entrepreneurship, finance, management of organizations, marketing, operations and information technology management, real estate. *Unit head:* Dr. Martin Lettau, Director, 510-643-6349, Fax: 510-643-4255, E-mail: kimg@haas.berkeley.edu. *Application contact:* Kim Guilfoyle, Director, Student Affairs, 510-642-3944, Fax: 510-643-4255, E-mail: kimg@haas.berkeley.edu.
Website: http://www.haas.berkeley.edu/Phd/.

University of California, Los Angeles, Graduate Division, UCLA Anderson School of Management, Los Angeles, CA 90095-1481. Offers accounting (PhD); Americas

(EMBA); Asia Pacific (EMBA); business administration (EMBA, MBA); decisions, operations and technology management (PhD); finance (PhD); financial engineering (MFE); global economics and management (PhD); management and organizations (PhD); marketing (PhD); strategy and policy (PhD); DDS/MBA; MBA/JD; MBA/MD; MBA/MLAS; MBA/MLIS; MBA/MPH; MBA/MPP; MBA/MSCS; MBA/MSN; MBA/MUP. *Accreditation:* AACSB. Part-time programs available. *Faculty:* 104 full-time (20 women), 28 part-time/adjunct (4 women). *Students:* 1,069 full-time (324 women), 879 part-time (251 women); includes 664 minority (37 Black or African American, non-Hispanic/Latino; 1 American Indian or Alaska Native, non-Hispanic/Latino; 470 Asian, non-Hispanic/Latino; 34 Hispanic/Latino; 2 Native Hawaiian or other Pacific Islander, non-Hispanic/Latino; 120 Two or more races, non-Hispanic/Latino), 444 international. Average age 30. 5,084 applicants, 27% accepted, 845 enrolled. In 2013, 801 master's, 14 doctorates awarded. *Degree requirements:* For master's, comprehensive exam, field study consulting project (for MBA); thesis (for MFE); for doctorate, comprehensive exam, thesis/dissertation, oral and written qualifying exams. *Entrance requirements:* For master's, GMAT (for MBA); GMAT or GRE General Test (for MFE), 4-year bachelor's degree or equivalent; recommendation letters (1 for MBA, 2 for MFE); two essays; interview (by invitation only for MBA); for doctorate, GMAT or GRE General Test, bachelor's degree from college or university of fully-recognized standing; minimum B average in undergraduate coursework or B+ average in prior graduate work; statement of purpose; three recommendation letters. Additional exam requirements/recommendations for international students: Required—TOEFL (minimum score 560 paper-based; 87 iBT). *Application deadline:* For fall admission, 10/22 priority date for domestic and international students; for winter admission, 1/7 for domestic and international students; for spring admission, 4/15 for domestic and international students. Applications are processed on a rolling basis. Application fee: $200. Electronic applications accepted. *Expenses:* Contact institution. *Financial support:* In 2013–14, 522 students received support. Fellowships, research assistantships with partial tuition reimbursements available, teaching assistantships with partial tuition reimbursements available, career-related internships or fieldwork, institutionally sponsored loans, scholarships/grants, health care benefits, and tuition waivers (partial) available. Financial award application deadline: 4/15; financial award applicants required to submit FAFSA. *Faculty research:* Asset pricing, decision-making, behavioral finance, international finance and economics, global macroeconomics. *Total annual research expenditures:* $368,086. *Unit head:* Dr. Judy D. Olian, Dean/Chair in Management, 310-825-7982, Fax: 310-206-2073, E-mail: judy.olian@anderson.ucla.edu. *Application contact:* Alex Lawrence, Assistant Dean, MBA Admissions and Financial Aid, 310-825-6944, Fax: 310-825-8582, E-mail: mba.admissions@anderson.ucla.edu.
Website: http://www.anderson.ucla.edu/.

See Display on page 145 and Close-Up on page 191.

University of Central Missouri, The Graduate School, Warrensburg, MO 6409. Offers accountancy (MA); accounting (MBA); applied mathematics (MS); aviation safety (MA); biology (MS); business administration (MBA); career and technical education leadership (MS); college student personnel administration (MS); communication (MA); computer science (MS); counseling (MS); criminal justice (MS); educational leadership (Ed D); educational technology (MS); elementary and early childhood education (MSE); English (MA); environmental studies (MA); finance (MBA); history (MA); human services/educational technology (Ed S); human services/learning resources (Ed S); human services/professional counseling (Ed S); industrial hygiene (MS); industrial management (MS); information systems (MBA); information technology (MS); kinesiology (MS); library science and information services (MS); literacy education (MSE); marketing (MBA); mathematics (MS); music (MA); occupational safety management (MS); psychology (MS); rural family nursing (MS); school administration (MSE); social gerontology (MS); sociology (MA); special education (MSE); speech language pathology (MS); superintendency (Ed S); teaching (MAT); teaching English as a second language (MA); technology (MS); technology management (PhD); theatre (MA). Part-time programs available. *Faculty:* 233. *Students:* 890 full-time (396 women), 1,486 part-time (1,001 women); includes 192 minority (97 Black or African American, non-Hispanic/Latino; 9 American Indian or Alaska Native, non-Hispanic/Latino; 32 Asian, non-Hispanic/Latino; 40 Hispanic/Latino; 3 Native Hawaiian or other Pacific Islander, non-Hispanic/Latino; 11 Two or more races, non-Hispanic/Latino), 539 international. Average age 31. 1,953 applicants, 75% accepted. In 2013, 719 master's, 58 other advanced degrees awarded. *Degree requirements:* For master's and Ed S, comprehensive exam (for some programs), thesis (for some programs). *Entrance requirements:* Additional exam requirements/recommendations for international students: Required—TOEFL (minimum score 550 paper-based; 79 iBT). *Application deadline:* For fall admission, 6/1 for domestic students; for spring admission, 10/1 for domestic and international students. Applications are processed on a rolling basis. Application fee: $30 ($75 for international students). Electronic applications accepted. *Expenses:* Tuition, state resident: full-time $7326; part-time $276.25 per credit hour. Tuition, nonresident: full-time $13,956; part-time $552.50 per credit hour. *Required fees:* $29 per credit hour. *Financial support:* In 2013–14, 118 students received support, including 271 research assistantships with full and partial tuition reimbursements available (averaging $7,500 per year), 109 teaching assistantships with full and partial tuition reimbursements available (averaging $7,500 per year); career-related internships or fieldwork, Federal Work-Study, scholarships/grants, and administrative and laboratory assistantships also available. Support available to part-time students. Financial award application deadline: 3/1; financial award applicants required to submit FAFSA. *Unit head:* Dr. Joseph Vaughn, Assistant Provost for Research/Dean, 660-543-4092, Fax: 660-543-4778, E-mail: vaughn@ucmo.edu. *Application contact:* Brittany Lawrence, Graduate Student Services Coordinator, 660-543-4621, Fax: 660-543-4778, E-mail: gradinfo@ucmo.edu.
Website: http://www.ucmo.edu/graduate/.

University of Cincinnati, Graduate School, Carl H. Lindner College of Business, PhD Programs, Cincinnati, OH 45221. Offers accounting (PhD); economics (PhD); finance (PhD); information systems (PhD); management (PhD); marketing (PhD); operations and business analytics (PhD). *Faculty:* 62 full-time (13 women). *Students:* 27 full-time (15 women), 9 part-time (1 woman); includes 2 minority (1 Asian, non-Hispanic/Latino; 1 Hispanic/Latino), 16 international. Average age 29. 86 applicants, 13% accepted, 6 enrolled. In 2013, 8 doctorates awarded. *Degree requirements:* For doctorate, comprehensive exam, thesis/dissertation. *Entrance requirements:* For doctorate, GMAT, GRE, transcripts, essays, resume, letters of recommendation. Additional exam requirements/recommendations for international students: Required—TOEFL (minimum score 600 paper-based; 100 iBT), IELTS (minimum score 6.5). *Application deadline:* For fall admission, 1/15 for domestic and international students. Application fee: $65 ($70 for international students). Electronic applications accepted. *Expenses:* Contact institution. *Financial support:* In 2013–14, 33 students received support, including 25 research assistantships with full and partial tuition reimbursements available (averaging $23,250 per year); scholarships/grants, tuition waivers (full and partial), and unspecified assistantships also available. Financial award application deadline: 1/15; financial award applicants required to submit FAFSA. *Unit head:* Dr. Suzanne Masterson, Director, 513-556-7125, Fax: 513-556-5499, E-mail: suzanne.masterson@uc.edu. *Application contact:* Angel Elvin, Assistant Director, 513-556-7190, Fax: 513-558-7006, E-mail: angel.elvin@uc.edu.
Website: http://www.business.uc.edu/phd.

The University of Manchester, School of Mechanical, Aerospace and Civil Engineering, Manchester, United Kingdom. Offers advanced manufacturing technology (M Ent); aerospace engineering (M Phil, M Sc, PhD); civil engineering (M Phil, M Sc, PhD); environmental engineering (M Phil, PhD); management of projects (M Phil, M Sc, PhD); mechanical engineering (M Phil, M Sc, PhD); mechanical engineering design (M Ent); nuclear engineering (M Phil, D Eng, PhD).

University of Michigan–Flint, School of Management, Flint, MI 48502-1950. Offers accounting (MBA, MSA); business (Graduate Certificate); computer information systems (MBA); finance (MBA); health care management (MBA); international business (MBA); lean manufacturing (MBA); marketing (MBA); organizational leadership (MBA). *Accreditation:* AACSB. Part-time and evening/weekend programs available. Postbaccalaureate distance learning degree programs offered (minimal on-campus study). *Faculty:* 13 full-time (3 women), 4 part-time/adjunct (0 women). *Students:* 19 full-time (6 women), 234 part-time (72 women); includes 50 minority (21 Black or African American, non-Hispanic/Latino; 5 American Indian or Alaska Native, non-Hispanic/Latino; 12 Asian, non-Hispanic/Latino; 5 Hispanic/Latino; 7 Two or more races, non-Hispanic/Latino), 30 international. Average age 32. 195 applicants, 56% accepted, 88 enrolled. In 2013, 73 master's awarded. *Degree requirements:* For master's, thesis or alternative. *Entrance requirements:* For master's, GMAT or GRE, minimum GPA of 3.0. Additional exam requirements/recommendations for international students: Required—TOEFL (minimum score 560 paper-based; 84 iBT), IELTS (minimum score 6.5). *Application deadline:* For fall admission, 8/1 for domestic students, 5/1 for international students; for winter admission, 11/1 for domestic students, 9/1 for international students; for spring admission, 2/15 for domestic students, 1/15 for international students. Applications are processed on a rolling basis. Application fee: $55. Electronic applications accepted. *Financial support:* Federal Work-Study, scholarships/grants, and unspecified assistantships available. Support available to part-time students. Financial award application deadline: 3/1; financial award applicants required to submit FAFSA. *Unit head:* Dr. Scott Johnson, Dean, School of Management, 810-762-3164, Fax: 810-237-6685, E-mail: scotjohn@umflint.edu. *Application contact:* Jeremiah Cook, Marketing Communications Specialist, 810-424-5583, Fax: 810-766-6789, E-mail: jecook@umflint.edu.
Website: http://www.umflint.edu/som/.

University of Minnesota, Twin Cities Campus, Carlson School of Management, Doctoral Program in Business Administration, Minneapolis, MN 55455-0213. Offers accounting (PhD); finance (PhD); information and decision sciences (PhD); marketing (PhD); operations and management science (PhD); strategic management and entrepreneurship (PhD). *Faculty:* 102 full-time (31 women). *Students:* 74 full-time (25 women); includes 8 minority (1 Black or African American, non-Hispanic/Latino; 5 Asian, non-Hispanic/Latino; 2 Hispanic/Latino), 46 international. Average age 30. 274 applicants, 8% accepted, 15 enrolled. In 2013, 10 doctorates awarded. *Degree requirements:* For doctorate, comprehensive exam, thesis/dissertation, written and oral preliminary exams, proposal defense, final defense. *Entrance requirements:* For doctorate, GMAT, GRE General Test. Additional exam requirements/recommendations for international students: Required—TOEFL (minimum score 600 paper-based; 100 iBT); Recommended—IELTS (minimum score 7.5). *Application deadline:* For fall admission, 12/31 for domestic students, 12/31 priority date for international students. Applications are processed on a rolling basis. Application fee: $75 ($95 for international students). Electronic applications accepted. *Expenses:* Contact institution. *Financial support:* In 2013–14, 68 students received support, including 96 fellowships with full tuition reimbursements available (averaging $6,300 per year), 65 research assistantships with full tuition reimbursements available (averaging $12,500 per year), 64 teaching assistantships with full tuition reimbursements available (averaging $12,500 per year); institutionally sponsored loans, scholarships/grants, health care benefits, unspecified assistantships, and full student fee waivers also available. Financial award application deadline: 12/31. *Faculty research:* Corporate strategy, finance, entrepreneurship, marketing, information and decision science, operations, accounting, supply chain. *Unit head:* Dr. Shawn P. Curley, Director, 612-624-6546, Fax: 612-624-8221, E-mail: curley@umn.edu. *Application contact:* Earlene K. Bronson, Assistant Director, 612-624-0875, Fax: 612-624-8221, E-mail: brons003@umn.edu.
Website: http://www.csom.umn.edu/phd-BA/.

University of Missouri–St. Louis, College of Business Administration, Program in Business Administration, St. Louis, MO 63121. Offers accounting (MBA); business administration (Certificate); business intelligence (Certificate); finance (MBA); human resource management (Certificate); information systems (MBA); logistics and supply chain management (MBA, PhD, Certificate); marketing (MBA); marketing management (Certificate); operations management (MBA). *Accreditation:* AACSB. Part-time and evening/weekend programs available. *Faculty:* 30 full-time (5 women), 20 part-time/adjunct (8 women). *Students:* 114 full-time (51 women), 269 part-time (100 women); includes 43 minority (16 Black or African American, non-Hispanic/Latino; 14 Asian, non-Hispanic/Latino; 11 Hispanic/Latino; 1 Native Hawaiian or other Pacific Islander, non-Hispanic/Latino; 1 Two or more races, non-Hispanic/Latino), 56 international. Average age 31. 153 applicants, 91% accepted, 110 enrolled. In 2013, 136 master's, 7 other advanced degrees awarded. *Degree requirements:* For doctorate, thesis/dissertation. *Entrance requirements:* For master's, GMAT, 2 letters of recommendation. Additional exam requirements/recommendations for international students: Recommended—TOEFL (minimum score 550 paper-based; 79 iBT), IELTS (minimum score 6.5). *Application deadline:* For fall admission, 7/1 for domestic and international students; for spring admission, 12/1 for domestic and international students. Applications are processed on a rolling basis. Application fee: $50 ($40 for international students). Electronic applications accepted. *Expenses:* Tuition, state resident: full-time $7364; part-time $409.10 per credit hour. Tuition, nonresident: full-time $19,162; part-time $1008.50 per credit hour. *Financial support:* In 2013–14, 14 research assistantships with full and partial tuition reimbursements (averaging $5,625 per year), 6 teaching assistantships with full and partial tuition reimbursements (averaging $9,403 per year) were awarded; career-related internships or fieldwork, Federal Work-Study, and institutionally sponsored loans also available. Support available to part-time students. Financial award application deadline: 4/1; financial award applicants required to submit FAFSA. *Faculty research:* Human resources, strategic management, marketing strategy, consumer behavior product development, advertising. *Unit head:* Francesca Ferrari, Assistant Director, 314-516-5885, Fax: 314-516-6420, E-mail: mba@umsl.edu. *Application contact:* 314-516-5458, Fax: 314-516-6996, E-mail: gradadm@umsl.edu.
Website: http://mba.umsl.edu/Degree%20Programs/index.html.

University of New Haven, Graduate School, Tagliatela College of Engineering, Program in Engineering and Operations Management, West Haven, CT 06516-1916. Offers engineering and operations management (MS); engineering management (MS); Lean/Six Sigma (Certificate). *Students:* 22 full-time (8 women), 66 part-time (10 women); includes 11 minority (4 Black or African American, non-Hispanic/Latino; 5 Asian, non-Hispanic/Latino; 2 Hispanic/Latino), 34 international. 100 applicants, 85% accepted, 38 enrolled. In 2013, 26 master's awarded. *Entrance requirements:* Additional exam requirements/recommendations for international students: Required—TOEFL (minimum score 75 iBT), IELTS, PTE (minimum score 50). *Application deadline:* For fall admission, 5/31 for international students; for winter admission, 10/15 for international students; for spring admission, 1/15 for international students. Applications are processed on a rolling

basis. Application fee: $75. Electronic applications accepted. Application fee is waived when completed online. *Expenses: Tuition:* Full-time $21,600; part-time $800 per credit hour. *Required fees:* $45 per trimester. *Unit head:* Dr. John Sarris, Chair, 203-932-7146, E-mail: jsarris@newhaven.edu. *Application contact:* Eloise Gormley, Director of Graduate Admissions, 203-932-7440, E-mail: gradinfo@newhaven.edu.
Website: http://www.newhaven.edu/88389/.

The University of North Carolina at Charlotte, The Graduate School, The William States Lee College of Engineering, Department of Systems Engineering and Engineering Management, Charlotte, NC 28223-0001. Offers energy analytics (Graduate Certificate); engineering management (MSEM); engineering science (MS); infrastructure and environmental systems (PhD); Lean Six Sigma (Graduate Certificate); logistics and supply chains (Graduate Certificate); systems analytics (Graduate Certificate). Part-time and evening/weekend programs available. Postbaccalaureate distance learning degree programs offered. *Faculty:* 6 full-time (1 woman), 1 (woman) part-time/adjunct. *Students:* 17 full-time (7 women), 39 part-time (11 women); includes 12 minority (6 Black or African American, non-Hispanic/Latino; 4 Asian, non-Hispanic/Latino; 2 Hispanic/Latino), 20 international. Average age 28. 86 applicants, 65% accepted, 23 enrolled. In 2013, 8 master's awarded. *Degree requirements:* For master's, thesis or alternative, project. *Entrance requirements:* For master's, GRE or GMAT, letters of recommendation. Additional exam requirements/recommendations for international students: Required—TOEFL (minimum score 557 paper-based; 83 iBT). *Application deadline:* For fall admission, 5/1 priority date for domestic students, 5/1 for international students; for spring admission, 10/1 priority date for domestic students, 10/1 for international students. Application fee: $75. Electronic applications accepted. *Expenses:* Tuition, state resident: full-time $3522. Tuition, nonresident: full-time $16,051. *Required fees:* $2585. Tuition and fees vary according to course load and program. *Financial support:* Applicants required to submit FAFSA. *Faculty research:* Sustainable material and renewable technology; thermal analysis; large scale optimization; project risk management; supply chains; leans systems; global product innovation; quality and reliability analysis and management; productivity and project management; business forecasting, market analyses and feasibility studies. *Unit head:* Dr. Robert E. Johnson, Dean, 704-687-8242, Fax: 704-687-2352, E-mail: robejohn@.uncc.edu. *Application contact:* Kathy B. Giddings, Director of Graduate Admissions, 704-687-5503, Fax: 704-687-1668, E-mail: gradadm@uncc.edu.

University of North Texas, Robert B. Toulouse School of Graduate Studies, Denton, TN 76203-5017. Offers accounting (MS, PhD); applied anthropology (MA, MS); applied behavior analysis (Certificate); applied technology and performance improvement (M Ed, MS, PhD); art education (MA, PhD); art history (MA); art museum education (Certificate); arts leadership (Certificate); audiology (Au D); behavior analysis (MS); biochemistry and molecular biology (MS, PhD); biology (MA, MS, PhD); business (PhD); business computer information systems (PhD); chemistry (MS, PhD); clinical psychology (PhD); communication studies (MA, MS); computer engineering (MS); computer science (MS); computer science and engineering (PhD); counseling (M Ed, MS, PhD), including clinical mental health counseling (MS), college and university counseling (M Ed, MS), elementary school counseling (M Ed, MS), secondary school counseling (M Ed, MS); counseling psychology (PhD); creative writing (MA); criminal justice (MS); curriculum and instruction (M Ed, PhD), including curriculum studies (PhD), early childhood studies (PhD), language and literacy studies (PhD); decision sciences (MBA); design (MA, MFA), including fashion design (MFA), innovation studies, interior design (MFA); early childhood studies (MS); economics (MS); educational leadership (M Ed, Ed D, PhD); educational psychology (MS), including family studies, gifted and talented (MS, PhD), human development, learning and cognition, research, measurement and evaluation; educational research (PhD), including gifted and talented (MS, PhD), human development and family studies, psychological aspects of sports and exercise, research, measurement and statistics; electrical engineering (MS); emergency management (MPA); engineering systems (MS); English (MA, PhD); environmental science (MS, PhD); experimental psychology (PhD); finance (MBA, MS, PhD); financial management (MPA); French (MA); health psychology and behavioral medicine (PhD); health services management (MBA); higher education (M Ed, Ed D, PhD); history (MA, MS, PhD), including European history (PhD), military history (PhD), United States history (PhD); hospitality management (MS); human resources management (MPA); information science (MS, PhD); information technologies (MBA); information technology and decision sciences (MS); interdisciplinary studies (MA, MS); international sustainable tourism (MS); jazz studies (MM); journalism (MA, MJ, Graduate Certificate), including interactive and virtual digital communication (Graduate Certificate), narrative journalism (Graduate Certificate), public relations (Graduate Certificate); kinesiology (MS); learning technologies (MS, PhD); library science (MS); local government management (MPA); logistics and supply chain management (MBA, PhD); long-term care, senior housing, and aging services (MA, MS); management science (PhD); marketing (MBA, PhD); materials science and engineering (MS, PhD); mathematics (MA, PhD); merchandising (MS); music (MA, MM Ed, PhD), including ethnomusicology (MA), music education (MM Ed, PhD), music theory (MA, PhD), musicology (MA, PhD), performance (MA); nonprofit management (MPA); operations and supply chain management (MBA); performance (MM, DMA); philosophy (MA, PhD); physics (MS, PhD); political science (MA, MS, PhD); public administration and management (PhD), including emergency management, nonprofit management, public financial management, urban management; radio, television and film (MA, MFA); recreation, event and sport management (MS); rehabilitation counseling (MS, Certificate); sociology (MA, MS, PhD); Spanish (MA); special education (M Ed, PhD), including autism intervention (PhD), emotional/behavioral disorders (PhD), mild/moderate disabilities (PhD); speech-language pathology (MA, MS); strategic management (MBA); studio art (MFA); taxation (MS); teaching (M Ed); MBA/MS; MS/MPH; MSES/MBA. Part-time and evening/weekend programs available. Postbaccalaureate distance learning degree programs offered. *Faculty:* 661 full-time (213 women), 240 part-time/adjunct (144 women). *Students:* 3,106 full-time (1,620 women), 3,543 part-time (2,221 women); includes 1,740 minority (533 Black or African American, non-Hispanic/Latino; 15 American Indian or Alaska Native, non-Hispanic/Latino; 286 Asian, non-Hispanic/Latino; 746 Hispanic/Latino; 3 Native Hawaiian or other Pacific Islander, non-Hispanic/Latino; 157 Two or more races, non-Hispanic/Latino), 1,145 international. Average age 32. 6,289 applicants, 43% accepted, 1751 enrolled. In 2013, 1,778 master's, 239 doctorates, 10 other advanced degrees awarded. Terminal master's awarded for partial completion of doctoral program. *Degree requirements:* For master's, variable foreign language requirement, comprehensive exam (for some programs), thesis (for some programs); for doctorate, variable foreign language requirement, comprehensive exam (for some programs), thesis/dissertation; for other advanced degree, variable foreign language requirement, comprehensive exam (for some programs). *Entrance requirements:* For master's and doctorate, GRE, GMAT. Additional exam requirements/recommendations for international students: Required—TOEFL (minimum score 550 paper-based; 79 iBT). *Application deadline:* For fall admission, 7/15 for domestic students, 3/15 for international students; for spring admission, 11/15 for domestic students, 9/15 for international students; for summer admission, 5/1 for domestic students. Applications are processed on a rolling basis. Application fee: $60. Electronic applications accepted. *Financial support:* Fellowships with partial tuition reimbursements, research assistantships with partial tuition reimbursements, teaching assistantships, career-related internships or fieldwork, Federal Work-Study, institutionally sponsored loans, scholarships/grants, health care benefits, and library assistantships available. Support available to part-time students. Financial award applicants required to submit FAFSA. *Unit head:* Mark Wardell, Dean, 940-565-2383, E-mail: mark.wardell@unt.edu. *Application contact:* Toulouse School of Graduate Studies, 940-565-2383, Fax: 940-565-2141, E-mail: gradsch@unt.edu.
Website: http://tsgs.unt.edu/.

University of Pittsburgh, Katz Graduate School of Business, Master of Business Administration Programs, Pittsburgh, PA 15260. Offers finance (MBA); information systems (MBA); marketing (MBA); operations management (MBA); organizational behavior and human resource management (MBA); strategy, environment and organizations (MBA); MBA/JD; MBA/MIB; MBA/MPIA; MBA/MSE; MBA/MSIS; MID/MBA. *Accreditation:* AACSB. Part-time and evening/weekend programs available. *Faculty:* 60 full-time (14 women), 21 part-time/adjunct (5 women). *Students:* 107 full-time (31 women), 428 part-time (155 women); includes 55 minority (15 Black or African American, non-Hispanic/Latino; 26 Asian, non-Hispanic/Latino; 10 Hispanic/Latino; 4 Two or more races, non-Hispanic/Latino), 83 international. Average age 30. 449 applicants, 23% accepted, 63 enrolled. In 2013, 279 master's awarded. *Degree requirements:* For master's, minimum GPA of 3.0. *Entrance requirements:* For master's, GMAT, recommendations, undergraduate transcripts, essay, resume, interview, bachelor's degree. Additional exam requirements/recommendations for international students: Required—TOEFL (minimum score 600 paper-based; 100 iBT) or IELTS. *Application deadline:* For fall admission, 4/1 priority date for domestic students, 2/1 priority date for international students. Application fee: $50. Electronic applications accepted. *Expenses:* Tuition, state resident: full-time $19,964; part-time $807 per credit. Tuition, nonresident: full-time $32,686; part-time $1337 per credit. *Required fees:* $740; $200. Tuition and fees vary according to program. *Financial support:* In 2013–14, 60 students received support. Career-related internships or fieldwork and scholarships/grants available. Financial award application deadline: 2/1. *Faculty research:* Accounting systems/financial reporting, corporate finance, shopper marketing/consumer behavior, management information systems, organizational behavior and entrepreneurship. *Unit head:* Tim Robison, Assistant Dean, 412-648-1700, Fax: 412-648-1659, E-mail: trobison@katz.pitt.edu. *Application contact:* Thomas Keller, Director of MBA Admissions, 412-648-1700, Fax: 412-648-1659, E-mail: mba@katz.pitt.edu.
Website: http://www.business.pitt.edu/katz/mba/.

University of Portland, Dr. Robert B. Pamplin, Jr. School of Business, Portland, OR 97203-5798. Offers entrepreneurship (MBA); finance (MBA, MS); health care management (MBA); marketing (MBA); nonprofit management (EMBA); operations and technology management (MBA, MS); sustainability (MBA). *Accreditation:* AACSB. Part-time and evening/weekend programs available. *Faculty:* 26 full-time (5 women), 8 part-time/adjunct (1 woman). *Students:* 37 full-time (11 women), 93 part-time (44 women); includes 15 minority (1 Black or African American, non-Hispanic/Latino; 7 Asian, non-Hispanic/Latino; 5 Hispanic/Latino; 2 Two or more races, non-Hispanic/Latino), 21 international. Average age 32. In 2013, 68 master's awarded. *Entrance requirements:* For master's, GMAT, minimum GPA of 3.0, resume, 2 letters of recommendation. Additional exam requirements/recommendations for international students: Required—TOEFL (minimum score 570 paper-based; 89 iBT), IELTS (minimum score 7). *Application deadline:* For fall admission, 7/15 priority date for domestic and international students; for spring admission, 12/15 priority date for domestic and international students. Applications are processed on a rolling basis. Application fee: $50. *Expenses:* Contact institution. *Financial support:* Federal Work-Study, scholarships/grants, and tuition waivers (partial) available. Support available to part-time students. Financial award application deadline: 3/1; financial award applicants required to submit FAFSA. *Unit head:* Melissa McCarthy, Director, 503-943-7224, E-mail: mba-up@up.edu.
Website: http://business.up.edu/mba/default.aspx?cid-1179&pid-6450.

University of Puerto Rico, Mayagüez Campus, Graduate Studies, College of Business Administration, Mayagüez, PR 00681-9000. Offers business administration (MBA); finance (MBA); human resources (MBA); industrial management (MBA). Part-time and evening/weekend programs available. *Faculty:* 42 full-time (26 women), 1 part-time/adjunct (0 women). *Students:* 36 full-time (18 women), 15 part-time (11 women). 26 applicants, 50% accepted, 10 enrolled. In 2013, 7 master's awarded. *Degree requirements:* For master's, comprehensive exam. *Entrance requirements:* For master's, GMAT or EXADEP, bachelor's degree with courses in calculus, microeconomics, accounting and statistics. Additional exam requirements/recommendations for international students: Required—TOEFL (minimum score 500 paper-based). *Application deadline:* For fall admission, 2/15 for domestic and international students; for spring admission, 9/15 for domestic and international students. Applications are processed on a rolling basis. Application fee: $25. *Expenses: Tuition, area resident:* Full-time $2466; part-time $822 per year. *International tuition:* $6371 full-time. *Required fees:* $1095; $1095. Tuition and fees vary according to course level, course load and reciprocity agreements. *Financial support:* In 2013–14, 7 students received support, including 2 research assistantships (averaging $8,725 per year), 5 teaching assistantships (averaging $4,106 per year); fellowships with full tuition reimbursements available, Federal Work-Study, institutionally sponsored loans, and unspecified assistantships also available. *Faculty research:* Organizational studies, management, accounting. *Total annual research expenditures:* $20,000. *Unit head:* Dr. Ana Martin, Graduate Student Coordinator, 787-832-4040 Ext. 3800, Fax: 787-832-5320, E-mail: ana.martin@upr.edu. *Application contact:* Milagros Soto, Student Administrator, 787-265-3887, Fax: 787-832-5320, E-mail: milagros.soto1@upr.edu.
Website: http://enterprise.uprm.edu/.

University of Puerto Rico, Río Piedras Campus, College of Business Administration, San Juan, PR 00931-3300. Offers accounting (MBA); finance (MBA, PhD); general business (MBA); human resources management (MBA); international trade and business (MBA, PhD); marketing (MBA); operations management (MBA); quantitative methods (MBA). Part-time programs available. *Degree requirements:* For master's, comprehensive exam, thesis or alternative, research project. *Entrance requirements:* For master's, GMAT or PAEG, minimum GPA of 3.0, letter of recommendation; for doctorate, GMAT, PAEG, minimum GPA of 3.0, master degree. *Faculty research:* Management.

University of Rhode Island, Graduate School, College of Business Administration, Kingston, RI 02881. Offers accounting (MS); business administration (MBA, PhD), including finance and insurance (PhD), management (PhD), marketing (PhD), operations and supply chain management (MBA); finance (MBA); general business (MBA); management (MBA); marketing (MBA); supply chain management (MBA). *Accreditation:* AACSB. Part-time and evening/weekend programs available. *Faculty:* 43 full-time (16 women). *Students:* 103 full-time (37 women), 196 part-time (82 women); includes 42 minority (6 Black or African American, non-Hispanic/Latino; 1 American Indian or Alaska Native, non-Hispanic/Latino; 16 Asian, non-Hispanic/Latino; 13 Hispanic/Latino; 6 Two or more races, non-Hispanic/Latino), 29 international. In 2013, 119 master's, 3 doctorates awarded. *Degree requirements:* For master's, comprehensive exam (for some programs), thesis optional; for doctorate, comprehensive exam, thesis/dissertation. *Entrance requirements:* For master's, GMAT or GRE, 2 letters of recommendation, resume; for doctorate, GMAT or GRE, 3 letters of

recommendation, resume. Additional exam requirements/recommendations for international students: Required—TOEFL (minimum score 575 paper-based; 91 iBT). *Application deadline:* For fall admission, 4/15 for domestic students, 2/15 for international students. Application fee: $65. Electronic applications accepted. *Expenses:* Tuition, state resident: full-time $11,532; part-time $641 per credit. Tuition, nonresident: full-time $23,606; part-time $1311 per credit. *Required fees:* $1388; $36 per credit. $35 per semester. One-time fee: $130. *Financial support:* In 2013–14, 14 teaching assistantships with full and partial tuition reimbursements (averaging $15,220 per year) were awarded. Financial award application deadline: 4/15; financial award applicants required to submit FAFSA. *Total annual research expenditures:* $66,948. *Unit head:* Dr. Mark Higgins, Dean, 401-874-4244, Fax: 401-874-4312, E-mail: markhiggins@uri.edu. *Application contact:* Lisa Lancellotta, Coordinator, MBA Programs, 401-874-4241, Fax: 401-874-4312, E-mail: mba@uri.edu.
Website: http://www.cba.uri.edu/.

University of Rochester, Simon Business School, Full-Time Master's Program in Business Administration, Rochester, NY 14627. Offers accounting and information systems (MBA); business environment and public policy (MBA); business systems consulting (MBA); competitive and organizational strategy - pricing (MBA); computers and information systems (MBA); corporate accounting (MBA); electronic commerce (MBA); entrepreneurship (MBA); finance (MBA); health sciences management (MBA); international management (MBA); marketing - brand management and pricing (MBA); operations management - manufacturing (MBA); operations management - services (MBA); public accounting (MBA). *Accreditation:* AACSB. Part-time and evening/weekend programs available. *Faculty:* 60 full-time (11 women), 23 part-time/adjunct (3 women). *Students:* 282 full-time (74 women); includes 55 minority (29 Black or African American, non-Hispanic/Latino; 1 American Indian or Alaska Native, non-Hispanic/Latino; 11 Asian, non-Hispanic/Latino; 12 Hispanic/Latino; 2 Two or more races, non-Hispanic/Latino), 144 international. 673 applicants, 33% accepted, 65 enrolled. In 2013, 176 master's awarded. *Entrance requirements:* For master's, GMAT/GRE, previous course work in calculus. Additional exam requirements/recommendations for international students: Required—TOEFL. *Application deadline:* For fall admission, 10/15 for domestic and international students; for winter admission, 1/5 for domestic and international students; for spring admission, 3/15 for domestic and international students; for summer admission, 5/15 for domestic students. Applications are processed on a rolling basis. Application fee: $150. Electronic applications accepted. *Expenses: Tuition:* Full-time $44,580; part-time $1394 per credit hour. *Required fees:* $492. *Financial support:* In 2013–14, 72 students received support. Fellowships, research assistantships, teaching assistantships, institutionally sponsored loans, scholarships/grants, and tuition waivers (partial) available. Financial award application deadline: 3/1; financial award applicants required to submit CSS PROFILE or FAFSA. *Unit head:* Mark Zupan, Dean, 585-275-3316. *Application contact:* Rebekah S. Lewin, Assistant Dean of Admissions and Student Engagement, 585-275-3533, E-mail: admissions@simon.rochester.edu.

University of Rochester, Simon Business School, Part-Time MBA Program, Rochester, NY 14627. Offers accounting and information systems (MBA); business environment and public policy (MBA); business systems consulting (MBA); competitive and organizational strategy (MBA); computers and information systems (MBA); corporate accounting (MBA); electronic commerce (MBA); entrepreneurship (MBA); finance (MBA); health sciences management (MBA); international management (MBA); manufacturing management (MBA); marketing (MBA); operations management - services (MBA); public accounting (MBA). Part-time and evening/weekend programs available. *Faculty:* 59 full-time (10 women), 23 part-time/adjunct (3 women). *Students:* 270 part-time (75 women); includes 38 minority (5 Black or African American, non-Hispanic/Latino; 1 American Indian or Alaska Native, non-Hispanic/Latino; 24 Asian, non-Hispanic/Latino; 5 Hispanic/Latino; 3 Two or more races, non-Hispanic/Latino). Average age 32. 56 applicants, 98% accepted, 51 enrolled. In 2013, 77 master's awarded. *Entrance requirements:* For master's, GRE or GMAT, resume, recommendation letters, essays, transcipts. *Application deadline:* For fall admission, 8/15 for domestic students; for winter admission, 11/15 for domestic students; for spring admission, 2/15 for domestic students; for summer admission, 5/15 for domestic students. Applications are processed on a rolling basis. Application fee: $150. Electronic applications accepted. *Expenses: Tuition:* Full-time $44,580; part-time $1394 per credit hour. *Required fees:* $492. *Financial support:* Scholarships/grants and tuition waivers available. Financial award applicants required to submit CSS PROFILE. *Unit head:* Mark Zupan, Dean, 585-275-3316, E-mail: mark.zupan@simon.rochester.edu. *Application contact:* Jennifer Mossotti, Associate Director of Part-Time Programs, 585-275-3803, E-mail: jennifer.mossotti@simon.rochester.edu.
Website: http://www.simon.rochester.edu/programs/part-time-mba-programs/index.aspx.

University of Southern Indiana, Graduate Studies, College of Science, Engineering, and Education, Program in Industrial Management, Evansville, IN 47712-3590. Offers MS. Part-time and evening/weekend programs available. *Faculty:* 1 full-time (0 women), 1 part-time/adjunct (0 women). *Students:* 12 part-time (1 woman), 1 international. Average age 32. 10 applicants, 50% accepted, 5 enrolled. In 2013, 4 master's awarded. *Degree requirements:* For master's, project. *Entrance requirements:* For master's, minimum GPA of 2.5, BS in engineering or engineering technology. Additional exam requirements/recommendations for international students: Required—TOEFL (minimum score 550 paper-based; 79 iBT), IELTS (minimum score 6). *Application deadline:* For fall admission, 8/15 priority date for domestic students, 3/1 priority date for international students. Applications are processed on a rolling basis. Application fee: $40. Electronic applications accepted. *Expenses:* Tuition, state resident: full-time $5567; part-time $309 per credit hour. Tuition, nonresident: full-time $10,977; part-time $610 per credit. *Required fees:* $23 per semester. *Financial support:* Federal Work-Study, scholarships/grants, tuition waivers (full and partial), and unspecified assistantships available. Financial award application deadline: 3/1; financial award applicants required to submit FAFSA. *Unit head:* Dr. David E. Schultz, Director, 812-464-1881, E-mail: dschultz@usi.edu. *Application contact:* Dr. Mayola Rowser, Director, Graduate Studies, 812-465-7016, Fax: 812-464-1956, E-mail: mrowser@usi.edu.
Website: http://www.usi.edu/science/engineering/programs/master-of-science-in-industrial-management.

The University of Tennessee, Graduate School, College of Business Administration, Program in Business Administration, Knoxville, TN 37996. Offers accounting (PhD); finance (MBA, PhD); logistics and transportation (MBA, PhD); management (PhD); marketing (MBA, PhD); operations management (MBA); professional business administration (MBA); statistics (PhD); JD/MBA; MS/MBA; Pharm D/MBA. Pharm D/MBA offered jointly with The University of Tennessee Health Science Center. *Accreditation:* AACSB. Postbaccalaureate distance learning degree programs offered. *Degree requirements:* For master's, thesis or alternative; for doctorate, thesis/dissertation. *Entrance requirements:* For master's and doctorate, GMAT, minimum GPA of 2.7. Additional exam requirements/recommendations for international students: Required—TOEFL. Electronic applications accepted. *Expenses:* Tuition, state resident: full-time $9540; part-time $531 per credit hour. Tuition, nonresident: full-time $27,728; part-time $1542 per credit hour. *Required fees:* $1404; $67 per credit hour.

The University of Texas at Arlington, Graduate School, College of Business, Program in Business Administration, Arlington, TX 76019. Offers accounting (PhD); business statistics (PhD); finance (MBA, PhD); information systems (MBA, PhD); management (MBA, PhD); marketing (MBA, PhD); operations management (MBA, PhD); real estate (MBA). *Accreditation:* AACSB. Part-time and evening/weekend programs available. *Degree requirements:* For master's, thesis optional; for doctorate, comprehensive exam, thesis/dissertation. *Entrance requirements:* For master's, GMAT or GRE; for doctorate, GMAT, minimum GPA of 3.0 (undergraduate), 3.4 (graduate); 30 hours of graduate course work. Additional exam requirements/recommendations for international students: Required—TOEFL (minimum score 550 paper-based; 79 iBT). Electronic applications accepted.

The University of Texas at Austin, Graduate School, McCombs School of Business, Department of Information, Risk, and Operations Management, Austin, TX 78712-1111. Offers information management (MBA); information systems (PhD); risk analysis and decision making (PhD); risk management (MBA); supply chain and operations management (MBA, PhD). *Degree requirements:* For doctorate, thesis/dissertation. *Entrance requirements:* For doctorate, GMAT or GRE. Electronic applications accepted. *Faculty research:* Stochastic processing and queuing, discrete nonlinear and large-scale optimization simulation, quality assurance logistics, distributed artificial intelligence, organizational modeling.

The University of Texas at Tyler, College of Business and Technology, School of Human Resource Development and Technology, Tyler, TX 75799-0001. Offers human resource development (MS, PhD); industrial management (MS). Part-time and evening/weekend programs available. Postbaccalaureate distance learning degree programs offered (no on-campus study). *Degree requirements:* For master's, comprehensive exam. *Entrance requirements:* For master's, GRE General Test or MAT. Additional exam requirements/recommendations for international students: Required—TOEFL. Electronic applications accepted. *Faculty research:* Human resource development.

University of Utah, Graduate School, David Eccles School of Business, Business Administration Program, Salt Lake City, UT 84112. Offers accounting (PhD); business administration (EMBA, MBA, PMBA); finance (PhD); information systems (PhD); marketing (PhD); operations management (PhD); organizational behavior (PhD); strategic management (PhD); MBA/JD; MBA/MHA; MBA/MS. Part-time and evening/weekend programs available. *Faculty:* 58 full-time (21 women), 37 part-time/adjunct (7 women). *Students:* 481 full-time (108 women), 109 part-time (19 women); includes 39 minority (2 Black or African American, non-Hispanic/Latino; 13 Asian, non-Hispanic/Latino; 18 Hispanic/Latino; 1 Native Hawaiian or other Pacific Islander, non-Hispanic/Latino; 5 Two or more races, non-Hispanic/Latino), 39 international. Average age 32. 486 applicants, 56% accepted, 215 enrolled. In 2013, 326 master's, 10 doctorates awarded. *Degree requirements:* For doctorate, comprehensive exam, thesis/dissertation. *Entrance requirements:* For master's, GMAT or GRE; for doctorate, GMAT. Additional exam requirements/recommendations for international students: Required—TOEFL (minimum score 600 paper-based; 100 iBT), IELTS (minimum score 7). *Application deadline:* For fall admission, 11/1 priority date for domestic students, 3/1 priority date for international students; for spring admission, 11/1 for domestic and international students. Applications are processed on a rolling basis. Application fee: $55 ($65 for international students). Electronic applications accepted. *Expenses:* Contact institution. *Financial support:* In 2013–14, 48 students received support, including 41 fellowships with partial tuition reimbursements available (averaging $8,600 per year), 35 research assistantships with partial tuition reimbursements available (averaging $6,378 per year), 57 teaching assistantships with full tuition reimbursements available (averaging $17,000 per year); scholarships/grants and unspecified assistantships also available. Financial award application deadline: 2/1; financial award applicants required to submit FAFSA. *Faculty research:* Corporate finance, strategy services, consumer behavior, financial disclosures, operations. *Unit head:* Dr. William Hesterly, Associate Dean, PhD Program, 801-581-7676, Fax: 801-581-3380, E-mail: mastersinfo@business.utah.edu. *Application contact:* Andrea Miller, Coordinator, 801-581-7785, Fax: 801-581-3666, E-mail: mastersinfo@business.utah.edu.
Website: http://business.utah.edu/full-time-mba.

University of Utah, Graduate School, David Eccles School of Business, Department of Operations and Information Systems, Salt Lake City, UT 84112. Offers information systems (MS, Graduate Certificate), including business intelligence and analytics, IT security, product and process management, software and systems architecture. Part-time and evening/weekend programs available. *Faculty:* 9 full-time (2 women), 6 part-time/adjunct (0 women). *Students:* 73 full-time (12 women), 53 part-time (4 women); includes 15 minority (2 Black or African American, non-Hispanic/Latino; 3 Asian, non-Hispanic/Latino; 9 Hispanic/Latino; 1 Two or more races, non-Hispanic/Latino), 12 international. Average age 32. 90 applicants, 86% accepted, 57 enrolled. In 2013, 59 master's awarded. *Degree requirements:* For master's, capstone project. *Entrance requirements:* For master's, GMAT/GRE, minimum undergraduate GPA of 3.0. Additional exam requirements/recommendations for international students: Required—TOEFL (minimum score 600 paper-based; 100 iBT), IELTS (minimum score 7). *Application deadline:* For fall admission, 7/28 for domestic students, 3/1 for international students; for spring admission, 12/7 for domestic students, 8/16 for international students. Applications are processed on a rolling basis. Application fee: $55 ($65 for international students). Electronic applications accepted. *Expenses:* Contact institution. *Financial support:* In 2013–14, 5 students received support, including 3 fellowships with partial tuition reimbursements available (averaging $5,160 per year), 2 teaching assistantships with partial tuition reimbursements available (averaging $5,160 per year); tuition waivers (partial) and unspecified assistantships also available. Financial award application deadline: 4/14; financial award applicants required to submit FAFSA. *Faculty research:* Business intelligence and analytics, software and system architecture, product and process management, IT security, Web and data mining, applications and management of IT in healthcare. *Unit head:* Bradden Blair, Director of the MSIS Program, 801-587-9489, Fax: 801-581-3666, E-mail: b.blair@business.utah.edu. *Application contact:* Jetta Harris, Academic Coordinator, 801-587-5878, Fax: 801-581-3666, E-mail: jetta.harris@business.utah.edu.
Website: http://msis.business.utah.edu.

Virginia Commonwealth University, Graduate School, da Vinci Center for Innovation, Richmond, VA 23284-9005. Offers product innovation (MPI). Part-time programs available. *Entrance requirements:* For master's, bachelor's degree or equivalent from accredited college or university; minimum undergraduate GPA of 3.0 for at least the last two years of undergraduate work; letter of recommendation; statement of intent; interview. Additional exam requirements/recommendations for international students: Required—TOEFL.

Wake Forest University, School of Business, Full-time MBA Program, Winston-Salem, NC 27106. Offers finance (MBA); marketing (MBA); operations management (MBA); JD/MBA; MD/MBA; MSA/MBA. *Accreditation:* AACSB. *Faculty:* 77 full-time (21 women), 32 part-time/adjunct (8 women). *Students:* 107 full-time (33 women); includes 22 minority (11 Black or African American, non-Hispanic/Latino; 4 Asian, non-Hispanic/Latino; 3 Hispanic/Latino; 4 Two or more races, non-Hispanic/Latino), 21 international. Average age 30. In 2013, 66 master's awarded. *Degree requirements:* For master's, 65.5 credit hours. *Entrance requirements:* For master's, GMAT or GRE, letters of recommendation,

Industrial and Manufacturing Management

official transcripts, current resume or curriculum vitae, 2 years of work experience. Additional exam requirements/recommendations for international students: Required—TOEFL (minimum score 600 paper-based; 100 iBT), PTE. *Application deadline:* For fall admission, 4/15 for domestic and international students. Applications are processed on a rolling basis. Application fee: $100. Electronic applications accepted. *Expenses:* Contact institution. *Financial support:* In 2013–14, 90 students received support. Career-related internships or fieldwork, scholarships/grants, and unspecified assistantships available. Financial award application deadline: 2/15; financial award applicants required to submit FAFSA. *Faculty research:* The influence of personal relationships on business decision-making and management of change; drivers of perceived value and consumer behavior; impact of accounting on auditing, financial, managerial, systems and taxation stakeholders; corporate governance and executive compensation; impact of operations strategies on competitiveness. *Unit head:* Scott Schaffer, Associate Dean, 336-758-5422, Fax: 336-758-5830, E-mail: busadmissions@wfu.edu. *Application contact:* Tamara Paquee, Administrative Assistant, 336-758-5422, Fax: 336-758-5830, E-mail: busadmissions@wfu.edu.
Website: http://www.business.wfu.edu/.

Washington State University, Graduate School, College of Business, Program in Operations Management and Decision Sciences, Pullman, WA 99164. Offers PhD. *Degree requirements:* For doctorate, qualifying exam.

Washington State University Spokane, Graduate Programs, Program in Engineering and Technology Management, Pullman, WA 99164-2785. Offers constraints management (Graduate Certificate); construction project management (Graduate Certificate); engineering and technology management (METM); facilities management (Graduate Certificate); logistics and supply chain management (Graduate Certificate); manufacturing leadership (Graduate Certificate); project management (Graduate Certificate); Six Sigma quality management (Graduate Certificate); systems engineering management (Graduate Certificate). *Degree requirements:* For master's, comprehensive exam (for some programs), thesis (for some programs), comprehensive exam or project. *Entrance requirements:* For master's, GMAT (for applicants with less than 3.0 GPA), minimum GPA of 3.0, 3 letters of reference, resume, personal statement, math through college algebra (prefer math through calculus I), experience in the engineering/technology area. Additional exam requirements/recommendations for international students: Required—TOEFL. *Expenses:* Contact institution. *Faculty research:* Operations research for decision analysis quality control and liability, analytical techniques to formulating decisions.

Wayne State University, College of Liberal Arts and Sciences, Department of Economics, Detroit, MI 48202. Offers health economics (MA, PhD); industrial organization (MA, PhD); international economics (MA, PhD); labor and human resources (MA, PhD); JD/MA. *Faculty:* 13 full-time (3 women). *Students:* 49 full-time (20 women), 11 part-time (3 women); includes 13 minority (7 Black or African American, non-Hispanic/Latino; 5 Asian, non-Hispanic/Latino; 1 Hispanic/Latino), 26 international. Average age 32. 80 applicants, 44% accepted, 14 enrolled. In 2013, 14 master's, 6 doctorates awarded. *Degree requirements:* For master's, comprehensive exam, thesis optional; for doctorate, thesis/dissertation, oral examination on research, completion of course work in quantitative methods. *Entrance requirements:* For master's, minimum upper-division GPA of 3.0, prior coursework in intermediate microeconomic and macroeconomic theory, statistics, and elementary calculus; for doctorate, GRE, minimum upper-division GPA of 3.0, prior coursework in intermediate microeconomic and macroeconomic theory, statistics, two courses in calculus, three letters of recommendation from officials or teaching staff at institution(s) most recently attended. Additional exam requirements/recommendations for international students: Required—TOEFL (minimum score 550 paper-based; 79 iBT), TWE (minimum score 5.5), Michigan English Language Assessment Battery (minimum score 85); Recommended—IELTS (minimum score 6.5). *Application deadline:* For fall admission, 6/1 priority date for domestic students, 5/1 priority date for international students; for winter admission, 10/1 priority date for domestic students, 9/1 priority date for international students; for spring admission, 2/1 priority date for domestic students, 1/1 priority date for international students. Applications are processed on a rolling basis. Application fee: $0. Electronic applications accepted. *Expenses:* Tuition, state resident: part-time $554.15 per credit. Tuition, nonresident: part-time $1200.35 per credit. *Required fees:* $42.15 per credit. $268.30 per semester. Tuition and fees vary according to course load and program. *Financial support:* In 2013–14, 22 students received support, including 2 fellowships with tuition reimbursements available (averaging $16,842 per year), 17 teaching assistantships with tuition reimbursements available (averaging $16,508 per year); research assistantships with tuition reimbursements available, scholarships/grants, health care benefits, and unspecified assistantships also available. Support available to part-time students. Financial award application deadline: 3/31; financial award applicants required to submit FAFSA. *Faculty research:* Health economics, international economics, macro economics, urban and labor economics, econometrics. *Unit head:* Dr. Stephen J. Spurr, Interim Chair, 313-577-3345, Fax: 313-577-9564, E-mail: sspurr@wayne.edu. *Application contact:* Dr. Allen Charles Goodman, Graduate Director, 313-577-3235, Fax: 313-577-9564, E-mail: allen.goodman@wayne.edu.
Website: http://clasweb.clas.wayne.edu/economics.

Wilkes University, College of Graduate and Professional Studies, Jay S. Sidhu School of Business and Leadership, Wilkes-Barre, PA 18766-0002. Offers accounting (MBA); entrepreneurship (MBA); finance (MBA); health care administration (MBA); human resource management (MBA); international business (MBA); marketing (MBA); operations management (MBA); organizational leadership and development (MBA). *Accreditation:* ACBSP. Part-time and evening/weekend programs available. *Students:* 41 full-time (20 women), 119 part-time (48 women); includes 20 minority (5 Black or African American, non-Hispanic/Latino; 3 Asian, non-Hispanic/Latino; 7 Hispanic/Latino; 5 Two or more races, non-Hispanic/Latino), 7 international. Average age 31. In 2013, 55 master's awarded. *Entrance requirements:* For master's, GMAT. Additional exam requirements/recommendations for international students: Required—TOEFL (minimum score 550 paper-based; 79 iBT). *Application deadline:* Applications are processed on a rolling basis. Application fee: $45 ($65 for international students). Electronic applications accepted. *Expenses:* Contact institution. *Financial support:* Federal Work-Study and unspecified assistantships available. Financial award application deadline: 3/1; financial award applicants required to submit FAFSA. *Unit head:* Dr. Jeffrey Alves, Dean, 570-408-4702, Fax: 570-408-7846, E-mail: jeffrey.alves@wilkes.edu. *Application contact:* Joanne Thomas, Interim Director of Graduate Enrollment, 570-408-4234, Fax: 570-408-7846, E-mail: joanne.thomas1@wilkes.edu.
Website: http://www.wilkes.edu/pages/457.asp.

Section 10
Insurance and Actuarial Science

This section contains a directory of institutions offering graduate work in insurance and actuarial science. Additional information about programs listed in the directory but not augmented by an in-depth entry may be obtained by writing directly to the dean of a graduate school or chair of a department at the address given in the directory.

For programs offering related work, see also in this book *Business Administration and Management*.

CONTENTS

Program Directories

Actuarial Science   402
Insurance   403

Actuarial Science

Ball State University, Graduate School, College of Sciences and Humanities, Department of Mathematical Sciences, Program in Actuarial Science, Muncie, IN 47306-1099. Offers MA. *Students:* 23 full-time (9 women), 9 part-time (2 women); includes 5 minority (3 Black or African American, non-Hispanic/Latino; 2 Asian, non-Hispanic/Latino), 14 international. Average age 27. 54 applicants, 63% accepted, 9 enrolled. In 2013, 12 master's awarded. *Entrance requirements:* For master's, GMAT. Application fee: $50. *Financial support:* In 2013–14, 16 students received support. Application deadline: 3/1. *Unit head:* Dr. Sheryl Stump, Director, 765-285-8640, Fax: 765-285-1721, E-mail: sstump@bsu.edu. *Application contact:* Dr. Hanspeter Fischer, Director of Graduate Programs, 765-285-8680, Fax: 765-285-1721, E-mail: hfischer@bsu.edu. Website: http://cms.bsu.edu/Academics/CollegesandDepartments/Math/AcademicsAdmissions/Programs/Masters/ActuarialScience.aspx.

Boston University, Metropolitan College, Department of Actuarial Science, Boston, MA 02215. Offers MS. Part-time and evening/weekend programs available. *Faculty:* 3 full-time (1 woman), 6 part-time/adjunct (1 woman). *Students:* 57 full-time (34 women), 43 part-time (20 women); includes 9 minority (1 Black or African American, non-Hispanic/Latino; 6 Asian, non-Hispanic/Latino; 1 Hispanic/Latino; 1 Two or more races, non-Hispanic/Latino), 64 international. Average age 26. 174 applicants, 79% accepted, 48 enrolled. In 2013, 33 master's awarded. *Entrance requirements:* For master's, prerequisite coursework in calculus. Additional exam requirements/recommendations for international students: Required—TOEFL (minimum score 84 iBT). *Application deadline:* For fall admission, 5/31 priority date for domestic students, 5/15 priority date for international students; for spring admission, 10/31 priority date for domestic students, 10/15 priority date for international students. Applications are processed on a rolling basis. Application fee: $80. Electronic applications accepted. *Expenses: Tuition:* Full-time $43,970; part-time $1374 per credit hour. *Required fees:* $60 per semester. Tuition and fees vary according to class time, course level and program. *Financial support:* In 2013–14, 1 research assistantship with full tuition reimbursement (averaging $19,300 per year), 6 teaching assistantships with full tuition reimbursements (averaging $19,300 per year) were awarded; career-related internships or fieldwork, scholarships/grants, and unspecified assistantships also available. *Faculty research:* Survival models, life contingencies, numerical analysis, operations research, compound interest. *Unit head:* Lois K. Horwitz, Chairman, 617-353-8758, Fax: 617-353-8757, E-mail: lhorwitz@bu.edu. *Application contact:* Andrea Cozzi, Administrative Coordinator, 617-353-8758, Fax: 617-353-8757, E-mail: actuary@bu.edu. Website: http://www.bu.edu/actuary/.

California State University, East Bay, Office of Academic Programs and Graduate Studies, College of Science, Department of Statistics and Biostatistics, Statistics Program, Hayward, CA 94542-3000. Offers actuarial science (MS); applied statistics (MS); computational statistics (MS); mathematical statistics (MS). Part-time and evening/weekend programs available. *Degree requirements:* For master's, comprehensive exam. *Entrance requirements:* For master's, letters of recommendation, minimum GPA of 3.0, math through lower-division calculus. Additional exam requirements/recommendations for international students: Required—TOEFL (minimum score 550 paper-based). Electronic applications accepted.

Central Connecticut State University, School of Graduate Studies, School of Arts and Sciences, Department of Mathematical Sciences, New Britain, CT 06050-4010. Offers data mining (MS, Certificate); mathematics (MA, MS, Certificate, Sixth Year Certificate), including actuarial science (MA), computer science (MA), statistics (MA). Part-time and evening/weekend programs available. *Faculty:* 13 full-time (4 women). *Students:* 14 full-time (9 women), 82 part-time (33 women); includes 19 minority (9 Black or African American, non-Hispanic/Latino; 6 Asian, non-Hispanic/Latino; 3 Hispanic/Latino; 1 Two or more races, non-Hispanic/Latino), 4 international. Average age 35. 81 applicants, 60% accepted, 29 enrolled. In 2013, 27 master's, 5 other advanced degrees awarded. *Degree requirements:* For master's, comprehensive exam, thesis or alternative; for other advanced degree, qualifying exam. *Entrance requirements:* For master's, minimum undergraduate GPA of 2.7; for other advanced degree, minimum undergraduate GPA of 3.0, essay, letters of recommendation. Additional exam requirements/recommendations for international students: Required—TOEFL (minimum score 550 paper-based; 79 iBT). *Application deadline:* For fall admission, 5/1 for domestic and international students; for spring admission, 11/1 for domestic and international students. Applications are processed on a rolling basis. Application fee: $50. Electronic applications accepted. Part-time tuition and fees vary according to degree level. *Financial support:* In 2013–14, 6 students received support. Career-related internships or fieldwork, Federal Work-Study, scholarships/grants, and unspecified assistantships available. Support available to part-time students. Financial award application deadline: 3/1; financial award applicants required to submit FAFSA. *Faculty research:* Statistics, actuarial mathematics, computer systems and engineering, computer programming techniques, operations research. *Unit head:* Dr. Jeffrey McGowan, Chair, 860-832-2835, E-mail: mcgowan@ccsu.edu. *Application contact:* Patricia Gardner, Associate Director of Graduate Studies, 860-832-2350, Fax: 860-832-2362, E-mail: graduateadmissions@ccsu.edu. Website: http://www.math.ccsu.edu/.

Columbia University, School of Continuing Education, Program in Actuarial Science, New York, NY 10027. Offers MS. Part-time programs available. *Degree requirements:* For master's, comprehensive exam. *Entrance requirements:* For master's, minimum GPA of 3.0, knowledge of economics, linear algebra, calculus. Additional exam requirements/recommendations for international students: Required—American Language Program placement test. Electronic applications accepted.

George Mason University, College of Science, Department of Mathematical Sciences, Fairfax, VA 22030. Offers actuarial sciences (Certificate); mathematics (MS, PhD). *Faculty:* 35 full-time (9 women), 12 part-time/adjunct (5 women). *Students:* 35 full-time (11 women), 32 part-time (11 women); includes 17 minority (1 Black or African American, non-Hispanic/Latino; 9 Asian, non-Hispanic/Latino; 5 Hispanic/Latino; 2 Two or more races, non-Hispanic/Latino), 8 international. Average age 31. 102 applicants, 45% accepted, 20 enrolled. In 2013, 11 master's, 2 doctorates awarded. *Degree requirements:* For master's, comprehensive exam, thesis optional; for doctorate, comprehensive exam, thesis/dissertation. *Entrance requirements:* For master's, GRE, 3 letters of recommendation; official college transcripts; expanded goals statement; resume; for doctorate, GRE (recommended), master's degree in math or undergraduate coursework with math preparation with minimum GPA of 3.0 in last 60 credits; 2 copies of official transcripts; 3 letters of recommendation; expanded goals statement; for Certificate, 3 letters of recommendation; official transcripts. Additional exam requirements/recommendations for international students: Required—TOEFL (minimum score 570 paper-based; 88 iBT), IELTS (minimum score 6.5), PTE. *Application deadline:* For fall admission, 4/15 priority date for domestic students; for spring admission, 11/1 priority date for domestic students. Application fee: $65 ($80 for international students).

Electronic applications accepted. *Expenses:* Tuition, state resident: full-time $9350; part-time $390 per credit. Tuition, nonresident: full-time $25,754; part-time $1073 per credit. *Required fees:* $2688; $112 per credit. *Financial support:* In 2013–14, 25 students received support, including 2 fellowships (averaging $8,000 per year), 10 research assistantships with full and partial tuition reimbursements available (averaging $20,309 per year), 15 teaching assistantships with full and partial tuition reimbursements available (averaging $15,941 per year); career-related internships or fieldwork, Federal Work-Study, scholarships/grants, unspecified assistantships, and health care benefits (for full-time research or teaching assistantship recipients) also available. Support available to part-time students. Financial award application deadline: 3/1; financial award applicants required to submit FAFSA. *Faculty research:* Nonlinear dynamics and topology, with an emphasis on global bifurcations and chaos; numerical and theoretical methods of dynamical systems. *Total annual research expenditures:* $1.4 million. *Unit head:* David Walnut, Chair, 703-993-1478, Fax: 703-993-1491, E-mail: dwalnut@gmu.edu. *Application contact:* Rebecca Goldin, Graduate Coordinator, 703-993-1480, Fax: 703-993-1491, E-mail: rgoldin@gmu.edu. Website: http://math.gmu.edu/.

Georgia State University, J. Mack Robinson College of Business, Department of Risk Management and Insurance, Program in Actuarial Science, Atlanta, GA 30302-3083. Offers MAS, MBA. Part-time and evening/weekend programs available. *Students:* Average age 0. *Entrance requirements:* For master's, GRE or GMAT, transcripts from all institutions attended, resume, essays. Additional exam requirements/recommendations for international students: Required—TOEFL (minimum score 610 paper-based; 101 iBT), IELTS (minimum score 7). *Application deadline:* For fall admission, 5/1 priority date for domestic students, 2/1 priority date for international students; for spring admission, 9/15 priority date for domestic students, 4/1 priority date for international students. Applications are processed on a rolling basis. Application fee: $50. Electronic applications accepted. *Expenses: Tuition, area resident:* Full-time $4176; part-time $348 per credit hour. Tuition, state resident: full-time $14,544; part-time $1212 per credit hour. Tuition, nonresident: full-time $14,544; part-time $1212 per credit hour. Tuition and fees vary according to course load and program. *Financial support:* Research assistantships, scholarships/grants, tuition waivers, and unspecified assistantships available. *Faculty research:* Quantification and pricing of risk, risk modeling, financial methods in insurance, economic theory, enterprise risk management. *Unit head:* Dr. Shaun Wang, Professor/Chair/Director, 404-413-7500, Fax: 404-413-7499. *Application contact:* Toby McChesney, Assistant Dean for Graduate Recruiting and Student Services, 404-413-7167, Fax: 404-413-7162, E-mail: rcbgradadmissions@gsu.edu. Website: http://www.rmi.gsu.edu/graduate/actuarial_science.shtml.

Maryville University of Saint Louis, College of Arts and Sciences, St. Louis, MO 63141-7299. Offers actuarial science (MS); organizational leadership (MA); strategic communication and leadership (MA). Part-time and evening/weekend programs available. *Faculty:* 5 full-time (4 women), 3 part-time/adjunct (2 women). *Students:* 21 full-time (15 women), 43 part-time (28 women); includes 19 minority (6 Black or African American, non-Hispanic/Latino; 6 Asian, non-Hispanic/Latino; 1 Hispanic/Latino; 6 Two or more races, non-Hispanic/Latino), 5 international. Average age 33. In 2013, 17 master's awarded. *Entrance requirements:* For master's, GRE with minimum score of 600 (for MS), strong mathematics background, 2 letters of recommendation, and personal statement (MS). Additional exam requirements/recommendations for international students: Required—TOEFL (minimum score 550 paper-based; 80 iBT). *Application deadline:* Applications are processed on a rolling basis. Application fee: $40 ($60 for international students). Electronic applications accepted. Application fee is waived when completed online. *Expenses: Tuition:* Full-time $23,812; part-time $728 per credit hour. *Required fees:* $395 per year. Tuition and fees vary according to course load, degree level and program. *Financial support:* Application deadline: 3/1; applicants required to submit FAFSA. *Unit head:* Dr. Candace Chambers, Dean, 314-529-9208, Fax: 314-529-9965, E-mail: cchambers@maryville.edu. *Application contact:* Crystal Jacobsmeyer, Assistant Director, Graduate Enrollment Advising, 314-529-9654, Fax: 314-529-9927, E-mail: cjacobsmeyer@maryville.edu. Website: http://www.maryville.edu/as/graduate-programs/.

Roosevelt University, Graduate Division, College of Arts and Sciences, Department of Mathematics and Actuarial Science, Program in Mathematics, Chicago, IL 60605. Offers mathematical sciences (MS), including actuarial science. Part-time and evening/weekend programs available. *Faculty research:* Statistics, mathematics education, finite groups, computers in mathematics.

St. John's University, The Peter J. Tobin College of Business, School of Risk Management and Actuarial Science, Queens, NY 11439. Offers enterprise risk management (MS); management of risk (MS); risk management (MBA). Postbaccalaureate distance learning degree programs offered (no on-campus study). *Students:* 43 full-time (23 women), 19 part-time (6 women); includes 3 minority (1 Black or African American, non-Hispanic/Latino; 1 Hispanic/Latino; 1 Two or more races, non-Hispanic/Latino), 42 international. Average age 25. 45 applicants, 76% accepted, 18 enrolled. In 2013, 37 master's awarded. *Degree requirements:* For master's, comprehensive exam (for some programs), thesis optional. *Entrance requirements:* For master's, GMAT or GRE (for MS), 2 letters of recommendation, resume, transcripts, essay. Additional exam requirements/recommendations for international students: Required—TOEFL (minimum score 600 paper-based; 100 iBT), IELTS (minimum score 7). *Application deadline:* For fall admission, 5/1 priority date for domestic and international students; for spring admission, 11/1 priority date for domestic and international students. Applications are processed on a rolling basis. Application fee: $50. Electronic applications accepted. *Expenses:* Contact institution. *Financial support:* Research assistantships, scholarships/grants, and unspecified assistantships available. Financial award applicants required to submit FAFSA. *Faculty research:* Insurance company operations and financial analysis, enterprise risk management, risk theory and modeling, credibility theory and actuarial price modeling, international insurance. *Unit head:* Dr. Mark Browne, Chair, 212-277-5175, E-mail: brownem1@stjohns.edu. *Application contact:* Carol J. Swanberg, Assistant Dean/Director of Graduate Admissions, 718-990-1345, Fax: 718-990-5242, E-mail: tobingradnyc@stjohns.edu.

Simon Fraser University, Office of Graduate Studies, Faculty of Science, Department of Statistics and Actuarial Science, Burnaby, BC V5A 1S6, Canada. Offers actuarial science (M Sc); statistics (M Sc, PhD). *Faculty:* 21 full-time (5 women). *Students:* 44 full-time (28 women). 183 applicants, 14% accepted, 14 enrolled. In 2013, 10 master's, 2 doctorates awarded. *Degree requirements:* For master's, participation in consulting, project; for doctorate, comprehensive exam, thesis/dissertation. *Entrance requirements:* For master's, minimum GPA of 3.0 (on scale of 4.33), or 3.33 based on last 60 credits of undergraduate courses; for doctorate, minimum GPA of 3.5 (on scale of 4.33). Additional exam requirements/recommendations for international students: Recommended—TOEFL (minimum score 580 paper-based; 93 iBT), IELTS (minimum

score 7), TWE (minimum score 5). *Application deadline:* For fall admission, 2/1 for domestic and international students. Application fee: $90 ($125 for international students). Electronic applications accepted. *Expenses: Tuition, area resident:* Full-time $5084 Canadian dollars. *Required fees:* $840 Canadian dollars. *Financial support:* In 2013–14, 27 students received support, including 31 fellowships (averaging $6,250 per year), teaching assistantships (averaging $5,608 per year); research assistantships, career-related internships or fieldwork, and scholarships/grants also available. *Faculty research:* Biostatistics, experimental design, envirometrics, statistical computing, statistical theory. *Unit head:* Dr. Tim Swartz, Graduate Chair, 778-782-4579, Fax: 778-782-4368, E-mail: stat-grad-chair@sfu.ca. *Application contact:* Kelly Jay, Graduate Secretary, 778-782-3801, Fax: 778-782-4368, E-mail: statgrad@sfu.ca.
Website: http://www.stat.sfu.ca/.

Temple University, Fox School of Business, Specialized Master's Programs, Philadelphia, PA 19122-6096. Offers accountancy (MS); actuarial science (MS); finance (MS); financial engineering (MS); human resource management (MS); innovation management and entrepreneurship (MS); marketing (MS); statistics (MS). MS in innovation management and entrepreneurship delivered jointly with College of Engineering. *Accreditation:* AACSB. Part-time programs available. *Entrance requirements:* For master's, GRE General Test or GMAT, minimum undergraduate GPA of 3.0. Additional exam requirements/recommendations for international students: Required—TOEFL (minimum score 600 paper-based; 100 iBT), IELTS (minimum score 7.5).

Université du Québec à Montréal, Graduate Programs, Program in Actuarial Sciences, Montréal, QC H3C 3P8, Canada. Offers Diploma. Part-time programs available. *Entrance requirements:* For degree, appropriate bachelor's degree or equivalent and proficiency in French.

University of Central Florida, College of Sciences, Department of Statistics and Actuarial Science, Orlando, FL 32816. Offers SAS data mining (Certificate); statistical computing (MS). Part-time and evening/weekend programs available. *Faculty:* 11 full-time (2 women), 1 part-time/adjunct (0 women). *Students:* 39 full-time (15 women), 26 part-time (7 women); includes 16 minority (6 Black or African American, non-Hispanic/Latino; 6 Asian, non-Hispanic/Latino; 4 Hispanic/Latino), 21 international. Average age 31. 69 applicants, 80% accepted, 39 enrolled. In 2013, 24 master's, 4 other advanced degrees awarded. *Degree requirements:* For master's, comprehensive exam. *Entrance requirements:* For master's, GRE General Test, minimum GPA of 3.0 in last 60 hours. Additional exam requirements/recommendations for international students: Required—TOEFL. *Application deadline:* For fall admission, 7/15 for domestic students; for spring admission, 12/1 for domestic students. Application fee: $30. Electronic applications accepted. *Financial support:* In 2013–14, 19 students received support, including 2 fellowships with partial tuition reimbursements available (averaging $4,000 per year), 1 research assistantship with partial tuition reimbursement available (averaging $14,700 per year), 18 teaching assistantships with partial tuition reimbursements available (averaging $12,300 per year); career-related internships or fieldwork, Federal Work-Study, institutionally sponsored loans, tuition waivers (partial), and unspecified assistantships also available. Financial award application deadline: 3/1; financial award applicants required to submit FAFSA. *Faculty research:* Multivariate analysis, quality control, shrinkage estimation. *Unit head:* Dr. David Nickerson, Chair, 407-823-2289, Fax: 407-823-5419, E-mail: david.nickerson@ucf.edu. *Application contact:* Barbara Rodriguez Lamas, Director, Admissions and Student Services, 407-823-2766, Fax: 407-823-6442, E-mail: gradadmissions@ucf.edu.
Website: http://statistics.cos.ucf.edu/.

University of Connecticut, Graduate School, College of Liberal Arts and Sciences, Department of Mathematics, Storrs, CT 06269. Offers applied financial mathematics (MS); mathematics (MS, PhD), including actuarial science, mathematics. *Degree requirements:* For doctorate, thesis/dissertation. *Entrance requirements:* For master's and doctorate, GRE General Test, GRE Subject Test. Additional exam requirements/recommendations for international students: Required—TOEFL (minimum score 550 paper-based). Electronic applications accepted.

University of Connecticut, Graduate School, College of Liberal Arts and Sciences, Department of Mathematics, Field of Mathematics, Program in Actuarial Science, Storrs, CT 06269. Offers MS, PhD. *Degree requirements:* For master's, comprehensive exam. *Entrance requirements:* Additional exam requirements/recommendations for international students: Required—TOEFL (minimum score 550 paper-based). Electronic applications accepted.

University of Illinois at Urbana–Champaign, Graduate College, College of Liberal Arts and Sciences, Department of Mathematics, Champaign, IL 61820. Offers applied mathematics (MS); applied mathematics: actuarial science (MS); mathematics (MS, PhD); teaching of mathematics (MS). *Students:* 211 (78 women). Application fee: $75 ($90 for international students). *Unit head:* Matthew Ando, Chair, 217-244-2846, Fax: 217-333-9576, E-mail: mando@illinois.edu. *Application contact:* Marci Blocher, Office Support Specialist, 217-333-5749, Fax: 217-333-9576, E-mail: mblocher@illinois.edu.
Website: http://math.illinois.edu/.

The University of Iowa, Graduate College, College of Liberal Arts and Sciences, Department of Statistics and Actuarial Science, Iowa City, IA 52242-1316. Offers actuarial science (MS); statistics (MS, PhD). *Degree requirements:* For master's, thesis optional, exam; for doctorate, comprehensive exam, thesis/dissertation. *Entrance requirements:* For master's and doctorate, GRE General Test, minimum GPA of 3.0. Additional exam requirements/recommendations for international students: Required—TOEFL (minimum score 550 paper-based; 81 iBT). Electronic applications accepted.

The University of Manchester, School of Mathematics, Manchester, United Kingdom. Offers actuarial science (PhD); applied mathematics (M Phil, PhD); applied numerical computing (M Phil, PhD); financial mathematics (M Phil, PhD); mathematical logic (M Phil); probability (M Phil, PhD); pure mathematics (M Phil, PhD); statistics (M Phil, PhD).

University of Nebraska–Lincoln, Graduate College, College of Business Administration, Interdepartmental Area of Actuarial Science, Lincoln, NE 68588. Offers MS. *Entrance requirements:* For master's, GRE. Additional exam requirements/recommendations for international students: Required—TOEFL (minimum score 550 paper-based). Electronic applications accepted. *Faculty research:* Risk theory, pensions, actuarial finance, decision theory, stochastic calculus.

University of Northern Iowa, Graduate College, College of Humanities, Arts and Sciences, Department of Mathematics, Program in Industrial Mathematics, Cedar Falls, IA 50614. Offers actuarial science (PSM); continuous quality improvement (PSM); mathematical computing and modeling (PSM). *Students:* 8 full-time (1 woman), 2 part-time (1 woman); includes 2 minority (1 Black or African American, non-Hispanic/Latino; 1 Hispanic/Latino), 1 international. 10 applicants, 90% accepted, 4 enrolled. In 2013, 3 master's awarded. Application fee: $50 ($70 for international students). *Unit head:* Dr. Syed Kirmani, Coordinator, 319-273-2940, Fax: 319-273-2546, E-mail: syed.kirmani@uni.edu. *Application contact:* Laurie S. Russell, Record Analyst, 319-273-2623, Fax: 319-273-2885, E-mail: laurie.russell@uni.edu.

The University of Texas at Austin, Graduate School, College of Natural Sciences, Department of Mathematics, Austin, TX 78712-1111. Offers MA, PhD. *Entrance requirements:* For master's and doctorate, GRE General Test. Electronic applications accepted.

The University of Texas at Dallas, School of Natural Sciences and Mathematics, Department of Mathematical Sciences, Richardson, TX 75080. Offers actuarial science (MS); applied mathematics (MS, PhD); engineering mathematics (MS); mathematics (MS); statistics (MS, PhD). Part-time and evening/weekend programs available. *Faculty:* 25 full-time (4 women). *Students:* 63 full-time (30 women), 28 part-time (10 women); includes 19 minority (2 Black or African American, non-Hispanic/Latino; 11 Asian, non-Hispanic/Latino; 5 Hispanic/Latino; 1 Two or more races, non-Hispanic/Latino), 43 international. Average age 30. 181 applicants, 33% accepted, 40 enrolled. In 2013, 16 master's, 7 doctorates awarded. *Degree requirements:* For master's, thesis optional; for doctorate, thesis/dissertation. *Entrance requirements:* For master's, GRE General Test, minimum GPA of 3.0 in upper-level course work in field; for doctorate, GRE General Test, minimum GPA of 3.5 in upper-level course work in field. Additional exam requirements/recommendations for international students: Required—TOEFL (minimum score 550 paper-based). *Application deadline:* For fall admission, 7/15 for domestic students, 5/1 priority date for international students; for spring admission, 11/15 for domestic students, 9/1 priority date for international students. Applications are processed on a rolling basis. Application fee: $50 ($100 for international students). Electronic applications accepted. *Expenses:* Tuition, state resident: full-time $11,940; part-time $663.33 per credit hour. Tuition, nonresident: full-time $21,606; part-time $1200.33 per credit hour. *Financial support:* In 2013–14, 59 students received support, including 2 research assistantships (averaging $20,104 per year), 40 teaching assistantships with partial tuition reimbursements available (averaging $15,300 per year); career-related internships or fieldwork, Federal Work-Study, institutionally sponsored loans, scholarships/grants, and unspecified assistantships also available. Support available to part-time students. Financial award application deadline: 4/30; financial award applicants required to submit FAFSA. *Faculty research:* Sequential analysis, applications in semiconductor manufacturing, medical image analysis, computational anatomy, information theory, probability theory. *Unit head:* Dr. Matthew Goeckner, Department Head, 972-883-4292, Fax: 972-883-6622, E-mail: goeckner@utdallas.edu. *Application contact:* Olivia Dao, Graduate Support Assistant, 972-883-2163, Fax: 972-883-6622, E-mail: utdmath@utdallas.edu.
Website: http://www.utdallas.edu/math.

University of Waterloo, Graduate Studies, Faculty of Mathematics, Department of Statistics and Actuarial Science, Waterloo, ON N2L 3G1, Canada. Offers actuarial science (M Math, PhD); biostatistics (PhD); statistics (M Math, PhD); statistics-biostatistics (M Math); statistics-computing (M Math); statistics-finance (M Math). *Degree requirements:* For master's, research paper or thesis; for doctorate, comprehensive exam, thesis/dissertation. *Entrance requirements:* For master's, honors degree in field, minimum B+ average; for doctorate, master's degree, minimum B+ average. Additional exam requirements/recommendations for international students: Required—TOEFL (minimum score 600 paper-based; 90 iBT), TWE (minimum score 4.5). Electronic applications accepted. *Faculty research:* Data analysis, risk theory, inference, stochastic processes, quantitative finance.

Insurance

California State University, Fullerton, Graduate Studies, College of Business and Economics, Program in Business Administration, Fullerton, CA 92834-9480. Offers business intelligence (MBA); general (MBA); international business (MBA); organizational leadership (MBA); risk management and insurance (MBA). *Accreditation:* AACSB. Part-time programs available. *Students:* 54 full-time (26 women), 119 part-time (48 women); includes 74 minority (46 Asian, non-Hispanic/Latino; 23 Hispanic/Latino; 5 Two or more races, non-Hispanic/Latino), 34 international. Average age 28. 500 applicants, 41% accepted, 78 enrolled. In 2013, 65 master's awarded. *Degree requirements:* For master's, project or thesis. *Entrance requirements:* For master's, GMAT. Application fee: $55. *Financial support:* Career-related internships or fieldwork, Federal Work-Study, institutionally sponsored loans, and scholarships/grants available. Support available to part-time students. Financial award application deadline: 3/1; financial award applicants required to submit FAFSA. *Unit head:* Dr. Anil Puri, Dean, 657-773-2592. *Application contact:* Admissions/Applications, 657-278-2371.

Florida State University, The Graduate School, College of Business, Tallahassee, FL 32306-1110. Offers accounting (M Acc), including accounting information services, assurance services, corporate accounting, taxation; business administration (MBA, PhD), including accounting (PhD), finance (PhD), management information systems (PhD), marketing (PhD), organizational behavior and human resources (PhD), risk management and insurance (PhD), strategic management (PhD); finance (MS); insurance (MSM); management information systems (MS); marketing (MS); JD/MBA; MSW/MBA. *Accreditation:* AACSB. Part-time programs available. Postbaccalaureate distance learning degree programs offered (no on-campus study). *Faculty:* 102 full-time (31 women), 5 part-time/adjunct (0 women). *Students:* 280 full-time (117 women), 278 part-time (88 women); includes 127 minority (26 Black or African American, non-Hispanic/Latino; 7 American Indian or Alaska Native, non-Hispanic/Latino; 44 Asian, non-Hispanic/Latino; 50 Hispanic/Latino). Average age 30. 630 applicants, 28% accepted, 103 enrolled. In 2013, 265 master's, 11 doctorates awarded. Terminal master's awarded for partial completion of doctoral program. *Degree requirements:* For doctorate, comprehensive exam, thesis/dissertation. *Entrance requirements:* For master's, GMAT, work experience (MBA, MS), minimum GPA of 3.0, letters of recommendation; for doctorate, GMAT, minimum graduate GPA of 3.5, letters of recommendation. Additional exam requirements/recommendations for international students: Required—TOEFL (minimum score 600 paper-based; 100 iBT); Recommended—IELTS (minimum score 6.5). *Application deadline:* For fall admission, 6/1 for domestic students, 5/1 for international students; for spring admission, 10/1 for

domestic students, 9/1 for international students. Applications are processed on a rolling basis. Application fee: $30. Electronic applications accepted. *Expenses:* Tuition, state resident: part-time $403.51 per credit hour. Tuition, nonresident: part-time $1004.85 per credit hour. *Required fees:* $75.81 per credit hour. One-time fee: $20 part-time. Tuition and fees vary according to course load, campus/location and student level. *Financial support:* In 2013–14, 92 students received support, including 10 fellowships with full tuition reimbursements available (averaging $1,500 per year), 20 research assistantships with full tuition reimbursements available (averaging $20,000 per year), 35 teaching assistantships with full tuition reimbursements available (averaging $20,000 per year); career-related internships or fieldwork, scholarships/grants, health care benefits, and unspecified assistantships also available. Financial award application deadline: 1/1. *Unit head:* Dr. Caryn Beck-Dudley, Dean, 850-644-3090, Fax: 850-644-0915. *Application contact:* Lisa Beverly, Director, Graduate Programs Admissions, 850-644-6458, Fax: 850-644-0588, E-mail: lbeverly@cob.fsu.edu.
Website: http://www.cob.fsu.edu/.

Georgia State University, J. Mack Robinson College of Business, Department of Risk Management and Insurance, Program in Risk Management and Insurance, Atlanta, GA 30302-3083. Offers enterprise risk management (MBA, Certificate); financial risk management (MBA); mathematical risk management (MS); risk and insurance (MS); risk management and insurance (MBA, PhD); MAS/MRM. Part-time and evening/weekend programs available. *Students:* Average age 0. *Degree requirements:* For doctorate, comprehensive exam, thesis/dissertation. *Entrance requirements:* For master's, GRE or GMAT, transcripts from all institutions attended, resume, essays. Additional exam requirements/recommendations for international students: Required—TOEFL (minimum score 610 paper-based; 101 iBT), IELTS (minimum score 7). *Application deadline:* For fall admission, 5/1 priority date for domestic students, 2/1 priority date for international students; for spring admission, 9/15 priority date for domestic students, 4/1 priority date for international students. Applications are processed on a rolling basis. Application fee: $50. Electronic applications accepted. *Expenses: Tuition, area resident:* Full-time $4176; part-time $348 per credit hour. Tuition, state resident: full-time $14,544; part-time $1212 per credit hour. Tuition, nonresident: full-time $14,544; part-time $1212 per credit hour. Tuition and fees vary according to course load and program. *Financial support:* Research assistantships, scholarships/grants, tuition waivers, and unspecified assistantships available. *Faculty research:* Insurance economics, structure and performance of insurance markets, regulation and policy in insurance markets, asset pricing theory, financial econometrics. *Unit head:* Dr. Martin Grace, Professor of Risk Management and Legal Studies/Chair of the Department of Risk Management and Insurance, 404-413-7500, Fax: 404-413-7499. *Application contact:* Toby McChesney, Graduate Recruiting Contact, 404-413-7167, Fax: 404-413-7162, E-mail: rcbgradadmissions@gsu.edu.
Website: http://www.rmi.gsu.edu/graduate/grad_rmi.shtml.

Pontificia Universidad Catolica Madre y Maestra, Graduate School, Faculty of Social and Administrative Sciences, Santiago, Dominican Republic. Offers business administration (MBA), including business development, finance, international business, management skills (M Mgmt, MBA), marketing, operations, strategic cost management, strategy, tourist destination planning and management; law (LL M), including civil law, corporate business law, criminal law, international relations, real estate law; management (M Mgmt), including higher financial management, insurance program administration, management skills (M Mgmt, MBA); psychology (MA), including clinical child and adolescent psychology, forensic psychology; strategic human resources (EMBA).

St. John's University, The Peter J. Tobin College of Business, School of Risk Management and Actuarial Science, Queens, NY 11439. Offers enterprise risk management (MS); management of risk (MS); risk management (MBA). Postbaccalaureate distance learning degree programs offered (no on-campus study). *Students:* 43 full-time (23 women), 19 part-time (6 women); includes 3 minority (1 Black or African American, non-Hispanic/Latino; 1 Hispanic/Latino; 1 Two or more races, non-Hispanic/Latino), 42 international. Average age 25. 45 applicants, 76% accepted, 18 enrolled. In 2013, 37 master's awarded. *Degree requirements:* For master's, comprehensive exam (for some programs), thesis optional. *Entrance requirements:* For master's, GMAT or GRE (for MS), 2 letters of recommendation, resume, transcripts, essay. Additional exam requirements/recommendations for international students: Required—TOEFL (minimum score 600 paper-based; 100 iBT), IELTS (minimum score 7). *Application deadline:* For fall admission, 5/1 priority date for domestic and international students; for spring admission, 11/1 priority date for domestic and international students. Applications are processed on a rolling basis. Application fee: $50. Electronic applications accepted. *Expenses:* Contact institution. *Financial support:* Research assistantships, scholarships/grants, and unspecified assistantships available. Financial award applicants required to submit FAFSA. *Faculty research:* Insurance company operations and financial analysis, enterprise risk management, risk theory and modeling, credibility theory and actuarial price modeling, international insurance. *Unit head:* Dr. Mark Browne, Chair, 212-277-5175, E-mail: brownem1@stjohns.edu. *Application contact:* Carol J. Swanberg, Assistant Dean/Director of Graduate Admissions, 718-990-1345, Fax: 718-990-5242, E-mail: tobingradnyc@stjohns.edu.

Temple University, Fox School of Business, Doctoral Programs in Business, Philadelphia, PA 19122-6096. Offers accounting (PhD); entrepreneurship (PhD); finance (PhD); international business (PhD); management information systems (PhD); marketing (PhD); risk management and insurance (PhD); statistics (PhD); strategic management (PhD); tourism and sport (PhD). *Accreditation:* AACSB. *Degree requirements:* For doctorate, thesis/dissertation. *Entrance requirements:* For doctorate, GRE General Test, GMAT, minimum GPA of 3.0, master's degree. Additional exam requirements/recommendations for international students: Required—TOEFL (minimum score 600 paper-based; 100 iBT), IELTS (minimum score 7.5). Electronic applications accepted.

Thomas M. Cooley Law School, JD and LL M Programs, Lansing, MI 48901-3038. Offers administrative law (public law) (JD); business transactions (JD); Canadian law practice (JD); Constitutional law and civil rights (public law) (JD); corporate law and finance (LL M); environmental law (public law) (JD); general practice (JD), including solo and small firm; homeland and national security law (LL M); insurance law (LL M); intellectual property (JD); intellectual property law (LL M); international law (JD); litigation (JD); self-directed (LL M, JD); tax law (LL M); taxation (JD); U.S. legal studies for foreign attorneys (LL M); JD/MBA; JD/MPA; JD/MSW. *Accreditation:* ABA. Part-time and evening/weekend programs available. Postbaccalaureate distance learning degree programs offered (no on-campus study). *Degree requirements:* For master's, thesis optional; for doctorate, minimum of 3 credits of clinical experience. *Entrance requirements:* For master's, JD or LL B; for doctorate, LSAT. Additional exam requirements/recommendations for international students: Required—TOEFL (for U.S. legal studies for foreign attorneys LL M program). Electronic applications accepted. *Faculty research:* Wrongful convictions, civil rights, environmental law, litigation techniques, data mining, intellectual property, practical and skills-based legal education.

University of Colorado Denver, Business School, Program in Finance, Denver, CO 80217. Offers economics (MS); finance (MS); financial analysis and management (MS); financial and commodities risk management (MS); risk management and insurance (MS); MS/MA; MS/MBA. Part-time and evening/weekend programs available. *Students:* 84 full-time (22 women), 29 part-time (6 women); includes 16 minority (2 Black or African American, non-Hispanic/Latino; 6 Asian, non-Hispanic/Latino; 6 Hispanic/Latino; 2 Two or more races, non-Hispanic/Latino), 36 international. Average age 28. 119 applicants, 68% accepted, 38 enrolled. In 2013, 36 master's awarded. *Degree requirements:* For master's, 30 semester hours (18 of required core courses, 9 of finance electives, and 3 of free elective). *Entrance requirements:* For master's, GMAT, essay, resume, two letters of recommendation, financial statements (for international students). Additional exam requirements/recommendations for international students: Required—TOEFL (minimum score 537 paper-based; 75 iBT); Recommended—IELTS (minimum score 6.5). *Application deadline:* For fall admission, 4/15 for domestic students, 3/15 for international students; for spring admission, 10/15 for domestic students, 9/15 for international students. Applications are processed on a rolling basis. Application fee: $50 ($75 for international students). Electronic applications accepted. *Expenses:* Contact institution. *Financial support:* In 2013–14, 20 students received support. Teaching assistantships, Federal Work-Study, institutionally sponsored loans, scholarships/grants, and traineeships available. Financial award application deadline: 4/1; financial award applicants required to submit FAFSA. *Faculty research:* Corporate governance, debt maturity policies, regulation and financial markets, option management strategies. *Unit head:* Dr. Ajeyo Banerjee, Associate Professor/Director of MS in Finance Program, 303-315-8456, E-mail: ajeyo.banerjee@ucdenver.edu. *Application contact:* Shelly Townley, Director of Graduate Admissions, 303-315-8202, E-mail: shelly.townley@ucdenver.edu.
Website: http://www.ucdenver.edu/academics/colleges/business/degrees/ms/finance/Pages/Finance.aspx.

University of Florida, Graduate School, Warrington College of Business Administration, Hough Graduate School of Business, Department of Finance, Insurance and Real Estate, Gainesville, FL 32611. Offers entrepreneurship (MS); finance (MS, PhD); financial services (Certificate); insurance (PhD); quantitative finance (PhD); real estate (MS); real estate and urban analysis (PhD); JD/MBA; JD/MS. *Faculty:* 17 full-time (0 women), 6 part-time/adjunct (0 women). *Students:* 77 full-time (20 women), 4 part-time (2 women); includes 11 minority (3 Black or African American, non-Hispanic/Latino; 1 American Indian or Alaska Native, non-Hispanic/Latino; 2 Asian, non-Hispanic/Latino; 5 Hispanic/Latino), 23 international. Average age 27. 226 applicants, 4% accepted, 8 enrolled. In 2013, 92 master's, 5 doctorates awarded. Terminal master's awarded for partial completion of doctoral program. *Degree requirements:* For master's, comprehensive exam, thesis; for doctorate, comprehensive exam, thesis/dissertation. *Entrance requirements:* For master's, GMAT (minimum score of 465) or GRE General Test, minimum GPA of 3.0 for last 60 hours of undergraduate degree, work experience (preferred); for doctorate, GMAT (minimum score of 465) or GRE General Test, minimum GPA of 3.0. Additional exam requirements/recommendations for international students: Required—TOEFL (minimum score 550 paper-based; 80 iBT), IELTS (minimum score 6). *Application deadline:* For fall admission, 1/15 priority date for domestic students, 1/15 for international students. Applications are processed on a rolling basis. Application fee: $30. Electronic applications accepted. *Expenses:* Tuition, state resident: full-time $12,640. Tuition, nonresident: full-time $30,000. *Financial support:* In 2013–14, 19 students received support, including 13 research assistantships (averaging $18,787 per year), 6 teaching assistantships (averaging $14,970 per year); career-related internships or fieldwork, scholarships/grants, and unspecified assistantships also available. Financial award application deadline: 1/15; financial award applicants required to submit FAFSA. *Faculty research:* Banking, empirical corporate finance, hedge funds. *Unit head:* Mahendrarajah Nimalendran, PhD, Chair, 352-392-9526, Fax: 352-392-0301, E-mail: nimal@ufl.edu. *Application contact:* Office of Admissions, 352-392-1365, E-mail: webrequests@admissions.ufl.edu.
Website: http://www.cba.ufl.edu/fire/.

University of Pennsylvania, Wharton School, Insurance and Risk Management Department, Philadelphia, PA 19104. Offers MBA, PhD. *Degree requirements:* For doctorate, thesis/dissertation. *Entrance requirements:* For master's, GMAT; for doctorate, GMAT or GRE. *Faculty research:* Fair rate of return in insurance economics of pension plans, insurance regulation, malpractice insurance, actuarial science, genetic testing and life insurance.

University of Wisconsin–Madison, Graduate School, Wisconsin School of Business, Doctoral Program in Actuarial Science, Risk Management and Insurance, Madison, WI 53706-1380. Offers PhD. *Faculty:* 5 full-time (2 women). *Students:* 10 full-time (6 women); includes 1 minority (Asian, non-Hispanic/Latino), 6 international. Average age 31. 30 applicants, 10% accepted, 3 enrolled. In 2013, 1 doctorate awarded. *Degree requirements:* For doctorate, comprehensive exam, thesis/dissertation. *Entrance requirements:* For doctorate, GMAT or GRE General Test. Additional exam requirements/recommendations for international students: Recommended—TOEFL (minimum score 623 paper-based; 106 iBT), IELTS (minimum score 7.5), TSE (minimum score 73). *Application deadline:* For fall admission, 12/15 priority date for domestic and international students. Application fee: $56. Electronic applications accepted. *Expenses:* Contact institution. *Financial support:* In 2013–14, 9 students received support, including 1 fellowship with full tuition reimbursement available (averaging $19,125 per year), 1 research assistantship with full tuition reimbursement available (averaging $14,746 per year), 7 teaching assistantships with full tuition reimbursements available (averaging $14,746 per year); Federal Work-Study, institutionally sponsored loans, scholarships/grants, health care benefits, and unspecified assistantships also available. Financial award application deadline: 12/15; financial award applicants required to submit FAFSA. *Faculty research:* Superfund, health insurance, workers compensation, employee benefits, fuzzy logic. *Unit head:* Prof. Edward Frees, Chair, 608-262-0429, E-mail: jfrees@bus.wisc.edu. *Application contact:* Belle Heberling, Assistant Director for Research Programs, 608-262-3749, Fax: 608-890-0180, E-mail: phd@bus.wisc.edu.
Website: http://www.bus.wisc.edu/phd.

University of Wisconsin–Madison, Graduate School, Wisconsin School of Business, Wisconsin Full-Time MBA Program, Madison, WI 53706. Offers applied security analysis (MBA); arts administration (MBA); brand and product management (MBA); corporate finance and investment banking (MBA); marketing research (MBA); operations and technology management (MBA); real estate (MBA); risk management and insurance (MBA); strategic human resource management (MBA); supply chain management (MBA). *Faculty:* 34 full-time (5 women), 30 part-time/adjunct (15 women). *Students:* 193 full-time (61 women); includes 37 minority (10 Black or African American, non-Hispanic/Latino; 14 Asian, non-Hispanic/Latino; 12 Hispanic/Latino; 1 Native Hawaiian or other Pacific Islander, non-Hispanic/Latino), 37 international. Average age 28. 460 applicants, 33% accepted, 101 enrolled. In 2013, 110 master's awarded. *Degree requirements:* For master's, thesis (for arts administration specialization). *Entrance requirements:* For master's, GMAT or GRE, bachelor's or equivalent degree, 2 years of work experience, letters of recommendation, resume. Additional exam requirements/recommendations for international students: Required—TOEFL (minimum score 600 paper-based; 100 iBT), IELTS. *Application deadline:* For fall admission, 11/5 for domestic and international students; for winter admission, 2/4 for domestic and international students; for spring admission, 4/28 for domestic students, 4/2 for international students. Applications are processed on a rolling basis. Application fee:

$56. Electronic applications accepted. *Expenses:* Contact institution. *Financial support:* In 2013–14, 176 students received support, including 12 fellowships with full tuition reimbursements available (averaging $37,956 per year), 42 research assistantships with full tuition reimbursements available (averaging $28,175 per year), 43 teaching assistantships with full tuition reimbursements available (averaging $28,175 per year); scholarships/grants, health care benefits, and unspecified assistantships also available. Financial award application deadline: 4/26; financial award applicants required to submit FAFSA. *Faculty research:* Market consequences of International Financial Reporting Standards (IFRS), inter-firm relationships and strategic partnerships, application of Bayesian statistical methods and applied probability models to understanding individuals' behaviors in the context of customer relationship management (CRM) applications, liquidity provision and the structure of financial markets, strategic management of global startups. *Unit head:* Prof. Larry W. Hunter, Associate Dean of Master's Programs, 608-265-3494, Fax: 608-265-4192, E-mail: lhunter@bus.wisc.edu. *Application contact:* William H. Wait, Assistant Director of MBA Marketing and Recruiting, 608-262-4000, Fax: 608-265-4192, E-mail: wwait@bus.wisc.edu. Website: http://www.bus.wisc.edu/mba.

Virginia Commonwealth University, Graduate School, School of Business, Program in Finance, Insurance, and Real Estate, Richmond, VA 23284-9005. Offers MS. *Entrance requirements:* For master's, GMAT. Additional exam requirements/recommendations for international students: Required—TOEFL (minimum score 600 paper-based; 100 iBT); Recommended—IELTS (minimum score 6.5). Electronic applications accepted.

Section 11
International Business

This section contains a directory of institutions offering graduate work in international business. Additional information about programs listed in the directory but not augmented by an in-depth entry may be obtained by writing directly to the dean of a graduate school or chair of a department at the address given in the directory.

For programs offering related work, see also in this book *Business Administration and Management, Entrepreneurship, Industrial and Manufacturing Management,* and *Organizational Behavior.* In another guide in this series:

Graduate Programs in the Humanities, Arts & Social Sciences

See *Political Science and International Affairs* and *Public, Regional, and Industrial Affairs*

CONTENTS

Program Directory
International Business   408

Display and Close-Up
See:
University of California, Los Angeles—Business
    Administration and Management   145, 191

International Business

Alliant International University–México City, School of Management, Mexico City, Mexico. Offers business administration (MBA); international business administration (MIBA); international studies (MA), including international relations. Part-time and evening/weekend programs available. *Faculty:* 7 part-time/adjunct (3 women). *Students:* 10 full-time (3 women), 9 international. Average age 31. 8 applicants, 75% accepted, 5 enrolled. In 2013, 9 master's awarded. *Degree requirements:* For master's, thesis (for some programs). *Entrance requirements:* For master's, GMAT or GRE (depending on program), minimum GPA of 3.0, letters of recommendation. Additional exam requirements/recommendations for international students: Required—TOEFL (minimum score 550 paper-based; 80 iBT), TWE (minimum score 5). *Application deadline:* For fall admission, 8/1 priority date for domestic and international students; for spring admission, 12/1 priority date for domestic and international students. Applications are processed on a rolling basis. Application fee: $55. Electronic applications accepted. *Financial support:* Research assistantships, teaching assistantships, career-related internships or fieldwork, Federal Work-Study, institutionally sponsored loans, and scholarships/grants available. Support available to part-time students. Financial award application deadline: 2/15; financial award applicants required to submit FAFSA. *Faculty research:* Global economy, international relations. *Unit head:* Dr. Lee White, Dean, 858-635-4495, E-mail: contacto@alliantmexico.com. *Application contact:* Lesly Gutierrez Garcia, Coordinator of Admissions and Student Services, 525 5525-7651, E-mail: contacto@alliantmexico.com.
Website: http://www.alliantmexico.com.

American InterContinental University Atlanta, Program in Global Technology Management, Atlanta, GA 30328. Offers MBA. Part-time and evening/weekend programs available. Postbaccalaureate distance learning degree programs offered. *Entrance requirements:* For master's, interview. Electronic applications accepted. *Faculty research:* E-commerce, service quality leadership, human resources management.

American InterContinental University Online, Program in Business Administration, Schaumburg, IL 60173. Offers accounting and finance (MBA); finance (MBA); healthcare management (MBA); human resource management (MBA); international business (MBA); management (MBA); marketing (MBA); operations management (MBA); organizational psychology and development (MBA); project management (MBA). *Accreditation:* ACBSP. Evening/weekend programs available. Postbaccalaureate distance learning degree programs offered (no on-campus study). *Entrance requirements:* Additional exam requirements/recommendations for international students: Required—TOEFL (minimum score 550 paper-based). Electronic applications accepted.

American InterContinental University South Florida, Program in International Business, Weston, FL 33326. Offers accounting and finance (MBA); human resource management (MBA); management (MBA); marketing (MBA). Part-time and evening/weekend programs available. Postbaccalaureate distance learning degree programs offered. Electronic applications accepted.

American Public University System, AMU/APU Graduate Programs, Charles Town, WV 25414. Offers accounting (MBA, MS); criminal justice (MA), including business administration, emergency and disaster management, general (MA, MS); educational leadership (M Ed); emergency and disaster management (MA); entrepreneurship (MBA); environmental policy and management (MS), including environmental planning, environmental sustainability, fish and wildlife management, general (MA, MS), global environmental management; finance (MBA); general (MBA); global business management (MBA); history (MA), including American history, ancient and classical history, European history, global history, public history; homeland security (MA), including business administration, counter-terrorism studies, criminal justice, cyber, emergency management and public health, intelligence studies, transportation security; homeland security resource allocation (MBA); humanities (MA); information technology (MS), including digital forensics, enterprise software development, information assurance and security, IT project management; information technology management (MBA); intelligence studies (MA), including criminal intelligence, cyber, general (MA, MS), homeland security, intelligence analysis, intelligence collection, intelligence management, intelligence operations, terrorism studies; international relations and conflict resolution (MA), including comparative and security issues, conflict resolution, international and transnational security issues, peacekeeping; legal studies (MA); management (MA), including defense management, general (MA, MS), human resource management, organizational leadership, public administration; marketing (MBA); military history (MA), including American military history, American Revolution, civil war, war since 1945, World War II; military studies (MA), including joint warfare, strategic leadership; national security studies (MA), including general (MA, MS), homeland security, regional security studies, security and intelligence analysis, terrorism studies; nonprofit management (MBA); political science (MA), including American politics and government, comparative government and development, general (MA, MS), international relations, public policy; psychology (MA), including general (MA, MS), maritime engineering management, reverse logistics management; public administration (MPA), including disaster management, environmental policy, health policy, human resources, national security, organizational management, security management; public health (MPH); reverse logistics management (MA); school counseling (M Ed); security management (MA); space studies (MS), including aerospace science, general (MA, MS), planetary science; sports and health sciences (MS); teaching (M Ed), including curriculum and instruction for elementary teachers, elementary reading, English language learners, instructional leadership, online learning, special education; transportation and logistics management (MA), including general (MA, MS), maritime engineering management, reverse logistics management. Programs offered via distance learning only. Part-time and evening/weekend programs available. Postbaccalaureate distance learning degree programs offered (no on-campus study). *Faculty:* 432 full-time (242 women), 1,722 part-time/adjunct (829 women). *Students:* 511 full-time (241 women), 10,947 part-time (4,294 women); includes 3,760 minority (2,058 Black or African American, non-Hispanic/Latino; 88 American Indian or Alaska Native, non-Hispanic/Latino; 293 Asian, non-Hispanic/Latino; 876 Hispanic/Latino; 91 Native Hawaiian or other Pacific Islander, non-Hispanic/Latino; 354 Two or more races, non-Hispanic/Latino), 134 international. Average age 36. In 2013, 3,323 master's awarded. *Degree requirements:* For master's, comprehensive exam or practicum. *Entrance requirements:* For master's, official transcript showing earned bachelor's degree from institution accredited by recognized accrediting body. Additional exam requirements/recommendations for international students: Required—TOEFL (minimum score 550 paper-based), IELTS (minimum score 6.5). *Application deadline:* Applications are processed on a rolling basis. Application fee: $0. Electronic applications accepted. *Expenses: Tuition:* Part-time $325 per semester hour. *Financial support:* Applicants required to submit FAFSA. *Faculty research:* Military history, criminal justice, management performance, national security. *Unit head:* Dr. Karan Powell, Executive Vice President and Provost, 877-468-6268, Fax: 304-724-3780. *Application contact:* Terry Grant, Vice President of Enrollment Management, 877-468-6268, Fax: 304-724-3780, E-mail: info@apus.edu.
Website: http://www.apus.edu.

The American University in Dubai, Graduate Programs, Dubai, United Arab Emirates. Offers construction management (MS); education (M Ed); finance (MBA); generalist (MBA); marketing (MBA). Part-time and evening/weekend programs available. *Degree requirements:* For master's, thesis optional. *Entrance requirements:* For master's, GMAT (for MBA); GRE (for M Ed and MS), minimum undergraduate GPA of 3.0, official transcripts, two reference forms, curriculum vitae/resume, statement of career objectives, work experience. Additional exam requirements/recommendations for international students: Required—TOEFL (minimum score 550 paper-based; 79 iBT). Electronic applications accepted.

The American University of Paris, Graduate Programs, Paris, France. Offers cross-cultural and sustainable business management (MA); cultural translation (MA); global communications (MA); global communications and civil society (MA); international affairs (MA); international affairs, conflict resolution and civil society development (MA); Middle East and Islamic studies (MA); Middle East and Islamic studies and international affairs (MA); public policy and international affairs (MA); public policy and international law (MA). *Faculty:* 17 full-time (4 women), 12 part-time/adjunct (4 women). *Students:* 86 full-time (70 women), 92 part-time (75 women). *Degree requirements:* For master's, thesis (for some programs). *Entrance requirements:* For master's, minimum undergraduate GPA of 3.0. Additional exam requirements/recommendations for international students: Recommended—TOEFL, IELTS. *Application deadline:* For fall admission, 4/15 priority date for international students; for spring admission, 11/15 priority date for international students. Applications are processed on a rolling basis. Application fee: $75. Electronic applications accepted. *Expenses: Tuition:* Full-time 12,990 euros; part-time 812 euros per credit. *Required fees:* 890 euros per year. One-time fee: 510 euros. *Financial support:* In 2013–14, 86 students received support. Scholarships/grants available. Financial award applicants required to submit FAFSA. *Unit head:* Oliver Feltham, Associate Dean of Graduate Studies, 33 1 40 62 06 67, E-mail: ofeltham@aup.edu. *Application contact:* International Admissions Counselor, 33 1 40 62 07 20, Fax: 33 1 47 05 34 32, E-mail: admissions@aup.edu.
Website: http://www.aup.edu/academics/graduate.

Anaheim University, Programs in Business Administration, Anaheim, CA 92806-5150. Offers entrepreneurship (ME, DBA); global sustainable management (MBA); international business (MBA, DBA, Certificate, Diploma); management (DBA); sustainable management (DBA, Certificate, Diploma). Postbaccalaureate distance learning degree programs offered.

Argosy University, Atlanta, College of Business, Atlanta, GA 30328. Offers accounting (DBA); corporate compliance (MBA); customized professional concentration (MBA, DBA); finance (MBA); healthcare administration (MBA); information systems (DBA); information systems management (MBA); international business (MBA, DBA); management (MBA, MSM, DBA); marketing (MBA, DBA).

Argosy University, Chicago, College of Business, Chicago, IL 60601. Offers accounting (DBA); customized professional concentration (MBA, DBA); finance (MBA); fraud examination (MBA); global business sustainability (DBA); healthcare administration (MBA); information systems (DBA); information systems management (MBA); international business (MBA, DBA); management (MBA, MSM, DBA); marketing (MBA, DBA); organizational leadership (Ed D); public administration (MBA); sustainable management (MBA). Postbaccalaureate distance learning degree programs offered (minimal on-campus study).

Argosy University, Dallas, College of Business, Farmers Branch, TX 75244. Offers accounting (DBA, AGC); corporate compliance (MBA, Graduate Certificate); customized professional concentration (MBA); finance (MBA, Graduate Certificate); fraud examination (MBA, Graduate Certificate); global business sustainability (DBA, AGC); healthcare administration (Graduate Certificate); healthcare management (MBA); information systems (MBA, DBA, AGC); information systems management (Graduate Certificate); international business (MBA, DBA, AGC, Graduate Certificate); management (MBA, DBA, AGC, Graduate Certificate); marketing (MBA, DBA, AGC, Graduate Certificate); public administration (MBA, Graduate Certificate); sustainable management (MBA, Graduate Certificate).

Argosy University, Denver, College of Business, Denver, CO 80231. Offers accounting (DBA); corporate compliance (MBA); customized professional concentration (MBA, DBA); finance (MBA); fraud examination (MBA); global business sustainability (DBA); healthcare administration (MBA); information systems (DBA); information systems management (MBA); international business (MBA, DBA); management (MBA, MSM, DBA); marketing (MBA, DBA); organizational leadership (Ed D); public administration (MBA); sustainable management (MBA).

Argosy University, Hawai`i, College of Business, Honolulu, HI 96813. Offers accounting (DBA); corporate compliance (MBA); customized professional concentration (MBA, DBA); finance (MBA, Certificate); fraud examination (MBA); global business sustainability (DBA); healthcare administration (MBA, Certificate); information systems (DBA); information systems management (MBA, Certificate); international business (MBA, DBA, Certificate); management (MBA, MSM, DBA); marketing (MBA, DBA, Certificate); organizational leadership (Ed D); public administration (MBA); sustainable management (MBA).

Argosy University, Inland Empire, College of Business, Ontario, CA 91761. Offers accounting (DBA); corporate compliance (MBA); customized professional concentration (MBA, DBA); finance (MBA); fraud examination (MBA); global business sustainability (DBA); healthcare administration (MBA); information systems (DBA); information systems management (MBA); international business (MBA, DBA); management (MBA, MSM, DBA); marketing (MBA, DBA); organizational leadership (Ed D); public administration (MBA); sustainable management (MBA).

Argosy University, Los Angeles, College of Business, Santa Monica, CA 90045. Offers accounting (DBA); corporate compliance (MBA); customized professional concentration (MBA, DBA); finance (MBA); fraud examination (MBA); global business sustainability (DBA); healthcare administration (MBA); information systems (DBA); information systems management (MBA); international business (MBA, DBA); management (MBA, MSM, DBA); marketing (MBA, DBA); organizational leadership (Ed D); public administration (MBA); sustainable management (MBA).

Argosy University, Nashville, College of Business, Nashville, TN 37214. Offers accounting (DBA); customized professional concentration (MBA, DBA); finance (MBA);

healthcare administration (MBA); information systems (MBA, DBA); international business (MBA, DBA); management (MBA, MSM, DBA); marketing (MBA, DBA).

Argosy University, Orange County, College of Business, Orange, CA 92868. Offers accounting (DBA, Adv C); corporate compliance (MBA); customized professional concentration (MBA, DBA); finance (MBA, Certificate); fraud examination (MBA); global business sustainability (DBA); healthcare administration (MBA, Certificate); information systems (DBA, Adv C, Certificate); information systems management (MBA); international business (MBA, DBA, Adv C, Certificate); management (MBA, MSM, DBA, Adv C); marketing (MBA, DBA, Adv C, Certificate); organizational leadership (Ed D); public administration (MBA, Certificate); sustainable management (MBA).

Argosy University, Phoenix, College of Business, Phoenix, AZ 85021. Offers accounting (DBA); corporate compliance (MBA); customized professional concentration (MBA, DBA); finance (MBA); fraud examination (MBA); global business sustainability (DBA); healthcare administration (MBA); information systems (DBA); information systems management (MBA); international business (MBA, DBA); management (MBA, DBA); marketing (MBA, DBA); public administration (MBA); sustainable management (MBA).

Argosy University, Salt Lake City, College of Business, Draper, UT 84020. Offers accounting (DBA); corporate compliance (MBA); customized professional concentration (MBA, DBA); finance (MBA); fraud examination (MBA); global business sustainability (DBA); healthcare administration (MBA); information systems (DBA); information systems management (MBA); international business (MBA, DBA); management (MBA, DBA); marketing (MBA, DBA); public administration (MBA); sustainable management (MBA).

Argosy University, San Diego, College of Business, San Diego, CA 92108. Offers accounting (DBA); corporate compliance (MBA); customized professional concentration (MBA, DBA); finance (MBA); fraud examination (MBA); global business sustainability (DBA); information systems (DBA); information systems management (MBA); international business (MBA, DBA); management (MBA, MSM, DBA); marketing (MBA, DBA); organizational leadership (Ed D); public administration (MBA).

Argosy University, San Francisco Bay Area, College of Business, Alameda, CA 94501. Offers accounting (DBA); corporate compliance (MBA); customized professional concentration (MBA, DBA); finance (MBA); fraud examination (MBA); global business sustainability (DBA); healthcare administration (MBA); information systems (DBA); information systems management (MBA); international business (MBA, DBA); management (MBA, MSM, DBA); marketing (MBA, DBA); organizational leadership (Ed D); public administration (MBA); sustainable management (MBA).

Argosy University, Sarasota, College of Business, Sarasota, FL 34235. Offers accounting (DBA, Adv C); corporate compliance (MBA, DBA, Certificate); customized professional concentration (MBA, DBA); finance (MBA, Certificate); fraud examination (MBA, Certificate); global business sustainability (DBA, Adv C); healthcare administration (MBA, Certificate); information systems (DBA, Adv C, Certificate); information systems management (MBA); international business (MBA, DBA, Adv C, Certificate); management (MBA, MSM, DBA, Adv C, Certificate); marketing (MBA, DBA, Adv C, Certificate); organizational leadership (Ed D); public administration (MBA, Certificate); sustainable management (MBA, Certificate).

Argosy University, Schaumburg, College of Business, Schaumburg, IL 60173-5403. Offers accounting (DBA, Adv C); customized professional concentration (MBA, DBA); finance (MBA, Certificate); fraud examination (MBA); global business sustainability (DBA); healthcare administration (MBA, Certificate); information systems (DBA, Adv C, Certificate); information systems management (MBA); international business (MBA, DBA, Adv C, Certificate); management (MBA, MSM, DBA, Adv C, Certificate); marketing (MBA, DBA, Adv C, Certificate); organizational leadership (Ed D); public administration (MBA); sustainable management (MBA).

Argosy University, Seattle, College of Business, Seattle, WA 98121. Offers accounting (DBA); corporate compliance (MBA); customized professional concentration (MBA, DBA); finance (MBA); fraud examination (MBA); global business sustainability (DBA); healthcare administration (MBA); information systems (DBA); information systems management (MBA); international business (MBA, DBA); management (MBA, MSM, DBA); marketing (MBA, DBA); organizational leadership (Ed D); public administration (MBA); sustainable management (MBA).

Argosy University, Tampa, College of Business, Tampa, FL 33607. Offers accounting (DBA); corporate compliance (MBA); customized professional concentration (MBA, DBA); finance (MBA); fraud examination (MBA); global business sustainability (DBA); healthcare administration (MBA); information systems (DBA); information systems management (MBA); international business (MBA, DBA); management (MBA, MSM, DBA); marketing (MBA, DBA); organizational leadership (Ed D); public administration (MBA); sustainable management (MBA).

Argosy University, Twin Cities, College of Business, Eagan, MN 55121. Offers accounting (DBA); customized professional concentration (MBA, DBA); finance (MBA); fraud examination (MBA); global business sustainability (DBA); healthcare administration (MBA); information systems (DBA); information systems management (MBA); international business (MBA, DBA); management (MBA, MSM, DBA); marketing (MBA, DBA); organizational leadership (Ed D); public administration (MBA); sustainable management (MBA).

Argosy University, Washington DC, College of Business, Arlington, VA 22209. Offers accounting (DBA); customized professional concentration (MBA, DBA); finance (MBA); fraud examination (MBA); global business sustainability (DBA); healthcare administration (MBA); information systems (DBA); information systems management (MBA); international business (MBA, DBA, Certificate); management (MBA, MSM, DBA); marketing (MBA, DBA, Certificate); organizational leadership (Ed D); public administration (MBA); sustainable management (MBA).

Ashworth College, Graduate Programs, Norcross, GA 30092. Offers business administration (MBA); criminal justice (MS); health care administration (MBA, MS); human resource management (MBA, MS); international business (MBA); management (MS); marketing (MBA, MS).

Assumption College, Graduate Studies, Department of Business Studies, Worcester, MA 01609-1296. Offers accounting (MBA); business administration (CAGS); finance/economics (MBA); frontline management (CGS); general business (MBA); human resources (MBA); international business (MBA); management (MBA); marketing (MBA); nonprofit leadership (MBA, CGS); organizational communication (CGS). Part-time and evening/weekend programs available. *Faculty:* 5 full-time (0 women), 20 part-time/adjunct (7 women). *Students:* 20 full-time (7 women), 130 part-time (68 women); includes 20 minority (8 Black or African American, non-Hispanic/Latino; 2 Asian, non-Hispanic/Latino; 8 Hispanic/Latino; 1 Native Hawaiian or other Pacific Islander, non-Hispanic/Latino; 1 Two or more races, non-Hispanic/Latino), 2 international. Average age 31. 63 applicants, 62% accepted, 22 enrolled. In 2013, 58 master's, 1 other advanced degree awarded. *Degree requirements:* For master's, thesis, capstone. *Entrance requirements:* For master's and other advanced degree, 3 letters of recommendation, resume, essay. Additional exam requirements/recommendations for international students: Required—TOEFL (minimum score 540 paper-based; 76 iBT), IELTS (minimum score 6). *Application deadline:* For fall admission, 10/1 for domestic and international students; for winter admission, 2/1 for domestic and international students; for spring admission, 4/1 for domestic and international students. Applications are processed on a rolling basis. Application fee: $30. Electronic applications accepted. *Expenses: Tuition:* Full-time $10,098; part-time $561 per credit. *Required fees:* $20 per term. Full-time tuition and fees vary according to course load and program. *Financial support:* In 2013–14, 15 students received support. Tuition waivers (full and partial), unspecified assistantships, and institutional discounts available. Financial award application deadline: 5/1; financial award applicants required to submit FAFSA. *Faculty research:* Workplace diversity, dynamics of team interaction, utilization of leased employees, experiential learning project on due diligence market for prostheses. *Unit head:* Dr. J. Bart Morrison, Director, 508-767-7458, Fax: 508-767-7252, E-mail: jmorrison@assumption.edu. *Application contact:* Laura Lawrence, Graduate Programs Operations Manager, 508-767-7387, Fax: 508-767-7030, E-mail: graduate@assumption.edu.
Website: http://graduate.assumption.edu/mba/assumption-mba.

Avila University, School of Business, Kansas City, MO 64145-1698. Offers accounting (MBA); finance (MBA); health care administration (MBA); international business (MBA); management (MBA); management information systems (MBA); marketing (MBA). Part-time and evening/weekend programs available. *Faculty:* 9 full-time (4 women), 12 part-time/adjunct (3 women). *Students:* 66 full-time (32 women), 46 part-time (27 women); includes 34 minority (22 Black or African American, non-Hispanic/Latino; 1 American Indian or Alaska Native, non-Hispanic/Latino; 4 Asian, non-Hispanic/Latino; 7 Hispanic/Latino), 27 international. Average age 32. 30 applicants, 80% accepted, 24 enrolled. In 2013, 61 master's awarded. *Degree requirements:* For master's, comprehensive exam, capstone course. *Entrance requirements:* For master's, GMAT (minimum score 420), minimum GPA of 3.0, interview. Additional exam requirements/recommendations for international students: Required—TOEFL (minimum score 550 paper-based). *Application deadline:* For fall admission, 7/30 priority date for domestic and international students; for winter admission, 11/30 priority date for domestic and international students; for spring admission, 2/28 priority date for domestic and international students; for summer admission, 6/1 priority date for domestic and international students. Applications are processed on a rolling basis. Application fee: $0. Electronic applications accepted. *Expenses:* Contact institution. *Financial support:* In 2013–14, 11 students received support. Career-related internships or fieldwork and scholarships/grants available. Support available to part-time students. Financial award applicants required to submit FAFSA. *Faculty research:* Leadership characteristics, financial hedging, group dynamics. *Unit head:* Dr. Richard Woodall, Dean, 816-501-3720, Fax: 816-501-2463, E-mail: richard.woodall@avila.edu. *Application contact:* Sarah Belanus, MBA Admissions Director, 816-501-3601, Fax: 816-501-2463, E-mail: sarah.belanus@avila.edu.
Website: http://www.avila.edu/mba.

Azusa Pacific University, School of Behavioral and Applied Sciences, Department of Higher Education and Organizational Leadership, Program in Global Leadership, Azusa, CA 91702-7000. Offers MA.

Azusa Pacific University, School of Business and Management, Azusa, CA 91702-7000. Offers business administration (MBA); diversity for strategic advantage (MA); entrepreneurship (MBA); finance (MBA); human and organizational development (MA); human resources and organizational development (MBA); human resources management (MA); international business (MBA); marketing (MBA); non-profit management (MA); organizational development and change (MA); performance improvement (MA); public administration (MA); strategic management (MBA). Part-time and evening/weekend programs available. *Degree requirements:* For master's, thesis (for some programs), final project. *Entrance requirements:* For master's, GMAT, minimum GPA of 3.0. Additional exam requirements/recommendations for international students: Required—TOEFL (minimum score 600 paper-based). *Expenses:* Contact institution. *Faculty research:* Gender issues, financial risk, leadership and ethics, marketing strategy.

Baldwin Wallace University, Graduate Programs, Division of Business, Program in International Management, Berea, OH 44017-2088. Offers MBA. Part-time and evening/weekend programs available. *Students:* 12 full-time (6 women), 9 part-time (4 women); includes 6 minority (1 Black or African American, non-Hispanic/Latino; 1 Asian, non-Hispanic/Latino; 4 Hispanic/Latino), 5 international. Average age 31. 8 applicants, 63% accepted, 5 enrolled. In 2013, 18 master's awarded. *Degree requirements:* For master's, one foreign language, minimum overall GPA of 3.0, completion of all required courses. *Entrance requirements:* For master's, GMAT or minimum undergraduate GPA of 3.0, interview, work experience, bachelor's degree in any field. Additional exam requirements/recommendations for international students: Required—TOEFL (minimum score 523 paper-based; 70 iBT). *Application deadline:* For fall admission, 7/25 priority date for domestic students, 4/30 priority date for international students; for spring admission, 12/15 priority date for domestic students, 9/30 priority date for international students. Applications are processed on a rolling basis. Application fee: $25. Electronic applications accepted. Application fee is waived when completed online. *Expenses:* Contact institution. *Financial support:* Application deadline: 5/1; applicants required to submit FAFSA. *Faculty research:* International finance, systems approach, international marketing. *Unit head:* Harvey Hopson, Director, 440-826-2137, Fax: 440-826-3868, E-mail: hhopson@bw.edu. *Application contact:* Laura Spencer, Graduate Application Specialist, 440-826-2191, Fax: 440-826-3868, E-mail: lspencer@bw.edu.
Website: http://www.bw.edu/academics/bus/programs/imba/.

Barry University, Andreas School of Business, Graduate Certificate Programs, Miami Shores, FL 33161-6695. Offers finance (Certificate); health services administration (Certificate); international business (Certificate); management (Certificate); management information systems (Certificate); marketing (Certificate).

Baruch College of the City University of New York, Zicklin School of Business, Department of Marketing and International Business, New York, NY 10010-5585. Offers international business (MBA); marketing (MBA, MS, PhD). PhD offered jointly with Graduate School and University Center of the City University of New York. Part-time and evening/weekend programs available. *Degree requirements:* For doctorate, comprehensive exam, thesis/dissertation. *Entrance requirements:* For master's, GMAT, 2 letters of recommendation, resume, 2 years of work experience; for doctorate, GMAT. Additional exam requirements/recommendations for international students: Required—TOEFL (minimum score 590 paper-based), TWE (minimum score 5).

Baruch College of the City University of New York, Zicklin School of Business, International Executive MS Programs, New York, NY 10010-5585. Offers entrepreneurship (MS). Part-time and evening/weekend programs available. *Entrance requirements:* For master's, GMAT, 2 letters of recommendation, resume, 2 years of work experience. Additional exam requirements/recommendations for international students: Required—TOEFL (minimum score 590 paper-based), TWE (minimum score 5).

Benedictine University, Graduate Programs, Program in Business Administration, Lisle, IL 60532-0900. Offers accounting (MBA); entrepreneurship and managing innovation (MBA); financial management (MBA); health administration (MBA); human

resource management (MBA); information systems security (MBA); international business (MBA); management consulting (MBA); management information systems (MBA); marketing management (MBA); operations management and logistics (MBA); organizational leadership (MBA). Part-time and evening/weekend programs available. Postbaccalaureate distance learning degree programs offered (minimal on-campus study). *Faculty:* 4 full-time (2 women), 24 part-time/adjunct (3 women). *Students:* 144 full-time (83 women), 599 part-time (328 women); includes 189 minority (115 Black or African American, non-Hispanic/Latino; 5 American Indian or Alaska Native, non-Hispanic/Latino; 43 Asian, non-Hispanic/Latino; 24 Hispanic/Latino; 2 Native Hawaiian or other Pacific Islander, non-Hispanic/Latino), 14 international. Average age 34. 211 applicants, 89% accepted, 155 enrolled. In 2013, 376 master's awarded. *Entrance requirements:* For master's, GMAT. Additional exam requirements/recommendations for international students: Required—TOEFL (minimum score 550 paper-based). *Application deadline:* For fall admission, 9/1 for domestic students; for winter admission, 12/1 for domestic students; for spring admission, 2/15 for domestic students. Applications are processed on a rolling basis. Application fee: $40. Electronic applications accepted. *Expenses: Tuition:* Part-time $590 per credit hour. *Financial support:* Career-related internships or fieldwork and health care benefits available. Support available to part-time students. *Faculty research:* Strategic leadership in professional organizations, sociology of professions, organizational change, social identity theory, applications to change management. *Unit head:* Dr. Sharon Borowicz, Director, 630-829-6219, E-mail: sborowicz@ben.edu. *Application contact:* Kari Gibbons, Director, Admissions, 630-829-6200, Fax: 630-829-6584, E-mail: kgibbons@ben.edu.

Boston University, Metropolitan College, Department of Administrative Sciences, Boston, MA 02215. Offers banking and financial management (MSM); business continuity in emergency management (MSM); economics development and tourism management (MSAS); electronic commerce, systems, and technology (MSAS); financial economics (MSAS); innovation and technology (MSAS); insurance management (MSM); international market management (MSM); multinational commerce (MSAS); project management (MS). *Accreditation:* AACSB. Part-time and evening/weekend programs available. Postbaccalaureate distance learning degree programs offered (no on-campus study). *Faculty:* 15 full-time (3 women), 22 part-time/adjunct (3 women). *Students:* 177 full-time (85 women), 560 part-time (293 women); includes 89 minority (31 Black or African American, non-Hispanic/Latino; 31 Asian, non-Hispanic/Latino; 25 Hispanic/Latino; 2 Two or more races, non-Hispanic/Latino), 242 international. Average age 31. 509 applicants, 71% accepted, 222 enrolled. In 2013, 158 master's awarded. *Degree requirements:* For master's, thesis optional. *Entrance requirements:* For master's, 1 year of work experience, minimum GPA of 3.0. Additional exam requirements/recommendations for international students: Required—TOEFL (minimum score 84 iBT). *Application deadline:* Applications are processed on a rolling basis. Application fee: $80. Electronic applications accepted. *Expenses: Tuition:* Full-time $43,970; part-time $1374 per credit hour. *Required fees:* $60 per semester. Tuition and fees vary according to class time, course level and program. *Financial support:* In 2013–14, 15 students received support, including 7 research assistantships (averaging $8,400 per year); career-related internships or fieldwork, Federal Work-Study, and unspecified assistantships also available. *Faculty research:* International business, innovative process. *Unit head:* Dr. Kip Becker, Chairman, 617-353-3016, E-mail: adminsc@bu.edu. *Application contact:* Fiona Niven, Administrative Sciences Department, 617-353-3016, E-mail: adminsc@bu.edu.
Website: http://www.bu.edu/met/academic-community/departments/administrative-sciences/.

Boston University, School of Law, Boston, MA 02215. Offers American law (LL M); banking (LL M); intellectual property law (LL M); international business law (LL M); law (JD); taxation (LL M); JD/LL M; JD/MA; JD/MBA; JD/MPH; JD/MS; JD/MSW. *Accreditation:* ABA. *Faculty:* 48 full-time (19 women), 91 part-time/adjunct (26 women). *Students:* 842 full-time (462 women), 118 part-time (54 women); includes 206 minority (19 Black or African American, non-Hispanic/Latino; 1 American Indian or Alaska Native, non-Hispanic/Latino; 83 Asian, non-Hispanic/Latino; 77 Hispanic/Latino; 26 Two or more races, non-Hispanic/Latino), 157 international. Average age 27. 4,584 applicants, 35% accepted, 220 enrolled. In 2013, 183 master's, 272 doctorates awarded. *Degree requirements:* For master's, thesis (for some programs); for doctorate, thesis/dissertation, research project resulting in a paper. *Entrance requirements:* For master's, JD; for doctorate, LSAT. Additional exam requirements/recommendations for international students: Required—TOEFL (minimum score 600 paper-based; 100 iBT). *Application deadline:* For fall admission, 4/1 for domestic and international students. Applications are processed on a rolling basis. Application fee: $80. Electronic applications accepted. *Expenses: Tuition:* Full-time $43,970; part-time $1374 per credit hour. *Required fees:* $60 per semester. Tuition and fees vary according to class time, course level and program. *Financial support:* In 2013–14, 600 students received support. Career-related internships or fieldwork, Federal Work-Study, institutionally sponsored loans, and scholarships/grants available. Financial award application deadline: 3/1; financial award applicants required to submit FAFSA. *Faculty research:* Health law, tax, intellectual property, Constitutional law, corporate law, business organizations and financial law, international law, and family law. *Unit head:* Maureen A. O'Rourke, Dean, 617-353-3112, Fax: 617-353-7400, E-mail: lawdean@bu.edu. *Application contact:* Alissa Leonard, Director of Admissions and Financial Aid, 617-353-3100, Fax: 617-353-0578, E-mail: bulawadm@bu.edu.
Website: http://www.bu.edu/law/.

Brandeis University, International Business School, Waltham, MA 02454-9110. Offers asset management (MBA); business economics (MBA); corporate finance (MBA); data analytics (MBA); finance (MSF), including asset management, corporate finance, real estate, risk management; international economic policy analysis (MBA); international economics and finance (MA, PhD); marketing (MBA); real estate (MBA); risk management (MBA); sustainability (MBA). Part-time and evening/weekend programs available. *Degree requirements:* For doctorate, thesis/dissertation. *Entrance requirements:* For master's, GMAT or GRE General Test (waived for applicants with at least 2 years of work experience applying to MSF); for doctorate, GRE General Test. Additional exam requirements/recommendations for international students: Required—TOEFL (minimum score 600 paper-based; 100 iBT), IELTS (minimum score 7). Electronic applications accepted. *Faculty research:* International economic policy analysis, U.S. economic policy analysis, real estate, strategy and municipal finance.

Brooklyn College of the City University of New York, Division of Graduate Studies, Department of Economics, Brooklyn, NY 11210-2889. Offers accounting (MS); business economics (MS), including economic analysis, global business and finance; economics (MA). Part-time and evening/weekend programs available. *Degree requirements:* For master's, comprehensive exam, thesis or alternative. *Entrance requirements:* For master's, GMAT (for MS), 2 letters of recommendation. Additional exam requirements/recommendations for international students: Required—TOEFL (minimum score 550 paper-based; 79 iBT). Electronic applications accepted. *Faculty research:* Econometrics, environmental economics, microeconomics, macroeconomics, taxation.

Bryant University, Graduate School of Business, Master of Business Administration Program, Smithfield, RI 02917. Offers general business (MBA); global finance (MBA); global supply chain management (MBA); international business (MBA). *Accreditation:* AACSB. Part-time and evening/weekend programs available. *Entrance requirements:* For master's, GMAT, transcripts, recommendation, resume, statement of objectives. Additional exam requirements/recommendations for international students: Required—TOEFL (minimum score 580 paper-based; 90 iBT). *Application deadline:* For fall admission, 7/15 for domestic and international students; for spring admission, 11/15 for domestic and international students. Applications are processed on a rolling basis. Application fee: $80. Electronic applications accepted. *Expenses: Tuition:* Full-time $26,832; part-time $1118 per credit hour. *Financial support:* In 2013–14, 11 research assistantships (averaging $6,708 per year) were awarded; unspecified assistantships also available. Financial award application deadline: 7/15; financial award applicants required to submit FAFSA. *Faculty research:* International business, information systems security, leadership, financial markets microstructure, commercial lending practice. *Unit head:* Richard S. Cheney, Director of Operations for Graduate Programs, School of Business, 401-232-6707, Fax: 401-232-6494, E-mail: rcheney@bryant.edu. *Application contact:* Linda Denzer, Assistant Director of Graduate Admission, 401-232-6529, Fax: 401-232-6494, E-mail: ldenzer@bryant.edu.

California Intercontinental University, School of Business, Diamond Bar, CA 91765. Offers banking and finance (MBA); entrepreneurship and business management (DBA); global business leadership (DBA); international management and marketing (MBA); organizational management and human resource management (MBA).

California Lutheran University, Graduate Studies, School of Management, Thousand Oaks, CA 91360-2787. Offers business (IMBA); computer science (MS); econometrics (MBA); economics (MS); entrepreneurship (MBA, Certificate); finance (MBA, Certificate); financial planning (MBA, Certificate); information systems and technology (MS); information technology management (MBA, Certificate); international business (MBA, Certificate); management and organization behavior (MBA); management and organizational behavior (Certificate); marketing (MBA, Certificate); microeconomics (MBA); nonprofit and social enterprise (MBA). Part-time and evening/weekend programs available. Postbaccalaureate distance learning degree programs offered (no on-campus study). *Faculty:* 26 full-time (9 women), 50 part-time/adjunct (11 women). *Students:* 426 full-time (175 women), 220 part-time (91 women); includes 114 minority (14 Black or African American, non-Hispanic/Latino; 30 Asian, non-Hispanic/Latino; 57 Hispanic/Latino; 13 Two or more races, non-Hispanic/Latino), 321 international. Average age 31. 495 applicants, 76% accepted, 119 enrolled. In 2013, 297 master's awarded. *Entrance requirements:* For master's, GMAT, interview, minimum GPA of 3.0. *Application deadline:* Applications are processed on a rolling basis. Application fee: $50. *Expenses:* Contact institution. *Unit head:* Dr. Gerhard Apfelthaler, Dean, 805-493-3360. *Application contact:* 805-493-3325, Fax: 805-493-3861, E-mail: clugrad@callutheran.edu.
Website: http://www.callutheran.edu/business/.

California State University, East Bay, Office of Academic Programs and Graduate Studies, College of Business and Economics, MBA Program, Hayward, CA 94542-3000. Offers entrepreneurship (MBA); finance (MBA); global innovators (MBA); human resources and organizational behavior (MBA); information technology management (MBA); marketing management (MBA); operations and supply chain management (MBA); strategy and international business (MBA). Part-time and evening/weekend programs available. *Degree requirements:* For master's, comprehensive exam or thesis. *Entrance requirements:* For master's, GMAT (minimum 20th percentile verbal and quantitative section), bachelor's degree, minimum GPA of 2.75. Additional exam requirements/recommendations for international students: Required—TOEFL (minimum score 550 paper-based; 79 iBT). Electronic applications accepted. *Expenses:* Contact institution.

California State University, East Bay, Office of Academic Programs and Graduate Studies, College of Business and Economics, Program in Information Technology Management, Option in Strategy and International Business, Hayward, CA 94542-3000. Offers MBA. Part-time and evening/weekend programs available. *Degree requirements:* For master's, comprehensive exam or thesis. *Entrance requirements:* For master's, GMAT, minimum GPA of 2.75. Additional exam requirements/recommendations for international students: Required—TOEFL (minimum score 550 paper-based).

California State University, Fullerton, Graduate Studies, College of Business and Economics, Program in Business Administration, Fullerton, CA 92834-9480. Offers business intelligence (MBA); general (MBA); international business (MBA); organizational leadership (MBA); risk management and insurance (MBA). *Accreditation:* AACSB. Part-time programs available. *Students:* 54 full-time (26 women), 119 part-time (48 women); includes 74 minority (46 Asian, non-Hispanic/Latino; 23 Hispanic/Latino; 5 Two or more races, non-Hispanic/Latino), 34 international. Average age 28. 500 applicants, 41% accepted, 78 enrolled. In 2013, 65 master's awarded. *Degree requirements:* For master's, project or thesis. *Entrance requirements:* For master's, GMAT. Application fee: $55. *Financial support:* Career-related internships or fieldwork, Federal Work-Study, institutionally sponsored loans, and scholarships/grants available. Support available to part-time students. Financial award application deadline: 3/1; financial award applicants required to submit FAFSA. *Unit head:* Dr. Anil Puri, Dean, 657-773-2592. *Application contact:* Admissions/Applications, 657-278-2371.

California State University, Los Angeles, Graduate Studies, College of Business and Economics, Department of Marketing, Los Angeles, CA 90032-8530. Offers international business (MBA, MS); marketing management (MBA, MS). Part-time and evening/weekend programs available. *Faculty:* 2 full-time (both women), 1 part-time/adjunct (0 women). *Students:* 1 full-time (0 women), 12 part-time (6 women); includes 3 minority (1 Asian, non-Hispanic/Latino; 1 Hispanic/Latino; 1 Two or more races, non-Hispanic/Latino), 9 international. Average age 28. In 2013, 11 master's awarded. *Degree requirements:* For master's, comprehensive exam (MBA), thesis (MS). *Entrance requirements:* For master's, GMAT, minimum GPA of 2.5 during previous 2 years of course work. Additional exam requirements/recommendations for international students: Required—TOEFL (minimum score 550 paper-based). *Application deadline:* For fall admission, 5/1 for domestic and international students. Applications are processed on a rolling basis. Application fee: $55. Electronic applications accepted. *Financial support:* Career-related internships or fieldwork and Federal Work-Study available. Support available to part-time students. Financial award application deadline: 3/1. *Unit head:* Dr. Tyrone Jackson, Chair, 323-343-2960, Fax: 323-343-5462, E-mail: tjackso4@calstatela.edu. *Application contact:* Dr. Larry Fritz, Dean of Graduate Studies, 323-343-3820, Fax: 323-343-5653, E-mail: lfritz@calstatela.edu.
Website: http://cbe.calstatela.edu/mkt/.

California University of Management and Sciences, Graduate Programs, Anaheim, CA 92801. Offers business administration (MBA, DBA); computer information systems (MS); economics (MS); international business (MS); sports management (MS).

Canisius College, Graduate Division, Richard J. Wehle School of Business, Department of Management, Buffalo, NY 14208-1098. Offers business administration (MBA); international business (MS). *Accreditation:* AACSB. Part-time and evening/weekend programs available. *Faculty:* 30 full-time (7 women), 8 part-time/adjunct (1 woman). *Students:* 99 full-time (43 women), 139 part-time (63 women); includes 22 minority (11 Black or African American, non-Hispanic/Latino; 2 American Indian or Alaska Native, non-Hispanic/Latino; 5 Asian, non-Hispanic/Latino; 2 Hispanic/Latino; 2 Two or more races, non-Hispanic/Latino), 3 international. Average age 28. 146

applicants, 68% accepted, 66 enrolled. In 2013, 113 master's awarded. *Entrance requirements:* For master's, GMAT, GRE, official transcript from colleges attended, current resume. Additional exam requirements/recommendations for international students: Required—TOEFL (minimum score 550 paper-based, 80 iBT), IELTS (minimum score 6.5), or CAEL (minimum score 70). *Application deadline:* For fall admission, 7/1 priority date for domestic students; for spring admission, 11/1 priority date for domestic students. Applications are processed on a rolling basis. Application fee: $25. Electronic applications accepted. Application fee is waived when completed online. *Expenses: Tuition:* Part-time $750 per credit hour. *Financial support:* Research assistantships, career-related internships or fieldwork, Federal Work-Study, scholarships/grants, and unspecified assistantships available. Support available to part-time students. Financial award application deadline: 4/30; financial award applicants required to submit FAFSA. *Faculty research:* Global leadership effectiveness, global supply chain management, quality management. *Unit head:* Dr. Gordon W. Meyer, Chair of Management, Entrepreneurship and International Business, 716-888-2634, E-mail: meyerg@canisius.edu. *Application contact:* Julie A. Zulewski, Director, Graduate Programs, 716-888-2548, Fax: 716-888-3195, E-mail: zulewskj@canisius.edu. Website: http://www.canisius.edu/graduate/.

Carlow University, School of Management, MBA Program, Pittsburgh, PA 15213-3165. Offers business administration (MBA); global business (MBA); healthcare management (MBA); project management (MBA). Part-time and evening/weekend programs available. Postbaccalaureate distance learning degree programs offered (no on-campus study). *Students:* 121 full-time (96 women), 26 part-time (17 women); includes 30 minority (22 Black or African American, non-Hispanic/Latino; 3 Asian, non-Hispanic/Latino; 3 Hispanic/Latino; 2 Two or more races, non-Hispanic/Latino), 5 international. Average age 32. 53 applicants, 96% accepted, 38 enrolled. In 2013, 41 master's awarded. *Entrance requirements:* For master's, minimum undergraduate GPA of 3.0; essay; resume; transcripts; two recommendations. Additional exam requirements/recommendations for international students: Required—TOEFL (minimum score 550 paper-based). *Application deadline:* Applications are processed on a rolling basis. Application fee: $20. Electronic applications accepted. Application fee is waived when completed online. *Expenses: Tuition:* Full-time $9523; part-time $744 per credit. Tuition and fees vary according to course load, degree level and program. *Unit head:* Dr. Enrique Mu, Chair, MBA Program, 412-578-8729, E-mail: emu@carlow.edu. *Application contact:* Jo Danhires, Administrative Assistant, Admissions, 412-578-6088, Fax: 412-578-6321, E-mail: gradstudies@carlow.edu. Website: http://gradstudies.carlow.edu/management/mba.html.

Central European University, Graduate Studies, Department of Legal Studies, Budapest, Hungary. Offers comparative Constitutional law (LL M); human rights (LL M, MA); international business law (LL M); law and economics (LL M, MA); legal studies (SJD). *Faculty:* 9 full-time (4 women), 16 part-time/adjunct (3 women). *Students:* 98 full-time (54 women). Average age 27. 324 applicants, 32% accepted, 67 enrolled. In 2013, 47 master's awarded. Terminal master's awarded for partial completion of doctoral program. *Degree requirements:* For master's, one foreign language, thesis; for doctorate, one foreign language, comprehensive exam, thesis/dissertation. *Entrance requirements:* For master's and doctorate, LSAT. Additional exam requirements/recommendations for international students: Required—TOEFL (minimum score 570 paper-based); Recommended—IELTS (minimum score 6.5). *Application deadline:* For fall admission, 1/24 for domestic and international students. Application fee: $40. Electronic applications accepted. *Expenses:* Contact institution. *Financial support:* In 2013–14, 77 students received support, including 77 fellowships with full and partial tuition reimbursements available (averaging $6,100 per year); career-related internships or fieldwork, institutionally sponsored loans, scholarships/grants, and tuition waivers (full and partial) also available. Financial award application deadline: 1/5. *Faculty research:* Institutional, constitutional and human rights in European Union law; biomedical law and reproductive rights; data protection law; Islamic banking and finance. *Unit head:* Dr. Renata Uitz, Head of Department, 36 1 327-3201, Fax: 361-327-3198, E-mail: legalst@ceu.hu. *Application contact:* Andrea Jenei, Department Coordinator, 361-327-3205, Fax: 361-327-3198, E-mail: jeneia@ceu.hu. Website: http://legal.ceu.hu/.

Central Michigan University, College of Graduate Studies, College of Business Administration, MBA Program, Mount Pleasant, MI 48859. Offers accounting (MBA); business economics (MBA); consulting (MBA); finance (MBA); general business (MBA); human resource management (MBA); information systems (MBA); international business (MBA); logistics management (MBA); marketing (MBA); value-driven organization (MBA). Part-time and evening/weekend programs available. Postbaccalaureate distance learning degree programs offered (no on-campus study). Electronic applications accepted. *Faculty research:* Accounting, consulting, international business, marketing, information systems.

Central Michigan University, College of Graduate Studies, Interdisciplinary Administration Programs, Mount Pleasant, MI 48859. Offers acquisitions administration (MSA, Graduate Certificate); general administration (MSA, Graduate Certificate); health services administration (MSA, Graduate Certificate); human resource administration (Graduate Certificate); human resources administration (MSA); information resource management (MSA, Graduate Certificate); international administration (MSA, Graduate Certificate); leadership (MSA, Graduate Certificate); public administration (MSA, Graduate Certificate); research administration (Graduate Certificate); sport administration (MSA). *Accreditation:* AACSB. Part-time and evening/weekend programs available. Postbaccalaureate distance learning degree programs offered (no on-campus study). *Degree requirements:* For master's, thesis or alternative. *Entrance requirements:* For master's, bachelor's degree with minimum GPA of 2.7. Electronic applications accepted. *Faculty research:* Interdisciplinary studies in acquisitions administration, health services administration, sport administration, recreation and park administration, and international administration.

Christian Brothers University, School of Business, Memphis, TN 38104-5581. Offers accountancy (M Acc); business (MBA); international business (MIB); project management (Certificate); MBA/MIB. Part-time and evening/weekend programs available. *Entrance requirements:* For master's, GMAT, GRE. Additional exam requirements/recommendations for international students: Required—TOEFL.

City University of Seattle, Graduate Division, School of Management, Bellevue, WA 98005. Offers accounting (Certificate); change leadership (MBA, Certificate); computer systems (MS); finance (Certificate); financial management (MBA); general management (MBA); general management-Europe (MBA); global marketing (MBA); human resources management (Certificate); individualized study (MBA); information security (MS); information systems (MBA); leadership (MA); marketing (MBA, Certificate); project management (MBA, MS, Certificate); sustainable business (Certificate); technology management (MBA, Certificate). Part-time and evening/weekend programs available. Postbaccalaureate distance learning degree programs offered (no on-campus study). *Degree requirements:* For master's, comprehensive exam (for some programs), thesis (for some programs). *Entrance requirements:* Additional exam requirements/recommendations for international students: Required—TOEFL (minimum score 567 paper-based; 87 iBT); Recommended—IELTS. Electronic applications accepted.

Clark University, Graduate School, Graduate School of Management, Business Administration Program, Worcester, MA 01610-1477. Offers accounting (MBA); finance (MBA); global business (MBA); information systems (MBA); management (MBA); marketing (MBA); social change (MBA); sustainability (MBA). *Accreditation:* AACSB. Part-time and evening/weekend programs available. *Students:* 109 full-time (50 women), 151 part-time (67 women); includes 16 minority (9 Black or African American, non-Hispanic/Latino; 3 Asian, non-Hispanic/Latino; 4 Hispanic/Latino), 74 international. Average age 30. 359 applicants, 50% accepted, 81 enrolled. In 2013, 125 master's awarded. *Degree requirements:* For master's, thesis optional. *Application deadline:* For fall admission, 6/1 priority date for domestic students; for spring admission, 12/1 priority date for domestic students. Applications are processed on a rolling basis. Application fee: $50. Electronic applications accepted. *Expenses: Tuition:* Full-time $39,200; part-time $1225 per credit hour. *Financial support:* In 2013–14, research assistantships with partial tuition reimbursements (averaging $4,800 per year), teaching assistantships with partial tuition reimbursements (averaging $4,800 per year) were awarded; fellowships, career-related internships or fieldwork, Federal Work-Study, institutionally sponsored loans, and tuition waivers (partial) also available. Support available to part-time students. Financial award application deadline: 5/31. *Faculty research:* Marketing, accounting, human resource management, management information systems, business finance. *Unit head:* Dr. Catherine Usoff, Dean, 508-793-8822, Fax: 508-793-8822, E-mail: clarkmba@clarku.edu. *Application contact:* Patrick Oroszko, Enrollment and Marketing Director, 508-793-8822, Fax: 508-793-8822, E-mail: clarkmba@clarku.edu. Website: http://www.clarku.edu/gsom/graduate/fulltime/.

Clayton State University, School of Graduate Studies, College of Business, Program in Business Administration, Morrow, GA 30260-0285. Offers accounting (MBA); international business (MBA); supply chain management (MBA). *Accreditation:* AACSB. Part-time and evening/weekend programs available. *Degree requirements:* For master's, thesis. *Entrance requirements:* For master's, GMAT, 3 letters of recommendation; statement of purpose; 2 official transcripts. Additional exam requirements/recommendations for international students: Required—TOEFL (minimum score 550 paper-based; 80 iBT). Electronic applications accepted. *Expenses:* Contact institution.

Cleveland State University, College of Graduate Studies, Monte Ahuja College of Business, Department of Marketing, Cleveland, OH 44115. Offers global business (Graduate Certificate); marketing (MBA, DBA); marketing analytics (Graduate Certificate). *Faculty:* 12 full-time (4 women), 6 part-time/adjunct (3 women). *Students:* 1 (woman) full-time, 16 part-time (4 women); includes 2 minority (both Black or African American, non-Hispanic/Latino), 2 international. Average age 40. 63 applicants, 25% accepted, 2 enrolled. *Expenses: Tuition,* state resident: full-time $8335; part-time $521 per credit hour. Tuition, nonresident: full-time $15,670; part-time $979 per credit hour. *Required fees:* $50; $25 per semester. *Financial support:* In 2013–14, research assistantships (averaging $9,744 per year) were awarded; tuition waivers (partial) also available. Financial award application deadline: 6/30; financial award applicants required to submit FAFSA. *Unit head:* Dr. Thomas W. Whipple, Chair, 216-687-4771, Fax: 216-687-5135, E-mail: t.whipple@csuohio.edu. *Application contact:* Kenneth Dippong, Director, Student Services, 216-523-7545, Fax: 216-687-9354, E-mail: k.dippong@csuohio.edu. Website: http://www.csuohio.edu/business/academics/mkt/.

Cleveland State University, College of Graduate Studies, Monte Ahuja College of Business, Doctor of Business Administration Program, Cleveland, OH 44115. Offers finance (DBA); global business (DBA); information systems (DBA); marketing (DBA); operations management (DBA). *Accreditation:* AACSB. Part-time and evening/weekend programs available. *Faculty:* 50 full-time (11 women). *Students:* 36 part-time (18 women); includes 6 minority (2 Black or African American, non-Hispanic/Latino; 4 Asian, non-Hispanic/Latino), 8 international. Average age 39. 96 applicants, 27% accepted, 6 enrolled. In 2013, 1 doctorate awarded. *Degree requirements:* For doctorate, comprehensive exam, thesis/dissertation, oral dissertation defense. *Entrance requirements:* For doctorate, GMAT, MBA or equivalent. Additional exam requirements/recommendations for international students: Required—TOEFL (minimum score 550 paper-based; 79 iBT). *Application deadline:* For spring admission, 2/28 priority date for domestic and international students. Application fee: $30. Electronic applications accepted. *Expenses:* Tuition, state resident: full-time $8335; part-time $521 per credit hour. Tuition, nonresident: full-time $15,670; part-time $979 per credit hour. *Required fees:* $50; $25 per semester. *Financial support:* In 2013–14, 5 research assistantships with full tuition reimbursements (averaging $12,700 per year), 4 teaching assistantships with full tuition reimbursements (averaging $12,700 per year) were awarded; tuition waivers (full) and unspecified assistantships also available. *Faculty research:* Supply chain management, international business, strategic management, risk analysis, consumer behavior. *Unit head:* Dr. Raj Shekhar G. Javalgi, Director, 216-687-3786, Fax: 216-687-9354, E-mail: r.javalgi@csuohio.edu. *Application contact:* Melinda J. Arnold, Administrative Secretary, 216-687-6952, Fax: 216-687-9257, E-mail: m.arnold@csuohio.edu. Website: http://www.csuohio.edu/business/academics/doctoral.html.

Columbia University, Graduate School of Business, Executive MBA Global Program, New York, NY 10027. Offers EMBA. Program offered jointly with London Business School. *Entrance requirements:* For master's, GMAT, 2 letters of reference, interview, minimum 5 years of work experience, curriculum vitae or resume, employer support. Additional exam requirements/recommendations for international students: Recommended—TOEFL, IELTS. Electronic applications accepted. *Expenses:* Contact institution.

Columbia University, Graduate School of Business, MBA Program, New York, NY 10027. Offers accounting (MBA); decision, risk, and operations (MBA); entrepreneurship (MBA); finance and economics (MBA); healthcare and pharmaceutical management (MBA); human resource management (MBA); international business (MBA); leadership and ethics (MBA); management (MBA); marketing (MBA); media (MBA); private equity (MBA); real estate (MBA); social enterprise (MBA); value investing (MBA); DDS/MBA; JD/MBA; MBA/MIA; MBA/MPH; MBA/MS; MD/MBA. *Entrance requirements:* For master's, GMAT, 2 letters of recommendation. Additional exam requirements/recommendations for international students: Required—TOEFL. Electronic applications accepted. *Expenses:* Contact institution. *Faculty research:* Human decision making and behavioral research; real estate market and mortgage defaults; financial crisis and corporate governance; international business; security analysis and accounting.

Concordia University Wisconsin, Graduate Programs, School of Business and Legal Studies, MBA Program, Mequon, WI 53097-2402. Offers finance (MBA); health care administration (MBA); human resource management (MBA); international business (MBA); international business-bilingual English/Chinese (MBA); management (MBA); management information systems (MBA); managerial communications (MBA); marketing (MBA); public administration (MBA); risk management (MBA). Postbaccalaureate distance learning degree programs offered (minimal on-campus study). *Degree requirements:* For master's, comprehensive exam, thesis or alternative. *Entrance requirements:* Additional exam requirements/recommendations for international students: Required—TOEFL. *Expenses:* Contact institution.

International Business

Copenhagen Business School, Graduate Programs, Copenhagen, Denmark. Offers business administration (Exec MBA, MBA, PhD); business administration and information systems (M Sc); business, language and culture (M Sc); economics and business administration (M Sc); health management (MHM); international business and politics (M Sc); public administration (MPA); shipping and logistics (Exec MBA); technology, market and organization (MBA).

Daemen College, Department of Accounting/Information Systems, Amherst, NY 14226-3592. Offers global business (MS), including accounting, global business, management information systems, marketing. Part-time and evening/weekend programs available. *Degree requirements:* For master's, minimum GPA of 3.0. *Entrance requirements:* For master's, GMAT if undergraduate GPA is less than 3.0, 2 letters of recommendation; goal statement; transcripts; demonstration of satisfactory oral and written English. Additional exam requirements/recommendations for international students: Required—TOEFL (minimum score 500 paper-based; 63 iBT), IELTS (minimum score 5.5). Electronic applications accepted. *Faculty research:* Internationalization of small business, cultural influences on business practices, international human resource practices.

Dallas Baptist University, College of Business, Business Administration Program, Dallas, TX 75211-9299. Offers accounting (MBA); business communication (MBA); conflict resolution management (MBA); entrepreneurship (MBA); finance (MBA); health care management (MBA); international business (MBA); leading the non-profit organization (MBA); management (MBA); management information systems (MBA); marketing (MBA); project management (MBA); technology and engineering (MBA). *Accreditation:* ACBSP. Part-time and evening/weekend programs available. *Entrance requirements:* For master's, GMAT, minimum GPA of 3.0. Additional exam requirements/recommendations for international students: Required—TOEFL, IELTS. *Application deadline:* Applications are processed on a rolling basis. Application fee: $25. Electronic applications accepted. *Expenses: Tuition:* Full-time $13,410; part-time $745 per credit hour. *Required fees:* $300; $150 per semester. Tuition and fees vary according to degree level. *Financial support:* Federal Work-Study, institutionally sponsored loans, scholarships/grants, and tuition waivers (full and partial) available. Support available to part-time students. Financial award applicants required to submit FAFSA. *Faculty research:* Sports management, services marketing, retailing, strategic management, financial planning/investments. *Unit head:* Dr. Sandra S. Reid, Chair, 214-333-5280, Fax: 214-333-5293, E-mail: graduate@dbu.edu. *Application contact:* Kit P. Montgomery, Director of Graduate Programs, 214-333-5242, Fax: 214-333-5579, E-mail: graduate@dbu.edu.
Website: http://www3.dbu.edu/graduate/mba.asp.

Dallas Baptist University, Gary Cook School of Leadership, Program in Global Leadership, Dallas, TX 75211-9299. Offers business communication (MA); East Asian studies (MA); ESL (MA); general studies (MA); global leadership (MA); global studies (MA); international business (MA); leading the nonprofit organization (MA); missions (MA); small group ministry (MA); MA/MA. Part-time and evening/weekend programs available. *Entrance requirements:* For master's, minimum GPA of 3.0. Additional exam requirements/recommendations for international students: Required—TOEFL, IELTS. Application fee: $25. *Expenses: Tuition:* Full-time $13,410; part-time $745 per credit hour. *Required fees:* $300; $150 per semester. Tuition and fees vary according to degree level. *Financial support:* Federal Work-Study, institutionally sponsored loans, scholarships/grants, and tuition waivers (full and partial) available. Support available to part-time students. Financial award applicants required to submit FAFSA. *Unit head:* Dr. Bob Garrett, Director, 214-333-5508, Fax: 214-333-5689, E-mail: graduate@dbu.edu. *Application contact:* Kit P. Montgomery, Director of Graduate Programs, 214-333-5242, Fax: 214-333-5579, E-mail: graduate@dbu.edu.
Website: http://www3.dbu.edu/leadership/globalleadership.asp.

Delaware Valley College, MBA Program, Doylestown, PA 18901-2697. Offers accounting (MBA); entrepreneurship (MBA); finance (MBA); food and agribusiness (MBA); general business (MBA); global executive leadership (MBA); human resource management (MBA); supply chain management (MBA). Part-time and evening/weekend programs available. Postbaccalaureate distance learning degree programs offered (no on-campus study). *Students:* 32 full-time (17 women), 183 part-time (99 women). Average age 34. 97 applicants, 78% accepted, 74 enrolled. *Entrance requirements:* For master's, minimum undergraduate GPA of 3.0. *Application deadline:* Applications are processed on a rolling basis. Application fee: $50. Electronic applications accepted. *Expenses:* Contact institution. *Financial support:* Applicants required to submit FAFSA. *Unit head:* Mike Prushan, Director of MBA Program, 215-489-2322, E-mail: michael.prushan@delval.edu. *Application contact:* Robin Mathews, Graduate and Continuing Studies Enrollment Manager, 215-489-2955, Fax: 215-489-4832, E-mail: robin.mathews@delval.edu.
Website: http://www.delval.edu/academics/graduate/master-of-business-administration.

Dominican University of California, Barowsky School of Business, San Rafael, CA 94901-2298. Offers global business (MBA); strategic leadership (MBA); sustainable enterprise (MBA). Part-time and evening/weekend programs available. *Faculty:* 7 full-time (3 women), 13 part-time/adjunct (5 women). *Students:* 53 full-time (35 women), 80 part-time (48 women); includes 28 minority (4 Black or African American, non-Hispanic/Latino; 6 Asian, non-Hispanic/Latino; 17 Hispanic/Latino; 1 Native Hawaiian or other Pacific Islander, non-Hispanic/Latino), 16 international. Average age 36. 136 applicants, 43% accepted, 36 enrolled. *Degree requirements:* For master's, thesis, capstone (for MBA). *Entrance requirements:* For master's, minimum GPA of 3.0. Additional exam requirements/recommendations for international students: Required—TOEFL (minimum score 550 paper-based; 80 iBT), IELTS (minimum score 6.5). *Application deadline:* For fall admission, 5/15 priority date for domestic and international students; for spring admission, 11/15 priority date for domestic and international students. Applications are processed on a rolling basis. Electronic applications accepted. Application fee is waived when completed online. *Expenses:* Contact institution. *Financial support:* Scholarships/grants and tuition discounts available. Support available to part-time students. Financial award application deadline: 3/2; financial award applicants required to submit FAFSA. *Unit head:* Dr. Sam Beldona, Dean, 415-458-3786, E-mail: sriam.beldona@dominican.edu. *Application contact:* Shannon Lovelace-White, Assistant Vice President, 415-485-3287, Fax: 415-485-3214, E-mail: shannon.lovelace-white@dominican.edu.
Website: http://www.dominican.edu/academics/barowskyschoolofbusiness.

Duke University, The Fuqua School of Business, Global Executive MBA Program, Durham, NC 27708-0586. Offers business administration (MBA); energy and the environment (MBA); entrepreneurship and innovation (MBA); finance (MBA); health sector management (Certificate); marketing (MBA); strategy (MBA). *Faculty:* 91 full-time (15 women), 53 part-time/adjunct (9 women). *Students:* 49 full-time (7 women); includes 7 minority (1 Black or African American, non-Hispanic/Latino; 3 Asian, non-Hispanic/Latino; 3 Hispanic/Latino), 17 international. Average age 39. In 2013, 51 master's awarded. *Entrance requirements:* For master's, transcripts, essays, resume, recommendation letters, interview. Additional exam requirements/recommendations for international students: Required—TOEFL, IELTS, PTE. *Application deadline:* For fall admission, 9/4 for domestic and international students; for winter admission, 10/16 for domestic and international students; for spring admission, 12/5 for domestic and international students; for summer admission, 1/13 for domestic and international students. Application fee: $225. *Financial support:* In 2013–14, 8 students received support. Institutionally sponsored loans and scholarships/grants available. Financial award applicants required to submit FAFSA. *Unit head:* John Gallagher, Associate Dean for Executive MBA Programs, 919-660-7728, E-mail: johng@duke.edu. *Application contact:* Liz Riley Hargrove, Director of EMBA Admissions, 919-660-7705, Fax: 919-681-8026, E-mail: admissions-info@fuqua.duke.edu.
Website: http://www.fuqua.duke.edu/programs/duke_mba/global-executive/.

Duke University, The Fuqua School of Business, MMS Program: Duke Kunshan University, Durham, NC 27708-0586. Offers MMS.

Duquesne University, School of Leadership and Professional Advancement, Pittsburgh, PA 15282-0001. Offers leadership (MS), including business ethics, community leadership, global leadership, health care, information technology, leadership, liberal studies, professional administration, sports leadership. Part-time and evening/weekend programs available. Postbaccalaureate distance learning degree programs offered (no on-campus study). *Faculty:* 15 full-time (7 women), 64 part-time/adjunct (26 women). *Students:* 213 full-time (106 women), 170 part-time (86 women); includes 89 minority (59 Black or African American, non-Hispanic/Latino; 2 American Indian or Alaska Native, non-Hispanic/Latino; 7 Asian, non-Hispanic/Latino; 9 Hispanic/Latino; 1 Native Hawaiian or other Pacific Islander, non-Hispanic/Latino; 11 Two or more races, non-Hispanic/Latino), 9 international. Average age 36. 204 applicants, 56% accepted, 103 enrolled. In 2013, 140 master's awarded. *Degree requirements:* For master's, capstone course. *Entrance requirements:* For master's, professional work experience, 500-word essay, resume, interview. Additional exam requirements/recommendations for international students: Required—TOEFL (minimum score 80 iBT). *Application deadline:* Applications are processed on a rolling basis. Application fee: $0. Electronic applications accepted. Application fee is waived when completed online. *Expenses: Tuition:* Full-time $18,162; part-time $1009 per credit. *Required fees:* $1728; $96 per credit. Tuition and fees vary according to program. *Financial support:* Scholarships/grants available. Financial award applicants required to submit FAFSA. *Unit head:* Dr. Dorothy Bassett, Dean, 412-396-2141, Fax: 412-396-4711, E-mail: bassettd@duq.edu. *Application contact:* Marianne Leister, Director of Student Services, 412-396-4933, Fax: 412-396-5072, E-mail: leister@duq.edu.
Website: http://www.duq.edu/academics/schools/leadership-and-professional-advancement.

D'Youville College, Department of Business, Buffalo, NY 14201-1084. Offers business administration (MBA); international business (MS). Part-time and evening/weekend programs available. *Students:* 61 full-time (20 women), 15 part-time (11 women); includes 10 minority (6 Black or African American, non-Hispanic/Latino; 3 Hispanic/Latino; 1 Two or more races, non-Hispanic/Latino), 12 international. Average age 27. 57 applicants, 46% accepted, 21 enrolled. In 2013, 15 master's awarded. *Degree requirements:* For master's, one foreign language, project or thesis. *Entrance requirements:* For master's, minimum GPA of 3.0. Additional exam requirements/recommendations for international students: Required—TOEFL (minimum score 500 paper-based). *Application deadline:* For fall admission, 5/1 priority date for international students; for spring admission, 9/1 priority date for international students. Applications are processed on a rolling basis. Application fee: $25. Electronic applications accepted. *Financial support:* Career-related internships or fieldwork, Federal Work-Study, and scholarships/grants available. Support available to part-time students. Financial award application deadline: 3/1; financial award applicants required to submit FAFSA. *Faculty research:* Assessment, accreditation, supply chain, online learning, adult learning. *Unit head:* Dr. Susan Kowaleski, Chair, 716-829-7839. *Application contact:* Mark Pavone, Graduate Admissions Director, 716-829-8400, Fax: 716-829-7900, E-mail: graduateadmissions@dyc.edu.
Website: http://www.dyc.edu/academics/business/index.asp.

Eastern Michigan University, Graduate School, College of Arts and Sciences, Department of World Languages, Program in Language and International Trade, Ypsilanti, MI 48197. Offers MA. Evening/weekend programs available. *Students:* 2 full-time (both women), 1 part-time (0 women); includes 1 minority (Black or African American, non-Hispanic/Latino), 1 international. Average age 25. 1 applicant, 100% accepted, 1 enrolled. In 2013, 1 master's awarded. *Degree requirements:* For master's, one foreign language. *Entrance requirements:* Additional exam requirements/recommendations for international students: Required—TOEFL. *Application deadline:* Applications are processed on a rolling basis. Application fee: $35. *Expenses:* Tuition, state resident: full-time $12,300; part-time $466 per credit hour. Tuition, nonresident: full-time $23,159; part-time $918 per credit hour. *Required fees:* $71 per credit hour. $46 per semester. One-time fee: $100. Tuition and fees vary according to course level and degree level. *Financial support:* Fellowships, research assistantships with full tuition reimbursements, teaching assistantships with full tuition reimbursements, career-related internships or fieldwork, Federal Work-Study, institutionally sponsored loans, scholarships/grants, tuition waivers (partial), and unspecified assistantships available. Support available to part-time students. Financial award applicants required to submit FAFSA. *Unit head:* Dr. Rosemary Weston-Gil, Department Head, 734-487-0130, Fax: 734-487-3411, E-mail: rweston3@emich.edu. *Application contact:* Dr. Margrit Zinggeler, Program Advisor, 734-487-1498, Fax: 734-487-3411, E-mail: mzinggele@emich.edu.

Eastern Michigan University, Graduate School, College of Arts and Sciences, Department of World Languages, Programs in Foreign Languages, Ypsilanti, MI 48197. Offers French (MA); German (MA); German for business (Graduate Certificate); Hispanic language and cultures (Graduate Certificate); Japanese business practices (Graduate Certificate); Spanish (MA). Part-time and evening/weekend programs available. Postbaccalaureate distance learning degree programs offered (minimal on-campus study). *Students:* 1 full-time (0 women), 16 part-time (11 women); includes 5 minority (2 Black or African American, non-Hispanic/Latino; 1 Asian, non-Hispanic/Latino; 2 Hispanic/Latino), 1 international. Average age 36. 6 applicants, 67% accepted, 3 enrolled. In 2013, 2 master's, 1 other advanced degree awarded. *Degree requirements:* For master's, one foreign language, thesis optional. *Entrance requirements:* Additional exam requirements/recommendations for international students: Required—TOEFL. *Application deadline:* Applications are processed on a rolling basis. Application fee: $35. *Expenses:* Tuition, state resident: full-time $12,300; part-time $466 per credit hour. Tuition, nonresident: full-time $23,159; part-time $918 per credit hour. *Required fees:* $71 per credit hour. $46 per semester. One-time fee: $100. Tuition and fees vary according to course level and degree level. *Financial support:* Fellowships, research assistantships with full tuition reimbursements, teaching assistantships with full tuition reimbursements, career-related internships or fieldwork, Federal Work-Study, institutionally sponsored loans, scholarships/grants, tuition waivers (partial), and unspecified assistantships available. Support available to part-time students. Financial award applicants required to submit FAFSA. *Unit head:* Dr. Rosemary Weston-Gil, Department Head, 734-487-0130, Fax: 734-487-3411, E-mail: rweston3@emich.edu. *Application contact:* Dr. Genevieve Peden, Program Advisor, 734-487-1498, Fax: 734-487-3411, E-mail: gpeden@emich.edu.

Eastern Michigan University, Graduate School, College of Business, Department of Marketing, Ypsilanti, MI 48197. Offers e-business (MBA); integrated marketing communications (MS); international business (MBA); marketing management (MBA); supply chain management (MBA). Part-time and evening/weekend programs available.

Postbaccalaureate distance learning degree programs offered (minimal on-campus study). *Faculty:* 15 full-time (8 women). *Students:* 25 full-time (20 women), 41 part-time (34 women); includes 16 minority (9 Black or African American, non-Hispanic/Latino; 1 Asian, non-Hispanic/Latino; 1 Hispanic/Latino; 5 Two or more races, non-Hispanic/Latino), 1 international. Average age 34. 41 applicants, 71% accepted, 16 enrolled. In 2013, 28 master's awarded. *Entrance requirements:* For master's, GMAT. Additional exam requirements/recommendations for international students: Required—TOEFL. *Application deadline:* For fall admission, 5/15 priority date for domestic and international students; for winter admission, 10/15 priority date for domestic and international students; for spring admission, 3/15 priority date for domestic and international students. Applications are processed on a rolling basis. Application fee: $35. *Expenses:* Tuition, state resident: full-time $12,300; part-time $466 per credit hour. Tuition, nonresident: full-time $23,159; part-time $918 per credit hour. *Required fees:* $71 per credit hour. $46 per semester. One-time fee: $100. Tuition and fees vary according to course level and degree level. *Financial support:* Fellowships, research assistantships with full tuition reimbursements, teaching assistantships with full tuition reimbursements, career-related internships or fieldwork, Federal Work-Study, institutionally sponsored loans, scholarships/grants, tuition waivers (partial), and unspecified assistantships available. Support available to part-time students. Financial award applicants required to submit FAFSA. *Unit head:* Dr. Paul Chao, Department Head, 734-487-3323, Fax: 734-487-7099, E-mail: pchao@emich.edu. *Application contact:* K. Michelle Henry, Director, Academic Services, 734-487-4444, Fax: 734-483-1316, E-mail: mhenry1@emich.edu. Website: http://www.mkt.emich.edu/index.html.

Eastern Michigan University, Graduate School, College of Business, Programs in Business Administration, Ypsilanti, MI 48197. Offers business administration (MBA, Graduate Certificate); computer information systems (Graduate Certificate); e-business (MBA, Graduate Certificate); enterprise business intelligence (MBA); entrepreneurship (MBA, Graduate Certificate); finance (MBA, Graduate Certificate); human resources (MBA); human resources management (Graduate Certificate); information systems (MBA); internal auditing (MBA); international business (MBA, Graduate Certificate); marketing management (Graduate Certificate); nonprofit management (MBA); organizational development (Graduate Certificate); supply chain management (MBA, Graduate Certificate). *Accreditation:* AACSB. Part-time programs available. Postbaccalaureate distance learning degree programs offered (no on-campus study). *Students:* 74 full-time (28 women), 342 part-time (183 women); includes 122 minority (84 Black or African American, non-Hispanic/Latino; 2 American Indian or Alaska Native, non-Hispanic/Latino; 19 Asian, non-Hispanic/Latino; 7 Hispanic/Latino; 10 Two or more races, non-Hispanic/Latino), 38 international. Average age 33. 305 applicants, 72% accepted, 131 enrolled. In 2013, 69 master's, 57 other advanced degrees awarded. *Entrance requirements:* For master's, GMAT (minimum score 450), minimum cumulative undergraduate GPA of 2.75. Additional exam requirements/recommendations for international students: Required—TOEFL. *Application deadline:* For fall admission, 5/15 for domestic students, 5/1 for international students; for winter admission, 10/15 for domestic students, 10/1 for international students; for spring admission, 3/15 for domestic students, 3/1 for international students. Applications are processed on a rolling basis. Application fee: $35. *Expenses:* Tuition, state resident: full-time $12,300; part-time $466 per credit hour. Tuition, nonresident: full-time $23,159; part-time $918 per credit hour. *Required fees:* $71 per credit hour. $46 per semester. One-time fee: $100. Tuition and fees vary according to course level and degree level. *Financial support:* Fellowships, research assistantships with full tuition reimbursements, teaching assistantships with full tuition reimbursements, career-related internships or fieldwork, Federal Work-Study, institutionally sponsored loans, scholarships/grants, tuition waivers (partial), and unspecified assistantships available. Support available to part-time students. Financial award applicants required to submit FAFSA. *Unit head:* K. Michelle Henry, Director, Academic Services, 734-487-4444, Fax: 734-483-1316, E-mail: mhenry1@emich.edu. *Application contact:* Beste Windes, Advisor, 734-487-4444, Fax: 734-483-1316, E-mail: bwindes@emich.edu. Website: http://www.emich.edu/public/cob/gr/grad.html.

Emerson College, Graduate Studies, School of Communication, Department of Marketing Communication, Program in Global Marketing Communication and Advertising, Boston, MA 02116-4624. Offers MA. *Faculty:* 16 full-time (7 women), 1 part-time/adjunct (0 women). *Students:* 29 full-time (20 women), 2 part-time (1 woman); includes 5 minority (3 Asian, non-Hispanic/Latino; 1 Hispanic/Latino; 1 Two or more races, non-Hispanic/Latino), 13 international. Average age 25. 78 applicants, 69% accepted, 29 enrolled. In 2013, 34 master's awarded. *Entrance requirements:* For master's, GMAT or GRE General Test. Additional exam requirements/recommendations for international students: Required—TOEFL (minimum score 550 paper-based; 80 iBT), IELTS (minimum score 6.5). *Application deadline:* For fall admission, 5/1 priority date for domestic and international students. Applications are processed on a rolling basis. Application fee: $60 ($75 for international students). Electronic applications accepted. *Expenses: Tuition:* Part-time $1145 per credit. *Financial support:* In 2013–14, 10 students received support, including 10 fellowships with partial tuition reimbursements available (averaging $10,000 per year), 5 research assistantships with partial tuition reimbursements available (averaging $10,000 per year); Federal Work-Study, scholarships/grants, and unspecified assistantships also available. Financial award application deadline: 3/1; financial award applicants required to submit FAFSA. *Faculty research:* International business, marketing. *Unit head:* Thomas Vogel, Graduate Program Director, 617-824-8492, E-mail: thomas_vogel@emerson.edu. *Application contact:* Sean Ganas, Office of Graduate Admission, 617-824-8610, Fax: 617-824-8614, E-mail: gradapp@emerson.edu. Website: http://www.emerson.edu/academics/departments/marketing-communication/graduate-degrees/global-marketing-communication-advertising.

ESSEC Business School, Graduate Programs, Paris, France. Offers business administration (PhD); executive business administration (MBA); global business administration (MBA); hospitality management (MBA); international luxury brand management (MBA); management (MSM).

Everest University, Department of Business Administration, Tampa, FL 33614-5899. Offers accounting (MBA); human resources (MBA); international business (MBA). Part-time and evening/weekend programs available. *Degree requirements:* For master's, thesis optional. *Entrance requirements:* For master's, GMAT or GRE General Test, minimum GPA of 3.0.

Everest University, Program in Business Administration, Largo, FL 33770. Offers accounting (MBA); human resources management (MBA); international business (MBA). *Faculty research:* Management fads, learning styles, effective use of technology.

Everest University, Program in Business Administration, Orlando, FL 32819. Offers accounting (MBA); general management (MBA); human resources (MBA); international management (MBA).

Fairleigh Dickinson University, College at Florham, Silberman College of Business, Department of Economics, Finance, and International Business, Program in International Business, Madison, NJ 07940-1099. Offers MBA, Certificate.

Fairleigh Dickinson University, Metropolitan Campus, Silberman College of Business, Department of Economics, Finance and International Business, Program in International Business, Teaneck, NJ 07666-1914. Offers MBA.

Florida Atlantic University, College of Business, Department of Management, Boca Raton, FL 33431-0991. Offers business administration (Exec MBA, MBA); entrepreneurship (MBA); health administration (MBA, MHA, MS); international business (MBA); management (PhD); sports management (MBA). *Faculty:* 22 full-time (10 women), 11 part-time/adjunct (6 women). *Students:* 267 full-time (120 women), 397 part-time (194 women); includes 279 minority (92 Black or African American, non-Hispanic/Latino; 31 Asian, non-Hispanic/Latino; 147 Hispanic/Latino; 9 Two or more races, non-Hispanic/Latino), 37 international. Average age 32. 551 applicants, 50% accepted, 216 enrolled. In 2013, 255 master's, 7 doctorates awarded. *Entrance requirements:* For master's, GMAT or GRE General Test, minimum GPA of 3.0 in last 60 hours of course work. Additional exam requirements/recommendations for international students: Required—TOEFL (minimum score 600 paper-based; 61 iBT), IELTS (minimum score 6). *Application deadline:* For fall admission, 7/25 for domestic students, 2/15 for international students; for spring admission, 12/10 for domestic students, 7/15 for international students. Applications are processed on a rolling basis. Application fee: $30. Electronic applications accepted. *Expenses:* Tuition, state resident: full-time $6660; part-time $370 per credit hour. Tuition, nonresident: full-time $18,450; part-time $1025 per credit hour. Tuition and fees vary according to course load. *Financial support:* Research assistantships with full tuition reimbursements, career-related internships or fieldwork, tuition waivers (partial), and unspecified assistantships available. *Faculty research:* Sports administration, healthcare, policy, finance, real estate, senior living. *Unit head:* Dr. Peggy Golden, Chair, 561-297-2675, E-mail: golden@fau.edu. *Application contact:* Dr. Marcy Krugel, Graduate Adviser, 561-297-3633, Fax: 561-297-1315, E-mail: krugel@fau.edu. Website: http://business.fau.edu/departments/management/index.aspx.

Florida Institute of Technology, Graduate Programs, Nathan M. Bisk College of Business, Online Programs, Melbourne, FL 32901-6975. Offers accounting (MBA); accounting and finance (MBA); business administration (MBA); finance (MBA); healthcare management (MBA); information assurance and cybersecurity (MS); information technology (MS); information technology cybersecurity (MS); information technology management (MBA); international business (MBA); Internet marketing (MBA); management (MBA); marketing (MBA); project management (MBA); supply chain management (MS). Part-time and evening/weekend programs available. Postbaccalaureate distance learning degree programs offered (no on-campus study). *Faculty:* 3 full-time (1 woman), 41 part-time/adjunct (13 women). *Students:* 6 full-time (1 woman), 1,121 part-time (530 women); includes 424 minority (276 Black or African American, non-Hispanic/Latino; 10 American Indian or Alaska Native, non-Hispanic/Latino; 45 Asian, non-Hispanic/Latino; 88 Hispanic/Latino; 5 Native Hawaiian or other Pacific Islander, non-Hispanic/Latino), 32 international. Average age 36. 348 applicants, 42% accepted, 146 enrolled. In 2013, 475 master's awarded. *Entrance requirements:* For master's, GMAT or resume showing 8 years of supervised experience, 2 letters of recommendation, resume, competency in math past college algebra. Additional exam requirements/recommendations for international students: Required—TOEFL (minimum score 550 paper-based; 79 iBT). *Application deadline:* For fall admission, 4/1 for international students; for spring admission, 9/30 for international students. Applications are processed on a rolling basis. Electronic applications accepted. *Expenses:* Contact institution. *Financial support:* Available to part-time students. Application deadline: 3/1; applicants required to submit FAFSA. *Unit head:* Brian Ehrlich, Associate Vice President/Director of Online Learning, 321-674-8202, E-mail: behrlich@fit.edu. *Application contact:* Carolyn Farrior, Director of Graduate Admissions, Online Learning and Off-Campus Programs, 321-674-7118. Website: http://online.fit.edu.

Florida International University, Alvah H. Chapman, Jr. Graduate School of Business, Department of Management and International Business, International Business Program, Miami, FL 33199. Offers MIB, PhD. Part-time and evening/weekend programs available. *Entrance requirements:* For master's, GRE or GMAT, minimum GPA of 3.0 (upper-level coursework), letter of intent, bachelor's degree in business administration or related area, resume, at least two years of work experience. Additional exam requirements/recommendations for international students: Required—TOEFL (minimum score 550 paper-based; 80 iBT) or IELTS (minimum score 6.5). Electronic applications accepted. *Expenses:* Contact institution. *Faculty research:* Strategy, international business, multinational corporations.

Florida State University, The Graduate School, College of Human Sciences, Department of Retail, Merchandising and Product Development, Tallahassee, FL 32306. Offers MS. Part-time programs available. *Faculty:* 6 full-time (all women). *Students:* 15 full-time (14 women); includes 6 minority (3 Black or African American, non-Hispanic/Latino; 3 Two or more races, non-Hispanic/Latino). 24 applicants, 33% accepted, 8 enrolled. In 2013, 6 master's awarded. *Degree requirements:* For master's, thesis optional. *Entrance requirements:* For master's, GRE General Test, minimum upper-division GPA of 3.0. Additional exam requirements/recommendations for international students: Required—TOEFL (minimum score 550 paper-based; 80 iBT). *Application deadline:* For fall admission, 7/1 for domestic and international students; for spring admission, 11/1 for domestic and international students. Applications are processed on a rolling basis. Application fee: $30. Electronic applications accepted. *Expenses:* Tuition, state resident: part-time $403.51 per credit hour. Tuition, nonresident: part-time $1004.85 per credit hour. *Required fees:* $75.81 per credit hour. One-time fee: $20 part-time. Tuition and fees vary according to course load, campus/location and student level. *Financial support:* In 2013–14, 19 teaching assistantships with full tuition reimbursements (averaging $5,642 per year) were awarded; career-related internships or fieldwork, institutionally sponsored loans, scholarships/grants, and unspecified assistantships also available. Financial award application deadline: 1/15; financial award applicants required to submit FAFSA. *Faculty research:* Global merchandising and product development. *Total annual research expenditures:* $34,011. *Unit head:* Dr. Mary Ann Moore, Interim Department Chair, 850-644-2498, Fax: 850-645-4673, E-mail: mmoore@fsu.edu. *Application contact:* Kristen Lawrance, Academic Support Assistant, 850-644-2498, Fax: 850-645-4673, E-mail: klawrance@fsu.edu. Website: http://www.chs.fsu.edu/Retail-Merchandising-Product-Development.

Franklin University Switzerland, The Taylor Institute for Global Enterprise Management, 6924 Sorengo, Switzerland. Offers international management (MS).

Fresno Pacific University, Graduate Programs, Global MBA Program, Fresno, CA 93702-4709. Offers MBA. *Faculty:* 3 full-time, 1 part-time/adjunct. *Students:* 21 full-time (14 women), 7 part-time (5 women); includes 16 minority (4 Black or African American, non-Hispanic/Latino; 1 American Indian or Alaska Native, non-Hispanic/Latino; 3 Asian, non-Hispanic/Latino; 7 Hispanic/Latino; 1 Two or more races, non-Hispanic/Latino). Average age 33. In 2013, 17 master's awarded. *Entrance requirements:* For master's, GMAT or GRE, three references; resume; official transcripts verifying BA/BS; minimum GPA of 3.0, prerequisite courses in economics, statistics, and accounting. Application fee: $90. *Expenses: Tuition:* Full-time $8910; part-time $495 per unit. *Required fees:* $270. Tuition and fees vary according to course load and program. *Unit head:* John Kilroy, PhD, Program Director, 559-453-3683, E-mail: john.kilroy@fresno.edu.

International Business

Application contact: Amanda Krum-Stovall, Director of Graduate Admissions, 559-453-2016, E-mail: amanda.krum-stovall@fresno.edu. Website: http://grad.fresno.edu/programs/global-mba.

George Mason University, College of Humanities and Social Sciences, Program in Global Affairs, Fairfax, VA 22030. Offers MA. *Faculty:* 16 full-time (6 women), 1 part-time/adjunct (0 women). *Students:* 22 full-time (18 women), 35 part-time (25 women); includes 12 minority (3 Black or African American, non-Hispanic/Latino; 2 Asian, non-Hispanic/Latino; 6 Hispanic/Latino; 1 Two or more races, non-Hispanic/Latino), 2 international. Average age 27. 86 applicants, 55% accepted, 16 enrolled. In 2013, 19 master's awarded. *Degree requirements:* For master's, capstone seminar. *Entrance requirements:* For master's, GRE, expanded goals statement, 2 letters of recommendation, evidence of professional competency in a second language tested through Language Testing International or other means approved by the department. Additional exam requirements/recommendations for international students: Required—TOEFL (minimum score 575 paper-based; 88 iBT), IELTS (minimum score 6.5), PTE. *Application deadline:* For fall admission, 3/15 for domestic students, 2/15 for international students; for spring admission, 10/15 for domestic students, 9/15 for international students. Application fee: $65 ($80 for international students). *Expenses:* Tuition, state resident: full-time $9350; part-time $390 per credit. Tuition, nonresident: full-time $25,754; part-time $1073 per credit. *Required fees:* $2688; $112 per credit. *Financial support:* Career-related internships or fieldwork, Federal Work-Study, and health care benefits (for full-time research or teaching assistantship recipients) available. Financial award application deadline: 3/1; financial award applicants required to submit FAFSA. *Unit head:* Lisa C. Breglia, Director, 703-993-9184, Fax: 703-993-1244, E-mail: lbreglia@gmu.edu. *Application contact:* Erin McSherry, Graduate Coordinator/Academic Advisor/Program Assistant, 703-993-5056, Fax: 703-993-1244, E-mail: emcsherr@gmu.edu.

Georgetown University, Graduate School of Arts and Sciences, Department of Economics, Washington, DC 20057. Offers econometrics (PhD); economic development (PhD); economic theory (PhD); industrial organization (PhD); international macro and finance (PhD); international trade (PhD); labor economics (PhD); macroeconomics (PhD); public economics and political economics (PhD); MA/PhD; MS/MA. *Degree requirements:* For doctorate, comprehensive exam, thesis/dissertation. *Entrance requirements:* For doctorate, GRE General Test. Additional exam requirements/recommendations for international students: Required—TOEFL. *Faculty research:* International economics, economic development.

Georgetown University, Graduate School of Arts and Sciences, McDonough School of Business, Washington, DC 20057. Offers business administration (IEMBA, MBA). *Accreditation:* AACSB. *Entrance requirements:* For master's, GMAT. Additional exam requirements/recommendations for international students: Required—TOEFL. *Expenses:* Contact institution.

Georgetown University, Law Center, Washington, DC 20001. Offers global health law (LL M); individualized study (LL M); international business and economic law (LL M); law (JD, SJD); national security law (LL M); securities and financial regulation (LL M); taxation (LL M); JD/LL M; JD/MA; JD/MBA; JD/MPH; JD/PhD. *Accreditation:* ABA. Part-time and evening/weekend programs available. *Degree requirements:* For master's, thesis; for doctorate, thesis/dissertation (for some programs). *Entrance requirements:* For master's, JD, LL B, or first law degree earned in country of origin; for doctorate, LSAT (for JD). Additional exam requirements/recommendations for international students: Required—TOEFL. *Expenses:* Contact institution. *Faculty research:* Constitutional law, legal history, jurisprudence.

The George Washington University, Elliott School of International Affairs, Program in International Trade and Investment Policy, Washington, DC 20052. Offers MA, JD/MA, MBA/MA. Part-time and evening/weekend programs available. *Students:* 31 full-time (18 women), 12 part-time (7 women); includes 11 minority (2 Black or African American, non-Hispanic/Latino; 4 Asian, non-Hispanic/Latino; 4 Hispanic/Latino; 1 Two or more races, non-Hispanic/Latino), 13 international. Average age 26. 72 applicants, 76% accepted, 20 enrolled. In 2013, 30 master's awarded. *Degree requirements:* For master's, one foreign language, capstone project. *Entrance requirements:* For master's, GRE General Test, 2 years of a modern foreign language, 2 semesters of introductory economics. Additional exam requirements/recommendations for international students: Required—TOEFL. *Application deadline:* For fall admission, 2/1 for domestic students; for spring admission, 10/1 for domestic students. Application fee: $75. Electronic applications accepted. *Financial support:* In 2013–14, 11 students received support. Fellowships with tuition reimbursements available, research assistantships with tuition reimbursements available, career-related internships or fieldwork, Federal Work-Study, institutionally sponsored loans, and tuition waivers available. Financial award application deadline: 1/15. *Unit head:* Steven Suranovic, Director, 202-994-7579, Fax: 202-994-5477, E-mail: smsuran@gwu.edu. *Application contact:* Jeff V. Miles, Director of Graduate Admissions, 202-994-7050, Fax: 202-994-9537, E-mail: esiagrad@gwu.edu. Website: http://elliott.gwu.edu/international-trade-investment-policy.

The George Washington University, School of Business, Department of International Business, Washington, DC 20052. Offers MBA, PhD, MBA/MA. Part-time and evening/weekend programs available. *Degree requirements:* For doctorate, thesis/dissertation. *Entrance requirements:* For master's, GMAT; for doctorate, GMAT or GRE. Additional exam requirements/recommendations for international students: Required—TOEFL. *Faculty research:* International trade, competitiveness, business management.

Georgia Institute of Technology, Graduate Studies and Research, College of Management, Program in Business Administration, Atlanta, GA 30332-0001. Offers accounting (MBA); e-commerce (Certificate); engineering entrepreneurship (MBA); entrepreneurship (Certificate); finance (MBA); information technology management (MBA); international business (MBA, Certificate); management of technology (Certificate); marketing (MBA); operations management (MBA); organizational behavior (MBA); strategic management (MBA). *Accreditation:* AACSB.

Georgia State University, J. Mack Robinson College of Business, Institute of International Business, Atlanta, GA 30303. Offers international business (GMBA, MBA, MIB); international business and information technology (MBA); international entrepreneurship (MBA); MIB/MIA. Part-time and evening/weekend programs available. *Faculty:* 7 full-time (3 women). *Students:* 41 full-time (29 women), 22 part-time (13 women); includes 26 minority (14 Black or African American, non-Hispanic/Latino; 1 Asian, non-Hispanic/Latino; 11 Hispanic/Latino), 15 international. Average age 32. 60 applicants, 52% accepted, 21 enrolled. In 2013, 25 master's awarded. *Entrance requirements:* For master's, GRE or GMAT, transcripts from all institutions attended, resume, essays. Additional exam requirements/recommendations for international students: Required—TOEFL (minimum score 610 paper-based; 101 iBT), IELTS (minimum score 7). *Application deadline:* For fall admission, 5/1 priority date for domestic students, 2/1 priority date for international students; for spring admission, 9/15 priority date for domestic students, 5/1 priority date for international students. Applications are processed on a rolling basis. Application fee: $50. Electronic applications accepted. *Expenses:* Tuition, area resident: Full-time $4176; part-time $348 per credit hour. Tuition, state resident: full-time $14,544; part-time $1212 per credit hour. Tuition, nonresident: full-time $14,544; part-time $1212 per credit hour. Tuition

and fees vary according to course load and program. *Financial support:* Research assistantships, teaching assistantships, scholarships/grants, tuition waivers (partial), and unspecified assistantships available. Financial award application deadline: 5/1. *Faculty research:* Business challenges in emerging markets (especially in India and China); interorganizational relationships in an international context, such as strategic alliances and global supply chain relations; globalization and entry mode strategy or new (or emerging) multinationals; emerging market development and business environments; cross-cultural effects on business processes and performance. *Unit head:* Dr. Daniel Bello, Professor/Director of the Institute of International Business, 404-413-7275, Fax: 404-413-7276. *Application contact:* Toby McChesney, Assistant Dean for Graduate Recruiting and Student Services, 404-413-7167, Fax: 404-413-7162, E-mail: rcbgradadmissions@gsu.edu. Website: http://iib.gsu.edu/.

Golden Gate University, Ageno School of Business, San Francisco, CA 94105-2968. Offers accounting (MBA); business administration (EMBA, MBA, PMBA, DBA); finance (MBA, MS, Certificate); financial planning (MS, Certificate); healthcare information systems (Certificate); human resource management (MBA, MS); human resources management (Certificate); information systems (MS); information technology (MBA); information technology management (Certificate); integrated marketing and communications (MS, Certificate); international business (MBA); management (MBA); marketing (MBA, MS, Certificate); operations supply chain management (Certificate); psychology (MA, Certificate); public administration (EMPA); public relations (MS, Certificate); technical market analysis (Certificate); JD/MBA. Part-time and evening/weekend programs available. *Degree requirements:* For doctorate, thesis/dissertation, qualifying examination. *Entrance requirements:* For master's, GMAT (MBA), minimum GPA of 2.5 (MS). Additional exam requirements/recommendations for international students: Required—TOEFL (minimum score 550 paper-based; 79 iBT). Electronic applications accepted. *Expenses:* Contact institution.

Goldey-Beacom College, Graduate Program, Wilmington, DE 19808-1999. Offers business administration (MBA); finance (MS); financial management (MBA); health care management (MBA); human resource management (MBA); information technology (MBA); international business management (MBA); major finance (MBA); major taxation (MBA); management (MM); marketing management (MBA); taxation (MBA, MS). *Accreditation:* ACBSP. Part-time and evening/weekend programs available. *Entrance requirements:* For master's, GMAT, MAT, GRE, minimum GPA of 3.0. Additional exam requirements/recommendations for international students: Required—TOEFL (minimum score 65 iBT); Recommended—IELTS (minimum score 6). Electronic applications accepted.

Harding University, Paul R. Carter College of Business Administration, Searcy, AR 72149-0001. Offers health care management (MBA); information technology management (MBA); international business (MBA); leadership and organizational management (MBA). *Accreditation:* ACBSP. Part-time and evening/weekend programs available. Postbaccalaureate distance learning degree programs offered (no on-campus study). *Faculty:* 25 part-time/adjunct (5 women). *Students:* 55 full-time (36 women), 115 part-time (50 women); includes 22 minority (17 Black or African American, non-Hispanic/Latino; 2 American Indian or Alaska Native, non-Hispanic/Latino; 3 Asian, non-Hispanic/Latino), 27 international. Average age 34. 48 applicants, 100% accepted, 48 enrolled. In 2013, 88 master's awarded. *Degree requirements:* For master's, portfolio. *Entrance requirements:* For master's, GMAT (minimum score of 500) or GRE (minimum score of 300), minimum GPA of 3.0, 2 letters of recommendation, resume, 3 essays, all official transcripts. Additional exam requirements/recommendations for international students: Required—TOEFL (minimum score 550 paper-based; 79 iBT). *Application deadline:* For fall admission, 8/1 priority date for domestic and international students; for spring admission, 12/1 priority date for domestic and international students. Applications are processed on a rolling basis. Application fee: $40. *Expenses: Tuition:* Full-time $11,574; part-time $643 per credit hour. *Required fees:* $432; $24 per credit hour. Tuition and fees vary according to course load, degree level and program. *Financial support:* Unspecified assistantships available. Financial award application deadline: 7/30; financial award applicants required to submit FAFSA. *Unit head:* Glen Metheny, Director of Graduate Studies, 501-279-5851, Fax: 501-279-4805, E-mail: gmetheny@harding.edu. *Application contact:* Melanie Kiihnl, Recruiting Manager/Director of Marketing, 501-279-4523, Fax: 501-279-4805, E-mail: mba@harding.edu. Website: http://www.harding.edu/mba.

Hawai`i Pacific University, College of Business Administration, Honolulu, HI 96813. Offers accounting/CPA (MBA); e-business (MBA); economics (MBA); finance (MBA); healthcare management (MBA); human resource management (MA, MBA); information systems (MBA, MSIS); international business (MBA); management (MBA); marketing (MBA); organizational change (MA, MBA); travel industry management (MBA). Part-time and evening/weekend programs available. *Faculty:* 22 full-time (9 women), 6 part-time/adjunct (0 women). *Students:* 232 full-time (100 women), 174 part-time (84 women); includes 241 minority (18 Black or African American, non-Hispanic/Latino; 112 Asian, non-Hispanic/Latino; 33 Hispanic/Latino; 11 Native Hawaiian or other Pacific Islander, non-Hispanic/Latino; 67 Two or more races, non-Hispanic/Latino). Average age 31. 240 applicants, 81% accepted, 102 enrolled. In 2013, 206 master's awarded. *Degree requirements:* For master's, thesis. *Entrance requirements:* For master's, GMAT. Additional exam requirements/recommendations for international students: Recommended—TOEFL (minimum score 550 paper-based; 80 iBT), TWE (minimum score 5). *Application deadline:* For fall admission, 2/15 priority date for domestic students; for spring admission, 10/15 priority date for domestic students. Applications are processed on a rolling basis. Application fee: $50. Electronic applications accepted. *Financial support:* In 2013–14, 90 students received support. Research assistantships, career-related internships or fieldwork, Federal Work-Study, scholarships/grants, tuition waivers, and unspecified assistantships available. Financial award application deadline: 3/1; financial award applicants required to submit FAFSA. *Faculty research:* Statistical control process as used by management, studies in comparative cross-cultural management styles, not-for-profit management. *Unit head:* Dr. Deborah Crown, Dean, 808-544-0275, Fax: 808-544-0283, E-mail: dcrown@hpu.edu. *Application contact:* Rumi Yoshida, Associate Director of Graduate Admissions, 808-543-8034, Fax: 808-544-0280, E-mail: grad@hpu.edu. Website: http://www.hpu.edu/CBA/Graduate/index.html.

HEC Montreal, School of Business Administration, Master of Science Programs in Administration, Program in International Business, Montréal, QC H3T 2A7, Canada. Offers M Sc. Specialization offered in French or English. *Students:* 61 full-time (32 women), 11 part-time (9 women). 58 applicants, 55% accepted, 16 enrolled. In 2013, 29 master's awarded. *Degree requirements:* For master's, one foreign language, thesis. *Entrance requirements:* For master's, Test de francais international (TFI) with minimum score of 850 (for those who have never studied in French), BBA, undergraduate degree in another field, degree deemed equivalent by program director and minimum GPA of 3.0 on 4.3 scale. *Application deadline:* For fall admission, 3/15 for domestic and international students; for winter admission, 9/15 for domestic and international students. Application fee: $83. Electronic applications accepted. *Expenses: Tuition, area resident:* Part-time $74.14 per credit. Tuition, state resident: full-time $2669.04; part-time $201.83 per credit. Tuition, nonresident: full-time $7266; part-time $500.59 per

credit. *International tuition:* $18,021.24 full-time. *Required fees:* $1529.70; $36.20 per credit. $65.50 per term. Tuition and fees vary according to degree level and program. *Financial support:* In 2013–14, 1,007 students received support. Research assistantships and teaching assistantships available. Financial award application deadline: 9/2. *Unit head:* Dr. Anne Bourhis, Director, 514-340-6873, Fax: 514-340-6880, E-mail: anne.bourhis@hec.ca. *Application contact:* Marianne de Moura, Administrative Director, 514-340-7106, Fax: 514-340-6411, E-mail: marianne.de-moura@hec.ca. Website: http://www.hec.ca/programmes_formations/msc/options/gestion_rh/index.html.

Hofstra University, Frank G. Zarb School of Business, Programs in Marketing and International Business, Hempstead, NY 11549. Offers business administration (MBA), including international business, marketing; international business (Advanced Certificate); marketing (MS, Advanced Certificate); marketing research (MS).

Hope International University, School of Graduate and Professional Studies, Program in Business Administration, Fullerton, CA 92831-3138. Offers general management (MBA, MSM); international development (MBA, MSM); marketing management (MBA, MSM); non-profit management (MBA, MSM). Part-time programs available. Postbaccalaureate distance learning degree programs offered (no on-campus study). *Degree requirements:* For master's, comprehensive exam (for some programs), thesis (for some programs), project. *Entrance requirements:* For master's, minimum GPA of 3.0; 2 references. Additional exam requirements/recommendations for international students: Required—TOEFL (minimum score 550 paper-based; 86 iBT); Recommended—IELTS (minimum score 6.5). Electronic applications accepted. *Expenses:* Contact institution.

Howard University, School of Business, Graduate Programs in Business, Washington, DC 20059-0002. Offers accounting (MBA); entrepreneurship (MBA); finance (MBA); general management (MBA); human resources management (MBA); information systems (MBA); international business (MBA); marketing (MBA); supply chain management (MBA); JD/MBA. *Accreditation:* AACSB. Part-time and evening/weekend programs available. Postbaccalaureate distance learning degree programs offered (no on-campus study). *Entrance requirements:* For master's, GMAT, minimum 1 year post undergraduate work experience, resume, 3 letters of recommendation, advanced college algebra. Additional exam requirements/recommendations for international students: Required—TOEFL. *Faculty research:* Marketing research in multi-ethnic populations, U.S. trade policies and international relations, risk management (finance).

Hult International Business School, Program in Business Administration - Hult London Campus, London WC 1B 4JP, United Kingdom. Offers entrepreneurship (MBA); international business (MBA); international finance (MBA); marketing (MBA). Part-time programs available. *Degree requirements:* For master's, comprehensive exam, thesis, internship. *Entrance requirements:* Additional exam requirements/recommendations for international students: Required—TOEFL (minimum score 580 paper-based), TWE (minimum score 5). Electronic applications accepted.

Hult International Business School, Program in International Business, Cambridge, MA 02141. Offers MIB.

Hult International Business School, Program in International Business - Hult Dubai Campus, Dubai, MA 02141, United Arab Emirates. Offers MIB.

Hult International Business School, Program in International Business - Hult London Campus, London WC 1B 4JP, United Kingdom. Offers MIB.

Hult International Business School, Program in International Business - Hult San Francisco Campus, San Francisco, CA 94133. Offers MIB.

Indiana Tech, Program in Global Leadership, Fort Wayne, IN 46803-1297. Offers PhD. Part-time and evening/weekend programs available. Postbaccalaureate distance learning degree programs offered (minimal on-campus study). *Faculty:* 5 full-time (1 woman), 10 part-time/adjunct (6 women). *Students:* 14 full-time (3 women), 118 part-time (43 women); includes 48 minority (37 Black or African American, non-Hispanic/Latino; 1 American Indian or Alaska Native, non-Hispanic/Latino; 1 Asian, non-Hispanic/Latino; 6 Hispanic/Latino; 1 Native Hawaiian or other Pacific Islander, non-Hispanic/Latino; 2 Two or more races, non-Hispanic/Latino), 4 international. Average age 42. *Entrance requirements:* For doctorate, GMAT, LSAT, GRE, or MAT, official transcripts of all previous undergraduate and graduate work including evidence of completion of a master's degree at regionally-accredited institution; original essay addressing the candidate's interest in the program and intended goals; current resume including educational record, employment history and relevant accomplishments. *Application deadline:* Applications are processed on a rolling basis. Application fee: $50. Electronic applications accepted. *Expenses: Tuition:* Full-time $8910; part-time $495 per credit. Tuition and fees vary according to course load, degree level and program. *Unit head:* Dr. Kenneth E. Rauch, PhD Director, 260-422-5561 Ext. 2446, E-mail: kerauch@indianatech.edu.

Instituto Tecnologico de Santo Domingo, Graduate School, Area of Business, Santo Domingo, Dominican Republic. Offers banking and securities markets (M Mgmt); corporate finance (M Mgmt); human resources management (M Mgmt, Certificate); international trade management (M Mgmt); marketing (M Mgmt); organizational development (M Mgmt); quality and productivity management (Certificate); tax management and planning (M Mgmt); upper management (M Mgmt).

Instituto Tecnologico de Santo Domingo, Graduate School, Area of Humanities and Social Sciences, Santo Domingo, Dominican Republic. Offers accounting (Certificate); adult education (Certificate); applied linguistics (MA); economics (MA); education (M Ed); educational psychology (MA, Certificate); gender and development (MA, Certificate); humanistic studies (MA); international marketing management (Certificate); international relations in the Caribbean basin (Certificate); intervention systems in family therapy (MA); linguistic and literary communication (Certificate); pedagogical support (MA); social science education (M Ed); sustainable human development (MA); terminal illness and death psychology (Certificate); youth and adult education (M Ed).

Instituto Tecnológico y de Estudios Superiores de Monterrey, Campus Central de Veracruz, Graduate Programs, Córdoba, Mexico. Offers administration (MA); administration of information technologies (MTI); computer sciences (MCC); education (MEE); educational institution administration (MAD); educational technology (MTE); electronic commerce (MCE); finance (MAF); humanistic studies (MEH); international business for Latin America (MNL); marketing (MMT); science (MCP). Part-time and evening/weekend programs available. Postbaccalaureate distance learning degree programs offered (minimal on-campus study). *Degree requirements:* For master's, thesis (for some programs). *Entrance requirements:* For master's, PAEP College Board. Electronic applications accepted.

Instituto Tecnológico y de Estudios Superiores de Monterrey, Campus Chihuahua, Graduate Programs, Chihuahua, Mexico. Offers computer systems engineering (Ingeniero); electrical engineering (Ingeniero); electromechanical engineering (Ingeniero); electronic engineering (Ingeniero); engineering administration (MEA); industrial engineering (MIE, Ingeniero); international trade (MIT); mechanical engineering (Ingeniero).

Instituto Tecnológico y de Estudios Superiores de Monterrey, Campus Ciudad de México, Virtual University Division, Ciudad de Mexico, Mexico. Offers administration of information technologies (MA); computer sciences (MA); education (MA, PhD); educational technology (MA); environmental engineering (MA); environmental systems (MA); humanistic studies (MA); industrial engineering (MA); international business for Latin America (MA); quality systems (MA); quality systems and productivity (MA). Part-time and evening/weekend programs available. Postbaccalaureate distance learning degree programs offered (minimal on-campus study). *Entrance requirements:* For master's and doctorate, Instituto entrance exam. Additional exam requirements/recommendations for international students: Required—TOEFL.

Instituto Tecnológico y de Estudios Superiores de Monterrey, Campus Cuernavaca, Programs in Business Administration, Temixco, Mexico. Offers finance (MA); human resources management (MA); international business (MA); marketing (MA).

Instituto Tecnológico y de Estudios Superiores de Monterrey, Campus Irapuato, Graduate Programs, Irapuato, Mexico. Offers administration (MBA); administration of information technology (MAIT); administration of telecommunications (MAT); architecture (M Arch); computer science (MCS); education (M Ed); educational administration (MEA); educational innovation and technology (DEIT); educational technology (MET); electronic commerce (MBA); environmental administration and planning (MEAP); environmental systems (MES); finances (MBA); humanistic studies (MHS); international management for Latin American executives (MIMLAE); library and information science (MLIS); manufacturing quality management (MMQM); marketing research (MBA).

Instituto Tecnológico y de Estudios Superiores de Monterrey, Campus Monterrey, Graduate School of Business Administration and Leadership, Program in Business Administration, Monterrey, Mexico. Offers business administration (MA, MBA); finance (M Sc); international business (M Sc); marketing (M Sc). *Accreditation:* AACSB. Part-time programs available. *Degree requirements:* For master's, one foreign language, thesis. *Entrance requirements:* For master's, GMAT. Additional exam requirements/recommendations for international students: Required—TOEFL. *Faculty research:* Technology management, quality management, organizational theory and behavior.

Inter American University of Puerto Rico, Metropolitan Campus, Graduate Programs, Program in International Business, San Juan, PR 00919-1293. Offers international business (MIB); interregional and international business (PhD).

Inter American University of Puerto Rico, San Germán Campus, Graduate Studies Center, Program in Business Administration, San Germán, PR 00683-5008. Offers accounting (MBA); finance (MBA); general business administration (MBA); human resources (MBA, PhD); industrial relations (MBA); information systems (MBA); international and interregional business (PhD); management (MBA); marketing (MBA). Part-time and evening/weekend programs available. *Faculty:* 8 full-time (2 women), 4 part-time/adjunct (3 women). *Students:* 138 full-time (80 women), 35 part-time (21 women); includes 172 minority (all Hispanic/Latino). 60 applicants, 65% accepted, 38 enrolled. In 2013, 38 master's, 3 doctorates awarded. *Degree requirements:* For master's, comprehensive exam. *Entrance requirements:* For master's, GRE General Test or EXADEP, minimum GPA of 3.0. *Application deadline:* For fall admission, 4/30 priority date for domestic students; for spring admission, 11/15 for domestic students. Applications are processed on a rolling basis. Application fee: $31. *Expenses: Tuition:* Full-time $2424; part-time $202 per credit hour. *Required fees:* $260 per semester. Tuition and fees vary according to course level, course load, degree level and program. *Financial support:* Teaching assistantships, Federal Work-Study, and unspecified assistantships available. *Unit head:* Dr. Elba T. Irizarry, Director of Graduate Studies Center, 787-264-1912 Ext. 7357, Fax: 787-892-6350, E-mail: elbat@sg.inter.edu. *Application contact:* Dr. Ailin Padilla, Coordinator, 787-264-1912 Ext. 7355, E-mail: ailin_padilla@intersg.edu.

The International University of Monaco, Graduate Programs, Monte Carlo, Monaco. Offers entrepreneurship (EMBA, MBA); financial engineering (M Sc); hedge fund and private equity (M Sc); international marketing (EMBA, MBA); international wealth management (M Sc); luxury goods and services (EMBA, M Sc, MBA); wealth and asset management (EMBA, MBA). Part-time programs available. *Degree requirements:* For master's, comprehensive exam (for some programs), applied research project. *Entrance requirements:* Additional exam requirements/recommendations for international students: Required—TOEFL (minimum score 550 paper-based), IELTS. Electronic applications accepted. *Faculty research:* Gaming, leadership, disintermediation.

Iona College, Hagan School of Business, Department of Finance, Business Economics and Legal Studies, New Rochelle, NY 10801-1890. Offers finance (MS); financial management (MBA, PMC); financial services (MS); international finance (MS). Part-time and evening/weekend programs available. *Faculty:* 8 full-time (2 women), 7 part-time/adjunct (1 woman). *Students:* 41 full-time (16 women), 62 part-time (23 women); includes 10 minority (2 Black or African American, non-Hispanic/Latino; 4 Asian, non-Hispanic/Latino; 4 Hispanic/Latino), 11 international. Average age 27. 30 applicants, 90% accepted, 19 enrolled. In 2013, 71 master's awarded. *Entrance requirements:* For master's, GMAT, 2 letters of recommendation, minimum GPA of 3.0; for PMC, minimum GPA of 3.0. Additional exam requirements/recommendations for international students: Required—TOEFL (minimum score 550 paper-based; 80 iBT), IELTS (minimum score 6.5). *Application deadline:* For fall admission, 8/15 priority date for domestic students, 8/1 priority date for international students; for winter admission, 11/15 priority date for domestic students, 11/1 priority date for international students; for spring admission, 2/15 priority date for domestic students, 2/1 priority date for international students; for summer admission, 5/15 priority date for domestic students, 5/1 priority date for international students. Applications are processed on a rolling basis. Application fee: $50. Electronic applications accepted. *Expenses:* Contact institution. *Financial support:* In 2013–14, 41 students received support. Scholarships/grants, tuition waivers (partial), and unspecified assistantships available. Support available to part-time students. Financial award application deadline: 4/15; financial award applicants required to submit FAFSA. *Faculty research:* Options, insurance financing, asset depreciation ranges, international finance, emerging markets. *Unit head:* Dr. Anand Shetty, Chairman, 914-633-2284, E-mail: ashetty@iona.edu. *Application contact:* Cameron Hudson, Director of MBA Admissions, 914-633-2288, Fax: 914-637-2708, E-mail: chudson@iona.edu. Website: http://www.iona.edu/Academics/Hagan-School-of-Business/Departments/Finance-Business-Economics-Legal-Studies/Graduate-Programs.aspx.

Iona College, Hagan School of Business, Department of Marketing and International Business, New Rochelle, NY 10801-1890. Offers international business (AC, PMC); marketing (MBA); sports and entertainment management (AC). Part-time and evening/weekend programs available. *Faculty:* 2 full-time (both women), 1 (woman) part-time/adjunct. *Students:* 17 full-time (9 women), 24 part-time (16 women); includes 4 minority (2 Black or African American, non-Hispanic/Latino; 2 Hispanic/Latino), 5 international. Average age 27. 15 applicants, 100% accepted, 9 enrolled. In 2013, 28 master's, 114 other advanced degrees awarded. *Entrance requirements:* For master's, GMAT, 2 letters of recommendation, minimum GPA of 3.0; for other advanced degree, GMAT, minimum GPA of 3.0. Additional exam requirements/recommendations for international students: Required—TOEFL (minimum score 550 paper-based; 80 iBT), IELTS (minimum score 6.5). *Application deadline:* For fall admission, 8/15 priority date for domestic students, 8/1 priority date for international students; for winter admission, 11/

15 priority date for domestic students, 11/1 priority date for international students; for spring admission, 2/15 priority date for domestic students, 2/1 priority date for international students; for summer admission, 5/15 for domestic students, 5/1 priority date for international students. Applications are processed on a rolling basis. Application fee: $50. Electronic applications accepted. *Expenses:* Contact institution. *Financial support:* In 2013–14, 23 students received support. Scholarships/grants, tuition waivers (partial), and unspecified assistantships available. Support available to part-time students. Financial award application deadline: 4/15; financial award applicants required to submit FAFSA. *Faculty research:* Business ethics, international retailing, mega-marketing, consumer behavior and consumer confidence. *Unit head:* Dr. Frederica E. Rudell, Chair, 914-637-2748, E-mail: frudell@iona.edu. *Application contact:* Cameron Hudson, Director of MBA Admissions, 914-633-2288, Fax: 914-637-2708, E-mail: chudson@iona.edu.
Website: http://www.iona.edu/Academics/Hagan-School-of-Business/Departments/Marketing/Graduate-Programs.aspx.

John Hancock University, MBA Program, Oakbrook Terrace, IL 60181. Offers e-commerce (MBA); finance (MBA); general business (MBA); global management (MBA); health care administration (MBA); leadership (MBA); management of information systems (MBA); marketing (MBA); professional accounting (MBA); project management (MBA); public accounting (MBA); risk management (MBA).

John Marshall Law School, Graduate and Professional Programs, Chicago, IL 60604-3968. Offers employee benefits (LL M, MS); estate planning (LL M); global legal studies (LL M); information technology (MS); information technology and privacy law (LL M); intellectual property (LL M, MS); international business and trade (LL M); law (JD); real estate (LL M, MS); taxation (LL M, MS); trial advocacy (LL M); JD/LL M; JD/MA; JD/MBA; JD/MPA. JD/MBA offered jointly with Dominican University; JD/MA and JD/MPA with Roosevelt University. *Accreditation:* ABA. Part-time and evening/weekend programs available. *Faculty:* 71 full-time (26 women), 132 part-time/adjunct (49 women). *Students:* 1,045 full-time (512 women), 421 part-time (211 women); includes 403 minority (152 Black or African American, non-Hispanic/Latino; 8 American Indian or Alaska Native, non-Hispanic/Latino; 89 Asian, non-Hispanic/Latino; 138 Hispanic/Latino; 3 Native Hawaiian or other Pacific Islander, non-Hispanic/Latino; 13 Two or more races, non-Hispanic/Latino), 57 international. Average age 27. 2,694 applicants, 73% accepted, 419 enrolled. In 2013, 81 master's, 445 doctorates awarded. *Degree requirements:* For master's, 24 credits; for doctorate, 90 credits. *Entrance requirements:* For master's, JD; for doctorate, LSAT. Additional exam requirements/recommendations for international students: Required—TOEFL. *Application deadline:* For fall admission, 3/1 priority date for domestic and international students; for spring admission, 10/15 priority date for domestic and international students. Applications are processed on a rolling basis. Application fee: $0. Electronic applications accepted. *Expenses:* Contact institution. *Financial support:* In 2013–14, 1,275 students received support. Scholarships/grants and tuition waivers (full and partial) available. Support available to part-time students. Financial award application deadline: 4/1; financial award applicants required to submit FAFSA. *Unit head:* John Corkery, Dean, 312-427-2737. *Application contact:* William B. Powers, Associate Dean of Admission and Student Affairs, 800-537-4280, Fax: 312-427-5136, E-mail: admission@jmls.edu.

Kaplan University, Davenport Campus, School of Business, Davenport, IA 52807-2095. Offers business administration (MBA); change leadership (MS); entrepreneurship (MBA); finance (MBA); health care management (MBA, MS); human resource (MBA); international business (MBA); management (MS); marketing (MBA); project management (MBA, MS); supply chain management and logistics (MBA, MS). *Accreditation:* ACBSP. Part-time and evening/weekend programs available. Postbaccalaureate distance learning degree programs offered (no on-campus study). *Entrance requirements:* Additional exam requirements/recommendations for international students: Required—TOEFL (minimum score 550 paper-based; 80 iBT). Electronic applications accepted.

Kean University, Nathan Weiss Graduate College, Program in Global Management, Union, NJ 07083. Offers executive management (MBA); global management (MBA). Part-time programs available. *Faculty:* 3 full-time (0 women). *Students:* 41 full-time (22 women), 29 part-time (13 women); includes 33 minority (8 Black or African American, non-Hispanic/Latino; 7 Asian, non-Hispanic/Latino; 18 Hispanic/Latino), 12 international. Average age 33. 36 applicants, 81% accepted, 20 enrolled. In 2013, 17 master's awarded. *Degree requirements:* For master's, one foreign language, internship or study abroad. *Entrance requirements:* For master's, GMAT, minimum GPA of 3.0, 3 letters of recommendation, prerequisite business courses, transcripts, personal essay, interview; 5 years of experience, resume, and personal statement (for executive management option). Additional exam requirements/recommendations for international students: Required—TOEFL (minimum score 550 paper-based; 79 iBT). *Application deadline:* For fall admission, 6/1 for domestic and international students; for spring admission, 12/1 for domestic and international students. Applications are processed on a rolling basis. Application fee: $75 ($150 for international students). Electronic applications accepted. *Expenses:* Tuition, state resident: full-time $12,099; part-time $589 per credit. Tuition, nonresident: full-time $16,399; part-time $722 per credit. *Required fees:* $3050; $139 per credit. Part-time tuition and fees vary according to course level, course load, degree level and program. *Financial support:* In 2013–14, 10 research assistantships with full tuition reimbursements (averaging $3,713 per year) were awarded; unspecified assistantships also available. Financial award applicants required to submit FAFSA. *Unit head:* Dr. Veysel Yucetepe, Program Coordinator, 908-737-5980, E-mail: vyucetep@kean.edu. *Application contact:* Reenat Hasan, Admissions Counselor, 908-737-5923, Fax: 908-737-5925, E-mail: rhasan@exchange.kean.edu.
Website: http://grad.kean.edu/masters-programs/mba-global-management.

Keiser University, Doctor of Business Administration Program, Ft. Lauderdale, FL 33309. Offers global business (DBA); global organizational leadership (DBA); marketing (DBA).

Keiser University, Master of Business Administration Program, Ft. Lauderdale, FL 33309. Offers accounting (MBA); health services management (MBA); information security management (MBA); international business (MBA); leadership for managers (MBA); marketing (MBA). All concentrations except information security management also offered in Mandarin; leadership for managers and international business also offered in Spanish. Part-time programs available. Postbaccalaureate distance learning degree programs offered (minimal on-campus study).

Lake Forest Graduate School of Management, The Immersion MBA Program (iMBA), Lake Forest, IL 60045. Offers global business (MBA). Postbaccalaureate distance learning degree programs offered (no on-campus study).

Lake Forest Graduate School of Management, The Leadership MBA Program, Lake Forest, IL 60045. Offers finance (MBA); global business (MBA); healthcare management (MBA); management (MBA); marketing (MBA); organizational behavior (MBA). Part-time and evening/weekend programs available. *Entrance requirements:* For master's, 4 years of work experience in field, interview, 2 letters of recommendation. Electronic applications accepted.

La Salle University, School of Business, Philadelphia, PA 19141-1199. Offers accounting (MBA, Post-MBA Certificate); business systems and analytics (MBA, Post-MBA Certificate); finance (MBA, Post-MBA Certificate); general business administration (MBA); human resource management (MBA, Post-MBA Certificate); international business (Post-MBA Certificate); management (MBA, Post-MBA Certificate); marketing (MBA, Post-MBA Certificate); MSN/MBA. *Accreditation:* AACSB. Part-time and evening/weekend programs available. Postbaccalaureate distance learning degree programs offered (minimal on-campus study). *Faculty:* 27 full-time (13 women), 15 part-time/adjunct (4 women). *Students:* 81 full-time (30 women), 428 part-time (211 women); includes 109 minority (47 Black or African American, non-Hispanic/Latino; 39 Asian, non-Hispanic/Latino; 18 Hispanic/Latino; 5 Two or more races, non-Hispanic/Latino), 6 international. Average age 30. 215 applicants, 90% accepted, 120 enrolled. In 2013, 182 master's, 1 other advanced degree awarded. *Entrance requirements:* For master's, GMAT or GRE, two letters of reference; resume; for Post-MBA Certificate, MBA with minimum GPA of 3.0. Additional exam requirements/recommendations for international students: Required—TOEFL. *Application deadline:* For fall admission, 8/15 priority date for domestic students, 7/15 for international students; for spring admission, 12/15 priority date for domestic students, 11/15 for international students; for summer admission, 4/15 priority date for domestic students, 3/15 for international students. Applications are processed on a rolling basis. Application fee: $35. Electronic applications accepted. Application fee is waived when completed online. *Expenses:* Contact institution. *Financial support:* In 2013–14, 88 students received support. Career-related internships or fieldwork, Federal Work-Study, scholarships/grants, and unspecified assistantships available. Support available to part-time students. Financial award application deadline: 8/31; financial award applicants required to submit FAFSA. *Unit head:* Dr. Gary Giamartino, Dean, 215-951-1040, Fax: 215-951-1886, E-mail: giamartino@lasalle.edu. *Application contact:* Paul J. Reilly, Assistant Vice President, Enrollment Services, 215-951-1946, Fax: 215-951-1462, E-mail: reilly@lasalle.edu.
Website: http://www.lasalle.edu/grad/index.php?section-mba&page-index.

Lehigh University, College of Business and Economics, Department of Management, Bethlehem, PA 18015. Offers business administration (MBA); corporate entrepreneurship (MBA); international business (MBA); marketing (MBA); project management (MBA); supply chain management (MBA); MBA/E; MBA/M Ed. *Accreditation:* AACSB. Part-time and evening/weekend programs available. Postbaccalaureate distance learning degree programs offered (minimal on-campus study). *Faculty:* 11 full-time (4 women), 13 part-time/adjunct (4 women). *Students:* 28 full-time (10 women), 171 part-time (54 women); includes 32 minority (2 Black or African American, non-Hispanic/Latino; 21 Asian, non-Hispanic/Latino; 6 Hispanic/Latino; 3 Two or more races, non-Hispanic/Latino), 21 international. Average age 33. 108 applicants, 63% accepted, 25 enrolled. In 2013, 79 master's awarded. *Entrance requirements:* For master's, GMAT or GRE. Additional exam requirements/recommendations for international students: Required—TOEFL (minimum score 600 paper-based; 94 iBT). *Application deadline:* For fall admission, 7/15 for domestic students, 5/1 for international students; for spring admission, 12/1 for domestic students. Applications are processed on a rolling basis. Application fee: $100. Electronic applications accepted. *Financial support:* In 2013–14, 33 students received support, including 10 teaching assistantships with full and partial tuition reimbursements available (averaging $14,200 per year); career-related internships or fieldwork, scholarships/grants, health care benefits, tuition waivers (full and partial), and unspecified assistantships also available. Support available to part-time students. Financial award application deadline: 1/15. *Faculty research:* Information systems, organizational behavior, supply chain management, strategic management, entrepreneurship. *Total annual research expenditures:* $77,886. *Unit head:* Dr. Robert J. Trent, Department Chair, 610-758-4952, Fax: 610-758-6941, E-mail: rjt2@lehigh.edu. *Application contact:* Jen Giordano, Director of Recruitment and Admissions, 610-758-3418, Fax: 610-758-5283, E-mail: jlg210@lehigh.edu.
Website: http://www4.lehigh.edu/business/academics/depts/management.

Lewis University, College of Business, Graduate School of Management, Program in Business Administration, Romeoville, IL 60446. Offers accounting (MBA); custom elective option (MBA); e-business (MBA); finance (MBA); healthcare management (MBA); human resources management (MBA); international business (MBA); management information systems (MBA); marketing (MBA); project management (MBA); technology and operations management (MBA). Part-time and evening/weekend programs available. *Students:* 115 full-time (55 women), 227 part-time (129 women); includes 128 minority (74 Black or African American, non-Hispanic/Latino; 1 American Indian or Alaska Native, non-Hispanic/Latino; 9 Asian, non-Hispanic/Latino; 40 Hispanic/Latino; 4 Two or more races, non-Hispanic/Latino), 10 international. Average age 31. In 2013, 99 master's awarded. *Entrance requirements:* For master's, interview, bachelor's degree, resume, 2 recommendations. Additional exam requirements/recommendations for international students: Required—TOEFL (minimum score 550 paper-based). *Application deadline:* For fall admission, 8/15 priority date for domestic students, 5/1 priority date for international students; for spring admission, 11/15 priority date for international students. Applications are processed on a rolling basis. Application fee: $40. Electronic applications accepted. *Financial support:* Career-related internships or fieldwork, Federal Work-Study, scholarships/grants, and unspecified assistantships available. Financial award application deadline: 5/1; financial award applicants required to submit FAFSA. *Unit head:* Dr. Maureen Culleeney, Academic Program Director, 815-838-0500 Ext. 5631, E-mail: culleema@lewisu.edu. *Application contact:* Michele Ryan, Director of Admission, 815-838-0500 Ext. 5384, E-mail: gsm@lewisu.edu.

Liberty University, School of Business, Lynchburg, VA 24515. Offers accounting (MBA, MS, DBA); business administration (MBA); criminal justice (MBA); cyber security (MS); executive leadership (MA); healthcare (MBA); human resources (DBA); information systems (MS), including information assurance, technology management; international business (MBA, DBA); leadership (MBA, DBA); management and leadership (MA); marketing (MBA, MS, DBA), including digital marketing and advertising (MS), project management (MS), public relations (MS), sports marketing and media (MS); project management (MBA, DBA); public administration (MBA); public relations (MBA). Part-time programs available. Postbaccalaureate distance learning degree programs offered (minimal on-campus study). *Students:* 1,342 full-time (749 women), 3,704 part-time (1,820 women); includes 1,657 minority (1,221 Black or African American, non-Hispanic/Latino; 11 American Indian or Alaska Native, non-Hispanic/Latino; 74 Asian, non-Hispanic/Latino; 209 Hispanic/Latino; 13 Native Hawaiian or other Pacific Islander, non-Hispanic/Latino; 129 Two or more races, non-Hispanic/Latino), 40 international. Average age 35. 5,899 applicants, 48% accepted, 1716 enrolled. In 2013, 1,535 master's awarded. *Entrance requirements:* For master's, minimum undergraduate GPA of 3.0, 15 hours of upper-level business courses. Additional exam requirements/recommendations for international students: Required—TOEFL (minimum score 600 paper-based; 100 iBT). *Application deadline:* Applications are processed on a rolling basis. Application fee: $50. Electronic applications accepted. *Expenses:* Contact institution. *Unit head:* Dr. Scott Hicks, Dean, 434-592-4808, Fax: 434-582-2366, E-mail: smhicks@liberty.edu. *Application contact:* Jay Bridge, Director of Graduate Admissions, 800-424-9595, Fax: 800-628-7977, E-mail: gradadmissions@liberty.edu.
Website: http://www.liberty.edu/academics/business/index.cfm?PID-149.

Lincoln University, Graduate Studies, Oakland, CA 94612. Offers finance and investments (DBA); finance management and investment banking (MBA); general business (MBA); human resource management (MBA, DBA); international business (MBA); management information systems (MBA). Part-time and evening/weekend

programs available. *Faculty:* 8 full-time (2 women), 22 part-time/adjunct (7 women). *Students:* 372 full-time (171 women), 4 part-time (1 woman); includes 8 minority (2 Black or African American, non-Hispanic/Latino; 6 Asian, non-Hispanic/Latino), 363 international. Average age 26. 421 applicants, 71% accepted, 133 enrolled. *Degree requirements:* For master's, research project (thesis), internship report, or comprehensive exam; for doctorate, comprehensive exam, thesis/dissertation. *Entrance requirements:* For master's, minimum GPA of 2.7; for doctorate, GMAT (minimum score: 550), GRE (minimum score: 1000), or equivalent test results (waived for master's degree with minimum cumulative GPA of 3.3). Additional exam requirements/recommendations for international students: Required—TOEFL (minimum score 525 paper-based; 71 iBT) or IELTS (minimum score 5.5) for MBA; TOEFL (minimum score 550 paper-based; 79 iBT) or IELTS (minimum score 6) for DBA. *Application deadline:* For fall admission, 7/1 priority date for domestic and international students; for spring admission, 11/1 priority date for domestic and international students; for summer admission, 5/1 for domestic and international students. Applications are processed on a rolling basis. Application fee: $75. Electronic applications accepted. *Expenses: Tuition:* Full-time $7290; part-time $405 per unit. *Required fees:* $375; $405 per unit. $375 per year. Tuition and fees vary according to course level and degree level. *Financial support:* Teaching assistantships with tuition reimbursements, career-related internships or fieldwork, and scholarships/grants available. Financial award application deadline: 7/31; financial award applicants required to submit FAFSA. *Unit head:* Dr. Marshall Burak, Director of Graduate Programs, 510-628-8016, Fax: 510-628-8012, E-mail: mburak@lincolnuca.edu. *Application contact:* Reenu Shrestha, Admissions Officer, 510-628-8010 Ext. 8030, Fax: 510-628-8012, E-mail: admissions@lincolnuca.edu.
Website: http://www.lincolnuca.edu/.

Lindenwood University, Graduate Programs, School of Business and Entrepreneurship, St. Charles, MO 63301-1695. Offers accountancy (MA); accounting (MBA); business administration (MBA); entrepreneurial studies (MBA); finance (MBA, MS); human resource management (MBA); international business (MBA); leadership (MA); management (MBA); marketing (MBA, MS); public management (MBA); sport management (MA); supply chain management (MBA). *Accreditation:* ACBSP. Part-time and evening/weekend programs available. Postbaccalaureate distance learning degree programs offered (no on-campus study). *Faculty:* 18 full-time (8 women), 33 part-time/adjunct (8 women). *Students:* 292 full-time (130 women), 111 part-time (46 women); includes 59 minority (42 Black or African American, non-Hispanic/Latino; 5 American Indian or Alaska Native, non-Hispanic/Latino; 1 Asian, non-Hispanic/Latino; 5 Hispanic/Latino; 6 Two or more races, non-Hispanic/Latino), 112 international. Average age 29. 212 applicants, 51% accepted, 102 enrolled. In 2013, 221 master's awarded. *Degree requirements:* For master's, comprehensive exam (for some programs), thesis (for some programs), minimum GPA of 3.0. *Entrance requirements:* For master's, interview, minimum GPA of 3.0, letter of recommendation. Additional exam requirements/recommendations for international students: Required—TOEFL (minimum score 550 paper-based; 80 iBT). *Application deadline:* For fall admission, 8/12 priority date for domestic and international students; for winter admission, 1/6 priority date for domestic and international students; for spring admission, 3/10 priority date for domestic and international students; for summer admission, 5/27 priority date for domestic and international students. Applications are processed on a rolling basis. Application fee: $30 ($100 for international students). Electronic applications accepted. *Expenses: Tuition:* Full-time $14,800; part-time $428 per credit hour. *Required fees:* $350. Tuition and fees vary according to course level and course load. *Financial support:* In 2013–14, 268 students received support. Career-related internships or fieldwork, Federal Work-Study, institutionally sponsored loans, scholarships/grants, tuition waivers (partial), and unspecified assistantships available. Financial award application deadline: 6/30; financial award applicants required to submit FAFSA. *Unit head:* Roger Ellis, Dean, 636-949-4839, E-mail: rellis@lindenwood.edu. *Application contact:* Brett Barger, Dean of Evening Admissions and Extension Campuses, 636-949-4934, Fax: 636-949-4109, E-mail: adultadmissions@lindenwood.edu.
Website: http://www.lindenwood.edu.

Long Island University–LIU Post, College of Management, School of Business, Brookville, NY 11548-1300. Offers accounting and taxation (Certificate); business administration (Certificate); finance (MBA, Certificate); general business administration (MBA); international business (MBA, Certificate); management (MBA, Certificate); management information systems (MBA, Certificate); marketing (MBA, Certificate). *Accreditation:* AACSB. Part-time and evening/weekend programs available. *Entrance requirements:* For master's, GMAT, resume, minimum GPA of 3.0, 2 letters of recommendation. Additional exam requirements/recommendations for international students: Required—TOEFL (minimum score 527 paper-based). Electronic applications accepted. *Faculty research:* Financial markets, consumer behavior.

Loyola University Chicago, Quinlan School of Business, MBA Programs, Chicago, IL 60610. Offers accounting (MBA); business ethics (MBA); derivative markets (MBA); economics (MBA); entrepreneurship (MBA); executive (MBA); finance (MBA); healthcare management (MBA); human resources management (MBA); information systems management (MBA); intercontinental (MBA); international business (MBA); marketing (MBA); operations management (MBA); risk management (MBA); JD/MBA. Part-time and evening/weekend programs available. *Faculty:* 76 full-time (20 women), 10 part-time/adjunct (4 women). *Students:* 73 full-time (34 women), 294 part-time (129 women); includes 60 minority (18 Black or African American, non-Hispanic/Latino; 28 Asian, non-Hispanic/Latino; 14 Hispanic/Latino), 19 international. Average age 31. 529 applicants, 51% accepted, 153 enrolled. In 2013, 229 master's awarded. *Entrance requirements:* For master's, GMAT or GRE, official transcripts, two letters of recommendation, statement of purpose, resume. Additional exam requirements/recommendations for international students: Required—TOEFL (minimum score 90 iBT) or IELTS (minimum score 6.5). *Application deadline:* For fall admission, 7/15 for domestic and international students; for winter admission, 10/1 for domestic and international students; for spring admission, 1/15 for domestic and international students; for summer admission, 4/1 for domestic and international students. Applications are processed on a rolling basis. Application fee: $50. Electronic applications accepted. Application fee is waived when completed online. *Expenses: Tuition:* Full-time $16,740; part-time $930 per credit. *Required fees:* $135 per semester. *Financial support:* Scholarships/grants and unspecified assistantships available. *Faculty research:* Social enterprise and responsibility, emerging markets, supply chain management, risk management. *Unit head:* Jennifer Huntley, Assistant Dean for Graduate Programs, 312-915-6124, Fax: 312-915-7207, E-mail: jhuntle@luc.edu. *Application contact:* Jessica Gagle, Enrollment Advisor, Quinlan School of Business Graduate Programs, 312-915-8908, Fax: 312-915-7207, E-mail: jgagle@luc.edu.

Loyola University Maryland, Graduate Programs, Sellinger School of Business and Management, Program in Business Administration, Baltimore, MD 21210-2699. Offers accounting (MBA); finance (MBA); general business (MBA); information systems operations management (MBA); international business (MBA); management (MBA); marketing (MBA). *Accreditation:* AACSB. Part-time and evening/weekend programs available. *Entrance requirements:* For master's, GMAT, letter of recommendation, resume, essay. Additional exam requirements/recommendations for international students: Required—TOEFL (minimum score 550 paper-based).

Lynn University, College of Business and Management, Boca Raton, FL 33431-5598. Offers aviation management (MBA); financial valuation and investment management (MBA); hospitality management (MBA); international business (MBA); marketing (MBA); mass communication and media management (MBA); sports and athletics administration (MBA). Part-time and evening/weekend programs available. Postbaccalaureate distance learning degree programs offered. *Faculty:* 16 full-time (6 women), 8 part-time/adjunct (3 women). *Students:* 181 full-time (95 women), 83 part-time (37 women); includes 41 minority (22 Black or African American, non-Hispanic/Latino; 1 Asian, non-Hispanic/Latino; 17 Hispanic/Latino; 1 Two or more races, non-Hispanic/Latino), 77 international. Average age 28. 137 applicants, 100% accepted, 107 enrolled. In 2013, 149 master's awarded. *Degree requirements:* For master's, projects. *Entrance requirements:* For master's, GMAT or GRE, bachelor's degree from accredited institution, minimum undergraduate GPA of 2.5, resume, 2 letters of recommendation. Additional exam requirements/recommendations for international students: Required—TOEFL (minimum score 550 paper-based). *Application deadline:* Applications are processed on a rolling basis. Application fee: $45. Electronic applications accepted. *Expenses: Tuition:* Full-time $23,760; part-time $660 per credit. *Required fees:* $300; $50 per term. Tuition and fees vary according to degree level and program. *Financial support:* Career-related internships or fieldwork, Federal Work-Study, institutionally sponsored loans, scholarships/grants, tuition waivers (full and partial), and unspecified assistantships available. Support available to part-time students. Financial award application deadline: 8/1; financial award applicants required to submit FAFSA. *Faculty research:* Labor relations, dynamic balance in leisure-time skills, ethics in athletics, hotel development. *Unit head:* Dr. Ralph Norcio, Senior Associate Dean, 561-237-7010, Fax: 561-237-7014, E-mail: rnorcio@lynn.edu. *Application contact:* Steven Pruitt, Director of Graduate and Undergraduate Evening Admission, 561-237-7834, Fax: 561-237-7100, E-mail: spruitt@lynn.edu.
Website: http://www.lynn.edu/academics/colleges/business-and-management.

Madonna University, School of Business, Livonia, MI 48150-1173. Offers business administration (MBA); international business (MSBA); leadership studies (MSBA); leadership studies in criminal justice (MSBA); quality and operations management (MSBA). Part-time and evening/weekend programs available. Postbaccalaureate distance learning degree programs offered (minimal on-campus study). *Degree requirements:* For master's, thesis (for some programs), foreign language proficiency (international business). *Entrance requirements:* For master's, GMAT, GRE General Test, minimum GPA of 3.0. Electronic applications accepted. *Faculty research:* Management, women in management, future studies.

Maine Maritime Academy, Loeb-Sullivan School of International Business and Logistics, Castine, ME 04420. Offers global logistics and maritime management (MS); international logistics management (MS). Part-time programs available. *Faculty:* 6 full-time (1 woman), 2 part-time/adjunct (0 women). *Students:* 11 full-time (8 women). *Degree requirements:* For master's, capstone course. *Entrance requirements:* For master's, GMAT or GRE, letter of recommendation. Additional exam requirements/recommendations for international students: Required—TOEFL. *Application deadline:* For fall admission, 6/1 for domestic and international students; for spring admission, 3/15 for domestic and international students. Application fee: $40. Application fee is waived when completed online. *Financial support:* In 2013–14, teaching assistantships with full tuition reimbursements (averaging $6,000 per year) were awarded; career-related internships or fieldwork, Federal Work-Study, and institutionally sponsored loans also available. Support available to part-time students. Financial award application deadline: 4/15. *Unit head:* Dr. William DeWitt, Dean, 207-326-2454, Fax: 207-326-4311, E-mail: william.dewitt@mma.edu. *Application contact:* Patrick Haugen, Program Coordinator, 207-326-2212, Fax: 207-326-2411, E-mail: info.ls@mma.edu.
Website: http://ibl.mainemaritime.edu.

Manhattanville College, School of Business, Program in International Management, Purchase, NY 10577-2132. Offers MS. Part-time and evening/weekend programs available. *Degree requirements:* For master's, final project. *Entrance requirements:* Additional exam requirements/recommendations for international students: Required—TOEFL.

Marquette University, Graduate School of Management, Executive MBA Program, Milwaukee, WI 53201-1881. Offers economics (MBA); finance (MBA); human resources (MBA); international business (MBA); management information systems (MBA); marketing (MBA); operations and supply chain management (MBA); sports business (MBA). *Accreditation:* AACSB. *Students:* 38 full-time (12 women), 1 international. Average age 36. 36 applicants. In 2013, 21 master's awarded. *Degree requirements:* For master's, international trip. *Entrance requirements:* For master's, GMAT or GRE, two letters of recommendation, official transcripts from current and previous colleges/universities. Additional exam requirements/recommendations for international students: Required—TOEFL (minimum score 550 paper-based; 88 iBT), IELTS (minimum score 6.5), PTE. *Application deadline:* For fall admission, 2/15 for domestic and international students. Application fee: $50. Electronic applications accepted. *Expenses:* Contact institution. *Financial support:* Application deadline: 2/15. *Faculty research:* International trade and finance, customer relationship management, consumer satisfaction, customer service. *Unit head:* Dr. Mark Eppli, Dean, 414-288-5724. *Application contact:* Dr. Jeanne Simmons, Associate Dean, 414-288-7145.
Website: http://www.busadm.mu.edu/emba/.

Marquette University, Graduate School of Management, Program in Business Administration, Milwaukee, WI 53201-1881. Offers business administration (MBA); economics (MBA); entrepreneurship (Certificate); finance (MBA); human resources (MBA); international business (MBA); management information systems (MBA); marketing (MBA); operations and supply chain management (MBA); sports business (MBA); JD/MBA; MBA/MA; MBA/MSN. *Accreditation:* AACSB. Part-time and evening/weekend programs available. *Students:* 28 full-time (13 women), 265 part-time (66 women); includes 20 minority (7 Black or African American, non-Hispanic/Latino; 8 Asian, non-Hispanic/Latino; 5 Hispanic/Latino), 11 international. Average age 31. 185 applicants. In 2013, 129 master's, 2 other advanced degrees awarded. *Degree requirements:* For Certificate, business plan. *Entrance requirements:* For master's, GMAT or GRE, letters of recommendation. Additional exam requirements/recommendations for international students: Required—TOEFL (minimum score 550 paper-based; 88 iBT), IELTS (minimum score 6.5), PTE. *Application deadline:* For fall admission, 2/15 for domestic and international students. Applications are processed on a rolling basis. Application fee: $50. Electronic applications accepted. *Financial support:* In 2013–14, 4 fellowships, 11 teaching assistantships were awarded; research assistantships, Federal Work-Study, institutionally sponsored loans, scholarships/grants, and tuition waivers (full and partial) also available. Support available to part-time students. Financial award application deadline: 2/15. *Faculty research:* Ethics in the professions, services marketing, technology impact on decision-making, mentoring. *Unit head:* Dr. Mark Eppli, Dean, 414-288-5724. *Application contact:* Dr. Jeanne Simmons, Associate Dean, 414-288-7145.
Website: http://business.marquette.edu/academics/mba.

McGill University, Faculty of Graduate and Postdoctoral Studies, Desautels Faculty of Management, Montréal, QC H3A 2T5, Canada. Offers administration (PhD); entrepreneurial studies (MBA); finance (MBA); general management (Post Master's

Certificate); information systems (MBA); international business (MBA); international practicing management (MM); management (MBA); management for development (MBA); manufacturing management (MMM); marketing (MBA); operations management (MBA); public accountancy (Diploma); strategic management (MBA); MBA/LL B; MD/ MBA. MMM offered jointly with Faculty of Engineering; PhD with Concordia University, HEC Montreal, Université de Montréal, Université du Québec à Montréal.

McKendree University, Graduate Programs, Master of Business Administration Program, Lebanon, IL 62254-1299. Offers business administration (MBA); human resource management (MBA); international business (MBA). Part-time and evening/ weekend programs available. Postbaccalaureate distance learning degree programs offered (no on-campus study). *Entrance requirements:* For master's, official transcripts from all institutions attended, essay, minimum GPA of 3.0, three references, resume. Additional exam requirements/recommendations for international students: Required—TOEFL. Electronic applications accepted.

MidAmerica Nazarene University, Graduate Studies in Management, Olathe, KS 66062-1899. Offers management (MBA); organizational administration (MA), including finance, international business, leadership, non-profit. Evening/weekend programs available. *Entrance requirements:* For master's, mathematical assessment, minimum undergraduate GPA of 3.0, letters of recommendation. Additional exam requirements/ recommendations for international students: Required—TOEFL. Electronic applications accepted. *Faculty research:* Economic development, international finance, business development, employee evaluation.

Milwaukee School of Engineering, Rader School of Business, Program in Marketing and Export Management, Milwaukee, WI 53202-3109. Offers MS. Part-time and evening/weekend programs available. *Faculty:* 1 full-time (0 women), 1 part-time/adjunct (0 women). *Students:* 2 full-time (1 woman), 4 part-time (2 women); includes 1 minority (Asian, non-Hispanic/Latino). Average age 27. 4 applicants, 75% accepted, 2 enrolled. In 2013, 2 master's awarded. *Degree requirements:* For master's, thesis, thesis defense or capstone project. *Entrance requirements:* For master's, GRE or GMAT if undergraduate GPA less than 2.8, 2 letters of recommendation. Additional exam requirements/recommendations for international students: Required—TOEFL (minimum score 79 iBT), IELTS (minimum score 6.5). *Application deadline:* Applications are processed on a rolling basis. Application fee: $0. Electronic applications accepted. Application fee is waived when completed online. *Expenses: Tuition:* Full-time $6939; part-time $771 per credit. *Financial support:* In 2013–14, 2 students received support. Career-related internships or fieldwork, institutionally sponsored loans, and scholarships/grants available. Financial award application deadline: 3/15; financial award applicants required to submit FAFSA. *Unit head:* David Schmitz, Graduate Management Program Director, 414-277-2487, Fax: 414-277-2487, E-mail: schmitz@ msoe.edu. *Application contact:* Katie Weinschenk, Graduate Admissions Director, 800-321-6763, Fax: 414-277-7208, E-mail: weinschenk@msoe.edu.

Montclair State University, The Graduate School, School of Business, Post Master's Certificate Program in International Business, Montclair, NJ 07043-1624. Offers Post Master's Certificate. *Entrance requirements:* For degree, essay. Additional exam requirements/recommendations for international students: Required—TOEFL (minimum score 83 iBT) or IELTS. Electronic applications accepted.

Monterey Institute of International Studies, Graduate School of International Policy and Management, Fisher International MBA Program, Monterey, CA 93940-2691. Offers MBA. *Accreditation:* AACSB. *Degree requirements:* For master's, one foreign language, thesis. *Entrance requirements:* For master's, GMAT, minimum GPA of 3.0, proficiency in a foreign language. Additional exam requirements/recommendations for international students: Required—TOEFL (minimum score 550 paper-based; 80 iBT). Electronic applications accepted. *Expenses: Tuition:* Full-time $34,970; part-time $1665 per credit. *Required fees:* $28 per semester. *Faculty research:* Cross-cultural consumer behavior, foreign direct investment, marketing and entrepreneurial orientation, political risk analysis and area studies, managing international human resources.

National University, Academic Affairs, School of Business and Management, La Jolla, CA 92037-1011. Offers accountancy (Certificate); business administration (GMBA, MBA), including financial management (MBA), human resource management (MBA), integrated marketing communications (MBA), international business (MBA), management accounting (MBA), marketing (MBA), mobile marketing and social media (MBA), organizational leadership (MA, MBA), professional golf management (MBA); global management (MGM); human resource management (MA), including organizational development and change, organizational leadership (MA, MBA); international business (Certificate); management information systems (MS); organizational leadership (MS), including community development; sustainability management (MS). Part-time and evening/weekend programs available. Postbaccalaureate distance learning degree programs offered (no on-campus study). *Faculty:* 30 full-time (8 women), 88 part-time/adjunct (25 women). *Students:* 688 full-time (357 women), 331 part-time (161 women); includes 453 minority (105 Black or African American, non-Hispanic/Latino; 2 American Indian or Alaska Native, non-Hispanic/ Latino; 143 Asian, non-Hispanic/Latino; 162 Hispanic/Latino; 13 Native Hawaiian or other Pacific Islander, non-Hispanic/Latino; 28 Two or more races, non-Hispanic/Latino), 165 international. Average age 33. 286 applicants, 100% accepted, 217 enrolled. In 2013, 641 master's awarded. *Degree requirements:* For master's, thesis (for some programs). *Entrance requirements:* For master's, interview, minimum GPA of 2.5. Additional exam requirements/recommendations for international students: Required—TOEFL (minimum score 550 paper-based; 79 iBT), IELTS (minimum score 6). *Application deadline:* Applications are processed on a rolling basis. Application fee: $60 ($65 for international students). Electronic applications accepted. *Expenses: Tuition:* Full-time $13,824; part-time $1728 per course. One-time fee: $160. *Financial support:* Career-related internships or fieldwork, scholarships/grants, and tuition waivers (partial) available. Support available to part-time students. Financial award application deadline: 6/30; financial award applicants required to submit FAFSA. *Unit head:* School of Business and Management, 800-628-8648, Fax: 858-642-8719, E-mail: sobm@nu.edu. *Application contact:* Louis Cruz, Interim Vice President for Enrollment Services, 800-628-8648, E-mail: advisor@nu.edu.
Website: http://www.nu.edu/OurPrograms/SchoolOfBusinessAndManagement.html.

Newman University, MBA Program, Wichita, KS 67213-2097. Offers finance (MBA); international business (MBA); leadership (MBA); management (MBA); management information technology (MBA). Part-time programs available. *Faculty:* 7 full-time (1 woman), 7 part-time/adjunct (4 women). *Students:* 31 full-time (19 women), 56 part-time (24 women); includes 24 minority (6 Black or African American, non-Hispanic/Latino; 1 American Indian or Alaska Native, non-Hispanic/Latino; 9 Asian, non-Hispanic/Latino; 5 Hispanic/Latino; 3 Two or more races, non-Hispanic/Latino), 9 international. Average age 31. 83 applicants, 63% accepted, 32 enrolled. In 2013, 47 master's awarded. *Degree requirements:* For master's, thesis optional. *Entrance requirements:* For master's, minimum GPA of 3.0; 2 letters of recommendation; course work in algebra, statistics, macroeconomics, and financial accounting. Additional exam requirements/ recommendations for international students: Required—TOEFL (minimum score 600 paper-based; 100 iBT). *Application deadline:* For fall admission, 8/1 priority date for domestic students, 7/15 priority date for international students; for winter admission, 1/1 priority date for domestic students; for spring admission, 1/1 priority date for domestic students, 11/15 priority date for international students. Applications are processed on a rolling basis. Application fee: $25 ($40 for international students). Electronic applications accepted. *Expenses:* Contact institution. *Financial support:* In 2013–14, 8 students received support. Scholarships/grants available. Financial award application deadline: 8/ 15; financial award applicants required to submit FAFSA. *Unit head:* Dr. Wendy Munday, Director of MBA Program, 316-942-4291 Ext. 2296, Fax: 316-942-4483, E-mail: mundayw@newmanu.edu. *Application contact:* Linda Kay Sabala, Director of Graduate Admissions, 316-942-4291 Ext. 2230, Fax: 316-942-4483, E-mail: sabalal@ newmanu.edu.
Website: http://www.newmanu.edu.

New Mexico Highlands University, Graduate Studies, School of Business, Media and Technology, Las Vegas, NM 87701. Offers business administration (MBA), including government nonprofit management, human resource management, international business, management, management information systems; media arts and technology (MA), including media arts and computer science. *Accreditation:* ACBSP. *Faculty:* 13 full-time (5 women). *Students:* 65 full-time (34 women), 146 part-time (89 women); includes 137 minority (3 Black or African American, non-Hispanic/Latino; 9 American Indian or Alaska Native, non-Hispanic/Latino; 1 Asian, non-Hispanic/Latino; 120 Hispanic/Latino; 2 Native Hawaiian or other Pacific Islander, non-Hispanic/Latino; 2 Two or more races, non-Hispanic/Latino), 23 international. Average age 34. In 2013, 56 master's awarded. *Degree requirements:* For master's, comprehensive exam, thesis or alternative. *Entrance requirements:* For master's, minimum undergraduate GPA of 3.0. Additional exam requirements/recommendations for international students: Required—TOEFL (minimum score 540 paper-based). *Application deadline:* For fall admission, 8/1 priority date for domestic students. Applications are processed on a rolling basis. Application fee: $15. *Expenses:* Tuition, state resident: full-time $4278; part-time $178 per credit hour. Tuition, nonresident: full-time $6716; part-time $281 per credit hour. One-time fee: $15. *Financial support:* Career-related internships or fieldwork, Federal Work-Study, institutionally sponsored loans, scholarships/grants, tuition waivers (full and partial), and unspecified assistantships available. Support available to part-time students. Financial award application deadline: 3/1; financial award applicants required to submit FAFSA. *Faculty research:* Real estate valuation, studying expert judgments in complex accounting, decision environments, green marketing, environmentalism, marketing research methodology. *Unit head:* Dr. Margaret Young, Dean, 505-454-3522, Fax: 505-454-3354, E-mail: young_m@nmhu.edu. *Application contact:* Diane Trujillo, Administrative Assistant, Graduate Studies, 505-454-3266, Fax: 505-426-2117, E-mail: dtrujillo@nmhu.edu.

New York University, Graduate School of Arts and Science, Department of Politics, New York, NY 10012-1019. Offers political campaign management (MA); politics (MA, PhD); JD/MA; MBA/MA. Part-time programs available. *Faculty:* 30 full-time (4 women). *Students:* 240 full-time (129 women), 50 part-time (22 women); includes 39 minority (6 Black or African American, non-Hispanic/Latino; 1 American Indian or Alaska Native, non-Hispanic/Latino; 15 Asian, non-Hispanic/Latino; 12 Hispanic/Latino; 5 Two or more races, non-Hispanic/Latino), 167 international. Average age 27. 722 applicants, 56% accepted, 112 enrolled. In 2013, 89 master's, 14 doctorates awarded. Terminal master's awarded for partial completion of doctoral program. *Degree requirements:* For master's, one foreign language, thesis or alternative; for doctorate, 2 foreign languages, comprehensive exam, thesis/dissertation. *Entrance requirements:* For master's and doctorate, GRE General Test. Additional exam requirements/recommendations for international students: Required—TOEFL. *Application deadline:* For fall admission, 12/ 18 priority date for domestic students, 12/18 for international students. Application fee: $95. *Expenses: Tuition:* Full-time $35,856; part-time $1494 per unit. *Required fees:* $1408; $64 per unit. $473 per term. Tuition and fees vary according to course load and program. *Financial support:* Fellowships with tuition reimbursements, teaching assistantships with tuition reimbursements, career-related internships or fieldwork, Federal Work-Study, and institutionally sponsored loans available. Financial award application deadline: 12/18; financial award applicants required to submit FAFSA. *Faculty research:* Comparative politics, democratic theory and practice, rational choice, political economy, international relations. *Unit head:* Sanford Gordon, Director of Graduate Studies, PhD Program, 212-998-8500, Fax: 212-995-4184, E-mail: politics.phd@nyu.edu. *Application contact:* Shinasi Rama, Director of Graduate Studies, Master's Program, 212-998-8500, Fax: 212-995-4184, E-mail: politics.masters@ nyu.edu.
Website: http://www.nyu.edu/gsas/dept/politics/.

North Central College, Graduate and Continuing Studies Programs, Department of Business, Program in Business Administration, Naperville, IL 60566-7063. Offers change management (MBA); finance (MBA); human resource management (MBA); international business administration (MIBA); management (MBA); marketing (MBA). Part-time and evening/weekend programs available. *Faculty:* 13 full-time (4 women), 8 part-time/adjunct (0 women). *Students:* 31 full-time (8 women), 67 part-time (32 women); includes 16 minority (6 Black or African American, non-Hispanic/Latino; 5 Asian, non-Hispanic/Latino; 5 Hispanic/Latino), 3 international. Average age 30. 99 applicants, 54% accepted, 29 enrolled. In 2013, 51 master's awarded. *Degree requirements:* For master's, thesis optional, project. *Entrance requirements:* For master's, interview. Additional exam requirements/recommendations for international students: Required—TOEFL (minimum score 577 paper-based; 90 iBT). *Application deadline:* For fall admission, 8/15 for domestic students; for winter admission, 12/1 for domestic students; for spring admission, 2/1 for domestic students. Application fee: $25. *Expenses: Tuition:* Full-time $4716; part-time $786 per credit hour. *Financial support:* Scholarships/grants available. Support available to part-time students. *Unit head:* Dr. Robert Moussetis, Program Coordinator, 630-637-5475, E-mail: rcmoussetis@noctrl.edu. *Application contact:* Wendy Kulpinski, Director of Graduate and Continuing Education Admission, 630-637-5808, Fax: 630-637-5844, E-mail: wekulpinski@noctrl.edu.

Northeastern University, D'Amore-McKim School of Business, Boston, MA 02115-5096. Offers accounting (MS); business administration (EMBA, MBA); finance (MS); international business (MS); taxation (MS); technological entrepreneurship (MS); JD/ MBA; MBA/MSN; MS/MBA. Part-time and evening/weekend programs available. Postbaccalaureate distance learning degree programs offered (no on-campus study). *Entrance requirements:* For master's, GMAT or GRE, interview. Additional exam requirements/recommendations for international students: Required—TOEFL (minimum score 600 paper-based; 100 iBT). Electronic applications accepted. *Expenses:* Contact institution.

Northwestern University, The Graduate School, Kellogg School of Management, Management Programs, Evanston, IL 60208. Offers accounting information and management (MBA, PhD); analytical finance (MBA); business administration (MBA); decision sciences (MBA); entrepreneurship and innovation (MBA); finance (MBA, PhD); health enterprise management (MBA); human resources management (MBA); international business (MBA); management and organizations (MBA, PhD); management and organizations and sociology (PhD); management and strategy (MBA); management studies (MS); managerial analytics (MBA); managerial economics (MBA); managerial economics and strategy (PhD); marketing (MBA, PhD); marketing management (MBA); media management (MBA); operations management (MBA, PhD); real estate (MBA); social enterprise at Kellogg (MBA); JD/MBA. Part-time and evening/

weekend programs available. Terminal master's awarded for partial completion of doctoral program. *Degree requirements:* For doctorate, thesis/dissertation, 2 years of coursework, qualifying (field) exam and candidacy, summer research papers and presentations to faculty, proposal defense, final exam/defense. *Entrance requirements:* For master's, GMAT, GRE, interview, 2 letters of recommendation, college transcripts, resume, essays, Kellogg honor code; for doctorate, GMAT, GRE, statement of purpose, transcripts, 2 letters of recommendation, resume, interview. Additional exam requirements/recommendations for international students: Required—TOEFL, IELTS. Electronic applications accepted. *Expenses:* Contact institution. *Faculty research:* Business cycles and international finance, health policy, networks, non-market strategy, consumer psychology.

Northwest University, School of Business and Management, Kirkland, WA 98033. Offers business administration (MBA); international business (MBA); project management (MBA); social entrepreneurship (MBA). *Accreditation:* ACBSP. Part-time and evening/weekend programs available. *Degree requirements:* For master's, formalized research. *Entrance requirements:* For master's, GMAT. Additional exam requirements/recommendations for international students: Required—TOEFL (minimum score 550 paper-based; 75 iBT). *Application deadline:* For fall admission, 8/1 for domestic and international students; for spring admission, 12/1 for domestic and international students. Application fee: $75. Electronic applications accepted. *Expenses:* Contact institution. *Financial support:* Federal Work-Study, scholarships/grants, health care benefits, and tuition waivers (full and partial) available. Financial award applicants required to submit FAFSA. *Unit head:* Dr. Teresa Gillespie, Dean, 425-889-5290, E-mail: teresa.gillespie@northwestu.edu. *Application contact:* Aaron Oosterwyk, Director of Graduate and Professional Studies Enrollment, 425-889-7792, Fax: 425-803-3059, E-mail: aaron.oosterwyk@northwestu.edu.
Website: http://www.northwestu.edu/business/.

Norwich University, College of Graduate and Continuing Studies, Master of Arts in Diplomacy Program, Northfield, VT 05663. Offers international commerce (MA); international conflict management (MA); international terrorism (MA). Evening/weekend programs available. Postbaccalaureate distance learning degree programs offered (minimal on-campus study). *Faculty:* 19 part-time/adjunct (2 women). *Students:* 212 full-time (52 women); includes 55 minority (34 Black or African American, non-Hispanic/Latino; 1 American Indian or Alaska Native, non-Hispanic/Latino; 7 Asian, non-Hispanic/Latino; 6 Hispanic/Latino; 1 Native Hawaiian or other Pacific Islander, non-Hispanic/Latino; 6 Two or more races, non-Hispanic/Latino). Average age 36. 291 applicants, 34% accepted, 96 enrolled. In 2013, 125 master's awarded. *Degree requirements:* For master's, comprehensive exam, thesis optional. *Entrance requirements:* For master's, minimum undergraduate GPA of 2.75. Additional exam requirements/recommendations for international students: Required—TOEFL (minimum score 600 paper-based; 94 iBT). *Application deadline:* For fall admission, 8/1 for domestic and international students; for winter admission, 11/1 for domestic and international students; for spring admission, 2/1 for domestic and international students; for summer admission, 5/1 for domestic and international students. Applications are processed on a rolling basis. Application fee: $50. Electronic applications accepted. *Expenses:* Contact institution. *Financial support:* In 2013–14, 89 students received support. Scholarships/grants available. Financial award applicants required to submit FAFSA. *Unit head:* Dr. Lasha Tchantouridze, Program Director, 802-485-2095, Fax: 802-485-2533, E-mail: ltchanto@norwich.edu. *Application contact:* Fianna Verret, Associate Program Director, 802-485-2783, Fax: 802-485-2533, E-mail: fverret@norwich.edu.
Website: http://online.norwich.edu/degree-programs/masters/master-arts-diplomacy/overview.

Nova Southeastern University, H. Wayne Huizenga School of Business and Entrepreneurship, Fort Lauderdale, FL 33314-7796. Offers accounting (M Acc); business administration (MBA, DBA); human resource management (MSHRM); international business administration (MIBA); leadership (MS); public administration (MPA, DPA); real estate development (MS); taxation (M Tax); JD/MBA; Pharm D/MBA. Part-time and evening/weekend programs available. Postbaccalaureate distance learning degree programs offered (minimal on-campus study). *Faculty:* 67 full-time (24 women), 135 part-time/adjunct (37 women). *Students:* 207 full-time (110 women), 3,069 part-time (1,888 women); includes 2,213 minority (1,077 Black or African American, non-Hispanic/Latino; 2 American Indian or Alaska Native, non-Hispanic/Latino; 108 Asian, non-Hispanic/Latino; 975 Hispanic/Latino; 2 Native Hawaiian or other Pacific Islander, non-Hispanic/Latino; 49 Two or more races, non-Hispanic/Latino), 190 international. Average age 33. 1,291 applicants, 68% accepted, 636 enrolled. In 2013, 1,146 master's, 17 doctorates awarded. *Degree requirements:* For master's, thesis optional; for doctorate, comprehensive exam, thesis/dissertation. *Entrance requirements:* For doctorate, GMAT. Additional exam requirements/recommendations for international students: Required—TOEFL (minimum score 550 paper-based; 79 iBT), IELTS (minimum score 6). *Application deadline:* Applications are processed on a rolling basis. Application fee: $50. Electronic applications accepted. *Financial support:* In 2013–14, 2 students received support. Federal Work-Study and scholarships/grants available. Support available to part-time students. Financial award applicants required to submit FAFSA. *Faculty research:* Reputation management, call centers, international social capital, corporate earnings guidance, corporate governance. *Unit head:* Dr. J. Preston Jones, Dean, 954-262-5127, E-mail: fieldsm@nova.edu. *Application contact:* Karen Goldberg, Associate Director of Recruitment and Special Events, 954-262-5039, Fax: 954-262-3822, E-mail: karen@nova.edu.
Website: http://www.huizenga.nova.edu.

Oakland University, Graduate Study and Lifelong Learning, School of Business Administration, Department of Management and Marketing, Rochester, MI 48309-4401. Offers business administration (MBA); entrepreneurship (Certificate); general management (Certificate); human resource management (Certificate); international business (Certificate); marketing (Certificate). *Faculty:* 11 full-time (4 women), 2 part-time/adjunct (both women). *Students:* 72 full-time (28 women), 232 part-time (63 women); includes 51 minority (17 Black or African American, non-Hispanic/Latino; 2 American Indian or Alaska Native, non-Hispanic/Latino; 25 Asian, non-Hispanic/Latino; 7 Hispanic/Latino), 25 international. Average age 32. 238 applicants, 43% accepted, 88 enrolled. In 2013, 144 master's, 4 other advanced degrees awarded. Application fee: $0. *Unit head:* Ravi Parameswaran, Chair, 238-370-3279, Fax: 249-370-4275. *Application contact:* Donna Free, Coordinator, 248-370-3281.

Oklahoma Christian University, Graduate School of Business, Oklahoma City, OK 73136-1100. Offers accounting (MBA); electronic business (MBA); financial services (MBA); health services management (MBA); human resources (MBA); international business (MBA); leadership and organizational development (MBA); marketing (MBA); project management (MBA). Postbaccalaureate distance learning degree programs offered (no on-campus study). *Entrance requirements:* For master's, bachelor's degree. Electronic applications accepted.

Old Dominion University, College of Business and Public Administration, MBA Program, Norfolk, VA 23529. Offers business and economic forecasting (MBA); financial analysis and valuation (MBA); health sciences administration (MBA); information technology and enterprise integration (MBA); international business (MBA); maritime and port management (MBA); public administration (MBA). *Accreditation:* AACSB. Part-time and evening/weekend programs available. Postbaccalaureate distance learning degree programs offered (no on-campus study). *Faculty:* 83 full-time (19 women), 5 part-time/adjunct (2 women). *Students:* 42 full-time (20 women), 103 part-time (42 women); includes 18 minority (8 Black or African American, non-Hispanic/Latino; 4 Asian, non-Hispanic/Latino; 1 Hispanic/Latino; 1 Native Hawaiian or other Pacific Islander, non-Hispanic/Latino; 4 Two or more races, non-Hispanic/Latino), 16 international. Average age 30. 161 applicants, 71% accepted, 75 enrolled. In 2013, 61 master's awarded. *Entrance requirements:* For master's, GMAT, GRE, letter of reference, resume, essay. Additional exam requirements/recommendations for international students: Required—TOEFL (minimum score 550 paper-based; 80 iBT). *Application deadline:* For fall admission, 6/1 priority date for domestic students, 4/15 priority date for international students; for spring admission, 11/1 priority date for domestic students, 10/1 priority date for international students. Applications are processed on a rolling basis. Application fee: $50. Electronic applications accepted. *Expenses:* Tuition, state resident: full-time $9888; part-time $412 per credit. Tuition, nonresident: full-time $25,152; part-time $1048 per credit. *Required fees:* $59 per semester. One-time fee: $50. *Financial support:* In 2013–14, 47 students received support, including 94 research assistantships with partial tuition reimbursements available (averaging $8,900 per year); career-related internships or fieldwork, scholarships/grants, and unspecified assistantships also available. Support available to part-time students. Financial award application deadline: 2/15; financial award applicants required to submit FAFSA. *Faculty research:* International business, buyer behavior, financial markets, strategy, operations research, maritime and transportation economics. *Unit head:* Dr. Kiran Karaude, Graduate Program Director, 757-683-3585, Fax: 757-683-5750, E-mail: mbainfo@odu.edu. *Application contact:* Sandi Phillips, MBA Program Assistant, 757-683-3585, Fax: 757-683-5750, E-mail: mbainfo@odu.edu.
Website: http://www.odu.edu/mba/.

Oral Roberts University, School of Business, Tulsa, OK 74171. Offers accounting (MBA); entrepreneurship (MBA); finance (MBA); international business (MBA); management (MBA); marketing (MBA); non-profit management (MBA); not for profit management (MNM). *Accreditation:* ACBSP. Part-time programs available. Postbaccalaureate distance learning degree programs offered (minimal on-campus study). *Degree requirements:* For master's, thesis optional. *Entrance requirements:* For master's, minimum cumulative GPA of 3.0. Additional exam requirements/recommendations for international students: Required—TOEFL (minimum score 550 paper-based; 79 iBT). Electronic applications accepted. *Faculty research:* Social media, international business and marketing.

Pace University, Lubin School of Business, International Business Program, New York, NY 10038. Offers MBA. Part-time and evening/weekend programs available. *Students:* 10 full-time (4 women), 28 part-time (16 women); includes 15 minority (5 Black or African American, non-Hispanic/Latino; 8 Asian, non-Hispanic/Latino; 2 Hispanic/Latino), 16 international. Average age 26. 83 applicants, 23% accepted, 12 enrolled. In 2013, 13 master's awarded. *Entrance requirements:* For master's, GMAT, GRE. Additional exam requirements/recommendations for international students: Required—TOEFL. *Application deadline:* For fall admission, 8/1 priority date for domestic students, 6/1 for international students; for spring admission, 12/1 for domestic students, 10/1 for international students. Applications are processed on a rolling basis. Application fee: $70. Electronic applications accepted. *Expenses: Tuition:* Part-time $1075 per credit. *Required fees:* $192 per semester. Tuition and fees vary according to course load, degree level and program. *Financial support:* Research assistantships, career-related internships or fieldwork, and Federal Work-Study available. Support available to part-time students. Financial award applicants required to submit FAFSA. *Unit head:* Dr. Alvin Hwang, Chairperson, 212-618-6573, E-mail: ahwang@pace.edu. *Application contact:* Susan Ford-Goldschein, Director of Graduate Admissions, 212-346-1531, Fax: 212-346-1585, E-mail: gradnyc@pace.edu.
Website: http://www.pace.edu/lubin.

Pacific States University, College of Business, Los Angeles, CA 90006. Offers accounting (MBA); finance (MBA); international business (MBA, DBA); management of information technology (MBA); real estate management (MBA). Part-time and evening/weekend programs available. Postbaccalaureate distance learning degree programs offered (no on-campus study). *Degree requirements:* For doctorate, comprehensive exam, thesis/dissertation. *Entrance requirements:* For master's, minimum undergraduate GPA of 2.5 during last 90 hours of course work. Additional exam requirements/recommendations for international students: Required—TOEFL (minimum score 500 paper-based; 61 iBT), IELTS (minimum score 5.5).

Park University, School of Graduate and Professional Studies, Kansas City, MO 54105. Offers adult education (M Ed); business and government leadership (Graduate Certificate); business, government, and global society (MPA); communication and leadership (MA); creative and life writing (Graduate Certificate); disaster and emergency management (MPA, Graduate Certificate); educational leadership (M Ed); finance (MBA, Graduate Certificate); general business (MBA); global business (Graduate Certificate); healthcare administration (MHA); healthcare services management and leadership (Graduate Certificate); international business (MBA); language and literacy (M Ed), including English for speakers of other languages, special reading teacher/literacy coach; leadership of international healthcare organizations (Graduate Certificate); management information systems (MBA, Graduate Certificate); music performance (ADP, Graduate Certificate), including cello (MM, ADP), piano (MM, ADP), viola (MM, ADP), violin (MM, ADP); nonprofit and community services management (MPA); nonprofit leadership (Graduate Certificate); performance (MM), including cello (MM, ADP), piano (MM, ADP), viola (MM, ADP), violin (MM, ADP); public management (MPA); social work (MSW); teacher leadership (M Ed), including curriculum and assessment, instructional leader. Part-time and evening/weekend programs available. Postbaccalaureate distance learning degree programs offered (no on-campus study). *Students:* 862 full-time (482 women); includes 55 minority (30 Black or African American, non-Hispanic/Latino; 2 American Indian or Alaska Native, non-Hispanic/Latino; 4 Asian, non-Hispanic/Latino; 14 Hispanic/Latino; 5 Two or more races, non-Hispanic/Latino), 141 international. Average age 34. 497 applicants, 62% accepted, 119 enrolled. In 2013, 281 master's, 14 other advanced degrees awarded. *Degree requirements:* For master's, comprehensive exam (for some programs), thesis (for some programs), internship (for some programs); exam (for some programs). *Entrance requirements:* For master's, GRE or GMAT (for some programs), teacher certification (for some M Ed programs), letters of recommendation, essay, resume (for some programs). Additional exam requirements/recommendations for international students: Required—TOEFL (minimum score 550 paper-based; 79 iBT), IELTS (minimum score 6). *Application deadline:* For fall admission, 8/1 priority date for domestic students, 7/15 priority date for international students; for spring admission, 1/1 priority date for domestic students, 11/1 priority date for international students. Applications are processed on a rolling basis. Application fee: $50 ($100 for international students). Electronic applications accepted. *Financial support:* In 2013–14, 2 research assistantships with full tuition reimbursements (averaging $15,760 per year) were awarded. Financial award applicants required to submit FAFSA. *Unit head:* Dr. Laurie Dipadova-Stocks, Dean of Graduate and Professional Studies, 816-559-5624, Fax: 816-472-1173, E-mail: ldipadovastocks@park.edu. *Application contact:* Judith Appollis, Director of Graduate

International Business

Admissions and Internationalization, School of Graduate and Professional Studies, 816-559-5627, Fax: 816-472-1173, E-mail: gradschool@park.edu. Website: http://www.park.edu/grad.

Pepperdine University, Graziadio School of Business and Management, International MBA Program, Malibu, CA 90263. Offers IMBA. *Students:* 9 full-time (7 women); includes 3 minority (1 Black or African American, non-Hispanic/Latino; 2 Asian, non-Hispanic/Latino), 1 international. *Entrance requirements:* For master's, GMAT or GRE, two letters of recommendation. Additional exam requirements/recommendations for international students: Required—TOEFL. *Application deadline:* For fall admission, 5/1 for domestic students, 4/1 for international students. Application fee: $75. Electronic applications accepted. Tuition and fees vary according to program. *Unit head:* Dr. Linda A. Livingstone, Dean, Graziadio School of Business and Management, 310-568-5689, Fax: 310-568-5766, E-mail: linda.livingstone@pepperdine.edu. *Application contact:* Darrell Eriksen, Director of Admission and Student Accounts, Graziadio School of Business and Management, 310-568-5525, E-mail: darrell.eriksen@pepperdine.edu. Website: http://bschool.pepperdine.edu/programs/international-mba/.

Pepperdine University, Graziadio School of Business and Management, MS in Global Business Program, Malibu, CA 90263. Offers MS. *Students:* 72 full-time (46 women); includes 1 minority (Black or African American, non-Hispanic/Latino), 68 international. *Entrance requirements:* For master's, GMAT or GRE, two letters of recommendation. Additional exam requirements/recommendations for international students: Required—TOEFL. *Application deadline:* For fall admission, 5/1 for domestic students. Application fee: $75. Tuition and fees vary according to program. *Unit head:* Dr. Linda A. Livingstone, Dean, Graziadio School of Business and Management, 310-568-5689, Fax: 310-568-5766, E-mail: linda.livingstone@pepperdine.edu. *Application contact:* Darrell Eriksen, Director of Admission and Student Accounts, Graziadio School of Business and Management, 310-568-5525, E-mail: darrell.eriksen@pepperdine.edu. Website: http://bschool.pepperdine.edu/programs/masters-global-business/.

Polytechnic University of Puerto Rico, Graduate School, Hato Rey, PR 00919. Offers business administration (MBA), including computer information systems, general management, management of information systems, management of international enterprises; civil engineering (ME, MS); computer engineering (ME, MS); computer science (MCS, MS); electrical engineering (ME, MS); engineering management (MEM); environmental management (MEM); landscape architecture (M Land Arch); manufacturing competitiveness (MMC, MS); manufacturing engineering (ME, MS); mechanical engineering (M Mech E). Part-time and evening/weekend programs available. *Entrance requirements:* For master's, 3 letters of recommendation.

Polytechnic University of Puerto Rico, Miami Campus, Graduate School, Miami, FL 33166. Offers accounting (MBA); business administration (MBA); construction management (MEM); environmental management (MEM); finance (MBA); human resources management (MBA); logistics and supply chain management (MBA); management of international enterprises (MBA); manufacturing management (MEM); marketing management (MBA); project management (MBA). Part-time and evening/weekend programs available. Postbaccalaureate distance learning degree programs offered (no on-campus study). *Entrance requirements:* For master's, minimum GPA of 3.0. Electronic applications accepted.

Polytechnic University of Puerto Rico, Orlando Campus, Graduate School, Winter Park, FL 32792. Offers accounting (MBA); business administration (MBA); construction management (MEM); engineering management (MEM); environmental management (MEM); finance (MBA); human resources management (MBA); management of international enterprises (MBA); management of technology (MBA); manufacturing management (MEM). Part-time and evening/weekend programs available. Postbaccalaureate distance learning degree programs offered (no on-campus study). *Entrance requirements:* For master's, minimum GPA of 3.0. Additional exam requirements/recommendations for international students: Recommended—TOEFL. Electronic applications accepted.

Pontifical Catholic University of Puerto Rico, College of Business Administration, Program in International Business, Ponce, PR 00717-0777. Offers MBA. Part-time and evening/weekend programs available. *Entrance requirements:* For master's, GRE, interview, minimum GPA of 2.75.

Pontificia Universidad Catolica Madre y Maestra, Graduate School, Faculty of Social and Administrative Sciences, Santiago, Dominican Republic. Offers business administration (MBA), including business development, finance, international business, management skills (M Mgmt, MBA), marketing, operations, strategic cost management, strategy, tourist destination planning and management; law (LL M), including civil law, corporate business law, criminal law, international relations, real estate law; management (M Mgmt), including higher financial management, insurance program administration, management skills (M Mgmt, MBA); psychology (MA), including clinical child and adolescent psychology, forensic psychology; strategic human resources (EMBA).

Portland State University, Graduate Studies, School of Business Administration, Program in International Management, Portland, OR 97207-0751. Offers MIM. Part-time and evening/weekend programs available. *Students:* 85 full-time (41 women), 2 part-time (1 woman); includes 11 minority (2 Black or African American, non-Hispanic/Latino; 1 American Indian or Alaska Native, non-Hispanic/Latino; 3 Asian, non-Hispanic/Latino; 4 Hispanic/Latino; 1 Two or more races, non-Hispanic/Latino), 49 international. Average age 28. 50 applicants, 46% accepted, 15 enrolled. In 2013, 40 master's awarded. *Degree requirements:* For master's, field study trip to China and Japan. *Entrance requirements:* For master's, GMAT, GRE General Test, minimum GPA of 2.75, resume, 2 letters of recommendation. Additional exam requirements/recommendations for international students: Required—TOEFL (minimum score 550 paper-based). *Application deadline:* For fall admission, 4/30 priority date for domestic students, 3/1 priority date for international students. Applications are processed on a rolling basis. Application fee: $50. *Expenses:* Tuition: state resident: full-time $9207; part-time $341 per credit. Tuition, nonresident: full-time $14,391; part-time $533 per credit. *Required fees:* $1263; $22 per credit. $98 per quarter. One-time fee: $150. Tuition and fees vary according to program. *Financial support:* Research assistantships with tuition reimbursements, teaching assistantships, career-related internships or fieldwork, Federal Work-Study, and institutionally sponsored loans available. Support available to part-time students. Financial award application deadline: 3/1; financial award applicants required to submit FAFSA. *Total annual research expenditures:* $43,877. *Unit head:* Cliff Allen, Director, 503-725-5053, Fax: 503-725-2290, E-mail: cliffa@sba.pdx.edu. *Application contact:* 503-725-3712, E-mail: info@sba.pdx.edu. Website: http://www.mim.pdx.edu/.

Providence College, School of Business, Providence, RI 02918. Offers accounting (MBA); finance (MBA); international business (MBA); management (MBA); marketing (MBA); not-for-profit organizations (MBA). Part-time and evening/weekend programs available. *Faculty:* 14 full-time (5 women), 3 part-time/adjunct (1 woman). *Students:* 68 full-time (25 women), 54 part-time (25 women); includes 12 minority (3 Black or African American, non-Hispanic/Latino; 1 Asian, non-Hispanic/Latino; 6 Hispanic/Latino; 2 Two or more races, non-Hispanic/Latino), 7 international. Average age 25. 43 applicants, 95% accepted, 36 enrolled. In 2013, 38 master's awarded. *Degree requirements:* For

master's, thesis optional. *Entrance requirements:* For master's, GMAT. Additional exam requirements/recommendations for international students: Required—TOEFL (minimum score 550 paper-based; 80 iBT). *Application deadline:* For fall admission, 7/15 priority date for domestic and international students; for spring admission, 11/15 priority date for domestic and international students; for summer admission, 4/15 priority date for domestic students. Applications are processed on a rolling basis. Application fee: $55. *Expenses:* Contact institution. *Financial support:* Federal Work-Study, institutionally sponsored loans, and unspecified assistantships available. Support available to part-time students. Financial award application deadline: 8/1; financial award applicants required to submit FAFSA. *Unit head:* Jacqueline Elcik, Director, 401-865-2131, E-mail: jelcik@providence.edu. *Application contact:* MBA Program, 401-865-2294, E-mail: mba@providence.edu. Website: http://www.providence.edu/business/Pages/default.aspx.

Purdue University, Graduate School, Krannert School of Management, International Master's in Management Program, West Lafayette, IN 47907. Offers MBA. *Entrance requirements:* For master's, letters of recommendation, essays, transcripts, resume. Electronic applications accepted. *Faculty research:* Dimensions of trust, communities of practice and networks, business in Latin America.

Regent's University London, Webster Graduate School, London, United Kingdom. Offers business (MBA); finance (MS); human resources (MA); information technology management (MA); international business (MA); international non-governmental organizations (MA); international relations (MA); management and leadership (MA); marketing (MA). Part-time programs available.

Rochester Institute of Technology, Graduate Enrollment Services, Saunders College of Business, Program in Management, Rochester, NY 14623-5603. Offers MS. Part-time programs available. *Students:* 4 full-time (3 women), 2 part-time (0 women), 4 international. Average age 25. 40 applicants, 18% accepted, 3 enrolled. In 2013, 10 master's awarded. *Degree requirements:* For master's, comprehensive exam (for some programs), thesis (for some programs). *Entrance requirements:* For master's, GMAT or GRE. Additional exam requirements/recommendations for international students: Required—TOEFL (minimum score 580 paper-based; 92 iBT), IELTS (minimum score 7), or PTE (minimum score 61). *Application deadline:* For fall admission, 2/15 for domestic and international students; for winter admission, 11/1 for domestic students, 10/1 for international students; for spring admission, 2/1 for domestic students, 1/1 for international students. Applications are processed on a rolling basis. Application fee: $60. Electronic applications accepted. *Expenses: Tuition:* Full-time $37,236; part-time $1552 per credit hour. *Required fees:* $250. *Financial support:* Research assistantships with partial tuition reimbursements, teaching assistantships with partial tuition reimbursements, career-related internships or fieldwork, scholarships/grants, and unspecified assistantships available. Support available to part-time students. Financial award applicants required to submit FAFSA. *Faculty research:* Strategic and managerial issues associated with manufacturing and production systems, total quality management (TQM), technology-based entrepreneurship. *Unit head:* Charles Ackley, Graduate Program Director, 585-475-6916, E-mail: cackley@saunders.rit.edu. *Application contact:* Diane Ellison, Assistant Vice President, Graduate Enrollment Services, 585-475-2229, Fax: 585-475-7164, E-mail: gradinfo@rit.edu. Website: http://saunders.rit.edu/graduate/index.php.

Rollins College, Crummer Graduate School of Business, Winter Park, FL 32789-4499. Offers business administration (EDBA); entrepreneurship (MBA); finance (MBA); international business (MBA); management (MBA); marketing (MBA); operations and technology management (MBA). *Accreditation:* AACSB. Part-time and evening/weekend programs available. Postbaccalaureate distance learning degree programs offered (minimal on-campus study). *Faculty:* 21 full-time (3 women), 2 part-time/adjunct (1 woman). *Students:* 157 full-time (86 women), 135 part-time (83 women); includes 60 minority (12 Black or African American, non-Hispanic/Latino; 1 American Indian or Alaska Native, non-Hispanic/Latino; 17 Asian, non-Hispanic/Latino; 23 Hispanic/Latino; 1 Native Hawaiian or other Pacific Islander, non-Hispanic/Latino; 6 Two or more races, non-Hispanic/Latino), 19 international. Average age 37. 264 applicants, 53% accepted, 105 enrolled. In 2013, 169 master's awarded. *Degree requirements:* For master's, minimum GPA of 2.85; for doctorate, thesis/dissertation, minimum GPA of 3.0. *Entrance requirements:* For master's, GMAT or GRE, official transcripts, two letters of recommendation, essay, current resume/curriculum vitae, interview; for doctorate, official transcripts, two letters of recommendation, essays, current resume/curriculum vitae, interview with EDBA academic committee. Additional exam requirements/recommendations for international students: Required—TOEFL (minimum score 100 iBT) or IELTS (minimum score 7). *Application deadline:* Applications are processed on a rolling basis. Application fee: $50. Electronic applications accepted. *Expenses:* Contact institution. *Financial support:* In 2013–14, 87 students received support. Federal Work-Study and scholarships/grants available. Support available to part-time students. Financial award applicants required to submit FAFSA. *Faculty research:* Sustainability, world financial markets, international business, market research, strategic marketing. *Unit head:* Dr. Craig M. McAllaster, Dean, 407-646-2249, Fax: 407-646-1550, E-mail: cmcallaster@rollins.edu. *Application contact:* Eva Gauthier Oleksiw, Admissions Coordinator, 407-646-2405, Fax: 407-646-1550, E-mail: mbaadmissions@rollins.edu. Website: http://www.rollins.edu/mba/.

Roosevelt University, Graduate Division, Walter E. Heller College of Business Administration, Program in International Business, Chicago, IL 60605. Offers MSIB. Part-time and evening/weekend programs available. *Degree requirements:* For master's, one foreign language. *Entrance requirements:* For master's, GMAT.

Rutgers, The State University of New Jersey, Newark, Graduate School, Program in Management, Newark, NJ 07102. Offers accounting (PhD); accounting information systems (PhD); computer information systems (PhD); finance (PhD); information technology (PhD); international business (PhD); management science (PhD); marketing (PhD); organization management (PhD). Program offered jointly with New Jersey Institute of Technology. *Accreditation:* AACSB. *Degree requirements:* For doctorate, thesis/dissertation, cumulative exams. *Entrance requirements:* For doctorate, GMAT or GRE General Test, minimum undergraduate B average. Additional exam requirements/recommendations for international students: Required—TOEFL. Electronic applications accepted. *Faculty research:* Technology management, leadership and teams, consumer behavior, financial and markets, logistics.

Rutgers, The State University of New Jersey, Newark, Rutgers Business School–Newark and New Brunswick, Doctoral Programs in Management, Newark, NJ 07102. Offers accounting (PhD); accounting information systems (PhD); economics (PhD); finance (PhD); individualized study (PhD); information technology (PhD); international business (PhD); management science (PhD); marketing science (PhD); organizational management (PhD); science, technology and management (PhD); supply chain management (PhD). *Degree requirements:* For doctorate, comprehensive exam, thesis/dissertation. *Entrance requirements:* For doctorate, GRE or GMAT. Additional exam requirements/recommendations for international students: Required—TOEFL (minimum score 550 paper-based; 79 iBT). Electronic applications accepted.

Sacred Heart University, Graduate Programs, John F. Welch College of Business, Department of Management, Fairfield, CT 06825-1000. Offers accounting (Certificate);

business (MBA); human resource management (MS); international business (Certificate); leadership (Certificate); marketing (Certificate). *Faculty:* 6 full-time (3 women), 2 part-time/adjunct (both women). *Students:* 24 full-time (9 women), 141 part-time (81 women); includes 29 minority (11 Black or African American, non-Hispanic/Latino; 5 Asian, non-Hispanic/Latino; 13 Hispanic/Latino), 4 international. Average age 32. 14 applicants, 79% accepted, 9 enrolled. In 2013, 81 master's awarded. *Entrance requirements:* For master's, GMAT (minimum score of 400), bachelor's degree in related field of business, microeconomics, macroeconomics or statistics; minimum GPA of 3.0. Additional exam requirements/recommendations for international students: Required—PTE; Recommended—TOEFL (minimum score 570 paper-based; 80 iBT), IELTS (minimum score 6.5). *Application deadline:* Applications are processed on a rolling basis. Application fee: $60. Electronic applications accepted. *Expenses: Tuition:* Full-time $22,775; part-time $617 per credit. *Financial support:* Applicants required to submit FAFSA. *Unit head:* Dr. John Chalykoff, Dean, 203-396-8084, E-mail: chalykoffj@sacredheart.edu. *Application contact:* Kathy Dilks, Executive Director of Graduate Admissions, 203-365-7619, Fax: 203-365-4732, E-mail: dilksk@sacredheart.edu.
Website: http://www.sacredheart.edu/academics/johnfwelchcollegeofbusiness/.

St. Edward's University, School of Management and Business, Area of Business Administration, Austin, TX 78704. Offers accounting (MBA); business management (MBA); finance (Certificate); global entrepreneurship (MBA); marketing (MBA). Part-time and evening/weekend programs available. *Students:* 29 full-time (12 women), 181 part-time (85 women); includes 88 minority (15 Black or African American, non-Hispanic/Latino; 1 American Indian or Alaska Native, non-Hispanic/Latino; 4 Asian, non-Hispanic/Latino; 61 Hispanic/Latino; 7 Two or more races, non-Hispanic/Latino), 10 international. Average age 33. 85 applicants, 79% accepted, 38 enrolled. In 2013, 79 master's awarded. *Degree requirements:* For master's, minimum of 24 resident hours. *Entrance requirements:* For master's, GMAT or GRE General Test, minimum GPA of 2.75 in last 60 hours of course work. Additional exam requirements/recommendations for international students: Required—TOEFL (minimum score 79 iBT) or IELTS (minimum score 6). *Application deadline:* For fall admission, 6/1 priority date for domestic and international students; for spring admission, 10/1 priority date for domestic and international students; for summer admission, 3/1 priority date for domestic and international students. Applications are processed on a rolling basis. Application fee: $50. Electronic applications accepted. *Expenses: Tuition:* Full-time $20,664; part-time $1148 per credit hour. *Required fees:* $50 per trimester. Full-time tuition and fees vary according to course load and program. *Unit head:* Dr. Stan Horner, Director, 512-428-1279, Fax: 512-448-8492, E-mail: stanleyh@stedwards.edu. *Application contact:* Office of Admission, 512-448-8500, Fax: 512-464-8877, E-mail: seu.admit@stedwards.edu.
Website: http://www.stedwards.edu.

St. John's University, The Peter J. Tobin College of Business, Program in International Business, Queens, NY 11439. Offers MBA, Adv C. Part-time and evening/weekend programs available. *Students:* 27 full-time (18 women), 11 part-time (4 women); includes 10 minority (3 Black or African American, non-Hispanic/Latino; 3 Asian, non-Hispanic/Latino; 4 Hispanic/Latino), 15 international. Average age 27. 38 applicants, 76% accepted, 15 enrolled. In 2013, 10 master's awarded. *Degree requirements:* For master's, comprehensive exam (for some programs), thesis optional. *Entrance requirements:* For master's, GMAT, 2 letters of recommendation, resume, transcripts, essay; for Adv C, 2 letters of recommendation, resume, undergraduate and graduate transcripts, essay, MBA. Additional exam requirements/recommendations for international students: Required—TOEFL (minimum score 600 paper-based; 100 iBT), IELTS (minimum score 7). *Application deadline:* For fall admission, 5/1 priority date for domestic and international students; for spring admission, 11/1 priority date for domestic and international students. Applications are processed on a rolling basis. Application fee: $50. Electronic applications accepted. *Expenses:* Contact institution. *Financial support:* Research assistantships, scholarships/grants, and unspecified assistantships available. Support available to part-time students. Financial award application deadline: 3/1; financial award applicants required to submit FAFSA. *Unit head:* Dr. Victoria L. Shoaf, Dean, 718-990-6800, E-mail: shoafv@stjohns.edu. *Application contact:* Carol J. Swanberg, Assistant Dean/Director of Graduate Admissions, 718-990-1345, Fax: 718-990-5242, E-mail: tobingradnyc@stjohns.edu.

Saint Joseph's University, Erivan K. Haub School of Business, MS Program in International Marketing, Philadelphia, PA 19131-1395. Offers MS. Part-time and evening/weekend programs available. *Students:* 45 full-time (29 women), 15 part-time (6 women); includes 1 minority (Black or African American, non-Hispanic/Latino), 50 international. Average age 25. In 2013, 32 master's awarded. *Degree requirements:* For master's, minimum GPA of 3.0. *Entrance requirements:* For master's, GMAT or GRE, 2 letters of recommendation, resume, personal statement, official undergraduate and graduate transcripts. Additional exam requirements/recommendations for international students: Required—TOEFL (minimum score 550 paper-based, 80 iBT), IELTS (minimum score 6.5), or PTE (minimum score 60). *Application deadline:* For fall admission, 7/15 priority date for domestic students, 5/15 priority date for international students; for spring admission, 11/15 priority date for domestic students, 10/15 priority date for international students; for summer admission, 4/15 priority date for domestic students. Applications are processed on a rolling basis. Application fee: $35. Electronic applications accepted. *Expenses: Tuition:* Part-time $786 per credit hour. Tuition and fees vary according to degree level and program. *Financial support:* In 2013–14, 1 research assistantship with partial tuition reimbursement (averaging $8,000 per year) was awarded; scholarships/grants and unspecified assistantships also available. Support available to part-time students. Financial award application deadline: 5/1; financial award applicants required to submit FAFSA. *Faculty research:* Export marketing, global marketing, international marketing research, new product development, emerging markets, international consumer behavior. *Unit head:* David Benglian, Director, 610-660-1626, Fax: 610-660-1599, E-mail: david.benglian@sju.edu. *Application contact:* Karena Whitmore, Administrative Assistant, MS Programs, 610-660-3211, Fax: 610-660-1599, E-mail: kwhitmor@sju.edu.
Website: http://www.sju.edu/academics/hsb/grad/mim/.

Saint Joseph's University, Erivan K. Haub School of Business, Professional MBA Program, Philadelphia, PA 19131-1395. Offers accounting (MBA, Postbaccalaureate Certificate); business intelligence (MBA); finance (MBA); general business (MBA); health and medical services administration (MBA); international business (MBA); international marketing (MBA); managing human capital (MBA); marketing (MBA); DO/MBA. DO/MBA offered jointly with Philadelphia College of Osteopathic Medicine. Part-time and evening/weekend programs available. *Students:* 81 full-time (37 women), 478 part-time (195 women); includes 85 minority (35 Black or African American, non-Hispanic/Latino; 1 American Indian or Alaska Native, non-Hispanic/Latino; 23 Asian, non-Hispanic/Latino; 13 Hispanic/Latino; 1 Native Hawaiian or other Pacific Islander, non-Hispanic/Latino; 12 Two or more races, non-Hispanic/Latino), 44 international. Average age 30. In 2013, 195 master's awarded. *Degree requirements:* For master's and Postbaccalaureate Certificate, minimum GPA of 3.0. *Entrance requirements:* For master's, GMAT or GRE, 2 letters of recommendation, resume, personal statement, official undergraduate and graduate transcripts; for Postbaccalaureate Certificate, official master's-level transcripts. Additional exam requirements/recommendations for international students: Required—TOEFL (minimum score 550 paper-based, 80 iBT), IELTS (minimum score 6.5), or PTE (minimum score 60). *Application deadline:* For fall admission, 7/15 priority date for domestic students, 5/15 priority date for international students; for spring admission, 11/15 priority date for domestic students, 10/15 priority date for international students; for summer admission, 4/15 priority date for domestic students, 2/15 priority date for international students. Applications are processed on a rolling basis. Application fee: $35. Electronic applications accepted. *Expenses: Tuition:* Part-time $786 per credit hour. Tuition and fees vary according to degree level and program. *Financial support:* In 2013–14, 2 research assistantships with partial tuition reimbursements (averaging $4,000 per year) were awarded; scholarships/grants and unspecified assistantships also available. Support available to part-time students. Financial award application deadline: 5/1; financial award applicants required to submit FAFSA. *Unit head:* Christine Hartmann, Director, MBA Program, 610-660-1659, Fax: 610-660-1599, E-mail: chartman@sju.edu. *Application contact:* Jeannine Lajeunesse, Assistant Director, MBA Program, 610-660-1695, Fax: 610-660-1599, E-mail: jlajeune@sju.edu.
Website: http://www.sju.edu/haubmba.

Saint Louis University, Graduate Education, John Cook School of Business, Boeing Institute of International Business, St. Louis, MO 63103-2097. Offers business administration (PhD), including international business and marketing; executive international business (EMIB); international business (MBA). Part-time and evening/weekend programs available. *Degree requirements:* For master's, thesis, study abroad; for doctorate, comprehensive exam, thesis/dissertation. *Entrance requirements:* For master's, GMAT, work experience. Additional exam requirements/recommendations for international students: Required—TOEFL (minimum score 525 paper-based). *Expenses:* Contact institution. *Faculty research:* Foreign direct investment, technology transfer, emerging markets, Asian business, Latin American business.

St. Mary's University, Graduate School, Bill Greehey School of Business, MBA Program, San Antonio, TX 78228-8507. Offers finance (MBA); international business (MBA); management (MBA). Part-time and evening/weekend programs available. Postbaccalaureate distance learning degree programs offered (minimal on-campus study). *Degree requirements:* For master's, comprehensive exam. *Entrance requirements:* For master's, GMAT. Additional exam requirements/recommendations for international students: Required—TOEFL (minimum score 570 paper-based; 80 iBT).

Saint Mary's University of Minnesota, Schools of Graduate and Professional Programs, Graduate School of Business and Technology, International Business Program, Winona, MN 55987-1399. Offers MA. *Unit head:* Dushan Knezevich, Director, 612-728-5156, E-mail: dknezevi@smumn.edu. *Application contact:* Russell Kreager, Director of Admissions for Graduate and Professional Programs, 612-728-5207, E-mail: rkreager@smumn.edu.
Website: http://www.smumn.edu/graduate-home/areas-of-study/graduate-school-of-business-technology/ma-in-international-business-twin-cities.

Saint Peter's University, Graduate Business Programs, MBA Program, Jersey City, NJ 07306-5997. Offers finance (MBA); health care administration (MBA); human resource management (MBA); international business (MBA); management (MBA); management information systems (MBA); marketing (MBA); risk management (MBA); MBA/MS. Part-time and evening/weekend programs available. *Entrance requirements:* Additional exam requirements/recommendations for international students: Required—TOEFL. Electronic applications accepted. *Faculty research:* Finance, health care management, human resource management, international business, management, management information systems, marketing, risk management.

St. Thomas University, School of Business, Department of Management, Miami Gardens, FL 33054-6459. Offers accounting (MBA); general management (MSM, Certificate); health management (MBA, MSM, Certificate); human resource management (MBA, MSM, Certificate); international business (MBA, MIB, MSM, Certificate); justice administration (MSM, Certificate); management accounting (MSM, Certificate); public management (MSM, Certificate); sports administration (MS). Part-time and evening/weekend programs available. *Degree requirements:* For master's, comprehensive exam. *Entrance requirements:* For master's, interview, minimum GPA of 3.0 or GMAT. Additional exam requirements/recommendations for international students: Required—TOEFL (minimum score 550 paper-based; 79 iBT). Electronic applications accepted.

Salem International University, School of Business, Salem, WV 26426-0500. Offers information security (MBA); international business (MBA). Part-time programs available. Postbaccalaureate distance learning degree programs offered (no on-campus study). *Entrance requirements:* For master's, minimum undergraduate GPA of 2.5, course work in business, resume. Additional exam requirements/recommendations for international students: Recommended—TOEFL (minimum score 550 paper-based), IELTS (minimum score 6.5). Electronic applications accepted. *Expenses:* Contact institution. *Faculty research:* Organizational behavior strategy, marketing services.

Schiller International University, MBA Program, Madrid, Spain, Madrid, Spain. Offers international business (MBA). Part-time programs available. *Degree requirements:* For master's, comprehensive exam, thesis optional. *Entrance requirements:* Additional exam requirements/recommendations for international students: Required—TOEFL (minimum score 550 paper-based).

Schiller International University, MBA Program Paris, France, Paris, France. Offers international business (MBA). Bilingual French/English MBA available for native French speakers. Part-time and evening/weekend programs available. Postbaccalaureate distance learning degree programs offered (no on-campus study). *Degree requirements:* For master's, comprehensive exam, thesis or alternative. *Entrance requirements:* Additional exam requirements/recommendations for international students: Required—TOEFL (minimum score 550 paper-based).

Schiller International University, MBA Programs, Florida, Program in International Business, Largo, FL 33771. Offers MBA. Part-time and evening/weekend programs available. Postbaccalaureate distance learning degree programs offered (no on-campus study). *Degree requirements:* For master's, thesis optional. *Entrance requirements:* Additional exam requirements/recommendations for international students: Required—TOEFL (minimum score 550 paper-based).

Schiller International University, MBA Programs, Heidelberg, Germany, Heidelberg, Germany. Offers international business (MBA, MIM); management of information technology (MBA). Part-time and evening/weekend programs available. *Degree requirements:* For master's, thesis optional. *Entrance requirements:* Additional exam requirements/recommendations for international students: Required—TOEFL (minimum score 550 paper-based). *Faculty research:* Leadership, international economy, foreign direct investment.

Seattle University, Albers School of Business and Economics, Master of International Business Program, Seattle, WA 98122-1090. Offers MIB, Certificate, JD/MIB. Part-time and evening/weekend programs available. *Faculty:* 16 full-time (4 women), 1 (woman) part-time/adjunct. *Students:* 1 (woman) full-time, 13 part-time (2 women); includes 5 minority (1 Asian, non-Hispanic/Latino; 4 Hispanic/Latino), 1 international. Average age 39. 9 applicants, 11% accepted. In 2013, 3 master's awarded. *Degree requirements:* For master's, one foreign language, international experience. *Entrance requirements:* For master's, GMAT, minimum GPA of 3.0, 1 year of related work experience. Additional

exam requirements/recommendations for international students: Required—TOEFL. *Application deadline:* For fall admission, 8/20 for domestic students; for winter admission, 11/20 for domestic students; for spring admission, 2/20 for domestic students. Applications are processed on a rolling basis. Application fee: $55. *Financial support:* In 2013–14, 3 students received support. Career-related internships or fieldwork and Federal Work-Study available. Support available to part-time students. Financial award applicants required to submit FAFSA. *Unit head:* Dr. Peter Raven, Director, 206-296-5763, E-mail: pvraven@seattleu.edu. *Application contact:* Janet Shandley, Associate Dean of Graduate Admissions, 206-296-5900, Fax: 206-298-5656, E-mail: grad_admissions@seattleu.edu.

Seton Hall University, Stillman School of Business, Department of International Business, South Orange, NJ 07079-2697. Offers MBA, Certificate. Part-time and evening/weekend programs available. *Faculty:* 6 full-time (1 woman), 1 part-time/adjunct (0 women). *Students:* 3 full-time (all women), 13 part-time (7 women); includes 5 minority (3 Black or African American, non-Hispanic/Latino; 2 Native Hawaiian or other Pacific Islander, non-Hispanic/Latino). Average age 33. 8 applicants, 63% accepted, 5 enrolled. In 2013, 1 master's awarded. *Entrance requirements:* For master's, GMAT, GRE or CPA, advanced degree from AACSB institution, MS in a business discipline, professional degree (MD, JD, PhD, DVM, DDS, etc.), minimum undergraduate GPA of 3.0; for Certificate, master's degree. Additional exam requirements/recommendations for international students: Required—TOEFL (minimum score 102 iBT), IELTS or PTE. *Application deadline:* For fall admission, 5/31 priority date for domestic students, 3/31 priority date for international students; for spring admission, 10/31 priority date for domestic students. Applications are processed on a rolling basis. Application fee: $75. Electronic applications accepted. *Expenses:* Contact institution. *Financial support:* In 2013–14, 1 student received support, including research assistantships with full tuition reimbursements available (averaging $23,956 per year); career-related internships or fieldwork, scholarships/grants, and unspecified assistantships also available. Support available to part-time students. Financial award application deadline: 6/30; financial award applicants required to submit FAFSA. *Faculty research:* International marketing, Asian financial markets, economics in eastern Europe, accounting in the Middle East. *Total annual research expenditures:* $22,000. *Unit head:* Dr. Laurence McCarthy, Director, 973-275-2957, Fax: 973-275-2465, E-mail: laurence.mccarthy@shu.edu. *Application contact:* Catherine Bianchi, Director of Graduate Admissions, 973-761-9262, Fax: 973-761-9208, E-mail: catherine.bianchi@shu.edu.
Website: http://www.shu.edu/academics/business/international-business.

Seton Hall University, Stillman School of Business, Programs in Business Administration, South Orange, NJ 07079-2697. Offers accounting (MBA); finance (MBA); information technology management (MBA); international business (MBA); management (MBA); marketing (MBA); sport management (MBA); supply chain management (MBA). Part-time and evening/weekend programs available. *Faculty:* 32 full-time (6 women), 20 part-time/adjunct (3 women). *Students:* 67 full-time (23 women), 162 part-time (66 women); includes 28 minority (7 Black or African American, non-Hispanic/Latino; 7 Asian, non-Hispanic/Latino; 6 Hispanic/Latino; 8 Native Hawaiian or other Pacific Islander, non-Hispanic/Latino). Average age 31. 216 applicants, 28% accepted, 39 enrolled. In 2013, 139 master's awarded. *Degree requirements:* For master's, 20 hours of community service (Social Responsibility Project). *Entrance requirements:* For master's, GMAT, GRE or CPA, advanced degree from AACSB institution, MS in a business discipline, professional degree (MD, JD, PhD, DVM, DDS, etc.), minimum undergraduate GPA of 3.0. Additional exam requirements/recommendations for international students: Required—TOEFL (minimum score 102 iBT), IELTS or PTE. *Application deadline:* For fall admission, 5/31 priority date for domestic students, 3/31 priority date for international students; for spring admission, 10/31 priority date for domestic students, 9/30 priority date for international students. Applications are processed on a rolling basis. Application fee: $75. Electronic applications accepted. *Financial support:* In 2013–14, research assistantships with full tuition reimbursements (averaging $23,956 per year) were awarded; career-related internships or fieldwork, Federal Work-Study, scholarships/grants, and unspecified assistantships also available. Support available to part-time students. Financial award application deadline: 6/30; financial award applicants required to submit FAFSA. *Faculty research:* Sport, hedge funds, international business, legal issues, disclosure and branding. *Total annual research expenditures:* $68,000. *Unit head:* Dr. Joyce Strawser, Dean, 973-761-9013, Fax: 973-761-9217, E-mail: joyce.strawser@shu.edu. *Application contact:* Catherine Bianchi, Director of Graduate Admissions, 973-761-9262, Fax: 973-761-9208, E-mail: catherine.bianchi@shu.edu.
Website: http://www.shu.edu/academics/business.

SIT Graduate Institute, Graduate Programs, Master's Programs in Intercultural Service, Leadership, and Management, Brattleboro, VT 05302-0676. Offers conflict transformation (MA); intercultural service, leadership, and management (MA); international education (MA); sustainable development (MA). Postbaccalaureate distance learning degree programs offered (minimal on-campus study). *Degree requirements:* For master's, one foreign language, thesis. *Entrance requirements:* For master's, 4 letters of reference. Additional exam requirements/recommendations for international students: Required—TOEFL, IELTS. *Faculty research:* Intercultural communication, conflict resolution, international education, world issues, international affairs.

Sonoma State University, School of Business and Economics, Rohnert Park, CA 94928. Offers business administration (MBA), including contemporary business issues, international business and global issues, leadership and ethics; executive business administration (MBA); wine business (MBA), including contemporary business issues, international business and global issues, leadership and ethics. *Accreditation:* AACSB. Part-time and evening/weekend programs available. *Faculty:* 8 full-time (3 women). *Students:* 45 part-time (20 women); includes 10 minority (3 Black or African American, non-Hispanic/Latino; 2 Asian, non-Hispanic/Latino; 3 Hispanic/Latino; 2 Two or more races, non-Hispanic/Latino). Average age 31. 35 applicants, 83% accepted, 10 enrolled. In 2013, 49 master's awarded. *Degree requirements:* For master's, thesis or alternative. *Entrance requirements:* For master's, GMAT. Additional exam requirements/recommendations for international students: Required—TOEFL (minimum score 500 paper-based). *Application deadline:* For fall admission, 1/31 priority date for domestic students; for spring admission, 8/31 for domestic students. Applications are processed on a rolling basis. Application fee: $55. *Expenses:* Tuition, state resident: full-time $8500. Tuition, nonresident: full-time $12,964. *Required fees:* $1762. *Financial support:* Career-related internships or fieldwork, Federal Work-Study, institutionally sponsored loans, and scholarships/grants available. Support available to part-time students. Financial award application deadline: 3/2; financial award applicants required to submit FAFSA. *Unit head:* Dr. Terry Lease, Department Chair, 707-664-2377, E-mail: terry.lease@sonoma.edu. *Application contact:* Kris Wright, Associate Vice Provost, Academic Programs and Graduate Studies, 707-664-3954, E-mail: wright@sonoma.edu.
Website: http://www.sonoma.edu/busadmin/mba/.

Southeast Missouri State University, School of Graduate Studies, Harrison College of Business, Cape Girardeau, MO 63701-4799. Offers accounting (MBA); entrepreneurship (MBA); environmental management (MBA); financial management (MBA); general management (MBA); health administration (MBA); industrial management (MBA); international business (MBA); organizational management (MS); sport management (MBA). *Accreditation:* AACSB. Part-time and evening/weekend programs available. Postbaccalaureate distance learning degree programs offered (no on-campus study). *Faculty:* 27 full-time (7 women), 1 (woman) part-time/adjunct. *Students:* 59 full-time (27 women), 83 part-time (28 women); includes 10 minority (5 Black or African American, non-Hispanic/Latino; 3 Asian, non-Hispanic/Latino; 1 Hispanic/Latino; 1 Two or more races, non-Hispanic/Latino), 40 international. Average age 28. 77 applicants, 79% accepted, 48 enrolled. In 2013, 50 master's awarded. *Degree requirements:* For master's, variable foreign language requirement, comprehensive exam (for some programs), thesis or alternative, applied research project. *Entrance requirements:* For master's, GMAT or GRE, minimum undergraduate GPA of 2.5, C or better in prerequisite courses. Additional exam requirements/recommendations for international students: Required—TOEFL (minimum score 550 paper-based; 79 iBT), IELTS (minimum score 6), PTE (minimum score 53). *Application deadline:* For fall admission, 8/1 for domestic students, 6/1 for international students; for spring admission, 11/21 for domestic students, 10/1 for international students; for summer admission, 5/15 for domestic students. Applications are processed on a rolling basis. Application fee: $30 ($40 for international students). Electronic applications accepted. *Expenses:* Tuition, state resident: full-time $5139; part-time $285.50 per credit hour. Tuition, nonresident: full-time $9099; part-time $505.50 per credit hour. *Financial support:* In 2013–14, 52 students received support, including 12 teaching assistantships with full tuition reimbursements available (averaging $8,144 per year); career-related internships or fieldwork, Federal Work-Study, scholarships/grants, traineeships, tuition waivers (full), and unspecified assistantships also available. Financial award application deadline: 6/30; financial award applicants required to submit FAFSA. *Faculty research:* Ethics, corporate finance, generational difference, leadership, organizational justice. *Unit head:* Dr. Kenneth A. Heischmidt, Director, Graduate Business Studies, 573-651-2912, Fax: 573-651-5032, E-mail: kheischmidt@semo.edu. *Application contact:* Gail Amick, Admissions Specialist, 573-651-2590, Fax: 573-651-5936, E-mail: gamick@semo.edu.
Website: http://www.semo.edu/mba.

Southern New Hampshire University, School of Business, Manchester, NH 03106-1045. Offers accounting (MBA, MS, Graduate Certificate); accounting finance (MS); accounting/auditing (MS); accounting/forensic accounting (MS); accounting/taxation (MS); athletic administration (MBA, Graduate Certificate); business administration (IMBA, MBA, Certificate, Graduate Certificate), including accounting (Certificate), business administration (MBA), business information systems (Graduate Certificate); human resource management (Certificate); corporate social responsibility (MBA); entrepreneurship (MBA); finance (MBA, MS, Graduate Certificate); finance/corporate finance (MS); finance/investments and securities (MS); forensic accounting (MBA); healthcare informatics (MBA); healthcare management (MBA); human resource management (Graduate Certificate); information technology (MS, Graduate Certificate); information technology management (MBA); international business (Graduate Certificate); international business and information technology (Graduate Certificate); international finance (Graduate Certificate); international sport management (Graduate Certificate); justice studies (MBA); leadership of nonprofit organizations (Graduate Certificate); marketing (MBA, MS, Graduate Certificate); operations and project management (MS); operations and supply chain management (MBA, Graduate Certificate); organizational leadership (MS); project management (MBA, Graduate Certificate); Six Sigma (MBA); Six Sigma quality (Graduate Certificate); social media marketing (MBA); sport management (MBA, MS, Graduate Certificate); sustainability and environmental compliance (MBA); workplace conflict management (MBA); MBA/Certificate. *Accreditation:* ACBSP. Part-time and evening/weekend programs available. Postbaccalaureate distance learning degree programs offered (no on-campus study). Terminal master's awarded for partial completion of doctoral program. *Degree requirements:* For master's, one foreign language, comprehensive exam (for some programs), thesis or alternative. *Entrance requirements:* For master's, minimum GPA of 2.5. Additional exam requirements/recommendations for international students: Required—TOEFL (minimum score 500 paper-based). Electronic applications accepted.

Southern Oregon University, Graduate Studies, School of Business, Ashland, OR 97520. Offers accounting (Postbaccalaureate Certificate); business administration (MBA); international management (MIM). *Accreditation:* ACBSP. Part-time and evening/weekend programs available. Postbaccalaureate distance learning degree programs offered (minimal on-campus study). *Faculty:* 19 full-time (5 women), 7 part-time/adjunct (2 women). *Students:* 37 full-time (16 women), 75 part-time (31 women); includes 11 minority (2 Black or African American, non-Hispanic/Latino; 2 American Indian or Alaska Native, non-Hispanic/Latino; 2 Hispanic/Latino; 5 Two or more races, non-Hispanic/Latino), 26 international. Average age 35. 83 applicants, 71% accepted, 34 enrolled. *Degree requirements:* For master's, comprehensive exam. *Entrance requirements:* For master's, GMAT, minimum cumulative GPA of 3.0 in the last 90 quarter credits (60 semester credits) of undergraduate coursework. Additional exam requirements/recommendations for international students: Required—TOEFL (minimum score 540 paper-based; 76 iBT), IELTS (minimum score 6), ELPT (minimum score 964) or ELS (minimum score 112). *Application deadline:* For fall admission, 7/31 priority date for domestic and international students; for winter admission, 11/15 priority date for domestic students, 11/14 priority date for international students; for spring admission, 1/7 priority date for domestic and international students. Applications are processed on a rolling basis. Application fee: $50. Electronic applications accepted. *Expenses:* Tuition, state resident: full-time $13,635; part-time $378.72 per credit hour. Tuition, nonresident: full-time $17,042; part-time $473.40 per credit hour. *Required fees:* $408 per quarter. *Financial support:* In 2013–14, 7 students received support, including 7 research assistantships with partial tuition reimbursements available; career-related internships or fieldwork, institutionally sponsored loans, scholarships/grants, and unspecified assistantships also available. *Unit head:* Dr. Mark Siders, Graduate Program Coordinator, 541-552-6709, E-mail: sidersm@sou.edu. *Application contact:* Kelly Moutsatson, Director of Admissions, 541-552-6411, Fax: 541-552-8403, E-mail: admissions@sou.edu.
Website: http://www.sou.edu/business/graduate-programs.html.

State University of New York Empire State College, School for Graduate Studies, Program in Business Administration, Saratoga Springs, NY 12866-4391. Offers global leadership (MBA); management (MBA). Part-time programs available. Postbaccalaureate distance learning degree programs offered (minimal on-campus study). *Degree requirements:* For master's, thesis or alternative. *Entrance requirements:* For master's, previous course work in statistics, macroeconomics, microeconomics, and accounting. Additional exam requirements/recommendations for international students: Required—TOEFL (minimum score 600 paper-based). Electronic applications accepted. *Expenses:* Contact institution. *Faculty research:* Corporate strategy, managerial competencies, decision analysis, economics in transition, organizational communication.

Stevens Institute of Technology, Graduate School, Wesley J. Howe School of Technology Management, Program in Management, Hoboken, NJ 07030. Offers general management (MS); global innovation management (MS); human resource management (MS); information management (MS); project management (MS);

technology commercialization (MS); technology management (MS). Part-time programs available. *Degree requirements:* For master's, thesis optional. *Entrance requirements:* For master's, GMAT, GRE General Test. Additional exam requirements/recommendations for international students: Required—TOEFL. Electronic applications accepted. *Faculty research:* Industrial economics.

Suffolk University, College of Arts and Sciences, Department of Economics, Boston, MA 02108-2770. Offers economic policy (MSEP); economics (MSE); international economics (MSIE); JD/MSIE. Part-time and evening/weekend programs available. *Faculty:* 5 full-time (1 woman), 1 part-time/adjunct (0 women). *Students:* 15 full-time (6 women), 16 part-time (3 women); includes 6 minority (1 Black or African American, non-Hispanic/Latino; 4 Asian, non-Hispanic/Latino; 1 Hispanic/Latino), 11 international. Average age 30. 47 applicants, 57% accepted, 9 enrolled. In 2013, 12 master's awarded. *Entrance requirements:* For master's, GRE General Test or GMAT, 2 letters of recommendation, resume. Additional exam requirements/recommendations for international students: Required—TOEFL (minimum score 550 paper-based; 80 iBT). *Application deadline:* For fall admission, 6/15 priority date for domestic students, 6/15 for international students; for spring admission, 11/1 priority date for domestic students, 11/1 for international students. Applications are processed on a rolling basis. Application fee: $50. Electronic applications accepted. *Expenses:* Contact institution. *Financial support:* In 2013–14, 21 students received support, including 20 fellowships (averaging $9,998 per year); career-related internships or fieldwork, Federal Work-Study, and institutionally sponsored loans also available. Support available to part-time students. Financial award application deadline: 4/1; financial award applicants required to submit FAFSA. *Faculty research:* Travel demands, decisions in multinational firms and in research production in higher education, charitable giving of fair tax, smoking, fair tax. *Unit head:* Dr. Shahruz Mohtadi, Chairperson, 617-573-8670, Fax: 617-994-4216, E-mail: smohtadi@suffolk.edu. *Application contact:* Cory Meyers, Director of Graduate Admissions, 617-573-8302, Fax: 617-305-1733, E-mail: grad.admission@suffolk.edu. Website: http://www.suffolk.edu/economics.

Suffolk University, Sawyer Business School, Master of Business Administration Program, Boston, MA 02108-2770. Offers accounting (MBA); business administration (APC); entrepreneurship (MBA); executive business administration (EMBA); finance (MBA); global business administration (GMBA); health administration (MBA); international business (MBA); marketing (MBA); nonprofit management (MBA); organizational behavior (MBA); strategic management (MBA); supply chain management (MBA); taxation (MBA); JD/MBA; MBA/GDPA; MBA/MHA; MBA/MSA; MBA/MSF; MBA/MST. *Accreditation:* AACSB. Part-time and evening/weekend programs available. Postbaccalaureate distance learning degree programs offered (no on-campus study). *Faculty:* 29 full-time (9 women), 12 part-time/adjunct (2 women). *Students:* 106 full-time (44 women), 334 part-time (184 women); includes 57 minority (20 Black or African American, non-Hispanic/Latino; 1 American Indian or Alaska Native, non-Hispanic/Latino; 18 Asian, non-Hispanic/Latino; 14 Hispanic/Latino; 4 Two or more races, non-Hispanic/Latino), 61 international. Average age 30. 448 applicants, 61% accepted, 135 enrolled. In 2013, 217 master's awarded. *Entrance requirements:* For master's, GMAT, minimum undergraduate GPA of 2.75 (MBA), 5 years of managerial experience (EMBA). Additional exam requirements/recommendations for international students: Required—TOEFL (minimum score 550 paper-based; 80 iBT). *Application deadline:* For fall admission, 6/15 priority date for domestic students, 6/15 for international students; for spring admission, 11/1 priority date for domestic students, 11/1 for international students. Applications are processed on a rolling basis. Application fee: $50. Electronic applications accepted. *Expenses: Tuition:* Full-time $38,374; part-time $1279 per credit. *Required fees:* $40; $20 per semester. Tuition and fees vary according to program. *Financial support:* In 2013–14, 107 students received support, including 91 fellowships with full and partial tuition reimbursements available (averaging $12,428 per year); career-related internships or fieldwork, Federal Work-Study, and institutionally sponsored loans also available. Support available to part-time students. Financial award application deadline: 4/1; financial award applicants required to submit FAFSA. *Faculty research:* Foreign investments; career strategies and boundaryless careers; corporate ethics codes; interest rates, inflation, and growth options; innovation and product development performance. *Unit head:* Heather Hewitt, Assistant Dean of Graduate Programs/Director of MBA Programs, 617-573-8306, E-mail: hhewitt@suffolk.edu. *Application contact:* Cory Meyers, Director of Graduate Admissions, 617-573-8302, Fax: 617-305-1733, E-mail: grad.admission@suffolk.edu. Website: http://www.suffolk.edu/mba.

Taylor University, Master of Business Administration Program, Upland, IN 46989-1001. Offers emerging business strategies (MBA); global leadership (MBA). Part-time programs available.

Temple University, Fox School of Business, Doctoral Programs in Business, Philadelphia, PA 19122-6096. Offers accounting (PhD); entrepreneurship (PhD); finance (PhD); international business (PhD); management information systems (PhD); marketing (PhD); risk management and insurance (PhD); statistics (PhD); strategic management (PhD); tourism and sport (PhD). *Accreditation:* AACSB. *Degree requirements:* For doctorate, thesis/dissertation. *Entrance requirements:* For doctorate, GRE General Test, GMAT, minimum GPA of 3.0, master's degree. Additional exam requirements/recommendations for international students: Required—TOEFL (minimum score 600 paper-based; 100 iBT), IELTS (minimum score 7.5). Electronic applications accepted.

Temple University, Fox School of Business, MBA Programs, Philadelphia, PA 19122-6096. Offers accounting (MBA); business management (MBA); financial management (MBA); healthcare and life sciences innovation (MBA); human resource management (MBA); international business (IMBA); IT management (MBA); marketing management (MBA); pharmaceutical management (MBA); strategic management (EMBA, MBA). EMBA offered in Philadelphia, PA and Tokyo, Japan. *Accreditation:* AACSB. Part-time and evening/weekend programs available. Postbaccalaureate distance learning degree programs offered (minimal on-campus study). *Entrance requirements:* For master's, GMAT, minimum undergraduate GPA of 3.0. Additional exam requirements/recommendations for international students: Required—TOEFL (minimum score 600 paper-based; 100 iBT), IELTS (minimum score 7.5).

Tennessee Technological University, College of Graduate Studies, College of Business, Cookeville, TN 38505. Offers accounting (MBA); finance (MBA); human resource management (MBA); international business (MBA); management information systems (MBA). *Accreditation:* AACSB. Part-time and evening/weekend programs available. Postbaccalaureate distance learning degree programs offered (no on-campus study). *Faculty:* 28 full-time (5 women). *Students:* 54 full-time (22 women), 115 part-time (44 women); includes 11 minority (5 Black or African American, non-Hispanic/Latino; 1 Asian, non-Hispanic/Latino; 1 Hispanic/Latino; 4 Two or more races, non-Hispanic/Latino), 8 international. Average age 25. 171 applicants, 47% accepted, 50 enrolled. In 2013, 87 master's awarded. *Entrance requirements:* For master's, GMAT, GRE. Additional exam requirements/recommendations for international students: Required—TOEFL (minimum score 550 paper-based; 79 iBT), IELTS (minimum score 5.5), PTE (minimum score 53), or TOEIC (Test of English as an International Communication). *Application deadline:* For fall admission, 8/1 for domestic students, 5/1 for international students; for spring admission, 12/1 for domestic students, 10/1 for international

students. Applications are processed on a rolling basis. Application fee: $35 ($40 for international students). Electronic applications accepted. *Expenses:* Tuition, state resident: full-time $9347; part-time $465 per credit hour. Tuition, nonresident: full-time $23,635; part-time $1152 per credit hour. *Financial support:* In 2013–14, 5 fellowships (averaging $10,000 per year), 18 research assistantships (averaging $4,000 per year), teaching assistantships (averaging $4,000 per year) were awarded. Support available to part-time students. Financial award application deadline: 4/1. *Unit head:* Amanda L. Brown, Interim Director, 931-372-3600, Fax: 931-372-6249, E-mail: albrown@tntech.edu. *Application contact:* Shelia K. Kendrick, Coordinator of Graduate Studies, 931-372-3808, Fax: 931-372-3497, E-mail: skendrick@tntech.edu. Website: http://www.tntech.edu/mba.

Texas A&M International University, Office of Graduate Studies and Research, A.R. Sanchez School of Business, Division of International Business and Technology Studies, Laredo, TX 78041-1900. Offers information systems (MSIS); international business management (MBA, PhD). *Faculty:* 10 full-time (2 women), 1 part-time/adjunct (0 women). *Students:* 47 full-time (13 women), 176 part-time (79 women); includes 137 minority (10 Black or African American, non-Hispanic/Latino; 2 Asian, non-Hispanic/Latino; 125 Hispanic/Latino), 78 international. Average age 29. 78 applicants, 96% accepted, 78 enrolled. In 2013, 65 master's, 3 doctorates awarded. *Degree requirements:* For master's, thesis (for some programs). *Entrance requirements:* For master's, GMAT or GRE General Test. Additional exam requirements/recommendations for international students: Required—TOEFL (minimum score 550 paper-based; 79 iBT). *Application deadline:* For fall admission, 4/30 priority date for domestic students, 4/30 for international students; for spring admission, 11/30 for domestic students, 10/1 for international students. Applications are processed on a rolling basis. Application fee: $35 ($50 for international students). *Expenses:* Tuition, state resident: full-time $5184. *International tuition:* $11,556 full-time. *Financial support:* In 2013–14, 8 students received support, including 5 research assistantships, 2 teaching assistantships; fellowships, Federal Work-Study, institutionally sponsored loans, and scholarships/grants also available. Support available to part-time students. *Unit head:* Dr. Nereu Kock, Chair, 956-326-2521, Fax: 956-326-2494, E-mail: nedkock@tamiu.edu. *Application contact:* Imelda Lopez, Graduate Admissions Counselor, 956-326-2485, Fax: 956-326-2459, E-mail: lopez@tamiu.edu.

Texas A&M University–Corpus Christi, Graduate Studies and Research, College of Business, Corpus Christi, TX 78412-5503. Offers accounting (M Acc); health care administration (MBA); international business (MBA). *Accreditation:* AACSB. Part-time and evening/weekend programs available. *Degree requirements:* For master's, comprehensive exam, thesis (for some programs). *Entrance requirements:* For master's, GMAT. Additional exam requirements/recommendations for international students: Required—TOEFL. Electronic applications accepted.

Texas A&M University–San Antonio, School of Business, San Antonio, TX 78224. Offers business administration (MBA); enterprise resource planning systems (MBA); finance (MBA); healthcare management (MBA); human resources management (MBA); information assurance and security (MBA); international business (MBA); professional accounting (MPA); project management (MBA); supply chain management (MBA). Part-time and evening/weekend programs available. *Entrance requirements:* For master's, GMAT. Additional exam requirements/recommendations for international students: Required—TOEFL (minimum score 550 paper-based; 80 iBT), IELTS (minimum score 6). Electronic applications accepted.

Thunderbird School of Global Management, Executive MBA Program–Glendale, Glendale, AZ 85306. Offers global management (MBA). Part-time and evening/weekend programs available. *Degree requirements:* For master's, one foreign language. *Entrance requirements:* For master's, 8 years of full-time work experience, 3 years of management experience, company sponsorship, mid-management position. Additional exam requirements/recommendations for international students: Recommended—TOEFL. Electronic applications accepted. *Expenses:* Contact institution. *Faculty research:* Management, social enterprise, cross-cultural communication, finance, marketing.

Thunderbird School of Global Management, Global MBA Program for Latin American Managers, Glendale, AZ 85306. Offers GMBA. Offered jointly with Instituto Technológico y de Estudios Superiores de Monterrey. Part-time and evening/weekend programs available. Postbaccalaureate distance learning degree programs offered. *Entrance requirements:* For master's, GMAT or PAEP (Pruebade Admisiona Estudios Posgrado), minimum GPA of 3.0, 2 years of work experience. Additional exam requirements/recommendations for international students: Required—TOEFL (minimum score 550 paper-based; 79 iBT). *Expenses:* Contact institution. *Faculty research:* Globalization impact on Latin American business, doing business in Latin America, international marketing in Latin America.

Thunderbird School of Global Management, GMBA - On Demand Program, Glendale, AZ 85306-6000. Offers GMBA. Part-time programs available. Postbaccalaureate distance learning degree programs offered (minimal on-campus study). *Entrance requirements:* For master's, GMAT. Additional exam requirements/recommendations for international students: Required—TOEFL.

Thunderbird School of Global Management, Master's Programs in Global Management, Glendale, AZ 85306. Offers global affairs and management (MA); global management (MS). *Accreditation:* AACSB. *Degree requirements:* For master's, one foreign language. *Entrance requirements:* For master's, GMAT/GRE. Additional exam requirements/recommendations for international students: Required—TOEFL.

Tiffin University, Program in Business Administration, Tiffin, OH 44883-2161. Offers finance (MBA); general management (MBA); healthcare administration (MBA); human resources (MBA); international business (MBA); leadership (MBA); marketing (MBA); sports management (MBA). *Accreditation:* ACBSP. Part-time and evening/weekend programs available. Postbaccalaureate distance learning degree programs offered (no on-campus study). *Entrance requirements:* For master's, minimum undergraduate GPA of 2.5, work experience. Additional exam requirements/recommendations for international students: Required—TOEFL (minimum score 550 paper-based; 79 iBT). Electronic applications accepted. *Faculty research:* Small business, executive development operations, research and statistical analysis, market research, management information systems.

Trident University International, College of Business Administration, Program in Business Administration, Cypress, CA 90630. Offers business administration (PhD); conflict and negotiation management (MBA); criminal justice administration (MBA); entrepreneurship (MBA); finance (MBA); general management (MBA); government accounting (MBA); human resource management (MBA); information security and digital assurance management (MBA); information technology management (MBA); international business (MBA); logistics management (MBA); marketing (MBA); project management (MBA); public management (MBA); quality management (MBA); strategic leadership (MBA). Part-time and evening/weekend programs available. Postbaccalaureate distance learning degree programs offered (no on-campus study). *Degree requirements:* For doctorate, comprehensive exam, thesis/dissertation, defense of dissertation. *Entrance requirements:* For master's, minimum GPA of 2.5 (students with GPA 3.0 or greater may transfer up to 30% of graduate level credits); for doctorate,

minimum GPA of 3.4, curriculum vitae, course work in research methods or statistics. Additional exam requirements/recommendations for international students: Required—TOEFL. Electronic applications accepted.

Trinity Western University, School of Graduate Studies, Program in Business Administration, Langley, BC V2Y 1Y1, Canada. Offers international business (MBA); management of the growing enterprise (MBA); non-profit and charitable organization management (MBA). Part-time programs available. Postbaccalaureate distance learning degree programs offered (minimal on-campus study). *Degree requirements:* For master's, thesis or alternative, applied project. *Entrance requirements:* For master's, GMAT (minimum score of 550 recommended). Additional exam requirements/ recommendations for international students: Required—TOEFL (minimum score 600 paper-based; 100 iBT), IELTS. Electronic applications accepted.

Troy University, Graduate School, College of Business, Program in Management, Troy, AL 36082. Offers applied management (MSM); healthcare management (MSM); human resources management (MSM); information systems (MSM); international hospitality management (MSM); international management (MSM); leadership and organizational effectiveness (MSM); public management (MS, MSM). *Accreditation:* ACBSP. Part-time and evening/weekend programs available. *Faculty:* 15 full-time (8 women), 3 part-time/adjunct (0 women). *Students:* 18 full-time (14 women), 148 part-time (86 women); includes 95 minority (75 Black or African American, non-Hispanic/ Latino; 1 American Indian or Alaska Native, non-Hispanic/Latino; 4 Asian, non-Hispanic/ Latino; 8 Hispanic/Latino; 7 Two or more races, non-Hispanic/Latino). Average age 35. 124 applicants, 79% accepted, 30 enrolled. In 2013, 75 master's awarded. *Degree requirements:* For master's, Graduate Educational Testing Service Major Field Test, capstone exam, minimum GPA of 3.0. *Entrance requirements:* For master's, GRE (minimum score of 900 on old exam or 294 on new exam) or GMAT (minimum score of 500), bachelor's degree; minimum undergraduate GPA of 2.5 or 3.0 on last 30 semester hours, letter of recommendation. Additional exam requirements/recommendations for international students: Required—TOEFL (minimum score 523 paper-based; 70 iBT), IELTS (minimum score 6). *Application deadline:* Applications are processed on a rolling basis. Application fee: $50. Electronic applications accepted. *Expenses:* Contact institution. *Unit head:* Dr. Bob Wheatley, Director, Graduate Business Programs, 334-670-3143, Fax: 334-670-3599, E-mail: rwheat@troy.edu. *Application contact:* Brenda K. Campbell, Director of Graduate Admissions, 334-670-3178, Fax: 334-670-3733, E-mail: bcamp@troy.edu.

Tufts University, The Fletcher School of Law and Diplomacy, Medford, MA 02155. Offers LL M, MA, MALD, MIB, PhD, DVM/MA, JD/MALD, MALD/MA, MALD/MBA, MALD/MS, MD/MA. Postbaccalaureate distance learning degree programs offered (minimal on-campus study). *Faculty:* 43 full-time, 42 part-time/adjunct. *Students:* 615 full-time (310 women), 12 part-time (5 women); includes 116 minority (17 Black or African American, non-Hispanic/Latino; 50 Asian, non-Hispanic/Latino; 27 Hispanic/ Latino; 22 Two or more races, non-Hispanic/Latino), 211 international. Average age 31. In 2013, 313 master's, 12 doctorates awarded. *Degree requirements:* For master's, one foreign language, thesis; for doctorate, one foreign language, comprehensive exam, thesis/dissertation, dissertation defense. *Entrance requirements:* For master's and doctorate, GMAT or GRE General Test. Additional exam requirements/ recommendations for international students: Required—TOEFL (minimum score 600 paper-based; 100 iBT), IELTS (minimum score 7). *Application deadline:* For fall admission, 1/10 for domestic and international students; for spring admission, 10/15 for domestic and international students. Application fee: $80. Electronic applications accepted. *Expenses:* Contact institution. *Financial support:* Career-related internships or fieldwork, Federal Work-Study, institutionally sponsored loans, scholarships/grants, and tuition waivers (partial) available. Financial award application deadline: 1/10; financial award applicants required to submit FAFSA. *Faculty research:* Negotiation and conflict resolution, international organizations, international business and economic law, security studies, development economics. *Unit head:* Dr. James Stavridis, Dean, 617-627-3050, Fax: 617-627-3712. *Application contact:* Laurie A. Hurley, Director of Admissions and Financial Aid, 617-627-3040, E-mail: fletcheradmissions@tufts.edu. Website: http://www.fletcher.tufts.edu.

United States International University, School of Business Administration, Nairobi, Kenya. Offers business administration (GEMBA); entrepreneurship (MBA); finance (MBA); human resource management (MBA); information technology management (MBA); integrated studies (MBA); international business administration (MBA); management and organizational development (MS); marketing (MBA); organizational development (EMS); strategic management (MBA). Part-time and evening/weekend programs available. *Degree requirements:* For master's, thesis. *Entrance requirements:* For master's, GMAT, 2 letters of reference, resume. Additional exam requirements/ recommendations for international students: Required—TOEFL (minimum score 550 paper-based). *Faculty research:* Marketing in small business enterprises, total quality management in Kenya.

Universidad Autonoma de Guadalajara, Graduate Programs, Guadalajara, Mexico. Offers administrative law and justice (LL M); advertising and corporate communications (MA); architecture (M Arch); business (MBA); computational science (MCC); education (Ed M, Ed D); English-Spanish translation (MA); entrepreneurship and management (MBA); integrated management of digital animation (MA); international business (MIB); international corporate law (LL M); internet technologies (MS); manufacturing systems (MMS); occupational health (MS); philosophy (MA, PhD); power electronics (MS); quality systems (MQS); renewable energy (MS); social evaluation of projects (MBA); strategic market research (MBA); tax law (MA); teaching mathematics (MA).

Universidad Metropolitana, School of Business Administration, Program in International Business, San Juan, PR 00928-1150. Offers MBA.

Université de Sherbrooke, Faculty of Administration, Program in International Business, Sherbrooke, QC J1K 2R1, Canada. Offers M Sc. *Degree requirements:* For master's, one foreign language, thesis. *Entrance requirements:* For master's, bachelor's degree in related field, minimum GPA of 3.0 (on 4.3 scale). Electronic applications accepted.

Université du Québec, École nationale d'administration publique, Graduate Program in Public Administration, Program in International Administration, Quebec, QC G1K 9E5, Canada. Offers MAP, Diploma. Part-time programs available. *Entrance requirements:* For degree, appropriate bachelor's degree, proficiency in French.

Université Laval, Faculty of Administrative Sciences, Programs in Business Administration, Québec, QC G1K 7P4, Canada. Offers accounting (MBA); agri-food management (MBA); electronic business (MBA, Diploma); factory management and logistics (MBA); finance (MBA); firm management (MBA); geomatic management (MBA); information technology management (MBA); international management (MBA); management (MBA); management accounting (MBA, Diploma); marketing (MBA); modeling and organizational decision (MBA); occupational health and safety management (MBA); pharmacy management (MBA); social and environmental responsibility (MBA); technological entrepreneurship (Diploma). *Accreditation:* AACSB. Part-time and evening/weekend programs available. Postbaccalaureate distance learning degree programs offered (no on-campus study). *Entrance requirements:* For master's and Diploma, knowledge of French and English. Electronic applications accepted.

University at Buffalo, the State University of New York, Graduate School, College of Arts and Sciences, Department of Geography, Buffalo, NY 14260. Offers Canadian studies (Certificate); earth systems science (MA, MS); economic geography and business geographics (MS); environmental modeling and analysis (MA); geographic information science (MA, MS); geography (MA, PhD); GIS and environmental analysis (Certificate); health geography (MS); international trade (MA); transportation and business geographics (MA); urban and regional analysis (MA). Part-time programs available. *Faculty:* 16 full-time (7 women), 1 part-time/adjunct (0 women). *Students:* 86 full-time (39 women), 23 part-time (8 women); includes 76 minority (72 Asian, non-Hispanic/Latino; 4 Hispanic/Latino). Average age 29. 161 applicants, 65% accepted, 43 enrolled. In 2013, 30 master's, 10 doctorates awarded. Terminal master's awarded for partial completion of doctoral program. *Degree requirements:* For master's, thesis (for some programs), project or portfolio; for doctorate, thesis/dissertation. *Entrance requirements:* For master's, GRE General Test, minimum GPA of 2.9; for doctorate, GRE General Test, minimum GPA of 3.0. Additional exam requirements/ recommendations for international students: Required—TOEFL (minimum score 550 paper-based; 79 iBT). *Application deadline:* For fall admission, 5/1 priority date for domestic students, 3/10 priority date for international students; for spring admission, 11/ 1 priority date for domestic students, 9/1 priority date for international students. Applications are processed on a rolling basis. Application fee: $75. Electronic applications accepted. *Financial support:* In 2013–14, 13 students received support, including 8 fellowships with full tuition reimbursements available (averaging $5,500 per year), 13 teaching assistantships with full tuition reimbursements available (averaging $13,520 per year); research assistantships with full tuition reimbursements available, career-related internships or fieldwork, Federal Work-Study, institutionally sponsored loans, traineeships, health care benefits, and unspecified assistantships also available. Financial award application deadline: 1/10. *Faculty research:* International business and world trade, geographic information systems and cartography, transportation, urban and regional analysis, physical and environmental geography. *Total annual research expenditures:* $2.6 million. *Unit head:* Dr. Sharmistha Bagchi-Sen, Chairman, 716-645-0473, Fax: 716-645-2329, E-mail: geosbs@buffalo.edu. *Application contact:* Betsy Crooks, Graduate Secretary, 716-645-0471, Fax: 716-645-2329, E-mail: babraham@buffalo.edu.
Website: http://www.geog.buffalo.edu/.

The University of Akron, Graduate School, College of Business Administration, Department of Marketing, Akron, OH 44325. Offers direct interactive marketing (MBA); international business (MBA); strategic marketing (MBA). Part-time and evening/ weekend programs available. *Faculty:* 10 full-time (1 woman), 6 part-time/adjunct (2 women). *Students:* 17 full-time (7 women), 22 part-time (15 women); includes 6 minority (3 Asian, non-Hispanic/Latino; 2 Hispanic/Latino; 1 Two or more races, non-Hispanic/ Latino), 7 international. Average age 28. 24 applicants, 42% accepted, 4 enrolled. In 2013, 12 master's awarded. *Entrance requirements:* For master's, GMAT, minimum GPA of 2.75, two letters of recommendation, statement of purpose, resume. Additional exam requirements/recommendations for international students: Required—TOEFL (minimum score 550 paper-based; 79 iBT). *Application deadline:* For fall admission, 7/15 for domestic and international students; for spring admission, 11/15 for domestic and international students. Application fee: $30 ($40 for international students). Electronic applications accepted. *Expenses:* Tuition, state resident: full-time $7430; part-time $412.80 per credit hour. Tuition, nonresident: full-time $12,722; part-time $706.80 per credit hour. *Required fees:* $53 per credit hour. $12 per semester. Tuition and fees vary according to course load and program. *Financial support:* In 2013–14, 2 research assistantships with full tuition reimbursements, 8 teaching assistantships with full tuition reimbursements were awarded. *Faculty research:* Multi-channel marketing, direct interactive marketing, strategic retailing, marketing strategy and telemarketing. *Total annual research expenditures:* $9,233. *Unit head:* Dr. William Baker, Chair, 330-972-8466, E-mail: wbaker@uakron.edu. *Application contact:* Dr. William Hauser, Director of Graduate Business Programs, 330-972-7043, Fax: 330-972-6588, E-mail: whauser@uakron.edu.
Website: http://www.uakron.edu/cba/departments/marketing/.

The University of Akron, Graduate School, College of Business Administration, Program in International Business, Akron, OH 44325. Offers MBA, JD/MBA. Part-time and evening/weekend programs available. *Students:* 4 full-time (1 woman), 5 part-time (2 women); includes 2 minority (1 Asian, non-Hispanic/Latino; 1 Hispanic/Latino), 4 international. Average age 29. 7 applicants, 57% accepted, 1 enrolled. In 2013, 2 master's awarded. *Entrance requirements:* For master's, GMAT, minimum GPA of 2.75, two letters of recommendation, resume, statement of purpose. Additional exam requirements/recommendations for international students: Required—TOEFL (minimum score 550 paper-based; 79 iBT). *Application deadline:* For fall admission, 7/15 for domestic and international students; for spring admission, 11/15 for domestic and international students. Application fee: $30 ($40 for international students). Electronic applications accepted. *Expenses:* Tuition, state resident: full-time $7430; part-time $412.80 per credit hour. Tuition, nonresident: full-time $12,722; part-time $706.80 per credit hour. *Required fees:* $53 per credit hour. $12 per semester. Tuition and fees vary according to course load and program. *Financial support:* In 2013–14, 1 teaching assistantship with full tuition reimbursement was awarded. *Unit head:* Dr. William Baker, Chair, 330-972-8466, E-mail: wbaker@uakron.edu. *Application contact:* Dr. William Hauser, Director of Graduate Business Programs, 330-972-7043, Fax: 330-972-6588, E-mail: whauser@uakron.edu.

University of Alberta, Faculty of Graduate Studies and Research, Program in Business Administration, Edmonton, AB T6G 2E1, Canada. Offers international business (MBA); leisure and sport management (MBA); natural resources and energy (MBA); technology commercialization (MBA); MBA/LL B; MBA/M Ag; MBA/M Eng; MBA/MF; MBA/PhD. *Accreditation:* AACSB. Part-time and evening/weekend programs available. *Degree requirements:* For master's, thesis or alternative. *Entrance requirements:* For master's, GMAT. Additional exam requirements/recommendations for international students: Required—TOEFL (minimum score 600 paper-based). Electronic applications accepted. *Faculty research:* Natural resources and energy/management and policy/family enterprise/international business/healthcare research management.

University of Bridgeport, School of Business, Bridgeport, CT 06604. Offers accounting (MBA); finance (MBA); general business (MBA); global financial services (MBA); human resource management (MBA); information systems and knowledge management (MBA); international business (MBA); management (MBA); marketing (MBA); operations management (MBA); small business and entrepreneurship (MBA); specialized business (MBA). *Accreditation:* ACBSP. Part-time and evening/weekend programs available. *Faculty:* 11 full-time (2 women), 39 part-time/adjunct (8 women). *Students:* 162 full-time (90 women), 69 part-time (45 women); includes 44 minority (20 Black or African American, non-Hispanic/Latino; 7 Asian, non-Hispanic/Latino; 15 Hispanic/Latino; 2 Two or more races, non-Hispanic/Latino), 163 international. Average age 28. 492 applicants, 48% accepted, 55 enrolled. In 2013, 144 master's awarded. *Degree requirements:* For master's, thesis optional. *Entrance requirements:* For master's, GMAT. Additional exam requirements/recommendations for international students: Recommended—TOEFL

(minimum score 550 paper-based; 80 iBT), IELTS (minimum score 6.5). *Application deadline:* For fall admission, 8/1 priority date for domestic and international students; for spring admission, 12/1 priority date for domestic and international students. Applications are processed on a rolling basis. Application fee: $50. Electronic applications accepted. *Expenses:* Contact institution. *Financial support:* In 2013–14, 69 students received support. Fellowships, research assistantships, teaching assistantships, career-related internships or fieldwork, Federal Work-Study, institutionally sponsored loans, and tuition waivers (partial) available. Support available to part-time students. Financial award application deadline: 6/1; financial award applicants required to submit FAFSA. *Unit head:* Dr. Lloyd G. Gibson, Dean, 203-576-4384, Fax: 203-576-4388, E-mail: llgibson@bridgeport.edu. *Application contact:* Leanne Proctor, Director of Graduate Admissions, 203-576-4552, Fax: 203-576-4941, E-mail: mba@bridgeport.edu.
Website: http://www.bridgeport.edu.

University of California, Berkeley, UC Berkeley Extension, International Diploma Programs, Berkeley, CA 94720-1500. Offers business administration (Certificate); finance (Certificate); global business management (Certificate); marketing (Certificate); project management (Certificate). *Accreditation:* AACSB.

University of California, Los Angeles, Graduate Division, UCLA Anderson School of Management, Los Angeles, CA 90095-1481. Offers accounting (PhD); Americas (EMBA); Asia Pacific (EMBA); business administration (EMBA, MBA); decisions, operations and technology management (PhD); finance (PhD); financial engineering (MFE); global economics and management (PhD); management and organizations (PhD); marketing (PhD); strategy and policy (PhD); DDS/MBA; MBA/JD; MBA/MD; MBA/MLAS; MBA/MLIS; MBA/MPH; MBA/MPP; MBA/MSCS; MBA/MSN; MBA/MUP. *Accreditation:* AACSB. Part-time programs available. *Faculty:* 104 full-time (20 women), 28 part-time/adjunct (4 women). *Students:* 1,069 full-time (324 women), 879 part-time (251 women); includes 664 minority (37 Black or African American, non-Hispanic/Latino; 1 American Indian or Alaska Native, non-Hispanic/Latino; 470 Asian, non-Hispanic/Latino; 34 Hispanic/Latino; 2 Native Hawaiian or other Pacific Islander, non-Hispanic/Latino; 120 Two or more races, non-Hispanic/Latino), 444 international. Average age 30. 5,084 applicants, 27% accepted, 845 enrolled. In 2013, 801 master's, 14 doctorates awarded. *Degree requirements:* For master's, comprehensive exam, field study consulting project (for MBA); thesis (for MFE); for doctorate, comprehensive exam, thesis/dissertation, oral and written qualifying exams. *Entrance requirements:* For master's, GMAT (for MBA); GMAT or GRE General Test (for MFE), 4-year bachelor's degree or equivalent; recommendation letters (1 for MBA, 2 for MFE); two essays; interview (by invitation only for MBA); for doctorate, GMAT or GRE General Test, bachelor's degree from college or university of fully-recognized standing; minimum B average in undergraduate coursework or B+ average in prior graduate work; statement of purpose; three recommendation letters. Additional exam requirements/recommendations for international students: Required—TOEFL (minimum score 560 paper-based; 87 iBT). *Application deadline:* For fall admission, 10/22 priority date for domestic and international students; for winter admission, 1/7 for domestic and international students; for spring admission, 4/15 for domestic and international students. Applications are processed on a rolling basis. Application fee: $200. Electronic applications accepted. *Expenses:* Contact institution. *Financial support:* In 2013–14, 522 students received support. Fellowships, research assistantships with partial tuition reimbursements available, teaching assistantships with partial tuition reimbursements available, career-related internships or fieldwork, institutionally sponsored loans, scholarships/grants, health care benefits, and tuition waivers (partial) available. Financial award application deadline: 4/15; financial award applicants required to submit FAFSA. *Faculty research:* Asset pricing, decision-making, behavioral finance, international finance and economics, global macroeconomics. *Total annual research expenditures:* $368,086. *Unit head:* Dr. Judy D. Olian, Dean/Chair in Management, 310-825-7982, Fax: 310-206-2073, E-mail: judy.olian@anderson.ucla.edu. *Application contact:* Alex Lawrence, Assistant Dean, MBA Admissions and Financial Aid, 310-825-6944, Fax: 310-825-8582, E-mail: mba.admissions@anderson.ucla.edu.
Website: http://www.anderson.ucla.edu/.

See Display on page 145 and Close-Up on page 191.

University of Chicago, Booth School of Business, Executive MBA Program Asia, Singapore 238 466, Singapore. Offers MBA. Part-time programs available. *Entrance requirements:* For master's, interview, letter of company support, 3 letters of recommendation, resume. Additional exam requirements/recommendations for international students: Recommended—TOEFL (minimum score 600 paper-based). Electronic applications accepted. *Expenses:* Contact institution. *Faculty research:* Finance, marketing, international business, general management, strategy.

University of Chicago, Booth School of Business, Executive MBA Program Europe, London EC2V 5HA, United Kingdom. Offers MBA. Part-time programs available. *Entrance requirements:* For master's, interview, 3 letters of recommendation, letter of company support, resume. Additional exam requirements/recommendations for international students: Recommended—TOEFL (minimum score 600 paper-based). Electronic applications accepted. *Expenses:* Contact institution. *Faculty research:* Finance, marketing, international business, general management, strategy.

University of Chicago, Booth School of Business, Executive MBA Program North America, Chicago, IL 60611. Offers MBA. Part-time programs available. *Entrance requirements:* For master's, interview, company-sponsored letter, 3 letters of recommendation, resume. Additional exam requirements/recommendations for international students: Required—TOEFL (minimum score 600 paper-based), IELTS. Electronic applications accepted. *Expenses:* Contact institution. *Faculty research:* Finance, marketing, international business, general management, strategy.

University of Chicago, Booth School of Business, Full-Time MBA Program, Chicago, IL 60637. Offers accounting (MBA); analytic finance (MBA); analytic management (MBA); econometrics and statistics (MBA); economics (MBA); entrepreneurship (MBA); finance (MBA); general management (MBA); health administration and policy (Certificate); human resource management (MBA); international business (MBA); managerial and organizational behavior (MBA); marketing management (MBA); operations management (MBA); strategic management (MBA); MBA/AM; MBA/JD; MBA/MA; MBA/MD; MBA/MPP. *Accreditation:* AACSB. Part-time and evening/weekend programs available. Terminal master's awarded for partial completion of doctoral program. *Entrance requirements:* For master's, GMAT, 2 letters of recommendation, 3 essays, resume, interview. Additional exam requirements/recommendations for international students: Required—TOEFL (minimum score 600 paper-based; 104 iBT), IELTS. Electronic applications accepted. *Expenses:* Contact institution. *Faculty research:* Finance, marketing, economics, entrepreneurship, strategy, management.

University of Chicago, Booth School of Business, International MBA Program, Chicago, IL 60637-1513. Offers IMBA. *Accreditation:* AACSB. *Degree requirements:* For master's, one foreign language, study abroad. *Entrance requirements:* For master's, GMAT, 2 letters of recommendation. Additional exam requirements/recommendations for international students: Required—TOEFL (minimum score 600 paper-based), IELTS. Electronic applications accepted.

University of Colorado Denver, Business School, Master of Business Administration Program, Denver, CO 80217. Offers bioinnovation and entrepreneurship (MBA); business intelligence (MBA); business strategy (MBA); business to business marketing (MBA); business to consumer marketing (MBA); change management (MBA); corporate financial management (MBA); enterprise technology management (MBA); entrepreneurship (MBA); health administration (MBA), including financial management, health administration, health information technologies, international health management and policy; human resources management (MBA); international business (MBA); investment management (MBA); managing for sustainability (MBA); sports and entertainment management (MBA). *Accreditation:* AACSB. Part-time and evening/weekend programs available. Postbaccalaureate distance learning degree programs offered (no on-campus study). *Students:* 611 full-time (246 women), 144 part-time (58 women); includes 102 minority (14 Black or African American, non-Hispanic/Latino; 2 American Indian or Alaska Native, non-Hispanic/Latino; 38 Asian, non-Hispanic/Latino; 42 Hispanic/Latino; 6 Two or more races, non-Hispanic/Latino), 26 international. Average age 32. 330 applicants, 64% accepted, 125 enrolled. In 2013, 398 master's awarded. *Degree requirements:* For master's, 48 semester hours, including 30 of core courses, 3 in international business, and 15 in electives from over 50 other graduate business courses. *Entrance requirements:* For master's, GMAT, resume, official transcripts, essay, two letters of recommendation, financial statements (for international applicants). Additional exam requirements/recommendations for international students: Required—TOEFL (minimum score 560 paper-based; 83 iBT); Recommended—IELTS (minimum score 6.5). *Application deadline:* For fall admission, 4/15 priority date for domestic students, 3/15 priority date for international students; for spring admission, 10/15 priority date for domestic students, 9/15 priority date for international students. Applications are processed on a rolling basis. Application fee: $50 ($75 for international students). Electronic applications accepted. *Expenses:* Contact institution. *Financial support:* In 2013–14, 62 students received support. Fellowships, research assistantships, teaching assistantships, Federal Work-Study, institutionally sponsored loans, scholarships/grants, traineeships, and unspecified assistantships available. Financial award application deadline: 4/1; financial award applicants required to submit FAFSA. *Faculty research:* Marketing, management, entrepreneurship, finance, health administration. *Unit head:* Elizabeth Cooperman, Professor of Finance and Managing for Sustainability/MBA Program Director, 303-315-8422, E-mail: elizabeth.cooperman@ucdenver.edu. *Application contact:* Shelly Townley, Admissions Director, Graduate Programs, 303-315-8202, E-mail: shelly.townley@ucdenver.edu.
Website: http://www.ucdenver.edu/academics/colleges/business/degrees/mba/Pages/MBA.aspx.

University of Colorado Denver, Business School, Program in Global Energy Management, Denver, CO 80217. Offers MS. Postbaccalaureate distance learning degree programs offered (minimal on-campus study). *Students:* 81 full-time (21 women), 3 part-time (0 women); includes 11 minority (5 Black or African American, non-Hispanic/Latino; 1 Asian, non-Hispanic/Latino; 4 Hispanic/Latino; 1 Two or more races, non-Hispanic/Latino), 10 international. Average age 33. 46 applicants, 80% accepted, 29 enrolled. In 2013, 38 master's awarded. *Degree requirements:* For master's, 36 semester credit hours. *Entrance requirements:* For master's, GMAT if less than three years of experience in the energy industry (waived for students already holding a graduate degree), minimum of 5 years' experience in energy industry; resume; letters of recommendation; essays. Additional exam requirements/recommendations for international students: Required—TOEFL (minimum score 525 paper-based; 71 iBT); Recommended—IELTS (minimum score 6). *Application deadline:* For fall admission, 6/1 for domestic and international students; for winter admission, 12/1 for domestic and international students; for spring admission, 12/1 for domestic and international students. Application fee: $50 ($75 for international students). Electronic applications accepted. *Expenses:* Contact institution. *Financial support:* Fellowships, research assistantships, teaching assistantships, Federal Work-Study, institutionally sponsored loans, scholarships/grants, and traineeships available. Financial award application deadline: 4/1; financial award applicants required to submit FAFSA. *Unit head:* Wayne Cascio, Chair in Global Leadership Management, 303-315-8434, E-mail: wayne.cascio@ucdenver.edu. *Application contact:* Shelly Townley, Director of Graduate Admissions, 303-315-8202, Fax: 303-556-5904, E-mail: shelly.townley@ucdenver.edu.
Website: http://www.ucdenver.edu/academics/colleges/business/degrees/ms/gem/Pages/Overview.aspx.

University of Colorado Denver, Business School, Program in International Business, Denver, CO 80217. Offers MSIB. Part-time and evening/weekend programs available. *Students:* 26 full-time (8 women), 2 part-time (both women); includes 6 minority (1 Black or African American, non-Hispanic/Latino; 2 Asian, non-Hispanic/Latino; 1 Hispanic/Latino; 2 Two or more races, non-Hispanic/Latino), 3 international. Average age 34. 6 applicants, 100% accepted, 3 enrolled. In 2013, 12 master's awarded. *Degree requirements:* For master's, one foreign language, thesis optional, 42 credit hours; thesis, internship or international field study. *Entrance requirements:* For master's, GMAT, resume, essay, two letters of recommendation, financial statements (for international applicants). Additional exam requirements/recommendations for international students: Required—TOEFL (minimum score 537 paper-based; 75 iBT); Recommended—IELTS (minimum score 6.5). *Application deadline:* For fall admission, 4/15 for domestic students, 3/15 for international students; for spring admission, 10/15 for domestic students, 9/15 for international students. Applications are processed on a rolling basis. Application fee: $50 ($75 for international students). Electronic applications accepted. *Expenses:* Contact institution. *Financial support:* In 2013–14, 2 students received support. Fellowships, research assistantships, teaching assistantships, Federal Work-Study, institutionally sponsored loans, scholarships/grants, and traineeships available. Financial award application deadline: 4/1; financial award applicants required to submit FAFSA. *Faculty research:* Foreign direct investment, international business strategies, cross-cultural management, internationalization of research and development, global leadership development. *Unit head:* Dr. Manuel Serapio, Associate Professor/Director of MS in International Business, 303-315-8436, E-mail: manuel.serapio@ucdenver.edu. *Application contact:* Shelly Townley, Admissions Director, Graduate Programs, 303-315-8202, E-mail: shelly.townley@ucdenver.edu.
Website: http://www.ucdenver.edu/academics/colleges/business/degrees/ms/ib/Pages/default.aspx.

University of Colorado Denver, Business School, Program in Management and Organization, Denver, CO 80217. Offers business strategy (MS); change and innovation (MS); enterprise technology management (MS); entrepreneurship and innovation (MS); global management (MS); human resources management (MS); leadership and management (MS); quantitative decision methods (MS); sports and entertainment management (MS); sustainability management (MS). *Accreditation:* AACSB. Part-time and evening/weekend programs available. Postbaccalaureate distance learning degree programs offered (no on-campus study). *Students:* 27 full-time (19 women), 14 part-time (7 women); includes 4 minority (1 Black or African American, non-Hispanic/Latino; 2 Hispanic/Latino; 1 Two or more races, non-Hispanic/Latino), 6 international. Average age 29. 38 applicants, 45% accepted, 8 enrolled. In 2013, 28 master's awarded. *Degree requirements:* For master's, 30 semester hours (12 of required courses, 12 of management electives, and 6 of free electives). *Entrance requirements:* For master's, GMAT, resume, two letters of recommendation, essay, financial statements (for international applicants). Additional exam requirements/recommendations for international students: Required—TOEFL (minimum score 537 paper-based; 75 iBT);

Recommended—IELTS (minimum score 6.5). *Application deadline:* For fall admission, 4/15 for domestic students, 3/15 for international students; for spring admission, 10/15 for domestic students, 9/15 for international students. Applications are processed on a rolling basis. Application fee: $50 ($75 for international students). Electronic applications accepted. *Expenses:* Contact institution. *Financial support:* In 2013–14, 5 students received support. Fellowships, research assistantships, teaching assistantships, Federal Work-Study, institutionally sponsored loans, scholarships/grants, and traineeships available. Financial award application deadline: 4/1; financial award applicants required to submit FAFSA. *Faculty research:* Human resource management, management of catastrophe, turnaround strategies. *Unit head:* Dr. Kenneth Bettenhausen, Associate Professor/Director of MS in Management, 303-315-8425, E-mail: kenneth.bettenhausen@ucdenver.edu. *Application contact:* Shelly Townley, Admissions Director, Graduate Programs, 303-315-8202, E-mail: shelly.townley@ucdenver.edu.
Website: http://www.ucdenver.edu/academics/colleges/business/degrees/ms/management/Pages/Management.aspx.

University of Colorado Denver, Business School, Program in Marketing, Denver, CO 80217. Offers brand management and marketing communication (MS); global marketing (MS); high-tech and entrepreneurial marketing (MS); Internet marketing (MS); marketing for sustainability (MS); marketing research (MS); sports and entertainment marketing (MS). Part-time and evening/weekend programs available. *Students:* 36 full-time (15 women), 12 part-time (4 women); includes 3 minority (1 Asian, non-Hispanic/Latino; 1 Hispanic/Latino; 1 Two or more races, non-Hispanic/Latino), 11 international. Average age 29. 47 applicants, 55% accepted, 11 enrolled. In 2013, 20 master's awarded. *Degree requirements:* For master's, 30 semester hours (21 of marketing core courses, 9 of marketing electives). *Entrance requirements:* For master's, GMAT, resume, essay, two letters of recommendation, financial statements (for international applicants). Additional exam requirements/recommendations for international students: Required—TOEFL (minimum score 537 paper-based; 75 iBT); Recommended—IELTS (minimum score 6.5). *Application deadline:* For fall admission, 4/15 for domestic students, 3/15 for international students; for spring admission, 10/15 for domestic students, 9/15 for international students. Applications are processed on a rolling basis. Application fee: $50 ($75 for international students). Electronic applications accepted. *Expenses:* Contact institution. *Financial support:* In 2013–14, 7 students received support. Fellowships, research assistantships, teaching assistantships, Federal Work-Study, institutionally sponsored loans, scholarships/grants, and traineeships available. Financial award application deadline: 4/1; financial award applicants required to submit FAFSA. *Faculty research:* Marketing issues in the Chinese environment, impact of individual difference and contextual factors on the risk-taking behaviors of managers making new-business creation decisions, attribution theory perspective of conflict between marketers and engineers, organizational identity and identification, international market entry strategies. *Unit head:* Dr. David Forlani, Associate Professor/Director of Marketing Programs, 303-315-8420, E-mail: david.forlani@ucdenver.edu. *Application contact:* Shelly Townley, Admissions Director, Graduate Programs, 303-315-8202, E-mail: shelly.townley@ucdenver.edu.
Website: http://www.ucdenver.edu/academics/colleges/business/degrees/ms/marketing/Pages/Marketing.aspx.

University of Dallas, Graduate School of Management, Irving, TX 75062-4736. Offers accounting (MBA, MM, MS); business management (MBA, MM); corporate finance (MBA, MM); financial services (MBA); global business (MBA, MM); health services management (MBA, MM); human resource management (MBA, MM); information assurance (MBA, MM, MS); information technology (MBA, MM, MS); information technology service management (MBA, MM, MS); marketing management (MBA, MM); organization development (MBA, MM); project management (MBA, MM); sports and entertainment management (MBA, MM); strategic leadership (MBA, MM); supply chain management (MBA); supply chain management and market logistics (MM). *Accreditation:* ACBSP. Part-time and evening/weekend programs available. Postbaccalaureate distance learning degree programs offered (no on-campus study). *Entrance requirements:* Additional exam requirements/recommendations for international students: Required—TOEFL. Electronic applications accepted. *Expenses:* Contact institution.

University of Denver, Daniels College of Business, International MBA Program, Denver, CO 80208. Offers IMBA, MBA. *Accreditation:* AACSB. *Students:* 40 full-time (20 women), 10 part-time (7 women); includes 5 minority (1 Black or African American, non-Hispanic/Latino; 3 Hispanic/Latino; 1 Two or more races, non-Hispanic/Latino), 10 international. Average age 27. 51 applicants, 88% accepted, 21 enrolled. In 2013, 40 master's awarded. *Degree requirements:* For master's, one foreign language. *Entrance requirements:* For master's, GRE General Test or GMAT, bachelor's degree, transcripts, resume, two letters of recommendation, essays, interview. Additional exam requirements/recommendations for international students: Required—TOEFL (minimum score 570 paper-based; 88 iBT). *Application deadline:* For fall admission, 11/15 priority date for domestic and international students; for spring admission, 10/1 priority date for domestic and international students. Applications are processed on a rolling basis. Application fee: $100. Electronic applications accepted. *Financial support:* In 2013–14, 35 students received support, including 12 teaching assistantships with full and partial tuition reimbursements available (averaging $9,384 per year); career-related internships or fieldwork, Federal Work-Study, institutionally sponsored loans, scholarships/grants, and unspecified assistantships also available. Support available to part-time students. Financial award application deadline: 2/15; financial award applicants required to submit FAFSA. *Unit head:* Leslie Carter, Associate Director, 303-871-2037, E-mail: leslie.carter@du.edu. *Application contact:* Lindsay Lauman, Graduate Admissions Manager, 303-871-4211, E-mail: lindsey.lauman@du.edu.
Website: http://daniels.du.edu/graduate/international-mba/.

University of Denver, Josef Korbel School of International Studies, Denver, CO 80210. Offers conflict resolution (MA); global finance, trade and economic integration (MA); global health affairs (Certificate); homeland security (Certificate); humanitarian assistance (Certificate); international administration (MA); international development (MA); international human rights (MA); international law and human rights (Certificate); international security (MA); international studies (MA, PhD). Part-time programs available. *Faculty:* 37 full-time (12 women), 18 part-time/adjunct (9 women). *Students:* 430 full-time (258 women), 23 part-time (11 women); includes 78 minority (14 Black or African American, non-Hispanic/Latino; 11 Asian, non-Hispanic/Latino; 43 Hispanic/Latino; 1 Native Hawaiian or other Pacific Islander, non-Hispanic/Latino; 9 Two or more races, non-Hispanic/Latino), 48 international. Average age 27. 841 applicants, 90% accepted, 227 enrolled. In 2013, 204 master's, 6 doctorates, 32 other advanced degrees awarded. *Degree requirements:* For master's, one foreign language, thesis (for some programs); for doctorate, one foreign language, comprehensive exam, thesis/dissertation, two extended research papers. *Entrance requirements:* For master's, GRE General Test, bachelor's degree, transcripts, two letters of recommendation, statement of purpose, resume or curriculum vitae; for doctorate, GRE General Test, master's degree, transcripts, three letters of recommendation, statement of purpose, resume or curriculum vitae, writing sample; for Certificate, bachelor's degree, transcripts, two letters of recommendation, statement of purpose, resume or curriculum vitae. Additional exam requirements/recommendations for international students: Required—TOEFL (minimum score 587 paper-based; 95 iBT). *Application deadline:* For fall admission, 1/15 priority date for domestic students, 12/15 priority date for international students; for winter admission, 11/1 priority date for domestic and international students. Application fee: $65. Electronic applications accepted. *Financial support:* In 2013–14, 216 students received support, including 1 research assistantship, 2 teaching assistantships with full and partial tuition reimbursements available (averaging $8,280 per year); career-related internships or fieldwork, Federal Work-Study, institutionally sponsored loans, scholarships/grants, and unspecified assistantships also available. Support available to part-time students. Financial award application deadline: 2/15; financial award applicants required to submit FAFSA. *Faculty research:* Human rights and international security, international politics and economics, economic-social and political development, international technology analysis and management. *Unit head:* Christopher R. Hill, Dean, 303-871-2359, Fax: 303-871-2456, E-mail: christopher.r.hill@du.edu. *Application contact:* Brad Miller, Director of Graduate Admissions, 303-871-2989, Fax: 303-871-2124, E-mail: brad.miller@du.edu.
Website: http://www.du.edu/korbel/.

University of Florida, Graduate School, Warrington College of Business Administration, Hough Graduate School of Business, Department of Management, Gainesville, FL 32611. Offers health care risk management (MS); international business (MA); management (MS, PhD). *Accreditation:* AACSB. Postbaccalaureate distance learning degree programs offered. *Faculty:* 8 full-time (3 women), 1 part-time/adjunct (0 women). *Students:* 114 full-time (67 women), 40 part-time (9 women); includes 45 minority (10 Black or African American, non-Hispanic/Latino; 2 American Indian or Alaska Native, non-Hispanic/Latino; 9 Asian, non-Hispanic/Latino; 24 Hispanic/Latino), 42 international. Average age 25. 211 applicants, 33% accepted, 43 enrolled. In 2013, 212 master's, 3 doctorates awarded. *Degree requirements:* For master's, comprehensive exam, thesis; for doctorate, comprehensive exam, thesis/dissertation. *Entrance requirements:* For master's and doctorate, GMAT (minimum score of 465) or GRE General Test, minimum GPA of 3.0. Additional exam requirements/recommendations for international students: Required—TOEFL (minimum score 550 paper-based; 80 iBT), IELTS (minimum score 6). *Application deadline:* For fall admission, 1/1 for domestic and international students. Applications are processed on a rolling basis. Application fee: $30. Electronic applications accepted. *Expenses:* Tuition, state resident: full-time $12,640. Tuition, nonresident: full-time $30,000. *Financial support:* In 2013–14, 10 students received support, including 10 teaching assistantships (averaging $21,605 per year); unspecified assistantships also available. Financial award applicants required to submit FAFSA. *Faculty research:* Job attitudes, personality and individual differences, organizational entry and exit, knowledge management, competitive dynamics. *Unit head:* Robert E. Thomas, PhD, Chair, 352-392-0136, Fax: 352-392-6020, E-mail: rethomas@ufl.edu. *Application contact:* Office of Admissions, 352-392-1365, E-mail: webrequests@admissions.ufl.edu.
Website: http://www.cba.ufl.edu/mang/.

University of Florida, Graduate School, Warrington College of Business Administration, Hough Graduate School of Business, Programs in Business Administration, Gainesville, FL 32611. Offers business administration (MBA); competitive strategy (MBA); entrepreneurship (MBA); finance (MBA); global management (MBA); Graham-Buffett security analysis (MBA); human resource management (MBA); information systems and operations management (MBA); international studies (MBA); Latin American business (MBA); management (MBA); marketing (MBA); real estate (MBA); sports administration (MBA); JD/MBA; MBA/MS; MBA/PhD; MBA/Pharm D; MD/MBA. *Accreditation:* AACSB. Part-time and evening/weekend programs available. Postbaccalaureate distance learning degree programs offered. *Faculty:* 72 full-time (10 women), 29 part-time/adjunct (7 women). *Students:* 440 full-time (122 women), 472 part-time (159 women); includes 203 minority (43 Black or African American, non-Hispanic/Latino; 3 American Indian or Alaska Native, non-Hispanic/Latino; 64 Asian, non-Hispanic/Latino; 92 Hispanic/Latino; 1 Native Hawaiian or other Pacific Islander, non-Hispanic/Latino), 39 international. Average age 32. 568 applicants, 58% accepted, 261 enrolled. In 2013, 405 master's awarded. *Degree requirements:* For master's, capstone course. *Entrance requirements:* For master's, GMAT (minimum score 465), minimum GPA of 3.0, interview. Additional exam requirements/recommendations for international students: Required—TOEFL (minimum score 550 paper-based; 80 iBT), IELTS (minimum score 6). *Application deadline:* For fall admission, 7/1 for domestic students, 1/1 for international students; for spring admission, 12/1 for domestic and international students. Applications are processed on a rolling basis. Application fee: $30. Electronic applications accepted. *Expenses:* Tuition, state resident: full-time $12,640. Tuition, nonresident: full-time $30,000. *Financial support:* In 2013–14, 24 students received support, including 24 teaching assistantships (averaging $6,143 per year); career-related internships or fieldwork, scholarships/grants, and unspecified assistantships also available. Support available to part-time students. Financial award applicants required to submit FAFSA. *Faculty research:* Accounting, finance, insurance, management, real estate, urban analysis marketing. *Unit head:* Alexander D. Sevilla, Assistant Dean/Director of MBA Program, 352-273-3252, Fax: 352-392-8791, E-mail: alex.sevilla@warrington.ufl.edu. *Application contact:* Andrew S. Lord, Senior Director of Admissions, 352-273-3241, Fax: 352-392-8791, E-mail: andrew.lord@warrington.ufl.edu.
Website: http://www.floridamba.ufl.edu/.

University of Florida, Levin College of Law, Gainesville, FL 32611. Offers comparative law (LL M); environmental law (LL M); international taxation (LL M); law (JD); taxation (LL M, SJD). *Accreditation:* ABA. *Faculty:* 77 full-time (37 women), 36 part-time/adjunct (10 women). *Students:* 1,072 full-time (452 women); includes 283 minority (69 Black or African American, non-Hispanic/Latino; 13 American Indian or Alaska Native, non-Hispanic/Latino; 45 Asian, non-Hispanic/Latino; 115 Hispanic/Latino; 41 Two or more races, non-Hispanic/Latino), 37 international. Average age 24. 2,686 applicants, 33% accepted, 284 enrolled. In 2013, 356 doctorates awarded. *Entrance requirements:* For doctorate, LSAT (for JD). *Application deadline:* For fall admission, 3/15 for domestic and international students. Applications are processed on a rolling basis. Application fee: $30. Electronic applications accepted. *Expenses:* Tuition, state resident: full-time $12,640. Tuition, nonresident: full-time $30,000. *Financial support:* In 2013–14, 446 students received support, including 42 research assistantships (averaging $9,261 per year); Federal Work-Study, institutionally sponsored loans, scholarships/grants, health care benefits, and unspecified assistantships also available. Financial award application deadline: 3/15; financial award applicants required to submit FAFSA. *Faculty research:* Environmental and land use law, taxation, dispute resolution, family law, Constitutional law. *Unit head:* Robert Jerry, Dean, 352-273-0600, Fax: 352-392-8727, E-mail: jerryr@law.ufl.edu. *Application contact:* Michelle Adorno, Assistant Dean for Admissions, 352-273-0890, Fax: 352-392-4087, E-mail: madorno@law.ufl.edu.
Website: http://www.law.ufl.edu/.

University of Hawaii at Manoa, Graduate Division, Shidler College of Business, Program in Business Administration, Honolulu, HI 96822. Offers Asian business studies (MBA); Chinese business studies (MBA); decision sciences (MBA); entrepreneurship (MBA); finance (MBA); finance and banking (MBA); human resources management (MBA); information management (MBA); information technology (MBA); international business (MBA); Japanese business studies (MBA); marketing (MBA); organizational behavior (MBA); organizational management (MBA); real estate (MBA); student-designed track (MBA). *Accreditation:* AACSB. Part-time and evening/weekend programs

available. *Degree requirements:* For master's, thesis optional. *Entrance requirements:* For master's, GMAT, minimum GPA of 3.0. Additional exam requirements/recommendations for international students: Required—TOEFL (minimum score 600 paper-based; 100 iBT), IELTS (minimum score 7). *Expenses:* Contact institution.

University of Hawaii at Manoa, Graduate Division, Shidler College of Business, Program in International Management, Honolulu, HI 96822. Offers Asian finance (PhD); global information technology management (PhD); international accounting (PhD); international marketing (PhD); international organization and strategy (PhD). Part-time programs available. *Degree requirements:* For doctorate, comprehensive exam, thesis/dissertation. *Entrance requirements:* For doctorate, GMAT or GRE General Test, minimum GPA of 3.0. Additional exam requirements/recommendations for international students: Required—TOEFL (minimum score 600 paper-based; 100 iBT), IELTS (minimum score 7). *Expenses:* Contact institution.

University of Houston–Victoria, School of Business Administration, Victoria, TX 77901-4450. Offers accounting (MBA); economic development and entrepreneurship (MS); finance (GMBA, MBA); general business (MBA); international business (MBA); management (GMBA, MBA); marketing (MBA). *Accreditation:* AACSB. Part-time and evening/weekend programs available. Postbaccalaureate distance learning degree programs offered (minimal on-campus study). *Faculty:* 45 full-time (15 women). *Students:* 193 full-time (93 women), 673 part-time (325 women); includes 489 minority (185 Black or African American, non-Hispanic/Latino; 169 Asian, non-Hispanic/Latino; 114 Hispanic/Latino; 1 Native Hawaiian or other Pacific Islander, non-Hispanic/Latino; 20 Two or more races, non-Hispanic/Latino), 94 international. *Entrance requirements:* For master's, GMAT. Additional exam requirements/recommendations for international students: Required—TOEFL (minimum score 550 paper-based). *Application deadline:* For fall admission, 6/1 for international students; for spring admission, 10/1 for international students. Applications are processed on a rolling basis. Application fee: $0. Electronic applications accepted. *Expenses:* Tuition, state resident: full-time $4534; part-time $251 per credit hour. Tuition, nonresident: full-time $10,906; part-time $606 per contact hour. *Required fees:* $68 per semester hour. Tuition and fees vary according to course load. *Financial support:* In 2013–14, research assistantships with partial tuition reimbursements (averaging $2,000 per year), teaching assistantships with partial tuition reimbursements (averaging $2,000 per year) were awarded; Federal Work-Study, scholarships/grants, and unspecified assistantships also available. Support available to part-time students. Financial award application deadline: 4/15; financial award applicants required to submit FAFSA. *Faculty research:* Economic development, marketing, finance. *Unit head:* Dr. Farhang Niroomand, Dean, 361-570-4230, Fax: 361-580-5599, E-mail: niroomandf@uhv.edu. *Application contact:* Admissions and Records, 361-570-4359, Fax: 361-580-5500, E-mail: admissions@uhv.edu.
Website: http://www.uhv.edu/bus/.

University of Kentucky, Graduate School, Patterson School of Diplomacy and International Commerce, Lexington, KY 40506-0027. Offers MA. *Degree requirements:* For master's, one foreign language, comprehensive exam, statistics. *Entrance requirements:* For master's, GRE General Test, minimum undergraduate GPA of 3.0. Additional exam requirements/recommendations for international students: Required—TOEFL (minimum score 550 paper-based; 79 iBT). Electronic applications accepted. *Faculty research:* International relations, foreign and defense policy, cross-cultural negotiation, international science and technology, diplomacy, international economics and development, geopolitical modeling.

University of La Verne, College of Business and Public Management, Graduate Programs in Business Administration, La Verne, CA 91750-4443. Offers accounting (MBA); executive management (MBA-EP); finance (MBA, MBA-EP); health services management (MBA); information technology (MBA, MBA-EP); international business (MBA, MBA-EP); leadership (MBA-EP); managed care (MBA); management (MBA, MBA-EP); marketing (MBA, MBA-EP). Part-time and evening/weekend programs available. *Faculty:* 22 full-time (9 women), 37 part-time/adjunct (10 women). *Students:* 793 full-time (356 women), 164 part-time (80 women); includes 153 minority (17 Black or African American, non-Hispanic/Latino; 21 Asian, non-Hispanic/Latino; 110 Hispanic/Latino; 5 Two or more races, non-Hispanic/Latino), 691 international. Average age 27. In 2013, 514 master's awarded. *Entrance requirements:* For master's, GMAT, MAT, or GRE, minimum undergraduate GPA of 3.0, 2 letters of recommendation, resume, statement of purpose. Additional exam requirements/recommendations for international students: Required—TOEFL (minimum score 550 paper-based; 85 iBT). *Application deadline:* Applications are processed on a rolling basis. Application fee: $50. *Expenses:* Contact institution. *Financial support:* Career-related internships or fieldwork, institutionally sponsored loans, and scholarships/grants available. Financial award application deadline: 3/2; financial award applicants required to submit FAFSA. *Unit head:* Dr. Abe Helou, Chairperson, 909-593-3511 Ext. 4211, Fax: 909-392-2704, E-mail: ihelou@laverne.edu. *Application contact:* Rina Lazarian-Chehab, Senior Associate Director of Graduate Admissions, 909-593-3511 Ext. 4317, Fax: 909-392-2704, E-mail: rlazarian@laverne.edu.

University of La Verne, Regional and Online Campuses, Graduate Programs, Inland Empire Campus, Ontario, CA 91761. Offers business administration (MBA, MBA-EP), including accounting (MBA), finance (MBA), health services management (MBA-EP), information technology (MBA-EP), international business (MBA), managed care (MBA), management and leadership (MBA-EP), marketing (MBA-EP), supply chain management (MBA); leadership and management (MS), including human resource management, nonprofit management, organizational development. Part-time and evening/weekend programs available. *Faculty:* 1 full-time (0 women), 14 part-time/adjunct (6 women). *Students:* 26 full-time (15 women), 106 part-time (65 women); includes 92 minority (15 Black or African American, non-Hispanic/Latino; 29 Asian, non-Hispanic/Latino; 43 Hispanic/Latino; 1 Native Hawaiian or other Pacific Islander, non-Hispanic/Latino; 4 Two or more races, non-Hispanic/Latino). Average age 37. In 2013, 49 master's awarded. *Application deadline:* Applications are processed on a rolling basis. Application fee: $50. *Expenses:* Contact institution. *Financial support:* Institutionally sponsored loans available. Financial award application deadline: 3/2; financial award applicants required to submit FAFSA. *Unit head:* Allen Stout, Campus Director, Inland Empire Regional Campus in Ontario, 909-937-6987, E-mail: astout@laverne.edu. *Application contact:* Karen Schumann, Senior Associate Director of Admissions, Inland Empire Regional Campus in Ontario, 909-937-6991, E-mail: kschumann@laverne.edu.
Website: http://laverne.edu/locations/inland-empire/.

University of Lethbridge, School of Graduate Studies, Lethbridge, AB T1K 3M4, Canada. Offers accounting (MScM); addictions counseling (M Sc); agricultural biotechnology (M Sc); agricultural studies (M Sc, MA); anthropology (MA); archaeology (M Sc, MA); art (MA, MFA); biochemistry (M Sc); biological sciences (M Sc); biomolecular science (PhD); biosystems and biodiversity (PhD); Canadian studies (MA); chemistry (M Sc); computer science (M Sc); computer science and geographical information science (M Sc); counseling (MC); counseling psychology (M Ed); dramatic arts (MA); earth, space, and physical science (PhD); economics (MA); education (MA); educational leadership (M Ed); English (MA); environmental science (M Sc); evolution and behavior (PhD); exercise science (M Sc); finance (MScM); French (MA); French/German (MA); French/Spanish (MA); general education (M Ed); general management (MScM); geography (M Sc, MA); German (MA); health sciences (M Sc); human resource management and labour relations (MScM); individualized multidisciplinary (M Sc, MA); information systems (MScM); international management (MScM); kinesiology (M Sc, MA); marketing (MScM); mathematics (M Sc); modern languages (MA); music (M Mus, MA); Native American studies (MA); neuroscience (M Sc, PhD); new media (MA, MFA); nursing (M Sc); philosophy (MA); physics (M Sc); policy and strategy (MScM); political science (MA); psychology (M Sc, MA); religious studies (MA); sociology (MA); theatre and dramatic arts (MFA); theoretical and computational science (PhD); urban and regional studies (MA); women and gender studies (MA). Part-time and evening/weekend programs available. *Degree requirements:* For doctorate, comprehensive exam, thesis/dissertation. *Entrance requirements:* For master's, GMAT (for M Sc in management), bachelor's degree in related field, minimum GPA of 3.0 during previous 20 graded semester courses, 2 years teaching or related experience (M Ed); for doctorate, master's degree, minimum graduate GPA of 3.5. Additional exam requirements/recommendations for international students: Required—TOEFL. Application fee: $60 Canadian dollars. *Financial support:* Fellowships, research assistantships, teaching assistantships, scholarships/grants, health care benefits, and unspecified assistantships available. *Faculty research:* Movement and brain plasticity, gibberellin physiology, photosynthesis, carbon cycling, molecular properties of main-group ring components. *Application contact:* School of Graduate Studies, 403-329-2793, Fax: 403-332-5239, E-mail: sgsinquiries@uleth.ca.
Website: http://www.uleth.ca/graduatestudies/.

University of Louisville, Graduate School, College of Business, MBA Programs, Louisville, KY 40292-0001. Offers entrepreneurship (MBA); global business (MBA); health sector management (MBA). *Accreditation:* AACSB. Part-time and evening/weekend programs available. *Students:* 202 full-time (65 women), 42 part-time (15 women); includes 21 minority (9 Black or African American, non-Hispanic/Latino; 1 American Indian or Alaska Native, non-Hispanic/Latino; 7 Asian, non-Hispanic/Latino; 3 Hispanic/Latino; 1 Two or more races, non-Hispanic/Latino), 38 international. Average age 29. 314 applicants, 42% accepted, 116 enrolled. In 2013, 61 master's awarded. *Degree requirements:* For master's, international learning experience. *Entrance requirements:* For master's, GMAT, 2 letters of reference, personal interview, resume, personal statement, college transcript(s). Additional exam requirements/recommendations for international students: Required—TOEFL (minimum score 83 iBT). *Application deadline:* For fall admission, 7/1 for domestic students; for spring admission, 12/1 for domestic students. Applications are processed on a rolling basis. Application fee: $60. *Expenses:* Tuition, state resident: full-time $10,788; part-time $599 per credit hour. Tuition, nonresident: full-time $22,446; part-time $1247 per credit hour. *Required fees:* $196. Tuition and fees vary according to program and reciprocity agreements. *Financial support:* Fellowships with full tuition reimbursements, research assistantships with full tuition reimbursements, health care benefits, and unspecified assistantships available. Financial award application deadline: 3/31; financial award applicants required to submit FAFSA. *Faculty research:* Entrepreneurship, venture capital, retailing/franchising, corporate governance and leadership, supply chain management. *Unit head:* Dr. Carolyn M. Callahan, Dean, 502-852-6440, Fax: 502-852-7557, E-mail: cmcall04@louisville.edu. *Application contact:* Susan E. Hildebrand, Program Director, 502-852-7257, Fax: 502-852-4901, E-mail: s.hildebrand@louisville.edu.
Website: http://business.louisville.edu/mba.

University of Maine, Graduate School, The Maine Business School, Orono, ME 04469. Offers accounting (MBA); business administration (CGS); business and sustainability (MBA); finance (MBA); international business (MBA); management (MBA). *Accreditation:* AACSB. Part-time and evening/weekend programs available. Postbaccalaureate distance learning degree programs offered. *Faculty:* 23 full-time (7 women). *Students:* 31 full-time (12 women), 12 part-time (9 women); includes 5 minority (1 Black or African American, non-Hispanic/Latino; 3 Asian, non-Hispanic/Latino; 1 Hispanic/Latino), 4 international. Average age 29. 41 applicants, 71% accepted, 24 enrolled. In 2013, 28 master's awarded. *Entrance requirements:* For master's, GMAT. Additional exam requirements/recommendations for international students: Required—TOEFL (minimum score 550 paper-based). *Application deadline:* For fall admission, 6/1 priority date for domestic and international students; for spring admission, 11/15 priority date for domestic and international students. Applications are processed on a rolling basis. Application fee: $65. Electronic applications accepted. *Expenses:* Contact institution. *Financial support:* In 2013–14, 14 students received support, including 3 teaching assistantships with full tuition reimbursements available (averaging $14,100 per year); career-related internships or fieldwork, Federal Work-Study, institutionally sponsored loans, scholarships/grants, tuition waivers (full and partial), and unspecified assistantships also available. Financial award application deadline: 3/1. *Faculty research:* Entrepreneurship, investment management, international markets, decision support systems, strategic planning. *Total annual research expenditures:* $5,089. *Unit head:* Carol Mandzik, Manager of MBA Programs, Executive Education and Internships, 207-581-1971, Fax: 207-581-1930, E-mail: carol.mandzik@maine.edu. *Application contact:* Scott G. Delcourt, Associate Dean of the Graduate School, 207-581-3291, Fax: 207-581-3232, E-mail: graduate@maine.edu.
Website: http://www.umaine.edu/business/.

University of Mary Hardin-Baylor, Graduate Studies in Business Administration, Belton, TX 76513. Offers accounting (MBA); information systems management (MBA); international business (MBA); management (MBA). Part-time and evening/weekend programs available. *Faculty:* 10 full-time (4 women), 2 part-time/adjunct (1 woman). *Students:* 26 full-time (11 women), 52 part-time (19 women); includes 20 minority (7 Black or African American, non-Hispanic/Latino; 3 Asian, non-Hispanic/Latino; 9 Hispanic/Latino; 1 Two or more races, non-Hispanic/Latino), 21 international. Average age 30. 55 applicants, 75% accepted, 27 enrolled. In 2013, 23 master's awarded. *Degree requirements:* For master's, comprehensive exam. *Entrance requirements:* For master's, minimum GPA of 3.0, interview. Additional exam requirements/recommendations for international students: Required—TOEFL (minimum score 550 paper-based; 80 iBT), IELTS (minimum score 6). *Application deadline:* For fall admission, 6/1 for domestic students, 6/15 priority date for international students; for spring admission, 11/1 for domestic students, 10/15 priority date for international students. Applications are processed on a rolling basis. Application fee: $35 ($135 for international students). Electronic applications accepted. *Expenses: Tuition:* Full-time $14,130; part-time $785 per credit hour. *Required fees:* $1350; $75 per credit hour. $50 per term. *Financial support:* Federal Work-Study, unspecified assistantships, and scholarships (for some active duty military personnel only) available. Financial award applicants required to submit FAFSA. *Unit head:* Dr. Nancy Bonner, Assistant Professor/Program Director, 254-295-5405, E-mail: nbonner@umhb.edu. *Application contact:* Melissa Ford, Director of Graduate Admissions, 254-295-4020, Fax: 254-295-5038, E-mail: mford@umhb.edu.
Website: http://www.graduate.umhb.edu/mba.

University of Maryland University College, Graduate School of Management and Technology, Program in International Management, Adelphi, MD 20783. Offers MIM, Certificate. Program offered evenings and weekends only. Part-time programs available. Postbaccalaureate distance learning degree programs offered (no on-campus study). *Students:* 5 full-time (all women), 217 part-time (113 women); includes 116 minority (76

Black or African American, non-Hispanic/Latino; 2 American Indian or Alaska Native, non-Hispanic/Latino; 11 Asian, non-Hispanic/Latino; 17 Hispanic/Latino; 10 Two or more races, non-Hispanic/Latino), 11 international. Average age 35. 58 applicants, 100% accepted, 38 enrolled. In 2013, 45 master's, 10 Certificates awarded. *Degree requirements:* For master's, thesis or alternative. *Application deadline:* Applications are processed on a rolling basis. Application fee: $50. Electronic applications accepted. *Financial support:* Federal Work-Study and scholarships/grants available. Support available to part-time students. Financial award application deadline: 6/1; financial award applicants required to submit FAFSA. *Unit head:* Dr. Robert Jerome, Director, 240-684-2400, Fax: 240-684-2401, E-mail: robert.jerome@umuc.edu. *Application contact:* Coordinator, Graduate Admissions, 800-888-8682, Fax: 240-684-2151, E-mail: newgrad@umuc.edu.
Website: http://www.umuc.edu/grad/iman.shtml.

University of Massachusetts Dartmouth, Graduate School, Charlton College of Business, Program in Business Administration, North Dartmouth, MA 02747-2300. Offers accounting (Postbaccalaureate Certificate); business administration (MBA); business foundations (Graduate Certificate); finance (Postbaccalaureate Certificate); international business (Graduate Certificate); management (Postbaccalaureate Certificate); marketing (Postbaccalaureate Certificate); organizational leadership (Graduate Certificate); supply chain management (Postbaccalaureate Certificate). *Accreditation:* AACSB. Part-time programs available. Postbaccalaureate distance learning degree programs offered (no on-campus study). *Faculty:* 36 full-time (12 women), 27 part-time/adjunct (10 women). *Students:* 154 full-time (73 women), 120 part-time (55 women); includes 28 minority (2 Black or African American, non-Hispanic/Latino; 1 American Indian or Alaska Native, non-Hispanic/Latino; 6 Asian, non-Hispanic/Latino; 11 Hispanic/Latino; 8 Two or more races, non-Hispanic/Latino), 129 international. Average age 29. 204 applicants, 82% accepted, 112 enrolled. In 2013, 71 master's, 15 other advanced degrees awarded. *Degree requirements:* For master's, portfolio of MBA course work. *Entrance requirements:* For master's, GMAT, statement of purpose (minimum of 300 words), resume, 2 letters of recommendation, official transcripts; for other advanced degree, statement of purpose (minimum of 300 words), resume, official transcripts. Additional exam requirements/recommendations for international students: Required—TOEFL (minimum score 500 paper-based; 72 iBT), IELTS (minimum score 6). *Application deadline:* For fall admission, 8/1 priority date for domestic students, 5/1 priority date for international students; for spring admission, 1/1 priority date for domestic students, 10/1 priority date for international students. Applications are processed on a rolling basis. Application fee: $60. Electronic applications accepted. *Expenses:* Tuition, state resident: full-time $2071; part-time $86.29 per credit. Tuition, nonresident: full-time $8099; part-time $337.46 per credit. Tuition and fees vary according to course load and reciprocity agreements. *Financial support:* Federal Work-Study and unspecified assistantships available. Support available to part-time students. Financial award application deadline: 3/1; financial award applicants required to submit FAFSA. *Faculty research:* E-commerce, managing diversity, agile manufacturing, green business, activity-based management, build-to-order supply chain management. *Total annual research expenditures:* $330,000. *Unit head:* Toby Stapleton, Assistant Dean for Graduate Studies, 508-999-8543, Fax: 508-999-8646, E-mail: tstapleton@umassd.edu. *Application contact:* Steven Briggs, Director of Marketing and Recruitment for Graduate Studies, 508-999-8604, Fax: 508-999-8183, E-mail: graduate@umassd.edu.
Website: http://www.umassd.edu/charlton/.

University of Memphis, Graduate School, Fogelman College of Business and Economics, Program in Business Administration, Memphis, TN 38152. Offers accounting (MBA, PhD); economics (MBA, PhD); executive business administration (MBA); finance (PhD); finance, insurance, and real estate (MBA, MS); international business administration (IMBA); management (MBA, MS, PhD); management information systems (MBA, MS, PhD); management science (MBA); marketing (MBA, MS); marketing and supply chain management (PhD); real estate development (MS); JD/MBA. *Accreditation:* AACSB. *Faculty:* 44 full-time (9 women), 5 part-time/adjunct (0 women). *Students:* 238 full-time (101 women), 315 part-time (113 women); includes 146 minority (80 Black or African American, non-Hispanic/Latino; 1 American Indian or Alaska Native, non-Hispanic/Latino; 46 Asian, non-Hispanic/Latino; 13 Hispanic/Latino; 2 Native Hawaiian or other Pacific Islander, non-Hispanic/Latino; 4 Two or more races, non-Hispanic/Latino), 104 international. Average age 32. 343 applicants, 62% accepted, 102 enrolled. In 2013, 140 master's, 17 doctorates awarded. *Degree requirements:* For master's, comprehensive exam; for doctorate, comprehensive exam, thesis/dissertation. *Entrance requirements:* For master's, GMAT, resume; for doctorate, GMAT, interview, minimum GPA of 3.4, resume, letter of recommendation. Additional exam requirements/recommendations for international students: Required—TOEFL (minimum score 550 paper-based). *Application deadline:* For fall admission, 8/1 for domestic students; for spring admission, 12/1 for domestic students. Application fee: $35 ($60 for international students). *Financial support:* In 2013–14, 164 students received support. Research assistantships with full tuition reimbursements available, teaching assistantships with full tuition reimbursements available, career-related internships or fieldwork, Federal Work-Study, scholarships/grants, and unspecified assistantships available. Financial award application deadline: 2/15; financial award applicants required to submit FAFSA. *Faculty research:* Competitive business strategy, finance microstructures, supply chain management innovations, health care economics, litigation risks and corporate audits. *Unit head:* Rajiv Grover, Dean, 901-678-3759, E-mail: rgrover@memphis.edu. *Application contact:* Dr. Carol V. Danehower, Associate Dean, 901-678-5402, Fax: 901-678-3579, E-mail: fcbegp@memphis.edu.
Website: http://www.memphis.edu/fcbe/grad_programs.php.

University of Miami, Graduate School, School of Business Administration, Program in Business Administration, Coral Gables, FL 33124. Offers accounting (MBA); computer information systems (MBA); executive and professional (MBA), including international business, management; finance (MBA); international business (MBA); management (MBA); management science (MBA); marketing (MBA); professional management (MSPM); JD/MBA; MBA/MSIE. *Accreditation:* AACSB. Evening/weekend programs available. *Degree requirements:* For master's, comprehensive exam. *Entrance requirements:* For master's, GMAT. Additional exam requirements/recommendations for international students: Required—TOEFL (minimum score 550 paper-based; 59 iBT). Electronic applications accepted. *Faculty research:* Leadership, e-commerce, supply chain management.

University of Michigan–Dearborn, College of Business, Dearborn, MI 48128-1491. Offers accounting (MBA, MS); business analytics (MS); finance (MBA, MS); human resource management (MBA); information systems (MS); international business (MBA); investment (MBA); management (MBA); management information systems (MBA); marketing (MBA); supply chain management (MBA, MS); taxation (MBA); MBA/MHSA; MBA/MSE; MBA/MSF; MBA/MSIS; MBA/MSSCM; MSF/MSA. *Accreditation:* AACSB. Part-time and evening/weekend programs available. Postbaccalaureate distance learning degree programs offered (no on-campus study). *Faculty:* 24 full-time (8 women), 5 part-time/adjunct (2 women). *Students:* 82 full-time (31 women), 323 part-time (116 women); includes 72 minority (17 Black or African American, non-Hispanic/Latino; 2 American Indian or Alaska Native, non-Hispanic/Latino; 30 Asian, non-Hispanic/Latino; 15 Hispanic/Latino; 8 Two or more races, non-Hispanic/Latino), 65 international. Average age 32. 290 applicants, 44% accepted, 99 enrolled. In 2013, 143 master's awarded. *Entrance requirements:* For master's, GMAT or GRE, pre-calculus or finite mathematics; 18 credits of accounting course work beyond introductory courses (MS in accounting). Additional exam requirements/recommendations for international students: Required—TOEFL (minimum score 560 paper-based; 84 iBT), IELTS. *Application deadline:* For fall admission, 8/1 priority date for domestic students, 5/1 priority date for international students; for winter admission, 12/1 priority date for domestic students, 9/1 priority date for international students; for spring admission, 4/1 priority date for domestic students, 1/1 priority date for international students. Applications are processed on a rolling basis. Application fee: $60. Electronic applications accepted. *Expenses:* Contact institution. *Financial support:* Career-related internships or fieldwork, Federal Work-Study, and scholarships/grants available. Support available to part-time students. Financial award application deadline: 9/1; financial award applicants required to submit FAFSA. *Faculty research:* Cultural diversity, buyer-supplier relations, error detection in data, economic evolution. *Unit head:* Dr. Raju Balakrishnan, Dean, 313-593-5248, Fax: 313-271-9835, E-mail: rajub@umich.edu. *Application contact:* Joan Doherty, Academic Advisor/Counselor, 313-593-5460, Fax: 313-271-9838, E-mail: umd-gradbusiness@umich.edu.
Website: http://www.cob.umd.umich.edu.

University of Michigan–Flint, School of Management, Flint, MI 48502-1950. Offers accounting (MBA, MSA); business (Graduate Certificate); computer information systems (MBA); finance (MBA); health care management (MBA); international business (MBA); lean manufacturing (MBA); marketing (MBA); organizational leadership (MBA). *Accreditation:* AACSB. Part-time and evening/weekend programs available. Postbaccalaureate distance learning degree programs offered (minimal on-campus study). *Faculty:* 13 full-time (3 women), 4 part-time/adjunct (0 women). *Students:* 19 full-time (6 women), 234 part-time (72 women); includes 50 minority (21 Black or African American, non-Hispanic/Latino; 5 American Indian or Alaska Native, non-Hispanic/Latino; 12 Asian, non-Hispanic/Latino; 5 Hispanic/Latino; 7 Two or more races, non-Hispanic/Latino), 30 international. Average age 32. 195 applicants, 56% accepted, 88 enrolled. In 2013, 73 master's awarded. *Degree requirements:* For master's, thesis or alternative. *Entrance requirements:* For master's, GMAT or GRE, minimum GPA of 3.0. Additional exam requirements/recommendations for international students: Required—TOEFL (minimum score 560 paper-based; 84 iBT), IELTS (minimum score 6.5). *Application deadline:* For fall admission, 8/1 for domestic students, 5/1 for international students; for winter admission, 11/1 for domestic students, 9/1 for international students; for spring admission, 2/15 for domestic students, 1/15 for international students. Applications are processed on a rolling basis. Application fee: $55. Electronic applications accepted. *Financial support:* Federal Work-Study, scholarships/grants, and unspecified assistantships available. Support available to part-time students. Financial award application deadline: 3/1; financial award applicants required to submit FAFSA. *Unit head:* Dr. Scott Johnson, Dean, School of Management, 810-762-3164, Fax: 810-237-6685, E-mail: scotjohn@umflint.edu. *Application contact:* Jeremiah Cook, Marketing Communications Specialist, 810-424-5583, Fax: 810-766-6789, E-mail: jecook@umflint.edu.
Website: http://www.umflint.edu/som/.

University of New Brunswick Saint John, Faculty of Business, Saint John, NB E2L 4L5, Canada. Offers administration (MBA); electronic commerce (MBA); international business (MBA); natural resource management (MBA). Part-time programs available. *Faculty:* 7 full-time (3 women), 2 part-time/adjunct (1 woman). *Students:* 72 full-time (28 women), 100 part-time (47 women). In 2013, 102 master's awarded. *Entrance requirements:* For master's, GMAT (minimum score of 550) or GRE (minimum 54th percentile), minimum GPA of 3.0. Additional exam requirements/recommendations for international students: Required—TOEFL (minimum score 580 paper-based; 93 iBT), TWE (minimum score 4.5). *Application deadline:* For fall admission, 5/31 for domestic students, 7/15 for international students. Application fee: $100. Electronic applications accepted. *Expenses:* Contact institution. *Financial support:* In 2013–14, 4 students received support. Career-related internships or fieldwork and scholarships/grants available. *Faculty research:* International business, project management, innovation and technology management; business use of Weblogs and podcasts to communicate; corporate governance; high-involvement work systems; international competitiveness; supply chain management and logistics. *Unit head:* Dr. Shelley Rinehart, Director of Graduate Studies, 506-648-5902, Fax: 506-648-5574, E-mail: rinehart@unb.ca. *Application contact:* Tammy Morin, Secretary, 506-648-5746, Fax: 506-648-5574, E-mail: tmorin@unbsj.ca.
Website: http://go.unb.ca/gradprograms.

University of New Haven, Graduate School, College of Business, Program in Business Administration, West Haven, CT 06516-1916. Offers accounting (MBA, Certificate), including CPA (MBA); business administration (MBA); business management (Certificate); business policy and strategic leadership (MBA); finance (MBA), including CFA; global marketing (MBA); human resource management (Certificate); human resources management (MBA); international business (Certificate); marketing (MBA, Certificate); sports management (MBA). Part-time and evening/weekend programs available. *Students:* 125 full-time (55 women), 88 part-time (30 women); includes 31 minority (16 Black or African American, non-Hispanic/Latino; 1 American Indian or Alaska Native, non-Hispanic/Latino; 8 Asian, non-Hispanic/Latino; 5 Hispanic/Latino; 1 Native Hawaiian or other Pacific Islander, non-Hispanic/Latino), 72 international. 196 applicants, 89% accepted, 72 enrolled. In 2013, 143 master's, 24 other advanced degrees awarded. *Degree requirements:* For master's, thesis optional. *Entrance requirements:* For master's, GMAT. Additional exam requirements/recommendations for international students: Required—TOEFL (minimum score 80 iBT), IELTS, PTE (minimum score 53). *Application deadline:* For fall admission, 5/31 for international students; for winter admission, 10/15 for international students; for spring admission, 1/15 for international students. Applications are processed on a rolling basis. Application fee: $75. Electronic applications accepted. Application fee is waived when completed online. *Expenses: Tuition:* Full-time $21,600; part-time $800 per credit hour. *Required fees:* $45 per trimester. *Financial support:* Research assistantships with partial tuition reimbursements, teaching assistantships with partial tuition reimbursements, career-related internships or fieldwork, Federal Work-Study, scholarships/grants, and unspecified assistantships available. Support available to part-time students. Financial award applicants required to submit FAFSA. *Unit head:* Dr. Armando Rodriguez, Director, 203-932-7372, E-mail: arodriguez@newhaven.edu. *Application contact:* Eloise Gormley, Director of Graduate Admissions, 203-932-7440, E-mail: gradinfo@newhaven.edu.
Website: http://www.newhaven.edu/7433/.

University of New Mexico, Anderson Graduate School of Management, Department of Finance, International, Technology and Entrepreneurship, Albuquerque, NM 87131-1221. Offers entrepreneurship (MBA); finance (MBA); international management (MBA); international management in Latin America (MBA); management of technology (MBA). Part-time and evening/weekend programs available. *Faculty:* 16 full-time (2 women), 5 part-time/adjunct (1 woman). In 2013, 72 master's awarded. *Entrance requirements:* For master's, GMAT or GRE, minimum GPA of 3.0 on last 60 hours of coursework. Additional exam requirements/recommendations for international students: Required—TOEFL (minimum score 550 paper-based; 79 iBT). *Application deadline:* For fall

admission, 4/1 priority date for domestic and international students; for spring admission, 10/1 priority date for domestic and international students. Applications are processed on a rolling basis. Application fee: $50. Electronic applications accepted. *Expenses:* Contact institution. *Financial support:* Fellowships, research assistantships, career-related internships or fieldwork, Federal Work-Study, scholarships/grants, and unspecified assistantships available. Support available to part-time students. Financial award application deadline: 6/1; financial award applicants required to submit FAFSA. *Faculty research:* Corporate finance, investments, management in Latin America, management of technology, entrepreneurship. *Unit head:* Dr. Leslie Boni, Chair, 505-277-6471, Fax: 505-277-7108, E-mail: boni01@unm.edu. *Application contact:* Tracy Wilkey, Manager, Academic Advisement, 505-277-3290, Fax: 505-277-8436, E-mail: andersonadvising@unm.edu.
Website: http://mba.mgt.unm.edu/default.asp.

University of North Florida, Coggin College of Business, MBA Program, Jacksonville, FL 32224. Offers accounting (MBA); construction management (MBA); e-commerce (MBA); economics (MBA); finance (MBA); human resource management (MBA); international business (MBA); logistics (MBA); management applications (MBA). *Accreditation:* AACSB. Part-time and evening/weekend programs available. *Faculty:* 14 full-time (6 women), 1 part-time/adjunct (0 women). *Students:* 90 full-time (41 women), 231 part-time (84 women); includes 47 minority (18 Black or African American, non-Hispanic/Latino; 8 Asian, non-Hispanic/Latino; 16 Hispanic/Latino; 5 Two or more races, non-Hispanic/Latino), 29 international. Average age 29. 222 applicants, 47% accepted, 80 enrolled. In 2013, 152 master's awarded. *Entrance requirements:* For master's, GMAT or GRE, U.S. bachelor's degree from regionally-accredited university or equivalent foreign degree. Additional exam requirements/recommendations for international students: Required—TOEFL (minimum score 550 paper-based; 79 iBT). *Application deadline:* For fall admission, 7/1 priority date for domestic students, 5/1 for international students; for spring admission, 11/1 priority date for domestic students, 10/1 for international students. Application fee: $30. *Expenses:* Tuition, state resident: full-time $9794; part-time $408.10 per credit hour. Tuition, nonresident: full-time $22,383; part-time $932.61 per credit hour. *Required fees:* $2020; $84.20 per credit hour. Tuition and fees vary according to course load and program. *Financial support:* In 2013–14, 35 students received support, including 1 research assistantship (averaging $2,700 per year); teaching assistantships, Federal Work-Study, and tuition waivers (partial) also available. Support available to part-time students. Financial award application deadline: 4/1; financial award applicants required to submit FAFSA. *Faculty research:* Performance measures, costing, and inventory issues in logistics and supply chain management; inter-organizational systems; international management and marketing practices; e-commerce; organizational learning and socialization processes. *Total annual research expenditures:* $12,025. *Application contact:* Cheryl Campbell, Graduate Advisor, 904-620-2575, Fax: 904-620-2832, E-mail: ccampbell@unf.edu.
Website: http://www.unf.edu/coggin/academics/graduate/mba.aspx.

University of Pennsylvania, School of Arts and Sciences and Wharton School, Joseph H. Lauder Institute of Management and International Studies, Philadelphia, PA 19104. Offers international studies (MA); management and international studies (MBA); MBA/MA. Applications must be made concurrently and separately to the Wharton MBA program. *Degree requirements:* For master's, one foreign language, thesis. *Entrance requirements:* For master's, GMAT or GRE, advanced proficiency in a non-native language (Arabic, Chinese, French, German, Hindi, Japanese, Portuguese, Russian, or Spanish). Additional exam requirements/recommendations for international students: Required—TOEFL. Electronic applications accepted. *Expenses:* Contact institution. *Faculty research:* Finance, marketing, strategy, operations management, multinational management.

University of Phoenix–Atlanta Campus, School of Business, Sandy Springs, GA 30350-4153. Offers accounting (MBA); business administration (MBA); global management (MBA); human resources management (MBA, MM); management (MM); marketing (MBA); public administration (MM). Evening/weekend programs available. Postbaccalaureate distance learning degree programs offered. *Degree requirements:* For master's, thesis (for some programs). *Entrance requirements:* For master's, minimum undergraduate GPA of 3.0, 3 years of work experience. Additional exam requirements/recommendations for international students: Required—TOEFL (minimum score 550 paper-based; 79 iBT).

University of Phoenix–Augusta Campus, School of Business, Augusta, GA 30909-4583. Offers accounting (MBA); business administration (MBA); business and management (MBA, MM); global management (MBA); human resources management (MBA, MM); management (MM); marketing (MBA); public administration (MBA, MM). Postbaccalaureate distance learning degree programs offered.

University of Phoenix–Austin Campus, School of Business, Austin, TX 78759. Offers accounting (MBA); business administration (MBA); business and management (MBA); e-business (MBA); global management (MBA); human resources management (MBA, MM); management (MM); marketing (MBA); public administration (MBA). Postbaccalaureate distance learning degree programs offered.

University of Phoenix–Bay Area Campus, School of Business, San Jose, CA 95134-1805. Offers accountancy (MS); accounting (MBA); business administration (MBA, DBA); energy management (MBA); global management (MBA); health care management (MBA); human resource management (MBA); human resources management (MM); management (MM); marketing (MBA); organizational leadership (DM); project management (MBA); public administration (MPA); technology management (MBA). Evening/weekend programs available. Postbaccalaureate distance learning degree programs offered (no on-campus study). *Degree requirements:* For master's, thesis (for some programs). *Entrance requirements:* For master's, minimum undergraduate GPA of 3.0, 3 years of work experience. Additional exam requirements/recommendations for international students: Required—TOEFL (minimum score 550 paper-based; 79 iBT). Electronic applications accepted.

University of Phoenix–Birmingham Campus, College of Graduate Business and Management, Birmingham, AL 35242. Offers accounting (MBA); business administration (MBA); global management (MBA); human resources management (MBA, MM); management (MM); marketing (MBA); public administration (MM).

University of Phoenix–Boston Campus, School of Business, Braintree, MA 02184. Offers administration (MBA); global management (MBA). Evening/weekend programs available. *Degree requirements:* For master's, thesis (for some programs). *Entrance requirements:* For master's, 3 years of work experience, minimum undergraduate GPA of 3.0. Additional exam requirements/recommendations for international students: Required—TOEFL (minimum score 550 paper-based; 79 iBT).

University of Phoenix–Central Valley Campus, School of Business, Fresno, CA 93720-1562. Offers accounting (MBA); business administration (MBA); global management (MBA); human resources management (MBA, MM); management (MM); marketing (MBA); public administration (MBA, MM).

University of Phoenix–Charlotte Campus, School of Business, Charlotte, NC 28273-3409. Offers accounting (MBA); business administration (MBA); global management (MBA). Evening/weekend programs available. *Degree requirements:* For master's, thesis (for some programs). *Entrance requirements:* For master's, minimum undergraduate GPA of 3.0, 3 years work experience. Additional exam requirements/recommendations for international students: Required—TOEFL (minimum score 550 paper-based; 79 iBT). Electronic applications accepted.

University of Phoenix–Chattanooga Campus, School of Business, Chattanooga, TN 37421-3707. Offers accounting (MBA); business administration (MBA); business and management (MBA); global management (MBA); human resources management (MBA, MM); management (MM); marketing (MBA); public administration (MBA, MM). Postbaccalaureate distance learning degree programs offered.

University of Phoenix–Cheyenne Campus, School of Business, Cheyenne, WY 82009. Offers global management (MBA); human resources management (MBA, MM); management (MM); marketing (MBA); public administration (MBA, MM). Postbaccalaureate distance learning degree programs offered.

University of Phoenix–Chicago Campus, School of Business, Schaumburg, IL 60173-4399. Offers business administration (MBA); global management (MBA); human resources management (MBA); information systems (MIS); management (MM). Evening/weekend programs available. *Degree requirements:* For master's, thesis (for some programs). *Entrance requirements:* For master's, minimum undergraduate GPA of 3.0, 3 years of work experience. Additional exam requirements/recommendations for international students: Required—TOEFL (minimum score 550 paper-based; 79 iBT). Electronic applications accepted.

University of Phoenix–Cincinnati Campus, School of Business, West Chester, OH 45069-4875. Offers accounting (MBA); business administration (MBA); global management (MBA); human resources management (MBA, MM); management (MM); marketing (MBA); public administration (MM). Evening/weekend programs available. *Degree requirements:* For master's, thesis (for some programs). *Entrance requirements:* For master's, minimum undergraduate GPA of 3.0, 3 years of work experience. Additional exam requirements/recommendations for international students: Required—TOEFL (minimum score 550 paper-based; 79 iBT). Electronic applications accepted.

University of Phoenix–Cleveland Campus, School of Business, Independence, OH 44131-2194. Offers accounting (MBA); business administration (MBA); global management (MBA); human resources management (MBA, MM); management (MM); marketing (MBA); public administration (MBA, MM). Evening/weekend programs available. Postbaccalaureate distance learning degree programs offered (no on-campus study). *Degree requirements:* For master's, thesis (for some programs). *Entrance requirements:* For master's, minimum undergraduate GPA of 3.0, 3 years of work experience. Additional exam requirements/recommendations for international students: Required—TOEFL (minimum score 550 paper-based; 79 iBT). Electronic applications accepted.

University of Phoenix–Columbus Georgia Campus, School of Business, Columbus, GA 31909. Offers accounting (MBA); business administration (MBA); global management (MBA); human resources management (MBA, MM); management (MM); marketing (MBA); public administration (MBA). Evening/weekend programs available. *Degree requirements:* For master's, thesis (for some programs). *Entrance requirements:* For master's, minimum undergraduate GPA of 3.0, 3 years of work experience. Additional exam requirements/recommendations for international students: Required—TOEFL (minimum score 550 paper-based; 79 iBT). Electronic applications accepted.

University of Phoenix–Columbus Ohio Campus, School of Business, Columbus, OH 43240-4032. Offers accounting (MBA); business administration (MBA); global management (MBA); human resources management (MBA, MM); management (MM); marketing (MBA); public administration (MM). Evening/weekend programs available. Postbaccalaureate distance learning degree programs offered. *Degree requirements:* For master's, thesis (for some programs). *Entrance requirements:* For master's, minimum undergraduate GPA of 3.0, 3 years of work experience. Additional exam requirements/recommendations for international students: Required—TOEFL (minimum score 550 paper-based; 79 iBT). Electronic applications accepted.

University of Phoenix–Dallas Campus, School of Business, Dallas, TX 75251. Offers accounting (MBA); business administration (MBA); global management (MBA); human resources management (MBA, MM); management (MM); marketing (MBA); public administration (MBA, MM). Evening/weekend programs available. Postbaccalaureate distance learning degree programs offered. *Degree requirements:* For master's, thesis (for some programs). *Entrance requirements:* For master's, 3 years of work experience, minimum undergraduate GPA of 3.0. Additional exam requirements/recommendations for international students: Required—TOEFL (minimum score 550 paper-based; 79 iBT). Electronic applications accepted.

University of Phoenix–Denver Campus, School of Business, Lone Tree, CO 80124-5453. Offers accountancy (MSA); accounting (MBA); business administration (MBA); e-business (MBA); global management (MBA); human resources management (MBA, MM); management (MM); marketing (MBA); public administration (MBA, MM). Evening/weekend programs available. Postbaccalaureate distance learning degree programs offered. *Degree requirements:* For master's, thesis (for some programs). *Entrance requirements:* For master's, minimum undergraduate GPA of 3.0, 3 years work experience. Additional exam requirements/recommendations for international students: Required—TOEFL (minimum score 550 paper-based; 79 iBT). Electronic applications accepted.

University of Phoenix–Des Moines Campus, School of Business, Des Moines, IA 50309. Offers accounting (MBA); business administration (MBA); global management (MBA); human resources management (MBA, MM); management (MM); marketing (MBA); public administration (MBA, MM). Postbaccalaureate distance learning degree programs offered.

University of Phoenix–Hawaii Campus, School of Business, Honolulu, HI 96813-4317. Offers accounting (MBA); business administration (MBA); global management (MBA); human resources management (MBA, MM); management (MM); marketing (MBA); public administration (MBA, MM). Evening/weekend programs available. *Degree requirements:* For master's, thesis (for some programs). *Entrance requirements:* For master's, minimum undergraduate GPA of 3.0, 3 years of work experience. Additional exam requirements/recommendations for international students: Required—TOEFL (minimum score 550 paper-based; 79 iBT). Electronic applications accepted.

University of Phoenix–Houston Campus, School of Business, Houston, TX 77079-2004. Offers accounting (MBA); business administration (MBA); global management (MBA); human resources management (MBA, MM); management (MM); marketing (MBA); public administration (MBA, MM). Evening/weekend programs available. Postbaccalaureate distance learning degree programs offered. *Degree requirements:* For master's, thesis (for some programs). *Entrance requirements:* For master's, 3 years of work experience, minimum undergraduate GPA of 3.0. Additional exam requirements/recommendations for international students: Required—TOEFL (minimum score 550 paper-based; 79 iBT). Electronic applications accepted.

University of Phoenix–Idaho Campus, School of Business, Meridian, ID 83642-5114. Offers accounting (MBA); administration (MBA); global management (MBA); human resources management (MBA, MM); management (MM); marketing (MBA); public administration (MM). Evening/weekend programs available. Postbaccalaureate distance learning degree programs offered. *Degree requirements:* For master's, thesis (for some

programs). *Entrance requirements:* For master's, 3 years of work experience, minimum undergraduate GPA of 3.0. Additional exam requirements/recommendations for international students: Required—TOEFL (minimum score 550 paper-based). Electronic applications accepted.

University of Phoenix–Indianapolis Campus, School of Business, Indianapolis, IN 46250-932. Offers accounting (MBA); business administration (MBA); global management (MBA); human resources management (MBA, MM); management (MM); marketing (MBA); public administration (MM). Evening/weekend programs available. *Degree requirements:* For master's, thesis (for some programs). *Entrance requirements:* For master's, minimum undergraduate GPA of 3.0, 3 years of work experience. Additional exam requirements/recommendations for international students: Required—TOEFL (minimum score 550 paper-based). Electronic applications accepted.

University of Phoenix–Jersey City Campus, School of Business, Jersey City, NJ 07310. Offers accounting (MBA); business administration (MBA); global management (MBA); human resources management (MBA, MM); management (MM); marketing (MBA); public administration (MBA, MM).

University of Phoenix–Kansas City Campus, School of Business, Kansas City, MO 64131. Offers accounting (MBA); business administration (MBA); global management (MBA); human resources management (MBA, MM); management (MM); marketing (MBA); public administration (MBA). Evening/weekend programs available. *Degree requirements:* For master's, thesis (for some programs). *Entrance requirements:* For master's, minimum undergraduate GPA of 3.0, 3 years of work experience. Additional exam requirements/recommendations for international students: Required—TOEFL (minimum score 550 paper-based). Electronic applications accepted.

University of Phoenix–Las Vegas Campus, School of Business, Las Vegas, NV 89135. Offers accounting (MBA); business administration (MBA); global management (MBA); human resources management (MBA, MM); management (MM); marketing (MBA); public administration (MM). Evening/weekend programs available. Postbaccalaureate distance learning degree programs offered (no on-campus study). *Degree requirements:* For master's, thesis (for some programs). *Entrance requirements:* For master's, minimum undergraduate GPA of 3.0, 3 years of work experience. Additional exam requirements/recommendations for international students: Required—TOEFL (minimum score 550 paper-based; 79 iBT). Electronic applications accepted.

University of Phoenix–Louisiana Campus, School of Business, Metairie, LA 70001-2082. Offers accounting (MBA); business administration (MBA); global management (MBA); human resources management (MBA, MM); management (MM); marketing (MBA); public administration (MBA). Evening/weekend programs available. *Degree requirements:* For master's, thesis (for some programs). *Entrance requirements:* For master's, minimum undergraduate GPA of 3.0, 3 years work experience. Additional exam requirements/recommendations for international students: Required—TOEFL (minimum score 550 paper-based; 79 iBT). Electronic applications accepted.

University of Phoenix–Madison Campus, School of Business, Madison, WI 53718-2416. Offers accounting (MBA); business and management (MBA); e-business (MBA); global management (MBA); human resources management (MBA, MM); management (MM); marketing (MBA); public administration (MBA).

University of Phoenix–Maryland Campus, School of Business, Columbia, MD 21045-5424. Offers business administration (MBA); global management (MBA); technology management (MBA). Evening/weekend programs available. Postbaccalaureate distance learning degree programs offered. *Entrance requirements:* Additional exam requirements/recommendations for international students: Required—TOEFL, TOEIC (Test of English as an International Communication), Berlitz Online English Proficiency Exam, PTE, or IELTS. Electronic applications accepted. *Expenses:* Contact institution.

University of Phoenix–Memphis Campus, School of Business, Cordova, TN 38018. Offers accounting (MBA); business and management (MBA); e-business (MBA); global management (MBA); human resources management (MBA, MM); management (MM); marketing (MBA); public administration (MBA, MM).

University of Phoenix–Milwaukee Campus, School of Business, Milwaukee, WI 53224. Offers accounting (MBA); business administration (MBA); energy management (MBA); global management (MBA); health care management (MBA); human resource management (MBA); management (MM); marketing (MBA); project management (MBA); technology management (MBA). Evening/weekend programs available. Postbaccalaureate distance learning degree programs offered. *Entrance requirements:* Additional exam requirements/recommendations for international students: Required—TOEFL, TOEIC (Test of English as an International Communication), Berlitz Online English Proficiency Exam, PTE, or IELTS. Electronic applications accepted. *Expenses:* Contact institution.

University of Phoenix–Minneapolis/St. Louis Park Campus, School of Business, St. Louis Park, MN 55426. Offers accounting (MBA); business administration (MBA); global management (MBA); human resources management (MBA); management (MM); marketing (MBA); public administration (MBA).

University of Phoenix–New Mexico Campus, School of Business, Albuquerque, NM 87113-1570. Offers accounting (MBA); business administration (MBA); global management (MBA); human resources management (MBA, MM); management (MM); marketing (MBA). Evening/weekend programs available. *Degree requirements:* For master's, thesis (for some programs). *Entrance requirements:* For master's, 3 years of work experience, minimum undergraduate GPA of 3.0. Additional exam requirements/recommendations for international students: Required—TOEFL (minimum score 550 paper-based; 79 iBT). Electronic applications accepted.

University of Phoenix–North Florida Campus, School of Business, Jacksonville, FL 32216-0959. Offers accounting (MBA); business administration (MBA); global management (MBA); human resources management (MBA, MM); management (MM); marketing (MBA); public administration (MBA, MM). Evening/weekend programs available. *Degree requirements:* For master's, thesis (for some programs). *Entrance requirements:* For master's, minimum undergraduate GPA of 3.0, 3 years work experience. Additional exam requirements/recommendations for international students: Required—TOEFL (minimum score 550 paper-based; 79 iBT). Electronic applications accepted.

University of Phoenix–Northwest Arkansas Campus, School of Business, Rogers, AR 72756-9615. Offers accounting (MBA); business and management (MBA); global management (MBA); human resources management (MBA, MM); management (MM); marketing (MBA); public administration (MBA, MM).

University of Phoenix–Oklahoma City Campus, School of Business, Oklahoma City, OK 73116-8244. Offers accounting (MBA); business administration (MBA); global management (MBA); human resource management (MBA); management (MM); marketing (MBA). Evening/weekend programs available. *Degree requirements:* For master's, thesis (for some programs). *Entrance requirements:* For master's, minimum undergraduate GPA of 3.0, 3 years of work experience. Additional exam requirements/recommendations for international students: Required—TOEFL (minimum score 550 paper-based; 79 iBT). Electronic applications accepted.

University of Phoenix–Omaha Campus, School of Business, Omaha, NE 68154-5240. Offers accounting (MBA); business and management (MBA); global management (MBA); human resources management (MBA, MM); management (MM); marketing (MBA); public administration (MBA, MM).

University of Phoenix–Online Campus, School of Business, Phoenix, AZ 85034-7209. Offers accountancy (MS); accounting (MBA, Certificate); business administration (MBA); energy management (MBA); global management (MBA); health care management (MBA); human resource management (MBA, Certificate); human resources management (MM); management (MM); marketing (MBA, Certificate); project management (MBA, Certificate); public administration (MBA, MM); technology management (MBA). Evening/weekend programs available. Postbaccalaureate distance learning degree programs offered. *Entrance requirements:* Additional exam requirements/recommendations for international students: Required—TOEFL, TOEIC (Test of English as an International Communication), Berlitz Online English Proficiency Exam, PTE, or IELTS. Electronic applications accepted. *Expenses:* Contact institution.

University of Phoenix–Oregon Campus, School of Business, Tigard, OR 97223. Offers accounting (MBA); business administration (MBA); global management (MBA); human resource management (MM); human resources management (MBA); management (MM); marketing (MBA); public administration (MM). Evening/weekend programs available. *Degree requirements:* For master's, thesis (for some programs). *Entrance requirements:* For master's, minimum undergraduate GPA of 3.0, 3 years of work experience. Additional exam requirements/recommendations for international students: Required—TOEFL (minimum score 550 paper-based; 79 iBT). Electronic applications accepted.

University of Phoenix–Philadelphia Campus, School of Business, Wayne, PA 19087-2121. Offers accounting (MBA); business administration (MBA); global management (MBA); human resources management (MBA, MM); management (MM); marketing (MBA); public administration (MM). Evening/weekend programs available. *Degree requirements:* For master's, thesis (for some programs). *Entrance requirements:* For master's, minimum undergraduate GPA of 3.0, 3 years work experience. Additional exam requirements/recommendations for international students: Required—TOEFL (minimum score 550 paper-based; 79 iBT). Electronic applications accepted.

University of Phoenix–Phoenix Campus, School of Business, Tempe, AZ 85282-2371. Offers accounting (MBA, MS, Certificate); business administration (MBA); energy management (MBA); global management (MBA); health care management (MBA); human resource management (MBA, Certificate); management (MM); marketing (MBA); project management (MBA); technology management (MBA). Evening/weekend programs available. Postbaccalaureate distance learning degree programs offered. *Entrance requirements:* Additional exam requirements/recommendations for international students: Required—TOEFL, TOEIC (Test of English as an International Communication), Berlitz Online English Proficiency Exam, PTE, or IELTS. Electronic applications accepted. *Expenses:* Contact institution.

University of Phoenix–Pittsburgh Campus, School of Business, Pittsburgh, PA 15276. Offers accounting (MBA); business administration (MBA); global management (MBA); human resources management (MBA, MM); management (MM); marketing (MBA); public administration (MBA, MM). Evening/weekend programs available. *Degree requirements:* For master's, thesis (for some programs). *Entrance requirements:* For master's, minimum undergraduate GPA of 3.0, 3 years work experience. Additional exam requirements/recommendations for international students: Required—TOEFL (minimum score 550 paper-based; 79 iBT). Electronic applications accepted.

University of Phoenix–Puerto Rico Campus, School of Business, Guaynabo, PR 00968. Offers accounting (MBA); energy management (MBA); global management (MBA); human resource management (MBA); marketing (MBA); project management (MBA); small business administration (MBA). Evening/weekend programs available. *Degree requirements:* For master's, thesis (for some programs). *Entrance requirements:* For master's, minimum undergraduate GPA of 3.0, 3 years work experience. Additional exam requirements/recommendations for international students: Required—TOEFL (minimum score 550 paper-based; 79 iBT). Electronic applications accepted.

University of Phoenix–Richmond-Virginia Beach Campus, School of Business, Glen Allen, VA 23060. Offers accounting (MBA); business administration (MBA); global management (MBA); human resources management (MBA, MM); management (MM); marketing (MBA); public administration (MBA, MM). Evening/weekend programs available. *Degree requirements:* For master's, thesis (for some programs). *Entrance requirements:* For master's, minimum undergraduate GPA of 3.0, 3 years work experience. Additional exam requirements/recommendations for international students: Required—TOEFL (minimum score 550 paper-based; 79 iBT). Electronic applications accepted.

University of Phoenix–Sacramento Valley Campus, School of Business, Sacramento, CA 95833-3632. Offers accounting (MBA); business administration (MBA); global management (MBA); human resources management (MBA, MM); management (MM); marketing (MBA); public administration (MBA, MM). Evening/weekend programs available. *Degree requirements:* For master's, thesis (for some programs). *Entrance requirements:* For master's, minimum undergraduate GPA of 3.0, 3 years work experience. Additional exam requirements/recommendations for international students: Required—TOEFL (minimum score 550 paper-based; 79 iBT). Electronic applications accepted.

University of Phoenix–St. Louis Campus, School of Business, St. Louis, MO 63043. Offers accounting (MBA); business administration (MBA); global management (MBA); human resources management (MBA, MM); management (MM); marketing (MBA); public administration (MM). Evening/weekend programs available. *Degree requirements:* For master's, thesis (for some programs). *Entrance requirements:* For master's, 3 years of work experience, minimum undergraduate GPA of 3.0. Additional exam requirements/recommendations for international students: Required—TOEFL (minimum score 550 paper-based; 79 iBT). Electronic applications accepted.

University of Phoenix–San Antonio Campus, School of Business, San Antonio, TX 78230. Offers accounting (MBA); business administration (MBA); e-business (MBA); global management (MBA); human resources management (MBA, MM); management (MM); marketing (MBA); public administration (MBA, MM).

University of Phoenix–San Diego Campus, School of Business, San Diego, CA 92123. Offers accounting (MBA); business administration (MBA); global management (MBA); human resources management (MBA, MM); management (MM); marketing (MBA); public administration (MBA). Evening/weekend programs available. *Degree requirements:* For master's, thesis (for some programs). *Entrance requirements:* For master's, 3 years of work experience, minimum undergraduate GPA of 3.0. Additional exam requirements/recommendations for international students: Required—TOEFL (minimum score 550 paper-based; 79 iBT). Electronic applications accepted.

University of Phoenix–Savannah Campus, School of Business, Savannah, GA 31405-7400. Offers accounting (MBA); business administration (MBA); global management (MBA); human resources management (MBA, MM); management (MM); marketing (MBA); public administration (MBA, MM).

University of Phoenix–Southern Arizona Campus, School of Business, Tucson, AZ 85711. Offers accountancy (MS); accounting (MBA); business administration (MBA); global management (MBA); human resources management (MBA); management (MM); marketing (MBA). Evening/weekend programs available. *Degree requirements:* For master's, thesis (for some programs). *Entrance requirements:* For master's, minimum undergraduate GPA of 3.0, 3 years of work experience. Additional exam requirements/recommendations for international students: Required—TOEFL (minimum score 550 paper-based; 79 iBT). Electronic applications accepted.

University of Phoenix–Southern California Campus, School of Business, Costa Mesa, CA 92626. Offers accounting (MBA); business administration (MBA); energy management (MBA); global management (MBA); health care management (MBA); human resource management (MBA); management (MM); marketing (MBA); project management (MBA); technology management (MBA). Evening/weekend programs available. Postbaccalaureate distance learning degree programs offered. *Entrance requirements:* Additional exam requirements/recommendations for international students: Required—TOEFL, TOEIC (Test of English as an International Communication), Berlitz Online English Proficiency Exam, PTE, or IELTS. Electronic applications accepted. *Expenses:* Contact institution.

University of Phoenix–Southern Colorado Campus, School of Business, Colorado Springs, CO 80903. Offers accounting (MBA); business administration (MBA); global management (MBA); human resources management (MBA, MM); management (MM); marketing (MBA); public administration (MM). Evening/weekend programs available. *Degree requirements:* For master's, thesis (for some programs). *Entrance requirements:* For master's, minimum undergraduate GPA of 3.0, 3 years of work experience. Additional exam requirements/recommendations for international students: Required—TOEFL (minimum score 550 paper-based; 79 iBT). Electronic applications accepted.

University of Phoenix–South Florida Campus, School of Business, Miramar, FL 33030. Offers accounting (MBA); business administration (MBA); global management (MBA); human resource management (MBA); human resources management (MM); management (MM); marketing (MBA); public administration (MBA, MM). Evening/weekend programs available. *Degree requirements:* For master's, thesis (for some programs). *Entrance requirements:* For master's, minimum undergraduate GPA of 3.0, 3 years work experience. Additional exam requirements/recommendations for international students: Required—TOEFL (minimum score 550 paper-based; 79 iBT). Electronic applications accepted.

University of Phoenix–Springfield Campus, School of Business, Springfield, MO 65804-7211. Offers accounting (MBA); business administration (MBA); global management (MBA); human resources management (MBA, MM); management (MM); marketing (MBA); public administration (MBA, MM).

University of Phoenix–Tulsa Campus, School of Business, Tulsa, OK 74134-1412. Offers accounting (MBA); business (MM); business administration (MBA); global management (MBA); human resources management (MBA); marketing (MBA). Evening/weekend programs available. *Degree requirements:* For master's, thesis (for some programs). *Entrance requirements:* For master's, minimum undergraduate GPA of 3.0, 3 years work experience. Additional exam requirements/recommendations for international students: Required—TOEFL (minimum score 550 paper-based; 79 iBT).

University of Phoenix–Utah Campus, School of Business, Salt Lake City, UT 84123-4617. Offers accounting (MBA); business administration (MBA); global management (MBA); human resource management (MBA, MM); management (MM); marketing (MBA); technology management (MBA). Evening/weekend programs available. *Degree requirements:* For master's, thesis (for some programs). *Entrance requirements:* For master's, minimum undergraduate GPA of 3.0, 3 years of work experience. Additional exam requirements/recommendations for international students: Required—TOEFL (minimum score 550 paper-based; 79 iBT). Electronic applications accepted.

University of Phoenix–West Florida Campus, School of Business, Temple Terrace, FL 33637. Offers accounting (MBA); business administration (MBA); global management (MBA); human resources management (MBA, MM); management (MM); marketing (MBA); public administration (MBA, MM). Evening/weekend programs available. *Degree requirements:* For master's, thesis (for some programs). *Entrance requirements:* For master's, 3 years of work experience, minimum undergraduate GPA of 3.0. Additional exam requirements/recommendations for international students: Required—TOEFL (minimum score 550 paper-based; 79 iBT). Electronic applications accepted.

University of Pittsburgh, Katz Graduate School of Business, Augsburg Executive Fellows Program, Pittsburgh, PA 15260. Offers MBA. *Faculty:* 61 full-time (15 women), 21 part-time/adjunct (5 women). *Students:* 15 full-time (all women), 5 part-time (all women). 20 applicants, 100% accepted, 20 enrolled. *Degree requirements:* For master's, one foreign language. *Entrance requirements:* For master's, Augsburg nominates students and Katz accepts them. They earn their MBA there and a certificate here. *Application deadline:* For spring admission, 7/1 priority date for international students. *Expenses:* Contact institution. *Faculty research:* Accounting systems/financial reporting, corporate finance, shopper marketing/consumer behavior, management information systems, organizational behavior and entrepreneurship. *Unit head:* Tim Robison, Assistant Dean, MBA Programs, 412-648-1610, Fax: 412-648-1659, E-mail: trobison@katz.pitt.edu. *Application contact:* Patricia Sablosky, Director, Special International and Dual Degree Programs, 412-383-8835, Fax: 412-648-1659, E-mail: psablosky@katz.pitt.edu.

University of Pittsburgh, Katz Graduate School of Business, MBA/Master of International Business Dual Degree Program, Pittsburgh, PA 15260. Offers MBA/MIB. Part-time and evening/weekend programs available. *Faculty:* 61 full-time (15 women), 21 part-time/adjunct (5 women). *Students:* 1 full-time (0 women), 6 part-time (3 women). Average age 29. 15 applicants, 20% accepted, 1 enrolled. *Entrance requirements:* Additional exam requirements/recommendations for international students: Required—TOEFL (minimum score 600 paper-based; 100 iBT) or IELTS. *Application deadline:* For fall admission, 4/1 priority date for domestic students, 2/1 priority date for international students. Application fee: $50. Electronic applications accepted. *Expenses:* Tuition, state resident: full-time $19,964; part-time $807 per credit. Tuition, nonresident: full-time $32,686; part-time $1337 per credit. *Required fees:* $740; $200. Tuition and fees vary according to program. *Financial support:* In 2013–14, 1 student received support. Career-related internships or fieldwork and scholarships/grants available. Financial award application deadline: 2/1. *Faculty research:* Accounting systems/financial reporting, corporate finance, shopper marketing/consumer behavior, management information systems, organizational behavior and entrepreneurship. *Unit head:* Tim Robison, Assistant Dean/Director, 412-648-1700, Fax: 412-648-1659, E-mail: trobison@katz.pitt.edu. *Application contact:* Thomas Keller, Director of MBA Admissions, 412-648-1700, Fax: 412-648-1659, E-mail: mba@katz.pitt.edu.
Website: http://www.business.pitt.edu/katz/mba/academics/programs/mba-mib.php.

University of Puerto Rico, Río Piedras Campus, College of Business Administration, San Juan, PR 00931-3300. Offers accounting (MBA); finance (MBA, PhD); general business (MBA); human resources management (MBA); international trade and business (MBA, PhD); marketing (MBA); operations management (MBA); quantitative methods (MBA). Part-time programs available. *Degree requirements:* For master's,

comprehensive exam, thesis or alternative, research project. *Entrance requirements:* For master's, GMAT or PAEG, minimum GPA of 3.0, letter of recommendation; for doctorate, GMAT, PAEG, minimum GPA of 3.0, master degree. *Faculty research:* Management.

University of Regina, Faculty of Graduate Studies and Research, Kenneth Levene Graduate School of Business, Program in Business Administration, Regina, SK S4S 0A2, Canada. Offers business foundations (PGD); engineering management (MBA); executive business administration (EMBA); general management (MBA); international business (MBA); leadership (M Admin); organizational leadership (Master's Certificate); project management (Master's Certificate). Part-time and evening/weekend programs available. *Faculty:* 39 full-time (14 women), 7 part-time/adjunct (0 women). *Students:* 86 full-time (30 women), 65 part-time (32 women). 123 applicants, 25% accepted. In 2013, 59 master's, 23 other advanced degrees awarded. *Degree requirements:* For master's, project (for some programs). *Entrance requirements:* For master's, GMAT, three years of relevant work experience, four-year undergraduate degree; for other advanced degree, GMAT (for PGD), four-year undergraduate degree and two years of relevant work experience (for Certificates); three years' work experience (for Postgraduate Diploma). Additional exam requirements/recommendations for international students: Required—TOEFL (minimum score 580 paper-based; 80 iBT), IELTS (minimum score 6.5). *Application deadline:* Applications are processed on a rolling basis. Application fee: $100. Electronic applications accepted. *Expenses:* Contact institution. *Financial support:* In 2013–14, 7 fellowships (averaging $6,000 per year), 1 research assistantship (averaging $5,500 per year), 7 teaching assistantships (averaging $2,356 per year) were awarded; scholarships/grants also available. Financial award application deadline: 6/15. *Faculty research:* Business policy and strategy, production and operations management, human behavior in organizations, financial management, social issues in business. *Unit head:* Dr. Andrew Gaudes, Dean, 306-585-4162, Fax: 306-585-5361, E-mail: andrew.gaudes@uregina.ca. *Application contact:* Steve Wield, Manager, Graduate Programs, 306-337-8463, Fax: 306-585-5361, E-mail: steve.wield@uregina.ca.
Website: http://www.uregina.ca/business/levene/.

University of Rochester, Simon Business School, Full-Time Master's Program in Business Administration, Rochester, NY 14627. Offers accounting and information systems (MBA); business environment and public policy (MBA); business systems consulting (MBA); competitive and organizational strategy - pricing (MBA); computers and information systems (MBA); corporate accounting (MBA); electronic commerce (MBA); entrepreneurship (MBA); finance (MBA); health sciences management (MBA); international management (MBA); marketing - brand management and pricing (MBA); operations management - manufacturing (MBA); operations management - services (MBA); public accounting (MBA). *Accreditation:* AACSB. Part-time and evening/weekend programs available. *Faculty:* 60 full-time (11 women), 23 part-time/adjunct (3 women). *Students:* 282 full-time (74 women); includes 55 minority (29 Black or African American, non-Hispanic/Latino; 1 American Indian or Alaska Native, non-Hispanic/Latino; 11 Asian, non-Hispanic/Latino; 12 Hispanic/Latino; 2 Two or more races, non-Hispanic/Latino), 144 international. 673 applicants, 33% accepted, 65 enrolled. In 2013, 176 master's awarded. *Entrance requirements:* For master's, GMAT/GRE, previous course work in calculus. Additional exam requirements/recommendations for international students: Required—TOEFL. *Application deadline:* For fall admission, 10/15 for domestic and international students; for winter admission, 1/5 for domestic and international students; for spring admission, 3/15 for domestic and international students; for summer admission, 5/15 for domestic students. Applications are processed on a rolling basis. Application fee: $150. Electronic applications accepted. *Expenses:* Tuition: Full-time $44,580; part-time $1394 per credit hour. *Required fees:* $492. *Financial support:* In 2013–14, 72 students received support. Fellowships, research assistantships, teaching assistantships, institutionally sponsored loans, scholarships/grants, and tuition waivers (partial) available. Financial award application deadline: 3/1; financial award applicants required to submit CSS PROFILE or FAFSA. *Unit head:* Mark Zupan, Dean, 585-275-3316. *Application contact:* Rebekah S. Lewin, Assistant Dean of Admissions and Student Engagement, 585-275-3533, E-mail: admissions@simon.rochester.edu.

University of Rochester, Simon Business School, Part-Time MBA Program, Rochester, NY 14627. Offers accounting and information systems (MBA); business environment and public policy (MBA); business systems consulting (MBA); competitive and organizational strategy (MBA); computers and information systems (MBA); corporate accounting (MBA); electronic commerce (MBA); entrepreneurship (MBA); finance (MBA); health sciences management (MBA); international management (MBA); manufacturing management (MBA); marketing (MBA); operations management - services (MBA); public accounting (MBA). Part-time and evening/weekend programs available. *Faculty:* 59 full-time (10 women), 23 part-time/adjunct (3 women). *Students:* 270 part-time (75 women); includes 38 minority (5 Black or African American, non-Hispanic/Latino; 1 American Indian or Alaska Native, non-Hispanic/Latino; 24 Asian, non-Hispanic/Latino; 5 Hispanic/Latino; 3 Two or more races, non-Hispanic/Latino). Average age 32. 56 applicants, 98% accepted, 51 enrolled. In 2013, 77 master's awarded. *Entrance requirements:* For master's, GRE or GMAT, resume, recommendation letters, essays, transcipts. *Application deadline:* For fall admission, 8/15 for domestic students; for winter admission, 11/15 for domestic students; for spring admission, 2/15 for domestic students; for summer admission, 5/15 for domestic students. Applications are processed on a rolling basis. Application fee: $150. Electronic applications accepted. *Expenses:* Tuition: Full-time $44,580; part-time $1394 per credit hour. *Required fees:* $492. *Financial support:* Scholarships/grants and tuition waivers available. Financial award applicants required to submit CSS PROFILE. *Unit head:* Mark Zupan, Dean, 585-275-3316, E-mail: mark.zupan@simon.rochester.edu. *Application contact:* Jennifer Mossotti, Associate Director of Part-Time Programs, 585-275-3803, E-mail: jennifer.mossotti@simon.rochester.edu.
Website: http://www.simon.rochester.edu/programs/part-time-mba-programs/index.aspx.

University of San Diego, School of Business Administration, Program in Global Leadership, San Diego, CA 92110-2492. Offers MS. Postbaccalaureate distance learning degree programs offered (minimal on-campus study). *Students:* 20 full-time (8 women), 51 part-time (14 women); includes 26 minority (5 Asian, non-Hispanic/Latino; 15 Hispanic/Latino; 6 Two or more races, non-Hispanic/Latino), 1 international. Average age 35. In 2013, 54 master's awarded. *Entrance requirements:* For master's, minimum GPA of 3.0, minimum 2 years of work experience. Additional exam requirements/recommendations for international students: Required—TOEFL (minimum score 580 paper-based; 92 iBT), TWE. *Application deadline:* For fall admission, 7/1 for domestic students; for spring admission, 11/1 for domestic students. Applications are processed on a rolling basis. Application fee: $80. Electronic applications accepted. *Expenses:* Tuition: Full-time $23,580; part-time $1310 per credit. *Required fees:* $350. *Financial support:* In 2013–14, 31 students received support. Scholarships/grants available. Financial award application deadline: 4/1; financial award applicants required to submit FAFSA. *Unit head:* Stephanie Kiesel, Director, 619-260-8850, E-mail: skiesel@sandiego.edu. *Application contact:* Monica Mahon, Associate Director of Graduate Admissions, 619-260-4524, Fax: 619-260-4158, E-mail: grads@sandiego.edu.
Website: http://www.sandiego.edu/business/programs/ms-global-leadership/.

International Business

University of San Francisco, School of Law, Master of Law Program, San Francisco, CA 94117-1080. Offers intellectual property and technology law (LL M); international transactions and comparative law (LL M). *Faculty:* 25 full-time (18 women), 61 part-time/adjunct (22 women). *Students:* 13 full-time (8 women), 4 part-time (2 women); includes 1 minority (Black or African American, non-Hispanic/Latino), 13 international. Average age 28. 122 applicants, 77% accepted, 14 enrolled. In 2013, 12 master's awarded. *Entrance requirements:* For master's, law degree from U.S. or foreign school (intellectual property and technology law); law degree from foreign school (international transactions and comparative law). Application fee: $60. *Expenses: Tuition:* Full-time $21,150; part-time $1175 per unit. Tuition and fees vary according to course load, campus/location and program. *Financial support:* In 2013–14, 6 students received support. *Unit head:* Constance De La Vega, Director, 650-728-6658. *Application contact:* Julianne Traylor, Program Assistant, 415-422-6658, E-mail: masterlaws@usfca.edu. Website: http://www.usfca.edu/law/llm/.

University of San Francisco, School of Management, Master in Global Entrepreneurial Management Program, San Francisco, CA 94105. Offers MGEM. Program offered jointly with IQS in Barcelona, Spain and Fu Jen Catholic University in Taipei, Taiwan. *Faculty:* 2 full-time (both women), 2 part-time/adjunct (0 women). *Students:* 40 full-time (19 women); includes 6 minority (3 Asian, non-Hispanic/Latino; 2 Hispanic/Latino; 1 Two or more races, non-Hispanic/Latino), 27 international. Average age 24. 73 applicants, 66% accepted, 35 enrolled. In 2013, 34 master's awarded. *Entrance requirements:* For master's, resume, transcripts from each college or university attended, two letters of recommendation, personal statement. Additional exam requirements/recommendations for international students: Required—TOEFL (minimum score 550 paper-based, 79 iBT), IELTS (minimum score 6), or PTE (minimum score 53). *Application deadline:* For fall admission, 5/15 for domestic students. Application fee: $55. Electronic applications accepted. *Expenses: Tuition:* Full-time $21,150; part-time $1175 per unit. Tuition and fees vary according to course load, campus/location and program. *Financial support:* In 2013–14, 3 students received support. Application deadline: 3/2; applicants required to submit FAFSA. *Unit head:* Dr. Jennifer Walske, Director, 415-422-2221, E-mail: management@usfca.edu. *Application contact:* Office of Graduate Recruiting and Admissions, 415-422-2221, Fax: 415-422-6315, E-mail: management@usfca.edu. Website: http://www.usfca.edu/mgem.

University of San Francisco, School of Management, Master of Business Administration Program, San Francisco, CA 94105. Offers entrepreneurship and innovation (MBA); finance (MBA); international business (MBA); marketing (MBA); organization development (MBA); DDS/MBA; JD/MBA; MBA/MAPS. *Accreditation:* AACSB. Part-time and evening/weekend programs available. *Faculty:* 18 full-time (4 women), 20 part-time/adjunct (10 women). *Students:* 157 full-time (69 women), 14 part-time (7 women); includes 57 minority (7 Black or African American, non-Hispanic/Latino; 31 Asian, non-Hispanic/Latino; 14 Hispanic/Latino; 5 Two or more races, non-Hispanic/Latino), 30 international. Average age 29. 345 applicants, 68% accepted, 79 enrolled. In 2013, 131 master's awarded. *Entrance requirements:* For master's, GMAT or GRE, resume (two years of professional work experience required for Part-Time MBA, preferred for Full-Time MBA), transcripts from each college or university attended, two letters of recommendation, a personal statement and an interview. Additional exam requirements/recommendations for international students: Required—TOEFL (minimum score 600 paper-based, 100 iBT), IELTS (minimum score 7) or PTE (minimum score 68). *Application deadline:* For fall admission, 6/5 for domestic students, 5/15 for international students; for spring admission, 11/30 for domestic students. Application fee: $55. Electronic applications accepted. *Expenses: Tuition:* Full-time $21,150; part-time $1175 per unit. Tuition and fees vary according to course load, campus/location and program. *Financial support:* In 2013–14, 42 students received support. Fellowships and scholarships/grants available. Financial award application deadline: 3/2; financial award applicants required to submit FAFSA. *Faculty research:* International financial markets, technology transfer licensing, international marketing, strategic planning. *Total annual research expenditures:* $50,000. *Unit head:* Dr. John Veitch, Associate Dean and Program Director, 415-422-2221, Fax: 415-422-6315, E-mail: management@usfca.edu. *Application contact:* Office of Graduate Recruiting and Admissions, 415-422-2221, Fax: 415-422-6315, E-mail: management@usfca.edu. Website: http://www.usfca.edu/mba.

University of Saskatchewan, College of Graduate Studies and Research, Edwards School of Business, Program in Business Administration, Saskatoon, SK S7N 5A2, Canada. Offers agribusiness management (MBA); biotechnology management (MBA); health services management (MBA); indigenous management (MBA); international business management (MBA). *Expenses: Tuition,* area resident: Full-time $3585 Canadian dollars; part-time $585 Canadian dollars per course. Tuition, nonresident: part-time $877 Canadian dollars per course. *International tuition:* $5377 Canadian dollars full-time. *Required fees:* $889.51 Canadian dollars.

University of Saskatchewan, College of Graduate Studies and Research, School of Public Policy, Saskatoon, SK S7N 5A2, Canada. Offers MIT, MPA, MPP, PhD. *Expenses: Tuition,* area resident: Full-time $3585 Canadian dollars; part-time $585 Canadian dollars per course. Tuition, nonresident: part-time $877 Canadian dollars per course. *International tuition:* $5377 Canadian dollars full-time. *Required fees:* $889.51 Canadian dollars.

The University of Scranton, College of Graduate and Continuing Education, Program in Business Administration, Scranton, PA 18510. Offers accounting (MBA); finance (MBA); general business administration (MBA); health care management (MBA); international business (MBA); management information systems (MBA); marketing (MBA); operations management (MBA). *Accreditation:* AACSB. Part-time and evening/weekend programs available. Postbaccalaureate distance learning degree programs offered (no on-campus study). *Faculty:* 34 full-time (8 women). *Students:* 316 full-time (134 women), 241 part-time (94 women); includes 104 minority (43 Black or African American, non-Hispanic/Latino; 3 American Indian or Alaska Native, non-Hispanic/Latino; 29 Asian, non-Hispanic/Latino; 27 Hispanic/Latino; 2 Two or more races, non-Hispanic/Latino), 47 international. Average age 34. 249 applicants, 85% accepted. In 2013, 200 master's awarded. *Degree requirements:* For master's, capstone experience. *Entrance requirements:* For master's, GMAT, minimum GPA of 3.0. Additional exam requirements/recommendations for international students: Required—TOEFL (minimum score 500 paper-based), IELTS (minimum score 6). *Application deadline:* Applications are processed on a rolling basis. Application fee: $0. *Financial support:* In 2013–14, 13 students received support, including 13 teaching assistantships with full and partial tuition reimbursements available (averaging $8,800 per year); fellowships, career-related internships or fieldwork, Federal Work-Study, and unspecified assistantships also available. Support available to part-time students. Financial award application deadline: 3/1. *Faculty research:* Financial markets, strategic impact of total quality management, internal accounting controls, consumer preference, information systems and the Internet. *Unit head:* Dr. Murli Rajan, Director, 570-941-4043, Fax: 570-941-4342. *Application contact:* Joseph M. Roback, Director of Admissions, 570-941-4385, Fax: 570-941-5928, E-mail: robackj2@scranton.edu. Website: http://www.scranton.edu/academics/cgce/busad.shtml.

University of South Carolina, The Graduate School, Darla Moore School of Business, International Business Administration Program, Columbia, SC 29208. Offers IMBA.

Degree requirements: For master's, one foreign language, field consulting project/internship. *Entrance requirements:* For master's, GMAT or GRE, minimum two years of work experience. Additional exam requirements/recommendations for international students: Required—TOEFL (minimum score 100 iBT); Recommended—IELTS. Electronic applications accepted. *Expenses:* Contact institution.

The University of Tampa, John H. Sykes College of Business, Tampa, FL 33606-1490. Offers accounting (MS); entrepreneurship (MBA); finance (MBA, MS); information systems management (MBA); innovation management (MBA); international business (MBA); marketing (MBA, MS); nonprofit management (MBA). *Accreditation:* AACSB. Part-time and evening/weekend programs available. *Faculty:* 41 full-time (15 women), 5 part-time/adjunct (1 woman). *Students:* 406 full-time (171 women), 152 part-time (61 women); includes 104 minority (18 Black or African American, non-Hispanic/Latino; 1 American Indian or Alaska Native, non-Hispanic/Latino; 20 Asian, non-Hispanic/Latino; 59 Hispanic/Latino; 6 Two or more races, non-Hispanic/Latino), 154 international. Average age 33. 1,341 applicants, 37% accepted, 256 enrolled. In 2013, 218 master's awarded. *Degree requirements:* For master's, capstone. *Entrance requirements:* For master's, GMAT or GRE, 4-year undergraduate degree, minimum GPA of 3.0, professional experience (for Executive MBA). Additional exam requirements/recommendations for international students: Required—TOEFL (minimum score 577 paper-based; 90 iBT); Recommended—IELTS (minimum score 7.5). *Application deadline:* Applications are processed on a rolling basis. Application fee: $40. Electronic applications accepted. *Expenses: Tuition:* Full-time $8928; part-time $558 per credit hour. *Required fees:* $80; $80 $40 per term. Tuition and fees vary according to program. *Financial support:* In 2013–14, 110 students received support. Career-related internships or fieldwork, scholarships/grants, and unspecified assistantships available. Financial award applicants required to submit FAFSA. *Faculty research:* Job market signaling, on-line shopping behaviors and social media, the Tampa Bay economy, digital literacy, entrepreneurship in small businesses. *Unit head:* Dr. Stephanie Thomason, Associate Dean, 813-253-6289, E-mail: sthomason@ut.edu. *Application contact:* Charlene Tobie, Associate Director of Admissions, 813-257-3566, E-mail: ctobie@ut.edu. Website: http://www.ut.edu/business/.

The University of Texas at Dallas, Naveen Jindal School of Management, Program in Business Administration, Richardson, TX 75080. Offers business administration (MBA, PMBA); executive business administration (EMBA); global leadership (EMBA); healthcare management for physicians (EMBA); product lifecycle and supply chain management (EMBA); project management (EMBA); real estate (MBA). *Accreditation:* AACSB. Part-time and evening/weekend programs available. Postbaccalaureate distance learning degree programs offered (no on-campus study). *Faculty:* 100 full-time (21 women), 52 part-time/adjunct (18 women). *Students:* 421 full-time (196 women), 630 part-time (398 women); includes 295 minority (45 Black or African American, non-Hispanic/Latino; 4 American Indian or Alaska Native, non-Hispanic/Latino; 151 Asian, non-Hispanic/Latino; 76 Hispanic/Latino; 19 Two or more races, non-Hispanic/Latino), 275 international. Average age 31. 940 applicants, 44% accepted, 375 enrolled. In 2013, 384 master's awarded. *Degree requirements:* For master's, thesis optional. *Entrance requirements:* For master's, GMAT, 10 years of business experience (EMBA), minimum GPA of 3.0. Additional exam requirements/recommendations for international students: Required—TOEFL (minimum score 550 paper-based). *Application deadline:* For fall admission, 7/15 for domestic students, 5/1 priority date for international students; for spring admission, 11/15 for domestic students, 9/1 priority date for international students. Applications are processed on a rolling basis. Application fee: $50 ($100 for international students). Electronic applications accepted. *Expenses:* Contact institution. *Financial support:* In 2013–14, 336 students received support. Research assistantships with partial tuition reimbursements available, teaching assistantships with partial tuition reimbursements available, career-related internships or fieldwork, Federal Work-Study, institutionally sponsored loans, scholarships/grants, and unspecified assistantships available. Support available to part-time students. Financial award application deadline: 4/30; financial award applicants required to submit FAFSA. *Faculty research:* Production scheduling, trade and finance, organizational decision-making, life/work planning. *Unit head:* Lisa Shatz, Assistant Dean, MBA Programs, 972-883-6191, E-mail: lisa.shatz@utdallas.edu. *Application contact:* Anna Walls, Enrollment Services Advisor, MBA Programs, 972-883-5951, E-mail: anna.walls@utdallas.edu. Website: http://jindal.utdallas.edu/academic-programs/mba-programs/.

The University of Texas at Dallas, Naveen Jindal School of Management, Program in Organizations, Strategy and International Management, Richardson, TX 75080. Offers healthcare management (MS); international management studies (MS, PhD); management and administrative sciences (MS); project management (MS). Part-time and evening/weekend programs available. *Faculty:* 13 full-time (4 women), 8 part-time/adjunct (4 women). *Students:* 101 full-time (59 women), 198 part-time (119 women); includes 88 minority (27 Black or African American, non-Hispanic/Latino; 38 Asian, non-Hispanic/Latino; 19 Hispanic/Latino; 1 Native Hawaiian or other Pacific Islander, non-Hispanic/Latino; 3 Two or more races, non-Hispanic/Latino), 72 international. Average age 35. 282 applicants, 53% accepted, 139 enrolled. In 2013, 131 master's, 5 doctorates awarded. *Degree requirements:* For doctorate, thesis/dissertation. *Entrance requirements:* For master's and doctorate, GMAT. Additional exam requirements/recommendations for international students: Required—TOEFL (minimum score 550 paper-based). *Application deadline:* For fall admission, 7/15 for domestic students, 5/1 priority date for international students; for spring admission, 11/15 for domestic students, 9/1 priority date for international students. Applications are processed on a rolling basis. Application fee: $50 ($100 for international students). Electronic applications accepted. *Expenses:* Tuition, state resident: full-time $11,940; part-time $663.33 per credit hour. Tuition, nonresident: full-time $21,606; part-time $1200.33 per credit hour. *Financial support:* In 2013–14, 58 students received support. Research assistantships with partial tuition reimbursements available, teaching assistantships with partial tuition reimbursements available, Federal Work-Study, institutionally sponsored loans, scholarships/grants, and unspecified assistantships available. Support available to part-time students. Financial award application deadline: 4/30; financial award applicants required to submit FAFSA. *Faculty research:* International accounting, international trade and finance, economic development, international economics. *Unit head:* Dr. Mike Peng, Area Coordinator, 972-883-2714, Fax: 972-883-5977, E-mail: mikepeng@utdallas.edu. *Application contact:* Dr. Habte Woldu, Director, International Management Studies, 972-883-6357, Fax: 972-883-5977, E-mail: wolduh@utdallas.edu. Website: http://jindal.utdallas.edu/academic-areas/organizations-strategy-and-international-management/.

The University of Texas at El Paso, Graduate School, College of Business Administration, Programs in Business Administration, El Paso, TX 79968-0001. Offers business administration (MBA, Certificate); international business (PhD). *Accreditation:* AACSB. Part-time and evening/weekend programs available. Postbaccalaureate distance learning degree programs offered (no on-campus study). *Degree requirements:* For master's, comprehensive exam. *Entrance requirements:* For master's and doctorate, GMAT. Additional exam requirements/recommendations for international students: Required—TOEFL. Electronic applications accepted. *Faculty research:* Cross-border modeling, human resources, and outsourcing and manufacturing; global information technology transfer; international investments and risk management.

University of the Incarnate Word, Extended Academic Programs, Program in Business Administration, San Antonio, TX 78209-6397. Offers business administration (MS); general business (MBA); international business (MBA). Part-time and evening/weekend programs available. Postbaccalaureate distance learning degree programs offered (minimal on-campus study). *Faculty:* 3 full-time (0 women), 20 part-time/adjunct (8 women). *Students:* 221 part-time (113 women); includes 138 minority (17 Black or African American, non-Hispanic/Latino; 1 American Indian or Alaska Native, non-Hispanic/Latino; 10 Asian, non-Hispanic/Latino; 109 Hispanic/Latino; 1 Two or more races, non-Hispanic/Latino). Average age 35. 105 applicants, 86% accepted, 66 enrolled. In 2013, 74 master's awarded. *Entrance requirements:* For master's, GMAT (minimum score of 450), baccalaureate degree with minimum GPA of 3.0. Additional exam requirements/recommendations for international students: Required—TOEFL (minimum score 560 paper-based; 83 iBT). *Application deadline:* Applications are processed on a rolling basis. Electronic applications accepted. *Expenses: Tuition:* Part-time $815 per credit hour. *Required fees:* $86 per credit hour. One-time fee: $40 part-time. Tuition and fees vary according to degree level and program. *Financial support:* Applicants required to submit FAFSA. *Unit head:* Dr. Cyndi Porter, Vice President, 877-603-1130, E-mail: porter@uiwtx.edu. *Application contact:* Julie Weber, Director of Marketing and Recruitment, 210-832-2100, Fax: 210-829-2756, E-mail: eapadmission@uiwtx.edu.

University of the Incarnate Word, School of Graduate Studies and Research, H-E-B School of Business and Administration, Programs in Business Administration, San Antonio, TX 78209-6397. Offers general business (MBA); international business (MBA); marketing (MBA); sports management (MBA). *Accreditation:* ACBSP. Part-time and evening/weekend programs available. Postbaccalaureate distance learning degree programs offered. *Faculty:* 20 full-time (10 women), 14 part-time/adjunct (6 women). *Students:* 95 full-time (33 women), 74 part-time (40 women); includes 93 minority (11 Black or African American, non-Hispanic/Latino; 1 American Indian or Alaska Native, non-Hispanic/Latino; 4 Asian, non-Hispanic/Latino; 71 Hispanic/Latino; 2 Native Hawaiian or other Pacific Islander, non-Hispanic/Latino; 4 Two or more races, non-Hispanic/Latino), 41 international. Average age 28. 183 applicants, 66% accepted, 51 enrolled. In 2013, 75 master's awarded. *Degree requirements:* For master's, capstone. *Entrance requirements:* For master's, GMAT (minimum score 450), undergraduate degree with minimum overall GPA of 2.5. Additional exam requirements/recommendations for international students: Required—TOEFL (minimum score 560 paper-based; 83 iBT). *Application deadline:* Applications are processed on a rolling basis. Application fee: $20. Electronic applications accepted. *Expenses: Tuition:* Part-time $815 per credit hour. *Required fees:* $86 per credit hour. One-time fee: $40 part-time. Tuition and fees vary according to degree level and program. *Financial support:* Federal Work-Study and scholarships/grants available. Financial award applicants required to submit FAFSA. *Unit head:* Dr. Jeannie Scott, Acting Dean, 210-283-5002, Fax: 210-805-3564, E-mail: scott@uiwtx.edu. *Application contact:* Andrea Cyterski-Acosta, Dean of Enrollment, 210-829-6005, Fax: 210-829-3921, E-mail: admis@uiwtx.edu.
Website: http://www.uiw.edu/mba/index.htm and http://www.uiw.edu/mba/admission.html.

University of the West, Department of Business Administration, Rosemead, CA 91770. Offers business administration (EMBA); computer information systems (MBA); finance (MBA); international business (MBA); nonprofit organization management (MBA). Part-time and evening/weekend programs available. *Entrance requirements:* Additional exam requirements/recommendations for international students: Required—TOEFL. *Application deadline:* For fall admission, 6/15 for domestic and international students; for winter admission, 4/1 for domestic and international students; for spring admission, 11/15 for domestic and international students. Applications are processed on a rolling basis. Application fee: $50 ($100 for international students). *Expenses: Tuition:* Full-time $7200; part-time $400 per credit hour. *Required fees:* $750; $400 per credit hour. $275 per semester. One-time fee: $75. Tuition and fees vary according to course level and program. *Financial support:* Career-related internships or fieldwork, Federal Work-Study, scholarships/grants, and tuition waivers (partial) available. Financial award applicants required to submit FAFSA. *Unit head:* Dr. Bill Y. Chen, Chair, 626-656-2125, Fax: 626-571-1413, E-mail: billchen@uwest.edu. *Application contact:* Jason Kosareff, Enrollment Counselor, 626-571-8811 Ext. 311, Fax: 626-571-1413, E-mail: jasonk@uwest.edu.

The University of Toledo, College of Graduate Studies, College of Business and Innovation, Department of Marketing and International Business, Toledo, OH 43606-3390. Offers MBA. Part-time and evening/weekend programs available. *Faculty:* 15. *Students:* 24 full-time (12 women), 19 part-time (11 women); includes 8 minority (5 Black or African American, non-Hispanic/Latino; 1 Asian, non-Hispanic/Latino; 1 Hispanic/Latino; 1 Two or more races, non-Hispanic/Latino), 19 international. Average age 26. 15 applicants, 93% accepted, 9 enrolled. In 2013, 67 master's awarded. *Entrance requirements:* For master's, GMAT, GRE, or LSAT, minimum GPA of 2.7 for all prior academic work, three letters of recommendation, statement of purpose, transcripts from all prior institutions attended. Additional exam requirements/recommendations for international students: Required—TOEFL (minimum score 550 paper-based; 80 iBT). *Application deadline:* For fall admission, 8/1 for domestic students, 5/1 for international students; for spring admission, 11/15 for domestic students, 10/1 for international students; for summer admission, 4/15 for domestic students, 3/1 for international students. Applications are processed on a rolling basis. Application fee: $45 ($75 for international students). Electronic applications accepted. *Financial support:* In 2013–14, 3 research assistantships with full and partial tuition reimbursements (averaging $4,375 per year) were awarded; career-related internships or fieldwork, Federal Work-Study, scholarships/grants, tuition waivers (full and partial), unspecified assistantships, and administrative assistantships also available. Financial award applicants required to submit FAFSA. *Unit head:* Dr. Iryna Pentina, Chair, 419-530-2093, E-mail: iryna.pentina@utoledo.edu. *Application contact:* Graduate School Office, 419-530-4723, Fax: 419-530-4724, E-mail: grdsch@utnet.utoledo.edu.
Website: http://www.utoledo.edu/business/index.html.

The University of Tulsa, Graduate School, Collins College of Business, Master of Business Administration Program, Tulsa, OK 74104-3189. Offers accounting (MBA); business administration (MBA); energy management (MBA); finance (MBA); international business (MBA); management information systems (MBA); taxation (MBA); JD/MBA; MBA/MSCS; MBA/MSF. *Accreditation:* AACSB. Part-time and evening/weekend programs available. *Faculty:* 32 full-time (6 women). *Students:* 59 full-time (28 women), 29 part-time (9 women); includes 11 minority (1 Black or African American, non-Hispanic/Latino; 5 American Indian or Alaska Native, non-Hispanic/Latino; 3 Asian, non-Hispanic/Latino; 1 Hispanic/Latino; 1 Two or more races, non-Hispanic/Latino), 16 international. Average age 27. 53 applicants, 81% accepted, 28 enrolled. In 2013, 39 master's awarded. *Entrance requirements:* For master's, GMAT. Additional exam requirements/recommendations for international students: Required—TOEFL (minimum score 577 paper-based; 91 iBT), IELTS (minimum score 6.5). *Application deadline:* Applications are processed on a rolling basis. Application fee: $40. Electronic applications accepted. *Expenses: Tuition:* Full-time $19,566; part-time $1087 per credit hour. *Required fees:* $1690; $5 per credit hour. $160 per semester. Tuition and fees vary according to course load. *Financial support:* In 2013–14, 31 students received

support, including 1 research assistantship (averaging $1,500 per year), 30 teaching assistantships (averaging $10,112 per year); fellowships, career-related internships or fieldwork, institutionally sponsored loans, scholarships/grants, health care benefits, tuition waivers (full and partial), and unspecified assistantships also available. Support available to part-time students. Financial award application deadline: 2/1; financial award applicants required to submit FAFSA. *Faculty research:* Accounting, energy management, finance, international business, management information systems, taxation. *Unit head:* Dr. Linda Nichols, Associate Dean of the Collins College of Business, 918-631-2242, Fax: 918-631-2142, E-mail: linda-nichols@utulsa.edu. *Application contact:* Information Contact, 918-631-2242, E-mail: graduate-business@utulsa.edu.
Website: http://www.utulsa.edu/academics/colleges/collins-college-of-business/bus-dept-schools/graduate-business-programs/degree-programs/MBA-Programs.aspx.

University of Washington, Graduate School, Interdisciplinary Program in Global Trade, Transportation and Logistics Studies, Seattle, WA 98195. Offers Certificate.

University of Washington, Graduate School, Michael G. Foster School of Business, Seattle, WA 98195-3200. Offers auditing and assurance (MP Acc); business administration (MBA, PhD); executive business administration (MBA); global executive business administration (MBA); taxation (MP Acc); technology management (MBA); JD/MBA; MBA/MAIS; MBA/MHA. *Accreditation:* AACSB. Part-time and evening/weekend programs available. *Faculty:* 100 full-time (28 women), 55 part-time/adjunct (22 women). *Students:* 407 full-time (130 women), 369 part-time (110 women); includes 199 minority (16 Black or African American, non-Hispanic/Latino; 5 American Indian or Alaska Native, non-Hispanic/Latino; 139 Asian, non-Hispanic/Latino; 25 Hispanic/Latino; 7 Native Hawaiian or other Pacific Islander, non-Hispanic/Latino; 7 Two or more races, non-Hispanic/Latino), 178 international. Average age 32. 2,474 applicants, 40% accepted, 776 enrolled. In 2013, 468 master's, 8 doctorates awarded. Terminal master's awarded for partial completion of doctoral program. *Degree requirements:* For doctorate, comprehensive exam, thesis/dissertation. *Entrance requirements:* For master's, GMAT; for doctorate, GMAT, GRE. Additional exam requirements/recommendations for international students: Required—TOEFL (minimum score 600 paper-based; 100 iBT). *Application deadline:* For fall admission, 3/15 for domestic students, 1/20 for international students. Application fee: $85. Electronic applications accepted. *Expenses:* Contact institution. *Financial support:* Fellowships with partial tuition reimbursements, research assistantships with partial tuition reimbursements, teaching assistantships with partial tuition reimbursements, Federal Work-Study, institutionally sponsored loans, and scholarships/grants available. Financial award application deadline: 2/28; financial award applicants required to submit FAFSA. *Faculty research:* Finance, marketing, organizational behavior, information technology, strategy. *Unit head:* Dr. James Jiambalvo, Dean, 206-543-4750. *Application contact:* Erin Town, Director of Admissions, 206-543-4661, Fax: 206-616-7351, E-mail: mba@uw.edu.
Website: http://www.foster.washington.edu/.

The University of Western Ontario, Richard Ivey School of Business, London, ON N6A 3K7, Canada. Offers business (EMBA, PhD); corporate strategy and leadership elective (MBA); entrepreneurship elective (MBA); finance elective (MBA); health sector stream (MBA); international management elective (MBA); marketing elective (MBA); JD/MBA. *Degree requirements:* For master's, thesis (for some programs); for doctorate, thesis/dissertation. *Entrance requirements:* For master's, GMAT, 2 years of full-time work experience, interview. Additional exam requirements/recommendations for international students: Required—TOEFL (minimum score 100 iBT) or IELTS (minimum score 6). Electronic applications accepted. *Faculty research:* Strategy, organizational behavior, international business, finance, operations management.

University of Wisconsin–Milwaukee, Graduate School, College of Letters and Sciences, Interdepartmental Program in Human Resources and Labor Relations, Milwaukee, WI 53201-0413. Offers human resources and labor relations (MHRLR); international human resources and labor relations (Certificate); mediation and negotiation (Certificate). Part-time programs available. *Faculty:* 2 full-time (0 women). *Students:* 16 full-time (10 women), 28 part-time (23 women); includes 11 minority (5 Black or African American, non-Hispanic/Latino; 3 Asian, non-Hispanic/Latino; 2 Hispanic/Latino; 1 Two or more races, non-Hispanic/Latino), 5 international. Average age 32. 31 applicants, 45% accepted, 7 enrolled. In 2013, 20 master's awarded. *Entrance requirements:* For master's, GMAT or GRE General Test. Additional exam requirements/recommendations for international students: Required—TOEFL (minimum score 550 paper-based; 79 iBT), IELTS (minimum score 6.5). *Application deadline:* For fall admission, 1/1 priority date for domestic students; for spring admission, 9/1 for domestic students. Applications are processed on a rolling basis. Application fee: $56 ($96 for international students). Electronic applications accepted. *Financial support:* Career-related internships or fieldwork available. Support available to part-time students. Financial award application deadline: 4/15; financial award applicants required to submit FAFSA. *Unit head:* Susan M. Donohue-Davies, Representative, 414-299-4009, Fax: 414-229-5915, E-mail: suedono@uwm.edu. *Application contact:* General Information Contact, 414-229-4982, Fax: 414-229-6967, E-mail: gradschool@uwm.edu.
Website: http://www.uwm.edu/dept/MHRLR/.

University of Wisconsin–Oshkosh, Graduate Studies, College of Business, Program in Global Business Administration, Oshkosh, WI 54901. Offers GMBA. *Degree requirements:* For master's, integrative seminar, study abroad. *Entrance requirements:* For master's, GMAT, GRE, letters of recommendation. Additional exam requirements/recommendations for international students: Required—TOEFL (minimum score 79 iBT).

University of Wisconsin–Whitewater, School of Graduate Studies, College of Business and Economics, Program in Business Administration, Whitewater, WI 53190-1790. Offers finance (MBA); human resource management (MBA); information technology management (MBA); international business (MBA); management (MBA); marketing (MBA); operations and supply chain management (MBA). *Accreditation:* AACSB. Part-time and evening/weekend programs available. Postbaccalaureate distance learning degree programs offered (no on-campus study). *Entrance requirements:* For master's, GMAT or GRE, minimum AACSB index of 1000, minimum GPA of 2.75. Additional exam requirements/recommendations for international students: Required—TOEFL (minimum score 550 paper-based; 80 iBT), IELTS (minimum score 6). Electronic applications accepted. *Faculty research:* Interface between social institutions and individual behavior, technology and innovation management, occupational mental health, workplace deviance and workplace romance.

Upper Iowa University, Online Master's Programs, Fayette, IA 52142-1857. Offers accounting (MBA); corporate financial management (MBA); global business (MBA); health and human services (MPA); higher education administration (MHEA); homeland security (MPA); human resources management (MBA); justice administration (MPA); organizational development (MBA); public personnel management (MPA); quality management (MBA). MBA also available at Madison, WI campus. Part-time programs available. Postbaccalaureate distance learning degree programs offered (no on-campus study). *Degree requirements:* For master's, research project. *Entrance requirements:* For master's, GMAT, GRE, or minimum GPA of 2.7 during last 60 hours. Additional exam requirements/recommendations for international students: Required—TOEFL

(minimum score 570 paper-based). Electronic applications accepted. *Faculty research:* Total quality management, CQI, teams, organization culture and climate, management.

Valparaiso University, Graduate School, Program in International Commerce and Policy, Valparaiso, IN 46383. Offers MS, JD/MS. Part-time and evening/weekend programs available. *Students:* 29 full-time (7 women), 22 part-time (4 women); includes 6 minority (4 Black or African American, non-Hispanic/Latino; 1 Asian, non-Hispanic/Latino; 1 Hispanic/Latino), 33 international. Average age 27. In 2013, 22 master's awarded. *Entrance requirements:* For master's, minimum GPA of 3.0. Additional exam requirements/recommendations for international students: Required—TOEFL (minimum score 550 paper-based; 80 iBT), IELTS (minimum score 6). *Application deadline:* Applications are processed on a rolling basis. Application fee: $30 ($50 for international students). Electronic applications accepted. *Expenses: Tuition:* Full-time $10,350; part-time $575 per credit hour. *Required fees:* $378; $101 per term. Tuition and fees vary according to course load and program. *Financial support:* Available to part-time students. Applicants required to submit FAFSA. *Unit head:* Dr. Jennifer A. Ziegler, Dean, Graduate School and Continuing Education, 219-464-5313, Fax: 219-464-5381, E-mail: jennifer.ziegler@valpo.edu. *Application contact:* Jessica Choquette, Graduate Admissions Specialist, 219-464-5313, Fax: 219-464-5381, E-mail: jessica.choquette@valpo.edu.
Website: http://www.valpo.edu/grad/icp/.

Vancouver Island University, Master of Business Administration Program, Nanaimo, BC V9R 5S5, Canada. Offers international business (MBA), including finance, marketing. Program offered jointly with University of Hertfordshire. *Accreditation:* ACBSP. Part-time programs available. *Degree requirements:* For master's, thesis. *Entrance requirements:* Additional exam requirements/recommendations for international students: Required—TOEFL (minimum score 550 paper-based). Electronic applications accepted. *Faculty research:* Tourism development, entrepreneurship, organizational development, strategic planning, international business strategy, intercultural team work.

Villanova University, Villanova School of Business, MBA - The Fast Track Program, Villanova, PA 19085. Offers finance (MBA); health care management (MBA); international business (MBA); management information systems (MBA); marketing (MBA); real estate (MBA); strategic management (MBA). *Accreditation:* AACSB. Part-time and evening/weekend programs available. *Faculty:* 101 full-time (33 women), 36 part-time/adjunct (3 women). *Students:* 140 part-time (44 women); includes 22 minority (1 Black or African American, non-Hispanic/Latino; 17 Asian, non-Hispanic/Latino; 3 Hispanic/Latino; 1 Two or more races, non-Hispanic/Latino), 3 international. Average age 29. 127 applicants, 72% accepted, 75 enrolled. In 2013, 61 master's awarded. *Degree requirements:* For master's, minimum GPA of 3.0. *Entrance requirements:* For master's, GMAT or GRE, work experience. Additional exam requirements/recommendations for international students: Required—TOEFL (minimum score 550 paper-based; 90 iBT). *Application deadline:* For fall admission, 6/30 for domestic and international students. Application fee: $50. Electronic applications accepted. *Financial support:* Scholarships/grants available. Financial award application deadline: 6/30; financial award applicants required to submit FAFSA. *Faculty research:* Business analytics; creativity, innovation and entrepreneurship; global leadership; real estate; church management; business ethics. *Unit head:* Zelon Crawford, Director of Graduate Business Programs, 610-519-6283, Fax: 610-519-6273, E-mail: zelon.crawford@villanova.edu. *Application contact:* Meredith L. Lockyer, Manager of Recruiting, 610-519-7016, Fax: 610-519-6273, E-mail: meredith.lockyer@villanova.edu.
Website: http://www1.villanova.edu/villanova/business/graduate/mba/fasttrack.html.

Villanova University, Villanova School of Business, MBA - The Flex Track Program, Villanova, PA 19085. Offers finance (MBA); health care management (MBA); international business (MBA); management information systems (MBA); marketing (MBA); real estate (MBA); strategic management (MBA); JD/MBA. *Accreditation:* AACSB. Part-time and evening/weekend programs available. Postbaccalaureate distance learning degree programs offered (minimal on-campus study). *Faculty:* 101 full-time (33 women), 36 part-time/adjunct (3 women). *Students:* 13 full-time (5 women), 413 part-time (127 women); includes 63 minority (13 Black or African American, non-Hispanic/Latino; 1 American Indian or Alaska Native, non-Hispanic/Latino; 29 Asian, non-Hispanic/Latino; 14 Hispanic/Latino; 1 Native Hawaiian or other Pacific Islander, non-Hispanic/Latino; 5 Two or more races, non-Hispanic/Latino), 9 international. Average age 29. 84 applicants, 83% accepted, 66 enrolled. In 2013, 133 master's awarded. *Degree requirements:* For master's, minimum GPA of 3.0. *Entrance requirements:* For master's, GMAT or GRE, work experience. Additional exam requirements/recommendations for international students: Required—TOEFL (minimum score 550 paper-based; 90 iBT). *Application deadline:* For fall admission, 6/30 for domestic and international students; for winter admission, 11/15 for domestic and international students; for spring admission, 11/15 for domestic and international students; for summer admission, 3/31 for domestic and international students. Applications are processed on a rolling basis. Application fee: $50. Electronic applications accepted. *Financial support:* In 2013–14, 13 research assistantships with full tuition reimbursements (averaging $13,100 per year) were awarded; scholarships/grants and unspecified assistantships also available. Financial award application deadline: 6/30; financial award applicants required to submit FAFSA. *Faculty research:* Business analytics; creativity, innovation and entrepreneurship; global leadership; real estate; church management; business ethics. *Unit head:* Zelon Crawford, Director of Graduate Business Programs, 610-610-6283, Fax: 610-519-6273, E-mail: zelon.crawford@villanova.edu. *Application contact:* Meredith L. Lockyer, Manager of Recruiting, 610-519-7016, Fax: 610-519-6273, E-mail: meredith.lockyer@villanova.edu.
Website: http://www1.villanova.edu/villanova/business/graduate/mba/flextrack.html.

Virginia International University, School of Business, Fairfax, VA 22030. Offers accounting (MBA); executive management (Graduate Certificate); global logistics (MBA); health care management (MBA); human resources management (MBA); international business management (MBA); international finance (MBA); marketing management (MBA). Part-time programs available. *Entrance requirements:* For master's and Graduate Certificate, bachelor's degree. Additional exam requirements/recommendations for international students: Required—TOEFL (minimum score 550 paper-based; 80 iBT), IELTS (minimum score 6). Electronic applications accepted.

Viterbo University, Master of Business Administration Program, La Crosse, WI 54601-4797. Offers general business administration (MBA); health care management (MBA); international business (MBA); leadership (MBA); project management (MBA). *Accreditation:* ACBSP. Part-time and evening/weekend programs available. *Faculty:* 3 full-time (2 women), 4 part-time/adjunct (2 women). *Students:* 86 full-time (47 women), 11 part-time (8 women); includes 5 minority (1 Black or African American, non-Hispanic/Latino; 3 Asian, non-Hispanic/Latino; 1 Hispanic/Latino), 11 international. Average age 34. In 2013, 59 master's awarded. *Degree requirements:* For master's, 34 credits. *Entrance requirements:* For master's, BS, transcripts, minimum undergraduate cumulative GPA of 3.0, 2 letters of reference, 3-5 page essay. Additional exam requirements/recommendations for international students: Recommended—TOEFL (minimum score 550 paper-based). Application fee: $50. Electronic applications accepted. *Expenses: Tuition:* Full-time $7140; part-time $444 per credit hour. *Required fees:* $100. *Unit head:* Dr. Barbara Gayle, Dean of Graduate Studies, 608-796-3080, E-mail: bmgayle@viterbo.edu. *Application contact:* Tiffany Morey, MBA Coordinator, 608-796-3379, E-mail: tlmorey@viterbo.edu.

Wagner College, Division of Graduate Studies, Department of Business Administration, Program in International Business, Staten Island, NY 10301-4495. Offers MBA. Part-time and evening/weekend programs available. *Faculty:* 1 (woman) full-time, 2 part-time/adjunct (1 woman). *Students:* 6 full-time (1 woman), 5 part-time (2 women); includes 3 minority (2 Black or African American, non-Hispanic/Latino; 1 Hispanic/Latino), 1 international. Average age 24. 5 applicants, 80% accepted, 4 enrolled. In 2013, 2 master's awarded. *Degree requirements:* For master's, thesis optional. *Entrance requirements:* For master's, GMAT, minimum GPA of 2.6. Additional exam requirements/recommendations for international students: Required—TOEFL (minimum score 550 paper-based; 79 iBT). *Application deadline:* For fall admission, 5/1 priority date for domestic students, 3/1 priority date for international students; for spring admission, 11/1 priority date for domestic students, 10/1 priority date for international students. Applications are processed on a rolling basis. Application fee: $50. *Expenses: Tuition:* Full-time $17,496; part-time $972 per credit. Tuition and fees vary according to course load. *Financial support:* In 2013–14, 7 students received support. Career-related internships or fieldwork, unspecified assistantships, and alumni fellowship grants available. Financial award applicants required to submit FAFSA. *Unit head:* Dr. John J. Moran, Director, 718-390-3255, Fax: 718-390-3255, E-mail: jmoran@wagner.edu. *Application contact:* Patricia Clancy, Assistant Coordinator of Graduate Studies, 718-420-4464, Fax: 718-390-3105, E-mail: patricia.clancy@wagner.edu.

Walden University, Graduate Programs, School of Management, Minneapolis, MN 55401. Offers accounting (MBA, MS, DBA), including accounting for the professional (MS), accounting with CPA emphasis (MS), self-designed (MS, PhD); accounting and management (MS), including accountants as strategic managers, self-designed (MS, PhD); advanced project management (Graduate Certificate); applied project management (Graduate Certificate); bridge to business administration (Post-Doctoral Certificate); bridge to management (Post-Doctoral Certificate); business administration (EMBA); business management (Graduate Certificate); communication (MS, Graduate Certificate); corporate finance (MBA); entrepreneurship (DBA); entrepreneurship and small business (MBA); finance (DBA); global supply chain management (DBA); healthcare management (MBA, DBA); human resource management (MBA, MS, Graduate Certificate), including functional human resource management (MS), general program (MS), integrating functional and strategic human resource management (MS), organizational strategy (MS); human resources management (DBA); information systems management (DBA); international business (MBA, DBA); leadership (MBA, MS, DBA), including general program (MS), human resources leadership (MS), leader development (MS), self-designed (MS, PhD); management (MS, PhD), including accounting (PhD), engineering management (PhD), finance (PhD), general program (MS), healthcare management (MS), human resource management (MS), human resources management (PhD), information systems management (PhD), leadership (MS), leadership and organizational change (PhD), marketing (MS), operations research (PhD), project management (MS), self-designed, strategy and operations (MS); marketing (MBA, DBA); project management (MBA, MS, DBA); self-designed (MBA, DBA); social impact management (DBA); technology entrepreneurship (DBA). Part-time and evening/weekend programs available. Postbaccalaureate distance learning degree programs offered (minimal on-campus study). *Faculty:* 24 full-time (9 women), 337 part-time/adjunct (127 women). *Students:* 4,369 full-time (2,379 women), 2,181 part-time (1,304 women); includes 3,669 minority (3,020 Black or African American, non-Hispanic/Latino; 22 American Indian or Alaska Native, non-Hispanic/Latino; 156 Asian, non-Hispanic/Latino; 331 Hispanic/Latino; 11 Native Hawaiian or other Pacific Islander, non-Hispanic/Latino; 129 Two or more races, non-Hispanic/Latino), 107 international. Average age 41. 2,030 applicants, 94% accepted, 1436 enrolled. In 2013, 757 master's, 128 doctorates, 32 other advanced degrees awarded. *Degree requirements:* For master's, residency (for some programs); for doctorate, thesis/dissertation (for some programs), residency. *Entrance requirements:* For master's, bachelor's degree or higher; minimum GPA of 2.5; official transcripts; goal statement (for some programs); access to computer and Internet; for doctorate, master's degree or higher; three years of related professional or academic experience (preferred); minimum GPA of 3.0; goal statement and current resume (select programs); official transcripts; access to computer and Internet; for other advanced degree, relevant work experience; access to computer and Internet. Additional exam requirements/recommendations for international students: Required—TOEFL (minimum score 550 paper-based; 79 iBT), IELTS (minimum score 6.5), Michigan English Language Assessment Battery (minimum score 82), or PTE. *Application deadline:* Applications are processed on a rolling basis. Application fee: $0. Electronic applications accepted. *Expenses: Tuition:* Full-time $11,813.55; part-time $500 per credit. *Required fees:* $618.76. *Financial support:* Fellowships, Federal Work-Study, scholarships/grants, unspecified assistantships, and family tuition reduction, active duty/veteran tuition reduction, group tuition reduction, interest-free payment plans, employee tuition reduction available. Support available to part-time students. Financial award applicants required to submit FAFSA. *Unit head:* Dr. Ward Ulmer, III, Associate Dean, 800-925-3368. *Application contact:* Jennifer Hall, Vice President of Enrollment Management, 866-4-WALDEN, E-mail: info@waldenu.edu.
Website: http://www.waldenu.edu/programs/colleges-schools/management.

Washington State University, Graduate School, College of Business, Online MBA Program, Pullman, WA 99164. Offers finance (MBA); general business (MBA); international business (MBA); marketing (MBA). Postbaccalaureate distance learning degree programs offered (no on-campus study).

Wayland Baptist University, Graduate Programs, Programs in Business Administration/Management, Plainview, TX 79072-6998. Offers accounting (MBA); general business (MBA); health care administration (MAM, MBA); healthcare administration (MBA); human resource management (MAM, MBA); international management (MBA); management (MBA); management information systems (MBA); organization management (MAM); project management (MBA). Part-time and evening/weekend programs available. Postbaccalaureate distance learning degree programs offered (no on-campus study). *Faculty:* 30 full-time (5 women), 38 part-time/adjunct (9 women). *Students:* 44 full-time (20 women), 702 part-time (315 women); includes 348 minority (149 Black or African American, non-Hispanic/Latino; 4 American Indian or Alaska Native, non-Hispanic/Latino; 23 Asian, non-Hispanic/Latino; 139 Hispanic/Latino; 9 Native Hawaiian or other Pacific Islander, non-Hispanic/Latino; 24 Two or more races, non-Hispanic/Latino), 5 international. Average age 40. 147 applicants, 94% accepted, 73 enrolled. In 2013, 296 master's awarded. *Degree requirements:* For master's, capstone course. *Entrance requirements:* For master's, GMAT, GRE or MAT. Additional exam requirements/recommendations for international students: Required—TOEFL (minimum score 500 paper-based; 61 iBT). *Application deadline:* Applications are processed on a rolling basis. Application fee: $50. Electronic applications accepted. *Expenses: Tuition:* Full-time $8190; part-time $455 per credit hour. *Required fees:* $970; $455 per credit hour. $485 per semester. *Financial support:* Federal Work-Study, institutionally sponsored loans, and scholarships/grants available. Support available to part-time students. Financial award application deadline: 5/1; financial award applicants required to submit FAFSA. *Unit head:* Dr. Otto Schacht, Chairman, 806-291-1020, Fax: 806-291-1957, E-mail: schachto@wbu.edu. *Application contact:* Amanda Stanton, Graduate Studies, 806-291-3423, Fax: 806-291-1950, E-mail: stanton@wbu.edu.

Webster University, George Herbert Walker School of Business and Technology, Department of Business, St. Louis, MO 63119-3194. Offers business and organizational security management (MBA); decision support systems (MBA); environmental management (MBA); finance (MBA, MS); forensic accounting (MS); gerontology (MBA); human resources development (MBA); human resources management (MBA); information technology management (MBA); international business (MA, MBA); international relations (MBA); management and leadership (MBA); marketing (MBA); media communications (MBA); procurement and acquisitions management (MBA); Web services (MBA). *Accreditation:* ACBSP. Part-time and evening/weekend programs available. Postbaccalaureate distance learning degree programs offered (no on-campus study). *Degree requirements:* For master's, comprehensive exam (for some programs), thesis (for some programs). *Entrance requirements:* Additional exam requirements/recommendations for international students: Required—TOEFL. *Expenses: Tuition:* Full-time $11,610; part-time $645 per credit hour. Tuition and fees vary according to campus/location and program.

Western International University, Graduate Programs in Business, Master of Business Administration Program in International Business, Phoenix, AZ 85021-2718. Offers MBA. Part-time and evening/weekend programs available. Postbaccalaureate distance learning degree programs offered (no on-campus study). *Entrance requirements:* For master's, minimum GPA of 2.75. Additional exam requirements/recommendations for international students: Required—TOEFL (minimum score 550 paper-based; 79 iBT), TWE (minimum score 5), or IELTS (minimum score 6.5). Electronic applications accepted.

Whitworth University, School of Business, Spokane, WA 99251-0001. Offers international management (MBA). Part-time and evening/weekend programs available. *Faculty:* 5 full-time (1 woman), 9 part-time/adjunct (2 women). *Students:* 5 full-time (1 woman), 30 part-time (17 women); includes 5 minority (2 Black or African American, non-Hispanic/Latino; 1 American Indian or Alaska Native, non-Hispanic/Latino; 2 Asian, non-Hispanic/Latino). Average age 29. 33 applicants, 67% accepted, 20 enrolled. In 2013, 12 master's awarded. *Degree requirements:* For master's, foreign language (for MBA in international management). *Entrance requirements:* For master's, GMAT or GRE, minimum GPA of 3.0; two letters of recommendation; resume; completion of prerequisite courses in micro-economics, macro-economics, financial accounting, finance, and marketing, interview with director. Additional exam requirements/recommendations for international students: Required—TOEFL (minimum score 88 iBT), TWE. *Application deadline:* For fall admission, 8/1 priority date for domestic and international students; for spring admission, 1/6 priority date for domestic students, 1/6 for international students. Applications are processed on a rolling basis. Application fee: $35. Electronic applications accepted. *Financial support:* In 2013–14, 9 students received support. Scholarships/grants available. Financial award applicants required to submit FAFSA. *Faculty research:* International business (European, Central America and Asian topics), entrepreneurship and business plan development. *Unit head:* John Hengesh, Director, Graduate Studies in Business, 509-777-4455, Fax: 509-777-3723, E-mail: jhengesh@whitworth.edu. *Application contact:* Susan Cook, Admissions Manager, Graduate Studies, 509-777-4298, Fax: 509-777-3723, E-mail: scook@whitworth.edu.
Website: http://www.whitworth.edu/schoolofbusiness.

Wilkes University, College of Graduate and Professional Studies, Jay S. Sidhu School of Business and Leadership, Wilkes-Barre, PA 18766-0002. Offers accounting (MBA); entrepreneurship (MBA); finance (MBA); health care administration (MBA); human resource management (MBA); international business (MBA); marketing (MBA); operations management (MBA); organizational leadership and development (MBA). *Accreditation:* ACBSP. Part-time and evening/weekend programs available. *Students:* 41 full-time (20 women), 119 part-time (48 women); includes 20 minority (5 Black or African American, non-Hispanic/Latino; 3 Asian, non-Hispanic/Latino; 7 Hispanic/Latino; 5 Two or more races, non-Hispanic/Latino), 7 international. Average age 31. In 2013, 55 master's awarded. *Entrance requirements:* For master's, GMAT. Additional exam requirements/recommendations for international students: Required—TOEFL (minimum score 550 paper-based; 79 iBT). *Application deadline:* Applications are processed on a rolling basis. Application fee: $45 ($65 for international students). Electronic applications accepted. *Expenses:* Contact institution. *Financial support:* Federal Work-Study and unspecified assistantships available. Financial award application deadline: 3/1; financial award applicants required to submit FAFSA. *Unit head:* Dr. Jeffrey Alves, Dean, 570-408-4702, Fax: 570-408-7846, E-mail: jeffrey.alves@wilkes.edu. *Application contact:* Joanne Thomas, Interim Director of Graduate Enrollment, 570-408-4234, Fax: 570-408-7846, E-mail: joanne.thomas1@wilkes.edu.
Website: http://www.wilkes.edu/pages/457.asp.

Wright State University, School of Graduate Studies, Raj Soin College of Business, Department of Management, Dayton, OH 45435. Offers flexible business (MBA); health care management (MBA); international business (MBA); management, innovation and change (MBA); project management (MBA); supply chain management (MBA); MBA/MS. *Entrance requirements:* For master's, GMAT, minimum AACSB index of 1000. Additional exam requirements/recommendations for international students: Required—TOEFL.

Xavier University, Williams College of Business, Master of Business Administration Program, Cincinnati, OH 45207-3221. Offers business administration (Exec MBA, MBA); business intelligence (MBA); finance (MBA); health industry (MBA); international business (MBA); marketing (MBA); values-based leadership (MBA); MBA/MHSA; MSN/MBA. *Accreditation:* AACSB. Part-time and evening/weekend programs available. *Faculty:* 39 full-time (17 women), 12 part-time/adjunct (2 women). *Students:* 163 full-time (47 women), 483 part-time (162 women); includes 91 minority (28 Black or African American, non-Hispanic/Latino; 3 American Indian or Alaska Native, non-Hispanic/Latino; 42 Asian, non-Hispanic/Latino; 14 Hispanic/Latino; 4 Two or more races, non-Hispanic/Latino), 33 international. Average age 30. 190 applicants, 86% accepted, 110 enrolled. In 2013, 319 master's awarded. *Degree requirements:* For master's, capstone course. *Entrance requirements:* For master's, GMAT or GRE. Additional exam requirements/recommendations for international students: Required—TOEFL (minimum score 550 paper-based; 79 iBT). *Application deadline:* For fall admission, 8/1 priority date for domestic students, 5/1 for international students; for spring admission, 12/1 priority date for domestic students, 9/1 for international students. Applications are processed on a rolling basis. Application fee: $0. Electronic applications accepted. *Expenses:* Contact institution. *Financial support:* In 2013–14, 115 students received support. Scholarships/grants, tuition waivers (partial), and unspecified assistantships available. Financial award application deadline: 3/1; financial award applicants required to submit FAFSA. *Unit head:* Jennifer Bush, Assistant Dean of Graduate Programs, Williams College of Business, 513-745-3527, Fax: 513-745-2929, E-mail: bush@xavier.edu. *Application contact:* Lauren Parcell, MBA Advisor, 513-745-1014, Fax: 513-745-2929, E-mail: parcelll@xavier.edu.
Website: http://www.xavier.edu/williams/mba/.

York University, Faculty of Graduate Studies, Schulich School of Business, Toronto, ON M3J 1P3, Canada. Offers accounting (M Acc); administration (PhD); business (MBA); business analytics (MBA); finance (MF); international business (IMBA); MBA/JD; MBA/MA; MBA/MFA. Part-time and evening/weekend programs available. *Students:* 683 full-time (255 women), 407 part-time (125 women). Average age 29. 1,498 applicants, 30% accepted, 409 enrolled. In 2013, 587 master's, 96 doctorates awarded. *Median time to degree:* Of those who began their doctoral program in fall 2005, 55% received their degree in 8 years or less. *Degree requirements:* For master's, advanced proficiency in a second language, work term (IMBA); for doctorate, comprehensive exam, thesis/dissertation. *Entrance requirements:* For master's, GMAT or GRE, minimum GPA of 3.0 (3.3 for MF, MBA in business analytics, and IMBA); for doctorate, GMAT or GRE, minimum GPA of 3.3. Additional exam requirements/recommendations for international students: Required—TOEFL (minimum score 600 paper-based; 100 iBT), IELTS (minimum score 7), York English Language Test (minimum score 1); PearsonVUE (minimum score 64). *Application deadline:* For fall admission, 4/30 for domestic students, 2/28 for international students; for winter admission, 9/1 for domestic and international students. Applications are processed on a rolling basis. Application fee: $150. Electronic applications accepted. *Financial support:* In 2013–14, 800 students received support, including fellowships (averaging $5,000 per year), research assistantships (averaging $3,000 per year), teaching assistantships (averaging $7,000 per year); career-related internships or fieldwork, scholarships/grants, and bursaries (for part-time students) also available. Financial award application deadline: 2/1. *Faculty research:* Accounting, finance, marketing, operations management and information systems, organizational studies, strategic management. *Unit head:* Dezso Horvath, Dean, 416-736-5070, E-mail: dhorvath@schulich.yorku.ca. *Application contact:* Graduate Admissions, 416-736-5060, Fax: 416-650-8174, E-mail: admissions@schulich.yorku.ca.
Website: http://www.schulich.yorku.ca.

Section 12
Management Information Systems

This section contains a directory of institutions offering graduate work in management information systems. Additional information about programs listed in the directory but not augmented by an in-depth entry may be obtained by writing directly to the dean of a graduate school or chair of a department at the address given in the directory.

For programs offering related work, see also in this book *Business Administration and Management.* In another guide in this series:

Graduate Programs in Engineering & Applied Sciences

See *Computer Science and Information Technology* and *Management of Engineering and Technology*

CONTENTS

Program Directory

Management Information Systems   438

Displays and Close-Ups

See:

Adelphi University—Business Administration and
   Management   70, 181
Syracuse University—Library and Information Studies   1583, 1599
University of California, Los Angeles—Business
   Administration and Management   145, 191
University of Oklahoma—Business Administration and
   Management   158, 193

Management Information Systems

Adelphi University, Robert B. Willumstad School of Business, MBA Program, Garden City, NY 11530-0701. Offers finance (MBA); management information systems (MBA); management/human resource management (MBA); marketing/e-commerce (MBA). *Accreditation:* AACSB. Part-time and evening/weekend programs available. *Students:* 254 full-time (129 women), 118 part-time (63 women); includes 60 minority (13 Black or African American, non-Hispanic/Latino; 18 Asian, non-Hispanic/Latino; 28 Hispanic/ Latino; 1 Native Hawaiian or other Pacific Islander, non-Hispanic/Latino), 200 international. Average age 28. In 2013, 182 master's awarded. *Degree requirements:* For master's, capstone course. *Entrance requirements:* For master's, GMAT, 2 letters of recommendation. Additional exam requirements/recommendations for international students: Required—TOEFL (minimum score 550 paper-based; 80 iBT). *Application deadline:* For fall admission, 4/1 for international students; for spring admission, 11/1 for international students. Applications are processed on a rolling basis. Application fee: $50. Electronic applications accepted. *Expenses: Tuition:* Full-time $32,530; part-time $1010 per credit. *Required fees:* $1150. Tuition and fees vary according to degree level and program. *Financial support:* Research assistantships with partial tuition reimbursements, career-related internships or fieldwork, Federal Work-Study, institutionally sponsored loans, scholarships/grants, tuition waivers (partial), and unspecified assistantships available. Financial award application deadline: 3/1; financial award applicants required to submit FAFSA. *Faculty research:* Supply chain management, distribution channels, productivity benchmark analysis, data envelopment analysis, financial portfolio analysis. *Unit head:* Dr. Rakesh Gupta, Associate Dean, 516-877-4629. *Application contact:* Christine Murphy, Director of Admissions, 516-877-3050, Fax: 516-877-3039, E-mail: graduateadmissions@adelphi.edu.
Website: http://business.adelphi.edu/degree-programs/graduate-degree-programs/m-b-a/.

See Display on page 70 and Close-Up on page 181.

Air Force Institute of Technology, Graduate School of Engineering and Management, Department of Systems and Engineering Management, Dayton, OH 45433-7765. Offers cost analysis (MS); environmental and engineering management (MS); environmental engineering science (MS); information resource/systems management (MS). *Accreditation:* ABET. Part-time programs available. *Degree requirements:* For master's, thesis. *Entrance requirements:* For master's, GRE, GMAT, minimum GPA of 3.0.

American InterContinental University Atlanta, Program in Information Technology, Atlanta, GA 30328. Offers MIT. Part-time and evening/weekend programs available. *Degree requirements:* For master's, technical proficiency demonstration. *Entrance requirements:* For master's, Computer Programmer Aptitude Battery Exam, interview. Electronic applications accepted. *Faculty research:* Operating systems, security issues, networks and routing, computer hardware.

American Public University System, AMU/APU Graduate Programs, Charles Town, WV 25414. Offers accounting (MBA, MS); criminal justice (MA), including business administration, emergency and disaster management, general (MA, MS); educational leadership (M Ed); emergency and disaster management (MA); entrepreneurship (MBA); environmental policy and management (MS), including environmental planning, environmental sustainability, fish and wildlife management, general (MA, MS), global environmental management; finance (MBA); general (MBA); global business management (MBA); history (MA), including American history, ancient and classical history, European history, global history, public history; homeland security (MA), including business administration, counter-terrorism studies, criminal justice, cyber, emergency management and public health, intelligence studies, transportation security; homeland security resource allocation (MBA); humanities (MA); information technology (MS), including digital forensics, enterprise software development, information assurance and security, IT project management; information technology management (MBA); intelligence studies (MA), including criminal intelligence, cyber, general (MA, MS), homeland security, intelligence analysis, intelligence collection, intelligence management, intelligence operations, terrorism studies; international relations and conflict resolution (MA), including comparative and security issues, conflict resolution, international and transnational security issues, peacekeeping; legal studies (MA); management (MA), including defense management, general (MA, MS), human resource management, organizational leadership, public administration; marketing (MBA); military history (MA), including American military history, American Revolution, civil war, war since 1945, World War II; military studies (MA), including joint warfare, strategic leadership; national security studies (MA), including general (MA, MS), homeland security, regional security studies, security and intelligence analysis, terrorism studies; nonprofit management (MBA); political science (MA), including American politics and government, comparative government and development, general (MA, MS), international relations, public policy; psychology (MA), including general (MA, MS), maritime engineering management, reverse logistics management; public administration (MPA), including disaster management, environmental policy, health policy, human resources, national security, organizational management, security management; public health (MPH); reverse logistics management (MA); school counseling (M Ed); security management (MA); space studies (MS), including aerospace science, general (MA, MS), planetary science; sports and health sciences (MS); teaching (M Ed), including curriculum and instruction for elementary teachers, elementary reading, English language learners, instructional leadership, online learning, special education; transportation and logistics management (MA), including general (MA, MS), maritime engineering management, reverse logistics management. Programs offered via distance learning only. Part-time and evening/weekend programs available. Postbaccalaureate distance learning degree programs offered (no on-campus study). *Faculty:* 432 full-time (242 women), 1,722 part-time/adjunct (829 women). *Students:* 511 full-time (241 women), 10,947 part-time (4,294 women); includes 3,760 minority (2,058 Black or African American, non-Hispanic/Latino; 88 American Indian or Alaska Native, non-Hispanic/Latino; 293 Asian, non-Hispanic/Latino; 876 Hispanic/Latino; 91 Native Hawaiian or other Pacific Islander, non-Hispanic/Latino; 354 Two or more races, non-Hispanic/Latino), 134 international. Average age 36. In 2013, 3,323 master's awarded. *Degree requirements:* For master's, comprehensive exam or practicum. *Entrance requirements:* For master's, official transcript showing earned bachelor's degree from institution accredited by recognized accrediting body. Additional exam requirements/ recommendations for international students: Required—TOEFL (minimum score 550 paper-based), IELTS (minimum score 6.5). *Application deadline:* Applications are processed on a rolling basis. Application fee: $0. Electronic applications accepted. *Expenses: Tuition:* Part-time $325 per semester hour. *Financial support:* Applicants required to submit FAFSA. *Faculty research:* Military history, criminal justice, management performance, national security. *Unit head:* Dr. Karan Powell, Executive Vice President and Provost, 877-468-6268, Fax: 304-724-3780. *Application contact:* Terry Grant, Vice President of Enrollment Management, 877-468-6268, Fax: 304-724-3780, E-mail: info@apus.edu.
Website: http://www.apus.edu.

American Sentinel University, Graduate Programs, Aurora, CO 80014. Offers business administration (MBA); business intelligence (MS); computer science (MSCS); health information management (MS); healthcare (MBA); information systems (MSIS); nursing (MSN). Part-time and evening/weekend programs available. Postbaccalaureate distance learning degree programs offered (no on-campus study). *Entrance requirements:* Additional exam requirements/recommendations for international students: Required—TOEFL (minimum score 600 paper-based). Electronic applications accepted.

American University, School of International Service, Washington, DC 20016-8071. Offers comparative and international disability policy (MA); comparative and regional studies (Certificate); cross-cultural communication (Certificate); development management (MS); ethics, peace, and global affairs (MA); European studies (Certificate); global environmental policy (MA, Certificate); global information technology (Certificate); international affairs (MA), including comparative and international disability policy, comparative and regional studies, international economic relations, international politics, natural resources and sustainable development, U.S. foreign policy; international communication (MA, Certificate); international development (MA, Certificate); international economic policy (Certificate); international economic relations (Certificate); international media (MA); international peace and conflict resolution (MA, Certificate); international politics (Certificate); international relations (PhD); international service (MIS); peacebuilding (Certificate); social enterprise (MA); the Americas (Certificate); United States foreign policy (Certificate); JD/MA. Part-time and evening/ weekend programs available. Postbaccalaureate distance learning degree programs offered (no on-campus study). *Faculty:* 116 full-time (43 women), 49 part-time/adjunct (19 women). *Students:* 598 full-time (362 women), 382 part-time (233 women); includes 239 minority (85 Black or African American, non-Hispanic/Latino; 8 American Indian or Alaska Native, non-Hispanic/Latino; 54 Asian, non-Hispanic/Latino; 77 Hispanic/Latino; 1 Native Hawaiian or other Pacific Islander, non-Hispanic/Latino; 14 Two or more races, non-Hispanic/Latino), 125 international. Average age 27. In 2013, 443 master's, 7 doctorates, 14 other advanced degrees awarded. Terminal master's awarded for partial completion of doctoral program. *Degree requirements:* For master's, one foreign language, comprehensive exam, thesis or alternative; for doctorate, one foreign language, comprehensive exam, thesis/dissertation. *Entrance requirements:* For master's, GRE, transcripts, resume, 2 letters of recommendation, statement of purpose; for doctorate, GRE, transcripts, resume, 3 letters of recommendation, statement of purpose. Additional exam requirements/recommendations for international students: Required—TOEFL (minimum score 600 paper-based; 100 iBT). *Application deadline:* For fall admission, 1/15 for domestic students; for spring admission, 10/1 for domestic students. Electronic applications accepted. *Expenses: Tuition:* Full-time $25,920; part-time $1482 per credit hour. *Required fees:* $430. Tuition and fees vary according to course load and program. *Financial support:* Fellowships with partial tuition reimbursements, research assistantships with partial tuition reimbursements, career-related internships or fieldwork, Federal Work-Study, institutionally sponsored loans, and scholarships/grants available. Financial award application deadline: 1/15. *Unit head:* Dr. James Goldgeier, Dean, 202-885-1603, E-mail: jgoldgei@american.edu. *Application contact:* Jia Jiang, Associate Director, Graduate Education Enrollment, 202-885-1689, E-mail: jiang@american.edu.
Website: http://www.american.edu/sis/.

The American University in Cairo, School of Sciences and Engineering, Department of Mechanical Engineering, Cairo, Egypt. Offers mechanical engineering (MS); product development and systems management (M Eng). Tuition and fees vary according to course level, course load and program.

American University of Armenia, Graduate Programs, Yerevan, Armenia. Offers business administration (MBA); computer and information science (MS), including business management, design and manufacturing, energy (ME, MS), industrial engineering and systems management; economics (MS); industrial engineering and systems management (ME), including business, computer aided design/manufacturing, energy (ME, MS), information technology; law (LL M); political science and international affairs (MPSIA); public health (MPH); teaching English as a foreign language (MA). Part-time and evening/weekend programs available. *Faculty:* 30 full-time (10 women), 42 part-time/adjunct (13 women). *Students:* 398 full-time (272 women), 138 part-time (84 women). Average age 24. 351 applicants, 77% accepted, 247 enrolled. In 2013, 215 master's awarded. *Degree requirements:* For master's, thesis (for some programs), capstone/project. *Entrance requirements:* For master's, GRE, GMAT, or LSAT. Additional exam requirements/recommendations for international students: Recommended—TOEFL (minimum score 79 iBT), IELTS (minimum score 6.5). *Application deadline:* For fall admission, 3/31 for domestic and international students; for spring admission, 12/20 for domestic and international students. Applications are processed on a rolling basis. Application fee: $30 ($70 for international students). *Expenses: Tuition:* Full-time $2683; part-time $122 per credit. Full-time tuition and fees vary according to program. *Financial support:* In 2013–14, 199 students received support. Teaching assistantships with partial tuition reimbursements available, career-related internships or fieldwork, institutionally sponsored loans, scholarships/grants, unspecified assistantships, and tuition assistance, institutionally-sponsored work study available. Support available to part-time students. Financial award application deadline: 6/30. *Faculty research:* Microfinance, finance (rural/development, international, corporate), firm life cycle theory, TESOL, language proficiency testing, public policy, administrative law, economic development, cryptography, artificial intelligence, energy efficiency/renewable energy, computer-aided design/manufacturing, health financing, tuberculosis control, mother/child health, preventive ophthalmology, post-earthquake psychopathological investigations, tobacco control, environmental health risk assessments. *Total annual research expenditures:* $465,763. *Unit head:* Dr. Dennis Leavens, Provost, 374 10512526, E-mail: provost@aua.am. *Application contact:* Karine Satamyan, Admissions Coordinator, 374-10324040, E-mail: grad@aua.am.
Website: http://www.aua.am.

Argosy University, Atlanta, College of Business, Atlanta, GA 30328. Offers accounting (DBA); corporate compliance (MBA); customized professional concentration (MBA, DBA); finance (MBA); healthcare administration (MBA); information systems (DBA); information systems management (MBA); international business (MBA, DBA); management (MBA, MSM, DBA); marketing (MBA, DBA).

Argosy University, Chicago, College of Business, Chicago, IL 60601. Offers accounting (DBA); customized professional concentration (MBA, DBA); finance (MBA); fraud examination (MBA); global business sustainability (DBA); healthcare

administration (MBA); information systems (DBA); information systems management (MBA); international business (MBA, DBA); management (MBA, MSM, DBA); marketing (MBA, DBA); organizational leadership (Ed D); public administration (MBA); sustainable management (MBA). Postbaccalaureate distance learning degree programs offered (minimal on-campus study).

Argosy University, Dallas, College of Business, Farmers Branch, TX 75244. Offers accounting (DBA, AGC); corporate compliance (MBA, Graduate Certificate); customized professional concentration (MBA); finance (MBA, Graduate Certificate); fraud examination (MBA, Graduate Certificate); global business sustainability (DBA, AGC); healthcare administration (Graduate Certificate); healthcare management (MBA); information systems (MBA, DBA, AGC); information systems management (Graduate Certificate); international business (MBA, DBA, AGC, Graduate Certificate); management (MBA, DBA, AGC, Graduate Certificate); marketing (MBA, DBA, AGC, Graduate Certificate); public administration (MBA, Graduate Certificate); sustainable management (MBA, Graduate Certificate).

Argosy University, Denver, College of Business, Denver, CO 80231. Offers accounting (DBA); corporate compliance (MBA); customized professional concentration (MBA, DBA); finance (MBA); fraud examination (MBA); global business sustainability (DBA); healthcare administration (MBA); information systems (DBA); information systems management (MBA); international business (MBA, DBA); management (MBA, MSM, DBA); marketing (MBA, DBA); organizational leadership (Ed D); public administration (MBA); sustainable management (MBA).

Argosy University, Hawai`i, College of Business, Honolulu, HI 96813. Offers accounting (DBA); corporate compliance (MBA); customized professional concentration (MBA, DBA); finance (MBA, Certificate); fraud examination (MBA); global business sustainability (DBA); healthcare administration (MBA, Certificate); information systems (DBA); information systems management (MBA, Certificate); international business (MBA, DBA, Certificate); management (MBA, MSM, DBA); marketing (MBA, DBA, Certificate); organizational leadership (Ed D); public administration (MBA); sustainable management (MBA).

Argosy University, Inland Empire, College of Business, Ontario, CA 91761. Offers accounting (DBA); corporate compliance (MBA); customized professional concentration (MBA, DBA); finance (MBA); fraud examination (MBA); global business sustainability (DBA); healthcare administration (MBA); information systems (DBA); information systems management (MBA); international business (MBA, DBA); management (MBA, MSM, DBA); marketing (MBA, DBA); organizational leadership (Ed D); public administration (MBA); sustainable management (MBA).

Argosy University, Los Angeles, College of Business, Santa Monica, CA 90045. Offers accounting (DBA); corporate compliance (MBA); customized professional concentration (MBA, DBA); finance (MBA); fraud examination (MBA); global business sustainability (DBA); healthcare administration (MBA); information systems (DBA); information systems management (MBA); international business (MBA, DBA); management (MBA, MSM, DBA); marketing (MBA, DBA); organizational leadership (Ed D); public administration (MBA); sustainable management (MBA).

Argosy University, Nashville, College of Business, Nashville, TN 37214. Offers accounting (DBA); customized professional concentration (MBA, DBA); finance (MBA); healthcare administration (MBA); information systems (MBA, DBA); international business (MBA, DBA); management (MBA, MSM, DBA); marketing (MBA, DBA).

Argosy University, Orange County, College of Business, Orange, CA 92868. Offers accounting (DBA, Adv C); corporate compliance (MBA); customized professional concentration (MBA, DBA); finance (MBA, Certificate); fraud examination (MBA); global business sustainability (DBA); healthcare administration (MBA, Certificate); information systems (DBA, Adv C, Certificate); information systems management (MBA); international business (MBA, DBA, Adv C, Certificate); management (MBA, MSM, DBA, Adv C); marketing (MBA, DBA, Adv C, Certificate); organizational leadership (Ed D); public administration (MBA, Certificate); sustainable management (MBA).

Argosy University, Phoenix, College of Business, Phoenix, AZ 85021. Offers accounting (DBA); corporate compliance (MBA); customized professional concentration (MBA, DBA); finance (MBA); fraud examination (MBA); global business sustainability (DBA); healthcare administration (MBA); information systems (DBA); information systems management (MBA); international business (MBA, DBA); management (MBA, DBA); marketing (MBA, DBA); public administration (MBA); sustainable management (MBA).

Argosy University, Salt Lake City, College of Business, Draper, UT 84020. Offers accounting (DBA); corporate compliance (MBA); customized professional concentration (MBA, DBA); finance (MBA); fraud examination (MBA); global business sustainability (DBA); healthcare administration (MBA); information systems (DBA); information systems management (MBA); international business (MBA, DBA); management (MBA, DBA); marketing (MBA, DBA); public administration (MBA); sustainable management (MBA).

Argosy University, San Diego, College of Business, San Diego, CA 92108. Offers accounting (DBA); corporate compliance (MBA); customized professional concentration (MBA, DBA); finance (MBA); fraud examination (MBA); global business sustainability (DBA); information systems (DBA); information systems management (MBA); international business (MBA, DBA); management (MBA, MSM, DBA); marketing (MBA, DBA); organizational leadership (Ed D); public administration (MBA).

Argosy University, San Francisco Bay Area, College of Business, Alameda, CA 94501. Offers accounting (DBA); corporate compliance (MBA); customized professional concentration (MBA, DBA); finance (MBA); fraud examination (MBA); global business sustainability (DBA); healthcare administration (MBA); information systems (DBA); information systems management (MBA); international business (MBA, DBA); management (MBA, MSM, DBA); marketing (MBA, DBA); organizational leadership (Ed D); public administration (MBA); sustainable management (MBA).

Argosy University, Sarasota, College of Business, Sarasota, FL 34235. Offers accounting (DBA, Adv C); corporate compliance (MBA, DBA, Certificate); customized professional concentration (MBA, DBA); finance (MBA, Certificate); fraud examination (MBA, Certificate); global business sustainability (DBA, Adv C); healthcare administration (MBA, Certificate); information systems (DBA, Adv C, Certificate); information systems management (MBA); international business (MBA, DBA, Adv C, Certificate); management (MBA, MSM, DBA, Adv C, Certificate); marketing (MBA, DBA, Adv C, Certificate); organizational leadership (Ed D); public administration (MBA, Certificate); sustainable management (MBA, Certificate).

Argosy University, Schaumburg, College of Business, Schaumburg, IL 60173-5403. Offers accounting (DBA, Adv C); customized professional concentration (MBA, DBA); finance (MBA, Certificate); fraud examination (MBA); global business sustainability (DBA); healthcare administration (MBA, Certificate); information systems (DBA, Adv C, Certificate); information systems management (MBA); international business (MBA, DBA, Adv C, Certificate); management (MBA, MSM, DBA, Adv C, Certificate); marketing (MBA, DBA, Adv C, Certificate); organizational leadership (Ed D); public administration (MBA); sustainable management (MBA).

Argosy University, Seattle, College of Business, Seattle, WA 98121. Offers accounting (DBA); corporate compliance (MBA); customized professional concentration (MBA, DBA); finance (MBA); fraud examination (MBA); global business sustainability (DBA); healthcare administration (MBA); information systems (DBA); information systems management (MBA); international business (MBA, DBA); management (MBA, MSM, DBA); marketing (MBA, DBA); organizational leadership (Ed D); public administration (MBA); sustainable management (MBA).

Argosy University, Tampa, College of Business, Tampa, FL 33607. Offers accounting (DBA); corporate compliance (MBA); customized professional concentration (MBA, DBA); finance (MBA); fraud examination (MBA); global business sustainability (DBA); healthcare administration (MBA); information systems (DBA); information systems management (MBA); international business (MBA, DBA); management (MBA, MSM, DBA); marketing (MBA, DBA); organizational leadership (Ed D); public administration (MBA); sustainable management (MBA).

Argosy University, Twin Cities, College of Business, Eagan, MN 55121. Offers accounting (DBA); customized professional concentration (MBA, DBA); finance (MBA); fraud examination (MBA); global business sustainability (DBA); healthcare administration (MBA); information systems (DBA); information systems management (MBA); international business (MBA, DBA); management (MBA, MSM, DBA); marketing (MBA, DBA); organizational leadership (Ed D); public administration (MBA); sustainable management (MBA).

Argosy University, Washington DC, College of Business, Arlington, VA 22209. Offers accounting (DBA); customized professional concentration (MBA, DBA); finance (MBA); fraud examination (MBA); global business sustainability (DBA); healthcare administration (MBA); information systems (DBA); information systems management (MBA); international business (MBA, DBA, Certificate); management (MBA, MSM, DBA); marketing (MBA, DBA, Certificate); organizational leadership (Ed D); public administration (MBA); sustainable management (MBA).

Arizona State University at the Tempe campus, College of Technology and Innovation, Department of Technology Management, Mesa, AZ 85212. Offers technology (aviation management and human factors) (MS); technology (environmental technology management) (MS); technology (global technology and development) (MS); technology (graphic information technology) (MS); technology (management of technology) (MS). Part-time and evening/weekend programs available. Postbaccalaureate distance learning degree programs offered (minimal on-campus study). *Degree requirements:* For master's, thesis or applied project and oral defense; interactive Program of Study (iPOS) submitted before completing 50 percent of required credit hours. *Entrance requirements:* For master's, GRE, minimum GPA of 3.0 or equivalent in last 2 years of work leading to bachelor's degree. Additional exam requirements/recommendations for international students: Required—TOEFL (minimum score 83 iBT), TOEFL, IELTS, or PTE. Electronic applications accepted. *Faculty research:* Digital imaging, digital publishing, Internet development/e-commerce, information aviation human factors, pilot selection, databases, multimedia, commercial digital photography, digital workflow, computer graphics modeling and animation, information design, sociotechnology, visual and technical literacy, environmental management, quality management, project management, industrial ethics, hazardous materials, environmental chemistry.

Arizona State University at the Tempe campus, W. P. Carey School of Business, Department of Information Systems, Tempe, AZ 85287-4606. Offers business administration (computer information systems) (PhD); information management (MS); MBA/MS. Evening/weekend programs available. Postbaccalaureate distance learning degree programs offered (no on-campus study). Terminal master's awarded for partial completion of doctoral program. *Degree requirements:* For master's, thesis or alternative, applied project, interactive Program of Study (iPOS) submitted before completing 50 percent of required credit hours; for doctorate, comprehensive exam, thesis/dissertation, interactive Program of Study (iPOS) submitted before completing 50 percent of required credit hours. *Entrance requirements:* For master's, 2 years of full-time related work experience, bachelor's degree in related field from accredited university, resume, essay, 2 letters of recommendation, official transcripts; for doctorate, GMAT, MBA, 2 years of full-time related work experience (recommended), bachelor's degree in related field from accredited university, 3 letters of recommendation, resume, personal statement. Additional exam requirements/recommendations for international students: Required—TOEFL (minimum score 550 paper-based; 80 iBT), IELTS (minimum score 6.5). Electronic applications accepted. *Expenses:* Contact institution. *Faculty research:* Strategy and technology, technology investments and firm valuation, Internet e-commerce, IT enablement for emergency preparedness and response, information supply chain, collaborative computing and security/privacy issues for e-health, enterprise information systems and their application to management control systems.

Arizona State University at the Tempe campus, W. P. Carey School of Business, Program in Business Administration, Tempe, AZ 85287-4906. Offers accountancy (PhD); agribusiness (PhD); business administration (MBA); finance (PhD); financial management and markets (MBA); information management (MBA); information systems (PhD); management (PhD); marketing (PhD); strategic marketing and services leadership (MBA); supply chain financial management (MBA); supply chain management (MBA, PhD); JD/MBA; MBA/M Acc; MBA/M Arch. *Accreditation:* AACSB. Part-time and evening/weekend programs available. Postbaccalaureate distance learning degree programs offered (minimal on-campus study). Terminal master's awarded for partial completion of doctoral program. *Degree requirements:* For master's, thesis or alternative, internship, interactive Program of Study (iPOS) submitted before completing 50 percent of required credit hours; for doctorate, comprehensive exam, thesis/dissertation, interactive Program of Study (iPOS) submitted before completing 50 percent of required credit hours. *Entrance requirements:* For master's, GMAT, minimum GPA of 3.0 in last 2 years of work leading to bachelor's degree, 2 letters of recommendation, professional resume, official transcripts, 3 essays; for doctorate, GMAT or GRE, minimum GPA of 3.0 in last 2 years of work leading to bachelor's degree, 3 letters of recommendation, resume, personal statement/essay. Additional exam requirements/recommendations for international students: Required—TOEFL (minimum score 550 paper-based; 80 iBT), IELTS (minimum score 6.5). Electronic applications accepted. *Expenses:* Contact institution.

Arkansas State University, Graduate School, College of Business, Department of Computer and Information Technology, Jonesboro, AR 72467. Offers business administration education (SCCT); business education (SCCT); business technology education (MSE, SCCT). Part-time programs available. *Faculty:* 9 full-time (1 woman). *Students:* 6 part-time (4 women); includes 4 minority (all Black or African American, non-Hispanic/Latino). Average age 36. 6 applicants, 83% accepted, 4 enrolled. In 2013, 8 master's awarded. *Degree requirements:* For master's, comprehensive exam, thesis or alternative. *Entrance requirements:* For master's, GRE General Test or MAT, appropriate bachelor's degree, official transcript, immunization records. Additional exam requirements/recommendations for international students: Required—TOEFL (minimum score 550 paper-based; 79 iBT), IELTS (minimum score 6), PTE (minimum score 56). *Application deadline:* For fall admission, 7/1 for domestic and international students; for spring admission, 11/15 for domestic students, 11/14 for international students.

Management Information Systems

Applications are processed on a rolling basis. Application fee: $30 ($40 for international students). Electronic applications accepted. *Expenses:* Contact institution. *Financial support:* Career-related internships or fieldwork, scholarships/grants, and unspecified assistantships available. Financial award application deadline: 7/1; financial award applicants required to submit FAFSA. *Unit head:* Dr. John Robertson, Chair, 870-972-3416, Fax: 870-972-3868, E-mail: jfrobert@astate.edu. *Application contact:* Vickey Ring, Graduate Admissions Coordinator, 870-972-3029, Fax: 870-972-3857, E-mail: vickeyring@astate.edu.
Website: http://www.astate.edu/college/business/faculty-staff/computer-information-technology/.

Aspen University, Programs in Information Management, Denver, CO 80246-1930. Offers information management (MS); information systems (Certificate). Part-time and evening/weekend programs available. Postbaccalaureate distance learning degree programs offered (no on-campus study). Electronic applications accepted.

Auburn University, Graduate School, College of Business, Department of Management, Auburn University, AL 36849. Offers human resource management (PhD); management (MS, PhD); management information systems (MS, PhD). *Accreditation:* AACSB. Part-time programs available. *Faculty:* 42 full-time (9 women), 10 part-time/adjunct (2 women). *Students:* 94 full-time (43 women), 329 part-time (61 women); includes 77 minority (40 Black or African American, non-Hispanic/Latino; 2 American Indian or Alaska Native, non-Hispanic/Latino; 22 Asian, non-Hispanic/Latino; 13 Hispanic/Latino), 46 international. Average age 34. 408 applicants, 55% accepted, 126 enrolled. In 2013, 173 master's, 6 doctorates awarded. *Degree requirements:* For master's, thesis (for some programs); for doctorate, thesis/dissertation. *Entrance requirements:* For master's, GMAT, GRE General Test (MS); for doctorate, GMAT, GRE General Test. Additional exam requirements/recommendations for international students: Required—TOEFL. *Application deadline:* For fall admission, 7/7 for domestic students; for spring admission, 11/24 for domestic students. Applications are processed on a rolling basis. Application fee: $50 ($60 for international students). Electronic applications accepted. *Expenses:* Tuition, state resident: full-time $8262; part-time $459 per credit hour. Tuition, nonresident: full-time $24,786; part-time $1377 per credit hour. Tuition and fees vary according to degree level and program. *Financial support:* Teaching assistantships and Federal Work-Study available. Support available to part-time students. Financial award application deadline: 3/15; financial award applicants required to submit FAFSA. *Unit head:* Dr. Christopher Shook, Head, 334-844-9565. *Application contact:* Dr. George Flowers, Dean of the Graduate School, 334-844-2125.
Website: http://business.auburn.edu/academics/departments/department-of-management/.

Auburn University at Montgomery, School of Business, Department of Information Systems and Decision Science, Montgomery, AL 36124-4023. Offers MSISM. *Faculty:* 2 full-time (0 women). *Students:* 1 full-time (0 women), 6 part-time (1 woman); includes 2 minority (1 Black or African American, non-Hispanic/Latino; 1 Asian, non-Hispanic/Latino). Average age 31. In 2013, 2 master's awarded. *Expenses:* Tuition, state resident: full-time $5994; part-time $333 per credit hour. Tuition, nonresident: full-time $17,982; part-time $999 per credit hour. *Unit head:* Dr. Rhea Ingram, Dean, 334-244-3476, Fax: 334-244-3792, E-mail: wingram4@aum.edu. *Application contact:* Dr. Evan Moore, Associate Dean of Graduate Programs, 334-244-3364, Fax: 334-277-3792, E-mail: emoore1@aum.edu.

Avila University, School of Business, Kansas City, MO 64145-1698. Offers accounting (MBA); finance (MBA); health care administration (MBA); international business (MBA); management (MBA); management information systems (MBA); marketing (MBA). Part-time and evening/weekend programs available. *Faculty:* 9 full-time (4 women), 12 part-time/adjunct (3 women). *Students:* 66 full-time (32 women), 46 part-time (27 women); includes 34 minority (22 Black or African American, non-Hispanic/Latino; 1 American Indian or Alaska Native, non-Hispanic/Latino; 4 Asian, non-Hispanic/Latino; 7 Hispanic/Latino), 27 international. Average age 32. 30 applicants, 80% accepted, 24 enrolled. In 2013, 61 master's awarded. *Degree requirements:* For master's, comprehensive exam, capstone course. *Entrance requirements:* For master's, GMAT (minimum score 420), minimum GPA of 3.0, interview. Additional exam requirements/recommendations for international students: Required—TOEFL (minimum score 550 paper-based). *Application deadline:* For fall admission, 7/30 priority date for domestic and international students; for winter admission, 11/30 priority date for domestic and international students; for spring admission, 2/28 priority date for domestic and international students; for summer admission, 6/1 priority date for domestic and international students. Applications are processed on a rolling basis. Application fee: $0. Electronic applications accepted. *Expenses:* Contact institution. *Financial support:* In 2013–14, 11 students received support. Career-related internships or fieldwork and scholarships/grants available. Support available to part-time students. Financial award applicants required to submit FAFSA. *Faculty research:* Leadership characteristics, financial hedging, group dynamics. *Unit head:* Dr. Richard Woodall, Dean, 816-501-3720, Fax: 816-501-2463, E-mail: richard.woodall@avila.edu. *Application contact:* Sarah Belanus, MBA Admissions Director, 816-501-3601, Fax: 816-501-2463, E-mail: sarah.belanus@avila.edu.
Website: http://www.avila.edu/mba.

Baker College Center for Graduate Studies - Online, Graduate Programs, Flint, MI 48507-9843. Offers accounting (MBA); business administration (DBA); finance (MBA); general business (MBA); health care management (MBA); human resources management (MBA); information management (MBA); leadership studies (MBA); management information systems (MSIS); marketing (MBA). Part-time and evening/weekend programs available. Postbaccalaureate distance learning degree programs offered. *Degree requirements:* For master's, portfolio. *Entrance requirements:* For master's, 3 years of work experience, minimum undergraduate GPA of 2.5, writing sample, 3 letters of recommendation; for doctorate, MBA or acceptable related master's degree from accredited association, 5 years work experience, minimum graduate GPA of 3.25, writing sample, 3 professional references. Additional exam requirements/recommendations for international students: Required—TOEFL (minimum score 550 paper-based). Electronic applications accepted.

Barry University, Andreas School of Business, Graduate Certificate Programs, Miami Shores, FL 33161-6695. Offers finance (Certificate); health services administration (Certificate); international business (Certificate); management (Certificate); management information systems (Certificate); marketing (Certificate).

Baruch College of the City University of New York, Zicklin School of Business, Department of Statistics and Computer Information Systems, Program in Information Systems, New York, NY 10010-5585. Offers MBA, MS, PhD. Part-time and evening/weekend programs available. Terminal master's awarded for partial completion of doctoral program. *Degree requirements:* For master's, thesis or alternative; for doctorate, comprehensive exam, thesis/dissertation. *Entrance requirements:* For master's, GMAT, 2 letters of recommendation, resume, 2 years of work experience; for doctorate, GMAT. Additional exam requirements/recommendations for international students: Required—TOEFL (minimum score 590 paper-based), TWE (minimum score 5).

Baylor University, Graduate School, Hankamer School of Business, Department of Information Systems, Waco, TX 76798. Offers information systems (MSIS, PhD); information systems management (MBA); MBA/MSIS. *Faculty:* 12 full-time (4 women). *Students:* 20 full-time (6 women), 10 part-time (2 women); includes 2 minority (1 Black or African American, non-Hispanic/Latino; 1 Asian, non-Hispanic/Latino), 15 international. In 2013, 15 master's, 1 doctorate awarded. *Entrance requirements:* For master's, GMAT; for doctorate, GMAT, GRE. Additional exam requirements/recommendations for international students: Required—TOEFL. *Application deadline:* For fall admission, 8/1 for domestic students; for spring admission, 12/1 for domestic students. Applications are processed on a rolling basis. Application fee: $25. *Expenses: Tuition:* Full-time $25,866; part-time $1437 per credit hour. *Required fees:* $2736; $152 per credit hour. Tuition and fees vary according to course load and program. *Financial support:* Research assistantships, career-related internships or fieldwork, and Federal Work-Study available. *Faculty research:* Computer personnel, group systems, information technology standards and infrastructure, international information systems, technology and the learning environment. *Unit head:* Dr. Gary Carini, Associate Dean, 254-710-4091, Fax: 254-710-1091, E-mail: gary_carini@baylor.edu. *Application contact:* Laurie Wilson, Director, Graduate Business Programs, 254-710-4163, Fax: 254-710-1066, E-mail: laurie_wilson@baylor.edu.
Website: http://hsb.baylor.edu/isy/.

Bay Path College, Program in Communications and Information Management, Longmeadow, MA 01106-2292. Offers MS. Part-time and evening/weekend programs available. Postbaccalaureate distance learning degree programs offered (no on-campus study). *Students:* 16 full-time (12 women), 33 part-time (31 women); includes 12 minority (9 Black or African American, non-Hispanic/Latino; 3 Hispanic/Latino). Average age 35. 44 applicants, 77% accepted, 28 enrolled. In 2013, 23 master's awarded. *Degree requirements:* For master's, eight core courses and four electives (each course is eight weeks long). *Application deadline:* Applications are processed on a rolling basis. Application fee: $45. Electronic applications accepted. Application fee is waived when completed online. *Financial support:* In 2013–14, 7 students received support. Scholarships/grants available. Financial award applicants required to submit FAFSA. *Unit head:* Richard Briotta, Program Director, 413-565-1332. *Application contact:* Lisa Adams, Director of Graduate Admissions, 413-565-1317, Fax: 413-565-1250, E-mail: ladams@baypath.edu.
Website: http://graduate.baypath.edu/Graduate-Programs/Programs-On-Campus/MS-Programs/Communications-And-Information-Management.

Bellarmine University, School of Continuing and Professional Studies, Louisville, KY 40205-0671. Offers MAIT. Part-time and evening/weekend programs available. *Faculty:* 1 part-time/adjunct (0 women). *Students:* 3 part-time (0 women). Average age 41. In 2013, 10 master's awarded. *Entrance requirements:* For master's, GRE or GMAT, minimum GPA of 2.75, two letters of recommendation. Additional exam requirements/recommendations for international students: Required—TOEFL (minimum score 550 paper-based; 80 iBT). Application fee: $25. *Expenses:* Contact institution. *Unit head:* Dr. Sean Ryan, Vice President of Enrollment Management/Dean of the School of Professional and Continuing Studies, 502-272-8376, E-mail: sryan@bellarmine.edu. *Application contact:* Dr. Sara Pettingill, Dean of Graduate Admission, 502-272-8401, E-mail: spettingill@bellarmine.edu.
Website: http://www.bellarmine.edu/ce/MAIT.asp.

Bellevue University, Graduate School, College of Information Technology, Bellevue, NE 68005-3098. Offers computer information systems (MS); cybersecurity (MS); management of information systems (MS); project management (MPM).

Benedictine University, Graduate Programs, Program in Business Administration, Lisle, IL 60532-0900. Offers accounting (MBA); entrepreneurship and managing innovation (MBA); financial management (MBA); health administration (MBA); human resource management (MBA); information systems security (MBA); international business (MBA); management consulting (MBA); management information systems (MBA); marketing management (MBA); operations management and logistics (MBA); organizational leadership (MBA). Part-time and evening/weekend programs available. Postbaccalaureate distance learning degree programs offered (minimal on-campus study). *Faculty:* 4 full-time (2 women), 24 part-time/adjunct (3 women). *Students:* 144 full-time (83 women), 599 part-time (328 women); includes 189 minority (115 Black or African American, non-Hispanic/Latino; 5 American Indian or Alaska Native, non-Hispanic/Latino; 43 Asian, non-Hispanic/Latino; 24 Hispanic/Latino; 2 Native Hawaiian or other Pacific Islander, non-Hispanic/Latino), 14 international. Average age 34. 211 applicants, 89% accepted, 155 enrolled. In 2013, 376 master's awarded. *Entrance requirements:* For master's, GMAT. Additional exam requirements/recommendations for international students: Required—TOEFL (minimum score 550 paper-based). *Application deadline:* For fall admission, 9/1 for domestic students; for winter admission, 12/1 for domestic students; for spring admission, 2/15 for domestic students. Applications are processed on a rolling basis. Application fee: $40. Electronic applications accepted. *Expenses: Tuition:* Part-time $590 per credit hour. *Financial support:* Career-related internships or fieldwork and health care benefits available. Support available to part-time students. *Faculty research:* Strategic leadership in professional organizations, sociology of professions, organizational change, social identity theory, applications to change management. *Unit head:* Dr. Sharon Borowicz, Director, 630-829-6219, E-mail: sborowicz@ben.edu. *Application contact:* Kari Gibbons, Director, Admissions, 630-829-6200, Fax: 630-829-6584, E-mail: kgibbons@ben.edu.

Benedictine University, Graduate Programs, Program in Management Information Systems, Lisle, IL 60532-0900. Offers MS, MBA/MS, MPH/MS. Part-time programs available. *Faculty:* 2 full-time (1 woman), 6 part-time/adjunct (1 woman). *Students:* 84 full-time (20 women), 17 part-time (10 women); includes 9 minority (2 Black or African American, non-Hispanic/Latino; 6 Asian, non-Hispanic/Latino; 1 Hispanic/Latino), 6 international. Average age 36. 102 applicants, 94% accepted, 84 enrolled. In 2013, 90 master's awarded. *Entrance requirements:* For master's, GMAT. Additional exam requirements/recommendations for international students: Required—TOEFL (minimum score 550 paper-based). *Application deadline:* For fall admission, 9/1 for domestic students; for winter admission, 12/1 for domestic students; for spring admission, 2/15 for domestic students. Applications are processed on a rolling basis. Application fee: $40. Electronic applications accepted. *Expenses: Tuition:* Part-time $590 per credit hour. *Financial support:* Career-related internships or fieldwork and health care benefits available. Support available to part-time students. *Faculty research:* Technology management, knowledge management, electronic commerce, information security. *Unit head:* Dr. Barbara Ozog, Director, 630-829-6218, E-mail: bozog@ben.edu. *Application contact:* Kari Gibbons, Associate Vice President, Enrollment Center, 630-829-6200, Fax: 630-829-6584, E-mail: kgibbons@ben.edu.

Boston University, Metropolitan College, Department of Computer Science, Boston, MA 02215. Offers advanced information technology (Certificate); computer information systems (MS), including computer networks, database management and business intelligence, health informatics, IT project management, security, Web application development; computer networks (Certificate); computer science (MS), including computer networks, security; database management and business intelligence (Certificate); digital forensics (Certificate); health informatics (Certificate); information security (Certificate); information technology (Certificate); information technology project

management (Certificate); medical information security and privacy (Certificate); software engineering (Certificate); software engineering in health care systems (Certificate); telecommunications (MS), including security; Web application development (Certificate). Part-time and evening/weekend programs available. Postbaccalaureate distance learning degree programs offered (no on-campus study). *Faculty:* 13 full-time (3 women), 35 part-time/adjunct (2 women). *Students:* 48 full-time (14 women), 720 part-time (174 women); includes 215 minority (51 Black or African American, non-Hispanic/Latino; 111 Asian, non-Hispanic/Latino; 44 Hispanic/Latino; 9 Two or more races, non-Hispanic/Latino), 113 international. Average age 35. 360 applicants, 71% accepted, 221 enrolled. In 2013, 246 master's, 25 other advanced degrees awarded. *Degree requirements:* For master's, thesis optional. *Entrance requirements:* For master's and Certificate, official transcripts from regionally-accredited bachelor's degree program, 3 letters of recommendation, professional resume, personal statement. Additional exam requirements/recommendations for international students: Required—TOEFL (minimum score 84 iBT), IELTS. *Application deadline:* For fall admission, 6/1 priority date for international students; for spring admission, 10/1 priority date for international students. Applications are processed on a rolling basis. Application fee: $80. Electronic applications accepted. *Expenses: Tuition:* Full-time $43,970; part-time $1374 per credit hour. *Required fees:* $60 per semester. Tuition and fees vary according to class time, course level and program. *Financial support:* In 2013–14, 12 research assistantships (averaging $5,000 per year) were awarded; unspecified assistantships also available. Support available to part-time students. Financial award applicants required to submit FAFSA. *Faculty research:* Medical informatics, Web technologies, telecom and networks, security and forensics, software engineering, programming languages, multimedia and artificial intelligence (AI), information systems and IT project management. *Unit head:* Dr. Anatoly Temkin, Chairman, 617-353-2566, Fax: 617-353-2367, E-mail: csinfo@bu.edu. *Application contact:* Kim Richards, Program Coordinator, 617-353-2566, Fax: 617-353-2367, E-mail: kimrich@bu.edu.
Website: http://www.bu.edu/csmet/.

Bowie State University, Graduate Programs, Program in Management Information Systems, Bowie, MD 20715-9465. Offers information systems analyst (Certificate); management information systems (MS). Part-time and evening/weekend programs available. *Degree requirements:* For master's, comprehensive exam, thesis optional, research paper. *Entrance requirements:* For master's, minimum GPA of 2.5. Electronic applications accepted. *Expenses:* Tuition, state resident: full-time $8665. Tuition, nonresident: full-time $16,007. *Required fees:* $1927.

Brandeis University, Rabb School of Continuing Studies, Division of Graduate Professional Studies, Master of Science in Information Technology Management Program, Waltham, MA 02454-9110. Offers MS. Part-time programs available. Postbaccalaureate distance learning degree programs offered (no on-campus study). *Faculty:* 2 full-time (1 woman), 33 part-time/adjunct (10 women). *Students:* 40 part-time (7 women); includes 9 minority (2 Black or African American, non-Hispanic/Latino; 5 Asian, non-Hispanic/Latino; 2 Hispanic/Latino). Average age 35. 6 applicants, 67% accepted, 4 enrolled. In 2013, 22 master's awarded. *Entrance requirements:* For master's, four-year bachelor's degree from regionally-accredited U.S. institution or equivalent; official transcript(s) from every college or university attended; resume or curriculum vitae; statement of goals; letter of recommendation. Additional exam requirements/recommendations for international students: Required—TOEFL (minimum scores: 600 paper-based, 100 iBT), IELTS (7), or PTE. *Application deadline:* For fall admission, 7/15 priority date for domestic and international students; for winter admission, 11/15 for domestic students; for spring admission, 11/15 priority date for domestic and international students; for summer admission, 3/15 priority date for domestic and international students. Applications are processed on a rolling basis. Application fee: $50. Electronic applications accepted. *Unit head:* Dr. Cynthia Phillips, Program Chair, 781-736-8787, Fax: 781-736-3420, E-mail: cynthiap@brandeis.edu. *Application contact:* Frances Stearns, Associate Director of Admissions and Student Services, 781-736-8785, Fax: 781-736-3420, E-mail: fstearns@brandeis.edu.
Website: http://www.brandeis.edu/gps.

Brigham Young University, Graduate Studies, Marriott School of Management, Master of Information Systems Program, Provo, UT 84602. Offers MISM. *Entrance requirements:* For master's, GMAT, minimum GPA of 3.0 in last 60 hours of course work. Additional exam requirements/recommendations for international students: Required—TOEFL (minimum score 580 paper-based). Electronic applications accepted. *Expenses: Tuition:* Full-time $6130; part-time $340 per credit hour. Tuition and fees vary according to program and student's religious affiliation. *Faculty research:* Research standards - faculty career development in information systems, electronic commerce technology and standards, collaborative tools and methods, technology for fraud detection and prevention, ethical issues in the information systems field.

Broadview University–West Jordan, Graduate Programs, West Jordan, UT 84088. Offers business administration (MBA); health care management (MSM); information technology (MSM); managerial leadership (MSM).

California Intercontinental University, School of Information Technology, Diamond Bar, CA 91765. Offers information systems and enterprise resource management (DBA); information systems and knowledge management (MBA); project and quality management (MBA).

California Lutheran University, Graduate Studies, School of Management, Thousand Oaks, CA 91360-2787. Offers business (IMBA); computer science (MS); econometrics (MBA); economics (MS); entrepreneurship (MBA, Certificate); finance (MBA, Certificate); financial planning (MBA, Certificate); information systems and technology (MS); information technology management (MBA, Certificate); international business (MBA, Certificate); management and organization behavior (MBA); management and organizational behavior (Certificate); marketing (MBA, Certificate); microeconomics (MBA); nonprofit and social enterprise (MBA). Part-time and evening/weekend programs available. Postbaccalaureate distance learning degree programs offered (no on-campus study). *Faculty:* 26 full-time (9 women), 50 part-time/adjunct (11 women). *Students:* 426 full-time (175 women), 220 part-time (91 women); includes 114 minority (14 Black or African American, non-Hispanic/Latino; 30 Asian, non-Hispanic/Latino; 57 Hispanic/Latino; 13 Two or more races, non-Hispanic/Latino), 321 international. Average age 31. 495 applicants, 76% accepted, 119 enrolled. In 2013, 297 master's awarded. *Entrance requirements:* For master's, GMAT, interview, minimum GPA of 3.0. *Application deadline:* Applications are processed on a rolling basis. Application fee: $50. *Expenses:* Contact institution. *Unit head:* Dr. Gerhard Apfelthaler, Dean, 805-493-3360. *Application contact:* 805-493-3325, Fax: 805-493-3861, E-mail: clugrad@callutheran.edu.
Website: http://www.callutheran.edu/business/.

California State Polytechnic University, Pomona, Academic Affairs, College of Business Administration, Master of Science in Business Administration Program, Pomona, CA 91768-2557. Offers information systems auditing (MS). *Students:* 3 full-time (2 women), 8 part-time (4 women); includes 7 minority (6 Asian, non-Hispanic/Latino; 1 Hispanic/Latino), 1 international. Average age 28. 28 applicants, 32% accepted, 5 enrolled. In 2013, 5 master's awarded. *Application deadline:* Applications are processed on a rolling basis. Application fee: $55. Electronic applications accepted. *Expenses:* Tuition, state resident: full-time $6738. Tuition, nonresident: full-time

$12,690. *Required fees:* $878; $248 per credit hour. *Unit head:* Dr. Richard S. Lapidus, Dean, 909-869-2400, Fax: 909-869-6799, E-mail: rslapidus@csupomona.edu. *Application contact:* Tricia Alicante, Graduate Coordinator, 909-869-4894, E-mail: taalicante@csupomona.edu.
Website: http://cba.csupomona.edu/graduateprograms/.

California State University, East Bay, Office of Academic Programs and Graduate Studies, College of Business and Economics, MBA Program, Hayward, CA 94542-3000. Offers entrepreneurship (MBA); finance (MBA); global innovators (MBA); human resources and organizational behavior (MBA); information technology management (MBA); marketing management (MBA); operations and supply chain management (MBA); strategy and international business (MBA). Part-time and evening/weekend programs available. *Degree requirements:* For master's, comprehensive exam or thesis. *Entrance requirements:* For master's, GMAT (minimum 20th percentile verbal and quantitative section), bachelor's degree, minimum GPA of 2.75. Additional exam requirements/recommendations for international students: Required—TOEFL (minimum score 550 paper-based; 79 iBT). Electronic applications accepted. *Expenses:* Contact institution.

California State University, East Bay, Office of Academic Programs and Graduate Studies, College of Business and Economics, Program in Information Technology Management, Hayward, CA 94542-3000. Offers MBA. Part-time and evening/weekend programs available. *Degree requirements:* For master's, comprehensive exam or thesis. *Entrance requirements:* For master's, GMAT, minimum GPA of 2.75. Additional exam requirements/recommendations for international students: Required—TOEFL (minimum score 550 paper-based). Electronic applications accepted.

California State University, Fullerton, Graduate Studies, College of Business and Economics, Department of Information Systems and Decision Sciences, Fullerton, CA 92834-9480. Offers decision science (MBA); information systems (MBA, MS); information systems and decision sciences (MS); information systems and e-commerce (MS); information technology (MS). Part-time programs available. *Students:* 28 full-time (12 women), 74 part-time (17 women); includes 50 minority (4 Black or African American, non-Hispanic/Latino; 27 Asian, non-Hispanic/Latino; 15 Hispanic/Latino; 4 Two or more races, non-Hispanic/Latino), 22 international. Average age 31. 146 applicants, 55% accepted, 42 enrolled. In 2013, 26 master's awarded. *Degree requirements:* For master's, project or thesis. *Entrance requirements:* For master's, GMAT, minimum AACSB index of 950. Application fee: $55. *Financial support:* Career-related internships or fieldwork, Federal Work-Study, institutionally sponsored loans, and scholarships/grants available. Support available to part-time students. Financial award application deadline: 3/1; financial award applicants required to submit FAFSA. *Unit head:* Dr. Bhushan Kapoor, Chair, 657-278-2221. *Application contact:* Admissions/Applications, 657-278-2371.
Website: http://business.fullerton.edu/isds/.

California State University, Los Angeles, Graduate Studies, College of Business and Economics, Department of Information Systems, Los Angeles, CA 90032-8530. Offers business information systems (MBA); management (MS); management information systems (MS); office management (MBA). Part-time and evening/weekend programs available. *Faculty:* 3 full-time (0 women), 3 part-time/adjunct (1 woman). *Students:* 16 full-time (5 women), 13 part-time (5 women); includes 7 minority (2 Black or African American, non-Hispanic/Latino; 4 Asian, non-Hispanic/Latino; 1 Hispanic/Latino), 16 international. Average age 30. 60 applicants, 43% accepted, 6 enrolled. In 2013, 5 master's awarded. *Degree requirements:* For master's, comprehensive exam (MBA), thesis (MS). *Entrance requirements:* For master's, GMAT, minimum GPA of 2.5 during previous 2 years of course work. Additional exam requirements/recommendations for international students: Required—TOEFL (minimum score 550 paper-based). *Application deadline:* For fall admission, 5/1 for domestic and international students. Applications are processed on a rolling basis. Application fee: $55. Electronic applications accepted. *Financial support:* Career-related internships or fieldwork and Federal Work-Study available. Support available to part-time students. Financial award application deadline: 3/1. *Unit head:* Dr. Nanda Ganesen, Chair, 323-343-2983, E-mail: nganesa@calstatela.edu. *Application contact:* Dr. Larry Fritz, Dean of Graduate Studies, 323-343-3820, Fax: 323-343-5653, E-mail: lfritz@calstatela.edu.

California State University, Monterey Bay, College of Science, Media Arts and Technology, School of Information Technology and Communication Design, Seaside, CA 93955-8001. Offers interdisciplinary studies (MA), including instructional science and technology; management and information technology (MA). *Degree requirements:* For master's, capstone or thesis. *Entrance requirements:* For master's, GRE, 2 letters of recommendation, minimum GPA of 3.0, technology screening assessment. Additional exam requirements/recommendations for international students: Required—TOEFL (minimum score 550 paper-based; 71 iBT). Electronic applications accepted. *Faculty research:* Electronic commerce, e-learning, knowledge management, international business, business and public policy.

California State University, San Bernardino, Graduate Studies, College of Business and Public Administration, Master in Business Administration Program, San Bernardino, CA 92407. Offers accounting (MBA); cyber security (MBA); entrepreneurship (MBA); finance (MBA); information systems and technology (MBA); management (MBA); marketing management (MBA); supply chain management (MBA). MBA is also offered online. *Accreditation:* AACSB. Part-time and evening/weekend programs available. Postbaccalaureate distance learning degree programs offered (no on-campus study). *Faculty:* 27 full-time (6 women), 8 part-time/adjunct (1 woman). *Students:* 161 full-time (59 women), 47 part-time (18 women); includes 74 minority (12 Black or African American, non-Hispanic/Latino; 19 Asian, non-Hispanic/Latino; 42 Hispanic/Latino; 1 Two or more races, non-Hispanic/Latino), 74 international. Average age 29. 281 applicants, 38% accepted, 67 enrolled. In 2013, 79 master's awarded. *Degree requirements:* For master's, comprehensive exam, thesis, portfolio, 60 units, minimum GPA of 3.0. *Entrance requirements:* For master's, GMAT or GRE, minimum GPA of 2.5. Additional exam requirements/recommendations for international students: Required—TOEFL (minimum score 550 paper-based; 79 iBT). *Application deadline:* For fall admission, 7/20 for domestic and international students; for winter admission, 10/20 for domestic and international students; for spring admission, 1/20 for domestic and international students. Applications are processed on a rolling basis. Application fee: $55. Electronic applications accepted. *Expenses:* Contact institution. *Financial support:* In 2013–14, 79 students received support, including 21 fellowships (averaging $4,867 per year), 29 research assistantships (averaging $2,748 per year), 6 teaching assistantships (averaging $5,162 per year); career-related internships or fieldwork, Federal Work-Study, institutionally sponsored loans, scholarships/grants, and unspecified assistantships also available. Support available to part-time students. Financial award application deadline: 3/1; financial award applicants required to submit FAFSA. *Faculty research:* Market reaction to Form 20-F, tax Constitutional questions in Obamacare, the performance of the faith and ethical investment products prior to and following the 2008 meltdown, capital appreciation bonds: a ruinous decision for an unborn generation, the effects of calorie count display on consumer eating behavior, local government bankruptcy. *Total annual research expenditures:* $2.3 million. *Unit head:* Dr. Lawrence C. Rose, Dean, 909-537-3703, Fax: 909-537-7026, E-mail: lrose@

csusb.edu. *Application contact:* Dr. Vipin Gupta, Associate Dean/MBA Director, 909-537-7380, Fax: 909-537-7026, E-mail: vgupta@csusb.edu.
Website: http://mba.csusb.edu/.

California University of Management and Sciences, Graduate Programs, Anaheim, CA 92801. Offers business administration (MBA, DBA); computer information systems (MS); economics (MS); international business (MS); sports management (MS).

Capella University, School of Business and Technology, Doctoral Programs in Technology, Minneapolis, MN 55402. Offers general information technology (PhD); global operations and supply chain management (DBA); information assurance and security (PhD); information technology education (PhD); information technology management (DBA, PhD).

Capella University, School of Business and Technology, Master's Programs in Technology, Minneapolis, MN 55402. Offers enterprise software architecture (MS); general information systems and technology management (MS); global operations and supply chain management (MBA); information assurance and security (MS); information technology management (MBA); network management (MS).

Capitol College, Graduate Programs, Laurel, MD 20708-9759. Offers business administration (MBA); computer science (MS); electrical engineering (MS); information and telecommunications systems management (MS); information architecture (MS); network security (MS). Part-time and evening/weekend programs available. Postbaccalaureate distance learning degree programs offered (no on-campus study). *Entrance requirements:* For master's, minimum GPA of 3.0. Electronic applications accepted.

Carnegie Mellon University, Heinz College Australia, Master of Science in Information Technology Program (Adelaide, South Australia), Adelaide, South Australia 5000, Australia. Offers MSIT. *Entrance requirements:* For master's, GRE or GMAT, college-level course in advanced algebra/pre-calculus; college-level courses in economics and statistics (recommended). Additional exam requirements/recommendations for international students: Required—TOEFL or IELTS.

Carnegie Mellon University, Heinz College, School of Information Systems and Management, Master of Information Systems Management Program, Pittsburgh, PA 15213-3891. Offers MISM. *Entrance requirements:* For master's, GRE or GMAT, college-level course in advanced algebra/pre-calculus; college-level courses in economics and statistics (recommended). Additional exam requirements/recommendations for international students: Required—TOEFL or IELTS.

Carnegie Mellon University, Heinz College, School of Information Systems and Management, Master of Science in Information Security Policy and Management Program, Pittsburgh, PA 15213-3891. Offers MSISPM. *Entrance requirements:* For master's, GRE or GMAT, college-level course in advanced algebra/pre-calculus; college-level courses in economics and statistics (recommended). Additional exam requirements/recommendations for international students: Required—TOEFL or IELTS.

Carnegie Mellon University, Heinz College, School of Information Systems and Management, Program in Information Technology, Pittsburgh, PA 15213-3891. Offers MSIT.

Carnegie Mellon University, Tepper School of Business, Program in Information Systems, Pittsburgh, PA 15213-3891. Offers PhD. *Degree requirements:* For doctorate, thesis/dissertation. *Entrance requirements:* For doctorate, GRE General Test.

Case Western Reserve University, Weatherhead School of Management, Department of Information Systems, Cleveland, OH 44106. Offers MBA. Part-time and evening/weekend programs available. *Entrance requirements:* For master's, GMAT. *Faculty research:* Decision support, business forecasting systems, design and use of information systems, artificial intelligence, executive information systems.

Case Western Reserve University, Weatherhead School of Management, Department of Operations, Cleveland, OH 44106. Offers management (MS, MSM), including finance (MS), information systems (MS), marketing (MS), operations research, quality management (MS), supply chain (MSM); management for liberal arts graduates (MSM); operations research (PhD); MBA/MSM. Part-time programs available. *Degree requirements:* For doctorate, thesis/dissertation. *Entrance requirements:* For master's, GRE General Test; for doctorate, GMAT, GRE General Test. *Faculty research:* Mathematical finance, mathematical programming, scheduling, stochastic optimization, environmental/energy models.

Central European University, CEU Business School, Budapest, Hungary. Offers executive business administration (EMBA); finance (MBA); general management (MBA); information technology management (M Sc); marketing (MBA). Part-time and evening/weekend programs available. *Faculty:* 18 full-time (5 women), 6 part-time/adjunct (1 woman). *Students:* 37 full-time (16 women), 82 part-time (20 women). Average age 32. 219 applicants, 34% accepted, 35 enrolled. In 2013, 69 master's awarded. *Degree requirements:* For master's, one foreign language. *Entrance requirements:* For master's, GMAT. Additional exam requirements/recommendations for international students: Required—TOEFL (minimum score 570 paper-based); Recommended—IELTS (minimum score 6.5). *Application deadline:* For fall admission, 5/15 for domestic students, 5/22 for international students; for winter admission, 11/15 for domestic students, 11/10 for international students. Applications are processed on a rolling basis. Application fee: $40. Electronic applications accepted. *Expenses: Tuition:* Full-time 62,700 Hungarian forints. *Financial support:* Tuition waivers (partial) available. *Faculty research:* Social and ethical business, marketing, international business, international trade and investment, management development in Central and East Europe, non-market strategies of emerging-market multinationals, macro and micro analysis of the business environment, international competitive analysis, the transition process from emerging economies to established market economies and its social impact, the regulation of natural monopolies. *Unit head:* Dr. Mel Horwitch, Dean and Managing Director, 361-887-5050, E-mail: mhorwitch@ceubusiness.com. *Application contact:* Miao Tan, Recruitment Coordinator, 361-887-5061, Fax: 361-887-5133, E-mail: tanm@ceubusiness.org.
Website: http://business.ceu.hu/.

Central Michigan University, Central Michigan University Global Campus, Program in Administration, Mount Pleasant, MI 48859. Offers acquisitions administration (MSA, Certificate); engineering management administration (MSA, Certificate); general administration (MSA, Certificate); health services administration (MSA, Certificate); human resources administration (MSA, Certificate); information resource management (MSA); information resource management administration (Certificate); international administration (MSA, Certificate); leadership (MSA, Certificate); philanthropy and fundraising administration (MSA, Certificate); public administration (MSA, Certificate); recreation and park administration (MSA); research administration (MSA, Certificate). Part-time and evening/weekend programs available. Postbaccalaureate distance learning degree programs offered (no on-campus study). *Students:* Average age 38. *Entrance requirements:* For master's, minimum GPA of 2.7 in major. *Application deadline:* Applications are processed on a rolling basis. Application fee: $50. Electronic applications accepted. *Financial support:* Scholarships/grants available. Support available to part-time students. Financial award applicants required to submit FAFSA. *Unit head:* Dr. Patricia Chase, Director, 989-774-1845, E-mail: chase1pb@cmich.edu. *Application contact:* 877-268-4636, E-mail: cmuglobal@cmich.edu.

Central Michigan University, College of Graduate Studies, College of Business Administration, Department of Business Information Systems, Mount Pleasant, MI 48859. Offers business computing (Graduate Certificate); information systems (MS), including accounting information systems, business informatics, enterprise systems using SAP software, information systems. Part-time and evening/weekend programs available. *Degree requirements:* For master's, thesis or alternative. Electronic applications accepted. *Faculty research:* Enterprise software, electronic commerce, decision support systems, ethical issues in information systems, information technology management and teaching issues.

Central Michigan University, College of Graduate Studies, College of Business Administration, MBA Program, Mount Pleasant, MI 48859. Offers accounting (MBA); business economics (MBA); consulting (MBA); finance (MBA); general business (MBA); human resource management (MBA); information systems (MBA); international business (MBA); logistics management (MBA); marketing (MBA); value-driven organization (MBA). Part-time and evening/weekend programs available. Postbaccalaureate distance learning degree programs offered (no on-campus study). Electronic applications accepted. *Faculty research:* Accounting, consulting, international business, marketing, information systems.

Central Michigan University, College of Graduate Studies, Interdisciplinary Administration Programs, Mount Pleasant, MI 48859. Offers acquisitions administration (MSA, Graduate Certificate); general administration (MSA, Graduate Certificate); health services administration (MSA, Graduate Certificate); human resource administration (Graduate Certificate); human resources administration (MSA); information resource management (MSA, Graduate Certificate); international administration (MSA, Graduate Certificate); leadership (MSA, Graduate Certificate); public administration (MSA, Graduate Certificate); research administration (Graduate Certificate); sport administration (MSA). *Accreditation:* AACSB. Part-time and evening/weekend programs available. Postbaccalaureate distance learning degree programs offered (no on-campus study). *Degree requirements:* For master's, thesis or alternative. *Entrance requirements:* For master's, bachelor's degree with minimum GPA of 2.7. Electronic applications accepted. *Faculty research:* Interdisciplinary studies in acquisitions administration, health services administration, sport administration, recreation and park administration, and international administration.

Central Penn College, Graduate Programs, Summerdale, PA 17093-0309. Offers information systems management (MPS); organizational development (MPS). Programs offered in Harrisburg, PA. Evening/weekend programs available.

Charleston Southern University, School of Business, Charleston, SC 29423-8087. Offers accounting (MBA); finance (MBA); general management (MBA); leadership (MBA); management information systems (MBA). Part-time and evening/weekend programs available. *Degree requirements:* For master's, thesis optional. *Entrance requirements:* For master's, GMAT. Additional exam requirements/recommendations for international students: Required—TOEFL (minimum score 550 paper-based; 79 iBT).

City University of Seattle, Graduate Division, School of Management, Bellevue, WA 98005. Offers accounting (Certificate); change leadership (MBA, Certificate); computer systems (MS); finance (Certificate); financial management (MBA); general management (MBA); general management-Europe (MBA); global marketing (MBA); human resources management (Certificate); individualized study (MBA); information security (MS); information systems (MBA); leadership (MA); marketing (MBA, Certificate); project management (MBA, MS, Certificate); sustainable business (Certificate); technology management (MBA, Certificate). Part-time and evening/weekend programs available. Postbaccalaureate distance learning degree programs offered (no on-campus study). *Degree requirements:* For master's, comprehensive exam (for some programs), thesis (for some programs). *Entrance requirements:* Additional exam requirements/recommendations for international students: Required—TOEFL (minimum score 567 paper-based; 87 iBT); Recommended—IELTS. Electronic applications accepted.

Claremont Graduate University, Graduate Programs, Center for Information Systems and Technology, Claremont, CA 91711-6160. Offers electronic commerce (MS, PhD); health information management (MS); information systems (Certificate); knowledge management (MS, PhD); systems development (MS, PhD); telecommunications and networking (MS, PhD); MBA/MS. Part-time programs available. *Faculty:* 6 full-time (1 woman). *Students:* 52 full-time (21 women), 62 part-time (18 women); includes 27 minority (9 Black or African American, non-Hispanic/Latino; 14 Asian, non-Hispanic/Latino; 4 Hispanic/Latino), 49 international. Average age 38. In 2013, 14 master's, 1 doctorate awarded. *Degree requirements:* For doctorate, comprehensive exam, thesis/dissertation, portfolio. *Entrance requirements:* For master's and doctorate, GMAT, GRE General Test. Additional exam requirements/recommendations for international students: Required—TOEFL (minimum score 550 paper-based; 80 iBT). *Application deadline:* For fall admission, 2/1 priority date for domestic and international students. Applications are processed on a rolling basis. Application fee: $80. Electronic applications accepted. *Expenses: Tuition:* Full-time $40,560; part-time $1690 per credit. *Required fees:* $275 per semester. Tuition and fees vary according to program. *Financial support:* Fellowships, research assistantships, teaching assistantships, Federal Work-Study, institutionally sponsored loans, and scholarships/grants available. Support available to part-time students. Financial award application deadline: 2/15; financial award applicants required to submit FAFSA. *Faculty research:* Man-machine interaction, organizational aspects of computing, implementation of information systems, information systems practice. *Unit head:* Tom Horan, Dean, 909-607-9302, Fax: 909-621-8564, E-mail: tom.horan@cgu.edu. *Application contact:* Leah Litwack, CISAT/Kay Center Administrative Assistant, 909-621-8209, E-mail: leah.litwack@cgu.edu.
Website: http://www.cgu.edu/pages/153.asp.

Clark University, Graduate School, Graduate School of Management, Business Administration Program, Worcester, MA 01610-1477. Offers accounting (MBA); finance (MBA); global business (MBA); information systems (MBA); management (MBA); marketing (MBA); social change (MBA); sustainability (MBA). *Accreditation:* AACSB. Part-time and evening/weekend programs available. *Students:* 109 full-time (50 women), 151 part-time (67 women); includes 16 minority (9 Black or African American, non-Hispanic/Latino; 3 Asian, non-Hispanic/Latino; 4 Hispanic/Latino), 74 international. Average age 30. 359 applicants, 50% accepted, 81 enrolled. In 2013, 125 master's awarded. *Degree requirements:* For master's, thesis optional. *Application deadline:* For fall admission, 6/1 priority date for domestic students; for spring admission, 12/1 priority date for domestic students. Applications are processed on a rolling basis. Application fee: $50. Electronic applications accepted. *Expenses: Tuition:* Full-time $39,200; part-time $1225 per credit hour. *Financial support:* In 2013–14, research assistantships with partial tuition reimbursements (averaging $4,800 per year), teaching assistantships with partial tuition reimbursements (averaging $4,800 per year) were awarded; fellowships, career-related internships or fieldwork, Federal Work-Study, institutionally sponsored loans, and tuition waivers (partial) also available. Support available to part-time students. Financial award application deadline: 5/31. *Faculty research:* Marketing, accounting, human resource management, management information systems, business finance. *Unit head:* Dr. Catherine Usoff, Dean, 508-793-8822, Fax: 508-793-8822,

E-mail: clarkmba@clarku.edu. *Application contact:* Patrick Oroszko, Enrollment and Marketing Director, 508-793-8822, Fax: 508-793-8822, E-mail: clarkmba@clarku.edu. Website: http://www.clarku.edu/gsom/graduate/fulltime/.

Cleveland State University, College of Graduate Studies, Monte Ahuja College of Business, Department of Computer and Information Science, Cleveland, OH 44115. Offers computer and information science (MCIS); information systems (DBA). Part-time and evening/weekend programs available. *Faculty:* 12 full-time (2 women), 3 part-time/adjunct (2 women). *Students:* 18 full-time (6 women), 83 part-time (32 women); includes 2 minority (both Asian, non-Hispanic/Latino), 65 international. Average age 28. 541 applicants, 46% accepted, 47 enrolled. In 2013, 24 master's awarded. Terminal master's awarded for partial completion of doctoral program. *Degree requirements:* For master's, thesis optional; for doctorate, comprehensive exam, thesis/dissertation. *Entrance requirements:* For master's, GRE or GMAT, minimum GPA of 2.75; for doctorate, GRE or GMAT, MBA, MCIS or equivalent. Additional exam requirements/recommendations for international students: Required—TOEFL (minimum score 525 paper-based; 78 iBT). *Application deadline:* For fall admission, 7/15 priority date for domestic students, 5/15 priority date for international students; for spring admission, 12/15 priority date for domestic students. Applications are processed on a rolling basis. Application fee: $30. Electronic applications accepted. *Expenses:* Tuition, state resident: full-time $8335; part-time $521 per credit hour. Tuition, nonresident: full-time $15,670; part-time $979 per credit hour. *Required fees:* $50; $25 per semester. *Financial support:* In 2013–14, 21 students received support, including 7 research assistantships with full and partial tuition reimbursements available (averaging $7,800 per year), 2 teaching assistantships with full and partial tuition reimbursements available (averaging $16,000 per year); career-related internships or fieldwork, tuition waivers (full), and unspecified assistantships also available. *Faculty research:* Artificial intelligence, object-oriented analysis, database design, software efficiency, distributed system, geographical information systems. *Total annual research expenditures:* $7,500. *Unit head:* Dr. Santosh K. Misra, Chairman, 216-687-4760, Fax: 216-687-5448, E-mail: s.misra@csuohio.edu. *Application contact:* 216-687-4760, Fax: 216-687-9354, E-mail: s.misra@csuohio.edu.
Website: http://cis.csuohio.edu/.

Cleveland State University, College of Graduate Studies, Monte Ahuja College of Business, Doctor of Business Administration Program, Cleveland, OH 44115. Offers finance (DBA); global business (DBA); information systems (DBA); marketing (DBA); operations management (DBA). *Accreditation:* AACSB. Part-time and evening/weekend programs available. *Faculty:* 50 full-time (11 women). *Students:* 36 part-time (18 women); includes 6 minority (2 Black or African American, non-Hispanic/Latino; 4 Asian, non-Hispanic/Latino), 8 international. Average age 39. 96 applicants, 27% accepted, 6 enrolled. In 2013, 1 doctorate awarded. *Degree requirements:* For doctorate, comprehensive exam, thesis/dissertation, oral dissertation defense. *Entrance requirements:* For doctorate, GMAT, MBA or equivalent. Additional exam requirements/recommendations for international students: Required—TOEFL (minimum score 550 paper-based; 79 iBT). *Application deadline:* For spring admission, 2/28 priority date for domestic and international students. Application fee: $30. Electronic applications accepted. *Expenses:* Tuition, state resident: full-time $8335; part-time $521 per credit hour. Tuition, nonresident: full-time $15,670; part-time $979 per credit hour. *Required fees:* $50; $25 per semester. *Financial support:* In 2013–14, 5 research assistantships with full tuition reimbursements (averaging $12,700 per year), 4 teaching assistantships with full tuition reimbursements (averaging $12,700 per year) were awarded; tuition waivers (full) and unspecified assistantships also available. *Faculty research:* Supply chain management, international business, strategic management, risk analysis, consumer behavior. *Unit head:* Dr. Raj Shekhar G. Javalgi, Director, 216-687-3786, Fax: 216-687-9354, E-mail: r.javalgi@csuohio.edu. *Application contact:* Melinda J. Arnold, Administrative Secretary, 216-687-6952, Fax: 216-687-9257, E-mail: m.arnold@csuohio.edu.
Website: http://www.csuohio.edu/business/academics/doctoral.html.

Coastal Carolina University, College of Science, Conway, SC 29528-6054. Offers applied computing and information systems (Certificate); coastal marine and wetland studies (MS). Part-time and evening/weekend programs available. *Faculty:* 21 full-time (4 women). *Students:* 21 full-time (9 women), 14 part-time (9 women); includes 1 minority (Hispanic/Latino), 1 international. Average age 27. 33 applicants, 67% accepted, 11 enrolled. In 2013, 9 master's, 1 other advanced degree awarded. *Degree requirements:* For master's, thesis optional, thesis or internship. *Entrance requirements:* For master's, GRE, 3 letters of recommendation, resume, official transcripts, written statement of educational and career goals, baccalaureate degree; for Certificate, 2 letters of reference, official transcripts. Additional exam requirements/recommendations for international students: Required—TOEFL (minimum score 575 paper-based; 89 iBT). *Application deadline:* For fall admission, 3/1 priority date for domestic and international students; for spring admission, 11/1 priority date for domestic and international students. Applications are processed on a rolling basis. Application fee: $45. Electronic applications accepted. *Expenses:* Tuition, state resident: full-time $11,976; part-time $499 per credit hour. Tuition, nonresident: full-time $18,936; part-time $789 per credit hour. *Required fees:* $80; $40 per term. Tuition and fees vary according to program. *Financial support:* Fellowships, research assistantships, and unspecified assistantships available. Support available to part-time students. Financial award application deadline: 3/1; financial award applicants required to submit FAFSA. *Unit head:* Dr. Michael H. Roberts, Dean, 843-349-2282, Fax: 843-349-2545, E-mail: mroberts@coastal.edu. *Application contact:* Dr. James O. Luken, Associate Provost/Director of Graduate Studies, 843-349-2235, Fax: 843-349-6444, E-mail: joluken@coastal.edu.
Website: http://www.coastal.edu/science/.

College of Charleston, Graduate School, School of Sciences and Mathematics, Program in Computer and Information Sciences, Charleston, SC 29424-0001. Offers MS. Program offered jointly with The Citadel, The Military College of South Carolina. Part-time and evening/weekend programs available. *Degree requirements:* For master's, thesis optional. *Entrance requirements:* For master's, GRE. Additional exam requirements/recommendations for international students: Required—TOEFL (minimum score 81 iBT). Electronic applications accepted.

The College of St. Scholastica, Graduate Studies, Department of Computer Information Systems, Duluth, MN 55811-4199. Offers MA, Certificate. Part-time programs available. Postbaccalaureate distance learning degree programs offered. *Faculty:* 1 full-time (0 women), 4 part-time/adjunct (0 women). *Students:* 23 full-time (9 women), 6 part-time (2 women); includes 3 minority (1 Black or African American, non-Hispanic/Latino; 1 Asian, non-Hispanic/Latino; 1 Hispanic/Latino), 2 international. Average age 36. 15 applicants, 80% accepted, 4 enrolled. In 2013, 7 master's awarded. *Degree requirements:* For master's, thesis. *Entrance requirements:* Additional exam requirements/recommendations for international students: Required—TOEFL (minimum score 550 paper-based; 79 iBT). *Application deadline:* For fall admission, 8/15 priority date for domestic and international students; for spring admission, 11/15 priority date for domestic students, 11/15 for international students; for summer admission, 5/15 priority date for domestic and international students. Applications are processed on a rolling basis. Electronic applications accepted. Application fee is waived when completed online. *Expenses:* Contact institution. *Financial support:* Scholarships/grants available.

Support available to part-time students. Financial award applicants required to submit FAFSA. *Faculty research:* Organization acceptance of software development methodologies. *Unit head:* Brandon Olson, Program Coordinator, 218-723-6199, E-mail: bolson@css.edu. *Application contact:* Lindsay Lahti, Director of Graduate and Extended Studies Recruitment, 218-733-2240, Fax: 218-733-2275, E-mail: gradstudies@css.edu. Website: http://www.css.edu/Graduate/Masters-Doctoral-and-Professional-Programs/Areas-of-Study/MA-IT-Leadership.html.

Colorado State University, Graduate School, College of Business, Department of Computer Information Systems, Fort Collins, CO 80523-1277. Offers MSBA. Part-time programs available. *Faculty:* 12 full-time (3 women). *Students:* 42 full-time (8 women), 25 part-time (11 women); includes 5 minority (2 Asian, non-Hispanic/Latino; 2 Hispanic/Latino; 1 Two or more races, non-Hispanic/Latino), 35 international. Average age 36. 62 applicants, 92% accepted, 36 enrolled. *Degree requirements:* For master's, thesis or alternative, project. *Entrance requirements:* For master's, GMAT or GRE, minimum GPA of 3.0, bachelor's degree. Additional exam requirements/recommendations for international students: Required—TOEFL (minimum score 565 paper-based; 86 iBT). *Application deadline:* For fall admission, 7/15 for domestic students, 4/1 for international students. Applications are processed on a rolling basis. Application fee: $50. Electronic applications accepted. *Expenses:* Tuition, state resident: full-time $9075.40; part-time $504 per credit. Tuition, nonresident: full-time $22,248; part-time $1236 per credit. *Required fees:* $1819; $60 per credit. *Financial support:* Fellowships, research assistantships, teaching assistantships with full and partial tuition reimbursements, career-related internships or fieldwork, Federal Work-Study, scholarships/grants, traineeships, and unspecified assistantships available. Support available to part-time students. Financial award application deadline: 3/1; financial award applicants required to submit FAFSA. *Faculty research:* Decision-making, object-oriented design, database research, electronic marketing, e-commerce. *Total annual research expenditures:* $142,503. *Unit head:* Dr. Jon D. Clark, Chair, 970-491-1618, Fax: 970-491-5205, E-mail: jon.clark@colostate.edu. *Application contact:* Janet Estes, Graduate Programs Contact, 970-491-4612, Fax: 970-491-5205, E-mail: janet.estes@colostate.edu.
Website: http://www.biz.colostate.edu/cis/Pages/default.aspx.

Concordia University Wisconsin, Graduate Programs, School of Business and Legal Studies, MBA Program, Mequon, WI 53097-2402. Offers finance (MBA); health care administration (MBA); human resource management (MBA); international business (MBA); international business-bilingual English/Chinese (MBA); management (MBA); management information systems (MBA); managerial communications (MBA); marketing (MBA); public administration (MBA); risk management (MBA). Postbaccalaureate distance learning degree programs offered (minimal on-campus study). *Degree requirements:* For master's, comprehensive exam, thesis or alternative. *Entrance requirements:* Additional exam requirements/recommendations for international students: Required—TOEFL. *Expenses:* Contact institution.

Copenhagen Business School, Graduate Programs, Copenhagen, Denmark. Offers business administration (Exec MBA, MBA, PhD); business administration and information systems (M Sc); business, language and culture (M Sc); economics and business administration (M Sc); health management (MHM); international business and politics (M Sc); public administration (MPA); shipping and logistics (Exec MBA); technology, market and organization (MBA).

Creighton University, Graduate School, Eugene C. Eppley College of Business Administration, Omaha, NE 68178-0001. Offers business administration (MBA); information technology management (MS); securities and portfolio management (MSAPM); JD/MBA; MBA/MS-ITM; MBA/MSAPM; MD/MBA; MS ITM/JD; Pharm D/MBA. *Accreditation:* AACSB. Part-time and evening/weekend programs available. Postbaccalaureate distance learning degree programs offered (no on-campus study). *Faculty:* 37 full-time (7 women). *Students:* 17 full-time (6 women), 298 part-time (75 women); includes 45 minority (21 Black or African American, non-Hispanic/Latino; 2 American Indian or Alaska Native, non-Hispanic/Latino; 14 Asian, non-Hispanic/Latino; 7 Hispanic/Latino; 1 Native Hawaiian or other Pacific Islander, non-Hispanic/Latino), 23 international. Average age 32. 113 applicants, 88% accepted, 98 enrolled. In 2013, 138 master's awarded. *Degree requirements:* For master's, thesis optional. *Entrance requirements:* For master's, GMAT, resume, 2 letters of recommendation. Additional exam requirements/recommendations for international students: Required—TOEFL (minimum score 550 paper-based; 80 iBT). *Application deadline:* For fall admission, 7/1 priority date for domestic students, 3/1 for international students; for winter admission, 10/1 priority date for domestic students, 7/1 for international students; for spring admission, 4/1 priority date for domestic students, 10/1 for international students; for summer admission, 5/1 for domestic and international students. Applications are processed on a rolling basis. Application fee: $50. Electronic applications accepted. *Expenses:* Tuition: Full-time $13,608; part-time $756 per credit hour. *Required fees:* $149 per semester. Tuition and fees vary according to course load, campus/location, program, reciprocity agreements and student's religious affiliation. *Financial support:* In 2013–14, 10 fellowships with partial tuition reimbursements (averaging $8,448 per year) were awarded; career-related internships or fieldwork, tuition waivers (partial), and unspecified assistantships also available. Financial award application deadline: 3/1. *Faculty research:* Small business issues, economics. *Unit head:* Dr. Deborah Wells, Associate Dean for Graduate Programs, 402-280-2841, E-mail: deborahwells@creighton.edu. *Application contact:* Gail Hafer, Assistant Dean, 402-280-2829, Fax: 402-280-2172, E-mail: ghafer@creighton.edu.
Website: http://business.creighton.edu.

Daemen College, Department of Accounting/Information Systems, Amherst, NY 14226-3592. Offers global business (MS), including accounting, global business, management information systems, marketing. Part-time and evening/weekend programs available. *Degree requirements:* For master's, minimum GPA of 3.0. *Entrance requirements:* For master's, GMAT if undergraduate GPA is less than 3.0, 2 letters of recommendation; goal statement; transcripts; demonstration of satisfactory oral and written English. Additional exam requirements/recommendations for international students: Required—TOEFL (minimum score 500 paper-based; 63 iBT), IELTS (minimum score 5.5). Electronic applications accepted. *Faculty research:* Internationalization of small business, cultural influences on business practices, international human resource practices.

Dakota State University, College of Business and Information Systems, Madison, SD 57042-1799. Offers applied computer science (MSACS); general management (MBA); health informatics (MSHI); information assurance (MSIA); information systems (MSIS, D Sc IS). *Accreditation:* ACBSP. Part-time and evening/weekend programs available. Postbaccalaureate distance learning degree programs offered (minimal on-campus study). *Faculty:* 20 full-time (6 women), 1 part-time/adjunct (0 women). *Students:* 47 full-time (12 women), 146 part-time (31 women); includes 38 minority (10 Black or African American, non-Hispanic/Latino; 1 American Indian or Alaska Native, non-Hispanic/Latino; 12 Asian, non-Hispanic/Latino; 7 Hispanic/Latino; 1 Native Hawaiian or other Pacific Islander, non-Hispanic/Latino; 7 Two or more races, non-Hispanic/Latino), 48 international. Average age 37. 167 applicants, 58% accepted, 62 enrolled. In 2013, 57 master's, 4 doctorates awarded. *Degree requirements:* For master's, comprehensive exam, thesis optional, examination, integrative project; for doctorate, comprehensive exam, thesis/dissertation, portfolio. *Entrance requirements:* For master's, GRE General

Management Information Systems

Test, demonstration of information systems skills, minimum GPA of 2.7; for doctorate, GRE General Test, demonstration of information systems skills. Additional exam requirements/recommendations for international students: Required—TOEFL (minimum score 550 paper-based; 79 iBT), IELTS (minimum score 6.5). *Application deadline:* For fall admission, 6/15 for domestic and international students; for spring admission, 11/15 for domestic and international students. Applications are processed on a rolling basis. Application fee: $35 ($85 for international students). *Financial support:* In 2013–14, 47 students received support, including 13 fellowships with partial tuition reimbursements available (averaging $32,782 per year), 10 research assistantships with partial tuition reimbursements available (averaging $12,956 per year), 1 teaching assistantship with partial tuition reimbursement available (averaging $12,956 per year); Federal Work-Study, scholarships/grants, unspecified assistantships, and administrative assistantships also available. Support available to part-time students. Financial award applicants required to submit FAFSA. *Faculty research:* E-commerce, data mining and data warehousing, effectiveness of hybrid learning environments, biometrics and information assurance, decision support systems. *Unit head:* Dr. Omar El-Gayar, Dean of Graduate Studies and Research, 605-256-5799, Fax: 605-256-5093, E-mail: omar.el-gayar@dsu.edu. *Application contact:* Erin Blankespoor, Secretary, Office of Graduate Studies and Research, 605-256-5799, Fax: 605-256-5093, E-mail: erin.blankespoor@dsu.edu.
Website: http://www.dsu.edu/bis/index.aspx.

Dalhousie University, Faculty of Management, Centre for Advanced Management Education, Halifax, NS B3H 3J5, Canada. Offers financial services (MBA); information management (MIM); management (MPA); natural resources (MBA). Part-time programs available. Postbaccalaureate distance learning degree programs offered. *Entrance requirements:* For master's, GMAT, minimum GPA of 3.0, resume. Additional exam requirements/recommendations for international students: Required—TOEFL, IELTS, CANTEST, CAEL, or Michigan English Language Assessment Battery. Electronic applications accepted.

Dallas Baptist University, College of Business, Business Administration Program, Dallas, TX 75211-9299. Offers accounting (MBA); business communication (MBA); conflict resolution management (MBA); entrepreneurship (MBA); finance (MBA); health care management (MBA); international business (MBA); leading the non-profit organization (MBA); management (MBA); management information systems (MBA); marketing (MBA); project management (MBA); technology and engineering (MBA). *Accreditation:* ACBSP. Part-time and evening/weekend programs available. *Entrance requirements:* For master's, GMAT, minimum GPA of 3.0. Additional exam requirements/recommendations for international students: Required—TOEFL, IELTS. *Application deadline:* Applications are processed on a rolling basis. Application fee: $25. Electronic applications accepted. *Expenses: Tuition:* Full-time $13,410; part-time $745 per credit hour. *Required fees:* $300; $150 per semester. Tuition and fees vary according to degree level. *Financial support:* Federal Work-Study, institutionally sponsored loans, scholarships/grants, and tuition waivers (full and partial) available. Support available to part-time students. Financial award applicants required to submit FAFSA. *Faculty research:* Sports management, services marketing, retailing, strategic management, financial planning/investments. *Unit head:* Dr. Sandra S. Reid, Chair, 214-333-5280, Fax: 214-333-5293, E-mail: graduate@dbu.edu. *Application contact:* Kit P. Montgomery, Director of Graduate Programs, 214-333-5242, Fax: 214-333-5579, E-mail: graduate@dbu.edu.
Website: http://www3.dbu.edu/graduate/mba.asp.

DePaul University, Charles H. Kellstadt Graduate School of Business, Chicago, IL 60604. Offers accountancy (M Acc, MS, MSA); applied economics (MBA); banking (MBA); behavioral finance (MBA); brand and product management (MBA); business development (MBA); business information technology (MS); business strategy and decision-making (MBA); computational finance (MS); consumer insights (MBA); corporate finance (MBA); economic policy analysis (MS); entrepreneurship (MBA, MS); finance (MBA, MS); financial analysis (MBA); general business (MBA); health sector management (MBA); hospitality leadership (MBA); hospitality leadership and operational performance (MS); human resource management (MBA); human resources (MS); investment management (MBA); leadership and change management (MBA); management accounting (MBA); marketing (MBA, MS); marketing analysis (MS); marketing strategy and planning (MBA); operations management (MBA); organizational diversity (MBA); real estate (MS); real estate finance and investment (MBA); revenue management (MBA); sports management (MBA); strategic global marketing (MBA); strategy, execution and valuation (MBA); sustainable management (MBA, MS); taxation (MS); wealth management (MS); JD/MBA. *Accreditation:* AACSB. Part-time and evening/weekend programs available. Postbaccalaureate distance learning degree programs offered (no on-campus study). *Faculty:* 81 full-time (20 women), 45 part-time/adjunct (8 women). *Students:* 1,238 full-time (605 women), 617 part-time (223 women); includes 295 minority (71 Black or African American, non-Hispanic/Latino; 129 Asian, non-Hispanic/Latino; 74 Hispanic/Latino; 4 Native Hawaiian or other Pacific Islander, non-Hispanic/Latino; 17 Two or more races, non-Hispanic/Latino), 462 international. Average age 29. In 2013, 911 master's awarded. *Entrance requirements:* For master's, GMAT, 2 letters of recommendation, resume, essay, official transcripts. Additional exam requirements/recommendations for international students: Required—TOEFL (minimum score 550 paper-based; 80 iBT). *Application deadline:* For fall admission, 7/1 for domestic students, 6/1 for international students; for winter admission, 10/1 for domestic students, 9/1 for international students; for spring admission, 2/1 for domestic students, 1/1 for international students. Applications are processed on a rolling basis. Application fee: $60. Electronic applications accepted. *Expenses:* Contact institution. *Financial support:* Application deadline: 4/1; applicants required to submit FAFSA. *Unit head:* Robert T. Ryan, Assistant Dean and Director, 312-362-8810, Fax: 312-362-6677, E-mail: rryan1@depaul.edu. *Application contact:* James Parker, Director of Recruitment and Admission, 312-362-8810, Fax: 312-362-6677, E-mail: kgsb@depaul.edu.
Website: http://kellstadt.depaul.edu.

DePaul University, College of Computing and Digital Media, Chicago, IL 60604. Offers animation (MA, MFA); business information technology (MS); cinema (MFA); cinema production (MS); computational finance (MS); computer and information sciences (PhD); computer game development (MS); computer information and network security (MS); computer science (MS); e-commerce technology (MS); health informatics (MS); human-computer interaction (MS); information systems (MS); information technology project management (MS); network engineering and management (MS); predictive analytics (MS); screenwriting (MFA); software engineering (MS); JD/MS. Part-time and evening/weekend programs available. Postbaccalaureate distance learning degree programs offered (no on-campus study). *Faculty:* 77 full-time (28 women), 44 part-time/adjunct (7 women). *Students:* 1,063 full-time (329 women), 877 part-time (248 women); includes 631 minority (240 Black or African American, non-Hispanic/Latino; 2 American Indian or Alaska Native, non-Hispanic/Latino; 186 Asian, non-Hispanic/Latino; 143 Hispanic/Latino; 9 Native Hawaiian or other Pacific Islander, non-Hispanic/Latino; 51 Two or more races, non-Hispanic/Latino), 288 international. Average age 32. In 2013, 511 master's, 3 doctorates awarded. *Degree requirements:* For master's, thesis (for some programs); for doctorate, comprehensive exam, thesis/dissertation. *Entrance requirements:* For master's, GRE or GMAT (for MS in computational finance only), bachelor's degree, resume (MS in predictive analytics only), IT experience (MS in information technology project management only), portfolio review (all MFA programs and MA in animation); for doctorate, GRE, master's degree in computer science. Additional exam requirements/recommendations for international students: Required—TOEFL (minimum score 590 paper-based; 80 iBT), IELTS (minimum score 6.5), PTE (minimum score 53). *Application deadline:* For fall admission, 8/1 priority date for domestic students, 6/15 priority date for international students; for winter admission, 12/1 priority date for domestic students, 10/15 priority date for international students; for spring admission, 3/1 priority date for domestic students, 1/15 priority date for international students; for summer admission, 5/1 for domestic students, 4/15 for international students. Applications are processed on a rolling basis. Application fee: $25. Electronic applications accepted. *Expenses:* Contact institution. *Financial support:* In 2013–14, 102 students received support, including 3 fellowships with full tuition reimbursements available (averaging $30,000 per year), 5 research assistantships with full and partial tuition reimbursements available (averaging $20,400 per year), 94 teaching assistantships with full and partial tuition reimbursements available (averaging $4,334 per year); Federal Work-Study, scholarships/grants, tuition waivers (full and partial), and unspecified assistantships also available. Support available to part-time students. Financial award application deadline: 4/20; financial award applicants required to submit FAFSA. *Faculty research:* Data mining, computer science, human-computer interaction, security, animation and film. *Total annual research expenditures:* $3.6 million. *Unit head:* Elly Kafritsas-Wessels, Senior Administrative Assistant, 312-362-5816, Fax: 312-362-5185, E-mail: ekafrits@cdm.depaul.edu. *Application contact:* Office of Admission, 312-362-8714, E-mail: admission@cdm.depaul.edu.
Website: http://cdm.depaul.edu.

DeSales University, Graduate Division, Division of Business, Center Valley, PA 18034-9568. Offers accounting (MBA); computer information systems (MBA); finance (MBA); health care systems management (MBA); human resources management (MBA); management (MBA); marketing (MBA); project management (MBA); self-design (MBA). *Accreditation:* ACBSP. Part-time and evening/weekend programs available. Postbaccalaureate distance learning degree programs offered (no on-campus study). *Students:* 444 part-time. Average age 37. In 2013, 1 master's awarded. *Entrance requirements:* For master's, GMAT, minimum GPA of 3.0, 2 years of work experience. Additional exam requirements/recommendations for international students: Required—TOEFL. *Application deadline:* Applications are processed on a rolling basis. Application fee: $50. Electronic applications accepted. *Expenses: Tuition:* Part-time $790 per credit. *Financial support:* Applicants required to submit FAFSA. *Faculty research:* Quality improvement, executive development, productivity, cross-cultural managerial differences, leadership. *Unit head:* Dr. David Gilfoil, Director, 610-282-1100 Ext. 1828, Fax: 610-282-2869, E-mail: david.gilfoil@desales.edu. *Application contact:* Abigail Wernicki, Director of Graduate Admissions, 610-282-1100 Ext. 1768, E-mail: gradadmissions@desales.edu.

DeVry University, Graduate Programs, Downers Grove, IL 60515. Offers accounting and financial management (MAFM); business administration (MBA); education (MS); educational technology (MS); electrical engineering (MS); human resources management (MHRM); information systems management (MISM); network and communications management (MNCM); project management (MPM); public administration (MPA).

Dowling College, School of Business, Oakdale, NY 11769. Offers aviation management (MBA, Certificate); corporate finance (MBA, Certificate); health care management (MBA); human resource management (Certificate); information systems management (MBA); management and leadership (MBA); marketing (Certificate); project management (Certificate); public management (MBA); school district business leader (MBA); sport, event and entertainment management (Certificate); JD/MBA. Part-time and evening/weekend programs available. Postbaccalaureate distance learning degree programs offered (minimal on-campus study). *Faculty:* 7 full-time (2 women), 43 part-time/adjunct (7 women). *Students:* 183 full-time (79 women), 299 part-time (142 women); includes 137 minority (84 Black or African American, non-Hispanic/Latino; 14 Asian, non-Hispanic/Latino; 20 Hispanic/Latino; 19 Native Hawaiian or other Pacific Islander, non-Hispanic/Latino). Average age 32. 360 applicants, 58% accepted, 127 enrolled. In 2013, 235 master's, 15 other advanced degrees awarded. *Degree requirements:* For master's, comprehensive exam, thesis optional. *Entrance requirements:* For master's, minimum GPA of 2.8, 2 letters of recommendation, courses or seminar in accounting and finance, resume. Additional exam requirements/recommendations for international students: Required—TOEFL (minimum score 550 paper-based). *Application deadline:* For fall admission, 9/1 priority date for domestic students; for winter admission, 1/1 priority date for domestic students; for spring admission, 2/1 priority date for domestic students. Applications are processed on a rolling basis. Application fee: $50. Electronic applications accepted. *Expenses: Tuition:* Full-time $22,731; part-time $1029 per credit. *Required fees:* $956; $956. *Financial support:* Career-related internships or fieldwork and Federal Work-Study available. Support available to part-time students. Financial award application deadline: 6/30; financial award applicants required to submit FAFSA. *Faculty research:* International finance, computer applications, labor relations, executive development. *Unit head:* Dr. Elana Zolfo, Dean, 631-244-3266, Fax: 631-244-1018, E-mail: zolfoe@dowling.edu. *Application contact:* Mary Boullianne, Dean of Admissions, 631-244-3274, Fax: 631-244-1059, E-mail: boulliam@dowling.edu.

Duquesne University, John F. Donahue Graduate School of Business, Pittsburgh, PA 15282-0001. Offers accounting (M Acc); finance (MBA); information systems management (MBA, MSISM); management (MBA); marketing (MBA); supply chain management (MBA); sustainability (MBA); JD/MBA; MBA/M Acc; MBA/MA; MBA/MES; MBA/MHMS; MBA/MSN; MSISM/MBA; Pharm D/MBA. *Accreditation:* AACSB. Part-time and evening/weekend programs available. *Faculty:* 58 full-time (17 women), 40 part-time/adjunct (8 women). *Students:* 117 full-time (59 women), 147 part-time (54 women); includes 14 minority (7 Black or African American, non-Hispanic/Latino; 1 Asian, non-Hispanic/Latino; 6 Hispanic/Latino), 53 international. Average age 27. 418 applicants, 46% accepted, 109 enrolled. In 2013, 133 master's awarded. *Entrance requirements:* For master's, GMAT, undergraduate transcripts, 2 letters of recommendation, current resume, personal statement. Additional exam requirements/recommendations for international students: Required—TOEFL (minimum score 577 paper-based; 90 iBT), IELTS (minimum score 7). *Application deadline:* For fall admission, 7/1 priority date for domestic students, 6/1 for international students; for spring admission, 11/1 for domestic and international students. Applications are processed on a rolling basis. Application fee: $0. Electronic applications accepted. *Expenses: Tuition:* Full-time $18,162; part-time $1009 per credit. *Required fees:* $1728; $96 per credit. Tuition and fees vary according to program. *Financial support:* In 2013–14, 39 students received support, including 6 fellowships with partial tuition reimbursements available (averaging $4,541 per year), 33 research assistantships with partial tuition reimbursements available (averaging $9,081 per year); career-related internships or fieldwork, scholarships/grants, and unspecified assistantships also available. Support available to part-time students. Financial award application deadline: 7/1; financial award applicants required to submit FAFSA. *Faculty research:* International business, investment management, business ethics, technology management, supply chain management, business strategy, finance. *Unit head:* Thomas J. Nist, Director of Graduate Programs, 412-396-6276, Fax: 412-396-1726, E-mail: nist@duq.edu. *Application contact:* Maria W.

DeCrosta, Enrollment Manager, 412-396-5529, Fax: 412-396-1726, E-mail: decrostam@duq.edu.
Website: http://www.duq.edu/business/grad.

Duquesne University, School of Leadership and Professional Advancement, Pittsburgh, PA 15282-0001. Offers leadership (MS), including business ethics, community leadership, global leadership, health care, information technology, leadership, liberal studies, professional administration, sports leadership. Part-time and evening/weekend programs available. Postbaccalaureate distance learning degree programs offered (no on-campus study). *Faculty:* 15 full-time (7 women), 64 part-time/adjunct (26 women). *Students:* 213 full-time (106 women), 170 part-time (86 women); includes 89 minority (59 Black or African American, non-Hispanic/Latino; 2 American Indian or Alaska Native, non-Hispanic/Latino; 7 Asian, non-Hispanic/Latino; 9 Hispanic/Latino; 1 Native Hawaiian or other Pacific Islander, non-Hispanic/Latino; 11 Two or more races, non-Hispanic/Latino), 9 international. Average age 36. 204 applicants, 56% accepted, 103 enrolled. In 2013, 140 master's awarded. *Degree requirements:* For master's, capstone course. *Entrance requirements:* For master's, professional work experience, 500-word essay, resume, interview. Additional exam requirements/recommendations for international students: Required—TOEFL (minimum score 80 iBT). *Application deadline:* Applications are processed on a rolling basis. Application fee: $0. Electronic applications accepted. Application fee is waived when completed online. *Expenses: Tuition:* Full-time $18,162; part-time $1009 per credit. *Required fees:* $1728; $96 per credit. Tuition and fees vary according to program. *Financial support:* Scholarships/grants available. Financial award applicants required to submit FAFSA. *Unit head:* Dr. Dorothy Bassett, Dean, 412-396-2141, Fax: 412-396-4711, E-mail: bassettd@duq.edu. *Application contact:* Marianne Leister, Director of Student Services, 412-396-4933, Fax: 412-396-5072, E-mail: leister@duq.edu.
Website: http://www.duq.edu/academics/schools/leadership-and-professional-advancement.

East Carolina University, Graduate School, College of Technology and Computer Science, Department of Technology Systems, Greenville, NC 27858-4353. Offers computer network professional (Certificate); industrial technology (MS), including computer networking management, digital communications, industrial distribution and logistics, information security, manufacturing, performance improvement, quality systems; information assurance (Certificate); Lean Six Sigma Black Belt (Certificate); occupational safety (MS); technology management (PhD); Website developer (Certificate). *Entrance requirements:* For master's and Certificate, GRE General Test or MAT, minimum GPA of 2.5; for doctorate, GRE General Test, related work experience. *Expenses:* Tuition, state resident: full-time $4223. Tuition, nonresident: full-time $16,540. *Required fees:* $2184.

Eastern Michigan University, Graduate School, College of Business, Department of Computer Information Systems, Ypsilanti, MI 48197. Offers MS. Part-time and evening/weekend programs available. *Faculty:* 12 full-time (2 women). *Students:* 36 full-time (19 women), 21 part-time (10 women); includes 7 minority (3 Black or African American, non-Hispanic/Latino; 4 Asian, non-Hispanic/Latino), 39 international. Average age 28. 66 applicants, 65% accepted, 15 enrolled. In 2013, 37 master's awarded. *Entrance requirements:* Additional exam requirements/recommendations for international students: Required—TOEFL. *Application deadline:* For fall admission, 5/15 priority date for domestic students, 5/1 priority date for international students; for winter admission, 10/15 priority date for domestic students, 10/1 priority date for international students; for spring admission, 3/15 priority date for domestic students, 3/1 priority date for international students. Applications are processed on a rolling basis. Application fee: $35. *Expenses:* Tuition, state resident: full-time $12,300; part-time $466 per credit hour. Tuition, nonresident: full-time $23,159; part-time $918 per credit hour. *Required fees:* $71 per credit hour. $46 per semester. One-time fee: $100. Tuition and fees vary according to course level and degree level. *Financial support:* Fellowships, research assistantships with full tuition reimbursements, teaching assistantships with full tuition reimbursements, career-related internships or fieldwork, Federal Work-Study, institutionally sponsored loans, scholarships/grants, tuition waivers (partial), and unspecified assistantships available. Support available to part-time students. Financial award applicants required to submit FAFSA. *Unit head:* Dr. LaVerne Higgins, Interim Department Head, 734-487-4140, Fax: 734-487-1941, E-mail: lhiggins@emich.edu. *Application contact:* K. Michelle Henry, Director, Academic Services, 734-487-4444, Fax: 734-483-1316, E-mail: mhenry1@emich.edu.
Website: http://www.cis.emich.edu.

Eastern Michigan University, Graduate School, College of Business, Programs in Business Administration, Ypsilanti, MI 48197. Offers business administration (MBA, Graduate Certificate); computer information systems (Graduate Certificate); e-business (MBA, Graduate Certificate); enterprise business intelligence (MBA); entrepreneurship (MBA, Graduate Certificate); finance (MBA, Graduate Certificate); human resources (MBA); human resources management (Graduate Certificate); information systems (MBA); internal auditing (MBA); international business (MBA, Graduate Certificate); marketing management (Graduate Certificate); nonprofit management (MBA); organizational development (Graduate Certificate); supply chain management (MBA, Graduate Certificate). *Accreditation:* AACSB. Part-time programs available. Postbaccalaureate distance learning degree programs offered (no on-campus study). *Students:* 74 full-time (28 women), 342 part-time (183 women); includes 122 minority (84 Black or African American, non-Hispanic/Latino; 2 American Indian or Alaska Native, non-Hispanic/Latino; 19 Asian, non-Hispanic/Latino; 7 Hispanic/Latino; 10 Two or more races, non-Hispanic/Latino), 38 international. Average age 33. 305 applicants, 72% accepted, 131 enrolled. In 2013, 69 master's, 57 other advanced degrees awarded. *Entrance requirements:* For master's, GMAT (minimum score 450), minimum cumulative undergraduate GPA of 2.75. Additional exam requirements/recommendations for international students: Required—TOEFL. *Application deadline:* For fall admission, 5/15 for domestic students, 5/1 for international students; for winter admission, 10/15 for domestic students, 10/1 for international students; for spring admission, 3/15 for domestic students, 3/1 for international students. Applications are processed on a rolling basis. Application fee: $35. *Expenses:* Tuition, state resident: full-time $12,300; part-time $466 per credit hour. Tuition, nonresident: full-time $23,159; part-time $918 per credit hour. *Required fees:* $71 per credit hour. $46 per semester. One-time fee: $100. Tuition and fees vary according to course level and degree level. *Financial support:* Fellowships, research assistantships with full tuition reimbursements, teaching assistantships with full tuition reimbursements, career-related internships or fieldwork, Federal Work-Study, institutionally sponsored loans, scholarships/grants, tuition waivers (partial), and unspecified assistantships available. Support available to part-time students. Financial award applicants required to submit FAFSA. *Unit head:* K. Michelle Henry, Director, Academic Services, 734-487-4444, Fax: 734-483-1316, E-mail: mhenry1@emich.edu. *Application contact:* Beste Windes, Advisor, 734-487-4444, Fax: 734-483-1316, E-mail: bwindes@emich.edu.
Website: http://www.emich.edu/public/cob/gr/grad.html.

East Tennessee State University, School of Graduate Studies, College of Business and Technology, Department of Computer and Information Sciences, Johnson City, TN 37614. Offers applied computer science (MS); information technology (MS). Part-time and evening/weekend programs available. *Faculty:* 16 full-time (2 women). *Students:* 27 full-time (2 women), 12 part-time (2 women); includes 7 minority (4 Black or African American, non-Hispanic/Latino; 1 Hispanic/Latino; 2 Two or more races, non-Hispanic/Latino), 3 international. Average age 30. 57 applicants, 42% accepted, 21 enrolled. In 2013, 19 master's awarded. *Degree requirements:* For master's, comprehensive exam, thesis optional, capstone. *Entrance requirements:* For master's, GRE General Test, minimum GPA of 2.5, three letters of recommendation. Additional exam requirements/recommendations for international students: Required—TOEFL (minimum score 550 paper-based; 79 iBT). *Application deadline:* For fall admission, 6/1 for domestic students, 4/30 for international students; for spring admission, 11/1 for domestic students, 9/30 for international students. Application fee: $35 ($45 for international students). Electronic applications accepted. *Expenses:* Tuition, state resident: full-time $7900; part-time $395 per credit hour. Tuition, nonresident: full-time $21,960; part-time $1098 per credit hour. *Required fees:* $1345; $84 per credit hour. *Financial support:* In 2013–14, 27 students received support, including 10 research assistantships with full tuition reimbursements available (averaging $9,000 per year), 15 teaching assistantships with full tuition reimbursements available (averaging $10,000 per year); career-related internships or fieldwork, institutionally sponsored loans, scholarships/grants, and unspecified assistantships also available. Financial award application deadline: 7/1; financial award applicants required to submit FAFSA. *Faculty research:* Data mining, security and forensics, numerical optimization, computer gaming, enterprise resource planning. *Unit head:* Dr. Terry Countermine, Chair, 423-439-5328, Fax: 423-439-7119, E-mail: counter@etsu.edu. *Application contact:* Kimberly Brockman, Graduate Specialist, 423-439-6165, Fax: 423-439-5624, E-mail: brockmank@etsu.edu.

Elmhurst College, Graduate Programs, Program in Computer Information Systems, Elmhurst, IL 60126-3296. Offers MS. Part-time and evening/weekend programs available. Postbaccalaureate distance learning degree programs offered (minimal on-campus study). *Faculty:* 2 full-time (1 woman). *Students:* 13 part-time (5 women); includes 1 minority (Asian, non-Hispanic/Latino). Average age 33. 17 applicants, 35% accepted, 4 enrolled. In 2013, 7 master's awarded. *Entrance requirements:* For master's, 3 recommendations, resume, statement of purpose. Additional exam requirements/recommendations for international students: Required—TOEFL (minimum score 550 paper-based; 79 iBT). *Application deadline:* Applications are processed on a rolling basis. Application fee: $0. Electronic applications accepted. *Financial support:* In 2013–14, 1 student received support. Federal Work-Study and scholarships/grants available. Support available to part-time students. Financial award application deadline: 6/1; financial award applicants required to submit FAFSA. *Application contact:* Timothy J. Panfil, Director of Enrollment Management, School for Professional Studies, 630-617-3300 Ext. 3256, Fax: 630-617-6471, E-mail: panfilt@elmhurst.edu.

Emory University, Goizueta Business School, Doctoral Program in Business, Atlanta, GA 30322-1100. Offers accounting (PhD); finance (PhD); information systems (PhD); marketing (PhD); organization and management (PhD). *Faculty:* 53 full-time (12 women). *Students:* 41 full-time (15 women); includes 28 minority (all Asian, non-Hispanic/Latino). Average age 29. 195 applicants, 9% accepted, 9 enrolled. In 2013, 1 doctorate awarded. *Degree requirements:* For doctorate, comprehensive exam, thesis/dissertation. *Entrance requirements:* For doctorate, GMAT (strongly preferred) or GRE. Additional exam requirements/recommendations for international students: Required—TOEFL. *Application deadline:* For fall admission, 1/3 priority date for domestic and international students. Application fee: $75. Electronic applications accepted. *Financial support:* In 2013–14, 35 students received support, including 3 fellowships (averaging $1,166 per year). *Unit head:* Dr. Anand Swaminathan, Associate Dean, Doctoral Program, 404-727-2306, Fax: 404-727-5337, E-mail: anand.swaminathan@emory.edu. *Application contact:* Allison Gilmore, Director of Admissions and Student Services, 404-727-6353, Fax: 404-727-5337, E-mail: phd@bus.emory.edu.

Endicott College, Van Loan School of Graduate and Professional Studies, Program in Information Technology, Beverly, MA 01915-2096. Offers MSIT. *Faculty:* 1 full-time (0 women), 5 part-time/adjunct (0 women). *Students:* 12 full-time (6 women), 14 part-time (3 women); includes 2 minority (1 Black or African American, non-Hispanic/Latino; 1 Two or more races, non-Hispanic/Latino), 5 international. Average age 32. 14 applicants, 71% accepted, 6 enrolled. In 2013, 12 master's awarded. *Degree requirements:* For master's, thesis. *Entrance requirements:* For master's, GRE or MAT, two letters of recommendation. Additional exam requirements/recommendations for international students: Required—TOEFL. *Application deadline:* Applications are processed on a rolling basis. Application fee: $50. Electronic applications accepted. *Expenses:* Contact institution. *Financial support:* Applicants required to submit FAFSA. *Unit head:* Dr. Mary Huegel, Dean, 978-232-2084, Fax: 978-232-3000, E-mail: mhuegel@endicott.edu. *Application contact:* Richard Benedetto, Associate Dean of Graduate School, 978-232-2744, Fax: 978-232-3000, E-mail: rbenedet@endicott.edu.

Fairfield University, Charles F. Dolan School of Business, Fairfield, CT 06824-5195. Offers accounting (MBA, MS, CAS); accounting information systems (MBA, CAS); entrepreneurship (MBA, CAS); finance (MBA, MS, CAS); general management (MBA, CAS); human resource management (MBA, CAS); information systems and operations (MBA); information systems and operations management (CAS); marketing (MBA, CAS); taxation (MBA, CAS). *Accreditation:* AACSB. Part-time and evening/weekend programs available. *Faculty:* 18 full-time (9 women), 15 part-time/adjunct (4 women). *Students:* 94 full-time (45 women), 72 part-time (26 women); includes 49 minority (7 Black or African American, non-Hispanic/Latino; 33 Asian, non-Hispanic/Latino; 8 Hispanic/Latino; 1 Two or more races, non-Hispanic/Latino), 9 international. Average age 29. 116 applicants, 43% accepted, 26 enrolled. In 2013, 100 master's awarded. *Degree requirements:* For master's, capstone course. *Entrance requirements:* For master's, GMAT (minimum score 500), 2 letters of reference, resume, minimum GPA of 3.0. Additional exam requirements/recommendations for international students: Required—TOEFL (minimum score 550 paper-based; 80 iBT) or IELTS (minimum score 6.5). *Application deadline:* For fall admission, 5/15 for international students; for spring admission, 10/15 for international students. Applications are processed on a rolling basis. Application fee: $60. Electronic applications accepted. *Expenses:* Contact institution. *Financial support:* In 2013–14, 28 students received support. Scholarships/grants, unspecified assistantships, and merit-based one-time entrance scholarships available. Financial award applicants required to submit FAFSA. *Faculty research:* International finance, leadership and careers, ethics in accounting, emotions in consumer behavior, supply chain analysis, organizational leadership attributes, emotions in the workplace, real estate finance, effect of social media on stock prices. *Unit head:* Dr. Donald Gibson, Dean, 203-254-4070, Fax: 203-254-4105, E-mail: dgibson@fairfield.edu. *Application contact:* Marianne Gumpper, Director of Graduate and Continuing Studies Admission, 203-254-4184, Fax: 203-254-4073, E-mail: gradadmis@fairfield.edu.
Website: http://fairfield.edu/mba.

Fairleigh Dickinson University, Metropolitan Campus, Silberman College of Business, Departments of Management, Marketing, and Entrepreneurial Studies, Program in Management, Teaneck, NJ 07666-1914. Offers management (MBA); management information systems (Certificate). *Accreditation:* AACSB.

Fairleigh Dickinson University, Metropolitan Campus, University College: Arts, Sciences, and Professional Studies, School of Computer Sciences and Engineering, Program in Management Information Systems, Teaneck, NJ 07666-1914. Offers MS.

Management Information Systems

Ferris State University, College of Business, Big Rapids, MI 49307. Offers business intelligence (MBA); design and innovation management (MBA); incident response (MBA); information security and intelligence (MS), including business intelligence, incident response, project management; management tools and concepts (MBA); project management (MBA). *Accreditation:* ACBSP. Part-time and evening/weekend programs available. Postbaccalaureate distance learning degree programs offered (minimal on-campus study). *Faculty:* 9 full-time (3 women), 6 part-time/adjunct (2 women). *Students:* 30 full-time (9 women), 101 part-time (51 women); includes 18 minority (5 Black or African American, non-Hispanic/Latino; 1 American Indian or Alaska Native, non-Hispanic/Latino; 2 Asian, non-Hispanic/Latino; 6 Hispanic/Latino; 4 Two or more races, non-Hispanic/Latino), 13 international. Average age 34. 72 applicants, 82% accepted, 31 enrolled. In 2013, 47 master's awarded. *Degree requirements:* For master's, comprehensive exam, thesis (for MS). *Entrance requirements:* For master's, GRE or GMAT (waived if GPA is 3.5 or better), minimum GPA of 3.0 in junior/senior level classes, 2.75 overall; statement of purpose; 3 letters of reference; resume. Additional exam requirements/recommendations for international students: Required—TOEFL (minimum score 500 paper-based; 67 iBT). *Application deadline:* For fall admission, 7/1 priority date for domestic students, 6/15 for international students; for winter admission, 11/1 priority date for domestic students, 10/15 for international students; for spring admission, 3/1 priority date for domestic students, 2/15 for international students. Applications are processed on a rolling basis. Application fee: $0 ($30 for international students). Electronic applications accepted. Application fee is waived when completed online. *Financial support:* Career-related internships or fieldwork, Federal Work-Study, scholarships/grants, and unspecified assistantships available. Support available to part-time students. Financial award application deadline: 3/15; financial award applicants required to submit FAFSA. *Faculty research:* Quality improvement, client/server end-user computing, security and digital forensics, performance metrics and sustainability. *Unit head:* Dr. David Nicol, College of Business Dean, 231-591-2168, Fax: 231-591-3521, E-mail: davidnicol@ferris.edu. *Application contact:* Shannon Yost, Department Secretary, 231-591-2168, Fax: 231-591-3521, E-mail: yosts@ferris.edu.
Website: http://cbgp.ferris.edu/.

Florida Agricultural and Mechanical University, Division of Graduate Studies, Research, and Continuing Education, School of Business and Industry, Tallahassee, FL 32307-3200. Offers accounting (MBA); finance (MBA); management information systems (MBA); marketing (MBA). *Accreditation:* ACBSP. *Degree requirements:* For master's, residency. *Entrance requirements:* For master's, GMAT, minimum GPA of 3.0.

Florida Atlantic University, College of Business, Department of Information Technology and Operations Management, Boca Raton, FL 33431-0991. Offers information technology (PhD); information technology management (MS); management information systems (MBA); operations management (MBA). *Faculty:* 12 full-time (4 women). *Students:* 5 full-time (0 women), 18 part-time (6 women); includes 11 minority (5 Black or African American, non-Hispanic/Latino; 1 Asian, non-Hispanic/Latino; 4 Hispanic/Latino; 1 Two or more races, non-Hispanic/Latino), 3 international. Average age 32. 31 applicants, 29% accepted, 6 enrolled. In 2013, 4 master's awarded. *Degree requirements:* For master's, thesis optional. *Entrance requirements:* For master's, GMAT, minimum GPA of 3.0. Additional exam requirements/recommendations for international students: Required—TOEFL (minimum score 600 paper-based; 61 iBT), IELTS (minimum score 6). *Application deadline:* For fall admission, 7/1 priority date for domestic students, 2/15 priority date for international students; for spring admission, 4/1 priority date for domestic students, 1/15 priority date for international students. Applications are processed on a rolling basis. Application fee: $30. Electronic applications accepted. *Expenses:* Tuition, state resident: full-time $6660; part-time $370 per credit hour. Tuition, nonresident: full-time $18,450; part-time $1025 per credit hour. Tuition and fees vary according to course load. *Financial support:* Research assistantships, teaching assistantships, career-related internships or fieldwork, Federal Work-Study, institutionally sponsored loans, tuition waivers (partial), and unspecified assistantships available. Support available to part-time students. Financial award application deadline: 3/1; financial award applicants required to submit FAFSA. *Unit head:* Dr. Tamara Dinev, Chair, 561-297-3675. *Application contact:* Dr. Marcy Krugel, Graduate Adviser, 561-297-3363, Fax: 561-297-1315, E-mail: krugel@fau.edu.
Website: http://business.fau.edu/departments/information-technology-operations-management/index.aspx.

Florida Atlantic University, College of Engineering and Computer Science, Department of Computer and Electrical Engineering and Computer Science, Boca Raton, FL 33431-0991. Offers bioengineering (MS); computer engineering (MS, PhD); computer science (MS, PhD); electrical engineering (MS, PhD); information technology and management (MS). Part-time and evening/weekend programs available. *Faculty:* 28 full-time (4 women), 2 part-time/adjunct (1 woman). *Students:* 98 full-time (31 women), 133 part-time (18 women); includes 97 minority (21 Black or African American, non-Hispanic/Latino; 22 Asian, non-Hispanic/Latino; 51 Hispanic/Latino; 1 Native Hawaiian or other Pacific Islander, non-Hispanic/Latino; 2 Two or more races, non-Hispanic/Latino), 59 international. Average age 34. 151 applicants, 40% accepted, 49 enrolled. In 2013, 54 master's, 7 doctorates awarded. Terminal master's awarded for partial completion of doctoral program. *Degree requirements:* For master's, thesis optional; for doctorate, thesis/dissertation, qualifying exam. *Entrance requirements:* For master's, GRE General Test, minimum GPA of 3.0; for doctorate, GRE General Test, master's degree, minimum GPA of 3.5. Additional exam requirements/recommendations for international students: Required—TOEFL (minimum score 500 paper-based; 61 iBT), IELTS (minimum score 6). *Application deadline:* For fall admission, 7/1 priority date for domestic students, 2/15 for international students; for spring admission, 11/1 for domestic students, 7/15 for international students. Applications are processed on a rolling basis. Application fee: $30. *Expenses:* Tuition, state resident: full-time $6660; part-time $370 per credit hour. Tuition, nonresident: full-time $18,450; part-time $1025 per credit hour. Tuition and fees vary according to course load. *Financial support:* Fellowships, research assistantships with partial tuition reimbursements, teaching assistantships with full tuition reimbursements, career-related internships or fieldwork, and Federal Work-Study available. Support available to part-time students. Financial award application deadline: 4/1; financial award applicants required to submit FAFSA. *Faculty research:* VLSI and neural networks, communication networks, software engineering, computer architecture, multimedia and video processing. *Unit head:* Dr. Borko Furht, Chairman, 561-297-3855, Fax: 561-297-2800. *Application contact:* Joanna Arlington, Manager, Graduate Admissions, 561-297-2428, Fax: 561-297-2117, E-mail: arlingto@fau.edu.
Website: http://www.ceecs.fau.edu/.

Florida Institute of Technology, Graduate Programs, College of Engineering, Computer Science and Cybersecurity Department, Melbourne, FL 32901-6975. Offers computer information systems (MS); computer science (MS, PhD); information assurance and cybersecurity (MS); software engineering (MS). Part-time and evening/weekend programs available. *Faculty:* 17 full-time (2 women), 8 part-time/adjunct (1 woman). *Students:* 115 full-time (26 women), 96 part-time (21 women); includes 19 minority (7 Black or African American, non-Hispanic/Latino; 2 Asian, non-Hispanic/Latino; 9 Hispanic/Latino; 1 Two or more races, non-Hispanic/Latino), 137 international. Average age 29. 502 applicants, 59% accepted, 65 enrolled. In 2013, 42 master's, 1 doctorate awarded. *Degree requirements:* For master's, comprehensive exam (for some programs), thesis optional, final exam, seminar, or internship (for non-thesis option); for doctorate, comprehensive exam, thesis/dissertation, publication in journal, teaching experience (strongly encouraged), specialized research program. *Entrance requirements:* For master's, GRE General Test, minimum GPA of 3.0, 3 letters of recommendation; for doctorate, GRE General Test, GRE Subject Test in computer science (recommended), 3 letters of recommendation, minimum GPA of 3.5, resume, statement of objectives. Additional exam requirements/recommendations for international students: Required—TOEFL (minimum score 550 paper-based; 79 iBT). *Application deadline:* For fall admission, 4/1 for international students; for spring admission, 9/30 for international students. Applications are processed on a rolling basis. Electronic applications accepted. *Expenses:* Tuition: Full-time $20,214; part-time $1123 per credit. Tuition and fees vary according to campus/location. *Financial support:* In 2013–14, 4 research assistantships with full and partial tuition reimbursements (averaging $9,900 per year), 12 teaching assistantships with full and partial tuition reimbursements (averaging $13,313 per year) were awarded; career-related internships or fieldwork, institutionally sponsored loans, tuition waivers (partial), unspecified assistantships, and tuition remissions also available. Support available to part-time students. Financial award application deadline: 3/1; financial award applicants required to submit FAFSA. *Faculty research:* Artificial intelligence, software engineering, management and processes, programming languages, database systems. *Total annual research expenditures:* $1.1 million. *Unit head:* Dr. Richard Ford, Department Head, 321-674-8763, Fax: 321-674-7046, E-mail: rford@fit.edu. *Application contact:* Cheryl A. Brown, Associate Director of Graduate Admissions, 321-674-7581, Fax: 321-723-9468, E-mail: cbrown@fit.edu.
Website: http://coe.fit.edu/cs.

Florida Institute of Technology, Graduate Programs, Extended Studies Division, Melbourne, FL 32901-6975. Offers acquisition and contract management (MS); aerospace engineering (MS); business administration (MBA, DBA); computer information systems (MS); computer science (MS); electrical engineering (MS); engineering management (MS); human resources management (MS); logistics management (MS), including humanitarian and disaster relief logistics; management (MS), including acquisition and contract management, e-business, human resources management, information systems, logistics management, management, transportation management; material acquisition management (MS); mechanical engineering (MS); operations research (MS); project management (MS), including information systems, operations research; public administration (MPA); quality management (MS); software engineering (MS); space systems (MS); space systems management (MS); supply chain management (MS); systems management (MS), including information systems, operations research; technology management (MS). Part-time and evening/weekend programs available. Postbaccalaureate distance learning degree programs offered (no on-campus study). *Faculty:* 8 full-time (1 woman), 96 part-time/adjunct (25 women). *Students:* 94 full-time (46 women), 912 part-time (397 women); includes 436 minority (290 Black or African American, non-Hispanic/Latino; 18 American Indian or Alaska Native, non-Hispanic/Latino; 38 Asian, non-Hispanic/Latino; 62 Hispanic/Latino; 2 Native Hawaiian or other Pacific Islander, non-Hispanic/Latino; 26 Two or more races, non-Hispanic/Latino), 9 international. Average age 37. 591 applicants, 44% accepted, 220 enrolled. In 2013, 522 master's awarded. *Degree requirements:* For master's, comprehensive exam (for some programs), capstone course. *Entrance requirements:* For master's, GMAT or resume showing 8 years of supervised experience, minimum GPA of 3.0, 2 letters of recommendation, resume. Additional exam requirements/recommendations for international students: Required—TOEFL (minimum score 550 paper-based; 79 iBT). *Application deadline:* For fall admission, 4/1 for international students; for spring admission, 9/30 for international students. Applications are processed on a rolling basis. Electronic applications accepted. *Expenses:* Contact institution. *Financial support:* Application deadline: 3/1; applicants required to submit FAFSA. *Unit head:* Dr. Theodore R. Richardson, III, Senior Associate Dean, 321-674-8123, Fax: 321-674-7597, E-mail: trichardson@fit.edu. *Application contact:* Carolyn Farrior, Director of Graduate Admissions, Online Learning and Off-Campus Programs, 321-674-7118, Fax: 321-674-8216, E-mail: cfarrior@fit.edu.
Website: http://es.fit.edu.

Florida Institute of Technology, Graduate Programs, Nathan M. Bisk College of Business, Online Programs, Melbourne, FL 32901-6975. Offers accounting (MBA); accounting and finance (MBA); business administration (MBA); finance (MBA); healthcare management (MBA); information assurance and cybersecurity (MS); information technology (MS); information technology cybersecurity (MS); information technology management (MBA); international business (MBA); Internet marketing (MBA); management (MBA); marketing (MBA); project management (MBA); supply chain management (MS). Part-time and evening/weekend programs available. Postbaccalaureate distance learning degree programs offered (no on-campus study). *Faculty:* 3 full-time (1 woman), 41 part-time/adjunct (13 women). *Students:* 6 full-time (1 woman), 1,121 part-time (530 women); includes 424 minority (276 Black or African American, non-Hispanic/Latino; 10 American Indian or Alaska Native, non-Hispanic/Latino; 45 Asian, non-Hispanic/Latino; 88 Hispanic/Latino; 5 Native Hawaiian or other Pacific Islander, non-Hispanic/Latino), 32 international. Average age 36. 348 applicants, 42% accepted, 146 enrolled. In 2013, 475 master's awarded. *Entrance requirements:* For master's, GMAT or resume showing 8 years of supervised experience, 2 letters of recommendation, resume, competency in math past college algebra. Additional exam requirements/recommendations for international students: Required—TOEFL (minimum score 550 paper-based; 79 iBT). *Application deadline:* For fall admission, 4/1 for international students; for spring admission, 9/30 for international students. Applications are processed on a rolling basis. Electronic applications accepted. *Expenses:* Contact institution. *Financial support:* Available to part-time students. Application deadline: 3/1; applicants required to submit FAFSA. *Unit head:* Brian Ehrlich, Associate Vice President/Director of Online Learning, 321-674-8202, E-mail: behrlich@fit.edu. *Application contact:* Carolyn Farrior, Director of Graduate Admissions, Online Learning and Off-Campus Programs, 321-674-7118.
Website: http://online.fit.edu.

Florida International University, Alvah H. Chapman, Jr. Graduate School of Business, Department of Decision Sciences and Information Systems, Miami, FL 33199. Offers MSMIS, PhD. Part-time and evening/weekend programs available. *Entrance requirements:* For master's, GMAT or GRE, minimum GPA of 3.0 (upper-level coursework); letter of intent; resume. Additional exam requirements/recommendations for international students: Required—TOEFL (minimum score 550 paper-based; 80 iBT) or IELTS. Electronic applications accepted. *Expenses:* Contact institution. *Faculty research:* Artificial intelligence, data warehouses, operations management.

Florida International University, College of Engineering and Computing, School of Computing and Information Sciences, Miami, FL 33199. Offers computer science (MS, PhD); information technology (MS); telecommunications and networking (MS). Part-time and evening/weekend programs available. *Degree requirements:* For master's, thesis or alternative; for doctorate, comprehensive exam, thesis/dissertation. *Entrance requirements:* For master's and doctorate, GRE General Test, 3 letters of recommendation, minimum GPA of 3.0. Additional exam requirements/recommendations for international students: Required—TOEFL (minimum score 550

paper-based; 80 iBT). Electronic applications accepted. *Faculty research:* Database systems, software engineering, operating systems, networks, bioinformatics and computational biology.

Florida State University, The Graduate School, College of Business, Tallahassee, FL 32306-1110. Offers accounting (M Acc), including accounting information services, assurance services, corporate accounting, taxation; business administration (MBA, PhD), including accounting (PhD), finance (PhD), management information systems (PhD), marketing (PhD), organizational behavior and human resources (PhD), risk management and insurance (PhD), strategic management (PhD); finance (MS); insurance (MSM); management information systems (MS); marketing (MS); JD/MBA; MSW/MBA. *Accreditation:* AACSB. Part-time programs available. Postbaccalaureate distance learning degree programs offered (no on-campus study). *Faculty:* 102 full-time (31 women), 5 part-time/adjunct (0 women). *Students:* 280 full-time (117 women), 278 part-time (88 women); includes 127 minority (26 Black or African American, non-Hispanic/Latino; 7 American Indian or Alaska Native, non-Hispanic/Latino; 44 Asian, non-Hispanic/Latino; 50 Hispanic/Latino). Average age 30. 630 applicants, 28% accepted, 103 enrolled. In 2013, 265 master's, 11 doctorates awarded. Terminal master's awarded for partial completion of doctoral program. *Degree requirements:* For doctorate, comprehensive exam, thesis/dissertation. *Entrance requirements:* For master's, GMAT, work experience (MBA, MS), minimum GPA of 3.0, letters of recommendation; for doctorate, GMAT, minimum graduate GPA of 3.5, letters of recommendation. Additional exam requirements/recommendations for international students: Required—TOEFL (minimum score 600 paper-based; 100 iBT); Recommended—IELTS (minimum score 6.5). *Application deadline:* For fall admission, 6/1 for domestic students, 5/1 for international students; for spring admission, 10/1 for domestic students, 9/1 for international students. Applications are processed on a rolling basis. Application fee: $30. Electronic applications accepted. *Expenses:* Tuition, state resident: part-time $403.51 per credit hour. Tuition, nonresident: part-time $1004.85 per credit hour. *Required fees:* $75.81 per credit hour. One-time fee: $20 part-time. Tuition and fees vary according to course load, campus/location and student level. *Financial support:* In 2013–14, 92 students received support, including 10 fellowships with full tuition reimbursements available (averaging $1,500 per year), 20 research assistantships with full tuition reimbursements available (averaging $20,000 per year), 35 teaching assistantships with full tuition reimbursements available (averaging $20,000 per year); career-related internships or fieldwork, scholarships/grants, health care benefits, and unspecified assistantships also available. Financial award application deadline: 1/1. *Unit head:* Dr. Caryn Beck-Dudley, Dean, 850-644-3090, Fax: 850-644-0915. *Application contact:* Lisa Beverly, Director, Graduate Programs Admissions, 850-644-6458, Fax: 850-644-0588, E-mail: lbeverly@cob.fsu.edu. Website: http://www.cob.fsu.edu/.

Florida State University, The Graduate School, College of Communication and Information, School of Information, Tallahassee, FL 32306-2100. Offers general information studies (MA); information studies (Specialist); information technology (MS); library and information studies (PhD). *Accreditation:* ALA (one or more programs are accredited). Part-time and evening/weekend programs available. Postbaccalaureate distance learning degree programs offered (no on-campus study). *Faculty:* 31 full-time (18 women), 11 part-time/adjunct (5 women). *Students:* 108 full-time (82 women), 305 part-time (230 women); includes 99 minority (36 Black or African American, non-Hispanic/Latino; 20 Asian, non-Hispanic/Latino; 34 Hispanic/Latino; 9 Two or more races, non-Hispanic/Latino). Average age 35. 195 applicants, 78% accepted, 103 enrolled. In 2013, 166 master's, 4 doctorates, 4 other advanced degrees awarded. Terminal master's awarded for partial completion of doctoral program. *Degree requirements:* For master's, thesis optional, minimum GPA of 3.0, 36 hours (MSLIS); 32 hours (MSIT); for doctorate, comprehensive exam, thesis/dissertation, dissertation defense, manuscript clearance, minimum GPA of 3.0; for Specialist, minimum GPA of 3.0; 30 hours. *Entrance requirements:* For master's, GRE (recommended minimum percentile of 50 on each of the verbal and quantitative portions and writing score of 4.0), minimum GPA of 3.0 on last 2 years of baccalaureate degree, resume, statement of goals, two letters of recommendation, official transcripts from every college-level institution attended; for doctorate, GRE (recommended minimum percentile of 50 on each of the verbal and quantitative portions and writing score of 4.0), minimum GPA of 3.0 on last degree program, resume, 3 letters of recommendation, personal/goals statement, writing sample, brief digital video, official transcripts from all college-level institutions attended; for Specialist, GRE (recommended minimum percentile of 50 on each of the verbal and quantitative portions and writing score of 4.0), minimum graduate GPA of 3.2, resume, statement of goals, 2 letters of recommendation, writing sample, official transcripts from every college-level institution attended. Additional exam requirements/recommendations for international students: Required—TOEFL (minimum score 585 paper-based; 94 iBT), IELTS (minimum score 6.5). *Application deadline:* For fall admission, 7/1 for domestic and international students; for spring admission, 11/1 for domestic and international students. Applications are processed on a rolling basis. Application fee: $30. Electronic applications accepted. *Expenses:* Contact institution. *Financial support:* In 2013–14, 54 students received support, including 7 fellowships with full tuition reimbursements available (averaging $16,000 per year), 24 research assistantships with full tuition reimbursements available (averaging $16,000 per year), 23 teaching assistantships with full tuition reimbursements available (averaging $16,000 per year); career-related internships or fieldwork, Federal Work-Study, scholarships/grants, health care benefits, tuition waivers, and unspecified assistantships also available. Financial award application deadline: 3/1; financial award applicants required to submit FAFSA. *Faculty research:* Needs assessment, social informatics, usability analysis, human information behavior, youth services. *Total annual research expenditures:* $2 million. *Unit head:* Dr. Kathleen Burnett, Interim Director and Professor, 850-644-8124, Fax: 850-644-9763, E-mail: kathleen.burnett@cci.fsu.edu. *Application contact:* Graduate Student Services, 850-645-3280, Fax: 850-644-9763, E-mail: slisgradadmissions@admin.fsu.edu. Website: http://slis.fsu.edu/.

Fordham University, Graduate School of Business, New York, NY 10023. Offers accounting (MBA); communications and media management (MBA); executive business administration (EMBA); finance (MBA, MS); information systems (MBA, MS); management systems (MBA); marketing (MBA); media management (MS); taxation (MS); taxation and accounting (MTA); JD/MBA; MBA/MIM; MS/MBA. MBA/MIM offered jointly with Thunderbird School of Global Management. *Accreditation:* AACSB. Part-time and evening/weekend programs available. *Entrance requirements:* For master's, GMAT, 2 letters of recommendation, resume. Additional exam requirements/recommendations for international students: Required—TOEFL (minimum score 600 paper-based; 100 iBT). Electronic applications accepted. *Expenses:* Contact institution.

Franklin Pierce University, Graduate Studies, Rindge, NH 03461-0060. Offers curriculum and instruction (M Ed); emerging network technologies (Graduate Certificate); energy and sustainability studies (MBA); health administration (MBA, Graduate Certificate); human resource management (MBA, Graduate Certificate); information technology (MBA); information technology management (MS); leadership (MBA, DA); nursing (MS); physical therapy (DPT); physician assistant studies (MPAS); special education (M Ed); sports management (MBA). *Accreditation:* APTA. Part-time programs available. Postbaccalaureate distance learning degree programs offered (no

on-campus study). *Degree requirements:* For master's, concentrated original research projects; student teaching; fieldwork and/or internship; leadership project; PRAXIS I and II (for M Ed); for doctorate, concentrated original research projects, clinical fieldwork and/or internship, leadership project. *Entrance requirements:* For master's, minimum GPA of 2.5, 3 letters of recommendation; competencies in accounting, economics, statistics, and computer skills through life experience or undergraduate coursework (for MBA); certification/e-portfolio, minimum C grade in all education courses (for M Ed); license to practice as RN (for MS in nursing); for doctorate, GRE, BA/BS, 3 letters of recommendation, personal mission statement, interview, writing sample, minimum cumulative GPA of 2.8, master's degree (for DA); 80 hours of observation/work in PT settings, completion of anatomy, chemistry, physics, and statistics, minimum GPA of 3.0 (for DPT). Additional exam requirements/recommendations for international students: Required—TOEFL (minimum score 550 paper-based; 61 iBT). Electronic applications accepted. *Faculty research:* Evidence-based practice in sports physical therapy, human resource management in economic crisis, leadership in nursing, innovation in sports facility management, differentiated learning and understanding by design.

Friends University, Graduate School, Wichita, KS 67213. Offers business law (MBL); Christian ministry (MACM); family therapy (MSFT); global (MBA), including accounting, business law, change management, health care leadership, management information systems, supply chain management and logistics; health care leadership (MHCL); management information systems (MMIS); operations management (MSOM); professional (MBA), including accounting, business law, change management, health care leadership, management information systems, supply chain management and logistics; teaching (MAT). Part-time and evening/weekend programs available. Postbaccalaureate distance learning degree programs offered (no on-campus study). *Faculty:* 18 full-time (8 women), 62 part-time/adjunct (28 women). *Students:* 161 full-time (111 women), 408 part-time (258 women); includes 157 minority (68 Black or African American, non-Hispanic/Latino; 7 American Indian or Alaska Native, non-Hispanic/Latino; 28 Asian, non-Hispanic/Latino; 18 Hispanic/Latino; 1 Native Hawaiian or other Pacific Islander, non-Hispanic/Latino; 35 Two or more races, non-Hispanic/Latino). Average age 36. 371 applicants, 90% accepted, 178 enrolled. In 2013, 432 master's awarded. *Degree requirements:* For master's, research project. *Entrance requirements:* For master's, bachelor's degree from accredited institution, official transcripts, interview with program director, letter(s) of recommendation. Additional exam requirements/recommendations for international students: Required—TOEFL (minimum score 560 paper-based). *Application deadline:* Applications are processed on a rolling basis. Application fee: $35 ($50 for international students). Electronic applications accepted. *Expenses: Tuition:* Part-time $631 per credit hour. Tuition and fees vary according to program. *Financial support:* In 2013–14, 30 students received support. Applicants required to submit FAFSA. *Unit head:* Dr. David Hofmeister, Dean of the Graduate School, 800-794-6945 Ext. 5858, Fax: 316-295-5040, E-mail: david_hofmeister@friends.edu. *Application contact:* Rachel Steiner, Manager, Graduate Recruiting Services, 800-794-6945, Fax: 316-295-5872, E-mail: rachel_steiner@friends.edu. Website: http://www.friends.edu/.

George Mason University, School of Business, Fairfax, VA 22030. Offers accounting (MS, Certificate), including accounting (MS), forensic accounting (Certificate); business administration (EMBA, MBA); management of secure information systems (MS); real estate development (MS); technology management (MS). Part-time and evening/weekend programs available. Postbaccalaureate distance learning degree programs offered. *Faculty:* 82 full-time (24 women), 55 part-time/adjunct (18 women). *Students:* 275 full-time (95 women), 267 part-time (94 women); includes 140 minority (42 Black or African American, non-Hispanic/Latino; 2 American Indian or Alaska Native, non-Hispanic/Latino; 53 Asian, non-Hispanic/Latino; 31 Hispanic/Latino; 3 Native Hawaiian or other Pacific Islander, non-Hispanic/Latino; 9 Two or more races, non-Hispanic/Latino); 43 international. Average age 32. 492 applicants, 48% accepted, 134 enrolled. In 2013, 243 master's awarded. *Entrance requirements:* For master's, GMAT. Additional exam requirements/recommendations for international students: Required—TOEFL (minimum score 570 paper-based; 88 iBT), IELTS (minimum score 6.5), PTE. *Application deadline:* Applications are processed on a rolling basis. Application fee: $65 ($80 for international students). Electronic applications accepted. *Expenses:* Contact institution. *Financial support:* In 2013–14, 28 students received support, including 22 research assistantships with full and partial tuition reimbursements available (averaging $7,075 per year), 12 teaching assistantships with full and partial tuition reimbursements available (averaging $8,411 per year); career-related internships or fieldwork, Federal Work-Study, scholarships/grants, unspecified assistantships, and health care benefits (for full-time research or teaching assistantship recipients) also available. Support available to part-time students. Financial award application deadline: 3/1; financial award applicants required to submit FAFSA. *Faculty research:* Current leading global issues: offshore outsourcing, international financial risk, comparative systems of innovation. *Total annual research expenditures:* $73,719. *Unit head:* Sarah E. Nutter, Dean, 703-993-1860, Fax: 703-993-1809, E-mail: snutter@gmu.edu. *Application contact:* Nancy Doernhoefer, Admissions Specialist, 703-993-4128, Fax: 703-993-1778, E-mail: ndoernho@gmu.edu. Website: http://business.gmu.edu/.

George Mason University, Volgenau School of Engineering, Department of Computer Science, Fairfax, VA 22030. Offers computer networking (Certificate); computer science (MS, PhD); e-commerce (Certificate); foundations of information systems (Certificate); information engineering (Certificate); information security and assurance (MS, Certificate); information systems (MS); software architecture (Certificate); software engineering (MS, Certificate); software engineering for C41 (Certificate); Web-based software engineering (Certificate). MS program offered jointly with Old Dominion University, University of Virginia, Virginia Commonwealth University, and Virginia Polytechnic Institute and State University. *Faculty:* 46 full-time (10 women), 13 part-time/adjunct (0 women). *Students:* 230 full-time (63 women), 303 part-time (57 women); includes 100 minority (15 Black or African American, non-Hispanic/Latino; 66 Asian, non-Hispanic/Latino; 14 Hispanic/Latino; 5 Two or more races, non-Hispanic/Latino); 215 international. Average age 30. 977 applicants, 49% accepted, 152 enrolled. In 2013, 183 master's, 8 doctorates, 26 other advanced degrees awarded. *Degree requirements:* For master's, thesis optional; for doctorate, comprehensive exam, thesis/dissertation. *Entrance requirements:* For master's, GRE, proof of financial support; 2 official college transcripts; resume; self-evaluation form; official bank statement; photocopy of passport; 3 letters of recommendation; baccalaureate degree related to computer science; minimum GPA of 3.0 in last 2 years of undergraduate work; 1 year beyond 1st-year calculus; personal goals statement; for doctorate, GRE, personal goals statement; 2 official copies of transcripts; self-evaluation form; 3 letters of recommendation; photocopy of passport; proof of financial support; official bank statement; resume; 4-year baccalaureate degree with strong background in computer science. Additional exam requirements/recommendations for international students: Required—TOEFL (minimum score 575 paper-based; 88 iBT), IELTS (minimum score 6.5), PTE. *Application deadline:* For fall admission, 1/15 priority date for domestic students; for spring admission, 8/15 priority date for domestic students. Application fee: $65 ($80 for international students). Electronic applications accepted. *Expenses:* Contact institution. *Financial support:* In 2013–14, 109 students received support, including 3 fellowships (averaging $5,267 per year), 53 research assistantships (averaging $16,866 per year), 56 teaching

Management Information Systems

assistantships (averaging $13,625 per year); career-related internships or fieldwork, Federal Work-Study, scholarships/grants, unspecified assistantships, and health care benefits (for full-time research or teaching assistantship recipients) also available. Support available to part-time students. Financial award application deadline: 3/1; financial award applicants required to submit FAFSA. *Faculty research:* Artificial intelligence, image processing/graphics, parallel/distributed systems, software engineering systems. *Total annual research expenditures:* $2.8 million. *Unit head:* Sanjeev Setia, Chair, 703-993-4098, Fax: 703-993-1710, E-mail: setia@gmu.edu. *Application contact:* Michele Pieper, Office Manager, 703-993-9483, Fax: 703-993-1710, E-mail: mpieper@gmu.edu.
Website: http://cs.gmu.edu/.

The George Washington University, School of Business, Department of Information Systems and Technology Management, Washington, DC 20052. Offers information and decision systems (PhD); information systems (MSIST); information systems development (MSIST); information systems management (MBA); information systems project management (MSIST); management information systems (MSIST); management of science, technology, and innovation (MBA, PhD). Programs also offered in Ashburn and Arlington, VA. Part-time and evening/weekend programs available. Postbaccalaureate distance learning degree programs offered (no on-campus study). *Faculty:* 9 full-time (2 women). *Students:* 115 full-time (44 women), 105 part-time (40 women); includes 61 minority (26 Black or African American, non-Hispanic/Latino; 22 Asian, non-Hispanic/Latino; 10 Hispanic/Latino; 3 Two or more races, non-Hispanic/Latino), 86 international. Average age 31. 363 applicants, 70% accepted, 94 enrolled. In 2013, 114 degrees awarded. *Entrance requirements:* For master's, GMAT. Additional exam requirements/recommendations for international students: Required—TOEFL. *Application deadline:* For fall admission, 4/1 priority date for domestic students; for spring admission, 10/1 for domestic students. Applications are processed on a rolling basis. Application fee: $75. *Financial support:* In 2013–14, 35 students received support. Fellowships, teaching assistantships, career-related internships or fieldwork, Federal Work-Study, institutionally sponsored loans, and tuition waivers available. Financial award application deadline: 4/1. *Faculty research:* Expert systems, decision support systems. *Unit head:* Subhasish Dasgupta, Chair, 202-994-7408, E-mail: dasgupta@gwu.edu. *Application contact:* Kristin Williams, Assistant Vice President for Graduate and Special Enrollment Management, 202-994-0467, Fax: 202-994-0371, E-mail: ksw@gwu.edu.

Georgia College & State University, Graduate School, The J. Whitney Bunting School of Business, Program in Management Information Systems, Milledgeville, GA 31061. Offers MMIS. Part-time programs available. *Students:* 3 full-time (2 women), 10 part-time (3 women); includes 4 minority (all Black or African American, non-Hispanic/Latino), 1 international. Average age 30. In 2013, 10 master's awarded. *Degree requirements:* For master's, minimum GPA of 3.0, complete program within 7 years of start date. *Entrance requirements:* For master's, GRE or GMAT. Additional exam requirements/recommendations for international students: Recommended—TOEFL (minimum score 500 paper-based; 61 iBT), IELTS (minimum score 6). *Application deadline:* For fall admission, 7/1 for domestic students; for spring admission, 11/14 for domestic students; for summer admission, 4/1 for domestic students. Applications are processed on a rolling basis. Application fee: $35. Electronic applications accepted. *Financial support:* Unspecified assistantships available. *Unit head:* Dr. Dale Young, Interim Dean, 478-445-5497, E-mail: dale.young@gcsu.edu. *Application contact:* Lynn Hanson, Director of Graduate Programs, 478-445-5115, E-mail: lynn.hanson@gcsu.edu.
Website: http://www.gcsu.edu/business/graduateprograms/mmis.htm.

Georgia Institute of Technology, Graduate Studies and Research, College of Management, Program in Business Administration, Atlanta, GA 30332-0001. Offers accounting (MBA); e-commerce (Certificate); engineering entrepreneurship (MBA); entrepreneurship (Certificate); finance (MBA); information technology management (MBA); international business (MBA, Certificate); management of technology (Certificate); marketing (MBA); operations management (MBA); organizational behavior (MBA); strategic management (MBA). *Accreditation:* AACSB.

Georgia Institute of Technology, Graduate Studies and Research, College of Management, Program in Management, Atlanta, GA 30332-0001. Offers accounting (PhD); finance (PhD); information technology management (PhD); marketing (PhD); operations management (PhD); organizational behavior (PhD); quantitative and computational finance (MS); strategic management (PhD). *Accreditation:* AACSB. *Degree requirements:* For doctorate, comprehensive exam, thesis/dissertation, oral exams. *Entrance requirements:* For master's and doctorate, GMAT. Additional exam requirements/recommendations for international students: Required—TOEFL. *Faculty research:* Management information systems, management of technology, international business, entrepreneurship, operations management.

Georgia Southern University, Jack N. Averitt College of Graduate Studies, Allen E. Paulson College of Engineering and Information Technology, Department of Information Technology, Statesboro, GA 30460. Offers MSAE. *Students:* 5 full-time (1 woman), 6 part-time (2 women); includes 3 minority (2 Black or African American, non-Hispanic/Latino; 1 Hispanic/Latino), 2 international. Average age 30. 2 applicants, 50% accepted, 1 enrolled. In 2013, 4 master's awarded. *Expenses:* Tuition, state resident: full-time $7068; part-time $270 per semester hour. Tuition, nonresident: full-time $26,446; part-time $1077 per semester hour. *Required fees:* $2092. *Financial support:* In 2013–14, 2 students received support. *Faculty research:* Big data, business intelligence, network security/disaster recovery, server/storage consolidation and virtualization, information systems and security. *Total annual research expenditures:* $22,323. *Unit head:* Art Gowan, Chair, 912-478-7679, E-mail: artgowan@georgiasouthern.edu. *Application contact:* Amanda Gilliland, Coordinator of Graduate Student Recruitment, 912-478-5384, Fax: 912-478-0740, E-mail: gradadmissions@georgiasouthern.edu.
Website: http://ceit.georgiasouthern.edu/it/.

Georgia Southern University, Jack N. Averitt College of Graduate Studies, College of Business Administration, Enterprise Resources Planning Certificate Program, Statesboro, GA 30460. Offers Graduate Certificate. Postbaccalaureate distance learning degree programs offered. *Students:* 19 part-time (10 women); includes 12 minority (8 Black or African American, non-Hispanic/Latino; 3 Asian, non-Hispanic/Latino; 1 Hispanic/Latino), 2 international. Average age 41. 29 applicants, 83% accepted, 15 enrolled. *Entrance requirements:* For degree, bachelor's degree or equivalent with minimum cumulative GPA of 2.7; official copies of all transcripts; resume with three references; personal statement. Additional exam requirements/recommendations for international students: Required—IELTS (minimum score 6). Application fee: $50. *Expenses:* Tuition, state resident: full-time $7068; part-time $270 per semester hour. Tuition, nonresident: full-time $26,446; part-time $1077 per semester hour. *Required fees:* $2092. *Faculty research:* Enterprise resource planning (ERP) and business intelligence (BI) synergies, cloud-based and on-demand ERP solutions, IT artifact in ERP-centered supply chain information systems, impact of bring your own device (BYOD) policies on deployment of enterprise systems mobile applications, career readiness of SAP University Alliances students for positions in ERP user and consulting firms. *Unit head:* Dr. Camille Rogers, Program Coordinator, 912-478-0194, E-mail: cfrogers@georgiasouthern.edu. *Application contact:* Amanda Gilliland, Coordinator for Graduate Student Recruitment, 912-478-5384, Fax: 912-478-0740, E-mail: gradadmissions@georgiasouthern.edu.
Website: http://cit.georgiasouthern.edu/is/erp-certificate.html.

Georgia State University, J. Mack Robinson College of Business, Department of Computer Information Systems, Atlanta, GA 30302-3083. Offers computer information systems (PhD); health informatics (MBA, MS); information systems (MSIS, Certificate); information systems development and project management (MBA); information systems management (MBA); managing information technology (Exec MS); the wireless organization (MBA). Part-time and evening/weekend programs available. *Faculty:* 15 full-time (2 women). *Students:* 91 full-time (32 women), 13 part-time (7 women); includes 36 minority (17 Black or African American, non-Hispanic/Latino; 17 Asian, non-Hispanic/Latino; 2 Two or more races, non-Hispanic/Latino), 38 international. Average age 32. 299 applicants, 49% accepted, 65 enrolled. In 2013, 62 master's, 3 doctorates awarded. *Degree requirements:* For master's, thesis optional; for doctorate, comprehensive exam, thesis/dissertation. *Entrance requirements:* For master's, GRE or GMAT, transcripts from all institutions attended, resume, essays; for doctorate, GRE or GMAT, three letters of recommendation, personal statement, transcripts from all institutions attended, resume. Additional exam requirements/recommendations for international students: Required—TOEFL (minimum score 610 paper-based; 101 iBT), IELTS (minimum score 7). *Application deadline:* For fall admission, 5/1 priority date for domestic students, 2/1 priority date for international students; for spring admission, 9/15 priority date for domestic students, 4/1 priority date for international students. Applications are processed on a rolling basis. Application fee: $50. Electronic applications accepted. *Expenses: Tuition, area resident:* Full-time $4176; part-time $348 per credit hour. Tuition, state resident: full-time $14,544; part-time $1212 per credit hour. Tuition, nonresident: full-time $14,544; part-time $1212 per credit hour. Tuition and fees vary according to course load and program. *Financial support:* Research assistantships, teaching assistantships, scholarships/grants, tuition waivers, and unspecified assistantships available. *Faculty research:* Process and technological innovation, strategic IT management, intelligent systems, information systems security, software project risk. *Unit head:* Dr. Ephraim R. McLean, Professor/Chair, 404-413-7360, Fax: 404-413-7394. *Application contact:* Toby McChesney, Assistant Dean for Graduate Recruiting and Student Services, 404-413-7167, Fax: 404-413-7167, E-mail: rcbgradadmissions@gsu.edu.
Website: http://cis.robinson.gsu.edu/.

Georgia State University, J. Mack Robinson College of Business, Institute of International Business, Atlanta, GA 30303. Offers international business (GMBA, MBA, MIB); international business and information technology (MBA); international entrepreneurship (MBA); MIB/MIA. Part-time and evening/weekend programs available. *Faculty:* 7 full-time (3 women). *Students:* 41 full-time (29 women), 22 part-time (13 women); includes 26 minority (14 Black or African American, non-Hispanic/Latino; 1 Asian, non-Hispanic/Latino; 11 Hispanic/Latino), 15 international. Average age 32. 60 applicants, 52% accepted, 21 enrolled. In 2013, 25 master's awarded. *Entrance requirements:* For master's, GRE or GMAT, transcripts from all institutions attended, resume, essays. Additional exam requirements/recommendations for international students: Required—TOEFL (minimum score 610 paper-based; 101 iBT), IELTS (minimum score 7). *Application deadline:* For fall admission, 5/1 priority date for domestic students, 2/1 priority date for international students; for spring admission, 9/15 priority date for domestic students, 5/1 priority date for international students. Applications are processed on a rolling basis. Application fee: $50. Electronic applications accepted. *Expenses: Tuition, area resident:* Full-time $4176; part-time $348 per credit hour. Tuition, state resident: full-time $14,544; part-time $1212 per credit hour. Tuition, nonresident: full-time $14,544; part-time $1212 per credit hour. Tuition and fees vary according to course load and program. *Financial support:* Research assistantships, teaching assistantships, scholarships/grants, tuition waivers (partial), and unspecified assistantships available. Financial award application deadline: 5/1. *Faculty research:* Business challenges in emerging markets (especially in India and China); interorganizational relationships in an international context, such as strategic alliances and global supply chain relations; globalization and entry mode strategy or new (or emerging) multinationals; emerging market development and business environments; cross-cultural effects on business processes and performance. *Unit head:* Dr. Daniel Bello, Professor/Director of the Institute of International Business, 404-413-7275, Fax: 404-413-7276. *Application contact:* Toby McChesney, Assistant Dean for Graduate Recruiting and Student Services, 404-413-7167, Fax: 404-413-7162, E-mail: rcbgradadmissions@gsu.edu.
Website: http://iib.gsu.edu/.

Globe University–Woodbury, Minnesota School of Business, Woodbury, MN 55125. Offers business administration (MBA); health care management (MSM); information technology (MSM); managerial leadership (MSM).

Golden Gate University, Ageno School of Business, San Francisco, CA 94105-2968. Offers accounting (MBA); business administration (EMBA, MBA, PMBA, DBA); finance (MBA, MS, Certificate); financial planning (MS, Certificate); healthcare information systems (Certificate); human resource management (MBA, MS); human resources management (Certificate); information systems (MS); information technology (MBA); information technology management (Certificate); integrated marketing and communications (MS, Certificate); international business (MBA); management (MBA); marketing (MBA, MS, Certificate); operations supply chain management (Certificate); psychology (MA, Certificate); public administration (EMPA); public relations (MS, Certificate); technical market analysis (Certificate); JD/MBA. Part-time and evening/weekend programs available. *Degree requirements:* For doctorate, thesis/dissertation, qualifying examination. *Entrance requirements:* For master's, GMAT (MBA), minimum GPA of 2.5 (MS). Additional exam requirements/recommendations for international students: Required—TOEFL (minimum score 550 paper-based; 79 iBT). Electronic applications accepted. *Expenses:* Contact institution.

Goldey-Beacom College, Graduate Program, Wilmington, DE 19808-1999. Offers business administration (MBA); finance (MS); financial management (MBA); health care management (MBA); human resource management (MBA); information technology (MBA); international business management (MBA); major finance (MBA); major taxation (MBA); management (MM); marketing management (MBA); taxation (MBA, MS). *Accreditation:* ACBSP. Part-time and evening/weekend programs available. *Entrance requirements:* For master's, GMAT, MAT, GRE, minimum GPA of 3.0. Additional exam requirements/recommendations for international students: Required—TOEFL (minimum score 65 iBT); Recommended—IELTS (minimum score 6). Electronic applications accepted.

Governors State University, College of Business and Public Administration, Program in Management Information Systems, University Park, IL 60484. Offers MS.

The Graduate Center, City University of New York, Graduate Studies, Program in Business, New York, NY 10016-4039. Offers accounting (PhD); behavioral science (PhD); finance (PhD); management planning systems (PhD). *Degree requirements:* For doctorate, thesis/dissertation. *Entrance requirements:* For doctorate, GMAT, writing sample (15 pages). Additional exam requirements/recommendations for international students: Required—TOEFL. Electronic applications accepted.

Grand Canyon University, College of Business, Phoenix, AZ 85017-1097. Offers accounting (MBA); corporate business administration (MBA); disaster preparedness and crisis management (MBA); executive fire service leadership (MS); finance (MBA); general management (MBA); government and policy (MPA); health care management (MPA); health systems management (MBA); human resource management (MBA); innovation (MBA); leadership (MBA, MS); management of information system (MBA); marketing (MBA); project-based (MBA); six sigma (MBA); strategic human resource management (MBA). *Accreditation:* ACBSP. Part-time and evening/weekend programs available. Postbaccalaureate distance learning degree programs offered (no on-campus study). *Entrance requirements:* For master's, equivalent of two years full-time professional work experience. Additional exam requirements/recommendations for international students: Required—TOEFL (minimum score 575 paper-based; 90 iBT), IELTS (minimum score 7). Electronic applications accepted.

Grand Valley State University, Padnos College of Engineering and Computing, School of Computing and Information Systems, Allendale, MI 49401-9403. Offers computer information systems (MS), including databases, distributed systems, management of information systems, object-oriented systems, software engineering. Part-time and evening/weekend programs available. *Degree requirements:* For master's, thesis or alternative. *Entrance requirements:* For master's, GMAT or GRE General Test. Additional exam requirements/recommendations for international students: Required—TOEFL. Electronic applications accepted. *Faculty research:* Object technology, distributed computing, information systems management database, software engineering.

Grantham University, Mark Skousen School of Business, Lenexa, KS 66219. Offers business administration (MBA); business intelligence (MS); information management (MBA); information management technology (MS); information technology (MS); performance improvement (MS); project management (MBA, MS). Part-time and evening/weekend programs available. Postbaccalaureate distance learning degree programs offered (no on-campus study). *Faculty:* 3 full-time (2 women), 35 part-time/adjunct (11 women). *Students:* 233 full-time (75 women), 559 part-time (207 women); includes 399 minority (296 Black or African American, non-Hispanic/Latino; 6 American Indian or Alaska Native, non-Hispanic/Latino; 14 Asian, non-Hispanic/Latino; 58 Hispanic/Latino; 1 Native Hawaiian or other Pacific Islander, non-Hispanic/Latino; 24 Two or more races, non-Hispanic/Latino). Average age 40. 792 applicants, 100% accepted, 792 enrolled. In 2013, 404 master's awarded. *Degree requirements:* For master's, thesis, capstone project, simulation game. *Entrance requirements:* For master's, bachelor's degree from accredited degree-granting institution with minimum GPA of 2.5. Additional exam requirements/recommendations for international students: Required—TOEFL (minimum score 530 paper-based; 71 iBT). *Application deadline:* Applications are processed on a rolling basis. Application fee: $30. Electronic applications accepted. *Expenses: Tuition:* Full-time $3900; part-time $325 per credit hour. *Required fees:* $35 per term. One-time fee: $100. *Financial support:* In 2013–14, 792 students received support. Scholarships/grants available. *Faculty research:* Relationship between media choices and teaching experience in online courses, online best teaching practices, strategy for co-creation of value with consumers, political identity and party polarization in the American Electorate, political participation and Web 2.0. *Unit head:* Dr. Niccole Buckley, Dean, Mark Skousen School of Business, 800-955-2527, E-mail: admissions@grantham.edu. *Application contact:* Jared Parlette, Vice President of Admissions, 800-955-2527, E-mail: admissions@grantham.edu. Website: http://www.grantham.edu/colleges-and-schools/school-of-business/.

Harrisburg University of Science and Technology, Program in Information Systems Engineering and Management, Harrisburg, PA 17101. Offers digital government (MS); digital health (MS); entrepreneurship (MS). Part-time programs available. *Degree requirements:* For master's, comprehensive exam, thesis optional. *Entrance requirements:* For master's, baccalaureate degree. Additional exam requirements/recommendations for international students: Required—TOEFL (minimum score 520 paper-based; 80 iBT). Electronic applications accepted.

Hawai`i Pacific University, College of Business Administration, Program in Information Systems, Honolulu, HI 96813. Offers MSIS. Part-time and evening/weekend programs available. *Faculty:* 12 full-time (6 women), 2 part-time/adjunct (0 women). *Students:* 61 full-time (12 women), 50 part-time (7 women); includes 77 minority (8 Black or African American, non-Hispanic/Latino; 39 Asian, non-Hispanic/Latino; 9 Hispanic/Latino; 2 Native Hawaiian or other Pacific Islander, non-Hispanic/Latino; 19 Two or more races, non-Hispanic/Latino). Average age 33. 66 applicants, 92% accepted, 25 enrolled. In 2013, 23 master's awarded. *Financial support:* In 2013–14, 15 students received support. Career-related internships or fieldwork, Federal Work-Study, scholarships/grants, tuition waivers, and unspecified assistantships available. *Unit head:* Dr. Lawrence Rowland, Department Chair, 808-544-1468, E-mail: lrowland@hpu.edu. *Application contact:* Rumi Yoshida, Associate Director of Graduate Admissions, 808-543-8034, Fax: 808-544-0280, E-mail: grad@hpu.edu. Website: http://www.hpu.edu/CBA/Graduate/MSIS.html.

HEC Montreal, School of Business Administration, Master of Science Programs in Administration, Program in Information Technologies, Montréal, QC H3T 2A7, Canada. Offers M Sc. All courses are given in French. *Students:* 32 full-time (7 women), 6 part-time (0 women). 26 applicants, 65% accepted, 11 enrolled. In 2013, 16 master's awarded. *Degree requirements:* For master's, one foreign language, thesis. *Entrance requirements:* For master's, Test de francais international (TFI) with minimum score of 850 (for those who have never studied in French), BBA, undergraduate degree in another field, degree deemed equivalent by program director and minimum GPA of 3.0 on 4.3 scale. *Application deadline:* For fall admission, 3/15 for domestic and international students; for winter admission, 9/15 for domestic and international students. Application fee: $83 Canadian dollars. Electronic applications accepted. *Expenses: Tuition, area resident:* Part-time $74.14 per credit. Tuition, state resident: full-time $2669.04; part-time $201.83 per credit. Tuition, nonresident: full-time $7266; part-time $500.59 per credit. *International tuition:* $18,021.24 full-time. *Required fees:* $1529.70; $36.20 per credit. $65.50 per term. Tuition and fees vary according to degree level and program. *Financial support:* In 2013–14, 1,007 students received support. Research assistantships, teaching assistantships, and scholarships/grants available. Financial award application deadline: 9/2. *Unit head:* Dr. Anne Bourhis, Director, 514-340-6873, Fax: 514-340-6880, E-mail: anne.bourhis@hec.ca. *Application contact:* Marianne de Moura, Administrative Director, 514-340-7106, Fax: 514-340-6411, E-mail: marianne.de-moura@hec.ca. Website: http://www.hec.ca/programmes_formations/msc/options/technologies_information/index.html.

Hodges University, Graduate Programs, Naples, FL 34119. Offers business administration (MBA); clinical mental health counseling (MS); criminal justice (MS); education (MPS); information systems management (MIS); legal studies (MS); management (MSM); public administration (MPA). Part-time and evening/weekend programs available. Postbaccalaureate distance learning degree programs offered (no on-campus study). *Faculty:* 17 full-time (5 women), 5 part-time/adjunct (3 women). *Students:* 20 full-time (13 women), 182 part-time (131 women); includes 75 minority (18 Black or African American, non-Hispanic/Latino; 1 American Indian or Alaska Native, non-Hispanic/Latino; 7 Asian, non-Hispanic/Latino; 48 Hispanic/Latino; 1 Two or more

races, non-Hispanic/Latino). Average age 35. 58 applicants, 100% accepted, 58 enrolled. In 2013, 88 master's awarded. *Degree requirements:* For master's, comprehensive exam (for some programs), thesis (for some programs). *Entrance requirements:* For master's, in-house entrance exam. Additional exam requirements/recommendations for international students: Recommended—TOEFL. *Application deadline:* Applications are processed on a rolling basis. Application fee: $50. Electronic applications accepted. *Financial support:* In 2013–14, 153 students received support. Federal Work-Study and scholarships/grants available. Financial award application deadline: 7/9; financial award applicants required to submit FAFSA. *Unit head:* Dr. Jeanette Brock, President, 239-513-1122, Fax: 239-598-6253, E-mail: jbrock@hodges.edu. *Application contact:* Christy Saunders, Director of Admissions, 239-513-1122, Fax: 239-598-6253, E-mail: csaunders@hodges.edu.

Hofstra University, Frank G. Zarb School of Business, Programs in Information Technology, Hempstead, NY 11549. Offers business administration (MBA), including information technology, quality management; information technology (MS, Advanced Certificate).

Holy Family University, Graduate School, School of Business Administration, Program in Information Systems Management, Philadelphia, PA 19114. Offers MS. Part-time and evening/weekend programs available. *Faculty:* 1 full-time (0 women), 2 part-time/adjunct (0 women). *Students:* 1 full-time (0 women), 14 part-time (3 women); includes 4 minority (1 Black or African American, non-Hispanic/Latino; 1 Asian, non-Hispanic/Latino; 2 Hispanic/Latino). Average age 31. 15 applicants, 40% accepted, 4 enrolled. In 2013, 8 master's awarded. *Degree requirements:* For master's, thesis optional. *Entrance requirements:* For master's, minimum GPA of 3.0, interview, essay/personal statement, current resume, official transcript of all college or university work. Additional exam requirements/recommendations for international students: Required—TOEFL (minimum score 550 paper-based; 79 iBT), IELTS (minimum score 6), PTE (minimum score 54). *Application deadline:* For fall admission, 7/1 priority date for domestic and international students; for winter admission, 1/1 for domestic students; for spring admission, 11/1 priority date for domestic and international students; for summer admission, 4/1 priority date for domestic and international students. Applications are processed on a rolling basis. Application fee: $25. Electronic applications accepted. *Expenses: Tuition:* Full-time $12,060. *Required fees:* $250. Tuition and fees vary according to degree level. *Financial support:* Available to part-time students. Application deadline: 5/1; applicants required to submit FAFSA. *Unit head:* Dr. Barry Dickinson, Dean of the School of Business, 267-341-3440, Fax: 215-637-5937, E-mail: jdickinson@holyfamily.edu. *Application contact:* Gidget Marie Montelibano, Graduate Admissions Counselor, 267-341-3558, Fax: 215-637-1478, E-mail: gmontelibano@holyfamily.edu. Website: http://www.holyfamily.edu/choosing-holy-family-u/academics/schools-of-study/school-of-business-administration/graduate-programs/357-information-system.

Hood College, Graduate School, Department of Economics and Business Administration, Frederick, MD 21701-8575. Offers accounting (MBA); administration and management (MBA); finance (MBA); human resource management (MBA); information systems (MBA); marketing (MBA); public management (MBA). *Accreditation:* ACBSP. Part-time and evening/weekend programs available. *Faculty:* 6 full-time (2 women), 7 part-time/adjunct (1 woman). *Students:* 31 full-time (21 women), 131 part-time (66 women); includes 36 minority (18 Black or African American, non-Hispanic/Latino; 7 Asian, non-Hispanic/Latino; 8 Hispanic/Latino; 3 Two or more races, non-Hispanic/Latino), 12 international. Average age 31. 78 applicants, 56% accepted, 33 enrolled. In 2013, 35 master's awarded. *Degree requirements:* For master's, capstone/final research project. *Entrance requirements:* For master's, minimum GPA of 2.75, resume, letters of recommendation. Additional exam requirements/recommendations for international students: Required—TOEFL (minimum score 575 paper-based; 89 iBT), IELTS (minimum score 6.5). *Application deadline:* For fall admission, 7/15 priority date for domestic students, 7/15 for international students; for spring admission, 12/1 priority date for domestic students, 12/1 for international students. Applications are processed on a rolling basis. Application fee: $35. Electronic applications accepted. Application fee is waived when completed online. *Expenses: Tuition:* Part-time $405 per credit. *Required fees:* $100 per semester. *Financial support:* In 2013–14, 11 students received support. Tuition waivers (partial) and unspecified assistantships available. Financial award applicants required to submit FAFSA. *Faculty research:* Corporate strategy and sustainable competitive advantages, business ethics, entrepreneurship, investments management, economic development. *Unit head:* Dr. Anita Jose, Program Director, 301-696-3691, Fax: 301-696-3597, E-mail: jose@hood.edu. *Application contact:* Dr. Maria Green Cowles, Dean of Graduate School, 301-696-3811, Fax: 301-696-3597, E-mail: gofurther@hood.edu.

Howard University, School of Business, Graduate Programs in Business, Washington, DC 20059-0002. Offers accounting (MBA); entrepreneurship (MBA); finance (MBA); general management (MBA); human resources management (MBA); information systems (MBA); international business (MBA); marketing (MBA); supply chain management (MBA); JD/MBA. *Accreditation:* AACSB. Part-time and evening/weekend programs available. Postbaccalaureate distance learning degree programs offered (no on-campus study). *Entrance requirements:* For master's, GMAT, minimum 1 year post undergraduate work experience, resume, 3 letters of recommendation, advanced college algebra. Additional exam requirements/recommendations for international students: Required—TOEFL. *Faculty research:* Marketing research in multi-ethnic populations, U.S. trade policies and international relations, risk management (finance).

Idaho State University, Office of Graduate Studies, College of Business, Pocatello, ID 83209-8020. Offers business administration (MBA, Postbaccalaureate Certificate); computer information systems (MS, Postbaccalaureate Certificate). *Accreditation:* AACSB. Part-time programs available. *Degree requirements:* For master's, comprehensive exam, thesis (for some programs), oral exam; for Postbaccalaureate Certificate, comprehensive exam, thesis (for some programs), 6 hours of clerkship. *Entrance requirements:* For master's, GMAT, GRE General Test, minimum GPA of 3.0, resume outlining work experience, 2 letters of reference; for Postbaccalaureate Certificate, GMAT, GRE General Test, minimum upper-level GPA of 3.0, resume of work experience. Additional exam requirements/recommendations for international students: Required—TOEFL (minimum score 550 paper-based; 80 iBT). Electronic applications accepted. *Faculty research:* Information assurance, computer information technology, finance management, marketing.

Illinois Institute of Technology, Graduate College, College of Science and Letters, Department of Computer Science, Chicago, IL 60616. Offers business (MCS); computational intelligence (MCS); computer networking and telecommunications (MCS); computer science (MCS, MS, PhD); cyber-physical systems (MCS); data analytics (MCS); distributed and cloud computing (MCS); education (MCS); finance (MCS); information security and assurance (MCS); information systems (MCS); software engineering (MCS); teaching (MST). Part-time and evening/weekend programs available. Postbaccalaureate distance learning degree programs offered (no on-campus study). Terminal master's awarded for partial completion of doctoral program. *Degree requirements:* For master's, thesis optional; for doctorate, comprehensive exam, thesis/dissertation. *Entrance requirements:* For master's, GRE General Test (minimum scores: 1000 Quantitative and Verbal, 3.0 Analytical Writing), minimum undergraduate GPA of 3.0; for doctorate, GRE General Test (minimum scores: 1100 Quantitative and Verbal,

3.5 Analytical Writing), minimum undergraduate GPA of 3.0. Additional exam requirements/recommendations for international students: Required—TOEFL (minimum score 523 paper-based; 70 iBT). Electronic applications accepted. *Faculty research:* Algorithms, data structures, artificial intelligence, computer architecture, computer graphics, computer networking and telecommunications, computer vision, database systems, distributed and parallel processing, I/O systems, image processing, information retrieval, natural language processing, software engineering and system software, machine learning, cloud computing.

Illinois Institute of Technology, Graduate College, College of Science and Letters, Lewis Department of Humanities, Chicago, IL 60616. Offers information architecture (MS); technical communication (PhD); technical communication and information design (MS). Part-time programs available. *Degree requirements:* For master's, comprehensive exam, thesis or alternative; for doctorate, comprehensive exam, thesis/dissertation. *Entrance requirements:* For master's and doctorate, GRE General Test (minimum score 500 Quantitative, 500 Verbal, and 3.0 Analytical Writing), minimum undergraduate GPA of 3.0. Additional exam requirements/recommendations for international students: Required—TOEFL (minimum score 523 paper-based; 70 iBT). Electronic applications accepted. *Faculty research:* Aesthetics, document and online design, ethics in the professions, history of art and architecture, humanizing technology, information seeking and retrieval, instructional design, intellectual property, knowledge management, linguistics, philosophy of science, rhetorical theory, social media, text analysis, usability testing.

Illinois Institute of Technology, Graduate College, School of Applied Technology, Program in Information Technology and Management, Wheaton, IL 60189. Offers cyber forensics and security (MS); information technology and management (MITM). Part-time and evening/weekend programs available. Postbaccalaureate distance learning degree programs offered (no on-campus study). *Entrance requirements:* For master's, GRE (minimum score 900 Quantitative and Verbal, 2.5 Analytical Writing), bachelor's degree with minimum cumulative undergraduate GPA of 3.0 (or its equivalent) from accredited institution. Additional exam requirements/recommendations for international students: Required—TOEFL (minimum score 523 paper-based; 70 iBT); Recommended—IELTS (minimum score 5.5). Electronic applications accepted. *Faculty research:* Database design, voice over IP, process engineering, object-oriented programming, computer networking, online design, system administration.

Illinois State University, Graduate School, College of Applied Science and Technology, School of Information Technology, Normal, IL 61790-2200. Offers MS. *Entrance requirements:* For master's, GRE General Test, minimum GPA of 3.0 in last 60 hours; proficiency in COBOL, FORTRAN, Pascal, or P12. *Faculty research:* Graduate practicum training in network support.

Indiana University Bloomington, School of Public and Environmental Affairs, Public Affairs Programs, Bloomington, IN 47405. Offers economic development (MPA); energy (MPA); environmental policy (PhD); environmental policy and natural resource management (MPA); information systems (MPA); international development (MPA); local government management (MPA); nonprofit management (MPA, Certificate); policy analysis (MPA); public budgeting and financial management (Certificate); public finance (PhD); public financial administration (MPA); public management (MPA, PhD, Certificate); public policy analysis (PhD); social entrepreneurship (Certificate); specialized public affairs (MPA); sustainability and sustainable development (MPA); JD/MPA; MPA/MA; MPA/MIS; MPA/MLS; MSES/MPA. *Accreditation:* NASPAA (one or more programs are accredited). Part-time programs available. *Faculty:* 79 full-time (32 women), 8 part-time/adjunct (3 women). *Students:* 433 full-time (232 women), 75 part-time (39 women); includes 90 minority (19 Black or African American, non-Hispanic/Latino; 1 American Indian or Alaska Native, non-Hispanic/Latino; 49 Asian, non-Hispanic/Latino; 14 Hispanic/Latino; 2 Native Hawaiian or other Pacific Islander, non-Hispanic/Latino; 5 Two or more races, non-Hispanic/Latino), 70 international. Average age 27. 714 applicants, 73% accepted, 253 enrolled. In 2013, 171 master's, 3 doctorates, 4 other advanced degrees awarded. *Degree requirements:* For master's, capstone, internship; for doctorate, comprehensive exam, thesis/dissertation. *Entrance requirements:* For master's, GRE General Test or GMAT, official transcripts, 3 letters of recommendation, resume, personal statement; for doctorate, GRE General Test, official transcripts, 3 letters of recommendation, statement of purpose. Additional exam requirements/recommendations for international students: Required—TOEFL (minimum score 600 paper-based; 96 iBT); Recommended—IELTS (minimum score 7). *Application deadline:* For fall admission, 2/1 priority date for domestic students, 12/1 priority date for international students; for spring admission, 11/15 for domestic students, 9/1 for international students. Applications are processed on a rolling basis. Application fee: $55 ($65 for international students). Electronic applications accepted. *Financial support:* Fellowships with partial tuition reimbursements, research assistantships with full and partial tuition reimbursements, teaching assistantships with full and partial tuition reimbursements, career-related internships or fieldwork, Federal Work-Study, scholarships/grants, health care benefits, unspecified assistantships, and Service Corps Program; Educational Opportunity Fellowships available. Financial award application deadline: 2/1; financial award applicants required to submit FAFSA. *Faculty research:* International development, environmental policy and resource management, policy analysis, public finance, public management, urban management, nonprofit management, energy policy, social policy, public finance. *Unit head:* Megan Siehl, Assistant Director, Admissions and Financial Aid, 812-855-9485, Fax: 812-856-3665, E-mail: speampo@indiana.edu. *Application contact:* Lane Bowman, Admissions Services Coordinator, 812-855-2840, Fax: 812-856-3665, E-mail: speaapps@indiana.edu.
Website: http://www.indiana.edu/~spea/prospective_students/masters/.

Indiana University South Bend, Judd Leighton School of Business and Economics, South Bend, IN 46634-7111. Offers accounting (MSA); business administration (MBA); management of information technologies (MS). Part-time and evening/weekend programs available. *Faculty:* 17 full-time (2 women), 3 part-time/adjunct (1 woman). *Students:* 34 full-time (18 women), 101 part-time (38 women); includes 13 minority (7 Black or African American, non-Hispanic/Latino; 3 Asian, non-Hispanic/Latino; 2 Hispanic/Latino; 1 Two or more races, non-Hispanic/Latino), 30 international. Average age 32. 48 applicants, 79% accepted, 18 enrolled. In 2013, 42 master's awarded. *Entrance requirements:* For master's, GMAT. Additional exam requirements/recommendations for international students: Required—TOEFL (minimum score 550 paper-based). *Application deadline:* For fall admission, 7/1 priority date for domestic and international students; for spring admission, 11/1 priority date for domestic and international students. Applications are processed on a rolling basis. *Expenses:* Contact institution. *Financial support:* Fellowships, Federal Work-Study, and institutionally sponsored loans available. Support available to part-time students. Financial award applicants required to submit FAFSA. *Faculty research:* Financial accounting, consumer research, capital budgeting research, business strategy research. *Unit head:* Robert H. Ducoffe, Dean, 574-520-4228, Fax: 574-520-4866. *Application contact:* Tracy White, Assistant Director of Graduate Business Program, 574-520-4138, E-mail: whitet@iusb.edu.
Website: https://www.iusb.edu/buse/graduate_programs/.

Instituto Tecnológico y de Estudios Superiores de Monterrey, Campus Central de Veracruz, Graduate Programs, Córdoba, Mexico. Offers administration (MA); administration of information technologies (MTI); computer sciences (MCC); education (MEE); educational institution administration (MAD); educational technology (MTE); electronic commerce (MCE); finance (MAF); humanistic studies (MEH); international business for Latin America (MNL); marketing (MMT); science (MCP). Part-time and evening/weekend programs available. Postbaccalaureate distance learning degree programs offered (minimal on-campus study). *Degree requirements:* For master's, thesis (for some programs). *Entrance requirements:* For master's, PAEP College Board. Electronic applications accepted.

Instituto Tecnológico y de Estudios Superiores de Monterrey, Campus Ciudad de México, Virtual University Division, Ciudad de Mexico, Mexico. Offers administration of information technologies (MA); computer sciences (MA); education (MA, PhD); educational technology (MA); environmental engineering (MA); environmental systems (MA); humanistic studies (MA); industrial engineering (MA); international business for Latin America (MA); quality systems (MA); quality systems and productivity (MA). Part-time and evening/weekend programs available. Postbaccalaureate distance learning degree programs offered (minimal on-campus study). *Entrance requirements:* For master's and doctorate, Instituto entrance exam. Additional exam requirements/recommendations for international students: Required—TOEFL.

Instituto Tecnológico y de Estudios Superiores de Monterrey, Campus Ciudad Juárez, Program in Administration of Information Technology, Ciudad Juárez, Mexico. Offers MAIT.

Instituto Tecnológico y de Estudios Superiores de Monterrey, Campus Ciudad Obregón, Program in Administration of Information Technology, Ciudad Obregón, Mexico. Offers MATI.

Instituto Tecnológico y de Estudios Superiores de Monterrey, Campus Estado de México, Professional and Graduate Division, Estado de Mexico, Mexico. Offers administration of information technologies (MITA); architecture (M Arch); business administration (GMBA, MBA); computer sciences (MCS, PhD); education (M Ed); educational institution administration (MAD); educational technology and innovation (PhD); electronic commerce (MEC); environmental systems (MS); finance (MAF); humanistic studies (MHS); information sciences and knowledge management (MISKM); information systems (MS); manufacturing systems (MS); marketing (MEM); quality systems and productivity (MS); science and materials engineering (PhD); telecommunications management (MTM). Part-time programs available. Postbaccalaureate distance learning degree programs offered (minimal on-campus study). *Degree requirements:* For master's, one foreign language, thesis (for some programs); for doctorate, one foreign language, thesis/dissertation. *Entrance requirements:* For master's, E-PAEP 500, interview; for doctorate, E-PAEP 500, research proposal. Additional exam requirements/recommendations for international students: Required—TOEFL (minimum score 550 paper-based). *Faculty research:* Surface treatments by plasmas, mechanical properties, robotics, graphical computing, mechatronics security protocols.

Instituto Tecnológico y de Estudios Superiores de Monterrey, Campus Irapuato, Graduate Programs, Irapuato, Mexico. Offers administration (MBA); administration of information technology (MAIT); administration of telecommunications (MAT); architecture (M Arch); computer science (MCS); education (M Ed); educational administration (MEA); educational innovation and technology (DEIT); educational technology (MET); electronic commerce (MBA); environmental administration and planning (MEAP); environmental systems (MES); finances (MBA); humanistic studies (MHS); international management for Latin American executives (MIMLAE); library and information science (MLIS); manufacturing quality management (MMQM); marketing research (MBA).

Instituto Tecnológico y de Estudios Superiores de Monterrey, Campus Laguna, Graduate School, Torreón, Mexico. Offers business administration (MBA); industrial engineering (MIE); management information systems (MS). Part-time programs available. *Entrance requirements:* For master's, GMAT. *Faculty research:* Computer communications from home to the university.

Inter American University of Puerto Rico, Aguadilla Campus, Graduate School, Aguadilla, PR 00605. Offers accounting (MBA); counseling psychology specializing in family (MS); criminal justice (MA); educative management and leadership (MA); elementary education (M Ed); finance (MBA); human resources (MBA); industrial management (MBA); management information systems (MBA); marketing (MBA). Part-time and evening/weekend programs available. *Degree requirements:* For master's, comprehensive exam. *Entrance requirements:* For master's, EXADEP, 2 letters of recommendation, minimum GPA of 2.5. Electronic applications accepted.

Inter American University of Puerto Rico, Metropolitan Campus, Graduate Programs, Program in Management Information Systems, San Juan, PR 00919-1293. Offers MBA.

Inter American University of Puerto Rico, San Germán Campus, Graduate Studies Center, Program in Business Administration, San Germán, PR 00683-5008. Offers accounting (MBA); finance (MBA); general business administration (MBA); human resources (MBA, PhD); industrial relations (MBA); information systems (MBA); international and interregional business (PhD); management (MBA); marketing (MBA). Part-time and evening/weekend programs available. *Faculty:* 8 full-time (2 women), 4 part-time/adjunct (3 women). *Students:* 138 full-time (80 women), 35 part-time (21 women); includes 172 minority (all Hispanic/Latino). 60 applicants, 65% accepted, 38 enrolled. In 2013, 38 master's, 3 doctorates awarded. *Degree requirements:* For master's, comprehensive exam. *Entrance requirements:* For master's, GRE General Test or EXADEP, minimum GPA of 3.0. *Application deadline:* For fall admission, 4/30 priority date for domestic students; for spring admission, 11/15 for domestic students. Applications are processed on a rolling basis. Application fee: $31. *Expenses: Tuition:* Full-time $2424; part-time $202 per credit hour. *Required fees:* $260 per semester. Tuition and fees vary according to course level, course load, degree level and program. *Financial support:* Teaching assistantships, Federal Work-Study, and unspecified assistantships available. *Unit head:* Dr. Elba T. Irizarry, Director of Graduate Studies Center, 787-264-1912 Ext. 7357, Fax: 787-892-6350, E-mail: elbat@sg.inter.edu. *Application contact:* Dr. Ailin Padilla, Coordinator, 787-264-1912 Ext. 7355, E-mail: ailin_padilla@intersg.edu.

Iowa State University of Science and Technology, Program in Business and Technology, Ames, IA 50011. Offers PhD. *Entrance requirements:* Additional exam requirements/recommendations for international students: Required—TOEFL (minimum score 600 paper-based; 100 iBT), IELTS (minimum score 7). Electronic applications accepted.

Iowa State University of Science and Technology, Program in Logistics, Operations, and Management Information Systems, Ames, IA 50011. Offers information systems (MS). *Degree requirements:* For master's, thesis or alternative. *Entrance requirements:* For master's, GMAT. Additional exam requirements/recommendations for international students: Recommended—TOEFL (minimum score 600 paper-based; 100 iBT), IELTS (minimum score 7). Electronic applications accepted.

John Hancock University, MBA Program, Oakbrook Terrace, IL 60181. Offers e-commerce (MBA); finance (MBA); general business (MBA); global management (MBA); health care administration (MBA); leadership (MBA); management of information systems (MBA); marketing (MBA); professional accounting (MBA); project management (MBA); public accounting (MBA); risk management (MBA).

John Marshall Law School, Graduate and Professional Programs, Chicago, IL 60604-3968. Offers employee benefits (LL M, MS); estate planning (LL M); global legal studies (LL M); information technology (MS); information technology and privacy law (LL M); intellectual property (LL M, MS); international business and trade (LL M); law (JD); real estate (LL M, MS); taxation (LL M, MS); trial advocacy (LL M); JD/LL M; JD/MA; JD/MBA; JD/MPA. JD/MBA offered jointly with Dominican University; JD/MA and JD/MPA with Roosevelt University. *Accreditation:* ABA. Part-time and evening/weekend programs available. *Faculty:* 71 full-time (26 women), 132 part-time/adjunct (49 women). *Students:* 1,045 full-time (512 women), 421 part-time (211 women); includes 403 minority (152 Black or African American, non-Hispanic/Latino; 8 American Indian or Alaska Native, non-Hispanic/Latino; 89 Asian, non-Hispanic/Latino; 138 Hispanic/Latino; 3 Native Hawaiian or other Pacific Islander, non-Hispanic/Latino; 13 Two or more races, non-Hispanic/Latino), 57 international. Average age 27. 2,694 applicants, 73% accepted, 419 enrolled. In 2013, 81 master's, 445 doctorates awarded. *Degree requirements:* For master's, 24 credits; for doctorate, 90 credits. *Entrance requirements:* For master's, JD; for doctorate, LSAT. Additional exam requirements/recommendations for international students: Required—TOEFL. *Application deadline:* For fall admission, 3/1 priority date for domestic and international students; for spring admission, 10/15 priority date for domestic and international students. Applications are processed on a rolling basis. Application fee: $0. Electronic applications accepted. *Expenses:* Contact institution. *Financial support:* In 2013–14, 1,275 students received support. Scholarships/grants and tuition waivers (full and partial) available. Support available to part-time students. Financial award application deadline: 4/1; financial award applicants required to submit FAFSA. *Unit head:* John Corkery, Dean, 312-427-2737. *Application contact:* William B. Powers, Associate Dean of Admission and Student Affairs, 800-537-4280, Fax: 312-427-5136, E-mail: admission@jmls.edu.

Johns Hopkins University, Carey Business School, Information Systems Program, Baltimore, MD 21218-2699. Offers MS. Part-time and evening/weekend programs available. *Faculty:* 29 full-time (6 women), 135 part-time/adjunct (29 women). *Students:* 13 full-time (6 women), 45 part-time (11 women); includes 20 minority (5 Black or African American, non-Hispanic/Latino; 7 Asian, non-Hispanic/Latino; 4 Hispanic/Latino; 4 Two or more races, non-Hispanic/Latino), 16 international. Average age 31. 37 applicants, 68% accepted, 13 enrolled. In 2013, 54 master's awarded. *Degree requirements:* For master's, 36 credits including final project. *Entrance requirements:* For master's, minimum GPA of 3.0, resume, work experience, two letters of recommendation. Additional exam requirements/recommendations for international students: Required—TOEFL (minimum score 600 paper-based; 100 iBT). *Application deadline:* For fall admission, 4/1 for international students; for spring admission, 9/15 for international students. Applications are processed on a rolling basis. Application fee: $100. Electronic applications accepted. *Financial support:* In 2013–14, 5 students received support. Scholarships/grants available. Support available to part-time students. Financial award application deadline: 4/15; financial award applicants required to submit FAFSA. *Faculty research:* Information security, healthcare information systems. *Total annual research expenditures:* $89,653. *Unit head:* Dr. Dipankar Chakravarti, Vice Dean of Programs, 410-234-9311, E-mail: dipankar.chakravarti@jhu.edu. *Application contact:* Robin Greenberg, Admissions Coordinator, 410-234-9227, Fax: 443-529-1554, E-mail: carey.admissions@jhu.edu.
Website: http://carey.jhu.edu/academics/master-of-science/ms-in-information-systems/.

Johns Hopkins University, Engineering Program for Professionals, Part-time Program in Information Systems and Technology, Baltimore, MD 21218-2699. Offers MS, Post-Master's Certificate. Part-time and evening/weekend programs available. *Faculty:* 9 part-time/adjunct (1 woman). *Students:* 4 full-time (1 woman), 146 part-time (33 women); includes 38 minority (13 Black or African American, non-Hispanic/Latino; 17 Asian, non-Hispanic/Latino; 6 Hispanic/Latino; 2 Two or more races, non-Hispanic/Latino), 2 international. Average age 31. 21 applicants, 90% accepted, 16 enrolled. In 2013, 2 master's awarded. *Application deadline:* Applications are processed on a rolling basis. Application fee: $75. Electronic applications accepted. *Financial support:* In 2013–14, 1 fellowship (averaging $6,660 per year) was awarded; institutionally sponsored loans also available. *Unit head:* Dr. Thomas A. Longstaff, Program Chair, 443-778-9389, E-mail: thomas.longstaff@jhuapl.edu. *Application contact:* Doug Schiller, Admissions Director, 410-516-2300, Fax: 410-579-8049, E-mail: schiller@jhu.edu.
Website: http://www.ep.jhu.edu/.

Kaplan University, Davenport Campus, School of Information Technology, Davenport, IA 52807-2095. Offers decision support systems (MS); information security and assurance (MS). Part-time and evening/weekend programs available. Postbaccalaureate distance learning degree programs offered (no on-campus study). *Entrance requirements:* Additional exam requirements/recommendations for international students: Required—TOEFL (minimum score 550 paper-based; 80 iBT).

Kean University, College of Natural, Applied and Health Sciences, Program in Computer Information Systems, Union, NJ 07083. Offers MS. Part-time programs available. *Faculty:* 8 full-time (3 women). *Students:* 15 full-time (4 women), 4 part-time (1 woman); includes 8 minority (2 Black or African American, non-Hispanic/Latino; 3 Asian, non-Hispanic/Latino; 2 Hispanic/Latino; 1 Two or more races, non-Hispanic/Latino), 9 international. Average age 27. 28 applicants, 82% accepted, 12 enrolled. In 2013, 3 master's awarded. *Entrance requirements:* For master's, baccalaureate degree in computer science or closely-related field from accredited college or university; minimum cumulative GPA of 3.0; official transcripts from all institutions attended; two letters of recommendation; professional resume/curriculum vitae; personal statement. Additional exam requirements/recommendations for international students: Required—TOEFL (minimum score 550 paper-based; 79 iBT). *Application deadline:* For fall admission, 6/1 for domestic and international students; for spring admission, 12/1 for domestic and international students. Applications are processed on a rolling basis. Application fee: $75 ($150 for international students). Electronic applications accepted. *Expenses:* Tuition, state resident: full-time $12,099; part-time $589 per credit. Tuition, nonresident: full-time $16,399; part-time $722 per credit. *Required fees:* $3050; $139 per credit. Part-time tuition and fees vary according to course level, course load, degree level and program. *Financial support:* In 2013–14, 2 research assistantships with full tuition reimbursements (averaging $3,713 per year) were awarded; unspecified assistantships also available. Financial award applicants required to submit FAFSA. *Unit head:* Dr. Jing-Chiou Liou, Program Coordinator, 908-737-3803, E-mail: jliou@kean.edu. *Application contact:* Reenat Hasan, Admissions Counselor, 908-737-5923, Fax: 908-737-5925, E-mail: hasanr@kean.edu.
Website: http://grad.kean.edu/masters-programs/computer-information-systems.

Keiser University, MS in Information Technology Leadership Program, Ft. Lauderdale, FL 33309. Offers MS.

Kent State University, College of Business Administration, Doctoral Program in Management Systems, Kent, OH 44242. Offers PhD. *Faculty:* 13 full-time (5 women). *Students:* 10 full-time (3 women), 6 international. Average age 36. 18 applicants, 22% accepted, 4 enrolled. In 2013, 1 doctorate awarded. *Degree requirements:* For doctorate, comprehensive exam, thesis/dissertation, oral defense. *Entrance requirements:* For doctorate, GMAT or GRE. Additional exam requirements/recommendations for international students: Required—TOEFL (minimum score 600 paper-based; 100 iBT). *Application deadline:* For fall admission, 2/1 for domestic students, 1/1 for international students. Application fee: $30 ($70 for international students). Electronic applications accepted. *Financial support:* In 2013–14, 10 students received support, including 10 teaching assistantships with full tuition reimbursements available (averaging $29,500 per year); Federal Work-Study also available. Financial award application deadline: 2/1; financial award applicants required to submit FAFSA. *Unit head:* Dr. O. Felix Offodile, Chair and Professor, 330-672-2750, Fax: 330-672-2953, E-mail: foffodil@kent.edu. *Application contact:* Felecia A. Urbanek, Coordinator, Graduate Programs, 330-672-2282, Fax: 330-672-7303, E-mail: gradbus@kent.edu.
Website: http://www.kent.edu/business/Grad/phd/index.cfm.

Kentucky State University, College of Professional Studies, Frankfort, KY 40601. Offers public administration (MPA), including human resource management, international development, management information systems, nonprofit management; special education (MA). Part-time and evening/weekend programs available. Postbaccalaureate distance learning degree programs offered (minimal on-campus study). *Degree requirements:* For master's, comprehensive exam, thesis optional. *Entrance requirements:* For master's, GMAT, GRE. Additional exam requirements/recommendations for international students: Required—TOEFL (minimum score 525 paper-based). Electronic applications accepted.

Lawrence Technological University, College of Management, Southfield, MI 48075-1058. Offers business administration (MBA, DBA); information systems (MS); management (PhD). *Accreditation:* ACBSP. Part-time and evening/weekend programs available. *Faculty:* 15 full-time (5 women), 19 part-time/adjunct (4 women). *Students:* 3 full-time (2 women), 406 part-time (147 women); includes 149 minority (70 Black or African American, non-Hispanic/Latino; 2 American Indian or Alaska Native, non-Hispanic/Latino; 63 Asian, non-Hispanic/Latino; 10 Hispanic/Latino; 1 Native Hawaiian or other Pacific Islander, non-Hispanic/Latino; 3 Two or more races, non-Hispanic/Latino), 25 international. Average age 36. 325 applicants, 51% accepted, 99 enrolled. In 2013, 174 master's, 14 doctorates awarded. *Degree requirements:* For master's, thesis (for some programs). *Entrance requirements:* Additional exam requirements/recommendations for international students: Required—TOEFL (minimum score 550 paper-based; 79 iBT). *Application deadline:* For fall admission, 8/1 priority date for domestic students, 5/29 for international students; for spring admission, 12/1 priority date for domestic students, 10/15 for international students. Applications are processed on a rolling basis. Application fee: $50. Electronic applications accepted. *Expenses:* *Tuition:* Full-time $14,112; part-time $1008 per credit hour. *Required fees:* $519. One-time fee: $519 part-time. *Financial support:* In 2013–14, 57 students received support, including 8 research assistantships (averaging $7,853 per year); Federal Work-Study and institutionally sponsored loans also available. Support available to part-time students. Financial award application deadline: 4/1; financial award applicants required to submit FAFSA. *Unit head:* Dr. Bahman Mirshab, Dean, 248-204-3050, E-mail: mgtdean@ltu.edu. *Application contact:* Jane Rohrback, Director of Admissions, 248-204-3160, Fax: 248-204-2228, E-mail: admissions@ltu.edu.
Website: http://www.ltu.edu/management/index.asp.

Lewis University, College of Business, Graduate School of Management, Program in Business Administration, Romeoville, IL 60446. Offers accounting (MBA); custom elective option (MBA); e-business (MBA); finance (MBA); healthcare management (MBA); human resources management (MBA); international business (MBA); management information systems (MBA); marketing (MBA); project management (MBA); technology and operations management (MBA). Part-time and evening/weekend programs available. *Students:* 115 full-time (55 women), 227 part-time (129 women); includes 128 minority (74 Black or African American, non-Hispanic/Latino; 1 American Indian or Alaska Native, non-Hispanic/Latino; 9 Asian, non-Hispanic/Latino; 40 Hispanic/Latino; 4 Two or more races, non-Hispanic/Latino), 10 international. Average age 31. In 2013, 99 master's awarded. *Entrance requirements:* For master's, interview, bachelor's degree, resume, 2 recommendations. Additional exam requirements/recommendations for international students: Required—TOEFL (minimum score 550 paper-based). *Application deadline:* For fall admission, 8/15 priority date for domestic students, 5/1 priority date for international students; for spring admission, 11/15 priority date for international students. Applications are processed on a rolling basis. Application fee: $40. Electronic applications accepted. *Financial support:* Career-related internships or fieldwork, Federal Work-Study, scholarships/grants, and unspecified assistantships available. Financial award application deadline: 5/1; financial award applicants required to submit FAFSA. *Unit head:* Dr. Maureen Culleeney, Academic Program Director, 815-838-0500 Ext. 5631, E-mail: culleema@lewisu.edu. *Application contact:* Michele Ryan, Director of Admission, 815-838-0500 Ext. 5384, E-mail: gsm@lewisu.edu.

Liberty University, School of Business, Lynchburg, VA 24515. Offers accounting (MBA, MS, DBA); business administration (MBA); criminal justice (MBA); cyber security (MS); executive leadership (MA); healthcare (MBA); human resources (DBA); information systems (MS), including information assurance, technology management; international business (MBA, DBA); leadership (MBA, DBA); management and leadership (MA); marketing (MBA, MS, DBA), including digital marketing and advertising (MS), project management (MS), public relations (MS), sports marketing and media (MS); project management (MBA, DBA); public administration (MBA); public relations (MBA). Part-time programs available. Postbaccalaureate distance learning degree programs offered (minimal on-campus study). *Students:* 1,342 full-time (749 women), 3,704 part-time (1,820 women); includes 1,657 minority (1,221 Black or African American, non-Hispanic/Latino; 11 American Indian or Alaska Native, non-Hispanic/Latino; 74 Asian, non-Hispanic/Latino; 209 Hispanic/Latino; 13 Native Hawaiian or other Pacific Islander, non-Hispanic/Latino; 129 Two or more races, non-Hispanic/Latino), 40 international. Average age 35. 5,899 applicants, 48% accepted, 1716 enrolled. In 2013, 1,535 master's awarded. *Entrance requirements:* For master's, minimum undergraduate GPA of 3.0, 15 hours of upper-level business courses. Additional exam requirements/recommendations for international students: Required—TOEFL (minimum score 600 paper-based; 100 iBT). *Application deadline:* Applications are processed on a rolling basis. Application fee: $50. Electronic applications accepted. *Expenses:* Contact institution. *Unit head:* Dr. Scott Hicks, Dean, 434-592-4808, Fax: 434-582-2366, E-mail: smhicks@liberty.edu. *Application contact:* Jay Bridge, Director of Graduate Admissions, 800-424-9595, Fax: 800-628-7977, E-mail: gradadmissions@liberty.edu.
Website: http://www.liberty.edu/academics/business/index.cfm?PID-149.

Lincoln University, Graduate Studies, Oakland, CA 94612. Offers finance and investments (DBA); finance management and investment banking (MBA); general business (MBA); human resource management (MBA, DBA); international business (MBA); management information systems (MBA). Part-time and evening/weekend programs available. *Faculty:* 8 full-time (2 women), 22 part-time/adjunct (7 women). *Students:* 372 full-time (171 women), 4 part-time (1 woman); includes 8 minority (2 Black or African American, non-Hispanic/Latino; 6 Asian, non-Hispanic/Latino), 363 international. Average age 26. 421 applicants, 71% accepted, 133 enrolled. *Degree requirements:* For master's, research project (thesis), internship report, or

comprehensive exam; for doctorate, comprehensive exam, thesis/dissertation. *Entrance requirements:* For master's, minimum GPA of 2.7; for doctorate, GMAT (minimum score: 550), GRE (minimum score: 1000), or equivalent test results (waived for master's degree with minimum cumulative GPA of 3.3). Additional exam requirements/recommendations for international students: Required—TOEFL (minimum score 525 paper-based; 71 iBT) or IELTS (minimum score 5.5) for MBA; TOEFL (minimum score 550 paper-based; 79 iBT) or IELTS (minimum score 6) for DBA. *Application deadline:* For fall admission, 7/1 priority date for domestic and international students; for spring admission, 11/1 priority date for domestic and international students; for summer admission, 5/1 for domestic and international students. Applications are processed on a rolling basis. Application fee: $75. Electronic applications accepted. *Expenses: Tuition:* Full-time $7290; part-time $405 per unit. *Required fees:* $375; $405 per unit. $375 per year. Tuition and fees vary according to course level and degree level. *Financial support:* Teaching assistantships with tuition reimbursements, career-related internships or fieldwork, and scholarships/grants available. Financial award application deadline: 7/31; financial award applicants required to submit FAFSA. *Unit head:* Dr. Marshall Burak, Director of Graduate Programs, 510-628-8016, Fax: 510-628-8012, E-mail: mburak@lincolnuca.edu. *Application contact:* Reenu Shrestha, Admissions Officer, 510-628-8010 Ext. 8030, Fax: 510-628-8012, E-mail: admissions@lincolnuca.edu.
Website: http://www.lincolnuca.edu/.

Lindenwood University, Graduate Programs, College of Individualized Education, St. Charles, MO 63301-1695. Offers administration (MSA); business administration (MBA); communications (MA); criminal justice and administration (MS); gerontology (MA); healthcare administration (MS); human resource management (MS); information technology (MBA, Certificate); managing information technology (MS); writing (MFA). Part-time and evening/weekend programs available. *Faculty:* 20 full-time (7 women), 96 part-time/adjunct (36 women). *Students:* 928 full-time (587 women), 85 part-time (53 women); includes 394 minority (336 Black or African American, non-Hispanic/Latino; 2 American Indian or Alaska Native, non-Hispanic/Latino; 7 Asian, non-Hispanic/Latino; 24 Hispanic/Latino; 2 Native Hawaiian or other Pacific Islander, non-Hispanic/Latino; 23 Two or more races, non-Hispanic/Latino), 33 international. Average age 34. 569 applicants, 62% accepted, 331 enrolled. In 2013, 487 master's awarded. *Degree requirements:* For master's, thesis (for some programs). *Entrance requirements:* For master's, interview, minimum GPA of 3.0. Additional exam requirements/recommendations for international students: Required—TOEFL (minimum score 550 paper-based; 80 iBT). *Application deadline:* For fall admission, 10/5 priority date for domestic and international students; for winter admission, 1/6 priority date for domestic and international students; for spring admission, 4/7 priority date for domestic and international students. Applications are processed on a rolling basis. Application fee: $30 ($100 for international students). Electronic applications accepted. *Expenses: Tuition:* Full-time $14,800; part-time $428 per credit hour. *Required fees:* $350. Tuition and fees vary according to course level and course load. *Financial support:* In 2013–14, 654 students received support. Career-related internships or fieldwork, institutionally sponsored loans, scholarships/grants, tuition waivers (partial), and unspecified assistantships available. Financial award application deadline: 6/30; financial award applicants required to submit FAFSA. *Unit head:* Dan Kemper, Dean, 636-949-4501, Fax: 636-949-4505, E-mail: dkemper@lindenwood.edu. *Application contact:* Brett Barger, Dean of Evening Admissions and Extension Campuses, 636-949-4934, Fax: 636-949-4109, E-mail: adultadmissions@lindenwood.edu.

Long Island University–LIU Post, College of Management, School of Business, Brookville, NY 11548-1300. Offers accounting and taxation (Certificate); business administration (Certificate); finance (MBA, Certificate); general business administration (MBA); international business (MBA, Certificate); management (MBA, Certificate); management information systems (MBA, Certificate); marketing (MBA, Certificate). *Accreditation:* AACSB. Part-time and evening/weekend programs available. *Entrance requirements:* For master's, GMAT, resume, minimum GPA of 3.0, 2 letters of recommendation. Additional exam requirements/recommendations for international students: Required—TOEFL (minimum score 527 paper-based). Electronic applications accepted. *Faculty research:* Financial markets, consumer behavior.

Louisiana State University and Agricultural & Mechanical College, Graduate School, E. J. Ourso College of Business, Department of Information Systems and Decision Sciences, Baton Rouge, LA 70803. Offers MS, PhD. *Faculty:* 12 full-time (3 women). *Students:* 29 full-time (7 women), 2 part-time (0 women); includes 2 minority (1 Black or African American, non-Hispanic/Latino; 1 Two or more races, non-Hispanic/Latino), 8 international. Average age 28. 4 applicants, 25% accepted. In 2013, 18 master's, 2 doctorates awarded. Terminal master's awarded for partial completion of doctoral program. *Degree requirements:* For master's, comprehensive exam, thesis optional; for doctorate, comprehensive exam, thesis/dissertation. *Entrance requirements:* For master's, GMAT or GRE General Test; for doctorate, GMAT or GRE. Additional exam requirements/recommendations for international students: Required—TOEFL (minimum score 550 paper-based; 79 IBT), IELTS (minimum score 6.5), or PTE (minimum score 59). *Application deadline:* For fall admission, 1/25 priority date for domestic students, 5/15 for international students; for spring admission, 10/15 for international students. Applications are processed on a rolling basis. Application fee: $50 ($70 for international students). Electronic applications accepted. *Financial support:* In 2013–14, 21 students received support, including 1 fellowship (averaging $39,805 per year), 2 research assistantships with full and partial tuition reimbursements available (averaging $20,000 per year), 3 teaching assistantships with full and partial tuition reimbursements available (averaging $7,000 per year); Federal Work-Study, institutionally sponsored loans, scholarships/grants, health care benefits, tuition waivers (full and partial), and unspecified assistantships also available. Support available to part-time students. Financial award applicants required to submit FAFSA. *Faculty research:* Healthcare informatics, outsourcing, information systems management, operations management. *Total annual research expenditures:* $305,401. *Unit head:* Dr. Helmut Schneider, Department Head, 225-578-2516, Fax: 225-578-2511, E-mail: hschnei@lsu.edu. *Application contact:* Dr. Rudy Hirschheim, Graduate Adviser, 225-578-2514, Fax: 225-578-2511, E-mail: rudy@lsu.edu.
Website: http://business.lsu.edu/isds.

Louisiana Tech University, Graduate School, College of Business, School of Accounting and Information Systems, Ruston, LA 71272. Offers accounting (MBA, MPA); accounting and information systems (DBA). *Accreditation:* AACSB. Part-time programs available. *Degree requirements:* For doctorate, thesis/dissertation. *Entrance requirements:* For master's and doctorate, GMAT. *Application deadline:* For fall admission, 7/29 for domestic students; for spring admission, 2/3 for domestic students. Application fee: $20 ($30 for international students). *Financial support:* Fellowships, research assistantships, and teaching assistantships available. Financial award application deadline: 2/1. *Unit head:* Dr. Andrea Drake, Interim Director, 318-257-2822, Fax: 318-257-4253, E-mail: adrake@latech.edu. *Application contact:* Marilyn J. Robinson, Assistant to the Dean, 318-257-2924, Fax: 318-257-4487.
Website: http://www.business.latech.edu/accounting/.

Loyola University Chicago, Quinlan School of Business, MBA Programs, Chicago, IL 60610. Offers accounting (MBA); business ethics (MBA); derivative markets (MBA); economics (MBA); entrepreneurship (MBA); executive (MBA); finance (MBA); healthcare management (MBA); human resources management (MBA); information systems management (MBA); intercontinental (MBA); international business (MBA); marketing (MBA); operations management (MBA); risk management (MBA); JD/MBA. Part-time and evening/weekend programs available. *Faculty:* 76 full-time (20 women), 10 part-time/adjunct (4 women). *Students:* 73 full-time (34 women), 294 part-time (129 women); includes 60 minority (18 Black or African American, non-Hispanic/Latino; 28 Asian, non-Hispanic/Latino; 14 Hispanic/Latino), 19 international. Average age 31. 529 applicants, 51% accepted, 153 enrolled. In 2013, 229 master's awarded. *Entrance requirements:* For master's, GMAT or GRE, official transcripts, two letters of recommendation, statement of purpose, resume. Additional exam requirements/recommendations for international students: Required—TOEFL (minimum score 90 iBT) or IELTS (minimum score 6.5). *Application deadline:* For fall admission, 7/15 for domestic and international students; for winter admission, 10/1 for domestic and international students; for spring admission, 1/15 for domestic and international students; for summer admission, 4/1 for domestic and international students. Applications are processed on a rolling basis. Application fee: $50. Electronic applications accepted. Application fee is waived when completed online. *Expenses: Tuition:* Full-time $16,740; part-time $930 per credit. *Required fees:* $135 per semester. *Financial support:* Scholarships/grants and unspecified assistantships available. *Faculty research:* Social enterprise and responsibility, emerging markets, supply chain management, risk management. *Unit head:* Jennifer Huntley, Assistant Dean for Graduate Programs, 312-915-6124, Fax: 312-915-7207, E-mail: jhuntle@luc.edu. *Application contact:* Jessica Gagle, Enrollment Advisor, Quinlan School of Business Graduate Programs, 312-915-8908, Fax: 312-915-7207, E-mail: jgagle@luc.edu.

Loyola University Maryland, Graduate Programs, Sellinger School of Business and Management, Program in Business Administration, Baltimore, MD 21210-2699. Offers accounting (MBA); finance (MBA); general business (MBA); information systems operations management (MBA); international business (MBA); management (MBA); marketing (MBA). *Accreditation:* AACSB. Part-time and evening/weekend programs available. *Entrance requirements:* For master's, GMAT, letter of recommendation, resume, essay. Additional exam requirements/recommendations for international students: Required—TOEFL (minimum score 550 paper-based).

Marist College, Graduate Programs, School of Computer Science and Mathematics, Poughkeepsie, NY 12601-1387. Offers computer science/software development (MS); information systems (MS, Adv C); technology management (MS). Part-time and evening/weekend programs available. Postbaccalaureate distance learning degree programs offered (minimal on-campus study). *Entrance requirements:* For master's, resume. Additional exam requirements/recommendations for international students: Required—TOEFL (minimum score 550 paper-based; 80 iBT); Recommended—IELTS (minimum score 6.5). Electronic applications accepted. *Faculty research:* Data quality, artificial intelligence, imaging, analysis of algorithms, distributed systems and applications.

Marquette University, Graduate School of Management, Executive MBA Program, Milwaukee, WI 53201-1881. Offers economics (MBA); finance (MBA); human resources (MBA); international business (MBA); management information systems (MBA); marketing (MBA); operations and supply chain management (MBA); sports business (MBA). *Accreditation:* AACSB. *Students:* 38 full-time (12 women), 1 international. Average age 36. 36 applicants. In 2013, 21 master's awarded. *Degree requirements:* For master's, international trip. *Entrance requirements:* For master's, GMAT or GRE, two letters of recommendation, official transcripts from current and previous colleges/universities. Additional exam requirements/recommendations for international students: Required—TOEFL (minimum score 550 paper-based; 88 iBT), IELTS (minimum score 6.5), PTE. *Application deadline:* For fall admission, 2/15 for domestic and international students. Application fee: $50. Electronic applications accepted. *Expenses:* Contact institution. *Financial support:* Application deadline: 2/15. *Faculty research:* International trade and finance, customer relationship management, consumer satisfaction, customer service. *Unit head:* Dr. Mark Eppli, Dean, 414-288-5724. *Application contact:* Dr. Jeanne Simmons, Associate Dean, 414-288-7145.
Website: http://www.busadm.mu.edu/emba/.

Marquette University, Graduate School of Management, Program in Business Administration, Milwaukee, WI 53201-1881. Offers business administration (MBA); economics (MBA); entrepreneurship (Certificate); finance (MBA); human resources (MBA); international business (MBA); management information systems (MBA); marketing (MBA); operations and supply chain management (MBA); sports business (MBA); JD/MBA; MBA/MA; MBA/MSN. *Accreditation:* AACSB. Part-time and evening/weekend programs available. *Students:* 28 full-time (13 women), 265 part-time (66 women); includes 20 minority (7 Black or African American, non-Hispanic/Latino; 8 Asian, non-Hispanic/Latino; 5 Hispanic/Latino), 11 international. Average age 31. 185 applicants. In 2013, 129 master's, 2 other advanced degrees awarded. *Degree requirements:* For Certificate, business plan. *Entrance requirements:* For master's, GMAT or GRE, letters of recommendation. Additional exam requirements/recommendations for international students: Required—TOEFL (minimum score 550 paper-based; 88 iBT), IELTS (minimum score 6.5), PTE. *Application deadline:* For fall admission, 2/15 for domestic and international students. Applications are processed on a rolling basis. Application fee: $50. Electronic applications accepted. *Financial support:* In 2013–14, 4 fellowships, 11 teaching assistantships were awarded; research assistantships, Federal Work-Study, institutionally sponsored loans, scholarships/grants, and tuition waivers (full and partial) also available. Support available to part-time students. Financial award application deadline: 2/15. *Faculty research:* Ethics in the professions, services marketing, technology impact on decision-making, mentoring. *Unit head:* Dr. Mark Eppli, Dean, 414-288-5724. *Application contact:* Dr. Jeanne Simmons, Associate Dean, 414-288-7145.
Website: http://business.marquette.edu/academics/mba.

Marymount University, School of Business Administration, Program in Information Technology, Arlington, VA 22207-4299. Offers computer security and information assurance (Certificate); health care informatics (Certificate); information technology (MS, Certificate); information technology project management: technology leadership (Certificate). Part-time and evening/weekend programs available. *Faculty:* 5 full-time (2 women), 9 part-time/adjunct (0 women). *Students:* 29 full-time (14 women), 33 part-time (8 women); includes 25 minority (16 Black or African American, non-Hispanic/Latino; 5 Asian, non-Hispanic/Latino; 3 Hispanic/Latino; 1 Two or more races, non-Hispanic/Latino), 18 international. Average age 31. 42 applicants, 100% accepted, 27 enrolled. In 2013, 30 master's, 5 other advanced degrees awarded. *Degree requirements:* For master's, thesis or alternative. *Entrance requirements:* For master's, interview, resume, bachelor's degree in computer-related field or degree in another subject with a post-baccalaureate certificate in a computer-related field; for Certificate, resume. Additional exam requirements/recommendations for international students: Required—TOEFL (minimum score 600 paper-based; 96 iBT), IELTS (minimum score 6.5). *Application deadline:* For fall admission, 7/15 priority date for domestic students, 7/1 for international students; for spring admission, 11/15 priority date for domestic students, 11/15 for international students. Applications are processed on a rolling basis. Application fee: $40. Electronic applications accepted. *Expenses:* Contact institution. *Financial support:*

In 2013–14, 13 students received support, including 1 research assistantship with full and partial tuition reimbursement available, 1 teaching assistantship; career-related internships or fieldwork, Federal Work-Study, scholarships/grants, and unspecified assistantships also available. Support available to part-time students. Financial award applicants required to submit FAFSA. *Unit head:* Dr. Diane Murphy, Chair, 703-284-5958, Fax: 703-527-3830, E-mail: diane.murphy@marymount.edu. *Application contact:* Francesca Reed, Director, Graduate Admissions, 703-284-5901, Fax: 703-527-3815, E-mail: grad.admissions@marymount.edu.
Website: http://www.marymount.edu/academics/programs/infoTechMS.

Marywood University, Academic Affairs, College of Liberal Arts and Sciences, School of Business and Global Innovation, Emphasis in Management Information Systems, Scranton, PA 18509-1598. Offers MBA, MS. *Entrance requirements:* Additional exam requirements/recommendations for international students: Required—TOEFL (minimum score 550 paper-based; 79 iBT). *Application deadline:* For fall admission, 4/1 priority date for domestic students, 3/31 priority date for international students; for spring admission, 11/1 priority date for domestic students, 8/31 priority date for international students. Applications are processed on a rolling basis. Application fee: $35. Electronic applications accepted. *Expenses: Tuition:* Part-time $775 per credit. Tuition and fees vary according to degree level. *Financial support:* Career-related internships or fieldwork, scholarships/grants, and unspecified assistantships available. Support available to part-time students. Financial award application deadline: 6/30; financial award applicants required to submit FAFSA. *Faculty research:* Systems design. *Unit head:* Dr. Arthur Comstock, Chairman, 570-248-6211 Ext. 2449, E-mail: comstock@marywood.edu. *Application contact:* Tammy Manka, Assistant Director of Graduate Admissions, 570-348-6211 Ext. 2322, E-mail: tmanka@marywood.edu.
Website: http://www.marywood.edu/business/graduate/mis.html.

McGill University, Faculty of Graduate and Postdoctoral Studies, Desautels Faculty of Management, Montréal, QC H3A 2T5, Canada. Offers administration (PhD); entrepreneurial studies (MBA); finance (MBA); general management (Post Master's Certificate); information systems (MBA); international business (MBA); international practicing management (MM); management (MBA); management for development (MBA); manufacturing management (MMM); marketing (MBA); operations management (MBA); public accountancy (Diploma); strategic management (MBA); MBA/LL B; MD/MBA. MMM offered jointly with Faculty of Engineering; PhD with Concordia University, HEC Montreal, Université de Montréal, Université du Québec à Montréal.

McMaster University, School of Graduate Studies, Faculty of Business, Program in Information Systems, Hamilton, ON L8S 4M2, Canada. Offers PhD. Part-time programs available. *Degree requirements:* For doctorate, comprehensive exam, thesis/dissertation. *Entrance requirements:* For doctorate, GMAT or GRE General Test, master's degree, minimum B+ average. Additional exam requirements/recommendations for international students: Required—TOEFL (minimum score 580 paper-based). *Faculty research:* Information systems, operations management, web-based decision support systems, web-based agents, financial engineering.

Metropolitan State University, College of Management, St. Paul, MN 55106-5000. Offers business administration (MBA, DBA); database administration (Graduate Certificate); healthcare information technology management (Graduate Certificate); information assurance security (Graduate Certificate); management information systems (MMIS); MIS generalist (Graduate Certificate); MIS systems analysis and design (Graduate Certificate); project management (Graduate Certificate); public and nonprofit administration (MPNA). Part-time and evening/weekend programs available. *Degree requirements:* For master's, thesis optional, computer language (MMIS). *Entrance requirements:* For master's, GMAT (for MBA), resume. Additional exam requirements/recommendations for international students: Required—TOEFL (minimum score 550 paper-based). Electronic applications accepted. *Expenses:* Tuition, state resident: full-time $5548. Tuition, nonresident: full-time $10,929. *Faculty research:* Yugoslav economic system, workers' cooperatives, participative management and job enrichment, global business systems.

Michigan State University, The Graduate School, College of Communication Arts and Sciences, Department of Telecommunication, Information Studies, and Media, East Lansing, MI 48824. Offers digital media arts and technology (MA); information and telecommunication management (MA); information, policy and society (MA); serious game design (MA). *Entrance requirements:* Additional exam requirements/recommendations for international students: Required—TOEFL. Electronic applications accepted.

Michigan State University, The Graduate School, Eli Broad College of Business, Department of Accounting and Information Systems, East Lansing, MI 48824. Offers accounting (MS, PhD), including information systems (MS), public and corporate accounting (MS), taxation (MS); business information systems (PhD). *Accreditation:* AACSB. *Faculty:* 36. *Students:* 193. 500 applicants, 34% accepted. In 2013, 123 master's awarded. *Degree requirements:* For doctorate, comprehensive exam, thesis/dissertation. *Entrance requirements:* For master's, GMAT (minimum score 550), bachelor's degree in accounting; minimum cumulative GPA of 3.0 at any institution attended and in any junior-/senior-level accounting courses taken; 3 letters of recommendation (at least 1 from faculty); working knowledge of computers including word processing, spreadsheets, networking, and database management system; for doctorate, GMAT (minimum score 600), bachelor's degree; transcripts; 3 letters of recommendation; statement of purpose; resume; on-campus interview; personal qualifications of sound character, perseverance, intellectual curiosity, and interest in scholarly research. Additional exam requirements/recommendations for international students: Required—TOEFL (minimum score 600 paper-based; 100 iBT), IELTS (minimum score 7) accepted for MS only. *Application deadline:* For fall admission, 1/1 for domestic and international students; for spring admission, 10/1 for domestic and international students; for summer admission, 1/1 for domestic and international students. Applications are processed on a rolling basis. Electronic applications accepted. *Financial support:* Research assistantships with tuition reimbursements, teaching assistantships with tuition reimbursements, scholarships/grants, and unspecified assistantships available. Financial award application deadline: 1/1. *Unit head:* Dr. Sanjay Gupta, Associate Dean for MBA and Professional Master's Programs, 517-432-6488, Fax: 517-432-1101, E-mail: gupta@broad.msu.edu. *Application contact:* Program Information Contact, 517-355-7486, Fax: 517-432-1101, E-mail: acct@broad.msu.edu.
Website: http://accounting.broad.msu.edu.

Middle Tennessee State University, College of Graduate Studies, Jennings A. Jones College of Business, Department of Computer Information Systems, Murfreesboro, TN 37132. Offers MS. Part-time and evening/weekend programs available. Postbaccalaureate distance learning degree programs offered. *Faculty:* 15 full-time (6 women). *Students:* 38 full-time (9 women), 38 part-time (9 women); includes 20 minority (8 Black or African American, non-Hispanic/Latino; 8 Asian, non-Hispanic/Latino; 2 Hispanic/Latino; 2 Two or more races, non-Hispanic/Latino). 90 applicants, 41% accepted. In 2013, 28 master's awarded. *Entrance requirements:* Additional exam requirements/recommendations for international students: Required—TOEFL (minimum score 525 paper-based; 71 iBT) or IELTS (minimum score 6). *Application deadline:* For fall admission, 6/1 for domestic and international students. Applications are processed

on a rolling basis. Application fee: $25 ($30 for international students). Electronic applications accepted. *Financial support:* In 2013–14, 8 students received support. Tuition waivers available. Support available to part-time students. Financial award application deadline: 5/1; financial award applicants required to submit FAFSA. *Faculty research:* Safety and security, project management. *Unit head:* Dr. Charles Apigian, Interim Chair, 615-898-2375, Fax: 615-898-5187, E-mail: charles.apigian@mtsu.edu. *Application contact:* Dr. Michael D. Allen, Vice Provost for Research and Dean, 615-898-2840, Fax: 615-904-8020, E-mail: michael.allen@mtsu.edu.

Minnesota State University Mankato, College of Graduate Studies, College of Science, Engineering and Technology, Department of Information Systems and Technology, Mankato, MN 56001. Offers database technologies (Certificate); information technology (MS). *Students:* 15 full-time (4 women), 20 part-time (8 women). *Degree requirements:* For master's, comprehensive exam, thesis or alternative. *Entrance requirements:* For master's, GRE General Test, minimum GPA of 3.0 during previous 2 years. Additional exam requirements/recommendations for international students: Required—TOEFL (minimum score 550 paper-based; 80 iBT). *Application deadline:* For fall admission, 7/1 priority date for domestic students; for spring admission, 11/1 for domestic students. Applications are processed on a rolling basis. Electronic applications accepted. *Financial support:* Research assistantships with full tuition reimbursements, teaching assistantships with full tuition reimbursements, and unspecified assistantships available. Financial award application deadline: 3/15; financial award applicants required to submit FAFSA. *Unit head:* Dr. Mahbubur Syed, Graduate Coordinator, 507-389-3226. *Application contact:* 507-389-2321, E-mail: grad@mnsu.edu.
Website: http://cset.mnsu.edu/ist/.

Minot State University, Graduate School, Information Systems Program, Minot, ND 58707-0002. Offers MSIS. Part-time programs available. Postbaccalaureate distance learning degree programs offered (minimal on-campus study).

Misericordia University, College of Professional Studies and Social Sciences, Program in Organizational Management, Dallas, PA 18612-1098. Offers human resource management (MS); information technology management (MS); management (MS); not-for-profit management (MS). Part-time and evening/weekend programs available. Postbaccalaureate distance learning degree programs offered (no on-campus study). *Faculty:* 3 full-time (0 women), 6 part-time/adjunct (0 women). *Students:* 82 part-time (53 women); includes 2 minority (1 Hispanic/Latino; 1 Native Hawaiian or other Pacific Islander, non-Hispanic/Latino). Average age 33. In 2013, 25 master's awarded. *Entrance requirements:* For master's, GRE General Test, MAT (35th percentile or higher), or minimum undergraduate GPA of 3.0. Additional exam requirements/recommendations for international students: Required—TOEFL. *Application deadline:* Applications are processed on a rolling basis. Application fee: $35. Electronic applications accepted. Application fee is waived when completed online. *Expenses:* Contact institution. *Financial support:* In 2013–14, 55 students received support. Scholarships/grants available. Support available to part-time students. Financial award application deadline: 6/30; financial award applicants required to submit FAFSA. *Unit head:* Dr. Timothy Kearney, Chair of Business Department, 570-674-1487, E-mail: tkearney@misericordia.edu. *Application contact:* David Pasquini, Assistant Director of Admissions, 570-674-8183, Fax: 570-674-6232, E-mail: dpasquin@misericordia.edu.
Website: http://www.misericordia.edu/om.

Mississippi State University, College of Business, Department of Management and Information Systems, Mississippi State, MS 39762. Offers business administration (MBA, PhD), including accounting, business administration (MBA), business information systems (PhD), finance (PhD), management (PhD), marketing (PhD); information systems (MSIS); project management (MBA). Part-time programs available. *Faculty:* 12 full-time (4 women). *Students:* 69 full-time (20 women), 245 part-time (69 women); includes 34 minority (9 Black or African American, non-Hispanic/Latino; 12 Asian, non-Hispanic/Latino; 7 Hispanic/Latino; 1 Native Hawaiian or other Pacific Islander, non-Hispanic/Latino; 5 Two or more races, non-Hispanic/Latino), 20 international. Average age 31. 367 applicants, 29% accepted, 73 enrolled. In 2013, 127 master's, 2 doctorates awarded. *Degree requirements:* For master's, comprehensive exam; for doctorate, comprehensive exam, thesis/dissertation. *Entrance requirements:* For master's, GMAT, minimum GPA of 3.0 in last 60 hours of undergraduate course work; for doctorate, GMAT (minimum score of 550), minimum GPA of 3.25 on all graduate work; BS with minimum GPA of 3.0 cumulative and last 60 hours. Additional exam requirements/recommendations for international students: Required—TOEFL (minimum score 575 paper-based; 84 iBT); Recommended—IELTS (minimum score 7). *Application deadline:* For fall admission, 7/1 for domestic students, 5/1 for international students; for spring admission, 11/1 for domestic students, 9/1 for international students. Applications are processed on a rolling basis. Application fee: $60. Electronic applications accepted. *Financial support:* In 2013–14, 1 teaching assistantship (averaging $13,497 per year) was awarded; career-related internships or fieldwork, Federal Work-Study, institutionally sponsored loans, scholarships/grants, and unspecified assistantships also available. Financial award applicants required to submit FAFSA. *Faculty research:* Electronic commerce, management of information technology. *Unit head:* Dr. Tim Barnett, Department Chairperson and Professor of Management, 662-325-3928, Fax: 662-325-8651, E-mail: tim.barnett@msstate.edu. *Application contact:* Dr. Rebecca Long, Graduate Coordinator, 662-325-3928, E-mail: gsb@cobian.msstate.edu.
Website: http://www.business.msstate.edu/programs/mis/index.php.

Missouri State University, Graduate College, College of Business Administration, Department of Computer Information Systems, Springfield, MO 65897. Offers computer information systems (MS); secondary education (MS Ed), including business. Part-time and evening/weekend programs available. Postbaccalaureate distance learning degree programs offered (no on-campus study). *Faculty:* 13 full-time (2 women), 6 part-time/adjunct (0 women). *Students:* 22 full-time (3 women); includes 4 minority (2 Black or African American, non-Hispanic/Latino; 1 Hispanic/Latino; 1 Two or more races, non-Hispanic/Latino), 21 international. Average age 38. 20 applicants, 70% accepted, 12 enrolled. In 2013, 15 master's awarded. *Degree requirements:* For master's, thesis optional. *Entrance requirements:* For master's, GMAT, 3 years of work experience in computer information systems, minimum GPA of 2.75 (MS), 9-12 teaching certification (MS Ed). Additional exam requirements/recommendations for international students: Required—TOEFL (minimum score 550 paper-based; 79 iBT). *Application deadline:* For fall admission, 7/20 priority date for domestic students, 5/1 for international students; for spring admission, 12/20 priority date for domestic students, 9/1 for international students. Applications are processed on a rolling basis. Application fee: $35 ($50 for international students). Electronic applications accepted. *Expenses:* Contact institution. *Financial support:* Federal Work-Study, institutionally sponsored loans, scholarships/grants, and unspecified assistantships available. Support available to part-time students. Financial award application deadline: 3/31; financial award applicants required to submit FAFSA. *Faculty research:* Decision support systems, algorithms in Visual Basic, end-user satisfaction, information security. *Unit head:* Dr. Jerry Chin, Head, 417-836-4131, Fax: 417-836-6907, E-mail: jerrychin@missouristate.edu. *Application contact:* Misty Stewart, Coordinator of Graduate Admissions and Recruitment, 417-836-6079, Fax: 417-836-6200, E-mail: mistystewart@missouristate.edu.
Website: http://cis.missouristate.edu/.

Management Information Systems

Missouri Western State University, Program in Applied Science, St. Joseph, MO 64507-2294. Offers chemistry (MAS); engineering technology management (MAS); human factors and usability testing (MAS); industrial life science (MAS); information technology management (MAS); sport and fitness management (MAS). Part-time programs available. *Students:* 38 full-time (11 women), 24 part-time (10 women); includes 7 minority (4 Black or African American, non-Hispanic/Latino; 1 Asian, non-Hispanic/Latino; 1 Hispanic/Latino; 1 Two or more races, non-Hispanic/Latino), 21 international. Average age 28. 60 applicants, 90% accepted, 37 enrolled. In 2013, 15 master's awarded. *Entrance requirements:* Additional exam requirements/recommendations for international students: Recommended—TOEFL (minimum score 500 paper-based; 61 iBT), IELTS (minimum score 5.5). *Application deadline:* For fall admission, 7/15 for domestic students, 6/15 for international students; for spring admission, 10/1 for domestic students, 10/15 for international students. Applications are processed on a rolling basis. Application fee: $45 ($50 for international students). Electronic applications accepted. *Expenses:* Tuition, state resident: full-time $6019; part-time $300.96 per credit hour. Tuition, nonresident: full-time $11,194; part-time $559.71 per credit hour. *Required fees:* $542; $99 per credit hour. $176 per semester. Tuition and fees vary according to course load and program. *Financial support:* Scholarships/grants and unspecified assistantships available. Support available to part-time students. *Unit head:* Dr. Benjamin D. Caldwell, Dean of the Graduate School, 816-271-4394, Fax: 816-271-4525, E-mail: graduate@missouriwestern.edu. *Application contact:* Dr. Benjamin D. Caldwell, Dean of the Graduate School, 816-271-4394, Fax: 816-271-4525, E-mail: graduate@missouriwestern.edu.

Monmouth University, The Graduate School, Department of Computer Science, West Long Branch, NJ 07764-1898. Offers computer science (MS); computer science software design and development (Certificate); information systems (MS). Part-time and evening/weekend programs available. *Faculty:* 4 full-time (2 women), 4 part-time/adjunct (0 women). *Students:* 41 full-time (17 women), 18 part-time (8 women); includes 2 minority (1 Asian, non-Hispanic/Latino; 1 Hispanic/Latino), 48 international. Average age 25. 107 applicants, 88% accepted, 31 enrolled. In 2013, 23 master's awarded. *Degree requirements:* For master's, thesis optional. *Entrance requirements:* For master's and Certificate, minimum GPA of 3.0 in major, 2.75 overall; two letters of recommendation; calculus I and II with minimum C grade; two semesters of computer programming courses within the past five years with minimum B grade. Additional exam requirements/recommendations for international students: Required—TOEFL (minimum score 550 paper-based, 79 iBT), IELTS (minimum score 6) or Michigan English Language Assessment Battery (minimum score 77). *Application deadline:* For fall admission, 7/15 priority date for domestic students, 6/1 for international students; for spring admission, 11/15 priority date for domestic students, 11/1 for international students. Applications are processed on a rolling basis. Application fee: $50. Electronic applications accepted. *Expenses: Tuition:* Part-time $1004 per credit hour. *Required fees:* $157 per semester. *Financial support:* In 2013–14, 47 students received support, including 45 fellowships (averaging $2,817 per year), 17 research assistantships (averaging $6,248 per year); career-related internships or fieldwork, scholarships/grants, and unspecified assistantships also available. Support available to part-time students. Financial award application deadline: 3/1; financial award applicants required to submit FAFSA. *Faculty research:* Databases, natural language processing, protocols, performance analysis, communications networks (systems), telecommunications. *Unit head:* Dr. Cui Yu, Program Director, 732-571-4460, Fax: 732-263-5202, E-mail: cyu@monmouth.edu. *Application contact:* Lauren Vento Cifelli, Associate Vice President of Undergraduate and Graduate Admission, 732-571-3452, Fax: 732-263-5123, E-mail: gradadm@monmouth.edu.
Website: http://www.monmouth.edu/academics/CSSE/mscs.asp.

Montclair State University, The Graduate School, School of Business, Post Master's Certificate Program in Management Information Systems, Montclair, NJ 07043-1624. Offers Post Master's Certificate. Part-time and evening/weekend programs available. *Entrance requirements:* For degree, essay. Additional exam requirements/recommendations for international students: Required—TOEFL (minimum score 83 iBT) or IELTS (minimum score 6.5). Electronic applications accepted. *Faculty research:* Search engine optimization; trust and privacy online; data mining; teaching in hybrid and online environments; counterproductive work behavior and its effect on organizations, employees and customers; social identity and identification in organizations.

Morehead State University, Graduate Programs, College of Business and Public Affairs, Department of Information Systems, Morehead, KY 40351. Offers MSIS. *Entrance requirements:* For master's, GRE, GMAT. Additional exam requirements/recommendations for international students: Required—TOEFL (minimum score 525 paper-based). Electronic applications accepted.

Morehead State University, Graduate Programs, College of Business and Public Affairs, School of Business Administration, Morehead, KY 40351. Offers business administration (MBA); information systems (MSIS); sport management (MA). Part-time and evening/weekend programs available. *Entrance requirements:* For master's, GRE or GMAT. Additional exam requirements/recommendations for international students: Required—TOEFL (minimum score 500 paper-based). Electronic applications accepted.

National University, Academic Affairs, School of Business and Management, La Jolla, CA 92037-1011. Offers accountancy (Certificate); business administration (GMBA, MBA), including financial management (MBA), human resource management (MBA), integrated marketing communications (MBA), international business (MBA), management accounting (MBA), marketing (MBA), mobile marketing and social media (MBA), organizational leadership (MA, MBA), professional golf management (MBA); global management (MGM); human resource management (MA), including organizational development and change, organizational leadership (MA, MBA); international business (Certificate); management information systems (MS); organizational leadership (MS), including community development; sustainability management (MS). Part-time and evening/weekend programs available. Postbaccalaureate distance learning degree programs offered (no on-campus study). *Faculty:* 30 full-time (8 women), 88 part-time/adjunct (25 women). *Students:* 688 full-time (357 women), 331 part-time (161 women); includes 453 minority (105 Black or African American, non-Hispanic/Latino; 2 American Indian or Alaska Native, non-Hispanic/Latino; 143 Asian, non-Hispanic/Latino; 162 Hispanic/Latino; 13 Native Hawaiian or other Pacific Islander, non-Hispanic/Latino; 28 Two or more races, non-Hispanic/Latino), 165 international. Average age 33. 286 applicants, 100% accepted, 217 enrolled. In 2013, 641 master's awarded. *Degree requirements:* For master's, thesis (for some programs). *Entrance requirements:* For master's, interview, minimum GPA of 2.5. Additional exam requirements/recommendations for international students: Required—TOEFL (minimum score 550 paper-based; 79 iBT), IELTS (minimum score 6). *Application deadline:* Applications are processed on a rolling basis. Application fee: $60 ($65 for international students). Electronic applications accepted. *Expenses: Tuition:* Full-time $13,824; part-time $1728 per course. One-time fee: $160. *Financial support:* Career-related internships or fieldwork, scholarships/grants, and tuition waivers (partial) available. Support available to part-time students. Financial award application deadline: 6/30; financial award applicants required to submit FAFSA. *Unit head:* School of Business and Management, 800-628-8648, Fax: 858-642-8719, E-mail: sobm@nu.edu.

Application contact: Louis Cruz, Interim Vice President for Enrollment Services, 800-628-8648, E-mail: advisor@nu.edu.
Website: http://www.nu.edu/OurPrograms/SchoolOfBusinessAndManagement.html.

National University, Academic Affairs, School of Engineering, Technology and Media, La Jolla, CA 92037-1011. Offers computer science (MS), including advanced computing, database engineering, software engineering; cyber security and information assurance (MS), including computer forensics, ethical hacking and penetration testing, health information assurance, information assurance and security; data analytics (MS); engineering management (MS), including enterprise architecture, project management, systems engineering, technology management; environmental engineering (MS); homeland security and emergency management (MS); management information systems (MS); project management (Certificate); sustainability management (MS); wireless communications (MS). Part-time and evening/weekend programs available. Postbaccalaureate distance learning degree programs offered (no on-campus study). *Faculty:* 19 full-time (4 women), 28 part-time/adjunct (5 women). *Students:* 294 full-time (90 women), 100 part-time (29 women); includes 198 minority (49 Black or African American, non-Hispanic/Latino; 69 Asian, non-Hispanic/Latino; 60 Hispanic/Latino; 3 Native Hawaiian or other Pacific Islander, non-Hispanic/Latino; 17 Two or more races, non-Hispanic/Latino), 50 international. Average age 34. 160 applicants, 100% accepted, 123 enrolled. In 2013, 174 master's awarded. *Degree requirements:* For master's, thesis (for some programs). *Entrance requirements:* For master's, interview, minimum GPA of 2.5. Additional exam requirements/recommendations for international students: Required—TOEFL (minimum score 550 paper-based; 79 iBT), IELTS (minimum score 6). *Application deadline:* Applications are processed on a rolling basis. Application fee: $60 ($65 for international students). Electronic applications accepted. *Expenses: Tuition:* Full-time $13,824; part-time $1728 per course. One-time fee: $160. *Financial support:* Career-related internships or fieldwork, institutionally sponsored loans, scholarships/grants, and tuition waivers (partial) available. Support available to part-time students. Financial award application deadline: 6/30; financial award applicants required to submit FAFSA. *Faculty research:* Educational technology, scholarships in science. *Unit head:* School of Engineering, Technology, and Media, 800-628-8648, E-mail: setm@nu.edu. *Application contact:* Louis Cruz, Interim Vice President for Enrollment Services, 800-628-8648, E-mail: advisor@nu.edu.
Website: http://www.nu.edu/OurPrograms/SchoolOfEngineeringAndTechnology.html.

Naval Postgraduate School, Departments and Academic Groups, Department of Information Sciences, Monterey, CA 93943. Offers electronic warfare systems engineering (MS); information sciences (PhD); information systems and operations (MS); information technology management (MS); information warfare systems engineering (MS); knowledge superiority (Certificate); remote sensing intelligence (MS); system technology (command, control and communications) (MS). Program open only to commissioned officers of the United States and friendly nations and selected United States federal civilian employees. Part-time programs available. *Degree requirements:* For master's, thesis (for some programs); for doctorate, thesis/dissertation. *Faculty research:* Designing inter-organisational collectivities for dynamic fit: stability, manoeuvrability and application in disaster relief endeavours; system self-awareness and related methods for Improving the use and understanding of data within DoD; evaluating a macrocognition model of team collaboration using real-world data from the Haiti relief effort; cyber distortion in command and control; performance and QoS in service-based systems.

Naval Postgraduate School, Departments and Academic Groups, Graduate School of Business and Public Policy, Monterey, CA 93943. Offers acquisition and contract management (MBA); business administration (EMBA, MBA); contract management (MS); defense business management (MBA); defense systems analysis (MS), including management; defense systems management (international) (MBA); financial management (MBA); information management (MBA); manpower systems analysis (MS); material logistics support management (MBA); program management (MS); resource planning and management for international defense (MBA); supply chain management (MBA); systems acquisition management (MBA); transportation management (MBA). Program only open to commissioned officers of the United States and friendly nations and selected United States federal civilian employees. *Accreditation:* AACSB; NASPAA. Part-time programs available. Postbaccalaureate distance learning degree programs offered (minimal on-campus study). *Degree requirements:* For master's, thesis (for some programs), terminal project/capstone (for some programs). *Faculty research:* U.S. and European public procurement policies for small and medium-sized enterprises, examining external validity criticisms in the choice of students as subjects in accounting experiment studies, assurance of learning in contract management education, contracting for cloud computing: opportunities and risks, NPS, Apple App Store as a business model supporting U. S. Navy requirements.

New England Institute of Technology, Program in Information Technology, East Greenwich, RI 02818. Offers MS. Part-time and evening/weekend programs available. *Students:* 3 full-time (0 women), 25 part-time (5 women); includes 3 minority (1 Asian, non-Hispanic/Latino; 2 Hispanic/Latino), 3 international. Average age 31. *Degree requirements:* For master's, project. *Application deadline:* For fall admission, 10/1 for domestic students. Applications are processed on a rolling basis. Application fee: $25. Electronic applications accepted. *Application contact:* James Jessup, Director of Admissions, 401-467-7744 Ext. 3339, E-mail: jjessup@neit.edu.
Website: http://www.neit.edu/Programs/Masters-Degree/Information-Technology.

New Jersey Institute of Technology, College of Computing Science, Newark, NJ 07102. Offers computer science (MS, PhD), including bioinformatics (MS), computer science, computing and business (MS), cyber security and privacy (MS), software engineering (MS); information systems (MS, PhD), including business and information systems (MS), emergency management and business continuity (MS), information systems; information technology administration and security (MS). Part-time and evening/weekend programs available. *Faculty:* 50 full-time (7 women), 22 part-time/adjunct (2 women). *Students:* 315 full-time (110 women), 317 part-time (86 women); includes 196 minority (53 Black or African American, non-Hispanic/Latino; 3 American Indian or Alaska Native, non-Hispanic/Latino; 78 Asian, non-Hispanic/Latino; 62 Hispanic/Latino), 605 international. Average age 30. 1,559 applicants, 63% accepted, 227 enrolled. In 2013, 239 master's, 4 doctorates awarded. Terminal master's awarded for partial completion of doctoral program. *Degree requirements:* For master's, thesis optional; for doctorate, thesis/dissertation. *Entrance requirements:* For master's, GRE General Test; for doctorate, GRE General Test, minimum graduate GPA of 3.5. Additional exam requirements/recommendations for international students: Required—TOEFL (minimum score 550 paper-based; 79 iBT). *Application deadline:* For fall admission, 6/1 priority date for domestic students, 5/1 priority date for international students; for spring admission, 11/15 priority date for domestic and international students. Applications are processed on a rolling basis. Application fee: $65. Electronic applications accepted. *Expenses:* Tuition, state resident: full-time $17,384; part-time $945 per credit. Tuition, nonresident: full-time $25,404; part-time $1341 per credit. *Required fees:* $2396; $118 per credit. *Financial support:* Fellowships with full and partial tuition reimbursements, research assistantships with full and partial tuition reimbursements, teaching assistantships with full and partial tuition reimbursements, career-related internships or fieldwork, Federal Work-Study, institutionally sponsored

loans, and unspecified assistantships available. Financial award application deadline: 1/15. *Faculty research:* Computer systems, communications and networking, artificial intelligence, database engineering, systems analysis. *Total annual research expenditures:* $984,200. *Unit head:* Dr. Narain Gehani, Dean, 973-542-5488, Fax: 973-596-5777, E-mail: narain.gehani@njit.edu. *Application contact:* Kathryn Kelly, Director of Admissions, 973-596-3300, Fax: 973-596-3461, E-mail: admissions@njit.edu. Website: http://ccs.njit.edu.

Newman University, MBA Program, Wichita, KS 67213-2097. Offers finance (MBA); international business (MBA); leadership (MBA); management (MBA); management information technology (MBA). Part-time programs available. *Faculty:* 7 full-time (1 woman), 7 part-time/adjunct (4 women). *Students:* 31 full-time (19 women), 56 part-time (24 women); includes 24 minority (6 Black or African American, non-Hispanic/Latino; 1 American Indian or Alaska Native, non-Hispanic/Latino; 9 Asian, non-Hispanic/Latino; 5 Hispanic/Latino; 3 Two or more races, non-Hispanic/Latino), 9 international. Average age 31. 83 applicants, 63% accepted, 32 enrolled. In 2013, 47 master's awarded. *Degree requirements:* For master's, thesis optional. *Entrance requirements:* For master's, minimum GPA of 3.0; 2 letters of recommendation; course work in algebra, statistics, macroeconomics, and financial accounting. Additional exam requirements/recommendations for international students: Required—TOEFL (minimum score 600 paper-based; 100 iBT). *Application deadline:* For fall admission, 8/1 priority date for domestic students, 7/15 priority date for international students; for winter admission, 1/1 priority date for domestic students; for spring admission, 1/1 priority date for domestic students, 11/15 priority date for international students. Applications are processed on a rolling basis. Application fee: $25 ($40 for international students). Electronic applications accepted. *Expenses:* Contact institution. *Financial support:* In 2013–14, 8 students received support. Scholarships/grants available. Financial award application deadline: 8/15; financial award applicants required to submit FAFSA. *Unit head:* Dr. Wendy Munday, Director of MBA Program, 316-942-4291 Ext. 2296, Fax: 316-942-4483, E-mail: mundayw@newmanu.edu. *Application contact:* Linda Kay Sabala, Director of Graduate Admissions, 316-942-4291 Ext. 2230, Fax: 316-942-4483, E-mail: sabalal@newmanu.edu.
Website: http://www.newmanu.edu.

New Mexico Highlands University, Graduate Studies, School of Business, Media and Technology, Las Vegas, NM 87701. Offers business administration (MBA), including government nonprofit management, human resource management, international business, management, management information systems; media arts and technology (MA), including media arts and computer science. *Accreditation:* ACBSP. *Faculty:* 13 full-time (5 women). *Students:* 65 full-time (34 women), 146 part-time (89 women); includes 137 minority (3 Black or African American, non-Hispanic/Latino; 9 American Indian or Alaska Native, non-Hispanic/Latino; 1 Asian, non-Hispanic/Latino; 120 Hispanic/Latino; 2 Native Hawaiian or other Pacific Islander, non-Hispanic/Latino; 2 Two or more races, non-Hispanic/Latino), 23 international. Average age 34. In 2013, 56 master's awarded. *Degree requirements:* For master's, comprehensive exam, thesis or alternative. *Entrance requirements:* For master's, minimum undergraduate GPA of 3.0. Additional exam requirements/recommendations for international students: Required—TOEFL (minimum score 540 paper-based). *Application deadline:* For fall admission, 8/1 priority date for domestic students. Applications are processed on a rolling basis. Application fee: $15. *Expenses:* Tuition, state resident: full-time $4278; part-time $178 per credit hour. Tuition, nonresident: full-time $6716; part-time $281 per credit hour. One-time fee: $15. *Financial support:* Career-related internships or fieldwork, Federal Work-Study, institutionally sponsored loans, scholarships/grants, tuition waivers (full and partial), and unspecified assistantships available. Support available to part-time students. Financial award application deadline: 3/1; financial award applicants required to submit FAFSA. *Faculty research:* Real estate valuation, studying expert judgments in complex accounting, decision environments, green marketing, environmentalism, marketing research methodology. *Unit head:* Dr. Margaret Young, Dean, 505-454-3522, Fax: 505-454-3354, E-mail: young_m@nmhu.edu. *Application contact:* Diane Trujillo, Administrative Assistant, Graduate Studies, 505-454-3266, Fax: 505-426-2117, E-mail: dtrujillo@nmhu.edu.

New York University, Leonard N. Stern School of Business, Department of Information, Operations and Management Sciences, New York, NY 10012-1019. Offers information systems (MBA, PhD); operations management (MBA, PhD); statistics (MBA, PhD). *Expenses:* Tuition: Full-time $35,856; part-time $1494 per unit. *Required fees:* $1408; $64 per unit. $473 per term. Tuition and fees vary according to course load and program. *Faculty research:* Knowledge management, economics of information, computer-supported groups and communities financial information systems, data mining and business intelligence.

New York University, Polytechnic School of Engineering, Department of Technology Management, New York, NY 10012-1019. Offers construction management (Advanced Certificate); electronic business management (Advanced Certificate); entrepreneurship (Advanced Certificate); human resources management (Advanced Certificate); industrial engineering (MS); information management (Advanced Certificate); management (MS); management of technology (MS); manufacturing engineering (MS); organizational behavior (MS, Advanced Certificate); project management (Advanced Certificate); technology management (MBA, PhD, Advanced Certificate); telecommunications management (Advanced Certificate). Part-time and evening/weekend programs available. *Faculty:* 7 full-time (1 woman), 41 part-time/adjunct (2 women). *Students:* 285 full-time (132 women), 116 part-time (45 women); includes 50 minority (10 Black or African American, non-Hispanic/Latino; 29 Asian, non-Hispanic/Latino; 11 Hispanic/Latino), 284 international. Average age 30. 726 applicants, 60% accepted, 140 enrolled. In 2013, 137 master's awarded. *Degree requirements:* For master's, comprehensive exam (for some programs), thesis (for some programs); for doctorate, comprehensive exam, thesis/dissertation. *Entrance requirements:* For master's, GMAT, minimum B average in undergraduate course work. Additional exam requirements/recommendations for international students: Required—TOEFL (minimum score 550 paper-based; 80 iBT); Recommended—IELTS (minimum score 6.5). *Application deadline:* For fall admission, 7/31 priority date for domestic students, 4/30 priority date for international students; for spring admission, 12/31 priority date for domestic students, 11/30 priority date for international students. Applications are processed on a rolling basis. Application fee: $75. Electronic applications accepted. *Expenses:* Tuition: Full-time $35,856; part-time $1494 per unit. *Required fees:* $1408; $64 per unit. $473 per term. Tuition and fees vary according to course load and program. *Financial support:* In 2013–14, 1 fellowship (averaging $26,400 per year) was awarded; research assistantships, teaching assistantships, institutionally sponsored loans, scholarships/grants, and unspecified assistantships also available. Support available to part-time students. *Faculty research:* Global innovation and research and development strategy, managing emerging technologies, technology and development, service design and innovation, tech entrepreneurship and commercialization, sustainable and clean-tech innovation, impacts of information technology upon individuals, organizations and society. *Total annual research expenditures:* $692,936. *Unit head:* Prof. Bharadwaj Rao, Head, 718-260-3617, Fax: 718-260-3874, E-mail: brao@poly.edu. *Application contact:* Raymond Lutzky, Director of Graduate Enrollment Management, 718-637-5984, Fax: 718-260-3624, E-mail: rlutzky@poly.edu.
Website: http://www.poly.edu/academics/departments/technology/.

New York University, School of Continuing and Professional Studies, Division of Programs in Business, Graduate Programs in Management and Systems, New York, NY 10012-1019. Offers core business competencies (Advanced Certificate); database technologies (MS); enterprise risk management (MS, Advanced Certificate); information technologies (Advanced Certificate); strategy and leadership (MS, Advanced Certificate); systems management (MS). Part-time and evening/weekend programs available. Postbaccalaureate distance learning degree programs offered (no on-campus study). *Faculty:* 1 full-time (0 women), 28 part-time/adjunct (7 women). *Students:* 59 full-time (30 women), 213 part-time (91 women); includes 75 minority (31 Black or African American, non-Hispanic/Latino; 30 Asian, non-Hispanic/Latino; 13 Hispanic/Latino; 1 Two or more races, non-Hispanic/Latino), 67 international. Average age 33. 213 applicants, 70% accepted, 58 enrolled. In 2013, 60 master's, 15 other advanced degrees awarded. *Degree requirements:* For master's, thesis, capstone project. *Entrance requirements:* For master's, bachelor's degree, resume with relevant professional work, internship or volunteer experience, two letters of recommendation, statement of purpose. Additional exam requirements/recommendations for international students: Required—TOEFL (minimum score 600 paper-based; 100 iBT), IELTS (minimum score 7). *Application deadline:* For fall admission, 2/1 priority date for domestic and international students; for spring admission, 10/15 priority date for domestic students, 8/15 priority date for international students. Applications are processed on a rolling basis. Application fee: $150. Electronic applications accepted. *Expenses:* Tuition: Full-time $35,856; part-time $1494 per unit. *Required fees:* $1408; $64 per unit. $473 per term. Tuition and fees vary according to course load and program. *Financial support:* In 2013–14, 60 students received support, including 60 fellowships (averaging $2,242 per year). *Unit head:* Vish Ganpati, Academic Director, 212-998-7112, E-mail: vg36@nyu.edu. *Application contact:* Admissions Office, 212-998-7100, E-mail: scps.gradadmissions@nyu.edu.
Website: http://www.scps.nyu.edu/areas-of-study/information-technology/.

North Carolina Agricultural and Technical State University, School of Graduate Studies, School of Technology, Department of Electronics, Computer, and Information Technology, Greensboro, NC 27411. Offers electronics and computer technology (MSIT, MSTM); information technology (MSIT, MSTM).

North Central College, Graduate and Continuing Studies Programs, Department of Business, Program in Management Information Systems, Naperville, IL 60566-7063. Offers MS. Part-time and evening/weekend programs available. *Faculty:* 15 full-time (5 women), 8 part-time/adjunct (0 women). *Students:* 1 full-time (0 women), 5 part-time (0 women); includes 1 minority (Black or African American, non-Hispanic/Latino), 1 international. Average age 38. 14 applicants, 7% accepted. In 2013, 2 master's awarded. *Degree requirements:* For master's, thesis optional, project. *Entrance requirements:* For master's, interview. Additional exam requirements/recommendations for international students: Required—TOEFL (minimum score 577 paper-based; 90 iBT). *Application deadline:* For fall admission, 8/15 for domestic students; for winter admission, 12/1 for domestic students; for spring admission, 2/1 for domestic students. Applications are processed on a rolling basis. Application fee: $25. *Expenses:* Contact institution. *Financial support:* Scholarships/grants available. Support available to part-time students. *Unit head:* Dr. Caroline St. Clair, Program Coordinator, Management Information Systems, 630-637-5171, Fax: 630-637-5172, E-mail: cstclair@noctrl.edu. *Application contact:* Wendy Kulpinski, Director of Graduate and Continuing Education Admission, 630-637-5808, Fax: 630-637-5844, E-mail: wekulpinski@noctrl.edu.

Northeastern University, College of Computer and Information Science, Boston, MA 02115-5096. Offers computer science (MS, PhD); health informatics (MS); information assurance (MS, PhD). Part-time and evening/weekend programs available. Terminal master's awarded for partial completion of doctoral program. *Degree requirements:* For master's, thesis optional; for doctorate, comprehensive exam, thesis/dissertation.

Northern Illinois University, Graduate School, College of Business, Department of Operations Management and Information Systems, De Kalb, IL 60115-2854. Offers management information systems (MS). Part-time programs available. *Faculty:* 11 full-time (3 women), 3 part-time/adjunct (0 women). *Students:* 48 full-time (19 women), 37 part-time (9 women); includes 11 minority (6 Black or African American, non-Hispanic/Latino; 4 Asian, non-Hispanic/Latino; 1 Hispanic/Latino), 44 international. Average age 30. 128 applicants, 65% accepted, 29 enrolled. In 2013, 37 master's awarded. *Degree requirements:* For master's, computer language. *Entrance requirements:* For master's, GMAT, minimum GPA of 2.75. Additional exam requirements/recommendations for international students: Required—TOEFL (minimum score 550 paper-based). *Application deadline:* For fall admission, 6/1 for domestic students, 5/1 for international students; for spring admission, 11/1 for domestic students, 10/1 for international students. Applications are processed on a rolling basis. Application fee: $40. Electronic applications accepted. *Financial support:* In 2013–14, 5 research assistantships with full tuition reimbursements, 16 teaching assistantships with full tuition reimbursements were awarded; fellowships with full tuition reimbursements, career-related internships or fieldwork, Federal Work-Study, scholarships/grants, tuition waivers (full), and unspecified assistantships also available. Support available to part-time students. Financial award applicants required to submit FAFSA. *Faculty research:* Affordability of home ownership, Web portal competition intranet, electronic commerce, corporate-academic alliances. *Unit head:* Dr. Chang Liu, Chair, 815-753-3021, Fax: 815-753-7460. *Application contact:* Steve Kispert, Office of Graduate Studies in Business, 815-753-6372, E-mail: skispert@niu.edu.
Website: http://www.cob.niu.edu/omis/.

Northwestern University, School of Professional Studies, Program in Information Systems, Evanston, IL 60208. Offers analytics and business intelligence (MS); database and Internet technologies (MS); information systems (MS); information systems management (MS); information systems security (MS); medical informatics (MS); software project management and development (MS).

Northwest Missouri State University, Graduate School, Melvin and Valorie Booth College of Business and Professional Studies, Program in Information Technology Management, Maryville, MO 64468-6001. Offers MBA. Part-time programs available. *Degree requirements:* For master's, comprehensive exam. *Entrance requirements:* For master's, GMAT/GRE, minimum GPA of 2.5. Additional exam requirements/recommendations for international students: Required—TOEFL (minimum score 550 paper-based).

Norwich University, College of Graduate and Continuing Studies, Master of Science in Information Assurance Program, Northfield, VT 05663. Offers information security and assurance (MS), including computer forensics, investigation/incident response team management, project management. Evening/weekend programs available. Postbaccalaureate distance learning degree programs offered (minimal on-campus study). *Faculty:* 9 part-time/adjunct (2 women). *Students:* 47 full-time (6 women); includes 8 minority (3 Black or African American, non-Hispanic/Latino; 1 American Indian or Alaska Native, non-Hispanic/Latino; 4 Asian, non-Hispanic/Latino). Average age 40. 77 applicants, 38% accepted, 23 enrolled. In 2013, 41 master's awarded. *Entrance requirements:* For master's, minimum undergraduate GPA of 2.75. Additional exam requirements/recommendations for international students: Required—TOEFL (minimum score 600 paper-based; 94 iBT). *Application deadline:* For fall admission, 8/1 for domestic and international students; for winter admission, 11/1 for domestic and

international students; for spring admission, 2/1 for domestic and international students; for summer admission, 5/1 for domestic and international students. Applications are processed on a rolling basis. Application fee: $50. Electronic applications accepted. *Expenses:* Contact institution. *Financial support:* In 2013–14, 13 students received support. Scholarships/grants available. Financial award applicants required to submit FAFSA. *Unit head:* Dr. Rosemarie Pelletier, Program Director, 802-485-2767, Fax: 802-485-2533, E-mail: rpellet2@norwich.edu. *Application contact:* Elizabeth Templeton, Associate Program Director, 802-485-2757, Fax: 802-485-2533, E-mail: etemplet@norwich.edu.
Website: http://online.norwich.edu/degree-programs/masters/master-science-information-security-assurance/overview.

Nova Southeastern University, Graduate School of Computer and Information Sciences, Fort Lauderdale, FL 33314-7796. Offers computer science (MS, PhD); information assurance (PhD); information security (MS); information systems (PhD); information technology (MS); management information systems (MS); software engineering (MS). Part-time and evening/weekend programs available. Postbaccalaureate distance learning degree programs offered (minimal on-campus study). *Faculty:* 20 full-time (6 women), 24 part-time/adjunct (3 women). *Students:* 99 full-time (30 women), 823 part-time (241 women); includes 422 minority (186 Black or African American, non-Hispanic/Latino; 2 American Indian or Alaska Native, non-Hispanic/Latino; 56 Asian, non-Hispanic/Latino; 161 Hispanic/Latino; 17 Two or more races, non-Hispanic/Latino), 67 international. Average age 41. 332 applicants, 69% accepted. In 2013, 177 master's, 69 doctorates awarded. Terminal master's awarded for partial completion of doctoral program. *Degree requirements:* For master's, thesis optional; for doctorate, thesis/dissertation. *Entrance requirements:* For master's, minimum undergraduate GPA of 2.5; 3.0 in major; for doctorate, master's degree, minimum graduate GPA of 3.25. Additional exam requirements/recommendations for international students: Required—TOEFL (minimum score 80 iBT), IELTS (minimum score 6). *Application deadline:* Applications are processed on a rolling basis. Application fee: $50. Electronic applications accepted. *Expenses:* Contact institution. *Financial support:* Application deadline: 5/1; applicants required to submit FAFSA. *Faculty research:* Artificial intelligence, database management, human-computer interaction, distance education, information security. *Unit head:* Dr. Eric S. Ackerman, Dean, 954-262-2000, Fax: 954-262-2752, E-mail: esa@nova.edu. *Application contact:* Nancy Ruidiaz, Director, Admissions, 954-262-2026, Fax: 954-262-2752, E-mail: azoulayn@nova.edu.
Website: http://www.scis.nova.edu/.

Oakland University, Graduate Study and Lifelong Learning, School of Business Administration, Department of Decision and Information Sciences, Rochester, MI 48309-4401. Offers information technology management (MS); management information systems (Certificate); production and operations management (Certificate). *Faculty:* 8 full-time (1 woman), 1 part-time/adjunct (0 women). *Students:* 17 full-time (6 women), 25 part-time (9 women); includes 9 minority (2 Black or African American, non-Hispanic/Latino; 7 Asian, non-Hispanic/Latino), 11 international. Average age 32. 78 applicants, 31% accepted, 24 enrolled. In 2013, 6 master's, 2 other advanced degrees awarded. Application fee: $0. *Unit head:* Dr. Thomas Lauer, Chair, 248-370-3283, Fax: 248-370-4604. *Application contact:* Donna Free, Coordinator, 248-370-3281.

The Ohio State University, Graduate School, Max M. Fisher College of Business, Department of Accounting and Management Information Systems, Columbus, OH 43210. Offers M Acc, PhD. *Accreditation:* AACSB. *Faculty:* 23. *Students:* 89 full-time (44 women), 2 part-time (1 woman); includes 10 minority (1 Black or African American, non-Hispanic/Latino; 4 Asian, non-Hispanic/Latino; 2 Hispanic/Latino; 1 Native Hawaiian or other Pacific Islander, non-Hispanic/Latino; 2 Two or more races, non-Hispanic/Latino), 35 international. Average age 24. In 2013, 85 master's, 2 doctorates awarded. Terminal master's awarded for partial completion of doctoral program. *Degree requirements:* For doctorate, thesis/dissertation. *Entrance requirements:* For master's and doctorate, GMAT (preferred) or GRE. Additional exam requirements/recommendations for international students: Required—TOEFL (minimum score 600 paper-based; 100 iBT), Michigan English Language Assessment Battery (minimum score 86); Recommended—IELTS (minimum score 7.5). *Application deadline:* For fall admission, 11/15 priority date for domestic students, 11/1 priority date for international students; for winter admission, 12/1 for domestic students, 11/1 for international students; for spring admission, 3/1 for domestic students, 2/1 for international students. Applications are processed on a rolling basis. Application fee: $60 ($70 for international students). Electronic applications accepted. *Financial support:* Fellowships with tuition reimbursements, research assistantships with tuition reimbursements, teaching assistantships with tuition reimbursements, career-related internships or fieldwork, Federal Work-Study, and institutionally sponsored loans available. Support available to part-time students. *Faculty research:* Artificial intelligence, protocol analysis, database design in decision-supporting systems. *Unit head:* Waleed Muhanna, Chair, 614-292-2082, Fax: 614-292-2118, E-mail: muhanna.1@osu.edu. *Application contact:* Graduate Admissions, 614-292-6031, Fax: 614-292-3656, E-mail: gradadmissions@osu.edu.
Website: http://fisher.osu.edu/departments/accounting-and-mis/.

Oklahoma State University, Spears School of Business, Department of Management Science and Information Systems, Stillwater, OK 74078. Offers management information systems (MS); management science and information systems (PhD); telecommunications management (MS). Part-time programs available. Postbaccalaureate distance learning degree programs offered. *Faculty:* 15 full-time (1 woman), 2 part-time/adjunct (1 woman). *Students:* 164 full-time (48 women), 104 part-time (20 women); includes 16 minority (5 Black or African American, non-Hispanic/Latino; 3 Asian, non-Hispanic/Latino; 3 Hispanic/Latino; 5 Two or more races, non-Hispanic/Latino), 176 international. Average age 28. 693 applicants, 33% accepted, 98 enrolled. In 2013, 103 master's, 3 doctorates awarded. *Degree requirements:* For master's, thesis or alternative; for doctorate, comprehensive exam, thesis/dissertation. *Entrance requirements:* For master's and doctorate, GRE or GMAT. Additional exam requirements/recommendations for international students: Required—TOEFL (minimum score 550 paper-based; 79 iBT). *Application deadline:* For fall admission, 3/1 priority date for international students; for spring admission, 8/1 priority date for international students. Applications are processed on a rolling basis. Application fee: $40 ($75 for international students). Electronic applications accepted. *Expenses:* Tuition, state resident: full-time $4272; part-time $178 per credit hour. Tuition, nonresident: full-time $17,472; part-time $709 per credit hour. *Required fees:* $2413.20; $100.55 per credit hour. One-time fee: $50 full-time. Part-time tuition and fees vary according to course load and campus/location. *Financial support:* In 2013–14, 4 research assistantships (averaging $12,193 per year), 12 teaching assistantships (averaging $12,990 per year) were awarded; career-related internships or fieldwork, Federal Work-Study, scholarships/grants, health care benefits, tuition waivers (partial), and unspecified assistantships also available. Support available to part-time students. Financial award application deadline: 3/1; financial award applicants required to submit FAFSA. *Unit head:* Dr. Rick Wilson, Department Head, 405-744-3551, Fax: 405-744-5180, E-mail: rick.wilson@okstate.edu. *Application contact:* Dr. Rathin Sarathy, Graduate Coordinator, 405-744-8646, Fax: 405-744-5180, E-mail: rathin.sarathy@okstate.edu.
Website: http://spears.okstate.edu/msis.

Old Dominion University, College of Business and Public Administration, MBA Program, Norfolk, VA 23529. Offers business and economic forecasting (MBA); financial analysis and valuation (MBA); health sciences administration (MBA); information technology and enterprise integration (MBA); international business (MBA); maritime and port management (MBA); public administration (MBA). *Accreditation:* AACSB. Part-time and evening/weekend programs available. Postbaccalaureate distance learning degree programs offered (no on-campus study). *Faculty:* 83 full-time (19 women), 5 part-time/adjunct (2 women). *Students:* 42 full-time (20 women), 103 part-time (42 women); includes 18 minority (8 Black or African American, non-Hispanic/Latino; 4 Asian, non-Hispanic/Latino; 1 Hispanic/Latino; 1 Native Hawaiian or other Pacific Islander, non-Hispanic/Latino; 4 Two or more races, non-Hispanic/Latino), 16 international. Average age 30. 161 applicants, 71% accepted, 75 enrolled. In 2013, 61 master's awarded. *Entrance requirements:* For master's, GMAT, GRE, letter of reference, resume, essay. Additional exam requirements/recommendations for international students: Required—TOEFL (minimum score 550 paper-based; 80 iBT). *Application deadline:* For fall admission, 6/1 priority date for domestic students, 4/15 priority date for international students; for spring admission, 11/1 priority date for domestic students, 10/1 priority date for international students. Applications are processed on a rolling basis. Application fee: $50. Electronic applications accepted. *Expenses:* Tuition, state resident: full-time $9888; part-time $412 per credit. Tuition, nonresident: full-time $25,152; part-time $1048 per credit. *Required fees:* $59 per semester. One-time fee: $50. *Financial support:* In 2013–14, 47 students received support, including 94 research assistantships with partial tuition reimbursements available (averaging $8,900 per year); career-related internships or fieldwork, scholarships/grants, and unspecified assistantships also available. Support available to part-time students. Financial award application deadline: 2/15; financial award applicants required to submit FAFSA. *Faculty research:* International business, buyer behavior, financial markets, strategy, operations research, maritime and transportation economics. *Unit head:* Dr. Kiran Karaude, Graduate Program Director, 757-683-3585, Fax: 757-683-5750, E-mail: mbainfo@odu.edu. *Application contact:* Sandi Phillips, MBA Program Assistant, 757-683-3585, Fax: 757-683-5750, E-mail: mbainfo@odu.edu.
Website: http://www.odu.edu/mba/.

Our Lady of the Lake University of San Antonio, School of Business and Leadership, Program in Information Systems and Security, San Antonio, TX 78207-4689. Offers MS. Part-time programs available. Postbaccalaureate distance learning degree programs offered (no on-campus study). *Faculty:* 2 full-time (0 women), 3 part-time/adjunct (0 women). *Students:* 55 full-time (15 women), 9 part-time (4 women); includes 36 minority (2 Black or African American, non-Hispanic/Latino; 1 American Indian or Alaska Native, non-Hispanic/Latino; 1 Asian, non-Hispanic/Latino; 32 Hispanic/Latino). Average age 35. 46 applicants, 89% accepted, 23 enrolled. In 2013, 17 master's awarded. *Entrance requirements:* For master's, GMAT, GRE General Test, or MAT. Additional exam requirements/recommendations for international students: Required—TOEFL. *Application deadline:* Applications are processed on a rolling basis. Application fee: $25 ($50 for international students). Electronic applications accepted. *Expenses: Tuition:* Full-time $9120; part-time $760 per credit. *Required fees:* $698; $334 per trimester. Tuition and fees vary according to course load, degree level, campus/location and program. *Financial support:* Fellowships, career-related internships or fieldwork, Federal Work-Study, institutionally sponsored loans, scholarships/grants, and tuition waivers (partial) available. Support available to part-time students. Financial award application deadline: 4/15. *Faculty research:* Innovative programming, data management, systems analysis, computer network security, information assurance. *Unit head:* Dr. Carol Jeffries-Horner, Chair of the Computer Information Systems and Security Department, 210-434-6711 Ext. 8155, Fax: 210-434-0821, E-mail: cjeffries@lake.ollusa.edu. *Application contact:* Graduate Admission, 210-431-3961, Fax: 210-431-4013, E-mail: gradadm@ollusa.edu.
Website: http://www.ollusa.edu/s/1190/ollu-3-column-noads.aspx?sid=1190&gid=1&pgid=1420.

Pace University, Lubin School of Business, Information Systems Program, New York, NY 10038. Offers MBA. Part-time and evening/weekend programs available. *Students:* 1 full-time (0 women), 13 part-time (4 women); includes 1 minority (Hispanic/Latino), 4 international. Average age 30. 32 applicants, 31% accepted, 4 enrolled. In 2013, 8 master's awarded. *Entrance requirements:* For master's, GMAT, GRE. Additional exam requirements/recommendations for international students: Required—TOEFL. *Application deadline:* For fall admission, 8/1 priority date for domestic students, 6/1 for international students; for spring admission, 12/1 for domestic students, 10/1 for international students. Applications are processed on a rolling basis. Application fee: $70. Electronic applications accepted. *Expenses: Tuition:* Part-time $1075 per credit. *Required fees:* $192 per semester. Tuition and fees vary according to course load, degree level and program. *Financial support:* Research assistantships, career-related internships or fieldwork, and Federal Work-Study available. Support available to part-time students. Financial award applicants required to submit FAFSA. *Unit head:* Dr. John Molluzzo, Chair, 212-346-1780, E-mail: jmulluzzo@pace.edu. *Application contact:* Susan Ford-Goldschein, Director of Graduate Admissions, 212-346-1531, Fax: 212-346-1585, E-mail: gradnyc@pace.edu.
Website: http://www.pace.edu/lubin.

Pacific States University, College of Business, Los Angeles, CA 90006. Offers accounting (MBA); finance (MBA); international business (MBA, DBA); management of information technology (MBA); real estate management (MBA). Part-time and evening/weekend programs available. Postbaccalaureate distance learning degree programs offered (no on-campus study). *Degree requirements:* For doctorate, comprehensive exam, thesis/dissertation. *Entrance requirements:* For master's, minimum undergraduate GPA of 2.5 during last 90 hours of course work. Additional exam requirements/recommendations for international students: Required—TOEFL (minimum score 500 paper-based; 61 iBT), IELTS (minimum score 5.5).

Pacific States University, College of Computer Science and Information Systems, Los Angeles, CA 90006. Offers computer science (MS); information systems (MS). Part-time and evening/weekend programs available. *Entrance requirements:* For master's, bachelor's degree in physics, engineering, computer science, or applied mathematics; minimum undergraduate GPA of 2.5 during last 90 hours of course work. Additional exam requirements/recommendations for international students: Required—TOEFL (minimum score 500 paper-based; 61 iBT), IELTS (minimum score 5.5).

Park University, School of Graduate and Professional Studies, Kansas City, MO 54105. Offers adult education (M Ed); business and government leadership (Graduate Certificate); business, government, and global society (MPA); communication and leadership (MA); creative and life writing (Graduate Certificate); disaster and emergency management (MPA, Graduate Certificate); educational leadership (M Ed); finance (MBA, Graduate Certificate); general business (MBA); global business (Graduate Certificate); healthcare administration (MHA); healthcare services management and leadership (Graduate Certificate); international business (MBA); language and literacy (M Ed), including English for speakers of other languages, special reading teacher/literacy coach; leadership of international healthcare organizations (Graduate Certificate); management information systems (MBA, Graduate Certificate); music performance (ADP, Graduate Certificate), including cello (MM, ADP), piano (MM, ADP),

viola (MM, ADP), violin (MM, ADP); nonprofit and community services management (MPA); nonprofit leadership (Graduate Certificate); performance (MM), including cello (MM, ADP), piano (MM, ADP), viola (MM, ADP), violin (MM, ADP); public management (MPA); social work (MSW); teacher leadership (M Ed), including curriculum and assessment, instructional leader. Part-time and evening/weekend programs available. Postbaccalaureate distance learning degree programs offered (no on-campus study). *Students:* 862 full-time (482 women); includes 55 minority (30 Black or African American, non-Hispanic/Latino; 2 American Indian or Alaska Native, non-Hispanic/Latino; 4 Asian, non-Hispanic/Latino; 14 Hispanic/Latino; 5 Two or more races, non-Hispanic/Latino), 141 international. Average age 34. 497 applicants, 62% accepted, 119 enrolled. In 2013, 281 master's, 14 other advanced degrees awarded. *Degree requirements:* For master's, comprehensive exam (for some programs), thesis (for some programs), internship (for some programs); exam (for some programs). *Entrance requirements:* For master's, GRE or GMAT (for some programs), teacher certification (for some M Ed programs), letters of recommendation, essay, resume (for some programs). Additional exam requirements/recommendations for international students: Required—TOEFL (minimum score 550 paper-based; 79 iBT), IELTS (minimum score 6). *Application deadline:* For fall admission, 8/1 priority date for domestic students, 7/15 priority date for international students; for spring admission, 1/1 priority date for domestic students, 11/1 priority date for international students. Applications are processed on a rolling basis. Application fee: $50 ($100 for international students). Electronic applications accepted. *Financial support:* In 2013–14, 2 research assistantships with full tuition reimbursements (averaging $15,760 per year) were awarded. Financial award applicants required to submit FAFSA. *Unit head:* Dr. Laurie Dipadova-Stocks, Dean of Graduate and Professional Studies, 816-559-5624, Fax: 816-472-1173, E-mail: ldipadovastocks@park.edu. *Application contact:* Judith Appollis, Director of Graduate Admissions and Internationalization, School of Graduate and Professional Studies, 816-559-5627, Fax: 816-472-1173, E-mail: gradschool@park.edu.
Website: http://www.park.edu/grad.

Penn State Harrisburg, Graduate School, School of Business Administration, Middletown, PA 17057-4898. Offers business administration (MBA); information systems (MS). Part-time and evening/weekend programs available. *Unit head:* Dr. Mukund S. Kulkarni, Chancellor, 717-948-6105, Fax: 717-948-6452, E-mail: msk5@psu.edu. *Application contact:* Robert W. Coffman, Jr., Director of Enrollment Management, Admissions, 717-948-6250, Fax: 717-948-6325, E-mail: ric1@psu.edu.
Website: http://harrisburg.psu.edu/business-administration/.

Penn State University Park, Graduate School, College of Information Sciences and Technology, State College, PA 16802. Offers enterprise architecture (MPS); information sciences (MPS); information sciences and technology (MS, PhD). Part-time and evening/weekend programs available. *Students:* 105 full-time (33 women), 11 part-time (4 women); includes 10 minority (3 Black or African American, non-Hispanic/Latino; 3 Asian, non-Hispanic/Latino; 3 Hispanic/Latino; 1 Two or more races, non-Hispanic/Latino), 79 international. Average age 29. 178 applicants, 37% accepted, 40 enrolled. In 2013, 6 master's, 22 doctorates awarded. *Entrance requirements:* Additional exam requirements/recommendations for international students: Required—TOEFL (minimum score 550 paper-based; 80 iBT). *Application deadline:* Applications are processed on a rolling basis. Application fee: $65. Electronic applications accepted. *Financial support:* Fellowships, research assistantships, teaching assistantships, career-related internships or fieldwork, Federal Work-Study, and unspecified assistantships available. Support available to part-time students. Financial award application deadline: 2/15; financial award applicants required to submit FAFSA. *Unit head:* Dr. David L. Hall, Dean, 814-865-3528, Fax: 814-865-7485, E-mail: dlh28@psu.edu. *Application contact:* Cynthia E. Nicosia, Director, Graduate Enrollment Services, 814-865-1834, Fax: 814-863-4627, E-mail: cey1@psu.edu.
Website: http://ist.psu.edu/.

Polytechnic University of Puerto Rico, Graduate School, Hato Rey, PR 00919. Offers business administration (MBA), including computer information systems, general management, management of information systems, management of international enterprises; civil engineering (ME, MS); computer engineering (ME, MS); computer science (MCS, MS); electrical engineering (ME, MS); engineering management (MEM); environmental management (MEM); landscape architecture (M Land Arch); manufacturing competitiveness (MMC, MS); manufacturing engineering (ME, MS); mechanical engineering (M Mech E). Part-time and evening/weekend programs available. *Entrance requirements:* For master's, 3 letters of recommendation.

Pontifical Catholic University of Puerto Rico, College of Business Administration, Program in Management Information Systems, Ponce, PR 00717-0777. Offers MBA, Professional Certificate. Part-time and evening/weekend programs available. *Degree requirements:* For master's, thesis. *Entrance requirements:* For master's, GRE, interview, minimum GPA of 2.75.

Prairie View A&M University, College of Engineering, Prairie View, TX 77446-0519. Offers computer information systems (MSCIS); computer science (MSCS); electrical engineering (MSEE, PhDEE); engineering (MS Engr). Part-time and evening/weekend programs available. *Faculty:* 12 full-time (3 women), 1 (woman) part-time/adjunct. *Students:* 91 full-time (32 women), 47 part-time (16 women); includes 67 minority (51 Black or African American, non-Hispanic/Latino; 1 American Indian or Alaska Native, non-Hispanic/Latino; 13 Asian, non-Hispanic/Latino; 2 Hispanic/Latino), 57 international. Average age 32. 141 applicants, 50% accepted, 45 enrolled. In 2013, 25 master's, 1 doctorate awarded. *Degree requirements:* For master's, thesis (for some programs); for doctorate, comprehensive exam, thesis/dissertation. *Entrance requirements:* For master's, GRE General Test, bachelor's degree in engineering from an ABET accredited institution; for doctorate, GRE. Additional exam requirements/recommendations for international students: Required—TOEFL (minimum score 550 paper-based). *Application deadline:* For fall admission, 7/1 priority date for domestic and international students; for spring admission, 11/1 priority date for domestic and international students. Application fee: $50. Electronic applications accepted. *Expenses:* Tuition, state resident: full-time $3776; part-time $209.77 per credit hour. Tuition, nonresident: full-time $10,183; part-time $565.77 per credit hour. *Required fees:* $2037; $446.50 per credit hour. *Financial support:* In 2013–14, 80 students received support, including 14 fellowships (averaging $1,050 per year), 16 research assistantships (averaging $16,150 per year), 13 teaching assistantships (averaging $14,000 per year); career-related internships or fieldwork, institutionally sponsored loans, scholarships/grants, health care benefits, tuition waivers (partial), and unspecified assistantships also available. Financial award application deadline: 3/1; financial award applicants required to submit FAFSA. *Faculty research:* Applied radiation research, thermal science, computational fluid dynamics, analog mixed signal, aerial space battlefield. *Total annual research expenditures:* $439,054. *Unit head:* Dr. Kendall T. Harris, Dean, 936-261-9956, Fax: 936-261-9869, E-mail: tharris@pvamu.edu. *Application contact:* Barbara A. Thompson, Administrative Assistant, 936-261-9896, Fax: 936-261-9869, E-mail: bathompson@pvamu.edu.

Purdue University, Graduate School, College of Technology, Department of Computer and Information Technology, West Lafayette, IN 47907. Offers MS. *Faculty:* 25 full-time (8 women), 4 part-time/adjunct (0 women). *Students:* 42 full-time (16 women), 30 part-time (6 women); includes 11 minority (4 Black or African American, non-Hispanic/Latino; 5 Asian, non-Hispanic/Latino; 2 Hispanic/Latino), 28 international. Average age 29. 199 applicants, 24% accepted, 35 enrolled. In 2013, 20 master's awarded. *Entrance requirements:* For master's, GRE, minimum GPA of 3.0 or equivalent. *Application deadline:* For fall admission, 4/1 for domestic and international students; for spring admission, 10/1 for domestic students, 9/1 for international students; for summer admission, 4/1 for domestic students, 2/15 for international students. Applications are processed on a rolling basis. Application fee: $60 ($75 for international students). Electronic applications accepted. *Unit head:* Jeffrey Whitten, Head, 765-494-2566, E-mail: jwhitten@purdue.edu. *Application contact:* Stacy M. Lane, Graduate Contact, 765-494-4545, E-mail: smlane@purdue.edu.
Website: http://www.tech.purdue.edu/cit/.

Quinnipiac University, School of Business and Engineering, Program in Business Administration, Hamden, CT 06518-1940. Offers chartered financial analyst (MBA); finance (MBA); healthcare management (MBA); information systems management (MBA); marketing (MBA); supply chain management (MBA); JD/MBA. *Accreditation:* AACSB. Part-time and evening/weekend programs available. Postbaccalaureate distance learning degree programs offered (no on-campus study). *Faculty:* 33 full-time (10 women), 7 part-time/adjunct (3 women). *Students:* 109 full-time (48 women), 225 part-time (101 women); includes 44 minority (14 Black or African American, non-Hispanic/Latino; 2 American Indian or Alaska Native, non-Hispanic/Latino; 12 Asian, non-Hispanic/Latino; 15 Hispanic/Latino; 1 Two or more races, non-Hispanic/Latino), 17 international. 230 applicants, 80% accepted, 154 enrolled. In 2013, 124 master's awarded. *Entrance requirements:* For master's, GMAT or GRE, minimum GPA of 3.0. Additional exam requirements/recommendations for international students: Required—TOEFL (minimum score 575 paper-based; 90 iBT), IELTS (minimum score 6.5). *Application deadline:* For fall admission, 7/30 priority date for domestic students, 4/30 priority date for international students; for spring admission, 12/15 priority date for domestic students, 9/15 priority date for international students. Applications are processed on a rolling basis. Application fee: $45. Electronic applications accepted. *Expenses: Tuition:* Part-time $920 per credit. *Required fees:* $37 per credit. *Financial support:* In 2013–14, 41 students received support. Career-related internships or fieldwork, Federal Work-Study, scholarships/grants, and unspecified assistantships available. Support available to part-time students. Financial award application deadline: 6/1; financial award applicants required to submit FAFSA. *Faculty research:* Financial markets and investments, international business, supply chain management, health care management, corporate governance. *Unit head:* Lisa Braiewa, MBA Program Director, E-mail: lisa.braiewa@quinnipiac.edu. *Application contact:* Office of Graduate Admissions, 800-462-1944, Fax: 203-582-3443, E-mail: graduate@quinnipiac.edu.
Website: http://www.quinnipiac.edu/mba.

Quinnipiac University, School of Business and Engineering, Program in Information Technology, Hamden, CT 06518-1940. Offers MS. Part-time and evening/weekend programs available. Postbaccalaureate distance learning degree programs offered (no on-campus study). *Faculty:* 4 full-time (0 women), 1 part-time/adjunct (0 women). *Students:* 4 full-time (1 woman), 39 part-time (8 women); includes 12 minority (6 Black or African American, non-Hispanic/Latino; 4 Asian, non-Hispanic/Latino; 2 Hispanic/Latino). 20 applicants, 85% accepted, 13 enrolled. In 2013, 16 master's awarded. *Entrance requirements:* For master's, minimum GPA of 2.7; course work in computer language programming, management, accounting foundation. Additional exam requirements/recommendations for international students: Required—TOEFL (minimum score 575 paper-based; 90 iBT), IELTS (minimum score 6.5). *Application deadline:* For fall admission, 7/30 priority date for domestic students, 4/30 priority date for international students; for spring admission, 12/30 priority date for domestic students, 9/15 priority date for international students; for summer admission, 4/30 priority date for domestic students. Applications are processed on a rolling basis. Application fee: $45. Electronic applications accepted. *Expenses: Tuition:* Part-time $920 per credit. *Required fees:* $37 per credit. *Financial support:* Federal Work-Study and unspecified assistantships available. Support available to part-time students. Financial award application deadline: 6/1; financial award applicants required to submit FAFSA. *Faculty research:* Data management and warehousing, peer-to-peer counseling, decision support systems. *Unit head:* Michael Taylor, Program Director, E-mail: michael.taylor@quinnipiac.edu. *Application contact:* Quinnipiac University Online Admissions Office, 203-582-3918, Fax: 203-582-3352, E-mail: quonlineadmissions@quinnipiac.edu.
Website: http://www.quinnipiac.edu/qu-online/academics/degree-programs/ms-in-information-technology.

Regent's University London, Webster Graduate School, London, United Kingdom. Offers business (MBA); finance (MS); human resources (MA); information technology management (MA); international business (MA); international non-governmental organizations (MA); international relations (MA); management and leadership (MA); marketing (MA). Part-time programs available.

Regis University, College for Professional Studies, School of Computer and Information Sciences, Denver, CO 80221-1099. Offers database administration with Oracle (Certificate); database development (Certificate); database technologies (M Sc); enterprise Java software development (Certificate); enterprise resource planning (Certificate); executive information technology (Certificate); information assurance (M Sc, Certificate); information technology management (M Sc); software engineering (M Sc, Certificate); software engineering and database technologies (M Sc); storage area networks (Certificate); systems engineering (M Sc, Certificate). Offered at Boulder Campus, Northwest Denver Campus, Southeast Denver Campus, Fort Collins Campus, Colorado Springs Campus, and Broomfield Campus. Part-time and evening/weekend programs available. Postbaccalaureate distance learning degree programs offered (no on-campus study). *Faculty:* 8 full-time (2 women), 51 part-time/adjunct (13 women). *Students:* 282 full-time (74 women), 252 part-time (69 women); includes 168 minority (67 Black or African American, non-Hispanic/Latino; 3 American Indian or Alaska Native, non-Hispanic/Latino; 34 Asian, non-Hispanic/Latino; 53 Hispanic/Latino; 1 Native Hawaiian or other Pacific Islander, non-Hispanic/Latino; 10 Two or more races, non-Hispanic/Latino), 28 international. Average age 42. 447 applicants, 91% accepted, 308 enrolled. In 2013, 142 master's awarded. *Degree requirements:* For master's, thesis (for some programs), final research project. *Entrance requirements:* For master's, official transcript reflecting baccalaureate degree awarded from regionally-accredited college or university, 2 years of related experience, resume, interview. Additional exam requirements/recommendations for international students: Required—TOEFL (minimum score 550 paper-based; 82 iBT). *Application deadline:* For fall admission, 8/13 for domestic students, 7/13 for international students; for winter admission, 10/8 for domestic students, 9/8 for international students; for spring admission, 12/17 for domestic students, 11/17 for international students. Applications are processed on a rolling basis. Application fee: $75. Electronic applications accepted. *Expenses:* Contact institution. *Financial support:* In 2013–14, 18 students received support. Federal Work-Study and scholarships/grants available. Financial award application deadline: 4/15; financial award applicants required to submit FAFSA. *Faculty research:* Information policy, knowledge management, software architectures. *Unit head:* Donald Archer, Interim Dean, 303-458-4335, E-mail: archer@regis.edu. *Application contact:* Sarah

Management Information Systems

Engel, Information Contact, 303-458-4900, Fax: 303-964-5534, E-mail: regisadm@regis.edu.
Website: http://regis.edu/CPS/Schools/School-of-Computer-and-Information-Sciences.aspx.

Rensselaer Polytechnic Institute, Graduate School, Lally School of Management, Program in Business Analytics, Troy, NY 12180-3590. Offers MS. Part-time programs available. *Faculty:* 17 full-time (3 women), 4 part-time/adjunct (0 women). *Students:* 13 full-time (11 women), 1 part-time (0 women); includes 4 minority (1 Black or African American, non-Hispanic/Latino; 1 Asian, non-Hispanic/Latino; 2 Two or more races, non-Hispanic/Latino), 10 international. Average age 26. 33 applicants, 73% accepted, 11 enrolled. *Entrance requirements:* For master's, GMAT or GRE. Additional exam requirements/recommendations for international students: Required—TOEFL (minimum score 570 paper-based; 88 iBT), IELTS (minimum score 6.5), PTE (minimum score 60). *Application deadline:* For fall admission, 1/1 priority date for domestic and international students. Applications are processed on a rolling basis. Application fee: $75. Electronic applications accepted. *Expenses: Tuition:* Full-time $45,100; part-time $1879 per credit hour. *Required fees:* $1983. *Financial support:* In 2013–14, 14 students received support. Scholarships/grants available. Financial award application deadline: 1/1. *Total annual research expenditures:* $106,192. *Unit head:* Dr. Gina O'Connor, Graduate Admissions Director, 518-276-6842, E-mail: connog@rpi.edu. *Application contact:* Office of Graduate Admissions, 518-276-6276, E-mail: gradadmissions@rpi.edu.
Website: http://lallyschool.rpi.edu/academics/ms_ba.html.

Rivier University, School of Graduate Studies, Department of Computer Information Systems, Nashua, NH 03060. Offers MS. Part-time programs available.

Robert Morris University, Graduate Studies, School of Communications and Information Systems, Moon Township, PA 15108-1189. Offers communication and information systems (MS); competitive intelligence systems (MS); information security and assurance (MS); information systems and communications (D Sc); information systems management (MS); information technology project management (MS); Internet information systems (MS); organizational leadership (MS). Part-time and evening/weekend programs available. Postbaccalaureate distance learning degree programs offered (no on-campus study). *Faculty:* 26 full-time (10 women), 14 part-time/adjunct (4 women). *Students:* 311 part-time (111 women); includes 57 minority (35 Black or African American, non-Hispanic/Latino; 1 American Indian or Alaska Native, non-Hispanic/Latino; 4 Asian, non-Hispanic/Latino; 3 Hispanic/Latino; 14 Two or more races, non-Hispanic/Latino), 37 international. 337 applicants, 39% accepted, 102 enrolled. In 2013, 90 master's, 15 doctorates awarded. *Degree requirements:* For doctorate, thesis/dissertation. *Entrance requirements:* For doctorate, employer letter of endorsement, interview. Additional exam requirements/recommendations for international students: Required—TOEFL (minimum score 550 paper-based; 79 iBT). *Application deadline:* For fall admission, 7/1 priority date for domestic and international students; for spring admission, 11/1 priority date for domestic and international students. Applications are processed on a rolling basis. Application fee: $35. Electronic applications accepted. *Expenses:* Contact institution. *Financial support:* Research assistantships with partial tuition reimbursements, institutionally sponsored loans, and unspecified assistantships available. Support available to part-time students. Financial award application deadline: 5/1. *Unit head:* Dr. Barbara J. Levine, Dean, 412-397-2591, Fax: 412-397-2481, E-mail: levine@rmu.edu. *Application contact:* 412-397-5200, Fax: 412-397-5915, E-mail: graduateadmissions@rmu.edu.
Website: http://www.rmu.edu/web/cms/schools/scis/Pages/default.aspx.

Robert Morris University Illinois, Morris Graduate School of Management, Chicago, IL 60605. Offers accounting (MBA); accounting/finance (MBA); business analytics (MIS); design and media (MM); educational technology (MM); health care administration (MM); higher education administration (MM); human resource management (MBA); information security (MIS); information systems (MIS); law enforcement administration (MM); management (MBA); management/finance (MBA); management/human resource management (MBA); mobile computing (MIS); sports administration (MM). Part-time and evening/weekend programs available. *Faculty:* 12 full-time (5 women), 18 part-time/adjunct (4 women). *Students:* 240 full-time (128 women), 195 part-time (127 women); includes 242 minority (147 Black or African American, non-Hispanic/Latino; 2 American Indian or Alaska Native, non-Hispanic/Latino; 24 Asian, non-Hispanic/Latino; 63 Hispanic/Latino; 1 Native Hawaiian or other Pacific Islander, non-Hispanic/Latino; 5 Two or more races, non-Hispanic/Latino), 26 international. Average age 33. 210 applicants, 63% accepted, 116 enrolled. In 2013, 278 master's awarded. *Entrance requirements:* For master's, official transcripts, two letters of recommendation. Additional exam requirements/recommendations for international students: Required—TOEFL (minimum score 550 paper-based). *Application deadline:* Applications are processed on a rolling basis. Application fee: $20 ($100 for international students). Electronic applications accepted. *Expenses: Tuition:* Full-time $14,400; part-time $2400 per course. *Financial support:* In 2013–14, 488 students received support. Federal Work-Study and scholarships/grants available. Support available to part-time students. Financial award applicants required to submit FAFSA. *Unit head:* Kayed Akkawi, Dean for Morris Graduate School of Management, 312-935-6050, Fax: 312-935-6020, E-mail: kakkawi@robertmorris.edu. *Application contact:* Fernando Villeda, Dean of Graduate Enrollment, 312-935-6050, Fax: 312-935-6020, E-mail: fvilleda@robertmorris.edu.

Rochester Institute of Technology, Graduate Enrollment Services, B. Thomas Golisano College of Computing and Information Sciences, Department of Computing Security, Rochester, NY 14623-5603. Offers MS. Part-time programs available. *Students:* 18 full-time (3 women), 8 part-time (0 women); includes 2 minority (both Asian, non-Hispanic/Latino), 19 international. Average age 26. 85 applicants, 44% accepted, 14 enrolled. In 2013, 7 master's awarded. *Degree requirements:* For master's, thesis. *Entrance requirements:* For master's, GRE, minimum GPA of 3.0. Additional exam requirements/recommendations for international students: Required—TOEFL (minimum score 600 paper-based; 100 iBT) or IELTS (minimum score 7). *Application deadline:* Applications are processed on a rolling basis. Application fee: $60. Electronic applications accepted. *Expenses: Tuition:* Full-time $37,236; part-time $1552 per credit hour. *Required fees:* $250. *Financial support:* Research assistantships with partial tuition reimbursements, teaching assistantships with partial tuition reimbursements, career-related internships or fieldwork, scholarships/grants, and unspecified assistantships available. Support available to part-time students. Financial award applicants required to submit FAFSA. *Unit head:* Sylvia Perez-Hardy, Graduate Program Director, Fax: 585-475-6584, E-mail: sphics@rit.edu. *Application contact:* Diane Ellison, Assistant Vice President, Graduate Enrollment Services, 585-475-2229, Fax: 585-475-7164, E-mail: gradinfo@rit.edu.
Website: http://csec.rit.edu/.

Roosevelt University, Graduate Division, Walter E. Heller College of Business Administration, Program in Information Systems, Chicago, IL 60605. Offers MSIS. Part-time and evening/weekend programs available. *Entrance requirements:* For master's, GMAT.

Rose-Hulman Institute of Technology, Faculty of Engineering and Applied Sciences, Department of Electrical and Computer Engineering, Terre Haute, IN 47803-3999. Offers electrical and computer engineering (M Eng); electrical engineering (MS); systems engineering and management (MS). Part-time programs available. Postbaccalaureate distance learning degree programs offered (minimal on-campus study). *Faculty:* 18 full-time (3 women), 1 (woman) part-time/adjunct. *Students:* 18 full-time (2 women), 5 part-time (0 women); includes 4 minority (all Asian, non-Hispanic/Latino), 13 international. Average age 24. 24 applicants, 79% accepted, 13 enrolled. *Degree requirements:* For master's, thesis (for some programs). *Entrance requirements:* For master's, GRE, minimum GPA of 3.0. Additional exam requirements/recommendations for international students: Required—TOEFL (minimum score 580 paper-based; 92 iBT). *Application deadline:* For fall admission, 2/1 priority date for domestic students. Applications are processed on a rolling basis. Application fee: $0. *Expenses: Tuition:* Full-time $39,462; part-time $1152 per credit hour. *Financial support:* In 2013–14, 9 students received support. Fellowships with full and partial tuition reimbursements available, research assistantships with full and partial tuition reimbursements available, institutionally sponsored loans, scholarships/grants, and tuition waivers (full and partial) available. *Faculty research:* VLSI, DSP, power systems, analog electronics, communications, electromagnetics. *Total annual research expenditures:* $31,273. *Unit head:* Dr. Robert Throne, Interim Chairman, 812-877-8414, Fax: 812-877-8895, E-mail: robert.d.throne@rose-hulman.edu. *Application contact:* Dr. Azad Siahmakoun, Associate Dean of the Faculty, 812-877-8400, Fax: 812-877-8061, E-mail: siahmako@rose-hulman.edu.
Website: http://www.rose-hulman.edu/academics/academic-departments/electrical-computer-engineering.aspx.

Rutgers, The State University of New Jersey, Newark, Graduate School, Program in Management, Newark, NJ 07102. Offers accounting (PhD); accounting information systems (PhD); computer information systems (PhD); finance (PhD); information technology (PhD); international business (PhD); management science (PhD); marketing (PhD); organization management (PhD). Program offered jointly with New Jersey Institute of Technology. *Accreditation:* AACSB. *Degree requirements:* For doctorate, thesis/dissertation, cumulative exams. *Entrance requirements:* For doctorate, GMAT or GRE General Test, minimum undergraduate B average. Additional exam requirements/recommendations for international students: Required—TOEFL. Electronic applications accepted. *Faculty research:* Technology management, leadership and teams, consumer behavior, financial and markets, logistics.

Rutgers, The State University of New Jersey, Newark, Rutgers Business School–Newark and New Brunswick, Doctoral Programs in Management, Newark, NJ 07102. Offers accounting (PhD); accounting information systems (PhD); economics (PhD); finance (PhD); individualized study (PhD); information technology (PhD); international business (PhD); management science (PhD); marketing science (PhD); organizational management (PhD); science, technology and management (PhD); supply chain management (PhD). *Degree requirements:* For doctorate, comprehensive exam, thesis/dissertation. *Entrance requirements:* For doctorate, GRE or GMAT. Additional exam requirements/recommendations for international students: Required—TOEFL (minimum score 550 paper-based; 79 iBT). Electronic applications accepted.

Sacred Heart University, Graduate Programs, College of Arts and Sciences, Department of Computer Science and Information Technology, Fairfield, CT 06825-1000. Offers computer science (MS); cybersecurity (MS); database design (CPS); game design (CPS); information technology (MS, CPS); information technology and network security (CPS); interactive multimedia (CPS); Web development (CPS). Part-time and evening/weekend programs available. *Faculty:* 7 full-time (3 women), 7 part-time/adjunct (0 women). *Students:* 51 full-time (9 women), 52 part-time (13 women); includes 13 minority (5 Black or African American, non-Hispanic/Latino; 3 Asian, non-Hispanic/Latino; 5 Hispanic/Latino), 52 international. Average age 30. 121 applicants, 93% accepted, 43 enrolled. In 2013, 35 master's awarded. *Degree requirements:* For master's, thesis optional. *Entrance requirements:* For master's, bachelor's degree, minimum GPA of 3.0. Additional exam requirements/recommendations for international students: Required—PTE; Recommended—TOEFL (minimum score 570 paper-based; 80 iBT), IELTS (minimum score 6.5). *Application deadline:* Applications are processed on a rolling basis. Application fee: $60. Electronic applications accepted. *Expenses: Tuition:* Full-time $22,775; part-time $617 per credit. *Financial support:* Career-related internships or fieldwork, institutionally sponsored loans, and unspecified assistantships available. Support available to part-time students. Financial award applicants required to submit FAFSA. *Unit head:* Domenick Pinto, Academic Director and Chairperson, 203-371-7789, Fax: 203-371-0506, E-mail: pintod@sacredheart.edu. *Application contact:* Kathy Dilks, Executive Director of Graduate Admissions, 203-365-7619, Fax: 203-365-4732, E-mail: gradstudies@sacredheart.edu.
Website: http://www.sacredheart.edu/academics/collegeofartssciences/academicdepartments/computerscienceinformationtechnology/graduatedegreesandcertificates/.

St. Edward's University, School of Management and Business, Program in Computer Information Systems, Austin, TX 78704. Offers MS. Part-time and evening/weekend programs available. *Students:* 16 full-time (4 women), 1 part-time (0 women); includes 7 minority (2 Black or African American, non-Hispanic/Latino; 5 Hispanic/Latino), 1 international. Average age 33. 29 applicants, 55% accepted, 10 enrolled. In 2013, 12 master's awarded. *Degree requirements:* For master's, minimum of 24 resident hours. *Entrance requirements:* For master's, GMAT or GRE General Test, minimum GPA of 2.75 in last 60 hours of course work. Additional exam requirements/recommendations for international students: Required—TOEFL (minimum score 79 iBT) or IELTS (minimum score 6). *Application deadline:* For fall admission, 6/1 priority date for domestic and international students; for spring admission, 10/1 priority date for domestic and international students; for summer admission, 3/1 priority date for domestic and international students. Applications are processed on a rolling basis. Application fee: $50. Electronic applications accepted. *Expenses: Tuition:* Full-time $20,664; part-time $1148 per credit hour. *Required fees:* $50 per trimester. Full-time tuition and fees vary according to course load and program. *Unit head:* Dwight D. Daniel, Director, 512-448-8599, Fax: 512-428-8492, E-mail: dwightd@stedwards.edu. *Application contact:* Office of Admission, 512-448-8500, Fax: 512-464-8877, E-mail: seu.admit@stedwards.edu.
Website: http://www.stedwards.edu.

St. John's University, The Peter J. Tobin College of Business, Department of Computer Information Systems and Decision Sciences, Queens, NY 11439. Offers business analytics (MBA); computer information systems for managers (Adv C). Part-time and evening/weekend programs available. *Students:* 8 full-time (1 woman), 8 part-time (3 women); includes 6 minority (2 Black or African American, non-Hispanic/Latino; 2 Asian, non-Hispanic/Latino; 2 Hispanic/Latino), 5 international. Average age 27. 7 applicants, 71% accepted, 3 enrolled. In 2013, 3 master's awarded. *Degree requirements:* For master's, comprehensive exam (for some programs), thesis optional. *Entrance requirements:* For master's, GMAT, 2 letters of recommendation, resume, transcripts, essay. Additional exam requirements/recommendations for international students: Required—TOEFL (minimum score 600 paper-based; 100 iBT), IELTS (minimum score 7). *Application deadline:* For fall admission, 5/1 priority date for domestic and international students; for spring admission, 11/1 priority date for domestic and international students. Applications are processed on a rolling basis. Application fee: $50. Electronic applications accepted. *Expenses:* Contact institution. *Financial support:* Research assistantships, scholarships/grants, and unspecified assistantships available. Support available to part-time students. Financial award application deadline:

3/1; financial award applicants required to submit FAFSA. *Unit head:* Dr. Victor Lu, Chair, 718-990-6392, E-mail: luf@stjohns.edu. *Application contact:* Carol J. Swanberg, Assistant Dean/Director of Graduate Admissions, 718-990-2599, E-mail: tobingradnyc@stjohns.edu.

Saint Joseph's University, Erivan K. Haub School of Business, MS Program in Business Intelligence, Philadelphia, PA 19131-1395. Offers MS. Part-time and evening/weekend programs available. Postbaccalaureate distance learning degree programs offered. *Students:* 34 full-time (10 women), 112 part-time (37 women); includes 23 minority (9 Black or African American, non-Hispanic/Latino; 1 American Indian or Alaska Native, non-Hispanic/Latino; 7 Asian, non-Hispanic/Latino; 4 Hispanic/Latino; 2 Two or more races, non-Hispanic/Latino), 29 international. Average age 31. In 2013, 42 master's awarded. *Degree requirements:* For master's, minimum GPA of 3.0. *Entrance requirements:* For master's, GMAT or GRE, 2 letters of recommendation, resume, personal statement, official undergraduate and graduate transcripts. Additional exam requirements/recommendations for international students: Required—TOEFL (minimum score 550 paper-based, 80 iBT), IELTS (minimum score 6.5), or PTE (minimum score 60). *Application deadline:* For fall admission, 7/15 priority date for domestic students, 5/15 priority date for international students; for spring admission, 11/15 priority date for domestic students, 10/15 priority date for international students; for summer admission, 4/15 priority date for domestic students. Applications are processed on a rolling basis. Application fee: $35. Electronic applications accepted. *Expenses: Tuition:* Part-time $786 per credit hour. Tuition and fees vary according to degree level and program. *Financial support:* Scholarships/grants available. Support available to part-time students. Financial award application deadline: 5/1; financial award applicants required to submit FAFSA. *Unit head:* Dr. Patricia Rafferty, Director, MS in Business Intelligence and Analytics and MS in Managing Human Capital Programs, 610-660-1318, Fax: 610-660-1229, E-mail: patricia.rafferty@sju.edu. *Application contact:* Dr. Patricia Rafferty, Director, MS in Business Intelligence and Analytics and MS in Managing Human Capital Programs, 610-660-1318, Fax: 610-660-1599, E-mail: patricia.rafferty@sju.edu.
Website: http://www.sju.edu/hsb/bi/.

Saint Peter's University, Graduate Business Programs, MBA Program, Jersey City, NJ 07306-5997. Offers finance (MBA); health care administration (MBA); human resource management (MBA); international business (MBA); management (MBA); management information systems (MBA); marketing (MBA); risk management (MBA); MBA/MS. Part-time and evening/weekend programs available. *Entrance requirements:* Additional exam requirements/recommendations for international students: Required—TOEFL. Electronic applications accepted. *Faculty research:* Finance, health care management, human resource management, international business, management, management information systems, marketing, risk management.

San Diego State University, Graduate and Research Affairs, College of Business Administration, Department of Management Information Systems, San Diego, CA 92182. Offers information systems (MS). Evening/weekend programs available. *Degree requirements:* For master's, thesis or alternative. *Entrance requirements:* For master's, GMAT, resume, letters of reference. Additional exam requirements/recommendations for international students: Required—TOEFL. Electronic applications accepted.

San Francisco State University, Division of Graduate Studies, College of Business, Program in Business Administration, San Francisco, CA 94132-1722. Offers decision sciences/operations research (MBA); finance (MBA); information systems (MBA); leadership (MBA); management (MBA); marketing (MBA); sustainable business (MBA). *Accreditation:* AACSB. Part-time and evening/weekend programs available. *Faculty:* 100. *Students:* 850 (408 women). 839 applicants, 56% accepted, 241 enrolled. *Degree requirements:* For master's, thesis, essay test. *Entrance requirements:* For master's, GMAT, minimum GPA of 2.7 in last 60 units. Additional exam requirements/recommendations for international students: Required—TOEFL (minimum score 550 paper-based). *Application deadline:* For fall admission, 5/1 priority date for domestic students, 4/1 for international students; for spring admission, 11/1 for domestic students, 10/15 for international students. Applications are processed on a rolling basis. Application fee: $55. *Financial support:* Application deadline: 3/1. *Unit head:* Linda Oubre, Dean, 415-817-4300, E-mail: loubre@sfsu.edu. *Application contact:* Armaan Moattari, Assistant Director, Graduate Programs, 415-817-4314, Fax: 817-4340, E-mail: amoatt@sfsu.edu.
Website: http://cob.sfsu.edu/.

San Jose State University, Graduate Studies and Research, Lucas Graduate School of Business, Programs in Business Administration, San Jose, CA 95192-0001. Offers MBA. *Accreditation:* AACSB. *Degree requirements:* For master's, comprehensive exam, thesis or alternative. *Entrance requirements:* For master's, GMAT, minimum GPA of 3.0. Electronic applications accepted.

Santa Clara University, Leavey School of Business, Santa Clara, CA 95053. Offers accelerated business administration (MBA); business administration (MBA); emerging professional business administration (MBA); entrepreneurship (MS); executive business administration (MBA); finance (MSF); information systems (MSIS); JD/MBA; MSIS/JD. *Accreditation:* AACSB. Part-time and evening/weekend programs available. *Faculty:* 85 full-time (21 women), 64 part-time/adjunct (20 women). *Students:* 292 full-time (154 women), 543 part-time (196 women); includes 262 minority (9 Black or African American, non-Hispanic/Latino; 203 Asian, non-Hispanic/Latino; 43 Hispanic/Latino; 2 Native Hawaiian or other Pacific Islander, non-Hispanic/Latino; 5 Two or more races, non-Hispanic/Latino), 260 international. Average age 30. 428 applicants, 77% accepted, 212 enrolled. In 2013, 345 master's awarded. *Degree requirements:* For master's, thesis or alternative. *Entrance requirements:* For master's, GMAT, GRE. Additional exam requirements/recommendations for international students: Required—TOEFL (minimum score 600 paper-based; 100 iBT). *Application deadline:* For fall admission, 6/1 for domestic and international students; for spring admission, 1/19 for domestic and international students. Applications are processed on a rolling basis. Application fee: $100 ($150 for international students). Electronic applications accepted. *Expenses:* Contact institution. *Financial support:* In 2013–14, 348 students received support. Career-related internships or fieldwork, Federal Work-Study, institutionally sponsored loans, and scholarships/grants available. Support available to part-time students. Financial award applicants required to submit FAFSA. *Faculty research:* Sovereign debt default, empire, and trade during the gold standard; CISE pathways to revitalized undergraduate computing education. *Unit head:* Elizabeth B. Ford, Senior Assistant Dean, 408-554-2752, Fax: 408-554-4571, E-mail: eford@scu.edu. *Application contact:* Tammy Fox, Director, Graduate Admissions and Financial Aid, 408-554-7858, E-mail: mbaadmissions@scu.edu.
Website: http://www.scu.edu/business/graduates.

Schiller International University, MBA Programs, Florida, Program in Information Technology, Largo, FL 33771. Offers MBA. *Entrance requirements:* Additional exam requirements/recommendations for international students: Required—TOEFL.

Schiller International University, MBA Programs, Heidelberg, Germany, Heidelberg, Germany. Offers international business (MBA, MIM); management of information technology (MBA). Part-time and evening/weekend programs available. *Degree requirements:* For master's, thesis optional. *Entrance requirements:* Additional exam requirements/recommendations for international students: Required—TOEFL (minimum score 550 paper-based). *Faculty research:* Leadership, international economy, foreign direct investment.

Seattle Pacific University, Master's Degree in Information Systems Management (MS-ISM) Program, Seattle, WA 98119-1997. Offers MS. Part-time programs available. *Students:* 4 full-time (3 women), 19 part-time (12 women); includes 2 minority (both Asian, non-Hispanic/Latino), 10 international. Average age 32. 24 applicants, 17% accepted, 4 enrolled. In 2013, 10 master's awarded. *Entrance requirements:* For master's, GMAT (minimum score of 500 preferred; 25 verbal, 30 quantitative, 4.4 analytical writing); GRE (minimum score of 295 preferred; 150 verbal/450 old scoring, 145 quantitative/525 old scoring), BA, resume as evidence of substantive work experience. Additional exam requirements/recommendations for international students: Required—TOEFL. *Application deadline:* For fall admission, 8/1 for domestic students, 6/1 for international students; for winter admission, 11/1 for domestic and international students; for spring admission, 2/1 for domestic students, 12/1 for international students; for summer admission, 5/1 for domestic students. Applications are processed on a rolling basis. Application fee: $50. Electronic applications accepted. *Financial support:* Applicants required to submit FAFSA. *Unit head:* Gary Karns, Associate Dean for Graduate Studies, 206-281-2948, Fax: 206-281-2733. *Application contact:* 206-281-2091.
Website: http://www.spu.edu/academics/school-of-business-and-economics/graduate-programs/ms-ism.

Shippensburg University of Pennsylvania, School of Graduate Studies, College of Arts and Sciences, Department of Sociology and Anthropology, Shippensburg, PA 17257-2299. Offers organizational development and leadership (MS), including business, communications, environmental management, higher education structure and policy, historical administration, individual and organizational development, management information systems, public organizations, social structures and organizations. Part-time and evening/weekend programs available. *Faculty:* 4 full-time (all women). *Students:* 19 full-time (11 women), 40 part-time (23 women); includes 7 minority (all Black or African American, non-Hispanic/Latino), 4 international. Average age 32. 63 applicants, 49% accepted, 19 enrolled. In 2013, 24 master's awarded. *Degree requirements:* For master's, capstone experience including internship. *Entrance requirements:* For master's, interview (if GPA less than 2.75), resume, personal goals statement. Additional exam requirements/recommendations for international students: Required—TOEFL (minimum score 580 paper-based); Recommended—IELTS (minimum score 6). *Application deadline:* For fall admission, 4/30 for international students; for spring admission, 9/30 for international students. Applications are processed on a rolling basis. Application fee: $45. Electronic applications accepted. *Expenses: Tuition, area resident:* Part-time $442 per credit. Tuition, state resident: part-time $442 per credit. Tuition, nonresident: part-time $663 per credit. *Required fees:* $127 per credit. *Financial support:* In 2013–14, 10 research assistantships with full tuition reimbursements (averaging $5,000 per year) were awarded; career-related internships or fieldwork, scholarships/grants, unspecified assistantships, and resident hall director and student payroll positions also available. Support available to part-time students. Financial award applicants required to submit FAFSA. *Unit head:* Dr. Barbara Denison, Program Coordinator, 717-477-1735, Fax: 717-477-4011, E-mail: bjdeni@ship.edu. *Application contact:* Jeremy R. Goshorn, Assistant Dean of Graduate Admissions, 717-477-1231, Fax: 717-477-4016, E-mail: jrgoshorn@ship.edu.
Website: http://www.ship.edu/odl/.

Southeastern Oklahoma State University, School of Arts and Sciences, Durant, OK 74701-0609. Offers biology (MT); computer information systems (MT); occupational safety and health (MT). Part-time and evening/weekend programs available. *Degree requirements:* For master's, thesis optional. *Entrance requirements:* For master's, minimum GPA of 3.0 in last 60 hours or 2.75 overall. Additional exam requirements/recommendations for international students: Required—TOEFL (minimum score 550 paper-based; 79 iBT). Electronic applications accepted.

Southern Illinois University Edwardsville, Graduate School, School of Business, Department of Computer Management and Information Systems, Edwardsville, IL 62026. Offers MS. Part-time and evening/weekend programs available. *Faculty:* 8 full-time (5 women). *Students:* 5 full-time (4 women), 16 part-time (5 women); includes 4 minority (3 Black or African American, non-Hispanic/Latino; 1 Asian, non-Hispanic/Latino), 5 international. 10 applicants, 40% accepted. In 2013, 14 master's awarded. *Degree requirements:* For master's, thesis or alternative, final exam. *Entrance requirements:* For master's, GMAT. Additional exam requirements/recommendations for international students: Required—TOEFL (minimum score 550 paper-based, 79 iBT), IELTS (minimum score 6.5), Michigan Test of English Language Proficiency or PTE. *Application deadline:* For fall admission, 7/18 for domestic students, 6/1 for international students; for spring admission, 12/12 for domestic students, 10/1 for international students; for summer admission, 4/24 for domestic students, 3/1 for international students. Applications are processed on a rolling basis. Application fee: $30. Electronic applications accepted. *Expenses:* Tuition, state resident: full-time $3551. Tuition, nonresident: full-time $8378. *Financial support:* In 2013–14, 3 students received support, including 3 teaching assistantships with tuition reimbursements available (averaging $9,585 per year); fellowships, research assistantships, institutionally sponsored loans, scholarships/grants, and unspecified assistantships also available. Financial award application deadline: 3/1; financial award applicants required to submit FAFSA. *Unit head:* Dr. Anne Powell, Chair, 618-650-2506, E-mail: apowell@siue.edu. *Application contact:* Dr. Jo Ellen Moore, Program Director, 618-650-5816, E-mail: joemoor@siue.edu.
Website: http://www.siue.edu/business/cmis/.

Southern Illinois University Edwardsville, Graduate School, School of Business, Program in Business Administration, Specialization in Management Information Systems, Edwardsville, IL 62026. Offers MBA. Part-time programs available. *Students:* 2 full-time (1 woman), 5 part-time (2 women); includes 1 minority (Hispanic/Latino). 5 applicants, 40% accepted. In 2013, 3 master's awarded. *Degree requirements:* For master's, thesis or alternative, final exam. *Entrance requirements:* For master's, GMAT. Additional exam requirements/recommendations for international students: Required—TOEFL (minimum score 550 paper-based; 79 iBT), IELTS (minimum score 6.5). *Application deadline:* For fall admission, 7/18 for domestic students, 6/1 for international students; for spring admission, 12/12 for domestic students, 10/1 for international students; for summer admission, 4/24 for domestic students, 3/1 for international students. Applications are processed on a rolling basis. Application fee: $30. Electronic applications accepted. *Expenses:* Tuition, state resident: full-time $3551. Tuition, nonresident: full-time $8378. *Financial support:* Fellowships with full tuition reimbursements, research assistantships with full tuition reimbursements, teaching assistantships with full tuition reimbursements, career-related internships or fieldwork, Federal Work-Study, institutionally sponsored loans, scholarships/grants, traineeships, and unspecified assistantships available. Support available to part-time students. Financial award application deadline: 3/1; financial award applicants required to submit FAFSA. *Unit head:* Dr. Janice Joplin, Director, 618-650-3412, E-mail: jjoplin@siue.edu. *Application contact:* Melissa K. Mace, Assistant Director of Graduate and International Recruitment, 618-650-2756, Fax: 618-650-3618, E-mail: mmace@siue.edu.
Website: http://www.siue.edu/business/mba/mis-specialization.shtml.

Management Information Systems

Southern Methodist University, Cox School of Business, MBA Program, Dallas, TX 75275. Offers accounting (MBA, PMBA); business administration (EMBA); finance (MBA); financial statement analysis (PMBA); general business (MBA); information technology and operations management (MBA); management (MBA); marketing (MBA); real estate (MBA); strategy (MBA); strategy and entrepreneurship (MBA); JD/MBA; MA/MBA. Part-time and evening/weekend programs available. *Entrance requirements:* For master's, GMAT. Additional exam requirements/recommendations for international students: Required—TOEFL. Electronic applications accepted. *Expenses:* Contact institution. *Faculty research:* Corporate finance, financial reporting, modeling consumer decision-making, competition between national brands and store brands, institutional determinants of firms' strategy.

Southern New Hampshire University, School of Business, Manchester, NH 03106-1045. Offers accounting (MBA, MS, Graduate Certificate); accounting finance (MS); accounting/auditing (MS); accounting/forensic accounting (MS); accounting/taxation (MS); athletic administration (MBA, Graduate Certificate); business administration (IMBA, MBA, Certificate, Graduate Certificate), including accounting (Certificate), business administration (MBA), business information systems (Graduate Certificate), human resource management (Certificate); corporate social responsibility (MBA); entrepreneurship (MBA); finance (MBA, MS, Graduate Certificate); finance/corporate finance (MS); finance/investments and securities (MS); forensic accounting (MBA); healthcare informatics (MBA); healthcare management (MBA); human resource management (Graduate Certificate); information technology (MS, Graduate Certificate); information technology management (MBA); international business (Graduate Certificate); international business and information technology (Graduate Certificate); international finance (Graduate Certificate); international sport management (Graduate Certificate); justice studies (MBA); leadership of nonprofit organizations (Graduate Certificate); marketing (MBA, MS, Graduate Certificate); operations and project management (MS); operations and supply chain management (MBA, Graduate Certificate); organizational leadership (MS); project management (MBA, Graduate Certificate); Six Sigma (MBA); Six Sigma quality (Graduate Certificate); social media marketing (MBA); sport management (MBA, MS, Graduate Certificate); sustainability and environmental compliance (MBA); workplace conflict management (MBA); MBA/Certificate. *Accreditation:* ACBSP. Part-time and evening/weekend programs available. Postbaccalaureate distance learning degree programs offered (no on-campus study). Terminal master's awarded for partial completion of doctoral program. *Degree requirements:* For master's, one foreign language, comprehensive exam (for some programs), thesis or alternative. *Entrance requirements:* For master's, minimum GPA of 2.5. Additional exam requirements/recommendations for international students: Required—TOEFL (minimum score 500 paper-based). Electronic applications accepted.

Southern Polytechnic State University, School of Engineering Technology and Management, Department of Business Administration, Marietta, GA 30060-2896. Offers accounting (MBA, MSA); business administration (Graduate Transition Certificate); finance (MBA); general (MBA); management (MBA); management information systems (MBA); marketing (MBA); operations and technology management (MBA). *Accreditation:* ACBSP. Part-time and evening/weekend programs available. Postbaccalaureate distance learning degree programs offered (no on-campus study). *Degree requirements:* For master's, comprehensive exam (for some programs), capstone course and major field exam (for MBA); 30 semester hours of course work (for MSA). *Entrance requirements:* For master's, GMAT or GRE, letters of recommendation, statement of purpose, resume, minimum GPA of 2.75 or undergraduate degree in business with up to 6 transition courses; undergraduate degree in accounting from regionally-accredited school (for MSA). Additional exam requirements/recommendations for international students: Required—TOEFL (minimum score 550 paper-based; 79 iBT), IELTS (minimum score 6.5). Electronic applications accepted. *Faculty research:* Ethics, virtual reality, sustainability, management of technology, quality management, capacity planning, human-computer interaction/interface, enterprise integration planning, economic impact of educational institutions, behavioral accounting, accounting ethics, taxation, information security, visualization simulation, human-computer interaction, supply chain, logistics, economics.

Southern University at New Orleans, School of Graduate Studies, New Orleans, LA 70126-1009. Offers criminal justice (MA); management information systems (MS); museum studies (MA); social work (MSW). *Accreditation:* CSWE. Part-time and evening/weekend programs available. *Degree requirements:* For master's, thesis. *Entrance requirements:* For master's, GRE/GMAT. Additional exam requirements/recommendations for international students: Required—TOEFL.

South University, Program in Information Systems and Technology, Austin, TX 78729. Offers MS.

South University, Program in Information Systems and Technology, Montgomery, AL 36116-1120. Offers MS.

South University, Program in Information Systems and Technology, Tampa, FL 33614. Offers MS.

South University, Program in Information Systems and Technology, Virginia Beach, VA 23452. Offers MS.

South University, Program in Information Systems and Technology, Royal Palm Beach, FL 33411. Offers MS.

Stevens Institute of Technology, Graduate School, Wesley J. Howe School of Technology Management, Doctoral Program in Technology Management, Hoboken, NJ 07030. Offers information management (PhD); technology management (PhD); telecommunications management (PhD). Part-time and evening/weekend programs available. Postbaccalaureate distance learning degree programs offered (minimal on-campus study). *Entrance requirements:* Additional exam requirements/recommendations for international students: Required—TOEFL. Electronic applications accepted.

Stevens Institute of Technology, Graduate School, Wesley J. Howe School of Technology Management, Program in Business Administration, Hoboken, NJ 07030. Offers engineering management (MBA); financial engineering (MBA); information management (MBA); information technology in financial services (MBA); information technology in the pharmaceutical industry (MBA); information technology outsourcing (MBA); pharmaceutical management (MBA); project management (MBA); technology management (MBA); telecommunications management (MBA).

Stevens Institute of Technology, Graduate School, Wesley J. Howe School of Technology Management, Program in Information Systems, Hoboken, NJ 07030. Offers computer science (MS); e-commerce (MS); enterprise systems (MS); entrepreneurial information technology (MS); information architecture (MS); information management (MS, Certificate); information security (MS); information technology in financial services industry (MS); information technology in the pharmaceutical industry (MS); information technology outsourcing management (MS); project management (MS, Certificate); software engineering (MS); telecommunications (MS). *Degree requirements:* For master's, thesis optional. *Entrance requirements:* For master's, GMAT, GRE General Test. Additional exam requirements/recommendations for international students: Required—TOEFL. Electronic applications accepted.

Stevens Institute of Technology, Graduate School, Wesley J. Howe School of Technology Management, Program in Management, Hoboken, NJ 07030. Offers general management (MS); global innovation management (MS); human resource management (MS); information management (MS); project management (MS); technology commercialization (MS); technology management (MS). Part-time programs available. *Degree requirements:* For master's, thesis optional. *Entrance requirements:* For master's, GMAT, GRE General Test. Additional exam requirements/recommendations for international students: Required—TOEFL. Electronic applications accepted. *Faculty research:* Industrial economics.

Stony Brook University, State University of New York, Graduate School, College of Business, Program in Business Administration, Stony Brook, NY 11794. Offers finance (MBA, Certificate); health care management (MBA, Certificate); human resource management (Certificate); human resources (MBA); information systems management (MBA, Certificate); management (MBA); marketing (MBA). *Faculty:* 32 full-time (7 women), 29 part-time/adjunct (8 women). *Students:* 189 full-time (102 women), 111 part-time (40 women); includes 50 minority (10 Black or African American, non-Hispanic/Latino; 1 American Indian or Alaska Native, non-Hispanic/Latino; 25 Asian, non-Hispanic/Latino; 14 Hispanic/Latino), 114 international. 255 applicants, 53% accepted, 70 enrolled. In 2013, 157 master's, 1 other advanced degree awarded. *Entrance requirements:* For master's, GMAT, 3 letters of recommendation from current or former employers or professors, transcripts, personal statement, resume. Additional exam requirements/recommendations for international students: Required—TOEFL (minimum score 550 paper-based; 90 iBT), IELTS (minimum score 6.5). *Application deadline:* For fall admission, 6/1 for domestic students, 3/15 for international students; for spring admission, 12/1 for domestic students, 11/1 for international students. Application fee: $100. *Expenses:* Tuition, state resident: full-time $9870; part-time $411 per credit. Tuition, nonresident: full-time $18,350; part-time $765 per credit. *Financial support:* Teaching assistantships available. *Total annual research expenditures:* $53,718. *Unit head:* Dr. Manuel London, Dean and Director, Center for Human Resource Management, 631-632-7159, Fax: 631-632-8181, E-mail: manuel.london@stonybrook.edu. *Application contact:* Dr. Dmytro Holod, Interim Associate Dean/Graduate Program Director, 631-632-7183, Fax: 631-632-8181, E-mail: dmytro.holod@stonybrook.edu.

Stony Brook University, State University of New York, Graduate School, College of Engineering and Applied Sciences, Department of Computer Science, Stony Brook, NY 11794. Offers computer science (MS, PhD); information systems (Certificate); information systems engineering (MS); software engineering (Certificate). *Faculty:* 43 full-time (8 women), 1 part-time/adjunct (0 women). *Students:* 326 full-time (65 women), 69 part-time (13 women); includes 18 minority (15 Asian, non-Hispanic/Latino; 3 Hispanic/Latino), 351 international. Average age 25. 1,875 applicants, 28% accepted, 150 enrolled. In 2013, 162 master's, 18 doctorates awarded. *Degree requirements:* For master's, thesis or alternative; for doctorate, comprehensive exam, thesis/dissertation. *Entrance requirements:* For master's and doctorate, GRE General Test. Additional exam requirements/recommendations for international students: Required—TOEFL. *Application deadline:* For fall admission, 1/15 for domestic students; for spring admission, 10/1 for domestic students. Application fee: $100. *Expenses:* Tuition, state resident: full-time $9870; part-time $411 per credit. Tuition, nonresident: full-time $18,350; part-time $765 per credit. *Financial support:* In 2013–14, 14 fellowships, 81 research assistantships, 40 teaching assistantships were awarded. *Faculty research:* Artificial intelligence, computer architecture, database management systems, VLSI, operating systems. *Total annual research expenditures:* $7.7 million. *Unit head:* Prof. Arie Kauffman, Chairman, 631-632-8428, Fax: 631-632-8334, E-mail: arie.kaufman@stonybrook.edu. *Application contact:* Cynthia Scalzo, Coordinator, 631-632-1521, Fax: 631-632-8334, E-mail: graduate@cs.stonybrook.edu.
Website: http://www.cs.sunysb.edu/.

Stony Brook University, State University of New York, School of Professional Development, Stony Brook, NY 11794. Offers biology (MAT); chemistry (MAT); coaching (Graduate Certificate); earth science (MAT); educational computing (Graduate Certificate); educational leadership (Advanced Certificate); English (MAT); environmental management (Graduate Certificate); French (MAT); German (MAT); higher education administration (MA, Certificate); human resource management (MS, Graduate Certificate); industrial management (Graduate Certificate); information systems management (Graduate Certificate); Italian (MAT); liberal studies (MA); mathematics (MAT); operations research (Graduate Certificate); physics (MAT); school district business leadership (Advanced Certificate); social science and the professions (MPS), including environmental management, human resource management; social studies (MAT); Spanish (MAT). Part-time and evening/weekend programs available. Postbaccalaureate distance learning degree programs offered. *Faculty:* 2 full-time (1 woman), 70 part-time/adjunct (30 women). *Students:* 241 full-time (135 women), 954 part-time (673 women); includes 209 minority (65 Black or African American, non-Hispanic/Latino; 2 American Indian or Alaska Native, non-Hispanic/Latino; 32 Asian, non-Hispanic/Latino; 104 Hispanic/Latino; 6 Two or more races, non-Hispanic/Latino), 7 international. Average age 28. 353 applicants, 92% accepted, 248 enrolled. In 2013, 312 master's, 131 other advanced degrees awarded. *Degree requirements:* For master's, one foreign language, thesis or alternative. *Application deadline:* For fall admission, 1/15 for domestic students; for spring admission, 10/1 for domestic students. Applications are processed on a rolling basis. Application fee: $100. *Expenses:* Tuition, state resident: full-time $9870; part-time $411 per credit. Tuition, nonresident: full-time $18,350; part-time $765 per credit. *Financial support:* Fellowships, research assistantships, teaching assistantships, and career-related internships or fieldwork available. Support available to part-time students. *Unit head:* Dr. Thomas Sexton, Interim Dean, 631-632-7181, Fax: 631-632-9046, E-mail: thomas.sexton@stonybrook.edu. *Application contact:* 631-632-7050 Ext. 1, E-mail: spd@stonybrook.edu.
Website: http://www.stonybrook.edu/spd/.

Stratford University, School of Graduate Studies, Falls Church, VA 22043. Offers accounting (MS); business administration (IMBA, MBA); enterprise business management (MS); entrepreneurial management (MS); information assurance (MS); information systems (MS); software engineering (MS); telecommunications (MS). Part-time and evening/weekend programs available. Postbaccalaureate distance learning degree programs offered (no on-campus study). *Degree requirements:* For master's, comprehensive exam, capstone project. *Entrance requirements:* For master's, GRE or GMAT, baccalaureate degree. Additional exam requirements/recommendations for international students: Required—TOEFL (minimum score 79 iBT) or IELTS (6.5). Electronic applications accepted.

Strayer University, Graduate Studies, Washington, DC 20005-2603. Offers accounting (MS); acquisition (MBA); business administration (MBA); communications technology (MS); educational management (M Ed); finance (MBA); health services administration (MHSA); hospitality and tourism management (MBA); human resource management (MBA); information systems (MS), including computer security management, decision support system management, enterprise resource management, network management, software engineering management, systems development management; management (MBA); management information systems (MS); marketing (MBA); professional accounting (MS), including accounting information systems, controllership, taxation;

public administration (MPA); supply chain management (MBA); technology in education (M Ed). Programs also offered at campus locations in Birmingham, AL; Chamblee, GA; Cobb County, GA; Morrow, GA; White Marsh, MD; Charleston, SC; Columbia, SC; Greensboro, NC; Greenville, SC; Lexington, KY; Louisville, KY; Nashville, TN; North Raleigh, NC; Washington, DC. Part-time and evening/weekend programs available. Postbaccalaureate distance learning degree programs offered (minimal on-campus study). *Degree requirements:* For master's, thesis. *Entrance requirements:* For master's, GMAT, GRE General Test, bachelor's degree from an accredited college or university, minimum undergraduate GPA of 2.75. Electronic applications accepted.

Syracuse University, Martin J. Whitman School of Management, PhD Program in Business Administration, Syracuse, NY 13244. Offers accounting (PhD); finance (PhD); management information systems (PhD); managerial statistics (PhD); marketing (PhD); operations management (PhD); organizational behavior (PhD); strategy and human resources (PhD); supply chain management (PhD). *Faculty:* 79 full-time (20 women), 25 part-time/adjunct (6 women). *Students:* 26 full-time (8 women), 1 part-time (0 women); includes 2 minority (1 Black or African American, non-Hispanic/Latino; 1 Asian, non-Hispanic/Latino), 20 international. Average age 30. 130 applicants, 9% accepted, 7 enrolled. In 2013, 15 doctorates awarded. *Degree requirements:* For doctorate, comprehensive exam, thesis/dissertation, summer research paper. *Entrance requirements:* For doctorate, GMAT or GRE General Test, 3 recommendations. Additional exam requirements/recommendations for international students: Required—TOEFL (minimum score 600 paper-based; 100 iBT). *Application deadline:* For fall admission, 1/15 priority date for domestic and international students. Applications are processed on a rolling basis. Application fee: $75. Electronic applications accepted. *Financial support:* In 2013–14, 1 fellowship with full tuition reimbursement (averaging $19,570 per year), 30 teaching assistantships with full tuition reimbursements (averaging $17,000 per year) were awarded; research assistantships with full tuition reimbursements also available. Financial award application deadline: 1/15. *Faculty research:* Marketing models, market microstructure, supply chain, auditing, corporate governance. *Unit head:* Dr. Michel Benaroch, Director of the PhD Program, 315-443-3429, E-mail: mbeanaroc@syr.edu. *Application contact:* Carol Hilleges, Administrative Specialist, 315-443-9601, Fax: 315-443-3671, E-mail: clhilleg@syr.edu. Website: http://whitman.syr.edu/phd/.

Syracuse University, School of Information Studies, Program in Data Science, Syracuse, NY 13244. Offers CAS. Part-time and evening/weekend programs available. Postbaccalaureate distance learning degree programs offered. *Students:* 1 full-time (0 women), 32 part-time (6 women); includes 5 minority (1 Black or African American, non-Hispanic/Latino; 3 Asian, non-Hispanic/Latino; 1 Hispanic/Latino), 10 international. Average age 36. 44 applicants, 91% accepted, 10 enrolled. In 2013, 13 CASs awarded. *Entrance requirements:* Additional exam requirements/recommendations for international students: Required—TOEFL (minimum score 100 iBT). *Application deadline:* For fall admission, 1/1 for domestic students, 1/1 priority date for international students. Applications are processed on a rolling basis. Application fee: $75. Electronic applications accepted. *Unit head:* Prof. Art Thomas, Program Director, 315-443-2911, E-mail: igrad@syr.edu. *Application contact:* Susan Corieri, Director of Enrollment Management, 315-443-2575, E-mail: ischool@syr.edu. Website: http://ischool.syr.edu/.

See Display on page 1583 and Close-Up on page 1599.

Syracuse University, School of Information Studies, Program in Information Management, Syracuse, NY 13244. Offers MS, DPS. Part-time and evening/weekend programs available. Postbaccalaureate distance learning degree programs offered (minimal on-campus study). *Students:* 225 full-time (102 women), 72 part-time (20 women); includes 46 minority (15 Black or African American, non-Hispanic/Latino; 1 American Indian or Alaska Native, non-Hispanic/Latino; 10 Asian, non-Hispanic/Latino; 14 Hispanic/Latino; 6 Two or more races, non-Hispanic/Latino), 170 international. Average age 27. 842 applicants, 40% accepted, 127 enrolled. In 2013, 142 master's awarded. *Degree requirements:* For doctorate, thesis/dissertation. *Entrance requirements:* For master's and doctorate, GRE General Test. Additional exam requirements/recommendations for international students: Required—TOEFL (minimum score 100 iBT). *Application deadline:* For fall admission, 1/15 priority date for domestic and international students; for spring admission, 10/15 priority date for domestic and international students. Applications are processed on a rolling basis. Application fee: $75. Electronic applications accepted. *Financial support:* Fellowships with full tuition reimbursements, research assistantships with partial tuition reimbursements, teaching assistantships with partial tuition reimbursements, and scholarships/grants available. Financial award application deadline: 1/1; financial award applicants required to submit FAFSA. *Unit head:* Art Thomas, Program Director, 315-443-2911, Fax: 315-443-6886, E-mail: igrad@syr.edu. *Application contact:* Susan Corieri, Director of Enrollment Management, 315-443-2575, E-mail: ischool@syr.edu. Website: http://ischool.syr.edu/.

See Display on page 1583 and Close-Up on page 1599.

Syracuse University, School of Information Studies, Program in Information Security Management, Syracuse, NY 13244. Offers CAS. Part-time and evening/weekend programs available. Postbaccalaureate distance learning degree programs offered. *Students:* 2 full-time (0 women), 5 part-time (0 women); includes 1 minority (Asian, non-Hispanic/Latino). Average age 33. 29 applicants, 76% accepted, 3 enrolled. In 2013, 35 CASs awarded. *Entrance requirements:* Additional exam requirements/recommendations for international students: Required—TOEFL (minimum score 100 iBT). *Application deadline:* For fall admission, 1/1 priority date for domestic and international students; for spring admission, 10/15 priority date for domestic and international students. Applications are processed on a rolling basis. Application fee: $75. Electronic applications accepted. *Financial support:* Application deadline: 1/1. *Unit head:* Art Thomas, Program Director, 315-443-2911, E-mail: igrad@syr.edu. *Application contact:* Susan Corieri, Director of Enrollment Management, 315-443-2575, E-mail: ischool@syr.edu. Website: http://ischool.syr.edu/.

See Display on page 1583 and Close-Up on page 1599.

Syracuse University, School of Information Studies, Program in Information Systems and Telecommunications Management, Syracuse, NY 13244. Offers CAS. Part-time and evening/weekend programs available. Postbaccalaureate distance learning degree programs offered. *Students:* 4 part-time (1 woman). Average age 41. 3 applicants, 33% accepted. In 2013, 13 CASs awarded. *Entrance requirements:* Additional exam requirements/recommendations for international students: Required—TOEFL (minimum score 100 iBT). *Application deadline:* For fall admission, 1/1 priority date for domestic and international students; for spring admission, 10/15 priority date for domestic and international students. Applications are processed on a rolling basis. Application fee: $75. Electronic applications accepted. *Financial support:* Application deadline: 1/1. *Unit head:* Art Thomas, Program Director, 315-443-2911, Fax: 315-443-6886, E-mail: igrad@syr.edu. *Application contact:* Susan Corieri, Director of Enrollment Management, 315-443-2575, E-mail: ischool@syr.edu. Website: http://ischool.syr.edu/.

See Display on page 1583 and Close-Up on page 1599.

Tarleton State University, College of Graduate Studies, College of Business Administration, Department of Computer Information Systems, Stephenville, TX 76402. Offers information systems (MS). Part-time and evening/weekend programs available. *Faculty:* 5 full-time (1 woman). *Students:* 11 full-time (3 women), 38 part-time (10 women); includes 7 minority (2 Black or African American, non-Hispanic/Latino; 2 Asian, non-Hispanic/Latino; 2 Hispanic/Latino; 1 Two or more races, non-Hispanic/Latino). Average age 37. 18 applicants, 72% accepted, 11 enrolled. In 2013, 25 master's awarded. *Degree requirements:* For master's, comprehensive exam. *Entrance requirements:* For master's, GRE, minimum GPA of 3.0. Additional exam requirements/recommendations for international students: Required—TOEFL (minimum score 550 paper-based; 80 iBT). *Application deadline:* For fall admission, 8/15 priority date for domestic students; for spring admission, 1/7 for domestic students. Applications are processed on a rolling basis. Application fee: $30 ($130 for international students). Electronic applications accepted. *Expenses:* Tuition, state resident: full-time $3312; part-time $184 per credit hour. Tuition, nonresident: full-time $9144; part-time $508 per credit hour. *Required fees:* $1916. Tuition and fees vary according to course load and campus/location. *Financial support:* Research assistantships and teaching assistantships available. Financial award application deadline: 5/1; financial award applicants required to submit FAFSA. *Unit head:* Dr. Leah Shultz, Department Head, 254-968-9169, Fax: 254-968-9345, E-mail: lschult@tarleton.edu. *Application contact:* Information Contact, 254-968-9104, Fax: 254-968-9670, E-mail: gradoffice@tarleton.edu. Website: http://www.tarleton.edu/cis/index.html.

Temple University, College of Education, Department of Curriculum, Instruction, and Technology in Education, Philadelphia, PA 19122-6096. Offers career and technical education (Ed M), including business, computing, and information technology, industrial education, marketing education; middle grades education (Ed M), including math and language arts, math and science, science and language arts; secondary education (Ed M), including English, math, social studies; teaching English to speakers of other languages (MS Ed); urban education (Ed M). Part-time and evening/weekend programs available. *Students:* 66 full-time (48 women), 120 part-time (67 women); includes 50 minority (35 Black or African American, non-Hispanic/Latino; 1 American Indian or Alaska Native, non-Hispanic/Latino; 2 Asian, non-Hispanic/Latino; 7 Hispanic/Latino; 5 Two or more races, non-Hispanic/Latino), 1 international. 229 applicants, 41% accepted, 60 enrolled. In 2013, 41 master's awarded. Terminal master's awarded for partial completion of doctoral program. *Degree requirements:* For master's, thesis or alternative. *Entrance requirements:* Additional exam requirements/recommendations for international students: Required—TOEFL (minimum score 550 paper-based; 79 iBT). *Application deadline:* For fall admission, 4/1 for domestic students, 12/15 for international students; for spring admission, 10/1 for domestic students, 8/1 for international students. Application fee: $60. Electronic applications accepted. *Financial support:* Fellowships, research assistantships, and teaching assistantships available. Financial award application deadline: 1/15; financial award applicants required to submit FAFSA. *Faculty research:* Workforce development, vocational education, technical education, industrial education, professional development, literacy, classroom management, school communities, curriculum development, instruction, applied linguistics, crosslinguistic influence, bilingual education, oral proficiency, multilingualism. *Application contact:* Felicia Neuber, Enrollment Management, 215-204-8011, E-mail: educate@temple.edu. Website: http://www.temple.edu/education/tl/.

Temple University, Fox School of Business, Doctoral Programs in Business, Philadelphia, PA 19122-6096. Offers accounting (PhD); entrepreneurship (PhD); finance (PhD); international business (PhD); management information systems (PhD); marketing (PhD); risk management and insurance (PhD); statistics (PhD); strategic management (PhD); tourism and sport (PhD). *Accreditation:* AACSB. *Degree requirements:* For doctorate, thesis/dissertation. *Entrance requirements:* For doctorate, GRE General Test, GMAT, minimum GPA of 3.0, master's degree. Additional exam requirements/recommendations for international students: Required—TOEFL (minimum score 600 paper-based; 100 iBT), IELTS (minimum score 7.5). Electronic applications accepted.

Tennessee Technological University, College of Graduate Studies, College of Business, Cookeville, TN 38505. Offers accounting (MBA); finance (MBA); human resource management (MBA); international business (MBA); management information systems (MBA). *Accreditation:* AACSB. Part-time and evening/weekend programs available. Postbaccalaureate distance learning degree programs offered (no on-campus study). *Faculty:* 28 full-time (5 women). *Students:* 54 full-time (22 women), 115 part-time (44 women); includes 11 minority (5 Black or African American, non-Hispanic/Latino; 1 Asian, non-Hispanic/Latino; 1 Hispanic/Latino; 4 Two or more races, non-Hispanic/Latino), 8 international. Average age 25. 171 applicants, 47% accepted, 50 enrolled. In 2013, 87 master's awarded. *Entrance requirements:* For master's, GMAT, GRE. Additional exam requirements/recommendations for international students: Required—TOEFL (minimum score 550 paper-based; 79 iBT), IELTS (minimum score 5.5), PTE (minimum score 53), or TOEIC (Test of English as an International Communication). *Application deadline:* For fall admission, 8/1 for domestic students, 5/1 for international students; for spring admission, 12/1 for domestic students, 10/1 for international students. Applications are processed on a rolling basis. Application fee: $35 ($40 for international students). Electronic applications accepted. *Expenses:* Tuition, state resident: full-time $9347; part-time $465 per credit hour. Tuition, nonresident: full-time $23,635; part-time $1152 per credit hour. *Financial support:* In 2013–14, 5 fellowships (averaging $10,000 per year), 18 research assistantships (averaging $4,000 per year), teaching assistantships (averaging $4,000 per year) were awarded. Support available to part-time students. Financial award application deadline: 4/1. *Unit head:* Amanda L. Brown, Interim Director, 931-372-3600, Fax: 931-372-6249, E-mail: albrown@tntech.edu. *Application contact:* Shelia K. Kendrick, Coordinator of Graduate Studies, 931-372-3808, Fax: 931-372-3497, E-mail: skendrick@tntech.edu. Website: http://www.tntech.edu/mba.

Texas A&M International University, Office of Graduate Studies and Research, A.R. Sanchez School of Business, Division of International Business and Technology Studies, Laredo, TX 78041-1900. Offers information systems (MSIS); international business management (MBA, PhD). *Faculty:* 10 full-time (2 women), 1 part-time/adjunct (0 women). *Students:* 47 full-time (13 women), 176 part-time (79 women); includes 137 minority (10 Black or African American, non-Hispanic/Latino; 2 Asian, non-Hispanic/Latino; 125 Hispanic/Latino), 78 international. Average age 29. 78 applicants, 96% accepted, 78 enrolled. In 2013, 65 master's, 3 doctorates awarded. *Degree requirements:* For master's, thesis (for some programs). *Entrance requirements:* For master's, GMAT or GRE General Test. Additional exam requirements/recommendations for international students: Required—TOEFL (minimum score 550 paper-based; 79 iBT). *Application deadline:* For fall admission, 4/30 priority date for domestic students, 4/30 for international students; for spring admission, 11/30 for domestic students, 10/1 for international students. Applications are processed on a rolling basis. Application fee: $35 ($50 for international students). *Expenses:* Tuition, state resident: full-time $5184. *International tuition:* $11,556 full-time. *Financial support:* In 2013–14, 8 students received support, including 5 research assistantships, 2 teaching assistantships; fellowships, Federal Work-Study, institutionally sponsored loans, and scholarships/

grants also available. Support available to part-time students. *Unit head:* Dr. Nereu Kock, Chair, 956-326-2521, Fax: 956-326-2494, E-mail: nedkock@tamiu.edu. *Application contact:* Imelda Lopez, Graduate Admissions Counselor, 956-326-2485, Fax: 956-326-2459, E-mail: lopez@tamiu.edu.

Texas A&M University, Mays Business School, Department of Information and Operations Management, College Station, TX 77843. Offers management information systems (MS). *Faculty:* 17. *Students:* 188 full-time (62 women), 1 part-time (0 women); includes 7 minority (1 Black or African American, non-Hispanic/Latino; 2 Asian, non-Hispanic/Latino; 2 Hispanic/Latino; 2 Two or more races, non-Hispanic/Latino), 139 international. Average age 25. 639 applicants, 23% accepted, 69 enrolled. In 2013, 119 master's awarded. Terminal master's awarded for partial completion of doctoral program. *Degree requirements:* For master's, comprehensive exam. *Entrance requirements:* For master's, GMAT. Additional exam requirements/recommendations for international students: Required—TOEFL. *Application deadline:* For fall admission, 3/1 priority date for domestic students; for spring admission, 8/1 for domestic students. Applications are processed on a rolling basis. Application fee: $50 ($75 for international students). *Expenses:* Tuition, state resident: full-time $4078; part-time $226.55 per credit hour. Tuition, nonresident: full-time $10,450; part-time $580.55 per credit hour. *Required fees:* $2328; $278.50 per credit hour. $642.45 per semester. *Financial support:* Fellowships, research assistantships, teaching assistantships, career-related internships or fieldwork, Federal Work-Study, and institutionally sponsored loans available. Financial award application deadline: 2/1. *Unit head:* Dr. Rich Metters, Head, 979-845-1148, Fax: 979-845-1148, E-mail: rmetters@mays.tamu.edu. *Application contact:* Ted Boone, Graduate Advisor, 979-845-0809, Fax: 979-845-1148, E-mail: tboone@mays.tamu.edu.
Website: http://mays.tamu.edu/info/.

Texas A&M University–San Antonio, School of Business, San Antonio, TX 78224. Offers business administration (MBA); enterprise resource planning systems (MBA); finance (MBA); healthcare management (MBA); human resources management (MBA); information assurance and security (MBA); international business (MBA); professional accounting (MPA); project management (MBA); supply chain management (MBA). Part-time and evening/weekend programs available. *Entrance requirements:* For master's, GMAT. Additional exam requirements/recommendations for international students: Required—TOEFL (minimum score 550 paper-based; 80 iBT), IELTS (minimum score 6). Electronic applications accepted.

Texas Southern University, Jesse H. Jones School of Business, Program in Management Information Systems, Houston, TX 77004-4584. Offers MS. *Faculty:* 14 full-time (7 women), 8 part-time/adjunct (1 woman). *Students:* 19 full-time (7 women), 13 part-time (5 women); includes 30 minority (27 Black or African American, non-Hispanic/Latino; 3 Asian, non-Hispanic/Latino), 2 international. Average age 30. 26 applicants, 50% accepted, 9 enrolled. In 2013, 11 master's awarded. *Application deadline:* For fall admission, 7/1 for domestic and international students; for spring admission, 11/1 for domestic and international students. Applications are processed on a rolling basis. Application fee: $50 ($75 for international students). Electronic applications accepted. *Financial support:* Teaching assistantships, career-related internships or fieldwork, scholarships/grants, and unspecified assistantships available. Financial award applicants required to submit FAFSA. *Unit head:* Dr. S. Srinivasan, Associate Dean for Academic Affairs and Research, 713-313-7776, E-mail: srinis@tsu.edu. *Application contact:* Dr. Gregory Maddox, Dean of the Graduate School, 713-313-7011, E-mail: maddox_gh@tsu.edu.
Website: http://www.tsu.edu/academics/colleges__schools/Jesse_H_Jones_School_of_Business/mmis.php.

Texas State University, Graduate School, Emmett and Miriam McCoy College of Business Administration, Program in Accounting and Information Technology, San Marcos, TX 78666. Offers MS. *Faculty:* 8 full-time (1 woman), 1 part-time/adjunct (0 women). *Students:* 6 full-time (2 women), 10 part-time (4 women); includes 3 minority (2 Asian, non-Hispanic/Latino; 1 Hispanic/Latino), 1 international. Average age 32. 14 applicants, 36% accepted, 2 enrolled. In 2013, 7 master's awarded. *Degree requirements:* For master's, comprehensive exam. *Entrance requirements:* For master's, GMAT, official transcript from each college or university attended, 2 letters of recommendation, resume. Additional exam requirements/recommendations for international students: Required—TOEFL (minimum score 550 paper-based; 78 iBT). *Application deadline:* For fall admission, 6/1 for domestic and international students; for spring admission, 10/1 for domestic and international students. Application fee: $40 ($90 for international students). *Expenses:* Tuition, state resident: full-time $6663; part-time $278 per credit hour. Tuition, nonresident: full-time $15,159; part-time $632 per credit hour. *Required fees:* $1872; $54 per credit hour. $306 per term. Tuition and fees vary according to course load. *Financial support:* In 2013–14, 5 students received support, including 1 research assistantship (averaging $10,950 per year), 3 teaching assistantships (averaging $11,280 per year); Federal Work-Study, institutionally sponsored loans, scholarships/grants, health care benefits, and unspecified assistantships also available. Support available to part-time students. *Unit head:* Dr. William Chittenden, Graduate Advisor, 512-245-3591, Fax: 512-245-7973, E-mail: wc10@txstate.edu. *Application contact:* Dr. Andrea Golato, Dean of Graduate School, 512-245-2581, Fax: 512-245-8365, E-mail: gradcollege@txstate.edu.

Texas Tech University, Graduate School, Rawls College of Business Administration, Area of Information Systems and Quantitative Sciences, Lubbock, TX 79409. Offers business statistics (MS, PhD); healthcare management (MS); management information systems (MS, PhD); production and operations management (PhD). Part-time programs available. *Faculty:* 13 full-time (0 women). *Students:* 107 full-time (24 women); includes 3 minority (1 Black or African American, non-Hispanic/Latino; 1 American Indian or Alaska Native, non-Hispanic/Latino; 1 Asian, non-Hispanic/Latino), 79 international. Average age 27. 125 applicants, 55% accepted, 40 enrolled. In 2013, 17 master's, 5 doctorates awarded. Terminal master's awarded for partial completion of doctoral program. *Degree requirements:* For master's, comprehensive exam or capstone course; for doctorate, thesis/dissertation, qualifying exams. *Entrance requirements:* For master's and doctorate, GMAT, holistic profile of academic credentials. Additional exam requirements/recommendations for international students: Required—TOEFL (minimum score 550 paper-based; 79 iBT). *Application deadline:* For fall admission, 7/1 priority date for domestic students, 1/15 for international students; for spring admission, 11/1 priority date for domestic students, 6/15 priority date for international students. Applications are processed on a rolling basis. Application fee: $60. Electronic applications accepted. *Expenses:* Tuition, state resident: full-time $6062; part-time $252.57 per credit hour. Tuition, nonresident: full-time $14,558; part-time $606.57 per credit hour. *Required fees:* $2655; $35 per credit hour. $907.50 per semester. Tuition and fees vary according to course load. *Financial support:* In 2013–14, 5 research assistantships (averaging $16,160 per year), 5 teaching assistantships (averaging $18,000 per year) were awarded; Federal Work-Study, scholarships/grants, and unspecified assistantships also available. Financial award applicants required to submit FAFSA. *Faculty research:* Database management systems, systems management and engineering, expert systems and adaptive knowledge-based sciences, statistical analysis and design. *Unit head:* Dr. Glenn Browne, Area Coordinator, 806-834-0969, Fax: 806-742-3193, E-mail: glenn.browne@ttu.edu. *Application contact:* Terri Boston, Applications Manager, Graduate and Professional Programs, 806-742-3184, Fax: 806-742-3958, E-mail: rawlsgrad@ttu.edu.
Website: http://is.ba.ttu.edu.

Touro College, Graduate School of Technology, New York, NY 10010. Offers information systems (MS); instructional technology (MS); Web and multimedia design (MA). *Students:* 10 full-time (6 women), 226 part-time (111 women); includes 104 minority (39 Black or African American, non-Hispanic/Latino; 1 American Indian or Alaska Native, non-Hispanic/Latino; 39 Asian, non-Hispanic/Latino; 21 Hispanic/Latino; 4 Two or more races, non-Hispanic/Latino), 6 international. *Unit head:* Dr. Isaac Herskowitz, Dean of the Graduate School of Technology, 202-463-0400 Ext. 5231, E-mail: issac.herskowitz@touro.edu.
Website: http://www.touro.edu/gst/.

Towson University, Program in Applied Information Technology, Towson, MD 21252-0001. Offers applied information technology (MS, D Sc); database management systems (Postbaccalaureate Certificate); information security and assurance (Postbaccalaureate Certificate); information systems management (Postbaccalaureate Certificate); Internet applications development (Postbaccalaureate Certificate); networking technologies (Postbaccalaureate Certificate); software engineering (Postbaccalaureate Certificate). *Students:* 129 full-time (42 women), 227 part-time (78 women); includes 125 minority (77 Black or African American, non-Hispanic/Latino; 28 Asian, non-Hispanic/Latino; 11 Hispanic/Latino; 3 Native Hawaiian or other Pacific Islander, non-Hispanic/Latino; 6 Two or more races, non-Hispanic/Latino), 84 international. *Entrance requirements:* For master's and Postbaccalaureate Certificate, bachelor's degree, minimum GPA of 3.0; for doctorate, master's degree in computer science, information systems, information technology, or closely-related areas; minimum GPA of 3.0; 2 letters of recommendation; resume. Additional exam requirements/recommendations for international students: Required—TOEFL. *Application deadline:* Applications are processed on a rolling basis. Application fee: $45. Electronic applications accepted. *Unit head:* Dr. Darush Davani, Graduate Program Director, 410-704-2774, E-mail: ddavani@towson.edu. *Application contact:* Alicia Arkell-Kleis, Information Contact, 410-704-6004, E-mail: grads@towson.edu.
Website: http://grad.towson.edu/program/master/ait-ms/.

Trevecca Nazarene University, Graduate Business Programs, Nashville, TN 37210-2877. Offers business administration (MBA); healthcare administration (Certificate); information technology (MBA, MS, Certificate); management (MSM); management and leadership (Certificate); project management (Certificate). Evening/weekend programs available. Postbaccalaureate distance learning degree programs offered. *Faculty:* 7 full-time (0 women), 3 part-time/adjunct (0 women). *Students:* 101 full-time (55 women), 21 part-time (8 women); includes 30 minority (27 Black or African American, non-Hispanic/Latino; 2 Asian, non-Hispanic/Latino; 1 Hispanic/Latino), 3 international. Average age 36. In 2013, 33 master's awarded. *Entrance requirements:* For master's, minimum GPA of 2.75, resume, official transcript from regionally-accredited institution, minimum math grade of C, minimum English composition grade of C, MS-IT requires undergraduate computing degree. Additional exam requirements/recommendations for international students: Required—TOEFL (minimum score 550 paper-based; 80 iBT). *Application deadline:* Applications are processed on a rolling basis. Application fee: $25. *Expenses:* Contact institution. *Financial support:* Applicants required to submit FAFSA. *Unit head:* Dr. Rick Mann, Director of Graduate and Professional Programs for School of Business, 615-248-1529, E-mail: management@trevecca.edu. *Application contact:* 615-248-1529, E-mail: cll@trevecca.edu.

Trident University International, College of Business Administration, Program in Business Administration, Cypress, CA 90630. Offers business administration (PhD); conflict and negotiation management (MBA); criminal justice administration (MBA); entrepreneurship (MBA); finance (MBA); general management (MBA); government accounting (MBA); human resource management (MBA); information security and digital assurance management (MBA); information technology management (MBA); international business (MBA); logistics management (MBA); marketing (MBA); project management (MBA); public management (MBA); quality management (MBA); strategic leadership (MBA). Part-time and evening/weekend programs available. Postbaccalaureate distance learning degree programs offered (no on-campus study). *Degree requirements:* For doctorate, comprehensive exam, thesis/dissertation, defense of dissertation. *Entrance requirements:* For master's, minimum GPA of 2.5 (students with GPA 3.0 or greater may transfer up to 30% of graduate level credits); for doctorate, minimum GPA of 3.4, curriculum vitae, course work in research methods or statistics. Additional exam requirements/recommendations for international students: Required—TOEFL. Electronic applications accepted.

Trident University International, College of Information Systems, Cypress, CA 90630. Offers business intelligence (Certificate); information technology management (MS). Part-time and evening/weekend programs available. Postbaccalaureate distance learning degree programs offered (no on-campus study). *Entrance requirements:* For master's, minimum GPA of 2.5 (students with GPA 3.0 or greater may transfer up to 30% of graduate level credits); undergraduate degree completed within the past 5 years. Additional exam requirements/recommendations for international students: Required—TOEFL (minimum score 525 paper-based). Electronic applications accepted.

Troy University, Graduate School, College of Business, Program in Business Administration, Troy, AL 36082. Offers accounting (EMBA, MBA); criminal justice (EMBA); finance (MBA); general management (EMBA, MBA); healthcare management (EMBA); information systems (EMBA, MBA); international economic development (MBA). *Accreditation:* ACBSP. Part-time and evening/weekend programs available. *Faculty:* 56 full-time (20 women), 3 part-time/adjunct (0 women). *Students:* 142 full-time (89 women), 310 part-time (192 women); includes 265 minority (185 Black or African American, non-Hispanic/Latino; 3 American Indian or Alaska Native, non-Hispanic/Latino; 62 Asian, non-Hispanic/Latino; 8 Hispanic/Latino; 1 Native Hawaiian or other Pacific Islander, non-Hispanic/Latino; 6 Two or more races, non-Hispanic/Latino). Average age 29. 472 applicants, 68% accepted, 51 enrolled. In 2013, 293 master's awarded. *Degree requirements:* For master's, minimum GPA of 3.0, capstone course, research course. *Entrance requirements:* For master's, GMAT (minimum score 500) or GRE General Test (minimum score 900 on old exam or 294 on new exam), bachelor's degree; minimum undergraduate GPA of 2.5 or 3.0 on last 30 semester hours, letter of recommendation. Additional exam requirements/recommendations for international students: Required—TOEFL (minimum score 523 paper-based; 70 iBT), IELTS (minimum score 6). *Application deadline:* Applications are processed on a rolling basis. Application fee: $50. *Expenses:* Tuition, state resident: full-time $6084; part-time $338 per credit hour. Tuition, nonresident: full-time $12,168; part-time $676 per credit hour. *Required fees:* $630; $35 per credit hour. $50 per semester. *Unit head:* Dr. Bob Wheatley, Director, Graduate Business Programs, 334-670-3194, Fax: 334-670-3599, E-mail: rwheat@troy.edu. *Application contact:* Brenda K. Campbell, Director of Graduate Admissions, 334-670-3178, Fax: 334-670-3733, E-mail: bcamp@troy.edu.

Troy University, Graduate School, College of Business, Program in Management, Troy, AL 36082. Offers applied management (MSM); healthcare management (MSM); human resources management (MSM); information systems (MSM); international hospitality management (MSM); international management (MSM); leadership and organizational effectiveness (MSM); public management (MS, MSM). *Accreditation:*

ACBSP. Part-time and evening/weekend programs available. *Faculty:* 15 full-time (8 women), 3 part-time/adjunct (0 women). *Students:* 18 full-time (14 women), 148 part-time (86 women); includes 95 minority (75 Black or African American, non-Hispanic/Latino; 1 American Indian or Alaska Native, non-Hispanic/Latino; 4 Asian, non-Hispanic/Latino; 8 Hispanic/Latino; 7 Two or more races, non-Hispanic/Latino). Average age 35. 124 applicants, 79% accepted, 30 enrolled. In 2013, 75 master's awarded. *Degree requirements:* For master's, Graduate Educational Testing Service Major Field Test, capstone exam, minimum GPA of 3.0. *Entrance requirements:* For master's, GRE (minimum score of 900 on old exam or 294 on new exam) or GMAT (minimum score of 500), bachelor's degree; minimum undergraduate GPA of 2.5 or 3.0 on last 30 semester hours, letter of recommendation. Additional exam requirements/recommendations for international students: Required—TOEFL (minimum score 523 paper-based; 70 iBT), IELTS (minimum score 6). *Application deadline:* Applications are processed on a rolling basis. Application fee: $50. Electronic applications accepted. *Expenses:* Contact institution. *Unit head:* Dr. Bob Wheatley, Director, Graduate Business Programs, 334-670-3143, Fax: 334-670-3599, E-mail: rwheat@troy.edu. *Application contact:* Brenda K. Campbell, Director of Graduate Admissions, 334-670-3178, Fax: 334-670-3733, E-mail: bcamp@troy.edu.

United States International University, School of Business Administration, Nairobi, Kenya. Offers business administration (GEMBA); entrepreneurship (MBA); finance (MBA); human resource management (MBA); information technology management (MBA); integrated studies (MBA); international business administration (MBA); management and organizational development (MS); marketing (MBA); organizational development (EMS); strategic management (MBA). Part-time and evening/weekend programs available. *Degree requirements:* For master's, thesis. *Entrance requirements:* For master's, GMAT, 2 letters of reference, resume. Additional exam requirements/recommendations for international students: Required—TOEFL (minimum score 550 paper-based). *Faculty research:* Marketing in small business enterprises, total quality management in Kenya.

Universidad del Este, Graduate School, Carolina, PR 00984. Offers accounting (MBA); adult education (M Ed); agribusiness (MBA); criminal justice and criminology (MA); curriculum and instruction - early education (M Ed); curriculum and instruction - elementary (M Ed); curriculum and instruction - English (M Ed); curriculum and instruction - Spanish (M Ed); human resources (MBA); information security management (MBA); information technology and Web business development (MBA); management (MBA); public policy (MPA); social work (MA), including clinical social work; special education (M Ed); strategic leadership (MBA). *Students:* 464 full-time (322 women), 669 part-time (499 women); all minorities (all Hispanic/Latino). Average age 35. 693 applicants, 61% accepted, 332 enrolled. In 2013, 228 master's awarded. *Unit head:* Jose R. Clintron, Dean, 787-257-7373 Ext. 3007, E-mail: ue_jcintron@suagm.edu. *Application contact:* Clotilde Santiago, Director of Admissions, 787-257-7373 Ext. 3400, E-mail: ue_csantiago@suagm.edu.

Universidad del Turabo, Graduate Programs, School in Business Administration, Program in Management of Information Systems, Gurabo, PR 00778-3030. Offers DBA.

Universidad Metropolitana, School of Business Administration, Program in Management Information Systems, San Juan, PR 00928-1150. Offers MBA.

Université de Sherbrooke, Faculty of Administration, Program in Governance, Audit and Security of Information Technology, Longueuil, QC J4K0A8, Canada. Offers M Adm. Part-time and evening/weekend programs available. Postbaccalaureate distance learning degree programs offered. *Degree requirements:* For master's, thesis. *Entrance requirements:* For master's, bachelor's degree, related work experience. Electronic applications accepted.

Université de Sherbrooke, Faculty of Administration, Program in Management Information Systems, Sherbrooke, QC J1K 2R1, Canada. Offers M Sc. *Degree requirements:* For master's, one foreign language, thesis. *Entrance requirements:* For master's, bachelor's degree in related field, minimum GPA of 3.0 (on 4.3 scale). Electronic applications accepted. *Faculty research:* Project management in IT, IT governance, business intelligence, IT performance.

Université de Sherbrooke, Faculty of Sciences, Centre de Formation en Technologies de L'information, Sherbrooke, QC J1K 2R1, Canada. Offers M Sc, Diploma. Electronic applications accepted.

Université du Québec à Montréal, Graduate Programs, Program in Management Information Systems, Montréal, QC H3C 3P8, Canada. Offers M Sc, M Sc A. Part-time programs available. *Entrance requirements:* For master's, appropriate bachelor's degree or equivalent and proficiency in French.

Université Laval, Faculty of Administrative Sciences, Programs in Business Administration, Québec, QC G1K 7P4, Canada. Offers accounting (MBA); agri-food management (MBA); electronic business (MBA, Diploma); factory management and logistics (MBA); finance (MBA); firm management (MBA); geomatic management (MBA); information technology management (MBA); international management (MBA); management (MBA); management accounting (MBA, Diploma); marketing (MBA); modeling and organizational decision (MBA); occupational health and safety management (MBA); pharmacy management (MBA); social and environmental responsibility (MBA); technological entrepreneurship (Diploma). *Accreditation:* AACSB. Part-time and evening/weekend programs available. Postbaccalaureate distance learning degree programs offered (no on-campus study). *Entrance requirements:* For master's and Diploma, knowledge of French and English. Electronic applications accepted.

University at Buffalo, the State University of New York, Graduate School, School of Engineering and Applied Sciences, Department of Computer Science and Engineering, Buffalo, NY 14260. Offers computer science and engineering (MS, PhD); information assurance (Certificate). Part-time programs available. *Faculty:* 37 full-time (4 women). *Students:* 595 full-time (105 women), 10 part-time (0 women); includes 13 minority (3 Black or African American, non-Hispanic/Latino; 9 Asian, non-Hispanic/Latino; 1 Hispanic/Latino), 558 international. Average age 24. 2,454 applicants, 31% accepted, 325 enrolled. In 2013, 153 master's, 13 doctorates awarded. Terminal master's awarded for partial completion of doctoral program. *Degree requirements:* For master's, thesis or alternative; for doctorate, thesis/dissertation, comprehensive qualifying exam. *Entrance requirements:* For master's and doctorate, GRE General Test. Additional exam requirements/recommendations for international students: Required—TOEFL (minimum score 550 paper-based; 79 iBT). *Application deadline:* For fall admission, 2/1 priority date for domestic and international students; for spring admission, 10/1 priority date for domestic and international students. Applications are processed on a rolling basis. Application fee: $75. Electronic applications accepted. *Financial support:* In 2013–14, 111 students received support, including 4 fellowships with full and partial tuition reimbursements available (averaging $26,150 per year), 43 research assistantships with full and partial tuition reimbursements available (averaging $20,400 per year), 64 teaching assistantships with full and partial tuition reimbursements available (averaging $21,100 per year); career-related internships or fieldwork, Federal Work-Study, institutionally sponsored loans, health care benefits, tuition waivers (partial), and unspecified assistantships also available. Financial award application deadline: 12/15; financial award applicants required to submit FAFSA. *Faculty research:* Bioinformatics, pattern recognition, computer networks and security, theory and algorithms, databases and data mining. *Total annual research expenditures:* $7.7 million. *Unit head:* Dr. Aidong Zhang, Chairman, 716-645-3180, Fax: 716-645-3464, E-mail: azhang@buffalo.edu. *Application contact:* Dr. Hung Ngo, Director of Graduate Studies, 716-645-4750, Fax: 716-645-3464, E-mail: hungngo@buffalo.edu.
Website: http://www.cse.buffalo.edu/.

University at Buffalo, the State University of New York, Graduate School, School of Management, Buffalo, NY 14260. Offers accounting (MS); business administration (EMBA, MBA, PMBA); finance (MS), including financial management, quantitative finance; management (PhD); management information systems (MS); supply chains and operations management (MS); Au D/MBA; DDS/MBA; JD/MBA; M Arch/MBA; MA/MBA; MD/MBA; MPH/MBA; MSW/MBA; Pharm D/MBA. *Accreditation:* AACSB. Part-time and evening/weekend programs available. *Faculty:* 72 full-time (23 women), 51 part-time/adjunct (13 women). *Students:* 627 full-time (266 women), 181 part-time (65 women); includes 50 minority (16 Black or African American, non-Hispanic/Latino; 5 American Indian or Alaska Native, non-Hispanic/Latino; 5 Asian, non-Hispanic/Latino; 3 Hispanic/Latino; 21 Native Hawaiian or other Pacific Islander, non-Hispanic/Latino), 332 international. Average age 28. 2,083 applicants, 52% accepted, 432 enrolled. In 2013, 476 master's, 10 doctorates awarded. *Degree requirements:* For master's, thesis (for some programs); for doctorate, comprehensive exam, thesis/dissertation. *Entrance requirements:* For master's, GMAT (for MS in accounting); GRE or GMAT (for MBA and all other MS concentrations), essays, letters of recommendation; for doctorate, GMAT or GRE, essays, writing sample, letters of recommendation. Additional exam requirements/recommendations for international students: Required—IELTS or PTE; Recommended—TOEFL (minimum score 95 iBT). *Application deadline:* For fall admission, 5/2 priority date for domestic students, 2/1 priority date for international students. Applications are processed on a rolling basis. Application fee: $100. Electronic applications accepted. *Expenses:* Contact institution. *Financial support:* In 2013–14, 115 students received support, including 40 fellowships (averaging $5,250 per year), 33 research assistantships with full and partial tuition reimbursements available (averaging $18,000 per year), 42 teaching assistantships with partial tuition reimbursements available (averaging $10,255 per year); career-related internships or fieldwork, Federal Work-Study, institutionally sponsored loans, scholarships/grants, health care benefits, and unspecified assistantships also available. Financial award application deadline: 2/15; financial award applicants required to submit FAFSA. *Faculty research:* Earnings management and electronic information assurance, supply chain and operations management, corporate financing and asset pricing, consumer behavior and quantitative modeling of marketing behavior, leadership and politics in organizations. *Total annual research expenditures:* $155,000. *Unit head:* Erin K. O'Brien, Assistant Dean and Director of Graduate Programs, 716-645-3204, Fax: 716-645-2341, E-mail: ekobrien@buffalo.edu. *Application contact:* Meghan Felser, Associate Director of Admissions and Recruiting, 716-645-3204, Fax: 716-645-2341, E-mail: mpwood@buffalo.edu.
Website: http://mgt.buffalo.edu/.

The University of Akron, Graduate School, College of Business Administration, Department of Management, Program in Information Systems Management, Akron, OH 44325. Offers MSM. *Students:* 16 full-time (6 women), 10 part-time (1 woman); includes 3 minority (2 Asian, non-Hispanic/Latino; 1 Hispanic/Latino), 15 international. Average age 29. 25 applicants, 76% accepted, 8 enrolled. In 2013, 9 master's awarded. *Entrance requirements:* For master's, GMAT, undergraduate degree in information systems, minimum GPA of 3.0, two letters of recommendation, statement of purpose, resume. Additional exam requirements/recommendations for international students: Required—TOEFL (minimum score 550 paper-based; 79 iBT). *Application deadline:* For fall admission, 7/15 for domestic students, 7/1 for international students; for spring admission, 11/15 for domestic and international students. Application fee: $30 ($40 for international students). Electronic applications accepted. *Expenses:* Tuition, state resident: full-time $7430; part-time $412.80 per credit hour. Tuition, nonresident: full-time $12,722; part-time $706.80 per credit hour. *Required fees:* $53 per credit hour. $12 per semester. Tuition and fees vary according to course load and program. *Unit head:* Dr. Steve Ash, Department Chair, 330-972-6429, E-mail: ash@uakron.edu. *Application contact:* Dr. William Hauser, Director of Graduate Business Programs, 330-972-7043, Fax: 330-972-6588, E-mail: whauser@uakron.edu.

The University of Alabama at Birmingham, School of Business, Program in Business Administration, Birmingham, AL 35294-4460. Offers business administration (MBA), including finance, health care management, information technology management, marketing. Part-time and evening/weekend programs available. *Students:* 59 full-time (25 women), 249 part-time (93 women); includes 74 minority (53 Black or African American, non-Hispanic/Latino; 13 Asian, non-Hispanic/Latino; 7 Hispanic/Latino; 1 Two or more races, non-Hispanic/Latino), 16 international. Average age 32. In 2013, 128 master's awarded. *Entrance requirements:* For master's, GMAT. Additional exam requirements/recommendations for international students: Required—TOEFL. *Application deadline:* For fall admission, 7/1 for domestic and international students; for spring admission, 11/1 for domestic and international students; for summer admission, 4/1 for domestic and international students. Application fee: $60 ($75 for international students). *Unit head:* Dr. Ken Miller, Executive Director, MBA Programs, 205-934-8855, E-mail: klmiller@uab.edu. *Application contact:* Christy Manning, Coordinator of Graduate Programs in Business, 205-934-8817, E-mail: cmanning@uab.edu.
Website: http://www.uab.edu/business/degrees-certificates/MBA.

The University of Alabama at Birmingham, School of Business, Program in Management Information Systems, Birmingham, AL 35294. Offers management information systems (MS), including information security, information technology management, Web and mobile development. Part-time programs available. Postbaccalaureate distance learning degree programs offered (no on-campus study). *Students:* 12 part-time (6 women); includes 7 minority (5 Black or African American, non-Hispanic/Latino; 2 Two or more races, non-Hispanic/Latino). Average age 39. *Entrance requirements:* For master's, GMAT. Additional exam requirements/recommendations for international students: Required—TOEFL. *Application deadline:* For fall admission, 7/15 for domestic and international students; for spring admission, 11/15 for domestic students, 12/15 for international students; for summer admission, 4/15 for domestic and international students. Application fee: $45 ($60 for international students). *Unit head:* Dr. Eric Jack, Dean, 205-934-8800, Fax: 205-934-8886, E-mail: ejack@uab.edu. *Application contact:* Wendy England, Online Program Coordinator, 205-934-8813, Fax: 205-975-4429.
Website: http://businessdegrees.uab.edu/mis-degree/.

The University of Alabama in Huntsville, School of Graduate Studies, College of Business Administration, Program in Accounting, Huntsville, AL 35899. Offers accounting (M Acc), including CPA preparatory with an emphasis in taxation, CPA preparatory with emphasis in assurance and financial reporting, general accounting, information systems audit and control (ISAC). *Accreditation:* AACSB. Part-time and evening/weekend programs available. *Faculty:* 9 full-time (3 women). *Students:* 14 full-time (6 women), 27 part-time (16 women); includes 8 minority (6 Black or African American, non-Hispanic/Latino; 2 Asian, non-Hispanic/Latino), 6 international. Average age 30. 24 applicants, 63% accepted, 8 enrolled. In 2013, 29 master's awarded. *Degree*

requirements: For master's, comprehensive exam, thesis or alternative. *Entrance requirements:* For master's, GMAT (minimum score 500), minimum AACSB index of 1080. Additional exam requirements/recommendations for international students: Required—TOEFL (minimum score 550 paper-based; 80 iBT), IELTS (minimum score 6.5). *Application deadline:* For fall admission, 7/15 priority date for domestic students, 4/1 priority date for international students; for spring admission, 11/30 priority date for domestic students, 9/1 priority date for international students. Applications are processed on a rolling basis. Application fee: $50. Electronic applications accepted. *Expenses:* Tuition, state resident: full-time $8912; part-time $540 per credit hour. Tuition, nonresident: full-time $20,774; part-time $1252 per credit hour. *Required fees:* $148 per semester. One-time fee: $150. *Financial support:* Teaching assistantships, career-related internships or fieldwork, Federal Work-Study, institutionally sponsored loans, scholarships/grants, health care benefits, and unspecified assistantships available. Support available to part-time students. Financial award application deadline: 4/1; financial award applicants required to submit FAFSA. *Faculty research:* Accounting information systems, managerial accounting, behavioral accounting, state and local taxation, financial accounting. *Unit head:* Dr. Allen Wilhite, Interim Chair, 256-824-6591, Fax: 256-824-2929, E-mail: allen.wilhite@uah.edu. *Application contact:* Jennifer Pettitt, Director of Graduate Programs, 256-824-6681, Fax: 256-824-7571, E-mail: jennifer.pettitt@uah.edu.

The University of Alabama in Huntsville, School of Graduate Studies, College of Business Administration, Programs in Information Systems, Huntsville, AL 35899. Offers enterprise resource planning (Certificate); information assurance (MS, Certificate); information systems (MSIS); supply chain management (Certificate). Part-time and evening/weekend programs available. *Faculty:* 8 full-time (1 woman). *Students:* 13 full-time (7 women), 21 part-time (10 women); includes 8 minority (5 Black or African American, non-Hispanic/Latino; 3 Asian, non-Hispanic/Latino), 3 international. Average age 34. 35 applicants, 54% accepted, 10 enrolled. In 2013, 8 master's awarded. *Degree requirements:* For master's, comprehensive exam, thesis or alternative. *Entrance requirements:* For master's, GMAT (minimum score 500), minimum AACSB index of 1080. Additional exam requirements/recommendations for international students: Required—TOEFL (minimum score 550 paper-based; 80 iBT), IELTS (minimum score 6.5). *Application deadline:* For fall admission, 7/15 priority date for domestic students, 4/1 priority date for international students; for spring admission, 11/30 priority date for domestic students, 9/1 priority date for international students. Applications are processed on a rolling basis. Application fee: $50. Electronic applications accepted. *Expenses:* Tuition, state resident: full-time $8912; part-time $540 per credit hour. Tuition, nonresident: full-time $20,774; part-time $1252 per credit hour. *Required fees:* $148 per semester. One-time fee: $150. *Financial support:* In 2013–14, 4 students received support, including 1 research assistantship with full tuition reimbursement available (averaging $9,000 per year), 3 teaching assistantships with full and partial tuition reimbursements available (averaging $6,000 per year); career-related internships or fieldwork, Federal Work-Study, institutionally sponsored loans, scholarships/grants, health care benefits, and unspecified assistantships also available. Support available to part-time students. Financial award application deadline: 4/1; financial award applicants required to submit FAFSA. *Faculty research:* Supply chain information systems, information assurance and security, databases and conceptual schema, workflow management, inter-organizational information sharing. *Total annual research expenditures:* $375,942. *Unit head:* Dr. Cynthia Gramm, Chair, 256-824-6913, Fax: 256-824-6328, E-mail: cynthia.gramm@uah.edu. *Application contact:* Jennifer Pettitt, Director of Graduate Programs, 256-824-6681, Fax: 256-824-7571, E-mail: jennifer.pettitt@uah.edu.

The University of Alabama in Huntsville, School of Graduate Studies, Interdisciplinary Studies, Interdisciplinary Program in Information Assurance and Security, Huntsville, AL 35899. Offers computer engineering (MS), including computer science; information systems (Certificate). Part-time and evening/weekend programs available. *Faculty:* 13 full-time (2 women). *Students:* 4 full-time (2 women), 17 part-time (5 women); includes 5 minority (1 Black or African American, non-Hispanic/Latino; 2 Asian, non-Hispanic/Latino; 1 Hispanic/Latino; 1 Two or more races, non-Hispanic/Latino), 1 international. Average age 42. 20 applicants, 70% accepted, 6 enrolled. In 2013, 9 master's, 10 other advanced degrees awarded. *Degree requirements:* For master's, comprehensive exam, thesis. *Entrance requirements:* For master's, GRE General Test, minimum GPA of 3.0; for Certificate, GMAT, minimum GPA of 3.0. Additional exam requirements/recommendations for international students: Required—TOEFL (minimum score 550 paper-based; 80 iBT), IELTS (minimum score 6.5). *Application deadline:* For fall admission, 7/15 priority date for domestic students, 4/1 priority date for international students; for spring admission, 11/30 priority date for domestic students, 9/1 priority date for international students. Applications are processed on a rolling basis. Application fee: $50. Electronic applications accepted. *Expenses:* Tuition, state resident: full-time $8912; part-time $540 per credit hour. Tuition, nonresident: full-time $20,774; part-time $1252 per credit hour. *Required fees:* $148 per semester. One-time fee: $150. *Financial support:* In 2013–14, 1 student received support, including 1 research assistantship with full and partial tuition reimbursement available (averaging $10,000 per year); career-related internships or fieldwork, Federal Work-Study, institutionally sponsored loans, scholarships/grants, health care benefits, and unspecified assistantships also available. Support available to part-time students. Financial award application deadline: 4/1; financial award applicants required to submit FAFSA. *Faculty research:* Service discovery, enterprise security, security metrics, cryptography, network security. *Total annual research expenditures:* $2.5 million. *Unit head:* Dr. David Berkowitz, Dean of Graduate Studies, 256-824-6002, Fax: 256-824-6405, E-mail: deangrad@uah.edu. *Application contact:* Jennifer Pettitt, College of Business Administration Director of Graduate Programs, 256-824-6681, Fax: 256-824-7572, E-mail: jennifer.pettitt@uah.edu.
Website: http://www.uah.edu/graduate/programs/masters-degrees/62-main/graduate-studies/982-grad-infoassurance.

The University of Arizona, Eller College of Management, Department of Management Information Systems, Tucson, AZ 85721. Offers MS. *Faculty:* 13 full-time (5 women). *Students:* 144 full-time (36 women), 70 part-time (18 women); includes 22 minority (3 Black or African American, non-Hispanic/Latino; 1 American Indian or Alaska Native, non-Hispanic/Latino; 7 Asian, non-Hispanic/Latino; 6 Hispanic/Latino; 5 Two or more races, non-Hispanic/Latino), 152 international. Average age 30. 986 applicants, 44% accepted, 114 enrolled. In 2013, 76 master's awarded. *Degree requirements:* For master's, thesis or alternative. *Entrance requirements:* For master's, GMAT or GRE General Test, 2 letters of recommendation, resume. Additional exam requirements/recommendations for international students: Required—TOEFL (minimum score 550 paper-based; 80 iBT). *Application deadline:* For fall admission, 1/15 for domestic and international students. Applications are processed on a rolling basis. Application fee: $75. Electronic applications accepted. *Expenses:* Tuition, state resident: full-time $11,526. Tuition, nonresident: full-time $27,398. *Financial support:* In 2013–14, 10 research assistantships with full tuition reimbursements (averaging $21,024 per year), 17 teaching assistantships with full tuition reimbursements (averaging $21,024 per year) were awarded; career-related internships or fieldwork, Federal Work-Study, scholarships/grants, health care benefits, tuition waivers (partial), and unspecified assistantships also available. Financial award application deadline: 3/15. *Faculty research:* Group decision support systems, domestic and international computing issues, expert systems, data management and structures. *Total annual research expenditures:* $2.7 million. *Unit head:* Dr. Paulo Goes, Department Head, 520-621-2429, Fax: 520-621-2775, E-mail: pgoes@eller.arizona.edu. *Application contact:* Cinda Van Winkle, Program Coordinator, 520-621-2387, E-mail: admissions_mis@eller.arizona.edu.
Website: http://mis.eller.arizona.edu/.

University of Arkansas, Graduate School, Sam M. Walton College of Business Administration, Department of Information Systems, Fayetteville, AR 72701-1201. Offers MIS. Part-time and evening/weekend programs available. *Entrance requirements:* For master's, GMAT.

University of Arkansas at Little Rock, Graduate School, College of Business Administration, Little Rock, AR 72204-1099. Offers accountancy (M Acc, Graduate Certificate); business administration (MBA); construction management (Graduate Certificate); management (Graduate Certificate); management information system (MIS); management information systems (Graduate Certificate); management information systems leadership (Graduate Certificate); taxation (MS, Graduate Certificate). *Accreditation:* AACSB. Part-time and evening/weekend programs available. *Entrance requirements:* For master's, GMAT, minimum undergraduate GPA of 2.7. Additional exam requirements/recommendations for international students: Required—TOEFL (minimum score 525 paper-based). *Expenses:* Tuition, state resident: full-time $5690; part-time $284.50 per credit hour. Tuition, nonresident: full-time $13,030; part-time $651.50 per credit hour. *Required fees:* $1121; $672 per term. One-time fee: $40 full-time.

University of Baltimore, Graduate School, Merrick School of Business, Department of Accounting and Management Information Systems, Baltimore, MD 21201-5779. Offers accounting and business advisory services (MS); accounting fundamentals (Graduate Certificate); forensic accounting (Graduate Certificate). Part-time and evening/weekend programs available. *Entrance requirements:* For master's, GMAT. Additional exam requirements/recommendations for international students: Required—TOEFL (minimum score 550 paper-based). Electronic applications accepted. *Faculty research:* Health care, accounting and administration, managerial accounting, financial accounting theory, accounting information.

University of Bridgeport, School of Business, Bridgeport, CT 06604. Offers accounting (MBA); finance (MBA); general business (MBA); global financial services (MBA); human resource management (MBA); information systems and knowledge management (MBA); international business (MBA); management (MBA); marketing (MBA); operations management (MBA); small business and entrepreneurship (MBA); specialized business (MBA). *Accreditation:* ACBSP. Part-time and evening/weekend programs available. *Faculty:* 11 full-time (2 women), 39 part-time/adjunct (8 women). *Students:* 162 full-time (90 women), 69 part-time (45 women); includes 44 minority (20 Black or African American, non-Hispanic/Latino; 7 Asian, non-Hispanic/Latino; 15 Hispanic/Latino; 2 Two or more races, non-Hispanic/Latino), 163 international. Average age 28. 492 applicants, 48% accepted, 55 enrolled. In 2013, 144 master's awarded. *Degree requirements:* For master's, thesis optional. *Entrance requirements:* For master's, GMAT. Additional exam requirements/recommendations for international students: Recommended—TOEFL (minimum score 550 paper-based; 80 iBT), IELTS (minimum score 6.5). *Application deadline:* For fall admission, 8/1 priority date for domestic and international students; for spring admission, 12/1 priority date for domestic and international students. Applications are processed on a rolling basis. Application fee: $50. Electronic applications accepted. *Expenses:* Contact institution. *Financial support:* In 2013–14, 69 students received support. Fellowships, research assistantships, teaching assistantships, career-related internships or fieldwork, Federal Work-Study, institutionally sponsored loans, and tuition waivers (partial) available. Support available to part-time students. Financial award application deadline: 6/1; financial award applicants required to submit FAFSA. *Unit head:* Dr. Lloyd G. Gibson, Dean, 203-576-4384, Fax: 203-576-4388, E-mail: llgibson@bridgeport.edu. *Application contact:* Leanne Proctor, Director of Graduate Admissions, 203-576-4552, Fax: 203-576-4941, E-mail: mba@bridgeport.edu.
Website: http://www.bridgeport.edu.

The University of British Columbia, Sauder School of Business, Doctoral Program in Commerce and Business Administration, Vancouver, BC V6T 1Z1, Canada. Offers accounting (PhD); finance (PhD); management information systems (PhD); management science (PhD); marketing (PhD); organizational behavior (PhD); strategy and business economics (PhD); transportation and logistics (PhD); urban land economics (PhD). *Faculty:* 91 full-time (22 women). *Students:* 66 full-time (24 women). Average age 30. 418 applicants, 2% accepted, 8 enrolled. In 2013, 7 doctorates awarded. *Degree requirements:* For doctorate, comprehensive exam, thesis/dissertation. *Entrance requirements:* For doctorate, GMAT or GRE. Additional exam requirements/recommendations for international students: Required—TOEFL (minimum score 600 paper-based; 100 iBT). *Application deadline:* For fall admission, 1/31 for domestic students, 12/31 for international students. Applications are processed on a rolling basis. Application fee: $95 Canadian dollars ($153 Canadian dollars for international students). Electronic applications accepted. *Expenses: Tuition, area resident:* Full-time $8000 Canadian dollars. *Financial support:* In 2013–14, fellowships with full tuition reimbursements (averaging $17,500 per year), research assistantships with full tuition reimbursements (averaging $8,500 per year), teaching assistantships with full tuition reimbursements (averaging $17,500 per year) were awarded. Financial award application deadline: 12/31. *Unit head:* Dr. Ralph Winter, Director, 604-822-8366, Fax: 604-822-8755. *Application contact:* Elaine Cho, Administrator, PhD and M Sc Programs, 604-822-8366, Fax: 604-822-8755, E-mail: phd.program@sauder.ubc.ca.
Website: http://www.sauder.ubc.ca/.

University of California, Berkeley, UC Berkeley Extension, Certificate Programs in Computer Technology and Information Management, Berkeley, CA 94720-1500. Offers information systems and management (Postbaccalaureate Certificate); UNIX/LINUX system administration (Certificate). Postbaccalaureate distance learning degree programs offered.

University of California, Los Angeles, Graduate Division, UCLA Anderson School of Management, Los Angeles, CA 90095-1481. Offers accounting (PhD); Americas (EMBA); Asia Pacific (EMBA); business administration (EMBA, MBA); decisions, operations and technology management (PhD); finance (PhD); financial engineering (MFE); global economics and management (PhD); management and organizations (PhD); marketing (PhD); strategy and policy (PhD); DDS/MBA; MBA/JD; MBA/MD; MBA/MLAS; MBA/MLIS; MBA/MPH; MBA/MPP; MBA/MSCS; MBA/MSN; MBA/MUP. *Accreditation:* AACSB. Part-time programs available. *Faculty:* 104 full-time (20 women), 28 part-time/adjunct (4 women). *Students:* 1,069 full-time (324 women), 879 part-time (251 women); includes 664 minority (37 Black or African American, non-Hispanic/Latino; 1 American Indian or Alaska Native, non-Hispanic/Latino; 470 Asian, non-Hispanic/Latino; 34 Hispanic/Latino; 2 Native Hawaiian or other Pacific Islander, non-Hispanic/Latino; 120 Two or more races, non-Hispanic/Latino), 444 international. Average age 30. 5,084 applicants, 27% accepted, 845 enrolled. In 2013, 801 master's, 14 doctorates awarded. *Degree requirements:* For master's, comprehensive exam, field study consulting project (for MBA); thesis (for MFE); for doctorate, comprehensive exam, thesis/dissertation, oral and written qualifying exams. *Entrance requirements:* For

master's, GMAT (for MBA); GMAT or GRE General Test (for MFE), 4-year bachelor's degree or equivalent; recommendation letters (1 for MBA, 2 for MFE); two essays; interview (by invitation only for MBA); for doctorate, GMAT or GRE General Test, bachelor's degree from college or university of fully-recognized standing; minimum B average in undergraduate coursework or B+ average in prior graduate work; statement of purpose; three recommendation letters. Additional exam requirements/recommendations for international students: Required—TOEFL (minimum score 560 paper-based; 87 iBT). *Application deadline:* For fall admission, 10/22 priority date for domestic and international students; for winter admission, 1/7 for domestic and international students; for spring admission, 4/15 for domestic and international students. Applications are processed on a rolling basis. Application fee: $200. Electronic applications accepted. *Expenses:* Contact institution. *Financial support:* In 2013–14, 522 students received support. Fellowships, research assistantships with partial tuition reimbursements available, teaching assistantships with partial tuition reimbursements available, career-related internships or fieldwork, institutionally sponsored loans, scholarships/grants, health care benefits, and tuition waivers (partial) available. Financial award application deadline: 4/15; financial award applicants required to submit FAFSA. *Faculty research:* Asset pricing, decision-making, behavioral finance, international finance and economics, global macroeconomics. *Total annual research expenditures:* $368,086. *Unit head:* Dr. Judy D. Olian, Dean/Chair in Management, 310-825-7982, Fax: 310-206-2073, E-mail: judy.olian@anderson.ucla.edu. *Application contact:* Alex Lawrence, Assistant Dean, MBA Admissions and Financial Aid, 310-825-6944, Fax: 310-825-8582, E-mail: mba.admissions@anderson.ucla.edu.
Website: http://www.anderson.ucla.edu/.

See Display on page 145 and Close-Up on page 191.

University of California, Santa Cruz, Division of Graduate Studies, Jack Baskin School of Engineering, Department of Technology and Information Management, Santa Cruz, CA 95064. Offers MS, PhD. Terminal master's awarded for partial completion of doctoral program. *Degree requirements:* For master's, thesis, 2 seminars; for doctorate, thesis/dissertation, 2 seminars. *Entrance requirements:* For master's and doctorate, GRE General Test; GRE Subject Test preferably in computer science, engineering, physics, or mathematics (highly recommended), minimum GPA of 3.5. Additional exam requirements/recommendations for international students: Required—TOEFL (minimum score 570 paper-based; 89 iBT); Recommended—IELTS (minimum score 8). Electronic applications accepted. *Faculty research:* Integration of information systems, technology, and business management.

University of Central Missouri, The Graduate School, Warrensburg, MO 6409. Offers accountancy (MA); accounting (MBA); applied mathematics (MS); aviation safety (MA); biology (MS); business administration (MBA); career and technical education leadership (MS); college student personnel administration (MS); communication (MA); computer science (MS); counseling (MS); criminal justice (MS); educational leadership (Ed D); educational technology (MS); elementary and early childhood education (MSE); English (MA); environmental studies (MA); finance (MBA); history (MA); human services/educational technology (Ed S); human services/learning resources (Ed S); human services/professional counseling (Ed S); industrial hygiene (MS); industrial management (MS); information systems (MBA); information technology (MS); kinesiology (MS); library science and information services (MS); literacy education (MSE); marketing (MBA); mathematics (MS); music (MA); occupational safety management (MS); psychology (MS); rural family nursing (MS); school administration (MSE); social gerontology (MS); sociology (MA); special education (MSE); speech language pathology (MS); superintendency (Ed S); teaching (MAT); teaching English as a second language (MA); technology (MS); technology management (PhD); theatre (MA). Part-time programs available. *Faculty:* 233. *Students:* 890 full-time (396 women), 1,486 part-time (1,001 women); includes 192 minority (97 Black or African American, non-Hispanic/Latino; 9 American Indian or Alaska Native, non-Hispanic/Latino; 32 Asian, non-Hispanic/Latino; 40 Hispanic/Latino; 3 Native Hawaiian or other Pacific Islander, non-Hispanic/Latino; 11 Two or more races, non-Hispanic/Latino), 539 international. Average age 31. 1,953 applicants, 75% accepted. In 2013, 719 master's, 58 other advanced degrees awarded. *Degree requirements:* For master's and Ed S, comprehensive exam (for some programs), thesis (for some programs). *Entrance requirements:* Additional exam requirements/recommendations for international students: Required—TOEFL (minimum score 550 paper-based; 79 iBT). *Application deadline:* For fall admission, 6/1 for domestic students; for spring admission, 10/1 for domestic and international students. Applications are processed on a rolling basis. Application fee: $30 ($75 for international students). Electronic applications accepted. *Expenses:* Tuition, state resident: full-time $7326; part-time $276.25 per credit hour. Tuition, nonresident: full-time $13,956; part-time $552.50 per credit hour. *Required fees:* $29 per credit hour. *Financial support:* In 2013–14, 118 students received support, including 271 research assistantships with full and partial tuition reimbursements available (averaging $7,500 per year), 109 teaching assistantships with full and partial tuition reimbursements available (averaging $7,500 per year); career-related internships or fieldwork, Federal Work-Study, scholarships/grants, and administrative and laboratory assistantships also available. Support available to part-time students. Financial award application deadline: 3/1; financial award applicants required to submit FAFSA. *Unit head:* Dr. Joseph Vaughn, Assistant Provost for Research/Dean, 660-543-4092, Fax: 660-543-4778, E-mail: vaughn@ucmo.edu. *Application contact:* Brittany Lawrence, Graduate Student Services Coordinator, 660-543-4621, Fax: 660-543-4778, E-mail: gradinfo@ucmo.edu.
Website: http://www.ucmo.edu/graduate/.

University of Cincinnati, Graduate School, Carl H. Lindner College of Business, MS Program, Cincinnati, OH 45221. Offers accounting (MS); business analytics (MS); finance (MS); information systems (MS); marketing (MS); taxation (MS). Part-time and evening/weekend programs available. *Faculty:* 39 full-time (11 women), 11 part-time/adjunct (3 women). *Students:* 275 full-time (105 women), 165 part-time (69 women); includes 29 minority (14 Black or African American, non-Hispanic/Latino; 9 Asian, non-Hispanic/Latino; 1 Native Hawaiian or other Pacific Islander, non-Hispanic/Latino; 5 Two or more races, non-Hispanic/Latino), 273 international. 953 applicants, 37% accepted, 258 enrolled. In 2013, 144 master's awarded. *Degree requirements:* For master's, thesis (for some programs). *Entrance requirements:* For master's, GMAT, GRE, resume, transcripts, essays, letters of recommendation. Additional exam requirements/recommendations for international students: Required—TOEFL (minimum score 600 paper-based; 100 iBT), IELTS (minimum score 6.5). *Application deadline:* For fall admission, 3/15 priority date for domestic students, 4/1 for international students. Applications are processed on a rolling basis. Application fee: $65 ($70 for international students). Electronic applications accepted. *Expenses:* Contact institution. *Financial support:* In 2013–14, 124 students received support, including 12 teaching assistantships with full and partial tuition reimbursements available (averaging $3,500 per year); scholarships/grants, tuition waivers (full and partial), and unspecified assistantships also available. Financial award application deadline: 2/1; financial award applicants required to submit FAFSA. *Faculty research:* Real estate, empirical pricing, organization information pricing, strategic management, portfolio choice in institutional investment. *Unit head:* Dr. David Szymanski, Dean, 513-556-7001, Fax: 513-556-4891, E-mail: david.szymanski@uc.edu. *Application contact:* Dona Clary, Director, Graduate Programs, 513-556-3546, Fax: 513-558-7006, E-mail: dona.clary@uc.edu.

University of Cincinnati, Graduate School, Carl H. Lindner College of Business, PhD Programs, Cincinnati, OH 45221. Offers accounting (PhD); economics (PhD); finance (PhD); information systems (PhD); management (PhD); marketing (PhD); operations and business analytics (PhD). *Faculty:* 62 full-time (13 women). *Students:* 27 full-time (15 women), 9 part-time (1 woman); includes 2 minority (1 Asian, non-Hispanic/Latino; 1 Hispanic/Latino), 16 international. Average age 29. 86 applicants, 13% accepted, 6 enrolled. In 2013, 8 doctorates awarded. *Degree requirements:* For doctorate, comprehensive exam, thesis/dissertation. *Entrance requirements:* For doctorate, GMAT, GRE, transcripts, essays, resume, letters of recommendation. Additional exam requirements/recommendations for international students: Required—TOEFL (minimum score 600 paper-based; 100 iBT), IELTS (minimum score 6.5). *Application deadline:* For fall admission, 1/15 for domestic and international students. Application fee: $65 ($70 for international students). Electronic applications accepted. *Expenses:* Contact institution. *Financial support:* In 2013–14, 33 students received support, including 25 research assistantships with full and partial tuition reimbursements available (averaging $23,250 per year); scholarships/grants, tuition waivers (full and partial), and unspecified assistantships also available. Financial award application deadline: 1/15; financial award applicants required to submit FAFSA. *Unit head:* Dr. Suzanne Masterson, Director, 513-556-7125, Fax: 513-556-5499, E-mail: suzanne.masterson@uc.edu. *Application contact:* Angel Elvin, Assistant Director, 513-556-7190, Fax: 513-558-7006, E-mail: angel.elvin@uc.edu.
Website: http://www.business.uc.edu/phd.

University of Colorado Boulder, Leeds School of Business, Division of Business Administration, Boulder, CO 80309. Offers accounting (MS, PhD); finance (PhD); information systems (PhD); marketing (PhD); operations (PhD); strategic, organizational, and entrepreneurial studies (PhD). *Students:* 143 full-time (72 women), 2 part-time (1 woman); includes 15 minority (1 Black or African American, non-Hispanic/Latino; 2 American Indian or Alaska Native, non-Hispanic/Latino; 5 Asian, non-Hispanic/Latino; 6 Hispanic/Latino; 1 Two or more races, non-Hispanic/Latino), 37 international. Average age 25. 281 applicants, 12% accepted, 19 enrolled. In 2013, 50 master's, 8 doctorates awarded. *Entrance requirements:* For master's, GMAT, minimum undergraduate GPA of 3.0. *Application deadline:* For fall admission, 3/31 for domestic students, 3/1 for international students; for spring admission, 10/31 for domestic and international students. Application fee: $50 ($60 for international students). Electronic applications accepted. *Financial support:* In 2013–14, 145 students received support, including 37 fellowships (averaging $3,977 per year), 27 research assistantships with full and partial tuition reimbursements available (averaging $40,893 per year), 12 teaching assistantships with full and partial tuition reimbursements available (averaging $38,197 per year); institutionally sponsored loans, scholarships/grants, health care benefits, and unspecified assistantships also available. Financial award applicants required to submit FAFSA.

University of Colorado Denver, Business School, Program in Computer Science and Information Systems, Denver, CO 80217. Offers PhD. *Students:* 13 full-time (3 women), 7 part-time (2 women); includes 2 minority (1 Black or African American, non-Hispanic/Latino; 1 Asian, non-Hispanic/Latino), 8 international. Average age 38. 20 applicants, 20% accepted, 4 enrolled. In 2013, 4 doctorates awarded. *Degree requirements:* For doctorate, comprehensive exam, thesis/dissertation. *Entrance requirements:* For doctorate, GMAT or GRE General Test, letters of recommendation, portfolio essay describing applicant's motivation and initial plan for doctoral study; resume. Additional exam requirements/recommendations for international students: Required—TOEFL (minimum score 525 paper-based; 71 iBT); Recommended—IELTS (minimum score 6.5). *Application deadline:* For fall admission, 3/1 priority date for domestic and international students; for spring admission, 10/15 for domestic students, 10/1 for international students. Applications are processed on a rolling basis. Application fee: $50 ($75 for international students). Electronic applications accepted. *Expenses:* Contact institution. *Financial support:* In 2013–14, 14 students received support. Fellowships, research assistantships, teaching assistantships, Federal Work-Study, institutionally sponsored loans, scholarships/grants, and traineeships available. Financial award application deadline: 4/1; financial award applicants required to submit FAFSA. *Faculty research:* Design science of information systems, information system economics, organizational impacts of information technology, high performance parallel and distributed systems, performance measurement and prediction. *Unit head:* Dr. Michael Mannino, Associate Professor/Co-Director, 303-315-8427, E-mail: michael.mannino@ucdenver.edu. *Application contact:* Shelly Townley, Director of Graduate Admissions, Business School, 303-315-8202, Fax: 303-556-5904, E-mail: shelly.townley@ucdenver.edu.
Website: http://www.ucdenver.edu/academics/colleges/business/degrees/phd/Pages/default.aspx.

University of Colorado Denver, Business School, Program in Information Systems, Denver, CO 80217. Offers accounting and information systems audit and control (MS); business intelligence systems (MS); ehealth and healthcare service entrepreneurship (MS); enterprise risk management (MS); enterprise technology management (MS); geographic information systems (MS); health information technology (MS); technology innovation and entrepreneurship (MS); Web and mobile computing (MS). Part-time and evening/weekend programs available. Postbaccalaureate distance learning degree programs offered (no on-campus study). *Students:* 55 full-time (14 women), 23 part-time (8 women); includes 10 minority (2 Black or African American, non-Hispanic/Latino; 7 Asian, non-Hispanic/Latino; 1 Hispanic/Latino), 15 international. Average age 33. 54 applicants, 78% accepted, 14 enrolled. In 2013, 27 master's awarded. *Degree requirements:* For master's, 30 credit hours. *Entrance requirements:* For master's, GMAT, resume, essay, two letters of recommendation, financial statements (for international applicants). Additional exam requirements/recommendations for international students: Required—TOEFL (minimum score 537 paper-based; 75 iBT); Recommended—IELTS (minimum score 6.5). *Application deadline:* For fall admission, 4/15 for domestic students, 3/15 for international students; for spring admission, 10/15 for domestic students, 9/15 for international students. Applications are processed on a rolling basis. Application fee: $50 ($75 for international students). Electronic applications accepted. *Expenses:* Contact institution. *Financial support:* In 2013–14, 18 students received support. Fellowships, research assistantships, teaching assistantships, Federal Work-Study, institutionally sponsored loans, scholarships/grants, and traineeships available. Financial award application deadline: 4/1; financial award applicants required to submit FAFSA. *Faculty research:* Human-computer interaction, expert systems, database management, electronic commerce, object-oriented software development. *Unit head:* Dr. Jahangir Karimi, Director of Information Systems Programs, 303-315-8430, E-mail: jahangir.karimi@ucdenver.edu. *Application contact:* Shelly Townley, Admissions Director, Graduate Programs, 303-315-8202, E-mail: shelly.townley@ucdenver.edu.
Website: http://www.ucdenver.edu/academics/colleges/business/degrees/ms/IS/Pages/Information-Systems.aspx.

University of Dallas, Graduate School of Management, Irving, TX 75062-4736. Offers accounting (MBA, MM, MS); business management (MBA, MM); corporate finance (MBA, MM); financial services (MBA); global business (MBA, MM); health services management (MBA, MM); human resource management (MBA, MM); information assurance (MBA, MM, MS); information technology (MBA, MM, MS); information

technology service management (MBA, MM, MS); marketing management (MBA, MM); organization development (MBA, MM); project management (MBA, MM); sports and entertainment management (MBA, MM); strategic leadership (MBA, MM); supply chain management (MBA); supply chain management and market logistics (MM). *Accreditation:* ACBSP. Part-time and evening/weekend programs available. Postbaccalaureate distance learning degree programs offered (no on-campus study). *Entrance requirements:* Additional exam requirements/recommendations for international students: Required—TOEFL. Electronic applications accepted. *Expenses:* Contact institution.

University of Delaware, Alfred Lerner College of Business and Economics, Department of Accounting and Management Information Systems and Department of Electrical and Computer Engineering, Program in Information Systems and Technology Management, Newark, DE 19716. Offers MS. Part-time and evening/weekend programs available. *Entrance requirements:* For master's, GRE or GMAT, 2 letters of recommendation, resume, minimum GPA of 2.75. Additional exam requirements/recommendations for international students: Required—TOEFL (minimum score 600 paper-based). *Faculty research:* Security, developer trust, XML.

University of Denver, University College, Denver, CO 80208. Offers arts and culture (MLS, Certificate), including art, literature, and culture, arts development and program management (Certificate), creative writing; environmental policy and management (MAS, Certificate), including energy and sustainability (Certificate), environmental assessment of nuclear power (Certificate), environmental health and safety (Certificate), environmental management, natural resource management (Certificate); geographic information systems (MAS, Certificate); global affairs (MLS, Certificate), including translation studies, world history and culture; healthcare leadership (MPH, Certificate), including healthcare policy, law, and ethics, medical and healthcare information technologies, strategic management of healthcare; information and communications technology (MCIS, Certificate), including database design and administration (Certificate), geographic information systems (MCIS), information security systems security (Certificate), information systems security (MCIS), project management (MCIS, MPS, Certificate), software design and administration (Certificate), software design and programming (MCIS), technology management, telecommunications technology (MCIS), Web design and development; leadership and organizations (MPS, Certificate), including human capital in organizations, philanthropic leadership, project management (MCIS, MPS, Certificate), strategic innovation and change; organizational and professional communication (MPS, Certificate), including alternative dispute resolution, organizational communication, organizational development and training, public relations and marketing; security management (MAS, Certificate), including emergency planning and response, information security (MAS), organizational security; strategic human resource management (MPS, Certificate), including global human resources (MPS), human resource management and development (MPS). Part-time and evening/weekend programs available. Postbaccalaureate distance learning degree programs offered (no on-campus study). *Faculty:* 139 part-time/adjunct (61 women). *Students:* 49 full-time (16 women), 1,297 part-time (732 women); includes 272 minority (92 Black or African American, non-Hispanic/Latino; 5 American Indian or Alaska Native, non-Hispanic/Latino; 30 Asian, non-Hispanic/Latino; 114 Hispanic/Latino; 3 Native Hawaiian or other Pacific Islander, non-Hispanic/Latino; 28 Two or more races, non-Hispanic/Latino), 92 international. Average age 35. 542 applicants, 95% accepted, 362 enrolled. In 2013, 374 master's, 128 other advanced degrees awarded. *Degree requirements:* For master's, capstone project. *Entrance requirements:* For master's, transcripts, two letters of recommendation, personal statement, resume. Additional exam requirements/recommendations for international students: Required—TOEFL (minimum score 550 paper-based; 80 iBT). *Application deadline:* For fall admission, 7/18 priority date for domestic students, 5/2 priority date for international students; for winter admission, 10/24 priority date for domestic students, 9/19 priority date for international students; for spring admission, 2/1 for domestic students, 12/14 for international students; for summer admission, 4/18 priority date for domestic students, 3/7 priority date for international students. Applications are processed on a rolling basis. Application fee: $75. Electronic applications accepted. *Expenses:* Contact institution. *Financial support:* In 2013–14, 28 students received support. Applicants required to submit FAFSA. *Unit head:* Dr. Michael McGuire, Interim Dean, 303-871-3518, E-mail: mmcguire@du.edu. *Application contact:* Information Contact, 303-871-2291, E-mail: ucoladm@du.edu.
Website: http://www.universitycollege.du.edu/.

University of Detroit Mercy, College of Business Administration, Program in Computer Information Systems, Detroit, MI 48221. Offers MSCIS. Part-time and evening/weekend programs available. *Degree requirements:* For master's, thesis or alternative. *Entrance requirements:* For master's, minimum GPA of 3.75.

University of Florida, Graduate School, Warrington College of Business Administration, Hough Graduate School of Business, Department of Information Systems and Operations Management, Gainesville, FL 32611. Offers information systems and operations management (MS, PhD); supply chain management (Certificate). *Faculty:* 13 full-time (3 women), 6 part-time/adjunct (1 woman). *Students:* 294 full-time (127 women), 9 part-time (all women); includes 31 minority (10 Black or African American, non-Hispanic/Latino; 17 Asian, non-Hispanic/Latino; 4 Hispanic/Latino), 254 international. Average age 25. 705 applicants, 65% accepted, 138 enrolled. In 2013, 118 master's, 2 doctorates awarded. Terminal master's awarded for partial completion of doctoral program. *Degree requirements:* For doctorate, thesis/dissertation. *Entrance requirements:* For master's, GMAT or GRE General Test, minimum GPA of 3.0; for doctorate, GMAT (minimum score 650) or GRE General Test, minimum GPA of 3.0. Additional exam requirements/recommendations for international students: Required—TOEFL (minimum score 550 paper-based; 80 iBT), IELTS (minimum score 6). *Application deadline:* For fall admission, 4/1 priority date for domestic students, 3/1 for international students; for spring admission, 10/15 for domestic students, 10/1 for international students. Applications are processed on a rolling basis. Application fee: $30. *Expenses:* Tuition, state resident: full-time $12,640. Tuition, nonresident: full-time $30,000. *Financial support:* In 2013–14, 13 students received support, including 3 fellowships (averaging $3,257 per year), 10 research assistantships (averaging $23,165 per year), 3 teaching assistantships (averaging $21,505 per year); unspecified assistantships also available. Financial award application deadline: 2/1; financial award applicants required to submit FAFSA. *Faculty research:* Expert systems, nonconvex optimization, manufacturing management, production and operation management, telecommunication. *Unit head:* Hsing Cheng, PharmD, Chair, 352-392-7068, Fax: 352-392-5438, E-mail: hkcheng@ufl.edu. *Application contact:* Praveen A. Pathak, PhD, Graduate Coordinator, 352-392-9599, Fax: 352-392-5438, E-mail: praveen@ufl.edu.
Website: http://www.cba.ufl.edu/isom/.

University of Florida, Graduate School, Warrington College of Business Administration, Hough Graduate School of Business, Programs in Business Administration, Gainesville, FL 32611. Offers business administration (MBA); competitive strategy (MBA); entrepreneurship (MBA); finance (MBA); global management (MBA); Graham-Buffett security analysis (MBA); human resource management (MBA); information systems and operations management (MBA); international studies (MBA); Latin American business (MBA); management (MBA); marketing (MBA); real estate (MBA); sports administration (MBA); JD/MBA; MBA/MS; MBA/PhD; MBA/Pharm D; MD/MBA. *Accreditation:* AACSB. Part-time and evening/weekend programs available. Postbaccalaureate distance learning degree programs offered. *Faculty:* 72 full-time (10 women), 29 part-time/adjunct (7 women). *Students:* 440 full-time (122 women), 472 part-time (159 women); includes 203 minority (43 Black or African American, non-Hispanic/Latino; 3 American Indian or Alaska Native, non-Hispanic/Latino; 64 Asian, non-Hispanic/Latino; 92 Hispanic/Latino; 1 Native Hawaiian or other Pacific Islander, non-Hispanic/Latino), 39 international. Average age 32. 568 applicants, 58% accepted, 261 enrolled. In 2013, 405 master's awarded. *Degree requirements:* For master's, capstone course. *Entrance requirements:* For master's, GMAT (minimum score 465), minimum GPA of 3.0, interview. Additional exam requirements/recommendations for international students: Required—TOEFL (minimum score 550 paper-based; 80 iBT), IELTS (minimum score 6). *Application deadline:* For fall admission, 7/1 for domestic students, 1/1 for international students; for spring admission, 12/1 for domestic and international students. Applications are processed on a rolling basis. Application fee: $30. Electronic applications accepted. *Expenses:* Tuition, state resident: full-time $12,640. Tuition, nonresident: full-time $30,000. *Financial support:* In 2013–14, 24 students received support, including 24 teaching assistantships (averaging $6,143 per year); career-related internships or fieldwork, scholarships/grants, and unspecified assistantships also available. Support available to part-time students. Financial award applicants required to submit FAFSA. *Faculty research:* Accounting, finance, insurance, management, real estate, urban analysis marketing. *Unit head:* Alexander D. Sevilla, Assistant Dean/Director of MBA Program, 352-273-3252, Fax: 352-392-8791, E-mail: alex.sevilla@warrington.ufl.edu. *Application contact:* Andrew S. Lord, Senior Director of Admissions, 352-273-3241, Fax: 352-392-8791, E-mail: andrew.lord@warrington.ufl.edu.
Website: http://www.floridamba.ufl.edu/.

University of Georgia, Terry College of Business, Department of Management Information Systems, Athens, GA 30602. Offers PhD.

University of Hawaii at Manoa, Graduate Division, College of Social Sciences, School of Communications, Program in Telecommunication and Information Resource Management, Honolulu, HI 96822. Offers Graduate Certificate. Part-time programs available. *Entrance requirements:* Additional exam requirements/recommendations for international students: Required—TOEFL (minimum score 500 paper-based; 61 iBT), IELTS (minimum score 5).

University of Hawaii at Manoa, Graduate Division, Shidler College of Business, Program in Accounting, Honolulu, HI 96822. Offers accounting (M Acc); accounting law (M Acc); information systems (M Acc); taxation (M Acc). Part-time programs available. *Entrance requirements:* For master's, GMAT, bachelor's degree in accounting, minimum GPA of 3.0. Additional exam requirements/recommendations for international students: Required—TOEFL (minimum score 550 paper-based; 79 iBT), IELTS (minimum score 5). *Faculty research:* International accounting, current tax topics, insurance industry financial reporting, behavioral accounting, auditing.

University of Hawaii at Manoa, Graduate Division, Shidler College of Business, Program in Business Administration, Honolulu, HI 96822. Offers Asian business studies (MBA); Chinese business studies (MBA); decision sciences (MBA); entrepreneurship (MBA); finance (MBA); finance and banking (MBA); human resources management (MBA); information management (MBA); information technology (MBA); international business (MBA); Japanese business studies (MBA); marketing (MBA); organizational behavior (MBA); organizational management (MBA); real estate (MBA); student-designed track (MBA). *Accreditation:* AACSB. Part-time and evening/weekend programs available. *Degree requirements:* For master's, thesis optional. *Entrance requirements:* For master's, GMAT, minimum GPA of 3.0. Additional exam requirements/recommendations for international students: Required—TOEFL (minimum score 600 paper-based; 100 iBT), IELTS (minimum score 7). *Expenses:* Contact institution.

University of Hawaii at Manoa, Graduate Division, Shidler College of Business, Program in International Management, Honolulu, HI 96822. Offers Asian finance (PhD); global information technology management (PhD); international accounting (PhD); international marketing (PhD); international organization and strategy (PhD). Part-time programs available. *Degree requirements:* For doctorate, comprehensive exam, thesis/dissertation. *Entrance requirements:* For doctorate, GMAT or GRE General Test, minimum GPA of 3.0. Additional exam requirements/recommendations for international students: Required—TOEFL (minimum score 600 paper-based; 100 iBT), IELTS (minimum score 7). *Expenses:* Contact institution.

University of Houston–Clear Lake, School of Business, Program in Management Information Systems, Houston, TX 77058-1002. Offers MS. Part-time programs available. *Entrance requirements:* For master's, GMAT. Additional exam requirements/recommendations for international students: Required—TOEFL (minimum score 550 paper-based).

University of Houston–Victoria, School of Arts and Sciences, Department of Computer Science, Victoria, TX 77901-4450. Offers computer information systems (MS); computer science (MS). Part-time and evening/weekend programs available. Postbaccalaureate distance learning degree programs offered (no on-campus study). *Degree requirements:* For master's, comprehensive exam (for some programs), thesis (for some programs). *Entrance requirements:* For master's, GRE. Additional exam requirements/recommendations for international students: Required—TOEFL (minimum score 550 paper-based). *Application deadline:* Applications are processed on a rolling basis. Application fee: $0. *Expenses:* Tuition, state resident: full-time $4534; part-time $251 per credit hour. Tuition, nonresident: full-time $10,906; part-time $606 per contact hour. *Required fees:* $68 per semester hour. Tuition and fees vary according to course load. *Financial support:* Research assistantships, career-related internships or fieldwork, scholarships/grants, and unspecified assistantships available. Support available to part-time students. Financial award application deadline: 4/15. *Unit head:* Dr. Li Chao, Chair, Science, Technology and Mathematics Division, 281-275-8828, E-mail: chaol@uhv.edu. *Application contact:* Tracey Fox, Director of Services, 361-570-4233, E-mail: foxt@uhv.edu.

University of Illinois at Chicago, Graduate College, Liautaud Graduate School of Business, Department of Information and Decision Sciences, Chicago, IL 60607-7128. Offers management information systems (MS, PhD). Part-time and evening/weekend programs available. *Faculty:* 17 full-time (3 women), 2 part-time/adjunct (1 woman). *Students:* 141 full-time (47 women), 15 part-time (6 women); includes 7 minority (5 Asian, non-Hispanic/Latino; 1 Hispanic/Latino; 1 Two or more races, non-Hispanic/Latino), 134 international. Average age 26. 989 applicants, 35% accepted, 77 enrolled. In 2013, 71 master's awarded. *Degree requirements:* For doctorate, thesis/dissertation. *Entrance requirements:* For doctorate, GMAT, minimum GPA of 2.75. Additional exam requirements/recommendations for international students: Required—TOEFL. *Application deadline:* For fall admission, 2/15 for domestic and international students; for spring admission, 11/1 for domestic students, 7/15 for international students. Applications are processed on a rolling basis. Application fee: $40 ($50 for international students). Electronic applications accepted. *Expenses:* Tuition, state resident: full-time $11,066; part-time $3689 per term. Tuition, nonresident: full-time $23,064; part-time $7688 per term. *Required fees:* $3004; $1190 per term. Tuition and fees vary according

to course level and program. *Financial support:* In 2013–14, 40 students received support, including 1 fellowship with full tuition reimbursement available; research assistantships with full tuition reimbursements available, teaching assistantships with full tuition reimbursements available, Federal Work-Study, traineeships, tuition waivers (full), and unspecified assistantships also available. Financial award application deadline: 3/1; financial award applicants required to submit FAFSA. *Total annual research expenditures:* $17,000. *Unit head:* Sid Bhattacharyya, Interim Head, 312-996-8794, E-mail: sidb@uic.edu. *Application contact:* Ann Rosi, Application Contact, 312-996-4751.
Website: http://business.uic.edu/academic-departments-and-faculty/academic-departments/department-of-ids.

University of Illinois at Springfield, Graduate Programs, College of Business and Management, Program in Management Information Systems, Springfield, IL 62703-5407. Offers MS. Part-time and evening/weekend programs available. Postbaccalaureate distance learning degree programs offered (no on-campus study). *Faculty:* 5 full-time (0 women), 3 part-time/adjunct (2 women). *Students:* 83 full-time (34 women), 144 part-time (44 women); includes 55 minority (23 Black or African American, non-Hispanic/Latino; 2 American Indian or Alaska Native, non-Hispanic/Latino; 16 Asian, non-Hispanic/Latino; 9 Hispanic/Latino; 2 Native Hawaiian or other Pacific Islander, non-Hispanic/Latino; 3 Two or more races, non-Hispanic/Latino), 72 international. Average age 33. 328 applicants, 50% accepted, 80 enrolled. In 2013, 50 master's awarded. *Degree requirements:* For master's, project, closure seminar. *Entrance requirements:* For master's, GMAT or GRE General Test, competency in a structured, high-level programming language; minimum undergraduate GPA of 3.0. Additional exam requirements/recommendations for international students: Required—TOEFL (minimum score 500 paper-based; 61 iBT). *Application deadline:* Applications are processed on a rolling basis. Application fee: $60 ($75 for international students). Electronic applications accepted. *Expenses:* Tuition, state resident: full-time $7440. Tuition, nonresident: full-time $15,744. *Required fees:* $2985.60. *Financial support:* In 2013–14, fellowships with full tuition reimbursements (averaging $9,900 per year), research assistantships with full tuition reimbursements (averaging $9,000 per year), teaching assistantships with full tuition reimbursements (averaging $9,000 per year) were awarded; career-related internships or fieldwork, Federal Work-Study, scholarships/grants, health care benefits, and unspecified assistantships also available. Support available to part-time students. Financial award application deadline: 11/15; financial award applicants required to submit FAFSA. *Unit head:* Dr. Rassule Hadidi, Program Administrator, 217-206-6067, Fax: 217-206-7541, E-mail: rhadi1@uis.edu. *Application contact:* Dr. Lynn Pardie, Office of Graduate Studies, 800-252-8533, Fax: 217-206-7623, E-mail: lpard1@uis.edu.

The University of Kansas, Graduate Studies, School of Engineering, Program in Information Technology, Lawrence, KS 66045. Offers MS. Part-time and evening/weekend programs available. *Faculty:* 34. *Students:* 2 full-time (both women), 18 part-time (1 woman); includes 4 minority (1 Black or African American, non-Hispanic/Latino; 2 Asian, non-Hispanic/Latino; 1 Two or more races, non-Hispanic/Latino), 3 international. Average age 35. 12 applicants, 75% accepted, 4 enrolled. In 2013, 6 master's awarded. *Degree requirements:* For master's, thesis optional, exam. *Entrance requirements:* For master's, GRE. Additional exam requirements/recommendations for international students: Required—TOEFL (minimum score 600 paper-based; 100 iBT). *Application deadline:* For fall admission, 3/1 priority date for domestic students, 3/1 for international students; for spring admission, 10/1 priority date for domestic students, 10/1 for international students. Applications are processed on a rolling basis. Application fee: $55 ($65 for international students). Electronic applications accepted. *Faculty research:* Information security and privacy, game theory, graph theory, software process improvement, resilient and survivable networks, object orientation technology. *Unit head:* Glenn Prescott, Department Chair, 785-864-4486, Fax: 785-864-3226, E-mail: prescott@ku.edu. *Application contact:* Pam Shadoin, Assistant to Graduate Director, 785-864-4487, Fax: 785-864-3226, E-mail: eecs_graduate@ku.edu.
Website: http://eecs.ku.edu/prospective_students/graduate/masters#information_technology.

University of La Verne, College of Business and Public Management, Graduate Programs in Business Administration, La Verne, CA 91750-4443. Offers accounting (MBA); executive management (MBA-EP); finance (MBA, MBA-EP); health services management (MBA); information technology (MBA, MBA-EP); international business (MBA, MBA-EP); leadership (MBA-EP); managed care (MBA); management (MBA, MBA-EP); marketing (MBA, MBA-EP). Part-time and evening/weekend programs available. *Faculty:* 22 full-time (9 women), 37 part-time/adjunct (10 women). *Students:* 793 full-time (356 women), 164 part-time (80 women); includes 153 minority (17 Black or African American, non-Hispanic/Latino; 21 Asian, non-Hispanic/Latino; 110 Hispanic/Latino; 5 Two or more races, non-Hispanic/Latino), 691 international. Average age 27. In 2013, 514 master's awarded. *Entrance requirements:* For master's, GMAT, MAT, or GRE, minimum undergraduate GPA of 3.0, 2 letters of recommendation, resume, statement of purpose. Additional exam requirements/recommendations for international students: Required—TOEFL (minimum score 550 paper-based; 85 iBT). *Application deadline:* Applications are processed on a rolling basis. Application fee: $50. *Expenses:* Contact institution. *Financial support:* Career-related internships or fieldwork, institutionally sponsored loans, and scholarships/grants available. Financial award application deadline: 3/2; financial award applicants required to submit FAFSA. *Unit head:* Dr. Abe Helou, Chairperson, 909-593-3511 Ext. 4211, Fax: 909-392-2704, E-mail: ihelou@laverne.edu. *Application contact:* Rina Lazarian-Chehab, Senior Associate Director of Graduate Admissions, 909-593-3511 Ext. 4317, Fax: 909-392-2704, E-mail: rlazarian@laverne.edu.

University of La Verne, Regional and Online Campuses, Graduate Programs, Central Coast/Vandenberg Air Force Base Campuses, La Verne, CA 91750-4443. Offers business administration for experienced professionals (MBA), including health services management, information technology; education (special emphasis) (M Ed); educational counseling (MS); educational leadership (M Ed); multiple subject (elementary) (Credential); preliminary administrative services (Credential); pupil personnel services (Credential); single subject (secondary) (Credential). Part-time programs available. *Faculty:* 11 part-time/adjunct (2 women). *Students:* 17 full-time (7 women), 34 part-time (22 women); includes 15 minority (1 Black or African American, non-Hispanic/Latino; 1 American Indian or Alaska Native, non-Hispanic/Latino; 1 Asian, non-Hispanic/Latino; 10 Hispanic/Latino; 2 Two or more races, non-Hispanic/Latino). Average age 38. In 2013, 25 master's awarded. *Application deadline:* Applications are processed on a rolling basis. Application fee: $50. *Expenses:* Contact institution. *Financial support:* Institutionally sponsored loans available. Financial award application deadline: 3/2; financial award applicants required to submit FAFSA. *Unit head:* Kitt Vincent, Director, Central Coast Campus, 805-788-6202, Fax: 805-788-6201, E-mail: kvincent@laverne.edu. *Application contact:* Gene Teal, Admissions, 805-788-6205, Fax: 805-788-6201, E-mail: eteal@laverne.edu.
Website: http://www.laverne.edu/locations.

University of La Verne, Regional and Online Campuses, Graduate Programs, Inland Empire Campus, Ontario, CA 91761. Offers business administration (MBA, MBA-EP), including accounting (MBA), finance (MBA), health services management (MBA-EP), information technology (MBA-EP), international business (MBA), managed care (MBA), management and leadership (MBA-EP), marketing (MBA-EP), supply chain management (MBA); leadership and management (MS), including human resource management, nonprofit management, organizational development. Part-time and evening/weekend programs available. *Faculty:* 1 full-time (0 women), 14 part-time/adjunct (6 women). *Students:* 26 full-time (15 women), 106 part-time (65 women); includes 92 minority (15 Black or African American, non-Hispanic/Latino; 29 Asian, non-Hispanic/Latino; 43 Hispanic/Latino; 1 Native Hawaiian or other Pacific Islander, non-Hispanic/Latino; 4 Two or more races, non-Hispanic/Latino). Average age 37. In 2013, 49 master's awarded. *Application deadline:* Applications are processed on a rolling basis. Application fee: $50. *Expenses:* Contact institution. *Financial support:* Institutionally sponsored loans available. Financial award application deadline: 3/2; financial award applicants required to submit FAFSA. *Unit head:* Allen Stout, Campus Director, Inland Empire Regional Campus in Ontario, 909-937-6987, E-mail: astout@laverne.edu. *Application contact:* Karen Schumann, Senior Associate Director of Admissions, Inland Empire Regional Campus in Ontario, 909-937-6991, E-mail: kschumann@laverne.edu.
Website: http://laverne.edu/locations/inland-empire/.

University of Lethbridge, School of Graduate Studies, Lethbridge, AB T1K 3M4, Canada. Offers accounting (MScM); addictions counseling (M Sc); agricultural biotechnology (M Sc); agricultural studies (M Sc, MA); anthropology (MA); archaeology (M Sc, MA); art (MA, MFA); biochemistry (M Sc); biological sciences (M Sc); biomolecular science (PhD); biosystems and biodiversity (PhD); Canadian studies (MA); chemistry (M Sc); computer science (M Sc); computer science and geographical information science (M Sc); counseling (MC); counseling psychology (M Ed); dramatic arts (MA); earth, space, and physical science (PhD); economics (MA); education (MA); educational leadership (M Ed); English (MA); environmental science (M Sc); evolution and behavior (PhD); exercise science (M Sc); finance (MScM); French (MA); French/German (MA); French/Spanish (MA); general education (M Ed); general management (MScM); geography (M Sc, MA); German (MA); health sciences (M Sc); human resource management and labour relations (MScM); individualized multidisciplinary (M Sc, MA); information systems (MScM); international management (MScM); kinesiology (M Sc, MA); marketing (MScM); mathematics (M Sc); modern languages (MA); music (M Mus, MA); Native American studies (MA); neuroscience (M Sc, PhD); new media (MA, MFA); nursing (M Sc); philosophy (MA); physics (M Sc); policy and strategy (MScM); political science (MA); psychology (M Sc, MA); religious studies (MA); sociology (MA); theatre and dramatic arts (MFA); theoretical and computational science (PhD); urban and regional studies (MA); women and gender studies (MA). Part-time and evening/weekend programs available. *Degree requirements:* For doctorate, comprehensive exam, thesis/dissertation. *Entrance requirements:* For master's, GMAT (for M Sc in management), bachelor's degree in related field, minimum GPA of 3.0 during previous 20 graded semester courses, 2 years teaching or related experience (M Ed); for doctorate, master's degree, minimum graduate GPA of 3.5. Additional exam requirements/recommendations for international students: Required—TOEFL. Application fee: $60 Canadian dollars. *Financial support:* Fellowships, research assistantships, teaching assistantships, scholarships/grants, health care benefits, and unspecified assistantships available. *Faculty research:* Movement and brain plasticity, gibberellin physiology, photosynthesis, carbon cycling, molecular properties of main-group ring components. *Application contact:* School of Graduate Studies, 403-329-2793, Fax: 403-332-5239, E-mail: sgsinquiries@uleth.ca.
Website: http://www.uleth.ca/graduatestudies/.

University of Maine, Graduate School, College of Liberal Arts and Sciences, School of Computing and Information Science, Orono, ME 04469. Offers computer science (MS, PhD); geographic information systems (CGS); information systems (MS); spatial information science and engineering (MS, PhD). Part-time programs available. *Faculty:* 14 full-time (2 women), 5 part-time/adjunct (1 woman). *Students:* 36 full-time (7 women), 7 part-time (1 woman); includes 1 minority (Asian, non-Hispanic/Latino), 12 international. Average age 35. 36 applicants, 42% accepted, 9 enrolled. In 2013, 3 master's awarded. *Degree requirements:* For master's, thesis (for some programs); for doctorate, comprehensive exam, thesis/dissertation. *Entrance requirements:* For master's and doctorate, GRE General Test, GRE Subject Test. Additional exam requirements/recommendations for international students: Required—TOEFL. *Application deadline:* For fall admission, 2/1 priority date for domestic students. Applications are processed on a rolling basis. Application fee: $65. Electronic applications accepted. *Expenses:* Tuition, state resident: full-time $7524. Tuition, nonresident: full-time $23,112. *Required fees:* $1970. *Financial support:* In 2013–14, 27 students received support, including 5 research assistantships with full tuition reimbursements available (averaging $14,600 per year), 13 teaching assistantships with full tuition reimbursements available (averaging $14,600 per year); career-related internships or fieldwork, Federal Work-Study, institutionally sponsored loans, and tuition waivers (full) also available. Financial award application deadline: 3/1. *Faculty research:* Theory, software engineering, graphics, applications, artificial intelligence. *Total annual research expenditures:* $42,204. *Unit head:* Dr. Max Egenhofer, Acting Director, 207-581-2114, Fax: 207-581-2206. *Application contact:* Scott G. Delcourt, Associate Dean of the Graduate School, 207-581-3291, Fax: 207-581-3232, E-mail: graduate@maine.edu.
Website: http://umaine.edu/cis/.

University of Management and Technology, Program in Information Technology, Arlington, VA 22209. Offers MS, Advanced Certificate.

University of Mary Hardin-Baylor, Graduate Studies in Business Administration, Belton, TX 76513. Offers accounting (MBA); information systems management (MBA); international business (MBA); management (MBA). Part-time and evening/weekend programs available. *Faculty:* 10 full-time (4 women), 2 part-time/adjunct (1 woman). *Students:* 26 full-time (11 women), 52 part-time (19 women); includes 20 minority (7 Black or African American, non-Hispanic/Latino; 3 Asian, non-Hispanic/Latino; 9 Hispanic/Latino; 1 Two or more races, non-Hispanic/Latino), 21 international. Average age 30. 55 applicants, 75% accepted, 27 enrolled. In 2013, 23 master's awarded. *Degree requirements:* For master's, comprehensive exam. *Entrance requirements:* For master's, minimum GPA of 3.0, interview. Additional exam requirements/recommendations for international students: Required—TOEFL (minimum score 550 paper-based; 80 iBT), IELTS (minimum score 6). *Application deadline:* For fall admission, 6/1 for domestic students, 6/15 priority date for international students; for spring admission, 11/1 for domestic students, 10/15 priority date for international students. Applications are processed on a rolling basis. Application fee: $35 ($135 for international students). Electronic applications accepted. *Expenses: Tuition:* Full-time $14,130; part-time $785 per credit hour. *Required fees:* $1350; $75 per credit hour. $50 per term. *Financial support:* Federal Work-Study, unspecified assistantships, and scholarships (for some active duty military personnel only) available. Financial award applicants required to submit FAFSA. *Unit head:* Dr. Nancy Bonner, Assistant Professor/Program Director, 254-295-5405, E-mail: nbonner@umhb.edu. *Application contact:* Melissa Ford, Director of Graduate Admissions, 254-295-4020, Fax: 254-295-5038, E-mail: mford@umhb.edu.
Website: http://www.graduate.umhb.edu/mba.

Management Information Systems

University of Mary Hardin-Baylor, Graduate Studies in Information Systems, Belton, TX 76513. Offers computer technology (MS); systems management (MS). Part-time and evening/weekend programs available. *Faculty:* 3 full-time (1 woman), 1 part-time/adjunct (0 women). *Students:* 24 full-time (18 women), 69 part-time (53 women); includes 3 minority (1 Asian, non-Hispanic/Latino; 2 Two or more races, non-Hispanic/Latino), 82 international. Average age 24. 251 applicants, 85% accepted, 69 enrolled. In 2013, 18 master's awarded. *Degree requirements:* For master's, comprehensive exam. *Entrance requirements:* For master's, minimum GPA of 3.0, interview. Additional exam requirements/recommendations for international students: Required—TOEFL (minimum score 550 paper-based; 80 iBT), IELTS (minimum score 6). *Application deadline:* For fall admission, 6/1 for domestic students, 6/15 priority date for international students; for spring admission, 11/1 for domestic students, 10/15 priority date for international students. Applications are processed on a rolling basis. Application fee: $35 ($135 for international students). Electronic applications accepted. *Expenses: Tuition:* Full-time $14,130; part-time $785 per credit hour. *Required fees:* $1350; $75 per credit hour. $50 per term. *Financial support:* Federal Work-Study, unspecified assistantships, and scholarships (for some active duty military personnel only) available. Support available to part-time students. Financial award applicants required to submit FAFSA. *Unit head:* Dr. Nancy Bonner, Assistant Professor/Program Director, Master of Science in Information Systems, 254-295-5405, E-mail: nbonner@umhb.edu. *Application contact:* Melissa Ford, Director of Graduate Admissions, 254-295-4020, Fax: 254-295-5038, E-mail: mford@umhb.edu.
Website: http://www.graduate.umhb.edu/msis.

University of Maryland University College, Graduate School of Management and Technology, Program in Accounting and Information Systems, Adelphi, MD 20783. Offers MS, Certificate. *Accreditation:* AACSB. Part-time and evening/weekend programs available. Postbaccalaureate distance learning degree programs offered (no on-campus study). *Students:* 2 full-time (1 woman), 145 part-time (89 women); includes 99 minority (79 Black or African American, non-Hispanic/Latino; 9 Asian, non-Hispanic/Latino; 10 Hispanic/Latino; 1 Native Hawaiian or other Pacific Islander, non-Hispanic/Latino), 4 international. Average age 36. 64 applicants, 100% accepted, 35 enrolled. In 2013, 40 master's, 3 other advanced degrees awarded. *Degree requirements:* For master's, thesis or alternative, capstone course. *Application deadline:* Applications are processed on a rolling basis. Application fee: $50. Electronic applications accepted. *Financial support:* Federal Work-Study and scholarships/grants available. Support available to part-time students. Financial award application deadline: 6/1; financial award applicants required to submit FAFSA. *Unit head:* Dr. Kathryn Klose, Director, 240-684-2400, Fax: 240-684-2401, E-mail: kathryn.klose@umuc.edu. *Application contact:* Coordinator, Graduate Admissions, 800-888-8682, Fax: 240-684-2151, E-mail: newgrad@umuc.edu.

University of Maryland University College, Graduate School of Management and Technology, Program in Financial Management and Information Systems, Adelphi, MD 20783. Offers MS, Certificate. Part-time and evening/weekend programs available. Postbaccalaureate distance learning degree programs offered (no on-campus study). *Students:* 135 part-time (60 women); includes 91 minority (67 Black or African American, non-Hispanic/Latino; 14 Asian, non-Hispanic/Latino; 5 Hispanic/Latino; 5 Two or more races, non-Hispanic/Latino), 5 international. Average age 34. 43 applicants, 100% accepted, 22 enrolled. In 2013, 44 master's awarded. *Degree requirements:* For master's, thesis or alternative. *Application deadline:* Applications are processed on a rolling basis. Application fee: $50. Electronic applications accepted. *Financial support:* Federal Work-Study and scholarships/grants available. Support available to part-time students. Financial award application deadline: 6/1; financial award applicants required to submit FAFSA. *Unit head:* Dr. Jayanta Sen, Director, 240-684-2400, Fax: 240-684-2401, E-mail: jayanta.sen@umuc.edu. *Application contact:* Coordinator, Graduate Admissions, 800-888-8682, Fax: 240-684-2151, E-mail: newgrad@umuc.edu.
Website: http://www.umuc.edu/programs/grad/fmis/.

University of Mary Washington, College of Business, Fredericksburg, VA 22401-5300. Offers business administration (MBA); management information systems (MSMIS). Part-time and evening/weekend programs available. *Faculty:* 12 full-time (4 women), 5 part-time/adjunct (0 women). *Students:* 45 full-time (19 women), 125 part-time (64 women); includes 48 minority (30 Black or African American, non-Hispanic/Latino; 2 American Indian or Alaska Native, non-Hispanic/Latino; 8 Asian, non-Hispanic/Latino; 8 Hispanic/Latino), 47 international. Average age 36. 51 applicants, 73% accepted, 21 enrolled. In 2013, 104 master's awarded. *Entrance requirements:* For master's, GMAT or GRE, minimum GPA of 3.0. Additional exam requirements/recommendations for international students: Required—TOEFL (minimum score 570 paper-based; 88 iBT), IELTS (minimum score 6.5). *Application deadline:* For fall admission, 6/1 priority date for domestic students, 6/1 for international students; for spring admission, 10/1 for domestic and international students. Application fee: $50. Electronic applications accepted. *Expenses: Tuition, area resident:* Part-time $444 per credit hour. Tuition, state resident: part-time $444 per credit hour. Tuition, nonresident: part-time $883 per credit hour. *Required fees:* $30 per semester. *Financial support:* Available to part-time students. Application deadline: 3/15; applicants required to submit FAFSA. *Faculty research:* Power laws/CEO compensation, sustainable competitive advantage, resistance to security implementation, profiling sustainable curriculums, perceived customer value. *Unit head:* Dr. Lynne D. Richardson, Dean, 540-654-2470, Fax: 540-654-2430, E-mail: lynne.richardson@umw.edu. *Application contact:* Dre N. Anthes, Associate Dean of Admissions, 540-286-8086, Fax: 540-286-8085, E-mail: aanthes@umw.edu.
Website: http://business.umw.edu/.

University of Memphis, Graduate School, Fogelman College of Business and Economics, Program in Business Administration, Memphis, TN 38152. Offers accounting (MBA, PhD); economics (MBA, PhD); executive business administration (MBA); finance (PhD); finance, insurance, and real estate (MBA, MS); international business administration (IMBA); management (MBA, MS, PhD); management information systems (MBA, MS, PhD); management science (MBA); marketing (MBA, MS); marketing and supply chain management (PhD); real estate development (MS); JD/MBA. *Accreditation:* AACSB. *Faculty:* 44 full-time (9 women), 5 part-time/adjunct (0 women). *Students:* 238 full-time (101 women), 315 part-time (113 women); includes 146 minority (80 Black or African American, non-Hispanic/Latino; 1 American Indian or Alaska Native, non-Hispanic/Latino; 46 Asian, non-Hispanic/Latino; 13 Hispanic/Latino; 2 Native Hawaiian or other Pacific Islander, non-Hispanic/Latino; 4 Two or more races, non-Hispanic/Latino), 104 international. Average age 32. 343 applicants, 62% accepted, 102 enrolled. In 2013, 140 master's, 17 doctorates awarded. *Degree requirements:* For master's, comprehensive exam; for doctorate, comprehensive exam, thesis/dissertation. *Entrance requirements:* For master's, GMAT, resume; for doctorate, GMAT, interview, minimum GPA of 3.4, resume, letter of recommendation. Additional exam requirements/recommendations for international students: Required—TOEFL (minimum score 550 paper-based). *Application deadline:* For fall admission, 8/1 for domestic students; for spring admission, 12/1 for domestic students. Application fee: $35 ($60 for international students). *Financial support:* In 2013–14, 164 students received support. Research assistantships with full tuition reimbursements available, teaching assistantships with full tuition reimbursements available, career-related internships or fieldwork, Federal Work-Study, scholarships/grants, and unspecified assistantships available. Financial award application deadline: 2/15; financial award applicants required to submit FAFSA. *Faculty research:* Competitive business strategy, finance microstructures, supply chain management innovations, health care economics, litigation risks and corporate audits. *Unit head:* Rajiv Grover, Dean, 901-678-3759, E-mail: rgrover@memphis.edu. *Application contact:* Dr. Carol V. Danehower, Associate Dean, 901-678-5402, Fax: 901-678-3579, E-mail: fcbegp@memphis.edu.
Website: http://www.memphis.edu/fcbe/grad_programs.php.

University of Miami, Graduate School, School of Business Administration, Program in Business Administration, Coral Gables, FL 33124. Offers accounting (MBA); computer information systems (MBA); executive and professional (MBA), including international business, management; finance (MBA); international business (MBA); management (MBA); management science (MBA); marketing (MBA); professional management (MSPM); JD/MBA; MBA/MSIE. *Accreditation:* AACSB. Evening/weekend programs available. *Degree requirements:* For master's, comprehensive exam. *Entrance requirements:* For master's, GMAT. Additional exam requirements/recommendations for international students: Required—TOEFL (minimum score 550 paper-based; 59 iBT). Electronic applications accepted. *Faculty research:* Leadership, e-commerce, supply chain management.

University of Michigan–Dearborn, College of Business, Dearborn, MI 48128-1491. Offers accounting (MBA, MS); business analytics (MS); finance (MBA, MS); human resource management (MBA); information systems (MS); international business (MBA); investment (MBA); management (MBA); management information systems (MBA); marketing (MBA); supply chain management (MBA, MS); taxation (MBA); MBA/MHSA; MBA/MSE; MBA/MSF; MBA/MSIS; MBA/MSSCM; MSF/MSA. *Accreditation:* AACSB. Part-time and evening/weekend programs available. Postbaccalaureate distance learning degree programs offered (no on-campus study). *Faculty:* 24 full-time (8 women), 5 part-time/adjunct (2 women). *Students:* 82 full-time (31 women), 323 part-time (116 women); includes 72 minority (17 Black or African American, non-Hispanic/Latino; 2 American Indian or Alaska Native, non-Hispanic/Latino; 30 Asian, non-Hispanic/Latino; 15 Hispanic/Latino; 8 Two or more races, non-Hispanic/Latino), 65 international. Average age 32. 290 applicants, 44% accepted, 99 enrolled. In 2013, 143 master's awarded. *Entrance requirements:* For master's, GMAT or GRE, pre-calculus or finite mathematics; 18 credits of accounting course work beyond introductory courses (MS in accounting). Additional exam requirements/recommendations for international students: Required—TOEFL (minimum score 560 paper-based; 84 iBT), IELTS. *Application deadline:* For fall admission, 8/1 priority date for domestic students, 5/1 priority date for international students; for winter admission, 12/1 priority date for domestic students, 9/1 priority date for international students; for spring admission, 4/1 priority date for domestic students, 1/1 priority date for international students. Applications are processed on a rolling basis. Application fee: $60. Electronic applications accepted. *Expenses:* Contact institution. *Financial support:* Career-related internships or fieldwork, Federal Work-Study, and scholarships/grants available. Support available to part-time students. Financial award application deadline: 9/1; financial award applicants required to submit FAFSA. *Faculty research:* Cultural diversity, buyer-supplier relations, error detection in data, economic evolution. *Unit head:* Dr. Raju Balakrishnan, Dean, 313-593-5248, Fax: 313-271-9835, E-mail: rajub@umich.edu. *Application contact:* Joan Doherty, Academic Advisor/Counselor, 313-593-5460, Fax: 313-271-9838, E-mail: umd-gradbusiness@umich.edu.
Website: http://www.cob.umd.umich.edu.

University of Michigan–Flint, School of Management, Flint, MI 48502-1950. Offers accounting (MBA, MSA); business (Graduate Certificate); computer information systems (MBA); finance (MBA); health care management (MBA); international business (MBA); lean manufacturing (MBA); marketing (MBA); organizational leadership (MBA). *Accreditation:* AACSB. Part-time and evening/weekend programs available. Postbaccalaureate distance learning degree programs offered (minimal on-campus study). *Faculty:* 13 full-time (3 women), 4 part-time/adjunct (0 women). *Students:* 19 full-time (6 women), 234 part-time (72 women); includes 50 minority (21 Black or African American, non-Hispanic/Latino; 5 American Indian or Alaska Native, non-Hispanic/Latino; 12 Asian, non-Hispanic/Latino; 5 Hispanic/Latino; 7 Two or more races, non-Hispanic/Latino), 30 international. Average age 32. 195 applicants, 56% accepted, 88 enrolled. In 2013, 73 master's awarded. *Degree requirements:* For master's, thesis or alternative. *Entrance requirements:* For master's, GMAT or GRE, minimum GPA of 3.0. Additional exam requirements/recommendations for international students: Required—TOEFL (minimum score 560 paper-based; 84 iBT), IELTS (minimum score 6.5). *Application deadline:* For fall admission, 8/1 for domestic students, 5/1 for international students; for winter admission, 11/1 for domestic students, 9/1 for international students; for spring admission, 2/15 for domestic students, 1/15 for international students. Applications are processed on a rolling basis. Application fee: $55. Electronic applications accepted. *Financial support:* Federal Work-Study, scholarships/grants, and unspecified assistantships available. Support available to part-time students. Financial award application deadline: 3/1; financial award applicants required to submit FAFSA. *Unit head:* Dr. Scott Johnson, Dean, School of Management, 810-762-3164, Fax: 810-237-6685, E-mail: scotjohn@umflint.edu. *Application contact:* Jeremiah Cook, Marketing Communications Specialist, 810-424-5583, Fax: 810-766-6789, E-mail: jecook@umflint.edu.
Website: http://www.umflint.edu/som/.

University of Minnesota, Twin Cities Campus, Carlson School of Management, Carlson Full-Time MBA Program, Minneapolis, MN 55455. Offers finance (MBA); information technology (MBA); management (MBA); marketing (MBA); medical industry orientation (MBA); supply chain and operations (MBA); JD/MBA; MBA/MPP; MD/MBA; MHA/MBA; Pharm D/MBA. *Accreditation:* AACSB. *Faculty:* 137 full-time (42 women), 16 part-time/adjunct (5 women). *Students:* 222 full-time (62 women); includes 30 minority (2 Black or African American, non-Hispanic/Latino; 17 Asian, non-Hispanic/Latino; 5 Hispanic/Latino; 6 Two or more races, non-Hispanic/Latino), 60 international. Average age 28. 565 applicants, 44% accepted, 113 enrolled. In 2013, 96 master's awarded. *Entrance requirements:* For master's, GMAT or GRE. Additional exam requirements/recommendations for international students: Required—TOEFL (minimum score 580 paper-based; 84 iBT), IELTS (minimum score 7), PTE. *Application deadline:* For fall admission, 4/1 for domestic students, 2/1 for international students. Application fee: $60 ($90 for international students). Electronic applications accepted. *Expenses:* Contact institution. *Financial support:* In 2013–14, 133 students received support, including 133 fellowships with full and partial tuition reimbursements available (averaging $29,445 per year); research assistantships with partial tuition reimbursements available, teaching assistantships with partial tuition reimbursements available, career-related internships or fieldwork, Federal Work-Study, institutionally sponsored loans, scholarships/grants, health care benefits, and unspecified assistantships also available. Financial award application deadline: 4/1; financial award applicants required to submit FAFSA. *Faculty research:* Finance and accounting: financial reporting, asset pricing models and corporate finance; information and decision sciences: on-line auctions, information transparency and recommender systems; marketing: psychological influences on consumer behavior, brand equity, pricing and marketing channels; operations: lean manufacturing, quality management and global supply chains; strategic management and organization: global strategy, networks, entrepreneurship and innovation, sustainability. *Unit head:* Philip J. Miller, Assistant Dean, MBA Programs and Graduate Business Career Center, 612-625-5555, Fax: 612-625-1012, E-mail: mba@umn.edu.

Application contact: Linh Gilles, Director of Admissions and Recruiting, 612-625-5555, Fax: 612-625-1012, E-mail: ftmba@umn.edu.
Website: http://www.csom.umn.edu/MBA/full-time/.

University of Minnesota, Twin Cities Campus, Carlson School of Management, Carlson Part-Time MBA Program, Minneapolis, MN 55455. Offers finance (MBA); information technology (MBA); management (MBA); marketing (MBA); medical industry orientation (MBA); supply chain and operations (MBA). Part-time and evening/weekend programs available. *Faculty:* 137 full-time (42 women), 15 part-time/adjunct (3 women). *Students:* 1,207 part-time (393 women); includes 108 minority (21 Black or African American, non-Hispanic/Latino; 4 American Indian or Alaska Native, non-Hispanic/Latino; 72 Asian, non-Hispanic/Latino; 5 Hispanic/Latino; 1 Native Hawaiian or other Pacific Islander, non-Hispanic/Latino; 5 Two or more races, non-Hispanic/Latino), 66 international. Average age 28. 291 applicants, 86% accepted, 205 enrolled. In 2013, 372 master's awarded. *Entrance requirements:* For master's, GMAT or GRE. Additional exam requirements/recommendations for international students: Required—TOEFL (minimum score 580 paper-based; 84 iBT), IELTS (minimum score 7), PTE. *Application deadline:* For fall admission, 5/1 priority date for domestic and international students; for spring admission, 10/1 priority date for domestic and international students. Applications are processed on a rolling basis. Application fee: $60 ($90 for international students). Electronic applications accepted. *Expenses:* Contact institution. *Financial support:* Applicants required to submit FAFSA. *Faculty research:* Finance and accounting: financial reporting, asset pricing models and corporate finance; information and decision sciences: on-line auctions, information transparency and recommender systems; marketing: psychological influences on consumer behavior, brand equity, pricing and marketing channels; operations: lean manufacturing, quality management and global supply chains; strategic management and organization: global strategy, networks, entrepreneurship and innovation, sustainability. *Unit head:* Philip J. Miller, Assistant Dean, MBA Programs and Graduate Business Career Center, 612-624-2039, Fax: 612-625-1012, E-mail: mba@umn.edu. *Application contact:* Linh Gilles, Director of Admissions and Recruiting, 612-625-5555, Fax: 612-625-1012, E-mail: ptmba@umn.edu.
Website: http://www.carlsonschool.umn.edu/ptmba.

University of Minnesota, Twin Cities Campus, Carlson School of Management, Doctoral Program in Business Administration, Minneapolis, MN 55455-0213. Offers accounting (PhD); finance (PhD); information and decision sciences (PhD); marketing (PhD); operations and management science (PhD); strategic management and entrepreneurship (PhD). *Faculty:* 102 full-time (31 women). *Students:* 74 full-time (25 women); includes 8 minority (1 Black or African American, non-Hispanic/Latino; 5 Asian, non-Hispanic/Latino; 2 Hispanic/Latino), 46 international. Average age 30. 274 applicants, 8% accepted, 15 enrolled. In 2013, 10 doctorates awarded. *Degree requirements:* For doctorate, comprehensive exam, thesis/dissertation, written and oral preliminary exams, proposal defense, final defense. *Entrance requirements:* For doctorate, GMAT, GRE General Test. Additional exam requirements/recommendations for international students: Required—TOEFL (minimum score 600 paper-based; 100 iBT); Recommended—IELTS (minimum score 7.5). *Application deadline:* For fall admission, 12/31 for domestic students, 12/31 priority date for international students. Applications are processed on a rolling basis. Application fee: $75 ($95 for international students). Electronic applications accepted. *Expenses:* Contact institution. *Financial support:* In 2013–14, 68 students received support, including 96 fellowships with full tuition reimbursements available (averaging $6,300 per year), 65 research assistantships with full tuition reimbursements available (averaging $12,500 per year), 64 teaching assistantships with full tuition reimbursements available (averaging $12,500 per year); institutionally sponsored loans, scholarships/grants, health care benefits, unspecified assistantships, and full student fee waivers also available. Financial award application deadline: 12/31. *Faculty research:* Corporate strategy, finance, entrepreneurship, marketing, information and decision science, operations, accounting, supply chain. *Unit head:* Dr. Shawn P. Curley, Director, 612-624-6546, Fax: 612-624-8221, E-mail: curley@umn.edu. *Application contact:* Earlene K. Bronson, Assistant Director, 612-624-0875, Fax: 612-624-8221, E-mail: brons003@umn.edu.
Website: http://www.csom.umn.edu/phd-BA/.

University of Mississippi, Graduate School, School of Business Administration, Oxford, MS 38677. Offers business administration (MBA, PhD); systems management (MS); JD/MBA. *Accreditation:* AACSB. *Faculty:* 53 full-time (16 women), 5 part-time/adjunct (1 woman). *Students:* 87 full-time (34 women), 105 part-time (37 women); includes 23 minority (7 Black or African American, non-Hispanic/Latino; 4 Asian, non-Hispanic/Latino; 5 Hispanic/Latino; 1 Native Hawaiian or other Pacific Islander, non-Hispanic/Latino; 6 Two or more races, non-Hispanic/Latino), 15 international. In 2013, 71 master's, 7 doctorates awarded. *Degree requirements:* For doctorate, thesis/dissertation. *Entrance requirements:* For master's, GMAT, minimum GPA of 3.0; for doctorate, GMAT. Additional exam requirements/recommendations for international students: Required—TOEFL. *Application deadline:* For fall admission, 2/1 for domestic students; for spring admission, 10/1 for domestic students. Applications are processed on a rolling basis. Application fee: $40. Electronic applications accepted. *Financial support:* Fellowships, career-related internships or fieldwork, scholarships/grants, tuition waivers (full), and unspecified assistantships available. Financial award application deadline: 3/1; financial award applicants required to submit FAFSA. *Unit head:* Dr. Ken Cyree, Dean, 662-915-5820, Fax: 662-915-5821, E-mail: info@bus.olemiss.edu. *Application contact:* Dr. Christy M. Wyandt, Associate Dean, 662-915-7474, Fax: 662-915-7577, E-mail: cwyandt@olemiss.edu.
Website: http://www.olemissbusiness.com/.

University of Missouri–St. Louis, College of Business Administration, Program in Business Administration, St. Louis, MO 63121. Offers accounting (MBA); business administration (Certificate); business intelligence (Certificate); finance (MBA); human resource management (Certificate); information systems (MBA); logistics and supply chain management (MBA, PhD, Certificate); marketing (MBA); marketing management (Certificate); operations management (MBA). *Accreditation:* AACSB. Part-time and evening/weekend programs available. *Faculty:* 30 full-time (5 women), 20 part-time/adjunct (8 women). *Students:* 114 full-time (51 women), 269 part-time (100 women); includes 43 minority (16 Black or African American, non-Hispanic/Latino; 14 Asian, non-Hispanic/Latino; 11 Hispanic/Latino; 1 Native Hawaiian or other Pacific Islander, non-Hispanic/Latino; 1 Two or more races, non-Hispanic/Latino), 56 international. Average age 31. 153 applicants, 91% accepted, 110 enrolled. In 2013, 136 master's, 7 other advanced degrees awarded. *Degree requirements:* For doctorate, thesis/dissertation. *Entrance requirements:* For master's, GMAT, 2 letters of recommendation. Additional exam requirements/recommendations for international students: Recommended—TOEFL (minimum score 550 paper-based; 79 iBT), IELTS (minimum score 6.5). *Application deadline:* For fall admission, 7/1 for domestic and international students; for spring admission, 12/1 for domestic and international students. Applications are processed on a rolling basis. Application fee: $50 ($40 for international students). Electronic applications accepted. *Expenses:* Tuition, state resident: full-time $7364; part-time $409.10 per credit hour. Tuition, nonresident: full-time $19,162; part-time $1008.50 per credit hour. *Financial support:* In 2013–14, 14 research assistantships with full and partial tuition reimbursements (averaging $5,625 per year), 6 teaching assistantships with full and partial tuition reimbursements (averaging $9,403 per year) were awarded; career-related internships or fieldwork, Federal Work-Study, and institutionally sponsored loans also available. Support available to part-time students. Financial award application deadline: 4/1; financial award applicants required to submit FAFSA. *Faculty research:* Human resources, strategic management, marketing strategy, consumer behavior product development, advertising. *Unit head:* Francesca Ferrari, Assistant Director, 314-516-5885, Fax: 314-516-6420, E-mail: mba@umsl.edu. *Application contact:* 314-516-5458, Fax: 314-516-6996, E-mail: gradadm@umsl.edu.
Website: http://mba.umsl.edu/Degree%20Programs/index.html.

University of Missouri–St. Louis, College of Business Administration, Program in Information Systems, St. Louis, MO 63121. Offers MS. Part-time and evening/weekend programs available. *Faculty:* 7 full-time (2 women), 4 part-time/adjunct (0 women). *Students:* 12 full-time (4 women), 19 part-time (4 women); includes 3 minority (1 Black or African American, non-Hispanic/Latino; 2 Asian, non-Hispanic/Latino), 9 international. Average age 31. 28 applicants, 75% accepted, 10 enrolled. In 2013, 10 master's awarded. *Entrance requirements:* For master's, GMAT, 2 letters of recommendation. Additional exam requirements/recommendations for international students: Recommended—TOEFL (minimum score 550 paper-based; 79 iBT), IELTS (minimum score 6.5). *Application deadline:* For fall admission, 7/1 priority date for domestic and international students; for spring admission, 12/1 priority date for domestic and international students. Applications are processed on a rolling basis. Application fee: $50 ($40 for international students). Electronic applications accepted. *Expenses:* Tuition, state resident: full-time $7364; part-time $409.10 per credit hour. Tuition, nonresident: full-time $19,162; part-time $1008.50 per credit hour. *Financial support:* Career-related internships or fieldwork, Federal Work-Study, and institutionally sponsored loans available. Support available to part-time students. Financial award application deadline: 4/1; financial award applicants required to submit FAFSA. *Faculty research:* International information systems, telecommunications, systems development, information systems sourcing. *Unit head:* Francesca Ferrari, Assistant Director, 314-516-5885, Fax: 314-516-6420, E-mail: mba@umsl.edu. *Application contact:* 314-516-5458, Fax: 314-516-6996, E-mail: gradadm@umsl.edu.

University of Nebraska at Kearney, Graduate Programs, College of Education, Department of Teacher Education, Kearney, NE 68849-0001. Offers curriculum and instruction (MA Ed), including early childhood education, elementary education, English as a second language, instructional effectiveness, reading/special education, secondary education; instructional technology (MS Ed), including information technology, instructional technology, school librarian; reading PK-12 (MA Ed); special education (MA Ed), including advanced practitioner, gifted, mild/moderate. Part-time and evening/weekend programs available. *Degree requirements:* For master's, comprehensive exam, thesis optional. *Entrance requirements:* For master's, portfolio or GRE. Additional exam requirements/recommendations for international students: Required—TOEFL (minimum score 550 paper-based). Electronic applications accepted.

University of Nebraska at Omaha, Graduate Studies, College of Information Science and Technology, Department of Information Systems and Quantitative Analysis, Omaha, NE 68182. Offers biomedical informatics (MS, PhD); information assurance (MS, Certificate); information technology (PhD); management information systems (MS); project management (Certificate); systems analysis and design (Certificate). Part-time and evening/weekend programs available. *Faculty:* 15 full-time (7 women). *Students:* 77 full-time (27 women), 117 part-time (27 women); includes 32 minority (10 Black or African American, non-Hispanic/Latino; 15 Asian, non-Hispanic/Latino; 4 Hispanic/Latino; 3 Two or more races, non-Hispanic/Latino), 74 international. Average age 31. 274 applicants, 48% accepted, 63 enrolled. In 2013, 37 master's, 2 doctorates, 22 other advanced degrees awarded. *Degree requirements:* For master's, comprehensive exam, thesis (for some programs); for doctorate, comprehensive exam, thesis/dissertation. *Entrance requirements:* For master's, GRE General Test, minimum GPA of 3.0, 3 letters of recommendation, writing sample, resume, official transcripts; for doctorate, GMAT or GRE General Test, minimum GPA of 3.0, 3 letters of recommendation, writing sample, resume, official transcripts; for Certificate, minimum GPA of 3.0, official transcripts. Additional exam requirements/recommendations for international students: Required—TOEFL, IELTS, PTE. *Application deadline:* For fall admission, 2/15 for domestic students; for spring admission, 9/15 for domestic students. Applications are processed on a rolling basis. Application fee: $45. Electronic applications accepted. *Financial support:* In 2013–14, 31 students received support, including 27 research assistantships with tuition reimbursements available, 4 teaching assistantships with tuition reimbursements available; fellowships, career-related internships or fieldwork, Federal Work-Study, scholarships/grants, tuition waivers (partial), and unspecified assistantships also available. Financial award application deadline: 3/1; financial award applicants required to submit FAFSA. *Unit head:* Dr. Peter Wolcott, Chairperson, 402-554-3770, E-mail: graduate@unomaha.edu. *Application contact:* Dr. Leah Pietron, Graduate Program Chair, 402-554-2801, E-mail: graduate@unomaha.edu.

University of Nebraska–Lincoln, Graduate College, College of Agricultural Sciences and Natural Resources, Program in Mechanized Systems Management, Lincoln, NE 68588. Offers MS. *Degree requirements:* For master's, thesis optional. *Entrance requirements:* For master's, GRE General Test. Additional exam requirements/recommendations for international students: Required—TOEFL (minimum score 550 paper-based). Electronic applications accepted. *Faculty research:* Irrigation management, agricultural power and machinery systems, sensors and controls, food/industrial materials handling and processing systems.

University of Nevada, Las Vegas, Graduate College, College of Business, Department of Management, Entrepreneurship and Technology, Las Vegas, NV 89154-6034. Offers management (Certificate); management information systems (MS, Certificate); new venture management (Certificate); MS/MS. Part-time and evening/weekend programs available. *Faculty:* 9 full-time (1 woman), 1 (woman) part-time/adjunct. *Students:* 30 full-time (8 women), 19 part-time (6 women); includes 11 minority (2 Black or African American, non-Hispanic/Latino; 3 Asian, non-Hispanic/Latino; 4 Hispanic/Latino; 1 Native Hawaiian or other Pacific Islander, non-Hispanic/Latino; 1 Two or more races, non-Hispanic/Latino), 18 international. Average age 31. 55 applicants, 82% accepted, 19 enrolled. In 2013, 21 master's, 1 other advanced degree awarded. *Entrance requirements:* For master's and Certificate, GMAT or GRE. Additional exam requirements/recommendations for international students: Required—TOEFL (minimum score 550 paper-based; 80 iBT), IELTS (minimum score 7). *Application deadline:* For fall admission, 8/1 for domestic students, 5/1 for international students; for spring admission, 11/15 for domestic students, 10/1 for international students. Application fee: $60 ($95 for international students). Electronic applications accepted. *Expenses:* Tuition, state resident: full-time $4752; part-time $264 per credit. Tuition, nonresident: full-time $18,662; part-time $554.50 per credit. *International tuition:* $18,952 full-time. *Required fees:* $532; $12 per credit. $266 per semester. One-time fee: $35. Tuition and fees vary according to course load and program. *Financial support:* In 2013–14, 8 students received support, including 5 research assistantships with partial tuition reimbursements available (averaging $8,000 per year), 3 teaching assistantships with partial tuition reimbursements available (averaging $8,333 per year); institutionally sponsored loans, scholarships/grants, health care benefits, and unspecified assistantships also available. Financial award application deadline: 3/1. *Faculty research:* Decision-making, publish or perish, ethical issues in information systems, IT-

enabled decision making, business ethics. *Unit head:* Alan Miller, Chair/Associate Professor, 702-895-1724, E-mail: alan.miller@unlv.edu. *Application contact:* Graduate College Admissions Evaluator, 702-895-3320, Fax: 702-895-4180, E-mail: gradcollege@unlv.edu.
Website: http://business.unlv.edu/met/.

University of Nevada, Reno, Graduate School, College of Business Administration, Department of Information Systems, Reno, NV 89557. Offers MS. *Degree requirements:* For master's, thesis optional. *Entrance requirements:* For master's, GRE or GMAT, minimum GPA of 2.75. Additional exam requirements/recommendations for international students: Required—TOEFL (minimum score 500 paper-based; 61 iBT), IELTS (minimum score 6). Electronic applications accepted.

University of New Hampshire, Graduate School Manchester Campus, Manchester, NH 03101. Offers business administration (MBA); counseling (M Ed); education (M Ed, MAT); educational administration and supervision (M Ed, Ed S); information technology (MS); management of technology (MS); public administration (MPA); public health (MPH, Certificate); social work (MSW); software systems engineering (Certificate). Part-time and evening/weekend programs available. *Students:* 2 full-time (0 women), 5 part-time (0 women), 2 international. Average age 38. 6 applicants, 17% accepted, 1 enrolled. In 2013, 1 master's awarded. *Degree requirements:* For master's, thesis or alternative. *Entrance requirements:* Additional exam requirements/recommendations for international students: Required—TOEFL (minimum score 550 paper-based; 80 iBT). *Application deadline:* For fall admission, 6/1 for domestic students, 4/1 for international students; for spring admission, 12/1 for domestic students. Applications are processed on a rolling basis. Application fee: $65. Electronic applications accepted. *Expenses:* Tuition, state resident: full-time $13,500; part-time $750 per credit hour. Tuition, nonresident: full-time $26,200; part-time $1100 per credit hour. *Required fees:* $1741; $435.25 per term. Tuition and fees vary according to course level, course load, campus/location and program. *Financial support:* Fellowships, research assistantships, teaching assistantships, Federal Work-Study, scholarships/grants, health care benefits, and unspecified assistantships available. Support available to part-time students. Financial award application deadline: 3/1; financial award applicants required to submit FAFSA. *Unit head:* Candice Brown, Director, 603-641-4313, E-mail: unhm.gradcenter@unh.edu. *Application contact:* Graduate Admissions Office, 603-862-3000, Fax: 603-862-0275, E-mail: grad.school@unh.edu.
Website: http://www.gradschool.unh.edu/manchester/.

University of New Mexico, Anderson Graduate School of Management, Department of Marketing, Information Systems, Information Assurance and Operations Management, Albuquerque, NM 87131. Offers information assurance (MBA); management information systems (MBA); marketing management (MBA); operations management (MBA). Part-time and evening/weekend programs available. *Faculty:* 15 full-time (3 women), 6 part-time/adjunct (1 woman). In 2013, 82 master's awarded. *Entrance requirements:* For master's, GMAT or GRE, minimum GPA of 3.0 on last 60 hours of coursework. Additional exam requirements/recommendations for international students: Required—TOEFL (minimum score 550 paper-based; 79 iBT). *Application deadline:* For fall admission, 4/1 priority date for domestic and international students; for spring admission, 10/1 priority date for domestic and international students. Applications are processed on a rolling basis. Application fee: $50. Electronic applications accepted. *Expenses:* Contact institution. *Financial support:* Fellowships, research assistantships, career-related internships or fieldwork, Federal Work-Study, scholarships/grants, and unspecified assistantships available. Support available to part-time students. Financial award application deadline: 6/1; financial award applicants required to submit FAFSA. *Faculty research:* Marketing, operations management, information systems, information assurance. *Unit head:* Dr. Steve Yourstone, Chair, 505-277-6471, Fax: 505-277-7108, E-mail: yourstone@unm.edu. *Application contact:* Tracy Wilkey, Manager, Academic Advisement, 505-277-3290, Fax: 505-277-8436, E-mail: andersonadvising@unm.edu.
Website: http://mba.mgt.unm.edu/default.asp.

University of North Alabama, College of Business, Florence, AL 35632-0001. Offers accounting (MBA); enterprise resource planning systems (MBA); finance (MBA); health care management (MBA); information systems (MBA); professional (MBA); project management (MBA). *Accreditation:* ACBSP. Part-time and evening/weekend programs available. *Faculty:* 20 full-time (2 women). *Students:* 118 full-time (50 women), 273 part-time (130 women); includes 115 minority (37 Black or African American, non-Hispanic/Latino; 4 American Indian or Alaska Native, non-Hispanic/Latino; 68 Asian, non-Hispanic/Latino; 4 Hispanic/Latino; 2 Two or more races, non-Hispanic/Latino), 36 international. Average age 34. 296 applicants, 82% accepted, 149 enrolled. In 2013, 179 master's awarded. *Entrance requirements:* For master's, GMAT, GRE, minimum GPA of 2.75 in last 60 hours, 2.5 overall on a 3.0 scale; 27 hours of course work in business and economics. Additional exam requirements/recommendations for international students: Required—TOEFL (minimum score 500 paper-based; 79 iBT), IELTS (minimum score 6). *Application deadline:* For fall admission, 7/1 priority date for domestic students, 7/1 for international students; for spring admission, 12/1 for domestic and international students. Applications are processed on a rolling basis. Application fee: $25 ($50 for international students). Electronic applications accepted. *Expenses:* Tuition, state resident: full-time $4968; part-time $3312 per year. Tuition, nonresident: full-time $9936; part-time $6624 per year. *Required fees:* $970; $60.33 per credit. $362 per semester. *Financial support:* Federal Work-Study available. Support available to part-time students. Financial award application deadline: 4/1; financial award applicants required to submit FAFSA. *Unit head:* Dr. Kerry Gatlin, Dean, 256-765-4261, Fax: 256-765-4170, E-mail: kpgatlin@una.edu. *Application contact:* Russ Darracott, Graduate Admissions Counselor, 256-765-4447, E-mail: erdarracott@una.edu.
Website: http://www.una.edu/business/.

University of North Alabama, Office of Professional and Interdisciplinary Studies, Florence, AL 35632-0001. Offers community development (MPS); information technology (MPS); security and safety leadership (MPS). Part-time and evening/weekend programs available. *Students:* 9 full-time (4 women), 24 part-time (10 women); includes 9 minority (8 Black or African American, non-Hispanic/Latino; 1 Hispanic/Latino), 1 international. Average age 36. 28 applicants, 79% accepted, 17 enrolled. *Degree requirements:* For master's, comprehensive exam (for some programs), thesis optional. *Entrance requirements:* For master's, ETS PPI, baccalaureate degree from accredited institution; minimum cumulative GPA of 2.75 or 3.0 in last 60 hours of undergraduate study; personal statement. Additional exam requirements/recommendations for international students: Required—TOEFL (minimum score 550 paper-based; 79 iBT), IELTS (minimum score 6). *Application deadline:* For fall admission, 7/1 for domestic and international students; for spring admission, 12/1 for domestic and international students. Applications are processed on a rolling basis. Application fee: $25 ($50 for international students). Electronic applications accepted. *Expenses:* Tuition, state resident: full-time $4968; part-time $3312 per year. Tuition, nonresident: full-time $9936; part-time $6624 per year. *Required fees:* $970; $60.33 per credit. $362 per semester. *Financial support:* Applicants required to submit FAFSA. *Unit head:* Dr. Craig T. Robertson, Director, 256-765-5003, E-mail: ctrobertson@una.edu. *Application contact:* Russ Durracott, Graduate Admissions Counselor, 256-765-4447, E-mail: erdarracott@una.edu.
Website: http://www.una.edu/masters-professional-studies/index.html.

The University of North Carolina at Chapel Hill, Kenan-Flagler Business School, Doctoral Program in Business Administration, Chapel Hill, NC 27599. Offers accounting (PhD); finance (PhD); marketing (PhD); operations management (PhD); organizational behavior (PhD); strategy (PhD). *Accreditation:* AACSB. *Degree requirements:* For doctorate, thesis/dissertation. *Entrance requirements:* For doctorate, GMAT or GRE General Test. Electronic applications accepted. *Expenses:* Contact institution.

The University of North Carolina at Charlotte, The Graduate School, College of Computing and Informatics, Department of Software and Information Systems, Charlotte, NC 28223-0001. Offers computing and information systems (PhD); information security/privacy (Graduate Certificate); information technology (MS, Graduate Certificate); management of information technology (Graduate Certificate). Part-time and evening/weekend programs available. *Faculty:* 19 full-time (6 women), 6 part-time/adjunct (0 women). *Students:* 107 full-time (28 women), 66 part-time (22 women); includes 25 minority (15 Black or African American, non-Hispanic/Latino; 5 Asian, non-Hispanic/Latino; 3 Hispanic/Latino; 2 Two or more races, non-Hispanic/Latino), 88 international. Average age 30. 219 applicants, 49% accepted, 48 enrolled. In 2013, 39 master's, 21 doctorates, 35 other advanced degrees awarded. Terminal master's awarded for partial completion of doctoral program. *Degree requirements:* For master's, thesis or alternative, practica; for doctorate, comprehensive exam, thesis/dissertation. *Entrance requirements:* For master's, GRE or GMAT, minimum undergraduate GPA of 2.8 overall, 2.0 in last 2 years; for doctorate, GRE or GMAT, working knowledge of 2 high-level programming languages, letters of recommendation. Additional exam requirements/recommendations for international students: Required—TOEFL (minimum score 557 paper-based; 83 iBT). *Application deadline:* For fall admission, 5/1 for domestic and international students; for spring admission, 10/1 for domestic and international students. Applications are processed on a rolling basis. Application fee: $75. Electronic applications accepted. *Expenses:* Tuition, state resident: full-time $3522. Tuition, nonresident: full-time $16,051. *Required fees:* $2585. Tuition and fees vary according to course load and program. *Financial support:* In 2013–14, 33 students received support, including 1 fellowship (averaging $50,000 per year), 17 research assistantships (averaging $10,320 per year), 15 teaching assistantships (averaging $11,506 per year); career-related internships or fieldwork, institutionally sponsored loans, scholarships/grants, and unspecified assistantships also available. Support available to part-time students. Financial award application deadline: 4/1; financial award applicants required to submit FAFSA. *Faculty research:* Information security, information privacy, information assurance, cryptography, software engineering, enterprise integration, intelligent information systems, human-computer interaction. *Total annual research expenditures:* $1.9 million. *Unit head:* Dr. Mary Lou Maher, Chair, 704-687-1940, E-mail: mmaher9@uncc.edu. *Application contact:* Kathy B. Giddings, Director of Graduate Admissions, 704-687-5503, Fax: 704-687-1668, E-mail: gradadm@uncc.edu.
Website: http://sis.uncc.edu/.

The University of North Carolina at Greensboro, Graduate School, Bryan School of Business and Economics, Department of Information Systems and Operations Management, Greensboro, NC 27412-5001. Offers information systems (PhD); information technology (Certificate); information technology and management (MS); supply chain management (Certificate). *Entrance requirements:* For master's, GMAT, GRE General Test. Additional exam requirements/recommendations for international students: Required—TOEFL. Electronic applications accepted.

University of North Florida, College of Computing, Engineering, and Construction, School of Computing, Jacksonville, FL 32224. Offers computer science (MS); information systems (MS); software engineering (MS). Part-time programs available. *Faculty:* 12 full-time (2 women). *Students:* 17 full-time (4 women), 51 part-time (16 women); includes 18 minority (6 Black or African American, non-Hispanic/Latino; 8 Asian, non-Hispanic/Latino; 3 Hispanic/Latino; 1 Two or more races, non-Hispanic/Latino), 15 international. Average age 31. 74 applicants, 53% accepted, 22 enrolled. In 2013, 4 master's awarded. *Degree requirements:* For master's, thesis. *Entrance requirements:* For master's, GRE General Test, minimum GPA of 3.0 in last 60 hours of course work. Additional exam requirements/recommendations for international students: Required—TOEFL (minimum score 500 paper-based; 61 iBT). *Application deadline:* For fall admission, 7/1 for domestic students, 5/1 for international students; for spring admission, 11/1 for domestic students, 10/1 for international students. Application fee: $30. Electronic applications accepted. *Expenses:* Tuition, state resident: full-time $9794; part-time $408.10 per credit hour. Tuition, nonresident: full-time $22,383; part-time $932.61 per credit hour. *Required fees:* $2020; $84.20 per credit hour. Tuition and fees vary according to course load and program. *Financial support:* In 2013–14, 7 students received support. Research assistantships, teaching assistantships, Federal Work-Study, scholarships/grants, and unspecified assistantships available. Financial award application deadline: 4/1; financial award applicants required to submit FAFSA. *Total annual research expenditures:* $76,471. *Unit head:* Dr. Asai Asaithambi, Dean, 904-620-2985, E-mail: asai.asaithambi@unf.edu. *Application contact:* Dr. Amanda Pascale, Director, The Graduate School, 904-620-1360, Fax: 904-620-1362, E-mail: graduateschool@unf.edu.
Website: http://www.unf.edu/ccec/computing/.

University of North Texas, Robert B. Toulouse School of Graduate Studies, Denton, TN 76203-5017. Offers accounting (MS, PhD); applied anthropology (MA, MS); applied behavior analysis (Certificate); applied technology and performance improvement (M Ed, MS, PhD); art education (MA, PhD); art history (MA); art museum education (Certificate); arts leadership (Certificate); audiology (Au D); behavior analysis (MS); biochemistry and molecular biology (MS, PhD); biology (MA, MS, PhD); business (PhD); business computer information systems (PhD); chemistry (MS, PhD); clinical psychology (PhD); communication studies (MA, MS); computer engineering (MS); computer science (MS); computer science and engineering (PhD); counseling (M Ed, MS, PhD), including clinical mental health counseling (MS), college and university counseling (M Ed, MS), elementary school counseling (M Ed, MS), secondary school counseling (M Ed, MS); counseling psychology (PhD); creative writing (MA); criminal justice (MS); curriculum and instruction (M Ed, PhD), including curriculum studies (PhD), early childhood studies (PhD), language and literacy studies (PhD); decision sciences (MBA); design (MA, MFA), including fashion design (MFA), innovation studies, interior design (MFA); early childhood studies (MS); economics (MS); educational leadership (M Ed, Ed D, PhD); educational psychology (MS), including family studies, gifted and talented (MS, PhD), human development, learning and cognition, research, measurement and evaluation; educational research (PhD), including gifted and talented (MS, PhD), human development and family studies, psychological aspects of sports and exercise, research, measurement and statistics; electrical engineering (MS); emergency management (MPA); engineering systems (MS); English (MA, PhD); environmental science (MS, PhD); experimental psychology (PhD); finance (MBA, MS, PhD); financial management (MPA); French (MA); health psychology and behavioral medicine (PhD); health services management (MBA); higher education (M Ed, Ed D, PhD); history (MA, MS, PhD), including European history (PhD), military history (PhD), United States history (PhD); hospitality management (MS); human resources management (MPA); information science (MS, PhD); information technologies (MBA); information technology and decision sciences (MS); interdisciplinary studies (MA, MS); international sustainable tourism (MS); jazz studies (MM); journalism (MA, MJ, Graduate Certificate), including

interactive and virtual digital communication (Graduate Certificate), narrative journalism (Graduate Certificate), public relations (Graduate Certificate); kinesiology (MS); learning technologies (MS, PhD); library science (MS); local government management (MPA); logistics and supply chain management (MBA, PhD); long-term care, senior housing, and aging services (MA, MS); management science (PhD); marketing (MBA, PhD); materials science and engineering (MS, PhD); mathematics (MA, PhD); merchandising (MS); music (MA, MM Ed, PhD), including ethnomusicology (MA), music education (MM Ed, PhD), music theory (MA, PhD), musicology (MA, PhD), performance (MA); nonprofit management (MPA); operations and supply chain management (MBA); performance (MM, DMA); philosophy (MA, PhD); physics (MS, PhD); political science (MA, MS, PhD); public administration and management (PhD), including emergency management, nonprofit management, public financial management, urban management; radio, television and film (MA, MFA); recreation, event and sport management (MS); rehabilitation counseling (MS, Certificate); sociology (MA, MS, PhD); Spanish (MA); special education (M Ed, PhD), including autism intervention (PhD), emotional/behavioral disorders (PhD), mild/moderate disabilities (PhD); speech-language pathology (MA, MS); strategic management (MBA); studio art (MFA); taxation (MS); teaching (M Ed); MBA/MS; MS/MPH; MSES/MBA. Part-time and evening/weekend programs available. Postbaccalaureate distance learning degree programs offered. *Faculty:* 661 full-time (213 women), 240 part-time/adjunct (144 women). *Students:* 3,106 full-time (1,620 women), 3,543 part-time (2,221 women); includes 1,740 minority (533 Black or African American, non-Hispanic/Latino; 15 American Indian or Alaska Native, non-Hispanic/Latino; 286 Asian, non-Hispanic/Latino; 746 Hispanic/Latino; 3 Native Hawaiian or other Pacific Islander, non-Hispanic/Latino; 157 Two or more races, non-Hispanic/Latino), 1,145 international. Average age 32. 6,289 applicants, 43% accepted, 1751 enrolled. In 2013, 1,778 master's, 239 doctorates, 10 other advanced degrees awarded. Terminal master's awarded for partial completion of doctoral program. *Degree requirements:* For master's, variable foreign language requirement, comprehensive exam (for some programs), thesis (for some programs); for doctorate, variable foreign language requirement, comprehensive exam (for some programs), thesis/dissertation; for other advanced degree, variable foreign language requirement, comprehensive exam (for some programs). *Entrance requirements:* For master's and doctorate, GRE, GMAT. Additional exam requirements/recommendations for international students: Required—TOEFL (minimum score 550 paper-based; 79 iBT). *Application deadline:* For fall admission, 7/15 for domestic students, 3/15 for international students; for spring admission, 11/15 for domestic students, 9/15 for international students; for summer admission, 5/1 for domestic students. Applications are processed on a rolling basis. Application fee: $60. Electronic applications accepted. *Financial support:* Fellowships with partial tuition reimbursements, research assistantships with partial tuition reimbursements, teaching assistantships, career-related internships or fieldwork, Federal Work-Study, institutionally sponsored loans, scholarships/grants, health care benefits, and library assistantships available. Support available to part-time students. Financial award applicants required to submit FAFSA. *Unit head:* Mark Wardell, Dean, 940-565-2383, E-mail: mark.wardell@unt.edu. *Application contact:* Toulouse School of Graduate Studies, 940-565-2383, Fax: 940-565-2141, E-mail: gradsch@unt.edu.
Website: http://tsgs.unt.edu/.

University of Oklahoma, Michael F. Price College of Business, Division of Management Information Systems, Norman, OK 73019. Offers MS, PhD, Graduate Certificate. Part-time programs available. *Faculty:* 11 full-time (5 women), 1 part-time/adjunct (0 women). *Students:* 12 full-time (4 women), 16 part-time (2 women); includes 4 minority (2 Asian, non-Hispanic/Latino; 1 Hispanic/Latino; 1 Two or more races, non-Hispanic/Latino), 4 international. Average age 30. 20 applicants, 30% accepted, 5 enrolled. In 2013, 7 master's, 5 other advanced degrees awarded. Terminal master's awarded for partial completion of doctoral program. *Degree requirements:* For master's, comprehensive exam; for doctorate, comprehensive exam, thesis/dissertation. *Entrance requirements:* For master's and doctorate, GMAT. Additional exam requirements/recommendations for international students: Required—TOEFL (minimum score 100 iBT). *Application deadline:* For fall admission, 3/15 for domestic students, 3/1 for international students; for spring admission, 11/1 for domestic students, 9/1 for international students. Application fee: $50 ($100 for international students). Electronic applications accepted. *Expenses:* Tuition, state resident: full-time $4205; part-time $175.20 per credit hour. Tuition, nonresident: full-time $16,205; part-time $675.20 per credit hour. *Required fees:* $2745; $103.85 per credit hour. $126.50 per semester. *Financial support:* In 2013–14, 15 students received support, including 6 research assistantships with full tuition reimbursements available (averaging $11,148 per year), 6 teaching assistantships with full tuition reimbursements available (averaging $14,834 per year); career-related internships or fieldwork, scholarships/grants, health care benefits, and unspecified assistantships also available. Support available to part-time students. Financial award application deadline: 6/1; financial award applicants required to submit FAFSA. *Faculty research:* Human-computer interaction and cognition, "gamification" in employee learning and training, detection in IT-mediated contexts, computer-mediated collaboration and communication, meaning in discourse about IT and discourse through IT. *Total annual research expenditures:* $653,548. *Unit head:* Laku Chidambaram, Director, 405-325-8013, E-mail: laku@ou.edu. *Application contact:* Callen Brehm, Academic Counselor, 405-325-2074, Fax: 405-325-7753, E-mail: cbrehm@ou.edu.
Website: http://price.ou.edu/mis.

See Display on page 159 and Close-Up on page 193.

University of Oregon, Graduate School, Interdisciplinary Program in Applied Information Management, Eugene, OR 97403. Offers MS. Part-time programs available. Postbaccalaureate distance learning degree programs offered (no on-campus study). *Degree requirements:* For master's, project. *Entrance requirements:* Additional exam requirements/recommendations for international students: Required—TOEFL. Electronic applications accepted. *Expenses:* Contact institution. *Faculty research:* Business management, information design.

University of Pennsylvania, Wharton School, Operations and Information Management Department, Philadelphia, PA 19104. Offers MBA, PhD. Terminal master's awarded for partial completion of doctoral program. *Degree requirements:* For master's, thesis, preliminary exams; for doctorate, thesis/dissertation, preliminary exams. *Entrance requirements:* For master's, GMAT, GRE; for doctorate, GRE. Electronic applications accepted. *Faculty research:* Supply chain management, operations research, economics of information systems, risk analysis, electronic commerce.

University of Phoenix–Atlanta Campus, College of Information Systems and Technology, Sandy Springs, GA 30350-4153. Offers information systems (MIS); technology management (MBA). Evening/weekend programs available. *Degree requirements:* For master's, thesis (for some programs). *Entrance requirements:* For master's, 3 years of work experience, minimum undergraduate GPA of 3.0. Additional exam requirements/recommendations for international students: Required—TOEFL (minimum score 550 paper-based; 79 iBT). Electronic applications accepted.

University of Phoenix–Augusta Campus, College of Information Systems and Technology, Augusta, GA 30909-4583. Offers information systems (MIS); technology management (MBA).

University of Phoenix–Austin Campus, College of Information Systems and Technology, Austin, TX 78759. Offers information systems (MIS); technology management (MBA).

University of Phoenix–Bay Area Campus, College of Information Systems and Technology, San Jose, CA 95134-1805. Offers information systems (MIS); organizational leadership/information systems and technology (DM). Evening/weekend programs available. *Degree requirements:* For master's, thesis (for some programs). *Entrance requirements:* For master's, minimum undergraduate GPA of 3.0, 3 years of work experience. Additional exam requirements/recommendations for international students: Required—TOEFL (minimum score 550 paper-based; 79 iBT). Electronic applications accepted.

University of Phoenix–Birmingham Campus, College of Information Systems and Technology, Birmingham, AL 35242. Offers information systems (MIS); technology management (MBA).

University of Phoenix–Boston Campus, College of Information Systems and Technology, Braintree, MA 02184. Offers technology management (MBA). Evening/weekend programs available. *Degree requirements:* For master's, thesis (for some programs). *Entrance requirements:* For master's, minimum GPA of 3.0, 3 years of work experience. Additional exam requirements/recommendations for international students: Required—TOEFL (minimum score 550 paper-based; 79 iBT). Electronic applications accepted.

University of Phoenix–Central Valley Campus, College of Information Systems and Technology, Fresno, CA 93720-1562. Offers information systems (MIS); technology management (MBA).

University of Phoenix–Charlotte Campus, College of Information Systems and Technology, Charlotte, NC 28273-3409. Offers information systems (MIS); information systems management (MISM); technology management (MBA). Evening/weekend programs available. *Degree requirements:* For master's, thesis (for some programs). *Entrance requirements:* For master's, minimum undergraduate GPA of 3.0, 3 years work experience. Additional exam requirements/recommendations for international students: Required—TOEFL (minimum score 550 paper-based; 79 iBT). Electronic applications accepted.

University of Phoenix–Chattanooga Campus, College of Information Systems and Technology, Chattanooga, TN 37421-3707. Offers information systems (MIS); technology management (MBA). Postbaccalaureate distance learning degree programs offered.

University of Phoenix–Cheyenne Campus, College of Information Systems and Technology, Cheyenne, WY 82009. Offers information systems (MIS); technology management (MBA).

University of Phoenix–Chicago Campus, College of Information Systems and Technology, Schaumburg, IL 60173-4399. Offers e-business (MBA); information systems (MIS); management (MM); technology management (MBA). Evening/weekend programs available. *Degree requirements:* For master's, thesis (for some programs). *Entrance requirements:* For master's, 3 years of work experience, minimum undergraduate GPA of 3.0. Additional exam requirements/recommendations for international students: Required—TOEFL (minimum score 550 paper-based; 79 iBT). Electronic applications accepted.

University of Phoenix–Cincinnati Campus, College of Information Systems and Technology, West Chester, OH 45069-4875. Offers electronic business (MBA); information systems (MIS); technology management (MBA). Evening/weekend programs available. Postbaccalaureate distance learning degree programs offered. *Degree requirements:* For master's, thesis (for some programs). *Entrance requirements:* For master's, minimum undergraduate GPA of 2.5, 3 years of work experience. Additional exam requirements/recommendations for international students: Required—TOEFL (minimum score 550 paper-based; 79 iBT). Electronic applications accepted.

University of Phoenix–Cleveland Campus, College of Information Systems and Technology, Independence, OH 44131-2194. Offers information management (MIS); technology management (MBA). Evening/weekend programs available. Postbaccalaureate distance learning degree programs offered (no on-campus study). *Degree requirements:* For master's, thesis (for some programs). *Entrance requirements:* For master's, minimum undergraduate GPA of 3.0, 3 years of work experience. Additional exam requirements/recommendations for international students: Required—TOEFL (minimum score 550 paper-based; 79 iBT). Electronic applications accepted.

University of Phoenix–Columbus Georgia Campus, College of Information Systems and Technology, Columbus, GA 31909. Offers e-business (MBA); information systems (MIS); technology management (MBA). Evening/weekend programs available. Postbaccalaureate distance learning degree programs offered. *Degree requirements:* For master's, thesis (for some programs). *Entrance requirements:* For master's, minimum undergraduate GPA of 3.0, 3 years of work experience. Additional exam requirements/recommendations for international students: Required—TOEFL (minimum score 550 paper-based; 79 iBT). Electronic applications accepted.

University of Phoenix–Columbus Ohio Campus, College of Information Systems and Technology, Columbus, OH 43240-4032. Offers information systems (MIS); technology management (MBA). Postbaccalaureate distance learning degree programs offered.

University of Phoenix–Dallas Campus, College of Information Systems and Technology, Dallas, TX 75251. Offers e-business (MBA); information systems (MIS); technology management (MBA). Evening/weekend programs available. *Degree requirements:* For master's, thesis (for some programs). *Entrance requirements:* For master's, minimum undergraduate GPA of 3.0, 3 years of work experience. Additional exam requirements/recommendations for international students: Required—TOEFL (minimum score 550 paper-based; 79 iBT). Electronic applications accepted.

University of Phoenix–Denver Campus, College of Information Systems and Technology, Lone Tree, CO 80124-5453. Offers e-business (MBA); management (MIS); technology management (MBA). Evening/weekend programs available. Postbaccalaureate distance learning degree programs offered. *Degree requirements:* For master's, thesis (for some programs). *Entrance requirements:* For master's, minimum undergraduate GPA of 3.0, 3 years of work experience. Additional exam requirements/recommendations for international students: Required—TOEFL (minimum score 550 paper-based; 79 iBT). Electronic applications accepted.

University of Phoenix–Des Moines Campus, College of Information Systems and Technology, Des Moines, IA 50309. Offers information systems (MIS); technology management (MBA). Postbaccalaureate distance learning degree programs offered.

University of Phoenix–Eastern Washington Campus, College of Information Systems and Technology, Spokane, WA 99212-2531. Offers technology management (MBA).

University of Phoenix–Hawaii Campus, College of Information Systems and Technology, Honolulu, HI 96813-4317. Offers information systems (MIS); technology management (MBA). Evening/weekend programs available. *Degree requirements:* For master's, thesis (for some programs). *Entrance requirements:* For master's, minimum undergraduate GPA of 3.0, 3 years of work experience. Additional exam requirements/

recommendations for international students: Required—TOEFL (minimum score 550 paper-based; 79 iBT). Electronic applications accepted.

University of Phoenix–Houston Campus, College of Information Systems and Technology, Houston, TX 77079-2004. Offers e-business (MBA); information systems (MIS); technology management (MBA). Evening/weekend programs available. Postbaccalaureate distance learning degree programs offered. *Degree requirements:* For master's, comprehensive exam (for some programs), thesis. *Entrance requirements:* For master's, minimum undergraduate GPA of 3.0, 3 years of work experience. Additional exam requirements/recommendations for international students: Required—TOEFL (minimum score 550 paper-based; 79 iBT). Electronic applications accepted.

University of Phoenix–Idaho Campus, College of Information Systems and Technology, Meridian, ID 83642-5114. Offers information systems (MIS); technology management (MBA). Evening/weekend programs available. *Degree requirements:* For master's, thesis (for some programs). *Entrance requirements:* For master's, minimum undergraduate GPA of 3.0, 3 years of work experience. Additional exam requirements/recommendations for international students: Required—TOEFL (minimum score 550 paper-based). Electronic applications accepted.

University of Phoenix–Indianapolis Campus, College of Information Systems and Technology, Indianapolis, IN 46250-932. Offers information systems (MIS); technology management (MBA). Evening/weekend programs available. *Degree requirements:* For master's, thesis (for some programs). *Entrance requirements:* For master's, minimum undergraduate GPA of 3.0, 3 years of work experience. Additional exam requirements/recommendations for international students: Required—TOEFL (minimum score 550 paper-based). Electronic applications accepted.

University of Phoenix–Jersey City Campus, College of Information Systems and Technology, Jersey City, NJ 07310. Offers information systems (MIS); technology management (MBA). Postbaccalaureate distance learning degree programs offered.

University of Phoenix–Las Vegas Campus, College of Information Systems and Technology, Las Vegas, NV 89135. Offers information systems (MIS); technology management (MBA). Evening/weekend programs available. *Degree requirements:* For master's, thesis (for some programs). *Entrance requirements:* For master's, minimum undergraduate GPA of 3.0, 3 years of work experience. Additional exam requirements/recommendations for international students: Required—TOEFL (minimum score 550 paper-based; 79 iBT). Electronic applications accepted.

University of Phoenix–Louisiana Campus, College of Information Systems and Technology, Metairie, LA 70001-2082. Offers information systems/management (MIS); technology management (MBA). Evening/weekend programs available. *Degree requirements:* For master's, thesis (for some programs). *Entrance requirements:* For master's, minimum undergraduate GPA of 3.0, 3 years work experience. Additional exam requirements/recommendations for international students: Required—TOEFL (minimum score 550 paper-based). Electronic applications accepted.

University of Phoenix–Madison Campus, College of Information Systems and Technology, Madison, WI 53718-2416. Offers information systems (MIS); management (MIS); technology management (MBA).

University of Phoenix–Memphis Campus, College of Information Systems and Technology, Cordova, TN 38018. Offers information systems (MIS); technology management (MBA).

University of Phoenix–Milwaukee Campus, School of Business, Milwaukee, WI 53224. Offers accounting (MBA); business administration (MBA); energy management (MBA); global management (MBA); health care management (MBA); human resource management (MBA); management (MM); marketing (MBA); project management (MBA); technology management (MBA). Evening/weekend programs available. Postbaccalaureate distance learning degree programs offered. *Entrance requirements:* Additional exam requirements/recommendations for international students: Required—TOEFL, TOEIC (Test of English as an International Communication), Berlitz Online English Proficiency Exam, PTE, or IELTS. Electronic applications accepted. *Expenses:* Contact institution.

University of Phoenix–Nashville Campus, College of Information Systems and Technology, Nashville, TN 37214-5048. Offers technology management (MBA). Evening/weekend programs available. *Degree requirements:* For master's, thesis (for some programs). *Entrance requirements:* For master's, 3 years of work experience, minimum undergraduate GPA of 3.0. Additional exam requirements/recommendations for international students: Required—TOEFL (minimum score 550 paper-based; 79 iBT). Electronic applications accepted.

University of Phoenix–New Mexico Campus, College of Information Systems and Technology, Albuquerque, NM 87113-1570. Offers e-business (MBA); information systems (MS); technology management (MBA). Evening/weekend programs available. *Degree requirements:* For master's, thesis (for some programs). *Entrance requirements:* For master's, minimum undergraduate GPA of 3.0, 3 years of work experience. Additional exam requirements/recommendations for international students: Required—TOEFL (minimum score 550 paper-based; 79 iBT). Electronic applications accepted.

University of Phoenix–North Florida Campus, College of Information Systems and Technology, Jacksonville, FL 32216-0959. Offers information systems (MIS); management (MIS). Evening/weekend programs available. *Degree requirements:* For master's, thesis (for some programs). *Entrance requirements:* For master's, minimum undergraduate GPA of 3.0, 3 years work experience. Additional exam requirements/recommendations for international students: Required—TOEFL (minimum score 550 paper-based; 79 iBT). Electronic applications accepted.

University of Phoenix–Northwest Arkansas Campus, College of Information Systems and Technology, Rogers, AR 72756-9615. Offers information systems (MIS); technology management (MBA).

University of Phoenix–Oklahoma City Campus, College of Information Systems and Technology, Oklahoma City, OK 73116-8244. Offers e-business (MBA); technology management (MBA). Evening/weekend programs available. *Degree requirements:* For master's, thesis (for some programs). *Entrance requirements:* For master's, minimum undergraduate GPA of 3.0, 3 years of work experience. Additional exam requirements/recommendations for international students: Required—TOEFL (minimum score 550 paper-based; 79 iBT). Electronic applications accepted.

University of Phoenix–Omaha Campus, College of Information Systems and Technology, Omaha, NE 68154-5240. Offers information systems (MIS); technology management (MBA).

University of Phoenix–Online Campus, College of Information Systems and Technology, Phoenix, AZ 85034-7209. Offers MIS. Evening/weekend programs available. Postbaccalaureate distance learning degree programs offered. *Entrance requirements:* Additional exam requirements/recommendations for international students: Required—TOEFL, TOEIC (Test of English as an International Communication), Berlitz Online English Proficiency Exam, PTE, or IELTS. Electronic applications accepted. *Expenses:* Contact institution.

University of Phoenix–Oregon Campus, College of Information Systems and Technology, Tigard, OR 97223. Offers information systems (MIS); technology management (MBA). Evening/weekend programs available. *Degree requirements:* For master's, thesis (for some programs). *Entrance requirements:* For master's, minimum undergraduate GPA of 2.5, 3 years work experience. Additional exam requirements/recommendations for international students: Required—TOEFL (minimum score 550 paper-based; 79 iBT). Electronic applications accepted.

University of Phoenix–Philadelphia Campus, College of Information Systems and Technology, Wayne, PA 19087-2121. Offers information systems (MIS); technology management (MBA). Evening/weekend programs available. *Degree requirements:* For master's, thesis (for some programs). *Entrance requirements:* For master's, 3 years of work experience, minimum undergraduate GPA of 3.0. Additional exam requirements/recommendations for international students: Required—TOEFL (minimum score 550 paper-based; 79 iBT). Electronic applications accepted.

University of Phoenix–Pittsburgh Campus, College of Information Systems and Technology, Pittsburgh, PA 15276. Offers e-business (MBA); information systems (MIS); technology management (MBA). Evening/weekend programs available. *Degree requirements:* For master's, thesis (for some programs). *Entrance requirements:* For master's, minimum undergraduate GPA of 3.0, 3 years work experience. Additional exam requirements/recommendations for international students: Required—TOEFL (minimum score 550 paper-based; 79 iBT). Electronic applications accepted.

University of Phoenix–Richmond-Virginia Beach Campus, College of Information Systems and Technology, Glen Allen, VA 23060. Offers information systems (MIS); technology management (MBA). Evening/weekend programs available. *Degree requirements:* For master's, thesis (for some programs). *Entrance requirements:* For master's, minimum undergraduate GPA of 3.0, 3 years work experience. Additional exam requirements/recommendations for international students: Required—TOEFL (minimum score 500 paper-based; 79 iBT). Electronic applications accepted.

University of Phoenix–Sacramento Valley Campus, College of Information Systems and Technology, Sacramento, CA 95833-3632. Offers management (MIS); technology management (MBA). Evening/weekend programs available. *Degree requirements:* For master's, thesis (for some programs). *Entrance requirements:* For master's, minimum undergraduate GPA of 3.0, 3 years work experience. Additional exam requirements/recommendations for international students: Required—TOEFL (minimum score 550 paper-based; 79 iBT). Electronic applications accepted.

University of Phoenix–St. Louis Campus, College of Information Systems and Technology, St. Louis, MO 63043. Offers information systems (MIS); technology management (MBA). Evening/weekend programs available. *Degree requirements:* For master's, thesis (for some programs). *Entrance requirements:* For master's, minimum undergraduate GPA of 3.0, 3 years of work experience. Additional exam requirements/recommendations for international students: Required—TOEFL (minimum score 550 paper-based). Electronic applications accepted.

University of Phoenix–San Antonio Campus, College of Information Systems and Technology, San Antonio, TX 78230. Offers information systems (MIS); technology management (MBA).

University of Phoenix–San Diego Campus, College of Information Systems and Technology, San Diego, CA 92123. Offers management (MIS); technology management (MBA). Evening/weekend programs available. *Degree requirements:* For master's, thesis (for some programs). *Entrance requirements:* For master's, minimum undergraduate GPA of 3.0, 3 years work experience. Additional exam requirements/recommendations for international students: Required—TOEFL (minimum score 550 paper-based; 79 iBT). Electronic applications accepted.

University of Phoenix–Savannah Campus, College of Information Systems and Technology, Savannah, GA 31405-7400. Offers information systems and technology (MIS); technology management (MBA).

University of Phoenix–Southern Arizona Campus, College of Information Systems and Technology, Tucson, AZ 85711. Offers information systems (MIS); technology management (MBA). Evening/weekend programs available. *Degree requirements:* For master's, thesis (for some programs). *Entrance requirements:* For master's, minimum undergraduate GPA of 3.0, 3 years of work experience. Additional exam requirements/recommendations for international students: Required—TOEFL (minimum score 550 paper-based; 79 iBT). Electronic applications accepted.

University of Phoenix–Southern Colorado Campus, College of Information Systems and Technology, Colorado Springs, CO 80903. Offers technology management (MBA). Evening/weekend programs available. *Degree requirements:* For master's, thesis (for some programs). *Entrance requirements:* For master's, minimum undergraduate GPA of 3.0, 3 years of work experience. Additional exam requirements/recommendations for international students: Required—TOEFL (minimum score 550 paper-based; 79 iBT). Electronic applications accepted.

University of Phoenix–South Florida Campus, College of Information Systems and Technology, Miramar, FL 33030. Offers management (MIS); technology management (MBA). Evening/weekend programs available. *Degree requirements:* For master's, thesis (for some programs). *Entrance requirements:* For master's, minimum undergraduate GPA of 3.0, 3 years of work experience. Additional exam requirements/recommendations for international students: Required—TOEFL (minimum score 550 paper-based; 79 iBT). Electronic applications accepted.

University of Phoenix–Springfield Campus, College of Information Systems and Technology, Springfield, MO 65804-7211. Offers information systems (MIS); technology management (MBA).

University of Phoenix–Tulsa Campus, College of Information Systems and Technology, Tulsa, OK 74134-1412. Offers information systems and technology (MIS); technology management (MBA).

University of Phoenix–Utah Campus, College of Information Systems and Technology, Salt Lake City, UT 84123-4617. Offers MIS. Evening/weekend programs available. *Degree requirements:* For master's, thesis (for some programs). *Entrance requirements:* For master's, minimum undergraduate GPA of 2.5, 3 years work experience. Additional exam requirements/recommendations for international students: Required—TOEFL (minimum score 550 paper-based; 79 iBT). Electronic applications accepted.

University of Phoenix–Washington D.C. Campus, College of Information Systems and Technology, Washington, DC 20001. Offers information systems (MIS); organizational leadership/information systems and technology (DM).

University of Phoenix–West Florida Campus, College of Information Systems and Technology, Temple Terrace, FL 33637. Offers information systems (MIS); technology management (MBA). Evening/weekend programs available. *Degree requirements:* For master's, thesis (for some programs). *Entrance requirements:* For master's, minimum undergraduate GPA of 3.0, 3 years work experience. Additional exam requirements/recommendations for international students: Required—TOEFL (minimum score 550 paper-based; 79 iBT). Electronic applications accepted.

University of Pittsburgh, Katz Graduate School of Business, Doctoral Program in Business Administration, Pittsburgh, PA 15260. Offers accounting (PhD); finance (PhD); information systems (PhD); marketing (PhD); operations/decision sciences/artificial

intelligence (PhD); organizational behavior and human resource management (PhD); strategic planning (PhD). *Accreditation:* AACSB. *Faculty:* 60 full-time (17 women). *Students:* 50 full-time (22 women); includes 4 minority (2 Black or African American, non-Hispanic/Latino; 2 Asian, non-Hispanic/Latino), 27 international. 321 applicants, 7% accepted, 14 enrolled. In 2013, 10 doctorates awarded. *Degree requirements:* For doctorate, comprehensive exam, thesis/dissertation. *Entrance requirements:* For doctorate, GMAT or GRE, 3 recommendations, statement of purpose, transcripts of all previous course work and degrees. Additional exam requirements/recommendations for international students: Required—TOEFL. *Application deadline:* For fall admission, 1/1 priority date for domestic and international students. Applications are processed on a rolling basis. Application fee: $50. Electronic applications accepted. *Expenses:* Tuition, state resident: full-time $19,964; part-time $807 per credit. Tuition, nonresident: full-time $32,686; part-time $1337 per credit. *Required fees:* $740; $200. Tuition and fees vary according to program. *Financial support:* In 2013–14, 40 students received support, including 30 research assistantships with full tuition reimbursements available (averaging $23,045 per year), 10 teaching assistantships with full tuition reimbursements available (averaging $26,055 per year); fellowships, Federal Work-Study, scholarships/grants, health care benefits, and unspecified assistantships also available. Financial award application deadline: 1/1. *Faculty research:* Accounting systems/financial reporting, corporate finance, shopper marketing/consumer behavior, management information systems, organizational behavior and entrepreneurship. *Unit head:* Dr. Dennis Galletta, Director, 412-648-1699, Fax: 412-624-3633, E-mail: galletta@katz.pitt.edu. *Application contact:* Carrie Woods, Assistant Director, 412-648-1525, Fax: 412-624-3633, E-mail: cawoods@katz.pitt.edu.
Website: http://www.business.pitt.edu/katz/phd/.

University of Pittsburgh, Katz Graduate School of Business, Master of Business Administration Programs, Pittsburgh, PA 15260. Offers finance (MBA); information systems (MBA); marketing (MBA); operations management (MBA); organizational behavior and human resource management (MBA); strategy, environment and organizations (MBA); MBA/JD; MBA/MIB; MBA/MPIA; MBA/MSE; MBA/MSIS; MID/MBA. *Accreditation:* AACSB. Part-time and evening/weekend programs available. *Faculty:* 60 full-time (14 women), 21 part-time/adjunct (5 women). *Students:* 107 full-time (31 women), 428 part-time (155 women); includes 55 minority (15 Black or African American, non-Hispanic/Latino; 26 Asian, non-Hispanic/Latino; 10 Hispanic/Latino; 4 Two or more races, non-Hispanic/Latino), 83 international. Average age 30. 449 applicants, 23% accepted, 63 enrolled. In 2013, 279 master's awarded. *Degree requirements:* For master's, minimum GPA of 3.0. *Entrance requirements:* For master's, GMAT, recommendations, undergraduate transcripts, essay, resume, interview, bachelor's degree. Additional exam requirements/recommendations for international students: Required—TOEFL (minimum score 600 paper-based; 100 iBT) or IELTS. *Application deadline:* For fall admission, 4/1 priority date for domestic students, 2/1 priority date for international students. Application fee: $50. Electronic applications accepted. *Expenses:* Tuition, state resident: full-time $19,964; part-time $807 per credit. Tuition, nonresident: full-time $32,686; part-time $1337 per credit. *Required fees:* $740; $200. Tuition and fees vary according to program. *Financial support:* In 2013–14, 60 students received support. Career-related internships or fieldwork and scholarships/grants available. Financial award application deadline: 2/1. *Faculty research:* Accounting systems/financial reporting, corporate finance, shopper marketing/consumer behavior, management information systems, organizational behavior and entrepreneurship. *Unit head:* Tim Robison, Assistant Dean, 412-648-1700, Fax: 412-648-1659, E-mail: trobison@katz.pitt.edu. *Application contact:* Thomas Keller, Director of MBA Admissions, 412-648-1700, Fax: 412-648-1659, E-mail: mba@katz.pitt.edu.
Website: http://www.business.pitt.edu/katz/mba/.

University of Pittsburgh, Katz Graduate School of Business, MBA/MS in Management of Information Systems Program, Pittsburgh, PA 15260. Offers MBA/MS. Part-time and evening/weekend programs available. *Faculty:* 61 full-time (15 women), 21 part-time/adjunct (5 women). *Students:* 4 full-time (0 women), 16 part-time (4 women); includes 4 minority (2 Black or African American, non-Hispanic/Latino; 2 Hispanic/Latino). Average age 30. 23 applicants, 35% accepted, 4 enrolled. *Entrance requirements:* Additional exam requirements/recommendations for international students: Required—TOEFL (minimum score 600 paper-based; 100 iBT) or IELTS. *Application deadline:* For fall admission, 4/1 priority date for domestic students, 2/1 priority date for international students. Application fee: $50. Electronic applications accepted. *Expenses:* Tuition, state resident: full-time $19,964; part-time $807 per credit. Tuition, nonresident: full-time $32,686; part-time $1337 per credit. *Required fees:* $740; $200. Tuition and fees vary according to program. *Financial support:* In 2013–14, 2 students received support. Career-related internships or fieldwork and scholarships/grants available. Financial award application deadline: 2/1; financial award applicants required to submit FAFSA. *Faculty research:* Accounting systems/financial reporting, corporate finance, shopper marketing/consumer behavior, management information systems, organizational behavior and entrepreneurship. *Unit head:* Tim Robison, Assistant Dean/Director of MBA Programs, 412-648-1700, Fax: 412-648-1659, E-mail: trobison@katz.pitt.edu. *Application contact:* Thomas Keller, Director, MBA Admissions, 412-648-1700, Fax: 412-648-1659, E-mail: mba@katz.pitt.edu.
Website: http://www.business.pitt.edu/katz/mba/academics/programs/mba-mis.php.

University of Redlands, School of Business, Redlands, CA 92373-0999. Offers business (MBA); information technology (MS); management (MA). Evening/weekend programs available. *Entrance requirements:* For master's, minimum GPA of 3.0, 2 letters of recommendation. *Faculty research:* Human resources management, educational leadership, humanities, teacher education.

University of Rochester, Simon Business School, Full-Time Master's Program in Business Administration, Rochester, NY 14627. Offers accounting and information systems (MBA); business environment and public policy (MBA); business systems consulting (MBA); competitive and organizational strategy - pricing (MBA); computers and information systems (MBA); corporate accounting (MBA); electronic commerce (MBA); entrepreneurship (MBA); finance (MBA); health sciences management (MBA); international management (MBA); marketing - brand management and pricing (MBA); operations management - manufacturing (MBA); operations management - services (MBA); public accounting (MBA). *Accreditation:* AACSB. Part-time and evening/weekend programs available. *Faculty:* 60 full-time (11 women), 23 part-time/adjunct (3 women). *Students:* 282 full-time (74 women); includes 55 minority (29 Black or African American, non-Hispanic/Latino; 1 American Indian or Alaska Native, non-Hispanic/Latino; 11 Asian, non-Hispanic/Latino; 12 Hispanic/Latino; 2 Two or more races, non-Hispanic/Latino), 144 international. 673 applicants, 33% accepted, 65 enrolled. In 2013, 176 master's awarded. *Entrance requirements:* For master's, GMAT/GRE, previous course work in calculus. Additional exam requirements/recommendations for international students: Required—TOEFL. *Application deadline:* For fall admission, 10/15 for domestic and international students; for winter admission, 1/5 for domestic and international students; for spring admission, 3/15 for domestic and international students; for summer admission, 5/15 for domestic students. Applications are processed on a rolling basis. Application fee: $150. Electronic applications accepted. *Expenses: Tuition:* Full-time $44,580; part-time $1394 per credit hour. *Required fees:* $492. *Financial support:* In 2013–14, 72 students received support. Fellowships, research assistantships, teaching assistantships, institutionally sponsored loans, scholarships/grants, and tuition waivers (partial) available. Financial award application deadline: 3/1; financial award applicants required to submit CSS PROFILE or FAFSA. *Unit head:* Mark Zupan, Dean, 585-275-3316. *Application contact:* Rebekah S. Lewin, Assistant Dean of Admissions and Student Engagement, 585-275-3533, E-mail: admissions@simon.rochester.edu.

University of Rochester, Simon Business School, Part-Time MBA Program, Rochester, NY 14627. Offers accounting and information systems (MBA); business environment and public policy (MBA); business systems consulting (MBA); competitive and organizational strategy (MBA); computers and information systems (MBA); corporate accounting (MBA); electronic commerce (MBA); entrepreneurship (MBA); finance (MBA); health sciences management (MBA); international management (MBA); manufacturing management (MBA); marketing (MBA); operations management - services (MBA); public accounting (MBA). Part-time and evening/weekend programs available. *Faculty:* 59 full-time (10 women), 23 part-time/adjunct (3 women). *Students:* 270 part-time (75 women); includes 38 minority (5 Black or African American, non-Hispanic/Latino; 1 American Indian or Alaska Native, non-Hispanic/Latino; 24 Asian, non-Hispanic/Latino; 5 Hispanic/Latino; 3 Two or more races, non-Hispanic/Latino). Average age 32. 56 applicants, 98% accepted, 51 enrolled. In 2013, 77 master's awarded. *Entrance requirements:* For master's, GRE or GMAT, resume, recommendation letters, essays, transcipts. *Application deadline:* For fall admission, 8/15 for domestic students; for winter admission, 11/15 for domestic students; for spring admission, 2/15 for domestic students; for summer admission, 5/15 for domestic students. Applications are processed on a rolling basis. Application fee: $150. Electronic applications accepted. *Expenses: Tuition:* Full-time $44,580; part-time $1394 per credit hour. *Required fees:* $492. *Financial support:* Scholarships/grants and tuition waivers available. Financial award applicants required to submit CSS PROFILE. *Unit head:* Mark Zupan, Dean, 585-275-3316, E-mail: mark.zupan@simon.rochester.edu. *Application contact:* Jennifer Mossotti, Associate Director of Part-Time Programs, 585-275-3803, E-mail: jennifer.mossotti@simon.rochester.edu.
Website: http://www.simon.rochester.edu/programs/part-time-mba-programs/index.aspx.

University of St. Thomas, Graduate Studies, Graduate Programs in Software, Saint Paul, MN 55105. Offers advanced studies in software engineering (Certificate); big data (Certificate); business analysis (Certificate); computer security (Certificate); information systems (Certificate); information technology (MS); software design and development (Certificate); software engineering (MS); software management (MS); software systems (MSS); MS/MBA. Part-time and evening/weekend programs available. *Faculty:* 6 full-time (0 women), 12 part-time/adjunct (1 woman). *Students:* 35 full-time (8 women), 371 part-time (104 women); includes 108 minority (53 Black or African American, non-Hispanic/Latino; 53 Asian, non-Hispanic/Latino; 2 Two or more races, non-Hispanic/Latino), 116 international. Average age 35. 151 applicants, 87% accepted, 74 enrolled. In 2013, 86 master's, 8 other advanced degrees awarded. *Degree requirements:* For master's, thesis optional. *Entrance requirements:* For master's, bachelor's degree earned in U.S. or equivalent international degree. Additional exam requirements/recommendations for international students: Required—TOEFL (minimum score 80 iBT). *Application deadline:* For fall admission, 8/1 priority date for domestic students, 5/1 priority date for international students; for spring admission, 1/1 priority date for domestic students, 10/1 priority date for international students. Applications are processed on a rolling basis. Application fee: $50. Electronic applications accepted. *Expenses:* Contact institution. *Financial support:* Federal Work-Study, institutionally sponsored loans, and scholarships/grants available. Financial award application deadline: 4/1. *Faculty research:* Data mining, distributed databases, computer security, big data. *Unit head:* Dr. Bhabani Misra, Director, 651-962-5508, Fax: 651-962-5543, E-mail: bsmisra@stthomas.edu. *Application contact:* Douglas J. Stubeda, Assistant Director, 651-962-5503, Fax: 651-962-5543, E-mail: djstubeda@stthomas.edu.
Website: http://www.stthomas.edu/software.

University of San Francisco, School of Management, Master of Science in Information Systems Program, San Francisco, CA 94105. Offers MS. Part-time and evening/weekend programs available. *Faculty:* 1 full-time (0 women), 4 part-time/adjunct (1 woman). *Students:* 47 full-time (14 women), 1 (woman) part-time; includes 31 minority (2 Black or African American, non-Hispanic/Latino; 1 American Indian or Alaska Native, non-Hispanic/Latino; 21 Asian, non-Hispanic/Latino; 4 Hispanic/Latino; 2 Native Hawaiian or other Pacific Islander, non-Hispanic/Latino; 1 Two or more races, non-Hispanic/Latino), 3 international. Average age 35. 37 applicants, 68% accepted, 14 enrolled. In 2013, 16 master's awarded. *Degree requirements:* For master's, thesis. *Entrance requirements:* For master's, resume demonstrating minimum of two years of professional work experience, transcripts from each college or university attended, two letters of recommendation, personal statement. Additional exam requirements/recommendations for international students: Required—TOEFL (minimum score 600 paper-based, 100 iBT), IELTS (minimum score 7) or PTE (minimum score 68). *Application deadline:* For fall admission, 6/15 for domestic students, 5/15 for international students. Application fee: $55. Electronic applications accepted. *Expenses: Tuition:* Full-time $21,150; part-time $1175 per unit. Tuition and fees vary according to course load, campus/location and program. *Financial support:* Scholarships/grants available. Financial award application deadline: 3/2; financial award applicants required to submit FAFSA. *Unit head:* Dr. Stephen Morris, Director, 415-422-2221, E-mail: management@usfca.edu. *Application contact:* Office of Graduate Recruiting and Admissions, 415-422-2221, Fax: 415-422-6315, E-mail: management@usfca.edu.
Website: http://www.usfca.edu/msis.

The University of Scranton, College of Graduate and Continuing Education, Program in Business Administration, Scranton, PA 18510. Offers accounting (MBA); finance (MBA); general business administration (MBA); health care management (MBA); international business (MBA); management information systems (MBA); marketing (MBA); operations management (MBA). *Accreditation:* AACSB. Part-time and evening/weekend programs available. Postbaccalaureate distance learning degree programs offered (no on-campus study). *Faculty:* 34 full-time (8 women). *Students:* 316 full-time (134 women), 241 part-time (94 women); includes 104 minority (43 Black or African American, non-Hispanic/Latino; 3 American Indian or Alaska Native, non-Hispanic/Latino; 29 Asian, non-Hispanic/Latino; 27 Hispanic/Latino; 2 Two or more races, non-Hispanic/Latino), 47 international. Average age 34. 249 applicants, 85% accepted. In 2013, 200 master's awarded. *Degree requirements:* For master's, capstone experience. *Entrance requirements:* For master's, GMAT, minimum GPA of 3.0. Additional exam requirements/recommendations for international students: Required—TOEFL (minimum score 500 paper-based), IELTS (minimum score 6). *Application deadline:* Applications are processed on a rolling basis. Application fee: $0. *Financial support:* In 2013–14, 13 students received support, including 13 teaching assistantships with full and partial tuition reimbursements available (averaging $8,800 per year); fellowships, career-related internships or fieldwork, Federal Work-Study, and unspecified assistantships also available. Support available to part-time students. Financial award application deadline: 3/1. *Faculty research:* Financial markets, strategic impact of total quality management, internal accounting controls, consumer preference, information systems and the Internet. *Unit head:* Dr. Murli Rajan, Director, 570-941-4043, Fax: 570-941-

4342. *Application contact:* Joseph M. Roback, Director of Admissions, 570-941-4385, Fax: 570-941-5928, E-mail: robackj2@scranton.edu.
Website: http://www.scranton.edu/academics/cgce/busad.shtml.

University of South Africa, College of Science, Engineering and Technology, Pretoria, South Africa. Offers chemical engineering (M Tech); information technology (M Tech).

University of South Alabama, Graduate School, School of Computer and Information Sciences, Mobile, AL 36688-0002. Offers computer science (MS); information systems (MS). Part-time and evening/weekend programs available. *Faculty:* 13 full-time (1 woman). *Students:* 85 full-time (23 women), 12 part-time (4 women); includes 13 minority (5 Black or African American, non-Hispanic/Latino; 5 Asian, non-Hispanic/Latino; 2 Hispanic/Latino; 1 Native Hawaiian or other Pacific Islander, non-Hispanic/Latino), 47 international. 209 applicants, 61% accepted, 38 enrolled. In 2013, 24 master's awarded. *Degree requirements:* For master's, thesis optional, project. *Entrance requirements:* For master's, GRE General Test. *Application deadline:* For fall admission, 7/15 priority date for domestic students, 6/15 priority date for international students; for spring admission, 12/1 for domestic students, 11/1 priority date for international students. Applications are processed on a rolling basis. Application fee: $35. *Expenses:* Tuition, state resident: full-time $8976; part-time $374 per credit hour. Tuition, nonresident: full-time $17,952; part-time $748 per credit hour. *Financial support:* Research assistantships, career-related internships or fieldwork, and institutionally sponsored loans available. Support available to part-time students. Financial award application deadline: 4/1. *Faculty research:* Numerical analysis, artificial intelligence, simulation, medical applications, software engineering. *Unit head:* Dr. Alec Yasinsac, Dean, 251-460-6390.
Website: http://www.cis.usouthal.edu.

University of Southern Mississippi, Graduate School, College of Business, School of Accountancy and Information Systems, Hattiesburg, MS 39406-0001. Offers accountancy (MPA). *Accreditation:* AACSB. Part-time and evening/weekend programs available. *Faculty:* 7 full-time (4 women), 2 part-time/adjunct (both women). *Students:* 14 full-time (8 women), 5 part-time (2 women); includes 2 minority (both Black or African American, non-Hispanic/Latino). Average age 30. 17 applicants, 94% accepted, 14 enrolled. In 2013, 20 master's awarded. *Degree requirements:* For master's, comprehensive exam. *Entrance requirements:* For master's, GMAT, minimum GPA of 2.75 on last 60 hours. Additional exam requirements/recommendations for international students: Required—TOEFL, IELTS. *Application deadline:* For fall admission, 7/15 priority date for domestic students, 7/15 for international students; for spring admission, 11/15 priority date for domestic students, 11/15 for international students. Applications are processed on a rolling basis. Application fee: $50. Electronic applications accepted. *Financial support:* In 2013–14, 7 research assistantships with full tuition reimbursements (averaging $7,200 per year) were awarded; Federal Work-Study, institutionally sponsored loans, scholarships/grants, health care benefits, and unspecified assistantships also available. Support available to part-time students. Financial award application deadline: 3/15; financial award applicants required to submit FAFSA. *Faculty research:* Bank liquidity, subchapter S corporations, internal auditing, governmental accounting, inflation accounting. *Unit head:* Dr. Skip Hughes, Director, 601-266-4322, Fax: 601-266-4639. *Application contact:* Dr. Michael Dugan, Director of Graduate Studies, 601-266-4641, Fax: 601-266-5814.
Website: http://www.usm.edu/graduateschool/table.php.

University of South Florida, College of Business, Department of Information Systems and Decision Sciences, Tampa, FL 33620-9951. Offers business administration (PhD), including information systems; management information systems (MS). Part-time programs available. *Faculty:* 15 full-time (2 women), 2 part-time/adjunct (0 women). *Students:* 98 full-time (23 women), 40 part-time (16 women); includes 23 minority (6 Black or African American, non-Hispanic/Latino; 1 American Indian or Alaska Native, non-Hispanic/Latino; 8 Asian, non-Hispanic/Latino; 7 Hispanic/Latino; 1 Native Hawaiian or other Pacific Islander, non-Hispanic/Latino), 78 international. Average age 29. 541 applicants, 51% accepted, 71 enrolled. In 2013, 46 master's awarded. Terminal master's awarded for partial completion of doctoral program. *Degree requirements:* For master's, thesis or practicum project; for doctorate, comprehensive exam, thesis/dissertation. *Entrance requirements:* For master's, GMAT or GRE, letters of recommendation, statement of purpose, relevant work experience; for doctorate, GMAT or GRE, letters of recommendation, personal statement, interview. Additional exam requirements/recommendations for international students: Required—TOEFL (minimum score 550 paper-based; 79 iBT) or IELTS (minimum score 6.5). *Application deadline:* For fall admission, 6/1 for domestic students, 1/2 for international students; for spring admission, 10/30 for domestic students, 6/1 for international students. Applications are processed on a rolling basis. Application fee: $30. Electronic applications accepted. *Financial support:* In 2013–14, 30 students received support, including 8 research assistantships with tuition reimbursements available (averaging $11,972 per year), 22 teaching assistantships with tuition reimbursements available (averaging $9,002 per year); scholarships/grants, health care benefits, and unspecified assistantships also available. Financial award applicants required to submit FAFSA. *Faculty research:* Data mining, business intelligence, bioterrorism surveillance, health informatics/informatics, software engineering, agent-based modeling, distributed systems, statistics, electronic markets, e-commerce, business process improvement, operations management, supply chain, LEAN management, global information systems, organizational impacts of IT, enterprise resource planning, business intelligence, Web and mobile technologies, social networks, information security. *Total annual research expenditures:* $139,660. *Unit head:* Dr. Kaushal Chari, Chair and Professor, 813-974-6768, Fax: 813-974-6749, E-mail: kchari@usf.edu. *Application contact:* Judy Oates, Office Assistant, 813-974-5524, Fax: 813-974-6749, E-mail: joates@usf.edu.
Website: http://business.usf.edu/departments/isds/.

University of South Florida, College of Engineering, Department of Industrial and Management Systems Engineering, Tampa, FL 33620-9951. Offers engineering management (MSEM); industrial engineering (MIE, MSIE, PhD); information technology (MSIT). Part-time programs available. Postbaccalaureate distance learning degree programs offered (minimal on-campus study). *Faculty:* 11 full-time (2 women), 5 part-time/adjunct (0 women). *Students:* 60 full-time (13 women), 85 part-time (22 women); includes 40 minority (9 Black or African American, non-Hispanic/Latino; 6 Asian, non-Hispanic/Latino; 23 Hispanic/Latino; 2 Two or more races, non-Hispanic/Latino), 52 international. Average age 31. 172 applicants, 47% accepted, 31 enrolled. In 2013, 44 master's, 3 doctorates awarded. Terminal master's awarded for partial completion of doctoral program. *Degree requirements:* For master's, comprehensive exam, thesis (for some programs); for doctorate, comprehensive exam, thesis/dissertation, 2 tools of research as specified by dissertation committee. *Entrance requirements:* For master's, GRE General Test, BS in engineering (or equivalent) with minimum GPA of 3.0 in last 60 hours of coursework, letter of recommendation, resume; for doctorate, GRE General Test, minimum GPA of 3.0 in last 60 hours of undergraduate/graduate coursework, three letters of recommendation, statement of purpose, strong background in scientific and engineering principles. Additional exam requirements/recommendations for international students: Required—TOEFL (minimum score 550 paper-based; 79 iBT) or IELTS (minimum score 6.5). *Application deadline:* For fall admission, 2/15 for domestic students, 1/2 for international students; for spring admission, 10/15 for domestic students, 6/1 for international students. Application fee: $30. Electronic applications accepted. *Financial support:* In 2013–14, 31 students received support, including 20 research assistantships with partial tuition reimbursements available (averaging $16,748 per year), 11 teaching assistantships with partial tuition reimbursements available (averaging $15,000 per year); tuition waivers (partial) also available. Financial award applicants required to submit FAFSA. *Faculty research:* Healthcare, healthcare systems, public health policies, energy and environment, manufacturing, logistics, transportation. *Total annual research expenditures:* $345,496. *Unit head:* Dr. Tapas K. Das, Professor/Chair, 813-974-5585, Fax: 813-974-5953, E-mail: das@usf.edu. *Application contact:* Dr. Alex Savachkin, Associate Professor/Graduate Director, 813-974-5577, Fax: 813-974-5953, E-mail: alexs@usf.edu.
Website: http://imse.eng.usf.edu.

University of South Florida, University College/Distance Education, Tampa, FL 33620-9951. *Unit head:* Kathy Barnes, Interdisciplinary Programs Coordinator, 813-974-8031, Fax: 813-974-7061, E-mail: barnesk@usf.edu. *Application contact:* Karen Tylinski, Metro Initiatives, 813-974-9943, Fax: 813-974-7061, E-mail: ktylinsk@usf.edu.
Website: http://uc.usf.edu/.

The University of Tampa, John H. Sykes College of Business, Tampa, FL 33606-1490. Offers accounting (MS); entrepreneurship (MBA); finance (MBA, MS); information systems management (MBA); innovation management (MBA); international business (MBA); marketing (MBA, MS); nonprofit management (MBA). *Accreditation:* AACSB. Part-time and evening/weekend programs available. *Faculty:* 41 full-time (15 women), 5 part-time/adjunct (1 woman). *Students:* 406 full-time (171 women), 152 part-time (61 women); includes 104 minority (18 Black or African American, non-Hispanic/Latino; 1 American Indian or Alaska Native, non-Hispanic/Latino; 20 Asian, non-Hispanic/Latino; 59 Hispanic/Latino; 6 Two or more races, non-Hispanic/Latino), 154 international. Average age 33. 1,341 applicants, 37% accepted, 256 enrolled. In 2013, 218 master's awarded. *Degree requirements:* For master's, capstone. *Entrance requirements:* For master's, GMAT or GRE, 4-year undergraduate degree, minimum GPA of 3.0, professional experience (for Executive MBA). Additional exam requirements/recommendations for international students: Required—TOEFL (minimum score 577 paper-based; 90 iBT); Recommended—IELTS (minimum score 7.5). *Application deadline:* Applications are processed on a rolling basis. Application fee: $40. Electronic applications accepted. *Expenses: Tuition:* Full-time $8928; part-time $558 per credit hour. *Required fees:* $80; $80 $40 per term. Tuition and fees vary according to program. *Financial support:* In 2013–14, 110 students received support. Career-related internships or fieldwork, scholarships/grants, and unspecified assistantships available. Financial award applicants required to submit FAFSA. *Faculty research:* Job market signaling, on-line shopping behaviors and social media, the Tampa Bay economy, digital literacy, entrepreneurship in small businesses. *Unit head:* Dr. Stephanie Thomason, Associate Dean, 813-253-6289, E-mail: sthomason@ut.edu. *Application contact:* Charlene Tobie, Associate Director of Admissions, 813-257-3566, E-mail: ctobie@ut.edu.
Website: http://www.ut.edu/business/.

The University of Texas at Arlington, Graduate School, College of Business, Department of Information Systems and Operations Management, Arlington, TX 76019. Offers information systems (MS, PhD). Part-time and evening/weekend programs available. *Degree requirements:* For master's, thesis optional; for doctorate, comprehensive exam, thesis/dissertation. *Entrance requirements:* For master's, GMAT, minimum GPA of 3.0; for doctorate, GMAT/GRE. Additional exam requirements/recommendations for international students: Required—TOEFL (minimum score 550 paper-based; 79 iBT). *Faculty research:* Database modeling, strategic issues in information systems, simulations, production operations management.

The University of Texas at Arlington, Graduate School, College of Business, Program in Business Administration, Arlington, TX 76019. Offers accounting (PhD); business statistics (PhD); finance (MBA, PhD); information systems (MBA, PhD); management (MBA, PhD); marketing (MBA, PhD); operations management (MBA, PhD); real estate (MBA). *Accreditation:* AACSB. Part-time and evening/weekend programs available. *Degree requirements:* For master's, thesis optional; for doctorate, comprehensive exam, thesis/dissertation. *Entrance requirements:* For master's, GMAT or GRE; for doctorate, GMAT, minimum GPA of 3.0 (undergraduate), 3.4 (graduate); 30 hours of graduate course work. Additional exam requirements/recommendations for international students: Required—TOEFL (minimum score 550 paper-based; 79 iBT). Electronic applications accepted.

The University of Texas at Austin, Graduate School, McCombs School of Business, Department of Information, Risk, and Operations Management, Austin, TX 78712-1111. Offers information management (MBA); information systems (PhD); risk analysis and decision making (PhD); risk management (MBA); supply chain and operations management (MBA, PhD). *Degree requirements:* For doctorate, thesis/dissertation. *Entrance requirements:* For doctorate, GMAT or GRE. Electronic applications accepted. *Faculty research:* Stochastic processing and queuing, discrete nonlinear and large-scale optimization simulation, quality assurance logistics, distributed artificial intelligence, organizational modeling.

The University of Texas at Dallas, Naveen Jindal School of Management, Program in Information Systems and Operations Management, Richardson, TX 75080. Offers business analytics (MS); information technology and management (MS); supply chain management (MS). Part-time and evening/weekend programs available. *Faculty:* 14 full-time (0 women), 9 part-time/adjunct (3 women). *Students:* 668 full-time (258 women), 222 part-time (80 women); includes 78 minority (15 Black or African American, non-Hispanic/Latino; 51 Asian, non-Hispanic/Latino; 10 Hispanic/Latino; 2 Two or more races, non-Hispanic/Latino), 734 international. Average age 26. 1,622 applicants, 56% accepted, 364 enrolled. In 2013, 296 master's awarded. *Degree requirements:* For master's, thesis optional. *Entrance requirements:* For master's, GMAT. Additional exam requirements/recommendations for international students: Required—TOEFL (minimum score 550 paper-based). *Application deadline:* For fall admission, 7/15 for domestic students, 5/1 priority date for international students; for spring admission, 11/15 for domestic students, 9/1 priority date for international students. Applications are processed on a rolling basis. Application fee: $50 ($100 for international students). Electronic applications accepted. *Expenses:* Tuition, state resident: full-time $11,940; part-time $663.33 per credit hour. Tuition, nonresident: full-time $21,606; part-time $1200.33 per credit hour. *Financial support:* In 2013–14, 183 students received support, including 3 research assistantships with partial tuition reimbursements available (averaging $13,750 per year), 18 teaching assistantships with partial tuition reimbursements available (averaging $10,340 per year); career-related internships or fieldwork, Federal Work-Study, institutionally sponsored loans, scholarships/grants, and unspecified assistantships also available. Support available to part-time students. Financial award application deadline: 4/30; financial award applicants required to submit FAFSA. *Faculty research:* Technology marketing, measuring information work productivity, electronic commerce, decision support systems, data quality. *Unit head:* Dr. Srinivasan Raghunathan, Area Coordinator, Information Systems, 972-883-4377,

E-mail: sraghu@utdallas.edu. *Application contact:* Dr. Milind Dawande, Area Coordinator, Supply Chain Management, 972-883-2793, E-mail: milind@utdallas.edu. Website: http://jindal.utdallas.edu/academic-areas/information-systems-and-operations-management/.

The University of Texas at Dallas, Naveen Jindal School of Management, Programs in Management Science, Richardson, TX 75080. Offers accounting (PhD); finance (PhD); information systems (PhD); marketing (PhD); operations management (PhD). *Accreditation:* AACSB. Part-time and evening/weekend programs available. *Faculty:* 13 full-time (3 women), 7 part-time/adjunct (2 women). *Students:* 78 full-time (27 women), 9 part-time (3 women); includes 6 minority (all Asian, non-Hispanic/Latino), 73 international. Average age 30. 258 applicants, 9% accepted, 16 enrolled. In 2013, 14 doctorates awarded. *Degree requirements:* For doctorate, thesis/dissertation. *Entrance requirements:* For doctorate, GMAT, minimum GPA of 3.0. Additional exam requirements/recommendations for international students: Required—TOEFL (minimum score 550 paper-based). *Application deadline:* For fall admission, 7/15 for domestic students, 5/1 priority date for international students; for spring admission, 11/15 for domestic students, 9/1 priority date for international students. Applications are processed on a rolling basis. Application fee: $50 ($100 for international students). Electronic applications accepted. *Expenses:* Tuition, state resident: full-time $11,940; part-time $663.33 per credit hour. Tuition, nonresident: full-time $21,606; part-time $1200.33 per credit hour. *Financial support:* In 2013–14, 81 students received support. Research assistantships with partial tuition reimbursements available, teaching assistantships with partial tuition reimbursements available, career-related internships or fieldwork, Federal Work-Study, institutionally sponsored loans, scholarships/grants, and unspecified assistantships available. Support available to part-time students. Financial award application deadline: 4/30; financial award applicants required to submit FAFSA. *Faculty research:* Empirical generalizations in marketing, diffusion of generations of technology, stochastic brand-choice theory, acceptance of trade deals by supermarkets, nonparametric estimations of market share response. *Unit head:* Dr. Sumit Sarkar, Program Director, 972-883-2745, Fax: 972-883-5977, E-mail: som_phd.@utdallas.edu. *Application contact:* Ashley J. Desouza, Program Administrator, 972-883-2745, Fax: 972-883-5977, E-mail: ashley.desouza@utdallas.edu.
Website: http://jindal.utdallas.edu/academic-programs/phd-programs/management-science/.

The University of Texas–Pan American, College of Engineering and Computer Science, Department of Computer Science, Edinburg, TX 78539. Offers computer science (MS); information technology (MS). Part-time and evening/weekend programs available. Postbaccalaureate distance learning degree programs offered (minimal on-campus study). *Degree requirements:* For master's, final written exam, project. *Entrance requirements:* For master's, GRE General Test, minimum GPA of 3.0 in last 60 hours. Additional exam requirements/recommendations for international students: Required—TOEFL. *Expenses:* Tuition, state resident: full-time $5986; part-time $333 per credit hour. Tuition, nonresident: full-time $12,358; part-time $687 per credit hour. *Required fees:* $782. Tuition and fees vary according to program. *Faculty research:* Artificial intelligence, distributed systems, Internet computing, theoretical computer sciences, information visualization.

University of the Sacred Heart, Graduate Programs, Department of Business Administration, Program in Information Systems Management, San Juan, PR 00914-0383. Offers MBA. Part-time and evening/weekend programs available. *Degree requirements:* For master's, thesis. *Entrance requirements:* For master's, EXADEP, minimum undergraduate GPA of 2.75, interview.

University of the West, Department of Business Administration, Rosemead, CA 91770. Offers business administration (EMBA); computer information systems (MBA); finance (MBA); international business (MBA); nonprofit organization management (MBA). Part-time and evening/weekend programs available. *Entrance requirements:* Additional exam requirements/recommendations for international students: Required—TOEFL. *Application deadline:* For fall admission, 6/15 for domestic and international students; for winter admission, 4/1 for domestic and international students; for spring admission, 11/15 for domestic and international students. Applications are processed on a rolling basis. Application fee: $50 ($100 for international students). *Expenses: Tuition:* Full-time $7200; part-time $400 per credit hour. *Required fees:* $750; $400 per credit hour. $275 per semester. One-time fee: $75. Tuition and fees vary according to course level and program. *Financial support:* Career-related internships or fieldwork, Federal Work-Study, scholarships/grants, and tuition waivers (partial) available. Financial award applicants required to submit FAFSA. *Unit head:* Dr. Bill Y. Chen, Chair, 626-656-2125, Fax: 626-571-1413, E-mail: billchen@uwest.edu. *Application contact:* Jason Kosareff, Enrollment Counselor, 626-571-8811 Ext. 311, Fax: 626-571-1413, E-mail: jasonk@uwest.edu.

The University of Tulsa, Graduate School, Collins College of Business, Master of Business Administration Program, Tulsa, OK 74104-3189. Offers accounting (MBA); business administration (MBA); energy management (MBA); finance (MBA); international business (MBA); management information systems (MBA); taxation (MBA); JD/MBA; MBA/MSCS; MBA/MSF. *Accreditation:* AACSB. Part-time and evening/weekend programs available. *Faculty:* 32 full-time (6 women). *Students:* 59 full-time (28 women), 29 part-time (9 women); includes 11 minority (1 Black or African American, non-Hispanic/Latino; 5 American Indian or Alaska Native, non-Hispanic/Latino; 3 Asian, non-Hispanic/Latino; 1 Hispanic/Latino; 1 Two or more races, non-Hispanic/Latino), 16 international. Average age 27. 53 applicants, 81% accepted, 28 enrolled. In 2013, 39 master's awarded. *Entrance requirements:* For master's, GMAT. Additional exam requirements/recommendations for international students: Required—TOEFL (minimum score 577 paper-based; 91 iBT), IELTS (minimum score 6.5). *Application deadline:* Applications are processed on a rolling basis. Application fee: $40. Electronic applications accepted. *Expenses: Tuition:* Full-time $19,566; part-time $1087 per credit hour. *Required fees:* $1690; $5 per credit hour. $160 per semester. Tuition and fees vary according to course load. *Financial support:* In 2013–14, 31 students received support, including 1 research assistantship (averaging $1,500 per year), 30 teaching assistantships (averaging $10,112 per year); fellowships, career-related internships or fieldwork, institutionally sponsored loans, scholarships/grants, health care benefits, tuition waivers (full and partial), and unspecified assistantships also available. Support available to part-time students. Financial award application deadline: 2/1; financial award applicants required to submit FAFSA. *Faculty research:* Accounting, energy management, finance, international business, management information systems, taxation. *Unit head:* Dr. Linda Nichols, Associate Dean of the Collins College of Business, 918-631-2242, Fax: 918-631-2142, E-mail: linda-nichols@utulsa.edu. *Application contact:* Information Contact, 918-631-2242, E-mail: graduate-business@utulsa.edu.
Website: http://www.utulsa.edu/academics/colleges/collins-college-of-business/bus-dept-schools/graduate-business-programs/degree-programs/MBA-Programs.aspx.

University of Utah, Graduate School, David Eccles School of Business, Business Administration Program, Salt Lake City, UT 84112. Offers accounting (PhD); business administration (EMBA, MBA, PMBA); finance (PhD); information systems (PhD); marketing (PhD); operations management (PhD); organizational behavior (PhD); strategic management (PhD); MBA/JD; MBA/MHA; MBA/MS. Part-time and evening/weekend programs available. *Faculty:* 58 full-time (21 women), 37 part-time/adjunct (7 women). *Students:* 481 full-time (108 women), 109 part-time (19 women); includes 39 minority (2 Black or African American, non-Hispanic/Latino; 13 Asian, non-Hispanic/Latino; 18 Hispanic/Latino; 1 Native Hawaiian or other Pacific Islander, non-Hispanic/Latino; 5 Two or more races, non-Hispanic/Latino), 39 international. Average age 32. 486 applicants, 56% accepted, 215 enrolled. In 2013, 326 master's, 10 doctorates awarded. *Degree requirements:* For doctorate, comprehensive exam, thesis/dissertation. *Entrance requirements:* For master's, GMAT or GRE; for doctorate, GMAT. Additional exam requirements/recommendations for international students: Required—TOEFL (minimum score 600 paper-based; 100 iBT), IELTS (minimum score 7). *Application deadline:* For fall admission, 11/1 priority date for domestic students, 3/1 priority date for international students; for spring admission, 11/1 for domestic and international students. Applications are processed on a rolling basis. Application fee: $55 ($65 for international students). Electronic applications accepted. *Expenses:* Contact institution. *Financial support:* In 2013–14, 48 students received support, including 41 fellowships with partial tuition reimbursements available (averaging $8,600 per year), 35 research assistantships with partial tuition reimbursements available (averaging $6,378 per year), 57 teaching assistantships with full tuition reimbursements available (averaging $17,000 per year); scholarships/grants and unspecified assistantships also available. Financial award application deadline: 2/1; financial award applicants required to submit FAFSA. *Faculty research:* Corporate finance, strategy services, consumer behavior, financial disclosures, operations. *Unit head:* Dr. William Hesterly, Associate Dean, PhD Program, 801-581-7676, Fax: 801-581-3380, E-mail: mastersinfo@business.utah.edu. *Application contact:* Andrea Miller, Coordinator, 801-581-7785, Fax: 801-581-3666, E-mail: mastersinfo@business.utah.edu.
Website: http://business.utah.edu/full-time-mba.

University of Utah, Graduate School, David Eccles School of Business, Department of Operations and Information Systems, Salt Lake City, UT 84112. Offers information systems (MS, Graduate Certificate), including business intelligence and analytics, IT security, product and process management, software and systems architecture. Part-time and evening/weekend programs available. *Faculty:* 9 full-time (2 women), 6 part-time/adjunct (0 women). *Students:* 73 full-time (12 women), 53 part-time (4 women); includes 15 minority (2 Black or African American, non-Hispanic/Latino; 3 Asian, non-Hispanic/Latino; 9 Hispanic/Latino; 1 Two or more races, non-Hispanic/Latino), 12 international. Average age 32. 90 applicants, 86% accepted, 57 enrolled. In 2013, 59 master's awarded. *Degree requirements:* For master's, capstone project. *Entrance requirements:* For master's, GMAT/GRE, minimum undergraduate GPA of 3.0. Additional exam requirements/recommendations for international students: Required—TOEFL (minimum score 600 paper-based; 100 iBT), IELTS (minimum score 7). *Application deadline:* For fall admission, 7/28 for domestic students, 3/1 for international students; for spring admission, 12/7 for domestic students, 8/16 for international students. Applications are processed on a rolling basis. Application fee: $55 ($65 for international students). Electronic applications accepted. *Expenses:* Contact institution. *Financial support:* In 2013–14, 5 students received support, including 3 fellowships with partial tuition reimbursements available (averaging $5,160 per year), 2 teaching assistantships with partial tuition reimbursements available (averaging $5,160 per year); tuition waivers (partial) and unspecified assistantships also available. Financial award application deadline: 4/14; financial award applicants required to submit FAFSA. *Faculty research:* Business intelligence and analytics, software and system architecture, product and process management, IT security, Web and data mining, applications and management of IT in healthcare. *Unit head:* Bradden Blair, Director of the MSIS Program, 801-587-9489, Fax: 801-581-3666, E-mail: b.blair@business.utah.edu. *Application contact:* Jetta Harris, Academic Coordinator, 801-587-5878, Fax: 801-581-3666, E-mail: jetta.harris@business.utah.edu.
Website: http://msis.business.utah.edu.

University of Virginia, McIntire School of Commerce, Program in Management of Information Technology, Charlottesville, VA 22903. Offers MS. *Students:* 73 full-time (15 women), 1 (woman) part-time; includes 22 minority (6 Black or African American, non-Hispanic/Latino; 1 American Indian or Alaska Native, non-Hispanic/Latino; 8 Asian, non-Hispanic/Latino; 5 Hispanic/Latino; 1 Native Hawaiian or other Pacific Islander, non-Hispanic/Latino; 1 Two or more races, non-Hispanic/Latino), 3 international. Average age 37. 127 applicants, 66% accepted, 73 enrolled. In 2013, 35 master's awarded. *Entrance requirements:* For master's, GMAT, 2 recommendations. Additional exam requirements/recommendations for international students: Required—TOEFL (minimum score 620 paper-based). *Application deadline:* For fall admission, 9/15 priority date for domestic students, 1/15 for international students. Applications are processed on a rolling basis. Application fee: $75. Electronic applications accepted. *Expenses:* Contact institution. *Financial support:* Fellowships and Federal Work-Study available. Financial award application deadline: 2/15; financial award applicants required to submit FAFSA. *Unit head:* Stefano Grazioli, Director, 434-982-2973, E-mail: grazioli@virginia.edu. *Application contact:* Emma Candalier, Associate Director of Graduate Recruiting, 434-243-4992, Fax: 434-924-4511, E-mail: ecandalier@virginia.edu.
Website: http://www.commerce.virginia.edu/msmit/Pages/default.aspx.

University of Wisconsin–Madison, Graduate School, Wisconsin School of Business, Doctoral Program in Accounting and Information Systems, Madison, WI 53706-1380. Offers PhD. *Accreditation:* AACSB. *Faculty:* 11 full-time (3 women). *Students:* 14 full-time (7 women); includes 1 minority (American Indian or Alaska Native, non-Hispanic/Latino), 1 international. Average age 31. 43 applicants, 12% accepted, 3 enrolled. In 2013, 1 doctorate awarded. *Degree requirements:* For doctorate, comprehensive exam, thesis/dissertation. *Entrance requirements:* For doctorate, GMAT or GRE. Additional exam requirements/recommendations for international students: Recommended—TOEFL (minimum score 623 paper-based; 106 iBT), IELTS (minimum score 7.5). *Application deadline:* For fall admission, 12/15 priority date for domestic and international students. Application fee: $56. Electronic applications accepted. *Expenses:* Contact institution. *Financial support:* In 2013–14, 14 students received support, including 1 fellowship with full tuition reimbursement available (averaging $19,125 per year), 4 research assistantships with full tuition reimbursements available (averaging $14,746 per year), 9 teaching assistantships with full tuition reimbursements available (averaging $14,746 per year); Federal Work-Study, institutionally sponsored loans, scholarships/grants, health care benefits, and unspecified assistantships also available. Financial award application deadline: 12/15. *Faculty research:* Auditing, financial reporting, economic theory, strategy, computer models. *Unit head:* Prof. Terry Warfield, Chair, 608-262-1028, E-mail: twarfield@bus.wisc.edu. *Application contact:* Belle Heberling, Assistant Director for Research Programs, 608-262-3749, Fax: 608-890-0180, E-mail: phd@bus.wisc.edu.
Website: http://www.bus.wisc.edu/phd.

University of Wisconsin–Madison, Graduate School, Wisconsin School of Business, Doctoral Program in Operations and Information Management, Madison, WI 53706-1380. Offers information systems (PhD); operations management (PhD). *Faculty:* 10 full-time (0 women). *Students:* 3 full-time (0 women), 2 international. Average age 32. 8 applicants, 13% accepted. *Degree requirements:* For doctorate, comprehensive exam, thesis/dissertation. *Entrance requirements:* For doctorate, GMAT or GRE General Test. Additional exam requirements/recommendations for international students: Recommended—TOEFL (minimum score 623 paper-based; 106 iBT), IELTS (minimum

score 7.5), TSE (minimum score 73). *Application deadline:* For fall admission, 12/15 priority date for domestic and international students. Application fee: $56. Electronic applications accepted. *Expenses:* Tuition, state resident: full-time $10,728; part-time $790 per credit. Tuition, nonresident: full-time $24,054; part-time $1623 per credit. *Required fees:* $1130; $119 per credit. *Financial support:* In 2013–14, 3 students received support, including 2 fellowships with full tuition reimbursements available (averaging $19,125 per year), research assistantships with full tuition reimbursements available (averaging $14,746 per year), 1 teaching assistantship with full tuition reimbursement available (averaging $14,746 per year); Federal Work-Study, institutionally sponsored loans, scholarships/grants, health care benefits, and unspecified assistantships also available. Financial award application deadline: 12/15; financial award applicants required to submit FAFSA. *Faculty research:* Supply chain management, reorganization of the factory, creating continuous innovation, transportation economics, organizational economics. *Unit head:* Prof. James G. Morris, Chair, 608-262-1284, E-mail: jmorris@bus.wisc.edu. *Application contact:* Belle Heberling, Assistant Director for Research Programs, 608-262-3749, Fax: 608-890-0180, E-mail: phd@bus.wisc.edu.
Website: http://bus.wisc.edu/phd.

Utah State University, School of Graduate Studies, College of Business, Department of Business Information Systems, Logan, UT 84322. Offers business education (MS); business information systems (MS); business information systems and education (Ed D); education (PhD). Part-time programs available. Terminal master's awarded for partial completion of doctoral program. *Degree requirements:* For master's, thesis optional; for doctorate, thesis/dissertation. *Entrance requirements:* For master's, GMAT, minimum GPA of 3.2; for doctorate, GRE General Test, minimum GPA of 3.0. Additional exam requirements/recommendations for international students: Required—TOEFL. *Faculty research:* Oral and written communication, methods of teaching, CASE tools, object-oriented programming, decision support systems.

Valparaiso University, Graduate School, Program in Information Technology and Management, Valparaiso, IN 46383. Offers MS. Part-time and evening/weekend programs available. *Students:* 95 full-time (13 women), 10 part-time (0 women); includes 1 minority (Black or African American, non-Hispanic/Latino), 99 international. Average age 25. In 2013, 15 master's awarded. *Entrance requirements:* For master's, minimum GPA of 3.0; minor or equivalent in computer science, information technology, or a related field. Additional exam requirements/recommendations for international students: Required—TOEFL (minimum score 550 paper-based; 80 iBT), IELTS (minimum score 6). *Application deadline:* Applications are processed on a rolling basis. Application fee: $30 ($50 for international students). Electronic applications accepted. *Expenses: Tuition:* Full-time $10,350; part-time $575 per credit hour. *Required fees:* $378; $101 per term. Tuition and fees vary according to course load and program. *Financial support:* Available to part-time students. Applicants required to submit FAFSA. *Unit head:* Dr. Jennifer A. Ziegler, Dean, Graduate School and Continuing Education, 219-464-5313, Fax: 219-464-5381, E-mail: jennifer.ziegler@valpo.edu. *Application contact:* Jessica Choquette, Graduate Admissions Specialist, 219-464-5313, Fax: 219-464-5381, E-mail: jessica.choquette@valpo.edu.
Website: http://www.valpo.edu/grad/it/.

Villanova University, Villanova School of Business, MBA - The Fast Track Program, Villanova, PA 19085. Offers finance (MBA); health care management (MBA); international business (MBA); management information systems (MBA); marketing (MBA); real estate (MBA); strategic management (MBA). *Accreditation:* AACSB. Part-time and evening/weekend programs available. *Faculty:* 101 full-time (33 women), 36 part-time/adjunct (3 women). *Students:* 140 part-time (44 women); includes 22 minority (1 Black or African American, non-Hispanic/Latino; 17 Asian, non-Hispanic/Latino; 3 Hispanic/Latino; 1 Two or more races, non-Hispanic/Latino), 3 international. Average age 29. 127 applicants, 72% accepted, 75 enrolled. In 2013, 61 master's awarded. *Degree requirements:* For master's, minimum GPA of 3.0. *Entrance requirements:* For master's, GMAT or GRE, work experience. Additional exam requirements/recommendations for international students: Required—TOEFL (minimum score 550 paper-based; 90 iBT). *Application deadline:* For fall admission, 6/30 for domestic and international students. Application fee: $50. Electronic applications accepted. *Financial support:* Scholarships/grants available. Financial award application deadline: 6/30; financial award applicants required to submit FAFSA. *Faculty research:* Business analytics; creativity, innovation and entrepreneurship; global leadership; real estate; church management; business ethics. *Unit head:* Zelon Crawford, Director of Graduate Business Programs, 610-519-6283, Fax: 610-519-6273, E-mail: zelon.crawford@villanova.edu. *Application contact:* Meredith L. Lockyer, Manager of Recruiting, 610-519-7016, Fax: 610-519-6273, E-mail: meredith.lockyer@villanova.edu.
Website: http://www1.villanova.edu/villanova/business/graduate/mba/fasttrack.html.

Villanova University, Villanova School of Business, MBA - The Flex Track Program, Villanova, PA 19085. Offers finance (MBA); health care management (MBA); international business (MBA); management information systems (MBA); marketing (MBA); real estate (MBA); strategic management (MBA); JD/MBA. *Accreditation:* AACSB. Part-time and evening/weekend programs available. Postbaccalaureate distance learning degree programs offered (minimal on-campus study). *Faculty:* 101 full-time (33 women), 36 part-time/adjunct (3 women). *Students:* 13 full-time (5 women), 413 part-time (127 women); includes 63 minority (13 Black or African American, non-Hispanic/Latino; 1 American Indian or Alaska Native, non-Hispanic/Latino; 29 Asian, non-Hispanic/Latino; 14 Hispanic/Latino; 1 Native Hawaiian or other Pacific Islander, non-Hispanic/Latino; 5 Two or more races, non-Hispanic/Latino), 9 international. Average age 29. 84 applicants, 83% accepted, 66 enrolled. In 2013, 133 master's awarded. *Degree requirements:* For master's, minimum GPA of 3.0. *Entrance requirements:* For master's, GMAT or GRE, work experience. Additional exam requirements/recommendations for international students: Required—TOEFL (minimum score 550 paper-based; 90 iBT). *Application deadline:* For fall admission, 6/30 for domestic and international students; for winter admission, 11/15 for domestic and international students; for spring admission, 11/15 for domestic and international students; for summer admission, 3/31 for domestic and international students. Applications are processed on a rolling basis. Application fee: $50. Electronic applications accepted. *Financial support:* In 2013–14, 13 research assistantships with full tuition reimbursements (averaging $13,100 per year) were awarded; scholarships/grants and unspecified assistantships also available. Financial award application deadline: 6/30; financial award applicants required to submit FAFSA. *Faculty research:* Business analytics; creativity, innovation and entrepreneurship; global leadership; real estate; church management; business ethics. *Unit head:* Zelon Crawford, Director of Graduate Business Programs, 610-610-6283, Fax: 610-519-6273, E-mail: zelon.crawford@villanova.edu. *Application contact:* Meredith L. Lockyer, Manager of Recruiting, 610-519-7016, Fax: 610-519-6273, E-mail: meredith.lockyer@villanova.edu.
Website: http://www1.villanova.edu/villanova/business/graduate/mba/flextrack.html.

Virginia Commonwealth University, Graduate School, School of Business, Program in Information Systems, Richmond, VA 23284-9005. Offers MS, PhD. *Degree requirements:* For doctorate, thesis/dissertation. *Entrance requirements:* For master's, GMAT. Additional exam requirements/recommendations for international students: Required—TOEFL (minimum score 600 paper-based; 100 iBT); Recommended—IELTS (minimum score 6.5). Electronic applications accepted.

Virginia International University, School of Computer Information Systems, Fairfax, VA 22030. Offers computer science (MS); information systems (MS). Part-time programs available. *Entrance requirements:* For master's, bachelor's degree. Additional exam requirements/recommendations for international students: Required—TOEFL (minimum score 550 paper-based; 80 iBT), IELTS. Electronic applications accepted.

Virginia Polytechnic Institute and State University, Graduate School, Intercollege, Blacksburg, VA 24061. Offers genetics, bioinformatics and computational biology (PhD); information technology (MIT); macromolecular science and engineering (MS, PhD). *Students:* 154 full-time (68 women), 720 part-time (261 women); includes 196 minority (61 Black or African American, non-Hispanic/Latino; 1 American Indian or Alaska Native, non-Hispanic/Latino; 80 Asian, non-Hispanic/Latino; 35 Hispanic/Latino; 19 Two or more races, non-Hispanic/Latino), 103 international. Average age 33. 700 applicants, 76% accepted, 374 enrolled. In 2013, 114 master's, 8 doctorates awarded. *Degree requirements:* For master's, comprehensive exam (for some programs), thesis (for some programs); for doctorate, comprehensive exam (for some programs), thesis/dissertation (for some programs). *Entrance requirements:* For master's and doctorate, GRE/GMAT (may vary by department). Additional exam requirements/recommendations for international students: Required—TOEFL (minimum score 550 paper-based). *Application deadline:* For fall admission, 8/1 for domestic students, 4/1 for international students; for spring admission, 1/1 for domestic students, 9/1 for international students. Applications are processed on a rolling basis. Application fee: $75. Electronic applications accepted. *Expenses:* Tuition, state resident: full-time $11,185; part-time $621.50 per credit hour. Tuition, nonresident: full-time $22,146; part-time $1230.25 per credit hour. *Required fees:* $2442; $449.25 per semester. Tuition and fees vary according to course load, campus/location and program. *Financial support:* In 2013–14, 85 research assistantships with full tuition reimbursements (averaging $22,512 per year), 16 teaching assistantships with full tuition reimbursements (averaging $18,419 per year) were awarded. Financial award application deadline: 3/1; financial award applicants required to submit FAFSA. *Unit head:* Dr. Karen P. DePauw, Vice President and Dean for Graduate Education, 540-231-7581, Fax: 540-231-1670, E-mail: kpdepauw@vt.edu. *Application contact:* Graduate Admissions and Academic Progress, 540-231-8636, Fax: 540-231-2039, E-mail: grads@vt.edu.
Website: http://www.graduateschool.vt.edu/graduate_catalog/colleges.htm.

Virginia Polytechnic Institute and State University, Graduate School, Pamplin College of Business, Blacksburg, VA 24061. Offers accounting and information systems (MACIS); business (PhD); business administration (MBA, MS); hospitality and tourism management (MS, PhD). *Faculty:* 118 full-time (35 women), 1 part-time/adjunct (0 women). *Students:* 333 full-time (149 women), 129 part-time (47 women); includes 75 minority (14 Black or African American, non-Hispanic/Latino; 42 Asian, non-Hispanic/Latino; 12 Hispanic/Latino; 7 Two or more races, non-Hispanic/Latino), 115 international. Average age 30. 520 applicants, 38% accepted, 157 enrolled. In 2013, 199 master's, 12 doctorates awarded. *Degree requirements:* For master's, comprehensive exam (for some programs), thesis (for some programs); for doctorate, comprehensive exam (for some programs), thesis/dissertation (for some programs). *Entrance requirements:* For master's and doctorate, GRE/GMAT (may vary by department). Additional exam requirements/recommendations for international students: Required—TOEFL (minimum score 550 paper-based). *Application deadline:* For fall admission, 8/1 for domestic students, 4/1 for international students; for spring admission, 1/1 for domestic students, 9/1 for international students. Applications are processed on a rolling basis. Application fee: $75. Electronic applications accepted. *Expenses:* Tuition, state resident: full-time $11,185; part-time $621.50 per credit hour. Tuition, nonresident: full-time $22,146; part-time $1230.25 per credit hour. *Required fees:* $2442; $449.25 per semester. Tuition and fees vary according to course load, campus/location and program. *Financial support:* In 2013–14, 5 fellowships with full tuition reimbursements (averaging $19,435 per year), 61 teaching assistantships with full tuition reimbursements (averaging $15,805 per year) were awarded. Financial award application deadline: 3/1; financial award applicants required to submit FAFSA. *Total annual research expenditures:* $2.5 million. *Unit head:* Dr. Robert T. Sumichrast, Dean, 540-231-6601, Fax: 540-231-4487, E-mail: busdean@vt.edu. *Application contact:* Martha Hilton, Executive Assistant to the Dean, 540-231-9647, Fax: 540-231-4487, E-mail: cartermc@vt.edu.
Website: http://www.pamplin.vt.edu/.

Virginia Polytechnic Institute and State University, VT Online, Blacksburg, VA 24061. Offers advanced transportation systems (Certificate); aerospace engineering (MS); agricultural and life sciences (MSLFS); business information systems (Graduate Certificate); career and technical education (MS); civil engineering (MS); computer engineering (M Eng, MS); decision support systems (Graduate Certificate); eLearning leadership (MA); electrical engineering (M Eng, MS); engineering administration (MEA); environmental engineering (Certificate); environmental politics and policy (Graduate Certificate); environmental sciences and engineering (MS); foundations of political analysis (Graduate Certificate); health product risk management (Graduate Certificate); industrial and systems engineering (MS); information policy and society (Graduate Certificate); information security (Graduate Certificate); information technology (MIT); instructional technology (MA); integrative STEM education (MA Ed); liberal arts (Graduate Certificate); life sciences: health product risk management (MS); natural resources (MNR, Graduate Certificate); networking (Graduate Certificate); nonprofit and nongovernmental organization management (Graduate Certificate); ocean engineering (MS); political science (MA); security studies (Graduate Certificate); software development (Graduate Certificate). *Expenses:* Tuition, state resident: full-time $11,185; part-time $621.50 per credit hour. Tuition, nonresident: full-time $22,146; part-time $1230.25 per credit hour. *Required fees:* $2442; $449.25 per semester. Tuition and fees vary according to course load, campus/location and program.

Walden University, Graduate Programs, School of Information Systems and Technology, Minneapolis, MN 55401. Offers information systems (Graduate Certificate); information systems and technology (MISM, DIT); information technology (MS), including health informatics, information assurance and cyber security, information systems, software engineering. Part-time and evening/weekend programs available. Postbaccalaureate distance learning degree programs offered (minimal on-campus study). *Faculty:* 2 full-time (0 women), 38 part-time/adjunct (11 women). *Students:* 209 full-time (71 women), 153 part-time (56 women); includes 187 minority (140 Black or African American, non-Hispanic/Latino; 15 Asian, non-Hispanic/Latino; 17 Hispanic/Latino; 15 Two or more races, non-Hispanic/Latino), 11 international. Average age 37. 215 applicants, 94% accepted, 152 enrolled. In 2013, 77 master's, 20 other advanced degrees awarded. *Degree requirements:* For doctorate, residency. *Entrance requirements:* For master's, bachelor's degree or higher; minimum GPA of 2.5; official transcripts; goal statement (for some programs); access to computer and Internet; for doctorate, master's degree or higher; three years of related professional or academic experience (preferred); minimum GPA of 3.0; goal statement and current resume (select programs); official transcripts; access to computer and Internet; for Graduate Certificate, relevant work experience; access to computer and Internet. Additional exam requirements/recommendations for international students: Required—TOEFL (minimum

score 550 paper-based; 79 iBT), IELTS (minimum score 6.5), Michigan English Language Assessment Battery (minimum score 82), or PTE. *Application deadline:* Applications are processed on a rolling basis. Application fee: $0. Electronic applications accepted. *Expenses: Tuition:* Full-time $11,813.55; part-time $500 per credit. *Required fees:* $618.76. *Financial support:* Fellowships, Federal Work-Study, scholarships/grants, unspecified assistantships, and family tuition reduction, active duty/veteran tuition reduction, group tuition reduction, interest-free payment plans, employee tuition reduction available. Support available to part-time students. Financial award applicants required to submit FAFSA. *Unit head:* Dr. Ward Ulmer, III, Associate Dean, 800-925-3368. *Application contact:* Jennifer Hall, Vice President of Enrollment Management, 866-4-WALDEN, E-mail: info@waldenu.edu. Website: http://www.waldenu.edu/programs/colleges-schools/information-systems-and-technology.

Walden University, Graduate Programs, School of Management, Minneapolis, MN 55401. Offers accounting (MBA, MS, DBA), including accounting for the professional (MS), accounting with CPA emphasis (MS), self-designed (MS, PhD); accounting and management (MS), including accountants as strategic managers, self-designed (MS, PhD); advanced project management (Graduate Certificate); applied project management (Graduate Certificate); bridge to business administration (Post-Doctoral Certificate); bridge to management (Post-Doctoral Certificate); business administration (EMBA); business management (Graduate Certificate); communication (MS, Graduate Certificate); corporate finance (MBA); entrepreneurship (DBA); entrepreneurship and small business (MBA); finance (DBA); global supply chain management (DBA); healthcare management (MBA, DBA); human resource management (MBA, MS, Graduate Certificate), including functional human resource management (MS), general program (MS), integrating functional and strategic human resource management (MS), organizational strategy (MS); human resources management (DBA); information systems management (DBA); international business (MBA, DBA); leadership (MBA, MS, DBA), including general program (MS), human resources leadership (MS), leader development (MS), self-designed (MS, PhD); management (MS, PhD), including accounting (PhD), engineering management (PhD), finance (PhD), general program (MS), healthcare management (MS), human resource management (MS), human resources management (PhD), information systems management (PhD), leadership (MS), leadership and organizational change (PhD), marketing (MS), operations research (PhD), project management (MS), self-designed, strategy and operations (MS); marketing (MBA, DBA); project management (MBA, MS, DBA); self-designed (MBA, DBA); social impact management (DBA); technology entrepreneurship (DBA). Part-time and evening/weekend programs available. Postbaccalaureate distance learning degree programs offered (minimal on-campus study). *Faculty:* 24 full-time (9 women), 337 part-time/adjunct (127 women). *Students:* 4,369 full-time (2,379 women), 2,181 part-time (1,304 women); includes 3,669 minority (3,020 Black or African American, non-Hispanic/Latino; 22 American Indian or Alaska Native, non-Hispanic/Latino; 156 Asian, non-Hispanic/Latino; 331 Hispanic/Latino; 11 Native Hawaiian or other Pacific Islander, non-Hispanic/Latino; 129 Two or more races, non-Hispanic/Latino), 107 international. Average age 41. 2,030 applicants, 94% accepted, 1436 enrolled. In 2013, 757 master's, 128 doctorates, 32 other advanced degrees awarded. *Degree requirements:* For master's, residency (for some programs); for doctorate, thesis/dissertation (for some programs), residency. *Entrance requirements:* For master's, bachelor's degree or higher; minimum GPA of 2.5; official transcripts; goal statement (for some programs); access to computer and Internet; for doctorate, master's degree or higher; three years of related professional or academic experience (preferred); minimum GPA of 3.0; goal statement and current resume (select programs); official transcripts; access to computer and Internet; for other advanced degree, relevant work experience; access to computer and Internet. Additional exam requirements/recommendations for international students: Required—TOEFL (minimum score 550 paper-based; 79 iBT), IELTS (minimum score 6.5), Michigan English Language Assessment Battery (minimum score 82), or PTE. *Application deadline:* Applications are processed on a rolling basis. Application fee: $0. Electronic applications accepted. *Expenses: Tuition:* Full-time $11,813.55; part-time $500 per credit. *Required fees:* $618.76. *Financial support:* Fellowships, Federal Work-Study, scholarships/grants, unspecified assistantships, and family tuition reduction, active duty/veteran tuition reduction, group tuition reduction, interest-free payment plans, employee tuition reduction available. Support available to part-time students. Financial award applicants required to submit FAFSA. *Unit head:* Dr. Ward Ulmer, III, Associate Dean, 800-925-3368. *Application contact:* Jennifer Hall, Vice President of Enrollment Management, 866-4-WALDEN, E-mail: info@waldenu.edu. Website: http://www.waldenu.edu/programs/colleges-schools/management.

Walsh College of Accountancy and Business Administration, Graduate Programs, Program in Business Information Technology, Troy, MI 48007-7006. Offers MSBIT.

Washington State University, Graduate School, College of Business, PhD Program in Information Systems, Pullman, WA 99164. Offers PhD.

Wayland Baptist University, Graduate Programs, Programs in Business Administration/Management, Plainview, TX 79072-6998. Offers accounting (MBA); general business (MBA); health care administration (MAM, MBA); healthcare administration (MBA); human resource management (MAM, MBA); international management (MBA); management (MBA); management information systems (MBA); organization management (MAM); project management (MBA). Part-time and evening/weekend programs available. Postbaccalaureate distance learning degree programs offered (no on-campus study). *Faculty:* 30 full-time (5 women), 38 part-time/adjunct (9 women). *Students:* 44 full-time (20 women), 702 part-time (315 women); includes 348 minority (149 Black or African American, non-Hispanic/Latino; 4 American Indian or Alaska Native, non-Hispanic/Latino; 23 Asian, non-Hispanic/Latino; 139 Hispanic/Latino; 9 Native Hawaiian or other Pacific Islander, non-Hispanic/Latino; 24 Two or more races, non-Hispanic/Latino), 5 international. Average age 40. 147 applicants, 94% accepted, 73 enrolled. In 2013, 296 master's awarded. *Degree requirements:* For master's, capstone course. *Entrance requirements:* For master's, GMAT, GRE or MAT. Additional exam requirements/recommendations for international students: Required—TOEFL (minimum score 500 paper-based; 61 iBT). *Application deadline:* Applications are processed on a rolling basis. Application fee: $50. Electronic applications accepted. *Expenses: Tuition:* Full-time $8190; part-time $455 per credit hour. *Required fees:* $970; $455 per credit hour. $485 per semester. *Financial support:* Federal Work-Study, institutionally sponsored loans, and scholarships/grants available. Support available to part-time students. Financial award application deadline: 5/1; financial award applicants required to submit FAFSA. *Unit head:* Dr. Otto Schacht, Chairman, 806-291-1020, Fax: 806-291-1957, E-mail: schachto@wbu.edu. *Application contact:* Amanda Stanton, Graduate Studies, 806-291-3423, Fax: 806-291-1950, E-mail: stanton@wbu.edu.

Wayne State University, College of Liberal Arts and Sciences, Department of Political Science, Program in Public Administration, Detroit, MI 48202. Offers aging policy and management (MPA); criminal justice policy and management (MPA); economic development policy and management (MPA); health and human services policy and management (MPA); human and fiscal resource management (MPA); information technology management (MPA); nonprofit policy and management (MPA); organizational behavior and management (MPA); public budgeting and financial management (MPA); public policy analysis and program evaluation (MPA); social

welfare policy and management (MPA); urban and metropolitan policy and management (MPA). Accreditation: NASPAA. Evening/weekend programs available. *Students:* 11 full-time (5 women), 55 part-time (43 women); includes 20 minority (14 Black or African American, non-Hispanic/Latino; 2 Asian, non-Hispanic/Latino; 2 Hispanic/Latino; 2 Two or more races, non-Hispanic/Latino), 1 international. Average age 33. 83 applicants, 34% accepted, 17 enrolled. In 2013, 19 master's awarded. *Degree requirements:* For master's, comprehensive exam. *Entrance requirements:* For master's, GRE General Test, minimum undergraduate upper-division GPA of 3.0 or master's degree. Additional exam requirements/recommendations for international students: Required—TOEFL (minimum score 550 paper-based; 79 iBT), TWE (minimum score 5.5), Michigan English Language Assessment Battery (minimum score 85); Recommended—IELTS (minimum score 6.5). *Application deadline:* For fall admission, 6/1 priority date for domestic students, 5/1 priority date for international students; for winter admission, 10/1 priority date for domestic students, 9/1 priority date for international students; for spring admission, 2/1 priority date for domestic students, 1/1 priority date for international students. Applications are processed on a rolling basis. Application fee: $0. Electronic applications accepted. *Expenses: Tuition,* state resident: part-time $554.15 per credit. Tuition, nonresident: part-time $1200.35 per credit. *Required fees:* $42.15 per credit. $268.30 per semester. Tuition and fees vary according to course load and program. *Financial support:* In 2013–14, 21 students received support. Fellowships, teaching assistantships, scholarships/grants, and unspecified assistantships available. Financial award application deadline: 3/31; financial award applicants required to submit FAFSA. *Faculty research:* Urban politics, urban education, state administration. *Unit head:* Dr. Daniel Geller, Department Chair, 313-577-6328, E-mail: dgeller@wayne.edu. *Application contact:* Dr. Brady Baybeck, Associate Professor/Director, Graduate Program in Public Administration, E-mail: mpa@wayne.edu. Website: http://clasweb.clas.wayne.edu/mpa.

Wayne State University, School of Library and Information Science, Detroit, MI 48202. Offers academic libraries (MLIS); archival administration (MLIS, Certificate); general librarianship (MLIS); health sciences librarianship (MLIS); information management for librarians (Certificate); information science (MLIS); law librarianship (MLIS); library and information science (Spec); organization of information (MLIS); public libraries (MLIS); public library services to children and young adults (MLIS, Certificate); records management (MLIS); references services (MLIS); school library media specialist endorsement (MLIS); special libraries (MLIS); urban libraries (MLIS); MLIS/MA. Accreditation: ALA (one or more programs are accredited). Part-time and evening/weekend programs available. Postbaccalaureate distance learning degree programs offered (no on-campus study). *Faculty:* 13 full-time (9 women), 17 part-time/adjunct (13 women). *Students:* 112 full-time (80 women), 372 part-time (296 women); includes 65 minority (26 Black or African American, non-Hispanic/Latino; 11 Asian, non-Hispanic/Latino; 18 Hispanic/Latino; 10 Two or more races, non-Hispanic/Latino), 2 international. Average age 33. 275 applicants, 61% accepted, 109 enrolled. In 2013, 179 master's, 42 other advanced degrees awarded. *Entrance requirements:* For master's and other advanced degree, GRE or MAT (if undergraduate GPA is between 2.5 and 2.99), minimum undergraduate GPA of 3.0 or graduate degree, personal statement, resume or curriculum vitae. Additional exam requirements/recommendations for international students: Required—TOEFL (minimum score 550 paper-based; 79 iBT); Recommended—IELTS (minimum score 6.5), TWE (minimum score 5.5). *Application deadline:* For fall admission, 7/1 for domestic students, 5/1 priority date for international students; for winter admission, 10/1 for domestic students, 9/1 priority date for international students; for spring admission, 3/15 for domestic students, 1/1 priority date for international students. Applications are processed on a rolling basis. Application fee: $0. Electronic applications accepted. *Expenses:* Contact institution. *Financial support:* In 2013–14, 65 students received support. Fellowships with tuition reimbursements available, research assistantships with tuition reimbursements available, institutionally sponsored loans, scholarships/grants, and unspecified assistantships available. Support available to part-time students. Financial award application deadline: 3/31; financial award applicants required to submit FAFSA. *Faculty research:* Library services, information management issues, digital content management, library/community engagement, archives and preservation. *Unit head:* Dr. Stephen Bajjaly, Associate Dean and Professor, 313-577-0350, Fax: 313-577-7563, E-mail: bajjaly@wayne.edu. *Application contact:* Matthew Fredericks, Academic Services Officer I, 313-577-2446, Fax: 313-577-7563, E-mail: mfredericks@wayne.edu. Website: http://slis.wayne.edu/.

Webster University, George Herbert Walker School of Business and Technology, Department of Business, St. Louis, MO 63119-3194. Offers business and organizational security management (MBA); decision support systems (MBA); environmental management (MBA); finance (MBA, MS); forensic accounting (MS); gerontology (MBA); human resources development (MBA); human resources management (MBA); information technology management (MBA); international business (MA, MBA); international relations (MBA); management and leadership (MBA); marketing (MBA); media communications (MBA); procurement and acquisitions management (MBA); Web services (MBA). Accreditation: ACBSP. Part-time and evening/weekend programs available. Postbaccalaureate distance learning degree programs offered (no on-campus study). *Degree requirements:* For master's, comprehensive exam (for some programs), thesis (for some programs). *Entrance requirements:* Additional exam requirements/recommendations for international students: Required—TOEFL. *Expenses: Tuition:* Full-time $11,610; part-time $645 per credit hour. Tuition and fees vary according to campus/location and program.

Webster University, George Herbert Walker School of Business and Technology, Department of Management, St. Louis, MO 63119-3194. Offers business and organizational security management (MA); health administration (MHA); health care management (MA); health services management (MA); human resources development (MA); human resources management (MA); information technology management (MS); management and leadership (MA); marketing (MA); nonprofit leadership (MA); procurement and acquisitions management (MA); public administration (MPA); space systems operations management (MS). Part-time and evening/weekend programs available. Postbaccalaureate distance learning degree programs offered (no on-campus study). *Degree requirements:* For master's, thesis (for some programs). *Entrance requirements:* Additional exam requirements/recommendations for international students: Required—TOEFL. *Expenses: Tuition:* Full-time $11,610; part-time $645 per credit hour. Tuition and fees vary according to campus/location and program.

Webster University, George Herbert Walker School of Business and Technology, Department of Mathematics and Computer Science, St. Louis, MO 63119-3194. Offers computer science/distributed systems (MS). Part-time and evening/weekend programs available. Postbaccalaureate distance learning degree programs offered (no on-campus study). *Entrance requirements:* For master's, 36 hours of graduate course work. Additional exam requirements/recommendations for international students: Required—TOEFL. *Expenses: Tuition:* Full-time $11,610; part-time $645 per credit hour. Tuition and fees vary according to campus/location and program. *Faculty research:* Databases, computer information systems networks, operating systems, computer architecture.

West Chester University of Pennsylvania, College of Arts and Sciences, Department of Computer Science, West Chester, PA 19383. Offers computer science (MS);

Management Information Systems

computer security (Certificate); information systems (Certificate); Web technology (Certificate). Part-time and evening/weekend programs available. *Faculty:* 5 full-time (2 women). *Students:* 10 full-time (1 woman), 24 part-time (4 women); includes 6 minority (1 Black or African American, non-Hispanic/Latino; 5 Asian, non-Hispanic/Latino), 10 international. Average age 28. 27 applicants, 81% accepted, 12 enrolled. In 2013, 5 master's awarded. *Degree requirements:* For master's, thesis optional. *Entrance requirements:* For master's, GRE, two letters of recommendation; for Certificate, BS. Additional exam requirements/recommendations for international students: Required— TOEFL (minimum score 550 paper-based; 80 iBT). *Application deadline:* For fall admission, 4/15 priority date for domestic students, 3/15 for international students; for spring admission, 10/15 priority date for domestic students, 9/1 for international students. Applications are processed on a rolling basis. Application fee: $45. Electronic applications accepted. *Expenses:* Tuition, state resident: full-time $7956; part-time $442 per credit. Tuition, nonresident: full-time $11,934; part-time $663 per credit. *Required fees:* $2134.20; $106.24 per credit. Tuition and fees vary according to campus/location and program. *Financial support:* Unspecified assistantships available. Support available to part-time students. Financial award application deadline: 2/15; financial award applicants required to submit FAFSA. *Faculty research:* Automata theory, compilers, non well-founded sets, security in sensor and mobile ad-hoc networks, intrusion detection, security and trust in pervasive computing, economic modeling of security protocols. *Unit head:* Dr. James Fabrey, Chair, 610-436-2204, E-mail: jfabrey@wcupa.edu. *Application contact:* Dr. Afrand Agah, Graduate Coordinator, 610-430-4419, E-mail: aagah@wcupa.edu.
Website: http://www.cs.wcupa.edu/.

Western Governors University, College of Business, Salt Lake City, UT 84107. Offers information technology management (MBA); management and strategy (MBA); strategic leadership (MBA). Evening/weekend programs available. *Degree requirements:* For master's, capstone project. *Entrance requirements:* For master's, Readiness Assessment, transcripts. Additional exam requirements/recommendations for international students: Required—TOEFL (minimum score 450 paper-based; 80 iBT). Electronic applications accepted.

Western International University, Graduate Programs in Business, MBA Program in Information Technology, Phoenix, AZ 85021-2718. Offers MBA. Evening/weekend programs available. Postbaccalaureate distance learning degree programs offered (no on-campus study). *Degree requirements:* For master's, thesis. *Entrance requirements:* For master's, minimum GPA of 2.75.

Wilmington University, College of Business, New Castle, DE 19720-6491. Offers accounting (MBA, MS); business administration (MBA, DBA); environmental stewardship (MBA); finance (MBA); health care administration (MBA, MSM); homeland security (MBA, MSM); human resource management (MSM); management information systems (MBA, MSN); marketing (MSM); marketing management (MBA); military leadership (MSM); organizational leadership (MBA, MSM); public administration (MSM). Part-time and evening/weekend programs available. *Entrance requirements:* Additional exam requirements/recommendations for international students: Required—TOEFL (minimum score 500 paper-based). Electronic applications accepted.

Wilmington University, College of Technology, New Castle, DE 19720-6491. Offers corporate training skills (MS); information assurance (MS); information systems technologies (MS); Internet/Web design (MS); management and management information systems (MS). Part-time and evening/weekend programs available. *Entrance requirements:* Additional exam requirements/recommendations for international students: Required—TOEFL (minimum score 500 paper-based). Electronic applications accepted.

Winston-Salem State University, Program in Computer Science and Information Technology, Winston-Salem, NC 27110-0003. Offers MS. Part-time programs available. *Degree requirements:* For master's, thesis optional. *Entrance requirements:* For master's, GRE, resume. Electronic applications accepted. *Faculty research:* Artificial intelligence, network protocols, software engineering.

Worcester Polytechnic Institute, Graduate Studies and Research, School of Business, Worcester, MA 01609-2280. Offers information technology (MS), including information security management; management (Graduate Certificate); marketing and technological innovation (MS); operations design and leadership (MS); technology (MBA, MS). *Accreditation:* AACSB. Part-time and evening/weekend programs available. Postbaccalaureate distance learning degree programs offered (minimal on-campus study). *Faculty:* 28 full-time (12 women), 17 part-time/adjunct (3 women). *Students:* 123 full-time (77 women), 282 part-time (88 women); includes 34 minority (3 Black or African American, non-Hispanic/Latino; 15 Asian, non-Hispanic/Latino; 10 Hispanic/Latino; 6 Two or more races, non-Hispanic/Latino), 146 international. 747 applicants, 56% accepted, 111 enrolled. In 2013, 110 master's awarded. *Degree requirements:* For master's, thesis optional. *Entrance requirements:* For master's, GMAT (MBA); GMAT or GRE General Test (MS), statement of purpose, 3 letters of recommendation, resume; for Graduate Certificate, GMAT or GRE General Test, statement of purpose, 3 letters of recommendation. Additional exam requirements/recommendations for international students: Required—TOEFL (minimum score 563 paper-based; 84 iBT), IELTS (minimum score 7). *Application deadline:* For fall admission, 6/1 priority date for domestic and international students; for spring admission, 11/1 priority date for domestic students, 10/1 priority date for international students. Applications are processed on a rolling basis. Application fee: $70. Electronic applications accepted. *Financial support:* Career-related internships or fieldwork, institutionally sponsored loans, scholarships/grants, and unspecified assistantships available. Financial award application deadline: 6/1; financial award applicants required to submit FAFSA. *Unit head:* Dr. Paul Mack, Dean, 508-831-4665, Fax: 508-831-4665, E-mail: biz@wpi.edu. *Application contact:* Eileen Dagostino, Recruiting Operations Coordinator, 508-831-4665, Fax: 508-831-5720, E-mail: edag@wpi.edu.
Website: http://www.wpi.edu/academics/business/about.html.

Wright State University, School of Graduate Studies, Raj Soin College of Business, Department of Information Systems and Operations Management, Information Systems Program, Dayton, OH 45435. Offers MIS.

Section 13
Management Strategy and Policy

This section contains a directory of institutions offering graduate work in management strategy and policy. Additional information about programs listed in the directory but not augmented by an in-depth entry may be obtained by writing directly to the dean of a graduate school or chair of a department at the address given in the directory.

For programs offering related work, see also in this book *Business Administration and Management.* In another guide in this series:

Graduate Programs in the Humanities, Arts & Social Sciences

See *Public, Regional, and Industrial Affairs (Industrial and Labor Relations)*

CONTENTS

Program Directories

Management Strategy and Policy   480
Sustainability Management   491

Display and Close-Up

See:

University of California, Los Angeles—Business
    Administration and Management   145, 191

Management Strategy and Policy

Amberton University, Graduate School, Department of Business Administration, Garland, TX 75041-5595. Offers general business (MBA); management (MBA); project management (MBA); strategic leadership (MBA). Part-time and evening/weekend programs available. *Entrance requirements:* For master's, minimum GPA of 3.0. *Expenses: Tuition:* Full-time $5808; part-time $242 per credit hour.

American Public University System, AMU/APU Graduate Programs, Charles Town, WV 25414. Offers accounting (MBA, MS); criminal justice (MA), including business administration, emergency and disaster management, general (MA, MS); educational leadership (M Ed); emergency and disaster management (MA); entrepreneurship (MBA); environmental policy and management (MS), including environmental planning, environmental sustainability, fish and wildlife management, general (MA, MS), global environmental management; finance (MBA); general (MBA); global business management (MBA); history (MA), including American history, ancient and classical history, European history, global history, public history; homeland security (MA), including business administration, counter-terrorism studies, criminal justice, cyber, emergency management and public health, intelligence studies, transportation security; homeland security resource allocation (MBA); humanities (MA); information technology (MS), including digital forensics, enterprise software development, information assurance and security, IT project management; information technology management (MBA); intelligence studies (MA), including criminal intelligence, cyber, general (MA, MS), homeland security, intelligence analysis, intelligence collection, intelligence management, intelligence operations, terrorism studies; international relations and conflict resolution (MA), including comparative and security issues, conflict resolution, international and transnational security issues, peacekeeping; legal studies (MA); management (MA), including defense management, general (MA, MS), human resource management, organizational leadership, public administration; marketing (MBA); military history (MA), including American military history, American Revolution, civil war, war since 1945, World War II; military studies (MA), including joint warfare, strategic leadership; national security studies (MA), including general (MA, MS), homeland security, regional security studies, security and intelligence analysis, terrorism studies; nonprofit management (MBA); political science (MA), including American politics and government, comparative government and development, general (MA, MS), international relations, public policy; psychology (MA), including general (MA, MS), maritime engineering management, reverse logistics management; public administration (MPA), including disaster management, environmental policy, health policy, human resources, national security, organizational management, security management; public health (MPH); reverse logistics management (MA); school counseling (M Ed); security management (MA); space studies (MS), including aerospace science, general (MA, MS), planetary science; sports and health sciences (MS); teaching (M Ed), including curriculum and instruction for elementary teachers, elementary reading, English language learners, instructional leadership, online learning, special education; transportation and logistics management (MA), including general (MA, MS), maritime engineering management, reverse logistics management. Programs offered via distance learning only. Part-time and evening/weekend programs available. Postbaccalaureate distance learning degree programs offered (no on-campus study). *Faculty:* 432 full-time (242 women), 1,722 part-time/adjunct (829 women). *Students:* 511 full-time (241 women), 10,947 part-time (4,294 women); includes 3,760 minority (2,058 Black or African American, non-Hispanic/Latino; 88 American Indian or Alaska Native, non-Hispanic/Latino; 293 Asian, non-Hispanic/Latino; 876 Hispanic/Latino; 91 Native Hawaiian or other Pacific Islander, non-Hispanic/Latino; 354 Two or more races, non-Hispanic/Latino), 134 international. Average age 36. In 2013, 3,323 master's awarded. *Degree requirements:* For master's, comprehensive exam or practicum. *Entrance requirements:* For master's, official transcript showing earned bachelor's degree from institution accredited by recognized accrediting body. Additional exam requirements/recommendations for international students: Required—TOEFL (minimum score 550 paper-based), IELTS (minimum score 6.5). *Application deadline:* Applications are processed on a rolling basis. Application fee: $0. Electronic applications accepted. *Expenses: Tuition:* Part-time $325 per semester hour. *Financial support:* Applicants required to submit FAFSA. *Faculty research:* Military history, criminal justice, management performance, national security. *Unit head:* Dr. Karan Powell, Executive Vice President and Provost, 877-468-6268, Fax: 304-724-3780. *Application contact:* Terry Grant, Vice President of Enrollment Management, 877-468-6268, Fax: 304-724-3780, E-mail: info@apus.edu.
Website: http://www.apus.edu.

Antioch University Midwest, Graduate Programs, Program in Management and Leading Change, Yellow Springs, OH 45387-1609. Offers MA. Part-time and evening/weekend programs available. Postbaccalaureate distance learning degree programs offered (minimal on-campus study). *Entrance requirements:* For master's, resume, goal statement, interview. Electronic applications accepted. *Expenses:* Contact institution.

Austin Peay State University, College of Graduate Studies, The Austin Peay Center at Ft. Campbell, Department of Professional Studies, Clarksville, TN 37044. Offers strategic leadership (MPS). *Degree requirements:* For master's, project. *Expenses:* Tuition, state resident: full-time $7500; part-time $375 per credit hour. Tuition, nonresident: full-time $20,800; part-time $1040 per credit hour. *Required fees:* $1284; $64.20 per credit hour.

Azusa Pacific University, School of Business and Management, Azusa, CA 91702-7000. Offers business administration (MBA); diversity for strategic advantage (MA); entrepreneurship (MBA); finance (MBA); human and organizational development (MA); human resources and organizational development (MBA); human resources management (MA); international business (MBA); marketing (MBA); non-profit management (MA); organizational development and change (MA); performance improvement (MA); public administration (MA); strategic management (MBA). Part-time and evening/weekend programs available. *Degree requirements:* For master's, thesis (for some programs), final project. *Entrance requirements:* For master's, GMAT, minimum GPA of 3.0. Additional exam requirements/recommendations for international students: Required—TOEFL (minimum score 600 paper-based). *Expenses:* Contact institution. *Faculty research:* Gender issues, financial risk, leadership and ethics, marketing strategy.

Bentley University, McCallum Graduate School of Business, Graduate Business Certificate Program, Waltham, MA 02452-4705. Offers accounting (GBC); business analytics (GBC); business ethics (GBC); financial planning (GBC); fraud and forensic accounting (GBC); marketing analytics (GBC); taxation (GBC). *Accreditation:* AACSB. Part-time and evening/weekend programs available. *Faculty:* 91 full-time (29 women), 22 part-time/adjunct (4 women). *Students:* 29 part-time (15 women); includes 3 minority (2 Asian, non-Hispanic/Latino; 1 Hispanic/Latino), 3 international. Average age 36. 16 applicants, 94% accepted, 9 enrolled. *Entrance requirements:* For degree, GMAT or GRE General Test. Additional exam requirements/recommendations for international students: Required—TOEFL (minimum score 600 paper-based; 100 iBT) or IELTS (minimum score 7). *Application deadline:* For fall admission, 11/1 priority date for domestic and international students; for spring admission, 10/1 priority date for domestic and international students. Applications are processed on a rolling basis. Application fee: $50. Electronic applications accepted. *Expenses: Tuition:* Full-time $30,400; part-time $1267 per credit. *Required fees:* $404. Tuition and fees vary according to course load and program. *Financial support:* Application deadline: 6/1. *Unit head:* Dr. Roy A. Wiggins, III, Dean, 781-891-3166. *Application contact:* Sharon Hill, Director of Graduate Admissions, 781-891-2108, Fax: 781-891-2464, E-mail: bentleygraduateadmissions@bentley.edu.
Website: http://www.bentley.edu/graduate/degree-programs/special-programs/graduate-certificate-programs.

Black Hills State University, Graduate Studies, Program in Strategic Leadership, Spearfish, SD 57799. Offers MS. Part-time and evening/weekend programs available. *Faculty:* 2 full-time (0 women), 9 part-time/adjunct (2 women). *Students:* 44 part-time (24 women); includes 6 minority (3 Black or African American, non-Hispanic/Latino; 1 Asian, non-Hispanic/Latino; 2 Hispanic/Latino). Average age 35. 30 applicants, 100% accepted, 18 enrolled. In 2013, 12 master's awarded. *Entrance requirements:* Additional exam requirements/recommendations for international students: Required—TOEFL (minimum score 500 paper-based; 60 iBT). Application fee: $35. *Expenses: Tuition,* state resident: full-time $3718; part-time $201.85 per credit hour. Tuition, nonresident: full-time $7686; part-time $427.30 per credit hour. Tuition and fees vary according to course load, program and reciprocity agreements. *Unit head:* Dr. Mitch Hopewell, Coordinator of Strategic Leadership Program, 605-642-6258, E-mail: thomas.hopewell@bhsu.edu.

Boston University, Metropolitan College, Department of Computer Science, Boston, MA 02215. Offers advanced information technology (Certificate); computer information systems (MS), including computer networks, database management and business intelligence, health informatics, IT project management, security, Web application development; computer networks (Certificate); computer science (MS), including computer networks, security; database management and business intelligence (Certificate); digital forensics (Certificate); health informatics (Certificate); information security (Certificate); information technology (Certificate); information technology project management (Certificate); medical information security and privacy (Certificate); software engineering (Certificate); software engineering in health care systems (Certificate); telecommunications (MS), including security; Web application development (Certificate). Part-time and evening/weekend programs available. Postbaccalaureate distance learning degree programs offered (no on-campus study). *Faculty:* 13 full-time (3 women), 35 part-time/adjunct (2 women). *Students:* 48 full-time (14 women), 720 part-time (174 women); includes 215 minority (51 Black or African American, non-Hispanic/Latino; 111 Asian, non-Hispanic/Latino; 44 Hispanic/Latino; 9 Two or more races, non-Hispanic/Latino), 113 international. Average age 35. 360 applicants, 71% accepted, 221 enrolled. In 2013, 246 master's, 25 other advanced degrees awarded. *Degree requirements:* For master's, thesis optional. *Entrance requirements:* For master's and Certificate, official transcripts from regionally-accredited bachelor's degree program, 3 letters of recommendation, professional resume, personal statement. Additional exam requirements/recommendations for international students: Required—TOEFL (minimum score 84 iBT), IELTS. *Application deadline:* For fall admission, 6/1 priority date for international students; for spring admission, 10/1 priority date for international students. Applications are processed on a rolling basis. Application fee: $80. Electronic applications accepted. *Expenses: Tuition:* Full-time $43,970; part-time $1374 per credit hour. *Required fees:* $60 per semester. Tuition and fees vary according to class time, course level and program. *Financial support:* In 2013–14, 12 research assistantships (averaging $5,000 per year) were awarded; unspecified assistantships also available. Support available to part-time students. Financial award applicants required to submit FAFSA. *Faculty research:* Medical informatics, Web technologies, telecom and networks, security and forensics, software engineering, programming languages, multimedia and artificial intelligence (AI), information systems and IT project management. *Unit head:* Dr. Anatoly Temkin, Chairman, 617-353-2566, Fax: 617-353-2367, E-mail: csinfo@bu.edu. *Application contact:* Kim Richards, Program Coordinator, 617-353-2566, Fax: 617-353-2367, E-mail: kimrich@bu.edu.
Website: http://www.bu.edu/csmet/.

Brandeis University, Rabb School of Continuing Studies, Division of Graduate Professional Studies, Master of Science in Strategic Analytics Program, Waltham, MA 02454-9110. Offers MS. Part-time programs available. Postbaccalaureate distance learning degree programs offered (no on-campus study). *Faculty:* 2 full-time (1 woman), 33 part-time/adjunct (10 women). *Students:* 1 part-time (0 women). Average age 35. *Entrance requirements:* For master's, four-year bachelor's degree from regionally-accredited U.S. institution or equivalent; official transcript(s) from every college or university attended; resume or curriculum vitae; statement of goals; letter of recommendation. Additional exam requirements/recommendations for international students: Required—TOEFL (minimum scores: 600 paper-based, 100 iBT), IELTS (7), or PTE. *Application deadline:* For fall admission, 7/15 priority date for domestic and international students; for spring admission, 11/15 priority date for domestic and international students; for summer admission, 3/15 priority date for domestic and international students. Application fee: $50. Electronic applications accepted. *Unit head:* Leanne Bateman, Program Chair, 781-736-8787, Fax: 781-736-3420, E-mail: lbateman@brandeis.edu. *Application contact:* Frances Stearns, Associate Director of Admissions and Student Services, 781-736-8785, Fax: 781-736-3420, E-mail: fstearns@brandeis.edu.
Website: http://www.brandeis.edu/gps/.

California Miramar University, Program in Strategic Leadership, San Diego, CA 92126. Offers MS. *Degree requirements:* For master's, capstone project.

California State University, East Bay, Office of Academic Programs and Graduate Studies, College of Business and Economics, MBA Program, Hayward, CA 94542-3000. Offers entrepreneurship (MBA); finance (MBA); global innovators (MBA); human resources and organizational behavior (MBA); information technology management (MBA); marketing management (MBA); operations and supply chain management (MBA); strategy and international business (MBA). Part-time and evening/weekend programs available. *Degree requirements:* For master's, comprehensive exam or thesis. *Entrance requirements:* For master's, GMAT (minimum 20th percentile verbal and quantitative section), bachelor's degree, minimum GPA of 2.75. Additional exam requirements/recommendations for international students: Required—TOEFL (minimum score 550 paper-based; 79 iBT). Electronic applications accepted. *Expenses:* Contact institution.

California State University, East Bay, Office of Academic Programs and Graduate Studies, College of Business and Economics, Program in Information Technology Management, Option in Strategy and International Business, Hayward, CA 94542-3000. Offers MBA. Part-time and evening/weekend programs available. *Degree requirements:* For master's, comprehensive exam or thesis. *Entrance requirements:* For master's, GMAT, minimum GPA of 2.75. Additional exam requirements/recommendations for international students: Required—TOEFL (minimum score 550 paper-based).

Capella University, School of Business and Technology, Doctoral Programs in Business, Minneapolis, MN 55402. Offers accounting (DBA, PhD); business intelligence (DBA); finance (DBA, PhD); general business management (PhD); human resource management (DBA, PhD); leadership (DBA, PhD); management education (PhD); marketing (DBA, PhD); project management (DBA, PhD); strategy and innovation (DBA, PhD).

Capella University, School of Business and Technology, Master's Programs in Business, Minneapolis, MN 55402. Offers accounting (MBA); business analysis (MS); business intelligence (MBA); entrepreneurship (MBA); finance (MBA); general business administration (MBA); general human resource management (MS); general leadership (MS); health care management (MBA); human resource management (MBA); marketing (MBA); project management (MBA, MS).

Case Western Reserve University, Weatherhead School of Management, Department of Marketing and Policy Studies, Cleveland, OH 44106. Offers labor and human resource policy (MBA); management policy (MBA); marketing (MBA). Part-time and evening/weekend programs available. *Entrance requirements:* For master's, GMAT.

Claremont Graduate University, Graduate Programs, Peter F. Drucker and Masatoshi Ito Graduate School of Management, Program in Executive Management, Claremont, CA 91711-6160. Offers advanced management (MS); executive management (EMBA); leadership (Certificate); management (MA, PhD, Certificate); strategy (Certificate). *Accreditation:* AACSB. Part-time programs available. *Students:* 4 full-time (2 women), 80 part-time (31 women); includes 44 minority (6 Black or African American, non-Hispanic/Latino; 16 Asian, non-Hispanic/Latino; 17 Hispanic/Latino; 1 Native Hawaiian or other Pacific Islander, non-Hispanic/Latino; 4 Two or more races, non-Hispanic/Latino), 2 international. Average age 43. In 2013, 35 master's, 104 other advanced degrees awarded. *Entrance requirements:* Additional exam requirements/recommendations for international students: Required—TOEFL (minimum score 550 paper-based; 80 iBT). *Application deadline:* For fall admission, 7/1 for domestic and international students. Applications are processed on a rolling basis. Application fee: $80. Electronic applications accepted. *Expenses:* Contact institution. *Financial support:* Federal Work-Study, institutionally sponsored loans, and scholarships/grants available. Support available to part-time students. Financial award application deadline: 2/15; financial award applicants required to submit FAFSA. *Faculty research:* Strategy and leadership, brand management, cost management and control, organizational transformation, general management. *Unit head:* Jay Prag, Clinical Associate Professor/EMP Academic Director, 909-607-2576, Fax: 909-607-9104, E-mail: jay.prag@cgu.edu. *Application contact:* Loren Bryant, Admissions Coordinator, 909-621-8067, E-mail: loren.bryant@cgu.edu.
Website: http://www.cgu.edu/pages/1247.asp.

Davenport University, Sneden Graduate School, Grand Rapids, MI 49512. Offers accounting (MBA); business administration (EMBA); finance (MBA); health care management (MBA); human resources (MBA); information assurance (MS); public health (MPH); strategic management (MBA). Evening/weekend programs available. *Entrance requirements:* For master's, GMAT, minimum undergraduate GPA of 2.75. Additional exam requirements/recommendations for international students: Required—TOEFL. Electronic applications accepted. *Faculty research:* Leadership, management, marketing, organizational culture.

Defiance College, Program in Business Administration, Defiance, OH 43512-1610. Offers criminal justice (MBA); health care (MBA); leadership (MBA); sport management (MBA). Part-time and evening/weekend programs available. *Degree requirements:* For master's, thesis. *Entrance requirements:* For master's, minimum GPA of 2.5. Additional exam requirements/recommendations for international students: Recommended—TOEFL.

DePaul University, Charles H. Kellstadt Graduate School of Business, Chicago, IL 60604. Offers accountancy (M Acc, MS, MSA); applied economics (MBA); banking (MBA); behavioral finance (MBA); brand and product management (MBA); business development (MBA); business information technology (MS); business strategy and decision-making (MBA); computational finance (MS); consumer insights (MBA); corporate finance (MBA); economic policy analysis (MS); entrepreneurship (MBA, MS); finance (MBA, MS); financial analysis (MBA); general business (MBA); health sector management (MBA); hospitality leadership (MBA); hospitality leadership and operational performance (MS); human resource management (MBA); human resources (MS); investment management (MBA); leadership and change management (MBA); management accounting (MBA); marketing (MBA, MS); marketing analysis (MS); marketing strategy and planning (MBA); operations management (MBA); organizational diversity (MBA); real estate (MS); real estate finance and investment (MBA); revenue management (MBA); sports management (MBA); strategic global marketing (MBA); strategy, execution and valuation (MBA); sustainable management (MBA, MS); taxation (MS); wealth management (MS); JD/MBA. *Accreditation:* AACSB. Part-time and evening/weekend programs available. Postbaccalaureate distance learning degree programs offered (no on-campus study). *Faculty:* 81 full-time (20 women), 45 part-time/adjunct (8 women). *Students:* 1,238 full-time (605 women), 617 part-time (223 women); includes 295 minority (71 Black or African American, non-Hispanic/Latino; 129 Asian, non-Hispanic/Latino; 74 Hispanic/Latino; 4 Native Hawaiian or other Pacific Islander, non-Hispanic/Latino; 17 Two or more races, non-Hispanic/Latino), 462 international. Average age 29. In 2013, 911 master's awarded. *Entrance requirements:* For master's, GMAT, 2 letters of recommendation, resume, essay, official transcripts. Additional exam requirements/recommendations for international students: Required—TOEFL (minimum score 550 paper-based; 80 iBT). *Application deadline:* For fall admission, 7/1 for domestic students, 6/1 for international students; for winter admission, 10/1 for domestic students, 9/1 for international students; for spring admission, 2/1 for domestic students, 1/1 for international students. Applications are processed on a rolling basis. Application fee: $60. Electronic applications accepted. *Expenses:* Contact institution. *Financial support:* Application deadline: 4/1; applicants required to submit FAFSA. *Unit head:* Robert T. Ryan, Assistant Dean and Director, 312-362-8810, Fax: 312-362-6677, E-mail: rryan1@depaul.edu. *Application contact:* James Parker, Director of Recruitment and Admission, 312-362-8810, Fax: 312-362-6677, E-mail: kgsb@depaul.edu.
Website: http://kellstadt.depaul.edu.

Dominican University of California, Barowsky School of Business, San Rafael, CA 94901-2298. Offers global business (MBA); strategic leadership (MBA); sustainable enterprise (MBA). Part-time and evening/weekend programs available. *Faculty:* 7 full-time (3 women), 13 part-time/adjunct (5 women). *Students:* 53 full-time (35 women), 80 part-time (48 women); includes 28 minority (4 Black or African American, non-Hispanic/Latino; 6 Asian, non-Hispanic/Latino; 17 Hispanic/Latino; 1 Native Hawaiian or other Pacific Islander, non-Hispanic/Latino), 16 international. Average age 36. 136 applicants, 43% accepted, 36 enrolled. *Degree requirements:* For master's, thesis, capstone (for MBA). *Entrance requirements:* For master's, minimum GPA of 3.0. Additional exam requirements/recommendations for international students: Required—TOEFL (minimum score 550 paper-based; 80 iBT), IELTS (minimum score 6.5). *Application deadline:* For fall admission, 5/15 priority date for domestic and international students; for spring admission, 11/15 priority date for domestic and international students. Applications are processed on a rolling basis. Electronic applications accepted. Application fee is waived when completed online. *Expenses:* Contact institution. *Financial support:* Scholarships/grants and tuition discounts available. Support available to part-time students. Financial award application deadline: 3/2; financial award applicants required to submit FAFSA. *Unit head:* Dr. Sam Beldona, Dean, 415-458-3786, E-mail: sriam.beldona@dominican.edu. *Application contact:* Shannon Lovelace-White, Assistant Vice President, 415-485-3287, Fax: 415-485-3214, E-mail: shannon.lovelace-white@dominican.edu.
Website: http://www.dominican.edu/academics/barowskyschoolofbusiness.

Drexel University, LeBow College of Business, Program in Business Administration, Philadelphia, PA 19104-2875. Offers business administration (MBA, PhD, APC), including accounting (MBA, PhD), decision sciences (PhD), economics (MBA, PhD), finance (MBA, PhD), legal studies (MBA), management (MBA), marketing (MBA, PhD), organizational sciences (PhD), quantitative methods (MBA), strategic management (PhD). *Accreditation:* AACSB. Part-time and evening/weekend programs available. Postbaccalaureate distance learning degree programs offered (minimal on-campus study). Terminal master's awarded for partial completion of doctoral program. *Entrance requirements:* For master's, GMAT, minimum GPA of 2.75; for doctorate, GMAT. Additional exam requirements/recommendations for international students: Required—TOEFL. Electronic applications accepted. *Faculty research:* Decision support systems, individual and group behavior, operations research, techniques and strategy.

Duke University, The Fuqua School of Business, Cross Continent Executive MBA Program, Durham, NC 27708-0586. Offers business administration (MBA); energy and the environment (MBA); entrepreneurship and innovation (MBA); finance (MBA); health sector management (Certificate); marketing (MBA); strategy (MBA). *Faculty:* 91 full-time (15 women), 53 part-time/adjunct (9 women). *Students:* 121 full-time (34 women); includes 23 minority (3 Black or African American, non-Hispanic/Latino; 15 Asian, non-Hispanic/Latino; 4 Hispanic/Latino; 1 Native Hawaiian or other Pacific Islander, non-Hispanic/Latino), 31 international. Average age 30. In 2013, 147 master's awarded. *Degree requirements:* For master's, one foreign language. *Entrance requirements:* For master's, GMAT or GRE, transcripts, essays, resume, recommendation letters, interview. Additional exam requirements/recommendations for international students: Required—TOEFL, IELTS, PTE. *Application deadline:* For fall admission, 10/16 for domestic students, 10/6 for international students; for winter admission, 2/12 for domestic and international students; for spring admission, 5/6 for domestic and international students; for summer admission, 6/4 for domestic students. Application fee: $225. Electronic applications accepted. *Financial support:* In 2013–14, 16 students received support. Institutionally sponsored loans and scholarships/grants available. Financial award applicants required to submit FAFSA. *Unit head:* John Gallagher, Associate Dean for Executive MBA Programs, 919-660-7641, E-mail: johng@duke.edu. *Application contact:* Liz Riley Hargrove, Associate Dean for Admissions, 919-660-1956, Fax: 919-681-8026, E-mail: admissions-info@fuqua.duke.edu.
Website: http://www.fuqua.duke.edu/programs/duke_mba/cross_continent/.

Duke University, The Fuqua School of Business, Daytime MBA Program, Durham, NC 27708-0586. Offers academic excellence in finance (Certificate); business administration (MBA); decision sciences (MBA); energy and environment (MBA); energy finance (MBA); entrepreneurship and innovation (MBA); finance (MBA); financial analysis (MBA); health sector management (Certificate); leadership and ethics (MBA); management (MBA); marketing (MBA); operations management (MBA); social entrepreneurship (MBA); strategy (MBA). *Faculty:* 91 full-time (15 women), 53 part-time/adjunct (9 women). *Students:* 862 full-time (283 women); includes 179 minority (34 Black or African American, non-Hispanic/Latino; 1 American Indian or Alaska Native, non-Hispanic/Latino; 92 Asian, non-Hispanic/Latino; 42 Hispanic/Latino; 2 Native Hawaiian or other Pacific Islander, non-Hispanic/Latino; 8 Two or more races, non-Hispanic/Latino), 342 international. Average age 29. In 2013, 437 master's awarded. *Entrance requirements:* For master's, GMAT or GRE, transcripts, essays, resume, recommendation letters, interview. Additional exam requirements/recommendations for international students: Required—TOEFL, IELTS, PTE. *Application deadline:* For fall admission, 9/18 for domestic and international students; for winter admission, 10/21 for domestic and international students; for spring admission, 1/6 for domestic and international students; for summer admission, 3/20 for domestic and international students. Application fee: $225. Electronic applications accepted. *Financial support:* In 2013–14, 331 students received support. Institutionally sponsored loans and scholarships/grants available. Financial award applicants required to submit FAFSA. *Unit head:* Russ Morgan, Associate Dean for the Daytime MBA Program, 919-660-2931, Fax: 919-684-8742, E-mail: ruskin.morgan@duke.edu. *Application contact:* Liz Riley Hargrove, Associate Dean of Admissions, 919-660-7705, Fax: 919-681-8026, E-mail: liz.riley@duke.edu.
Website: http://www.fuqua.duke.edu/daytime-mba/.

Duke University, The Fuqua School of Business, Global Executive MBA Program, Durham, NC 27708-0586. Offers business administration (MBA); energy and the environment (MBA); entrepreneurship and innovation (MBA); finance (MBA); health sector management (Certificate); marketing (MBA); strategy (MBA). *Faculty:* 91 full-time (15 women), 53 part-time/adjunct (9 women). *Students:* 49 full-time (7 women); includes 7 minority (1 Black or African American, non-Hispanic/Latino; 3 Asian, non-Hispanic/Latino; 3 Hispanic/Latino), 17 international. Average age 39. In 2013, 51 master's awarded. *Entrance requirements:* For master's, transcripts, essays, resume, recommendation letters, interview. Additional exam requirements/recommendations for international students: Required—TOEFL, IELTS, PTE. *Application deadline:* For fall admission, 9/4 for domestic and international students; for winter admission, 10/16 for domestic and international students; for spring admission, 12/5 for domestic and international students; for summer admission, 1/13 for domestic and international students. Application fee: $225. *Financial support:* In 2013–14, 8 students received support. Institutionally sponsored loans and scholarships/grants available. Financial award applicants required to submit FAFSA. *Unit head:* John Gallagher, Associate Dean for Executive MBA Programs, 919-660-7728, E-mail: johng@duke.edu. *Application contact:* Liz Riley Hargrove, Director of EMBA Admissions, 919-660-7705, Fax: 919-681-8026, E-mail: admissions-info@fuqua.duke.edu.
Website: http://www.fuqua.duke.edu/programs/duke_mba/global-executive/.

Duke University, The Fuqua School of Business, PhD Program, Durham, NC 27708-0586. Offers accounting (PhD); decision sciences (PhD); finance (PhD); management and organizations (PhD); marketing (PhD); operations management (PhD); strategy (PhD). *Faculty:* 91 full-time (15 women). *Students:* 78 full-time (27 women); includes 4 minority (1 Black or African American, non-Hispanic/Latino; 3 Asian, non-Hispanic/Latino), 49 international. 589 applicants, 5% accepted, 16 enrolled. In 2013, 26 doctorates awarded. *Degree requirements:* For doctorate, thesis/dissertation, major field requirement (exam or major paper, depending upon the area). *Entrance requirements:* For doctorate, GMAT or GRE, transcripts, essays, recommendation letters, statement of

purpose. Additional exam requirements/recommendations for international students: Required—TOEFL (minimum score 577 paper-based; 90 iBT), IELTS (minimum score 7). *Application deadline:* For fall admission, 12/8 priority date for domestic and international students. Application fee: $80. Electronic applications accepted. *Financial support:* In 2013–14, 70 fellowships with full tuition reimbursements (averaging $25,300 per year), 56 research assistantships with full tuition reimbursements (averaging $7,000 per year) were awarded; institutionally sponsored loans, scholarships/grants, and tuition waivers (full) also available. Financial award applicants required to submit FAFSA. *Unit head:* William Boulding, Dean, 919-660-7822, Fax: 919-684-8742, E-mail: bb1@duke.edu. *Application contact:* Dr. James R. Bettman, Director of Graduate Studies, 919-660-7851, Fax: 919-681-6245, E-mail: jrb12@mail.duke.edu.

Duke University, The Fuqua School of Business, Weekend Executive MBA Program, Durham, NC 27708-0586. Offers business administration (MBA); energy and environment (MBA); entrepreneurship and innovation (MBA); finance (MBA); health sector management (Certificate); marketing (MBA); strategy (MBA). *Faculty:* 91 full-time (15 women), 53 part-time/adjunct (9 women). *Students:* 93 full-time (14 women); includes 33 minority (5 Black or African American, non-Hispanic/Latino; 24 Asian, non-Hispanic/Latino; 3 Hispanic/Latino; 1 Two or more races, non-Hispanic/Latino), 15 international. Average age 36. In 2013, 103 master's awarded. *Degree requirements:* For master's, one foreign language. *Entrance requirements:* For master's, GMAT (preferred) or GRE, transcripts, essays, resume, recommendation letters, interview. Additional exam requirements/recommendations for international students: Required—TOEFL, IELTS, PTE. *Application deadline:* For fall admission, 9/4 for domestic and international students; for winter admission, 10/16 for domestic and international students; for spring admission, 2/12 for domestic and international students; for summer admission, 4/2 for domestic and international students. Application fee: $225. Electronic applications accepted. *Financial support:* In 2013–14, 14 students received support. Institutionally sponsored loans and scholarships/grants available. Financial award applicants required to submit FAFSA. *Unit head:* John Gallagher, Associate Dean for Executive MBA Programs, 919-660-7728, E-mail: johng@duke.edu. *Application contact:* Liz Riley Hargrove, Director of EMBA Admissions, 919-660-7705, Fax: 919-681-8026, E-mail: admissions-info@fuqua.duke.edu.
Website: http://www.fuqua.duke.edu/programs/duke_mba/weekend_executive/.

Duquesne University, School of Leadership and Professional Advancement, Pittsburgh, PA 15282-0001. Offers leadership (MS), including business ethics, community leadership, global leadership, health care, information technology, leadership, liberal studies, professional administration, sports leadership. Part-time and evening/weekend programs available. Postbaccalaureate distance learning degree programs offered (no on-campus study). *Faculty:* 15 full-time (7 women), 64 part-time/adjunct (26 women). *Students:* 213 full-time (106 women), 170 part-time (86 women); includes 89 minority (59 Black or African American, non-Hispanic/Latino; 2 American Indian or Alaska Native, non-Hispanic/Latino; 7 Asian, non-Hispanic/Latino; 9 Hispanic/Latino; 1 Native Hawaiian or other Pacific Islander, non-Hispanic/Latino; 11 Two or more races, non-Hispanic/Latino), 9 international. Average age 36. 204 applicants, 56% accepted, 103 enrolled. In 2013, 140 master's awarded. *Degree requirements:* For master's, capstone course. *Entrance requirements:* For master's, professional work experience, 500-word essay, resume, interview. Additional exam requirements/recommendations for international students: Required—TOEFL (minimum score 80 iBT). *Application deadline:* Applications are processed on a rolling basis. Application fee: $0. Electronic applications accepted. Application fee is waived when completed online. *Expenses: Tuition:* Full-time $18,162; part-time $1009 per credit. *Required fees:* $1728; $96 per credit. Tuition and fees vary according to program. *Financial support:* Scholarships/grants available. Financial award applicants required to submit FAFSA. *Unit head:* Dr. Dorothy Bassett, Dean, 412-396-2141, Fax: 412-396-4711, E-mail: bassettd@duq.edu. *Application contact:* Marianne Leister, Director of Student Services, 412-396-4933, Fax: 412-396-5072, E-mail: leister@duq.edu.
Website: http://www.duq.edu/academics/schools/leadership-and-professional-advancement.

East Tennessee State University, School of Graduate Studies, School of Continuing Studies and Academic Outreach, Johnson City, TN 37614. Offers archival studies (MALS, Postbaccalaureate Certificate); gender and diversity (MALS); regional and community studies (MALS); strategic leadership (MPS); training and development (MPS). Part-time programs available. Postbaccalaureate distance learning degree programs offered (no on-campus study). *Faculty:* 4 full-time (all women), 2 part-time/adjunct (1 woman). *Students:* 20 full-time (14 women), 41 part-time (33 women); includes 8 minority (2 Black or African American, non-Hispanic/Latino; 1 Asian, non-Hispanic/Latino; 2 Hispanic/Latino; 3 Two or more races, non-Hispanic/Latino), 2 international. Average age 39. 42 applicants, 50% accepted, 19 enrolled. In 2013, 11 master's, 5 other advanced degrees awarded. *Degree requirements:* For master's, comprehensive exam, thesis optional, professional project. *Entrance requirements:* For master's, GRE General Test, minimum GPA of 2.75, professional portfolio, three letters of recommendation, interview, writing sample; for Postbaccalaureate Certificate, minimum GPA of 2.5, three letters of recommendation, interview. Additional exam requirements/recommendations for international students: Required—TOEFL (minimum score 550 paper-based; 79 iBT). *Application deadline:* For fall admission, 6/1 for domestic students, 4/30 for international students; for spring admission, 11/1 for domestic students, 9/30 for international students. Application fee: $35 ($45 for international students). Electronic applications accepted. *Expenses:* Tuition, state resident: full-time $7900; part-time $395 per credit hour. Tuition, nonresident: full-time $21,960; part-time $1098 per credit hour. *Required fees:* $1345; $84 per credit hour. *Financial support:* In 2013–14, 14 students received support, including 3 research assistantships with full tuition reimbursements available (averaging $6,000 per year), 1 teaching assistantship with full tuition reimbursement available (averaging $9,000 per year); institutionally sponsored loans, scholarships/grants, tuition waivers, and unspecified assistantships also available. Financial award application deadline: 7/1; financial award applicants required to submit FAFSA. *Faculty research:* Appalachian studies, women's and gender studies, interdisciplinary theory, regional and Southern cultures. *Unit head:* Dr. Rick E. Osborn, Dean, 423-439-4223, Fax: 423-439-7091, E-mail: osbornr@etsu.edu. *Application contact:* Mary Duncan, Graduate Specialist, 423-439-4302, Fax: 423-439-5624, E-mail: duncanm@etsu.edu.
Website: http://www.etsu.edu/academicaffairs/scs/.

Florida State University, The Graduate School, College of Business, Tallahassee, FL 32306-1110. Offers accounting (M Acc), including accounting information services, assurance services, corporate accounting, taxation; business administration (MBA, PhD), including accounting (PhD), finance (PhD), management information systems (PhD), marketing (PhD), organizational behavior and human resources (PhD), risk management and insurance (PhD), strategic management (PhD); finance (MS); insurance (MSM); management information systems (MS); marketing (MS); JD/MBA; MSW/MBA. *Accreditation:* AACSB. Part-time programs available. Postbaccalaureate distance learning degree programs offered (no on-campus study). *Faculty:* 102 full-time (31 women), 5 part-time/adjunct (0 women). *Students:* 280 full-time (117 women), 278 part-time (88 women); includes 127 minority (26 Black or African American, non-Hispanic/Latino; 7 American Indian or Alaska Native, non-Hispanic/Latino; 44 Asian, non-Hispanic/Latino; 50 Hispanic/Latino). Average age 30. 630 applicants, 28% accepted, 103 enrolled. In 2013, 265 master's, 11 doctorates awarded. Terminal master's awarded for partial completion of doctoral program. *Degree requirements:* For doctorate, comprehensive exam, thesis/dissertation. *Entrance requirements:* For master's, GMAT, work experience (MBA, MS), minimum GPA of 3.0, letters of recommendation; for doctorate, GMAT, minimum graduate GPA of 3.5, letters of recommendation. Additional exam requirements/recommendations for international students: Required—TOEFL (minimum score 600 paper-based; 100 iBT); Recommended—IELTS (minimum score 6.5). *Application deadline:* For fall admission, 6/1 for domestic students, 5/1 for international students; for spring admission, 10/1 for domestic students, 9/1 for international students. Applications are processed on a rolling basis. Application fee: $30. Electronic applications accepted. *Expenses:* Tuition, state resident: part-time $403.51 per credit hour. Tuition, nonresident: part-time $1004.85 per credit hour. *Required fees:* $75.81 per credit hour. One-time fee: $20 part-time. Tuition and fees vary according to course load, campus/location and student level. *Financial support:* In 2013–14, 92 students received support, including 10 fellowships with full tuition reimbursements available (averaging $1,500 per year), 20 research assistantships with full tuition reimbursements available (averaging $20,000 per year), 35 teaching assistantships with full tuition reimbursements available (averaging $20,000 per year); career-related internships or fieldwork, scholarships/grants, health care benefits, and unspecified assistantships also available. Financial award application deadline: 1/1. *Unit head:* Dr. Caryn Beck-Dudley, Dean, 850-644-3090, Fax: 850-644-0915. *Application contact:* Lisa Beverly, Director, Graduate Programs Admissions, 850-644-6458, Fax: 850-644-0588, E-mail: lbeverly@cob.fsu.edu.
Website: http://www.cob.fsu.edu/.

Franklin Pierce University, Graduate Studies, Rindge, NH 03461-0060. Offers curriculum and instruction (M Ed); emerging network technologies (Graduate Certificate); energy and sustainability studies (MBA); health administration (MBA, Graduate Certificate); human resource management (MBA, Graduate Certificate); information technology (MBA); information technology management (MS); leadership (MBA, DA); nursing (MS); physical therapy (DPT); physician assistant studies (MPAS); special education (M Ed); sports management (MBA). *Accreditation:* APTA. Part-time programs available. Postbaccalaureate distance learning degree programs offered (no on-campus study). *Degree requirements:* For master's, concentrated original research projects; student teaching; fieldwork and/or internship; leadership project; PRAXIS I and II (for M Ed); for doctorate, concentrated original research projects, clinical fieldwork and/or internship, leadership project. *Entrance requirements:* For master's, minimum GPA of 2.5, 3 letters of recommendation; competencies in accounting, economics, statistics, and computer skills through life experience or undergraduate coursework (for MBA); certification/e-portfolio, minimum C grade in all education courses (for M Ed); license to practice as RN (for MS in nursing); for doctorate, GRE, BA/BS, 3 letters of recommendation, personal mission statement, interview, writing sample, minimum cumulative GPA of 2.8, master's degree (for DA); 80 hours of observation/work in PT settings, completion of anatomy, chemistry, physics, and statistics, minimum GPA of 3.0 (for DPT). Additional exam requirements/recommendations for international students: Required—TOEFL (minimum score 550 paper-based; 61 iBT). Electronic applications accepted. *Faculty research:* Evidence-based practice in sports physical therapy, human resource management in economic crisis, leadership in nursing, innovation in sports facility management, differentiated learning and understanding by design.

Freed-Hardeman University, Program in Business Administration, Henderson, TN 38340-2399. Offers accounting (MBA); corporate responsibility (MBA); leadership (MBA). *Accreditation:* ACBSP. Part-time and evening/weekend programs available. Postbaccalaureate distance learning degree programs offered (no on-campus study). *Entrance requirements:* For master's, GMAT. Additional exam requirements/recommendations for international students: Required—TOEFL (minimum score 500 paper-based).

Friends University, Graduate School, Wichita, KS 67213. Offers business law (MBL); Christian ministry (MACM); family therapy (MSFT); global (MBA), including accounting, business law, change management, health care leadership, management information systems, supply chain management and logistics; health care leadership (MHCL); management information systems (MMIS); operations management (MSOM); professional (MBA), including accounting, business law, change management, health care leadership, management information systems, supply chain management and logistics; teaching (MAT). Part-time and evening/weekend programs available. Postbaccalaureate distance learning degree programs offered (no on-campus study). *Faculty:* 18 full-time (8 women), 62 part-time/adjunct (28 women). *Students:* 161 full-time (111 women), 408 part-time (258 women); includes 157 minority (68 Black or African American, non-Hispanic/Latino; 7 American Indian or Alaska Native, non-Hispanic/Latino; 28 Asian, non-Hispanic/Latino; 18 Hispanic/Latino; 1 Native Hawaiian or other Pacific Islander, non-Hispanic/Latino; 35 Two or more races, non-Hispanic/Latino). Average age 36. 371 applicants, 90% accepted, 178 enrolled. In 2013, 432 master's awarded. *Degree requirements:* For master's, research project. *Entrance requirements:* For master's, bachelor's degree from accredited institution, official transcripts, interview with program director, letter(s) of recommendation. Additional exam requirements/recommendations for international students: Required—TOEFL (minimum score 560 paper-based). *Application deadline:* Applications are processed on a rolling basis. Application fee: $35 ($50 for international students). Electronic applications accepted. *Expenses: Tuition:* Part-time $631 per credit hour. Tuition and fees vary according to program. *Financial support:* In 2013–14, 30 students received support. Applicants required to submit FAFSA. *Unit head:* Dr. David Hofmeister, Dean of the Graduate School, 800-794-6945 Ext. 5858, Fax: 316-295-5040, E-mail: david_hofmeister@friends.edu. *Application contact:* Rachel Steiner, Manager, Graduate Recruiting Services, 800-794-6945, Fax: 316-295-5872, E-mail: rachel_steiner@friends.edu.
Website: http://www.friends.edu/.

The George Washington University, School of Business, Department of Strategic Management and Public Policy, Washington, DC 20052. Offers MBA, PhD. *Accreditation:* NASPAA. Part-time and evening/weekend programs available. *Faculty:* 16 full-time (4 women). *Students:* 197 full-time (78 women), 3 part-time (2 women); includes 31 minority (10 Black or African American, non-Hispanic/Latino; 14 Asian, non-Hispanic/Latino; 3 Hispanic/Latino; 4 Two or more races, non-Hispanic/Latino), 74 international. Average age 29. 617 applicants, 46% accepted. In 2013, 120 master's awarded. *Degree requirements:* For doctorate, thesis/dissertation. *Entrance requirements:* For master's, GMAT; for doctorate, GMAT or GRE. Additional exam requirements/recommendations for international students: Required—TOEFL. *Application deadline:* For fall admission, 4/1 priority date for domestic students; for spring admission, 10/1 for domestic students. Applications are processed on a rolling basis. Application fee: $75. *Financial support:* In 2013–14, 1 student received support. Fellowships, teaching assistantships, career-related internships or fieldwork, Federal Work-Study, and institutionally sponsored loans available. Financial award application deadline: 4/1. *Unit head:* Dr. Jennifer Griffin, Chair, 202-994-7872, E-mail: jgriffin@gwu.edu. *Application contact:* Kristin Williams, Assistant Vice President for Graduate and Special Enrollment Management, 202-994-0467, Fax: 202-994-0371, E-mail: ksw@gwu.edu.
Website: http://business.gwu.edu/smpp/.

Georgia Institute of Technology, Graduate Studies and Research, College of Management, Program in Business Administration, Atlanta, GA 30332-0001. Offers accounting (MBA); e-commerce (Certificate); engineering entrepreneurship (MBA); entrepreneurship (Certificate); finance (MBA); information technology management (MBA); international business (MBA, Certificate); management of technology (Certificate); marketing (MBA); operations management (MBA); organizational behavior (MBA); strategic management (MBA). *Accreditation:* AACSB.

Georgia Institute of Technology, Graduate Studies and Research, College of Management, Program in Management, Atlanta, GA 30332-0001. Offers accounting (PhD); finance (PhD); information technology management (PhD); marketing (PhD); operations management (PhD); organizational behavior (PhD); quantitative and computational finance (MS); strategic management (PhD). *Accreditation:* AACSB. *Degree requirements:* For doctorate, comprehensive exam, thesis/dissertation, oral exams. *Entrance requirements:* For master's and doctorate, GMAT. Additional exam requirements/recommendations for international students: Required—TOEFL. *Faculty research:* Management information systems, management of technology, international business, entrepreneurship, operations management.

Georgia State University, J. Mack Robinson College of Business, Department of Managerial Sciences, Atlanta, GA 30302-3083. Offers business analysis (MBA, MS); entrepreneurship (MBA); human resources management (MBA, MS); operations management (MBA, MS); organization behavior/human resource management (PhD); organization management (MBA); organizational change (MS); strategic management (PhD). *Accreditation:* AACSB. Part-time and evening/weekend programs available. *Faculty:* 18 full-time (6 women). *Students:* 31 full-time (15 women), 22 part-time (14 women); includes 20 minority (11 Black or African American, non-Hispanic/Latino; 1 American Indian or Alaska Native, non-Hispanic/Latino; 2 Asian, non-Hispanic/Latino; 2 Hispanic/Latino; 4 Two or more races, non-Hispanic/Latino), 16 international. Average age 31. 92 applicants, 20% accepted, 13 enrolled. In 2013, 45 master's, 2 doctorates awarded. *Degree requirements:* For doctorate, comprehensive exam, thesis/dissertation. *Entrance requirements:* For master's, GRE or GMAT, transcripts from all institutions attended, resume, essays; for doctorate, GMAT, three letters of recommendation, personal statement, transcripts from all institutions attended, resume. Additional exam requirements/recommendations for international students: Required—TOEFL (minimum score 610 paper-based; 101 iBT), IELTS (minimum score 7). *Application deadline:* For fall admission, 5/1 priority date for domestic students, 2/1 priority date for international students; for spring admission, 9/15 priority date for domestic students, 4/1 priority date for international students. Applications are processed on a rolling basis. Application fee: $50. Electronic applications accepted. *Expenses: Tuition, area resident:* Full-time $4176; part-time $348 per credit hour. Tuition, state resident: full-time $14,544; part-time $1212 per credit hour. Tuition, nonresident: full-time $14,544; part-time $1212 per credit hour. Tuition and fees vary according to course load and program. *Financial support:* Research assistantships, teaching assistantships, scholarships/grants, tuition waivers, and unspecified assistantships available. *Faculty research:* Entrepreneurship and Innovation; strategy process; workplace interactions, relationships, and processes; leadership and culture; supply chain management. *Unit head:* Dr. Pamela S. Barr, Interim Chair, 404-413-7525, Fax: 404-413-7571. *Application contact:* Toby McChesney, Assistant Dean for Graduate Recruiting and Student Services, 404-413-7167, Fax: 404-413-7162, E-mail: rcbgradadmissions@gsu.edu.
Website: http://mgmt.robinson.gsu.edu/.

Grantham University, Mark Skousen School of Business, Lenexa, KS 66219. Offers business administration (MBA); business intelligence (MS); information management (MBA); information management technology (MS); information technology (MS); performance improvement (MS); project management (MBA, MS). Part-time and evening/weekend programs available. Postbaccalaureate distance learning degree programs offered (no on-campus study). *Faculty:* 3 full-time (2 women), 35 part-time/adjunct (11 women). *Students:* 233 full-time (75 women), 559 part-time (207 women); includes 399 minority (296 Black or African American, non-Hispanic/Latino; 6 American Indian or Alaska Native, non-Hispanic/Latino; 14 Asian, non-Hispanic/Latino; 58 Hispanic/Latino; 1 Native Hawaiian or other Pacific Islander, non-Hispanic/Latino; 24 Two or more races, non-Hispanic/Latino). Average age 40. 792 applicants, 100% accepted, 792 enrolled. In 2013, 404 master's awarded. *Degree requirements:* For master's, thesis, capstone project, simulation game. *Entrance requirements:* For master's, bachelor's degree from accredited degree-granting institution with minimum GPA of 2.5. Additional exam requirements/recommendations for international students: Required—TOEFL (minimum score 530 paper-based; 71 iBT). *Application deadline:* Applications are processed on a rolling basis. Application fee: $30. Electronic applications accepted. *Expenses: Tuition:* Full-time $3900; part-time $325 per credit hour. *Required fees:* $35 per term. One-time fee: $100. *Financial support:* In 2013–14, 792 students received support. Scholarships/grants available. *Faculty research:* Relationship between media choices and teaching experience in online courses, online best teaching practices, strategy for co-creation of value with consumers, political identity and party polarization in the American Electorate, political participation and Web 2.0. *Unit head:* Dr. Niccole Buckley, Dean, Mark Skousen School of Business, 800-955-2527, E-mail: admissions@grantham.edu. *Application contact:* Jared Parlette, Vice President of Admissions, 800-955-2527, E-mail: admissions@grantham.edu.
Website: http://www.grantham.edu/colleges-and-schools/school-of-business/.

Harvard University, Harvard Business School, Doctoral Programs in Management, Boston, MA 02163. Offers accounting and management (DBA); business economics (PhD); health policy management (PhD); management (DBA); marketing (DBA); organizational behavior (PhD); science, technology and management (PhD); strategy (DBA); technology and operations management (DBA). *Degree requirements:* For doctorate, comprehensive exam (for some programs), thesis/dissertation. *Entrance requirements:* For doctorate, GRE General Test or GMAT. Additional exam requirements/recommendations for international students: Required—TOEFL. *Expenses: Tuition:* Full-time $38,888. *Required fees:* $958. Tuition and fees vary according to campus/location, program and student level.

HEC Montreal, School of Business Administration, Master of Science Programs in Administration, Program in Business Intelligence, Montréal, QC H3T 2A7, Canada. Offers M Sc. All courses are given in French. *Students:* 32 full-time (14 women), 11 part-time (4 women). 17 applicants, 76% accepted, 9 enrolled. In 2013, 3 master's awarded. *Degree requirements:* For master's, one foreign language, thesis. *Entrance requirements:* For master's, Test de francais international (TFI) with minimum score of 850 (for those who have never studied in French), BBA, undergraduate degree in another field, degree deemed equivalent by program director and minimum GPA of 3.0 on 4.3 scale. *Application deadline:* For fall admission, 3/15 for domestic and international students; for winter admission, 9/15 for domestic and international students. Application fee: $83 Canadian dollars. Electronic applications accepted. *Expenses: Tuition, area resident:* Part-time $74.14 per credit. Tuition, state resident: full-time $2669.04; part-time $201.83 per credit. Tuition, nonresident: full-time $7266; part-time $500.59 per credit. *International tuition:* $18,021.24 full-time. *Required fees:* $1529.70; $36.20 per credit. $65.50 per term. Tuition and fees vary according to degree level and program. *Financial support:* In 2013–14, 1,007 students received support.

Research assistantships, teaching assistantships, and scholarships/grants available. Financial award application deadline: 9/2. *Unit head:* Dr. Anne Bourhis, Director, 514-340-6873, Fax: 514-340-6880, E-mail: anne.bourhis@hec.ca. *Application contact:* Marianne de Moura, Administrative Director, 514-340-7106, Fax: 514-340-6411, E-mail: marianne.de-moura@hec.ca.
Website: http://www.hec.ca/programmes_formations/msc/options/finance/ingenierie_financiere/index.html.

HEC Montreal, School of Business Administration, Master of Science Programs in Administration, Program in Strategy, Montréal, QC H3T 2A7, Canada. Offers M Sc. All courses are given in French. *Students:* 63 full-time (28 women), 20 part-time (5 women). 63 applicants, 83% accepted, 32 enrolled. In 2013, 18 master's awarded. *Degree requirements:* For master's, one foreign language, thesis. *Entrance requirements:* For master's, Test de francais international (TFI) with minimum score of 850 (for those who have never studied in French), BBA, undergraduate degree in another field, degree deemed equivalent by program director and minimum GPA of 3.0 on 4.3 scale. *Application deadline:* For fall admission, 3/15 for domestic and international students; for winter admission, 9/15 for domestic and international students. Application fee: $83. Electronic applications accepted. *Expenses: Tuition, area resident:* Part-time $74.14 per credit. Tuition, state resident: full-time $2669.04; part-time $201.83 per credit. Tuition, nonresident: full-time $7266; part-time $500.59 per credit. *International tuition:* $18,021.24 full-time. *Required fees:* $1529.70; $36.20 per credit. $65.50 per term. Tuition and fees vary according to degree level and program. *Financial support:* In 2013–14, 1,007 students received support. Research assistantships, teaching assistantships, and scholarships/grants available. Financial award application deadline: 9/2. *Unit head:* Dr. Anne Bourhis, Director, 514-340-6873, Fax: 514-340-6880, E-mail: anne.bourhis@hec.ca. *Application contact:* Marianne de Moura, Administrative Director, 514-340-7106, Fax: 514-340-6411, E-mail: marianne.de-moura@hec.ca.
Website: http://www.hec.ca/programmes_formations/msc/options/strategie/index.html.

Lamar University, College of Graduate Studies, College of Business, Beaumont, TX 77710. Offers accounting (MBA); experiential business and entrepreneurship (MBA); financial management (MBA); healthcare administration (MBA); information systems (MBA); management (MBA). *Accreditation:* AACSB. Part-time and evening/weekend programs available. *Degree requirements:* For master's, comprehensive exam (for some programs), thesis optional. *Entrance requirements:* For master's, GMAT. Additional exam requirements/recommendations for international students: Required—TOEFL (minimum score 525 paper-based). *Faculty research:* Marketing, finance, quantitative methods, management information systems, legal, environmental.

LeTourneau University, Graduate Programs, Longview, TX 75607-7001. Offers business administration (MBA); counseling (MA); education (M Ed); engineering (MS); health care administration (MS); marriage and family therapy (MA); psychology (MA); strategic leadership (MSL). Part-time programs available. Postbaccalaureate distance learning degree programs offered (no on-campus study). *Faculty:* 15 full-time (7 women), 54 part-time/adjunct (23 women). *Students:* 58 full-time (45 women), 365 part-time (287 women); includes 106 minority (51 Black or African American, non-Hispanic/Latino; 3 American Indian or Alaska Native, non-Hispanic/Latino; 1 Asian, non-Hispanic/Latino; 45 Hispanic/Latino; 6 Two or more races, non-Hispanic/Latino), 4 international. Average age 38. 263 applicants, 68% accepted, 116 enrolled. In 2013, 112 master's awarded. *Degree requirements:* For master's, thesis (for some programs). *Entrance requirements:* For master's, GRE (for engineering programs), minimum GPA of 2.8 (3.0 for counseling and engineering programs). Additional exam requirements/recommendations for international students: Required—TOEFL. *Application deadline:* For fall admission, 8/22 for domestic students, 8/29 for international students; for winter admission, 10/10 for domestic students; for spring admission, 1/2 for domestic students, 1/10 for international students; for summer admission, 5/1 for domestic and international students. Applications are processed on a rolling basis. Electronic applications accepted. Application fee is waived when completed online. *Financial support:* In 2013–14, 11 students received support, including 13 research assistantships (averaging $9,122 per year); institutionally sponsored loans and unspecified assistantships also available. Financial award applicants required to submit FAFSA. *Unit head:* Dr. Robert Hudson, Vice President and Dean of the Graduate School, 903-233-1110, E-mail: roberthudson@letu.edu. *Application contact:* Chris Fontaine, Assistant Vice President for Global Campus Admissions, 903-233-4312, E-mail: chrisfontaine@letu.edu.
Website: http://www.adults.letu.edu/.

Manhattanville College, School of Business, Program in Business Leadership, Purchase, NY 10577-2132. Offers MS. Part-time and evening/weekend programs available. *Degree requirements:* For master's, thesis, final project. *Entrance requirements:* For master's, 2 letters of recommendation, interview. Additional exam requirements/recommendations for international students: Required—TOEFL.

McGill University, Faculty of Graduate and Postdoctoral Studies, Desautels Faculty of Management, Montréal, QC H3A 2T5, Canada. Offers administration (PhD); entrepreneurial studies (MBA); finance (MBA); general management (Post Master's Certificate); information systems (MBA); international business (MBA); international practicing management (MM); management (MBA); management for development (MBA); manufacturing management (MMM); marketing (MBA); operations management (MBA); public accountancy (Diploma); strategic management (MBA); MBA/LL B; MD/MBA. MMM offered jointly with Faculty of Engineering; PhD with Concordia University, HEC Montreal, Université de Montréal, Université du Québec à Montréal.

Michigan State University, The Graduate School, Eli Broad College of Business, Department of Management, East Lansing, MI 48824. Offers management (PhD); management, strategy, and leadership (MS). Part-time programs available. Postbaccalaureate distance learning degree programs offered (no on-campus study). *Faculty:* 24. *Degree requirements:* For doctorate, comprehensive exam, thesis/dissertation. *Entrance requirements:* For master's, full-time managerial experience in a supervisory role; for doctorate, GMAT or GRE, letters of recommendation, experience in teaching and conducting research, work experience in business contexts, personal essay. Additional exam requirements/recommendations for international students: Required—TOEFL (minimum score 600 paper-based). Electronic applications accepted. *Financial support:* Research assistantships with tuition reimbursements and teaching assistantships with tuition reimbursements available. Financial award application deadline: 1/1; financial award applicants required to submit FAFSA. *Unit head:* Dr. Robert Wiseman, Chairperson, 517-355-1878, Fax: 517-432-1111, E-mail: wiseman@broad.msu.edu. *Application contact:* Program Information Contact, 517-355-1878, Fax: 517-432-1111, E-mail: mgt@msu.edu.
Website: http://management.broad.msu.edu/.

Michigan State University, The Graduate School, Eli Broad College of Business, Program in Business Analytics, East Lansing, MI 48824. Offers MS. Program offered in collaboration with MSU's College of Engineering and College of Natural Science. *Students:* 9 full-time. *Entrance requirements:* For master's, GMAT or GRE, bachelor's degree; minimum cumulative GPA of 3.0 in undergraduate course work and in college-level courses in introductory calculus and statistics; working knowledge of personal computers; knowledge of programming languages; experience in using statistical software program packages; recent laptop computer with MS Office. Additional exam requirements/recommendations for international students: Required—PTE (minimum

score 70), TOEFL or IELTS. *Application deadline:* For fall admission, 11/1 for international students; for winter admission, 11/1 for domestic students. Applications are processed on a rolling basis. Application fee: $50. Electronic applications accepted. *Unit head:* Dr. Sanjay Gupta, Associate Dean for MBA and Professional Master's Programs, 517-432-6488, Fax: 517-353-6395, E-mail: gupta@broad.msu.edu. *Application contact:* Betsey Voorhees, Program Director, 517-432-2917, Fax: 517-353-6395, E-mail: voorheesb@broad.msu.edu.
Website: http://broad.msu.edu/businessanalytics/.

Middle Tennessee State University, College of Graduate Studies, University College, Murfreesboro, TN 37132. Offers M Ed, MPS, MSN, Graduate Certificate. Part-time and evening/weekend programs available. Postbaccalaureate distance learning degree programs offered. *Students:* 58 full-time (52 women), 263 part-time (222 women). *Entrance requirements:* Additional exam requirements/recommendations for international students: Required—TOEFL (minimum score 525 paper-based; 71 iBT) or IELTS (minimum score 6). *Application deadline:* For fall admission, 6/1 for domestic and international students. Applications are processed on a rolling basis. Application fee: $25 ($30 for international students). *Financial support:* In 2013–14, 2 students received support. Tuition waivers available. Support available to part-time students. Financial award application deadline: 5/1. *Unit head:* Dr. Mike Boyle, Dean, 615-494-8877, Fax: 615-896-7925, E-mail: mike.boyle@mtsu.edu. *Application contact:* Dr. Michael D. Allen, Dean and Vice Provost for Research, 615-898-2840, Fax: 615-904-8020, E-mail: michael.allen@mtsu.edu.

Neumann University, Program in Strategic Leadership, Aston, PA 19014-1298. Offers MS. Electronic applications accepted.

New England College, Program in Management, Henniker, NH 03242-3293. Offers accounting (MSA); healthcare administration (MS); international relations (MA); marketing management (MS); nonprofit leadership (MS); project management (MS); strategic leadership (MS). Part-time and evening/weekend programs available. *Degree requirements:* For master's, independent research project. Electronic applications accepted.

New York University, Leonard N. Stern School of Business, Department of Management and Organizations, New York, NY 10012-1019. Offers management organizations (MBA); organization theory (PhD); organizational behavior (PhD); strategy (PhD). *Expenses: Tuition:* Full-time $35,856; part-time $1494 per unit. *Required fees:* $1408; $64 per unit. $473 per term. Tuition and fees vary according to course load and program. *Faculty research:* Strategic management, managerial cognition, interpersonal processes, conflict and negotiation.

New York University, School of Continuing and Professional Studies, Division of Programs in Business, Graduate Programs in Management and Systems, New York, NY 10012-1019. Offers core business competencies (Advanced Certificate); database technologies (MS); enterprise risk management (MS, Advanced Certificate); information technologies (Advanced Certificate); strategy and leadership (MS, Advanced Certificate); systems management (MS). Part-time and evening/weekend programs available. Postbaccalaureate distance learning degree programs offered (no on-campus study). *Faculty:* 1 full-time (0 women), 28 part-time/adjunct (7 women). *Students:* 59 full-time (30 women), 213 part-time (91 women); includes 75 minority (31 Black or African American, non-Hispanic/Latino; 30 Asian, non-Hispanic/Latino; 13 Hispanic/Latino; 1 Two or more races, non-Hispanic/Latino), 67 international. Average age 33. 213 applicants, 70% accepted, 58 enrolled. In 2013, 60 master's, 15 other advanced degrees awarded. *Degree requirements:* For master's, thesis, capstone project. *Entrance requirements:* For master's, bachelor's degree, resume with relevant professional work, internship or volunteer experience, two letters of recommendation, statement of purpose. Additional exam requirements/recommendations for international students: Required—TOEFL (minimum score 600 paper-based; 100 iBT), IELTS (minimum score 7). *Application deadline:* For fall admission, 2/1 priority date for domestic and international students; for spring admission, 10/15 priority date for domestic students, 8/15 priority date for international students. Applications are processed on a rolling basis. Application fee: $150. Electronic applications accepted. *Expenses: Tuition:* Full-time $35,856; part-time $1494 per unit. *Required fees:* $1408; $64 per unit. $473 per term. Tuition and fees vary according to course load and program. *Financial support:* In 2013–14, 60 students received support, including 60 fellowships (averaging $2,242 per year). *Unit head:* Vish Ganpati, Academic Director, 212-998-7112, E-mail: vg36@nyu.edu. *Application contact:* Admissions Office, 212-998-7100, E-mail: scps.gradadmissions@nyu.edu.
Website: http://www.scps.nyu.edu/areas-of-study/information-technology/.

New York University, School of Continuing and Professional Studies, Schack Institute of Real Estate, Program in Real Estate, New York, NY 10012-1019. Offers real estate (Advanced Certificate); strategic real estate management (MS). Part-time and evening/weekend programs available. *Faculty:* 10 full-time (4 women), 60 part-time/adjunct (6 women). *Students:* 103 full-time (36 women), 235 part-time (48 women); includes 36 minority (8 Black or African American, non-Hispanic/Latino; 1 American Indian or Alaska Native, non-Hispanic/Latino; 20 Asian, non-Hispanic/Latino; 4 Hispanic/Latino; 3 Two or more races, non-Hispanic/Latino), 75 international. Average age 30. 212 applicants, 79% accepted, 102 enrolled. In 2013, 129 master's, 15 other advanced degrees awarded. *Degree requirements:* For master's, thesis, capstone. *Entrance requirements:* For master's, bachelor's degree, resume with relevant professional work, internship or volunteer experience, two letters of recommendation, statement of purpose. Additional exam requirements/recommendations for international students: Required—TOEFL (minimum score 600 paper-based; 100 iBT), IELTS (minimum score 7). *Application deadline:* For fall admission, 2/1 priority date for domestic and international students; for spring admission, 10/15 priority date for domestic students, 8/15 priority date for international students. Applications are processed on a rolling basis. Application fee: $150. Electronic applications accepted. *Expenses: Tuition:* Full-time $35,856; part-time $1494 per unit. *Required fees:* $1408; $64 per unit. $473 per term. Tuition and fees vary according to course load and program. *Financial support:* In 2013–14, 83 students received support, including 83 fellowships (averaging $2,116 per year); scholarships/grants also available. Support available to part-time students. Financial award application deadline: 3/2. *Faculty research:* Economics and market cycles, international property rights, comparative metropolitan economies, current market trends. *Unit head:* Rosemary Scanlon, Divisional Dean, 212-992-3250. *Application contact:* Office of Admissions, 212-998-7100, E-mail: scps.gradadmissions@nyu.edu.
Website: http://www.scps.nyu.edu/areas-of-study/real-estate/graduate-programs/.

North Central College, Graduate and Continuing Studies Programs, Department of Business, Program in Business Administration, Naperville, IL 60566-7063. Offers change management (MBA); finance (MBA); human resource management (MBA); international business administration (MIBA); management (MBA); marketing (MBA). Part-time and evening/weekend programs available. *Faculty:* 13 full-time (4 women), 8 part-time/adjunct (0 women). *Students:* 31 full-time (8 women), 67 part-time (32 women); includes 16 minority (6 Black or African American, non-Hispanic/Latino; 5 Asian, non-Hispanic/Latino; 5 Hispanic/Latino), 3 international. Average age 30. 99 applicants, 54% accepted, 29 enrolled. In 2013, 51 master's awarded. *Degree requirements:* For master's, thesis optional, project. *Entrance requirements:* For master's, interview. Additional exam requirements/recommendations for international students: Required—TOEFL (minimum score 577 paper-based; 90 iBT). *Application deadline:* For fall admission, 8/15 for domestic students; for winter admission, 12/1 for domestic students; for spring admission, 2/1 for domestic students. Application fee: $25. *Expenses: Tuition:* Full-time $4716; part-time $786 per credit hour. *Financial support:* Scholarships/grants available. Support available to part-time students. *Unit head:* Dr. Robert Moussetis, Program Coordinator, 630-637-5475, E-mail: rcmoussetis@noctrl.edu. *Application contact:* Wendy Kulpinski, Director of Graduate and Continuing Education Admission, 630-637-5808, Fax: 630-637-5844, E-mail: wekulpinski@noctrl.edu.

Northwestern University, The Graduate School, Kellogg School of Management, Department of Management and Strategy, Evanston, IL 60208. Offers PhD.

Northwestern University, The Graduate School, Kellogg School of Management, Department of Managerial Economics and Decision Sciences, Evanston, IL 60208. Offers PhD. Admissions and degree offered through The Graduate School. *Degree requirements:* For doctorate, comprehensive exam, thesis/dissertation. *Entrance requirements:* For doctorate, GMAT or GRE General Test. Additional exam requirements/recommendations for international students: Required—TOEFL. Electronic applications accepted. *Faculty research:* Competitive strategy and organization, managerial economics, decision sciences, game theory, operations management.

Northwestern University, The Graduate School, Kellogg School of Management, Management Programs, Evanston, IL 60208. Offers accounting information and management (MBA, PhD); analytical finance (MBA); business administration (MBA); decision sciences (MBA); entrepreneurship and innovation (MBA); finance (MBA, PhD); health enterprise management (MBA); human resources management (MBA); international business (MBA); management and organizations (MBA, PhD); management and organizations and sociology (PhD); management and strategy (MBA); management studies (MS); managerial analytics (MBA); managerial economics (MBA); managerial economics and strategy (PhD); marketing (MBA, PhD); marketing management (MBA); media management (MBA); operations management (MBA, PhD); real estate (MBA); social enterprise at Kellogg (MBA); JD/MBA. Part-time and evening/weekend programs available. Terminal master's awarded for partial completion of doctoral program. *Degree requirements:* For doctorate, thesis/dissertation, 2 years of coursework, qualifying (field) exam and candidacy, summer research papers and presentations to faculty, proposal defense, final exam/defense. *Entrance requirements:* For master's, GMAT, GRE, interview, 2 letters of recommendation, college transcripts, resume, essays, Kellogg honor code; for doctorate, GMAT, GRE, statement of purpose, transcripts, 2 letters of recommendation, resume, interview. Additional exam requirements/recommendations for international students: Required—TOEFL, IELTS. Electronic applications accepted. *Expenses:* Contact institution. *Faculty research:* Business cycles and international finance, health policy, networks, non-market strategy, consumer psychology.

Northwestern University, School of Professional Studies, Program in Information Systems, Evanston, IL 60208. Offers analytics and business intelligence (MS); database and Internet technologies (MS); information systems (MS); information systems management (MS); information systems security (MS); medical informatics (MS); software project management and development (MS).

Northwestern University, School of Professional Studies, Program in Predictive Analytics, Evanston, IL 60208. Offers computer-based data mining (MS); marketing analytics (MS); predictive modeling (MS); risk analytics (MS); Web analytics (MS). Postbaccalaureate distance learning degree programs offered. *Entrance requirements:* For master's, official transcripts, two letters of recommendation, statement of purpose, current resume or curriculum vitae. Additional exam requirements/recommendations for international students: Required—TOEFL (minimum score 600 paper-based; 100 iBT) or IELTS (minimum score 7).

Pace University, Lubin School of Business, Program in Management, New York, NY 10038. Offers entrepreneurial studies (MBA); executive management (MBA); human resource management (MBA, MS); management (MBA); strategic management (MBA). Part-time and evening/weekend programs available. *Students:* 20 full-time (9 women), 141 part-time (78 women); includes 40 minority (19 Black or African American, non-Hispanic/Latino; 15 Asian, non-Hispanic/Latino; 6 Hispanic/Latino), 44 international. Average age 29. 343 applicants, 39% accepted, 69 enrolled. In 2013, 44 master's awarded. *Entrance requirements:* For master's, GMAT, GRE. Additional exam requirements/recommendations for international students: Required—TOEFL. *Application deadline:* For fall admission, 8/1 priority date for domestic students, 6/1 for international students; for spring admission, 12/1 for domestic students, 10/1 for international students. Applications are processed on a rolling basis. Application fee: $70. Electronic applications accepted. *Expenses: Tuition:* Part-time $1075 per credit. *Required fees:* $192 per semester. Tuition and fees vary according to course load, degree level and program. *Financial support:* Research assistantships, career-related internships or fieldwork, and Federal Work-Study available. Support available to part-time students. Financial award applicants required to submit FAFSA. *Unit head:* Dr. John C. Byrne, Chairperson, 212-618-6581, E-mail: jbyrne@pace.edu. *Application contact:* Susan Ford-Goldschein, Director of Graduate Admissions, 212-346-1531, Fax: 212-346-1585, E-mail: gradnyc@pace.edu.
Website: http://www.pace.edu/lubin.

Philadelphia University, School of Business Administration, Program in Business Administration, Philadelphia, PA 19144. Offers general business (MBA); innovation (MBA); management (MBA); marketing (MBA); strategic design (MBA); MBA/MS. Part-time and evening/weekend programs available. Postbaccalaureate distance learning degree programs offered (no on-campus study). *Entrance requirements:* For master's, GMAT. Additional exam requirements/recommendations for international students: Required—TOEFL (minimum score 550 paper-based; 79 iBT).

Philadelphia University, School of Business Administration, Program in Strategic Design Business Administration, Philadelphia, PA 19144. Offers MBA. Evening/weekend programs available.

Pontificia Universidad Catolica Madre y Maestra, Graduate School, Faculty of Social and Administrative Sciences, Santiago, Dominican Republic. Offers business administration (MBA), including business development, finance, international business, management skills (M Mgmt, MBA), marketing, operations, strategic cost management, strategy, tourist destination planning and management; law (LL M), including civil law, corporate business law, criminal law, international relations, real estate law; management (M Mgmt), including higher financial management, insurance program administration, management skills (M Mgmt, MBA); psychology (MA), including clinical child and adolescent psychology, forensic psychology; strategic human resources (EMBA).

Regent University, Graduate School, School of Business and Leadership, Virginia Beach, VA 23464-9800. Offers business administration (MBA); leadership (Certificate); organizational leadership (MA, PhD), including ecclesial leadership (PhD), entrepreneurial leadership (PhD), human resource development (PhD); strategic foresight (MA); strategic leadership (DSL), including global consulting, leadership coaching, strategic foresight. Part-time and evening/weekend programs available. Postbaccalaureate distance learning degree programs offered (minimal on-campus

study). *Faculty:* 11 full-time (4 women), 6 part-time/adjunct (3 women). *Students:* 34 full-time (19 women), 655 part-time (276 women); includes 222 minority (175 Black or African American, non-Hispanic/Latino; 2 American Indian or Alaska Native, non-Hispanic/Latino; 16 Asian, non-Hispanic/Latino; 29 Hispanic/Latino), 117 international. Average age 42. 384 applicants, 53% accepted, 120 enrolled. In 2013, 74 master's, 72 doctorates awarded. *Degree requirements:* For master's, thesis or alternative, 3 credit hour culminating experience; for doctorate, thesis/dissertation. *Entrance requirements:* For master's, GRE, GMAT, minimum undergraduate GPA of 2.75, computer literacy survey, 2 recommendations, resume, transcripts, essay; for doctorate, GRE, GMAT, sample of writing, minimum 3 years of relevant experience, computer literacy survey, 2 recommendations, resume, essay, transcripts; for Certificate, writing sample, resume, transcripts. Additional exam requirements/recommendations for international students: Required—TOEFL (minimum score 577 paper-based). *Application deadline:* For fall admission, 5/1 priority date for domestic students; for spring admission, 10/1 priority date for domestic students. Applications are processed on a rolling basis. Application fee: $50. Electronic applications accepted. *Expenses:* Contact institution. *Financial support:* Career-related internships or fieldwork, scholarships/grants, and tuition waivers (full and partial) available. Support available to part-time students. Financial award application deadline: 9/1. *Faculty research:* Servant leadership, ethics and values, telecommuting and family values, organizational communications, distance education. *Unit head:* Dr. Doris Gomez, Interim Dean, 757-352-4686, Fax: 757-352-4634, E-mail: dorigom@regent.edu. *Application contact:* Matthew Chadwick, Director of Enrollment Support Services, 800-373-5504, Fax: 757-352-4381, E-mail: admissions@regent.edu.
Website: http://www.regent.edu/acad/global/.

Regis University, College for Professional Studies, School of Management, MBA Program, Denver, CO 80221-1099. Offers finance and accounting (MBA); general business (MBA); health industry leadership (MBA); marketing (MBA); operations management (MBA); organizational performance management (MBA); strategic management (MBA). Part-time and evening/weekend programs available. Postbaccalaureate distance learning degree programs offered (no on-campus study). *Faculty:* 10 full-time (3 women), 74 part-time/adjunct (17 women). *Students:* 386 full-time (183 women), 269 part-time (134 women); includes 190 minority (38 Black or African American, non-Hispanic/Latino; 2 American Indian or Alaska Native, non-Hispanic/Latino; 30 Asian, non-Hispanic/Latino; 109 Hispanic/Latino; 1 Native Hawaiian or other Pacific Islander, non-Hispanic/Latino; 10 Two or more races, non-Hispanic/Latino), 11 international. Average age 42. 152 applicants, 91% accepted, 112 enrolled. In 2013, 318 master's awarded. *Degree requirements:* For master's, thesis (for some programs), final research project. *Entrance requirements:* For master's, official transcript reflecting baccalaureate degree awarded from regionally-accredited college or university, work experience, resume, letters of recommendation. Additional exam requirements/recommendations for international students: Required—TOEFL (minimum score 550 paper-based; 82 iBT). *Application deadline:* Applications are processed on a rolling basis. Application fee: $75. Electronic applications accepted. *Expenses:* Contact institution. *Financial support:* In 2013–14, 22 students received support. Federal Work-Study and scholarships/grants available. Financial award application deadline: 4/15; financial award applicants required to submit FAFSA. *Unit head:* Dr. Anthony Vrba, Interim Dean, 303-964-5384, Fax: 303-964-5538, E-mail: avrba@regis.edu. *Application contact:* Sarah Engel, Director of Admissions, 303-458-4900, Fax: 303-964-5534, E-mail: regisadm@regis.edu.
Website: http://www.regis.edu/CPS/Academics/Degrees-and-Programs/Graduate-Programs/MBA-College-for-Professional-Studies.aspx.

Robert Morris University Illinois, Morris Graduate School of Management, Chicago, IL 60605. Offers accounting (MBA); accounting/finance (MBA); business analytics (MIS); design and media (MM); educational technology (MM); health care administration (MM); higher education administration (MM); human resource management (MBA); information security (MIS); information systems (MIS); law enforcement administration (MM); management (MBA); management/finance (MBA); management/human resource management (MBA); mobile computing (MIS); sports administration (MM). Part-time and evening/weekend programs available. *Faculty:* 12 full-time (5 women), 18 part-time/adjunct (4 women). *Students:* 240 full-time (128 women), 195 part-time (127 women); includes 242 minority (147 Black or African American, non-Hispanic/Latino; 2 American Indian or Alaska Native, non-Hispanic/Latino; 24 Asian, non-Hispanic/Latino; 63 Hispanic/Latino; 1 Native Hawaiian or other Pacific Islander, non-Hispanic/Latino; 5 Two or more races, non-Hispanic/Latino), 26 international. Average age 33. 210 applicants, 63% accepted, 116 enrolled. In 2013, 278 master's awarded. *Entrance requirements:* For master's, official transcripts, two letters of recommendation. Additional exam requirements/recommendations for international students: Required—TOEFL (minimum score 550 paper-based). *Application deadline:* Applications are processed on a rolling basis. Application fee: $20 ($100 for international students). Electronic applications accepted. *Expenses: Tuition:* Full-time $14,400; part-time $2400 per course. *Financial support:* In 2013–14, 488 students received support. Federal Work-Study and scholarships/grants available. Support available to part-time students. Financial award applicants required to submit FAFSA. *Unit head:* Kayed Akkawi, Dean for Morris Graduate School of Management, 312-935-6050, Fax: 312-935-6020, E-mail: kakkawi@robertmorris.edu. *Application contact:* Fernando Villeda, Dean of Graduate Enrollment, 312-935-6050, Fax: 312-935-6020, E-mail: fvilleda@robertmorris.edu.

Roberts Wesleyan College, Graduate Business Programs, Rochester, NY 14624-1997. Offers strategic leadership (MS); strategic marketing (MS). Evening/weekend programs available. *Degree requirements:* For master's, thesis or alternative. *Entrance requirements:* For master's, GMAT, minimum GPA of 2.75, verifiable work experience. *Application deadline:* Applications are processed on a rolling basis. Application fee: $35. *Expenses:* Contact institution. *Financial support:* Applicants required to submit FAFSA. *Unit head:* Dr. Steven Bovee, Co-Director, 585-594-6763, Fax: 716-594-6316, E-mail: bovees@roberts.edu. *Application contact:* Office of Admissions, 800-777-4RWC, E-mail: admissions@roberts.edu.
Website: http://www.roberts.edu/graduate-business-programs.aspx.

Sage Graduate School, School of Management, Program in Business Administration, Troy, NY 12180-4115. Offers business strategy (MBA); finance (MBA); human resources (MBA); marketing (MBA); JD/MBA. Part-time and evening/weekend programs available. *Faculty:* 2 full-time (both women), 9 part-time/adjunct (2 women). *Students:* 10 full-time (5 women), 53 part-time (33 women); includes 14 minority (5 Black or African American, non-Hispanic/Latino; 6 Asian, non-Hispanic/Latino; 2 Hispanic/Latino; 1 Two or more races, non-Hispanic/Latino). Average age 30. 52 applicants, 54% accepted, 16 enrolled. In 2013, 22 master's awarded. *Entrance requirements:* For master's, minimum GPA of 2.75, resume, 2 letters of recommendation. Additional exam requirements/recommendations for international students: Required—TOEFL (minimum score 550 paper-based). *Application deadline:* Applications are processed on a rolling basis. Application fee: $40. *Expenses: Tuition:* Full-time $11,880; part-time $660 per credit hour. *Financial support:* Fellowships, research assistantships, Federal Work-Study, scholarships/grants, and unspecified assistantships available. Support available to part-time students. Financial award application deadline: 3/1; financial award applicants required to submit FAFSA. *Unit head:* Dr. Daniel Robeson, Dean, School of Management, 518-292-8657, Fax: 518-292-1964, E-mail: robesd@sage.edu.

Application contact: Wendy D. Diefendorf, Director of Graduate and Adult Admission, 518-244-2443, Fax: 518-244-6880, E-mail: diefew@sage.edu.

St. John's University, The Peter J. Tobin College of Business, Department of Computer Information Systems and Decision Sciences, Queens, NY 11439. Offers business analytics (MBA); computer information systems for managers (Adv C). Part-time and evening/weekend programs available. *Students:* 8 full-time (1 woman), 8 part-time (3 women); includes 6 minority (2 Black or African American, non-Hispanic/Latino; 2 Asian, non-Hispanic/Latino; 2 Hispanic/Latino), 5 international. Average age 27. 7 applicants, 71% accepted, 3 enrolled. In 2013, 3 master's awarded. *Degree requirements:* For master's, comprehensive exam (for some programs), thesis optional. *Entrance requirements:* For master's, GMAT, 2 letters of recommendation, resume, transcripts, essay. Additional exam requirements/recommendations for international students: Required—TOEFL (minimum score 600 paper-based; 100 iBT), IELTS (minimum score 7). *Application deadline:* For fall admission, 5/1 priority date for domestic and international students; for spring admission, 11/1 priority date for domestic and international students. Applications are processed on a rolling basis. Application fee: $50. Electronic applications accepted. *Expenses:* Contact institution. *Financial support:* Research assistantships, scholarships/grants, and unspecified assistantships available. Support available to part-time students. Financial award application deadline: 3/1; financial award applicants required to submit FAFSA. *Unit head:* Dr. Victor Lu, Chair, 718-990-6392, E-mail: luf@stjohns.edu. *Application contact:* Carol J. Swanberg, Assistant Dean/Director of Graduate Admissions, 718-990-2599, E-mail: tobingradnyc@stjohns.edu.

Saint Joseph's University, Erivan K. Haub School of Business, MS Program in Business Intelligence, Philadelphia, PA 19131-1395. Offers MS. Part-time and evening/weekend programs available. Postbaccalaureate distance learning degree programs offered. *Students:* 34 full-time (10 women), 112 part-time (37 women); includes 23 minority (9 Black or African American, non-Hispanic/Latino; 1 American Indian or Alaska Native, non-Hispanic/Latino; 7 Asian, non-Hispanic/Latino; 4 Hispanic/Latino; 2 Two or more races, non-Hispanic/Latino), 29 international. Average age 31. In 2013, 42 master's awarded. *Degree requirements:* For master's, minimum GPA of 3.0. *Entrance requirements:* For master's, GMAT or GRE, 2 letters of recommendation, resume, personal statement, official undergraduate and graduate transcripts. Additional exam requirements/recommendations for international students: Required—TOEFL (minimum score 550 paper-based, 80 iBT), IELTS (minimum score 6.5), or PTE (minimum score 60). *Application deadline:* For fall admission, 7/15 priority date for domestic students, 5/15 priority date for international students; for spring admission, 11/15 priority date for domestic students, 10/15 priority date for international students; for summer admission, 4/15 priority date for domestic students. Applications are processed on a rolling basis. Application fee: $35. Electronic applications accepted. *Expenses: Tuition:* Part-time $786 per credit hour. Tuition and fees vary according to degree level and program. *Financial support:* Scholarships/grants available. Support available to part-time students. Financial award application deadline: 5/1; financial award applicants required to submit FAFSA. *Unit head:* Dr. Patricia Rafferty, Director, MS in Business Intelligence and Analytics and MS in Managing Human Capital Programs, 610-660-1318, Fax: 610-660-1229, E-mail: patricia.rafferty@sju.edu. *Application contact:* Dr. Patricia Rafferty, Director, MS in Business Intelligence and Analytics and MS in Managing Human Capital Programs, 610-660-1318, Fax: 610-660-1599, E-mail: patricia.rafferty@sju.edu.
Website: http://www.sju.edu/hsb/bi/.

Saint Joseph's University, Erivan K. Haub School of Business, MS Program in Managing Human Capital, Philadelphia, PA 19131-1395. Offers MS. Part-time and evening/weekend programs available. *Students:* 3 full-time (all women), 22 part-time (15 women); includes 13 minority (11 Black or African American, non-Hispanic/Latino; 1 Asian, non-Hispanic/Latino; 1 Hispanic/Latino). Average age 28. In 2013, 11 master's awarded. *Degree requirements:* For master's, minimum GPA of 3.0. *Entrance requirements:* For master's, MAT, GRE, or GMAT, 2 letters of recommendation, resume, personal statement, official undergraduate and graduate transcripts. *Application deadline:* For fall admission, 7/15 priority date for domestic students; for spring admission, 11/15 priority date for domestic students. Application fee: $35. *Expenses: Tuition:* Part-time $786 per credit hour. Tuition and fees vary according to degree level and program. *Financial support:* Scholarships/grants available. Support available to part-time students. Financial award application deadline: 5/1; financial award applicants required to submit FAFSA. *Unit head:* Dr. Patricia Rafferty, Director, MS in Business Intelligence and Analytics and MS in Managing Human Capital Programs, 610-660-1318, Fax: 610-660-1229, E-mail: patricia.rafferty@sju.edu. *Application contact:* Dr. Patricia Rafferty, Director, MS in Business Intelligence and Analytics and MS in Managing Human Capital Programs, 610-660-1318, Fax: 610-660-1229, E-mail: patricia.rafferty@sju.edu.
Website: http://sju.edu/majors-programs/graduate-business/master-degrees/managing-human-capital-ms.

Saint Mary-of-the-Woods College, Program in Leadership Development, Saint Mary of the Woods, IN 47876. Offers MLD.

Salve Regina University, Holistic Graduate Programs, Newport, RI 02840-4192. Offers expressive and creative arts (CAGS, Certificate); holistic counseling (MA); holistic leadership (MA, CAGS, Certificate); holistic leadership and change management (Certificate); holistic studies (Certificate); substance abuse and treatment (CAGS); substance abuse foundations in holistic studies (Certificate). Part-time and evening/weekend programs available. *Faculty:* 3 full-time (2 women), 9 part-time/adjunct (7 women). *Students:* 17 full-time (all women), 69 part-time (59 women); includes 7 minority (3 Black or African American, non-Hispanic/Latino; 2 American Indian or Alaska Native, non-Hispanic/Latino; 1 Asian, non-Hispanic/Latino; 1 Two or more races, non-Hispanic/Latino). Average age 41. 23 applicants, 96% accepted, 17 enrolled. In 2013, 17 master's, 10 other advanced degrees awarded. *Degree requirements:* For master's, internship, project. *Entrance requirements:* For master's, GMAT, GRE General Test, or MAT. Additional exam requirements/recommendations for international students: Required—TOEFL (minimum score 600 paper-based; 100 iBT) or IELTS. *Application deadline:* For fall admission, 3/15 priority date for domestic and international students; for spring admission, 9/15 priority date for domestic and international students. Applications are processed on a rolling basis. Application fee: $60. Electronic applications accepted. *Expenses: Tuition:* Full-time $8280; part-time $460 per credit. *Required fees:* $40 per term. Tuition and fees vary according to course level, course load, degree level and program. *Financial support:* Career-related internships or fieldwork and Federal Work-Study available. Support available to part-time students. Financial award application deadline: 3/1; financial award applicants required to submit FAFSA. *Unit head:* Dr. Nancy Gordon, Director, 401-341-3290, E-mail: nancy.gordon@salve.edu. *Application contact:* Kelly Alverson, Director of Graduate Admissions, 401-341-2153, Fax: 401-341-2973, E-mail: kelly.alverson@salve.edu.
Website: http://www.salve.edu/graduate-studies/holistic-studies.

Simmons College, School of Management, Boston, MA 02115. Offers business administration (MBA); business and financial analytics (MBA); corporate social responsibility and sustainability (MBA); entrepreneurship (MBA); healthcare management (MBA); management (MS), including communications management, non-profit management; marketing (MBA); nonprofit management (MBA); organizational

Management Strategy and Policy

leadership (MBA); MBA/MSW; MS/MA. *Accreditation:* AACSB. Part-time and evening/weekend programs available. *Students:* 34 full-time (33 women), 233 part-time (214 women); includes 67 minority (41 Black or African American, non-Hispanic/Latino; 1 American Indian or Alaska Native, non-Hispanic/Latino; 9 Asian, non-Hispanic/Latino; 10 Hispanic/Latino; 2 Native Hawaiian or other Pacific Islander, non-Hispanic/Latino; 4 Two or more races, non-Hispanic/Latino), 7 international. In 2013, 133 master's awarded. *Entrance requirements:* For master's, GMAT or GRE. Additional exam requirements/recommendations for international students: Required—TOEFL. *Application deadline:* Applications are processed on a rolling basis. Application fee: $75. Electronic applications accepted. *Financial support:* Scholarships/grants and unspecified assistantships available. Financial award applicants required to submit FAFSA. *Faculty research:* Gender and organizations, leadership, health care management. *Unit head:* Cathy Minehan, Dean, 617-521-2846. *Application contact:* Melissa Terrio, Director of Graduate Admissions, 617-521-3840, Fax: 617-521-3880, E-mail: somadm@simmons.edu.
Website: http://www.simmons.edu/som.

Southern Methodist University, Cox School of Business, MBA Program, Dallas, TX 75275. Offers accounting (MBA, PMBA); business administration (EMBA); finance (MBA); financial statement analysis (PMBA); general business (MBA); information technology and operations management (MBA); management (MBA); marketing (MBA); real estate (MBA); strategy (MBA); strategy and entrepreneurship (MBA); JD/MBA; MA/MBA. Part-time and evening/weekend programs available. *Entrance requirements:* For master's, GMAT. Additional exam requirements/recommendations for international students: Required—TOEFL. Electronic applications accepted. *Expenses:* Contact institution. *Faculty research:* Corporate finance, financial reporting, modeling consumer decision-making, competition between national brands and store brands, institutional determinants of firms' strategy.

Stevens Institute of Technology, Graduate School, Wesley J. Howe School of Technology Management, Program in Management, Hoboken, NJ 07030. Offers general management (MS); global innovation management (MS); human resource management (MS); information management (MS); project management (MS); technology commercialization (MS); technology management (MS). Part-time programs available. *Degree requirements:* For master's, thesis optional. *Entrance requirements:* For master's, GMAT, GRE General Test. Additional exam requirements/recommendations for international students: Required—TOEFL. Electronic applications accepted. *Faculty research:* Industrial economics.

Suffolk University, Sawyer Business School, Master of Business Administration Program, Boston, MA 02108-2770. Offers accounting (MBA); business administration (APC); entrepreneurship (MBA); executive business administration (EMBA); finance (MBA); global business administration (GMBA); health administration (MBA); international business (MBA); marketing (MBA); nonprofit management (MBA); organizational behavior (MBA); strategic management (MBA); supply chain management (MBA); taxation (MBA); JD/MBA; MBA/GDPA; MBA/MHA; MBA/MSA; MBA/MSF; MBA/MST. *Accreditation:* AACSB. Part-time and evening/weekend programs available. Postbaccalaureate distance learning degree programs offered (no on-campus study). *Faculty:* 29 full-time (9 women), 12 part-time/adjunct (2 women). *Students:* 106 full-time (44 women), 334 part-time (184 women); includes 57 minority (20 Black or African American, non-Hispanic/Latino; 1 American Indian or Alaska Native, non-Hispanic/Latino; 18 Asian, non-Hispanic/Latino; 14 Hispanic/Latino; 4 Two or more races, non-Hispanic/Latino), 61 international. Average age 30. 448 applicants, 61% accepted, 135 enrolled. In 2013, 217 master's awarded. *Entrance requirements:* For master's, GMAT, minimum undergraduate GPA of 2.75 (MBA), 5 years of managerial experience (EMBA). Additional exam requirements/recommendations for international students: Required—TOEFL (minimum score 550 paper-based; 80 iBT). *Application deadline:* For fall admission, 6/15 priority date for domestic students, 6/15 for international students; for spring admission, 11/1 priority date for domestic students, 11/1 for international students. Applications are processed on a rolling basis. Application fee: $50. Electronic applications accepted. *Expenses: Tuition:* Full-time $38,374; part-time $1279 per credit. *Required fees:* $40; $20 per semester. Tuition and fees vary according to program. *Financial support:* In 2013–14, 107 students received support, including 91 fellowships with full and partial tuition reimbursements available (averaging $12,428 per year); career-related internships or fieldwork, Federal Work-Study, and institutionally sponsored loans also available. Support available to part-time students. Financial award application deadline: 4/1; financial award applicants required to submit FAFSA. *Faculty research:* Foreign investments; career strategies and boundaryless careers; corporate ethics codes; interest rates, inflation, and growth options; innovation and product development performance. *Unit head:* Heather Hewitt, Assistant Dean of Graduate Programs/Director of MBA Programs, 617-573-8306, E-mail: hhewitt@suffolk.edu. *Application contact:* Cory Meyers, Director of Graduate Admissions, 617-573-8302, Fax: 617-305-1733, E-mail: grad.admission@suffolk.edu.
Website: http://www.suffolk.edu/mba.

Syracuse University, Martin J. Whitman School of Management, PhD Program in Business Administration, Syracuse, NY 13244. Offers accounting (PhD); finance (PhD); management information systems (PhD); managerial statistics (PhD); marketing (PhD); operations management (PhD); organizational behavior (PhD); strategy and human resources (PhD); supply chain management (PhD). *Faculty:* 79 full-time (20 women), 25 part-time/adjunct (6 women). *Students:* 26 full-time (8 women), 1 part-time (0 women); includes 2 minority (1 Black or African American, non-Hispanic/Latino; 1 Asian, non-Hispanic/Latino), 20 international. Average age 30. 130 applicants, 9% accepted, 7 enrolled. In 2013, 15 doctorates awarded. *Degree requirements:* For doctorate, comprehensive exam, thesis/dissertation, summer research paper. *Entrance requirements:* For doctorate, GMAT or GRE General Test, 3 recommendations. Additional exam requirements/recommendations for international students: Required—TOEFL (minimum score 600 paper-based; 100 iBT). *Application deadline:* For fall admission, 1/15 priority date for domestic and international students. Applications are processed on a rolling basis. Application fee: $75. Electronic applications accepted. *Financial support:* In 2013–14, 1 fellowship with full tuition reimbursement (averaging $19,570 per year), 30 teaching assistantships with full tuition reimbursements (averaging $17,000 per year) were awarded; research assistantships with full tuition reimbursements also available. Financial award application deadline: 1/15. *Faculty research:* Marketing models, market microstructure, supply chain, auditing, corporate governance. *Unit head:* Dr. Michel Benaroc, Director of the PhD Program, 315-443-3429, E-mail: mbeanaroc@syr.edu. *Application contact:* Carol Hilleges, Administrative Specialist, 315-443-9601, Fax: 315-443-3671, E-mail: clhilleg@syr.edu.
Website: http://whitman.syr.edu/phd/.

Taylor University, Master of Business Administration Program, Upland, IN 46989-1001. Offers emerging business strategies (MBA); global leadership (MBA). Part-time programs available.

Temple University, Fox School of Business, Doctoral Programs in Business, Philadelphia, PA 19122-6096. Offers accounting (PhD); entrepreneurship (PhD); finance (PhD); international business (PhD); management information systems (PhD); marketing (PhD); risk management and insurance (PhD); statistics (PhD); strategic management (PhD); tourism and sport (PhD). *Accreditation:* AACSB. *Degree*

requirements: For doctorate, thesis/dissertation. *Entrance requirements:* For doctorate, GRE General Test, GMAT, minimum GPA of 3.0, master's degree. Additional exam requirements/recommendations for international students: Required—TOEFL (minimum score 600 paper-based; 100 iBT), IELTS (minimum score 7.5). Electronic applications accepted.

Tennessee State University, The School of Graduate Studies and Research, College of Public Service and Urban Affairs, Nashville, TN 37209-1561. Offers human resource management (MPS); public administration (MPA, PhD); social work (MSW); strategic leadership (MPS); training and development (MPS). *Accreditation:* NASPAA (one or more programs are accredited). Part-time and evening/weekend programs available. *Students:* 49 full-time (28 women), 108 part-time (67 women); includes 90 minority (86 Black or African American, non-Hispanic/Latino; 2 American Indian or Alaska Native, non-Hispanic/Latino; 1 Asian, non-Hispanic/Latino; 1 Hispanic/Latino). Average age 35. *Degree requirements:* For master's, comprehensive exam, thesis optional; for doctorate, comprehensive exam, thesis/dissertation. *Entrance requirements:* For master's, GRE General Test, minimum GPA of 2.5, writing sample; for doctorate, GRE General Test, minimum GPA of 3.25, writing sample. *Application deadline:* For fall admission, 3/1 priority date for domestic students. Application fee: $25. *Financial support:* Research assistantships and teaching assistantships available. Support available to part-time students. *Faculty research:* Total quality management and process improvement, national health care policy and administration, starting non-profit ventures, public service ethics, state education financing across the U.S. public. *Unit head:* Dr. Michael Harris, Dean, 615-963-7201, Fax: 615-963-7275, E-mail: mharris50@tnstate.edu. *Application contact:* Deborah Chisom, Director of Graduate Admissions, 615-963-5962, Fax: 615-963-5963, E-mail: dchiscom@tnstate.edu.
Website: http://www.tnstate.edu/cpsua/.

Tennessee Technological University, College of Graduate Studies, School of Professional Studies, Cookeville, TN 38505. Offers human resources leadership (MPS); strategic leadership (MPS); training and development (MPS). Part-time and evening/weekend programs available. Postbaccalaureate distance learning degree programs offered (no on-campus study). *Students:* 4 full-time (1 woman), 31 part-time (18 women); includes 4 minority (all Black or African American, non-Hispanic/Latino). 21 applicants, 71% accepted, 8 enrolled. In 2013, 8 master's awarded. *Degree requirements:* For master's, comprehensive exam, thesis or alternative. *Entrance requirements:* For master's, GRE. Additional exam requirements/recommendations for international students: Required—TOEFL (minimum score 527 paper-based; 71 iBT), IELTS (minimum score 5.5), PTE (minimum score 48), or TOEIC (Test of English as an International Communication). *Application deadline:* For fall admission, 8/1 for domestic students, 5/1 for international students; for spring admission, 12/1 for domestic students, 10/1 for international students. Applications are processed on a rolling basis. Application fee: $35 ($40 for international students). Electronic applications accepted. *Expenses:* Tuition, state resident: full-time $9347; part-time $465 per credit hour. Tuition, nonresident: full-time $23,635; part-time $1152 per credit hour. *Financial support:* Application deadline: 4/1. *Unit head:* Dr. Melissa J. Geist, Interim Dean, College of Interdisciplinary Studies, 931-372-3394, Fax: 372-372-3499, E-mail: mgeist@tntech.edu. *Application contact:* Shelia K. Kendrick, Coordinator of Graduate Studies, 931-372-3808, Fax: 931-372-3497, E-mail: skendrick@tntech.edu.
Website: https://www.tntech.edu/is/sps/.

Towson University, Program in Management and Leadership Development, Towson, MD 21252-0001. Offers Postbaccalaureate Certificate. Part-time and evening/weekend programs available. *Students:* 3 full-time (all women), 14 part-time (11 women); includes 6 minority (4 Black or African American, non-Hispanic/Latino; 1 Asian, non-Hispanic/Latino; 1 Hispanic/Latino). *Entrance requirements:* For degree, minimum GPA of 3.0, letter of intent. *Application deadline:* Applications are processed on a rolling basis. Application fee: $45. Electronic applications accepted. *Unit head:* Dr. Alan Clardy, Graduate Program Director, 410-704-3069, E-mail: aclardy@towson.edu. *Application contact:* Alicia Arkell-Kleis, Information Contact, 410-704-6004, Fax: 410-704-4675, E-mail: grads@towson.edu.

Tufts University, Graduate School of Arts and Sciences, Graduate Certificate Programs, Program Evaluation Program, Medford, MA 02155. Offers Certificate. Part-time and evening/weekend programs available. Electronic applications accepted. *Expenses:* Contact institution.

United States International University, School of Business Administration, Nairobi, Kenya. Offers business administration (GEMBA); entrepreneurship (MBA); finance (MBA); human resource management (MBA); information technology management (MBA); integrated studies (MBA); international business administration (MBA); management and organizational development (MS); marketing (MBA); organizational development (EMS); strategic management (MBA). Part-time and evening/weekend programs available. *Degree requirements:* For master's, thesis. *Entrance requirements:* For master's, GMAT, 2 letters of reference, resume. Additional exam requirements/recommendations for international students: Required—TOEFL (minimum score 550 paper-based). *Faculty research:* Marketing in small business enterprises, total quality management in Kenya.

Universidad del Este, Graduate School, Carolina, PR 00984. Offers accounting (MBA); adult education (M Ed); agribusiness (MBA); criminal justice and criminology (MA); curriculum and instruction - early education (M Ed); curriculum and instruction - elementary (M Ed); curriculum and instruction - English (M Ed); curriculum and instruction - Spanish (M Ed); human resources (MBA); information security management (MBA); information technology and Web business development (MBA); management (MBA); public policy (MPA); social work (MA), including clinical social work; special education (M Ed); strategic leadership (MBA). *Students:* 464 full-time (322 women), 669 part-time (499 women); all minorities (all Hispanic/Latino). Average age 35. 693 applicants, 61% accepted, 332 enrolled. In 2013, 228 master's awarded. *Unit head:* Jose R. Clintron, Dean, 787-257-7373 Ext. 3007, E-mail: ue_jcintron@suagm.edu. *Application contact:* Clotilde Santiago, Director of Admissions, 787-257-7373 Ext. 3400, E-mail: ue_csantiago@suagm.edu.

The University of Arizona, Eller College of Management, Department of Management, Tucson, AZ 85721. Offers PhD. Evening/weekend programs available. *Faculty:* 10 full-time (2 women), 1 (woman) part-time/adjunct. *Students:* 108 full-time (41 women), 14 part-time (5 women); includes 9 minority (5 Asian, non-Hispanic/Latino; 1 Hispanic/Latino; 3 Two or more races, non-Hispanic/Latino), 65 international. Average age 30. 361 applicants, 30% accepted, 27 enrolled. In 2013, 14 doctorates awarded. *Entrance requirements:* Additional exam requirements/recommendations for international students: Required—TOEFL (minimum score 550 paper-based; 79 iBT). *Application deadline:* For fall admission, 1/15 for domestic and international students. Applications are processed on a rolling basis. Application fee: $75. Electronic applications accepted. *Expenses:* Tuition, state resident: full-time $11,526. Tuition, nonresident: full-time $27,398. *Financial support:* In 2013–14, 8 research assistantships with full tuition reimbursements (averaging $26,000 per year), 10 teaching assistantships with full tuition reimbursements (averaging $26,000 per year) were awarded; career-related internships or fieldwork, Federal Work-Study, institutionally sponsored loans, scholarships/grants, health care benefits, tuition waivers (partial), and unspecified assistantships also available. Financial award application deadline: 3/15. *Faculty*

research: Organizational behavior, human resources, decision-making, health economics and finance, immigration. *Total annual research expenditures:* $251,243. *Unit head:* Dr. Stephen Gilliland, Department Head, 520-621-9324, Fax: 520-621-4171, E-mail: sgill@eller.arizona.edu. *Application contact:* Information Contact, 520-621-1053, Fax: 520-621-4171.
Website: http://management.eller.arizona.edu/doctoral/.

The University of British Columbia, Sauder School of Business, Doctoral Program in Commerce and Business Administration, Vancouver, BC V6T 1Z1, Canada. Offers accounting (PhD); finance (PhD); management information systems (PhD); management science (PhD); marketing (PhD); organizational behavior (PhD); strategy and business economics (PhD); transportation and logistics (PhD); urban land economics (PhD). *Faculty:* 91 full-time (22 women). *Students:* 66 full-time (24 women). Average age 30. 418 applicants, 2% accepted, 8 enrolled. In 2013, 7 doctorates awarded. *Degree requirements:* For doctorate, comprehensive exam, thesis/dissertation. *Entrance requirements:* For doctorate, GMAT or GRE. Additional exam requirements/recommendations for international students: Required—TOEFL (minimum score 600 paper-based; 100 iBT). *Application deadline:* For fall admission, 1/31 for domestic students, 12/31 for international students. Applications are processed on a rolling basis. Application fee: $95 Canadian dollars ($153 Canadian dollars for international students). Electronic applications accepted. *Expenses: Tuition, area resident:* Full-time $8000 Canadian dollars. *Financial support:* In 2013–14, fellowships with full tuition reimbursements (averaging $17,500 per year), research assistantships with full tuition reimbursements (averaging $8,500 per year), teaching assistantships with full tuition reimbursements (averaging $17,500 per year) were awarded. Financial award application deadline: 12/31. *Unit head:* Dr. Ralph Winter, Director, 604-822-8366, Fax: 604-822-8755. *Application contact:* Elaine Cho, Administrator, PhD and M Sc Programs, 604-822-8366, Fax: 604-822-8755, E-mail: phd.program@sauder.ubc.ca.
Website: http://www.sauder.ubc.ca/.

University of Calgary, Faculty of Graduate Studies, Centre for Military and Strategic Studies, Calgary, AB T2N 1N4, Canada. Offers MSS, PhD. PhD offered in special cases only. Part-time programs available. *Degree requirements:* For master's, thesis; for doctorate, comprehensive exam, thesis/dissertation. *Entrance requirements:* For master's, minimum GPA of 3.4. Additional exam requirements/recommendations for international students: Recommended—TOEFL (minimum score 550 paper-based). *Faculty research:* Military history, Israeli studies, strategic studies, int'l relations, Arctic security.

University of California, Los Angeles, Graduate Division, UCLA Anderson School of Management, Los Angeles, CA 90095-1481. Offers accounting (PhD); Americas (EMBA); Asia Pacific (EMBA); business administration (EMBA, MBA); decisions, operations and technology management (PhD); finance (PhD); financial engineering (MFE); global economics and management (PhD); management and organizations (PhD); marketing (PhD); strategy and policy (PhD); DDS/MBA; MBA/JD; MBA/MD; MBA/MLAS; MBA/MLIS; MBA/MPH; MBA/MPP; MBA/MSCS; MBA/MSN; MBA/MUP. *Accreditation:* AACSB. Part-time programs available. *Faculty:* 104 full-time (20 women), 28 part-time/adjunct (4 women). *Students:* 1,069 full-time (324 women), 879 part-time (251 women); includes 664 minority (37 Black or African American, non-Hispanic/Latino; 1 American Indian or Alaska Native, non-Hispanic/Latino; 470 Asian, non-Hispanic/Latino; 34 Hispanic/Latino; 2 Native Hawaiian or other Pacific Islander, non-Hispanic/Latino; 120 Two or more races, non-Hispanic/Latino), 444 international. Average age 30. 5,084 applicants, 27% accepted, 845 enrolled. In 2013, 801 master's, 14 doctorates awarded. *Degree requirements:* For master's, comprehensive exam, field study consulting project (for MBA); thesis (for MFE); for doctorate, comprehensive exam, thesis/dissertation, oral and written qualifying exams. *Entrance requirements:* For master's, GMAT (for MBA); GMAT or GRE General Test (for MFE), 4-year bachelor's degree or equivalent; recommendation letters (1 for MBA, 2 for MFE); two essays; interview (by invitation only for MBA); for doctorate, GMAT or GRE General Test, bachelor's degree from college or university of fully-recognized standing; minimum B average in undergraduate coursework or B+ average in prior graduate work; statement of purpose; three recommendation letters. Additional exam requirements/recommendations for international students: Required—TOEFL (minimum score 560 paper-based; 87 iBT). *Application deadline:* For fall admission, 10/22 priority date for domestic and international students; for winter admission, 1/7 for domestic and international students; for spring admission, 4/15 for domestic and international students. Applications are processed on a rolling basis. Application fee: $200. Electronic applications accepted. *Expenses:* Contact institution. *Financial support:* In 2013–14, 522 students received support. Fellowships, research assistantships with partial tuition reimbursements available, teaching assistantships with partial tuition reimbursements available, career-related internships or fieldwork, institutionally sponsored loans, scholarships/grants, health care benefits, and tuition waivers (partial) available. Financial award application deadline: 4/15; financial award applicants required to submit FAFSA. *Faculty research:* Asset pricing, decision-making, behavioral finance, international finance and economics, global macroeconomics. *Total annual research expenditures:* $368,086. *Unit head:* Dr. Judy D. Olian, Dean/Chair in Management, 310-825-7982, Fax: 310-206-2073, E-mail: judy.olian@anderson.ucla.edu. *Application contact:* Alex Lawrence, Assistant Dean, MBA Admissions and Financial Aid, 310-825-6944, Fax: 310-825-8582, E-mail: mba.admissions@anderson.ucla.edu.
Website: http://www.anderson.ucla.edu/.

See Display on page 145 and Close-Up on page 191.

University of Charleston, Master of Science in Strategic Leadership Program, Charleston, WV 25304-1099. Offers MS. *Students:* 63 full-time (22 women), 2 part-time (1 woman); includes 11 minority (10 Black or African American, non-Hispanic/Latino; 1 Two or more races, non-Hispanic/Latino), 5 international. Average age 36. *Entrance requirements:* For master's, bachelor's degree from regionally-accredited college or university with minimum GPA of 3.0. *Unit head:* Dr. John Barnette, Associate Dean of Leadership, 304-720-6688, E-mail: johnbarnette@ucwv.edu. *Application contact:* Bobby Redd, Admissions Representative, 304-860-5621, E-mail: bobbyredd@ucwv.edu.
Website: http://www.ucwv.edu/business/StrategicLeadership/.

University of Chicago, Booth School of Business, Full-Time MBA Program, Chicago, IL 60637. Offers accounting (MBA); analytic finance (MBA); analytic management (MBA); econometrics and statistics (MBA); economics (MBA); entrepreneurship (MBA); finance (MBA); general management (MBA); health administration and policy (Certificate); human resource management (MBA); international business (MBA); managerial and organizational behavior (MBA); marketing management (MBA); operations management (MBA); strategic management (MBA); MBA/AM; MBA/JD; MBA/MA; MBA/MD; MBA/MPP. *Accreditation:* AACSB. Part-time and evening/weekend programs available. Terminal master's awarded for partial completion of doctoral program. *Entrance requirements:* For master's, GMAT, 2 letters of recommendation, 3 essays, resume, interview. Additional exam requirements/recommendations for international students: Required—TOEFL (minimum score 600 paper-based; 104 iBT), IELTS. Electronic applications accepted. *Expenses:* Contact institution. *Faculty research:* Finance, marketing, economics, entrepreneurship, strategy, management.

University of Colorado Denver, Business School, Master of Business Administration Program, Denver, CO 80217. Offers bioinnovation and entrepreneurship (MBA); business intelligence (MBA); business strategy (MBA); business to business marketing (MBA); business to consumer marketing (MBA); change management (MBA); corporate financial management (MBA); enterprise technology management (MBA); entrepreneurship (MBA); health administration (MBA), including financial management, health administration, health information technologies, international health management and policy; human resources management (MBA); international business (MBA); investment management (MBA); managing for sustainability (MBA); sports and entertainment management (MBA). *Accreditation:* AACSB. Part-time and evening/weekend programs available. Postbaccalaureate distance learning degree programs offered (no on-campus study). *Students:* 611 full-time (246 women), 144 part-time (58 women); includes 102 minority (14 Black or African American, non-Hispanic/Latino; 2 American Indian or Alaska Native, non-Hispanic/Latino; 38 Asian, non-Hispanic/Latino; 42 Hispanic/Latino; 6 Two or more races, non-Hispanic/Latino), 26 international. Average age 32. 330 applicants, 64% accepted, 125 enrolled. In 2013, 398 master's awarded. *Degree requirements:* For master's, 48 semester hours, including 30 of core courses, 3 in international business, and 15 in electives from over 50 other graduate business courses. *Entrance requirements:* For master's, GMAT, resume, official transcripts, essay, two letters of recommendation, financial statements (for international applicants). Additional exam requirements/recommendations for international students: Required—TOEFL (minimum score 560 paper-based; 83 iBT); Recommended—IELTS (minimum score 6.5). *Application deadline:* For fall admission, 4/15 priority date for domestic students, 3/15 priority date for international students; for spring admission, 10/15 priority date for domestic students, 9/15 priority date for international students. Applications are processed on a rolling basis. Application fee: $50 ($75 for international students). Electronic applications accepted. *Expenses:* Contact institution. *Financial support:* In 2013–14, 62 students received support. Fellowships, research assistantships, teaching assistantships, Federal Work-Study, institutionally sponsored loans, scholarships/grants, traineeships, and unspecified assistantships available. Financial award application deadline: 4/1; financial award applicants required to submit FAFSA. *Faculty research:* Marketing, management, entrepreneurship, finance, health administration. *Unit head:* Elizabeth Cooperman, Professor of Finance and Managing for Sustainability/MBA Program Director, 303-315-8422, E-mail: elizabeth.cooperman@ucdenver.edu. *Application contact:* Shelly Townley, Admissions Director, Graduate Programs, 303-315-8202, E-mail: shelly.townley@ucdenver.edu.
Website: http://www.ucdenver.edu/academics/colleges/business/degrees/mba/Pages/MBA.aspx.

University of Colorado Denver, Business School, Program in Management and Organization, Denver, CO 80217. Offers business strategy (MS); change and innovation (MS); enterprise technology management (MS); entrepreneurship and innovation (MS); global management (MS); human resources management (MS); leadership and management (MS); quantitative decision methods (MS); sports and entertainment management (MS); sustainability management (MS). *Accreditation:* AACSB. Part-time and evening/weekend programs available. Postbaccalaureate distance learning degree programs offered (no on-campus study). *Students:* 27 full-time (19 women), 14 part-time (7 women); includes 4 minority (1 Black or African American, non-Hispanic/Latino; 2 Hispanic/Latino; 1 Two or more races, non-Hispanic/Latino), 6 international. Average age 29. 38 applicants, 45% accepted, 8 enrolled. In 2013, 28 master's awarded. *Degree requirements:* For master's, 30 semester hours (12 of required courses, 12 of management electives, and 6 of free electives). *Entrance requirements:* For master's, GMAT, resume, two letters of recommendation, essay, financial statements (for international applicants). Additional exam requirements/recommendations for international students: Required—TOEFL (minimum score 537 paper-based; 75 iBT); Recommended—IELTS (minimum score 6.5). *Application deadline:* For fall admission, 4/15 for domestic students, 3/15 for international students; for spring admission, 10/15 for domestic students, 9/15 for international students. Applications are processed on a rolling basis. Application fee: $50 ($75 for international students). Electronic applications accepted. *Expenses:* Contact institution. *Financial support:* In 2013–14, 5 students received support. Fellowships, research assistantships, teaching assistantships, Federal Work-Study, institutionally sponsored loans, scholarships/grants, and traineeships available. Financial award application deadline: 4/1; financial award applicants required to submit FAFSA. *Faculty research:* Human resource management, management of catastrophe, turnaround strategies. *Unit head:* Dr. Kenneth Bettenhausen, Associate Professor/Director of MS in Management, 303-315-8425, E-mail: kenneth.bettenhausen@ucdenver.edu. *Application contact:* Shelly Townley, Admissions Director, Graduate Programs, 303-315-8202, E-mail: shelly.townley@ucdenver.edu.
Website: http://www.ucdenver.edu/academics/colleges/business/degrees/ms/management/Pages/Management.aspx.

University of Dallas, Graduate School of Management, Irving, TX 75062-4736. Offers accounting (MBA, MM, MS); business management (MBA, MM); corporate finance (MBA, MM); financial services (MBA); global business (MBA, MM); health services management (MBA, MM); human resource management (MBA, MM); information assurance (MBA, MM, MS); information technology (MBA, MM, MS); information technology service management (MBA, MM, MS); marketing management (MBA, MM); organization development (MBA, MM); project management (MBA, MM); sports and entertainment management (MBA, MM); strategic leadership (MBA, MM); supply chain management (MBA); supply chain management and market logistics (MM). *Accreditation:* ACBSP. Part-time and evening/weekend programs available. Postbaccalaureate distance learning degree programs offered (no on-campus study). *Entrance requirements:* Additional exam requirements/recommendations for international students: Required—TOEFL. Electronic applications accepted. *Expenses:* Contact institution.

University of Denver, Daniels College of Business, Department of Business Information and Analytics, Denver, CO 80208. Offers business analytics (MS); business information and analytics (IMBA, MBA). *Faculty:* 15 full-time (4 women), 6 part-time/adjunct (2 women). *Students:* 14 full-time (8 women), 11 part-time (7 women); includes 2 minority (1 Hispanic/Latino; 1 Two or more races, non-Hispanic/Latino), 15 international. Average age 25. 45 applicants, 73% accepted, 13 enrolled. In 2013, 4 master's awarded. *Entrance requirements:* For master's, GRE General Test or GMAT, bachelor's degree, transcripts, essays, resume, interview. Additional exam requirements/recommendations for international students: Required—TOEFL (minimum score 570 paper-based; 88 iBT). *Application deadline:* For fall admission, 11/15 priority date for domestic and international students; for spring admission, 10/1 priority date for domestic and international students. Applications are processed on a rolling basis. Application fee: $100. Electronic applications accepted. *Financial support:* In 2013–14, 15 students received support, including 5 teaching assistantships with full and partial tuition reimbursements available (averaging $7,949 per year); career-related internships or fieldwork, Federal Work-Study, institutionally sponsored loans, scholarships/grants, and unspecified assistantships also available. Support available to part-time students. Financial award application deadline: 2/15; financial award applicants required to submit FAFSA. *Faculty research:* Information technology strategy, project management, healthcare information systems, distributed knowledge work, complex adaptive systems. *Total annual research expenditures:* $5,000. *Unit head:* Dr. Andrew Urbaczewski, Chair,

303-871-4802, E-mail: andrew.urbaczewski@du.edu. *Application contact:* Lynn Noel, Graduate Admissions Manager, 303-871-7895, E-mail: lynn.noel@du.edu.
Website: http://daniels.du.edu/masters-degrees/business-analytics/.

University of Illinois at Urbana–Champaign, Graduate College, College of Education, Department of Education Policy, Organization, and Leadership, Champaign, IL 61820. Offers educational organization and leadership (Ed M, MS, Ed D, PhD, CAS); educational policy studies (Ed M, MA, PhD); human resource education (Ed M, MS, Ed D, PhD, CAS). Part-time programs available. Postbaccalaureate distance learning degree programs offered (no on-campus study). *Students:* 518 (342 women). Application fee: $75 ($90 for international students). *Unit head:* James Anderson, Head, 217-333-2446, Fax: 217-244-5632, E-mail: janders@illinois.edu. *Application contact:* Rebecca Grady, Office Support Specialist, 217-265-5404, Fax: 217-244-5632, E-mail: rgrady@illinois.edu.
Website: http://education.illinois.edu/epol.

The University of Iowa, Henry B. Tippie College of Business, Henry B. Tippie School of Management, Iowa City, IA 52242-1316. Offers corporate finance (MBA); investment management (MBA); marketing (MBA); strategic management and innovation (MBA); supply chain and analytics (MBA); JD/MBA; MBA/MA; MBA/MD; MBA/MHA; MBA/MSN. *Accreditation:* AACSB. Part-time and evening/weekend programs available. *Faculty:* 113 full-time (27 women), 89 part-time/adjunct (23 women). *Students:* 110 full-time (28 women), 786 part-time (236 women); includes 51 minority (13 Black or African American, non-Hispanic/Latino; 3 American Indian or Alaska Native, non-Hispanic/Latino; 23 Asian, non-Hispanic/Latino; 12 Hispanic/Latino), 162 international. Average age 33. 622 applicants, 73% accepted, 383 enrolled. In 2013, 333 master's awarded. *Degree requirements:* For master's, minimum GPA of 2.75. *Entrance requirements:* For master's, GMAT, GRE, quality work experience and leadership as shown through resume, references, and essays. Additional exam requirements/recommendations for international students: Required—TOEFL (minimum score 600 paper-based; 100 iBT), IELTS (minimum score 7). *Application deadline:* For fall admission, 7/30 for domestic students, 4/1 for international students; for spring admission, 12/30 for domestic and international students. Applications are processed on a rolling basis. Application fee: $60 ($100 for international students). Electronic applications accepted. *Expenses:* Contact institution. *Financial support:* In 2013–14, 96 students received support, including 102 fellowships (averaging $9,519 per year), 83 research assistantships with partial tuition reimbursements available (averaging $8,893 per year), 14 teaching assistantships with partial tuition reimbursements available (averaging $17,049 per year); career-related internships or fieldwork, scholarships/grants, health care benefits, and unspecified assistantships also available. Financial award application deadline: 7/30; financial award applicants required to submit FAFSA. *Faculty research:* Capital markets, econometrics, optimization, investments and empirical corporate finance, Iowa electronic markets. *Unit head:* Prof. David W. Frasier, Associate Dean, Tippie School of Management, 800-622-4692, Fax: 319-335-3604, E-mail: david-frasier@uiowa.edu. *Application contact:* Jodi Schafer, Director, MBA Admissions and Financial Aid, 319-335-0864, Fax: 319-335-3604, E-mail: jodi-schafer@uiowa.edu.
Website: http://tippie.uiowa.edu/mba.

University of Lethbridge, School of Graduate Studies, Lethbridge, AB T1K 3M4, Canada. Offers accounting (MScM); addictions counseling (M Sc); agricultural biotechnology (M Sc); agricultural studies (M Sc, MA); anthropology (MA); archaeology (M Sc, MA); art (MA, MFA); biochemistry (M Sc); biological sciences (M Sc); biomolecular science (PhD); biosystems and biodiversity (PhD); Canadian studies (MA); chemistry (M Sc); computer science (M Sc); computer science and geographical information science (M Sc); counseling (MC); counseling psychology (M Ed); dramatic arts (MA); earth, space, and physical science (PhD); economics (MA); education (MA); educational leadership (M Ed); English (MA); environmental science (M Sc); evolution and behavior (PhD); exercise science (M Sc); finance (MScM); French (MA); French/German (MA); French/Spanish (MA); general education (M Ed); general management (MScM); geography (M Sc, MA); German (MA); health sciences (M Sc); human resource management and labour relations (MScM); individualized multidisciplinary (M Sc, MA); information systems (MScM); international management (MScM); kinesiology (M Sc, MA); marketing (MScM); mathematics (M Sc); modern languages (MA); music (M Mus, MA); Native American studies (MA); neuroscience (M Sc, PhD); new media (MA, MFA); nursing (M Sc); philosophy (MA); physics (M Sc); policy and strategy (MScM); political science (MA); psychology (M Sc, MA); religious studies (MA); sociology (MA); theatre and dramatic arts (MFA); theoretical and computational science (PhD); urban and regional studies (MA); women and gender studies (MA). Part-time and evening/weekend programs available. *Degree requirements:* For doctorate, comprehensive exam, thesis/dissertation. *Entrance requirements:* For master's, GMAT (for M Sc in management), bachelor's degree in related field, minimum GPA of 3.0 during previous 20 graded semester courses, 2 years teaching or related experience (M Ed); for doctorate, master's degree, minimum graduate GPA of 3.5. Additional exam requirements/recommendations for international students: Required—TOEFL. Application fee: $60 Canadian dollars. *Financial support:* Fellowships, research assistantships, teaching assistantships, scholarships/grants, health care benefits, and unspecified assistantships available. *Faculty research:* Movement and brain plasticity, gibberellin physiology, photosynthesis, carbon cycling, molecular properties of main-group ring components. *Application contact:* School of Graduate Studies, 403-329-2793, Fax: 403-332-5239, E-mail: sgsinquiries@uleth.ca.
Website: http://www.uleth.ca/graduatestudies/.

University of Mary, Gary Tharaldson School of Business, Bismarck, ND 58504-9652. Offers accountancy (MBA); business administration (MBA); health care (MBA); human resource management (MBA); management (MBA); project management (MPM); strategic leadership (MSSL). Part-time and evening/weekend programs available. *Degree requirements:* For master's, strategic planning seminar. *Entrance requirements:* For master's, minimum GPA of 2.5. Additional exam requirements/recommendations for international students: Required—TOEFL (minimum score 500 paper-based; 71 iBT).

University of Massachusetts Amherst, Graduate School, Isenberg School of Management, Program in Management, Amherst, MA 01003. Offers accounting (PhD); business administration (MBA); entrepreneurship (MBA); finance (MBA, PhD); healthcare administration (MBA); hospitality and tourism management (PhD); management science (PhD); marketing (MBA, PhD); organization studies (PhD); sport management (PhD); strategic management (PhD); MBA/MS. *Accreditation:* AACSB. Part-time and evening/weekend programs available. Postbaccalaureate distance learning degree programs offered. *Faculty:* 68 full-time (14 women). *Students:* 140 full-time (59 women), 1,127 part-time (319 women); includes 229 minority (24 Black or African American, non-Hispanic/Latino; 2 American Indian or Alaska Native, non-Hispanic/Latino; 135 Asian, non-Hispanic/Latino; 51 Hispanic/Latino; 6 Native Hawaiian or other Pacific Islander, non-Hispanic/Latino; 11 Two or more races, non-Hispanic/Latino), 131 international. Average age 36. 828 applicants, 56% accepted, 351 enrolled. In 2013, 361 master's, 12 doctorates awarded. Terminal master's awarded for partial completion of doctoral program. *Degree requirements:* For doctorate, comprehensive exam, thesis/dissertation. *Entrance requirements:* For master's and doctorate, GMAT or GRE General Test. Additional exam requirements/recommendations for international students: Required—TOEFL (minimum score 550 paper-based; 80 iBT), IELTS (minimum score 6.5). *Application deadline:* For fall admission, 1/20 for domestic and international students. Applications are processed on a rolling basis. Application fee: $75. Electronic applications accepted. *Financial support:* Fellowships with full and partial tuition reimbursements, research assistantships with full and partial tuition reimbursements, teaching assistantships with full and partial tuition reimbursements, career-related internships or fieldwork, Federal Work-Study, scholarships/grants, traineeships, health care benefits, tuition waivers (full and partial), and unspecified assistantships available. Support available to part-time students. Financial award application deadline: 1/20; financial award applicants required to submit FAFSA. *Unit head:* Dr. John Wells, Chair, 413-545-7609, Fax: 413-577-2234. *Application contact:* Lindsay DeSantis, Supervisor of Admissions, 413-545-0722, Fax: 413-577-0010, E-mail: gradadm@grad.umass.edu.
Website: http://www.isenberg.umass.edu/.

University of Michigan–Dearborn, College of Business, Dearborn, MI 48128-1491. Offers accounting (MBA, MS); business analytics (MS); finance (MBA, MS); human resource management (MBA); information systems (MS); international business (MBA); investment (MBA); management (MBA); management information systems (MBA); marketing (MBA); supply chain management (MBA, MS); taxation (MBA); MBA/MHSA; MBA/MSE; MBA/MSF; MBA/MSIS; MBA/MSSCM; MSF/MSA. *Accreditation:* AACSB. Part-time and evening/weekend programs available. Postbaccalaureate distance learning degree programs offered (no on-campus study). *Faculty:* 24 full-time (8 women), 5 part-time/adjunct (2 women). *Students:* 82 full-time (31 women), 323 part-time (116 women); includes 72 minority (17 Black or African American, non-Hispanic/Latino; 2 American Indian or Alaska Native, non-Hispanic/Latino; 30 Asian, non-Hispanic/Latino; 15 Hispanic/Latino; 8 Two or more races, non-Hispanic/Latino), 65 international. Average age 32. 290 applicants, 44% accepted, 99 enrolled. In 2013, 143 master's awarded. *Entrance requirements:* For master's, GMAT or GRE, pre-calculus or finite mathematics; 18 credits of accounting course work beyond introductory courses (MS in accounting). Additional exam requirements/recommendations for international students: Required—TOEFL (minimum score 560 paper-based; 84 iBT), IELTS. *Application deadline:* For fall admission, 8/1 priority date for domestic students, 5/1 priority date for international students; for winter admission, 12/1 priority date for domestic students, 9/1 priority date for international students; for spring admission, 4/1 priority date for domestic students, 1/1 priority date for international students. Applications are processed on a rolling basis. Application fee: $60. Electronic applications accepted. *Expenses:* Contact institution. *Financial support:* Career-related internships or fieldwork, Federal Work-Study, and scholarships/grants available. Support available to part-time students. Financial award application deadline: 9/1; financial award applicants required to submit FAFSA. *Faculty research:* Cultural diversity, buyer-supplier relations, error detection in data, economic evolution. *Unit head:* Dr. Raju Balakrishnan, Dean, 313-593-5248, Fax: 313-271-9835, E-mail: rajub@umich.edu. *Application contact:* Joan Doherty, Academic Advisor/Counselor, 313-593-5460, Fax: 313-271-9838, E-mail: umd-gradbusiness@umich.edu.
Website: http://www.cob.umd.umich.edu.

University of Minnesota, Twin Cities Campus, Carlson School of Management, Doctoral Program in Business Administration, Minneapolis, MN 55455-0213. Offers accounting (PhD); finance (PhD); information and decision sciences (PhD); marketing (PhD); operations and management science (PhD); strategic management and entrepreneurship (PhD). *Faculty:* 102 full-time (31 women). *Students:* 74 full-time (25 women); includes 8 minority (1 Black or African American, non-Hispanic/Latino; 5 Asian, non-Hispanic/Latino; 2 Hispanic/Latino), 46 international. Average age 30. 274 applicants, 8% accepted, 15 enrolled. In 2013, 10 doctorates awarded. *Degree requirements:* For doctorate, comprehensive exam, thesis/dissertation, written and oral preliminary exams, proposal defense, final defense. *Entrance requirements:* For doctorate, GMAT, GRE General Test. Additional exam requirements/recommendations for international students: Required—TOEFL (minimum score 600 paper-based; 100 iBT); Recommended—IELTS (minimum score 7.5). *Application deadline:* For fall admission, 12/31 for domestic students, 12/31 priority date for international students. Applications are processed on a rolling basis. Application fee: $75 ($95 for international students). Electronic applications accepted. *Expenses:* Contact institution. *Financial support:* In 2013–14, 68 students received support, including 96 fellowships with full tuition reimbursements available (averaging $6,300 per year), 65 research assistantships with full tuition reimbursements available (averaging $12,500 per year), 64 teaching assistantships with full tuition reimbursements available (averaging $12,500 per year); institutionally sponsored loans, scholarships/grants, health care benefits, unspecified assistantships, and full student fee waivers also available. Financial award application deadline: 12/31. *Faculty research:* Corporate strategy, finance, entrepreneurship, marketing, information and decision science, operations, accounting, supply chain. *Unit head:* Dr. Shawn P. Curley, Director, 612-624-6546, Fax: 612-624-8221, E-mail: curley@umn.edu. *Application contact:* Earlene K. Bronson, Assistant Director, 612-624-0875, Fax: 612-624-8221, E-mail: brons003@umn.edu.
Website: http://www.csom.umn.edu/phd-BA/.

University of Missouri–St. Louis, College of Business Administration, Program in Business Administration, St. Louis, MO 63121. Offers accounting (MBA); business administration (Certificate); business intelligence (Certificate); finance (MBA); human resource management (Certificate); information systems (MBA); logistics and supply chain management (MBA, PhD, Certificate); marketing (MBA); marketing management (Certificate); operations management (MBA). *Accreditation:* AACSB. Part-time and evening/weekend programs available. *Faculty:* 30 full-time (5 women), 20 part-time/adjunct (8 women). *Students:* 114 full-time (51 women), 269 part-time (100 women); includes 43 minority (16 Black or African American, non-Hispanic/Latino; 14 Asian, non-Hispanic/Latino; 11 Hispanic/Latino; 1 Native Hawaiian or other Pacific Islander, non-Hispanic/Latino; 1 Two or more races, non-Hispanic/Latino), 56 international. Average age 31. 153 applicants, 91% accepted, 110 enrolled. In 2013, 136 master's, 7 other advanced degrees awarded. *Degree requirements:* For doctorate, thesis/dissertation. *Entrance requirements:* For master's, GMAT, 2 letters of recommendation. Additional exam requirements/recommendations for international students: Recommended—TOEFL (minimum score 550 paper-based; 79 iBT), IELTS (minimum score 6.5). *Application deadline:* For fall admission, 7/1 for domestic and international students; for spring admission, 12/1 for domestic and international students. Applications are processed on a rolling basis. Application fee: $50 ($40 for international students). Electronic applications accepted. *Expenses:* Tuition, state resident: full-time $7364; part-time $409.10 per credit hour. Tuition, nonresident: full-time $19,162; part-time $1008.50 per credit hour. *Financial support:* In 2013–14, 14 research assistantships with full and partial tuition reimbursements (averaging $5,625 per year), 6 teaching assistantships with full and partial tuition reimbursements (averaging $9,403 per year) were awarded; career-related internships or fieldwork, Federal Work-Study, and institutionally sponsored loans also available. Support available to part-time students. Financial award application deadline: 4/1; financial award applicants required to submit FAFSA. *Faculty research:* Human resources, strategic management, marketing strategy, consumer behavior product development, advertising. *Unit head:* Francesca Ferrari, Assistant Director, 314-516-5885, Fax: 314-516-6420, E-mail: mba@umsl.edu. *Application contact:* 314-516-5458, Fax: 314-516-6996, E-mail: gradadm@umsl.edu.
Website: http://mba.umsl.edu/Degree%20Programs/index.html.

University of New Haven, Graduate School, College of Business, Program in Business Administration, West Haven, CT 06516-1916. Offers accounting (MBA, Certificate), including CPA (MBA); business administration (MBA); business management (Certificate); business policy and strategic leadership (MBA); finance (MBA), including CFA; global marketing (MBA); human resource management (Certificate); human resources management (MBA); international business (Certificate); marketing (MBA, Certificate); sports management (MBA). Part-time and evening/weekend programs available. *Students:* 125 full-time (55 women), 88 part-time (30 women); includes 31 minority (16 Black or African American, non-Hispanic/Latino; 1 American Indian or Alaska Native, non-Hispanic/Latino; 8 Asian, non-Hispanic/Latino; 5 Hispanic/Latino; 1 Native Hawaiian or other Pacific Islander, non-Hispanic/Latino), 72 international. 196 applicants, 89% accepted, 72 enrolled. In 2013, 143 master's, 24 other advanced degrees awarded. *Degree requirements:* For master's, thesis optional. *Entrance requirements:* For master's, GMAT. Additional exam requirements/recommendations for international students: Required—TOEFL (minimum score 80 iBT), IELTS, PTE (minimum score 53). *Application deadline:* For fall admission, 5/31 for international students; for winter admission, 10/15 for international students; for spring admission, 1/15 for international students. Applications are processed on a rolling basis. Application fee: $75. Electronic applications accepted. Application fee is waived when completed online. *Expenses: Tuition:* Full-time $21,600; part-time $800 per credit hour. *Required fees:* $45 per trimester. *Financial support:* Research assistantships with partial tuition reimbursements, teaching assistantships with partial tuition reimbursements, career-related internships or fieldwork, Federal Work-Study, scholarships/grants, and unspecified assistantships available. Support available to part-time students. Financial award applicants required to submit FAFSA. *Unit head:* Dr. Armando Rodriguez, Director, 203-932-7372, E-mail: arodriguez@newhaven.edu. *Application contact:* Eloise Gormley, Director of Graduate Admissions, 203-932-7440, E-mail: gradinfo@newhaven.edu.
Website: http://www.newhaven.edu/7433/.

University of New Mexico, Anderson Graduate School of Management, Department of Marketing, Information Systems, Information Assurance and Operations Management, Albuquerque, NM 87131. Offers information assurance (MBA); management information systems (MBA); marketing management (MBA); operations management (MBA). Part-time and evening/weekend programs available. *Faculty:* 15 full-time (3 women), 6 part-time/adjunct (1 woman). In 2013, 82 master's awarded. *Entrance requirements:* For master's, GMAT or GRE, minimum GPA of 3.0 on last 60 hours of coursework. Additional exam requirements/recommendations for international students: Required—TOEFL (minimum score 550 paper-based; 79 iBT). *Application deadline:* For fall admission, 4/1 priority date for domestic and international students; for spring admission, 10/1 priority date for domestic and international students. Applications are processed on a rolling basis. Application fee: $50. Electronic applications accepted. *Expenses:* Contact institution. *Financial support:* Fellowships, research assistantships, career-related internships or fieldwork, Federal Work-Study, scholarships/grants, and unspecified assistantships available. Support available to part-time students. Financial award application deadline: 6/1; financial award applicants required to submit FAFSA. *Faculty research:* Marketing, operations management, information systems, information assurance. *Unit head:* Dr. Steve Yourstone, Chair, 505-277-6471, Fax: 505-277-7108, E-mail: yourstone@unm.edu. *Application contact:* Tracy Wilkey, Manager, Academic Advisement, 505-277-3290, Fax: 505-277-8436, E-mail: andersonadvising@unm.edu. Website: http://mba.mgt.unm.edu/default.asp.

University of New Mexico, Anderson Graduate School of Management, Department of Organizational Studies, Albuquerque, NM 87131. Offers human resources management (MBA); policy and planning (MBA). Part-time and evening/weekend programs available. *Faculty:* 11 full-time (5 women), 11 part-time/adjunct (5 women). In 2013, 56 master's awarded. *Entrance requirements:* For master's, GMAT or GRE, minimum GPA of 3.0 on last 60 hours of coursework. Additional exam requirements/recommendations for international students: Required—TOEFL (minimum score 550 paper-based; 79 iBT). *Application deadline:* For fall admission, 4/1 priority date for domestic and international students; for spring admission, 10/1 priority date for domestic and international students. Applications are processed on a rolling basis. Application fee: $50. Electronic applications accepted. *Expenses:* Contact institution. *Financial support:* Fellowships, research assistantships, career-related internships or fieldwork, Federal Work-Study, scholarships/grants, and unspecified assistantships available. Support available to part-time students. Financial award application deadline: 6/1; financial award applicants required to submit FAFSA. *Faculty research:* Business ethics and social corporate responsibility, diversity, human resources, organizational strategy, organizational behavior. *Unit head:* Dr. Jacqueline Hood, Chair, 505-277-6471, Fax: 505-277-7108, E-mail: jnhood@unm.edu. *Application contact:* Tracy Wilkey, Manager, Academic Advisement, 505-277-3290, Fax: 505-277-8436, E-mail: andersonadvising@unm.edu. Website: http://mba.mgt.unm.edu/default.asp.

The University of North Carolina at Chapel Hill, Kenan-Flagler Business School, Doctoral Program in Business Administration, Chapel Hill, NC 27599. Offers accounting (PhD); finance (PhD); marketing (PhD); operations management (PhD); organizational behavior (PhD); strategy (PhD). *Accreditation:* AACSB. *Degree requirements:* For doctorate, thesis/dissertation. *Entrance requirements:* For doctorate, GMAT or GRE General Test. Electronic applications accepted. *Expenses:* Contact institution.

University of North Texas, Robert B. Toulouse School of Graduate Studies, Denton, TN 76203-5017. Offers accounting (MS, PhD); applied anthropology (MA, MS); applied behavior analysis (Certificate); applied technology and performance improvement (M Ed, MS, PhD); art education (MA, PhD); art history (MA); art museum education (Certificate); arts leadership (Certificate); audiology (Au D); behavior analysis (MS); biochemistry and molecular biology (MS, PhD); biology (MA, MS, PhD); business (PhD); business computer information systems (PhD); chemistry (MS, PhD); clinical psychology (PhD); communication studies (MA, MS); computer engineering (MS); computer science (MS); computer science and engineering (PhD); counseling (M Ed, MS, PhD), including clinical mental health counseling (MS), college and university counseling (M Ed, MS), elementary school counseling (M Ed, MS), secondary school counseling (M Ed, MS); counseling psychology (PhD); creative writing (MA); criminal justice (MS); curriculum and instruction (M Ed, PhD), including curriculum studies (PhD), early childhood studies (PhD), language and literacy studies (PhD); decision sciences (MBA); design (MA, MFA), including fashion design (MFA), innovation studies, interior design (MFA); early childhood studies (MS); economics (MS); educational leadership (M Ed, Ed D, PhD); educational psychology (MS), including family studies, gifted and talented (MS, PhD); human development, learning and cognition, research, measurement and evaluation; educational research (PhD), including gifted and talented (MS, PhD), human development and family studies, psychological aspects of sports and exercise, research, measurement and statistics; electrical engineering (MS); emergency management (MPA); engineering systems (MS); English (MA, PhD); environmental science (MS, PhD); experimental psychology (PhD); finance (MBA, MS, PhD); financial management (MPA); French (MA); health psychology and behavioral medicine (PhD); health services management (MBA); higher education (M Ed, Ed D, PhD); history (MA, MS, PhD), including European history (PhD), military history (PhD), United States history (PhD); hospitality management (MS); human resources management (MPA); information science (MS, PhD); information technologies (MBA); information technology and

decision sciences (MS); interdisciplinary studies (MA, MS); international sustainable tourism (MS); jazz studies (MM); journalism (MA, MJ, Graduate Certificate), including interactive and virtual digital communication (Graduate Certificate), narrative journalism (Graduate Certificate), public relations (Graduate Certificate); kinesiology (MS); learning technologies (MS, PhD); library science (MS); local government management (MPA); logistics and supply chain management (MBA, PhD); long-term care, senior housing, and aging services (MA, MS); management science (PhD); marketing (MBA, PhD); materials science and engineering (MS, PhD); mathematics (MA, PhD); merchandising (MS); music (MA, MM Ed, PhD), including ethnomusicology (MA), music education (MM Ed, PhD), music theory (MA, PhD), musicology (MA, PhD), performance (MA); nonprofit management (MPA); operations and supply chain management (MBA); performance (MM, DMA); philosophy (MA, PhD); physics (MS, PhD); political science (MA, MS, PhD); public administration and management (PhD), including emergency management, nonprofit management, public financial management, urban management; radio, television and film (MA, MFA); recreation, event and sport management (MS); rehabilitation counseling (MS, Certificate); sociology (MA, MS, PhD); Spanish (MA); special education (M Ed, PhD), including autism intervention (PhD), emotional/behavioral disorders (PhD), mild/moderate disabilities (PhD); speech-language pathology (MA, MS); strategic management (MBA); studio art (MFA); taxation (MS); teaching (M Ed); MBA/MS; MS/MPH; MSES/MBA. Part-time and evening/weekend programs available. Postbaccalaureate distance learning degree programs offered. *Faculty:* 661 full-time (213 women), 240 part-time/adjunct (144 women). *Students:* 3,106 full-time (1,620 women), 3,543 part-time (2,221 women); includes 1,740 minority (533 Black or African American, non-Hispanic/Latino; 15 American Indian or Alaska Native, non-Hispanic/Latino; 286 Asian, non-Hispanic/Latino; 746 Hispanic/Latino; 3 Native Hawaiian or other Pacific Islander, non-Hispanic/Latino; 157 Two or more races, non-Hispanic/Latino), 1,145 international. Average age 32. 6,289 applicants, 43% accepted, 1751 enrolled. In 2013, 1,778 master's, 239 doctorates, 10 other advanced degrees awarded. Terminal master's awarded for partial completion of doctoral program. *Degree requirements:* For master's, variable foreign language requirement, comprehensive exam (for some programs), thesis (for some programs); for doctorate, variable foreign language requirement, comprehensive exam (for some programs), thesis/dissertation; for other advanced degree, variable foreign language requirement, comprehensive exam (for some programs). *Entrance requirements:* For master's and doctorate, GRE, GMAT. Additional exam requirements/recommendations for international students: Required—TOEFL (minimum score 550 paper-based; 79 iBT). *Application deadline:* For fall admission, 7/15 for domestic students, 3/15 for international students; for spring admission, 11/15 for domestic students, 9/15 for international students; for summer admission, 5/1 for domestic students. Applications are processed on a rolling basis. Application fee: $60. Electronic applications accepted. *Financial support:* Fellowships with partial tuition reimbursements, research assistantships with partial tuition reimbursements, teaching assistantships, career-related internships or fieldwork, Federal Work-Study, institutionally sponsored loans, scholarships/grants, health care benefits, and library assistantships available. Support available to part-time students. Financial award applicants required to submit FAFSA. *Unit head:* Mark Wardell, Dean, 940-565-2383, E-mail: mark.wardell@unt.edu. *Application contact:* Toulouse School of Graduate Studies, 940-565-2383, Fax: 940-565-2141, E-mail: gradsch@unt.edu.
Website: http://tsgs.unt.edu/.

University of Pittsburgh, Katz Graduate School of Business, Master of Business Administration Programs, Pittsburgh, PA 15260. Offers finance (MBA); information systems (MBA); marketing (MBA); operations management (MBA); organizational behavior and human resource management (MBA); strategy, environment and organizations (MBA); MBA/JD; MBA/MIB; MBA/MPIA; MBA/MSE; MBA/MSIS; MID/MBA. *Accreditation:* AACSB. Part-time and evening/weekend programs available. *Faculty:* 60 full-time (14 women), 21 part-time/adjunct (5 women). *Students:* 107 full-time (31 women), 428 part-time (155 women); includes 55 minority (15 Black or African American, non-Hispanic/Latino; 26 Asian, non-Hispanic/Latino; 10 Hispanic/Latino; 4 Two or more races, non-Hispanic/Latino), 83 international. Average age 30. 449 applicants, 23% accepted, 63 enrolled. In 2013, 279 master's awarded. *Degree requirements:* For master's, minimum GPA of 3.0. *Entrance requirements:* For master's, GMAT, recommendations, undergraduate transcripts, essay, resume, interview, bachelor's degree. Additional exam requirements/recommendations for international students: Required—TOEFL (minimum score 600 paper-based; 100 iBT) or IELTS. *Application deadline:* For fall admission, 4/1 priority date for domestic students, 2/1 priority date for international students. Application fee: $50. Electronic applications accepted. *Expenses:* Tuition, state resident: full-time $19,964; part-time $807 per credit. Tuition, nonresident: full-time $32,686; part-time $1337 per credit. *Required fees:* $740; $200. Tuition and fees vary according to program. *Financial support:* In 2013–14, 60 students received support. Career-related internships or fieldwork and scholarships/grants available. Financial award application deadline: 2/1. *Faculty research:* Accounting systems/financial reporting, corporate finance, shopper marketing/consumer behavior, management information systems, organizational behavior and entrepreneurship. *Unit head:* Tim Robison, Assistant Dean, 412-648-1700, Fax: 412-648-1659, E-mail: trobison@katz.pitt.edu. *Application contact:* Thomas Keller, Director of MBA Admissions, 412-648-1700, Fax: 412-648-1659, E-mail: mba@katz.pitt.edu.
Website: http://www.business.pitt.edu/katz/mba/.

University of Rochester, Simon Business School, Full-Time Master's Program in Business Administration, Rochester, NY 14627. Offers accounting and information systems (MBA); business environment and public policy (MBA); business systems consulting (MBA); competitive and organizational strategy - pricing (MBA); computers and information systems (MBA); corporate accounting (MBA); electronic commerce (MBA); entrepreneurship (MBA); finance (MBA); health sciences management (MBA); international management (MBA); marketing - brand management and pricing (MBA); operations management - manufacturing (MBA); operations management - services (MBA); public accounting (MBA). *Accreditation:* AACSB. Part-time and evening/weekend programs available. *Faculty:* 60 full-time (11 women), 23 part-time/adjunct (3 women). *Students:* 282 full-time (74 women); includes 55 minority (29 Black or African American, non-Hispanic/Latino; 1 American Indian or Alaska Native, non-Hispanic/Latino; 11 Asian, non-Hispanic/Latino; 12 Hispanic/Latino; 2 Two or more races, non-Hispanic/Latino), 144 international. 673 applicants, 33% accepted, 65 enrolled. In 2013, 176 master's awarded. *Entrance requirements:* For master's, GMAT/GRE, previous course work in calculus. Additional exam requirements/recommendations for international students: Required—TOEFL. *Application deadline:* For fall admission, 10/15 for domestic and international students; for winter admission, 1/5 for domestic and international students; for spring admission, 3/15 for domestic and international students; for summer admission, 5/15 for domestic students. Applications are processed on a rolling basis. Application fee: $150. Electronic applications accepted. *Expenses: Tuition:* Full-time $44,580; part-time $1394 per credit hour. *Required fees:* $492. *Financial support:* In 2013–14, 72 students received support. Fellowships, research assistantships, teaching assistantships, institutionally sponsored loans, scholarships/grants, and tuition waivers (partial) available. Financial award application deadline: 3/1; financial award applicants required to submit CSS PROFILE or FAFSA. *Unit head:* Mark Zupan, Dean, 585-275-3316. *Application contact:* Rebekah S. Lewin, Assistant Dean of

Management Strategy and Policy

Admissions and Student Engagement, 585-275-3533, E-mail: admissions@simon.rochester.edu.

University of Rochester, Simon Business School, Part-Time MBA Program, Rochester, NY 14627. Offers accounting and information systems (MBA); business environment and public policy (MBA); business systems consulting (MBA); competitive and organizational strategy (MBA); computers and information systems (MBA); corporate accounting (MBA); electronic commerce (MBA); entrepreneurship (MBA); finance (MBA); health sciences management (MBA); international management (MBA); manufacturing management (MBA); marketing (MBA); operations management - services (MBA); public accounting (MBA). Part-time and evening/weekend programs available. *Faculty:* 59 full-time (10 women), 23 part-time/adjunct (3 women). *Students:* 270 part-time (75 women); includes 38 minority (5 Black or African American, non-Hispanic/Latino; 1 American Indian or Alaska Native, non-Hispanic/Latino; 24 Asian, non-Hispanic/Latino; 5 Hispanic/Latino; 3 Two or more races, non-Hispanic/Latino). Average age 32. 56 applicants, 98% accepted, 51 enrolled. In 2013, 77 master's awarded. *Entrance requirements:* For master's, GRE or GMAT, resume, recommendation letters, essays, transcipts. *Application deadline:* For fall admission, 8/15 for domestic students; for winter admission, 11/15 for domestic students; for spring admission, 2/15 for domestic students; for summer admission, 5/15 for domestic students. Applications are processed on a rolling basis. Application fee: $150. Electronic applications accepted. *Expenses: Tuition:* Full-time $44,580; part-time $1394 per credit hour. *Required fees:* $492. *Financial support:* Scholarships/grants and tuition waivers available. Financial award applicants required to submit CSS PROFILE. *Unit head:* Mark Zupan, Dean, 585-275-3316, E-mail: mark.zupan@simon.rochester.edu. *Application contact:* Jennifer Mossotti, Associate Director of Part-Time Programs, 585-275-3803, E-mail: jennifer.mossotti@simon.rochester.edu.
Website: http://www.simon.rochester.edu/programs/part-time-mba-programs/index.aspx.

University of South Florida, University College/Distance Education, Tampa, FL 33620-9951. *Unit head:* Kathy Barnes, Interdisciplinary Programs Coordinator, 813-974-8031, Fax: 813-974-7061, E-mail: barnesk@usf.edu. *Application contact:* Karen Tylinski, Metro Initiatives, 813-974-9943, Fax: 813-974-7061, E-mail: ktylinsk@usf.edu.
Website: http://uc.usf.edu/.

The University of Texas at Dallas, Naveen Jindal School of Management, Program in Information Systems and Operations Management, Richardson, TX 75080. Offers business analytics (MS); information technology and management (MS); supply chain management (MS). Part-time and evening/weekend programs available. *Faculty:* 14 full-time (0 women), 9 part-time/adjunct (3 women). *Students:* 668 full-time (258 women), 222 part-time (80 women); includes 78 minority (15 Black or African American, non-Hispanic/Latino; 51 Asian, non-Hispanic/Latino; 10 Hispanic/Latino; 2 Two or more races, non-Hispanic/Latino), 734 international. Average age 26. 1,622 applicants, 56% accepted, 364 enrolled. In 2013, 296 master's awarded. *Degree requirements:* For master's, thesis optional. *Entrance requirements:* For master's, GMAT. Additional exam requirements/recommendations for international students: Required—TOEFL (minimum score 550 paper-based). *Application deadline:* For fall admission, 7/15 for domestic students, 5/1 priority date for international students; for spring admission, 11/15 for domestic students, 9/1 priority date for international students. Applications are processed on a rolling basis. Application fee: $50 ($100 for international students). Electronic applications accepted. *Expenses:* Tuition, state resident: full-time $11,940; part-time $663.33 per credit hour. Tuition, nonresident: full-time $21,606; part-time $1200.33 per credit hour. *Financial support:* In 2013–14, 183 students received support, including 3 research assistantships with partial tuition reimbursements available (averaging $13,750 per year), 18 teaching assistantships with partial tuition reimbursements available (averaging $10,340 per year); career-related internships or fieldwork, Federal Work-Study, institutionally sponsored loans, scholarships/grants, and unspecified assistantships also available. Support available to part-time students. Financial award application deadline: 4/30; financial award applicants required to submit FAFSA. *Faculty research:* Technology marketing, measuring information work productivity, electronic commerce, decision support systems, data quality. *Unit head:* Dr. Srinivasan Raghunathan, Area Coordinator, Information Systems, 972-883-4377, E-mail: sraghu@utdallas.edu. *Application contact:* Dr. Milind Dawande, Area Coordinator, Supply Chain Management, 972-883-2793, E-mail: milind@utdallas.edu.
Website: http://jindal.utdallas.edu/academic-areas/information-systems-and-operations-management/.

The University of Texas at Dallas, Naveen Jindal School of Management, Programs in Management Science, Richardson, TX 75080. Offers accounting (PhD); finance (PhD); information systems (PhD); marketing (PhD); operations management (PhD). *Accreditation:* AACSB. Part-time and evening/weekend programs available. *Faculty:* 13 full-time (3 women), 7 part-time/adjunct (2 women). *Students:* 78 full-time (27 women), 9 part-time (3 women); includes 6 minority (all Asian, non-Hispanic/Latino), 73 international. Average age 30. 258 applicants, 9% accepted, 16 enrolled. In 2013, 14 doctorates awarded. *Degree requirements:* For doctorate, thesis/dissertation. *Entrance requirements:* For doctorate, GMAT, minimum GPA of 3.0. Additional exam requirements/recommendations for international students: Required—TOEFL (minimum score 550 paper-based). *Application deadline:* For fall admission, 7/15 for domestic students, 5/1 priority date for international students; for spring admission, 11/15 for domestic students, 9/1 priority date for international students. Applications are processed on a rolling basis. Application fee: $50 ($100 for international students). Electronic applications accepted. *Expenses:* Tuition, state resident: full-time $11,940; part-time $663.33 per credit hour. Tuition, nonresident: full-time $21,606; part-time $1200.33 per credit hour. *Financial support:* In 2013–14, 81 students received support. Research assistantships with partial tuition reimbursements available, teaching assistantships with partial tuition reimbursements available, career-related internships or fieldwork, Federal Work-Study, institutionally sponsored loans, scholarships/grants, and unspecified assistantships available. Support available to part-time students. Financial award application deadline: 4/30; financial award applicants required to submit FAFSA. *Faculty research:* Empirical generalizations in marketing, diffusion of generations of technology, stochastic brand-choice theory, acceptance of trade deals by supermarkets, nonparametric estimations of market share response. *Unit head:* Dr. Sumit Sarkar, Program Director, 972-883-2745, Fax: 972-883-5977, E-mail: som_phd.@utdallas.edu. *Application contact:* Ashley J. Desouza, Program Administrator, 972-883-2745, Fax: 972-883-5977, E-mail: ashley.desouza@utdallas.edu.
Website: http://jindal.utdallas.edu/academic-programs/phd-programs/management-science/.

University of Utah, Graduate School, David Eccles School of Business, Business Administration Program, Salt Lake City, UT 84112. Offers accounting (PhD); business administration (EMBA, MBA, PMBA); finance (PhD); information systems (PhD); marketing (PhD); operations management (PhD); organizational behavior (PhD); strategic management (PhD); MBA/JD; MBA/MHA; MBA/MS. Part-time and evening/weekend programs available. *Faculty:* 58 full-time (21 women), 37 part-time/adjunct (7 women). *Students:* 481 full-time (108 women), 109 part-time (19 women); includes 39 minority (2 Black or African American, non-Hispanic/Latino; 13 Asian, non-Hispanic/Latino; 18 Hispanic/Latino; 1 Native Hawaiian or other Pacific Islander, non-Hispanic/Latino; 5 Two or more races, non-Hispanic/Latino), 39 international. Average age 32. 486 applicants, 56% accepted, 215 enrolled. In 2013, 326 master's, 10 doctorates awarded. *Degree requirements:* For doctorate, comprehensive exam, thesis/dissertation. *Entrance requirements:* For master's, GMAT or GRE; for doctorate, GMAT. Additional exam requirements/recommendations for international students: Required—TOEFL (minimum score 600 paper-based; 100 iBT), IELTS (minimum score 7). *Application deadline:* For fall admission, 11/1 priority date for domestic students, 3/1 priority date for international students; for spring admission, 11/1 for domestic and international students. Applications are processed on a rolling basis. Application fee: $55 ($65 for international students). Electronic applications accepted. *Expenses:* Contact institution. *Financial support:* In 2013–14, 48 students received support, including 41 fellowships with partial tuition reimbursements available (averaging $8,600 per year), 35 research assistantships with partial tuition reimbursements available (averaging $6,378 per year), 57 teaching assistantships with full tuition reimbursements available (averaging $17,000 per year); scholarships/grants and unspecified assistantships also available. Financial award application deadline: 2/1; financial award applicants required to submit FAFSA. *Faculty research:* Corporate finance, strategy services, consumer behavior, financial disclosures, operations. *Unit head:* Dr. William Hesterly, Associate Dean, PhD Program, 801-581-7676, Fax: 801-581-3380, E-mail: mastersinfo@business.utah.edu. *Application contact:* Andrea Miller, Coordinator, 801-581-7785, Fax: 801-581-3666, E-mail: mastersinfo@business.utah.edu.
Website: http://business.utah.edu/full-time-mba.

University of Utah, Graduate School, David Eccles School of Business, Department of Operations and Information Systems, Salt Lake City, UT 84112. Offers information systems (MS, Graduate Certificate), including business intelligence and analytics, IT security, product and process management, software and systems architecture. Part-time and evening/weekend programs available. *Faculty:* 9 full-time (2 women), 6 part-time/adjunct (0 women). *Students:* 73 full-time (12 women), 53 part-time (4 women); includes 15 minority (2 Black or African American, non-Hispanic/Latino; 3 Asian, non-Hispanic/Latino; 9 Hispanic/Latino; 1 Two or more races, non-Hispanic/Latino), 12 international. Average age 32. 90 applicants, 86% accepted, 57 enrolled. In 2013, 59 master's awarded. *Degree requirements:* For master's, capstone project. *Entrance requirements:* For master's, GMAT/GRE, minimum undergraduate GPA of 3.0. Additional exam requirements/recommendations for international students: Required—TOEFL (minimum score 600 paper-based; 100 iBT), IELTS (minimum score 7). *Application deadline:* For fall admission, 7/28 for domestic students, 3/1 for international students; for spring admission, 12/7 for domestic students, 8/16 for international students. Applications are processed on a rolling basis. Application fee: $55 ($65 for international students). Electronic applications accepted. *Expenses:* Contact institution. *Financial support:* In 2013–14, 5 students received support, including 3 fellowships with partial tuition reimbursements available (averaging $5,160 per year), 2 teaching assistantships with partial tuition reimbursements available (averaging $5,160 per year); tuition waivers (partial) and unspecified assistantships also available. Financial award application deadline: 4/14; financial award applicants required to submit FAFSA. *Faculty research:* Business intelligence and analytics, software and system architecture, product and process management, IT security, Web and data mining, applications and management of IT in healthcare. *Unit head:* Bradden Blair, Director of the MSIS Program, 801-587-9489, Fax: 801-581-3666, E-mail: b.blair@business.utah.edu. *Application contact:* Jetta Harris, Academic Coordinator, 801-587-5878, Fax: 801-581-3666, E-mail: jetta.harris@business.utah.edu.
Website: http://msis.business.utah.edu.

The University of Western Ontario, Richard Ivey School of Business, London, ON N6A 3K7, Canada. Offers business (EMBA, PhD); corporate strategy and leadership elective (MBA); entrepreneurship elective (MBA); finance elective (MBA); health sector stream (MBA); international management elective (MBA); marketing elective (MBA); JD/MBA. *Degree requirements:* For master's, thesis (for some programs); for doctorate, thesis/dissertation. *Entrance requirements:* For master's, GMAT, 2 years of full-time work experience, interview. Additional exam requirements/recommendations for international students: Required—TOEFL (minimum score 100 iBT) or IELTS (minimum score 6). Electronic applications accepted. *Faculty research:* Strategy, organizational behavior, international business, finance, operations management.

University of West Florida, College of Professional Studies, Department of Research and Advanced Studies, Pensacola, FL 32514-5750. Offers administration (MSA), including acquisition and contract administration, biomedical/pharmaceutical, criminal justice administration, database administration, education leadership, healthcare administration, human performance technology, leadership, nursing administration, public administration, software engineering and administration; college student personnel administration (M Ed), including college personnel administration, guidance and counseling; curriculum and instruction (M Ed, Ed S); educational leadership (M Ed); middle and secondary level education and ESOL (M Ed). Part-time and evening/weekend programs available. *Entrance requirements:* For master's, GRE or MAT, official transcripts; minimum undergraduate GPA of 3.0; letter of intent; three letters of recommendation; resume. Additional exam requirements/recommendations for international students: Required—TOEFL (minimum score 550 paper-based).

University of West Florida, College of Professional Studies, Program in Administration, Pensacola, FL 32514-5750. Offers acquisition and contract administration (MSA); database administration (MSA); health care administration (MSA); human performance technology (MSA); leadership (MSA); public administration (MSA); software engineering administration (MSA). Part-time and evening/weekend programs available. Postbaccalaureate distance learning degree programs offered (no on-campus study). *Entrance requirements:* For master's, GRE General Test, letter of intent, names of references. Additional exam requirements/recommendations for international students: Required—TOEFL (minimum score 550 paper-based).

Valparaiso University, Graduate School, College of Business, Valparaiso, IN 46383. Offers business administration (MBA); business intelligence (Certificate); engineering management (Certificate); entrepreneurship (Certificate); finance (Certificate); general business (Certificate); management (Certificate); marketing (Certificate); sustainability (Certificate); JD/MBA; MSN/MBA. *Accreditation:* AACSB. Part-time and evening/weekend programs available. Postbaccalaureate distance learning degree programs offered (minimal on-campus study). *Faculty:* 11 part-time/adjunct (2 women). *Students:* 13 full-time (3 women), 48 part-time (21 women); includes 6 minority (3 Black or African American, non-Hispanic/Latino; 2 Hispanic/Latino; 1 Two or more races, non-Hispanic/Latino), 5 international. Average age 33. In 2013, 19 master's, 3 other advanced degrees awarded. *Entrance requirements:* For master's, GMAT, GRE, minimum GPA of 3.0. Additional exam requirements/recommendations for international students: Required—TOEFL (minimum score 550 paper-based; 80 iBT), IELTS (minimum score 6). *Application deadline:* Applications are processed on a rolling basis. Application fee: $30 ($50 for international students). Electronic applications accepted. *Expenses:* Contact institution. *Financial support:* Available to part-time students. Applicants required to submit FAFSA. *Unit head:* Bruce MacLean, Director of Graduate Programs in Management, 219-465-7952, Fax: 219-464-5789, E-mail: bruce.maclean@valpo.edu.

Application contact: Cindy Scanlan, Assistant Director of Graduate Programs in Management, 219-465-7952, Fax: 219-464-5789, E-mail: cindy.scanlan@valpo.edu. Website: http://www.valpo.edu/mba/.

Vanderbilt University, Vanderbilt Graduate School of Management, Vanderbilt MBA Program (Full-time), Nashville, TN 37203. Offers accounting (MBA); finance (MBA); general management (MBA); human and organizational performance (MBA); marketing (MBA); operations (MBA); strategy (MBA); MBA/JD; MBA/M Div; MBA/MD; MBA/MTS; MBA/PhD. *Accreditation:* AACSB. *Students:* 341 full-time (119 women); includes 42 minority (20 Black or African American, non-Hispanic/Latino; 12 Asian, non-Hispanic/Latino; 5 Hispanic/Latino; 5 Two or more races, non-Hispanic/Latino), 73 international. Average age 28. 1,059 applicants, 38% accepted, 166 enrolled. In 2013, 161 master's awarded. *Entrance requirements:* For master's, GMAT (preferred) or GRE, 2 years of work experience (recommended). Additional exam requirements/recommendations for international students: Required—TOEFL. *Application deadline:* For fall admission, 10/1 priority date for domestic and international students; for winter admission, 1/6 priority date for domestic and international students; for spring admission, 3/3 priority date for domestic students, 3/5 priority date for international students; for summer admission, 4/5 for domestic students, 5/5 for international students. Applications are processed on a rolling basis. Application fee: $75 ($175 for international students). Electronic applications accepted. *Financial support:* In 2013–14, 237 students received support. Scholarships/grants and tuition waivers (full and partial) available. Financial award application deadline: 5/15; financial award applicants required to submit FAFSA. *Unit head:* Nancy Lea Hyer, Associate Dean, 615-322-2530, Fax: 615-343-7110, E-mail: nancy.lea.hyer@owen.vanderbilt.edu. *Application contact:* Dinah Webster, Administrative Assistant, 615-322-6469, Fax: 615-343-1175, E-mail: mba@owen.vanderbilt.edu. Website: http://www.owen.vanderbilt.edu.

Villanova University, Villanova School of Business, MBA - The Fast Track Program, Villanova, PA 19085. Offers finance (MBA); health care management (MBA); international business (MBA); management information systems (MBA); marketing (MBA); real estate (MBA); strategic management (MBA). *Accreditation:* AACSB. Part-time and evening/weekend programs available. *Faculty:* 101 full-time (33 women), 36 part-time/adjunct (3 women). *Students:* 140 part-time (44 women); includes 22 minority (1 Black or African American, non-Hispanic/Latino; 17 Asian, non-Hispanic/Latino; 3 Hispanic/Latino; 1 Two or more races, non-Hispanic/Latino), 3 international. Average age 29. 127 applicants, 72% accepted, 75 enrolled. In 2013, 61 master's awarded. *Degree requirements:* For master's, minimum GPA of 3.0. *Entrance requirements:* For master's, GMAT or GRE, work experience. Additional exam requirements/recommendations for international students: Required—TOEFL (minimum score 550 paper-based; 90 iBT). *Application deadline:* For fall admission, 6/30 for domestic and international students. Application fee: $50. Electronic applications accepted. *Financial support:* Scholarships/grants available. Financial award application deadline: 6/30; financial award applicants required to submit FAFSA. *Faculty research:* Business analytics; creativity, innovation and entrepreneurship; global leadership; real estate; church management; business ethics. *Unit head:* Zelon Crawford, Director of Graduate Business Programs, 610-519-6283, Fax: 610-519-6273, E-mail: zelon.crawford@villanova.edu. *Application contact:* Meredith L. Lockyer, Manager of Recruiting, 610-519-7016, Fax: 610-519-6273, E-mail: meredith.lockyer@villanova.edu. Website: http://www1.villanova.edu/villanova/business/graduate/mba/fasttrack.html.

Villanova University, Villanova School of Business, MBA - The Flex Track Program, Villanova, PA 19085. Offers finance (MBA); health care management (MBA); international business (MBA); management information systems (MBA); marketing (MBA); real estate (MBA); strategic management (MBA); JD/MBA. *Accreditation:* AACSB. Part-time and evening/weekend programs available. Postbaccalaureate distance learning degree programs offered (minimal on-campus study). *Faculty:* 101 full-time (33 women), 36 part-time/adjunct (3 women). *Students:* 13 full-time (5 women), 413 part-time (127 women); includes 63 minority (13 Black or African American, non-Hispanic/Latino; 1 American Indian or Alaska Native, non-Hispanic/Latino; 29 Asian, non-Hispanic/Latino; 14 Hispanic/Latino; 1 Native Hawaiian or other Pacific Islander, non-Hispanic/Latino; 5 Two or more races, non-Hispanic/Latino), 9 international. Average age 29. 84 applicants, 83% accepted, 66 enrolled. In 2013, 133 master's awarded. *Degree requirements:* For master's, minimum GPA of 3.0. *Entrance requirements:* For master's, GMAT or GRE, work experience. Additional exam requirements/recommendations for international students: Required—TOEFL (minimum score 550 paper-based; 90 iBT). *Application deadline:* For fall admission, 6/30 for domestic and international students; for winter admission, 11/15 for domestic and international students; for spring admission, 11/15 for domestic and international students; for summer admission, 3/31 for domestic and international students. Applications are processed on a rolling basis. Application fee: $50. Electronic applications accepted. *Financial support:* In 2013–14, 13 research assistantships with full tuition reimbursements (averaging $13,100 per year) were awarded; scholarships/grants and unspecified assistantships also available. Financial award application deadline: 6/30; financial award applicants required to submit FAFSA. *Faculty research:* Business analytics; creativity, innovation and entrepreneurship; global leadership; real estate; church management; business ethics. *Unit head:* Zelon Crawford, Director of Graduate Business Programs, 610-610-6283, Fax: 610-519-6273, E-mail: zelon.crawford@villanova.edu. *Application contact:* Meredith L. Lockyer, Manager of Recruiting, 610-519-7016, Fax: 610-519-6273, E-mail: meredith.lockyer@villanova.edu. Website: http://www1.villanova.edu/villanova/business/graduate/mba/flextrack.html.

Virginia Commonwealth University, Graduate School, School of Business, Program in Decision Sciences and Business Analytics, Richmond, VA 23284-9005. Offers MBA, MS. *Entrance requirements:* For master's, GMAT. Additional exam requirements/recommendations for international students: Required—TOEFL (minimum score 600 paper-based; 100 iBT). Electronic applications accepted.

Walden University, Graduate Programs, School of Management, Minneapolis, MN 55401. Offers accounting (MBA, MS, DBA), including accounting for the professional (MS), accounting with CPA emphasis (MS), self-designed (MS, PhD); accounting and management (MS), including accountants as strategic managers, self-designed (MS, PhD); advanced project management (Graduate Certificate); applied project management (Graduate Certificate); bridge to business administration (Post-Doctoral Certificate); bridge to management (Post-Doctoral Certificate); business administration (EMBA); business management (Graduate Certificate); communication (MS, Graduate Certificate); corporate finance (MBA); entrepreneurship (DBA); entrepreneurship and small business (MBA); finance (DBA); global supply chain management (DBA); healthcare management (MBA, DBA); human resource management (MBA, MS, Graduate Certificate), including functional human resource management (MS), general program (MS), integrating functional and strategic human resource management (MS), organizational strategy (MS); human resources management (DBA); information systems management (DBA); international business (MBA, DBA); leadership (MBA, MS, DBA), including general program (MS), human resources leadership (MS), leader development (MS), self-designed (MS, PhD); management (MS, PhD), including accounting (PhD), engineering management (PhD), finance (PhD), general program (MS), healthcare management (MS), human resource management (MS), human resources management (PhD), information systems management (PhD), leadership (MS), leadership and organizational change (PhD), marketing (MS), operations research (PhD), project management (MS), self-designed, strategy and operations (MS); marketing (MBA, DBA); project management (MBA, MS, DBA); self-designed (MBA, DBA); social impact management (DBA); technology entrepreneurship (DBA). Part-time and evening/weekend programs available. Postbaccalaureate distance learning degree programs offered (minimal on-campus study). *Faculty:* 24 full-time (9 women), 337 part-time/adjunct (127 women). *Students:* 4,369 full-time (2,379 women), 2,181 part-time (1,304 women); includes 3,669 minority (3,020 Black or African American, non-Hispanic/Latino; 22 American Indian or Alaska Native, non-Hispanic/Latino; 156 Asian, non-Hispanic/Latino; 331 Hispanic/Latino; 11 Native Hawaiian or other Pacific Islander, non-Hispanic/Latino; 129 Two or more races, non-Hispanic/Latino), 107 international. Average age 41. 2,030 applicants, 94% accepted, 1436 enrolled. In 2013, 757 master's, 128 doctorates, 32 other advanced degrees awarded. *Degree requirements:* For master's, residency (for some programs); for doctorate, thesis/dissertation (for some programs), residency. *Entrance requirements:* For master's, bachelor's degree or higher; minimum GPA of 2.5; official transcripts; goal statement (for some programs); access to computer and Internet; for doctorate, master's degree or higher; three years of related professional or academic experience (preferred); minimum GPA of 3.0; goal statement and current resume (select programs); official transcripts; access to computer and Internet; for other advanced degree, relevant work experience; access to computer and Internet. Additional exam requirements/recommendations for international students: Required—TOEFL (minimum score 550 paper-based; 79 iBT), IELTS (minimum score 6.5), Michigan English Language Assessment Battery (minimum score 82), or PTE. *Application deadline:* Applications are processed on a rolling basis. Application fee: $0. Electronic applications accepted. *Expenses:* Tuition: Full-time $11,813.55; part-time $500 per credit. Required fees: $618.76. *Financial support:* Fellowships, Federal Work-Study, scholarships/grants, unspecified assistantships, and family tuition reduction, active duty/veteran tuition reduction, group tuition reduction, interest-free payment plans, employee tuition reduction available. Support available to part-time students. Financial award applicants required to submit FAFSA. *Unit head:* Dr. Ward Ulmer, III, Associate Dean, 800-925-3368. *Application contact:* Jennifer Hall, Vice President of Enrollment Management, 866-4-WALDEN, E-mail: info@waldenu.edu. Website: http://www.waldenu.edu/programs/colleges-schools/management.

Western Governors University, College of Business, Salt Lake City, UT 84107. Offers information technology management (MBA); management and strategy (MBA); strategic leadership (MBA). Evening/weekend programs available. *Degree requirements:* For master's, capstone project. *Entrance requirements:* For master's, Readiness Assessment, transcripts. Additional exam requirements/recommendations for international students: Required—TOEFL (minimum score 450 paper-based; 80 iBT). Electronic applications accepted.

Western International University, Graduate Programs in Business, Master of Arts Program in Innovative Leadership, Phoenix, AZ 85021-2718. Offers MA. Part-time and evening/weekend programs available. Postbaccalaureate distance learning degree programs offered (no on-campus study). *Entrance requirements:* For master's, minimum GPA of 2.75. Additional exam requirements/recommendations for international students: Required—TOEFL (minimum score 550 paper-based; 79 iBT), TWE (minimum score 5), or IELTS (minimum score 6.5). Electronic applications accepted.

Xavier University, Williams College of Business, Master of Business Administration Program, Cincinnati, OH 45207-3221. Offers business administration (Exec MBA, MBA); business intelligence (MBA); finance (MBA); health industry (MBA); international business (MBA); marketing (MBA); values-based leadership (MBA); MBA/MHSA; MSN/MBA. *Accreditation:* AACSB. Part-time and evening/weekend programs available. *Faculty:* 39 full-time (17 women), 12 part-time/adjunct (2 women). *Students:* 163 full-time (47 women), 483 part-time (162 women); includes 91 minority (28 Black or African American, non-Hispanic/Latino; 3 American Indian or Alaska Native, non-Hispanic/Latino; 42 Asian, non-Hispanic/Latino; 14 Hispanic/Latino; 4 Two or more races, non-Hispanic/Latino), 33 international. Average age 30. 190 applicants, 86% accepted, 110 enrolled. In 2013, 319 master's awarded. *Degree requirements:* For master's, capstone course. *Entrance requirements:* For master's, GMAT or GRE. Additional exam requirements/recommendations for international students: Required—TOEFL (minimum score 550 paper-based; 79 iBT). *Application deadline:* For fall admission, 8/1 priority date for domestic students, 5/1 for international students; for spring admission, 12/1 priority date for domestic students, 9/1 for international students. Applications are processed on a rolling basis. Application fee: $0. Electronic applications accepted. *Expenses:* Contact institution. *Financial support:* In 2013–14, 115 students received support. Scholarships/grants, tuition waivers (partial), and unspecified assistantships available. Financial award application deadline: 3/1; financial award applicants required to submit FAFSA. *Unit head:* Jennifer Bush, Assistant Dean of Graduate Programs, Williams College of Business, 513-745-3527, Fax: 513-745-2929, E-mail: bush@xavier.edu. *Application contact:* Lauren Parcell, MBA Advisor, 513-745-1014, Fax: 513-745-2929, E-mail: parcelll@xavier.edu. Website: http://www.xavier.edu/williams/mba/.

Sustainability Management

American University, Kogod School of Business, Washington, DC 20016-8044. Offers accounting (MS); business administration (MBA); business fundamentals (Certificate); entrepreneurship (Certificate); finance (MS); forensic accounting (Certificate); management (MS); marketing (MS); real estate (MS, Certificate); sustainability management (MS); tax (Certificate); taxation (MS). *Accreditation:* AACSB. Part-time and evening/weekend programs available. Postbaccalaureate distance learning degree programs offered. *Faculty:* 75 full-time (24 women), 36 part-time/adjunct (7 women). *Students:* 194 full-time (95 women), 370 part-time (184 women); includes 168 minority (69 Black or African American, non-Hispanic/Latino; 60 Asian, non-Hispanic/Latino; 33 Hispanic/Latino; 2 Native Hawaiian or other Pacific Islander, non-Hispanic/Latino; 4 Two

or more races, non-Hispanic/Latino), 108 international. Average age 30. 940 applicants, 46% accepted, 193 enrolled. In 2013, 221 master's, 4 other advanced degrees awarded. *Entrance requirements:* For master's, GMAT, resume, personal statement, interview, 2 letters of recommendation, transcripts. Additional exam requirements/recommendations for international students: Required—TOEFL (minimum score 100 iBT). *Application deadline:* Applications are processed on a rolling basis. Application fee: $100. Electronic applications accepted. *Expenses:* Contact institution. *Financial support:* Fellowships, career-related internships or fieldwork, Federal Work-Study, institutionally sponsored loans, and tuition waivers (partial) available. Support available to part-time students. Financial award application deadline: 2/1. *Unit head:* Dr. Michael Ginzberg, Dean, 202-885-1985, E-mail: ginzberg@american.edu. *Application contact:* Jason Kennedy, Associate Director of Graduate Admissions, 202-885-1968, E-mail: jkennedy@american.edu.
Website: http://www.kogod.american.edu/.

Anaheim University, Programs in Business Administration, Anaheim, CA 92806-5150. Offers entrepreneurship (ME, DBA); global sustainable management (MBA); international business (MBA, DBA, Certificate, Diploma); management (DBA); sustainable management (DBA, Certificate, Diploma). Postbaccalaureate distance learning degree programs offered.

Antioch University New England, Graduate School, Department of Management, Program in Sustainability (Green MBA), Keene, NH 03431-3552. Offers MBA. Part-time programs available. *Entrance requirements:* For master's, GRE, resume, 3 letters of recommendation. Additional exam requirements/recommendations for international students: Required—TOEFL (minimum score 600 paper-based).

Aquinas College, School of Management, Grand Rapids, MI 49506-1799. Offers health care administration (MM); marketing management (MM); organizational leadership (MM); sustainable business (MM, MSB). Part-time and evening/weekend programs available. *Students:* 13 full-time (10 women), 56 part-time (38 women); includes 10 minority (4 Black or African American, non-Hispanic/Latino; 1 American Indian or Alaska Native, non-Hispanic/Latino; 4 Hispanic/Latino; 1 Two or more races, non-Hispanic/Latino), 1 international. Average age 33. In 2013, 18 master's awarded. *Entrance requirements:* For master's, GMAT, minimum undergraduate GPA of 2.75, 2 years of work experience. Additional exam requirements/recommendations for international students: Required—TOEFL (minimum score 550 paper-based). *Application deadline:* Applications are processed on a rolling basis. Application fee: $0. *Expenses:* Contact institution. *Financial support:* Scholarships/grants available. Support available to part-time students. Financial award application deadline: 3/15; financial award applicants required to submit FAFSA. *Unit head:* Brian DiVita, Director, 616-632-2922, Fax: 616-732-4489. *Application contact:* Lynn Atkins-Rykert, Administrative Assistant, 616-632-2924, Fax: 616-732-4489, E-mail: atkinlyn@aquinas.edu.

Argosy University, Chicago, College of Business, Chicago, IL 60601. Offers accounting (DBA); customized professional concentration (MBA, DBA); finance (MBA); fraud examination (MBA); global business sustainability (DBA); healthcare administration (MBA); information systems (DBA); information systems management (MBA); international business (MBA, DBA); management (MBA, MSM, DBA); marketing (MBA, DBA); organizational leadership (Ed D); public administration (MBA); sustainable management (MBA). Postbaccalaureate distance learning degree programs offered (minimal on-campus study).

Argosy University, Dallas, College of Business, Farmers Branch, TX 75244. Offers accounting (DBA, AGC); corporate compliance (MBA, Graduate Certificate); customized professional concentration (MBA); finance (MBA, Graduate Certificate); fraud examination (MBA, Graduate Certificate); global business sustainability (DBA, AGC); healthcare administration (Graduate Certificate); healthcare management (MBA); information systems (MBA, DBA, AGC); information systems management (Graduate Certificate); international business (MBA, DBA, AGC, Graduate Certificate); management (MBA, DBA, AGC, Graduate Certificate); marketing (MBA, DBA, AGC, Graduate Certificate); public administration (MBA, Graduate Certificate); sustainable management (MBA, Graduate Certificate).

Argosy University, Denver, College of Business, Denver, CO 80231. Offers accounting (DBA); corporate compliance (MBA); customized professional concentration (MBA, DBA); finance (MBA); fraud examination (MBA); global business sustainability (DBA); healthcare administration (MBA); information systems (DBA); information systems management (MBA); international business (MBA, DBA); management (MBA, MSM, DBA); marketing (MBA, DBA); organizational leadership (Ed D); public administration (MBA); sustainable management (MBA).

Argosy University, Hawai`i, College of Business, Honolulu, HI 96813. Offers accounting (DBA); corporate compliance (MBA); customized professional concentration (MBA, DBA); finance (MBA, Certificate); fraud examination (MBA); global business sustainability (DBA); healthcare administration (MBA, Certificate); information systems (DBA); information systems management (MBA, Certificate); international business (MBA, DBA, Certificate); management (MBA, MSM, DBA); marketing (MBA, DBA, Certificate); organizational leadership (Ed D); public administration (MBA); sustainable management (MBA).

Argosy University, Inland Empire, College of Business, Ontario, CA 91761. Offers accounting (DBA); corporate compliance (MBA); customized professional concentration (MBA, DBA); finance (MBA); fraud examination (MBA); global business sustainability (DBA); healthcare administration (MBA); information systems (DBA); information systems management (MBA); international business (MBA, DBA); management (MBA, MSM, DBA); marketing (MBA, DBA); organizational leadership (Ed D); public administration (MBA); sustainable management (MBA).

Argosy University, Los Angeles, College of Business, Santa Monica, CA 90045. Offers accounting (DBA); corporate compliance (MBA); customized professional concentration (MBA, DBA); finance (MBA); fraud examination (MBA); global business sustainability (DBA); healthcare administration (MBA); information systems (DBA); information systems management (MBA); international business (MBA, DBA); management (MBA, MSM, DBA); marketing (MBA, DBA); organizational leadership (Ed D); public administration (MBA); sustainable management (MBA).

Argosy University, Orange County, College of Business, Orange, CA 92868. Offers accounting (DBA, Adv C); corporate compliance (MBA); customized professional concentration (MBA, DBA); finance (MBA, Certificate); fraud examination (MBA); global business sustainability (DBA); healthcare administration (MBA, Certificate); information systems (DBA, Adv C, Certificate); information systems management (MBA); international business (MBA, DBA, Adv C, Certificate); management (MBA, MSM, DBA, Adv C); marketing (MBA, DBA, Adv C, Certificate); organizational leadership (Ed D); public administration (MBA, Certificate); sustainable management (MBA).

Argosy University, Phoenix, College of Business, Phoenix, AZ 85021. Offers accounting (DBA); corporate compliance (MBA); customized professional concentration (MBA, DBA); finance (MBA); fraud examination (MBA); global business sustainability (DBA); healthcare administration (MBA); information systems (DBA); information systems management (MBA); international business (MBA, DBA); management (MBA, DBA); marketing (MBA, DBA); public administration (MBA); sustainable management (MBA).

Argosy University, Salt Lake City, College of Business, Draper, UT 84020. Offers accounting (DBA); corporate compliance (MBA); customized professional concentration (MBA, DBA); finance (MBA); fraud examination (MBA); global business sustainability (DBA); healthcare administration (MBA); information systems (DBA); information systems management (MBA); international business (MBA, DBA); management (MBA, DBA); marketing (MBA, DBA); public administration (MBA); sustainable management (MBA).

Argosy University, San Francisco Bay Area, College of Business, Alameda, CA 94501. Offers accounting (DBA); corporate compliance (MBA); customized professional concentration (MBA, DBA); finance (MBA); fraud examination (MBA); global business sustainability (DBA); healthcare administration (MBA); information systems (DBA); information systems management (MBA); international business (MBA, DBA); management (MBA, MSM, DBA); marketing (MBA, DBA); organizational leadership (Ed D); public administration (MBA); sustainable management (MBA).

Argosy University, Sarasota, College of Business, Sarasota, FL 34235. Offers accounting (DBA, Adv C); corporate compliance (MBA, DBA, Certificate); customized professional concentration (MBA, DBA); finance (MBA, Certificate); fraud examination (MBA, Certificate); global business sustainability (DBA, Adv C); healthcare administration (MBA, Certificate); information systems (DBA, Adv C, Certificate); information systems management (MBA); international business (MBA, DBA, Adv C, Certificate); management (MBA, MSM, DBA, Adv C, Certificate); marketing (MBA, DBA, Adv C, Certificate); organizational leadership (Ed D); public administration (MBA, Certificate); sustainable management (MBA, Certificate).

Argosy University, Schaumburg, College of Business, Schaumburg, IL 60173-5403. Offers accounting (DBA, Adv C); customized professional concentration (MBA, DBA); finance (MBA, Certificate); fraud examination (MBA); global business sustainability (DBA); healthcare administration (MBA, Certificate); information systems (DBA, Adv C, Certificate); information systems management (MBA); international business (MBA, DBA, Adv C, Certificate); management (MBA, MSM, DBA, Adv C, Certificate); marketing (MBA, DBA, Adv C, Certificate); organizational leadership (Ed D); public administration (MBA); sustainable management (MBA).

Argosy University, Seattle, College of Business, Seattle, WA 98121. Offers accounting (DBA); corporate compliance (MBA); customized professional concentration (MBA, DBA); finance (MBA); fraud examination (MBA); global business sustainability (DBA); healthcare administration (MBA); information systems (DBA); information systems management (MBA); international business (MBA, DBA); management (MBA, MSM, DBA); marketing (MBA, DBA); organizational leadership (Ed D); public administration (MBA); sustainable management (MBA).

Argosy University, Tampa, College of Business, Tampa, FL 33607. Offers accounting (DBA); corporate compliance (MBA); customized professional concentration (MBA, DBA); finance (MBA); fraud examination (MBA); global business sustainability (DBA); healthcare administration (MBA); information systems (DBA); information systems management (MBA); international business (MBA, DBA); management (MBA, MSM, DBA); marketing (MBA, DBA); organizational leadership (Ed D); public administration (MBA); sustainable management (MBA).

Argosy University, Twin Cities, College of Business, Eagan, MN 55121. Offers accounting (DBA); customized professional concentration (MBA, DBA); finance (MBA); fraud examination (MBA); global business sustainability (DBA); healthcare administration (MBA); information systems (DBA); information systems management (MBA); international business (MBA, DBA); management (MBA, MSM, DBA); marketing (MBA, DBA); organizational leadership (Ed D); public administration (MBA); sustainable management (MBA).

Argosy University, Washington DC, College of Business, Arlington, VA 22209. Offers accounting (DBA); customized professional concentration (MBA, DBA); finance (MBA); fraud examination (MBA); global business sustainability (DBA); healthcare administration (MBA); information systems (DBA); information systems management (MBA); international business (MBA, DBA, Certificate); management (MBA, MSM, DBA); marketing (MBA, DBA, Certificate); organizational leadership (Ed D); public administration (MBA); sustainable management (MBA).

Baldwin Wallace University, Graduate Programs, Division of Business, Program in Sustainability, Berea, OH 44017-2088. Offers MBA. Part-time and evening/weekend programs available. *Students:* 7 full-time (2 women), 8 part-time (6 women); includes 1 minority (Black or African American, non-Hispanic/Latino). Average age 34. 7 applicants, 71% accepted, 2 enrolled. In 2013, 3 master's awarded. *Degree requirements:* For master's, minimum overall GPA of 3.0, completion of all required courses. *Entrance requirements:* For master's, GMAT or minimum GPA of 3.0, bachelor's degree. Additional exam requirements/recommendations for international students: Required—TOEFL (minimum score 523 paper-based; 70 iBT). *Application deadline:* For fall admission, 7/25 for domestic students, 4/30 for international students; for spring admission, 12/15 for domestic students, 9/30 for international students. Applications are processed on a rolling basis. Application fee: $25. Electronic applications accepted. Application fee is waived when completed online. *Expenses:* Contact institution. *Financial support:* Application deadline: 5/1; applicants required to submit FAFSA. *Unit head:* Ven Ochaya, Director, 440-826-2391, Fax: 440-826-3868, E-mail: vochaya@bw.edu. *Application contact:* Laura Spencer, Graduate Application Specialist, 440-826-2191, Fax: 440-826-3868, E-mail: lspencer@bw.edu.
Website: http://www.bw.edu/academics/bus/programs/smba/.

Bard College, Bard Center for Environmental Policy, Annandale-on-Hudson, NY 12504. Offers climate science and policy (MS, Professional Certificate), including agriculture (MS), ecosystems (MS); environmental policy (MS, Professional Certificate); sustainability (MBA); MS/JD; MS/MAT. Part-time programs available. *Degree requirements:* For master's, thesis, 4-month, full-time internship. *Entrance requirements:* For master's, GRE, coursework in statistics, chemistry and one other semester of college science; personal statement; curriculum vitae; 3 letters of recommendation; sample of written work. Additional exam requirements/recommendations for international students: Required—TOEFL (minimum score 600 paper-based; 100 iBT). Electronic applications accepted. *Expenses:* Contact institution. *Faculty research:* Climate and agriculture, alternative energy, environmental economics, environmental toxicology, EPA law, sustainable development, international relations, literature and composition, human rights, agronomy, advocacy, leadership.

Baruch College of the City University of New York, Zicklin School of Business, Department of Management, New York, NY 10010-5585. Offers entrepreneurship (MBA); management (PhD); operations management (MBA); organizational behavior/human resources management (MBA); sustainable business (MBA). PhD offered jointly with Graduate School and University Center of the City University of New York. Part-time and evening/weekend programs available. *Degree requirements:* For doctorate, comprehensive exam, thesis/dissertation. *Entrance requirements:* For master's, GMAT, 2 letters of recommendation, resume, 2 years of work experience; for doctorate, GMAT.

Additional exam requirements/recommendations for international students: Required—TOEFL (minimum score 590 paper-based), TWE.

Brandeis University, International Business School, Waltham, MA 02454-9110. Offers asset management (MBA); business economics (MBA); corporate finance (MBA); data analytics (MBA); finance (MSF), including asset management, corporate finance, real estate, risk management; international economic policy analysis (MBA); international economics and finance (MA, PhD); marketing (MBA); real estate (MBA); risk management (MBA); sustainability (MBA). Part-time and evening/weekend programs available. *Degree requirements:* For doctorate, thesis/dissertation. *Entrance requirements:* For master's, GMAT or GRE General Test (waived for applicants with at least 2 years of work experience applying to MSF); for doctorate, GRE General Test. Additional exam requirements/recommendations for international students: Required—TOEFL (minimum score 600 paper-based; 100 iBT), IELTS (minimum score 7). Electronic applications accepted. *Faculty research:* International economic policy analysis, U.S. economic policy analysis, real estate, strategy and municipal finance.

Chatham University, Program in Business Administration, Pittsburgh, PA 15232-2826. Offers business administration (MBA); healthcare management (MBA); sustainability (MBA); women's leadership (MBA). Part-time and evening/weekend programs available. *Faculty:* 11 part-time/adjunct (8 women). *Students:* 17 full-time (12 women), 43 part-time (30 women); includes 10 minority (6 Black or African American, non-Hispanic/Latino; 1 American Indian or Alaska Native, non-Hispanic/Latino; 1 Asian, non-Hispanic/Latino; 1 Hispanic/Latino; 1 Two or more races, non-Hispanic/Latino), 11 international. Average age 29. 34 applicants, 79% accepted, 17 enrolled. In 2013, 28 master's awarded. *Entrance requirements:* For master's, minimum GPA of 3.0, letters of recommendation. Additional exam requirements/recommendations for international students: Required—TOEFL (minimum score 600 paper-based; 100 iBT), IELTS (minimum score 7), TWE. *Application deadline:* For fall admission, 4/1 for domestic and international students; for spring admission, 11/1 for domestic students, 10/1 for international students. Applications are processed on a rolling basis. Application fee: $45. Electronic applications accepted. Application fee is waived when completed online. *Expenses: Tuition:* Full-time $14,886; part-time $827 per credit hour. One-time fee: $396 full-time. *Financial support:* Applicants required to submit FAFSA. *Unit head:* Dr. Rachel Chung, Director of Business and Entrepreneurship Program, 412-365-2433. *Application contact:* Katie Noel, Assistant Director of Graduate Admission, 412-365-2758, Fax: 412-365-1609, E-mail: gradadmissions@chatham.edu.
Website: http://www.chatham.edu/mba.

City University of Seattle, Graduate Division, School of Management, Bellevue, WA 98005. Offers accounting (Certificate); change leadership (MBA, Certificate); computer systems (MS); finance (Certificate); financial management (MBA); general management (MBA); general management-Europe (MBA); global marketing (MBA); human resources management (Certificate); individualized study (MBA); information security (MS); information systems (MBA); leadership (MA); marketing (MBA, Certificate); project management (MBA, MS, Certificate); sustainable business (Certificate); technology management (MBA, Certificate). Part-time and evening/weekend programs available. Postbaccalaureate distance learning degree programs offered (no on-campus study). *Degree requirements:* For master's, comprehensive exam (for some programs), thesis (for some programs). *Entrance requirements:* Additional exam requirements/recommendations for international students: Required—TOEFL (minimum score 567 paper-based; 87 iBT); Recommended—IELTS. Electronic applications accepted.

Clark University, Graduate School, Graduate School of Management, Business Administration Program, Worcester, MA 01610-1477. Offers accounting (MBA); finance (MBA); global business (MBA); information systems (MBA); management (MBA); marketing (MBA); social change (MBA); sustainability (MBA). *Accreditation:* AACSB. Part-time and evening/weekend programs available. *Students:* 109 full-time (50 women), 151 part-time (67 women); includes 16 minority (9 Black or African American, non-Hispanic/Latino; 3 Asian, non-Hispanic/Latino; 4 Hispanic/Latino), 74 international. Average age 30. 359 applicants, 50% accepted, 81 enrolled. In 2013, 125 master's awarded. *Degree requirements:* For master's, thesis optional. *Application deadline:* For fall admission, 6/1 priority date for domestic students; for spring admission, 12/1 priority date for domestic students. Applications are processed on a rolling basis. Application fee: $50. Electronic applications accepted. *Expenses: Tuition:* Full-time $39,200; part-time $1225 per credit hour. *Financial support:* In 2013–14, research assistantships with partial tuition reimbursements (averaging $4,800 per year), teaching assistantships with partial tuition reimbursements (averaging $4,800 per year) were awarded; fellowships, career-related internships or fieldwork, Federal Work-Study, institutionally sponsored loans, and tuition waivers (partial) also available. Support available to part-time students. Financial award application deadline: 5/31. *Faculty research:* Marketing, accounting, human resource management, management information systems, business finance. *Unit head:* Dr. Catherine Usoff, Dean, 508-793-8822, Fax: 508-793-8822, E-mail: clarkmba@clarku.edu. *Application contact:* Patrick Oroszko, Enrollment and Marketing Director, 508-793-8822, Fax: 508-793-8822, E-mail: clarkmba@clarku.edu.
Website: http://www.clarku.edu/gsom/graduate/fulltime/.

Cleary University, Online Program in Business Administration, Ann Arbor, MI 48105-2659. Offers accounting (MBA); financial planning (MBA); financial planning (Graduate Certificate); green business strategy (MBA, Graduate Certificate); health care leadership (MBA); management (MBA); nonprofit management (MBA, Graduate Certificate); organizational leadership (MBA). Part-time and evening/weekend programs available. Postbaccalaureate distance learning degree programs offered (no on-campus study). *Degree requirements:* For master's, thesis. *Entrance requirements:* For master's, bachelor's degree; minimum GPA of 2.5; professional resume indicating minimum of 2 years of management or related experience; undergraduate degree from accredited college or university with at least 18 quarter hours (or 12 semester hours) of accounting study (for MBA in accounting). Additional exam requirements/recommendations for international students: Required—TOEFL (minimum score 550 paper-based; 79 iBT), Michigan English Language Assessment Battery (minimum score 75). Electronic applications accepted.

Colorado State University, Graduate School, College of Business, Program in Global Social and Sustainable Enterprise, Fort Collins, CO 80523-1201. Offers MSBA. *Students:* 52 full-time (27 women); includes 6 minority (1 Black or African American, non-Hispanic/Latino; 1 Asian, non-Hispanic/Latino; 4 Hispanic/Latino), 16 international. Average age 30. 32 applicants, 91% accepted, 24 enrolled. In 2013, 20 master's awarded. *Degree requirements:* For master's, variable foreign language requirement, comprehensive exam (for some programs), thesis, practicum. *Entrance requirements:* For master's, GMAT or GRE, 3 recommendations, current resume, minimum cumulative GPA of 3.0, essays, transcripts. Additional exam requirements/recommendations for international students: Required—TOEFL (minimum score 567 paper-based; 80 iBT); Recommended—IELTS (minimum score 6). *Application deadline:* For fall admission, 3/31 priority date for domestic students, 3/30 priority date for international students. Application fee: $50. *Expenses:* Tuition, state resident: full-time $9075.40; part-time $504 per credit. Tuition, nonresident: full-time $22,248; part-time $1236 per credit. *Required fees:* $1819; $60 per credit. *Financial support:* Fellowships with tuition reimbursements, research assistantships with tuition reimbursements, teaching assistantships, scholarships/grants, and unspecified assistantships available. Financial

award application deadline: 3/31; financial award applicants required to submit FAFSA. *Faculty research:* Entrepreneurial and collective decision-making, entrepreneurship and sustainability, cooperative business analysis, organizational behavior, risk management. *Unit head:* Dr. Carl Hammerdorfer, Director, 970-492-4955, E-mail: carl.hammerdorfer@business.colostate.edu. *Application contact:* Sandy Dahlberg, Admissions Counselor, 970-491-6937, E-mail: sandy.dahlberg@colostate.edu.
Website: http://www.biz.colostate.edu/gsse/pages/default.aspx.

Columbia University, School of Continuing Education, Program in Sustainability Management, New York, NY 10027. Offers MS. Program offered in collaboration with Columbia University's Earth Institute. Part-time programs available. Electronic applications accepted.

DePaul University, Charles H. Kellstadt Graduate School of Business, Chicago, IL 60604. Offers accountancy (M Acc, MS, MSA); applied economics (MBA); banking (MBA); behavioral finance (MBA); brand and product management (MBA); business development (MBA); business information technology (MS); business strategy and decision-making (MBA); computational finance (MS); consumer insights (MBA); corporate finance (MBA); economic policy analysis (MS); entrepreneurship (MBA, MS); finance (MBA, MS); financial analysis (MBA); general business (MBA); health sector management (MBA); hospitality leadership (MBA); hospitality leadership and operational performance (MS); human resource management (MBA); human resources (MS); investment management (MBA); leadership and change management (MBA); management accounting (MBA); marketing (MBA, MS); marketing analysis (MS); marketing strategy and planning (MBA); operations management (MBA); organizational diversity (MBA); real estate (MS); real estate finance and investment (MBA); revenue management (MBA); sports management (MBA); strategic global marketing (MBA); strategy, execution and valuation (MBA); sustainable management (MBA, MS); taxation (MS); wealth management (MS); JD/MBA. *Accreditation:* AACSB. Part-time and evening/weekend programs available. Postbaccalaureate distance learning degree programs offered (no on-campus study). *Faculty:* 81 full-time (20 women), 45 part-time/adjunct (8 women). *Students:* 1,238 full-time (605 women), 617 part-time (223 women); includes 295 minority (71 Black or African American, non-Hispanic/Latino; 129 Asian, non-Hispanic/Latino; 74 Hispanic/Latino; 4 Native Hawaiian or other Pacific Islander, non-Hispanic/Latino; 17 Two or more races, non-Hispanic/Latino), 462 international. Average age 29. In 2013, 911 master's awarded. *Entrance requirements:* For master's, GMAT, 2 letters of recommendation, resume, essay, official transcripts. Additional exam requirements/recommendations for international students: Required—TOEFL (minimum score 550 paper-based; 80 iBT). *Application deadline:* For fall admission, 7/1 for domestic students, 6/1 for international students; for winter admission, 10/1 for domestic students, 9/1 for international students; for spring admission, 2/1 for domestic students, 1/1 for international students. Applications are processed on a rolling basis. Application fee: $60. Electronic applications accepted. *Expenses:* Contact institution. *Financial support:* Application deadline: 4/1; applicants required to submit FAFSA. *Unit head:* Robert T. Ryan, Assistant Dean and Director, 312-362-8810, Fax: 312-362-6677, E-mail: rryan1@depaul.edu. *Application contact:* James Parker, Director of Recruitment and Admission, 312-362-8810, Fax: 312-362-6677, E-mail: kgsb@depaul.edu.
Website: http://kellstadt.depaul.edu.

Dominican University of California, Barowsky School of Business, San Rafael, CA 94901-2298. Offers global business (MBA); strategic leadership (MBA); sustainable enterprise (MBA). Part-time and evening/weekend programs available. *Faculty:* 7 full-time (3 women), 13 part-time/adjunct (5 women). *Students:* 53 full-time (35 women), 80 part-time (48 women); includes 28 minority (4 Black or African American, non-Hispanic/Latino; 6 Asian, non-Hispanic/Latino; 17 Hispanic/Latino; 1 Native Hawaiian or other Pacific Islander, non-Hispanic/Latino), 16 international. Average age 36. 136 applicants, 43% accepted, 36 enrolled. *Degree requirements:* For master's, thesis, capstone (for MBA). *Entrance requirements:* For master's, minimum GPA of 3.0. Additional exam requirements/recommendations for international students: Required—TOEFL (minimum score 550 paper-based; 80 iBT), IELTS (minimum score 6.5). *Application deadline:* For fall admission, 5/15 priority date for domestic and international students; for spring admission, 11/15 priority date for domestic and international students. Applications are processed on a rolling basis. Electronic applications accepted. Application fee is waived when completed online. *Expenses:* Contact institution. *Financial support:* Scholarships/grants and tuition discounts available. Support available to part-time students. Financial award application deadline: 3/2; financial award applicants required to submit FAFSA. *Unit head:* Dr. Sam Beldona, Dean, 415-458-3786, E-mail: sriam.beldona@dominican.edu. *Application contact:* Shannon Lovelace-White, Assistant Vice President, 415-485-3287, Fax: 415-485-3214, E-mail: shannon.lovelace-white@dominican.edu.
Website: http://www.dominican.edu/academics/barowskyschoolofbusiness.

Duquesne University, John F. Donahue Graduate School of Business, Pittsburgh, PA 15282-0001. Offers accounting (M Acc); finance (MBA); information systems management (MBA, MSISM); management (MBA); marketing (MBA); supply chain management (MBA); sustainability (MBA); JD/MBA; MBA/M Acc; MBA/MA; MBA/MES; MBA/MHMS; MBA/MSN; MSISM/MBA; Pharm D/MBA. *Accreditation:* AACSB. Part-time and evening/weekend programs available. *Faculty:* 58 full-time (17 women), 40 part-time/adjunct (8 women). *Students:* 117 full-time (59 women), 147 part-time (54 women); includes 14 minority (7 Black or African American, non-Hispanic/Latino; 1 Asian, non-Hispanic/Latino; 6 Hispanic/Latino), 53 international. Average age 27. 418 applicants, 46% accepted, 109 enrolled. In 2013, 133 master's awarded. *Entrance requirements:* For master's, GMAT, undergraduate transcripts, 2 letters of recommendation, current resume, personal statement. Additional exam requirements/recommendations for international students: Required—TOEFL (minimum score 577 paper-based; 90 iBT), IELTS (minimum score 7). *Application deadline:* For fall admission, 7/1 priority date for domestic students, 6/1 for international students; for spring admission, 11/1 for domestic and international students. Applications are processed on a rolling basis. Application fee: $0. Electronic applications accepted. *Expenses: Tuition:* Full-time $18,162; part-time $1009 per credit. *Required fees:* $1728; $96 per credit. Tuition and fees vary according to program. *Financial support:* In 2013–14, 39 students received support, including 6 fellowships with partial tuition reimbursements available (averaging $4,541 per year), 33 research assistantships with partial tuition reimbursements available (averaging $9,081 per year); career-related internships or fieldwork, scholarships/grants, and unspecified assistantships also available. Support available to part-time students. Financial award application deadline: 7/1; financial award applicants required to submit FAFSA. *Faculty research:* International business, investment management, business ethics, technology management, supply chain management, business strategy, finance. *Unit head:* Thomas J. Nist, Director of Graduate Programs, 412-396-6276, Fax: 412-396-1726, E-mail: nist@duq.edu. *Application contact:* Maria W. DeCrosta, Enrollment Manager, 412-396-5529, Fax: 412-396-1726, E-mail: decrostam@duq.edu.
Website: http://www.duq.edu/business/grad.

Edgewood College, Program in Business, Madison, WI 53711-1997. Offers accountancy (MS); accounting (MBA); business administration (MBA); finance (MBA); management (MBA); marketing (MBA); organization development (MS); sustainability leadership (MBA). *Accreditation:* ACBSP. Part-time and evening/weekend programs available. *Students:* 24 full-time (8 women), 136 part-time (82 women); includes 18

minority (5 Black or African American, non-Hispanic/Latino; 1 American Indian or Alaska Native, non-Hispanic/Latino; 4 Asian, non-Hispanic/Latino; 4 Hispanic/Latino; 4 Two or more races, non-Hispanic/Latino), 10 international. Average age 33. In 2013, 55 master's awarded. *Entrance requirements:* For master's, GMAT (minimum score 430), minimum GPA of 2.75, 2 letters of recommendation. Additional exam requirements/recommendations for international students: Required—TOEFL. *Application deadline:* For fall admission, 8/15 for domestic students, 5/1 for international students; for spring admission, 1/8 for domestic students, 11/1 for international students. Applications are processed on a rolling basis. Application fee: $30. Electronic applications accepted. *Financial support:* Career-related internships or fieldwork and scholarships/grants available. *Unit head:* Martin Preizler, Dean, 608-663-2898, Fax: 608-663-3291, E-mail: martinpreizler@edgewood.edu. *Application contact:* Joann Eastman, Admissions Counselor, 608-663-3250, Fax: 608-663-2214, E-mail: gps@edgewood.edu.
Website: http://www.edgewood.edu/Academics/School-of-Business.

Edgewood College, Program in Education, Madison, WI 53711-1997. Offers adult learning (MA Ed); bilingual teaching and learning (MA Ed); director of instruction (Certificate); director of special education and pupil services (Certificate); education (MA Ed); educational administration (MA Ed); educational leadership (Ed D); professional studies (MA Ed); program coordinator (Certificate); reading administration (MA Ed); school business administration (Certificate); school principalship K-12 (Certificate); special education (MA Ed); sustainability leadership (MA Ed); teaching and learning (MA Ed); teaching English to speakers of other languages (TESOL) (MA Ed). *Accreditation:* NCATE (one or more programs are accredited). Part-time and evening/weekend programs available. *Students:* 159 full-time (95 women), 164 part-time (121 women); includes 61 minority (19 Black or African American, non-Hispanic/Latino; 9 Asian, non-Hispanic/Latino; 25 Hispanic/Latino; 8 Two or more races, non-Hispanic/Latino), 27 international. Average age 36. In 2013, 51 master's, 22 doctorates awarded. *Degree requirements:* For master's, practicum, research project; for doctorate, comprehensive exam, thesis/dissertation. *Entrance requirements:* For master's, minimum GPA of 2.75, 2 letters of recommendation, personal statement; for doctorate, resume, letter of intent, 2 letters of recommendation, interview, writing sample. Additional exam requirements/recommendations for international students: Required—TOEFL (minimum score 525 paper-based; 72 iBT). *Application deadline:* For fall admission, 8/15 for domestic students, 5/1 for international students; for spring admission, 1/8 for domestic students, 11/1 for international students. Applications are processed on a rolling basis. Application fee: $30. Electronic applications accepted. *Unit head:* Dr. Timothy Slekar, Dean, E-mail: tslekar@edgewood.edu. *Application contact:* Joann Eastman, Admissions Counselor, 608-663-3250, Fax: 608-663-2214, E-mail: gps@edgewood.edu.
Website: http://www.edgewood.edu/Academics/School-of-Education.

Fairleigh Dickinson University, College at Florham, Silberman College of Business, Certificate Program in Managing Sustainability, Madison, NJ 07940-1099. Offers Certificate.

Franklin Pierce University, Graduate Studies, Rindge, NH 03461-0060. Offers curriculum and instruction (M Ed); emerging network technologies (Graduate Certificate); energy and sustainability studies (MBA); health administration (MBA, Graduate Certificate); human resource management (MBA, Graduate Certificate); information technology (MBA); information technology management (MS); leadership (MBA, DA); nursing (MS); physical therapy (DPT); physician assistant studies (MPAS); special education (M Ed); sports management (MBA). *Accreditation:* APTA. Part-time programs available. Postbaccalaureate distance learning degree programs offered (no on-campus study). *Degree requirements:* For master's, concentrated original research projects; student teaching; fieldwork and/or internship; leadership project; PRAXIS I and II (for M Ed); for doctorate, concentrated original research projects, clinical fieldwork and/or internship, leadership project. *Entrance requirements:* For master's, minimum GPA of 2.5, 3 letters of recommendation; competencies in accounting, economics, statistics, and computer skills through life experience or undergraduate coursework (for MBA); certification/e-portfolio, minimum C grade in all education courses (for M Ed); license to practice as RN (for MS in nursing); for doctorate, GRE, BA/BS, 3 letters of recommendation, personal mission statement, interview, writing sample, minimum cumulative GPA of 2.8, master's degree (for DA); 80 hours of observation/work in PT settings, completion of anatomy, chemistry, physics, and statistics, minimum GPA of 3.0 (for DPT). Additional exam requirements/recommendations for international students: Required—TOEFL (minimum score 550 paper-based; 61 iBT). Electronic applications accepted. *Faculty research:* Evidence-based practice in sports physical therapy, human resource management in economic crisis, leadership in nursing, innovation in sports facility management, differentiated learning and understanding by design.

George Mason University, College of Humanities and Social Sciences, Interdisciplinary Studies Program, Fairfax, VA 22030. Offers community college teaching (MAIS); computational social science (MAIS); energy and sustainability (MAIS); film and video studies (MAIS); folklore studies (MAIS); higher education administration (MAIS); neuroethics (MAIS); religion, culture and values (MAIS); social entrepreneurship (MAIS); war and military in society (MAIS); women and gender studies (MAIS). *Faculty:* 10 full-time (3 women), 7 part-time/adjunct (3 women). *Students:* 31 full-time (17 women), 79 part-time (50 women); includes 30 minority (17 Black or African American, non-Hispanic/Latino; 4 Asian, non-Hispanic/Latino; 6 Hispanic/Latino; 3 Two or more races, non-Hispanic/Latino), 3 international. Average age 33. 78 applicants, 59% accepted, 25 enrolled. In 2013, 32 master's awarded. *Degree requirements:* For master's, project or thesis. *Entrance requirements:* For master's, 3 letters of recommendation; writing sample; official transcript; resume. Additional exam requirements/recommendations for international students: Required—TOEFL (minimum score 570 paper-based; 88 iBT), IELTS (minimum score 6.5), PTE. *Application deadline:* For fall admission, 3/1 priority date for domestic students; for spring admission, 10/15 for domestic students. Application fee: $65 ($80 for international students). Electronic applications accepted. *Expenses:* Tuition, state resident: full-time $9350; part-time $390 per credit. Tuition, nonresident: full-time $25,754; part-time $1073 per credit. *Required fees:* $2688; $112 per credit. *Financial support:* In 2013–14, 8 students received support, including 3 research assistantships with full and partial tuition reimbursements available (averaging $10,238 per year), 5 teaching assistantships with full and partial tuition reimbursements available (averaging $7,655 per year); career-related internships or fieldwork, Federal Work-Study, scholarships/grants, unspecified assistantships, and health care benefits (for full-time research or teaching assistantship recipients) also available. Support available to part-time students. Financial award application deadline: 3/1; financial award applicants required to submit FAFSA. *Faculty research:* Combined English and folklore, religious and cultural studies (Christianity and Muslim society). *Unit head:* Jan Arminio, Interim Director, 703-993-2064, Fax: 703-993-2307, E-mail: jarminio@gmu.edu. *Application contact:* Becky Durham, Administrative Coordinator, 703-993-8762, Fax: 703-993-5585, E-mail: rdurham4@gmu.edu.
Website: http://mais.gmu.edu.

Goddard College, Graduate Division, Master of Arts in Sustainable Business and Communities Program, Plainfield, VT 05667-9432. Offers MA. Postbaccalaureate distance learning degree programs offered (minimal on-campus study). *Degree requirements:* For master's, thesis. *Entrance requirements:* For master's, 3 letters of recommendation, study plan and resource list, interview.

Illinois Institute of Technology, Stuart School of Business, Program in Business Administration, Chicago, IL 60661. Offers financial management (MBA); innovation and emerging enterprises (MBA); management science (MBA); marketing (MBA); sustainability (MBA); JD/MBA; M Des/MBA; MBA/MS. *Accreditation:* AACSB. Part-time and evening/weekend programs available. *Entrance requirements:* For master's, GRE (minimum score 1000) or GMAT (500). Additional exam requirements/recommendations for international students: Required—TOEFL (minimum score 600 paper-based; 85 iBT); Recommended—IELTS (minimum score 7). Electronic applications accepted. *Expenses:* Contact institution. *Faculty research:* Global management and marketing strategy, technological innovation, management science, financial management, knowledge management.

Indiana University Bloomington, School of Public and Environmental Affairs, Public Affairs Programs, Bloomington, IN 47405. Offers economic development (MPA); energy (MPA); environmental policy (PhD); environmental policy and natural resource management (MPA); information systems (MPA); international development (MPA); local government management (MPA); nonprofit management (MPA, Certificate); policy analysis (MPA); public budgeting and financial management (Certificate); public finance (PhD); public financial administration (MPA); public management (MPA, PhD, Certificate); public policy analysis (PhD); social entrepreneurship (Certificate); specialized public affairs (MPA); sustainability and sustainable development (MPA); JD/MPA; MPA/MA; MPA/MIS; MPA/MLS; MSES/MPA. *Accreditation:* NASPAA (one or more programs are accredited). Part-time programs available. *Faculty:* 79 full-time (32 women), 8 part-time/adjunct (3 women). *Students:* 433 full-time (232 women), 75 part-time (39 women); includes 90 minority (19 Black or African American, non-Hispanic/Latino; 1 American Indian or Alaska Native, non-Hispanic/Latino; 49 Asian, non-Hispanic/Latino; 14 Hispanic/Latino; 2 Native Hawaiian or other Pacific Islander, non-Hispanic/Latino; 5 Two or more races, non-Hispanic/Latino), 70 international. Average age 27. 714 applicants, 73% accepted, 253 enrolled. In 2013, 171 master's, 3 doctorates, 4 other advanced degrees awarded. *Degree requirements:* For master's, capstone, internship; for doctorate, comprehensive exam, thesis/dissertation. *Entrance requirements:* For master's, GRE General Test or GMAT, official transcripts, 3 letters of recommendation, resume, personal statement; for doctorate, GRE General Test, official transcripts, 3 letters of recommendation, statement of purpose. Additional exam requirements/recommendations for international students: Required—TOEFL (minimum score 600 paper-based; 96 iBT); Recommended—IELTS (minimum score 7). *Application deadline:* For fall admission, 2/1 priority date for domestic students, 12/1 priority date for international students; for spring admission, 11/15 for domestic students, 9/1 for international students. Applications are processed on a rolling basis. Application fee: $55 ($65 for international students). Electronic applications accepted. *Financial support:* Fellowships with partial tuition reimbursements, research assistantships with full and partial tuition reimbursements, teaching assistantships with full and partial tuition reimbursements, career-related internships or fieldwork, Federal Work-Study, scholarships/grants, health care benefits, unspecified assistantships, and Service Corps Program; Educational Opportunity Fellowships available. Financial award application deadline: 2/1; financial award applicants required to submit FAFSA. *Faculty research:* International development, environmental policy and resource management, policy analysis, public finance, public management, urban management, nonprofit management, energy policy, social policy, public finance. *Unit head:* Megan Siehl, Assistant Director, Admissions and Financial Aid, 812-855-9485, Fax: 812-856-3665, E-mail: speampo@indiana.edu. *Application contact:* Lane Bowman, Admissions Services Coordinator, 812-855-2840, Fax: 812-856-3665, E-mail: speaapps@indiana.edu.
Website: http://www.indiana.edu/~spea/prospective_students/masters/.

Lipscomb University, Graduate School of Business, Nashville, TN 37204-3951. Offers accountancy (M Acc); accounting (MBA); conflict management (MBA); distributive (general) (MBA); financial services (MBA); health care informatics (MBA); healthcare management (MBA); human resources (MHR); information security (MBA); leadership (MBA); nonprofit management (MBA); professional accountancy (Certificate); sports management (MBA); strategic human resources (MBA); sustainability (MBA); MBA/MS. *Accreditation:* ACBSP. Part-time and evening/weekend programs available. *Faculty:* 12 full-time (1 woman), 12 part-time/adjunct (2 women). *Students:* 90 full-time (44 women), 104 part-time (51 women); includes 28 minority (24 Black or African American, non-Hispanic/Latino; 3 Hispanic/Latino; 1 Two or more races, non-Hispanic/Latino), 6 international. Average age 33. 145 applicants, 79% accepted, 69 enrolled. In 2013, 98 master's, 1 other advanced degree awarded. *Entrance requirements:* For master's, GMAT, transcripts, interview, 2 references, resume. Additional exam requirements/recommendations for international students: Required—TOEFL (minimum score 570 paper-based). *Application deadline:* For fall admission, 6/15 for domestic students, 2/1 for international students; for winter admission, 6/1 for international students; for spring admission, 11/15 for domestic students. Applications are processed on a rolling basis. Application fee: $50 ($75 for international students). Electronic applications accepted. *Expenses:* Contact institution. *Financial support:* Career-related internships or fieldwork, scholarships/grants, tuition waivers (partial), and unspecified assistantships available. Support available to part-time students. Financial award application deadline: 7/1; financial award applicants required to submit FAFSA. *Faculty research:* Impact of spirituality on organization commitment, women in corporate leadership, psychological empowerment, training. *Unit head:* Joe Ivey, Associate Dean of Graduate Business Programs, 615-966-6229, Fax: 615-966-1818, E-mail: joe.ivey@lipscomb.edu. *Application contact:* Lisa Shacklett, Assistant Dean of Enrollment and Marketing, 615-966-5968, E-mail: lisa.shacklett@lipscomb.edu.
Website: http://www.lipscomb.edu/business/Graduate-Programs.

Maastricht School of Management, Graduate Programs, Maastricht, Netherlands. Offers business administration (MBA, DBA, PhD); facility management (Exec MBA); management (M Sc); sustainability (Exec MBA).

Maharishi University of Management, Graduate Studies, Program in Business Administration, Fairfield, IA 52557. Offers accounting (MBA); business administration (PhD); sustainability (MBA). Evening/weekend programs available. Postbaccalaureate distance learning degree programs offered (minimal on-campus study). *Degree requirements:* For doctorate, thesis/dissertation. *Entrance requirements:* For master's, GMAT, minimum GPA of 3.0; for doctorate, minimum GPA of 3.0. Additional exam requirements/recommendations for international students: Required—TOEFL. *Faculty research:* Leadership, effects of the group dynamics of consciousness on the economy, innovation, employee development, cooperative strategy.

Marlboro College, Graduate and Professional Studies, Program in Business Administration, Marlboro, VT 05344. Offers managing for sustainability (MBA). Part-time and evening/weekend programs available. Postbaccalaureate distance learning degree programs offered (minimal on-campus study). *Faculty:* 14 part-time/adjunct (6 women). *Students:* 5 full-time (4 women), 11 part-time (9 women); includes 1 minority (Asian, non-Hispanic/Latino). Average age 35. 7 applicants, 71% accepted, 4 enrolled. In 2013, 7 master's awarded. *Degree requirements:* For master's, 60 credits including capstone project. *Entrance requirements:* For master's, letter of intent, essay, transcripts, 2 letters

of recommendation. *Application deadline:* For fall admission, 7/1 priority date for domestic students; for winter admission, 11/1 priority date for domestic students. Applications are processed on a rolling basis. Application fee: $0. Electronic applications accepted. *Expenses: Tuition:* Part-time $685 per credit. Tuition and fees vary according to course load and program. *Financial support:* Applicants required to submit FAFSA. *Unit head:* Patricia Daniel, Degree Chair, 802-451-7511, Fax: 802-258-9201, E-mail: pdaniel@gradschool.marlboro.edu. *Application contact:* Matthew Livingston, Director of Graduate Admissions, 802-258-9209, Fax: 802-258-9201, E-mail: mlivingston@marlboro.edu.
Website: https://www.marlboro.edu/academics/graduate/mba.

Michigan Technological University, Graduate School, Sustainable Futures Institute, Houghton, MI 49931. Offers sustainability (Graduate Certificate). Part-time programs available. *Entrance requirements:* For degree, official transcripts, statement of purpose, 2 letters of recommendation. Additional exam requirements/recommendations for international students: Required—TOEFL (minimum score 79 iBT) or IELTS.

National University, Academic Affairs, School of Business and Management, La Jolla, CA 92037-1011. Offers accountancy (Certificate); business administration (GMBA, MBA), including financial management (MBA), human resource management (MBA), integrated marketing communications (MBA), international business (MBA), management accounting (MBA), marketing (MBA), mobile marketing and social media (MBA), organizational leadership (MA, MBA), professional golf management (MBA); global management (MGM); human resource management (MA), including organizational development and change, organizational leadership (MA, MBA); international business (Certificate); management information systems (MS); organizational leadership (MS), including community development; sustainability management (MS). Part-time and evening/weekend programs available. Postbaccalaureate distance learning degree programs offered (no on-campus study). *Faculty:* 30 full-time (8 women), 88 part-time/adjunct (25 women). *Students:* 688 full-time (357 women), 331 part-time (161 women); includes 453 minority (105 Black or African American, non-Hispanic/Latino; 2 American Indian or Alaska Native, non-Hispanic/Latino; 143 Asian, non-Hispanic/Latino; 162 Hispanic/Latino; 13 Native Hawaiian or other Pacific Islander, non-Hispanic/Latino; 28 Two or more races, non-Hispanic/Latino), 165 international. Average age 33. 286 applicants, 100% accepted, 217 enrolled. In 2013, 641 master's awarded. *Degree requirements:* For master's, thesis (for some programs). *Entrance requirements:* For master's, interview, minimum GPA of 2.5. Additional exam requirements/recommendations for international students: Required—TOEFL (minimum score 550 paper-based; 79 iBT), IELTS (minimum score 6). *Application deadline:* Applications are processed on a rolling basis. Application fee: $60 ($65 for international students). Electronic applications accepted. *Expenses: Tuition:* Full-time $13,824; part-time $1728 per course. One-time fee: $160. *Financial support:* Career-related internships or fieldwork, scholarships/grants, and tuition waivers (partial) available. Support available to part-time students. Financial award application deadline: 6/30; financial award applicants required to submit FAFSA. *Unit head:* School of Business and Management, 800-628-8648, Fax: 858-642-8719, E-mail: sobm@nu.edu. *Application contact:* Louis Cruz, Interim Vice President for Enrollment Services, 800-628-8648, E-mail: advisor@nu.edu.
Website: http://www.nu.edu/OurPrograms/SchoolOfBusinessAndManagement.html.

National University, Academic Affairs, School of Engineering, Technology and Media, La Jolla, CA 92037-1011. Offers computer science (MS), including advanced computing, database engineering, software engineering; cyber security and information assurance (MS), including computer forensics, ethical hacking and penetration testing, health information assurance, information assurance and security; data analytics (MS); engineering management (MS), including enterprise architecture, project management, systems engineering, technology management; environmental engineering (MS); homeland security and emergency management (MS); management information systems (MS); project management (Certificate); sustainability management (MS); wireless communications (MS). Part-time and evening/weekend programs available. Postbaccalaureate distance learning degree programs offered (no on-campus study). *Faculty:* 19 full-time (4 women), 28 part-time/adjunct (5 women). *Students:* 294 full-time (90 women), 100 part-time (29 women); includes 198 minority (49 Black or African American, non-Hispanic/Latino; 69 Asian, non-Hispanic/Latino; 60 Hispanic/Latino; 3 Native Hawaiian or other Pacific Islander, non-Hispanic/Latino; 17 Two or more races, non-Hispanic/Latino), 50 international. Average age 34. 160 applicants, 100% accepted, 123 enrolled. In 2013, 174 master's awarded. *Degree requirements:* For master's, thesis (for some programs). *Entrance requirements:* For master's, interview, minimum GPA of 2.5. Additional exam requirements/recommendations for international students: Required—TOEFL (minimum score 550 paper-based; 79 iBT), IELTS (minimum score 6). *Application deadline:* Applications are processed on a rolling basis. Application fee: $60 ($65 for international students). Electronic applications accepted. *Expenses: Tuition:* Full-time $13,824; part-time $1728 per course. One-time fee: $160. *Financial support:* Career-related internships or fieldwork, institutionally sponsored loans, scholarships/grants, and tuition waivers (partial) available. Support available to part-time students. Financial award application deadline: 6/30; financial award applicants required to submit FAFSA. *Faculty research:* Educational technology, scholarships in science. *Unit head:* School of Engineering, Technology, and Media, 800-628-8648, E-mail: setm@nu.edu. *Application contact:* Louis Cruz, Interim Vice President for Enrollment Services, 800-628-8648, E-mail: advisor@nu.edu.
Website: http://www.nu.edu/OurPrograms/SchoolOfEngineeringAndTechnology.html.

The New School, Milano The New School for Management and Urban Policy, Program in Environmental Policy and Sustainability Management, New York, NY 10011. Offers MS.

Oklahoma State University, Graduate College, Stillwater, OK 74078. Offers aerospace security (Graduate Certificate); bioenergy and sustainable technology (Graduate Certificate); bioinformatics (Graduate Certificate); business data mining (Graduate Certificate); business sustainability (Graduate Certificate); engineering and technology management (Graduate Certificate); entrepreneurship (Graduate Certificate); environmental science (MS); global issues (Graduate Certificate); grassland management (Graduate Certificate); information assurance (Graduate Certificate); interdisciplinary sciences (MS); interdisciplinary toxicology (Graduate Certificate); international studies (MS); non-profit management (Graduate Certificate); online teaching (Graduate Certificate); photonics (PhD); plant science (PhD); teaching English to speakers of other languages (Graduate Certificate); telecommunications management (MS). Programs are interdisciplinary. *Faculty:* 4 full-time (2 women), 2 part-time/adjunct (1 woman). *Students:* 74 full-time (58 women), 147 part-time (74 women); includes 44 minority (12 Black or African American, non-Hispanic/Latino; 8 American Indian or Alaska Native, non-Hispanic/Latino; 10 Asian, non-Hispanic/Latino; 6 Hispanic/Latino; 8 Two or more races, non-Hispanic/Latino), 43 international. Average age 32. 495 applicants, 70% accepted, 75 enrolled. In 2013, 55 master's, 11 doctorates awarded. *Degree requirements:* For master's, thesis (for some programs); for doctorate, comprehensive exam, thesis/dissertation. *Entrance requirements:* For master's and doctorate, GRE or GMAT. Additional exam requirements/recommendations for international students: Required—TOEFL (minimum score 550 paper-based; 79 iBT). *Application deadline:* For fall admission, 3/1 priority date for international students; for

spring admission, 8/1 priority date for international students. Applications are processed on a rolling basis. Application fee: $40 ($75 for international students). Electronic applications accepted. *Expenses:* Tuition, state resident: full-time $4272; part-time $178 per credit hour. Tuition, nonresident: full-time $17,472; part-time $709 per credit hour. *Required fees:* $2413.20; $100.55 per credit hour. One-time fee: $50 full-time. Part-time tuition and fees vary according to course load and campus/location. *Financial support:* Career-related internships or fieldwork, Federal Work-Study, scholarships/grants, health care benefits, tuition waivers (partial), and unspecified assistantships available. Support available to part-time students. Financial award application deadline: 3/1; financial award applicants required to submit FAFSA. *Unit head:* Dr. Sheryl Tucker, Dean, 405-744-7099, Fax: 405-744-0355, E-mail: grad-i@okstate.edu. *Application contact:* Dr. Susan Mathew, Coordinator of Admissions, 405-744-6368, Fax: 405-744-0355, E-mail: grad-i@okstate.edu.
Website: http://gradcollege.okstate.edu/.

Oregon State University, College of Business, Program in Business Administration, Corvallis, OR 97331. Offers clean technology (MBA); commercialization (MBA); executive leadership (MBA); global operations (MBA); marketing (MBA); research thesis (MBA); wealth management (MBA). Part-time programs available. *Faculty:* 34 full-time (13 women), 2 part-time/adjunct (1 woman). *Students:* 153 full-time (67 women), 44 part-time (18 women); includes 20 minority (1 Black or African American, non-Hispanic/Latino; 12 Asian, non-Hispanic/Latino; 3 Hispanic/Latino; 1 Native Hawaiian or other Pacific Islander, non-Hispanic/Latino; 3 Two or more races, non-Hispanic/Latino), 97 international. Average age 29. 194 applicants, 64% accepted, 106 enrolled. In 2013, 61 degrees awarded. *Degree requirements:* For master's, thesis optional. *Entrance requirements:* For master's, GMAT. Additional exam requirements/recommendations for international students: Required—TOEFL (minimum score 91 iBT), IELTS (minimum score 7). *Application deadline:* Applications are processed on a rolling basis. Application fee: $60. *Expenses:* Contact institution. *Unit head:* Dr. David Baldridge, Director for Business Master's Program, 541-737-6062, E-mail: david.baldridge@bus.oregonstate.edu.
Website: http://business.oregonstate.edu/mba/degrees.

Oregon State University, College of Forestry, Program in Sustainable Forest Management, Corvallis, OR 97331. Offers MAIS, MF, MS, PhD. Part-time programs available. *Faculty:* 17 full-time (2 women), 2 part-time/adjunct (0 women). *Students:* 33 full-time (12 women), 3 part-time (1 woman); includes 2 minority (1 Hispanic/Latino; 1 Two or more races, non-Hispanic/Latino), 10 international. Average age 29. 30 applicants, 63% accepted, 12 enrolled. In 2013, 1 master's awarded. *Entrance requirements:* For master's and doctorate, GRE. Additional exam requirements/recommendations for international students: Required—TOEFL (minimum score 80 iBT), IELTS (minimum score 6.5). *Application deadline:* For fall admission, 6/1 for domestic students, 4/1 for international students; for winter admission, 9/1 for domestic students, 7/1 for international students; for spring admission, 12/1 for domestic students, 10/1 for international students; for summer admission, 3/1 for domestic students, 1/1 for international students. Application fee: $60. *Expenses:* Tuition, state resident: full-time $11,664; part-time $432 per credit hour. Tuition, nonresident: full-time $19,197; part-time $711 per credit hour. *Required fees:* $1446; $443 per quarter. One-time fee: $300. Tuition and fees vary according to course load and program. *Unit head:* Dr. Claire Montgomery, Professor and Interim Department Head, 541-737-5533, E-mail: claire.montgomery@oregonstate.edu. *Application contact:* Dr. John Sessions, Professor/Chair of Forest Operations Management, 541-737-2818, E-mail: john.sessions@oregonstate.edu.
Website: http://ferm.forestry.oregonstate.edu/academic-programs/graduate-degree.

Point Loma Nazarene University, Fermanian School of Business, San Diego, CA 92106-2899. Offers general business (MBA); healthcare (MBA); not-for-profit management (MBA); organizational leadership (MBA); sustainability (MBA). *Accreditation:* ACBSP. Part-time and evening/weekend programs available. *Students:* 37 full-time (12 women), 70 part-time (35 women); includes 33 minority (3 Black or African American, non-Hispanic/Latino; 9 Asian, non-Hispanic/Latino; 14 Hispanic/Latino; 1 Native Hawaiian or other Pacific Islander, non-Hispanic/Latino; 6 Two or more races, non-Hispanic/Latino), 1 international. Average age 29. 51 applicants, 65% accepted, 28 enrolled. In 2013, 59 master's awarded. *Entrance requirements:* For master's, GMAT, letters of recommendation, essay, interview. Additional exam requirements/recommendations for international students: Required—TOEFL. *Application deadline:* For fall admission, 8/4 priority date for domestic students; for spring admission, 12/8 priority date for domestic students; for summer admission, 4/13 priority date for domestic students. Applications are processed on a rolling basis. Application fee: $50. Electronic applications accepted. *Expenses: Tuition:* Full-time $6900; part-time $567 per credit hour. *Financial support:* Applicants required to submit FAFSA. *Unit head:* Dr. Ken Armstrong, Interim Dean, 619-849-2290, E-mail: kenarmstrong@pointloma.edu. *Application contact:* Laura Leinweber, Director of Graduate Admission, 866-692-4723, E-mail: lauraleinweber@pointloma.edu.
Website: http://www.pointloma.edu/discover/graduate-school-san-diego/san-diego-graduate-programs-masters-degree-san-diego/mba.

Rochester Institute of Technology, Graduate Enrollment Services, Golisano Institute for Sustainability, Rochester, NY 14623-5603. Offers M Arch, MS, PhD. *Students:* 60 full-time (31 women), 9 part-time (3 women); includes 7 minority (1 Black or African American, non-Hispanic/Latino; 1 Asian, non-Hispanic/Latino; 5 Hispanic/Latino), 19 international. Average age 28. 164 applicants, 46% accepted, 35 enrolled. In 2013, 1 master's, 4 doctorates awarded. *Degree requirements:* For master's, comprehensive exam, thesis. *Entrance requirements:* For master's, GRE. Additional exam requirements/recommendations for international students: Required—TOEFL (minimum score 600 paper-based; 100 iBT) or IELTS (minimum score 6.5). *Application deadline:* For fall admission, 1/15 priority date for domestic and international students. Applications are processed on a rolling basis. Application fee: $60. Electronic applications accepted. *Expenses: Tuition:* Full-time $37,236; part-time $1552 per credit hour. *Required fees:* $250. *Faculty research:* Remanufacturing and resource recovery, sustainable production, sustainable mobility, systems modernization and sustainment, pollution prevention. *Unit head:* Dr. Nabil Nasr, Assistant Provost and Director, 585-475-2602, E-mail: info@sustainability.rit.edu. *Application contact:* Diane Ellison, Assistant Vice President, Graduate Enrollment Services, 585-475-2229, Fax: 585-475-7164, E-mail: gradinfo@rit.edu.
Website: http://www.sustainability.rit.edu/.

San Francisco State University, Division of Graduate Studies, College of Business, Program in Business Administration, San Francisco, CA 94132-1722. Offers decision sciences/operations research (MBA); finance (MBA); information systems (MBA); leadership (MBA); management (MBA); marketing (MBA); sustainable business (MBA). *Accreditation:* AACSB. Part-time and evening/weekend programs available. *Faculty:* 100. *Students:* 850 (408 women). 839 applicants, 56% accepted, 241 enrolled. *Degree requirements:* For master's, thesis, essay, test. *Entrance requirements:* For master's, GMAT, minimum GPA of 2.7 in last 60 units. Additional exam requirements/recommendations for international students: Required—TOEFL (minimum score 550 paper-based). *Application deadline:* For fall admission, 5/1 priority date for domestic students, 4/1 for international students; for spring admission, 11/1 for domestic students,

10/15 for international students. Applications are processed on a rolling basis. Application fee: $55. *Financial support:* Application deadline: 3/1. *Unit head:* Linda Oubre, Dean, 415-817-4300, E-mail: loubre@sfsu.edu. *Application contact:* Armaan Moattari, Assistant Director, Graduate Programs, 415-817-4314, Fax: 817-4340, E-mail: amoatt@sfsu.edu.
Website: http://cob.sfsu.edu/.

Seattle Pacific University, Master of Arts in Management Program, Seattle, WA 98119-1997. Offers faith and business (MA); human resources (MA); social and sustainable management (MA). *Entrance requirements:* For master's, GMAT or GRE (waived with cumulative GPA of 3.3 or above), bachelor's degree from accredited college or university, resume, essay, official transcript. *Application deadline:* For fall admission, 6/15 for domestic students. Application fee: $50. *Unit head:* Vicki Eveland, Program Director, 206-281-2088, E-mail: evelav@spu.edu. *Application contact:* John Glancy, Director, Graduate Admissions and Marketing, 206-281-2325, Fax: 206-281-2877, E-mail: jglancy@spu.edu.
Website: http://spu.edu/academics/school-of-business-and-economics/graduate-programs/ma-management/massm.

Seattle Pacific University, Master's Degree in Business Administration (MBA) Program, Seattle, WA 98119-1997. Offers business administration (MBA); social and sustainable enterprise (MBA). *Accreditation:* AACSB. Part-time programs available. *Students:* 24 full-time (15 women), 63 part-time (25 women); includes 26 minority (3 Black or African American, non-Hispanic/Latino; 14 Asian, non-Hispanic/Latino; 5 Hispanic/Latino; 4 Two or more races, non-Hispanic/Latino), 7 international. Average age 31. 35 applicants, 23% accepted, 8 enrolled. In 2013, 37 master's awarded. *Entrance requirements:* For master's, GMAT (minimum score of 500 preferred; 25 verbal, 30 quantitative, 4.4 analytical writing); GRE (minimum score of 295 preferred; 150 verbal/450 old scoring, 145 quantitative/525 old scoring), BA, resume as evidence of substantive work experience. Additional exam requirements/recommendations for international students: Required—TOEFL. *Application deadline:* For fall admission, 8/1 for domestic and international students; for winter admission, 11/1 for domestic and international students; for spring admission, 2/1 for domestic and international students. Applications are processed on a rolling basis. Application fee: $50. Electronic applications accepted. *Financial support:* Scholarships/grants available. Financial award applicants required to submit FAFSA. *Unit head:* Gary Karns, Associate Dean for Graduate Studies, 206-281-2948, Fax: 206-281-2733. *Application contact:* 206-281-2091.
Website: http://www.spu.edu/academics/school-of-business-and-economics/graduate-programs/mba.

Southern New Hampshire University, School of Business, Manchester, NH 03106-1045. Offers accounting (MBA, MS, Graduate Certificate); accounting finance (MS); accounting/auditing (MS); accounting/forensic accounting (MS); accounting/taxation (MS); athletic administration (MBA, Graduate Certificate); business administration (IMBA, MBA, Certificate, Graduate Certificate), including accounting (Certificate), business administration (MBA), business information systems (Graduate Certificate), human resource management (Certificate); corporate social responsibility (MBA); entrepreneurship (MBA); finance (MBA, MS, Graduate Certificate); finance/corporate finance (MS); finance/investments and securities (MS); forensic accounting (MBA); healthcare informatics (MBA); healthcare management (MBA); human resource management (Graduate Certificate); information technology (MS, Graduate Certificate); information technology management (MBA); international business (Graduate Certificate); international business and information technology (Graduate Certificate); international finance (Graduate Certificate); international sport management (Graduate Certificate); justice studies (MBA); leadership of nonprofit organizations (Graduate Certificate); marketing (MBA, MS, Graduate Certificate); operations and project management (MS); operations and supply chain management (MBA, Graduate Certificate); organizational leadership (MS); project management (MBA, Graduate Certificate); Six Sigma (MBA); Six Sigma quality (Graduate Certificate); social media marketing (MBA); sport management (MBA, MS, Graduate Certificate); sustainability and environmental compliance (MBA); workplace conflict management (MBA); MBA/Certificate. *Accreditation:* ACBSP. Part-time and evening/weekend programs available. Postbaccalaureate distance learning degree programs offered (no on-campus study). Terminal master's awarded for partial completion of doctoral program. *Degree requirements:* For master's, one foreign language, comprehensive exam (for some programs), thesis or alternative. *Entrance requirements:* For master's, minimum GPA of 2.5. Additional exam requirements/recommendations for international students: Required—TOEFL (minimum score 500 paper-based). Electronic applications accepted.

South University, Graduate Programs, College of Business, Savannah, GA 31406. Offers corrections (MBA); entrepreneurship and small business (MBA); healthcare administration (MBA); hospitality management (MBA); leadership (MS); public administration (MPA); sustainability (MBA).

State University of New York College of Environmental Science and Forestry, Department of Paper and Bioprocess Engineering, Syracuse, NY 13210-2779. Offers biomaterials engineering (MS, PhD); bioprocess engineering (MPS, MS, PhD); bioprocessing (Advanced Certificate); paper science and engineering (MPS, MS, PhD); sustainable engineering management (MPS). *Faculty:* 9 full-time (1 woman), 3 part-time/adjunct (0 women). *Students:* 37 full-time (11 women), 1 part-time (0 women); includes 2 minority (1 Black or African American, non-Hispanic/Latino; 1 Hispanic/Latino), 21 international. Average age 25. 14 applicants, 57% accepted, 4 enrolled. In 2013, 2 master's, 3 doctorates, 4 other advanced degrees awarded. *Degree requirements:* For master's, thesis; for doctorate, comprehensive exam, thesis/dissertation; for Advanced Certificate, 15 credit hours. *Entrance requirements:* For master's and doctorate, GRE General Test, minimum GPA of 3.0; for Advanced Certificate, BS, calculus plus science major. Additional exam requirements/recommendations for international students: Required—TOEFL (minimum score 550 paper-based; 80 iBT), IELTS (minimum score 6). *Application deadline:* For fall admission, 2/1 priority date for domestic and international students; for spring admission, 11/1 priority date for domestic and international students. Applications are processed on a rolling basis. Application fee: $60. *Expenses:* Tuition, state resident: full-time $10,370; part-time $432 per credit hour. Tuition, nonresident: full-time $20,190; part-time $841 per credit hour. *Required fees:* $44 per credit hour. *Financial support:* In 2013–14, 17 students received support, including 11 research assistantships with full tuition reimbursements available (averaging $14,000 per year), 9 teaching assistantships with full tuition reimbursements available (averaging $12,000 per year); fellowships with full tuition reimbursements available, career-related internships or fieldwork, Federal Work-Study, institutionally sponsored loans, scholarships/grants, health care benefits, and unspecified assistantships also available. Support available to part-time students. Financial award application deadline: 6/30; financial award applicants required to submit FAFSA. *Faculty research:* Sustainable products and processes, biorefinery, pulping and papermaking, nanocellulose, bioconversions, process control and modeling. *Total annual research expenditures:* $604,516. *Unit head:* Dr. Gary M. Scott, Chair, 315-470-6501, Fax: 315-470-6945, E-mail: gscott@esf.edu. *Application contact:* Scott Shannon, Associate Provost and Dean, Instruction and Graduate Studies, 315-470-6599, Fax: 315-470-6978, E-mail: esfgrad@esf.edu.
Website: http://www.esf.edu/pbe/.

University of California, Berkeley, UC Berkeley Extension, Certificate Programs in Sustainability Studies, Berkeley, CA 94720-1500. Offers leadership in sustainability and environmental management (Professional Certificate); solar energy and green building (Professional Certificate); sustainable design (Professional Certificate).

University of Colorado Denver, Business School, Master of Business Administration Program, Denver, CO 80217. Offers bioinnovation and entrepreneurship (MBA); business intelligence (MBA); business strategy (MBA); business to business marketing (MBA); business to consumer marketing (MBA); change management (MBA); corporate financial management (MBA); enterprise technology management (MBA); entrepreneurship (MBA); health administration (MBA), including financial management, health administration, health information technologies, international health management and policy; human resources management (MBA); international business (MBA); investment management (MBA); managing for sustainability (MBA); sports and entertainment management (MBA). *Accreditation:* AACSB. Part-time and evening/weekend programs available. Postbaccalaureate distance learning degree programs offered (no on-campus study). *Students:* 611 full-time (246 women), 144 part-time (58 women); includes 102 minority (14 Black or African American, non-Hispanic/Latino; 2 American Indian or Alaska Native, non-Hispanic/Latino; 38 Asian, non-Hispanic/Latino; 42 Hispanic/Latino; 6 Two or more races, non-Hispanic/Latino), 26 international. Average age 32. 330 applicants, 64% accepted, 125 enrolled. In 2013, 398 master's awarded. *Degree requirements:* For master's, 48 semester hours, including 30 of core courses, 3 in international business, and 15 in electives from over 50 other graduate business courses. *Entrance requirements:* For master's, GMAT, resume, official transcripts, essay, two letters of recommendation, financial statements (for international applicants). Additional exam requirements/recommendations for international students: Required—TOEFL (minimum score 560 paper-based; 83 iBT); Recommended—IELTS (minimum score 6.5). *Application deadline:* For fall admission, 4/15 priority date for domestic students, 3/15 priority date for international students; for spring admission, 10/15 priority date for domestic students, 9/15 priority date for international students. Applications are processed on a rolling basis. Application fee: $50 ($75 for international students). Electronic applications accepted. *Expenses:* Contact institution. *Financial support:* In 2013–14, 62 students received support. Fellowships, research assistantships, teaching assistantships, Federal Work-Study, institutionally sponsored loans, scholarships/grants, traineeships, and unspecified assistantships available. Financial award application deadline: 4/1; financial award applicants required to submit FAFSA. *Faculty research:* Marketing, management, entrepreneurship, finance, health administration. *Unit head:* Elizabeth Cooperman, Professor of Finance and Managing for Sustainability/MBA Program Director, 303-315-8422, E-mail: elizabeth.cooperman@ucdenver.edu. *Application contact:* Shelly Townley, Admissions Director, Graduate Programs, 303-315-8202, E-mail: shelly.townley@ucdenver.edu.
Website: http://www.ucdenver.edu/academics/colleges/business/degrees/mba/Pages/MBA.aspx.

University of Colorado Denver, Business School, Program in Management and Organization, Denver, CO 80217. Offers business strategy (MS); change and innovation (MS); enterprise technology management (MS); entrepreneurship and innovation (MS); global management (MS); human resources management (MS); leadership and management (MS); quantitative decision methods (MS); sports and entertainment management (MS); sustainability management (MS). *Accreditation:* AACSB. Part-time and evening/weekend programs available. Postbaccalaureate distance learning degree programs offered (no on-campus study). *Students:* 27 full-time (19 women), 14 part-time (7 women); includes 4 minority (1 Black or African American, non-Hispanic/Latino; 2 Hispanic/Latino; 1 Two or more races, non-Hispanic/Latino), 6 international. Average age 29. 38 applicants, 45% accepted, 8 enrolled. In 2013, 28 master's awarded. *Degree requirements:* For master's, 30 semester hours (12 of required courses, 12 of management electives, and 6 of free electives). *Entrance requirements:* For master's, GMAT, resume, two letters of recommendation, essay, financial statements (for international applicants). Additional exam requirements/recommendations for international students: Required—TOEFL (minimum score 537 paper-based; 75 iBT); Recommended—IELTS (minimum score 6.5). *Application deadline:* For fall admission, 4/15 for domestic students, 3/15 for international students; for spring admission, 10/15 for domestic students, 9/15 for international students. Applications are processed on a rolling basis. Application fee: $50 ($75 for international students). Electronic applications accepted. *Expenses:* Contact institution. *Financial support:* In 2013–14, 5 students received support. Fellowships, research assistantships, teaching assistantships, Federal Work-Study, institutionally sponsored loans, scholarships/grants, and traineeships available. Financial award application deadline: 4/1; financial award applicants required to submit FAFSA. *Faculty research:* Human resource management, management of catastrophe, turnaround strategies. *Unit head:* Dr. Kenneth Bettenhausen, Associate Professor/Director of MS in Management, 303-315-8425, E-mail: kenneth.bettenhausen@ucdenver.edu. *Application contact:* Shelly Townley, Admissions Director, Graduate Programs, 303-315-8202, E-mail: shelly.townley@ucdenver.edu.
Website: http://www.ucdenver.edu/academics/colleges/business/degrees/ms/management/Pages/Management.aspx.

University of Maine, Graduate School, The Maine Business School, Orono, ME 04469. Offers accounting (MBA); business administration (CGS); business and sustainability (MBA); finance (MBA); international business (MBA); management (MBA). *Accreditation:* AACSB. Part-time and evening/weekend programs available. Postbaccalaureate distance learning degree programs offered. *Faculty:* 23 full-time (7 women). *Students:* 31 full-time (12 women), 12 part-time (9 women); includes 5 minority (1 Black or African American, non-Hispanic/Latino; 3 Asian, non-Hispanic/Latino; 1 Hispanic/Latino), 4 international. Average age 29. 41 applicants, 71% accepted, 24 enrolled. In 2013, 28 master's awarded. *Entrance requirements:* For master's, GMAT. Additional exam requirements/recommendations for international students: Required—TOEFL (minimum score 550 paper-based). *Application deadline:* For fall admission, 6/1 priority date for domestic and international students; for spring admission, 11/15 priority date for domestic and international students. Applications are processed on a rolling basis. Application fee: $65. Electronic applications accepted. *Expenses:* Contact institution. *Financial support:* In 2013–14, 14 students received support, including 3 teaching assistantships with full tuition reimbursements available (averaging $14,100 per year); career-related internships or fieldwork, Federal Work-Study, institutionally sponsored loans, scholarships/grants, tuition waivers (full and partial), and unspecified assistantships also available. Financial award application deadline: 3/1. *Faculty research:* Entrepreneurship, investment management, international markets, decision support systems, strategic planning. *Total annual research expenditures:* $5,089. *Unit head:* Carol Mandzik, Manager of MBA Programs, Executive Education and Internships, 207-581-1971, Fax: 207-581-1930, E-mail: carol.mandzik@maine.edu. *Application contact:* Scott G. Delcourt, Associate Dean of the Graduate School, 207-581-3291, Fax: 207-581-3232, E-mail: graduate@maine.edu.
Website: http://www.umaine.edu/business/.

University of New Hampshire, Graduate School, College of Liberal Arts, Department of Political Science, Program in Political Science, Durham, NH 03824. Offers political science (MA); sustainability (Postbaccalaureate Certificate). Part-time programs available. *Students:* 11 full-time (4 women), 9 part-time (3 women); includes 1 minority (Black or African American, non-Hispanic/Latino). Average age 31. 19 applicants, 89% accepted, 11 enrolled. In 2013, 2 master's awarded. *Degree requirements:* For master's, thesis. *Entrance requirements:* For master's, GRE General Test. Additional exam requirements/recommendations for international students: Required—TOEFL (minimum score 550 paper-based; 80 iBT). *Application deadline:* For fall admission, 6/1 priority date for domestic students, 4/1 for international students; for spring admission, 12/1 for domestic students. Applications are processed on a rolling basis. Application fee: $65. Electronic applications accepted. *Expenses:* Tuition, state resident: full-time $13,500; part-time $750 per credit hour. Tuition, nonresident: full-time $26,200; part-time $1100 per credit hour. *Required fees:* $1741; $435.25 per term. Tuition and fees vary according to course level, course load, campus/location and program. *Financial support:* In 2013–14, 5 students received support, including 5 teaching assistantships; fellowships, research assistantships, career-related internships or fieldwork, Federal Work-Study, scholarships/grants, and tuition waivers (full and partial) also available. Support available to part-time students. Financial award application deadline: 2/15. *Unit head:* Stacy VanDeever, Chairperson, 603-862-0167. *Application contact:* Tama Andrews, Administrative Assistant, 603-862-2321, E-mail: mpa.ma.political.science.grad@unh.edu.
Website: http://www.unh.edu/political-science/.

University of Portland, Dr. Robert B. Pamplin, Jr. School of Business, Portland, OR 97203-5798. Offers entrepreneurship (MBA); finance (MBA, MS); health care management (MBA); marketing (MBA); nonprofit management (EMBA); operations and technology management (MBA, MS); sustainability (MBA). *Accreditation:* AACSB. Part-time and evening/weekend programs available. *Faculty:* 26 full-time (5 women), 8 part-time/adjunct (1 woman). *Students:* 37 full-time (11 women), 93 part-time (44 women); includes 15 minority (1 Black or African American, non-Hispanic/Latino; 7 Asian, non-Hispanic/Latino; 5 Hispanic/Latino; 2 Two or more races, non-Hispanic/Latino), 21 international. Average age 32. In 2013, 68 master's awarded. *Entrance requirements:* For master's, GMAT, minimum GPA of 3.0, resume, 2 letters of recommendation. Additional exam requirements/recommendations for international students: Required—TOEFL (minimum score 570 paper-based; 89 iBT), IELTS (minimum score 7). *Application deadline:* For fall admission, 7/15 priority date for domestic and international students; for spring admission, 12/15 priority date for domestic and international students. Applications are processed on a rolling basis. Application fee: $50. *Expenses:* Contact institution. *Financial support:* Federal Work-Study, scholarships/grants, and tuition waivers (partial) available. Support available to part-time students. Financial award application deadline: 3/1; financial award applicants required to submit FAFSA. *Unit head:* Melissa McCarthy, Director, 503-943-7224, E-mail: mba-up@up.edu. Website: http://business.up.edu/mba/default.aspx?cid-1179&pid-6450.

University of Saint Francis, Graduate School, Keith Busse School of Business and Entrepreneurial Leadership, Fort Wayne, IN 46808-3994. Offers business administration (MBA); environmental health (MEH); healthcare administration (MHA); sustainability (MBA). *Accreditation:* ACBSP. Part-time and evening/weekend programs available. Postbaccalaureate distance learning degree programs offered (no on-campus study). *Faculty:* 8. *Students:* 74 full-time (38 women), 69 part-time (35 women); includes 22 minority (12 Black or African American, non-Hispanic/Latino; 2 Asian, non-Hispanic/Latino; 7 Hispanic/Latino; 1 Two or more races, non-Hispanic/Latino), 3 international. Average age 34. 73 applicants, 97% accepted, 71 enrolled. In 2013, 12 master's awarded. *Entrance requirements:* For master's, minimum undergraduate GPA of 2.75. *Application deadline:* For fall admission, 7/1 priority date for domestic students; for spring admission, 11/1 priority date for domestic students. Applications are processed on a rolling basis. Application fee: $20. Application fee is waived when completed online. *Financial support:* Federal Work-Study, scholarships/grants, and unspecified assistantships available. Support available to part-time students. Financial award application deadline: 3/10; financial award applicants required to submit FAFSA. *Unit head:* Dr. Karen Palumbo, Professor/Graduate Program Director, 260-399-7700 Ext. 8312, Fax: 260-399-8174, E-mail: kpalumbo@sf.edu. *Application contact:* James Cashdollar, Admissions Counselor, 260-399-7700 Ext. 6302, Fax: 260-399-8152, E-mail: jcashdollar@sf.edu.
Website: http://www.sf.edu/sf/graduate/business.

University of Saskatchewan, College of Graduate Studies and Research, School of Environment and Sustainability, Saskatoon, SK S7N 5A2, Canada. Offers MES. *Expenses: Tuition, area resident:* Full-time $3585 Canadian dollars; part-time $585 Canadian dollars per course. Tuition, nonresident: part-time $877 Canadian dollars per course. *International tuition:* $5377 Canadian dollars full-time. *Required fees:* $889.51 Canadian dollars.

University of Southern Maine, College of Management and Human Service, School of Business, Portland, ME 04104-9300. Offers accounting (MBA); business administration (MBA); finance (MBA); health management and policy (MBA); sustainability (MBA); JD/MBA; MBA/MSA; MBA/MSN; MS/MBA. *Accreditation:* AACSB. Part-time and evening/weekend programs available. *Faculty:* 10 part-time/adjunct (2 women). *Students:* 89 part-time (37 women); includes 4 minority (3 American Indian or Alaska Native, non-Hispanic/Latino; 1 Asian, non-Hispanic/Latino), 2 international. Average age 31. 36 applicants, 56% accepted, 16 enrolled. In 2013, 34 master's awarded. *Entrance requirements:* For master's, GMAT or GRE, minimum AACSB index of 1100. Additional exam requirements/recommendations for international students: Required—TOEFL (minimum score 550 paper-based; 79 iBT). *Application deadline:* For fall admission, 8/1 priority date for domestic students, 5/1 priority date for international students; for spring admission, 12/1 priority date for domestic students, 9/1 priority date for international students. Applications are processed on a rolling basis. Application fee: $65. Electronic applications accepted. *Expenses:* Tuition, state resident: part-time $380 per credit.

Tuition, nonresident: part-time $1026 per credit. Part-time tuition and fees vary according to program. *Financial support:* In 2013–14, 3 research assistantships with partial tuition reimbursements (averaging $9,000 per year), 3 teaching assistantships with partial tuition reimbursements (averaging $9,000 per year) were awarded; career-related internships or fieldwork, Federal Work-Study, scholarships/grants, tuition waivers (full and partial), and unspecified assistantships also available. Support available to part-time students. Financial award application deadline: 2/15; financial award applicants required to submit FAFSA. *Faculty research:* Economic development, management information systems, real options, system dynamics, simulation. *Unit head:* Joseph W. McDonnell, Dean, 207-228-8002, Fax: 207-780-4060, E-mail: jmcdonnell@usm.maine.edu. *Application contact:* Alice B. Cash, Assistant Director for Student Affairs, 207-780-4184, Fax: 207-780-4662, E-mail: acash@usm.maine.edu.
Website: http://www.usm.maine.edu/sb.

University of South Florida, College of Global Sustainability, Tampa, FL 33620-9951. Offers entrepreneurship (MA); sustainable energy (MA); sustainable tourism (MA); water (MA); MA/MS. *Faculty:* 7 full-time (2 women), 1 (woman) part-time/adjunct. *Students:* 39 full-time (27 women), 26 part-time (15 women); includes 15 minority (3 Black or African American, non-Hispanic/Latino; 1 American Indian or Alaska Native, non-Hispanic/Latino; 8 Hispanic/Latino; 3 Two or more races, non-Hispanic/Latino), 13 international. Average age 39. 58 applicants, 59% accepted, 8 enrolled. In 2013, 10 master's awarded. *Degree requirements:* For master's, comprehensive exam (for some programs), thesis or alternative, internship. *Entrance requirements:* For master's, minimum GPA of 3.0 in undergraduate coursework; at least two letters of recommendation (one must be academic); 200-250-word essay on student's background, professional goals, and reasons for seeking degree. Additional exam requirements/recommendations for international students: Required—TOEFL (minimum score 550 paper-based; 79 iBT). *Faculty research:* Global sustainability, integrated resource management, systems thinking, green communities, entrepreneurship, ecotourism. *Total annual research expenditures:* $564,596. *Unit head:* Dr. Kalanithy Vairavamoorthy, Dean, 813-974-9694, E-mail: vairavk@grad.usf.edu. *Application contact:* Dr. Carl Herndl, Associate Dean, 813-974-5397, E-mail: cgh@usf.edu.
Website: http://psgs.usf.edu/.

University of Wisconsin–Green Bay, Graduate Studies, Program in Sustainable Management, Green Bay, WI 54311-7001. Offers MS. Program held jointly with four other University of Wisconsin System campuses: Oshkosh, Parkside, Stout, and Superior. Part-time programs available. Postbaccalaureate distance learning degree programs offered (no on-campus study). *Faculty:* 2 full-time (1 woman), 1 part-time/adjunct (0 women). *Students:* 3 full-time (2 women), 11 part-time (5 women). Average age 41. 23 applicants, 52% accepted, 10 enrolled. *Degree requirements:* For master's, capstone project. *Entrance requirements:* For master's, bachelor's degree from nationally-accredited university with minimum cumulative GPA of 3.0. Additional exam requirements/recommendations for international students: Required—TOEFL. *Application deadline:* Applications are processed on a rolling basis. Application fee: $56. *Expenses:* Tuition, state resident: full-time $7640; part-time $424 per credit. Tuition, nonresident: full-time $16,772; part-time $932 per credit. *Required fees:* $1378. Full-time tuition and fees vary according to course load and reciprocity agreements. *Unit head:* Dr. John Katers, Director, 920-465-2278, E-mail: katersj@uwgb.edu. *Application contact:* Mary Valitchka, Graduate Studies Coordinator, 920-465-2123, Fax: 920-465-5043, E-mail: valitchm@uwgb.edu.
Website: http://sustain.wisconsin.edu/degrees-and-certificates/masters/.

University of Wisconsin–Superior, Graduate Division, Department of Business and Economics, Superior, WI 54880-4500. Offers sustainable management (MS). *Students:* 9 full-time (4 women), 1 (woman) part-time. Average age 32. 9 applicants, 89% accepted, 6 enrolled. *Application deadline:* For fall admission, 4/1 priority date for domestic students; for spring admission, 10/15 priority date for domestic students. Applications are processed on a rolling basis. Application fee: $56. Electronic applications accepted. *Expenses:* Tuition, state resident: full-time $4526; part-time $649.24 per credit. Tuition, nonresident: full-time $9091; part-time $1156.51 per credit. *Unit head:* Dr. Jerry Hembd, Professor, 715-394-8208, Fax: 715-394-8371, E-mail: jhembd@uwsuper.edu. *Application contact:* Suzie Finckler, Student Status Examiner, 715-394-8295, Fax: 715-394-8371, E-mail: gradstudy@uwsuper.edu.
Website: http://www.uwsuper.edu/dl/facts/sustainable-management—online-masters_fact_1_1479488.

Valparaiso University, Graduate School, College of Business, Valparaiso, IN 46383. Offers business administration (MBA); business intelligence (Certificate); engineering management (Certificate); entrepreneurship (Certificate); finance (Certificate); general business (Certificate); management (Certificate); marketing (Certificate); sustainability (Certificate); JD/MBA; MSN/MBA. *Accreditation:* AACSB. Part-time and evening/weekend programs available. Postbaccalaureate distance learning degree programs offered (minimal on-campus study). *Faculty:* 11 part-time/adjunct (2 women). *Students:* 13 full-time (3 women), 48 part-time (21 women); includes 6 minority (3 Black or African American, non-Hispanic/Latino; 2 Hispanic/Latino; 1 Two or more races, non-Hispanic/Latino), 5 international. Average age 33. In 2013, 19 master's, 3 other advanced degrees awarded. *Entrance requirements:* For master's, GMAT, GRE, minimum GPA of 3.0. Additional exam requirements/recommendations for international students: Required—TOEFL (minimum score 550 paper-based; 80 iBT), IELTS (minimum score 6). *Application deadline:* Applications are processed on a rolling basis. Application fee: $30 ($50 for international students). Electronic applications accepted. *Expenses:* Contact institution. *Financial support:* Available to part-time students. Applicants required to submit FAFSA. *Unit head:* Bruce MacLean, Director of Graduate Programs in Management, 219-465-7952, Fax: 219-464-5789, E-mail: bruce.maclean@valpo.edu. *Application contact:* Cindy Scanlan, Assistant Director of Graduate Programs in Management, 219-465-7952, Fax: 219-464-5789, E-mail: cindy.scanlan@valpo.edu.
Website: http://www.valpo.edu/mba/.

Section 14
Marketing

This section contains a directory of institutions offering graduate work in marketing, followed by an in-depth entry submitted by an institution that chose to prepare a detailed program description. Additional information about programs listed in the directory but not augmented by an in-depth entry may be obtained by writing directly to the dean of a graduate school or chair of a department at the address given in the directory.

For programs offering related work, see also in this book *Advertising and Public Relations, Business Administration and Management,* and *Hospitality Management.* In another guide in this series:

Graduate Programs in the Humanities, Arts & Social Sciences

See *Communication and Media* and *Public, Regional, and Industrial Affairs*

CONTENTS

Program Directories
Marketing   500
Marketing Research   533

Displays and Close-Ups
Fashion Institute of Technology   507, 535

See also:
Adelphi University—Business Administration and
    Management   70, 181
University of California, Los Angeles—Business
    Administration and Management   145, 191

Marketing

Adelphi University, Robert B. Willumstad School of Business, MBA Program, Garden City, NY 11530-0701. Offers finance (MBA); management information systems (MBA); management/human resource management (MBA); marketing/e-commerce (MBA). *Accreditation:* AACSB. Part-time and evening/weekend programs available. *Students:* 254 full-time (129 women), 118 part-time (63 women); includes 60 minority (13 Black or African American, non-Hispanic/Latino; 18 Asian, non-Hispanic/Latino; 28 Hispanic/Latino; 1 Native Hawaiian or other Pacific Islander, non-Hispanic/Latino), 200 international. Average age 28. In 2013, 182 master's awarded. *Degree requirements:* For master's, capstone course. *Entrance requirements:* For master's, GMAT, 2 letters of recommendation. Additional exam requirements/recommendations for international students: Required—TOEFL (minimum score 550 paper-based; 80 iBT). *Application deadline:* For fall admission, 4/1 for international students; for spring admission, 11/1 for international students. Applications are processed on a rolling basis. Application fee: $50. Electronic applications accepted. *Expenses: Tuition:* Full-time $32,530; part-time $1010 per credit. *Required fees:* $1150. Tuition and fees vary according to degree level and program. *Financial support:* Research assistantships with partial tuition reimbursements, career-related internships or fieldwork, Federal Work-Study, institutionally sponsored loans, scholarships/grants, tuition waivers (partial), and unspecified assistantships available. Financial award application deadline: 3/1; financial award applicants required to submit FAFSA. *Faculty research:* Supply chain management, distribution channels, productivity benchmark analysis, data envelopment analysis, financial portfolio analysis. *Unit head:* Dr. Rakesh Gupta, Associate Dean, 516-877-4629. *Application contact:* Christine Murphy, Director of Admissions, 516-877-3050, Fax: 516-877-3039, E-mail: graduateadmissions@adelphi.edu.
Website: http://business.adelphi.edu/degree-programs/graduate-degree-programs/m-b-a/.
See Display on page 70 and Close-Up on page 181.

Alabama Agricultural and Mechanical University, School of Graduate Studies, School of Business, Department of Management and Marketing, Huntsville, AL 35811. Offers MBA. Part-time and evening/weekend programs available. *Degree requirements:* For master's, comprehensive exam, thesis optional. *Entrance requirements:* For master's, GMAT, minimum undergraduate GPA of 2.5. Additional exam requirements/recommendations for international students: Required—TOEFL (minimum score 500 paper-based; 61 iBT). Electronic applications accepted. *Faculty research:* Consumer behavior of blacks, small business marketing, economics of education, China in transition, international economics.

American College of Thessaloniki, Department of Business Administration, Pylea-Thessaloniki, Greece. Offers banking and finance (MBA); entrepreneurship (MBA, Certificate); finance (Certificate); management (MBA, Certificate); marketing (MBA, Certificate). Part-time and evening/weekend programs available. *Degree requirements:* For master's, thesis. *Entrance requirements:* For master's, bachelor's degree. Additional exam requirements/recommendations for international students: Recommended—TOEFL. Electronic applications accepted.

American InterContinental University Online, Program in Business Administration, Schaumburg, IL 60173. Offers accounting and finance (MBA); finance (MBA); healthcare management (MBA); human resource management (MBA); international business (MBA); management (MBA); marketing (MBA); operations management (MBA); organizational psychology and development (MBA); project management (MBA). *Accreditation:* ACBSP. Evening/weekend programs available. Postbaccalaureate distance learning degree programs offered (no on-campus study). *Entrance requirements:* Additional exam requirements/recommendations for international students: Required—TOEFL (minimum score 550 paper-based). Electronic applications accepted.

American InterContinental University South Florida, Program in International Business, Weston, FL 33326. Offers accounting and finance (MBA); human resource management (MBA); management (MBA); marketing (MBA). Part-time and evening/weekend programs available. Postbaccalaureate distance learning degree programs offered. Electronic applications accepted.

American Public University System, AMU/APU Graduate Programs, Charles Town, WV 25414. Offers accounting (MBA, MS); criminal justice (MA), including business administration, emergency and disaster management, general (MA, MS); educational leadership (M Ed); emergency and disaster management (MA); entrepreneurship (MBA); environmental policy and management (MS), including environmental planning, environmental sustainability, fish and wildlife management, general (MA, MS), global environmental management; finance (MBA); general (MBA); global business management (MBA); history (MA), including American history, ancient and classical history, European history, global history, public history; homeland security (MA), including business administration, counter-terrorism studies, criminal justice, cyber, emergency management and public health, intelligence studies, transportation security; homeland security resource allocation (MBA); humanities (MA); information technology (MS), including digital forensics, enterprise software development, information assurance and security, IT project management; information technology management (MBA); intelligence studies (MA), including criminal intelligence, cyber, general (MA, MS), homeland security, intelligence analysis, intelligence collection, intelligence management, intelligence operations, terrorism studies; international relations and conflict resolution (MA), including comparative and security issues, conflict resolution, international and transnational security issues, peacekeeping; legal studies (MA); management (MA), including defense management, general (MA, MS), human resource management, organizational leadership, public administration; marketing (MBA); military history (MA), including American military history, American Revolution, civil war, war since 1945, World War II; military studies (MA), including joint warfare, strategic leadership; national security studies (MA), including general (MA, MS), homeland security, regional security studies, security and intelligence analysis, terrorism studies; nonprofit management (MBA); political science (MA), including American politics and government, comparative government and development, general (MA, MS), international relations, public policy; psychology (MA), including general (MA, MS); maritime engineering management, reverse logistics management; public administration (MPA), including disaster management, environmental policy, health policy, human resources, national security, organizational management, security management; public health (MPH); reverse logistics management (MA); school counseling (M Ed); security management (MA); space studies (MS), including aerospace science, general (MA, MS), planetary science; sports and health sciences (MS); teaching (M Ed), including curriculum and instruction for elementary teachers, elementary reading, English language learners, instructional leadership, online learning, special education; transportation and logistics management (MA), including general (MA, MS), maritime engineering management, reverse logistics management. Programs offered via distance

learning only. Part-time and evening/weekend programs available. Postbaccalaureate distance learning degree programs offered (no on-campus study). *Faculty:* 432 full-time (242 women), 1,722 part-time/adjunct (829 women). *Students:* 511 full-time (241 women), 10,947 part-time (4,294 women); includes 3,760 minority (2,058 Black or African American, non-Hispanic/Latino; 88 American Indian or Alaska Native, non-Hispanic/Latino; 293 Asian, non-Hispanic/Latino; 876 Hispanic/Latino; 91 Native Hawaiian or other Pacific Islander, non-Hispanic/Latino; 354 Two or more races, non-Hispanic/Latino), 134 international. Average age 36. In 2013, 3,323 master's awarded. *Degree requirements:* For master's, comprehensive exam or practicum. *Entrance requirements:* For master's, official transcript showing earned bachelor's degree from institution accredited by recognized accrediting body. Additional exam requirements/recommendations for international students: Required—TOEFL (minimum score 550 paper-based), IELTS (minimum score 6.5). *Application deadline:* Applications are processed on a rolling basis. Application fee: $0. Electronic applications accepted. *Expenses: Tuition:* Part-time $325 per semester hour. *Financial support:* Applicants required to submit FAFSA. *Faculty research:* Military history, criminal justice, management performance, national security. *Unit head:* Dr. Karan Powell, Executive Vice President and Provost, 877-468-6268, Fax: 304-724-3780. *Application contact:* Terry Grant, Vice President of Enrollment Management, 877-468-6268, Fax: 304-724-3780, E-mail: info@apus.edu.
Website: http://www.apus.edu.

American University, Kogod School of Business, Washington, DC 20016-8044. Offers accounting (MS); business administration (MBA); business fundamentals (Certificate); entrepreneurship (Certificate); finance (MS); forensic accounting (Certificate); management (MS); marketing (MS); real estate (MS, Certificate); sustainability management (MS); tax (Certificate); taxation (MS). *Accreditation:* AACSB. Part-time and evening/weekend programs available. Postbaccalaureate distance learning degree programs offered. *Faculty:* 75 full-time (24 women), 36 part-time/adjunct (7 women). *Students:* 194 full-time (95 women), 370 part-time (184 women); includes 168 minority (69 Black or African American, non-Hispanic/Latino; 60 Asian, non-Hispanic/Latino; 33 Hispanic/Latino; 2 Native Hawaiian or other Pacific Islander, non-Hispanic/Latino; 4 Two or more races, non-Hispanic/Latino), 108 international. Average age 30. 940 applicants, 46% accepted, 193 enrolled. In 2013, 221 master's, 4 other advanced degrees awarded. *Entrance requirements:* For master's, GMAT, resume, personal statement, interview, 2 letters of recommendation, transcripts. Additional exam requirements/recommendations for international students: Required—TOEFL (minimum score 100 iBT). *Application deadline:* Applications are processed on a rolling basis. Application fee: $100. Electronic applications accepted. *Expenses:* Contact institution. *Financial support:* Fellowships, career-related internships or fieldwork, Federal Work-Study, institutionally sponsored loans, and tuition waivers (partial) available. Support available to part-time students. Financial award application deadline: 2/1. *Unit head:* Dr. Michael Ginzberg, Dean, 202-885-1985, E-mail: ginzberg@american.edu. *Application contact:* Jason Kennedy, Associate Director of Graduate Admissions, 202-885-1968, E-mail: jkennedy@american.edu.
Website: http://www.kogod.american.edu/.

The American University in Dubai, Graduate Programs, Dubai, United Arab Emirates. Offers construction management (MS); education (M Ed); finance (MBA); generalist (MBA); marketing (MBA). Part-time and evening/weekend programs available. *Degree requirements:* For master's, thesis optional. *Entrance requirements:* For master's, GMAT (for MBA); GRE (for M Ed and MS), minimum undergraduate GPA of 3.0, official transcripts, two reference forms, curriculum vitae/resume, statement of career objectives, work experience. Additional exam requirements/recommendations for international students: Required—TOEFL (minimum score 550 paper-based; 79 iBT). Electronic applications accepted.

Aquinas College, School of Management, Grand Rapids, MI 49506-1799. Offers health care administration (MM); marketing management (MM); organizational leadership (MM); sustainable business (MM, MSB). Part-time and evening/weekend programs available. *Students:* 13 full-time (10 women), 56 part-time (38 women); includes 10 minority (4 Black or African American, non-Hispanic/Latino; 1 American Indian or Alaska Native, non-Hispanic/Latino; 4 Hispanic/Latino; 1 Two or more races, non-Hispanic/Latino), 1 international. Average age 33. In 2013, 18 master's awarded. *Entrance requirements:* For master's, GMAT, minimum undergraduate GPA of 2.75, 2 years of work experience. Additional exam requirements/recommendations for international students: Required—TOEFL (minimum score 550 paper-based). *Application deadline:* Applications are processed on a rolling basis. Application fee: $0. *Expenses:* Contact institution. *Financial support:* Scholarships/grants available. Support available to part-time students. Financial award application deadline: 3/15; financial award applicants required to submit FAFSA. *Unit head:* Brian DiVita, Director, 616-632-2922, Fax: 616-732-4489. *Application contact:* Lynn Atkins-Rykert, Administrative Assistant, 616-632-2924, Fax: 616-732-4489, E-mail: atkinlyn@aquinas.edu.

Argosy University, Atlanta, College of Business, Atlanta, GA 30328. Offers accounting (DBA); corporate compliance (MBA); customized professional concentration (MBA, DBA); finance (MBA); healthcare administration (MBA); information systems (DBA); information systems management (MBA); international business (MBA, DBA); management (MBA, MSM, DBA); marketing (MBA, DBA).

Argosy University, Chicago, College of Business, Chicago, IL 60601. Offers accounting (DBA); customized professional concentration (MBA, DBA); finance (MBA); fraud examination (MBA); global business sustainability (DBA); healthcare administration (MBA); information systems (DBA); information systems management (MBA); international business (MBA, DBA); management (MBA, MSM, DBA); marketing (MBA, DBA); organizational leadership (Ed D); public administration (MBA); sustainable management (MBA). Postbaccalaureate distance learning degree programs offered (minimal on-campus study).

Argosy University, Dallas, College of Business, Farmers Branch, TX 75244. Offers accounting (DBA, AGC); corporate compliance (MBA, Graduate Certificate); customized professional concentration (MBA); finance (MBA, Graduate Certificate); fraud examination (MBA, Graduate Certificate); global business sustainability (DBA, AGC); healthcare administration (Graduate Certificate); healthcare management (MBA); information systems (MBA, DBA, AGC); information systems management (Graduate Certificate); international business (MBA, DBA, AGC, Graduate Certificate); management (MBA, DBA, AGC, Graduate Certificate); marketing (MBA, DBA, AGC, Graduate Certificate); public administration (MBA, Graduate Certificate); sustainable management (MBA, Graduate Certificate).

Argosy University, Denver, College of Business, Denver, CO 80231. Offers accounting (DBA); corporate compliance (MBA); customized professional concentration (MBA, DBA); finance (MBA); fraud examination (MBA); global business sustainability

(DBA); healthcare administration (MBA); information systems (DBA); information systems management (MBA); international business (MBA, DBA); management (MBA, MSM, DBA); marketing (MBA, DBA); organizational leadership (Ed D); public administration (MBA); sustainable management (MBA).

Argosy University, Hawai`i, College of Business, Honolulu, HI 96813. Offers accounting (DBA); corporate compliance (MBA); customized professional concentration (MBA, DBA); finance (MBA, Certificate); fraud examination (MBA); global business sustainability (DBA); healthcare administration (MBA, Certificate); information systems (DBA); information systems management (MBA, Certificate); international business (MBA, DBA, Certificate); management (MBA, MSM, DBA); marketing (MBA, DBA, Certificate); organizational leadership (Ed D); public administration (MBA); sustainable management (MBA).

Argosy University, Inland Empire, College of Business, Ontario, CA 91761. Offers accounting (DBA); corporate compliance (MBA); customized professional concentration (MBA, DBA); finance (MBA); fraud examination (MBA); global business sustainability (DBA); healthcare administration (MBA); information systems (DBA); information systems management (MBA); international business (MBA, DBA); management (MBA, MSM, DBA); marketing (MBA, DBA); organizational leadership (Ed D); public administration (MBA); sustainable management (MBA).

Argosy University, Los Angeles, College of Business, Santa Monica, CA 90045. Offers accounting (DBA); corporate compliance (MBA); customized professional concentration (MBA, DBA); finance (MBA); fraud examination (MBA); global business sustainability (DBA); healthcare administration (MBA); information systems (DBA); information systems management (MBA); international business (MBA, DBA); management (MBA, MSM, DBA); marketing (MBA, DBA); organizational leadership (Ed D); public administration (MBA); sustainable management (MBA).

Argosy University, Nashville, College of Business, Nashville, TN 37214. Offers accounting (DBA); customized professional concentration (MBA, DBA); finance (MBA); healthcare administration (MBA); information systems (MBA, DBA); international business (MBA, DBA); management (MBA, MSM, DBA); marketing (MBA, DBA).

Argosy University, Orange County, College of Business, Orange, CA 92868. Offers accounting (DBA, Adv C); corporate compliance (MBA); customized professional concentration (MBA, DBA); finance (MBA, Certificate); fraud examination (MBA); global business sustainability (DBA); healthcare administration (MBA, Certificate); information systems (DBA, Adv C, Certificate); information systems management (MBA); international business (MBA, DBA, Adv C, Certificate); management (MBA, MSM, DBA, Adv C); marketing (MBA, DBA, Adv C, Certificate); organizational leadership (Ed D); public administration (MBA, Certificate); sustainable management (MBA).

Argosy University, Phoenix, College of Business, Phoenix, AZ 85021. Offers accounting (DBA); corporate compliance (MBA); customized professional concentration (MBA, DBA); finance (MBA); fraud examination (MBA); global business sustainability (DBA); healthcare administration (MBA); information systems (DBA); information systems management (MBA); international business (MBA, DBA); management (MBA, DBA); marketing (MBA, DBA); public administration (MBA); sustainable management (MBA).

Argosy University, Salt Lake City, College of Business, Draper, UT 84020. Offers accounting (DBA); corporate compliance (MBA); customized professional concentration (MBA, DBA); finance (MBA); fraud examination (MBA); global business sustainability (DBA); healthcare administration (MBA); information systems (DBA); information systems management (MBA); international business (MBA, DBA); management (MBA, DBA); marketing (MBA, DBA); public administration (MBA); sustainable management (MBA).

Argosy University, San Diego, College of Business, San Diego, CA 92108. Offers accounting (DBA); corporate compliance (MBA); customized professional concentration (MBA, DBA); finance (MBA); fraud examination (MBA); global business sustainability (DBA); information systems (DBA); information systems management (MBA); international business (MBA, DBA); management (MBA, MSM, DBA); marketing (MBA, DBA); organizational leadership (Ed D); public administration (MBA).

Argosy University, San Francisco Bay Area, College of Business, Alameda, CA 94501. Offers accounting (DBA); corporate compliance (MBA); customized professional concentration (MBA, DBA); finance (MBA); fraud examination (MBA); global business sustainability (DBA); healthcare administration (MBA); information systems (DBA); information systems management (MBA); international business (MBA, DBA); management (MBA, MSM, DBA); marketing (MBA, DBA); organizational leadership (Ed D); public administration (MBA); sustainable management (MBA).

Argosy University, Sarasota, College of Business, Sarasota, FL 34235. Offers accounting (DBA, Adv C); corporate compliance (MBA, DBA, Certificate); customized professional concentration (MBA, DBA); finance (MBA, Certificate); fraud examination (MBA, Certificate); global business sustainability (DBA, Adv C); healthcare administration (MBA, Certificate); information systems (DBA, Adv C, Certificate); information systems management (MBA); international business (MBA, DBA, Adv C, Certificate); management (MBA, MSM, DBA, Adv C, Certificate); marketing (MBA, DBA, Adv C, Certificate); organizational leadership (Ed D); public administration (MBA, Certificate); sustainable management (MBA, Certificate).

Argosy University, Schaumburg, College of Business, Schaumburg, IL 60173-5403. Offers accounting (DBA, Adv C); customized professional concentration (MBA, DBA); finance (MBA, Certificate); fraud examination (MBA); global business sustainability (DBA); healthcare administration (MBA, Certificate); information systems (DBA, Adv C, Certificate); information systems management (MBA); international business (MBA, DBA, Adv C, Certificate); management (MBA, MSM, DBA, Adv C, Certificate); marketing (MBA, DBA, Adv C, Certificate); organizational leadership (Ed D); public administration (MBA); sustainable management (MBA).

Argosy University, Seattle, College of Business, Seattle, WA 98121. Offers accounting (DBA); corporate compliance (MBA); customized professional concentration (MBA, DBA); finance (MBA); fraud examination (MBA); global business sustainability (DBA); healthcare administration (MBA); information systems (DBA); information systems management (MBA); international business (MBA, DBA); management (MBA, MSM, DBA); marketing (MBA, DBA); organizational leadership (Ed D); public administration (MBA); sustainable management (MBA).

Argosy University, Tampa, College of Business, Tampa, FL 33607. Offers accounting (DBA); corporate compliance (MBA); customized professional concentration (MBA, DBA); finance (MBA); fraud examination (MBA); global business sustainability (DBA); healthcare administration (MBA); information systems (DBA); information systems management (MBA); international business (MBA, DBA); management (MBA, MSM, DBA); marketing (MBA, DBA); organizational leadership (Ed D); public administration (MBA); sustainable management (MBA).

Argosy University, Twin Cities, College of Business, Eagan, MN 55121. Offers accounting (DBA); customized professional concentration (MBA, DBA); finance (MBA); fraud examination (MBA); global business sustainability (DBA); healthcare administration (MBA); information systems (DBA); information systems management (MBA); international business (MBA, DBA); management (MBA, MSM, DBA); marketing (MBA, DBA); organizational leadership (Ed D); public administration (MBA); sustainable management (MBA).

Argosy University, Washington DC, College of Business, Arlington, VA 22209. Offers accounting (DBA); customized professional concentration (MBA, DBA); finance (MBA); fraud examination (MBA); global business sustainability (DBA); healthcare administration (MBA); information systems (DBA); information systems management (MBA); international business (MBA, DBA, Certificate); management (MBA, MSM, DBA); marketing (MBA, DBA, Certificate); organizational leadership (Ed D); public administration (MBA); sustainable management (MBA).

Arizona State University at the Tempe campus, W. P. Carey School of Business, Department of Marketing, Tempe, AZ 85287-4106. Offers business administration (marketing) (PhD); real estate development (MRED). Part-time and evening/weekend programs available. Postbaccalaureate distance learning degree programs offered. *Degree requirements:* For master's, thesis or alternative, capstone project, interactive Program of Study (iPOS) submitted before completing 50 percent of required credit hours; for doctorate, comprehensive exam, thesis/dissertation, interactive Program of Study (iPOS) submitted before completing 50 percent of required credit hours. *Entrance requirements:* For master's, GMAT, GRE, or LSAT, minimum GPA of 3.0 in last 2 years of work leading to bachelor's degree, 3 personal references, resume, official transcripts, personal statement; for doctorate, GMAT, minimum GPA of 3.0 in last 2 years of work leading to bachelor's degree, 3 letters of recommendation, personal statement/essay. Additional exam requirements/recommendations for international students: Required—TOEFL (minimum score 550 paper-based; 80 iBT), IELTS (minimum score 6.5). Electronic applications accepted. *Expenses:* Contact institution. *Faculty research:* Service marketing and management, strategic marketing, customer portfolio management, characteristics and skills of high-performing managers, market orientation, market segmentation, consumer behavior, marketing strategy, new product development, management of innovation, social influences on consumption, e-commerce, market research methodology.

Arizona State University at the Tempe campus, W. P. Carey School of Business, Program in Business Administration, Tempe, AZ 85287-4906. Offers accountancy (PhD); agribusiness (PhD); business administration (MBA); finance (PhD); financial management and markets (MBA); information management (MBA); information systems (PhD); management (PhD); marketing (PhD); strategic marketing and services leadership (MBA); supply chain financial management (MBA); supply chain management (MBA, PhD); JD/MBA; MBA/M Acc; MBA/M Arch. *Accreditation:* AACSB. Part-time and evening/weekend programs available. Postbaccalaureate distance learning degree programs offered (minimal on-campus study). Terminal master's awarded for partial completion of doctoral program. *Degree requirements:* For master's, thesis or alternative, internship, interactive Program of Study (iPOS) submitted before completing 50 percent of required credit hours; for doctorate, comprehensive exam, thesis/dissertation, interactive Program of Study (iPOS) submitted before completing 50 percent of required credit hours. *Entrance requirements:* For master's, GMAT, minimum GPA of 3.0 in last 2 years of work leading to bachelor's degree, 2 letters of recommendation, professional resume, official transcripts, 3 essays; for doctorate, GMAT or GRE, minimum GPA of 3.0 in last 2 years of work leading to bachelor's degree, 3 letters of recommendation, resume, personal statement/essay. Additional exam requirements/recommendations for international students: Required—TOEFL (minimum score 550 paper-based; 80 iBT), IELTS (minimum score 6.5). Electronic applications accepted. *Expenses:* Contact institution.

Ashworth College, Graduate Programs, Norcross, GA 30092. Offers business administration (MBA); criminal justice (MS); health care administration (MBA, MS); human resource management (MBA, MS); international business (MBA); management (MS); marketing (MBA, MS).

Assumption College, Graduate Studies, Department of Business Studies, Worcester, MA 01609-1296. Offers accounting (MBA); business administration (CAGS); finance/economics (MBA); frontline management (CGS); general business (MBA); human resources (MBA); international business (MBA); management (MBA); marketing (MBA); nonprofit leadership (MBA, CGS); organizational communication (CGS). Part-time and evening/weekend programs available. *Faculty:* 5 full-time (0 women), 20 part-time/adjunct (7 women). *Students:* 20 full-time (7 women), 130 part-time (68 women); includes 20 minority (8 Black or African American, non-Hispanic/Latino; 2 Asian, non-Hispanic/Latino; 8 Hispanic/Latino; 1 Native Hawaiian or other Pacific Islander, non-Hispanic/Latino; 1 Two or more races, non-Hispanic/Latino), 2 international. Average age 31. 63 applicants, 62% accepted, 22 enrolled. In 2013, 58 master's, 1 other advanced degree awarded. *Degree requirements:* For master's, thesis, capstone. *Entrance requirements:* For master's and other advanced degree, 3 letters of recommendation, resume, essay. Additional exam requirements/recommendations for international students: Required—TOEFL (minimum score 540 paper-based; 76 iBT), IELTS (minimum score 6). *Application deadline:* For fall admission, 10/1 for domestic and international students; for winter admission, 2/1 for domestic and international students; for spring admission, 4/1 for domestic and international students. Applications are processed on a rolling basis. Application fee: $30. Electronic applications accepted. *Expenses: Tuition:* Full-time $10,098; part-time $561 per credit. *Required fees:* $20 per term. Full-time tuition and fees vary according to course load and program. *Financial support:* In 2013–14, 15 students received support. Tuition waivers (full and partial), unspecified assistantships, and institutional discounts available. Financial award application deadline: 5/1; financial award applicants required to submit FAFSA. *Faculty research:* Workplace diversity, dynamics of team interaction, utilization of leased employees, experiential learning project on due diligence market for prostheses. *Unit head:* Dr. J. Bart Morrison, Director, 508-767-7458, Fax: 508-767-7252, E-mail: jmorrison@assumption.edu. *Application contact:* Laura Lawrence, Graduate Programs Operations Manager, 508-767-7387, Fax: 508-767-7030, E-mail: graduate@assumption.edu.
Website: http://graduate.assumption.edu/mba/assumption-mba.

Avila University, School of Business, Kansas City, MO 64145-1698. Offers accounting (MBA); finance (MBA); health care administration (MBA); international business (MBA); management (MBA); management information systems (MBA); marketing (MBA). Part-time and evening/weekend programs available. *Faculty:* 9 full-time (4 women), 12 part-time/adjunct (3 women). *Students:* 66 full-time (32 women), 46 part-time (27 women); includes 34 minority (22 Black or African American, non-Hispanic/Latino; 1 American Indian or Alaska Native, non-Hispanic/Latino; 4 Asian, non-Hispanic/Latino; 7 Hispanic/Latino), 27 international. Average age 32. 30 applicants, 80% accepted, 24 enrolled. In 2013, 61 master's awarded. *Degree requirements:* For master's, comprehensive exam, capstone course. *Entrance requirements:* For master's, GMAT (minimum score 420), minimum GPA of 3.0, interview. Additional exam requirements/recommendations for international students: Required—TOEFL (minimum score 550 paper-based). *Application deadline:* For fall admission, 7/30 priority date for domestic and international students; for winter admission, 11/30 priority date for domestic and international students; for spring admission, 2/28 priority date for domestic and international students; for summer admission, 6/1 priority date for domestic and international students. Applications are processed on a rolling basis. Application fee: $0. Electronic applications

Marketing

accepted. *Expenses:* Contact institution. *Financial support:* In 2013–14, 11 students received support. Career-related internships or fieldwork and scholarships/grants available. Support available to part-time students. Financial award applicants required to submit FAFSA. *Faculty research:* Leadership characteristics, financial hedging, group dynamics. *Unit head:* Dr. Richard Woodall, Dean, 816-501-3720, Fax: 816-501-2463, E-mail: richard.woodall@avila.edu. *Application contact:* Sarah Belanus, MBA Admissions Director, 816-501-3601, Fax: 816-501-2463, E-mail: sarah.belanus@avila.edu.
Website: http://www.avila.edu/mba.

Azusa Pacific University, School of Business and Management, Azusa, CA 91702-7000. Offers business administration (MBA); diversity for strategic advantage (MA); entrepreneurship (MBA); finance (MBA); human and organizational development (MA); human resources and organizational development (MBA); human resources management (MA); international business (MBA); marketing (MBA); non-profit management (MA); organizational development and change (MA); performance improvement (MA); public administration (MA); strategic management (MBA). Part-time and evening/weekend programs available. *Degree requirements:* For master's, thesis (for some programs), final project. *Entrance requirements:* For master's, GMAT, minimum GPA of 3.0. Additional exam requirements/recommendations for international students: Required—TOEFL (minimum score 600 paper-based). *Expenses:* Contact institution. *Faculty research:* Gender issues, financial risk, leadership and ethics, marketing strategy.

Baker College Center for Graduate Studies - Online, Graduate Programs, Flint, MI 48507-9843. Offers accounting (MBA); business administration (DBA); finance (MBA); general business (MBA); health care management (MBA); human resources management (MBA); information management (MBA); leadership studies (MBA); management information systems (MSIS); marketing (MBA). Part-time and evening/weekend programs available. Postbaccalaureate distance learning degree programs offered. *Degree requirements:* For master's, portfolio. *Entrance requirements:* For master's, 3 years of work experience, minimum undergraduate GPA of 2.5, writing sample, 3 letters of recommendation; for doctorate, MBA or acceptable related master's degree from accredited association, 5 years work experience, minimum graduate GPA of 3.25, writing sample, 3 professional references. Additional exam requirements/recommendations for international students: Required—TOEFL (minimum score 550 paper-based). Electronic applications accepted.

Barry University, Andreas School of Business, Graduate Certificate Programs, Miami Shores, FL 33161-6695. Offers finance (Certificate); health services administration (Certificate); international business (Certificate); management (Certificate); management information systems (Certificate); marketing (Certificate).

Baruch College of the City University of New York, Zicklin School of Business, Department of Marketing and International Business, New York, NY 10010-5585. Offers international business (MBA); marketing (MBA, MS, PhD). PhD offered jointly with Graduate School and University Center of the City University of New York. Part-time and evening/weekend programs available. *Degree requirements:* For doctorate, comprehensive exam, thesis/dissertation. *Entrance requirements:* For master's, GMAT, 2 letters of recommendation, resume, 2 years of work experience; for doctorate, GMAT. Additional exam requirements/recommendations for international students: Required—TOEFL (minimum score 590 paper-based), TWE (minimum score 5).

Bayamón Central University, Graduate Programs, Program in Business Administration, Bayamón, PR 00960-1725. Offers accounting (MBA); finance (MBA); general business (MBA); management (MBA); marketing (MBA). Part-time and evening/weekend programs available. *Degree requirements:* For master's, comprehensive exam (for some programs). *Entrance requirements:* For master's, EXADEP, bachelor's degree in business or related field.

Benedictine University, Graduate Programs, Program in Business Administration, Lisle, IL 60532-0900. Offers accounting (MBA); entrepreneurship and managing innovation (MBA); financial management (MBA); health administration (MBA); human resource management (MBA); information systems security (MBA); international business (MBA); management consulting (MBA); management information systems (MBA); marketing management (MBA); operations management and logistics (MBA); organizational leadership (MBA). Part-time and evening/weekend programs available. Postbaccalaureate distance learning degree programs offered (minimal on-campus study). *Faculty:* 4 full-time (2 women), 24 part-time/adjunct (3 women). *Students:* 144 full-time (83 women), 599 part-time (328 women); includes 189 minority (115 Black or African American, non-Hispanic/Latino; 5 American Indian or Alaska Native, non-Hispanic/Latino; 43 Asian, non-Hispanic/Latino; 24 Hispanic/Latino; 2 Native Hawaiian or other Pacific Islander, non-Hispanic/Latino), 14 international. Average age 34. 211 applicants, 89% accepted, 155 enrolled. In 2013, 376 master's awarded. *Entrance requirements:* For master's, GMAT. Additional exam requirements/recommendations for international students: Required—TOEFL (minimum score 550 paper-based). *Application deadline:* For fall admission, 9/1 for domestic students; for winter admission, 12/1 for domestic students; for spring admission, 2/15 for domestic students. Applications are processed on a rolling basis. Application fee: $40. Electronic applications accepted. *Expenses: Tuition:* Part-time $590 per credit hour. *Financial support:* Career-related internships or fieldwork and health care benefits available. Support available to part-time students. *Faculty research:* Strategic leadership in professional organizations, sociology of professions, organizational change, social identity theory, applications to change management. *Unit head:* Dr. Sharon Borowicz, Director, 630-829-6219, E-mail: sborowicz@ben.edu. *Application contact:* Kari Gibbons, Director, Admissions, 630-829-6200, Fax: 630-829-6584, E-mail: kgibbons@ben.edu.

Bentley University, McCallum Graduate School of Business, Program in Marketing Analytics, Waltham, MA 02452-4705. Offers MSMA. Part-time and evening/weekend programs available. *Faculty:* 91 full-time (29 women), 22 part-time/adjunct (4 women). *Students:* 80 full-time (58 women), 13 part-time (7 women); includes 1 minority (Two or more races, non-Hispanic/Latino), 75 international. Average age 26. 206 applicants, 68% accepted, 43 enrolled. In 2013, 45 master's awarded. *Entrance requirements:* For master's, GMAT or GRE General Test. Additional exam requirements/recommendations for international students: Required—TOEFL (minimum score 600 paper-based; 100 iBT) or IELTS (minimum score 7). *Application deadline:* For fall admission, 12/1 priority date for domestic and international students; for spring admission, 10/1 priority date for domestic and international students. Application fee: $50. Electronic applications accepted. *Expenses: Tuition:* Full-time $30,400; part-time $1267 per credit. *Required fees:* $404. Tuition and fees vary according to course load and program. *Financial support:* In 2013–14, 12 students received support. Scholarships/grants and unspecified assistantships available. Financial award application deadline: 6/1; financial award applicants required to submit CSS PROFILE or FAFSA. *Faculty research:* Marketing information processing, blogging and social media, customer lifetime value and customer relationship management, measuring and improving productivity, online consumer behavior. *Unit head:* Dr. Paul Berger, Director, 781-891-2746, E-mail: pberger@bentley.edu. *Application contact:* Sharon Hill, Director of Graduate Admissions, 781-891-2108, Fax: 781-891-2464, E-mail: bentleygraduateadmissions@bentley.edu.
Website: http://www.bentley.edu/graduate/degree-programs/ms-programs/marketing-analytics.

Brandeis University, International Business School, Waltham, MA 02454-9110. Offers asset management (MBA); business economics (MBA); corporate finance (MBA); data analytics (MBA); finance (MSF), including asset management, corporate finance, real estate, risk management; international economic policy analysis (MBA); international economics and finance (MA, PhD); marketing (MBA); real estate (MBA); risk management (MBA); sustainability (MBA). Part-time and evening/weekend programs available. *Degree requirements:* For doctorate, thesis/dissertation. *Entrance requirements:* For master's, GMAT or GRE General Test (waived for applicants with at least 2 years of work experience applying to MSF); for doctorate, GRE General Test. Additional exam requirements/recommendations for international students: Required—TOEFL (minimum score 600 paper-based; 100 iBT), IELTS (minimum score 7). Electronic applications accepted. *Faculty research:* International economic policy analysis, U.S. economic policy analysis, real estate, strategy and municipal finance.

California Coast University, School of Administration and Management, Santa Ana, CA 92701. Offers business marketing (MBA); health care management (MBA); human resource management (MBA); management (MBA, MS). Postbaccalaureate distance learning degree programs offered (no on-campus study). Electronic applications accepted.

California Intercontinental University, School of Business, Diamond Bar, CA 91765. Offers banking and finance (MBA); entrepreneurship and business management (DBA); global business leadership (DBA); international management and marketing (MBA); organizational management and human resource management (MBA).

California Lutheran University, Graduate Studies, School of Management, Thousand Oaks, CA 91360-2787. Offers business (IMBA); computer science (MS); econometrics (MBA); economics (MS); entrepreneurship (MBA, Certificate); finance (MBA, Certificate); financial planning (MBA, Certificate); information systems and technology (MS); information technology management (MBA, Certificate); international business (MBA, Certificate); management and organization behavior (MBA); management and organizational behavior (Certificate); marketing (MBA, Certificate); microeconomics (MBA); nonprofit and social enterprise (MBA). Part-time and evening/weekend programs available. Postbaccalaureate distance learning degree programs offered (no on-campus study). *Faculty:* 26 full-time (9 women), 50 part-time/adjunct (11 women). *Students:* 426 full-time (175 women), 220 part-time (91 women); includes 114 minority (14 Black or African American, non-Hispanic/Latino; 30 Asian, non-Hispanic/Latino; 57 Hispanic/Latino; 13 Two or more races, non-Hispanic/Latino), 321 international. Average age 31. 495 applicants, 76% accepted, 119 enrolled. In 2013, 297 master's awarded. *Entrance requirements:* For master's, GMAT, interview, minimum GPA of 3.0. *Application deadline:* Applications are processed on a rolling basis. Application fee: $50. *Expenses:* Contact institution. *Unit head:* Dr. Gerhard Apfelthaler, Dean, 805-493-3360. *Application contact:* 805-493-3325, Fax: 805-493-3861, E-mail: clugrad@callutheran.edu.
Website: http://www.callutheran.edu/business/.

California State University, East Bay, Office of Academic Programs and Graduate Studies, College of Business and Economics, Department of Marketing, Option in Marketing, Hayward, CA 94542-3000. Offers MBA. Part-time and evening/weekend programs available. *Degree requirements:* For master's, comprehensive exam or thesis. *Entrance requirements:* For master's, GMAT, minimum GPA of 2.75. Additional exam requirements/recommendations for international students: Required—TOEFL (minimum score 550 paper-based). Electronic applications accepted.

California State University, East Bay, Office of Academic Programs and Graduate Studies, College of Business and Economics, MBA Program, Hayward, CA 94542-3000. Offers entrepreneurship (MBA); finance (MBA); global innovators (MBA); human resources and organizational behavior (MBA); information technology management (MBA); marketing management (MBA); operations and supply chain management (MBA); strategy and international business (MBA). Part-time and evening/weekend programs available. *Degree requirements:* For master's, comprehensive exam or thesis. *Entrance requirements:* For master's, GMAT (minimum 20th percentile verbal and quantitative section), bachelor's degree, minimum GPA of 2.75. Additional exam requirements/recommendations for international students: Required—TOEFL (minimum score 550 paper-based; 79 iBT). Electronic applications accepted. *Expenses:* Contact institution.

California State University, Fullerton, Graduate Studies, College of Business and Economics, Department of Marketing, Fullerton, CA 92834-9480. Offers marketing (MBA). Part-time programs available. *Students:* 5 full-time (all women), 12 part-time (6 women); includes 8 minority (4 Asian, non-Hispanic/Latino; 4 Hispanic/Latino), 3 international. Average age 27. In 2013, 19 master's awarded. *Degree requirements:* For master's, project or thesis. *Entrance requirements:* For master's, GMAT, minimum AACSB index of 950. Application fee: $55. *Financial support:* Career-related internships or fieldwork, Federal Work-Study, institutionally sponsored loans, and scholarships/grants available. Support available to part-time students. Financial award application deadline: 3/1; financial award applicants required to submit FAFSA. *Unit head:* Dr. Irene Lange, Chair, 657-278-2223. *Application contact:* Admissions/Applications, 657-278-2371.

California State University, Los Angeles, Graduate Studies, College of Business and Economics, Department of Marketing, Los Angeles, CA 90032-8530. Offers international business (MBA, MS); marketing management (MBA, MS). Part-time and evening/weekend programs available. *Faculty:* 2 full-time (both women), 1 part-time/adjunct (0 women). *Students:* 1 full-time (0 women), 12 part-time (6 women); includes 3 minority (1 Asian, non-Hispanic/Latino; 1 Hispanic/Latino; 1 Two or more races, non-Hispanic/Latino), 9 international. Average age 28. In 2013, 11 master's awarded. *Degree requirements:* For master's, comprehensive exam (MBA), thesis (MS). *Entrance requirements:* For master's, GMAT, minimum GPA of 2.5 during previous 2 years of course work. Additional exam requirements/recommendations for international students: Required—TOEFL (minimum score 550 paper-based). *Application deadline:* For fall admission, 5/1 for domestic and international students. Applications are processed on a rolling basis. Application fee: $55. Electronic applications accepted. *Financial support:* Career-related internships or fieldwork and Federal Work-Study available. Support available to part-time students. Financial award application deadline: 3/1. *Unit head:* Dr. Tyrone Jackson, Chair, 323-343-2960, Fax: 323-343-5462, E-mail: tjackso4@calstatela.edu. *Application contact:* Dr. Larry Fritz, Dean of Graduate Studies, 323-343-3820, Fax: 323-343-5653, E-mail: lfritz@calstatela.edu.
Website: http://cbe.calstatela.edu/mkt/.

California State University, San Bernardino, Graduate Studies, College of Arts and Letters, Department of Communication Studies, San Bernardino, CA 92407-2397. Offers communication studies (MA); integrated marketing communication (MA). *Students:* 7 full-time (5 women), 16 part-time (11 women); includes 7 minority (2 Black or African American, non-Hispanic/Latino; 2 Asian, non-Hispanic/Latino; 3 Hispanic/Latino), 5 international. Average age 28. 45 applicants, 53% accepted, 12 enrolled. In 2013, 9 master's awarded. *Degree requirements:* For master's, comprehensive exam,

advancement to candidacy. *Entrance requirements:* Additional exam requirements/recommendations for international students: Required—TOEFL. *Application deadline:* For fall admission, 8/31 priority date for domestic students. Application fee: $55. *Unit head:* Dr. Michael Salvador, Chair, 909-537-5820, Fax: 909-537-7009, E-mail: salvador@csusb.edu. *Application contact:* Dr. Jeffrey Thompson, Dean of Graduate Studies, 909-537-5058, Fax: 909-537-7034, E-mail: jthompso@csusb.edu.

California State University, San Bernardino, Graduate Studies, College of Business and Public Administration, Master in Business Administration Program, San Bernardino, CA 92407. Offers accounting (MBA); cyber security (MBA); entrepreneurship (MBA); finance (MBA); information systems and technology (MBA); management (MBA); marketing management (MBA); supply chain management (MBA). MBA is also offered online. *Accreditation:* AACSB. Part-time and evening/weekend programs available. Postbaccalaureate distance learning degree programs offered (no on-campus study). *Faculty:* 27 full-time (6 women), 8 part-time/adjunct (1 woman). *Students:* 161 full-time (59 women), 47 part-time (18 women); includes 74 minority (12 Black or African American, non-Hispanic/Latino; 19 Asian, non-Hispanic/Latino; 42 Hispanic/Latino; 1 Two or more races, non-Hispanic/Latino), 74 international. Average age 29. 281 applicants, 38% accepted, 67 enrolled. In 2013, 79 master's awarded. *Degree requirements:* For master's, comprehensive exam, thesis, portfolio, 60 units, minimum GPA of 3.0. *Entrance requirements:* For master's, GMAT or GRE, minimum GPA of 2.5. Additional exam requirements/recommendations for international students: Required—TOEFL (minimum score 550 paper-based; 79 iBT). *Application deadline:* For fall admission, 7/20 for domestic and international students; for winter admission, 10/20 for domestic and international students; for spring admission, 1/20 for domestic and international students. Applications are processed on a rolling basis. Application fee: $55. Electronic applications accepted. *Expenses:* Contact institution. *Financial support:* In 2013–14, 79 students received support, including 21 fellowships (averaging $4,867 per year), 29 research assistantships (averaging $2,748 per year), 6 teaching assistantships (averaging $5,162 per year); career-related internships or fieldwork, Federal Work-Study, institutionally sponsored loans, scholarships/grants, and unspecified assistantships also available. Support available to part-time students. Financial award application deadline: 3/1; financial award applicants required to submit FAFSA. *Faculty research:* Market reaction to Form 20-F, tax Constitutional questions in Obamacare, the performance of the faith and ethical investment products prior to and following the 2008 meltdown, capital appreciation bonds: a ruinous decision for an unborn generation, the effects of calorie count display on consumer eating behavior, local government bankruptcy. *Total annual research expenditures:* $2.3 million. *Unit head:* Dr. Lawrence C. Rose, Dean, 909-537-3703, Fax: 909-537-7026, E-mail: lrose@csusb.edu. *Application contact:* Dr. Vipin Gupta, Associate Dean/MBA Director, 909-537-7380, Fax: 909-537-7026, E-mail: vgupta@csusb.edu.
Website: http://mba.csusb.edu/.

Capella University, School of Business and Technology, Doctoral Programs in Business, Minneapolis, MN 55402. Offers accounting (DBA, PhD); business intelligence (DBA); finance (DBA, PhD); general business management (PhD); human resource management (DBA, PhD); leadership (DBA, PhD); management education (PhD); marketing (DBA, PhD); project management (DBA, PhD); strategy and innovation (DBA, PhD).

Capella University, School of Business and Technology, Master's Programs in Business, Minneapolis, MN 55402. Offers accounting (MBA); business analysis (MS); business intelligence (MBA); entrepreneurship (MBA); finance (MBA); general business administration (MBA); general human resource management (MS); general leadership (MS); health care management (MBA); human resource management (MBA); marketing (MBA); project management (MBA, MS).

Capital University, School of Management, Columbus, OH 43209-2394. Offers entrepreneurship (MBA); finance (MBA); leadership (MBA); marketing (MBA); MBA/JD; MBA/LL M; MBA/MSN; MBA/MT. *Accreditation:* ACBSP. Part-time and evening/weekend programs available. *Faculty:* 17 full-time (7 women), 23 part-time/adjunct (1 woman). *Students:* 192 (77 women). Average age 31. 34 applicants, 74% accepted, 20 enrolled. In 2013, 1 master's awarded. *Entrance requirements:* For master's, GMAT, 2 years of work experience. Additional exam requirements/recommendations for international students: Required—TOEFL (minimum score 550 paper-based); Recommended—IELTS (minimum score 6.5). *Application deadline:* For fall admission, 7/1 priority date for domestic students; for winter admission, 11/1 for domestic students; for spring admission, 11/1 priority date for domestic students; for summer admission, 4/1 priority date for domestic students. Applications are processed on a rolling basis. Electronic applications accepted. *Financial support:* Application deadline: 8/1; applicants required to submit FAFSA. *Faculty research:* Taxation, public policy, health care, management of non-profits. *Unit head:* Dr. David Schwantes, MBA Director, 614-236-6984, Fax: 614-236-6923, E-mail: dschwant@capital.edu. *Application contact:* Carli Isgrigg, Assistant Director of Adult and Graduate Education Recruitment, 614-236-6546, Fax: 614-236-6923, E-mail: cisgrigg@capital.edu.
Website: http://www.capital.edu/capital-mba/.

Carnegie Mellon University, Tepper School of Business, Program in Marketing, Pittsburgh, PA 15213-3891. Offers PhD. *Degree requirements:* For doctorate, thesis/dissertation.

Case Western Reserve University, Weatherhead School of Management, Department of Marketing and Policy Studies, Division of Marketing, Cleveland, OH 44106. Offers MBA. *Entrance requirements:* For master's, GMAT. *Faculty research:* Consumer decision making, global marketing, brand equity management, supply chain management, industrial and new technology marketing.

Case Western Reserve University, Weatherhead School of Management, Department of Operations, Cleveland, OH 44106. Offers management (MS, MSM), including finance (MS), information systems (MS), marketing (MS), operations research, quality management (MS), supply chain (MSM); management for liberal arts graduates (MSM); operations research (PhD); MBA/MSM. Part-time programs available. *Degree requirements:* For doctorate, thesis/dissertation. *Entrance requirements:* For master's, GRE General Test; for doctorate, GMAT, GRE General Test. *Faculty research:* Mathematical finance, mathematical programming, scheduling, stochastic optimization, environmental/energy models.

Central European University, CEU Business School, Budapest, Hungary. Offers executive business administration (EMBA); finance (MBA); general management (MBA); information technology management (M Sc); marketing (MBA). Part-time and evening/weekend programs available. *Faculty:* 18 full-time (5 women), 6 part-time/adjunct (1 woman). *Students:* 37 full-time (16 women), 82 part-time (20 women). Average age 32. 219 applicants, 34% accepted, 35 enrolled. In 2013, 69 master's awarded. *Degree requirements:* For master's, one foreign language. *Entrance requirements:* For master's, GMAT. Additional exam requirements/recommendations for international students: Required—TOEFL (minimum score 570 paper-based); Recommended—IELTS (minimum score 6.5). *Application deadline:* For fall admission, 5/15 for domestic students, 5/22 for international students; for winter admission, 11/15 for domestic students, 11/10 for international students. Applications are processed on a rolling basis. Application fee: $40. Electronic applications accepted. *Expenses: Tuition:* Full-time 62,700 Hungarian forints. *Financial support:* Tuition waivers (partial) available. *Faculty research:* Social and ethical business, marketing, international business, international trade and investment, management development in Central and East Europe, non-market strategies of emerging-market multinationals, macro and micro analysis of the business environment, international competitive analysis, the transition process from emerging economies to established market economies and its social impact, the regulation of natural monopolies. *Unit head:* Dr. Mel Horwitch, Dean and Managing Director, 361-887-5050, E-mail: mhorwitch@ceubusiness.com. *Application contact:* Miao Tan, Recruitment Coordinator, 361-887-5061, Fax: 361-887-5133, E-mail: tanm@ceubusiness.org.
Website: http://business.ceu.hu/.

Central Michigan University, Central Michigan University Global Campus, Program in Business Administration, Mount Pleasant, MI 48859. Offers enterprise resource planning (MBA, Certificate); human resource management (MBA); logistics management (MBA, Certificate); marketing (MBA); value-driven organization (MBA). Part-time and evening/weekend programs available. *Entrance requirements:* For master's, GMAT. *Financial support:* Scholarships/grants available. Support available to part-time students. *Unit head:* Dr. Debasish Chakraborty, 989-774-3678, E-mail: chakt1d@cmich.edu. *Application contact:* Global Campus Student Services Call Center, 877-268-4636, E-mail: cmuglobal@cmich.edu.

Central Michigan University, College of Graduate Studies, College of Business Administration, MBA Program, Mount Pleasant, MI 48859. Offers accounting (MBA); business economics (MBA); consulting (MBA); finance (MBA); general business (MBA); human resource management (MBA); information systems (MBA); international business (MBA); logistics management (MBA); marketing (MBA); value-driven organization (MBA). Part-time and evening/weekend programs available. Postbaccalaureate distance learning degree programs offered (no on-campus study). Electronic applications accepted. *Faculty research:* Accounting, consulting, international business, marketing, information systems.

City College of the City University of New York, Graduate School, College of Liberal Arts and Science, Division of the Humanities and Arts, Department of Media and Communication Arts, Program in Branding and Integrated Communications, New York, NY 10031. Offers MPS.

City University of Seattle, Graduate Division, School of Management, Bellevue, WA 98005. Offers accounting (Certificate); change leadership (MBA, Certificate); computer systems (MS); finance (Certificate); financial management (MBA); general management (MBA); general management-Europe (MBA); global marketing (MBA); human resources management (Certificate); individualized study (MBA); information security (MS); information systems (MBA); leadership (MA); marketing (MBA, Certificate); project management (MBA, MS, Certificate); sustainable business (Certificate); technology management (MBA, Certificate). Part-time and evening/weekend programs available. Postbaccalaureate distance learning degree programs offered (no on-campus study). *Degree requirements:* For master's, comprehensive exam (for some programs), thesis (for some programs). *Entrance requirements:* Additional exam requirements/recommendations for international students: Required—TOEFL (minimum score 567 paper-based; 87 iBT); Recommended—IELTS. Electronic applications accepted.

Clark University, Graduate School, Graduate School of Management, Business Administration Program, Worcester, MA 01610-1477. Offers accounting (MBA); finance (MBA); global business (MBA); information systems (MBA); management (MBA); marketing (MBA); social change (MBA); sustainability (MBA). *Accreditation:* AACSB. Part-time and evening/weekend programs available. *Students:* 109 full-time (50 women), 151 part-time (67 women); includes 16 minority (9 Black or African American, non-Hispanic/Latino; 3 Asian, non-Hispanic/Latino; 4 Hispanic/Latino), 74 international. Average age 30. 359 applicants, 50% accepted, 81 enrolled. In 2013, 125 master's awarded. *Degree requirements:* For master's, thesis optional. *Application deadline:* For fall admission, 6/1 priority date for domestic students; for spring admission, 12/1 priority date for domestic students. Applications are processed on a rolling basis. Application fee: $50. Electronic applications accepted. *Expenses: Tuition:* Full-time $39,200; part-time $1225 per credit hour. *Financial support:* In 2013–14, research assistantships with partial tuition reimbursements (averaging $4,800 per year), teaching assistantships with partial tuition reimbursements (averaging $4,800 per year) were awarded; fellowships, career-related internships or fieldwork, Federal Work-Study, institutionally sponsored loans, and tuition waivers (partial) also available. Support available to part-time students. Financial award application deadline: 5/31. *Faculty research:* Marketing, accounting, human resource management, management information systems, business finance. *Unit head:* Dr. Catherine Usoff, Dean, 508-793-8822, Fax: 508-793-8822, E-mail: clarkmba@clarku.edu. *Application contact:* Patrick Oroszko, Enrollment and Marketing Director, 508-793-8822, Fax: 508-793-8822, E-mail: clarkmba@clarku.edu.
Website: http://www.clarku.edu/gsom/graduate/fulltime/.

Clemson University, Graduate School, College of Business and Behavioral Science, Department of Marketing, Clemson, SC 29634. Offers marketing (MS). Part-time programs available. *Faculty:* 11 full-time (3 women), 1 part-time/adjunct (0 women). *Students:* 13 full-time (7 women); includes 6 minority (1 Black or African American, non-Hispanic/Latino; 4 Asian, non-Hispanic/Latino; 1 Native Hawaiian or other Pacific Islander, non-Hispanic/Latino), 5 international. Average age 24. 198 applicants, 18% accepted, 13 enrolled. In 2013, 7 master's awarded. *Entrance requirements:* For master's, GMAT or GRE, minimum GPA of 3.0, letters of recommendation, personal statement, resume. Additional exam requirements/recommendations for international students: Required—TOEFL. *Application deadline:* Applications are processed on a rolling basis. Application fee: $70 ($80 for international students). Electronic applications accepted. *Financial support:* Career-related internships or fieldwork, institutionally sponsored loans, scholarships/grants, health care benefits, and unspecified assistantships available. Support available to part-time students. Financial award applicants required to submit FAFSA. *Faculty research:* Marketing decision-making, marketing analysis, marketing strategy. *Unit head:* Dr. Mary Anne Raymond, Chair, 864-656-6782, E-mail: mar@clemson.edu. *Application contact:* Dr. Michael J. Dorsch, Program Director, 864-656-5288, Fax: 864-656-0138, E-mail: mdorsch@clemson.edu.
Website: http://business.clemson.edu/departments/marketing/mkt_about.htm.

Cleveland State University, College of Graduate Studies, Monte Ahuja College of Business, Department of Marketing, Cleveland, OH 44115. Offers global business (Graduate Certificate); marketing (MBA, DBA); marketing analytics (Graduate Certificate). *Faculty:* 12 full-time (4 women), 6 part-time/adjunct (3 women). *Students:* 1 (woman) full-time, 16 part-time (4 women); includes 2 minority (both Black or African American, non-Hispanic/Latino), 2 international. Average age 40. 63 applicants, 25% accepted, 2 enrolled. *Expenses: Tuition,* state resident: full-time $8335; part-time $521 per credit hour. Tuition, nonresident: full-time $15,670; part-time $979 per credit hour. *Required fees:* $50; $25 per semester. *Financial support:* In 2013–14, research assistantships (averaging $9,744 per year) were awarded; tuition waivers (partial) also available. Financial award application deadline: 6/30; financial award applicants required to submit FAFSA. *Unit head:* Dr. Thomas W. Whipple, Chair, 216-687-4771, Fax: 216-687-5135, E-mail: t.whipple@csuohio.edu. *Application contact:* Kenneth Dippong,

Director, Student Services, 216-523-7545, Fax: 216-687-9354, E-mail: k.dippong@csuohio.edu.
Website: http://www.csuohio.edu/business/academics/mkt/.

Cleveland State University, College of Graduate Studies, Monte Ahuja College of Business, Doctor of Business Administration Program, Cleveland, OH 44115. Offers finance (DBA); global business (DBA); information systems (DBA); marketing (DBA); operations management (DBA). *Accreditation:* AACSB. Part-time and evening/weekend programs available. *Faculty:* 50 full-time (11 women). *Students:* 36 part-time (18 women); includes 6 minority (2 Black or African American, non-Hispanic/Latino; 4 Asian, non-Hispanic/Latino), 8 international. Average age 39. 96 applicants, 27% accepted, 6 enrolled. In 2013, 1 doctorate awarded. *Degree requirements:* For doctorate, comprehensive exam, thesis/dissertation, oral dissertation defense. *Entrance requirements:* For doctorate, GMAT, MBA or equivalent. Additional exam requirements/recommendations for international students: Required—TOEFL (minimum score 550 paper-based; 79 iBT). *Application deadline:* For spring admission, 2/28 priority date for domestic and international students. Application fee: $30. Electronic applications accepted. *Expenses:* Tuition, state resident: full-time $8335; part-time $521 per credit hour. Tuition, nonresident: full-time $15,670; part-time $979 per credit hour. *Required fees:* $50; $25 per semester. *Financial support:* In 2013–14, 5 research assistantships with full tuition reimbursements (averaging $12,700 per year), 4 teaching assistantships with full tuition reimbursements (averaging $12,700 per year) were awarded; tuition waivers (full) and unspecified assistantships also available. *Faculty research:* Supply chain management, international business, strategic management, risk analysis, consumer behavior. *Unit head:* Dr. Raj Shekhar G. Javalgi, Director, 216-687-3786, Fax: 216-687-9354, E-mail: r.javalgi@csuohio.edu. *Application contact:* Melinda J. Arnold, Administrative Secretary, 216-687-6952, Fax: 216-687-9257, E-mail: m.arnold@csuohio.edu.
Website: http://www.csuohio.edu/business/academics/doctoral.html.

Colorado Technical University Colorado Springs, Graduate Studies, Program in Management, Colorado Springs, CO 80907-3896. Offers accounting (MBA, MSA); business administration (MBA); finance (MBA); human resources management (MBA); logistics/supply chain management (MBA); management (DM); marketing (MBA); mediation and dispute resolution (MBA); operations management (MBA); project management (MBA); technology management (MBA). Part-time and evening/weekend programs available. Postbaccalaureate distance learning degree programs offered. *Degree requirements:* For master's, thesis or alternative; for doctorate, thesis/dissertation. *Entrance requirements:* For doctorate, minimum graduate GPA of 3.0, 5 years of related work experience. *Faculty research:* Sexual harassment, performance evaluation, critical thinking.

Colorado Technical University Denver South, Programs in Business Administration and Management, Aurora, CO 80014. Offers accounting (MBA); business administration (MBA); business administration and management (EMBA); finance (MBA); human resource management (MBA); marketing (MBA); mediation and dispute resolution (MBA); operations management (MBA); project management (MBA); technology management (MBA). Part-time and evening/weekend programs available. *Degree requirements:* For master's, thesis or alternative. *Entrance requirements:* For master's, minimum undergraduate GPA of 3.0, resume.

Columbia Southern University, MBA Program, Orange Beach, AL 36561. Offers finance (MBA); health care management (MBA); human resource management (MBA); marketing (MBA); project management (MBA); public administration (MBA). Part-time and evening/weekend programs available. Postbaccalaureate distance learning degree programs offered (no on-campus study). *Entrance requirements:* For master's, bachelor's degree from accredited/approved institution. Additional exam requirements/recommendations for international students: Required—TOEFL. Electronic applications accepted.

Columbia University, Graduate School of Business, Doctoral Program in Business, New York, NY 10027. Offers business (PhD), including accounting, decision, risk, and operations, finance and economics, management, marketing. *Accreditation:* AACSB. *Degree requirements:* For doctorate, comprehensive exam, thesis/dissertation, major field exam, research paper, thesis proposal. *Entrance requirements:* For doctorate, GMAT or GRE (finance), 2 letters of reference, resume. Additional exam requirements/recommendations for international students: Required—TOEFL. Electronic applications accepted. *Expenses:* Contact institution. *Faculty research:* Human decision making and behavioral research; real estate market and mortgage defaults; financial crisis and corporate governance; international business; security analysis and accounting.

Columbia University, Graduate School of Business, MBA Program, New York, NY 10027. Offers accounting (MBA); decision, risk, and operations (MBA); entrepreneurship (MBA); finance and economics (MBA); healthcare and pharmaceutical management (MBA); human resource management (MBA); international business (MBA); leadership and ethics (MBA); management (MBA); marketing (MBA); media (MBA); private equity (MBA); real estate (MBA); social enterprise (MBA); value investing (MBA); DDS/MBA; JD/MBA; MBA/MIA; MBA/MPH; MBA/MS; MD/MBA. *Entrance requirements:* For master's, GMAT, 2 letters of recommendation. Additional exam requirements/recommendations for international students: Required—TOEFL. Electronic applications accepted. *Expenses:* Contact institution. *Faculty research:* Human decision making and behavioral research; real estate market and mortgage defaults; financial crisis and corporate governance; international business; security analysis and accounting.

Concordia University, School of Graduate Studies, John Molson School of Business, Montreal, QC H3G 1M8, Canada. Offers administration (M Sc), including finance, management, marketing; business administration (MBA, PhD, Certificate, Diploma); executive business administration (EMBA); investment management (MBA). PhD program offered jointly with HEC Montreal, McGill University, and Université du Québec à Montréal. *Accreditation:* AACSB. Part-time and evening/weekend programs available. *Degree requirements:* For master's, one foreign language, thesis (for some programs), research project; for doctorate, one foreign language, thesis/dissertation; for other advanced degree, one foreign language. *Entrance requirements:* For master's, GMAT, minimum 2 years of work experience (for MBA); letters of recommendation, bachelor's degree from recognized university with minimum GPA of 3.0, curriculum vitae; for doctorate, GMAT (minimum score of 600), official transcripts, curriculum vitae, 3 letters of reference, statement of purpose; for other advanced degree, minimum GPA of 2.7, 2 letters of reference, statement of purpose, resume. Additional exam requirements/recommendations for international students: Required—TOEFL (minimum score 90 iBT), IELTS (minimum score 7). Electronic applications accepted. *Expenses:* Contact institution. *Faculty research:* General business, capital markets, international business.

Concordia University Wisconsin, Graduate Programs, School of Business and Legal Studies, MBA Program, Mequon, WI 53097-2402. Offers finance (MBA); health care administration (MBA); human resource management (MBA); international business (MBA); international business-bilingual English/Chinese (MBA); management (MBA); management information systems (MBA); managerial communications (MBA); marketing (MBA); public administration (MBA); risk management (MBA). Postbaccalaureate distance learning degree programs offered (minimal on-campus study). *Degree requirements:* For master's, comprehensive exam, thesis or alternative. *Entrance requirements:* Additional exam requirements/recommendations for international students: Required—TOEFL. *Expenses:* Contact institution.

Cornell University, Graduate School, Graduate Field of Management, Ithaca, NY 14853. Offers accounting (PhD); finance (PhD); marketing (PhD); organizational behavior (PhD); production and operations management (PhD). *Accreditation:* AACSB. *Faculty:* 54 full-time (7 women). *Students:* 37 full-time (13 women); includes 5 minority (4 Asian, non-Hispanic/Latino; 1 Two or more races, non-Hispanic/Latino), 24 international. Average age 29. 486 applicants, 4% accepted, 11 enrolled. In 2013, 8 doctorates awarded. *Degree requirements:* For doctorate, comprehensive exam, thesis/dissertation. *Entrance requirements:* For doctorate, GMAT or GRE General Test. Additional exam requirements/recommendations for international students: Required—TOEFL (minimum score 600 paper-based; 77 iBT). *Application deadline:* For fall admission, 1/3 for domestic students. Application fee: $95. Electronic applications accepted. *Expenses:* Contact institution. *Financial support:* In 2013–14, 33 students received support, including 31 research assistantships with full tuition reimbursements available, 2 teaching assistantships with full tuition reimbursements available; fellowships with full tuition reimbursements available, institutionally sponsored loans, scholarships/grants, health care benefits, tuition waivers (full and partial), and unspecified assistantships also available. Financial award applicants required to submit FAFSA. *Faculty research:* Operations and manufacturing. *Unit head:* Director of Graduate Studies, 607-255-3669. *Application contact:* Graduate Field Assistant, 607-255-9431, E-mail: js_phd@cornell.edu.
Website: http://www.gradschool.cornell.edu/fields.php?id-91&a-2.

Daemen College, Department of Accounting/Information Systems, Amherst, NY 14226-3592. Offers global business (MS), including accounting, global business, management information systems, marketing. Part-time and evening/weekend programs available. *Degree requirements:* For master's, minimum GPA of 3.0. *Entrance requirements:* For master's, GMAT if undergraduate GPA is less than 3.0, 2 letters of recommendation; goal statement; transcripts; demonstration of satisfactory oral and written English. Additional exam requirements/recommendations for international students: Required—TOEFL (minimum score 500 paper-based; 63 iBT), IELTS (minimum score 5.5). Electronic applications accepted. *Faculty research:* Internationalization of small business, cultural influences on business practices, international human resource practices.

Dallas Baptist University, College of Business, Business Administration Program, Dallas, TX 75211-9299. Offers accounting (MBA); business communication (MBA); conflict resolution management (MBA); entrepreneurship (MBA); finance (MBA); health care management (MBA); international business (MBA); leading the non-profit organization (MBA); management (MBA); management information systems (MBA); marketing (MBA); project management (MBA); technology and engineering (MBA). *Accreditation:* ACBSP. Part-time and evening/weekend programs available. *Entrance requirements:* For master's, GMAT, minimum GPA of 3.0. Additional exam requirements/recommendations for international students: Required—TOEFL, IELTS. *Application deadline:* Applications are processed on a rolling basis. Application fee: $25. Electronic applications accepted. *Expenses: Tuition:* Full-time $13,410; part-time $745 per credit hour. *Required fees:* $300; $150 per semester. Tuition and fees vary according to degree level. *Financial support:* Federal Work-Study, institutionally sponsored loans, scholarships/grants, and tuition waivers (full and partial) available. Support available to part-time students. Financial award applicants required to submit FAFSA. *Faculty research:* Sports management, services marketing, retailing, strategic management, financial planning/investments. *Unit head:* Dr. Sandra S. Reid, Chair, 214-333-5280, Fax: 214-333-5293, E-mail: graduate@dbu.edu. *Application contact:* Kit P. Montgomery, Director of Graduate Programs, 214-333-5242, Fax: 214-333-5579, E-mail: graduate@dbu.edu.
Website: http://www3.dbu.edu/graduate/mba.asp.

DePaul University, Charles H. Kellstadt Graduate School of Business, Chicago, IL 60604. Offers accountancy (M Acc, MS, MSA); applied economics (MBA); banking (MBA); behavioral finance (MBA); brand and product management (MBA); business development (MBA); business information technology (MS); business strategy and decision-making (MBA); computational finance (MS); consumer insights (MBA); corporate finance (MBA); economic policy analysis (MS); entrepreneurship (MBA, MS); finance (MBA, MS); financial analysis (MBA); general business (MBA); health sector management (MBA); hospitality leadership (MBA); hospitality leadership and operational performance (MS); human resource management (MBA); human resources (MS); investment management (MBA); leadership and change management (MBA); management accounting (MBA); marketing (MBA, MS); marketing analysis (MS); marketing strategy and planning (MBA); operations management (MBA); organizational diversity (MBA); real estate (MS); real estate finance and investment (MBA); revenue management (MBA); sports management (MBA); strategic global marketing (MBA); strategy, execution and valuation (MBA); sustainable management (MBA, MS); taxation (MS); wealth management (MS); JD/MBA. *Accreditation:* AACSB. Part-time and evening/weekend programs available. Postbaccalaureate distance learning degree programs offered (no on-campus study). *Faculty:* 81 full-time (20 women), 45 part-time/adjunct (8 women). *Students:* 1,238 full-time (605 women), 617 part-time (223 women); includes 295 minority (71 Black or African American, non-Hispanic/Latino; 129 Asian, non-Hispanic/Latino; 74 Hispanic/Latino; 4 Native Hawaiian or other Pacific Islander, non-Hispanic/Latino; 17 Two or more races, non-Hispanic/Latino), 462 international. Average age 29. In 2013, 911 master's awarded. *Entrance requirements:* For master's, GMAT, 2 letters of recommendation, resume, essay, official transcripts. Additional exam requirements/recommendations for international students: Required—TOEFL (minimum score 550 paper-based; 80 iBT). *Application deadline:* For fall admission, 7/1 for domestic students, 6/1 for international students; for winter admission, 10/1 for domestic students, 9/1 for international students; for spring admission, 2/1 for domestic students, 1/1 for international students. Applications are processed on a rolling basis. Application fee: $60. Electronic applications accepted. *Expenses:* Contact institution. *Financial support:* Application deadline: 4/1; applicants required to submit FAFSA. *Unit head:* Robert T. Ryan, Assistant Dean and Director, 312-362-8810, Fax: 312-362-6677, E-mail: rryan1@depaul.edu. *Application contact:* James Parker, Director of Recruitment and Admission, 312-362-8810, Fax: 312-362-6677, E-mail: kgsb@depaul.edu.
Website: http://kellstadt.depaul.edu.

DEREE - The American College of Greece, Graduate Programs, Athens, Greece. Offers applied psychology (MS); communication (MA); leadership (MS); marketing (MS).

DeSales University, Graduate Division, Division of Business, Center Valley, PA 18034-9568. Offers accounting (MBA); computer information systems (MBA); finance (MBA); health care systems management (MBA); human resources management (MBA); management (MBA); marketing (MBA); project management (MBA); self-design (MBA). *Accreditation:* ACBSP. Part-time and evening/weekend programs available. Postbaccalaureate distance learning degree programs offered (no on-campus study). *Students:* 444 part-time. Average age 37. In 2013, 1 master's awarded. *Entrance requirements:* For master's, GMAT, minimum GPA of 3.0, 2 years of work experience. Additional exam requirements/recommendations for international students: Required—TOEFL. *Application deadline:* Applications are processed on a rolling basis. Application fee: $50. Electronic applications accepted. *Expenses: Tuition:* Part-time $790 per credit.

Financial support: Applicants required to submit FAFSA. *Faculty research:* Quality improvement, executive development, productivity, cross-cultural managerial differences, leadership. *Unit head:* Dr. David Gilfoil, Director, 610-282-1100 Ext. 1828, Fax: 610-282-2869, E-mail: david.gilfoil@desales.edu. *Application contact:* Abigail Wernicki, Director of Graduate Admissions, 610-282-1100 Ext. 1768, E-mail: gradadmissions@desales.edu.

Dowling College, School of Business, Oakdale, NY 11769. Offers aviation management (MBA, Certificate); corporate finance (MBA, Certificate); health care management (MBA); human resource management (Certificate); information systems management (MBA); management and leadership (MBA); marketing (Certificate); project management (Certificate); public management (MBA); school district business leader (MBA); sport, event and entertainment management (Certificate); JD/MBA. Part-time and evening/weekend programs available. Postbaccalaureate distance learning degree programs offered (minimal on-campus study). *Faculty:* 7 full-time (2 women), 43 part-time/adjunct (7 women). *Students:* 183 full-time (79 women), 299 part-time (142 women); includes 137 minority (84 Black or African American, non-Hispanic/Latino; 14 Asian, non-Hispanic/Latino; 20 Hispanic/Latino; 19 Native Hawaiian or other Pacific Islander, non-Hispanic/Latino). Average age 32. 360 applicants, 58% accepted, 127 enrolled. In 2013, 235 master's, 15 other advanced degrees awarded. *Degree requirements:* For master's, comprehensive exam, thesis optional. *Entrance requirements:* For master's, minimum GPA of 2.8, 2 letters of recommendation, courses or seminar in accounting and finance, resume. Additional exam requirements/recommendations for international students: Required—TOEFL (minimum score 550 paper-based). *Application deadline:* For fall admission, 9/1 priority date for domestic students; for winter admission, 1/1 priority date for domestic students; for spring admission, 2/1 priority date for domestic students. Applications are processed on a rolling basis. Application fee: $50. Electronic applications accepted. *Expenses: Tuition:* Full-time $22,731; part-time $1029 per credit. *Required fees:* $956; $956. *Financial support:* Career-related internships or fieldwork and Federal Work-Study available. Support available to part-time students. Financial award application deadline: 6/30; financial award applicants required to submit FAFSA. *Faculty research:* International finance, computer applications, labor relations, executive development. *Unit head:* Dr. Elana Zolfo, Dean, 631-244-3266, Fax: 631-244-1018, E-mail: zolfoe@dowling.edu. *Application contact:* Mary Boullianne, Dean of Admissions, 631-244-3274, Fax: 631-244-1059, E-mail: boulliam@dowling.edu.

Drexel University, LeBow College of Business, Program in Business Administration, Philadelphia, PA 19104-2875. Offers business administration (MBA, PhD, APC), including accounting (MBA, PhD), decision sciences (PhD), economics (MBA, PhD), finance (MBA, PhD), legal studies (MBA), management (MBA), marketing (MBA, PhD), organizational sciences (PhD), quantitative methods (MBA), strategic management (PhD). *Accreditation:* AACSB. Part-time and evening/weekend programs available. Postbaccalaureate distance learning degree programs offered (minimal on-campus study). Terminal master's awarded for partial completion of doctoral program. *Entrance requirements:* For master's, GMAT, minimum GPA of 2.75; for doctorate, GMAT. Additional exam requirements/recommendations for international students: Required—TOEFL. Electronic applications accepted. *Faculty research:* Decision support systems, individual and group behavior, operations research, techniques and strategy.

Duke University, The Fuqua School of Business, Cross Continent Executive MBA Program, Durham, NC 27708-0586. Offers business administration (MBA); energy and the environment (MBA); entrepreneurship and innovation (MBA); finance (MBA); health sector management (Certificate); marketing (MBA); strategy (MBA). *Faculty:* 91 full-time (15 women), 53 part-time/adjunct (9 women). *Students:* 121 full-time (34 women); includes 23 minority (3 Black or African American, non-Hispanic/Latino; 15 Asian, non-Hispanic/Latino; 4 Hispanic/Latino; 1 Native Hawaiian or other Pacific Islander, non-Hispanic/Latino), 31 international. Average age 30. In 2013, 147 master's awarded. *Degree requirements:* For master's, one foreign language. *Entrance requirements:* For master's, GMAT or GRE, transcripts, essays, resume, recommendation letters, interview. Additional exam requirements/recommendations for international students: Required—TOEFL, IELTS, PTE. *Application deadline:* For fall admission, 10/16 for domestic students, 10/6 for international students; for winter admission, 2/12 for domestic and international students; for spring admission, 5/6 for domestic and international students; for summer admission, 6/4 for domestic students. Application fee: $225. Electronic applications accepted. *Financial support:* In 2013–14, 16 students received support. Institutionally sponsored loans and scholarships/grants available. Financial award applicants required to submit FAFSA. *Unit head:* John Gallagher, Associate Dean for Executive MBA Programs, 919-660-7641, E-mail: johng@duke.edu. *Application contact:* Liz Riley Hargrove, Associate Dean for Admissions, 919-660-1956, Fax: 919-681-8026, E-mail: admissions-info@fuqua.duke.edu.
Website: http://www.fuqua.duke.edu/programs/duke_mba/cross_continent/.

Duke University, The Fuqua School of Business, Daytime MBA Program, Durham, NC 27708-0586. Offers academic excellence in finance (Certificate); business administration (MBA); decision sciences (MBA); energy and environment (MBA); energy finance (MBA); entrepreneurship and innovation (MBA); finance (MBA); financial analysis (MBA); health sector management (Certificate); leadership and ethics (MBA); management (MBA); marketing (MBA); operations management (MBA); social entrepreneurship (MBA); strategy (MBA). *Faculty:* 91 full-time (15 women), 53 part-time/adjunct (9 women). *Students:* 862 full-time (283 women); includes 179 minority (34 Black or African American, non-Hispanic/Latino; 1 American Indian or Alaska Native, non-Hispanic/Latino; 92 Asian, non-Hispanic/Latino; 42 Hispanic/Latino; 2 Native Hawaiian or other Pacific Islander, non-Hispanic/Latino; 8 Two or more races, non-Hispanic/Latino), 342 international. Average age 29. In 2013, 437 master's awarded. *Entrance requirements:* For master's, GMAT or GRE, transcripts, essays, resume, recommendation letters, interview. Additional exam requirements/recommendations for international students: Required—TOEFL, IELTS, PTE. *Application deadline:* For fall admission, 9/18 for domestic and international students; for winter admission, 10/21 for domestic and international students; for spring admission, 1/6 for domestic and international students; for summer admission, 3/20 for domestic and international students. Application fee: $225. Electronic applications accepted. *Financial support:* In 2013–14, 331 students received support. Institutionally sponsored loans and scholarships/grants available. Financial award applicants required to submit FAFSA. *Unit head:* Russ Morgan, Associate Dean for the Daytime MBA Program, 919-660-2931, Fax: 919-684-8742, E-mail: ruskin.morgan@duke.edu. *Application contact:* Liz Riley Hargrove, Associate Dean of Admissions, 919-660-7705, Fax: 919-681-8026, E-mail: liz.riley@duke.edu.
Website: http://www.fuqua.duke.edu/daytime-mba/.

Duke University, The Fuqua School of Business, Global Executive MBA Program, Durham, NC 27708-0586. Offers business administration (MBA); energy and the environment (MBA); entrepreneurship and innovation (MBA); finance (MBA); health sector management (Certificate); marketing (MBA); strategy (MBA). *Faculty:* 91 full-time (15 women), 53 part-time/adjunct (9 women). *Students:* 49 full-time (7 women); includes 7 minority (1 Black or African American, non-Hispanic/Latino; 3 Asian, non-Hispanic/Latino; 3 Hispanic/Latino), 17 international. Average age 39. In 2013, 51 master's awarded. *Entrance requirements:* For master's, transcripts, essays, resume, recommendation letters, interview. Additional exam requirements/recommendations for international students: Required—TOEFL, IELTS, PTE. *Application deadline:* For fall admission, 9/4 for domestic and international students; for winter admission, 10/16 for domestic and international students; for spring admission, 12/5 for domestic and international students; for summer admission, 1/13 for domestic and international students. Application fee: $225. *Financial support:* In 2013–14, 8 students received support. Institutionally sponsored loans and scholarships/grants available. Financial award applicants required to submit FAFSA. *Unit head:* John Gallagher, Associate Dean for Executive MBA Programs, 919-660-7728, E-mail: johng@duke.edu. *Application contact:* Liz Riley Hargrove, Director of EMBA Admissions, 919-660-7705, Fax: 919-681-8026, E-mail: admissions-info@fuqua.duke.edu.
Website: http://www.fuqua.duke.edu/programs/duke_mba/global-executive/.

Duke University, The Fuqua School of Business, PhD Program, Durham, NC 27708-0586. Offers accounting (PhD); decision sciences (PhD); finance (PhD); management and organizations (PhD); marketing (PhD); operations management (PhD); strategy (PhD). *Faculty:* 91 full-time (15 women). *Students:* 78 full-time (27 women); includes 4 minority (1 Black or African American, non-Hispanic/Latino; 3 Asian, non-Hispanic/Latino), 49 international. 589 applicants, 5% accepted, 16 enrolled. In 2013, 26 doctorates awarded. *Degree requirements:* For doctorate, thesis/dissertation, major field requirement (exam or major paper, depending upon the area). *Entrance requirements:* For doctorate, GMAT or GRE, transcripts, essays, recommendation letters, statement of purpose. Additional exam requirements/recommendations for international students: Required—TOEFL (minimum score 577 paper-based; 90 iBT), IELTS (minimum score 7). *Application deadline:* For fall admission, 12/8 priority date for domestic and international students. Application fee: $80. Electronic applications accepted. *Financial support:* In 2013–14, 70 fellowships with full tuition reimbursements (averaging $25,300 per year), 56 research assistantships with full tuition reimbursements (averaging $7,000 per year) were awarded; institutionally sponsored loans, scholarships/grants, and tuition waivers (full) also available. Financial award applicants required to submit FAFSA. *Unit head:* William Boulding, Dean, 919-660-7822, Fax: 919-684-8742, E-mail: bb1@duke.edu. *Application contact:* Dr. James R. Bettman, Director of Graduate Studies, 919-660-7851, Fax: 919-681-6245, E-mail: jrb12@mail.duke.edu.

Duke University, The Fuqua School of Business, Weekend Executive MBA Program, Durham, NC 27708-0586. Offers business administration (MBA); energy and environment (MBA); entrepreneurship and innovation (MBA); finance (MBA); health sector management (Certificate); marketing (MBA); strategy (MBA). *Faculty:* 91 full-time (15 women), 53 part-time/adjunct (9 women). *Students:* 93 full-time (14 women); includes 33 minority (5 Black or African American, non-Hispanic/Latino; 24 Asian, non-Hispanic/Latino; 3 Hispanic/Latino; 1 Two or more races, non-Hispanic/Latino), 15 international. Average age 36. In 2013, 103 master's awarded. *Degree requirements:* For master's, one foreign language. *Entrance requirements:* For master's, GMAT (preferred) or GRE, transcripts, essays, resume, recommendation letters, interview. Additional exam requirements/recommendations for international students: Required—TOEFL, IELTS, PTE. *Application deadline:* For fall admission, 9/4 for domestic and international students; for winter admission, 10/16 for domestic and international students; for spring admission, 2/12 for domestic and international students; for summer admission, 4/2 for domestic and international students. Application fee: $225. Electronic applications accepted. *Financial support:* In 2013–14, 14 students received support. Institutionally sponsored loans and scholarships/grants available. Financial award applicants required to submit FAFSA. *Unit head:* John Gallagher, Associate Dean for Executive MBA Programs, 919-660-7728, E-mail: johng@duke.edu. *Application contact:* Liz Riley Hargrove, Director of EMBA Admissions, 919-660-7705, Fax: 919-681-8026, E-mail: admissions-info@fuqua.duke.edu.
Website: http://www.fuqua.duke.edu/programs/duke_mba/weekend_executive/.

Duquesne University, John F. Donahue Graduate School of Business, Pittsburgh, PA 15282-0001. Offers accounting (M Acc); finance (MBA); information systems management (MBA, MSISM); management (MBA); marketing (MBA); supply chain management (MBA); sustainability (MBA); JD/MBA; MBA/M Acc; MBA/MA; MBA/MES; MBA/MHMS; MBA/MSN; MSISM/MBA; Pharm D/MBA. *Accreditation:* AACSB. Part-time and evening/weekend programs available. *Faculty:* 58 full-time (17 women), 40 part-time/adjunct (8 women). *Students:* 117 full-time (59 women), 147 part-time (54 women); includes 14 minority (7 Black or African American, non-Hispanic/Latino; 1 Asian, non-Hispanic/Latino; 6 Hispanic/Latino), 53 international. Average age 27. 418 applicants, 46% accepted, 109 enrolled. In 2013, 133 master's awarded. *Entrance requirements:* For master's, GMAT, undergraduate transcripts, 2 letters of recommendation, current resume, personal statement. Additional exam requirements/recommendations for international students: Required—TOEFL (minimum score 577 paper-based; 90 iBT), IELTS (minimum score 7). *Application deadline:* For fall admission, 7/1 priority date for domestic students, 6/1 for international students; for spring admission, 11/1 for domestic and international students. Applications are processed on a rolling basis. Application fee: $0. Electronic applications accepted. *Expenses: Tuition:* Full-time $18,162; part-time $1009 per credit. *Required fees:* $1728; $96 per credit. Tuition and fees vary according to program. *Financial support:* In 2013–14, 39 students received support, including 6 fellowships with partial tuition reimbursements available (averaging $4,541 per year), 33 research assistantships with partial tuition reimbursements available (averaging $9,081 per year); career-related internships or fieldwork, scholarships/grants, and unspecified assistantships also available. Support available to part-time students. Financial award application deadline: 7/1; financial award applicants required to submit FAFSA. *Faculty research:* International business, investment management, business ethics, technology management, supply chain management, business strategy, finance. *Unit head:* Thomas J. Nist, Director of Graduate Programs, 412-396-6276, Fax: 412-396-1726, E-mail: nist@duq.edu. *Application contact:* Maria W. DeCrosta, Enrollment Manager, 412-396-5529, Fax: 412-396-1726, E-mail: decrostam@duq.edu.
Website: http://www.duq.edu/business/grad.

Eastern Michigan University, Graduate School, Academic Affairs Division, Ypsilanti, MI 48197. Offers individualized studies (MA, MS); integrated marketing communications (MS). *Students:* 1 full-time (0 women), 18 part-time (13 women); includes 12 minority (11 Black or African American, non-Hispanic/Latino; 1 Hispanic/Latino), 2 international. Average age 39. 226 applicants, 92% accepted, 43 enrolled. In 2013, 7 master's awarded. *Entrance requirements:* Additional exam requirements/recommendations for international students: Required—TOEFL. *Expenses:* Tuition, state resident: full-time $12,300; part-time $466 per credit hour. Tuition, nonresident: full-time $23,159; part-time $918 per credit hour. *Required fees:* $71 per credit hour. $46 per semester. One-time fee: $100. Tuition and fees vary according to course level and degree level. *Unit head:* Dr. Jeffrey Kentor, Dean, 734-487-0042, Fax: 734-487-0050, E-mail: jkentor@emich.edu. *Application contact:* Graduate Admissions, 734-487-2400, Fax: 734-487-6559, E-mail: graduate.admissions@emich.edu.

Eastern Michigan University, Graduate School, College of Business, Department of Marketing, Program in Integrated Marketing Communications, Ypsilanti, MI 48197. Offers MS. *Students:* 25 full-time (20 women), 41 part-time (34 women); includes 16 minority (9 Black or African American, non-Hispanic/Latino; 1 Asian, non-Hispanic/Latino; 1 Hispanic/Latino; 5 Two or more races, non-Hispanic/Latino), 1 international.

Average age 34. 41 applicants, 71% accepted, 16 enrolled. In 2013, 28 master's awarded. *Expenses:* Tuition, state resident: full-time $12,300; part-time $466 per credit hour. Tuition, nonresident: full-time $23,159; part-time $918 per credit hour. *Required fees:* $71 per credit hour. $46 per semester. One-time fee: $100. Tuition and fees vary according to course level and degree level. *Unit head:* Dr. Paul Chao, Department Head, 734-487-3323, Fax: 734-487-7099, E-mail: pchao@emich.edu. *Application contact:* K. Michelle Henry, Director, Academic Services, 734-487-4444, Fax: 734-478-1316, E-mail: cob.graduate@emich.edu.

Eastern Michigan University, Graduate School, College of Business, Programs in Business Administration, Ypsilanti, MI 48197. Offers business administration (MBA, Graduate Certificate); computer information systems (Graduate Certificate); e-business (MBA, Graduate Certificate); enterprise business intelligence (MBA); entrepreneurship (MBA, Graduate Certificate); finance (MBA, Graduate Certificate); human resources (MBA); human resources management (Graduate Certificate); information systems (MBA); internal auditing (MBA); international business (MBA, Graduate Certificate); marketing management (Graduate Certificate); nonprofit management (MBA); organizational development (Graduate Certificate); supply chain management (MBA, Graduate Certificate). *Accreditation:* AACSB. Part-time programs available. Postbaccalaureate distance learning degree programs offered (no on-campus study). *Students:* 74 full-time (28 women), 342 part-time (183 women); includes 122 minority (84 Black or African American, non-Hispanic/Latino; 2 American Indian or Alaska Native, non-Hispanic/Latino; 19 Asian, non-Hispanic/Latino; 7 Hispanic/Latino; 10 Two or more races, non-Hispanic/Latino), 38 international. Average age 33. 305 applicants, 72% accepted, 131 enrolled. In 2013, 69 master's, 57 other advanced degrees awarded. *Entrance requirements:* For master's, GMAT (minimum score 450), minimum cumulative undergraduate GPA of 2.75. Additional exam requirements/recommendations for international students: Required—TOEFL. *Application deadline:* For fall admission, 5/15 for domestic students, 5/1 for international students; for winter admission, 10/15 for domestic students, 10/1 for international students; for spring admission, 3/15 for domestic students, 3/1 for international students. Applications are processed on a rolling basis. Application fee: $35. *Expenses:* Tuition, state resident: full-time $12,300; part-time $466 per credit hour. Tuition, nonresident: full-time $23,159; part-time $918 per credit hour. *Required fees:* $71 per credit hour. $46 per semester. One-time fee: $100. Tuition and fees vary according to course level and degree level. *Financial support:* Fellowships, research assistantships with full tuition reimbursements, teaching assistantships with full tuition reimbursements, career-related internships or fieldwork, Federal Work-Study, institutionally sponsored loans, scholarships/grants, tuition waivers (partial), and unspecified assistantships available. Support available to part-time students. Financial award applicants required to submit FAFSA. *Unit head:* K. Michelle Henry, Director, Academic Services, 734-487-4444, Fax: 734-483-1316, E-mail: mhenry1@emich.edu. *Application contact:* Beste Windes, Advisor, 734-487-4444, Fax: 734-483-1316, E-mail: bwindes@emich.edu.
Website: http://www.emich.edu/public/cob/gr/grad.html.

Edgewood College, Program in Business, Madison, WI 53711-1997. Offers accountancy (MS); accounting (MBA); business administration (MBA); finance (MBA); management (MBA); marketing (MBA); organization development (MS); sustainability leadership (MBA). *Accreditation:* ACBSP. Part-time and evening/weekend programs available. *Students:* 24 full-time (8 women), 136 part-time (82 women); includes 18 minority (5 Black or African American, non-Hispanic/Latino; 1 American Indian or Alaska Native, non-Hispanic/Latino; 4 Asian, non-Hispanic/Latino; 4 Hispanic/Latino; 4 Two or more races, non-Hispanic/Latino), 10 international. Average age 33. In 2013, 55 master's awarded. *Entrance requirements:* For master's, GMAT (minimum score 430), minimum GPA of 2.75, 2 letters of recommendation. Additional exam requirements/recommendations for international students: Required—TOEFL. *Application deadline:* For fall admission, 8/15 for domestic students, 5/1 for international students; for spring admission, 1/8 for domestic students, 11/1 for international students. Applications are processed on a rolling basis. Application fee: $30. Electronic applications accepted. *Financial support:* Career-related internships or fieldwork and scholarships/grants available. *Unit head:* Martin Preizler, Dean, 608-663-2898, Fax: 608-663-3291, E-mail: martinpreizler@edgewood.edu. *Application contact:* Joann Eastman, Admissions Counselor, 608-663-3250, Fax: 608-663-2214, E-mail: gps@edgewood.edu.
Website: http://www.edgewood.edu/Academics/School-of-Business.

Emerson College, Graduate Studies, School of Communication, Department of Marketing Communication, Program in Integrated Marketing Communication, Boston, MA 02116-4624. Offers MA. Part-time and evening/weekend programs available. *Faculty:* 16 full-time (7 women), 7 part-time/adjunct (2 women). *Students:* 131 full-time (99 women), 22 part-time (18 women); includes 9 minority (4 Black or African American, non-Hispanic/Latino; 1 Asian, non-Hispanic/Latino; 4 Hispanic/Latino), 90 international. Average age 24. 263 applicants, 72% accepted, 53 enrolled. In 2013, 68 master's awarded. *Entrance requirements:* For master's, GMAT or GRE General Test. Additional exam requirements/recommendations for international students: Required—TOEFL (minimum score 550 paper-based; 80 iBT), IELTS (minimum score 6.5). *Application deadline:* For fall admission, 6/1 priority date for domestic students, 5/1 priority date for international students; for spring admission, 11/1 priority date for domestic students. Applications are processed on a rolling basis. Application fee: $60 ($75 for international students). Electronic applications accepted. *Expenses: Tuition:* Part-time $1145 per credit. *Financial support:* In 2013–14, 17 students received support, including 17 fellowships with partial tuition reimbursements available (averaging $9,300 per year), 16 research assistantships with partial tuition reimbursements available (averaging $10,000 per year); Federal Work-Study, scholarships/grants, and unspecified assistantships also available. Financial award application deadline: 3/1; financial award applicants required to submit FAFSA. *Faculty research:* Marketing, international business. *Unit head:* Prof. Lu An Reeb, Graduate Program Director, 617-824-8492, E-mail: cathy_waters@emerson.edu. *Application contact:* Sean Ganas, Office of Graduate Admission, 617-824-8610, Fax: 617-824-8614, E-mail: gradapp@emerson.edu.
Website: http://www.emerson.edu/graduate_admission.

Emory University, Goizueta Business School, Doctoral Program in Business, Atlanta, GA 30322-1100. Offers accounting (PhD); finance (PhD); information systems (PhD); marketing (PhD); organization and management (PhD). *Faculty:* 53 full-time (12 women). *Students:* 41 full-time (15 women); includes 28 minority (all Asian, non-Hispanic/Latino). Average age 29. 195 applicants, 9% accepted, 9 enrolled. In 2013, 1 doctorate awarded. *Degree requirements:* For doctorate, comprehensive exam, thesis/dissertation. *Entrance requirements:* For doctorate, GMAT (strongly preferred) or GRE. Additional exam requirements/recommendations for international students: Required—TOEFL. *Application deadline:* For fall admission, 1/3 priority date for domestic and international students. Application fee: $75. Electronic applications accepted. *Financial support:* In 2013–14, 35 students received support, including 3 fellowships (averaging $1,166 per year). *Unit head:* Dr. Anand Swaminathan, Associate Dean, Doctoral Program, 404-727-2306, Fax: 404-727-5337, E-mail: anand.swaminathan@emory.edu. *Application contact:* Allison Gilmore, Director of Admissions and Student Services, 404-727-6353, Fax: 404-727-5337, E-mail: phd@bus.emory.edu.

Fairfield University, Charles F. Dolan School of Business, Fairfield, CT 06824-5195. Offers accounting (MBA, MS, CAS); accounting information systems (MBA, CAS); entrepreneurship (MBA, CAS); finance (MBA, MS, CAS); general management (MBA, CAS); human resource management (MBA, CAS); information systems and operations (MBA); information systems and operations management (CAS); marketing (MBA, CAS); taxation (MBA, CAS). *Accreditation:* AACSB. Part-time and evening/weekend programs available. *Faculty:* 18 full-time (9 women), 15 part-time/adjunct (4 women). *Students:* 94 full-time (45 women), 72 part-time (26 women); includes 49 minority (7 Black or African American, non-Hispanic/Latino; 33 Asian, non-Hispanic/Latino; 8 Hispanic/Latino; 1 Two or more races, non-Hispanic/Latino), 9 international. Average age 29. 116 applicants, 43% accepted, 26 enrolled. In 2013, 100 master's awarded. *Degree requirements:* For master's, capstone course. *Entrance requirements:* For master's, GMAT (minimum score 500), 2 letters of reference, resume, minimum GPA of 3.0. Additional exam requirements/recommendations for international students: Required—TOEFL (minimum score 550 paper-based; 80 iBT) or IELTS (minimum score 6.5). *Application deadline:* For fall admission, 5/15 for international students; for spring admission, 10/15 for international students. Applications are processed on a rolling basis. Application fee: $60. Electronic applications accepted. *Expenses:* Contact institution. *Financial support:* In 2013–14, 28 students received support. Scholarships/grants, unspecified assistantships, and merit-based one-time entrance scholarships available. Financial award applicants required to submit FAFSA. *Faculty research:* International finance, leadership and careers, ethics in accounting, emotions in consumer behavior, supply chain analysis, organizational leadership attributes, emotions in the workplace, real estate finance, effect of social media on stock prices. *Unit head:* Dr. Donald Gibson, Dean, 203-254-4070, Fax: 203-254-4105, E-mail: dgibson@fairfield.edu. *Application contact:* Marianne Gumpper, Director of Graduate and Continuing Studies Admission, 203-254-4184, Fax: 203-254-4073, E-mail: gradadmis@fairfield.edu.
Website: http://fairfield.edu/mba.

Fairleigh Dickinson University, College at Florham, Silberman College of Business, Departments of Management, Marketing, and Entrepreneurial Studies, Program in Marketing, Madison, NJ 07940-1099. Offers MBA, Certificate. *Entrance requirements:* For master's, GMAT.

Fairleigh Dickinson University, Metropolitan Campus, Silberman College of Business, Departments of Management, Marketing, and Entrepreneurial Studies, Program in Marketing, Teaneck, NJ 07666-1914. Offers MBA, Certificate.

Fashion Institute of Technology, School of Graduate Studies, Program in Cosmetics and Fragrance Marketing and Management, New York, NY 10001-5992. Offers MPS. *Degree requirements:* For master's, capstone seminar. *Entrance requirements:* Additional exam requirements/recommendations for international students: Required—TOEFL (minimum score 550 paper-based). Electronic applications accepted.
See Display on next page and Close-Up on page 535.

Florida Agricultural and Mechanical University, Division of Graduate Studies, Research, and Continuing Education, School of Business and Industry, Tallahassee, FL 32307-3200. Offers accounting (MBA); finance (MBA); management information systems (MBA); marketing (MBA). *Accreditation:* ACBSP. *Degree requirements:* For master's, residency. *Entrance requirements:* For master's, GMAT, minimum GPA of 3.0.

Florida Atlantic University, College of Business, Department of Marketing, Boca Raton, FL 33431-0991. Offers PhD. *Expenses:* Tuition, state resident: full-time $6660; part-time $370 per credit hour. Tuition, nonresident: full-time $18,450; part-time $1025 per credit hour. Tuition and fees vary according to course load. *Unit head:* Dr. Daniel Gropper, Dean, 561-297-3629, Fax: 561-297-3686, E-mail: vhale4@fau.edu. *Application contact:* Dr. Marcy Krugel, Graduate Adviser, 561-297-3940, Fax: 561-297-0801, E-mail: krugel@fau.edu.

Florida Institute of Technology, Graduate Programs, Nathan M. Bisk College of Business, Online Programs, Melbourne, FL 32901-6975. Offers accounting (MBA); accounting and finance (MBA); business administration (MBA); finance (MBA); healthcare management (MBA); information assurance and cybersecurity (MS); information technology (MS); information technology cybersecurity (MS); information technology management (MBA); international business (MBA); Internet marketing (MBA); management (MBA); marketing (MBA); project management (MBA); supply chain management (MS). Part-time and evening/weekend programs available. Postbaccalaureate distance learning degree programs offered (no on-campus study). *Faculty:* 3 full-time (1 woman), 41 part-time/adjunct (13 women). *Students:* 6 full-time (1 woman), 1,121 part-time (530 women); includes 424 minority (276 Black or African American, non-Hispanic/Latino; 10 American Indian or Alaska Native, non-Hispanic/Latino; 45 Asian, non-Hispanic/Latino; 88 Hispanic/Latino; 5 Native Hawaiian or other Pacific Islander, non-Hispanic/Latino), 32 international. Average age 36. 348 applicants, 42% accepted, 146 enrolled. In 2013, 475 master's awarded. *Entrance requirements:* For master's, GMAT or resume showing 8 years of supervised experience, 2 letters of recommendation, resume, competency in math past college algebra. Additional exam requirements/recommendations for international students: Required—TOEFL (minimum score 550 paper-based; 79 iBT). *Application deadline:* For fall admission, 4/1 for international students; for spring admission, 9/30 for international students. Applications are processed on a rolling basis. Electronic applications accepted. *Expenses:* Contact institution. *Financial support:* Available to part-time students. Application deadline: 3/1; applicants required to submit FAFSA. *Unit head:* Brian Ehrlich, Associate Vice President/Director of Online Learning, 321-674-8202, E-mail: behrlich@fit.edu. *Application contact:* Carolyn Farrior, Director of Graduate Admissions, Online Learning and Off-Campus Programs, 321-674-7118.
Website: http://online.fit.edu.

Florida National University, Program in Business Administration, Hialeah, FL 33012. Offers finance (MBA); general management (MBA); marketing (MBA). Postbaccalaureate distance learning degree programs offered (no on-campus study). *Degree requirements:* For master's, capstone.

Florida State University, The Graduate School, College of Business, Tallahassee, FL 32306-1110. Offers accounting (M Acc), including accounting information services, assurance services, corporate accounting, taxation; business administration (MBA, PhD), including accounting (PhD), finance (PhD), management information systems (PhD), marketing (PhD), organizational behavior and human resources (PhD), risk management and insurance (PhD), strategic management (PhD); finance (MS); insurance (MSM); management information systems (MS); marketing (MS); JD/MBA; MSW/MBA. *Accreditation:* AACSB. Part-time programs available. Postbaccalaureate distance learning degree programs offered (no on-campus study). *Faculty:* 102 full-time (31 women), 5 part-time/adjunct (0 women). *Students:* 280 full-time (117 women), 278 part-time (88 women); includes 127 minority (26 Black or African American, non-Hispanic/Latino; 7 American Indian or Alaska Native, non-Hispanic/Latino; 44 Asian, non-Hispanic/Latino; 50 Hispanic/Latino). Average age 30. 630 applicants, 28% accepted, 103 enrolled. In 2013, 265 master's, 11 doctorates awarded. Terminal master's awarded for partial completion of doctoral program. *Degree requirements:* For doctorate, comprehensive exam, thesis/dissertation. *Entrance requirements:* For master's, GMAT, work experience (MBA, MS), minimum GPA of 3.0, letters of recommendation; for doctorate, GMAT, minimum graduate GPA of 3.5, letters of recommendation. Additional exam requirements/recommendations for international

students: Required—TOEFL (minimum score 600 paper-based; 100 iBT); Recommended—IELTS (minimum score 6.5). *Application deadline:* For fall admission, 6/1 for domestic students, 5/1 for international students; for spring admission, 10/1 for domestic students, 9/1 for international students. Applications are processed on a rolling basis. Application fee: $30. Electronic applications accepted. *Expenses:* Tuition, state resident: part-time $403.51 per credit hour. Tuition, nonresident: part-time $1004.85 per credit hour. *Required fees:* $75.81 per credit hour. One-time fee: $20 part-time. Tuition and fees vary according to course load, campus/location and student level. *Financial support:* In 2013–14, 92 students received support, including 10 fellowships with full tuition reimbursements available (averaging $1,500 per year), 20 research assistantships with full tuition reimbursements available (averaging $20,000 per year), 35 teaching assistantships with full tuition reimbursements available (averaging $20,000 per year); career-related internships or fieldwork, scholarships/grants, health care benefits, and unspecified assistantships also available. Financial award application deadline: 1/1. *Unit head:* Dr. Caryn Beck-Dudley, Dean, 850-644-3090, Fax: 850-644-0915. *Application contact:* Lisa Beverly, Director, Graduate Programs Admissions, 850-644-6458, Fax: 850-644-0588, E-mail: lbeverly@cob.fsu.edu. Website: http://www.cob.fsu.edu/.

Florida State University, The Graduate School, College of Communication and Information, School of Communication, Tallahassee, FL 32306. Offers communication theory and research (PhD); integrated marketing communication (MA, MS); media and communication studies (MA, MS). Part-time programs available. *Faculty:* 23 full-time (9 women), 17 part-time/adjunct (11 women). *Students:* 134 full-time (97 women), 42 part-time (28 women); includes 86 minority (17 Black or African American, non-Hispanic/Latino; 49 Asian, non-Hispanic/Latino; 17 Hispanic/Latino; 3 Two or more races, non-Hispanic/Latino). Average age 24. 216 applicants, 44% accepted, 56 enrolled. In 2013, 69 master's, 4 doctorates awarded. *Degree requirements:* For master's, thesis (for some programs); for doctorate, comprehensive exam, thesis/dissertation. *Entrance requirements:* For master's, GRE General Test, minimum GPA of 3.0; for doctorate, GRE General Test, minimum GPA of 3.3 in graduate course work. Additional exam requirements/recommendations for international students: Required—TOEFL (minimum score 600 paper-based; 100 iBT), IELTS (minimum score 7). *Application deadline:* For fall admission, 7/1 priority date for domestic students, 5/1 priority date for international students; for spring admission, 11/1 priority date for domestic and international students; for summer admission, 3/1 priority date for domestic and international students. Applications are processed on a rolling basis. Application fee: $30. Electronic applications accepted. *Expenses:* Tuition, state resident: part-time $403.51 per credit hour. Tuition, nonresident: part-time $1004.85 per credit hour. *Required fees:* $75.81 per credit hour. One-time fee: $20 part-time. Tuition and fees vary according to course load, campus/location and student level. *Financial support:* In 2013–14, 87 students received support, including 3 fellowships (averaging $7,779 per year), 13 research assistantships with full tuition reimbursements available (averaging $7,779 per year), 71 teaching assistantships with full tuition reimbursements available (averaging $7,779 per year); career-related internships or fieldwork, Federal Work-Study, institutionally sponsored loans, scholarships/grants, tuition waivers (partial), and unspecified assistantships also available. Support available to part-time students. Financial award application deadline: 2/1; financial award applicants required to submit FAFSA. *Faculty research:* Communication technology and policy, marketing communication, communication content and effect, new communication/information technologies. *Total annual research expenditures:* $19,001. *Unit head:* Dr. Ulla Sypher, Director, 850-644-1809, Fax: 850-644-8642, E-mail: ulla.sypher@cci.fsu.edu. *Application contact:* Natashia Hinson-Turner, Graduate Coordinator, 850-644-8746, Fax: 850-644-8642, E-mail: natashia.turner@cci.fsu.edu. Website: http://www.cci.fsu.edu.

Fordham University, Graduate School of Business, New York, NY 10023. Offers accounting (MBA); communications and media management (MBA); executive business administration (EMBA); finance (MBA, MS); information systems (MBA, MS); management systems (MBA); marketing (MBA); media management (MS); taxation (MS); taxation and accounting (MTA); JD/MBA; MBA/MIM; MS/MBA. MBA/MIM offered jointly with Thunderbird School of Global Management. *Accreditation:* AACSB. Part-time and evening/weekend programs available. *Entrance requirements:* For master's, GMAT, 2 letters of recommendation, resume. Additional exam requirements/recommendations for international students: Required—TOEFL (minimum score 600 paper-based; 100 iBT). Electronic applications accepted. *Expenses:* Contact institution.

Franklin University, Marketing and Communication Program, Columbus, OH 43215-5399. Offers MS. Part-time and evening/weekend programs available. *Entrance requirements:* For master's, minimum undergraduate GPA of 2.75. Additional exam requirements/recommendations for international students: Required—TOEFL (minimum score 550 paper-based). Electronic applications accepted.

Full Sail University, Internet Marketing Master of Science Program - Online, Winter Park, FL 32792-7437. Offers MS. Postbaccalaureate distance learning degree programs offered.

Gannon University, School of Graduate Studies, College of Engineering and Business, Dahlkemper School of Business, Program in Business Administration, Erie, PA 16541-0001. Offers business administration (MBA); finance (MBA); human resources management (MBA); marketing (MBA). *Accreditation:* ACBSP. Part-time and evening/weekend programs available. Postbaccalaureate distance learning degree programs offered (no on-campus study). *Students:* 44 full-time (20 women), 87 part-time (30 women); includes 7 minority (4 Black or African American, non-Hispanic/Latino; 1 Asian, non-Hispanic/Latino; 2 Hispanic/Latino), 22 international. Average age 28. 279 applicants, 84% accepted, 59 enrolled. In 2013, 40 master's awarded. *Degree requirements:* For master's, comprehensive exam, thesis. *Entrance requirements:* For master's, GMAT, resume, transcripts, 3 letters of recommendation. Additional exam requirements/recommendations for international students: Required—TOEFL (minimum score 79 iBT). *Application deadline:* Applications are processed on a rolling basis. Application fee: $25. Electronic applications accepted. *Expenses:* Tuition: Full-time $15,930; part-time $885 per credit. *Required fees:* $430; $18 per credit. Tuition and fees vary according to course load, degree level and program. *Financial support:* Administrative assistantships available. Financial award application deadline: 7/1; financial award applicants required to submit FAFSA. *Unit head:* Dr. Donna Mottilla, Director, 814-871-7780, E-mail: mottilla001@gannon.edu. *Application contact:* Kara Morgan, Director of Graduate Admissions, 814-871-5831, Fax: 814-871-5827, E-mail: graduate@gannon.edu.

Geneva College, Program in Business Administration, Beaver Falls, PA 15010-3599. Offers business administration (MBA); finance (MBA); marketing (MBA); operations (MBA). *Accreditation:* ACBSP. Part-time and evening/weekend programs available. *Faculty:* 5 full-time (1 woman), 1 part-time/adjunct (0 women). *Students:* 1 (woman) full-time, 19 part-time (8 women); includes 3 minority (1 Black or African American, non-Hispanic/Latino; 2 Asian, non-Hispanic/Latino). Average age 33. 9 applicants, 100% accepted, 6 enrolled. In 2013, 9 master's awarded. *Degree requirements:* For master's, 36 credit hours of course work (30 of which are required of all students). *Entrance requirements:* For master's, GMAT (if college GPA less than 2.5), undergraduate transcript, 2 letters of recommendation, resume, goals statement. Additional exam requirements/recommendations for international students: Required—TOEFL. *Application deadline:* For fall admission, 3/1 priority date for domestic students; for spring admission, 11/1 priority date for domestic students. Applications are processed on a rolling basis. Electronic applications accepted. *Expenses:* Contact institution.

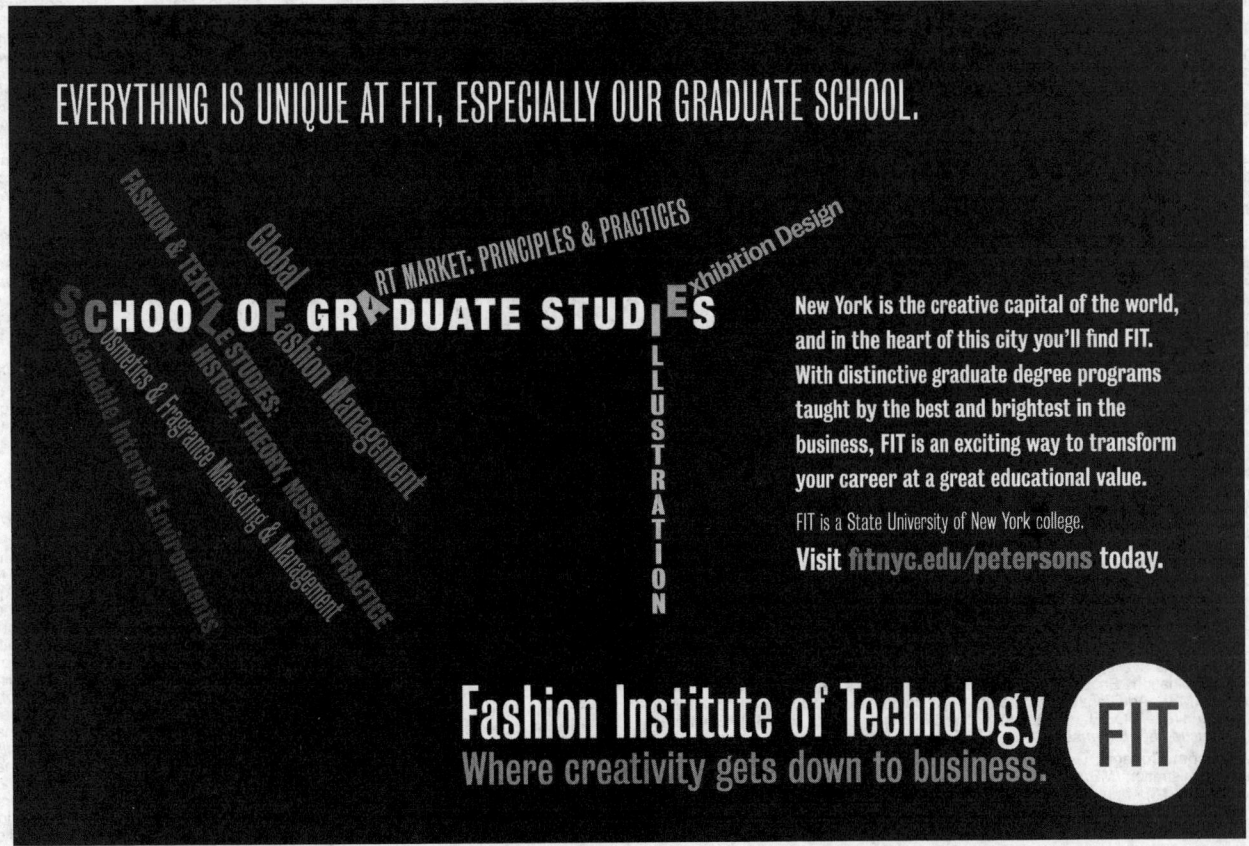

Marketing

Financial support: In 2013–14, 1 student received support. Scholarships/grants available. Financial award application deadline: 8/1; financial award applicants required to submit FAFSA. *Unit head:* Dr. Gary Vander Plaats, Director of the MBA Program, 724-847-6619, E-mail: gpvander@geneva.edu. *Application contact:* Marina Frazier, Director of Graduate Enrollment, 724-847-6697, E-mail: mba@geneva.edu.
Website: http://www.geneva.edu/page/masters_business.

George Fox University, College of Business, Newberg, OR 97132-2697. Offers finance (MBA); management (DBA); management and leadership (MBA); marketing (DBA); organizational strategy (MBA); strategic human resource management (MBA). MBA offered in Newberg, OR and in Portland, OR. *Accreditation:* ACBSP. Part-time and evening/weekend programs available. Postbaccalaureate distance learning degree programs offered (minimal on-campus study). *Faculty:* 8 full-time (2 women), 5 part-time/adjunct (2 women). *Students:* 31 full-time (15 women), 194 part-time (76 women); includes 21 minority (6 Black or African American, non-Hispanic/Latino; 4 American Indian or Alaska Native, non-Hispanic/Latino; 6 Asian, non-Hispanic/Latino; 3 Hispanic/Latino; 2 Two or more races, non-Hispanic/Latino), 15 international. Average age 39. 98 applicants, 79% accepted, 62 enrolled. In 2013, 98 master's, 2 doctorates awarded. *Degree requirements:* For master's, capstone project; for doctorate, credit-applied research project. *Entrance requirements:* For master's, resume (5 years of professional experience); 3 professional references; interview; financial e-learning course, official transcripts; for doctorate, GRE or GMAT, resume; personal mission statement; academic research writing sample; official transcript from each college/university attended; three professional references. Additional exam requirements/recommendations for international students: Required—TOEFL (minimum score 577 paper-based; 90 iBT) or IELTS (minimum score 7). *Application deadline:* For fall admission, 8/1 for domestic and international students; for spring admission, 12/1 for domestic and international students. Applications are processed on a rolling basis. Application fee: $40. Electronic applications accepted. *Expenses:* Contact institution. *Financial support:* Applicants required to submit FAFSA. *Unit head:* Dr. Chris Meade, Professor/Dean, 800-631-0921. *Application contact:* Ty Sohlman, Admissions Counselor, 800-493-4937, Fax: 503-554-6111, E-mail: business@georgefox.edu.
Website: http://www.georgefox.edu/business/index.html.

The George Washington University, School of Business, Department of Marketing, Washington, DC 20052. Offers MBA, PhD. Part-time and evening/weekend programs available. *Degree requirements:* For doctorate, thesis/dissertation. *Entrance requirements:* For master's, GMAT; for doctorate, GMAT or GRE. Additional exam requirements/recommendations for international students: Required—TOEFL. *Faculty research:* Strategic marketing, marketing and public policy, marketing management.

Georgia Institute of Technology, Graduate Studies and Research, College of Management, Program in Business Administration, Atlanta, GA 30332-0001. Offers accounting (MBA); e-commerce (Certificate); engineering entrepreneurship (MBA); entrepreneurship (Certificate); finance (MBA); information technology management (MBA); international business (MBA, Certificate); management of technology (Certificate); marketing (MBA); operations management (MBA); organizational behavior (MBA); strategic management (MBA). *Accreditation:* AACSB.

Georgia Institute of Technology, Graduate Studies and Research, College of Management, Program in Management, Atlanta, GA 30332-0001. Offers accounting (PhD); finance (PhD); information technology management (PhD); marketing (PhD); operations management (PhD); organizational behavior (PhD); quantitative and computational finance (MS); strategic management (PhD). *Accreditation:* AACSB. *Degree requirements:* For doctorate, comprehensive exam, thesis/dissertation, oral exams. *Entrance requirements:* For master's and doctorate, GMAT. Additional exam requirements/recommendations for international students: Required—TOEFL. *Faculty research:* Management information systems, management of technology, international business, entrepreneurship, operations management.

Georgia State University, J. Mack Robinson College of Business, Department of Marketing, Atlanta, GA 30302-3083. Offers MBA, MS, PhD. Part-time and evening/weekend programs available. *Faculty:* 24 full-time (9 women). *Students:* 56 full-time (41 women), 6 part-time (5 women); includes 29 minority (20 Black or African American, non-Hispanic/Latino; 6 Asian, non-Hispanic/Latino; 2 Hispanic/Latino; 1 Two or more races, non-Hispanic/Latino), 16 international. Average age 31. 39 applicants, 8% accepted, 2 enrolled. In 2013, 36 master's, 3 doctorates awarded. *Degree requirements:* For doctorate, comprehensive exam, thesis/dissertation. *Entrance requirements:* For master's, GRE or GMAT, transcripts from all institutions attended, resume, essays; for doctorate, GRE or GMAT, three letters of recommendation, personal statement, transcripts from all institutions attended, resume. Additional exam requirements/recommendations for international students: Required—TOEFL (minimum score 610 paper-based; 101 iBT), IELTS (minimum score 7). *Application deadline:* For fall admission, 5/1 priority date for domestic students, 2/1 priority date for international students; for spring admission, 9/15 priority date for domestic students, 4/1 priority date for international students. Applications are processed on a rolling basis. Application fee: $50. Electronic applications accepted. *Expenses: Tuition, area resident:* Full-time $4176; part-time $348 per credit hour. Tuition, state resident: full-time $14,544; part-time $1212 per credit hour. Tuition, nonresident: full-time $14,544; part-time $1212 per credit hour. Tuition and fees vary according to course load and program. *Financial support:* Research assistantships, teaching assistantships, scholarships/grants, tuition waivers (partial), and unspecified assistantships available. *Faculty research:* Marketing strategy, market in science, brand and customer management, digital and social media marketing, global marketing. *Unit head:* Dr. Naveen Donthu, Professor/Chair of the Department of Marketing, 404-413-7650, Fax: 404-413-7699. *Application contact:* Toby McChesney, Assistant Dean for Graduate Recruiting and Student Services, 404-413-7167, Fax: 404-413-7162, E-mail: rcbgradadmissions@gsu.edu.
Website: http://robinson.gsu.edu/marketing/.

Golden Gate University, Ageno School of Business, San Francisco, CA 94105-2968. Offers accounting (MBA); business administration (EMBA, MBA, PMBA, DBA); finance (MBA, MS, Certificate); financial planning (MS, Certificate); healthcare information systems (Certificate); human resource management (MBA, MS); human resources management (Certificate); information systems (MS); information technology (MBA); information technology management (Certificate); integrated marketing and communications (MS, Certificate); international business (MBA); management (MBA); marketing (MBA, MS, Certificate); operations supply chain management (Certificate); psychology (MA, Certificate); public administration (EMPA); public relations (MS, Certificate); technical market analysis (Certificate); JD/MBA. Part-time and evening/weekend programs available. *Degree requirements:* For doctorate, thesis/dissertation, qualifying examination. *Entrance requirements:* For master's, GMAT (MBA), minimum GPA of 2.5 (MS). Additional exam requirements/recommendations for international students: Required—TOEFL (minimum score 550 paper-based; 79 iBT). Electronic applications accepted. *Expenses:* Contact institution.

Goldey-Beacom College, Graduate Program, Wilmington, DE 19808-1999. Offers business administration (MBA); finance (MS); financial management (MBA); health care management (MBA); human resource management (MBA); information technology (MBA); international business management (MBA); major finance (MBA); major taxation (MBA); management (MM); marketing management (MBA); taxation (MBA, MS). *Accreditation:* ACBSP. Part-time and evening/weekend programs available. *Entrance requirements:* For master's, GMAT, MAT, GRE, minimum GPA of 3.0. Additional exam requirements/recommendations for international students: Required—TOEFL (minimum score 65 iBT); Recommended—IELTS (minimum score 6). Electronic applications accepted.

Grand Canyon University, College of Business, Phoenix, AZ 85017-1097. Offers accounting (MBA); corporate business administration (MBA); disaster preparedness and crisis management (MBA); executive fire service leadership (MS); finance (MBA); general management (MBA); government and policy (MPA); health care management (MPA); health systems management (MBA); human resource management (MBA); innovation (MBA); leadership (MBA, MS); management of information system (MBA); marketing (MBA); project-based (MBA); six sigma (MBA); strategic human resource management (MBA). *Accreditation:* ACBSP. Part-time and evening/weekend programs available. Postbaccalaureate distance learning degree programs offered (no on-campus study). *Entrance requirements:* For master's, equivalent of two years full-time professional work experience. Additional exam requirements/recommendations for international students: Required—TOEFL (minimum score 575 paper-based; 90 iBT), IELTS (minimum score 7). Electronic applications accepted.

Harvard University, Harvard Business School, Doctoral Programs in Management, Boston, MA 02163. Offers accounting and management (DBA); business economics (PhD); health policy management (PhD); management (DBA); marketing (DBA); organizational behavior (PhD); science, technology and management (PhD); strategy (DBA); technology and operations management (DBA). *Degree requirements:* For doctorate, comprehensive exam (for some programs), thesis/dissertation. *Entrance requirements:* For doctorate, GRE General Test or GMAT. Additional exam requirements/recommendations for international students: Required—TOEFL. *Expenses: Tuition:* Full-time $38,888. *Required fees:* $958. Tuition and fees vary according to campus/location, program and student level.

Hawai`i Pacific University, College of Business Administration, Honolulu, HI 96813. Offers accounting/CPA (MBA); e-business (MBA); economics (MBA); finance (MBA); healthcare management (MBA); human resource management (MA, MBA); information systems (MBA, MSIS); international business (MBA); management (MBA); marketing (MBA); organizational change (MA, MBA); travel industry management (MBA). Part-time and evening/weekend programs available. *Faculty:* 22 full-time (9 women), 6 part-time/adjunct (0 women). *Students:* 232 full-time (100 women), 174 part-time (84 women); includes 241 minority (18 Black or African American, non-Hispanic/Latino; 112 Asian, non-Hispanic/Latino; 33 Hispanic/Latino; 11 Native Hawaiian or other Pacific Islander, non-Hispanic/Latino; 67 Two or more races, non-Hispanic/Latino). Average age 31. 240 applicants, 81% accepted, 102 enrolled. In 2013, 206 master's awarded. *Degree requirements:* For master's, thesis. *Entrance requirements:* For master's, GMAT. Additional exam requirements/recommendations for international students: Recommended—TOEFL (minimum score 550 paper-based; 80 iBT), TWE (minimum score 5). *Application deadline:* For fall admission, 2/15 priority date for domestic students; for spring admission, 10/15 priority date for domestic students. Applications are processed on a rolling basis. Application fee: $50. Electronic applications accepted. *Financial support:* In 2013–14, 90 students received support. Research assistantships, career-related internships or fieldwork, Federal Work-Study, scholarships/grants, tuition waivers, and unspecified assistantships available. Financial award application deadline: 3/1; financial award applicants required to submit FAFSA. *Faculty research:* Statistical control process as used by management, studies in comparative cross-cultural management styles, not-for-profit management. *Unit head:* Dr. Deborah Crown, Dean, 808-544-0275, Fax: 808-544-0283, E-mail: dcrown@hpu.edu. *Application contact:* Rumi Yoshida, Associate Director of Graduate Admissions, 808-543-8034, Fax: 808-544-0280, E-mail: grad@hpu.edu.
Website: http://www.hpu.edu/CBA/Graduate/index.html.

HEC Montreal, School of Business Administration, Master of Science Programs in Administration, Program in Marketing, Montréal, QC H3T 2A7, Canada. Offers M Sc. All courses are given in French. *Students:* 106 full-time (72 women), 28 part-time (22 women). 99 applicants, 66% accepted, 40 enrolled. In 2013, 48 master's awarded. *Degree requirements:* For master's, one foreign language, thesis. *Entrance requirements:* For master's, Test de francais international (TFI) with minimum score of 850 (for those who have never studied in French), BBA, undergraduate degree in another field, degree deemed equivalent by program director and minimum GPA of 3.0 on 4.3 scale. *Application deadline:* For fall admission, 3/15 for domestic and international students; for winter admission, 9/15 for domestic and international students. Application fee: $83 Canadian dollars. Electronic applications accepted. *Expenses: Tuition, area resident:* Part-time $74.14 per credit. Tuition, state resident: full-time $2669.04; part-time $201.83 per credit. Tuition, nonresident: full-time $7266; part-time $500.59 per credit. *International tuition:* $18,021.24 full-time. *Required fees:* $1529.70; $36.20 per credit. $65.50 per term. Tuition and fees vary according to degree level and program. *Financial support:* In 2013–14, 1,007 students received support. Research assistantships, teaching assistantships, and scholarships/grants available. Financial award application deadline: 9/2. *Unit head:* Dr. Anne Bourhis, Director, 514-340-6873, Fax: 514-340-6880, E-mail: anne.bourhis@hec.ca. *Application contact:* Marianne de Moura, Administrative Director, 514-340-7106, Fax: 514-340-6411, E-mail: marianne.de-moura@hec.ca.
Website: http://www.hec.ca/programmes_formations/msc/options/marketing/index.html.

Herzing University Online, Program in Business Administration, Milwaukee, WI 53203. Offers accounting (MBA); business administration (MBA); business management (MBA); healthcare management (MBA); human resources (MBA); marketing (MBA); project management (MBA); technology management (MBA). Postbaccalaureate distance learning degree programs offered (no on-campus study).

Hofstra University, Frank G. Zarb School of Business, Programs in Marketing and International Business, Hempstead, NY 11549. Offers business administration (MBA), including international business, marketing; international business (Advanced Certificate); marketing (MS, Advanced Certificate); marketing research (MS).

Holy Names University, Graduate Division, Department of Business, Oakland, CA 94619-1699. Offers energy and environment management (MBA); finance (MBA); management and leadership (MBA); marketing (MBA); sports management (MBA). Part-time and evening/weekend programs available. *Faculty:* 4 full-time, 12 part-time/adjunct. *Students:* 23 full-time (14 women), 20 part-time (12 women); includes 30 minority (19 Black or African American, non-Hispanic/Latino; 4 Asian, non-Hispanic/Latino; 7 Hispanic/Latino), 4 international. Average age 32. 35 applicants, 31% accepted, 7 enrolled. In 2013, 30 master's awarded. *Entrance requirements:* For master's, minimum undergraduate GPA of 2.6 overall, 3.0 in major; two recommendations (letter or form) from previous professors or current or previous work supervisors, 1-3 page personal statement, resume. Additional exam requirements/recommendations for international students: Required—TOEFL (minimum score 550 paper-based; 79 iBT). *Application deadline:* For fall admission, 8/1 priority date for domestic students, 7/15 for international students; for spring admission, 12/1 priority date for domestic students, 12/1 for international students; for summer admission, 5/1 priority date for domestic students, 5/1 for international students. Applications are processed on a rolling basis. Application fee: $65. Electronic applications accepted. Application fee is waived when completed online.

Expenses: Tuition: Part-time $866 per unit. *Financial support:* Career-related internships or fieldwork, Federal Work-Study, scholarships/grants, and unspecified assistantships available. Support available to part-time students. Financial award application deadline: 3/2; financial award applicants required to submit FAFSA. *Faculty research:* Business ethics, sustainable economics, accounting models, cross-cultural management, diversity in organizations. *Unit head:* Dr. Hector Saez, MBA Program Director, 510-436-1622, E-mail: saez@hnu.edu. *Application contact:* 800-430-1321, Fax: 510-436-1325, E-mail: graduateadmissions@hnu.edu. Website: http://www.hnu.edu.

Hood College, Graduate School, Department of Economics and Business Administration, Frederick, MD 21701-8575. Offers accounting (MBA); administration and management (MBA); finance (MBA); human resource management (MBA); information systems (MBA); marketing (MBA); public management (MBA). *Accreditation:* ACBSP. Part-time and evening/weekend programs available. *Faculty:* 6 full-time (2 women), 7 part-time/adjunct (1 woman). *Students:* 31 full-time (21 women), 131 part-time (66 women); includes 36 minority (18 Black or African American, non-Hispanic/Latino; 7 Asian, non-Hispanic/Latino; 8 Hispanic/Latino; 3 Two or more races, non-Hispanic/Latino), 12 international. Average age 31. 78 applicants, 56% accepted, 33 enrolled. In 2013, 35 master's awarded. *Degree requirements:* For master's, capstone/final research project. *Entrance requirements:* For master's, minimum GPA of 2.75, resume, letters of recommendation. Additional exam requirements/recommendations for international students: Required—TOEFL (minimum score 575 paper-based; 89 iBT), IELTS (minimum score 6.5). *Application deadline:* For fall admission, 7/15 priority date for domestic students, 7/15 for international students; for spring admission, 12/1 priority date for domestic students, 12/1 for international students. Applications are processed on a rolling basis. Application fee: $35. Electronic applications accepted. Application fee is waived when completed online. *Expenses: Tuition:* Part-time $405 per credit. *Required fees:* $100 per semester. *Financial support:* In 2013–14, 11 students received support. Tuition waivers (partial) and unspecified assistantships available. Financial award applicants required to submit FAFSA. *Faculty research:* Corporate strategy and sustainable competitive advantages, business ethics, entrepreneurship, investments management, economic development. *Unit head:* Dr. Anita Jose, Program Director, 301-696-3691, Fax: 301-696-3597, E-mail: jose@hood.edu. *Application contact:* Dr. Maria Green Cowles, Dean of Graduate School, 301-696-3811, Fax: 301-696-3597, E-mail: gofurther@hood.edu.

Hope International University, School of Graduate and Professional Studies, Program in Business Administration, Fullerton, CA 92831-3138. Offers general management (MBA, MSM); international development (MBA, MSM); marketing management (MBA, MSM); non-profit management (MBA, MSM). Part-time programs available. Postbaccalaureate distance learning degree programs offered (no on-campus study). *Degree requirements:* For master's, comprehensive exam (for some programs), thesis (for some programs), project. *Entrance requirements:* For master's, minimum GPA of 3.0; 2 references. Additional exam requirements/recommendations for international students: Required—TOEFL (minimum score 550 paper-based; 86 iBT); Recommended—IELTS (minimum score 6.5). Electronic applications accepted. *Expenses:* Contact institution.

Howard University, School of Business, Graduate Programs in Business, Washington, DC 20059-0002. Offers accounting (MBA); entrepreneurship (MBA); finance (MBA); general management (MBA); human resources management (MBA); information systems (MBA); international business (MBA); marketing (MBA); supply chain management (MBA); JD/MBA. *Accreditation:* AACSB. Part-time and evening/weekend programs available. Postbaccalaureate distance learning degree programs offered (no on-campus study). *Entrance requirements:* For master's, GMAT, minimum 1 year post undergraduate work experience, resume, 3 letters of recommendation, advanced college algebra. Additional exam requirements/recommendations for international students: Required—TOEFL. *Faculty research:* Marketing research in multi-ethnic populations, U.S. trade policies and international relations, risk management (finance).

Hult International Business School, Program in Business Administration - Hult London Campus, London WC1B 4JP, United Kingdom. Offers entrepreneurship (MBA); international business (MBA); international finance (MBA); marketing (MBA). Part-time programs available. *Degree requirements:* For master's, comprehensive exam, thesis, internship. *Entrance requirements:* Additional exam requirements/recommendations for international students: Required—TOEFL (minimum score 580 paper-based), TWE (minimum score 5). Electronic applications accepted.

Illinois Institute of Technology, Stuart School of Business, Program in Business Administration, Chicago, IL 60661. Offers financial management (MBA); innovation and emerging enterprises (MBA); management science (MBA); marketing (MBA); sustainability (MBA); JD/MBA; M Des/MBA; MBA/MS. *Accreditation:* AACSB. Part-time and evening/weekend programs available. *Entrance requirements:* For master's, GRE (minimum score 1000) or GMAT (500). Additional exam requirements/recommendations for international students: Required—TOEFL (minimum score 600 paper-based; 85 iBT); Recommended—IELTS (minimum score 7). Electronic applications accepted. *Expenses:* Contact institution. *Faculty research:* Global management and marketing strategy, technological innovation, management science, financial management, knowledge management.

Illinois Institute of Technology, Stuart School of Business, Program in Marketing Analytics and Communication, Chicago, IL 60661. Offers MS, MBA/MS. Part-time and evening/weekend programs available. *Entrance requirements:* For master's, GRE (minimum score 1000) or GMAT (500). Additional exam requirements/recommendations for international students: Required—TOEFL (minimum score 600 paper-based; 85 iBT); Recommended—IELTS (minimum score 7). Electronic applications accepted. *Expenses:* Contact institution.

Indiana Tech, Program in Business Administration, Fort Wayne, IN 46803-1297. Offers accounting (MBA); health care administration (MBA); human resources (MBA); management (MBA); marketing (MBA). Part-time and evening/weekend programs available. Postbaccalaureate distance learning degree programs offered (no on-campus study). *Students:* 160 full-time (94 women), 97 part-time (53 women); includes 69 minority (58 Black or African American, non-Hispanic/Latino; 1 Asian, non-Hispanic/Latino; 8 Hispanic/Latino; 2 Two or more races, non-Hispanic/Latino), 11 international. Average age 36. *Entrance requirements:* For master's, GMAT, bachelor's degree from regionally-accredited university; minimum undergraduate GPA of 2.5; 2 years of significant work experience; 3 letters of recommendation. *Application deadline:* Applications are processed on a rolling basis. Application fee: $25. Electronic applications accepted. *Expenses: Tuition:* Full-time $8910; part-time $495 per credit. Tuition and fees vary according to course load, degree level and program. *Financial support:* Applicants required to submit FAFSA. *Unit head:* Dr. Andrew I. Nwanne, Associate Dean of Business/Academic Coordinator, 260-422-5561 Ext. 2214, E-mail: ainwanne@indianatech.edu. Website: http://www.indianatech.edu/.

Instituto Tecnologico de Santo Domingo, Graduate School, Area of Business, Santo Domingo, Dominican Republic. Offers banking and securities markets (M Mgmt); corporate finance (M Mgmt); human resources management (M Mgmt, Certificate); international trade management (M Mgmt); marketing (M Mgmt); organizational development (M Mgmt); quality and productivity management (Certificate); tax management and planning (M Mgmt); upper management (M Mgmt).

Instituto Tecnologico de Santo Domingo, Graduate School, Area of Humanities and Social Sciences, Santo Domingo, Dominican Republic. Offers accounting (Certificate); adult education (Certificate); applied linguistics (MA); economics (MA); education (M Ed); educational psychology (MA, Certificate); gender and development (MA, Certificate); humanistic studies (MA); international marketing management (Certificate); international relations in the Caribbean basin (Certificate); intervention systems in family therapy (MA); linguistic and literary communication (Certificate); pedagogical support (MA); social science education (M Ed); sustainable human development (MA); terminal illness and death psychology (Certificate); youth and adult education (M Ed).

Instituto Tecnológico y de Estudios Superiores de Monterrey, Campus Central de Veracruz, Graduate Programs, Córdoba, Mexico. Offers administration (MA); administration of information technologies (MTI); computer sciences (MCC); education (MEE); educational institution administration (MAD); educational technology (MTE); electronic commerce (MCE); finance (MAF); humanistic studies (MEH); international business for Latin America (MNL); marketing (MMT); science (MCP). Part-time and evening/weekend programs available. Postbaccalaureate distance learning degree programs offered (minimal on-campus study). *Degree requirements:* For master's, thesis (for some programs). *Entrance requirements:* For master's, PAEP College Board. Electronic applications accepted.

Instituto Tecnológico y de Estudios Superiores de Monterrey, Campus Ciudad Obregón, Program in Marketing Technology, Ciudad Obregón, Mexico. Offers MMT.

Instituto Tecnológico y de Estudios Superiores de Monterrey, Campus Cuernavaca, Programs in Business Administration, Temixco, Mexico. Offers finance (MA); human resources management (MA); international business (MA); marketing (MA).

Instituto Tecnológico y de Estudios Superiores de Monterrey, Campus Estado de México, Professional and Graduate Division, Estado de Mexico, Mexico. Offers administration of information technologies (MITA); architecture (M Arch); business administration (GMBA, MBA); computer sciences (MCS, PhD); education (M Ed); educational institution administration (MAD); educational technology and innovation (PhD); electronic commerce (MEC); environmental systems (MS); finance (MAF); humanistic studies (MHS); information sciences and knowledge management (MISKM); information systems (MS); manufacturing systems (MS); marketing (MEM); quality systems and productivity (MS); science and materials engineering (PhD); telecommunications management (MTM). Part-time programs available. Postbaccalaureate distance learning degree programs offered (minimal on-campus study). *Degree requirements:* For master's, one foreign language, thesis (for some programs); for doctorate, one foreign language, thesis/dissertation. *Entrance requirements:* For master's, E-PAEP 500, interview; for doctorate, E-PAEP 500, research proposal. Additional exam requirements/recommendations for international students: Required—TOEFL (minimum score 550 paper-based). *Faculty research:* Surface treatments by plasmas, mechanical properties, robotics, graphical computing, mechatronics security protocols.

Instituto Tecnológico y de Estudios Superiores de Monterrey, Campus Monterrey, Graduate School of Business Administration and Leadership, Program in Business Administration, Monterrey, Mexico. Offers business administration (MA, MBA); finance (M Sc); international business (M Sc); marketing (M Sc). *Accreditation:* AACSB. Part-time programs available. *Degree requirements:* For master's, one foreign language, thesis. *Entrance requirements:* For master's, GMAT. Additional exam requirements/recommendations for international students: Required—TOEFL. *Faculty research:* Technology management, quality management, organizational theory and behavior.

Inter American University of Puerto Rico, Aguadilla Campus, Graduate School, Aguadilla, PR 00605. Offers accounting (MBA); counseling psychology specializing in family (MS); criminal justice (MA); educative management and leadership (MA); elementary education (M Ed); finance (MBA); human resources (MBA); industrial management (MBA); management information systems (MBA); marketing (MBA). Part-time and evening/weekend programs available. *Degree requirements:* For master's, comprehensive exam. *Entrance requirements:* For master's, EXADEP, 2 letters of recommendation, minimum GPA of 2.5. Electronic applications accepted.

Inter American University of Puerto Rico, Guayama Campus, Department of Business Administration, Guayama, PR 00785. Offers marketing (MBA).

Inter American University of Puerto Rico, Metropolitan Campus, Graduate Programs, Program in Marketing, San Juan, PR 00919-1293. Offers MBA. *Degree requirements:* For master's, comprehensive exam. *Entrance requirements:* For master's, GRE or EXADEP, interview. Electronic applications accepted.

Inter American University of Puerto Rico, Ponce Campus, Graduate School, Mercedita, PR 00715-1602. Offers accounting (MBA); biology (M Ed); chemistry (M Ed); criminal justice (MA); elementary education (M Ed); English as a Second Language (M Ed); finance (MBA); history (M Ed); human resources (MBA); marketing (MBA); mathematics (M Ed); Spanish (M Ed). *Entrance requirements:* For master's, minimum GPA of 2.5.

Inter American University of Puerto Rico, San Germán Campus, Graduate Studies Center, Program in Business Administration, San Germán, PR 00683-5008. Offers accounting (MBA); finance (MBA); general business administration (MBA); human resources (MBA, PhD); industrial relations (MBA); information systems (MBA); international and interregional business (PhD); management (MBA); marketing (MBA). Part-time and evening/weekend programs available. *Faculty:* 8 full-time (2 women), 4 part-time/adjunct (3 women). *Students:* 138 full-time (80 women), 35 part-time (21 women); includes 172 minority (all Hispanic/Latino). 60 applicants, 65% accepted, 38 enrolled. In 2013, 38 master's, 3 doctorates awarded. *Degree requirements:* For master's, comprehensive exam. *Entrance requirements:* For master's, GRE General Test or EXADEP, minimum GPA of 3.0. *Application deadline:* For fall admission, 4/30 priority date for domestic students; for spring admission, 11/15 for domestic students. Applications are processed on a rolling basis. Application fee: $31. *Expenses: Tuition:* Full-time $2424; part-time $202 per credit hour. *Required fees:* $260 per semester. Tuition and fees vary according to course level, course load, degree level and program. *Financial support:* Teaching assistantships, Federal Work-Study, and unspecified assistantships available. *Unit head:* Dr. Elba T. Irizarry, Director of Graduate Studies Center, 787-264-1912 Ext. 7357, Fax: 787-892-6350, E-mail: elbat@sg.inter.edu. *Application contact:* Dr. Ailin Padilla, Coordinator, 787-264-1912 Ext. 7355, E-mail: ailin_padilla@intersg.edu.

The International University of Monaco, Graduate Programs, Monte Carlo, Monaco. Offers entrepreneurship (EMBA, MBA); financial engineering (M Sc); hedge fund and private equity (M Sc); international marketing (EMBA, MBA); international wealth management (M Sc); luxury goods and services (EMBA, M Sc, MBA); wealth and asset management (EMBA, MBA). Part-time programs available. *Degree requirements:* For master's, comprehensive exam (for some programs), applied research project. *Entrance requirements:* Additional exam requirements/recommendations for international

students: Required—TOEFL (minimum score 550 paper-based), IELTS. Electronic applications accepted. *Faculty research:* Gaming, leadership, disintermediation.

Iona College, Hagan School of Business, Department of Marketing and International Business, New Rochelle, NY 10801-1890. Offers international business (AC, PMC); marketing (MBA); sports and entertainment management (AC). Part-time and evening/weekend programs available. *Faculty:* 2 full-time (both women), 1 (woman) part-time/adjunct. *Students:* 17 full-time (9 women), 24 part-time (16 women); includes 4 minority (2 Black or African American, non-Hispanic/Latino; 2 Hispanic/Latino), 5 international. Average age 27. 15 applicants, 100% accepted, 9 enrolled. In 2013, 28 master's, 114 other advanced degrees awarded. *Entrance requirements:* For master's, GMAT, 2 letters of recommendation, minimum GPA of 3.0; for other advanced degree, GMAT, minimum GPA of 3.0. Additional exam requirements/recommendations for international students: Required—TOEFL (minimum score 550 paper-based; 80 iBT), IELTS (minimum score 6.5). *Application deadline:* For fall admission, 8/15 priority date for domestic students, 8/1 priority date for international students; for winter admission, 11/15 priority date for domestic students, 11/1 priority date for international students; for spring admission, 2/15 priority date for domestic students, 2/1 priority date for international students; for summer admission, 5/15 for domestic students, 5/1 priority date for international students. Applications are processed on a rolling basis. Application fee: $50. Electronic applications accepted. *Expenses:* Contact institution. *Financial support:* In 2013–14, 23 students received support. Scholarships/grants, tuition waivers (partial), and unspecified assistantships available. Support available to part-time students. Financial award application deadline: 4/15; financial award applicants required to submit FAFSA. *Faculty research:* Business ethics, international retailing, mega-marketing, consumer behavior and consumer confidence. *Unit head:* Dr. Frederica E. Rudell, Chair, 914-637-2748, E-mail: frudell@iona.edu. *Application contact:* Cameron Hudson, Director of MBA Admissions, 914-633-2288, Fax: 914-637-2708, E-mail: chudson@iona.edu.
Website: http://www.iona.edu/Academics/Hagan-School-of-Business/Departments/Marketing/Graduate-Programs.aspx.

John Hancock University, MBA Program, Oakbrook Terrace, IL 60181. Offers e-commerce (MBA); finance (MBA); general business (MBA); global management (MBA); health care administration (MBA); leadership (MBA); management of information systems (MBA); marketing (MBA); professional accounting (MBA); project management (MBA); public accounting (MBA); risk management (MBA).

Johns Hopkins University, Carey Business School, Marketing Program, Baltimore, MD 21218-2699. Offers MS. Part-time and evening/weekend programs available. *Faculty:* 29 full-time (6 women), 135 part-time/adjunct (29 women). *Students:* 86 full-time (54 women), 52 part-time (45 women); includes 18 minority (2 Black or African American, non-Hispanic/Latino; 12 Asian, non-Hispanic/Latino; 1 Hispanic/Latino; 3 Two or more races, non-Hispanic/Latino), 89 international. Average age 26. 211 applicants, 60% accepted, 77 enrolled. In 2013, 35 master's awarded. *Degree requirements:* For master's, research project (MS). *Entrance requirements:* For master's, minimum GPA of 3.0, resume, work experience, two letters of recommendation. Additional exam requirements/recommendations for international students: Required—TOEFL (minimum score 600 paper-based; 100 iBT). *Application deadline:* For fall admission, 4/1 for international students; for spring admission, 9/15 for international students. Applications are processed on a rolling basis. Application fee: $100. Electronic applications accepted. *Financial support:* Scholarships/grants available. Support available to part-time students. Financial award application deadline: 4/15; financial award applicants required to submit FAFSA. *Faculty research:* Consumer behavior and advertising. *Unit head:* Dr. Dipankar Chakravarti, Vice Dean of Programs, 410-234-9311, E-mail: dipankar.chakravarti@jhu.edu. *Application contact:* Robin Greenberg, Admissions Coordinator, 410-234-9227, Fax: 443-529-1554, E-mail: carey.admissions@jhu.edu.
Website: http://carey.jhu.edu/academics/master-of-science/ms-in-marketing/.

Kansas State University, Graduate School, College of Human Ecology, Department of Apparel, Textiles, and Interior Design, Manhattan, KS 66506. Offers apparel and textiles (MS), including design, general apparel and textiles, marketing, merchandising, product development. Postbaccalaureate distance learning degree programs offered (no on-campus study). *Faculty:* 11 full-time (9 women). *Students:* 7 full-time (6 women), 19 part-time (18 women); includes 7 minority (3 Black or African American, non-Hispanic/Latino; 2 Asian, non-Hispanic/Latino; 2 Hispanic/Latino), 6 international. Average age 28. 12 applicants, 75% accepted, 5 enrolled. In 2013, 9 master's awarded. *Degree requirements:* For master's, comprehensive exam (for some programs), thesis (for some programs). *Entrance requirements:* For master's, GRE General Test (except for merchandising applicants), minimum undergraduate GPA of 3.0. Additional exam requirements/recommendations for international students: Required—TOEFL (minimum score 550 paper-based; 79 iBT), IELTS (minimum score 6.1). *Application deadline:* For fall admission, 1/1 priority date for domestic and international students; for spring admission, 8/1 priority date for domestic and international students; for summer admission, 12/1 priority date for domestic and international students. Applications are processed on a rolling basis. Application fee: $50 ($75 for international students). Electronic applications accepted. *Financial support:* In 2013–14, 6 students received support, including 1 fellowship (averaging $8,652 per year), 2 research assistantships (averaging $17,674 per year), 3 teaching assistantships with full tuition reimbursements available (averaging $11,760 per year); career-related internships or fieldwork, Federal Work-Study, institutionally sponsored loans, scholarships/grants, and unspecified assistantships also available. Support available to part-time students. Financial award application deadline: 2/1; financial award applicants required to submit FAFSA. *Faculty research:* Apparel marketing and consumer behavior, social and environmental responsibility, apparel design, new product development. *Total annual research expenditures:* $76,055. *Unit head:* Prof. Barbara G. Anderson, Head, 785-532-6993, Fax: 785-532-3796, E-mail: barbara@ksu.edu. *Application contact:* Gina Jackson, Application Contact, 785-532-6693, Fax: 785-532-3796, E-mail: gjackson@ksu.edu.
Website: http://www.he.k-state.edu/atid/.

Kaplan University, Davenport Campus, School of Business, Davenport, IA 52807-2095. Offers business administration (MBA); change leadership (MS); entrepreneurship (MBA); finance (MBA); health care management (MBA, MS); human resource (MBA); international business (MBA); management (MS); marketing (MBA); project management (MBA, MS); supply chain management and logistics (MBA, MS). *Accreditation:* ACBSP. Part-time and evening/weekend programs available. Postbaccalaureate distance learning degree programs offered (no on-campus study). *Entrance requirements:* Additional exam requirements/recommendations for international students: Required—TOEFL (minimum score 550 paper-based; 80 iBT). Electronic applications accepted.

Keiser University, Doctor of Business Administration Program, Ft. Lauderdale, FL 33309. Offers global business (DBA); global organizational leadership (DBA); marketing (DBA).

Keiser University, Master of Business Administration Program, Ft. Lauderdale, FL 33309. Offers accounting (MBA); health services management (MBA); information security management (MBA); international business (MBA); leadership for managers (MBA); marketing (MBA). All concentrations except information security management also offered in Mandarin; leadership for managers and international business also offered in Spanish. Part-time programs available. Postbaccalaureate distance learning degree programs offered (minimal on-campus study).

Kent State University, College of Business Administration, Doctoral Program in Marketing, Kent, OH 44242. Offers PhD. *Faculty:* 9 full-time (3 women). *Students:* 12 full-time (5 women), 5 international. Average age 32. 13 applicants, 31% accepted, 4 enrolled. In 2013, 3 doctorates awarded. *Degree requirements:* For doctorate, comprehensive exam, thesis/dissertation, oral defense. *Entrance requirements:* For doctorate, GMAT or GRE. Additional exam requirements/recommendations for international students: Required—TOEFL (minimum score 600 paper-based; 100 iBT). *Application deadline:* For fall admission, 2/1 for domestic students, 1/1 for international students. Application fee: $30 ($70 for international students). Electronic applications accepted. *Financial support:* In 2013–14, 12 students received support, including 12 teaching assistantships with full tuition reimbursements available (averaging $29,500 per year); Federal Work-Study also available. Financial award application deadline: 2/1; financial award applicants required to submit FAFSA. *Faculty research:* Advertising effects, satisfaction, international marketing, high-tech marketing, personality and consumer behavior. *Unit head:* Dr. Pamela Grimm, Chair and Associate Professor, 330-672-2170, Fax: 330-672-5006, E-mail: pgrimm@kent.edu. *Application contact:* Felecia A. Urbanek, Coordinator, Graduate Programs, 330-672-2282, Fax: 330-672-7303, E-mail: gradbus@kent.edu.
Website: http://www.kent.edu/business/Grad/phd/index.cfm.

Lake Forest Graduate School of Management, The Leadership MBA Program, Lake Forest, IL 60045. Offers finance (MBA); global business (MBA); healthcare management (MBA); management (MBA); marketing (MBA); organizational behavior (MBA). Part-time and evening/weekend programs available. *Entrance requirements:* For master's, 4 years of work experience in field, interview, 2 letters of recommendation. Electronic applications accepted.

La Salle University, School of Business, Philadelphia, PA 19141-1199. Offers accounting (MBA, Post-MBA Certificate); business systems and analytics (MBA, Post-MBA Certificate); finance (MBA, Post-MBA Certificate); general business administration (MBA); human resource management (MBA, Post-MBA Certificate); international business (Post-MBA Certificate); management (MBA, Post-MBA Certificate); marketing (MBA, Post-MBA Certificate); MSN/MBA. *Accreditation:* AACSB. Part-time and evening/weekend programs available. Postbaccalaureate distance learning degree programs offered (minimal on-campus study). *Faculty:* 27 full-time (13 women), 15 part-time/adjunct (4 women). *Students:* 81 full-time (30 women), 428 part-time (211 women); includes 109 minority (47 Black or African American, non-Hispanic/Latino; 39 Asian, non-Hispanic/Latino; 18 Hispanic/Latino; 5 Two or more races, non-Hispanic/Latino), 6 international. Average age 30. 215 applicants, 90% accepted, 120 enrolled. In 2013, 182 master's, 1 other advanced degree awarded. *Entrance requirements:* For master's, GMAT or GRE, two letters of reference; resume; for Post-MBA Certificate, MBA with minimum GPA of 3.0. Additional exam requirements/recommendations for international students: Required—TOEFL. *Application deadline:* For fall admission, 8/15 priority date for domestic students, 7/15 for international students; for spring admission, 12/15 priority date for domestic students, 11/15 for international students; for summer admission, 4/15 priority date for domestic students, 3/15 for international students. Applications are processed on a rolling basis. Application fee: $35. Electronic applications accepted. Application fee is waived when completed online. *Expenses:* Contact institution. *Financial support:* In 2013–14, 88 students received support. Career-related internships or fieldwork, Federal Work-Study, scholarships/grants, and unspecified assistantships available. Support available to part-time students. Financial award application deadline: 8/31; financial award applicants required to submit FAFSA. *Unit head:* Dr. Gary Giamartino, Dean, 215-951-1040, Fax: 215-951-1886, E-mail: giamartino@lasalle.edu. *Application contact:* Paul J. Reilly, Assistant Vice President, Enrollment Services, 215-951-1946, Fax: 215-951-1462, E-mail: reilly@lasalle.edu.
Website: http://www.lasalle.edu/grad/index.php?section-mba&page-index.

Lasell College, Graduate and Professional Studies in Communication, Newton, MA 02466-2709. Offers health communication (MSC, Graduate Certificate); integrated marketing communication (MSC, Graduate Certificate); public relations (MSC, Graduate Certificate). Part-time and evening/weekend programs available. Postbaccalaureate distance learning degree programs offered (minimal on-campus study). *Faculty:* 5 full-time (3 women), 10 part-time/adjunct (5 women). *Students:* 48 full-time (35 women), 92 part-time (72 women); includes 40 minority (25 Black or African American, non-Hispanic/Latino; 2 American Indian or Alaska Native, non-Hispanic/Latino; 4 Asian, non-Hispanic/Latino; 8 Hispanic/Latino; 1 Two or more races, non-Hispanic/Latino), 19 international. Average age 30. 124 applicants, 66% accepted, 43 enrolled. In 2013, 22 master's awarded. *Entrance requirements:* For master's and Graduate Certificate, bachelor's degree from an accredited institution. Additional exam requirements/recommendations for international students: Required—TOEFL (minimum score 550 paper-based; 79 iBT), IELTS. *Application deadline:* For fall admission, 8/31 priority date for domestic students, 6/30 priority date for international students; for spring admission, 12/31 priority date for domestic students, 10/31 priority date for international students. Applications are processed on a rolling basis. Electronic applications accepted. *Expenses: Tuition:* Part-time $575 per credit. *Required fees:* $80 per semester. *Financial support:* Available to part-time students. Application deadline: 8/31; applicants required to submit FAFSA. *Unit head:* Dr. Joan Dolamore, Dean of Graduate and Professional Studies, 617-243-2485, Fax: 617-243-2450, E-mail: gradinfo@lasell.edu. *Application contact:* Adrienne Franciosi, Director of Graduate Admission, 617-243-2214, Fax: 617-243-2450, E-mail: gradinfo@lasell.edu.
Website: http://www.lasell.edu/Academics/Graduate-and-Professional-Studies/MS-in-Communication.html.

Lasell College, Graduate and Professional Studies in Management, Newton, MA 02466-2709. Offers business administration (PMBA); elder care management (MSM, Graduate Certificate); elder care marketing (MSM); human resource management (Graduate Certificate); human resources management (MSM); integrated marketing communication (Graduate Certificate); management (MSM, Graduate Certificate); marketing (MSM, Graduate Certificate); non-profit management (MSM, Graduate Certificate); project management (MSM, Graduate Certificate); public relations (Graduate Certificate). Part-time and evening/weekend programs available. Postbaccalaureate distance learning degree programs offered (no on-campus study). *Faculty:* 3 full-time (1 woman), 16 part-time/adjunct (9 women). *Students:* 46 full-time (33 women), 105 part-time (73 women); includes 35 minority (24 Black or African American, non-Hispanic/Latino; 1 American Indian or Alaska Native, non-Hispanic/Latino; 3 Asian, non-Hispanic/Latino; 7 Hispanic/Latino), 22 international. Average age 32. 88 applicants, 55% accepted, 29 enrolled. In 2013, 61 master's awarded. *Entrance requirements:* For master's and Graduate Certificate, bachelor's degree from an accredited institution. Additional exam requirements/recommendations for international students: Required—TOEFL (minimum score 550 paper-based; 79 iBT). *Application deadline:* For fall admission, 8/31 priority date for domestic students, 6/30 priority date for international students; for spring admission, 12/31 priority date for domestic students, 10/31 priority date for international students. Applications are processed on a rolling basis. Electronic applications accepted. *Expenses: Tuition:* Part-time $575 per credit. *Required fees:* $80 per semester. *Financial support:* Available to part-time students.

Application deadline: 8/31; applicants required to submit FAFSA. *Unit head:* Dr. Joan Dolamore, Dean of Graduate and Professional Studies, 617-243-2485, Fax: 617-243-2450, E-mail: gradinfo@lasell.edu. *Application contact:* Adrienne Franciosi, Director of Graduate Admission, 617-243-2214, Fax: 617-243-2450, E-mail: gradinfo@lasell.edu.
Website: http://www.lasell.edu/Academics/Graduate-and-Professional-Studies/MS-in-Management.html.

La Sierra University, School of Business and Management, Riverside, CA 92515. Offers accounting (MBA); finance (MBA); general management (MBA); human resources management (MBA); leadership, values, and ethics for business and management (Certificate); marketing (MBA). *Degree requirements:* For master's, research project. *Entrance requirements:* For master's, GMAT, minimum GPA of 3.0. Additional exam requirements/recommendations for international students: Required—TOEFL. *Faculty research:* Financial econometrics, institutional assessment and strategic planning, legal issues in management, behavioral finance, content of financial reports.

Lehigh University, College of Business and Economics, Department of Management, Bethlehem, PA 18015. Offers business administration (MBA); corporate entrepreneurship (MBA); international business (MBA); marketing (MBA); project management (MBA); supply chain management (MBA); MBA/E; MBA/M Ed. *Accreditation:* AACSB. Part-time and evening/weekend programs available. Postbaccalaureate distance learning degree programs offered (minimal on-campus study). *Faculty:* 11 full-time (4 women), 13 part-time/adjunct (4 women). *Students:* 28 full-time (10 women), 171 part-time (54 women); includes 32 minority (2 Black or African American, non-Hispanic/Latino; 21 Asian, non-Hispanic/Latino; 6 Hispanic/Latino; 3 Two or more races, non-Hispanic/Latino), 21 international. Average age 33. 108 applicants, 63% accepted, 25 enrolled. In 2013, 79 master's awarded. *Entrance requirements:* For master's, GMAT or GRE. Additional exam requirements/recommendations for international students: Required—TOEFL (minimum score 600 paper-based; 94 iBT). *Application deadline:* For fall admission, 7/15 for domestic students, 5/1 for international students; for spring admission, 12/1 for domestic students. Applications are processed on a rolling basis. Application fee: $100. Electronic applications accepted. *Financial support:* In 2013–14, 33 students received support, including 10 teaching assistantships with full and partial tuition reimbursements available (averaging $14,200 per year); career-related internships or fieldwork, scholarships/grants, health care benefits, tuition waivers (full and partial), and unspecified assistantships also available. Support available to part-time students. Financial award application deadline: 1/15. *Faculty research:* Information systems, organizational behavior, supply chain management, strategic management, entrepreneurship. *Total annual research expenditures:* $77,886. *Unit head:* Dr. Robert J. Trent, Department Chair, 610-758-4952, Fax: 610-758-6941, E-mail: rjt2@lehigh.edu. *Application contact:* Jen Giordano, Director of Recruitment and Admissions, 610-758-3418, Fax: 610-758-5283, E-mail: jlg210@lehigh.edu.
Website: http://www4.lehigh.edu/business/academics/depts/management.

Lewis University, College of Business, Graduate School of Management, Program in Business Administration, Romeoville, IL 60446. Offers accounting (MBA); custom elective option (MBA); e-business (MBA); finance (MBA); healthcare management (MBA); human resources management (MBA); international business (MBA); management information systems (MBA); marketing (MBA); project management (MBA); technology and operations management (MBA). Part-time and evening/weekend programs available. *Students:* 115 full-time (55 women), 227 part-time (129 women); includes 128 minority (74 Black or African American, non-Hispanic/Latino; 1 American Indian or Alaska Native, non-Hispanic/Latino; 9 Asian, non-Hispanic/Latino; 40 Hispanic/Latino; 4 Two or more races, non-Hispanic/Latino), 10 international. Average age 31. In 2013, 99 master's awarded. *Entrance requirements:* For master's, interview, bachelor's degree, resume, 2 recommendations. Additional exam requirements/recommendations for international students: Required—TOEFL (minimum score 550 paper-based). *Application deadline:* For fall admission, 8/15 priority date for domestic students, 5/1 priority date for international students; for spring admission, 11/15 priority date for international students. Applications are processed on a rolling basis. Application fee: $40. Electronic applications accepted. *Financial support:* Career-related internships or fieldwork, Federal Work-Study, scholarships/grants, and unspecified assistantships available. Financial award application deadline: 5/1; financial award applicants required to submit FAFSA. *Unit head:* Dr. Maureen Culleeney, Academic Program Director, 815-838-0500 Ext. 5631, E-mail: culleema@lewisu.edu. *Application contact:* Michele Ryan, Director of Admission, 815-838-0500 Ext. 5384, E-mail: gsm@lewisu.edu.

Liberty University, School of Business, Lynchburg, VA 24515. Offers accounting (MBA, MS, DBA); business administration (MBA); criminal justice (MBA); cyber security (MS); executive leadership (MA); healthcare (MBA); human resources (DBA); information systems (MS), including information assurance, technology management; international business (MBA, DBA); leadership (MBA, DBA); management and leadership (MA); marketing (MBA, MS, DBA), including digital marketing and advertising (MS), project management (MS), public relations (MS), sports marketing and media (MS); project management (MBA, DBA); public administration (MBA); public relations (MBA). Part-time programs available. Postbaccalaureate distance learning degree programs offered (minimal on-campus study). *Students:* 1,342 full-time (749 women), 3,704 part-time (1,820 women); includes 1,657 minority (1,221 Black or African American, non-Hispanic/Latino; 11 American Indian or Alaska Native, non-Hispanic/Latino; 74 Asian, non-Hispanic/Latino; 209 Hispanic/Latino; 13 Native Hawaiian or other Pacific Islander, non-Hispanic/Latino; 129 Two or more races, non-Hispanic/Latino), 40 international. Average age 35. 5,899 applicants, 48% accepted, 1716 enrolled. In 2013, 1,535 master's awarded. *Entrance requirements:* For master's, minimum undergraduate GPA of 3.0, 15 hours of upper-level business courses. Additional exam requirements/recommendations for international students: Required—TOEFL (minimum score 600 paper-based; 100 iBT). *Application deadline:* Applications are processed on a rolling basis. Application fee: $50. Electronic applications accepted. *Expenses:* Contact institution. *Unit head:* Dr. Scott Hicks, Dean, 434-592-4808, Fax: 434-582-2366, E-mail: smhicks@liberty.edu. *Application contact:* Jay Bridge, Director of Graduate Admissions, 800-424-9595, Fax: 800-628-7977, E-mail: gradadmissions@liberty.edu.
Website: http://www.liberty.edu/academics/business/index.cfm?PID-149.

LIM College, MPS Program, New York, NY 10022-5268. Offers fashion marketing (MPS); fashion merchandising and retail management (MPS); visual merchandising (MPS). *Faculty:* 21. *Students:* 58 full-time (53 women), 8 part-time (all women). *Expenses: Tuition:* Full-time $25,050; part-time $835 per credit hour. Tuition and fees vary according to course load. *Application contact:* Paul Mucciarone, Associate Director of Graduate Admissions, 646-218-4124, Fax: 212-750-3779, E-mail: paul.mucciarone@limcollege.edu.

Lindenwood University, Graduate Programs, School of Business and Entrepreneurship, St. Charles, MO 63301-1695. Offers accountancy (MA); accounting (MBA); business administration (MBA); entrepreneurial studies (MBA); finance (MBA, MS); human resource management (MBA); international business (MBA); leadership (MA); management (MBA); marketing (MBA, MS); public management (MBA); sport management (MA); supply chain management (MBA). *Accreditation:* ACBSP. Part-time and evening/weekend programs available. Postbaccalaureate distance learning degree programs offered (no on-campus study). *Faculty:* 18 full-time (8 women), 33 part-time/adjunct (8 women). *Students:* 292 full-time (130 women), 111 part-time (46 women); includes 59 minority (42 Black or African American, non-Hispanic/Latino; 5 American Indian or Alaska Native, non-Hispanic/Latino; 1 Asian, non-Hispanic/Latino; 5 Hispanic/Latino; 6 Two or more races, non-Hispanic/Latino), 112 international. Average age 29. 212 applicants, 51% accepted, 102 enrolled. In 2013, 221 master's awarded. *Degree requirements:* For master's, comprehensive exam (for some programs), thesis (for some programs), minimum GPA of 3.0. *Entrance requirements:* For master's, interview, minimum GPA of 3.0, letter of recommendation. Additional exam requirements/recommendations for international students: Required—TOEFL (minimum score 550 paper-based; 80 iBT). *Application deadline:* For fall admission, 8/12 priority date for domestic and international students; for winter admission, 1/6 priority date for domestic and international students; for spring admission, 3/10 priority date for domestic and international students; for summer admission, 5/27 priority date for domestic and international students. Applications are processed on a rolling basis. Application fee: $30 ($100 for international students). Electronic applications accepted. *Expenses: Tuition:* Full-time $14,800; part-time $428 per credit hour. *Required fees:* $350. Tuition and fees vary according to course level and course load. *Financial support:* In 2013–14, 268 students received support. Career-related internships or fieldwork, Federal Work-Study, institutionally sponsored loans, scholarships/grants, tuition waivers (partial), and unspecified assistantships available. Financial award application deadline: 6/30; financial award applicants required to submit FAFSA. *Unit head:* Roger Ellis, Dean, 636-949-4839, E-mail: rellis@lindenwood.edu. *Application contact:* Brett Barger, Dean of Evening Admissions and Extension Campuses, 636-949-4934, Fax: 636-949-4109, E-mail: adultadmissions@lindenwood.edu.
Website: http://www.lindenwood.edu.

Long Island University–LIU Post, College of Management, School of Business, Brookville, NY 11548-1300. Offers accounting and taxation (Certificate); business administration (Certificate); finance (MBA, Certificate); general business administration (MBA); international business (MBA, Certificate); management (MBA, Certificate); management information systems (MBA, Certificate); marketing (MBA, Certificate). *Accreditation:* AACSB. Part-time and evening/weekend programs available. *Entrance requirements:* For master's, GMAT, resume, minimum GPA of 3.0, 2 letters of recommendation. Additional exam requirements/recommendations for international students: Required—TOEFL (minimum score 527 paper-based). Electronic applications accepted. *Faculty research:* Financial markets, consumer behavior.

Louisiana State University and Agricultural & Mechanical College, Graduate School, E. J. Ourso College of Business, Department of Marketing, Baton Rouge, LA 70803. Offers business administration (PhD), including marketing. Part-time programs available. *Faculty:* 9 full-time (1 woman). *Students:* 1 (woman) part-time, all international. Average age 32. *Degree requirements:* For doctorate, thesis/dissertation. *Entrance requirements:* Additional exam requirements/recommendations for international students: Required—TOEFL (minimum score 550 paper-based; 79 IBT), IELTS (minimum score 6.5), or PTE (minimum score 59). *Application deadline:* For fall admission, 1/25 priority date for domestic students, 5/15 for international students; for spring admission, 10/15 for international students. Applications are processed on a rolling basis. Application fee: $50 ($70 for international students). Electronic applications accepted. *Financial support:* Fellowships, research assistantships with partial tuition reimbursements, teaching assistantships with full and partial tuition reimbursements, career-related internships or fieldwork, Federal Work-Study, institutionally sponsored loans, scholarships/grants, health care benefits, and unspecified assistantships available. Support available to part-time students. Financial award applicants required to submit FAFSA. *Faculty research:* Consumer behavior, marketing strategy, global marketing, e-commerce, branding/brand equity. *Total annual research expenditures:* $20,956. *Unit head:* Dr. Ronald Niedrich, Chair, 225-578-8684, Fax: 225-578-8616, E-mail: niedrich@lsu.edu. *Application contact:* Dr. Judith Garretson Folse, Graduate Adviser, 225-578-6539, Fax: 225-578-8616, E-mail: folse@lsu.edu.
Website: http://www.business.lsu.edu/marketing.

Loyola University Chicago, Quinlan School of Business, Marketing Department, Chicago, IL 60610. Offers integrated marketing communications (MSIMC); MSIMC/MBA. Part-time and evening/weekend programs available. *Faculty:* 10 full-time (6 women), 9 part-time/adjunct (5 women). *Students:* 15 full-time (11 women), 22 part-time (13 women); includes 5 minority (2 Black or African American, non-Hispanic/Latino; 1 Asian, non-Hispanic/Latino; 1 Hispanic/Latino; 1 Native Hawaiian or other Pacific Islander, non-Hispanic/Latino), 21 international. Average age 25. 107 applicants, 44% accepted, 11 enrolled. In 2013, 27 master's awarded. *Entrance requirements:* For master's, GMAT or GRE, official transcripts, letters of recommendation, statement of purpose, resume. Additional exam requirements/recommendations for international students: Required—TOEFL (minimum score 90 iBT) or IELTS (minimum score 6.5). *Application deadline:* For fall admission, 7/15 for domestic and international students; for winter admission, 10/1 for domestic and international students; for spring admission, 1/15 for domestic and international students; for summer admission, 4/1 for domestic and international students. Applications are processed on a rolling basis. Application fee: $50. Electronic applications accepted. Application fee is waived when completed online. *Expenses: Tuition:* Full-time $16,740; part-time $930 per credit. *Required fees:* $135 per semester. *Financial support:* Scholarships/grants and unspecified assistantships available. Financial award application deadline: 3/15. *Faculty research:* Web performance metrics, new venture marketing strategies over consumption, benefit segmentation strategies. *Unit head:* Dr. Keith Lambrecht, Chair, Marketing Department, 312-915-6514, E-mail: klambre@luc.edu. *Application contact:* Jessica Gagle, Enrollment Advisor, Quinlan School of Business Graduate Programs, 312-915-8908, Fax: 312-915-7207, E-mail: jgagle@luc.edu.
Website: http://www.luc.edu/quinlan/mba/masters-in-marketing/index.shtml.

Loyola University Chicago, Quinlan School of Business, MBA Programs, Chicago, IL 60610. Offers accounting (MBA); business ethics (MBA); derivative markets (MBA); economics (MBA); entrepreneurship (MBA); executive (MBA); finance (MBA); healthcare management (MBA); human resources management (MBA); information systems management (MBA); intercontinental (MBA); international business (MBA); marketing (MBA); operations management (MBA); risk management (MBA); JD/MBA. Part-time and evening/weekend programs available. *Faculty:* 76 full-time (20 women), 10 part-time/adjunct (4 women). *Students:* 73 full-time (34 women), 294 part-time (129 women); includes 60 minority (18 Black or African American, non-Hispanic/Latino; 28 Asian, non-Hispanic/Latino; 14 Hispanic/Latino), 19 international. Average age 31. 529 applicants, 51% accepted, 153 enrolled. In 2013, 229 master's awarded. *Entrance requirements:* For master's, GMAT or GRE, official transcripts, two letters of recommendation, statement of purpose, resume. Additional exam requirements/recommendations for international students: Required—TOEFL (minimum score 90 iBT) or IELTS (minimum score 6.5). *Application deadline:* For fall admission, 7/15 for domestic and international students; for winter admission, 10/1 for domestic and international students; for spring admission, 1/15 for domestic and international students; for summer admission, 4/1 for domestic and international students. Applications are processed on a rolling basis. Application fee: $50. Electronic applications accepted. Application fee is waived when completed online. *Expenses: Tuition:* Full-time $16,740; part-time $930 per credit. *Required fees:* $135 per semester. *Financial support:* Scholarships/grants and unspecified assistantships available.

Faculty research: Social enterprise and responsibility, emerging markets, supply chain management, risk management. *Unit head:* Jennifer Huntley, Assistant Dean for Graduate Programs, 312-915-6124, Fax: 312-915-7207, E-mail: jhuntle@luc.edu. *Application contact:* Jessica Gagle, Enrollment Advisor, Quinlan School of Business Graduate Programs, 312-915-8908, Fax: 312-915-7207, E-mail: jgagle@luc.edu.

Loyola University Maryland, Graduate Programs, Sellinger School of Business and Management, Program in Business Administration, Baltimore, MD 21210-2699. Offers accounting (MBA); finance (MBA); general business (MBA); information systems operations management (MBA); international business (MBA); management (MBA); marketing (MBA). *Accreditation:* AACSB. Part-time and evening/weekend programs available. *Entrance requirements:* For master's, GMAT, letter of recommendation, resume, essay. Additional exam requirements/recommendations for international students: Required—TOEFL (minimum score 550 paper-based).

Lynn University, College of Business and Management, Boca Raton, FL 33431-5598. Offers aviation management (MBA); financial valuation and investment management (MBA); hospitality management (MBA); international business (MBA); marketing (MBA); mass communication and media management (MBA); sports and athletics administration (MBA). Part-time and evening/weekend programs available. Postbaccalaureate distance learning degree programs offered. *Faculty:* 16 full-time (6 women), 8 part-time/adjunct (3 women). *Students:* 181 full-time (95 women), 83 part-time (37 women); includes 41 minority (22 Black or African American, non-Hispanic/Latino; 1 Asian, non-Hispanic/Latino; 17 Hispanic/Latino; 1 Two or more races, non-Hispanic/Latino), 77 international. Average age 28. 137 applicants, 100% accepted, 107 enrolled. In 2013, 149 master's awarded. *Degree requirements:* For master's, projects. *Entrance requirements:* For master's, GMAT or GRE, bachelor's degree from accredited institution, minimum undergraduate GPA of 2.5, resume, 2 letters of recommendation. Additional exam requirements/recommendations for international students: Required—TOEFL (minimum score 550 paper-based). *Application deadline:* Applications are processed on a rolling basis. Application fee: $45. Electronic applications accepted. *Expenses: Tuition:* Full-time $23,760; part-time $660 per credit. *Required fees:* $300; $50 per term. Tuition and fees vary according to degree level and program. *Financial support:* Career-related internships or fieldwork, Federal Work-Study, institutionally sponsored loans, scholarships/grants, tuition waivers (full and partial), and unspecified assistantships available. Support available to part-time students. Financial award application deadline: 8/1; financial award applicants required to submit FAFSA. *Faculty research:* Labor relations, dynamic balance in leisure-time skills, ethics in athletics, hotel development. *Unit head:* Dr. Ralph Norcio, Senior Associate Dean, 561-237-7010, Fax: 561-237-7014, E-mail: rnorcio@lynn.edu. *Application contact:* Steven Pruitt, Director of Graduate and Undergraduate Evening Admission, 561-237-7834, Fax: 561-237-7100, E-mail: spruitt@lynn.edu.
Website: http://www.lynn.edu/academics/colleges/business-and-management.

Manhattanville College, School of Business, Program in Marketing Communication Management, Purchase, NY 10577-2132. Offers MS. Part-time and evening/weekend programs available. *Degree requirements:* For master's, final project. *Entrance requirements:* Additional exam requirements/recommendations for international students: Required—TOEFL.

Marist College, Graduate Programs, School of Communication and the Arts, Program in Integrated Marketing Communication, Poughkeepsie, NY 12601-1387. Offers MA. *Entrance requirements:* For master's, GRE or GMAT, official undergraduate/graduate transcripts from all institutions attended; current resume; completed recommendation forms for three references; personal statement.

Marquette University, Graduate School of Management, Executive MBA Program, Milwaukee, WI 53201-1881. Offers economics (MBA); finance (MBA); human resources (MBA); international business (MBA); management information systems (MBA); marketing (MBA); operations and supply chain management (MBA); sports business (MBA). *Accreditation:* AACSB. *Students:* 38 full-time (12 women), 1 international. Average age 36. 36 applicants. In 2013, 21 master's awarded. *Degree requirements:* For master's, international trip. *Entrance requirements:* For master's, GMAT or GRE, two letters of recommendation, official transcripts from current and previous colleges/universities. Additional exam requirements/recommendations for international students: Required—TOEFL (minimum score 550 paper-based; 88 iBT), IELTS (minimum score 6.5), PTE. *Application deadline:* For fall admission, 2/15 for domestic and international students. Application fee: $50. Electronic applications accepted. *Expenses:* Contact institution. *Financial support:* Application deadline: 2/15. *Faculty research:* International trade and finance, customer relationship management, consumer satisfaction, customer service. *Unit head:* Dr. Mark Eppli, Dean, 414-288-5724. *Application contact:* Dr. Jeanne Simmons, Associate Dean, 414-288-7145.
Website: http://www.busadm.mu.edu/emba/.

Marquette University, Graduate School of Management, Program in Business Administration, Milwaukee, WI 53201-1881. Offers business administration (MBA); economics (MBA); entrepreneurship (Certificate); finance (MBA); human resources (MBA); international business (MBA); management information systems (MBA); marketing (MBA); operations and supply chain management (MBA); sports business (MBA); JD/MBA; MBA/MA; MBA/MSN. *Accreditation:* AACSB. Part-time and evening/weekend programs available. *Students:* 28 full-time (13 women), 265 part-time (66 women); includes 20 minority (7 Black or African American, non-Hispanic/Latino; 8 Asian, non-Hispanic/Latino; 5 Hispanic/Latino), 11 international. Average age 31. 185 applicants. In 2013, 129 master's, 2 other advanced degrees awarded. *Degree requirements:* For Certificate, business plan. *Entrance requirements:* For master's, GMAT or GRE, letters of recommendation. Additional exam requirements/recommendations for international students: Required—TOEFL (minimum score 550 paper-based; 88 iBT), IELTS (minimum score 6.5), PTE. *Application deadline:* For fall admission, 2/15 for domestic and international students. Applications are processed on a rolling basis. Application fee: $50. Electronic applications accepted. *Financial support:* In 2013–14, 4 fellowships, 11 teaching assistantships were awarded; research assistantships, Federal Work-Study, institutionally sponsored loans, scholarships/grants, and tuition waivers (full and partial) also available. Support available to part-time students. Financial award application deadline: 2/15. *Faculty research:* Ethics in the professions, services marketing, technology impact on decision-making, mentoring. *Unit head:* Dr. Mark Eppli, Dean, 414-288-5724. *Application contact:* Dr. Jeanne Simmons, Associate Dean, 414-288-7145.
Website: http://business.marquette.edu/academics/mba.

Marylhurst University, Department of Business Administration, Marylhurst, OR 97036-0261. Offers finance (MBA); general management (MBA); government policy and administration (MBA); green development (MBA); health care management (MBA); marketing (MBA); natural and organic resources (MBA); nonprofit management (MBA); organizational behavior (MBA); real estate (MBA); renewable energy (MBA); sustainable business (MBA). Part-time and evening/weekend programs available. Postbaccalaureate distance learning degree programs offered (no on-campus study). *Degree requirements:* For master's, comprehensive exam, capstone course. *Entrance requirements:* For master's, GMAT (if GPA less than 3.0 and fewer than 5 years of work experience), interview, resume, 2 letters of recommendation. Additional exam requirements/recommendations for international students: Recommended—TOEFL (minimum score 550 paper-based; 80 iBT). Electronic applications accepted.

Maryville University of Saint Louis, The John E. Simon School of Business, St. Louis, MO 63141-7299. Offers accounting (MBA, PGC); management (MBA, PGC); marketing (MBA, PGC); process and project management (MBA, PGC); sport and entertainment management (MBA, PGC). *Accreditation:* ACBSP. Part-time and evening/weekend programs available. *Faculty:* 5 full-time (3 women), 14 part-time/adjunct (4 women). *Students:* 21 full-time (12 women), 85 part-time (41 women); includes 22 minority (8 Black or African American, non-Hispanic/Latino; 2 Asian, non-Hispanic/Latino; 7 Hispanic/Latino; 5 Two or more races, non-Hispanic/Latino), 3 international. Average age 31. In 2013, 39 master's awarded. *Entrance requirements:* For master's, GMAT (unless applicant possesses undergraduate business degree with minimum cumulative GPA of 3.0, or has completed master's degree from accredited university or one early access course prior to undergraduate degree). Additional exam requirements/recommendations for international students: Required—TOEFL (minimum score 85 iBT). *Application deadline:* Applications are processed on a rolling basis. Application fee: $40 ($60 for international students). Electronic applications accepted. Application fee is waived when completed online. *Expenses: Tuition:* Full-time $23,812; part-time $728 per credit hour. *Required fees:* $395 per year. Tuition and fees vary according to course load, degree level and program. *Financial support:* Career-related internships or fieldwork, Federal Work-Study, tuition waivers (partial), and campus employment available. Financial award application deadline: 3/1; financial award applicants required to submit FAFSA. *Faculty research:* International business, e-marketing, strategic planning, interpersonal management skills, financial analysis. *Unit head:* Dr. Pamela Horwitz, Dean, 314-529-9418, Fax: 314-529-9975, E-mail: horwitz@maryville.edu. *Application contact:* Kathy Dougherty, Director of MBA Programs, 314-529-9382, Fax: 314-529-9975, E-mail: business@maryville.edu.
Website: http://www.maryville.edu/bu/business-administration-masters/.

McGill University, Faculty of Graduate and Postdoctoral Studies, Desautels Faculty of Management, Montréal, QC H3A 2T5, Canada. Offers administration (PhD); entrepreneurial studies (MBA); finance (MBA); general management (Post Master's Certificate); information systems (MBA); international business (MBA); international practicing management (MM); management (MBA); management for development (MBA); manufacturing management (MMM); marketing (MBA); operations management (MBA); public accountancy (Diploma); strategic management (MBA); MBA/LL B; MD/MBA. MMM offered jointly with Faculty of Engineering; PhD with Concordia University, HEC Montreal, Université de Montréal, Université du Québec à Montréal.

Melbourne Business School, Graduate Programs, Carlton, Australia. Offers business administration (Exec MBA, MBA); management (PhD); management science (PhD); marketing (PhD); social impact (Graduate Certificate); JD/MBA.

Michigan State University, The Graduate School, Eli Broad College of Business, Department of Marketing, East Lansing, MI 48824. Offers marketing (PhD); marketing research (MS). *Faculty:* 22. *Students:* 29. *Degree requirements:* For doctorate, comprehensive exam, thesis/dissertation. *Entrance requirements:* For master's, GMAT, bachelor's degree with minimum GPA of 3.0 in last 2 years of undergraduate work; transcripts; 3 letters of recommendation; statement of purpose; resume; working knowledge of computers; basic understanding of accounting, finance, marketing, and the management of people; laptop capable of running Windows software; for doctorate, GMAT (taken within past 5 years), bachelor's degree; letters of recommendation; statement of purpose; previous work experience; personal qualifications of sound character, perseverance, intellectual curiosity, and an interest in scholarly research. Additional exam requirements/recommendations for international students: Required—TOEFL (minimum score 100 iBT), PTE (minimum score 70), IELTS (minimum score 7) accepted for MS only. *Financial support:* Research assistantships with tuition reimbursements and teaching assistantships with tuition reimbursements available. Financial award application deadline: 1/10. *Unit head:* Dr. R. Dale Wilson, Chairperson, 517-432-6403, Fax: 517-432-8048, E-mail: wilsonrr@broad.msu.edu. *Application contact:* Jessica Bunce, Office Supervisor, 517-355-2241, Fax: 517-432-8048, E-mail: bunce@broad.msu.edu.
Website: http://marketing.broad.msu.edu/.

Michigan State University, The Graduate School, Eli Broad College of Business, Program in Business Administration, East Lansing, MI 48824. Offers finance (MBA); human resource management (MBA); integrative management (MBA); marketing (MBA); supply chain management (MBA). MBA in integrative management is through Weekend MBA Program; other 4 concentrations are through Full-Time MBA Program. Evening/weekend programs available. *Students:* 432. In 2013, 241 degrees awarded. *Degree requirements:* For master's, enrichment experience. *Entrance requirements:* For master's, GMAT or GRE, 4-year bachelor's degree; resume; work experience (minimum of 5 years for Weekend MBA); 2-3 personal essays; 2 letters of recommendation; personal interview. Additional exam requirements/recommendations for international students: Required—PTE (minimum score 70), TOEFL (minimum score 100 iBT) or IELTS (minimum score 7) for Full-Time MBA applicants. *Application deadline:* Applications are processed on a rolling basis. Application fee: $50. Electronic applications accepted. *Expenses:* Contact institution. *Financial support:* Fellowships with tuition reimbursements, research assistantships with tuition reimbursements, teaching assistantships with tuition reimbursements, scholarships/grants, unspecified assistantships, and non-resident tuition waivers (for all military veterans and their dependents in the Full-Time MBA Program) available. Financial award applicants required to submit FAFSA. *Unit head:* Dr. Sanjay Gupta, Associate Dean for MBA and Professional Master's Programs, 517-432-6488, Fax: 517-353-6395, E-mail: gupta@broad.msu.edu. *Application contact:* Program Information Contact, 517-355-7604, Fax: 517-353-1649, E-mail: mba@msu.edu.
Website: http://mba.broad.msu.edu.

Milwaukee School of Engineering, Rader School of Business, Program in Marketing and Export Management, Milwaukee, WI 53202-3109. Offers MS. Part-time and evening/weekend programs available. *Faculty:* 1 full-time (0 women), 1 part-time/adjunct (0 women). *Students:* 2 full-time (1 woman), 4 part-time (2 women); includes 1 minority (Asian, non-Hispanic/Latino). Average age 27. 4 applicants, 75% accepted, 2 enrolled. In 2013, 2 master's awarded. *Degree requirements:* For master's, thesis, thesis defense or capstone project. *Entrance requirements:* For master's, GRE or GMAT if undergraduate GPA less than 2.8, 2 letters of recommendation. Additional exam requirements/recommendations for international students: Required—TOEFL (minimum score 79 iBT), IELTS (minimum score 6.5). *Application deadline:* Applications are processed on a rolling basis. Application fee: $0. Electronic applications accepted. Application fee is waived when completed online. *Expenses: Tuition:* Full-time $6939; part-time $771 per credit. *Financial support:* In 2013–14, 2 students received support. Career-related internships or fieldwork, institutionally sponsored loans, and scholarships/grants available. Financial award application deadline: 3/15; financial award applicants required to submit FAFSA. *Unit head:* David Schmitz, Graduate Management Program Director, 414-277-2487, Fax: 414-277-2487, E-mail: schmitz@msoe.edu. *Application contact:* Katie Weinschenk, Graduate Admissions Director, 800-321-6763, Fax: 414-277-7208, E-mail: weinschenk@msoe.edu.

Mississippi State University, College of Business, Department of Management and Information Systems, Mississippi State, MS 39762. Offers business administration (MBA, PhD), including accounting, business administration (MBA), business information systems (PhD), finance (PhD), management (PhD), marketing (PhD); information systems (MSIS); project management (MBA). Part-time programs available. *Faculty:* 12 full-time (4 women). *Students:* 69 full-time (20 women), 245 part-time (69 women); includes 34 minority (9 Black or African American, non-Hispanic/Latino; 12 Asian, non-Hispanic/Latino; 7 Hispanic/Latino; 1 Native Hawaiian or other Pacific Islander, non-Hispanic/Latino; 5 Two or more races, non-Hispanic/Latino), 20 international. Average age 31. 367 applicants, 29% accepted, 73 enrolled. In 2013, 127 master's, 2 doctorates awarded. *Degree requirements:* For master's, comprehensive exam; for doctorate, comprehensive exam, thesis/dissertation. *Entrance requirements:* For master's, GMAT, minimum GPA of 3.0 in last 60 hours of undergraduate course work; for doctorate, GMAT (minimum score of 550), minimum GPA of 3.25 on all graduate work; BS with minimum GPA of 3.0 cumulative and last 60 hours. Additional exam requirements/recommendations for international students: Required—TOEFL (minimum score 575 paper-based; 84 iBT); Recommended—IELTS (minimum score 7). *Application deadline:* For fall admission, 7/1 for domestic students, 5/1 for international students; for spring admission, 11/1 for domestic students, 9/1 for international students. Applications are processed on a rolling basis. Application fee: $60. Electronic applications accepted. *Financial support:* In 2013–14, 1 teaching assistantship (averaging $13,497 per year) was awarded; career-related internships or fieldwork, Federal Work-Study, institutionally sponsored loans, scholarships/grants, and unspecified assistantships also available. Financial award applicants required to submit FAFSA. *Faculty research:* Electronic commerce, management of information technology. *Unit head:* Dr. Tim Barnett, Department Chairperson and Professor of Management, 662-325-3928, Fax: 662-325-8651, E-mail: tim.barnett@msstate.edu. *Application contact:* Dr. Rebecca Long, Graduate Coordinator, 662-325-3928, E-mail: gsb@cobian.msstate.edu.
Website: http://www.business.msstate.edu/programs/mis/index.php.

Molloy College, Graduate Business Program, Rockville Centre, NY 11571-5002. Offers accounting (MBA); accounting and finance (MBA); accounting and management (MBA); finance (MBA); finance and management (MBA); finance and personal financial planning (MBA); healthcare administration (MBA); management (MBA); management and personal financial planning (MBA); marketing (MBA); personal financial planning (MBA). Part-time programs available. *Faculty:* 8 full-time (3 women), 7 part-time/adjunct (1 woman). *Students:* 41 full-time (19 women), 104 part-time (36 women); includes 45 minority (21 Black or African American, non-Hispanic/Latino; 8 Asian, non-Hispanic/Latino; 14 Hispanic/Latino; 1 Native Hawaiian or other Pacific Islander, non-Hispanic/Latino; 1 Two or more races, non-Hispanic/Latino), 4 international. Average age 29. 48 applicants, 71% accepted, 27 enrolled. In 2013, 33 master's awarded. *Application deadline:* Applications are processed on a rolling basis. Application fee: $60. *Expenses: Tuition:* Full-time $16,920; part-time $940 per credit. *Required fees:* $880. *Faculty research:* Leadership, marketing, accounting, finance, international. *Unit head:* Dr. Daniel Cillis, Associate Dean and Director, MBA Program, 516-323-3080, E-mail: dcillis@molloy.edu. *Application contact:* Alina Haitz, Assistant Director of Graduate Admissions, 516-323-4008, E-mail: ahaitz@molloy.edu.

Montclair State University, The Graduate School, School of Business, Post Master's Certificate Program in Marketing, Montclair, NJ 07043-1624. Offers Post Master's Certificate. Part-time and evening/weekend programs available. *Entrance requirements:* For degree, essay. Additional exam requirements/recommendations for international students: Required—TOEFL (minimum score 83 iBT) or IELTS (minimum score 6.5). Electronic applications accepted. *Faculty research:* Converting service marketing to tangibility, mathematical approaches to solving marketing problems, system dynamic modeling of brand management, attitudes toward safety in leisure facilities, marketing/retailing strategy and instruction.

National University, Academic Affairs, School of Business and Management, La Jolla, CA 92037-1011. Offers accountancy (Certificate); business administration (GMBA, MBA), including financial management (MBA), human resource management (MBA), integrated marketing communications (MBA), international business (MBA), management accounting (MBA), marketing (MBA), mobile marketing and social media (MBA), organizational leadership (MA, MBA), professional golf management (MBA); global management (MGM); human resource management (MA), including organizational development and change, organizational leadership (MA, MBA); international business (Certificate); management information systems (MS); organizational leadership (MS), including community development; sustainability management (MS). Part-time and evening/weekend programs available. Postbaccalaureate distance learning degree programs offered (no on-campus study). *Faculty:* 30 full-time (8 women), 88 part-time/adjunct (25 women). *Students:* 688 full-time (357 women), 331 part-time (161 women); includes 453 minority (105 Black or African American, non-Hispanic/Latino; 2 American Indian or Alaska Native, non-Hispanic/Latino; 143 Asian, non-Hispanic/Latino; 162 Hispanic/Latino; 13 Native Hawaiian or other Pacific Islander, non-Hispanic/Latino; 28 Two or more races, non-Hispanic/Latino), 165 international. Average age 33. 286 applicants, 100% accepted, 217 enrolled. In 2013, 641 master's awarded. *Degree requirements:* For master's, thesis (for some programs). *Entrance requirements:* For master's, interview, minimum GPA of 2.5. Additional exam requirements/recommendations for international students: Required—TOEFL (minimum score 550 paper-based; 79 iBT), IELTS (minimum score 6). *Application deadline:* Applications are processed on a rolling basis. Application fee: $60 ($65 for international students). Electronic applications accepted. *Expenses: Tuition:* Full-time $13,824; part-time $1728 per course. One-time fee: $160. *Financial support:* Career-related internships or fieldwork, scholarships/grants, and tuition waivers (partial) available. Support available to part-time students. Financial award application deadline: 6/30; financial award applicants required to submit FAFSA. *Unit head:* School of Business and Management, 800-628-8648, Fax: 858-642-8719, E-mail: sobm@nu.edu. *Application contact:* Louis Cruz, Interim Vice President for Enrollment Services, 800-628-8648, E-mail: advisor@nu.edu.
Website: http://www.nu.edu/OurPrograms/SchoolOfBusinessAndManagement.html.

New England College, Program in Management, Henniker, NH 03242-3293. Offers accounting (MSA); healthcare administration (MS); international relations (MA); marketing management (MS); nonprofit leadership (MS); project management (MS); strategic leadership (MS). Part-time and evening/weekend programs available. *Degree requirements:* For master's, independent research project. Electronic applications accepted.

New Mexico State University, Graduate School, College of Business, Department of Marketing, Las Cruces, NM 88003. Offers PhD. *Faculty:* 9 full-time (2 women). *Students:* 5 full-time (1 woman), 1 part-time (0 women); includes 2 minority (both Hispanic/Latino), 3 international. Average age 32. 51 applicants, 12% accepted, 4 enrolled. In 2013, 2 doctorates awarded. *Degree requirements:* For doctorate, comprehensive exam, thesis/dissertation. *Entrance requirements:* For doctorate, GMAT or GRE. Additional exam requirements/recommendations for international students: Required—TOEFL (minimum score 550 paper-based; 79 iBT), IELTS (minimum score 6.5). *Application deadline:* For fall admission, 2/1 for domestic and international students. Application fee: $40 ($50 for international students). Electronic applications accepted. *Expenses:* Tuition, state resident: full-time $5398; part-time $224.90 per credit. Tuition, nonresident: full-time $18,821; part-time $784.20 per credit. *Required fees:* $1310; $54.60 per credit. *Financial support:* In 2013–14, 5 students received support, including 2 fellowships (averaging $4,050 per year), 5 teaching assistantships (averaging $20,554 per year); Federal Work-Study, scholarships/grants, health care benefits, and unspecified assistantships also available. Financial award application deadline: 3/1. *Faculty research:* Consumer behavior, nutrition, ethics, advertising, public policy. *Unit head:* Dr. Michael R. Hyman, PhD Coordinator, 575-646-5238, Fax: 575-646-1498, E-mail: mhyman@nmsu.edu. *Application contact:* Dr. Mike R. Hyman, Coordinator/Recruiting Contact, 575-646-5238, Fax: 575-646-1498, E-mail: mhyman@nmsu.edu.
Website: http://business.nmsu.edu/academics/marketing/marketing-programs/phd/.

New York Institute of Technology, School of Management, Department of Business Administration, Old Westbury, NY 11568-8000. Offers management (MBA), including decision science, finance, management, marketing; professional accounting (MBA). Part-time and evening/weekend programs available. *Faculty:* 22 full-time (6 women), 17 part-time/adjunct (3 women). *Students:* 151 full-time (74 women), 120 part-time (47 women); includes 44 minority (13 Black or African American, non-Hispanic/Latino; 23 Asian, non-Hispanic/Latino; 4 Hispanic/Latino; 4 Two or more races, non-Hispanic/Latino), 177 international. Average age 27. 355 applicants, 66% accepted, 110 enrolled. In 2013, 151 master's awarded. *Degree requirements:* For master's, thesis (for some programs). *Entrance requirements:* For master's, minimum QPA of 2.85. Additional exam requirements/recommendations for international students: Required—TOEFL (minimum score 550 paper-based; 79 iBT), IELTS (minimum score 6). *Application deadline:* For fall admission, 7/1 priority date for domestic students, 6/1 for international students; for spring admission, 12/1 priority date for domestic students, 12/1 for international students. Applications are processed on a rolling basis. Application fee: $50. Electronic applications accepted. *Expenses: Tuition:* Full-time $18,900; part-time $1050 per credit. *Financial support:* Research assistantships with partial tuition reimbursements, career-related internships or fieldwork, scholarships/grants, health care benefits, tuition waivers (full and partial), and unspecified assistantships available. Support available to part-time students. Financial award applicants required to submit FAFSA. *Faculty research:* Accounting, economics, finance, management, marketing. *Unit head:* Dr. Diamando Afxentiou, Director, 212-261-1602, E-mail: dafxenti@nyit.edu. *Application contact:* Alice Dolitsky, Director, Graduate Admissions, 516-686-7520, Fax: 516-686-1116, E-mail: nyitgrad@nyit.edu.
Website: http://www.nyit.edu/management/mba.

New York University, Leonard N. Stern School of Business, Department of Marketing, New York, NY 10012-1019. Offers entertainment, media and technology (MBA); general marketing (MBA); marketing (PhD); product management (MBA). *Expenses: Tuition:* Full-time $35,856; part-time $1494 per unit. *Required fees:* $1408; $64 per unit. $473 per term. Tuition and fees vary according to course load and program.

New York University, School of Continuing and Professional Studies, Division of Programs in Business, Program in Integrated Marketing, New York, NY 10012-1019. Offers brand management (MS); digital marketing (MS); marketing analytics (MS). Part-time and evening/weekend programs available. *Faculty:* 2 full-time (both women), 74 part-time/adjunct (28 women). *Students:* 272 full-time (216 women), 147 part-time (113 women); includes 51 minority (11 Black or African American, non-Hispanic/Latino; 23 Asian, non-Hispanic/Latino; 14 Hispanic/Latino; 3 Two or more races, non-Hispanic/Latino), 285 international. Average age 26. 715 applicants, 64% accepted, 177 enrolled. In 2013, 91 master's awarded. *Degree requirements:* For master's, comprehensive exam, thesis, capstone; writing of complete business plan. *Entrance requirements:* For master's, bachelor's degree, resume with relevant professional work, internship or volunteer experience, two letters of recommendation, statement of purpose. Additional exam requirements/recommendations for international students: Required—TOEFL (minimum score 600 paper-based; 100 iBT), IELTS (minimum score 7). *Application deadline:* For fall admission, 2/1 priority date for domestic and international students; for spring admission, 10/15 priority date for domestic students, 8/15 priority date for international students. Applications are processed on a rolling basis. Application fee: $150. Electronic applications accepted. *Expenses: Tuition:* Full-time $35,856; part-time $1494 per unit. *Required fees:* $1408; $64 per unit. $473 per term. Tuition and fees vary according to course load and program. *Financial support:* In 2013–14, 71 students received support, including 71 fellowships (averaging $2,982 per year); institutionally sponsored loans and scholarships/grants also available. Financial award application deadline: 3/1; financial award applicants required to submit FAFSA. *Faculty research:* Branding, digital marketing, Web analytics, consumer behavior, customer loyalty, campaign planning and management. *Unit head:* Paula Payton, Academic Director, 212-992-3228, E-mail: pp64@nyu.edu. *Application contact:* Admissions Office, 212-998-7100, E-mail: scps.gradadmissions@nyu.edu.
Website: http://www.scps.nyu.edu/areas-of-study/marketing/graduate-programs/ms-integrated-marketing/.

New York University, School of Continuing and Professional Studies, The Preston Robert Tisch Center for Hospitality, Tourism, and Sports Management, Program in Sports Business, New York, NY 10012-1019. Offers global sports media (MS); professional and collegiate sports operations (MS); sports business (Advanced Certificate); sports law (MS); sports marketing and sales (MS). Part-time and evening/weekend programs available. *Faculty:* 8 full-time (3 women), 24 part-time/adjunct (7 women). *Students:* 75 full-time (27 women), 56 part-time (17 women); includes 23 minority (8 Black or African American, non-Hispanic/Latino; 6 Asian, non-Hispanic/Latino; 7 Hispanic/Latino; 2 Two or more races, non-Hispanic/Latino), 39 international. Average age 26. 136 applicants, 79% accepted, 59 enrolled. In 2013, 32 master's, 5 other advanced degrees awarded. *Degree requirements:* For master's, thesis. *Entrance requirements:* For master's, bachelor's degree, resume with relevant professional work, internship or volunteer experience, two letters of recommendation, statement of purpose. Additional exam requirements/recommendations for international students: Required—TOEFL (minimum score 600 paper-based; 100 iBT), IELTS (minimum score 7). *Application deadline:* For fall admission, 2/1 priority date for domestic and international students; for spring admission, 10/15 priority date for domestic students, 8/15 priority date for international students. Applications are processed on a rolling basis. Application fee: $150. Electronic applications accepted. *Expenses: Tuition:* Full-time $35,856; part-time $1494 per unit. *Required fees:* $1408; $64 per unit. $473 per term. Tuition and fees vary according to course load and program. *Financial support:* In 2013–14, 51 students received support, including 50 fellowships (averaging $3,118 per year); scholarships/grants also available. Support available to part-time students. Financial award application deadline: 2/15. *Faculty research:* Implications of college football's bowl coalition series from a legal, economic, and academic perspective; social history of sports. *Unit head:* Bjorn Hanson, Division Dean and Clinical Professor, 212-998-7100. *Application contact:* Admissions Office, 212-998-7100, E-mail: scps.gradadmissions@nyu.edu.
Website: http://www.scps.nyu.edu/areas-of-study/tisch/graduate-programs/ms-sports-business/.

North Central College, Graduate and Continuing Studies Programs, Department of Business, Program in Business Administration, Naperville, IL 60566-7063. Offers change management (MBA); finance (MBA); human resource management (MBA);

international business administration (MIBA); management (MBA); marketing (MBA). Part-time and evening/weekend programs available. *Faculty:* 13 full-time (4 women), 8 part-time/adjunct (0 women). *Students:* 31 full-time (8 women), 67 part-time (32 women); includes 16 minority (6 Black or African American, non-Hispanic/Latino; 5 Asian, non-Hispanic/Latino; 5 Hispanic/Latino), 3 international. Average age 30. 99 applicants, 54% accepted, 29 enrolled. In 2013, 51 master's awarded. *Degree requirements:* For master's, thesis optional, project. *Entrance requirements:* For master's, interview. Additional exam requirements/recommendations for international students: Required—TOEFL (minimum score 577 paper-based; 90 iBT). *Application deadline:* For fall admission, 8/15 for domestic students; for winter admission, 12/1 for domestic students; for spring admission, 2/1 for domestic students. Application fee: $25. *Expenses: Tuition:* Full-time $4716; part-time $786 per credit hour. *Financial support:* Scholarships/grants available. Support available to part-time students. *Unit head:* Dr. Robert Moussetis, Program Coordinator, 630-637-5475, E-mail: rcmoussetis@noctrl.edu. *Application contact:* Wendy Kulpinski, Director of Graduate and Continuing Education Admission, 630-637-5808, Fax: 630-637-5844, E-mail: wekulpinski@noctrl.edu.

Northeastern Illinois University, College of Graduate Studies and Research, College of Business and Management, Chicago, IL 60625-4699. Offers accounting (MSA); business administration (MBA); finance (MBA); management (MBA); marketing (MBA). Part-time and evening/weekend programs available. *Degree requirements:* For master's, thesis optional. *Entrance requirements:* For master's, GMAT, minimum GPA of 2.75. Additional exam requirements/recommendations for international students: Required—TOEFL (minimum score 550 paper-based; 79 iBT). Electronic applications accepted. *Faculty research:* Perception of accountants and non-accountants toward the future of the accounting industry, asynchronous learning outcomes, cost and efficiency of financial markets, impact of deregulation on airline industry, analysis of derivational instruments.

Northwestern University, The Graduate School, Kellogg School of Management, Department of Marketing, Evanston, IL 60208. Offers PhD. Admissions and degree offered through The Graduate School. *Degree requirements:* For doctorate, comprehensive exam, thesis/dissertation. *Entrance requirements:* For doctorate, GMAT or GRE General Test. Additional exam requirements/recommendations for international students: Required—TOEFL. Electronic applications accepted. *Faculty research:* Choice models, database and high-tech marketing, consumer information processing, ethnographic analysis of consumption, psychometric analysis of consumer behavior.

Northwestern University, The Graduate School, Kellogg School of Management, Management Programs, Evanston, IL 60208. Offers accounting information and management (MBA, PhD); analytical finance (MBA); business administration (MBA); decision sciences (MBA); entrepreneurship and innovation (MBA); finance (MBA, PhD); health enterprise management (MBA); human resources management (MBA); international business (MBA); management and organizations (MBA, PhD); management and organizations and sociology (PhD); management and strategy (MBA); management studies (MS); managerial analytics (MBA); managerial economics (MBA); managerial economics and strategy (PhD); marketing (MBA, PhD); marketing management (MBA); media management (MBA); operations management (MBA, PhD); real estate (MBA); social enterprise at Kellogg (MBA); JD/MBA. Part-time and evening/weekend programs available. Terminal master's awarded for partial completion of doctoral program. *Degree requirements:* For doctorate, thesis/dissertation, 2 years of coursework, qualifying (field) exam and candidacy, summer research papers and presentations to faculty, proposal defense, final exam/defense. *Entrance requirements:* For master's, GMAT, GRE, interview, 2 letters of recommendation, college transcripts, resume, essays, Kellogg honor code; for doctorate, GMAT, GRE, statement of purpose, transcripts, 2 letters of recommendation, resume, interview. Additional exam requirements/recommendations for international students: Required—TOEFL, IELTS. Electronic applications accepted. *Expenses:* Contact institution. *Faculty research:* Business cycles and international finance, health policy, networks, non-market strategy, consumer psychology.

Northwestern University, Medill School of Journalism, Media, and Integrated Marketing Communications, Integrated Marketing Communications Program, Evanston, IL 60208. Offers brand strategy (MSIMC); content marketing (MSIMC); direct and interactive marketing (MSIMC); marketing analytics (MSIMC); strategic communications (MSIMC). Part-time programs available. *Entrance requirements:* For master's, GRE General Test or GMAT, full-time work experience (preferred). Additional exam requirements/recommendations for international students: Required—TOEFL. Electronic applications accepted. *Faculty research:* Data mining, business to business marketing, values in advertising, political advertising.

Notre Dame de Namur University, Division of Academic Affairs, School of Business and Management, Program in Business Administration, Belmont, CA 94002-1908. Offers business administration (MBA); entrepreneurship (MBA); finance (MBA); human resource management (MBA); marketing (MBA); media and promotion (MBA); technology and operations management (MBA). *Accreditation:* ACBSP. Part-time and evening/weekend programs available. *Entrance requirements:* For master's, minimum GPA of 2.5. Additional exam requirements/recommendations for international students: Required—TOEFL (minimum score 550 paper-based; 79 iBT). Electronic applications accepted.

Oakland University, Graduate Study and Lifelong Learning, School of Business Administration, Department of Management and Marketing, Rochester, MI 48309-4401. Offers business administration (MBA); entrepreneurship (Certificate); general management (Certificate); human resource management (Certificate); international business (Certificate); marketing (Certificate). *Faculty:* 11 full-time (4 women), 2 part-time/adjunct (both women). *Students:* 72 full-time (28 women), 232 part-time (63 women); includes 51 minority (17 Black or African American, non-Hispanic/Latino; 2 American Indian or Alaska Native, non-Hispanic/Latino; 25 Asian, non-Hispanic/Latino; 7 Hispanic/Latino), 25 international. Average age 32. 238 applicants, 43% accepted, 88 enrolled. In 2013, 144 master's, 4 other advanced degrees awarded. Application fee: $0. *Unit head:* Ravi Parameswaran, Chair, 238-370-3279, Fax: 249-370-4275. *Application contact:* Donna Free, Coordinator, 248-370-3281.

The Ohio State University, Graduate School, Max M. Fisher College of Business, Program in Marketing, Columbus, OH 43210. Offers MBA, MS, PhD. *Students:* 3 part-time (1 woman); includes 1 minority (Asian, non-Hispanic/Latino). In 2013, 8 master's awarded. *Entrance requirements:* Additional exam requirements/recommendations for international students: Required—TOEFL. *Unit head:* Walter Zinn, Chair, 614-292-0797, E-mail: zinn.13@osu.edu. *Application contact:* Graduate Admissions, 614-292-6031, Fax: 614-292-3656, E-mail: gradadmissions@osu.edu.

Oklahoma Christian University, Graduate School of Business, Oklahoma City, OK 73136-1100. Offers accounting (MBA); electronic business (MBA); financial services (MBA); health services management (MBA); human resources (MBA); international business (MBA); leadership and organizational development (MBA); marketing (MBA); project management (MBA). Postbaccalaureate distance learning degree programs offered (no on-campus study). *Entrance requirements:* For master's, bachelor's degree. Electronic applications accepted.

Oklahoma City University, Meinders School of Business, Program in Business Administration, Oklahoma City, OK 73106-1402. Offers accounting (MBA); finance (MBA); general (MBA); marketing (MBA); JD/MBA; MSN/MBA. *Accreditation:* ACBSP. Part-time and evening/weekend programs available. *Students:* 82 full-time (39 women), 101 part-time (41 women); includes 18 minority (7 Black or African American, non-Hispanic/Latino; 6 American Indian or Alaska Native, non-Hispanic/Latino; 3 Asian, non-Hispanic/Latino; 2 Two or more races, non-Hispanic/Latino), 50 international. Average age 31. 109 applicants, 61% accepted, 19 enrolled. In 2013, 114 master's awarded. *Degree requirements:* For master's, comprehensive exam. *Entrance requirements:* For master's, GRE or GMAT, bachelor's degree from accredited institution, minimum GPA of 3.0, essay, recommendation letters. Additional exam requirements/recommendations for international students: Required—TOEFL (minimum score 550 paper-based; 80 iBT). *Application deadline:* Applications are processed on a rolling basis. Application fee: $50. Electronic applications accepted. *Expenses: Tuition:* Full-time $16,848; part-time $936 per credit hour. Tuition and fees vary according to course load, degree level and program. *Financial support:* Career-related internships or fieldwork, Federal Work-Study, institutionally sponsored loans, scholarships/grants, and tuition waivers (partial) available. Support available to part-time students. Financial award application deadline: 6/1; financial award applicants required to submit FAFSA. *Faculty research:* Management information systems, international business strategies. *Unit head:* Dr. Steve Agee, Dean, 405-208-5130, Fax: 405-208-5098, E-mail: sagee@okcu.edu. *Application contact:* Heidi Puckett, Director of Graduate Admissions, 800-633-7242, Fax: 405-208-5916, E-mail: gadmissions@okcu.edu.
Website: http://msb.okcu.edu/graduate/.

Oklahoma State University, Spears School of Business, Department of Marketing, Stillwater, OK 74078. Offers business administration (PhD), including marketing; marketing (MBA). Part-time programs available. *Faculty:* 18 full-time (2 women), 7 part-time/adjunct (3 women). *Students:* 2 full-time (both women), 4 part-time (1 woman), 4 international. Average age 34. 21 applicants, 10% accepted, 2 enrolled. In 2013, 3 doctorates awarded. *Degree requirements:* For master's, thesis or alternative; for doctorate, comprehensive exam, thesis/dissertation. *Entrance requirements:* For master's and doctorate, GRE or GMAT. Additional exam requirements/recommendations for international students: Required—TOEFL (minimum score 550 paper-based; 79 iBT). *Application deadline:* For fall admission, 3/1 priority date for international students; for spring admission, 8/1 priority date for international students. Applications are processed on a rolling basis. Application fee: $40 ($75 for international students). Electronic applications accepted. *Expenses:* Tuition, state resident: full-time $4272; part-time $178 per credit hour. Tuition, nonresident: full-time $17,472; part-time $709 per credit hour. *Required fees:* $2413.20; $100.55 per credit hour. One-time fee: $50 full-time. Part-time tuition and fees vary according to course load and campus/location. *Financial support:* In 2013–14, 3 research assistantships (averaging $17,704 per year), 3 teaching assistantships (averaging $23,556 per year) were awarded; career-related internships or fieldwork, Federal Work-Study, scholarships/grants, health care benefits, tuition waivers (partial), and unspecified assistantships also available. Support available to part-time students. Financial award application deadline: 3/1; financial award applicants required to submit FAFSA. *Faculty research:* Decision-making (consumer, managerial, cross-functional), communication effects, services marketing, public policy and marketing, corporate image. *Unit head:* Dr. Joshua L. Wiener, Department Head, 405-744-5192, Fax: 405-744-5180, E-mail: josh.wiener@okstate.edu.
Website: http://spears.okstate.edu/marketing.

Old Dominion University, College of Business and Public Administration, Doctoral Program in Business Administration, Norfolk, VA 23529. Offers finance (PhD); information technology (PhD); marketing (PhD); strategic management (PhD). *Accreditation:* AACSB. *Faculty:* 29 full-time (6 women). *Students:* 29 full-time (8 women), 29 part-time (13 women); includes 3 minority (1 Black or African American, non-Hispanic/Latino; 1 Asian, non-Hispanic/Latino; 1 Native Hawaiian or other Pacific Islander, non-Hispanic/Latino), 41 international. Average age 33. 77 applicants, 35% accepted, 12 enrolled. In 2013, 8 doctorates awarded. *Degree requirements:* For doctorate, comprehensive exam, thesis/dissertation. *Entrance requirements:* For doctorate, GMAT. Additional exam requirements/recommendations for international students: Required—TOEFL (minimum score 550 paper-based; 79 iBT). *Application deadline:* For fall admission, 3/1 priority date for domestic and international students. Application fee: $50. Electronic applications accepted. *Expenses:* Tuition, state resident: full-time $9888; part-time $412 per credit. Tuition, nonresident: full-time $25,152; part-time $1048 per credit. *Required fees:* $59 per semester. One-time fee: $50. *Financial support:* In 2013–14, 27 students received support, including 14 fellowships with full tuition reimbursements available (averaging $7,500 per year), 24 research assistantships with full tuition reimbursements available (averaging $7,500 per year), 16 teaching assistantships with full tuition reimbursements available (averaging $7,500 per year); scholarships/grants and unspecified assistantships also available. Financial award application deadline: 3/1; financial award applicants required to submit FAFSA. *Faculty research:* International business, buyer behavior, financial markets, strategy, operations research. *Unit head:* Dr. John B. Ford, Graduate Program Director, 757-683-3587, Fax: 757-683-4076, E-mail: jbford@odu.edu. *Application contact:* Katrina Davenport, Program Coordinator, 757-683-5138, Fax: 757-683-4076, E-mail: kdavenpo@odu.edu.
Website: http://bpa.odu.edu/bpa/academics/baphd.shtml.

Oral Roberts University, School of Business, Tulsa, OK 74171. Offers accounting (MBA); entrepreneurship (MBA); finance (MBA); international business (MBA); management (MBA); marketing (MBA); non-profit management (MBA); not for profit management (MNM). *Accreditation:* ACBSP. Part-time programs available. Postbaccalaureate distance learning degree programs offered (minimal on-campus study). *Degree requirements:* For master's, thesis optional. *Entrance requirements:* For master's, minimum cumulative GPA of 3.0. Additional exam requirements/recommendations for international students: Required—TOEFL (minimum score 550 paper-based; 79 iBT). Electronic applications accepted. *Faculty research:* Social media, international business and marketing.

Oregon State University, College of Business, Program in Business Administration, Corvallis, OR 97331. Offers clean technology (MBA); commercialization (MBA); executive leadership (MBA); global operations (MBA); marketing (MBA); research thesis (MBA); wealth management (MBA). Part-time programs available. *Faculty:* 34 full-time (13 women), 2 part-time/adjunct (1 woman). *Students:* 153 full-time (67 women), 44 part-time (18 women); includes 20 minority (1 Black or African American, non-Hispanic/Latino; 12 Asian, non-Hispanic/Latino; 3 Hispanic/Latino; 1 Native Hawaiian or other Pacific Islander, non-Hispanic/Latino; 3 Two or more races, non-Hispanic/Latino), 97 international. Average age 29. 194 applicants, 64% accepted, 106 enrolled. In 2013, 61 degrees awarded. *Degree requirements:* For master's, thesis optional. *Entrance requirements:* For master's, GMAT. Additional exam requirements/recommendations for international students: Required—TOEFL (minimum score 91 iBT), IELTS (minimum score 7). *Application deadline:* Applications are processed on a rolling basis. Application fee: $60. *Expenses:* Contact institution. *Unit head:* Dr. David Baldridge, Director for

Business Master's Program, 541-737-6062, E-mail: david.baldridge@bus.oregonstate.edu.
Website: http://business.oregonstate.edu/mba/degrees.

Ottawa University, Graduate Studies-Arizona, Programs in Business, Ottawa, KS 66067-3399. Offers business administration (MBA); finance (MBA); human resources (MA, MBA); leadership (MBA); marketing (MBA). Programs offered in Mesa, Phoenix, Tempe and West Valley, AZ. Part-time and evening/weekend programs available. Postbaccalaureate distance learning degree programs offered. *Degree requirements:* For master's, thesis or alternative. *Entrance requirements:* For master's, minimum undergraduate GPA of 3.0. Additional exam requirements/recommendations for international students: Required—TOEFL (minimum score 550 paper-based). Electronic applications accepted.

Pace University, Lubin School of Business, Marketing Program, New York, NY 10038. Offers marketing management (MBA); marketing research (MBA). Part-time and evening/weekend programs available. *Students:* 24 full-time (14 women), 66 part-time (38 women); includes 15 minority (3 Black or African American, non-Hispanic/Latino; 1 American Indian or Alaska Native, non-Hispanic/Latino; 5 Asian, non-Hispanic/Latino; 3 Hispanic/Latino; 3 Two or more races, non-Hispanic/Latino), 42 international. Average age 26. 148 applicants, 32% accepted, 34 enrolled. In 2013, 26 master's awarded. *Entrance requirements:* For master's, GMAT, GRE. Additional exam requirements/recommendations for international students: Required—TOEFL. *Application deadline:* For fall admission, 8/1 priority date for domestic students, 6/1 for international students; for spring admission, 12/1 for domestic students, 10/1 for international students. Applications are processed on a rolling basis. Application fee: $70. Electronic applications accepted. *Expenses: Tuition:* Part-time $1075 per credit. *Required fees:* $192 per semester. Tuition and fees vary according to course load, degree level and program. *Financial support:* Research assistantships, career-related internships or fieldwork, and Federal Work-Study available. Support available to part-time students. Financial award applicants required to submit FAFSA. *Unit head:* Dr. Mary M. Long, Chairperson, 212-618-6453, E-mail: mlong@pace.edu. *Application contact:* Susan Ford-Goldschein, Director of Graduate Admissions, 212-346-1531, Fax: 212-346-1585, E-mail: gradnyc@pace.edu.
Website: http://www.pace.edu/lubin.

Philadelphia University, School of Business Administration, Program in Business Administration, Philadelphia, PA 19144. Offers general business (MBA); innovation (MBA); management (MBA); marketing (MBA); strategic design (MBA); MBA/MS. Part-time and evening/weekend programs available. Postbaccalaureate distance learning degree programs offered (no on-campus study). *Entrance requirements:* For master's, GMAT. Additional exam requirements/recommendations for international students: Required—TOEFL (minimum score 550 paper-based; 79 iBT).

Polytechnic University of Puerto Rico, Miami Campus, Graduate School, Miami, FL 33166. Offers accounting (MBA); business administration (MBA); construction management (MEM); environmental management (MEM); finance (MBA); human resources management (MBA); logistics and supply chain management (MBA); management of international enterprises (MBA); manufacturing management (MEM); marketing management (MBA); project management (MBA). Part-time and evening/weekend programs available. Postbaccalaureate distance learning degree programs offered (no on-campus study). *Entrance requirements:* For master's, minimum GPA of 3.0. Electronic applications accepted.

Pontifical Catholic University of Puerto Rico, College of Business Administration, Program in Marketing, Ponce, PR 00717-0777. Offers MBA. Part-time and evening/weekend programs available. *Degree requirements:* For master's, thesis. *Entrance requirements:* For master's, GRE, interview, minimum GPA of 2.75.

Pontificia Universidad Catolica Madre y Maestra, Graduate School, Faculty of Social and Administrative Sciences, Santiago, Dominican Republic. Offers business administration (MBA), including business development, finance, international business, management skills (M Mgmt, MBA), marketing, operations, strategic cost management, strategy, tourist destination planning and management; law (LL M), including civil law, corporate business law, criminal law, international relations, real estate law; management (M Mgmt), including higher financial management, insurance program administration, management skills (M Mgmt, MBA); psychology (MA), including clinical child and adolescent psychology, forensic psychology; strategic human resources (EMBA).

Post University, Program in Business Administration, Waterbury, CT 06723-2540. Offers accounting (MSA); business administration (MBA); corporate innovation (MBA); entrepreneurship (MBA); finance (MBA); healthcare (MBA); leadership (MBA); marketing (MBA); project management (MBA). *Accreditation:* ACBSP. Postbaccalaureate distance learning degree programs offered.

Providence College, School of Business, Providence, RI 02918. Offers accounting (MBA); finance (MBA); international business (MBA); management (MBA); marketing (MBA); not-for-profit organizations (MBA). Part-time and evening/weekend programs available. *Faculty:* 14 full-time (5 women), 3 part-time/adjunct (1 woman). *Students:* 68 full-time (25 women), 54 part-time (25 women); includes 12 minority (3 Black or African American, non-Hispanic/Latino; 1 Asian, non-Hispanic/Latino; 6 Hispanic/Latino; 2 Two or more races, non-Hispanic/Latino), 7 international. Average age 25. 43 applicants, 95% accepted, 36 enrolled. In 2013, 38 master's awarded. *Degree requirements:* For master's, thesis optional. *Entrance requirements:* For master's, GMAT. Additional exam requirements/recommendations for international students: Required—TOEFL (minimum score 550 paper-based; 80 iBT). *Application deadline:* For fall admission, 7/15 priority date for domestic and international students; for spring admission, 11/15 priority date for domestic and international students; for summer admission, 4/15 priority date for domestic students. Applications are processed on a rolling basis. Application fee: $55. *Expenses:* Contact institution. *Financial support:* Federal Work-Study, institutionally sponsored loans, and unspecified assistantships available. Support available to part-time students. Financial award application deadline: 8/1; financial award applicants required to submit FAFSA. *Unit head:* Jacqueline Elcik, Director, 401-865-2131, E-mail: jelcik@providence.edu. *Application contact:* MBA Program, 401-865-2294, E-mail: mba@providence.edu.
Website: http://www.providence.edu/business/Pages/default.aspx.

Queen's University at Kingston, Queens School of Business, Program in Business Administration, Kingston, ON K7L 3N6, Canada. Offers consulting and project management (MBA); finance (MBA); innovation and entrepreneurship (MBA); marketing (MBA). *Accreditation:* AACSB. *Degree requirements:* For master's, thesis optional, research project. *Entrance requirements:* For master's, GMAT, minimum B+ average. Additional exam requirements/recommendations for international students: Required—TOEFL. Electronic applications accepted. *Faculty research:* Management fundamentals, strategic thinking, global business, innovation and change, leadership.

Quinnipiac University, School of Business and Engineering, Program in Business Administration, Hamden, CT 06518-1940. Offers chartered financial analyst (MBA); finance (MBA); healthcare management (MBA); information systems management (MBA); marketing (MBA); supply chain management (MBA); JD/MBA. *Accreditation:* AACSB. Part-time and evening/weekend programs available. Postbaccalaureate distance learning degree programs offered (no on-campus study). *Faculty:* 33 full-time (10 women), 7 part-time/adjunct (3 women). *Students:* 109 full-time (48 women), 225 part-time (101 women); includes 44 minority (14 Black or African American, non-Hispanic/Latino; 2 American Indian or Alaska Native, non-Hispanic/Latino; 12 Asian, non-Hispanic/Latino; 15 Hispanic/Latino; 1 Two or more races, non-Hispanic/Latino), 17 international. 230 applicants, 80% accepted, 154 enrolled. In 2013, 124 master's awarded. *Entrance requirements:* For master's, GMAT or GRE, minimum GPA of 3.0. Additional exam requirements/recommendations for international students: Required—TOEFL (minimum score 575 paper-based; 90 iBT), IELTS (minimum score 6.5). *Application deadline:* For fall admission, 7/30 priority date for domestic students, 4/30 priority date for international students; for spring admission, 12/15 priority date for domestic students, 9/15 priority date for international students. Applications are processed on a rolling basis. Application fee: $45. Electronic applications accepted. *Expenses: Tuition:* Part-time $920 per credit. *Required fees:* $37 per credit. *Financial support:* In 2013–14, 41 students received support. Career-related internships or fieldwork, Federal Work-Study, scholarships/grants, and unspecified assistantships available. Support available to part-time students. Financial award application deadline: 6/1; financial award applicants required to submit FAFSA. *Faculty research:* Financial markets and investments, international business, supply chain management, health care management, corporate governance. *Unit head:* Lisa Braiewa, MBA Program Director, E-mail: lisa.braiewa@quinnipiac.edu. *Application contact:* Office of Graduate Admissions, 800-462-1944, Fax: 203-582-3443, E-mail: graduate@quinnipiac.edu.
Website: http://www.quinnipiac.edu/mba.

Regent's University London, Webster Graduate School, London, United Kingdom. Offers business (MBA); finance (MS); human resources (MA); information technology management (MA); international business (MA); international non-governmental organizations (MA); international relations (MA); management and leadership (MA); marketing (MA). Part-time programs available.

Regis University, College for Professional Studies, School of Management, MBA Program, Denver, CO 80221-1099. Offers finance and accounting (MBA); general business (MBA); health industry leadership (MBA); marketing (MBA); operations management (MBA); organizational performance management (MBA); strategic management (MBA). Part-time and evening/weekend programs available. Postbaccalaureate distance learning degree programs offered (no on-campus study). *Faculty:* 10 full-time (3 women), 74 part-time/adjunct (17 women). *Students:* 386 full-time (183 women), 269 part-time (134 women); includes 190 minority (38 Black or African American, non-Hispanic/Latino; 2 American Indian or Alaska Native, non-Hispanic/Latino; 30 Asian, non-Hispanic/Latino; 109 Hispanic/Latino; 1 Native Hawaiian or other Pacific Islander, non-Hispanic/Latino; 10 Two or more races, non-Hispanic/Latino), 11 international. Average age 42. 152 applicants, 91% accepted, 112 enrolled. In 2013, 318 master's awarded. *Degree requirements:* For master's, thesis (for some programs), final research project. *Entrance requirements:* For master's, official transcript reflecting baccalaureate degree awarded from regionally-accredited college or university, work experience, resume, letters of recommendation. Additional exam requirements/recommendations for international students: Required—TOEFL (minimum score 550 paper-based; 82 iBT). *Application deadline:* Applications are processed on a rolling basis. Application fee: $75. Electronic applications accepted. *Expenses:* Contact institution. *Financial support:* In 2013–14, 22 students received support. Federal Work-Study and scholarships/grants available. Financial award application deadline: 4/15; financial award applicants required to submit FAFSA. *Unit head:* Dr. Anthony Vrba, Interim Dean, 303-964-5384, Fax: 303-964-5538, E-mail: avrba@regis.edu. *Application contact:* Sarah Engel, Director of Admissions, 303-458-4900, Fax: 303-964-5534, E-mail: regisadm@regis.edu.
Website: http://www.regis.edu/CPS/Academics/Degrees-and-Programs/Graduate-Programs/MBA-College-for-Professional-Studies.aspx.

Roberts Wesleyan College, Graduate Business Programs, Rochester, NY 14624-1997. Offers strategic leadership (MS); strategic marketing (MS). Evening/weekend programs available. *Degree requirements:* For master's, thesis or alternative. *Entrance requirements:* For master's, GMAT, minimum GPA of 2.75, verifiable work experience. *Application deadline:* Applications are processed on a rolling basis. Application fee: $35. *Expenses:* Contact institution. *Financial support:* Applicants required to submit FAFSA. *Unit head:* Dr. Steven Bovee, Co-Director, 585-594-6763, Fax: 716-594-6316, E-mail: bovees@roberts.edu. *Application contact:* Office of Admissions, 800-777-4RWC, E-mail: admissions@roberts.edu.
Website: http://www.roberts.edu/graduate-business-programs.aspx.

Rollins College, Crummer Graduate School of Business, Winter Park, FL 32789-4499. Offers business administration (EDBA); entrepreneurship (MBA); finance (MBA); international business (MBA); management (MBA); marketing (MBA); operations and technology management (MBA). *Accreditation:* AACSB. Part-time and evening/weekend programs available. Postbaccalaureate distance learning degree programs offered (minimal on-campus study). *Faculty:* 21 full-time (3 women), 2 part-time/adjunct (1 woman). *Students:* 157 full-time (86 women), 135 part-time (83 women); includes 60 minority (12 Black or African American, non-Hispanic/Latino; 1 American Indian or Alaska Native, non-Hispanic/Latino; 17 Asian, non-Hispanic/Latino; 23 Hispanic/Latino; 1 Native Hawaiian or other Pacific Islander, non-Hispanic/Latino; 6 Two or more races, non-Hispanic/Latino), 19 international. Average age 37. 264 applicants, 53% accepted, 105 enrolled. In 2013, 169 master's awarded. *Degree requirements:* For master's, minimum GPA of 2.85; for doctorate, thesis/dissertation, minimum GPA of 3.0. *Entrance requirements:* For master's, GMAT or GRE, official transcripts, two letters of recommendation, essay, current resume/curriculum vitae, interview; for doctorate, official transcripts, two letters of recommendation, essays, current resume/curriculum vitae, interview with EDBA academic committee. Additional exam requirements/recommendations for international students: Required—TOEFL (minimum score 100 iBT) or IELTS (minimum score 7). *Application deadline:* Applications are processed on a rolling basis. Application fee: $50. Electronic applications accepted. *Expenses:* Contact institution. *Financial support:* In 2013–14, 87 students received support. Federal Work-Study and scholarships/grants available. Support available to part-time students. Financial award applicants required to submit FAFSA. *Faculty research:* Sustainability, world financial markets, international business, market research, strategic marketing. *Unit head:* Dr. Craig M. McAllaster, Dean, 407-646-2249, Fax: 407-646-1550, E-mail: cmcallaster@rollins.edu. *Application contact:* Eva Gauthier Oleksiw, Admissions Coordinator, 407-646-2405, Fax: 407-646-1550, E-mail: mbaadmissions@rollins.edu.
Website: http://www.rollins.edu/mba/.

Roosevelt University, Graduate Division, College of Arts and Sciences, Department of Communication, Program in Integrated Marketing Communications, Chicago, IL 60605. Offers MSIMC. Part-time and evening/weekend programs available. *Faculty research:* Print journalism, urban high school journalism.

Rowan University, Graduate School, College of Communication and Creative Arts, Integrated Marketing Communication and New Media Certificate of Graduate Study Program, Glassboro, NJ 08028-1701. Offers CGS. *Students:* 1 (woman) part-time. Average age 38. 1 applicant, 100% accepted, 1 enrolled. *Application deadline:* For spring admission, 2/15 for domestic and international students; for summer admission, 4/1 for domestic and international students. Application fee: $65. *Expenses: Tuition,*

area resident: Part-time $638 per credit. Tuition, state resident: full-time $5742. *Required fees:* $142 per credit. Tuition and fees vary according to course level and program. *Unit head:* Dr. Horacio Sosa, Dean, College of Graduate and Continuing Education, 856-256-4747, Fax: 856-256-5638, E-mail: sosa@rowan.edu. *Application contact:* Admissions and Enrollment Services, 856-256-5435, Fax: 856-256-5637, E-mail: cgceadmissions@rowan.edu.

Rutgers, The State University of New Jersey, Newark, Graduate School, Program in Management, Newark, NJ 07102. Offers accounting (PhD); accounting information systems (PhD); computer information systems (PhD); finance (PhD); information technology (PhD); international business (PhD); management science (PhD); marketing (PhD); organization management (PhD). Program offered jointly with New Jersey Institute of Technology. *Accreditation:* AACSB. *Degree requirements:* For doctorate, thesis/dissertation, cumulative exams. *Entrance requirements:* For doctorate, GMAT or GRE General Test, minimum undergraduate B average. Additional exam requirements/recommendations for international students: Required—TOEFL. Electronic applications accepted. *Faculty research:* Technology management, leadership and teams, consumer behavior, financial and markets, logistics.

Rutgers, The State University of New Jersey, Newark, Rutgers Business School–Newark and New Brunswick, Doctoral Programs in Management, Newark, NJ 07102. Offers accounting (PhD); accounting information systems (PhD); economics (PhD); finance (PhD); individualized study (PhD); information technology (PhD); international business (PhD); management science (PhD); marketing science (PhD); organizational management (PhD); science, technology and management (PhD); supply chain management (PhD). *Degree requirements:* For doctorate, comprehensive exam, thesis/dissertation. *Entrance requirements:* For doctorate, GRE or GMAT. Additional exam requirements/recommendations for international students: Required—TOEFL (minimum score 550 paper-based; 79 iBT). Electronic applications accepted.

Sacred Heart University, Graduate Programs, John F. Welch College of Business, Department of Management, Fairfield, CT 06825-1000. Offers accounting (Certificate); business (MBA); human resource management (MS); international business (Certificate); leadership (Certificate); marketing (Certificate). *Faculty:* 6 full-time (3 women), 2 part-time/adjunct (both women). *Students:* 24 full-time (9 women), 141 part-time (81 women); includes 29 minority (11 Black or African American, non-Hispanic/Latino; 5 Asian, non-Hispanic/Latino; 13 Hispanic/Latino), 4 international. Average age 32. 14 applicants, 79% accepted, 9 enrolled. In 2013, 81 master's awarded. *Entrance requirements:* For master's, GMAT (minimum score of 400), bachelor's degree in related field of business, microeconomics, macroeconomics or statistics; minimum GPA of 3.0. Additional exam requirements/recommendations for international students: Required—PTE; Recommended—TOEFL (minimum score 570 paper-based; 80 iBT), IELTS (minimum score 6.5). *Application deadline:* Applications are processed on a rolling basis. Application fee: $60. Electronic applications accepted. *Expenses: Tuition:* Full-time $22,775; part-time $617 per credit. *Financial support:* Applicants required to submit FAFSA. *Unit head:* Dr. John Chalykoff, Dean, 203-396-8084, E-mail: chalykoffj@sacredheart.edu. *Application contact:* Kathy Dilks, Executive Director of Graduate Admissions, 203-365-7619, Fax: 203-365-4732, E-mail: dilksk@sacredheart.edu. Website: http://www.sacredheart.edu/academics/johnfwelchcollegeofbusiness/.

Sacred Heart University, Graduate Programs, John F. Welch College of Business, Department of Marketing, Fairfield, CT 06825-1000. Offers digital marketing (MS). *Faculty:* 2 full-time (0 women). *Students:* 2 full-time (1 woman), 9 part-time (6 women); includes 1 minority (Hispanic/Latino). Average age 33. 13 applicants, 77% accepted, 8 enrolled. *Entrance requirements:* For master's, GMAT (minimum score of 400), bachelor's degree with minimum GPA of 3.0. Additional exam requirements/recommendations for international students: Required—PTE; Recommended—TOEFL (minimum score 570 paper-based; 80 iBT), IELTS (minimum score 6.5). *Expenses: Tuition:* Full-time $22,775; part-time $617 per credit. *Unit head:* Dr. Joshua Shuart, Department Chair, 203-371-7875, Fax: 203-365-7538, E-mail: marketing@sacredheart.edu. *Application contact:* Kathy Dilks, Executive Director of Graduate Admissions, 203-365-7619, Fax: 203-365-4732, E-mail: dilksk@sacredheart.edu. Website: http://www.sacredheart.edu/academics/johnfwelchcollegeofbusiness/graduateprogramscertificates/msindigitalmarketing/.

Sage Graduate School, School of Management, Program in Business Administration, Troy, NY 12180-4115. Offers business strategy (MBA); finance (MBA); human resources (MBA); marketing (MBA); JD/MBA. Part-time and evening/weekend programs available. *Faculty:* 2 full-time (both women), 9 part-time/adjunct (2 women). *Students:* 10 full-time (5 women), 53 part-time (33 women); includes 14 minority (5 Black or African American, non-Hispanic/Latino; 6 Asian, non-Hispanic/Latino; 2 Hispanic/Latino; 1 Two or more races, non-Hispanic/Latino). Average age 30. 52 applicants, 54% accepted, 16 enrolled. In 2013, 22 master's awarded. *Entrance requirements:* For master's, minimum GPA of 2.75, resume, 2 letters of recommendation. Additional exam requirements/recommendations for international students: Required—TOEFL (minimum score 550 paper-based). *Application deadline:* Applications are processed on a rolling basis. Application fee: $40. *Expenses: Tuition:* Full-time $11,880; part-time $660 per credit hour. *Financial support:* Fellowships, research assistantships, Federal Work-Study, scholarships/grants, and unspecified assistantships available. Support available to part-time students. Financial award application deadline: 3/1; financial award applicants required to submit FAFSA. *Unit head:* Dr. Daniel Robeson, Dean, School of Management, 518-292-8657, Fax: 518-292-1964, E-mail: robesd@sage.edu. *Application contact:* Wendy D. Diefendorf, Director of Graduate and Adult Admission, 518-244-2443, Fax: 518-244-6880, E-mail: diefew@sage.edu.

St. Bonaventure University, School of Graduate Studies, Russell J. Jandoli School of Journalism and Mass Communication, Program in Integrated Marketing Communications, St. Bonaventure, NY 14778-2284. Offers MA. Weekend format option offered at Buffalo Center (Hamburg, NY). Evening/weekend programs available. *Faculty:* 5 full-time (2 women), 7 part-time/adjunct (3 women). *Students:* 51 full-time (29 women), 18 part-time (13 women); includes 5 minority (3 Black or African American, non-Hispanic/Latino; 1 American Indian or Alaska Native, non-Hispanic/Latino; 1 Two or more races, non-Hispanic/Latino), 2 international. Average age 25. 52 applicants, 90% accepted, 37 enrolled. In 2013, 35 master's awarded. *Entrance requirements:* For master's, transcripts, two letters of recommendation, essay. Additional exam requirements/recommendations for international students: Required—TOEFL (minimum score 550 paper-based; 79 iBT). *Application deadline:* For fall admission, 6/5 for domestic students, 2/1 for international students; for spring admission, 10/15 for domestic students, 7/1 for international students. Applications are processed on a rolling basis. Application fee: $0. Electronic applications accepted. *Financial support:* In 2013–14, 2 research assistantships were awarded; Federal Work-Study, scholarships/grants, health care benefits, and unspecified assistantships also available. Support available to part-time students. *Unit head:* Br. Basil Valente, Director, 716-375-2585, Fax: 716-646-1825, E-mail: bvalente@sbu.edu. *Application contact:* Bruce Campbell, Director of Graduate Admissions, 716-375-2429, Fax: 716-375-4015, E-mail: gradsch@sbu.edu. Website: http://www.sbu.edu/academics/schools/journalism-and-mass-communications/graduate-degrees/ma-integrated-marketing-communications.

St. Edward's University, School of Management and Business, Area of Business Administration, Austin, TX 78704. Offers accounting (MBA); business management (MBA); finance (Certificate); global entrepreneurship (MBA); marketing (MBA). Part-time and evening/weekend programs available. *Students:* 29 full-time (12 women), 181 part-time (85 women); includes 88 minority (15 Black or African American, non-Hispanic/Latino; 1 American Indian or Alaska Native, non-Hispanic/Latino; 4 Asian, non-Hispanic/Latino; 61 Hispanic/Latino; 7 Two or more races, non-Hispanic/Latino), 10 international. Average age 33. 85 applicants, 79% accepted, 38 enrolled. In 2013, 79 master's awarded. *Degree requirements:* For master's, minimum of 24 resident hours. *Entrance requirements:* For master's, GMAT or GRE General Test, minimum GPA of 2.75 in last 60 hours of course work. Additional exam requirements/recommendations for international students: Required—TOEFL (minimum score 79 iBT) or IELTS (minimum score 6). *Application deadline:* For fall admission, 6/1 priority date for domestic and international students; for spring admission, 10/1 priority date for domestic and international students; for summer admission, 3/1 priority date for domestic and international students. Applications are processed on a rolling basis. Application fee: $50. Electronic applications accepted. *Expenses: Tuition:* Full-time $20,664; part-time $1148 per credit hour. *Required fees:* $50 per trimester. Full-time tuition and fees vary according to course load and program. *Unit head:* Dr. Stan Horner, Director, 512-428-1279, Fax: 512-448-8492, E-mail: stanleyh@stedwards.edu. *Application contact:* Office of Admission, 512-448-8500, Fax: 512-464-8877, E-mail: seu.admit@stedwards.edu. Website: http://www.stedwards.edu.

St. John's University, The Peter J. Tobin College of Business, Department of Marketing, Queens, NY 11439. Offers MBA, Adv C. Part-time and evening/weekend programs available. *Students:* 37 full-time (23 women), 15 part-time (7 women); includes 10 minority (2 Black or African American, non-Hispanic/Latino; 4 Asian, non-Hispanic/Latino; 2 Hispanic/Latino; 2 Two or more races, non-Hispanic/Latino), 17 international. Average age 26. 47 applicants, 81% accepted, 19 enrolled. In 2013, 34 master's awarded. *Degree requirements:* For master's, comprehensive exam (for some programs), thesis optional. *Entrance requirements:* For master's, GMAT, 2 letters of recommendation, resume, transcripts, essay; for Adv C, GMAT, 2 letters of recommendation, resume, undergraduate and graduate transcripts, essay, MBA. Additional exam requirements/recommendations for international students: Required—TOEFL (minimum score 600 paper-based; 100 iBT), IELTS (minimum score 7). *Application deadline:* For fall admission, 5/1 priority date for domestic and international students; for spring admission, 11/1 priority date for domestic and international students. Applications are processed on a rolling basis. Application fee: $50. Electronic applications accepted. *Expenses:* Contact institution. *Financial support:* Research assistantships, scholarships/grants, and unspecified assistantships available. Support available to part-time students. Financial award application deadline: 3/1; financial award applicants required to submit FAFSA. *Faculty research:* Global brand management, China's stimulus plan, measuring attitude, marketing in India, consumer decision-making. *Unit head:* Dr. Noel Doherty, Chair, 718-990-7370, E-mail: dohertya@stjohns.edu. *Application contact:* Carol J. Swanberg, Assistant Dean/Director of Graduate Admissions, 718-990-1345, Fax: 718-990-5242, E-mail: tobingradnyc@stjohns.edu.

Saint Joseph's University, Erivan K. Haub School of Business, Executive Master's in Food Marketing Program, Philadelphia, PA 19131-1395. Offers MBA, MS. Part-time programs available. *Students:* 5 full-time (3 women), 62 part-time (30 women); includes 7 minority (1 Black or African American, non-Hispanic/Latino; 2 Asian, non-Hispanic/Latino; 4 Hispanic/Latino), 1 international. Average age 32. In 2013, 12 master's awarded. *Degree requirements:* For master's, minimum GPA of 3.0. *Entrance requirements:* For master's, 4 years of industry experience, interview or GMAT/GRE, 2 letters of recommendation, resume, official transcripts, personal statement, 2 business writing samples. Additional exam requirements/recommendations for international students: Required—TOEFL (minimum score 550 paper-based, 80 iBT), IELTS (minimum score 6.5), or PTE (minimum score 60). *Application deadline:* For fall admission, 7/15 for domestic students, 4/15 for international students; for spring admission, 11/15 for domestic students, 10/15 for international students. Applications are processed on a rolling basis. Application fee: $0. Electronic applications accepted. *Expenses:* Contact institution. *Financial support:* Institutionally sponsored loans and scholarships/grants available. Support available to part-time students. Financial award application deadline: 5/1; financial award applicants required to submit FAFSA. *Faculty research:* Organic food marketing, marketing vitamin D, mushrooms: nutrition marketing for specialty groups, transforming food marketing education. *Unit head:* Bryant Wynes, Director, 610-660-3056, Fax: 610-660-3153, E-mail: wwynes@sju.edu. *Application contact:* Amanda Basile, Marketing Development Manager, 610-660-3156, Fax: 610-660-3153, E-mail: abasile@sju.edu. Website: http://www.sju.edu/academics/hsb/grad/efm/.

Saint Joseph's University, Erivan K. Haub School of Business, MS Program in International Marketing, Philadelphia, PA 19131-1395. Offers MS. Part-time and evening/weekend programs available. *Students:* 45 full-time (29 women), 15 part-time (6 women); includes 1 minority (Black or African American, non-Hispanic/Latino), 50 international. Average age 25. In 2013, 32 master's awarded. *Degree requirements:* For master's, minimum GPA of 3.0. *Entrance requirements:* For master's, GMAT or GRE, 2 letters of recommendation, resume, personal statement, official undergraduate and graduate transcripts. Additional exam requirements/recommendations for international students: Required—TOEFL (minimum score 550 paper-based, 80 iBT), IELTS (minimum score 6.5), or PTE (minimum score 60). *Application deadline:* For fall admission, 7/15 priority date for domestic students, 5/15 priority date for international students; for spring admission, 11/15 priority date for domestic students, 10/15 priority date for international students; for summer admission, 4/15 priority date for domestic students. Applications are processed on a rolling basis. Application fee: $35. Electronic applications accepted. *Expenses: Tuition:* Part-time $786 per credit hour. Tuition and fees vary according to degree level and program. *Financial support:* In 2013–14, 1 research assistantship with partial tuition reimbursement (averaging $8,000 per year) was awarded; scholarships/grants and unspecified assistantships also available. Support available to part-time students. Financial award application deadline: 5/1; financial award applicants required to submit FAFSA. *Faculty research:* Export marketing, global marketing, international marketing research, new product development, emerging markets, international consumer behavior. *Unit head:* David Benglian, Director, 610-660-1626, Fax: 610-660-1599, E-mail: david.benglian@sju.edu. *Application contact:* Karena Whitmore, Administrative Assistant, MS Programs, 610-660-3211, Fax: 610-660-1599, E-mail: kwhitmor@sju.edu. Website: http://www.sju.edu/academics/hsb/grad/mim/.

Saint Joseph's University, Erivan K. Haub School of Business, Pharmaceutical and Healthcare Marketing MBA for Executives Program, Philadelphia, PA 19131-1395. Offers executive pharmaceutical marketing (Post Master's Certificate); pharmaceutical marketing (MBA). Part-time and evening/weekend programs available. Postbaccalaureate distance learning degree programs offered. *Students:* 9 full-time (7 women), 137 part-time (72 women); includes 42 minority (19 Black or African American, non-Hispanic/Latino; 14 Asian, non-Hispanic/Latino; 6 Hispanic/Latino; 1 Native Hawaiian or other Pacific Islander, non-Hispanic/Latino; 2 Two or more races, non-Hispanic/Latino), 2 international. Average age 38. In 2013, 40 master's awarded. *Degree requirements:* For master's and Post Master's Certificate, minimum GPA of 3.0. *Entrance requirements:* For master's, 4 years of industry experience, letter of

recommendation, resume, interview, official transcripts; for Post Master's Certificate, MBA, 4 years of industry experience, resume. Additional exam requirements/recommendations for international students: Required—TOEFL (minimum score 550 paper-based, 80 iBT), IELTS (minimum score 6.5), or PTE (minimum score 60). *Application deadline:* For fall admission, 7/15 for domestic students, 4/15 for international students; for spring admission, 11/15 for domestic students, 10/15 for international students. Applications are processed on a rolling basis. Electronic applications accepted. *Expenses:* Contact institution. *Financial support:* In 2013–14, research assistantships with partial tuition reimbursements (averaging $4,000 per year) were awarded; scholarships/grants and unspecified assistantships also available. Support available to part-time students. Financial award application deadline: 5/1; financial award applicants required to submit FAFSA. *Faculty research:* Pharmaceutical strategy, Internet and pharmaceuticals, pharmaceutical promotion. *Unit head:* Terese W. Waldron, Director, 610-660-3150, Fax: 610-660-5160, E-mail: twaldron@sju.edu. *Application contact:* Christine Anderson, Senior Manager, Executive Relations and Industry Outreach, 610-660-3157, Fax: 610-660-3160, E-mail: christine.anderson@sju.edu.
Website: http://www.sju.edu/epharma.

Saint Joseph's University, Erivan K. Haub School of Business, Professional MBA Program, Philadelphia, PA 19131-1395. Offers accounting (MBA, Postbaccalaureate Certificate); business intelligence (MBA); finance (MBA); general business (MBA); health and medical services administration (MBA); international business (MBA); international marketing (MBA); managing human capital (MBA); marketing (MBA); DO/MBA. DO/MBA offered jointly with Philadelphia College of Osteopathic Medicine. Part-time and evening/weekend programs available. *Students:* 81 full-time (37 women), 478 part-time (195 women); includes 85 minority (35 Black or African American, non-Hispanic/Latino; 1 American Indian or Alaska Native, non-Hispanic/Latino; 23 Asian, non-Hispanic/Latino; 13 Hispanic/Latino; 1 Native Hawaiian or other Pacific Islander, non-Hispanic/Latino; 12 Two or more races, non-Hispanic/Latino), 44 international. Average age 30. In 2013, 195 master's awarded. *Degree requirements:* For master's and Postbaccalaureate Certificate, minimum GPA of 3.0. *Entrance requirements:* For master's, GMAT or GRE, 2 letters of recommendation, resume, personal statement, official undergraduate and graduate transcripts; for Postbaccalaureate Certificate, official master's-level transcripts. Additional exam requirements/recommendations for international students: Required—TOEFL (minimum score 550 paper-based, 80 iBT), IELTS (minimum score 6.5), or PTE (minimum score 60). *Application deadline:* For fall admission, 7/15 priority date for domestic students, 5/15 priority date for international students; for spring admission, 11/15 priority date for domestic students, 10/15 priority date for international students; for summer admission, 4/15 priority date for domestic students, 2/15 priority date for international students. Applications are processed on a rolling basis. Application fee: $35. Electronic applications accepted. *Expenses: Tuition:* Part-time $786 per credit hour. Tuition and fees vary according to degree level and program. *Financial support:* In 2013–14, 2 research assistantships with partial tuition reimbursements (averaging $4,000 per year) were awarded; scholarships/grants and unspecified assistantships also available. Support available to part-time students. Financial award application deadline: 5/1; financial award applicants required to submit FAFSA. *Unit head:* Christine Hartmann, Director, MBA Program, 610-660-1659, Fax: 610-660-1599, E-mail: chartman@sju.edu. *Application contact:* Jeannine Lajeunesse, Assistant Director, MBA Program, 610-660-1695, Fax: 610-660-1599, E-mail: jlajeune@sju.edu.
Website: http://www.sju.edu/haubmba.

Saint Leo University, Graduate Business Studies, Saint Leo, FL 33574-6665. Offers accounting (M Acc, MBA); business (MBA); health care management (MBA); human resource management (MBA); information security management (MBA); marketing (MBA); marketing research and social media analytics (MBA); project management (MBA); sport business (MBA). Part-time and evening/weekend programs available. Postbaccalaureate distance learning degree programs offered (no on-campus study). *Faculty:* 48 full-time (12 women), 61 part-time/adjunct (21 women). *Students:* 1,855 full-time (1,020 women); includes 810 minority (587 Black or African American, non-Hispanic/Latino; 7 American Indian or Alaska Native, non-Hispanic/Latino; 36 Asian, non-Hispanic/Latino; 161 Hispanic/Latino; 3 Native Hawaiian or other Pacific Islander, non-Hispanic/Latino; 16 Two or more races, non-Hispanic/Latino), 33 international. Average age 38. In 2013, 905 master's awarded. *Entrance requirements:* For master's, GMAT (minimum score 500 if applicant has less than 3.0 in the last two years of undergraduate study), bachelor's degree with minimum GPA of 3.0 in the last 60 hours of coursework from regionally-accredited college or university; 2 years of professional work experience; resume; 2 letters of recommendation. Additional exam requirements/recommendations for international students: Required—TOEFL (minimum score 550 paper-based; 80 iBT). *Application deadline:* For fall admission, 7/1 priority date for domestic and international students; for spring admission, 11/12 priority date for domestic students, 11/1 for international students. Applications are processed on a rolling basis. Application fee: $80. Electronic applications accepted. *Expenses: Tuition:* Full-time $12,114; part-time $673 per semester hour. Tuition and fees vary according to degree level, campus/location and program. *Financial support:* In 2013–14, 116 students received support. Career-related internships or fieldwork, Federal Work-Study, scholarships/grants; and health care benefits available. Financial award application deadline: 3/1; financial award applicants required to submit FAFSA. *Unit head:* Dr. Lorrie McGovern, Assistant Dean, Graduate Studies in Business, 352-588-7390, Fax: 352-588-8585, E-mail: mbaslu@saintleo.edu. *Application contact:* Joshua Stagner, Director of Graduate Admission, 800-707-8846, Fax: 352-588-7873, E-mail: grad.admissions@saintleo.edu.
Website: http://www.saintleo.edu/academics/graduate.aspx.

Saint Peter's University, Graduate Business Programs, MBA Program, Jersey City, NJ 07306-5997. Offers finance (MBA); health care administration (MBA); human resource management (MBA); international business (MBA); management (MBA); management information systems (MBA); marketing (MBA); risk management (MBA); MBA/MS. Part-time and evening/weekend programs available. *Entrance requirements:* Additional exam requirements/recommendations for international students: Required—TOEFL. Electronic applications accepted. *Faculty research:* Finance, health care management, human resource management, international business, management, management information systems, marketing, risk management.

St. Thomas Aquinas College, Division of Business Administration, Sparkill, NY 10976. Offers business administration (MBA); finance (MBA); management (MBA); marketing (MBA). Part-time and evening/weekend programs available. *Entrance requirements:* For master's, GMAT. Additional exam requirements/recommendations for international students: Required—TOEFL. Electronic applications accepted.

Saint Xavier University, Graduate Studies, Graham School of Management, Chicago, IL 60655-3105. Offers employee health benefits (Certificate); finance (MBA); financial fraud examination and management (MBA, Certificate); financial planning (MBA, Certificate); generalist/individualized (MBA); health administration (MBA); managed care (Certificate); management (MBA); marketing (MBA); project management (MBA, Certificate); MBA/MS. *Accreditation:* ACBSP. Part-time and evening/weekend programs

available. *Entrance requirements:* For master's, GMAT, minimum GPA of 3.0, 2 years of work experience. Electronic applications accepted. *Expenses:* Contact institution.

San Diego State University, Graduate and Research Affairs, College of Business Administration, Department of Marketing, San Diego, CA 92182. Offers MS. Part-time and evening/weekend programs available. *Degree requirements:* For master's, thesis or alternative. *Entrance requirements:* For master's, GMAT, resume, letters of reference. Additional exam requirements/recommendations for international students: Required—TOEFL. Electronic applications accepted.

San Francisco State University, Division of Graduate Studies, College of Business, Program in Business Administration, San Francisco, CA 94132-1722. Offers decision sciences/operations research (MBA); finance (MBA); information systems (MBA); leadership (MBA); management (MBA); marketing (MBA); sustainable business (MBA). *Accreditation:* AACSB. Part-time and evening/weekend programs available. *Faculty:* 100. *Students:* 850 (408 women). 839 applicants, 56% accepted, 241 enrolled. *Degree requirements:* For master's, thesis, essay test. *Entrance requirements:* For master's, GMAT, minimum GPA of 2.7 in last 60 units. Additional exam requirements/recommendations for international students: Required—TOEFL (minimum score 550 paper-based). *Application deadline:* For fall admission, 5/1 priority date for domestic students, 4/1 for international students; for spring admission, 11/1 for domestic students, 10/15 for international students. Applications are processed on a rolling basis. Application fee: $55. *Financial support:* Application deadline: 3/1. *Unit head:* Linda Oubre, Dean, 415-817-4300, E-mail: loubre@sfsu.edu. *Application contact:* Armaan Moattari, Assistant Director, Graduate Programs, 415-817-4314, Fax: 817-4340, E-mail: amoatt@sfsu.edu.
Website: http://cob.sfsu.edu/.

Seton Hall University, Stillman School of Business, Programs in Business Administration, South Orange, NJ 07079-2697. Offers accounting (MBA); finance (MBA); information technology management (MBA); international business (MBA); management (MBA); marketing (MBA); sport management (MBA); supply chain management (MBA). Part-time and evening/weekend programs available. *Faculty:* 32 full-time (6 women), 20 part-time/adjunct (3 women). *Students:* 67 full-time (23 women), 162 part-time (66 women); includes 28 minority (7 Black or African American, non-Hispanic/Latino; 7 Asian, non-Hispanic/Latino; 6 Hispanic/Latino; 8 Native Hawaiian or other Pacific Islander, non-Hispanic/Latino). Average age 31. 216 applicants, 28% accepted, 39 enrolled. In 2013, 139 master's awarded. *Degree requirements:* For master's, 20 hours of community service (Social Responsibility Project). *Entrance requirements:* For master's, GMAT, GRE or CPA, advanced degree from AACSB institution, MS in a business discipline, professional degree (MD, JD, PhD, DVM, DDS, etc.), minimum undergraduate GPA of 3.0. Additional exam requirements/recommendations for international students: Required—TOEFL (minimum score 102 iBT), IELTS or PTE. *Application deadline:* For fall admission, 5/31 priority date for domestic students, 3/31 priority date for international students; for spring admission, 10/31 priority date for domestic students, 9/30 priority date for international students. Applications are processed on a rolling basis. Application fee: $75. Electronic applications accepted. *Financial support:* In 2013–14, research assistantships with full tuition reimbursements (averaging $23,956 per year) were awarded; career-related internships or fieldwork, Federal Work-Study, scholarships/grants, and unspecified assistantships also available. Support available to part-time students. Financial award application deadline: 6/30; financial award applicants required to submit FAFSA. *Faculty research:* Sport, hedge funds, international business, legal issues, disclosure and branding. *Total annual research expenditures:* $68,000. *Unit head:* Dr. Joyce Strawser, Dean, 973-761-9013, Fax: 973-761-9217, E-mail: joyce.strawser@shu.edu. *Application contact:* Catherine Bianchi, Director of Graduate Admissions, 973-761-9262, Fax: 973-761-9208, E-mail: catherine.bianchi@shu.edu.
Website: http://www.shu.edu/academics/business.

Simmons College, School of Management, Boston, MA 02115. Offers business administration (MBA); business and financial analytics (MBA); corporate social responsibility and sustainability (MBA); entrepreneurship (MBA); healthcare management (MBA); management (MS), including communications management, non-profit management; marketing (MBA); nonprofit management (MBA); organizational leadership (MBA); MBA/MSW; MS/MA. *Accreditation:* AACSB. Part-time and evening/weekend programs available. *Students:* 34 full-time (33 women), 233 part-time (214 women); includes 67 minority (41 Black or African American, non-Hispanic/Latino; 1 American Indian or Alaska Native, non-Hispanic/Latino; 9 Asian, non-Hispanic/Latino; 10 Hispanic/Latino; 2 Native Hawaiian or other Pacific Islander, non-Hispanic/Latino; 4 Two or more races, non-Hispanic/Latino), 7 international. In 2013, 133 master's awarded. *Entrance requirements:* For master's, GMAT or GRE. Additional exam requirements/recommendations for international students: Required—TOEFL. *Application deadline:* Applications are processed on a rolling basis. Application fee: $75. Electronic applications accepted. *Financial support:* Scholarships/grants and unspecified assistantships available. Financial award applicants required to submit FAFSA. *Faculty research:* Gender and organizations, leadership, health care management. *Unit head:* Cathy Minehan, Dean, 617-521-2846. *Application contact:* Melissa Terrio, Director of Graduate Admissions, 617-521-3840, Fax: 617-521-3880, E-mail: somadm@simmons.edu.
Website: http://www.simmons.edu/som.

Southern Adventist University, School of Business and Management, Collegedale, TN 37315-0370. Offers accounting (MBA); church administration (MSA); church and nonprofit leadership (MBA); financial management (MFM); healthcare administration (MBA); management (MBA); marketing management (MBA); outdoor education (MSA). Part-time and evening/weekend programs available. Postbaccalaureate distance learning degree programs offered (no on-campus study). *Entrance requirements:* For master's, GMAT. Additional exam requirements/recommendations for international students: Required—TOEFL (minimum score 600 paper-based; 100 iBT). Electronic applications accepted.

Southern Methodist University, Cox School of Business, MBA Program, Dallas, TX 75275. Offers accounting (MBA, PMBA); business administration (EMBA); finance (MBA); financial statement analysis (PMBA); general business (MBA); information technology and operations management (MBA); management (MBA); marketing (MBA); real estate (MBA); strategy (MBA); strategy and entrepreneurship (MBA); JD/MBA; MA/MBA. Part-time and evening/weekend programs available. *Entrance requirements:* For master's, GMAT. Additional exam requirements/recommendations for international students: Required—TOEFL. Electronic applications accepted. *Expenses:* Contact institution. *Faculty research:* Corporate finance, financial reporting, modeling consumer decision-making, competition between national brands and store brands, institutional determinants of firms' strategy.

Southern New Hampshire University, School of Business, Manchester, NH 03106-1045. Offers accounting (MBA, MS, Graduate Certificate); accounting finance (MS); accounting/auditing (MS); accounting/forensic accounting (MS); accounting/taxation (MS); athletic administration (MBA, Graduate Certificate); business administration (IMBA, MBA, Certificate, Graduate Certificate), including accounting (Certificate), business administration (MBA), business information systems (Graduate Certificate), human resource management (Certificate); corporate social responsibility (MBA);

entrepreneurship (MBA); finance (MBA, MS, Graduate Certificate); finance/corporate finance (MS); finance/investments and securities (MS); forensic accounting (MBA); healthcare informatics (MBA); healthcare management (MBA); human resource management (Graduate Certificate); information technology (MS, Graduate Certificate); information technology management (MBA); international business (Graduate Certificate); international business and information technology (Graduate Certificate); international finance (Graduate Certificate); international sport management (Graduate Certificate); justice studies (MBA); leadership of nonprofit organizations (Graduate Certificate); marketing (MBA, MS, Graduate Certificate); operations and project management (MS); operations and supply chain management (MBA, Graduate Certificate); organizational leadership (MS); project management (MBA, Graduate Certificate); Six Sigma (MBA); Six Sigma quality (Graduate Certificate); social media marketing (MBA); sport management (MBA, MS, Graduate Certificate); sustainability and environmental compliance (MBA); workplace conflict management (MBA); MBA/Certificate. *Accreditation:* ACBSP. Part-time and evening/weekend programs available. Postbaccalaureate distance learning degree programs offered (no on-campus study). Terminal master's awarded for partial completion of doctoral program. *Degree requirements:* For master's, one foreign language, comprehensive exam (for some programs), thesis or alternative. *Entrance requirements:* For master's, minimum GPA of 2.5. Additional exam requirements/recommendations for international students: Required—TOEFL (minimum score 500 paper-based). Electronic applications accepted.

Southern Polytechnic State University, School of Engineering Technology and Management, Department of Business Administration, Marietta, GA 30060-2896. Offers accounting (MBA, MSA); business administration (Graduate Transition Certificate); finance (MBA); general (MBA); management (MBA); management information systems (MBA); marketing (MBA); operations and technology management (MBA). *Accreditation:* ACBSP. Part-time and evening/weekend programs available. Postbaccalaureate distance learning degree programs offered (no on-campus study). *Degree requirements:* For master's, comprehensive exam (for some programs), capstone course and major field exam (for MBA); 30 semester hours of course work (for MSA). *Entrance requirements:* For master's, GMAT or GRE, letters of recommendation, statement of purpose, resume, minimum GPA of 2.75 or undergraduate degree in business with up to 6 transition courses; undergraduate degree in accounting from regionally-accredited school (for MSA). Additional exam requirements/recommendations for international students: Required—TOEFL (minimum score 550 paper-based; 79 iBT), IELTS (minimum score 6.5). Electronic applications accepted. *Faculty research:* Ethics, virtual reality, sustainability, management of technology, quality management, capacity planning, human-computer interaction/interface, enterprise integration planning, economic impact of educational institutions, behavioral accounting, accounting ethics, taxation, information security, visualization simulation, human-computer interaction, supply chain, logistics, economics.

Southwest Minnesota State University, Department of Business and Public Affairs, Marshall, MN 56258. Offers leadership (MBA); management (MBA); marketing (MBA). Part-time and evening/weekend programs available. Postbaccalaureate distance learning degree programs offered (no on-campus study). *Degree requirements:* For master's, thesis. *Entrance requirements:* For master's, GMAT (minimum score: 450). Additional exam requirements/recommendations for international students: Recommended—TOEFL (minimum score 550 paper-based; 79 iBT), IELTS. Electronic applications accepted.

State University of New York Institute of Technology, Program in Business Administration in Technology Management, Utica, NY 13504-3050. Offers accounting and finance (MBA); business management (MBA); health services management (MBA); human resource management (MBA); marketing management (MBA). Part-time programs available. Postbaccalaureate distance learning degree programs offered (no on-campus study). *Faculty:* 10 full-time (2 women), 2 part-time/adjunct (1 woman). *Students:* 29 full-time (13 women), 89 part-time (26 women); includes 17 minority (5 Black or African American, non-Hispanic/Latino; 8 Asian, non-Hispanic/Latino; 3 Hispanic/Latino; 1 Two or more races, non-Hispanic/Latino), 1 international. Average age 33. 78 applicants, 54% accepted, 29 enrolled. In 2013, 57 master's awarded. *Degree requirements:* For master's, capstone course. *Entrance requirements:* For master's, GMAT, resume, one letter of reference. Additional exam requirements/recommendations for international students: Required—TOEFL (minimum score 550 paper-based; 79 iBT), IELTS (minimum score 6.5). *Application deadline:* For fall admission, 8/1 priority date for domestic students, 7/1 for international students; for spring admission, 12/1 for domestic students, 11/1 for international students. Applications are processed on a rolling basis. Application fee: $60. Electronic applications accepted. *Expenses:* Tuition, state resident: full-time $9870; part-time $411 per credit hour. Tuition, nonresident: full-time $20,150; part-time $765 per credit hour. *Required fees:* $1180; $50.73 per credit hour. *Financial support:* In 2013–14, 3 students received support, including 1 fellowship with full tuition reimbursement available (averaging $5,545 per year), 2 research assistantships with partial tuition reimbursements available (averaging $4,000 per year); unspecified assistantships also available. Financial award application deadline: 6/1; financial award applicants required to submit FAFSA. *Faculty research:* Technology management, writing schools, leadership, new products. *Unit head:* Dr. Rafael Romero, Program Coordinator and Associate Professor, 315-792-7337, Fax: 315-792-7138, E-mail: rafael.romero@sunyit.edu. *Application contact:* Maryrose Raab, Coordinator of Graduate Center, 315-792-7347, Fax: 315-792-7221, E-mail: maryrose.raab@sunyit.edu.
Website: http://www.sunyit.edu/programs/graduate/mbatm/.

Stephen F. Austin State University, Graduate School, College of Business, Program in Business Administration, Nacogdoches, TX 75962. Offers business (MBA); management and marketing (MBA). *Accreditation:* AACSB. Part-time and evening/weekend programs available. *Degree requirements:* For master's, comprehensive exam. *Entrance requirements:* For master's, GMAT, minimum AACSB index of 1000. Additional exam requirements/recommendations for international students: Required—TOEFL (minimum score 550 paper-based). *Faculty research:* Strategic implications, information search, multinational firms, philosophical guidance.

Stony Brook University, State University of New York, Graduate School, College of Business, Program in Business Administration, Stony Brook, NY 11794. Offers finance (MBA, Certificate); health care management (MBA, Certificate); human resource management (Certificate); human resources (MBA); information systems management (MBA, Certificate); management (MBA); marketing (MBA). *Faculty:* 32 full-time (7 women), 29 part-time/adjunct (8 women). *Students:* 189 full-time (102 women), 111 part-time (40 women); includes 50 minority (10 Black or African American, non-Hispanic/Latino; 1 American Indian or Alaska Native, non-Hispanic/Latino; 25 Asian, non-Hispanic/Latino; 14 Hispanic/Latino), 114 international. 255 applicants, 53% accepted, 70 enrolled. In 2013, 157 master's, 1 other advanced degree awarded. *Entrance requirements:* For master's, GMAT, 3 letters of recommendation from current or former employers or professors, transcripts, personal statement, resume. Additional exam requirements/recommendations for international students: Required—TOEFL (minimum score 550 paper-based; 90 iBT), IELTS (minimum score 6.5). *Application deadline:* For fall admission, 6/1 for domestic students, 3/15 for international students; for spring admission, 12/1 for domestic students, 11/1 for international students. Application fee: $100. *Expenses:* Tuition, state resident: full-time $9870; part-time $411 per credit. Tuition, nonresident: full-time $18,350; part-time $765 per credit. *Financial support:* Teaching assistantships available. *Total annual research expenditures:* $53,718. *Unit head:* Dr. Manuel London, Dean and Director, Center for Human Resource Management, 631-632-7159, Fax: 631-632-8181, E-mail: manuel.london@stonybrook.edu. *Application contact:* Dr. Dmytro Holod, Interim Associate Dean/Graduate Program Director, 631-632-7183, Fax: 631-632-8181, E-mail: dmytro.holod@stonybrook.edu.

Strayer University, Graduate Studies, Washington, DC 20005-2603. Offers accounting (MS); acquisition (MBA); business administration (MBA); communications technology (MS); educational management (M Ed); finance (MBA); health services administration (MHSA); hospitality and tourism management (MBA); human resource management (MBA); information systems (MS), including computer security management, decision support system management, enterprise resource management, network management, software engineering management, systems development management; management (MBA); management information systems (MS); marketing (MBA); professional accounting (MS), including accounting information systems, controllership, taxation; public administration (MPA); supply chain management (MBA); technology in education (M Ed). Programs also offered at campus locations in Birmingham, AL; Chamblee, GA; Cobb County, GA; Morrow, GA; White Marsh, MD; Charleston, SC; Columbia, SC; Greensboro, NC; Greenville, SC; Lexington, KY; Louisville, KY; Nashville, TN; North Raleigh, NC; Washington, DC. Part-time and evening/weekend programs available. Postbaccalaureate distance learning degree programs offered (minimal on-campus study). *Degree requirements:* For master's, thesis. *Entrance requirements:* For master's, GMAT, GRE General Test, bachelor's degree from an accredited college or university, minimum undergraduate GPA of 2.75. Electronic applications accepted.

Suffolk University, College of Arts and Sciences, Department of Communication and Journalism, Boston, MA 02108-2770. Offers communication studies (MAC); integrated marketing communication (MAC); public relations and advertising (MAC). Part-time and evening/weekend programs available. *Faculty:* 9 full-time (6 women). *Students:* 27 full-time (21 women), 19 part-time (15 women); includes 5 minority (1 Black or African American, non-Hispanic/Latino; 1 Asian, non-Hispanic/Latino; 3 Hispanic/Latino), 18 international. Average age 24. 98 applicants, 66% accepted, 19 enrolled. In 2013, 23 master's awarded. *Degree requirements:* For master's, thesis optional. *Entrance requirements:* For master's, GRE General Test, MAT, or GMAT, 2 letters of recommendation, resume. Additional exam requirements/recommendations for international students: Required—TOEFL (minimum score 550 paper-based; 80 iBT). *Application deadline:* For fall admission, 6/15 priority date for domestic students, 6/15 for international students; for spring admission, 11/1 priority date for domestic students, 11/1 for international students. Applications are processed on a rolling basis. Application fee: $50. Electronic applications accepted. *Expenses:* Contact institution. *Financial support:* In 2013–14, 38 students received support, including 36 fellowships (averaging $7,982 per year); career-related internships or fieldwork, Federal Work-Study, and institutionally sponsored loans also available. Support available to part-time students. Financial award application deadline: 4/1; financial award applicants required to submit FAFSA. *Faculty research:* Branding law and management, health care communication, gender roles and violence in video games, new media, political communication. *Unit head:* Dr. Robert Rosenthal, Chair, 617-573-8502, Fax: 617-742-6982, E-mail: rrosenth@suffolk.edu. *Application contact:* Cory Meyers, Director of Graduate Admissions, 617-573-8302, Fax: 617-305-1733, E-mail: grad.admission@suffolk.edu.
Website: http://www.suffolk.edu/college/departments/10483.php.

Suffolk University, Sawyer Business School, Master of Business Administration Program, Boston, MA 02108-2770. Offers accounting (MBA); business administration (APC); entrepreneurship (MBA); executive business administration (EMBA); finance (MBA); global business administration (GMBA); health administration (MBA); international business (MBA); marketing (MBA); nonprofit management (MBA); organizational behavior (MBA); strategic management (MBA); supply chain management (MBA); taxation (MBA); JD/MBA; MBA/GDPA; MBA/MHA; MBA/MSA; MBA/MSF; MBA/MST. *Accreditation:* AACSB. Part-time and evening/weekend programs available. Postbaccalaureate distance learning degree programs offered (no on-campus study). *Faculty:* 29 full-time (9 women), 12 part-time/adjunct (2 women). *Students:* 106 full-time (44 women), 334 part-time (184 women); includes 57 minority (20 Black or African American, non-Hispanic/Latino; 1 American Indian or Alaska Native, non-Hispanic/Latino; 18 Asian, non-Hispanic/Latino; 14 Hispanic/Latino; 4 Two or more races, non-Hispanic/Latino), 61 international. Average age 30. 448 applicants, 61% accepted, 135 enrolled. In 2013, 217 master's awarded. *Entrance requirements:* For master's, GMAT, minimum undergraduate GPA of 2.75 (MBA), 5 years of managerial experience (EMBA). Additional exam requirements/recommendations for international students: Required—TOEFL (minimum score 550 paper-based; 80 iBT). *Application deadline:* For fall admission, 6/15 priority date for domestic students, 6/15 for international students; for spring admission, 11/1 priority date for domestic students, 11/1 for international students. Applications are processed on a rolling basis. Application fee: $50. Electronic applications accepted. *Expenses: Tuition:* Full-time $38,374; part-time $1279 per credit. *Required fees:* $40; $20 per semester. Tuition and fees vary according to program. *Financial support:* In 2013–14, 107 students received support, including 91 fellowships with full and partial tuition reimbursements available (averaging $12,428 per year); career-related internships or fieldwork, Federal Work-Study, and institutionally sponsored loans also available. Support available to part-time students. Financial award application deadline: 4/1; financial award applicants required to submit FAFSA. *Faculty research:* Foreign investments; career strategies and boundaryless careers; corporate ethics codes; interest rates, inflation, and growth options; innovation and product development performance. *Unit head:* Heather Hewitt, Assistant Dean of Graduate Programs/Director of MBA Programs, 617-573-8306, E-mail: hhewitt@suffolk.edu. *Application contact:* Cory Meyers, Director of Graduate Admissions, 617-573-8302, Fax: 617-305-1733, E-mail: grad.admission@suffolk.edu.
Website: http://www.suffolk.edu/mba.

Syracuse University, Martin J. Whitman School of Management, PhD Program in Business Administration, Syracuse, NY 13244. Offers accounting (PhD); finance (PhD); management information systems (PhD); managerial statistics (PhD); marketing (PhD); operations management (PhD); organizational behavior (PhD); strategy and human resources (PhD); supply chain management (PhD). *Faculty:* 79 full-time (20 women), 25 part-time/adjunct (6 women). *Students:* 26 full-time (8 women), 1 part-time (0 women); includes 2 minority (1 Black or African American, non-Hispanic/Latino; 1 Asian, non-Hispanic/Latino), 20 international. Average age 30. 130 applicants, 9% accepted, 7 enrolled. In 2013, 15 doctorates awarded. *Degree requirements:* For doctorate, comprehensive exam, thesis/dissertation, summer research paper. *Entrance requirements:* For doctorate, GMAT or GRE General Test, 3 recommendations. Additional exam requirements/recommendations for international students: Required—TOEFL (minimum score 600 paper-based; 100 iBT). *Application deadline:* For fall admission, 1/15 priority date for domestic and international students. Applications are processed on a rolling basis. Application fee: $75. Electronic applications accepted. *Financial support:* In 2013–14, 1 fellowship with full tuition reimbursement (averaging $19,570 per year), 30 teaching assistantships with full tuition reimbursements (averaging $17,000 per year) were awarded; research assistantships with full tuition

reimbursements also available. Financial award application deadline: 1/15. *Faculty research:* Marketing models, market microstructure, supply chain, auditing, corporate governance. *Unit head:* Dr. Michel Benarock, Director of the PhD Program, 315-443-3429, E-mail: mbeanaroc@syr.edu. *Application contact:* Carol Hilleges, Administrative Specialist, 315-443-9601, Fax: 315-443-3671, E-mail: clhilleg@syr.edu.
Website: http://whitman.syr.edu/phd/.

Syracuse University, Martin J. Whitman School of Management, Program in Business Administration, Syracuse, NY 13244. Offers accounting (MBA); entrepreneurship (MBA); finance (MBA); marketing (MBA); supply chain management (MBA). Postbaccalaureate distance learning degree programs offered (minimal on-campus study). *Faculty:* 79 full-time (20 women), 25 part-time/adjunct (6 women). *Students:* 112 full-time (41 women), 181 part-time (49 women); includes 52 minority (19 Black or African American, non-Hispanic/Latino; 18 Asian, non-Hispanic/Latino; 11 Hispanic/Latino; 4 Two or more races, non-Hispanic/Latino), 56 international. Average age 33. 179 applicants, 50% accepted, 36 enrolled. In 2013, 115 master's awarded. *Entrance requirements:* For master's, GMAT, 2 letters of recommendation. Additional exam requirements/recommendations for international students: Required—TOEFL (minimum score 600 paper-based; 100 iBT). *Application deadline:* For fall admission, 11/30 priority date for domestic and international students. Applications are processed on a rolling basis. Application fee: $75. Electronic applications accepted. *Financial support:* In 2013–14, 17 students received support. Fellowships with full and partial tuition reimbursements available, teaching assistantships with partial tuition reimbursements available, career-related internships or fieldwork, scholarships/grants, tuition waivers (partial), and unspecified assistantships available. Support available to part-time students. Financial award application deadline: 3/1. *Unit head:* Dr. Don Harter, Associate Dean for Master's Programs, 315-443-3502, Fax: 315-443-9517, E-mail: dharter@syr.edu. *Application contact:* Danielle Goodroe, Director, Graduate Enrollment, 315-443-3006, Fax: 315-443-9517, E-mail: mbainfo@syr.edu.
Website: http://whitman.syr.edu/ftmba/.

Temple University, Fox School of Business, Doctoral Programs in Business, Philadelphia, PA 19122-6096. Offers accounting (PhD); entrepreneurship (PhD); finance (PhD); international business (PhD); management information systems (PhD); marketing (PhD); risk management and insurance (PhD); statistics (PhD); strategic management (PhD); tourism and sport (PhD). *Accreditation:* AACSB. *Degree requirements:* For doctorate, thesis/dissertation. *Entrance requirements:* For doctorate, GRE General Test, GMAT, minimum GPA of 3.0, master's degree. Additional exam requirements/recommendations for international students: Required—TOEFL (minimum score 600 paper-based; 100 iBT), IELTS (minimum score 7.5). Electronic applications accepted.

Temple University, Fox School of Business, MBA Programs, Philadelphia, PA 19122-6096. Offers accounting (MBA); business management (MBA); financial management (MBA); healthcare and life sciences innovation (MBA); human resource management (MBA); international business (IMBA); IT management (MBA); marketing management (MBA); pharmaceutical management (MBA); strategic management (EMBA, MBA). EMBA offered in Philadelphia, PA and Tokyo, Japan. *Accreditation:* AACSB. Part-time and evening/weekend programs available. Postbaccalaureate distance learning degree programs offered (minimal on-campus study). *Entrance requirements:* For master's, GMAT, minimum undergraduate GPA of 3.0. Additional exam requirements/recommendations for international students: Required—TOEFL (minimum score 600 paper-based; 100 iBT), IELTS (minimum score 7.5).

Temple University, Fox School of Business, Specialized Master's Programs, Philadelphia, PA 19122-6096. Offers accountancy (MS); actuarial science (MS); finance (MS); financial engineering (MS); human resource management (MS); innovation management and entrepreneurship (MS); marketing (MS); statistics (MS). MS in innovation management and entrepreneurship delivered jointly with College of Engineering. *Accreditation:* AACSB. Part-time programs available. *Entrance requirements:* For master's, GRE General Test or GMAT, minimum undergraduate GPA of 3.0. Additional exam requirements/recommendations for international students: Required—TOEFL (minimum score 600 paper-based; 100 iBT), IELTS (minimum score 7.5).

Temple University, School of Tourism and Hospitality Management, Program in Sport Business, Philadelphia, PA 19122-6096. Offers athletics administration (MS); recreation and event management (MS); sport analytics (MS); sport marketing and promotions (MS). Part-time programs available. *Faculty:* 12 full-time (2 women), 3 part-time/adjunct (1 woman). *Students:* 19 full-time (10 women), 7 part-time (4 women); includes 2 minority (both Black or African American, non-Hispanic/Latino). 54 applicants, 54% accepted, 20 enrolled. *Degree requirements:* For master's, thesis optional, internship or project. *Entrance requirements:* For master's, GRE General Test, GMAT, or MAT, bachelor's degree or equivalent with minimum GPA of 3.0, 500-word essay, 2 letters of recommendation, resume. Additional exam requirements/recommendations for international students: Required—TOEFL (minimum score 550 paper-based; 79 iBT), IELTS (minimum score 6.5). *Application deadline:* For fall admission, 3/1 priority date for domestic students, 1/15 priority date for international students; for spring admission, 8/15 priority date for domestic students, 6/30 priority date for international students. Applications are processed on a rolling basis. Application fee: $60. Electronic applications accepted. *Expenses:* Contact institution. *Financial support:* In 2013–14, 1 teaching assistantship with full tuition reimbursement (averaging $18,000 per year) was awarded. Financial award application deadline: 3/1; financial award applicants required to submit FAFSA. *Faculty research:* Industrial/organization management, corporate social responsibility, diversity/inclusion, sport/recreation for persons with disabilities, youth sport development, sport pricing, sport consumer behavior, marketing/advertising assessment, facility design and operation, participant sport behavior, mass participant sport events, brand evaluation, sport marketing communication, sport economics, recreation programming and assessment, non-profit development and management. *Unit head:* Dr. Joris Drayer, Associate Professor/Director of Programs in Sport and Recreation, 215-204-8701, Fax: 215-204-8705, E-mail: joris.drayer@temple.edu. *Application contact:* Michael J. Usino, Senior Associate Director of Recruitment, 215-204-3103, Fax: 215-204-8705, E-mail: musino@temple.edu.
Website: http://sthm.temple.edu/grad/explore-ma-sports.html.

Temple University, School of Tourism and Hospitality Management, Program in Tourism and Hospitality Management, Philadelphia, PA 19122-6096. Offers hospitality operations (MTHM); tourism and hospitality marketing (MTHM). Part-time and evening/weekend programs available. *Faculty:* 10 full-time (3 women), 3 part-time/adjunct (0 women). *Students:* 23 full-time (21 women), 4 part-time (2 women); includes 2 minority (1 Asian, non-Hispanic/Latino; 1 Two or more races, non-Hispanic/Latino), 22 international. 57 applicants, 58% accepted, 8 enrolled. In 2013, 11 master's awarded. *Degree requirements:* For master's, thesis optional, internship or project. *Entrance requirements:* For master's, GRE General Test, GMAT, or MAT, bachelor's degree or equivalent with minimum GPA of 3.0, 500-word essay, 2 letters of recommendation, resume. Additional exam requirements/recommendations for international students: Required—TOEFL (minimum score 550 paper-based; 79 iBT), IELTS (minimum score 6.5). *Application deadline:* For fall admission, 3/1 priority date for domestic students, 1/15 priority date for international students; for spring admission, 8/15 priority date for domestic students, 6/30 priority date for international students. Applications are processed on a rolling basis. Application fee: $60. Electronic applications accepted. *Expenses:* Contact institution. *Financial support:* In 2013–14, 1 research assistantship with full tuition reimbursement (averaging $18,000 per year) was awarded. Financial award application deadline: 3/1; financial award applicants required to submit FAFSA. *Faculty research:* Consumer behavior, revenue management, tourism marketing, advertising evaluation and information technology, brand management, service management, customer relationship management, emotional labor and emotional intelligence, employee knowledge sharing, event management, destination marketing evaluation. *Unit head:* Dr. Ceridwyn King, Assistant Professor/Director of Programs in Tourism and Hospitality Management, 215-204-8701, Fax: 215-204-8705, E-mail: ceridwyn.king@temple.edu. *Application contact:* Michael J. Usino, Senior Associate Director of Recruitment, 215-204-3103, Fax: 215-204-8705, E-mail: musino@temple.edu.
Website: http://sthm.temple.edu/cms/main/graduate-programs/.

Texas A&M University, Mays Business School, Department of Marketing, College Station, TX 77843. Offers MS, PhD. *Faculty:* 11. *Students:* 77 full-time (51 women), 1 (woman) part-time; includes 15 minority (1 Black or African American, non-Hispanic/Latino; 4 Asian, non-Hispanic/Latino; 9 Hispanic/Latino; 1 Two or more races, non-Hispanic/Latino), 17 international. Average age 25. 220 applicants, 15% accepted, 29 enrolled. In 2013, 24 master's awarded. Terminal master's awarded for partial completion of doctoral program. *Degree requirements:* For master's, comprehensive exam; for doctorate, thesis/dissertation. *Entrance requirements:* For master's, GMAT; for doctorate, GMAT or GRE General Test. Additional exam requirements/recommendations for international students: Required—TOEFL. *Application deadline:* For fall admission, 3/1 priority date for domestic students. Applications are processed on a rolling basis. Application fee: $50 ($75 for international students). *Expenses:* Tuition, state resident: full-time $4078; part-time $226.55 per credit hour. Tuition, nonresident: full-time $10,450; part-time $580.55 per credit hour. *Required fees:* $2328; $278.50 per credit hour. $642.45 per semester. *Financial support:* Fellowships, research assistantships, teaching assistantships, career-related internships or fieldwork, and institutionally sponsored loans available. Financial award application deadline: 2/1. *Faculty research:* Consumer behavior, innovation and product management, international marketing, marketing management and strategy, services marketing. *Unit head:* Dr. Rajan Varadarajan, Head, 979-845-5809, E-mail: rvaradarajan@mays.tamu.edu. *Application contact:* Stephen W. McDaniel, Master's Advisor, 979-845-5801, E-mail: smcdaniel@mays.tamu.edu.
Website: http://mays.tamu.edu/mktg/.

Texas A&M University–Commerce, Graduate School, College of Business, MS Programs, Commerce, TX 75429-3011. Offers accounting (MS); economics (MA); finance (MS); management (MS); marketing (MS). Part-time programs available. *Degree requirements:* For master's, comprehensive exam, thesis (for some programs). *Entrance requirements:* For master's, GMAT or GRE General Test. Electronic applications accepted. *Expenses:* Tuition, state resident: full-time $3630; part-time $2420 per year. Tuition, nonresident: full-time $9948; part-time $6632.16 per year. *Required fees:* $1006 per year. Tuition and fees vary according to course load. *Faculty research:* Economic activity, forensic economics, volatility and finance, international economics.

Texas Tech University, Graduate School, Rawls College of Business Administration, Area of Marketing, Lubbock, TX 79409. Offers PhD. Part-time programs available. *Faculty:* 11 full-time (3 women). *Students:* 11 full-time (2 women). Average age 36. 8 applicants, 75% accepted, 6 enrolled. In 2013, 3 doctorates awarded. *Degree requirements:* For doctorate, thesis/dissertation, qualifying exams. *Entrance requirements:* For doctorate, GMAT, holistic profile of academic credentials. Additional exam requirements/recommendations for international students: Required—TOEFL (minimum score 550 paper-based; 79 iBT). *Application deadline:* For fall admission, 7/1 priority date for domestic students, 1/15 for international students. Applications are processed on a rolling basis. Application fee: $60. Electronic applications accepted. *Expenses:* Tuition, state resident: full-time $6062; part-time $252.57 per credit hour. Tuition, nonresident: full-time $14,558; part-time $606.57 per credit hour. *Required fees:* $2655; $35 per credit hour. $907.50 per semester. Tuition and fees vary according to course load. *Financial support:* In 2013–14, 11 research assistantships (averaging $14,655 per year), 3 teaching assistantships (averaging $18,000 per year) were awarded; Federal Work-Study and scholarships/grants also available. Financial award applicants required to submit FAFSA. *Faculty research:* Consumer behavior, macromarketing, marketing strategy and strategic planning. *Unit head:* Dr. Debbie Laverie, Area Coordinator, 806-742-3188, E-mail: debbie.laverie@ttu.edu. *Application contact:* Terri Boston, Applications Manager, Graduate and Professional Programs, 806-742-3184, Fax: 806-742-3958, E-mail: rawlsgrad@ttu.edu.
Website: http://marketing.ba.ttu.edu.

Tiffin University, Program in Business Administration, Tiffin, OH 44883-2161. Offers finance (MBA); general management (MBA); healthcare administration (MBA); human resources (MBA); international business (MBA); leadership (MBA); marketing (MBA); sports management (MBA). *Accreditation:* ACBSP. Part-time and evening/weekend programs available. Postbaccalaureate distance learning degree programs offered (no on-campus study). *Entrance requirements:* For master's, minimum undergraduate GPA of 2.5, work experience. Additional exam requirements/recommendations for international students: Required—TOEFL (minimum score 550 paper-based; 79 iBT). Electronic applications accepted. *Faculty research:* Small business, executive development operations, research and statistical analysis, market research, management information systems.

Trident University International, College of Business Administration, Program in Business Administration, Cypress, CA 90630. Offers business administration (PhD); conflict and negotiation management (MBA); criminal justice administration (MBA); entrepreneurship (MBA); finance (MBA); general management (MBA); government accounting (MBA); human resource management (MBA); information security and digital assurance management (MBA); information technology management (MBA); international business (MBA); logistics management (MBA); marketing (MBA); project management (MBA); public management (MBA); quality management (MBA); strategic leadership (MBA). Part-time and evening/weekend programs available. Postbaccalaureate distance learning degree programs offered (no on-campus study). *Degree requirements:* For doctorate, comprehensive exam, thesis/dissertation, defense of dissertation. *Entrance requirements:* For master's, minimum GPA of 2.5 (students with GPA 3.0 or greater may transfer up to 30% of graduate level credits); for doctorate, minimum GPA of 3.4, curriculum vitae, course work in research methods or statistics. Additional exam requirements/recommendations for international students: Required—TOEFL. Electronic applications accepted.

United States International University, School of Business Administration, Nairobi, Kenya. Offers business administration (GEMBA); entrepreneurship (MBA); finance (MBA); human resource management (MBA); information technology management (MBA); integrated studies (MBA); international business administration (MBA); management and organizational development (MS); marketing (MBA); organizational development (EMS); strategic management (MBA). Part-time and evening/weekend programs available. *Degree requirements:* For master's, thesis. *Entrance requirements:*

Marketing

For master's, GMAT, 2 letters of reference, resume. Additional exam requirements/recommendations for international students: Required—TOEFL (minimum score 550 paper-based). *Faculty research:* Marketing in small business enterprises, total quality management in Kenya.

Universidad del Turabo, Graduate Programs, School in Business Administration, Program in Marketing, Gurabo, PR 00778-3030. Offers MBA. Part-time and evening/weekend programs available. *Entrance requirements:* For master's, GRE, EXADEP, interview.

Universidad Iberoamericana, Graduate School, Santo Domingo D.N., Dominican Republic. Offers business administration (MBA, PMBA); constitutional law (LL M); dentistry (DMD); educational management (MA); integrated marketing communication (MA); psychopedagogical intervention (M Ed); real estate law (LL M); strategic management of human talent (MM).

Universidad Metropolitana, School of Business Administration, Program in Marketing, San Juan, PR 00928-1150. Offers MBA. Part-time programs available. *Degree requirements:* For master's, thesis or alternative. *Entrance requirements:* For master's, GMAT, PAEG, interview. Electronic applications accepted.

Université de Sherbrooke, Faculty of Administration, Program in Marketing, Sherbrooke, QC J1K 2R1, Canada. Offers M Sc. *Degree requirements:* For master's, one foreign language, thesis. *Entrance requirements:* For master's, bachelor's degree in related field, minimum GPA of 3.0 (on 4.3 scale). Electronic applications accepted. *Faculty research:* Consumer behavior, sales force, branding, prices management.

Université Laval, Faculty of Administrative Sciences, Programs in Business Administration, Québec, QC G1K 7P4, Canada. Offers accounting (MBA); agri-food management (MBA); electronic business (MBA, Diploma); factory management and logistics (MBA); finance (MBA); firm management (MBA); geomatic management (MBA); information technology management (MBA); international management (MBA); management (MBA); management accounting (MBA, Diploma); marketing (MBA); modeling and organizational decision (MBA); occupational health and safety management (MBA); pharmacy management (MBA); social and environmental responsibility (MBA); technological entrepreneurship (Diploma). *Accreditation:* AACSB. Part-time and evening/weekend programs available. Postbaccalaureate distance learning degree programs offered (no on-campus study). *Entrance requirements:* For master's and Diploma, knowledge of French and English. Electronic applications accepted.

The University of Akron, Graduate School, College of Business Administration, Department of Marketing, Akron, OH 44325. Offers direct interactive marketing (MBA); international business (MBA); strategic marketing (MBA). Part-time and evening/weekend programs available. *Faculty:* 10 full-time (1 woman), 6 part-time/adjunct (2 women). *Students:* 17 full-time (7 women), 22 part-time (15 women); includes 6 minority (3 Asian, non-Hispanic/Latino; 2 Hispanic/Latino; 1 Two or more races, non-Hispanic/Latino), 7 international. Average age 28. 24 applicants, 42% accepted, 4 enrolled. In 2013, 12 master's awarded. *Entrance requirements:* For master's, GMAT, minimum GPA of 2.75, two letters of recommendation, statement of purpose, resume. Additional exam requirements/recommendations for international students: Required—TOEFL (minimum score 550 paper-based; 79 iBT). *Application deadline:* For fall admission, 7/15 for domestic and international students; for spring admission, 11/15 for domestic and international students. Application fee: $30 ($40 for international students). Electronic applications accepted. *Expenses:* Tuition, state resident: full-time $7430; part-time $412.80 per credit hour. Tuition, nonresident: full-time $12,722; part-time $706.80 per credit hour. *Required fees:* $53 per credit hour. $12 per semester. Tuition and fees vary according to course load and program. *Financial support:* In 2013–14, 2 research assistantships with full tuition reimbursements, 8 teaching assistantships with full tuition reimbursements were awarded. *Faculty research:* Multi-channel marketing, direct interactive marketing, strategic retailing, marketing strategy and telemarketing. *Total annual research expenditures:* $9,233. *Unit head:* Dr. William Baker, Chair, 330-972-8466, E-mail: wbaker@uakron.edu. *Application contact:* Dr. William Hauser, Director of Graduate Business Programs, 330-972-7043, Fax: 330-972-6588, E-mail: whauser@uakron.edu.
Website: http://www.uakron.edu/cba/departments/marketing/.

The University of Alabama, Graduate School, Manderson Graduate School of Business, Department of Marketing, Tuscaloosa, AL 35487. Offers MS, PhD. *Accreditation:* AACSB. *Faculty:* 19 full-time (4 women), 1 part-time/adjunct (0 women). *Students:* 61 full-time (31 women), 6 part-time (5 women); includes 7 minority (4 Black or African American, non-Hispanic/Latino; 1 Asian, non-Hispanic/Latino; 1 Hispanic/Latino; 1 Two or more races, non-Hispanic/Latino), 13 international. Average age 25. 134 applicants, 54% accepted, 28 enrolled. In 2013, 35 master's, 4 doctorates awarded. Terminal master's awarded for partial completion of doctoral program. *Degree requirements:* For master's, internship; for doctorate, comprehensive exam, thesis/dissertation. *Entrance requirements:* For master's, GRE or GMAT; for doctorate, GRE or GMAT, minimum GPA of 3.0. Additional exam requirements/recommendations for international students: Required—TOEFL (minimum score 600 paper-based) or IELTS (minimum score 6.5). *Application deadline:* For fall admission, 4/1 priority date for domestic and international students; for spring admission, 2/1 priority date for domestic and international students. Applications are processed on a rolling basis. Application fee: $50 ($60 for international students). Electronic applications accepted. *Expenses:* Tuition, state resident: full-time $9450. Tuition, nonresident: full-time $23,950. *Financial support:* In 2013–14, 1 fellowship with full tuition reimbursement (averaging $15,000 per year), 5 research assistantships with full tuition reimbursements (averaging $25,000 per year), 5 teaching assistantships with full tuition reimbursements (averaging $25,000 per year) were awarded; scholarships/grants, health care benefits, and unspecified assistantships also available. *Faculty research:* Relationship marketing, consumer behavior, services marketing, professional selling, supply chain management. *Unit head:* Dr. Robert M. Morgan, Department Head, 205-348-6183, Fax: 205-348-6695, E-mail: rmorgan@cba.ua.edu. *Application contact:* Courtney Cox, Office Associate II, 205-348-6183, Fax: 205-348-6695, E-mail: crhodes@cba.ua.edu.
Website: http://cba.ua.edu/mkt.

The University of Alabama at Birmingham, School of Business, Program in Business Administration, Birmingham, AL 35294-4460. Offers business administration (MBA), including finance, health care management, information technology management, marketing. Part-time and evening/weekend programs available. *Students:* 59 full-time (25 women), 249 part-time (93 women); includes 74 minority (53 Black or African American, non-Hispanic/Latino; 13 Asian, non-Hispanic/Latino; 7 Hispanic/Latino; 1 Two or more races, non-Hispanic/Latino), 16 international. Average age 32. In 2013, 128 master's awarded. *Entrance requirements:* For master's, GMAT. Additional exam requirements/recommendations for international students: Required—TOEFL. *Application deadline:* For fall admission, 7/1 for domestic and international students; for spring admission, 11/1 for domestic and international students; for summer admission, 4/1 for domestic and international students. Application fee: $60 ($75 for international students). *Unit head:* Dr. Ken Miller, Executive Director, MBA Programs, 205-934-8855, E-mail: klmiller@uab.edu. *Application contact:* Christy Manning, Coordinator of Graduate Programs in Business, 205-934-8817, E-mail: cmanning@uab.edu.
Website: http://www.uab.edu/business/degrees-certificates/MBA.

The University of Alabama in Huntsville, School of Graduate Studies, College of Business Administration, Programs in Business and Management, Huntsville, AL 35899. Offers federal contracting and procurement management (Certificate); management (MBA), including acquisition management, entrepreneurship, federal contract accounting, finance, human resource management, logistics and supply chain management, marketing, project management; supply chain management (Certificate); technology and innovation management (Certificate). *Accreditation:* AACSB. Part-time and evening/weekend programs available. *Faculty:* 13 full-time (3 women), 5 part-time/adjunct (0 women). *Students:* 41 full-time (19 women), 144 part-time (59 women); includes 35 minority (13 Black or African American, non-Hispanic/Latino; 1 American Indian or Alaska Native, non-Hispanic/Latino; 9 Asian, non-Hispanic/Latino; 11 Hispanic/Latino; 1 Two or more races, non-Hispanic/Latino), 13 international. Average age 33. 131 applicants, 78% accepted, 67 enrolled. In 2013, 83 master's, 5 other advanced degrees awarded. *Degree requirements:* For master's, comprehensive exam, thesis or alternative. *Entrance requirements:* For master's, GMAT (minimum score 500), minimum AACSB index of 1080. Additional exam requirements/recommendations for international students: Required—TOEFL (minimum score 550 paper-based; 80 iBT), IELTS (minimum score 6.5). *Application deadline:* For fall admission, 7/15 priority date for domestic students, 4/1 priority date for international students; for spring admission, 11/30 priority date for domestic students, 9/1 priority date for international students. Applications are processed on a rolling basis. Application fee: $50. Electronic applications accepted. *Expenses:* Tuition, state resident: full-time $8912; part-time $540 per credit hour. Tuition, nonresident: full-time $20,774; part-time $1252 per credit hour. *Required fees:* $148 per semester. One-time fee: $150. *Financial support:* In 2013–14, 10 students received support, including 4 research assistantships with full and partial tuition reimbursements available (averaging $7,750 per year), 5 teaching assistantships with full and partial tuition reimbursements available (averaging $9,000 per year); career-related internships or fieldwork, Federal Work-Study, institutionally sponsored loans, scholarships/grants, health care benefits, tuition waivers (full and partial), and unspecified assistantships also available. Support available to part-time students. Financial award application deadline: 4/1; financial award applicants required to submit FAFSA. *Faculty research:* Supply chain management, management of research and development, international marketing and branding, organizational behavior and human resource management, social networks and computational economics. *Total annual research expenditures:* $2.1 million. *Unit head:* Dr. Cynthia Gramm, Chair, 256-824-6913, Fax: 256-824-6328, E-mail: cynthia.gramm@uah.edu. *Application contact:* Jennifer Pettitt, Director of Graduate Programs, 256-824-6681, Fax: 256-824-7571, E-mail: jennifer.pettitt@uah.edu.

University of Alberta, Faculty of Graduate Studies and Research, Doctoral Program in Business, Edmonton, AB T6G 2E1, Canada. Offers accounting (PhD); finance (PhD); human resources/industrial relations (PhD); management science (PhD); marketing (PhD); organizational analysis (PhD); MBA/PhD. *Accreditation:* AACSB. Part-time programs available. *Degree requirements:* For doctorate, comprehensive exam, thesis/dissertation. *Entrance requirements:* For doctorate, GMAT. Additional exam requirements/recommendations for international students: Required—TOEFL (minimum score 550 paper-based). Electronic applications accepted. *Faculty research:* Accounting, capital markets and corporate finance, organizational change and human resource management, marketing, strategic management.

The University of Arizona, Eller College of Management, Department of Marketing, Tucson, AZ 85721. Offers MS, PhD. *Faculty:* 7 full-time (3 women), 2 part-time/adjunct (0 women). *Degree requirements:* For doctorate, comprehensive exam, thesis/dissertation. *Entrance requirements:* For doctorate, GMAT (minimum score 600). Additional exam requirements/recommendations for international students: Required—TOEFL (minimum score 600 paper-based). *Application deadline:* For fall admission, 3/1 for domestic students, 12/1 for international students. Applications are processed on a rolling basis. Application fee: $75. Electronic applications accepted. *Expenses:* Tuition, state resident: full-time $11,526. Tuition, nonresident: full-time $27,398. *Financial support:* In 2013–14, 11 teaching assistantships with full tuition reimbursements (averaging $24,387 per year) were awarded; research assistantships with full tuition reimbursements, career-related internships or fieldwork, Federal Work-Study, scholarships/grants, health care benefits, tuition waivers (partial), and unspecified assistantships also available. Financial award application deadline: 2/1. *Faculty research:* Consumer behavior, customer relationship management, research methods, brand strategy, public policy. *Unit head:* Dr. Linda Price, Head, 520-621-7479, Fax: 520-621-7483, E-mail: llprice@eller.arizona.edu. *Application contact:* Ashley L. Vallet, Graduate Secretary, 520-621-0991, Fax: 520-621-7483, E-mail: avallet@eller.arizona.edu.
Website: http://marketing.eller.arizona.edu/.

University of Baltimore, Graduate School, Merrick School of Business, Department of Marketing, Baltimore, MD 21201-5779. Offers business/marketing and venturing (MS). Part-time and evening/weekend programs available. *Entrance requirements:* For master's, GMAT. Additional exam requirements/recommendations for international students: Required—TOEFL (minimum score 550 paper-based). Electronic applications accepted.

University of Bridgeport, School of Business, Bridgeport, CT 06604. Offers accounting (MBA); finance (MBA); general business (MBA); global financial services (MBA); human resource management (MBA); information systems and knowledge management (MBA); international business (MBA); management (MBA); marketing (MBA); operations management (MBA); small business and entrepreneurship (MBA); specialized business (MBA). *Accreditation:* ACBSP. Part-time and evening/weekend programs available. *Faculty:* 11 full-time (2 women), 39 part-time/adjunct (8 women). *Students:* 162 full-time (90 women), 69 part-time (45 women); includes 44 minority (20 Black or African American, non-Hispanic/Latino; 7 Asian, non-Hispanic/Latino; 15 Hispanic/Latino; 2 Two or more races, non-Hispanic/Latino), 163 international. Average age 28. 492 applicants, 48% accepted, 55 enrolled. In 2013, 144 master's awarded. *Degree requirements:* For master's, thesis optional. *Entrance requirements:* For master's, GMAT. Additional exam requirements/recommendations for international students: Recommended—TOEFL (minimum score 550 paper-based; 80 iBT), IELTS (minimum score 6.5). *Application deadline:* For fall admission, 8/1 priority date for domestic and international students; for spring admission, 12/1 priority date for domestic and international students. Applications are processed on a rolling basis. Application fee: $50. Electronic applications accepted. *Expenses:* Contact institution. *Financial support:* In 2013–14, 69 students received support. Fellowships, research assistantships, teaching assistantships, career-related internships or fieldwork, Federal Work-Study, institutionally sponsored loans, and tuition waivers (partial) available. Support available to part-time students. Financial award application deadline: 6/1; financial award applicants required to submit FAFSA. *Unit head:* Dr. Lloyd G. Gibson, Dean, 203-576-4384, Fax: 203-576-4388, E-mail: llgibson@bridgeport.edu. *Application contact:* Leanne Proctor, Director of Graduate Admissions, 203-576-4552, Fax: 203-576-4941, E-mail: mba@bridgeport.edu.
Website: http://www.bridgeport.edu.

The University of British Columbia, Sauder School of Business, Doctoral Program in Commerce and Business Administration, Vancouver, BC V6T 1Z1, Canada. Offers accounting (PhD); finance (PhD); management information systems (PhD); management science (PhD); marketing (PhD); organizational behavior (PhD); strategy and business economics (PhD); transportation and logistics (PhD); urban land economics (PhD). *Faculty:* 91 full-time (22 women). *Students:* 66 full-time (24 women). Average age 30. 418 applicants, 2% accepted, 8 enrolled. In 2013, 7 doctorates awarded. *Degree requirements:* For doctorate, comprehensive exam, thesis/dissertation. *Entrance requirements:* For doctorate, GMAT or GRE. Additional exam requirements/recommendations for international students: Required—TOEFL (minimum score 600 paper-based; 100 iBT). *Application deadline:* For fall admission, 1/31 for domestic students, 12/31 for international students. Applications are processed on a rolling basis. Application fee: $95 Canadian dollars ($153 Canadian dollars for international students). Electronic applications accepted. *Expenses: Tuition, area resident:* Full-time $8000 Canadian dollars. *Financial support:* In 2013–14, fellowships with full tuition reimbursements (averaging $17,500 per year), research assistantships with full tuition reimbursements (averaging $8,500 per year), teaching assistantships with full tuition reimbursements (averaging $17,500 per year) were awarded. Financial award application deadline: 12/31. *Unit head:* Dr. Ralph Winter, Director, 604-822-8366, Fax: 604-822-8755. *Application contact:* Elaine Cho, Administrator, PhD and M Sc Programs, 604-822-8366, Fax: 604-822-8755, E-mail: phd.program@sauder.ubc.ca.
Website: http://www.sauder.ubc.ca/.

University of California, Berkeley, Graduate Division, Haas School of Business, PhD in Business Administration Program, Berkeley, CA 94720-1500. Offers accounting (PhD); business and public policy (PhD); finance (PhD); management of organizations (PhD); marketing (PhD); operations management (PhD); real estate (PhD). *Accreditation:* AACSB. *Students:* 74 full-time (28 women); includes 11 minority (9 Asian, non-Hispanic/Latino; 2 Hispanic/Latino), 38 international. Average age 27. 490 applicants, 6% accepted, 14 enrolled. In 2013, 14 doctorates awarded. *Degree requirements:* For doctorate, comprehensive exam, thesis/dissertation, written preliminary exams, oral qualifying exam. *Entrance requirements:* For doctorate, GMAT or GRE, minimum GPA of 3.0 in undergraduate and graduate coursework. Additional exam requirements/recommendations for international students: Required—TOEFL (minimum score 570 paper-based; 70 iBT), IELTS (minimum score 7). *Application deadline:* For fall admission, 12/10 for domestic and international students. Application fee: $80 ($100 for international students). Electronic applications accepted. *Financial support:* In 2013–14, 74 students received support, including 62 fellowships with full and partial tuition reimbursements available (averaging $30,000 per year), research assistantships with full and partial tuition reimbursements available (averaging $12,000 per year), teaching assistantships with full and partial tuition reimbursements available (averaging $13,000 per year); scholarships/grants, health care benefits, tuition waivers (full), unspecified assistantships, and transit passes, travel grants also available. Financial award application deadline: 12/10; financial award applicants required to submit FAFSA. *Faculty research:* Accounting, business and public policy, entrepreneurship, finance, management of organizations, marketing, operations and information technology management, real estate. *Unit head:* Dr. Martin Lettau, Director, 510-643-6349, Fax: 510-643-4255, E-mail: kimg@haas.berkeley.edu. *Application contact:* Kim Guilfoyle, Director, Student Affairs, 510-642-3944, Fax: 510-643-4255, E-mail: kimg@haas.berkeley.edu.
Website: http://www.haas.berkeley.edu/Phd/.

University of California, Berkeley, UC Berkeley Extension, Certificate Programs in Business, Berkeley, CA 94720-1500. Offers accounting (Certificate); business administration (Certificate); finance (Certificate); human resource management (Certificate); management (Certificate); marketing (Certificate); project management (Certificate). *Accreditation:* AACSB. Postbaccalaureate distance learning degree programs offered.

University of California, Berkeley, UC Berkeley Extension, International Diploma Programs, Berkeley, CA 94720-1500. Offers business administration (Certificate); finance (Certificate); global business management (Certificate); marketing (Certificate); project management (Certificate). *Accreditation:* AACSB.

University of California, Los Angeles, Graduate Division, UCLA Anderson School of Management, Los Angeles, CA 90095-1481. Offers accounting (PhD); Americas (EMBA); Asia Pacific (EMBA); business administration (EMBA, MBA); decisions, operations and technology management (PhD); finance (PhD); financial engineering (MFE); global economics and management (PhD); management and organizations (PhD); marketing (PhD); strategy and policy (PhD); DDS/MBA; MBA/JD; MBA/MD; MBA/MLAS; MBA/MLIS; MBA/MPH; MBA/MPP; MBA/MSCS; MBA/MSN; MBA/MUP. *Accreditation:* AACSB. Part-time programs available. *Faculty:* 104 full-time (20 women), 28 part-time/adjunct (4 women). *Students:* 1,069 full-time (324 women), 879 part-time (251 women); includes 664 minority (37 Black or African American, non-Hispanic/Latino; 1 American Indian or Alaska Native, non-Hispanic/Latino; 470 Asian, non-Hispanic/Latino; 34 Hispanic/Latino; 2 Native Hawaiian or other Pacific Islander, non-Hispanic/Latino; 120 Two or more races, non-Hispanic/Latino), 444 international. Average age 30. 5,084 applicants, 27% accepted, 845 enrolled. In 2013, 801 master's, 14 doctorates awarded. *Degree requirements:* For master's, comprehensive exam, field study consulting project (for MBA); thesis (for MFE); for doctorate, comprehensive exam, thesis/dissertation, oral and written qualifying exams. *Entrance requirements:* For master's, GMAT (for MBA); GMAT or GRE General Test (for MFE), 4-year bachelor's degree or equivalent; recommendation letters (1 for MBA, 2 for MFE); two essays; interview (by invitation only for MBA); for doctorate, GMAT or GRE General Test, bachelor's degree from college or university of fully-recognized standing; minimum B average in undergraduate coursework or B+ average in prior graduate work; statement of purpose; three recommendation letters. Additional exam requirements/recommendations for international students: Required—TOEFL (minimum score 560 paper-based; 87 iBT). *Application deadline:* For fall admission, 10/22 priority date for domestic and international students; for winter admission, 1/7 for domestic and international students; for spring admission, 4/15 for domestic and international students. Applications are processed on a rolling basis. Application fee: $200. Electronic applications accepted. *Expenses:* Contact institution. *Financial support:* In 2013–14, 522 students received support. Fellowships, research assistantships with partial tuition reimbursements available, teaching assistantships with partial tuition reimbursements available, career-related internships or fieldwork, institutionally sponsored loans, scholarships/grants, health care benefits, and tuition waivers (partial) available. Financial award application deadline: 4/15; financial award applicants required to submit FAFSA. *Faculty research:* Asset pricing, decision-making, behavioral finance, international finance and economics, global macroeconomics. *Total annual research expenditures:* $368,086. *Unit head:* Dr. Judy D. Olian, Dean/Chair in Management, 310-825-7982, Fax: 310-206-2073, E-mail: judy.olian@anderson.ucla.edu. *Application contact:* Alex Lawrence, Assistant Dean, MBA Admissions and Financial Aid, 310-825-6944, Fax: 310-825-8582, E-mail: mba.admissions@anderson.ucla.edu.
Website: http://www.anderson.ucla.edu/.

See Display on page 145 and Close-Up on page 191.

University of Central Missouri, The Graduate School, Warrensburg, MO 6409. Offers accountancy (MA); accounting (MBA); applied mathematics (MS); aviation safety (MA); biology (MS); business administration (MBA); career and technical education leadership (MS); college student personnel administration (MS); communication (MA); computer science (MS); counseling (MS); criminal justice (MS); educational leadership (Ed D); educational technology (MS); elementary and early childhood education (MSE); English (MA); environmental studies (MA); finance (MBA); history (MA); human services/educational technology (Ed S); human services/learning resources (Ed S); human services/professional counseling (Ed S); industrial hygiene (MS); industrial management (MS); information systems (MBA); information technology (MS); kinesiology (MS); library science and information services (MS); literacy education (MSE); marketing (MBA); mathematics (MS); music (MA); occupational safety management (MS); psychology (MS); rural family nursing (MS); school administration (MSE); social gerontology (MS); sociology (MA); special education (MSE); speech language pathology (MS); superintendency (Ed S); teaching (MAT); teaching English as a second language (MA); technology (MS); technology management (PhD); theatre (MA). Part-time programs available. *Faculty:* 233. *Students:* 890 full-time (396 women), 1,486 part-time (1,001 women); includes 192 minority (97 Black or African American, non-Hispanic/Latino; 9 American Indian or Alaska Native, non-Hispanic/Latino; 32 Asian, non-Hispanic/Latino; 40 Hispanic/Latino; 3 Native Hawaiian or other Pacific Islander, non-Hispanic/Latino; 11 Two or more races, non-Hispanic/Latino), 539 international. Average age 31. 1,953 applicants, 75% accepted. In 2013, 719 master's, 58 other advanced degrees awarded. *Degree requirements:* For master's and Ed S, comprehensive exam (for some programs), thesis (for some programs). *Entrance requirements:* Additional exam requirements/recommendations for international students: Required—TOEFL (minimum score 550 paper-based; 79 iBT). *Application deadline:* For fall admission, 6/1 for domestic students; for spring admission, 10/1 for domestic and international students. Applications are processed on a rolling basis. Application fee: $30 ($75 for international students). Electronic applications accepted. *Expenses:* Tuition, state resident: full-time $7326; part-time $276.25 per credit hour. Tuition, nonresident: full-time $13,956; part-time $552.50 per credit hour. *Required fees:* $29 per credit hour. *Financial support:* In 2013–14, 118 students received support, including 271 research assistantships with full and partial tuition reimbursements available (averaging $7,500 per year), 109 teaching assistantships with full and partial tuition reimbursements available (averaging $7,500 per year); career-related internships or fieldwork, Federal Work-Study, scholarships/grants, and administrative and laboratory assistantships also available. Support available to part-time students. Financial award application deadline: 3/1; financial award applicants required to submit FAFSA. *Unit head:* Dr. Joseph Vaughn, Assistant Provost for Research/Dean, 660-543-4092, Fax: 660-543-4778, E-mail: vaughn@ucmo.edu. *Application contact:* Brittany Lawrence, Graduate Student Services Coordinator, 660-543-4621, Fax: 660-543-4778, E-mail: gradinfo@ucmo.edu.
Website: http://www.ucmo.edu/graduate/.

University of Chicago, Booth School of Business, Full-Time MBA Program, Chicago, IL 60637. Offers accounting (MBA); analytic finance (MBA); analytic management (MBA); econometrics and statistics (MBA); economics (MBA); entrepreneurship (MBA); finance (MBA); general management (MBA); health administration and policy (Certificate); human resource management (MBA); international business (MBA); managerial and organizational behavior (MBA); marketing management (MBA); operations management (MBA); strategic management (MBA); MBA/AM; MBA/JD; MBA/MA; MBA/MD; MBA/MPP. *Accreditation:* AACSB. Part-time and evening/weekend programs available. Terminal master's awarded for partial completion of doctoral program. *Entrance requirements:* For master's, GMAT, 2 letters of recommendation, 3 essays, resume, interview. Additional exam requirements/recommendations for international students: Required—TOEFL (minimum score 600 paper-based; 104 iBT), IELTS. Electronic applications accepted. *Expenses:* Contact institution. *Faculty research:* Finance, marketing, economics, entrepreneurship, strategy, management.

University of Cincinnati, Graduate School, Carl H. Lindner College of Business, MS Program, Cincinnati, OH 45221. Offers accounting (MS); business analytics (MS); finance (MS); information systems (MS); marketing (MS); taxation (MS). Part-time and evening/weekend programs available. *Faculty:* 39 full-time (11 women), 11 part-time/adjunct (3 women). *Students:* 275 full-time (105 women), 165 part-time (69 women); includes 29 minority (14 Black or African American, non-Hispanic/Latino; 9 Asian, non-Hispanic/Latino; 1 Native Hawaiian or other Pacific Islander, non-Hispanic/Latino; 5 Two or more races, non-Hispanic/Latino), 273 international. 953 applicants, 37% accepted, 258 enrolled. In 2013, 144 master's awarded. *Degree requirements:* For master's, thesis (for some programs). *Entrance requirements:* For master's, GMAT, GRE, resume, transcripts, essays, letters of recommendation. Additional exam requirements/recommendations for international students: Required—TOEFL (minimum score 600 paper-based; 100 iBT), IELTS (minimum score 6.5). *Application deadline:* For fall admission, 3/15 priority date for domestic students, 4/1 for international students. Applications are processed on a rolling basis. Application fee: $65 ($70 for international students). Electronic applications accepted. *Expenses:* Contact institution. *Financial support:* In 2013–14, 124 students received support, including 12 teaching assistantships with full and partial tuition reimbursements available (averaging $3,500 per year); scholarships/grants, tuition waivers (full and partial), and unspecified assistantships also available. Financial award application deadline: 2/1; financial award applicants required to submit FAFSA. *Faculty research:* Real estate, empirical pricing, organization information pricing, strategic management, portfolio choice in institutional investment. *Unit head:* Dr. David Szymanski, Dean, 513-556-7001, Fax: 513-556-4891, E-mail: david.szymanski@uc.edu. *Application contact:* Dona Clary, Director, Graduate Programs, 513-556-3546, Fax: 513-558-7006, E-mail: dona.clary@uc.edu.

University of Cincinnati, Graduate School, Carl H. Lindner College of Business, PhD Programs, Cincinnati, OH 45221. Offers accounting (PhD); economics (PhD); finance (PhD); information systems (PhD); management (PhD); marketing (PhD); operations and business analytics (PhD). *Faculty:* 62 full-time (13 women). *Students:* 27 full-time (15 women), 9 part-time (1 woman); includes 2 minority (1 Asian, non-Hispanic/Latino; 1 Hispanic/Latino), 16 international. Average age 29. 86 applicants, 13% accepted, 6 enrolled. In 2013, 8 doctorates awarded. *Degree requirements:* For doctorate, comprehensive exam, thesis/dissertation. *Entrance requirements:* For doctorate, GMAT, GRE, transcripts, essays, resume, letters of recommendation. Additional exam requirements/recommendations for international students: Required—TOEFL (minimum score 600 paper-based; 100 iBT), IELTS (minimum score 6.5). *Application deadline:* For fall admission, 1/15 for domestic and international students. Application fee: $65 ($70 for international students). Electronic applications accepted. *Expenses:* Contact institution. *Financial support:* In 2013–14, 33 students received support, including 25 research assistantships with full and partial tuition reimbursements available (averaging $23,250 per year); scholarships/grants, tuition waivers (full and partial), and unspecified assistantships also available. Financial award application deadline: 1/15; financial award applicants required to submit FAFSA. *Unit head:* Dr. Suzanne Masterson, Director, 513-556-7125, Fax: 513-556-5499, E-mail: suzanne.masterson@uc.edu. *Application contact:* Angel Elvin, Assistant Director, 513-556-7190, Fax: 513-558-7006, E-mail: angel.elvin@uc.edu.
Website: http://www.business.uc.edu/phd.

Marketing

University of Colorado Boulder, Leeds School of Business, Division of Business Administration, Boulder, CO 80309. Offers accounting (MS, PhD); finance (PhD); information systems (PhD); marketing (PhD); operations (PhD); strategic, organizational, and entrepreneurial studies (PhD). *Students:* 143 full-time (72 women), 2 part-time (1 woman); includes 15 minority (1 Black or African American, non-Hispanic/Latino; 2 American Indian or Alaska Native, non-Hispanic/Latino; 5 Asian, non-Hispanic/Latino; 6 Hispanic/Latino; 1 Two or more races, non-Hispanic/Latino), 37 international. Average age 25. 281 applicants, 12% accepted, 19 enrolled. In 2013, 50 master's, 8 doctorates awarded. *Entrance requirements:* For master's, GMAT, minimum undergraduate GPA of 3.0. *Application deadline:* For fall admission, 3/31 for domestic students, 3/1 for international students; for spring admission, 10/31 for domestic and international students. Application fee: $50 ($60 for international students). Electronic applications accepted. *Financial support:* In 2013–14, 145 students received support, including 37 fellowships (averaging $3,977 per year), 27 research assistantships with full and partial tuition reimbursements available (averaging $40,893 per year), 12 teaching assistantships with full and partial tuition reimbursements available (averaging $38,197 per year); institutionally sponsored loans, scholarships/grants, health care benefits, and unspecified assistantships also available. Financial award applicants required to submit FAFSA.

University of Colorado Denver, Business School, Master of Business Administration Program, Denver, CO 80217. Offers bioinnovation and entrepreneurship (MBA); business intelligence (MBA); business strategy (MBA); business to business marketing (MBA); business to consumer marketing (MBA); change management (MBA); corporate financial management (MBA); enterprise technology management (MBA); entrepreneurship (MBA); health administration (MBA), including financial management, health administration, health information technologies, international health management and policy; human resources management (MBA); international business (MBA); investment management (MBA); managing for sustainability (MBA); sports and entertainment management (MBA). *Accreditation:* AACSB. Part-time and evening/weekend programs available. Postbaccalaureate distance learning degree programs offered (no on-campus study). *Students:* 611 full-time (246 women), 144 part-time (58 women); includes 102 minority (14 Black or African American, non-Hispanic/Latino; 2 American Indian or Alaska Native, non-Hispanic/Latino; 38 Asian, non-Hispanic/Latino; 42 Hispanic/Latino; 6 Two or more races, non-Hispanic/Latino), 26 international. Average age 32. 330 applicants, 64% accepted, 125 enrolled. In 2013, 398 master's awarded. *Degree requirements:* For master's, 48 semester hours, including 30 of core courses, 3 in international business, and 15 in electives from over 50 other graduate business courses. *Entrance requirements:* For master's, GMAT, resume, official transcripts, essay, two letters of recommendation, financial statements (for international applicants). Additional exam requirements/recommendations for international students: Required—TOEFL (minimum score 560 paper-based; 83 iBT); Recommended—IELTS (minimum score 6.5). *Application deadline:* For fall admission, 4/15 priority date for domestic students, 3/15 priority date for international students; for spring admission, 10/15 priority date for domestic students, 9/15 priority date for international students. Applications are processed on a rolling basis. Application fee: $50 ($75 for international students). Electronic applications accepted. *Expenses:* Contact institution. *Financial support:* In 2013–14, 62 students received support. Fellowships, research assistantships, teaching assistantships, Federal Work-Study, institutionally sponsored loans, scholarships/grants, traineeships, and unspecified assistantships available. Financial award application deadline: 4/1; financial award applicants required to submit FAFSA. *Faculty research:* Marketing, management, entrepreneurship, finance, health administration. *Unit head:* Elizabeth Cooperman, Professor of Finance and Managing for Sustainability/MBA Program Director, 303-315-8422, E-mail: elizabeth.cooperman@ucdenver.edu. *Application contact:* Shelly Townley, Admissions Director, Graduate Programs, 303-315-8202, E-mail: shelly.townley@ucdenver.edu.
Website: http://www.ucdenver.edu/academics/colleges/business/degrees/mba/Pages/MBA.aspx.

University of Colorado Denver, Business School, Program in Marketing, Denver, CO 80217. Offers brand management and marketing communication (MS); global marketing (MS); high-tech and entrepreneurial marketing (MS); Internet marketing (MS); marketing for sustainability (MS); marketing research (MS); sports and entertainment marketing (MS). Part-time and evening/weekend programs available. *Students:* 36 full-time (15 women), 12 part-time (4 women); includes 3 minority (1 Asian, non-Hispanic/Latino; 1 Hispanic/Latino; 1 Two or more races, non-Hispanic/Latino), 11 international. Average age 29. 47 applicants, 55% accepted, 11 enrolled. In 2013, 20 master's awarded. *Degree requirements:* For master's, 30 semester hours (21 of marketing core courses, 9 of marketing electives). *Entrance requirements:* For master's, GMAT, resume, essay, two letters of recommendation, financial statements (for international applicants). Additional exam requirements/recommendations for international students: Required—TOEFL (minimum score 537 paper-based; 75 iBT); Recommended—IELTS (minimum score 6.5). *Application deadline:* For fall admission, 4/15 for domestic students, 3/15 for international students; for spring admission, 10/15 for domestic students, 9/15 for international students. Applications are processed on a rolling basis. Application fee: $50 ($75 for international students). Electronic applications accepted. *Expenses:* Contact institution. *Financial support:* In 2013–14, 7 students received support. Fellowships, research assistantships, teaching assistantships, Federal Work-Study, institutionally sponsored loans, scholarships/grants, and traineeships available. Financial award application deadline: 4/1; financial award applicants required to submit FAFSA. *Faculty research:* Marketing issues in the Chinese environment, impact of individual difference and contextual factors on the risk-taking behaviors of managers making new-business creation decisions, attribution theory perspective of conflict between marketers and engineers, organizational identity and identification, international market entry strategies. *Unit head:* Dr. David Forlani, Associate Professor/Director of Marketing Programs, 303-315-8420, E-mail: david.forlani@ucdenver.edu. *Application contact:* Shelly Townley, Admissions Director, Graduate Programs, 303-315-8202, E-mail: shelly.townley@ucdenver.edu.
Website: http://www.ucdenver.edu/academics/colleges/business/degrees/ms/marketing/Pages/Marketing.aspx.

University of Connecticut, Graduate School, School of Business, Storrs, CT 06269. Offers accounting (MS, PhD); business administration (Exec MBA, MBA, PhD); finance (PhD); health care management and insurance studies (MBA); management (PhD); management consulting (MBA); marketing (PhD); marketing intelligence (MBA); MA/MBA; MBA/MSW. *Accreditation:* AACSB. *Degree requirements:* For master's, comprehensive exam; for doctorate, thesis/dissertation. *Entrance requirements:* For master's and doctorate, GMAT. Additional exam requirements/recommendations for international students: Required—TOEFL (minimum score 550 paper-based). Electronic applications accepted.

University of Dallas, Graduate School of Management, Irving, TX 75062-4736. Offers accounting (MBA, MM, MS); business management (MBA, MM); corporate finance (MBA, MM); financial services (MBA); global business (MBA, MM); health services management (MBA, MM); human resource management (MBA, MM); information assurance (MBA, MM, MS); information technology (MBA, MM, MS); information technology service management (MBA, MM, MS); marketing management (MBA, MM); organization development (MBA, MM); project management (MBA, MM); sports and entertainment management (MBA, MM); strategic leadership (MBA, MM); supply chain management (MBA); supply chain management and market logistics (MM). *Accreditation:* ACBSP. Part-time and evening/weekend programs available. Postbaccalaureate distance learning degree programs offered (no on-campus study). *Entrance requirements:* Additional exam requirements/recommendations for international students: Required—TOEFL. Electronic applications accepted. *Expenses:* Contact institution.

University of Dayton, School of Business Administration, Dayton, OH 45469-1300. Offers accounting (MBA); cyber security (MBA); finance (MBA); marketing (MBA); JD/MBA. *Accreditation:* AACSB. Part-time and evening/weekend programs available. *Faculty:* 20 full-time (7 women), 8 part-time/adjunct (1 woman). *Students:* 166 full-time (76 women), 85 part-time (43 women); includes 10 minority (4 Black or African American, non-Hispanic/Latino; 4 Asian, non-Hispanic/Latino; 2 Hispanic/Latino), 96 international. Average age 27. 437 applicants, 44% accepted, 53 enrolled. In 2013, 119 master's awarded. *Entrance requirements:* For master's, GMAT or GRE. Additional exam requirements/recommendations for international students: Required—TOEFL (minimum score 550 paper-based; 80 iBT); Recommended—IELTS (minimum score 6.5). *Application deadline:* For fall admission, 5/1 priority date for international students; for winter admission, 7/1 for international students; for spring admission, 11/1 priority date for international students. Applications are processed on a rolling basis. Application fee: $0 ($50 for international students). Electronic applications accepted. *Expenses:* Contact institution. *Financial support:* In 2013–14, 10 research assistantships with partial tuition reimbursements (averaging $7,020 per year) were awarded; institutionally sponsored loans, health care benefits, and unspecified assistantships also available. Financial award application deadline: 3/1; financial award applicants required to submit FAFSA. *Faculty research:* Management information systems, economics, finance, entrepreneurship, marketing, accounting and cyber security. *Unit head:* John M. Gentner, Director, MBA Program, 937-229-3733, Fax: 937-229-3882, E-mail: jgentner1@udayton.edu. *Application contact:* Mandy Schrank, Assistant Director, MBA Program, 937-229-3733, Fax: 937-229-3882, E-mail: mschrank2@udayton.edu.
Website: http://business.udayton.edu/mba/.

University of Denver, Daniels College of Business, Department of Marketing, Denver, CO 80208. Offers IMBA, MBA, MS. Part-time and evening/weekend programs available. *Faculty:* 13 full-time (5 women), 6 part-time/adjunct (4 women). *Students:* 19 full-time (7 women), 28 part-time (15 women); includes 5 minority (1 Black or African American, non-Hispanic/Latino; 1 Asian, non-Hispanic/Latino; 2 Hispanic/Latino; 1 Two or more races, non-Hispanic/Latino), 27 international. Average age 26. 225 applicants, 49% accepted, 21 enrolled. In 2013, 29 master's awarded. *Entrance requirements:* For master's, GRE General Test or GMAT, bachelor's degree, transcripts, essays, resume, interview. Additional exam requirements/recommendations for international students: Required—TOEFL (minimum score 570 paper-based; 88 iBT). *Application deadline:* For fall admission, 11/15 priority date for domestic and international students; for spring admission, 10/1 priority date for domestic and international students. Applications are processed on a rolling basis. Application fee: $100. Electronic applications accepted. *Financial support:* In 2013–14, 22 students received support, including 5 teaching assistantships with full and partial tuition reimbursements available (averaging $9,936 per year); career-related internships or fieldwork, Federal Work-Study, institutionally sponsored loans, scholarships/grants, and unspecified assistantships also available. Support available to part-time students. Financial award application deadline: 2/15; financial award applicants required to submit FAFSA. *Faculty research:* Social policy issues in marketing, price bundling, marketing to persons with disabilities, marketing to older persons, international marketing and logistics. *Unit head:* Dr. Carol Johnson, Associate Professor and Chair, 303-871-2276, Fax: 303-871-2323, E-mail: carol.johnson@du.edu. *Application contact:* Jessica Hanna, Graduate Admissions Manager, 303-871-2204, E-mail: jessica.hanna@du.edu.
Website: http://daniels.du.edu/masters-degrees/marketing/.

University of Florida, Graduate School, Warrington College of Business Administration, Hough Graduate School of Business, Department of Marketing, Gainesville, FL 32611. Offers MA, MS, PhD. *Faculty:* 12 full-time (2 women), 5 part-time/adjunct (1 woman). *Students:* 11 full-time (5 women), 1 (woman) part-time, 9 international. Average age 30. 76 applicants, 5% accepted, 3 enrolled. In 2013, 2 doctorates awarded. Terminal master's awarded for partial completion of doctoral program. *Degree requirements:* For master's, comprehensive exam, thesis optional; for doctorate, comprehensive exam, thesis/dissertation. *Entrance requirements:* For master's and doctorate, GMAT (minimum score of 465) or GRE General Test, minimum GPA of 3.0. Additional exam requirements/recommendations for international students: Required—TOEFL (minimum score 550 paper-based; 80 iBT), IELTS (minimum score 6). *Application deadline:* For fall admission, 2/1 for domestic and international students. Applications are processed on a rolling basis. Application fee: $30. Electronic applications accepted. *Expenses:* Tuition, state resident: full-time $12,640. Tuition, nonresident: full-time $30,000. *Financial support:* In 2013–14, 11 students received support, including 3 fellowships (averaging $3,450 per year), 10 research assistantships (averaging $27,970 per year), 1 teaching assistantship (averaging $24,730 per year); career-related internships or fieldwork, institutionally sponsored loans, and unspecified assistantships also available. Financial award application deadline: 2/1; financial award applicants required to submit FAFSA. *Faculty research:* Consumer behavior, decision-making, behavioral decision theory, marketing models, marketing strategy. *Unit head:* Jinhong Xie, PhD, Chair, 352-273-3270, Fax: 352-846-0457, E-mail: jinhong.xie@warrington.ufl.edu. *Application contact:* Lyle A. Brenner, PhD, Graduate Coordinator, 352-273-3272, Fax: 352-846-0457, E-mail: lbrenner@ufl.edu.
Website: http://www.cba.ufl.edu/mkt/.

University of Florida, Graduate School, Warrington College of Business Administration, Hough Graduate School of Business, Programs in Business Administration, Gainesville, FL 32611. Offers business administration (MBA); competitive strategy (MBA); entrepreneurship (MBA); finance (MBA); global management (MBA); Graham-Buffett security analysis (MBA); human resource management (MBA); information systems and operations management (MBA); international studies (MBA); Latin American business (MBA); management (MBA); marketing (MBA); real estate (MBA); sports administration (MBA); JD/MBA; MBA/MS; MBA/PhD; MBA/Pharm D; MD/MBA. *Accreditation:* AACSB. Part-time and evening/weekend programs available. Postbaccalaureate distance learning degree programs offered. *Faculty:* 72 full-time (10 women), 29 part-time/adjunct (7 women). *Students:* 440 full-time (122 women), 472 part-time (159 women); includes 203 minority (43 Black or African American, non-Hispanic/Latino; 3 American Indian or Alaska Native, non-Hispanic/Latino; 64 Asian, non-Hispanic/Latino; 92 Hispanic/Latino; 1 Native Hawaiian or other Pacific Islander, non-Hispanic/Latino), 39 international. Average age 32. 568 applicants, 58% accepted, 261 enrolled. In 2013, 405 master's awarded. *Degree requirements:* For master's, capstone course. *Entrance requirements:* For master's, GMAT (minimum score 465), minimum GPA of 3.0, interview. Additional exam requirements/recommendations for international students: Required—TOEFL (minimum score 550 paper-based; 80 iBT), IELTS (minimum score 6). *Application deadline:* For fall admission, 7/1 for domestic students, 1/1 for international students; for spring admission, 12/1 for domestic and international students. Applications are processed on a rolling basis. Application fee: $30. Electronic applications accepted. *Expenses:*

Tuition, state resident: full-time $12,640. Tuition, nonresident: full-time $30,000. *Financial support:* In 2013–14, 24 students received support, including 24 teaching assistantships (averaging $6,143 per year); career-related internships or fieldwork, scholarships/grants, and unspecified assistantships also available. Support available to part-time students. Financial award applicants required to submit FAFSA. *Faculty research:* Accounting, finance, insurance, management, real estate, urban analysis marketing. *Unit head:* Alexander D. Sevilla, Assistant Dean/Director of MBA Program, 352-273-3252, Fax: 352-392-8791, E-mail: alex.sevilla@warrington.ufl.edu. *Application contact:* Andrew S. Lord, Senior Director of Admissions, 352-273-3241, Fax: 352-392-8791, E-mail: andrew.lord@warrington.ufl.edu.
Website: http://www.floridamba.ufl.edu/.

University of Hawaii at Manoa, Graduate Division, Shidler College of Business, Program in Business Administration, Honolulu, HI 96822. Offers Asian business studies (MBA); Chinese business studies (MBA); decision sciences (MBA); entrepreneurship (MBA); finance (MBA); finance and banking (MBA); human resources management (MBA); information management (MBA); information technology (MBA); international business (MBA); Japanese business studies (MBA); marketing (MBA); organizational behavior (MBA); organizational management (MBA); real estate (MBA); student-designed track (MBA). *Accreditation:* AACSB. Part-time and evening/weekend programs available. *Degree requirements:* For master's, thesis optional. *Entrance requirements:* For master's, GMAT, minimum GPA of 3.0. Additional exam requirements/recommendations for international students: Required—TOEFL (minimum score 600 paper-based; 100 iBT), IELTS (minimum score 7). *Expenses:* Contact institution.

University of Hawaii at Manoa, Graduate Division, Shidler College of Business, Program in International Management, Honolulu, HI 96822. Offers Asian finance (PhD); global information technology management (PhD); international accounting (PhD); international marketing (PhD); international organization and strategy (PhD). Part-time programs available. *Degree requirements:* For doctorate, comprehensive exam, thesis/dissertation. *Entrance requirements:* For doctorate, GMAT or GRE General Test, minimum GPA of 3.0. Additional exam requirements/recommendations for international students: Required—TOEFL (minimum score 600 paper-based; 100 iBT), IELTS (minimum score 7). *Expenses:* Contact institution.

University of Houston, Bauer College of Business, Marketing Program, Houston, TX 77204. Offers PhD. Part-time and evening/weekend programs available. *Degree requirements:* For doctorate, comprehensive exam, thesis/dissertation. *Entrance requirements:* For doctorate, GMAT or GRE. *Faculty research:* Accountancy and taxation, finance, international business, management.

University of Houston–Victoria, School of Business Administration, Victoria, TX 77901-4450. Offers accounting (MBA); economic development and entrepreneurship (MS); finance (GMBA, MBA); general business (MBA); international business (MBA); management (GMBA, MBA); marketing (MBA). *Accreditation:* AACSB. Part-time and evening/weekend programs available. Postbaccalaureate distance learning degree programs offered (minimal on-campus study). *Faculty:* 45 full-time (15 women). *Students:* 193 full-time (93 women), 673 part-time (325 women); includes 489 minority (185 Black or African American, non-Hispanic/Latino; 169 Asian, non-Hispanic/Latino; 114 Hispanic/Latino; 1 Native Hawaiian or other Pacific Islander, non-Hispanic/Latino; 20 Two or more races, non-Hispanic/Latino), 94 international. *Entrance requirements:* For master's, GMAT. Additional exam requirements/recommendations for international students: Required—TOEFL (minimum score 550 paper-based). *Application deadline:* For fall admission, 6/1 for international students; for spring admission, 10/1 for international students. Applications are processed on a rolling basis. Application fee: $0. Electronic applications accepted. *Expenses:* Tuition, state resident: full-time $4534; part-time $251 per credit hour. Tuition, nonresident: full-time $10,906; part-time $606 per contact hour. *Required fees:* $68 per semester hour. Tuition and fees vary according to course load. *Financial support:* In 2013–14, research assistantships with partial tuition reimbursements (averaging $2,000 per year), teaching assistantships with partial tuition reimbursements (averaging $2,000 per year) were awarded; Federal Work-Study, scholarships/grants, and unspecified assistantships also available. Support available to part-time students. Financial award application deadline: 4/15; financial award applicants required to submit FAFSA. *Faculty research:* Economic development, marketing, finance. *Unit head:* Dr. Farhang Niroomand, Dean, 361-570-4230, Fax: 361-580-5599, E-mail: niroomandf@uhv.edu. *Application contact:* Admissions and Records, 361-570-4359, Fax: 361-580-5500, E-mail: admissions@uhv.edu.
Website: http://www.uhv.edu/bus/.

The University of Iowa, Henry B. Tippie College of Business, Department of Marketing, Iowa City, IA 52242-1316. Offers PhD. *Faculty:* 15 full-time (6 women), 16 part-time/adjunct (5 women). *Students:* 10 full-time (3 women), 8 international. Average age 34. 28 applicants, 11% accepted, 2 enrolled. In 2013, 2 doctorates awarded. *Degree requirements:* For doctorate, comprehensive exam, thesis/dissertation, thesis defense. *Entrance requirements:* For doctorate, GMAT or GRE. Additional exam requirements/recommendations for international students: Required—TOEFL (minimum score 600 paper-based; 100 iBT) or IELTS (minimum score 7). *Application deadline:* For fall admission, 1/15 for domestic and international students. Applications are processed on a rolling basis. Application fee: $60 ($100 for international students). Electronic applications accepted. *Financial support:* In 2013–14, 10 students received support, including 1 fellowship with full tuition reimbursement available (averaging $17,680 per year), 9 teaching assistantships with full tuition reimbursements available (averaging $17,680 per year); institutionally sponsored loans, scholarships/grants, health care benefits, and unspecified assistantships also available. Financial award application deadline: 1/15. *Faculty research:* Judgments and decision-making under certainty; consumer behavior: cognitive neuroscience, attitudes and evaluation; hierarchical Bayesian estimation; marketing-finance interface; advertising effects. *Unit head:* Prof. Gary J. Russell, Department Executive Officer, 319-335-1013, Fax: 319-335-1956, E-mail: gary-j-russell@uiowa.edu. *Application contact:* Renea L. Jay, PhD Program Coordinator, 319-335-0830, Fax: 319-335-1956, E-mail: renea-jay@uiowa.edu.
Website: http://tippie.uiowa.edu/marketing/.

The University of Iowa, Henry B. Tippie College of Business, Henry B. Tippie School of Management, Iowa City, IA 52242-1316. Offers corporate finance (MBA); investment management (MBA); marketing (MBA); strategic management and innovation (MBA); supply chain and analytics (MBA); JD/MBA; MBA/MA; MBA/MD; MBA/MHA, MBA/MSN. *Accreditation:* AACSB. Part-time and evening/weekend programs available. *Faculty:* 113 full-time (27 women), 89 part-time/adjunct (23 women). *Students:* 110 full-time (28 women), 786 part-time (236 women); includes 51 minority (13 Black or African American, non-Hispanic/Latino; 3 American Indian or Alaska Native, non-Hispanic/Latino; 23 Asian, non-Hispanic/Latino; 12 Hispanic/Latino), 162 international. Average age 33. 622 applicants, 73% accepted, 383 enrolled. In 2013, 333 master's awarded. *Degree requirements:* For master's, minimum GPA of 2.75. *Entrance requirements:* For master's, GMAT, GRE, quality work experience and leadership as shown through resume, references, and essays. Additional exam requirements/recommendations for international students: Required—TOEFL (minimum score 600 paper-based; 100 iBT), IELTS (minimum score 7). *Application deadline:* For fall admission, 7/30 for domestic students, 4/1 for international students; for spring admission, 12/30 for domestic and international students. Applications are processed on a rolling basis. Application fee:

$60 ($100 for international students). Electronic applications accepted. *Expenses:* Contact institution. *Financial support:* In 2013–14, 96 students received support, including 102 fellowships (averaging $9,519 per year), 83 research assistantships with partial tuition reimbursements available (averaging $8,893 per year), 14 teaching assistantships with partial tuition reimbursements available (averaging $17,049 per year); career-related internships or fieldwork, scholarships/grants, health care benefits, and unspecified assistantships also available. Financial award application deadline: 7/30; financial award applicants required to submit FAFSA. *Faculty research:* Capital markets, econometrics, optimization, investments and empirical corporate finance, Iowa electronic markets. *Unit head:* Prof. David W. Frasier, Associate Dean, Tippie School of Management, 800-622-4692, Fax: 319-335-3604, E-mail: david-frasier@uiowa.edu. *Application contact:* Jodi Schafer, Director, MBA Admissions and Financial Aid, 319-335-0864, Fax: 319-335-3604, E-mail: jodi-schafer@uiowa.edu.
Website: http://tippie.uiowa.edu/mba.

University of La Verne, College of Business and Public Management, Graduate Programs in Business Administration, La Verne, CA 91750-4443. Offers accounting (MBA); executive management (MBA-EP); finance (MBA, MBA-EP); health services management (MBA); information technology (MBA, MBA-EP); international business (MBA, MBA-EP); leadership (MBA-EP); managed care (MBA); management (MBA, MBA-EP); marketing (MBA, MBA-EP). Part-time and evening/weekend programs available. *Faculty:* 22 full-time (9 women), 37 part-time/adjunct (10 women). *Students:* 793 full-time (356 women), 164 part-time (80 women); includes 153 minority (17 Black or African American, non-Hispanic/Latino; 21 Asian, non-Hispanic/Latino; 110 Hispanic/Latino; 5 Two or more races, non-Hispanic/Latino), 691 international. Average age 27. In 2013, 514 master's awarded. *Entrance requirements:* For master's, GMAT, MAT, or GRE, minimum undergraduate GPA of 3.0, 2 letters of recommendation, resume, statement of purpose. Additional exam requirements/recommendations for international students: Required—TOEFL (minimum score 550 paper-based; 85 iBT). *Application deadline:* Applications are processed on a rolling basis. Application fee: $50. *Expenses:* Contact institution. *Financial support:* Career-related internships or fieldwork, institutionally sponsored loans, and scholarships/grants available. Financial award application deadline: 3/2; financial award applicants required to submit FAFSA. *Unit head:* Dr. Abe Helou, Chairperson, 909-593-3511 Ext. 4211, Fax: 909-392-2704, E-mail: ihelou@laverne.edu. *Application contact:* Rina Lazarian-Chehab, Senior Associate Director of Graduate Admissions, 909-593-3511 Ext. 4317, Fax: 909-392-2704, E-mail: rlazarian@laverne.edu.

University of La Verne, Regional and Online Campuses, Graduate Programs, Inland Empire Campus, Ontario, CA 91761. Offers business administration (MBA, MBA-EP), including accounting (MBA), finance (MBA), health services management (MBA-EP), information technology (MBA-EP), international business (MBA), managed care (MBA), management and leadership (MBA-EP), marketing (MBA-EP), supply chain management (MBA); leadership and management (MS), including human resource management, nonprofit management, organizational development. Part-time and evening/weekend programs available. *Faculty:* 1 full-time (0 women), 14 part-time/adjunct (6 women). *Students:* 26 full-time (15 women), 106 part-time (65 women); includes 92 minority (15 Black or African American, non-Hispanic/Latino; 29 Asian, non-Hispanic/Latino; 43 Hispanic/Latino; 1 Native Hawaiian or other Pacific Islander, non-Hispanic/Latino; 4 Two or more races, non-Hispanic/Latino). Average age 37. In 2013, 49 master's awarded. *Application deadline:* Applications are processed on a rolling basis. Application fee: $50. *Expenses:* Contact institution. *Financial support:* Institutionally sponsored loans available. Financial award application deadline: 3/2; financial award applicants required to submit FAFSA. *Unit head:* Allen Stout, Campus Director, Inland Empire Regional Campus in Ontario, 909-937-6987, E-mail: astout@laverne.edu. *Application contact:* Karen Schumann, Senior Associate Director of Admissions, Inland Empire Regional Campus in Ontario, 909-937-6991, E-mail: kschumann@laverne.edu.
Website: http://laverne.edu/locations/inland-empire/.

University of Massachusetts Amherst, Graduate School, Isenberg School of Management, Program in Management, Amherst, MA 01003. Offers accounting (PhD); business administration (MBA); entrepreneurship (MBA); finance (MBA, PhD); healthcare administration (MBA); hospitality and tourism management (PhD); management science (PhD); marketing (MBA, PhD); organization studies (PhD); sport management (PhD); strategic management (PhD); MBA/MS. *Accreditation:* AACSB. Part-time and evening/weekend programs available. Postbaccalaureate distance learning degree programs offered. *Faculty:* 68 full-time (14 women). *Students:* 140 full-time (59 women), 1,127 part-time (319 women); includes 229 minority (24 Black or African American, non-Hispanic/Latino; 2 American Indian or Alaska Native, non-Hispanic/Latino; 135 Asian, non-Hispanic/Latino; 51 Hispanic/Latino; 6 Native Hawaiian or other Pacific Islander, non-Hispanic/Latino; 11 Two or more races, non-Hispanic/Latino), 131 international. Average age 36. 828 applicants, 56% accepted, 351 enrolled. In 2013, 361 master's, 12 doctorates awarded. Terminal master's awarded for partial completion of doctoral program. *Degree requirements:* For doctorate, comprehensive exam, thesis/dissertation. *Entrance requirements:* For master's and doctorate, GMAT or GRE General Test. Additional exam requirements/recommendations for international students: Required—TOEFL (minimum score 550 paper-based; 80 iBT), IELTS (minimum score 6.5). *Application deadline:* For fall admission, 1/20 for domestic and international students. Applications are processed on a rolling basis. Application fee: $75. Electronic applications accepted. *Financial support:* Fellowships with full and partial tuition reimbursements, research assistantships with full and partial tuition reimbursements, teaching assistantships with full and partial tuition reimbursements, career-related internships or fieldwork, Federal Work-Study, scholarships/grants, traineeships, health care benefits, tuition waivers (full and partial), and unspecified assistantships available. Support available to part-time students. Financial award application deadline: 1/20; financial award applicants required to submit FAFSA. *Unit head:* Dr. John Wells, Chair, 413-545-7609, Fax: 413-577-2234. *Application contact:* Lindsay DeSantis, Supervisor of Admissions, 413-545-0722, Fax: 413-577-0010, E-mail: gradadm@grad.umass.edu.
Website: http://www.isenberg.umass.edu/.

University of Massachusetts Dartmouth, Graduate School, Charlton College of Business, Program in Business Administration, North Dartmouth, MA 02747-2300. Offers accounting (Postbaccalaureate Certificate); business administration (MBA); business foundations (Graduate Certificate); finance (Postbaccalaureate Certificate); international business (Graduate Certificate); management (Postbaccalaureate Certificate); marketing (Postbaccalaureate Certificate); organizational leadership (Graduate Certificate); supply chain management (Postbaccalaureate Certificate). *Accreditation:* AACSB. Part-time programs available. Postbaccalaureate distance learning degree programs offered (no on-campus study). *Faculty:* 36 full-time (12 women), 27 part-time/adjunct (10 women). *Students:* 154 full-time (73 women), 120 part-time (55 women); includes 28 minority (2 Black or African American, non-Hispanic/Latino; 1 American Indian or Alaska Native, non-Hispanic/Latino; 6 Asian, non-Hispanic/Latino; 11 Hispanic/Latino; 8 Two or more races, non-Hispanic/Latino), 129 international. Average age 29. 204 applicants, 82% accepted, 112 enrolled. In 2013, 71 master's, 15 other advanced degrees awarded. *Degree requirements:* For master's, portfolio of MBA course work. *Entrance requirements:* For master's, GMAT, statement of

purpose (minimum of 300 words), resume, 2 letters of recommendation, official transcripts; for other advanced degree, statement of purpose (minimum of 300 words), resume, official transcripts. Additional exam requirements/recommendations for international students: Required—TOEFL (minimum score 500 paper-based; 72 iBT), IELTS (minimum score 6). *Application deadline:* For fall admission, 8/1 priority date for domestic students, 5/1 priority date for international students; for spring admission, 1/1 priority date for domestic students, 10/1 priority date for international students. Applications are processed on a rolling basis. Application fee: $60. Electronic applications accepted. *Expenses:* Tuition, state resident: full-time $2071; part-time $86.29 per credit. Tuition, nonresident: full-time $8099; part-time $337.46 per credit. Tuition and fees vary according to course load and reciprocity agreements. *Financial support:* Federal Work-Study and unspecified assistantships available. Support available to part-time students. Financial award application deadline: 3/1; financial award applicants required to submit FAFSA. *Faculty research:* E-commerce, managing diversity, agile manufacturing, green business, activity-based management, build-to-order supply chain management. *Total annual research expenditures:* $330,000. *Unit head:* Toby Stapleton, Assistant Dean for Graduate Studies, 508-999-8543, Fax: 508-999-8646, E-mail: tstapleton@umassd.edu. *Application contact:* Steven Briggs, Director of Marketing and Recruitment for Graduate Studies, 508-999-8604, Fax: 508-999-8183, E-mail: graduate@umassd.edu.
Website: http://www.umassd.edu/charlton/.

University of Memphis, Graduate School, Fogelman College of Business and Economics, Program in Business Administration, Memphis, TN 38152. Offers accounting (MBA, PhD); economics (MBA, PhD); executive business administration (MBA); finance (PhD); finance, insurance, and real estate (MBA, MS); international business administration (IMBA); management (MBA, MS, PhD); management information systems (MBA, MS, PhD); management science (MBA); marketing (MBA, MS); marketing and supply chain management (PhD); real estate development (MS); JD/MBA. *Accreditation:* AACSB. *Faculty:* 44 full-time (9 women), 5 part-time/adjunct (0 women). *Students:* 238 full-time (101 women), 315 part-time (113 women); includes 146 minority (80 Black or African American, non-Hispanic/Latino; 1 American Indian or Alaska Native, non-Hispanic/Latino; 46 Asian, non-Hispanic/Latino; 13 Hispanic/Latino; 2 Native Hawaiian or other Pacific Islander, non-Hispanic/Latino; 4 Two or more races, non-Hispanic/Latino), 104 international. Average age 32. 343 applicants, 62% accepted, 102 enrolled. In 2013, 140 master's, 17 doctorates awarded. *Degree requirements:* For master's, comprehensive exam; for doctorate, comprehensive exam, thesis/dissertation. *Entrance requirements:* For master's, GMAT, resume; for doctorate, GMAT, interview, minimum GPA of 3.4, resume, letter of recommendation. Additional exam requirements/recommendations for international students: Required—TOEFL (minimum score 550 paper-based). *Application deadline:* For fall admission, 8/1 for domestic students; for spring admission, 12/1 for domestic students. Application fee: $35 ($60 for international students). *Financial support:* In 2013–14, 164 students received support. Research assistantships with full tuition reimbursements available, teaching assistantships with full tuition reimbursements available, career-related internships or fieldwork, Federal Work-Study, scholarships/grants, and unspecified assistantships available. Financial award application deadline: 2/15; financial award applicants required to submit FAFSA. *Faculty research:* Competitive business strategy, finance microstructures, supply chain management innovations, health care economics, litigation risks and corporate audits. *Unit head:* Rajiv Grover, Dean, 901-678-3759, E-mail: rgrover@memphis.edu. *Application contact:* Dr. Carol V. Danehower, Associate Dean, 901-678-5402, Fax: 901-678-3579, E-mail: fcbegp@memphis.edu.
Website: http://www.memphis.edu/fcbe/grad_programs.php.

University of Miami, Graduate School, School of Business Administration, Program in Business Administration, Coral Gables, FL 33124. Offers accounting (MBA); computer information systems (MBA); executive and professional (MBA), including international business, management; finance (MBA); international business (MBA); management (MBA); management science (MBA); marketing (MBA); professional management (MSPM); JD/MBA; MBA/MSIE. *Accreditation:* AACSB. Evening/weekend programs available. *Degree requirements:* For master's, comprehensive exam. *Entrance requirements:* For master's, GMAT. Additional exam requirements/recommendations for international students: Required—TOEFL (minimum score 550 paper-based; 59 iBT). Electronic applications accepted. *Faculty research:* Leadership, e-commerce, supply chain management.

University of Michigan–Dearborn, College of Business, Dearborn, MI 48128-1491. Offers accounting (MBA, MS); business analytics (MS); finance (MBA, MS); human resource management (MBA); information systems (MS); international business (MBA); investment (MBA); management (MBA); management information systems (MBA); marketing (MBA); supply chain management (MBA, MS); taxation (MBA); MBA/MHSA; MBA/MSE; MBA/MSF; MBA/MSIS; MBA/MSSCM; MSF/MSA. *Accreditation:* AACSB. Part-time and evening/weekend programs available. Postbaccalaureate distance learning degree programs offered (no on-campus study). *Faculty:* 24 full-time (8 women), 5 part-time/adjunct (2 women). *Students:* 82 full-time (31 women), 323 part-time (116 women); includes 72 minority (17 Black or African American, non-Hispanic/Latino; 2 American Indian or Alaska Native, non-Hispanic/Latino; 30 Asian, non-Hispanic/Latino; 15 Hispanic/Latino; 8 Two or more races, non-Hispanic/Latino), 65 international. Average age 32. 290 applicants, 44% accepted, 99 enrolled. In 2013, 143 master's awarded. *Entrance requirements:* For master's, GMAT or GRE, pre-calculus or finite mathematics; 18 credits of accounting course work beyond introductory courses (MS in accounting). Additional exam requirements/recommendations for international students: Required—TOEFL (minimum score 560 paper-based; 84 iBT), IELTS. *Application deadline:* For fall admission, 8/1 priority date for domestic students, 5/1 priority date for international students; for winter admission, 12/1 priority date for domestic students, 9/1 priority date for international students; for spring admission, 4/1 priority date for domestic students, 1/1 priority date for international students. Applications are processed on a rolling basis. Application fee: $60. Electronic applications accepted. *Expenses:* Contact institution. *Financial support:* Career-related internships or fieldwork, Federal Work-Study, and scholarships/grants available. Support available to part-time students. Financial award application deadline: 9/1; financial award applicants required to submit FAFSA. *Faculty research:* Cultural diversity, buyer-supplier relations, error detection in data, economic evolution. *Unit head:* Dr. Raju Balakrishnan, Dean, 313-593-5248, Fax: 313-271-9835, E-mail: rajub@umich.edu. *Application contact:* Joan Doherty, Academic Advisor/Counselor, 313-593-5460, Fax: 313-271-9838, E-mail: umd-gradbusiness@umich.edu.
Website: http://www.cob.umd.umich.edu.

University of Michigan–Flint, School of Management, Flint, MI 48502-1950. Offers accounting (MBA, MSA); business (Graduate Certificate); computer information systems (MBA); finance (MBA); health care management (MBA); international business (MBA); lean manufacturing (MBA); marketing (MBA); organizational leadership (MBA). *Accreditation:* AACSB. Part-time and evening/weekend programs available. Postbaccalaureate distance learning degree programs offered (minimal on-campus study). *Faculty:* 13 full-time (3 women), 4 part-time/adjunct (0 women). *Students:* 19 full-time (6 women), 234 part-time (72 women); includes 50 minority (21 Black or African American, non-Hispanic/Latino; 5 American Indian or Alaska Native, non-Hispanic/Latino; 12 Asian, non-Hispanic/Latino; 5 Hispanic/Latino; 7 Two or more races, non-Hispanic/Latino), 30 international. Average age 32. 195 applicants, 56% accepted, 88 enrolled. In 2013, 73 master's awarded. *Degree requirements:* For master's, thesis or alternative. *Entrance requirements:* For master's, GMAT or GRE, minimum GPA of 3.0. Additional exam requirements/recommendations for international students: Required—TOEFL (minimum score 560 paper-based; 84 iBT), IELTS (minimum score 6.5). *Application deadline:* For fall admission, 8/1 for domestic students, 5/1 for international students; for winter admission, 11/1 for domestic students, 9/1 for international students; for spring admission, 2/15 for domestic students, 1/15 for international students. Applications are processed on a rolling basis. Application fee: $55. Electronic applications accepted. *Financial support:* Federal Work-Study, scholarships/grants, and unspecified assistantships available. Support available to part-time students. Financial award application deadline: 3/1; financial award applicants required to submit FAFSA. *Unit head:* Dr. Scott Johnson, Dean, School of Management, 810-762-3164, Fax: 810-237-6685, E-mail: scotjohn@umflint.edu. *Application contact:* Jeremiah Cook, Marketing Communications Specialist, 810-424-5583, Fax: 810-766-6789, E-mail: jecook@umflint.edu.
Website: http://www.umflint.edu/som/.

University of Minnesota, Twin Cities Campus, Carlson School of Management, Carlson Full-Time MBA Program, Minneapolis, MN 55455. Offers finance (MBA); information technology (MBA); management (MBA); marketing (MBA); medical industry orientation (MBA); supply chain and operations (MBA); JD/MBA; MBA/MPP; MD/MBA; MHA/MBA; Pharm D/MBA. *Accreditation:* AACSB. *Faculty:* 137 full-time (42 women), 16 part-time/adjunct (5 women). *Students:* 222 full-time (62 women); includes 30 minority (2 Black or African American, non-Hispanic/Latino; 17 Asian, non-Hispanic/Latino; 5 Hispanic/Latino; 6 Two or more races, non-Hispanic/Latino), 60 international. Average age 28. 565 applicants, 44% accepted, 113 enrolled. In 2013, 96 master's awarded. *Entrance requirements:* For master's, GMAT or GRE. Additional exam requirements/recommendations for international students: Required—TOEFL (minimum score 580 paper-based; 84 iBT), IELTS (minimum score 7), PTE. *Application deadline:* For fall admission, 4/1 for domestic students, 2/1 for international students. Application fee: $60 ($90 for international students). Electronic applications accepted. *Expenses:* Contact institution. *Financial support:* In 2013–14, 133 students received support, including 133 fellowships with full and partial tuition reimbursements available (averaging $29,445 per year); research assistantships with partial tuition reimbursements available, teaching assistantships with partial tuition reimbursements available, career-related internships or fieldwork, Federal Work-Study, institutionally sponsored loans, scholarships/grants, health care benefits, and unspecified assistantships also available. Financial award application deadline: 4/1; financial award applicants required to submit FAFSA. *Faculty research:* Finance and accounting: financial reporting, asset pricing models and corporate finance; information and decision sciences: on-line auctions, information transparency and recommender systems; marketing: psychological influences on consumer behavior, brand equity, pricing and marketing channels; operations: lean manufacturing, quality management and global supply chains; strategic management and organization: global strategy, networks, entrepreneurship and innovation, sustainability. *Unit head:* Philip J. Miller, Assistant Dean, MBA Programs and Graduate Business Career Center, 612-625-5555, Fax: 612-625-1012, E-mail: mba@umn.edu. *Application contact:* Linh Gilles, Director of Admissions and Recruiting, 612-625-5555, Fax: 612-625-1012, E-mail: ftmba@umn.edu.
Website: http://www.csom.umn.edu/MBA/full-time/.

University of Minnesota, Twin Cities Campus, Carlson School of Management, Carlson Part-Time MBA Program, Minneapolis, MN 55455. Offers finance (MBA); information technology (MBA); management (MBA); marketing (MBA); medical industry orientation (MBA); supply chain and operations (MBA). Part-time and evening/weekend programs available. *Faculty:* 137 full-time (42 women), 15 part-time/adjunct (3 women). *Students:* 1,207 part-time (393 women); includes 108 minority (21 Black or African American, non-Hispanic/Latino; 4 American Indian or Alaska Native, non-Hispanic/Latino; 72 Asian, non-Hispanic/Latino; 5 Hispanic/Latino; 1 Native Hawaiian or other Pacific Islander, non-Hispanic/Latino; 5 Two or more races, non-Hispanic/Latino), 66 international. Average age 28. 291 applicants, 86% accepted, 205 enrolled. In 2013, 372 master's awarded. *Entrance requirements:* For master's, GMAT or GRE. Additional exam requirements/recommendations for international students: Required—TOEFL (minimum score 580 paper-based; 84 iBT), IELTS (minimum score 7), PTE. *Application deadline:* For fall admission, 5/1 priority date for domestic and international students; for spring admission, 10/1 priority date for domestic and international students. Applications are processed on a rolling basis. Application fee: $60 ($90 for international students). Electronic applications accepted. *Expenses:* Contact institution. *Financial support:* Applicants required to submit FAFSA. *Faculty research:* Finance and accounting: financial reporting, asset pricing models and corporate finance; information and decision sciences: on-line auctions, information transparency and recommender systems; marketing: psychological influences on consumer behavior, brand equity, pricing and marketing channels; operations: lean manufacturing, quality management and global supply chains; strategic management and organization: global strategy, networks, entrepreneurship and innovation, sustainability. *Unit head:* Philip J. Miller, Assistant Dean, MBA Programs and Graduate Business Career Center, 612-624-2039, Fax: 612-625-1012, E-mail: mba@umn.edu. *Application contact:* Linh Gilles, Director of Admissions and Recruiting, 612-625-5555, Fax: 612-625-1012, E-mail: ptmba@umn.edu.
Website: http://www.carlsonschool.umn.edu/ptmba.

University of Minnesota, Twin Cities Campus, Carlson School of Management, Doctoral Program in Business Administration, Minneapolis, MN 55455-0213. Offers accounting (PhD); finance (PhD); information and decision sciences (PhD); marketing (PhD); operations and management science (PhD); strategic management and entrepreneurship (PhD). *Faculty:* 102 full-time (31 women). *Students:* 74 full-time (25 women); includes 8 minority (1 Black or African American, non-Hispanic/Latino; 5 Asian, non-Hispanic/Latino; 2 Hispanic/Latino), 46 international. Average age 30. 274 applicants, 8% accepted, 15 enrolled. In 2013, 10 doctorates awarded. *Degree requirements:* For doctorate, comprehensive exam, thesis/dissertation, written and oral preliminary exams, proposal defense, final defense. *Entrance requirements:* For doctorate, GMAT, GRE General Test. Additional exam requirements/recommendations for international students: Required—TOEFL (minimum score 600 paper-based; 100 iBT); Recommended—IELTS (minimum score 7.5). *Application deadline:* For fall admission, 12/31 for domestic students, 12/31 priority date for international students. Applications are processed on a rolling basis. Application fee: $75 ($95 for international students). Electronic applications accepted. *Expenses:* Contact institution. *Financial support:* In 2013–14, 68 students received support, including 96 fellowships with full tuition reimbursements available (averaging $6,300 per year), 65 research assistantships with full tuition reimbursements available (averaging $12,500 per year), 64 teaching assistantships with full tuition reimbursements available (averaging $12,500 per year); institutionally sponsored loans, scholarships/grants, health care benefits, unspecified assistantships, and full student fee waivers also available. Financial award application deadline: 12/31. *Faculty research:* Corporate strategy, finance, entrepreneurship, marketing, information and decision science, operations, accounting, supply chain. *Unit head:* Dr. Shawn P. Curley, Director, 612-624-6546, Fax: 612-624-

8221, E-mail: curley@umn.edu. *Application contact:* Earlene K. Bronson, Assistant Director, 612-624-0875, Fax: 612-624-8221, E-mail: brons003@umn.edu. Website: http://www.csom.umn.edu/phd-BA/.

University of Missouri, Graduate School, Robert J. Trulaske, Sr. College of Business, Program in Business Administration, Columbia, MO 65211. Offers business administration (MBA); executive (MBA); finance (PhD); management (PhD); marketing (PhD); MBA/JD; MBA/MHA; MBA/MSIE. *Accreditation:* AACSB. *Faculty:* 42 full-time (9 women), 4 part-time/adjunct (2 women). *Students:* 208 full-time (69 women), 16 part-time (6 women); includes 9 minority (2 Black or African American, non-Hispanic/Latino; 1 Asian, non-Hispanic/Latino; 4 Hispanic/Latino; 2 Two or more races, non-Hispanic/Latino), 63 international. Average age 29. 435 applicants, 30% accepted, 86 enrolled. In 2013, 101 master's, 6 doctorates awarded. *Degree requirements:* For doctorate, thesis/dissertation. *Entrance requirements:* For master's and doctorate, GMAT, minimum GPA of 3.0. Additional exam requirements/recommendations for international students: Required—TOEFL (minimum score 500 paper-based; 61 iBT). *Application deadline:* For fall admission, 2/1 priority date for domestic and international students. Applications are processed on a rolling basis. Application fee: $55 ($75 for international students). Electronic applications accepted. *Financial support:* Fellowships with full and partial tuition reimbursements, research assistantships with full and partial tuition reimbursements, teaching assistantships with full and partial tuition reimbursements, institutionally sponsored loans, scholarships/grants, health care benefits, and unspecified assistantships available. Support available to part-time students. *Faculty research:* International relations, management, finance, marketing, entrepreneurship, organization and process theory, mentoring and networking processes, capital market regulation, corporate governance, bankruptcy. *Unit head:* Joan T.A. Gabel, Dean, 573-882-6688, E-mail: gabelj@missouri.edu. *Application contact:* Jan Curry, Administrative Assistant, 573-882-2750, E-mail: curryja@missouri.edu. Website: http://business.missouri.edu/.

University of Missouri–St. Louis, College of Business Administration, Program in Business Administration, St. Louis, MO 63121. Offers accounting (MBA); business administration (Certificate); business intelligence (Certificate); finance (MBA); human resource management (Certificate); information systems (MBA); logistics and supply chain management (MBA, PhD, Certificate); marketing (MBA); marketing management (Certificate); operations management (MBA). *Accreditation:* AACSB. Part-time and evening/weekend programs available. *Faculty:* 30 full-time (5 women), 20 part-time/adjunct (8 women). *Students:* 114 full-time (51 women), 269 part-time (100 women); includes 43 minority (16 Black or African American, non-Hispanic/Latino; 14 Asian, non-Hispanic/Latino; 11 Hispanic/Latino; 1 Native Hawaiian or other Pacific Islander, non-Hispanic/Latino; 1 Two or more races, non-Hispanic/Latino), 56 international. Average age 31. 153 applicants, 91% accepted, 110 enrolled. In 2013, 136 master's, 7 other advanced degrees awarded. *Degree requirements:* For doctorate, thesis/dissertation. *Entrance requirements:* For master's, GMAT, 2 letters of recommendation. Additional exam requirements/recommendations for international students: Recommended—TOEFL (minimum score 550 paper-based; 79 iBT), IELTS (minimum score 6.5). *Application deadline:* For fall admission, 7/1 for domestic and international students; for spring admission, 12/1 for domestic and international students. Applications are processed on a rolling basis. Application fee: $50 ($40 for international students). Electronic applications accepted. *Expenses:* Tuition, state resident: full-time $7364; part-time $409.10 per credit hour. Tuition, nonresident: full-time $19,162; part-time $1008.50 per credit hour. *Financial support:* In 2013–14, 14 research assistantships with full and partial tuition reimbursements (averaging $5,625 per year), 6 teaching assistantships with full and partial tuition reimbursements (averaging $9,403 per year) were awarded; career-related internships or fieldwork, Federal Work-Study, and institutionally sponsored loans also available. Support available to part-time students. Financial award application deadline: 4/1; financial award applicants required to submit FAFSA. *Faculty research:* Human resources, strategic management, marketing strategy, consumer behavior product development, advertising. *Unit head:* Francesca Ferrari, Assistant Director, 314-516-5885, Fax: 314-516-6420, E-mail: mba@umsl.edu. *Application contact:* 314-516-5458, Fax: 314-516-6996, E-mail: gradadm@umsl.edu. Website: http://mba.umsl.edu/Degree%20Programs/index.html.

University of Nebraska at Kearney, Graduate Programs, College of Business and Technology, Department of Business, Kearney, NE 68849-0001. Offers accounting (MBA); generalist (MBA); human resources (MBA); human services (MBA); marketing (MBA). *Accreditation:* AACSB. Part-time and evening/weekend programs available. *Degree requirements:* For master's, thesis optional. *Entrance requirements:* For master's, GMAT or GRE, letters of recommendation, work history, letter of interest, resume. Additional exam requirements/recommendations for international students: Required—TOEFL (minimum score 550 paper-based; 79 iBT). Electronic applications accepted. *Faculty research:* Small business financial management, employment law, expert systems, international trade and marketing, environmental economics.

University of Nebraska–Lincoln, Graduate College, College of Arts and Sciences, Department of Communication Studies, Lincoln, NE 68588. Offers instructional communication (MA, PhD); interpersonal communication (MA, PhD); marketing communication studies, and advertising (MA, PhD); organizational communication (MA, PhD); rhetoric and culture (MA, PhD). *Degree requirements:* For master's, thesis optional; for doctorate, comprehensive exam, thesis/dissertation. *Entrance requirements:* For master's and doctorate, GRE General Test, writing sample. Additional exam requirements/recommendations for international students: Required—TOEFL (minimum score 600 paper-based). Electronic applications accepted. *Faculty research:* Message strategies, gender communication, political communication, organizational communication, instructional communication.

University of Nebraska–Lincoln, Graduate College, College of Business Administration, Interdepartmental Area of Business, Department of Marketing, Lincoln, NE 68588. Offers business (MA, PhD). *Degree requirements:* For doctorate, comprehensive exam, thesis/dissertation. *Entrance requirements:* For master's and doctorate, GMAT. Additional exam requirements/recommendations for international students: Required—TOEFL. Electronic applications accepted. *Faculty research:* Channel information, marketing research methodology, sales management, cross-cultural marketing, impact of new technology.

University of Nebraska–Lincoln, Graduate College, College of Journalism and Mass Communications, Lincoln, NE 68588. Offers marketing, communication and advertising (MA); professional journalism (MA). Postbaccalaureate distance learning degree programs offered (no on-campus study). *Degree requirements:* For master's, thesis. *Entrance requirements:* For master's, samples of work. Additional exam requirements/recommendations for international students: Required—TOEFL (minimum score 600 paper-based). Electronic applications accepted. *Faculty research:* Interactive media and the Internet, community newspapers, children's radio, advertising involvement, telecommunications policy.

University of New Brunswick Fredericton, School of Graduate Studies, Faculty of Forestry and Environmental Management, Fredericton, NB E3B 5A3, Canada. Offers ecological foundations of forest management (PhD); environmental management (MEM); forest engineering (M Sc FE, MFE); forest products marketing (MBA); forest resources (M Sc F, MF, PhD). Part-time programs available. *Faculty:* 27 full-time (2

women). *Students:* 58 full-time (18 women), 13 part-time (8 women). In 2013, 21 master's, 6 doctorates awarded. *Degree requirements:* For master's, thesis; for doctorate, thesis/dissertation. *Entrance requirements:* For master's and doctorate, minimum GPA of 3.0. Additional exam requirements/recommendations for international students: Required—TOEFL (minimum score 550 paper-based; 80 iBT), IELTS (minimum score 7), TWE (minimum score 4). *Application deadline:* For fall admission, 3/1 for domestic students. Applications are processed on a rolling basis. Application fee: $50 Canadian dollars. Electronic applications accepted. *Financial support:* In 2013–14, 98 research assistantships, 36 teaching assistantships were awarded; fellowships also available. *Faculty research:* Forest machines, soils, and ecosystems; integrated forest management; forest meteorology; wood engineering; stream ecosystems dynamics; forest and natural resources policy; forest operations planning; wood technology and mechanics; forest road construction and engineering; forest, wildlife, insect, bird, and fire ecology; remote sensing; insect impacts; Silviculture; LiDAR analytics; integrated pest management; forest tree genetics; genetic resource conservation and sustainable management. *Unit head:* Dr. Marek Krasowski, Director of Graduate Studies, 506-453-4915, Fax: 506-453-3538, E-mail: marek@unb.ca. *Application contact:* Faith Sharpe, Graduate Secretary, 506-458-7520, Fax: 506-453-3538, E-mail: fsharpe@unb.ca. Website: http://go.unb.ca/gradprograms.

University of New Haven, Graduate School, College of Business, Program in Business Administration, West Haven, CT 06516-1916. Offers accounting (MBA, Certificate), including CPA (MBA); business administration (MBA); business management (Certificate); business policy and strategic leadership (MBA); finance (MBA), including CFA; global marketing (MBA); human resource management (Certificate); human resources management (MBA); international business (Certificate); marketing (MBA, Certificate); sports management (MBA). Part-time and evening/weekend programs available. *Students:* 125 full-time (55 women), 88 part-time (30 women); includes 31 minority (16 Black or African American, non-Hispanic/Latino; 1 American Indian or Alaska Native, non-Hispanic/Latino; 8 Asian, non-Hispanic/Latino; 5 Hispanic/Latino; 1 Native Hawaiian or other Pacific Islander, non-Hispanic/Latino), 72 international. 196 applicants, 89% accepted, 72 enrolled. In 2013, 143 master's, 24 other advanced degrees awarded. *Degree requirements:* For master's, thesis optional. *Entrance requirements:* For master's, GMAT. Additional exam requirements/recommendations for international students: Required—TOEFL (minimum score 80 iBT), IELTS, PTE (minimum score 53). *Application deadline:* For fall admission, 5/31 for international students; for winter admission, 10/15 for international students; for spring admission, 1/15 for international students. Applications are processed on a rolling basis. Application fee: $75. Electronic applications accepted. Application fee is waived when completed online. *Expenses:* Tuition: Full-time $21,600; part-time $800 per credit hour. *Required fees:* $45 per trimester. *Financial support:* Research assistantships with partial tuition reimbursements, teaching assistantships with partial tuition reimbursements, career-related internships or fieldwork, Federal Work-Study, scholarships/grants, and unspecified assistantships available. Support available to part-time students. Financial award applicants required to submit FAFSA. *Unit head:* Dr. Armando Rodriguez, Director, 203-932-7372, E-mail: arodriguez@newhaven.edu. *Application contact:* Eloise Gormley, Director of Graduate Admissions, 203-932-7440, E-mail: gradinfo@newhaven.edu. Website: http://www.newhaven.edu/7433/.

University of New Mexico, Anderson Graduate School of Management, Department of Marketing, Information Systems, Information Assurance and Operations Management, Albuquerque, NM 87131. Offers information assurance (MBA); management information systems (MBA); marketing management (MBA); operations management (MBA). Part-time and evening/weekend programs available. *Faculty:* 15 full-time (3 women), 6 part-time/adjunct (1 woman). In 2013, 82 master's awarded. *Entrance requirements:* For master's, GMAT or GRE, minimum GPA of 3.0 on last 60 hours of coursework. Additional exam requirements/recommendations for international students: Required—TOEFL (minimum score 550 paper-based; 79 iBT). *Application deadline:* For fall admission, 4/1 priority date for domestic and international students; for spring admission, 10/1 priority date for domestic and international students. Applications are processed on a rolling basis. Application fee: $50. Electronic applications accepted. *Expenses:* Contact institution. *Financial support:* Fellowships, research assistantships, career-related internships or fieldwork, Federal Work-Study, scholarships/grants, and unspecified assistantships available. Support available to part-time students. Financial award application deadline: 6/1; financial award applicants required to submit FAFSA. *Faculty research:* Marketing, operations management, information systems, information assurance. *Unit head:* Dr. Steve Yourstone, Chair, 505-277-6471, Fax: 505-277-7108, E-mail: yourstone@unm.edu. *Application contact:* Tracy Wilkey, Manager, Academic Advisement, 505-277-3290, Fax: 505-277-8436, E-mail: andersonadvising@unm.edu. Website: http://mba.mgt.unm.edu/default.asp.

The University of North Carolina at Chapel Hill, Kenan-Flagler Business School, Doctoral Program in Business Administration, Chapel Hill, NC 27599. Offers accounting (PhD); finance (PhD); marketing (PhD); operations management (PhD); organizational behavior (PhD); strategy (PhD). *Accreditation:* AACSB. *Degree requirements:* For doctorate, thesis/dissertation. *Entrance requirements:* For doctorate, GMAT or GRE General Test. Electronic applications accepted. *Expenses:* Contact institution.

The University of North Carolina at Greensboro, Graduate School, School of Human Environmental Sciences, Department of Consumer, Apparel, and Retail Studies, Greensboro, NC 27412-5001. Offers MS, PhD. *Degree requirements:* For master's, one foreign language; for doctorate, one foreign language, thesis/dissertation. *Entrance requirements:* For master's and doctorate, GRE General Test. Additional exam requirements/recommendations for international students: Required—TOEFL. Electronic applications accepted. *Faculty research:* Impact of phosphate removal, protective clothing for pesticide workers, fabric hand: subjective and objective measurements.

University of North Texas, Robert B. Toulouse School of Graduate Studies, Denton, TN 76203-5017. Offers accounting (MS, PhD); applied anthropology (MA, MS); applied behavior analysis (Certificate); applied technology and performance improvement (M Ed, MS, PhD); art education (MA, PhD); art history (MA); art museum education (Certificate); arts leadership (Certificate); audiology (Au D); behavior analysis (MS); biochemistry and molecular biology (MS, PhD); biology (MA, MS, PhD); business (PhD); business computer information systems (PhD); chemistry (MS, PhD); clinical psychology (PhD); communication studies (MA, MS); computer engineering (MS); computer science (MS); computer science and engineering (PhD); counseling (M Ed, MS, PhD), including clinical mental health counseling (MS), college and university counseling (M Ed, MS), elementary school counseling (M Ed, MS), secondary school counseling (M Ed, MS); counseling psychology (PhD); creative writing (MA); criminal justice (MS); curriculum and instruction (M Ed, PhD), including curriculum studies (PhD), early childhood studies (PhD), language and literacy studies (PhD); decision sciences (MBA); design (MA, MFA), including fashion design (MFA), innovation studies, interior design (MFA); early childhood studies (MS); economics (MS); educational leadership (M Ed, Ed D, PhD); educational psychology (MS), including family studies, gifted and talented (MS, PhD), human development, learning and cognition, research, measurement and evaluation; educational research (PhD), including gifted and talented (MS, PhD), human

development and family studies, psychological aspects of sports and exercise, research, measurement and statistics; electrical engineering (MS); emergency management (MPA); engineering systems (MS); English (MA, PhD); environmental science (MS, PhD); experimental psychology (PhD); finance (MBA, MS, PhD); financial management (MPA); French (MA); health psychology and behavioral medicine (PhD); health services management (MBA); higher education (M Ed, Ed D, PhD); history (MA, MS, PhD), including European history (PhD), military history (PhD), United States history (PhD); hospitality management (MS); human resources management (MPA); information science (MS, PhD); information technologies (MBA); information technology and decision sciences (MS); interdisciplinary studies (MA, MS); international sustainable tourism (MS); jazz studies (MM); journalism (MA, MJ, Graduate Certificate), including interactive and virtual digital communication (Graduate Certificate), narrative journalism (Graduate Certificate), public relations (Graduate Certificate); kinesiology (MS); learning technologies (MS, PhD); library science (MS); local government management (MPA); logistics and supply chain management (MBA, PhD); long-term care, senior housing, and aging services (MA, MS); management science (PhD); marketing (MBA, PhD); materials science and engineering (MS, PhD); mathematics (MA, PhD); merchandising (MS); music (MA, MM Ed, PhD), including ethnomusicology (MA), music education (MM Ed, PhD), music theory (MA, PhD), musicology (MA, PhD), performance (MA); nonprofit management (MPA); operations and supply chain management (MBA); performance (MM, DMA); philosophy (MA, PhD); physics (MS, PhD); political science (MA, MS, PhD); public administration and management (PhD), including emergency management, nonprofit management, public financial management, urban management; radio, television and film (MA, MFA); recreation, event and sport management (MS); rehabilitation counseling (MS, Certificate); sociology (MA, MS, PhD); Spanish (MA); special education (M Ed, PhD), including autism intervention (PhD), emotional/behavioral disorders (PhD), mild/moderate disabilities (PhD); speech-language pathology (MA, MS); strategic management (MBA); studio art (MFA); taxation (MS); teaching (M Ed); MBA/MS; MS/MPH; MSES/MBA. Part-time and evening/weekend programs available. Postbaccalaureate distance learning degree programs offered. *Faculty:* 661 full-time (213 women), 240 part-time/adjunct (144 women). *Students:* 3,106 full-time (1,620 women), 3,543 part-time (2,221 women); includes 1,740 minority (533 Black or African American, non-Hispanic/Latino; 15 American Indian or Alaska Native, non-Hispanic/Latino; 286 Asian, non-Hispanic/Latino; 746 Hispanic/Latino; 3 Native Hawaiian or other Pacific Islander, non-Hispanic/Latino; 157 Two or more races, non-Hispanic/Latino), 1,145 international. Average age 32. 6,289 applicants, 43% accepted, 1751 enrolled. In 2013, 1,778 master's, 239 doctorates, 10 other advanced degrees awarded. Terminal master's awarded for partial completion of doctoral program. *Degree requirements:* For master's, variable foreign language requirement, comprehensive exam (for some programs), thesis (for some programs); for doctorate, variable foreign language requirement, comprehensive exam (for some programs), thesis/dissertation; for other advanced degree, variable foreign language requirement, comprehensive exam (for some programs). *Entrance requirements:* For master's and doctorate, GRE, GMAT. Additional exam requirements/recommendations for international students: Required—TOEFL (minimum score 550 paper-based; 79 iBT). *Application deadline:* For fall admission, 7/15 for domestic students, 3/15 for international students; for spring admission, 11/15 for domestic students, 9/15 for international students; for summer admission, 5/1 for domestic students. Applications are processed on a rolling basis. Application fee: $60. Electronic applications accepted. *Financial support:* Fellowships with partial tuition reimbursements, research assistantships with partial tuition reimbursements, teaching assistantships, career-related internships or fieldwork, Federal Work-Study, institutionally sponsored loans, scholarships/grants, health care benefits, and library assistantships available. Support available to part-time students. Financial award applicants required to submit FAFSA. *Unit head:* Mark Wardell, Dean, 940-565-2383, E-mail: mark.wardell@unt.edu. *Application contact:* Toulouse School of Graduate Studies, 940-565-2383, Fax: 940-565-2141, E-mail: gradsch@unt.edu.
Website: http://tsgs.unt.edu/.

University of Oregon, Graduate School, Charles H. Lundquist College of Business, Department of Marketing, Eugene, OR 97403. Offers PhD. Part-time programs available. *Degree requirements:* For doctorate, thesis/dissertation, 2 comprehensive exams. *Entrance requirements:* For doctorate, GMAT. Additional exam requirements/recommendations for international students: Required—TOEFL. *Faculty research:* Consumer behavior, marketing research, international marketing, marketing management, price quality.

University of Pennsylvania, Wharton School, Marketing Department, Philadelphia, PA 19104. Offers MBA, PhD. Terminal master's awarded for partial completion of doctoral program. *Degree requirements:* For master's, thesis optional; for doctorate, thesis/dissertation. *Entrance requirements:* For doctorate, GMAT or GRE. *Faculty research:* Scanner data, consumer preferences, decision-making theory, modeling for marketing and e-business.

University of Phoenix–Atlanta Campus, School of Business, Sandy Springs, GA 30350-4153. Offers accounting (MBA); business administration (MBA); global management (MBA); human resources management (MBA, MM); management (MM); marketing (MBA); public administration (MM). Evening/weekend programs available. Postbaccalaureate distance learning degree programs offered. *Degree requirements:* For master's, thesis (for some programs). *Entrance requirements:* For master's, minimum undergraduate GPA of 3.0, 3 years of work experience. Additional exam requirements/recommendations for international students: Required—TOEFL (minimum score 550 paper-based; 79 iBT).

University of Phoenix–Augusta Campus, School of Business, Augusta, GA 30909-4583. Offers accounting (MBA); business administration (MBA); business and management (MBA, MM); global management (MBA); human resources management (MBA, MM); management (MM); marketing (MBA); public administration (MBA, MM). Postbaccalaureate distance learning degree programs offered.

University of Phoenix–Austin Campus, School of Business, Austin, TX 78759. Offers accounting (MBA); business administration (MBA); business and management (MBA); e-business (MBA); global management (MBA); human resources management (MBA, MM); management (MM); marketing (MBA); public administration (MBA). Postbaccalaureate distance learning degree programs offered.

University of Phoenix–Bay Area Campus, School of Business, San Jose, CA 95134-1805. Offers accountancy (MS); accounting (MBA); business administration (MBA, DBA); energy management (MBA); global management (MBA); health care management (MBA); human resource management (MBA); human resources management (MM); management (MM); marketing (MBA); organizational leadership (DM); project management (MBA); public administration (MPA); technology management (MBA). Evening/weekend programs available. Postbaccalaureate distance learning degree programs offered (no on-campus study). *Degree requirements:* For master's, thesis (for some programs). *Entrance requirements:* For master's, minimum undergraduate GPA of 3.0, 3 years of work experience. Additional exam requirements/recommendations for international students: Required—TOEFL (minimum score 550 paper-based; 79 iBT). Electronic applications accepted.

University of Phoenix–Birmingham Campus, College of Graduate Business and Management, Birmingham, AL 35242. Offers accounting (MBA); business administration (MBA); global management (MBA); human resources management (MBA, MM); management (MM); marketing (MBA); public administration (MM).

University of Phoenix–Central Valley Campus, School of Business, Fresno, CA 93720-1562. Offers accounting (MBA); business administration (MBA); global management (MBA); human resources management (MBA, MM); management (MM); marketing (MBA); public administration (MBA, MM).

University of Phoenix–Chattanooga Campus, School of Business, Chattanooga, TN 37421-3707. Offers accounting (MBA); business administration (MBA); business and management (MBA); global management (MBA); human resources management (MBA, MM); management (MM); marketing (MBA); public administration (MBA, MM). Postbaccalaureate distance learning degree programs offered.

University of Phoenix–Cheyenne Campus, School of Business, Cheyenne, WY 82009. Offers global management (MBA); human resources management (MBA, MM); management (MM); marketing (MBA); public administration (MBA, MM). Postbaccalaureate distance learning degree programs offered.

University of Phoenix–Cincinnati Campus, School of Business, West Chester, OH 45069-4875. Offers accounting (MBA); business administration (MBA); global management (MBA); human resources management (MBA, MM); management (MM); marketing (MBA); public administration (MM). Evening/weekend programs available. *Degree requirements:* For master's, thesis (for some programs). *Entrance requirements:* For master's, minimum undergraduate GPA of 3.0, 3 years of work experience. Additional exam requirements/recommendations for international students: Required—TOEFL (minimum score 550 paper-based; 79 iBT). Electronic applications accepted.

University of Phoenix–Cleveland Campus, School of Business, Independence, OH 44131-2194. Offers accounting (MBA); business administration (MBA); global management (MBA); human resources management (MBA, MM); management (MM); marketing (MBA); public administration (MBA, MM). Evening/weekend programs available. Postbaccalaureate distance learning degree programs offered (no on-campus study). *Degree requirements:* For master's, thesis (for some programs). *Entrance requirements:* For master's, minimum undergraduate GPA of 3.0, 3 years of work experience. Additional exam requirements/recommendations for international students: Required—TOEFL (minimum score 550 paper-based; 79 iBT). Electronic applications accepted.

University of Phoenix–Columbus Georgia Campus, School of Business, Columbus, GA 31909. Offers accounting (MBA); business administration (MBA); global management (MBA); human resources management (MBA, MM); management (MM); marketing (MBA); public administration (MBA). Evening/weekend programs available. *Degree requirements:* For master's, thesis (for some programs). *Entrance requirements:* For master's, minimum undergraduate GPA of 3.0, 3 years of work experience. Additional exam requirements/recommendations for international students: Required—TOEFL (minimum score 550 paper-based; 79 iBT). Electronic applications accepted.

University of Phoenix–Columbus Ohio Campus, School of Business, Columbus, OH 43240-4032. Offers accounting (MBA); business administration (MBA); global management (MBA); human resources management (MBA, MM); management (MM); marketing (MBA); public administration (MM). Evening/weekend programs available. Postbaccalaureate distance learning degree programs offered. *Degree requirements:* For master's, thesis (for some programs). *Entrance requirements:* For master's, minimum undergraduate GPA of 3.0, 3 years of work experience. Additional exam requirements/recommendations for international students: Required—TOEFL (minimum score 550 paper-based; 79 iBT). Electronic applications accepted.

University of Phoenix–Dallas Campus, School of Business, Dallas, TX 75251. Offers accounting (MBA); business administration (MBA); global management (MBA); human resources management (MBA, MM); management (MM); marketing (MBA); public administration (MBA, MM). Evening/weekend programs available. Postbaccalaureate distance learning degree programs offered. *Degree requirements:* For master's, thesis (for some programs). *Entrance requirements:* For master's, 3 years of work experience, minimum undergraduate GPA of 3.0. Additional exam requirements/recommendations for international students: Required—TOEFL (minimum score 550 paper-based; 79 iBT). Electronic applications accepted.

University of Phoenix–Denver Campus, School of Business, Lone Tree, CO 80124-5453. Offers accountancy (MSA); accounting (MBA); business administration (MBA); e-business (MBA); global management (MBA); human resources management (MBA, MM); management (MM); marketing (MBA); public administration (MBA, MM). Evening/weekend programs available. Postbaccalaureate distance learning degree programs offered. *Degree requirements:* For master's, thesis (for some programs). *Entrance requirements:* For master's, minimum undergraduate GPA of 3.0, 3 years work experience. Additional exam requirements/recommendations for international students: Required—TOEFL (minimum score 550 paper-based; 79 iBT). Electronic applications accepted.

University of Phoenix–Des Moines Campus, School of Business, Des Moines, IA 50309. Offers accounting (MBA); business administration (MBA); global management (MBA); human resources management (MBA, MM); management (MM); marketing (MBA); public administration (MBA, MM). Postbaccalaureate distance learning degree programs offered.

University of Phoenix–Eastern Washington Campus, School of Business, Spokane, WA 99212-2531. Offers accounting (MBA); business administration (MBA); human resources management (MBA); marketing (MBA); public administration (MBA). Evening/weekend programs available. *Degree requirements:* For master's, thesis (for some programs). *Entrance requirements:* For master's, minimum undergraduate GPA of 3.0, 3 years of work experience. Additional exam requirements/recommendations for international students: Required—TOEFL (minimum score 550 paper-based; 79 iBT). Electronic applications accepted.

University of Phoenix–Hawaii Campus, School of Business, Honolulu, HI 96813-4317. Offers accounting (MBA); business administration (MBA); global management (MBA); human resources management (MBA, MM); management (MM); marketing (MBA); public administration (MBA, MM). Evening/weekend programs available. *Degree requirements:* For master's, thesis (for some programs). *Entrance requirements:* For master's, minimum undergraduate GPA of 3.0, 3 years of work experience. Additional exam requirements/recommendations for international students: Required—TOEFL (minimum score 550 paper-based; 79 iBT). Electronic applications accepted.

University of Phoenix–Houston Campus, School of Business, Houston, TX 77079-2004. Offers accounting (MBA); business administration (MBA); global management (MBA); human resources management (MBA, MM); management (MM); marketing (MBA); public administration (MBA, MM). Evening/weekend programs available. Postbaccalaureate distance learning degree programs offered. *Degree requirements:* For master's, thesis (for some programs). *Entrance requirements:* For master's, 3 years of work experience, minimum undergraduate GPA of 3.0. Additional exam requirements/recommendations for international students: Required—TOEFL (minimum score 550 paper-based; 79 iBT). Electronic applications accepted.

University of Phoenix–Idaho Campus, School of Business, Meridian, ID 83642-5114. Offers accounting (MBA); administration (MBA); global management (MBA); human resources management (MBA, MM); management (MM); marketing (MBA); public administration (MM). Evening/weekend programs available. Postbaccalaureate distance learning degree programs offered. *Degree requirements:* For master's, thesis (for some programs). *Entrance requirements:* For master's, 3 years of work experience, minimum undergraduate GPA of 3.0. Additional exam requirements/recommendations for international students: Required—TOEFL (minimum score 550 paper-based). Electronic applications accepted.

University of Phoenix–Indianapolis Campus, School of Business, Indianapolis, IN 46250-932. Offers accounting (MBA); business administration (MBA); global management (MBA); human resources management (MBA, MM); management (MM); marketing (MBA); public administration (MM). Evening/weekend programs available. *Degree requirements:* For master's, thesis (for some programs). *Entrance requirements:* For master's, minimum undergraduate GPA of 3.0, 3 years of work experience. Additional exam requirements/recommendations for international students: Required—TOEFL (minimum score 550 paper-based). Electronic applications accepted.

University of Phoenix–Jersey City Campus, School of Business, Jersey City, NJ 07310. Offers accounting (MBA); business administration (MBA); global management (MBA); human resources management (MBA, MM); management (MM); marketing (MBA); public administration (MBA, MM).

University of Phoenix–Kansas City Campus, School of Business, Kansas City, MO 64131. Offers accounting (MBA); business administration (MBA); global management (MBA); human resources management (MBA, MM); management (MM); marketing (MBA); public administration (MBA). Evening/weekend programs available. *Degree requirements:* For master's, thesis (for some programs). *Entrance requirements:* For master's, minimum undergraduate GPA of 3.0, 3 years of work experience. Additional exam requirements/recommendations for international students: Required—TOEFL (minimum score 550 paper-based). Electronic applications accepted.

University of Phoenix–Las Vegas Campus, School of Business, Las Vegas, NV 89135. Offers accounting (MBA); business administration (MBA); global management (MBA); human resources management (MBA, MM); management (MM); marketing (MBA); public administration (MM). Evening/weekend programs available. Postbaccalaureate distance learning degree programs offered (no on-campus study). *Degree requirements:* For master's, thesis (for some programs). *Entrance requirements:* For master's, minimum undergraduate GPA of 3.0, 3 years of work experience. Additional exam requirements/recommendations for international students: Required—TOEFL (minimum score 550 paper-based; 79 iBT). Electronic applications accepted.

University of Phoenix–Louisiana Campus, School of Business, Metairie, LA 70001-2082. Offers accounting (MBA); business administration (MBA); global management (MBA); human resources management (MBA, MM); management (MM); marketing (MBA); public administration (MBA). Evening/weekend programs available. *Degree requirements:* For master's, thesis (for some programs). *Entrance requirements:* For master's, minimum undergraduate GPA of 3.0, 3 years work experience. Additional exam requirements/recommendations for international students: Required—TOEFL (minimum score 550 paper-based; 79 iBT). Electronic applications accepted.

University of Phoenix–Madison Campus, School of Business, Madison, WI 53718-2416. Offers accounting (MBA); business and management (MBA); e-business (MBA); global management (MBA); human resources management (MBA, MM); management (MM); marketing (MBA); public administration (MBA).

University of Phoenix–Memphis Campus, School of Business, Cordova, TN 38018. Offers accounting (MBA); business and management (MBA); e-business (MBA); global management (MBA); human resources management (MBA, MM); management (MM); marketing (MBA); public administration (MBA, MM).

University of Phoenix–Milwaukee Campus, School of Business, Milwaukee, WI 53224. Offers accounting (MBA); business administration (MBA); energy management (MBA); global management (MBA); health care management (MBA); human resource management (MBA); management (MM); marketing (MBA); project management (MBA); technology management (MBA). Evening/weekend programs available. Postbaccalaureate distance learning degree programs offered. *Entrance requirements:* Additional exam requirements/recommendations for international students: Required—TOEFL, TOEIC (Test of English as an International Communication), Berlitz Online English Proficiency Exam, PTE, or IELTS. Electronic applications accepted. *Expenses:* Contact institution.

University of Phoenix–Minneapolis/St. Louis Park Campus, School of Business, St. Louis Park, MN 55426. Offers accounting (MBA); business administration (MBA); global management (MBA); human resources management (MBA); management (MM); marketing (MBA); public administration (MBA).

University of Phoenix–New Mexico Campus, School of Business, Albuquerque, NM 87113-1570. Offers accounting (MBA); business administration (MBA); global management (MBA); human resources management (MBA, MM); management (MM); marketing (MBA). Evening/weekend programs available. *Degree requirements:* For master's, thesis (for some programs). *Entrance requirements:* For master's, 3 years of work experience, minimum undergraduate GPA of 3.0. Additional exam requirements/recommendations for international students: Required—TOEFL (minimum score 550 paper-based; 79 iBT). Electronic applications accepted.

University of Phoenix–North Florida Campus, School of Business, Jacksonville, FL 32216-0959. Offers accounting (MBA); business administration (MBA); global management (MBA); human resources management (MBA, MM); management (MM); marketing (MBA); public administration (MBA, MM). Evening/weekend programs available. *Degree requirements:* For master's, thesis (for some programs). *Entrance requirements:* For master's, minimum undergraduate GPA of 3.0, 3 years work experience. Additional exam requirements/recommendations for international students: Required—TOEFL (minimum score 550 paper-based; 79 iBT). Electronic applications accepted.

University of Phoenix–Northwest Arkansas Campus, School of Business, Rogers, AR 72756-9615. Offers accounting (MBA); business and management (MBA); global management (MBA); human resources management (MBA, MM); management (MM); marketing (MBA); public administration (MBA, MM).

University of Phoenix–Oklahoma City Campus, School of Business, Oklahoma City, OK 73116-8244. Offers accounting (MBA); business administration (MBA); global management (MBA); human resource management (MBA); management (MM); marketing (MBA). Evening/weekend programs available. *Degree requirements:* For master's, thesis (for some programs). *Entrance requirements:* For master's, minimum undergraduate GPA of 3.0, 3 years of work experience. Additional exam requirements/recommendations for international students: Required—TOEFL (minimum score 550 paper-based; 79 iBT). Electronic applications accepted.

University of Phoenix–Omaha Campus, School of Business, Omaha, NE 68154-5240. Offers accounting (MBA); business and management (MBA); global management (MBA); human resources management (MBA, MM); management (MM); marketing (MBA); public administration (MBA, MM).

University of Phoenix–Online Campus, School of Business, Phoenix, AZ 85034-7209. Offers accountancy (MS); accounting (MBA, Certificate); business administration (MBA); energy management (MBA); global management (MBA); health care management (MBA); human resource management (MBA, Certificate); human resources management (MM); management (MM); marketing (MBA, Certificate); project management (MBA, Certificate); public administration (MBA, MM); technology management (MBA). Evening/weekend programs available. Postbaccalaureate distance learning degree programs offered. *Entrance requirements:* Additional exam requirements/recommendations for international students: Required—TOEFL, TOEIC (Test of English as an International Communication), Berlitz Online English Proficiency Exam, PTE, or IELTS. Electronic applications accepted. *Expenses:* Contact institution.

University of Phoenix–Oregon Campus, School of Business, Tigard, OR 97223. Offers accounting (MBA); business administration (MBA); global management (MBA); human resource management (MM); human resources management (MBA); management (MM); marketing (MBA); public administration (MM). Evening/weekend programs available. *Degree requirements:* For master's, thesis (for some programs). *Entrance requirements:* For master's, minimum undergraduate GPA of 3.0, 3 years of work experience. Additional exam requirements/recommendations for international students: Required—TOEFL (minimum score 550 paper-based; 79 iBT). Electronic applications accepted.

University of Phoenix–Philadelphia Campus, School of Business, Wayne, PA 19087-2121. Offers accounting (MBA); business administration (MBA); global management (MBA); human resources management (MBA, MM); management (MM); marketing (MBA); public administration (MM). Evening/weekend programs available. *Degree requirements:* For master's, thesis (for some programs). *Entrance requirements:* For master's, minimum undergraduate GPA of 3.0, 3 years work experience. Additional exam requirements/recommendations for international students: Required—TOEFL (minimum score 550 paper-based; 79 iBT). Electronic applications accepted.

University of Phoenix–Phoenix Campus, School of Business, Tempe, AZ 85282-2371. Offers accounting (MBA, MS, Certificate); business administration (MBA); energy management (MBA); global management (MBA); health care management (MBA); human resource management (MBA, Certificate); management (MM); marketing (MBA); project management (MBA); technology management (MBA). Evening/weekend programs available. Postbaccalaureate distance learning degree programs offered. *Entrance requirements:* Additional exam requirements/recommendations for international students: Required—TOEFL, TOEIC (Test of English as an International Communication), Berlitz Online English Proficiency Exam, PTE, or IELTS. Electronic applications accepted. *Expenses:* Contact institution.

University of Phoenix–Pittsburgh Campus, School of Business, Pittsburgh, PA 15276. Offers accounting (MBA); business administration (MBA); global management (MBA); human resources management (MBA, MM); management (MM); marketing (MBA); public administration (MBA, MM). Evening/weekend programs available. *Degree requirements:* For master's, thesis (for some programs). *Entrance requirements:* For master's, minimum undergraduate GPA of 3.0, 3 years work experience. Additional exam requirements/recommendations for international students: Required—TOEFL (minimum score 550 paper-based; 79 iBT). Electronic applications accepted.

University of Phoenix–Puerto Rico Campus, School of Business, Guaynabo, PR 00968. Offers accounting (MBA); energy management (MBA); global management (MBA); human resource management (MBA); marketing (MBA); project management (MBA); small business administration (MBA). Evening/weekend programs available. *Degree requirements:* For master's, thesis (for some programs). *Entrance requirements:* For master's, minimum undergraduate GPA of 3.0, 3 years work experience. Additional exam requirements/recommendations for international students: Required—TOEFL (minimum score 550 paper-based; 79 iBT). Electronic applications accepted.

University of Phoenix–Richmond-Virginia Beach Campus, School of Business, Glen Allen, VA 23060. Offers accounting (MBA); business administration (MBA); global management (MBA); human resources management (MBA, MM); management (MM); marketing (MBA); public administration (MBA, MM). Evening/weekend programs available. *Degree requirements:* For master's, thesis (for some programs). *Entrance requirements:* For master's, minimum undergraduate GPA of 3.0, 3 years work experience. Additional exam requirements/recommendations for international students: Required—TOEFL (minimum score 550 paper-based; 79 iBT). Electronic applications accepted.

University of Phoenix–Sacramento Valley Campus, School of Business, Sacramento, CA 95833-3632. Offers accounting (MBA); business administration (MBA); global management (MBA); human resources management (MBA, MM); management (MM); marketing (MBA); public administration (MBA, MM). Evening/weekend programs available. *Degree requirements:* For master's, thesis (for some programs). *Entrance requirements:* For master's, minimum undergraduate GPA of 3.0, 3 years work experience. Additional exam requirements/recommendations for international students: Required—TOEFL (minimum score 550 paper-based; 79 iBT). Electronic applications accepted.

University of Phoenix–St. Louis Campus, School of Business, St. Louis, MO 63043. Offers accounting (MBA); business administration (MBA); global management (MBA); human resources management (MBA, MM); management (MM); marketing (MBA); public administration (MM). Evening/weekend programs available. *Degree requirements:* For master's, thesis (for some programs). *Entrance requirements:* For master's, 3 years of work experience, minimum undergraduate GPA of 3.0. Additional exam requirements/recommendations for international students: Required—TOEFL (minimum score 550 paper-based; 79 iBT). Electronic applications accepted.

University of Phoenix–San Antonio Campus, School of Business, San Antonio, TX 78230. Offers accounting (MBA); business administration (MBA); e-business (MBA); global management (MBA); human resources management (MBA, MM); management (MM); marketing (MBA); public administration (MBA, MM).

University of Phoenix–San Diego Campus, School of Business, San Diego, CA 92123. Offers accounting (MBA); business administration (MBA); global management (MBA); human resources management (MBA, MM); management (MM); marketing (MBA); public administration (MBA). Evening/weekend programs available. *Degree requirements:* For master's, thesis (for some programs). *Entrance requirements:* For master's, 3 years of work experience, minimum undergraduate GPA of 3.0. Additional exam requirements/recommendations for international students: Required—TOEFL (minimum score 550 paper-based; 79 iBT). Electronic applications accepted.

University of Phoenix–Savannah Campus, School of Business, Savannah, GA 31405-7400. Offers accounting (MBA); business administration (MBA); global management (MBA); human resources management (MBA, MM); management (MM); marketing (MBA); public administration (MBA, MM).

University of Phoenix–Southern Arizona Campus, School of Business, Tucson, AZ 85711. Offers accountancy (MS); accounting (MBA); business administration (MBA); global management (MBA); human resources management (MBA); management (MM);

marketing (MBA). Evening/weekend programs available. *Degree requirements:* For master's, thesis (for some programs). *Entrance requirements:* For master's, minimum undergraduate GPA of 3.0, 3 years of work experience. Additional exam requirements/recommendations for international students: Required—TOEFL (minimum score 550 paper-based; 79 iBT). Electronic applications accepted.

University of Phoenix–Southern California Campus, School of Business, Costa Mesa, CA 92626. Offers accounting (MBA); business administration (MBA); energy management (MBA); global management (MBA); health care management (MBA); human resource management (MBA); management (MM); marketing (MBA); project management (MBA); technology management (MBA). Evening/weekend programs available. Postbaccalaureate distance learning degree programs offered. *Entrance requirements:* Additional exam requirements/recommendations for international students: Required—TOEFL, TOEIC (Test of English as an International Communication), Berlitz Online English Proficiency Exam, PTE, or IELTS. Electronic applications accepted. *Expenses:* Contact institution.

University of Phoenix–Southern Colorado Campus, School of Business, Colorado Springs, CO 80903. Offers accounting (MBA); business administration (MBA); global management (MBA); human resources management (MBA, MM); management (MM); marketing (MBA); public administration (MM). Evening/weekend programs available. *Degree requirements:* For master's, thesis (for some programs). *Entrance requirements:* For master's, minimum undergraduate GPA of 3.0, 3 years of work experience. Additional exam requirements/recommendations for international students: Required—TOEFL (minimum score 550 paper-based; 79 iBT). Electronic applications accepted.

University of Phoenix–South Florida Campus, School of Business, Miramar, FL 33030. Offers accounting (MBA); business administration (MBA); global management (MBA); human resource management (MBA); human resources management (MM); management (MM); marketing (MBA); public administration (MBA, MM). Evening/weekend programs available. *Degree requirements:* For master's, thesis (for some programs). *Entrance requirements:* For master's, minimum undergraduate GPA of 3.0, 3 years work experience. Additional exam requirements/recommendations for international students: Required—TOEFL (minimum score 550 paper-based; 79 iBT). Electronic applications accepted.

University of Phoenix–Springfield Campus, School of Business, Springfield, MO 65804-7211. Offers accounting (MBA); business administration (MBA); global management (MBA); human resources management (MBA, MM); management (MM); marketing (MBA); public administration (MBA, MM).

University of Phoenix–Tulsa Campus, School of Business, Tulsa, OK 74134-1412. Offers accounting (MBA); business (MM); business administration (MBA); global management (MBA); human resources management (MBA); marketing (MBA). Evening/weekend programs available. *Degree requirements:* For master's, thesis (for some programs). *Entrance requirements:* For master's, minimum undergraduate GPA of 3.0, 3 years work experience. Additional exam requirements/recommendations for international students: Required—TOEFL (minimum score 550 paper-based; 79 iBT).

University of Phoenix–Utah Campus, School of Business, Salt Lake City, UT 84123-4617. Offers accounting (MBA); business administration (MBA); global management (MBA); human resource management (MBA, MM); management (MM); marketing (MBA); technology management (MBA). Evening/weekend programs available. *Degree requirements:* For master's, thesis (for some programs). *Entrance requirements:* For master's, minimum undergraduate GPA of 3.0, 3 years of work experience. Additional exam requirements/recommendations for international students: Required—TOEFL (minimum score 550 paper-based; 79 iBT). Electronic applications accepted.

University of Phoenix–West Florida Campus, School of Business, Temple Terrace, FL 33637. Offers accounting (MBA); business administration (MBA); global management (MBA); human resources management (MBA, MM); management (MM); marketing (MBA); public administration (MBA, MM). Evening/weekend programs available. *Degree requirements:* For master's, thesis (for some programs). *Entrance requirements:* For master's, 3 years of work experience, minimum undergraduate GPA of 3.0. Additional exam requirements/recommendations for international students: Required—TOEFL (minimum score 550 paper-based; 79 iBT). Electronic applications accepted.

University of Pittsburgh, Katz Graduate School of Business, Doctoral Program in Business Administration, Pittsburgh, PA 15260. Offers accounting (PhD); finance (PhD); information systems (PhD); marketing (PhD); operations/decision sciences/artificial intelligence (PhD); organizational behavior and human resource management (PhD); strategic planning (PhD). *Accreditation:* AACSB. *Faculty:* 60 full-time (17 women). *Students:* 50 full-time (22 women); includes 4 minority (2 Black or African American, non-Hispanic/Latino; 2 Asian, non-Hispanic/Latino), 27 international. 321 applicants, 7% accepted, 14 enrolled. In 2013, 10 doctorates awarded. *Degree requirements:* For doctorate, comprehensive exam, thesis/dissertation. *Entrance requirements:* For doctorate, GMAT or GRE, 3 recommendations, statement of purpose, transcripts of all previous course work and degrees. Additional exam requirements/recommendations for international students: Required—TOEFL. *Application deadline:* For fall admission, 1/1 priority date for domestic and international students. Applications are processed on a rolling basis. Application fee: $50. Electronic applications accepted. *Expenses:* Tuition, state resident: full-time $19,964; part-time $807 per credit. Tuition, nonresident: full-time $32,686; part-time $1337 per credit. *Required fees:* $740; $200. Tuition and fees vary according to program. *Financial support:* In 2013–14, 40 students received support, including 30 research assistantships with full tuition reimbursements available (averaging $23,045 per year), 10 teaching assistantships with full tuition reimbursements available (averaging $26,055 per year); fellowships, Federal Work-Study, scholarships/grants, health care benefits, and unspecified assistantships also available. Financial award application deadline: 1/1. *Faculty research:* Accounting systems/financial reporting, corporate finance, shopper marketing/consumer behavior, management information systems, organizational behavior and entrepreneurship. *Unit head:* Dr. Dennis Galletta, Director, 412-648-1699, Fax: 412-624-3633, E-mail: galletta@katz.pitt.edu. *Application contact:* Carrie Woods, Assistant Director, 412-648-1525, Fax: 412-624-3633, E-mail: cawoods@katz.pitt.edu.
Website: http://www.business.pitt.edu/katz/phd/.

University of Pittsburgh, Katz Graduate School of Business, Master of Business Administration Programs, Pittsburgh, PA 15260. Offers finance (MBA); information systems (MBA); marketing (MBA); operations management (MBA); organizational behavior and human resource management (MBA); strategy, environment and organizations (MBA); MBA/JD; MBA/MIB; MBA/MPIA; MBA/MSE; MBA/MSIS; MID/MBA. *Accreditation:* AACSB. Part-time and evening/weekend programs available. *Faculty:* 60 full-time (14 women), 21 part-time/adjunct (5 women). *Students:* 107 full-time (31 women), 428 part-time (155 women); includes 55 minority (15 Black or African American, non-Hispanic/Latino; 26 Asian, non-Hispanic/Latino; 10 Hispanic/Latino; 4 Two or more races, non-Hispanic/Latino), 83 international. Average age 30. 449 applicants, 23% accepted, 63 enrolled. In 2013, 279 master's awarded. *Degree requirements:* For master's, minimum GPA of 3.0. *Entrance requirements:* For master's, GMAT, recommendations, undergraduate transcripts, essay, resume, interview, bachelor's degree. Additional exam requirements/recommendations for international students: Required—TOEFL (minimum score 600 paper-based; 100 iBT) or IELTS. *Application deadline:* For fall admission, 4/1 priority date for domestic students, 2/1 priority date for international students. Application fee: $50. Electronic applications accepted. *Expenses:* Tuition, state resident: full-time $19,964; part-time $807 per credit. Tuition, nonresident: full-time $32,686; part-time $1337 per credit. *Required fees:* $740; $200. Tuition and fees vary according to program. *Financial support:* In 2013–14, 60 students received support. Career-related internships or fieldwork and scholarships/grants available. Financial award application deadline: 2/1. *Faculty research:* Accounting systems/financial reporting, corporate finance, shopper marketing/consumer behavior, management information systems, organizational behavior and entrepreneurship. *Unit head:* Tim Robison, Assistant Dean, 412-648-1700, Fax: 412-648-1659, E-mail: trobison@katz.pitt.edu. *Application contact:* Thomas Keller, Director of MBA Admissions, 412-648-1700, Fax: 412-648-1659, E-mail: mba@katz.pitt.edu.
Website: http://www.business.pitt.edu/katz/mba/.

University of Portland, Dr. Robert B. Pamplin, Jr. School of Business, Portland, OR 97203-5798. Offers entrepreneurship (MBA); finance (MBA, MS); health care management (MBA); marketing (MBA); nonprofit management (EMBA); operations and technology management (MBA, MS); sustainability (MBA). *Accreditation:* AACSB. Part-time and evening/weekend programs available. *Faculty:* 26 full-time (5 women), 8 part-time/adjunct (1 woman). *Students:* 37 full-time (11 women), 93 part-time (44 women); includes 15 minority (1 Black or African American, non-Hispanic/Latino; 7 Asian, non-Hispanic/Latino; 5 Hispanic/Latino; 2 Two or more races, non-Hispanic/Latino), 21 international. Average age 32. In 2013, 68 master's awarded. *Entrance requirements:* For master's, GMAT, minimum GPA of 3.0, resume, 2 letters of recommendation. Additional exam requirements/recommendations for international students: Required—TOEFL (minimum score 570 paper-based; 89 iBT), IELTS (minimum score 7). *Application deadline:* For fall admission, 7/15 priority date for domestic and international students; for spring admission, 12/15 priority date for domestic and international students. Applications are processed on a rolling basis. Application fee: $50. *Expenses:* Contact institution. *Financial support:* Federal Work-Study, scholarships/grants, and tuition waivers (partial) available. Support available to part-time students. Financial award application deadline: 3/1; financial award applicants required to submit FAFSA. *Unit head:* Melissa McCarthy, Director, 503-943-7224, E-mail: mba-up@up.edu.
Website: http://business.up.edu/mba/default.aspx?cid-1179&pid-6450.

University of Puerto Rico, Río Piedras Campus, College of Business Administration, San Juan, PR 00931-3300. Offers accounting (MBA); finance (MBA, PhD); general business (MBA); human resources management (MBA); international trade and business (MBA, PhD); marketing (MBA); operations management (MBA); quantitative methods (MBA). Part-time programs available. *Degree requirements:* For master's, comprehensive exam, thesis or alternative, research project. *Entrance requirements:* For master's, GMAT or PAEG, minimum GPA of 3.0, letter of recommendation; for doctorate, GMAT, PAEG, minimum GPA of 3.0, master degree. *Faculty research:* Management.

University of Rhode Island, Graduate School, College of Business Administration, Kingston, RI 02881. Offers accounting (MS); business administration (MBA, PhD), including finance and insurance (PhD), management (PhD), marketing (PhD), operations and supply chain management (MBA); finance (MBA); general business (MBA); management (MBA); marketing (MBA); supply chain management (MBA). *Accreditation:* AACSB. Part-time and evening/weekend programs available. *Faculty:* 43 full-time (16 women). *Students:* 103 full-time (37 women), 196 part-time (82 women); includes 42 minority (6 Black or African American, non-Hispanic/Latino; 1 American Indian or Alaska Native, non-Hispanic/Latino; 16 Asian, non-Hispanic/Latino; 13 Hispanic/Latino; 6 Two or more races, non-Hispanic/Latino), 29 international. In 2013, 119 master's, 3 doctorates awarded. *Degree requirements:* For master's, comprehensive exam (for some programs), thesis optional; for doctorate, comprehensive exam, thesis/dissertation. *Entrance requirements:* For master's, GMAT or GRE, 2 letters of recommendation, resume; for doctorate, GMAT or GRE, 3 letters of recommendation, resume. Additional exam requirements/recommendations for international students: Required—TOEFL (minimum score 575 paper-based; 91 iBT). *Application deadline:* For fall admission, 4/15 for domestic students, 2/15 for international students. Application fee: $65. Electronic applications accepted. *Expenses:* Tuition, state resident: full-time $11,532; part-time $641 per credit. Tuition, nonresident: full-time $23,606; part-time $1311 per credit. *Required fees:* $1388; $36 per credit. $35 per semester. One-time fee: $130. *Financial support:* In 2013–14, 14 teaching assistantships with full and partial tuition reimbursements (averaging $15,220 per year) were awarded. Financial award application deadline: 4/15; financial award applicants required to submit FAFSA. *Total annual research expenditures:* $66,948. *Unit head:* Dr. Mark Higgins, Dean, 401-874-4244, Fax: 401-874-4312, E-mail: markhiggins@uri.edu. *Application contact:* Lisa Lancellotta, Coordinator, MBA Programs, 401-874-4241, Fax: 401-874-4312, E-mail: mba@uri.edu.
Website: http://www.cba.uri.edu/.

University of Rochester, Simon Business School, Full-Time Master's Program in Business Administration, Rochester, NY 14627. Offers accounting and information systems (MBA); business environment and public policy (MBA); business systems consulting (MBA); competitive and organizational strategy - pricing (MBA); computers and information systems (MBA); corporate accounting (MBA); electronic commerce (MBA); entrepreneurship (MBA); finance (MBA); health sciences management (MBA); international management (MBA); marketing - brand management and pricing (MBA); operations management - manufacturing (MBA); operations management - services (MBA); public accounting (MBA). *Accreditation:* AACSB. Part-time and evening/weekend programs available. *Faculty:* 60 full-time (11 women), 23 part-time/adjunct (3 women). *Students:* 282 full-time (74 women); includes 55 minority (29 Black or African American, non-Hispanic/Latino; 1 American Indian or Alaska Native, non-Hispanic/Latino; 11 Asian, non-Hispanic/Latino; 12 Hispanic/Latino; 2 Two or more races, non-Hispanic/Latino), 144 international. 673 applicants, 33% accepted, 65 enrolled. In 2013, 176 master's awarded. *Entrance requirements:* For master's, GMAT/GRE, previous course work in calculus. Additional exam requirements/recommendations for international students: Required—TOEFL. *Application deadline:* For fall admission, 10/15 for domestic and international students; for winter admission, 1/5 for domestic and international students; for spring admission, 3/15 for domestic and international students; for summer admission, 5/15 for domestic students. Applications are processed on a rolling basis. Application fee: $150. Electronic applications accepted. *Expenses:* *Tuition:* Full-time $44,580; part-time $1394 per credit hour. *Required fees:* $492. *Financial support:* In 2013–14, 72 students received support. Fellowships, research assistantships, teaching assistantships, institutionally sponsored loans, scholarships/grants, and tuition waivers (partial) available. Financial award application deadline: 3/1; financial award applicants required to submit CSS PROFILE or FAFSA. *Unit head:* Mark Zupan, Dean, 585-275-3316. *Application contact:* Rebekah S. Lewin, Assistant Dean of Admissions and Student Engagement, 585-275-3533, E-mail: admissions@simon.rochester.edu.

University of Rochester, Simon Business School, Part-Time MBA Program, Rochester, NY 14627. Offers accounting and information systems (MBA); business environment and public policy (MBA); business systems consulting (MBA); competitive

and organizational strategy (MBA); computers and information systems (MBA); corporate accounting (MBA); electronic commerce (MBA); entrepreneurship (MBA); finance (MBA); health sciences management (MBA); international management (MBA); manufacturing management (MBA); marketing (MBA); operations management - services (MBA); public accounting (MBA). Part-time and evening/weekend programs available. *Faculty:* 59 full-time (10 women), 23 part-time/adjunct (3 women). *Students:* 270 part-time (75 women); includes 38 minority (5 Black or African American, non-Hispanic/Latino; 1 American Indian or Alaska Native, non-Hispanic/Latino; 24 Asian, non-Hispanic/Latino; 5 Hispanic/Latino; 3 Two or more races, non-Hispanic/Latino). Average age 32. 56 applicants, 98% accepted, 51 enrolled. In 2013, 77 master's awarded. *Entrance requirements:* For master's, GRE or GMAT, resume, recommendation letters, essays, transcipts. *Application deadline:* For fall admission, 8/15 for domestic students; for winter admission, 11/15 for domestic students; for spring admission, 2/15 for domestic students; for summer admission, 5/15 for domestic students. Applications are processed on a rolling basis. Application fee: $150. Electronic applications accepted. *Expenses: Tuition:* Full-time $44,580; part-time $1394 per credit hour. *Required fees:* $492. *Financial support:* Scholarships/grants and tuition waivers available. Financial award applicants required to submit CSS PROFILE. *Unit head:* Mark Zupan, Dean, 585-275-3316, E-mail: mark.zupan@simon.rochester.edu. *Application contact:* Jennifer Mossotti, Associate Director of Part-Time Programs, 585-275-3803, E-mail: jennifer.mossotti@simon.rochester.edu.
Website: http://www.simon.rochester.edu/programs/part-time-mba-programs/index.aspx.

University of Saint Mary, Graduate Programs, Program in Business Administration, Leavenworth, KS 66048-5082. Offers enterprise risk management (MBA); finance (MBA); general management (MBA); health care management (MBA); human resource management (MBA); marketing and advertising management (MBA). Part-time and evening/weekend programs available. Postbaccalaureate distance learning degree programs offered (no on-campus study). *Students:* 151 full-time (87 women), 61 part-time (39 women); includes 60 minority (38 Black or African American, non-Hispanic/Latino; 1 American Indian or Alaska Native, non-Hispanic/Latino; 10 Asian, non-Hispanic/Latino; 11 Hispanic/Latino). *Degree requirements:* For master's, thesis. *Entrance requirements:* For master's, minimum undergraduate GPA of 2.75, official transcripts, two letters of recommendation. *Application deadline:* Applications are processed on a rolling basis. Application fee: $25. *Expenses: Tuition:* Part-time $550 per credit hour. *Unit head:* Rick Gunter, Director, 913-319-3007. *Application contact:* Patrick Smith, Coordinator of Business Programs, 913-319-3007, E-mail: smithp@stmary.edu.

University of San Francisco, School of Management, Master of Business Administration Program, San Francisco, CA 94105. Offers entrepreneurship and innovation (MBA); finance (MBA); international business (MBA); marketing (MBA); organization development (MBA); DDS/MBA; JD/MBA; MBA/MAPS. *Accreditation:* AACSB. Part-time and evening/weekend programs available. *Faculty:* 18 full-time (4 women), 20 part-time/adjunct (10 women). *Students:* 157 full-time (69 women), 14 part-time (7 women); includes 57 minority (7 Black or African American, non-Hispanic/Latino; 31 Asian, non-Hispanic/Latino; 14 Hispanic/Latino; 5 Two or more races, non-Hispanic/Latino), 30 international. Average age 29. 345 applicants, 68% accepted, 79 enrolled. In 2013, 131 master's awarded. *Entrance requirements:* For master's, GMAT or GRE, resume (two years of professional work experience required for Part-Time MBA, preferred for Full-Time MBA), transcripts from each college or university attended, two letters of recommendation, a personal statement and an interview. Additional exam requirements/recommendations for international students: Required—TOEFL (minimum score 600 paper-based, 100 iBT), IELTS (minimum score 7) or PTE (minimum score 68). *Application deadline:* For fall admission, 6/5 for domestic students, 5/15 for international students; for spring admission, 11/30 for domestic students. Application fee: $55. Electronic applications accepted. *Expenses: Tuition:* Full-time $21,150; part-time $1175 per unit. Tuition and fees vary according to course load, campus/location and program. *Financial support:* In 2013–14, 42 students received support. Fellowships and scholarships/grants available. Financial award application deadline: 3/2; financial award applicants required to submit FAFSA. *Faculty research:* International financial markets, technology transfer licensing, international marketing, strategic planning. *Total annual research expenditures:* $50,000. *Unit head:* Dr. John Veitch, Associate Dean and Program Director, 415-422-2221, Fax: 415-422-6315, E-mail: management@usfca.edu. *Application contact:* Office of Graduate Recruiting and Admissions, 415-422-2221, Fax: 415-422-6315, E-mail: management@usfca.edu.
Website: http://www.usfca.edu/mba.

University of Saskatchewan, College of Graduate Studies and Research, Edwards School of Business, Department of Management and Marketing, Saskatoon, SK S7N 5A2, Canada. Offers marketing (M Sc). Part-time programs available. *Degree requirements:* For master's, thesis. *Entrance requirements:* For master's, GMAT. Additional exam requirements/recommendations for international students: Required—TOEFL. *Expenses: Tuition, area resident:* Full-time $3585 Canadian dollars; part-time $585 Canadian dollars per course. Tuition, nonresident: part-time $877 Canadian dollars per course. *International tuition:* $5377 Canadian dollars full-time. *Required fees:* $889.51 Canadian dollars.

The University of Scranton, College of Graduate and Continuing Education, Program in Business Administration, Scranton, PA 18510. Offers accounting (MBA); finance (MBA); general business administration (MBA); health care management (MBA); international business (MBA); management information systems (MBA); marketing (MBA); operations management (MBA). *Accreditation:* AACSB. Part-time and evening/weekend programs available. Postbaccalaureate distance learning degree programs offered (no on-campus study). *Faculty:* 34 full-time (8 women). *Students:* 316 full-time (134 women), 241 part-time (94 women); includes 104 minority (43 Black or African American, non-Hispanic/Latino; 3 American Indian or Alaska Native, non-Hispanic/Latino; 29 Asian, non-Hispanic/Latino; 27 Hispanic/Latino; 2 Two or more races, non-Hispanic/Latino), 47 international. Average age 34. 249 applicants, 85% accepted. In 2013, 200 master's awarded. *Degree requirements:* For master's, capstone experience. *Entrance requirements:* For master's, GMAT, minimum GPA of 3.0. Additional exam requirements/recommendations for international students: Required—TOEFL (minimum score 500 paper-based), IELTS (minimum score 6). *Application deadline:* Applications are processed on a rolling basis. Application fee: $0. *Financial support:* In 2013–14, 13 students received support, including 13 teaching assistantships with full and partial tuition reimbursements available (averaging $8,800 per year); fellowships, career-related internships or fieldwork, Federal Work-Study, and unspecified assistantships also available. Support available to part-time students. Financial award application deadline: 3/1. *Faculty research:* Financial markets, strategic impact of total quality management, internal accounting controls, consumer preference, information systems and the Internet. *Unit head:* Dr. Murli Rajan, Director, 570-941-4043, Fax: 570-941-4342. *Application contact:* Joseph M. Roback, Director of Admissions, 570-941-4385, Fax: 570-941-5928, E-mail: robackj2@scranton.edu.
Website: http://www.scranton.edu/academics/cgce/busad.shtml.

University of Sioux Falls, Vucurevich School of Business, Sioux Falls, SD 57105-1699. Offers entrepreneurial leadership (MBA); general management (MBA); health care management (MBA); marketing (MBA). Part-time and evening/weekend programs available. *Degree requirements:* For master's, project. *Entrance requirements:* For master's, minimum GPA of 3.0. Additional exam requirements/recommendations for international students: Required—TOEFL. *Expenses:* Contact institution.

University of South Africa, College of Economic and Management Sciences, Pretoria, South Africa. Offers accounting (D Admin, D Com); accounting science (DA); auditing (D Admin, D Com); business administration (M Tech); business economics (D Admin); business leadership (DBL); business management (D Admin, D Com); economic management analysis (M Tech); economics (D Admin, D Com, PhD); human resource development (M Tech); industrial psychology (D Admin, D Com, PhD); logistics (D Com); marketing (M Tech); public administration (D Admin, D Com, DPA, PhD); public management (M Tech); quantitative management (D Admin, D Com); real estate (M Tech); statistics (D Admin, PhD); tourism management (D Admin, D Com); transport economics (D Admin, D Com).

University of South Florida, College of Business, Department of Marketing, Tampa, FL 33620-9951. Offers business administration (PhD), including marketing; marketing (MSM). Part-time and evening/weekend programs available. *Faculty:* 10 full-time (3 women). *Students:* 47 full-time (32 women), 10 part-time (3 women); includes 5 minority (2 Black or African American, non-Hispanic/Latino; 1 Asian, non-Hispanic/Latino; 2 Hispanic/Latino), 43 international. Average age 26. 101 applicants, 54% accepted, 30 enrolled. In 2013, 27 master's, 1 doctorate awarded. Terminal master's awarded for partial completion of doctoral program. *Degree requirements:* For master's, thesis or alternative; for doctorate, comprehensive exam, thesis/dissertation, 90 credit hours, minimum GPA of 3.0. *Entrance requirements:* For master's, GMAT (minimum score of 500) or GRE (in some cases), minimum GPA of 3.0 in upper-division undergraduate and marketing coursework, two letters of recommendation; for doctorate, GMAT or GRE, personal statement, recommendations, interview. Additional exam requirements/recommendations for international students: Required—TOEFL (minimum score 550 paper-based; 79 iBT) or IELTS (minimum score 6.5). *Application deadline:* For fall admission, 6/1 for domestic students, 1/2 for international students; for spring admission, 10/15 for domestic students, 6/1 for international students. Applications are processed on a rolling basis. Application fee: $30. Electronic applications accepted. *Financial support:* In 2013–14, 11 students received support, including 5 research assistantships (averaging $14,943 per year), 6 teaching assistantships (averaging $11,972 per year); health care benefits and unspecified assistantships also available. *Faculty research:* Branding; consumer behavior; marketing communications' effectiveness; customer satisfaction; customer delight; consumer reactions to new technology, products and services; consumer emotions; brand strategies; communications; advertising effectiveness; green alliances; strategic marketing; international business; international marketing; consumer research; customer service branding; focus group research; market surveys; market research; promotion; services marketing; strategic planning. *Unit head:* Dr. Anand Kumar, Interim Department Chair and Associate Professor, 813-974-6205, Fax: 813-974-6175, E-mail: akumar@usf.edu. *Application contact:* Dr. James Stock, Area Coordinator and Professor, 813-974-6173, Fax: 813-974-6175, E-mail: jstock@usf.edu.
Website: http://business.usf.edu/departments/marketing/.

The University of Tampa, John H. Sykes College of Business, Tampa, FL 33606-1490. Offers accounting (MS); entrepreneurship (MBA); finance (MBA, MS); information systems management (MBA); innovation management (MBA); international business (MBA); marketing (MBA, MS); nonprofit management (MBA). *Accreditation:* AACSB. Part-time and evening/weekend programs available. *Faculty:* 41 full-time (15 women), 5 part-time/adjunct (1 woman). *Students:* 406 full-time (171 women), 152 part-time (61 women); includes 104 minority (18 Black or African American, non-Hispanic/Latino; 1 American Indian or Alaska Native, non-Hispanic/Latino; 20 Asian, non-Hispanic/Latino; 59 Hispanic/Latino; 6 Two or more races, non-Hispanic/Latino), 154 international. Average age 33. 1,341 applicants, 37% accepted, 256 enrolled. In 2013, 218 master's awarded. *Degree requirements:* For master's, capstone. *Entrance requirements:* For master's, GMAT or GRE, 4-year undergraduate degree, minimum GPA of 3.0, professional experience (for Executive MBA). Additional exam requirements/recommendations for international students: Required—TOEFL (minimum score 577 paper-based; 90 iBT); Recommended—IELTS (minimum score 7.5). *Application deadline:* Applications are processed on a rolling basis. Application fee: $40. Electronic applications accepted. *Expenses: Tuition:* Full-time $8928; part-time $558 per credit hour. *Required fees:* $80; $80 $40 per term. Tuition and fees vary according to program. *Financial support:* In 2013–14, 110 students received support. Career-related internships or fieldwork, scholarships/grants, and unspecified assistantships available. Financial award applicants required to submit FAFSA. *Faculty research:* Job market signaling, on-line shopping behaviors and social media, the Tampa Bay economy, digital literacy, entrepreneurship in small businesses. *Unit head:* Dr. Stephanie Thomason, Associate Dean, 813-253-6289, E-mail: sthomason@ut.edu. *Application contact:* Charlene Tobie, Associate Director of Admissions, 813-257-3566, E-mail: ctobie@ut.edu.
Website: http://www.ut.edu/business/.

The University of Tennessee, Graduate School, College of Business Administration, Program in Business Administration, Knoxville, TN 37996. Offers accounting (PhD); finance (MBA, PhD); logistics and transportation (MBA, PhD); management (PhD); marketing (MBA, PhD); operations management (MBA); professional business administration (MBA); statistics (PhD); JD/MBA; MS/MBA; Pharm D/MBA. Pharm D/MBA offered jointly with The University of Tennessee Health Science Center. *Accreditation:* AACSB. Postbaccalaureate distance learning degree programs offered. *Degree requirements:* For master's, thesis or alternative; for doctorate, thesis/dissertation. *Entrance requirements:* For master's and doctorate, GMAT, minimum GPA of 2.7. Additional exam requirements/recommendations for international students: Required—TOEFL. Electronic applications accepted. *Expenses:* Tuition, state resident: full-time $9540; part-time $531 per credit hour. Tuition, nonresident: full-time $27,728; part-time $1542 per credit hour. *Required fees:* $1404; $67 per credit hour.

The University of Texas at Arlington, Graduate School, College of Business, Department of Marketing, Arlington, TX 76019. Offers marketing (PhD); marketing research (MS). Part-time and evening/weekend programs available. *Degree requirements:* For master's, thesis optional; for doctorate, comprehensive exam, thesis/dissertation. *Entrance requirements:* For master's and doctorate, GMAT, GRE. Additional exam requirements/recommendations for international students: Required—TOEFL (minimum score 550 paper-based; 79 iBT). Electronic applications accepted. *Faculty research:* Marketing strategy, marketing research, international marketing.

The University of Texas at Arlington, Graduate School, College of Business, Program in Business Administration, Arlington, TX 76019. Offers accounting (PhD); business statistics (PhD); finance (MBA, PhD); information systems (MBA, PhD); management (MBA, PhD); marketing (MBA, PhD); operations management (MBA, PhD); real estate (MBA). *Accreditation:* AACSB. Part-time and evening/weekend programs available. *Degree requirements:* For master's, thesis optional; for doctorate, comprehensive exam, thesis/dissertation. *Entrance requirements:* For master's, GMAT or GRE; for doctorate, GMAT, minimum GPA of 3.0 (undergraduate), 3.4 (graduate); 30 hours of graduate course work. Additional exam requirements/recommendations for international students:

Required—TOEFL (minimum score 550 paper-based; 79 iBT). Electronic applications accepted.

The University of Texas at Austin, Graduate School, McCombs School of Business, Department of Marketing, Austin, TX 78712-1111. Offers MBA, PhD. *Degree requirements:* For doctorate, comprehensive exam, thesis/dissertation. *Entrance requirements:* For doctorate, GMAT or GRE. Electronic applications accepted. *Faculty research:* Internet marketing, strategic marketing, buy behavior.

The University of Texas at Dallas, Naveen Jindal School of Management, Program in Marketing, Richardson, TX 75080. Offers marketing (MS); professional sales (MS). Part-time and evening/weekend programs available. *Faculty:* 15 full-time (5 women), 3 part-time/adjunct (0 women). *Students:* 141 full-time (94 women), 26 part-time (19 women); includes 19 minority (11 Asian, non-Hispanic/Latino; 7 Hispanic/Latino; 1 Two or more races, non-Hispanic/Latino), 116 international. Average age 25. 337 applicants, 49% accepted, 67 enrolled. In 2013, 32 master's awarded. *Degree requirements:* For master's, thesis optional. *Entrance requirements:* For master's, GMAT, minimum GPA of 3.0 in upper-level coursework in field. Additional exam requirements/recommendations for international students: Required—TOEFL (minimum score 550 paper-based). *Application deadline:* For fall admission, 7/15 for domestic students, 5/1 priority date for international students; for spring admission, 11/15 for domestic students, 9/1 priority date for international students. Applications are processed on a rolling basis. Application fee: $50 ($100 for international students). Electronic applications accepted. *Expenses:* Tuition, state resident: full-time $11,940; part-time $663.33 per credit hour. Tuition, nonresident: full-time $21,606; part-time $1200.33 per credit hour. *Financial support:* In 2013–14, 27 students received support. Research assistantships with partial tuition reimbursements available, teaching assistantships with partial tuition reimbursements available, career-related internships or fieldwork, Federal Work-Study, institutionally sponsored loans, scholarships/grants, and unspecified assistantships available. Support available to part-time students. Financial award application deadline: 4/30; financial award applicants required to submit FAFSA. *Faculty research:* Inventory control and risk management. *Unit head:* Dr. Ernan Haruvy, Area Coordinator, 972-883-4865, E-mail: eharuvy@utdallas.edu. *Application contact:* Alexander Edsel, Director, Graduate Marketing Program, 972-883-4421, E-mail: alexander.edsel@utdallas.edu.
Website: http://jindal.utdallas.edu/academic-areas/marketing/.

The University of Texas at Dallas, Naveen Jindal School of Management, Programs in Management Science, Richardson, TX 75080. Offers accounting (PhD); finance (PhD); information systems (PhD); marketing (PhD); operations management (PhD). *Accreditation:* AACSB. Part-time and evening/weekend programs available. *Faculty:* 13 full-time (3 women), 7 part-time/adjunct (2 women). *Students:* 78 full-time (27 women), 9 part-time (3 women); includes 6 minority (all Asian, non-Hispanic/Latino), 73 international. Average age 30. 258 applicants, 9% accepted, 16 enrolled. In 2013, 14 doctorates awarded. *Degree requirements:* For doctorate, thesis/dissertation. *Entrance requirements:* For doctorate, GMAT, minimum GPA of 3.0. Additional exam requirements/recommendations for international students: Required—TOEFL (minimum score 550 paper-based). *Application deadline:* For fall admission, 7/15 for domestic students, 5/1 priority date for international students; for spring admission, 11/15 for domestic students, 9/1 priority date for international students. Applications are processed on a rolling basis. Application fee: $50 ($100 for international students). Electronic applications accepted. *Expenses:* Tuition, state resident: full-time $11,940; part-time $663.33 per credit hour. Tuition, nonresident: full-time $21,606; part-time $1200.33 per credit hour. *Financial support:* In 2013–14, 81 students received support. Research assistantships with partial tuition reimbursements available, teaching assistantships with partial tuition reimbursements available, career-related internships or fieldwork, Federal Work-Study, institutionally sponsored loans, scholarships/grants, and unspecified assistantships available. Support available to part-time students. Financial award application deadline: 4/30; financial award applicants required to submit FAFSA. *Faculty research:* Empirical generalizations in marketing, diffusion of generations of technology, stochastic brand-choice theory, acceptance of trade deals by supermarkets, nonparametric estimations of market share response. *Unit head:* Dr. Sumit Sarkar, Program Director, 972-883-2745, Fax: 972-883-5977, E-mail: som_phd.@utdallas.edu. *Application contact:* Ashley J. Desouza, Program Administrator, 972-883-2745, Fax: 972-883-5977, E-mail: ashley.desouza@utdallas.edu.
Website: http://jindal.utdallas.edu/academic-programs/phd-programs/management-science/.

The University of Texas at San Antonio, College of Business, Department of Marketing, San Antonio, TX 78249-0617. Offers marketing (PhD); marketing management (MBA); tourism destination development (MBA). Part-time and evening/weekend programs available. *Faculty:* 5 full-time (2 women), 1 part-time/adjunct (0 women). *Students:* 17 full-time (8 women), 12 part-time (7 women); includes 9 minority (2 Asian, non-Hispanic/Latino; 6 Hispanic/Latino; 1 Two or more races, non-Hispanic/Latino), 8 international. Average age 29. 8 applicants, 100% accepted, 8 enrolled. In 2013, 5 master's, 1 doctorate awarded. *Degree requirements:* For master's, comprehensive exam (for some programs), thesis (for some programs). *Entrance requirements:* For master's, GMAT, minimum GPA of 3.0. Additional exam requirements/recommendations for international students: Required—TOEFL (minimum score 550 paper-based; 79 iBT). *Application deadline:* For fall admission, 7/1 for domestic students, 4/1 for international students; for spring admission, 11/1 for domestic students, 9/1 for international students. Applications are processed on a rolling basis. Application fee: $45 ($80 for international students). Electronic applications accepted. *Expenses:* Tuition, state resident: full-time $4671. Tuition, nonresident: full-time $8708. *International tuition:* $17,415 full-time. *Required fees:* $1924.60. Tuition and fees vary according to course load and degree level. *Financial support:* Career-related internships or fieldwork, Federal Work-Study, scholarships/grants, and unspecified assistantships available. Support available to part-time students. *Faculty research:* Consumer behavior, cross-cultural research, psycholinguistics, pricing, mass media and materialism. *Unit head:* Dr. L. J. Shrum, Department Chair, 210-458-5374, Fax: 210-458-6335, E-mail: lj.shrum@utsa.edu. *Application contact:* Veronica Ramirez, Assistant Dean of the Graduate School, 210-458-7841, Fax: 210-458-4332, E-mail: graduatestudies@utsa.edu.
Website: http://business.utsa.edu/marketing/.

The University of Texas–Pan American, College of Business Administration, Program in Business Administration, Edinburg, TX 78539. Offers business administration (MBA); finance (PhD); management (PhD); marketing (PhD). Part-time and evening/weekend programs available. Postbaccalaureate distance learning degree programs offered (no on-campus study). *Degree requirements:* For master's, thesis optional. *Entrance requirements:* For master's, GMAT, minimum GPA of 3.0. Additional exam requirements/recommendations for international students: Required—TOEFL (minimum score 500 paper-based). Electronic applications accepted. *Expenses:* Tuition, state resident: full-time $5986; part-time $333 per credit hour. Tuition, nonresident: full-time $12,358; part-time $687 per credit hour. *Required fees:* $782. Tuition and fees vary according to program. *Faculty research:* Human resources, border region, entrepreneurship, marketing.

University of the Cumberlands, Graduate Programs in Education, Williamsburg, KY 40769-1372. Offers all grades (P-12) (M Ed); business and marketing (MA Ed, MAT); counselor education and supervision (Ed D); director of pupil personnel (Certificate); director of special education (Certificate); educational administration and supervision (Ed S); educational leadership (Ed D); elementary education (MA Ed, MAT); instructional leadership - principalship (MA Ed); instructional leadership - school principal (Certificate); middle school education (MA Ed, MAT); reading and writing (MA Ed); school counseling (MA Ed); school superintendent (Certificate); secondary education (MA Ed, MAT); special education (MAT); supervisor of instruction (Certificate); teacher leader (MA Ed). Part-time and evening/weekend programs available. Postbaccalaureate distance learning degree programs offered. *Degree requirements:* For master's, comprehensive exam. Electronic applications accepted.

University of the Incarnate Word, School of Graduate Studies and Research, H-E-B School of Business and Administration, Programs in Business Administration, San Antonio, TX 78209-6397. Offers general business (MBA); international business (MBA); marketing (MBA); sports management (MBA). *Accreditation:* ACBSP. Part-time and evening/weekend programs available. Postbaccalaureate distance learning degree programs offered. *Faculty:* 20 full-time (10 women), 14 part-time/adjunct (6 women). *Students:* 95 full-time (33 women), 74 part-time (40 women); includes 93 minority (11 Black or African American, non-Hispanic/Latino; 1 American Indian or Alaska Native, non-Hispanic/Latino; 4 Asian, non-Hispanic/Latino; 71 Hispanic/Latino; 2 Native Hawaiian or other Pacific Islander, non-Hispanic/Latino; 4 Two or more races, non-Hispanic/Latino), 41 international. Average age 28. 183 applicants, 66% accepted, 51 enrolled. In 2013, 75 master's awarded. *Degree requirements:* For master's, capstone. *Entrance requirements:* For master's, GMAT (minimum score 450), undergraduate degree with minimum overall GPA of 2.5. Additional exam requirements/recommendations for international students: Required—TOEFL (minimum score 560 paper-based; 83 iBT). *Application deadline:* Applications are processed on a rolling basis. Application fee: $20. Electronic applications accepted. *Expenses: Tuition:* Part-time $815 per credit hour. *Required fees:* $86 per credit hour. One-time fee: $40 part-time. Tuition and fees vary according to degree level and program. *Financial support:* Federal Work-Study and scholarships/grants available. Financial award applicants required to submit FAFSA. *Unit head:* Dr. Jeannie Scott, Acting Dean, 210-283-5002, Fax: 210-805-3564, E-mail: scott@uiwtx.edu. *Application contact:* Andrea Cyterski-Acosta, Dean of Enrollment, 210-829-6005, Fax: 210-829-3921, E-mail: admis@uiwtx.edu.
Website: http://www.uiw.edu/mba/index.htm and http://www.uiw.edu/mba/admission.html.

University of the Sacred Heart, Graduate Programs, Department of Business Administration, Program in International Marketing, San Juan, PR 00914-0383. Offers MBA. Part-time and evening/weekend programs available. *Degree requirements:* For master's, thesis. *Entrance requirements:* For master's, EXADEP, minimum undergraduate GPA of 2.75, interview.

The University of Toledo, College of Graduate Studies, College of Business and Innovation, Department of Marketing and International Business, Toledo, OH 43606-3390. Offers MBA. Part-time and evening/weekend programs available. *Faculty:* 15. *Students:* 24 full-time (12 women), 19 part-time (11 women); includes 8 minority (5 Black or African American, non-Hispanic/Latino; 1 Asian, non-Hispanic/Latino; 1 Hispanic/Latino; 1 Two or more races, non-Hispanic/Latino), 19 international. Average age 26. 15 applicants, 93% accepted, 9 enrolled. In 2013, 67 master's awarded. *Entrance requirements:* For master's, GMAT, GRE, or LSAT, minimum GPA of 2.7 for all prior academic work, three letters of recommendation, statement of purpose, transcripts from all prior institutions attended. Additional exam requirements/recommendations for international students: Required—TOEFL (minimum score 550 paper-based; 80 iBT). *Application deadline:* For fall admission, 8/1 for domestic students, 5/1 for international students; for spring admission, 11/15 for domestic students, 10/1 for international students; for summer admission, 4/15 for domestic students, 3/1 for international students. Applications are processed on a rolling basis. Application fee: $45 ($75 for international students). Electronic applications accepted. *Financial support:* In 2013–14, 3 research assistantships with full and partial tuition reimbursements (averaging $4,375 per year) were awarded; career-related internships or fieldwork, Federal Work-Study, scholarships/grants, tuition waivers (full and partial), unspecified assistantships, and administrative assistantships also available. Financial award applicants required to submit FAFSA. *Unit head:* Dr. Iryna Pentina, Chair, 419-530-2093, E-mail: iryna.pentina@utoledo.edu. *Application contact:* Graduate School Office, 419-530-4723, Fax: 419-530-4724, E-mail: grdsch@utnet.utoledo.edu.
Website: http://www.utoledo.edu/business/index.html.

University of Utah, Graduate School, David Eccles School of Business, Business Administration Program, Salt Lake City, UT 84112. Offers accounting (PhD); business administration (EMBA, MBA, PMBA); finance (PhD); information systems (PhD); marketing (PhD); operations management (PhD); organizational behavior (PhD); strategic management (PhD); MBA/JD; MBA/MHA; MBA/MS. Part-time and evening/weekend programs available. *Faculty:* 58 full-time (21 women), 37 part-time/adjunct (7 women). *Students:* 481 full-time (108 women), 109 part-time (19 women); includes 39 minority (2 Black or African American, non-Hispanic/Latino; 13 Asian, non-Hispanic/Latino; 18 Hispanic/Latino; 1 Native Hawaiian or other Pacific Islander, non-Hispanic/Latino; 5 Two or more races, non-Hispanic/Latino), 39 international. Average age 32. 486 applicants, 56% accepted, 215 enrolled. In 2013, 326 master's, 10 doctorates awarded. *Degree requirements:* For doctorate, comprehensive exam, thesis/dissertation. *Entrance requirements:* For master's, GMAT or GRE; for doctorate, GMAT. Additional exam requirements/recommendations for international students: Required—TOEFL (minimum score 600 paper-based; 100 iBT), IELTS (minimum score 7). *Application deadline:* For fall admission, 11/1 priority date for domestic students, 3/1 priority date for international students; for spring admission, 11/1 for domestic and international students. Applications are processed on a rolling basis. Application fee: $55 ($65 for international students). Electronic applications accepted. *Expenses:* Contact institution. *Financial support:* In 2013–14, 48 students received support, including 41 fellowships with partial tuition reimbursements available (averaging $8,600 per year), 35 research assistantships with partial tuition reimbursements available (averaging $6,378 per year), 57 teaching assistantships with full tuition reimbursements available (averaging $17,000 per year); scholarships/grants and unspecified assistantships also available. Financial award application deadline: 2/1; financial award applicants required to submit FAFSA. *Faculty research:* Corporate finance, strategy services, consumer behavior, financial disclosures, operations. *Unit head:* Dr. William Hesterly, Associate Dean, PhD Program, 801-581-7676, Fax: 801-581-3380, E-mail: mastersinfo@business.utah.edu. *Application contact:* Andrea Miller, Coordinator, 801-581-7785, Fax: 801-581-3666, E-mail: mastersinfo@business.utah.edu.
Website: http://business.utah.edu/full-time-mba.

University of Virginia, McIntire School of Commerce, Program in Commerce, Charlottesville, VA 22903. Offers financial services (MSC); marketing and management (MSC). *Students:* 103 full-time (44 women), 1 part-time (0 women); includes 19 minority (2 Black or African American, non-Hispanic/Latino; 11 Asian, non-Hispanic/Latino; 3 Hispanic/Latino; 3 Two or more races, non-Hispanic/Latino), 18 international. Average age 22. 317 applicants, 47% accepted, 105 enrolled. In 2013, 92 master's awarded. *Entrance requirements:* For master's, GMAT, 2 letters of recommendation; prerequisite

course work in financial accounting, microeconomics, and introduction to business. Additional exam requirements/recommendations for international students: Required—TOEFL (minimum score 600 paper-based; 100 iBT), IELTS (minimum score 7). *Application deadline:* For fall admission, 9/15 priority date for domestic students, 1/15 priority date for international students. Applications are processed on a rolling basis. Application fee: $75. Electronic applications accepted. *Expenses:* Contact institution. *Financial support:* Scholarships/grants available. Financial award application deadline: 3/1; financial award applicants required to submit CSS PROFILE or FAFSA. *Unit head:* Ira C. Harris, Head, 434-924-8816, Fax: 434-924-7074, E-mail: ich3x@comm.virginia.edu. *Application contact:* Emma Candalier, Associate Director of Graduate Recruiting, 434-243-4992, Fax: 434-924-4511, E-mail: ecandalier@virginia.edu.
Website: http://www.commerce.virginia.edu/academic_programs/MSCommerce/Pages/index.aspx.

The University of Western Ontario, Richard Ivey School of Business, London, ON N6A 3K7, Canada. Offers business (EMBA, PhD); corporate strategy and leadership elective (MBA); entrepreneurship elective (MBA); finance elective (MBA); health sector stream (MBA); international management elective (MBA); marketing elective (MBA); JD/MBA. *Degree requirements:* For master's, thesis (for some programs); for doctorate, thesis/dissertation. *Entrance requirements:* For master's, GMAT, 2 years of full-time work experience, interview. Additional exam requirements/recommendations for international students: Required—TOEFL (minimum score 100 iBT) or IELTS (minimium score 6). Electronic applications accepted. *Faculty research:* Strategy, organizational behavior, international business, finance, operations management.

University of Wisconsin–Madison, Graduate School, Wisconsin School of Business, Doctoral Program in Marketing, Madison, WI 53706-1380. Offers PhD. *Faculty:* 14 full-time (4 women). *Students:* 7 full-time (6 women); includes 1 minority (American Indian or Alaska Native, non-Hispanic/Latino), 3 international. Average age 30. 38 applicants, 13% accepted, 1 enrolled. In 2013, 2 doctorates awarded. *Degree requirements:* For doctorate, comprehensive exam, thesis/dissertation. *Entrance requirements:* For doctorate, GMAT or GRE. Additional exam requirements/recommendations for international students: Recommended—TOEFL (minimum score 623 paper-based; 106 iBT), IELTS (minimum score 7.5), TSE (minimum score 73). *Application deadline:* For fall admission, 12/15 priority date for domestic and international students. Application fee: $56. Electronic applications accepted. *Expenses:* Contact institution. *Financial support:* In 2013–14, 7 students received support, including fellowships with full tuition reimbursements available (averaging $19,125 per year), 2 research assistantships with full tuition reimbursements available (averaging $14,746 per year), 5 teaching assistantships with full tuition reimbursements available (averaging $14,746 per year); Federal Work-Study, institutionally sponsored loans, scholarships/grants, health care benefits, and unspecified assistantships also available. Financial award application deadline: 12/15; financial award applicants required to submit FAFSA. *Faculty research:* Marketing strategy, consumer behavior, channels of distribution, advertising, price promotions. *Unit head:* Prof. Neeraj Arora, Chair, 608-262-1990, Fax: 608-262-0394, E-mail: narora@bus.wisc.edu. *Application contact:* Belle Heberling, Assistant Director for Research Programs, 608-262-3749, Fax: 608-890-0180, E-mail: phd@bus.wisc.edu.
Website: http://www.bus.wisc.edu/phd.

University of Wisconsin–Whitewater, School of Graduate Studies, College of Business and Economics, Program in Business Administration, Whitewater, WI 53190-1790. Offers finance (MBA); human resource management (MBA); information technology management (MBA); international business (MBA); management (MBA); marketing (MBA); operations and supply chain management (MBA). *Accreditation:* AACSB. Part-time and evening/weekend programs available. Postbaccalaureate distance learning degree programs offered (no on-campus study). *Entrance requirements:* For master's, GMAT or GRE, minimum AACSB index of 1000, minimum GPA of 2.75. Additional exam requirements/recommendations for international students: Required—TOEFL (minimum score 550 paper-based; 80 iBT), IELTS (minimum score 6). Electronic applications accepted. *Faculty research:* Interface between social institutions and individual behavior, technology and innovation management, occupational mental health, workplace deviance and workplace romance.

University of Wisconsin–Whitewater, School of Graduate Studies, College of Business and Economics, Program in Business and Marketing Education, Whitewater, WI 53190-1790. Offers MS. *Accreditation:* NCATE. Part-time and evening/weekend programs available. Postbaccalaureate distance learning degree programs offered (no on-campus study). *Degree requirements:* For master's, thesis or alternative. *Entrance requirements:* For master's, interview, teaching license. Additional exam requirements/recommendations for international students: Required—TOEFL (minimum score 550 paper-based; 80 iBT), IELTS (minimum score 6). Electronic applications accepted. *Faculty research:* Active learning and performance strategies, technology-enhanced formative assessment, computer-supported cooperative work, privacy surveillance.

Valparaiso University, Graduate School, College of Business, Valparaiso, IN 46383. Offers business administration (MBA); business intelligence (Certificate); engineering management (Certificate); entrepreneurship (Certificate); finance (Certificate); general business (Certificate); management (Certificate); marketing (Certificate); sustainability (Certificate); JD/MBA; MSN/MBA. *Accreditation:* AACSB. Part-time and evening/weekend programs available. Postbaccalaureate distance learning degree programs offered (minimal on-campus study). *Faculty:* 11 part-time/adjunct (2 women). *Students:* 13 full-time (3 women), 48 part-time (21 women); includes 6 minority (3 Black or African American, non-Hispanic/Latino; 2 Hispanic/Latino; 1 Two or more races, non-Hispanic/Latino), 5 international. Average age 33. In 2013, 19 master's, 3 other advanced degrees awarded. *Entrance requirements:* For master's, GMAT, GRE, minimum GPA of 3.0. Additional exam requirements/recommendations for international students: Required—TOEFL (minimum score 550 paper-based; 80 iBT), IELTS (minimum score 6). *Application deadline:* Applications are processed on a rolling basis. Application fee: $30 ($50 for international students). Electronic applications accepted. *Expenses:* Contact institution. *Financial support:* Available to part-time students. Applicants required to submit FAFSA. *Unit head:* Bruce MacLean, Director of Graduate Programs in Management, 219-465-7952, Fax: 219-464-5789, E-mail: bruce.maclean@valpo.edu. *Application contact:* Cindy Scanlan, Assistant Director of Graduate Programs in Management, 219-465-7952, Fax: 219-464-5789, E-mail: cindy.scanlan@valpo.edu.
Website: http://www.valpo.edu/mba/.

Vancouver Island University, Master of Business Administration Program, Nanaimo, BC V9R 5S5, Canada. Offers international business (MBA), including finance, marketing. Program offered jointly with University of Hertfordshire. *Accreditation:* ACBSP. Part-time programs available. *Degree requirements:* For master's, thesis. *Entrance requirements:* Additional exam requirements/recommendations for international students: Required—TOEFL (minimum score 550 paper-based). Electronic applications accepted. *Faculty research:* Tourism development, entrepreneurship, organizational development, strategic planning, international business strategy, intercultural team work.

Vanderbilt University, Vanderbilt Graduate School of Management, Vanderbilt MBA Program (Full-time), Nashville, TN 37203. Offers accounting (MBA); finance (MBA); general management (MBA); human and organizational performance (MBA); marketing (MBA); operations (MBA); strategy (MBA); MBA/JD; MBA/M Div; MBA/MD; MBA/MTS; MBA/PhD. *Accreditation:* AACSB. *Students:* 341 full-time (119 women); includes 42 minority (20 Black or African American, non-Hispanic/Latino; 12 Asian, non-Hispanic/Latino; 5 Hispanic/Latino; 5 Two or more races, non-Hispanic/Latino), 73 international. Average age 28. 1,059 applicants, 38% accepted, 166 enrolled. In 2013, 161 master's awarded. *Entrance requirements:* For master's, GMAT (preferred) or GRE, 2 years of work experience (recommended). Additional exam requirements/recommendations for international students: Required—TOEFL. *Application deadline:* For fall admission, 10/1 priority date for domestic and international students; for winter admission, 1/6 priority date for domestic and international students; for spring admission, 3/3 priority date for domestic students, 3/5 priority date for international students; for summer admission, 4/5 for domestic students, 5/5 for international students. Applications are processed on a rolling basis. Application fee: $75 ($175 for international students). Electronic applications accepted. *Financial support:* In 2013–14, 237 students received support. Scholarships/grants and tuition waivers (full and partial) available. Financial award application deadline: 5/15; financial award applicants required to submit FAFSA. *Unit head:* Nancy Lea Hyer, Associate Dean, 615-322-2530, Fax: 615-343-7110, E-mail: nancy.lea.hyer@owen.vanderbilt.edu. *Application contact:* Dinah Webster, Administrative Assistant, 615-322-6469, Fax: 615-343-1175, E-mail: mba@owen.vanderbilt.edu.
Website: http://www.owen.vanderbilt.edu.

Villanova University, Villanova School of Business, MBA - The Fast Track Program, Villanova, PA 19085. Offers finance (MBA); health care management (MBA); international business (MBA); management information systems (MBA); marketing (MBA); real estate (MBA); strategic management (MBA). *Accreditation:* AACSB. Part-time and evening/weekend programs available. *Faculty:* 101 full-time (33 women), 36 part-time/adjunct (3 women). *Students:* 140 part-time (44 women); includes 22 minority (1 Black or African American, non-Hispanic/Latino; 17 Asian, non-Hispanic/Latino; 3 Hispanic/Latino; 1 Two or more races, non-Hispanic/Latino), 3 international. Average age 29. 127 applicants, 72% accepted, 75 enrolled. In 2013, 61 master's awarded. *Degree requirements:* For master's, minimum GPA of 3.0. *Entrance requirements:* For master's, GMAT or GRE, work experience. Additional exam requirements/recommendations for international students: Required—TOEFL (minimum score 550 paper-based; 90 iBT). *Application deadline:* For fall admission, 6/30 for domestic and international students. Application fee: $50. Electronic applications accepted. *Financial support:* Scholarships/grants available. Financial award application deadline: 6/30; financial award applicants required to submit FAFSA. *Faculty research:* Business analytics; creativity, innovation and entrepreneurship; global leadership; real estate; church management; business ethics. *Unit head:* Zelon Crawford, Director of Graduate Business Programs, 610-519-6283, Fax: 610-519-6273, E-mail: zelon.crawford@villanova.edu. *Application contact:* Meredith L. Lockyer, Manager of Recruiting, 610-519-7016, Fax: 610-519-6273, E-mail: meredith.lockyer@villanova.edu.
Website: http://www1.villanova.edu/villanova/business/graduate/mba/fasttrack.html.

Villanova University, Villanova School of Business, MBA - The Flex Track Program, Villanova, PA 19085. Offers finance (MBA); health care management (MBA); international business (MBA); management information systems (MBA); marketing (MBA); real estate (MBA); strategic management (MBA); JD/MBA. *Accreditation:* AACSB. Part-time and evening/weekend programs available. Postbaccalaureate distance learning degree programs offered (minimal on-campus study). *Faculty:* 101 full-time (33 women), 36 part-time/adjunct (3 women). *Students:* 13 full-time (5 women), 413 part-time (127 women); includes 63 minority (13 Black or African American, non-Hispanic/Latino; 1 American Indian or Alaska Native, non-Hispanic/Latino; 29 Asian, non-Hispanic/Latino; 14 Hispanic/Latino; 1 Native Hawaiian or other Pacific Islander, non-Hispanic/Latino; 5 Two or more races, non-Hispanic/Latino), 9 international. Average age 29. 84 applicants, 83% accepted, 66 enrolled. In 2013, 133 master's awarded. *Degree requirements:* For master's, minimum GPA of 3.0. *Entrance requirements:* For master's, GMAT or GRE, work experience. Additional exam requirements/recommendations for international students: Required—TOEFL (minimum score 550 paper-based; 90 iBT). *Application deadline:* For fall admission, 6/30 for domestic and international students; for winter admission, 11/15 for domestic and international students; for spring admission, 11/15 for domestic and international students; for summer admission, 3/31 for domestic and international students. Applications are processed on a rolling basis. Application fee: $50. Electronic applications accepted. *Financial support:* In 2013–14, 13 research assistantships with full tuition reimbursements (averaging $13,100 per year) were awarded; scholarships/grants and unspecified assistantships also available. Financial award application deadline: 6/30; financial award applicants required to submit FAFSA. *Faculty research:* Business analytics; creativity, innovation and entrepreneurship; global leadership; real estate; church management; business ethics. *Unit head:* Zelon Crawford, Director of Graduate Business Programs, 610-610-6283, Fax: 610-519-6273, E-mail: zelon.crawford@villanova.edu. *Application contact:* Meredith L. Lockyer, Manager of Recruiting, 610-519-7016, Fax: 610-519-6273, E-mail: meredith.lockyer@villanova.edu.
Website: http://www1.villanova.edu/villanova/business/graduate/mba/flextrack.html.

Virginia Commonwealth University, Graduate School, School of Business, Program in Marketing and Business Law, Richmond, VA 23284-9005. Offers MS. *Entrance requirements:* For master's, GMAT. Additional exam requirements/recommendations for international students: Required—TOEFL (minimum score 600 paper-based; 100 iBT); Recommended—IELTS (minimum score 6.5). Electronic applications accepted.

Virginia International University, School of Business, Fairfax, VA 22030. Offers accounting (MBA); executive management (Graduate Certificate); global logistics (MBA); health care management (MBA); human resources management (MBA); international business management (MBA); international finance (MBA); marketing management (MBA). Part-time programs available. *Entrance requirements:* For master's and Graduate Certificate, bachelor's degree. Additional exam requirements/recommendations for international students: Required—TOEFL (minimum score 550 paper-based; 80 iBT), IELTS (minimum score 6). Electronic applications accepted.

Wagner College, Division of Graduate Studies, Department of Business Administration, Program in Marketing, Staten Island, NY 10301-4495. Offers MBA. Part-time and evening/weekend programs available. *Faculty:* 1 (woman) part-time/adjunct. *Students:* 11 full-time (6 women), 6 part-time (2 women); includes 2 minority (1 Black or African American, non-Hispanic/Latino; 1 Native Hawaiian or other Pacific Islander, non-Hispanic/Latino). Average age 25. 8 applicants, 100% accepted, 7 enrolled. In 2013, 9 master's awarded. *Degree requirements:* For master's, thesis optional. *Entrance requirements:* For master's, GMAT, minimum GPA of 2.6. Additional exam requirements/recommendations for international students: Required—TOEFL (minimum score 550 paper-based; 79 iBT). *Application deadline:* For fall admission, 4/1 priority date for domestic students, 3/1 priority date for international students; for spring admission, 11/1 priority date for domestic students, 10/1 priority date for international students. Applications are processed on a rolling basis. Application fee: $50. *Expenses: Tuition:* Full-time $17,496; part-time $972 per credit. Tuition and fees vary according to course load. *Financial support:* In 2013–14, 15 students received support. Career-related internships or fieldwork, unspecified assistantships, and alumni fellowship grants available. Financial award applicants required to submit FAFSA. *Unit head:* Dr. John J.

Marketing

Moran, Director, 718-390-3255, Fax: 718-390-3255, E-mail: jmoran@wagner.edu. *Application contact:* Patricia Clancy, Assistant Coordinator of Graduate Studies, 718-420-4464, Fax: 718-390-3105, E-mail: patricia.clancy@wagner.edu.

Wake Forest University, School of Business, Full-time MBA Program, Winston-Salem, NC 27106. Offers finance (MBA); marketing (MBA); operations management (MBA); JD/MBA; MD/MBA; MSA/MBA. *Accreditation:* AACSB. *Faculty:* 77 full-time (21 women), 32 part-time/adjunct (8 women). *Students:* 107 full-time (33 women); includes 22 minority (11 Black or African American, non-Hispanic/Latino; 4 Asian, non-Hispanic/Latino; 3 Hispanic/Latino; 4 Two or more races, non-Hispanic/Latino), 21 international. Average age 30. In 2013, 66 master's awarded. *Degree requirements:* For master's, 65.5 credit hours. *Entrance requirements:* For master's, GMAT or GRE, letters of recommendation, official transcripts, current resume or curriculum vitae, 2 years of work experience. Additional exam requirements/recommendations for international students: Required—TOEFL (minimum score 600 paper-based; 100 iBT), PTE. *Application deadline:* For fall admission, 4/15 for domestic and international students. Applications are processed on a rolling basis. Application fee: $100. Electronic applications accepted. *Expenses:* Contact institution. *Financial support:* In 2013–14, 90 students received support. Career-related internships or fieldwork, scholarships/grants, and unspecified assistantships available. Financial award application deadline: 2/15; financial award applicants required to submit FAFSA. *Faculty research:* The influence of personal relationships on business decision-making and management of change; drivers of perceived value and consumer behavior; impact of accounting on auditing, financial, managerial, systems and taxation stakeholders; corporate governance and executive compensation; impact of operations strategies on competitiveness. *Unit head:* Scott Schaffer, Associate Dean, 336-758-5422, Fax: 336-758-5830, E-mail: busadmissions@wfu.edu. *Application contact:* Tamara Paquee, Administrative Assistant, 336-758-5422, Fax: 336-758-5830, E-mail: busadmissions@wfu.edu.
Website: http://www.business.wfu.edu/.

Walden University, Graduate Programs, School of Management, Minneapolis, MN 55401. Offers accounting (MBA, MS, DBA), including accounting for the professional (MS), accounting with CPA emphasis (MS), self-designed (MS, PhD); accounting and management (MS), including accountants as strategic managers, self-designed (MS, PhD); advanced project management (Graduate Certificate); applied project management (Graduate Certificate); bridge to business administration (Post-Doctoral Certificate); bridge to management (Post-Doctoral Certificate); business administration (EMBA); business management (Graduate Certificate); communication (MS, Graduate Certificate; corporate finance (MBA); entrepreneurship (DBA); entrepreneurship and small business (MBA); finance (DBA); global supply chain management (DBA); healthcare management (MBA, DBA); human resource management (MBA, MS, Graduate Certificate), including functional human resource management (MS), general program (MS), integrating functional and strategic human resource management (MS), organizational strategy (MS); human resources management (DBA); information systems management (DBA); international business (MBA, DBA); leadership (MBA, MS, DBA), including general program (MS), human resources leadership (MS), leader development (MS), self-designed (MS, PhD); management (MS, PhD), including accounting (PhD), engineering management (PhD), finance (PhD), general program (MS), healthcare management (MS), human resource management (MS), human resources management (PhD), information systems management (PhD), leadership (MS), leadership and organizational change (PhD), marketing (MS), operations research (PhD), project management (MS), self-designed, strategy and operations (MS); marketing (MBA, DBA); project management (MBA, MS, DBA); self-designed (MBA, DBA); social impact management (DBA); technology entrepreneurship (DBA). Part-time and evening/weekend programs available. Postbaccalaureate distance learning degree programs offered (minimal on-campus study). *Faculty:* 24 full-time (9 women), 337 part-time/adjunct (127 women). *Students:* 4,369 full-time (2,379 women), 2,181 part-time (1,304 women); includes 3,669 minority (3,020 Black or African American, non-Hispanic/Latino; 22 American Indian or Alaska Native, non-Hispanic/Latino; 156 Asian, non-Hispanic/Latino; 331 Hispanic/Latino; 11 Native Hawaiian or other Pacific Islander, non-Hispanic/Latino; 129 Two or more races, non-Hispanic/Latino), 107 international. Average age 41. 2,030 applicants, 94% accepted, 1436 enrolled. In 2013, 757 master's, 128 doctorates, 32 other advanced degrees awarded. *Degree requirements:* For master's, residency (for some programs); for doctorate, thesis/dissertation (for some programs), residency. *Entrance requirements:* For master's, bachelor's degree or higher; minimum GPA of 2.5; official transcripts; goal statement, (for some programs); access to computer and Internet; for doctorate, master's degree or higher; three years of related professional or academic experience (preferred); minimum GPA of 3.0; goal statement and current resume (select programs); official transcripts; access to computer and Internet; for other advanced degree, relevant work experience; access to computer and Internet. Additional exam requirements/recommendations for international students: Required—TOEFL (minimum score 550 paper-based; 79 iBT), IELTS (minimum score 6.5), Michigan English Language Assessment Battery (minimum score 82), or PTE. *Application deadline:* Applications are processed on a rolling basis. Application fee: $0. Electronic applications accepted. *Expenses: Tuition:* Full-time $11,813.55; part-time $500 per credit. *Required fees:* $618.76. *Financial support:* Fellowships, Federal Work-Study, scholarships/grants, unspecified assistantships, and family tuition reduction, active duty/veteran tuition reduction, group tuition reduction, interest-free payment plans, employee tuition reduction available. Support available to part-time students. Financial award applicants required to submit FAFSA. *Unit head:* Dr. Ward Ulmer, III, Associate Dean, 800-925-3368. *Application contact:* Jennifer Hall, Vice President of Enrollment Management, 866-4-WALDEN, E-mail: info@waldenu.edu.
Website: http://www.waldenu.edu/programs/colleges-schools/management.

Walsh University, Graduate Studies, MBA Program, North Canton, OH 44720-3396. Offers entrepreneurship (MBA); healthcare management (MBA); management (MBA); marketing (MBA). Part-time and evening/weekend programs available. Postbaccalaureate distance learning degree programs offered (no on-campus study). *Faculty:* 5 full-time (1 woman), 16 part-time/adjunct (4 women). *Students:* 29 full-time (15 women), 147 part-time (77 women); includes 6 minority (5 Black or African American, non-Hispanic/Latino; 1 American Indian or Alaska Native, non-Hispanic/Latino), 2 international. Average age 34. 69 applicants, 94% accepted, 31 enrolled. In 2013, 63 master's awarded. *Degree requirements:* For master's, capstone course in strategic management. *Entrance requirements:* For master's, GMAT (minimum score of 490), minimum GPA of 3.0. Additional exam requirements/recommendations for international students: Required—TOEFL (minimum score 500 paper-based; 61 iBT). *Application deadline:* For fall admission, 7/15 priority date for domestic students. Applications are processed on a rolling basis. Application fee: $25. Electronic applications accepted. *Expenses: Tuition:* Full-time $10,890; part-time $605 per credit hour. *Required fees:* $100; $100. *Financial support:* In 2013–14, 91 students received support, including 4 research assistantships with partial tuition reimbursements available (averaging $8,088 per year), 4 teaching assistantships (averaging $6,806 per year); scholarships/grants, tuition waivers (partial), unspecified assistantships, and tuition discounts also available. Support available to part-time students. Financial award application deadline: 12/31; financial award applicants required to submit FAFSA. *Faculty research:* Patient and physician satisfaction, advancing and improving learning with information technology, consumer-driven healthcare, branding and the service industry, service provider training and customer satisfaction, entrepreneurship, business strategy, social media, curriculum redesign, leadership, educational funding. *Total annual research expenditures:* $3,100. *Unit head:* Dr. Michael A. Petrochuk, Director of the MBA Program/Assistant Professor, 330-244-4764, Fax: 330-490-7359, E-mail: mpetrochuk@walsh.edu. *Application contact:* Audra Dice, Graduate and Transfer Admissions Counselor, 330-490-7181, Fax: 330-244-4925, E-mail: adice@walsh.edu.
Website: http://www.walsh.edu/mba-program.

Washington State University, Graduate School, College of Business, Online MBA Program, Pullman, WA 99164. Offers finance (MBA); general business (MBA); international business (MBA); marketing (MBA). Postbaccalaureate distance learning degree programs offered (no on-campus study).

Washington State University, Graduate School, College of Business, PhD Program in Marketing, Pullman, WA 99164-4730. Offers PhD. *Degree requirements:* For doctorate, comprehensive exam, thesis/dissertation. *Entrance requirements:* For doctorate, GMAT or GRE with GMAT preferred. Additional exam requirements/recommendations for international students: Required—TOEFL. Electronic applications accepted.

Webster University, George Herbert Walker School of Business and Technology, Department of Business, St. Louis, MO 63119-3194. Offers business and organizational security management (MBA); decision support systems (MBA); environmental management (MBA); finance (MBA, MS); forensic accounting (MS); gerontology (MBA); human resources development (MBA); human resources management (MBA); information technology management (MBA); international business (MA, MBA); international relations (MBA); management and leadership (MBA); marketing (MBA); media communications (MBA); procurement and acquisitions management (MBA); Web services (MBA). *Accreditation:* ACBSP. Part-time and evening/weekend programs available. Postbaccalaureate distance learning degree programs offered (no on-campus study). *Degree requirements:* For master's, comprehensive exam (for some programs), thesis (for some programs). *Entrance requirements:* Additional exam requirements/recommendations for international students: Required—TOEFL. *Expenses: Tuition:* Full-time $11,610; part-time $645 per credit hour. Tuition and fees vary according to campus/location and program.

Webster University, George Herbert Walker School of Business and Technology, Department of Management, St. Louis, MO 63119-3194. Offers business and organizational security management (MA); health administration (MHA); health care management (MA); health services management (MA); human resources development (MA); human resources management (MA); information technology management (MS); management and leadership (MA); marketing (MA); nonprofit leadership (MA); procurement and acquisitions management (MA); public administration (MPA); space systems operations management (MS). Part-time and evening/weekend programs available. Postbaccalaureate distance learning degree programs offered (no on-campus study). *Degree requirements:* For master's, thesis (for some programs). *Entrance requirements:* Additional exam requirements/recommendations for international students: Required—TOEFL. *Expenses: Tuition:* Full-time $11,610; part-time $645 per credit hour. Tuition and fees vary according to campus/location and program.

Western International University, Graduate Programs in Business, Master of Business Administration Program in Marketing, Phoenix, AZ 85021-2718. Offers MBA. Part-time and evening/weekend programs available. Postbaccalaureate distance learning degree programs offered (no on-campus study). *Entrance requirements:* For master's, minimum GPA of 2.75. Additional exam requirements/recommendations for international students: Required—TOEFL (minimum score 550 paper-based; 79 iBT), TWE (minimum score 5), or IELTS (minimum score 6.5). Electronic applications accepted.

West Virginia University, Reed College of Media, Program in Integrated Marketing Communications, Morgantown, WV 26501. Offers MS, Graduate Certificate. Part-time programs available. Postbaccalaureate distance learning degree programs offered (no on-campus study). *Entrance requirements:* For master's, GRE or GMAT (waived with minimum undergraduate GPA of 3.3 or at least 6 years of related professional experience), undergraduate transcript, resume; letters of recommendation (strongly recommended). Additional exam requirements/recommendations for international students: Required—TOEFL.

Wilfrid Laurier University, Faculty of Graduate and Postdoctoral Studies, School of Business and Economics, Department of Business, Waterloo, ON N2L 3C5, Canada. Offers accounting (PhD); finance (M Fin); financial economics (PhD); marketing (PhD); operations and supply chain management (PhD); organizational behavior and human resource management (M Sc); organizational behaviour and human resource management (PhD); supply chain management (M Sc); technology management (EMTM). *Accreditation:* AACSB. Part-time and evening/weekend programs available. *Degree requirements:* For master's, thesis optional; for doctorate, comprehensive exam, thesis/dissertation. *Entrance requirements:* For master's, GMAT, 4-year honors degree with minimum B+ average; for doctorate, GMAT, master's degree, minimum B+ average. Additional exam requirements/recommendations for international students: Required—TOEFL (minimum score 89 iBT). Electronic applications accepted. *Faculty research:* Financial economics, management and organizational behavior, operations and supply chain management.

Wilkes University, College of Graduate and Professional Studies, Jay S. Sidhu School of Business and Leadership, Wilkes-Barre, PA 18766-0002. Offers accounting (MBA); entrepreneurship (MBA); finance (MBA); health care administration (MBA); human resource management (MBA); international business (MBA); marketing (MBA); operations management (MBA); organizational leadership and development (MBA). *Accreditation:* ACBSP. Part-time and evening/weekend programs available. *Students:* 41 full-time (20 women), 119 part-time (48 women); includes 20 minority (5 Black or African American, non-Hispanic/Latino; 3 Asian, non-Hispanic/Latino; 7 Hispanic/Latino; 5 Two or more races, non-Hispanic/Latino), 7 international. Average age 31. In 2013, 55 master's awarded. *Entrance requirements:* For master's, GMAT. Additional exam requirements/recommendations for international students: Required—TOEFL (minimum score 550 paper-based; 79 iBT). *Application deadline:* Applications are processed on a rolling basis. Application fee: $45 ($65 for international students). Electronic applications accepted. *Expenses:* Contact institution. *Financial support:* Federal Work-Study and unspecified assistantships available. Financial award application deadline: 3/1; financial award applicants required to submit FAFSA. *Unit head:* Dr. Jeffrey Alves, Dean, 570-408-4702, Fax: 570-408-7846, E-mail: jeffrey.alves@wilkes.edu. *Application contact:* Joanne Thomas, Interim Director of Graduate Enrollment, 570-408-4234, Fax: 570-408-7846, E-mail: joanne.thomas1@wilkes.edu.
Website: http://www.wilkes.edu/pages/457.asp.

William Woods University, Graduate and Adult Studies, Fulton, MO 65251-1098. Offers administration (M Ed, Ed S); athletic/activities administration (M Ed); curriculum and instruction (M Ed, Ed S); educational leadership (Ed D); equestrian education (M Ed); health management (MBA); human resources (MBA); leadership (MBA); marketing, advertising, and public relations (MBA); teaching and technology (M Ed). Part-time and evening/weekend programs available. *Faculty:* 231 part-time/adjunct (87 women). *Students:* 418 full-time (276 women), 716 part-time (433 women); includes 51 minority (34 Black or African American, non-Hispanic/Latino; 4 American Indian or

Alaska Native, non-Hispanic/Latino; 5 Asian, non-Hispanic/Latino; 3 Hispanic/Latino; 5 Two or more races, non-Hispanic/Latino), 4 international. Average age 35. In 2013, 507 master's, 8 doctorates, 143 other advanced degrees awarded. *Degree requirements:* For master's, capstone course (MBA), action research (M Ed); for Ed S, field experience. *Entrance requirements:* Additional exam requirements/recommendations for international students: Required—TOEFL (minimum score 550 paper-based). *Application deadline:* Applications are processed on a rolling basis. Application fee: $0. Electronic applications accepted. *Expenses:* Contact institution. *Financial support:* Institutionally sponsored loans available. Financial award applicants required to submit FAFSA. *Unit head:* Dr. Michael Westerfield, Vice President and Dean of the Graduate College, 573-592-4383, Fax: 573-592-1164. *Application contact:* Jessica Brush, Director of Operations, 573-592-4227, Fax: 573-592-1164, E-mail: jessica.brush@williamwoods.ede.
Website: http://www.williamwoods.edu/evening_programs/index.asp.

Wilmington University, College of Business, New Castle, DE 19720-6491. Offers accounting (MBA, MS); business administration (MBA, DBA); environmental stewardship (MBA); finance (MBA); health care administration (MBA, MSM); homeland security (MBA, MSM); human resource management (MSM); management information systems (MBA, MSN); marketing (MSM); marketing management (MBA); military leadership (MSM); organizational leadership (MBA, MSM); public administration (MSM). Part-time and evening/weekend programs available. *Entrance requirements:* Additional exam requirements/recommendations for international students: Required—TOEFL (minimum score 500 paper-based). Electronic applications accepted.

Worcester Polytechnic Institute, Graduate Studies and Research, School of Business, Worcester, MA 01609-2280. Offers information technology (MS), including information security management; management (Graduate Certificate); marketing and technological innovation (MS); operations design and leadership (MS); technology (MBA, MS). *Accreditation:* AACSB. Part-time and evening/weekend programs available. Postbaccalaureate distance learning degree programs offered (minimal on-campus study). *Faculty:* 28 full-time (12 women), 17 part-time/adjunct (3 women). *Students:* 123 full-time (77 women), 282 part-time (88 women); includes 34 minority (3 Black or African American, non-Hispanic/Latino; 15 Asian, non-Hispanic/Latino; 10 Hispanic/Latino; 6 Two or more races, non-Hispanic/Latino), 146 international. 747 applicants, 56% accepted, 111 enrolled. In 2013, 110 master's awarded. *Degree requirements:* For master's, thesis optional. *Entrance requirements:* For master's, GMAT (MBA); GMAT or GRE General Test (MS), statement of purpose, 3 letters of recommendation, resume; for Graduate Certificate, GMAT or GRE General Test, statement of purpose, 3 letters of recommendation. Additional exam requirements/recommendations for international students: Required—TOEFL (minimum score 563 paper-based; 84 iBT), IELTS (minimum score 7). *Application deadline:* For fall admission, 6/1 priority date for domestic and international students; for spring admission, 11/1 priority date for domestic students, 10/1 priority date for international students. Applications are processed on a rolling basis. Application fee: $70. Electronic applications accepted. *Financial support:* Career-related internships or fieldwork, institutionally sponsored loans, scholarships/grants, and unspecified assistantships available. Financial award application deadline: 6/1; financial award applicants required to submit FAFSA. *Unit head:* Dr. Paul Mack, Dean, 508-831-4665, Fax: 508-831-4665, E-mail: biz@wpi.edu. *Application contact:* Eileen Dagostino, Recruiting Operations Coordinator, 508-831-4665, Fax: 508-831-5720, E-mail: edag@wpi.edu.
Website: http://www.wpi.edu/academics/business/about.html.

Wright State University, School of Graduate Studies, Raj Soin College of Business, Department of Marketing, Dayton, OH 45435. Offers MBA, MBA/MS. *Entrance requirements:* For master's, GMAT, minimum AACSB index of 1000. Additional exam requirements/recommendations for international students: Required—TOEFL.

Xavier University, Williams College of Business, Master of Business Administration Program, Cincinnati, OH 45207-3221. Offers business administration (Exec MBA, MBA); business intelligence (MBA); finance (MBA); health industry (MBA); international business (MBA); marketing (MBA); values-based leadership (MBA); MBA/MHSA; MSN/MBA. *Accreditation:* AACSB. Part-time and evening/weekend programs available. *Faculty:* 39 full-time (17 women), 12 part-time/adjunct (2 women). *Students:* 163 full-time (47 women), 483 part-time (162 women); includes 91 minority (28 Black or African American, non-Hispanic/Latino; 3 American Indian or Alaska Native, non-Hispanic/Latino; 42 Asian, non-Hispanic/Latino; 14 Hispanic/Latino; 4 Two or more races, non-Hispanic/Latino), 33 international. Average age 30. 190 applicants, 86% accepted, 110 enrolled. In 2013, 319 master's awarded. *Degree requirements:* For master's, capstone course. *Entrance requirements:* For master's, GMAT or GRE. Additional exam requirements/recommendations for international students: Required—TOEFL (minimum score 550 paper-based; 79 iBT). *Application deadline:* For fall admission, 8/1 priority date for domestic students, 5/1 for international students; for spring admission, 12/1 priority date for domestic students, 9/1 for international students. Applications are processed on a rolling basis. Application fee: $0. Electronic applications accepted. *Expenses:* Contact institution. *Financial support:* In 2013–14, 115 students received support. Scholarships/grants, tuition waivers (partial), and unspecified assistantships available. Financial award application deadline: 3/1; financial award applicants required to submit FAFSA. *Unit head:* Jennifer Bush, Assistant Dean of Graduate Programs, Williams College of Business, 513-745-3527, Fax: 513-745-2929, E-mail: bush@xavier.edu. *Application contact:* Lauren Parcell, MBA Advisor, 513-745-1014, Fax: 513-745-2929, E-mail: parcell@xavier.edu.
Website: http://www.xavier.edu/williams/mba/.

Yale University, Yale School of Management and Graduate School of Arts and Sciences, Doctoral Program in Management, New Haven, CT 06520. Offers accounting (PhD); financial economics (PhD); marketing (PhD); organizations and management (PhD). *Accreditation:* AACSB. *Degree requirements:* For doctorate, comprehensive exam, thesis/dissertation. *Entrance requirements:* For doctorate, GMAT or GRE General Test. Additional exam requirements/recommendations for international students: Required—TOEFL or IELTS. Electronic applications accepted. *Expenses:* Contact institution. *Faculty research:* Pricing of options and futures, term structure of interest rates, use of accounting numbers in debt contracts, product differentiation, e-commerce and marketing, behavioral finance.

York College of Pennsylvania, Graham School of Business, York, PA 17405-7199. Offers continuous improvement (MBA); financial management (MBA); health care management (MBA); management (MBA); marketing (MBA); self-designed focus (MBA). *Accreditation:* ACBSP. Part-time and evening/weekend programs available. *Faculty:* 13 full-time (3 women), 2 part-time/adjunct (0 women). *Students:* 6 full-time (all women), 109 part-time (40 women); includes 8 minority (2 Black or African American, non-Hispanic/Latino; 1 Asian, non-Hispanic/Latino; 1 Hispanic/Latino; 4 Two or more races, non-Hispanic/Latino), 3 international. Average age 30. 62 applicants, 63% accepted, 23 enrolled. In 2013, 24 master's awarded. *Entrance requirements:* For master's, GMAT. Additional exam requirements/recommendations for international students: Required—TOEFL (minimum score 530 paper-based; 72 iBT). *Application deadline:* For fall admission, 7/15 priority date for domestic students; for spring admission, 12/15 priority date for domestic students. Applications are processed on a rolling basis. Application fee: $50. Electronic applications accepted. *Expenses: Tuition:* Full-time $12,870; part-time $715 per credit. *Required fees:* $1660; $360 per semester. Tuition and fees vary according to degree level. *Financial support:* In 2013–14, 4 students received support. Scholarships/grants available. Financial award application deadline: 4/15; financial award applicants required to submit FAFSA. *Unit head:* Dr. David Greisler, MBA Director, 717-815-6410, Fax: 717-600-3999, E-mail: dgreisle@ycp.edu. *Application contact:* Brenda Adams, Assistant Director, MBA Program, 717-815-1749, Fax: 717-600-3999, E-mail: badams@ycp.edu.
Website: http://www.ycp.edu/mba.

Youngstown State University, Graduate School, Williamson College of Business Administration, Department of Marketing, Youngstown, OH 44555-0001. Offers MBA. Part-time and evening/weekend programs available. *Degree requirements:* For master's, thesis optional. *Entrance requirements:* For master's, GMAT, minimum GPA of 2.7. Additional exam requirements/recommendations for international students: Required—TOEFL. *Faculty research:* Media, international marketing, advanced marketing simulations, ethics in business.

Marketing Research

Hofstra University, Frank G. Zarb School of Business, Programs in Marketing and International Business, Hempstead, NY 11549. Offers business administration (MBA), including international business, marketing; international business (Advanced Certificate); marketing (MS, Advanced Certificate); marketing research (MS).

Instituto Tecnológico y de Estudios Superiores de Monterrey, Campus Irapuato, Graduate Programs, Irapuato, Mexico. Offers administration (MBA); administration of information technology (MAIT); administration of telecommunications (MAT); architecture (M Arch); computer science (MCS); education (M Ed); educational administration (MEA); educational innovation and technology (DEIT); educational technology (MET); electronic commerce (MBA); environmental administration and planning (MEAP); environmental systems (MES); finances (MBA); humanistic studies (MHS); international management for Latin American executives (MIMLAE); library and information science (MLIS); manufacturing quality management (MMQM); marketing research (MBA).

Marquette University, Graduate School of Management, Department of Economics, Milwaukee, WI 53201-1881. Offers business economics (MSAE); financial economics (MSAE); international economics (MSAE); marketing research (MSAE); real estate economics (MSAE). Part-time and evening/weekend programs available. *Faculty:* 15 full-time (5 women), 2 part-time/adjunct (1 woman). *Students:* 25 full-time (7 women), 34 part-time (11 women); includes 6 minority (2 Black or African American, non-Hispanic/Latino; 2 Asian, non-Hispanic/Latino; 2 Hispanic/Latino), 24 international. Average age 25. 81 applicants, 47% accepted, 27 enrolled. In 2013, 26 master's awarded. *Degree requirements:* For master's, comprehensive exam, professional project. *Entrance requirements:* For master's, GMAT or GRE General Test. Additional exam requirements/recommendations for international students: Required—TOEFL (minimum score 550 paper-based; 88 iBT), IELTS (minimum score 6.5), PTE. *Application deadline:* For fall admission, 2/15 for domestic and international students. Applications are processed on a rolling basis. Application fee: $50. Electronic applications accepted. *Financial support:* In 2013–14, 2 fellowships, 7 teaching assistantships were awarded; research assistantships, Federal Work-Study, institutionally sponsored loans, scholarships/grants, and tuition waivers (full and partial) also available. Support available to part-time students. Financial award application deadline: 2/15. *Faculty research:* Monetary and fiscal policy in open economy, housing and regional migration, political economy of taxation and state/local government. *Unit head:* Dr. Mark Eppli, Dean, 414-288-5724. *Application contact:* Dr. Jeanne Simmons, Associate Dean, 414-288-7145.
Website: http://business.marquette.edu/academics/msae.

Michigan State University, The Graduate School, Eli Broad College of Business, Department of Marketing, East Lansing, MI 48824. Offers marketing (PhD); marketing research (MS). *Faculty:* 22. *Students:* 29. *Degree requirements:* For doctorate, comprehensive exam, thesis/dissertation. *Entrance requirements:* For master's, GMAT, bachelor's degree with minimum GPA of 3.0 in last 2 years of undergraduate work; transcripts; 3 letters of recommendation; statement of purpose; resume; working knowledge of computers; basic understanding of accounting, finance, marketing, and the management of people; laptop capable of running Windows software; for doctorate, GMAT (taken within past 5 years), bachelor's degree; letters of recommendation; statement of purpose; previous work experience; personal qualifications of sound character, perseverance, intellectual curiosity, and an interest in scholarly research. Additional exam requirements/recommendations for international students: Required—TOEFL (minimum score 100 iBT), PTE (minimum score 70), IELTS (minimum score 7) accepted for MS only. *Financial support:* Research assistantships with tuition reimbursements and teaching assistantships with tuition reimbursements available. Financial award application deadline: 1/10. *Unit head:* Dr. R. Dale Wilson, Chairperson, 517-432-6403, Fax: 517-432-8048, E-mail: wilsonrr@broad.msu.edu. *Application contact:* Jessica Bunce, Office Supervisor, 517-355-2241, Fax: 517-432-8048, E-mail: bunce@broad.msu.edu.
Website: http://marketing.broad.msu.edu/.

Pace University, Lubin School of Business, Marketing Program, New York, NY 10038. Offers marketing management (MBA); marketing research (MBA). Part-time and evening/weekend programs available. *Students:* 24 full-time (14 women), 66 part-time (38 women); includes 15 minority (3 Black or African American, non-Hispanic/Latino; 1 American Indian or Alaska Native, non-Hispanic/Latino; 5 Asian, non-Hispanic/Latino; 3 Hispanic/Latino; 3 Two or more races, non-Hispanic/Latino), 42 international. Average age 26. 148 applicants, 32% accepted, 34 enrolled. In 2013, 26 master's awarded. *Entrance requirements:* For master's, GMAT, GRE. Additional exam requirements/recommendations for international students: Required—TOEFL. *Application deadline:* For fall admission, 8/1 priority date for domestic students, 6/1 for international students; for spring admission, 12/1 for domestic students, 10/1 for international students.

Marketing Research

Applications are processed on a rolling basis. Application fee: $70. Electronic applications accepted. *Expenses: Tuition:* Part-time $1075 per credit. *Required fees:* $192 per semester. Tuition and fees vary according to course load, degree level and program. *Financial support:* Research assistantships, career-related internships or fieldwork, and Federal Work-Study available. Support available to part-time students. Financial award applicants required to submit FAFSA. *Unit head:* Dr. Mary M. Long, Chairperson, 212-618-6453, E-mail: mlong@pace.edu. *Application contact:* Susan Ford-Goldschein, Director of Graduate Admissions, 212-346-1531, Fax: 212-346-1585, E-mail: gradnyc@pace.edu.
Website: http://www.pace.edu/lubin.

Saint Leo University, Graduate Business Studies, Saint Leo, FL 33574-6665. Offers accounting (M Acc, MBA); business (MBA); health care management (MBA); human resource management (MBA); information security management (MBA); marketing (MBA); marketing research and social media analytics (MBA); project management (MBA); sport business (MBA). Part-time and evening/weekend programs available. Postbaccalaureate distance learning degree programs offered (no on-campus study). *Faculty:* 48 full-time (12 women), 61 part-time/adjunct (21 women). *Students:* 1,855 full-time (1,020 women); includes 810 minority (587 Black or African American, non-Hispanic/Latino; 7 American Indian or Alaska Native, non-Hispanic/Latino; 36 Asian, non-Hispanic/Latino; 161 Hispanic/Latino; 3 Native Hawaiian or other Pacific Islander, non-Hispanic/Latino; 16 Two or more races, non-Hispanic/Latino), 33 international. Average age 38. In 2013, 905 master's awarded. *Entrance requirements:* For master's, GMAT (minimum score 500 if applicant has less than 3.0 in the last two years of undergraduate study), bachelor's degree with minimum GPA of 3.0 in the last 60 hours of coursework from regionally-accredited college or university; 2 years of professional work experience; resume; 2 letters of recommendation. Additional exam requirements/recommendations for international students: Required—TOEFL (minimum score 550 paper-based; 80 iBT). *Application deadline:* For fall admission, 7/1 priority date for domestic and international students; for spring admission, 11/12 priority date for domestic students, 11/1 for international students. Applications are processed on a rolling basis. Application fee: $80. Electronic applications accepted. *Expenses: Tuition:* Full-time $12,114; part-time $673 per semester hour. Tuition and fees vary according to degree level, campus/location and program. *Financial support:* In 2013–14, 116 students received support. Career-related internships or fieldwork, Federal Work-Study, scholarships/grants, and health care benefits available. Financial award application deadline: 3/1; financial award applicants required to submit FAFSA. *Unit head:* Dr. Lorrie McGovern, Assistant Dean, Graduate Studies in Business, 352-588-7390, Fax: 352-588-8585, E-mail: mbaslu@saintleo.edu. *Application contact:* Joshua Stagner, Director of Graduate Admission, 800-707-8846, Fax: 352-588-7873, E-mail: grad.admissions@saintleo.edu.
Website: http://www.saintleo.edu/academics/graduate.aspx.

Southern Illinois University Edwardsville, Graduate School, School of Business, Department of Management and Marketing, Edwardsville, IL 62026. Offers marketing research (MMR). Part-time and evening/weekend programs available. *Faculty:* 15 full-time (7 women). *Students:* 2 full-time (0 women), 21 part-time (10 women); includes 4 minority (3 Black or African American, non-Hispanic/Latino; 1 Two or more races, non-Hispanic/Latino), 6 international. 16 applicants, 63% accepted. In 2013, 19 master's awarded. *Degree requirements:* For master's, comprehensive exam, final exam. *Entrance requirements:* For master's, GMAT. Additional exam requirements/recommendations for international students: Required—TOEFL (minimum score 550 paper-based, 79 iBT), IELTS (minimum score 6.5), Michigan Test of English Language Proficiency or PTE. *Application deadline:* For fall admission, 7/18 for domestic students, 6/1 for international students; for spring admission, 12/12 for domestic students, 10/1 for international students; for summer admission, 4/24 for domestic students, 3/1 for international students. Applications are processed on a rolling basis. Application fee: $30. Electronic applications accepted. *Expenses:* Tuition, state resident: full-time $3551. Tuition, nonresident: full-time $8378. *Financial support:* In 2013–14, 23 students received support, including 22 research assistantships with full tuition reimbursements available (averaging $9,585 per year), 1 teaching assistantship with full tuition reimbursement available (averaging $9,585 per year); fellowships with full tuition reimbursements available, career-related internships or fieldwork, institutionally sponsored loans, scholarships/grants, and unspecified assistantships also available. Financial award application deadline: 3/1; financial award applicants required to submit FAFSA. *Unit head:* Dr. Edmund Hershberger, Chair, 618-650-3224, E-mail: ehershb@siue.edu. *Application contact:* Dr. Ramana Madupalli, Program Director, 618-650-2701, E-mail: rmadupa@siue.edu.
Website: http://www.siue.edu/business/managementandmarketing/.

Universidad Autonoma de Guadalajara, Graduate Programs, Guadalajara, Mexico. Offers administrative law and justice (LL M); advertising and corporate communications (MA); architecture (M Arch); business (MBA); computational science (MCC); education (Ed M, Ed D); English-Spanish translation (MA); entrepreneurship and management (MBA); integrated management of digital animation (MA); international business (MIB); international corporate law (LL M); internet technologies (MS); manufacturing systems (MMS); occupational health (MS); philosophy (MA, PhD); power electronics (MS); quality systems (MQS); renewable energy (MS); social evaluation of projects (MBA); strategic market research (MBA); tax law (MA); teaching mathematics (MA).

Universidad de las Americas, A.C., Program in Business Administration, Mexico City, Mexico. Offers finance (MBA); marketing research (MBA); production and quality (MBA).

University of Colorado Denver, Business School, Program in Marketing, Denver, CO 80217. Offers brand management and marketing communication (MS); global marketing (MS); high-tech and entrepreneurial marketing (MS); Internet marketing (MS); marketing for sustainability (MS); marketing research (MS); sports and entertainment marketing (MS). Part-time and evening/weekend programs available. *Students:* 36 full-time (15 women), 12 part-time (4 women); includes 3 minority (1 Asian, non-Hispanic/Latino; 1 Hispanic/Latino; 1 Two or more races, non-Hispanic/Latino), 11 international. Average age 29. 47 applicants, 55% accepted, 11 enrolled. In 2013, 20 master's awarded. *Degree requirements:* For master's, 30 semester hours (21 of marketing core courses, 9 of marketing electives). *Entrance requirements:* For master's, GMAT, resume, essay, two letters of recommendation, financial statements (for international applicants). Additional exam requirements/recommendations for international students: Required—TOEFL (minimum score 537 paper-based; 75 iBT); Recommended—IELTS (minimum score 6.5). *Application deadline:* For fall admission, 4/15 for domestic students, 3/15 for international students; for spring admission, 10/15 for domestic students, 9/15 for international students. Applications are processed on a rolling basis. Application fee: $50 ($75 for international students). Electronic applications accepted. *Expenses:* Contact institution. *Financial support:* In 2013–14, 7 students received support. Fellowships, research assistantships, teaching assistantships, Federal Work-Study, institutionally sponsored loans, scholarships/grants, and traineeships available. Financial award application deadline: 4/1; financial award applicants required to submit FAFSA. *Faculty research:* Marketing issues in the Chinese environment, impact of individual difference and contextual factors on the risk-taking behaviors of managers making new-business creation decisions, attribution theory perspective of conflict between marketers and engineers, organizational identity and identification, international market entry strategies. *Unit head:* Dr. David Forlani, Associate Professor/Director of Marketing Programs, 303-315-8420, E-mail: david.forlani@ucdenver.edu. *Application contact:* Shelly Townley, Admissions Director, Graduate Programs, 303-315-8202, E-mail: shelly.townley@ucdenver.edu.
Website: http://www.ucdenver.edu/academics/colleges/business/degrees/ms/marketing/Pages/Marketing.aspx.

The University of Texas at Arlington, Graduate School, College of Business, Department of Marketing, Arlington, TX 76019. Offers marketing (PhD); marketing research (MS). Part-time and evening/weekend programs available. *Degree requirements:* For master's, thesis optional; for doctorate, comprehensive exam, thesis/dissertation. *Entrance requirements:* For master's and doctorate, GMAT, GRE. Additional exam requirements/recommendations for international students: Required—TOEFL (minimum score 550 paper-based; 79 iBT). Electronic applications accepted. *Faculty research:* Marketing strategy, marketing research, international marketing.

University of Wisconsin–Madison, Graduate School, Wisconsin School of Business, Wisconsin Full-Time MBA Program, Madison, WI 53706. Offers applied security analysis (MBA); arts administration (MBA); brand and product management (MBA); corporate finance and investment banking (MBA); marketing research (MBA); operations and technology management (MBA); real estate (MBA); risk management and insurance (MBA); strategic human resource management (MBA); supply chain management (MBA). *Faculty:* 34 full-time (5 women), 30 part-time/adjunct (15 women). *Students:* 193 full-time (61 women); includes 37 minority (10 Black or African American, non-Hispanic/Latino; 14 Asian, non-Hispanic/Latino; 12 Hispanic/Latino; 1 Native Hawaiian or other Pacific Islander, non-Hispanic/Latino), 37 international. Average age 28. 460 applicants, 33% accepted, 101 enrolled. In 2013, 110 master's awarded. *Degree requirements:* For master's, thesis (for arts administration specialization). *Entrance requirements:* For master's, GMAT or GRE, bachelor's or equivalent degree, 2 years of work experience, letters of recommendation, resume. Additional exam requirements/recommendations for international students: Required—TOEFL (minimum score 600 paper-based; 100 iBT), IELTS. *Application deadline:* For fall admission, 11/5 for domestic and international students; for winter admission, 2/4 for domestic and international students; for spring admission, 4/28 for domestic students, 4/2 for international students. Applications are processed on a rolling basis. Application fee: $56. Electronic applications accepted. *Expenses:* Contact institution. *Financial support:* In 2013–14, 176 students received support, including 12 fellowships with full tuition reimbursements available (averaging $37,956 per year), 42 research assistantships with full tuition reimbursements available (averaging $28,175 per year), 43 teaching assistantships with full tuition reimbursements available (averaging $28,175 per year); scholarships/grants, health care benefits, and unspecified assistantships also available. Financial award application deadline: 4/26; financial award applicants required to submit FAFSA. *Faculty research:* Market consequences of International Financial Reporting Standards (IFRS), inter-firm relationships and strategic partnerships, application of Bayesian statistical methods and applied probability models to understanding individuals' behaviors in the context of customer relationship management (CRM) applications, liquidity provision and the structure of financial markets, strategic management of global startups. *Unit head:* Prof. Larry W. Hunter, Associate Dean of Master's Programs, 608-265-3494, Fax: 608-265-4192, E-mail: lhunter@bus.wisc.edu. *Application contact:* William H. Wait, Assistant Director of MBA Marketing and Recruiting, 608-262-4000, Fax: 608-265-4192, E-mail: wwait@bus.wisc.edu.
Website: http://www.bus.wisc.edu/mba.

FASHION INSTITUTE OF TECHNOLOGY
State University of New York

M.P.S. in Cosmetics and Fragrance Marketing and Management

Program of Study

The Fashion Institute of Technology (FIT), a State University of New York (SUNY) college of art and design, business, and technology, is home to a mix of innovative achievers, creative thinkers, and industry pioneers. FIT fosters interdisciplinary initiatives, advances research, and provides access to an international network of professionals. With a reputation for excellence, FIT offers its diverse student body access to world-class faculty, dynamic and relevant curricula, and a superior education at an affordable cost. It offers seven programs of graduate study. The programs in Art Market: Principles and Practices; Exhibition Design; Fashion and Textile Studies: History, Theory, Museum Practice; and Sustainable Interior Environments lead to the Master of Arts (M.A.) degree. The Illustration program leads to the Master of Fine Arts (M.F.A.) degree. The Master of Professional Studies (M.P.S.) degree programs are Cosmetics and Fragrance Marketing and Management, and Global Fashion Management.

Cosmetics and Fragrance Marketing and Management is a 38-credit, part-time M.P.S. program designed to provide industry professionals with intensive training in marketing and leadership skills while helping them build interdisciplinary, global perspectives. The curriculum focuses on building three skill sets that leaders in the cosmetics and fragrance industries have identified as crucial to managerial success: core business skills, such as leadership, corporate finance, supply chain management, and management communication; marketing skills, such as advanced marketing theory, consumer insights, and digital marketing strategy; and technical and creative competencies, such as cosmetics and fragrance product knowledge, retail and creative management, and an intellectual foundation in beauty and fashion culture. An international field study component sends students to Europe and Asia to meet with industry leaders, talk with market research analysts, and visit diverse retail environments to develop a global business and cultural perspective. The program culminates in a capstone seminar with students producing cutting-edge research on leading business topics.

Research Facilities

The School of Graduate Studies is primarily located in the campus's Shirley Goodman Resource Center, which also houses the Gladys Marcus Library and The Museum at FIT. School of Graduate Studies facilities include conference rooms; a fully equipped conservation laboratory; a multipurpose laboratory for conservation projects and the dressing of mannequins; storage facilities for costume and textile materials; a graduate student lounge with computer and printer access; a graduate student library reading room with computers, reference materials, and copies of past classes' qualifying and thesis papers; specialized wireless classrooms; traditional and digital illustration studios; and classrooms equipped with model stands, easels, and drafting tables. The college has the only working cosmetics and fragrance laboratory on a college campus in the United States.

The Gladys Marcus Library houses more than 300,000 volumes of print, nonprint, and digital resources. Specialized holdings include industry reference materials, manufacturers' catalogues, original fashion sketches and scrapbooks, photographs, portfolios of plates, and sample books. The FIT Digital Library provides access to over 90 searchable online databases.

The Museum at FIT houses one of the world's most important collections of clothing and textiles and is the only museum in New York City dedicated to the art of fashion. The permanent collection encompasses more than 50,000 garments and accessories dating from the eighteenth century to the present, with particular strength in twentieth-century fashion, as well as 30,000 textiles and 100,000 textile swatches. Each year, nearly 100,000 visitors are drawn to the museum's award-winning exhibitions and public programs.

Financial Aid

FIT directly administers its institutional grants, scholarships, and loans. Federal funding administered by the college may include Federal Perkins Loans, federally subsidized and unsubsidized Direct Loans for students, Grad PLUS loans, and the Federal Work-Study Program. Priority for institutionally administered funds is given to students enrolled and designated as full-time.

Cost of Study

Tuition for New York State residents is $5,185 per semester, or $432 per credit. Out-of-state residents' tuition is $10,095 per semester, or $841 per credit. Full-time programs adhere to semester tuition rates and part-time graduate programs charge by credit. Tuition and fees are subject to change at the discretion of FIT's Board of Trustees. Additional expenses—for class materials, textbooks, and travel—may apply and vary per program.

Living and Housing Costs

On-campus housing is available to graduate students. Traditional residence hall accommodations (including meal plan) cost from $6,485 to $6,688 per semester. Apartment-style housing options (not including meal plan) cost from $6,060 to $10,095 per semester.

Student Group

Enrollment in the School of Graduate Studies is approximately 200 students per academic year, allowing considerable individualized advisement. Students come to FIT from throughout the country and around the world.

Student Outcomes

Students in the Cosmetics and Fragrance Marketing and Management program maintain full-time employment in the industry while working toward their degree, which provides the basis for advancement to positions of upper-level managerial responsibility.

Fashion Institute of Technology

Location

FIT is located in Manhattan's Chelsea neighborhood, at the heart of the advertising, visual arts, marketing, fashion, business, design, and communications industries. Students are connected to New York City and gain unparalleled exposure to their field through guest lectures, field trips, internships, and sponsored competitions. The location provides access to major museums, galleries, and auction houses as well as dining, entertainment, and shopping options. The campus is near subway, bus, and commuter rail lines.

Applying

Applicants to all School of Graduate Studies programs must hold a baccalaureate degree in an appropriate major from a college or university, with a cumulative GPA of 3.0 or higher. International students from non-English-speaking countries are required to submit minimum TOEFL scores of 550 on the written test, 213 on the computer test, or 80 on the Internet test. Each major has additional, specialized prerequisites for admission; for detailed information, students should visit the School of Graduate Studies on FIT's website.

Domestic and international students use the same application when seeking admission. The deadline for Cosmetics and Fragrance Marketing and Management is March 15. After the deadline date, applicants are considered on a rolling admissions basis. Candidates may apply online at fitnyc.edu/gradstudies.

Correspondence and Information

School of Graduate Studies
Shirley Goodman Resource Center, Room E315
Fashion Institute of Technology
227 West 27 Street
New York, New York 10001-5992
Phone: 212-217-4300
Fax: 212-217-4301
E-mail: gradinfo@fitnyc.edu
Websites: http://www.fitnyc.edu/gradstudies
http://www.fitnyc.edu/CFMM

THE FACULTY

A partial listing of faculty members is below. Guest lecturers are not included.

Stephan Kanlian, Chairperson; M.P.A., Pennsylvania.
Brooke Carlson, Sc.D., New Haven.
Mark Polson, M.P.S., Fashion Institute of Technology.
Mary Tumolo, former Vice President, Promotional Marketing, Lancôme, L'Oreal USA.
Pamela Vaile, M.B.A., Pace.
Karen Young, B.A., Denver.

Section 15
Nonprofit Management

This section contains a directory of institutions offering graduate work in nonprofit management. Additional information about programs listed in the directory may be obtained by writing directly to the dean of a graduate school or chair of a department at the address given in the directory.

For programs offering related work, see also in this book *Accounting and Finance* and *Business Administration and Management.* In another guide in this series:

Graduate Programs in the Humanities, Arts & Social Sciences
See *Public, Regional, and Industrial Affairs*

CONTENTS

Program Directory

Nonprofit Management   538

Nonprofit Management

Adler School of Professional Psychology, Programs in Psychology, Chicago, IL 60602. Offers advanced Adlerian psychotherapy (Certificate); art therapy (MA); clinical neuropsychology (Certificate); clinical psychology (Psy D); community psychology (MA); counseling and organizational psychology (MA); counseling psychology (MA); criminology (MA); emergency management leadership (MA); forensic psychology (MA); marriage and family counseling (MA); marriage and family therapy (Certificate); military psychology (MA); nonprofit management (MA); organizational psychology (MA); police psychology (MA); public policy and administration (MA); rehabilitation counseling (MA); sport and health psychology (MA); substance abuse counseling (Certificate); Psy D/Certificate; Psy D/MACAT; Psy D/MACP; Psy D/MAMFC; Psy D/MASAC. *Accreditation:* APA. Part-time and evening/weekend programs available. Postbaccalaureate distance learning degree programs offered (minimal on-campus study). Terminal master's awarded for partial completion of doctoral program. *Degree requirements:* For master's, thesis or alternative, oral exam, practicum; for doctorate, thesis/dissertation, clinical exam, internship, oral exam, practicum, written qualifying exam. *Entrance requirements:* For master's, 12 semester hours in psychology, minimum GPA of 3.0; for doctorate, 18 semester hours in psychology, minimum GPA of 3.25; for Certificate, appropriate master's or doctoral degree. Additional exam requirements/recommendations for international students: Required—TOEFL (minimum score 550 paper-based; 79 iBT). Electronic applications accepted.

American Jewish University, Graduate School of Nonprofit Management, Program in Business Administration, Bel Air, CA 90077-1599. Offers general nonprofit administration (MBA); Jewish nonprofit administration (MBA). Part-time and evening/weekend programs available. *Degree requirements:* For master's, thesis, internship. *Entrance requirements:* For master's, GMAT or GRE General Test, interview, minimum undergraduate GPA of 3.0. Additional exam requirements/recommendations for international students: Required—TOEFL (minimum score 550 paper-based).

American Public University System, AMU/APU Graduate Programs, Charles Town, WV 25414. Offers accounting (MBA, MS); criminal justice (MA), including business administration, emergency and disaster management, general (MA, MS); educational leadership (M Ed); emergency and disaster management (MA); entrepreneurship (MBA); environmental policy and management (MS), including environmental planning, environmental sustainability, fish and wildlife management, general (MA, MS), global environmental management; finance (MBA); general (MBA); global business management (MBA); history (MA), including American history, ancient and classical history, European history, global history, public history; homeland security (MA), including business administration, counter-terrorism studies, criminal justice, cyber, emergency management and public health, intelligence studies, transportation security; homeland security resource allocation (MBA); humanities (MA); information technology (MS), including digital forensics, enterprise software development, information assurance and security, IT project management; information technology management (MBA); intelligence studies (MA), including criminal intelligence, cyber, general (MA, MS), homeland security, intelligence analysis, intelligence collection, intelligence management, intelligence operations, terrorism studies; international relations and conflict resolution (MA), including comparative and security issues, conflict resolution, international and transnational security issues, peacekeeping; legal studies (MA); management (MA), including defense management, general (MA, MS), human resource management, organizational leadership, public administration; marketing (MBA); military history (MA), including American military history, American Revolution, civil war, war since 1945, World War II; military studies (MA), including joint warfare, strategic leadership; national security studies (MA), including general (MA, MS), homeland security, regional security studies, security and intelligence analysis, terrorism studies; nonprofit management (MBA); political science (MA), including American politics and government, comparative government and development, general (MA, MS), international relations, public policy; psychology (MA), including general (MA, MS), maritime engineering management, reverse logistics management; public administration (MPA), including disaster management, environmental policy, health policy, human resources, national security, organizational management, security management; public health (MPH); reverse logistics management (MA); school counseling (M Ed); security management (MA); space studies (MS), including aerospace science, general (MA, MS), planetary science; sports and health sciences (MS); teaching (M Ed), including curriculum and instruction for elementary teachers, elementary reading, English language learners, instructional leadership, online learning, special education; transportation and logistics management (MA), including general (MA, MS), maritime engineering management, reverse logistics management. Programs offered via distance learning only. Part-time and evening/weekend programs available. Postbaccalaureate distance learning degree programs offered (no on-campus study). *Faculty:* 432 full-time (242 women), 1,722 part-time/adjunct (829 women). *Students:* 511 full-time (241 women), 10,947 part-time (4,294 women); includes 3,760 minority (2,058 Black or African American, non-Hispanic/Latino; 88 American Indian or Alaska Native, non-Hispanic/Latino; 293 Asian, non-Hispanic/Latino; 876 Hispanic/Latino; 91 Native Hawaiian or other Pacific Islander, non-Hispanic/Latino; 354 Two or more races, non-Hispanic/Latino; 134 international. Average age 36. In 2013, 3,323 master's awarded. *Degree requirements:* For master's, comprehensive exam or practicum. *Entrance requirements:* For master's, official transcript showing earned bachelor's degree from institution accredited by recognized accrediting body. Additional exam requirements/recommendations for international students: Required—TOEFL (minimum score 550 paper-based), IELTS (minimum score 6.5). *Application deadline:* Applications are processed on a rolling basis. Application fee: $0. Electronic applications accepted. *Expenses: Tuition:* Part-time $325 per semester hour. *Financial support:* Applicants required to submit FAFSA. *Faculty research:* Military history, criminal justice, management performance, national security. *Unit head:* Dr. Karan Powell, Executive Vice President and Provost, 877-468-6268, Fax: 304-724-3780. *Application contact:* Terry Grant, Vice President of Enrollment Management, 877-468-6268, Fax: 304-724-3780, E-mail: info@apus.edu.
Website: http://www.apus.edu.

American University, School of Public Affairs, Washington, DC 20016-8022. Offers justice, law and criminology (MS, PhD); leadership for organizational change (Certificate); nonprofit management (Certificate); organization development (MS); political communication (MA); political science (MA, PhD); public administration (MPA, PhD); public administration: key executive leadership (MPA); public financial management (Certificate); public management (Certificate); public policy (MPP); public policy analysis (Certificate); terrorism and homeland security policy (MS); women, policy and political leadership (Certificate). Part-time and evening/weekend programs available. *Faculty:* 82 full-time (36 women), 56 part-time/adjunct (16 women). *Students:* 364 full-time (220 women), 238 part-time (146 women); includes 158 minority (76 Black or African American, non-Hispanic/Latino; 7 American Indian or Alaska Native, non-

Hispanic/Latino; 26 Asian, non-Hispanic/Latino; 40 Hispanic/Latino; 2 Native Hawaiian or other Pacific Islander, non-Hispanic/Latino; 7 Two or more races, non-Hispanic/Latino), 39 international. Average age 28. In 2013, 239 master's, 10 doctorates, 7 other advanced degrees awarded. Terminal master's awarded for partial completion of doctoral program. *Degree requirements:* For master's, comprehensive exam; for doctorate, comprehensive exam, thesis/dissertation. *Entrance requirements:* For master's, GRE, statement of purpose; 2 recommendations, resume, transcript; for doctorate, GRE, 3 recommendations, statement of purpose, resume, writing sample, transcript. Additional exam requirements/recommendations for international students: Required—TOEFL (minimum score 100 iBT). *Application deadline:* For fall admission, 2/1 for domestic and international students. Application fee: $55. Electronic applications accepted. *Expenses: Tuition:* Full-time $25,920; part-time $1482 per credit hour. *Required fees:* $430. Tuition and fees vary according to course load and program. *Financial support:* Fellowships with tuition reimbursements, research assistantships with tuition reimbursements, teaching assistantships with tuition reimbursements, career-related internships or fieldwork, Federal Work-Study, institutionally sponsored loans, scholarships/grants, and tuition waivers (full and partial) available. Financial award application deadline: 2/1. *Unit head:* Dr. Barbara Romzek, Dean, 202-885-2940, E-mail: bromzek@american.edu. *Application contact:* Brenda Manley, Director of Graduate Admissions, 202-885-6202, E-mail: bmanley@american.edu.
Website: http://www.american.edu/spa/.

Antioch University Los Angeles, Graduate Programs, Program in Nonprofit Management, Culver City, CA 90230. Offers MA. Evening/weekend programs available. *Entrance requirements:* For master's, official transcripts, interview. Electronic applications accepted.

Arizona State University at the Tempe campus, College of Public Programs, School of Community Resources and Development, Phoenix, AZ 85004-0685. Offers community resources and development (PhD); nonprofit leadership and management (Graduate Certificate); nonprofit studies (MNpS); recreation and tourism studies (MS). *Accreditation:* ACSP. Part-time and evening/weekend programs available. Terminal master's awarded for partial completion of doctoral program. *Degree requirements:* For master's, thesis or alternative, interactive Program of Study (iPOS) submitted before completing 50 percent of required credit hours; for doctorate, comprehensive exam, thesis/dissertation, interactive Program of Study (iPOS) submitted before completing 50 percent of required credit hours. *Entrance requirements:* For master's and doctorate, GRE, minimum GPA of 3.0 or equivalent in last 2 years of work leading to bachelor's degree. Additional exam requirements/recommendations for international students: Required—TOEFL (minimum score 80 iBT), TOEFL, IELTS, or PTE. Electronic applications accepted. *Expenses:* Contact institution.

Arizona State University at the Tempe campus, College of Public Programs, School of Public Affairs, Phoenix, AZ 85004-0687. Offers public administration (nonprofit administration) (MPA); public administration (urban management) (MPA); public affairs (PhD); public policy (MPP); MPA/MSW. *Accreditation:* NASPAA (one or more programs are accredited). Part-time and evening/weekend programs available. Terminal master's awarded for partial completion of doctoral program. *Degree requirements:* For master's, thesis or alternative, policy analysis or capstone project; interactive Program of Study (iPOS) submitted before completing 50 percent of required credit hours; for doctorate, comprehensive exam, thesis/dissertation, interactive Program of Study (iPOS) submitted before completing 50 percent of required credit hours. *Entrance requirements:* For master's, GRE, minimum GPA of 3.0 or equivalent in last 2 years of work leading to bachelor's degree; for doctorate, GRE, minimum GPA of 3.0 or equivalent in last 2 years of work leading to bachelor's degree, 3 letters of recommendation, resume, statement of goals, samples of research reports. Additional exam requirements/recommendations for international students: Required—TOEFL (minimum score 600 paper-based; 100 iBT), IELTS (minimum score 6.5). Electronic applications accepted. *Expenses:* Contact institution.

Assumption College, Graduate Studies, Department of Business Studies, Worcester, MA 01609-1296. Offers accounting (MBA); business administration (CAGS); finance/economics (MBA); frontline management (CGS); general business (MBA); human resources (MBA); international business (MBA); management (MBA); marketing (MBA); nonprofit leadership (MBA, CGS); organizational communication (CGS). Part-time and evening/weekend programs available. *Faculty:* 5 full-time (0 women), 20 part-time/adjunct (7 women). *Students:* 20 full-time (7 women), 130 part-time (68 women); includes 20 minority (8 Black or African American, non-Hispanic/Latino; 2 Asian, non-Hispanic/Latino; 8 Hispanic/Latino; 1 Native Hawaiian or other Pacific Islander, non-Hispanic/Latino; 1 Two or more races, non-Hispanic/Latino), 2 international. Average age 31. 63 applicants, 62% accepted, 22 enrolled. In 2013, 58 master's, 1 other advanced degree awarded. *Degree requirements:* For master's, thesis, capstone. *Entrance requirements:* For master's and other advanced degree, 3 letters of recommendation, resume, essay. Additional exam requirements/recommendations for international students: Required—TOEFL (minimum score 540 paper-based; 76 iBT), IELTS (minimum score 6). *Application deadline:* For fall admission, 10/1 for domestic and international students; for winter admission, 2/1 for domestic and international students; for spring admission, 4/1 for domestic and international students. Applications are processed on a rolling basis. Application fee: $30. Electronic applications accepted. *Expenses: Tuition:* Full-time $10,098; part-time $561 per credit. *Required fees:* $20 per term. Full-time tuition and fees vary according to course load and program. *Financial support:* In 2013–14, 15 students received support. Tuition waivers (full and partial), unspecified assistantships, and institutional discounts available. Financial award application deadline: 5/1; financial award applicants required to submit FAFSA. *Faculty research:* Workplace diversity, dynamics of team interaction, utilization of leased employees, experiential learning project on due diligence market for prostheses. *Unit head:* Dr. J. Bart Morrison, Director, 508-767-7458, Fax: 508-767-7252, E-mail: jmorrison@assumption.edu. *Application contact:* Laura Lawrence, Graduate Programs Operations Manager, 508-767-7387, Fax: 508-767-7030, E-mail: graduate@assumption.edu.
Website: http://graduate.assumption.edu/mba/assumption-mba.

Auburn University at Montgomery, School of Sciences, Department of Public Administration and Political Science, Montgomery, AL 36124-4023. Offers international relations (MIR); nonprofit management and leadership (Certificate); political science (MPS); public administration (MPA); public administration and public policy (PhD); public health care administration and policy (Certificate). PhD offered jointly with Auburn University. *Accreditation:* NASPAA (one or more programs are accredited). Part-time and evening/weekend programs available. *Faculty:* 3 full-time (1 woman), 1 part-time/adjunct (0 women). *Students:* 11 full-time (7 women), 66 part-time (44 women); includes 31 minority (29 Black or African American, non-Hispanic/Latino; 2 Hispanic/Latino), 1 international. Average age 37. In 2013, 24 master's awarded. *Degree requirements:* For

master's, comprehensive exam; for doctorate, thesis/dissertation. *Entrance requirements:* For master's, GRE General Test or MAT; for doctorate, GRE General Test. *Application deadline:* Applications are processed on a rolling basis. Electronic applications accepted. *Expenses:* Tuition, state resident: full-time $5994; part-time $333 per credit hour. Tuition, nonresident: full-time $17,982; part-time $999 per credit hour. *Financial support:* Research assistantships, career-related internships or fieldwork, and scholarships/grants available. Support available to part-time students. Financial award application deadline: 3/1; financial award applicants required to submit FAFSA. *Unit head:* Dr. Andrew Cortell, Department Head, 334-244-3622, E-mail: acortell@aum.edu. *Application contact:* Dr. William Ellis, Graduate Coordinator, 334-244-3177, Fax: 334-244-3992, E-mail: wellis3@aum.edu.
Website: http://sciences.aum.edu/departments/political-science-and-public-administration.

Azusa Pacific University, School of Business and Management, Azusa, CA 91702-7000. Offers business administration (MBA); diversity for strategic advantage (MA); entrepreneurship (MBA); finance (MBA); human and organizational development (MA); human resources and organizational development (MBA); human resources management (MA); international business (MBA); marketing (MBA); non-profit management (MA); organizational development and change (MA); performance improvement (MA); public administration (MA); strategic management (MBA). Part-time and evening/weekend programs available. *Degree requirements:* For master's, thesis (for some programs), final project. *Entrance requirements:* For master's, GMAT, minimum GPA of 3.0. Additional exam requirements/recommendations for international students: Required—TOEFL (minimum score 600 paper-based). *Expenses:* Contact institution. *Faculty research:* Gender issues, financial risk, leadership and ethics, marketing strategy.

Baruch College of the City University of New York, School of Public Affairs, Program in Public Administration, New York, NY 10010-5585. Offers general public administration (MPA); health care policy (MPA); nonprofit administration (MPA); policy analysis and evaluation (MPA); public management (MPA); MS/MPA. *Accreditation:* NASPAA. Part-time and evening/weekend programs available. *Degree requirements:* For master's, thesis, capstone. *Entrance requirements:* For master's, GRE General Test. Additional exam requirements/recommendations for international students: Required—TOEFL. Electronic applications accepted. *Expenses:* Contact institution. *Faculty research:* Urbanization, population and poverty in the developing world, housing and community development, labor unions and housing, government-nongovernment relations, immigration policy, social network analysis, cross-sectoral governance, comparative healthcare systems, program evaluation, social welfare policy, health outcomes, educational policy and leadership, transnationalism, infant health, welfare reform, racial/ethnic disparities in health, urban politics, homelessness, race and ethnic relations.

Bay Path College, Program in Nonprofit Management and Philanthropy, Longmeadow, MA 01106-2292. Offers MS. Part-time and evening/weekend programs available. Postbaccalaureate distance learning degree programs offered (no on-campus study). *Students:* 9 full-time (all women), 49 part-time (44 women); includes 17 minority (12 Black or African American, non-Hispanic/Latino; 5 Hispanic/Latino), 1 international. Average age 37. 53 applicants, 79% accepted, 29 enrolled. In 2013, 25 master's awarded. *Degree requirements:* For master's, eight required courses (24 credits) and four electives (12 credits) for a total of 36 credits; capstone paper. *Application deadline:* Applications are processed on a rolling basis. Application fee: $45. Electronic applications accepted. Application fee is waived when completed online. *Expenses:* Contact institution. *Financial support:* In 2013–14, 16 students received support. Scholarships/grants available. Financial award applicants required to submit FAFSA. *Unit head:* Jeffrey Greim, Program Director, 413-565-1010, Fax: 413-565-1116, E-mail: mmolson@baypath.edu. *Application contact:* Lisa Adams, Director of Graduate Admissions, 413-565-1317, Fax: 413-565-1250, E-mail: ladams@baypath.edu.
Website: http://graduate.baypath.edu/Graduate-Programs/Programs-On-Campus/MS-Programs/Nonprofit-Management-and-Philanthropy.

Bay Path College, Program in Strategic Fundraising and Philanthropy, Longmeadow, MA 01106-2292. Offers higher education (MS); non-profit fundraising administration (MS). Part-time and evening/weekend programs available. Postbaccalaureate distance learning degree programs offered (no on-campus study). *Students:* 9 part-time (8 women). Average age 33. 7 applicants, 71% accepted, 2 enrolled. In 2013, 13 master's awarded. *Degree requirements:* For master's, 36 hours of coursework inluding portfolio. *Application deadline:* Applications are processed on a rolling basis. Application fee: $45. Electronic applications accepted. Application fee is waived when completed online. *Expenses:* Contact institution. *Financial support:* In 2013–14, 6 students received support. Scholarships/grants available. Financial award applicants required to submit FAFSA. *Unit head:* Jeffrey Greim, Program Director, 413-565-1045. *Application contact:* Lisa Adams, Director of Graduate Admissions, 413-565-1317, Fax: 413-565-1250, E-mail: ladams@baypath.edu.
Website: http://graduate.baypath.edu/Graduate-Programs/Programs-On-Campus/MS-Programs/Strategic-Fundraising-and-Philanthropy.

Brandeis University, The Heller School for Social Policy and Management, Program in Nonprofit Management, Waltham, MA 02454-9110. Offers child, youth, and family management (MBA); health care management (MBA); social impact management (MBA); social policy and management (MBA); sustainable development (MBA); MBA/MA; MBA/MD. MBA/MD program offered in conjunction with Tufts University School of Medicine. *Accreditation:* AACSB. Part-time programs available. *Degree requirements:* For master's, team consulting project. *Entrance requirements:* For master's, GMAT (preferred) or GRE, 2 letters of recommendation, problem statement analysis, 3-5 years of professional experience. Additional exam requirements/recommendations for international students: Required—TOEFL (minimum score 600 paper-based; 100 iBT). Electronic applications accepted. *Expenses:* Contact institution. *Faculty research:* Health care; children and families; elder and disabled services; social impact management; organizations in the non-profit, for-profit, or public sector.

Brigham Young University, Graduate Studies, Marriott School of Management, Master of Public Administration Program, Provo, UT 84602. Offers finance (MPA); human resources (MPA); local government (MPA); nonprofit management (MPA); JD/MPA. *Entrance requirements:* For master's, GRE or GMAT, minimum GPA of 3.0. Additional exam requirements/recommendations for international students: Required—TOEFL (minimum score 580 paper-based; 85 iBT), IELTS (minimum score 7). Electronic applications accepted. *Expenses: Tuition:* Full-time $6130; part-time $340 per credit hour. Tuition and fees vary according to program and student's religious affiliation. *Faculty research:* Taxes, budgeting, nonprofit, ethics, decision modeling, work balance, organizational behavior.

California Lutheran University, Graduate Studies, School of Management, Thousand Oaks, CA 91360-2787. Offers business (IMBA); computer science (MS); econometrics (MBA); economics (MS); entrepreneurship (MBA, Certificate); finance (MBA, Certificate); financial planning (MBA, Certificate); information systems and technology (MS); information technology management (MBA, Certificate); international business (MBA, Certificate); management and organization behavior (MBA); management and organizational behavior (Certificate); marketing (MBA, Certificate); microeconomics (MBA); nonprofit and social enterprise (MBA). Part-time and evening/weekend programs available. Postbaccalaureate distance learning degree programs offered (no on-campus study). *Faculty:* 26 full-time (9 women), 50 part-time/adjunct (11 women). *Students:* 426 full-time (175 women), 220 part-time (91 women); includes 114 minority (14 Black or African American, non-Hispanic/Latino; 30 Asian, non-Hispanic/Latino; 57 Hispanic/Latino; 13 Two or more races, non-Hispanic/Latino), 321 international. Average age 31. 495 applicants, 76% accepted, 119 enrolled. In 2013, 297 master's awarded. *Entrance requirements:* For master's, GMAT, interview, minimum GPA of 3.0. *Application deadline:* Applications are processed on a rolling basis. Application fee: $50. *Expenses:* Contact institution. *Unit head:* Dr. Gerhard Apfelthaler, Dean, 805-493-3360. *Application contact:* 805-493-3325, Fax: 805-493-3861, E-mail: clugrad@callutheran.edu.
Website: http://www.callutheran.edu/business/.

California State University, Northridge, Graduate Studies, The Tseng College of Extended Learning, Program in Nonprofit-Sector Management, Northridge, CA 91330. Offers Graduate Certificate. Offered in collaboration with College of Social and Behavioral Sciences. *Entrance requirements:* For degree, bachelor's degree from accredited college or university with minimum GPA of 2.5 in last 60 semester units or 90 quarter units; at least one year of work experience in the public or non-profit sector.

Cambridge College, School of Management, Cambridge, MA 02138-5304. Offers business negotiation and conflict resolution (M Mgt); general business (M Mgt); health care informatics (M Mgt); health care management (M Mgt); leadership in human and organizational dynamics (M Mgt); non-profit and public organization management (M Mgt); small business development (M Mgt); technology management (M Mgt). Part-time and evening/weekend programs available. *Degree requirements:* For master's, thesis, seminars. *Entrance requirements:* For master's, resume, 2 professional references. Additional exam requirements/recommendations for international students: Required—TOEFL (minimum score 550 paper-based; 79 iBT), Michigan English Language Assessment Battery (minimum score 85); Recommended—IELTS (minimum score 6). Electronic applications accepted. *Expenses:* Contact institution. *Faculty research:* Negotiation, mediation and conflict resolution; leadership; management of diverse organizations; case studies and simulation methodologies for management education, digital as a second language: social networking for digital immigrants, non-profit and public management.

Capella University, School of Public Service Leadership, Doctoral Programs in Healthcare, Minneapolis, MN 55402. Offers criminal justice (PhD); emergency management (PhD); epidemiology (Dr PH); general health administration (DHA); general public administration (DPA); health advocacy and leadership (Dr PH); health care administration (PhD); health care leadership (DHA); health policy advocacy (DHA); multidisciplinary human services (PhD); nonprofit management and leadership (PhD); public safety leadership (PhD); social and community services (PhD).

Carlos Albizu University, Miami Campus, Graduate Programs, Miami, FL 33172-2209. Offers clinical psychology (Psy D); entrepreneurship (MBA); exceptional student education (MS); human services (PhD); industrial/organizational psychology (MS); marriage and family therapy (MS); mental health counseling (MS); nonprofit management (MBA); organizational management (MBA); psychology (MS); school counseling (MS); teaching English as a second language (MS). *Accreditation:* APA. Part-time and evening/weekend programs available. *Faculty:* 26 full-time (20 women), 34 part-time/adjunct (16 women). *Students:* 416 full-time (335 women), 281 part-time (237 women); includes 604 minority (57 Black or African American, non-Hispanic/Latino; 1 American Indian or Alaska Native, non-Hispanic/Latino; 13 Asian, non-Hispanic/Latino; 533 Hispanic/Latino), 14 international. Average age 36. 176 applicants, 59% accepted, 96 enrolled. In 2013, 176 master's, 37 doctorates awarded. Terminal master's awarded for partial completion of doctoral program. *Degree requirements:* For master's, one foreign language, comprehensive exam, integrative project (MBA), research project (exceptional student education, teaching English as a second language); for doctorate, one foreign language, comprehensive exam, internship, project. *Entrance requirements:* For master's, 3 letters of recommendation, interview, minimum GPA of 3.0, resume, statement of purpose, official transcripts; for doctorate, 3 letters of recommendation, minimum GPA of 3.0, resume, interview, statement of purpose, official transcripts. Additional exam requirements/recommendations for international students: Required—Michigan Test of English Language Proficiency. *Application deadline:* For fall admission, 4/1 priority date for domestic students, 5/1 priority date for international students; for spring admission, 11/1 priority date for domestic students, 9/1 priority date for international students. Applications are processed on a rolling basis. Application fee: $50. Electronic applications accepted. *Expenses: Tuition:* Full-time $9360; part-time $520 per credit. *Required fees:* $298 per term. Tuition and fees vary according to course load, degree level and program. *Financial support:* In 2013–14, 62 students received support. Federal Work-Study, scholarships/grants, and tuition discounts available. Financial award application deadline: 6/1; financial award applicants required to submit FAFSA. *Faculty research:* Psychotherapy, forensic psychology, neuropsychology, marketing strategy, entrepreneurship, special education. *Unit head:* Peter M. Rubio, Interim Chancellor, 305-593-1223 Ext. 3120, Fax: 305-592-7930, E-mail: prubio@albizu.edu. *Application contact:* Vanessa Almendarez, Administrative Assistant, 305-593-1223 Ext. 3137, Fax: 305-593-1854, E-mail: valmendarez@albizu.edu.

Case Western Reserve University, Jack, Joseph and Morton Mandel School of Applied Social Sciences, Cleveland, OH 44106. Offers nonprofit management (MNO); social welfare (PhD); social work (MSSA); JD/MSSA; MSSA/MA; MSSA/MBA; MSSA/MNO. *Accreditation:* CSWE (one or more programs are accredited). Evening/weekend programs available. Postbaccalaureate distance learning degree programs offered (no on-campus study). *Faculty:* 40 full-time (23 women), 52 part-time/adjunct (34 women). *Students:* 310 full-time (255 women), 76 part-time (62 women); includes 106 minority (70 Black or African American, non-Hispanic/Latino; 3 American Indian or Alaska Native, non-Hispanic/Latino; 10 Asian, non-Hispanic/Latino; 11 Hispanic/Latino; 12 Two or more races, non-Hispanic/Latino), 27 international. Average age 30. 429 applicants, 81% accepted, 199 enrolled. In 2013, 136 master's, 3 doctorates awarded. *Degree requirements:* For master's, fieldwork; for doctorate, thesis/dissertation. *Entrance requirements:* For master's, GRE General Test, MAT, or minimum GPA of 2.7; for doctorate, GRE General Test. Additional exam requirements/recommendations for international students: Required—TOEFL (minimum score 557 paper-based, 90 iBT) or IELTS (minimum score 7). *Application deadline:* For fall admission, 4/18 for domestic students, 3/14 for international students; for spring admission, 11/22 for domestic students; for summer admission, 3/7 for domestic students. Applications are processed on a rolling basis. Application fee: $0. Electronic applications accepted. *Expenses:* Contact institution. *Financial support:* In 2013–14, 352 students received support, including 352 fellowships with full tuition reimbursements available (averaging $11,000 per year); career-related internships or fieldwork, Federal Work-Study, institutionally sponsored loans, scholarships/grants, tuition waivers (partial), and paid field placement (for MSSA students) also available. Support available to part-time students. Financial award application deadline: 4/30; financial award applicants required to submit FAFSA. *Faculty research:* Urban poverty, community social development, substance abuse, health, child welfare, aging, mental health. *Total annual research expenditures:* $3.8 million. *Unit head:* Dr. Grover Cleveland Gilmore, Dean, 216-368-2256, E-mail:

msassdean@case.edu. *Application contact:* Richard Sigg, Admissions/Recruitment, 216-368-1655, Fax: 216-368-6624, E-mail: msassadmit@po.cwru.edu. Website: http://msass.case.edu/.

Case Western Reserve University, Weatherhead School of Management, Mandel Center for Nonprofit Organizations, Cleveland, OH 44106-7167. Offers MNO, CNM, JD/MNO, MNO/MSSA, MSSA/MNO. *Entrance requirements:* For master's, GMAT or GRE. Additional exam requirements/recommendations for international students: Required—TOEFL. *Expenses:* Contact institution. *Faculty research:* Leadership management of non-profit organizations, strategic alliances, economic analysis of non-profit organizations.

Central Michigan University, Central Michigan University Global Campus, Program in Administration, Mount Pleasant, MI 48859. Offers acquisitions administration (MSA, Certificate); engineering management administration (MSA, Certificate); general administration (MSA, Certificate); health services administration (MSA, Certificate); human resources administration (MSA, Certificate); information resource management (MSA); information resource management administration (Certificate); international administration (MSA, Certificate); leadership (MSA, Certificate); philanthropy and fundraising administration (MSA, Certificate); public administration (MSA, Certificate); recreation and park administration (MSA); research administration (MSA, Certificate). Part-time and evening/weekend programs available. Postbaccalaureate distance learning degree programs offered (no on-campus study). *Students:* Average age 38. *Entrance requirements:* For master's, minimum GPA of 2.7 in major. *Application deadline:* Applications are processed on a rolling basis. Application fee: $50. Electronic applications accepted. *Financial support:* Scholarships/grants available. Support available to part-time students. Financial award applicants required to submit FAFSA. *Unit head:* Dr. Patricia Chase, Director, 989-774-1845, E-mail: chase1pb@cmich.edu. *Application contact:* 877-268-4636, E-mail: cmuglobal@cmich.edu.

Chaminade University of Honolulu, Graduate Services, Program in Business Administration, Honolulu, HI 96816-1578. Offers accounting (MBA); business (MBA); not-for-profit (MBA); public sector (MBA). Part-time and evening/weekend programs available. *Entrance requirements:* For master's, minimum GPA of 3.0, resume. Additional exam requirements/recommendations for international students: Required—TOEFL (minimum score 650 paper-based). Electronic applications accepted. *Faculty research:* Total quality management, international finance, not-for-profit accounting, service-learning in business contexts.

Cleary University, Online Program in Business Administration, Ann Arbor, MI 48105-2659. Offers accounting (MBA); financial planning (MBA); financial planning (Graduate Certificate); green business strategy (MBA, Graduate Certificate); health care leadership (MBA); management (MBA); nonprofit management (MBA, Graduate Certificate); organizational leadership (MBA). Part-time and evening/weekend programs available. Postbaccalaureate distance learning degree programs offered (no on-campus study). *Degree requirements:* For master's, thesis. *Entrance requirements:* For master's, bachelor's degree; minimum GPA of 2.5; professional resume indicating minimum of 2 years of management or related experience; undergraduate degree from accredited college or university with at least 18 quarter hours (or 12 semester hours) of accounting study (for MBA in accounting). Additional exam requirements/recommendations for international students: Required—TOEFL (minimum score 550 paper-based; 79 iBT), Michigan English Language Assessment Battery (minimum score 75). Electronic applications accepted.

Cleveland State University, College of Graduate Studies, Maxine Goodman Levin College of Urban Affairs, Program in Environmental Studies, Cleveland, OH 44115. Offers environmental nonprofit management (MAES); environmental planning (MAES); geographic information systems (Certificate); policy and administration (MAES); sustainable economic development (MAES); urban economic development (Certificate); urban real estate development and finance (Certificate); JD/MAES. Part-time and evening/weekend programs available. *Faculty:* 21 full-time (10 women), 11 part-time/adjunct (3 women). *Students:* 2 full-time (both women), 5 part-time (3 women); includes 1 minority (Hispanic/Latino). Average age 34. 4 applicants, 25% accepted. In 2013, 11 master's awarded. *Degree requirements:* For master's, thesis or alternative, exit project. *Entrance requirements:* For master's, GRE General Test (minimum score: verbal and quantitative combined 40th percentile, analytical writing 4.0), minimum GPA of 3.0. Additional exam requirements/recommendations for international students: Required—TOEFL (minimum score 525 paper-based; 65 iBT), IELTS or ITEP. *Application deadline:* For fall admission, 7/15 priority date for domestic students, 5/15 for international students; for spring admission, 11/1 for international students. Applications are processed on a rolling basis. Application fee: $30. Electronic applications accepted. *Expenses:* Tuition, state resident: full-time $8335; part-time $521 per credit hour. Tuition, nonresident: full-time $15,670; part-time $979 per credit hour. *Required fees:* $50; $25 per semester. *Financial support:* In 2013–14, 4 students received support, including 4 research assistantships with full and partial tuition reimbursements available (averaging $3,625 per year); career-related internships or fieldwork, scholarships/grants, traineeships, and unspecified assistantships also available. Support available to part-time students. Financial award application deadline: 3/1; financial award applicants required to submit FAFSA. *Faculty research:* Environmental policy and administration, environmental planning, geographic information systems (GIS), urban sustainability planning and management, energy policy, land re-use. *Unit head:* Dr. Sanda Kaufman, Director, 216-687-2367, Fax: 216-687-9342, E-mail: s.kaufman@csuohio.edu. *Application contact:* David Arrighi, Graduate Academic Advisor, 216-523-7522, Fax: 216-687-5398, E-mail: urbanprograms@csuohio.edu. Website: http://urban.csuohio.edu/academics/graduate/maes/.

Cleveland State University, College of Graduate Studies, Maxine Goodman Levin College of Urban Affairs, Program in Nonprofit Administration and Leadership, Cleveland, OH 44115. Offers advanced fundraising (Certificate); local and urban management (Certificate); nonprofit administration and leadership (MNAL); nonprofit management (Certificate). Part-time and evening/weekend programs available. *Faculty:* 21 full-time (10 women), 11 part-time/adjunct (3 women). *Students:* 6 full-time (all women), 16 part-time (14 women); includes 10 minority (8 Black or African American, non-Hispanic/Latino; 1 Hispanic/Latino; 1 Two or more races, non-Hispanic/Latino), 3 international. Average age 35. 23 applicants, 52% accepted, 3 enrolled. In 2013, 12 master's awarded. *Degree requirements:* For master's, thesis or alternative, capstone course. *Entrance requirements:* For master's, GRE (minimum score: verbal and quantitative combined 40th percentile, analytical writing 4.0), minimum GPA of 3.0. Additional exam requirements/recommendations for international students: Required—TOEFL (minimum score 525 paper-based; 65 iBT), IELTS or ITEP. *Application deadline:* For fall admission, 7/15 priority date for domestic students, 5/15 for international students; for spring admission, 11/1 for international students. Applications are processed on a rolling basis. Application fee: $30. Electronic applications accepted. *Expenses:* Tuition, state resident: full-time $8335; part-time $521 per credit hour. Tuition, nonresident: full-time $15,670; part-time $979 per credit hour. *Required fees:* $50; $25 per semester. *Financial support:* In 2013–14, 3 students received support, including 1 research assistantship with full and partial tuition reimbursement available (averaging $7,200 per year), 2 teaching assistantships with full tuition reimbursements available (averaging $4,800 per year); career-related internships or fieldwork, scholarships/grants, traineeships, and unspecified assistantships also available. Support available to part-time students. Financial award application deadline: 3/1; financial award applicants required to submit FAFSA. *Faculty research:* Human resource management, volunteerism, performance measurement in nonprofits, government-nonprofit partnerships. *Unit head:* Dr. Mittie Davis Jones, Assistant Dean and Program Director, 216-687-3861, Fax: 216-687-9342, E-mail: m.d.jones97@csuohio.edu. *Application contact:* David Arrighi, Graduate Academic Advisor, 216-523-7522, Fax: 216-687-5398, E-mail: urbanprograms@csuohio.edu. Website: http://urban.csuohio.edu/academics/graduate/mnal/.

Cleveland State University, College of Graduate Studies, Maxine Goodman Levin College of Urban Affairs, Program in Public Administration, Cleveland, OH 44115. Offers city management (MPA); economic development (MPA); healthcare administration (MPA); local and urban management (Certificate); non-profit management (MPA, Certificate); public financial management (MPA); public management (MPA); urban economic development (Certificate); JD/MPA. *Accreditation:* NASPAA. Part-time and evening/weekend programs available. *Faculty:* 21 full-time (10 women), 11 part-time/adjunct (3 women). *Students:* 16 full-time (11 women), 64 part-time (40 women); includes 23 minority (19 Black or African American, non-Hispanic/Latino; 3 Hispanic/Latino; 1 Two or more races, non-Hispanic/Latino), 3 international. Average age 36. 67 applicants, 51% accepted, 13 enrolled. In 2013, 56 master's awarded. *Degree requirements:* For master's, thesis or alternative, capstone course. *Entrance requirements:* For master's, GRE General Test (minimum scores in 40th percentile verbal and quantitative, 4.0 writing), minimum GPA of 3.0. Additional exam requirements/recommendations for international students: Required—TOEFL (minimum score 525 paper-based; 65 iBT), IELTS or ITEP. *Application deadline:* For fall admission, 7/15 priority date for domestic students, 5/15 for international students; for spring admission, 11/1 for international students. Applications are processed on a rolling basis. Application fee: $30. Electronic applications accepted. *Expenses:* Tuition, state resident: full-time $8335; part-time $521 per credit hour. Tuition, nonresident: full-time $15,670; part-time $979 per credit hour. *Required fees:* $50; $25 per semester. *Financial support:* In 2013–14, 16 students received support, including 12 research assistantships with full and partial tuition reimbursements available (averaging $4,800 per year), 4 teaching assistantships with full and partial tuition reimbursements available (averaging $3,300 per year); career-related internships or fieldwork, scholarships/grants, traineeships, and unspecified assistantships also available. Support available to part-time students. Financial award application deadline: 3/1; financial award applicants required to submit FAFSA. *Faculty research:* City management, nonprofit management, health care administration, public management, economic development. *Unit head:* Dr. Nicholas Zingale, Director, 216-802-3398, Fax: 216-687-9342, E-mail: n.zingale@csuohio.edu. *Application contact:* David Arrighi, Graduate Academic Advisor, 216-523-7522, Fax: 216-687-5398, E-mail: urbanprograms@csuohio.edu. Website: http://urban.csuohio.edu/academics/graduate/mpa/.

The College at Brockport, State University of New York, School of Education and Human Services, Department of Public Administration, Brockport, NY 14420-2997. Offers arts administration (AGC); nonprofit management (AGC); public administration (MPA), including general public administration, health care management, nonprofit management. *Accreditation:* NASPAA. Part-time and evening/weekend programs available. *Faculty:* 5 full-time (2 women), 1 part-time/adjunct (0 women). *Students:* 24 full-time (16 women), 50 part-time (36 women); includes 11 minority (all Black or African American, non-Hispanic/Latino), 2 international. 38 applicants, 87% accepted, 19 enrolled. In 2013, 32 master's, 7 other advanced degrees awarded. *Degree requirements:* For master's, thesis or alternative. *Entrance requirements:* For master's, GRE or minimum GPA of 3.0, letters of recommendation, statement of objectives, current resume. Additional exam requirements/recommendations for international students: Required—TOEFL (minimum score 550 paper-based; 79 iBT), IELTS (minimum score 6.5). *Application deadline:* For fall admission, 8/15 priority date for domestic and international students; for spring admission, 1/15 priority date for domestic and international students. Application fee: $50. Electronic applications accepted. *Expenses:* Tuition, state resident: full-time $9870. Tuition, nonresident: full-time $18,350. *Required fees:* $1848. *Financial support:* In 2013–14, 1 fellowship with full tuition reimbursement (averaging $7,500 per year), 1 teaching assistantship with full tuition reimbursement (averaging $6,000 per year) were awarded; Federal Work-Study, scholarships/grants, and unspecified assistantships also available. Support available to part-time students. Financial award application deadline: 3/15; financial award applicants required to submit FAFSA. *Faculty research:* E-government, performance management, nonprofits and policy implementation, Medicaid and disabilities. *Unit head:* Dr. Celia Watt, Graduate Director, 585-395-5538, Fax: 585-395-2172, E-mail: cwatt@brockport.edu. *Application contact:* Danielle A. Welch, Graduate Admissions Counselor, 585-395-2525, Fax: 585-395-2515. Website: http://www.brockport.edu/pubadmin.

The College of Saint Rose, Graduate Studies, School of Business, Department of Not-for-Profit Management, Albany, NY 12203-1419. Offers Certificate. Part-time and evening/weekend programs available. *Entrance requirements:* For degree, minimum undergraduate GPA of 3.0 or GMAT. Additional exam requirements/recommendations for international students: Required—TOEFL (minimum score 550 paper-based). Electronic applications accepted.

Columbia University, School of Continuing Education, Program in Fundraising Management, New York, NY 10027. Offers MS. Part-time and evening/weekend programs available. *Degree requirements:* For master's, internship. *Entrance requirements:* For master's, BA with minimum GPA of 3.0. Additional exam requirements/recommendations for international students: Required—American Language Program placement test; Recommended—TOEFL. Electronic applications accepted. *Faculty research:* Fundraising for annual campaigns, capital campaigns, nonprofit financial management, research for fundraising and planned giving.

Corban University, Graduate School, The Corban MBA, Salem, OR 97301-9392. Offers management (MBA); non-profit management (MBA). Postbaccalaureate distance learning degree programs offered (no on-campus study).

Daemen College, Program in Executive Leadership and Change, Amherst, NY 14226-3592. Offers business (MS); health professions (MS); not-for-profit organizations (MS). Part-time and evening/weekend programs available. *Degree requirements:* For master's, thesis, cohort learning sequence (2 years for weekend cohort; 3 years for weeknight cohort). *Entrance requirements:* For master's, 2 letters of recommendation, interview, goal statement, official transcripts, resume. Additional exam requirements/recommendations for international students: Required—TOEFL (minimum score 500 paper-based; 63 iBT), IELTS (minimum score 5.5). Electronic applications accepted.

Dallas Baptist University, College of Business, Business Administration Program, Dallas, TX 75211-9299. Offers accounting (MBA); business communication (MBA); conflict resolution management (MBA); entrepreneurship (MBA); finance (MBA); health care management (MBA); international business (MBA); leading the non-profit organization (MBA); management (MBA); management information systems (MBA); marketing (MBA); project management (MBA); technology and engineering (MBA). *Accreditation:* ACBSP. Part-time and evening/weekend programs available. *Entrance requirements:* For master's, GMAT, minimum GPA of 3.0. Additional exam

requirements/recommendations for international students: Required—TOEFL, IELTS. *Application deadline:* Applications are processed on a rolling basis. Application fee: $25. Electronic applications accepted. *Expenses: Tuition:* Full-time $13,410; part-time $745 per credit hour. *Required fees:* $300; $150 per semester. Tuition and fees vary according to degree level. *Financial support:* Federal Work-Study, institutionally sponsored loans, scholarships/grants, and tuition waivers (full and partial) available. Support available to part-time students. Financial award applicants required to submit FAFSA. *Faculty research:* Sports management, services marketing, retailing, strategic management, financial planning/investments. *Unit head:* Dr. Sandra S. Reid, Chair, 214-333-5280, Fax: 214-333-5293, E-mail: graduate@dbu.edu. *Application contact:* Kit P. Montgomery, Director of Graduate Programs, 214-333-5242, Fax: 214-333-5579, E-mail: graduate@dbu.edu.
Website: http://www3.dbu.edu/graduate/mba.asp.

Dallas Baptist University, Gary Cook School of Leadership, Program in Christian Education, Dallas, TX 75211-9299. Offers adult ministry (MA); business ministry (MA); Christian studies (MA); collegiate ministry (MA); communication ministry (MA); counseling ministry (MA); family ministry (MA); general ministry (MA); leading the nonprofit organization (MA); missions ministry (MA); small group ministry (MA); student ministry (MA); worship ministry (MA); MA/MA. Part-time and evening/weekend programs available. *Entrance requirements:* For master's, minimum GPA of 3.0. Additional exam requirements/recommendations for international students: Required—TOEFL. *Application deadline:* Applications are processed on a rolling basis. Application fee: $25. Electronic applications accepted. *Expenses: Tuition:* Full-time $13,410; part-time $745 per credit hour. *Required fees:* $300; $150 per semester. Tuition and fees vary according to degree level. *Financial support:* Federal Work-Study, institutionally sponsored loans, scholarships/grants, and tuition waivers (full and partial) available. Support available to part-time students. Financial award applicants required to submit FAFSA. *Unit head:* Dr. Judy Morris, Director, 214-333-5246, Fax: 214-333-5115, E-mail: graduate@dbu.edu. *Application contact:* Kit P. Montgomery, Director of Graduate Programs, 214-333-5242, Fax: 214-333-5579, E-mail: graduate@dbu.edu.
Website: http://www3.dbu.edu/leadership/mace/.

Dallas Baptist University, Gary Cook School of Leadership, Program in Global Leadership, Dallas, TX 75211-9299. Offers business communication (MA); East Asian studies (MA); ESL (MA); general studies (MA); global leadership (MA); global studies (MA); international business (MA); leading the nonprofit organization (MA); missions (MA); small group ministry (MA); MA/MA. Part-time and evening/weekend programs available. *Entrance requirements:* For master's, minimum GPA of 3.0. Additional exam requirements/recommendations for international students: Required—TOEFL, IELTS. Application fee: $25. *Expenses: Tuition:* Full-time $13,410; part-time $745 per credit hour. *Required fees:* $300; $150 per semester. Tuition and fees vary according to degree level. *Financial support:* Federal Work-Study, institutionally sponsored loans, scholarships/grants, and tuition waivers (full and partial) available. Support available to part-time students. Financial award applicants required to submit FAFSA. *Unit head:* Dr. Bob Garrett, Director, 214-333-5508, Fax: 214-333-5689, E-mail: graduate@dbu.edu. *Application contact:* Kit P. Montgomery, Director of Graduate Programs, 214-333-5242, Fax: 214-333-5579, E-mail: graduate@dbu.edu.
Website: http://www3.dbu.edu/leadership/globalleadership.asp.

DePaul University, College of Liberal Arts and Social Sciences, Chicago, IL 60614. Offers Arabic (MA); Chinese (MA); English (MA); French (MA); German (MA); history (MA); interdisciplinary studies (MA, MS); international public service (MS); international studies (MA); Italian (MA); Japanese (MA); leadership and policy studies (MS); liberal studies (MA); new media studies (MA); nonprofit management (MNM); public administration (MPA); public health (MPH); public service management (MS); social work (MSW); sociology (MA); Spanish (MA); sustainable urban development (MA); women and gender studies (MA); writing and publishing (MA); writing, rhetoric, and discourse (MA); MA/PhD. Part-time and evening/weekend programs available. Postbaccalaureate distance learning degree programs offered (no on-campus study). *Faculty:* 75 full-time (38 women), 26 part-time/adjunct (15 women). *Students:* 539 full-time (382 women), 391 part-time (255 women); includes 302 minority (150 Black or African American, non-Hispanic/Latino; 30 Asian, non-Hispanic/Latino; 91 Hispanic/Latino; 1 Native Hawaiian or other Pacific Islander, non-Hispanic/Latino; 30 Two or more races, non-Hispanic/Latino), 33 international. Average age 29. In 2013, 419 master's awarded. Terminal master's awarded for partial completion of doctoral program. *Degree requirements:* For master's, variable foreign language requirement, comprehensive exam (for some programs), thesis (for some programs). *Application deadline:* Applications are processed on a rolling basis. Application fee: $40. Electronic applications accepted. Tuition and fees vary according to course level, course load and degree level. *Financial support:* Applicants required to submit FAFSA. *Unit head:* Dr. Charles Suchar, Dean, 773-325-7305. *Application contact:* Ann Spittle, Director of Graduate Admission, 773-325-7315, Fax: 312-476-3244, E-mail: graddepaul@depaul.edu.
Website: http://las.depaul.edu/.

Eastern Mennonite University, Program in Business Administration, Harrisonburg, VA 22802-2462. Offers business administration (MBA); health services administration (MBA); non-profit management (MBA). Part-time and evening/weekend programs available. *Degree requirements:* For master's, final capstone course. *Entrance requirements:* For master's, GMAT, minimum GPA of 2.5, 2 years of work experience, 2 letters of reference. Additional exam requirements/recommendations for international students: Required—TOEFL (minimum score 500 paper-based). Electronic applications accepted. *Expenses:* Contact institution. *Faculty research:* Information security, Anabaptist/Mennonite experiences and perspectives, limits of multi-cultural education, international development performance criteria.

Eastern Michigan University, Graduate School, College of Business, Programs in Business Administration, Ypsilanti, MI 48197. Offers business administration (MBA, Graduate Certificate); computer information systems (Graduate Certificate); e-business (MBA, Graduate Certificate); enterprise business intelligence (MBA); entrepreneurship (MBA, Graduate Certificate); finance (MBA, Graduate Certificate); human resources (MBA); human resources management (Graduate Certificate); information systems (MBA); internal auditing (MBA); international business (MBA, Graduate Certificate); marketing management (Graduate Certificate); nonprofit management (MBA); organizational development (Graduate Certificate); supply chain management (MBA, Graduate Certificate). *Accreditation:* AACSB. Part-time programs available. Postbaccalaureate distance learning degree programs offered (no on-campus study). *Students:* 74 full-time (28 women), 342 part-time (183 women); includes 122 minority (84 Black or African American, non-Hispanic/Latino; 2 American Indian or Alaska Native, non-Hispanic/Latino; 19 Asian, non-Hispanic/Latino; 7 Hispanic/Latino; 10 Two or more races, non-Hispanic/Latino), 38 international. Average age 33. 305 applicants, 72% accepted, 131 enrolled. In 2013, 69 master's, 57 other advanced degrees awarded. *Entrance requirements:* For master's, GMAT (minimum score 450), minimum cumulative undergraduate GPA of 2.75. Additional exam requirements/recommendations for international students: Required—TOEFL. *Application deadline:* For fall admission, 5/15 for domestic students, 5/1 for international students; for winter admission, 10/15 for domestic students, 10/1 for international students; for spring admission, 3/15 for

domestic students, 3/1 for international students. Applications are processed on a rolling basis. Application fee: $35. *Expenses:* Tuition, state resident: full-time $12,300; part-time $466 per credit hour. Tuition, nonresident: full-time $23,159; part-time $918 per credit hour. *Required fees:* $71 per credit hour. $46 per semester. One-time fee: $100. Tuition and fees vary according to course level and degree level. *Financial support:* Fellowships, research assistantships with full tuition reimbursements, teaching assistantships with full tuition reimbursements, career-related internships or fieldwork, Federal Work-Study, institutionally sponsored loans, scholarships/grants, tuition waivers (partial), and unspecified assistantships available. Support available to part-time students. Financial award applicants required to submit FAFSA. *Unit head:* K. Michelle Henry, Director, Academic Services, 734-487-4444, Fax: 734-483-1316, E-mail: mhenry1@emich.edu. *Application contact:* Beste Windes, Advisor, 734-487-4444, Fax: 734-483-1316, E-mail: bwindes@emich.edu.
Website: http://www.emich.edu/public/cob/gr/grad.html.

Eastern Michigan University, Graduate School, College of Health and Human Services, Interdisciplinary Program in Non-Profit Management, Ypsilanti, MI 48197. Offers Graduate Certificate. *Expenses:* Tuition, state resident: full-time $12,300; part-time $466 per credit hour. Tuition, nonresident: full-time $23,159; part-time $918 per credit hour. *Required fees:* $71 per credit hour. $46 per semester. One-time fee: $100. Tuition and fees vary according to course level and degree level. *Unit head:* Dr. Marcia Bombyk, Program Coordinator, 734-487-4173, Fax: 734-487-8536, E-mail: marcia.bombyk@emich.edu. *Application contact:* Graduate Admissions, 734-487-2400, Fax: 734-487-6559, E-mail: graduate.admissions@emich.edu.

Eastern University, School of Leadership and Development, St. Davids, PA 19087-3696. Offers economic development (MBA), including international development, urban development (MA, MBA); international development (MA), including global development, urban development (MA, MBA); nonprofit management (MS); organizational leadership (MA); M Div/MBA. Part-time and evening/weekend programs available. Postbaccalaureate distance learning degree programs offered (minimal on-campus study). *Faculty:* 6 full-time (3 women), 19 part-time/adjunct (8 women). *Students:* 131 full-time (77 women), 67 part-time (42 women); includes 43 minority (29 Black or African American, non-Hispanic/Latino; 1 American Indian or Alaska Native, non-Hispanic/Latino; 6 Asian, non-Hispanic/Latino; 6 Hispanic/Latino; 1 Two or more races, non-Hispanic/Latino), 13 international. Average age 34. 45 applicants, 100% accepted, 33 enrolled. In 2013, 91 master's awarded. *Degree requirements:* For master's, thesis (for some programs). *Entrance requirements:* For master's, GMAT (MBA), minimum GPA of 2.5. Additional exam requirements/recommendations for international students: Required—TOEFL (minimum score 550 paper-based; 79 iBT). *Application deadline:* For fall admission, 8/14 for domestic students. Applications are processed on a rolling basis. Application fee: $35. Application fee is waived when completed online. *Expenses:* Contact institution. *Financial support:* In 2013–14, 131 students received support, including 3 fellowships with partial tuition reimbursements available (averaging $2,500 per year), 7 research assistantships with partial tuition reimbursements available (averaging $1,500 per year); scholarships/grants and unspecified assistantships also available. Financial award application deadline: 3/15; financial award applicants required to submit FAFSA. *Faculty research:* Micro-level economic development, China welfare and economic development, macroethics, micro- and macro-level economic development in transitional economics, organizational effectiveness. *Unit head:* Beth Birmingham, Chair, 610-341-4380. *Application contact:* Lindsey Perry, Enrollment Counselor, 484-581-1311, Fax: 484-581-1276, E-mail: lperry@eastern.edu.
Website: http://www.eastern.edu/academics/programs/school-leadership-and-development.

East Tennessee State University, School of Graduate Studies, College of Arts and Sciences, Department of Political Science, International Affairs and Public Administration, Johnson City, TN 37614. Offers economic development (Postbaccalaureate Certificate); not-for-profit administration (MPA); planning and development (MPA); public financial management (MPA); urban planning (Postbaccalaureate Certificate). Part-time programs available. *Faculty:* 6 full-time (2 women), 3 part-time/adjunct (2 women). *Students:* 17 full-time (4 women), 8 part-time (2 women); includes 2 minority (both Black or African American, non-Hispanic/Latino), 4 international. Average age 29. 32 applicants, 50% accepted, 13 enrolled. In 2013, 11 master's awarded. *Degree requirements:* For master's, internship. *Entrance requirements:* For master's, GRE General Test, three letters of recommendation; for Postbaccalaureate Certificate, GRE General Test. Additional exam requirements/recommendations for international students: Required—TOEFL (minimum score 550 paper-based; 79 iBT). *Application deadline:* For fall admission, 6/1 for domestic students, 4/29 for international students; for spring admission, 11/1 for domestic students, 9/30 for international students. Application fee: $35 ($45 for international students). Electronic applications accepted. *Expenses:* Tuition, state resident: full-time $7900; part-time $395 per credit hour. Tuition, nonresident: full-time $21,960; part-time $1098 per credit hour. *Required fees:* $1345; $84 per credit hour. *Financial support:* In 2013–14, 16 students received support, including 7 research assistantships with full tuition reimbursements available (averaging $6,000 per year), 1 teaching assistantship with full tuition reimbursement available (averaging $6,000 per year); career-related internships or fieldwork, institutionally sponsored loans, scholarships/grants, and unspecified assistantships also available. Financial award application deadline: 7/1; financial award applicants required to submit FAFSA. *Faculty research:* Labor issues, presidency, public law in American politics, East Asian politics, European politics, Middle Eastern politics, development in comparative politics, international political economy, international relations, world politics in international affairs. *Unit head:* Dr. Weixing Chen, Chair, 423-439-4217, Fax: 423-439-4348, E-mail: chen@etsu.edu. *Application contact:* Gail Powers, Graduate Specialist, 423-439-4703, Fax: 423-439-5624, E-mail: pwersg@etsu.edu.
Website: http://www.etsu.edu/cas/PoliSci/.

Fairleigh Dickinson University, Metropolitan Campus, Anthony J. Petrocelli College of Continuing Studies, Public Administration Institute, Teaneck, NJ 07666-1914. Offers public administration (MPA, Certificate); public non-profit management (Certificate).

Fielding Graduate University, Graduate Programs, School of Human and Organization Development, Santa Barbara, CA 93105-3814. Offers comprehensive evidence-based coaching (Certificate); evidence based coaching for education leadership (Certificate); evidence based coaching for organization leadership (Certificate); evidence based coaching for personal development (Certificate); human and organizational systems (PhD), including aging, culture and society, information society and knowledge organizations, transformative learning for social justice; human development (PhD), including aging, culture and society, information society and knowledge organizations, transformative learning for social justice; leadership and management effectiveness (Certificate); leadership for sustainability (Certificate); nonprofit leadership (Certificate); organization consulting (Certificate); organizational development and leadership (MA). Postbaccalaureate distance learning degree programs offered (minimal on-campus study). *Faculty:* 19 full-time (11 women), 38 part-time/adjunct (20 women). *Students:* 321 full-time (225 women), 135 part-time (101 women); includes 103 minority (55 Black or African American, non-Hispanic/Latino; 3 American Indian or Alaska Native, non-

Nonprofit Management

Hispanic/Latino; 12 Asian, non-Hispanic/Latino; 23 Hispanic/Latino; 1 Native Hawaiian or other Pacific Islander, non-Hispanic/Latino; 9 Two or more races, non-Hispanic/Latino); 1 international. Average age 49. 106 applicants, 96% accepted, 70 enrolled. In 2013, 35 master's, 58 doctorates, 60 other advanced degrees awarded. Terminal master's awarded for partial completion of doctoral program. *Degree requirements:* For master's, thesis or alternative; for doctorate, comprehensive exam, thesis/dissertation. *Entrance requirements:* For master's and Certificate, BA from regionally-accredited institution or equivalent; for doctorate, BA or MA from regionally-accredited institution or equivalent. *Application deadline:* For fall admission, 3/1 for domestic and international students; for spring admission, 9/1 for domestic and international students. Application fee: $75. Electronic applications accepted. *Expenses:* Contact institution. *Financial support:* In 2013–14, 35 students received support, including 1 research assistantship (averaging $1,600 per year); scholarships/grants, health care benefits, and unspecified assistantships also available. Support available to part-time students. Financial award applicants required to submit FAFSA. *Unit head:* Dr. Mario Borunda, Dean, 805-898-2940, Fax: 805-687-9793, E-mail: mborunda@fielding.edu. *Application contact:* Kathy Wells, Admission Counselor, 800-340-1099 Ext. 4098, Fax: 805-687-9793, E-mail: hodadmissions@fielding.edu.
Website: http://www.fielding.edu/programs/hod/default.aspx.

Florida Atlantic University, College of Design and Social Inquiry, School of Public Administration, Boca Raton, FL 33431-0991. Offers MNM, MPA, PhD. *Accreditation:* NASPAA (one or more programs are accredited). Part-time and evening/weekend programs available. *Faculty:* 11 full-time (4 women), 4 part-time/adjunct (1 woman). *Students:* 74 full-time (44 women), 176 part-time (115 women); includes 136 minority (89 Black or African American, non-Hispanic/Latino; 3 Asian, non-Hispanic/Latino; 42 Hispanic/Latino; 2 Two or more races, non-Hispanic/Latino), 8 international. Average age 36. 191 applicants, 53% accepted, 68 enrolled. In 2013, 66 master's, 4 doctorates awarded. *Degree requirements:* For master's, thesis optional; for doctorate, comprehensive exam, thesis/dissertation. *Entrance requirements:* For master's, GRE General Test, minimum GPA of 3.0; for doctorate, GRE General Test, faculty reference, scholarly writing samples, letters of recommendation. Additional exam requirements/recommendations for international students: Required—TOEFL (minimum score 500 paper-based; 61 iBT), IELTS (minimum score 6). *Application deadline:* For fall admission, 5/1 priority date for domestic students, 2/15 for international students; for spring admission, 11/1 for domestic students, 7/15 for international students. Applications are processed on a rolling basis. Application fee: $30. *Expenses:* Tuition, state resident: full-time $6660; part-time $370 per credit hour. Tuition, nonresident: full-time $18,450; part-time $1025 per credit hour. Tuition and fees vary according to course load. *Financial support:* Fellowships with full tuition reimbursements, research assistantships with partial tuition reimbursements, teaching assistantships with partial tuition reimbursements, career-related internships or fieldwork, Federal Work-Study, institutionally sponsored loans, and tuition waivers (partial) available. Support available to part-time students. Financial award application deadline: 4/1. *Faculty research:* Public finance and budgeting, public management, evaluation, criminal justice, postmodern public administration. *Unit head:* Dr. Khi Thai, Director, 954-762-5650, Fax: 954-762-5693, E-mail: thai@fau.edu. *Application contact:* Joanna Arlington, Manager, Graduate Admissions, 561-297-2428, Fax: 561-297-2117, E-mail: arlingto@fau.edu.
Website: http://www.fau.edu/spa/.

George Mason University, School of Policy, Government, and International Affairs, Department of Public and International Affairs, Fairfax, VA 22030. Offers administration of justice (Certificate); association management (Certificate); biodefense (MS, PhD); critical analysis and strategic response to terrorism (Certificate); emergency management and homeland security (Certificate); nonprofit management (Certificate); political science (MA, PhD); public administration (MPA); public management (Certificate). *Accreditation:* NASPAA (one or more programs are accredited). *Faculty:* 39 full-time (10 women), 35 part-time/adjunct (10 women). *Students:* 174 full-time (89 women), 281 part-time (162 women); includes 105 minority (34 Black or African American, non-Hispanic/Latino; 22 Asian, non-Hispanic/Latino; 35 Hispanic/Latino; 2 Native Hawaiian or other Pacific Islander, non-Hispanic/Latino; 12 Two or more races, non-Hispanic/Latino), 19 international. Average age 30. 415 applicants, 68% accepted, 144 enrolled. In 2013, 136 master's, 3 doctorates, 8 other advanced degrees awarded. *Entrance requirements:* For master's, GRE, GMAT or LSAT (for MPA); GRE (for MS in biodefense and MA in political science), expanded goals statement; 3 letters of recommendation; official transcripts; resume (for MPA); writing sample (for MS, MA); for doctorate, GRE (taken within the last 5 years), 3 letters of recommendation; expanded goals statement; resume; official transcript; writing sample; for Certificate, GRE, GMAT or LSAT, expanded goals statement; 3 letters of recommendation; official transcripts; resume. Additional exam requirements/recommendations for international students: Required—TOEFL (minimum score 570 paper-based; 88 iBT), IELTS (minimum score 6.5), PTE. Application fee: $65 ($80 for international students). Electronic applications accepted. *Expenses:* Contact institution. *Financial support:* In 2013–14, 32 students received support, including 1 fellowship (averaging $2,500 per year), 14 research assistantships with full and partial tuition reimbursements available (averaging $15,364 per year), 18 teaching assistantships with full and partial tuition reimbursements available (averaging $12,562 per year); career-related internships or fieldwork, Federal Work-Study, scholarships/grants, unspecified assistantships, and health care benefits (for full-time research or teaching assistantship recipients) also available. Support available to part-time students. Financial award application deadline: 3/1; financial award applicants required to submit FAFSA. *Faculty research:* The Rehnquist Court and economic liberties; intersection of economic development with high-tech industry, telecommunications, and entrepreneurism; political economy of development; violence, terrorism and U.S. foreign policy; international security issues. *Total annual research expenditures:* $503,888. *Unit head:* Dr. Priscilla Regan, Chair, 703-993-1419, Fax: 703-993-1399, E-mail: pregan@gmu.edu. *Application contact:* Peg Koback, Education Support Specialist, 703-993-3707, Fax: 703-993-1399, E-mail: mkoback@gmu.edu.
Website: http://pia.gmu.edu/.

The George Washington University, School of Business, Department of Management, Washington, DC 20052. Offers business administration (MBA, PhD); corporate social responsibility (Certificate); nonprofit management (Certificate). *Accreditation:* AACSB. Part-time and evening/weekend programs available. Postbaccalaureate distance learning degree programs offered (no on-campus study). *Degree requirements:* For doctorate, thesis/dissertation. *Entrance requirements:* For master's, GMAT; for doctorate, GMAT or GRE. Additional exam requirements/recommendations for international students: Required—TOEFL. *Application deadline:* For fall admission, 4/1 priority date for domestic students; for spring admission, 10/1 for domestic students. Applications are processed on a rolling basis. Application fee: $60. *Financial support:* Fellowships, teaching assistantships, career-related internships or fieldwork, Federal Work-Study, and institutionally sponsored loans available. Financial award application deadline: 4/1. *Faculty research:* Artificial intelligence, technological entrepreneurship, expert systems, strategic planning/management. *Unit head:* Paul M. Swiercz, Chair, 202-994-7375, E-mail: prof1@gwu.edu. *Application contact:* Kristin Williams, Assistant Vice President for Graduate and Special Enrollment Management, 202-994-0467, Fax: 202-994-0371, E-mail: ksw@gwu.edu.

Georgia Southern University, Jack N. Averitt College of Graduate Studies, College of Liberal Arts and Social Sciences, Department of Non-Profit and Public Studies, Program in Public and Nonprofit Management, Statesboro, GA 30460. Offers Graduate Certificate. Postbaccalaureate distance learning degree programs offered (no on-campus study). *Students:* 13 part-time (11 women); includes 2 minority (1 Black or African American, non-Hispanic/Latino; 1 Two or more races, non-Hispanic/Latino). Average age 35. 10 applicants, 70% accepted, 6 enrolled. *Entrance requirements:* For degree, GRE, three years of work experience in the public or nonprofit sector, bachelor's degree, minimum cumulative undergraduate GPA of 2.75, three letters of recommendation, statement of career goals and objectives. *Application deadline:* For fall admission, 7/1 for domestic students. *Expenses:* Tuition, state resident: full-time $7068; part-time $270 per semester hour. Tuition, nonresident: full-time $26,446; part-time $1077 per semester hour. *Required fees:* $2092. *Unit head:* Dr. Trenton Davis, Director, 912-478-5430, Fax: 912-478-8029, E-mail: tjdavis@georgiasouthern.edu. *Application contact:* Amanda Gilliland, Coordinator for Graduate Student Recruitment, 912-478-5384, Fax: 912-478-0740, E-mail: gradadmissions@georgiasouthern.edu.
Website: http://class.georgiasouthern.edu/ipns/online-certificate/.

Georgia State University, Andrew Young School of Policy Studies, Department of Public Management and Policy, Atlanta, GA 30303. Offers criminal justice (MPA); disaster management (Certificate); disaster policy (MPA); environmental policy (PhD); health policy (PhD); management and finance (MPA); nonprofit management (MPA, Certificate); nonprofit policy (MPA); planning and economic development (MPP, Certificate); policy analysis and evaluation (MPA), including planning and economic development; public and nonprofit management (PhD); public finance and budgeting (PhD), including science and technology policy, urban and regional economic development; public finance policy (MPA), including social policy; public health (MPA). *Accreditation:* NASPAA (one or more programs are accredited). Part-time programs available. *Faculty:* 17 full-time (8 women), 3 part-time/adjunct (0 women). *Students:* 139 full-time (76 women), 95 part-time (59 women); includes 98 minority (69 Black or African American, non-Hispanic/Latino; 9 Asian, non-Hispanic/Latino; 11 Hispanic/Latino; 9 Two or more races, non-Hispanic/Latino), 19 international. Average age 29. 310 applicants, 55% accepted, 68 enrolled. In 2013, 68 master's, 9 other advanced degrees awarded. Terminal master's awarded for partial completion of doctoral program. *Degree requirements:* For master's, thesis optional; for doctorate, comprehensive exam, thesis/dissertation. *Entrance requirements:* For master's and doctorate, GRE. Additional exam requirements/recommendations for international students: Required—TOEFL (minimum score 603 paper-based; 100 iBT) or IELTS (minimum score 7). *Application deadline:* For fall admission, 2/15 for domestic and international students; for spring admission, 10/1 for domestic and international students. Application fee: $50. Electronic applications accepted. *Expenses:* Tuition, area resident: Full-time $4176; part-time $348 per credit hour. Tuition, state resident: full-time $14,544; part-time $1212 per credit hour. Tuition, nonresident: full-time $14,544; part-time $1212 per credit hour. Tuition and fees vary according to course load and program. *Financial support:* In 2013–14, fellowships (averaging $8,194 per year), research assistantships (averaging $8,068 per year), teaching assistantships (averaging $3,600 per year) were awarded; institutionally sponsored loans, scholarships/grants, health care benefits, and unspecified assistantships also available. Financial award application deadline: 2/1. *Faculty research:* Public budgeting and finance, public management, nonprofit management, performance measurement and management, urban development. *Unit head:* Dr. Gregory Burr Lewis, Chair and Professor, 404-413-0114, Fax: 404-413-0104, E-mail: glewis@gsu.edu. *Application contact:* Charisma Parker, Admissions Coordinator, 404-413-0030, Fax: 404-413-0023, E-mail: cparker28@gsu.edu.
Website: http://aysps.gsu.edu/pmap/.

Gratz College, Graduate Programs, Program in Jewish Non-Profit Management, Melrose Park, PA 19027. Offers Graduate Certificate.

Hamline University, School of Business, St. Paul, MN 55104-1284. Offers business administration (MBA); nonprofit management (MA); public administration (MA, DPA); JD/MA; JD/MBA; LL M/MA; LL M/MBA; MBA/MA. Part-time and evening/weekend programs available. Postbaccalaureate distance learning degree programs offered (minimal on-campus study). *Faculty:* 13 full-time (4 women), 26 part-time/adjunct (7 women). *Students:* 114 full-time (55 women), 325 part-time (148 women); includes 39 minority (17 Black or African American, non-Hispanic/Latino; 2 American Indian or Alaska Native, non-Hispanic/Latino; 13 Asian, non-Hispanic/Latino; 5 Hispanic/Latino; 2 Two or more races, non-Hispanic/Latino), 26 international. Average age 32. 216 applicants, 80% accepted, 134 enrolled. In 2013, 203 master's, 3 doctorates awarded. *Degree requirements:* For master's, thesis (for some programs); for doctorate, comprehensive exam, thesis/dissertation. *Entrance requirements:* For master's, personal statement, official transcripts, curriculum vitae, letters of recommendation, writing sample; for doctorate, personal statement, curriculum vitae, official transcripts, letters of recommendation, writing sample. Additional exam requirements/recommendations for international students: Required—TOEFL (minimum score 550 paper-based; 80 iBT). *Application deadline:* Applications are processed on a rolling basis. Application fee: $0 ($100 for international students). Electronic applications accepted. *Financial support:* Career-related internships or fieldwork, Federal Work-Study, scholarships/grants, and unspecified assistantships available. Support available to part-time students. Financial award applicants required to submit FAFSA. *Faculty research:* Liberal arts-based business programs, experiential learning, organizational process/politics, gender differences, social equity. *Unit head:* Dr. Anne McCarthy, Dean, 651-523-2284, Fax: 651-523-3098, E-mail: amccarthy02@hamline.edu. *Application contact:* Shawn Skoog, Director of Graduate Recruitment and Admission, 651-523-2900, Fax: 651-523-3058, E-mail: sskoog03@hamline.edu.
Website: http://www.hamline.edu/business.

Hebrew Union College–Jewish Institute of Religion, School of Jewish Nonprofit Management, Los Angeles, CA 90007. Offers MA.

High Point University, Norcross Graduate School, High Point, NC 27262-3598. Offers business administration (MBA); educational leadership (M Ed); elementary education (M Ed); history (MA); nonprofit management (MA); secondary math (M Ed); special education (M Ed); strategic communication (MA); teaching elementary education k-6 (MAT); teaching secondary mathematics 9-12 (MAT). *Accreditation:* NCATE. Part-time and evening/weekend programs available. *Degree requirements:* For master's, comprehensive exam (for some programs), thesis (for some programs). *Entrance requirements:* For master's, GMAT (MBA), GRE, MAT, minimum GPA of 3.0. Additional exam requirements/recommendations for international students: Required—TOEFL (minimum score 550 paper-based). Electronic applications accepted.

Hope International University, School of Graduate and Professional Studies, Program in Business Administration, Fullerton, CA 92831-3138. Offers general management (MBA, MSM); international development (MBA, MSM); marketing management (MBA, MSM); non-profit management (MBA, MSM). Part-time programs available. Postbaccalaureate distance learning degree programs offered (no on-campus study). *Degree requirements:* For master's, comprehensive exam (for some programs), thesis (for some programs), project. *Entrance requirements:* For master's, minimum GPA of 3.0; 2 references. Additional exam requirements/recommendations for international students: Required—TOEFL (minimum score 550 paper-based; 86 iBT);

Recommended—IELTS (minimum score 6.5). Electronic applications accepted. *Expenses:* Contact institution.

Husson University, Master of Business Administration Program, Bangor, ME 04401-2999. Offers general business administration (MBA); healthcare management (MBA); hospitality and tourism management (MBA); non-profit management (MBA). Part-time and evening/weekend programs available. *Faculty:* 7 full-time (4 women), 16 part-time/adjunct (3 women). *Students:* 91 full-time (55 women), 87 part-time (47 women); includes 21 minority (7 Black or African American, non-Hispanic/Latino; 11 Asian, non-Hispanic/Latino; 3 Two or more races, non-Hispanic/Latino), 4 international. 112 applicants, 88% accepted, 86 enrolled. In 2013, 163 master's awarded. *Degree requirements:* For master's, comprehensive exam (for some programs), thesis optional. *Entrance requirements:* For master's, GMAT or GRE, minimum GPA of 3.0. Additional exam requirements/recommendations for international students: Required—TOEFL (minimum score 550 paper-based). *Application deadline:* Applications are processed on a rolling basis. Application fee: $40. Electronic applications accepted. *Expenses:* Contact institution. *Financial support:* In 2013–14, 6 students received support. Career-related internships or fieldwork, Federal Work-Study, scholarships/grants, and unspecified assistantships available. Financial award application deadline: 4/15; financial award applicants required to submit FAFSA. *Unit head:* Prof. Stephanie Shayne, Director, Graduate and Online Programs, 207-404-5632, Fax: 207-992-4987, E-mail: shaynes@husson.edu. *Application contact:* Kristen Card, Director of Graduate Admissions, 207-404-5660, Fax: 207-941-7935, E-mail: cardk@husson.edu.
Website: http://www.husson.edu/mba.

Indiana University Bloomington, School of Public and Environmental Affairs, Public Affairs Programs, Bloomington, IN 47405. Offers economic development (MPA); energy (MPA); environmental policy (PhD); environmental policy and natural resource management (MPA); information systems (MPA); international development (MPA); local government management (MPA); nonprofit management (MPA, Certificate); policy analysis (MPA); public budgeting and financial management (Certificate); public finance (PhD); public financial administration (MPA); public management (MPA, PhD, Certificate); public policy analysis (PhD); social entrepreneurship (Certificate); specialized public affairs (MPA); sustainability and sustainable development (MPA); JD/MPA; MPA/MA; MPA/MIS; MPA/MLS; MSES/MPA. *Accreditation:* NASPAA (one or more programs are accredited). Part-time programs available. *Faculty:* 79 full-time (32 women), 8 part-time/adjunct (3 women). *Students:* 433 full-time (232 women), 75 part-time (39 women); includes 90 minority (19 Black or African American, non-Hispanic/Latino; 1 American Indian or Alaska Native, non-Hispanic/Latino; 49 Asian, non-Hispanic/Latino; 14 Hispanic/Latino; 2 Native Hawaiian or other Pacific Islander, non-Hispanic/Latino; 5 Two or more races, non-Hispanic/Latino), 70 international. Average age 27. 714 applicants, 73% accepted, 253 enrolled. In 2013, 171 master's, 3 doctorates, 4 other advanced degrees awarded. *Degree requirements:* For master's, capstone, internship; for doctorate, comprehensive exam, thesis/dissertation. *Entrance requirements:* For master's, GRE General Test or GMAT, official transcripts, 3 letters of recommendation, resume, personal statement; for doctorate, GRE General Test, official transcripts, 3 letters of recommendation, statement of purpose. Additional exam requirements/recommendations for international students: Required—TOEFL (minimum score 600 paper-based; 96 iBT); Recommended—IELTS (minimum score 7). *Application deadline:* For fall admission, 2/1 priority date for domestic students, 12/1 priority date for international students; for spring admission, 11/15 for domestic students, 9/1 for international students. Applications are processed on a rolling basis. Application fee: $55 ($65 for international students). Electronic applications accepted. *Financial support:* Fellowships with partial tuition reimbursements, research assistantships with full and partial tuition reimbursements, teaching assistantships with full and partial tuition reimbursements, career-related internships or fieldwork, Federal Work-Study, scholarships/grants, health care benefits, unspecified assistantships, and Service Corps Program; Educational Opportunity Fellowships available. Financial award application deadline: 2/1; financial award applicants required to submit FAFSA. *Faculty research:* International development, environmental policy and resource management, policy analysis, public finance, public management, urban management, nonprofit management, energy policy, social policy, public finance. *Unit head:* Megan Siehl, Assistant Director, Admissions and Financial Aid, 812-855-9485, Fax: 812-856-3665, E-mail: speampo@indiana.edu. *Application contact:* Lane Bowman, Admissions Services Coordinator, 812-855-2840, Fax: 812-856-3665, E-mail: speaapps@indiana.edu.
Website: http://www.indiana.edu/~spea/prospective_students/masters/.

Indiana University Northwest, School of Public and Environmental Affairs, Gary, IN 46408-1197. Offers criminal justice (MPA); environmental affairs (Graduate Certificate); health services (MPA); human services (MPA); nonprofit management (Certificate); public management (MPA). *Accreditation:* NASPAA (one or more programs are accredited). Part-time programs available. *Faculty:* 5 full-time (3 women). *Students:* 17 full-time (13 women), 73 part-time (49 women); includes 62 minority (48 Black or African American, non-Hispanic/Latino; 2 Asian, non-Hispanic/Latino; 12 Hispanic/Latino). Average age 38. 25 applicants, 92% accepted, 21 enrolled. In 2013, 27 master's, 26 other advanced degrees awarded. *Entrance requirements:* For master's, GRE General Test or GMAT, letters of recommendation. *Application deadline:* For fall admission, 8/15 priority date for domestic students. Applications are processed on a rolling basis. *Financial support:* Career-related internships or fieldwork, Federal Work-Study, and tuition waivers (partial) available. Support available to part-time students. Financial award application deadline: 3/1. *Faculty research:* Employment in income security policies, evidence in criminal justice, equal employment law, social welfare policy and welfare reform, public finance in developing countries. *Unit head:* Dr. Barbara Peat, Department Chair, 219-981-5645. *Application contact:* Tierra Jackson, Senior Secretary, 219-981-5616, E-mail: jacksoti@iun.edu.
Website: http://www.iun.edu/spea/index.htm.

Indiana University–Purdue University Indianapolis, School of Public and Environmental Affairs, Indianapolis, IN 46202. Offers criminal justice and public safety (MS); homeland security and emergency management (Graduate Certificate); library management (Graduate Certificate); nonprofit management (Graduate Certificate); public affairs (MPA); public management (Graduate Certificate); social entrepreneurship: nonprofit and public benefit organizations (Graduate Certificate); JD/MPA; MLS/NMC; MLS/PMC; MPA/MA. *Accreditation:* CAHME (one or more programs are accredited); NASPAA. Part-time and evening/weekend programs available. Postbaccalaureate distance learning degree programs offered (no on-campus study). *Entrance requirements:* For master's, GRE General Test, GMAT or LSAT, minimum GPA of 3.0 (preferred). Additional exam requirements/recommendations for international students: Required—TOEFL (minimum score 93 iBT), IELTS (minimum score 6.5). Electronic applications accepted. *Faculty research:* Nonprofit and public management, public policy, urban policy, sustainability policy, disaster preparedness and recovery, vehicular safety, homicide, offender rehabilitation and re-entry.

Iona College, School of Arts and Science, Department of Mass Communication, New Rochelle, NY 10801-1890. Offers non-profit public relations (Certificate); public relations (MA). *Accreditation:* ACEJMC (one or more programs are accredited). Part-time and evening/weekend programs available. *Faculty:* 3 full-time (0 women), 2 part-time/adjunct (both women). *Students:* 12 full-time (8 women), 24 part-time (19 women); includes 8 minority (5 Black or African American, non-Hispanic/Latino; 3 Hispanic/Latino), 9 international. Average age 27. 29 applicants, 86% accepted, 17 enrolled. In 2013, 16 master's, 6 other advanced degrees awarded. *Degree requirements:* For master's, comprehensive exam (for some programs), thesis or alternative. *Entrance requirements:* For master's, GRE General Test, Required if undergraduate GPA is below 3.0. Additional exam requirements/recommendations for international students: Required—TOEFL (minimum score 550 paper-based; 80 iBT), IELTS (minimum score 6). *Application deadline:* For fall admission, 8/1 for domestic students, 5/1 for international students; for spring admission, 1/1 for domestic students, 9/1 for international students. Applications are processed on a rolling basis. Application fee: $50. Electronic applications accepted. *Expenses:* Contact institution. *Financial support:* In 2013–14, 13 students received support. Scholarships/grants, tuition waivers (partial), and unspecified assistantships available. Support available to part-time students. Financial award application deadline: 4/15; financial award applicants required to submit FAFSA. *Faculty research:* Media ecology, new media, corporate communication, media images, organizational learning in public relations. *Unit head:* Robert Petrausch, PhD, Chair, 914-633-2354, E-mail: rpetausch@iona.edu. *Application contact:* Veronica Jarek-Prinz, Director, Graduate Admissions, 914-633-2420, Fax: 914-633-2277, E-mail: vjarekprinz@iona.edu.
Website: http://www.iona.edu/Academics/School-of-Arts-Science/Departments/Mass-Communication/Graduate-Programs.aspx.

John Carroll University, Graduate School, Program in Nonprofit Administration, University Heights, OH 44118-4581. Offers MA. Part-time and evening/weekend programs available. *Degree requirements:* For master's, thesis optional. *Entrance requirements:* For master's, minimum GPA of 3.0, interview. Additional exam requirements/recommendations for international students: Required—TOEFL. Electronic applications accepted.

Johns Hopkins University, Zanvyl Krieger School of Arts and Sciences, Advanced Academic Programs, Program in Government, Washington, DC 20036. Offers global security studies (MA); government (MA); national securities study (Certificate); nonprofit management (Certificate); public management (MA); research administration (MS); MA/MBA. Part-time and evening/weekend programs available. Postbaccalaureate distance learning degree programs offered (minimal on-campus study). *Faculty:* 4 full-time (2 women), 35 part-time/adjunct (5 women). *Students:* 81 full-time (40 women), 77 part-time (37 women); includes 40 minority (13 Black or African American, non-Hispanic/Latino; 14 Asian, non-Hispanic/Latino; 10 Hispanic/Latino; 3 Two or more races, non-Hispanic/Latino), 8 international. Average age 28. 30 applicants, 97% accepted, 26 enrolled. In 2013, 89 master's awarded. *Degree requirements:* For master's, thesis. *Entrance requirements:* For master's, minimum GPA of 3.0. Additional exam requirements/recommendations for international students: Required—TOEFL (minimum score 100 iBT). *Application deadline:* For fall admission, 5/31 priority date for domestic students, 4/30 priority date for international students; for spring admission, 10/31 priority date for domestic and international students. Applications are processed on a rolling basis. Application fee: $75. Electronic applications accepted. *Financial support:* Applicants required to submit FAFSA. *Unit head:* Dr. Kathy Wagner, Program Director, 202-452-1953, E-mail: kwagner@jhu.edu. *Application contact:* Melissa Edwards, Admissions Manager, 202-452-1941, Fax: 202-452-1970, E-mail: aapadmissions@jhu.edu.
Website: http://advanced.jhu.edu/academics/graduate-degree-programs/government/.

Kean University, College of Business and Public Management, Program in Public Administration, Union, NJ 07083. Offers environmental management (MPA); health services administration (MPA); non-profit management (MPA); public administration (MPA). *Accreditation:* NASPAA. Part-time programs available. *Faculty:* 13 full-time (4 women). *Students:* 64 full-time (38 women), 81 part-time (47 women); includes 100 minority (69 Black or African American, non-Hispanic/Latino; 7 Asian, non-Hispanic/Latino; 22 Hispanic/Latino; 2 Two or more races, non-Hispanic/Latino), 3 international. Average age 32. 76 applicants, 82% accepted, 40 enrolled. In 2013, 48 master's awarded. *Degree requirements:* For master's, thesis, internship, research seminar. *Entrance requirements:* For master's, minimum cumulative GPA of 3.0, official transcripts from all institutions attended, two letters of recommendation, personal statement, writing sample, professional resume/curriculum vitae. Additional exam requirements/recommendations for international students: Required—TOEFL (minimum score 550 paper-based; 79 iBT). *Application deadline:* For fall admission, 6/1 for domestic and international students; for spring admission, 12/1 for domestic and international students. Applications are processed on a rolling basis. Application fee: $75 ($150 for international students). Electronic applications accepted. *Expenses:* Tuition, state resident: full-time $12,099; part-time $589 per credit. Tuition, nonresident: full-time $16,399; part-time $722 per credit. *Required fees:* $3050; $139 per credit. Part-time tuition and fees vary according to course level, course load, degree level and program. *Financial support:* In 2013–14, 17 research assistantships with full tuition reimbursements (averaging $3,713 per year) were awarded; unspecified assistantships also available. Financial award applicants required to submit FAFSA. *Unit head:* Dr. Patricia Moore, Program Coordinator, 908-737-4314, E-mail: pmoore@kean.edu. *Application contact:* Reenat Hasan, Admissions Counselor, 908-737-5923, Fax: 908-737-5925, E-mail: hasanr@kean.edu.
Website: http://grad.kean.edu/masters-programs/public-administration.

Kentucky State University, College of Professional Studies, Frankfort, KY 40601. Offers public administration (MPA), including human resource management, international development, management information systems, nonprofit management; special education (MA). Part-time and evening/weekend programs available. Postbaccalaureate distance learning degree programs offered (minimal on-campus study). *Degree requirements:* For master's, comprehensive exam, thesis optional. *Entrance requirements:* For master's, GMAT, GRE. Additional exam requirements/recommendations for international students: Required—TOEFL (minimum score 525 paper-based). Electronic applications accepted.

La Salle University, College of Professional and Continuing Studies, Program in Nonprofit Leadership, Philadelphia, PA 19141-1199. Offers MS. Part-time and evening/weekend programs available. Postbaccalaureate distance learning degree programs offered. *Degree requirements:* For master's, successful completion of all required courses within seven-year period; minimum cumulative GPA of 3.0. *Entrance requirements:* For master's, professional resume; personal statement explaining the applicant's interest in and goals for pursuit of this degree; 2 letters of recommendation. Additional exam requirements/recommendations for international students: Required—TOEFL. *Application deadline:* For fall admission, 8/15 priority date for domestic students, 7/15 for international students; for spring admission, 12/15 priority date for domestic students, 11/15 for international students; for summer admission, 4/15 priority date for domestic students, 3/15 for international students. Applications are processed on a rolling basis. Application fee: $35. Electronic applications accepted. Application fee is waived when completed online. *Expenses: Tuition:* Full-time $20,750; part-time $695 per credit hour. *Required fees:* $300; $200 per year. Tuition and fees vary according to program. *Financial support:* Federal Work-Study and scholarships/grants available. Support available to part-time students. Financial award application deadline: 8/31;

financial award applicants required to submit FAFSA. *Unit head:* Laura Otten, Director, 215-991-3682, Fax: 215-951-1960, E-mail: npl@lasalle.edu. *Application contact:* Lynnette Clement, Online Program Coordinator, Nonprofit Leadership, 215-991-3682, Fax: 215-951-1960, E-mail: clementl@lasalle.edu.
Website: http://www.lasalle.edu/grad/index.php?section=nonprofit&page=index.

Lasell College, Graduate and Professional Studies in Management, Newton, MA 02466-2709. Offers business administration (PMBA); elder care management (MSM, Graduate Certificate); elder care marketing (MSM); human resource management (Graduate Certificate); human resources management (MSM); integrated marketing communication (Graduate Certificate); management (MSM, Graduate Certificate); marketing (MSM, Graduate Certificate); non-profit management (MSM, Graduate Certificate); project management (MSM, Graduate Certificate); public relations (Graduate Certificate). Part-time and evening/weekend programs available. Postbaccalaureate distance learning degree programs offered (no on-campus study). *Faculty:* 3 full-time (1 woman), 16 part-time/adjunct (9 women). *Students:* 46 full-time (33 women), 105 part-time (73 women); includes 35 minority (24 Black or African American, non-Hispanic/Latino; 1 American Indian or Alaska Native, non-Hispanic/Latino; 3 Asian, non-Hispanic/Latino; 7 Hispanic/Latino), 22 international. Average age 32. 88 applicants, 55% accepted, 29 enrolled. In 2013, 61 master's awarded. *Entrance requirements:* For master's and Graduate Certificate, bachelor's degree from an accredited institution. Additional exam requirements/recommendations for international students: Required—TOEFL (minimum score 550 paper-based; 79 iBT). *Application deadline:* For fall admission, 8/31 priority date for domestic students, 6/30 priority date for international students; for spring admission, 12/31 priority date for domestic students, 10/31 priority date for international students. Applications are processed on a rolling basis. Electronic applications accepted. *Expenses: Tuition:* Part-time $575 per credit. *Required fees:* $80 per semester. *Financial support:* Available to part-time students. Application deadline: 8/31; applicants required to submit FAFSA. *Unit head:* Dr. Joan Dolamore, Dean of Graduate and Professional Studies, 617-243-2485, Fax: 617-243-2450, E-mail: gradinfo@lasell.edu. *Application contact:* Adrienne Franciosi, Director of Graduate Admission, 617-243-2214, Fax: 617-243-2450, E-mail: gradinfo@lasell.edu.
Website: http://www.lasell.edu/Academics/Graduate-and-Professional-Studies/MS-in-Management.html.

Lasell College, Graduate and Professional Studies in Sport Management, Newton, MA 02466-2709. Offers sport hospitality management (MS, Graduate Certificate); sport leadership (MS, Graduate Certificate); sport non-profit management (MS, Graduate Certificate). Part-time programs available. Postbaccalaureate distance learning degree programs offered (no on-campus study). *Faculty:* 2 full-time (0 women), 6 part-time/adjunct (5 women). *Students:* 13 full-time (4 women), 42 part-time (16 women); includes 17 minority (11 Black or African American, non-Hispanic/Latino; 3 American Indian or Alaska Native, non-Hispanic/Latino; 2 Hispanic/Latino; 1 Two or more races, non-Hispanic/Latino). Average age 30. 34 applicants, 62% accepted, 11 enrolled. In 2013, 11 master's awarded. *Entrance requirements:* For master's and Graduate Certificate, bachelor's degree from an accredited institution. Additional exam requirements/recommendations for international students: Required—TOEFL (minimum score 550 paper-based; 79 iBT), IELTS. *Application deadline:* For fall admission, 8/31 priority date for domestic students, 6/30 priority date for international students; for spring admission, 12/31 priority date for domestic students, 10/31 priority date for international students. Applications are processed on a rolling basis. Electronic applications accepted. *Expenses: Tuition:* Part-time $575 per credit. *Required fees:* $80 per semester. *Financial support:* Available to part-time students. Application deadline: 8/31; applicants required to submit FAFSA. *Unit head:* Dr. Joan Dolamore, Dean of Graduate and Professional Studies, 617-243-2485, Fax: 617-243-2450, E-mail: gradinfo@lasell.edu. *Application contact:* Adrienne Franciosi, Director of Graduate Admission, 617-243-2214, Fax: 617-243-2450, E-mail: gradinfo@lasell.edu.
Website: http://www.lasell.edu/Academics/Graduate-and-Professional-Studies/MS-in-Sport-Management-.html.

Lewis University, College of Arts and Sciences, Program in Organizational Leadership, Romeoville, IL 60446. Offers coaching (MA); higher education/student services (MA); non-for-profit management (MA); organizational management (MA); public administration (MA); training and development (MA). Part-time and evening/weekend programs available. Postbaccalaureate distance learning degree programs offered (no on-campus study). *Students:* 24 full-time (21 women), 200 part-time (152 women); includes 87 minority (60 Black or African American, non-Hispanic/Latino; 2 American Indian or Alaska Native, non-Hispanic/Latino; 4 Asian, non-Hispanic/Latino; 20 Hispanic/Latino; 1 Two or more races, non-Hispanic/Latino), 1 international. Average age 36. *Entrance requirements:* For master's, bachelor's degree, at least 24 years of age, minimum of 3 years of work experience, minimum GPA of 3.0, letter of recommendation. Additional exam requirements/recommendations for international students: Required—TOEFL (minimum score 550 paper-based; 80 iBT). *Application deadline:* For fall admission, 5/1 priority date for international students; for spring admission, 11/15 priority date for international students. Applications are processed on a rolling basis. Application fee: $40. Electronic applications accepted. *Financial support:* Tuition waivers and unspecified assistantships available. Financial award application deadline: 5/1; financial award applicants required to submit FAFSA. *Unit head:* Dr. Keith Lavine, Chair of Organizational Leadership, 815-838-0500, E-mail: lavineke@lewisu.edu. *Application contact:* Julie Branchaw, Assistant Director, Graduate and Adult Admission, 815-836-5574, Fax: 815-836-5578, E-mail: branchju@lewisu.edu.

Lindenwood University, Graduate Programs, School of Human Services, St. Charles, MO 63301-1695. Offers nonprofit administration (MA); public administration (MPA). Part-time programs available. Postbaccalaureate distance learning degree programs offered (no on-campus study). *Faculty:* 3 full-time (1 woman), 2 part-time/adjunct (1 woman). *Students:* 26 full-time (18 women), 42 part-time (28 women); includes 35 minority (33 Black or African American, non-Hispanic/Latino; 1 American Indian or Alaska Native, non-Hispanic/Latino; 1 Two or more races, non-Hispanic/Latino), 4 international. Average age 35. 48 applicants, 63% accepted, 25 enrolled. In 2013, 11 master's awarded. *Degree requirements:* For master's, minimum cumulative GPA of 3.0, directed internship, capstone project. *Entrance requirements:* Additional exam requirements/recommendations for international students: Required—TOEFL (minimum score 550 paper-based; 80 iBT). *Application deadline:* For fall admission, 8/26 priority date for domestic and international students; for spring admission, 1/27 priority date for domestic and international students. Applications are processed on a rolling basis. Application fee: $30 ($100 for international students). Electronic applications accepted. *Expenses: Tuition:* Full-time $14,800; part-time $428 per credit hour. *Required fees:* $350. Tuition and fees vary according to course level and course load. *Financial support:* In 2013–14, 42 students received support. Career-related internships or fieldwork, institutionally sponsored loans, scholarships/grants, tuition waivers, and unspecified assistantships available. Financial award application deadline: 6/30; financial award applicants required to submit FAFSA. *Unit head:* Carla Mueller, Dean, 636-949-4731, E-mail: cmueller@lindenwood.edu. *Application contact:* Brett Barger, Dean of Evening Admissions and Extension Campuses, 636-949-4934, Fax: 636-949-4109, E-mail: adultadmissions@lindenwood.edu.
Website: http://www.lindenwood.edu/humanServices/.

Lipscomb University, Graduate School of Business, Nashville, TN 37204-3951. Offers accountancy (M Acc); accounting (MBA); conflict management (MBA); distributive (general) (MBA); financial services (MBA); health care informatics (MBA); healthcare management (MBA); human resources (MHR); information security (MBA); leadership (MBA); nonprofit management (MBA); professional accountancy (Certificate); sports management (MBA); strategic human resources (MBA); sustainability (MBA); MBA/MS. *Accreditation:* ACBSP. Part-time and evening/weekend programs available. *Faculty:* 12 full-time (1 woman), 12 part-time/adjunct (2 women). *Students:* 90 full-time (44 women), 104 part-time (51 women); includes 28 minority (24 Black or African American, non-Hispanic/Latino; 3 Hispanic/Latino; 1 Two or more races, non-Hispanic/Latino), 6 international. Average age 33. 145 applicants, 79% accepted, 69 enrolled. In 2013, 98 master's, 1 other advanced degree awarded. *Entrance requirements:* For master's, GMAT, transcripts, interview, 2 references, resume. Additional exam requirements/recommendations for international students: Required—TOEFL (minimum score 570 paper-based). *Application deadline:* For fall admission, 6/15 for domestic students, 2/1 for international students; for winter admission, 6/1 for international students; for spring admission, 11/15 for domestic students. Applications are processed on a rolling basis. Application fee: $50 ($75 for international students). Electronic applications accepted. *Expenses:* Contact institution. *Financial support:* Career-related internships or fieldwork, scholarships/grants, tuition waivers (partial), and unspecified assistantships available. Support available to part-time students. Financial award application deadline: 7/1; financial award applicants required to submit FAFSA. *Faculty research:* Impact of spirituality on organization commitment, women in corporate leadership, psychological empowerment, training. *Unit head:* Joe Ivey, Associate Dean of Graduate Business Programs, 615-966-6229, Fax: 615-966-1818, E-mail: joe.ivey@lipscomb.edu. *Application contact:* Lisa Shacklett, Assistant Dean of Enrollment and Marketing, 615-966-5968, E-mail: lisa.shacklett@lipscomb.edu.
Website: http://www.lipscomb.edu/business/Graduate-Programs.

Long Island University–LIU Post, College of Management, Department of Health Care and Public Administration, Brookville, NY 11548-1300. Offers gerontology (Certificate); health care administration (MPA); health care administration/gerontology (MPA); nonprofit management (MPA, Certificate); public administration (MPA). *Accreditation:* NASPAA (one or more programs are accredited). Part-time and evening/weekend programs available. *Degree requirements:* For master's, thesis. *Entrance requirements:* For master's, GMAT, minimum GPA of 2.5; for Certificate, minimum GPA of 2.5. Electronic applications accepted. *Faculty research:* Critical issues in sexuality, social work in religious communities, gerontological social work.

Long Island University–LIU Post, School of Health Professions and Nursing, Master of Social Work Program, Brookville, NY 11548-1300. Offers alcohol and substance abuse (MSW); child and family welfare (MSW); forensic social work (MSW); gerontology (MSW); nonprofit management (MSW). *Accreditation:* CSWE.

Marlboro College, Graduate and Professional Studies, Program in Managing Mission-Driven Organizations, Brattleboro, VT 05301. Offers MSM. Part-time and evening/weekend programs available. Postbaccalaureate distance learning degree programs offered (minimal on-campus study). *Faculty:* 1 (woman) full-time, 13 part-time/adjunct (8 women). *Students:* 7 full-time (3 women), 10 part-time (9 women). Average age 35. 14 applicants, 71% accepted, 5 enrolled. In 2013, 4 master's awarded. *Degree requirements:* For master's, 36 credits including capstone project. *Entrance requirements:* For master's, letter of intent, 2 letters of recommendation, transcripts. *Application deadline:* For fall admission, 7/1 priority date for domestic students; for winter admission, 11/1 priority date for domestic students; for spring admission, 3/1 priority date for domestic students. Applications are processed on a rolling basis. Application fee: $0. Electronic applications accepted. *Expenses: Tuition:* Part-time $685 per credit. Tuition and fees vary according to course load and program. *Financial support:* Applicants required to submit FAFSA. *Unit head:* Kate Jellema, Degree Chair, 802-451-7510, Fax: 802-258-9201, E-mail: katej@marlboro.edu. *Application contact:* Matthew Livingston, Director of Graduate Admissions, 802-258-9209, Fax: 802-258-9201, E-mail: mlivingston@marlboro.edu.
Website: https://www.marlboro.edu/academics/graduate/mdo.

Marquette University, Graduate School, College of Professional Studies, Milwaukee, WI 53201-1881. Offers criminal justice administration (MLS, Certificate); dispute resolution (MDR, MLS); health care administration (MLS); leadership studies (Certificate); non-profit sector administration (MLS); public service (MAPS, MLS); sports leadership (MLS). Part-time and evening/weekend programs available. Postbaccalaureate distance learning degree programs offered (no on-campus study). *Faculty:* 3 full-time (2 women), 25 part-time/adjunct (11 women). *Students:* 29 full-time (14 women), 109 part-time (61 women); includes 28 minority (17 Black or African American, non-Hispanic/Latino; 2 American Indian or Alaska Native, non-Hispanic/Latino; 2 Asian, non-Hispanic/Latino; 5 Hispanic/Latino; 2 Two or more races, non-Hispanic/Latino), 1 international. Average age 36. 81 applicants, 81% accepted, 36 enrolled. In 2013, 42 master's, 18 Certificates awarded. *Degree requirements:* For master's, comprehensive exam (for some programs). *Entrance requirements:* For master's, GRE General Test (preferred), GMAT, or LSAT, official transcripts from all current and previous colleges/universities except Marquette, three letters of recommendation, statement of purpose. Additional exam requirements/recommendations for international students: Required—TOEFL. *Application deadline:* Applications are processed on a rolling basis. Electronic applications accepted. *Financial support:* In 2013–14, 9 students received support, including 8 fellowships with full tuition reimbursements available (averaging $16,247 per year). Financial award application deadline: 2/15. *Unit head:* Dr. Robert Deahl, Dean/Assistant Professor, 414-288-3156. *Application contact:* Eva Soeka, Director and Associate Professor, 414-288-5535.

Marylhurst University, Department of Business Administration, Marylhurst, OR 97036-0261. Offers finance (MBA); general management (MBA); government policy and administration (MBA); green development (MBA); health care management (MBA); marketing (MBA); natural and organic resources (MBA); nonprofit management (MBA); organizational behavior (MBA); real estate (MBA); renewable energy (MBA); sustainable business (MBA). Part-time and evening/weekend programs available. Postbaccalaureate distance learning degree programs offered (no on-campus study). *Degree requirements:* For master's, comprehensive exam, capstone course. *Entrance requirements:* For master's, GMAT (if GPA less than 3.0 and fewer than 5 years of work experience), interview, resume, 2 letters of recommendation. Additional exam requirements/recommendations for international students: Recommended—TOEFL (minimum score 550 paper-based; 80 iBT). Electronic applications accepted.

Marymount University, School of Business Administration, Program in Leadership and Management, Arlington, VA 22207-4299. Offers leadership (Certificate); management (MS); non-profit management (Certificate); project management (Certificate). Part-time and evening/weekend programs available. *Faculty:* 5 full-time (2 women), 1 (woman) part-time/adjunct. *Students:* 1 full-time (0 women), 22 part-time (16 women); includes 8 minority (4 Black or African American, non-Hispanic/Latino; 2 Asian, non-Hispanic/Latino; 2 Hispanic/Latino). Average age 37. 14 applicants, 93% accepted, 11 enrolled. In 2013, 7 master's, 13 other advanced degrees awarded. *Degree requirements:* For master's, thesis or alternative. *Entrance requirements:* For master's, GMAT or GRE

General Test, resume, at least 3 years of managerial experience, essay; for Certificate, resume, at least 3 years of managerial experience. Additional exam requirements/recommendations for international students: Required—TOEFL (minimum score 600 paper-based; 96 iBT), IELTS (minimum score 6.5). *Application deadline:* For fall admission, 7/15 priority date for domestic students, 7/1 for international students; for spring admission, 11/15 priority date for domestic students, 11/15 for international students. Applications are processed on a rolling basis. Application fee: $40. Electronic applications accepted. *Expenses: Tuition:* Part-time $850 per credit. *Required fees:* $10 per credit. One-time fee: $200 part-time. Tuition and fees vary according to program. *Financial support:* Research assistantships with full and partial tuition reimbursements, career-related internships or fieldwork, Federal Work-Study, scholarships/grants, and unspecified assistantships available. Support available to part-time students. Financial award applicants required to submit FAFSA. *Unit head:* Dr. Lorri Cooper, Director, Master's in Management Program, 703-284-5950, Fax: 703-527-3830, E-mail: lorri.cooper@marymount.edu. *Application contact:* Francesca Reed, Director, Graduate Admissions, 703-284-5901, Fax: 703-527-3815, E-mail: grad.admissions@marymount.edu.

Mercyhurst University, Graduate Studies, Program in Organizational Leadership, Erie, PA 16546. Offers accounting (MS); entrepreneurship (MS); higher education administration (MS); human resources (MS); nonprofit management (MS); organizational leadership (Certificate); sports leadership (MS). Part-time and evening/weekend programs available. *Degree requirements:* For master's, thesis. *Entrance requirements:* For master's, GRE General Test or MAT, interview, resume, essay, three professional references, transcripts. Additional exam requirements/recommendations for international students: Required—TOEFL. Electronic applications accepted. *Faculty research:* Leadership training, organizational communication, leadership pedagogy.

Metropolitan State University, College of Management, St. Paul, MN 55106-5000. Offers business administration (MBA, DBA); database administration (Graduate Certificate); healthcare information technology management (Graduate Certificate); information assurance security (Graduate Certificate); management information systems (MMIS); MIS generalist (Graduate Certificate); MIS systems analysis and design (Graduate Certificate); project management (Graduate Certificate); public and nonprofit administration (MPNA). Part-time and evening/weekend programs available. *Degree requirements:* For master's, thesis optional, computer language (MMIS). *Entrance requirements:* For master's, GMAT (for MBA), resume. Additional exam requirements/recommendations for international students: Required—TOEFL (minimum score 550 paper-based). Electronic applications accepted. *Expenses:* Tuition, state resident: full-time $5548. Tuition, nonresident: full-time $10,929. *Faculty research:* Yugoslav economic system, workers' cooperatives, participative management and job enrichment, global business systems.

MidAmerica Nazarene University, Graduate Studies in Management, Olathe, KS 66062-1899. Offers management (MBA); organizational administration (MA), including finance, international business, leadership, non-profit. Evening/weekend programs available. *Entrance requirements:* For master's, mathematical assessment, minimum undergraduate GPA of 3.0, letters of recommendation. Additional exam requirements/recommendations for international students: Required—TOEFL. Electronic applications accepted. *Faculty research:* Economic development, international finance, business development, employee evaluation.

Misericordia University, College of Professional Studies and Social Sciences, Program in Organizational Management, Dallas, PA 18612-1098. Offers human resource management (MS); information technology management (MS); management (MS); not-for-profit management (MS). Part-time and evening/weekend programs available. Postbaccalaureate distance learning degree programs offered (no on-campus study). *Faculty:* 3 full-time (0 women), 6 part-time/adjunct (0 women). *Students:* 82 part-time (53 women); includes 2 minority (1 Hispanic/Latino; 1 Native Hawaiian or other Pacific Islander, non-Hispanic/Latino). Average age 33. In 2013, 25 master's awarded. *Entrance requirements:* For master's, GRE General Test, MAT (35th percentile or higher), or minimum undergraduate GPA of 3.0. Additional exam requirements/recommendations for international students: Required—TOEFL. *Application deadline:* Applications are processed on a rolling basis. Application fee: $35. Electronic applications accepted. Application fee is waived when completed online. *Expenses:* Contact institution. *Financial support:* In 2013–14, 55 students received support. Scholarships/grants available. Support available to part-time students. Financial award application deadline: 6/30; financial award applicants required to submit FAFSA. *Unit head:* Dr. Timothy Kearney, Chair of Business Department, 570-674-1487, E-mail: tkearney@misericordia.edu. *Application contact:* David Pasquini, Assistant Director of Admissions, 570-674-8183, Fax: 570-674-6232, E-mail: dpasquin@misericordia.edu. Website: http://www.misericordia.edu/om.

New England College, Program in Management, Henniker, NH 03242-3293. Offers accounting (MSA); healthcare administration (MS); international relations (MA); marketing management (MS); nonprofit leadership (MS); project management (MS); strategic leadership (MS). Part-time and evening/weekend programs available. *Degree requirements:* For master's, independent research project. Electronic applications accepted.

New Mexico Highlands University, Graduate Studies, School of Business, Media and Technology, Las Vegas, NM 87701. Offers business administration (MBA), including government nonprofit management, human resource management, international business, management, management information systems; media arts and technology (MA), including media arts and computer science. *Accreditation:* ACBSP. *Faculty:* 13 full-time (5 women). *Students:* 65 full-time (34 women), 146 part-time (89 women); includes 137 minority (3 Black or African American, non-Hispanic/Latino; 9 American Indian or Alaska Native, non-Hispanic/Latino; 1 Asian, non-Hispanic/Latino; 120 Hispanic/Latino; 2 Native Hawaiian or other Pacific Islander, non-Hispanic/Latino; 2 Two or more races, non-Hispanic/Latino), 23 international. Average age 34. In 2013, 56 master's awarded. *Degree requirements:* For master's, comprehensive exam, thesis or alternative. *Entrance requirements:* For master's, minimum undergraduate GPA of 3.0. Additional exam requirements/recommendations for international students: Required—TOEFL (minimum score 540 paper-based). *Application deadline:* For fall admission, 8/1 priority date for domestic students. Applications are processed on a rolling basis. Application fee: $15. *Expenses:* Tuition, state resident: full-time $4278; part-time $178 per credit hour. Tuition, nonresident: full-time $6716; part-time $281 per credit hour. One-time fee: $15. *Financial support:* Career-related internships or fieldwork, Federal Work-Study, institutionally sponsored loans, scholarships/grants, tuition waivers (full and partial), and unspecified assistantships available. Support available to part-time students. Financial award application deadline: 3/1; financial award applicants required to submit FAFSA. *Faculty research:* Real estate valuation, studying expert judgments in complex accounting, decision environments, green marketing, environmentalism, marketing research methodology. *Unit head:* Dr. Margaret Young, Dean, 505-454-3522, Fax: 505-454-3354, E-mail: young_m@nmhu.edu. *Application contact:* Diane Trujillo, Administrative Assistant, Graduate Studies, 505-454-3266, Fax: 505-426-2117, E-mail: dtrujillo@nmhu.edu.

New Mexico Highlands University, Graduate Studies, School of Social Work, Las Vegas, NM 87701. Offers bilingual/bicultural clinical practice (MSW); clinical practice (MSW); government non-profit management (MSW). *Accreditation:* CSWE. Part-time programs available. *Faculty:* 19 full-time (9 women), 49 part-time/adjunct (32 women). *Students:* 65 full-time (34 women), 146 part-time (89 women); includes 137 minority (3 Black or African American, non-Hispanic/Latino; 9 American Indian or Alaska Native, non-Hispanic/Latino; 1 Asian, non-Hispanic/Latino; 120 Hispanic/Latino; 2 Native Hawaiian or other Pacific Islander, non-Hispanic/Latino; 2 Two or more races, non-Hispanic/Latino), 23 international. Average age 34. 259 applicants, 98% accepted, 148 enrolled. In 2013, 145 master's awarded. *Degree requirements:* For master's, comprehensive exam, thesis or alternative. *Entrance requirements:* For master's, minimum undergraduate GPA of 3.0. Additional exam requirements/recommendations for international students: Required—TOEFL (minimum score 540 paper-based). *Application deadline:* For fall admission, 1/15 priority date for domestic students. Applications are processed on a rolling basis. Application fee: $15. *Expenses:* Tuition, state resident: full-time $4278; part-time $178 per credit hour. Tuition, nonresident: full-time $6716; part-time $281 per credit hour. One-time fee: $15. *Financial support:* Career-related internships or fieldwork, Federal Work-Study, institutionally sponsored loans, scholarships/grants, tuition waivers (partial), and unspecified assistantships available. Support available to part-time students. Financial award application deadline: 3/1; financial award applicants required to submit FAFSA. *Faculty research:* Treatment attrition among domestic violence batterers, children's health and mental health, Dejando Huellas: meeting the bilingual/bicultural needs of the Latino mental health patient, impact of culture on the therapeutic process, effects of generational gang involvement on adolescents' future. *Unit head:* Dr. Alfredo Garcia, Dean, 505-891-9053, Fax: 505-454-3290, E-mail: a_garcia@nmhu.edu. *Application contact:* LouAnn Romero, Administrative Assistant, Graduate Studies, 505-454-3087, E-mail: laromero@nmhu.edu.

The New School, Milano The New School for Management and Urban Policy, Program in Nonprofit Management, New York, NY 10011. Offers MS. Part-time and evening/weekend programs available. *Degree requirements:* For master's, thesis. *Entrance requirements:* For master's, interview. Additional exam requirements/recommendations for international students: Required—TOEFL (minimum score 600 paper-based; 100 iBT). Electronic applications accepted. *Faculty research:* Management of nonprofit organizations, fundraising in minority nonprofit organizations.

New York University, Robert F. Wagner Graduate School of Public Service, Program in Public Administration, New York, NY 10012. Offers public administration (PhD); public and nonprofit management and policy (MPA, Advanced Certificate), including developmental administration (Advanced Certificate), financial management and public finance, human resources management (Advanced Certificate), international administration (Advanced Certificate), management (MPA), management for public and nonprofit organizations (Advanced Certificate), public policy analysis, quantitative analysis and computer applications (Advanced Certificate), urban public policy (Advanced Certificate); JD/MPA; MBA/MPA; MPA/MA. *Accreditation:* NASPAA (one or more programs are accredited). Part-time programs available. *Faculty:* 29 full-time (13 women), 41 part-time/adjunct (21 women). *Students:* 373 full-time (275 women), 245 part-time (176 women); includes 207 minority (56 Black or African American, non-Hispanic/Latino; 2 American Indian or Alaska Native, non-Hispanic/Latino; 70 Asian, non-Hispanic/Latino; 64 Hispanic/Latino; 2 Native Hawaiian or other Pacific Islander, non-Hispanic/Latino; 13 Two or more races, non-Hispanic/Latino), 122 international. Average age 28. 1,163 applicants, 61% accepted, 250 enrolled. In 2013, 233 master's, 6 doctorates, 1 other advanced degree awarded. *Degree requirements:* For master's, thesis or alternative, capstone end event; for doctorate, one foreign language, comprehensive exam, thesis/dissertation, preliminary qualifying examination. *Entrance requirements:* Additional exam requirements/recommendations for international students: Required—TOEFL (minimum score 100 iBT), IELTS (minimum score 7.5), TWE. *Application deadline:* For fall admission, 1/6 for domestic and international students; for spring admission, 10/1 for domestic and international students. Application fee: $85. Electronic applications accepted. *Expenses:* Contact institution. *Financial support:* In 2013–14, 152 students received support, including 141 fellowships with full and partial tuition reimbursements available (averaging $10,100 per year), 5 research assistantships with full tuition reimbursements available (averaging $39,643 per year); career-related internships or fieldwork, Federal Work-Study, scholarships/grants, health care benefits, and unspecified assistantships also available. Support available to part-time students. Financial award application deadline: 1/5; financial award applicants required to submit FAFSA. *Unit head:* Prof. Katherine O'Regan, Associate Professor of Public Policy, 212-998-7498, E-mail: katherine.oregan@nyu.edu. *Application contact:* Janet Barzilay, Admissions Officer, 212-998-7414, Fax: 212-995-4611, E-mail: wagner.admissions@nyu.edu. Website: http://wagner.nyu.edu/.

New York University, School of Continuing and Professional Studies, The George Heyman Jr. Center for Philanthropy and Fundraising, New York, NY 10012-1019. Offers fundraising and grantmaking (MS), including fundraising, grantmaking. Part-time and evening/weekend programs available. *Faculty:* 1 full-time (0 women), 9 part-time/adjunct (5 women). *Students:* 7 full-time (5 women), 34 part-time (29 women); includes 7 minority (3 Black or African American, non-Hispanic/Latino; 2 Asian, non-Hispanic/Latino; 1 Hispanic/Latino; 1 Two or more races, non-Hispanic/Latino), 3 international. Average age 34. 17 applicants, 71% accepted, 4 enrolled. In 2013, 17 master's awarded. *Degree requirements:* For master's, thesis, capstone project. *Entrance requirements:* For master's, bachelor's degree, resume with relevant professional work, internship or volunteer experience, two letters of recommendation, statement of purpose. Additional exam requirements/recommendations for international students: Required—TOEFL (minimum score 600 paper-based; 100 iBT), IELTS (minimum score 7). *Application deadline:* For fall admission, 2/1 priority date for domestic and international students; for spring admission, 10/15 priority date for domestic students, 8/15 priority date for international students. Applications are processed on a rolling basis. Application fee: $150. Electronic applications accepted. *Expenses: Tuition:* Full-time $35,856; part-time $1494 per unit. *Required fees:* $1408; $64 per unit. $473 per term. Tuition and fees vary according to course load and program. *Financial support:* In 2013–14, 18 students received support, including 17 fellowships (averaging $2,247 per year); scholarships/grants also available. Support available to part-time students. Financial award application deadline: 8/15; financial award applicants required to submit FAFSA. *Unit head:* Naomi Levine, Executive Director, 212-998-7100. *Application contact:* Admissions Office, 212-998-7100, E-mail: scps.gradadmissions@nyu.edu. Website: http://www.scps.nyu.edu/academics/departments/heyman-center.html.

North Carolina State University, Graduate School, College of Humanities and Social Sciences, School of Public and International Affairs, Raleigh, NC 27695. Offers international studies (MIS); nonprofit management (Certificate); public administration (MPA, PhD). *Accreditation:* NASPAA (one or more programs are accredited). Part-time and evening/weekend programs available. *Entrance requirements:* For master's, GRE General Test, minimum GPA of 3.0 during previous 2 years. Electronic applications accepted. *Faculty research:* Public sector leadership and ethics, financial management, management systems evaluation, computer applications, service delivery.

North Central College, Graduate and Continuing Studies Programs, Program in Leadership Studies, Naperville, IL 60566-7063. Offers higher education leadership

(MLD); professional leadership (MLD); social entrepreneurship (MLD); sports leadership (MLD). Part-time and evening/weekend programs available. *Faculty:* 9 full-time (1 woman), 16 part-time/adjunct (9 women). *Students:* 42 full-time (24 women), 24 part-time (8 women); includes 16 minority (10 Black or African American, non-Hispanic/Latino; 6 Hispanic/Latino), 4 international. Average age 28. 104 applicants, 51% accepted, 23 enrolled. In 2013, 36 master's awarded. *Degree requirements:* For master's, thesis optional, project. *Entrance requirements:* For master's, interview. Additional exam requirements/recommendations for international students: Required—TOEFL (minimum score 570 paper-based; 90 iBT). *Application deadline:* For fall admission, 8/15 for domestic students; for winter admission, 12/1 for domestic students; for spring admission, 2/1 for domestic students. Applications are processed on a rolling basis. Application fee: $25. *Expenses:* Contact institution. *Financial support:* In 2013–14, 1 student received support. Scholarships/grants available. Support available to part-time students. *Unit head:* Dr. Thomas Cavenagh, Program Coordinator, Leadership Studies, 630-637-5285. *Application contact:* Wendy Kulpinski, Director of Graduate and Continuing Education Admission, 630-637-5808, Fax: 630-637-5844, E-mail: wekulpinski@noctrl.edu.

Northeastern University, College of Professional Studies, Boston, MA 02115-5096. Offers applied nutrition (MS); commerce and economic development (MS); corporate and organizational communication (MS); digital media (MPS); geographic information technology (MPS); global studies and international affairs (MS); homeland security (MA); human services (MS); informatics (MPS); leadership (MS); nonprofit management (MS); project management (MS); regulatory affairs for drugs, biologics, and medical devices (MS); regulatory affairs of food and food industries (MS); respiratory care leadership (MS); technical communication (MS). Postbaccalaureate distance learning degree programs offered (no on-campus study).

Northern Kentucky University, Office of Graduate Programs, College of Arts and Sciences, Program in Public Administration, Highland Heights, KY 41099. Offers non-profit management (Certificate); public administration (MPA). *Accreditation:* NASPAA. Part-time and evening/weekend programs available. *Faculty:* 8 full-time (3 women), 2 part-time/adjunct (both women). *Students:* 6 full-time (2 women), 66 part-time (37 women); includes 9 minority (5 Black or African American, non-Hispanic/Latino; 1 Asian, non-Hispanic/Latino; 2 Hispanic/Latino; 1 Two or more races, non-Hispanic/Latino). Average age 33. 49 applicants, 55% accepted, 19 enrolled. In 2013, 38 master's, 8 other advanced degrees awarded. *Degree requirements:* For master's, capstone. *Entrance requirements:* For master's, GRE, GMAT or MAT, 2 letters of recommendation, writing sample, minimum GPA of 2.75, essay, resume (for those in-career). Additional exam requirements/recommendations for international students: Required—TOEFL (minimum score 550 paper-based; 79 iBT); Recommended—IELTS (minimum score 6.5). *Application deadline:* For fall admission, 7/1 priority date for domestic students, 6/1 for international students; for spring admission, 12/1 priority date for domestic students, 10/1 for international students; for summer admission, 4/1 for domestic students. Applications are processed on a rolling basis. Application fee: $40. Electronic applications accepted. *Expenses:* Tuition, state resident: full-time $4446; part-time $494 per credit hour. Tuition, nonresident: full-time $6885; part-time $765 per credit hour. *Required fees:* $72 per semester. One-time fee: $125.50. Part-time tuition and fees vary according to course load, degree level, program and reciprocity agreements. *Financial support:* In 2013–14, 20 students received support. Unspecified assistantships available. Financial award applicants required to submit FAFSA. *Unit head:* Dr. Julie Olberding, Program Director, 859-572-1953, Fax: 859-572-6184, E-mail: olberdingj@nku.edu. *Application contact:* Beth Devantier, MPA Coordinator, 859-572-5326, Fax: 859-572-6184, E-mail: devantier@nku.edu.
Website: http://psc-cj.nku.edu/programs/public/masters/index.php.

North Park University, School of Business and Nonprofit Management, Chicago, IL 60625-4895. Offers MBA, MHEA, MHRM, MM, MNA. Part-time and evening/weekend programs available. Postbaccalaureate distance learning degree programs offered (no on-campus study). *Entrance requirements:* For master's, GMAT, GRE. Additional exam requirements/recommendations for international students: Required—TOEFL. *Expenses:* Contact institution.

Notre Dame of Maryland University, Graduate Studies, Program in Nonprofit Management, Baltimore, MD 21210-2476. Offers MA. Part-time and evening/weekend programs available. *Degree requirements:* For master's, thesis optional. *Entrance requirements:* For master's, minimum GPA of 3.0. Additional exam requirements/recommendations for international students: Required—TOEFL (minimum score 500 paper-based; 61 iBT). Electronic applications accepted.

Oklahoma City University, Petree College of Arts and Sciences, Division of Sociology and Justice Studies, Oklahoma City, OK 73106-1402. Offers applied sociology (MA), including nonprofit leadership; criminology (MS). Part-time and evening/weekend programs available. *Students:* 15 full-time (12 women), 14 part-time (9 women); includes 7 minority (3 Black or African American, non-Hispanic/Latino; 2 Hispanic/Latino; 2 Two or more races, non-Hispanic/Latino), 3 international. Average age 30. 32 applicants, 78% accepted, 13 enrolled. In 2013, 19 master's awarded. *Degree requirements:* For master's, thesis or alternative. *Entrance requirements:* For master's, minimum GPA of 3.0, two letters of recommendation. Additional exam requirements/recommendations for international students: Required—TOEFL (minimum score 550 paper-based; 80 iBT). *Application deadline:* Applications are processed on a rolling basis. Application fee: $50. Electronic applications accepted. *Expenses: Tuition:* Full-time $16,848; part-time $936 per credit hour. Tuition and fees vary according to course load, degree level and program. *Financial support:* Career-related internships or fieldwork, Federal Work-Study, institutionally sponsored loans, scholarships/grants, and tuition waivers available. Support available to part-time students. Financial award application deadline: 6/1; financial award applicants required to submit FAFSA. *Faculty research:* Victims, police, corrections, security, women and crime. *Unit head:* Robert Spinks, Director, 405-208-5368, Fax: 405-208-5447, E-mail: bspinks@okcu.edu. *Application contact:* Heidi Puckett, Director, Admissions, 800-633-7242, Fax: 405-208-5916, E-mail: gadmissions@okcu.edu.
Website: http://www.okcu.edu/petree/soc/.

Oklahoma State University, Graduate College, Stillwater, OK 74078. Offers aerospace security (Graduate Certificate); bioenergy and sustainable technology (Graduate Certificate); bioinformatics (Graduate Certificate); business data mining (Graduate Certificate); business sustainability (Graduate Certificate); engineering and technology management (Graduate Certificate); entrepreneurship (Graduate Certificate); environmental science (MS); global issues (Graduate Certificate); grassland management (Graduate Certificate); information assurance (Graduate Certificate); interdisciplinary sciences (MS); interdisciplinary toxicology (Graduate Certificate); international studies (MS); non-profit management (Graduate Certificate); online teaching (Graduate Certificate); photonics (PhD); plant science (PhD); teaching English to speakers of other languages (Graduate Certificate); telecommunications management (MS). Programs are interdisciplinary. *Faculty:* 4 full-time (2 women), 2 part-time/adjunct (1 woman). *Students:* 74 full-time (58 women), 147 part-time (74 women); includes 44 minority (12 Black or African American, non-Hispanic/Latino; 8 American Indian or Alaska Native, non-Hispanic/Latino; 10 Asian, non-Hispanic/Latino; 6 Hispanic/Latino; 8 Two or more races, non-Hispanic/Latino), 43 international. Average age 32. 495 applicants, 70% accepted, 75 enrolled. In 2013, 55 master's, 11 doctorates awarded. *Degree requirements:* For master's, thesis (for some programs); for doctorate, comprehensive exam, thesis/dissertation. *Entrance requirements:* For master's and doctorate, GRE or GMAT. Additional exam requirements/recommendations for international students: Required—TOEFL (minimum score 550 paper-based; 79 iBT). *Application deadline:* For fall admission, 3/1 priority date for international students; for spring admission, 8/1 priority date for international students. Applications are processed on a rolling basis. Application fee: $40 ($75 for international students). Electronic applications accepted. *Expenses:* Tuition, state resident: full-time $4272; part-time $178 per credit hour. Tuition, nonresident: full-time $17,472; part-time $709 per credit hour. *Required fees:* $2413.20; $100.55 per credit hour. One-time fee: $50 full-time. Part-time tuition and fees vary according to course load and campus/location. *Financial support:* Career-related internships or fieldwork, Federal Work-Study, scholarships/grants, health care benefits, tuition waivers (partial), and unspecified assistantships available. Support available to part-time students. Financial award application deadline: 3/1; financial award applicants required to submit FAFSA. *Unit head:* Dr. Sheryl Tucker, Dean, 405-744-7099, Fax: 405-744-0355, E-mail: grad-i@okstate.edu. *Application contact:* Dr. Susan Mathew, Coordinator of Admissions, 405-744-6368, Fax: 405-744-0355, E-mail: grad-i@okstate.edu.
Website: http://gradcollege.okstate.edu/.

Oral Roberts University, School of Business, Tulsa, OK 74171. Offers accounting (MBA); entrepreneurship (MBA); finance (MBA); international business (MBA); management (MBA); marketing (MBA); non-profit management (MBA); not for profit management (MNM). *Accreditation:* ACBSP. Part-time programs available. Postbaccalaureate distance learning degree programs offered (minimal on-campus study). *Degree requirements:* For master's, thesis optional. *Entrance requirements:* For master's, minimum cumulative GPA of 3.0. Additional exam requirements/recommendations for international students: Required—TOEFL (minimum score 550 paper-based; 79 iBT). Electronic applications accepted. *Faculty research:* Social media, international business and marketing.

Our Lady of the Lake University of San Antonio, School of Business and Leadership, Program in Nonprofit Management, San Antonio, TX 78207-4689. Offers MS. Part-time and evening/weekend programs available. Postbaccalaureate distance learning degree programs offered. *Faculty:* 3 full-time (0 women), 1 (woman) part-time/adjunct. *Students:* 24 full-time (17 women), 1 (woman) part-time; includes 16 minority (2 Black or African American, non-Hispanic/Latino; 13 Hispanic/Latino; 1 Native Hawaiian or other Pacific Islander, non-Hispanic/Latino). Average age 36. 31 applicants, 61% accepted, 12 enrolled. In 2013, 16 master's awarded. *Entrance requirements:* For master's, GMAT, GRE General Test, or MAT. Additional exam requirements/recommendations for international students: Required—TOEFL. *Application deadline:* Applications are processed on a rolling basis. Application fee: $25 ($50 for international students). Electronic applications accepted. *Expenses: Tuition:* Full-time $9120; part-time $760 per credit. *Required fees:* $698; $334 per trimester. Tuition and fees vary according to course load, degree level, campus/location and program. *Financial support:* Fellowships, career-related internships or fieldwork, Federal Work-Study, institutionally sponsored loans, scholarships/grants, and tuition waivers (partial) available. Support available to part-time students. *Faculty research:* Learning about the nonprofit industry while learning how to manage and lead a nonprofit entity with business acumen. *Unit head:* Dr. Kathryn Winney, Dean, 210-434-6711 Ext. 2297, E-mail: kmwinney@lake.ollusa.edu. *Application contact:* Graduate Admission, 210-431-3961, Fax: 210-431-4013, E-mail: gradadm@ollusa.edu.
Website: http://www.ollusa.edu/s/1190/ollu-3-column-noads.aspx?sid=1190&gid=1&pgid=2401.

Pace University, Dyson College of Arts and Sciences, Department of Public Administration, New York, NY 10038. Offers environmental management (MPA); government management (MPA); health care administration (MPA); management for public safety and homeland security (MA); nonprofit management (MPA); JD/MPA. Offered at White Plains, NY location only. Part-time and evening/weekend programs available. *Faculty:* 5 full-time (2 women), 5 part-time/adjunct (1 woman). *Students:* 78 full-time (60 women), 68 part-time (37 women); includes 82 minority (49 Black or African American, non-Hispanic/Latino; 1 American Indian or Alaska Native, non-Hispanic/Latino; 5 Asian, non-Hispanic/Latino; 22 Hispanic/Latino; 5 Two or more races, non-Hispanic/Latino), 31 international. Average age 29. 101 applicants, 86% accepted, 51 enrolled. In 2013, 43 master's awarded. *Degree requirements:* For master's, capstone project. *Entrance requirements:* For master's, GRE General Test. Additional exam requirements/recommendations for international students: Required—TOEFL. *Application deadline:* For fall admission, 8/1 priority date for domestic students, 6/1 for international students; for spring admission, 12/1 priority date for domestic students, 10/1 for international students. Applications are processed on a rolling basis. Application fee: $70. Electronic applications accepted. *Expenses: Tuition:* Part-time $1075 per credit. *Required fees:* $192 per semester. Tuition and fees vary according to course load, degree level and program. *Financial support:* Research assistantships, career-related internships or fieldwork, Federal Work-Study, and tuition waivers (partial) available. Support available to part-time students. Financial award applicants required to submit FAFSA. *Unit head:* Dr. Farrokh Hormozi, Chairperson, 914-422-4285, E-mail: fhormozi@pace.edu. *Application contact:* Susan Ford-Goldschein, Director of Admissions, 914-422-4283, Fax: 914-422-4287, E-mail: gradwp@pace.edu.
Website: http://www.pace.edu/dyson/academic-departments-and-programs/public-admin.

Park University, School of Graduate and Professional Studies, Kansas City, MO 54105. Offers adult education (M Ed); business and government leadership (Graduate Certificate); business, government, and global society (MPA); communication and leadership (MA); creative and life writing (Graduate Certificate); disaster and emergency management (MPA, Graduate Certificate); educational leadership (M Ed); finance (MBA, Graduate Certificate); general business (MBA); global business (Graduate Certificate); healthcare administration (MHA); healthcare services management and leadership (Graduate Certificate); international business (MBA); language and literacy (M Ed), including English for speakers of other languages, special reading teacher/literacy coach; leadership of international healthcare organizations (Graduate Certificate); management information systems (MBA, Graduate Certificate); music performance (ADP, Graduate Certificate), including cello (MM, ADP), piano (MM, ADP), viola (MM, ADP), violin (MM, ADP); nonprofit and community services management (MPA); nonprofit leadership (Graduate Certificate); performance (MM), including cello (MM, ADP), piano (MM, ADP), viola (MM, ADP), violin (MM, ADP); public management (MPA); social work (MSW); teacher leadership (M Ed), including curriculum and assessment, instructional leader. Part-time and evening/weekend programs available. Postbaccalaureate distance learning degree programs offered (no on-campus study). *Students:* 862 full-time (482 women); includes 55 minority (30 Black or African American, non-Hispanic/Latino; 2 American Indian or Alaska Native, non-Hispanic/Latino; 4 Asian, non-Hispanic/Latino; 14 Hispanic/Latino; 5 Two or more races, non-Hispanic/Latino), 141 international. Average age 34. 497 applicants, 62% accepted, 119 enrolled. In 2013, 281 master's, 14 other advanced degrees awarded. *Degree requirements:* For master's, comprehensive exam (for some programs), thesis (for some programs), internship (for some programs); exam (for some programs). *Entrance*

requirements: For master's, GRE or GMAT (for some programs), teacher certification (for some M Ed programs), letters of recommendation, essay, resume (for some programs). Additional exam requirements/recommendations for international students: Required—TOEFL (minimum score 550 paper-based; 79 iBT), IELTS (minimum score 6). *Application deadline:* For fall admission, 8/1 priority date for domestic students, 7/15 priority date for international students; for spring admission, 1/1 priority date for domestic students, 11/1 priority date for international students. Applications are processed on a rolling basis. Application fee: $50 ($100 for international students). Electronic applications accepted. *Financial support:* In 2013–14, 2 research assistantships with full tuition reimbursements (averaging $15,760 per year) were awarded. Financial award applicants required to submit FAFSA. *Unit head:* Dr. Laurie Dipadova-Stocks, Dean of Graduate and Professional Studies, 816-559-5624, Fax: 816-472-1173, E-mail: ldipadovastocks@park.edu. *Application contact:* Judith Appollis, Director of Graduate Admissions and Internationalization, School of Graduate and Professional Studies, 816-559-5627, Fax: 816-472-1173, E-mail: gradschool@park.edu.
Website: http://www.park.edu/grad.

Point Loma Nazarene University, Fermanian School of Business, San Diego, CA 92106-2899. Offers general business (MBA); healthcare (MBA); not-for-profit management (MBA); organizational leadership (MBA); sustainability (MBA). *Accreditation:* ACBSP. Part-time and evening/weekend programs available. *Students:* 37 full-time (12 women), 70 part-time (35 women); includes 33 minority (3 Black or African American, non-Hispanic/Latino; 9 Asian, non-Hispanic/Latino; 14 Hispanic/Latino; 1 Native Hawaiian or other Pacific Islander, non-Hispanic/Latino; 6 Two or more races, non-Hispanic/Latino), 1 international. Average age 29. 51 applicants, 65% accepted, 28 enrolled. In 2013, 59 master's awarded. *Entrance requirements:* For master's, GMAT, letters of recommendation, essay, interview. Additional exam requirements/recommendations for international students: Required—TOEFL. *Application deadline:* For fall admission, 8/4 priority date for domestic students; for spring admission, 12/8 priority date for domestic students; for summer admission, 4/13 priority date for domestic students. Applications are processed on a rolling basis. Application fee: $50. Electronic applications accepted. *Expenses: Tuition:* Full-time $6900; part-time $567 per credit hour. *Financial support:* Applicants required to submit FAFSA. *Unit head:* Dr. Ken Armstrong, Interim Dean, 619-849-2290, E-mail: kenarmstrong@pointloma.edu. *Application contact:* Laura Leinweber, Director of Graduate Admission, 866-692-4723, E-mail: lauraleinweber@pointloma.edu.
Website: http://www.pointloma.edu/discover/graduate-school-san-diego/san-diego-graduate-programs-masters-degree-san-diego/mba.

Post University, Program in Human Services, Waterbury, CT 06723-2540. Offers human services (MS); human services/alcohol and drug counseling (MS); human services/clinical counseling (MS); human services/non-profit management (MS). Part-time and evening/weekend programs available. Postbaccalaureate distance learning degree programs offered.

Providence College, School of Business, Providence, RI 02918. Offers accounting (MBA); finance (MBA); international business (MBA); management (MBA); marketing (MBA); not-for-profit organizations (MBA). Part-time and evening/weekend programs available. *Faculty:* 14 full-time (5 women), 3 part-time/adjunct (1 woman). *Students:* 68 full-time (25 women), 54 part-time (25 women); includes 12 minority (3 Black or African American, non-Hispanic/Latino; 1 Asian, non-Hispanic/Latino; 6 Hispanic/Latino; 2 Two or more races, non-Hispanic/Latino), 7 international. Average age 25. 43 applicants, 95% accepted, 36 enrolled. In 2013, 38 master's awarded. *Degree requirements:* For master's, thesis optional. *Entrance requirements:* For master's, GMAT. Additional exam requirements/recommendations for international students: Required—TOEFL (minimum score 550 paper-based; 80 iBT). *Application deadline:* For fall admission, 7/15 priority date for domestic and international students; for spring admission, 11/15 priority date for domestic and international students; for summer admission, 4/15 priority date for domestic students. Applications are processed on a rolling basis. Application fee: $55. *Expenses:* Contact institution. *Financial support:* Federal Work-Study, institutionally sponsored loans, and unspecified assistantships available. Support available to part-time students. Financial award application deadline: 8/1; financial award applicants required to submit FAFSA. *Unit head:* Jacqueline Elcik, Director, 401-865-2131, E-mail: jelcik@providence.edu. *Application contact:* MBA Program, 401-865-2294, E-mail: mba@providence.edu.
Website: http://www.providence.edu/business/Pages/default.aspx.

Regent University, Graduate School, Robertson School of Government, Virginia Beach, VA 23464. Offers government (MA), including American government, international politics, political theory; public administration (MPA), including emergency management and homeland security, general public administration, nonprofit administration and civil society organizations, public leadership and management. Part-time and evening/weekend programs available. Postbaccalaureate distance learning degree programs offered (minimal on-campus study). *Faculty:* 10 full-time (1 woman), 8 part-time/adjunct (1 woman). *Students:* 43 full-time (24 women), 69 part-time (28 women); includes 34 minority (27 Black or African American, non-Hispanic/Latino; 7 Hispanic/Latino), 6 international. Average age 33. 82 applicants, 63% accepted, 32 enrolled. In 2013, 41 master's awarded. *Degree requirements:* For master's, thesis optional, internship. *Entrance requirements:* For master's, GRE General Test or LSAT, minimum undergraduate GPA of 3.0, writing sample, resume, interview, references. Additional exam requirements/recommendations for international students: Required—TOEFL (minimum score 577 paper-based). *Application deadline:* For fall admission, 5/1 priority date for domestic students; for spring admission, 11/1 priority date for domestic students. Applications are processed on a rolling basis. Application fee: $50. Electronic applications accepted. *Expenses:* Contact institution. *Financial support:* Career-related internships or fieldwork, scholarships/grants, tuition waivers (full and partial), and unspecified assistantships available. Support available to part-time students. Financial award application deadline: 9/1; financial award applicants required to submit FAFSA. *Faculty research:* Education reform, political character issues, social capital concerns, administrative ethics, Biblical law and public policy. *Unit head:* Dr. Eric Patterson, Dean, 757-352-4616, Fax: 757-352-4735, E-mail: epatterson@regent.edu. *Application contact:* Matthew Chadwick, Director of Enrollment Support Services, 800-373-5504, Fax: 757-352-4381, E-mail: admissions@regent.edu.
Website: http://www.regent.edu/government/.

Regis University, College for Professional Studies, School of Humanities and Social Sciences, Program in Nonprofit Management, Denver, CO 80221-1099. Offers executive nonprofit leadership (Post-Graduate Certificate); nonprofit management (MNM); nonprofit organizational capacity building (Certificate). Offered at Northwest Denver Campus and Southeast Denver Campus. Part-time and evening/weekend programs available. Postbaccalaureate distance learning degree programs offered (no on-campus study). *Faculty:* 3 full-time (0 women), 30 part-time/adjunct (21 women). *Students:* 115 full-time (91 women), 86 part-time (72 women); includes 54 minority (20 Black or African American, non-Hispanic/Latino; 4 American Indian or Alaska Native, non-Hispanic/Latino; 4 Asian, non-Hispanic/Latino; 21 Hispanic/Latino; 5 Two or more races, non-Hispanic/Latino), 2 international. Average age 42. 53 applicants, 85% accepted, 39 enrolled. In 2013, 87 master's awarded. *Degree requirements:* For master's, thesis optional, professional research project, field experience; for other advanced degree, thesis optional, professional research project. *Entrance requirements:* For master's, official transcript reflecting baccalaureate degree awarded from regionally-accredited college or university, essay, letters of recommendation, resume, interview; for other advanced degree, resume. Additional exam requirements/recommendations for international students: Required—TOEFL (minimum score 550 paper-based, 82 iBT), TWE (minimum score 5) or university-based test. *Application deadline:* For fall admission, 8/13 for domestic students, 7/13 for international students; for winter admission, 10/8 for domestic students, 9/8 for international students; for spring admission, 12/17 for domestic students, 11/17 priority date for international students. Applications are processed on a rolling basis. Application fee: $75. Electronic applications accepted. *Expenses:* Contact institution. *Financial support:* In 2013–14, 16 students received support. Fellowships, Federal Work-Study, and scholarships/grants available. Financial award application deadline: 4/15; financial award applicants required to submit FAFSA. *Faculty research:* International nonprofits, enterprise, grass roots nonprofits, leadership in nonprofit organizations. *Unit head:* Dr. Elisa Robyn, Dean, 303-458-4081, Fax: 303-964-5539, E-mail: erobyn@regis.edu. *Application contact:* Sarah Engel, Director of Admissions, 303-458-4900, Fax: 303-964-5534, E-mail: regisadm@regis.edu.
Website: http://www.regis.edu/CPS/Academics/Degrees-and-Programs/Graduate-Programs/Master-Nonprofit-Management.aspx.

Robert Morris University, Graduate Studies, School of Business, Moon Township, PA 15108-1189. Offers business administration (MBA); human resource management (MS); nonprofit management (MS); taxation (MS). *Accreditation:* AACSB. Part-time and evening/weekend programs available. Postbaccalaureate distance learning degree programs offered (no on-campus study). *Faculty:* 25 full-time (10 women), 8 part-time/adjunct (2 women). *Students:* 247 part-time (99 women); includes 10 minority (1 Black or African American, non-Hispanic/Latino; 2 Asian, non-Hispanic/Latino; 7 Two or more races, non-Hispanic/Latino), 5 international. Average age 26. 214 applicants, 40% accepted, 62 enrolled. In 2013, 187 master's awarded. *Entrance requirements:* For master's, GMAT, letters of recommendation. Additional exam requirements/recommendations for international students: Required—TOEFL (minimum score 550 paper-based; 79 iBT). *Application deadline:* For fall admission, 7/1 priority date for domestic and international students; for spring admission, 11/1 priority date for domestic and international students. Applications are processed on a rolling basis. Application fee: $35. Electronic applications accepted. *Expenses: Tuition:* Part-time $825 per credit. Part-time tuition and fees vary according to degree level and program. *Financial support:* Research assistantships with partial tuition reimbursements, Federal Work-Study, institutionally sponsored loans, and unspecified assistantships available. Support available to part-time students. Financial award application deadline: 5/1; financial award applicants required to submit FAFSA. *Unit head:* Dr. John M. Beehler, Dean, 412-397-5445, Fax: 412-397-2172, E-mail: beehler@rmu.edu. *Application contact:* 412-397-5200, Fax: 412-397-5915, E-mail: graduateadmissions@rmu.edu.
Website: http://www.rmu.edu/web/cms/schools/sbus/Pages/default.aspx.

St. Cloud State University, School of Graduate Studies, College of Social Sciences, Department of Economics, Program in Public and Nonprofit Institutions, St. Cloud, MN 56301-4498. Offers MS. Part-time programs available. *Degree requirements:* For master's, thesis or alternative. *Entrance requirements:* For master's, GRE General Test, minimum GPA of 2.75. Additional exam requirements/recommendations for international students: Required—Michigan English Language Assessment Battery; Recommended—TOEFL (minimum score 550 paper-based), IELTS (minimum score 6.5). Electronic applications accepted.

Salve Regina University, Program in Management, Newport, RI 02840-4192. Offers law enforcement leadership (MS); nonprofit management (MS, Certificate). Part-time and evening/weekend programs available. Postbaccalaureate distance learning degree programs offered (no on-campus study). *Faculty:* 3 full-time (2 women), 12 part-time/adjunct (5 women). *Students:* 6 full-time (4 women), 24 part-time (13 women); includes 3 minority (1 Black or African American, non-Hispanic/Latino; 2 Hispanic/Latino). Average age 38. 7 applicants, 86% accepted, 4 enrolled. In 2013, 13 master's awarded. *Entrance requirements:* For master's, GMAT, GRE General Test, or MAT. Additional exam requirements/recommendations for international students: Required—TOEFL (minimum score 600 paper-based; 100 iBT). *Application deadline:* For fall admission, 3/15 priority date for domestic students, 3/5 priority date for international students; for spring admission, 9/15 priority date for domestic and international students. Applications are processed on a rolling basis. Application fee: $60. Electronic applications accepted. *Expenses: Tuition:* Full-time $8280; part-time $460 per credit. *Required fees:* $40 per term. Tuition and fees vary according to course level, course load, degree level and program. *Financial support:* Career-related internships or fieldwork and Federal Work-Study available. Support available to part-time students. Financial award application deadline: 3/1; financial award applicants required to submit FAFSA. *Unit head:* Dr. Arlene Nicholas, Director, 401-341-3280, E-mail: arlene.nicholas@salve.edu. *Application contact:* Kelly Alverson, Director of Graduate Admissions, 401-341-2153, Fax: 401-341-2973, E-mail: kelly.alverson@salve.edu.
Website: http://salve.edu/graduate-studies/business-administration-and-management.

San Francisco State University, Division of Graduate Studies, College of Health and Social Sciences, Public Administration Program, San Francisco, CA 94132-1722. Offers criminal justice administration (MPA); environmental administration and policy (MPA); nonprofit administration (MPA); public management (MPA); public policy (MPA); urban administration (MPA). *Accreditation:* NASPAA. *Unit head:* Dr. Gerald Eisman, Director of the School of Public Affairs and Civic Engagement, 415-338-1149, E-mail: pace@sfsu.edu. *Application contact:* Dr. Genie Sowers, Graduate Coordinator, 415-817-4455, E-mail: gstowers@sfsu.edu.
Website: http://mpa.sfsu.edu/.

Savannah State University, Master of Public Administration Program, Savannah, GA 31404. Offers city management (MPA); general public administration (MPA); human resources (MPA); non-profit management (MPA). *Accreditation:* NASPAA. Part-time programs available. *Faculty:* 4 full-time (1 woman). *Students:* 8 full-time (6 women), 11 part-time (7 women); includes 14 minority (13 Black or African American, non-Hispanic/Latino; 1 Hispanic/Latino), 1 international. Average age 34. 7 applicants, 57% accepted, 3 enrolled. In 2013, 22 master's awarded. *Degree requirements:* For master's, comprehensive exam, thesis, public service internship, capstone seminar. *Entrance requirements:* For master's, GRE General Test, GMAT, or MAT, minimum cumulative GPA of 2.5, 3 letters of recommendation, essay, official transcripts, resume, essay of 500-1000 words detailing reasons for pursuing degree. Additional exam requirements/recommendations for international students: Required—TOEFL. *Application deadline:* For fall admission, 5/23 for domestic students, 5/15 for international students; for spring admission, 10/31 for domestic students, 10/1 for international students. Applications are processed on a rolling basis. Application fee: $25. *Expenses:* Tuition, state resident: full-time $4482; part-time $187 per credit hour. Tuition, nonresident: full-time $16,660; part-time $694 per credit hour. *Required fees:* $1716; $858 per term. *Financial support:* Career-related internships or fieldwork, Federal Work-Study, institutionally sponsored loans, scholarships/grants, health care benefits, and unspecified assistantships available. Financial award applicants required to submit FAFSA. *Faculty research:* Community development, human resources, leadership, conflict resolution, city

management, non-profit management. *Unit head:* Dr. David Bell, MPA Program Coordinator, 912-358-3211, E-mail: mpa@savannahstate.edu. *Application contact:* Dr. Nat Hardy, Director of Graduate Studies, 912-358-4195, E-mail: grad@savannahstate.edu.
Website: http://www.savannahstate.edu/prospective-student/degrees-grad-pa.shtml.

Seton Hall University, College of Arts and Sciences, Department of Political Science and Public Affairs, South Orange, NJ 07079-2697. Offers healthcare administration (MHA, Graduate Certificate); nonprofit organization management (Graduate Certificate); public administration (MPA), including health policy and management, nonprofit organization management, public service: leadership, governance, and policy. *Accreditation:* NASPAA. Part-time and evening/weekend programs available. Postbaccalaureate distance learning degree programs offered (minimal on-campus study). *Degree requirements:* For master's, thesis or alternative, internship or practicum. *Entrance requirements:* Additional exam requirements/recommendations for international students: Required—TOEFL. Electronic applications accepted.

Simmons College, School of Management, Boston, MA 02115. Offers business administration (MBA); business and financial analytics (MBA); corporate social responsibility and sustainability (MBA); entrepreneurship (MBA); healthcare management (MBA); management (MS), including communications management, non-profit management; marketing (MBA); nonprofit management (MBA); organizational leadership (MBA); MBA/MSW; MS/MA. *Accreditation:* AACSB. Part-time and evening/weekend programs available. *Students:* 34 full-time (33 women), 233 part-time (214 women); includes 67 minority (41 Black or African American, non-Hispanic/Latino; 1 American Indian or Alaska Native, non-Hispanic/Latino; 9 Asian, non-Hispanic/Latino; 10 Hispanic/Latino; 2 Native Hawaiian or other Pacific Islander, non-Hispanic/Latino; 4 Two or more races, non-Hispanic/Latino), 7 international. In 2013, 133 master's awarded. *Entrance requirements:* For master's, GMAT or GRE. Additional exam requirements/recommendations for international students: Required—TOEFL. *Application deadline:* Applications are processed on a rolling basis. Application fee: $75. Electronic applications accepted. *Financial support:* Scholarships/grants and unspecified assistantships available. Financial award applicants required to submit FAFSA. *Faculty research:* Gender and organizations, leadership, health care management. *Unit head:* Cathy Minehan, Dean, 617-521-2846. *Application contact:* Melissa Terrio, Director of Graduate Admissions, 617-521-3840, Fax: 617-521-3880, E-mail: somadm@simmons.edu.
Website: http://www.simmons.edu/som.

Sonoma State University, School of Social Sciences, Department of Political Science, Rohnert Park, CA 94928. Offers administration of nonprofit agencies (Certificate); public administration (MPA). Part-time and evening/weekend programs available. *Faculty:* 1 full-time (0 women), 4 part-time/adjunct (all women). *Students:* 7 full-time (6 women), 33 part-time (21 women); includes 9 minority (1 Black or African American, non-Hispanic/Latino; 1 Asian, non-Hispanic/Latino; 5 Hispanic/Latino; 2 Two or more races, non-Hispanic/Latino). Average age 30. 17 applicants, 94% accepted, 6 enrolled. In 2013, 13 master's awarded. *Degree requirements:* For master's, thesis or alternative. *Entrance requirements:* For master's, GRE General Test, minimum GPA of 3.0. Additional exam requirements/recommendations for international students: Required—TOEFL (minimum score 500 paper-based). *Application deadline:* For fall admission, 11/30 for domestic students; for spring admission, 8/31 for domestic students. Application fee: $55. *Expenses:* Tuition, state resident: full-time $8500. Tuition, nonresident: full-time $12,964. *Required fees:* $1762. *Financial support:* Research assistantships, teaching assistantships, career-related internships or fieldwork, and Federal Work-Study available. Support available to part-time students. Financial award application deadline: 3/2; financial award applicants required to submit FAFSA. *Unit head:* Dr. Robert McNamara, Chair, 707-664-2676. *Application contact:* Diane Brown, Graduate Program Coordinator, 707-664-2731, Fax: 707-664-3920, E-mail: diane.brown@sonoma.edu.
Website: http://www.sonoma.edu/polisci/.

Southern Adventist University, School of Business and Management, Collegedale, TN 37315-0370. Offers accounting (MBA); church administration (MSA); church and nonprofit leadership (MBA); financial management (MFM); healthcare administration (MBA); management (MBA); marketing management (MBA); outdoor education (MSA). Part-time and evening/weekend programs available. Postbaccalaureate distance learning degree programs offered (no on-campus study). *Entrance requirements:* For master's, GMAT. Additional exam requirements/recommendations for international students: Required—TOEFL (minimum score 600 paper-based; 100 iBT). Electronic applications accepted.

Southern New Hampshire University, School of Business, Manchester, NH 03106-1045. Offers accounting (MBA, MS, Graduate Certificate); accounting finance (MS); accounting/auditing (MS); accounting/forensic accounting (MS); accounting/taxation (MS); athletic administration (MBA, Graduate Certificate); business administration (IMBA, MBA, Certificate, Graduate Certificate), including accounting (Certificate), business administration (MBA), business information systems (Graduate Certificate), human resource management (Certificate); corporate social responsibility (MBA); entrepreneurship (MBA); finance (MBA, MS, Graduate Certificate); finance/corporate finance (MS); finance/investments and securities (MS); forensic accounting (MBA); healthcare informatics (MBA); healthcare management (MBA); human resource management (Graduate Certificate); information technology (MS, Graduate Certificate); information technology management (MBA); international business (Graduate Certificate); international business and information technology (Graduate Certificate); international finance (Graduate Certificate); international sport management (Graduate Certificate); justice studies (MBA); leadership of nonprofit organizations (Graduate Certificate); marketing (MBA, MS, Graduate Certificate); operations and project management (MS); operations and supply chain management (MBA, Graduate Certificate); organizational leadership (MS); project management (MBA, Graduate Certificate); Six Sigma (MBA); Six Sigma quality (Graduate Certificate); social media marketing (MBA); sport management (MBA, MS, Graduate Certificate); sustainability and environmental compliance (MBA); workplace conflict management (MBA); MBA/Certificate. *Accreditation:* ACBSP. Part-time and evening/weekend programs available. Postbaccalaureate distance learning degree programs offered (no on-campus study). Terminal master's awarded for partial completion of doctoral program. *Degree requirements:* For master's, one foreign language, comprehensive exam (for some programs), thesis or alternative. *Entrance requirements:* For master's, minimum GPA of 2.5. Additional exam requirements/recommendations for international students: Required—TOEFL (minimum score 500 paper-based). Electronic applications accepted.

Spertus Institute for Jewish Learning and Leadership, Graduate Programs, Program in Nonprofit Management, Chicago, IL 60605-1901. Offers MSNM. Part-time and evening/weekend programs available. *Degree requirements:* For master's, one foreign language, thesis optional. *Entrance requirements:* For master's, interview, minimum GPA of 2.75, graduation from accredited undergraduate program. Electronic applications accepted.

Suffolk University, Sawyer Business School, Department of Public Administration, Boston, MA 02108-2770. Offers nonprofit management (MPA); public administration (CASPA); state and local government (MPA); JD/MPA; MPA/MS. *Accreditation:* NASPAA (one or more programs are accredited). Part-time and evening/weekend programs available. *Faculty:* 7 full-time (3 women), 1 (woman) part-time/adjunct. *Students:* 23 full-time (15 women), 85 part-time (48 women); includes 23 minority (17 Black or African American, non-Hispanic/Latino; 1 Asian, non-Hispanic/Latino; 2 Hispanic/Latino; 3 Two or more races, non-Hispanic/Latino), 5 international. Average age 33. 133 applicants, 76% accepted, 35 enrolled. In 2013, 58 master's awarded. *Entrance requirements:* Additional exam requirements/recommendations for international students: Required—TOEFL (minimum score 550 paper-based; 80 iBT). *Application deadline:* For fall admission, 6/15 priority date for domestic students, 6/15 for international students; for spring admission, 11/1 priority date for domestic students, 11/1 for international students. Applications are processed on a rolling basis. Application fee: $50. Electronic applications accepted. *Expenses:* Contact institution. *Financial support:* In 2013–14, 46 students received support, including 42 fellowships (averaging $8,036 per year); career-related internships or fieldwork and Federal Work-Study also available. Support available to part-time students. Financial award application deadline: 4/1; financial award applicants required to submit FAFSA. *Faculty research:* Local government, health care, federal policy, mental health, HIV/AIDS. *Unit head:* Dr. Richard Beinecke, Chair of The Institute for Public Service, 617-573-8062, Fax: 617-227-4618, E-mail: rbeineck@suffolk.edu. *Application contact:* Cory Meyers, Director of Graduate Admissions, 617-573-8302, Fax: 617-305-1733, E-mail: grad.admission@suffolk.edu.
Website: http://www.suffolk.edu/mpa.

Suffolk University, Sawyer Business School, Master of Business Administration Program, Boston, MA 02108-2770. Offers accounting (MBA); business administration (APC); entrepreneurship (MBA); executive business administration (EMBA); finance (MBA); global business administration (GMBA); health administration (MBA); international business (MBA); marketing (MBA); nonprofit management (MBA); organizational behavior (MBA); strategic management (MBA); supply chain management (MBA); taxation (MBA); JD/MBA; MBA/GDPA; MBA/MHA; MBA/MSA; MBA/MSF; MBA/MST. *Accreditation:* AACSB. Part-time and evening/weekend programs available. Postbaccalaureate distance learning degree programs offered (no on-campus study). *Faculty:* 29 full-time (9 women), 12 part-time/adjunct (2 women). *Students:* 106 full-time (44 women), 334 part-time (184 women); includes 57 minority (20 Black or African American, non-Hispanic/Latino; 1 American Indian or Alaska Native, non-Hispanic/Latino; 18 Asian, non-Hispanic/Latino; 14 Hispanic/Latino; 4 Two or more races, non-Hispanic/Latino), 61 international. Average age 30. 448 applicants, 61% accepted, 135 enrolled. In 2013, 217 master's awarded. *Entrance requirements:* For master's, GMAT, minimum undergraduate GPA of 2.75 (MBA), 5 years of managerial experience (EMBA). Additional exam requirements/recommendations for international students: Required—TOEFL (minimum score 550 paper-based; 80 iBT). *Application deadline:* For fall admission, 6/15 priority date for domestic students, 6/15 for international students; for spring admission, 11/1 priority date for domestic students, 11/1 for international students. Applications are processed on a rolling basis. Application fee: $50. Electronic applications accepted. *Expenses:* *Tuition:* Full-time $38,374; part-time $1279 per credit. *Required fees:* $40; $20 per semester. Tuition and fees vary according to program. *Financial support:* In 2013–14, 107 students received support, including 91 fellowships with full and partial tuition reimbursements available (averaging $12,428 per year); career-related internships or fieldwork, Federal Work-Study, and institutionally sponsored loans also available. Support available to part-time students. Financial award application deadline: 4/1; financial award applicants required to submit FAFSA. *Faculty research:* Foreign investments; career strategies and boundaryless careers; corporate ethics codes; interest rates, inflation, and growth options; innovation and product development performance. *Unit head:* Heather Hewitt, Assistant Dean of Graduate Programs/Director of MBA Programs, 617-573-8306, E-mail: hhewitt@suffolk.edu. *Application contact:* Cory Meyers, Director of Graduate Admissions, 617-573-8302, Fax: 617-305-1733, E-mail: grad.admission@suffolk.edu.
Website: http://www.suffolk.edu/mba.

Texas A&M University, Bush School of Government and Public Service, College Station, TX 77843. Offers homeland security (Certificate); international affairs (MIA, Certificate); national security affairs (Certificate); non-profit management (Certificate); public service and administration (MPSA). *Accreditation:* NASPAA. *Faculty:* 55. *Students:* 275 full-time (121 women), 10 part-time (4 women); includes 56 minority (12 Black or African American, non-Hispanic/Latino; 7 Asian, non-Hispanic/Latino; 28 Hispanic/Latino; 1 Native Hawaiian or other Pacific Islander, non-Hispanic/Latino; 8 Two or more races, non-Hispanic/Latino), 37 international. Average age 26. 257 applicants, 81% accepted, 138 enrolled. In 2013, 112 master's awarded. *Degree requirements:* For master's, summer internship. *Entrance requirements:* For master's, GRE (preferred) or GMAT. Additional exam requirements/recommendations for international students: Recommended—TOEFL. *Application deadline:* For fall admission, 1/24 for domestic and international students. Application fee: $50 ($75 for international students). Electronic applications accepted. *Expenses:* Tuition, state resident: full-time $4078; part-time $226.55 per credit hour. Tuition, nonresident: full-time $10,450; part-time $580.55 per credit hour. *Required fees:* $2328; $278.50 per credit hour. $642.45 per semester. *Financial support:* In 2013–14, fellowships (averaging $11,000 per year), research assistantships (averaging $11,250 per year) were awarded; career-related internships or fieldwork, Federal Work-Study, and institutionally sponsored loans also available. Financial award application deadline: 2/1; financial award applicants required to submit FAFSA. *Faculty research:* Public policy, Presidential studies, public leadership, economic policy, social policy. *Unit head:* Dr. Ryan Crocker, Dean, 979-862-8007, E-mail: rcrocker@tamu.edu. *Application contact:* Kathryn Meyer, Director of Recruitment and Admissions, 979-458-4767, Fax: 979-845-4155, E-mail: bushschooladmissions@tamu.edu.
Website: http://bush.tamu.edu/.

Trinity Washington University, School of Business and Graduate Studies, Washington, DC 20017-1094. Offers business administration (MBA); communication (MA); international security studies (MA); organizational management (MSA), including federal program management, human resource management, nonprofit management, organizational development, public and community health. Part-time and evening/weekend programs available. *Degree requirements:* For master's, thesis (for some programs), capstone project (MSA). *Entrance requirements:* For master's, minimum GPA of 2.5. Additional exam requirements/recommendations for international students: Required—TOEFL (minimum score 550 paper-based). *Application deadline:* For fall admission, 4/1 priority date for domestic students; for winter admission, 11/1 priority date for domestic students; for spring admission, 11/1 priority date for domestic students. Applications are processed on a rolling basis. Application fee: $40. *Expenses:* *Tuition:* Part-time $715 per credit. *Financial support:* Career-related internships or fieldwork and unspecified assistantships available. Support available to part-time students. Financial award application deadline: 4/1; financial award applicants required to submit FAFSA. *Unit head:* Dr. Peggy Lewis, Associate Dean, 202-884-9204, E-mail: lewisp@trinitydc.edu. *Application contact:* Alesha Tyson, Director of Admissions for School of Business and Graduate Studies, 202-884-9400, Fax: 202-884-9229, E-mail: tysona@trinitydc.edu.
Website: http://www.trinitydc.edu/bgs/.

Trinity Western University, School of Graduate Studies, Program in Business Administration, Langley, BC V2Y 1Y1, Canada. Offers international business (MBA); management of the growing enterprise (MBA); non-profit and charitable organization

management (MBA). Part-time programs available. Postbaccalaureate distance learning degree programs offered (minimal on-campus study). *Degree requirements:* For master's, thesis or alternative, applied project. *Entrance requirements:* For master's, GMAT (minimum score of 550 recommended). Additional exam requirements/recommendations for international students: Required—TOEFL (minimum score 600 paper-based; 100 iBT), IELTS. Electronic applications accepted.

Trinity Western University, School of Graduate Studies, Program in Leadership, Langley, BC V2Y 1Y1, Canada. Offers business (MA, Certificate); Christian ministry (MA); education (MA, Certificate); healthcare (MA, Certificate); non-profit (MA, Certificate). Postbaccalaureate distance learning degree programs offered (minimal on-campus study). *Degree requirements:* For master's, major project. *Entrance requirements:* For master's, minimum GPA of 2.7. Additional exam requirements/recommendations for international students: Required—TOEFL (minimum score 620 paper-based; 105 iBT). Electronic applications accepted. *Expenses:* Contact institution. *Faculty research:* Servant leadership.

Troy University, Graduate School, College of Arts and Sciences, Program in Public Administration, Troy, AL 36082. Offers education (MPA); environmental management (MPA); government contracting (MPA); health care administration (MPA); justice administration (MPA); national security affairs (MPA); nonprofit management (MPA); public human resources management (MPA); public management (MPA). *Accreditation:* NASPAA. Part-time and evening/weekend programs available. Postbaccalaureate distance learning degree programs offered (no on-campus study). *Faculty:* 15 full-time (9 women), 7 part-time/adjunct (4 women). *Students:* 95 full-time (62 women), 307 part-time (204 women); includes 231 minority (195 Black or African American, non-Hispanic/Latino; 3 American Indian or Alaska Native, non-Hispanic/Latino; 5 Asian, non-Hispanic/Latino; 15 Hispanic/Latino; 13 Two or more races, non-Hispanic/Latino). Average age 32. 172 applicants, 87% accepted, 107 enrolled. In 2013, 159 master's awarded. *Degree requirements:* For master's, capstone course with minimum B grade, minimum GPA of 3.0, admission to candidacy. *Entrance requirements:* For master's, GRE (minimum score of 850 on old exam or 294 on new exam), MAT (minimum score of 400) or GMAT (minimum score of 490), bachelor's degree; minimum undergraduate GPA of 2.5 or 3.0 on last 30 semester hours, letter of recommendation; essay. Additional exam requirements/recommendations for international students: Required—TOEFL (minimum score 523 paper-based; 70 iBT), IELTS (minimum score 6). *Application deadline:* Applications are processed on a rolling basis. Application fee: $50. Electronic applications accepted. *Expenses:* Tuition, state resident: full-time $6084; part-time $338 per credit hour. Tuition, nonresident: full-time $12,168; part-time $676 per credit hour. *Required fees:* $630; $35 per credit hour. $50 per semester. *Financial support:* Available to part-time students. Applicants required to submit FAFSA. *Unit head:* Dr. Sam Shelton, Chairman, 334-670-3754, Fax: 334-670-5647, E-mail: sshelton1@troy.edu. *Application contact:* Brenda K. Campbell, Director of Graduate Admissions, 334-670-3178, Fax: 334-670-3733, E-mail: bcamp@troy.edu.

Tufts University, Graduate School of Arts and Sciences, Graduate Certificate Programs, Management of Community Organizations Program, Medford, MA 02155. Offers Certificate. Part-time and evening/weekend programs available. Electronic applications accepted. *Expenses:* Contact institution.

University of Arkansas at Little Rock, Graduate School, College of Professional Studies, Program in Nonprofit Management, Little Rock, AR 72204-1099. Offers Graduate Certificate. *Expenses:* Tuition, state resident: full-time $5690; part-time $284.50 per credit hour. Tuition, nonresident: full-time $13,030; part-time $651.50 per credit hour. *Required fees:* $1121; $672 per term. One-time fee: $40 full-time.

University of Central Florida, College of Health and Public Affairs, School of Public Administration, Orlando, FL 32816. Offers emergency management and homeland security (Certificate); fundraising (Certificate); non-profit management (MNM, Certificate); public administration (MPA, Certificate); urban and regional planning (MS, Certificate). *Accreditation:* NASPAA. Part-time and evening/weekend programs available. *Faculty:* 19 full-time (10 women), 11 part-time/adjunct (4 women). *Students:* 100 full-time (71 women), 272 part-time (190 women); includes 137 minority (63 Black or African American, non-Hispanic/Latino; 6 Asian, non-Hispanic/Latino; 61 Hispanic/Latino; 7 Two or more races, non-Hispanic/Latino), 4 international. Average age 32. 251 applicants, 80% accepted, 144 enrolled. In 2013, 121 master's, 23 other advanced degrees awarded. *Degree requirements:* For master's, comprehensive exam, thesis or alternative, research report. *Entrance requirements:* For master's, GRE General Test. *Application deadline:* For fall admission, 7/1 for domestic students; for spring admission, 12/1 for domestic students. Application fee: $30. Electronic applications accepted. *Financial support:* In 2013–14, 2 students received support, including 1 fellowship with partial tuition reimbursement available (averaging $10,000 per year), 1 research assistantship with partial tuition reimbursement available (averaging $10,400 per year); teaching assistantships, career-related internships or fieldwork, Federal Work-Study, institutionally sponsored loans, tuition waivers (partial), and unspecified assistantships also available. Financial award application deadline: 3/1; financial award applicants required to submit FAFSA. *Unit head:* Dr. Mary Ann Feldheim, Director, 407-823-3693, Fax: 407-823-5651, E-mail: mary.feldheim@ucf.edu. *Application contact:* Barbara Rodriguez Lamas, Director, Admissions and Student Services, 407-823-2766, Fax: 407-823-6442, E-mail: gradadmissions@ucf.edu.
Website: http://www.cohpa.ucf.edu/pubadm/

University of Colorado Denver, School of Public Affairs, Program in Public Affairs and Administration, Denver, CO 80127. Offers public administration (MPA), including domestic violence, emergency management and homeland security, environmental policy, management and law, homeland security and defense, local government, nonprofit management, public administration; public affairs (PhD). *Accreditation:* NASPAA. Part-time and evening/weekend programs available. Postbaccalaureate distance learning degree programs offered (no on-campus study). *Students:* 268 full-time (168 women), 162 part-time (100 women); includes 60 minority (8 Black or African American, non-Hispanic/Latino; 6 American Indian or Alaska Native, non-Hispanic/Latino; 9 Asian, non-Hispanic/Latino; 34 Hispanic/Latino; 1 Native Hawaiian or other Pacific Islander, non-Hispanic/Latino; 2 Two or more races, non-Hispanic/Latino), 31 international. Average age 34. 293 applicants, 64% accepted, 109 enrolled. In 2013, 133 master's, 3 doctorates awarded. *Degree requirements:* For master's, thesis or alternative, 36-39 credit hours; for doctorate, comprehensive exam, thesis/dissertation, minimum of 66 semester hours, including at least 30 hours of dissertation. *Entrance requirements:* For master's, GRE, GMAT or LSAT, resume, essay, transcripts, recommendations; for doctorate, GRE, resume, essay, transcripts, recommendations. Additional exam requirements/recommendations for international students: Required—TOEFL (minimum score 550 paper-based; 80 iBT); Recommended—IELTS (minimum score 6.5). *Application deadline:* For fall admission, 2/1 priority date for domestic students, 1/15 priority date for international students; for spring admission, 10/15 priority date for domestic students, 10/1 priority date for international students. Application fee: $50 ($75 for international students). Electronic applications accepted. *Expenses:* Contact institution. *Financial support:* In 2013–14, 54 students received support. Fellowships with partial tuition reimbursements available, research assistantships with partial tuition reimbursements available, teaching assistantships with partial tuition reimbursements available, Federal Work-Study, institutionally sponsored loans,

scholarships/grants, traineeships, and unspecified assistantships available. Financial award application deadline: 4/1; financial award applicants required to submit FAFSA. *Faculty research:* Housing, education and the social and economic issues of vulnerable populations; nonprofit governance and management; education finance, effectiveness and reform; P-20 education initiatives; municipal government accountability. *Unit head:* Dr. Christine Martell, Director of MPA Program, 303-315-2716, Fax: 303-315-2229, E-mail: christine.martell@ucdenver.edu. *Application contact:* Dawn Savage, Student Services Coordinator, 303-315-2743, Fax: 303-315-2229, E-mail: dawn.savage@ucdenver.edu.
Website: http://www.ucdenver.edu/academics/colleges/SPA/Academics/programs/PublicAffairsAdmin/Pages/index.aspx.

University of Connecticut, Graduate School, College of Liberal Arts and Sciences, Department of Public Policy, Field of Public Administration, Storrs, CT 06269. Offers nonprofit management (Graduate Certificate); public administration (MPA); public financial management (Graduate Certificate); JD/MPA; MPA/MSW. *Accreditation:* NASPAA. *Degree requirements:* For master's, comprehensive exam, internship. *Entrance requirements:* For master's, GRE General Test. Additional exam requirements/recommendations for international students: Required—TOEFL (minimum score 550 paper-based). Electronic applications accepted.

University of Florida, Graduate School, College of Agricultural and Life Sciences, Department of Family, Youth, and Community Sciences, Gainesville, FL 32611. Offers community studies (MS); family and youth development (MS); family, youth and community services (MS); nonprofit organization development (MS). Part-time programs available. Postbaccalaureate distance learning degree programs offered (no on-campus study). *Faculty:* 21 full-time (11 women), 4 part-time/adjunct (2 women). *Students:* 10 full-time (7 women), 17 part-time (13 women); includes 10 minority (4 Black or African American, non-Hispanic/Latino; 1 American Indian or Alaska Native, non-Hispanic/Latino; 5 Hispanic/Latino), 4 international. Average age 26. 32 applicants, 41% accepted, 10 enrolled. In 2013, 9 master's awarded. *Degree requirements:* For master's, comprehensive exam (for some programs), thesis (for some programs). *Entrance requirements:* For master's, GRE General Test, minimum GPA of 3.0. Additional exam requirements/recommendations for international students: Required—TOEFL (minimum score 550 paper-based; 80 iBT), IELTS (minimum score 6). *Application deadline:* For fall admission, 7/1 for domestic students, 11/1 for international students; for spring admission, 11/1 for domestic and international students. Applications are processed on a rolling basis. Application fee: $30. Electronic applications accepted. *Expenses:* Tuition, state resident: full-time $12,640. Tuition, nonresident: full-time $30,000. *Financial support:* In 2013–14, 5 students received support, including 2 fellowships (averaging $8,500 per year), 4 teaching assistantships (averaging $14,980 per year). Financial award applicants required to submit FAFSA. *Faculty research:* Family financial management, family nutrition and wellness, community-based interventions, family and youth relations, nonprofit organizations. *Unit head:* Traci Irani, PhD, Professor and Interim Chair, 352-273-3446, E-mail: irani@ufl.edu. *Application contact:* Gregg Henderschiedt, Academic Coordinator, Graduate Program, 352-273-3514, Fax: 352-392-8196, E-mail: ghenderschiedt@ufl.edu.
Website: http://fycs.ifas.ufl.edu/.

University of Georgia, School of Social Work, Athens, GA 30602. Offers MA, MSW, PhD, Certificate. *Accreditation:* CSWE (one or more programs are accredited). Part-time and evening/weekend programs available. *Degree requirements:* For master's, thesis or alternative; for doctorate, one foreign language, thesis/dissertation. *Entrance requirements:* For master's and doctorate, GRE General Test. Electronic applications accepted. *Faculty research:* Juvenile justice, substance abuse, civil rights and social justice, gerontology, social policy.

University of Houston–Downtown, College of Humanities and Social Sciences, Department of Social Sciences, Houston, TX 77002. Offers MA. Postbaccalaureate distance learning degree programs offered (no on-campus study). *Faculty:* 1 full-time (0 women), 2 part-time/adjunct (0 women). *Students:* 20 full-time (17 women), 3 part-time (2 women); includes 15 minority (10 Black or African American, non-Hispanic/Latino; 5 Hispanic/Latino). 24 applicants, 100% accepted, 23 enrolled. *Degree requirements:* For master's, thesis or capstone project. *Entrance requirements:* For master's, GRE, essay, resume, 2 letters of recommendation, transcripts. Additional exam requirements/recommendations for international students: Required—TOEFL (minimum score 600 paper-based; 86 iBT). *Application deadline:* For fall admission, 4/1 for domestic and international students; for spring admission, 11/15 for domestic and international students. Application fee: $35 ($60 for international students). Electronic applications accepted. *Expenses:* Tuition, state resident: full-time $4212; part-time $234 per credit hour. Tuition, nonresident: full-time $9684; part-time $538 per credit hour. *Required fees:* $1074. Tuition and fees vary according to program. *Unit head:* Dr. Jeffrey Jackson, Chair, 713-221-2793, Fax: 713-226-5205, E-mail: jacksonjef@uhd.edu. *Application contact:* Ceshia Love, Assistant Director of Graduate Admissions, 713-221-8093, Fax: 713-223-7408, E-mail: gradadmissions@uhd.edu.
Website: http://www.uhd.edu/academic/colleges/humanities/sos/ma/index.html.

University of La Verne, College of Business and Public Management, Master's Program in Public Administration, La Verne, CA 91750-4443. Offers governance concentration (MPA); non-profit concentration (MPA). *Accreditation:* NASPAA. Part-time programs available. *Faculty:* 13 full-time (6 women), 4 part-time/adjunct (2 women). *Students:* 29 full-time (15 women), 54 part-time (31 women); includes 55 minority (9 Black or African American, non-Hispanic/Latino; 1 American Indian or Alaska Native, non-Hispanic/Latino; 5 Asian, non-Hispanic/Latino; 37 Hispanic/Latino; 3 Two or more races, non-Hispanic/Latino), 6 international. Average age 34. In 2013, 31 master's awarded. *Entrance requirements:* For master's, minimum undergraduate GPA of 3.0, statement of purpose, 2 letters of recommendation, resume. Additional exam requirements/recommendations for international students: Required—TOEFL (minimum score 550 paper-based). *Application deadline:* Applications are processed on a rolling basis. Application fee: $50. *Expenses:* Contact institution. *Financial support:* Fellowships and research assistantships available. Financial award application deadline: 3/2; financial award applicants required to submit FAFSA. *Unit head:* Dr. Jack Meek, Chairperson, 909-593-3511 Ext. 4941, E-mail: jmeek@laverne.edu. *Application contact:* Erma Cross, Associate Director of Graduate Admissions, 909-593-3511 Ext. 4948, Fax: 909-392-2761, E-mail: ecross@laverne.edu.
Website: http://www.laverne.edu/business-and-public-administration/public-administration/.

University of La Verne, College of Business and Public Management, Program in Organizational Management and Leadership, La Verne, CA 91750-4443. Offers leadership and management (MS), including human resource management, nonprofit management, organizational development; nonprofit management (Certificate); organizational leadership (Certificate). Part-time programs available. *Faculty:* 2 full-time (1 woman), 8 part-time/adjunct (6 women). *Students:* 77 full-time (39 women), 67 part-time (47 women); includes 69 minority (7 Black or African American, non-Hispanic/Latino; 3 Asian, non-Hispanic/Latino; 55 Hispanic/Latino; 2 Native Hawaiian or other Pacific Islander, non-Hispanic/Latino; 2 Two or more races, non-Hispanic/Latino), 38 international. Average age 32. In 2013, 183 master's awarded. *Degree requirements:* For master's, thesis or research project. *Entrance requirements:* For master's, minimum

undergraduate GPA of 2.75, 2 letters of recommendation, interview, resume. Additional exam requirements/recommendations for international students: Required—TOEFL (minimum score 550 paper-based). *Application deadline:* Applications are processed on a rolling basis. Application fee: $50. *Expenses:* Contact institution. *Financial support:* Institutionally sponsored loans available. Financial award application deadline: 3/2; financial award applicants required to submit FAFSA. *Unit head:* Dr. Kathy Duncan, Program Director, 909-593-3511 Ext. 4415, E-mail: kduncan2@laverne.edu. *Application contact:* Rina Lazarian-Chehab, Senior Associate Director of Graduate Admissions, 909-593-3511 Ext. 4317, Fax: 909-392-2761, E-mail: rlazarian@laverne.edu.
Website: http://www.laverne.edu/business-and-public-administration/org-mgmt/.

University of La Verne, Regional and Online Campuses, Graduate Programs, Inland Empire Campus, Ontario, CA 91761. Offers business administration (MBA, MBA-EP), including accounting (MBA), finance (MBA), health services management (MBA-EP), information technology (MBA-EP), international business (MBA), managed care (MBA), management and leadership (MBA-EP), marketing (MBA-EP), supply chain management (MBA); leadership and management (MS), including human resource management, nonprofit management, organizational development. Part-time and evening/weekend programs available. *Faculty:* 1 full-time (0 women), 14 part-time/adjunct (6 women). *Students:* 26 full-time (15 women), 106 part-time (65 women); includes 92 minority (15 Black or African American, non-Hispanic/Latino; 29 Asian, non-Hispanic/Latino; 43 Hispanic/Latino; 1 Native Hawaiian or other Pacific Islander, non-Hispanic/Latino; 4 Two or more races, non-Hispanic/Latino). Average age 37. In 2013, 49 master's awarded. *Application deadline:* Applications are processed on a rolling basis. Application fee: $50. *Expenses:* Contact institution. *Financial support:* Institutionally sponsored loans available. Financial award application deadline: 3/2; financial award applicants required to submit FAFSA. *Unit head:* Allen Stout, Campus Director, Inland Empire Regional Campus in Ontario, 909-937-6987, E-mail: astout@laverne.edu. *Application contact:* Karen Schumann, Senior Associate Director of Admissions, Inland Empire Regional Campus in Ontario, 909-937-6991, E-mail: kschumann@laverne.edu.
Website: http://laverne.edu/locations/inland-empire/.

University of Louisville, Graduate School, College of Arts and Sciences, Department of Urban and Public Affairs, Louisville, KY 40208. Offers public administration (MPA), including human resources management, non-profit management, public policy and administration; urban and public affairs (PhD), including urban planning and development, urban policy and administration; urban planning (MUP), including administration of planning organizations, housing and community development, land use and environmental planning, spatial analysis. Part-time and evening/weekend programs available. *Students:* 65 full-time (31 women), 27 part-time (16 women); includes 10 minority (5 Black or African American, non-Hispanic/Latino; 2 Asian, non-Hispanic/Latino; 2 Hispanic/Latino; 1 Two or more races, non-Hispanic/Latino), 7 international. Average age 31. 93 applicants, 62% accepted, 30 enrolled. In 2013, 17 master's, 3 doctorates awarded. Terminal master's awarded for partial completion of doctoral program. *Degree requirements:* For master's, internship; for doctorate, comprehensive exam, thesis/dissertation. *Entrance requirements:* For master's, GRE General Test, minimum GPA of 3.0; for doctorate, GRE General Test, master's degree in appropriate field. Additional exam requirements/recommendations for international students: Required—TOEFL (minimum score 550 paper-based; 79 iBT). *Application deadline:* For fall admission, 7/15 for domestic students, 5/1 priority date for international students; for spring admission, 11/15 for domestic students, 11/1 priority date for international students; for summer admission, 4/1 priority date for international students. Applications are processed on a rolling basis. Application fee: $60. Electronic applications accepted. *Expenses:* Tuition, state resident: full-time $10,788; part-time $599 per credit hour. Tuition, nonresident: full-time $22,446; part-time $1247 per credit hour. *Required fees:* $196. Tuition and fees vary according to program and reciprocity agreements. *Financial support:* Fellowships, research assistantships, and health care benefits available. Financial award application deadline: 3/1. *Faculty research:* Housing and community development, performance-based budgeting, environmental policy and natural hazards, sustainability, real estate development, comparative urban development. *Unit head:* Dr. David Simpson, Chair, 502-852-8019, Fax: 502-852-4558, E-mail: dave.simpson@louisville.edu. *Application contact:* Libby Leggett, Director, Graduate Admissions, 502-852-3101, Fax: 502-852-4558, E-mail: gradadm@louisville.edu.
Website: http://supa.louisville.edu.

University of Memphis, Graduate School, College of Arts and Sciences, Division of Public and Nonprofit Administration, Memphis, TN 38152. Offers nonprofit administration (MPA); public management and policy (MPA); urban management and planning (MPA). *Accreditation:* NASPAA. Part-time and evening/weekend programs available. Postbaccalaureate distance learning degree programs offered (minimal on-campus study). *Faculty:* 6 full-time (3 women), 1 (woman) part-time/adjunct. *Students:* 22 full-time (17 women), 34 part-time (29 women); includes 37 minority (36 Black or African American, non-Hispanic/Latino; 1 Two or more races, non-Hispanic/Latino), 2 international. Average age 37. 17 applicants, 94% accepted, 3 enrolled. In 2013, 17 master's awarded. *Degree requirements:* For master's, comprehensive exam, thesis or alternative, internship. *Entrance requirements:* For master's, GRE General Test, GMAT, or MAT, minimum GPA of 3.0. Additional exam requirements/recommendations for international students: Required—TOEFL. *Application deadline:* For fall admission, 7/1 for domestic students, 5/15 for international students; for spring admission, 12/1 for domestic students, 9/15 for international students. Applications are processed on a rolling basis. Application fee: $35 ($60 for international students). *Financial support:* In 2013–14, 37 students received support. Fellowships, research assistantships with full tuition reimbursements available, career-related internships or fieldwork, Federal Work-Study, scholarships/grants, and unspecified assistantships available. Support available to part-time students. Financial award application deadline: 2/15; financial award applicants required to submit FAFSA. *Faculty research:* Nonprofit organization governance, local government management, community collaboration, urban problems, accountability. *Unit head:* Dr. Charles Menifield, Director, 901-678-5527, Fax: 901-678-2981, E-mail: cmenifld@memphis.edu. *Application contact:* Dr. Charles Menifield, Graduate Admissions Coordinator, 901-678-3360, Fax: 901-678-2981, E-mail: cmenifld@memphis.edu.
Website: http://www.memphis.edu/padm/.

University of Michigan–Flint, Graduate Programs, Program in Public Administration, Flint, MI 48502-1950. Offers administration of non-profit agencies (MPA); criminal justice administration (MPA); educational administration (MPA); healthcare administration (MPA). Part-time programs available. *Faculty:* 6 full-time (2 women), 12 part-time/adjunct (4 women). *Students:* 16 full-time (6 women), 112 part-time (74 women); includes 34 minority (24 Black or African American, non-Hispanic/Latino; 1 American Indian or Alaska Native, non-Hispanic/Latino; 1 Asian, non-Hispanic/Latino; 5 Hispanic/Latino; 3 Two or more races, non-Hispanic/Latino), 4 international. Average age 33. 75 applicants, 65% accepted, 44 enrolled. In 2013, 59 master's awarded. *Degree requirements:* For master's, thesis or alternative, internship. *Entrance requirements:* For master's, minimum GPA of 3.0, 1 course each in American government, microeconomics and statistics. Additional exam requirements/recommendations for international students: Required—TOEFL (minimum score 560 paper-based; 84 iBT), IELTS (minimum score 6.5). *Application deadline:* For fall admission, 8/1 for domestic students, 5/1 for international students; for winter admission, 11/15 for domestic students, 9/1 for international students; for spring admission, 3/15 for domestic students, 1/1 for international students; for summer admission, 5/15 for domestic students. Applications are processed on a rolling basis. Application fee: $55. Electronic applications accepted. *Expenses:* Contact institution. *Financial support:* Career-related internships or fieldwork, Federal Work-Study, and scholarships/grants available. Support available to part-time students. Financial award application deadline: 3/1; financial award applicants required to submit FAFSA. *Unit head:* Dr. Kathryn Schellenberg, Director, 810-762-3340, E-mail: kathsch@umflint.edu. *Application contact:* Bradley T. Maki, Director of Graduate Admissions, 810-762-3171, Fax: 810-766-6789, E-mail: bmaki@umflint.edu.
Website: http://www.umflint.edu/graduateprograms/public-administration-mpa.

University of Missouri, Graduate School, Harry S Truman School of Public Affairs, Columbia, MO 65211. Offers grantsmanship (Graduate Certificate); nonprofit management (Graduate Certificate); organizational change (Graduate Certificate); public affairs (MPA, PhD); public management (Graduate Certificate); science and public policy (Graduate Certificate). *Accreditation:* NASPAA. *Faculty:* 12 full-time (5 women). *Students:* 91 full-time (54 women), 60 part-time (30 women); includes 14 minority (10 Black or African American, non-Hispanic/Latino; 1 Asian, non-Hispanic/Latino; 2 Hispanic/Latino; 1 Two or more races, non-Hispanic/Latino), 47 international. Average age 31. 152 applicants, 53% accepted, 51 enrolled. In 2013, 53 master's, 1 doctorate, 19 other advanced degrees awarded. *Entrance requirements:* For master's, GRE General Test, minimum GPA of 3.0. Additional exam requirements/recommendations for international students: Required—TOEFL (minimum score 550 paper-based; 79 iBT). *Application deadline:* For fall admission, 2/1 priority date for domestic and international students. Applications are processed on a rolling basis. Application fee: $55 ($75 for international students). Electronic applications accepted. *Financial support:* Fellowships, research assistantships, teaching assistantships, institutionally sponsored loans, scholarships/grants, traineeships, health care benefits, and unspecified assistantships available. Support available to part-time students. *Faculty research:* Public service ethics, history and theory, organizational symbolism and culture; program evaluation and social policy, with special emphasis on child development, education and health policies; organization theory and applied psychoanalytic theory; foreign policy and international political economy; health care delivery for persons with disabilities and health policy; survival strategies employed by low-income households; rural economic development, fiscal and economic impact analysis. *Unit head:* Dr. Bart Wechsler, Director, 573-882-3304, E-mail: wechslerb@missouri.edu. *Application contact:* Nicole Harris, Assistant Program Director for Student Services, 573-882-3471, E-mail: harrisnr@missouri.edu.
Website: http://truman.missouri.edu/.

University of Missouri–St. Louis, Graduate School, Program in Public Policy Administration, St. Louis, MO 63121. Offers local government management (MPPA, Certificate); managing human resources and organization (MPPA); nonprofit organization management (MPPA); nonprofit organization management and leadership (Certificate); policy research and analysis (MPPA). *Accreditation:* NASPAA. Part-time and evening/weekend programs available. *Faculty:* 9 full-time (4 women), 13 part-time/adjunct (9 women). *Students:* 19 full-time (12 women), 59 part-time (36 women); includes 20 minority (17 Black or African American, non-Hispanic/Latino; 1 Asian, non-Hispanic/Latino; 1 Hispanic/Latino; 1 Two or more races, non-Hispanic/Latino), 4 international. Average age 33. 39 applicants, 74% accepted, 16 enrolled. In 2013, 25 master's, 27 Certificates awarded. *Degree requirements:* For master's, exit project. *Entrance requirements:* For master's, 3 letters of recommendation. Additional exam requirements/recommendations for international students: Recommended—TOEFL (minimum score 550 paper-based), IELTS (minimum score 6.5). *Application deadline:* For fall admission, 7/1 priority date for domestic and international students; for spring admission, 12/1 priority date for domestic and international students. Applications are processed on a rolling basis. Application fee: $50 ($40 for international students). Electronic applications accepted. *Expenses:* Tuition, state resident: full-time $7364; part-time $409.10 per credit hour. Tuition, nonresident: full-time $19,162; part-time $1008.50 per credit hour. *Financial support:* In 2013–14, 2 research assistantships with full and partial tuition reimbursements (averaging $12,000 per year) were awarded; career-related internships or fieldwork also available. Financial award application deadline: 4/1; financial award applicants required to submit FAFSA. *Faculty research:* Urban policy, public finance, evaluation. *Unit head:* Dr. Deborah Balser, Director, 314-516-5145, Fax: 314-516-5210, E-mail: balserd@msx.umsl.edu. *Application contact:* 314-516-5458, Fax: 314-516-6996, E-mail: gradadm@umsl.edu.
Website: http://www.umsl.edu/divisions/graduate/mppa/.

University of Nevada, Las Vegas, Graduate College, Greenspun College of Urban Affairs, School of Environmental and Public Affairs, Las Vegas, NV 89154-4030. Offers environmental science (MS, PhD); non-profit management (Certificate); public administration (MPA, MS), including crisis and emergency management (MS); public affairs (PhD); public management (Certificate); solar and renewable energy (Certificate); urban leadership (MA); workforce development and organizational leadership (PhD). Part-time programs available. *Faculty:* 8 full-time (6 women), 6 part-time/adjunct (5 women). *Students:* 73 full-time (35 women), 133 part-time (63 women); includes 81 minority (29 Black or African American, non-Hispanic/Latino; 2 American Indian or Alaska Native, non-Hispanic/Latino; 5 Asian, non-Hispanic/Latino; 29 Hispanic/Latino; 2 Native Hawaiian or other Pacific Islander, non-Hispanic/Latino; 14 Two or more races, non-Hispanic/Latino), 7 international. Average age 37. 86 applicants, 71% accepted, 53 enrolled. In 2013, 60 master's, 6 doctorates, 17 other advanced degrees awarded. *Degree requirements:* For master's, comprehensive exam (for some programs), thesis; for doctorate, comprehensive exam (for some programs), thesis/dissertation. *Entrance requirements:* Additional exam requirements/recommendations for international students: Required—TOEFL (minimum score 550 paper-based; 80 iBT), IELTS (minimum score 7). *Application deadline:* For fall admission, 2/15 for domestic students, 5/1 for international students; for spring admission, 11/1 for domestic students, 10/1 for international students. Application fee: $60 ($95 for international students). Electronic applications accepted. *Expenses:* Tuition, state resident: full-time $4752; part-time $264 per credit. Tuition, nonresident: full-time $18,662; part-time $554.50 per credit. *International tuition:* $18,952 full-time. *Required fees:* $532; $12 per credit. $266 per semester. One-time fee: $35. Tuition and fees vary according to course load and program. *Financial support:* In 2013–14, 28 students received support, including 19 research assistantships with partial tuition reimbursements available (averaging $11,301 per year), 9 teaching assistantships with partial tuition reimbursements available (averaging $12,028 per year); institutionally sponsored loans, scholarships/grants, health care benefits, and unspecified assistantships also available. Financial award application deadline: 3/1. *Faculty research:* Community and organizational resilience; environmental decision-making and management; budgeting and human resource/workforce management; urban design, sustainability and governance; public and non-profit management. *Total annual research expenditures:* $333,798. *Unit head:* Dr. Christopher Stream, Chair/Associate Professor, 702-895-5120, Fax: 702-895-4436, E-mail: chris.stream@unlv.edu. *Application contact:* Graduate College Admissions Evaluator, 702-895-3320, Fax: 702-895-4180, E-mail: gradcollege@unlv.edu.
Website: http://sepa.unlv.edu/.

The University of North Carolina at Charlotte, The Graduate School, College of Liberal Arts and Sciences, Department of Political Science and Public Administration, Charlotte, NC 28223-0001. Offers emergency management (Graduate Certificate); non-profit management (Graduate Certificate); public administration (MPA), including arts administration, emergency management, non-profit management, public finance; public finance (Graduate Certificate); urban management and policy (Graduate Certificate). *Accreditation:* NASPAA. Part-time and evening/weekend programs available. *Faculty:* 16 full-time (8 women), 4 part-time/adjunct (0 women). *Students:* 24 full-time (14 women), 80 part-time (47 women); includes 37 minority (27 Black or African American, non-Hispanic/Latino; 1 American Indian or Alaska Native, non-Hispanic/Latino; 1 Asian, non-Hispanic/Latino; 6 Hispanic/Latino; 2 Two or more races, non-Hispanic/Latino), 1 international. Average age 29. 68 applicants, 72% accepted, 35 enrolled. In 2013, 24 master's, 9 other advanced degrees awarded. Terminal master's awarded for partial completion of doctoral program. *Degree requirements:* For master's, thesis or alternative. *Entrance requirements:* For master's, GRE General Test or MAT, minimum GPA of 3.0 in undergraduate major, 2.75 overall. Additional exam requirements/recommendations for international students: Required—TOEFL (minimum score 557 paper-based; 83 iBT). *Application deadline:* For fall admission, 5/1 priority date for domestic students, 5/1 for international students; for spring admission, 10/1 priority date for domestic students, 10/1 for international students. Applications are processed on a rolling basis. Application fee: $75. Electronic applications accepted. *Expenses:* Tuition, state resident: full-time $3522. Tuition, nonresident: full-time $16,051. *Required fees:* $2585. Tuition and fees vary according to course load and program. *Financial support:* In 2013–14, 9 students received support, including 9 research assistantships (averaging $9,444 per year); career-related internships or fieldwork, Federal Work-Study, institutionally sponsored loans, scholarships/grants, and unspecified assistantships also available. Support available to part-time students. Financial award application deadline: 4/1; financial award applicants required to submit FAFSA. *Faculty research:* Health policy and politics, managed care, issues of ethnic and racial disparities in health, aging policies, Central Asia. *Total annual research expenditures:* $276,620. *Unit head:* Dr. Greg Weeks, Chair, 704-687-7574, Fax: 704-687-1400, E-mail: gbweeks@uncc.edu. *Application contact:* Kathy B. Giddings, Director of Graduate Admissions, 704-687-5503, Fax: 704-687-1668, E-mail: gradadm@uncc.edu.
Website: https://politicalscience.uncc.edu/graduate.

The University of North Carolina at Greensboro, Graduate School, College of Arts and Sciences, Department of Political Science, Greensboro, NC 27412-5001. Offers nonprofit management (Certificate); public affairs (MPA); urban and economic development (Certificate). *Accreditation:* NASPAA. *Degree requirements:* For master's, comprehensive exam. *Entrance requirements:* For master's, GRE General Test. Additional exam requirements/recommendations for international students: Required—TOEFL. Electronic applications accepted. *Faculty research:* U.S. Constitution, Canadian parliament, public management, ethical challenge of public service.

University of Northern Iowa, Graduate College, MA Program in Philanthropy and Nonprofit Development, Cedar Falls, IA 50614. Offers MA. *Students:* 19 part-time (15 women); includes 2 minority (1 Hispanic/Latino; 1 Two or more races, non-Hispanic/Latino). 3 applicants. In 2013, 1 master's awarded. *Entrance requirements:* For master's, minimum GPA of 3.0; 3 letters of recommendation; experience in the philanthropy and/or nonprofit areas. Additional exam requirements/recommendations for international students: Required—TOEFL (minimum score 500 paper-based; 61 iBT). *Application deadline:* Applications are processed on a rolling basis. Application fee: $50 ($70 for international students). Electronic applications accepted. *Financial support:* Application deadline: 2/1. *Unit head:* Dr. Rodney Dieser, Coordinator, 319-273-7775, Fax: 319-273-5958, E-mail: rodney.dieser@uni.edu. *Application contact:* Laurie S. Russell, Record Analyst, 319-273-2623, Fax: 319-273-2885, E-mail: laurie.russell@uni.edu.
Website: http://www.grad.uni.edu/degrees-programs/programs/philanthropy-and-nonprofit-development-ma.

University of North Florida, College of Arts and Sciences, Department of Political Science and Public Administration, Jacksonville, FL 32224. Offers nonprofit management (Graduate Certificate); public administration (MPA). *Accreditation:* NASPAA. Part-time programs available. *Faculty:* 11 full-time (5 women), 1 part-time/adjunct (0 women). *Students:* 21 full-time (14 women), 45 part-time (24 women); includes 26 minority (16 Black or African American, non-Hispanic/Latino; 1 Asian, non-Hispanic/Latino; 8 Hispanic/Latino; 1 Two or more races, non-Hispanic/Latino), 1 international. Average age 31. 34 applicants, 41% accepted, 8 enrolled. In 2013, 26 master's awarded. *Degree requirements:* For master's, thesis or alternative, internship. *Entrance requirements:* For master's, GRE General Test, minimum GPA of 3.0 in last 60 hours, 2 letters of recommendation, interview. Additional exam requirements/recommendations for international students: Required—TOEFL (minimum score 500 paper-based; 61 iBT). *Application deadline:* For fall admission, 7/1 priority date for domestic students, 5/1 for international students; for spring admission, 11/1 priority date for domestic students, 10/1 for international students. Application fee: $30. Electronic applications accepted. *Expenses:* Tuition, state resident: full-time $9794; part-time $408.10 per credit hour. Tuition, nonresident: full-time $22,383; part-time $932.61 per credit hour. *Required fees:* $2020; $84.20 per credit hour. Tuition and fees vary according to course load and program. *Financial support:* In 2013–14, 12 students received support, including 2 teaching assistantships (averaging $6,042 per year); research assistantships, career-related internships or fieldwork, Federal Work-Study, scholarships/grants, tuition waivers (partial), and unspecified assistantships also available. Financial award application deadline: 4/1; financial award applicants required to submit FAFSA. *Faculty research:* America's usage of the Internet, use of information communication technologies by educators and children. *Total annual research expenditures:* $2,415. *Unit head:* Dr. Matthew T. Corrigan, Chair, 904-620-2977, Fax: 904-620-2979, E-mail: mcorriga@unf.edu. *Application contact:* Dr. Amanda Pascale, Director, The Graduate School, 904-620-1360, Fax: 907-620-1362, E-mail: graduateschool@unf.edu.
Website: http://www.unf.edu/coas/pspa/.

University of North Texas, Robert B. Toulouse School of Graduate Studies, Denton, TN 76203-5017. Offers accounting (MS, PhD); applied anthropology (MA, MS); applied behavior analysis (Certificate); applied technology and performance improvement (M Ed, MS, PhD); art education (MA, PhD); art history (MA); art museum education (Certificate); arts leadership (Certificate); audiology (Au D); behavior analysis (MS); biochemistry and molecular biology (MS, PhD); biology (MA, MS, PhD); business (PhD); business computer information systems (PhD); chemistry (MS, PhD); clinical psychology (PhD); communication studies (MA, MS); computer engineering (MS); computer science (MS); computer science and engineering (PhD); counseling (M Ed, MS, PhD), including clinical mental health counseling (MS), college and university counseling (M Ed, MS), elementary school counseling (M Ed, MS), secondary school counseling (M Ed, MS); counseling psychology (PhD); creative writing (MA); criminal justice (MS); curriculum and instruction (M Ed, PhD), including curriculum studies (PhD), early childhood studies (PhD), language and literacy studies (PhD); decision sciences (MBA); design (MA, MFA), including fashion design (MFA), innovation studies, interior design (MFA); early childhood studies (MS); economics (MS); educational leadership (M Ed, Ed D, PhD); educational psychology (MS), including family studies, gifted and talented (MS, PhD);

human development, learning and cognition, research, measurement and evaluation; educational research (PhD), including gifted and talented (MS, PhD), human development and family studies, psychological aspects of sports and exercise, research, measurement and statistics; electrical engineering (MS); emergency management (MPA); engineering systems (MS); English (MA, PhD); environmental science (MS, PhD); experimental psychology (PhD); finance (MBA, MS, PhD); financial management (MPA); French (MA); health psychology and behavioral medicine (PhD); health services management (MBA); higher education (M Ed, Ed D, PhD); history (MA, MS, PhD), including European history (PhD), military history (PhD), United States history (PhD); hospitality management (MS); human resources management (MPA); information science (MS, PhD); information technologies (MBA); information technology and decision sciences (MS); interdisciplinary studies (MA, MS); international sustainable tourism (MS); jazz studies (MM); journalism (MA, MJ, Graduate Certificate), including interactive and virtual digital communication (Graduate Certificate), narrative journalism (Graduate Certificate), public relations (Graduate Certificate); kinesiology (MS); learning technologies (MS, PhD); library science (MS); local government management (MPA); logistics and supply chain management (MBA, PhD); long-term care, senior housing, and aging services (MA, MS); management science (PhD); marketing (MBA, PhD); materials science and engineering (MS, PhD); mathematics (MA, PhD); merchandising (MS); music (MA, MM Ed, PhD), including ethnomusicology (MA), music education (MM Ed, PhD), music theory (MA, PhD), musicology (MA, PhD), performance (MA); nonprofit management (MPA); operations and supply chain management (MBA); performance (MM, DMA); philosophy (MA, PhD); physics (MS, PhD); political science (MA, MS, PhD); public administration and management (PhD), including emergency management, nonprofit management, public financial management, urban management; radio, television and film (MA, MFA); recreation, event and sport management (MS); rehabilitation counseling (MS, Certificate); sociology (MA, MS, PhD); Spanish (MA); special education (M Ed, PhD), including autism intervention (PhD), emotional/behavioral disorders (PhD), mild/moderate disabilities (PhD); speech-language pathology (MA, MS); strategic management (MBA); studio art (MFA); taxation (MS); teaching (M Ed); MBA/MS; MS/MPH; MSES/MBA. Part-time and evening/weekend programs available. Postbaccalaureate distance learning degree programs offered. *Faculty:* 661 full-time (213 women), 240 part-time/adjunct (144 women). *Students:* 3,106 full-time (1,620 women), 3,543 part-time (2,221 women); includes 1,740 minority (533 Black or African American, non-Hispanic/Latino; 15 American Indian or Alaska Native, non-Hispanic/Latino; 286 Asian, non-Hispanic/Latino; 746 Hispanic/Latino; 3 Native Hawaiian or other Pacific Islander, non-Hispanic/Latino; 157 Two or more races, non-Hispanic/Latino), 1,145 international. Average age 32. 6,289 applicants, 43% accepted, 1751 enrolled. In 2013, 1,778 master's, 239 doctorates, 10 other advanced degrees awarded. Terminal master's awarded for partial completion of doctoral program. *Degree requirements:* For master's, variable foreign language requirement, comprehensive exam (for some programs), thesis (for some programs); for doctorate, variable foreign language requirement, comprehensive exam (for some programs), thesis/dissertation; for other advanced degree, variable foreign language requirement, comprehensive exam (for some programs). *Entrance requirements:* For master's and doctorate, GRE, GMAT. Additional exam requirements/recommendations for international students: Required—TOEFL (minimum score 550 paper-based; 79 iBT). *Application deadline:* For fall admission, 7/15 for domestic students, 3/15 for international students; for spring admission, 11/15 for domestic students, 9/15 for international students; for summer admission, 5/1 for domestic students. Applications are processed on a rolling basis. Application fee: $60. Electronic applications accepted. *Financial support:* Fellowships with partial tuition reimbursements, research assistantships with partial tuition reimbursements, teaching assistantships, career-related internships or fieldwork, Federal Work-Study, institutionally sponsored loans, scholarships/grants, health care benefits, and library assistantships available. Support available to part-time students. Financial award applicants required to submit FAFSA. *Unit head:* Mark Wardell, Dean, 940-565-2383, E-mail: mark.wardell@unt.edu. *Application contact:* Toulouse School of Graduate Studies, 940-565-2383, Fax: 940-565-2141, E-mail: gradsch@unt.edu.
Website: http://tsgs.unt.edu/.

University of Notre Dame, Mendoza College of Business, Program in Nonprofit Administration, Notre Dame, IN 46556. Offers MNA. *Accreditation:* AACSB. Part-time programs available. Postbaccalaureate distance learning degree programs offered (minimal on-campus study). *Faculty:* 8 full-time (0 women), 10 part-time/adjunct (5 women). *Students:* 11 full-time (7 women), 61 part-time (36 women); includes 12 minority (2 Black or African American, non-Hispanic/Latino; 4 Asian, non-Hispanic/Latino; 1 Hispanic/Latino; 5 Two or more races, non-Hispanic/Latino). Average age 30. 100 applicants, 42% accepted, 35 enrolled. In 2013, 32 master's awarded. *Degree requirements:* For master's, thesis. *Entrance requirements:* For master's, GRE General Test; GMAT, work experience. Additional exam requirements/recommendations for international students: Required—TOEFL (minimum score 600 paper-based; 100 iBT). *Application deadline:* For winter admission, 1/15 for domestic students; for spring admission, 3/31 for domestic students. Application fee: $60. Electronic applications accepted. *Expenses:* Contact institution. *Financial support:* In 2013–14, 47 students received support, including 47 fellowships (averaging $3,700 per year); institutionally sponsored loans and scholarships/grants also available. Support available to part-time students. *Unit head:* Thomas J. Harvey, Director, 574-631-7593, Fax: 574-631-6532, E-mail: harvey.18@nd.edu. *Application contact:* Kimberly M. Brennan, Program Manager, 574-631-3639, Fax: 574-631-6532, E-mail: brennan.53@nd.edu.
Website: http://business.nd.edu/mna/.

University of Oklahoma, College of Arts and Sciences, Department of Political Science, Program in Public Administration, Norman, OK 73019. Offers non-profit management (MPA); public administration (MPA); public policy (MPA). Part-time and evening/weekend programs available. *Students:* 20 full-time (7 women), 36 part-time (14 women); includes 17 minority (6 Black or African American, non-Hispanic/Latino; 2 American Indian or Alaska Native, non-Hispanic/Latino; 4 Hispanic/Latino; 5 Two or more races, non-Hispanic/Latino). Average age 31. 29 applicants, 83% accepted, 19 enrolled. In 2013, 39 master's awarded. Terminal master's awarded for partial completion of doctoral program. *Degree requirements:* For master's, comprehensive exam, thesis or alternative, 36 hours (12 required, 12 area coursework, 12 electives). *Entrance requirements:* For master's, GRE, statement of purpose, two letters of recommendation. Additional exam requirements/recommendations for international students: Required—TOEFL (minimum score 100 iBT). *Application deadline:* For fall admission, 2/15 for domestic students, 4/1 for international students; for spring admission, 10/1 for domestic students, 9/1 for international students; for summer admission, 2/1 for international students. Applications are processed on a rolling basis. Application fee: $50 ($100 for international students). Electronic applications accepted. *Expenses:* Tuition, state resident: full-time $4205; part-time $175.20 per credit hour. Tuition, nonresident: full-time $16,205; part-time $675.20 per credit hour. *Required fees:* $2745; $103.85 per credit hour. $126.50 per semester. *Financial support:* In 2013–14, 25 students received support. Career-related internships or fieldwork, scholarships/grants, health care benefits, and unspecified assistantships available. Support available to part-time students. Financial award application deadline: 6/1; financial award applicants required to submit FAFSA. *Faculty research:* Public management, nonprofit

administration, public policy, policy analysis, program evaluation. *Unit head:* Dr. Alisa Fryar, Interim Director, Graduate Programs in Public Administration, 405-325-0107, Fax: 405-325-0718, E-mail: ahicklin@ou.edu. *Application contact:* Jeff Alexander, Graduate Programs Coordinator, 405-325-1845, Fax: 405-325-0718, E-mail: jjalexander@ou.edu.
Website: http://psc.ou.edu/.

University of Pennsylvania, School of Arts and Sciences, Fels Institute of Government, Philadelphia, PA 19104. Offers economic development and growth (Certificate); government administration (MGA); nonprofit administration (Certificate); organization dynamics (MS); politics (Certificate); public administration (MPA); public finance (Certificate). Part-time and evening/weekend programs available. *Students:* 55 full-time (27 women), 70 part-time (40 women); includes 26 minority (10 Black or African American, non-Hispanic/Latino; 1 American Indian or Alaska Native, non-Hispanic/Latino; 6 Asian, non-Hispanic/Latino; 4 Hispanic/Latino; 5 Two or more races, non-Hispanic/Latino), 17 international. 519 applicants, 34% accepted, 111 enrolled. In 2013, 56 master's, 31 other advanced degrees awarded. *Entrance requirements:* For master's, GRE, GMAT, or LSAT. Additional exam requirements/recommendations for international students: Required—TOEFL, IELTS. *Application deadline:* For fall admission, 1/15 for domestic students. Applications are processed on a rolling basis. Application fee: $70. *Financial support:* Fellowships, institutionally sponsored loans, and scholarships/grants available. Financial award application deadline: 1/15; financial award applicants required to submit FAFSA. *Unit head:* David B Thornburgh, Executive Director, 215-746-2800, E-mail: david_thornburgh@sas.upenn.edu. *Application contact:* 215-746-6684, Fax: 215-898-6238, E-mail: felsinstitute@sas.upenn.edu.
Website: http://www.fels.upenn.edu/.

University of Portland, Dr. Robert B. Pamplin, Jr. School of Business, Portland, OR 97203-5798. Offers entrepreneurship (MBA); finance (MBA, MS); health care management (MBA); marketing (MBA); nonprofit management (EMBA); operations and technology management (MBA, MS); sustainability (MBA). *Accreditation:* AACSB. Part-time and evening/weekend programs available. *Faculty:* 26 full-time (5 women), 8 part-time/adjunct (1 woman). *Students:* 37 full-time (11 women), 93 part-time (44 women); includes 15 minority (1 Black or African American, non-Hispanic/Latino; 7 Asian, non-Hispanic/Latino; 5 Hispanic/Latino; 2 Two or more races, non-Hispanic/Latino), 21 international. Average age 32. In 2013, 68 master's awarded. *Entrance requirements:* For master's, GMAT, minimum GPA of 3.0, resume, 2 letters of recommendation. Additional exam requirements/recommendations for international students: Required—TOEFL (minimum score 570 paper-based; 89 iBT), IELTS (minimum score 7). *Application deadline:* For fall admission, 7/15 priority date for domestic and international students; for spring admission, 12/15 priority date for domestic and international students. Applications are processed on a rolling basis. Application fee: $50. *Expenses:* Contact institution. *Financial support:* Federal Work-Study, scholarships/grants, and tuition waivers (partial) available. Support available to part-time students. Financial award application deadline: 3/1; financial award applicants required to submit FAFSA. *Unit head:* Melissa McCarthy, Director, 503-943-7224, E-mail: mba-up@up.edu.
Website: http://business.up.edu/mba/default.aspx?cid-1179&pid-6450.

University of San Diego, School of Leadership and Education Sciences, Department of Leadership Studies, San Diego, CA 92110-2492. Offers higher education leadership (MA); leadership studies (MA, PhD); nonprofit leadership and management (MA, Certificate). Part-time and evening/weekend programs available. *Faculty:* 10 full-time (6 women), 25 part-time/adjunct (17 women). *Students:* 25 full-time (17 women), 193 part-time (134 women); includes 115 minority (13 Black or African American, non-Hispanic/Latino; 2 American Indian or Alaska Native, non-Hispanic/Latino; 22 Asian, non-Hispanic/Latino; 23 Hispanic/Latino; 18 Native Hawaiian or other Pacific Islander, non-Hispanic/Latino; 37 Two or more races, non-Hispanic/Latino), 16 international. Average age 35. 254 applicants, 58% accepted, 85 enrolled. In 2013, 63 master's, 11 doctorates awarded. *Degree requirements:* For master's, thesis (for some programs), international experience; for doctorate, comprehensive exam, thesis/dissertation, international experience. *Entrance requirements:* For master's, minimum GPA of 3.0, interview; for doctorate, GRE, master's degree, minimum GPA of 3.5 (recommended), interview, resume. Additional exam requirements/recommendations for international students: Required—TOEFL (minimum score 580 paper-based; 83 iBT), TWE. *Application deadline:* For fall admission, 12/1 for domestic and international students. Application fee: $45. Electronic applications accepted. *Expenses: Tuition:* Full-time $23,580; part-time $1310 per credit. *Required fees:* $350. *Financial support:* In 2013–14, 160 students received support. Career-related internships or fieldwork, Federal Work-Study, institutionally sponsored loans, unspecified assistantships, and stipends available. Support available to part-time students. Financial award application deadline: 4/1; financial award applicants required to submit FAFSA. *Faculty research:* Higher education administration policy and relations, organizational leadership, nonprofits and philanthropy, student affairs leadership. *Unit head:* Dr. Afsaneh Nahavandi, Graduate Program Director, 619-260-4181, E-mail: anahavandi@sandiego.edu. *Application contact:* Monica Mahon, Associate Director of Graduate Admissions, 619-260-4524, Fax: 619-260-4158, E-mail: grads@sandiego.edu.
Website: http://www.sandiego.edu/soles/departments/leadership-studies/.

University of San Francisco, School of Management, Master of Nonprofit Administration Program, San Francisco, CA 94105. Offers MNA. Part-time and evening/weekend programs available. *Faculty:* 1 full-time (0 women), 7 part-time/adjunct (4 women). *Students:* 60 full-time (46 women), 2 part-time (both women); includes 19 minority (4 Black or African American, non-Hispanic/Latino; 1 American Indian or Alaska Native, non-Hispanic/Latino; 5 Asian, non-Hispanic/Latino; 9 Hispanic/Latino), 2 international. Average age 33. 25 applicants, 84% accepted, 14 enrolled. In 2013, 29 master's awarded. *Degree requirements:* For master's, thesis optional. *Entrance requirements:* For master's, resume demonstrating minimum of two years of professional work experience, transcripts from each college or university attended, two letters of recommendation, personal statement. Additional exam requirements/recommendations for international students: Required—TOEFL (minimum score 600 paper-based, 100 iBT), IELTS (minimum score 7) or PTE (minimum score 68). *Application deadline:* For fall admission, 6/15 for domestic students, 5/15 for international students. Application fee: $55. Electronic applications accepted. *Expenses: Tuition:* Full-time $21,150; part-time $1175 per unit. Tuition and fees vary according to course load, campus/location and program. *Financial support:* In 2013–14, 11 students received support. Scholarships/grants available. Financial award application deadline: 3/2; financial award applicants required to submit FAFSA. *Faculty research:* Philanthropy in ethnic communities. *Unit head:* Dr. Richard Waters, Program Director, 415-422-2221, E-mail: management@usfca.edu. *Application contact:* Office of Graduate Recruiting and Admissions, 415-422-2221, Fax: 415-422-6315, E-mail: management@usfca.edu.
Website: http://www.usfca.edu/mna.

University of Southern California, Graduate School, School of Policy, Planning, and Development, Master of Public Administration Program, Los Angeles, CA 90089. Offers nonprofit management and policy (Graduate Certificate); political management (Graduate Certificate); public administration (MPA); public management (Graduate Certificate); MPA/JD; MPA/M Pl; MPA/MA; MPA/MAJCS; MPA/MS; MPA/MSW. *Accreditation:* NASPAA (one or more programs are accredited). Part-time and evening/weekend programs available. Postbaccalaureate distance learning degree programs offered (minimal on-campus study). Terminal master's awarded for partial completion of doctoral program. *Degree requirements:* For master's, capstone, internship. *Entrance requirements:* For master's, GRE, GMAT. Additional exam requirements/recommendations for international students: Required—TOEFL (minimum score 600 paper-based; 100 iBT). Electronic applications accepted. *Faculty research:* Collaborative governance and decision-making, nonprofit management, environmental management, institutional analysis, local government, civic engagement.

University of Southern Maine, College of Management and Human Service, Muskie School of Public Service, Program in Public Policy and Management, Portland, ME 04104-9300. Offers applied research and evaluation methods (CGS); non-profit management (CGS); performance management and measurement (CGS); practice management (CGS); public management (CGS); public policy and management (MPPM); social policy analysis (CGS); JD/MPPM. Part-time and evening/weekend programs available. Postbaccalaureate distance learning degree programs offered (minimal on-campus study). *Faculty:* 7 full-time (5 women). *Students:* 18 full-time (9 women), 53 part-time (28 women); includes 5 minority (1 American Indian or Alaska Native, non-Hispanic/Latino; 2 Asian, non-Hispanic/Latino; 2 Hispanic/Latino), 1 international. Average age 36. 24 applicants, 96% accepted, 14 enrolled. In 2013, 10 master's awarded. *Degree requirements:* For master's, thesis, capstone project, field experience. *Entrance requirements:* For master's, GRE General Test or LSAT. Additional exam requirements/recommendations for international students: Required—TOEFL. *Application deadline:* For fall admission, 2/1 priority date for domestic and international students; for spring admission, 12/1 for domestic and international students. Applications are processed on a rolling basis. Application fee: $65. Electronic applications accepted. *Expenses:* Tuition, state resident: part-time $380 per credit. Tuition, nonresident: part-time $1026 per credit. Part-time tuition and fees vary according to program. *Financial support:* Fellowships, research assistantships, teaching assistantships, career-related internships or fieldwork, Federal Work-Study, scholarships/grants, tuition waivers (partial), and unspecified assistantships available. Financial award application deadline: 4/1; financial award applicants required to submit FAFSA. *Faculty research:* State and local public finance, education finance, applied social science methodology, nonprofit and higher education organizational management, public service ethics, comparative public policy. *Unit head:* Dr. Josephine LaPlante, Chair, 207-780-4863, E-mail: jlaplante@usm.maine.edu. *Application contact:* Mary Sloan, Assistant Dean of Graduate Studies and Director of Graduate Admissions, 207-780-4812, E-mail: gradstudies@usm.maine.edu.

University of South Florida, University College/Distance Education, Tampa, FL 33620-9951. *Unit head:* Kathy Barnes, Interdisciplinary Programs Coordinator, 813-974-8031, Fax: 813-974-7061, E-mail: barnesk@usf.edu. *Application contact:* Karen Tylinski, Metro Initiatives, 813-974-9943, Fax: 813-974-7061, E-mail: ktylinsk@usf.edu.
Website: http://uc.usf.edu/.

The University of Tampa, John H. Sykes College of Business, Tampa, FL 33606-1490. Offers accounting (MS); entrepreneurship (MBA); finance (MBA, MS); information systems management (MBA); innovation management (MBA); international business (MBA); marketing (MBA, MS); nonprofit management (MBA). *Accreditation:* AACSB. Part-time and evening/weekend programs available. *Faculty:* 41 full-time (15 women), 5 part-time/adjunct (1 woman). *Students:* 406 full-time (171 women), 152 part-time (61 women); includes 104 minority (18 Black or African American, non-Hispanic/Latino; 1 American Indian or Alaska Native, non-Hispanic/Latino; 20 Asian, non-Hispanic/Latino; 59 Hispanic/Latino; 6 Two or more races, non-Hispanic/Latino), 154 international. Average age 33. 1,341 applicants, 37% accepted, 256 enrolled. In 2013, 218 master's awarded. *Degree requirements:* For master's, capstone. *Entrance requirements:* For master's, GMAT or GRE, 4-year undergraduate degree, minimum GPA of 3.0, professional experience (for Executive MBA). Additional exam requirements/recommendations for international students: Required—TOEFL (minimum score 577 paper-based; 90 iBT); Recommended—IELTS (minimum score 7.5). *Application deadline:* Applications are processed on a rolling basis. Application fee: $40. Electronic applications accepted. *Expenses: Tuition:* Full-time $8928; part-time $558 per credit hour. *Required fees:* $80; $80 $40 per term. Tuition and fees vary according to program. *Financial support:* In 2013–14, 110 students received support. Career-related internships or fieldwork, scholarships/grants, and unspecified assistantships available. Financial award applicants required to submit FAFSA. *Faculty research:* Job market signaling, on-line shopping behaviors and social media, the Tampa Bay economy, digital literacy, entrepreneurship in small businesses. *Unit head:* Dr. Stephanie Thomason, Associate Dean, 813-253-6289, E-mail: sthomason@ut.edu. *Application contact:* Charlene Tobie, Associate Director of Admissions, 813-257-3566, E-mail: ctobie@ut.edu.
Website: http://www.ut.edu/business/.

The University of Tennessee at Chattanooga, Graduate School, College of Arts and Sciences, Department of Political Science, Chattanooga, TN 37403. Offers local government management (MPA); non profit management (MPA); public administration (MPA); public administration and non-profit management (Postbaccalaureate Certificate). Part-time and evening/weekend programs available. *Faculty:* 3 full-time (0 women). *Students:* 13 full-time (6 women), 18 part-time (12 women); includes 4 minority (3 Black or African American, non-Hispanic/Latino; 1 Hispanic/Latino). Average age 29. 16 applicants, 88% accepted, 11 enrolled. In 2013, 12 master's awarded. *Degree requirements:* For master's, comprehensive exam, thesis or alternative, internship. *Entrance requirements:* For master's, GRE General Test. Additional exam requirements/recommendations for international students: Required—TOEFL (minimum score 550 paper-based; 79 iBT), IELTS (minimum score 6). *Application deadline:* For fall admission, 6/13 priority date for domestic students, 6/1 for international students; for spring admission, 10/15 priority date for domestic students, 10/1 for international students. Applications are processed on a rolling basis. Application fee: $30 ($35 for international students). Electronic applications accepted. *Financial support:* In 2013–14, 3 research assistantships with tuition reimbursements (averaging $6,860 per year) were awarded; career-related internships or fieldwork, scholarships/grants, and unspecified assistantships also available. Support available to part-time students. *Faculty research:* Organizational cultures and renewal, management theory, public policy, policy analysis, nonprofit organization. *Unit head:* Dr. Michelle D. Deardorf, Department Head, 423-425-4231, Fax: 423-425-2373, E-mail: michelle-deardorff@utc.edu. *Application contact:* Dr. J. Randy Walker, Interim Dean of Graduate Studies, 423-425-4478, Fax: 423-425-5223, E-mail: randy-walker@utc.edu.
Website: http://www.utc.edu/Academic/PoliticalScience/.

University of the Sacred Heart, Graduate Programs, Program in Nonprofit Organization Administration, San Juan, PR 00914-0383. Offers MBA.

University of the West, Department of Business Administration, Rosemead, CA 91770. Offers business administration (EMBA); computer information systems (MBA); finance (MBA); international business (MBA); nonprofit organization management (MBA). Part-time and evening/weekend programs available. *Entrance requirements:* Additional exam requirements/recommendations for international students: Required—TOEFL. *Application deadline:* For fall admission, 6/15 for domestic and international students; for winter admission, 4/1 for domestic and international students; for spring admission, 11/15 for domestic and international students. Applications are processed on a rolling

basis. Application fee: $50 ($100 for international students). *Expenses: Tuition:* Full-time $7200; part-time $400 per credit hour. *Required fees:* $750; $400 per credit hour. $275 per semester. One-time fee: $75. Tuition and fees vary according to course level and program. *Financial support:* Career-related internships or fieldwork, Federal Work-Study, scholarships/grants, and tuition waivers (partial) available. Financial award applicants required to submit FAFSA. *Unit head:* Dr. Bill Y. Chen, Chair, 626-656-2125, Fax: 626-571-1413, E-mail: billchen@uwest.edu. *Application contact:* Jason Kosareff, Enrollment Counselor, 626-571-8811 Ext. 311, Fax: 626-571-1413, E-mail: jasonk@uwest.edu.

The University of Toledo, College of Graduate Studies, College of Language, Literature and Social Sciences, Department of Political Science and Public Administration, Toledo, OH 43606-3390. Offers health care policy and administration (Certificate); management of non-profit organizations (Certificate); municipal administration (Certificate); political science (MA); public administration (MPA); JD/MPA. Part-time programs available. *Faculty:* 8. *Students:* 15 full-time (11 women), 18 part-time (12 women); includes 7 minority (4 Black or African American, non-Hispanic/Latino; 1 Asian, non-Hispanic/Latino; 2 Hispanic/Latino), 2 international. Average age 31. 27 applicants, 89% accepted, 19 enrolled. In 2013, 13 master's, 9 other advanced degrees awarded. *Degree requirements:* For master's, comprehensive exam (for some programs), thesis. *Entrance requirements:* For master's, GRE General Test, minimum cumulative point-hour ratio of 2.7 (3.0 for MPA) for all previous academic work, three letters of recommendation, statement of purpose, transcripts from all prior institutions attended; for Certificate, minimum cumulative point-hour ratio of 2.7 for all previous academic work, three letters of recommendation, statement of purpose, transcripts from all prior institutions attended. Additional exam requirements/recommendations for international students: Required—TOEFL (minimum score 550 paper-based; 80 iBT). *Application deadline:* For fall admission, 1/15 priority date for domestic and international students. Applications are processed on a rolling basis. Application fee: $45 ($75 for international students). Electronic applications accepted. *Financial support:* In 2013–14, 11 teaching assistantships with full and partial tuition reimbursements (averaging $6,682 per year) were awarded; career-related internships or fieldwork, Federal Work-Study, institutionally sponsored loans, scholarships/grants, tuition waivers (full), unspecified assistantships, and administrative assistantships also available. Support available to part-time students. *Faculty research:* Economic development, health care, Third World, criminal justice, Eastern Europe. *Unit head:* Dr. Sam Nelson, Chair, 419-530-4974, E-mail: sam.nelson@utoledo.edu. *Application contact:* Graduate School Office, 419-530-4723, Fax: 419-530-4724, E-mail: grdsch@utnet.utoledo.edu.
Website: http://www.utoledo.edu/llss/.

University of Wisconsin–Milwaukee, Graduate School, School of Social Welfare, Department of Social Work, Milwaukee, WI 53201-0413. Offers applied gerontology (Certificate); marriage and family therapy (Certificate); non-profit management (Certificate); social work (MSW, PhD). *Accreditation:* CSWE. Part-time programs available. *Faculty:* 14 full-time (8 women). *Students:* 186 full-time (165 women), 87 part-time (79 women); includes 63 minority (35 Black or African American, non-Hispanic/Latino; 1 American Indian or Alaska Native, non-Hispanic/Latino; 4 Asian, non-Hispanic/Latino; 4 Hispanic/Latino; 19 Two or more races, non-Hispanic/Latino), 2 international. Average age 30. 323 applicants, 56% accepted, 106 enrolled. In 2013, 123 master's awarded. *Degree requirements:* For master's, thesis or alternative. *Entrance requirements:* For doctorate, GRE, bachelor's degree. Additional exam requirements/recommendations for international students: Required—TOEFL (minimum score 550 paper-based; 79 iBT), IELTS (minimum score 6.5). *Application deadline:* For fall admission, 1/1 priority date for domestic students; for spring admission, 9/1 for domestic students. Applications are processed on a rolling basis. Application fee: $56 ($96 for international students). Electronic applications accepted. *Financial support:* In 2013–14, 5 fellowships, 4 research assistantships, 3 teaching assistantships were awarded; career-related internships or fieldwork, health care benefits, unspecified assistantships, and project assistantships also available. Support available to part-time students. Financial award application deadline: 4/15; financial award applicants required to submit FAFSA. *Unit head:* Deborah Padgett, Department Chair, 414-229-6452, E-mail: dpadgett@uwm.edu. *Application contact:* General Information Contact, 414-229-4982, Fax: 414-229-6967, E-mail: gradschool@uwm.edu.
Website: http://www.uwm.edu/Dept/SSW/sw/.

University of Wisconsin–Milwaukee, Graduate School, Sheldon B. Lubar School of Business, Program in Nonprofit Management and Leadership, Milwaukee, WI 53201-0413. Offers MS, Certificate. *Students:* 19 full-time (13 women), 22 part-time (18 women); includes 11 minority (5 Black or African American, non-Hispanic/Latino; 2 Asian, non-Hispanic/Latino; 4 Two or more races, non-Hispanic/Latino). Average age 33. 18 applicants, 78% accepted, 12 enrolled. In 2013, 16 master's awarded. *Entrance requirements:* For master's, GRE/GMAT. Additional exam requirements/recommendations for international students: Required—TOEFL (minimum score 550 paper-based; 79 iBT), IELTS (minimum score 6.5). *Application deadline:* Applications are processed on a rolling basis. Application fee: $56 ($96 for international students). Electronic applications accepted. *Financial support:* Fellowships, research assistantships, teaching assistantships, health care benefits, and unspecified assistantships available. Financial award applicants required to submit FAFSA. *Unit head:* Douglas Ihrke, Representative, 414-229-3176, E-mail: dihrke@uwm.edu. *Application contact:* Matthew Jensen, Administrative Program Manager III, 414-229-5403, E-mail: mba-ms@uwm.edu.

Virginia Commonwealth University, Graduate School, College of Humanities and Sciences, Program in Nonprofit Management, Richmond, VA 23284-9005. Offers Graduate Certificate. Part-time programs available. *Entrance requirements:* Additional exam requirements/recommendations for international students: Required—TOEFL (minimum score 600 paper-based; 100 iBT); Recommended—IELTS (minimum score 6.5). Electronic applications accepted.

Virginia Commonwealth University, Graduate School, College of Humanities and Sciences, Wilder School of Government and Public Affairs, Department of Political Science and Public Administration, Richmond, VA 23284-9005. Offers nonprofit management (CPM); public administration (MPA); public management (CPM). *Accreditation:* NASPAA (one or more programs are accredited). Part-time programs available. *Entrance requirements:* For master's, GRE, GMAT or LSAT. Additional exam requirements/recommendations for international students: Required—TOEFL (minimum score 600 paper-based; 100 iBT); Recommended—IELTS (minimum score 6.5). Electronic applications accepted. *Faculty research:* Environmental policy, executive leadership, human resource management, local government management, nonprofit management, public financial management, public policy analysis and evaluation.

Virginia Polytechnic Institute and State University, VT Online, Blacksburg, VA 24061. Offers advanced transportation systems (Certificate); aerospace engineering (MS); agricultural and life sciences (MSLFS); business information systems (Graduate Certificate); career and technical education (MS); civil engineering (MS); computer engineering (M Eng, MS); decision support systems (Graduate Certificate); eLearning leadership (MA); electrical engineering (M Eng, MS); engineering administration (MEA); environmental engineering (Certificate); environmental politics and policy (Graduate Certificate); environmental sciences and engineering (MS); foundations of political analysis (Graduate Certificate); health product risk management (Graduate Certificate); industrial and systems engineering (MS); information policy and society (Graduate Certificate); information security (Graduate Certificate); information technology (MIT); instructional technology (MA); integrative STEM education (MA Ed); liberal arts (Graduate Certificate); life sciences: health product risk management (MS); natural resources (MNR, Graduate Certificate); networking (Graduate Certificate); nonprofit and nongovernmental organization management (Graduate Certificate); ocean engineering (MS); political science (MA); security studies (Graduate Certificate); software development (Graduate Certificate). *Expenses:* Tuition, state resident: full-time $11,185; part-time $621.50 per credit hour. Tuition, nonresident: full-time $22,146; part-time $1230.25 per credit hour. *Required fees:* $2442; $449.25 per semester. Tuition and fees vary according to course load, campus/location and program.

Walden University, Graduate Programs, School of Counseling, Minneapolis, MN 55401. Offers addiction counseling (MS), including addictions and public health, child and adolescent counseling, family studies and interventions, forensic counseling, general program (MS, PhD), trauma and crisis counseling; counselor education and supervision (PhD), including consultation, counseling and social change, forensic mental health counseling, general program (MS, PhD), nonprofit management and leadership, trauma and crisis; marriage, couple, and family counseling (MS), including forensic counseling, general program (MS, PhD), trauma and crisis counseling; mental health counseling (MS), including forensic counseling, general program (MS, PhD), trauma and crisis counseling; school counseling (MS), including addictions counseling, crisis and trauma, general program (MS, PhD), military. Part-time and evening/weekend programs available. Postbaccalaureate distance learning degree programs offered (minimal on-campus study). *Faculty:* 50 full-time (38 women), 238 part-time/adjunct (172 women). *Students:* 2,019 full-time (1,709 women), 1,566 part-time (1,345 women); includes 1,622 minority (1,223 Black or African American, non-Hispanic/Latino; 21 American Indian or Alaska Native, non-Hispanic/Latino; 36 Asian, non-Hispanic/Latino; 231 Hispanic/Latino; 8 Native Hawaiian or other Pacific Islander, non-Hispanic/Latino; 103 Two or more races, non-Hispanic/Latino), 19 international. Average age 38. 789 applicants, 90% accepted, 623 enrolled. In 2013, 410 master's awarded. *Degree requirements:* For master's, residency, field experience, professional development plan, licensure plan; for doctorate, thesis/dissertation, residency, practicum, internship. *Entrance requirements:* For master's, bachelor's degree or higher; minimum GPA of 2.5; official transcripts; goal statement (for some programs); access to computer and Internet; for doctorate, master's degree or higher; three years of related professional or academic experience (preferred); minimum GPA of 3.0; goal statement and current resume (select programs); official transcripts; access to computer and Internet. Additional exam requirements/recommendations for international students: Required—TOEFL (minimum score 550 paper-based; 79 iBT), IELTS (minimum score 6.5), Michigan English Language Assessment Battery (minimum score 82), or PTE. *Application deadline:* Applications are processed on a rolling basis. Application fee: $0. Electronic applications accepted. *Expenses: Tuition:* Full-time $11,813.55; part-time $500 per credit. *Required fees:* $618.76. *Financial support:* Federal Work-Study, scholarships/grants, unspecified assistantships, and family tuition reduction, active duty/veteran tuition reduction, group tuition reduction, interest-free payment plans, employee tuition reduction available. Support available to part-time students. Financial award applicants required to submit FAFSA. *Unit head:* Dr. Savitri Dixon-Saxon, Associate Dean, 800-925-3368. *Application contact:* Jennifer Hall, Vice President of Enrollment Management, 866-4-WALDEN, E-mail: info@waldenu.edu.

Walden University, Graduate Programs, School of Psychology, Minneapolis, MN 55401. Offers clinical psychology (MS), including counseling, general program; forensic psychology (MS), including forensic psychology in the community, general program, mental health applications, program planning and evaluation in forensic settings, psychology and legal systems; organizational psychology and development (Postbaccalaureate Certificate); psychology (MS, PhD), including applied psychology (MS), clinical psychology (PhD), counseling psychology (PhD), crisis management and response (MS), educational psychology, forensic psychology (PhD), general psychology, health psychology, leadership development and coaching (MS), media psychology (MS), organizational psychology, organizational psychology and nonprofit management (MS), psychology of culture (MS), psychology, public administration, and social change (MS), social psychology, terrorism and security (MS); psychology respecialization (Post-Doctoral Certificate); teaching online (Post-Master's Certificate). Part-time and evening/weekend programs available. Postbaccalaureate distance learning degree programs offered (minimal on-campus study). *Faculty:* 25 full-time (16 women), 272 part-time/adjunct (143 women). *Students:* 2,997 full-time (2,366 women), 1,450 part-time (1,149 women); includes 1,931 minority (1,326 Black or African American, non-Hispanic/Latino; 40 American Indian or Alaska Native, non-Hispanic/Latino; 88 Asian, non-Hispanic/Latino; 354 Hispanic/Latino; 11 Native Hawaiian or other Pacific Islander, non-Hispanic/Latino; 112 Two or more races, non-Hispanic/Latino), 30 international. Average age 41. 856 applicants, 94% accepted, 623 enrolled. In 2013, 483 master's, 146 doctorates, 5 other advanced degrees awarded. Terminal master's awarded for partial completion of doctoral program. *Degree requirements:* For master's, thesis optional; for doctorate, thesis/dissertation, residency. *Entrance requirements:* For master's, bachelor's degree or higher; minimum GPA of 2.5; official transcripts; goal statement (for some programs); access to computer and Internet; for doctorate, master's degree or higher; three years of related professional or academic experience (preferred); minimum GPA of 3.0; goal statement and current resume (select programs); official transcripts; access to computer and Internet; for other advanced degree, relevant work experience; access to computer and Internet. Additional exam requirements/recommendations for international students: Required—TOEFL (minimum score 550 paper-based; 79 iBT), IELTS (minimum score 6.5), Michigan English Language Assessment Battery (minimum score 82), or PTE. *Application deadline:* Applications are processed on a rolling basis. Application fee: $0. Electronic applications accepted. *Expenses: Tuition:* Full-time $11,813.55; part-time $500 per credit. *Required fees:* $618.76. *Financial support:* Fellowships, Federal Work-Study, scholarships/grants, unspecified assistantships, and family tuition reduction, active duty/veteran tuition reduction, group tuition reduction, interest-free payment plans, employee tuition reduction available. Support available to part-time students. Financial award applicants required to submit FAFSA. *Unit head:* Dr. Marilyn Powell, Associate Dean, 800-925-3368. *Application contact:* Jennifer Hall, Vice President of Enrollment Management, 866-4-WALDEN, E-mail: info@waldenu.edu.
Website: http://www.waldenu.edu/programs/colleges-schools/psychology.

Walden University, Graduate Programs, School of Public Policy and Administration, Minneapolis, MN 55401. Offers criminal justice (MPA, MPP, MS, Graduate Certificate), including emergency management (MS, PhD), general program (MS, PhD), homeland security and policy coordination (MS, PhD), law and public policy (MS, PhD), policy analysis (MS, PhD), public management and leadership (MS, PhD), self-designed (MS), terrorism, mediation, and peace (MS, PhD); criminal justice leadership and executive management (MS), including emergency management (MS, PhD), general program (MS, PhD), homeland security and policy coordination (MS, PhD), law and public policy (MS, PhD), policy analysis (MS, PhD), public management and leadership (MS, PhD), self-designed, terrorism, mediation, and peace (MS, PhD); emergency management (MPA, MPP, MS), including criminal justice (MS, PhD), general program (MS, PhD),

homeland security (MS), public management and leadership (MS, PhD), terrorism and emergency management (MS); general program (MPA, MPP); government management (Graduate Certificate); health policy (MPA, MPP); homeland security (Graduate Certificate); homeland security and policy coordination (MPA, MPP); international nongovernmental organizations (MPA, MPP); law and public policy (MPA, MPP); local government management for sustainable communities (MPA, MPP); nonprofit management (Graduate Certificate); nonprofit management and leadership (MPA, MPP, MS); policy analysis (MPA); public management and leadership (MPA, MPP, Graduate Certificate); public policy (Graduate Certificate); public policy and administration (PhD), including criminal justice (MS, PhD), emergency management (MS, PhD), general program (MS, PhD), health policy, homeland security and policy coordination (MS, PhD), international nongovernmental organizations, law and public policy (MS, PhD), local government management for sustainable communities, nonprofit management and leadership, policy analysis (MS, PhD), public management and leadership (MS, PhD), terrorism, mediation, and peace (MS, PhD); strategic planning and public policy (Graduate Certificate); terrorism, mediation, and peace (MPA, MPP). Part-time and evening/weekend programs available. Postbaccalaureate distance learning degree programs offered (minimal on-campus study). *Faculty:* 10 full-time (4 women), 123 part-time/adjunct (55 women). *Students:* 1,029 full-time (640 women), 1,601 part-time (981 women); includes 1,579 minority (1,326 Black or African American, non-Hispanic/Latino; 18 American Indian or Alaska Native, non-Hispanic/Latino; 39 Asian, non-Hispanic/Latino; 127 Hispanic/Latino; 3 Native Hawaiian or other Pacific Islander, non-Hispanic/Latino; 66 Two or more races, non-Hispanic/Latino), 27 international. Average age 42. 566 applicants, 93% accepted, 412 enrolled. In 2013, 257 master's, 44 doctorates, 18 other advanced degrees awarded. *Degree requirements:* For doctorate, thesis/dissertation, residency. *Entrance requirements:* For master's, bachelor's degree or higher; minimum GPA of 2.5; official transcripts; goal statement (for some programs); access to computer and Internet; for doctorate, master's degree or higher; three years of related professional or academic experience (preferred); minimum GPA of 3.0; goal statement and current resume (select programs); official transcripts; access to computer and Internet; for Graduate Certificate, relevant work experience; access to computer and Internet. Additional exam requirements/recommendations for international students: Required—TOEFL (minimum score 550 paper-based; 79 iBT), IELTS (minimum score 6.5), Michigan English Language Assessment Battery (minimum score 82), or PTE. *Application deadline:* Applications are processed on a rolling basis. Application fee: $0. Electronic applications accepted. *Expenses: Tuition:* Full-time $11,813.55; part-time $500 per credit. *Required fees:* $618.76. *Financial support:* Fellowships, Federal Work-Study, scholarships/grants, unspecified assistantships, and family tuition reduction, active duty/veteran tuition reduction, group tuition reduction, interest-free payment plans, employee tuition reduction available. Support available to part-time students. Financial award applicants required to submit FAFSA. *Unit head:* Dr. Mark Gordon, Associate Dean, 800-925-3368. *Application contact:* Jennifer Hall, Vice President of Enrollment Management, 866-4-WALDEN, E-mail: info@waldenu.edu.
Website: http://www.waldenu.edu/programs/colleges-schools/public-policy-and-administration.

Warner Pacific College, Graduate Programs, Portland, OR 97215-4099. Offers Biblical and theological studies (MA); Biblical studies (M Rel); education (M Ed); management and organizational leadership (MS); not-for-profit leadership (MSM); pastoral ministries (M Rel); religion and ethics (M Rel); teaching (MAT); theology (M Rel). Part-time programs available. *Faculty:* 20 part-time/adjunct (6 women). *Students:* 57 full-time (26 women), 4 part-time (2 women); includes 5 minority (4 Black or African American, non-Hispanic/Latino; 1 Asian, non-Hispanic/Latino). *Degree requirements:* For master's, thesis or alternative, presentation of defense. *Entrance requirements:* For master's, interview, minimum GPA of 2.5, letters of recommendation. *Application deadline:* Applications are processed on a rolling basis. *Expenses: Tuition:* Part-time $630 per credit hour. *Financial support:* Application deadline: 7/1; applicants required to submit FAFSA. *Faculty research:* New Testament studies, nineteenth-century Wesleyan theology, preaching and church growth, Christian ethics. *Unit head:* Dr. Andrea P. Cook, President, 503-517-1045, Fax: 503-517-1350. *Application contact:* Dr. John Fazio, Professor, 503-517-1043, Fax: 503-517-1350, E-mail: jfazio@warnerpacific.edu.

Wayne State University, College of Liberal Arts and Sciences, Department of Political Science, Program in Public Administration, Detroit, MI 48202. Offers aging policy and management (MPA); criminal justice policy and management (MPA); economic development policy and management (MPA); health and human services policy and management (MPA); human and fiscal resource management (MPA); information technology management (MPA); nonprofit policy and management (MPA); organizational behavior and management (MPA); public budgeting and financial management (MPA); public policy analysis and program evaluation (MPA); social welfare policy and management (MPA); urban and metropolitan policy and management (MPA). *Accreditation:* NASPAA. Evening/weekend programs available. *Students:* 11 full-time (5 women), 55 part-time (43 women); includes 20 minority (14 Black or African American, non-Hispanic/Latino; 2 Asian, non-Hispanic/Latino; 2 Hispanic/Latino; 2 Two or more races, non-Hispanic/Latino), 1 international. Average age 33. 83 applicants, 34% accepted, 17 enrolled. In 2013, 19 master's awarded. *Degree requirements:* For master's, comprehensive exam. *Entrance requirements:* For master's, GRE General Test, minimum undergraduate upper-division GPA of 3.0 or master's degree. Additional exam requirements/recommendations for international students: Required—TOEFL (minimum score 550 paper-based; 79 iBT), TWE (minimum score 5.5), Michigan English Language Assessment Battery (minimum score 85); Recommended—IELTS (minimum score 6.5). *Application deadline:* For fall admission, 6/1 priority date for domestic students, 5/1 priority date for international students; for winter admission, 10/1 priority date for domestic students, 9/1 priority date for international students; for spring admission, 2/1 priority date for domestic students, 1/1 priority date for international students. Applications are processed on a rolling basis. Application fee: $0. Electronic applications accepted. *Expenses:* Tuition, state resident: part-time $554.15 per credit. Tuition, nonresident: part-time $1200.35 per credit. *Required fees:* $42.15 per credit. $268.30 per semester. Tuition and fees vary according to course load and program. *Financial support:* In 2013–14, 21 students received support. Fellowships, teaching assistantships, scholarships/grants, and unspecified assistantships available. Financial award application deadline: 3/31; financial award applicants required to submit FAFSA. *Faculty research:* Urban politics, urban education, state administration. *Unit head:* Dr. Daniel Geller, Department Chair, 313-577-6328, E-mail: dgeller@wayne.edu. *Application contact:* Dr. Brady Baybeck, Associate Professor/Director, Graduate Program in Public Administration, E-mail: mpa@wayne.edu.
Website: http://clasweb.clas.wayne.edu/mpa.

Webster University, George Herbert Walker School of Business and Technology, Department of Management, St. Louis, MO 63119-3194. Offers business and organizational security management (MA); health administration (MHA); health care management (MA); health services management (MA); human resources development (MA); human resources management (MA); information technology management (MS); management and leadership (MA); marketing (MA); nonprofit leadership (MA); procurement and acquisitions management (MA); public administration (MPA); space systems operations management (MS). Part-time and evening/weekend programs available. Postbaccalaureate distance learning degree programs offered (no on-campus study). *Degree requirements:* For master's, thesis (for some programs). *Entrance requirements:* Additional exam requirements/recommendations for international students: Required—TOEFL. *Expenses: Tuition:* Full-time $11,610; part-time $645 per credit hour. Tuition and fees vary according to campus/location and program.

West Chester University of Pennsylvania, College of Business and Public Affairs, Department of Public Policy and Administration, West Chester, PA 19383. Offers general public administration (MPA); human resource management (MPA, Certificate); non profit administration (Certificate); nonprofit administration (MPA); public administration (Certificate). Part-time and evening/weekend programs available. *Faculty:* 6 full-time (3 women), 3 part-time/adjunct (0 women). *Students:* 58 full-time (37 women), 94 part-time (54 women); includes 55 minority (44 Black or African American, non-Hispanic/Latino; 3 Asian, non-Hispanic/Latino; 8 Hispanic/Latino), 3 international. Average age 29. 84 applicants, 88% accepted, 52 enrolled. In 2013, 54 master's, 8 other advanced degrees awarded. *Degree requirements:* For master's, capstone project. *Entrance requirements:* For master's and Certificate, statement of professional goals, resume, two letters of reference, academic transcripts. Additional exam requirements/recommendations for international students: Required—TOEFL (minimum score 550 paper-based; 80 iBT). *Application deadline:* For fall admission, 4/15 priority date for domestic students, 3/15 for international students; for spring admission, 10/15 priority date for domestic students, 9/1 for international students. Applications are processed on a rolling basis. Application fee: $45. Electronic applications accepted. *Expenses:* Tuition, state resident: full-time $7956; part-time $442 per credit. Tuition, nonresident: full-time $11,934; part-time $663 per credit. *Required fees:* $2134.20; $106.24 per credit. Tuition and fees vary according to campus/location and program. *Financial support:* Unspecified assistantships available. Support available to part-time students. Financial award application deadline: 2/15; financial award applicants required to submit FAFSA. *Faculty research:* Public policy, economic development, research methodology, urban politics, public administration. *Unit head:* Dr. Jeffery Osgoods, Department Chair and Graduate Coordinator, 610-436-2286, E-mail: josgood@wcupa.edu.
Website: http://www.wcupa.edu/_ACADEMICS/sch_sba/g-mpa.html.

Western Michigan University, Graduate College, College of Arts and Sciences, School of Public Affairs and Administration, Kalamazoo, MI 49008. Offers health care administration (Graduate Certificate); nonprofit leadership and administration (Graduate Certificate); public administration (MPA, PhD). *Accreditation:* NASPAA (one or more programs are accredited). *Degree requirements:* For doctorate, thesis/dissertation, oral exams. *Entrance requirements:* For doctorate, GRE General Test.

Worcester State University, Graduate Studies, Program in Non-Profit Management, Worcester, MA 01602-2597. Offers MS. Part-time and evening/weekend programs available. *Faculty:* 1 (woman) full-time, 1 part-time/adjunct (0 women). *Students:* 2 full-time (0 women), 17 part-time (14 women), 1 international. Average age 38. 17 applicants, 53% accepted, 4 enrolled. In 2013, 12 master's awarded. *Degree requirements:* For master's, comprehensive exam (for some programs), thesis optional. *Entrance requirements:* For master's, GRE General Test or MAT. Additional exam requirements/recommendations for international students: Required—TOEFL (minimum score 500 paper-based; 61 iBT). *Application deadline:* For fall admission, 6/15 for domestic and international students; for spring admission, 4/1 for domestic and international students. Applications are processed on a rolling basis. Application fee: $40. Electronic applications accepted. *Expenses: Tuition, area resident:* Part-time $150 per credit. Tuition, state resident: part-time $150 per credit. Tuition, nonresident: part-time $150 per credit. *Required fees:* $114.50 per credit. *Financial support:* In 2013–14, 1 student received support, including 1 research assistantship with full tuition reimbursement available (averaging $4,800 per year); career-related internships or fieldwork, scholarships/grants, and unspecified assistantships also available. Financial award application deadline: 3/1; financial award applicants required to submit FAFSA. *Faculty research:* Politics of human services, models of supervision. *Unit head:* Dr. Shiko Gathuo, Coordinator, 508-929-8892, Fax: 508-929-8144, E-mail: agathuo@worcester.edu. *Application contact:* Sara Grady, Assistant Dean of Continuing Education, 508-929-8787, Fax: 508-929-8100, E-mail: sara.grady@worcester.edu.

Section 16
Organizational Studies

This section contains a directory of institutions offering graduate work in organizational studies. Additional information about programs listed in the directory but not augmented by an in-depth entry may be obtained by writing directly to the dean of a graduate school or chair of a department at the address given in the directory.

For programs offering related work, see also in this book *Business Administration and Management, Human Resources,* and *Industrial and Manufacturing Management.* In another guide in this series:

Graduate Programs in the Humanities, Arts & Social Sciences

See *Communication and Media* and *Public, Regional, and Industrial Affairs*

CONTENTS

Program Directories

Organizational Behavior   556
Organizational Management   560

Display and Close-Up

See:

University of California, Los Angeles—Business
Administration and Management   145, 191

Organizational Behavior

Amridge University, Graduate and Professional Programs, Montgomery, AL 36117. Offers behavioral leadership and management (MA); Biblical studies (MA, PhD); family therapy (D Min); leadership and management (MS); marriage and family therapy (M Div, MA, PhD); ministerial leadership (M Div, MS); pastoral counseling (M Div, MS); practical ministry (MA); professional counseling (M Div, MA, PhD); theology (M Div, D Min). Part-time and evening/weekend programs available. Postbaccalaureate distance learning degree programs offered (no on-campus study). *Faculty:* 48 full-time (9 women), 27 part-time/adjunct (12 women). *Students:* 124 full-time (62 women), 189 part-time (112 women); includes 196 minority (189 Black or African American, non-Hispanic/Latino; 3 Asian, non-Hispanic/Latino; 4 Hispanic/Latino). Average age 35. *Degree requirements:* For master's, one foreign language, comprehensive exam (for some programs), thesis (for some programs); for doctorate, comprehensive exam (for some programs), thesis/dissertation. *Entrance requirements:* For master's and doctorate, GRE General Test or MAT. Additional exam requirements/recommendations for international students: Required—TOEFL. *Application deadline:* For fall admission, 9/1 priority date for domestic students; for spring admission, 1/1 priority date for domestic students. Applications are processed on a rolling basis. Application fee: $50. Electronic applications accepted. *Financial support:* Federal Work-Study and scholarships/grants available. Support available to part-time students. Financial award applicants required to submit FAFSA. *Faculty research:* Homiletics, hermeneutics, ancient Near Eastern history. *Unit head:* Carl Byrd, Student Affairs Coordinator, 800-351-4040 Ext. 7569, Fax: 334-387-3878. *Application contact:* Ora Davis, Admissions Officer, 334-387-3877 Ext. 7524, Fax: 334-387-3878, E-mail: admissions@amridgeuniversity.edu.

Argosy University, Chicago, College of Psychology and Behavioral Sciences, Doctoral Program in Clinical Psychology, Chicago, IL 60601. Offers child and adolescent psychology (Psy D); client-centered and experiential psychotherapies (Psy D); diversity and multicultural psychology (Psy D); family psychology (Psy D); forensic psychology (Psy D); health psychology (Psy D); neuropsychology (Psy D); organizational consulting (Psy D); psychoanalytic psychology (Psy D); psychology and spirituality (Psy D). *Accreditation:* APA.

Baruch College of the City University of New York, Zicklin School of Business, Department of Management, New York, NY 10010-5585. Offers entrepreneurship (MBA); management (PhD); operations management (MBA); organizational behavior/human resources management (MBA); sustainable business (MBA). PhD offered jointly with Graduate School and University Center of the City University of New York. Part-time and evening/weekend programs available. *Degree requirements:* For doctorate, comprehensive exam, thesis/dissertation. *Entrance requirements:* For master's, GMAT, 2 letters of recommendation, resume, 2 years of work experience; for doctorate, GMAT. Additional exam requirements/recommendations for international students: Required—TOEFL (minimum score 590 paper-based), TWE.

Benedictine University, Graduate Programs, Program in Management and Organizational Behavior, Lisle, IL 60532-0900. Offers MS, MBA/MS, MPH/MS. Part-time and evening/weekend programs available. *Students:* 15 full-time (10 women), 113 part-time (79 women); includes 40 minority (27 Black or African American, non-Hispanic/Latino; 1 American Indian or Alaska Native, non-Hispanic/Latino; 4 Asian, non-Hispanic/Latino; 7 Hispanic/Latino; 1 Native Hawaiian or other Pacific Islander, non-Hispanic/Latino), 5 international. Average age 40. 45 applicants, 96% accepted, 28 enrolled. In 2013, 61 master's awarded. *Entrance requirements:* For master's, GMAT. Additional exam requirements/recommendations for international students: Required—TOEFL (minimum score 550 paper-based). *Application deadline:* For fall admission, 9/1 for domestic students; for winter admission, 12/1 for domestic students; for spring admission, 2/15 for domestic students. Applications are processed on a rolling basis. Application fee: $40. Electronic applications accepted. *Expenses: Tuition:* Part-time $590 per credit hour. *Financial support:* Career-related internships or fieldwork and health care benefits available. Support available to part-time students. *Faculty research:* Organizational change, transformation, development, learning organizations, career transitions for academics. *Unit head:* Dr. Peter F. Sorensen, Director, 630-829-6220, Fax: 630-960-1126, E-mail: psorensen@ben.edu. *Application contact:* Kari Gibbons, Associate Vice President, Enrollment Center, 630-829-6200, Fax: 630-829-6584, E-mail: kgibbons@ben.edu.

Benedictine University at Springfield, Program in Management and Organizational Behavior, Springfield, IL 62702. Offers MS. Evening/weekend programs available. *Entrance requirements:* For master's, official transcripts, 2 letters of reference, essay, resume, interview.

Boston College, Carroll School of Management, Department of Management and Organization, Chestnut Hill, MA 02467-3800. Offers PhD. *Faculty:* 10 full-time (5 women), 8 part-time/adjunct (3 women). *Students:* 15 full-time (11 women); includes 2 minority (1 Black or African American, non-Hispanic/Latino; 1 Hispanic/Latino), 6 international. Average age 31. 54 applicants, 9% accepted, 2 enrolled. In 2013, 2 doctorates awarded. *Degree requirements:* For doctorate, comprehensive exam, thesis/dissertation, teaching experience. *Entrance requirements:* For doctorate, GMAT or GRE, letters of recommendation, resume, transcripts. Additional exam requirements/recommendations for international students: Required—TOEFL (minimum score 100 iBT), IELTS (minimum score 7.5), or PTE (minimum score 68). *Application deadline:* For fall admission, 12/1 for domestic and international students; for spring admission, 2/1 for domestic and international students. Application fee: $100. Electronic applications accepted. *Financial support:* In 2013–14, 16 students received support, including 16 fellowships with full tuition reimbursements available (averaging $11,976 per year), 14 research assistantships (averaging $26,518 per year). Financial award application deadline: 3/1. *Faculty research:* Organizational transformation, mergers and acquisitions, managerial effectiveness, organizational change, organizational structure. *Unit head:* Dr. Jeffrey L. Ringuest, Associate Dean, Graduate Programs, 617-552-9100, Fax: 617-552-0514, E-mail: gsomdean@bc.edu. *Application contact:* Shelley A. Burt, Director of Graduate Enrollment, 617-552-3920, Fax: 617-552-8078, E-mail: bcmba@bc.edu.
Website: http://www.bc.edu/csom/.

Brooklyn College of the City University of New York, Division of Graduate Studies, Department of Psychology, Program in Industrial and Organizational Psychology, Brooklyn, NY 11210-2889. Offers human relations (MA); organizational behavior (MA). *Degree requirements:* For master's, comprehensive exam, thesis. *Entrance requirements:* For master's, 2 letters of recommendation. Additional exam requirements/recommendations for international students: Required—TOEFL (minimum score 520 paper-based; 69 iBT). Electronic applications accepted.

California Lutheran University, Graduate Studies, School of Management, Thousand Oaks, CA 91360-2787. Offers business (IMBA); computer science (MS); econometrics (MBA); economics (MS); entrepreneurship (MBA, Certificate); finance (MBA, Certificate); financial planning (MBA, Certificate); information systems and technology (MS); information technology management (MBA, Certificate); international business (MBA, Certificate); management and organization behavior (MBA); management and organizational behavior (Certificate); marketing (MBA, Certificate); microeconomics (MBA); nonprofit and social enterprise (MBA). Part-time and evening/weekend programs available. Postbaccalaureate distance learning degree programs offered (no on-campus study). *Faculty:* 26 full-time (9 women), 50 part-time/adjunct (11 women). *Students:* 426 full-time (175 women), 220 part-time (91 women); includes 114 minority (14 Black or African American, non-Hispanic/Latino; 30 Asian, non-Hispanic/Latino; 57 Hispanic/Latino; 13 Two or more races, non-Hispanic/Latino), 321 international. Average age 31. 495 applicants, 76% accepted, 119 enrolled. In 2013, 297 master's awarded. *Entrance requirements:* For master's, GMAT, interview, minimum GPA of 3.0. *Application deadline:* Applications are processed on a rolling basis. Application fee: $50. *Expenses:* Contact institution. *Unit head:* Dr. Gerhard Apfelthaler, Dean, 805-493-3360. *Application contact:* 805-493-3325, Fax: 805-493-3861, E-mail: clugrad@callutheran.edu.
Website: http://www.callutheran.edu/business/.

Carnegie Mellon University, College of Humanities and Social Sciences, Department of Social and Decision Sciences, Pittsburgh, PA 15213-3891. Offers behavioral decision research (PhD); behavioral decision research and psychology (PhD); social and decision science (PhD); strategy, entrepeneurship, and technological change (PhD). Terminal master's awarded for partial completion of doctoral program. *Degree requirements:* For doctorate, comprehensive exam, thesis/dissertation, research paper. *Entrance requirements:* For doctorate, GRE General Test. Additional exam requirements/recommendations for international students: Required—TOEFL. Electronic applications accepted. *Faculty research:* Organization theory, political science, sociology, technology studies.

Carnegie Mellon University, Tepper School of Business, Organizational Behavior and Theory Program, Pittsburgh, PA 15213-3891. Offers PhD. *Degree requirements:* For doctorate, thesis/dissertation. *Entrance requirements:* For doctorate, GMAT or GRE General Test. Additional exam requirements/recommendations for international students: Required—TOEFL. *Faculty research:* Negotiation, organizational learning, interorganizational relations and strategy, group process and performance, communication process and electronic media, group goal setting, uncertainty in organizations, creation and effect of institutions and psychological contracts.

Case Western Reserve University, Weatherhead School of Management, Department of Organizational Behavior and Analysis, Cleveland, OH 44106. Offers MBA, MPOD, MS. Part-time and evening/weekend programs available. *Entrance requirements:* For master's, GMAT. *Faculty research:* Social innovation in global management, competency-based learning, life-long learning, organizational theory, organizational change.

Columbia College, Graduate Programs, Department of Human Relations, Columbia, SC 29203-5998. Offers interpersonal relations/conflict management (Certificate); organizational behavior/conflict management (Certificate); organizational change and leadership (MA). Part-time and evening/weekend programs available. Postbaccalaureate distance learning degree programs offered. *Faculty:* 3 part-time/adjunct (2 women). *Students:* 32 full-time (31 women), 13 part-time (12 women); includes 23 minority (21 Black or African American, non-Hispanic/Latino; 1 Asian, non-Hispanic/Latino; 1 Hispanic/Latino). Average age 29. 51 applicants, 80% accepted, 37 enrolled. In 2013, 25 master's awarded. *Degree requirements:* For master's, thesis, practicum. *Entrance requirements:* For master's, GRE General Test, MAT, 2 letters of recommendation, minimum GPA of 3.2. Additional exam requirements/recommendations for international students: Required—TOEFL. *Application deadline:* For fall admission, 7/15 priority date for domestic students, 7/15 for international students. Applications are processed on a rolling basis. Application fee: $50. Electronic applications accepted. *Expenses:* Contact institution. *Financial support:* Available to part-time students. Application deadline: 7/1; applicants required to submit FAFSA. *Faculty research:* Envisioning and the resolution of conflict, environmental conflict resolution, crisis negotiation. *Unit head:* Dr. Elaine Ferraro, Chair, 803-786-3687, Fax: 803-786-3790, E-mail: eferraro@colacoll.edu. *Application contact:* Carolyn Emeneker, Director of Graduate School and Evening College Admissions, 803-786-3766, Fax: 803-786-3674, E-mail: emeneker@colacoll.edu.

Cornell University, Graduate School, Graduate Field of Management, Ithaca, NY 14853. Offers accounting (PhD); finance (PhD); marketing (PhD); organizational behavior (PhD); production and operations management (PhD). *Accreditation:* AACSB. *Faculty:* 54 full-time (7 women). *Students:* 37 full-time (13 women); includes 5 minority (4 Asian, non-Hispanic/Latino; 1 Two or more races, non-Hispanic/Latino), 24 international. Average age 29. 486 applicants, 4% accepted, 11 enrolled. In 2013, 8 doctorates awarded. *Degree requirements:* For doctorate, comprehensive exam, thesis/dissertation. *Entrance requirements:* For doctorate, GMAT or GRE General Test. Additional exam requirements/recommendations for international students: Required—TOEFL (minimum score 600 paper-based; 77 iBT). *Application deadline:* For fall admission, 1/3 for domestic students. Application fee: $95. Electronic applications accepted. *Expenses:* Contact institution. *Financial support:* In 2013–14, 33 students received support, including 31 research assistantships with full tuition reimbursements available, 2 teaching assistantships with full tuition reimbursements available; fellowships with full tuition reimbursements available, institutionally sponsored loans, scholarships/grants, health care benefits, tuition waivers (full and partial), and unspecified assistantships also available. Financial award applicants required to submit FAFSA. *Faculty research:* Operations and manufacturing. *Unit head:* Director of Graduate Studies, 607-255-3669. *Application contact:* Graduate Field Assistant, 607-255-9431, E-mail: js_phd@cornell.edu.
Website: http://www.gradschool.cornell.edu/fields.php?id-91&a-2.

Cornell University, Graduate School, Graduate Fields of Industrial and Labor Relations, Ithaca, NY 14853. Offers collective bargaining, labor law and labor history (MILR, MPS, MS, PhD); economic and social statistics (MILR); human resource studies (MILR, MPS, MS, PhD); industrial and labor relations problems (MILR, MPS, MS, PhD); international and comparative labor (MILR, MPS, MS, PhD); labor economics (MILR, MPS, MS, PhD); organizational behavior (MILR, MPS, MS, PhD). *Faculty:* 55 full-time (15 women). *Students:* 174 full-time (102 women); includes 30 minority (10 Black or African American, non-Hispanic/Latino; 11 Asian, non-Hispanic/Latino; 5 Hispanic/Latino; 4 Two or more races, non-Hispanic/Latino), 60 international. Average age 29. 353 applicants, 25% accepted, 77 enrolled. In 2013, 69 master's, 4 doctorates awarded. *Degree requirements:* For master's, thesis (MS); for doctorate, comprehensive exam, thesis/dissertation, teaching experience. *Entrance requirements:* For master's and doctorate, GMAT or GRE General Test, 2 academic recommendations. Additional exam requirements/recommendations for international students: Required—TOEFL (minimum

score 550 paper-based; 77 iBT). Application fee: $95. Electronic applications accepted. *Expenses:* Contact institution. *Financial support:* In 2013–14, 64 students received support, including 9 fellowships with full tuition reimbursements available, 24 research assistantships with full tuition reimbursements available, 31 teaching assistantships with full tuition reimbursements available; institutionally sponsored loans, scholarships/grants, health care benefits, tuition waivers (full and partial), and unspecified assistantships also available. Financial award applicants required to submit FAFSA. *Unit head:* Director of Graduate Studies, 607-255-1522. *Application contact:* Graduate Field Assistant, 607-255-1522, E-mail: ilrgradapplicant@cornell.edu.
Website: http://www.gradschool.cornell.edu/fields.php?id-85&a-2.

Drexel University, LeBow College of Business, Program in Business Administration, Philadelphia, PA 19104-2875. Offers business administration (MBA, PhD, APC), including accounting (MBA, PhD), decision sciences (PhD), economics (MBA, PhD), finance (MBA, PhD), legal studies (MBA), management (MBA), marketing (MBA, PhD), organizational sciences (PhD), quantitative methods (MBA), strategic management (PhD). *Accreditation:* AACSB. Part-time and evening/weekend programs available. Postbaccalaureate distance learning degree programs offered (minimal on-campus study). Terminal master's awarded for partial completion of doctoral program. *Entrance requirements:* For master's, GMAT, minimum GPA of 2.75; for doctorate, GMAT. Additional exam requirements/recommendations for international students: Required—TOEFL. Electronic applications accepted. *Faculty research:* Decision support systems, individual and group behavior, operations research, techniques and strategy.

Fairleigh Dickinson University, College at Florham, Maxwell Becton College of Arts and Sciences, Department of Psychology, Program in Organizational Behavior, Madison, NJ 07940-1099. Offers organizational behavior (MA); organizational leadership (Certificate).

Florida Institute of Technology, Graduate Programs, College of Psychology and Liberal Arts, School of Psychology, Melbourne, FL 32901-6975. Offers applied behavior analysis (MS); applied behavior analysis and organizational behavior management (MS); behavior analysis (PhD); clinical psychology (Psy D); industrial/organizational psychology (MS, PhD); organizational behavior management (MS); professional behavior analysis (MA); psychology (MS). *Accreditation:* APA (one or more programs are accredited). Part-time programs available. *Faculty:* 28 full-time (13 women), 13 part-time/adjunct (5 women). *Students:* 196 full-time (154 women), 13 part-time (10 women); includes 40 minority (10 Black or African American, non-Hispanic/Latino; 8 Asian, non-Hispanic/Latino; 14 Hispanic/Latino; 8 Two or more races, non-Hispanic/Latino), 15 international. Average age 27. 430 applicants, 33% accepted, 70 enrolled. In 2013, 65 master's, 25 doctorates awarded. Terminal master's awarded for partial completion of doctoral program. *Degree requirements:* For master's, comprehensive exam (for some programs), thesis (for some programs), BCBA certification, final exam; for doctorate, comprehensive exam, thesis/dissertation, internship, full-time resident of school for 4 years (8 semesters, 3 summers). *Entrance requirements:* For master's, GRE General Test, 3 letters of recommendation, minimum GPA of 3.0, resume, statement of objectives; for doctorate, GRE General Test, GRE Subject Test (psychology), 3 letters of recommendation, minimum GPA of 3.2, resume, statement of objectives. Additional exam requirements/recommendations for international students: Required—TOEFL (minimum score 550 paper-based; 79 iBT). *Application deadline:* For fall admission, 4/1 for international students; for spring admission, 9/30 for international students. Applications are processed on a rolling basis. Application fee: $0. Electronic applications accepted. *Expenses: Tuition:* Full-time $20,214; part-time $1123 per credit. Tuition and fees vary according to campus/location. *Financial support:* In 2013–14, 2 fellowships with full and partial tuition reimbursements (averaging $4,800 per year), 59 research assistantships with full and partial tuition reimbursements (averaging $2,556 per year), 11 teaching assistantships with full and partial tuition reimbursements (averaging $2,910 per year) were awarded; career-related internships or fieldwork, institutionally sponsored loans, tuition waivers (partial), unspecified assistantships, and tuition remissions also available. Support available to part-time students. Financial award application deadline: 3/1; financial award applicants required to submit FAFSA. *Faculty research:* Addictions, neuropsychology, child abuse, assessment, psychological trauma. *Total annual research expenditures:* $232,129. *Unit head:* Dr. Mary Beth Kenkel, Dean, 321-674-8142, Fax: 321-674-7105, E-mail: mkenkel@fit.edu. *Application contact:* Cheryl A. Brown, Associate Director of Graduate Admissions, 321-674-7581, Fax: 321-723-9468, E-mail: cbrown@fit.edu.
Website: http://cpla.fit.edu/psych/.

Florida State University, The Graduate School, College of Business, Tallahassee, FL 32306-1110. Offers accounting (M Acc), including accounting information services, assurance services, corporate accounting, taxation; business administration (MBA, PhD), including accounting (PhD), finance (PhD), management information systems (PhD), marketing (PhD), organizational behavior and human resources (PhD), risk management and insurance (PhD), strategic management (PhD); finance (MS); insurance (MSM); management information systems (MS); marketing (MS); JD/MBA; MSW/MBA. *Accreditation:* AACSB. Part-time programs available. Postbaccalaureate distance learning degree programs offered (no on-campus study). *Faculty:* 102 full-time (31 women), 5 part-time/adjunct (0 women). *Students:* 280 full-time (117 women), 278 part-time (88 women); includes 127 minority (26 Black or African American, non-Hispanic/Latino; 7 American Indian or Alaska Native, non-Hispanic/Latino; 44 Asian, non-Hispanic/Latino; 50 Hispanic/Latino). Average age 30. 630 applicants, 28% accepted, 103 enrolled. In 2013, 265 master's, 11 doctorates awarded. Terminal master's awarded for partial completion of doctoral program. *Degree requirements:* For doctorate, comprehensive exam, thesis/dissertation. *Entrance requirements:* For master's, GMAT, work experience (MBA, MS), minimum GPA of 3.0, letters of recommendation; for doctorate, GMAT, minimum graduate GPA of 3.5, letters of recommendation. Additional exam requirements/recommendations for international students: Required—TOEFL (minimum score 600 paper-based; 100 iBT); Recommended—IELTS (minimum score 6.5). *Application deadline:* For fall admission, 6/1 for domestic students, 5/1 for international students; for spring admission, 10/1 for domestic students, 9/1 for international students. Applications are processed on a rolling basis. Application fee: $30. Electronic applications accepted. *Expenses:* Tuition, state resident: part-time $403.51 per credit hour. Tuition, nonresident: part-time $1004.85 per credit hour. *Required fees:* $75.81 per credit hour. One-time fee: $20 part-time. Tuition and fees vary according to course load, campus/location and student level. *Financial support:* In 2013–14, 92 students received support, including 10 fellowships with full tuition reimbursements available (averaging $1,500 per year), 20 research assistantships with full tuition reimbursements available (averaging $20,000 per year), 35 teaching assistantships with full tuition reimbursements available (averaging $20,000 per year); career-related internships or fieldwork, scholarships/grants, health care benefits, and unspecified assistantships also available. Financial award application deadline: 1/1. *Unit head:* Dr. Caryn Beck-Dudley, Dean, 850-644-3090, Fax: 850-644-0915. *Application contact:* Lisa Beverly, Director, Graduate Programs Admissions, 850-644-6458, Fax: 850-644-0588, E-mail: lbeverly@cob.fsu.edu.
Website: http://www.cob.fsu.edu/.

Georgia Institute of Technology, Graduate Studies and Research, College of Management, Program in Business Administration, Atlanta, GA 30332-0001. Offers accounting (MBA); e-commerce (Certificate); engineering entrepreneurship (MBA); entrepreneurship (Certificate); finance (MBA); information technology management (MBA); international business (MBA, Certificate); management of technology (Certificate); marketing (MBA); operations management (MBA); organizational behavior (MBA); strategic management (MBA). *Accreditation:* AACSB.

Georgia Institute of Technology, Graduate Studies and Research, College of Management, Program in Management, Atlanta, GA 30332-0001. Offers accounting (PhD); finance (PhD); information technology management (PhD); marketing (PhD); operations management (PhD); organizational behavior (PhD); quantitative and computational finance (MS); strategic management (PhD). *Accreditation:* AACSB. *Degree requirements:* For doctorate, comprehensive exam, thesis/dissertation, oral exams. *Entrance requirements:* For master's and doctorate, GMAT. Additional exam requirements/recommendations for international students: Required—TOEFL. *Faculty research:* Management information systems, management of technology, international business, entrepreneurship, operations management.

The Graduate Center, City University of New York, Graduate Studies, Program in Business, New York, NY 10016-4039. Offers accounting (PhD); behavioral science (PhD); finance (PhD); management planning systems (PhD). *Degree requirements:* For doctorate, thesis/dissertation. *Entrance requirements:* For doctorate, GMAT, writing sample (15 pages). Additional exam requirements/recommendations for international students: Required—TOEFL. Electronic applications accepted.

Harvard University, Graduate School of Arts and Sciences and Doctoral Programs in Management, Committee on Organizational Behavior, Cambridge, MA 02138. Offers PhD. *Entrance requirements:* For doctorate, GRE General Test or GMAT, major in psychology or sociology, course work in statistics or mathematics. Additional exam requirements/recommendations for international students: Required—TOEFL. *Expenses: Tuition:* Full-time $38,888. *Required fees:* $958. Tuition and fees vary according to campus/location, program and student level.

Harvard University, Harvard Business School, Doctoral Programs in Management, Boston, MA 02163. Offers accounting and management (DBA); business economics (PhD); health policy management (PhD); management (DBA); marketing (DBA); organizational behavior (PhD); science, technology and management (PhD); strategy (DBA); technology and operations management (DBA). *Degree requirements:* For doctorate, comprehensive exam (for some programs), thesis/dissertation. *Entrance requirements:* For doctorate, GRE General Test or GMAT. Additional exam requirements/recommendations for international students: Required—TOEFL. *Expenses: Tuition:* Full-time $38,888. *Required fees:* $958. Tuition and fees vary according to campus/location, program and student level.

International Institute for Restorative Practices, Graduate Programs, Bethlehem, PA 18018. Offers MS, Certificate. Postbaccalaureate distance learning degree programs offered (minimal on-campus study).

John Jay College of Criminal Justice of the City University of New York, Graduate Studies, Programs in Criminal Justice, New York, NY 10019-1093. Offers criminal justice (MA, PhD); criminology and deviance (PhD); forensic psychology (PhD); forensic science (PhD); law and philosophy (PhD); organizational behavior (PhD); public policy (PhD). Part-time and evening/weekend programs available. Terminal master's awarded for partial completion of doctoral program. *Degree requirements:* For master's, thesis or alternative; for doctorate, one foreign language, thesis/dissertation. *Entrance requirements:* For master's, GRE General Test, minimum B average; for doctorate, GRE General Test. Additional exam requirements/recommendations for international students: Required—TOEFL (minimum score 500 paper-based).

Lake Forest Graduate School of Management, The Leadership MBA Program, Lake Forest, IL 60045. Offers finance (MBA); global business (MBA); healthcare management (MBA); management (MBA); marketing (MBA); organizational behavior (MBA). Part-time and evening/weekend programs available. *Entrance requirements:* For master's, 4 years of work experience in field, interview, 2 letters of recommendation. Electronic applications accepted.

Marylhurst University, Department of Business Administration, Marylhurst, OR 97036-0261. Offers finance (MBA); general management (MBA); government policy and administration (MBA); green development (MBA); health care management (MBA); marketing (MBA); natural and organic resources (MBA); nonprofit management (MBA); organizational behavior (MBA); real estate (MBA); renewable energy (MBA); sustainable business (MBA). Part-time and evening/weekend programs available. Postbaccalaureate distance learning degree programs offered (no on-campus study). *Degree requirements:* For master's, comprehensive exam, capstone course. *Entrance requirements:* For master's, GMAT (if GPA less than 3.0 and fewer than 5 years of work experience), interview, resume, 2 letters of recommendation. Additional exam requirements/recommendations for international students: Recommended—TOEFL (minimum score 550 paper-based; 80 iBT). Electronic applications accepted.

New York University, Leonard N. Stern School of Business, Department of Management and Organizations, New York, NY 10012-1019. Offers management organizations (MBA); organization theory (PhD); organizational behavior (PhD); strategy (PhD). *Expenses: Tuition:* Full-time $35,856; part-time $1494 per unit. *Required fees:* $1408; $64 per unit. $473 per term. Tuition and fees vary according to course load and program. *Faculty research:* Strategic management, managerial cognition, interpersonal processes, conflict and negotiation.

New York University, Polytechnic School of Engineering, Department of Finance and Risk Engineering, New York, NY 10012-1019. Offers financial engineering (MS, Advanced Certificate), including capital markets (MS), computational finance (MS), financial technology (MS); financial technology management (Advanced Certificate); organizational behavior (Advanced Certificate); risk management (Advanced Certificate); technology management (Advanced Certificate). MS program also offered in Manhattan. Part-time and evening/weekend programs available. *Faculty:* 8 full-time (3 women), 26 part-time/adjunct (5 women). *Students:* 232 full-time (76 women), 30 part-time (5 women); includes 19 minority (2 Black or African American, non-Hispanic/Latino; 15 Asian, non-Hispanic/Latino; 2 Hispanic/Latino), 221 international. Average age 25. 634 applicants, 57% accepted, 124 enrolled. In 2013, 111 master's awarded. *Degree requirements:* For master's, comprehensive exam (for some programs), thesis (for some programs). *Entrance requirements:* For master's, GMAT, minimum B average in undergraduate course work. Additional exam requirements/recommendations for international students: Required—TOEFL (minimum score 550 paper-based; 80 iBT); Recommended—IELTS (minimum score 6.5). *Application deadline:* For fall admission, 7/31 priority date for domestic students, 4/30 priority date for international students; for spring admission, 12/31 priority date for domestic students, 11/30 priority date for international students. Applications are processed on a rolling basis. Application fee: $75. Electronic applications accepted. *Expenses: Tuition:* Full-time $35,856; part-time $1494 per unit. *Required fees:* $1408; $64 per unit. $473 per term. Tuition and fees vary according to course load and program. *Financial support:* Institutionally sponsored loans, scholarships/grants, and unspecified assistantships available. Support available to part-time students. Financial award applicants required to submit FAFSA. *Faculty research:* Optimal control theory, general modeling and analysis, risk parity optimality, a new algorithmic approach to entangled political economy. *Total annual research*

expenditures: $176,428. *Unit head:* Prof. Charles S. Tapiero, Academic Director, 718-260-3653, Fax: 718-260-3874, E-mail: ctapiero@poly.edu. *Application contact:* Raymond Lutzky, Director, Graduate Enrollment Management, 718-637-5984, Fax: 718-260-3624, E-mail: rlutzky@poly.edu.

New York University, Polytechnic School of Engineering, Department of Technology Management, Major in Organizational Behavior, New York, NY 10012-1019. Offers MS. Part-time and evening/weekend programs available. *Students:* 37 full-time (25 women), 17 part-time (10 women); includes 11 minority (6 Asian, non-Hispanic/Latino; 5 Hispanic/Latino), 18 international. Average age 29. 45 applicants, 67% accepted, 13 enrolled. In 2013, 12 master's awarded. *Degree requirements:* For master's, comprehensive exam (for some programs), thesis (for some programs). *Entrance requirements:* For master's, GMAT, minimum B average in undergraduate course work. Additional exam requirements/recommendations for international students: Required—TOEFL (minimum score 550 paper-based; 80 iBT); Recommended—IELTS (minimum score 6.5). *Application deadline:* For fall admission, 7/31 priority date for domestic students, 4/30 priority date for international students; for spring admission, 12/31 priority date for domestic students, 11/30 priority date for international students. Applications are processed on a rolling basis. Application fee: $75. Electronic applications accepted. *Expenses: Tuition:* Full-time $35,856; part-time $1494 per unit. *Required fees:* $1408; $64 per unit. $473 per term. Tuition and fees vary according to course load and program. *Financial support:* Applicants required to submit FAFSA. *Unit head:* Prof. Bharadwaj Rao, Head, 718-260-3617, Fax: 718-260-3874, E-mail: brao@poly.edu. *Application contact:* Raymond Lutzky, Director of Graduate Enrollment Management, 718-637-5984, Fax: 718-260-3624, E-mail: rlutzky@poly.edu.

Northwestern University, The Graduate School, School of Education and Social Policy, Program in Learning and Organizational Change, Evanston, IL 60208. Offers MS. Part-time and evening/weekend programs available. Postbaccalaureate distance learning degree programs offered (minimal on-campus study). *Degree requirements:* For master's, thesis, practicum. *Entrance requirements:* For master's, GRE or GMAT (recommended), letters of recommendation. Additional exam requirements/recommendations for international students: Required—TOEFL (minimum score 600 paper-based; 100 iBT); Recommended—IELTS (minimum score 7). Electronic applications accepted. *Faculty research:* Strategic change, learning and performance, workplace learning, leadership development, cognitive design, knowledge management.

Phillips Graduate Institute, Program in Organizational Management and Consulting, Encino, CA 91316-1509. Offers Psy D. Evening/weekend programs available. *Degree requirements:* For doctorate, thesis/dissertation. *Entrance requirements:* For doctorate, minimum GPA of 3.0, interview. Electronic applications accepted.

Purdue University, Graduate School, Krannert School of Management, Doctoral Program in Organizational Behavior and Human Resource Management, West Lafayette, IN 47907-2056. Offers PhD. *Degree requirements:* For doctorate, comprehensive exam, thesis/dissertation, dissertation proposal, dissertation defense. *Entrance requirements:* For doctorate, GMAT or GRE, bachelor's degree, two semesters of calculus, one semester each of linear algebra and statistics. Additional exam requirements/recommendations for international students: Required—TOEFL (minimum score 575 paper-based); Recommended—TWE. Electronic applications accepted. *Faculty research:* Human resource management, organizational behavior.

Saybrook University, School of Organizational Leadership and Transformation, San Francisco, CA 94111-1920. Offers MA. Program offered jointly with Bastyr University. *Degree requirements:* For master's, thesis (for some programs), oral exams. *Entrance requirements:* For master's, bachelor's degree from an accredited college or university. *Expenses: Tuition:* Full-time $22,560. *Required fees:* $2200; $1000 per credit. $2200 per year. One-time fee: $450. *Faculty research:* Cross-functional work teams, communication, management authority, employee influence, systems theory.

Saybrook University, School of Psychology and Interdisciplinary Inquiry, San Francisco, CA 94111-1920. Offers human science (MA, PhD), including consciousness and spirituality, humanistic and transpersonal psychology, integrative health studies, organizational systems, social transformation; organizational systems (MA, PhD), including consciousness and spirituality, humanistic and transpersonal psychology, integrative health studies, leadership of sustainable systems (MA), organizational systems, social transformation; psychology (MA, PhD), including consciousness and spirituality, creativity studies (MA), humanistic and transpersonal psychology, integrative health studies, Jungian studies, marriage and family therapy (MA), organizational systems, social transformation. Postbaccalaureate distance learning degree programs offered (minimal on-campus study). Terminal master's awarded for partial completion of doctoral program. *Degree requirements:* For master's, thesis or alternative; for doctorate, thesis/dissertation. *Entrance requirements:* Additional exam requirements/recommendations for international students: Required—TOEFL (minimum score 580 paper-based; 93 iBT). Electronic applications accepted. *Expenses: Tuition:* Full-time $22,560. *Required fees:* $2200; $1000 per credit. $2200 per year. One-time fee: $450. *Faculty research:* Humanistic theory, health studies, organizational systems, consciousness and spirituality, social transformation.

Silver Lake College of the Holy Family, Division of Graduate Studies, Program in Management and Organizational Development, Manitowoc, WI 54220-9319. Offers MS. Part-time and evening/weekend programs available. Postbaccalaureate distance learning degree programs offered (minimal on-campus study). *Faculty:* 27 part-time/adjunct (14 women). *Students:* 15 full-time (13 women), 52 part-time (31 women); includes 7 minority (6 American Indian or Alaska Native, non-Hispanic/Latino; 1 Asian, non-Hispanic/Latino). Average age 38. 33 applicants, 94% accepted, 18 enrolled. In 2013, 39 master's awarded. *Degree requirements:* For master's, thesis optional. *Entrance requirements:* For master's, minimum undergraduate GPA of 3.0, statement of purpose, three letters of recommendation, professional resume. Additional exam requirements/recommendations for international students: Required—TOEFL. *Application deadline:* For fall admission, 8/1 priority date for domestic students; for spring admission, 12/1 priority date for domestic students. Applications are processed on a rolling basis. Application fee: $0. Electronic applications accepted. *Expenses: Tuition:* Part-time $500 per credit. *Financial support:* Career-related internships or fieldwork, Federal Work-Study, and scholarships/grants available. Support available to part-time students. Financial award application deadline: 6/30; financial award applicants required to submit FAFSA. *Application contact:* Ryan Roberts, Assistant Director of Admissions, 920-686-6204, Fax: 920-686-6350, E-mail: ryan.roberts@sl.edu. Website: https://www.sl.edu/adult-education/academics/graduate-program/master-of-science-in-management-and-organizational-development/.

Suffolk University, Sawyer Business School, Master of Business Administration Program, Boston, MA 02108-2770. Offers accounting (MBA); business administration (APC); entrepreneurship (MBA); executive business administration (EMBA); finance (MBA); global business administration (GMBA); health administration (MBA); international business (MBA); marketing (MBA); nonprofit management (MBA); organizational behavior (MBA); strategic management (MBA); supply chain management (MBA); taxation (MBA); JD/MBA; MBA/GDPA; MBA/MHA; MBA/MSA; MBA/MSF; MBA/MST. *Accreditation:* AACSB. Part-time and evening/weekend programs available. Postbaccalaureate distance learning degree programs offered (no on-campus study). *Faculty:* 29 full-time (9 women), 12 part-time/adjunct (2 women). *Students:* 106 full-time (44 women), 334 part-time (184 women); includes 57 minority (20 Black or African American, non-Hispanic/Latino; 1 American Indian or Alaska Native, non-Hispanic/Latino; 18 Asian, non-Hispanic/Latino; 14 Hispanic/Latino; 4 Two or more races, non-Hispanic/Latino), 61 international. Average age 30. 448 applicants, 61% accepted, 135 enrolled. In 2013, 217 master's awarded. *Entrance requirements:* For master's, GMAT, minimum undergraduate GPA of 2.75 (MBA), 5 years of managerial experience (EMBA). Additional exam requirements/recommendations for international students: Required—TOEFL (minimum score 550 paper-based; 80 iBT). *Application deadline:* For fall admission, 6/15 priority date for domestic students, 6/15 for international students; for spring admission, 11/1 priority date for domestic students, 11/1 for international students. Applications are processed on a rolling basis. Application fee: $50. Electronic applications accepted. *Expenses: Tuition:* Full-time $38,374; part-time $1279 per credit. *Required fees:* $40; $20 per semester. Tuition and fees vary according to program. *Financial support:* In 2013–14, 107 students received support, including 91 fellowships with full and partial tuition reimbursements available (averaging $12,428 per year); career-related internships or fieldwork, Federal Work-Study, and institutionally sponsored loans also available. Support available to part-time students. Financial award application deadline: 4/1; financial award applicants required to submit FAFSA. *Faculty research:* Foreign investments; career strategies and boundaryless careers; corporate ethics codes; interest rates, inflation, and growth options; innovation and product development performance. *Unit head:* Heather Hewitt, Assistant Dean of Graduate Programs/Director of MBA Programs, 617-573-8306, E-mail: hhewitt@suffolk.edu. *Application contact:* Cory Meyers, Director of Graduate Admissions, 617-573-8302, Fax: 617-305-1733, E-mail: grad.admission@suffolk.edu. Website: http://www.suffolk.edu/mba.

Syracuse University, Martin J. Whitman School of Management, PhD Program in Business Administration, Syracuse, NY 13244. Offers accounting (PhD); finance (PhD); management information systems (PhD); managerial statistics (PhD); marketing (PhD); operations management (PhD); organizational behavior (PhD); strategy and human resources (PhD); supply chain management (PhD). *Faculty:* 79 full-time (20 women), 25 part-time/adjunct (6 women). *Students:* 26 full-time (8 women), 1 part-time (0 women); includes 2 minority (1 Black or African American, non-Hispanic/Latino; 1 Asian, non-Hispanic/Latino), 20 international. Average age 30. 130 applicants, 9% accepted, 7 enrolled. In 2013, 15 doctorates awarded. *Degree requirements:* For doctorate, comprehensive exam, thesis/dissertation, summer research paper. *Entrance requirements:* For doctorate, GMAT or GRE General Test, 3 recommendations. Additional exam requirements/recommendations for international students: Required—TOEFL (minimum score 600 paper-based; 100 iBT). *Application deadline:* For fall admission, 1/15 priority date for domestic and international students. Applications are processed on a rolling basis. Application fee: $75. Electronic applications accepted. *Financial support:* In 2013–14, 1 fellowship with full tuition reimbursement (averaging $19,570 per year), 30 teaching assistantships with full tuition reimbursements (averaging $17,000 per year) were awarded; research assistantships with full tuition reimbursements also available. Financial award application deadline: 1/15. *Faculty research:* Marketing models, market microstructure, supply chain, auditing, corporate governance. *Unit head:* Dr. Michel Benarock, Director of the PhD Program, 315-443-3429, E-mail: mbenaroc@syr.edu. *Application contact:* Carol Hilleges, Administrative Specialist, 315-443-9601, Fax: 315-443-3671, E-mail: clhilleg@syr.edu. Website: http://whitman.syr.edu/phd/.

Towson University, Program in Organizational Change, Towson, MD 21252-0001. Offers CAS. *Students:* 3 full-time (all women), 100 part-time (82 women); includes 24 minority (20 Black or African American, non-Hispanic/Latino; 1 American Indian or Alaska Native, non-Hispanic/Latino; 2 Hispanic/Latino; 1 Two or more races, non-Hispanic/Latino), 1 international. *Entrance requirements:* For degree, minimum 3 years of teaching experience, 2 letters of recommendation, minimum GPA of 3.1, personal statement. *Application deadline:* Applications are processed on a rolling basis. Application fee: $45. Electronic applications accepted. *Unit head:* Dr. Jessica Shiller, Graduate Program Director, 410-704-5383, E-mail: jshiller@towson.edu. *Application contact:* Alicia Arkell-Kleis, Information Contact, 410-704-6004, E-mail: grads@towson.edu. Website: http://grad.towson.edu/program/certificate/orgc-cas/.

Universidad de las Americas, A.C., Program in International Organizations and Institutions, Mexico City, Mexico. Offers MA.

Université de Sherbrooke, Faculty of Administration, Program in Organizational Change and Intervention, Sherbrooke, QC J1K 2R1, Canada. Offers M Sc. *Degree requirements:* For master's, one foreign language, thesis. *Entrance requirements:* For master's, bachelor's degree in related field, minimum GPA of 3.0 (on 4.3 scale). Electronic applications accepted. *Faculty research:* Organizational change, organizational communication, process approaches and qualitative research, organizational behavior.

The University of British Columbia, Sauder School of Business, Doctoral Program in Commerce and Business Administration, Vancouver, BC V6T 1Z1, Canada. Offers accounting (PhD); finance (PhD); management information systems (PhD); management science (PhD); marketing (PhD); organizational behavior (PhD); strategy and business economics (PhD); transportation and logistics (PhD); urban land economics (PhD). *Faculty:* 91 full-time (22 women). *Students:* 66 full-time (24 women). Average age 30. 418 applicants, 2% accepted, 8 enrolled. In 2013, 7 doctorates awarded. *Degree requirements:* For doctorate, comprehensive exam, thesis/dissertation. *Entrance requirements:* For doctorate, GMAT or GRE. Additional exam requirements/recommendations for international students: Required—TOEFL (minimum score 600 paper-based; 100 iBT). *Application deadline:* For fall admission, 1/31 for domestic students, 12/31 for international students. Applications are processed on a rolling basis. Application fee: $95 Canadian dollars ($153 Canadian dollars for international students). Electronic applications accepted. *Expenses: Tuition, area resident:* Full-time $8000 Canadian dollars. *Financial support:* In 2013–14, fellowships with full tuition reimbursements (averaging $17,500 per year), research assistantships with full tuition reimbursements (averaging $8,500 per year), teaching assistantships with full tuition reimbursements (averaging $17,500 per year) were awarded. Financial award application deadline: 12/31. *Unit head:* Dr. Ralph Winter, Director, 604-822-8366, Fax: 604-822-8755. *Application contact:* Elaine Cho, Administrator, PhD and M Sc Programs, 604-822-8366, Fax: 604-822-8755, E-mail: phd.program@sauder.ubc.ca. Website: http://www.sauder.ubc.ca/.

University of California, Berkeley, Graduate Division, Haas School of Business, PhD in Business Administration Program, Berkeley, CA 94720-1500. Offers accounting (PhD); business and public policy (PhD); finance (PhD); management of organizations (PhD); marketing (PhD); operations management (PhD); real estate (PhD). *Accreditation:* AACSB. *Students:* 74 full-time (28 women); includes 11 minority (9 Asian, non-Hispanic/Latino; 2 Hispanic/Latino), 38 international. Average age 27. 490 applicants, 6% accepted, 14 enrolled. In 2013, 14 doctorates awarded. *Degree requirements:* For doctorate, comprehensive exam, thesis/dissertation, written preliminary exams, oral qualifying exam. *Entrance requirements:* For doctorate, GMAT or GRE, minimum GPA of 3.0 in undergraduate and graduate coursework. Additional

exam requirements/recommendations for international students: Required—TOEFL (minimum score 570 paper-based; 70 iBT), IELTS (minimum score 7). *Application deadline:* For fall admission, 12/10 for domestic and international students. Application fee: $80 ($100 for international students). Electronic applications accepted. *Financial support:* In 2013–14, 74 students received support, including 62 fellowships with full and partial tuition reimbursements available (averaging $30,000 per year), research assistantships with full and partial tuition reimbursements available (averaging $12,000 per year), teaching assistantships with full and partial tuition reimbursements available (averaging $13,000 per year); scholarships/grants, health care benefits, tuition waivers (full), unspecified assistantships, and transit passes, travel grants also available. Financial award application deadline: 12/10; financial award applicants required to submit FAFSA. *Faculty research:* Accounting, business and public policy, entrepreneurship, finance, management of organizations, marketing, operations and information technology management, real estate. *Unit head:* Dr. Martin Lettau, Director, 510-643-6349, Fax: 510-643-4255, E-mail: kimg@haas.berkeley.edu. *Application contact:* Kim Guilfoyle, Director, Student Affairs, 510-642-3944, Fax: 510-643-4255, E-mail: kimg@haas.berkeley.edu.
Website: http://www.haas.berkeley.edu/Phd/.

University of California, Los Angeles, Graduate Division, UCLA Anderson School of Management, Los Angeles, CA 90095-1481. Offers accounting (PhD); Americas (EMBA); Asia Pacific (EMBA); business administration (EMBA, MBA); decisions, operations and technology management (PhD); finance (PhD); financial engineering (MFE); global economics and management (PhD); management and organizations (PhD); marketing (PhD); strategy and policy (PhD); DDS/MBA; MBA/JD; MBA/MD; MBA/MLAS; MBA/MLIS; MBA/MPH; MBA/MPP; MBA/MSCS; MBA/MSN; MBA/MUP. *Accreditation:* AACSB. Part-time programs available. *Faculty:* 104 full-time (20 women), 28 part-time/adjunct (4 women). *Students:* 1,069 full-time (324 women), 879 part-time (251 women); includes 664 minority (37 Black or African American, non-Hispanic/Latino; 1 American Indian or Alaska Native, non-Hispanic/Latino; 470 Asian, non-Hispanic/Latino; 34 Hispanic/Latino; 2 Native Hawaiian or other Pacific Islander, non-Hispanic/Latino; 120 Two or more races, non-Hispanic/Latino), 444 international. Average age 30. 5,084 applicants, 27% accepted, 845 enrolled. In 2013, 801 master's, 14 doctorates awarded. *Degree requirements:* For master's, comprehensive exam, field study consulting project (for MBA); thesis (for MFE); for doctorate, comprehensive exam, thesis/dissertation, oral and written qualifying exams. *Entrance requirements:* For master's, GMAT (for MBA); GMAT or GRE General Test (for MFE), 4-year bachelor's degree or equivalent; recommendation letters (1 for MBA, 2 for MFE); two essays; interview (by invitation only for MBA); for doctorate, GMAT or GRE General Test, bachelor's degree from college or university of fully-recognized standing; minimum B average in undergraduate coursework or B+ average in prior graduate work; statement of purpose; three recommendation letters. Additional exam requirements/recommendations for international students: Required—TOEFL (minimum score 560 paper-based; 87 iBT). *Application deadline:* For fall admission, 10/22 priority date for domestic and international students; for winter admission, 1/7 for domestic and international students; for spring admission, 4/15 for domestic and international students. Applications are processed on a rolling basis. Application fee: $200. Electronic applications accepted. *Expenses:* Contact institution. *Financial support:* In 2013–14, 522 students received support. Fellowships, research assistantships with partial tuition reimbursements available, teaching assistantships with partial tuition reimbursements available, career-related internships or fieldwork, institutionally sponsored loans, scholarships/grants, health care benefits, and tuition waivers (partial) available. Financial award application deadline: 4/15; financial award applicants required to submit FAFSA. *Faculty research:* Asset pricing, decision-making, behavioral finance, international finance and economics, global macroeconomics. *Total annual research expenditures:* $368,086. *Unit head:* Dr. Judy D. Olian, Dean/Chair in Management, 310-825-7982, Fax: 310-206-2073, E-mail: judy.olian@anderson.ucla.edu. *Application contact:* Alex Lawrence, Assistant Dean, MBA Admissions and Financial Aid, 310-825-6944, Fax: 310-825-8582, E-mail: mba.admissions@anderson.ucla.edu.
Website: http://www.anderson.ucla.edu/.

See Display on page 145 and Close-Up on page 191.

University of Chicago, Booth School of Business, Full-Time MBA Program, Chicago, IL 60637. Offers accounting (MBA); analytic finance (MBA); analytic management (MBA); econometrics and statistics (MBA); economics (MBA); entrepreneurship (MBA); finance (MBA); general management (MBA); health administration and policy (Certificate); human resource management (MBA); international business (MBA); managerial and organizational behavior (MBA); marketing management (MBA); operations management (MBA); strategic management (MBA); MBA/AM; MBA/JD; MBA/MA; MBA/MD; MBA/MPP. *Accreditation:* AACSB. Part-time and evening/weekend programs available. Terminal master's awarded for partial completion of doctoral program. *Entrance requirements:* For master's, GMAT, 2 letters of recommendation, 3 essays, resume, interview. Additional exam requirements/recommendations for international students: Required—TOEFL (minimum score 600 paper-based; 104 iBT), IELTS. Electronic applications accepted. *Expenses:* Contact institution. *Faculty research:* Finance, marketing, economics, entrepreneurship, strategy, management.

University of Hartford, College of Arts and Sciences, Department of Psychology, Program in Organizational Behavior, West Hartford, CT 06117-1599. Offers MS. Part-time and evening/weekend programs available. *Entrance requirements:* Additional exam requirements/recommendations for international students: Required—TOEFL (minimum score 550 paper-based). Electronic applications accepted.

University of Hawaii at Manoa, Graduate Division, Shidler College of Business, Program in Business Administration, Honolulu, HI 96822. Offers Asian business studies (MBA); Chinese business studies (MBA); decision sciences (MBA); entrepreneurship (MBA); finance (MBA); finance and banking (MBA); human resources management (MBA); information management (MBA); information technology (MBA); international business (MBA); Japanese business studies (MBA); marketing (MBA); organizational behavior (MBA); organizational management (MBA); real estate (MBA); student-designed track (MBA). *Accreditation:* AACSB. Part-time and evening/weekend programs available. *Degree requirements:* For master's, thesis optional. *Entrance requirements:* For master's, GMAT, minimum GPA of 3.0. Additional exam requirements/recommendations for international students: Required—TOEFL (minimum score 600 paper-based; 100 iBT), IELTS (minimum score 7). *Expenses:* Contact institution.

The University of North Carolina at Chapel Hill, Kenan-Flagler Business School, Doctoral Program in Business Administration, Chapel Hill, NC 27599. Offers accounting (PhD); finance (PhD); marketing (PhD); operations management (PhD); organizational behavior (PhD); strategy (PhD). *Accreditation:* AACSB. *Degree requirements:* For doctorate, thesis/dissertation. *Entrance requirements:* For doctorate, GMAT or GRE General Test. Electronic applications accepted. *Expenses:* Contact institution.

University of Oklahoma, College of Arts and Sciences, Department of Psychology, Program in Organizational Dynamics, Tulsa, OK 74135. Offers technical project management (MA). Part-time and evening/weekend programs available. *Students:* 6 full-time (all women), 25 part-time (14 women); includes 10 minority (2 Black or African American, non-Hispanic/Latino; 2 American Indian or Alaska Native, non-Hispanic/

Latino; 1 Asian, non-Hispanic/Latino; 2 Hispanic/Latino; 3 Two or more races, non-Hispanic/Latino). Average age 37. 7 applicants, 86% accepted, 4 enrolled. In 2013, 18 master's awarded. Terminal master's awarded for partial completion of doctoral program. *Degree requirements:* For master's, capstone project, thesis, or comprehensive exam. *Entrance requirements:* For master's, interview, statement of purpose, 2 letters of recommendation, resume showing at least 2 years of professional work experience. Additional exam requirements/recommendations for international students: Required—TOEFL (minimum score 79 iBT). *Application deadline:* For fall admission, 1/1 for domestic and international students; for spring admission, 11/1 for domestic students, 10/1 for international students. Application fee: $50 ($100 for international students). Electronic applications accepted. *Expenses:* Tuition, state resident: full-time $4205; part-time $175.20 per credit hour. Tuition, nonresident: full-time $16,205; part-time $675.20 per credit hour. *Required fees:* $2745; $103.85 per credit hour. $126.50 per semester. *Financial support:* In 2013–14, 6 students received support. Health care benefits and unspecified assistantships available. Financial award application deadline: 6/1; financial award applicants required to submit FAFSA. *Faculty research:* Leadership, teamwork, organizational citizenship behavior, ethics, organizational assessment. *Unit head:* Dr. Jennifer Kisamore, Graduate Liaison and Associate Professor, 918-660-3603, Fax: 918-660-3383, E-mail: jkisamore@ou.edu. *Application contact:* Lauren McKinney, Staff Assistant, 918-660-3489, Fax: 918-660-3491, E-mail: lmckinney@ou.edu.
Website: http://odyn.ou.edu.

University of Pittsburgh, Katz Graduate School of Business, Doctoral Program in Business Administration, Pittsburgh, PA 15260. Offers accounting (PhD); finance (PhD); information systems (PhD); marketing (PhD); operations/decision sciences/artificial intelligence (PhD); organizational behavior and human resource management (PhD); strategic planning (PhD). *Accreditation:* AACSB. *Faculty:* 60 full-time (17 women). *Students:* 50 full-time (22 women); includes 4 minority (2 Black or African American, non-Hispanic/Latino; 2 Asian, non-Hispanic/Latino), 27 international. 321 applicants, 7% accepted, 14 enrolled. In 2013, 10 doctorates awarded. *Degree requirements:* For doctorate, comprehensive exam, thesis/dissertation. *Entrance requirements:* For doctorate, GMAT or GRE, 3 recommendations, statement of purpose, transcripts of all previous course work and degrees. Additional exam requirements/recommendations for international students: Required—TOEFL. *Application deadline:* For fall admission, 1/1 priority date for domestic and international students. Applications are processed on a rolling basis. Application fee: $50. Electronic applications accepted. *Expenses:* Tuition, state resident: full-time $19,964; part-time $807 per credit. Tuition, nonresident: full-time $32,686; part-time $1337 per credit. *Required fees:* $740; $200. Tuition and fees vary according to program. *Financial support:* In 2013–14, 40 students received support, including 30 research assistantships with full tuition reimbursements available (averaging $23,045 per year), 10 teaching assistantships with full tuition reimbursements available (averaging $26,055 per year); fellowships, Federal Work-Study, scholarships/grants, health care benefits, and unspecified assistantships also available. Financial award application deadline: 1/1. *Faculty research:* Accounting systems/financial reporting, corporate finance, shopper marketing/consumer behavior, management information systems, organizational behavior and entrepreneurship. *Unit head:* Dr. Dennis Galletta, Director, 412-648-1699, Fax: 412-624-3633, E-mail: galletta@katz.pitt.edu. *Application contact:* Carrie Woods, Assistant Director, 412-648-1525, Fax: 412-624-3633, E-mail: cawoods@katz.pitt.edu.
Website: http://www.business.pitt.edu/katz/phd/.

University of Pittsburgh, Katz Graduate School of Business, Master of Business Administration Programs, Pittsburgh, PA 15260. Offers finance (MBA); information systems (MBA); marketing (MBA); operations management (MBA); organizational behavior and human resource management (MBA); strategy, environment and organizations (MBA); MBA/JD; MBA/MIB; MBA/MPIA; MBA/MSE; MBA/MSIS; MID/MBA. *Accreditation:* AACSB. Part-time and evening/weekend programs available. *Faculty:* 60 full-time (14 women), 21 part-time/adjunct (5 women). *Students:* 107 full-time (31 women), 428 part-time (155 women); includes 55 minority (15 Black or African American, non-Hispanic/Latino; 26 Asian, non-Hispanic/Latino; 10 Hispanic/Latino; 4 Two or more races, non-Hispanic/Latino), 83 international. Average age 30. 449 applicants, 23% accepted, 63 enrolled. In 2013, 279 master's awarded. *Degree requirements:* For master's, minimum GPA of 3.0. *Entrance requirements:* For master's, GMAT, recommendations, undergraduate transcripts, essay, resume, interview, bachelor's degree. Additional exam requirements/recommendations for international students: Required—TOEFL (minimum score 600 paper-based; 100 iBT) or IELTS. *Application deadline:* For fall admission, 4/1 priority date for domestic students, 2/1 priority date for international students. Application fee: $50. Electronic applications accepted. *Expenses:* Tuition, state resident: full-time $19,964; part-time $807 per credit. Tuition, nonresident: full-time $32,686; part-time $1337 per credit. *Required fees:* $740; $200. Tuition and fees vary according to program. *Financial support:* In 2013–14, 60 students received support. Career-related internships or fieldwork and scholarships/grants available. Financial award application deadline: 2/1. *Faculty research:* Accounting systems/financial reporting, corporate finance, shopper marketing/consumer behavior, management information systems, organizational behavior and entrepreneurship. *Unit head:* Tim Robison, Assistant Dean, 412-648-1700, Fax: 412-648-1659, E-mail: trobison@katz.pitt.edu. *Application contact:* Thomas Keller, Director of MBA Admissions, 412-648-1700, Fax: 412-648-1659, E-mail: mba@katz.pitt.edu.
Website: http://www.business.pitt.edu/katz/mba/.

University of South Florida, University College/Distance Education, Tampa, FL 33620-9951. *Unit head:* Kathy Barnes, Interdisciplinary Programs Coordinator, 813-974-8031, Fax: 813-974-7061, E-mail: barnesk@usf.edu. *Application contact:* Karen Tylinski, Metro Initiatives, 813-974-9943, Fax: 813-974-7061, E-mail: ktylinsk@usf.edu.
Website: http://uc.usf.edu/.

The University of Texas at Austin, Graduate School, College of Liberal Arts, Program in Human Dimensions of Organizations, Austin, TX 78712-1111. Offers MA. Evening/weekend programs available. Postbaccalaureate distance learning degree programs offered (no on-campus study). *Degree requirements:* For master's, capstone project.

University of Utah, Graduate School, David Eccles School of Business, Business Administration Program, Salt Lake City, UT 84112. Offers accounting (PhD); business administration (EMBA, MBA, PMBA); finance (PhD); information systems (PhD); marketing (PhD); operations management (PhD); organizational behavior (PhD); strategic management (PhD); MBA/JD; MBA/MHA; MBA/MS. Part-time and evening/weekend programs available. *Faculty:* 58 full-time (21 women), 37 part-time/adjunct (7 women). *Students:* 481 full-time (108 women), 109 part-time (19 women); includes 39 minority (2 Black or African American, non-Hispanic/Latino; 13 Asian, non-Hispanic/Latino; 18 Hispanic/Latino; 1 Native Hawaiian or other Pacific Islander, non-Hispanic/Latino; 5 Two or more races, non-Hispanic/Latino), 39 international. Average age 32. 486 applicants, 56% accepted, 215 enrolled. In 2013, 326 master's, 10 doctorates awarded. *Degree requirements:* For doctorate, comprehensive exam, thesis/dissertation. *Entrance requirements:* For master's, GMAT or GRE; for doctorate, GMAT. Additional exam requirements/recommendations for international students: Required—TOEFL (minimum score 600 paper-based; 100 iBT), IELTS (minimum score 7). *Application deadline:* For fall admission, 11/1 priority date for domestic students, 3/1

priority date for international students; for spring admission, 11/1 for domestic and international students. Applications are processed on a rolling basis. Application fee: $55 ($65 for international students). Electronic applications accepted. *Expenses:* Contact institution. *Financial support:* In 2013–14, 48 students received support, including 41 fellowships with partial tuition reimbursements available (averaging $8,600 per year), 35 research assistantships with partial tuition reimbursements available (averaging $6,378 per year), 57 teaching assistantships with full tuition reimbursements available (averaging $17,000 per year); scholarships/grants and unspecified assistantships also available. Financial award application deadline: 2/1; financial award applicants required to submit FAFSA. *Faculty research:* Corporate finance, strategy services, consumer behavior, financial disclosures, operations. *Unit head:* Dr. William Hesterly, Associate Dean, PhD Program, 801-581-7676, Fax: 801-581-3380, E-mail: mastersinfo@business.utah.edu. *Application contact:* Andrea Miller, Coordinator, 801-581-7785, Fax: 801-581-3666, E-mail: mastersinfo@business.utah.edu.
Website: http://business.utah.edu/full-time-mba.

Wayne State University, College of Liberal Arts and Sciences, Department of Political Science, Program in Public Administration, Detroit, MI 48202. Offers aging policy and management (MPA); criminal justice policy and management (MPA); economic development policy and management (MPA); health and human services policy and management (MPA); human and fiscal resource management (MPA); information technology management (MPA); nonprofit policy and management (MPA); organizational behavior and management (MPA); public budgeting and financial management (MPA); public policy analysis and program evaluation (MPA); social welfare policy and management (MPA); urban and metropolitan policy and management (MPA). *Accreditation:* NASPAA. Evening/weekend programs available. *Students:* 11 full-time (5 women), 55 part-time (43 women); includes 20 minority (14 Black or African American, non-Hispanic/Latino; 2 Asian, non-Hispanic/Latino; 2 Hispanic/Latino; 2 Two or more races, non-Hispanic/Latino), 1 international. Average age 33. 83 applicants, 34% accepted, 17 enrolled. In 2013, 19 master's awarded. *Degree requirements:* For master's, comprehensive exam. *Entrance requirements:* For master's, GRE General Test, minimum undergraduate upper-division GPA of 3.0 or master's degree. Additional exam requirements/recommendations for international students: Required—TOEFL (minimum score 550 paper-based; 79 iBT), TWE (minimum score 5.5), Michigan English Language Assessment Battery (minimum score 85); Recommended—IELTS (minimum score 6.5). *Application deadline:* For fall admission, 6/1 priority date for domestic students, 5/1 priority date for international students; for winter admission, 10/1 priority date for domestic students, 9/1 priority date for international students; for spring admission, 2/1 priority date for domestic students, 1/1 priority date for international students. Applications are processed on a rolling basis. Application fee: $0. Electronic applications accepted. *Expenses:* Tuition, state resident: part-time $554.15 per credit. Tuition, nonresident: part-time $1200.35 per credit. *Required fees:* $42.15 per credit. $268.30 per semester. Tuition and fees vary according to course load and program. *Financial support:* In 2013–14, 21 students received support. Fellowships, teaching assistantships, scholarships/grants, and unspecified assistantships available. Financial award application deadline: 3/31; financial award applicants required to submit FAFSA. *Faculty research:* Urban politics, urban education, state administration. *Unit head:* Dr. Daniel Geller, Department Chair, 313-577-6328, E-mail: dgeller@wayne.edu. *Application contact:* Dr. Brady Baybeck, Associate Professor/Director, Graduate Program in Public Administration, E-mail: mpa@wayne.edu.
Website: http://clasweb.clas.wayne.edu/mpa.

Western International University, Graduate Programs in Business, Program in Human Dynamics, Phoenix, AZ 85021-2718. Offers MA. Evening/weekend programs available. Postbaccalaureate distance learning degree programs offered (no on-campus study). *Entrance requirements:* Additional exam requirements/recommendations for international students: Required—TOEFL (minimum score 550 paper-based; 79 iBT).

Wilfrid Laurier University, Faculty of Graduate and Postdoctoral Studies, School of Business and Economics, Department of Business, Waterloo, ON N2L 3C5, Canada. Offers accounting (PhD); finance (M Fin); financial economics (PhD); marketing (PhD); operations and supply chain management (PhD); organizational behavior and human resource management (M Sc); organizational behaviour and human resource management (PhD); supply chain management (M Sc); technology management (EMTM). *Accreditation:* AACSB. Part-time and evening/weekend programs available. *Degree requirements:* For master's, thesis optional; for doctorate, comprehensive exam, thesis/dissertation. *Entrance requirements:* For master's, GMAT, 4-year honors degree with minimum B+ average; for doctorate, GMAT, master's degree, minimum B+ average. Additional exam requirements/recommendations for international students: Required—TOEFL (minimum score 89 iBT). Electronic applications accepted. *Faculty research:* Financial economics, management and organizational behavior, operations and supply chain management.

Organizational Management

Albertus Magnus College, Program in Management and Organizational Leadership, New Haven, CT 06511-1189. Offers MS. *Degree requirements:* For master's, project. *Entrance requirements:* For master's, bachelor's degree from regionally-accredited college or university, minimum GPA of 2.5, three years of professional and/or related experience, official transcripts, essay. Additional exam requirements/recommendations for international students: Required—TOEFL (minimum score 600 paper-based). *Application contact:* Dr. Sean O'Connell, Interim Vice President for Academic Affairs, 203-777-8539, Fax: 203-777-3701, E-mail: soconnell@albertus.edu.
Website: http://www.albertus.edu/graduate-degrees/graduate-degree-programs/management-and-organizational-leadership/.

Alvernia University, Graduate Studies, Program in Leadership, Reading, PA 19607-1799. Offers PhD. *Degree requirements:* For doctorate, comprehensive exam, thesis/dissertation (for some programs). *Entrance requirements:* For doctorate, GRE, GMAT, or MAT, minimum GPA of 3.3, 3 letters of recommendation, resume, interview.

The American College, Graduate Programs, Bryn Mawr, PA 19010-2105. Offers financial services (MSFS); leadership (MSM). Part-time and evening/weekend programs available. Postbaccalaureate distance learning degree programs offered (minimal on-campus study). Electronic applications accepted. *Faculty research:* Retirement counseling, social security, aging, family composition, inflation.

American Public University System, AMU/APU Graduate Programs, Charles Town, WV 25414. Offers accounting (MBA, MS); criminal justice (MA), including business administration, emergency and disaster management, general (MA, MS); educational leadership (M Ed); emergency and disaster management (MA); entrepreneurship (MBA); environmental policy and management (MS), including environmental planning, environmental sustainability, fish and wildlife management, general (MA, MS), global environmental management; finance (MBA); general (MBA); global business management (MBA); history (MA), including American history, ancient and classical history, European history, global history, public history; homeland security (MA), including business administration, counter-terrorism studies, criminal justice, cyber, emergency management and public health, intelligence studies, transportation security; homeland security resource allocation (MBA); humanities (MA); information technology (MS), including digital forensics, enterprise software development, information assurance and security, IT project management; information technology management (MBA); intelligence studies (MA), including criminal intelligence, cyber, general (MA, MS), homeland security, intelligence analysis, intelligence collection, intelligence management, intelligence operations, terrorism studies; international relations and conflict resolution (MA), including comparative and security issues, conflict resolution, international and transnational security issues, peacekeeping; legal studies (MA); management (MA), including defense management, general (MA, MS), human resource management, organizational leadership, public administration; marketing (MBA); military history (MA), including American military history, American Revolution, civil war, war since 1945, World War II; military studies (MA), including joint warfare, strategic leadership; national security studies (MA), including general (MA, MS), homeland security, regional security studies, security and intelligence analysis, terrorism studies; nonprofit management (MBA); political science (MA), including American politics and government, comparative government and development, general (MA, MS), international relations, public policy; psychology (MA), including general (MA, MS), maritime engineering management, reverse logistics management; public administration (MPA), including disaster management, environmental policy, health policy, human resources, national security, organizational management, security management; public health (MPH); reverse logistics management (MA); school counseling (M Ed); security management (MA); space studies (MS), including aerospace science, general (MA, MS), planetary science; sports and health sciences (MS); teaching (M Ed), including curriculum and instruction for elementary teachers, elementary reading, English language learners, instructional leadership, online learning, special education; transportation and logistics management (MA), including general (MA, MS), maritime engineering management, reverse logistics management. Programs offered via distance learning only. Part-time and evening/weekend programs available. Postbaccalaureate distance learning degree programs offered (no on-campus study). *Faculty:* 432 full-time (242 women), 1,722 part-time/adjunct (829 women). *Students:* 511 full-time (241 women), 10,947 part-time (4,294 women); includes 3,760 minority (2,058 Black or African American, non-Hispanic/Latino; 88 American Indian or Alaska Native, non-Hispanic/Latino; 293 Asian, non-Hispanic/Latino; 876 Hispanic/Latino; 91 Native Hawaiian or other Pacific Islander, non-Hispanic/Latino; 354 Two or more races, non-Hispanic/Latino), 134 international. Average age 36. In 2013, 3,323 master's awarded. *Degree requirements:* For master's, comprehensive exam or practicum. *Entrance requirements:* For master's, official transcript showing earned bachelor's degree from institution accredited by recognized accrediting body. Additional exam requirements/recommendations for international students: Required—TOEFL (minimum score 550 paper-based), IELTS (minimum score 6.5). *Application deadline:* Applications are processed on a rolling basis. Application fee: $0. Electronic applications accepted. *Expenses: Tuition:* Part-time $325 per semester hour. *Financial support:* Applicants required to submit FAFSA. *Faculty research:* Military history, criminal justice, management performance, national security. *Unit head:* Dr. Karan Powell, Executive Vice President and Provost, 877-468-6268, Fax: 304-724-3780. *Application contact:* Terry Grant, Vice President of Enrollment Management, 877-468-6268, Fax: 304-724-3780, E-mail: info@apus.edu.
Website: http://www.apus.edu.

American University, School of Public Affairs, Washington, DC 20016-8022. Offers justice, law and criminology (MS, PhD); leadership for organizational change (Certificate); nonprofit management (Certificate); organization development (MS); political communication (MA); political science (MA, PhD); public administration (MPA, PhD); public administration: key executive leadership (MPA); public financial management (Certificate); public management (Certificate); public policy (MPP); public policy analysis (Certificate); terrorism and homeland security policy (MS); women, policy and political leadership (Certificate). Part-time and evening/weekend programs available. *Faculty:* 82 full-time (36 women), 56 part-time/adjunct (16 women). *Students:* 364 full-time (220 women), 238 part-time (146 women); includes 158 minority (76 Black or African American, non-Hispanic/Latino; 7 American Indian or Alaska Native, non-Hispanic/Latino; 26 Asian, non-Hispanic/Latino; 40 Hispanic/Latino; 2 Native Hawaiian or other Pacific Islander, non-Hispanic/Latino; 7 Two or more races, non-Hispanic/Latino), 39 international. Average age 28. In 2013, 239 master's, 10 doctorates, 7 other advanced degrees awarded. Terminal master's awarded for partial completion of doctoral program. *Degree requirements:* For master's, comprehensive exam; for doctorate, comprehensive exam, thesis/dissertation. *Entrance requirements:* For master's, GRE, statement of purpose; 2 recommendations, resume, transcript; for doctorate, GRE, 3 recommendations, statement of purpose, resume, writing sample, transcript. Additional exam requirements/recommendations for international students: Required—TOEFL (minimum score 100 iBT). *Application deadline:* For fall admission, 2/1 for domestic and international students. Application fee: $55. Electronic applications accepted. *Expenses: Tuition:* Full-time $25,920; part-time $1482 per credit hour. *Required fees:* $430. Tuition and fees vary according to course load and program. *Financial support:* Fellowships with tuition reimbursements, research assistantships with tuition reimbursements, teaching assistantships with tuition reimbursements, career-related internships or fieldwork, Federal Work-Study, institutionally sponsored loans, scholarships/grants, and tuition waivers (full and partial) available. Financial award application deadline: 2/1. *Unit head:* Dr. Barbara Romzek, Dean, 202-885-2940, E-mail: bromzek@american.edu. *Application contact:* Brenda Manley, Director of Graduate Admissions, 202-885-6202, E-mail: bmanley@american.edu.
Website: http://www.american.edu/spa/.

Amridge University, Graduate and Professional Programs, Montgomery, AL 36117. Offers behavioral leadership and management (MA); Biblical studies (MA, PhD); family therapy (D Min); leadership and management (MS); marriage and family therapy (M Div, MA, PhD); ministerial leadership (M Div, MS); pastoral counseling (M Div, MS); practical ministry (MA); professional counseling (M Div, MA, PhD); theology (M Div, D Min). Part-time and evening/weekend programs available. Postbaccalaureate distance learning degree programs offered (no on-campus study). *Faculty:* 48 full-time (9 women), 27

part-time/adjunct (12 women). *Students:* 124 full-time (62 women), 189 part-time (112 women); includes 196 minority (189 Black or African American, non-Hispanic/Latino; 3 Asian, non-Hispanic/Latino; 4 Hispanic/Latino). Average age 35. *Degree requirements:* For master's, one foreign language, comprehensive exam (for some programs), thesis (for some programs); for doctorate, comprehensive exam (for some programs), thesis/dissertation. *Entrance requirements:* For master's and doctorate, GRE General Test or MAT. Additional exam requirements/recommendations for international students: Required—TOEFL. *Application deadline:* For fall admission, 9/1 priority date for domestic students; for spring admission, 1/1 priority date for domestic students. Applications are processed on a rolling basis. Application fee: $50. Electronic applications accepted. *Financial support:* Federal Work-Study and scholarships/grants available. Support available to part-time students. Financial award applicants required to submit FAFSA. *Faculty research:* Homiletics, hermeneutics, ancient Near Eastern history. *Unit head:* Carl Byrd, Student Affairs Coordinator, 800-351-4040 Ext. 7569, Fax: 334-387-3878. *Application contact:* Ora Davis, Admissions Officer, 334-387-3877 Ext. 7524, Fax: 334-387-3878, E-mail: admissions@amridgeuniversity.edu.

Antioch University Los Angeles, Graduate Programs, Program in Organizational Management, Culver City, CA 90230. Offers human resource development (MA); leadership (MA); organizational development (MA). Part-time and evening/weekend programs available. *Entrance requirements:* For master's, interview. Additional exam requirements/recommendations for international students: Required—TOEFL. *Faculty research:* Systems thinking and chaos theory, technology and organizational structure, nonprofit management, power and empowerment.

Antioch University Santa Barbara, Program in Organizational Management, Santa Barbara, CA 93101-1581. Offers MA. Part-time and evening/weekend programs available. Postbaccalaureate distance learning degree programs offered (minimal on-campus study). Electronic applications accepted. *Faculty research:* Multicultural communication, organizational change.

Antioch University Seattle, Graduate Programs, Center for Creative Change, Seattle, WA 98121-1814. Offers environment and community (MA); organizational development (MA); whole system design (MA). Evening/weekend programs available. Electronic applications accepted. *Expenses:* Contact institution.

Aquinas College, School of Management, Grand Rapids, MI 49506-1799. Offers health care administration (MM); marketing management (MM); organizational leadership (MM); sustainable business (MM, MSB). Part-time and evening/weekend programs available. *Students:* 13 full-time (10 women), 56 part-time (38 women); includes 10 minority (4 Black or African American, non-Hispanic/Latino; 1 American Indian or Alaska Native, non-Hispanic/Latino; 4 Hispanic/Latino; 1 Two or more races, non-Hispanic/Latino), 1 international. Average age 33. In 2013, 18 master's awarded. *Entrance requirements:* For master's, GMAT, minimum undergraduate GPA of 2.75, 2 years of work experience. Additional exam requirements/recommendations for international students: Required—TOEFL (minimum score 550 paper-based). *Application deadline:* Applications are processed on a rolling basis. Application fee: $0. *Expenses:* Contact institution. *Financial support:* Scholarships/grants available. Support available to part-time students. Financial award application deadline: 3/15; financial award applicants required to submit FAFSA. *Unit head:* Brian DiVita, Director, 616-632-2922, Fax: 616-732-4489. *Application contact:* Lynn Atkins-Rykert, Administrative Assistant, 616-632-2924, Fax: 616-732-4489, E-mail: atkinlyn@aquinas.edu.

Argosy University, Chicago, College of Business, Program in Organizational Leadership, Chicago, IL 60601. Offers Ed D.

Argosy University, Denver, College of Business, Denver, CO 80231. Offers accounting (DBA); corporate compliance (MBA); customized professional concentration (MBA, DBA); finance (MBA); fraud examination (MBA); global business sustainability (DBA); healthcare administration (MBA); information systems (DBA); information systems management (MBA); international business (MBA, DBA); management (MBA, MSM, DBA); marketing (MBA, DBA); organizational leadership (Ed D); public administration (MBA); sustainable management (MBA).

Argosy University, Hawai`i, College of Business, Program in Organizational Leadership, Honolulu, HI 96813. Offers Ed D.

Argosy University, Inland Empire, College of Business, Ontario, CA 91761. Offers accounting (DBA); corporate compliance (MBA); customized professional concentration (MBA, DBA); finance (MBA); fraud examination (MBA); global business sustainability (DBA); healthcare administration (MBA); information systems (DBA); information systems management (MBA); international business (MBA, DBA); management (MBA, MSM, DBA); marketing (MBA, DBA); organizational leadership (Ed D); public administration (MBA); sustainable management (MBA).

Argosy University, Los Angeles, College of Business, Santa Monica, CA 90045. Offers accounting (DBA); corporate compliance (MBA); customized professional concentration (MBA, DBA); finance (MBA); fraud examination (MBA); global business sustainability (DBA); healthcare administration (MBA); information systems (DBA); information systems management (MBA); international business (MBA, DBA); management (MBA, MSM, DBA); marketing (MBA, DBA); organizational leadership (Ed D); public administration (MBA); sustainable management (MBA).

Argosy University, Orange County, College of Business, Program in Organizational Leadership, Orange, CA 92868. Offers Ed D.

Argosy University, San Diego, College of Business, San Diego, CA 92108. Offers accounting (DBA); corporate compliance (MBA); customized professional concentration (MBA, DBA); finance (MBA); fraud examination (MBA); global business sustainability (DBA); information systems (DBA); information systems management (MBA); international business (MBA, DBA); management (MBA, MSM, DBA); marketing (MBA, DBA); organizational leadership (Ed D); public administration (MBA).

Argosy University, San Francisco Bay Area, College of Business, Alameda, CA 94501. Offers accounting (DBA); corporate compliance (MBA); customized professional concentration (MBA, DBA); finance (MBA); fraud examination (MBA); global business sustainability (DBA); healthcare administration (MBA); information systems (DBA); information systems management (MBA); international business (MBA, DBA); management (MBA, MSM, DBA); marketing (MBA, DBA); organizational leadership (Ed D); public administration (MBA); sustainable management (MBA).

Argosy University, Sarasota, College of Business, Sarasota, FL 34235. Offers accounting (DBA, Adv C); corporate compliance (MBA, DBA, Certificate); customized professional concentration (MBA, DBA); finance (MBA, Certificate); fraud examination (MBA, Certificate); global business sustainability (DBA, Adv C); healthcare administration (MBA, Certificate); information systems (DBA, Adv C, Certificate); information systems management (MBA); international business (MBA, DBA, Adv C, Certificate); management (MBA, MSM, DBA, Adv C, Certificate); marketing (MBA, DBA, Adv C, Certificate); organizational leadership (Ed D); public administration (MBA, Certificate); sustainable management (MBA, Certificate).

Argosy University, Seattle, College of Business, Seattle, WA 98121. Offers accounting (DBA); corporate compliance (MBA); customized professional concentration (MBA, DBA); finance (MBA); fraud examination (MBA); global business sustainability (DBA); healthcare administration (MBA); information systems (DBA); information systems management (MBA); international business (MBA, DBA); management (MBA, MSM, DBA); marketing (MBA, DBA); organizational leadership (Ed D); public administration (MBA); sustainable management (MBA).

Argosy University, Tampa, College of Business, Tampa, FL 33607. Offers accounting (DBA); corporate compliance (MBA); customized professional concentration (MBA, DBA); finance (MBA); fraud examination (MBA); global business sustainability (DBA); healthcare administration (MBA); information systems (DBA); information systems management (MBA); international business (MBA, DBA); management (MBA, MSM, DBA); marketing (MBA, DBA); organizational leadership (Ed D); public administration (MBA); sustainable management (MBA).

Argosy University, Twin Cities, College of Business, Eagan, MN 55121. Offers accounting (DBA); customized professional concentration (MBA, DBA); finance (MBA); fraud examination (MBA); global business sustainability (DBA); healthcare administration (MBA); information systems (DBA); information systems management (MBA); international business (MBA, DBA); management (MBA, MSM, DBA); marketing (MBA, DBA); organizational leadership (Ed D); public administration (MBA); sustainable management (MBA).

Argosy University, Washington DC, College of Business, Arlington, VA 22209. Offers accounting (DBA); customized professional concentration (MBA, DBA); finance (MBA); fraud examination (MBA); global business sustainability (DBA); healthcare administration (MBA); information systems (DBA); information systems management (MBA); international business (MBA, DBA, Certificate); management (MBA, MSM, DBA); marketing (MBA, DBA, Certificate); organizational leadership (Ed D); public administration (MBA); sustainable management (MBA).

Athabasca University, Centre for Integrated Studies, Athabasca, AB T9S 3A3, Canada. Offers adult education (MA); community studies (MA); cultural studies (MA); educational studies (MA); global change (MA); work, organization, and leadership (MA). Part-time and evening/weekend programs available. Postbaccalaureate distance learning degree programs offered (no on-campus study). *Degree requirements:* For master's, project. *Entrance requirements:* Additional exam requirements/recommendations for international students: Required—TOEFL (minimum score 560 paper-based). Electronic applications accepted. *Faculty research:* Women's history, literature and culture studies, sustainable development, labor and education.

Auburn University at Montgomery, School of Sciences, Department of Justice and Public Safety, Montgomery, AL 36124-4023. Offers criminal studies (MSJPS); homeland security (MSJPS); homeland security and emergency management (MS); legal studies (MSJPS); organizational leadership (MSJPS); paralegal (Certificate). Part-time and evening/weekend programs available. *Faculty:* 4 full-time (1 woman), 3 part-time/adjunct (0 women). *Students:* 15 full-time (10 women), 53 part-time (35 women); includes 28 minority (27 Black or African American, non-Hispanic/Latino; 1 Asian, non-Hispanic/Latino). Average age 33. In 2013, 29 master's awarded. *Degree requirements:* For master's, comprehensive exam, thesis optional. *Entrance requirements:* For master's, GRE General Test or MAT. *Application deadline:* Applications are processed on a rolling basis. Electronic applications accepted. *Expenses:* Tuition, state resident: full-time $5994; part-time $333 per credit hour. Tuition, nonresident: full-time $17,982; part-time $999 per credit hour. *Financial support:* Career-related internships or fieldwork and scholarships/grants available. Support available to part-time students. Financial award application deadline: 3/1; financial award applicants required to submit FAFSA. *Faculty research:* Law enforcement, corrections, juvenile justice. *Unit head:* Dr. Ralph Ioimo, Head, 334-244-3691, Fax: 334-244-3244, E-mail: rioimo@aum.edu. *Application contact:* Jennifer Fuller, Administrative Associate, 334-244-3692, Fax: 334-244-3244, E-mail: jfuller@aum.edu.
Website: http://sciences.aum.edu/departments/justice-and-public-safety.

Augsburg College, Program in Leadership, Minneapolis, MN 55454-1351. Offers MA. Part-time and evening/weekend programs available. *Degree requirements:* For master's, thesis or alternative. *Entrance requirements:* For master's, MAT, minimum GPA of 3.0. Additional exam requirements/recommendations for international students: Required—TOEFL (minimum score 600 paper-based). *Faculty research:* Soviet leaders, artificial intelligence, homelessness.

Avila University, School of Professional Studies, Kansas City, MO 64145-1698. Offers executive leadership development (MS); fundraising (MA); instructional design and technology (MA); leadership coaching (MS); organizational development (MS); project management (MA); strategic human resources (MS). Part-time and evening/weekend programs available. Postbaccalaureate distance learning degree programs offered (no on-campus study). *Faculty:* 2 full-time (1 woman), 10 part-time/adjunct (7 women). *Students:* 73 full-time (50 women), 68 part-time (54 women); includes 46 minority (33 Black or African American, non-Hispanic/Latino; 1 Asian, non-Hispanic/Latino; 11 Hispanic/Latino; 1 Two or more races, non-Hispanic/Latino), 11 international. Average age 38. 47 applicants, 64% accepted, 27 enrolled. In 2013, 42 master's awarded. *Degree requirements:* For master's, thesis optional. *Entrance requirements:* For master's, 2 letters of recommendation, minimum GPA of 3.0 during last 60 hours, resume, statement of intent. Additional exam requirements/recommendations for international students: Required—TOEFL. *Application deadline:* Applications are processed on a rolling basis. Application fee: $0. Electronic applications accepted. *Expenses: Tuition:* Full-time $8430; part-time $468 per credit hour. *Required fees:* $648; $36 per credit hour. Tuition and fees vary according to program. *Financial support:* In 2013–14, 20 students received support. Unspecified assistantships available. Support available to part-time students. Financial award applicants required to submit FAFSA. *Unit head:* Dr. Steve Iliff, Dean, 816-501-3737, Fax: 816-941-4650, E-mail: advantage@avila.edu. *Application contact:* Linda Dubar, School of Professional Studies, 816-501-3737, Fax: 816-941-4650, E-mail: advantage@avila.edu.
Website: http://www.avila.edu/advantage.

Azusa Pacific University, Center for Adult and Professional Studies, Azusa, CA 91702-7000. Offers leadership and organizational studies (MA). Postbaccalaureate distance learning degree programs offered.

Azusa Pacific University, School of Behavioral and Applied Sciences, Department of Higher Education and Organizational Leadership, Program in Organizational Leadership, Azusa, CA 91702-7000. Offers MA.

Azusa Pacific University, School of Business and Management, Azusa, CA 91702-7000. Offers business administration (MBA); diversity for strategic advantage (MA); entrepreneurship (MBA); finance (MBA); human and organizational development (MA); human resources and organizational development (MBA); human resources management (MA); international business (MBA); marketing (MBA); non-profit management (MA); organizational development and change (MA); performance improvement (MA); public administration (MA); strategic management (MBA). Part-time and evening/weekend programs available. *Degree requirements:* For master's, thesis (for some programs), final project. *Entrance requirements:* For master's, GMAT, minimum GPA of 3.0. Additional exam requirements/recommendations for international students: Required—TOEFL (minimum score 600 paper-based). *Expenses:* Contact institution. *Faculty research:* Gender issues, financial risk, leadership and ethics, marketing strategy.

Organizational Management

Bainbridge Graduate Institute, Organization Systems Renewal Program, Bainbridge Island, WA 98110. Offers organizational leadership (MA). *Degree requirements:* For master's, capstone project. *Entrance requirements:* For master's, bachelor's degree from accredited institution.

Baker University, School of Professional and Graduate Studies, Programs in Business, Baldwin City, KS 66006-0065. Offers MAOL, MBA, MSM. Programs also offered in Lee's Summit, MO; Overland Park, KS; Topeka, KS; and Wichita, KS. *Accreditation:* ACBSP. Part-time and evening/weekend programs available. Postbaccalaureate distance learning degree programs offered (minimal on-campus study). *Students:* 186 full-time (97 women), 283 part-time (130 women); includes 110 minority (61 Black or African American, non-Hispanic/Latino; 15 American Indian or Alaska Native, non-Hispanic/Latino; 6 Asian, non-Hispanic/Latino; 23 Hispanic/Latino; 1 Native Hawaiian or other Pacific Islander, non-Hispanic/Latino; 4 Two or more races, non-Hispanic/Latino). Average age 34. In 2013, 217 master's awarded. *Entrance requirements:* For master's, 2 years of full-time work experience. Additional exam requirements/recommendations for international students: Required—TOEFL (minimum score 600 paper-based; 100 iBT). *Application deadline:* Applications are processed on a rolling basis. Application fee: $45. *Financial support:* Applicants required to submit FAFSA. *Unit head:* Dr. Brian Messer, Vice President and Dean of the School of Professional and Graduate Studies, 913-491-4432, E-mail: brian.messer@bakeru.edu. *Application contact:* Piper Childs, Enrollment Representative, 913-491-4432, E-mail: piper.childs@learn.bakeru.edu.

Baptist Bible College of Pennsylvania, Baptist Bible Seminary, Clarks Summit, PA 18411-1297. Offers Biblical apologetics (MA); church education (M Div, M Min); church planting (M Div, M Min); global ministry (M Div, M Min); leadership in communication (D Min); leadership in counseling and spiritual development (D Min); leadership in global ministry (D Min); leadership in pastoral ministry (D Min); leadership in theological studies (D Min); military chaplaincy (M Div); ministry (PhD); organizational leadership (M Min); outreach pastor (M Div, M Min); pastoral counseling (M Div, M Min); pastoral leadership (M Div, M Min); theology (Th M); worship ministries leadership (M Div, M Min); youth pastor (M Div, M Min). Part-time and evening/weekend programs available. Postbaccalaureate distance learning degree programs offered (minimal on-campus study). Terminal master's awarded for partial completion of doctoral program. *Degree requirements:* For master's, 2 foreign languages, thesis, oral exam (for M Div); for doctorate, 2 foreign languages, comprehensive exam (for some programs), thesis/dissertation, oral exam. *Entrance requirements:* For doctorate, Greek and Hebrew entrance exams (for PhD). Electronic applications accepted.

Baptist Bible College of Pennsylvania, Graduate Studies, Clarks Summit, PA 18411-1297. Offers Bible (MA); counseling (MA, MS); curriculum and instruction (M Ed); educational administration (M Ed); intercultural studies (MA); literature (MA); missions (MA); organizational leadership (MA); reading specialist (M Ed); secondary English/communications (M Ed); social entrepreneurship (MA); worldview studies (MA). MA in missions program available only for Association of Baptists for World Evangelism missionary personnel. Part-time and evening/weekend programs available. Postbaccalaureate distance learning degree programs offered (no on-campus study). *Entrance requirements:* Additional exam requirements/recommendations for international students: Required—TOEFL (minimum score 500 paper-based).

Bellevue University, Graduate School, College of Professional Studies, Bellevue, NE 68005-3098. Offers instructional design and development (MS); justice administration and criminal management (MS); leadership (MA); organizational performance (MS); public administration (MPA); security management (MS).

Benedictine University, Graduate Programs, Doctoral Program in Values-Driven Leadership, Lisle, IL 60532-0900. Offers DBA, PhD. *Faculty:* 2 full-time (0 women), 2 part-time/adjunct (1 woman). *Students:* 42 part-time (23 women); includes 11 minority (8 Black or African American, non-Hispanic/Latino; 1 American Indian or Alaska Native, non-Hispanic/Latino; 1 Asian, non-Hispanic/Latino; 1 Hispanic/Latino), 2 international. *Expenses: Tuition:* Part-time $590 per credit hour. *Unit head:* Dr. James Ludema, Director, 630-829-6229, E-mail: jludema@ben.edu. *Application contact:* Kari Gibbons, Associate Vice President, Enrollment Center, 630-829-6200, Fax: 630-829-6584, E-mail: kgibbons@ben.edu.
Website: http://www.cvdl.org/education/doctoral-program/.

Benedictine University, Graduate Programs, Program in Business Administration, Lisle, IL 60532-0900. Offers accounting (MBA); entrepreneurship and managing innovation (MBA); financial management (MBA); health administration (MBA); human resource management (MBA); information systems security (MBA); international business (MBA); management consulting (MBA); management information systems (MBA); marketing management (MBA); operations management and logistics (MBA); organizational leadership (MBA). Part-time and evening/weekend programs available. Postbaccalaureate distance learning degree programs offered (minimal on-campus study). *Faculty:* 4 full-time (2 women), 24 part-time/adjunct (3 women). *Students:* 144 full-time (83 women), 599 part-time (328 women); includes 189 minority (115 Black or African American, non-Hispanic/Latino; 5 American Indian or Alaska Native, non-Hispanic/Latino; 43 Asian, non-Hispanic/Latino; 24 Hispanic/Latino; 2 Native Hawaiian or other Pacific Islander, non-Hispanic/Latino), 14 international. Average age 34. 211 applicants, 89% accepted, 155 enrolled. In 2013, 376 master's awarded. *Entrance requirements:* For master's, GMAT. Additional exam requirements/recommendations for international students: Required—TOEFL (minimum score 550 paper-based). *Application deadline:* For fall admission, 9/1 for domestic students; for winter admission, 12/1 for domestic students; for spring admission, 2/15 for domestic students. Applications are processed on a rolling basis. Application fee: $40. Electronic applications accepted. *Expenses: Tuition:* Part-time $590 per credit hour. *Financial support:* Career-related internships or fieldwork and health care benefits available. Support available to part-time students. *Faculty research:* Strategic leadership in professional organizations, sociology of professions, organizational change, social identity theory, applications to change management. *Unit head:* Dr. Sharon Borowicz, Director, 630-829-6219, E-mail: sborowicz@ben.edu. *Application contact:* Kari Gibbons, Director, Admissions, 630-829-6200, Fax: 630-829-6584, E-mail: kgibbons@ben.edu.

Benedictine University, Graduate Programs, Program in Organization Development, Lisle, IL 60532-0900. Offers PhD. Evening/weekend programs available. *Students:* 14 full-time (7 women), 1 (woman) part-time; includes 6 minority (2 Black or African American, non-Hispanic/Latino; 3 Asian, non-Hispanic/Latino; 1 Hispanic/Latino). Average age 44. In 2013, 19 doctorates awarded. *Degree requirements:* For doctorate, thesis/dissertation. *Entrance requirements:* Additional exam requirements/recommendations for international students: Required—TOEFL (minimum score 550 paper-based). *Application deadline:* For fall admission, 9/1 for domestic students; for winter admission, 12/1 for domestic students; for spring admission, 2/15 for domestic students. Application fee: $40. Electronic applications accepted. *Expenses: Tuition:* Part-time $590 per credit hour. *Financial support:* Career-related internships or fieldwork and health care benefits available. *Faculty research:* Change management, appreciative inquiry, innovation and organization design, global and international organization development, organization renewal. *Unit head:* Dr. Peter F. Sorensen, Director, 630-829-6220, Fax: 630-960-1126, E-mail: psorensen@ben.edu. *Application contact:* Kari Gibbons, Associate Vice President, Enrollment Center, 630-829-6200, Fax: 630-829-6584, E-mail: kgibbons@ben.edu.

Benedictine University at Springfield, Program in Business Administration, Springfield, IL 62702. Offers health administration (MBA); organizational leadership (MBA). Part-time and evening/weekend programs available. *Entrance requirements:* For master's, GMAT.

Benedictine University at Springfield, Program in Organization Development, Springfield, IL 62702. Offers PhD. Evening/weekend programs available. *Degree requirements:* For doctorate, thesis/dissertation.

Bethel University, Graduate School, St. Paul, MN 55112-6999. Offers autism spectrum disorders (Certificate); business administration (MBA); communication (MA); counseling psychology (MA); educational leadership (Ed D); gerontology (MA); international baccalaureate education (Certificate); K-12 education (MA); literacy education (MA, Certificate); nurse educator (Certificate); nurse leader (Certificate); nurse-midwifery (MS); nursing (MS); physician assistant (MS); postsecondary teaching (Certificate); special education (MA); strategic leadership (MA); teaching (MA). Part-time and evening/weekend programs available. Postbaccalaureate distance learning degree programs offered (no on-campus study). *Faculty:* 13 full-time (7 women), 89 part-time/adjunct (43 women). *Students:* 692 full-time (457 women), 573 part-time (371 women); includes 170 minority (86 Black or African American, non-Hispanic/Latino; 1 American Indian or Alaska Native, non-Hispanic/Latino; 49 Asian, non-Hispanic/Latino; 20 Hispanic/Latino; 1 Native Hawaiian or other Pacific Islander, non-Hispanic/Latino; 13 Two or more races, non-Hispanic/Latino), 21 international. Average age 37. In 2013, 166 master's, 9 doctorates, 11 other advanced degrees awarded. *Degree requirements:* For master's, comprehensive exam (for some programs), thesis (for some programs); for doctorate, comprehensive exam, thesis/dissertation. *Entrance requirements:* Additional exam requirements/recommendations for international students: Required—TOEFL (minimum score 550 paper-based; 80 iBT). *Application deadline:* Applications are processed on a rolling basis. Electronic applications accepted. Tuition and fees vary according to course load, degree level and program. *Financial support:* Teaching assistantships, career-related internships or fieldwork, and scholarships/grants available. Support available to part-time students. Financial award applicants required to submit FAFSA. *Unit head:* Dick Crombie, Vice-President/Dean, 651-635-8000, Fax: 651-635-8004, E-mail: gs@bethel.edu. *Application contact:* Director of Admissions, 651-635-8000, Fax: 651-635-8004, E-mail: gs@bethel.edu.
Website: http://gs.bethel.edu/.

Bluffton University, Programs in Business, Bluffton, OH 45817. Offers business administration (MBA); organizational management (MA). Evening/weekend programs available. *Entrance requirements:* Additional exam requirements/recommendations for international students: Required—TOEFL. Electronic applications accepted.

Boston College, Carroll School of Management, Department of Management and Organization, Chestnut Hill, MA 02467-3800. Offers PhD. *Faculty:* 10 full-time (5 women), 8 part-time/adjunct (3 women). *Students:* 15 full-time (11 women); includes 2 minority (1 Black or African American, non-Hispanic/Latino; 1 Hispanic/Latino), 6 international. Average age 31. 54 applicants, 9% accepted, 2 enrolled. In 2013, 2 doctorates awarded. *Degree requirements:* For doctorate, comprehensive exam, thesis/dissertation, teaching experience. *Entrance requirements:* For doctorate, GMAT or GRE, letters of recommendation, resume, transcripts. Additional exam requirements/recommendations for international students: Required—TOEFL (minimum score 100 iBT), IELTS (minimum score 7.5), or PTE (minimum score 68). *Application deadline:* For fall admission, 12/1 for domestic and international students; for spring admission, 2/1 for domestic and international students. Application fee: $100. Electronic applications accepted. *Financial support:* In 2013–14, 16 students received support, including 16 fellowships with full tuition reimbursements available (averaging $11,976 per year), 14 research assistantships (averaging $26,518 per year). Financial award application deadline: 3/1. *Faculty research:* Organizational transformation, mergers and acquisitions, managerial effectiveness, organizational change, organizational structure. *Unit head:* Dr. Jeffrey L. Ringuest, Associate Dean, Graduate Programs, 617-552-9100, Fax: 617-552-0514, E-mail: gsomdean@bc.edu. *Application contact:* Shelley A. Burt, Director of Graduate Enrollment, 617-552-3920, Fax: 617-552-8078, E-mail: bcmba@bc.edu.
Website: http://www.bc.edu/csom/.

Boston University, Metropolitan College, Program in Leadership, Boston, MA 02215. Offers MS. Program offered on the Brussels Campus and at military locations in Massachusetts, North Carolina and Virginia. *Students:* 50 part-time (15 women); includes 5 minority (1 Black or African American, non-Hispanic/Latino; 4 Hispanic/Latino). Average age 35. *Expenses: Tuition:* Full-time $43,970; part-time $1374 per credit hour. *Required fees:* $60 per semester. Tuition and fees vary according to class time, course level and program. *Unit head:* Dr. Tanya Zlateva, Interim Dean, 617-353-3010, Fax: 617-353-6066, E-mail: metdean@bu.edu.
Website: http://www.bu.edu/met/subject/leadership/.

Bowling Green State University, Graduate College, College of Business Administration, Program in Organization Development, Bowling Green, OH 43403. Offers MOD. Part-time and evening/weekend programs available. *Degree requirements:* For master's, thesis or alternative, internship. *Entrance requirements:* For master's, GMAT or GRE General Test. Additional exam requirements/recommendations for international students: Required—TOEFL. Electronic applications accepted. *Faculty research:* Charismatic leadership, self-managing work teams, knowledge workers, stress, effects of change processes.

Brandman University, School of Business and Professional Studies, Irvine, CA 92618. Offers business administration (MBA); human resources (MS); organizational leadership (MA); public administration (MPA).

Brenau University, Sydney O. Smith Graduate School, School of Business and Mass Communication, Gainesville, GA 30501. Offers accounting (MBA); business administration (MBA); healthcare management (MBA); organizational leadership (MS); project management (MBA). *Accreditation:* ACBSP. Part-time and evening/weekend programs available. Postbaccalaureate distance learning degree programs offered (no on-campus study). *Degree requirements:* For master's, comprehensive exam (for some programs). *Entrance requirements:* For master's, resume, minimum undergraduate GPA of 2.5. Additional exam requirements/recommendations for international students: Required—TOEFL (minimum score 500 paper-based; 61 iBT); Recommended—IELTS (minimum score 5). Electronic applications accepted. *Expenses:* Contact institution.

Briercrest Seminary, Graduate Programs, Program in Leadership and Management, Caronport, SK S0H 0S0, Canada. Offers organizational leadership (MA). Part-time programs available. *Degree requirements:* For master's, comprehensive exam, thesis optional. *Entrance requirements:* Additional exam requirements/recommendations for international students: Required—TOEFL (minimum score 550 paper-based).

Cabrini College, Graduate Studies, Radnor, PA 19087-3698. Offers accounting (M Acc); education (M Ed); leadership (MS). Part-time and evening/weekend programs available. *Faculty:* 9 full-time (7 women), 81 part-time/adjunct (64 women). *Students:* 75 full-time (53 women), 1,031 part-time (789 women); includes 135 minority (95 Black or African American, non-Hispanic/Latino; 13 Asian, non-Hispanic/Latino; 24 Hispanic/Latino; 3 Two or more races, non-Hispanic/Latino). Average age 33. 417 applicants, 73% accepted, 261 enrolled. In 2013, 717 master's awarded. *Degree requirements:* For

master's, thesis optional. *Entrance requirements:* For master's, GRE and/or MAT (in some cases), bachelor's degree with minimum GPA of 3.0, one-page personal essay/statement, professional letter of recommendation. Additional exam requirements/recommendations for international students: Required—TOEFL. *Application deadline:* For fall admission, 7/29 priority date for domestic students, 7/29 for international students; for spring admission, 12/9 for domestic and international students. Applications are processed on a rolling basis. Application fee: $50. Electronic applications accepted. *Expenses: Tuition:* Part-time $595 per credit hour. *Financial support:* Career-related internships or fieldwork and unspecified assistantships available. Support available to part-time students. Financial award applicants required to submit FAFSA. *Unit head:* Dr. Jeffrey P. Gingerich, Vice Provost/Dean for Academic Affairs, 610-902-8302, Fax: 610-902-8552, E-mail: jeffrey.p.gingerich@cabrini.edu. *Application contact:* Bruce D. Bryde, Director of Enrollment and Recruiting, 610-902-8291, Fax: 610-902-8522, E-mail: bruce.d.bryde@cabrini.edu.
Website: http://cabrini.edu/graduate.

Cairn University, School of Business and Leadership, Langhorne, PA 19047-2990. Offers business administration (MBA); organizational leadership (MSOL, Postbaccalaureate Certificate). Part-time and evening/weekend programs available. *Faculty:* 2 full-time (0 women), 2 part-time/adjunct (0 women). *Students:* 4 full-time (3 women), 21 part-time (11 women); includes 11 minority (9 Black or African American, non-Hispanic/Latino; 1 Asian, non-Hispanic/Latino; 1 Hispanic/Latino), 1 international. Average age 33. 16 applicants, 81% accepted, 10 enrolled. In 2013, 13 master's awarded. *Entrance requirements:* Additional exam requirements/recommendations for international students: Required—TOEFL (minimum score 550 paper-based). *Application deadline:* Applications are processed on a rolling basis. Application fee: $25. Electronic applications accepted. *Expenses: Tuition:* Full-time $11,250; part-time $625 per credit. Tuition and fees vary according to program. *Financial support:* Scholarships/grants available. Support available to part-time students. Financial award applicants required to submit FAFSA. *Unit head:* Dr. William Bowles, Chair, Graduate Programs, 215-702-4871, Fax: 215-702-4248, E-mail: wbowles@cairn.edu. *Application contact:* Timothy Nessler, Assistant Director, Graduate Admissions, 800-572-2472, Fax: 215-702-4248, E-mail: tnessler@cairn.edu.
Website: http://cairn.edu/academics/business.

California Baptist University, Program in Leadership and Organizational Studies, Riverside, CA 92504-3206. Offers MA. Part-time and evening/weekend programs available. *Faculty:* 2 full-time (0 women), 2 part-time/adjunct (0 women). *Students:* 21 part-time (14 women); includes 11 minority (5 Black or African American, non-Hispanic/Latino; 6 Hispanic/Latino). Average age 44. 10 applicants, 90% accepted, 6 enrolled. *Degree requirements:* For master's, internship. *Entrance requirements:* For master's, minimum undergraduate GPA of 3.0; three recommendations; resume, 500-word essay. Additional exam requirements/recommendations for international students: Required—TOEFL (minimum score 80 iBT). *Application deadline:* For fall admission, 8/1 priority date for domestic students, 7/1 for international students; for spring admission, 11/1 priority date for domestic students, 11/1 for international students. Applications are processed on a rolling basis. Application fee: $45. Electronic applications accepted. *Expenses:* Contact institution. *Financial support:* Applicants required to submit CSS PROFILE or FAFSA. *Unit head:* Dr. John Shoup, Dean, School of Education, 951-343-4205, E-mail: jshoup@calbaptist.edu. *Application contact:* Dr. Kathryn Norwood, Associate Dean, School of Education, 951-343-4760, E-mail: knorwood@calbaptist.edu.
Website: http://www.calbaptist.edu/explore-cbu/schools-colleges/school-education/programs/graduate/master-arts-education/leadership-and-organizational-studies/.

California Coast University, School of Education, Santa Ana, CA 92701. Offers administration (M Ed); curriculum and instruction (M Ed); educational administration (Ed D); educational psychology (Ed D); organizational leadership (Ed D). Postbaccalaureate distance learning degree programs offered (no on-campus study).

California College of the Arts, Graduate Programs, MBA in Design Strategy Program, San Francisco, CA 94107. Offers MBA. *Accreditation:* NASAD. *Faculty:* 4 full-time (1 woman), 30 part-time/adjunct (11 women). *Students:* 113 full-time (69 women); includes 32 minority (5 Black or African American, non-Hispanic/Latino; 21 Asian, non-Hispanic/Latino; 6 Hispanic/Latino), 22 international. Average age 32. 150 applicants, 79% accepted, 59 enrolled. In 2013, 53 master's awarded. *Degree requirements:* For master's, thesis. *Entrance requirements:* Additional exam requirements/recommendations for international students: Required—TOEFL (minimum score 600 paper-based; 100 iBT). *Application deadline:* For fall admission, 1/5 for domestic and international students. Application fee: $70. *Expenses: Tuition:* Full-time $60,350; part-time $1445 per credit. *Required fees:* $350; $350 175. Full-time tuition and fees vary according to class time, course level, course load, degree level, campus/location and student level. *Financial support:* In 2013–14, 3 fellowships (averaging $20,000 per year) were awarded. *Unit head:* Nathan Shedroff, Program Chair, 800-447-1ART, E-mail: nshedroff@cca.edu. *Application contact:* Heidi Geis, Assistant Director of Graduate Admissions, 415-703-9533, Fax: 415-703-9539, E-mail: hgeis@cca.edu.

California Intercontinental University, School of Business, Diamond Bar, CA 91765. Offers banking and finance (MBA); entrepreneurship and business management (DBA); global business leadership (DBA); international management and marketing (MBA); organizational management and human resource management (MBA).

California State University, East Bay, Office of Academic Programs and Graduate Studies, College of Business and Economics, MBA Program, Hayward, CA 94542-3000. Offers entrepreneurship (MBA); finance (MBA); global innovators (MBA); human resources and organizational behavior (MBA); information technology management (MBA); marketing management (MBA); operations and supply chain management (MBA); strategy and international business (MBA). Part-time and evening/weekend programs available. *Degree requirements:* For master's, comprehensive exam or thesis. *Entrance requirements:* For master's, GMAT (minimum 20th percentile verbal and quantitative section), bachelor's degree, minimum GPA of 2.75. Additional exam requirements/recommendations for international students: Required—TOEFL (minimum score 550 paper-based; 79 iBT). Electronic applications accepted. *Expenses:* Contact institution.

California State University, Fullerton, Graduate Studies, College of Business and Economics, Program in Business Administration, Fullerton, CA 92834-9480. Offers business intelligence (MBA); general (MBA); international business (MBA); organizational leadership (MBA); risk management and insurance (MBA). *Accreditation:* AACSB. Part-time programs available. *Students:* 54 full-time (26 women), 119 part-time (48 women); includes 74 minority (46 Asian, non-Hispanic/Latino; 23 Hispanic/Latino; 5 Two or more races, non-Hispanic/Latino), 34 international. Average age 28. 500 applicants, 41% accepted, 78 enrolled. In 2013, 65 master's awarded. *Degree requirements:* For master's, project or thesis. *Entrance requirements:* For master's, GMAT. Application fee: $55. *Financial support:* Career-related internships or fieldwork, Federal Work-Study, institutionally sponsored loans, and scholarships/grants available. Support available to part-time students. Financial award application deadline: 3/1; financial award applicants required to submit FAFSA. *Unit head:* Dr. Anil Puri, Dean, 657-773-2592. *Application contact:* Admissions/Applications, 657-278-2371.

Cambridge College, School of Management, Cambridge, MA 02138-5304. Offers business negotiation and conflict resolution (M Mgt); general business (M Mgt); health care informatics (M Mgt); health care management (M Mgt); leadership in human and organizational dynamics (M Mgt); non-profit and public organization management (M Mgt); small business development (M Mgt); technology management (M Mgt). Part-time and evening/weekend programs available. *Degree requirements:* For master's, thesis, seminars. *Entrance requirements:* For master's, resume, 2 professional references. Additional exam requirements/recommendations for international students: Required—TOEFL (minimum score 550 paper-based; 79 iBT), Michigan English Language Assessment Battery (minimum score 85); Recommended—IELTS (minimum score 6). Electronic applications accepted. *Expenses:* Contact institution. *Faculty research:* Negotiation, mediation and conflict resolution; leadership; management of diverse organizations; case studies and simulation methodologies for management education, digital as a second language: social networking for digital immigrants, non-profit and public management.

Campbellsville University, School of Business and Economics, Campbellsville, KY 42718-2799. Offers business administration (MBA); business organizational management (MAOL). Part-time and evening/weekend programs available. *Entrance requirements:* For master's, GRE or GMAT. Additional exam requirements/recommendations for international students: Required—TOEFL (minimum score 550 paper-based). Electronic applications accepted. *Expenses:* Contact institution.

Capella University, School of Business and Technology, Doctoral Programs in Business, Minneapolis, MN 55402. Offers accounting (DBA, PhD); business intelligence (DBA); finance (DBA, PhD); general business management (PhD); human resource management (DBA, PhD); leadership (DBA, PhD); management education (PhD); marketing (DBA, PhD); project management (DBA, PhD); strategy and innovation (DBA, PhD).

Capella University, School of Business and Technology, Master's Programs in Business, Minneapolis, MN 55402. Offers accounting (MBA); business analysis (MS); business intelligence (MBA); entrepreneurship (MBA); finance (MBA); general business administration (MBA); general human resource management (MS); general leadership (MS); health care management (MBA); human resource management (MBA); marketing (MBA); project management (MBA, MS).

Carlos Albizu University, Miami Campus, Graduate Programs, Miami, FL 33172-2209. Offers clinical psychology (Psy D); entrepreneurship (MBA); exceptional student education (MS); human services (PhD); industrial/organizational psychology (MS); marriage and family therapy (MS); mental health counseling (MS); nonprofit management (MBA); organizational management (MBA); psychology (MS); school counseling (MS); teaching English as a second language (MS). *Accreditation:* APA. Part-time and evening/weekend programs available. *Faculty:* 26 full-time (20 women), 34 part-time/adjunct (16 women). *Students:* 416 full-time (335 women), 281 part-time (237 women); includes 604 minority (57 Black or African American, non-Hispanic/Latino; 1 American Indian or Alaska Native, non-Hispanic/Latino; 13 Asian, non-Hispanic/Latino; 533 Hispanic/Latino), 14 international. Average age 36. 176 applicants, 59% accepted, 96 enrolled. In 2013, 176 master's, 37 doctorates awarded. Terminal master's awarded for partial completion of doctoral program. *Degree requirements:* For master's, one foreign language, comprehensive exam, integrative project (MBA), research project (exceptional student education, teaching English as a second language); for doctorate, one foreign language, comprehensive exam, internship, project. *Entrance requirements:* For master's, 3 letters of recommendation, interview, minimum GPA of 3.0, resume, statement of purpose, official transcripts; for doctorate, 3 letters of recommendation, minimum GPA of 3.0, resume, interview, statement of purpose, official transcripts. Additional exam requirements/recommendations for international students: Required—Michigan Test of English Language Proficiency. *Application deadline:* For fall admission, 4/1 priority date for domestic students, 5/1 priority date for international students; for spring admission, 11/1 priority date for domestic students, 9/1 priority date for international students. Applications are processed on a rolling basis. Application fee: $50. Electronic applications accepted. *Expenses: Tuition:* Full-time $9360; part-time $520 per credit. *Required fees:* $298 per term. Tuition and fees vary according to course load, degree level and program. *Financial support:* In 2013–14, 62 students received support. Federal Work-Study, scholarships/grants, and tuition discounts available. Financial award application deadline: 6/1; financial award applicants required to submit FAFSA. *Faculty research:* Psychotherapy, forensic psychology, neuropsychology, marketing strategy, entrepreneurship, special education. *Unit head:* Peter M. Rubio, Interim Chancellor, 305-593-1223 Ext. 3120, Fax: 305-592-7930, E-mail: prubio@albizu.edu. *Application contact:* Vanessa Almendarez, Administrative Assistant, 305-593-1223 Ext. 3137, Fax: 305-593-1854, E-mail: valmendarez@albizu.edu.

Carlow University, School for Social Change, Pittsburgh, PA 15213-3165. Offers MS, Psy D, Certificate. Part-time and evening/weekend programs available. Postbaccalaureate distance learning degree programs offered (no on-campus study). *Students:* 222 full-time (183 women), 35 part-time (29 women); includes 47 minority (35 Black or African American, non-Hispanic/Latino; 3 Asian, non-Hispanic/Latino; 3 Hispanic/Latino; 6 Two or more races, non-Hispanic/Latino). Average age 32. 127 applicants, 91% accepted, 57 enrolled. In 2013, 63 master's, 12 doctorates, 13 other advanced degrees awarded. *Degree requirements:* For doctorate, thesis/dissertation, internship. *Entrance requirements:* For master's, personal essay; resume or curriculum vitae; three recommendations; official transcripts; interview; minimum undergraduate GPA of 3.0; undergraduate courses in statistics, abnormal psychology, and personality theory; undergraduate work or work experience in the helping professions; for doctorate, GRE, resume or curriculum vitae; personal essay; reflective essay; official transcripts from all previous undergraduate and graduate institutions; three letters of recommendation; master's degree in closely-related field. Additional exam requirements/recommendations for international students: Required—TOEFL (minimum score 550 paper-based). *Application deadline:* For fall admission, 6/15 priority date for domestic and international students; for spring admission, 11/15 priority date for domestic and international students. Applications are processed on a rolling basis. Application fee: $20. Electronic applications accepted. Application fee is waived when completed online. *Expenses: Tuition:* Full-time $9523; part-time $744 per credit. Tuition and fees vary according to course load, degree level and program. *Financial support:* Federal Work-Study available. Financial award application deadline: 4/1; financial award applicants required to submit FAFSA. *Unit head:* Dr. Robert A. Reed, Chair, Department of Psychology and Counseling, 412-575-6349, E-mail: reedra@carlow.edu. *Application contact:* Dr. Kathleen A. Chrisman, Associate Director, Graduate Admissions, 412-578-8812, Fax: 412-578-6321, E-mail: kachrisman@carlow.edu.
Website: http://www.carlow.edu/School_for_Social_Change.aspx.

Central Penn College, Graduate Programs, Summerdale, PA 17093-0309. Offers information systems management (MPS); organizational development (MPS). Programs offered in Harrisburg, PA. Evening/weekend programs available.

The Chicago School of Professional Psychology, Program in Business Psychology, Chicago, IL 60610. Offers business psychology (PhD); industrial and organizational business psychology (Psy D); industrial and organizational psychology (MA); organizational leadership (MA, PhD). *Students:* 63 full-time (35 women), 4 part-time (all women); includes 17 minority (10 Black or African American, non-Hispanic/Latino; 4

Asian, non-Hispanic/Latino; 3 Hispanic/Latino), 1 international. 33 applicants, 76% accepted, 19 enrolled. *Degree requirements:* For doctorate, thesis/dissertation optional. *Entrance requirements:* For doctorate, GRE. Additional exam requirements/recommendations for international students: Required—TOEFL. *Financial support:* In 2013–14, research assistantships (averaging $6,000 per year), teaching assistantships (averaging $6,000 per year) were awarded; Federal Work-Study and institutionally sponsored loans also available. Financial award application deadline: 3/1; financial award applicants required to submit FAFSA. *Unit head:* Dr. Ilianna Kwaske, Department Chair, 312-467-8601, E-mail: ikwaske@thechicagoschool.edu. *Application contact:* Andrea Schmoyer, Director of Admission, 312-329-6666, Fax: 312-644-3333, E-mail: admissions@thechicagoschool.edu.
Website: http://www.thechicagoschool.edu/Home/Our_Programs/Business_Psychology_Programs.

City University of Seattle, Graduate Division, Albright School of Education, Bellevue, WA 98005. Offers administrator certification (Certificate); curriculum and instruction (M Ed); educational leadership (Ed D); elementary education (MIT); guidance and counseling (M Ed); higher education leadership (Ed D); leadership (M Ed); leadership and school counseling (M Ed); organizational leadership (Ed D); reading and literacy (M Ed); special education (MIT); superintendent certification (Certificate). Part-time and evening/weekend programs available. Postbaccalaureate distance learning degree programs offered (no on-campus study). *Degree requirements:* For master's, comprehensive exam (for some programs), thesis (for some programs); for doctorate, comprehensive exam, thesis/dissertation. *Entrance requirements:* Additional exam requirements/recommendations for international students: Required—TOEFL (minimum score 567 paper-based; 87 iBT); Recommended—IELTS. Electronic applications accepted. *Expenses:* Contact institution.

City University of Seattle, Graduate Division, School of Management, Bellevue, WA 98005. Offers accounting (Certificate); change leadership (MBA, Certificate); computer systems (MS); finance (Certificate); financial management (MBA); general management (MBA); general management-Europe (MBA); global marketing (MBA); human resources management (Certificate); individualized study (MBA); information security (MS); information systems (MBA); leadership (MA); marketing (MBA, Certificate); project management (MBA, MS, Certificate); sustainable business (Certificate); technology management (MBA, Certificate). Part-time and evening/weekend programs available. Postbaccalaureate distance learning degree programs offered (no on-campus study). *Degree requirements:* For master's, comprehensive exam (for some programs), thesis (for some programs). *Entrance requirements:* Additional exam requirements/recommendations for international students: Required—TOEFL (minimum score 567 paper-based; 87 iBT); Recommended—IELTS. Electronic applications accepted.

Cleary University, Online Program in Business Administration, Ann Arbor, MI 48105-2659. Offers accounting (MBA); financial planning (MBA); financial planning (Graduate Certificate); green business strategy (MBA, Graduate Certificate); health care leadership (MBA); management (MBA); nonprofit management (MBA, Graduate Certificate); organizational leadership (MBA). Part-time and evening/weekend programs available. Postbaccalaureate distance learning degree programs offered (no on-campus study). *Degree requirements:* For master's, thesis. *Entrance requirements:* For master's, bachelor's degree; minimum GPA of 2.5; professional resume indicating minimum of 2 years of management or related experience; undergraduate degree from accredited college or university with at least 18 quarter hours (or 12 semester hours) of accounting study (for MBA in accounting). Additional exam requirements/recommendations for international students: Required—TOEFL (minimum score 550 paper-based; 79 iBT), Michigan English Language Assessment Battery (minimum score 75). Electronic applications accepted.

Cleveland State University, College of Graduate Studies, College of Education and Human Services, Department of Counseling, Administration, Supervision and Adult Learning (CASAL), Cleveland, OH 44115. Offers adult learning and development (M Ed); chemical dependency counseling (Certificate); clinical mental health counseling (M Ed); early childhood mental health counseling (Certificate); educational administration and supervision (M Ed); organizational leadership (M Ed); school administration (Ed S); school counseling (M Ed). *Accreditation:* ACA (one or more programs are accredited). Part-time and evening/weekend programs available. *Faculty:* 15 full-time (8 women), 19 part-time/adjunct (10 women). *Students:* 79 full-time (61 women), 237 part-time (188 women); includes 101 minority (86 Black or African American, non-Hispanic/Latino; 3 Asian, non-Hispanic/Latino; 11 Hispanic/Latino; 1 Two or more races, non-Hispanic/Latino), 8 international. Average age 36. 131 applicants, 69% accepted, 49 enrolled. In 2013, 99 master's, 7 Certificates awarded. *Degree requirements:* For master's, comprehensive exam (for some programs), thesis optional, internship. *Entrance requirements:* For master's, GRE General Test or MAT, letter of recommendation and minimum GPA of 2.75 (for counseling); 2 letters of recommendation and interviews (for organizational leadership). Additional exam requirements/recommendations for international students: Required—TOEFL (minimum score 525 paper-based), IELTS (minimum score 6). *Application deadline:* For fall admission, 6/21 for domestic students, 5/15 for international students; for spring admission, 8/31 for domestic students, 11/1 for international students. Application fee: $30. Electronic applications accepted. *Expenses:* Tuition, state resident: full-time $8335; part-time $521 per credit hour. Tuition, nonresident: full-time $15,670; part-time $979 per credit hour. *Required fees:* $50; $25 per semester. *Financial support:* In 2013–14, 19 students received support, including 10 research assistantships with full and partial tuition reimbursements available (averaging $11,882 per year), 5 teaching assistantships with full and partial tuition reimbursements available (averaging $11,882 per year); scholarships/grants and unspecified assistantships also available. Support available to part-time students. *Faculty research:* Education law, career development, bullying, psychopharmacology, counseling and spirituality. *Total annual research expenditures:* $225,821. *Unit head:* Dr. Ann L. Bauer, Chairperson, 216-687-4582, Fax: 216-687-5378, E-mail: a.l.bauer@csuohio.edu. *Application contact:* Deborah L. Brown, Interim Assistant Director, Graduate Admissions, 216-523-7572, Fax: 216-687-5400, E-mail: d.l.brown@csuohio.edu.
Website: http://www.csuohio.edu/cehs/departments/CASAL/casal_dept.html.

College of Saint Elizabeth, Department of Business Administration and Management, Morristown, NJ 07960-6989. Offers human resource management (MS); organizational change (MS). Part-time programs available. *Faculty:* 1 full-time (0 women), 2 part-time/adjunct (1 woman). *Students:* 6 full-time (5 women), 33 part-time (25 women); includes 14 minority (8 Black or African American, non-Hispanic/Latino; 1 Asian, non-Hispanic/Latino; 5 Hispanic/Latino), 1 international. Average age 34. In 2013, 17 master's awarded. *Entrance requirements:* For master's, minimum GPA of 3.0, personal statement/self-assessment. Additional exam requirements/recommendations for international students: Required—TOEFL. *Application deadline:* Applications are processed on a rolling basis. Application fee: $35. Electronic applications accepted. *Expenses: Tuition:* Full-time $19,152; part-time $1064 per credit. *Financial support:* Career-related internships or fieldwork, tuition waivers (partial), and unspecified assistantships available. Support available to part-time students. Financial award application deadline: 3/15; financial award applicants required to submit FAFSA. *Unit head:* Dr. Jonathan H. Silver, Professor, Graduate Program in Management, 973-290-4113, E-mail: jsilver@cse.edu. *Application contact:* Deborah S. Cobo, Associate Director of Graduate Admission, 973-290-4194, Fax: 973-290-4710, E-mail: dscobo@cse.edu.
Website: http://www.cse.edu/academics/catalog/academic-programs/business-administration.dot.

College of Saint Mary, Program in Organizational Leadership, Omaha, NE 68106. Offers MOL. Part-time and evening/weekend programs available. *Entrance requirements:* For master's, resume. Electronic applications accepted.

Colorado State University, Graduate School, College of Business, Program in Management Practice, Fort Collins, CO 80523-1201. Offers MMP. *Faculty:* 16 full-time (6 women). *Students:* 18 full-time (10 women), 17 part-time (9 women); includes 6 minority (2 Black or African American, non-Hispanic/Latino; 1 American Indian or Alaska Native, non-Hispanic/Latino; 1 Asian, non-Hispanic/Latino; 2 Hispanic/Latino), 6 international. Average age 33. 27 applicants, 96% accepted, 17 enrolled. In 2013, 22 master's awarded. *Entrance requirements:* For master's, GMAT or GRE, minimum cumulative GPA of 3.0, current resume, 3 recommendations, transcripts, resume. Additional exam requirements/recommendations for international students: Required—TOEFL (minimum score 565 paper-based; 86 iBT) or IELTS (minimum score 6.5). *Application deadline:* For fall admission, 7/15 for domestic students, 6/1 for international students; for spring admission, 12/5 for domestic students, 11/1 for international students. Applications are processed on a rolling basis. Application fee: $50. Electronic applications accepted. *Expenses:* Tuition, state resident: full-time $9075.40; part-time $504 per credit. Tuition, nonresident: full-time $22,248; part-time $1236 per credit. *Required fees:* $1819; $60 per credit. *Financial support:* Fellowships with partial tuition reimbursements, research assistantships with partial tuition reimbursements, teaching assistantships, and unspecified assistantships available. Financial award application deadline: 4/1; financial award applicants required to submit FAFSA. *Faculty research:* Ethical behavior in the marketplace, sustainable entrepreneurship, corporate entrepreneurship, logistics in market orientation, organizational communication. *Total annual research expenditures:* $11,003. *Unit head:* Dr. John Hoxmeier, Associate Dean, 970-491-2142, Fax: 970-491-0269, E-mail: john.hoxmeier@colostate.edu. *Application contact:* Tonja Rosales, Admissions Coordinator, 970-491-4661, Fax: 970-491-3481, E-mail: tonja.rosales@colostate.edu.
Website: http://www.biz.colostate.edu/mmp/.

Columbia Southern University, Program in Organizational Leadership, Orange Beach, AL 36561. Offers MS.

Columbus State University, Graduate Studies, D. Abbott Turner College of Business and Computer Science, Columbus, GA 31907-5645. Offers applied computer science (MS); business administration (MBA); information systems security (Certificate); modeling and simulation (Certificate); organizational leadership (MS). *Accreditation:* AACSB. *Faculty:* 16 full-time (2 women), 1 (woman) part-time/adjunct. *Students:* 94 full-time (28 women), 182 part-time (56 women); includes 79 minority (49 Black or African American, non-Hispanic/Latino; 13 Asian, non-Hispanic/Latino; 8 Hispanic/Latino; 1 Native Hawaiian or other Pacific Islander, non-Hispanic/Latino; 8 Two or more races, non-Hispanic/Latino), 22 international. Average age 32. 170 applicants, 49% accepted, 66 enrolled. In 2013, 82 master's awarded. *Entrance requirements:* For master's, GMAT, GRE, minimum undergraduate GPA of 2.75, letters of recommendation. Additional exam requirements/recommendations for international students: Required—TOEFL (minimum score 550 paper-based; 79 iBT). *Application deadline:* For fall admission, 6/30 for domestic students, 5/1 for international students; for spring admission, 11/1 for domestic and international students; for summer admission, 3/1 for domestic and international students. Applications are processed on a rolling basis. Application fee: $40. Electronic applications accepted. *Expenses:* Tuition, state resident: full-time $4572; part-time $382 per credit hour. Tuition, nonresident: full-time $18,292; part-time $1526 per credit hour. *Required fees:* $1800; $196 per credit hour. Tuition and fees vary according to campus/location and program. *Financial support:* In 2013–14, 111 students received support, including 19 research assistantships (averaging $3,000 per year). Financial award application deadline: 5/1; financial award applicants required to submit FAFSA. *Unit head:* Dr. Linda U. Hadley, Dean, 706-507-8153, Fax: 706-568-2184, E-mail: hadley_linda@columbusstate.edu. *Application contact:* Kristin Williams, Director of International and Graduate Recruitment, 706-507-8848, Fax: 706-568-5091, E-mail: thornton_katie@colstate.edu.
Website: http://turner.columbusstate.edu/.

Concordia College–New York, Program in Business Leadership, Bronxville, NY 10708-1998. Offers MS. *Degree requirements:* For master's, capstone seminar.

Concordia University, School of Graduate Studies, Faculty of Arts and Science, Department of Applied Human Sciences, Montréal, QC H3G 1M8, Canada. Offers human systems intervention (MA). *Degree requirements:* For master's, 2 week residential laboratory. *Entrance requirements:* For master's, 1 week residential laboratory, 2 full years of work experience. *Faculty research:* Health promotion, adult learning and transitions, applications of group development and small group leadership, adolescent development, generational issues in immigrant families.

Concordia University Ann Arbor, Graduate Programs, Ann Arbor, MI 48105-2797. Offers curriculum and instruction (MS); educational leadership (MS); organizational leadership and administration (MS). Part-time and evening/weekend programs available. *Degree requirements:* For master's, thesis. *Entrance requirements:* Additional exam requirements/recommendations for international students: Required—TOEFL (minimum score 80 iBT); Recommended—IELTS (minimum score 6.5). Electronic applications accepted.

Concordia University, St. Paul, College of Business and Organizational Leadership, St. Paul, MN 55104-5494. Offers business and organizational leadership (MBA); criminal justice leadership (MA); forensic mental health (MA); health care management (MBA); human resource management (MA); leadership and management (MA). *Accreditation:* ACBSP. Evening/weekend programs available. Postbaccalaureate distance learning degree programs offered (minimal on-campus study). *Faculty:* 10 full-time (3 women), 20 part-time/adjunct (9 women). *Students:* 336 full-time (222 women), 84 part-time (44 women); includes 82 minority (46 Black or African American, non-Hispanic/Latino; 1 American Indian or Alaska Native, non-Hispanic/Latino; 17 Asian, non-Hispanic/Latino; 9 Hispanic/Latino; 1 Native Hawaiian or other Pacific Islander, non-Hispanic/Latino; 8 Two or more races, non-Hispanic/Latino), 1 international. Average age 34. 405 applicants, 50% accepted, 187 enrolled. In 2013, 253 master's awarded. *Degree requirements:* For master's, thesis (for some programs). *Entrance requirements:* For master's, official transcripts from regionally-accredited institution stating the conferral of a bachelor's degree with minimum cumulative GPA of 3.0; personal statement; professional resume. Additional exam requirements/recommendations for international students: Recommended—TOEFL (minimum score 547 paper-based; 78 iBT), IELTS (minimum score 6). *Application deadline:* For fall admission, 8/1 for domestic and international students; for spring admission, 12/1 for domestic and international students; for summer admission, 5/1 for domestic and international students. Applications are processed on a rolling basis. Application fee: $50. Electronic applications accepted. *Expenses: Tuition:* Full-time $6200; part-time $425 per credit. Tuition and fees vary according to degree level and program. *Financial support:*

Applicants required to submit FAFSA. *Unit head:* Lonn Maly, Dean, 651-641-8203, Fax: 651-641-8807, E-mail: maly@csp.edu. *Application contact:* Kimberly Craig, Director of Graduate and Cohort Admission, 651-603-6223, Fax: 651-603-6320, E-mail: craig@csp.edu.

Dallas Baptist University, College of Business, Management Program, Dallas, TX 75211-9299. Offers conflict resolution management (MA); general management (MA); health care management (MA); human resource management (MA); organizational management (MA); performance management (MA); professional sales and management optimization (MA). Part-time and evening/weekend programs available. *Entrance requirements:* For master's, GRE General Test, minimum GPA of 3.0. Additional exam requirements/recommendations for international students: Required—TOEFL, IELTS. *Application deadline:* Applications are processed on a rolling basis. Application fee: $25. Electronic applications accepted. *Expenses: Tuition:* Full-time $13,410; part-time $745 per credit hour. *Required fees:* $300; $150 per semester. Tuition and fees vary according to degree level. *Financial support:* Federal Work-Study, institutionally sponsored loans, scholarships/grants, and tuition waivers (full and partial) available. Support available to part-time students. Financial award applicants required to submit FAFSA. *Faculty research:* Organizational behavior, conflict personalities. *Unit head:* Joanne Hix, Director, 214-333-5280, Fax: 214-333-5293, E-mail: graduate@dbu.edu. *Application contact:* Kit P. Montgomery, Director of Graduate Programs, 214-333-5242, Fax: 214-333-5579, E-mail: graduate@dbu.edu.
Website: http://www3.dbu.edu/graduate/maom.asp.

DePaul University, Charles H. Kellstadt Graduate School of Business, Chicago, IL 60604. Offers accountancy (M Acc, MS, MSA); applied economics (MBA); banking (MBA); behavioral finance (MBA); brand and product management (MBA); business development (MBA); business information technology (MS); business strategy and decision-making (MBA); computational finance (MS); consumer insights (MBA); corporate finance (MBA); economic policy analysis (MS); entrepreneurship (MBA, MS); finance (MBA, MS); financial analysis (MBA); general business (MBA); health sector management (MBA); hospitality leadership (MBA); hospitality leadership and operational performance (MS); human resource management (MBA); human resources (MS); investment management (MBA); leadership and change management (MBA); management accounting (MBA); marketing (MBA, MS); marketing analysis (MS); marketing strategy and planning (MBA); operations management (MBA); organizational diversity (MBA); real estate (MS); real estate finance and investment (MBA); revenue management (MBA); sports management (MBA); strategic global marketing (MBA); strategy, execution and valuation (MBA); sustainable management (MBA, MS); taxation (MS); wealth management (MS); JD/MBA. *Accreditation:* AACSB. Part-time and evening/weekend programs available. Postbaccalaureate distance learning degree programs offered (no on-campus study). *Faculty:* 81 full-time (20 women), 45 part-time/adjunct (8 women). *Students:* 1,238 full-time (605 women), 617 part-time (223 women); includes 295 minority (71 Black or African American, non-Hispanic/Latino; 129 Asian, non-Hispanic/Latino; 74 Hispanic/Latino; 4 Native Hawaiian or other Pacific Islander, non-Hispanic/Latino; 17 Two or more races, non-Hispanic/Latino), 462 international. Average age 29. In 2013, 911 master's awarded. *Entrance requirements:* For master's, GMAT, 2 letters of recommendation, resume, essay, official transcripts. Additional exam requirements/recommendations for international students: Required—TOEFL (minimum score 550 paper-based; 80 iBT). *Application deadline:* For fall admission, 7/1 for domestic students, 6/1 for international students; for winter admission, 10/1 for domestic students, 9/1 for international students; for spring admission, 2/1 for domestic students, 1/1 for international students. Applications are processed on a rolling basis. Application fee: $60. Electronic applications accepted. *Expenses:* Contact institution. *Financial support:* Application deadline: 4/1; applicants required to submit FAFSA. *Unit head:* Robert T. Ryan, Assistant Dean and Director, 312-362-8810, Fax: 312-362-6677, E-mail: rryan1@depaul.edu. *Application contact:* James Parker, Director of Recruitment and Admission, 312-362-8810, Fax: 312-362-6677, E-mail: kgsb@depaul.edu.
Website: http://kellstadt.depaul.edu.

Duke University, The Fuqua School of Business, Daytime MBA Program, Durham, NC 27708-0586. Offers academic excellence in finance (Certificate); business administration (MBA); decision sciences (MBA); energy and environment (MBA); energy finance (MBA); entrepreneurship and innovation (MBA); finance (MBA); financial analysis (MBA); health sector management (Certificate); leadership and ethics (MBA); management (MBA); marketing (MBA); operations management (MBA); social entrepreneurship (MBA); strategy (MBA). *Faculty:* 91 full-time (15 women), 53 part-time/adjunct (9 women). *Students:* 862 full-time (283 women); includes 179 minority (34 Black or African American, non-Hispanic/Latino; 1 American Indian or Alaska Native, non-Hispanic/Latino; 92 Asian, non-Hispanic/Latino; 42 Hispanic/Latino; 2 Native Hawaiian or other Pacific Islander, non-Hispanic/Latino; 8 Two or more races, non-Hispanic/Latino), 342 international. Average age 29. In 2013, 437 master's awarded. *Entrance requirements:* For master's, GMAT or GRE, transcripts, essays, resume, recommendation letters, interview. Additional exam requirements/recommendations for international students: Required—TOEFL, IELTS, PTE. *Application deadline:* For fall admission, 9/18 for domestic and international students; for winter admission, 10/21 for domestic and international students; for spring admission, 1/6 for domestic and international students; for summer admission, 3/20 for domestic and international students. Application fee: $225. Electronic applications accepted. *Financial support:* In 2013–14, 331 students received support. Institutionally sponsored loans and scholarships/grants available. Financial award applicants required to submit FAFSA. *Unit head:* Russ Morgan, Associate Dean for the Daytime MBA Program, 919-660-2931, Fax: 919-684-8742, E-mail: ruskin.morgan@duke.edu. *Application contact:* Liz Riley Hargrove, Associate Dean of Admissions, 919-660-7705, Fax: 919-681-8026, E-mail: liz.riley@duke.edu.
Website: http://www.fuqua.duke.edu/daytime-mba/.

Duke University, The Fuqua School of Business, PhD Program, Durham, NC 27708-0586. Offers accounting (PhD); decision sciences (PhD); finance (PhD); management and organizations (PhD); marketing (PhD); operations management (PhD); strategy (PhD). *Faculty:* 91 full-time (15 women). *Students:* 78 full-time (27 women); includes 4 minority (1 Black or African American, non-Hispanic/Latino; 3 Asian, non-Hispanic/Latino), 49 international. 589 applicants, 5% accepted, 16 enrolled. In 2013, 26 doctorates awarded. *Degree requirements:* For doctorate, thesis/dissertation, major field requirement (exam or major paper, depending upon the area). *Entrance requirements:* For doctorate, GMAT or GRE, transcripts, essays, recommendation letters, statement of purpose. Additional exam requirements/recommendations for international students: Required—TOEFL (minimum score 577 paper-based; 90 iBT), IELTS (minimum score 7). *Application deadline:* For fall admission, 12/8 priority date for domestic and international students. Application fee: $80. Electronic applications accepted. *Financial support:* In 2013–14, 70 fellowships with full tuition reimbursements (averaging $25,300 per year), 56 research assistantships with full tuition reimbursements (averaging $7,000 per year) were awarded; institutionally sponsored loans, scholarships/grants, and tuition waivers (full) also available. Financial award applicants required to submit FAFSA. *Unit head:* William Boulding, Dean, 919-660-7822, Fax: 919-684-8742, E-mail: bb1@duke.edu. *Application contact:* Dr. James R. Bettman, Director of Graduate Studies, 919-660-7851, Fax: 919-681-6245, E-mail: jrb12@mail.duke.edu.

Duquesne University, School of Leadership and Professional Advancement, Pittsburgh, PA 15282-0001. Offers leadership (MS), including business ethics, community leadership, global leadership, health care, information technology, leadership, liberal studies, professional administration, sports leadership. Part-time and evening/weekend programs available. Postbaccalaureate distance learning degree programs offered (no on-campus study). *Faculty:* 15 full-time (7 women), 64 part-time/adjunct (26 women). *Students:* 213 full-time (106 women), 170 part-time (86 women); includes 89 minority (59 Black or African American, non-Hispanic/Latino; 2 American Indian or Alaska Native, non-Hispanic/Latino; 7 Asian, non-Hispanic/Latino; 9 Hispanic/Latino; 1 Native Hawaiian or other Pacific Islander, non-Hispanic/Latino; 11 Two or more races, non-Hispanic/Latino), 9 international. Average age 36. 204 applicants, 56% accepted, 103 enrolled. In 2013, 140 master's awarded. *Degree requirements:* For master's, capstone course. *Entrance requirements:* For master's, professional work experience, 500-word essay, resume, interview. Additional exam requirements/recommendations for international students: Required—TOEFL (minimum score 80 iBT). *Application deadline:* Applications are processed on a rolling basis. Application fee: $0. Electronic applications accepted. Application fee is waived when completed online. *Expenses: Tuition:* Full-time $18,162; part-time $1009 per credit. *Required fees:* $1728; $96 per credit. Tuition and fees vary according to program. *Financial support:* Scholarships/grants available. Financial award applicants required to submit FAFSA. *Unit head:* Dr. Dorothy Bassett, Dean, 412-396-2141, Fax: 412-396-4711, E-mail: bassettd@duq.edu. *Application contact:* Marianne Leister, Director of Student Services, 412-396-4933, Fax: 412-396-5072, E-mail: leister@duq.edu.
Website: http://www.duq.edu/academics/schools/leadership-and-professional-advancement.

Eastern Connecticut State University, School of Education and Professional Studies/Graduate Division, Program in Organizational Management, Willimantic, CT 06226-2295. Offers MS. Part-time and evening/weekend programs available. *Degree requirements:* For master's, comprehensive exam or thesis. *Entrance requirements:* For master's, minimum GPA of 2.7. Additional exam requirements/recommendations for international students: Required—TOEFL (minimum score 550 paper-based).

Eastern Mennonite University, Program in Organizational Leadership, Harrisonburg, VA 22802-2462. Offers MA.

Eastern Michigan University, Graduate School, College of Business, Department of Management, Program in Human Resources Management and Organizational Development, Ypsilanti, MI 48197. Offers MSHROD. Part-time and evening/weekend programs available. Postbaccalaureate distance learning degree programs offered (minimal on-campus study). *Students:* 10 full-time (7 women), 60 part-time (46 women); includes 18 minority (13 Black or African American, non-Hispanic/Latino; 2 Asian, non-Hispanic/Latino; 2 Hispanic/Latino; 1 Two or more races, non-Hispanic/Latino), 9 international. Average age 30. 39 applicants, 59% accepted, 9 enrolled. In 2013, 83 master's awarded. *Degree requirements:* For master's, thesis optional. *Entrance requirements:* For master's, GMAT. Additional exam requirements/recommendations for international students: Required—TOEFL. *Application deadline:* Applications are processed on a rolling basis. Application fee: $35. *Expenses:* Tuition, state resident: full-time $12,300; part-time $466 per credit hour. Tuition, nonresident: full-time $23,159; part-time $918 per credit hour. *Required fees:* $71 per credit hour. $46 per semester. One-time fee: $100. Tuition and fees vary according to course level and degree level. *Financial support:* Fellowships, research assistantships with full tuition reimbursements, teaching assistantships with full tuition reimbursements, career-related internships or fieldwork, Federal Work-Study, institutionally sponsored loans, scholarships/grants, tuition waivers (partial), and unspecified assistantships available. Support available to part-time students. Financial award applicants required to submit FAFSA. *Unit head:* Dr. Fraya Wagner-Marsh, Department Head, 734-487-3240, Fax: 734-487-4100, E-mail: fraya.wagner@emich.edu. *Application contact:* Dr. Fraya Wagner-Marsh, Department Head/Advisor, 734-487-3240, Fax: 734-483-4100, E-mail: fray.wagner@emich.edu.
Website: http://www.emich.edu/public/cob/management/mshrod.

Eastern Michigan University, Graduate School, College of Business, Programs in Business Administration, Ypsilanti, MI 48197. Offers business administration (MBA, Graduate Certificate); computer information systems (Graduate Certificate); e-business (MBA, Graduate Certificate); enterprise business intelligence (MBA); entrepreneurship (MBA, Graduate Certificate); finance (MBA, Graduate Certificate); human resources (MBA); human resources management (Graduate Certificate); information systems (MBA); internal auditing (MBA); international business (MBA, Graduate Certificate); marketing management (Graduate Certificate); nonprofit management (MBA); organizational development (Graduate Certificate); supply chain management (MBA, Graduate Certificate). *Accreditation:* AACSB. Part-time programs available. Postbaccalaureate distance learning degree programs offered (no on-campus study). *Students:* 74 full-time (28 women), 342 part-time (183 women); includes 122 minority (84 Black or African American, non-Hispanic/Latino; 2 American Indian or Alaska Native, non-Hispanic/Latino; 19 Asian, non-Hispanic/Latino; 7 Hispanic/Latino; 10 Two or more races, non-Hispanic/Latino), 38 international. Average age 33. 305 applicants, 72% accepted, 131 enrolled. In 2013, 69 master's, 57 other advanced degrees awarded. *Entrance requirements:* For master's, GMAT (minimum score 450), minimum cumulative undergraduate GPA of 2.75. Additional exam requirements/recommendations for international students: Required—TOEFL. *Application deadline:* For fall admission, 5/15 for domestic students, 5/1 for international students; for winter admission, 10/15 for domestic students, 10/1 for international students; for spring admission, 3/15 for domestic students, 3/1 for international students. Applications are processed on a rolling basis. Application fee: $35. *Expenses:* Tuition, state resident: full-time $12,300; part-time $466 per credit hour. Tuition, nonresident: full-time $23,159; part-time $918 per credit hour. *Required fees:* $71 per credit hour. $46 per semester. One-time fee: $100. Tuition and fees vary according to course level and degree level. *Financial support:* Fellowships, research assistantships with full tuition reimbursements, teaching assistantships with full tuition reimbursements, career-related internships or fieldwork, Federal Work-Study, institutionally sponsored loans, scholarships/grants, tuition waivers (partial), and unspecified assistantships available. Support available to part-time students. Financial award applicants required to submit FAFSA. *Unit head:* K. Michelle Henry, Director, Academic Services, 734-487-4444, Fax: 734-483-1316, E-mail: mhenry1@emich.edu. *Application contact:* Beste Windes, Advisor, 734-487-4444, Fax: 734-483-1316, E-mail: bwindes@emich.edu.
Website: http://www.emich.edu/public/cob/gr/grad.html.

Eastern University, School of Leadership and Development, St. Davids, PA 19087-3696. Offers economic development (MBA), including international development, urban development (MA, MBA); international development (MA), including global development, urban development (MA, MBA); nonprofit management (MS); organizational leadership (MA); M Div/MBA. Part-time and evening/weekend programs available. Postbaccalaureate distance learning degree programs offered (minimal on-campus study). *Faculty:* 6 full-time (3 women), 19 part-time/adjunct (8 women). *Students:* 131 full-time (77 women), 67 part-time (42 women); includes 43 minority (29 Black or African American, non-Hispanic/Latino; 1 American Indian or Alaska Native, non-Hispanic/Latino; 6 Asian, non-Hispanic/Latino; 6 Hispanic/Latino; 1 Two or more races, non-Hispanic/Latino), 13 international. Average age 34. 45 applicants, 100%

accepted, 33 enrolled. In 2013, 91 master's awarded. *Degree requirements:* For master's, thesis (for some programs). *Entrance requirements:* For master's, GMAT (MBA), minimum GPA of 2.5. Additional exam requirements/recommendations for international students: Required—TOEFL (minimum score 550 paper-based; 79 iBT). *Application deadline:* For fall admission, 8/14 for domestic students. Applications are processed on a rolling basis. Application fee: $35. Application fee is waived when completed online. *Expenses:* Contact institution. *Financial support:* In 2013–14, 131 students received support, including 3 fellowships with partial tuition reimbursements available (averaging $2,500 per year), 7 research assistantships with partial tuition reimbursements available (averaging $1,500 per year); scholarships/grants and unspecified assistantships also available. Financial award application deadline: 3/15; financial award applicants required to submit FAFSA. *Faculty research:* Micro-level economic development, China welfare and economic development, macroethics, micro- and macro-level economic development in transitional economics, organizational effectiveness. *Unit head:* Beth Birmingham, Chair, 610-341-4380. *Application contact:* Lindsey Perry, Enrollment Counselor, 484-581-1311, Fax: 484-581-1276, E-mail: lperry@eastern.edu.
Website: http://www.eastern.edu/academics/programs/school-leadership-and-development.

Eastern University, East Central University, Program in Organizational Leadership, St. Davids, PA 19087-3696. Offers PhD. *Students:* 90 full-time (50 women); includes 23 minority (21 Black or African American, non-Hispanic/Latino; 2 Hispanic/Latino), 4 international. Average age 46. In 2013, 12 doctorates awarded. *Unit head:* Dr. Gwen White, Director, 610-341-1596. *Application contact:* Graduate Admissions Office, 800-732-7669, E-mail: gpsadm@eastern.edu.

Edgewood College, Program in Business, Madison, WI 53711-1997. Offers accountancy (MS); accounting (MBA); business administration (MBA); finance (MBA); management (MBA); marketing (MBA); organization development (MS); sustainability leadership (MBA). *Accreditation:* ACBSP. Part-time and evening/weekend programs available. *Students:* 24 full-time (8 women), 136 part-time (82 women); includes 18 minority (5 Black or African American, non-Hispanic/Latino; 1 American Indian or Alaska Native, non-Hispanic/Latino; 4 Asian, non-Hispanic/Latino; 4 Hispanic/Latino; 4 Two or more races, non-Hispanic/Latino), 10 international. Average age 33. In 2013, 55 master's awarded. *Entrance requirements:* For master's, GMAT (minimum score 430), minimum GPA of 2.75, 2 letters of recommendation. Additional exam requirements/recommendations for international students: Required—TOEFL. *Application deadline:* For fall admission, 8/15 for domestic students, 5/1 for international students; for spring admission, 1/8 for domestic students, 11/1 for international students. Applications are processed on a rolling basis. Application fee: $30. Electronic applications accepted. *Financial support:* Career-related internships or fieldwork and scholarships/grants available. *Unit head:* Martin Preizler, Dean, 608-663-2898, Fax: 608-663-3291, E-mail: martinpreizler@edgewood.edu. *Application contact:* Joann Eastman, Admissions Counselor, 608-663-3250, Fax: 608-663-2214, E-mail: gps@edgewood.edu.
Website: http://www.edgewood.edu/Academics/School-of-Business.

Edgewood College, Program in Organization Development, Madison, WI 53711-1997. Offers MS. Part-time and evening/weekend programs available. Postbaccalaureate distance learning degree programs offered (minimal on-campus study). *Application deadline:* For fall admission, 8/15 for domestic students, 5/1 for international students; for spring admission, 1/8 for domestic students, 11/1 for international students. Electronic applications accepted.
Website: http://www.edgewood.edu/Academics/Graduate/OrganizationalDevelopment.aspx.

Emory & Henry College, Graduate Programs, Emory, VA 24327-0947. Offers American history (MA Ed); organizational leadership (MCOL); professional studies (M Ed); reading specialist (MA Ed). Part-time and evening/weekend programs available. *Faculty:* 7 full-time (3 women). *Students:* 11 full-time (8 women), 32 part-time (22 women); includes 1 minority (Black or African American, non-Hispanic/Latino). Average age 36. 34 applicants, 85% accepted, 28 enrolled. In 2013, 36 master's awarded. *Entrance requirements:* For master's, GRE or PRAXIS I, recommendations, writing sample. Additional exam requirements/recommendations for international students: Recommended—TOEFL. *Application deadline:* Applications are processed on a rolling basis. Application fee: $30. *Financial support:* Applicants required to submit FAFSA. *Unit head:* Dr. Jack Roper, Director of Graduate Studies, 276-944-6188, Fax: 276-944-5223, E-mail: jroper@ehc.edu. *Application contact:* Dr. Jack Roper, Director of Graduate Studies, 276-944-6188, Fax: 276-944-5223, E-mail: jroper@ehc.edu.

Emory University, Goizueta Business School, Doctoral Program in Business, Atlanta, GA 30322-1100. Offers accounting (PhD); finance (PhD); information systems (PhD); marketing (PhD); organization and management (PhD). *Faculty:* 53 full-time (12 women). *Students:* 41 full-time (15 women); includes 28 minority (all Asian, non-Hispanic/Latino). Average age 29. 195 applicants, 9% accepted, 9 enrolled. In 2013, 1 doctorate awarded. *Degree requirements:* For doctorate, comprehensive exam, thesis/dissertation. *Entrance requirements:* For doctorate, GMAT (strongly preferred) or GRE. Additional exam requirements/recommendations for international students: Required—TOEFL. *Application deadline:* For fall admission, 1/3 priority date for domestic and international students. Application fee: $75. Electronic applications accepted. *Financial support:* In 2013–14, 35 students received support, including 3 fellowships (averaging $1,166 per year). *Unit head:* Dr. Anand Swaminathan, Associate Dean, Doctoral Program, 404-727-2306, Fax: 404-727-5337, E-mail: anand.swaminathan@emory.edu. *Application contact:* Allison Gilmore, Director of Admissions and Student Services, 404-727-6353, Fax: 404-727-5337, E-mail: phd@bus.emory.edu.

Endicott College, Apicius International School of Hospitality, Florence, 50122, Italy. Offers international tourism (MOM). Program held entirely in Florence, Italy. *Degree requirements:* For master's, thesis. *Entrance requirements:* For master's, MAT or GRE, 250-500 word essay explaining professional goals, official transcripts of all academic work, bachelor's degree, two letters of recommendation, personal interview. *Application deadline:* For fall admission, 6/30 for domestic and international students. Application fee: $50. *Financial support:* Applicants required to submit FAFSA. *Application contact:* E-mail: admissions@fua.it.
Website: http://www.apicius.it.

Endicott College, Van Loan School of Graduate and Professional Studies, Program in Organizational Management, Beverly, MA 01915-2096. Offers M Ed. Part-time and evening/weekend programs available. *Degree requirements:* For master's, thesis. *Entrance requirements:* For master's, GRE or MAT, two letters of recommendation, personal interview, 250-500 word essay, official transcripts of undergraduate and graduate course work. Additional exam requirements/recommendations for international students: Required—TOEFL. *Application deadline:* Applications are processed on a rolling basis. Application fee: $50. Electronic applications accepted. *Expenses:* Contact institution. *Financial support:* Career-related internships or fieldwork, Federal Work-Study, institutionally sponsored loans, and tuition waivers (partial) available. Financial award applicants required to submit FAFSA. *Unit head:* Kristy Walker, Assistant Director of Graduate Management Programs, 978-998-7790, Fax: 978-232-3000, E-mail: kwalker@endicott.edu.
Website: http://www.endicott.edu/VanLoan/Graduate-Studies/Master-Education/Organizational-Management.aspx.

Evangel University, Organizational Leadership Program, Springfield, MO 65802. Offers MOL. Part-time and evening/weekend programs available. Postbaccalaureate distance learning degree programs offered (minimal on-campus study). *Faculty:* 4 full-time (0 women), 5 part-time/adjunct (1 woman). *Students:* 56 full-time (29 women), 7 part-time (3 women); includes 8 minority (2 Black or African American, non-Hispanic/Latino; 1 American Indian or Alaska Native, non-Hispanic/Latino; 4 Hispanic/Latino; 1 Native Hawaiian or other Pacific Islander, non-Hispanic/Latino). Average age 36. 4 applicants, 50% accepted, 2 enrolled. In 2013, 21 master's awarded. *Degree requirements:* For master's, comprehensive exam, thesis. *Entrance requirements:* Additional exam requirements/recommendations for international students: Required—TOEFL (minimum score 550 paper-based). *Application deadline:* For fall admission, 7/15 priority date for domestic students, 8/1 for international students; for spring admission, 11/15 priority date for domestic students, 12/1 for international students. Applications are processed on a rolling basis. Application fee: $25. Electronic applications accepted. *Financial support:* In 2013–14, 15 students received support. Career-related internships or fieldwork and scholarships/grants available. Support available to part-time students. Financial award application deadline: 3/1; financial award applicants required to submit FAFSA. *Unit head:* Dr. Duane Praschan, Program Coordinator, 417-865-2815 Ext. 8118, Fax: 417-575-5484, E-mail: praschand@evangel.edu. *Application contact:* Karen Benitez, Admissions Representative, Graduate Studies, 417-865-2815 Ext. 7227, Fax: 417-575-5484, E-mail: benitezk@evangel.edu.
Website: http://www.evangel.edu/academics/graduate-studies/graduate-programs.

Fairleigh Dickinson University, College at Florham, Maxwell Becton College of Arts and Sciences, Department of Psychology, Program in Organizational Behavior, Madison, NJ 07940-1099. Offers organizational behavior (MA); organizational leadership (Certificate).

Fielding Graduate University, Graduate Programs, School of Human and Organization Development, Santa Barbara, CA 93105-3814. Offers comprehensive evidence-based coaching (Certificate); evidence based coaching for education leadership (Certificate); evidence based coaching for organization leadership (Certificate); evidence based coaching for personal development (Certificate); human and organizational systems (PhD), including aging, culture and society, information society and knowledge organizations, transformative learning for social justice; human development (PhD), including aging, culture and society, information society and knowledge organizations, transformative learning for social justice; leadership and management effectiveness (Certificate); leadership for sustainability (Certificate); nonprofit leadership (Certificate); organization consulting (Certificate); organizational development and leadership (MA). Postbaccalaureate distance learning degree programs offered (minimal on-campus study). *Faculty:* 19 full-time (11 women), 38 part-time/adjunct (20 women). *Students:* 321 full-time (225 women), 135 part-time (101 women); includes 103 minority (55 Black or African American, non-Hispanic/Latino; 3 American Indian or Alaska Native, non-Hispanic/Latino; 12 Asian, non-Hispanic/Latino; 23 Hispanic/Latino; 1 Native Hawaiian or other Pacific Islander, non-Hispanic/Latino; 9 Two or more races, non-Hispanic/Latino), 1 international. Average age 49. 106 applicants, 96% accepted, 70 enrolled. In 2013, 35 master's, 58 doctorates, 60 other advanced degrees awarded. Terminal master's awarded for partial completion of doctoral program. *Degree requirements:* For master's, thesis or alternative; for doctorate, comprehensive exam, thesis/dissertation. *Entrance requirements:* For master's and Certificate, BA from regionally-accredited institution or equivalent; for doctorate, BA or MA from regionally-accredited institution or equivalent. *Application deadline:* For fall admission, 3/1 for domestic and international students; for spring admission, 9/1 for domestic and international students. Application fee: $75. Electronic applications accepted. *Expenses:* Contact institution. *Financial support:* In 2013–14, 35 students received support, including 1 research assistantship (averaging $1,600 per year); scholarships/grants, health care benefits, and unspecified assistantships also available. Support available to part-time students. Financial award applicants required to submit FAFSA. *Unit head:* Dr. Mario Borunda, Dean, 805-898-2940, Fax: 805-687-9793, E-mail: mborunda@fielding.edu. *Application contact:* Kathy Wells, Admission Counselor, 800-340-1099 Ext. 4098, Fax: 805-687-9793, E-mail: hodadmissions@fielding.edu.
Website: http://www.fielding.edu/programs/hod/default.aspx.

Gannon University, School of Graduate Studies, College of Engineering and Business, Dahlkemper School of Business, Program in Organizational Leadership, Erie, PA 16541-0001. Offers Certificate. Part-time and evening/weekend programs available. *Students:* 1 applicant. *Entrance requirements:* Additional exam requirements/recommendations for international students: Required—TOEFL (minimum score 79 iBT). Application fee: $25. *Expenses: Tuition:* Full-time $15,930; part-time $885 per credit. *Required fees:* $430; $18 per credit. Tuition and fees vary according to course load, degree level and program. *Financial support:* Application deadline: 7/1; applicants required to submit FAFSA. *Unit head:* Dr. William L. Scheller, II, Dean, 814-871-7582, E-mail: scheller002@gannon.edu. *Application contact:* Kara Morgan, Director of Graduate Admissions, 814-871-5831, Fax: 814-871-5827, E-mail: graduate@gannon.edu.

Gannon University, School of Graduate Studies, College of Humanities, Education, and Social Sciences, School of Humanities, Program in Organizational Learning and Leadership, Erie, PA 16541-0001. Offers PhD. Part-time and evening/weekend programs available. *Students:* 5 full-time (2 women), 56 part-time (39 women); includes 2 minority (both Black or African American, non-Hispanic/Latino). Average age 42. 16 applicants, 81% accepted, 9 enrolled. In 2013, 6 doctorates awarded. *Degree requirements:* For doctorate, thesis/dissertation. *Entrance requirements:* For doctorate, GRE, minimum graduate GPA of 3.5, 2 years of post-baccalaureate work experience, letters of recommendation, statement of purpose. Additional exam requirements/recommendations for international students: Required—TOEFL (minimum score 79 iBT). *Application deadline:* For spring admission, 2/1 for domestic students. Applications are processed on a rolling basis. Application fee: $50. Electronic applications accepted. *Expenses: Tuition:* Full-time $15,930; part-time $885 per credit. *Required fees:* $430; $18 per credit. Tuition and fees vary according to course load, degree level and program. *Financial support:* Scholarships/grants and unspecified assistantships available. Financial award applicants required to submit FAFSA. *Unit head:* Dr. Gail Latta, Director, 814-871-5792, E-mail: latta001@gannon.edu. *Application contact:* Kara Morgan, Director of Graduate Admissions, 814-871-5831, Fax: 814-871-5827, E-mail: graduate@gannon.edu.

Geneva College, Program in Organizational Leadership, Beaver Falls, PA 15010-3599. Offers MS. Evening/weekend programs available. *Faculty:* 3 full-time (2 women), 10 part-time/adjunct (2 women). *Students:* 103 full-time (64 women); includes 31 minority (30 Black or African American, non-Hispanic/Latino; 1 Two or more races, non-Hispanic/Latino). Average age 42. 14 applicants, 64% accepted, 9 enrolled. In 2013, 59 master's awarded. *Degree requirements:* For master's, thesis. *Entrance requirements:* For master's, 3-5 years of professional experience, minimum GPA of 3.0 (preferred), resume, writing sample, interview, 3 recommendations. Additional exam requirements/

recommendations for international students: Required—TOEFL. *Application deadline:* Applications are processed on a rolling basis. Application fee: $15. Electronic applications accepted. Application fee is waived when completed online. *Expenses: Tuition:* Full-time $14,640; part-time $640 per credit hour. Tuition and fees vary according to program. *Financial support:* In 2013–14, 41 students received support. Scholarships/grants available. Financial award application deadline: 8/1; financial award applicants required to submit FAFSA. *Faculty research:* Servant leadership. *Unit head:* Dr. James K. Dittmar, Chair, 724-847-6853, Fax: 724-847-4198, E-mail: jkd@geneva.edu. *Application contact:* Linda Roundtree, Enrollment Counselor, 724-847-6856, Fax: 724-847-4198, E-mail: lroundtr@geneva.edu.
Website: http://www.geneva.edu/page/msol.

George Fox University, College of Business, Newberg, OR 97132-2697. Offers finance (MBA); management (DBA); management and leadership (MBA); marketing (DBA); organizational strategy (MBA); strategic human resource management (MBA). MBA offered in Newberg, OR and in Portland, OR. *Accreditation:* ACBSP. Part-time and evening/weekend programs available. Postbaccalaureate distance learning degree programs offered (minimal on-campus study). *Faculty:* 8 full-time (2 women), 5 part-time/adjunct (2 women). *Students:* 31 full-time (15 women), 194 part-time (76 women); includes 21 minority (6 Black or African American, non-Hispanic/Latino; 4 American Indian or Alaska Native, non-Hispanic/Latino; 6 Asian, non-Hispanic/Latino; 3 Hispanic/Latino; 2 Two or more races, non-Hispanic/Latino), 15 international. Average age 39. 98 applicants, 79% accepted, 62 enrolled. In 2013, 98 master's, 2 doctorates awarded. *Degree requirements:* For master's, capstone project; for doctorate, credit-applied research project. *Entrance requirements:* For master's, resume (5 years of professional experience); 3 professional references; interview; financial e-learning course, official transcripts; for doctorate, GRE or GMAT, resume; personal mission statement; academic research writing sample; official transcript from each college/university attended; three professional references. Additional exam requirements/recommendations for international students: Required—TOEFL (minimum score 577 paper-based; 90 iBT) or IELTS (minimum score 7). *Application deadline:* For fall admission, 8/1 for domestic and international students; for spring admission, 12/1 for domestic and international students. Applications are processed on a rolling basis. Application fee: $40. Electronic applications accepted. *Expenses:* Contact institution. *Financial support:* Applicants required to submit FAFSA. *Unit head:* Dr. Chris Meade, Professor/Dean, 800-631-0921. *Application contact:* Ty Sohlman, Admissions Counselor, 800-493-4937, Fax: 503-554-6111, E-mail: business@georgefox.edu.
Website: http://www.georgefox.edu/business/index.html.

George Mason University, College of Humanities and Social Sciences, Interdisciplinary Studies Program, Fairfax, VA 22030. Offers community college teaching (MAIS); computational social science (MAIS); energy and sustainability (MAIS); film and video studies (MAIS); folklore studies (MAIS); higher education administration (MAIS); neuroethics (MAIS); religion, culture and values (MAIS); social entrepreneurship (MAIS); war and military in society (MAIS); women and gender studies (MAIS). *Faculty:* 10 full-time (3 women), 7 part-time/adjunct (3 women). *Students:* 31 full-time (17 women), 79 part-time (50 women); includes 30 minority (17 Black or African American, non-Hispanic/Latino; 4 Asian, non-Hispanic/Latino; 6 Hispanic/Latino; 3 Two or more races, non-Hispanic/Latino), 3 international. Average age 33. 78 applicants, 59% accepted, 25 enrolled. In 2013, 32 master's awarded. *Degree requirements:* For master's, project or thesis. *Entrance requirements:* For master's, 3 letters of recommendation; writing sample; official transcript; resume. Additional exam requirements/recommendations for international students: Required—TOEFL (minimum score 570 paper-based; 88 iBT), IELTS (minimum score 6.5), PTE. *Application deadline:* For fall admission, 3/1 priority date for domestic students; for spring admission, 10/15 for domestic students. Application fee: $65 ($80 for international students). Electronic applications accepted. *Expenses:* Tuition, state resident: full-time $9350; part-time $390 per credit. Tuition, nonresident: full-time $25,754; part-time $1073 per credit. *Required fees:* $2688; $112 per credit. *Financial support:* In 2013–14, 8 students received support, including 3 research assistantships with full and partial tuition reimbursements available (averaging $10,238 per year), 5 teaching assistantships with full and partial tuition reimbursements available (averaging $7,655 per year); career-related internships or fieldwork, Federal Work-Study, scholarships/grants, unspecified assistantships, and health care benefits (for full-time research or teaching assistantship recipients) also available. Support available to part-time students. Financial award application deadline: 3/1; financial award applicants required to submit FAFSA. *Faculty research:* Combined English and folklore, religious and cultural studies (Christianity and Muslim society). *Unit head:* Jan Arminio, Interim Director, 703-993-2064, Fax: 703-993-2307, E-mail: jarminio@gmu.edu. *Application contact:* Becky Durham, Administrative Coordinator, 703-993-8762, Fax: 703-993-5585, E-mail: rdurham4@gmu.edu.
Website: http://mais.gmu.edu.

George Mason University, School of Policy, Government, and International Affairs, Program in Organization Development and Knowledge Management, Arlington, VA 22201. Offers MS. *Faculty:* 5 full-time (3 women), 4 part-time/adjunct (0 women). *Students:* 4 full-time (all women), 55 part-time (43 women); includes 20 minority (12 Black or African American, non-Hispanic/Latino; 4 Asian, non-Hispanic/Latino; 3 Hispanic/Latino; 1 Two or more races, non-Hispanic/Latino), 1 international. Average age 33. 64 applicants, 59% accepted, 27 enrolled. In 2013, 40 master's awarded. *Degree requirements:* For master's, thesis or alternative, internship. *Entrance requirements:* For master's, GRE (for students seeking merit-based scholarships), bachelor's degree with minimum GPA of 3.0, current resume, 2 letters of recommendation, expanded goals statement, 2 copies of official transcripts. Additional exam requirements/recommendations for international students: Required—TOEFL (minimum score 575 paper-based; 88 iBT), IELTS (minimum score 6.5), PTE. *Application deadline:* For fall admission, 6/1 priority date for domestic students, 5/1 priority date for international students; for spring admission, 12/1 priority date for domestic students, 11/1 priority date for international students. Applications are processed on a rolling basis. Application fee: $65 ($80 for international students). Electronic applications accepted. *Expenses:* Contact institution. *Financial support:* Career-related internships or fieldwork, Federal Work-Study, scholarships/grants, unspecified assistantships, and health care benefits (for full-time research or teaching assistantship recipients) available. Financial award application deadline: 3/1; financial award applicants required to submit FAFSA. *Unit head:* Tojo Joseph Thatchenkery, Director, 703-993-3808, Fax: 703-993-8215, E-mail: thatchen@gmu.edu. *Application contact:* Travis Major, Director of Graduate Admissions, 703-993-1383, E-mail: tmajor@gmu.edu.
Website: http://policy.gmu.edu/academic-professional-programs/masters-programs/organization-development-knowledge-management-odkm/.

The George Washington University, Columbian College of Arts and Sciences, Department of Organizational Sciences and Communication, Washington, DC 20052. Offers human resources management (MA); industrial/organizational psychology (PhD); organizational management (MA). Part-time and evening/weekend programs available. *Faculty:* 11 full-time (6 women). *Students:* 26 full-time (20 women), 41 part-time (30 women); includes 21 minority (9 Black or African American, non-Hispanic/Latino; 2 Asian, non-Hispanic/Latino; 5 Hispanic/Latino; 1 Native Hawaiian or other Pacific Islander, non-Hispanic/Latino; 4 Two or more races, non-Hispanic/Latino), 10 international. Average age 28. 78 applicants, 95% accepted, 24 enrolled. In 2013, 24 master's awarded. *Degree requirements:* For master's, comprehensive exam. *Entrance requirements:* For master's, GRE General Test, minimum GPA of 3.0. Additional exam requirements/recommendations for international students: Required—TOEFL (minimum score 500 paper-based; 80 iBT). *Application deadline:* For fall admission, 1/15 priority date for domestic and international students; for spring admission, 10/1 priority date for domestic students, 9/1 priority date for international students. Applications are processed on a rolling basis. Application fee: $75. Electronic applications accepted. *Financial support:* Federal Work-Study and institutionally sponsored loans available. *Unit head:* Dr. Clay Warren, Chair, 202-994-1870, Fax: 202-994-1881, E-mail: claywar@gwu.edu. *Application contact:* Information Contact, 202-994-1880, Fax: 202-994-1881.
Website: http://www.gwu.edu/~orgsci/.

The George Washington University, Graduate School of Education and Human Development, Department of Human and Organizational Learning, Program in Organizational Learning and Change, Washington, DC 20052. Offers Graduate Certificate. *Students:* 2 part-time (1 woman); includes 1 minority (Black or African American, non-Hispanic/Latino). Average age 54. 3 applicants, 100% accepted. In 2013, 2 Graduate Certificates awarded. *Entrance requirements:* For degree, two letters of recommendation, resume, statement of purpose. *Unit head:* Dr. Mary Hatwood Futrell, Dean, 202-994-6161, Fax: 202-994-7207, E-mail: mfutrell@gwu.edu. *Application contact:* Sarah Lang, Director of Graduate Admissions, 202-994-1447, Fax: 202-994-7207, E-mail: slang@gwu.edu.
Website: http://gsehd.gwu.edu/academics/programs/certificates/organizational-learning-and-change/overview.

Georgia State University, J. Mack Robinson College of Business, Department of Managerial Sciences, Atlanta, GA 30302-3083. Offers business analysis (MBA, MS); entrepreneurship (MBA); human resources management (MBA, MS); operations management (MBA, MS); organization behavior/human resource management (PhD); organization management (MBA); organizational change (MS); strategic management (PhD). *Accreditation:* AACSB. Part-time and evening/weekend programs available. *Faculty:* 18 full-time (6 women). *Students:* 31 full-time (15 women), 22 part-time (14 women); includes 20 minority (11 Black or African American, non-Hispanic/Latino; 1 American Indian or Alaska Native, non-Hispanic/Latino; 2 Asian, non-Hispanic/Latino; 2 Hispanic/Latino; 4 Two or more races, non-Hispanic/Latino), 16 international. Average age 31. 92 applicants, 20% accepted, 13 enrolled. In 2013, 45 master's, 2 doctorates awarded. *Degree requirements:* For doctorate, comprehensive exam, thesis/dissertation. *Entrance requirements:* For master's, GRE or GMAT, transcripts from all institutions attended, resume, essays; for doctorate, GMAT, three letters of recommendation, personal statement, transcripts from all institutions attended, resume. Additional exam requirements/recommendations for international students: Required—TOEFL (minimum score 610 paper-based; 101 iBT), IELTS (minimum score 7). *Application deadline:* For fall admission, 5/1 priority date for domestic students, 2/1 priority date for international students; for spring admission, 9/15 priority date for domestic students, 4/1 priority date for international students. Applications are processed on a rolling basis. Application fee: $50. Electronic applications accepted. *Expenses: Tuition, area resident:* Full-time $4176; part-time $348 per credit hour. Tuition, state resident: full-time $14,544; part-time $1212 per credit hour. Tuition, nonresident: full-time $14,544; part-time $1212 per credit hour. Tuition and fees vary according to course load and program. *Financial support:* Research assistantships, teaching assistantships, scholarships/grants, tuition waivers, and unspecified assistantships available. *Faculty research:* Entrepreneurship and Innovation; strategy process; workplace interactions, relationships, and processes; leadership and culture; supply chain management. *Unit head:* Dr. Pamela S. Barr, Interim Chair, 404-413-7525, Fax: 404-413-7571. *Application contact:* Toby McChesney, Assistant Dean for Graduate Recruiting and Student Services, 404-413-7167, Fax: 404-413-7162, E-mail: rcbgradadmissions@gsu.edu.
Website: http://mgmt.robinson.gsu.edu/.

Gonzaga University, School of Professional Studies, Program in Organizational Leadership, Spokane, WA 99258. Offers MOL. Part-time programs available. Postbaccalaureate distance learning degree programs offered (minimal on-campus study). *Faculty:* 7 full-time (3 women), 16 part-time/adjunct (6 women). *Students:* 40 full-time (21 women), 484 part-time (222 women); includes 74 minority (27 Black or African American, non-Hispanic/Latino; 9 American Indian or Alaska Native, non-Hispanic/Latino; 11 Asian, non-Hispanic/Latino; 17 Hispanic/Latino; 4 Native Hawaiian or other Pacific Islander, non-Hispanic/Latino; 6 Two or more races, non-Hispanic/Latino), 22 international. Average age 37. 156 applicants, 71% accepted, 80 enrolled. In 2013, 203 master's awarded. *Entrance requirements:* For master's, GRE General Test or MAT, minimum B average in undergraduate course work. Additional exam requirements/recommendations for international students: Required—TOEFL. *Application deadline:* For fall admission, 7/20 priority date for domestic students; for spring admission, 11/1 for domestic students. Applications are processed on a rolling basis. Application fee: $50. Electronic applications accepted. *Expenses:* Contact institution. *Financial support:* Application deadline: 2/1; applicants required to submit FAFSA. *Unit head:* Dr. Joseph Albert, Acting Dean, 509-328-4220 Ext. 3564. *Application contact:* Julie McCulloh, Dean of Admissions, 509-313-6592, Fax: 509-313-5780, E-mail: mcculloh@gu.gonzaga.edu.

Graceland University, School of Nursing, Independence, MO 64050-3434. Offers family nurse practitioner (MSN, PMC); nurse educator (MSN, PMC); organizational leadership (DNP). Part-time programs available. Postbaccalaureate distance learning degree programs offered (minimal on-campus study). *Faculty:* 13 full-time (all women), 9 part-time/adjunct (7 women). *Students:* 215 full-time (197 women), 339 part-time (303 women); includes 95 minority (37 Black or African American, non-Hispanic/Latino; 11 American Indian or Alaska Native, non-Hispanic/Latino; 15 Asian, non-Hispanic/Latino; 18 Hispanic/Latino; 2 Native Hawaiian or other Pacific Islander, non-Hispanic/Latino; 12 Two or more races, non-Hispanic/Latino), 4 international. Average age 44. 84 applicants, 89% accepted, 63 enrolled. In 2013, 71 master's awarded. *Degree requirements:* For master's, comprehensive exam (for some programs), thesis optional, scholarly project; for doctorate, capstone project. *Entrance requirements:* For master's, BSN from nationally-accredited program, RN license, minimum GPA of 3.0; satisfactory criminal background check; for doctorate, MSN from nationally-accredited program, RN license, minimum GPA of 3.2; satisfactory criminal background check. Additional exam requirements/recommendations for international students: Recommended—TOEFL. *Application deadline:* For fall admission, 6/1 priority date for domestic students; for winter admission, 10/1 priority date for domestic students; for spring admission, 3/1 priority date for domestic students. Application fee: $50. Electronic applications accepted. *Expenses:* Contact institution. *Financial support:* Institutionally sponsored loans available. Support available to part-time students. Financial award applicants required to submit FAFSA. *Faculty research:* International nursing, family care-giving, health promotion. *Unit head:* Dr. Claudia D. Horton, Dean, 816-423-4670, Fax: 816-423-4753, E-mail: horton@graceland.edu. *Application contact:* Nick Walker, Program Consultant, 816-423-4717, Fax: 816-833-2990, E-mail: nowalker@graceland.edu.
Website: http://www.graceland.edu/nursing.

Grand Canyon University, College of Doctoral Studies, Phoenix, AZ 85017-1097. Offers business administration (DBA); general psychology (PhD), including cognition

and instruction, industrial and organizational psychology; organizational leadership (Ed D, PhD), including behavioral health (PhD), education and effective schools (PhD), higher education (PhD), instructional leadership (PhD), organizational development (Ed D). *Degree requirements:* For doctorate, comprehensive exam, thesis/dissertation. *Entrance requirements:* For doctorate, minimum GPA of 3.4 on earned advanced degree from regionally-accredited institution; transcripts; goals statement.

Grand View University, Master of Science in Innovative Leadership Program, Des Moines, IA 50316-1599. Offers business (MS); education (MS); nursing (MS). Part-time and evening/weekend programs available. *Degree requirements:* For master's, completion of all required coursework in common core and selected track with minimum cumulative GPA of 3.0 and no more than two grades of C. *Entrance requirements:* For master's, GRE, GMAT, or essay, minimum undergraduate GPA of 3.0, professional resume, 3 letters of recommendation, interview. Additional exam requirements/recommendations for international students: Required—TOEFL (minimum score 550 paper-based). Electronic applications accepted.

Granite State College, Program in Leadership, Concord, NH 03301. Offers MS. Part-time programs available. Postbaccalaureate distance learning degree programs offered (no on-campus study). *Faculty:* 1 (woman) full-time, 16 part-time/adjunct (8 women). *Students:* 18 full-time (15 women), 26 part-time (19 women); includes 5 minority (1 Black or African American, non-Hispanic/Latino; 4 Hispanic/Latino). Average age 40. 22 applicants, 59% accepted, 11 enrolled. In 2013, 1 master's awarded. *Degree requirements:* For master's, capstone. *Entrance requirements:* For master's, bachelor's degree with minimum GPA of 3.0 on last 60 credit hours, 500-1000 word statement, two letters of professional or academic reference, resume, official transcripts. Additional exam requirements/recommendations for international students: Required—TOEFL, IELTS. *Application deadline:* Applications are processed on a rolling basis. Application fee: $0. Electronic applications accepted. *Expenses:* Tuition, state resident: full-time $8910; part-time $495 per credit. Tuition, nonresident: full-time $9090; part-time $515 per credit. *Unit head:* Johnna Herrick-Phelps, Director, 603-228-3000, E-mail: johnna.herrick-phelps@granite.edu. *Application contact:* Ana Gonzalez, Administrative Assistant, Office of Graduate Studies, 603-513-1334, Fax: 603-513-1387, E-mail: gsc.graduatestudies@granite.edu.
Website: http://www.granite.edu/academics/degrees/masters/leadership.php.

Grantham University, College of Nursing and Allied Health, Lenexa, KS 66219. Offers case management (MSN); health systems management (MS); healthcare administration (MHA); nursing education (MSN); nursing informatics (MSN); nursing management and organizational leadership (MSN). Part-time and evening/weekend programs available. Postbaccalaureate distance learning degree programs offered (no on-campus study). *Faculty:* 1 (woman) full-time, 11 part-time/adjunct (5 women). *Students:* 64 full-time (43 women), 166 part-time (123 women); includes 116 minority (94 Black or African American, non-Hispanic/Latino; 4 Asian, non-Hispanic/Latino; 9 Hispanic/Latino; 1 Native Hawaiian or other Pacific Islander, non-Hispanic/Latino; 8 Two or more races, non-Hispanic/Latino). Average age 40. 230 applicants, 100% accepted, 230 enrolled. In 2013, 61 master's awarded. *Degree requirements:* For master's, thesis, major applied research paper and practicum (MSN). *Entrance requirements:* For master's, bachelor's degree from accredited degree-granting institution with minimum GPA of 2.5, BSN from an accredited nursing program, valid RN license. Additional exam requirements/recommendations for international students: Required—TOEFL (minimum score 530 paper-based; 71 iBT). *Application deadline:* Applications are processed on a rolling basis. Application fee: $30. Electronic applications accepted. *Expenses: Tuition:* Full-time $3900; part-time $325 per credit hour. *Required fees:* $35 per term. One-time fee: $100. *Financial support:* In 2013–14, 230 students received support. Scholarships/grants available. *Faculty research:* Pharmacy licensure, vaccination certification. *Unit head:* Dr. Susan Fairchild, Dean, School of Nursing, 800-955-2527, E-mail: admissions@grantham.edu. *Application contact:* Jared Parlette, Vice President of Admissions, 800-955-2527, E-mail: admissions@grantham.edu.
Website: http://www.grantham.edu/colleges-and-schools/college-of-nursing-and-allied-health/.

Harding University, Paul R. Carter College of Business Administration, Searcy, AR 72149-0001. Offers health care management (MBA); information technology management (MBA); international business (MBA); leadership and organizational management (MBA). *Accreditation:* ACBSP. Part-time and evening/weekend programs available. Postbaccalaureate distance learning degree programs offered (no on-campus study). *Faculty:* 25 part-time/adjunct (5 women). *Students:* 55 full-time (36 women), 115 part-time (50 women); includes 22 minority (17 Black or African American, non-Hispanic/Latino; 2 American Indian or Alaska Native, non-Hispanic/Latino; 3 Asian, non-Hispanic/Latino), 27 international. Average age 34. 48 applicants, 100% accepted, 48 enrolled. In 2013, 88 master's awarded. *Degree requirements:* For master's, portfolio. *Entrance requirements:* For master's, GMAT (minimum score of 500) or GRE (minimum score of 300), minimum GPA of 3.0, 2 letters of recommendation, resume, 3 essays, all official transcripts. Additional exam requirements/recommendations for international students: Required—TOEFL (minimum score 550 paper-based; 79 iBT). *Application deadline:* For fall admission, 8/1 priority date for domestic and international students; for spring admission, 12/1 priority date for domestic and international students. Applications are processed on a rolling basis. Application fee: $40. *Expenses: Tuition:* Full-time $11,574; part-time $643 per credit hour. *Required fees:* $432; $24 per credit hour. Tuition and fees vary according to course load, degree level and program. *Financial support:* Unspecified assistantships available. Financial award application deadline: 7/30; financial award applicants required to submit FAFSA. *Unit head:* Glen Metheny, Director of Graduate Studies, 501-279-5851, Fax: 501-279-4805, E-mail: gmetheny@harding.edu. *Application contact:* Melanie Kiihnl, Recruiting Manager/Director of Marketing, 501-279-4523, Fax: 501-279-4805, E-mail: mba@harding.edu.
Website: http://www.harding.edu/mba.

Hawai`i Pacific University, College of Business Administration, Program in Organizational Change, Honolulu, HI 96813. Offers MA. Part-time and evening/weekend programs available. *Faculty:* 10 full-time (3 women), 4 part-time/adjunct (0 women). *Students:* 25 full-time (15 women), 33 part-time (25 women); includes 24 minority (1 Black or African American, non-Hispanic/Latino; 10 Asian, non-Hispanic/Latino; 5 Hispanic/Latino; 8 Two or more races, non-Hispanic/Latino). Average age 34. 33 applicants, 79% accepted, 17 enrolled. *Financial support:* In 2013–14, 12 students received support. Career-related internships or fieldwork, Federal Work-Study, scholarships/grants, tuition waivers, and unspecified assistantships available. *Unit head:* Dr. Deborah Crown, Dean, 808-544-0275, E-mail: dcrown@hpu.edu. *Application contact:* Rumi Yoshida, Associate Director of Graduate Admissions, 808-543-8034, Fax: 808-544-0280, E-mail: grad@hpu.edu.
Website: http://www.hpu.edu/CBA/Graduate/MAOC.html.

HEC Montreal, School of Business Administration, Master of Science Programs in Administration, Program in Cultural Enterprises, Montréal, QC H3T 2A7, Canada. Offers MM. Program offered in French only. *Students:* 8 full-time (6 women), 28 part-time (21 women). In 2013, 19 master's awarded. *Degree requirements:* For master's, one foreign language. *Entrance requirements:* For master's, bachelor's degree. *Application deadline:* For fall admission, 4/1 for domestic and international students. Application fee: $83. Electronic applications accepted. *Expenses: Tuition, area resident:* Part-time $74.14 per credit. Tuition, state resident: full-time $2669.04; part-time $201.83 per credit. Tuition, nonresident: full-time $7266; part-time $500.59 per credit. *International tuition:* $18,021.24 full-time. *Required fees:* $1529.70; $36.20 per credit. $65.50 per term. Tuition and fees vary according to degree level and program. *Financial support:* In 2013–14, 1,017 students received support. Research assistantships, teaching assistantships, and scholarships/grants available. Financial award application deadline: 9/2. *Unit head:* Silvia Ponce, Director, 514-340-6393, Fax: 514-340-6915, E-mail: silvia.ponce@hec.ca. *Application contact:* Jo Anne Audet, Administrative Director, 514-340-1315, Fax: 514-340-6411, E-mail: joanne.audet@hec.ca.
Website: http://www.hec.ca/programmes_formations/des/maitrises_professionnelles/mmec/index.html.

HEC Montreal, School of Business Administration, Master of Science Programs in Administration, Program in Management and Social Innovations, Montréal, QC H3T 2A7, Canada. Offers M Sc. All courses are given in French. *Students:* 12 full-time (11 women), 3 part-time (2 women). 6 applicants, 100% accepted, 4 enrolled. In 2013, 4 master's awarded. *Degree requirements:* For master's, one foreign language, thesis. *Entrance requirements:* For master's, Test de francais international (TFI) with minimum score of 850 (for those who have never studied in French), BBA, undergraduate degree in another field, degree deemed equivalent by program director and minimum GPA of 3.0 on 4.3 scale. *Application deadline:* For fall admission, 3/15 for domestic and international students; for winter admission, 9/15 for domestic and international students. Application fee: $83. Electronic applications accepted. *Expenses: Tuition, area resident:* Part-time $74.14 per credit. Tuition, state resident: full-time $2669.04; part-time $201.83 per credit. Tuition, nonresident: full-time $7266; part-time $500.59 per credit. *International tuition:* $18,021.24 full-time. *Required fees:* $1529.70; $36.20 per credit. $65.50 per term. Tuition and fees vary according to degree level and program. *Financial support:* In 2013–14, 1,007 students received support. Research assistantships, teaching assistantships, and scholarships/grants available. Financial award application deadline: 9/2. *Unit head:* Dr. Anne Bourhis, Director, 514-340-6873, Fax: 514-340-6880, E-mail: anne.bourhis@hec.ca. *Application contact:* Marianne de Moura, Administrative Director, 514-340-7106, Fax: 514-340-6411, E-mail: marianne.de-moura@hec.ca.
Website: http://www.hec.ca/programmes_formations/msc/options/gestions_innovations_sociales/index.html.

HEC Montreal, School of Business Administration, Master of Science Programs in Administration, Program in Organizational Development, Montréal, QC H3T 2A7, Canada. Offers M Sc. All courses are given in French. *Students:* 43 full-time (34 women), 28 part-time (23 women). 137 applicants, 26% accepted, 17 enrolled. In 2013, 19 master's awarded. *Degree requirements:* For master's, one foreign language, thesis. *Entrance requirements:* For master's, Test de francais international (TFI) with minimum score of 850 (for those who have never studied in French), BBA, undergraduate degree in another field, degree deemed equivalent by program director and minimum GPA of 3.0 on 4.3 scale. *Application deadline:* For fall admission, 3/15 for domestic and international students; for winter admission, 9/15 for domestic and international students. Application fee: $83. Electronic applications accepted. *Expenses: Tuition, area resident:* Part-time $74.14 per credit. Tuition, state resident: full-time $2669.04; part-time $201.83 per credit. Tuition, nonresident: full-time $7266; part-time $500.59 per credit. *International tuition:* $18,021.24 full-time. *Required fees:* $1529.70; $36.20 per credit. $65.50 per term. Tuition and fees vary according to degree level and program. *Financial support:* In 2013–14, 1,007 students received support. Research assistantships, teaching assistantships, and scholarships/grants available. Financial award application deadline: 9/2. *Unit head:* Dr. Anne Bourhis, Director, 514-340-6873, Fax: 514-340-6880, E-mail: anne.bourhis@hec.ca. *Application contact:* Marianne de Moura, Administrative Director, 514-340-7106, Fax: 514-340-6411, E-mail: marianne.de-moura@hec.ca.
Website: http://www.hec.ca/en/programs_training/executiveeducation/seminars/pido.html.

Immaculata University, College of Graduate Studies, Program in Organization Studies, Immaculata, PA 19345. Offers MA. Part-time and evening/weekend programs available. *Degree requirements:* For master's, comprehensive exam, thesis optional. *Entrance requirements:* For master's, GMAT, GRE General Test, MAT, minimum GPA of 3.0. Additional exam requirements/recommendations for international students: Required—TOEFL, IELTS. Electronic applications accepted.

Indiana Tech, Program in Organizational Leadership, Fort Wayne, IN 46803-1297. Offers MS. Part-time and evening/weekend programs available. Postbaccalaureate distance learning degree programs offered (minimal on-campus study). *Students:* 41 full-time (28 women), 34 part-time (25 women); includes 46 minority (42 Black or African American, non-Hispanic/Latino; 2 American Indian or Alaska Native, non-Hispanic/Latino; 1 Hispanic/Latino; 1 Two or more races, non-Hispanic/Latino). Average age 38. *Entrance requirements:* For master's, minimum GPA of 2.5, bachelor's degree from regionally-accredited university, minimum three years of work experience, three letters of recommendation, essay, current resume. *Application deadline:* Applications are processed on a rolling basis. Application fee: $25. Electronic applications accepted. *Expenses: Tuition:* Full-time $8910; part-time $495 per credit. Tuition and fees vary according to course load, degree level and program. *Financial support:* Applicants required to submit FAFSA. *Unit head:* Dr. Jeffrey A. Zimmerman, Dean of Business, 260-422-5561 Ext. 2117, E-mail: jazimmerman@indianatech.edu.

Indiana University Bloomington, School of Public and Environmental Affairs, Public Affairs Programs, Bloomington, IN 47405. Offers economic development (MPA); energy (MPA); environmental policy (PhD); environmental policy and natural resource management (MPA); information systems (MPA); international development (MPA); local government management (MPA); nonprofit management (MPA, Certificate); policy analysis (MPA); public budgeting and financial management (Certificate); public finance (PhD); public financial administration (MPA); public management (MPA, PhD, Certificate); public policy analysis (PhD); social entrepreneurship (Certificate); specialized public affairs (MPA); sustainability and sustainable development (MPA); JD/MPA; MPA/MA; MPA/MIS; MPA/MLS; MSES/MPA. *Accreditation:* NASPAA (one or more programs are accredited). Part-time programs available. *Faculty:* 79 full-time (32 women), 8 part-time/adjunct (3 women). *Students:* 433 full-time (232 women), 75 part-time (39 women); includes 90 minority (19 Black or African American, non-Hispanic/Latino; 1 American Indian or Alaska Native, non-Hispanic/Latino; 49 Asian, non-Hispanic/Latino; 14 Hispanic/Latino; 2 Native Hawaiian or other Pacific Islander, non-Hispanic/Latino; 5 Two or more races, non-Hispanic/Latino), 70 international. Average age 27. 714 applicants, 73% accepted, 253 enrolled. In 2013, 171 master's, 3 doctorates, 4 other advanced degrees awarded. *Degree requirements:* For master's, capstone, internship; for doctorate, comprehensive exam, thesis/dissertation. *Entrance requirements:* For master's, GRE General Test or GMAT, official transcripts, 3 letters of recommendation, resume, personal statement; for doctorate, GRE General Test, official transcripts, 3 letters of recommendation, statement of purpose. Additional exam requirements/recommendations for international students: Required—TOEFL (minimum score 600 paper-based; 96 iBT); Recommended—IELTS (minimum score 7). *Application deadline:* For fall admission, 2/1 priority date for domestic students, 12/1 priority date for international students; for spring admission, 11/15 for domestic students,

9/1 for international students. Applications are processed on a rolling basis. Application fee: $55 ($65 for international students). Electronic applications accepted. *Financial support:* Fellowships with partial tuition reimbursements, research assistantships with full and partial tuition reimbursements, teaching assistantships with full and partial tuition reimbursements, career-related internships or fieldwork, Federal Work-Study, scholarships/grants, health care benefits, unspecified assistantships, and Service Corps Program; Educational Opportunity Fellowships available. Financial award application deadline: 2/1; financial award applicants required to submit FAFSA. *Faculty research:* International development, environmental policy and resource management, policy analysis, public finance, public management, urban management, nonprofit management, energy policy, social policy, public finance. *Unit head:* Megan Siehl, Assistant Director, Admissions and Financial Aid, 812-855-9485, Fax: 812-856-3665, E-mail: speampo@indiana.edu. *Application contact:* Lane Bowman, Admissions Services Coordinator, 812-855-2840, Fax: 812-856-3665, E-mail: speaapps@indiana.edu.
Website: http://www.indiana.edu/~spea/prospective_students/masters/.

Indiana University–Purdue University Fort Wayne, College of Engineering, Technology, and Computer Science, Department of Organizational Leadership and Supervision, Fort Wayne, IN 46805-1499. Offers human resources (MS); leadership (MS); organizational leadership and supervision (Certificate). Part-time programs available. *Faculty:* 4 full-time (1 woman). *Students:* 7 full-time (all women), 22 part-time (13 women); includes 5 minority (2 Black or African American, non-Hispanic/Latino; 1 Asian, non-Hispanic/Latino; 1 Hispanic/Latino; 1 Two or more races, non-Hispanic/Latino), 3 international. Average age 38. 15 applicants, 100% accepted, 10 enrolled. In 2013, 5 master's awarded. *Entrance requirements:* For master's, GRE or GMAT (if undergraduate GPA is below 3.0), current resume, 2 recent letters of recommendation, essay. Additional exam requirements/recommendations for international students: Required—TOEFL (minimum score 550 paper-based; 79 iBT); Recommended—TWE. *Application deadline:* For fall admission, 5/15 for domestic students, 4/1 for international students; for spring admission, 11/15 for domestic students, 10/1 for international students. Applications are processed on a rolling basis. Application fee: $55 ($60 for international students). Electronic applications accepted. *Financial support:* In 2013–14, 3 teaching assistantships with partial tuition reimbursements (averaging $13,322 per year) were awarded; scholarships/grants also available. Support available to part-time students. Financial award application deadline: 3/1; financial award applicants required to submit FAFSA. *Faculty research:* Differentiating between unfairness and envy, affirmative action and cross-cultural conflict, Latina/o scholars. *Unit head:* Dr. Linda Hite, Chair/Professor, 260-481-6416, Fax: 260-481-6417, E-mail: hitel@ipfw.edu. *Application contact:* Dr. Max Montesino, Director of Graduate Studies/Associate Professor, 260-481-6413, Fax: 260-481-6880, E-mail: montesin@ipfw.edu.
Website: http://www.ipfw.edu/ols/.

Indiana University–Purdue University Indianapolis, School of Public and Environmental Affairs, Indianapolis, IN 46202. Offers criminal justice and public safety (MS); homeland security and emergency management (Graduate Certificate); library management (Graduate Certificate); nonprofit management (Graduate Certificate); public affairs (MPA); public management (Graduate Certificate); social entrepreneurship: nonprofit and public benefit organizations (Graduate Certificate); JD/MPA; MLS/NMC; MLS/PMC; MPA/MA. *Accreditation:* CAHME (one or more programs are accredited); NASPAA. Part-time and evening/weekend programs available. Postbaccalaureate distance learning degree programs offered (no on-campus study). *Entrance requirements:* For master's, GRE General Test, GMAT or LSAT, minimum GPA of 3.0 (preferred). Additional exam requirements/recommendations for international students: Required—TOEFL (minimum score 93 iBT), IELTS (minimum score 6.5). Electronic applications accepted. *Faculty research:* Nonprofit and public management, public policy, urban policy, sustainability policy, disaster preparedness and recovery, vehicular safety, homicide, offender rehabilitation and re-entry.

Indiana Wesleyan University, College of Adult and Professional Studies, Graduate Studies in Business, Marion, IN 46953. Offers accounting (MBA, Graduate Certificate); applied management (MBA); business administration (MBA); health care (MBA, Graduate Certificate); human resources (MBA, Graduate Certificate); management (MS); organizational leadership (MA). Part-time and evening/weekend programs available. Postbaccalaureate distance learning degree programs offered (no on-campus study). *Degree requirements:* For master's, applied business or management project. *Entrance requirements:* For master's, minimum GPA of 2.5, 2 years of related work experience. Additional exam requirements/recommendations for international students: Required—TOEFL (minimum score 550 paper-based). Electronic applications accepted. *Expenses:* Tuition: Full-time $8712; part-time $484 per credit hour. *Required fees:* $1673; $105 per credit hour. Tuition and fees vary according to course load, degree level, campus/location and program.

Indiana Wesleyan University, College of Adult and Professional Studies, Graduate Studies in Leadership, Marion, IN 46953. Offers organizational leadership (Ed D). Part-time programs available. Postbaccalaureate distance learning degree programs offered (minimal on-campus study). *Degree requirements:* For doctorate, comprehensive exam, thesis/dissertation, applied field project. *Entrance requirements:* For doctorate, GRE, GMAT. Additional exam requirements/recommendations for international students: Required—TOEFL. *Expenses:* Tuition: Full-time $8712; part-time $484 per credit hour. *Required fees:* $1673; $105 per credit hour. Tuition and fees vary according to course load, degree level, campus/location and program. *Faculty research:* Organizational leadership as a new structural model for research and teaching, wisdom and its application for leaders, stewardship and its application for leaders, followership and its application for leaders, the importance of a world view in establishing authenticity for leaders.

Instituto Tecnologico de Santo Domingo, Graduate School, Area of Business, Santo Domingo, Dominican Republic. Offers banking and securities markets (M Mgmt); corporate finance (M Mgmt); human resources management (M Mgmt, Certificate); international trade management (M Mgmt); marketing (M Mgmt); organizational development (M Mgmt); quality and productivity management (Certificate); tax management and planning (M Mgmt); upper management (M Mgmt).

Jacksonville University, Davis College of Business, Master of Science in Organizational Leadership Program, Jacksonville, FL 32211. Offers MS. Part-time and evening/weekend programs available. *Faculty:* 12 full-time (3 women). *Students:* 10 full-time (4 women), 6 part-time (4 women); includes 6 minority (3 Black or African American, non-Hispanic/Latino; 3 Hispanic/Latino). Average age 32. 13 applicants, 54% accepted, 4 enrolled. *Entrance requirements:* For master's, GMAT or GRE (may be waived for 3.3 or higher undergraduate GPA from AACSB-accredited institution). Additional exam requirements/recommendations for international students: Required—TOEFL, IELTS. *Application deadline:* For fall admission, 8/1 priority date for domestic students, 7/15 priority date for international students; for spring admission, 12/1 priority date for domestic students, 11/15 priority date for international students; for summer admission, 4/1 priority date for domestic students, 3/15 priority date for international students. Applications are processed on a rolling basis. Application fee: $50. Electronic applications accepted. *Expenses:* Contact institution. *Financial support:* In 2013–14, 1 student received support. Scholarships/grants available. Financial award applicants

required to submit FAFSA. *Faculty research:* Ethics; science of a start-up culture; organizational culture; sustainability. *Unit head:* Dr. Mohamad Sepehri, Associate Dean and Graduate Programs Director, 904-256-7435, Fax: 904-256-7168, E-mail: msepehr@ju.edu. *Application contact:* AnnaMaria Murphy, Admissions Counselor, 904-256-7426, Fax: 904-256-7168, E-mail: mba@ju.edu.
Website: http://www.ju.edu/dcob/AcademicPrograms/Pages/Master-of-Science-in-Organizational-Leadership.aspx.

Jacksonville University, School of Education, Jacksonville, FL 32211. Offers educational leadership (M Ed); instructional leadership and organizational development (M Ed); sport management and leadership (M Ed). Part-time and evening/weekend programs available. *Degree requirements:* For master's, comprehensive exam. *Entrance requirements:* For master's, GRE General Test, minimum GPA of 3.0. Additional exam requirements/recommendations for international students: Required—TOEFL (minimum score 550 paper-based), TWE. *Expenses:* Contact institution.

John F. Kennedy University, School of Management, Program in Business Administration, Pleasant Hill, CA 94523-4817. Offers business administration (MBA); organizational leadership (Certificate). Part-time and evening/weekend programs available. *Degree requirements:* For master's, thesis or alternative. *Entrance requirements:* For master's, interview. Additional exam requirements/recommendations for international students: Required—TOEFL.

Jones International University, School of Education, Centennial, CO 80112. Offers adult education (M Ed); corporate training and knowledge management (M Ed); curriculum and instruction (M Ed), including elementary teacher licensure, secondary teacher licensure; e-learning technology and design (M Ed); educational leadership and administration (M Ed); educational leadership and administration: principal and administrator licensure (M Ed); elementary curriculum instruction and assessment (M Ed); higher education leadership and administration (M Ed); K-12 instructional technology (M Ed); K-12 instructional technology: teacher licensure (M Ed); secondary curriculum instruction and assessment (M Ed); technology and design (M Ed). Part-time and evening/weekend programs available. Postbaccalaureate distance learning degree programs offered (no on-campus study). *Entrance requirements:* For master's, minimum cumulative GPA of 2.5. Additional exam requirements/recommendations for international students: Recommended—TOEFL (minimum score 550 paper-based). Electronic applications accepted.

Judson University, Graduate Programs, Program in Organizational Leadership, Elgin, IL 60123-1498. Offers MA. Part-time and evening/weekend programs available. Postbaccalaureate distance learning degree programs offered (no on-campus study). *Degree requirements:* For master's, thesis optional. *Entrance requirements:* For master's, bachelor's degree from regionally-accredited college or university with minimum GPA of 3.0; employment verification form; two letters of reference; essay. Additional exam requirements/recommendations for international students: Required—TOEFL (minimum score 550 paper-based). Electronic applications accepted. *Faculty research:* Leadership, human resource management, public affairs, international marketing.

Kaplan University, Davenport Campus, School of Business, Davenport, IA 52807-2095. Offers business administration (MBA); change leadership (MS); entrepreneurship (MBA); finance (MBA); health care management (MBA, MS); human resource (MBA); international business (MBA); management (MS); marketing (MBA); project management (MBA, MS); supply chain management and logistics (MBA, MS). *Accreditation:* ACBSP. Part-time and evening/weekend programs available. Postbaccalaureate distance learning degree programs offered (no on-campus study). *Entrance requirements:* Additional exam requirements/recommendations for international students: Required—TOEFL (minimum score 550 paper-based; 80 iBT). Electronic applications accepted.

Keiser University, Doctor of Business Administration Program, Ft. Lauderdale, FL 33309. Offers global business (DBA); global organizational leadership (DBA); marketing (DBA).

LaGrange College, Graduate Programs, Program in Organizational Leadership, LaGrange, GA 30240-2999. Offers MA. Program is held on Albany campus. Evening/weekend programs available. *Entrance requirements:* For master's, GRE or MAT, minimum GPA of 2.5, 3 letters of reference. Additional exam requirements/recommendations for international students: Required—TOEFL (minimum score 500 paper-based; 61 iBT). Electronic applications accepted.

Lewis University, College of Arts and Sciences, Program in Organizational Leadership, Romeoville, IL 60446. Offers coaching (MA); higher education/student services (MA); non-for-profit management (MA); organizational management (MA); public administration (MA); training and development (MA). Part-time and evening/weekend programs available. Postbaccalaureate distance learning degree programs offered (no on-campus study). *Students:* 24 full-time (21 women), 200 part-time (152 women); includes 87 minority (60 Black or African American, non-Hispanic/Latino; 2 American Indian or Alaska Native, non-Hispanic/Latino; 4 Asian, non-Hispanic/Latino; 20 Hispanic/Latino; 1 Two or more races, non-Hispanic/Latino), 1 international. Average age 36. *Entrance requirements:* For master's, bachelor's degree, at least 24 years of age, minimum of 3 years of work experience, minimum GPA of 3.0, letter of recommendation. Additional exam requirements/recommendations for international students: Required—TOEFL (minimum score 550 paper-based; 80 iBT). *Application deadline:* For fall admission, 5/1 priority date for international students; for spring admission, 11/15 priority date for international students. Applications are processed on a rolling basis. Application fee: $40. Electronic applications accepted. *Financial support:* Tuition waivers and unspecified assistantships available. Financial award application deadline: 5/1; financial award applicants required to submit FAFSA. *Unit head:* Dr. Keith Lavine, Chair of Organizational Leadership, 815-838-0500, E-mail: lavineke@lewisu.edu. *Application contact:* Julie Branchaw, Assistant Director, Graduate and Adult Admission, 815-836-5574, Fax: 815-836-5578, E-mail: branchju@lewisu.edu.

Lipscomb University, Nelson and Sue Andrews Institute for Civic Leadership, Nashville, TN 37204-3951. Offers MA. Part-time and evening/weekend programs available. *Faculty:* 2 full-time (both women), 1 (woman) part-time/adjunct. *Students:* 18 part-time (15 women); includes 6 minority (all Black or African American, non-Hispanic/Latino). Average age 36. 23 applicants, 100% accepted, 18 enrolled. In 2013, 21 master's awarded. *Degree requirements:* For master's, project, externship. *Entrance requirements:* For master's, GRE, GMAT or MAT, transcripts, 2 references, essay, resume. Additional exam requirements/recommendations for international students: Required—TOEFL (minimum score 570 paper-based). *Application deadline:* Applications are processed on a rolling basis. Application fee: $50 ($75 for international students). Electronic applications accepted. *Expenses:* Contact institution. *Financial support:* Applicants required to submit FAFSA. *Unit head:* Linda Peek Schacht, Executive Director, 615-966-1341, E-mail: linda.schacht@lipscomb.edu. *Application contact:* Melanie Matthews, Program Coordinator, 615-966-6155, E-mail: melanie.matthews@lipscomb.edu.
Website: http://lipscomb.edu/civicleadership.

Lourdes University, Graduate School, Sylvania, OH 43560-2898. Offers business (MBA); leadership (M Ed); nurse anesthesia (MSN); nurse educator (MSN); nurse

leader (MSN); organizational leadership (MOL); reading (M Ed); teaching and curriculum (M Ed); theology (MA). Evening/weekend programs available. *Entrance requirements:* Additional exam requirements/recommendations for international students: Required—TOEFL. *Application deadline:* For fall admission, 6/15 priority date for domestic students; for spring admission, 11/1 priority date for domestic students. Application fee: $25. *Application contact:* Melissa Bergfeld, Administrative Assistant, 419-824-3517, Fax: 419-824-3510, E-mail: mbergfeld2@lourdes.edu.
Website: http://www.lourdes.edu/gradschool.aspx.

Malone University, Graduate Program in Organizational Leadership, Canton, OH 44709. Offers MAOL. Part-time and evening/weekend programs available. *Faculty:* 4 full-time (2 women), 3 part-time/adjunct (0 women). *Students:* 13 full-time (9 women), 57 part-time (36 women); includes 6 minority (all Black or African American, non-Hispanic/Latino). Average age 38. In 2013, 21 master's awarded. *Entrance requirements:* For master's, minimum GPA of 3.0. Additional exam requirements/recommendations for international students: Required—TOEFL (minimum score 550 paper-based; 79 iBT). *Expenses:* Contact institution. *Financial support:* Tuition waivers (partial) available. Support available to part-time students. Financial award application deadline: 6/30. *Faculty research:* Graduates' perceptions of the impact of a Christian higher education. *Unit head:* Dr. Dennis D. Kincaid, Director, 330-471-8186, Fax: 330-471-8563, E-mail: dkincaid@malone.edu. *Application contact:* Natalie D. Denholm, Graduate Recruiter, 330-471-8207, Fax: 330-471-8570, E-mail: ndenholm@malone.edu.
Website: http://www.malone.edu/admissions/graduate/organizational-leadership/.

Manhattanville College, School of Business, Program in Human Resource Management and Organizational Effectiveness, Purchase, NY 10577-2132. Offers MS. Part-time and evening/weekend programs available. *Degree requirements:* For master's, thesis, final project. *Entrance requirements:* For master's, interview, 2 letters of recommendation. Additional exam requirements/recommendations for international students: Required—TOEFL.

Mansfield University of Pennsylvania, Graduate Studies, Program in Organizational Leadership, Mansfield, PA 16933. Offers MA. Postbaccalaureate distance learning degree programs offered.

Marian University, School of Business and Public Safety, Fond du Lac, WI 54935-4699. Offers criminal justice leadership (MS); organizational leadership and quality (MS). Part-time and evening/weekend programs available. *Faculty:* 1 full-time (0 women), 6 part-time/adjunct (2 women). *Students:* 1 full-time (0 women), 53 part-time (31 women); includes 7 minority (3 Black or African American, non-Hispanic/Latino; 1 American Indian or Alaska Native, non-Hispanic/Latino; 2 Asian, non-Hispanic/Latino; 1 Hispanic/Latino). Average age 37. In 2013, 45 master's awarded. *Degree requirements:* For master's, comprehensive group project. *Entrance requirements:* For master's, 3 years of managerial experience, minimum GPA of 2.75, letters of professional reference. Additional exam requirements/recommendations for international students: Required—TOEFL (minimum score 525 paper-based; 70 iBT). *Application deadline:* Applications are processed on a rolling basis. Application fee: $25. Electronic applications accepted. *Expenses:* Contact institution. *Financial support:* In 2013–14, 1 student received support. Institutionally sponsored loans available. Financial award application deadline: 3/1; financial award applicants required to submit FAFSA. *Faculty research:* Organizational values, statistical decision-making, learning organization, quality planning, customer research. *Unit head:* Dr. Jeffrey G. Reed, Dean, Marian School of Business, 920-923-8759, Fax: 920-923-7167, E-mail: jreed@marianuniversity.edu. *Application contact:* Jordan Baitinger, Admission Counselor, 920-923-8609, Fax: 920-923-7167, E-mail: jlbaitinger16@marianuniversity.edu.
Website: http://www.marianuniversity.edu/Academic-Programs/School-of-Business-and-Public-Safety/School-of-Business-and-Public-Safety/.

Maryville University of Saint Louis, College of Arts and Sciences, St. Louis, MO 63141-7299. Offers actuarial science (MS); organizational leadership (MA); strategic communication and leadership (MA). Part-time and evening/weekend programs available. *Faculty:* 5 full-time (4 women), 3 part-time/adjunct (2 women). *Students:* 21 full-time (15 women), 43 part-time (28 women); includes 19 minority (6 Black or African American, non-Hispanic/Latino; 6 Asian, non-Hispanic/Latino; 1 Hispanic/Latino; 6 Two or more races, non-Hispanic/Latino), 5 international. Average age 33. In 2013, 17 master's awarded. *Entrance requirements:* For master's, GRE with minimum score of 600 (for MS), strong mathematics background, 2 letters of recommendation, and personal statement (MS). Additional exam requirements/recommendations for international students: Required—TOEFL (minimum score 550 paper-based; 80 iBT). *Application deadline:* Applications are processed on a rolling basis. Application fee: $40 ($60 for international students). Electronic applications accepted. Application fee is waived when completed online. *Expenses: Tuition:* Full-time $23,812; part-time $728 per credit hour. *Required fees:* $395 per year. Tuition and fees vary according to course load, degree level and program. *Financial support:* Application deadline: 3/1; applicants required to submit FAFSA. *Unit head:* Dr. Candace Chambers, Dean, 314-529-9208, Fax: 314-529-9965, E-mail: cchambers@maryville.edu. *Application contact:* Crystal Jacobsmeyer, Assistant Director, Graduate Enrollment Advising, 314-529-9654, Fax: 314-529-9927, E-mail: cjacobsmeyer@maryville.edu.
Website: http://www.maryville.edu/as/graduate-programs/.

Medaille College, Program in Business Administration - Amherst, Amherst, NY 14221. Offers business administration (MBA); organizational leadership (MA). Evening/weekend programs available. *Faculty:* 20 full-time (17 women), 8 part-time/adjunct (6 women). *Students:* 116 full-time (72 women), 14 part-time (6 women); includes 42 minority (27 Black or African American, non-Hispanic/Latino; 1 American Indian or Alaska Native, non-Hispanic/Latino; 6 Asian, non-Hispanic/Latino; 8 Hispanic/Latino), 6 international. Average age 40. 92 applicants, 89% accepted, 29 enrolled. In 2013, 91 master's awarded. *Degree requirements:* For master's, thesis or alternative. *Entrance requirements:* For master's, GMAT, minimum undergraduate GPA of 2.7, 3 years of work experience. Additional exam requirements/recommendations for international students: Required—TOEFL (minimum score 550 paper-based). *Application deadline:* Applications are processed on a rolling basis. Application fee: $35. Electronic applications accepted. *Expenses:* Contact institution. *Financial support:* Federal Work-Study available. Financial award applicants required to submit FAFSA. *Unit head:* Jennifer Bavifard, Associate Dean for Special Programs, 716-631-1061 Ext. 150, Fax: 716-631-1380, E-mail: jbavifar@medaille.edu. *Application contact:* E-mail: sageadmissions@medaille.edu.
Website: http://www.medaille.edu/.

Medaille College, Program in Business Administration - Rochester, Rochester, NY 14623. Offers business administration (MBA); organizational leadership (MA). Evening/weekend programs available. *Students:* 16 full-time (12 women), 1 part-time (0 women); includes 10 minority (6 Black or African American, non-Hispanic/Latino; 1 Asian, non-Hispanic/Latino; 3 Hispanic/Latino). Average age 32. 19 applicants, 100% accepted, 13 enrolled. In 2013, 13 master's awarded. *Degree requirements:* For master's, thesis or alternative. *Entrance requirements:* For master's, GMAT, 3 years of work experience, minimum undergraduate GPA of 2.7. Additional exam requirements/recommendations for international students: Required—TOEFL (minimum score 550 paper-based). *Application deadline:* Applications are processed on a rolling basis. Application fee: $35. *Expenses:* Contact institution. *Financial support:* Federal Work-Study available. Financial award applicants required to submit FAFSA. *Unit head:* Jennifer Bavifard, Branch Campus Director, 716-932-2591, Fax: 716-631-1380, E-mail: jbavifard@medaille.edu. *Application contact:* E-mail: sageadmissions@medaille.edu.
Website: http://www.medaille.edu/.

Mercer University, Graduate Studies, Cecil B. Day Campus, Penfield College, Macon, GA 31207-0003. Offers clinical mental health (MS); counselor education and supervision (PhD); organizational leadership (MS); public safety leadership (MS); school counseling (MS). *Faculty:* 19 full-time (10 women), 16 part-time/adjunct (12 women). *Students:* 130 full-time (105 women), 233 part-time (188 women); includes 184 minority (159 Black or African American, non-Hispanic/Latino; 11 Asian, non-Hispanic/Latino; 11 Hispanic/Latino; 2 Native Hawaiian or other Pacific Islander, non-Hispanic/Latino; 1 Two or more races, non-Hispanic/Latino), 3 international. Average age 33. In 2013, 80 master's awarded. *Unit head:* Dr. Priscilla R. Danheiser, Dean, 678-547-6028, E-mail: danheiser_p@mercer.edu. *Application contact:* Tracey M. Wofford, Associate Director of Admissions, 678-547-6422, E-mail: wofford_tm@mercer.edu.
Website: http://ccps.mercer.edu/graduate/.

Mercy College, School of Business, Program in Organizational Leadership, Dobbs Ferry, NY 10522-1189. Offers MS. Part-time and evening/weekend programs available. Postbaccalaureate distance learning degree programs offered (no on-campus study). *Students:* 37 full-time (18 women), 2 part-time (1 woman); includes 24 minority (16 Black or African American, non-Hispanic/Latino; 2 Asian, non-Hispanic/Latino; 6 Hispanic/Latino), 1 international. Average age 32. 70 applicants, 79% accepted, 23 enrolled. In 2013, 59 master's awarded. *Entrance requirements:* For master's, interview by program director, resume, 2 letters of reference. Additional exam requirements/recommendations for international students: Required—TOEFL (minimum score 600 paper-based; 100 iBT), IELTS (minimum score 8). *Application deadline:* For fall admission, 8/1 for international students. Applications are processed on a rolling basis. Application fee: $40. Electronic applications accepted. *Expenses:* Contact institution. *Financial support:* Career-related internships or fieldwork, Federal Work-Study, scholarships/grants, and unspecified assistantships available. Support available to part-time students. Financial award applicants required to submit FAFSA. *Unit head:* Ed Weis, Dean, School of Business, 914-674-7490, E-mail: eweis@mercy.edu. *Application contact:* Allison Gurdineer, Senior Director of Admissions, 877-637-2946, E-mail: admissions@mercy.edu.
Website: https://www.mercy.edu/academics/school-of-business/department-of-business-administration/ms-in-organizational-leadership/.

Mercyhurst University, Graduate Studies, Program in Organizational Leadership, Erie, PA 16546. Offers accounting (MS); entrepreneurship (MS); higher education administration (MS); human resources (MS); nonprofit management (MS); organizational leadership (Certificate); sports leadership (MS). Part-time and evening/weekend programs available. *Degree requirements:* For master's, thesis. *Entrance requirements:* For master's, GRE General Test or MAT, interview, resume, essay, three professional references, transcripts. Additional exam requirements/recommendations for international students: Required—TOEFL. Electronic applications accepted. *Faculty research:* Leadership training, organizational communication, leadership pedagogy.

Mid-America Christian University, Program in Leadership, Oklahoma City, OK 73170-4504. Offers MA. *Entrance requirements:* For master's, bachelor's degree from a regionally accredited college or university, minimum overall cumulative GPA of 2.75 of bachelor course work. Additional exam requirements/recommendations for international students: Required—TOEFL (minimum score 550 paper-based).

MidAmerica Nazarene University, Graduate Studies in Management, Olathe, KS 66062-1899. Offers management (MBA); organizational administration (MA), including finance, international business, leadership, non-profit. Evening/weekend programs available. *Entrance requirements:* For master's, mathematical assessment, minimum undergraduate GPA of 3.0, letters of recommendation. Additional exam requirements/recommendations for international students: Required—TOEFL. Electronic applications accepted. *Faculty research:* Economic development, international finance, business development, employee evaluation.

Midway College, Graduate Programs, Midway, KY 40347-1120. Offers education (MAT); leadership (MBA). *Degree requirements:* For master's, capstone course. *Entrance requirements:* For master's, GMAT (for MBA); GRE or PRAXIS I (for MAT), bachelor's degree; interview; minimum GPA of 3.0 (for MBA), 2.75 (for MAT); 3 years of professional work experience (for MBA). Additional exam requirements/recommendations for international students: Required—TOEFL (minimum score 550 paper-based; 80 iBT).

Misericordia University, College of Professional Studies and Social Sciences, Program in Organizational Management, Dallas, PA 18612-1098. Offers human resource management (MS); information technology management (MS); management (MS); not-for-profit management (MS). Part-time and evening/weekend programs available. Postbaccalaureate distance learning degree programs offered (no on-campus study). *Faculty:* 3 full-time (0 women), 6 part-time/adjunct (0 women). *Students:* 82 part-time (53 women); includes 2 minority (1 Hispanic/Latino; 1 Native Hawaiian or other Pacific Islander, non-Hispanic/Latino). Average age 33. In 2013, 25 master's awarded. *Entrance requirements:* For master's, GRE General Test, MAT (35th percentile or higher), or minimum undergraduate GPA of 3.0. Additional exam requirements/recommendations for international students: Required—TOEFL. *Application deadline:* Applications are processed on a rolling basis. Application fee: $35. Electronic applications accepted. Application fee is waived when completed online. *Expenses:* Contact institution. *Financial support:* In 2013–14, 55 students received support. Scholarships/grants available. Support available to part-time students. Financial award application deadline: 6/30; financial award applicants required to submit FAFSA. *Unit head:* Dr. Timothy Kearney, Chair of Business Department, 570-674-1487, E-mail: tkearney@misericordia.edu. *Application contact:* David Pasquini, Assistant Director of Admissions, 570-674-8183, Fax: 570-674-6232, E-mail: dpasquin@misericordia.edu.
Website: http://www.misericordia.edu/om.

Mount St. Joseph University, Master of Science in Organizational Leadership Program, Cincinnati, OH 45233-1670. Offers MS. Part-time and evening/weekend programs available. *Faculty:* 7 full-time (4 women). *Students:* 1 full-time (0 women), 71 part-time (41 women); includes 8 minority (3 Black or African American, non-Hispanic/Latino; 2 Hispanic/Latino; 3 Two or more races, non-Hispanic/Latino). Average age 40. 83 applicants, 71% accepted, 35 enrolled. In 2013, 11 master's awarded. *Degree requirements:* For master's, integrative project. *Entrance requirements:* For master's, minimum GPA of 3.0, interview, 3 years of work experience, 3 letters of reference, resume, letter of intent, essay. Additional exam requirements/recommendations for international students: Required—TOEFL (minimum score 560 paper-based; 83 iBT). *Application deadline:* Applications are processed on a rolling basis. Application fee: $50. Electronic applications accepted. *Expenses:* Contact institution. *Financial support:* Application deadline: 6/1; applicants required to submit FAFSA. *Faculty research:* Gender and cultural effects on management education, group identity formation, leadership skill development, methods for improving instructional effectiveness, technology-based productivity improvement. *Unit head:* Daryl Smith, Chair, 513-244-4920, Fax: 513-244-4270, E-mail: daryl_smith@mail.msj.edu. *Application contact:* Mary

Brigham, Assistant Director of Graduate Recruitment, 513-244-4233, Fax: 513-244-4629, E-mail: mary_brigham@mail.msj.edu.
Website: http://www.msj.edu/academics/graduate-programs/master-of-science-in-organizational-leadership-program/.

National University, Academic Affairs, School of Business and Management, La Jolla, CA 92037-1011. Offers accountancy (Certificate); business administration (GMBA, MBA), including financial management (MBA), human resource management (MBA), integrated marketing communications (MBA), international business (MBA), management accounting (MBA), marketing (MBA), mobile marketing and social media (MBA), organizational leadership (MA, MBA), professional golf management (MBA); global management (MGM); human resource management (MA), including organizational development and change, organizational leadership (MA, MBA); international business (Certificate); management information systems (MS); organizational leadership (MS), including community development; sustainability management (MS). Part-time and evening/weekend programs available. Postbaccalaureate distance learning degree programs offered (no on-campus study). *Faculty:* 30 full-time (8 women), 88 part-time/adjunct (25 women). *Students:* 688 full-time (357 women), 331 part-time (161 women); includes 453 minority (105 Black or African American, non-Hispanic/Latino; 2 American Indian or Alaska Native, non-Hispanic/Latino; 143 Asian, non-Hispanic/Latino; 162 Hispanic/Latino; 13 Native Hawaiian or other Pacific Islander, non-Hispanic/Latino; 28 Two or more races, non-Hispanic/Latino), 165 international. Average age 33. 286 applicants, 100% accepted, 217 enrolled. In 2013, 641 master's awarded. *Degree requirements:* For master's, thesis (for some programs). *Entrance requirements:* For master's, interview, minimum GPA of 2.5. Additional exam requirements/recommendations for international students: Required—TOEFL (minimum score 550 paper-based; 79 iBT), IELTS (minimum score 6). *Application deadline:* Applications are processed on a rolling basis. Application fee: $60 ($65 for international students). Electronic applications accepted. *Expenses: Tuition:* Full-time $13,824; part-time $1728 per course. One-time fee: $160. *Financial support:* Career-related internships or fieldwork, scholarships/grants, and tuition waivers (partial) available. Support available to part-time students. Financial award application deadline: 6/30; financial award applicants required to submit FAFSA. *Unit head:* School of Business and Management, 800-628-8648, Fax: 858-642-8719, E-mail: sobm@nu.edu. *Application contact:* Louis Cruz, Interim Vice President for Enrollment Services, 800-628-8648, E-mail: advisor@nu.edu.
Website: http://www.nu.edu/OurPrograms/SchoolOfBusinessAndManagement.html.

National University, Academic Affairs, School of Professional Studies, La Jolla, CA 92037-1011. Offers criminal justice (MCJ); digital cinema (MFA); digital journalism (MA); juvenile justice (MS); professional screen writing (MFA); public administration (MPA), including human resource management, organizational leadership, public finance. Part-time and evening/weekend programs available. Postbaccalaureate distance learning degree programs offered (no on-campus study). *Faculty:* 14 full-time (6 women), 28 part-time/adjunct (8 women). *Students:* 265 full-time (140 women), 130 part-time (69 women); includes 233 minority (90 Black or African American, non-Hispanic/Latino; 3 American Indian or Alaska Native, non-Hispanic/Latino; 23 Asian, non-Hispanic/Latino; 92 Hispanic/Latino; 8 Native Hawaiian or other Pacific Islander, non-Hispanic/Latino; 17 Two or more races, non-Hispanic/Latino), 4 international. Average age 37. 89 applicants, 100% accepted, 70 enrolled. *Degree requirements:* For master's, thesis (for some programs). *Entrance requirements:* For master's, interview, minimum GPA of 2.5. Additional exam requirements/recommendations for international students: Required—TOEFL (minimum score 550 paper-based; 79 iBT), IELTS (minimum score 6). *Application deadline:* Applications are processed on a rolling basis. Application fee: $60 ($65 for international students). Electronic applications accepted. *Expenses: Tuition:* Full-time $13,824; part-time $1728 per course. One-time fee: $160. *Financial support:* Career-related internships or fieldwork, institutionally sponsored loans, scholarships/grants, and tuition waivers (partial) available. Support available to part-time students. Financial award application deadline: 6/30; financial award applicants required to submit FAFSA. *Unit head:* School of Professional Studies, 800-628-8648, E-mail: sops@nu.edu. *Application contact:* Louis Cruz, Interim Vice President for Enrollment Services, 800-628-8648, E-mail: advisor@nu.edu.
Website: http://www.nu.edu/OurPrograms/School-of-Professional-Studies.html.

Newman University, Master of Education Program, Wichita, KS 67213-2097. Offers building leadership (MS Ed); curriculum and instruction (MS Ed), including English as a second language, reading specialist; organizational leadership (MS Ed). *Accreditation:* NCATE. Part-time and evening/weekend programs available. Postbaccalaureate distance learning degree programs offered (no on-campus study). *Faculty:* 3 full-time (1 woman), 22 part-time/adjunct (all women). *Students:* 19 full-time (15 women), 498 part-time (407 women); includes 66 minority (19 Black or African American, non-Hispanic/Latino; 5 American Indian or Alaska Native, non-Hispanic/Latino; 10 Asian, non-Hispanic/Latino; 27 Hispanic/Latino; 1 Native Hawaiian or other Pacific Islander, non-Hispanic/Latino; 4 Two or more races, non-Hispanic/Latino). Average age 37. 67 applicants, 73% accepted, 35 enrolled. In 2013, 53 master's awarded. *Degree requirements:* For master's, thesis optional. *Entrance requirements:* For master's, 3 years' full-time teaching experience, minimum GPA of 3.0, writing sample, 2 letters of recommendation, evidence of teaching certification. Additional exam requirements/recommendations for international students: Required—TOEFL (minimum score 600 paper-based; 100 iBT). *Application deadline:* For fall admission, 8/15 priority date for domestic students, 7/15 priority date for international students; for spring admission, 1/10 priority date for domestic students, 11/15 priority date for international students. Applications are processed on a rolling basis. Application fee: $25 ($40 for international students). Electronic applications accepted. *Expenses:* Contact institution. *Financial support:* Application deadline: 8/15; applicants required to submit FAFSA. *Unit head:* Dr. Gina Marx, Director of Graduate Education, 316-942-4291 Ext. 2416, Fax: 316-942-4483, E-mail: marxg@newmanu.edu. *Application contact:* Linda Kay Sabala, Director of Graduate Admissions, 316-942-4291 Ext. 2230, Fax: 316-942-4483, E-mail: sabalal@newmanu.edu.
Website: http://www.newmanu.edu/studynu/graduate/master-science-education.

Newman University, MBA Program, Wichita, KS 67213-2097. Offers finance (MBA); international business (MBA); leadership (MBA); management (MBA); management information technology (MBA). Part-time programs available. *Faculty:* 7 full-time (1 woman), 7 part-time/adjunct (4 women). *Students:* 31 full-time (19 women), 56 part-time (24 women); includes 24 minority (6 Black or African American, non-Hispanic/Latino; 1 American Indian or Alaska Native, non-Hispanic/Latino; 9 Asian, non-Hispanic/Latino; 5 Hispanic/Latino; 3 Two or more races, non-Hispanic/Latino), 9 international. Average age 31. 83 applicants, 63% accepted, 32 enrolled. In 2013, 47 master's awarded. *Degree requirements:* For master's, thesis optional. *Entrance requirements:* For master's, minimum GPA of 3.0; 2 letters of recommendation; course work in algebra, statistics, macroeconomics, and financial accounting. Additional exam requirements/recommendations for international students: Required—TOEFL (minimum score 600 paper-based; 100 iBT). *Application deadline:* For fall admission, 8/1 priority date for domestic students, 7/15 priority date for international students; for winter admission, 1/1 priority date for domestic students; for spring admission, 1/1 priority date for domestic students, 11/15 priority date for international students. Applications are processed on a rolling basis. Application fee: $25 ($40 for international students). Electronic applications accepted. *Expenses:* Contact institution. *Financial support:* In 2013–14, 8 students received support. Scholarships/grants available. Financial award application deadline: 8/15; financial award applicants required to submit FAFSA. *Unit head:* Dr. Wendy Munday, Director of MBA Program, 316-942-4291 Ext. 2296, Fax: 316-942-4483, E-mail: mundayw@newmanu.edu. *Application contact:* Linda Kay Sabala, Director of Graduate Admissions, 316-942-4291 Ext. 2230, Fax: 316-942-4483, E-mail: sabalal@newmanu.edu.
Website: http://www.newmanu.edu.

The New School, Milano The New School for Management and Urban Policy, Program in Organizational Change Management, New York, NY 10011. Offers MS. Part-time and evening/weekend programs available. *Degree requirements:* For master's, thesis. *Entrance requirements:* For master's, 3 years of work experience, interview. Additional exam requirements/recommendations for international students: Required—TOEFL (minimum score 600 paper-based; 100 iBT). Electronic applications accepted.

New York University, Leonard N. Stern School of Business, Department of Management and Organizations, New York, NY 10012-1019. Offers management organizations (MBA); organization theory (PhD); organizational behavior (PhD); strategy (PhD). *Expenses: Tuition:* Full-time $35,856; part-time $1494 per unit. *Required fees:* $1408; $64 per unit. $473 per term. Tuition and fees vary according to course load and program. *Faculty research:* Strategic management, managerial cognition, interpersonal processes, conflict and negotiation.

New York University, School of Continuing and Professional Studies, Division of Programs in Business, Program in Leadership and Human Capital Management, New York, NY 10012-1019. Offers benefits and compensation (Advanced Certificate); human resource management (Advanced Certificate); human resource management and development (MS), including human resource development, human resource management, organizational effectiveness; organizational and executive coaching (Advanced Certificate). Part-time and evening/weekend programs available. Postbaccalaureate distance learning degree programs offered (no on-campus study). *Faculty:* 1 (woman) full-time, 49 part-time/adjunct (25 women). *Students:* 73 full-time (54 women), 161 part-time (140 women); includes 66 minority (25 Black or African American, non-Hispanic/Latino; 22 Asian, non-Hispanic/Latino; 14 Hispanic/Latino; 1 Native Hawaiian or other Pacific Islander, non-Hispanic/Latino; 4 Two or more races, non-Hispanic/Latino), 61 international. Average age 29. 239 applicants, 62% accepted, 72 enrolled. In 2013, 77 master's, 11 other advanced degrees awarded. *Degree requirements:* For master's, thesis. *Entrance requirements:* For master's, bachelor's degree, resume with relevant professional work, internship or volunteer experience, two letters of recommendation, statement of purpose. Additional exam requirements/recommendations for international students: Required—TOEFL (minimum score 600 paper-based; 100 iBT), IELTS (minimum score 7). *Application deadline:* For fall admission, 2/1 priority date for domestic and international students; for spring admission, 10/15 priority date for domestic students, 8/15 priority date for international students. Applications are processed on a rolling basis. Application fee: $150. Electronic applications accepted. *Expenses: Tuition:* Full-time $35,856; part-time $1494 per unit. *Required fees:* $1408; $64 per unit. $473 per term. Tuition and fees vary according to course load and program. *Financial support:* In 2013–14, 98 students received support, including 98 fellowships (averaging $1,944 per year). *Unit head:* Vish Ganpati, Academic Director, 212-998-7112, E-mail: vg36@nyu.edu. *Application contact:* Admissions Office, 212-998-7100, E-mail: scps.gradadmissions@nyu.edu.
Website: http://www.scps.nyu.edu/areas-of-study/leadership/.

Nichols College, Graduate and Professional Studies, Dudley, MA 01571-5000. Offers business administration (MBA); organizational leadership (MSOL). Part-time and evening/weekend programs available. Postbaccalaureate distance learning degree programs offered (no on-campus study). *Degree requirements:* For master's, project (for MOL). *Entrance requirements:* For master's, 2 letters of recommendation, current resume, official transcripts, 800-word personal statement. Additional exam requirements/recommendations for international students: Required—TOEFL (minimum score 500 paper-based). Electronic applications accepted.

North Central College, Graduate and Continuing Studies Programs, Program in Leadership Studies, Naperville, IL 60566-7063. Offers higher education leadership (MLD); professional leadership (MLD); social entrepreneurship (MLD); sports leadership (MLD). Part-time and evening/weekend programs available. *Faculty:* 9 full-time (1 woman), 16 part-time/adjunct (9 women). *Students:* 42 full-time (24 women), 24 part-time (8 women); includes 16 minority (10 Black or African American, non-Hispanic/Latino; 6 Hispanic/Latino), 4 international. Average age 28. 104 applicants, 51% accepted, 23 enrolled. In 2013, 36 master's awarded. *Degree requirements:* For master's, thesis optional, project. *Entrance requirements:* For master's, interview. Additional exam requirements/recommendations for international students: Required—TOEFL (minimum score 570 paper-based; 90 iBT). *Application deadline:* For fall admission, 8/15 for domestic students; for winter admission, 12/1 for domestic students; for spring admission, 2/1 for domestic students. Applications are processed on a rolling basis. Application fee: $25. *Expenses:* Contact institution. *Financial support:* In 2013–14, 1 student received support. Scholarships/grants available. Support available to part-time students. *Unit head:* Dr. Thomas Cavenagh, Program Coordinator, Leadership Studies, 630-637-5285. *Application contact:* Wendy Kulpinski, Director of Graduate and Continuing Education Admission, 630-637-5808, Fax: 630-637-5844, E-mail: wekulpinski@noctrl.edu.

Northeastern University, School of Education, Boston, MA 02115-5096. Offers curriculum, teaching, learning, and leadership (Ed D); elementary licensure (MAT); higher education administration (MAT, Ed D); Jewish education leadership (Ed D); learning and instruction (M Ed); organizational leadership studies (Ed D); secondary licensure (MAT); special education (M Ed). Part-time and evening/weekend programs available.

Northern Kentucky University, Office of Graduate Programs, College of Business, Program in Executive Leadership and Organizational Change, Highland Heights, KY 41099. Offers MS. Part-time and evening/weekend programs available. *Faculty:* 3 full-time (2 women), 1 part-time/adjunct (0 women). *Students:* 43 part-time (17 women); includes 8 minority (4 Black or African American, non-Hispanic/Latino; 2 Hispanic/Latino; 2 Two or more races, non-Hispanic/Latino). Average age 37. 40 applicants, 68% accepted, 24 enrolled. In 2013, 23 master's awarded. *Degree requirements:* For master's, field research project. *Entrance requirements:* For master's, minimum GPA of 2.5; essay on professional career objective; 3 letters of recommendation, 1 from a current organization; 3 years of professional or managerial work experience; full-time employment at time of entry. Additional exam requirements/recommendations for international students: Required—TOEFL (minimum score 600 paper-based; 79 iBT); Recommended—IELTS (minimum score 6.5). *Application deadline:* For fall admission, 6/15 for domestic students, 6/1 priority date for international students. Applications are processed on a rolling basis. Application fee: $40. Electronic applications accepted. *Expenses:* Contact institution. *Financial support:* In 2013–14, 9 students received support. Unspecified assistantships available. Financial award applicants required to submit FAFSA. *Faculty research:* Organizational change, assessment and development, strategy development and systems thinking, global leadership and sustainable changes. *Unit head:* Dr. Kenneth Rhee, Program Director, 859-572-6310,

Fax: 859-572-5150, E-mail: rhee@nku.edu. *Application contact:* Amberly Hurst-Nutini, Coordinator, 859-572-5947, Fax: 859-572-5150, E-mail: hurstam@nku.edu.
Website: http://cob.nku.edu/graduatedegrees/eloc.html.

Northwestern University, The Graduate School, Kellogg School of Management, Department of Management and Organizations, Evanston, IL 60208. Offers PhD. Admissions and degree offered through The Graduate School. *Degree requirements:* For doctorate, comprehensive exam, thesis/dissertation. *Entrance requirements:* For doctorate, GMAT or GRE General Test. Additional exam requirements/recommendations for international students: Required—TOEFL. Electronic applications accepted. *Faculty research:* Bargaining and negotiation, organizational design, decision-making, organizational change, strategic alliances.

Northwestern University, The Graduate School, Kellogg School of Management, Management Programs, Evanston, IL 60208. Offers accounting information and management (MBA, PhD); analytical finance (MBA); business administration (MBA); decision sciences (MBA); entrepreneurship and innovation (MBA); finance (MBA, PhD); health enterprise management (MBA); human resources management (MBA); international business (MBA); management and organizations (MBA, PhD); management and organizations and sociology (PhD); management and strategy (MBA); management studies (MS); managerial analytics (MBA); managerial economics (MBA); managerial economics and strategy (PhD); marketing (MBA, PhD); marketing management (MBA); media management (MBA); operations management (MBA, PhD); real estate (MBA); social enterprise at Kellogg (MBA); JD/MBA. Part-time and evening/weekend programs available. Terminal master's awarded for partial completion of doctoral program. *Degree requirements:* For doctorate, thesis/dissertation, 2 years of coursework, qualifying (field) exam and candidacy, summer research papers and presentations to faculty, proposal defense, final exam/defense. *Entrance requirements:* For master's, GMAT, GRE, interview, 2 letters of recommendation, college transcripts, resume, essays, Kellogg honor code; for doctorate, GMAT, GRE, statement of purpose, transcripts, 2 letters of recommendation, resume, interview. Additional exam requirements/recommendations for international students: Required—TOEFL, IELTS. Electronic applications accepted. *Expenses:* Contact institution. *Faculty research:* Business cycles and international finance, health policy, networks, non-market strategy, consumer psychology.

Northwestern University, The Graduate School, School of Education and Social Policy, Program in Learning and Organizational Change, Evanston, IL 60208. Offers MS. Part-time and evening/weekend programs available. Postbaccalaureate distance learning degree programs offered (minimal on-campus study). *Degree requirements:* For master's, thesis, practicum. *Entrance requirements:* For master's, GRE or GMAT (recommended), letters of recommendation. Additional exam requirements/recommendations for international students: Required—TOEFL (minimum score 600 paper-based; 100 iBT); Recommended—IELTS (minimum score 7). Electronic applications accepted. *Faculty research:* Strategic change, learning and performance, workplace learning, leadership development, cognitive design, knowledge management.

Northwest University, School of Business and Management, Kirkland, WA 98033. Offers business administration (MBA); international business (MBA); project management (MBA); social entrepreneurship (MBA). *Accreditation:* ACBSP. Part-time and evening/weekend programs available. *Degree requirements:* For master's, formalized research. *Entrance requirements:* For master's, GMAT. Additional exam requirements/recommendations for international students: Required—TOEFL (minimum score 550 paper-based; 75 iBT). *Application deadline:* For fall admission, 8/1 for domestic and international students; for spring admission, 12/1 for domestic and international students. Application fee: $75. Electronic applications accepted. *Expenses:* Contact institution. *Financial support:* Federal Work-Study, scholarships/grants, health care benefits, and tuition waivers (full and partial) available. Financial award applicants required to submit FAFSA. *Unit head:* Dr. Teresa Gillespie, Dean, 425-889-5290, E-mail: teresa.gillespie@northwestu.edu. *Application contact:* Aaron Oosterwyk, Director of Graduate and Professional Studies Enrollment, 425-889-7792, Fax: 425-803-3059, E-mail: aaron.oosterwyk@northwestu.edu.
Website: http://www.northwestu.edu/business/.

Norwich University, College of Graduate and Continuing Studies, Master of Business Administration Program, Northfield, VT 05663. Offers finance (MBA); organizational leadership (MBA); project management (MBA). *Accreditation:* ACBSP. Evening/weekend programs available. Postbaccalaureate distance learning degree programs offered (minimal on-campus study). *Faculty:* 16 part-time/adjunct (6 women). *Students:* 198 full-time (57 women); includes 33 minority (18 Black or African American, non-Hispanic/Latino; 9 Asian, non-Hispanic/Latino; 3 Hispanic/Latino; 3 Two or more races, non-Hispanic/Latino). Average age 36. 200 applicants, 41% accepted, 82 enrolled. In 2013, 89 master's awarded. *Degree requirements:* For master's, comprehensive exam, thesis optional. *Entrance requirements:* For master's, minimum undergraduate GPA of 2.75. Additional exam requirements/recommendations for international students: Required—TOEFL (minimum score 600 paper-based; 94 iBT). *Application deadline:* For fall admission, 8/1 for domestic and international students; for winter admission, 11/1 for domestic and international students; for spring admission, 2/1 for domestic and international students; for summer admission, 5/1 for domestic and international students. Applications are processed on a rolling basis. Application fee: $50. Electronic applications accepted. *Expenses:* Contact institution. *Financial support:* In 2013–14, 65 students received support. Scholarships/grants available. Financial award applicants required to submit FAFSA. *Unit head:* Dr. Jose Cordova, Program Director, 802-485-2567, Fax: 802-485-2533, E-mail: jcordova@norwich.edu. *Application contact:* Ashley Farren, Associate Program Director, 802-485-2748, Fax: 802-485-2533, E-mail: afarren@norwich.edu.
Website: http://online.norwich.edu/degree-programs/masters/master-business-administration/overview.

Norwich University, College of Graduate and Continuing Studies, Master of Public Administration Program, Northfield, VT 05663. Offers criminal justice studies (MPA); fiscal management (MPA); international development and influence (MPA); leadership (MPA); organizational leadership (MPA); public works administration (MPA). Evening/weekend programs available. Postbaccalaureate distance learning degree programs offered (minimal on-campus study). *Faculty:* 8 part-time/adjunct (6 women). *Students:* 97 full-time (33 women); includes 23 minority (9 Black or African American, non-Hispanic/Latino; 3 Asian, non-Hispanic/Latino; 3 Hispanic/Latino; 8 Two or more races, non-Hispanic/Latino). Average age 38. 101 applicants, 36% accepted, 35 enrolled. In 2013, 76 master's awarded. *Entrance requirements:* Additional exam requirements/recommendations for international students: Required—TOEFL (minimum score 600 paper-based; 94 iBT). *Application deadline:* For fall admission, 8/1 for domestic and international students; for winter admission, 11/1 for domestic and international students; for spring admission, 2/1 for domestic and international students; for summer admission, 5/1 for domestic and international students. Applications are processed on a rolling basis. Application fee: $50. Electronic applications accepted. *Expenses:* Contact institution. *Financial support:* In 2013–14, 35 students received support. Scholarships/grants available. Financial award applicants required to submit FAFSA. *Faculty research:* Pre-employment investigations for public safety professionals, sustainability programs and policy implementation, innovative voting procedures. *Unit head:* Dr. Rosemarie Pelletier, Program Director, 802-485-2767, Fax: 802-485-2533, E-mail: rpellet2@norwich.edu. *Application contact:* Elizabeth Templeton, Associate Program Director, 802-485-2757, Fax: 802-485-2533, E-mail: etemplet@norwich.edu.
Website: http://online.norwich.edu/degree-programs/masters/master-public-administration/overview.

Norwich University, College of Graduate and Continuing Studies, Master of Science in Organizational Leadership Program, Northfield, VT 05663. Offers leadership (MS). Evening/weekend programs available. Postbaccalaureate distance learning degree programs offered (minimal on-campus study). *Faculty:* 10 part-time/adjunct (3 women). *Students:* 94 full-time (35 women); includes 15 minority (9 Black or African American, non-Hispanic/Latino; 1 American Indian or Alaska Native, non-Hispanic/Latino; 2 Asian, non-Hispanic/Latino; 3 Two or more races, non-Hispanic/Latino). Average age 40. 106 applicants, 35% accepted, 37 enrolled. In 2013, 48 master's awarded. *Entrance requirements:* Additional exam requirements/recommendations for international students: Required—TOEFL (minimum score 600 paper-based; 94 iBT). *Application deadline:* For fall admission, 8/1 for domestic and international students; for winter admission, 11/1 for domestic and international students; for spring admission, 2/1 for domestic and international students; for summer admission, 5/1 for domestic and international students. Applications are processed on a rolling basis. Application fee: $50. Electronic applications accepted. *Expenses:* Contact institution. *Financial support:* In 2013–14, 46 students received support. Scholarships/grants available. Financial award applicants required to submit FAFSA. *Faculty research:* Portable computing in high risk team dynamics. *Unit head:* Dr. Stacie Morgan, Program Director, 802-485-2866, Fax: 802-485-2533, E-mail: smorgan3@norwich.edu. *Application contact:* Elizabeth Templeton, Associate Program Director, 802-485-2757, Fax: 802-485-2533, E-mail: etemplet@norwich.edu.
Website: http://online.norwich.edu/admissions/masters-admissions/master-science-leadership.

Nyack College, School of Business and Leadership, Nyack, NY 10960-3698. Offers business administration (MBA); organizational leadership (MS). Evening/weekend programs available. Postbaccalaureate distance learning degree programs offered (no on-campus study). *Students:* 75 full-time (40 women), 53 part-time (29 women); includes 95 minority (65 Black or African American, non-Hispanic/Latino; 1 American Indian or Alaska Native, non-Hispanic/Latino; 2 Asian, non-Hispanic/Latino; 24 Hispanic/Latino; 3 Two or more races, non-Hispanic/Latino), 13 international. Average age 35. In 2013, 95 master's awarded. *Degree requirements:* For master's, thesis (for some programs). *Entrance requirements:* For master's, GMAT (for MBA only), transcripts, personal goals statement, recommendations, resume, interview. Additional exam requirements/recommendations for international students: Required—TOEFL (minimum score 550 paper-based; 83 iBT). *Application deadline:* Applications are processed on a rolling basis. Application fee: $50. Electronic applications accepted. *Expenses:* Contact institution. *Financial support:* Applicants required to submit FAFSA. *Unit head:* Dr. Anita Underwood, Dean, 845-675-4511, Fax: 845-353-5812. *Application contact:* Traci Piescki, Director of Admissions, 800-541-6891, Fax: 845-348-3912, E-mail: admissions.grad@nyack.edu.
Website: http://www.nyack.edu/sbl.

Oklahoma Christian University, Graduate School of Business, Oklahoma City, OK 73136-1100. Offers accounting (MBA); electronic business (MBA); financial services (MBA); health services management (MBA); human resources (MBA); international business (MBA); leadership and organizational development (MBA); marketing (MBA); project management (MBA). Postbaccalaureate distance learning degree programs offered (no on-campus study). *Entrance requirements:* For master's, bachelor's degree. Electronic applications accepted.

Olivet Nazarene University, Program in Organizational Leadership, Bourbonnais, IL 60914. Offers MOL.

Our Lady of the Lake University of San Antonio, School of Business and Leadership, Program in Leadership Studies, San Antonio, TX 78207-4689. Offers PhD. Part-time and evening/weekend programs available. *Faculty:* 12 full-time (5 women), 4 part-time/adjunct (1 woman). *Students:* 239 full-time (140 women), 17 part-time (10 women); includes 193 minority (39 Black or African American, non-Hispanic/Latino; 1 American Indian or Alaska Native, non-Hispanic/Latino; 1 Asian, non-Hispanic/Latino; 151 Hispanic/Latino; 1 Native Hawaiian or other Pacific Islander, non-Hispanic/Latino). Average age 45. 176 applicants, 50% accepted, 54 enrolled. In 2013, 18 doctorates awarded. *Degree requirements:* For doctorate, thesis/dissertation, internship, qualifying exam. *Entrance requirements:* For doctorate, GRE General Test or MAT, interview. Additional exam requirements/recommendations for international students: Required—TOEFL. *Application deadline:* For fall admission, 3/1 for domestic students. Applications are processed on a rolling basis. Application fee: $25 ($50 for international students). Electronic applications accepted. *Expenses: Tuition:* Full-time $9120; part-time $760 per credit. *Required fees:* $698; $334 per trimester. Tuition and fees vary according to course load, degree level, campus/location and program. *Financial support:* Fellowships, career-related internships or fieldwork, and tuition waivers (partial) available. Financial award application deadline: 4/15. *Faculty research:* Teamwork, ethics, communication, strategy, research methodology. *Unit head:* Dr. Esther Gergen, Chair of Leadership Department, 210-434-6711 Ext. 2287, E-mail: esgergen@lake.ollusa.edu. *Application contact:* Graduate Admission, 210-434-3961, Fax: 210-431-4013, E-mail: gradadm@ollusa.edu.
Website: http://www.ollusa.edu/s/1190/ollu-3-column-noads.aspx?sid=1190&gid=1&pgid=1751.

Our Lady of the Lake University of San Antonio, School of Business and Leadership, Program in Organizational Leadership, San Antonio, TX 78207-4689. Offers MS. Part-time and evening/weekend programs available. Postbaccalaureate distance learning degree programs offered (no on-campus study). *Faculty:* 7 full-time (4 women), 5 part-time/adjunct (2 women). *Students:* 57 full-time (43 women), 10 part-time (7 women); includes 54 minority (5 Black or African American, non-Hispanic/Latino; 1 Asian, non-Hispanic/Latino; 48 Hispanic/Latino). Average age 37. 38 applicants, 84% accepted, 20 enrolled. In 2013, 35 master's awarded. *Entrance requirements:* For master's, GMAT, GRE General Test, or MAT. Additional exam requirements/recommendations for international students: Required—TOEFL. *Application deadline:* Applications are processed on a rolling basis. Application fee: $25 ($50 for international students). Electronic applications accepted. *Expenses: Tuition:* Full-time $9120; part-time $760 per credit. *Required fees:* $698; $334 per trimester. Tuition and fees vary according to course load, degree level, campus/location and program. *Financial support:* Fellowships, career-related internships or fieldwork, Federal Work-Study, institutionally sponsored loans, scholarships/grants, and tuition waivers (partial) available. Support available to part-time students. Financial award application deadline: 4/15. *Faculty research:* Leadership, management, interdisciplinary, critical thinking and strategizing skills, teamwork. *Unit head:* Dr. Esther Gergen, Dean, 210-434-6711 Ext. 2287, E-mail: esgergen@ollusa.edu. *Application contact:* Graduate Admission, 210-431-3961, Fax: 210-431-4013, E-mail: gradadm@ollusa.edu.
Website: http://www.ollusa.edu/s/1190/ollu-3-column-noads.aspx?sid=1190&gid=1&pgid=1153.

Oxford Graduate School, Graduate Programs, Dayton, TN 37321-6736. Offers family life education (M Litt); organizational leadership (M Litt); sociological integration of religion and society (D Phil).

Palm Beach Atlantic University, MacArthur School of Leadership, West Palm Beach, FL 33416-4708. Offers MS. Part-time and evening/weekend programs available. *Faculty:* 1 (woman) full-time, 7 part-time/adjunct (0 women). *Students:* 3 full-time (1 woman), 96 part-time (53 women); includes 53 minority (31 Black or African American, non-Hispanic/Latino; 1 American Indian or Alaska Native, non-Hispanic/Latino; 2 Asian, non-Hispanic/Latino; 16 Hispanic/Latino; 3 Two or more races, non-Hispanic/Latino), 1 international. Average age 39. 48 applicants, 92% accepted, 42 enrolled. In 2013, 34 master's awarded. *Entrance requirements:* For master's, minimum GPA of 3.0; essay. Additional exam requirements/recommendations for international students: Required—TOEFL (minimum score 550 paper-based; 79 iBT). *Application deadline:* For fall admission, 7/15 priority date for domestic students; for spring admission, 11/15 priority date for domestic students. Applications are processed on a rolling basis. Application fee: $45. Electronic applications accepted. *Expenses:* Tuition: Part-time $495 per credit hour. *Required fees:* $495 per credit hour. Part-time tuition and fees vary according to course load and program. *Financial support:* Scholarships/grants available. Financial award application deadline: 5/1; financial award applicants required to submit FAFSA. *Unit head:* Dr. Jim Laub, Dean, 561-803-2302, E-mail: jim_laub@pba.edu. *Application contact:* Graduate Admissions, 888-468-6722, E-mail: grad@pba.edu.
Website: http://www.pba.edu/masters-in-leadership.

Penn State University Park, Graduate School, College of Education, Department of Learning and Performance Systems, State College, PA 16802. Offers adult education (M Ed, D Ed, PhD, Certificate); instructional systems (Certificate); learning, design, and technology (M Ed, MS, D Ed, PhD, Certificate); organization development and change (MPS); workforce education and development (M Ed, MS, PhD). *Unit head:* Dr. David H. Monk, Dean, 814-865-2523, Fax: 814-865-0555, E-mail: dhm6@psu.edu. *Application contact:* Cynthia E. Nicosia, Director, Graduate Enrollment Services, 814-865-1834, Fax: 814-863-4627, E-mail: cey1@psu.edu.
Website: http://www.ed.psu.edu/educ/lps/dept-lps.

Pepperdine University, Graduate School of Education and Psychology, Division of Education, MA Program in Social Entrepreneurship and Change, Malibu, CA 90263. Offers MA. Part-time and evening/weekend programs available. *Students:* 34 part-time (26 women); includes 13 minority (6 Black or African American, non-Hispanic/Latino; 2 Asian, non-Hispanic/Latino; 5 Hispanic/Latino), 4 international. 46 applicants, 63% accepted, 18 enrolled. In 2013, 29 master's awarded. *Entrance requirements:* For master's, two letters of recommendation, one- to two-page statement of educational purpose. Additional exam requirements/recommendations for international students: Required—TOEFL. *Application deadline:* For fall admission, 6/1 priority date for domestic students. Application fee: $55. Tuition and fees vary according to program. *Unit head:* Dr. Margaret J. Weber, Dean, 310-568-5600, E-mail: margaret.weber@pepperdine.edu. *Application contact:* Jennifer Agatep, Admissions Manager, Education, 310-258-2849, E-mail: jennifer.agatep@pepperdine.edu.
Website: http://gsep.pepperdine.edu/masters-social-entrepreneurship-and-change/.

Pepperdine University, Graziadio School of Business and Management, MS in Organization Development Program, Malibu, CA 90263. Offers MSOD. Program consists of four week-long sessions per year at different locations in Northern California, Southern California and abroad. Part-time programs available. *Students:* 71 part-time (53 women); includes 1 minority (Asian, non-Hispanic/Latino), 10 international. 53 applicants, 79% accepted, 36 enrolled. In 2013, 25 master's awarded. *Entrance requirements:* For master's, GMAT or GRE, two letters of recommendation. Additional exam requirements/recommendations for international students: Required—TOEFL. Application fee: $75. Tuition and fees vary according to program. *Unit head:* Dr. Gary Mangiofico, Associate Dean of Fully-Employed and Executive Programs, Graziadio School of Business and Management, 310-568-5541, Fax: 310-568-5610, E-mail: gary.mangiofico@pepperdine.edu. *Application contact:* Shany Mahalu, Assistant Director, MSOD Marketing and Recruiting, 310-568-5639, E-mail: shany.mahalu@pepperdine.edu.
Website: http://bschool.pepperdine.edu/programs/masters-organization-development/.

Peru State College, Graduate Programs, Program in Organizational Management, Peru, NE 68421. Offers MS. Program offered online only. Part-time programs available. Postbaccalaureate distance learning degree programs offered (no on-campus study). *Faculty:* 6. *Students:* 48 part-time (22 women); includes 1 minority (Black or African American, non-Hispanic/Latino). Average age 34. 38 applicants, 95% accepted, 25 enrolled. *Degree requirements:* For master's, thesis (for some programs). *Application deadline:* For fall admission, 8/6 priority date for domestic students; for spring admission, 1/5 priority date for domestic students. Application fee: $0. *Expenses:* Contact institution. *Faculty research:* Emotional intelligence. *Unit head:* Dr. Greg Seay, Dean of Graduate Programs, 402-872-2283, Fax: 402-872-2413, E-mail: gseay@peru.edu. *Application contact:* Emily Volker, Program Coordinator, 402-872-2282, Fax: 402-872-2413, E-mail: evolker@peru.edu.

Pfeiffer University, Program in Leadership and Organizational Change, Misenheimer, NC 28109-0960. Offers MS, MBA/MS. *Entrance requirements:* For master's, GRE or GMAT.

Point Loma Nazarene University, Fermanian School of Business, San Diego, CA 92106-2899. Offers general business (MBA); healthcare (MBA); not-for-profit management (MBA); organizational leadership (MBA); sustainability (MBA). *Accreditation:* ACBSP. Part-time and evening/weekend programs available. *Students:* 37 full-time (12 women), 70 part-time (35 women); includes 33 minority (3 Black or African American, non-Hispanic/Latino; 9 Asian, non-Hispanic/Latino; 14 Hispanic/Latino; 1 Native Hawaiian or other Pacific Islander, non-Hispanic/Latino; 6 Two or more races, non-Hispanic/Latino), 1 international. Average age 29. 51 applicants, 65% accepted, 28 enrolled. In 2013, 59 master's awarded. *Entrance requirements:* For master's, GMAT, letters of recommendation, essay, interview. Additional exam requirements/recommendations for international students: Required—TOEFL. *Application deadline:* For fall admission, 8/4 priority date for domestic students; for spring admission, 12/8 priority date for domestic students; for summer admission, 4/13 priority date for domestic students. Applications are processed on a rolling basis. Application fee: $50. Electronic applications accepted. *Expenses:* Tuition: Full-time $6900; part-time $567 per credit hour. *Financial support:* Applicants required to submit FAFSA. *Unit head:* Dr. Ken Armstrong, Interim Dean, 619-849-2290, E-mail: kenarmstrong@pointloma.edu. *Application contact:* Laura Leinweber, Director of Graduate Admission, 866-692-4723, E-mail: lauraleinweber@pointloma.edu.
Website: http://www.pointloma.edu/discover/graduate-school-san-diego/san-diego-graduate-programs-masters-degree-san-diego/mba.

Point Park University, School of Business, Pittsburgh, PA 15222-1984. Offers business (MBA); organizational leadership (MA). Part-time and evening/weekend programs available. *Degree requirements:* For master's, comprehensive exam (for some programs), thesis or alternative. *Entrance requirements:* For master's, minimum QPA of 2.75; 2 letters of recommendation; resume (MA). Additional exam requirements/recommendations for international students: Required—TOEFL (minimum score 550

paper-based; 79 iBT). Electronic applications accepted. *Faculty research:* Technology issues, foreign direct investment, multinational corporate issues, cross-cultural international organizations/administrations, regional integration issues.

Quincy University, Program in Business Administration, Quincy, IL 62301-2699. Offers general business administration (MBA); operations management (MBA); organizational leadership (MBA). Part-time and evening/weekend programs available. Postbaccalaureate distance learning degree programs offered (no on-campus study). *Faculty:* 5 full-time (3 women). *Students:* 5 full-time (0 women), 18 part-time (5 women), 1 international. In 2013, 20 master's awarded. *Entrance requirements:* For master's, GMAT, previous course work in accounting, economics, finance, management or marketing, and statistics. Additional exam requirements/recommendations for international students: Required—TOEFL (minimum score 550 paper-based; 79 iBT). *Application deadline:* Applications are processed on a rolling basis. Application fee: $25. Electronic applications accepted. *Expenses:* Contact institution. *Financial support:* Applicants required to submit FAFSA. *Faculty research:* Macroeconomic forecasting. *Unit head:* Dr. Cynthia Haliemun, Director, 217-228-5432 Ext. 3067, E-mail: haliecy@quincy.edu. *Application contact:* Office of Admissions, 217-228-5210, Fax: 217-228-5479, E-mail: admissions@quincy.edu.
Website: http://www.quincy.edu/academics/graduate-programs/business-administration.

Quinnipiac University, School of Business and Engineering, Program in Organizational Leadership, Hamden, CT 06518-1940. Offers MS. Part-time and evening/weekend programs available. Postbaccalaureate distance learning degree programs offered (no on-campus study). *Faculty:* 4 full-time (1 woman), 2 part-time/adjunct (both women). *Students:* 12 full-time (all women), 185 part-time (128 women); includes 38 minority (20 Black or African American, non-Hispanic/Latino; 4 Asian, non-Hispanic/Latino; 12 Hispanic/Latino; 2 Two or more races, non-Hispanic/Latino), 1 international. 87 applicants, 92% accepted, 69 enrolled. In 2013, 66 master's awarded. *Entrance requirements:* For master's, four years of work experience. Additional exam requirements/recommendations for international students: Required—TOEFL (minimum score 575 paper-based; 90 iBT), IELTS (minimum score 6.5). *Application deadline:* For fall admission, 7/30 priority date for domestic students; for spring admission, 12/31 priority date for domestic students; for summer admission, 4/30 priority date for domestic students. Applications are processed on a rolling basis. Application fee: $45. Electronic applications accepted. *Expenses:* Tuition: Part-time $920 per credit. *Required fees:* $37 per credit. *Financial support:* Unspecified assistantships available. Support available to part-time students. Financial award application deadline: 6/1; financial award applicants required to submit FAFSA. *Faculty research:* Virtual teams, women and leadership, virtual human resources applications and practices, emotional intelligence and its application in the workplace. *Unit head:* Michael Taylor, Director of Online Master's Programs, School of Business, E-mail: michael.taylor@quinnipiac.edu. *Application contact:* QU Online Admissions, 203-582-3918, Fax: 203-582-3443, E-mail: quonlineadmissions@quinnipiac.edu.
Website: http://www.quinnipiac.edu/academics/qu-online/online-programs/online-graduate-programs/master-of-science-in-organizational-leadership/.

Regent University, Graduate School, School of Business and Leadership, Virginia Beach, VA 23464-9800. Offers business administration (MBA); leadership (Certificate); organizational leadership (MA, PhD), including ecclesial leadership (PhD), entrepreneurial leadership (PhD), human resource development (PhD); strategic foresight (MA); strategic leadership (DSL), including global consulting, leadership coaching, strategic foresight. Part-time and evening/weekend programs available. Postbaccalaureate distance learning degree programs offered (minimal on-campus study). *Faculty:* 11 full-time (4 women), 6 part-time/adjunct (3 women). *Students:* 34 full-time (19 women), 655 part-time (276 women); includes 222 minority (175 Black or African American, non-Hispanic/Latino; 2 American Indian or Alaska Native, non-Hispanic/Latino; 16 Asian, non-Hispanic/Latino; 29 Hispanic/Latino), 117 international. Average age 42. 384 applicants, 53% accepted, 120 enrolled. In 2013, 74 master's, 72 doctorates awarded. *Degree requirements:* For master's, thesis or alternative, 3 credit hour culminating experience; for doctorate, thesis/dissertation. *Entrance requirements:* For master's, GRE, GMAT, minimum undergraduate GPA of 2.75, computer literacy survey, 2 recommendations, resume, transcripts, essay; for doctorate, GRE, GMAT, sample of writing, minimum 3 years of relevant experience, computer literacy survey, 2 recommendations, resume, essay, transcripts; for Certificate, writing sample, resume, transcripts. Additional exam requirements/recommendations for international students: Required—TOEFL (minimum score 577 paper-based). *Application deadline:* For fall admission, 5/1 priority date for domestic students; for spring admission, 10/1 priority date for domestic students. Applications are processed on a rolling basis. Application fee: $50. Electronic applications accepted. *Expenses:* Contact institution. *Financial support:* Career-related internships or fieldwork, scholarships/grants, and tuition waivers (full and partial) available. Support available to part-time students. Financial award application deadline: 9/1. *Faculty research:* Servant leadership, ethics and values, telecommuting and family values, organizational communications, distance education. *Unit head:* Dr. Doris Gomez, Interim Dean, 757-352-4686, Fax: 757-352-4634, E-mail: dorigom@regent.edu. *Application contact:* Matthew Chadwick, Director of Enrollment Support Services, 800-373-5504, Fax: 757-352-4381, E-mail: admissions@regent.edu.
Website: http://www.regent.edu/acad/global/.

Regis University, College for Professional Studies, School of Management, MBA Program, Denver, CO 80221-1099. Offers finance and accounting (MBA); general business (MBA); health industry leadership (MBA); marketing (MBA); operations management (MBA); organizational performance management (MBA); strategic management (MBA). Part-time and evening/weekend programs available. Postbaccalaureate distance learning degree programs offered (no on-campus study). *Faculty:* 10 full-time (3 women), 74 part-time/adjunct (17 women). *Students:* 386 full-time (183 women), 269 part-time (134 women); includes 190 minority (38 Black or African American, non-Hispanic/Latino; 2 American Indian or Alaska Native, non-Hispanic/Latino; 30 Asian, non-Hispanic/Latino; 109 Hispanic/Latino; 1 Native Hawaiian or other Pacific Islander, non-Hispanic/Latino; 10 Two or more races, non-Hispanic/Latino), 11 international. Average age 42. 152 applicants, 91% accepted, 112 enrolled. In 2013, 318 master's awarded. *Degree requirements:* For master's, thesis (for some programs), final research project. *Entrance requirements:* For master's, official transcript reflecting baccalaureate degree awarded from regionally-accredited college or university, work experience, resume, letters of recommendation. Additional exam requirements/recommendations for international students: Required—TOEFL (minimum score 550 paper-based; 82 iBT). *Application deadline:* Applications are processed on a rolling basis. Application fee: $75. Electronic applications accepted. *Expenses:* Contact institution. *Financial support:* In 2013–14, 22 students received support. Federal Work-Study and scholarships/grants available. Financial award application deadline: 4/15; financial award applicants required to submit FAFSA. *Unit head:* Dr. Anthony Vrba, Interim Dean, 303-964-5384, Fax: 303-964-5538, E-mail: avrba@regis.edu. *Application contact:* Sarah Engel, Director of Admissions, 303-458-4900, Fax: 303-964-5534, E-mail: regisadm@regis.edu.
Website: http://www.regis.edu/CPS/Academics/Degrees-and-Programs/Graduate-Programs/MBA-College-for-Professional-Studies.aspx.

Organizational Management

Rider University, Department of Graduate Education, Leadership and Counseling, Program in Organizational Leadership, Lawrenceville, NJ 08648-3001. Offers MA. *Entrance requirements:* For master's, resume.

Robert Morris University, Graduate Studies, School of Communications and Information Systems, Moon Township, PA 15108-1189. Offers communication and information systems (MS); competitive intelligence systems (MS); information security and assurance (MS); information systems and communications (D Sc); information systems management (MS); information technology project management (MS); Internet information systems (MS); organizational leadership (MS). Part-time and evening/weekend programs available. Postbaccalaureate distance learning degree programs offered (no on-campus study). *Faculty:* 26 full-time (10 women), 14 part-time/adjunct (4 women). *Students:* 311 part-time (111 women); includes 57 minority (35 Black or African American, non-Hispanic/Latino; 1 American Indian or Alaska Native, non-Hispanic/Latino; 4 Asian, non-Hispanic/Latino; 3 Hispanic/Latino; 14 Two or more races, non-Hispanic/Latino), 37 international. 337 applicants, 39% accepted, 102 enrolled. In 2013, 90 master's, 15 doctorates awarded. *Degree requirements:* For doctorate, thesis/dissertation. *Entrance requirements:* For doctorate, employer letter of endorsement, interview. Additional exam requirements/recommendations for international students: Required—TOEFL (minimum score 550 paper-based; 79 iBT). *Application deadline:* For fall admission, 7/1 priority date for domestic and international students; for spring admission, 11/1 priority date for domestic and international students. Applications are processed on a rolling basis. Application fee: $35. Electronic applications accepted. *Expenses:* Contact institution. *Financial support:* Research assistantships with partial tuition reimbursements, institutionally sponsored loans, and unspecified assistantships available. Support available to part-time students. Financial award application deadline: 5/1. *Unit head:* Dr. Barbara J. Levine, Dean, 412-397-2591, Fax: 412-397-2481, E-mail: levine@rmu.edu. *Application contact:* 412-397-5200, Fax: 412-397-5915, E-mail: graduateadmissions@rmu.edu.
Website: http://www.rmu.edu/web/cms/schools/scis/Pages/default.aspx.

Roosevelt University, Graduate Division, College of Education, Program in Educational Leadership, Chicago, IL 60605. Offers MA, Ed D.

Rutgers, The State University of New Jersey, Newark, Rutgers Business School–Newark and New Brunswick, Doctoral Programs in Management, Newark, NJ 07102. Offers accounting (PhD); accounting information systems (PhD); economics (PhD); finance (PhD); individualized study (PhD); information technology (PhD); international business (PhD); management science (PhD); marketing science (PhD); organizational management (PhD); science, technology and management (PhD); supply chain management (PhD). *Degree requirements:* For doctorate, comprehensive exam, thesis/dissertation. *Entrance requirements:* For doctorate, GRE or GMAT. Additional exam requirements/recommendations for international students: Required—TOEFL (minimum score 550 paper-based; 79 iBT). Electronic applications accepted.

Sage Graduate School, School of Management, Program in Organization Management, Troy, NY 12180-4115. Offers organization management (MS); public administration (MS). Part-time and evening/weekend programs available. *Faculty:* 2 full-time (both women), 9 part-time/adjunct (2 women). *Students:* 6 full-time (5 women), 36 part-time (25 women); includes 7 minority (4 Black or African American, non-Hispanic/Latino; 1 American Indian or Alaska Native, non-Hispanic/Latino; 2 Asian, non-Hispanic/Latino), 1 international. Average age 36. 27 applicants, 63% accepted, 10 enrolled. In 2013, 23 master's awarded. *Degree requirements:* For master's, capstone seminar. *Entrance requirements:* For master's, minimum GPA of 2.75. Additional exam requirements/recommendations for international students: Required—TOEFL (minimum score 550 paper-based). *Application deadline:* Applications are processed on a rolling basis. Application fee: $40. *Expenses: Tuition:* Full-time $11,880; part-time $660 per credit hour. *Financial support:* Fellowships, research assistantships, Federal Work-Study, scholarships/grants, tuition waivers (partial), and unspecified assistantships available. Support available to part-time students. Financial award application deadline: 3/1; financial award applicants required to submit FAFSA. *Unit head:* Dr. Daniel Robeson, Dean, School of Management, 518-292-8657, Fax: 518-292-1964, E-mail: robesd@sage.edu. *Application contact:* Wendy D. Diefendorf, Director of Graduate and Adult Admission, 518-244-2443, Fax: 518-244-6880, E-mail: diefew@sage.edu.
Website: http://www.sage.edu/academics/management/programs/organization_management/.

St. Ambrose University, College of Business, Program in Organizational Leadership, Davenport, IA 52801. Offers MOL. Part-time and evening/weekend programs available. *Degree requirements:* For master's, comprehensive exam (for some programs), thesis or alternative, integration projects. *Entrance requirements:* Additional exam requirements/recommendations for international students: Required—TOEFL. Electronic applications accepted. *Expenses:* Contact institution.

St. Catharine College, School of Graduate Studies, St. Catharine, KY 40061-9499. Offers leadership (MA), including community and regional studies, health promotion. *Degree requirements:* For master's, thesis or alternative. *Entrance requirements:* For master's, GRE, official transcripts. Additional exam requirements/recommendations for international students: Required—TOEFL, IELTS, or Michigan English Language Assessment Battery. Electronic applications accepted.

St. Catherine University, Graduate Programs, Program in Organizational Leadership, St. Paul, MN 55105. Offers MA. Part-time and evening/weekend programs available. *Degree requirements:* For master's, thesis. *Entrance requirements:* For master's, GMAT, GRE General Test or MAT, 2 years of work experience, minimum GPA of 3.0. Additional exam requirements/recommendations for international students: Required—TOEFL (minimum score 600 paper-based; 100 iBT). *Faculty research:* Ethics.

St. Edward's University, School of Management and Business, Program in Organizational Leadership and Ethics, Austin, TX 78704. Offers MS. Part-time and evening/weekend programs available. *Students:* 28 part-time (19 women); includes 12 minority (5 Black or African American, non-Hispanic/Latino; 7 Hispanic/Latino). Average age 40. 17 applicants, 94% accepted, 12 enrolled. In 2013, 15 master's awarded. *Degree requirements:* For master's, minimum of 24 hours in residence. *Entrance requirements:* For master's, GMAT or GRE General Test, minimum GPA of 2.75 in last 60 hours of course work. Additional exam requirements/recommendations for international students: Required—TOEFL (minimum score 79 iBT) or IELTS (minimum score 6). *Application deadline:* For fall admission, 6/1 priority date for domestic and international students; for spring admission, 10/1 priority date for domestic and international students; for summer admission, 3/1 priority date for domestic and international students. Applications are processed on a rolling basis. Application fee: $50. Electronic applications accepted. *Expenses: Tuition:* Full-time $20,664; part-time $1148 per credit hour. *Required fees:* $50 per trimester. Full-time tuition and fees vary according to course load and program. *Unit head:* Dr. Tom Sechrest, Director, 512-637-1954, Fax: 512-448-8492, E-mail: thomasl@stedwards.edu. *Application contact:* Office of Admission, 512-448-8500, Fax: 512-464-8877, E-mail: seu.admit@stedwards.edu.
Website: http://www.stedwards.edu.

St. Edward's University, School of Management and Business, Program in Organization Development, Austin, TX 78704. Offers MA. Part-time and evening/weekend programs available. *Students:* 1 (woman) full-time, 22 part-time (18 women); includes 9 minority (3 Black or African American, non-Hispanic/Latino; 6 Hispanic/Latino), 1 international. Average age 36. 26 applicants, 73% accepted, 12 enrolled. *Degree requirements:* For master's, minimum of 24 hours in residence. *Entrance requirements:* For master's, GMAT or GRE General Test, minimum GPA of 2.75 in last 60 hours of course work. Additional exam requirements/recommendations for international students: Required—TOEFL (minimum score 79 iBT) or IELTS (minimum score 6). *Application deadline:* For fall admission, 6/1 priority date for domestic and international students; for spring admission, 10/1 priority date for domestic and international students; for summer admission, 3/1 priority date for domestic and international students. Applications are processed on a rolling basis. Application fee: $50. Electronic applications accepted. *Expenses: Tuition:* Full-time $20,664; part-time $1148 per credit hour. *Required fees:* $50 per trimester. Full-time tuition and fees vary according to course load and program. *Unit head:* Connie Porter, Director, 512-416-5827, Fax: 512-448-8492, E-mail: constanp@stedwards.edu. *Application contact:* Office of Admission, 512-448-8500, Fax: 512-464-8877, E-mail: seu.admit@stedwards.edu.
Website: http://www.stedwards.edu.

St. Joseph's College, Long Island Campus, Program in Management, Patchogue, NY 11772-2399. Offers health care (AC); health care management (MS); human resource management (AC); human resources management (MS); organizational management (MS).

Saint Joseph's University, College of Arts and Sciences, Organization Development and Leadership Programs, Philadelphia, PA 19131-1395. Offers adult learning and training (MS, Certificate); organization dynamics and leadership (MS, Certificate); organizational psychology and development (MS, Certificate). Part-time and evening/weekend programs available. Postbaccalaureate distance learning degree programs offered (no on-campus study). *Faculty:* 2 full-time (both women), 16 part-time/adjunct (9 women). *Students:* 7 full-time (3 women), 233 part-time (154 women); includes 94 minority (59 Black or African American, non-Hispanic/Latino; 17 American Indian or Alaska Native, non-Hispanic/Latino; 9 Asian, non-Hispanic/Latino; 7 Hispanic/Latino; 1 Native Hawaiian or other Pacific Islander, non-Hispanic/Latino; 1 Two or more races, non-Hispanic/Latino), 3 international. Average age 38. 100 applicants, 78% accepted, 50 enrolled. In 2013, 65 master's awarded. *Entrance requirements:* For master's, GRE (if GPA less than 2.7), minimum GPA of 2.7, 2 letters of recommendation, resume, personal statement. Additional exam requirements/recommendations for international students: Required—TOEFL (minimum score 550 paper-based; 80 iBT). *Application deadline:* For fall admission, 7/15 priority date for domestic students, 4/15 for international students; for winter admission, 1/15 for international students; for spring admission, 11/15 priority date for domestic students, 10/15 for international students. Applications are processed on a rolling basis. Application fee: $35. Electronic applications accepted. *Expenses: Tuition:* Part-time $786 per credit hour. Tuition and fees vary according to degree level and program. *Financial support:* Applicants required to submit FAFSA. *Unit head:* Dr. Felice Tilin, Director, 610-660-1575, E-mail: ftilin@sju.edu. *Application contact:* Elisabeth Woodward, Director of Marketing and Admissions, Graduate Arts and Sciences, 610-660-3131, Fax: 610-660-3230, E-mail: gradstudies@sju.edu.
Website: http://www.sju.edu/majors-programs/graduate-arts-sciences/masters/organization-development-and-leadership-ms.

Saint Louis University, Graduate Education, College of Education and Public Service, Department of Public Policy Studies, St. Louis, MO 63103-2097. Offers geographic information systems (Certificate); organizational development (Certificate); public administration (MAPA); public policy analysis (PhD); urban affairs (MAUA); urban planning and real estate development (MUPRED). *Accreditation:* NASPAA. Part-time programs available. *Degree requirements:* For master's, comprehensive exam (for some programs), thesis (for some programs); for doctorate, comprehensive exam, thesis/dissertation, preliminary exams. *Entrance requirements:* For master's, GMAT, GRE General Test, or LSAT, letters of recommendation, resume; for doctorate, GMAT, GRE General Test, or LSAT, letters of recommendation, resumé, interview, transcripts, goal statement. Additional exam requirements/recommendations for international students: Required—TOEFL (minimum score 525 paper-based). Electronic applications accepted. *Faculty research:* Urban politics, brown fields, e-government, and administration, evaluation research, community development, electronic government and governance.

Saint Mary's University of Minnesota, Schools of Graduate and Professional Programs, Graduate School of Business and Technology, Organizational Leadership Program, Winona, MN 55987-1399. Offers MA. Postbaccalaureate distance learning degree programs offered (no on-campus study). *Unit head:* Diana-Christine Teodorescu, Director, 507-238-4510, E-mail: dteodore@smumn.edu. *Application contact:* Russell Kreager, Director of Admissions for Graduate and Professional Programs, 612-728-5207, Fax: 612-728-5121, E-mail: rkreager@smumn.edu.
Website: http://www.smumn.edu/graduate-home/areas-of-study/graduate-school-of-business-technology/ma-in-organizational-leadership.

Saybrook University, LIOS MA Residential Programs, Kirkland, WA 98033. Offers leadership and organization development (MA); psychology counseling (MA). *Degree requirements:* For master's, thesis (for some programs), oral exams. *Entrance requirements:* For master's, bachelor's degree from an accredited university or college. Additional exam requirements/recommendations for international students: Recommended—TOEFL, IELTS, TWE. *Expenses: Tuition:* Full-time $22,560. *Required fees:* $2200; $1000 per credit. $2200 per year. One-time fee: $450.

Saybrook University, School of Organizational Leadership and Transformation, San Francisco, CA 94111-1920. Offers MA. Program offered jointly with Bastyr University. *Degree requirements:* For master's, thesis (for some programs), oral exams. *Entrance requirements:* For master's, bachelor's degree from an accredited college or university. *Expenses: Tuition:* Full-time $22,560. *Required fees:* $2200; $1000 per credit. $2200 per year. One-time fee: $450. *Faculty research:* Cross-functional work teams, communication, management authority, employee influence, systems theory.

Saybrook University, School of Psychology and Interdisciplinary Inquiry, San Francisco, CA 94111-1920. Offers human science (MA, PhD), including consciousness and spirituality, humanistic and transpersonal psychology, integrative health studies, organizational systems, social transformation; organizational systems (MA, PhD), including consciousness and spirituality, humanistic and transpersonal psychology, integrative health studies, leadership of sustainable systems (MA), organizational systems, social transformation; psychology (MA, PhD), including consciousness and spirituality, creativity studies (MA), humanistic and transpersonal psychology, integrative health studies, Jungian studies, marriage and family therapy (MA), organizational systems, social transformation. Postbaccalaureate distance learning degree programs offered (minimal on-campus study). Terminal master's awarded for partial completion of doctoral program. *Degree requirements:* For master's, thesis or alternative; for doctorate, thesis/dissertation. *Entrance requirements:* Additional exam requirements/recommendations for international students: Required—TOEFL (minimum score 580 paper-based; 93 iBT). Electronic applications accepted. *Expenses: Tuition:* Full-time $22,560. *Required fees:* $2200; $1000 per credit. $2200 per year. One-time fee: $450. *Faculty research:* Humanistic theory, health studies, organizational systems, consciousness and spirituality, social transformation.

Seattle University, Albers School of Business and Economics, Center for Leadership Formation, Seattle, WA 98122-1090. Offers health leadership (EMBA); leadership (EMBA, Certificate). Evening/weekend programs available. *Faculty:* 16 full-time (5 women), 6 part-time/adjunct (all women). *Students:* 52 full-time (26 women); includes 14 minority (5 Black or African American, non-Hispanic/Latino; 6 Asian, non-Hispanic/Latino; 1 Hispanic/Latino; 2 Two or more races, non-Hispanic/Latino). Average age 41. 46 applicants, 80% accepted, 31 enrolled. In 2013, 37 master's awarded. *Entrance requirements:* For master's, GMAT, 7 years of continuous professional experience, undergraduate degree with minimum GPA of 3.0, resume, writing sample, statement of intent/interest; for Certificate, 7 years of continuous professional experience, undergraduate degree with minimum GPA of 3.0. *Application deadline:* Applications are processed on a rolling basis. Application fee: $55. Electronic applications accepted. *Expenses:* Contact institution. *Financial support:* In 2013–14, 10 students received support. *Unit head:* Dr. Marilyn Gist, Executive Director, 206-296-5374, E-mail: gistm@seattleu.edu. *Application contact:* Sommer Harrison, Recruiting Coordinator, 206-296-2529, Fax: 206-296-2374, E-mail: emba@seattleu.edu.
Website: http://www.seattleu.edu/albers/executiveeducation/.

Shippensburg University of Pennsylvania, School of Graduate Studies, College of Arts and Sciences, Department of Sociology and Anthropology, Shippensburg, PA 17257-2299. Offers organizational development and leadership (MS), including business, communications, environmental management, higher education structure and policy, historical administration, individual and organizational development, management information systems, public organizations, social structures and organizations. Part-time and evening/weekend programs available. *Faculty:* 4 full-time (all women). *Students:* 19 full-time (11 women), 40 part-time (23 women); includes 7 minority (all Black or African American, non-Hispanic/Latino), 4 international. Average age 32. 63 applicants, 49% accepted, 19 enrolled. In 2013, 24 master's awarded. *Degree requirements:* For master's, capstone experience including internship. *Entrance requirements:* For master's, interview (if GPA less than 2.75), resume, personal goals statement. Additional exam requirements/recommendations for international students: Required—TOEFL (minimum score 580 paper-based); Recommended—IELTS (minimum score 6). *Application deadline:* For fall admission, 4/30 for international students; for spring admission, 9/30 for international students. Applications are processed on a rolling basis. Application fee: $45. Electronic applications accepted. *Expenses: Tuition, area resident:* Part-time $442 per credit. Tuition, state resident: part-time $442 per credit. Tuition, nonresident: part-time $663 per credit. *Required fees:* $127 per credit. *Financial support:* In 2013–14, 10 research assistantships with full tuition reimbursements (averaging $5,000 per year) were awarded; career-related internships or fieldwork, scholarships/grants, unspecified assistantships, and resident hall director and student payroll positions also available. Support available to part-time students. Financial award applicants required to submit FAFSA. *Unit head:* Dr. Barbara Denison, Program Coordinator, 717-477-1735, Fax: 717-477-4011, E-mail: bjdeni@ship.edu. *Application contact:* Jeremy R. Goshorn, Assistant Dean of Graduate Admissions, 717-477-1231, Fax: 717-477-4016, E-mail: jrgoshorn@ship.edu.
Website: http://www.ship.edu/odl/.

Siena Heights University, Graduate College, Adrian, MI 49221-1796. Offers clinical mental health counseling (MA); education leadership (Specialist); leadership (MA), including health care, higher education leadership, organizational; teacher education (MA), including early childhood, early childhood: Montessori-based, education leadership: principal, elementary education, K-12 reading, leadership: higher education, secondary education, K-12 reading, special education, K-12 cognitive impairment, special education, K-12 learning disabled. Part-time and evening/weekend programs available. *Faculty:* 37. *Students:* 9 full-time (7 women), 251 part-time (179 women). In 2013, 32 master's awarded. *Degree requirements:* For master's, thesis, presentation. *Entrance requirements:* For master's, minimum GPA of 3.0, current resume, essay, all post-secondary transcripts, 3 letters of reference, conviction disclosure form; copy of teaching certificate (for some education programs); for Specialist, master's degree, minimum GPA of 3.0, current resume, essay, all post-secondary transcripts, 3 letters of reference, conviction disclosure form; copy of teaching certificate (for some education programs). *Application deadline:* Applications are processed on a rolling basis. Application fee: $50. *Expenses: Tuition:* Part-time $535 per semester hour. *Required fees:* $130 per semester. *Financial support:* Career-related internships or fieldwork, Federal Work-Study, and resident assistantships available. Financial award application deadline: 9/1; financial award applicants required to submit FAFSA. *Unit head:* Dr. Linda S. Pettit, Dean, Graduate College, 517-264-7661, Fax: 517-264-7714, E-mail: lpettit@sienahts.edu.
Website: http://www.sienaheights.edu.

Simmons College, School of Management, Boston, MA 02115. Offers business administration (MBA); business and financial analytics (MBA); corporate social responsibility and sustainability (MBA); entrepreneurship (MBA); healthcare management (MBA); management (MS), including communications management, non-profit management; marketing (MBA); nonprofit management (MBA); organizational leadership (MBA); MBA/MSW; MS/MA. *Accreditation:* AACSB. Part-time and evening/weekend programs available. *Students:* 34 full-time (33 women), 233 part-time (214 women); includes 67 minority (41 Black or African American, non-Hispanic/Latino; 1 American Indian or Alaska Native, non-Hispanic/Latino; 9 Asian, non-Hispanic/Latino; 10 Hispanic/Latino; 2 Native Hawaiian or other Pacific Islander, non-Hispanic/Latino; 4 Two or more races, non-Hispanic/Latino), 7 international. In 2013, 133 master's awarded. *Entrance requirements:* For master's, GMAT or GRE. Additional exam requirements/recommendations for international students: Required—TOEFL. *Application deadline:* Applications are processed on a rolling basis. Application fee: $75. Electronic applications accepted. *Financial support:* Scholarships/grants and unspecified assistantships available. Financial award applicants required to submit FAFSA. *Faculty research:* Gender and organizations, leadership, health care management. *Unit head:* Cathy Minehan, Dean, 617-521-2846. *Application contact:* Melissa Terrio, Director of Graduate Admissions, 617-521-3840, Fax: 617-521-3880, E-mail: somadm@simmons.edu.
Website: http://www.simmons.edu/som.

Simpson University, School of Graduate Studies, Redding, CA 96003-8606. Offers counseling psychology (MA); organizational leadership (MA). Evening/weekend programs available. Postbaccalaureate distance learning degree programs offered (minimal on-campus study). *Faculty:* 3 full-time (all women), 24 part-time/adjunct (16 women). *Students:* 40 full-time (37 women), 3 part-time (2 women); includes 9 minority (1 American Indian or Alaska Native, non-Hispanic/Latino; 5 Asian, non-Hispanic/Latino; 3 Hispanic/Latino). Average age 34. 75 applicants, 51% accepted, 31 enrolled. In 2013, 14 master's awarded. *Degree requirements:* For master's, thesis optional, portfolio capstone and integrative essay. *Entrance requirements:* Additional exam requirements/recommendations for international students: Required—TOEFL (minimum score 550 paper-based; 79 iBT). *Application deadline:* For fall admission, 3/1 for domestic and international students; for winter admission, 9/15 for domestic and international students; for summer admission, 6/1 for domestic and international students. Application fee: $50. Electronic applications accepted. Tuition and fees vary according to program. *Financial support:* Applicants required to submit FAFSA. *Faculty research:* Development of executive functioning in young children, cognitive neuropsychology, historical issues in the neurosciences, neurotheology. *Unit head:* Adeline Jackson, Dean, 530-226-4788, E-mail: ajackson@simpsonu.edu. *Application contact:* Vanessa Buendia, Admissions Assistant, 530-226-4547, E-mail: vanessab@simpsonu.edu.
Website: http://gs.simpsonu.edu/.

Southeast Missouri State University, School of Graduate Studies, Harrison College of Business, Cape Girardeau, MO 63701-4799. Offers accounting (MBA); entrepreneurship (MBA); environmental management (MBA); financial management (MBA); general management (MBA); health administration (MBA); industrial management (MBA); international business (MBA); organizational management (MS); sport management (MBA). *Accreditation:* AACSB. Part-time and evening/weekend programs available. Postbaccalaureate distance learning degree programs offered (no on-campus study). *Faculty:* 27 full-time (7 women), 1 (woman) part-time/adjunct. *Students:* 59 full-time (27 women), 83 part-time (28 women); includes 10 minority (5 Black or African American, non-Hispanic/Latino; 3 Asian, non-Hispanic/Latino; 1 Hispanic/Latino; 1 Two or more races, non-Hispanic/Latino), 40 international. Average age 28. 77 applicants, 79% accepted, 48 enrolled. In 2013, 50 master's awarded. *Degree requirements:* For master's, variable foreign language requirement, comprehensive exam (for some programs), thesis or alternative, applied research project. *Entrance requirements:* For master's, GMAT or GRE, minimum undergraduate GPA of 2.5, C or better in prerequisite courses. Additional exam requirements/recommendations for international students: Required—TOEFL (minimum score 550 paper-based; 79 iBT), IELTS (minimum score 6), PTE (minimum score 53). *Application deadline:* For fall admission, 8/1 for domestic students, 6/1 for international students; for spring admission, 11/21 for domestic students, 10/1 for international students; for summer admission, 5/15 for domestic students. Applications are processed on a rolling basis. Application fee: $30 ($40 for international students). Electronic applications accepted. *Expenses:* Tuition, state resident: full-time $5139; part-time $285.50 per credit hour. Tuition, nonresident: full-time $9099; part-time $505.50 per credit hour. *Financial support:* In 2013–14, 52 students received support, including 12 teaching assistantships with full tuition reimbursements available (averaging $8,144 per year); career-related internships or fieldwork, Federal Work-Study, scholarships/grants, traineeships, tuition waivers (full), and unspecified assistantships also available. Financial award application deadline: 6/30; financial award applicants required to submit FAFSA. *Faculty research:* Ethics, corporate finance, generational difference, leadership, organizational justice. *Unit head:* Dr. Kenneth A. Heischmidt, Director, Graduate Business Studies, 573-651-2912, Fax: 573-651-5032, E-mail: kheischmidt@semo.edu. *Application contact:* Gail Amick, Admissions Specialist, 573-651-2590, Fax: 573-651-5936, E-mail: gamick@semo.edu.
Website: http://www.semo.edu/mba.

Southern New Hampshire University, School of Business, Manchester, NH 03106-1045. Offers accounting (MBA, MS, Graduate Certificate); accounting finance (MS); accounting/auditing (MS); accounting/forensic accounting (MS); accounting/taxation (MS); athletic administration (MBA, Graduate Certificate); business administration (IMBA, MBA, Certificate, Graduate Certificate), including accounting (Certificate), business administration (MBA), business information systems (Graduate Certificate), human resource management (Certificate); corporate social responsibility (MBA); entrepreneurship (MBA); finance (MBA, MS, Graduate Certificate); finance/corporate finance (MS); finance/investments and securities (MS); forensic accounting (MBA); healthcare informatics (MBA); healthcare management (MBA); human resource management (Graduate Certificate); information technology (MS, Graduate Certificate); information technology management (MBA); international business (Graduate Certificate); international business and information technology (Graduate Certificate); international finance (Graduate Certificate); international sport management (Graduate Certificate); justice studies (MBA); leadership of nonprofit organizations (Graduate Certificate); marketing (MBA, MS, Graduate Certificate); operations and project management (MS); operations and supply chain management (MBA, Graduate Certificate); organizational leadership (MS); project management (MBA, Graduate Certificate); Six Sigma (MBA); Six Sigma quality (Graduate Certificate); social media marketing (MBA); sport management (MBA, MS, Graduate Certificate); sustainability and environmental compliance (MBA); workplace conflict management (MBA); MBA/Certificate. *Accreditation:* ACBSP. Part-time and evening/weekend programs available. Postbaccalaureate distance learning degree programs offered (no on-campus study). Terminal master's awarded for partial completion of doctoral program. *Degree requirements:* For master's, one foreign language, comprehensive exam (for some programs), thesis or alternative. *Entrance requirements:* For master's, minimum GPA of 2.5. Additional exam requirements/recommendations for international students: Required—TOEFL (minimum score 500 paper-based). Electronic applications accepted.

South University, Graduate Programs, College of Business, Program in Leadership, Savannah, GA 31406. Offers MS.

South University, Program in Leadership, Virginia Beach, VA 23452. Offers MS.

South University, Program in Leadership, Columbia, SC 29203. Offers MS.

Southwest University, MBA Program, Kenner, LA 70062. Offers business administration (MBA); management (MBA); organizational management (MBA).

Southwest University, Program in Organizational Management, Kenner, LA 70062. Offers MA.

Spring Arbor University, School of Graduate and Professional Studies, Spring Arbor, MI 49283-9799. Offers counseling (MAC); family studies (MAFS); nursing (MSN); organizational management (MSM). Part-time and evening/weekend programs available. Postbaccalaureate distance learning degree programs offered (no on-campus study). *Faculty:* 12 full-time (5 women), 113 part-time/adjunct (67 women). *Students:* 225 full-time (185 women), 269 part-time (222 women); includes 166 minority (142 Black or African American, non-Hispanic/Latino; 4 American Indian or Alaska Native, non-Hispanic/Latino; 5 Asian, non-Hispanic/Latino; 13 Hispanic/Latino; 2 Two or more races, non-Hispanic/Latino), 1 international. Average age 40. In 2013, 276 master's awarded. *Entrance requirements:* For master's, bachelor's degree from regionally-accredited college or university, minimum GPA of 3.0 for at least the last two years of the bachelor's degree, at least two recommendations from professional/academic individuals. Additional exam requirements/recommendations for international students: Required—TOEFL (minimum score 600 paper-based). *Application deadline:* Applications are processed on a rolling basis. Application fee: $40. Electronic applications accepted. *Financial support:* Scholarships/grants available. Support available to part-time students. Financial award applicants required to submit FAFSA. *Unit head:* Natalie Gianetti, Dean, 517-750-1200 Ext. 1343, Fax: 517-750-6602, E-mail: gianetti@arbor.edu. *Application contact:* Greg Bentle, Coordinator of Graduate Recruitment, 517-750-6763, Fax: 517-750-6624, E-mail: gbentle@arbor.edu.
Website: http://www.arbor.edu/.

Springfield College, Graduate Programs, Program in Human Services, Springfield, MA 01109-3797. Offers human services (MS), including community counseling psychology, mental health counseling, organizational management and leadership. Part-time and evening/weekend programs available. *Faculty:* 14 full-time (7 women), 73 part-time/adjunct (41 women). *Students:* 428 full-time (315 women); includes 305 minority (238 Black or African American, non-Hispanic/Latino; 1 Asian, non-Hispanic/Latino; 36

Hispanic/Latino; 30 Two or more races, non-Hispanic/Latino), 1 international. Average age 37. 490 applicants, 99% accepted, 428 enrolled. In 2013, 274 master's awarded. *Degree requirements:* For master's, comprehensive exam, thesis (for some programs), Community Action Research Project. *Entrance requirements:* Additional exam requirements/recommendations for international students: Required—TOEFL (minimum score 550 paper-based). *Application deadline:* For fall admission, 8/31 for domestic and international students; for winter admission, 11/1 for domestic and international students; for spring admission, 12/31 for domestic and international students; for summer admission, 4/30 for domestic and international students. Applications are processed on a rolling basis. Application fee: $40. Electronic applications accepted. *Expenses:* Contact institution. *Financial support:* Application deadline: 3/1; applicants required to submit FAFSA. *Unit head:* Dr. Robert J. Willey, Dean, 413-748-3982, E-mail: rwilley@springfieldcollege.edu. *Application contact:* Marisol Guevara, Director of Recruitment and Admissions, 413-748-3742, E-mail: mguevara@springfieldcollege.edu. Website: http://www.springfieldcollege.edu/springfield-college-school-of-human-services/shs-programs/school-of-human-services-master-of-science-program/index.

State University of New York College at Potsdam, School of Education and Professional Studies, Program in Information and Communication Technology, Potsdam, NY 13676. Offers educational technology specialist (MS Ed); organizational performance, leadership and technology (MS Ed). Part-time and evening/weekend programs available. *Degree requirements:* For master's, culminating experience. *Entrance requirements:* For master's, minimum GPA of 3.0 in last 60 hours of course work. Additional exam requirements/recommendations for international students: Required—TOEFL (minimum score 550 paper-based; 80 iBT), IELTS (minimum score 6). Electronic applications accepted.

Syracuse University, Maxwell School of Citizenship and Public Affairs, Program in Leadership of International and Non-governmental Organizations, Syracuse, NY 13244. Offers CAS. Part-time programs available. *Students:* 16 applicants, 100% accepted. In 2013, 22 CASs awarded. *Degree requirements:* For CAS, seminar. *Entrance requirements:* Additional exam requirements/recommendations for international students: Required—TOEFL (minimum score 100 iBT). *Application deadline:* For fall admission, 2/1 for domestic and international students. Applications are processed on a rolling basis. Application fee: $75. Electronic applications accepted. *Unit head:* Dr. Michael Steinberg, Dean, 315-443-4000, Fax: 315-443-3385. *Application contact:* Tammy Salisbury, Office Coordinator III, 315-443-3159, E-mail: mtsalisb@maxwell.syr.edu.
Website: http://www.maxwell.syr.edu/.

Teachers College, Columbia University, Graduate Faculty of Education, Department of Organization and Leadership, Program in Social and Organizational Psychology, New York, NY 10027-6696. Offers change leadership (MA); social-organizational psychology (MA). *Faculty:* 11 full-time, 4 part-time/adjunct. *Students:* 143 full-time (85 women), 115 part-time (79 women); includes 69 minority (14 Black or African American, non-Hispanic/Latino; 26 Asian, non-Hispanic/Latino; 22 Hispanic/Latino; 7 Two or more races, non-Hispanic/Latino), 50 international. Average age 29. 256 applicants, 55% accepted, 72 enrolled. In 2013, 129 master's awarded. Terminal master's awarded for partial completion of doctoral program. *Degree requirements:* For master's, comprehensive exam. *Entrance requirements:* For master's, GRE, MAT, or GMAT, minimum GPA of 3.0. *Application deadline:* For fall admission, 12/15 for domestic students. Application fee: $65. Electronic applications accepted. *Financial support:* Fellowships, research assistantships, career-related internships or fieldwork, Federal Work-Study, institutionally sponsored loans, and tuition waivers (full and partial) available. Support available to part-time students. Financial award application deadline: 2/1. *Faculty research:* Conflict resolution, human resource and organization development, management competence, organizational culture, leadership. *Unit head:* Prof. Debra Noumair, Program Coordinator, 212-678-3395, E-mail: dn28@columbia.edu. *Application contact:* Lynda Hallmark, Program Manager, 212-678-3273, Fax: 212-678-3273, E-mail: hallmark@tc.edu.

Thomas Edison State College, School of Business and Management, Program in Organizational Leadership, Trenton, NJ 08608-1176. Offers Graduate Certificate. Part-time programs available. Postbaccalaureate distance learning degree programs offered (no on-campus study). *Entrance requirements:* Additional exam requirements/recommendations for international students: Required—TOEFL (minimum score 550 paper-based; 79 iBT). Electronic applications accepted.

Trevecca Nazarene University, Graduate Business Programs, Nashville, TN 37210-2877. Offers business administration (MBA); healthcare administration (Certificate); information technology (MBA, MS, Certificate); management (MSM); management and leadership (Certificate); project management (Certificate). Evening/weekend programs available. Postbaccalaureate distance learning degree programs offered. *Faculty:* 7 full-time (0 women), 3 part-time/adjunct (0 women). *Students:* 101 full-time (55 women), 21 part-time (8 women); includes 30 minority (27 Black or African American, non-Hispanic/Latino; 2 Asian, non-Hispanic/Latino; 1 Hispanic/Latino), 3 international. Average age 36. In 2013, 33 master's awarded. *Entrance requirements:* For master's, minimum GPA of 2.75, resume, official transcript from regionally-accredited institution, minimum math grade of C, minimum English composition grade of C, MS-IT requires undergraduate computing degree. Additional exam requirements/recommendations for international students: Required—TOEFL (minimum score 550 paper-based; 80 iBT). *Application deadline:* Applications are processed on a rolling basis. Application fee: $25. *Expenses:* Contact institution. *Financial support:* Applicants required to submit FAFSA. *Unit head:* Dr. Rick Mann, Director of Graduate and Professional Programs for School of Business, 615-248-1529, E-mail: management@trevecca.edu. *Application contact:* 615-248-1529, E-mail: cll@trevecca.edu.

Trevecca Nazarene University, Graduate Organizational Leadership Program, Nashville, TN 37210-2877. Offers independent school leadership (MOL); organizational leadership (MOL). Postbaccalaureate distance learning degree programs offered (minimal on-campus study). *Faculty:* 2 full-time (1 woman), 9 part-time/adjunct (2 women). *Students:* 110 full-time (65 women), 3 part-time (all women); includes 29 minority (26 Black or African American, non-Hispanic/Latino; 2 Hispanic/Latino; 1 Two or more races, non-Hispanic/Latino). Average age 39. In 2013, 10 master's awarded. *Degree requirements:* For master's, capstone course. *Entrance requirements:* For master's, minimum GPA of 2.5, official transcript from regionally accredited institution, resume, 500-600 word 5-paragraph essay (selected topic). Additional exam requirements/recommendations for international students: Required—TOEFL (minimum score 550 paper-based; 80 iBT). Tuition and fees vary according to degree level and program. *Financial support:* Applicants required to submit FAFSA. *Unit head:* Dr. Carol Maxson, Interim Dean, College of Lifelong Learning, 615-248-1259, E-mail: cll@trevecca.edu. *Application contact:* 615-248-1529, E-mail: mol@trevecca.edu.
Website: http://www.trevecca.edu/mol/.

Trinity Washington University, School of Business and Graduate Studies, Washington, DC 20017-1094. Offers business administration (MBA); communication (MA); international security studies (MA); organizational management (MSA), including federal program management, human resource management, nonprofit management, organizational development, public and community health. Part-time and evening/weekend programs available. *Degree requirements:* For master's, thesis (for some programs), capstone project (MSA). *Entrance requirements:* For master's, minimum GPA of 2.5. Additional exam requirements/recommendations for international students: Required—TOEFL (minimum score 550 paper-based). *Application deadline:* For fall admission, 4/1 priority date for domestic students; for winter admission, 11/1 priority date for domestic students; for spring admission, 11/1 priority date for domestic students. Applications are processed on a rolling basis. Application fee: $40. *Expenses:* *Tuition:* Part-time $715 per credit. *Financial support:* Career-related internships or fieldwork and unspecified assistantships available. Support available to part-time students. Financial award application deadline: 4/1; financial award applicants required to submit FAFSA. *Unit head:* Dr. Peggy Lewis, Associate Dean, 202-884-9204, E-mail: lewisp@trinitydc.edu. *Application contact:* Alesha Tyson, Director of Admissions for School of Business and Graduate Studies, 202-884-9400, Fax: 202-884-9229, E-mail: tysona@trinitydc.edu.
Website: http://www.trinitydc.edu/bgs/.

Trinity Western University, School of Graduate Studies, Program in Leadership, Langley, BC V2Y 1Y1, Canada. Offers business (MA, Certificate); Christian ministry (MA); education (MA, Certificate); healthcare (MA, Certificate); non-profit (MA, Certificate). Postbaccalaureate distance learning degree programs offered (minimal on-campus study). *Degree requirements:* For master's, major project. *Entrance requirements:* For master's, minimum GPA of 2.7. Additional exam requirements/recommendations for international students: Required—TOEFL (minimum score 620 paper-based; 105 iBT). Electronic applications accepted. *Expenses:* Contact institution. *Faculty research:* Servant leadership.

Troy University, Graduate School, College of Business, Program in Management, Troy, AL 36082. Offers applied management (MSM); healthcare management (MSM); human resources management (MSM); information systems (MSM); international hospitality management (MSM); international management (MSM); leadership and organizational effectiveness (MSM); public management (MS, MSM). *Accreditation:* ACBSP. Part-time and evening/weekend programs available. *Faculty:* 15 full-time (8 women), 3 part-time/adjunct (0 women). *Students:* 18 full-time (14 women), 148 part-time (86 women); includes 95 minority (75 Black or African American, non-Hispanic/Latino; 1 American Indian or Alaska Native, non-Hispanic/Latino; 4 Asian, non-Hispanic/Latino; 8 Hispanic/Latino; 7 Two or more races, non-Hispanic/Latino). Average age 35. 124 applicants, 79% accepted, 30 enrolled. In 2013, 75 master's awarded. *Degree requirements:* For master's, Graduate Educational Testing Service Major Field Test, capstone exam, minimum GPA of 3.0. *Entrance requirements:* For master's, GRE (minimum score of 900 on old exam or 294 on new exam) or GMAT (minimum score of 500), bachelor's degree; minimum undergraduate GPA of 2.5 or 3.0 on last 30 semester hours, letter of recommendation. Additional exam requirements/recommendations for international students: Required—TOEFL (minimum score 523 paper-based; 70 iBT), IELTS (minimum score 6). *Application deadline:* Applications are processed on a rolling basis. Application fee: $50. Electronic applications accepted. *Expenses:* Contact institution. *Unit head:* Dr. Bob Wheatley, Director, Graduate Business Programs, 334-670-3143, Fax: 334-670-3599, E-mail: rwheat@troy.edu. *Application contact:* Brenda K. Campbell, Director of Graduate Admissions, 334-670-3178, Fax: 334-670-3733, E-mail: bcamp@troy.edu.

Tusculum College, Graduate School, Program in Organizational Management, Greeneville, TN 37743-9997. Offers MAOM. *Degree requirements:* For master's, thesis or alternative. *Entrance requirements:* For master's, GMAT, GRE Subject Test, MAT, 3 years of work experience, minimum GPA of 2.75.

United States International University, School of Business Administration, Nairobi, Kenya. Offers business administration (GEMBA); entrepreneurship (MBA); finance (MBA); human resource management (MBA); information technology management (MBA); integrated studies (MBA); international business administration (MBA); management and organizational development (MS); marketing (MBA); organizational development (EMS); strategic management (MBA). Part-time and evening/weekend programs available. *Degree requirements:* For master's, thesis. *Entrance requirements:* For master's, GMAT, 2 letters of reference, resume. Additional exam requirements/recommendations for international students: Required—TOEFL (minimum score 550 paper-based). *Faculty research:* Marketing in small business enterprises, total quality management in Kenya.

Université Laval, Faculty of Administrative Sciences, Programs in Business Administration, Québec, QC G1K 7P4, Canada. Offers accounting (MBA); agri-food management (MBA); electronic business (MBA, Diploma); factory management and logistics (MBA); finance (MBA); firm management (MBA); geomatic management (MBA); information technology management (MBA); international management (MBA); management (MBA); management accounting (MBA, Diploma); marketing (MBA); modeling and organizational decision (MBA); occupational health and safety management (MBA); pharmacy management (MBA); social and environmental responsibility (MBA); technological entrepreneurship (Diploma). *Accreditation:* AACSB. Part-time and evening/weekend programs available. Postbaccalaureate distance learning degree programs offered (no on-campus study). *Entrance requirements:* For master's and Diploma, knowledge of French and English. Electronic applications accepted.

University of Alberta, Faculty of Graduate Studies and Research, Doctoral Program in Business, Edmonton, AB T6G 2E1, Canada. Offers accounting (PhD); finance (PhD); human resources/industrial relations (PhD); management science (PhD); marketing (PhD); organizational analysis (PhD); MBA/PhD. *Accreditation:* AACSB. Part-time programs available. *Degree requirements:* For doctorate, comprehensive exam, thesis/dissertation. *Entrance requirements:* For doctorate, GMAT. Additional exam requirements/recommendations for international students: Required—TOEFL (minimum score 550 paper-based). Electronic applications accepted. *Faculty research:* Accounting, capital markets and corporate finance, organizational change and human resource management, marketing, strategic management.

University of Central Arkansas, Graduate School, Interdisciplinary PhD Program in Leadership Studies, Conway, AR 72035-0001. Offers PhD. Part-time programs available. *Degree requirements:* For doctorate, thesis/dissertation. *Entrance requirements:* For doctorate, GRE. Additional exam requirements/recommendations for international students: Required—TOEFL. Electronic applications accepted.

University of Charleston, Doctor of Executive Leadership Program, Charleston, WV 25304-1099. Offers DEL. *Students:* 20 full-time (7 women), 9 part-time (5 women); includes 8 minority (6 Black or African American, non-Hispanic/Latino; 1 Asian, non-Hispanic/Latino; 1 Hispanic/Latino). Average age 45. *Unit head:* Dr. John Barnette, Associate Dean, 304-720-6688, E-mail: johnbarnette@ucwv.edu. *Application contact:* Bobby Redd, Application Coordinator, 304-860-5621, E-mail: bobbyredd@ucwv.edu.
Website: http://www.ucwv.edu/business/DEL/.

University of Cincinnati, Graduate School, McMicken College of Arts and Sciences, Center for Organizational Leadership, Cincinnati, OH 45221. Offers MALER. Part-time and evening/weekend programs available. *Entrance requirements:* For master's, GRE or GMAT. Additional exam requirements/recommendations for international students: Required—TOEFL (minimum score 520 paper-based; 68 iBT). Electronic applications accepted. *Faculty research:* Leadership and diversity.

University of Colorado Boulder, Leeds School of Business, Division of Business Administration, Boulder, CO 80309. Offers accounting (MS, PhD); finance (PhD); information systems (PhD); marketing (PhD); operations (PhD); strategic, organizational, and entrepreneurial studies (PhD). *Students:* 143 full-time (72 women), 2 part-time (1 woman); includes 15 minority (1 Black or African American, non-Hispanic/Latino; 2 American Indian or Alaska Native, non-Hispanic/Latino; 5 Asian, non-Hispanic/Latino; 6 Hispanic/Latino; 1 Two or more races, non-Hispanic/Latino), 37 international. Average age 25. 281 applicants, 12% accepted, 19 enrolled. In 2013, 50 master's, 8 doctorates awarded. *Entrance requirements:* For master's, GMAT, minimum undergraduate GPA of 3.0. *Application deadline:* For fall admission, 3/31 for domestic students, 3/1 for international students; for spring admission, 10/31 for domestic and international students. Application fee: $50 ($60 for international students). Electronic applications accepted. *Financial support:* In 2013–14, 145 students received support, including 37 fellowships (averaging $3,977 per year), 27 research assistantships with full and partial tuition reimbursements available (averaging $40,893 per year), 12 teaching assistantships with full and partial tuition reimbursements available (averaging $38,197 per year); institutionally sponsored loans, scholarships/grants, health care benefits, and unspecified assistantships also available. Financial award applicants required to submit FAFSA.

University of Dallas, Graduate School of Management, Irving, TX 75062-4736. Offers accounting (MBA, MM, MS); business management (MBA, MM); corporate finance (MBA, MM); financial services (MBA); global business (MBA, MM); health services management (MBA, MM); human resource management (MBA, MM); information assurance (MBA, MM, MS); information technology (MBA, MM, MS); information technology service management (MBA, MM, MS); marketing management (MBA, MM); organization development (MBA, MM); project management (MBA, MM); sports and entertainment management (MBA, MM); strategic leadership (MBA, MM); supply chain management (MBA); supply chain management and market logistics (MM). *Accreditation:* ACBSP. Part-time and evening/weekend programs available. Postbaccalaureate distance learning degree programs offered (no on-campus study). *Entrance requirements:* Additional exam requirements/recommendations for international students: Required—TOEFL. Electronic applications accepted. *Expenses:* Contact institution.

University of Denver, University College, Denver, CO 80208. Offers arts and culture (MLS, Certificate), including art, literature, and culture, arts development and program management (Certificate), creative writing; environmental policy and management (MAS, Certificate), including energy and sustainability (Certificate), environmental assessment of nuclear power (Certificate), environmental health and safety (Certificate), environmental management, natural resource management (Certificate); geographic information systems (MAS, Certificate); global affairs (MLS, Certificate), including translation studies, world history and culture; healthcare leadership (MPH, Certificate), including healthcare policy, law, and ethics, medical and healthcare information technologies, strategic management of healthcare; information and communications technology (MCIS, Certificate), including database design and administration (Certificate), geographic information systems (MCIS), information security systems security (Certificate), information systems security (MCIS), project management (MCIS, MPS, Certificate), software design and administration (Certificate), software design and programming (MCIS), technology management, telecommunications technology (MCIS), Web design and development; leadership and organizations (MPS, Certificate), including human capital in organizations, philanthropic leadership, project management (MCIS, MPS, Certificate), strategic innovation and change; organizational and professional communication (MPS, Certificate), including alternative dispute resolution, organizational communication, organizational development and training, public relations and marketing; security management (MAS, Certificate), including emergency planning and response, information security (MAS), organizational security; strategic human resource management (MPS, Certificate), including global human resources (MPS), human resource management and development (MPS). Part-time and evening/weekend programs available. Postbaccalaureate distance learning degree programs offered (no on-campus study). *Faculty:* 139 part-time/adjunct (61 women). *Students:* 49 full-time (16 women), 1,297 part-time (732 women); includes 272 minority (92 Black or African American, non-Hispanic/Latino; 5 American Indian or Alaska Native, non-Hispanic/Latino; 30 Asian, non-Hispanic/Latino; 114 Hispanic/Latino; 3 Native Hawaiian or other Pacific Islander, non-Hispanic/Latino; 28 Two or more races, non-Hispanic/Latino), 92 international. Average age 35. 542 applicants, 95% accepted, 362 enrolled. In 2013, 374 master's, 128 other advanced degrees awarded. *Degree requirements:* For master's, capstone project. *Entrance requirements:* For master's, transcripts, two letters of recommendation, personal statement, resume. Additional exam requirements/recommendations for international students: Required—TOEFL (minimum score 550 paper-based; 80 iBT). *Application deadline:* For fall admission, 7/18 priority date for domestic students, 5/2 priority date for international students; for winter admission, 10/24 priority date for domestic students, 9/19 priority date for international students; for spring admission, 2/1 for domestic students, 12/14 for international students; for summer admission, 4/18 priority date for domestic students, 3/7 priority date for international students. Applications are processed on a rolling basis. Application fee: $75. Electronic applications accepted. *Expenses:* Contact institution. *Financial support:* In 2013–14, 28 students received support. Applicants required to submit FAFSA. *Unit head:* Dr. Michael McGuire, Interim Dean, 303-871-3518, E-mail: mmcguire@du.edu. *Application contact:* Information Contact, 303-871-2291, E-mail: ucoladm@du.edu.
Website: http://www.universitycollege.du.edu/.

The University of Findlay, Office of Graduate Admissions, Findlay, OH 45840-3653. Offers athletic training (MAT); business (MBA), including health care management, hospitality management, organizational leadership, public management; education (MA Ed), including administration, children's literature, early childhood, human resource development, reading, science, special education, technology; environmental, safety and health management (MSEM); health informatics (MS); occupational therapy (MOT); pharmacy (Pharm D); physical therapy (DPT); physician assistant (MPA); rhetoric and writing (MA); teaching English to speakers of other languages (TESOL) and bilingual education (MA). Part-time and evening/weekend programs available. Postbaccalaureate distance learning degree programs offered (no on-campus study). *Faculty:* 209 full-time (98 women), 69 part-time/adjunct (38 women). *Students:* 551 full-time (332 women), 457 part-time (276 women); includes 77 minority (37 Black or African American, non-Hispanic/Latino; 1 American Indian or Alaska Native, non-Hispanic/Latino; 15 Asian, non-Hispanic/Latino; 23 Hispanic/Latino; 1 Native Hawaiian or other Pacific Islander, non-Hispanic/Latino), 135 international. Average age 28. 637 applicants, 66% accepted, 241 enrolled. In 2013, 267 master's, 91 doctorates awarded. *Degree requirements:* For master's, thesis, cumulative project, capstone project. *Entrance requirements:* For master's, GRE/GMAT, bachelor's degree from accredited institution, minimum undergraduate GPA of 2.5 in last 64 hours of course work; for doctorate, GRE, minimum cumulative GPA of 3.0. Additional exam requirements/recommendations for international students: Required—TOEFL (minimum score 80 iBT). *Application deadline:* Applications are processed on a rolling basis. Application fee: $25. Electronic applications accepted. *Expenses: Required fees:* $146 per semester. Tuition and fees vary according to degree level and program. *Financial support:* In 2013–14, 11 research assistantships with full and partial tuition reimbursements (averaging $4,000 per year),

10 teaching assistantships with full and partial tuition reimbursements (averaging $3,600 per year) were awarded; career-related internships or fieldwork, Federal Work-Study, health care benefits, and unspecified assistantships also available. Financial award application deadline: 4/1; financial award applicants required to submit FAFSA. *Unit head:* Christopher M. Harris, Director of Admissions, 419-434-4347, E-mail: harrisc1@findlay.edu. *Application contact:* Emily Ickes, Graduate Admissions Counselor, 419-434-6933, Fax: 419-434-4898, E-mail: ickese@findlay.edu.
Website: http://www.findlay.edu/admissions/graduate/Pages/default.aspx.

University of Guelph, Graduate Studies, College of Management and Economics, MA (Leadership) Program, Guelph, ON N1G 2W1, Canada. Offers MA. Part-time and evening/weekend programs available. Postbaccalaureate distance learning degree programs offered (minimal on-campus study). *Entrance requirements:* For master's, minimum B-average, minimum 5 years of relevant work experience. Additional exam requirements/recommendations for international students: Required—TOEFL (minimum score 550 paper-based). Electronic applications accepted. *Faculty research:* Theories of leadership, organizational change, ethics in leadership, decision making, politics of organizations.

University of Hawaii at Manoa, Graduate Division, Shidler College of Business, Program in Business Administration, Honolulu, HI 96822. Offers Asian business studies (MBA); Chinese business studies (MBA); decision sciences (MBA); entrepreneurship (MBA); finance (MBA); finance and banking (MBA); human resources management (MBA); information management (MBA); information technology (MBA); international business (MBA); Japanese business studies (MBA); marketing (MBA); organizational behavior (MBA); organizational management (MBA); real estate (MBA); student-designed track (MBA). *Accreditation:* AACSB. Part-time and evening/weekend programs available. *Degree requirements:* For master's, thesis optional. *Entrance requirements:* For master's, GMAT, minimum GPA of 3.0. Additional exam requirements/recommendations for international students: Required—TOEFL (minimum score 600 paper-based; 100 iBT), IELTS (minimum score 7). *Expenses:* Contact institution.

University of Hawaii at Manoa, Graduate Division, Shidler College of Business, Program in International Management, Honolulu, HI 96822. Offers Asian finance (PhD); global information technology management (PhD); international accounting (PhD); international marketing (PhD); international organization and strategy (PhD). Part-time programs available. *Degree requirements:* For doctorate, comprehensive exam, thesis/dissertation. *Entrance requirements:* For doctorate, GMAT or GRE General Test, minimum GPA of 3.0. Additional exam requirements/recommendations for international students: Required—TOEFL (minimum score 600 paper-based; 100 iBT), IELTS (minimum score 7). *Expenses:* Contact institution.

The University of Kansas, University of Kansas Medical Center, School of Nursing, Kansas City, KS 66160. Offers adult/gerontological clinical nurse specialist (PMC); adult/gerontological nurse practitioner (PMC); clinical research management (PMC); health care informatics (PMC); health professions educator (PMC); nurse midwife (PMC); nursing (MS, DNP, PhD); organizational leadership (PMC); psychiatric/mental health nurse practitioner (PMC); public health nursing (PMC). *Accreditation:* AACN; ACNM/ACME. Part-time programs available. Postbaccalaureate distance learning degree programs offered (minimal on-campus study). *Faculty:* 59. *Students:* 55 full-time (53 women), 323 part-time (303 women); includes 57 minority (23 Black or African American, non-Hispanic/Latino; 14 Asian, non-Hispanic/Latino; 16 Hispanic/Latino; 1 Native Hawaiian or other Pacific Islander, non-Hispanic/Latino; 3 Two or more races, non-Hispanic/Latino), 1 international. Average age 38. 113 applicants, 59% accepted, 61 enrolled. In 2013, 77 master's, 18 doctorates, 11 other advanced degrees awarded. Terminal master's awarded for partial completion of doctoral program. *Degree requirements:* For master's, comprehensive exam, thesis (for some programs), general oral exam; for doctorate, variable foreign language requirement, thesis/dissertation, comprehensive oral exam (for DNP); comprehensive written and oral exam (for PhD). *Entrance requirements:* For master's, bachelor's degree in nursing, minimum GPA of 3.0, 1 year of clinical experience, RN license in KS and MO; for doctorate, GRE General Test, bachelor's degree in nursing, minimum GPA of 3.5, RN license in KS and MO. Additional exam requirements/recommendations for international students: Required—TOEFL. *Application deadline:* For fall admission, 4/1 for domestic and international students; for spring admission, 9/1 for domestic and international students. Application fee: $60. Electronic applications accepted. *Financial support:* Research assistantships with full and partial tuition reimbursements, teaching assistantships with full and partial tuition reimbursements, scholarships/grants, and traineeships available. Financial award application deadline: 3/1; financial award applicants required to submit FAFSA. *Faculty research:* Breastfeeding practices of teen mothers, national database of nursing quality indicators, caregiving of families of patients using technology in the home, simulation in nursing education, diaphragm fatigue. *Total annual research expenditures:* $6.4 million. *Unit head:* Dr. Karen L. Miller, Dean, 913-588-1601, Fax: 913-588-1660, E-mail: kmiller@kumc.edu. *Application contact:* Dr. Pamela K. Barnes, Associate Dean, Student Affairs, 913-588-1619, Fax: 913-588-1615, E-mail: pbarnes2@kumc.edu.
Website: http://nursing.kumc.edu.

University of La Verne, College of Business and Public Management, Program in Organizational Management and Leadership, La Verne, CA 91750-4443. Offers leadership and management (MS), including human resource management, nonprofit management, organizational development; nonprofit management (Certificate); organizational leadership (Certificate). Part-time programs available. *Faculty:* 2 full-time (1 woman), 8 part-time/adjunct (6 women). *Students:* 77 full-time (39 women), 67 part-time (47 women); includes 69 minority (7 Black or African American, non-Hispanic/Latino; 3 Asian, non-Hispanic/Latino; 55 Hispanic/Latino; 2 Native Hawaiian or other Pacific Islander, non-Hispanic/Latino; 2 Two or more races, non-Hispanic/Latino), 38 international. Average age 32. In 2013, 183 master's awarded. *Degree requirements:* For master's, thesis or research project. *Entrance requirements:* For master's, minimum undergraduate GPA of 2.75, 2 letters of recommendation, interview, resume. Additional exam requirements/recommendations for international students: Required—TOEFL (minimum score 550 paper-based). *Application deadline:* Applications are processed on a rolling basis. Application fee: $50. *Expenses:* Contact institution. *Financial support:* Institutionally sponsored loans available. Financial award application deadline: 3/2; financial award applicants required to submit FAFSA. *Unit head:* Dr. Kathy Duncan, Program Director, 909-593-3511 Ext. 4415, E-mail: kduncan2@laverne.edu. *Application contact:* Rina Lazarian-Chehab, Senior Associate Director of Graduate Admissions, 909-593-3511 Ext. 4317, Fax: 909-392-2761, E-mail: rlazarian@laverne.edu.
Website: http://www.laverne.edu/business-and-public-administration/org-mgmt/.

University of La Verne, College of Education and Organizational Leadership, Doctoral Program in Organizational Leadership, La Verne, CA 91750-4443. Offers Ed D. Part-time programs available. *Faculty:* 10 part-time/adjunct (5 women). *Students:* 125 full-time (83 women), 68 part-time (46 women); includes 73 minority (23 Black or African American, non-Hispanic/Latino; 1 American Indian or Alaska Native, non-Hispanic/Latino; 4 Asian, non-Hispanic/Latino; 45 Hispanic/Latino), 1 international. Average age 45. In 2013, 62 doctorates awarded. *Degree requirements:* For doctorate, thesis/dissertation. *Entrance requirements:* For doctorate, GRE or MAT, minimum graduate GPA of 3.0, resume or curriculum vitae, 2 endorsement forms. Additional exam requirements/recommendations for international students: Required—TOEFL (minimum

score 550 paper-based). *Application deadline:* Applications are processed on a rolling basis. Application fee: $75. *Expenses:* Contact institution. *Financial support:* Institutionally sponsored loans available. Financial award application deadline: 3/2; financial award applicants required to submit FAFSA. *Unit head:* Dr. Laura Hyatt, Chairperson, 909-448-4583, E-mail: lhyatt@laverne.edu. *Application contact:* Christy Ranells, Program and Admission Specialist, 909-448-4644, Fax: 909-392-2744, E-mail: cranells@laverne.edu.
Website: http://laverne.edu/education/.

University of La Verne, Regional and Online Campuses, Graduate Programs, Inland Empire Campus, Ontario, CA 91761. Offers business administration (MBA, MBA-EP), including accounting (MBA), finance (MBA), health services management (MBA-EP), information technology (MBA-EP), international business (MBA), managed care (MBA), management and leadership (MBA-EP), marketing (MBA-EP), supply chain management (MBA); leadership and management (MS), including human resource management, nonprofit management, organizational development. Part-time and evening/weekend programs available. *Faculty:* 1 full-time (0 women), 14 part-time/adjunct (6 women). *Students:* 26 full-time (15 women), 106 part-time (65 women); includes 92 minority (15 Black or African American, non-Hispanic/Latino; 29 Asian, non-Hispanic/Latino; 43 Hispanic/Latino; 1 Native Hawaiian or other Pacific Islander, non-Hispanic/Latino; 4 Two or more races, non-Hispanic/Latino). Average age 37. In 2013, 49 master's awarded. *Application deadline:* Applications are processed on a rolling basis. Application fee: $50. *Expenses:* Contact institution. *Financial support:* Institutionally sponsored loans available. Financial award application deadline: 3/2; financial award applicants required to submit FAFSA. *Unit head:* Allen Stout, Campus Director, Inland Empire Regional Campus in Ontario, 909-937-6987, E-mail: astout@laverne.edu. *Application contact:* Karen Schumann, Senior Associate Director of Admissions, Inland Empire Regional Campus in Ontario, 909-937-6991, E-mail: kschumann@laverne.edu.
Website: http://laverne.edu/locations/inland-empire/.

University of La Verne, Regional and Online Campuses, Graduate Programs, Kern County Campus, Bakersfield, CA 93301. Offers business administration for experienced professionals (MBA-EP); education (special emphasis) (M Ed); educational counseling (MS); educational leadership (M Ed); health administration (MHA); leadership and management (MS); mild/moderate education specialist preliminary (Credential); multiple subject (elementary) (Credential); organizational leadership (Ed D); preliminary administrative services (Credential); single subject (secondary) (Credential); special education studies (MS). Part-time and evening/weekend programs available. *Faculty:* 2 part-time/adjunct (1 woman). *Students:* 1 (woman) full-time, 5 part-time (3 women); includes 4 minority (3 Hispanic/Latino; 1 Two or more races, non-Hispanic/Latino). Average age 36. In 2013, 4 master's awarded. *Application deadline:* Applications are processed on a rolling basis. Application fee: $50. *Expenses:* Contact institution. *Financial support:* Institutionally sponsored loans available. Financial award application deadline: 3/2; financial award applicants required to submit FAFSA. *Unit head:* Nora Dominguez, Regional Campus Director, 661-861-6802, E-mail: ndominguez@laverne.edu. *Application contact:* Regina Benavides, Associate Director of Admissions, 661-861-6807, E-mail: rbenavides@laverne.edu.
Website: http://laverne.edu/locations/bakersfield/.

University of Maryland Eastern Shore, Graduate Programs, Program in Organizational Leadership, Princess Anne, MD 21853-1299. Offers PhD. Evening/weekend programs available. *Degree requirements:* For doctorate, comprehensive exam, thesis/dissertation, internship. *Entrance requirements:* For doctorate, interview, writing sample, successful record of employment or career in organization/profession. Additional exam requirements/recommendations for international students: Required—TOEFL (minimum score 80 iBT). Electronic applications accepted.

University of Massachusetts Amherst, Graduate School, Isenberg School of Management, Program in Management, Amherst, MA 01003. Offers accounting (PhD); business administration (MBA); entrepreneurship (MBA); finance (MBA, PhD); healthcare administration (MBA); hospitality and tourism management (PhD); management science (PhD); marketing (MBA, PhD); organization studies (PhD); sport management (PhD); strategic management (PhD); MBA/MS. *Accreditation:* AACSB. Part-time and evening/weekend programs available. Postbaccalaureate distance learning degree programs offered. *Faculty:* 68 full-time (14 women). *Students:* 140 full-time (59 women), 1,127 part-time (319 women); includes 229 minority (24 Black or African American, non-Hispanic/Latino; 2 American Indian or Alaska Native, non-Hispanic/Latino; 135 Asian, non-Hispanic/Latino; 51 Hispanic/Latino; 6 Native Hawaiian or other Pacific Islander, non-Hispanic/Latino; 11 Two or more races, non-Hispanic/Latino), 131 international. Average age 36. 828 applicants, 56% accepted, 351 enrolled. In 2013, 361 master's, 12 doctorates awarded. Terminal master's awarded for partial completion of doctoral program. *Degree requirements:* For doctorate, comprehensive exam, thesis/dissertation. *Entrance requirements:* For master's and doctorate, GMAT or GRE General Test. Additional exam requirements/recommendations for international students: Required—TOEFL (minimum score 550 paper-based; 80 iBT), IELTS (minimum score 6.5). *Application deadline:* For fall admission, 1/20 for domestic and international students. Applications are processed on a rolling basis. Application fee: $75. Electronic applications accepted. *Financial support:* Fellowships with full and partial tuition reimbursements, research assistantships with full and partial tuition reimbursements, teaching assistantships with full and partial tuition reimbursements, career-related internships or fieldwork, Federal Work-Study, scholarships/grants, traineeships, health care benefits, tuition waivers (full and partial), and unspecified assistantships available. Support available to part-time students. Financial award application deadline: 1/20; financial award applicants required to submit FAFSA. *Unit head:* Dr. John Wells, Chair, 413-545-7609, Fax: 413-577-2234. *Application contact:* Lindsay DeSantis, Supervisor of Admissions, 413-545-0722, Fax: 413-577-0010, E-mail: gradadm@grad.umass.edu.
Website: http://www.isenberg.umass.edu/.

University of Massachusetts Dartmouth, Graduate School, Charlton College of Business, Program in Business Administration, North Dartmouth, MA 02747-2300. Offers accounting (Postbaccalaureate Certificate); business administration (MBA); business foundations (Graduate Certificate); finance (Postbaccalaureate Certificate); international business (Graduate Certificate); management (Postbaccalaureate Certificate); marketing (Postbaccalaureate Certificate); organizational leadership (Graduate Certificate); supply chain management (Postbaccalaureate Certificate). *Accreditation:* AACSB. Part-time programs available. Postbaccalaureate distance learning degree programs offered (no on-campus study). *Faculty:* 36 full-time (12 women), 27 part-time/adjunct (10 women). *Students:* 154 full-time (73 women), 120 part-time (55 women); includes 28 minority (2 Black or African American, non-Hispanic/Latino; 1 American Indian or Alaska Native, non-Hispanic/Latino; 6 Asian, non-Hispanic/Latino; 11 Hispanic/Latino; 8 Two or more races, non-Hispanic/Latino), 129 international. Average age 29. 204 applicants, 82% accepted, 112 enrolled. In 2013, 71 master's, 15 other advanced degrees awarded. *Degree requirements:* For master's, portfolio of MBA course work. *Entrance requirements:* For master's, GMAT, statement of purpose (minimum of 300 words), resume, 2 letters of recommendation, official transcripts; for other advanced degree, statement of purpose (minimum of 300 words), resume, official transcripts. Additional exam requirements/recommendations for international students: Required—TOEFL (minimum score 500 paper-based; 72 iBT), IELTS (minimum score 6). *Application deadline:* For fall admission, 8/1 priority date for domestic students, 5/1 priority date for international students; for spring admission, 1/1 priority date for domestic students, 10/1 priority date for international students. Applications are processed on a rolling basis. Application fee: $60. Electronic applications accepted. *Expenses:* Tuition, state resident: full-time $2071; part-time $86.29 per credit. Tuition, nonresident: full-time $8099; part-time $337.46 per credit. Tuition and fees vary according to course load and reciprocity agreements. *Financial support:* Federal Work-Study and unspecified assistantships available. Support available to part-time students. Financial award application deadline: 3/1; financial award applicants required to submit FAFSA. *Faculty research:* E-commerce, managing diversity, agile manufacturing, green business, activity-based management, build-to-order supply chain management. *Total annual research expenditures:* $330,000. *Unit head:* Toby Stapleton, Assistant Dean for Graduate Studies, 508-999-8543, Fax: 508-999-8646, E-mail: tstapleton@umassd.edu. *Application contact:* Steven Briggs, Director of Marketing and Recruitment for Graduate Studies, 508-999-8604, Fax: 508-999-8183, E-mail: graduate@umassd.edu.
Website: http://www.umassd.edu/charlton/.

University of Michigan–Flint, School of Management, Flint, MI 48502-1950. Offers accounting (MBA, MSA); business (Graduate Certificate); computer information systems (MBA); finance (MBA); health care management (MBA); international business (MBA); lean manufacturing (MBA); marketing (MBA); organizational leadership (MBA). *Accreditation:* AACSB. Part-time and evening/weekend programs available. Postbaccalaureate distance learning degree programs offered (minimal on-campus study). *Faculty:* 13 full-time (3 women), 4 part-time/adjunct (0 women). *Students:* 19 full-time (6 women), 234 part-time (72 women); includes 50 minority (21 Black or African American, non-Hispanic/Latino; 5 American Indian or Alaska Native, non-Hispanic/Latino; 12 Asian, non-Hispanic/Latino; 5 Hispanic/Latino; 7 Two or more races, non-Hispanic/Latino), 30 international. Average age 32. 195 applicants, 56% accepted, 88 enrolled. In 2013, 73 master's awarded. *Degree requirements:* For master's, thesis or alternative. *Entrance requirements:* For master's, GMAT or GRE, minimum GPA of 3.0. Additional exam requirements/recommendations for international students: Required—TOEFL (minimum score 560 paper-based; 84 iBT), IELTS (minimum score 6.5). *Application deadline:* For fall admission, 8/1 for domestic students, 5/1 for international students; for winter admission, 11/1 for domestic students, 9/1 for international students; for spring admission, 2/15 for domestic students, 1/15 for international students. Applications are processed on a rolling basis. Application fee: $55. Electronic applications accepted. *Financial support:* Federal Work-Study, scholarships/grants, and unspecified assistantships available. Support available to part-time students. Financial award application deadline: 3/1; financial award applicants required to submit FAFSA. *Unit head:* Dr. Scott Johnson, Dean, School of Management, 810-762-3164, Fax: 810-237-6685, E-mail: scotjohn@umflint.edu. *Application contact:* Jeremiah Cook, Marketing Communications Specialist, 810-424-5583, Fax: 810-766-6789, E-mail: jecook@umflint.edu.
Website: http://www.umflint.edu/som/.

University of Missouri, Graduate School, Harry S Truman School of Public Affairs, Columbia, MO 65211. Offers grantsmanship (Graduate Certificate); nonprofit management (Graduate Certificate); organizational change (Graduate Certificate); public affairs (MPA, PhD); public management (Graduate Certificate); science and public policy (Graduate Certificate). *Accreditation:* NASPAA. *Faculty:* 12 full-time (5 women). *Students:* 91 full-time (54 women), 60 part-time (30 women); includes 14 minority (10 Black or African American, non-Hispanic/Latino; 1 Asian, non-Hispanic/Latino; 2 Hispanic/Latino; 1 Two or more races, non-Hispanic/Latino), 47 international. Average age 31. 152 applicants, 53% accepted, 51 enrolled. In 2013, 53 master's, 1 doctorate, 19 other advanced degrees awarded. *Entrance requirements:* For master's, GRE General Test, minimum GPA of 3.0. Additional exam requirements/recommendations for international students: Required—TOEFL (minimum score 550 paper-based; 79 iBT). *Application deadline:* For fall admission, 2/1 priority date for domestic and international students. Applications are processed on a rolling basis. Application fee: $55 ($75 for international students). Electronic applications accepted. *Financial support:* Fellowships, research assistantships, teaching assistantships, institutionally sponsored loans, scholarships/grants, traineeships, health care benefits, and unspecified assistantships available. Support available to part-time students. *Faculty research:* Public service ethics, history and theory, organizational symbolism and culture; program evaluation and social policy, with special emphasis on child development, education and health policies; organization theory and applied psychoanalytic theory; foreign policy and international political economy; health care delivery for persons with disabilities and health policy; survival strategies employed by low-income households; rural economic development, fiscal and economic impact analysis. *Unit head:* Dr. Bart Wechsler, Director, 573-882-3304, E-mail: wechslerb@missouri.edu. *Application contact:* Nicole Harris, Assistant Program Director for Student Services, 573-882-3471, E-mail: harrisnr@missouri.edu.
Website: http://truman.missouri.edu/.

University of Nevada, Las Vegas, Graduate College, Greenspun College of Urban Affairs, School of Environmental and Public Affairs, Las Vegas, NV 89154-4030. Offers environmental science (MS, PhD); non-profit management (Certificate); public administration (MPA, MS), including crisis and emergency management (MS); public affairs (PhD); public management (Certificate); solar and renewable energy (Certificate); urban leadership (MA); workforce development and organizational leadership (PhD). Part-time programs available. *Faculty:* 8 full-time (6 women), 6 part-time/adjunct (5 women). *Students:* 73 full-time (35 women), 133 part-time (63 women); includes 81 minority (29 Black or African American, non-Hispanic/Latino; 2 American Indian or Alaska Native, non-Hispanic/Latino; 5 Asian, non-Hispanic/Latino; 29 Hispanic/Latino; 2 Native Hawaiian or other Pacific Islander, non-Hispanic/Latino; 14 Two or more races, non-Hispanic/Latino), 7 international. Average age 37. 86 applicants, 71% accepted, 53 enrolled. In 2013, 60 master's, 6 doctorates, 17 other advanced degrees awarded. *Degree requirements:* For master's, comprehensive exam (for some programs), thesis; for doctorate, comprehensive exam (for some programs), thesis/dissertation. *Entrance requirements:* Additional exam requirements/recommendations for international students: Required—TOEFL (minimum score 550 paper-based; 80 iBT), IELTS (minimum score 7). *Application deadline:* For fall admission, 2/15 for domestic students, 5/1 for international students; for spring admission, 11/1 for domestic students, 10/1 for international students. Application fee: $60 ($95 for international students). Electronic applications accepted. *Expenses:* Tuition, state resident: full-time $4752; part-time $264 per credit. Tuition, nonresident: full-time $18,662; part-time $554.50 per credit. *International tuition:* $18,952 full-time. *Required fees:* $532; $12 per credit. $266 per semester. One-time fee: $35. Tuition and fees vary according to course load and program. *Financial support:* In 2013–14, 28 students received support, including 19 research assistantships with partial tuition reimbursements available (averaging $11,301 per year), 9 teaching assistantships with partial tuition reimbursements available (averaging $12,028 per year); institutionally sponsored loans, scholarships/grants, health care benefits, and unspecified assistantships also available. Financial award application deadline: 3/1. *Faculty research:* Community and organizational resilience;

environmental decision-making and management; budgeting and human resource/workforce management; urban design, sustainability and governance; public and non-profit management. *Total annual research expenditures:* $333,798. *Unit head:* Dr. Christopher Stream, Chair/Associate Professor, 702-895-5120, Fax: 702-895-4436, E-mail: chris.stream@unlv.edu. *Application contact:* Graduate College Admissions Evaluator, 702-895-3320, Fax: 702-895-4180, E-mail: gradcollege@unlv.edu.
Website: http://sepa.unlv.edu/.

University of New Haven, Graduate School, College of Arts and Sciences, Program in Industrial and Organizational Psychology, West Haven, CT 06516-1916. Offers conflict management (MA); human resource management (MA); industrial organizational psychology (MA); organizational development (MA); psychology of conflict management (Certificate). Part-time and evening/weekend programs available. *Students:* 73 full-time (49 women), 20 part-time (15 women); includes 24 minority (11 Black or African American, non-Hispanic/Latino; 4 Asian, non-Hispanic/Latino; 6 Hispanic/Latino; 3 Two or more races, non-Hispanic/Latino), 10 international. 125 applicants, 95% accepted, 51 enrolled. In 2013, 49 master's, 1 other advanced degree awarded. *Degree requirements:* For master's, thesis or alternative, internship or practicum. *Entrance requirements:* Additional exam requirements/recommendations for international students: Required—TOEFL (minimum score 80 iBT), IELTS, PTE (minimum score 53). *Application deadline:* For fall admission, 5/31 for international students; for winter admission, 10/15 for international students; for spring admission, 1/15 for international students. Applications are processed on a rolling basis. Application fee: $75. Electronic applications accepted. Application fee is waived when completed online. *Expenses:* Contact institution. *Financial support:* Research assistantships with partial tuition reimbursements, teaching assistantships with partial tuition reimbursements, career-related internships or fieldwork, Federal Work-Study, scholarships/grants, and unspecified assistantships available. Support available to part-time students. Financial award applicants required to submit FAFSA. *Unit head:* Dr. Dennis McGough, Coordinator, 203-479-4986, E-mail: dmcgough@newhaven.edu. *Application contact:* Eloise Gormley, Information Contact, 203-932-7440.
Website: http://www.newhaven.edu/4730/.

University of New Mexico, Anderson Graduate School of Management, Department of Organizational Studies, Albuquerque, NM 87131. Offers human resources management (MBA); policy and planning (MBA). Part-time and evening/weekend programs available. *Faculty:* 11 full-time (5 women), 11 part-time/adjunct (5 women). In 2013, 56 master's awarded. *Entrance requirements:* For master's, GMAT or GRE, minimum GPA of 3.0 on last 60 hours of coursework. Additional exam requirements/recommendations for international students: Required—TOEFL (minimum score 550 paper-based; 79 iBT). *Application deadline:* For fall admission, 4/1 priority date for domestic and international students; for spring admission, 10/1 priority date for domestic and international students. Applications are processed on a rolling basis. Application fee: $50. Electronic applications accepted. *Expenses:* Contact institution. *Financial support:* Fellowships, research assistantships, career-related internships or fieldwork, Federal Work-Study, scholarships/grants, and unspecified assistantships available. Support available to part-time students. Financial award application deadline: 6/1; financial award applicants required to submit FAFSA. *Faculty research:* Business ethics and social corporate responsibility, diversity, human resources, organizational strategy, organizational behavior. *Unit head:* Dr. Jacqueline Hood, Chair, 505-277-6471, Fax: 505-277-7108, E-mail: jnhood@unm.edu. *Application contact:* Tracy Wilkey, Manager, Academic Advisement, 505-277-3290, Fax: 505-277-8436, E-mail: andersonadvising@unm.edu.
Website: http://mba.mgt.unm.edu/default.asp.

University of Northwestern–St. Paul, Program in Leadership, St. Paul, MN 55113-1598. Offers Graduate Certificate. Part-time and evening/weekend programs available. Postbaccalaureate distance learning degree programs offered (no on-campus study). *Expenses: Tuition:* Full-time $8820; part-time $490 per credit.
Website: http://www.unwsp.edu/web/grad-studies/graduate-certificate-in-leadership.

University of Northwestern–St. Paul, Program in Organizational Leadership, St. Paul, MN 55113-1598. Offers MOL. Part-time and evening/weekend programs available. *Expenses: Tuition:* Full-time $8820; part-time $490 per credit.

University of Pennsylvania, School of Arts and Sciences, College of Liberal and Professional Studies, Philadelphia, PA 19104. Offers applied geosciences (MSAG); applied positive psychology (MAP); chemical sciences (MCS); environmental studies (MES); individualized study (MLA); liberal arts (M Phil); medical physics (MMP); organization dynamics (M Phil). *Students:* 167 full-time (98 women), 310 part-time (165 women); includes 84 minority (29 Black or African American, non-Hispanic/Latino; 1 American Indian or Alaska Native, non-Hispanic/Latino; 25 Asian, non-Hispanic/Latino; 18 Hispanic/Latino; 11 Two or more races, non-Hispanic/Latino), 61 international. 718 applicants, 49% accepted, 281 enrolled. In 2013, 173 master's awarded. *Application deadline:* For fall admission, 12/1 priority date for domestic students. Application fee: $70. Electronic applications accepted. *Unit head:* Nora Lewis, Vice Dean, Professional and Liberal Education, 215-898-7326, E-mail: nlewis@sas.upenn.edu. *Application contact:* 215-898-7326, E-mail: lps@sas.upenn.edu.
Website: http://www.sas.upenn.edu/lps/graduate.

University of Pennsylvania, School of Arts and Sciences, Fels Institute of Government, Philadelphia, PA 19104. Offers economic development and growth (Certificate); government administration (MGA); nonprofit administration (Certificate); organization dynamics (MS); politics (Certificate); public administration (MPA); public finance (Certificate). Part-time and evening/weekend programs available. *Students:* 55 full-time (27 women), 70 part-time (40 women); includes 26 minority (10 Black or African American, non-Hispanic/Latino; 1 American Indian or Alaska Native, non-Hispanic/Latino; 6 Asian, non-Hispanic/Latino; 4 Hispanic/Latino; 5 Two or more races, non-Hispanic/Latino), 17 international. 519 applicants, 34% accepted, 111 enrolled. In 2013, 56 master's, 31 other advanced degrees awarded. *Entrance requirements:* For master's, GRE, GMAT, or LSAT. Additional exam requirements/recommendations for international students: Required—TOEFL, IELTS. *Application deadline:* For fall admission, 1/15 for domestic students. Applications are processed on a rolling basis. Application fee: $70. *Financial support:* Fellowships, institutionally sponsored loans, and scholarships/grants available. Financial award application deadline: 1/15; financial award applicants required to submit FAFSA. *Unit head:* David B Thornburgh, Executive Director, 215-746-2800, E-mail: david_thornburgh@sas.upenn.edu. *Application contact:* 215-746-6684, Fax: 215-898-6238, E-mail: felsinstitute@sas.upenn.edu.
Website: http://www.fels.upenn.edu/.

University of Phoenix–Bay Area Campus, College of Information Systems and Technology, San Jose, CA 95134-1805. Offers information systems (MIS); organizational leadership/information systems and technology (DM). Evening/weekend programs available. *Degree requirements:* For master's, thesis (for some programs). *Entrance requirements:* For master's, minimum undergraduate GPA of 3.0, 3 years of work experience. Additional exam requirements/recommendations for international students: Required—TOEFL (minimum score 550 paper-based; 79 iBT). Electronic applications accepted.

University of Phoenix–Bay Area Campus, School of Business, San Jose, CA 95134-1805. Offers accountancy (MS); accounting (MBA); business administration (MBA, DBA); energy management (MBA); global management (MBA); health care management (MBA); human resource management (MBA); human resources management (MM); management (MM); marketing (MBA); organizational leadership (DM); project management (MBA); public administration (MPA); technology management (MBA). Evening/weekend programs available. Postbaccalaureate distance learning degree programs offered (no on-campus study). *Degree requirements:* For master's, thesis (for some programs). *Entrance requirements:* For master's, minimum undergraduate GPA of 3.0, 3 years of work experience. Additional exam requirements/recommendations for international students: Required—TOEFL (minimum score 550 paper-based; 79 iBT). Electronic applications accepted.

University of Phoenix–Online Campus, School of Advanced Studies, Phoenix, AZ 85034-7209. Offers business administration (DBA); education (Ed S); educational leadership (Ed D), including curriculum and instruction, education technology, educational leadership; health administration (DHA); higher education administration (PhD); industrial/organizational psychology (PhD); nursing (PhD); organizational leadership (DM), including information systems and technology, organizational leadership. Evening/weekend programs available. Postbaccalaureate distance learning degree programs offered. *Degree requirements:* For doctorate, thesis/dissertation. *Entrance requirements:* Additional exam requirements/recommendations for international students: Required—TOEFL, TOEIC (Test of English as an International Communication), Berlitz Online English Proficiency Exam, PTE, or IELTS. Electronic applications accepted. *Expenses:* Contact institution.

University of Phoenix–Washington D.C. Campus, College of Information Systems and Technology, Washington, DC 20001. Offers information systems (MIS); organizational leadership/information systems and technology (DM).

University of Phoenix–Washington D.C. Campus, School of Business, Washington, DC 20001. Offers accountancy (MS); business administration (MBA, DBA); human resources management (MM); management (MM); organizational leadership (DM); public administration (MPA).

University of Portland, School of Education, Portland, OR 97203-5798. Offers education (MA, MAT); educational leadership (M Ed); English for speakers of other languages (M Ed); initial administrator licensure (M Ed); neuroeducation (Ed D); organizational leadership and development (Ed D); reading (M Ed); special education (M Ed). M Ed also available through the Graduate Outreach Program for teachers residing in the Oregon and Washington state areas. *Accreditation:* NCATE. Part-time and evening/weekend programs available. *Faculty:* 17 full-time (10 women), 12 part-time/adjunct (4 women). *Students:* 47 full-time (29 women), 214 part-time (155 women); includes 25 minority (1 Black or African American, non-Hispanic/Latino; 1 American Indian or Alaska Native, non-Hispanic/Latino; 8 Asian, non-Hispanic/Latino; 6 Hispanic/Latino; 6 Native Hawaiian or other Pacific Islander, non-Hispanic/Latino; 3 Two or more races, non-Hispanic/Latino), 63 international. Average age 32. In 2013, 96 master's awarded. *Entrance requirements:* For master's, minimum GPA of 3.0, teaching certificate, letters of recommendation, resume, statement of goals, official transcripts. Additional exam requirements/recommendations for international students: Required—TOEFL (minimum score 550 paper-based; 80 iBT), IELTS (minimum score 7). *Application deadline:* For fall admission, 7/15 priority date for domestic and international students; for spring admission, 12/15 priority date for domestic and international students. Applications are processed on a rolling basis. Application fee: $50. *Expenses: Tuition:* Part-time $1025 per credit hour. Tuition and fees vary according to program. *Financial support:* Federal Work-Study and scholarships/grants available. Support available to part-time students. Financial award application deadline: 3/1; financial award applicants required to submit FAFSA. *Faculty research:* Multicultural education, supervision/leadership. *Unit head:* Dr. Bruce Weitzel, Associate Dean, 503-943-7135, E-mail: soed@up.edu. *Application contact:* Dr. Matt Baasten, Assistant to the Provost and Dean of the Graduate School, 503-943-7107, Fax: 503-943-7315, E-mail: baasten@up.edu.
Website: http://education.up.edu/default.aspx?cid-4318&pid-5590.

University of Regina, Faculty of Graduate Studies and Research, Kenneth Levene Graduate School of Business, Program in Business Administration, Regina, SK S4S 0A2, Canada. Offers business foundations (PGD); engineering management (MBA); executive business administration (EMBA); general management (MBA); international business (MBA); leadership (M Admin); organizational leadership (Master's Certificate); project management (Master's Certificate). Part-time and evening/weekend programs available. *Faculty:* 39 full-time (14 women), 7 part-time/adjunct (0 women). *Students:* 86 full-time (30 women), 65 part-time (32 women). 123 applicants, 25% accepted. In 2013, 59 master's, 23 other advanced degrees awarded. *Degree requirements:* For master's, project (for some programs). *Entrance requirements:* For master's, GMAT, three years of relevant work experience, four-year undergraduate degree; for other advanced degree, GMAT (for PGD), four-year undergraduate degree and two years of relevant work experience (for Certificates); three years' work experience (for Postgraduate Diploma). Additional exam requirements/recommendations for international students: Required—TOEFL (minimum score 580 paper-based; 80 iBT), IELTS (minimum score 6.5). *Application deadline:* Applications are processed on a rolling basis. Application fee: $100. Electronic applications accepted. *Expenses:* Contact institution. *Financial support:* In 2013–14, 7 fellowships (averaging $6,000 per year), 1 research assistantship (averaging $5,500 per year), 7 teaching assistantships (averaging $2,356 per year) were awarded; scholarships/grants also available. Financial award application deadline: 6/15. *Faculty research:* Business policy and strategy, production and operations management, human behavior in organizations, financial management, social issues in business. *Unit head:* Dr. Andrew Gaudes, Dean, 306-585-4162, Fax: 306-585-5361, E-mail: andrew.gaudes@uregina.ca. *Application contact:* Steve Wield, Manager, Graduate Programs, 306-337-8463, Fax: 306-585-5361, E-mail: steve.wield@uregina.ca.
Website: http://www.uregina.ca/business/levene/.

University of St. Thomas, Graduate Studies, School of Education, Department of Organization Learning and Development, St. Paul, MN 55105-1096. Offers human resources and change leadership (MA); learning, performance and technology (MA); organization development (Ed D). Part-time and evening/weekend programs available. Postbaccalaureate distance learning degree programs offered (minimal on-campus study). *Degree requirements:* For master's, practicum; for doctorate, comprehensive exam, thesis/dissertation. *Entrance requirements:* For master's, minimum GPA of 3.0, 2 letters of reference, personal statement, 2-5 years of organization experience; for doctorate, minimum GPA of 3.5, interview, 5-7 years of OD or leadership experience. Additional exam requirements/recommendations for international students: Required—TOEFL (minimum score 550 paper-based). *Application deadline:* For fall admission, 8/1 priority date for domestic and international students; for winter admission, 12/1 priority date for domestic students, 12/1 for international students; for spring admission, 12/1 priority date for domestic and international students. Applications are processed on a rolling basis. Application fee: $50. Electronic applications accepted. *Expenses:* Contact institution. *Financial support:* Fellowships, research assistantships, institutionally sponsored loans, and scholarships/grants available. Support available to part-time students. Financial award applicants required to submit FAFSA. *Faculty research:* Workplace conflict, physician leaders, virtual teams, technology use in schools/

workplace, developing masterful practitioners. *Unit head:* Dr. David W. Jamieson, Chair, 651-962-4387, Fax: 651-962-4169, E-mail: djamieson@stthomas.edu. *Application contact:* Liz G. Knight, Program Manager, 651-962-4459, Fax: 651-962-4169, E-mail: egknight@stthomas.edu.

University of San Francisco, School of Management, Master of Business Administration Program, San Francisco, CA 94105. Offers entrepreneurship and innovation (MBA); finance (MBA); international business (MBA); marketing (MBA); organization development (MBA); DDS/MBA; JD/MBA; MBA/MAPS. *Accreditation:* AACSB. Part-time and evening/weekend programs available. *Faculty:* 18 full-time (4 women), 20 part-time/adjunct (10 women). *Students:* 157 full-time (69 women), 14 part-time (7 women); includes 57 minority (7 Black or African American, non-Hispanic/Latino; 31 Asian, non-Hispanic/Latino; 14 Hispanic/Latino; 5 Two or more races, non-Hispanic/Latino), 30 international. Average age 29. 345 applicants, 68% accepted, 79 enrolled. In 2013, 131 master's awarded. *Entrance requirements:* For master's, GMAT or GRE, resume (two years of professional work experience required for Part-Time MBA, preferred for Full-Time MBA), transcripts from each college or university attended, two letters of recommendation, a personal statement and an interview. Additional exam requirements/recommendations for international students: Required—TOEFL (minimum score 600 paper-based, 100 iBT), IELTS (minimum score 7) or PTE (minimum score 68). *Application deadline:* For fall admission, 6/5 for domestic students, 5/15 for international students; for spring admission, 11/30 for domestic students. Application fee: $55. Electronic applications accepted. *Expenses: Tuition:* Full-time $21,150; part-time $1175 per unit. Tuition and fees vary according to course load, campus/location and program. *Financial support:* In 2013–14, 42 students received support. Fellowships and scholarships/grants available. Financial award application deadline: 3/2; financial award applicants required to submit FAFSA. *Faculty research:* International financial markets, technology transfer licensing, international marketing, strategic planning. *Total annual research expenditures:* $50,000. *Unit head:* Dr. John Veitch, Associate Dean and Program Director, 415-422-2221, Fax: 415-422-6315, E-mail: management@usfca.edu. *Application contact:* Office of Graduate Recruiting and Admissions, 415-422-2221, Fax: 415-422-6315, E-mail: management@usfca.edu.
Website: http://www.usfca.edu/mba.

University of San Francisco, School of Management, Master of Science in Organization Development Program, San Francsico, CA 94105. Offers MSOD. Part-time and evening/weekend programs available. *Faculty:* 6 full-time (3 women), 4 part-time/adjunct (1 woman). *Students:* 104 full-time (73 women), 2 part-time (1 woman); includes 53 minority (14 Black or African American, non-Hispanic/Latino; 2 American Indian or Alaska Native, non-Hispanic/Latino; 18 Asian, non-Hispanic/Latino; 14 Hispanic/Latino; 5 Two or more races, non-Hispanic/Latino), 1 international. Average age 36. 80 applicants, 95% accepted, 52 enrolled. In 2013, 44 master's awarded. *Degree requirements:* For master's, thesis. *Entrance requirements:* For master's, resume demonstrating minimum of two years of professional work experience, transcripts from each college or university attended, two letters of recommendation, personal statement. Additional exam requirements/recommendations for international students: Required—TOEFL (minimum score 600 paper-based, 100 iBT), IELTS (minimum score 7) or PTE. *Application deadline:* For fall admission, 6/15 for domestic students, 5/15 for international students. Application fee: $55. Electronic applications accepted. *Expenses: Tuition:* Full-time $21,150; part-time $1175 per unit. Tuition and fees vary according to course load, campus/location and program. *Financial support:* In 2013–14, 17 students received support. Scholarships/grants available. Financial award application deadline: 3/2; financial award applicants required to submit FAFSA. *Unit head:* Dr. Jennifer Parlamis, Program Director, 415-422-2221, E-mail: management@usfca.edu. *Application contact:* Office of Graduate Recruiting and Admissions, 415-422-2221, Fax: 415-422-6315, E-mail: management@usfca.edu.
Website: http://www.usfca.edu/msod.

The University of Scranton, College of Graduate and Continuing Education, Department of Health Administration and Human Resources, Program in Human Resources Administration, Scranton, PA 18510. Offers human resources (MS); human resources development (MS); organizational leadership (MS). Part-time and evening/weekend programs available. *Students:* 1 (woman) part-time. Average age 39. *Degree requirements:* For master's, capstone experience. *Entrance requirements:* For master's, minimum GPA of 2.75. Additional exam requirements/recommendations for international students: Required—TOEFL (minimum score 500 paper-based), IELTS (minimum score 5.5). *Application deadline:* Applications are processed on a rolling basis. Application fee: $0. *Financial support:* Fellowships, teaching assistantships, career-related internships or fieldwork, Federal Work-Study, and unspecified assistantships available. Support available to part-time students. Financial award application deadline: 3/1. *Unit head:* Dr. Daniel J. West, Director, 570-941-6218, E-mail: westd1@scranton.edu. *Application contact:* Joseph M. Roback, Director of Admissions, 570-941-4385, Fax: 570-941-5928, E-mail: robackj2@scranton.edu.

The University of South Dakota, Graduate School, College of Arts and Sciences, Program in Administrative Studies, Vermillion, SD 57069-2390. Offers alcohol and drug studies (MSA); criminal justice (MSA); health services administration (MSA); human resource management (MSA); interdisciplinary (MSA); long term care administration (MSA); organizational leadership (MSA). Part-time and evening/weekend programs available. Postbaccalaureate distance learning degree programs offered (no on-campus study). *Degree requirements:* For master's, thesis or alternative. *Entrance requirements:* For master's, 3 years of work or experience, minimum GPA of 2.7, resume. Additional exam requirements/recommendations for international students: Required—TOEFL (minimum score 550 paper-based; 79 iBT). Electronic applications accepted.

University of Southern California, Graduate School, School of Policy, Planning, and Development, Executive Master of Leadership Program, Los Angeles, CA 90089. Offers EML. Part-time and evening/weekend programs available. *Entrance requirements:* Additional exam requirements/recommendations for international students: Required—TOEFL (minimum score 600 paper-based; 100 iBT). Electronic applications accepted. *Expenses:* Contact institution. *Faculty research:* Strategic planning, organizational transformation, strategic management, leadership.

The University of Texas at San Antonio, College of Business, Department of Management, San Antonio, TX 78249-0617. Offers management and organization studies (PhD). *Students:* 17 full-time (6 women); includes 5 minority (3 Black or African American, non-Hispanic/Latino; 1 American Indian or Alaska Native, non-Hispanic/Latino; 1 Hispanic/Latino), 1 international. Average age 24. 5 applicants, 80% accepted, 4 enrolled. In 2013, 17 doctorates awarded. Terminal master's awarded for partial completion of doctoral program. *Degree requirements:* For doctorate, comprehensive exam, thesis/dissertation. *Entrance requirements:* For doctorate, GMAT, GRE. Additional exam requirements/recommendations for international students: Required—TOEFL (minimum score 550 paper-based; 79 iBT), IELTS (minimum score 6.5). *Application deadline:* For fall admission, 7/1 for domestic students, 4/1 for international students; for spring admission, 11/1 for domestic students, 9/1 for international students. Application fee: $45 ($80 for international students). Electronic applications accepted. *Expenses:* Tuition, state resident: full-time $4671. Tuition, nonresident: full-time $8708. *International tuition:* $17,415 full-time. *Required fees:* $1924.60. Tuition and fees vary according to course load and degree level. *Financial support:* In 2013–14, 9 students received support, including 14 research assistantships with tuition reimbursements available (averaging $22,000 per year), 14 teaching assistantships with tuition reimbursements available (averaging $22,000 per year); fellowships with full tuition reimbursements available also available. Financial award application deadline: 3/31. *Total annual research expenditures:* $35. *Unit head:* Dr. William Gerard Sanders, Dean, 210-458-4317, Fax: 210-458-4308, E-mail: gerry.sanders@utsa.edu. *Application contact:* Caron Kiley, Assistant Director of Graduate Fiscal Services/PhD Program Manager, 210-458-7324, Fax: 210-458-4398, E-mail: caron.kiley@utsa.edu.
Website: http://business.utsa.edu/mgt/.

University of the Incarnate Word, Extended Academic Programs, Program in Administration, San Antonio, TX 78209-6397. Offers applied administration (MAA); organizational development (MAA). Part-time and evening/weekend programs available. *Faculty:* 12 part-time/adjunct (2 women). *Students:* 2 full-time (both women), 325 part-time (193 women); includes 215 minority (54 Black or African American, non-Hispanic/Latino; 3 American Indian or Alaska Native, non-Hispanic/Latino; 13 Asian, non-Hispanic/Latino; 143 Hispanic/Latino; 2 Native Hawaiian or other Pacific Islander, non-Hispanic/Latino). Average age 37. 138 applicants, 99% accepted, 98 enrolled. In 2013, 96 master's awarded. *Degree requirements:* For master's, capstone experience. *Entrance requirements:* For master's, GRE (minimum score of 800) or GMAT (minimum score of 450) if GPA is between 2.0 - 2.5. Additional exam requirements/recommendations for international students: Required—TOEFL (minimum score 560 paper-based; 83 iBT). *Expenses: Tuition:* Part-time $815 per credit hour. *Required fees:* $86 per credit hour. One-time fee: $40 part-time. Tuition and fees vary according to degree level and program. *Unit head:* Dr. Cyndi Porter, Vice President, 877-603-1130, E-mail: porter@uiwtx.edu. *Application contact:* Julie Weber, Director of Marketing and Recruitment, 210-832-2100, Fax: 210-829-2756, E-mail: eapadmission@uiwtx.edu.
Website: http://adcap.uiw.edu/academics/graduate_degrees/ma_administration.

University of the Incarnate Word, School of Graduate Studies and Research, Dreeben School of Education, Programs in Education, San Antonio, TX 78209-6397. Offers adult education (M Ed, MA); cross-cultural education (M Ed, MA); early childhood literacy (M Ed, MA); general education (M Ed, MA); higher education (PhD); instructional technology (M Ed, MA); international education and entrepreneurship (PhD); kinesiology (M Ed, MA); literacy (M Ed, MA); organizational leadership (PhD); organizational learning and learning (M Ed, MA); reading (M Ed, MA); special education (M Ed, MA); teacher leadership (M Ed, MA). Part-time and evening/weekend programs available. *Faculty:* 17 full-time (9 women), 6 part-time/adjunct (all women). *Students:* 23 full-time (13 women), 187 part-time (122 women); includes 114 minority (24 Black or African American, non-Hispanic/Latino; 1 American Indian or Alaska Native, non-Hispanic/Latino; 3 Asian, non-Hispanic/Latino; 85 Hispanic/Latino; 1 Two or more races, non-Hispanic/Latino), 30 international. Average age 41. 52 applicants, 67% accepted, 25 enrolled. In 2013, 12 master's, 14 doctorates awarded. *Degree requirements:* For master's, capstone; for doctorate, thesis/dissertation, qualifying exam. *Entrance requirements:* For master's, baccalaureate degree; minimum foundation GPA of 2.5; interview; for doctorate, master's degree; interview; supervised writing sample. Additional exam requirements/recommendations for international students: Required—TOEFL (minimum score 560 paper-based; 83 iBT). *Application deadline:* Applications are processed on a rolling basis. Application fee: $20. Electronic applications accepted. *Expenses: Tuition:* Part-time $815 per credit hour. *Required fees:* $86 per credit hour. One-time fee: $40 part-time. Tuition and fees vary according to degree level and program. *Financial support:* In 2013–14, 5 research assistantships were awarded; Federal Work-Study and scholarships/grants also available. Financial award applicants required to submit FAFSA. *Unit head:* Dr. Denise Staudt, Dean, Dreeben School of Education, 210-829-2762, E-mail: staudt@uiwtx.edu. *Application contact:* Andrea Cyterski-Acosta, Dean of Enrollment, 210-829-6005, Fax: 210-829-3921, E-mail: admis@uiwtx.edu.
Website: http://www.uiw.edu/education/index.htm.

University of the Incarnate Word, School of Graduate Studies and Research, H-E-B School of Business and Administration, Programs in Administration, San Antonio, TX 78209-6397. Offers adult education (MAA); communication arts (MAA); healthcare administration (MAA); instructional technology (MAA); nutrition (MAA); organizational development (MAA); sports management (MAA). Part-time and evening/weekend programs available. Postbaccalaureate distance learning degree programs offered (no on-campus study). *Faculty:* 20 full-time (10 women), 14 part-time/adjunct (6 women). *Students:* 31 full-time (22 women), 54 part-time (36 women); includes 61 minority (14 Black or African American, non-Hispanic/Latino; 1 Asian, non-Hispanic/Latino; 46 Hispanic/Latino), 6 international. Average age 31. 63 applicants, 68% accepted, 21 enrolled. In 2013, 35 master's awarded. *Degree requirements:* For master's, capstone. *Entrance requirements:* For master's, GRE, GMAT, undergraduate degree, minimum GPA of 2.5. Additional exam requirements/recommendations for international students: Required—TOEFL (minimum score 560 paper-based; 83 iBT). *Application deadline:* Applications are processed on a rolling basis. Application fee: $20. Electronic applications accepted. *Expenses: Tuition:* Part-time $815 per credit hour. *Required fees:* $86 per credit hour. One-time fee: $40 part-time. Tuition and fees vary according to degree level and program. *Financial support:* Federal Work-Study and scholarships/grants available. Financial award applicants required to submit FAFSA. *Unit head:* Dr. Mark Teachout, MAA Programs Director, 210-829-3177, Fax: 210-805-3564, E-mail: teachout@uiwtx.edu. *Application contact:* Andrea Cyterski-Acosta, Dean of Enrollment, 210-829-6005, Fax: 210-829-3921, E-mail: admis@uiwtx.edu.
Website: http://www.uiw.edu/maa/.

Upper Iowa University, Online Master's Programs, Fayette, IA 52142-1857. Offers accounting (MBA); corporate financial management (MBA); global business (MBA); health and human services (MPA); higher education administration (MHEA); homeland security (MPA); human resources management (MBA); justice administration (MPA); organizational development (MBA); public personnel management (MPA); quality management (MBA). MBA also available at Madison, WI campus. Part-time programs available. Postbaccalaureate distance learning degree programs offered (no on-campus study). *Degree requirements:* For master's, research project. *Entrance requirements:* For master's, GMAT, GRE, or minimum GPA of 2.7 during last 60 hours. Additional exam requirements/recommendations for international students: Required—TOEFL (minimum score 570 paper-based). Electronic applications accepted. *Faculty research:* Total quality management, CQI, teams, organization culture and climate, management.

Vanderbilt University, Peabody College, Department of Leadership, Policy, and Organizations, Nashville, TN 37240-1001. Offers education policy (MPP); educational leadership and policy (Ed D); higher education (M Ed); higher education, leadership and policy (Ed D); international education policy and management (M Ed); leadership and organizational performance (M Ed). Part-time and evening/weekend programs available. *Faculty:* 30 full-time (13 women), 13 part-time/adjunct (6 women). *Students:* 183 full-time (128 women), 92 part-time (49 women); includes 59 minority (32 Black or African American, non-Hispanic/Latino; 8 Asian, non-Hispanic/Latino; 14 Hispanic/Latino; 5 Two or more races, non-Hispanic/Latino), 21 international. Average age 28. 464 applicants, 62% accepted, 123 enrolled. In 2013, 91 master's, 24 doctorates awarded. *Degree requirements:* For master's, comprehensive exam, thesis optional; for doctorate, thesis/dissertation, qualifying exams, residency. *Entrance requirements:* For master's and

doctorate, GRE General Test. Additional exam requirements/recommendations for international students: Required—TOEFL (minimum score 550 paper-based; 80 iBT). *Application deadline:* For fall admission, 12/31 priority date for domestic and international students; for spring admission, 11/1 priority date for domestic and international students. Applications are processed on a rolling basis. Application fee: $0. Electronic applications accepted. *Financial support:* Fellowships with full and partial tuition reimbursements, research assistantships with full and partial tuition reimbursements, teaching assistantships with full and partial tuition reimbursements, Federal Work-Study, institutionally sponsored loans, scholarships/grants, tuition waivers (partial), and unspecified assistantships available. Support available to part-time students. Financial award application deadline: 1/15; financial award applicants required to submit FAFSA. *Faculty research:* Higher education, educational leadership, education policy, economics of education, education accountability, school choice. *Unit head:* Dr. Ellen B. Goldring, Chair, 615-322-8000, Fax: 615-343-7094, E-mail: ellen.b.goldring@vanderbilt.edu. *Application contact:* Rosie Moody, Educational Coordinator, 615-322-8019, Fax: 615-343-7094, E-mail: rosie.moody@vanderbilt.edu.

Vanderbilt University, Vanderbilt Graduate School of Management, Vanderbilt MBA Program (Full-time), Nashville, TN 37203. Offers accounting (MBA); finance (MBA); general management (MBA); human and organizational performance (MBA); marketing (MBA); operations (MBA); strategy (MBA); MBA/JD; MBA/M Div; MBA/MD; MBA/MTS; MBA/PhD. *Accreditation:* AACSB. *Students:* 341 full-time (119 women); includes 42 minority (20 Black or African American, non-Hispanic/Latino; 12 Asian, non-Hispanic/Latino; 5 Hispanic/Latino; 5 Two or more races, non-Hispanic/Latino), 73 international. Average age 28. 1,059 applicants, 38% accepted, 166 enrolled. In 2013, 161 master's awarded. *Entrance requirements:* For master's, GMAT (preferred) or GRE, 2 years of work experience (recommended). Additional exam requirements/recommendations for international students: Required—TOEFL. *Application deadline:* For fall admission, 10/1 priority date for domestic and international students; for winter admission, 1/6 priority date for domestic and international students; for spring admission, 3/3 priority date for domestic students, 3/5 priority date for international students; for summer admission, 4/5 for domestic students, 5/5 for international students. Applications are processed on a rolling basis. Application fee: $75 ($175 for international students). Electronic applications accepted. *Financial support:* In 2013–14, 237 students received support. Scholarships/grants and tuition waivers (full and partial) available. Financial award application deadline: 5/15; financial award applicants required to submit FAFSA. *Unit head:* Nancy Lea Hyer, Associate Dean, 615-322-2530, Fax: 615-343-7110, E-mail: nancy.lea.hyer@owen.vanderbilt.edu. *Application contact:* Dinah Webster, Administrative Assistant, 615-322-6469, Fax: 615-343-1175, E-mail: mba@owen.vanderbilt.edu.
Website: http://www.owen.vanderbilt.edu.

Viterbo University, Master of Arts in Servant Leadership Program, La Crosse, WI 54601-4797. Offers MA. Part-time and evening/weekend programs available. *Faculty:* 2 full-time (0 women), 1 part-time/adjunct (0 women). *Students:* 19 full-time (13 women), 30 part-time (25 women); includes 2 minority (1 Black or African American, non-Hispanic/Latino; 1 Hispanic/Latino), 1 international. Average age 43. In 2013, 8 master's awarded. *Degree requirements:* For master's, 32 credits, 18 of Servant Leadership core courses and 14 elective relevant to particular calling, interests, and needs. *Entrance requirements:* For master's, letter of reference, statement of goals, baccalaureate degree, transcript, interview. Additional exam requirements/recommendations for international students: Required—TOEFL (minimum score 525 paper-based). *Application deadline:* For fall admission, 8/1 for domestic students; for spring admission, 12/1 for domestic students; for summer admission, 5/1 for domestic students. Application fee: $50. Electronic applications accepted. *Expenses:* Contact institution. *Unit head:* Tom Thibodeau, Director, 608-796-3705, E-mail: tathibodeau@viterbo.edu. *Application contact:* Maureen Cooney, Administrative Assistant, 608-796-3082, E-mail: mjcooney@viterbo.edu.
Website: http://www.viterbo.edu/Academics/Letters_and_Sciences/graduate/masl/Master_of_Arts_in_Servant_Leadership.aspx.

Walden University, Graduate Programs, School of Management, Minneapolis, MN 55401. Offers accounting (MBA, MS, DBA), including accounting for the professional (MS), accounting with CPA emphasis (MS), self-designed (MS, PhD); accounting and management (MS), including accountants as strategic managers, self-designed (MS, PhD); advanced project management (Graduate Certificate); applied project management (Graduate Certificate); bridge to business administration (Post-Doctoral Certificate); bridge to management (Post-Doctoral Certificate); business administration (EMBA); business management (Graduate Certificate); communication (MS, Graduate Certificate); corporate finance (MBA); entrepreneurship (DBA); entrepreneurship and small business (MBA); finance (DBA); global supply chain management (DBA); healthcare management (MBA, DBA); human resource management (MBA, MS, Graduate Certificate), including functional human resource management (MS), general program (MS), integrating functional and strategic human resource management (MS), organizational strategy (MS); human resources management (DBA); information systems management (DBA); international business (MBA, DBA); leadership (MBA, MS, DBA), including general program (MS), human resources leadership (MS), leader development (MS), self-designed (MS, PhD); management (MS, PhD), including accounting (PhD), engineering management (PhD), finance (PhD), general program (MS), healthcare management (MS), human resource management (MS), human resources management (PhD), information systems management (PhD), leadership (MS), leadership and organizational change (PhD), marketing (MS), operations research (PhD), project management (MS), self-designed, strategy and operations (MS); marketing (MBA, DBA); project management (MBA, MS, DBA); self-designed (MBA, DBA); social impact management (DBA); technology entrepreneurship (DBA). Part-time and evening/weekend programs available. Postbaccalaureate distance learning degree programs offered (minimal on-campus study). *Faculty:* 24 full-time (9 women), 337 part-time/adjunct (127 women). *Students:* 4,369 full-time (2,379 women), 2,181 part-time (1,304 women); includes 3,669 minority (3,020 Black or African American, non-Hispanic/Latino; 22 American Indian or Alaska Native, non-Hispanic/Latino; 156 Asian, non-Hispanic/Latino; 331 Hispanic/Latino; 11 Native Hawaiian or other Pacific Islander, non-Hispanic/Latino; 129 Two or more races, non-Hispanic/Latino), 107 international. Average age 41. 2,030 applicants, 94% accepted, 1436 enrolled. In 2013, 757 master's, 128 doctorates, 32 other advanced degrees awarded. *Degree requirements:* For master's, residency (for some programs); for doctorate, thesis/dissertation (for some programs), residency. *Entrance requirements:* For master's, bachelor's degree or higher; minimum GPA of 2.5; official transcripts; goal statement (for some programs); access to computer and Internet; for doctorate, master's degree or higher; three years of related professional or academic experience (preferred); minimum GPA of 3.0; goal statement and current resume (select programs); official transcripts; access to computer and Internet; for other advanced degree, relevant work experience; access to computer and Internet. Additional exam requirements/recommendations for international students: Required—TOEFL (minimum score 550 paper-based; 79 iBT), IELTS (minimum score 6.5), Michigan English Language Assessment Battery (minimum score 82), or PTE. *Application deadline:* Applications are processed on a rolling basis. Application fee: $0. Electronic applications accepted. *Expenses:* *Tuition:* Full-time $11,813.55; part-time $500 per credit. *Required fees:* $618.76. *Financial support:* Fellowships, Federal Work-Study, scholarships/grants, unspecified assistantships, and family tuition reduction, active duty/veteran tuition reduction, group tuition reduction, interest-free payment plans, employee tuition reduction available. Support available to part-time students. Financial award applicants required to submit FAFSA. *Unit head:* Dr. Ward Ulmer, III, Associate Dean, 800-925-3368. *Application contact:* Jennifer Hall, Vice President of Enrollment Management, 866-4-WALDEN, E-mail: info@waldenu.edu.
Website: http://www.waldenu.edu/programs/colleges-schools/management.

Walden University, Graduate Programs, School of Public Policy and Administration, Minneapolis, MN 55401. Offers criminal justice (MPA, MPP, MS, Graduate Certificate), including emergency management (MS, PhD), general program (MS, PhD), homeland security and policy coordination (MS, PhD), law and public policy (MS, PhD), policy analysis (MS, PhD), public management and leadership (MS, PhD), self-designed (MS), terrorism, mediation, and peace (MS, PhD); criminal justice leadership and executive management (MS), including emergency management (MS, PhD), general program (MS, PhD), homeland security and policy coordination (MS, PhD), law and public policy (MS, PhD), policy analysis (MS, PhD), public management and leadership (MS, PhD), self-designed, terrorism, mediation, and peace (MS, PhD); emergency management (MPA, MPP, MS), including criminal justice (MS, PhD), general program (MS, PhD), homeland security (MS), public management and leadership (MS, PhD), terrorism and emergency management (MS); general program (MPA, MPP); government management (Graduate Certificate); health policy (MPA, MPP); homeland security (Graduate Certificate); homeland security and policy coordination (MPA, MPP); international nongovernmental organizations (MPA, MPP); law and public policy (MPA, MPP); local government management for sustainable communities (MPA, MPP); nonprofit management (Graduate Certificate); nonprofit management and leadership (MPA, MPP, MS); policy analysis (MPA); public management and leadership (MPA, MPP, Graduate Certificate); public policy (Graduate Certificate); public policy and administration (PhD), including criminal justice (MS, PhD), emergency management (MS, PhD), general program (MS, PhD), health policy, homeland security and policy coordination (MS, PhD), international nongovernmental organizations, law and public policy (MS, PhD), local government management for sustainable communities, nonprofit management and leadership, policy analysis (MS, PhD), public management and leadership (MS, PhD), terrorism, mediation, and peace (MS, PhD); strategic planning and public policy (Graduate Certificate); terrorism, mediation, and peace (MPA, MPP). Part-time and evening/weekend programs available. Postbaccalaureate distance learning degree programs offered (minimal on-campus study). *Faculty:* 10 full-time (4 women), 123 part-time/adjunct (55 women). *Students:* 1,029 full-time (640 women), 1,601 part-time (981 women); includes 1,579 minority (1,326 Black or African American, non-Hispanic/Latino; 18 American Indian or Alaska Native, non-Hispanic/Latino; 39 Asian, non-Hispanic/Latino; 127 Hispanic/Latino; 3 Native Hawaiian or other Pacific Islander, non-Hispanic/Latino; 66 Two or more races, non-Hispanic/Latino), 27 international. Average age 42. 566 applicants, 93% accepted, 412 enrolled. In 2013, 257 master's, 44 doctorates, 18 other advanced degrees awarded. *Degree requirements:* For doctorate, thesis/dissertation, residency. *Entrance requirements:* For master's, bachelor's degree or higher; minimum GPA of 2.5; official transcripts; goal statement (for some programs); access to computer and Internet; for doctorate, master's degree or higher; three years of related professional or academic experience (preferred); minimum GPA of 3.0; goal statement and current resume (select programs); official transcripts; access to computer and Internet; for Graduate Certificate, relevant work experience; access to computer and Internet. Additional exam requirements/recommendations for international students: Required—TOEFL (minimum score 550 paper-based; 79 iBT), IELTS (minimum score 6.5), Michigan English Language Assessment Battery (minimum score 82), or PTE. *Application deadline:* Applications are processed on a rolling basis. Application fee: $0. Electronic applications accepted. *Expenses:* *Tuition:* Full-time $11,813.55; part-time $500 per credit. *Required fees:* $618.76. *Financial support:* Fellowships, Federal Work-Study, scholarships/grants, unspecified assistantships, and family tuition reduction, active duty/veteran tuition reduction, group tuition reduction, interest-free payment plans, employee tuition reduction available. Support available to part-time students. Financial award applicants required to submit FAFSA. *Unit head:* Dr. Mark Gordon, Associate Dean, 800-925-3368. *Application contact:* Jennifer Hall, Vice President of Enrollment Management, 866-4-WALDEN, E-mail: info@waldenu.edu.
Website: http://www.waldenu.edu/programs/colleges-schools/public-policy-and-administration.

Warner Pacific College, Graduate Programs, Portland, OR 97215-4099. Offers Biblical and theological studies (MA); Biblical studies (M Rel); education (M Ed); management and organizational leadership (MS); not-for-profit leadership (MSM); pastoral ministries (M Rel); religion and ethics (M Rel); teaching (MAT); theology (M Rel). Part-time programs available. *Faculty:* 20 part-time/adjunct (6 women). *Students:* 57 full-time (26 women), 4 part-time (2 women); includes 5 minority (4 Black or African American, non-Hispanic/Latino; 1 Asian, non-Hispanic/Latino). *Degree requirements:* For master's, thesis or alternative, presentation of defense. *Entrance requirements:* For master's, interview, minimum GPA of 2.5, letters of recommendation. *Application deadline:* Applications are processed on a rolling basis. *Expenses:* *Tuition:* Part-time $630 per credit hour. *Financial support:* Application deadline: 7/1; applicants required to submit FAFSA. *Faculty research:* New Testament studies, nineteenth-century Wesleyan theology, preaching and church growth, Christian ethics. *Unit head:* Dr. Andrea P. Cook, President, 503-517-1045, Fax: 503-517-1350. *Application contact:* Dr. John Fazio, Professor, 503-517-1043, Fax: 503-517-1350, E-mail: jfazio@warnerpacific.edu.

Washington State University, Graduate School, College of Business, PhD Program in Organizational Management, Pullman, WA 99164. Offers PhD. *Entrance requirements:* Additional exam requirements/recommendations for international students: Required—TOEFL (minimum score 580 paper-based).

Wayland Baptist University, Graduate Programs, Programs in Business Administration/Management, Plainview, TX 79072-6998. Offers accounting (MBA); general business (MBA); health care administration (MAM, MBA); healthcare administration (MBA); human resource management (MAM, MBA); international management (MBA); management (MBA); management information systems (MBA); organization management (MAM); project management (MBA). Part-time and evening/weekend programs available. Postbaccalaureate distance learning degree programs offered (no on-campus study). *Faculty:* 30 full-time (5 women), 38 part-time/adjunct (9 women). *Students:* 44 full-time (20 women), 702 part-time (315 women); includes 348 minority (149 Black or African American, non-Hispanic/Latino; 4 American Indian or Alaska Native, non-Hispanic/Latino; 23 Asian, non-Hispanic/Latino; 139 Hispanic/Latino; 9 Native Hawaiian or other Pacific Islander, non-Hispanic/Latino; 24 Two or more races, non-Hispanic/Latino), 5 international. Average age 40. 147 applicants, 94% accepted, 73 enrolled. In 2013, 296 master's awarded. *Degree requirements:* For master's, capstone course. *Entrance requirements:* For master's, GMAT, GRE or MAT. Additional exam requirements/recommendations for international students: Required—TOEFL (minimum score 500 paper-based; 61 iBT). *Application deadline:* Applications are processed on a rolling basis. Application fee: $50. Electronic applications accepted. *Expenses:* *Tuition:* Full-time $8190; part-time $455 per credit hour. *Required fees:* $970; $455 per credit hour. $485 per semester. *Financial support:* Federal Work-Study, institutionally sponsored loans, and scholarships/grants available. Support available to part-time students. Financial award application deadline: 5/1; financial award applicants

required to submit FAFSA. *Unit head:* Dr. Otto Schacht, Chairman, 806-291-1020, Fax: 806-291-1957, E-mail: schachto@wbu.edu. *Application contact:* Amanda Stanton, Graduate Studies, 806-291-3423, Fax: 806-291-1950, E-mail: stanton@wbu.edu.

Waynesburg University, Graduate and Professional Studies, Canonsburg, PA 15370. Offers business (MBA), including energy management, finance, health systems, human resources, leadership, market development; counseling (MA), including addictions counseling, clinical mental health; education (M Ed, MAT), including autism (M Ed), curriculum and instruction (M Ed), educational leadership (M Ed), online teaching (M Ed); nursing (MSN), including administration, education, informatics; nursing practice (DNP); special education (M Ed); technology (M Ed); MSN/MBA. *Accreditation:* AACN. Part-time and evening/weekend programs available. *Faculty:* 11 full-time (5 women), 136 part-time/adjunct (80 women). *Students:* 146 full-time (99 women), 419 part-time (268 women). In 2013, 290 master's, 7 doctorates awarded. *Degree requirements:* For doctorate, thesis/dissertation. *Entrance requirements:* Additional exam requirements/recommendations for international students: Required—TOEFL. *Application deadline:* For fall admission, 8/1 priority date for domestic students. Applications are processed on a rolling basis. Electronic applications accepted. *Financial support:* Available to part-time students. Application deadline: 5/1. *Unit head:* David Mariner, Dean, 724-743-4420, Fax: 724-743-4425, E-mail: dmariner@waynesburg.edu. *Application contact:* Dr. Michael Bednarski, Director of Enrollment, 724-743-4420, Fax: 724-743-4425, E-mail: mbednars@waynesburg.edu.
Website: http://www.waynesburg.edu/.

Wayne State College, Department of Health, Human Performance and Sport, Wayne, NE 68787. Offers exercise science (MSE); organizational management (MS), including sport management. Part-time and evening/weekend programs available. *Degree requirements:* For master's, comprehensive exam, thesis optional. *Entrance requirements:* For master's, GRE General Test, minimum GPA of 3.0. Additional exam requirements/recommendations for international students: Required—TOEFL (minimum score 550 paper-based). Electronic applications accepted.

Wayne State University, College of Liberal Arts and Sciences, Department of Political Science, Program in Public Administration, Detroit, MI 48202. Offers aging policy and management (MPA); criminal justice policy and management (MPA); economic development policy and management (MPA); health and human services policy and management (MPA); human and fiscal resource management (MPA); information technology management (MPA); nonprofit policy and management (MPA); organizational behavior and management (MPA); public budgeting and financial management (MPA); public policy analysis and program evaluation (MPA); social welfare policy and management (MPA); urban and metropolitan policy and management (MPA). *Accreditation:* NASPAA. Evening/weekend programs available. *Students:* 11 full-time (5 women), 55 part-time (43 women); includes 20 minority (14 Black or African American, non-Hispanic/Latino; 2 Asian, non-Hispanic/Latino; 2 Hispanic/Latino; 2 Two or more races, non-Hispanic/Latino), 1 international. Average age 33. 83 applicants, 34% accepted, 17 enrolled. In 2013, 19 master's awarded. *Degree requirements:* For master's, comprehensive exam. *Entrance requirements:* For master's, GRE General Test, minimum undergraduate upper-division GPA of 3.0 or master's degree. Additional exam requirements/recommendations for international students: Required—TOEFL (minimum score 550 paper-based; 79 iBT), TWE (minimum score 5.5), Michigan English Language Assessment Battery (minimum score 85); Recommended—IELTS (minimum score 6.5). *Application deadline:* For fall admission, 6/1 priority date for domestic students, 5/1 priority date for international students; for winter admission, 10/1 priority date for domestic students, 9/1 priority date for international students; for spring admission, 2/1 priority date for domestic students, 1/1 priority date for international students. Applications are processed on a rolling basis. Application fee: $0. Electronic applications accepted. *Expenses:* Tuition, state resident: part-time $554.15 per credit. Tuition, nonresident: part-time $1200.35 per credit. *Required fees:* $42.15 per credit. $268.30 per semester. Tuition and fees vary according to course load and program. *Financial support:* In 2013–14, 21 students received support. Fellowships, teaching assistantships, scholarships/grants, and unspecified assistantships available. Financial award application deadline: 3/31; financial award applicants required to submit FAFSA. *Faculty research:* Urban politics, urban education, state administration. *Unit head:* Dr. Daniel Geller, Department Chair, 313-577-6328, E-mail: dgeller@wayne.edu. *Application contact:* Dr. Brady Baybeck, Associate Professor/Director, Graduate Program in Public Administration, E-mail: mpa@wayne.edu.
Website: http://clasweb.clas.wayne.edu/mpa.

Webster University, College of Arts and Sciences, Department of History, Politics and International Relations, Program in International Nongovernmental Organizations, St. Louis, MO 63119-3194. Offers global international nongovernmental organizations (MA); international nongovernmental organizations (MA). *Expenses: Tuition:* Full-time $11,610; part-time $645 per credit hour. Tuition and fees vary according to campus/location and program.

Western International University, Graduate Programs in Business, Program in Organization Development, Phoenix, AZ 85021-2718. Offers MBA. *Entrance requirements:* For master's, minimum GPA of 2.75.

Wheeling Jesuit University, Department of Social Sciences, Wheeling, WV 26003-6295. Offers MSOL. Part-time and evening/weekend programs available. *Degree requirements:* For master's, thesis. *Entrance requirements:* For master's, MAT, minimum GPA of 2.75, minimum of three years full-time professional work experience. Additional exam requirements/recommendations for international students: Required—TOEFL (minimum score 600 paper-based; 100 iBT). Electronic applications accepted. Application fee is waived when completed online. *Faculty research:* History, theory and philosophy of leadership; gender roles and leadership; spirituality and leadership.

Wilfrid Laurier University, Faculty of Graduate and Postdoctoral Studies, Lyle S. Hallman Faculty of Social Work, Waterloo, ON N2L 3C5, Canada. Offers Aboriginal studies (MSW); community, policy, planning and organizations (MSW); critical social policy and organizational studies (PhD); individuals, families and groups (MSW); social work practice (individuals, families, groups and communities) (PhD); social work practice: individuals, families, groups and communities (PhD). Part-time programs available. *Degree requirements:* For master's, thesis optional; for doctorate, thesis/dissertation. *Entrance requirements:* For master's, course work in social science, research methodology, and statistics; honors BA with a minimum B average; for doctorate, master's degree in social work, minimum A- average. Additional exam requirements/recommendations for international students: Required—TOEFL (minimum score 89 iBT). Electronic applications accepted. *Expenses:* Contact institution.

Wilkes University, College of Graduate and Professional Studies, Jay S. Sidhu School of Business and Leadership, Wilkes-Barre, PA 18766-0002. Offers accounting (MBA); entrepreneurship (MBA); finance (MBA); health care administration (MBA); human resource management (MBA); international business (MBA); marketing (MBA); operations management (MBA); organizational leadership and development (MBA). *Accreditation:* ACBSP. Part-time and evening/weekend programs available. *Students:* 41 full-time (20 women), 119 part-time (48 women); includes 20 minority (5 Black or African American, non-Hispanic/Latino; 3 Asian, non-Hispanic/Latino; 7 Hispanic/Latino; 5 Two or more races, non-Hispanic/Latino), 7 international. Average age 31. In 2013, 55 master's awarded. *Entrance requirements:* For master's, GMAT. Additional exam requirements/recommendations for international students: Required—TOEFL (minimum score 550 paper-based; 79 iBT). *Application deadline:* Applications are processed on a rolling basis. Application fee: $45 ($65 for international students). Electronic applications accepted. *Expenses:* Contact institution. *Financial support:* Federal Work-Study and unspecified assistantships available. Financial award application deadline: 3/1; financial award applicants required to submit FAFSA. *Unit head:* Dr. Jeffrey Alves, Dean, 570-408-4702, Fax: 570-408-7846, E-mail: jeffrey.alves@wilkes.edu. *Application contact:* Joanne Thomas, Interim Director of Graduate Enrollment, 570-408-4234, Fax: 570-408-7846, E-mail: joanne.thomas1@wilkes.edu.
Website: http://www.wilkes.edu/pages/457.asp.

William Penn University, College for Working Adults, Oskaloosa, IA 52577-1799. Offers business leadership (MBL). Postbaccalaureate distance learning degree programs offered (no on-campus study).

Wilmington University, College of Business, New Castle, DE 19720-6491. Offers accounting (MBA, MS); business administration (MBA, DBA); environmental stewardship (MBA); finance (MBA); health care administration (MBA, MSM); homeland security (MBA, MSM); human resource management (MSM); management information systems (MBA, MSN); marketing (MSM); marketing management (MBA); military leadership (MSM); organizational leadership (MBA, MSM); public administration (MSM). Part-time and evening/weekend programs available. *Entrance requirements:* Additional exam requirements/recommendations for international students: Required—TOEFL (minimum score 500 paper-based). Electronic applications accepted.

Woodbury University, School of Business and Management, Program in Organizational Leadership, Burbank, CA 91504-1099. Offers MA. Evening/weekend programs available. *Faculty:* 1 (woman) full-time, 12 part-time/adjunct (5 women). *Students:* 61 full-time (37 women), 4 part-time (0 women); includes 23 minority (4 Black or African American, non-Hispanic/Latino; 3 Asian, non-Hispanic/Latino; 16 Hispanic/Latino), 7 international. Average age 37. 88 applicants, 84% accepted, 62 enrolled. In 2013, 89 master's awarded. *Entrance requirements:* For master's, GRE General Test (if GPA less than 2.5), 3 recommendations, essay, resume, academic transcripts. Additional exam requirements/recommendations for international students: Required—TOEFL (minimum score 550 paper-based; 83 iBT), IELTS (minimum score 6.5). *Application deadline:* For fall admission, 8/1 priority date for domestic students; for spring admission, 12/1 priority date for domestic students. Applications are processed on a rolling basis. Application fee: $35. *Expenses: Tuition:* Full-time $30,120; part-time $1004 per unit. *Required fees:* $8 per unit. $195 per term. Tuition and fees vary according to course load and program. *Financial support:* Scholarships/grants available. *Unit head:* Eric H. Shockman, Chair, Center for Leadership, 818-394-3307, E-mail: eric.shockman@woodbury.edu. *Application contact:* Ruth Lorenzana, Director of Admissions, 800-784-9663, Fax: 818-767-7520, E-mail: admissions@woodbury.edu.

Worcester Polytechnic Institute, Graduate Studies and Research, School of Business, Worcester, MA 01609-2280. Offers information technology (MS), including information security management; management (Graduate Certificate); marketing and technological innovation (MS); operations design and leadership (MS); technology (MBA, MS). *Accreditation:* AACSB. Part-time and evening/weekend programs available. Postbaccalaureate distance learning degree programs offered (minimal on-campus study). *Faculty:* 28 full-time (12 women), 17 part-time/adjunct (3 women). *Students:* 123 full-time (77 women), 282 part-time (88 women); includes 34 minority (3 Black or African American, non-Hispanic/Latino; 15 Asian, non-Hispanic/Latino; 10 Hispanic/Latino; 6 Two or more races, non-Hispanic/Latino), 146 international. 747 applicants, 56% accepted, 111 enrolled. In 2013, 110 master's awarded. *Degree requirements:* For master's, thesis optional. *Entrance requirements:* For master's, GMAT (MBA); GMAT or GRE General Test (MS), statement of purpose, 3 letters of recommendation, resume; for Graduate Certificate, GMAT or GRE General Test, statement of purpose, 3 letters of recommendation. Additional exam requirements/recommendations for international students: Required—TOEFL (minimum score 563 paper-based; 84 iBT), IELTS (minimum score 7). *Application deadline:* For fall admission, 6/1 priority date for domestic and international students; for spring admission, 11/1 priority date for domestic students, 10/1 priority date for international students. Applications are processed on a rolling basis. Application fee: $70. Electronic applications accepted. *Financial support:* Career-related internships or fieldwork, institutionally sponsored loans, scholarships/grants, and unspecified assistantships available. Financial award application deadline: 6/1; financial award applicants required to submit FAFSA. *Unit head:* Dr. Paul Mack, Dean, 508-831-4665, Fax: 508-831-4665, E-mail: biz@wpi.edu. *Application contact:* Eileen Dagostino, Recruiting Operations Coordinator, 508-831-4665, Fax: 508-831-5720, E-mail: edag@wpi.edu.
Website: http://www.wpi.edu/academics/business/about.html.

Worcester State University, Graduate Studies, Program in Management, Worcester, MA 01602-2597. Offers accounting (MS); managerial leadership (MS). Part-time and evening/weekend programs available. *Faculty:* 4 full-time (3 women), 3 part-time/adjunct (0 women). *Students:* 6 full-time (4 women), 29 part-time (15 women); includes 12 minority (4 Black or African American, non-Hispanic/Latino; 3 Asian, non-Hispanic/Latino; 4 Hispanic/Latino; 1 Two or more races, non-Hispanic/Latino), 4 international. Average age 31. 30 applicants, 60% accepted, 7 enrolled. In 2013, 6 master's awarded. *Degree requirements:* For master's, comprehensive exam (for some programs), thesis optional. *Entrance requirements:* For master's, GMAT. Additional exam requirements/recommendations for international students: Required—TOEFL (minimum score 500 paper-based; 61 iBT). *Application deadline:* For fall admission, 6/15 for domestic and international students; for spring admission, 4/1 for domestic and international students. Applications are processed on a rolling basis. Application fee: $40. Electronic applications accepted. *Expenses: Tuition, area resident:* Part-time $150 per credit. Tuition, state resident: part-time $150 per credit. Tuition, nonresident: part-time $150 per credit. *Required fees:* $114.50 per credit. *Financial support:* In 2013–14, 2 students received support, including 2 research assistantships with full tuition reimbursements available (averaging $4,800 per year); career-related internships or fieldwork, scholarships/grants, and unspecified assistantships also available. Financial award application deadline: 3/1; financial award applicants required to submit FAFSA. *Unit head:* Dr. Rodney Oudan, Coordinator, 508-929-8751, Fax: 508-929-8048, E-mail: roudan@worcester.edu. *Application contact:* Sara Grady, Assistant Dean of Continuing Education, 508-929-8787, Fax: 508-929-8100, E-mail: sara.grady@worcester.edu.

Yale University, Yale School of Management and Graduate School of Arts and Sciences, Doctoral Program in Management, New Haven, CT 06520. Offers accounting (PhD); financial economics (PhD); marketing (PhD); organizations and management (PhD). *Accreditation:* AACSB. *Degree requirements:* For doctorate, comprehensive exam, thesis/dissertation. *Entrance requirements:* For doctorate, GMAT or GRE General Test. Additional exam requirements/recommendations for international students: Required—TOEFL or IELTS. Electronic applications accepted. *Expenses:* Contact institution. *Faculty research:* Pricing of options and futures, term structure of interest rates, use of accounting numbers in debt contracts, product differentiation, e-commerce and marketing, behavioral finance.

Section 17
Project Management

This section contains a directory of institutions offering graduate work in project management. Additional information about programs listed in the directory may be obtained by writing directly to the dean of a graduate school or chair of a department at the address given in the directory.

For programs offering related work, see also in this book *Business Administration and Management*.

CONTENTS

Program Directory

Project Management   584

Project Management

Amberton University, Graduate School, Department of Business Administration, Garland, TX 75041-5595. Offers general business (MBA); management (MBA); project management (MBA); strategic leadership (MBA). Part-time and evening/weekend programs available. *Entrance requirements:* For master's, minimum GPA of 3.0. *Expenses: Tuition:* Full-time $5808; part-time $242 per credit hour.

American Graduate University, Program in Business Administration, Covina, CA 91724. Offers acquisition and contracting (MBA); general management (MBA); program/project management (MBA); supply chain management (MBA). Part-time programs available. Postbaccalaureate distance learning degree programs offered (no on-campus study). *Degree requirements:* For master's, thesis. *Entrance requirements:* For master's, undergraduate degree from institution accredited by accrediting agency recognized by the U.S. Department of Education, photo identification, response to distance education survey. Additional exam requirements/recommendations for international students: Required—TOEFL. Electronic applications accepted.

American Graduate University, Program in Project Management, Covina, CA 91724. Offers MPM, Certificate. Part-time programs available. Postbaccalaureate distance learning degree programs offered (no on-campus study). *Entrance requirements:* For master's, undergraduate degree from institution accredited by accrediting agency recognized by the U.S. Department of Education. Additional exam requirements/recommendations for international students: Required—TOEFL. Electronic applications accepted.

American InterContinental University Online, Program in Business Administration, Schaumburg, IL 60173. Offers accounting and finance (MBA); finance (MBA); healthcare management (MBA); human resource management (MBA); international business (MBA); management (MBA); marketing (MBA); operations management (MBA); organizational psychology and development (MBA); project management (MBA). *Accreditation:* ACBSP. Evening/weekend programs available. Postbaccalaureate distance learning degree programs offered (no on-campus study). *Entrance requirements:* Additional exam requirements/recommendations for international students: Required—TOEFL (minimum score 550 paper-based). Electronic applications accepted.

American InterContinental University Online, Program in Information Technology, Schaumburg, IL 60173. Offers Internet security (MIT); IT project management (MIT). Evening/weekend programs available. Postbaccalaureate distance learning degree programs offered (no on-campus study). *Entrance requirements:* Additional exam requirements/recommendations for international students: Required—TOEFL (minimum score 550 paper-based). Electronic applications accepted.

American Public University System, AMU/APU Graduate Programs, Charles Town, WV 25414. Offers accounting (MBA, MS); criminal justice (MA), including business administration, emergency and disaster management, general (MA, MS); educational leadership (M Ed); emergency and disaster management (MA); entrepreneurship (MBA); environmental policy and management (MS), including environmental planning, environmental sustainability, fish and wildlife management, general (MA, MS), global environmental management; finance (MBA); general (MBA); global business management (MBA); history (MA), including American history, ancient and classical history, European history, global history, public history; homeland security (MA), including business administration, counter-terrorism studies, criminal justice, cyber, emergency management and public health, intelligence studies, transportation security; homeland security resource allocation (MBA); humanities (MA); information technology (MS), including digital forensics, enterprise software development, information assurance and security, IT project management; information technology management (MBA); intelligence studies (MA), including criminal intelligence, cyber, general (MA, MS), homeland security, intelligence analysis, intelligence collection, intelligence management, intelligence operations, terrorism studies; international relations and conflict resolution (MA), including comparative and security issues, conflict resolution, international and transnational security issues, peacekeeping; legal studies (MA); management (MA), including defense management, general (MA, MS), human resource management, organizational leadership, public administration; marketing (MBA); military history (MA), including American military history, American Revolution, civil war, war since 1945, World War II; military studies (MA), including joint warfare, strategic leadership; national security studies (MA), including general (MA, MS), homeland security, regional security studies, security and intelligence analysis, terrorism studies; nonprofit management (MBA); political science (MA), including American politics and government, comparative government and development, general (MA, MS), international relations, public policy; psychology (MA), including general (MA, MS), maritime engineering management, reverse logistics management; public administration (MPA), including disaster management, environmental policy, health policy, human resources, national security, organizational management, security management; public health (MPH); reverse logistics management (MA); school counseling (M Ed); security management (MA); space studies (MS), including aerospace science, general (MA, MS), planetary science; sports and health sciences (MS); teaching (M Ed), including curriculum and instruction for elementary teachers, elementary reading, English language learners, instructional leadership, online learning, special education; transportation and logistics management (MA), including general (MA, MS), maritime engineering management, reverse logistics management. Programs offered via distance learning only. Part-time and evening/weekend programs available. Postbaccalaureate distance learning degree programs offered (no on-campus study). *Faculty:* 432 full-time (242 women), 1,722 part-time/adjunct (829 women). *Students:* 511 full-time (241 women), 10,947 part-time (4,294 women); includes 3,760 minority (2,058 Black or African American, non-Hispanic/Latino; 88 American Indian or Alaska Native, non-Hispanic/Latino; 293 Asian, non-Hispanic/Latino; 876 Hispanic/Latino; 91 Native Hawaiian or other Pacific Islander, non-Hispanic/Latino; 354 Two or more races, non-Hispanic/Latino), 134 international. Average age 36. In 2013, 3,323 master's awarded. *Degree requirements:* For master's, comprehensive exam or practicum. *Entrance requirements:* For master's, official transcript showing earned bachelor's degree from institution accredited by recognized accrediting body. Additional exam requirements/recommendations for international students: Required—TOEFL (minimum score 550 paper-based), IELTS (minimum score 6.5). *Application deadline:* Applications are processed on a rolling basis. Application fee: $0. Electronic applications accepted. *Expenses: Tuition:* Part-time $325 per semester hour. *Financial support:* Applicants required to submit FAFSA. *Faculty research:* Military history, criminal justice, management performance, national security. *Unit head:* Dr. Karan Powell, Executive Vice President and Provost, 877-468-6268, Fax: 304-724-3780. *Application contact:* Terry Grant, Vice President of Enrollment Management, 877-468-6268, Fax: 304-724-3780, E-mail: info@apus.edu. Website: http://www.apus.edu.

Aspen University, Program in Business Administration, Denver, CO 80246-1930. Offers business administration (MBA); finance (MBA); information management (MBA); project management (MBA, Certificate). Part-time and evening/weekend programs available. Postbaccalaureate distance learning degree programs offered (no on-campus study). *Entrance requirements:* Additional exam requirements/recommendations for international students: Required—TOEFL (minimum score 530 paper-based). Electronic applications accepted.

Athabasca University, Centre for Innovative Management, St. Albert, AB T8N 1B4, Canada. Offers business administration (MBA); information technology management (MBA), including policing concentration; management (GDM); project management (MBA, GDM). Part-time and evening/weekend programs available. Postbaccalaureate distance learning degree programs offered (no on-campus study). *Degree requirements:* For master's, thesis or alternative, applied project. *Entrance requirements:* For master's, 3-8 years of managerial experience, 3 years with undergraduate degree, 5 years managerial experience with professional designation, 8-10 years management experience (on exception). Electronic applications accepted. *Expenses:* Contact institution. *Faculty research:* Human resources, project management, operations research, information technology management, corporate stewardship, energy management.

Avila University, School of Professional Studies, Kansas City, MO 64145-1698. Offers executive leadership development (MS); fundraising (MA); instructional design and technology (MA); leadership coaching (MS); organizational development (MS); project management (MA); strategic human resources (MS). Part-time and evening/weekend programs available. Postbaccalaureate distance learning degree programs offered (no on-campus study). *Faculty:* 2 full-time (1 woman), 10 part-time/adjunct (7 women). *Students:* 73 full-time (50 women), 68 part-time (54 women); includes 46 minority (33 Black or African American, non-Hispanic/Latino; 1 Asian, non-Hispanic/Latino; 11 Hispanic/Latino; 1 Two or more races, non-Hispanic/Latino), 11 international. Average age 38. 47 applicants, 64% accepted, 27 enrolled. In 2013, 42 master's awarded. *Degree requirements:* For master's, thesis optional. *Entrance requirements:* For master's, 2 letters of recommendation, minimum GPA of 3.0 during last 60 hours, resume, statement of intent. Additional exam requirements/recommendations for international students: Required—TOEFL. *Application deadline:* Applications are processed on a rolling basis. Application fee: $0. Electronic applications accepted. *Expenses: Tuition:* Full-time $8430; part-time $468 per credit hour. *Required fees:* $648; $36 per credit hour. Tuition and fees vary according to program. *Financial support:* In 2013–14, 20 students received support. Unspecified assistantships available. Support available to part-time students. Financial award applicants required to submit FAFSA. *Unit head:* Dr. Steve Iliff, Dean, 816-501-3737, Fax: 816-941-4650, E-mail: advantage@avila.edu. *Application contact:* Linda Dubar, School of Professional Studies, 816-501-3737, Fax: 816-941-4650, E-mail: advantage@avila.edu. Website: http://www.avila.edu/advantage.

Bellevue University, Graduate School, College of Information Technology, Bellevue, NE 68005-3098. Offers computer information systems (MS); cybersecurity (MS); management of information systems (MS); project management (MPM).

Boston University, Metropolitan College, Department of Administrative Sciences, Boston, MA 02215. Offers banking and financial management (MSM); business continuity in emergency management (MSM); economics development and tourism management (MSAS); electronic commerce, systems, and technology (MSAS); financial economics (MSAS); innovation and technology (MSAS); insurance management (MSM); international market management (MSM); multinational commerce (MSAS); project management (MS). *Accreditation:* AACSB. Part-time and evening/weekend programs available. Postbaccalaureate distance learning degree programs offered (no on-campus study). *Faculty:* 15 full-time (3 women), 22 part-time/adjunct (3 women). *Students:* 177 full-time (85 women), 560 part-time (293 women); includes 89 minority (31 Black or African American, non-Hispanic/Latino; 31 Asian, non-Hispanic/Latino; 25 Hispanic/Latino; 2 Two or more races, non-Hispanic/Latino), 242 international. Average age 31. 509 applicants, 71% accepted, 222 enrolled. In 2013, 158 master's awarded. *Degree requirements:* For master's, thesis optional. *Entrance requirements:* For master's, 1 year of work experience, minimum GPA of 3.0. Additional exam requirements/recommendations for international students: Required—TOEFL (minimum score 84 iBT). *Application deadline:* Applications are processed on a rolling basis. Application fee: $80. Electronic applications accepted. *Expenses: Tuition:* Full-time $43,970; part-time $1374 per credit hour. *Required fees:* $60 per semester. Tuition and fees vary according to class time, course level and program. *Financial support:* In 2013–14, 15 students received support, including 7 research assistantships (averaging $8,400 per year); career-related internships or fieldwork, Federal Work-Study, and unspecified assistantships also available. *Faculty research:* International business, innovative process. *Unit head:* Dr. Kip Becker, Chairman, 617-353-3016, E-mail: adminsc@bu.edu. *Application contact:* Fiona Niven, Administrative Sciences Department, 617-353-3016, E-mail: adminsc@bu.edu. Website: http://www.bu.edu/met/academic-community/departments/administrative-sciences/.

Boston University, Metropolitan College, Department of Computer Science, Boston, MA 02215. Offers advanced information technology (Certificate); computer information systems (MS), including computer networks, database management and business intelligence, health informatics, IT project management, security, Web application development; computer networks (Certificate); computer science (MS), including computer networks, security; database management and business intelligence (Certificate); digital forensics (Certificate); health informatics (Certificate); information security (Certificate); information technology (Certificate); information technology project management (Certificate); medical information security and privacy (Certificate); software engineering (Certificate); software engineering in health care systems (Certificate); telecommunications (MS), including security; Web application development (Certificate). Part-time and evening/weekend programs available. Postbaccalaureate distance learning degree programs offered (no on-campus study). *Faculty:* 13 full-time (3 women), 35 part-time/adjunct (2 women). *Students:* 48 full-time (14 women), 720 part-time (174 women); includes 215 minority (51 Black or African American, non-Hispanic/Latino; 111 Asian, non-Hispanic/Latino; 44 Hispanic/Latino; 9 Two or more races, non-Hispanic/Latino), 113 international. Average age 35. 360 applicants, 71% accepted, 221 enrolled. In 2013, 246 master's, 25 other advanced degrees awarded. *Degree requirements:* For master's, thesis optional. *Entrance requirements:* For master's and Certificate, official transcripts from regionally-accredited bachelor's degree program, 3 letters of recommendation, professional resume, personal statement. Additional exam requirements/recommendations for international students: Required—TOEFL (minimum score 84 iBT), IELTS. *Application deadline:* For fall admission, 6/1 priority date for international students; for spring admission, 10/1 priority date for

international students. Applications are processed on a rolling basis. Application fee: $80. Electronic applications accepted. *Expenses: Tuition:* Full-time $43,970; part-time $1374 per credit hour. *Required fees:* $60 per semester. Tuition and fees vary according to class time, course level and program. *Financial support:* In 2013–14, 12 research assistantships (averaging $5,000 per year) were awarded; unspecified assistantships also available. Support available to part-time students. Financial award applicants required to submit FAFSA. *Faculty research:* Medical informatics, Web technologies, telecom and networks, security and forensics, software engineering, programming languages, multimedia and artificial intelligence (AI), information systems and IT project management. *Unit head:* Dr. Anatoly Temkin, Chairman, 617-353-2566, Fax: 617-353-2367, E-mail: csinfo@bu.edu. *Application contact:* Kim Richards, Program Coordinator, 617-353-2566, Fax: 617-353-2367, E-mail: kimrich@bu.edu.
Website: http://www.bu.edu/csmet/.

Brandeis University, Rabb School of Continuing Studies, Division of Graduate Professional Studies, Master of Science in Virtual Management Program, Waltham, MA 02454-9110. Offers MS. Part-time programs available. Postbaccalaureate distance learning degree programs offered (no on-campus study). *Faculty:* 2 full-time (1 woman), 33 part-time/adjunct (10 women). *Students:* 5 part-time (all women); includes 3 minority (1 Black or African American, non-Hispanic/Latino; 1 Asian, non-Hispanic/Latino; 1 Hispanic/Latino). Average age 35. 1 applicant, 100% accepted, 1 enrolled. In 2013, 3 master's awarded. *Entrance requirements:* For master's, resume, official transcripts, recommendations, goal statements. Additional exam requirements/recommendations for international students: Required—TOEFL (minimum score 600 paper-based; 100 iBT), IELTS (minimum score 7). *Application deadline:* For fall admission, 7/15 priority date for domestic and international students; for winter admission, 11/15 for domestic students; for spring admission, 11/15 priority date for domestic and international students; for summer admission, 3/15 priority date for domestic and international students. Applications are processed on a rolling basis. Application fee: $50. Electronic applications accepted. *Unit head:* Dr. Aline Yurik, Program Chair, 781-736-8787, Fax: 781-736-3420, E-mail: ayurik@brandeis.edu. *Application contact:* Frances Stearns, Associate Director of Admissions and Student Services, 781-736-8785, Fax: 781-736-3420, E-mail: fstearns@brandeis.edu.
Website: http://www.brandeis.edu/gps.

Brandeis University, Rabb School of Continuing Studies, Division of Graduate Professional Studies, Master of Science Program in Project and Program Management, Waltham, MA 02454-9110. Offers MS. Part-time programs available. Postbaccalaureate distance learning degree programs offered (no on-campus study). *Faculty:* 2 full-time (1 woman), 33 part-time/adjunct (10 women). *Students:* 1 (woman) full-time, 97 part-time (49 women); includes 26 minority (8 Black or African American, non-Hispanic/Latino; 1 American Indian or Alaska Native, non-Hispanic/Latino; 9 Asian, non-Hispanic/Latino; 6 Hispanic/Latino; 2 Native Hawaiian or other Pacific Islander, non-Hispanic/Latino), 1 international. Average age 35. 31 applicants, 61% accepted, 15 enrolled. In 2013, 21 master's awarded. *Entrance requirements:* For master's, four-year bachelor's degree from regionally-accredited U.S. institution or equivalent; official transcript(s) from every college or university attended; resume or curriculum vitae; statement of goals; letter of recommendation. Additional exam requirements/recommendations for international students: Required—TOEFL (minimum scores: 600 paper-based, 100 iBT), IELTS (7), or PTE. *Application deadline:* For fall admission, 7/15 priority date for domestic and international students; for winter admission, 11/15 for domestic students; for spring admission, 11/15 priority date for domestic and international students; for summer admission, 3/15 priority date for domestic and international students. Applications are processed on a rolling basis. Application fee: $50. Electronic applications accepted. *Unit head:* Leanne Bateman, Program Chair, 781-736-8787, Fax: 781-736-3420, E-mail: lbateman@brandeis.edu. *Application contact:* Frances Stearns, Associate Director of Admissions and Student Services, 781-736-8785, Fax: 781-736-3420, E-mail: fstearns@brandeis.edu.
Website: http://www.brandeis.edu/gps.

Brenau University, Sydney O. Smith Graduate School, School of Business and Mass Communication, Gainesville, GA 30501. Offers accounting (MBA); business administration (MBA); healthcare management (MBA); organizational leadership (MS); project management (MBA). *Accreditation:* ACBSP. Part-time and evening/weekend programs available. Postbaccalaureate distance learning degree programs offered (no on-campus study). *Degree requirements:* For master's, comprehensive exam (for some programs). *Entrance requirements:* For master's, resume, minimum undergraduate GPA of 2.5. Additional exam requirements/recommendations for international students: Required—TOEFL (minimum score 500 paper-based; 61 iBT); Recommended—IELTS (minimum score 5). Electronic applications accepted. *Expenses:* Contact institution.

California Intercontinental University, School of Information Technology, Diamond Bar, CA 91765. Offers information systems and enterprise resource management (DBA); information systems and knowledge management (MBA); project and quality management (MBA).

Capella University, School of Business and Technology, Doctoral Programs in Business, Minneapolis, MN 55402. Offers accounting (DBA, PhD); business intelligence (DBA); finance (DBA, PhD); general business management (PhD); human resource management (DBA, PhD); leadership (DBA, PhD); management education (PhD); marketing (DBA, PhD); project management (DBA, PhD); strategy and innovation (DBA, PhD).

Capella University, School of Business and Technology, Master's Programs in Business, Minneapolis, MN 55402. Offers accounting (MBA); business analysis (MS); business intelligence (MBA); entrepreneurship (MBA); finance (MBA); general business administration (MBA); general human resource management (MS); general leadership (MS); health care management (MBA); human resource management (MBA); marketing (MBA); project management (MBA, MS).

Carlow University, School of Management, MBA Program, Pittsburgh, PA 15213-3165. Offers business administration (MBA); global business (MBA); healthcare management (MBA); project management (MBA). Part-time and evening/weekend programs available. Postbaccalaureate distance learning degree programs offered (no on-campus study). *Students:* 121 full-time (96 women), 26 part-time (17 women); includes 30 minority (22 Black or African American, non-Hispanic/Latino; 3 Asian, non-Hispanic/Latino; 3 Hispanic/Latino; 2 Two or more races, non-Hispanic/Latino), 5 international. Average age 32. 53 applicants, 96% accepted, 38 enrolled. In 2013, 41 master's awarded. *Entrance requirements:* For master's, minimum undergraduate GPA of 3.0; essay; resume; transcripts; two recommendations. Additional exam requirements/recommendations for international students: Required—TOEFL (minimum score 550 paper-based). *Application deadline:* Applications are processed on a rolling basis. Application fee: $20. Electronic applications accepted. Application fee is waived when completed online. *Expenses: Tuition:* Full-time $9523; part-time $744 per credit. Tuition and fees vary according to course load, degree level and program. *Unit head:* Dr. Enrique Mu, Chair, MBA Program, 412-578-8729, E-mail: emu@carlow.edu. *Application contact:* Jo Danhires, Administrative Assistant, Admissions, 412-578-6088, Fax: 412-578-6321, E-mail: gradstudies@carlow.edu.
Website: http://gradstudies.carlow.edu/management/mba.html.

Christian Brothers University, School of Business, Memphis, TN 38104-5581. Offers accountancy (M Acc); business (MBA); international business (MIB); project management (Certificate); MBA/MIB. Part-time and evening/weekend programs available. *Entrance requirements:* For master's, GMAT, GRE. Additional exam requirements/recommendations for international students: Required—TOEFL.

The Citadel, The Military College of South Carolina, Citadel Graduate College, Engineering Leadership and Program Management Department, Charleston, SC 29409. Offers technical project management (MS). Part-time and evening/weekend programs available. *Faculty:* 1 full-time (0 women). *Students:* 3 full-time (0 women), 54 part-time (19 women); includes 9 minority (5 Black or African American, non-Hispanic/Latino; 1 Asian, non-Hispanic/Latino; 1 Hispanic/Latino; 2 Two or more races, non-Hispanic/Latino). Average age 35. In 2013, 29 master's awarded. *Entrance requirements:* For master's, GRE or GMAT, evidence of a minimum of one year of professional experience, or permission from department head; two letters of reference; resume detailing previous work. Additional exam requirements/recommendations for international students: Required—TOEFL (minimum score 550 paper-based; 79 iBT). *Application deadline:* For fall admission, 8/1 priority date for domestic students. Applications are processed on a rolling basis. Application fee: $30. Electronic applications accepted. *Expenses: Tuition, area resident:* Part-time $525 per credit hour. Tuition, state resident: part-time $525 per credit hour. Tuition, nonresident: part-time $865 per credit hour. *Financial support:* Health care benefits available. Support available to part-time students. Financial award application deadline: 7/1; financial award applicants required to submit FAFSA. *Unit head:* Dr. Charles O. Skipper, Department Head, 843-953-9811, Fax: 843-953-6328, E-mail: charles.skipper@citadel.edu. *Application contact:* Maj. Keith Plemmons, Program Director, 843-953-7677, Fax: 843-953-6328, E-mail: keith.plemmons@citadel.edu.
Website: http://www.citadel.edu/pmgt/.

City University of Seattle, Graduate Division, School of Management, Bellevue, WA 98005. Offers accounting (Certificate); change leadership (MBA, Certificate); computer systems (MS); finance (Certificate); financial management (MBA); general management (MBA); general management-Europe (MBA); global marketing (MBA); human resources management (Certificate); individualized study (MBA); information security (MS); information systems (MBA); leadership (MA); marketing (MBA, Certificate); project management (MBA, MS, Certificate); sustainable business (Certificate); technology management (MBA, Certificate). Part-time and evening/weekend programs available. Postbaccalaureate distance learning degree programs offered (no on-campus study). *Degree requirements:* For master's, comprehensive exam (for some programs), thesis (for some programs). *Entrance requirements:* Additional exam requirements/recommendations for international students: Required—TOEFL (minimum score 567 paper-based; 87 iBT); Recommended—IELTS. Electronic applications accepted.

Colorado Christian University, Program in Business Administration, Lakewood, CO 80226. Offers corporate training (MBA); information security (MA); leadership (MBA); project management (MBA). Part-time and evening/weekend programs available. Postbaccalaureate distance learning degree programs offered (minimal on-campus study). *Degree requirements:* For master's, thesis optional. *Entrance requirements:* For master's, GMAT, 2 letters of recommendation, resume. Additional exam requirements/recommendations for international students: Required—TOEFL. Electronic applications accepted. *Expenses:* Contact institution.

Colorado Technical University Colorado Springs, Graduate Studies, Program in Management, Colorado Springs, CO 80907-3896. Offers accounting (MBA, MSA); business administration (MBA); finance (MBA); human resources management (MBA); logistics/supply chain management (MBA); management (DM); marketing (MBA); mediation and dispute resolution (MBA); operations management (MBA); project management (MBA); technology management (MBA). Part-time and evening/weekend programs available. Postbaccalaureate distance learning degree programs offered. *Degree requirements:* For master's, thesis or alternative; for doctorate, thesis/dissertation. *Entrance requirements:* For doctorate, minimum graduate GPA of 3.0, 5 years of related work experience. *Faculty research:* Sexual harassment, performance evaluation, critical thinking.

Colorado Technical University Denver South, Programs in Business Administration and Management, Aurora, CO 80014. Offers accounting (MBA); business administration (MBA); business administration and management (EMBA); finance (MBA); human resource management (MBA); marketing (MBA); mediation and dispute resolution (MBA); operations management (MBA); project management (MBA); technology management (MBA). Part-time and evening/weekend programs available. *Degree requirements:* For master's, thesis or alternative. *Entrance requirements:* For master's, minimum undergraduate GPA of 3.0, resume.

Dallas Baptist University, College of Business, Business Administration Program, Dallas, TX 75211-9299. Offers accounting (MBA); business communication (MBA); conflict resolution management (MBA); entrepreneurship (MBA); finance (MBA); health care management (MBA); international business (MBA); leading the non-profit organization (MBA); management (MBA); management information systems (MBA); marketing (MBA); project management (MBA); technology and engineering (MBA). *Accreditation:* ACBSP. Part-time and evening/weekend programs available. *Entrance requirements:* For master's, GMAT, minimum GPA of 3.0. Additional exam requirements/recommendations for international students: Required—TOEFL, IELTS. *Application deadline:* Applications are processed on a rolling basis. Application fee: $25. Electronic applications accepted. *Expenses: Tuition:* Full-time $13,410; part-time $745 per credit hour. *Required fees:* $300; $150 per semester. Tuition and fees vary according to degree level. *Financial support:* Federal Work-Study, institutionally sponsored loans, scholarships/grants, and tuition waivers (full and partial) available. Support available to part-time students. Financial award applicants required to submit FAFSA. *Faculty research:* Sports management, services marketing, retailing, strategic management, financial planning/investments. *Unit head:* Dr. Sandra S. Reid, Chair, 214-333-5280, Fax: 214-333-5293, E-mail: graduate@dbu.edu. *Application contact:* Kit P. Montgomery, Director of Graduate Programs, 214-333-5242, Fax: 214-333-5579, E-mail: graduate@dbu.edu.
Website: http://www3.dbu.edu/graduate/mba.asp.

DeSales University, Graduate Division, Division of Business, Center Valley, PA 18034-9568. Offers accounting (MBA); computer information systems (MBA); finance (MBA); health care systems management (MBA); human resources management (MBA); management (MBA); marketing (MBA); project management (MBA); self-design (MBA). *Accreditation:* ACBSP. Part-time and evening/weekend programs available. Postbaccalaureate distance learning degree programs offered (no on-campus study). *Students:* 444 part-time. Average age 37. In 2013, 1 master's awarded. *Entrance requirements:* For master's, GMAT, minimum GPA of 3.0, 2 years of work experience. Additional exam requirements/recommendations for international students: Required—TOEFL. *Application deadline:* Applications are processed on a rolling basis. Application fee: $50. Electronic applications accepted. *Expenses: Tuition:* Part-time $790 per credit. *Financial support:* Applicants required to submit FAFSA. *Faculty research:* Quality improvement, executive development, productivity, cross-cultural managerial differences, leadership. *Unit head:* Dr. David Gilfoil, Director, 610-282-1100 Ext. 1828, Fax: 610-282-2869, E-mail: david.gilfoil@desales.edu. *Application contact:* Abigail

Wernicki, Director of Graduate Admissions, 610-282-1100 Ext. 1768, E-mail: gradadmissions@desales.edu.

DeVry University, Graduate Programs, Downers Grove, IL 60515. Offers accounting and financial management (MAFM); business administration (MBA); education (MS); educational technology (MS); electrical engineering (MS); human resources management (MHRM); information systems management (MISM); network and communications management (MNCM); project management (MPM); public administration (MPA).

Dowling College, School of Business, Oakdale, NY 11769. Offers aviation management (MBA, Certificate); corporate finance (MBA, Certificate); health care management (MBA); human resource management (Certificate); information systems management (MBA); management and leadership (MBA); marketing (Certificate); project management (Certificate); public management (MBA); school district business leader (MBA); sport, event and entertainment management (Certificate); JD/MBA. Part-time and evening/weekend programs available. Postbaccalaureate distance learning degree programs offered (minimal on-campus study). *Faculty:* 7 full-time (2 women), 43 part-time/adjunct (7 women). *Students:* 183 full-time (79 women), 299 part-time (142 women); includes 137 minority (84 Black or African American, non-Hispanic/Latino; 14 Asian, non-Hispanic/Latino; 20 Hispanic/Latino; 19 Native Hawaiian or other Pacific Islander, non-Hispanic/Latino). Average age 32. 360 applicants, 58% accepted, 127 enrolled. In 2013, 235 master's, 15 other advanced degrees awarded. *Degree requirements:* For master's, comprehensive exam, thesis optional. *Entrance requirements:* For master's, minimum GPA of 2.8, 2 letters of recommendation, courses or seminar in accounting and finance, resume. Additional exam requirements/recommendations for international students: Required—TOEFL (minimum score 550 paper-based). *Application deadline:* For fall admission, 9/1 priority date for domestic students; for winter admission, 1/1 priority date for domestic students; for spring admission, 2/1 priority date for domestic students. Applications are processed on a rolling basis. Application fee: $50. Electronic applications accepted. *Expenses: Tuition:* Full-time $22,731; part-time $1029 per credit. *Required fees:* $956; $956. *Financial support:* Career-related internships or fieldwork and Federal Work-Study available. Support available to part-time students. Financial award application deadline: 6/30; financial award applicants required to submit FAFSA. *Faculty research:* International finance, computer applications, labor relations, executive development. *Unit head:* Dr. Elana Zolfo, Dean, 631-244-3266, Fax: 631-244-1018, E-mail: zolfoe@dowling.edu. *Application contact:* Mary Boullianne, Dean of Admissions, 631-244-3274, Fax: 631-244-1059, E-mail: boulliam@dowling.edu.

Drexel University, Goodwin College of Professional Studies, School of Technology and Professional Studies, Philadelphia, PA 19104-2875. Offers construction management (MS); creativity and innovation (MS); engineering technology (MS); food science (MS); hospitality management (MS); professional studies: creativity studies (MS); professional studies: e-learning leadership (MS); professional studies: homeland security management (MS); project management (MS); property management (MS); sport management (MS). Part-time and evening/weekend programs available. *Entrance requirements:* Additional exam requirements/recommendations for international students: Required—TOEFL, IELTS. Electronic applications accepted. Application fee is waived when completed online.

Embry-Riddle Aeronautical University–Worldwide, Worldwide Headquarters - Graduate Programs, Program in Business Administration and Management, Daytona Beach, FL 32114-3900. Offers air transportation management (Graduate Certificate); airport planning design and development (Graduate Certificate); aviation (MBAA); aviation enterprises in the global environment (Graduate Certificate); aviation-aerospace industrial management (Graduate Certificate); engineering management (MSEM); integrated logistics management (Graduate Certificate); leadership (MSL); logistics and supply chain management (MSLSCM); management (MSM); modeling and simulation management (Graduate Certificate); occupational safety management (MSOSM); project management (MSPM, Graduate Certificate). Part-time and evening/weekend programs available. Postbaccalaureate distance learning degree programs offered (no on-campus study). *Degree requirements:* For master's, comprehensive exam (for some programs), thesis (for some programs). *Entrance requirements:* Additional exam requirements/recommendations for international students: Recommended—TOEFL (minimum score 550 paper-based; 79 iBT). Electronic applications accepted. *Faculty research:* Healthcare operations management, humanitarian logistics, supply chain risk management, collaborative supply chain management, intersection of collaborative supply chain management and the learning organization, development of assessment tool measuring supply chain collaborative capacity, teaching effectiveness, teaching quality, management style effectiveness, aeronautics, small/medium-sized business leadership study, leadership factors, critical thinking, efficacy of ePortfolio.

Ferris State University, College of Business, Big Rapids, MI 49307. Offers business intelligence (MBA); design and innovation management (MBA); incident response (MBA); information security and intelligence (MS), including business intelligence, incident response, project management; management tools and concepts (MBA); project management (MBA). *Accreditation:* ACBSP. Part-time and evening/weekend programs available. Postbaccalaureate distance learning degree programs offered (minimal on-campus study). *Faculty:* 9 full-time (3 women), 6 part-time/adjunct (2 women). *Students:* 30 full-time (9 women), 101 part-time (51 women); includes 18 minority (5 Black or African American, non-Hispanic/Latino; 1 American Indian or Alaska Native, non-Hispanic/Latino; 2 Asian, non-Hispanic/Latino; 6 Hispanic/Latino; 4 Two or more races, non-Hispanic/Latino), 13 international. Average age 34. 72 applicants, 82% accepted, 31 enrolled. In 2013, 47 master's awarded. *Degree requirements:* For master's, comprehensive exam, thesis (for MS). *Entrance requirements:* For master's, GRE or GMAT (waived if GPA is 3.5 or better), minimum GPA of 3.0 in junior/senior level classes, 2.75 overall; statement of purpose; 3 letters of reference; resume. Additional exam requirements/recommendations for international students: Required—TOEFL (minimum score 500 paper-based; 67 iBT). *Application deadline:* For fall admission, 7/1 priority date for domestic students, 6/15 for international students; for winter admission, 11/1 priority date for domestic students, 10/15 for international students; for spring admission, 3/1 priority date for domestic students, 2/15 for international students. Applications are processed on a rolling basis. Application fee: $0 ($30 for international students). Electronic applications accepted. Application fee is waived when completed online. *Financial support:* Career-related internships or fieldwork, Federal Work-Study, scholarships/grants, and unspecified assistantships available. Support available to part-time students. Financial award application deadline: 3/15; financial award applicants required to submit FAFSA. *Faculty research:* Quality improvement, client/server end-user computing, security and digital forensics, performance metrics and sustainability. *Unit head:* Dr. David Nicol, College of Business Dean, 231-591-2168, Fax: 231-591-3521, E-mail: davidnicol@ferris.edu. *Application contact:* Shannon Yost, Department Secretary, 231-591-2168, Fax: 231-591-3521, E-mail: yosts@ferris.edu.
Website: http://cbgp.ferris.edu/.

Florida Institute of Technology, Graduate Programs, Extended Studies Division, Melbourne, FL 32901-6975. Offers acquisition and contract management (MS); aerospace engineering (MS); business administration (MBA, DBA); computer information systems (MS); computer science (MS); electrical engineering (MS); engineering management (MS); human resources management (MS); logistics management (MS), including humanitarian and disaster relief logistics; management (MS), including acquisition and contract management, e-business, human resources management, information systems, logistics management, management, transportation management; material acquisition management (MS); mechanical engineering (MS); operations research (MS); project management (MS), including information systems, operations research; public administration (MPA); quality management (MS); software engineering (MS); space systems (MS); space systems management (MS); supply chain management (MS); systems management (MS), including information systems, operations research; technology management (MS). Part-time and evening/weekend programs available. Postbaccalaureate distance learning degree programs offered (no on-campus study). *Faculty:* 8 full-time (1 woman), 96 part-time/adjunct (25 women). *Students:* 94 full-time (46 women), 912 part-time (397 women); includes 436 minority (290 Black or African American, non-Hispanic/Latino; 18 American Indian or Alaska Native, non-Hispanic/Latino; 38 Asian, non-Hispanic/Latino; 62 Hispanic/Latino; 2 Native Hawaiian or other Pacific Islander, non-Hispanic/Latino; 26 Two or more races, non-Hispanic/Latino), 9 international. Average age 37. 591 applicants, 44% accepted, 220 enrolled. In 2013, 522 master's awarded. *Degree requirements:* For master's, comprehensive exam (for some programs), capstone course. *Entrance requirements:* For master's, GMAT or resume showing 8 years of supervised experience, minimum GPA of 3.0, 2 letters of recommendation, resume. Additional exam requirements/recommendations for international students: Required—TOEFL (minimum score 550 paper-based; 79 iBT). *Application deadline:* For fall admission, 4/1 for international students; for spring admission, 9/30 for international students. Applications are processed on a rolling basis. Electronic applications accepted. *Expenses:* Contact institution. *Financial support:* Application deadline: 3/1; applicants required to submit FAFSA. *Unit head:* Dr. Theodore R. Richardson, III, Senior Associate Dean, 321-674-8123, Fax: 321-674-7597, E-mail: trichardson@fit.edu. *Application contact:* Carolyn Farrior, Director of Graduate Admissions, Online Learning and Off-Campus Programs, 321-674-7118, Fax: 321-674-8216, E-mail: cfarrior@fit.edu.
Website: http://es.fit.edu.

Florida Institute of Technology, Graduate Programs, Nathan M. Bisk College of Business, Online Programs, Melbourne, FL 32901-6975. Offers accounting (MBA); accounting and finance (MBA); business administration (MBA); finance (MBA); healthcare management (MBA); information assurance and cybersecurity (MS); information technology (MS); information technology cybersecurity (MS); information technology management (MBA); international business (MBA); Internet marketing (MBA); management (MBA); marketing (MBA); project management (MBA); supply chain management (MS). Part-time and evening/weekend programs available. Postbaccalaureate distance learning degree programs offered (no on-campus study). *Faculty:* 3 full-time (1 woman), 41 part-time/adjunct (13 women). *Students:* 6 full-time (1 woman), 1,121 part-time (530 women); includes 424 minority (276 Black or African American, non-Hispanic/Latino; 10 American Indian or Alaska Native, non-Hispanic/Latino; 45 Asian, non-Hispanic/Latino; 88 Hispanic/Latino; 5 Native Hawaiian or other Pacific Islander, non-Hispanic/Latino), 32 international. Average age 36. 348 applicants, 42% accepted, 146 enrolled. In 2013, 475 master's awarded. *Entrance requirements:* For master's, GMAT or resume showing 8 years of supervised experience, 2 letters of recommendation, resume, competency in math past college algebra. Additional exam requirements/recommendations for international students: Required—TOEFL (minimum score 550 paper-based; 79 iBT). *Application deadline:* For fall admission, 4/1 for international students; for spring admission, 9/30 for international students. Applications are processed on a rolling basis. Electronic applications accepted. *Expenses:* Contact institution. *Financial support:* Available to part-time students. Application deadline: 3/1; applicants required to submit FAFSA. *Unit head:* Brian Ehrlich, Associate Vice President/Director of Online Learning, 321-674-8202, E-mail: behrlich@fit.edu. *Application contact:* Carolyn Farrior, Director of Graduate Admissions, Online Learning and Off-Campus Programs, 321-674-7118.
Website: http://online.fit.edu.

George Mason University, College of Visual and Performing Arts, Program in Arts Management, Fairfax, VA 22030. Offers arts management (MA); entrepreneurship in the arts (Certificate); fund-raising and development in the arts (Certificate); marketing and public relations in the arts (Certificate); programming and project management (Certificate). *Accreditation:* NASAD. *Faculty:* 2 full-time (both women), 6 part-time/adjunct (5 women). *Students:* 38 full-time (36 women), 41 part-time (35 women); includes 15 minority (7 Black or African American, non-Hispanic/Latino; 3 Asian, non-Hispanic/Latino; 3 Hispanic/Latino; 2 Two or more races, non-Hispanic/Latino), 12 international. Average age 29. 106 applicants, 52% accepted, 22 enrolled. In 2013, 37 master's awarded. *Degree requirements:* For master's, internship. *Entrance requirements:* For master's and Certificate, GRE (recommended), undergraduate degree with minimum GPA of 3.0, official transcripts, 2 letters of recommendation, statement of purpose, resume. Additional exam requirements/recommendations for international students: Required—TOEFL (minimum score 570 paper-based; 88 iBT), IELTS (minimum score 6.5), PTE. *Application deadline:* For fall admission, 3/1 for domestic students, 2/15 for international students; for spring admission, 10/1 for domestic students, 9/15 for international students. Application fee: $65 ($80 for international students). Electronic applications accepted. *Expenses:* Tuition, state resident: full-time $9350; part-time $390 per credit. Tuition, nonresident: full-time $25,754; part-time $1073 per credit. *Required fees:* $2688; $112 per credit. *Financial support:* In 2013–14, 1 student received support, including 1 teaching assistantship with full and partial tuition reimbursement available (averaging $10,920 per year); career-related internships or fieldwork, Federal Work-Study, scholarships/grants, unspecified assistantships, and health care benefits (for full-time research or teaching assistantship recipients) also available. Support available to part-time students. Financial award application deadline: 3/1; financial award applicants required to submit FAFSA. *Faculty research:* Information technology for arts managers, special topics in arts management, directions in gallery management, arts in society, public relations/marketing strategies for art organizations. *Unit head:* Claire Huschle, Interim Program Director, 703-993-8719, Fax: 703-993-9829, E-mail: chuschle@gmu.edu. *Application contact:* Allison Byers, Administrative Assistant, 703-993-8926, Fax: 703-993-9829, E-mail: abyers3@gmu.edu.
Website: http://artsmanagement.gmu.edu/arts-management-ma/.

The George Washington University, School of Business, Department of Decision Sciences, Washington, DC 20052. Offers business analytics (MS, Certificate); project management (MS). Postbaccalaureate distance learning degree programs offered (no on-campus study). *Faculty:* 18 full-time (1 woman). *Students:* 27 full-time (15 women), 211 part-time (81 women); includes 83 minority (38 Black or African American, non-Hispanic/Latino; 21 Asian, non-Hispanic/Latino; 24 Hispanic/Latino), 22 international. Average age 38. 111 applicants, 88% accepted, 69 enrolled. In 2013, 46 degrees awarded. Application fee: $75. *Financial support:* Tuition waivers available. *Unit head:* Refik Soyer, Chair, 202-994-6445, Fax: 202-994-6382, E-mail: soyer@gwu.edu. *Application contact:* Kristin Williams, Assistant Vice President for Graduate and Special Enrollment Management, 202-994-0467, Fax: 202-994-0371, E-mail: ksw@gwu.edu.
Website: http://business.gwu.edu/decisionsciences/.

The George Washington University, School of Business, Department of Information Systems and Technology Management, Washington, DC 20052. Offers information and decision systems (PhD); information systems (MSIST); information systems development (MSIST); information systems management (MBA); information systems project management (MSIST); management information systems (MSIST); management of science, technology, and innovation (MBA, PhD). Programs also offered in Ashburn and Arlington, VA. Part-time and evening/weekend programs available. Postbaccalaureate distance learning degree programs offered (no on-campus study). *Faculty:* 9 full-time (2 women). *Students:* 115 full-time (44 women), 105 part-time (40 women); includes 61 minority (26 Black or African American, non-Hispanic/Latino; 22 Asian, non-Hispanic/Latino; 10 Hispanic/Latino; 3 Two or more races, non-Hispanic/Latino), 86 international. Average age 31. 363 applicants, 70% accepted, 94 enrolled. In 2013, 114 degrees awarded. *Entrance requirements:* For master's, GMAT. Additional exam requirements/recommendations for international students: Required—TOEFL. *Application deadline:* For fall admission, 4/1 priority date for domestic students; for spring admission, 10/1 for domestic students. Applications are processed on a rolling basis. Application fee: $75. *Financial support:* In 2013–14, 35 students received support. Fellowships, teaching assistantships, career-related internships or fieldwork, Federal Work-Study, institutionally sponsored loans, and tuition waivers available. Financial award application deadline: 4/1. *Faculty research:* Expert systems, decision support systems. *Unit head:* Subhasish Dasgupta, Chair, 202-994-7408, E-mail: dasgupta@gwu.edu. *Application contact:* Kristin Williams, Assistant Vice President for Graduate and Special Enrollment Management, 202-994-0467, Fax: 202-994-0371, E-mail: ksw@gwu.edu.

Granite State College, Program in Project Management, Concord, NH 03301. Offers MS. Part-time programs available. Postbaccalaureate distance learning degree programs offered (no on-campus study). *Faculty:* 1 (woman) full-time, 20 part-time/adjunct (10 women). *Students:* 24 full-time (14 women), 33 part-time (17 women); includes 5 minority (2 American Indian or Alaska Native, non-Hispanic/Latino; 1 Asian, non-Hispanic/Latino; 1 Hispanic/Latino; 1 Two or more races, non-Hispanic/Latino). Average age 42. 22 applicants, 59% accepted, 9 enrolled. In 2013, 29 master's awarded. *Degree requirements:* For master's, capstone. *Entrance requirements:* For master's, bachelor's degree with minimum GPA of 3.0 on last 60 credit hours, 500-1000 word statement, two letters of professional or academic reference, resume, official transcripts. Additional exam requirements/recommendations for international students: Required—TOEFL, IELTS. *Application deadline:* Applications are processed on a rolling basis. Application fee: $0. Electronic applications accepted. *Expenses:* Tuition, state resident: full-time $8910; part-time $495 per credit. Tuition, nonresident: full-time $9090; part-time $515 per credit. *Unit head:* Michelle Capozzoli, Director, 603-447-3970, E-mail: michelle.capozzoli@granite.edu. *Application contact:* Ana Gonzalez, Administrative Assistant, Office of Graduate Studies, 603-513-1334, Fax: 603-513-1387, E-mail: gsc.graduatestudies@granite.edu.
Website: http://www.granite.edu/academics/degrees/masters/project.php.

Grantham University, Mark Skousen School of Business, Lenexa, KS 66219. Offers business administration (MBA); business intelligence (MS); information management (MBA); information management technology (MS); information technology (MS); performance improvement (MS); project management (MBA, MS). Part-time and evening/weekend programs available. Postbaccalaureate distance learning degree programs offered (no on-campus study). *Faculty:* 3 full-time (2 women), 35 part-time/adjunct (11 women). *Students:* 233 full-time (75 women), 559 part-time (207 women); includes 399 minority (296 Black or African American, non-Hispanic/Latino; 6 American Indian or Alaska Native, non-Hispanic/Latino; 14 Asian, non-Hispanic/Latino; 58 Hispanic/Latino; 1 Native Hawaiian or other Pacific Islander, non-Hispanic/Latino; 24 Two or more races, non-Hispanic/Latino). Average age 40. 792 applicants, 100% accepted, 792 enrolled. In 2013, 404 master's awarded. *Degree requirements:* For master's, thesis, capstone project, simulation game. *Entrance requirements:* For master's, bachelor's degree from accredited degree-granting institution with minimum GPA of 2.5. Additional exam requirements/recommendations for international students: Required—TOEFL (minimum score 530 paper-based; 71 iBT). *Application deadline:* Applications are processed on a rolling basis. Application fee: $30. Electronic applications accepted. *Expenses: Tuition:* Full-time $3900; part-time $325 per credit hour. *Required fees:* $35 per term. One-time fee: $100. *Financial support:* In 2013–14, 792 students received support. Scholarships/grants available. *Faculty research:* Relationship between media choices and teaching experience in online courses, online best teaching practices, strategy for co-creation of value with consumers, political identity and party polarization in the American Electorate, political participation and Web 2.0. *Unit head:* Dr. Niccole Buckley, Dean, Mark Skousen School of Business, 800-955-2527, E-mail: admissions@grantham.edu. *Application contact:* Jared Parlette, Vice President of Admissions, 800-955-2527, E-mail: admissions@grantham.edu.
Website: http://www.grantham.edu/colleges-and-schools/school-of-business/.

Harrisburg University of Science and Technology, Program in Project Management, Harrisburg, PA 17101. Offers construction services (MS); governmental services (MS); information technology (MS). Part-time and evening/weekend programs available. *Entrance requirements:* For master's, BS, BBA. Additional exam requirements/recommendations for international students: Required—TOEFL (minimum score 520 paper-based; 80 iBT). Electronic applications accepted.

Herzing University Online, Program in Business Administration, Milwaukee, WI 53203. Offers accounting (MBA); business administration (MBA); business management (MBA); healthcare management (MBA); human resources (MBA); marketing (MBA); project management (MBA); technology management (MBA). Postbaccalaureate distance learning degree programs offered (no on-campus study).

Iona College, Hagan School of Business, Department of Information Systems, New Rochelle, NY 10801-1890. Offers business continuity and risk management (AC); healthcare information systems (AC); information systems (MBA, PMC); project management (AC). Part-time and evening/weekend programs available. *Faculty:* 5 full-time (0 women), 2 part-time/adjunct (0 women). *Students:* 6 full-time (2 women), 20 part-time (6 women); includes 6 minority (3 Black or African American, non-Hispanic/Latino; 3 Hispanic/Latino), 1 international. Average age 30. 8 applicants, 100% accepted, 8 enrolled. In 2013, 18 master's, 9 other advanced degrees awarded. *Entrance requirements:* For master's, GMAT, 2 letters of recommendation, minimum GPA of 3.0; for other advanced degree, GMAT, minimum GPA of 3.0. Additional exam requirements/recommendations for international students: Required—TOEFL (minimum score 550 paper-based; 80 iBT), IELTS (minimum score 6.5). *Application deadline:* For fall admission, 8/15 priority date for domestic students, 8/1 priority date for international students; for winter admission, 11/15 priority date for domestic students, 11/1 priority date for international students; for spring admission, 2/15 priority date for domestic students, 2/1 priority date for international students; for summer admission, 5/15 priority date for domestic students, 5/1 priority date for international students. Applications are processed on a rolling basis. Application fee: $50. Electronic applications accepted. *Expenses:* Contact institution. *Financial support:* In 2013–14, 11 students received support. Scholarships/grants, tuition waivers (partial), and unspecified assistantships available. Support available to part-time students. Financial award application deadline: 4/15; financial award applicants required to submit FAFSA. *Faculty research:* Fuzzy

sets, risk management, computer security, competence set analysis, investment strategies. *Unit head:* Dr. Robert Richardson, Chairman, 914-637-7726, E-mail: rrichardson@iona.edu. *Application contact:* Cameron Hudson, Director of MBA Admissions, 914-633-2289, Fax: 914-637-2708, E-mail: chudson@iona.edu.
Website: http://www.iona.edu/Academics/Hagan-School-of-Business/Departments/Information-Systems/Graduate-Programs.aspx.

John Hancock University, MBA Program, Oakbrook Terrace, IL 60181. Offers e-commerce (MBA); finance (MBA); general business (MBA); global management (MBA); health care administration (MBA); leadership (MBA); management of information systems (MBA); marketing (MBA); professional accounting (MBA); project management (MBA); public accounting (MBA); risk management (MBA).

Jones International University, School of Business, Centennial, CO 80112. Offers accounting (MBA); business communication (MABC); entrepreneurship (MABC, MBA); finance (MBA); global enterprise management (MBA); health care management (MBA); information security management (MBA); information technology management (MBA); leadership and influence (MABC); leading the customer-driven organization (MABC); negotiation and conflict management (MBA); project management (MABC, MBA). Program only offered online. Part-time and evening/weekend programs available. Postbaccalaureate distance learning degree programs offered (no on-campus study). *Degree requirements:* For master's, capstone project. *Entrance requirements:* For master's, minimum cumulative GPA of 2.5. Additional exam requirements/recommendations for international students: Recommended—TOEFL (minimum score 550 paper-based). Electronic applications accepted.

Kaplan University, Davenport Campus, School of Business, Davenport, IA 52807-2095. Offers business administration (MBA); change leadership (MS); entrepreneurship (MBA); finance (MBA); health care management (MBA, MS); human resource (MBA); international business (MBA); management (MS); marketing (MBA); project management (MBA, MS); supply chain management and logistics (MBA, MS). *Accreditation:* ACBSP. Part-time and evening/weekend programs available. Postbaccalaureate distance learning degree programs offered (no on-campus study). *Entrance requirements:* Additional exam requirements/recommendations for international students: Required—TOEFL (minimum score 550 paper-based; 80 iBT). Electronic applications accepted.

Lakeland College, Graduate Studies Division, Program in Business Administration, Sheboygan, WI 53082-0359. Offers accounting (MBA); finance (MBA); healthcare management (MBA); project management (MBA). *Entrance requirements:* For master's, GMAT. *Expenses:* Contact institution.

Lasell College, Graduate and Professional Studies in Management, Newton, MA 02466-2709. Offers business administration (PMBA); elder care management (MSM, Graduate Certificate); elder care marketing (MSM); human resource management (Graduate Certificate); human resources management (MSM); integrated marketing communication (Graduate Certificate); management (MSM, Graduate Certificate); marketing (MSM, Graduate Certificate); non-profit management (MSM, Graduate Certificate); project management (MSM, Graduate Certificate); public relations (Graduate Certificate). Part-time and evening/weekend programs available. Postbaccalaureate distance learning degree programs offered (no on-campus study). *Faculty:* 3 full-time (1 woman), 16 part-time/adjunct (9 women). *Students:* 46 full-time (33 women), 105 part-time (73 women); includes 35 minority (24 Black or African American, non-Hispanic/Latino; 1 American Indian or Alaska Native, non-Hispanic/Latino; 3 Asian, non-Hispanic/Latino; 7 Hispanic/Latino), 22 international. Average age 32. 88 applicants, 55% accepted, 29 enrolled. In 2013, 61 master's awarded. *Entrance requirements:* For master's and Graduate Certificate, bachelor's degree from an accredited institution. Additional exam requirements/recommendations for international students: Required—TOEFL (minimum score 550 paper-based; 79 iBT). *Application deadline:* For fall admission, 8/31 priority date for domestic students, 6/30 priority date for international students; for spring admission, 12/31 priority date for domestic students, 10/31 priority date for international students. Applications are processed on a rolling basis. Electronic applications accepted. *Expenses: Tuition:* Part-time $575 per credit. *Required fees:* $80 per semester. *Financial support:* Available to part-time students. Application deadline: 8/31; applicants required to submit FAFSA. *Unit head:* Dr. Joan Dolamore, Dean of Graduate and Professional Studies, 617-243-2485, Fax: 617-243-2450, E-mail: gradinfo@lasell.edu. *Application contact:* Adrienne Franciosi, Director of Graduate Admission, 617-243-2214, Fax: 617-243-2450, E-mail: gradinfo@lasell.edu.
Website: http://www.lasell.edu/Academics/Graduate-and-Professional-Studies/MS-in-Management.html.

Lehigh University, College of Business and Economics, Department of Management, Bethlehem, PA 18015. Offers business administration (MBA); corporate entrepreneurship (MBA); international business (MBA); marketing (MBA); project management (MBA); supply chain management (MBA); MBA/E; MBA/M Ed. *Accreditation:* AACSB. Part-time and evening/weekend programs available. Postbaccalaureate distance learning degree programs offered (minimal on-campus study). *Faculty:* 11 full-time (4 women), 13 part-time/adjunct (4 women). *Students:* 28 full-time (10 women), 171 part-time (54 women); includes 32 minority (2 Black or African American, non-Hispanic/Latino; 21 Asian, non-Hispanic/Latino; 6 Hispanic/Latino; 3 Two or more races, non-Hispanic/Latino), 21 international. Average age 33. 108 applicants, 63% accepted, 25 enrolled. In 2013, 79 master's awarded. *Entrance requirements:* For master's, GMAT or GRE. Additional exam requirements/recommendations for international students: Required—TOEFL (minimum score 600 paper-based; 94 iBT). *Application deadline:* For fall admission, 7/15 for domestic students, 5/1 for international students; for spring admission, 12/1 for domestic students. Applications are processed on a rolling basis. Application fee: $100. Electronic applications accepted. *Financial support:* In 2013–14, 33 students received support, including 10 teaching assistantships with full and partial tuition reimbursements available (averaging $14,200 per year); career-related internships or fieldwork, scholarships/grants, health care benefits, tuition waivers (full and partial), and unspecified assistantships also available. Support available to part-time students. Financial award application deadline: 1/15. *Faculty research:* Information systems, organizational behavior, supply chain management, strategic management, entrepreneurship. *Total annual research expenditures:* $77,886. *Unit head:* Dr. Robert J. Trent, Department Chair, 610-758-4952, Fax: 610-758-6941, E-mail: rjt2@lehigh.edu. *Application contact:* Jen Giordano, Director of Recruitment and Admissions, 610-758-3418, Fax: 610-758-5283, E-mail: jlg210@lehigh.edu.
Website: http://www4.lehigh.edu/business/academics/depts/management.

Lewis University, College of Business, Graduate School of Management, Program in Business Administration, Romeoville, IL 60446. Offers accounting (MBA); custom elective option (MBA); e-business (MBA); finance (MBA); healthcare management (MBA); human resources management (MBA); international business (MBA); management information systems (MBA); marketing (MBA); project management (MBA); technology and operations management (MBA). Part-time and evening/weekend programs available. *Students:* 115 full-time (55 women), 227 part-time (129 women); includes 128 minority (74 Black or African American, non-Hispanic/Latino; 1 American Indian or Alaska Native, non-Hispanic/Latino; 9 Asian, non-Hispanic/Latino; 40 Hispanic/Latino; 4 Two or more races, non-Hispanic/Latino), 10 international. Average age 31. In 2013, 99 master's awarded. *Entrance requirements:* For master's, interview, bachelor's

degree, resume, 2 recommendations. Additional exam requirements/recommendations for international students: Required—TOEFL (minimum score 550 paper-based). *Application deadline:* For fall admission, 8/15 priority date for domestic students, 5/1 priority date for international students; for spring admission, 11/15 priority date for international students. Applications are processed on a rolling basis. Application fee: $40. Electronic applications accepted. *Financial support:* Career-related internships or fieldwork, Federal Work-Study, scholarships/grants, and unspecified assistantships available. Financial award application deadline: 5/1; financial award applicants required to submit FAFSA. *Unit head:* Dr. Maureen Culleeney, Academic Program Director, 815-838-0500 Ext. 5631, E-mail: culleema@lewisu.edu. *Application contact:* Michele Ryan, Director of Admission, 815-838-0500 Ext. 5384, E-mail: gsm@lewisu.edu.

Lewis University, College of Business, Graduate School of Management, Program in Project Management, Romeoville, IL 60446. Offers MS. Part-time and evening/weekend programs available. *Students:* 8 full-time (4 women), 9 part-time (8 women); includes 3 minority (2 Asian, non-Hispanic/Latino; 1 Hispanic/Latino), 2 international. Average age 34. *Entrance requirements:* For master's, bachelor's degree, interview, resume, statement of purpose, 2 letters of recommendation, minimum GPA of 2.75. Additional exam requirements/recommendations for international students: Required—TOEFL (minimum score 550 paper-based; 80 iBT). *Application deadline:* For fall admission, 5/1 priority date for international students; for spring admission, 11/15 priority date for international students. Applications are processed on a rolling basis. Application fee: $40. Electronic applications accepted. *Financial support:* Federal Work-Study and unspecified assistantships available. Support available to part-time students. Financial award application deadline: 5/1; financial award applicants required to submit FAFSA. *Unit head:* Rev. Dr. Kevin Spiess, Academic Program Director, 815-838-0500 Ext. 5399, E-mail: spiesske@lewisu.edu. *Application contact:* Michele Ryan, Director of Admission, 815-838-0500 Ext. 5384, E-mail: gsm@lewisu.edu.

Liberty University, School of Business, Lynchburg, VA 24515. Offers accounting (MBA, MS, DBA); business administration (MBA); criminal justice (MBA); cyber security (MS); executive leadership (MA); healthcare (MBA); human resources (DBA); information systems (MS), including information assurance, technology management; international business (MBA, DBA); leadership (MBA, DBA); management and leadership (MA); marketing (MBA, MS, DBA), including digital marketing and advertising (MS), project management (MS), public relations (MS), sports marketing and media (MS); project management (MBA, DBA); public administration (MBA); public relations (MBA). Part-time programs available. Postbaccalaureate distance learning degree programs offered (minimal on-campus study). *Students:* 1,342 full-time (749 women), 3,704 part-time (1,820 women); includes 1,657 minority (1,221 Black or African American, non-Hispanic/Latino; 11 American Indian or Alaska Native, non-Hispanic/Latino; 74 Asian, non-Hispanic/Latino; 209 Hispanic/Latino; 13 Native Hawaiian or other Pacific Islander, non-Hispanic/Latino; 129 Two or more races, non-Hispanic/Latino), 40 international. Average age 35. 5,899 applicants, 48% accepted, 1716 enrolled. In 2013, 1,535 master's awarded. *Entrance requirements:* For master's, minimum undergraduate GPA of 3.0, 15 hours of upper-level business courses. Additional exam requirements/recommendations for international students: Required—TOEFL (minimum score 600 paper-based; 100 iBT). *Application deadline:* Applications are processed on a rolling basis. Application fee: $50. Electronic applications accepted. *Expenses:* Contact institution. *Unit head:* Dr. Scott Hicks, Dean, 434-592-4808, Fax: 434-582-2366, E-mail: smhicks@liberty.edu. *Application contact:* Jay Bridge, Director of Graduate Admissions, 800-424-9595, Fax: 800-628-7977, E-mail: gradadmissions@liberty.edu.
Website: http://www.liberty.edu/academics/business/index.cfm?PID-149.

Marlboro College, Graduate and Professional Studies, Program in Information Technologies, Marlboro, VT 05344. Offers information technologies (MS); open source Web development (Certificate); project management (MS, Certificate). Part-time and evening/weekend programs available. Postbaccalaureate distance learning degree programs offered (minimal on-campus study). *Faculty:* 6 part-time/adjunct (4 women). *Students:* 1 (woman) full-time, 4 part-time (3 women). Average age 38. 3 applicants. In 2013, 4 master's awarded. *Degree requirements:* For master's, 30 credits including capstone project. *Entrance requirements:* For master's, letter of intent, 2 letters of recommendation, transcripts. *Application deadline:* For fall admission, 7/1 priority date for domestic students; for winter admission, 11/1 priority date for domestic students; for spring admission, 3/1 priority date for domestic students. Applications are processed on a rolling basis. Application fee: $0. Electronic applications accepted. *Expenses: Tuition:* Part-time $685 per credit. Tuition and fees vary according to course load and program. *Financial support:* Applicants required to submit FAFSA. *Unit head:* Peter Crowell, Program Director, 802-258-9209, Fax: 802-258-9201, E-mail: pcrowell@gradschool.marlboro.edu. *Application contact:* Joe Heslin, Director of Admissions, 802-258-9209, Fax: 802-258-9201, E-mail: jheslin@gradschool.marlboro.edu.

Marymount University, School of Business Administration, Program in Information Technology, Arlington, VA 22207-4299. Offers computer security and information assurance (Certificate); health care informatics (Certificate); information technology (MS, Certificate); information technology project management: technology leadership (Certificate). Part-time and evening/weekend programs available. *Faculty:* 5 full-time (2 women), 9 part-time/adjunct (0 women). *Students:* 29 full-time (14 women), 33 part-time (8 women); includes 25 minority (16 Black or African American, non-Hispanic/Latino; 5 Asian, non-Hispanic/Latino; 3 Hispanic/Latino; 1 Two or more races, non-Hispanic/Latino), 18 international. Average age 31. 42 applicants, 100% accepted, 27 enrolled. In 2013, 30 master's, 5 other advanced degrees awarded. *Degree requirements:* For master's, thesis or alternative. *Entrance requirements:* For master's, interview, resume, bachelor's degree in computer-related field or degree in another subject with a post-baccalaureate certificate in a computer-related field; for Certificate, resume. Additional exam requirements/recommendations for international students: Required—TOEFL (minimum score 600 paper-based; 96 iBT), IELTS (minimum score 6.5). *Application deadline:* For fall admission, 7/15 priority date for domestic students, 7/1 for international students; for spring admission, 11/15 priority date for domestic students, 11/15 for international students. Applications are processed on a rolling basis. Application fee: $40. Electronic applications accepted. *Expenses:* Contact institution. *Financial support:* In 2013–14, 13 students received support, including 1 research assistantship with full and partial tuition reimbursement available, 1 teaching assistantship; career-related internships or fieldwork, Federal Work-Study, scholarships/grants, and unspecified assistantships also available. Support available to part-time students. Financial award applicants required to submit FAFSA. *Unit head:* Dr. Diane Murphy, Chair, 703-284-5958, Fax: 703-527-3830, E-mail: diane.murphy@marymount.edu. *Application contact:* Francesca Reed, Director, Graduate Admissions, 703-284-5901, Fax: 703-527-3815, E-mail: grad.admissions@marymount.edu.
Website: http://www.marymount.edu/academics/programs/infoTechMS.

Marymount University, School of Business Administration, Program in Leadership and Management, Arlington, VA 22207-4299. Offers leadership (Certificate); management (MS); non-profit management (Certificate); project management (Certificate). Part-time and evening/weekend programs available. *Faculty:* 5 full-time (2 women), 1 (woman) part-time/adjunct. *Students:* 1 full-time (0 women), 22 part-time (16 women); includes 8 minority (4 Black or African American, non-Hispanic/Latino; 2 Asian, non-Hispanic/Latino; 2 Hispanic/Latino). Average age 37. 14 applicants, 93% accepted, 11 enrolled. In 2013, 7 master's, 13 other advanced degrees awarded. *Degree requirements:* For master's, thesis or alternative. *Entrance requirements:* For master's, GMAT or GRE General Test, resume, at least 3 years of managerial experience, essay; for Certificate, resume, at least 3 years of managerial experience. Additional exam requirements/recommendations for international students: Required—TOEFL (minimum score 600 paper-based; 96 iBT), IELTS (minimum score 6.5). *Application deadline:* For fall admission, 7/15 priority date for domestic students, 7/1 for international students; for spring admission, 11/15 priority date for domestic students, 11/15 for international students. Applications are processed on a rolling basis. Application fee: $40. Electronic applications accepted. *Expenses: Tuition:* Part-time $850 per credit. *Required fees:* $10 per credit. One-time fee: $200 part-time. Tuition and fees vary according to program. *Financial support:* Research assistantships with full and partial tuition reimbursements, career-related internships or fieldwork, Federal Work-Study, scholarships/grants, and unspecified assistantships available. Support available to part-time students. Financial award applicants required to submit FAFSA. *Unit head:* Dr. Lorri Cooper, Director, Master's in Management Program, 703-284-5950, Fax: 703-527-3830, E-mail: lorri.cooper@marymount.edu. *Application contact:* Francesca Reed, Director, Graduate Admissions, 703-284-5901, Fax: 703-527-3815, E-mail: grad.admissions@marymount.edu.

Maryville University of Saint Louis, The John E. Simon School of Business, St. Louis, MO 63141-7299. Offers accounting (MBA, PGC); management (MBA, PGC); marketing (MBA, PGC); process and project management (MBA, PGC); sport and entertainment management (MBA, PGC). *Accreditation:* ACBSP. Part-time and evening/weekend programs available. *Faculty:* 5 full-time (3 women), 14 part-time/adjunct (4 women). *Students:* 21 full-time (12 women), 85 part-time (41 women); includes 22 minority (8 Black or African American, non-Hispanic/Latino; 2 Asian, non-Hispanic/Latino; 7 Hispanic/Latino; 5 Two or more races, non-Hispanic/Latino), 3 international. Average age 31. In 2013, 39 master's awarded. *Entrance requirements:* For master's, GMAT (unless applicant possesses undergraduate business degree with minimum cumulative GPA of 3.0, or has completed master's degree from accredited university or one early access course prior to undergraduate degree). Additional exam requirements/recommendations for international students: Required—TOEFL (minimum score 85 iBT). *Application deadline:* Applications are processed on a rolling basis. Application fee: $40 ($60 for international students). Electronic applications accepted. Application fee is waived when completed online. *Expenses: Tuition:* Full-time $23,812; part-time $728 per credit hour. *Required fees:* $395 per year. Tuition and fees vary according to course load, degree level and program. *Financial support:* Career-related internships or fieldwork, Federal Work-Study, tuition waivers (partial), and campus employment available. Financial award application deadline: 3/1; financial award applicants required to submit FAFSA. *Faculty research:* International business, e-marketing, strategic planning, interpersonal management skills, financial analysis. *Unit head:* Dr. Pamela Horwitz, Dean, 314-529-9418, Fax: 314-529-9975, E-mail: horwitz@maryville.edu. *Application contact:* Kathy Dougherty, Director of MBA Programs, 314-529-9382, Fax: 314-529-9975, E-mail: business@maryville.edu.
Website: http://www.maryville.edu/bu/business-administration-masters/.

Metropolitan State University, College of Management, St. Paul, MN 55106-5000. Offers business administration (MBA, DBA); database administration (Graduate Certificate); healthcare information technology management (Graduate Certificate); information assurance security (Graduate Certificate); management information systems (MMIS); MIS generalist (Graduate Certificate); MIS systems analysis and design (Graduate Certificate); project management (Graduate Certificate); public and nonprofit administration (MPNA). Part-time and evening/weekend programs available. *Degree requirements:* For master's, thesis optional, computer language (MMIS). *Entrance requirements:* For master's, GMAT (for MBA), resume. Additional exam requirements/recommendations for international students: Required—TOEFL (minimum score 550 paper-based). Electronic applications accepted. *Expenses:* Tuition, state resident: full-time $5548. Tuition, nonresident: full-time $10,929. *Faculty research:* Yugoslav economic system, workers' cooperatives, participative management and job enrichment, global business systems.

Mississippi State University, College of Business, Department of Management and Information Systems, Mississippi State, MS 39762. Offers business administration (MBA, PhD), including accounting, business administration (MBA), business information systems (PhD), finance (PhD), management (PhD), marketing (PhD); information systems (MSIS); project management (MBA). Part-time programs available. *Faculty:* 12 full-time (4 women). *Students:* 69 full-time (20 women), 245 part-time (69 women); includes 34 minority (9 Black or African American, non-Hispanic/Latino; 12 Asian, non-Hispanic/Latino; 7 Hispanic/Latino; 1 Native Hawaiian or other Pacific Islander, non-Hispanic/Latino; 5 Two or more races, non-Hispanic/Latino), 20 international. Average age 31. 367 applicants, 29% accepted, 73 enrolled. In 2013, 127 master's, 2 doctorates awarded. *Degree requirements:* For master's, comprehensive exam; for doctorate, comprehensive exam, thesis/dissertation. *Entrance requirements:* For master's, GMAT, minimum GPA of 3.0 in last 60 hours of undergraduate course work; for doctorate, GMAT (minimum score of 550), minimum GPA of 3.25 on all graduate work; BS with minimum GPA of 3.0 cumulative and last 60 hours. Additional exam requirements/recommendations for international students: Required—TOEFL (minimum score 575 paper-based; 84 iBT); Recommended—IELTS (minimum score 7). *Application deadline:* For fall admission, 7/1 for domestic students, 5/1 for international students; for spring admission, 11/1 for domestic students, 9/1 for international students. Applications are processed on a rolling basis. Application fee: $60. Electronic applications accepted. *Financial support:* In 2013–14, 1 teaching assistantship (averaging $13,497 per year) was awarded; career-related internships or fieldwork, Federal Work-Study, institutionally sponsored loans, scholarships/grants, and unspecified assistantships also available. Financial award applicants required to submit FAFSA. *Faculty research:* Electronic commerce, management of information technology. *Unit head:* Dr. Tim Barnett, Department Chairperson and Professor of Management, 662-325-3928, Fax: 662-325-8651, E-mail: tim.barnett@msstate.edu. *Application contact:* Dr. Rebecca Long, Graduate Coordinator, 662-325-3928, E-mail: gsb@cobian.msstate.edu.
Website: http://www.business.msstate.edu/programs/mis/index.php.

Missouri State University, Graduate College, College of Business Administration, Department of Technology and Construction Management, Springfield, MO 65897. Offers project management (MS). Part-time programs available. *Faculty:* 4 full-time (1 woman), 2 part-time/adjunct (1 woman). *Students:* 11 full-time (3 women), 47 part-time (14 women); includes 11 minority (5 Black or African American, non-Hispanic/Latino; 1 Asian, non-Hispanic/Latino; 3 Hispanic/Latino; 2 Two or more races, non-Hispanic/Latino), 3 international. Average age 34. 18 applicants, 94% accepted, 9 enrolled. In 2013, 35 master's awarded. *Degree requirements:* For master's, thesis or alternative. *Entrance requirements:* For master's, GRE or GMAT, minimum GPA of 2.75. Additional exam requirements/recommendations for international students: Required—TOEFL (minimum score 550 paper-based; 79 iBT). *Application deadline:* For fall admission, 7/20 for domestic students, 5/1 for international students; for spring admission, 12/20 for domestic students, 9/1 for international students. Applications are processed on a rolling basis. Application fee: $35 ($50 for international students). Electronic applications accepted. *Expenses:* Tuition, state resident: full-time $4500; part-time $250 per credit hour. Tuition, nonresident: full-time $9018; part-time $501 per credit hour. *Required*

fees: $361 per semester. Tuition and fees vary according to course level, course load and program. *Financial support:* Federal Work-Study, institutionally sponsored loans, scholarships/grants, and unspecified assistantships available. Financial award application deadline: 3/31; financial award applicants required to submit FAFSA. *Unit head:* Dr. Richard Callahan, Interim Department Head, 417-836-5121, Fax: 417-836-8556, E-mail: indmgt@missouristate.edu. *Application contact:* Misty Stewart, Coordinator of Graduate Admissions and Recruitment, 417-836-6079, Fax: 417-836-6200, E-mail: mistystewart@missouristate.edu.
Website: http://tcm.missouristate.edu/.

Missouri State University, Graduate College, Interdisciplinary Program in Administrative Studies, Springfield, MO 65897. Offers applied communication (MS); criminal justice (MS); environmental management (MS); homeland security (MS); project management (MS); sports management (MS). Part-time and evening/weekend programs available. Postbaccalaureate distance learning degree programs offered (no on-campus study). *Students:* 14 full-time (9 women), 67 part-time (31 women); includes 3 minority (1 Hispanic/Latino; 2 Two or more races, non-Hispanic/Latino), 4 international. Average age 32. 31 applicants, 87% accepted, 22 enrolled. In 2013, 30 master's awarded. *Degree requirements:* For master's, comprehensive exam, thesis or alternative. *Entrance requirements:* For master's, GRE, GMAT, 3 years of work experience. Additional exam requirements/recommendations for international students: Required—TOEFL (minimum score 550 paper-based; 79 iBT). *Application deadline:* For fall admission, 7/20 priority date for domestic students; for spring admission, 12/20 priority date for domestic students. Applications are processed on a rolling basis. Application fee: $35 ($50 for international students). Electronic applications accepted. *Expenses:* Tuition, state resident: full-time $4500; part-time $250 per credit hour. Tuition, nonresident: full-time $9018; part-time $501 per credit hour. *Required fees:* $361 per semester. Tuition and fees vary according to course level, course load and program. *Financial support:* Career-related internships or fieldwork, Federal Work-Study, institutionally sponsored loans, scholarships/grants, and unspecified assistantships available. Support available to part-time students. Financial award application deadline: 3/31; financial award applicants required to submit FAFSA. *Unit head:* Dr. Gerald Masterson, Program Coordinator, 417-836-5251, Fax: 417-836-6888, E-mail: msas@missouristate.edu. *Application contact:* Misty Stewart, Coordinator of Graduate Recruitment, 417-836-6079, Fax: 417-836-6200, E-mail: mistystewart@missouristate.edu.
Website: http://msas.missouristate.edu.

Montana Tech of The University of Montana, Graduate School, Project Engineering and Management Program, Butte, MT 59701-8997. Offers MPEM. Part-time and evening/weekend programs available. Postbaccalaureate distance learning degree programs offered (no on-campus study). *Faculty:* 1 full-time (0 women), 7 part-time/adjunct (1 woman). *Students:* 8 part-time (1 woman). 4 applicants, 100% accepted, 4 enrolled. In 2013, 2 master's awarded. *Degree requirements:* For master's, comprehensive exam, final project presentation. *Entrance requirements:* For master's, minimum GPA of 3.0. Additional exam requirements/recommendations for international students: Required—TOEFL (minimum score 550 paper-based; 71 iBT). *Application deadline:* For fall admission, 4/1 priority date for domestic students, 3/1 priority date for international students; for spring admission, 10/1 priority date for domestic students, 7/1 priority date for international students. Applications are processed on a rolling basis. Application fee: $30. Electronic applications accepted. *Expenses:* Tuition, state resident: full-time $2901; part-time $242 per credit hour. Tuition, nonresident: full-time $21,066; part-time $878 per credit hour. *Required fees:* $75 per credit hour. $30 per semester. Full-time tuition and fees vary according to course load, degree level and reciprocity agreements. *Financial support:* Application deadline: 4/1; applicants required to submit FAFSA. *Unit head:* Dr. Kumar Ganesan, Director, 406-496-4239, Fax: 406-496-4650, E-mail: kganesan@mtech.edu. *Application contact:* Fred Sullivan, Administrator, Graduate School, 406-496-4304, Fax: 406-496-4710, E-mail: fsullivan@mtech.edu.
Website: http://www.mtech.edu/academics/gradschool/distancelearning/distancelearning-pem.htm.

National University, Academic Affairs, School of Engineering, Technology and Media, La Jolla, CA 92037-1011. Offers computer science (MS), including advanced computing, database engineering, software engineering; cyber security and information assurance (MS), including computer forensics, ethical hacking and penetration testing, health information assurance, information assurance and security; data analytics (MS); engineering management (MS), including enterprise architecture, project management, systems engineering, technology management; environmental engineering (MS); homeland security and emergency management (MS); management information systems (MS); project management (Certificate); sustainability management (MS); wireless communications (MS). Part-time and evening/weekend programs available. Postbaccalaureate distance learning degree programs offered (no on-campus study). *Faculty:* 19 full-time (4 women), 28 part-time/adjunct (5 women). *Students:* 294 full-time (90 women), 100 part-time (29 women); includes 198 minority (49 Black or African American, non-Hispanic/Latino; 69 Asian, non-Hispanic/Latino; 60 Hispanic/Latino; 3 Native Hawaiian or other Pacific Islander, non-Hispanic/Latino; 17 Two or more races, non-Hispanic/Latino), 50 international. Average age 34. 160 applicants, 100% accepted, 123 enrolled. In 2013, 174 master's awarded. *Degree requirements:* For master's, thesis (for some programs). *Entrance requirements:* For master's, interview, minimum GPA of 2.5. Additional exam requirements/recommendations for international students: Required—TOEFL (minimum score 550 paper-based; 79 iBT), IELTS (minimum score 6). *Application deadline:* Applications are processed on a rolling basis. Application fee: $60 ($65 for international students). Electronic applications accepted. *Expenses:* Tuition: Full-time $13,824; part-time $1728 per course. One-time fee: $160. *Financial support:* Career-related internships or fieldwork, institutionally sponsored loans, scholarships/grants, and tuition waivers (partial) available. Support available to part-time students. Financial award application deadline: 6/30; financial award applicants required to submit FAFSA. *Faculty research:* Educational technology, scholarships in science. *Unit head:* School of Engineering, Technology, and Media, 800-628-8648, E-mail: setm@nu.edu. *Application contact:* Louis Cruz, Interim Vice President for Enrollment Services, 800-628-8648, E-mail: advisor@nu.edu.
Website: http://www.nu.edu/OurPrograms/SchoolOfEngineeringAndTechnology.html.

New England College, Program in Management, Henniker, NH 03242-3293. Offers accounting (MSA); healthcare administration (MS); international relations (MA); marketing management (MS); nonprofit leadership (MS); project management (MS); strategic leadership (MS). Part-time and evening/weekend programs available. *Degree requirements:* For master's, independent research project. Electronic applications accepted.

New York University, Polytechnic School of Engineering, Department of Technology Management, New York, NY 10012-1019. Offers construction management (Advanced Certificate); electronic business management (Advanced Certificate); entrepreneurship (Advanced Certificate); human resources management (Advanced Certificate); industrial engineering (MS); information management (Advanced Certificate); management (MS); management of technology (MS); manufacturing engineering (MS); organizational behavior (MS, Advanced Certificate); project management (Advanced Certificate);

technology management (MBA, PhD, Advanced Certificate); telecommunications management (Advanced Certificate). Part-time and evening/weekend programs available. *Faculty:* 7 full-time (1 woman), 41 part-time/adjunct (2 women). *Students:* 285 full-time (132 women), 116 part-time (45 women); includes 50 minority (10 Black or African American, non-Hispanic/Latino; 29 Asian, non-Hispanic/Latino; 11 Hispanic/Latino), 284 international. Average age 30. 726 applicants, 60% accepted, 140 enrolled. In 2013, 137 master's awarded. *Degree requirements:* For master's, comprehensive exam (for some programs), thesis (for some programs); for doctorate, comprehensive exam, thesis/dissertation. *Entrance requirements:* For master's, GMAT, minimum B average in undergraduate course work. Additional exam requirements/recommendations for international students: Required—TOEFL (minimum score 550 paper-based; 80 iBT); Recommended—IELTS (minimum score 6.5). *Application deadline:* For fall admission, 7/31 priority date for domestic students, 4/30 priority date for international students; for spring admission, 12/31 priority date for domestic students, 11/30 priority date for international students. Applications are processed on a rolling basis. Application fee: $75. Electronic applications accepted. *Expenses: Tuition:* Full-time $35,856; part-time $1494 per unit. *Required fees:* $1408; $64 per unit. $473 per term. Tuition and fees vary according to course load and program. *Financial support:* In 2013–14, 1 fellowship (averaging $26,400 per year) was awarded; research assistantships, teaching assistantships, institutionally sponsored loans, scholarships/grants, and unspecified assistantships also available. Support available to part-time students. *Faculty research:* Global innovation and research and development strategy, managing emerging technologies, technology and development, service design and innovation, tech entrepreneurship and commercialization, sustainable and clean-tech innovation, impacts of information technology upon individuals, organizations and society. Total annual research expenditures: $692,936. *Unit head:* Prof. Bharadwaj Rao, Head, 718-260-3617, Fax: 718-260-3874, E-mail: brao@poly.edu. *Application contact:* Raymond Lutzky, Director of Graduate Enrollment Management, 718-637-5984, Fax: 718-260-3624, E-mail: rlutzky@poly.edu.
Website: http://www.poly.edu/academics/departments/technology/.

Northeastern University, College of Professional Studies, Boston, MA 02115-5096. Offers applied nutrition (MS); commerce and economic development (MS); corporate and organizational communication (MS); digital media (MPS); geographic information technology (MPS); global studies and international affairs (MS); homeland security (MA); human services (MS); informatics (MPS); leadership (MS); nonprofit management (MS); project management (MS); regulatory affairs for drugs, biologics, and medical devices (MS); regulatory affairs of food and food industries (MS); respiratory care leadership (MS); technical communication (MS). Postbaccalaureate distance learning degree programs offered (no on-campus study).

Northwestern University, McCormick School of Engineering and Applied Science, Department of Civil and Environmental Engineering, Masters of Project Management Program, Evanston, IL 60208. Offers MS. Part-time and evening/weekend programs available. *Faculty:* 2 full-time (0 women), 22 part-time/adjunct (5 women). *Students:* 47 full-time (22 women), 34 part-time (11 women); includes 8 minority (1 Black or African American, non-Hispanic/Latino; 3 Asian, non-Hispanic/Latino; 4 Hispanic/Latino), 53 international. Average age 30. 93 applicants, 70% accepted, 40 enrolled. In 2013, 28 master's awarded. *Degree requirements:* For master's, capstone report. *Entrance requirements:* Additional exam requirements/recommendations for international students: Required—TOEFL (minimum score 560 paper-based; 83 iBT). *Application deadline:* For fall admission, 8/15 for domestic students, 6/15 for international students; for winter admission, 11/15 for domestic students, 9/15 for international students; for spring admission, 2/15 for domestic students, 12/15 for international students. Applications are processed on a rolling basis. Application fee: $50. Electronic applications accepted. *Financial support:* Institutionally sponsored loans and health care benefits available. Financial award applicants required to submit FAFSA. *Faculty research:* Construction management, environmental management, A/E/C business management and infrastructure management. *Unit head:* Prof. Raymond J. Krizek, Director, 847-491-4040, Fax: 847-491-4011, E-mail: rjkrizek@northwestern.edu. *Application contact:* Prof. Ahmad Hadavi, Associate Director, 847-467-3219, Fax: 847-491-4011, E-mail: a-hadavi@northwestern.edu.
Website: http://www.mpm.northwestern.edu/.

Northwestern University, School of Professional Studies, Program in Information Systems, Evanston, IL 60208. Offers analytics and business intelligence (MS); database and Internet technologies (MS); information systems (MS); information systems management (MS); information systems security (MS); medical informatics (MS); software project management and development (MS).

Northwest University, School of Business and Management, Kirkland, WA 98033. Offers business administration (MBA); international business (MBA); project management (MBA); social entrepreneurship (MBA). Accreditation: ACBSP. Part-time and evening/weekend programs available. *Degree requirements:* For master's, formalized research. *Entrance requirements:* For master's, GMAT. Additional exam requirements/recommendations for international students: Required—TOEFL (minimum score 550 paper-based; 75 iBT). *Application deadline:* For fall admission, 8/1 for domestic and international students; for spring admission, 12/1 for domestic and international students. Application fee: $75. Electronic applications accepted. *Expenses:* Contact institution. *Financial support:* Federal Work-Study, scholarships/grants, health care benefits, and tuition waivers (full and partial) available. Financial award applicants required to submit FAFSA. *Unit head:* Dr. Teresa Gillespie, Dean, 425-889-5290, E-mail: teresa.gillespie@northwestu.edu. *Application contact:* Aaron Oosterwyk, Director of Graduate and Professional Studies Enrollment, 425-889-7792, Fax: 425-803-3059, E-mail: aaron.oosterwyk@northwestu.edu.
Website: http://www.northwestu.edu/business/.

Norwich University, College of Graduate and Continuing Studies, Master of Business Administration Program, Northfield, VT 05663. Offers finance (MBA); organizational leadership (MBA); project management (MBA). Accreditation: ACBSP. Evening/weekend programs available. Postbaccalaureate distance learning degree programs offered (minimal on-campus study). *Faculty:* 16 part-time/adjunct (6 women). *Students:* 198 full-time (57 women); includes 33 minority (18 Black or African American, non-Hispanic/Latino; 9 Asian, non-Hispanic/Latino; 3 Hispanic/Latino; 3 Two or more races, non-Hispanic/Latino). Average age 36. 200 applicants, 41% accepted, 82 enrolled. In 2013, 89 master's awarded. *Degree requirements:* For master's, comprehensive exam, thesis optional. *Entrance requirements:* For master's, minimum undergraduate GPA of 2.75. Additional exam requirements/recommendations for international students: Required—TOEFL (minimum score 600 paper-based; 94 iBT). *Application deadline:* For fall admission, 8/1 for domestic and international students; for winter admission, 11/1 for domestic and international students; for spring admission, 2/1 for domestic and international students; for summer admission, 5/1 for domestic and international students. Applications are processed on a rolling basis. Application fee: $50. Electronic applications accepted. *Expenses:* Contact institution. *Financial support:* In 2013–14, 65 students received support. Scholarships/grants available. Financial award applicants required to submit FAFSA. *Unit head:* Dr. Jose Cordova, Program Director, 802-485-2567, Fax: 802-485-2533, E-mail: jcordova@norwich.edu. *Application contact:* Ashley

Farren, Associate Program Director, 802-485-2748, Fax: 802-485-2533, E-mail: afarren@norwich.edu.
Website: http://online.norwich.edu/degree-programs/masters/master-business-administration/overview.

Norwich University, College of Graduate and Continuing Studies, Master of Science in Information Assurance Program, Northfield, VT 05663. Offers information security and assurance (MS), including computer forensics, investigation/incident response team management, project management. Evening/weekend programs available. Postbaccalaureate distance learning degree programs offered (minimal on-campus study). *Faculty:* 9 part-time/adjunct (2 women). *Students:* 47 full-time (6 women); includes 8 minority (3 Black or African American, non-Hispanic/Latino; 1 American Indian or Alaska Native, non-Hispanic/Latino; 4 Asian, non-Hispanic/Latino). Average age 40. 77 applicants, 38% accepted, 23 enrolled. In 2013, 41 master's awarded. *Entrance requirements:* For master's, minimum undergraduate GPA of 2.75. Additional exam requirements/recommendations for international students: Required—TOEFL (minimum score 600 paper-based; 94 iBT). *Application deadline:* For fall admission, 8/1 for domestic and international students; for winter admission, 11/1 for domestic and international students; for spring admission, 2/1 for domestic and international students; for summer admission, 5/1 for domestic and international students. Applications are processed on a rolling basis. Application fee: $50. Electronic applications accepted. *Expenses:* Contact institution. *Financial support:* In 2013–14, 13 students received support. Scholarships/grants available. Financial award applicants required to submit FAFSA. *Unit head:* Dr. Rosemarie Pelletier, Program Director, 802-485-2767, Fax: 802-485-2533, E-mail: rpellet2@norwich.edu. *Application contact:* Elizabeth Templeton, Associate Program Director, 802-485-2757, Fax: 802-485-2533, E-mail: etemplet@norwich.edu.
Website: http://online.norwich.edu/degree-programs/masters/master-science-information-security-assurance/overview.

Oklahoma Christian University, Graduate School of Business, Oklahoma City, OK 73136-1100. Offers accounting (MBA); electronic business (MBA); financial services (MBA); health services management (MBA); human resources (MBA); international business (MBA); leadership and organizational development (MBA); marketing (MBA); project management (MBA). Postbaccalaureate distance learning degree programs offered (no on-campus study). *Entrance requirements:* For master's, bachelor's degree. Electronic applications accepted.

Penn State Erie, The Behrend College, Graduate School, Erie, PA 16563-0001. Offers business administration (MBA); project management (MPM); quality and manufacturing management (MMM). *Accreditation:* AACSB. Part-time programs available. *Students:* 31 full-time (10 women), 83 part-time (23 women); includes 8 minority (2 Black or African American, non-Hispanic/Latino; 3 Asian, non-Hispanic/Latino; 3 Hispanic/Latino), 3 international. Average age 29. 71 applicants, 79% accepted, 45 enrolled. In 2013, 52 master's awarded. *Entrance requirements:* Additional exam requirements/recommendations for international students: Required—TOEFL (minimum score 550 paper-based; 80 iBT). *Application deadline:* Applications are processed on a rolling basis. Application fee: $65. Electronic applications accepted. *Financial support:* Federal Work-Study available. Financial award application deadline: 2/15; financial award applicants required to submit FAFSA. *Unit head:* Dr. Donald L. Birx, Chancellor, 814-898-6160, Fax: 814-898-6461, E-mail: dlb69@psu.edu. *Application contact:* Ann M. Burbules, Assistant Director, Graduate Admissions, 866-374-3378, Fax: 814-898-6053, E-mail: psbehrendmba@psu.edu.
Website: http://psbehrend.psu.edu/.

Polytechnic University of Puerto Rico, Miami Campus, Graduate School, Miami, FL 33166. Offers accounting (MBA); business administration (MBA); construction management (MEM); environmental management (MEM); finance (MBA); human resources management (MBA); logistics and supply chain management (MBA); management of international enterprises (MBA); manufacturing management (MEM); marketing management (MBA); project management (MBA). Part-time and evening/weekend programs available. Postbaccalaureate distance learning degree programs offered (no on-campus study). *Entrance requirements:* For master's, minimum GPA of 3.0. Electronic applications accepted.

Post University, Program in Business Administration, Waterbury, CT 06723-2540. Offers accounting (MSA); business administration (MBA); corporate innovation (MBA); entrepreneurship (MBA); finance (MBA); healthcare (MBA); leadership (MBA); marketing (MBA); project management (MBA). *Accreditation:* ACBSP. Postbaccalaureate distance learning degree programs offered.

Queen's University at Kingston, Queens School of Business, Program in Business Administration, Kingston, ON K7L 3N6, Canada. Offers consulting and project management (MBA); finance (MBA); innovation and entrepreneurship (MBA); marketing (MBA). *Accreditation:* AACSB. *Degree requirements:* For master's, thesis optional, research project. *Entrance requirements:* For master's, GMAT, minimum B+ average. Additional exam requirements/recommendations for international students: Required—TOEFL. Electronic applications accepted. *Faculty research:* Management fundamentals, strategic thinking, global business, innovation and change, leadership.

Regis University, College for Professional Studies, School of Management, Denver, CO 80221-1099. Offers accounting (MS); business administration (MBA), including finance and accounting, general business, health industry leadership, marketing, operations management, organizational performance management, strategic management; emerging markets (MBA); enterprise resource leadership and planning (MSOL); human resource management and leadership (MSOL); organizational leadership (MSOL, Certificate), including executive project management (Certificate), organizational leadership and management (MSOL), strategic human resource integration (Certificate); organizational management (Certificate), including executive leadership; project leadership and management (MSOL). Offered at Colorado Springs Campus, Northwest Denver Campus, Southeast Denver Campus, Fort Collins Campus, Broomfield Campus, Henderson (Nevada) Campus, Summerlin (Nevada) Campus and online. Part-time and evening/weekend programs available. Postbaccalaureate distance learning degree programs offered (no on-campus study). *Faculty:* 14 full-time (5 women), 94 part-time/adjunct (30 women). *Students:* 594 full-time (313 women), 439 part-time (235 women); includes 307 minority (71 Black or African American, non-Hispanic/Latino; 3 American Indian or Alaska Native, non-Hispanic/Latino; 50 Asian, non-Hispanic/Latino; 162 Hispanic/Latino; 2 Native Hawaiian or other Pacific Islander, non-Hispanic/Latino; 19 Two or more races, non-Hispanic/Latino), 17 international. Average age 42. 502 applicants, 89% accepted, 330 enrolled. In 2013, 464 master's awarded. *Degree requirements:* For master's, thesis (for some programs), capstone or final research project. *Entrance requirements:* For master's, official transcript reflecting baccalaureate degree awarded from regionally-accredited college or university, interview, 2 years of full-time related work experience, resume, letters of recommendation. Additional exam requirements/recommendations for international students: Required—TOEFL (minimum score 550 paper-based, 82 iBT), TWE (minimum score 5) or university-based test. *Application deadline:* For fall admission, 8/13 for domestic and international students; for winter admission, 10/8 for domestic students, 9/8 for international students; for spring admission, 12/17 for domestic students, 11/17 for international students. Applications are processed on a rolling basis. Application fee: $75. Electronic applications accepted. *Expenses:* Contact institution. *Financial support:* In 2013–14, 45 students received support. Federal Work-Study and scholarships/grants available. Financial award application deadline: 4/15; financial award applicants required to submit FAFSA. *Faculty research:* Impact of information technology on small business regulation of accounting, international project financing, mineral development, delivery of healthcare to rural indigenous communities. *Unit head:* Dr. Peter Bemski, Chair, 303-458-1805, E-mail: pbemski@regis.edu. *Application contact:* Sarah Engel, Information Contact, 303-458-4900, Fax: 303-964-5534, E-mail: regisadm@regis.edu.
Website: http://www.regis.edu/CPS/Schools/School-of-Management.aspx.

Robert Morris University, Graduate Studies, School of Communications and Information Systems, Moon Township, PA 15108-1189. Offers communication and information systems (MS); competitive intelligence systems (MS); information security and assurance (MS); information systems and communications (D Sc); information systems management (MS); information technology project management (MS); Internet information systems (MS); organizational leadership (MS). Part-time and evening/weekend programs available. Postbaccalaureate distance learning degree programs offered (no on-campus study). *Faculty:* 26 full-time (10 women), 14 part-time/adjunct (4 women). *Students:* 311 part-time (111 women); includes 57 minority (35 Black or African American, non-Hispanic/Latino; 1 American Indian or Alaska Native, non-Hispanic/Latino; 4 Asian, non-Hispanic/Latino; 3 Hispanic/Latino; 14 Two or more races, non-Hispanic/Latino), 37 international. 337 applicants, 39% accepted, 102 enrolled. In 2013, 90 master's, 15 doctorates awarded. *Degree requirements:* For doctorate, thesis/dissertation. *Entrance requirements:* For doctorate, employer letter of endorsement, interview. Additional exam requirements/recommendations for international students: Required—TOEFL (minimum score 550 paper-based; 79 iBT). *Application deadline:* For fall admission, 7/1 priority date for domestic and international students; for spring admission, 11/1 priority date for domestic and international students. Applications are processed on a rolling basis. Application fee: $35. Electronic applications accepted. *Expenses:* Contact institution. *Financial support:* Research assistantships with partial tuition reimbursements, institutionally sponsored loans, and unspecified assistantships available. Support available to part-time students. Financial award application deadline: 5/1. *Unit head:* Dr. Barbara J. Levine, Dean, 412-397-2591, Fax: 412-397-2481, E-mail: levine@rmu.edu. *Application contact:* 412-397-5200, Fax: 412-397-5915, E-mail: graduateadmissions@rmu.edu.
Website: http://www.rmu.edu/web/cms/schools/scis/Pages/default.aspx.

Rochester Institute of Technology, Graduate Enrollment Services, Center for Multidisciplinary Studies, Program in Project Management, Rochester, NY 14623-5603. Offers Certificate. Part-time programs available. Postbaccalaureate distance learning degree programs offered (no on-campus study). *Students:* 4 part-time (3 women). Average age 30. 11 applicants, 27% accepted, 3 enrolled. In 2013, 47 Certificates awarded. *Entrance requirements:* Additional exam requirements/recommendations for international students: Required—TOEFL (minimum score 560 paper-based; 79 iBT) or IELTS (minimum score 6). *Application deadline:* Applications are processed on a rolling basis. Application fee: $60. Electronic applications accepted. *Expenses: Tuition:* Full-time $37,236; part-time $1552 per credit hour. *Required fees:* $250. *Unit head:* Dr. Samuel McQuade, Graduate Program Director, 585-475-2234, E-mail: cms1@rit.edu. *Application contact:* Diane Ellison, Assistant Vice President, Graduate Enrollment Services, 585-475-2229, Fax: 585-475-7164, E-mail: gradinfo@rit.edu.

Royal Roads University, Graduate Studies, Applied Leadership and Management Program, Victoria, BC V9B 5Y2, Canada. Offers executive coaching (Graduate Certificate); health systems leadership (Graduate Certificate); project management (Graduate Certificate); public relations management (Graduate Certificate); strategic human resources management (Graduate Certificate).

Saint Leo University, Graduate Business Studies, Saint Leo, FL 33574-6665. Offers accounting (M Acc, MBA); business (MBA); health care management (MBA); human resource management (MBA); information security management (MBA); marketing (MBA); marketing research and social media analytics (MBA); project management (MBA); sport business (MBA). Part-time and evening/weekend programs available. Postbaccalaureate distance learning degree programs offered (no on-campus study). *Faculty:* 48 full-time (12 women), 61 part-time/adjunct (21 women). *Students:* 1,855 full-time (1,020 women); includes 810 minority (587 Black or African American, non-Hispanic/Latino; 7 American Indian or Alaska Native, non-Hispanic/Latino; 36 Asian, non-Hispanic/Latino; 161 Hispanic/Latino; 3 Native Hawaiian or other Pacific Islander, non-Hispanic/Latino; 16 Two or more races, non-Hispanic/Latino), 33 international. Average age 38. In 2013, 905 master's awarded. *Entrance requirements:* For master's, GMAT (minimum score 500 if applicant has less than 3.0 in the last two years of undergraduate study), bachelor's degree with minimum GPA of 3.0 in the last 60 hours of coursework from regionally-accredited college or university; 2 years of professional work experience; resume; 2 letters of recommendation. Additional exam requirements/recommendations for international students: Required—TOEFL (minimum score 550 paper-based; 80 iBT). *Application deadline:* For fall admission, 7/1 priority date for domestic and international students; for spring admission, 11/12 priority date for domestic students, 11/1 for international students. Applications are processed on a rolling basis. Application fee: $80. Electronic applications accepted. *Expenses: Tuition:* Full-time $12,114; part-time $673 per semester hour. Tuition and fees vary according to degree level, campus/location and program. *Financial support:* In 2013–14, 116 students received support. Career-related internships or fieldwork, Federal Work-Study, scholarships/grants, and health care benefits available. Financial award application deadline: 3/1; financial award applicants required to submit FAFSA. *Unit head:* Dr. Lorrie McGovern, Assistant Dean, Graduate Studies in Business, 352-588-7390, Fax: 352-588-8585, E-mail: mbaslu@saintleo.edu. *Application contact:* Joshua Stagner, Director of Graduate Admission, 800-707-8846, Fax: 352-588-7873, E-mail: grad.admissions@saintleo.edu.
Website: http://www.saintleo.edu/academics/graduate.aspx.

Saint Mary's University of Minnesota, Schools of Graduate and Professional Programs, Graduate School of Business and Technology, Project Management Program, Winona, MN 55987-1399. Offers MS, Certificate. Part-time and evening/weekend programs available. Postbaccalaureate distance learning degree programs offered (no on-campus study). *Unit head:* Heather Wegwerth, Director, 612-728-5178, E-mail: hlwegw07@smumn.edu. *Application contact:* Russell Kreager, Director of Admissions for Graduate and Professional Programs, 612-728-5207, Fax: 612-728-5121, E-mail: rkreager@smumn.edu.
Website: http://www.smumn.edu/graduate-home/areas-of-study/graduate-school-of-business-technology/ms-in-project-management.

Saint Xavier University, Graduate Studies, Graham School of Management, Chicago, IL 60655-3105. Offers employee health benefits (Certificate); finance (MBA); financial fraud examination and management (MBA, Certificate); financial planning (MBA, Certificate); generalist/individualized (MBA); health administration (MBA); managed care (Certificate); management (MBA); marketing (MBA); project management (MBA, Certificate); MBA/MS. *Accreditation:* ACBSP. Part-time and evening/weekend programs available. *Entrance requirements:* For master's, GMAT, minimum GPA of 3.0, 2 years of work experience. Electronic applications accepted. *Expenses:* Contact institution.

Sam Houston State University, College of Business Administration, Department of General Business and Finance, Huntsville, TX 77341. Offers banking and financial institutions (EMBA); business administration (MBA); project management (MS). Part-time and evening/weekend programs available. Postbaccalaureate distance learning degree programs offered (minimal on-campus study). *Faculty:* 22 full-time (7 women). *Students:* 94 full-time (47 women), 283 part-time (122 women); includes 109 minority (39 Black or African American, non-Hispanic/Latino; 1 American Indian or Alaska Native, non-Hispanic/Latino; 17 Asian, non-Hispanic/Latino; 40 Hispanic/Latino; 2 Native Hawaiian or other Pacific Islander, non-Hispanic/Latino; 10 Two or more races, non-Hispanic/Latino), 29 international. Average age 35. 279 applicants, 89% accepted, 89 enrolled. In 2013, 92 master's awarded. *Degree requirements:* For master's, comprehensive exam. *Entrance requirements:* For master's, GMAT. Additional exam requirements/recommendations for international students: Required—TOEFL (minimum score 550 paper-based; 79 iBT), IELTS (minimum score 6.5). *Application deadline:* For fall admission, 8/1 for domestic students, 6/25 for international students; for spring admission, 12/1 for domestic students, 11/12 for international students. Applications are processed on a rolling basis. Application fee: $45 ($75 for international students). Electronic applications accepted. *Financial support:* Career-related internships or fieldwork, Federal Work-Study, institutionally sponsored loans, scholarships/grants, tuition waivers, and unspecified assistantships available. Support available to part-time students. Financial award application deadline: 5/31; financial award applicants required to submit FAFSA. *Unit head:* Dr. Kurt Jesswein, Chair, 936-294-4582, E-mail: kurt.jesswein@shsu.edu. *Application contact:* Rick Thaler, Associate Director, 936-294-1239, Fax: 936-294-3612, E-mail: busgrad@shsu.edu. Website: http://www.shsu.edu/~gba_www/.

Southern New Hampshire University, School of Business, Manchester, NH 03106-1045. Offers accounting (MBA, MS, Graduate Certificate); accounting finance (MS); accounting/auditing (MS); accounting/forensic accounting (MS); accounting/taxation (MS); athletic administration (MBA, Graduate Certificate); business administration (IMBA, MBA, Certificate, Graduate Certificate), including accounting (Certificate), business administration (MBA), business information systems (Graduate Certificate), human resource management (Certificate); corporate social responsibility (MBA); entrepreneurship (MBA); finance (MBA, MS, Graduate Certificate); finance/corporate finance (MS); finance/investments and securities (MS); forensic accounting (MBA); healthcare informatics (MBA); healthcare management (MBA); human resource management (Graduate Certificate); information technology (MS, Graduate Certificate); information technology management (MBA); international business (Graduate Certificate); international business and information technology (Graduate Certificate); international finance (Graduate Certificate); international sport management (Graduate Certificate); justice studies (MBA); leadership of nonprofit organizations (Graduate Certificate); marketing (MBA, MS, Graduate Certificate); operations and project management (MS); operations and supply chain management (MBA, Graduate Certificate); organizational leadership (MS); project management (MBA, Graduate Certificate); Six Sigma (MBA); Six Sigma quality (Graduate Certificate); social media marketing (MBA); sport management (MBA, MS, Graduate Certificate); sustainability and environmental compliance (MBA); workplace conflict management (MBA); MBA/Certificate. *Accreditation:* ACBSP. Part-time and evening/weekend programs available. Postbaccalaureate distance learning degree programs offered (no on-campus study). Terminal master's awarded for partial completion of doctoral program. *Degree requirements:* For master's, one foreign language, comprehensive exam (for some programs), thesis or alternative. *Entrance requirements:* For master's, minimum GPA of 2.5. Additional exam requirements/recommendations for international students: Required—TOEFL (minimum score 500 paper-based). Electronic applications accepted.

Stevens Institute of Technology, Graduate School, Wesley J. Howe School of Technology Management, Program in Business Administration, Hoboken, NJ 07030. Offers engineering management (MBA); financial engineering (MBA); information management (MBA); information technology in financial services (MBA); information technology in the pharmaceutical industry (MBA); information technology outsourcing (MBA); pharmaceutical management (MBA); project management (MBA); technology management (MBA); telecommunications management (MBA).

Stevens Institute of Technology, Graduate School, Wesley J. Howe School of Technology Management, Program in Information Systems, Hoboken, NJ 07030. Offers computer science (MS); e-commerce (MS); enterprise systems (MS); entrepreneurial information technology (MS); information architecture (MS); information management (MS, Certificate); information security (MS); information technology in financial services industry (MS); information technology in the pharmaceutical industry (MS); information technology outsourcing management (MS); project management (MS, Certificate); software engineering (MS); telecommunications (MS). *Degree requirements:* For master's, thesis optional. *Entrance requirements:* For master's, GMAT, GRE General Test. Additional exam requirements/recommendations for international students: Required—TOEFL. Electronic applications accepted.

Stevens Institute of Technology, Graduate School, Wesley J. Howe School of Technology Management, Program in Management, Hoboken, NJ 07030. Offers general management (MS); global innovation management (MS); human resource management (MS); information management (MS); project management (MS); technology commercialization (MS); technology management (MS). Part-time programs available. *Degree requirements:* For master's, thesis optional. *Entrance requirements:* For master's, GMAT, GRE General Test. Additional exam requirements/recommendations for international students: Required—TOEFL. Electronic applications accepted. *Faculty research:* Industrial economics.

Texas A&M University–San Antonio, School of Business, San Antonio, TX 78224. Offers business administration (MBA); enterprise resource planning systems (MBA); finance (MBA); healthcare management (MBA); human resources management (MBA); information assurance and security (MBA); international business (MBA); professional accounting (MPA); project management (MBA); supply chain management (MBA). Part-time and evening/weekend programs available. *Entrance requirements:* For master's, GMAT. Additional exam requirements/recommendations for international students: Required—TOEFL (minimum score 550 paper-based; 80 iBT), IELTS (minimum score 6). Electronic applications accepted.

Trevecca Nazarene University, Graduate Business Programs, Nashville, TN 37210-2877. Offers business administration (MBA); healthcare administration (Certificate); information technology (MBA, MS, Certificate); management (MSM); management and leadership (Certificate); project management (Certificate). Evening/weekend programs available. Postbaccalaureate distance learning degree programs offered. *Faculty:* 7 full-time (0 women), 3 part-time/adjunct (0 women). *Students:* 101 full-time (55 women), 21 part-time (8 women); includes 30 minority (27 Black or African American, non-Hispanic/Latino; 2 Asian, non-Hispanic/Latino; 1 Hispanic/Latino), 3 international. Average age 36. In 2013, 33 master's awarded. *Entrance requirements:* For master's, minimum GPA of 2.75, resume, official transcript from regionally-accredited institution, minimum math grade of C, minimum English composition grade of C, MS-IT requires undergraduate computing degree. Additional exam requirements/recommendations for international students: Required—TOEFL (minimum score 550 paper-based; 80 iBT). *Application deadline:* Applications are processed on a rolling basis. Application fee: $25. *Expenses:*

Contact institution. *Financial support:* Applicants required to submit FAFSA. *Unit head:* Dr. Rick Mann, Director of Graduate and Professional Programs for School of Business, 615-248-1529, E-mail: management@trevecca.edu. *Application contact:* 615-248-1529, E-mail: cll@trevecca.edu.

Trident University International, College of Business Administration, Program in Business Administration, Cypress, CA 90630. Offers business administration (PhD); conflict and negotiation management (MBA); criminal justice administration (MBA); entrepreneurship (MBA); finance (MBA); general management (MBA); government accounting (MBA); human resource management (MBA); information security and digital assurance management (MBA); information technology management (MBA); international business (MBA); logistics management (MBA); marketing (MBA); project management (MBA); public management (MBA); quality management (MBA); strategic leadership (MBA). Part-time and evening/weekend programs available. Postbaccalaureate distance learning degree programs offered (no on-campus study). *Degree requirements:* For doctorate, comprehensive exam, thesis/dissertation, defense of dissertation. *Entrance requirements:* For master's, minimum GPA of 2.5 (students with GPA 3.0 or greater may transfer up to 30% of graduate level credits); for doctorate, minimum GPA of 3.4, curriculum vitae, course work in research methods or statistics. Additional exam requirements/recommendations for international students: Required—TOEFL. Electronic applications accepted.

Universidad del Turabo, Graduate Programs, School in Business Administration, Program in Project Management, Gurabo, PR 00778-3030. Offers MBA.

Universidad Nacional Pedro Henriquez Urena, Graduate School, Santo Domingo, Dominican Republic. Offers agricultural diversity (MS), including horticultural/fruit production, tropical animal production; conservation of monuments and cultural assets (M Arch); ecology and environment (MS); environmental engineering (MEE); international relations (MA); natural resource management (MS); political science (MA); project optimization (MPM); project feasibility (MPM); project management (MPM); sanitation engineering (ME); science for teachers (MS); tropical Caribbean architecture (M Arch).

Université du Québec à Chicoutimi, Graduate Programs, Program in Project Management, Chicoutimi, QC G7H 2B1, Canada. Offers M Sc. Part-time programs available. *Entrance requirements:* For master's, appropriate bachelor's degree, proficiency in French.

Université du Québec à Montréal, Graduate Programs, Program in Project Management, Montréal, QC H3C 3P8, Canada. Offers MGP, Diploma. Part-time programs available. *Entrance requirements:* For master's and Diploma, appropriate bachelor's degree or equivalent, proficiency in French.

Université du Québec à Rimouski, Graduate Programs, Program in Project Management, Rimouski, QC G5L 3A1, Canada. Offers M Sc, Diploma. Programs offered jointly with Université du Québec à Chicoutimi, Université du Québec à Trois-Rivières, Université du Québec en Outaouais, Université du Québec en Abitibi-Témiscamingue, and Université du Québec à Montréal. Part-time programs available. *Entrance requirements:* For master's, proficiency in French, appropriate bachelor's degree.

Université du Québec en Abitibi-Témiscamingue, Graduate Programs, Program in Project Management, Rouyn-Noranda, QC J9X 5E4, Canada. Offers M Sc, DESS. M Sc offered jointly with Université du Québec à Chicoutimi, Université du Québec à Rimouski, Université du Québec à Trois-Rivières, Université du Québec en Outaouais, and Université du Québec à Montréal. Part-time programs available. *Entrance requirements:* For master's, appropriate bachelor's degree, proficiency in French.

Université du Québec en Outaouais, Graduate Programs, Program in Project Management, Gatineau, QC J8X 3X7, Canada. Offers M Sc, MA, DESS, Diploma. Programs offered jointly with Université du Québec à Chicoutimi, Université du Québec à Rimouski, Université du Québec à Trois-Rivières, Université du Québec en Abitibi-T'miscamingue, and Université du Québec à Montreal. Part-time and evening/weekend programs available. *Degree requirements:* For master's, thesis (for some programs). *Entrance requirements:* For master's, appropriate bachelor's degree, proficiency in French.

The University of Alabama in Huntsville, School of Graduate Studies, College of Business Administration, Programs in Business and Management, Huntsville, AL 35899. Offers federal contracting and procurement management (Certificate); management (MBA), including acquisition management, entrepreneurship, federal contract accounting, finance, human resource management, logistics and supply chain management, marketing, project management; supply chain management (Certificate); technology and innovation management (Certificate). *Accreditation:* AACSB. Part-time and evening/weekend programs available. *Faculty:* 13 full-time (3 women), 5 part-time/adjunct (0 women). *Students:* 41 full-time (19 women), 144 part-time (59 women); includes 35 minority (13 Black or African American, non-Hispanic/Latino; 1 American Indian or Alaska Native, non-Hispanic/Latino; 9 Asian, non-Hispanic/Latino; 11 Hispanic/Latino; 1 Two or more races, non-Hispanic/Latino), 13 international. Average age 33. 131 applicants, 78% accepted, 67 enrolled. In 2013, 83 master's, 5 other advanced degrees awarded. *Degree requirements:* For master's, comprehensive exam, thesis or alternative. *Entrance requirements:* For master's, GMAT (minimum score 500), minimum AACSB index of 1080. Additional exam requirements/recommendations for international students: Required—TOEFL (minimum score 550 paper-based; 80 iBT), IELTS (minimum score 6.5). *Application deadline:* For fall admission, 7/15 priority date for domestic students, 4/1 priority date for international students; for spring admission, 11/30 priority date for domestic students, 9/1 priority date for international students. Applications are processed on a rolling basis. Application fee: $50. Electronic applications accepted. *Expenses:* Tuition, state resident: full-time $8912; part-time $540 per credit hour. Tuition, nonresident: full-time $20,774; part-time $1252 per credit hour. *Required fees:* $148 per semester. One-time fee: $150. *Financial support:* In 2013–14, 10 students received support, including 4 research assistantships with full and partial tuition reimbursements available (averaging $7,750 per year), 5 teaching assistantships with full and partial tuition reimbursements available (averaging $9,000 per year); career-related internships or fieldwork, Federal Work-Study, institutionally sponsored loans, scholarships/grants, health care benefits, tuition waivers (full and partial), and unspecified assistantships also available. Support available to part-time students. Financial award application deadline: 4/1; financial award applicants required to submit FAFSA. *Faculty research:* Supply chain management, management of research and development, international marketing and branding, organizational behavior and human resource management, social networks and computational economics. *Total annual research expenditures:* $2.1 million. *Unit head:* Dr. Cynthia Gramm, Chair, 256-824-6913, Fax: 256-824-6328, E-mail: cynthia.gramm@uah.edu. *Application contact:* Jennifer Pettitt, Director of Graduate Programs, 256-824-6681, Fax: 256-824-7571, E-mail: jennifer.pettitt@uah.edu.

University of Alaska Anchorage, School of Engineering, Program in Project Management, Anchorage, AK 99508. Offers MS. Part-time and evening/weekend programs available. Postbaccalaureate distance learning degree programs offered (no on-campus study). *Degree requirements:* For master's, thesis or alternative, case study and research project. *Entrance requirements:* For master's, two years of project

management experience. Additional exam requirements/recommendations for international students: Required—TOEFL (minimum score 550 paper-based). *Expenses:* Contact institution.

University of Calgary, Faculty of Graduate Studies, Schulich School of Engineering, Department of Civil Engineering, Calgary, AB T2N 1N4, Canada. Offers avalanche mechanics (M Sc, PhD); civil engineering (M Eng, M Sc, PhD); energy and environment engineering (M Eng, M Sc, PhD); environmental engineering (M Eng, M Sc, PhD); geotechnical engineering (M Eng, M Sc, PhD); materials science (M Eng, M Sc, PhD); project management (M Eng, M Sc, PhD); structures and solid mechanics (M Eng, M Sc, PhD); transportation engineering (M Eng, M Sc, PhD); water resources (M Eng, M Sc, PhD). Part-time programs available. *Faculty:* 26 full-time (9 women), 9 part-time/adjunct (1 woman). *Students:* 115 full-time (29 women), 47 part-time (7 women). Average age 35. 124 applicants, 12% accepted, 11 enrolled. In 2013, 44 master's, 19 doctorates awarded. *Degree requirements:* For master's, thesis; for doctorate, thesis/dissertation, written and oral candidacy exam. *Entrance requirements:* For master's, minimum GPA of 3.0; for doctorate, minimum GPA of 3.5. Additional exam requirements/recommendations for international students: Required—TOEFL (minimum score 580 paper-based; 93 iBT), IELTS (minimum score 7). *Application deadline:* For fall admission, 5/1 priority date for domestic students, 4/1 priority date for international students; for winter admission, 9/1 priority date for domestic students, 8/1 priority date for international students; for spring admission, 1/1 for domestic students, 12/1 for international students. Applications are processed on a rolling basis. Application fee: $100 ($130 for international students). Electronic applications accepted. *Financial support:* In 2013–14, 49 students received support, including 9 fellowships (averaging $13,139 per year), 57 research assistantships (averaging $11,632 per year), 32 teaching assistantships (averaging $4,190 per year); scholarships/grants also available. *Faculty research:* Geotechnical engineering, energy and environment, transportation, project management, structures and solid mechanics. *Unit head:* Dr. Ron Wong, Department Head, 403-220-4821, Fax: 403-282-7026, E-mail: rckwong@ucalgary.ca. *Application contact:* Dr. Jocelyn Grozic, Associate Head, Graduate Studies, 403-220-5281, Fax: 403-282-7026, E-mail: ahgrad@ucalgary.ca.
Website: http://schulich.ucalgary.ca/Civil/.

University of California, Berkeley, UC Berkeley Extension, Certificate Programs in Business, Berkeley, CA 94720-1500. Offers accounting (Certificate); business administration (Certificate); finance (Certificate); human resource management (Certificate); management (Certificate); marketing (Certificate); project management (Certificate). *Accreditation:* AACSB. Postbaccalaureate distance learning degree programs offered.

University of California, Berkeley, UC Berkeley Extension, International Diploma Programs, Berkeley, CA 94720-1500. Offers business administration (Certificate); finance (Certificate); global business management (Certificate); marketing (Certificate); project management (Certificate). *Accreditation:* AACSB.

University of Dallas, Graduate School of Management, Irving, TX 75062-4736. Offers accounting (MBA, MM, MS); business management (MBA, MM); corporate finance (MBA, MM); financial services (MBA); global business (MBA, MM); health services management (MBA, MM); human resource management (MBA, MM); information assurance (MBA, MM, MS); information technology (MBA, MM, MS); information technology service management (MBA, MM, MS); marketing management (MBA, MM); organization development (MBA, MM); project management (MBA, MM); sports and entertainment management (MBA, MM); strategic leadership (MBA, MM); supply chain management (MBA); supply chain management and market logistics (MM). *Accreditation:* ACBSP. Part-time and evening/weekend programs available. Postbaccalaureate distance learning degree programs offered (no on-campus study). *Entrance requirements:* Additional exam requirements/recommendations for international students: Required—TOEFL. Electronic applications accepted. *Expenses:* Contact institution.

University of Denver, University College, Denver, CO 80208. Offers arts and culture (MLS, Certificate), including art, literature, and culture, arts development and program management (Certificate), creative writing; environmental policy and management (MAS, Certificate), including energy and sustainability (Certificate), environmental assessment of nuclear power (Certificate), environmental health and safety (Certificate), environmental management, natural resource management (Certificate); geographic information systems (MAS, Certificate); global affairs (MLS, Certificate), including translation studies, world history and culture; healthcare leadership (MPH, Certificate), including healthcare policy, law, and ethics, medical and healthcare information technologies, strategic management of healthcare; information and communications technology (MCIS, Certificate), including database design and administration (Certificate), geographic information systems (MCIS), information security systems security (Certificate), information systems security (MCIS), project management (MCIS, MPS, Certificate), software design and administration (Certificate), software design and programming (MCIS), technology management, telecommunications technology (MCIS), Web design and development; leadership and organizations (MPS, Certificate), including human capital in organizations, philanthropic leadership, project management (MCIS, MPS, Certificate), strategic innovation and change; organizational and professional communication (MPS, Certificate), including alternative dispute resolution, organizational communication, organizational development and training, public relations and marketing; security management (MAS, Certificate), including emergency planning and response, information security (MAS), organizational security; strategic human resource management (MPS, Certificate), including global human resources (MPS), human resource management and development (MPS). Part-time and evening/weekend programs available. Postbaccalaureate distance learning degree programs offered (no on-campus study). *Faculty:* 139 part-time/adjunct (61 women). *Students:* 49 full-time (16 women), 1,297 part-time (732 women); includes 272 minority (92 Black or African American, non-Hispanic/Latino; 5 American Indian or Alaska Native, non-Hispanic/Latino; 30 Asian, non-Hispanic/Latino; 114 Hispanic/Latino; 3 Native Hawaiian or other Pacific Islander, non-Hispanic/Latino; 28 Two or more races, non-Hispanic/Latino), 92 international. Average age 35. 542 applicants, 95% accepted, 362 enrolled. In 2013, 374 master's, 128 other advanced degrees awarded. *Degree requirements:* For master's, capstone project. *Entrance requirements:* For master's, transcripts, two letters of recommendation, personal statement, resume. Additional exam requirements/recommendations for international students: Required—TOEFL (minimum score 550 paper-based; 80 iBT). *Application deadline:* For fall admission, 7/18 priority date for domestic students, 5/2 priority date for international students; for winter admission, 10/24 priority date for domestic students, 9/19 priority date for international students; for spring admission, 2/1 for domestic students, 12/14 for international students; for summer admission, 4/18 priority date for domestic students, 3/7 priority date for international students. Applications are processed on a rolling basis. Application fee: $75. Electronic applications accepted. *Expenses:* Contact institution. *Financial support:* In 2013–14, 28 students received support. Applicants required to submit FAFSA. *Unit head:* Dr. Michael McGuire, Interim Dean, 303-871-3518, E-mail: mmcguire@du.edu. *Application contact:* Information Contact, 303-871-2291, E-mail: ucoladm@du.edu.
Website: http://www.universitycollege.du.edu/.

University of Houston, College of Technology, Department of Information and Logistics Technology, Houston, TX 77204. Offers information security (MS); supply chain and logistics technology (MS); technology project management (MS). Part-time programs available. *Degree requirements:* For master's, project or thesis (most programs). *Entrance requirements:* For master's, GMAT. Additional exam requirements/recommendations for international students: Required—TOEFL (minimum score 550 paper-based; 79 iBT). Electronic applications accepted.

The University of Kansas, Graduate Studies, School of Engineering, Program in Project Management, Overland Park, KS 66213. Offers ME, MS. *Faculty:* 10. *Students:* 18 part-time (4 women); includes 1 minority (Hispanic/Latino), 1 international. Average age 38. 12 applicants, 100% accepted, 12 enrolled. *Unit head:* Herbert R. Tuttle, Assistant Dean, 913-897-8561, E-mail: htuttle@ku.edu. *Application contact:* Natalie Rand, Program Coordinator, 913-897-8635, E-mail: nrand@ku.edu.
Website: https://pmgt.ku.edu/ms-pm.

University of Management and Technology, Program in Business Administration, Arlington, VA 22209. Offers acquisition management (DBA); general management (MBA, DBA); project management (MBA, DBA). Part-time and evening/weekend programs available. Postbaccalaureate distance learning degree programs offered (no on-campus study). *Degree requirements:* For master's, comprehensive exam. *Entrance requirements:* For master's, 3 recommendations, resume. Additional exam requirements/recommendations for international students: Required—TOEFL (minimum score 530 paper-based; 71 iBT). Electronic applications accepted.

University of Management and Technology, Program in Computer Science, Arlington, VA 22209. Offers computer science (MS); information technology (AC); project management (AC); software engineering (MS). Part-time and evening/weekend programs available. Postbaccalaureate distance learning degree programs offered (no on-campus study). *Entrance requirements:* For master's, 3 recommendations, resume. Additional exam requirements/recommendations for international students: Required—TOEFL (minimum score 530 paper-based; 71 iBT). Electronic applications accepted.

University of Management and Technology, Program in Management, Arlington, VA 22209. Offers acquisition management (MS, AC); criminal justice administration (MPA, MS); general management (MS); project management (MS, AC); public administration (MPA, MS, AC). Part-time and evening/weekend programs available. Postbaccalaureate distance learning degree programs offered (no on-campus study). *Entrance requirements:* For master's, 3 recommendations, resume. Additional exam requirements/recommendations for international students: Required—TOEFL (minimum score 530 paper-based; 71 iBT). Electronic applications accepted.

University of Mary, Gary Tharaldson School of Business, Bismarck, ND 58504-9652. Offers accountancy (MBA); business administration (MBA); health care (MBA); human resource management (MBA); management (MBA); project management (MPM); strategic leadership (MSSL). Part-time and evening/weekend programs available. *Degree requirements:* For master's, strategic planning seminar. *Entrance requirements:* For master's, minimum GPA of 2.5. Additional exam requirements/recommendations for international students: Required—TOEFL (minimum score 500 paper-based; 71 iBT).

University of Michigan–Dearborn, College of Engineering and Computer Science, Department of Industrial and Manufacturing Systems Engineering, Dearborn, MI 48128-1491. Offers engineering management (MS); industrial and systems engineering (MSE); information systems and technology (MS); program and project management (MS); MBA/MSE. Part-time and evening/weekend programs available. *Faculty:* 13 full-time (0 women), 5 part-time/adjunct (0 women). *Students:* 37 full-time (15 women), 162 part-time (42 women); includes 33 minority (11 Black or African American, non-Hispanic/Latino; 11 Asian, non-Hispanic/Latino; 8 Hispanic/Latino; 3 Two or more races, non-Hispanic/Latino), 44 international. Average age 36. 130 applicants, 62% accepted, 50 enrolled. In 2013, 58 master's awarded. *Degree requirements:* For master's, thesis optional. *Entrance requirements:* For master's, bachelor's degree in applied mathematics, computer science, engineering, or physical science; minimum GPA of 3.0. Additional exam requirements/recommendations for international students: Required—TOEFL (minimum score 560 paper-based; 84 iBT), IELTS (minimum score 6.5). *Application deadline:* For fall admission, 8/1 priority date for domestic students, 5/1 priority date for international students; for winter admission, 12/1 priority date for domestic students, 9/1 priority date for international students; for spring admission, 4/1 priority date for domestic students, 1/1 priority date for international students. Applications are processed on a rolling basis. Application fee: $60. *Expenses:* Tuition, state resident: full-time $11,838; part-time $686 per credit hour. Tuition, nonresident: full-time $20,926; part-time $1206 per credit hour. *Required fees:* $760; $286 per semester. Tuition and fees vary according to course load and program. *Financial support:* Fellowships, research assistantships, teaching assistantships, and Federal Work-Study available. Financial award application deadline: 4/1; financial award applicants required to submit FAFSA. *Faculty research:* Health care systems, data and knowledge management, human factors engineering, machine diagnostics, precision machining. *Unit head:* Dr. Armen Zakarian, Chair, 313-593-5361, Fax: 313-593-3692, E-mail: zakarian@umd.umich.edu. *Application contact:* Joey W. Woods, Graduate Program Assistant, 313-593-5361, Fax: 313-593-3692, E-mail: jwwoods@umd.umich.edu.
Website: http://www.engin.umd.umich.edu/IMSE/.

University of Nebraska at Omaha, Graduate Studies, College of Information Science and Technology, Department of Information Systems and Quantitative Analysis, Omaha, NE 68182. Offers biomedical informatics (MS, PhD); information assurance (MS, Certificate); information technology (PhD); management information systems (MS); project management (Certificate); systems analysis and design (Certificate). Part-time and evening/weekend programs available. *Faculty:* 15 full-time (7 women). *Students:* 77 full-time (27 women), 117 part-time (27 women); includes 32 minority (10 Black or African American, non-Hispanic/Latino; 15 Asian, non-Hispanic/Latino; 4 Hispanic/Latino; 3 Two or more races, non-Hispanic/Latino), 74 international. Average age 31. 274 applicants, 48% accepted, 63 enrolled. In 2013, 37 master's, 2 doctorates, 22 other advanced degrees awarded. *Degree requirements:* For master's, comprehensive exam, thesis (for some programs); for doctorate, comprehensive exam, thesis/dissertation. *Entrance requirements:* For master's, GRE General Test, minimum GPA of 3.0, 3 letters of recommendation, writing sample, resume, official transcripts; for doctorate, GMAT or GRE General Test, minimum GPA of 3.0, 3 letters of recommendation, writing sample, resume, official transcripts; for Certificate, minimum GPA of 3.0, official transcripts. Additional exam requirements/recommendations for international students: Required—TOEFL, IELTS, PTE. *Application deadline:* For fall admission, 2/15 for domestic students; for spring admission, 9/15 for domestic students. Applications are processed on a rolling basis. Application fee: $45. Electronic applications accepted. *Financial support:* In 2013–14, 31 students received support, including 27 research assistantships with tuition reimbursements available, 4 teaching assistantships with tuition reimbursements available; fellowships, career-related internships or fieldwork, Federal Work-Study, scholarships/grants, tuition waivers (partial), and unspecified assistantships also available. Financial award application deadline: 3/1; financial award applicants required to submit FAFSA. *Unit head:* Dr. Peter Wolcott, Chairperson, 402-554-3770, E-mail: graduate@unomaha.edu. *Application contact:* Dr. Leah Pietron, Graduate Program Chair, 402-554-2801, E-mail: graduate@unomaha.edu.

University of North Alabama, College of Business, Florence, AL 35632-0001. Offers accounting (MBA); enterprise resource planning systems (MBA); finance (MBA); health care management (MBA); information systems (MBA); professional (MBA); project management (MBA). *Accreditation:* ACBSP. Part-time and evening/weekend programs available. *Faculty:* 20 full-time (2 women). *Students:* 118 full-time (50 women), 273 part-time (130 women); includes 115 minority (37 Black or African American, non-Hispanic/Latino; 4 American Indian or Alaska Native, non-Hispanic/Latino; 68 Asian, non-Hispanic/Latino; 4 Hispanic/Latino; 2 Two or more races, non-Hispanic/Latino), 36 international. Average age 34. 296 applicants, 82% accepted, 149 enrolled. In 2013, 179 master's awarded. *Entrance requirements:* For master's, GMAT, GRE, minimum GPA of 2.75 in last 60 hours, 2.5 overall on a 3.0 scale; 27 hours of course work in business and economics. Additional exam requirements/recommendations for international students: Required—TOEFL (minimum score 500 paper-based; 79 iBT), IELTS (minimum score 6). *Application deadline:* For fall admission, 7/1 priority date for domestic students, 7/1 for international students; for spring admission, 12/1 for domestic and international students. Applications are processed on a rolling basis. Application fee: $25 ($50 for international students). Electronic applications accepted. *Expenses:* Tuition, state resident: full-time $4968; part-time $3312 per year. Tuition, nonresident: full-time $9936; part-time $6624 per year. *Required fees:* $970; $60.33 per credit. $362 per semester. *Financial support:* Federal Work-Study available. Support available to part-time students. Financial award application deadline: 4/1; financial award applicants required to submit FAFSA. *Unit head:* Dr. Kerry Gatlin, Dean, 256-765-4261, Fax: 256-765-4170, E-mail: kpgatlin@una.edu. *Application contact:* Russ Darracott, Graduate Admissions Counselor, 256-765-4447, E-mail: erdarracott@una.edu. Website: http://www.una.edu/business/.

University of Oklahoma, College of Arts and Sciences, Department of Psychology, Program in Organizational Dynamics, Tulsa, OK 74135. Offers technical project management (MA). Part-time and evening/weekend programs available. *Students:* 6 full-time (all women), 25 part-time (14 women); includes 10 minority (2 Black or African American, non-Hispanic/Latino; 2 American Indian or Alaska Native, non-Hispanic/Latino; 1 Asian, non-Hispanic/Latino; 2 Hispanic/Latino; 3 Two or more races, non-Hispanic/Latino). Average age 37. 7 applicants, 86% accepted, 4 enrolled. In 2013, 18 master's awarded. Terminal master's awarded for partial completion of doctoral program. *Degree requirements:* For master's, capstone project, thesis, or comprehensive exam. *Entrance requirements:* For master's, interview, statement of purpose, 2 letters of recommendation, resume showing at least 2 years of professional work experience. Additional exam requirements/recommendations for international students: Required—TOEFL (minimum score 79 iBT). *Application deadline:* For fall admission, 1/1 for domestic and international students; for spring admission, 11/1 for domestic students, 10/1 for international students. Application fee: $50 ($100 for international students). Electronic applications accepted. *Expenses:* Tuition, state resident: full-time $4205; part-time $175.20 per credit hour. Tuition, nonresident: full-time $16,205; part-time $675.20 per credit hour. *Required fees:* $2745; $103.85 per credit hour. $126.50 per semester. *Financial support:* In 2013–14, 6 students received support. Health care benefits and unspecified assistantships available. Financial award application deadline: 6/1; financial award applicants required to submit FAFSA. *Faculty research:* Leadership, teamwork, organizational citizenship behavior, ethics, organizational assessment. *Unit head:* Dr. Jennifer Kisamore, Graduate Liaison and Associate Professor, 918-660-3603, Fax: 918-660-3383, E-mail: jkisamore@ou.edu. *Application contact:* Lauren McKinney, Staff Assistant, 918-660-3489, Fax: 918-660-3491, E-mail: lmckinney@ou.edu. Website: http://odyn.ou.edu.

University of Ottawa, Faculty of Graduate and Postdoctoral Studies, Faculty of Engineering, Engineering Management Program, Ottawa, ON K1N 6N5, Canada. Offers engineering management (M Eng); information technology (Certificate); project management (Certificate). *Degree requirements:* For master's, thesis or alternative. *Entrance requirements:* For master's and Certificate, honors degree or equivalent, minimum B average. Electronic applications accepted.

University of Phoenix–Bay Area Campus, School of Business, San Jose, CA 95134-1805. Offers accountancy (MS); accounting (MBA); business administration (MBA, DBA); energy management (MBA); global management (MBA); health care management (MBA); human resource management (MBA); human resources management (MM); management (MM); marketing (MBA); organizational leadership (DM); project management (MBA); public administration (MPA); technology management (MBA). Evening/weekend programs available. Postbaccalaureate distance learning degree programs offered (no on-campus study). *Degree requirements:* For master's, thesis (for some programs). *Entrance requirements:* For master's, minimum undergraduate GPA of 3.0, 3 years of work experience. Additional exam requirements/recommendations for international students: Required—TOEFL (minimum score 550 paper-based; 79 iBT). Electronic applications accepted.

University of Phoenix–Milwaukee Campus, School of Business, Milwaukee, WI 53224. Offers accounting (MBA); business administration (MBA); energy management (MBA); global management (MBA); health care management (MBA); human resource management (MBA); management (MM); marketing (MBA); project management (MBA); technology management (MBA). Evening/weekend programs available. Postbaccalaureate distance learning degree programs offered. *Entrance requirements:* Additional exam requirements/recommendations for international students: Required—TOEFL, TOEIC (Test of English as an International Communication), Berlitz Online English Proficiency Exam, PTE, or IELTS. Electronic applications accepted. *Expenses:* Contact institution.

University of Phoenix–Online Campus, School of Business, Phoenix, AZ 85034-7209. Offers accountancy (MS); accounting (MBA, Certificate); business administration (MBA); energy management (MBA); global management (MBA); health care management (MBA); human resource management (MBA, Certificate); human resources management (MM); management (MM); marketing (MBA, Certificate); project management (MBA, Certificate); public administration (MBA, MM); technology management (MBA). Evening/weekend programs available. Postbaccalaureate distance learning degree programs offered. *Entrance requirements:* Additional exam requirements/recommendations for international students: Required—TOEFL, TOEIC (Test of English as an International Communication), Berlitz Online English Proficiency Exam, PTE, or IELTS. Electronic applications accepted. *Expenses:* Contact institution.

University of Phoenix–Phoenix Campus, School of Business, Tempe, AZ 85282-2371. Offers accounting (MBA, MS, Certificate); business administration (MBA); energy management (MBA); global management (MBA); health care management (MBA); human resource management (MBA, Certificate); management (MM); marketing (MBA); project management (MBA); technology management (MBA). Evening/weekend programs available. Postbaccalaureate distance learning degree programs offered. *Entrance requirements:* Additional exam requirements/recommendations for international students: Required—TOEFL, TOEIC (Test of English as an International Communication), Berlitz Online English Proficiency Exam, PTE, or IELTS. Electronic applications accepted. *Expenses:* Contact institution.

University of Phoenix–Puerto Rico Campus, School of Business, Guaynabo, PR 00968. Offers accounting (MBA); energy management (MBA); global management

(MBA); human resource management (MBA); marketing (MBA); project management (MBA); small business administration (MBA). Evening/weekend programs available. *Degree requirements:* For master's, thesis (for some programs). *Entrance requirements:* For master's, minimum undergraduate GPA of 3.0, 3 years work experience. Additional exam requirements/recommendations for international students: Required—TOEFL (minimum score 550 paper-based; 79 iBT). Electronic applications accepted.

University of Phoenix–Southern California Campus, School of Business, Costa Mesa, CA 92626. Offers accounting (MBA); business administration (MBA); energy management (MBA); global management (MBA); health care management (MBA); human resource management (MBA); management (MM); marketing (MBA); project management (MBA); technology management (MBA). Evening/weekend programs available. Postbaccalaureate distance learning degree programs offered. *Entrance requirements:* Additional exam requirements/recommendations for international students: Required—TOEFL, TOEIC (Test of English as an International Communication), Berlitz Online English Proficiency Exam, PTE, or IELTS. Electronic applications accepted. *Expenses:* Contact institution.

University of Regina, Faculty of Graduate Studies and Research, Kenneth Levene Graduate School of Business, Program in Business Administration, Regina, SK S4S 0A2, Canada. Offers business foundations (PGD); engineering management (MBA); executive business administration (EMBA); general management (MBA); international business (MBA); leadership (M Admin); organizational leadership (Master's Certificate); project management (Master's Certificate). Part-time and evening/weekend programs available. *Faculty:* 39 full-time (14 women), 7 part-time/adjunct (0 women). *Students:* 86 full-time (30 women), 65 part-time (32 women). 123 applicants, 25% accepted. In 2013, 59 master's, 23 other advanced degrees awarded. *Degree requirements:* For master's, project (for some programs). *Entrance requirements:* For master's, GMAT, three years of relevant work experience, four-year undergraduate degree; for other advanced degree, GMAT (for PGD), four-year undergraduate degree and two years of relevant work experience (for Certificates); three years' work experience (for Postgraduate Diploma). Additional exam requirements/recommendations for international students: Required—TOEFL (minimum score 580 paper-based; 80 iBT), IELTS (minimum score 6.5). *Application deadline:* Applications are processed on a rolling basis. Application fee: $100. Electronic applications accepted. *Expenses:* Contact institution. *Financial support:* In 2013–14, 7 fellowships (averaging $6,000 per year), 1 research assistantship (averaging $5,500 per year), 7 teaching assistantships (averaging $2,356 per year) were awarded; scholarships/grants also available. Financial award application deadline: 6/15. *Faculty research:* Business policy and strategy, production and operations management, human behavior in organizations, financial management, social issues in business. *Unit head:* Dr. Andrew Gaudes, Dean, 306-585-4162, Fax: 306-585-5361, E-mail: andrew.gaudes@uregina.ca. *Application contact:* Steve Wield, Manager, Graduate Programs, 306-337-8463, Fax: 306-585-5361, E-mail: steve.wield@uregina.ca. Website: http://www.uregina.ca/business/levene/.

The University of Tennessee at Chattanooga, Graduate School, College of Engineering and Computer Science, Department of Engineering Management, Chattanooga, TN 37403. Offers engineering management (MS); fundamentals of engineering management (Graduate Certificate); leadership and ethics (Graduate Certificate); logistics and supply chain management (Graduate Certificate); nuclear engineering (Graduate Certificate); power system protection (Graduate Certificate); power systems management (Graduate Certificate); project and value management (Graduate Certificate); quality management (Graduate Certificate); sustainable electric energy (Graduate Certificate). Postbaccalaureate distance learning degree programs offered (no on-campus study). *Faculty:* 5 full-time (1 woman). *Students:* 14 full-time (5 women), 67 part-time (14 women); includes 24 minority (13 Black or African American, non-Hispanic/Latino; 6 Asian, non-Hispanic/Latino; 4 Hispanic/Latino; 1 Two or more races, non-Hispanic/Latino), 6 international. Average age 31. 31 applicants, 45% accepted, 10 enrolled. In 2013, 31 master's, 17 other advanced degrees awarded. *Degree requirements:* For master's, thesis. *Entrance requirements:* For master's, GRE General Test, letters of recommendation; minimum undergraduate GPA of 2.5 overall or 3.0 in senior year. Additional exam requirements/recommendations for international students: Required—TOEFL (minimum score 550 paper-based; 79 iBT), IELTS (minimum score 6). *Application deadline:* For fall admission, 6/13 priority date for domestic students, 6/1 for international students; for spring admission, 10/15 priority date for domestic students, 10/1 for international students. Applications are processed on a rolling basis. Application fee: $30 ($35 for international students). Electronic applications accepted. *Financial support:* In 2013–14, 5 research assistantships (averaging $6,528 per year), 3 teaching assistantships (averaging $6,781 per year) were awarded; career-related internships or fieldwork, scholarships/grants, and unspecified assistantships also available. Support available to part-time students. Financial award applicants required to submit FAFSA. *Faculty research:* Plant layout design, lean manufacturing, Six Sigma, value management, product development. *Unit head:* Dr. Neslihan Alp, Department Head, 423-425-4032, Fax: 423-425-5229, E-mail: neslihan-alp@utc.edu. *Application contact:* Dr. J. Randy Walker, Interim Dean of Graduate Studies, 423-425-4478, Fax: 423-425-5223, E-mail: randy-walker@utc.edu. Website: http://www.utc.edu/Departments/engrcs/engm/index.php.

The University of Texas at Dallas, Naveen Jindal School of Management, Program in Business Administration, Richardson, TX 75080. Offers business administration (MBA, PMBA); executive business administration (EMBA); global leadership (EMBA); healthcare management for physicians (EMBA); product lifecycle and supply chain management (EMBA); project management (EMBA); real estate (MBA). *Accreditation:* AACSB. Part-time and evening/weekend programs available. Postbaccalaureate distance learning degree programs offered (no on-campus study). *Faculty:* 100 full-time (21 women), 52 part-time/adjunct (18 women). *Students:* 421 full-time (196 women), 630 part-time (398 women); includes 295 minority (45 Black or African American, non-Hispanic/Latino; 4 American Indian or Alaska Native, non-Hispanic/Latino; 151 Asian, non-Hispanic/Latino; 76 Hispanic/Latino; 19 Two or more races, non-Hispanic/Latino), 275 international. Average age 31. 940 applicants, 44% accepted, 375 enrolled. In 2013, 384 master's awarded. *Degree requirements:* For master's, thesis optional. *Entrance requirements:* For master's, GMAT, 10 years of business experience (EMBA), minimum GPA of 3.0. Additional exam requirements/recommendations for international students: Required—TOEFL (minimum score 550 paper-based). *Application deadline:* For fall admission, 7/15 for domestic students, 5/1 priority date for international students; for spring admission, 11/15 for domestic students, 9/1 priority date for international students. Applications are processed on a rolling basis. Application fee: $50 ($100 for international students). Electronic applications accepted. *Expenses:* Contact institution. *Financial support:* In 2013–14, 336 students received support. Research assistantships with partial tuition reimbursements available, teaching assistantships with partial tuition reimbursements available, career-related internships or fieldwork, Federal Work-Study, institutionally sponsored loans, scholarships/grants, and unspecified assistantships available. Support available to part-time students. Financial award application deadline: 4/30; financial award applicants required to submit FAFSA. *Faculty research:* Production scheduling, trade and finance, organizational decision-making, life/work planning. *Unit head:* Lisa Shatz, Assistant Dean, MBA Programs, 972-883-6191, E-mail: lisa.shatz@

utdallas.edu. *Application contact:* Anna Walls, Enrollment Services Advisor, MBA Programs, 972-883-5951, E-mail: anna.walls@utdallas.edu.
Website: http://jindal.utdallas.edu/academic-programs/mba-programs/.

The University of Texas at Dallas, Naveen Jindal School of Management, Program in Organizations, Strategy and International Management, Richardson, TX 75080. Offers healthcare management (MS); international management studies (MS, PhD); management and administrative sciences (MS); project management (MS). Part-time and evening/weekend programs available. *Faculty:* 13 full-time (4 women), 8 part-time/adjunct (4 women). *Students:* 101 full-time (59 women), 198 part-time (119 women); includes 88 minority (27 Black or African American, non-Hispanic/Latino; 38 Asian, non-Hispanic/Latino; 19 Hispanic/Latino; 1 Native Hawaiian or other Pacific Islander, non-Hispanic/Latino; 3 Two or more races, non-Hispanic/Latino), 72 international. Average age 35. 282 applicants, 53% accepted, 139 enrolled. In 2013, 131 master's, 5 doctorates awarded. *Degree requirements:* For doctorate, thesis/dissertation. *Entrance requirements:* For master's and doctorate, GMAT. Additional exam requirements/recommendations for international students: Required—TOEFL (minimum score 550 paper-based). *Application deadline:* For fall admission, 7/15 for domestic students, 5/1 priority date for international students; for spring admission, 11/15 for domestic students, 9/1 priority date for international students. Applications are processed on a rolling basis. Application fee: $50 ($100 for international students). Electronic applications accepted. *Expenses:* Tuition, state resident: full-time $11,940; part-time $663.33 per credit hour. Tuition, nonresident: full-time $21,606; part-time $1200.33 per credit hour. *Financial support:* In 2013–14, 58 students received support. Research assistantships with partial tuition reimbursements available, teaching assistantships with partial tuition reimbursements available, Federal Work-Study, institutionally sponsored loans, scholarships/grants, and unspecified assistantships available. Support available to part-time students. Financial award application deadline: 4/30; financial award applicants required to submit FAFSA. *Faculty research:* International accounting, international trade and finance, economic development, international economics. *Unit head:* Dr. Mike Peng, Area Coordinator, 972-883-2714, Fax: 972-883-5977, E-mail: mikepeng@utdallas.edu. *Application contact:* Dr. Habte Woldu, Director, International Management Studies, 972-883-6357, Fax: 972-883-5977, E-mail: wolduh@utdallas.edu.
Website: http://jindal.utdallas.edu/academic-areas/organizations-strategy-and-international-management/.

University of Wisconsin–Platteville, School of Graduate Studies, Distance Learning Center, Online Master of Science in Project Management Program, Platteville, WI 53818-3099. Offers MS. Part-time and evening/weekend programs available. Postbaccalaureate distance learning degree programs offered (no on-campus study). *Students:* 70 full-time (33 women), 156 part-time (55 women); includes 32 minority (12 Black or African American, non-Hispanic/Latino; 9 Asian, non-Hispanic/Latino; 10 Hispanic/Latino; 1 Native Hawaiian or other Pacific Islander, non-Hispanic/Latino). 59 applicants, 93% accepted, 33 enrolled. *Degree requirements:* For master's, thesis or alternative. *Entrance requirements:* Additional exam requirements/recommendations for international students: Required—TOEFL (minimum score 500 paper-based; 61 iBT), IELTS (minimum score 6). *Application deadline:* For fall admission, 7/1 priority date for domestic students; for spring admission, 11/1 priority date for domestic students. Applications are processed on a rolling basis. Application fee: $56. Electronic applications accepted. *Unit head:* William Haskins, Coordinator, 608-342-1961, Fax: 608-342-1466, E-mail: haskinsd@uwplatt.edu. *Application contact:* Karen Adams, Marketing Director, 800-362-5460, Fax: 608-342-1071, E-mail: adamskar@uwplatt.edu.
Website: http://www.uwplatt.edu/disted/project-management.html.

Viterbo University, Master of Business Administration Program, La Crosse, WI 54601-4797. Offers general business administration (MBA); health care management (MBA); international business (MBA); leadership (MBA); project management (MBA). *Accreditation:* ACBSP. Part-time and evening/weekend programs available. *Faculty:* 3 full-time (2 women), 4 part-time/adjunct (2 women). *Students:* 86 full-time (47 women), 11 part-time (8 women); includes 5 minority (1 Black or African American, non-Hispanic/Latino; 3 Asian, non-Hispanic/Latino; 1 Hispanic/Latino), 11 international. Average age 34. In 2013, 59 master's awarded. *Degree requirements:* For master's, 34 credits. *Entrance requirements:* For master's, BS, transcripts, minimum undergraduate cumulative GPA of 3.0, 2 letters of reference, 3-5 page essay. Additional exam requirements/recommendations for international students: Recommended—TOEFL (minimum score 550 paper-based). Application fee: $50. Electronic applications accepted. *Expenses: Tuition:* Full-time $7140; part-time $444 per credit hour. *Required fees:* $100. *Unit head:* Dr. Barbara Gayle, Dean of Graduate Studies, 608-796-3080, E-mail: bmgayle@viterbo.edu. *Application contact:* Tiffany Morey, MBA Coordinator, 608-796-3379, E-mail: tlmorey@viterbo.edu.

Walden University, Graduate Programs, School of Management, Minneapolis, MN 55401. Offers accounting (MBA, MS, DBA), including accounting for the professional (MS), accounting with CPA emphasis (MS), self-designed (MS, PhD); accounting and management (MS), including accountants as strategic managers, self-designed (MS, PhD); advanced project management (Graduate Certificate); applied project management (Graduate Certificate); bridge to business administration (Post-Doctoral Certificate); bridge to management (Post-Doctoral Certificate); business administration (EMBA); business management (Graduate Certificate); communication (MS, Graduate Certificate); corporate finance (MBA); entrepreneurship (DBA); entrepreneurship and small business (MBA); finance (DBA); global supply chain management (DBA); healthcare management (MBA, DBA); human resource management (MBA, MS, Graduate Certificate), including functional human resource management (MS), general program (MS), integrating functional and strategic human resource management (MS), organizational strategy (MS); human resources management (DBA); information systems management (DBA); international business (MBA, DBA); leadership (MBA, MS, DBA), including general program (MS), human resources leadership (MS), leader development (MS), self-designed (MS, PhD); management (MS, PhD), including accounting (PhD), engineering management (PhD), finance (PhD), general program (MS), healthcare management (MS), human resource management (MS), human resources management (PhD), information systems management (PhD), leadership (MS), leadership and organizational change (PhD), marketing (MS), operations research (PhD), project management (MS), self-designed, strategy and operations (MS); marketing (MBA, DBA); project management (MBA, MS, DBA); self-designed (MBA, DBA); social impact management (DBA); technology entrepreneurship (DBA). Part-time and evening/weekend programs available. Postbaccalaureate distance learning degree programs offered (minimal on-campus study). *Faculty:* 24 full-time (9 women), 337 part-time/adjunct (127 women). *Students:* 4,369 full-time (2,379 women), 2,181 part-time (1,304 women); includes 3,669 minority (3,020 Black or African American, non-Hispanic/Latino; 22 American Indian or Alaska Native, non-Hispanic/Latino; 156 Asian, non-Hispanic/Latino; 331 Hispanic/Latino; 11 Native Hawaiian or other Pacific Islander, non-Hispanic/Latino; 129 Two or more races, non-Hispanic/Latino), 107 international. Average age 41. 2,030 applicants, 94% accepted, 1436 enrolled. In 2013, 757 master's, 128 doctorates, 32 other advanced degrees awarded. *Degree requirements:* For master's, residency (for some programs); for doctorate, thesis/dissertation (for some programs), residency. *Entrance requirements:* For master's, bachelor's degree or higher; minimum GPA of 2.5; official transcripts; goal statement (for some programs); access to computer and Internet; for doctorate, master's degree or higher; three years of related professional or academic experience (preferred); minimum GPA of 3.0; goal statement and current resume (select programs); official transcripts; access to computer and Internet; for other advanced degree, relevant work experience; access to computer and Internet. Additional exam requirements/recommendations for international students: Required—TOEFL (minimum score 550 paper-based; 79 iBT), IELTS (minimum score 6.5), Michigan English Language Assessment Battery (minimum score 82), or PTE. *Application deadline:* Applications are processed on a rolling basis. Application fee: $0. Electronic applications accepted. *Expenses: Tuition:* Full-time $11,813.55; part-time $500 per credit. *Required fees:* $618.76. *Financial support:* Fellowships, Federal Work-Study, scholarships/grants, unspecified assistantships, and family tuition reduction, active duty/veteran tuition reduction, group tuition reduction, interest-free payment plans, employee tuition reduction available. Support available to part-time students. Financial award applicants required to submit FAFSA. *Unit head:* Dr. Ward Ulmer, III, Associate Dean, 800-925-3368. *Application contact:* Jennifer Hall, Vice President of Enrollment Management, 866-4-WALDEN, E-mail: info@waldenu.edu.
Website: http://www.waldenu.edu/programs/colleges-schools/management.

Washington State University, Graduate School, College of Engineering and Architecture, Online Program in Engineering and Technology Management, Pullman, WA 99164-2785. Offers constraints management (Graduate Certificate); construction project management (Graduate Certificate); engineering and technology management (METM); manufacturing leadership (Graduate Certificate); program and facilities management (Graduate Certificate); project management (Graduate Certificate); Six Sigma quality management (Graduate Certificate); supply chain management (Graduate Certificate); systems engineering management (Graduate Certificate). Part-time and evening/weekend programs available. Postbaccalaureate distance learning degree programs offered (no on-campus study). *Degree requirements:* For master's, one foreign language, comprehensive exam (for some programs). *Entrance requirements:* Additional exam requirements/recommendations for international students: Required—TOEFL. Electronic applications accepted. *Faculty research:* Constraints management, Six Sigma quality management, supply chain management, project management, construction management, systems engineering management, manufacturing leadership.

Washington State University Spokane, Graduate Programs, Program in Engineering and Technology Management, Pullman, WA 99164-2785. Offers constraints management (Graduate Certificate); construction project management (Graduate Certificate); engineering and technology management (METM); facilities management (Graduate Certificate); logistics and supply chain management (Graduate Certificate); manufacturing leadership (Graduate Certificate); project management (Graduate Certificate); Six Sigma quality management (Graduate Certificate); systems engineering management (Graduate Certificate). *Degree requirements:* For master's, comprehensive exam (for some programs), thesis (for some programs), comprehensive exam or project. *Entrance requirements:* For master's, GMAT (for applicants with less than 3.0 GPA), minimum GPA of 3.0, 3 letters of reference, resume, personal statement, math through college algebra (prefer math through calculus I), experience in the engineering/technology area. Additional exam requirements/recommendations for international students: Required—TOEFL. *Expenses:* Contact institution. *Faculty research:* Operations research for decision analysis quality control and liability, analytical techniques to formulating decisions.

Wayland Baptist University, Graduate Programs, Programs in Business Administration/Management, Plainview, TX 79072-6998. Offers accounting (MBA); general business (MBA); health care administration (MAM, MBA); healthcare administration (MBA); human resource management (MAM, MBA); international management (MBA); management (MBA); management information systems (MBA); organization management (MAM); project management (MBA). Part-time and evening/weekend programs available. Postbaccalaureate distance learning degree programs offered (no on-campus study). *Faculty:* 30 full-time (5 women), 38 part-time/adjunct (9 women). *Students:* 44 full-time (20 women), 702 part-time (315 women); includes 348 minority (149 Black or African American, non-Hispanic/Latino; 4 American Indian or Alaska Native, non-Hispanic/Latino; 23 Asian, non-Hispanic/Latino; 139 Hispanic/Latino; 9 Native Hawaiian or other Pacific Islander, non-Hispanic/Latino; 24 Two or more races, non-Hispanic/Latino), 5 international. Average age 40. 147 applicants, 94% accepted, 73 enrolled. In 2013, 296 master's awarded. *Degree requirements:* For master's, capstone course. *Entrance requirements:* For master's, GMAT, GRE or MAT. Additional exam requirements/recommendations for international students: Required—TOEFL (minimum score 500 paper-based; 61 iBT). *Application deadline:* Applications are processed on a rolling basis. Application fee: $50. Electronic applications accepted. *Expenses: Tuition:* Full-time $8190; part-time $455 per credit hour. *Required fees:* $970; $455 per credit hour. $485 per semester. *Financial support:* Federal Work-Study, institutionally sponsored loans, and scholarships/grants available. Support available to part-time students. Financial award application deadline: 5/1; financial award applicants required to submit FAFSA. *Unit head:* Dr. Otto Schacht, Chairman, 806-291-1020, Fax: 806-291-1957, E-mail: schachto@wbu.edu. *Application contact:* Amanda Stanton, Graduate Studies, 806-291-3423, Fax: 806-291-1950, E-mail: stanton@wbu.edu.

Western Carolina University, Graduate School, College of Business, Program in Project Management, Cullowhee, NC 28723. Offers MPM. Part-time and evening/weekend programs available. Postbaccalaureate distance learning degree programs offered (no on-campus study). *Entrance requirements:* For master's, GMAT or GRE, work experience in project management, appropriate undergraduate degree with minimum GPA of 3.0, employer recommendation, resume. Additional exam requirements/recommendations for international students: Required—TOEFL (minimum score 550 paper-based; 79 iBT).

Winthrop University, College of Business Administration, Program in Software Project Management, Rock Hill, SC 29733. Offers software development (MS); software project management (Certificate). *Entrance requirements:* For master's, GMAT.

Wright State University, School of Graduate Studies, Raj Soin College of Business, Department of Management, Dayton, OH 45435. Offers flexible business (MBA); health care management (MBA); international business (MBA); management, innovation and change (MBA); project management (MBA); supply chain management (MBA); MBA/MS. *Entrance requirements:* For master's, GMAT, minimum AACSB index of 1000. Additional exam requirements/recommendations for international students: Required—TOEFL.

Section 18
Quality Management

This section contains a directory of institutions offering graduate work in quality management. Additional information about programs listed in the directory may be obtained by writing directly to the dean of a graduate school or chair of a department at the address given in the directory.

For programs offering related work, see also in this book *Business Administration and Management*.

CONTENTS

Program Directory

Quality Management   596

Quality Management

California Intercontinental University, School of Information Technology, Diamond Bar, CA 91765. Offers information systems and enterprise resource management (DBA); information systems and knowledge management (MBA); project and quality management (MBA).

California State University, Dominguez Hills, College of Extended and International Education, Program in Quality Assurance, Carson, CA 90747-0001. Offers MS. Part-time and evening/weekend programs available. Postbaccalaureate distance learning degree programs offered (no on-campus study). *Faculty:* 16 part-time/adjunct (3 women). *Students:* 6 full-time (3 women), 293 part-time (160 women); includes 126 minority (28 Black or African American, non-Hispanic/Latino; 4 American Indian or Alaska Native, non-Hispanic/Latino; 55 Asian, non-Hispanic/Latino; 32 Hispanic/Latino; 1 Native Hawaiian or other Pacific Islander, non-Hispanic/Latino; 6 Two or more races, non-Hispanic/Latino), 33 international. Average age 39. 83 applicants, 94% accepted, 54 enrolled. In 2013, 24 master's awarded. *Degree requirements:* For master's, thesis. *Entrance requirements:* For master's, minimum GPA of 2.75. Additional exam requirements/recommendations for international students: Required—TOEFL. *Application deadline:* For fall admission, 6/1 priority date for domestic and international students; for spring admission, 10/1 priority date for domestic and international students. Application fee: $55. Electronic applications accepted. *Expenses:* Contact institution. *Faculty research:* Six Sigma, lean thinking, risk management, quality management. *Unit head:* Dr. Milton Krivokuca, Coordinator, 310-243-3880, Fax: 310-516-4423, E-mail: mkrivokuca@csudh.edu. *Application contact:* Rodger Hamrick, Program Assistant, 310-243-3880, Fax: 310-516-4423, E-mail: rhamrick@csudh.edu. Website: http://www.csudh.edu/msqa.

Calumet College of Saint Joseph, Program in Quality Assurance, Whiting, IN 46394-2195. Offers MS.

Case Western Reserve University, Weatherhead School of Management, Department of Operations, Cleveland, OH 44106. Offers management (MS, MSM), including finance (MS), information systems (MS), marketing (MS), operations research, quality management (MS), supply chain (MSM); management for liberal arts graduates (MSM); operations research (PhD); MBA/MSM. Part-time programs available. *Degree requirements:* For doctorate, thesis/dissertation. *Entrance requirements:* For master's, GRE General Test; for doctorate, GMAT, GRE General Test. *Faculty research:* Mathematical finance, mathematical programming, scheduling, stochastic optimization, environmental/energy models.

East Carolina University, Graduate School, College of Technology and Computer Science, Department of Technology Systems, Greenville, NC 27858-4353. Offers computer network professional (Certificate); industrial technology (MS), including computer networking management, digital communications, industrial distribution and logistics, information security, manufacturing, performance improvement, quality systems; information assurance (Certificate); Lean Six Sigma Black Belt (Certificate); occupational safety (MS); technology management (PhD); Website developer (Certificate). *Entrance requirements:* For master's and Certificate, GRE General Test or MAT, minimum GPA of 2.5; for doctorate, GRE General Test, related work experience. *Expenses:* Tuition, state resident: full-time $4223. Tuition, nonresident: full-time $16,540. *Required fees:* $2184.

Eastern Michigan University, Graduate School, College of Technology, School of Engineering Technology, Programs in Quality Management, Ypsilanti, MI 48197. Offers quality (MS, Graduate Certificate); quality management (MS). Part-time and evening/weekend programs available. Postbaccalaureate distance learning degree programs offered (minimal on-campus study). *Students:* 5 full-time (1 woman), 74 part-time (34 women); includes 21 minority (12 Black or African American, non-Hispanic/Latino; 3 Asian, non-Hispanic/Latino; 4 Hispanic/Latino; 1 Native Hawaiian or other Pacific Islander, non-Hispanic/Latino; 1 Two or more races, non-Hispanic/Latino), 3 international. Average age 39. 30 applicants, 80% accepted, 10 enrolled. In 2013, 26 master's, 2 other advanced degrees awarded. *Entrance requirements:* Additional exam requirements/recommendations for international students: Required—TOEFL. *Application deadline:* Applications are processed on a rolling basis. Application fee: $35. *Expenses:* Tuition, state resident: full-time $12,300; part-time $466 per credit hour. Tuition, nonresident: full-time $23,159; part-time $918 per credit hour. *Required fees:* $71 per credit hour. $46 per semester. One-time fee: $100. Tuition and fees vary according to course level and degree level. *Financial support:* Fellowships, research assistantships with full tuition reimbursements, teaching assistantships with full tuition reimbursements, career-related internships or fieldwork, Federal Work-Study, institutionally sponsored loans, scholarships/grants, tuition waivers (partial), and unspecified assistantships available. Support available to part-time students. Financial award applicants required to submit FAFSA. *Unit head:* Dr. Behrooz (Bob) Lahidji, Director, 734-487-2040, Fax: 734-487-8755, E-mail: bob.lahidji@emich.edu. *Application contact:* Dr. Walter Tucker, Program Coordinator, 734-487-2040, Fax: 734-487-8755, E-mail: walter.tucker@emich.edu.

Florida Institute of Technology, Graduate Programs, Extended Studies Division, Melbourne, FL 32901-6975. Offers acquisition and contract management (MS); aerospace engineering (MS); business administration (MBA, DBA); computer information systems (MS); computer science (MS); electrical engineering (MS); engineering management (MS); human resources management (MS); logistics management (MS), including humanitarian and disaster relief logistics; management (MS), including acquisition and contract management, e-business, human resources management, information systems, logistics management, management, transportation management; material acquisition management (MS); mechanical engineering (MS); operations research (MS); project management (MS), including information systems, operations research; public administration (MPA); quality management (MS); software engineering (MS); space systems (MS); space systems management (MS); supply chain management (MS); systems management (MS), including information systems, operations research; technology management (MS). Part-time and evening/weekend programs available. Postbaccalaureate distance learning degree programs offered (no on-campus study). *Faculty:* 8 full-time (1 woman), 96 part-time/adjunct (25 women). *Students:* 94 full-time (46 women), 912 part-time (397 women); includes 436 minority (290 Black or African American, non-Hispanic/Latino; 18 American Indian or Alaska Native, non-Hispanic/Latino; 38 Asian, non-Hispanic/Latino; 62 Hispanic/Latino; 2 Native Hawaiian or other Pacific Islander, non-Hispanic/Latino; 26 Two or more races, non-Hispanic/Latino), 9 international. Average age 37. 591 applicants, 44% accepted, 220 enrolled. In 2013, 522 master's awarded. *Degree requirements:* For master's, comprehensive exam (for some programs), capstone course. *Entrance requirements:* For master's, GMAT or resume showing 8 years of supervised experience, minimum GPA of 3.0, 2 letters of recommendation, resume. Additional exam requirements/recommendations for international students: Required—TOEFL (minimum score 550

paper-based; 79 iBT). *Application deadline:* For fall admission, 4/1 for international students; for spring admission, 9/30 for international students. Applications are processed on a rolling basis. Electronic applications accepted. *Expenses:* Contact institution. *Financial support:* Application deadline: 3/1; applicants required to submit FAFSA. *Unit head:* Dr. Theodore R. Richardson, III, Senior Associate Dean, 321-674-8123, Fax: 321-674-7597, E-mail: trichardson@fit.edu. *Application contact:* Carolyn Farrior, Director of Graduate Admissions, Online Learning and Off-Campus Programs, 321-674-7118, Fax: 321-674-8216, E-mail: cfarrior@fit.edu. Website: http://es.fit.edu.

Hofstra University, Frank G. Zarb School of Business, Programs in Information Technology, Hempstead, NY 11549. Offers business administration (MBA), including information technology, quality management; information technology (MS, Advanced Certificate).

Instituto Tecnologico de Santo Domingo, Graduate School, Area of Business, Santo Domingo, Dominican Republic. Offers banking and securities markets (M Mgmt); corporate finance (M Mgmt); human resources management (M Mgmt, Certificate); international trade management (M Mgmt); marketing (M Mgmt); organizational development (M Mgmt); quality and productivity management (Certificate); tax management and planning (M Mgmt); upper management (M Mgmt).

Instituto Tecnológico y de Estudios Superiores de Monterrey, Campus Ciudad de México, Virtual University Division, Ciudad de Mexico, Mexico. Offers administration of information technologies (MA); computer sciences (MA); education (MA, PhD); educational technology (MA); environmental engineering (MA); environmental systems (MA); humanistic studies (MA); industrial engineering (MA); international business for Latin America (MA); quality systems (MA); quality systems and productivity (MA). Part-time and evening/weekend programs available. Postbaccalaureate distance learning degree programs offered (minimal on-campus study). *Entrance requirements:* For master's and doctorate, Instituto entrance exam. Additional exam requirements/recommendations for international students: Required—TOEFL.

Instituto Tecnológico y de Estudios Superiores de Monterrey, Campus Ciudad Juárez, Program in Quality Management, Ciudad Juárez, Mexico. Offers MQM.

Instituto Tecnológico y de Estudios Superiores de Monterrey, Campus Estado de México, Professional and Graduate Division, Estado de Mexico, Mexico. Offers administration of information technologies (MITA); architecture (M Arch); business administration (GMBA, MBA); computer sciences (MCS, PhD); education (M Ed); educational institution administration (MAD); educational technology and innovation (PhD); electronic commerce (MEC); environmental systems (MS); finance (MAF); humanistic studies (MHS); information sciences and knowledge management (MISKM); information systems (MS); manufacturing systems (MS); marketing (MEM); quality systems and productivity (MS); science and materials engineering (PhD); telecommunications management (MTM). Part-time programs available. Postbaccalaureate distance learning degree programs offered (minimal on-campus study). *Degree requirements:* For master's, one foreign language, thesis (for some programs); for doctorate, one foreign language, thesis/dissertation. *Entrance requirements:* For master's, E-PAEP 500, interview; for doctorate, E-PAEP 500, research proposal. Additional exam requirements/recommendations for international students: Required—TOEFL (minimum score 550 paper-based). *Faculty research:* Surface treatments by plasmas, mechanical properties, robotics, graphical computing, mechatronics security protocols.

Instituto Tecnológico y de Estudios Superiores de Monterrey, Campus Irapuato, Graduate Programs, Irapuato, Mexico. Offers administration (MBA); administration of information technology (MAIT); administration of telecommunications (MAT); architecture (M Arch); computer science (MCS); education (M Ed); educational administration (MEA); educational innovation and technology (DEIT); educational technology (MET); electronic commerce (MBA); environmental administration and planning (MEAP); environmental systems (MES); finances (MBA); humanistic studies (MHS); international management for Latin American executives (MIMLAE); library and information science (MLIS); manufacturing quality management (MMQM); marketing research (MBA).

Madonna University, School of Business, Livonia, MI 48150-1173. Offers business administration (MBA); international business (MSBA); leadership studies (MSBA); leadership studies in criminal justice (MSBA); quality and operations management (MSBA). Part-time and evening/weekend programs available. Postbaccalaureate distance learning degree programs offered (minimal on-campus study). *Degree requirements:* For master's, thesis (for some programs), foreign language proficiency (international business). *Entrance requirements:* For master's, GMAT, GRE General Test, minimum GPA of 3.0. Electronic applications accepted. *Faculty research:* Management, women in management, future studies.

Marian University, School of Business and Public Safety, Fond du Lac, WI 54935-4699. Offers criminal justice leadership (MS); organizational leadership and quality (MS). Part-time and evening/weekend programs available. *Faculty:* 1 full-time (0 women), 6 part-time/adjunct (2 women). *Students:* 1 full-time (0 women), 53 part-time (31 women); includes 7 minority (3 Black or African American, non-Hispanic/Latino; 1 American Indian or Alaska Native, non-Hispanic/Latino; 2 Asian, non-Hispanic/Latino; 1 Hispanic/Latino). Average age 37. In 2013, 45 master's awarded. *Degree requirements:* For master's, comprehensive group project. *Entrance requirements:* For master's, 3 years of managerial experience, minimum GPA of 2.75, letters of professional reference. Additional exam requirements/recommendations for international students: Required—TOEFL (minimum score 525 paper-based; 70 iBT). *Application deadline:* Applications are processed on a rolling basis. Application fee: $25. Electronic applications accepted. *Expenses:* Contact institution. *Financial support:* In 2013–14, 1 student received support. Institutionally sponsored loans available. Financial award application deadline: 3/1; financial award applicants required to submit FAFSA. *Faculty research:* Organizational values, statistical decision-making, learning organization, quality planning, customer research. *Unit head:* Dr. Jeffrey G. Reed, Dean, Marian School of Business, 920-923-8759, Fax: 920-923-7167, E-mail: jreed@marianuniversity.edu. *Application contact:* Jordan Baitinger, Admission Counselor, 920-923-8609, Fax: 920-923-7167, E-mail: jlbaitinger16@marianuniversity.edu. Website: http://www.marianuniversity.edu/Academic-Programs/School-of-Business-and-Public-Safety/School-of-Business-and-Public-Safety/.

The National Graduate School of Quality Management, Graduate Programs, Falmouth, MA 02541. Offers homeland security (MS); quality systems management (MS, DBA).

Northwestern University, School of Professional Studies, Program in Regulatory Compliance, Evanston, IL 60208. Offers clinical research (MS); healthcare compliance

(MS); quality systems (MS). Offered in partnership with Northwestern Univesity's Clinical and Translational Sciences Institute.

Penn State Erie, The Behrend College, Graduate School, Erie, PA 16563-0001. Offers business administration (MBA); project management (MPM); quality and manufacturing management (MMM). *Accreditation:* AACSB. Part-time programs available. *Students:* 31 full-time (10 women), 83 part-time (23 women); includes 8 minority (2 Black or African American, non-Hispanic/Latino; 3 Asian, non-Hispanic/Latino; 3 Hispanic/Latino), 3 international. Average age 29. 71 applicants, 79% accepted, 45 enrolled. In 2013, 52 master's awarded. *Entrance requirements:* Additional exam requirements/ recommendations for international students: Required—TOEFL (minimum score 550 paper-based; 80 iBT). *Application deadline:* Applications are processed on a rolling basis. Application fee: $65. Electronic applications accepted. *Financial support:* Federal Work-Study available. Financial award application deadline: 2/15; financial award applicants required to submit FAFSA. *Unit head:* Dr. Donald L. Birx, Chancellor, 814-898-6160, Fax: 814-898-6461, E-mail: dlb69@psu.edu. *Application contact:* Ann M. Burbules, Assistant Director, Graduate Admissions, 866-374-3378, Fax: 814-898-6053, E-mail: psbehrendmba@psu.edu.
Website: http://psbehrend.psu.edu/.

Regis College, Program in Regulatory and Clinical Research Management, Weston, MA 02493. Offers MS. Part-time and evening/weekend programs available. *Degree requirements:* For master's, thesis optional, internship. *Entrance requirements:* For master's, GRE or MAT. Additional exam requirements/recommendations for international students: Required—TOEFL (minimum score 550 paper-based). *Expenses:* Contact institution. *Faculty research:* FDA regulatory affairs medical device.

Rutgers, The State University of New Jersey, New Brunswick, Graduate School-New Brunswick, Program in Statistics, Piscataway, NJ 08854-8097. Offers applied statistics (MS); biostatistics (MS); data mining (MS); quality and productivity management (MS); statistics (MS, PhD). Part-time programs available. Terminal master's awarded for partial completion of doctoral program. *Degree requirements:* For master's, comprehensive exam, essay, exam, non-thesis essay paper; for doctorate, one foreign language, thesis/dissertation, qualifying oral and written exams. *Entrance requirements:* For master's, GRE General Test; for doctorate, GRE General Test, GRE Subject Test (recommended). Additional exam requirements/recommendations for international students: Required—TOEFL (minimum score 550 paper-based). Electronic applications accepted. *Faculty research:* Probability, decision theory, linear models, multivariate statistics, statistical computing.

San Jose State University, Graduate Studies and Research, Charles W. Davidson College of Engineering, Department of Aviation and Technology, San Jose, CA 95192-0001. Offers quality assurance (MS). *Entrance requirements:* For master's, GRE. Electronic applications accepted.

Southern New Hampshire University, School of Business, Manchester, NH 03106-1045. Offers accounting (MBA, MS, Graduate Certificate); accounting finance (MS); accounting/auditing (MS); accounting/forensic accounting (MS); accounting/taxation (MS); athletic administration (MBA, Graduate Certificate); business administration (IMBA, MBA, Certificate, Graduate Certificate), including accounting (Certificate), business administration (MBA), business information systems (Graduate Certificate), human resource management (Certificate); corporate social responsibility (MBA); entrepreneurship (MBA); finance (MBA, MS, Graduate Certificate); finance/corporate finance (MS); finance/investments and securities (MS); forensic accounting (MBA); healthcare informatics (MBA); healthcare management (MBA); human resource management (Graduate Certificate); information technology (MS, Graduate Certificate); information technology management (MBA); international business (Graduate Certificate); international business and information technology (Graduate Certificate); international finance (Graduate Certificate); international sport management (Graduate Certificate); justice studies (MBA); leadership of nonprofit organizations (Graduate Certificate); marketing (MBA, MS, Graduate Certificate); operations and project management (MS); operations and supply chain management (MBA, Graduate Certificate); organizational leadership (MS); project management (MBA, Graduate Certificate); Six Sigma (MBA); Six Sigma quality (Graduate Certificate); social media marketing (MBA); sport management (MBA, MS, Graduate Certificate); sustainability and environmental compliance (MBA); workplace conflict management (MBA); MBA/ Certificate. *Accreditation:* ACBSP. Part-time and evening/weekend programs available. Postbaccalaureate distance learning degree programs offered (no on-campus study). Terminal master's awarded for partial completion of doctoral program. *Degree requirements:* For master's, one foreign language, comprehensive exam (for some programs), thesis or alternative. *Entrance requirements:* For master's, minimum GPA of 2.5. Additional exam requirements/recommendations for international students: Required—TOEFL (minimum score 500 paper-based). Electronic applications accepted.

Southern Polytechnic State University, School of Engineering Technology and Management, Department of Industrial Engineering Technology, Marietta, GA 30060-2896. Offers quality assurance (MS, Graduate Certificate). Part-time and evening/ weekend programs available. Postbaccalaureate distance learning degree programs offered (no on-campus study). *Degree requirements:* For master's and Graduate Certificate, comprehensive exam (for some programs). *Entrance requirements:* For master's, 3 reference forms, minimum GPA of 2.7, statement of purpose; for Graduate Certificate, minimum GPA of 2.7, statement of purpose. Additional exam requirements/ recommendations for international students: Required—TOEFL (minimum score 550 paper-based; 79 iBT), IELTS (minimum score 6.5). Electronic applications accepted. *Faculty research:* Assessing technical and non-technical workforce skills in a two-year college; analysis of the effectiveness of using exclusively workshop-style instruction in the college algebra classroom, focused on engineering and engineering technology; the human impact potential of engineering as outreach; comparison of an introductory level undergraduate statistics course taught with traditional, hybrid, and online delivery methods; reducing TB incidence.

Stevens Institute of Technology, Graduate School, Charles V. Schaefer Jr. School of Engineering, Department of Civil, Environmental, and Ocean Engineering, Program in Construction Management, Hoboken, NJ 07030. Offers construction accounting/ estimating (Certificate); construction engineering (Certificate); construction law/disputes (Certificate); construction management (MS); construction/quality management (Certificate). *Degree requirements:* For master's, thesis optional. *Entrance requirements:* For master's, GMAT, GRE General Test. Additional exam requirements/ recommendations for international students: Required—TOEFL. Electronic applications accepted.

Trident University International, College of Business Administration, Program in Business Administration, Cypress, CA 90630. Offers business administration (PhD); conflict and negotiation management (MBA); criminal justice administration (MBA); entrepreneurship (MBA); finance (MBA); general management (MBA); government accounting (MBA); human resource management (MBA); information security and digital assurance management (MBA); information technology management (MBA); international business (MBA); logistics management (MBA); marketing (MBA); project management (MBA); public management (MBA); quality management (MBA); strategic leadership (MBA). Part-time and evening/weekend programs available. Postbaccalaureate distance learning degree programs offered (no on-campus study). *Degree requirements:* For doctorate, comprehensive exam, thesis/dissertation, defense of dissertation. *Entrance requirements:* For master's, minimum GPA of 2.5 (students with GPA 3.0 or greater may transfer up to 30% of graduate level credits); for doctorate, minimum GPA of 3.4, curriculum vitae, course work in research methods or statistics. Additional exam requirements/recommendations for international students: Required—TOEFL. Electronic applications accepted.

Trident University International, College of Health Sciences, Program in Health Sciences, Cypress, CA 90630. Offers clinical research administration (MS, Certificate); emergency and disaster management (MS, Certificate); environmental health science (Certificate); health care administration (PhD); health care management (MS), including health informatics; health education (MS, Certificate); health informatics (Certificate); health sciences (PhD); international health (MS); international health: educator or researcher option (PhD); international health: practitioner option (PhD); law and expert witness studies (MS, Certificate); public health (MS); quality assurance (Certificate). Part-time and evening/weekend programs available. Postbaccalaureate distance learning degree programs offered (no on-campus study). *Degree requirements:* For doctorate, comprehensive exam, thesis/dissertation, defense of dissertation. *Entrance requirements:* For master's, minimum GPA of 2.5 (students with GPA 3.0 or greater may transfer up to 30% of graduate level credits); for doctorate, minimum GPA of 3.4, curriculum vitae, course work in research methods or statistics. Additional exam requirements/recommendations for international students: Required—TOEFL. Electronic applications accepted.

Universidad de las Americas, A.C., Program in Business Administration, Mexico City, Mexico. Offers finance (MBA); marketing research (MBA); production and quality (MBA).

Universidad del Turabo, Graduate Programs, School in Business Administration, Program in Quality Management, Gurabo, PR 00778-3030. Offers MBA.

The University of Alabama, Graduate School, College of Human Environmental Sciences, Program in Human Environmental Science, Tuscaloosa, AL 35487. Offers family financial planning and counseling (MS); interactive technology (MS); quality management (MS); restaurant and meeting management (MS); rural community health (MS); sport management (MS). *Faculty:* 1 full-time (0 women). *Students:* 55 full-time (34 women), 98 part-time (48 women); includes 41 minority (30 Black or African American, non-Hispanic/Latino; 2 American Indian or Alaska Native, non-Hispanic/Latino; 2 Asian, non-Hispanic/Latino; 2 Hispanic/Latino; 5 Two or more races, non-Hispanic/Latino), 1 international. Average age 34. 102 applicants, 69% accepted, 60 enrolled. In 2013, 88 master's awarded. *Degree requirements:* For master's, comprehensive exam. *Entrance requirements:* For master's, GRE (for some specializations), minimum GPA of 3.0. Additional exam requirements/recommendations for international students: Required—TOEFL. *Application deadline:* Applications are processed on a rolling basis. Application fee: $50 ($60 for international students). Electronic applications accepted. *Expenses:* Tuition, state resident: full-time $9450. Tuition, nonresident: full-time $23,950. *Faculty research:* Hospitality management, sports medicine education, technology and education. *Unit head:* Dr. Milla D. Boschung, Dean, 205-348-6250, Fax: 205-348-1786, E-mail: mboschun@ches.ua.edu. *Application contact:* Dr. Stuart Usdan, Associate Dean, 205-348-6150, Fax: 205-348-3789, E-mail: susdan@ches.ua.edu.

The University of Tennessee at Chattanooga, Graduate School, College of Engineering and Computer Science, Department of Engineering Management, Chattanooga, TN 37403. Offers engineering management (MS); fundamentals of engineering management (Graduate Certificate); leadership and ethics (Graduate Certificate); logistics and supply chain management (Graduate Certificate); nuclear engineering (Graduate Certificate); power system protection (Graduate Certificate); power systems management (Graduate Certificate); project and value management (Graduate Certificate); quality management (Graduate Certificate); sustainable electric energy (Graduate Certificate). Postbaccalaureate distance learning degree programs offered (no on-campus study). *Faculty:* 5 full-time (1 woman). *Students:* 14 full-time (5 women), 67 part-time (14 women); includes 24 minority (13 Black or African American, non-Hispanic/Latino; 6 Asian, non-Hispanic/Latino; 4 Hispanic/Latino; 1 Two or more races, non-Hispanic/Latino), 6 international. Average age 31. 31 applicants, 45% accepted, 10 enrolled. In 2013, 31 master's, 17 other advanced degrees awarded. *Degree requirements:* For master's, thesis. *Entrance requirements:* For master's, GRE General Test, letters of recommendation; minimum undergraduate GPA of 2.5 overall or 3.0 in senior year. Additional exam requirements/recommendations for international students: Required—TOEFL (minimum score 550 paper-based; 79 iBT), IELTS (minimum score 6). *Application deadline:* For fall admission, 6/13 priority date for domestic students, 6/1 for international students; for spring admission, 10/15 priority date for domestic students, 10/1 for international students. Applications are processed on a rolling basis. Application fee: $30 ($35 for international students). Electronic applications accepted. *Financial support:* In 2013–14, 5 research assistantships (averaging $6,528 per year), 3 teaching assistantships (averaging $6,781 per year) were awarded; career-related internships or fieldwork, scholarships/grants, and unspecified assistantships also available. Support available to part-time students. Financial award applicants required to submit FAFSA. *Faculty research:* Plant layout design, lean manufacturing, Six Sigma, value management, product development. *Unit head:* Dr. Neslihan Alp, Department Head, 423-425-4032, Fax: 423-425-5229, E-mail: neslihan-alp@utc.edu. *Application contact:* Dr. J. Randy Walker, Interim Dean of Graduate Studies, 423-425-4478, Fax: 423-425-5223, E-mail: randy-walker@utc.edu.
Website: http://www.utc.edu/Departments/engrcs/engm/index.php.

Upper Iowa University, Online Master's Programs, Fayette, IA 52142-1857. Offers accounting (MBA); corporate financial management (MBA); global business (MBA); health and human services (MPA); higher education administration (MHEA); homeland security (MPA); human resources management (MBA); justice administration (MPA); organizational development (MBA); public personnel management (MPA); quality management (MBA). MBA also available at Madison, WI campus. Part-time programs available. Postbaccalaureate distance learning degree programs offered (no on-campus study). *Degree requirements:* For master's, research project. *Entrance requirements:* For master's, GMAT, GRE, or minimum GPA of 2.7 during last 60 hours. Additional exam requirements/recommendations for international students: Required—TOEFL (minimum score 570 paper-based). Electronic applications accepted. *Faculty research:* Total quality management, CQI, teams, organization culture and climate, management.

Washington State University, Graduate School, College of Engineering and Architecture, Online Program in Engineering and Technology Management, Pullman, WA 99164-2785. Offers constraints management (Graduate Certificate); construction project management (Graduate Certificate); engineering and technology management (METM); manufacturing leadership (Graduate Certificate); program and facilities management (Graduate Certificate); project management (Graduate Certificate); Six Sigma quality management (Graduate Certificate); supply chain management (Graduate Certificate); systems engineering management (Graduate Certificate). Part-time and evening/weekend programs available. Postbaccalaureate distance learning degree programs offered (no on-campus study). *Degree requirements:* For master's, one foreign language, comprehensive exam (for some programs). *Entrance requirements:* Additional exam requirements/recommendations for international students: Required—TOEFL. Electronic applications accepted. *Faculty research:* Constraints management,

Quality Management

Six Sigma quality management, supply chain management, project management, construction management, systems engineering management, manufacturing leadership.

Washington State University Spokane, Graduate Programs, Program in Engineering and Technology Management, Pullman, WA 99164-2785. Offers constraints management (Graduate Certificate); construction project management (Graduate Certificate); engineering and technology management (METM); facilities management (Graduate Certificate); logistics and supply chain management (Graduate Certificate); manufacturing leadership (Graduate Certificate); project management (Graduate Certificate); Six Sigma quality management (Graduate Certificate); systems engineering management (Graduate Certificate). *Degree requirements:* For master's, comprehensive exam (for some programs), thesis (for some programs), comprehensive exam or project. *Entrance requirements:* For master's, GMAT (for applicants with less than 3.0 GPA), minimum GPA of 3.0, 3 letters of reference, resume, personal statement, math through college algebra (prefer math through calculus I), experience in the engineering/technology area. Additional exam requirements/recommendations for international students: Required—TOEFL. *Expenses:* Contact institution. *Faculty research:* Operations research for decision analysis quality control and liability, analytical techniques to formulating decisions.

Section 19
Quantitative Analysis

This section contains a directory of institutions offering graduate work in quantitative analysis. Additional information about programs listed in the directory may be obtained by writing directly to the dean of a graduate school or chair of a department at the address given in the directory.

For programs offering related work, see also in this book *Business Administration and Management*.

CONTENTS

Program Directory

Quantitative Analysis   600

Quantitative Analysis

American University, College of Arts and Sciences, Washington, DC 20016-8012. Offers addiction and addictive behavior (Certificate); anthropology (PhD); applied microeconomics (Certificate); applied statistics (Certificate); art history (MA); arts management (MA, Certificate); Asian studies (Certificate); audio production (Certificate); audio technology (MA); behavior, cognition, and neuroscience (PhD); bilingual education (MA, Certificate); biology (MA, MS); chemistry (MS); clinical psychology (PhD); computer science (MS, Certificate); creative writing (MFA); curriculum and instruction (M Ed, Certificate); economics (MA, PhD); environmental assessment (Certificate); environmental science (MS); ethics, peace, and global affairs (MA); gender analysis in economics (Certificate); health promotion management (MS); history (MA, PhD); international arts management (Certificate); international economic relations (Certificate); international economics (MA); international training and education (MA); literature (MA); mathematics (MA); North American studies (Certificate); nutrition education (MS, Certificate); philosophy (MA); professional science: biotechnology (MS); professional science: environmental assessment (MS); professional science: quantitative analysis (MS); psychobiology of healing (Certificate); psychology (MA); psychology: general (PhD); public anthropology (MA, Certificate); public sociology (Certificate); social research (Certificate); sociology (MA); Spanish: Latin American studies (MA); special education: learning disabilities (MA); statistics (MS); studio art (MFA); teaching (MAT); teaching English as a foreign language (MA); teaching: early childhood (Certificate); teaching: elementary (Certificate); teaching: ESOL (Certificate); teaching: secondary (Certificate); technology in arts management (Certificate); TESOL (MA); translation: French (Certificate); translation: Russian (Certificate); translation: Spanish (Certificate); women's, gender, and sexuality studies (Certificate). Part-time and evening/weekend programs available. Postbaccalaureate distance learning degree programs offered (no on-campus study). *Faculty:* 358 full-time (187 women), 254 part-time/adjunct (127 women). *Students:* 627 full-time (411 women), 416 part-time (300 women); includes 206 minority (91 Black or African American, non-Hispanic/Latino; 5 American Indian or Alaska Native, non-Hispanic/Latino; 32 Asian, non-Hispanic/Latino; 64 Hispanic/Latino; 1 Native Hawaiian or other Pacific Islander, non-Hispanic/Latino; 13 Two or more races, non-Hispanic/Latino), 124 international. Average age 29. 1,672 applicants, 52% accepted, 361 enrolled. In 2013, 382 master's, 38 doctorates, 33 other advanced degrees awarded. Terminal master's awarded for partial completion of doctoral program. *Degree requirements:* For master's, comprehensive exam (for some programs), thesis (for some programs); for doctorate, comprehensive exam (for some programs), thesis/dissertation. *Entrance requirements:* For master's, GRE, minimum GPA of 3.0 in last 60 credit hours, letter of recommendation, statement of purpose, resume, unofficial transcript; for doctorate, GRE, minimum GPA of 3.0 for all graduate work, letter of recommendation, statement of purpose, resume, unofficial transcript. Additional exam requirements/recommendations for international students: Required—TOEFL (minimum score 600 paper-based; 100 iBT), IELTS (minimum score 7). *Application deadline:* For fall admission, 2/1 for domestic students; for spring admission, 10/1 for domestic students. Applications are processed on a rolling basis. Application fee: $55. Electronic applications accepted. *Expenses: Tuition:* Full-time $25,920; part-time $1482 per credit hour. *Required fees:* $430. Tuition and fees vary according to course load and program. *Financial support:* Fellowships, research assistantships with full and partial tuition reimbursements, teaching assistantships with full and partial tuition reimbursements, career-related internships or fieldwork, Federal Work-Study, institutionally sponsored loans, scholarships/grants, traineeships, tuition waivers (full and partial), and unspecified assistantships available. Support available to part-time students. Financial award applicants required to submit FAFSA. *Unit head:* Dr. Peter Starr, Dean, 202-885-2446, Fax: 202-885-2429, E-mail: pstarr@american.edu. *Application contact:* Kathleen Clowery, Associate Director, Graduate Enrollment Management, 202-885-3621, Fax: 202-885-1505, E-mail: clowery@american.edu.
Website: http://www.american.edu/cas/.

Baruch College of the City University of New York, Zicklin School of Business, Department of Operations Research and Quantitative Methods, New York, NY 10010-5585. Offers quantitative methods and modeling (MBA, MS). Part-time programs available.

Baruch College of the City University of New York, Zicklin School of Business, Department of Statistics and Computer Information Systems, Program in Decision Sciences, New York, NY 10010-5585. Offers MBA. Part-time and evening/weekend programs available. *Entrance requirements:* For master's, GMAT, 2 letters of recommendation, resume, 2 years of work experience. Additional exam requirements/recommendations for international students: Required—TOEFL (minimum score 590 paper-based), TWE (minimum score 5).

Columbia University, Graduate School of Arts and Sciences, New York, NY 10027. Offers African-American studies (MA); American studies (MA); anthropology (MA, PhD); art history and archaeology (MA, PhD); astronomy (PhD); biological sciences (PhD); biotechnology (MA); chemical physics (PhD); chemistry (PhD); classical studies (MA, PhD); classics (MA, PhD); climate and society (MA); earth and environmental sciences (PhD); East Asia: regional studies (MA); East Asian languages and cultures (MA, PhD); ecology, evolution and environmental biology (MA), including conservation biology; ecology, evolution, and environmental biology (PhD), including ecology and evolutionary biology, evolutionary primatology; economics (PhD); English and comparative literature (MA, PhD); French and Romance philology (MA, PhD); Germanic languages (MA, PhD); global French studies (MA); Hispanic cultural studies (MA); history (PhD); history and literature (MA); human rights studies (MA); Islamic studies (MA); Italian (MA, PhD); Japanese pedagogy (MA); Jewish studies (MA); Latin America and the Caribbean: regional studies (MA); Latin American and Iberian cultures (PhD); mathematics (MA, PhD), including finance (MA); medieval and Renaissance studies (MA); Middle Eastern, South Asian, and African studies (MA, PhD); modern art: critical and curatorial studies (MA); modern European studies (MA); museum anthropology (MA); music (DMA, PhD); oral history (MA); philosophical foundations of physics (MA); philosophy (MA, PhD); physics (PhD); political science (MA, PhD); psychology (PhD); quantitative methods in the social sciences (MA); religion (MA, PhD); Russia, Eurasia and East Europe: regional studies (MA); Russian translation (MA); Slavic cultures (MA); Slavic languages (MA, PhD); sociology (MA, PhD); South Asian studies (MA); statistics (MA, PhD); theatre (PhD); JD/PhD; MA/MS; MD/PhD; MPA/MA. Dual-degree programs require admission to both Graduate School of Arts and Sciences and another Columbia school. Part-time and evening/weekend programs available. *Faculty:* 808 full-time (310 women). *Students:* 2,755 full-time, 354 part-time; includes 493 minority (80 Black or African American, non-Hispanic/Latino; 6 American Indian or Alaska Native, non-Hispanic/Latino; 215 Asian, non-Hispanic/Latino; 135 Hispanic/Latino; 3 Native Hawaiian or other Pacific Islander, non-Hispanic/Latino; 54 Two or more races, non-Hispanic/Latino), 1,433 international. 12,949 applicants, 19% accepted, 998 enrolled. In 2013, 969 master's, 461 doctorates awarded. Terminal master's awarded for partial completion of doctoral program. *Degree requirements:* For master's, thesis (for some programs); for doctorate, comprehensive exam, thesis/dissertation. *Entrance requirements:* For master's and doctorate, GRE General Test, GRE Subject Test (for some programs). Application fee: $105. Electronic applications accepted. *Financial support:* Application deadline: 12/15. *Faculty research:* Humanities, natural sciences, social sciences. *Unit head:* Carlos J. Alonso, Dean of the Graduate School of Arts and Sciences, 212-854-5177. *Application contact:* GSAS Office of Admissions, 212-854-8903, E-mail: gsas-admissions@columbia.edu.
Website: http://gsas.columbia.edu/.

Cornell University, Graduate School, Graduate Fields of Agriculture and Life Sciences, Field of Natural Resources, Ithaca, NY 14853-0001. Offers community-based natural resources management (MS, PhD); conservation biology (MS, PhD); ecosystem biology and biogeochemistry (MPS, MS, PhD); environmental management (MPS); fishery and aquatic science (MPS, MS, PhD); forest science (MPS, MS, PhD); human dimensions of natural resources management (MPS, MS, PhD); policy and institutional analysis (MS, PhD); program development and evaluation (MPS, MS, PhD); quantitative ecology (MS, PhD); wildlife science (MPS, MS, PhD). *Faculty:* 39 full-time (8 women). *Students:* 65 full-time (30 women); includes 2 minority (1 Asian, non-Hispanic/Latino; 1 Hispanic/Latino), 18 international. Average age 31. 93 applicants, 26% accepted, 20 enrolled. In 2013, 8 master's, 7 doctorates awarded. *Degree requirements:* For master's, thesis (MS), project paper (MPS); for doctorate, comprehensive exam, thesis/dissertation. *Entrance requirements:* For master's and doctorate, GRE General Test, 2 letters of recommendation. Additional exam requirements/recommendations for international students: Required—TOEFL (minimum score 550 paper-based; 77 iBT). *Application deadline:* For spring admission, 10/30 for domestic students. Applications are processed on a rolling basis. Application fee: $95. Electronic applications accepted. *Financial support:* In 2013–14, 48 students received support, including 10 fellowships with full tuition reimbursements available, 18 research assistantships with full tuition reimbursements available, 20 teaching assistantships with full tuition reimbursements available; institutionally sponsored loans, scholarships/grants, health care benefits, tuition waivers (full and partial), and unspecified assistantships also available. Financial award applicants required to submit FAFSA. *Faculty research:* Ecosystem-level dynamics, systems modeling, conservation biology/management, resource management's human dimensions, biogeochemistry. *Unit head:* Director of Graduate Studies, 607-255-2807, Fax: 607-255-0349. *Application contact:* Graduate Field Assistant, 607-255-2807, Fax: 607-255-0349, E-mail: nrgrad@cornell.edu.
Website: http://www.gradschool.cornell.edu/fields.php?id-54&a-2.

Drexel University, LeBow College of Business, Program in Business Administration, Philadelphia, PA 19104-2875. Offers business administration (MBA, PhD, APC), including accounting (MBA, PhD), decision sciences (PhD), economics (MBA, PhD), finance (MBA, PhD), legal studies (MBA), management (MBA), marketing (MBA, PhD), organizational sciences (PhD), quantitative methods (MBA), strategic management (PhD). *Accreditation:* AACSB. Part-time and evening/weekend programs available. Postbaccalaureate distance learning degree programs offered (minimal on-campus study). Terminal master's awarded for partial completion of doctoral program. *Entrance requirements:* For master's, GMAT, minimum GPA of 2.75; for doctorate, GMAT. Additional exam requirements/recommendations for international students: Required—TOEFL. Electronic applications accepted. *Faculty research:* Decision support systems, individual and group behavior, operations research, techniques and strategy.

Duke University, The Fuqua School of Business, Daytime MBA Program, Durham, NC 27708-0586. Offers academic excellence in finance (Certificate); business administration (MBA); decision sciences (MBA); energy and environment (MBA); energy finance (MBA); entrepreneurship and innovation (MBA); finance (MBA); financial analysis (MBA); health sector management (Certificate); leadership and ethics (MBA); management (MBA); marketing (MBA); operations management (MBA); social entrepreneurship (MBA); strategy (MBA). *Faculty:* 91 full-time (15 women), 53 part-time/adjunct (9 women). *Students:* 862 full-time (283 women); includes 179 minority (34 Black or African American, non-Hispanic/Latino; 1 American Indian or Alaska Native, non-Hispanic/Latino; 92 Asian, non-Hispanic/Latino; 42 Hispanic/Latino; 2 Native Hawaiian or other Pacific Islander, non-Hispanic/Latino; 8 Two or more races, non-Hispanic/Latino), 342 international. Average age 29. In 2013, 437 master's awarded. *Entrance requirements:* For master's, GMAT or GRE, transcripts, essays, resume, recommendation letters, interview. Additional exam requirements/recommendations for international students: Required—TOEFL, IELTS, PTE. *Application deadline:* For fall admission, 9/18 for domestic and international students; for winter admission, 10/21 for domestic and international students; for spring admission, 1/6 for domestic and international students; for summer admission, 3/20 for domestic and international students. Application fee: $225. Electronic applications accepted. *Financial support:* In 2013–14, 331 students received support. Institutionally sponsored loans and scholarships/grants available. Financial award applicants required to submit FAFSA. *Unit head:* Russ Morgan, Associate Dean for the Daytime MBA Program, 919-660-2931, Fax: 919-684-8742, E-mail: ruskin.morgan@duke.edu. *Application contact:* Liz Riley Hargrove, Associate Dean of Admissions, 919-660-7705, Fax: 919-681-8026, E-mail: liz.riley@duke.edu.
Website: http://www.fuqua.duke.edu/daytime-mba/.

Duke University, The Fuqua School of Business, PhD Program, Durham, NC 27708-0586. Offers accounting (PhD); decision sciences (PhD); finance (PhD); management and organizations (PhD); marketing (PhD); operations management (PhD); strategy (PhD). *Faculty:* 91 full-time (15 women). *Students:* 78 full-time (27 women); includes 4 minority (1 Black or African American, non-Hispanic/Latino; 3 Asian, non-Hispanic/Latino), 49 international. 589 applicants, 5% accepted, 16 enrolled. In 2013, 26 doctorates awarded. *Degree requirements:* For doctorate, thesis/dissertation, major field requirement (exam or major paper, depending upon the area). *Entrance requirements:* For doctorate, GMAT or GRE, transcripts, essays, recommendation letters, statement of purpose. Additional exam requirements/recommendations for international students: Required—TOEFL (minimum score 577 paper-based; 90 iBT), IELTS (minimum score 7). *Application deadline:* For fall admission, 12/8 priority date for domestic and international students. Application fee: $80. Electronic applications accepted. *Financial support:* In 2013–14, 70 fellowships with full tuition reimbursements (averaging $25,300 per year), 56 research assistantships with full tuition reimbursements (averaging $7,000 per year) were awarded; institutionally sponsored loans, scholarships/grants, and tuition waivers (full) also available. Financial award applicants required to submit FAFSA. *Unit head:* William Boulding, Dean, 919-660-7822, Fax: 919-684-8742, E-mail: bb1@duke.edu. *Application contact:* Dr. James R. Bettman, Director of Graduate Studies, 919-660-7851, Fax: 919-681-6245, E-mail: jrb12@mail.duke.edu.

Hofstra University, Frank G. Zarb School of Business, Programs in Finance, Hempstead, NY 11549. Offers business administration (MBA), including finance, real

estate management; corporate finance (Advanced Certificate); finance (MS); investment management (Advanced Certificate); quantitative finance (MS).

Instituto Tecnologico de Santo Domingo, Graduate School, Area of Engineering, Santo Domingo, Dominican Republic. Offers construction administration (MS, Certificate); data telecommunications (M Eng, MS, Certificate); industrial engineering (M Eng, Certificate); industrial management (M Mgmt); information technology (Certificate); maintenance engineering (M Eng); occupational hazard prevention (M Mgmt); production management (Certificate); quantitative methods (Certificate); sanitary and environmental engineering (M Eng); structural engineering (M Eng); systems engineering and electronic data processing (Certificate); transportation (Certificate).

La Salle University, School of Business, Philadelphia, PA 19141-1199. Offers accounting (MBA, Post-MBA Certificate); business systems and analytics (MBA, Post-MBA Certificate); finance (MBA, Post-MBA Certificate); general business administration (MBA); human resource management (MBA, Post-MBA Certificate); international business (Post-MBA Certificate); management (MBA, Post-MBA Certificate); marketing (MBA, Post-MBA Certificate); MSN/MBA. *Accreditation:* AACSB. Part-time and evening/weekend programs available. Postbaccalaureate distance learning degree programs offered (minimal on-campus study). *Faculty:* 27 full-time (13 women), 15 part-time/adjunct (4 women). *Students:* 81 full-time (30 women), 428 part-time (211 women); includes 109 minority (47 Black or African American, non-Hispanic/Latino; 39 Asian, non-Hispanic/Latino; 18 Hispanic/Latino; 5 Two or more races, non-Hispanic/Latino), 6 international. Average age 30. 215 applicants, 90% accepted, 120 enrolled. In 2013, 182 master's, 1 other advanced degree awarded. *Entrance requirements:* For master's, GMAT or GRE, two letters of reference; resume; for Post-MBA Certificate, MBA with minimum GPA of 3.0. Additional exam requirements/recommendations for international students: Required—TOEFL. *Application deadline:* For fall admission, 8/15 priority date for domestic students, 7/15 for international students; for spring admission, 12/15 priority date for domestic students, 11/15 for international students; for summer admission, 4/15 priority date for domestic students, 3/15 for international students. Applications are processed on a rolling basis. Application fee: $35. Electronic applications accepted. Application fee is waived when completed online. *Expenses:* Contact institution. *Financial support:* In 2013–14, 88 students received support. Career-related internships or fieldwork, Federal Work-Study, scholarships/grants, and unspecified assistantships available. Support available to part-time students. Financial award application deadline: 8/31; financial award applicants required to submit FAFSA. *Unit head:* Dr. Gary Giamartino, Dean, 215-951-1040, Fax: 215-951-1886, E-mail: giamartino@lasalle.edu. *Application contact:* Paul J. Reilly, Assistant Vice President, Enrollment Services, 215-951-1946, Fax: 215-951-1462, E-mail: reilly@lasalle.edu.
Website: http://www.lasalle.edu/grad/index.php?section-mba&page-index.

Lehigh University, College of Business and Economics, Department of Finance, Bethlehem, PA 18015. Offers analytical finance (MS). *Faculty:* 7 full-time (0 women), 1 part-time/adjunct (0 women). *Students:* 60 full-time (37 women), 7 part-time (4 women); includes 1 minority (Asian, non-Hispanic/Latino), 66 international. Average age 23. 510 applicants, 23% accepted, 35 enrolled. In 2013, 24 master's awarded. *Degree requirements:* For master's, capstone project. *Entrance requirements:* For master's, GMAT or GRE, bachelor's degree from a mathematically rigorous program, minimum GPA of 3.0. Additional exam requirements/recommendations for international students: Required—TOEFL (minimum score 600 paper-based; 94 iBT). *Application deadline:* For fall admission, 7/15 for domestic students, 2/15 for international students. Applications are processed on a rolling basis. Application fee: $100. Electronic applications accepted. *Financial support:* Application deadline: 1/15. *Unit head:* Richard Kish, Department Chair, 610-758-4205, E-mail: rjk7@lehigh.edu. *Application contact:* Jen Giordano, Director of Recruitment and Admissions, 610-758-3418, Fax: 610-758-5283, E-mail: jlg210@lehigh.edu.
Website: http://www4.lehigh.edu/business/academics/depts/finance.

New York University, Robert F. Wagner Graduate School of Public Service, Program in Public Administration, New York, NY 10012. Offers public administration (PhD); public and nonprofit management and policy (MPA, Advanced Certificate), including developmental administration (Advanced Certificate), financial management and public finance, human resources management (Advanced Certificate), international administration (Advanced Certificate), management (MPA), management for public and nonprofit organizations (Advanced Certificate), public policy analysis, quantitative analysis and computer applications (Advanced Certificate), urban public policy (Advanced Certificate); JD/MPA; MBA/MPA; MPA/MA. *Accreditation:* NASPAA (one or more programs are accredited). Part-time programs available. *Faculty:* 29 full-time (13 women), 41 part-time/adjunct (21 women). *Students:* 373 full-time (275 women), 245 part-time (176 women); includes 207 minority (56 Black or African American, non-Hispanic/Latino; 2 American Indian or Alaska Native, non-Hispanic/Latino; 70 Asian, non-Hispanic/Latino; 64 Hispanic/Latino; 2 Native Hawaiian or other Pacific Islander, non-Hispanic/Latino; 13 Two or more races, non-Hispanic/Latino), 122 international. Average age 28. 1,163 applicants, 61% accepted, 250 enrolled. In 2013, 233 master's, 6 doctorates, 1 other advanced degree awarded. *Degree requirements:* For master's, thesis or alternative, capstone end event; for doctorate, one foreign language, comprehensive exam, thesis/dissertation, preliminary qualifying examination. *Entrance requirements:* Additional exam requirements/recommendations for international students: Required—TOEFL (minimum score 100 iBT), IELTS (minimum score 7.5), TWE. *Application deadline:* For fall admission, 1/6 for domestic and international students; for spring admission, 10/1 for domestic and international students. Application fee: $85. Electronic applications accepted. *Expenses:* Contact institution. *Financial support:* In 2013–14, 152 students received support, including 141 fellowships with full and partial tuition reimbursements available (averaging $10,100 per year), 5 research assistantships with full tuition reimbursements available (averaging $39,643 per year); career-related internships or fieldwork, Federal Work-Study, scholarships/grants, health care benefits, and unspecified assistantships also available. Support available to part-time students. Financial award application deadline: 1/5; financial award applicants required to submit FAFSA. *Unit head:* Prof. Katherine O'Regan, Associate Professor of Public Policy, 212-998-7498, E-mail: katherine.oregan@nyu.edu. *Application contact:* Janet Barzilay, Admissions Officer, 212-998-7414, Fax: 212-995-4611, E-mail: wagner.admissions@nyu.edu.
Website: http://wagner.nyu.edu/.

Northwestern University, The Graduate School, Kellogg School of Management, Management Programs, Evanston, IL 60208. Offers accounting information and management (MBA, PhD); analytical finance (MBA); business administration (MBA); decision sciences (MBA); entrepreneurship and innovation (MBA); finance (MBA, PhD); health enterprise management (MBA); human resources management (MBA); international business (MBA); management and organizations (MBA, PhD); management and organizations and sociology (PhD); management and strategy (MBA); management studies (MS); managerial analytics (MBA); managerial economics (MBA); managerial economics and strategy (PhD); marketing (MBA, PhD); marketing management (MBA); media management (MBA); operations management (MBA, PhD); real estate (MBA); social enterprise at Kellogg (MBA); JD/MBA. Part-time and evening/weekend programs available. Terminal master's awarded for partial completion of

doctoral program. *Degree requirements:* For doctorate, thesis/dissertation, 2 years of coursework, qualifying (field) exam and candidacy, summer research papers and presentations to faculty, proposal defense, final exam/defense. *Entrance requirements:* For master's, GMAT, GRE, interview, 2 letters of recommendation, college transcripts, resume, essays, Kellogg honor code; for doctorate, GMAT, GRE, statement of purpose, transcripts, 2 letters of recommendation, resume, interview. Additional exam requirements/recommendations for international students: Required—TOEFL, IELTS. Electronic applications accepted. *Expenses:* Contact institution. *Faculty research:* Business cycles and international finance, health policy, networks, non-market strategy, consumer psychology.

Oklahoma State University, Spears School of Business, Department of Finance, Stillwater, OK 74078. Offers finance (PhD); quantitative financial economics (MS). Part-time programs available. *Faculty:* 13 full-time (1 woman), 2 part-time/adjunct (0 women). *Students:* 15 full-time (5 women), 11 part-time (4 women); includes 3 minority (2 Black or African American, non-Hispanic/Latino; 1 Hispanic/Latino), 13 international. Average age 29. 47 applicants, 32% accepted, 8 enrolled. In 2013, 5 master's awarded. *Degree requirements:* For master's, thesis or alternative; for doctorate, comprehensive exam, thesis/dissertation. *Entrance requirements:* For master's and doctorate, GRE or GMAT. Additional exam requirements/recommendations for international students: Required—TOEFL (minimum score 550 paper-based; 79 iBT). *Application deadline:* For fall admission, 3/1 priority date for international students; for spring admission, 8/1 priority date for international students. Applications are processed on a rolling basis. Application fee: $40 ($75 for international students). Electronic applications accepted. *Expenses:* Tuition, state resident: full-time $4272; part-time $178 per credit hour. Tuition, nonresident: full-time $17,472; part-time $709 per credit hour. *Required fees:* $2413.20; $100.55 per credit hour. One-time fee: $50 full-time. Part-time tuition and fees vary according to course load and campus/location. *Financial support:* In 2013–14, 18 research assistantships (averaging $11,565 per year), 2 teaching assistantships (averaging $22,304 per year) were awarded; career-related internships or fieldwork, Federal Work-Study, scholarships/grants, health care benefits, tuition waivers (partial), and unspecified assistantships also available. Support available to part-time students. Financial award application deadline: 3/1; financial award applicants required to submit FAFSA. *Faculty research:* Corporate risk management, derivatives banking, investments and securities issuance, corporate governance, banking. *Unit head:* Dr. John Polonchek, Department Head, 405-744-5199, Fax: 405-744-5180, E-mail: john.polonchek@okstate.edu.
Website: http://spears.okstate.edu/finance/.

Purdue University, Graduate School, College of Agriculture, Department of Forestry and Natural Resources, West Lafayette, IN 47907. Offers fisheries and aquatic sciences (MS, MSF, PhD); forest biology (MS, MSF, PhD); natural resource social science (MS, PhD); natural resources social science (MSF); quantitative ecology (MS, MSF, PhD); wildlife science (MS, MSF, PhD); wood products and wood products manufacturing (MS, MSF, PhD). *Faculty:* 25 full-time (5 women), 14 part-time/adjunct (2 women). *Students:* 59 full-time (23 women), 8 part-time (2 women); includes 4 minority (2 American Indian or Alaska Native, non-Hispanic/Latino; 1 Hispanic/Latino; 1 Two or more races, non-Hispanic/Latino), 19 international. Average age 28. 66 applicants, 15% accepted, 10 enrolled. In 2013, 16 master's, 16 doctorates awarded. *Degree requirements:* For master's, thesis; for doctorate, thesis/dissertation. *Entrance requirements:* For master's and doctorate, GRE General Test (minimum score: verbal 50th percentile; quantitative 50th percentile; analytical writing 4.0), minimum undergraduate GPA of 3.2 or equivalent. Additional exam requirements/recommendations for international students: Required—TOEFL (minimum score 550 paper-based; 77 iBT). *Application deadline:* For fall admission, 1/5 for domestic students, 1/15 for international students; for spring admission, 9/15 for domestic and international students. Applications are processed on a rolling basis. Application fee: $60 ($75 for international students). Electronic applications accepted. *Financial support:* In 2013–14, 10 research assistantships (averaging $15,259 per year) were awarded; fellowships, teaching assistantships, career-related internships or fieldwork, and scholarships/grants also available. Support available to part-time students. Financial award application deadline: 1/5; financial award applicants required to submit FAFSA. *Faculty research:* Wildlife management, forest management, forest ecology, forest soils, limnology. *Unit head:* Dr. Robert K. Swihart, Interim Head, 765-494-3590, Fax: 765-494-9461, E-mail: rswihart@purdue.edu. *Application contact:* Kelly J. Wrede, Graduate Secretary, 765-494-3572, Fax: 765-494-9461, E-mail: kgarrett@purdue.edu.
Website: https://ag.purdue.edu/fnr.

Rutgers, The State University of New Jersey, Newark, School of Public Health, Newark, NJ 07107-1709. Offers clinical epidemiology (Certificate); dental public health (MPH); general public health (Certificate); public policy and oral health services administration (Certificate); quantitative methods (MPH); urban health (MPH); DMD/MPH; MD/MPH; MS/MPH. *Accreditation:* CEPH. Part-time and evening/weekend programs available. *Degree requirements:* For master's, thesis, internship. *Entrance requirements:* For master's, GRE General Test. Additional exam requirements/recommendations for international students: Required—TOEFL. Electronic applications accepted.

St. John's University, The Peter J. Tobin College of Business, Department of Computer Information Systems and Decision Sciences, Queens, NY 11439. Offers business analytics (MBA); computer information systems for managers (Adv C). Part-time and evening/weekend programs available. *Students:* 8 full-time (1 woman), 8 part-time (3 women); includes 6 minority (2 Black or African American, non-Hispanic/Latino; 2 Asian, non-Hispanic/Latino; 2 Hispanic/Latino), 5 international. Average age 27. 7 applicants, 71% accepted, 3 enrolled. In 2013, 3 master's awarded. *Degree requirements:* For master's, comprehensive exam (for some programs), thesis optional. *Entrance requirements:* For master's, GMAT, 2 letters of recommendation, resume, transcripts, essay. Additional exam requirements/recommendations for international students: Required—TOEFL (minimum score 600 paper-based; 100 iBT), IELTS (minimum score 7). *Application deadline:* For fall admission, 5/1 priority date for domestic and international students; for spring admission, 11/1 priority date for domestic and international students. Applications are processed on a rolling basis. Application fee: $50. Electronic applications accepted. *Expenses:* Contact institution. *Financial support:* Research assistantships, scholarships/grants, and unspecified assistantships available. Support available to part-time students. Financial award application deadline: 3/1; financial award applicants required to submit FAFSA. *Unit head:* Dr. Victor Lu, Chair, 718-990-6392, E-mail: luf@stjohns.edu. *Application contact:* Carol J. Swanberg, Assistant Dean/Director of Graduate Admissions, 718-990-2599, E-mail: tobingradnyc@stjohns.edu.

San Francisco State University, Division of Graduate Studies, College of Business, Program in Business Administration, San Francisco, CA 94132-1722. Offers decision sciences/operations research (MBA); finance (MBA); information systems (MBA); leadership (MBA); management (MBA); marketing (MBA); sustainable business (MBA). *Accreditation:* AACSB. Part-time and evening/weekend programs available. *Faculty:* 100. *Students:* 850 (408 women). 839 applicants, 56% accepted, 241 enrolled. *Degree requirements:* For master's, thesis, essay test. *Entrance requirements:* For master's, GMAT, minimum GPA of 2.7 in last 60 units. Additional exam requirements/

recommendations for international students: Required—TOEFL (minimum score 550 paper-based). *Application deadline:* For fall admission, 5/1 priority date for domestic students, 4/1 for international students; for spring admission, 11/1 for domestic students, 10/15 for international students. Applications are processed on a rolling basis. Application fee: $55. *Financial support:* Application deadline: 3/1. *Unit head:* Linda Oubre, Dean, 415-817-4300, E-mail: loubre@sfsu.edu. *Application contact:* Armaan Moattari, Assistant Director, Graduate Programs, 415-817-4314, Fax: 817-4340, E-mail: amoatt@sfsu.edu.
Website: http://cob.sfsu.edu/.

Syracuse University, Martin J. Whitman School of Management, PhD Program in Business Administration, Syracuse, NY 13244. Offers accounting (PhD); finance (PhD); management information systems (PhD); managerial statistics (PhD); marketing (PhD); operations management (PhD); organizational behavior (PhD); strategy and human resources (PhD); supply chain management (PhD). *Faculty:* 79 full-time (20 women), 25 part-time/adjunct (6 women). *Students:* 26 full-time (8 women), 1 part-time (0 women); includes 2 minority (1 Black or African American, non-Hispanic/Latino; 1 Asian, non-Hispanic/Latino), 20 international. Average age 30. 130 applicants, 9% accepted, 7 enrolled. In 2013, 15 doctorates awarded. *Degree requirements:* For doctorate, comprehensive exam, thesis/dissertation, summer research paper. *Entrance requirements:* For doctorate, GMAT or GRE General Test, 3 recommendations. Additional exam requirements/recommendations for international students: Required—TOEFL (minimum score 600 paper-based; 100 iBT). *Application deadline:* For fall admission, 1/15 priority date for domestic and international students. Applications are processed on a rolling basis. Application fee: $75. Electronic applications accepted. *Financial support:* In 2013–14, 1 fellowship with full tuition reimbursement (averaging $19,570 per year), 30 teaching assistantships with full tuition reimbursements (averaging $17,000 per year) were awarded; research assistantships with full tuition reimbursements also available. Financial award application deadline: 1/15. *Faculty research:* Marketing models, market microstructure, supply chain, auditing, corporate governance. *Unit head:* Dr. Michel Benarock, Director of the PhD Program, 315-443-3429, E-mail: mbeanaroc@syr.edu. *Application contact:* Carol Hilleges, Administrative Specialist, 315-443-9601, Fax: 315-443-3671, E-mail: clhilleg@syr.edu.
Website: http://whitman.syr.edu/phd/.

Texas Tech University, Graduate School, Rawls College of Business Administration, Area of Information Systems and Quantitative Sciences, Lubbock, TX 79409. Offers business statistics (MS, PhD); healthcare management (MS); management information systems (MS, PhD); production and operations management (PhD). Part-time programs available. *Faculty:* 13 full-time (0 women). *Students:* 107 full-time (24 women); includes 3 minority (1 Black or African American, non-Hispanic/Latino; 1 American Indian or Alaska Native, non-Hispanic/Latino; 1 Asian, non-Hispanic/Latino), 79 international. Average age 27. 125 applicants, 55% accepted, 40 enrolled. In 2013, 17 master's, 5 doctorates awarded. Terminal master's awarded for partial completion of doctoral program. *Degree requirements:* For master's, comprehensive exam or capstone course; for doctorate, thesis/dissertation, qualifying exams. *Entrance requirements:* For master's and doctorate, GMAT, holistic profile of academic credentials. Additional exam requirements/recommendations for international students: Required—TOEFL (minimum score 550 paper-based; 79 iBT). *Application deadline:* For fall admission, 7/1 priority date for domestic students, 1/15 for international students; for spring admission, 11/1 priority date for domestic students, 6/15 priority date for international students. Applications are processed on a rolling basis. Application fee: $60. Electronic applications accepted. *Expenses:* Tuition, state resident: full-time $6062; part-time $252.57 per credit hour. Tuition, nonresident: full-time $14,558; part-time $606.57 per credit hour. *Required fees:* $2655; $35 per credit hour. $907.50 per semester. Tuition and fees vary according to course load. *Financial support:* In 2013–14, 5 research assistantships (averaging $16,160 per year), 5 teaching assistantships (averaging $18,000 per year) were awarded; Federal Work-Study, scholarships/grants, and unspecified assistantships also available. Financial award applicants required to submit FAFSA. *Faculty research:* Database management systems, systems management and engineering, expert systems and adaptive knowledge-based sciences, statistical analysis and design. *Unit head:* Dr. Glenn Browne, Area Coordinator, 806-834-0969, Fax: 806-742-3193, E-mail: glenn.browne@ttu.edu. *Application contact:* Terri Boston, Applications Manager, Graduate and Professional Programs, 806-742-3184, Fax: 806-742-3958, E-mail: rawlsgrad@ttu.edu.
Website: http://is.ba.ttu.edu.

University at Buffalo, the State University of New York, Graduate School, School of Management, Buffalo, NY 14260. Offers accounting (MS); business administration (EMBA, MBA, PMBA); finance (MS), including financial management, quantitative finance; management (PhD); management information systems (MS); supply chains and operations management (MS); Au D/MBA; DDS/MBA; JD/MBA; M Arch/MBA; MA/MBA; MD/MBA; MPH/MBA; MSW/MBA; Pharm D/MBA. *Accreditation:* AACSB. Part-time and evening/weekend programs available. *Faculty:* 72 full-time (23 women), 51 part-time/adjunct (13 women). *Students:* 627 full-time (266 women), 181 part-time (65 women); includes 50 minority (16 Black or African American, non-Hispanic/Latino; 5 American Indian or Alaska Native, non-Hispanic/Latino; 5 Asian, non-Hispanic/Latino; 3 Hispanic/Latino; 21 Native Hawaiian or other Pacific Islander, non-Hispanic/Latino), 332 international. Average age 28. 2,083 applicants, 52% accepted, 432 enrolled. In 2013, 476 master's, 10 doctorates awarded. *Degree requirements:* For master's, thesis (for some programs); for doctorate, comprehensive exam, thesis/dissertation. *Entrance requirements:* For master's, GMAT (for MS in accounting); GRE or GMAT (for MBA and all other MS concentrations), essays, letters of recommendation; for doctorate, GMAT or GRE, essays, writing sample, letters of recommendation. Additional exam requirements/recommendations for international students: Required—IELTS or PTE; Recommended—TOEFL (minimum score 95 iBT). *Application deadline:* For fall admission, 5/2 priority date for domestic students, 2/1 priority date for international students. Applications are processed on a rolling basis. Application fee: $100. Electronic applications accepted. *Expenses:* Contact institution. *Financial support:* In 2013–14, 115 students received support, including 40 fellowships (averaging $5,250 per year), 33 research assistantships with full and partial tuition reimbursements available (averaging $18,000 per year), 42 teaching assistantships with partial tuition reimbursements available (averaging $10,255 per year); career-related internships or fieldwork, Federal Work-Study, institutionally sponsored loans, scholarships/grants, health care benefits, and unspecified assistantships also available. Financial award application deadline: 2/15; financial award applicants required to submit FAFSA. *Faculty research:* Earnings management and electronic information assurance, supply chain and operations management, corporate financing and asset pricing, consumer behavior and quantitative modeling of marketing behavior, leadership and politics in organizations. *Total annual research expenditures:* $155,000. *Unit head:* Erin K. O'Brien, Assistant Dean and Director of Graduate Programs, 716-645-3204, Fax: 716-645-2341, E-mail: ekobrien@buffalo.edu. *Application contact:* Meghan Felser, Associate Director of Admissions and Recruiting, 716-645-3204, Fax: 716-645-2341, E-mail: mpwood@buffalo.edu.
Website: http://mgt.buffalo.edu/.

The University of Alabama at Birmingham, School of Public Health, Program in Public Health, Birmingham, AL 35294. Offers accelerated industrial hygiene (MPH); applied epidemiology (MSPH); biostatistics (MPH); clinical and translational science (MSPH); environmental health (MPH); environmental health and toxicology (MSPH); epidemiology (MPH); general theory and practice (MPH); health behavior (MPH); health care organization (MPH); health policy quantitative policy analysis (MPH); industrial hygiene (MPH, MSPH); maternal and child health policy (Dr PH); maternal and child health policy and leadership (MPH); occupational health and safety (MPH); outcomes research (MSPH, Dr PH); pharmacoepidemiology and comparative effectiveness research (MSPH); public health (PhD); public health management (Dr PH); public health preparedness management (MPH). *Accreditation:* CEPH. *Entrance requirements:* For master's and doctorate, GRE, evaluations. Additional exam requirements/recommendations for international students: Recommended—TOEFL (minimum score 550 paper-based; 79 iBT), IELTS (minimum score 6.5).

The University of British Columbia, Faculty of Arts and Faculty of Graduate Studies, Department of Psychology, Vancouver, BC V6T 1Z4, Canada. Offers behavioral neuroscience (MA, PhD); clinical psychology (MA, PhD); cognitive science (MA, PhD); developmental psychology (MA, PhD); health psychology (MA, PhD); quantitative methods (MA, PhD); social/personality psychology (MA, PhD). *Accreditation:* APA (one or more programs are accredited). Terminal master's awarded for partial completion of doctoral program. *Degree requirements:* For master's, thesis; for doctorate, comprehensive exam, thesis/dissertation. *Entrance requirements:* For master's and doctorate, GRE General Test. Additional exam requirements/recommendations for international students: Required—TOEFL (minimum score 550 paper-based; 80 iBT). Electronic applications accepted. *Expenses: Tuition, area resident:* Full-time $8000 Canadian dollars. *Faculty research:* Clinical, developmental, social/personality, cognition, behavioral neuroscience.

University of California, Santa Barbara, Graduate Division, College of Letters and Sciences, Division of Mathematics, Life, and Physical Sciences, Department of Geography, Santa Barbara, CA 93106-4060. Offers cognitive science (PhD); geography (MA, PhD); global studies (PhD); quantitative methods in the social sciences (PhD); technology and society (PhD); transportation (PhD); MA/PhD. *Faculty:* 21 full-time (4 women), 14 part-time/adjunct (4 women). *Students:* 66 full-time (32 women); includes 13 minority (2 Black or African American, non-Hispanic/Latino; 6 Asian, non-Hispanic/Latino; 5 Hispanic/Latino), 17 international. Average age 32. 153 applicants, 25% accepted, 16 enrolled. In 2013, 7 master's, 10 doctorates awarded. Terminal master's awarded for partial completion of doctoral program. *Degree requirements:* For master's, comprehensive exam (for some programs), thesis or alternative; for doctorate, comprehensive exam, thesis/dissertation, 1 quarter of teaching assistantship. *Entrance requirements:* For master's and doctorate, GRE (minimum combined verbal and quantitative scores of 1100 in old scoring system or 301 in new scoring system). Additional exam requirements/recommendations for international students: Required—TOEFL (minimum score 550 paper-based; 80 iBT), IELTS (minimum score 7). *Application deadline:* For fall admission, 12/15 for domestic and international students. Application fee: $80 ($100 for international students). Electronic applications accepted. *Expenses:* Tuition, state resident: part-time $5148.26 per quarter. Tuition, nonresident: part-time $10,182.26 per quarter. *Financial support:* In 2013–14, 60 students received support, including 32 fellowships with full and partial tuition reimbursements available (averaging $8,646 per year), 36 research assistantships with full and partial tuition reimbursements available (averaging $13,840 per year), 35 teaching assistantships with partial tuition reimbursements available (averaging $10,709 per year). Financial award applicants required to submit FAFSA. *Faculty research:* Earth system science; human environment relations; modeling, measurement, and computation. *Total annual research expenditures:* $3.9 million. *Unit head:* Dr. Dar Alexander Roberts, Professor/Chair, 805-880-2531, Fax: 805-893-2578, E-mail: dar@geog.ucsb.edu. *Application contact:* Karl Antonsson, Student Programs Manager, 805-456-2836, Fax: 805-893-2578, E-mail: karl@geog.ucsb.edu.
Website: http://www.geog.ucsb.edu/.

University of California, Santa Barbara, Graduate Division, College of Letters and Sciences, Division of Mathematics, Life, and Physical Sciences, Department of Statistics and Applied Probability, Santa Barbara, CA 93106-3110. Offers bioengineering (PhD); financial mathematics and statistics (PhD); quantitative methods in the social sciences (PhD); statistics (MA), including applied statistics, mathematical statistics; statistics and applied probability (PhD); MA/PhD. *Faculty:* 11 full-time (2 women), 8 part-time/adjunct (0 women). *Students:* 66 full-time (35 women); includes 2 minority (both Hispanic/Latino), 51 international. Average age 27. 377 applicants, 14% accepted, 19 enrolled. In 2013, 14 master's, 6 doctorates awarded. Terminal master's awarded for partial completion of doctoral program. *Degree requirements:* For master's, comprehensive exam, thesis optional; for doctorate, comprehensive exam, thesis/dissertation. *Entrance requirements:* For master's and doctorate, GRE General Test. Additional exam requirements/recommendations for international students: Required—TOEFL (minimum score 550 paper-based; 80 iBT), IELTS (minimum score 7). *Application deadline:* For fall admission, 12/15 priority date for domestic students, 12/1 priority date for international students; for winter admission, 11/1 priority date for domestic and international students; for spring admission, 2/1 priority date for domestic and international students. Application fee: $80 ($100 for international students). Electronic applications accepted. *Expenses:* Tuition, state resident: part-time $5148.26 per quarter. Tuition, nonresident: part-time $10,182.26 per quarter. *Financial support:* In 2013–14, 23 students received support, including 6 fellowships with full tuition reimbursements available (averaging $11,285 per year), 1 research assistantship with full and partial tuition reimbursement available (averaging $2,790 per year), 28 teaching assistantships with partial tuition reimbursements available (averaging $14,557 per year); Federal Work-Study, scholarships/grants, and health care benefits also available. Financial award application deadline: 12/15; financial award applicants required to submit FAFSA. *Faculty research:* Bayesian inference, financial mathematics, stochastic processes, environmental statistics, biostatistical modeling. *Total annual research expenditures:* $139,480. *Unit head:* Dr. John Hsu, Chair, 805-893-4055, E-mail: hsu@pstat.ucsb.edu. *Application contact:* Angelina M. Toporov, Graduate Program Assistant, 805-893-2129, Fax: 805-893-2334, E-mail: toporov@pstat.ucsb.edu.
Website: http://www.pstat.ucsb.edu/.

University of California, Santa Barbara, Graduate Division, College of Letters and Sciences, Division of Social Sciences, Department of Communication, Santa Barbara, CA 93106-4020. Offers cognitive science (PhD); communication (PhD); feminist studies (PhD); language, interaction and social organization (PhD); quantitative methods in the social sciences (PhD); society and technology (PhD); MA/PhD. *Faculty:* 20 full-time (9 women). *Students:* 32 full-time (19 women); includes 4 minority (all Hispanic/Latino), 1 international. Average age 30. 120 applicants, 12% accepted, 7 enrolled. In 2013, 7 doctorates awarded. Terminal master's awarded for partial completion of doctoral program. *Degree requirements:* For doctorate, comprehensive exam, thesis/dissertation. *Entrance requirements:* For doctorate, GRE. Additional exam requirements/recommendations for international students: Required—TOEFL (minimum score 80 iBT), IELTS (minimum score 7). *Application deadline:* For fall admission, 12/1 for domestic and international students. Application fee: $80 ($100 for international students). Electronic applications accepted. *Expenses:* Tuition, state resident: part-time $5148.26 per quarter. Tuition, nonresident: part-time $10,182.26 per quarter. *Financial support:* In 2013–14, 37 students received support, including 37 fellowships with full and

partial tuition reimbursements available (averaging $6,045 per year), 5 research assistantships with full and partial tuition reimbursements available (averaging $9,646 per year), 29 teaching assistantships with partial tuition reimbursements available (averaging $17,600 per year); career-related internships or fieldwork, health care benefits, and tuition waivers (full and partial) also available. Support available to part-time students. Financial award application deadline: 12/1; financial award applicants required to submit FAFSA. *Faculty research:* Interpersonal, intercultural, organizational, health, media. *Unit head:* Prof. Ronald E. Rice, Professor, 805-893-8696, Fax: 805-893-7102, E-mail: rrice@comm.ucsb.edu. *Application contact:* Tricia S. Taylor, Graduate Program Assistant, 805-893-3046, Fax: 805-893-7102, E-mail: ttaylor@comm.ucsb.edu. Website: http://www.comm.ucsb.edu/.

University of California, Santa Barbara, Graduate Division, College of Letters and Sciences, Division of Social Sciences, Department of Sociology, Santa Barbara, CA 93106-9430. Offers interdisciplinary emphasis: Black studies (PhD); interdisciplinary emphasis: environment and society (PhD); interdisciplinary emphasis: feminist studies (PhD); interdisciplinary emphasis: global studies (PhD); interdisciplinary emphasis: language, interaction and social organization (PhD); interdisciplinary emphasis: quantitative methods in social science (PhD); interdisciplinary emphasis: technology and society (PhD); sociology (PhD); MA/PhD. *Faculty:* 33 full-time (12 women). *Students:* 63 full-time (42 women); includes 30 minority (7 Black or African American, non-Hispanic/Latino; 4 Asian, non-Hispanic/Latino; 19 Hispanic/Latino), 1 international. Average age 31. 144 applicants, 10% accepted, 9 enrolled. In 2013, 5 doctorates awarded. Terminal master's awarded for partial completion of doctoral program. *Degree requirements:* For doctorate, comprehensive exam, thesis/dissertation. *Entrance requirements:* For doctorate, GRE General Test. Additional exam requirements/recommendations for international students: Required—TOEFL (minimum score 550 paper-based; 80 iBT), IELTS (minimum score 7). *Application deadline:* For fall admission, 12/1 for domestic and international students. Application fee: $80 ($100 for international students). Electronic applications accepted. *Expenses:* Tuition, state resident: part-time $5148.26 per quarter. Tuition, nonresident: part-time $10,182.26 per quarter. *Financial support:* In 2013–14, 52 students received support, including 52 fellowships with full and partial tuition reimbursements available (averaging $9,057 per year), 3 research assistantships (averaging $2,000 per year), 48 teaching assistantships with full and partial tuition reimbursements available (averaging $17,655 per year); career-related internships or fieldwork, Federal Work-Study, institutionally sponsored loans, scholarships/grants, health care benefits, tuition waivers (full and partial), and unspecified assistantships also available. Financial award application deadline: 12/1; financial award applicants required to submit FAFSA. *Faculty research:* Gender and sexualities, race/ethnicity, social movements, conversation analysis, global sociology. *Unit head:* Prof. Maria Charles, Chair, 805-893-3118, Fax: 805-893-3324. *Application contact:* Sharon Applegate, Graduate Program Advisor, 805-893-3328, Fax: 805-893-3324, E-mail: grad-soc@soc.ucsb.edu.
Website: http://www.soc.ucsb.edu/.

University of Cincinnati, Graduate School, Carl H. Lindner College of Business, MS Program, Cincinnati, OH 45221. Offers accounting (MS); business analytics (MS); finance (MS); information systems (MS); marketing (MS); taxation (MS). Part-time and evening/weekend programs available. *Faculty:* 39 full-time (11 women), 11 part-time/adjunct (3 women). *Students:* 275 full-time (105 women), 165 part-time (69 women); includes 29 minority (14 Black or African American, non-Hispanic/Latino; 9 Asian, non-Hispanic/Latino; 1 Native Hawaiian or other Pacific Islander, non-Hispanic/Latino; 5 Two or more races, non-Hispanic/Latino), 273 international. 953 applicants, 37% accepted, 258 enrolled. In 2013, 144 master's awarded. *Degree requirements:* For master's, thesis (for some programs). *Entrance requirements:* For master's, GMAT, GRE, resume, transcripts, essays, letters of recommendation. Additional exam requirements/recommendations for international students: Required—TOEFL (minimum score 600 paper-based; 100 iBT), IELTS (minimum score 6.5). *Application deadline:* For fall admission, 3/15 priority date for domestic students, 4/1 for international students. Applications are processed on a rolling basis. Application fee: $65 ($70 for international students). Electronic applications accepted. *Expenses:* Contact institution. *Financial support:* In 2013–14, 124 students received support, including 12 teaching assistantships with full and partial tuition reimbursements available (averaging $3,500 per year); scholarships/grants, tuition waivers (full and partial), and unspecified assistantships also available. Financial award application deadline: 2/1; financial award applicants required to submit FAFSA. *Faculty research:* Real estate, empirical pricing, organization information pricing, strategic management, portfolio choice in institutional investment. *Unit head:* Dr. David Szymanski, Dean, 513-556-7001, Fax: 513-556-4891, E-mail: david.szymanski@uc.edu. *Application contact:* Dona Clary, Director, Graduate Programs, 513-556-3546, Fax: 513-558-7006, E-mail: dona.clary@uc.edu.

University of Cincinnati, Graduate School, Carl H. Lindner College of Business, PhD Programs, Cincinnati, OH 45221. Offers accounting (PhD); economics (PhD); finance (PhD); information systems (PhD); management (PhD); marketing (PhD); operations and business analytics (PhD). *Faculty:* 62 full-time (13 women). *Students:* 27 full-time (15 women), 9 part-time (1 woman); includes 2 minority (1 Asian, non-Hispanic/Latino; 1 Hispanic/Latino), 16 international. Average age 29. 86 applicants, 13% accepted, 6 enrolled. In 2013, 8 doctorates awarded. *Degree requirements:* For doctorate, comprehensive exam, thesis/dissertation. *Entrance requirements:* For doctorate, GMAT, GRE, transcripts, essays, resume, letters of recommendation. Additional exam requirements/recommendations for international students: Required—TOEFL (minimum score 600 paper-based; 100 iBT), IELTS (minimum score 6.5). *Application deadline:* For fall admission, 1/15 for domestic and international students. Application fee: $65 ($70 for international students). Electronic applications accepted. *Expenses:* Contact institution. *Financial support:* In 2013–14, 33 students received support, including 25 research assistantships with full and partial tuition reimbursements available (averaging $23,250 per year); scholarships/grants, tuition waivers (full and partial), and unspecified assistantships also available. Financial award application deadline: 1/15; financial award applicants required to submit FAFSA. *Unit head:* Dr. Suzanne Masterson, Director, 513-556-7125, Fax: 513-556-5499, E-mail: suzanne.masterson@uc.edu. *Application contact:* Angel Elvin, Assistant Director, 513-556-7190, Fax: 513-558-7006, E-mail: angel.elvin@uc.edu.
Website: http://www.business.uc.edu/phd.

University of Colorado Denver, Business School, Program in Decision Sciences, Denver, CO 80217. Offers MS, MS/MBA. Part-time and evening/weekend programs available. *Students:* 11 full-time (4 women), 6 part-time (5 women); includes 3 minority (1 Black or African American, non-Hispanic/Latino; 1 Asian, non-Hispanic/Latino; 1 Two or more races, non-Hispanic/Latino). Average age 32. 8 applicants, 63% accepted, 3 enrolled. In 2013, 2 master's awarded. *Degree requirements:* For master's, 30 semester hours (18 of required courses and 12 of electives). *Entrance requirements:* For master's, GMAT, essay, resume, two letters of recommendation; financial statements (for international students). Additional exam requirements/recommendations for international students: Required—TOEFL (minimum score 537 paper-based; 75 iBT); Recommended—IELTS (minimum score 6.5). *Application deadline:* For fall admission, 4/15 for domestic students, 3/15 for international students; for spring admission, 10/15 for domestic students, 9/15 for international students. Applications are processed on a rolling basis. Application fee: $50 ($75 for international students). Electronic applications

accepted. *Expenses:* Contact institution. *Financial support:* In 2013–14, 3 students received support. Fellowships, research assistantships, teaching assistantships, Federal Work-Study, institutionally sponsored loans, scholarships/grants, and traineeships available. Financial award application deadline: 4/1; financial award applicants required to submit FAFSA. *Faculty research:* Quantitative business analysis, quantitative methods and modeling, business intelligence, forecasting, quality and Six Sigma, optimization, project management, data mining, supply chain management. *Unit head:* Marlene Smith, Associate Professor/Director of MS in Decision Sciences Program, 303-315-8421, E-mail: ma.smith@ucdenver.edu. *Application contact:* Shelly Townley, Director of Graduate Admissions, 303-315-8202, Fax: 303-556-5904, E-mail: shelly.townley@ucdenver.edu.
Website: http://www.ucdenver.edu/academics/colleges/business/degrees/ms/business-analytics/Pages/default.aspx.

University of Colorado Denver, Business School, Program in Management and Organization, Denver, CO 80217. Offers business strategy (MS); change and innovation (MS); enterprise technology management (MS); entrepreneurship and innovation (MS); global management (MS); human resources management (MS); leadership and management (MS); quantitative decision methods (MS); sports and entertainment management (MS); sustainability management (MS). Accreditation: AACSB. Part-time and evening/weekend programs available. Postbaccalaureate distance learning degree programs offered (no on-campus study). *Students:* 27 full-time (19 women), 14 part-time (7 women); includes 4 minority (1 Black or African American, non-Hispanic/Latino; 2 Hispanic/Latino; 1 Two or more races, non-Hispanic/Latino), 6 international. Average age 29. 38 applicants, 45% accepted, 8 enrolled. In 2013, 28 master's awarded. *Degree requirements:* For master's, 30 semester hours (12 of required courses, 12 of management electives, and 6 of free electives). *Entrance requirements:* For master's, GMAT, resume, two letters of recommendation, essay, financial statements (for international applicants). Additional exam requirements/recommendations for international students: Required—TOEFL (minimum score 537 paper-based; 75 iBT); Recommended—IELTS (minimum score 6.5). *Application deadline:* For fall admission, 4/15 for domestic students, 3/15 for international students; for spring admission, 10/15 for domestic students, 9/15 for international students. Applications are processed on a rolling basis. Application fee: $50 ($75 for international students). Electronic applications accepted. *Expenses:* Contact institution. *Financial support:* In 2013–14, 5 students received support. Fellowships, research assistantships, teaching assistantships, Federal Work-Study, institutionally sponsored loans, scholarships/grants, and traineeships available. Financial award application deadline: 4/1; financial award applicants required to submit FAFSA. *Faculty research:* Human resource management, management of catastrophe, turnaround strategies. *Unit head:* Dr. Kenneth Bettenhausen, Associate Professor/Director of MS in Management, 303-315-8425, E-mail: kenneth.bettenhausen@ucdenver.edu. *Application contact:* Shelly Townley, Admissions Director, Graduate Programs, 303-315-8202, E-mail: shelly.townley@ucdenver.edu.
Website: http://www.ucdenver.edu/academics/colleges/business/degrees/ms/management/Pages/Management.aspx.

University of Connecticut, Graduate School, College of Liberal Arts and Sciences, Department of Public Policy, Field of Survey Research, Storrs, CT 06269. Offers quantitative research methods (Graduate Certificate); survey research (MA). *Degree requirements:* For master's, comprehensive exam. *Entrance requirements:* For master's, GRE General Test. Additional exam requirements/recommendations for international students: Required—TOEFL (minimum score 550 paper-based). Electronic applications accepted.

University of Florida, Graduate School, College of Liberal Arts and Sciences, Department of Mathematics, Gainesville, FL 32611. Offers mathematics (MA, MAT, MS, MST, PhD), including imaging science and technology (PhD), mathematics (PhD), quantitative finance (PhD). Part-time programs available. *Faculty:* 36 full-time (3 women), 1 part-time/adjunct (0 women). *Students:* 77 full-time (23 women), 7 part-time (3 women); includes 15 minority (2 Black or African American, non-Hispanic/Latino; 8 Asian, non-Hispanic/Latino; 5 Hispanic/Latino), 30 international. Average age 29. 122 applicants, 30% accepted, 19 enrolled. In 2013, 19 master's, 14 doctorates awarded. Terminal master's awarded for partial completion of doctoral program. *Degree requirements:* For master's, comprehensive exam, thesis optional, first-year exam; for doctorate, one foreign language, comprehensive exam, thesis/dissertation. *Entrance requirements:* For master's and doctorate, GRE General Test, minimum GPA of 3.0. Additional exam requirements/recommendations for international students: Required—TOEFL (minimum score 550 paper-based; 80 iBT), IELTS (minimum score 6). *Application deadline:* For fall admission, 6/1 priority date for domestic students. Applications are processed on a rolling basis. Application fee: $30. Electronic applications accepted. *Expenses:* Tuition, state resident: full-time $12,640. Tuition, nonresident: full-time $30,000. *Financial support:* In 2013–14, 69 students received support, including 15 fellowships (averaging $16,130 per year), 3 research assistantships (averaging $6,745 per year), 68 teaching assistantships (averaging $13,395 per year); career-related internships or fieldwork and unspecified assistantships also available. Financial award applicants required to submit FAFSA. *Faculty research:* Combinatorics and number theory, group theory, probability theory, logic, differential geometry and mathematical physics. *Unit head:* Douglas Cenzer, PhD, Chairman, 352-294-2313, Fax: 352-392-8357, E-mail: cenzer@ufl.edu. *Application contact:* Jean Larson, Associate Chair and Graduate Coordinator, 352-294-2317, Fax: 352-392-8357, E-mail: jal@ufl.edu.
Website: http://www.math.ufl.edu/gradprog/.

University of Florida, Graduate School, College of Liberal Arts and Sciences, Department of Statistics, Gainesville, FL 32611. Offers quantitative finance (PhD); statistics (M Stat, MS Stat, PhD). Part-time programs available. *Faculty:* 9 full-time (2 women), 1 part-time/adjunct (0 women). *Students:* 68 full-time (27 women), 6 part-time (5 women); includes 5 minority (3 Asian, non-Hispanic/Latino; 2 Hispanic/Latino), 58 international. Average age 27. 381 applicants, 4% accepted, 9 enrolled. In 2013, 19 master's, 7 doctorates awarded. Terminal master's awarded for partial completion of doctoral program. *Degree requirements:* For master's, variable foreign language requirement, comprehensive exam, final oral exam; thesis (for MS Stat); for doctorate, comprehensive exam, thesis/dissertation. *Entrance requirements:* For master's and doctorate, GRE General Test, minimum GPA of 3.0. Additional exam requirements/recommendations for international students: Required—TOEFL (minimum score 550 paper-based; 80 iBT), IELTS (minimum score 6). *Application deadline:* For fall admission, 2/1 priority date for domestic students, 2/1 for international students. Applications are processed on a rolling basis. Application fee: $30. Electronic applications accepted. *Expenses:* Tuition, state resident: full-time $12,640. Tuition, nonresident: full-time $30,000. *Financial support:* In 2013–14, 48 students received support, including 9 fellowships (averaging $27,444 per year), 4 research assistantships (averaging $11,930 per year), 68 teaching assistantships (averaging $11,750 per year); unspecified assistantships also available. Financial award application deadline: 2/1; financial award applicants required to submit FAFSA. *Faculty research:* Bayesian statistics, biostatistics, Markov Chain Monte Carlo (MCMC), nonparametric statistics, statistical genetics/genomics. *Unit head:* Brett Presnell, PhD, Associate Professor and Department Chair, 352-273-2989, Fax: 352-392-5175, E-mail: presnell@stat.ufl.edu.

Quantitative Analysis

Application contact: James P. Hobert, PhD, Professor and Graduate Coordinator, 352-273-2990, Fax: 352-392-5175, E-mail: jhobert@stat.ufl.edu.
Website: http://www.stat.ufl.edu/.

University of Florida, Graduate School, Warrington College of Business Administration, Hough Graduate School of Business, Department of Finance, Insurance and Real Estate, Gainesville, FL 32611. Offers entrepreneurship (MS); finance (MS, PhD); financial services (Certificate); insurance (PhD); quantitative finance (PhD); real estate (MS); real estate and urban analysis (PhD); JD/MBA; JD/MS. *Faculty:* 17 full-time (0 women), 6 part-time/adjunct (0 women). *Students:* 77 full-time (20 women), 4 part-time (2 women); includes 11 minority (3 Black or African American, non-Hispanic/Latino; 1 American Indian or Alaska Native, non-Hispanic/Latino; 2 Asian, non-Hispanic/Latino; 5 Hispanic/Latino), 23 international. Average age 27. 226 applicants, 4% accepted, 8 enrolled. In 2013, 92 master's, 5 doctorates awarded. Terminal master's awarded for partial completion of doctoral program. *Degree requirements:* For master's, comprehensive exam, thesis; for doctorate, comprehensive exam, thesis/dissertation. *Entrance requirements:* For master's, GMAT (minimum score of 465) or GRE General Test, minimum GPA of 3.0 for last 60 hours of undergraduate degree, work experience (preferred); for doctorate, GMAT (minimum score of 465) or GRE General Test, minimum GPA of 3.0. Additional exam requirements/recommendations for international students: Required—TOEFL (minimum score 550 paper-based; 80 iBT), IELTS (minimum score 6). *Application deadline:* For fall admission, 1/15 priority date for domestic students, 1/15 for international students. Applications are processed on a rolling basis. Application fee: $30. Electronic applications accepted. *Expenses:* Tuition, state resident: full-time $12,640. Tuition, nonresident: full-time $30,000. *Financial support:* In 2013–14, 19 students received support, including 13 research assistantships (averaging $18,787 per year), 6 teaching assistantships (averaging $14,970 per year); career-related internships or fieldwork, scholarships/grants, and unspecified assistantships also available. Financial award application deadline: 1/15; financial award applicants required to submit FAFSA. *Faculty research:* Banking, empirical corporate finance, hedge funds. *Unit head:* Mahendrarajah Nimalendran, PhD, Chair, 352-392-9526, Fax: 352-392-0301, E-mail: nimal@ufl.edu. *Application contact:* Office of Admissions, 352-392-1365, E-mail: webrequests@admissions.ufl.edu.
Website: http://www.cba.ufl.edu/fire/.

The University of Iowa, Graduate College, College of Public Health, Department of Biostatistics, Iowa City, IA 52242-1316. Offers biostatistics (MS, PhD, Certificate); quantitative methods (MPH). *Degree requirements:* For master's, thesis optional, exam; for doctorate, comprehensive exam, thesis/dissertation. *Entrance requirements:* For master's and doctorate, GRE General Test, minimum GPA of 3.0. Additional exam requirements/recommendations for international students: Required—TOEFL (minimum score 600 paper-based; 100 iBT). Electronic applications accepted.

University of Maryland, College Park, Academic Affairs, College of Education, Department of Human Development and Quantitative Methodology, College Park, MD 20742. Offers MA, Ed D, PhD. *Faculty:* 56 full-time (47 women), 12 part-time/adjunct (10 women). *Students:* 73 full-time (60 women), 46 part-time (36 women); includes 29 minority (8 Black or African American, non-Hispanic/Latino; 7 Asian, non-Hispanic/Latino; 10 Hispanic/Latino; 1 Native Hawaiian or other Pacific Islander, non-Hispanic/Latino; 3 Two or more races, non-Hispanic/Latino), 22 international. 162 applicants, 26% accepted, 26 enrolled. In 2013, 16 master's, 18 doctorates awarded. *Entrance requirements:* Additional exam requirements/recommendations for international students: Required—TOEFL. *Application deadline:* For fall admission, 3/15 for domestic students, 12/15 for international students; for spring admission, 10/1 for domestic students, 6/1 for international students. Application fee: $75. *Expenses:* Tuition, state resident: full-time $10,314; part-time $573 per credit hour. Tuition, nonresident: full-time $22,248; part-time $1236 per credit. *Required fees:* $1446; $403.15 per semester. Tuition and fees vary according to program. *Financial support:* In 2013–14, 9 fellowships with full tuition reimbursements (averaging $32,282 per year), 39 teaching assistantships (averaging $17,585 per year) were awarded. *Total annual research expenditures:* $3.4 million. *Unit head:* Nathan Fox, Chair, 301-405-2827, E-mail: fox@umd.edu. *Application contact:* Dr. Charles A. Caramello, Dean of Graduate School, 301-405-0358, Fax: 301-314-9305, E-mail: ccaramel@umd.edu.
Website: http://www.education.umd.edu/EDHI/.

University of Minnesota, Twin Cities Campus, College of Science and Engineering, School of Mathematics, Minneapolis, MN 55455-0213. Offers mathematics (MS, PhD); quantitative finance (Certificate). Part-time programs available. *Faculty:* 71 full-time (6 women). *Students:* 230 (76 women); includes 22 minority (5 Black or African American, non-Hispanic/Latino; 12 Asian, non-Hispanic/Latino; 5 Hispanic/Latino), 102 international. 643 applicants, 27% accepted, 69 enrolled. In 2013, 44 master's, 30 doctorates awarded. Terminal master's awarded for partial completion of doctoral program. *Degree requirements:* For master's, thesis (for some programs); for doctorate, 2 foreign languages, thesis/dissertation. *Entrance requirements:* For master's, GRE Subject Test (recommended); for doctorate, GRE Subject Test. Additional exam requirements/recommendations for international students: Required—TOEFL. *Application deadline:* For fall admission, 12/15 priority date for domestic and international students. Applications are processed on a rolling basis. Application fee: $75 ($95 for international students). Electronic applications accepted. *Financial support:* Fellowships and teaching assistantships available. *Faculty research:* Partial and ordinary differential equations, algebra and number theory, geometry, combinatorics, numerical analysis, probability, financial mathematics. *Unit head:* Steven L. Crouch, Dean, 612-624-2006, Fax: 612-624-2841, E-mail: crouch@umn.edu. *Application contact:* Mathematics Graduate Program, E-mail: gradprog@math.umn.edu.
Website: http://www.math.umn.edu.

University of New Mexico, Graduate School, College of Arts and Sciences, Department of Psychology, Albuquerque, NM 87131-2039. Offers behavioral neuroscience (PhD); clinical psychology (PhD); cognitive neuroimaging (PhD); developmental psychology (PhD); evolution (PhD); health psychology (PhD); quantitative methodology (PhD). *Faculty:* 24 full-time (9 women), 2 part-time/adjunct (both women). *Students:* 67 full-time (42 women), 8 part-time (6 women); includes 20 minority (1 American Indian or Alaska Native, non-Hispanic/Latino; 4 Asian, non-Hispanic/Latino; 14 Hispanic/Latino; 1 Two or more races, non-Hispanic/Latino), 1 international. Average age 33. 123 applicants, 17% accepted, 12 enrolled. In 2013, 9 doctorates awarded. *Degree requirements:* For doctorate, comprehensive exam, thesis/dissertation. *Entrance requirements:* For doctorate, GRE General Test, GRE Subject Test (psychology), minimum GPA of 3.0. Additional exam requirements/recommendations for international students: Required—TOEFL (minimum score 550 paper-based; 79 iBT), IELTS (minimum score 6.5). *Application deadline:* For fall admission, 12/15 priority date for domestic and international students. Applications are processed on a rolling basis. Application fee: $50. Electronic applications accepted. *Financial support:* In 2013–14, 62 students received support, including 8 fellowships (averaging $13,124 per year), 37 research assistantships with full and partial tuition reimbursements available (averaging $11,655 per year), 67 teaching assistantships with full and partial tuition reimbursements available (averaging $13,600 per year); career-related internships or fieldwork, Federal Work-Study, institutionally sponsored loans, scholarships/grants, health care benefits, tuition waivers (partial), and unspecified assistantships also available. Financial award application deadline: 3/1; financial award applicants required to submit FAFSA. *Faculty research:* Addiction, cognition, brain and behavior, developmental, evolutionary, functioning neuroimaging, health psychology, learning and memory, neuroscience. *Unit head:* Dr. Jane Ellen Smith, Department Chair, 505-277-4121, Fax: 505-277-1394. *Application contact:* Rikk Murphy, Graduate Program Coordinator, 505-277-5009, Fax: 505-277-1394, E-mail: advising@unm.edu.
Website: http://psych.unm.edu.

University of North Texas, Robert B. Toulouse School of Graduate Studies, Denton, TN 76203-5017. Offers accounting (MS, PhD); applied anthropology (MA, MS); applied behavior analysis (Certificate); applied technology and performance improvement (M Ed, MS, PhD); art education (MA, PhD); art history (MA); art museum education (Certificate); arts leadership (Certificate); audiology (Au D); behavior analysis (MS); biochemistry and molecular biology (MS, PhD); biology (MA, MS, PhD); business (PhD); business computer information systems (PhD); chemistry (MS, PhD); clinical psychology (PhD); communication studies (MA, MS); computer engineering (MS); computer science (MS); computer science and engineering (PhD); counseling (M Ed, MS, PhD), including clinical mental health counseling (MS), college and university counseling (M Ed, MS), elementary school counseling (M Ed, MS), secondary school counseling (M Ed, MS); counseling psychology (PhD); creative writing (MA); criminal justice (MS); curriculum and instruction (M Ed, PhD), including curriculum studies (PhD), early childhood studies (PhD), language and literacy studies (PhD); decision sciences (MBA); design (MA, MFA), including fashion design (MFA), innovation studies, interior design (MFA); early childhood studies (MS); economics (MS); educational leadership (M Ed, Ed D, PhD); educational psychology (MS), including family studies, gifted and talented (MS, PhD), human development, learning and cognition, research, measurement and evaluation; educational research (PhD), including gifted and talented (MS, PhD), human development and family studies, psychological aspects of sports and exercise, research, measurement and statistics; electrical engineering (MS); emergency management (MPA); engineering systems (MS); English (MA, PhD); environmental science (MS, PhD); experimental psychology (PhD); finance (MBA, MS, PhD); financial management (MPA); French (MA); health psychology and behavioral medicine (PhD); health services management (MBA); higher education (M Ed, Ed D, PhD); history (MA, MS, PhD), including European history (PhD), military history (PhD), United States history (PhD); hospitality management (MS); human resources management (MPA); information science (MS, PhD); information technologies (MBA); information technology and decision sciences (MS); interdisciplinary studies (MA, MS); international sustainable tourism (MS); jazz studies (MM); journalism (MA, MJ, Graduate Certificate), including interactive and virtual digital communication (Graduate Certificate), narrative journalism (Graduate Certificate), public relations (Graduate Certificate); kinesiology (MS); learning technologies (MS, PhD); library science (MS); local government management (MPA); logistics and supply chain management (MBA, PhD); long-term care, senior housing, and aging services (MA, MS); management science (PhD); marketing (MBA, PhD); materials science and engineering (MS, PhD); mathematics (MA, PhD); merchandising (MS); music (MA, MM Ed, PhD), including ethnomusicology (MA), music education (MM Ed, PhD), music theory (MA, PhD), musicology (MA, PhD), performance (MA); nonprofit management (MPA); operations and supply chain management (MBA); performance (MM, DMA); philosophy (MA, PhD); physics (MS, PhD); political science (MA, MS, PhD); public administration and management (PhD), including emergency management, nonprofit management, public financial management, urban management; radio, television and film (MA, MFA); recreation, event and sport management (MS); rehabilitation counseling (MS, Certificate); sociology (MA, MS, PhD); Spanish (MA); special education (M Ed, PhD), including autism intervention (PhD), emotional/behavioral disorders (PhD), mild/moderate disabilities (PhD); speech-language pathology (MA, MS); strategic management (MBA); studio art (MFA); taxation (MS); teaching (M Ed); MBA/MS; MS/MPH; MSES/MBA. Part-time and evening/weekend programs available. Postbaccalaureate distance learning degree programs offered. *Faculty:* 661 full-time (213 women), 240 part-time/adjunct (144 women). *Students:* 3,106 full-time (1,620 women), 3,543 part-time (2,221 women); includes 1,740 minority (533 Black or African American, non-Hispanic/Latino; 15 American Indian or Alaska Native, non-Hispanic/Latino; 286 Asian, non-Hispanic/Latino; 746 Hispanic/Latino; 3 Native Hawaiian or other Pacific Islander, non-Hispanic/Latino; 157 Two or more races, non-Hispanic/Latino), 1,145 international. Average age 32. 6,289 applicants, 43% accepted, 1751 enrolled. In 2013, 1,778 master's, 239 doctorates, 10 other advanced degrees awarded. Terminal master's awarded for partial completion of doctoral program. *Degree requirements:* For master's, variable foreign language requirement, comprehensive exam (for some programs), thesis (for some programs); for doctorate, variable foreign language requirement, comprehensive exam (for some programs), thesis/dissertation; for other advanced degree, variable foreign language requirement, comprehensive exam (for some programs). *Entrance requirements:* For master's and doctorate, GRE, GMAT. Additional exam requirements/recommendations for international students: Required—TOEFL (minimum score 550 paper-based; 79 iBT). *Application deadline:* For fall admission, 7/15 for domestic students, 3/15 for international students; for spring admission, 11/15 for domestic students, 9/15 for international students; for summer admission, 5/1 for domestic students. Applications are processed on a rolling basis. Application fee: $60. Electronic applications accepted. *Financial support:* Fellowships with partial tuition reimbursements, research assistantships with partial tuition reimbursements, teaching assistantships, career-related internships or fieldwork, Federal Work-Study, institutionally sponsored loans, scholarships/grants, health care benefits, and library assistantships available. Support available to part-time students. Financial award applicants required to submit FAFSA. *Unit head:* Mark Wardell, Dean, 940-565-2383, E-mail: mark.wardell@unt.edu. *Application contact:* Toulouse School of Graduate Studies, 940-565-2383, Fax: 940-565-2141, E-mail: gradsch@unt.edu.
Website: http://tsgs.unt.edu/.

University of Oregon, Graduate School, Charles H. Lundquist College of Business, Department of Decision Sciences, Eugene, OR 97403. Offers MA, MS. *Entrance requirements:* For master's, GMAT. *Faculty research:* Time-series analysis, production scheduling, nonparametric methods, decision theory.

University of Pittsburgh, Katz Graduate School of Business, Doctoral Program in Business Administration, Pittsburgh, PA 15260. Offers accounting (PhD); finance (PhD); information systems (PhD); marketing (PhD); operations/decision sciences/artificial intelligence (PhD); organizational behavior and human resource management (PhD); strategic planning (PhD). *Accreditation:* AACSB. *Faculty:* 60 full-time (17 women). *Students:* 50 full-time (22 women); includes 4 minority (2 Black or African American, non-Hispanic/Latino; 2 Asian, non-Hispanic/Latino), 27 international. 321 applicants, 7% accepted, 14 enrolled. In 2013, 10 doctorates awarded. *Degree requirements:* For doctorate, comprehensive exam, thesis/dissertation. *Entrance requirements:* For doctorate, GMAT or GRE, 3 recommendations, statement of purpose, transcripts of all previous course work and degrees. Additional exam requirements/recommendations for international students: Required—TOEFL. *Application deadline:* For fall admission, 1/1 priority date for domestic and international students. Applications are processed on a rolling basis. Application fee: $50. Electronic applications accepted. *Expenses:* Tuition, state resident: full-time $19,964; part-time $807 per credit. Tuition, nonresident: full-time $32,686; part-time $1337 per credit. *Required fees:* $740; $200. Tuition and fees vary

according to program. *Financial support:* In 2013–14, 40 students received support, including 30 research assistantships with full tuition reimbursements available (averaging $23,045 per year), 10 teaching assistantships with full tuition reimbursements available (averaging $26,055 per year); fellowships, Federal Work-Study, scholarships/grants, health care benefits, and unspecified assistantships also available. Financial award application deadline: 1/1. *Faculty research:* Accounting systems/financial reporting, corporate finance, shopper marketing/consumer behavior, management information systems, organizational behavior and entrepreneurship. *Unit head:* Dr. Dennis Galletta, Director, 412-648-1699, Fax: 412-624-3633, E-mail: galletta@katz.pitt.edu. *Application contact:* Carrie Woods, Assistant Director, 412-648-1525, Fax: 412-624-3633, E-mail: cawoods@katz.pitt.edu.
Website: http://www.business.pitt.edu/katz/phd/.

University of Puerto Rico, Río Piedras Campus, College of Business Administration, San Juan, PR 00931-3300. Offers accounting (MBA); finance (MBA, PhD); general business (MBA); human resources management (MBA); international trade and business (MBA, PhD); marketing (MBA); operations management (MBA); quantitative methods (MBA). Part-time programs available. *Degree requirements:* For master's, comprehensive exam, thesis or alternative, research project. *Entrance requirements:* For master's, GMAT or PAEG, minimum GPA of 3.0, letter of recommendation; for doctorate, GMAT, PAEG, minimum GPA of 3.0, master degree. *Faculty research:* Management.

University of South Africa, College of Economic and Management Sciences, Pretoria, South Africa. Offers accounting (D Admin, D Com); accounting science (DA); auditing (D Admin, D Com); business administration (M Tech); business economics (D Admin); business leadership (DBL); business management (D Admin, D Com); economic management analysis (M Tech); economics (D Admin, D Com, PhD); human resource development (M Tech); industrial psychology (D Admin, D Com, PhD); logistics (D Com); marketing (M Tech); public administration (D Admin, D Com, DPA, PhD); public management (M Tech); quantitative management (D Admin, D Com); real estate (M Tech); statistics (D Admin, PhD); tourism management (D Admin, D Com); transport economics (D Admin, D Com).

University of Southern California, Graduate School, Dana and David Dornsife College of Letters, Arts and Sciences, Department of Psychology, Los Angeles, CA 90089. Offers brain and cognitive science (PhD); clinical science (PhD); developmental psychology (PhD); human behavior (MHB); quantitative methods (PhD); social psychology (PhD). *Accreditation:* APA. *Degree requirements:* For doctorate, comprehensive exam, thesis/dissertation, one-year internship (for clinical science students). *Entrance requirements:* For doctorate, GRE. Additional exam requirements/recommendations for international students: Recommended—TOEFL (minimum score 600 paper-based; 100 iBT). Electronic applications accepted. *Faculty research:* Affective neuroscience; children and families; vision, culture and ethnicity; intergroup relations; aggression and violence; language and reading development; substance abuse.

The University of Texas at Arlington, Graduate School, College of Business, Department of Finance and Real Estate, Arlington, TX 76019. Offers finance (PhD); quantitative finance (MS); real estate (MS). Part-time and evening/weekend programs available. *Degree requirements:* For master's, thesis optional; for doctorate, comprehensive exam, thesis/dissertation. *Entrance requirements:* For master's, GMAT/GRE, minimum GPA of 3.0; for doctorate, GMAT/GRE. Additional exam requirements/recommendations for international students: Required—TOEFL (minimum score 550 paper-based; 79 iBT).

The University of Texas at Arlington, Graduate School, College of Business, Program in Business Administration, Arlington, TX 76019. Offers accounting (PhD); business statistics (PhD); finance (MBA, PhD); information systems (MBA, PhD); management (MBA, PhD); marketing (MBA, PhD); operations management (MBA, PhD); real estate (MBA). *Accreditation:* AACSB. Part-time and evening/weekend programs available. *Degree requirements:* For master's, thesis optional; for doctorate, comprehensive exam, thesis/dissertation. *Entrance requirements:* For master's, GMAT or GRE; for doctorate, GMAT, minimum GPA of 3.0 (undergraduate), 3.4 (graduate); 30 hours of graduate course work. Additional exam requirements/recommendations for international students: Required—TOEFL (minimum score 550 paper-based; 79 iBT). Electronic applications accepted.

The University of Texas at Austin, Graduate School, College of Education, Department of Educational Psychology, Austin, TX 78712-1111. Offers academic educational psychology (M Ed, MA); counseling psychology (PhD); counselor education (M Ed); human development, culture and learning sciences (PhD); program evaluation (MA); quantitative methods (M Ed, MA, PhD); school psychology (MA, PhD). *Accreditation:* APA (one or more programs are accredited). *Degree requirements:* For master's, thesis optional; for doctorate, thesis/dissertation. *Entrance requirements:* For master's and doctorate, GRE General Test, 3 letters of recommendation. Additional exam requirements/recommendations for international students: Required—TOEFL.

Virginia Commonwealth University, Graduate School, School of Business, Program in Decision Sciences and Business Analytics, Richmond, VA 23284-9005. Offers MBA, MS. *Entrance requirements:* For master's, GMAT. Additional exam requirements/recommendations for international students: Required—TOEFL (minimum score 600 paper-based; 100 iBT). Electronic applications accepted.

Virginia Polytechnic Institute and State University, VT Online, Blacksburg, VA 24061. Offers advanced transportation systems (Certificate); aerospace engineering (MS); agricultural and life sciences (MSLFS); business information systems (Graduate Certificate); career and technical education (MS); civil engineering (MS); computer engineering (M Eng, MS); decision support systems (Graduate Certificate); eLearning leadership (MA); electrical engineering (M Eng, MS); engineering administration (MEA); environmental engineering (Certificate); environmental politics and policy (Graduate Certificate); environmental sciences and engineering (MS); foundations of political analysis (Graduate Certificate); health product risk management (Graduate Certificate); industrial and systems engineering (MS); information policy and society (Graduate Certificate); information security (Graduate Certificate); information technology (MIT); instructional technology (MA); integrative STEM education (MA Ed); liberal arts (Graduate Certificate); life sciences: health product risk management (MS); natural resources (MNR, Graduate Certificate); networking (Graduate Certificate); nonprofit and nongovernmental organization management (Graduate Certificate); ocean engineering (MS); political science (MA); security studies (Graduate Certificate); software development (Graduate Certificate). *Expenses:* Tuition, state resident: full-time $11,185; part-time $621.50 per credit hour. Tuition, nonresident: full-time $22,146; part-time $1230.25 per credit hour. *Required fees:* $2442; $449.25 per semester. Tuition and fees vary according to course load, campus/location and program.

Washington State University, Graduate School, College of Business, Program in Operations Management and Decision Sciences, Pullman, WA 99164. Offers PhD. *Degree requirements:* For doctorate, qualifying exam.

Wayne State University, School of Medicine, Graduate Programs in Medicine, Department of Family Medicine and Public Health Sciences, Detroit, MI 48202. Offers public health (MPH), including occupational and environmental health, public health practice, quantitative health sciences; public health practice (Graduate Certificate). *Students:* 22 full-time (13 women), 30 part-time (15 women); includes 15 minority (5 Black or African American, non-Hispanic/Latino; 8 Asian, non-Hispanic/Latino; 1 Hispanic/Latino; 1 Two or more races, non-Hispanic/Latino), 13 international. Average age 32. 187 applicants, 21% accepted, 22 enrolled. In 2013, 14 master's, 3 other advanced degrees awarded. *Degree requirements:* For master's, thesis (for some programs), project or thesis. *Entrance requirements:* For master's, GRE, undergraduate work in mathematics, natural sciences, and social sciences; experience in health-related position, admission to graduate school, minimum undergraduate GPA of 3.0 overall and in mathematics, social sciences, and natural sciences, college-level mathematics, personal statement, three letters of recommendation; for Graduate Certificate, undergraduate work in mathematics, natural sciences, and social sciences; experience in health-related position, admission to graduate school, minimum undergraduate GPA of 3.0 overall and in mathematics, social sciences, and natural sciences, college-level mathematics, personal statement, three letters of recommendation. Additional exam requirements/recommendations for international students: Required—TOEFL (minimum score 550 paper-based; 100 iBT), TWE (minimum score 6); Recommended—IELTS (minimum score 6.5). *Application deadline:* For fall admission, 2/1 for domestic students, 1/1 priority date for international students. Application fee: $0. Electronic applications accepted. *Expenses:* Contact institution. *Financial support:* In 2013–14, 7 students received support. Scholarships/grants available. Financial award application deadline: 3/31; financial award applicants required to submit FAFSA. *Faculty research:* Urban health disparities, community health promotion, substance abuse etiology and prevention, HIV/AIDS, interpersonal violence. *Unit head:* Dr. Kimberly Campbell-Voytal, Program Director, 313-577-1051, E-mail: kvoytal@med.wayne.edu.
Website: http://gradprograms.med.wayne.edu/program-spotlight.php?id=26.

Section 20
Real Estate

This section contains a directory of institutions offering graduate work in real estate. Additional information about programs listed in the directory but not augmented by an in-depth entry may be obtained by writing directly to the dean of a graduate school or chair of a department at the address given in the directory.

For programs offering related work, see also in this book *Business Administration and Management.*

CONTENTS

Program Directory
Real Estate   608

Display and Close-Up
See:
Monmouth University   116, 187

Real Estate

American University, Kogod School of Business, Washington, DC 20016-8044. Offers accounting (MS); business administration (MBA); business fundamentals (Certificate); entrepreneurship (Certificate); finance (MS); forensic accounting (Certificate); management (MS); marketing (MS); real estate (MS, Certificate); sustainability management (MS); tax (Certificate); taxation (MS). *Accreditation:* AACSB. Part-time and evening/weekend programs available. Postbaccalaureate distance learning degree programs offered. *Faculty:* 75 full-time (24 women), 36 part-time/adjunct (7 women). *Students:* 194 full-time (95 women), 370 part-time (184 women); includes 168 minority (69 Black or African American, non-Hispanic/Latino; 60 Asian, non-Hispanic/Latino; 33 Hispanic/Latino; 2 Native Hawaiian or other Pacific Islander, non-Hispanic/Latino; 4 Two or more races, non-Hispanic/Latino), 108 international. Average age 30. 940 applicants, 46% accepted, 193 enrolled. In 2013, 221 master's, 4 other advanced degrees awarded. *Entrance requirements:* For master's, GMAT, resume, personal statement, interview, 2 letters of recommendation, transcripts. Additional exam requirements/recommendations for international students: Required—TOEFL (minimum score 100 iBT). *Application deadline:* Applications are processed on a rolling basis. Application fee: $100. Electronic applications accepted. *Expenses:* Contact institution. *Financial support:* Fellowships, career-related internships or fieldwork, Federal Work-Study, institutionally sponsored loans, and tuition waivers (partial) available. Support available to part-time students. Financial award application deadline: 2/1. *Unit head:* Dr. Michael Ginzberg, Dean, 202-885-1985, E-mail: ginzberg@american.edu. *Application contact:* Jason Kennedy, Associate Director of Graduate Admissions, 202-885-1968, E-mail: jkennedy@american.edu.
Website: http://www.kogod.american.edu/.

Arizona State University at the Tempe campus, W. P. Carey School of Business, Department of Marketing, Tempe, AZ 85287-4106. Offers business administration (marketing) (PhD); real estate development (MRED). Part-time and evening/weekend programs available. Postbaccalaureate distance learning degree programs offered. *Degree requirements:* For master's, thesis or alternative, capstone project, interactive Program of Study (iPOS) submitted before completing 50 percent of required credit hours; for doctorate, comprehensive exam, thesis/dissertation, interactive Program of Study (iPOS) submitted before completing 50 percent of required credit hours. *Entrance requirements:* For master's, GMAT, GRE, or LSAT, minimum GPA of 3.0 in last 2 years of work leading to bachelor's degree, 3 personal references, resume, official transcripts, personal statement; for doctorate, GMAT, minimum GPA of 3.0 in last 2 years of work leading to bachelor's degree, 3 letters of recommendation, personal statement/essay. Additional exam requirements/recommendations for international students: Required—TOEFL (minimum score 550 paper-based; 80 iBT), IELTS (minimum score 6.5). Electronic applications accepted. *Expenses:* Contact institution. *Faculty research:* Service marketing and management, strategic marketing, customer portfolio management, characteristics and skills of high-performing managers, market orientation, market segmentation, consumer behavior, marketing strategy, new product development, management of innovation, social influences on consumption, e-commerce, market research methodology.

Auburn University, Graduate School, Interdepartmental Programs, Program in Real Estate Development, Auburn University, AL 36849. Offers MRED. *Faculty:* 10 full-time (1 woman). *Students:* 28 part-time (2 women); includes 7 minority (6 Black or African American, non-Hispanic/Latino; 1 American Indian or Alaska Native, non-Hispanic/Latino). Average age 38. 23 applicants, 87% accepted, 14 enrolled. In 2013, 14 master's awarded. *Expenses:* Tuition, state resident: full-time $8262; part-time $459 per credit hour. Tuition, nonresident: full-time $24,786; part-time $1377 per credit hour. Tuition and fees vary according to degree level and program. *Unit head:* Jana Smith, Assistant Director, 334-844-5078, E-mail: mred.info@auburn.edu. *Application contact:* Dr. George Flowers, Dean of the Graduate School, 334-844-2125.
Website: http://mred.auburn.edu/.

Baruch College of the City University of New York, Zicklin School of Business, Department of Real Estate, New York, NY 10010-5585. Offers MBA, MS.

Baylor University, School of Law, Waco, TX 76798-7288. Offers administrative practice (JD); business litigation (JD); business transactions (JD); criminal practice (JD); estate planning (JD); general civil litigation (JD); healthcare (JD); intellectual property (JD); law (JD); real estate and natural resources (JD); JD/M Tax; JD/MBA; JD/MPPA. *Accreditation:* ABA. *Faculty:* 30 full-time (7 women), 45 part-time/adjunct (5 women). *Students:* 371 full-time (163 women), 8 part-time (2 women); includes 71 minority (6 Black or African American, non-Hispanic/Latino; 9 American Indian or Alaska Native, non-Hispanic/Latino; 14 Asian, non-Hispanic/Latino; 28 Hispanic/Latino; 14 Two or more races, non-Hispanic/Latino). Average age 24. 2,226 applicants, 37% accepted, 86 enrolled. In 2013, 176 doctorates awarded. *Entrance requirements:* For doctorate, LSAT. Additional exam requirements/recommendations for international students: Recommended—TOEFL. *Application deadline:* For fall admission, 3/1 for domestic and international students; for spring admission, 11/1 for domestic and international students; for summer admission, 2/1 for domestic and international students. Applications are processed on a rolling basis. Application fee: $0. Electronic applications accepted. Application fee is waived when completed online. *Expenses:* Contact institution. *Financial support:* In 2013–14, 296 students received support. Career-related internships or fieldwork and scholarships/grants available. Financial award application deadline: 3/1; financial award applicants required to submit FAFSA. *Unit head:* Dr. Bradley J. B. Toben, Dean, 254-710-1911, Fax: 254-710-2316. *Application contact:* Nicole Neeley, Assistant Dean of Admissions, 254-710-1911, Fax: 254-710-2316, E-mail: nicole_neeley@baylor.edu.
Website: http://www.baylor.edu/law.

Brandeis University, International Business School, Waltham, MA 02454-9110. Offers asset management (MBA); business economics (MBA); corporate finance (MBA); data analytics (MBA); finance (MSF), including asset management, corporate finance, real estate, risk management; international economic policy analysis (MBA); international economics and finance (MA, PhD); marketing (MBA); real estate (MBA); risk management (MBA); sustainability (MBA). Part-time and evening/weekend programs available. *Degree requirements:* For doctorate, thesis/dissertation. *Entrance requirements:* For master's, GMAT or GRE General Test (waived for applicants with at least 2 years of work experience applying to MSF); for doctorate, GRE General Test. Additional exam requirements/recommendations for international students: Required—TOEFL (minimum score 600 paper-based; 100 iBT), IELTS (minimum score 7). Electronic applications accepted. *Faculty research:* International economic policy analysis, U.S. economic policy analysis, real estate, strategy and municipal finance.

California State University, Sacramento, Office of Graduate Studies, College of Business Administration, Sacramento, CA 95819. Offers accountancy (MS); business administration (IMBA, MBA); human resources (MBA); urban land development (MBA).

Accreditation: AACSB. Part-time and evening/weekend programs available. *Degree requirements:* For master's, thesis or alternative, writing proficiency exam. *Entrance requirements:* For master's, GMAT. Additional exam requirements/recommendations for international students: Required—TOEFL. *Application deadline:* For fall admission, 2/1 for domestic students, 3/1 for international students; for spring admission, 9/15 for domestic students, 9/30 for international students. Applications are processed on a rolling basis. Application fee: $55. Electronic applications accepted. *Financial support:* Research assistantships, teaching assistantships, career-related internships or fieldwork, and Federal Work-Study available. Support available to part-time students. Financial award applicants required to submit FAFSA. *Unit head:* Dr. Sanjay Varshney, Dean, 916-278-6942, Fax: 916-278-5793, E-mail: cba@csus.edu. *Application contact:* Jose Martinez, Graduate Admissions Supervisor, 916-278-7871, E-mail: martinj@skymail.csus.edu.
Website: http://www.cba.csus.edu.

Clemson University, Graduate School, College of Architecture, Arts, and Humanities, Department of Planning, Development and Preservation and College of Business and Behavioral Science, Program in Real Estate Development, Greenville, SC 29601. Offers MRED. *Faculty:* 6 full-time (1 woman), 2 part-time/adjunct (0 women). *Students:* 31 full-time (3 women), 1 (woman) part-time; includes 5 minority (2 Black or African American, non-Hispanic/Latino; 2 Asian, non-Hispanic/Latino; 1 Hispanic/Latino). Average age 26. 37 applicants, 62% accepted, 16 enrolled. In 2013, 14 master's awarded. *Entrance requirements:* For master's, GRE or GMAT, 3 letters of recommendation, resume, personal statement, transcripts. Additional exam requirements/recommendations for international students: Required—TOEFL (minimum score 600 paper-based). *Application deadline:* For fall admission, 2/15 priority date for domestic and international students. Applications are processed on a rolling basis. Application fee: $70 ($80 for international students). Electronic applications accepted. *Expenses:* Contact institution. *Financial support:* In 2013–14, 8 students received support, including 8 fellowships (averaging $1,719 per year); career-related internships or fieldwork, scholarships/grants, and health care benefits also available. *Faculty research:* Real estate education, real estate investment/finance, sustainability, public private partnership, historic preservation. *Unit head:* Dr. Robert C. Benedict, Director, 864-656-2476, Fax: 864-656-7519, E-mail: benedic@clemson.edu. *Application contact:* Amy Matthews, Program Coordinator, 864-656-4257, E-mail: matthe3@clemson.edu.
Website: http://www.clemson.edu/mred.

Cleveland State University, College of Graduate Studies, Maxine Goodman Levin College of Urban Affairs, Program in Environmental Studies, Cleveland, OH 44115. Offers environmental nonprofit management (MAES); environmental planning (MAES); geographic information systems (Certificate); policy and administration (MAES); sustainable economic development (MAES); urban economic development (Certificate); urban real estate development and finance (Certificate); JD/MAES. Part-time and evening/weekend programs available. *Faculty:* 21 full-time (10 women), 11 part-time/adjunct (3 women). *Students:* 2 full-time (both women), 5 part-time (3 women); includes 1 minority (Hispanic/Latino). Average age 34. 4 applicants, 25% accepted. In 2013, 11 master's awarded. *Degree requirements:* For master's, thesis or alternative, exit project. *Entrance requirements:* For master's, GRE General Test (minimum score: verbal and quantitative combined 40th percentile, analytical writing 4.0), minimum GPA of 3.0. Additional exam requirements/recommendations for international students: Required—TOEFL (minimum score 525 paper-based; 65 iBT), IELTS or ITEP. *Application deadline:* For fall admission, 7/15 priority date for domestic students, 5/15 for international students; for spring admission, 11/1 for international students. Applications are processed on a rolling basis. Application fee: $30. Electronic applications accepted. *Expenses:* Tuition, state resident: full-time $8335; part-time $521 per credit hour. Tuition, nonresident: full-time $15,670; part-time $979 per credit hour. *Required fees:* $50; $25 per semester. *Financial support:* In 2013–14, 4 students received support, including 4 research assistantships with full and partial tuition reimbursements available (averaging $3,625 per year); career-related internships or fieldwork, scholarships/grants, traineeships, and unspecified assistantships also available. Support available to part-time students. Financial award application deadline: 3/1; financial award applicants required to submit FAFSA. *Faculty research:* Environmental policy and administration, environmental planning, geographic information systems (GIS), urban sustainability planning and management, energy policy, land re-use. *Unit head:* Dr. Sanda Kaufman, Director, 216-687-2367, Fax: 216-687-9342, E-mail: s.kaufman@csuohio.edu. *Application contact:* David Arrighi, Graduate Academic Advisor, 216-523-7522, Fax: 216-687-5398, E-mail: urbanprograms@csuohio.edu.
Website: http://urban.csuohio.edu/academics/graduate/maes/.

Cleveland State University, College of Graduate Studies, Maxine Goodman Levin College of Urban Affairs, Program in Urban Planning, Design, and Development, Cleveland, OH 44115. Offers economic development (MUPDD); environmental sustainability (MUPDD); geographic information systems (MUPDD, Certificate); historic preservation (MUPDD); housing and neighborhood development (MUPDD); urban economic development (Certificate); urban real estate development and finance (MUPDD, Certificate); JD/MUPDD. *Accreditation:* ACSP. Part-time and evening/weekend programs available. *Faculty:* 21 full-time (10 women), 11 part-time/adjunct (3 women). *Students:* 11 full-time (5 women), 25 part-time (10 women); includes 8 minority (2 Black or African American, non-Hispanic/Latino; 1 Asian, non-Hispanic/Latino; 2 Hispanic/Latino; 3 Two or more races, non-Hispanic/Latino), 3 international. Average age 38. 48 applicants, 56% accepted, 5 enrolled. In 2013, 23 master's awarded. *Degree requirements:* For master's, thesis or alternative, planning studio. *Entrance requirements:* For master's, GRE General Test (minimum score: 50th percentile combined verbal and quantitative, 4.0 analytical writing), minimum GPA of 3.0. Additional exam requirements/recommendations for international students: Required—TOEFL (minimum score 525 paper-based; 65 iBT), IELTS or ITEP. *Application deadline:* For fall admission, 7/15 priority date for domestic students, 5/15 for international students; for spring admission, 11/1 for international students. Applications are processed on a rolling basis. Application fee: $30. Electronic applications accepted. *Expenses:* Tuition, state resident: full-time $8335; part-time $521 per credit hour. Tuition, nonresident: full-time $15,670; part-time $979 per credit hour. *Required fees:* $50; $25 per semester. *Financial support:* In 2013–14, 10 students received support, including 7 research assistantships with full and partial tuition reimbursements available (averaging $7,200 per year), 3 teaching assistantships with full and partial tuition reimbursements available (averaging $4,000 per year); career-related internships or fieldwork, Federal Work-Study, scholarships/grants, tuition waivers, and unspecified assistantships also available. Support available to part-time students. Financial award application deadline: 3/1; financial award applicants required to submit FAFSA. *Faculty research:* Housing and neighborhood development, urban housing policy, environmental sustainability, economic development, GIS and planning decision support. *Unit head:*

Dr. Dennis Keating, Director, 216-687-2298, Fax: 216-687-2013, E-mail: w.keating@csuohio.edu. *Application contact:* David Arrighi, Graduate Academic Advisor, 216-523-7522, Fax: 216-687-5398, E-mail: urbanprograms@csuohio.edu.
Website: http://urban.csuohio.edu/academics/graduate/mupdd/.

Cleveland State University, College of Graduate Studies, Maxine Goodman Levin College of Urban Affairs, Program in Urban Studies, Cleveland, OH 44115. Offers community and neighborhood development (MS); economic development (MS); law and public policy (MS); public finance (MS); urban economic development (Certificate); urban policy analysis (MS); urban real estate development (MS); urban real estate development and finance (Certificate). Part-time and evening/weekend programs available. *Faculty:* 21 full-time (10 women), 11 part-time/adjunct (3 women). *Students:* 5 full-time (1 woman), 8 part-time (2 women); includes 1 minority (Black or African American, non-Hispanic/Latino). Average age 34. 21 applicants, 29% accepted, 4 enrolled. In 2013, 8 master's awarded. *Degree requirements:* For master's, thesis or alternative, exit project. *Entrance requirements:* For master's, GRE General Test (minimum score: verbal and quantitative combined 40th percentile, analytical writing 4.0), minimum GPA of 3.0. Additional exam requirements/recommendations for international students: Required—TOEFL (minimum score 525 paper-based; 65 iBT), IELTS or ITEP. *Application deadline:* For fall admission, 1/15 priority date for domestic students, 1/15 for international students. Applications are processed on a rolling basis. Application fee: $30. Electronic applications accepted. *Expenses:* Tuition, state resident: full-time $8335; part-time $521 per credit hour. Tuition, nonresident: full-time $15,670; part-time $979 per credit hour. *Required fees:* $50; $25 per semester. *Financial support:* In 2013–14, 4 students received support, including 3 research assistantships with full and partial tuition reimbursements available (averaging $7,200 per year), 1 teaching assistantship with full and partial tuition reimbursement available (averaging $7,200 per year); career-related internships or fieldwork, scholarships/grants, traineeships, and unspecified assistantships also available. Support available to part-time students. Financial award application deadline: 3/1; financial award applicants required to submit FAFSA. *Faculty research:* Environmental issues, economic development, urban and public policy, public management. *Unit head:* Dr. Brian Mikelbank, Director, 216-875-9980, Fax: 216-687-9342, E-mail: b.mikelbank@csuohio.edu. *Application contact:* David Arrighi, Graduate Academic Advisor, 216-523-7522, Fax: 216-687-5398, E-mail: urbanprograms@csuohio.edu.
Website: http://urban.csuohio.edu/academics/graduate/msus/.

Columbia University, Graduate School of Architecture, Planning, and Preservation, Program in Real Estate Development, New York, NY 10027. Offers MS. *Degree requirements:* For master's, thesis. *Entrance requirements:* For master's, GRE General Test.

Columbia University, Graduate School of Business, MBA Program, New York, NY 10027. Offers accounting (MBA); decision, risk, and operations (MBA); entrepreneurship (MBA); finance and economics (MBA); healthcare and pharmaceutical management (MBA); human resource management (MBA); international business (MBA); leadership and ethics (MBA); management (MBA); marketing (MBA); media (MBA); private equity (MBA); real estate (MBA); social enterprise (MBA); value investing (MBA); DDS/MBA; JD/MBA; MBA/MIA; MBA/MPH; MBA/MS; MD/MBA. *Entrance requirements:* For master's, GMAT, 2 letters of recommendation. Additional exam requirements/recommendations for international students: Required—TOEFL. Electronic applications accepted. *Expenses:* Contact institution. *Faculty research:* Human decision making and behavioral research; real estate market and mortgage defaults; financial crisis and corporate governance; international business; security analysis and accounting.

Cornell University, Graduate School, Graduate Fields of Architecture, Art and Planning, Field of Real Estate, Ithaca, NY 14853-0001. Offers MPS. *Faculty:* 21 full-time (1 woman). *Students:* 45 full-time (9 women); includes 9 minority (3 Black or African American, non-Hispanic/Latino; 3 Asian, non-Hispanic/Latino; 2 Hispanic/Latino; 1 Two or more races, non-Hispanic/Latino), 23 international. Average age 29. 105 applicants, 37% accepted, 28 enrolled. In 2013, 25 master's awarded. *Degree requirements:* For master's, project paper. *Entrance requirements:* For master's, GMAT, 2 letters of recommendation, resume. Additional exam requirements/recommendations for international students: Required—TOEFL (minimum score 600 paper-based; 77 iBT). *Application deadline:* For fall admission, 1/15 for domestic students. Application fee: $95. Electronic applications accepted. *Financial support:* In 2013–14, 1 student received support, including 1 fellowship with full tuition reimbursement available; research assistantships with full tuition reimbursements available, teaching assistantships with full tuition reimbursements available, institutionally sponsored loans, scholarships/grants, health care benefits, and unspecified assistantships also available. Financial award applicants required to submit FAFSA. *Faculty research:* Smart growth, economic development, urban redevelopment, development financing, securitization of real estate. *Unit head:* Director of Graduate Studies, 607-255-7110, Fax: 607-255-0242. *Application contact:* Graduate Field Assistant, 607-255-7110, Fax: 607-255-0242, E-mail: real_estate@cornell.edu.
Website: http://www.gradschool.cornell.edu/fields.php?id-96&a-2.

DePaul University, Charles H. Kellstadt Graduate School of Business, Chicago, IL 60604. Offers accountancy (M Acc, MS, MSA); applied economics (MBA); banking (MBA); behavioral finance (MBA); brand and product management (MBA); business development (MBA); business information technology (MS); business strategy and decision-making (MBA); computational finance (MS); consumer insights (MBA); corporate finance (MBA); economic policy analysis (MS); entrepreneurship (MBA, MS); finance (MBA, MS); financial analysis (MBA); general business (MBA); health sector management (MBA); hospitality leadership (MBA); hospitality leadership and operational performance (MS); human resource management (MBA); human resources (MS); investment management (MBA); leadership and change management (MBA); management accounting (MBA); marketing (MBA, MS); marketing analysis (MS); marketing strategy and planning (MBA); operations management (MBA); organizational diversity (MBA); real estate (MS); real estate finance and investment (MBA); revenue management (MBA); sports management (MBA); strategic global marketing (MBA); strategy, execution and valuation (MBA); sustainable management (MBA, MS); taxation (MS); wealth management (MS); JD/MBA. *Accreditation:* AACSB. Part-time and evening/weekend programs available. Postbaccalaureate distance learning degree programs offered (no on-campus study). *Faculty:* 81 full-time (20 women), 45 part-time/adjunct (8 women). *Students:* 1,238 full-time (605 women), 617 part-time (223 women); includes 295 minority (71 Black or African American, non-Hispanic/Latino; 129 Asian, non-Hispanic/Latino; 74 Hispanic/Latino; 4 Native Hawaiian or other Pacific Islander, non-Hispanic/Latino; 17 Two or more races, non-Hispanic/Latino), 462 international. Average age 29. In 2013, 911 master's awarded. *Entrance requirements:* For master's, GMAT, 2 letters of recommendation, resume, essay, official transcripts. Additional exam requirements/recommendations for international students: Required—TOEFL (minimum score 550 paper-based; 80 iBT). *Application deadline:* For fall admission, 7/1 for domestic students, 6/1 for international students; for winter admission, 10/1 for domestic students, 9/1 for international students; for spring admission, 2/1 for domestic students, 1/1 for international students. Applications are processed on a rolling basis. Application fee: $60. Electronic applications accepted. *Expenses:* Contact institution. *Financial support:* Application deadline: 4/1; applicants required to submit FAFSA. *Unit head:* Robert T. Ryan, Assistant Dean and Director, 312-362-8810, Fax: 312-362-6677, E-mail: rryan1@depaul.edu. *Application contact:* James Parker, Director of Recruitment and Admission, 312-362-8810, Fax: 312-362-6677, E-mail: kgsb@depaul.edu.
Website: http://kellstadt.depaul.edu.

Drexel University, Goodwin College of Professional Studies, School of Technology and Professional Studies, Philadelphia, PA 19104-2875. Offers construction management (MS); creativity and innovation (MS); engineering technology (MS); food science (MS); hospitality management (MS); professional studies: creativity studies (MS); professional studies: e-learning leadership (MS); professional studies: homeland security management (MS); project management (MS); property management (MS); sport management (MS). Part-time and evening/weekend programs available. *Entrance requirements:* Additional exam requirements/recommendations for international students: Required—TOEFL, IELTS. Electronic applications accepted. Application fee is waived when completed online.

Florida International University, Alvah H. Chapman, Jr. Graduate School of Business, Program in Real Estate, Miami, FL 33199. Offers international real estate (MS). Part-time and evening/weekend programs available. *Entrance requirements:* For master's, GMAT or GRE, letter of intent; resume. Additional exam requirements/recommendations for international students: Required—TOEFL (minimum score 550 paper-based; 80 iBT) or IELTS (minimum score 6.5). Electronic applications accepted. *Expenses:* Contact institution. *Faculty research:* International real estate, real estate investments, commercial real estate.

George Mason University, School of Business, Fairfax, VA 22030. Offers accounting (MS, Certificate), including accounting (MS), forensic accounting (Certificate); business administration (EMBA, MBA); management of secure information systems (MS); real estate development (MS); technology management (MS). Part-time and evening/weekend programs available. Postbaccalaureate distance learning degree programs offered. *Faculty:* 82 full-time (24 women), 55 part-time/adjunct (18 women). *Students:* 275 full-time (95 women), 267 part-time (94 women); includes 140 minority (42 Black or African American, non-Hispanic/Latino; 2 American Indian or Alaska Native, non-Hispanic/Latino; 53 Asian, non-Hispanic/Latino; 31 Hispanic/Latino; 3 Native Hawaiian or other Pacific Islander, non-Hispanic/Latino; 9 Two or more races, non-Hispanic/Latino), 43 international. Average age 32. 492 applicants, 48% accepted, 134 enrolled. In 2013, 243 master's awarded. *Entrance requirements:* For master's, GMAT. Additional exam requirements/recommendations for international students: Required—TOEFL (minimum score 570 paper-based; 88 iBT), IELTS (minimum score 6.5), PTE. *Application deadline:* Applications are processed on a rolling basis. Application fee: $65 ($80 for international students). Electronic applications accepted. *Expenses:* Contact institution. *Financial support:* In 2013–14, 28 students received support, including 22 research assistantships with full and partial tuition reimbursements available (averaging $7,075 per year), 12 teaching assistantships with full and partial tuition reimbursements available (averaging $8,411 per year); career-related internships or fieldwork, Federal Work-Study, scholarships/grants, unspecified assistantships, and health care benefits (for full-time research or teaching assistantship recipients) also available. Support available to part-time students. Financial award application deadline: 3/1; financial award applicants required to submit FAFSA. *Faculty research:* Current leading global issues: offshore outsourcing, international financial risk, comparative systems of innovation. *Total annual research expenditures:* $73,719. *Unit head:* Sarah E. Nutter, Dean, 703-993-1860, Fax: 703-993-1809, E-mail: snutter@gmu.edu. *Application contact:* Nancy Doernhoefer, Admissions Specialist, 703-993-4128, Fax: 703-993-1778, E-mail: ndoernho@gmu.edu.
Website: http://business.gmu.edu/.

Georgetown University, Graduate School of Arts and Sciences, School of Continuing Studies, Washington, DC 20057. Offers American studies (MALS); Catholic studies (MALS); classical civilizations (MALS); emergency and disaster management (MPS); ethics and the professions (MALS); human resources management (MPS); humanities (MALS); individualized study (MALS); international affairs (MALS); Islam and Muslim-Christian relations (MALS); journalism (MPS); liberal studies (DLS); literature and society (MALS); medieval and early modern European studies (MALS); public relations and corporate communications (MPS); real estate (MPS); religious studies (MALS); social and public policy (MALS); sports industry management (MPS); systems engineering management (MPS); technology management (MPS); the theory and practice of American democracy (MALS); urban and regional planning (MPS); visual culture (MALS). MPS in systems engineering management offered in conjunction with Stevens Institute of Technology. *Entrance requirements:* Additional exam requirements/recommendations for international students: Required—TOEFL.

The George Washington University, School of Business, Department of Finance, Washington, DC 20052. Offers finance (MSF, PhD); finance and investments (MBA); real estate and urban development (MBA). Part-time and evening/weekend programs available. *Faculty:* 18 full-time (4 women). *Students:* 207 full-time (83 women), 11 part-time (3 women); includes 21 minority (9 Black or African American, non-Hispanic/Latino; 4 Asian, non-Hispanic/Latino; 7 Hispanic/Latino; 1 Two or more races, non-Hispanic/Latino), 164 international. Average age 28. 780 applicants, 25% accepted, 91 enrolled. In 2013, 115 master's awarded. *Degree requirements:* For doctorate, thesis/dissertation. *Entrance requirements:* For master's, GMAT; for doctorate, GMAT or GRE. Additional exam requirements/recommendations for international students: Required—TOEFL. *Application deadline:* For fall admission, 4/1 priority date for domestic students; for spring admission, 10/1 for domestic students. Applications are processed on a rolling basis. Application fee: $75. *Financial support:* In 2013–14, 38 students received support. Fellowships, teaching assistantships, career-related internships or fieldwork, Federal Work-Study, and institutionally sponsored loans available. Financial award application deadline: 4/1. *Unit head:* Robert Van Order, Chair, 202-994-2559, E-mail: rvo@gwu.edu. *Application contact:* Kristin Williams, Assistant Vice President for Graduate and Special Enrollment Management, 202-994-0467, Fax: 202-994-0371, E-mail: ksw@gwu.edu.

Georgia State University, J. Mack Robinson College of Business, Department of Real Estate, Atlanta, GA 30302-3083. Offers hotel real estate (MBA); real estate (MBA, MS, PhD, Certificate). Part-time and evening/weekend programs available. *Faculty:* 3 full-time (1 woman). *Students:* 15 full-time (2 women), 11 part-time (3 women); includes 3 minority (all Black or African American, non-Hispanic/Latino), 8 international. Average age 32. 30 applicants, 37% accepted, 9 enrolled. In 2013, 12 master's, 1 doctorate awarded. *Degree requirements:* For doctorate, comprehensive exam, thesis/dissertation. *Entrance requirements:* For master's, GRE or GMAT, transcripts from all institutions attended, resume, essays; for doctorate, GRE or GMAT, three letters of recommendation, personal statement, transcripts from all institutions attended, resume. Additional exam requirements/recommendations for international students: Required—TOEFL (minimum score 610 paper-based; 101 iBT), IELTS (minimum score 7). *Application deadline:* For fall admission, 5/1 priority date for domestic students, 2/1 priority date for international students; for spring admission, 9/15 priority date for domestic students, 4/1 priority date for international students. Applications are processed on a rolling basis. Application fee: $50. Electronic applications accepted. *Expenses: Tuition, area resident:* Full-time $4176; part-time $348 per credit hour. Tuition, state resident: full-time $14,544; part-time $1212 per credit hour. Tuition,

nonresident: full-time $14,544; part-time $1212 per credit hour. Tuition and fees vary according to course load and program. *Financial support:* Research assistantships, teaching assistantships, scholarships/grants, and unspecified assistantships available. *Faculty research:* International real estate investments, corporate real estate, capital formation, consumer behavior applied to real estate, real estate development. *Unit head:* Dr. Gerald Gay, III, Professor of Finance/Interim Chair of the Department of Real Estate, 404-413-7720, Fax: 404-413-7736. *Application contact:* Toby McChesney, Assistant Dean for Graduate Recruiting and Student Services, 404-413-7167, Fax: 404-413-7162, E-mail: rcbgradadmissions@gsu.edu.
Website: http://realestate.robinson.gsu.edu/.

Hofstra University, Frank G. Zarb School of Business, Programs in Finance, Hempstead, NY 11549. Offers business administration (MBA), including finance, real estate management; corporate finance (Advanced Certificate); finance (MS); investment management (Advanced Certificate); quantitative finance (MS).

Instituto Centroamericano de Administración de Empresas, Graduate Programs, La Garita, Costa Rica. Offers agribusiness management (MIAM); business administration (EMBA); finance (MBA); real estate management (MGREM); sustainable development (MBA); technology (MBA). *Degree requirements:* For master's, comprehensive exam, essay. *Entrance requirements:* For master's, GMAT or GRE General Test, fluency in Spanish, interview, letters of recommendation, minimum 1 year of work experience. Additional exam requirements/recommendations for international students: Recommended—TOEFL. Electronic applications accepted. *Faculty research:* Competitiveness, production.

John Marshall Law School, Graduate and Professional Programs, Chicago, IL 60604-3968. Offers employee benefits (LL M, MS); estate planning (LL M); global legal studies (LL M); information technology (MS); information technology and privacy law (LL M); intellectual property (LL M, MS); international business and trade (LL M); law (JD); real estate (LL M, MS); taxation (LL M, MS); trial advocacy (LL M); JD/LL M; JD/MA; JD/MBA; JD/MPA. JD/MBA offered jointly with Dominican University; JD/MA and JD/MPA with Roosevelt University. *Accreditation:* ABA. Part-time and evening/weekend programs available. *Faculty:* 71 full-time (26 women), 132 part-time/adjunct (49 women). *Students:* 1,045 full-time (512 women), 421 part-time (211 women); includes 403 minority (152 Black or African American, non-Hispanic/Latino; 8 American Indian or Alaska Native, non-Hispanic/Latino; 89 Asian, non-Hispanic/Latino; 138 Hispanic/Latino; 3 Native Hawaiian or other Pacific Islander, non-Hispanic/Latino; 13 Two or more races, non-Hispanic/Latino), 57 international. Average age 27. 2,694 applicants, 73% accepted, 419 enrolled. In 2013, 81 master's, 445 doctorates awarded. *Degree requirements:* For master's, 24 credits; for doctorate, 90 credits. *Entrance requirements:* For master's, JD; for doctorate, LSAT. Additional exam requirements/recommendations for international students: Required—TOEFL. *Application deadline:* For fall admission, 3/1 priority date for domestic and international students; for spring admission, 10/15 priority date for domestic and international students. Applications are processed on a rolling basis. Application fee: $0. Electronic applications accepted. *Expenses:* Contact institution. *Financial support:* In 2013–14, 1,275 students received support. Scholarships/grants and tuition waivers (full and partial) available. Support available to part-time students. Financial award application deadline: 4/1; financial award applicants required to submit FAFSA. *Unit head:* John Corkery, Dean, 312-427-2737. *Application contact:* William B. Powers, Associate Dean of Admission and Student Affairs, 800-537-4280, Fax: 312-427-5136, E-mail: admission@jmls.edu.

Johns Hopkins University, Carey Business School, Real Estate and Infrastructure Program, Baltimore, MD 21218-2699. Offers MS. Part-time and evening/weekend programs available. *Faculty:* 29 full-time (6 women), 135 part-time/adjunct (29 women). *Students:* 32 full-time (18 women), 65 part-time (20 women); includes 14 minority (6 Black or African American, non-Hispanic/Latino; 4 Asian, non-Hispanic/Latino; 3 Hispanic/Latino; 1 Two or more races, non-Hispanic/Latino), 22 international. Average age 29. 90 applicants, 77% accepted, 35 enrolled. In 2013, 57 degrees awarded. *Degree requirements:* For master's, 36 credits including final project. *Entrance requirements:* For master's, GMAT, GRE, or LSAT (for full-time students only), minimum GPA of 3.0, resume, work experience, two letters of recommendation. Additional exam requirements/recommendations for international students: Required—TOEFL (minimum score 600 paper-based; 100 iBT). *Application deadline:* For fall admission, 4/1 for international students; for spring admission, 9/15 for international students. Applications are processed on a rolling basis. Application fee: $100. Electronic applications accepted. *Financial support:* Scholarships/grants available. Support available to part-time students. Financial award application deadline: 4/15; financial award applicants required to submit FAFSA. *Unit head:* Dr. Michael Anikeeff, Program Director, 410-234-9404, E-mail: mikea@jhu.edu. *Application contact:* Robin Greenberg, Admissions Coordinator, 410-234-9227, Fax: 443-529-1554, E-mail: carey.admissions@jhu.edu.
Website: http://carey.jhu.edu/academics/master-of-science/ms-in-real-estate-infrastructure/.

Longwood University, College of Graduate and Professional Studies, College of Business and Economics, Farmville, VA 23909. Offers general business (MBA); real estate (MBA); retail management (MBA). *Accreditation:* AACSB. Part-time programs available. Postbaccalaureate distance learning degree programs offered (minimal on-campus study). *Faculty:* 15 full-time (6 women). *Students:* 1 full-time (0 women), 16 part-time (9 women); includes 1 minority (Two or more races, non-Hispanic/Latino). 7 applicants, 71% accepted, 5 enrolled. In 2013, 13 master's awarded. *Degree requirements:* For master's, internship. *Entrance requirements:* For master's, GMAT. Additional exam requirements/recommendations for international students: Required—TOEFL (minimum score 570 paper-based), IELTS (minimum score 6.5). *Application deadline:* For fall admission, 5/1 priority date for domestic students; for summer admission, 2/1 priority date for domestic students. Applications are processed on a rolling basis. Application fee: $50. Electronic applications accepted. *Expenses:* Tuition, state resident: full-time $7506; part-time $327 per credit hour. Tuition, nonresident: full-time $17,100; part-time $837 per credit hour. Tuition and fees vary according to course load and campus/location. *Unit head:* Abigail H. O'Connor, Assistant Dean and MBA Program Coordinator, 434-395-2043, E-mail: oconnorah@longwood.edu. *Application contact:* College of Graduate and Professional Studies, 434-395-2380, Fax: 434-395-2750, E-mail: graduate@longwood.edu.
Website: http://www.longwood.edu/business/mba.htm.

Marquette University, Graduate School of Management, Department of Economics, Milwaukee, WI 53201-1881. Offers business economics (MSAE); financial economics (MSAE); international economics (MSAE); marketing research (MSAE); real estate economics (MSAE). Part-time and evening/weekend programs available. *Faculty:* 15 full-time (5 women), 2 part-time/adjunct (1 woman). *Students:* 25 full-time (7 women), 34 part-time (11 women); includes 6 minority (2 Black or African American, non-Hispanic/Latino; 2 Asian, non-Hispanic/Latino; 2 Hispanic/Latino), 24 international. Average age 25. 81 applicants, 47% accepted, 27 enrolled. In 2013, 26 master's awarded. *Degree requirements:* For master's, comprehensive exam, professional project. *Entrance requirements:* For master's, GMAT or GRE General Test. Additional exam requirements/recommendations for international students: Required—TOEFL (minimum score 550 paper-based; 88 iBT), IELTS (minimum score 6.5), PTE. *Application deadline:* For fall admission, 2/15 for domestic and international students. Applications are processed on a rolling basis. Application fee: $50. Electronic applications accepted. *Financial support:* In 2013–14, 2 fellowships, 7 teaching assistantships were awarded; research assistantships, Federal Work-Study, institutionally sponsored loans, scholarships/grants, and tuition waivers (full and partial) also available. Support available to part-time students. Financial award application deadline: 2/15. *Faculty research:* Monetary and fiscal policy in open economy, housing and regional migration, political economy of taxation and state/local government. *Unit head:* Dr. Mark Eppli, Dean, 414-288-5724. *Application contact:* Dr. Jeanne Simmons, Associate Dean, 414-288-7145.
Website: http://business.marquette.edu/academics/msae.

Marylhurst University, Department of Business Administration, Marylhurst, OR 97036-0261. Offers finance (MBA); general management (MBA); government policy and administration (MBA); green development (MBA); health care management (MBA); marketing (MBA); natural and organic resources (MBA); nonprofit management (MBA); organizational behavior (MBA); real estate (MBA); renewable energy (MBA); sustainable business (MBA). Part-time and evening/weekend programs available. Postbaccalaureate distance learning degree programs offered (no on-campus study). *Degree requirements:* For master's, comprehensive exam, capstone course. *Entrance requirements:* For master's, GMAT (if GPA less than 3.0 and fewer than 5 years of work experience), interview, resume, 2 letters of recommendation. Additional exam requirements/recommendations for international students: Recommended—TOEFL (minimum score 550 paper-based; 80 iBT). Electronic applications accepted.

Massachusetts Institute of Technology, School of Architecture and Planning, Center for Real Estate, Cambridge, MA 02139-4307. Offers real estate development (MSRED). *Faculty:* 4 full-time (0 women), 5 part-time/adjunct (1 woman). *Students:* 26 full-time (6 women); includes 5 minority (3 Asian, non-Hispanic/Latino; 2 Hispanic/Latino), 15 international. Average age 31. 66 applicants, 50% accepted, 23 enrolled. In 2013, 21 master's awarded. *Degree requirements:* For master's, thesis. *Entrance requirements:* For master's, GMAT. Additional exam requirements/recommendations for international students: Required—TOEFL (minimum score 100 iBT), IELTS (minimum score 7.5). *Application deadline:* For fall admission, 1/5 for domestic and international students. Application fee: $75. Electronic applications accepted. *Expenses: Tuition:* Full-time $43,210; part-time $670 per credit hour. *Required fees:* $288. *Financial support:* In 2013–14, 9 students received support, including 2 fellowships, 1 research assistantship (averaging $31,500 per year); Federal Work-Study, institutionally sponsored loans, scholarships/grants, health care benefits, and unspecified assistantships also available. *Faculty research:* Real estate finance and investment, real estate development, urban design, planning, project management, infrastructure delivery methods, urban economics, entrepreneurship, strategic planning, housing, leadership development, international housing economics and finance, mortgage securitization. *Unit head:* W. Tod McGrath, Interim Chair, 617-253-4373, Fax: 617-258-6991, E-mail: mit-cre@mit.edu. *Application contact:* W. Tod McGrath, Interim Chair, 617-253-4373, Fax: 617-258-6991, E-mail: mit-cre@mit.edu.
Website: http://web.mit.edu/cre/.

Monmouth University, The Graduate School, Leon Hess Business School, West Long Branch, NJ 07764-1898. Offers accounting (MBA, Post-Master's Certificate); business (MBA); finance (MBA); real estate (MBA). *Accreditation:* AACSB. Part-time and evening/weekend programs available. *Faculty:* 32 full-time (10 women), 5 part-time/adjunct (0 women). *Students:* 92 full-time (35 women), 98 part-time (45 women); includes 30 minority (9 Black or African American, non-Hispanic/Latino; 12 Asian, non-Hispanic/Latino; 6 Hispanic/Latino; 3 Two or more races, non-Hispanic/Latino), 9 international. Average age 27. 157 applicants, 82% accepted, 84 enrolled. In 2013, 134 master's awarded. *Degree requirements:* For master's, capstone course. *Entrance requirements:* For master's, GMAT, minimum GPA of 3.0 in major, 2.75 overall. Additional exam requirements/recommendations for international students: Required—TOEFL (minimum score 550 paper-based; 79 iBT), IELTS (minimum score 6), Michigan English Language Assessment Battery (minimum score 77). *Application deadline:* For fall admission, 7/15 priority date for domestic students, 6/1 for international students; for spring admission, 11/15 priority date for domestic students, 11/1 for international students. Applications are processed on a rolling basis. Application fee: $50. Electronic applications accepted. *Expenses: Tuition:* Part-time $1004 per credit hour. *Required fees:* $157 per semester. *Financial support:* In 2013–14, 119 students received support, including 281 fellowships (averaging $1,244 per year), 27 research assistantships (averaging $6,273 per year); career-related internships or fieldwork, scholarships/grants, and unspecified assistantships also available. Support available to part-time students. Financial award applicants required to submit FAFSA. *Faculty research:* Information technology and marketing, behavioral research in accounting, human resources, management of technology. *Unit head:* Dr. Susan Gupta, MBA Program Director, 732-571-3639, Fax: 732-263-5517, E-mail: sgupta@monmouth.edu. *Application contact:* Lauren Vento-Cifelli, Associate Vice President of Undergraduate and Graduate Admission, 732-571-3452, Fax: 732-263-5123, E-mail: gradadm@monmouth.edu.
Website: http://www.monmouth.edu/mba.

See Display on page 116 and Close-Up on page 187.

New York University, School of Continuing and Professional Studies, Schack Institute of Real Estate, Program in Real Estate, New York, NY 10012-1019. Offers real estate (Advanced Certificate); strategic real estate management (MS). Part-time and evening/weekend programs available. *Faculty:* 10 full-time (4 women), 60 part-time/adjunct (6 women). *Students:* 103 full-time (36 women), 235 part-time (48 women); includes 36 minority (8 Black or African American, non-Hispanic/Latino; 1 American Indian or Alaska Native, non-Hispanic/Latino; 20 Asian, non-Hispanic/Latino; 4 Hispanic/Latino; 3 Two or more races, non-Hispanic/Latino), 75 international. Average age 30. 212 applicants, 79% accepted, 102 enrolled. In 2013, 129 master's, 15 other advanced degrees awarded. *Degree requirements:* For master's, thesis, capstone. *Entrance requirements:* For master's, bachelor's degree, resume with relevant professional work, internship or volunteer experience, two letters of recommendation, statement of purpose. Additional exam requirements/recommendations for international students: Required—TOEFL (minimum score 600 paper-based; 100 iBT), IELTS (minimum score 7). *Application deadline:* For fall admission, 2/1 priority date for domestic and international students; for spring admission, 10/15 priority date for domestic students, 8/15 priority date for international students. Applications are processed on a rolling basis. Application fee: $150. Electronic applications accepted. *Expenses: Tuition:* Full-time $35,856; part-time $1494 per unit. *Required fees:* $1408; $64 per unit. $473 per term. Tuition and fees vary according to course load and program. *Financial support:* In 2013–14, 83 students received support, including 83 fellowships (averaging $2,116 per year); scholarships/grants also available. Support available to part-time students. Financial award application deadline: 3/2. *Faculty research:* Economics and market cycles, international property rights, comparative metropolitan economies, current market trends. *Unit head:* Rosemary Scanlon, Divisional Dean, 212-992-3250. *Application contact:* Office of Admissions, 212-998-7100, E-mail: scps.gradadmissions@nyu.edu.
Website: http://www.scps.nyu.edu/areas-of-study/real-estate/graduate-programs/.

Northwestern University, The Graduate School, Kellogg School of Management, Management Programs, Evanston, IL 60208. Offers accounting information and management (MBA, PhD); analytical finance (MBA); business administration (MBA);

decision sciences (MBA); entrepreneurship and innovation (MBA); finance (MBA, PhD); health enterprise management (MBA); human resources management (MBA); international business (MBA); management and organizations (MBA, PhD); management and organizations and sociology (PhD); management and strategy (MBA); management studies (MS); managerial analytics (MBA); managerial economics (MBA); managerial economics and strategy (PhD); marketing (MBA, PhD); marketing management (MBA); media management (MBA); operations management (MBA, PhD); real estate (MBA); social enterprise at Kellogg (MBA); JD/MBA. Part-time and evening/weekend programs available. Terminal master's awarded for partial completion of doctoral program. *Degree requirements:* For doctorate, thesis/dissertation, 2 years of coursework, qualifying (field) exam and candidacy, summer research papers and presentations to faculty, proposal defense, final exam/defense. *Entrance requirements:* For master's, GMAT, GRE, interview, 2 letters of recommendation, college transcripts, resume, essays, Kellogg honor code; for doctorate, GMAT, GRE, statement of purpose, transcripts, 2 letters of recommendation, resume, interview. Additional exam requirements/recommendations for international students: Required—TOEFL, IELTS. Electronic applications accepted. *Expenses:* Contact institution. *Faculty research:* Business cycles and international finance, health policy, networks, non-market strategy, consumer psychology.

Nova Southeastern University, H. Wayne Huizenga School of Business and Entrepreneurship, Fort Lauderdale, FL 33314-7796. Offers accounting (M Acc); business administration (MBA, DBA); human resource management (MSHRM); international business administration (MIBA); leadership (MS); public administration (MPA, DPA); real estate development (MS); taxation (M Tax); JD/MBA; Pharm D/MBA. Part-time and evening/weekend programs available. Postbaccalaureate distance learning degree programs offered (minimal on-campus study). *Faculty:* 67 full-time (24 women), 135 part-time/adjunct (37 women). *Students:* 207 full-time (110 women), 3,069 part-time (1,888 women); includes 2,213 minority (1,077 Black or African American, non-Hispanic/Latino; 2 American Indian or Alaska Native, non-Hispanic/Latino; 108 Asian, non-Hispanic/Latino; 975 Hispanic/Latino; 2 Native Hawaiian or other Pacific Islander, non-Hispanic/Latino; 49 Two or more races, non-Hispanic/Latino), 190 international. Average age 33. 1,291 applicants, 68% accepted, 636 enrolled. In 2013, 1,146 master's, 17 doctorates awarded. *Degree requirements:* For master's, thesis optional; for doctorate, comprehensive exam, thesis/dissertation. *Entrance requirements:* For doctorate, GMAT. Additional exam requirements/recommendations for international students: Required—TOEFL (minimum score 550 paper-based; 79 iBT), IELTS (minimum score 6). *Application deadline:* Applications are processed on a rolling basis. Application fee: $50. Electronic applications accepted. *Financial support:* In 2013–14, 2 students received support. Federal Work-Study and scholarships/grants available. Support available to part-time students. Financial award applicants required to submit FAFSA. *Faculty research:* Reputation management, call centers, international social capital, corporate earnings guidance, corporate governance. *Unit head:* Dr. J. Preston Jones, Dean, 954-262-5127, E-mail: fieldsm@nova.edu. *Application contact:* Karen Goldberg, Associate Director of Recruitment and Special Events, 954-262-5039, Fax: 954-262-3822, E-mail: karen@nova.edu.
Website: http://www.huizenga.nova.edu.

Pacific States University, College of Business, Los Angeles, CA 90006. Offers accounting (MBA); finance (MBA); international business (MBA, DBA); management of information technology (MBA); real estate management (MBA). Part-time and evening/weekend programs available. Postbaccalaureate distance learning degree programs offered (no on-campus study). *Degree requirements:* For doctorate, comprehensive exam, thesis/dissertation. *Entrance requirements:* For master's, minimum undergraduate GPA of 2.5 during last 90 hours of course work. Additional exam requirements/recommendations for international students: Required—TOEFL (minimum score 500 paper-based; 61 iBT), IELTS (minimum score 5.5).

Pontificia Universidad Catolica Madre y Maestra, Graduate School, Faculty of Social and Administrative Sciences, Santiago, Dominican Republic. Offers business administration (MBA), including business development, finance, international business, management skills (M Mgmt, MBA), marketing, operations, strategic cost management, strategy, tourist destination planning and management; law (LL M), including civil law, corporate business law, criminal law, international relations, real estate law; management (M Mgmt), including higher financial management, insurance program administration, management skills (M Mgmt, MBA); psychology (MA), including clinical child and adolescent psychology, forensic psychology; strategic human resources (EMBA).

Roosevelt University, Graduate Division, Walter E. Heller College of Business Administration, School of Finance and Real Estate, Chicago, IL 60605. Offers commercial real estate development (Certificate); real estate (MBA, MS).

Southern Methodist University, Cox School of Business, MBA Program, Dallas, TX 75275. Offers accounting (MBA, PMBA); business administration (EMBA); finance (MBA); financial statement analysis (PMBA); general business (MBA); information technology and operations management (MBA); management (MBA); marketing (MBA); real estate (MBA); strategy (MBA); strategy and entrepreneurship (MBA); JD/MBA; MA/MBA. Part-time and evening/weekend programs available. *Entrance requirements:* For master's, GMAT. Additional exam requirements/recommendations for international students: Required—TOEFL. Electronic applications accepted. *Expenses:* Contact institution. *Faculty research:* Corporate finance, financial reporting, modeling consumer decision-making, competition between national brands and store brands, institutional determinants of firms' strategy.

Texas A&M University, Mays Business School, Department of Finance, College Station, TX 77843. Offers finance (MS, PhD); land economics and real estate (MRE). *Faculty:* 16. *Students:* 159 full-time (61 women), 1 part-time (0 women); includes 16 minority (7 Asian, non-Hispanic/Latino; 7 Hispanic/Latino; 2 Two or more races, non-Hispanic/Latino), 14 international. Average age 24. 127 applicants, 35% accepted, 36 enrolled. In 2013, 120 master's, 2 doctorates awarded. Terminal master's awarded for partial completion of doctoral program. *Degree requirements:* For master's, comprehensive exam; for doctorate, thesis/dissertation. *Entrance requirements:* For master's, GMAT; for doctorate, GMAT or GRE General Test. Additional exam requirements/recommendations for international students: Required—TOEFL. *Application deadline:* For fall admission, 3/1 priority date for domestic students; for spring admission, 8/1 for domestic students. Applications are processed on a rolling basis. Application fee: $50 ($75 for international students). *Expenses:* Tuition, state resident: full-time $4078; part-time $226.55 per credit hour. Tuition, nonresident: full-time $10,450; part-time $580.55 per credit hour. *Required fees:* $2328; $278.50 per credit hour. $642.45 per semester. *Financial support:* In 2013–14, 30 students received support. Fellowships, research assistantships, teaching assistantships, career-related internships or fieldwork, and institutionally sponsored loans available. Financial award application deadline: 2/1. *Unit head:* Dr. Sorin Sorescu, Head, 979-458-0380, Fax: 979-845-3884, E-mail: smsorescu@mays.tamu.edu. *Application contact:* Angela G. Degelman, Program Coordinator/Graduate Academic Advisor, 979-845-4858, Fax: 979-845-3884, E-mail: adegelman@mays.tamu.edu.
Website: http://mays.tamu.edu/finc/.

Universidad Iberoamericana, Graduate School, Santo Domingo D.N., Dominican Republic. Offers business administration (MBA, PMBA); constitutional law (LL M); dentistry (DMD); educational management (MA); integrated marketing communication (MA); psychopedagogical intervention (M Ed); real estate law (LL M); strategic management of human talent (MM).

University of California, Berkeley, Graduate Division, Haas School of Business, PhD in Business Administration Program, Berkeley, CA 94720-1500. Offers accounting (PhD); business and public policy (PhD); finance (PhD); management of organizations (PhD); marketing (PhD); operations management (PhD); real estate (PhD). *Accreditation:* AACSB. *Students:* 74 full-time (28 women); includes 11 minority (9 Asian, non-Hispanic/Latino; 2 Hispanic/Latino), 38 international. Average age 27. 490 applicants, 6% accepted, 14 enrolled. In 2013, 14 doctorates awarded. *Degree requirements:* For doctorate, comprehensive exam, thesis/dissertation, written preliminary exams, oral qualifying exam. *Entrance requirements:* For doctorate, GMAT or GRE, minimum GPA of 3.0 in undergraduate and graduate coursework. Additional exam requirements/recommendations for international students: Required—TOEFL (minimum score 570 paper-based; 70 iBT), IELTS (minimum score 7). *Application deadline:* For fall admission, 12/10 for domestic and international students. Application fee: $80 ($100 for international students). Electronic applications accepted. *Financial support:* In 2013–14, 74 students received support, including 62 fellowships with full and partial tuition reimbursements available (averaging $30,000 per year), research assistantships with full and partial tuition reimbursements available (averaging $12,000 per year), teaching assistantships with full and partial tuition reimbursements available (averaging $13,000 per year); scholarships/grants, health care benefits, tuition waivers (full), unspecified assistantships, and transit passes, travel grants also available. Financial award application deadline: 12/10; financial award applicants required to submit FAFSA. *Faculty research:* Accounting, business and public policy, entrepreneurship, finance, management of organizations, marketing, operations and information technology management, real estate. *Unit head:* Dr. Martin Lettau, Director, 510-643-6349, Fax: 510-643-4255, E-mail: kimg@haas.berkeley.edu. *Application contact:* Kim Guilfoyle, Director, Student Affairs, 510-642-3944, Fax: 510-643-4255, E-mail: kimg@haas.berkeley.edu.
Website: http://www.haas.berkeley.edu/Phd/.

University of Denver, Daniels College of Business, Franklin L. Burns School of Real Estate and Construction Management, Denver, CO 80208. Offers real estate (MBA); real estate and construction management (IMBA, MS). Part-time and evening/weekend programs available. *Faculty:* 8 full-time (1 woman). *Students:* 6 full-time (2 women), 66 part-time (21 women); includes 8 minority (2 Black or African American, non-Hispanic/Latino; 3 Hispanic/Latino; 3 Two or more races, non-Hispanic/Latino), 11 international. Average age 35. 61 applicants, 80% accepted, 26 enrolled. In 2013, 44 master's awarded. *Entrance requirements:* For master's, GRE General Test or GMAT, bachelor's degree, transcripts, essays, resume, interview. Additional exam requirements/recommendations for international students: Required—TOEFL (minimum score 570 paper-based; 88 iBT). *Application deadline:* For fall admission, 11/15 priority date for domestic and international students; for spring admission, 10/1 priority date for domestic and international students. Applications are processed on a rolling basis. Application fee: $100. Electronic applications accepted. *Financial support:* In 2013–14, 30 students received support, including 3 teaching assistantships with full and partial tuition reimbursements available (averaging $9,936 per year); career-related internships or fieldwork, Federal Work-Study, institutionally sponsored loans, scholarships/grants, and unspecified assistantships also available. Support available to part-time students. Financial award application deadline: 2/15; financial award applicants required to submit FAFSA. *Unit head:* Dr. Barbara Jackson, Director, 303-871-3470, E-mail: barbara.jackson@du.edu. *Application contact:* Lindsay Lauman, Graduate Admissions Manager, 303-871-4211, E-mail: lindsay.lauman@du.edu.
Website: http://daniels.du.edu/masters-degrees/real-estate-construction-management/.

University of Florida, Graduate School, Warrington College of Business Administration, Hough Graduate School of Business, Department of Finance, Insurance and Real Estate, Gainesville, FL 32611. Offers entrepreneurship (MS); finance (MS, PhD); financial services (Certificate); insurance (PhD); quantitative finance (PhD); real estate (MS); real estate and urban analysis (PhD); JD/MBA; JD/MS. *Faculty:* 17 full-time (0 women), 6 part-time/adjunct (0 women). *Students:* 77 full-time (20 women), 4 part-time (2 women); includes 11 minority (3 Black or African American, non-Hispanic/Latino; 1 American Indian or Alaska Native, non-Hispanic/Latino; 2 Asian, non-Hispanic/Latino; 5 Hispanic/Latino), 23 international. Average age 27. 226 applicants, 4% accepted, 8 enrolled. In 2013, 92 master's, 5 doctorates awarded. Terminal master's awarded for partial completion of doctoral program. *Degree requirements:* For master's, comprehensive exam, thesis; for doctorate, comprehensive exam, thesis/dissertation. *Entrance requirements:* For master's, GMAT (minimum score of 465) or GRE General Test, minimum GPA of 3.0 for last 60 hours of undergraduate degree, work experience (preferred); for doctorate, GMAT (minimum score of 465) or GRE General Test, minimum GPA of 3.0. Additional exam requirements/recommendations for international students: Required—TOEFL (minimum score 550 paper-based; 80 iBT), IELTS (minimum score 6). *Application deadline:* For fall admission, 1/15 priority date for domestic students, 1/15 for international students. Applications are processed on a rolling basis. Application fee: $30. Electronic applications accepted. *Expenses:* Tuition, state resident: full-time $12,640. Tuition, nonresident: full-time $30,000. *Financial support:* In 2013–14, 19 students received support, including 13 research assistantships (averaging $18,787 per year), 6 teaching assistantships (averaging $14,970 per year); career-related internships or fieldwork, scholarships/grants, and unspecified assistantships also available. Financial award application deadline: 1/15; financial award applicants required to submit FAFSA. *Faculty research:* Banking, empirical corporate finance, hedge funds. *Unit head:* Mahendrarajah Nimalendran, PhD, Chair, 352-392-9526, Fax: 352-392-0301, E-mail: nimal@ufl.edu. *Application contact:* Office of Admissions, 352-392-1365, E-mail: webrequests@admissions.ufl.edu.
Website: http://www.cba.ufl.edu/fire/.

University of Florida, Graduate School, Warrington College of Business Administration, Hough Graduate School of Business, Programs in Business Administration, Gainesville, FL 32611. Offers business administration (MBA); competitive strategy (MBA); entrepreneurship (MBA); finance (MBA); global management (MBA); Graham-Buffett security analysis (MBA); human resource management (MBA); information systems and operations management (MBA); international studies (MBA); Latin American business (MBA); management (MBA); marketing (MBA); real estate (MBA); sports administration (MBA); JD/MBA; MBA/MS; MBA/PhD; MBA/Pharm D; MD/MBA. *Accreditation:* AACSB. Part-time and evening/weekend programs available. Postbaccalaureate distance learning degree programs offered. *Faculty:* 72 full-time (10 women), 29 part-time/adjunct (7 women). *Students:* 440 full-time (122 women), 472 part-time (159 women); includes 203 minority (43 Black or African American, non-Hispanic/Latino; 3 American Indian or Alaska Native, non-Hispanic/Latino; 64 Asian, non-Hispanic/Latino; 92 Hispanic/Latino; 1 Native Hawaiian or other Pacific Islander, non-Hispanic/Latino), 39 international. Average age 32. 568 applicants, 58% accepted, 261 enrolled. In 2013, 405 master's awarded. *Degree requirements:* For master's, capstone course. *Entrance requirements:* For master's, GMAT (minimum score 465), minimum GPA of 3.0, interview. Additional exam

requirements/recommendations for international students: Required—TOEFL (minimum score 550 paper-based; 80 iBT), IELTS (minimum score 6). *Application deadline:* For fall admission, 7/1 for domestic students, 1/1 for international students; for spring admission, 12/1 for domestic and international students. Applications are processed on a rolling basis. Application fee: $30. Electronic applications accepted. *Expenses:* Tuition, state resident: full-time $12,640. Tuition, nonresident: full-time $30,000. *Financial support:* In 2013–14, 24 students received support, including 24 teaching assistantships (averaging $6,143 per year); career-related internships or fieldwork, scholarships/grants, and unspecified assistantships also available. Support available to part-time students. Financial award applicants required to submit FAFSA. *Faculty research:* Accounting, finance, insurance, management, real estate, urban analysis marketing. *Unit head:* Alexander D. Sevilla, Assistant Dean/Director of MBA Program, 352-273-3252, Fax: 352-392-8791, E-mail: alex.sevilla@warrington.ufl.edu. *Application contact:* Andrew S. Lord, Senior Director of Admissions, 352-273-3241, Fax: 352-392-8791, E-mail: andrew.lord@warrington.ufl.edu.
Website: http://www.floridamba.ufl.edu/.

University of Hawaii at Manoa, Graduate Division, Shidler College of Business, Program in Business Administration, Honolulu, HI 96822. Offers Asian business studies (MBA); Chinese business studies (MBA); decision sciences (MBA); entrepreneurship (MBA); finance (MBA); finance and banking (MBA); human resources management (MBA); information management (MBA); information technology (MBA); international business (MBA); Japanese business studies (MBA); marketing (MBA); organizational behavior (MBA); organizational management (MBA); real estate (MBA); student-designed track (MBA). *Accreditation:* AACSB. Part-time and evening/weekend programs available. *Degree requirements:* For master's, thesis optional. *Entrance requirements:* For master's, GMAT, minimum GPA of 3.0. Additional exam requirements/recommendations for international students: Required—TOEFL (minimum score 600 paper-based; 100 iBT), IELTS (minimum score 7). *Expenses:* Contact institution.

University of Illinois at Chicago, Graduate College, Liautaud Graduate School of Business, Program in Real Estate, Chicago, IL 60607-7128. Offers real estate (MA). *Expenses:* Tuition, state resident: full-time $11,066; part-time $3689 per term. Tuition, nonresident: full-time $23,064; part-time $7688 per term. *Required fees:* $3004; $1190 per term. Tuition and fees vary according to course level and program.

University of Maryland, College Park, Academic Affairs, School of Architecture, Planning and Preservation, Program in Real Estate Development, College Park, MD 20742. Offers MRED. *Students:* 29 full-time (13 women), 54 part-time (20 women); includes 33 minority (25 Black or African American, non-Hispanic/Latino; 1 American Indian or Alaska Native, non-Hispanic/Latino; 3 Asian, non-Hispanic/Latino; 4 Hispanic/Latino), 14 international. 78 applicants, 58% accepted, 28 enrolled. In 2013, 20 master's awarded. *Application deadline:* For fall admission, 8/1 for domestic students, 2/1 for international students; for spring admission, 10/15 for domestic students, 6/1 for international students. Application fee: $75. *Expenses:* Tuition, state resident: full-time $10,314; part-time $573 per credit hour. Tuition, nonresident: full-time $22,248; part-time $1236 per credit. *Required fees:* $1446; $403.15 per semester. Tuition and fees vary according to program. *Financial support:* In 2013–14, 13 fellowships with full and partial tuition reimbursements (averaging $14,015 per year), 5 teaching assistantships (averaging $15,158 per year) were awarded. *Unit head:* Dr. Margaret McFarland, Director, 301-405-6790, E-mail: mmcf@umd.edu. *Application contact:* Dr. Charles A. Caramello, Dean of Graduate School, 301-405-0358, Fax: 301-314-9305.
Website: http://www.arch.umd.edu/real_estate_development/.

University of Memphis, Graduate School, Fogelman College of Business and Economics, Program in Business Administration, Memphis, TN 38152. Offers accounting (MBA, PhD); economics (MBA, PhD); executive business administration (MBA); finance (PhD); finance, insurance, and real estate (MBA, MS); international business administration (IMBA); management (MBA, MS, PhD); management information systems (MBA, MS, PhD); management science (MBA); marketing (MBA, MS); marketing and supply chain management (PhD); real estate development (MS); JD/MBA. *Accreditation:* AACSB. *Faculty:* 44 full-time (9 women), 5 part-time/adjunct (0 women). *Students:* 238 full-time (101 women), 315 part-time (113 women); includes 146 minority (80 Black or African American, non-Hispanic/Latino; 1 American Indian or Alaska Native, non-Hispanic/Latino; 46 Asian, non-Hispanic/Latino; 13 Hispanic/Latino; 2 Native Hawaiian or other Pacific Islander, non-Hispanic/Latino; 4 Two or more races, non-Hispanic/Latino), 104 international. Average age 32. 343 applicants, 62% accepted, 102 enrolled. In 2013, 140 master's, 17 doctorates awarded. *Degree requirements:* For master's, comprehensive exam; for doctorate, comprehensive exam, thesis/dissertation. *Entrance requirements:* For master's, GMAT, resume; for doctorate, GMAT, interview, minimum GPA of 3.4, resume, letter of recommendation. Additional exam requirements/recommendations for international students: Required—TOEFL (minimum score 550 paper-based). *Application deadline:* For fall admission, 8/1 for domestic students; for spring admission, 12/1 for domestic students. Application fee: $35 ($60 for international students). *Financial support:* In 2013–14, 164 students received support. Research assistantships with full tuition reimbursements available, teaching assistantships with full tuition reimbursements available, career-related internships or fieldwork, Federal Work-Study, scholarships/grants, and unspecified assistantships available. Financial award application deadline: 2/15; financial award applicants required to submit FAFSA. *Faculty research:* Competitive business strategy, finance microstructures, supply chain management innovations, health care economics, litigation risks and corporate audits. *Unit head:* Rajiv Grover, Dean, 901-678-3759, E-mail: rgrover@memphis.edu. *Application contact:* Dr. Carol V. Danehower, Associate Dean, 901-678-5402, Fax: 901-678-3579, E-mail: fcbegp@memphis.edu.
Website: http://www.memphis.edu/fcbe/grad_programs.php.

University of Miami, Graduate School, School of Law, Coral Gables, FL 33124-8087. Offers business and financial, international, employment, labor and immigration law, litigation specialization (Certificate); employment, labor and immigration law (JD); estate planning (LL M); international law (LL M), including general international law, inter-American law, international arbitration, U.S. transnational law for foreign lawyers; law (JD); ocean and coastal law (LL M); real property development (real estate) (LL M); taxation (LL M); JD/LL M; JD/LL MMBA; JD/MA; JD/MBA; JD/MD; JD/MM; JD/MPH; JD/MPS; JD/MS Ed; JD/PhD. *Accreditation:* ABA. *Faculty:* 82 full-time (42 women), 108 part-time/adjunct (36 women). *Students:* 1,176 full-time (521 women); includes 402 minority (79 Black or African American, non-Hispanic/Latino; 7 American Indian or Alaska Native, non-Hispanic/Latino; 31 Asian, non-Hispanic/Latino; 266 Hispanic/Latino; 1 Native Hawaiian or other Pacific Islander, non-Hispanic/Latino; 18 Two or more races, non-Hispanic/Latino), 38 international. Average age 24. 3,300 applicants, 53% accepted, 308 enrolled. In 2013, 430 doctorates awarded. *Entrance requirements:* For doctorate, LSAT, 2 letters of recommendation. Additional exam requirements/recommendations for international students: Required—TOEFL (minimum score 580 paper-based; 92 iBT). *Application deadline:* For fall admission, 1/6 priority date for domestic and international students. Applications are processed on a rolling basis. Application fee: $60. Electronic applications accepted. *Expenses:* Contact institution. *Financial support:* Fellowships, research assistantships, career-related internships or fieldwork, Federal Work-Study, institutionally sponsored loans, scholarships/grants, and unspecified assistantships available. Financial award application deadline: 3/1; financial

award applicants required to submit FAFSA. *Faculty research:* National security law, international finance, Internet law/law of electronic commerce, law of the seas, art law/cultural heritage law. *Unit head:* Michael Goodnight, Associate Dean of Admissions and Enrollment Management, 305-284-2527, Fax: 305-284-3084, E-mail: mgoodnig@law.miami.edu. *Application contact:* Therese Lambert, Director of Student Recruitment, 305-284-6746, Fax: 305-284-3084, E-mail: tlambert@law.miami.edu.
Website: http://www.law.miami.edu/.

University of Michigan, Taubman College of Architecture and Urban Planning, Urban and Regional Planning Program, Ann Arbor, MI 48109. Offers real estate development (Certificate); urban planning (MUP); JD/MUP; M Arch/MUP; MBA/MUP; MLA/MUP; MPP/MUP. Offered through the Horace H. Rackham School of Graduate Studies; students in the Certificate program must either be currently enrolled in a graduate program or have earned a master's or PhD degree within the last five years. *Accreditation:* ACSP (one or more programs are accredited). Part-time programs available. *Faculty:* 7 full-time (3 women), 8 part-time/adjunct (2 women). *Students:* 106 full-time (48 women), 24 part-time (13 women); includes 22 minority (7 Black or African American, non-Hispanic/Latino; 5 Asian, non-Hispanic/Latino; 10 Hispanic/Latino), 22 international. Average age 25. 226 applicants, 78% accepted, 72 enrolled. In 2013, 45 master's awarded. *Degree requirements:* For master's, thesis or alternative, professional project, capstone studio. *Entrance requirements:* For master's, GRE General Test, LSAT or GMAT. Additional exam requirements/recommendations for international students: Required—TOEFL (minimum score 600 paper-based; 100 iBT). *Application deadline:* For fall admission, 1/5 priority date for domestic and international students; for winter admission, 11/15 priority date for domestic students, 10/15 priority date for international students. Applications are processed on a rolling basis. Application fee: $60 ($75 for international students). Electronic applications accepted. Tuition and fees vary according to course level, course load, degree level, program and student level. *Financial support:* In 2013–14, 39 students received support, including 25 fellowships with full and partial tuition reimbursements available (averaging $15,650 per year), 10 teaching assistantships with full and partial tuition reimbursements available (averaging $15,600 per year); research assistantships with full and partial tuition reimbursements available also available. Financial award application deadline: 1/5; financial award applicants required to submit FAFSA. *Faculty research:* Housing community and economic development, transportation planning, physical planning and urban design, planning in developing countries, land use and environmental planning. *Total annual research expenditures:* $755,000. *Unit head:* Prof. Jonathan Levine, Chair, 734-763-0039, Fax: 734-763-2322, E-mail: jnthnlvn@umich.edu. *Application contact:* Beverly A. Walter, Admissions Coordinator, 734-763-3075, Fax: 734-763-2322, E-mail: beverlyw@umich.edu.
Website: http://www.tcaup.umich.edu/.

University of Missouri–Kansas City, Henry W. Bloch School of Management, Kansas City, MO 64110-2499. Offers accounting (MS); business administration (MBA); entrepreneurial real estate (MERE); entrepreneurship and innovation (PhD); finance (MS); public affairs (MPA, PhD); JD/MBA; LL M/MPA. PhD (interdisciplinary) offered through the School of Graduate Studies. *Accreditation:* AACSB; NASPAA. Part-time and evening/weekend programs available. *Faculty:* 57 full-time (15 women), 32 part-time/adjunct (10 women). *Students:* 309 full-time (151 women), 377 part-time (163 women); includes 100 minority (39 Black or African American, non-Hispanic/Latino; 2 American Indian or Alaska Native, non-Hispanic/Latino; 27 Asian, non-Hispanic/Latino; 24 Hispanic/Latino; 1 Native Hawaiian or other Pacific Islander, non-Hispanic/Latino; 7 Two or more races, non-Hispanic/Latino), 93 international. Average age 30. 489 applicants, 54% accepted, 252 enrolled. In 2013, 252 master's, 1 doctorate awarded. Terminal master's awarded for partial completion of doctoral program. *Entrance requirements:* For master's, GMAT, GRE, 2 essays, 2 references, support of employer; for doctorate, GRE, minimum GPA of 3.0. Additional exam requirements/recommendations for international students: Required—TOEFL (minimum score 550 paper-based; 80 iBT). *Application deadline:* For fall admission, 5/1 priority date for domestic and international students; for spring admission, 10/1 priority date for domestic and international students. Applications are processed on a rolling basis. Application fee: $45 ($50 for international students). Electronic applications accepted. *Expenses:* Tuition, state resident: full-time $6073; part-time $337.40 per credit hour. Tuition, nonresident: full-time $15,680; part-time $871.10 per credit hour. *Required fees:* $97.59 per credit hour. Full-time tuition and fees vary according to program. *Financial support:* In 2013–14, 38 research assistantships with partial tuition reimbursements (averaging $10,499 per year), 6 teaching assistantships with partial tuition reimbursements (averaging $13,380 per year) were awarded; career-related internships or fieldwork, Federal Work-Study, institutionally sponsored loans, scholarships/grants, tuition waivers (full and partial), and unspecified assistantships also available. Support available to part-time students. Financial award application deadline: 3/1; financial award applicants required to submit FAFSA. *Faculty research:* Entrepreneurship, finance, non-profit, risk management. *Unit head:* Dr. David Donnelly, Dean, 816-235-1333, Fax: 816-235-2206, E-mail: donnellyd@umkc.edu. *Application contact:* 816-235-1111, E-mail: admit@umkc.edu.
Website: http://www.bloch.umkc.edu.

The University of North Carolina at Charlotte, The Graduate School, Belk College of Business, Department of Management, Charlotte, NC 28223-0001. Offers business administration (MBA, PhD); real estate finance and development (Graduate Certificate). Part-time and evening/weekend programs available. *Faculty:* 11 full-time (4 women), 1 part-time/adjunct (0 women). *Students:* 114 full-time (43 women), 266 part-time (86 women); includes 64 minority (28 Black or African American, non-Hispanic/Latino; 2 American Indian or Alaska Native, non-Hispanic/Latino; 11 Asian, non-Hispanic/Latino; 13 Hispanic/Latino; 10 Two or more races, non-Hispanic/Latino), 132 international. Average age 31. 286 applicants, 51% accepted, 98 enrolled. In 2013, 169 master's, 2 doctorates, 2 other advanced degrees awarded. Terminal master's awarded for partial completion of doctoral program. *Degree requirements:* For master's, thesis or alternative; for doctorate, thesis/dissertation. *Entrance requirements:* For master's, GMAT or GRE, 3 letters of recommendation, essay; for doctorate, GMAT (minimum score of 650), letters of recommendation, minimum GPA of 3.25. Additional exam requirements/recommendations for international students: Required—TOEFL (minimum score 557 paper-based; 83 iBT). *Application deadline:* For fall admission, 1/15 priority date for domestic and international students; for spring admission, 10/1 priority date for domestic and international students. Applications are processed on a rolling basis. Application fee: $75. Electronic applications accepted. *Expenses:* Tuition, state resident: full-time $3522. Tuition, nonresident: full-time $16,051. *Required fees:* $2585. Tuition and fees vary according to course load and program. *Financial support:* In 2013–14, 2 students received support, including 1 research assistantship (averaging $18,000 per year), 1 teaching assistantship (averaging $18,000 per year); career-related internships or fieldwork, institutionally sponsored loans, scholarships/grants, and unspecified assistantships also available. Support available to part-time students. Financial award application deadline: 4/1; financial award applicants required to submit FAFSA. *Total annual research expenditures:* $104,426. *Unit head:* Dr. Christie Amato, Associate Dean, 704-687-7712, Fax: 704-687-5309, E-mail: chamato@uncc.edu. *Application contact:* Kathy B. Giddings, Director of Graduate Admissions, 704-687-5503, Fax: 704-687-1668, E-mail: gradadm@uncc.edu.
Website: http://belkcollege.uncc.edu/about-college/departments/management.

The University of North Carolina at Charlotte, The Graduate School, Belk College of Business, Interdisciplinary Business Programs, Charlotte, NC 28223-0001. Offers mathematical finance (MS); real estate (MS). Part-time and evening/weekend programs available. *Faculty:* 15 full-time (2 women). *Students:* 75 full-time (29 women), 55 part-time (17 women); includes 18 minority (8 Black or African American, non-Hispanic/Latino; 8 Asian, non-Hispanic/Latino; 2 Two or more races, non-Hispanic/Latino), 70 international. Average age 28. 138 applicants, 74% accepted, 52 enrolled. In 2013, 43 master's awarded. *Degree requirements:* For master's, thesis or alternative, project. *Entrance requirements:* For master's, GRE or GMAT, minimum GPA of 2.75, letters of recommendation. Additional exam requirements/recommendations for international students: Required—TOEFL (minimum score 557 paper-based; 87 iBT). *Application deadline:* For fall admission, 1/15 for domestic and international students; for spring admission, 10/1 priority date for domestic and international students. Application fee: $75. Electronic applications accepted. *Expenses:* Tuition, state resident: full-time $3522. Tuition, nonresident: full-time $16,051. *Required fees:* $2585. Tuition and fees vary according to course load and program. *Financial support:* In 2013–14, 2 students received support, including 1 research assistantship (averaging $18,000 per year), 1 teaching assistantship (averaging $11,800 per year); career-related internships or fieldwork, scholarships/grants, and unspecified assistantships also available. Support available to part-time students. Financial award applicants required to submit FAFSA. *Unit head:* Dr. Christie Amato, Associate Dean for Graduate Programs, 704-687-7712, Fax: 704-687-4014, E-mail: chamato@uncc.edu. *Application contact:* Kathy B. Giddings, Director of Graduate Admissions, 704-687-5503, Fax: 704-687-1668, E-mail: gradadm@uncc.edu.
Website: http://belkcollege.uncc.edu/.

University of Pennsylvania, Wharton School, Real Estate Department, Philadelphia, PA 19104. Offers MBA, PhD. Terminal master's awarded for partial completion of doctoral program. *Degree requirements:* For doctorate, thesis/dissertation. *Entrance requirements:* For master's, GMAT; for doctorate, GRE General Test. *Faculty research:* Public economics and taxation economics and finance of real estate markets, economics of housing markets, real estate development.

University of St. Thomas, Graduate Studies, Opus College of Business, Master of Science in Real Estate Program, Minneapolis, MN 55403. Offers MS. Part-time and evening/weekend programs available. *Students:* 32 part-time (10 women); includes 2 minority (1 American Indian or Alaska Native, non-Hispanic/Latino; 1 Hispanic/Latino). Average age 36. In 2013, 3 master's awarded. *Entrance requirements:* For master's, GMAT. Additional exam requirements/recommendations for international students: Required—TOEFL (minimum score 80 iBT), IELTS (minimum score 6.5), or Michigan English Language Assessment Battery. *Application deadline:* For fall admission, 5/1 for domestic students, 4/15 for international students; for spring admission, 10/1 for domestic and international students. Applications are processed on a rolling basis. Application fee: $40. Electronic applications accepted. *Unit head:* Herb Tousley, Program Director, 651-962-4289, Fax: 651-962-4410, E-mail: msrealestate@stthomas.edu. *Application contact:* Jessica Kluntz, Manager of Marketing and Enrollment, 651-962-4289, Fax: 651-962-4410, E-mail: msrealestate@stthomas.edu.
Website: http://www.stthomas.edu/realestate.

University of San Diego, School of Business Administration, Program in Real Estate, San Diego, CA 92110-2492. Offers MS, MBA/MSRE. Part-time and evening/weekend programs available. *Students:* 20 full-time (3 women), 4 part-time (1 woman); includes 6 minority (3 Asian, non-Hispanic/Latino; 1 Hispanic/Latino; 1 Native Hawaiian or other Pacific Islander, non-Hispanic/Latino; 1 Two or more races, non-Hispanic/Latino), 2 international. Average age 29. In 2013, 15 master's awarded. *Degree requirements:* For master's, capstone course. *Entrance requirements:* For master's, GMAT (minimum score of 550), minimum GPA of 3.0, minimum 2 years of relevant work experience. Additional exam requirements/recommendations for international students: Required—TOEFL (minimum score 580 paper-based; 92 iBT), TWE. *Application deadline:* For fall admission, 12/15 priority date for domestic students. Application fee: $80. Electronic applications accepted. *Expenses: Tuition:* Full-time $23,580; part-time $1310 per credit. *Required fees:* $350. *Financial support:* In 2013–14, 18 students received support. Career-related internships or fieldwork, Federal Work-Study, institutionally sponsored loans, scholarships/grants, and unspecified assistantships available. Support available to part-time students. Financial award application deadline: 4/1; financial award applicants required to submit FAFSA. *Unit head:* Dr. Charles Tu, Academic Director, Real Estate Program, 619-260-5942, E-mail: realestate@sandiego.edu. *Application contact:* Monica Mahon, Associate Director of Graduate Admissions, 619-260-4524, Fax: 619-260-4158, E-mail: grads@sandiego.edu.
Website: http://www.sandiego.edu/business/programs/ms-real-estate/.

University of South Africa, College of Economic and Management Sciences, Pretoria, South Africa. Offers accounting (D Admin, D Com); accounting science (DA); auditing (D Admin, D Com); business administration (M Tech); business economics (D Admin); business leadership (DBL); business management (D Admin, D Com); economic management analysis (M Tech); economics (D Admin, D Com, PhD); human resource development (M Tech); industrial psychology (D Admin, D Com, PhD); logistics (D Com); marketing (M Tech); public administration (D Admin, D Com, DPA, PhD); public management (M Tech); quantitative management (D Admin, D Com); real estate (M Tech); statistics (D Admin, PhD); tourism management (D Admin, D Com); transport economics (D Admin, D Com).

University of Southern California, Graduate School, School of Policy, Planning, and Development, Master of Real Estate Development Program, Los Angeles, CA 90089. Offers MRED, JD/MRED, M Pl/MRED, MBA/MRED. Part-time programs available. *Degree requirements:* For master's, comprehensive exam. *Entrance requirements:* For master's, GRE, GMAT. Additional exam requirements/recommendations for international students: Required—TOEFL (minimum score 600 paper-based; 100 iBT). Electronic applications accepted. *Expenses:* Contact institution. *Faculty research:* Urban development, urban economics, real estate finance, housing markets.

University of South Florida, College of Business, Department of Finance, Tampa, FL 33620-9951. Offers business administration (PhD), including finance; finance (MS); real estate (MSRE). Part-time and evening/weekend programs available. *Faculty:* 14 full-time (2 women), 1 part-time/adjunct (0 women). *Students:* 90 full-time (37 women), 10 part-time (7 women); includes 1 minority (Two or more races, non-Hispanic/Latino), 80 international. Average age 26. 149 applicants, 57% accepted, 38 enrolled. In 2013, 37 master's, 3 doctorates awarded. Terminal master's awarded for partial completion of doctoral program. *Degree requirements:* For master's, thesis or alternative; for doctorate, comprehensive exam, thesis/dissertation. *Entrance requirements:* For master's, GMAT (minimum score of 550), minimum undergraduate GPA of 3.0 in upper-division coursework; for doctorate, GMAT or GRE, minimum undergraduate GPA of 3.0 in upper-division coursework, personal statement, recommendations, interview. Additional exam requirements/recommendations for international students: Required—TOEFL (minimum score 550 paper-based; 79 iBT) or IELTS (minimum score 6.5). *Application deadline:* For fall admission, 6/1 for domestic students, 1/2 for international students; for spring admission, 10/15 for domestic students, 6/1 for international students. Application fee: $30. Electronic applications accepted. *Financial support:* In 2013–14, 17 students received support, including 8 research assistantships (averaging $14,357 per year), 9 teaching assistantships with tuition reimbursements available (averaging $11,972 per year); scholarships/grants, health care benefits, and unspecified assistantships also available. Financial award application deadline: 6/30. *Faculty research:* International corporate finance, corporate finance, market efficiency, mergers and acquisitions, agency theory, corporate governance, investments, mutual fund industry, mergers and acquisitions, corporate creditworthiness, credit risk issues, empirical asset pricing, financial intermediation, corporate finance theory, public offerings, business strategy. *Total annual research expenditures:* $361,660. *Unit head:* Dr. Scott Besley, Chairperson and Associate Professor, 813-974-6341, Fax: 813-974-3084, E-mail: sbesley@usf.edu. *Application contact:* Amy Dunkel, Office Manager, Finance Department, 813-974-6294, Fax: 813-974-3084, E-mail: adunkel@usf.edu.
Website: http://business.usf.edu/departments/finance/.

The University of Texas at Arlington, Graduate School, College of Business, Department of Finance and Real Estate, Arlington, TX 76019. Offers finance (PhD); quantitative finance (MS); real estate (MS). Part-time and evening/weekend programs available. *Degree requirements:* For master's, thesis optional; for doctorate, comprehensive exam, thesis/dissertation. *Entrance requirements:* For master's, GMAT/GRE, minimum GPA of 3.0; for doctorate, GMAT/GRE. Additional exam requirements/recommendations for international students: Required—TOEFL (minimum score 550 paper-based; 79 iBT).

The University of Texas at Arlington, Graduate School, College of Business, Program in Business Administration, Arlington, TX 76019. Offers accounting (PhD); business statistics (PhD); finance (MBA, PhD); information systems (MBA, PhD); management (MBA, PhD); marketing (MBA, PhD); operations management (MBA, PhD); real estate (MBA). *Accreditation:* AACSB. Part-time and evening/weekend programs available. *Degree requirements:* For master's, thesis optional; for doctorate, comprehensive exam, thesis/dissertation. *Entrance requirements:* For master's, GMAT or GRE; for doctorate, GMAT, minimum GPA of 3.0 (undergraduate), 3.4 (graduate); 30 hours of graduate course work. Additional exam requirements/recommendations for international students: Required—TOEFL (minimum score 550 paper-based; 79 iBT). Electronic applications accepted.

The University of Texas at Dallas, Naveen Jindal School of Management, Program in Business Administration, Richardson, TX 75080. Offers business administration (MBA, PMBA); executive business administration (EMBA); global leadership (EMBA); healthcare management for physicians (EMBA); product lifecycle and supply chain management (EMBA); project management (EMBA); real estate (MBA). *Accreditation:* AACSB. Part-time and evening/weekend programs available. Postbaccalaureate distance learning degree programs offered (no on-campus study). *Faculty:* 100 full-time (21 women), 52 part-time/adjunct (18 women). *Students:* 421 full-time (196 women), 630 part-time (398 women); includes 295 minority (45 Black or African American, non-Hispanic/Latino; 4 American Indian or Alaska Native, non-Hispanic/Latino; 151 Asian, non-Hispanic/Latino; 76 Hispanic/Latino; 19 Two or more races, non-Hispanic/Latino), 275 international. Average age 31. 940 applicants, 44% accepted, 375 enrolled. In 2013, 384 master's awarded. *Degree requirements:* For master's, thesis optional. *Entrance requirements:* For master's, GMAT, 10 years of business experience (EMBA), minimum GPA of 3.0. Additional exam requirements/recommendations for international students: Required—TOEFL (minimum score 550 paper-based). *Application deadline:* For fall admission, 7/15 for domestic students, 5/1 priority date for international students; for spring admission, 11/15 for domestic students, 9/1 priority date for international students. Applications are processed on a rolling basis. Application fee: $50 ($100 for international students). Electronic applications accepted. *Expenses:* Contact institution. *Financial support:* In 2013–14, 336 students received support. Research assistantships with partial tuition reimbursements available, teaching assistantships with partial tuition reimbursements available, career-related internships or fieldwork, Federal Work-Study, institutionally sponsored loans, scholarships/grants, and unspecified assistantships available. Support available to part-time students. Financial award application deadline: 4/30; financial award applicants required to submit FAFSA. *Faculty research:* Production scheduling, trade and finance, organizational decision-making, life/work planning. *Unit head:* Lisa Shatz, Assistant Dean, MBA Programs, 972-883-6191, E-mail: lisa.shatz@utdallas.edu. *Application contact:* Anna Walls, Enrollment Services Advisor, MBA Programs, 972-883-5951, E-mail: anna.walls@utdallas.edu.
Website: http://jindal.utdallas.edu/academic-programs/mba-programs/.

University of Utah, Graduate School, David Eccles School of Business, Master in Real Estate Program, Salt Lake City, UT 84112. Offers MRED. Part-time programs available. *Students:* 26 full-time (4 women), 14 part-time (0 women); includes 3 minority (2 Asian, non-Hispanic/Latino; 1 Two or more races, non-Hispanic/Latino). Average age 34. 23 applicants, 83% accepted, 18 enrolled. In 2013, 18 master's awarded. *Degree requirements:* For master's, professional project. *Entrance requirements:* For master's, GMAT or GRE, minimum undergraduate GPA of 3.0. Additional exam requirements/recommendations for international students: Required—TOEFL (minimum score 600 paper-based; 100 iBT), IELTS (minimum score 7). *Application deadline:* For fall admission, 2/1 priority date for domestic and international students; for winter admission, 4/1 for domestic students. Applications are processed on a rolling basis. Application fee: $55 ($65 for international students). Electronic applications accepted. *Expenses:* Contact institution. *Financial support:* In 2013–14, 4 students received support, including 4 fellowships with partial tuition reimbursements available (averaging $9,375 per year); scholarships/grants and unspecified assistantships also available. Financial award application deadline: 2/1; financial award applicants required to submit FAFSA. *Unit head:* Danny Wall, Program Director, 801-581-8903, E-mail: buzz.welch@utah.edu. *Application contact:* Andrea Miller, Director of Graduate Admissions, 801-581-7785, Fax: 801-581-3666, E-mail: mastersinfo@business.utah.edu.
Website: http://mred.business.utah.edu/.

University of Wisconsin–Madison, Graduate School, Wisconsin School of Business, Doctoral Program in Real Estate and Urban Land Economics, Madison, WI 53706-1380. Offers PhD. *Faculty:* 8 full-time (0 women). *Students:* Average age 29. In 2013, 1 doctorate awarded. *Degree requirements:* For doctorate, comprehensive exam, thesis/dissertation. *Entrance requirements:* For doctorate, GMAT or GRE. Additional exam requirements/recommendations for international students: Recommended—TOEFL (minimum score 623 paper-based; 106 iBT), IELTS (minimum score 7.5), TSE (minimum score 73). *Application deadline:* For fall admission, 12/15 priority date for domestic and international students. Application fee: $56. Electronic applications accepted. *Expenses:* Tuition, state resident: full-time $10,728; part-time $790 per credit. Tuition, nonresident: full-time $24,054; part-time $1623 per credit. *Required fees:* $1130; $119 per credit. *Financial support:* In 2013–14, fellowships with full tuition reimbursements (averaging $19,125 per year), research assistantships with full tuition reimbursements (averaging $14,746 per year), teaching assistantships with full tuition reimbursements (averaging $14,746 per year) were awarded; career-related internships or fieldwork, Federal Work-Study, institutionally sponsored loans, scholarships/grants, health care benefits, and unspecified assistantships also available. Financial award application deadline: 2/1; financial award applicants required to submit FAFSA. *Faculty research:* Real estate finance, real estate equity investments, zoning restructurings, home ownership, international real estate and public policy. *Unit head:* Prof. Abdallah Yavas, Chair, 608-263-7651, Fax: 608-265-2738, E-mail: ayavas@bus.wisc.edu.

Real Estate

Application contact: Belle Heberling, Assistant Director for Research Programs, 608-262-3749, Fax: 608-890-0180, E-mail: phd@bus.wisc.edu. Website: http://www.bus.wisc.edu/phd.

University of Wisconsin–Madison, Graduate School, Wisconsin School of Business, Wisconsin Full-Time MBA Program, Madison, WI 53706. Offers applied security analysis (MBA); arts administration (MBA); brand and product management (MBA); corporate finance and investment banking (MBA); marketing research (MBA); operations and technology management (MBA); real estate (MBA); risk management and insurance (MBA); strategic human resource management (MBA); supply chain management (MBA). *Faculty:* 34 full-time (5 women), 30 part-time/adjunct (15 women). *Students:* 193 full-time (61 women); includes 37 minority (10 Black or African American, non-Hispanic/Latino; 14 Asian, non-Hispanic/Latino; 12 Hispanic/Latino; 1 Native Hawaiian or other Pacific Islander, non-Hispanic/Latino), 37 international. Average age 28. 460 applicants, 33% accepted, 101 enrolled. In 2013, 110 master's awarded. *Degree requirements:* For master's, thesis (for arts administration specialization). *Entrance requirements:* For master's, GMAT or GRE, bachelor's or equivalent degree, 2 years of work experience, letters of recommendation, resume. Additional exam requirements/recommendations for international students: Required—TOEFL (minimum score 600 paper-based; 100 iBT), IELTS. *Application deadline:* For fall admission, 11/5 for domestic and international students; for winter admission, 2/4 for domestic and international students; for spring admission, 4/28 for domestic students, 4/2 for international students. Applications are processed on a rolling basis. Application fee: $56. Electronic applications accepted. *Expenses:* Contact institution. *Financial support:* In 2013–14, 176 students received support, including 12 fellowships with full tuition reimbursements available (averaging $37,956 per year), 42 research assistantships with full tuition reimbursements available (averaging $28,175 per year), 43 teaching assistantships with full tuition reimbursements available (averaging $28,175 per year); scholarships/grants, health care benefits, and unspecified assistantships also available. Financial award application deadline: 4/26; financial award applicants required to submit FAFSA. *Faculty research:* Market consequences of International Financial Reporting Standards (IFRS), inter-firm relationships and strategic partnerships, application of Bayesian statistical methods and applied probability models to understanding individuals' behaviors in the context of customer relationship management (CRM) applications, liquidity provision and the structure of financial markets, strategic management of global startups. *Unit head:* Prof. Larry W. Hunter, Associate Dean of Master's Programs, 608-265-3494, Fax: 608-265-4192, E-mail: lhunter@bus.wisc.edu. *Application contact:* William H. Wait, Assistant Director of MBA Marketing and Recruiting, 608-262-4000, Fax: 608-265-4192, E-mail: wwait@bus.wisc.edu. Website: http://www.bus.wisc.edu/mba.

University of Wisconsin–Milwaukee, Graduate School, School of Architecture and Urban Planning, Department of Urban Planning, Milwaukee, WI 53201-0413. Offers geographic information systems (Certificate); real estate development (Certificate); urban planning (MUP); M Arch/MUP; MPA/MUP; MUP/MS. *Accreditation:* ACSP. Part-time programs available. *Faculty:* 4 full-time (2 women), 1 part-time/adjunct (0 women). *Students:* 32 full-time (8 women), 10 part-time (4 women); includes 9 minority (5 Black or African American, non-Hispanic/Latino; 2 Asian, non-Hispanic/Latino; 2 Two or more races, non-Hispanic/Latino), 1 international. Average age 29. 40 applicants, 63% accepted, 9 enrolled. In 2013, 22 master's awarded. *Degree requirements:* For master's, comprehensive exam, thesis or alternative. *Entrance requirements:* For master's, GRE General Test. Additional exam requirements/recommendations for international students: Required—TOEFL (minimum score 550 paper-based; 79 iBT), IELTS (minimum score 6.5). *Application deadline:* For fall admission, 1/1 priority date for domestic students; for spring admission, 9/1 for domestic students. Applications are processed on a rolling basis. Application fee: $56 ($96 for international students). Electronic applications accepted. *Financial support:* Fellowships, research assistantships, teaching assistantships, career-related internships or fieldwork, health care benefits, and unspecified assistantships available. Support available to part-time students. Financial award application deadline: 4/15; financial award applicants required to submit FAFSA. *Unit head:* William Huxhold, Department Chair, 414-229-6954, E-mail: hux@uwm.edu. *Application contact:* General Information Contact, 414-229-4982, Fax: 414-229-6967, E-mail: gradschool@uwm.edu. Website: http://www4.uwm.edu/sarup/program/planning/.

Villanova University, Villanova School of Business, MBA - The Fast Track Program, Villanova, PA 19085. Offers finance (MBA); health care management (MBA); international business (MBA); management information systems (MBA); marketing (MBA); real estate (MBA); strategic management (MBA). *Accreditation:* AACSB. Part-time and evening/weekend programs available. *Faculty:* 101 full-time (33 women), 36 part-time/adjunct (3 women). *Students:* 140 part-time (44 women); includes 22 minority (1 Black or African American, non-Hispanic/Latino; 17 Asian, non-Hispanic/Latino; 3 Hispanic/Latino; 1 Two or more races, non-Hispanic/Latino), 3 international. Average age 29. 127 applicants, 72% accepted, 75 enrolled. In 2013, 61 master's awarded. *Degree requirements:* For master's, minimum GPA of 3.0. *Entrance requirements:* For master's, GMAT or GRE, work experience. Additional exam requirements/recommendations for international students: Required—TOEFL (minimum score 550 paper-based; 90 iBT). *Application deadline:* For fall admission, 6/30 for domestic and international students. Application fee: $50. Electronic applications accepted. *Financial support:* Scholarships/grants available. Financial award application deadline: 6/30; financial award applicants required to submit FAFSA. *Faculty research:* Business analytics; creativity, innovation and entrepreneurship; global leadership; real estate; church management; business ethics. *Unit head:* Zelon Crawford, Director of Graduate Business Programs, 610-519-6283, Fax: 610-519-6273, E-mail: zelon.crawford@villanova.edu. *Application contact:* Meredith L. Lockyer, Manager of Recruiting, 610-519-7016, Fax: 610-519-6273, E-mail: meredith.lockyer@villanova.edu. Website: http://www1.villanova.edu/villanova/business/graduate/mba/fasttrack.html.

Villanova University, Villanova School of Business, MBA - The Flex Track Program, Villanova, PA 19085. Offers finance (MBA); health care management (MBA); international business (MBA); management information systems (MBA); marketing (MBA); real estate (MBA); strategic management (MBA); JD/MBA. *Accreditation:* AACSB. Part-time and evening/weekend programs available. Postbaccalaureate distance learning degree programs offered (minimal on-campus study). *Faculty:* 101 full-time (33 women), 36 part-time/adjunct (3 women). *Students:* 13 full-time (5 women), 413 part-time (127 women); includes 63 minority (13 Black or African American, non-Hispanic/Latino; 1 American Indian or Alaska Native, non-Hispanic/Latino; 29 Asian, non-Hispanic/Latino; 14 Hispanic/Latino; 1 Native Hawaiian or other Pacific Islander, non-Hispanic/Latino; 5 Two or more races, non-Hispanic/Latino), 9 international. Average age 29. 84 applicants, 83% accepted, 66 enrolled. In 2013, 133 master's awarded. *Degree requirements:* For master's, minimum GPA of 3.0. *Entrance requirements:* For master's, GMAT or GRE, work experience. Additional exam requirements/recommendations for international students: Required—TOEFL (minimum score 550 paper-based; 90 iBT). *Application deadline:* For fall admission, 6/30 for domestic and international students; for winter admission, 11/15 for domestic and international students; for spring admission, 11/15 for domestic and international students; for summer admission, 3/31 for domestic and international students. Applications are processed on a rolling basis. Application fee: $50. Electronic applications accepted. *Financial support:* In 2013–14, 13 research assistantships with full tuition reimbursements (averaging $13,100 per year) were awarded; scholarships/grants and unspecified assistantships also available. Financial award application deadline: 6/30; financial award applicants required to submit FAFSA. *Faculty research:* Business analytics; creativity, innovation and entrepreneurship; global leadership; real estate; church management; business ethics. *Unit head:* Zelon Crawford, Director of Graduate Business Programs, 610-610-6283, Fax: 610-519-6273, E-mail: zelon.crawford@villanova.edu. *Application contact:* Meredith L. Lockyer, Manager of Recruiting, 610-519-7016, Fax: 610-519-6273, E-mail: meredith.lockyer@villanova.edu. Website: http://www1.villanova.edu/villanova/business/graduate/mba/flextrack.html.

Virginia Commonwealth University, Graduate School, School of Business, Program in Finance, Insurance, and Real Estate, Richmond, VA 23284-9005. Offers MS. *Entrance requirements:* For master's, GMAT. Additional exam requirements/recommendations for international students: Required—TOEFL (minimum score 600 paper-based; 100 iBT); Recommended—IELTS (minimum score 6.5). Electronic applications accepted.

Virginia Commonwealth University, Graduate School, School of Business, Program in Real Estate and Urban Land Development, Richmond, VA 23284-9005. Offers Certificate. *Entrance requirements:* Additional exam requirements/recommendations for international students: Required—TOEFL (minimum score 600 paper-based; 100 iBT); Recommended—IELTS (minimum score 6.5). Electronic applications accepted.

Section 21
Transportation Management, Logistics, and Supply Chain Management

This section contains a directory of institutions offering graduate work in transportation management, logistics, and supply chain management, followed by an in-depth entry submitted by an institution that chose to prepare a detailed program description. Additional information about programs listed in the directory but not augmented by an in-depth entry may be obtained by writing directly to the dean of a graduate school or chair of a department at the address given in the directory.

For programs offering related work, see also in this book *Business Administration and Management.*

CONTENTS

Program Directories

Aviation Management 616
Logistics 617
Supply Chain Management 622
Transportation Management 632

Displays and Close-Ups

Embry-Riddle Aeronautical University–Daytona 616, 635

See also:

North Carolina State University—Business Administration 120, 189

Aviation Management

Aviation Management

Arizona State University at the Tempe campus, College of Technology and Innovation, Department of Technology Management, Mesa, AZ 85212. Offers technology (aviation management and human factors) (MS); technology (environmental technology management) (MS); technology (global technology and development) (MS); technology (graphic information technology) (MS); technology (management of technology) (MS). Part-time and evening/weekend programs available. Postbaccalaureate distance learning degree programs offered (minimal on-campus study). *Degree requirements:* For master's, thesis or applied project and oral defense; interactive Program of Study (iPOS) submitted before completing 50 percent of required credit hours. *Entrance requirements:* For master's, GRE, minimum GPA of 3.0 or equivalent in last 2 years of work leading to bachelor's degree. Additional exam requirements/recommendations for international students: Required—TOEFL (minimum score 83 iBT), TOEFL, IELTS, or PTE. Electronic applications accepted. *Faculty research:* Digital imaging, digital publishing, Internet development/e-commerce, information aviation human factors, pilot selection, databases, multimedia, commercial digital photography, digital workflow, computer graphics modeling and animation, information design, sociotechnology, visual and technical literacy, environmental management, quality management, project management, industrial ethics, hazardous materials, environmental chemistry.

Daniel Webster College, MBA Program for Aviation Professionals, Nashua, NH 03063-1300. Offers MBA. Part-time and evening/weekend programs available. *Degree requirements:* For master's, capstone research project. *Entrance requirements:* Additional exam requirements/recommendations for international students: Required—TOEFL (minimum score 550 paper-based; 79 iBT). Electronic applications accepted.

Delta State University, Graduate Programs, College of Business, Department of Commercial Aviation, Cleveland, MS 38733-0001. Offers MCA. Part-time and evening/weekend programs available. Postbaccalaureate distance learning degree programs offered (minimal on-campus study). *Faculty:* 1 (woman) full-time, 1 part-time/adjunct (0 women). *Students:* 15 full-time (6 women), 29 part-time (2 women); includes 7 minority (4 Black or African American, non-Hispanic/Latino; 1 Asian, non-Hispanic/Latino; 2 Hispanic/Latino), 3 international. Average age 34. 18 applicants, 100% accepted, 14 enrolled. In 2013, 20 master's awarded. *Degree requirements:* For master's, thesis or alternative. *Entrance requirements:* For master's, GMAT. *Application deadline:* For fall admission, 8/1 priority date for domestic students; for spring admission, 12/1 priority date for domestic students. Applications are processed on a rolling basis. Application fee: $0. *Expenses:* Tuition, state resident: full-time $3006; part-time $334 per credit hour. Tuition, nonresident: full-time $3006; part-time $334 per credit hour. *Financial support:* In 2013–14, research assistantships (averaging $4,000 per year) were awarded; career-related internships or fieldwork, Federal Work-Study, and institutionally sponsored loans also available. Support available to part-time students. Financial award application deadline: 6/1. *Unit head:* Dr. Tommy Sledge, Chair, 662-846-4205, Fax: 662-846-4214, E-mail: tsledge@deltastate.edu. *Application contact:* Carla Johnson, Coordinator, College of Business Graduate Programs, 662-846-4234, Fax: 662-846-4215, E-mail: cjohnson@deltastate.edu.
Website: http://www.deltastate.edu/pages/4457.asp.

Dowling College, School of Business, Oakdale, NY 11769. Offers aviation management (MBA, Certificate); corporate finance (MBA, Certificate); health care management (MBA); human resource management (Certificate); information systems management (MBA); management and leadership (MBA); marketing (Certificate); project management (Certificate); public management (MBA); school district business leader (MBA); sport, event and entertainment management (Certificate); JD/MBA. Part-time and evening/weekend programs available. Postbaccalaureate distance learning degree programs offered (minimal on-campus study). *Faculty:* 7 full-time (2 women), 43 part-time/adjunct (7 women). *Students:* 183 full-time (79 women), 299 part-time (142 women); includes 137 minority (84 Black or African American, non-Hispanic/Latino; 14 Asian, non-Hispanic/Latino; 20 Hispanic/Latino; 19 Native Hawaiian or other Pacific Islander, non-Hispanic/Latino). Average age 32. 360 applicants, 58% accepted, 127 enrolled. In 2013, 235 master's, 15 other advanced degrees awarded. *Degree requirements:* For master's, comprehensive exam, thesis optional. *Entrance requirements:* For master's, minimum GPA of 2.8, 2 letters of recommendation, courses or seminar in accounting and finance, resume. Additional exam requirements/recommendations for international students: Required—TOEFL (minimum score 550 paper-based). *Application deadline:* For fall admission, 9/1 priority date for domestic students; for winter admission, 1/1 priority date for domestic students; for spring admission, 2/1 priority date for domestic students. Applications are processed on a rolling basis. Application fee: $50. Electronic applications accepted. *Expenses:* Tuition: Full-time $22,731; part-time $1029 per credit. *Required fees:* $956; $956. *Financial support:* Career-related internships or fieldwork and Federal Work-Study available. Support available to part-time students. Financial award application deadline: 6/30; financial award applicants required to submit FAFSA. *Faculty research:* International finance, computer applications, labor relations, executive development. *Unit head:* Dr. Elana Zolfo, Dean, 631-244-3266, Fax: 631-244-1018, E-mail: zolfoe@dowling.edu. *Application contact:* Mary Boullianne, Dean of Admissions, 631-244-3274, Fax: 631-244-1059, E-mail: boulliam@dowling.edu.

Embry-Riddle Aeronautical University–Daytona, Daytona Beach Campus Graduate Program, Department of Business Administration, Daytona Beach, FL 32114-3900. Offers MBA, MBA-AM, MSAF. *Accreditation:* ACBSP. Part-time programs available. *Degree requirements:* For master's, thesis or alternative. *Entrance requirements:* For master's, GMAT, minimum GPA of 2.5. Additional exam requirements/recommendations for international students: Required—TOEFL (minimum score 550 paper-based; 79 iBT). Electronic applications accepted. *Faculty research:* Aircraft safety operations analysis, energy consumption analysis, statistical analysis of general aviation accidents, airport funding strategies, industry assessment and marketing analysis for ENAER aerospace.
See Display on this page and Close-Up on page 635.

Embry-Riddle Aeronautical University–Worldwide, Worldwide Headquarters - Graduate Programs, Program in Business Administration and Management, Daytona Beach, FL 32114-3900. Offers air transportation management (Graduate Certificate); airport planning design and development (Graduate Certificate); aviation (MBAA); aviation enterprises in the global environment (Graduate Certificate); aviation-aerospace industrial management (Graduate Certificate); engineering management (MSEM); integrated logistics management (Graduate Certificate); leadership (MSL); logistics and supply chain management (MSLSCM); management (MSM); modeling and simulation

management (Graduate Certificate); occupational safety management (MSOSM); project management (MSPM, Graduate Certificate). Part-time and evening/weekend programs available. Postbaccalaureate distance learning degree programs offered (no on-campus study). *Degree requirements:* For master's, comprehensive exam (for some programs), thesis (for some programs). *Entrance requirements:* Additional exam requirements/recommendations for international students: Recommended—TOEFL (minimum score 550 paper-based; 79 iBT). Electronic applications accepted. *Faculty research:* Healthcare operations management, humanitarian logistics, supply chain risk management, collaborative supply chain management, intersection of collaborative supply chain management and the learning organization, development of assessment tool measuring supply chain collaborative capacity, teaching effectiveness, teaching quality, management style effectiveness, aeronautics, small/medium-sized business leadership study, leadership factors, critical thinking, efficacy of ePortfolio.

Lewis University, College of Arts and Sciences, Program in Aviation and Transportation, Romeoville, IL 60446. Offers administration (MS); safety and security (MS). Part-time and evening/weekend programs available. Postbaccalaureate distance learning degree programs offered (no on-campus study). *Students:* 7 full-time (3 women), 18 part-time (7 women); includes 5 minority (3 Black or African American, non-Hispanic/Latino; 1 Hispanic/Latino; 1 Two or more races, non-Hispanic/Latino), 2 international. Average age 33. *Entrance requirements:* For master's, bachelor's degree, minimum GPA of 3.0, personal statement, 3 letters of recommendation. Additional exam requirements/recommendations for international students: Required—TOEFL (minimum score 550 paper-based; 80 iBT). *Application deadline:* For fall admission, 5/1 priority date for international students; for spring admission, 11/15 priority date for international students. Applications are processed on a rolling basis. Application fee: $40. Electronic applications accepted. *Financial support:* Application deadline: 5/1; applicants required to submit FAFSA. *Unit head:* Dr. Randal DeMik, Program Chair, 815-838-0500 Ext. 5559, E-mail: demikra@lewisu.edu. *Application contact:* Julie Branchaw, Assistant Director, Graduate and Adult Admission, 815-836-5574, E-mail: branchju@lewisu.edu.

Lynn University, College of Business and Management, Boca Raton, FL 33431-5598. Offers aviation management (MBA); financial valuation and investment management (MBA); hospitality management (MBA); international business (MBA); marketing (MBA); mass communication and media management (MBA); sports and athletics administration (MBA). Part-time and evening/weekend programs available. Postbaccalaureate distance learning degree programs offered. *Faculty:* 16 full-time (6 women), 8 part-time/adjunct (3 women). *Students:* 181 full-time (95 women), 83 part-time (37 women); includes 41 minority (22 Black or African American, non-Hispanic/Latino; 1 Asian, non-Hispanic/Latino; 17 Hispanic/Latino; 1 Two or more races, non-Hispanic/Latino), 77 international. Average age 28. 137 applicants, 100% accepted, 107 enrolled. In 2013, 149 master's awarded. *Degree requirements:* For master's, projects. *Entrance requirements:* For master's, GMAT or GRE, bachelor's degree from accredited institution, minimum undergraduate GPA of 2.5, resume, 2 letters of recommendation. Additional exam requirements/recommendations for international students: Required—TOEFL (minimum score 550 paper-based). *Application deadline:* Applications are processed on a rolling basis. Application fee: $45. Electronic applications accepted. *Expenses: Tuition:* Full-time $23,760; part-time $660 per credit. *Required fees:* $300; $50 per term. Tuition and fees vary according to degree level and program. *Financial support:* Career-related internships or fieldwork, Federal Work-Study, institutionally sponsored loans, scholarships/grants, tuition waivers (full and partial), and unspecified assistantships available. Support available to part-time students. Financial award application deadline: 8/1; financial award applicants required to submit FAFSA. *Faculty research:* Labor relations, dynamic balance in leisure-time skills, ethics in athletics, hotel development. *Unit head:* Dr. Ralph Norcio, Senior Associate Dean, 561-237-7010, Fax: 561-237-7014, E-mail: rnorcio@lynn.edu. *Application contact:* Steven Pruitt, Director of Graduate and Undergraduate Evening Admission, 561-237-7834, Fax: 561-237-7100, E-mail: spruitt@lynn.edu.
Website: http://www.lynn.edu/academics/colleges/business-and-management.

Middle Tennessee State University, College of Graduate Studies, College of Basic and Applied Sciences, Department of Aerospace, Program in Aviation Administration, Murfreesboro, TN 37132. Offers MS. Part-time and evening/weekend programs available. Postbaccalaureate distance learning degree programs offered. *Students:* 14 full-time (5 women), 20 part-time (2 women); includes 15 minority (6 Black or African American, non-Hispanic/Latino; 7 Asian, non-Hispanic/Latino; 1 Hispanic/Latino; 1 Two or more races, non-Hispanic/Latino). 19 applicants, 63% accepted. In 2013, 10 master's awarded. *Degree requirements:* For master's, comprehensive exam, thesis optional. *Entrance requirements:* For master's, GRE or MAT. Additional exam requirements/recommendations for international students: Required—TOEFL (minimum score 525 paper-based; 71 iBT) or IELTS (minimum score 6). *Application deadline:* For fall admission, 6/1 for domestic and international students. Applications are processed on a rolling basis. Application fee: $25 ($30 for international students). *Financial support:* In 2013–14, 4 students received support. Tuition waivers available. Support available to part-time students. Financial award application deadline: 5/1. *Unit head:* Dr. Ron Ferrara, Interim Chair, 615-898-2788, Fax: 615-904-8273, E-mail: ron.ferrara@mtsu.edu. *Application contact:* Dr. Michael D. Allen, Vice Provost for Research and Dean, 615-898-2840, Fax: 615-904-8020, E-mail: michael.allen@mtsu.edu.

Purdue University, Graduate School, College of Technology, Department of Aviation Technology, West Lafayette, IN 47907. Offers aviation and aerospace management (MS). *Faculty:* 28 full-time (4 women), 4 part-time/adjunct (0 women). *Students:* 24 full-time (4 women), 18 part-time (2 women); includes 7 minority (1 Black or African American, non-Hispanic/Latino; 5 Asian, non-Hispanic/Latino; 1 Hispanic/Latino), 9 international. Average age 29. 29 applicants, 90% accepted, 15 enrolled. In 2013, 17 master's awarded. *Entrance requirements:* For master's, GRE/GMAT, written and spoken communication skills; general knowledge of aviation industry operations and components; entry-level analytical tools and processes; group activity and interpersonal skills. Additional exam requirements/recommendations for international students: Required—TOEFL (minimum score 550 paper-based; 77 iBT); Recommended—TWE. *Application deadline:* For fall admission, 4/1 for domestic and international students; for spring admission, 10/1 for domestic students, 9/1 for international students; for summer admission, 4/1 for domestic students, 2/15 for international students. Applications are processed on a rolling basis. Application fee: $60 ($75 for international students). Electronic applications accepted. *Unit head:* Robert F. Cox, Head, E-mail: rfcox@purdue.edu. *Application contact:* Shannon M. Cassady, Graduate School Admissions, 765-494-2884, E-mail: scassady@purdue.edu.
Website: https://tech.purdue.edu/departments/aviation-technology.

Southeastern Oklahoma State University, Department of Aviation Science, Durant, OK 74701-0609. Offers aerospace administration and logistics (MS). Part-time and evening/weekend programs available. *Entrance requirements:* For master's, minimum GPA of 3.0 in last 60 hours or 2.75 overall. Additional exam requirements/recommendations for international students: Required—TOEFL (minimum score 550 paper-based; 79 iBT). Electronic applications accepted.

Vaughn College of Aeronautics and Technology, Graduate Programs, Flushing, NY 11369. Offers airport management (MS). *Degree requirements:* For master's, project or thesis.

Logistics

Air Force Institute of Technology, Graduate School of Engineering and Management, Department of Operational Sciences, Dayton, OH 45433-7765. Offers logistics management (MS); operations research (MS, PhD); space operations (MS). Part-time programs available. *Degree requirements:* For master's, thesis; for doctorate, thesis/dissertation. *Entrance requirements:* For doctorate, GRE General Test, minimum GPA of 3.0, U.S. citizenship. *Faculty research:* Optimization, simulation, combat modeling and analysis, reliability and maintainability, resource scheduling.

American Public University System, AMU/APU Graduate Programs, Charles Town, WV 25414. Offers accounting (MBA, MS); criminal justice (MA), including business administration, emergency and disaster management, general (MA, MS); educational leadership (M Ed); emergency and disaster management (MA); entrepreneurship (MBA); environmental policy and management (MS), including environmental planning, environmental sustainability, fish and wildlife management, general (MA, MS), global environmental management; finance (MBA); general (MBA); global business management (MBA); history (MA), including American history, ancient and classical history, European history, global history, public history; homeland security (MA), including business administration, counter-terrorism studies, criminal justice, cyber, emergency management and public health, intelligence studies, transportation security; homeland security resource allocation (MBA); humanities (MA); information technology (MS), including digital forensics, enterprise software development, information assurance and security, IT project management; information technology management (MBA); intelligence studies (MA), including criminal intelligence, cyber, general (MA, MS), homeland security, intelligence analysis, intelligence collection, intelligence management, intelligence operations, terrorism studies; international relations and conflict resolution (MA), including comparative and security issues, conflict resolution, international and transnational security issues, peacekeeping; legal studies (MA); management (MA), including defense management, general (MA, MS), human resource management, organizational leadership, public administration; marketing (MBA); military history (MA), including American military history, American Revolution, civil war, war since 1945, World War II; military studies (MA), including joint warfare, strategic leadership; national security studies (MA), including general (MA, MS), homeland security, regional security studies, security and intelligence analysis, terrorism studies; nonprofit management (MBA); political science (MA), including American politics and government, comparative government and development, general (MA, MS), international relations, public policy; psychology (MA), including general (MA, MS), maritime engineering management, reverse logistics management; public administration (MPA), including disaster management, environmental policy, health policy, human resources, national security, organizational management, security management; public health (MPH); reverse logistics management (MA); school counseling (M Ed); security management (MA); space studies (MS), including aerospace science, general (MA, MS), planetary science; sports and health sciences (MS); teaching (M Ed), including curriculum and instruction for elementary teachers, elementary reading, English language learners, instructional leadership, online learning, special education; transportation and logistics management (MA), including general (MA, MS), maritime engineering management, reverse logistics management. Programs offered via distance learning only. Part-time and evening/weekend programs available. Postbaccalaureate distance learning degree programs offered (no on-campus study). *Faculty:* 432 full-time (242 women), 1,722 part-time/adjunct (829 women). *Students:* 511 full-time (241 women), 10,947 part-time (4,294 women); includes 3,760 minority (2,058 Black or African American, non-Hispanic/Latino; 88 American Indian or Alaska Native, non-Hispanic/Latino; 293 Asian, non-Hispanic/Latino; 876 Hispanic/Latino; 91 Native Hawaiian or other Pacific Islander, non-Hispanic/Latino; 354 Two or more races, non-Hispanic/Latino), 134 international. Average age 36. In 2013, 3,323 master's awarded. *Degree requirements:* For master's, comprehensive exam or practicum. *Entrance requirements:* For master's, official transcript showing earned bachelor's degree from institution accredited by recognized accrediting body. Additional exam requirements/recommendations for international students: Required—TOEFL (minimum score 550 paper-based), IELTS (minimum score 6.5). *Application deadline:* Applications are processed on a rolling basis. Application fee: $0. Electronic applications accepted. *Expenses: Tuition:* Part-time $325 per semester hour. *Financial support:* Applicants required to submit FAFSA. *Faculty research:* Military history, criminal justice, management performance, national security. *Unit head:* Dr. Karan Powell, Executive Vice President and Provost, 877-468-6268, Fax: 304-724-3780. *Application contact:* Terry Grant, Vice President of Enrollment Management, 877-468-6268, Fax: 304-724-3780, E-mail: info@apus.edu.
Website: http://www.apus.edu.

Benedictine University, Graduate Programs, Program in Business Administration, Lisle, IL 60532-0900. Offers accounting (MBA); entrepreneurship and managing innovation (MBA); financial management (MBA); health administration (MBA); human resource management (MBA); information systems security (MBA); international business (MBA); management consulting (MBA); management information systems (MBA); marketing management (MBA); operations management and logistics (MBA); organizational leadership (MBA). Part-time and evening/weekend programs available. Postbaccalaureate distance learning degree programs offered (minimal on-campus study). *Faculty:* 4 full-time (2 women), 24 part-time/adjunct (3 women). *Students:* 144 full-time (83 women), 599 part-time (328 women); includes 189 minority (115 Black or African American, non-Hispanic/Latino; 5 American Indian or Alaska Native, non-Hispanic/Latino; 43 Asian, non-Hispanic/Latino; 24 Hispanic/Latino; 2 Native Hawaiian or other Pacific Islander, non-Hispanic/Latino), 14 international. Average age 34. 211 applicants, 89% accepted, 155 enrolled. In 2013, 376 master's awarded. *Entrance requirements:* For master's, GMAT. Additional exam requirements/recommendations for international students: Required—TOEFL (minimum score 550 paper-based). *Application deadline:* For fall admission, 9/1 for domestic students; for winter admission, 12/1 for domestic students; for spring admission, 2/15 for domestic students.

Logistics

Applications are processed on a rolling basis. Application fee: $40. Electronic applications accepted. *Expenses: Tuition:* Part-time $590 per credit hour. *Financial support:* Career-related internships or fieldwork and health care benefits available. Support available to part-time students. *Faculty research:* Strategic leadership in professional organizations, sociology of professions, organizational change, social identity theory, applications to change management. *Unit head:* Dr. Sharon Borowicz, Director, 630-829-6219, E-mail: sborowicz@ben.edu. *Application contact:* Kari Gibbons, Director, Admissions, 630-829-6200, Fax: 630-829-6584, E-mail: kgibbons@ben.edu.

California State University, Long Beach, Graduate Studies, College of Liberal Arts, Department of Economics, Long Beach, CA 90840. Offers economics (MA); global logistics (MA). Part-time programs available. *Degree requirements:* For master's, comprehensive exam or thesis. *Entrance requirements:* For master's, GRE General Test, GRE Subject Test, minimum GPA of 3.0. Electronic applications accepted. *Faculty research:* Trade and development, economic forecasting, resource economics.

Case Western Reserve University, School of Graduate Studies, Case School of Engineering, Department of Electrical Engineering and Computer Science, Cleveland, OH 44106. Offers computer engineering (MS, PhD); computing and information sciences (MS, PhD); electrical engineering (MS, PhD); systems and control engineering (MS, PhD). Part-time and evening/weekend programs available. Postbaccalaureate distance learning degree programs offered (minimal on-campus study). *Faculty:* 30 full-time (2 women). *Students:* 165 full-time (35 women), 25 part-time (7 women); includes 5 minority (2 Black or African American, non-Hispanic/Latino; 2 Asian, non-Hispanic/Latino; 1 Hispanic/Latino), 131 international. In 2013, 24 master's, 15 doctorates awarded. Terminal master's awarded for partial completion of doctoral program. *Degree requirements:* For master's, thesis; for doctorate, thesis/dissertation, qualifying exam, teaching experience. *Entrance requirements:* For master's and doctorate, GRE General Test. Additional exam requirements/recommendations for international students: Required—TOEFL. *Application deadline:* For fall admission, 2/1 for domestic students; for spring admission, 11/1 for domestic students. Applications are processed on a rolling basis. Application fee: $50. *Financial support:* In 2013–14, 6 fellowships with full and partial tuition reimbursements, 81 research assistantships with full and partial tuition reimbursements, 9 teaching assistantships were awarded; career-related internships or fieldwork, Federal Work-Study, and institutionally sponsored loans also available. Support available to part-time students. Financial award application deadline: 3/1; financial award applicants required to submit FAFSA. *Faculty research:* Micro/nano systems; robotics and haptics, applied artificial intelligence; automation, computer-aided design and testing of digital systems. *Unit head:* Dr. Kenneth Loparo, Department Chair, 216-368-4115, E-mail: kal4@case.edu. *Application contact:* David Easler, Student Affairs Coordinator, 216-368-4080, Fax: 216-368-2801, E-mail: david.easler@case.edu. Website: http://eecs.cwru.edu/.

Central Connecticut State University, School of Graduate Studies, School of Technology, Department of Manufacturing and Construction Management, New Britain, CT 06050-4010. Offers construction management (MS, Certificate); lean manufacturing and Six Sigma (Certificate); supply chain and logistics (Certificate); technology management (MS). Part-time and evening/weekend programs available. *Faculty:* 7 full-time (1 woman), 5 part-time/adjunct (0 women). *Students:* 23 full-time (5 women), 88 part-time (21 women); includes 24 minority (12 Black or African American, non-Hispanic/Latino; 8 Asian, non-Hispanic/Latino; 3 Hispanic/Latino; 1 Two or more races, non-Hispanic/Latino), 8 international. Average age 34. 63 applicants, 67% accepted, 28 enrolled. In 2013, 39 master's awarded. *Degree requirements:* For master's, comprehensive exam, thesis or alternative; for Certificate, qualifying exam. *Entrance requirements:* For master's, minimum undergraduate GPA of 2.7. Additional exam requirements/recommendations for international students: Required—TOEFL (minimum score 550 paper-based; 79 iBT). *Application deadline:* For fall admission, 6/1 for domestic students, 5/1 for international students; for spring admission, 11/1 for domestic and international students. Applications are processed on a rolling basis. Application fee: $50. Electronic applications accepted. Part-time tuition and fees vary according to degree level. *Financial support:* In 2013–14, 4 students received support, including 4 research assistantships; career-related internships or fieldwork, Federal Work-Study, scholarships/grants, and unspecified assistantships also available. Support available to part-time students. Financial award application deadline: 3/1; financial award applicants required to submit FAFSA. *Faculty research:* All aspects of middle management, technical supervision in the workplace. *Unit head:* Dr. Jacob Kovel, Chair, 860-832-1830, E-mail: kovelj@ccsu.edu. *Application contact:* Patricia Gardner, Associate Director of Graduate Studies, 860-832-2350, Fax: 860-832-2362, E-mail: graduateadmissions@ccsu.edu.
Website: http://www.ccsu.edu/page.cfm?p=6497.

Central Michigan University, Central Michigan University Global Campus, Program in Business Administration, Mount Pleasant, MI 48859. Offers enterprise resource planning (MBA, Certificate); human resource management (MBA); logistics management (MBA, Certificate); marketing (MBA); value-driven organization (MBA). Part-time and evening/weekend programs available. *Entrance requirements:* For master's, GMAT. *Financial support:* Scholarships/grants available. Support available to part-time students. *Unit head:* Dr. Debasish Chakraborty, 989-774-3678, E-mail: chakt1d@cmich.edu. *Application contact:* Global Campus Student Services Call Center, 877-268-4636, E-mail: cmuglobal@cmich.edu.

Central Michigan University, College of Graduate Studies, College of Business Administration, MBA Program, Mount Pleasant, MI 48859. Offers accounting (MBA); business economics (MBA); consulting (MBA); finance (MBA); general business (MBA); human resource management (MBA); information systems (MBA); international business (MBA); logistics management (MBA); marketing (MBA); value-driven organization (MBA). Part-time and evening/weekend programs available. Postbaccalaureate distance learning degree programs offered (no on-campus study). Electronic applications accepted. *Faculty research:* Accounting, consulting, international business, marketing, information systems.

Colorado Technical University Colorado Springs, Graduate Studies, Program in Management, Colorado Springs, CO 80907-3896. Offers accounting (MBA, MSA); business administration (MBA); finance (MBA); human resources management (MBA); logistics/supply chain management (MBA); management (DM); marketing (MBA); mediation and dispute resolution (MBA); operations management (MBA); project management (MBA); technology management (MBA). Part-time and evening/weekend programs available. Postbaccalaureate distance learning degree programs offered. *Degree requirements:* For master's, thesis or alternative; for doctorate, thesis/dissertation. *Entrance requirements:* For doctorate, minimum graduate GPA of 3.0, 5 years of related work experience. *Faculty research:* Sexual harassment, performance evaluation, critical thinking.

Copenhagen Business School, Graduate Programs, Copenhagen, Denmark. Offers business administration (Exec MBA, MBA, PhD); business administration and information systems (M Sc); business, language and culture (M Sc); economics and business administration (M Sc); health management (MHM); international business and politics (M Sc); public administration (MPA); shipping and logistics (Exec MBA); technology, market and organization (MBA).

East Carolina University, Graduate School, College of Technology and Computer Science, Department of Technology Systems, Greenville, NC 27858-4353. Offers computer network professional (Certificate); industrial technology (MS), including computer networking management, digital communications, industrial distribution and logistics, information security, manufacturing, performance improvement, quality systems; information assurance (Certificate); Lean Six Sigma Black Belt (Certificate); occupational safety (MS); technology management (PhD); Website developer (Certificate). *Entrance requirements:* For master's and Certificate, GRE General Test or MAT, minimum GPA of 2.5; for doctorate, GRE General Test, related work experience. *Expenses:* Tuition, state resident: full-time $4223. Tuition, nonresident: full-time $16,540. *Required fees:* $2184.

Embry-Riddle Aeronautical University–Worldwide, Worldwide Headquarters - Graduate Programs, Program in Business Administration and Management, Daytona Beach, FL 32114-3900. Offers air transportation management (Graduate Certificate); airport planning design and development (Graduate Certificate); aviation (MBAA); aviation enterprises in the global environment (Graduate Certificate); aviation-aerospace industrial management (Graduate Certificate); engineering management (MSEM); integrated logistics management (Graduate Certificate); leadership (MSL); logistics and supply chain management (MSLSCM); management (MSM); modeling and simulation management (Graduate Certificate); occupational safety management (MSOSM); project management (MSPM, Graduate Certificate). Part-time and evening/weekend programs available. Postbaccalaureate distance learning degree programs offered (no on-campus study). *Degree requirements:* For master's, comprehensive exam (for some programs), thesis (for some programs). *Entrance requirements:* Additional exam requirements/recommendations for international students: Recommended—TOEFL (minimum score 550 paper-based; 79 iBT). Electronic applications accepted. *Faculty research:* Healthcare operations management, humanitarian logistics, supply chain risk management, collaborative supply chain management, intersection of collaborative supply chain management and the learning organization, development of assessment tool measuring supply chain collaborative capacity, teaching effectiveness, teaching quality, management style effectiveness, aeronautics, small/medium-sized business leadership study, leadership factors, critical thinking, efficacy of ePortfolio.

Florida Institute of Technology, Graduate Programs, Extended Studies Division, Melbourne, FL 32901-6975. Offers acquisition and contract management (MS); aerospace engineering (MS); business administration (MBA, DBA); computer information systems (MS); computer science (MS); electrical engineering (MS); engineering management (MS); human resources management (MS); logistics management (MS), including humanitarian and disaster relief logistics; management (MS), including acquisition and contract management, e-business, human resources management, information systems, logistics management, management, transportation management; material acquisition management (MS); mechanical engineering (MS); operations research (MS); project management (MS), including information systems, operations research; public administration (MPA); quality management (MS); software engineering (MS); space systems (MS); space systems management (MS); supply chain management (MS); systems management (MS), including information systems, operations research; technology management (MS). Part-time and evening/weekend programs available. Postbaccalaureate distance learning degree programs offered (no on-campus study). *Faculty:* 8 full-time (1 woman), 96 part-time/adjunct (25 women). *Students:* 94 full-time (46 women), 912 part-time (397 women); includes 436 minority (290 Black or African American, non-Hispanic/Latino; 18 American Indian or Alaska Native, non-Hispanic/Latino; 38 Asian, non-Hispanic/Latino; 62 Hispanic/Latino; 2 Native Hawaiian or other Pacific Islander, non-Hispanic/Latino; 26 Two or more races, non-Hispanic/Latino), 9 international. Average age 37. 591 applicants, 44% accepted, 220 enrolled. In 2013, 522 master's awarded. *Degree requirements:* For master's, comprehensive exam (for some programs), capstone course. *Entrance requirements:* For master's, GMAT or resume showing 8 years of supervised experience, minimum GPA of 3.0, 2 letters of recommendation, resume. Additional exam requirements/recommendations for international students: Required—TOEFL (minimum score 550 paper-based; 79 iBT). *Application deadline:* For fall admission, 4/1 for international students; for spring admission, 9/30 for international students. Applications are processed on a rolling basis. Electronic applications accepted. *Expenses:* Contact institution. *Financial support:* Application deadline: 3/1; applicants required to submit FAFSA. *Unit head:* Dr. Theodore R. Richardson, III, Senior Associate Dean, 321-674-8123, Fax: 321-674-7597, E-mail: trichardson@fit.edu. *Application contact:* Carolyn Farrior, Director of Graduate Admissions, Online Learning and Off-Campus Programs, 321-674-7118, Fax: 321-674-8216, E-mail: cfarrior@fit.edu.
Website: http://es.fit.edu.

Friends University, Graduate School, Wichita, KS 67213. Offers business law (MBL); Christian ministry (MACM); family therapy (MSFT); global (MBA), including accounting, business law, change management, health care leadership, management information systems, supply chain management and logistics; health care leadership (MHCL); management information systems (MMIS); operations management (MSOM); professional (MBA), including accounting, business law, change management, health care leadership, management information systems, supply chain management and logistics; teaching (MAT). Part-time and evening/weekend programs available. Postbaccalaureate distance learning degree programs offered (no on-campus study). *Faculty:* 18 full-time (8 women), 62 part-time/adjunct (28 women). *Students:* 161 full-time (111 women), 408 part-time (258 women); includes 157 minority (68 Black or African American, non-Hispanic/Latino; 7 American Indian or Alaska Native, non-Hispanic/Latino; 28 Asian, non-Hispanic/Latino; 18 Hispanic/Latino; 1 Native Hawaiian or other Pacific Islander, non-Hispanic/Latino; 35 Two or more races, non-Hispanic/Latino). Average age 36. 371 applicants, 90% accepted, 178 enrolled. In 2013, 432 master's awarded. *Degree requirements:* For master's, research project. *Entrance requirements:* For master's, bachelor's degree from accredited institution, official transcripts, interview with program director, letter(s) of recommendation. Additional exam requirements/recommendations for international students: Required—TOEFL (minimum score 560 paper-based). *Application deadline:* Applications are processed on a rolling basis. Application fee: $35 ($50 for international students). Electronic applications accepted. *Expenses: Tuition:* Part-time $631 per credit hour. Tuition and fees vary according to program. *Financial support:* In 2013–14, 30 students received support. Applicants required to submit FAFSA. *Unit head:* Dr. David Hofmeister, Dean of the Graduate School, 800-794-6945 Ext. 5858, Fax: 316-295-5040, E-mail: david_hofmeister@friends.edu. *Application contact:* Rachel Steiner, Manager, Graduate Recruiting Services, 800-794-6945, Fax: 316-295-5872, E-mail: rachel_steiner@friends.edu.
Website: http://www.friends.edu/.

George Mason University, School of Policy, Government, and International Affairs, Program in Transportation Policy, Operations and Logistics, Arlington, VA 22201. Offers MA, Certificate. *Faculty:* 9 full-time (5 women), 3 part-time/adjunct (0 women). *Students:* 11 full-time (1 woman), 19 part-time (4 women); includes 8 minority (4 Black or African American, non-Hispanic/Latino; 1 Asian, non-Hispanic/Latino; 2 Hispanic/Latino; 1 Two or more races, non-Hispanic/Latino), 1 international. Average age 33. 26 applicants, 81% accepted, 12 enrolled. In 2013, 8 master's awarded. *Degree requirements:* For master's, thesis or alternative. *Entrance requirements:* For master's, GRE (for students seeking merit-based scholarships), bachelor's degree with minimum GPA of 3.0, current

resume, 2 letters of recommendation, expanded goals statement, 2 copies of official transcripts. Additional exam requirements/recommendations for international students: Required—TOEFL (minimum score 575 paper-based; 88 iBT), IELTS (minimum score 6.5), PTE. *Application deadline:* For fall admission, 6/1 priority date for domestic students, 5/1 priority date for international students; for spring admission, 12/1 priority date for domestic students, 11/1 priority date for international students. Applications are processed on a rolling basis. Application fee: $65 ($80 for international students). Electronic applications accepted. *Expenses:* Contact institution. *Financial support:* Career-related internships or fieldwork, Federal Work-Study, scholarships/grants, unspecified assistantships, and health care benefits (for full-time research or teaching assistantship recipients) available. Financial award application deadline: 3/1; financial award applicants required to submit FAFSA. *Unit head:* Laurie Schintler, Director, 703-993-2256, Fax: 703-993-4557, E-mail: lschintl@gmu.edu. *Application contact:* Travis Major, Director, Graduate Admissions, 703-993-1383, E-mail: tmajor@gmu.edu.
Website: http://policy.gmu.edu/academic-professional-programs/masters-programs/transportation-policy-operations-logistics-tpol/.

Georgia College & State University, Graduate School, The J. Whitney Bunting School of Business, Logistics Education Center, Milledgeville, GA 31061. Offers MLSCM. Part-time and evening/weekend programs available. *Students:* 5 full-time (2 women), 38 part-time (20 women); includes 15 minority (11 Black or African American, non-Hispanic/Latino; 1 American Indian or Alaska Native, non-Hispanic/Latino; 2 Hispanic/Latino; 1 Native Hawaiian or other Pacific Islander, non-Hispanic/Latino). Average age 32. In 2013, 34 master's awarded. *Entrance requirements:* For master's, MAT, GRE, GMAT, immunization record, transcripts. Additional exam requirements/recommendations for international students: Recommended—TOEFL (minimum score 550 paper-based; 79 iBT). *Application deadline:* For fall admission, 7/1 priority date for domestic students, 4/1 priority date for international students; for spring admission, 11/15 priority date for domestic students, 9/1 priority date for international students. Applications are processed on a rolling basis. Application fee: $40. Electronic applications accepted. *Financial support:* Application deadline: 3/1; applicants required to submit FAFSA. *Application contact:* Lynn Hanson, Director of Graduate Programs in Business, 478-445-5115, E-mail: lynn.hanson@gcsu.edu.

Georgia Southern University, Jack N. Averitt College of Graduate Studies, College of Business Administration, Program in Logistics/Supply Chain Management, Statesboro, GA 30460. Offers PhD. *Students:* 7 full-time (2 women), 5 part-time (2 women); includes 4 minority (1 Asian, non-Hispanic/Latino; 2 Hispanic/Latino; 1 Two or more races, non-Hispanic/Latino), 4 international. Average age 37. 22 applicants. In 2013, 1 doctorate awarded. *Degree requirements:* For doctorate, comprehensive exam, thesis/dissertation. *Entrance requirements:* For doctorate, GMAT, minimum of three letters of reference; statement of purpose; resume. Additional exam requirements/recommendations for international students: Required—TOEFL (minimum score 550 paper-based; 80 iBT), IELTS (minimum score 6). *Application deadline:* For fall admission, 3/15 priority date for domestic and international students. Application fee: $50. Electronic applications accepted. *Expenses:* Tuition, state resident: full-time $7068; part-time $270 per semester hour. Tuition, nonresident: full-time $26,446; part-time $1077 per semester hour. *Required fees:* $2092. *Financial support:* In 2013–14, 10 students received support. Research assistantships, teaching assistantships, career-related internships or fieldwork, Federal Work-Study, scholarships/grants, traineeships, and unspecified assistantships available. Support available to part-time students. Financial award application deadline: 4/15; financial award applicants required to submit FAFSA. *Faculty research:* Buyer-supplier relationships, retail supply chain management, military logistics/transportation/supply chain management, strategic sourcing/outsourcing, supply chain metrics, service scheduling, demand and supply planning, supply chain strategy, sustainability, operations and supply management, decision sciences. *Unit head:* Dr. Gordon Smith, Graduate Program Director, 912-478-2357, Fax: 912-478-0292, E-mail: gsmith@georgiasouthern.edu. *Application contact:* Amanda Gilliland, Communications Coordinator, 912-478-5384, Fax: 912-478-1523, E-mail: gradadmissions@georgiasouthern.edu.
Website: http://cogs.georgiasouthern.edu/admission/GraduatePrograms/phdlogistics.php.

HEC Montreal, School of Business Administration, Master of Science Programs in Administration, Program in International Logistics, Montréal, QC H3T 2A7, Canada. Offers M Sc. Specialization offered in French. *Students:* 25 full-time (12 women), 10 part-time (4 women). 30 applicants, 47% accepted, 8 enrolled. In 2013, 2 master's awarded. *Degree requirements:* For master's, one foreign language, thesis. *Entrance requirements:* For master's, Test de francais international (TFI) with minimum score of 850 (for those who have never studied in French), BBA, undergraduate degree in another field, degree deemed equivalent by program director and minimum GPA of 3.0 on 4.3 scale. *Application deadline:* For fall admission, 3/15 for domestic and international students; for winter admission, 9/15 for domestic and international students. Application fee: $83 Canadian dollars. Electronic applications accepted. *Expenses: Tuition, area resident:* Part-time $74.14 per credit. Tuition, state resident: full-time $2669.04; part-time $201.83 per credit. Tuition, nonresident: full-time $7266; part-time $500.59 per credit. *International tuition:* $18,021.24 full-time. *Required fees:* $1529.70; $36.20 per credit. $65.50 per term. Tuition and fees vary according to degree level and program. *Financial support:* In 2013–14, 1,007 students received support. Research assistantships, teaching assistantships, and scholarships/grants available. Financial award application deadline: 9/2. *Unit head:* Dr. Anne Bourhis, Director, 514-340-6873, Fax: 514-340-6880, E-mail: anne.bourhis@hec.ca. *Application contact:* Marianne de Moura, Administrative Director, 514-340-7106, Fax: 514-340-6411, E-mail: marianne.de-moura@hec.ca.
Website: http://www.hec.ca/programmes_formations/msc/options/logistique_internationale/index.html.

Kaplan University, Davenport Campus, School of Business, Davenport, IA 52807-2095. Offers business administration (MBA); change leadership (MS); entrepreneurship (MBA); finance (MBA); health care management (MBA, MS); human resource (MBA); international business (MBA); management (MS); marketing (MBA); project management (MBA, MS); supply chain management and logistics (MBA, MS). *Accreditation:* ACBSP. Part-time and evening/weekend programs available. Postbaccalaureate distance learning degree programs offered (no on-campus study). *Entrance requirements:* Additional exam requirements/recommendations for international students: Required—TOEFL (minimum score 550 paper-based; 80 iBT). Electronic applications accepted.

Massachusetts Institute of Technology, School of Engineering, Engineering Systems Division, Cambridge, MA 02139-4307. Offers engineering and management (SM); engineering systems (SM, PhD); logistics (M Eng); technology and policy (SM); technology, management and policy (PhD); SM/MBA. *Faculty:* 20 full-time (6 women). *Students:* 295 full-time (92 women); includes 48 minority (5 Black or African American, non-Hispanic/Latino; 26 Asian, non-Hispanic/Latino; 14 Hispanic/Latino; 3 Two or more races, non-Hispanic/Latino), 136 international. Average age 31. 930 applicants, 28% accepted, 180 enrolled. In 2013, 166 master's, 18 doctorates awarded. *Degree requirements:* For master's, thesis; for doctorate, comprehensive exam, thesis/dissertation. *Entrance requirements:* For master's, GRE General Test; for doctorate, GRE General Test. Additional exam requirements/recommendations for international students: Required—IELTS (minimum score 7.5). *Application deadline:* For fall admission, 12/15 for domestic and international students. Application fee: $75. Electronic applications accepted. *Expenses:* Contact institution. *Financial support:* In 2013–14, 221 students received support, including 65 fellowships (averaging $33,800 per year), 88 research assistantships (averaging $31,300 per year), 19 teaching assistantships (averaging $30,200 per year); Federal Work-Study, institutionally sponsored loans, scholarships/grants, traineeships, health care benefits, and unspecified assistantships also available. *Faculty research:* Critical infrastructures, extended enterprises, energy and sustainability, health care delivery, humans and technology, uncertainty and dynamics, design and implementation, networks and flows, policy and standards. *Total annual research expenditures:* $13.3 million. *Unit head:* Munther A. Dahleh, Acting Director, 617-258-8773, E-mail: esdinquiries@mit.edu. *Application contact:* Graduate Admissions, 617-253-1182, E-mail: esdgrad@mit.edu.
Website: http://esd.mit.edu/.

Michigan State University, The Graduate School, Eli Broad College of Business, Department of Supply Chain Management, East Lansing, MI 48824. Offers logistics (PhD); operations and sourcing management (PhD); supply chain management (MS), including logistics management, operations management, rail management, supply management. Part-time programs available. *Faculty:* 21. *Students:* 36. *Degree requirements:* For master's, field study/research project; for doctorate, comprehensive exam, thesis/dissertation. *Entrance requirements:* For master's, GMAT (taken within past 5 years), bachelor's degree, minimum GPA of 3.0 in junior/senior years, transcripts, at least 2 years of professional supply chain work experience, 3 letters of recommendation, essays, resume; for doctorate, GMAT or GRE, bachelor's or master's degree, transcripts, strong work experience, 3 letters of recommendation, statement of personal goals, interview. Additional exam requirements/recommendations for international students: Required—TOEFL (minimum score 600 paper-based). *Application deadline:* For fall admission, 12/1 for domestic and international students. Application fee: $50. Electronic applications accepted. *Expenses:* Contact institution. *Financial support:* Fellowships with tuition reimbursements, research assistantships with tuition reimbursements, and teaching assistantships with tuition reimbursements available. *Unit head:* Dr. David J. Closs, Chairperson, 517-432-6406, Fax: 517-432-8048, E-mail: closs@broad.msu.edu. *Application contact:* Nancy Taylor, Office Supervisor, 517-432-6458, Fax: 517-432-8048, E-mail: taylor@broad.msu.edu.
Website: http://supplychain.broad.msu.edu.

Naval Postgraduate School, Departments and Academic Groups, Graduate School of Business and Public Policy, Monterey, CA 93943. Offers acquisition and contract management (MBA); business administration (EMBA, MBA); contract management (MS); defense business management (MBA); defense systems analysis (MS), including management; defense systems management (international) (MBA); financial management (MBA); information management (MBA); manpower systems analysis (MS); material logistics support management (MBA); program management (MS); resource planning and management for international defense (MBA); supply chain management (MBA); systems acquisition management (MBA); transportation management (MBA). Program only open to commissioned officers of the United States and friendly nations and selected United States federal civilian employees. *Accreditation:* AACSB; NASPAA. Part-time programs available. Postbaccalaureate distance learning degree programs offered (minimal on-campus study). *Degree requirements:* For master's, thesis (for some programs), terminal project/capstone (for some programs). *Faculty research:* U.S. and European public procurement policies for small and medium-sized enterprises, examining external validity criticisms in the choice of students as subjects in accounting experiment studies, assurance of learning in contract management education, contracting for cloud computing: opportunities and risks, NPS, Apple App Store as a business model supporting U. S. Navy requirements.

North Dakota State University, College of Graduate and Interdisciplinary Studies, College of Engineering and Architecture, Department of Civil Engineering, Fargo, ND 58108. Offers civil engineering (MS, PhD); environmental engineering (MS, PhD); transportation and logistics (PhD). PhD in transportation and logistics offered jointly with Upper Great Plains Transportation Institute. Part-time programs available. Postbaccalaureate distance learning degree programs offered (minimal on-campus study). *Faculty:* 12 full-time (2 women), 1 part-time/adjunct (0 women). *Students:* 29 full-time (4 women), 19 part-time (1 woman); includes 3 minority (1 Black or African American, non-Hispanic/Latino; 1 American Indian or Alaska Native, non-Hispanic/Latino; 1 Two or more races, non-Hispanic/Latino), 27 international. Average age 29. 37 applicants, 32% accepted, 8 enrolled. In 2013, 5 master's, 2 doctorates awarded. *Degree requirements:* For master's, thesis; for doctorate, comprehensive exam, thesis/dissertation. *Entrance requirements:* Additional exam requirements/recommendations for international students: Required—TOEFL (minimum score 525 paper-based; 71 iBT). *Application deadline:* For fall admission, 2/15 priority date for domestic and international students; for spring admission, 9/15 priority date for domestic and international students. Applications are processed on a rolling basis. Application fee: $35. Electronic applications accepted. *Financial support:* Fellowships with full tuition reimbursements, research assistantships with full tuition reimbursements, teaching assistantships with full tuition reimbursements, career-related internships or fieldwork, Federal Work-Study, and institutionally sponsored loans available. Support available to part-time students. Financial award application deadline: 1/15. *Faculty research:* Wastewater, solid waste, composites, nanotechnology. *Unit head:* Dr. Eakalak Khan, Chair, 701-231-7244, Fax: 701-231-6185, E-mail: eakalak.khan@ndsu.edu. *Application contact:* Dr. Kalpana Katti, Professor and Graduate Program Coordinator, 701-231-9504, Fax: 701-231-6185, E-mail: kalpana.katti@ndsu.edu.
Website: http://www.ce.ndsu.nodak.edu/.

North Dakota State University, College of Graduate and Interdisciplinary Studies, Interdisciplinary Program in Transportation and Logistics, Fargo, ND 58108. Offers managerial logistics (MML); transportation and logistics (PhD); transportation and urban systems (MS). *Students:* 37 full-time (6 women), 15 part-time (2 women); includes 7 minority (5 Black or African American, non-Hispanic/Latino; 1 Asian, non-Hispanic/Latino; 1 Two or more races, non-Hispanic/Latino), 21 international. Average age 36. 26 applicants, 62% accepted, 12 enrolled. In 2013, 5 master's, 1 doctorate awarded. *Entrance requirements:* For doctorate, 1 year of calculus, statistics and probability, minimum GPA of 3.0. Additional exam requirements/recommendations for international students: Required—TOEFL (minimum score 550 paper-based; 79 iBT). *Application deadline:* For fall admission, 5/1 priority date for domestic students. Applications are processed on a rolling basis. Application fee: $35. *Financial support:* Research assistantships with full tuition reimbursements available. *Faculty research:* Supply chain optimization, spatial analysis of transportation networks, advanced traffic analysis, transportation demand, railroad/intermodal freight. *Unit head:* Dr. Denver Tolliver, Director, 701-231-7938, Fax: 701-231-1945, E-mail: denver.tolliver@ndsu.nodak.edu. *Application contact:* Sonya Goergen, Marketing, Recruitment, and Public Relations Coordinator, 701-231-7033, Fax: 701-231-6524.
Website: http://www.mountain-plains.org/education/tlprogram/.

The Ohio State University, Graduate School, Max M. Fisher College of Business, Program in Business Logistics Engineering, Columbus, OH 43210. Offers MBLE.

Students: 75 full-time (49 women); includes 1 minority (Asian, non-Hispanic/Latino), 73 international. Average age 23. In 2013, 38 master's awarded. *Entrance requirements:* For master's, GRE or GMAT. Additional exam requirements/recommendations for international students: Required—TOEFL (minimum score 550 paper-based; 79 iBT), Michigan English Language Assessment Battery (minimum score 82); Recommended—IELTS (minimum score 7). *Application deadline:* For fall admission, 7/15 for domestic students, 5/1 for international students; for spring admission, 5/15 for domestic students, 4/1 for international students. Applications are processed on a rolling basis. Application fee: $60 ($70 for international students). Electronic applications accepted. *Unit head:* Walter Zinn, Chair, 614-292-0797, E-mail: zinn.13@osu.edu. *Application contact:* Graduate Admissions, 614-292-6031, Fax: 614-292-3656, E-mail: gradadmissions@osu.edu.
Website: http://fisher.osu.edu/mble.

Polytechnic University of Puerto Rico, Miami Campus, Graduate School, Miami, FL 33166. Offers accounting (MBA); business administration (MBA); construction management (MEM); environmental management (MEM); finance (MBA); human resources management (MBA); logistics and supply chain management (MBA); management of international enterprises (MBA); manufacturing management (MEM); marketing management (MBA); project management (MBA). Part-time and evening/weekend programs available. Postbaccalaureate distance learning degree programs offered (no on-campus study). *Entrance requirements:* For master's, minimum GPA of 3.0. Electronic applications accepted.

Pontifical Catholic University of Puerto Rico, College of Business Administration, Program in Maritime Logistics and Transportation, Ponce, PR 00717-0777. Offers Professional Certificate.

Pontificia Universidad Catolica Madre y Maestra, Graduate School, Faculty of Engineering Sciences, Santiago, Dominican Republic. Offers earthquake engineering (ME); logistics management (ME).

Stevens Institute of Technology, Graduate School, School of Systems and Enterprises, Program in Systems Design and Operational Effectiveness, Hoboken, NJ 07030. Offers M Eng.

Stevens Institute of Technology, Graduate School, School of Systems and Enterprises, Program in Systems Engineering, Hoboken, NJ 07030. Offers agile systems and enterprises (Certificate); systems and supportability engineering (Certificate); systems engineering (M Eng, PhD); systems engineering management (Certificate).

Trident University International, College of Business Administration, Program in Business Administration, Cypress, CA 90630. Offers business administration (PhD); conflict and negotiation management (MBA); criminal justice administration (MBA); entrepreneurship (MBA); finance (MBA); general management (MBA); government accounting (MBA); human resource management (MBA); information security and digital assurance management (MBA); information technology management (MBA); international business (MBA); logistics management (MBA); marketing (MBA); project management (MBA); public management (MBA); quality management (MBA); strategic leadership (MBA). Part-time and evening/weekend programs available. Postbaccalaureate distance learning degree programs offered (no on-campus study). *Degree requirements:* For doctorate, comprehensive exam, thesis/dissertation, defense of dissertation. *Entrance requirements:* For master's, minimum GPA of 2.5 (students with GPA 3.0 or greater may transfer up to 30% of graduate level credits); for doctorate, minimum GPA of 3.4, curriculum vitae, course work in research methods or statistics. Additional exam requirements/recommendations for international students: Required—TOEFL. Electronic applications accepted.

Universidad del Turabo, Graduate Programs, School in Business Administration, Program in Logistics and Materials Management, Gurabo, PR 00778-3030. Offers MBA. Part-time and evening/weekend programs available. *Entrance requirements:* For master's, GRE, EXADEP, interview.

University at Buffalo, the State University of New York, Graduate School, School of Management, Buffalo, NY 14260. Offers accounting (MS); business administration (EMBA, MBA, PMBA); finance (MS), including financial management, quantitative finance; management (PhD); management information systems (MS); supply chains and operations management (MS); Au D/MBA; DDS/MBA; JD/MBA; M Arch/MBA; MA/MBA; MD/MBA; MPH/MBA; MSW/MBA; Pharm D/MBA. *Accreditation:* AACSB. Part-time and evening/weekend programs available. *Faculty:* 72 full-time (23 women), 51 part-time/adjunct (13 women). *Students:* 627 full-time (266 women), 181 part-time (65 women); includes 50 minority (16 Black or African American, non-Hispanic/Latino; 5 American Indian or Alaska Native, non-Hispanic/Latino; 5 Asian, non-Hispanic/Latino; 3 Hispanic/Latino; 21 Native Hawaiian or other Pacific Islander, non-Hispanic/Latino), 332 international. Average age 28. 2,083 applicants, 52% accepted, 432 enrolled. In 2013, 476 master's, 10 doctorates awarded. *Degree requirements:* For master's, thesis (for some programs); for doctorate, comprehensive exam, thesis/dissertation. *Entrance requirements:* For master's, GMAT (for MS in accounting); GRE or GMAT (for MBA and all other MS concentrations), essays, letters of recommendation; for doctorate, GMAT or GRE, essays, writing sample, letters of recommendation. Additional exam requirements/recommendations for international students: Required—IELTS or PTE; Recommended—TOEFL (minimum score 95 iBT). *Application deadline:* For fall admission, 5/2 priority date for domestic students, 2/1 priority date for international students. Applications are processed on a rolling basis. Application fee: $100. Electronic applications accepted. *Expenses:* Contact institution. *Financial support:* In 2013–14, 115 students received support, including 40 fellowships (averaging $5,250 per year), 33 research assistantships with full and partial tuition reimbursements available (averaging $18,000 per year), 42 teaching assistantships with partial tuition reimbursements available (averaging $10,255 per year); career-related internships or fieldwork, Federal Work-Study, institutionally sponsored loans, scholarships/grants, health care benefits, and unspecified assistantships also available. Financial award application deadline: 2/15; financial award applicants required to submit FAFSA. *Faculty research:* Earnings management and electronic information assurance, supply chain and operations management, corporate financing and asset pricing, consumer behavior and quantitative modeling of marketing behavior, leadership and politics in organizations. *Total annual research expenditures:* $155,000. *Unit head:* Erin K. O'Brien, Assistant Dean and Director of Graduate Programs, 716-645-3204, Fax: 716-645-2341, E-mail: ekobrien@buffalo.edu. *Application contact:* Meghan Felser, Associate Director of Admissions and Recruiting, 716-645-3204, Fax: 716-645-2341, E-mail: mpwood@buffalo.edu.
Website: http://mgt.buffalo.edu/.

The University of Alabama in Huntsville, School of Graduate Studies, College of Business Administration, Programs in Business and Management, Huntsville, AL 35899. Offers federal contracting and procurement management (Certificate); management (MBA), including acquisition management, entrepreneurship, federal contract accounting, finance, human resource management, logistics and supply chain management, marketing, project management; supply chain management (Certificate); technology and innovation management (Certificate). *Accreditation:* AACSB. Part-time and evening/weekend programs available. *Faculty:* 13 full-time (3 women), 5 part-time/adjunct (0 women). *Students:* 41 full-time (19 women), 144 part-time (59 women); includes 35 minority (13 Black or African American, non-Hispanic/Latino; 1 American Indian or Alaska Native, non-Hispanic/Latino; 9 Asian, non-Hispanic/Latino; 11 Hispanic/Latino; 1 Two or more races, non-Hispanic/Latino), 13 international. Average age 33. 131 applicants, 78% accepted, 67 enrolled. In 2013, 83 master's, 5 other advanced degrees awarded. *Degree requirements:* For master's, comprehensive exam, thesis or alternative. *Entrance requirements:* For master's, GMAT (minimum score 500), minimum AACSB index of 1080. Additional exam requirements/recommendations for international students: Required—TOEFL (minimum score 550 paper-based; 80 iBT), IELTS (minimum score 6.5). *Application deadline:* For fall admission, 7/15 priority date for domestic students, 4/1 priority date for international students; for spring admission, 11/30 priority date for domestic students, 9/1 priority date for international students. Applications are processed on a rolling basis. Application fee: $50. Electronic applications accepted. *Expenses:* Tuition, state resident: full-time $8912; part-time $540 per credit hour. Tuition, nonresident: full-time $20,774; part-time $1252 per credit hour. *Required fees:* $148 per semester. One-time fee: $150. *Financial support:* In 2013–14, 10 students received support, including 4 research assistantships with full and partial tuition reimbursements available (averaging $7,750 per year), 5 teaching assistantships with full and partial tuition reimbursements available (averaging $9,000 per year); career-related internships or fieldwork, Federal Work-Study, institutionally sponsored loans, scholarships/grants, health care benefits, tuition waivers (full and partial), and unspecified assistantships also available. Support available to part-time students. Financial award application deadline: 4/1; financial award applicants required to submit FAFSA. *Faculty research:* Supply chain management, management of research and development, international marketing and branding, organizational behavior and human resource management, social networks and computational economics. *Total annual research expenditures:* $2.1 million. *Unit head:* Dr. Cynthia Gramm, Chair, 256-824-6913, Fax: 256-824-6328, E-mail: cynthia.gramm@uah.edu. *Application contact:* Jennifer Pettitt, Director of Graduate Programs, 256-824-6681, Fax: 256-824-7571, E-mail: jennifer.pettitt@uah.edu.

University of Alaska Anchorage, College of Business and Public Policy, Program in Logistics, Anchorage, AK 99508. Offers global supply chain management (MS); supply chain management (Certificate). Part-time and evening/weekend programs available. Postbaccalaureate distance learning degree programs offered (no on-campus study). *Degree requirements:* For master's, thesis or alternative, research project. *Entrance requirements:* Additional exam requirements/recommendations for international students: Required—TOEFL (minimum score 550 paper-based).

University of Dallas, Graduate School of Management, Irving, TX 75062-4736. Offers accounting (MBA, MM, MS); business management (MBA, MM); corporate finance (MBA, MM); financial services (MBA); global business (MBA, MM); health services management (MBA, MM); human resource management (MBA, MM); information assurance (MBA, MM, MS); information technology (MBA, MM, MS); information technology service management (MBA, MM, MS); marketing management (MBA, MM); organization development (MBA, MM); project management (MBA, MM); sports and entertainment management (MBA, MM); strategic leadership (MBA, MM); supply chain management (MBA); supply chain management and market logistics (MM). *Accreditation:* ACBSP. Part-time and evening/weekend programs available. Postbaccalaureate distance learning degree programs offered (no on-campus study). *Entrance requirements:* Additional exam requirements/recommendations for international students: Required—TOEFL. Electronic applications accepted. *Expenses:* Contact institution.

University of Houston, College of Technology, Department of Information and Logistics Technology, Houston, TX 77204. Offers information security (MS); supply chain and logistics technology (MS); technology project management (MS). Part-time programs available. *Degree requirements:* For master's, project or thesis (most programs). *Entrance requirements:* For master's, GMAT. Additional exam requirements/recommendations for international students: Required—TOEFL (minimum score 550 paper-based; 79 iBT). Electronic applications accepted.

University of Louisville, J. B. Speed School of Engineering, Department of Industrial Engineering, Louisville, KY 40292-0001. Offers engineering management (M Eng); industrial engineering (M Eng, MS, PhD); logistics and distribution (Certificate). *Accreditation:* ABET (one or more programs are accredited). Part-time programs available. *Students:* 60 full-time (7 women), 54 part-time (10 women); includes 19 minority (2 Black or African American, non-Hispanic/Latino; 5 Asian, non-Hispanic/Latino; 7 Hispanic/Latino; 5 Two or more races, non-Hispanic/Latino), 16 international. Average age 27. 104 applicants, 73% accepted, 51 enrolled. In 2013, 11 master's awarded. Terminal master's awarded for partial completion of doctoral program. *Degree requirements:* For master's, comprehensive exam (for some programs), thesis or alternative; for doctorate, comprehensive exam, thesis/dissertation, minimum GPA of 3.0. *Entrance requirements:* For master's and doctorate, GRE General Test. Additional exam requirements/recommendations for international students: Required—TOEFL (minimum score 550 paper-based; 80 iBT), IELTS (minimum score 6.5). *Application deadline:* For fall admission, 5/1 priority date for domestic and international students; for spring admission, 11/1 priority date for domestic and international students. Applications are processed on a rolling basis. Application fee: $60. Electronic applications accepted. *Expenses:* Tuition, state resident: full-time $10,788; part-time $599 per credit hour. Tuition, nonresident: full-time $22,446; part-time $1247 per credit hour. *Required fees:* $196. Tuition and fees vary according to program and reciprocity agreements. *Financial support:* In 2013–14, 15 students received support, including 7 fellowships with full tuition reimbursements available (averaging $20,000 per year), 2 research assistantships with full tuition reimbursements available (averaging $20,000 per year), 6 teaching assistantships with full tuition reimbursements available (averaging $20,000 per year). Financial award application deadline: 1/25; financial award applicants required to submit FAFSA. *Faculty research:* Optimization, computer simulation, logistics and distribution, ergonomics and human factors, advanced manufacturing process. *Total annual research expenditures:* $748,000. *Unit head:* Dr. John S. Usher, Chair, 502-852-6342, Fax: 502-852-5633, E-mail: usher@louisville.edu. *Application contact:* Dr. Michael Day, Associate Dean, 502-852-6195, Fax: 502-852-7294, E-mail: day@louisville.edu.
Website: http://www.louisville.edu/speed/industrial/.

University of Missouri–St. Louis, College of Business Administration, Program in Business Administration, St. Louis, MO 63121. Offers accounting (MBA); business administration (Certificate); business intelligence (Certificate); finance (MBA); human resource management (Certificate); information systems (MBA); logistics and supply chain management (MBA, PhD, Certificate); marketing (MBA); marketing management (Certificate); operations management (MBA). *Accreditation:* AACSB. Part-time and evening/weekend programs available. *Faculty:* 30 full-time (5 women), 20 part-time/adjunct (8 women). *Students:* 114 full-time (51 women), 269 part-time (100 women); includes 43 minority (16 Black or African American, non-Hispanic/Latino; 14 Asian, non-Hispanic/Latino; 11 Hispanic/Latino; 1 Native Hawaiian or other Pacific Islander, non-Hispanic/Latino; 1 Two or more races, non-Hispanic/Latino), 56 international. Average age 31. 153 applicants, 91% accepted, 110 enrolled. In 2013, 136 master's, 7 other advanced degrees awarded. *Degree requirements:* For doctorate, thesis/dissertation.

Entrance requirements: For master's, GMAT, 2 letters of recommendation. Additional exam requirements/recommendations for international students: Recommended—TOEFL (minimum score 550 paper-based; 79 iBT), IELTS (minimum score 6.5). *Application deadline:* For fall admission, 7/1 for domestic and international students; for spring admission, 12/1 for domestic and international students. Applications are processed on a rolling basis. Application fee: $50 ($40 for international students). Electronic applications accepted. *Expenses:* Tuition, state resident: full-time $7364; part-time $409.10 per credit hour. Tuition, nonresident: full-time $19,162; part-time $1008.50 per credit hour. *Financial support:* In 2013–14, 14 research assistantships with full and partial tuition reimbursements (averaging $5,625 per year), 6 teaching assistantships with full and partial tuition reimbursements (averaging $9,403 per year) were awarded; career-related internships or fieldwork, Federal Work-Study, and institutionally sponsored loans also available. Support available to part-time students. Financial award application deadline: 4/1; financial award applicants required to submit FAFSA. *Faculty research:* Human resources, strategic management, marketing strategy, consumer behavior product development, advertising. *Unit head:* Francesca Ferrari, Assistant Director, 314-516-5885, Fax: 314-516-6420, E-mail: mba@umsl.edu. *Application contact:* 314-516-5458, Fax: 314-516-6996, E-mail: gradadm@umsl.edu.
Website: http://mba.umsl.edu/Degree%20Programs/index.html.

University of New Hampshire, Graduate School, College of Engineering and Physical Sciences, Department of Mechanical Engineering, Durham, NH 03824. Offers mechanical engineering (MS, PhD); systems design (PhD). Part-time programs available. *Faculty:* 19 full-time (2 women). *Students:* 23 full-time (2 women), 43 part-time (3 women); includes 4 minority (1 Black or African American, non-Hispanic/Latino; 1 Asian, non-Hispanic/Latino; 2 Two or more races, non-Hispanic/Latino), 21 international. Average age 26. 55 applicants, 71% accepted, 17 enrolled. In 2013, 10 master's, 3 doctorates awarded. *Degree requirements:* For master's, thesis or alternative; for doctorate, thesis/dissertation. *Entrance requirements:* For master's and doctorate, GRE. Additional exam requirements/recommendations for international students: Required—TOEFL (minimum score 550 paper-based; 80 iBT). *Application deadline:* For fall admission, 4/1 priority date for domestic students, 4/1 for international students; for spring admission, 12/1 for domestic students. Applications are processed on a rolling basis. Application fee: $65. Electronic applications accepted. *Expenses:* Tuition, state resident: full-time $13,500; part-time $750 per credit hour. Tuition, nonresident: full-time $26,200; part-time $1100 per credit hour. *Required fees:* $1741; $435.25 per term. Tuition and fees vary according to course level, course load, campus/location and program. *Financial support:* In 2013–14, 37 students received support, including 2 fellowships, 18 research assistantships, 16 teaching assistantships; Federal Work-Study, scholarships/grants, and tuition waivers (full and partial) also available. Support available to part-time students. Financial award application deadline: 2/15. *Faculty research:* Solid mechanics, dynamics, materials science, dynamic systems, automatic control. *Unit head:* Dr. Brad Kinsey, Chairperson, 603-862-1811. *Application contact:* Tracey Harvey, Administrative Assistant, 603-862-1353, E-mail: mechanical.engineering@unh.edu.
Website: http://www.unh.edu/mechanical-engineering/.

The University of North Carolina at Charlotte, The Graduate School, The William States Lee College of Engineering, Department of Systems Engineering and Engineering Management, Charlotte, NC 28223-0001. Offers energy analytics (Graduate Certificate); engineering management (MSEM); engineering science (MS); infrastructure and environmental systems (PhD); Lean Six Sigma (Graduate Certificate); logistics and supply chains (Graduate Certificate); systems analytics (Graduate Certificate). Part-time and evening/weekend programs available. Postbaccalaureate distance learning degree programs offered. *Faculty:* 6 full-time (1 woman), 1 (woman) part-time/adjunct. *Students:* 17 full-time (7 women), 39 part-time (11 women); includes 12 minority (6 Black or African American, non-Hispanic/Latino; 4 Asian, non-Hispanic/Latino; 2 Hispanic/Latino), 20 international. Average age 28. 86 applicants, 65% accepted, 23 enrolled. In 2013, 8 master's awarded. *Degree requirements:* For master's, thesis or alternative, project. *Entrance requirements:* For master's, GRE or GMAT, letters of recommendation. Additional exam requirements/recommendations for international students: Required—TOEFL (minimum score 557 paper-based; 83 iBT). *Application deadline:* For fall admission, 5/1 priority date for domestic students, 5/1 for international students; for spring admission, 10/1 priority date for domestic students, 10/1 for international students. Application fee: $75. Electronic applications accepted. *Expenses:* Tuition, state resident: full-time $3522. Tuition, nonresident: full-time $16,051. *Required fees:* $2585. Tuition and fees vary according to course load and program. *Financial support:* Applicants required to submit FAFSA. *Faculty research:* Sustainable material and renewable technology; thermal analysis; large scale optimization; project risk management; supply chains; leans systems; global product innovation; quality and reliability analysis and management; productivity and project management; business forecasting, market analyses and feasibility studies. *Unit head:* Dr. Robert E. Johnson, Dean, 704-687-8242, Fax: 704-687-2352, E-mail: robejohn@.uncc.edu. *Application contact:* Kathy B. Giddings, Director of Graduate Admissions, 704-687-5503, Fax: 704-687-1668, E-mail: gradadm@uncc.edu.

University of North Florida, Coggin College of Business, MBA Program, Jacksonville, FL 32224. Offers accounting (MBA); construction management (MBA); e-commerce (MBA); economics (MBA); finance (MBA); human resource management (MBA); international business (MBA); logistics (MBA); management applications (MBA). *Accreditation:* AACSB. Part-time and evening/weekend programs available. *Faculty:* 14 full-time (6 women), 1 part-time/adjunct (0 women). *Students:* 90 full-time (41 women), 231 part-time (84 women); includes 47 minority (18 Black or African American, non-Hispanic/Latino; 8 Asian, non-Hispanic/Latino; 16 Hispanic/Latino; 5 Two or more races, non-Hispanic/Latino), 29 international. Average age 29. 222 applicants, 47% accepted, 80 enrolled. In 2013, 152 master's awarded. *Entrance requirements:* For master's, GMAT or GRE, U.S. bachelor's degree from regionally-accredited university or equivalent foreign degree. Additional exam requirements/recommendations for international students: Required—TOEFL (minimum score 550 paper-based; 79 iBT). *Application deadline:* For fall admission, 7/1 priority date for domestic students, 5/1 for international students; for spring admission, 11/1 priority date for domestic students, 10/1 for international students. Application fee: $30. *Expenses:* Tuition, state resident: full-time $9794; part-time $408.10 per credit hour. Tuition, nonresident: full-time $22,383; part-time $932.61 per credit hour. *Required fees:* $2020; $84.20 per credit hour. Tuition and fees vary according to course load and program. *Financial support:* In 2013–14, 35 students received support, including 1 research assistantship (averaging $2,700 per year); teaching assistantships, Federal Work-Study, and tuition waivers (partial) also available. Support available to part-time students. Financial award application deadline: 4/1; financial award applicants required to submit FAFSA. *Faculty research:* Performance measures, costing, and inventory issues in logistics and supply chain management; inter-organizational systems; international management and marketing practices; e-commerce; organizational learning and socialization processes. *Total annual research expenditures:* $12,025. *Application contact:* Cheryl Campbell, Graduate Advisor, 904-620-2575, Fax: 904-620-2832, E-mail: ccampbell@unf.edu.
Website: http://www.unf.edu/coggin/academics/graduate/mba.aspx.

University of North Texas, Robert B. Toulouse School of Graduate Studies, Denton, TN 76203-5017. Offers accounting (MS, PhD); applied anthropology (MA, MS); applied behavior analysis (Certificate); applied technology and performance improvement (M Ed, MS, PhD); art education (MA, PhD); art history (MA); art museum education (Certificate); arts leadership (Certificate); audiology (Au D); behavior analysis (MS); biochemistry and molecular biology (MS, PhD); biology (MA, MS, PhD); business (PhD); business computer information systems (PhD); chemistry (MS, PhD); clinical psychology (PhD); communication studies (MA, MS); computer engineering (MS); computer science (MS); computer science and engineering (PhD); counseling (M Ed, MS, PhD), including clinical mental health counseling (MS), college and university counseling (M Ed, MS), elementary school counseling (M Ed, MS), secondary school counseling (M Ed, MS); counseling psychology (PhD); creative writing (MA); criminal justice (MS); curriculum and instruction (M Ed, PhD), including curriculum studies (PhD), early childhood studies (PhD), language and literacy studies (PhD); decision sciences (MBA); design (MA, MFA), including fashion design (MFA), innovation studies, interior design (MFA); early childhood studies (MS); economics (MS); educational leadership (M Ed, Ed D, PhD); educational psychology (MS), including family studies, gifted and talented (MS, PhD), human development, learning and cognition, research, measurement and evaluation; educational research (PhD), including gifted and talented (MS, PhD), human development and family studies, psychological aspects of sports and exercise, research, measurement and statistics; electrical engineering (MS); emergency management (MPA); engineering systems (MS); English (MA, PhD); environmental science (MS, PhD); experimental psychology (PhD); finance (MBA, MS, PhD); financial management (MPA); French (MA); health psychology and behavioral medicine (PhD); health services management (MBA); higher education (M Ed, Ed D, PhD); history (MA, MS, PhD), including European history (PhD), military history (PhD), United States history (PhD); hospitality management (MS); human resources management (MPA); information science (MS, PhD); information technologies (MBA); information technology and decision sciences (MS); interdisciplinary studies (MA, MS); international sustainable tourism (MS); jazz studies (MM); journalism (MA, MJ, Graduate Certificate), including interactive and virtual digital communication (Graduate Certificate), narrative journalism (Graduate Certificate), public relations (Graduate Certificate); kinesiology (MS); learning technologies (MS, PhD); library science (MS); local government management (MPA); logistics and supply chain management (MBA, PhD); long-term care, senior housing, and aging services (MA, MS); management science (PhD); marketing (MBA, PhD); materials science and engineering (MS, PhD); mathematics (MA, PhD); merchandising (MS); music (MA, MM Ed, PhD), including ethnomusicology (MA), music education (MM Ed, PhD), music theory (MA, PhD), musicology (MA, PhD), performance (MA); nonprofit management (MPA); operations and supply chain management (MBA); performance (MM, DMA); philosophy (MA, PhD); physics (MS, PhD); political science (MA, MS, PhD); public administration and management (PhD), including emergency management, nonprofit management, public financial management, urban management; radio, television and film (MA, MFA); recreation, event and sport management (MS); rehabilitation counseling (MS, Certificate); sociology (MA, MS, PhD); Spanish (MA); special education (M Ed, PhD), including autism intervention (PhD), emotional/behavioral disorders (PhD), mild/moderate disabilities (PhD); speech-language pathology (MA, MS); strategic management (MBA); studio art (MFA); taxation (MS); teaching (M Ed); MBA/MS; MS/MPH; MSES/MBA. Part-time and evening/weekend programs available. Postbaccalaureate distance learning degree programs offered. *Faculty:* 661 full-time (213 women), 240 part-time/adjunct (144 women). *Students:* 3,106 full-time (1,620 women), 3,543 part-time (2,221 women); includes 1,740 minority (533 Black or African American, non-Hispanic/Latino; 15 American Indian or Alaska Native, non-Hispanic/Latino; 286 Asian, non-Hispanic/Latino; 746 Hispanic/Latino; 3 Native Hawaiian or other Pacific Islander, non-Hispanic/Latino; 157 Two or more races, non-Hispanic/Latino), 1,145 international. Average age 32. 6,289 applicants, 43% accepted, 1751 enrolled. In 2013, 1,778 master's, 239 doctorates, 10 other advanced degrees awarded. Terminal master's awarded for partial completion of doctoral program. *Degree requirements:* For master's, variable foreign language requirement, comprehensive exam (for some programs), thesis (for some programs); for doctorate, variable foreign language requirement, comprehensive exam (for some programs), thesis/dissertation; for other advanced degree, variable foreign language requirement, comprehensive exam (for some programs). *Entrance requirements:* For master's and doctorate, GRE, GMAT. Additional exam requirements/recommendations for international students: Required—TOEFL (minimum score 550 paper-based; 79 iBT). *Application deadline:* For fall admission, 7/15 for domestic students, 3/15 for international students; for spring admission, 11/15 for domestic students, 9/15 for international students; for summer admission, 5/1 for domestic students. Applications are processed on a rolling basis. Application fee: $60. Electronic applications accepted. *Financial support:* Fellowships with partial tuition reimbursements, research assistantships with partial tuition reimbursements, teaching assistantships, career-related internships or fieldwork, Federal Work-Study, institutionally sponsored loans, scholarships/grants, health care benefits, and library assistantships available. Support available to part-time students. Financial award applicants required to submit FAFSA. *Unit head:* Mark Wardell, Dean, 940-565-2383, E-mail: mark.wardell@unt.edu. *Application contact:* Toulouse School of Graduate Studies, 940-565-2383, Fax: 940-565-2141, E-mail: gradsch@unt.edu.
Website: http://tsgs.unt.edu/.

University of St. Francis, College of Business and Health Administration, School of Business, Joliet, IL 60435-6169. Offers business administration (MBA); logistics (Certificate); management (MSM). Part-time and evening/weekend programs available. Postbaccalaureate distance learning degree programs offered (no on-campus study). *Faculty:* 8 full-time (4 women), 17 part-time/adjunct (9 women). *Students:* 32 full-time (16 women), 106 part-time (55 women); includes 38 minority (24 Black or African American, non-Hispanic/Latino; 3 Asian, non-Hispanic/Latino; 10 Hispanic/Latino; 1 Two or more races, non-Hispanic/Latino), 7 international. Average age 35. 118 applicants, 60% accepted, 53 enrolled. In 2013, 54 master's, 3 other advanced degrees awarded. *Entrance requirements:* For master's, GMAT or 2 years of managerial experience, minimum GPA of 2.75, 2 letters recommendation, personal essay, computer proficiency. Additional exam requirements/recommendations for international students: Required—TOEFL (minimum score 550 paper-based; 79 iBT), IELTS (minimum score 6.5). *Application deadline:* Applications are processed on a rolling basis. Application fee: $30. Electronic applications accepted. Application fee is waived when completed online. *Expenses: Tuition:* Part-time $710 per credit hour. *Required fees:* $125 per semester. Part-time tuition and fees vary according to degree level and program. *Financial support:* In 2013–14, 47 students received support. Scholarships/grants, tuition waivers (partial), and unspecified assistantships available. Support available to part-time students. Financial award applicants required to submit FAFSA. *Unit head:* Dr. Christopher Clott, Dean, 815-740-3395, Fax: 815-740-3537, E-mail: cclott@stfrancis.edu. *Application contact:* Sandra Sloka, Director of Admissions for Graduate and Degree Completion Programs, 800-735-7500, Fax: 815-740-3431, E-mail: ssloka@stfrancis.edu.
Website: http://www.stfrancis.edu/academics/college-of-business-health-administration/

University of South Africa, College of Economic and Management Sciences, Pretoria, South Africa. Offers accounting (D Admin, D Com); accounting science (DA); auditing (D Admin, D Com); business administration (M Tech); business economics (D Admin); business leadership (DBL); business management (D Admin, D Com); economic management analysis (M Tech); economics (D Admin, D Com, PhD); human resource

development (M Tech); industrial psychology (D Admin, D Com, PhD); logistics (D Com); marketing (M Tech); public administration (D Admin, D Com, DPA, PhD); public management (M Tech); quantitative management (D Admin, D Com); real estate (M Tech); statistics (D Admin, PhD); tourism management (D Admin, D Com); transport economics (D Admin, D Com).

University of Southern Mississippi, Graduate School, College of Science and Technology, School of Construction, Hattiesburg, MS 39406-0001. Offers logistics, trade and transportation (MS). Part-time programs available. *Faculty:* 6 full-time (0 women). *Students:* 15 full-time (7 women), 15 part-time (4 women); includes 5 minority (all Black or African American, non-Hispanic/Latino), 6 international. Average age 34. 18 applicants, 67% accepted, 8 enrolled. In 2013, 13 degrees awarded. *Degree requirements:* For master's, comprehensive exam, thesis optional. *Entrance requirements:* For master's, GMAT or GRE General Test, minimum GPA of 2.75 in last 60 hours. Additional exam requirements/recommendations for international students: Required—TOEFL, IELTS. *Application deadline:* For fall admission, 3/1 priority date for domestic students, 3/1 for international students. Applications are processed on a rolling basis. Application fee: $50. *Financial support:* In 2013–14, research assistantships with full tuition reimbursements (averaging $7,200 per year), 7 teaching assistantships with full tuition reimbursements (averaging $7,200 per year) were awarded; career-related internships or fieldwork, Federal Work-Study, scholarships/grants, health care benefits, and unspecified assistantships also available. Financial award application deadline: 3/15; financial award applicants required to submit FAFSA. *Faculty research:* Robotics; CAD/CAM; simulation; computer-integrated manufacturing processes; construction scheduling, estimating, and computer systems. *Unit head:* John Hannon, Director, 601-266-4895. *Application contact:* Dr. Tulio Sulbaran, Director, Graduate Studies, 601-266-6419.
Website: http://www.usm.edu/construction.

The University of Tennessee, Graduate School, College of Business Administration, Program in Business Administration, Knoxville, TN 37996. Offers accounting (PhD); finance (MBA, PhD); logistics and transportation (MBA, PhD); management (PhD); marketing (MBA, PhD); operations management (MBA); professional business administration (MBA); statistics (PhD); JD/MBA; MS/MBA; Pharm D/MBA. Pharm D/MBA offered jointly with The University of Tennessee Health Science Center. *Accreditation:* AACSB. Postbaccalaureate distance learning degree programs offered. *Degree requirements:* For master's, thesis or alternative; for doctorate, thesis/dissertation. *Entrance requirements:* For master's and doctorate, GMAT, minimum GPA of 2.7. Additional exam requirements/recommendations for international students: Required—TOEFL. Electronic applications accepted. *Expenses:* Tuition, state resident: full-time $9540; part-time $531 per credit hour. Tuition, nonresident: full-time $27,728; part-time $1542 per credit hour. *Required fees:* $1404; $67 per credit hour.

The University of Tennessee at Chattanooga, Graduate School, College of Engineering and Computer Science, Department of Engineering Management, Chattanooga, TN 37403. Offers engineering management (MS); fundamentals of engineering management (Graduate Certificate); leadership and ethics (Graduate Certificate); logistics and supply chain management (Graduate Certificate); nuclear engineering (Graduate Certificate); power system protection (Graduate Certificate); power systems management (Graduate Certificate); project and value management (Graduate Certificate); quality management (Graduate Certificate); sustainable electric energy (Graduate Certificate). Postbaccalaureate distance learning degree programs offered (no on-campus study). *Faculty:* 5 full-time (1 woman). *Students:* 14 full-time (5 women), 67 part-time (14 women); includes 24 minority (13 Black or African American, non-Hispanic/Latino; 6 Asian, non-Hispanic/Latino; 4 Hispanic/Latino; 1 Two or more races, non-Hispanic/Latino), 6 international. Average age 31. 31 applicants, 45% accepted, 10 enrolled. In 2013, 31 master's, 17 other advanced degrees awarded. *Degree requirements:* For master's, thesis. *Entrance requirements:* For master's, GRE General Test, letters of recommendation; minimum undergraduate GPA of 2.5 overall or 3.0 in senior year. Additional exam requirements/recommendations for international students: Required—TOEFL (minimum score 550 paper-based; 79 iBT), IELTS (minimum score 6). *Application deadline:* For fall admission, 6/13 priority date for domestic students, 6/1 for international students; for spring admission, 10/15 priority date for domestic students, 10/1 for international students. Applications are processed on a rolling basis. Application fee: $30 ($35 for international students). Electronic applications accepted. *Financial support:* In 2013–14, 5 research assistantships (averaging $6,528 per year), 3 teaching assistantships (averaging $6,781 per year) were awarded; career-related internships or fieldwork, scholarships/grants, and unspecified assistantships also available. Support available to part-time students. Financial award applicants required to submit FAFSA. *Faculty research:* Plant layout design, lean manufacturing, Six Sigma, value management, product development. *Unit head:* Dr. Neslihan Alp, Department Head, 423-425-4032, Fax: 423-425-5229, E-mail: neslihan-alp@utc.edu. *Application contact:* Dr. J. Randy Walker, Interim Dean of Graduate Studies, 423-425-4478, Fax: 423-425-5223, E-mail: randy-walker@utc.edu.
Website: http://www.utc.edu/Departments/engrcs/engm/index.php.

The University of Texas at Arlington, Graduate School, College of Engineering, Department of Industrial and Manufacturing Systems Engineering, Program in Logistics, Arlington, TX 76019. Offers MS. *Degree requirements:* For master's, comprehensive exam, thesis optional. *Entrance requirements:* For master's, GRE, GMAT, minimum GPA of 3.0. Additional exam requirements/recommendations for international students: Required—TOEFL (minimum score 550 paper-based).

University of Washington, Graduate School, Interdisciplinary Program in Global Trade, Transportation and Logistics Studies, Seattle, WA 98195. Offers Certificate.

Virginia International University, School of Business, Fairfax, VA 22030. Offers accounting (MBA); executive management (Graduate Certificate); global logistics (MBA); health care management (MBA); human resources management (MBA); international business management (MBA); international finance (MBA); marketing management (MBA). Part-time programs available. *Entrance requirements:* For master's and Graduate Certificate, bachelor's degree. Additional exam requirements/recommendations for international students: Required—TOEFL (minimum score 550 paper-based; 80 iBT), IELTS (minimum score 6). Electronic applications accepted.

Washington State University Spokane, Graduate Programs, Program in Engineering and Technology Management, Pullman, WA 99164-2785. Offers constraints management (Graduate Certificate); construction project management (Graduate Certificate); engineering and technology management (METM); facilities management (Graduate Certificate); logistics and supply chain management (Graduate Certificate); manufacturing leadership (Graduate Certificate); project management (Graduate Certificate); Six Sigma quality management (Graduate Certificate); systems engineering management (Graduate Certificate). *Degree requirements:* For master's, comprehensive exam (for some programs), thesis (for some programs), comprehensive exam or project. *Entrance requirements:* For master's, GMAT (for applicants with less than 3.0 GPA), minimum GPA of 3.0, 3 letters of reference, resume, personal statement, math through college algebra (prefer math through calculus I), experience in the engineering/technology area. Additional exam requirements/recommendations for international students: Required—TOEFL. *Expenses:* Contact institution. *Faculty research:* Operations research for decision analysis quality control and liability, analytical techniques to formulating decisions.

Wright State University, School of Graduate Studies, Raj Soin College of Business, Department of Information Systems and Operations Management, Logistics and Supply Chain Management Program, Dayton, OH 45435. Offers MS.

Supply Chain Management

American Graduate University, Master of Supply Management Program, Covina, CA 91724. Offers MSM, Certificate. Part-time programs available. Postbaccalaureate distance learning degree programs offered (no on-campus study). *Entrance requirements:* For master's, undergraduate degree from institution accredited by accrediting agency recognized by the U.S. Department of Education, photo identification and distance education survey. Additional exam requirements/recommendations for international students: Required—TOEFL.

American Graduate University, Program in Business Administration, Covina, CA 91724. Offers acquisition and contracting (MBA); general management (MBA); program/project management (MBA); supply chain management (MBA). Part-time programs available. Postbaccalaureate distance learning degree programs offered (no on-campus study). *Degree requirements:* For master's, thesis. *Entrance requirements:* For master's, undergraduate degree from institution accredited by accrediting agency recognized by the U.S. Department of Education, photo identification, response to distance education survey. Additional exam requirements/recommendations for international students: Required—TOEFL. Electronic applications accepted.

Arizona State University at the Tempe campus, W. P. Carey School of Business, Program in Business Administration, Tempe, AZ 85287-4906. Offers accountancy (PhD); agribusiness (PhD); business administration (MBA); finance (PhD); financial management and markets (MBA); information management (MBA); information systems (PhD); management (PhD); marketing (PhD); strategic marketing and services leadership (MBA); supply chain financial management (MBA); supply chain management (MBA, PhD); JD/MBA; MBA/M Acc; MBA/M Arch. *Accreditation:* AACSB. Part-time and evening/weekend programs available. Postbaccalaureate distance learning degree programs offered (minimal on-campus study). Terminal master's awarded for partial completion of doctoral program. *Degree requirements:* For master's, thesis or alternative, internship, interactive Program of Study (iPOS) submitted before completing 50 percent of required credit hours; for doctorate, comprehensive exam, thesis/dissertation, interactive Program of Study (iPOS) submitted before completing 50 percent of required credit hours. *Entrance requirements:* For master's, GMAT, minimum GPA of 3.0 in last 2 years of work leading to bachelor's degree, 2 letters of recommendation, professional resume, official transcripts, 3 essays; for doctorate, GMAT or GRE, minimum GPA of 3.0 in last 2 years of work leading to bachelor's degree, 3 letters of recommendation, resume, personal statement/essay. Additional exam requirements/recommendations for international students: Required—TOEFL (minimum score 550 paper-based; 80 iBT), IELTS (minimum score 6.5). Electronic applications accepted. *Expenses:* Contact institution.

Bryant University, Graduate School of Business, Master of Business Administration Program, Smithfield, RI 02917. Offers general business (MBA); global finance (MBA); global supply chain management (MBA); international business (MBA). *Accreditation:* AACSB. Part-time and evening/weekend programs available. *Entrance requirements:* For master's, GMAT, transcripts, recommendation, resume, statement of objectives. Additional exam requirements/recommendations for international students: Required—TOEFL (minimum score 580 paper-based; 90 iBT). *Application deadline:* For fall admission, 7/15 for domestic and international students; for spring admission, 11/15 for domestic and international students. Applications are processed on a rolling basis. Application fee: $80. Electronic applications accepted. *Expenses: Tuition:* Full-time $26,832; part-time $1118 per credit hour. *Financial support:* In 2013–14, 11 research assistantships (averaging $6,708 per year) were awarded; unspecified assistantships also available. Financial award application deadline: 7/15; financial award applicants required to submit FAFSA. *Faculty research:* International business, information systems security, leadership, financial markets microstructure, commercial lending practice. *Unit head:* Richard S. Cheney, Director of Operations for Graduate Programs, School of Business, 401-232-6707, Fax: 401-232-6494, E-mail: rcheney@bryant.edu. *Application contact:* Linda Denzer, Assistant Director of Graduate Admission, 401-232-6529, Fax: 401-232-6494, E-mail: ldenzer@bryant.edu.

California State University, East Bay, Office of Academic Programs and Graduate Studies, College of Business and Economics, MBA Program, Hayward, CA 94542-3000. Offers entrepreneurship (MBA); finance (MBA); global innovators (MBA); human resources and organizational behavior (MBA); information technology management (MBA); marketing management (MBA); operations and supply chain management (MBA); strategy and international business (MBA). Part-time and evening/weekend programs available. *Degree requirements:* For master's, comprehensive exam or thesis. *Entrance requirements:* For master's, GMAT (minimum 20th percentile verbal and quantitative section), bachelor's degree, minimum GPA of 2.75. Additional exam requirements/recommendations for international students: Required—TOEFL (minimum score 550 paper-based; 79 iBT). Electronic applications accepted. *Expenses:* Contact institution.

California State University, East Bay, Office of Academic Programs and Graduate Studies, College of Business and Economics, Program in Information Technology Management, Option in Operations and Supply Chain Management, Hayward, CA 94542-3000. Offers MBA. *Degree requirements:* For master's, comprehensive exam or thesis. *Entrance requirements:* For master's, GMAT, minimum GPA of 2.75. Additional exam requirements/recommendations for international students: Required—TOEFL (minimum score 550 paper-based). Electronic applications accepted.

California State University, San Bernardino, Graduate Studies, College of Business and Public Administration, Master in Business Administration Program, San Bernardino, CA 92407. Offers accounting (MBA); cyber security (MBA); entrepreneurship (MBA);

finance (MBA); information systems and technology (MBA); management (MBA); marketing management (MBA); supply chain management (MBA). MBA is also offered online. *Accreditation:* AACSB. Part-time and evening/weekend programs available. Postbaccalaureate distance learning degree programs offered (no on-campus study). *Faculty:* 27 full-time (6 women), 8 part-time/adjunct (1 woman). *Students:* 161 full-time (59 women), 47 part-time (18 women); includes 74 minority (12 Black or African American, non-Hispanic/Latino; 19 Asian, non-Hispanic/Latino; 42 Hispanic/Latino; 1 Two or more races, non-Hispanic/Latino), 74 international. Average age 29. 281 applicants, 38% accepted, 67 enrolled. In 2013, 79 master's awarded. *Degree requirements:* For master's, comprehensive exam, thesis, portfolio, 60 units, minimum GPA of 3.0. *Entrance requirements:* For master's, GMAT or GRE, minimum GPA of 2.5. Additional exam requirements/recommendations for international students: Required—TOEFL (minimum score 550 paper-based; 79 iBT). *Application deadline:* For fall admission, 7/20 for domestic and international students; for winter admission, 10/20 for domestic and international students; for spring admission, 1/20 for domestic and international students. Applications are processed on a rolling basis. Application fee: $55. Electronic applications accepted. *Expenses:* Contact institution. *Financial support:* In 2013–14, 79 students received support, including 21 fellowships (averaging $4,867 per year), 29 research assistantships (averaging $2,748 per year), 6 teaching assistantships (averaging $5,162 per year); career-related internships or fieldwork, Federal Work-Study, institutionally sponsored loans, scholarships/grants, and unspecified assistantships also available. Support available to part-time students. Financial award application deadline: 3/1; financial award applicants required to submit FAFSA. *Faculty research:* Market reaction to Form 20-F, tax Constitutional questions in Obamacare, the performance of the faith and ethical investment products prior to and following the 2008 meltdown, capital appreciation bonds: a ruinous decision for an unborn generation, the effects of calorie count display on consumer eating behavior, local government bankruptcy. *Total annual research expenditures:* $2.3 million. *Unit head:* Dr. Lawrence C. Rose, Dean, 909-537-3703, Fax: 909-537-7026, E-mail: lrose@csusb.edu. *Application contact:* Dr. Vipin Gupta, Associate Dean/MBA Director, 909-537-7380, Fax: 909-537-7026, E-mail: vgupta@csusb.edu.
Website: http://mba.csusb.edu/.

Capella University, School of Business and Technology, Doctoral Programs in Technology, Minneapolis, MN 55402. Offers general information technology (PhD); global operations and supply chain management (DBA); information assurance and security (PhD); information technology education (PhD); information technology management (DBA, PhD).

Capella University, School of Business and Technology, Master's Programs in Technology, Minneapolis, MN 55402. Offers enterprise software architecture (MS); general information systems and technology management (MS); global operations and supply chain management (MBA); information assurance and security (MS); information technology management (MBA); network management (MS).

Case Western Reserve University, Weatherhead School of Management, Department of Operations, Management Program, Cleveland, OH 44106. Offers operations research (MSM); supply chain (MSM); MBA/MSM. *Accreditation:* AACSB. Part-time and evening/weekend programs available. *Entrance requirements:* For master's, GMAT or GRE, 3 letters of recommendation, resume. Additional exam requirements/recommendations for international students: Required—TOEFL (minimum score 600 paper-based). *Faculty research:* Supply chain management, operations management, operations/finance interface optimization, scheduling.

Central Connecticut State University, School of Graduate Studies, School of Technology, Department of Manufacturing and Construction Management, New Britain, CT 06050-4010. Offers construction management (MS, Certificate); lean manufacturing and Six Sigma (Certificate); supply chain and logistics (Certificate); technology management (MS). Part-time and evening/weekend programs available. *Faculty:* 7 full-time (1 woman), 5 part-time/adjunct (0 women). *Students:* 23 full-time (5 women), 88 part-time (21 women); includes 24 minority (12 Black or African American, non-Hispanic/Latino; 8 Asian, non-Hispanic/Latino; 3 Hispanic/Latino; 1 Two or more races, non-Hispanic/Latino), 8 international. Average age 34. 63 applicants, 67% accepted, 28 enrolled. In 2013, 39 master's awarded. *Degree requirements:* For master's, comprehensive exam, thesis or alternative; for Certificate, qualifying exam. *Entrance requirements:* For master's, minimum undergraduate GPA of 2.7. Additional exam requirements/recommendations for international students: Required—TOEFL (minimum score 550 paper-based; 79 iBT). *Application deadline:* For fall admission, 6/1 for domestic students, 5/1 for international students; for spring admission, 11/1 for domestic and international students. Applications are processed on a rolling basis. Application fee: $50. Electronic applications accepted. Part-time tuition and fees vary according to degree level. *Financial support:* In 2013–14, 4 students received support, including 4 research assistantships; career-related internships or fieldwork, Federal Work-Study, scholarships/grants, and unspecified assistantships also available. Support available to part-time students. Financial award application deadline: 3/1; financial award applicants required to submit FAFSA. *Faculty research:* All aspects of middle management, technical supervision in the workplace. *Unit head:* Dr. Jacob Kovel, Chair, 860-832-1830, E-mail: kovelj@ccsu.edu. *Application contact:* Patricia Gardner, Associate Director of Graduate Studies, 860-832-2350, Fax: 860-832-2362, E-mail: graduateadmissions@ccsu.edu.
Website: http://www.ccsu.edu/page.cfm?p=6497.

Clayton State University, School of Graduate Studies, College of Business, Program in Business Administration, Morrow, GA 30260-0285. Offers accounting (MBA); international business (MBA); supply chain management (MBA). *Accreditation:* AACSB. Part-time and evening/weekend programs available. *Degree requirements:* For master's, thesis. *Entrance requirements:* For master's, GMAT, 3 letters of recommendation; statement of purpose; 2 official transcripts. Additional exam requirements/recommendations for international students: Required—TOEFL (minimum score 550 paper-based; 80 iBT). Electronic applications accepted. *Expenses:* Contact institution.

Delaware Valley College, MBA Program, Doylestown, PA 18901-2697. Offers accounting (MBA); entrepreneurship (MBA); finance (MBA); food and agribusiness (MBA); general business (MBA); global executive leadership (MBA); human resource management (MBA); supply chain management (MBA). Part-time and evening/weekend programs available. Postbaccalaureate distance learning degree programs offered (no on-campus study). *Students:* 32 full-time (17 women), 183 part-time (99 women). Average age 34. 97 applicants, 78% accepted, 74 enrolled. *Entrance requirements:* For master's, minimum undergraduate GPA of 3.0. *Application deadline:* Applications are processed on a rolling basis. Application fee: $50. Electronic applications accepted. *Expenses:* Contact institution. *Financial support:* Applicants required to submit FAFSA. *Unit head:* Mike Prushan, Director of MBA Program, 215-489-2322, E-mail: michael.prushan@delval.edu. *Application contact:* Robin Mathews, Graduate and Continuing Studies Enrollment Manager, 215-489-2955, Fax: 215-489-4832, E-mail: robin.mathews@delval.edu.
Website: http://www.delval.edu/academics/graduate/master-of-business-administration.

Duquesne University, John F. Donahue Graduate School of Business, Pittsburgh, PA 15282-0001. Offers accounting (M Acc); finance (MBA); information systems management (MBA, MSISM); management (MBA); marketing (MBA); supply chain management (MBA); sustainability (MBA); JD/MBA; MBA/M Acc; MBA/MA; MBA/MES; MBA/MHMS; MBA/MSN; MSISM/MBA; Pharm D/MBA. *Accreditation:* AACSB. Part-time and evening/weekend programs available. *Faculty:* 58 full-time (17 women), 40 part-time/adjunct (8 women). *Students:* 117 full-time (59 women), 147 part-time (54 women); includes 14 minority (7 Black or African American, non-Hispanic/Latino; 1 Asian, non-Hispanic/Latino; 6 Hispanic/Latino), 53 international. Average age 27. 418 applicants, 46% accepted, 109 enrolled. In 2013, 133 master's awarded. *Entrance requirements:* For master's, GMAT, undergraduate transcripts, 2 letters of recommendation, current resume, personal statement. Additional exam requirements/recommendations for international students: Required—TOEFL (minimum score 577 paper-based; 90 iBT), IELTS (minimum score 7). *Application deadline:* For fall admission, 7/1 priority date for domestic students, 6/1 for international students; for spring admission, 11/1 for domestic and international students. Applications are processed on a rolling basis. Application fee: $0. Electronic applications accepted. *Expenses: Tuition:* Full-time $18,162; part-time $1009 per credit. *Required fees:* $1728; $96 per credit. Tuition and fees vary according to program. *Financial support:* In 2013–14, 39 students received support, including 6 fellowships with partial tuition reimbursements available (averaging $4,541 per year), 33 research assistantships with partial tuition reimbursements available (averaging $9,081 per year); career-related internships or fieldwork, scholarships/grants, and unspecified assistantships also available. Support available to part-time students. Financial award application deadline: 7/1; financial award applicants required to submit FAFSA. *Faculty research:* International business, investment management, business ethics, technology management, supply chain management, business strategy, finance. *Unit head:* Thomas J. Nist, Director of Graduate Programs, 412-396-6276, Fax: 412-396-1726, E-mail: nist@duq.edu. *Application contact:* Maria W. DeCrosta, Enrollment Manager, 412-396-5529, Fax: 412-396-1726, E-mail: decrostam@duq.edu.
Website: http://www.duq.edu/business/grad.

Eastern Michigan University, Graduate School, College of Business, Department of Marketing, Ypsilanti, MI 48197. Offers e-business (MBA); integrated marketing communications (MS); international business (MBA); marketing management (MBA); supply chain management (MBA). Part-time and evening/weekend programs available. Postbaccalaureate distance learning degree programs offered (minimal on-campus study). *Faculty:* 15 full-time (8 women). *Students:* 25 full-time (20 women), 41 part-time (34 women); includes 16 minority (9 Black or African American, non-Hispanic/Latino; 1 Asian, non-Hispanic/Latino; 1 Hispanic/Latino; 5 Two or more races, non-Hispanic/Latino), 1 international. Average age 34. 41 applicants, 71% accepted, 16 enrolled. In 2013, 28 master's awarded. *Entrance requirements:* For master's, GMAT. Additional exam requirements/recommendations for international students: Required—TOEFL. *Application deadline:* For fall admission, 5/15 priority date for domestic and international students; for winter admission, 10/15 priority date for domestic and international students; for spring admission, 3/15 priority date for domestic and international students. Applications are processed on a rolling basis. Application fee: $35. *Expenses:* Tuition, state resident: full-time $12,300; part-time $466 per credit hour. Tuition, nonresident: full-time $23,159; part-time $918 per credit hour. *Required fees:* $71 per credit hour. $46 per semester. One-time fee: $100. Tuition and fees vary according to course level and degree level. *Financial support:* Fellowships, research assistantships with full tuition reimbursements, teaching assistantships with full tuition reimbursements, career-related internships or fieldwork, Federal Work-Study, institutionally sponsored loans, scholarships/grants, tuition waivers (partial), and unspecified assistantships available. Support available to part-time students. Financial award applicants required to submit FAFSA. *Unit head:* Dr. Paul Chao, Department Head, 734-487-3323, Fax: 734-487-7099, E-mail: pchao@emich.edu. *Application contact:* K. Michelle Henry, Director, Academic Services, 734-487-4444, Fax: 734-483-1316, E-mail: mhenry1@emich.edu.
Website: http://www.mkt.emich.edu/index.html.

Eastern Michigan University, Graduate School, College of Business, Programs in Business Administration, Ypsilanti, MI 48197. Offers business administration (MBA, Graduate Certificate); computer information systems (Graduate Certificate); e-business (MBA, Graduate Certificate); enterprise business intelligence (MBA); entrepreneurship (MBA, Graduate Certificate); finance (MBA, Graduate Certificate); human resources (MBA); human resources management (Graduate Certificate); information systems (MBA); internal auditing (MBA); international business (MBA, Graduate Certificate); marketing management (Graduate Certificate); nonprofit management (MBA); organizational development (Graduate Certificate); supply chain management (MBA, Graduate Certificate). *Accreditation:* AACSB. Part-time programs available. Postbaccalaureate distance learning degree programs offered (no on-campus study). *Students:* 74 full-time (28 women), 342 part-time (183 women); includes 122 minority (84 Black or African American, non-Hispanic/Latino; 2 American Indian or Alaska Native, non-Hispanic/Latino; 19 Asian, non-Hispanic/Latino; 7 Hispanic/Latino; 10 Two or more races, non-Hispanic/Latino), 38 international. Average age 33. 305 applicants, 72% accepted, 131 enrolled. In 2013, 69 master's, 57 other advanced degrees awarded. *Entrance requirements:* For master's, GMAT (minimum score 450), minimum cumulative undergraduate GPA of 2.75. Additional exam requirements/recommendations for international students: Required—TOEFL. *Application deadline:* For fall admission, 5/15 for domestic students, 5/1 for international students; for winter admission, 10/15 for domestic students, 10/1 for international students; for spring admission, 3/15 for domestic students, 3/1 for international students. Applications are processed on a rolling basis. Application fee: $35. *Expenses:* Tuition, state resident: full-time $12,300; part-time $466 per credit hour. Tuition, nonresident: full-time $23,159; part-time $918 per credit hour. *Required fees:* $71 per credit hour. $46 per semester. One-time fee: $100. Tuition and fees vary according to course level and degree level. *Financial support:* Fellowships, research assistantships with full tuition reimbursements, teaching assistantships with full tuition reimbursements, career-related internships or fieldwork, Federal Work-Study, institutionally sponsored loans, scholarships/grants, tuition waivers (partial), and unspecified assistantships available. Support available to part-time students. Financial award applicants required to submit FAFSA. *Unit head:* K. Michelle Henry, Director, Academic Services, 734-487-4444, Fax: 734-483-1316, E-mail: mhenry1@emich.edu. *Application contact:* Beste Windes, Advisor, 734-487-4444, Fax: 734-483-1316, E-mail: bwindes@emich.edu.
Website: http://www.emich.edu/public/cob/gr/grad.html.

Elmhurst College, Graduate Programs, Program in Supply Chain Management, Elmhurst, IL 60126-3296. Offers MS. Part-time and evening/weekend programs available. *Faculty:* 3 full-time (1 woman), 3 part-time/adjunct (0 women). *Students:* 39 part-time (13 women); includes 6 minority (1 Black or African American, non-Hispanic/Latino; 3 Asian, non-Hispanic/Latino; 2 Hispanic/Latino), 2 international. Average age 35. 53 applicants, 62% accepted, 21 enrolled. In 2013, 15 master's awarded. *Entrance requirements:* For master's, 3 recommendations, resume, statement of purpose. Additional exam requirements/recommendations for international students: Required—TOEFL (minimum score 550 paper-based; 79 iBT). *Application deadline:* Applications are processed on a rolling basis. Application fee: $0. Electronic applications accepted. *Expenses:* Contact institution. *Financial support:* In 2013–14, 4 students received support. Federal Work-Study and scholarships/grants available. Support available to part-time students. Financial award application deadline: 6/1; financial award applicants

required to submit FAFSA. *Application contact:* Timothy J. Panfil, Director of Enrollment Management, School for Professional Studies, 630-617-3300 Ext. 3256, Fax: 630-617-6471, E-mail: panfilt@elmhurst.edu.

Embry-Riddle Aeronautical University–Worldwide, Worldwide Headquarters - Graduate Programs, Program in Business Administration and Management, Daytona Beach, FL 32114-3900. Offers air transportation management (Graduate Certificate); airport planning design and development (Graduate Certificate); aviation (MBAA); aviation enterprises in the global environment (Graduate Certificate); aviation-aerospace industrial management (Graduate Certificate); engineering management (MSEM); integrated logistics management (Graduate Certificate); leadership (MSL); logistics and supply chain management (MSLSCM); management (MSM); modeling and simulation management (Graduate Certificate); occupational safety management (MSOSM); project management (MSPM, Graduate Certificate). Part-time and evening/weekend programs available. Postbaccalaureate distance learning degree programs offered (no on-campus study). *Degree requirements:* For master's, comprehensive exam (for some programs), thesis (for some programs). *Entrance requirements:* Additional exam requirements/recommendations for international students: Recommended—TOEFL (minimum score 550 paper-based; 79 iBT). Electronic applications accepted. *Faculty research:* Healthcare operations management, humanitarian logistics, supply chain risk management, collaborative supply chain management, intersection of collaborative supply chain management and the learning organization, development of assessment tool measuring supply chain collaborative capacity, teaching effectiveness, teaching quality, management style effectiveness, aeronautics, small/medium-sized business leadership study, leadership factors, critical thinking, efficacy of ePortfolio.

Florida Institute of Technology, Graduate Programs, Extended Studies Division, Melbourne, FL 32901-6975. Offers acquisition and contract management (MS); aerospace engineering (MS); business administration (MBA, DBA); computer information systems (MS); computer science (MS); electrical engineering (MS); engineering management (MS); human resources management (MS); logistics management (MS), including humanitarian and disaster relief logistics; management (MS), including acquisition and contract management, e-business, human resources management, information systems, logistics management, management, transportation management; material acquisition management (MS); mechanical engineering (MS); operations research (MS); project management (MS), including information systems, operations research; public administration (MPA); quality management (MS); software engineering (MS); space systems (MS); space systems management (MS); supply chain management (MS); systems management (MS), including information systems, operations research; technology management (MS). Part-time and evening/weekend programs available. Postbaccalaureate distance learning degree programs offered (no on-campus study). *Faculty:* 8 full-time (1 woman), 96 part-time/adjunct (25 women). *Students:* 94 full-time (46 women), 912 part-time (397 women); includes 436 minority (290 Black or African American, non-Hispanic/Latino; 18 American Indian or Alaska Native, non-Hispanic/Latino; 38 Asian, non-Hispanic/Latino; 62 Hispanic/Latino; 2 Native Hawaiian or other Pacific Islander, non-Hispanic/Latino; 26 Two or more races, non-Hispanic/Latino), 9 international. Average age 37. 591 applicants, 44% accepted, 220 enrolled. In 2013, 522 master's awarded. *Degree requirements:* For master's, comprehensive exam (for some programs), capstone course. *Entrance requirements:* For master's, GMAT or resume showing 8 years of supervised experience, minimum GPA of 3.0, 2 letters of recommendation, resume. Additional exam requirements/recommendations for international students: Required—TOEFL (minimum score 550 paper-based; 79 iBT). *Application deadline:* For fall admission, 4/1 for international students; for spring admission, 9/30 for international students. Applications are processed on a rolling basis. Electronic applications accepted. *Expenses:* Contact institution. *Financial support:* Application deadline: 3/1; applicants required to submit FAFSA. *Unit head:* Dr. Theodore R. Richardson, III, Senior Associate Dean, 321-674-8123, Fax: 321-674-7597, E-mail: trichardson@fit.edu. *Application contact:* Carolyn Farrior, Director of Graduate Admissions, Online Learning and Off-Campus Programs, 321-674-7118, Fax: 321-674-8216, E-mail: cfarrior@fit.edu.
Website: http://es.fit.edu.

Florida Institute of Technology, Graduate Programs, Nathan M. Bisk College of Business, Online Programs, Melbourne, FL 32901-6975. Offers accounting (MBA); accounting and finance (MBA); business administration (MBA); finance (MBA); healthcare management (MBA); information assurance and cybersecurity (MS); information technology (MS); information technology cybersecurity (MS); information technology management (MBA); international business (MBA); Internet marketing (MBA); management (MBA); marketing (MBA); project management (MBA); supply chain management (MS). Part-time and evening/weekend programs available. Postbaccalaureate distance learning degree programs offered (no on-campus study). *Faculty:* 3 full-time (1 woman), 41 part-time/adjunct (13 women). *Students:* 6 full-time (1 woman), 1,121 part-time (530 women); includes 424 minority (276 Black or African American, non-Hispanic/Latino; 10 American Indian or Alaska Native, non-Hispanic/Latino; 45 Asian, non-Hispanic/Latino; 88 Hispanic/Latino; 5 Native Hawaiian or other Pacific Islander, non-Hispanic/Latino), 32 international. Average age 36. 348 applicants, 42% accepted, 146 enrolled. In 2013, 475 master's awarded. *Entrance requirements:* For master's, GMAT or resume showing 8 years of supervised experience, 2 letters of recommendation, resume, competency in math past college algebra. Additional exam requirements/recommendations for international students: Required—TOEFL (minimum score 550 paper-based; 79 iBT). *Application deadline:* For fall admission, 4/1 for international students; for spring admission, 9/30 for international students. Applications are processed on a rolling basis. Electronic applications accepted. *Expenses:* Contact institution. *Financial support:* Available to part-time students. Application deadline: 3/1; applicants required to submit FAFSA. *Unit head:* Brian Ehrlich, Associate Vice President/Director of Online Learning, 321-674-8202, E-mail: behrlich@fit.edu. *Application contact:* Carolyn Farrior, Director of Graduate Admissions, Online Learning and Off-Campus Programs, 321-674-7118.
Website: http://online.fit.edu.

Friends University, Graduate School, Wichita, KS 67213. Offers business law (MBL); Christian ministry (MACM); family therapy (MSFT); global (MBA), including accounting, business law, change management, health care leadership, management information systems, supply chain management and logistics; health care leadership (MHCL); management information systems (MMIS); operations management (MSOM); professional (MBA), including accounting, business law, change management, health care leadership, management information systems, supply chain management and logistics; teaching (MAT). Part-time and evening/weekend programs available. Postbaccalaureate distance learning degree programs offered (no on-campus study). *Faculty:* 18 full-time (8 women), 62 part-time/adjunct (28 women). *Students:* 161 full-time (111 women), 408 part-time (258 women); includes 157 minority (68 Black or African American, non-Hispanic/Latino; 7 American Indian or Alaska Native, non-Hispanic/Latino; 28 Asian, non-Hispanic/Latino; 18 Hispanic/Latino; 1 Native Hawaiian or other Pacific Islander, non-Hispanic/Latino; 35 Two or more races, non-Hispanic/Latino). Average age 36. 371 applicants, 90% accepted, 178 enrolled. In 2013, 432 master's awarded. *Degree requirements:* For master's, research project. *Entrance requirements:* For master's, bachelor's degree from accredited institution, official transcripts, interview with program director, letter(s) of recommendation. Additional exam requirements/recommendations for international students: Required—TOEFL (minimum score 560 paper-based). *Application deadline:* Applications are processed on a rolling basis. Application fee: $35 ($50 for international students). Electronic applications accepted. *Expenses: Tuition:* Part-time $631 per credit hour. Tuition and fees vary according to program. *Financial support:* In 2013–14, 30 students received support. Applicants required to submit FAFSA. *Unit head:* Dr. David Hofmeister, Dean of the Graduate School, 800-794-6945 Ext. 5858, Fax: 316-295-5040, E-mail: david_hofmeister@friends.edu. *Application contact:* Rachel Steiner, Manager, Graduate Recruiting Services, 800-794-6945, Fax: 316-295-5872, E-mail: rachel_steiner@friends.edu.
Website: http://www.friends.edu/.

Georgia Southern University, Jack N. Averitt College of Graduate Studies, College of Business Administration, Program in Logistics/Supply Chain Management, Statesboro, GA 30460. Offers PhD. *Students:* 7 full-time (2 women), 5 part-time (2 women); includes 4 minority (1 Asian, non-Hispanic/Latino; 2 Hispanic/Latino; 1 Two or more races, non-Hispanic/Latino), 4 international. Average age 37. 22 applicants. In 2013, 1 doctorate awarded. *Degree requirements:* For doctorate, comprehensive exam, thesis/dissertation. *Entrance requirements:* For doctorate, GMAT, minimum of three letters of reference; statement of purpose; resume. Additional exam requirements/recommendations for international students: Required—TOEFL (minimum score 550 paper-based; 80 iBT), IELTS (minimum score 6). *Application deadline:* For fall admission, 3/15 priority date for domestic and international students. Application fee: $50. Electronic applications accepted. *Expenses:* Tuition, state resident: full-time $7068; part-time $270 per semester hour. Tuition, nonresident: full-time $26,446; part-time $1077 per semester hour. *Required fees:* $2092. *Financial support:* In 2013–14, 10 students received support. Research assistantships, teaching assistantships, career-related internships or fieldwork, Federal Work-Study, scholarships/grants, traineeships, and unspecified assistantships available. Support available to part-time students. Financial award application deadline: 4/15; financial award applicants required to submit FAFSA. *Faculty research:* Buyer-supplier relationships, retail supply chain management, military logistics/transportation/supply chain management, strategic sourcing/outsourcing, supply chain metrics, service scheduling, demand and supply planning, supply chain strategy, sustainability, operations and supply management, decision sciences. *Unit head:* Dr. Gordon Smith, Graduate Program Director, 912-478-2357, Fax: 912-478-0292, E-mail: gsmith@georgiasouthern.edu. *Application contact:* Amanda Gilliland, Communications Coordinator, 912-478-5384, Fax: 912-478-1523, E-mail: gradadmissions@georgiasouthern.edu.
Website: http://cogs.georgiasouthern.edu/admission/GraduatePrograms/phdlogistics.php.

Golden Gate University, Ageno School of Business, San Francisco, CA 94105-2968. Offers accounting (MBA); business administration (EMBA, MBA, PMBA, DBA); finance (MBA, MS, Certificate); financial planning (MS, Certificate); healthcare information systems (Certificate); human resource management (MBA, MS); human resources management (Certificate); information systems (MS); information technology (MBA); information technology management (Certificate); integrated marketing and communications (MS, Certificate); international business (MBA); management (MBA); marketing (MBA, MS, Certificate); operations supply chain management (Certificate); psychology (MA, Certificate); public administration (EMPA); public relations (MS, Certificate); technical market analysis (Certificate); JD/MBA. Part-time and evening/weekend programs available. *Degree requirements:* For doctorate, thesis/dissertation, qualifying examination. *Entrance requirements:* For master's, GMAT (MBA), minimum GPA of 2.5 (MS). Additional exam requirements/recommendations for international students: Required—TOEFL (minimum score 550 paper-based; 79 iBT). Electronic applications accepted. *Expenses:* Contact institution.

HEC Montreal, School of Business Administration, Graduate Diplomas Programs in Administration, Program in Supply Chain Management, Montréal, QC H3T 2A7, Canada. Offers Graduate Diploma. *Students:* 37 full-time (15 women), 108 part-time (32 women). 73 applicants, 75% accepted, 40 enrolled. In 2013, 29 Graduate Diplomas awarded. *Degree requirements:* For Graduate Diploma, one foreign language. *Entrance requirements:* For degree, bachelor's degree, two years of working experience, letters of recommendation. *Application deadline:* For fall admission, 4/15 for domestic and international students; for winter admission, 9/15 for domestic and international students. Application fee: $83 Canadian dollars. Electronic applications accepted. *Expenses: Tuition, area resident:* Part-time $74.14 per credit. Tuition, state resident: full-time $2669.04; part-time $201.83 per credit. Tuition, nonresident: full-time $7266; part-time $500.59 per credit. *International tuition:* $18,021.24 full-time. *Required fees:* $1529.70; $36.20 per credit. $65.50 per term. Tuition and fees vary according to degree level and program. *Financial support:* In 2013–14, 1,007 students received support. Research assistantships, teaching assistantships, and scholarships/grants available. Financial award application deadline: 9/2. *Unit head:* Silvia Ponce, Director, 514-340-6393, Fax: 514-340-6915, E-mail: silvia.ponce@hec.ca. *Application contact:* Jo Anne Audet, Administrative Director, 514-340-1315, Fax: 514-340-6411, E-mail: joanne.audet@hec.ca.
Website: http://www.hec.ca/programmes_formations/des/dess/dess_logistique/index.html.

HEC Montreal, School of Business Administration, Master of Science Programs in Administration, Program in Global Supply Chain Management, Montréal, QC H3T 2A7, Canada. Offers M Sc. Specialiszation offered in English. *Students:* 22 full-time (11 women). 36 applicants, 61% accepted, 13 enrolled. In 2013, 1 master's awarded. *Degree requirements:* For master's, one foreign language, thesis. *Entrance requirements:* For master's, BBA, undergraduate degree in another field, degree deemed equivalent by program director and minimum GPA of 3.0 on 4.3 scale. *Application deadline:* For fall admission, 3/15 for domestic and international students; for winter admission, 9/15 for domestic and international students. Application fee: $83. Electronic applications accepted. *Expenses: Tuition, area resident:* Part-time $74.14 per credit. Tuition, state resident: full-time $2669.04; part-time $201.83 per credit. Tuition, nonresident: full-time $7266; part-time $500.59 per credit. *International tuition:* $18,021.24 full-time. *Required fees:* $1529.70; $36.20 per credit. $65.50 per term. Tuition and fees vary according to degree level and program. *Financial support:* In 2013–14, 1,007 students received support. Research assistantships, teaching assistantships, and scholarships/grants available. Financial award application deadline: 9/2. *Unit head:* Dr. Anne Bourhis, Director, 514-340-6873, Fax: 514-340-6880, E-mail: anne.bourhis@hec.ca. *Application contact:* Marianne de Moura, Administrative Director, 514-340-7106, Fax: 514-340-6411, E-mail: marianne.de-moura@hec.ca.
Website: http://www.hec.ca/en/programs_training/msc/options/global_supply_chain_management/global_supply_chain_management.html.

Howard University, School of Business, Graduate Programs in Business, Washington, DC 20059-0002. Offers accounting (MBA); entrepreneurship (MBA); finance (MBA); general management (MBA); human resources management (MBA); information systems (MBA); international business (MBA); marketing (MBA); supply chain management (MBA); JD/MBA. *Accreditation:* AACSB. Part-time and evening/weekend programs available. Postbaccalaureate distance learning degree programs offered (no on-campus study). *Entrance requirements:* For master's, GMAT, minimum 1 year post undergraduate work experience, resume, 3 letters of recommendation, advanced

college algebra. Additional exam requirements/recommendations for international students: Required—TOEFL. *Faculty research:* Marketing research in multi-ethnic populations, U.S. trade policies and international relations, risk management (finance).

Kansas State University, Graduate School, College of Business Administration, Program in Business Administration, Manhattan, KS 66506. Offers enterprise information systems (MBA); entrepreneurial technology (MBA); finance (MBA); management (MBA); supply chain management (MBA). *Accreditation:* AACSB. Part-time programs available. *Faculty:* 1 full-time (0 women), 2 part-time/adjunct (0 women). *Students:* 54 full-time (25 women), 24 part-time (14 women); includes 9 minority (3 Black or African American, non-Hispanic/Latino; 2 Asian, non-Hispanic/Latino; 2 Hispanic/Latino; 2 Two or more races, non-Hispanic/Latino), 22 international. Average age 26. 121 applicants, 69% accepted, 23 enrolled. In 2013, 28 master's awarded. *Entrance requirements:* For master's, GMAT (minimum score of 500), minimum undergraduate GPA of 3.0. Additional exam requirements/recommendations for international students: Required—TOEFL (minimum score 550 paper-based; 79 iBT); Recommended—IELTS (minimum score 7). *Application deadline:* For fall admission, 2/1 priority date for domestic and international students; for spring admission, 10/1 priority date for domestic students, 8/1 priority date for international students. Applications are processed on a rolling basis. Application fee: $70 ($80 for international students). Electronic applications accepted. *Financial support:* In 2013–14, 1 research assistantship with partial tuition reimbursement (averaging $8,320 per year) was awarded; institutionally sponsored loans and scholarships/grants also available. Financial award application deadline: 3/1; financial award applicants required to submit FAFSA. *Faculty research:* Organizational citizenship behavior, service marketing, impression management, human resources management, lean manufacturing and supply chain management, financial market behavior and investment management. *Total annual research expenditures:* $11,288. *Unit head:* Dr. Ali Malekzadeh, Dean, 785-532-7227, Fax: 785-532-7216. *Application contact:* Dr. Stacy Kovar, Associate Dean for Academic Programs, 785-532-7190, Fax: 785-532-7809, E-mail: gradbusiness@ksu.edu.
Website: http://www.cba.k-state.edu/.

Kaplan University, Davenport Campus, School of Business, Davenport, IA 52807-2095. Offers business administration (MBA); change leadership (MS); entrepreneurship (MBA); finance (MBA); health care management (MBA, MS); human resource (MBA); international business (MBA); management (MS); marketing (MBA); project management (MBA, MS); supply chain management and logistics (MBA, MS). *Accreditation:* ACBSP. Part-time and evening/weekend programs available. Postbaccalaureate distance learning degree programs offered (no on-campus study). *Entrance requirements:* Additional exam requirements/recommendations for international students: Required—TOEFL (minimum score 550 paper-based; 80 iBT). Electronic applications accepted.

Lehigh University, College of Business and Economics, Department of Management, Bethlehem, PA 18015. Offers business administration (MBA); corporate entrepreneurship (MBA); international business (MBA); marketing (MBA); project management (MBA); supply chain management (MBA); MBA/E; MBA/M Ed. *Accreditation:* AACSB. Part-time and evening/weekend programs available. Postbaccalaureate distance learning degree programs offered (minimal on-campus study). *Faculty:* 11 full-time (4 women), 13 part-time/adjunct (4 women). *Students:* 28 full-time (10 women), 171 part-time (54 women); includes 32 minority (2 Black or African American, non-Hispanic/Latino; 21 Asian, non-Hispanic/Latino; 6 Hispanic/Latino; 3 Two or more races, non-Hispanic/Latino), 21 international. Average age 33. 108 applicants, 63% accepted, 25 enrolled. In 2013, 79 master's awarded. *Entrance requirements:* For master's, GMAT or GRE. Additional exam requirements/recommendations for international students: Required—TOEFL (minimum score 600 paper-based; 94 iBT). *Application deadline:* For fall admission, 7/15 for domestic students, 5/1 for international students; for spring admission, 12/1 for domestic students. Applications are processed on a rolling basis. Application fee: $100. Electronic applications accepted. *Financial support:* In 2013–14, 33 students received support, including 10 teaching assistantships with full and partial tuition reimbursements available (averaging $14,200 per year); career-related internships or fieldwork, scholarships/grants, health care benefits, tuition waivers (full and partial), and unspecified assistantships also available. Support available to part-time students. Financial award application deadline: 1/15. *Faculty research:* Information systems, organizational behavior, supply chain management, strategic management, entrepreneurship. *Total annual research expenditures:* $77,886. *Unit head:* Dr. Robert J. Trent, Department Chair, 610-758-4952, Fax: 610-758-6941, E-mail: rjt2@lehigh.edu. *Application contact:* Jen Giordano, Director of Recruitment and Admissions, 610-758-3418, Fax: 610-758-5283, E-mail: jlg210@lehigh.edu.
Website: http://www4.lehigh.edu/business/academics/depts/management.

Lindenwood University, Graduate Programs, School of Business and Entrepreneurship, St. Charles, MO 63301-1695. Offers accountancy (MA); accounting (MBA); business administration (MBA); entrepreneurial studies (MBA); finance (MBA, MS); human resource management (MBA); international business (MBA); leadership (MA); management (MBA); marketing (MBA, MS); public management (MBA); sport management (MA); supply chain management (MBA). *Accreditation:* ACBSP. Part-time and evening/weekend programs available. Postbaccalaureate distance learning degree programs offered (no on-campus study). *Faculty:* 18 full-time (8 women), 33 part-time/adjunct (8 women). *Students:* 292 full-time (130 women), 111 part-time (46 women); includes 59 minority (42 Black or African American, non-Hispanic/Latino; 5 American Indian or Alaska Native, non-Hispanic/Latino; 1 Asian, non-Hispanic/Latino; 5 Hispanic/Latino; 6 Two or more races, non-Hispanic/Latino), 112 international. Average age 29. 212 applicants, 51% accepted, 102 enrolled. In 2013, 221 master's awarded. *Degree requirements:* For master's, comprehensive exam (for some programs), thesis (for some programs), minimum GPA of 3.0. *Entrance requirements:* For master's, interview, minimum GPA of 3.0, letter of recommendation. Additional exam requirements/recommendations for international students: Required—TOEFL (minimum score 550 paper-based; 80 iBT). *Application deadline:* For fall admission, 8/12 priority date for domestic and international students; for winter admission, 1/6 priority date for domestic and international students; for spring admission, 3/10 priority date for domestic and international students; for summer admission, 5/27 priority date for domestic and international students. Applications are processed on a rolling basis. Application fee: $30 ($100 for international students). Electronic applications accepted. *Expenses: Tuition:* Full-time $14,800; part-time $428 per credit hour. *Required fees:* $350. Tuition and fees vary according to course level and course load. *Financial support:* In 2013–14, 268 students received support. Career-related internships or fieldwork, Federal Work-Study, institutionally sponsored loans, scholarships/grants, tuition waivers (partial), and unspecified assistantships available. Financial award application deadline: 6/30; financial award applicants required to submit FAFSA. *Unit head:* Roger Ellis, Dean, 636-949-4839, E-mail: rellis@lindenwood.edu. *Application contact:* Brett Barger, Dean of Evening Admissions and Extension Campuses, 636-949-4934, Fax: 636-949-4109, E-mail: adultadmissions@lindenwood.edu.
Website: http://www.lindenwood.edu.

Loyola University Chicago, Quinlan School of Business, Program in Supply Chain Management, Chicago, IL 60610. Offers MSSCM, MBA/MSSCM. Part-time and evening/weekend programs available. *Faculty:* 12 full-time (1 woman), 4 part-time/adjunct (1 woman). *Students:* 6 full-time (1 woman), 8 part-time (0 women); includes 2 minority (both Black or African American, non-Hispanic/Latino), 4 international. Average age 29. 28 applicants, 39% accepted, 5 enrolled. *Entrance requirements:* For master's, GMAT or GRE, official transcripts, two letters of recommendation, statement of purpose, resume. Additional exam requirements/recommendations for international students: Required—TOEFL (minimum score 90 iBT) or IELTS (minimum score 6.5). *Application deadline:* For fall admission, 7/15 for domestic and international students; for winter admission, 10/1 for domestic and international students; for spring admission, 1/15 for domestic students, 1/14 for international students; for summer admission, 4/1 for domestic and international students. Applications are processed on a rolling basis. Application fee: $50. Electronic applications accepted. Application fee is waived when completed online. *Expenses: Tuition:* Full-time $16,740; part-time $930 per credit. *Required fees:* $135 per semester. *Financial support:* Scholarships/grants and unspecified assistantships available. *Faculty research:* Vehicle research, tracking technology, logistics, purchasing management. *Unit head:* Dr. Mary Malliaris, Chair, ISOM Department, 312-915-7064, E-mail: mmallia@luc.edu. *Application contact:* Jessica Gagle, Enrollment Advisor, Quinlan School of Business Graduate Programs, 312-915-8908, Fax: 312-915-7202, E-mail: jgagle@luc.edu.
Website: http://www.luc.edu/quinlan/mba/supply-chain-management-degrees/index.shtml.

Maine Maritime Academy, Loeb-Sullivan School of International Business and Logistics, Castine, ME 04420. Offers global logistics and maritime management (MS); international logistics management (MS). Part-time programs available. *Faculty:* 6 full-time (1 woman), 2 part-time/adjunct (0 women). *Students:* 11 full-time (8 women). *Degree requirements:* For master's, capstone course. *Entrance requirements:* For master's, GMAT or GRE, letter of recommendation. Additional exam requirements/recommendations for international students: Required—TOEFL. *Application deadline:* For fall admission, 6/1 for domestic and international students; for spring admission, 3/15 for domestic and international students. Application fee: $40. Application fee is waived when completed online. *Financial support:* In 2013–14, teaching assistantships with full tuition reimbursements (averaging $6,000 per year) were awarded; career-related internships or fieldwork, Federal Work-Study, and institutionally sponsored loans also available. Support available to part-time students. Financial award application deadline: 4/15. *Unit head:* Dr. William DeWitt, Dean, 207-326-2454, Fax: 207-326-4311, E-mail: william.dewitt@mma.edu. *Application contact:* Patrick Haugen, Program Coordinator, 207-326-2212, Fax: 207-326-2411, E-mail: info.ls@mma.edu.
Website: http://ibl.mainemaritime.edu.

Marquette University, Graduate School of Management, Executive MBA Program, Milwaukee, WI 53201-1881. Offers economics (MBA); finance (MBA); human resources (MBA); international business (MBA); management information systems (MBA); marketing (MBA); operations and supply chain management (MBA); sports business (MBA). *Accreditation:* AACSB. *Students:* 38 full-time (12 women), 1 international. Average age 36. 36 applicants. In 2013, 21 master's awarded. *Degree requirements:* For master's, international trip. *Entrance requirements:* For master's, GMAT or GRE, two letters of recommendation, official transcripts from current and previous colleges/universities. Additional exam requirements/recommendations for international students: Required—TOEFL (minimum score 550 paper-based; 88 iBT), IELTS (minimum score 6.5), PTE. *Application deadline:* For fall admission, 2/15 for domestic and international students. Application fee: $50. Electronic applications accepted. *Expenses:* Contact institution. *Financial support:* Application deadline: 2/15. *Faculty research:* International trade and finance, customer relationship management, consumer satisfaction, customer service. *Unit head:* Dr. Mark Eppli, Dean, 414-288-5724. *Application contact:* Dr. Jeanne Simmons, Associate Dean, 414-288-7145.
Website: http://www.busadm.mu.edu/emba/.

Marquette University, Graduate School of Management, Program in Business Administration, Milwaukee, WI 53201-1881. Offers business administration (MBA); economics (MBA); entrepreneurship (Certificate); finance (MBA); human resources (MBA); international business (MBA); management information systems (MBA); marketing (MBA); operations and supply chain management (MBA); sports business (MBA); JD/MBA; MBA/MA; MBA/MSN. *Accreditation:* AACSB. Part-time and evening/weekend programs available. *Students:* 28 full-time (13 women), 265 part-time (66 women); includes 20 minority (7 Black or African American, non-Hispanic/Latino; 8 Asian, non-Hispanic/Latino; 5 Hispanic/Latino), 11 international. Average age 31. 185 applicants. In 2013, 129 master's, 2 other advanced degrees awarded. *Degree requirements:* For Certificate, business plan. *Entrance requirements:* For master's, GMAT or GRE, letters of recommendation. Additional exam requirements/recommendations for international students: Required—TOEFL (minimum score 550 paper-based; 88 iBT), IELTS (minimum score 6.5), PTE. *Application deadline:* For fall admission, 2/15 for domestic and international students. Applications are processed on a rolling basis. Application fee: $50. Electronic applications accepted. *Financial support:* In 2013–14, 4 fellowships, 11 teaching assistantships were awarded; research assistantships, Federal Work-Study, institutionally sponsored loans, scholarships/grants, and tuition waivers (full and partial) also available. Support available to part-time students. Financial award application deadline: 2/15. *Faculty research:* Ethics in the professions, services marketing, technology impact on decision-making, mentoring. *Unit head:* Dr. Mark Eppli, Dean, 414-288-5724. *Application contact:* Dr. Jeanne Simmons, Associate Dean, 414-288-7145.
Website: http://business.marquette.edu/academics/mba.

Michigan State University, The Graduate School, Eli Broad College of Business, Department of Supply Chain Management, East Lansing, MI 48824. Offers logistics (PhD); operations and sourcing management (PhD); supply chain management (MS), including logistics management, operations management, rail management, supply management. Part-time programs available. *Faculty:* 21. *Students:* 36. *Degree requirements:* For master's, field study/research project; for doctorate, comprehensive exam, thesis/dissertation. *Entrance requirements:* For master's, GMAT (taken within past 5 years), bachelor's degree, minimum GPA of 3.0 in junior/senior years, transcripts, at least 2 years of professional supply chain work experience, 3 letters of recommendation, essays, resume; for doctorate, GMAT or GRE, bachelor's or master's degree, transcripts, strong work experience, 3 letters of recommendation, statement of personal goals, interview. Additional exam requirements/recommendations for international students: Required—TOEFL (minimum score 600 paper-based). *Application deadline:* For fall admission, 12/1 for domestic and international students. Application fee: $50. Electronic applications accepted. *Expenses:* Contact institution. *Financial support:* Fellowships with tuition reimbursements, research assistantships with tuition reimbursements, and teaching assistantships with tuition reimbursements available. *Unit head:* Dr. David J. Closs, Chairperson, 517-432-6406, Fax: 517-432-8048, E-mail: closs@broad.msu.edu. *Application contact:* Nancy Taylor, Office Supervisor, 517-432-6458, Fax: 517-432-8048, E-mail: taylor@broad.msu.edu.
Website: http://supplychain.broad.msu.edu.

Michigan State University, The Graduate School, Eli Broad College of Business, Program in Business Administration, East Lansing, MI 48824. Offers finance (MBA); human resource management (MBA); integrative management (MBA); marketing (MBA); supply chain management (MBA). MBA in integrative management is through

Weekend MBA Program; other 4 concentrations are through Full-Time MBA Program. Evening/weekend programs available. *Students:* 432. In 2013, 241 degrees awarded. *Degree requirements:* For master's, enrichment experience. *Entrance requirements:* For master's, GMAT or GRE, 4-year bachelor's degree; resume; work experience (minimum of 5 years for Weekend MBA); 2-3 personal essays; 2 letters of recommendation; personal interview. Additional exam requirements/recommendations for international students: Required—PTE (minimum score 70), TOEFL (minimum score 100 iBT) or IELTS (minimum score 7) for Full-Time MBA applicants. *Application deadline:* Applications are processed on a rolling basis. Application fee: $50. Electronic applications accepted. *Expenses:* Contact institution. *Financial support:* Fellowships with tuition reimbursements, research assistantships with tuition reimbursements, teaching assistantships with tuition reimbursements, scholarships/grants, unspecified assistantships, and non-resident tuition waivers (for all military veterans and their dependents in the Full-Time MBA Program) available. Financial award applicants required to submit FAFSA. *Unit head:* Dr. Sanjay Gupta, Associate Dean for MBA and Professional Master's Programs, 517-432-6488, Fax: 517-353-6395, E-mail: gupta@broad.msu.edu. *Application contact:* Program Information Contact, 517-355-7604, Fax: 517-353-1649, E-mail: mba@msu.edu.
Website: http://mba.broad.msu.edu.

Moravian College, Moravian College Comenius Center, Business and Management Programs, Bethlehem, PA 18018-6650. Offers accounting (MBA); business analytics (MBA); general management (MBA); health administration (MHA); healthcare management (MBA); human resource management (MBA); leadership (MSHRM); learning and performance management (MSHRM); supply chain management (MBA). Part-time and evening/weekend programs available. *Entrance requirements:* For master's, GMAT. Additional exam requirements/recommendations for international students: Required—TOEFL (minimum score 550 paper-based; 90 iBT). Application fee is waived when completed online. *Expenses:* Contact institution. *Faculty research:* Leadership, change management, human resources.

Naval Postgraduate School, Departments and Academic Groups, Graduate School of Business and Public Policy, Monterey, CA 93943. Offers acquisition and contract management (MBA); business administration (EMBA, MBA); contract management (MS); defense business management (MBA); defense systems analysis (MS), including management; defense systems management (international) (MBA); financial management (MBA); information management (MBA); manpower systems analysis (MS); material logistics support management (MBA); program management (MS); resource planning and management for international defense (MBA); supply chain management (MBA); systems acquisition management (MBA); transportation management (MBA). Program only open to commissioned officers of the United States and friendly nations and selected United States federal civilian employees. *Accreditation:* AACSB; NASPAA. Part-time programs available. Postbaccalaureate distance learning degree programs offered (minimal on-campus study). *Degree requirements:* For master's, thesis (for some programs), terminal project/capstone (for some programs). *Faculty research:* U.S. and European public procurement policies for small and medium-sized enterprises, examining external validity criticisms in the choice of students as subjects in accounting experiment studies, assurance of learning in contract management education, contracting for cloud computing: opportunities and risks, NPS, Apple App Store as a business model supporting U. S. Navy requirements.

North Carolina Agricultural and Technical State University, School of Graduate Studies, School of Business and Economics, Greensboro, NC 27411. Offers accounting (MSM); business education (MAT); human resources management (MSM); supply chain systems (MSM).

North Carolina State University, Graduate School, Poole College of Management, Program in Business Administration, Raleigh, NC 27695. Offers biosciences management (MBA); entrepreneurship and technology commercialization (MBA); financial management (MBA); innovation management (MBA); marketing management (MBA); services management (MBA); supply chain management (MBA). *Accreditation:* AACSB. Part-time programs available. *Degree requirements:* For master's, thesis optional. *Entrance requirements:* For master's, GMAT, interview, 3 letters of recommendation. Additional exam requirements/recommendations for international students: Required—TOEFL (minimum score 600 paper-based; 100 iBT). Electronic applications accepted. *Faculty research:* Manufacturing strategy, information systems, technology commercialization, managing research and development, historical stock returns.

See Display on page 120 and Close-Up on page 189.

Oregon State University, College of Business, Program in Business Administration, Corvallis, OR 97331. Offers clean technology (MBA); commercialization (MBA); executive leadership (MBA); global operations (MBA); marketing (MBA); research thesis (MBA); wealth management (MBA). Part-time programs available. *Faculty:* 34 full-time (13 women), 2 part-time/adjunct (1 woman). *Students:* 153 full-time (67 women), 44 part-time (18 women); includes 20 minority (1 Black or African American, non-Hispanic/Latino; 12 Asian, non-Hispanic/Latino; 3 Hispanic/Latino; 1 Native Hawaiian or other Pacific Islander, non-Hispanic/Latino; 3 Two or more races, non-Hispanic/Latino), 97 international. Average age 29. 194 applicants, 64% accepted, 106 enrolled. In 2013, 61 degrees awarded. *Degree requirements:* For master's, thesis optional. *Entrance requirements:* For master's, GMAT. Additional exam requirements/recommendations for international students: Required—TOEFL (minimum score 91 iBT), IELTS (minimum score 7). *Application deadline:* Applications are processed on a rolling basis. Application fee: $60. *Expenses:* Contact institution. *Unit head:* Dr. David Baldridge, Director for Business Master's Program, 541-737-6062, E-mail: david.baldridge@bus.oregonstate.edu.
Website: http://business.oregonstate.edu/mba/degrees.

Penn State University Park, Graduate School, The Mary Jean and Frank P. Smeal College of Business Administration, State College, PA 16802. Offers accounting (M Acc); business administration (MBA, MS, PhD); supply chain management (MPS). *Accreditation:* AACSB. Part-time and evening/weekend programs available. *Students:* 297 full-time (94 women), 4 part-time (1 woman); includes 58 minority (19 Black or African American, non-Hispanic/Latino; 30 Asian, non-Hispanic/Latino; 9 Hispanic/Latino), 96 international. Average age 30. 1,153 applicants, 20% accepted, 141 enrolled. In 2013, 245 master's, 20 doctorates awarded. *Entrance requirements:* Additional exam requirements/recommendations for international students: Required—TOEFL (minimum score 550 paper-based; 80 iBT). *Application deadline:* Applications are processed on a rolling basis. Application fee: $65. Electronic applications accepted. *Financial support:* Fellowships, research assistantships, teaching assistantships, career-related internships or fieldwork, Federal Work-Study, and unspecified assistantships available. Support available to part-time students. Financial award application deadline: 2/15; financial award applicants required to submit FAFSA. *Unit head:* Dr. Charles H. Whiteman, Dean, 814-863-0448, Fax: 814-865-7064, E-mail: chw17@psu.edu. *Application contact:* Cynthia E. Nicosia, Director, Graduate Enrollment Services, 814-865-1834, Fax: 814-863-4627, E-mail: cey1@psu.edu.
Website: http://www.smeal.psu.edu/.

Polytechnic University of Puerto Rico, Miami Campus, Graduate School, Miami, FL 33166. Offers accounting (MBA); business administration (MBA); construction management (MEM); environmental management (MEM); finance (MBA); human resources management (MBA); logistics and supply chain management (MBA); management of international enterprises (MBA); manufacturing management (MEM); marketing management (MBA); project management (MBA). Part-time and evening/weekend programs available. Postbaccalaureate distance learning degree programs offered (no on-campus study). *Entrance requirements:* For master's, minimum GPA of 3.0. Electronic applications accepted.

Portland State University, Graduate Studies, School of Business Administration, MS in Global Supply Chain Management Program, Portland, OR 97207-0751. Offers MS. Part-time programs available. Postbaccalaureate distance learning degree programs offered (no on-campus study). *Students:* 1 full-time (0 women), 18 part-time (9 women); includes 5 minority (1 Black or African American, non-Hispanic/Latino; 3 Asian, non-Hispanic/Latino; 1 Hispanic/Latino), 1 international. Average age 36. 19 applicants, 95% accepted, 18 enrolled. *Entrance requirements:* For master's, GMAT, GRE General Test, minimum undergraduate GPA of 3.0; two academic references; unofficial transcript from each college or university attended. Additional exam requirements/recommendations for international students: Required—TOEFL (minimum score 550 paper-based). *Application deadline:* For fall admission, 5/1 priority date for domestic and international students; for winter admission, 12/1 priority date for domestic and international students; for spring admission, 2/1 priority date for domestic and international students; for summer admission, 5/1 priority date for domestic and international students. Application fee: $50. Electronic applications accepted. *Expenses:* Tuition, state resident: full-time $9207; part-time $341 per credit. Tuition, nonresident: full-time $14,391; part-time $533 per credit. *Required fees:* $1263; $22 per credit. $98 per quarter. One-time fee: $150. Tuition and fees vary according to program. *Unit head:* Cliff Allen, Academic Director, 503-725-5053, E-mail: cliffa@sba.pdx.edu. *Application contact:* Abby Messenger, Recruiting and Admissions Specialist, 503-725-2291, Fax: 503-725-5850, E-mail: a.g.messenger@sba.pdx.edu.
Website: http://www.pdx.edu/gradbusiness/ms-global-supply-chain-management.

Quinnipiac University, School of Business and Engineering, Program in Business Administration, Hamden, CT 06518-1940. Offers chartered financial analyst (MBA); finance (MBA); healthcare management (MBA); information systems management (MBA); marketing (MBA); supply chain management (MBA); JD/MBA. *Accreditation:* AACSB. Part-time and evening/weekend programs available. Postbaccalaureate distance learning degree programs offered (no on-campus study). *Faculty:* 33 full-time (10 women), 7 part-time/adjunct (3 women). *Students:* 109 full-time (48 women), 225 part-time (101 women); includes 44 minority (14 Black or African American, non-Hispanic/Latino; 2 American Indian or Alaska Native, non-Hispanic/Latino; 12 Asian, non-Hispanic/Latino; 15 Hispanic/Latino; 1 Two or more races, non-Hispanic/Latino), 17 international. 230 applicants, 80% accepted, 154 enrolled. In 2013, 124 master's awarded. *Entrance requirements:* For master's, GMAT or GRE, minimum GPA of 3.0. Additional exam requirements/recommendations for international students: Required—TOEFL (minimum score 575 paper-based; 90 iBT), IELTS (minimum score 6.5). *Application deadline:* For fall admission, 7/30 priority date for domestic students, 4/30 priority date for international students; for spring admission, 12/15 priority date for domestic students, 9/15 priority date for international students. Applications are processed on a rolling basis. Application fee: $45. Electronic applications accepted. *Expenses: Tuition:* Part-time $920 per credit. *Required fees:* $37 per credit. *Financial support:* In 2013–14, 41 students received support. Career-related internships or fieldwork, Federal Work-Study, scholarships/grants, and unspecified assistantships available. Support available to part-time students. Financial award application deadline: 6/1; financial award applicants required to submit FAFSA. *Faculty research:* Financial markets and investments, international business, supply chain management, health care management, corporate governance. *Unit head:* Lisa Braiewa, MBA Program Director, E-mail: lisa.braiewa@quinnipiac.edu. *Application contact:* Office of Graduate Admissions, 800-462-1944, Fax: 203-582-3443, E-mail: graduate@quinnipiac.edu.
Website: http://www.quinnipiac.edu/mba.

Rensselaer Polytechnic Institute, Graduate School, Lally School of Management, Program in Supply Chain Management, Troy, NY 12180-3590. Offers MS. Part-time programs available. *Faculty:* 15 full-time (3 women), 4 part-time/adjunct (1 woman). *Students:* 1 (woman) full-time. Average age 36. 10 applicants, 50% accepted, 1 enrolled. *Entrance requirements:* For master's, GMAT or GRE. Additional exam requirements/recommendations for international students: Required—TOEFL (minimum score 570 paper-based; 88 iBT), IELTS (minimum score 6.8), PTE (minimum score 60). *Application deadline:* For fall admission, 1/1 for domestic and international students. Applications are processed on a rolling basis. Application fee: $75. Electronic applications accepted. *Expenses: Tuition:* Full-time $45,100; part-time $1879 per credit hour. *Required fees:* $1983. *Financial support:* In 2013–14, 1 student received support. Scholarships/grants available. Financial award application deadline: 1/1. *Unit head:* Dr. Gina O'Connor, Graduate Program Director, 518-276-6842, E-mail: oconng@rpi.edu. *Application contact:* Office of Graduate Admissions, 518-576-6216, E-mail: gradadmissions@rpi.edu.
Website: http://lallyschool.rpi.edu/academics/ms_scm.html.

Rutgers, The State University of New Jersey, Newark, Rutgers Business School–Newark and New Brunswick, Doctoral Programs in Management, Newark, NJ 07102. Offers accounting (PhD); accounting information systems (PhD); economics (PhD); finance (PhD); individualized study (PhD); information technology (PhD); international business (PhD); management science (PhD); marketing science (PhD); organizational management (PhD); science, technology and management (PhD); supply chain management (PhD). *Degree requirements:* For doctorate, comprehensive exam, thesis/dissertation. *Entrance requirements:* For doctorate, GRE or GMAT. Additional exam requirements/recommendations for international students: Required—TOEFL (minimum score 550 paper-based; 79 iBT). Electronic applications accepted.

Seton Hall University, Stillman School of Business, Programs in Business Administration, South Orange, NJ 07079-2697. Offers accounting (MBA); finance (MBA); information technology management (MBA); international business (MBA); management (MBA); marketing (MBA); sport management (MBA); supply chain management (MBA). Part-time and evening/weekend programs available. *Faculty:* 32 full-time (6 women), 20 part-time/adjunct (3 women). *Students:* 67 full-time (23 women), 162 part-time (66 women); includes 28 minority (7 Black or African American, non-Hispanic/Latino; 7 Asian, non-Hispanic/Latino; 6 Hispanic/Latino; 8 Native Hawaiian or other Pacific Islander, non-Hispanic/Latino). Average age 31. 216 applicants, 28% accepted, 39 enrolled. In 2013, 139 master's awarded. *Degree requirements:* For master's, 20 hours of community service (Social Responsibility Project). *Entrance requirements:* For master's, GMAT, GRE or CPA, advanced degree from AACSB institution, MS in a business discipline, professional degree (MD, JD, PhD, DVM, DDS, etc.), minimum undergraduate GPA of 3.0. Additional exam requirements/recommendations for international students: Required—TOEFL (minimum score 102 iBT), IELTS or PTE. *Application deadline:* For fall admission, 5/31 priority date for domestic students, 3/31 priority date for international students; for spring admission, 10/31 priority date for domestic students, 9/30 priority date for international students.

Applications are processed on a rolling basis. Application fee: $75. Electronic applications accepted. *Financial support:* In 2013–14, research assistantships with full tuition reimbursements (averaging $23,956 per year) were awarded; career-related internships or fieldwork, Federal Work-Study, scholarships/grants, and unspecified assistantships also available. Support available to part-time students. Financial award application deadline: 6/30; financial award applicants required to submit FAFSA. *Faculty research:* Sport, hedge funds, international business, legal issues, disclosure and branding. *Total annual research expenditures:* $68,000. *Unit head:* Dr. Joyce Strawser, Dean, 973-761-9013, Fax: 973-761-9217, E-mail: joyce.strawser@shu.edu. *Application contact:* Catherine Bianchi, Director of Graduate Admissions, 973-761-9262, Fax: 973-761-9208, E-mail: catherine.bianchi@shu.edu.
Website: http://www.shu.edu/academics/business.

Southern New Hampshire University, School of Business, Manchester, NH 03106-1045. Offers accounting (MBA, MS, Graduate Certificate); accounting finance (MS); accounting/auditing (MS); accounting/forensic accounting (MS); accounting/taxation (MS); athletic administration (MBA, Graduate Certificate); business administration (IMBA, MBA, Certificate, Graduate Certificate), including accounting (Certificate), business administration (MBA), business information systems (Graduate Certificate); human resource management (Certificate); corporate social responsibility (MBA); entrepreneurship (MBA); finance (MBA, MS, Graduate Certificate); finance/corporate finance (MS); finance/investments and securities (MS); forensic accounting (MBA); healthcare informatics (MBA); healthcare management (MBA); human resource management (Graduate Certificate); information technology (MS, Graduate Certificate); information technology management (MBA); international business (Graduate Certificate); international business and information technology (Graduate Certificate); international finance (Graduate Certificate); international sport management (Graduate Certificate); justice studies (MBA); leadership of nonprofit organizations (Graduate Certificate); marketing (MBA, MS, Graduate Certificate); operations and project management (MS); operations and supply chain management (MBA, Graduate Certificate); organizational leadership (MS); project management (MBA, Graduate Certificate); Six Sigma (MBA); Six Sigma quality (Graduate Certificate); social media marketing (MBA); sport management (MBA, MS, Graduate Certificate); sustainability and environmental compliance (MBA); workplace conflict management (MBA); MBA/Certificate. *Accreditation:* ACBSP. Part-time and evening/weekend programs available. Postbaccalaureate distance learning degree programs offered (no on-campus study). Terminal master's awarded for partial completion of doctoral program. *Degree requirements:* For master's, one foreign language, comprehensive exam (for some programs), thesis or alternative. *Entrance requirements:* For master's, minimum GPA of 2.5. Additional exam requirements/recommendations for international students: Required—TOEFL (minimum score 500 paper-based). Electronic applications accepted.

Strayer University, Graduate Studies, Washington, DC 20005-2603. Offers accounting (MS); acquisition (MBA); business administration (MBA); communications technology (MS); educational management (M Ed); finance (MBA); health services administration (MHSA); hospitality and tourism management (MBA); human resource management (MBA); information systems (MS), including computer security management, decision support system management, enterprise resource management, network management, software engineering management, systems development management; management (MBA); management information systems (MS); marketing (MBA); professional accounting (MS), including accounting information systems, controllership, taxation; public administration (MPA); supply chain management (MBA); technology in education (M Ed). Programs also offered at campus locations in Birmingham, AL; Chamblee, GA; Cobb County, GA; Morrow, GA; White Marsh, MD; Charleston, SC; Columbia, SC; Greensboro, NC; Greenville, SC; Lexington, KY; Louisville, KY; Nashville, TN; North Raleigh, NC; Washington, DC. Part-time and evening/weekend programs available. Postbaccalaureate distance learning degree programs offered (minimal on-campus study). *Degree requirements:* For master's, thesis. *Entrance requirements:* For master's, GMAT, GRE General Test, bachelor's degree from an accredited college or university, minimum undergraduate GPA of 2.75. Electronic applications accepted.

Suffolk University, Sawyer Business School, Master of Business Administration Program, Boston, MA 02108-2770. Offers accounting (MBA); business administration (APC); entrepreneurship (MBA); executive business administration (EMBA); finance (MBA); global business administration (GMBA); health administration (MBA); international business (MBA); marketing (MBA); nonprofit management (MBA); organizational behavior (MBA); strategic management (MBA); supply chain management (MBA); taxation (MBA); JD/MBA; MBA/GDPA; MBA/MHA; MBA/MSA; MBA/MSF; MBA/MST. *Accreditation:* AACSB. Part-time and evening/weekend programs available. Postbaccalaureate distance learning degree programs offered (no on-campus study). *Faculty:* 29 full-time (9 women), 12 part-time/adjunct (2 women). *Students:* 106 full-time (44 women), 334 part-time (184 women); includes 57 minority (20 Black or African American, non-Hispanic/Latino; 1 American Indian or Alaska Native, non-Hispanic/Latino; 18 Asian, non-Hispanic/Latino; 14 Hispanic/Latino; 4 Two or more races, non-Hispanic/Latino), 61 international. Average age 30. 448 applicants, 61% accepted, 135 enrolled. In 2013, 217 master's awarded. *Entrance requirements:* For master's, GMAT, minimum undergraduate GPA of 2.75 (MBA), 5 years of managerial experience (EMBA). Additional exam requirements/recommendations for international students: Required—TOEFL (minimum score 550 paper-based; 80 iBT). *Application deadline:* For fall admission, 6/15 priority date for domestic students, 6/15 for international students; for spring admission, 11/1 priority date for domestic students, 11/1 for international students. Applications are processed on a rolling basis. Application fee: $50. Electronic applications accepted. *Expenses:* Tuition: Full-time $38,374; part-time $1279 per credit. *Required fees:* $40; $20 per semester. Tuition and fees vary according to program. *Financial support:* In 2013–14, 107 students received support, including 91 fellowships with full and partial tuition reimbursements available (averaging $12,428 per year); career-related internships or fieldwork, Federal Work-Study, and institutionally sponsored loans also available. Support available to part-time students. Financial award application deadline: 4/1; financial award applicants required to submit FAFSA. *Faculty research:* Foreign investments; career strategies and boundaryless careers; corporate ethics codes; interest rates, inflation, and growth options; innovation and product development performance. *Unit head:* Heather Hewitt, Assistant Dean of Graduate Programs/Director of MBA Programs, 617-573-8306, E-mail: hhewitt@suffolk.edu. *Application contact:* Cory Meyers, Director of Graduate Admissions, 617-573-8302, Fax: 617-305-1733, E-mail: grad.admission@suffolk.edu.
Website: http://www.suffolk.edu/mba.

Syracuse University, Martin J. Whitman School of Management, PhD Program in Business Administration, Syracuse, NY 13244. Offers accounting (PhD); finance (PhD); management information systems (PhD); managerial statistics (PhD); marketing (PhD); operations management (PhD); organizational behavior (PhD); strategy and human resources (PhD); supply chain management (PhD). *Faculty:* 79 full-time (20 women), 25 part-time/adjunct (6 women). *Students:* 26 full-time (8 women), 1 part-time (0 women); includes 2 minority (1 Black or African American, non-Hispanic/Latino; 1 Asian, non-Hispanic/Latino), 20 international. Average age 30. 130 applicants, 9% accepted, 7 enrolled. In 2013, 15 doctorates awarded. *Degree requirements:* For doctorate, comprehensive exam, thesis/dissertation, summer research paper. *Entrance requirements:* For doctorate, GMAT or GRE General Test, 3 recommendations.

Additional exam requirements/recommendations for international students: Required—TOEFL (minimum score 600 paper-based; 100 iBT). *Application deadline:* For fall admission, 1/15 priority date for domestic and international students. Applications are processed on a rolling basis. Application fee: $75. Electronic applications accepted. *Financial support:* In 2013–14, 1 fellowship with full tuition reimbursement (averaging $19,570 per year), 30 teaching assistantships with full tuition reimbursements (averaging $17,000 per year) were awarded; research assistantships with full tuition reimbursements also available. Financial award application deadline: 1/15. *Faculty research:* Marketing models, market microstructure, supply chain, auditing, corporate governance. *Unit head:* Dr. Michel Benarock, Director of the PhD Program, 315-443-3429, E-mail: mbeanaroc@syr.edu. *Application contact:* Carol Hilleges, Administrative Specialist, 315-443-9601, Fax: 315-443-3671, E-mail: clhilleg@syr.edu.
Website: http://whitman.syr.edu/phd/.

Syracuse University, Martin J. Whitman School of Management, Program in Business Administration, Syracuse, NY 13244. Offers accounting (MBA); entrepreneurship (MBA); finance (MBA); marketing (MBA); supply chain management (MBA). Postbaccalaureate distance learning degree programs offered (minimal on-campus study). *Faculty:* 79 full-time (20 women), 25 part-time/adjunct (6 women). *Students:* 112 full-time (41 women), 181 part-time (49 women); includes 52 minority (19 Black or African American, non-Hispanic/Latino; 18 Asian, non-Hispanic/Latino; 11 Hispanic/Latino; 4 Two or more races, non-Hispanic/Latino), 56 international. Average age 33. 179 applicants, 50% accepted, 36 enrolled. In 2013, 115 master's awarded. *Entrance requirements:* For master's, GMAT, 2 letters of recommendation. Additional exam requirements/recommendations for international students: Required—TOEFL (minimum score 600 paper-based; 100 iBT). *Application deadline:* For fall admission, 11/30 priority date for domestic and international students. Applications are processed on a rolling basis. Application fee: $75. Electronic applications accepted. *Financial support:* In 2013–14, 17 students received support. Fellowships with full and partial tuition reimbursements available, teaching assistantships with partial tuition reimbursements available, career-related internships or fieldwork, scholarships/grants, tuition waivers (partial), and unspecified assistantships available. Support available to part-time students. Financial award application deadline: 3/1. *Unit head:* Dr. Don Harter, Associate Dean for Master's Programs, 315-443-3502, Fax: 315-443-9517, E-mail: dharter@syr.edu. *Application contact:* Danielle Goodroe, Director, Graduate Enrollment, 315-443-3006, Fax: 315-443-9517, E-mail: mbainfo@syr.edu.
Website: http://whitman.syr.edu/ftmba/.

Syracuse University, Martin J. Whitman School of Management, Program in Supply Chain Management, Syracuse, NY 13244. Offers MBA. Part-time programs available. Postbaccalaureate distance learning degree programs offered (minimal on-campus study). *Students:* 1 (woman) full-time, 13 part-time (3 women); includes 1 minority (Asian, non-Hispanic/Latino), 1 international. Average age 34. In 2013, 11 master's awarded. *Entrance requirements:* For master's, GMAT. Additional exam requirements/recommendations for international students: Required—TOEFL (minimum score 100 iBT). *Application deadline:* For fall admission, 11/30 priority date for domestic and international students. Application fee: $75. Electronic applications accepted. *Unit head:* Prof. Fran Tucker, Chair/Associate Professor of Marketing and Supply Chain, 315-443-3442, E-mail: fgtucker@syr.edu. *Application contact:* Danielle Goodroe, Director of Graduate Enrollment, 315-443-3006, Fax: 315-443-9517, E-mail: mbainfo@syr.edu.
Website: http://whitman.syr.edu/Academics/Marketing/SupplyChain/.

Texas A&M University–San Antonio, School of Business, San Antonio, TX 78224. Offers business administration (MBA); enterprise resource planning systems (MBA); finance (MBA); healthcare management (MBA); human resources management (MBA); information assurance and security (MBA); international business (MBA); professional accounting (MPA); project management (MBA); supply chain management (MBA). Part-time and evening/weekend programs available. *Entrance requirements:* For master's, GMAT. Additional exam requirements/recommendations for international students: Required—TOEFL (minimum score 550 paper-based; 80 iBT), IELTS (minimum score 6). Electronic applications accepted.

Towson University, Program in e-Business and Technology Management, Towson, MD 21252-0001. Offers project, program and portfolio management (Postbaccalaureate Certificate); supply chain management (MS, Postbaccalaureate Certificate). *Students:* 5 full-time (1 woman), 68 part-time (33 women); includes 16 minority (12 Black or African American, non-Hispanic/Latino; 2 Asian, non-Hispanic/Latino; 2 Hispanic/Latino), 6 international. *Entrance requirements:* For master's and Postbaccalaureate Certificate, GRE or GMAT, bachelor's degree in relevant field and/or three years of post-bachelor's experience working in supply chain related areas; minimum cumulative GPA of 3.0; resume; 1-2 page statement; 2 reference letters. Additional exam requirements/recommendations for international students: Required—TOEFL (minimum score 550 paper-based). *Application deadline:* Applications are processed on a rolling basis. Application fee: $45. Electronic applications accepted. *Unit head:* Dr. Tobin Porterfield, Director, 410-704-3265, E-mail: tporterfield@towson.edu. *Application contact:* Jennifer Bethke, Information Contact, 410-704-6004, E-mail: grads@towson.edu.

The University of Akron, Graduate School, College of Business Administration, Department of Management, Program in Supply Chain Management, Akron, OH 44325. Offers MBA. *Students:* 9 full-time (3 women), 14 part-time (6 women); includes 2 minority (both Asian, non-Hispanic/Latino), 6 international. Average age 30. 11 applicants, 64% accepted, 6 enrolled. In 2013, 6 master's awarded. *Entrance requirements:* For master's, GMAT, minimum GPA of 2.75, two letters of recommendation, statement of purpose, resume. Additional exam requirements/recommendations for international students: Required—TOEFL (minimum score 550 paper-based; 79 iBT). *Application deadline:* For fall admission, 7/15 for domestic and international students; for spring admission, 11/15 for domestic and international students. Application fee: $30 ($40 for international students). Electronic applications accepted. *Expenses:* Tuition, state resident: full-time $7430; part-time $412.80 per credit hour. Tuition, nonresident: full-time $12,722; part-time $706.80 per credit hour. *Required fees:* $53 per credit hour. $12 per semester. Tuition and fees vary according to course load and program. *Unit head:* Dr. Steve Ash, Interim Chair, 330-972-6086, E-mail: ash@uakron.edu. *Application contact:* Dr. William Hauser, Director of Graduate Business Programs, 330-972-7043, Fax: 330-972-6588, E-mail: whauser@uakron.edu.

The University of Alabama in Huntsville, School of Graduate Studies, College of Business Administration, Programs in Business and Management, Huntsville, AL 35899. Offers federal contracting and procurement management (Certificate); management (MBA), including acquisition management, entrepreneurship, federal contract accounting, finance, human resource management, logistics and supply chain management, marketing, project management; supply chain management (Certificate); technology and innovation management (Certificate). *Accreditation:* AACSB. Part-time and evening/weekend programs available. *Faculty:* 13 full-time (3 women), 5 part-time/adjunct (0 women). *Students:* 41 full-time (19 women), 144 part-time (59 women); includes 35 minority (13 Black or African American, non-Hispanic/Latino; 1 American Indian or Alaska Native, non-Hispanic/Latino; 9 Asian, non-Hispanic/Latino; 11 Hispanic/Latino; 1 Two or more races, non-Hispanic/Latino), 13 international. Average age 33. 131 applicants, 78% accepted, 67 enrolled. In 2013, 83 master's, 5 other advanced degrees awarded. *Degree requirements:* For master's, comprehensive exam, thesis or

alternative. *Entrance requirements:* For master's, GMAT (minimum score 500), minimum AACSB index of 1080. Additional exam requirements/recommendations for international students: Required—TOEFL (minimum score 550 paper-based; 80 iBT), IELTS (minimum score 6.5). *Application deadline:* For fall admission, 7/15 priority date for domestic students, 4/1 priority date for international students; for spring admission, 11/30 priority date for domestic students, 9/1 priority date for international students. Applications are processed on a rolling basis. Application fee: $50. Electronic applications accepted. *Expenses:* Tuition, state resident: full-time $8912; part-time $540 per credit hour. Tuition, nonresident: full-time $20,774; part-time $1252 per credit hour. *Required fees:* $148 per semester. One-time fee: $150. *Financial support:* In 2013–14, 10 students received support, including 4 research assistantships with full and partial tuition reimbursements available (averaging $7,750 per year), 5 teaching assistantships with full and partial tuition reimbursements available (averaging $9,000 per year); career-related internships or fieldwork, Federal Work-Study, institutionally sponsored loans, scholarships/grants, health care benefits, tuition waivers (full and partial), and unspecified assistantships also available. Support available to part-time students. Financial award application deadline: 4/1; financial award applicants required to submit FAFSA. *Faculty research:* Supply chain management, management of research and development, international marketing and branding, organizational behavior and human resource management, social networks and computational economics. *Total annual research expenditures:* $2.1 million. *Unit head:* Dr. Cynthia Gramm, Chair, 256-824-6913, Fax: 256-824-6328, E-mail: cynthia.gramm@uah.edu. *Application contact:* Jennifer Pettitt, Director of Graduate Programs, 256-824-6681, Fax: 256-824-7571, E-mail: jennifer.pettitt@uah.edu.

The University of Alabama in Huntsville, School of Graduate Studies, College of Business Administration, Programs in Information Systems, Huntsville, AL 35899. Offers enterprise resource planning (Certificate); information assurance (MS, Certificate); information systems (MSIS); supply chain management (Certificate). Part-time and evening/weekend programs available. *Faculty:* 8 full-time (1 woman). *Students:* 13 full-time (7 women), 21 part-time (10 women); includes 8 minority (5 Black or African American, non-Hispanic/Latino; 3 Asian, non-Hispanic/Latino), 3 international. Average age 34. 35 applicants, 54% accepted, 10 enrolled. In 2013, 8 master's awarded. *Degree requirements:* For master's, comprehensive exam, thesis or alternative. *Entrance requirements:* For master's, GMAT (minimum score 500), minimum AACSB index of 1080. Additional exam requirements/recommendations for international students: Required—TOEFL (minimum score 550 paper-based; 80 iBT), IELTS (minimum score 6.5). *Application deadline:* For fall admission, 7/15 priority date for domestic students, 4/1 priority date for international students; for spring admission, 11/30 priority date for domestic students, 9/1 priority date for international students. Applications are processed on a rolling basis. Application fee: $50. Electronic applications accepted. *Expenses:* Tuition, state resident: full-time $8912; part-time $540 per credit hour. Tuition, nonresident: full-time $20,774; part-time $1252 per credit hour. *Required fees:* $148 per semester. One-time fee: $150. *Financial support:* In 2013–14, 4 students received support, including 1 research assistantship with full tuition reimbursement available (averaging $9,000 per year), 3 teaching assistantships with full and partial tuition reimbursements available (averaging $6,000 per year); career-related internships or fieldwork, Federal Work-Study, institutionally sponsored loans, scholarships/grants, health care benefits, and unspecified assistantships also available. Support available to part-time students. Financial award application deadline: 4/1; financial award applicants required to submit FAFSA. *Faculty research:* Supply chain information systems, information assurance and security, databases and conceptual schema, workflow management, inter-organizational information sharing. *Total annual research expenditures:* $375,942. *Unit head:* Dr. Cynthia Gramm, Chair, 256-824-6913, Fax: 256-824-6328, E-mail: cynthia.gramm@uah.edu. *Application contact:* Jennifer Pettitt, Director of Graduate Programs, 256-824-6681, Fax: 256-824-7571, E-mail: jennifer.pettitt@uah.edu.

University of Dallas, Graduate School of Management, Irving, TX 75062-4736. Offers accounting (MBA, MM, MS); business management (MBA, MM); corporate finance (MBA, MM); financial services (MBA); global business (MBA, MM); health services management (MBA, MM); human resource management (MBA, MM); information assurance (MBA, MM, MS); information technology (MBA, MM, MS); information technology service management (MBA, MM, MS); marketing management (MBA, MM); organization development (MBA, MM); project management (MBA, MM); sports and entertainment management (MBA, MM); strategic leadership (MBA, MM); supply chain management (MBA); supply chain management and market logistics (MM). *Accreditation:* ACBSP. Part-time and evening/weekend programs available. Postbaccalaureate distance learning degree programs offered (no on-campus study). *Entrance requirements:* Additional exam requirements/recommendations for international students: Required—TOEFL. Electronic applications accepted. *Expenses:* Contact institution.

University of Florida, Graduate School, Warrington College of Business Administration, Hough Graduate School of Business, Department of Information Systems and Operations Management, Gainesville, FL 32611. Offers information systems and operations management (MS, PhD); supply chain management (Certificate). *Faculty:* 13 full-time (3 women), 6 part-time/adjunct (1 woman). *Students:* 294 full-time (127 women), 9 part-time (all women); includes 31 minority (10 Black or African American, non-Hispanic/Latino; 17 Asian, non-Hispanic/Latino; 4 Hispanic/Latino), 254 international. Average age 25. 705 applicants, 65% accepted, 138 enrolled. In 2013, 118 master's, 2 doctorates awarded. Terminal master's awarded for partial completion of doctoral program. *Degree requirements:* For doctorate, thesis/dissertation. *Entrance requirements:* For master's, GMAT or GRE General Test, minimum GPA of 3.0; for doctorate, GMAT (minimum score 650) or GRE General Test, minimum GPA of 3.0. Additional exam requirements/recommendations for international students: Required—TOEFL (minimum score 550 paper-based; 80 iBT), IELTS (minimum score 6). *Application deadline:* For fall admission, 4/1 priority date for domestic students, 3/1 for international students; for spring admission, 10/15 for domestic students, 10/1 for international students. Applications are processed on a rolling basis. Application fee: $30. *Expenses:* Tuition, state resident: full-time $12,640. Tuition, nonresident: full-time $30,000. *Financial support:* In 2013–14, 13 students received support, including 3 fellowships (averaging $3,257 per year), 10 research assistantships (averaging $23,165 per year), 3 teaching assistantships (averaging $21,505 per year); unspecified assistantships also available. Financial award application deadline: 2/1; financial award applicants required to submit FAFSA. *Faculty research:* Expert systems, nonconvex optimization, manufacturing management, production and operation management, telecommunication. *Unit head:* Hsing Cheng, PharmD, Chair, 352-392-7068, Fax: 352-392-5438, E-mail: hkcheng@ufl.edu. *Application contact:* Praveen A. Pathak, PhD, Graduate Coordinator, 352-392-9599, Fax: 352-392-5438, E-mail: praveen@ufl.edu.
Website: http://www.cba.ufl.edu/isom/.

University of Houston, College of Technology, Department of Information and Logistics Technology, Houston, TX 77204. Offers information security (MS); supply chain and logistics technology (MS); technology project management (MS). Part-time programs available. *Degree requirements:* For master's, project or thesis (most programs). *Entrance requirements:* For master's, GMAT. Additional exam requirements/recommendations for international students: Required—TOEFL (minimum score 550 paper-based; 79 iBT). Electronic applications accepted.

University of Houston–Downtown, College of Business, Houston, TX 77002. Offers finance (MBA); general management (MBA); human resource management (MBA); leadership (MBA); sales management and business development (MBA); supply chain management (MBA). Evening/weekend programs available. *Faculty:* 18 full-time (7 women). *Students:* 1 (woman) full-time, 88 part-time (32 women); includes 60 minority (18 Black or African American, non-Hispanic/Latino; 10 Asian, non-Hispanic/Latino; 30 Hispanic/Latino; 1 Native Hawaiian or other Pacific Islander, non-Hispanic/Latino; 1 Two or more races, non-Hispanic/Latino), 2 international. Average age 33. 41 applicants, 63% accepted, 24 enrolled. *Entrance requirements:* For master's, GMAT, official transcripts, bachelor's degree or equivalent, resume, 2 professional references. Additional exam requirements/recommendations for international students: Required—TOEFL (minimum score 81 iBT). *Application deadline:* For fall admission, 7/15 for domestic and international students. Applications are processed on a rolling basis. Application fee: $35 ($60 for international students). Electronic applications accepted. *Expenses:* Contact institution. *Financial support:* In 2013–14, 2 fellowships (averaging $6,000 per year) were awarded. Financial award application deadline: 4/1; financial award applicants required to submit FAFSA. *Faculty research:* Corporate finance, sustainability, recruitment and selection, international strategic management, gender and race discrimination. *Unit head:* Dr. D. Michael Fields, Dean, College of Business, 713-221-8179, Fax: 713-221-8675, E-mail: fieldsd@uhd.edu. *Application contact:* Ceshia Love, Assistant Director of Graduate Admissions, 713-221-8093, Fax: 713-223-7408, E-mail: gradadmissions@uhd.edu.
Website: http://mba.uhd.edu/.

The University of Iowa, Henry B. Tippie College of Business, Henry B. Tippie School of Management, Iowa City, IA 52242-1316. Offers corporate finance (MBA); investment management (MBA); marketing (MBA); strategic management and innovation (MBA); supply chain and analytics (MBA); JD/MBA; MBA/MA; MBA/MD; MBA/MHA; MBA/MSN. *Accreditation:* AACSB. Part-time and evening/weekend programs available. *Faculty:* 113 full-time (27 women), 89 part-time/adjunct (23 women). *Students:* 110 full-time (28 women), 786 part-time (236 women); includes 51 minority (13 Black or African American, non-Hispanic/Latino; 3 American Indian or Alaska Native, non-Hispanic/Latino; 23 Asian, non-Hispanic/Latino; 12 Hispanic/Latino), 162 international. Average age 33. 622 applicants, 73% accepted, 383 enrolled. In 2013, 333 master's awarded. *Degree requirements:* For master's, minimum GPA of 2.75. *Entrance requirements:* For master's, GMAT, GRE, quality work experience and leadership as shown through resume, references, and essays. Additional exam requirements/recommendations for international students: Required—TOEFL (minimum score 600 paper-based; 100 iBT), IELTS (minimum score 7). *Application deadline:* For fall admission, 7/30 for domestic students, 4/1 for international students; for spring admission, 12/30 for domestic and international students. Applications are processed on a rolling basis. Application fee: $60 ($100 for international students). Electronic applications accepted. *Expenses:* Contact institution. *Financial support:* In 2013–14, 96 students received support, including 102 fellowships (averaging $9,519 per year), 83 research assistantships with partial tuition reimbursements available (averaging $8,893 per year), 14 teaching assistantships with partial tuition reimbursements available (averaging $17,049 per year); career-related internships or fieldwork, scholarships/grants, health care benefits, and unspecified assistantships also available. Financial award application deadline: 7/30; financial award applicants required to submit FAFSA. *Faculty research:* Capital markets, econometrics, optimization, investments and empirical corporate finance, Iowa electronic markets. *Unit head:* Prof. David W. Frasier, Associate Dean, Tippie School of Management, 800-622-4692, Fax: 319-335-3604, E-mail: david-frasier@uiowa.edu. *Application contact:* Jodi Schafer, Director, MBA Admissions and Financial Aid, 319-335-0864, Fax: 319-335-3604, E-mail: jodi-schafer@uiowa.edu.
Website: http://tippie.uiowa.edu/mba.

University of La Verne, Regional and Online Campuses, Graduate Programs, Inland Empire Campus, Ontario, CA 91761. Offers business administration (MBA, MBA-EP), including accounting (MBA), finance (MBA), health services management (MBA-EP), information technology (MBA-EP), international business (MBA), managed care (MBA), management and leadership (MBA-EP), marketing (MBA-EP), supply chain management (MBA); leadership and management (MS), including human resource management, nonprofit management, organizational development. Part-time and evening/weekend programs available. *Faculty:* 1 full-time (0 women), 14 part-time/adjunct (6 women). *Students:* 26 full-time (15 women), 106 part-time (65 women); includes 92 minority (15 Black or African American, non-Hispanic/Latino; 29 Asian, non-Hispanic/Latino; 43 Hispanic/Latino; 1 Native Hawaiian or other Pacific Islander, non-Hispanic/Latino; 4 Two or more races, non-Hispanic/Latino). Average age 37. In 2013, 49 master's awarded. *Application deadline:* Applications are processed on a rolling basis. Application fee: $50. *Expenses:* Contact institution. *Financial support:* Institutionally sponsored loans available. Financial award application deadline: 3/2; financial award applicants required to submit FAFSA. *Unit head:* Allen Stout, Campus Director, Inland Empire Regional Campus in Ontario, 909-937-6987, E-mail: astout@laverne.edu. *Application contact:* Karen Schumann, Senior Associate Director of Admissions, Inland Empire Regional Campus in Ontario, 909-937-6991, E-mail: kschumann@laverne.edu.
Website: http://laverne.edu/locations/inland-empire/.

University of Louisville, J. B. Speed School of Engineering, Department of Industrial Engineering, Louisville, KY 40292-0001. Offers engineering management (M Eng); industrial engineering (M Eng, MS, PhD); logistics and distribution (Certificate). *Accreditation:* ABET (one or more programs are accredited). Part-time programs available. *Students:* 60 full-time (7 women), 54 part-time (10 women); includes 19 minority (2 Black or African American, non-Hispanic/Latino; 5 Asian, non-Hispanic/Latino; 7 Hispanic/Latino; 5 Two or more races, non-Hispanic/Latino), 16 international. Average age 27. 104 applicants, 73% accepted, 51 enrolled. In 2013, 11 master's awarded. Terminal master's awarded for partial completion of doctoral program. *Degree requirements:* For master's, comprehensive exam (for some programs), thesis or alternative; for doctorate, comprehensive exam, thesis/dissertation, minimum GPA of 3.0. *Entrance requirements:* For master's and doctorate, GRE General Test. Additional exam requirements/recommendations for international students: Required—TOEFL (minimum score 550 paper-based; 80 iBT), IELTS (minimum score 6.5). *Application deadline:* For fall admission, 5/1 priority date for domestic and international students; for spring admission, 11/1 priority date for domestic and international students. Applications are processed on a rolling basis. Application fee: $60. Electronic applications accepted. *Expenses:* Tuition, state resident: full-time $10,788; part-time $599 per credit hour. Tuition, nonresident: full-time $22,446; part-time $1247 per credit hour. *Required fees:* $196. Tuition and fees vary according to program and reciprocity agreements. *Financial support:* In 2013–14, 15 students received support, including 7 fellowships with full tuition reimbursements available (averaging $20,000 per year), 2 research assistantships with full tuition reimbursements available (averaging $20,000 per year), 6 teaching assistantships with full tuition reimbursements available (averaging $20,000 per year). Financial award application deadline: 1/25; financial award applicants required to submit FAFSA. *Faculty research:* Optimization, computer simulation, logistics and distribution, ergonomics and human factors, advanced manufacturing

process. *Total annual research expenditures:* $748,000. *Unit head:* Dr. John S. Usher, Chair, 502-852-6342, Fax: 502-852-5633, E-mail: usher@louisville.edu. *Application contact:* Dr. Michael Day, Associate Dean, 502-852-6195, Fax: 502-852-7294, E-mail: day@louisville.edu.
Website: http://www.louisville.edu/speed/industrial/.

University of Massachusetts Dartmouth, Graduate School, Charlton College of Business, Program in Business Administration, North Dartmouth, MA 02747-2300. Offers accounting (Postbaccalaureate Certificate); business administration (MBA); business foundations (Graduate Certificate); finance (Postbaccalaureate Certificate); international business (Graduate Certificate); management (Postbaccalaureate Certificate); marketing (Postbaccalaureate Certificate); organizational leadership (Graduate Certificate); supply chain management (Postbaccalaureate Certificate). *Accreditation:* AACSB. Part-time programs available. Postbaccalaureate distance learning degree programs offered (no on-campus study). *Faculty:* 36 full-time (12 women), 27 part-time/adjunct (10 women). *Students:* 154 full-time (73 women), 120 part-time (55 women); includes 28 minority (2 Black or African American, non-Hispanic/Latino; 1 American Indian or Alaska Native, non-Hispanic/Latino; 6 Asian, non-Hispanic/Latino; 11 Hispanic/Latino; 8 Two or more races, non-Hispanic/Latino), 129 international. Average age 29. 204 applicants, 82% accepted, 112 enrolled. In 2013, 71 master's, 15 other advanced degrees awarded. *Degree requirements:* For master's, portfolio of MBA course work. *Entrance requirements:* For master's, GMAT, statement of purpose (minimum of 300 words), resume, 2 letters of recommendation, official transcripts; for other advanced degree, statement of purpose (minimum of 300 words), resume, official transcripts. Additional exam requirements/recommendations for international students: Required—TOEFL (minimum score 500 paper-based; 72 iBT), IELTS (minimum score 6). *Application deadline:* For fall admission, 8/1 priority date for domestic students, 5/1 priority date for international students; for spring admission, 1/1 priority date for domestic students, 10/1 priority date for international students. Applications are processed on a rolling basis. Application fee: $60. Electronic applications accepted. *Expenses:* Tuition, state resident: full-time $2071; part-time $86.29 per credit. Tuition, nonresident: full-time $8099; part-time $337.46 per credit. Tuition and fees vary according to course load and reciprocity agreements. *Financial support:* Federal Work-Study and unspecified assistantships available. Support available to part-time students. Financial award application deadline: 3/1; financial award applicants required to submit FAFSA. *Faculty research:* E-commerce, managing diversity, agile manufacturing, green business, activity-based management, build-to-order supply chain management. *Total annual research expenditures:* $330,000. *Unit head:* Toby Stapleton, Assistant Dean for Graduate Studies, 508-999-8543, Fax: 508-999-8646, E-mail: tstapleton@umassd.edu. *Application contact:* Steven Briggs, Director of Marketing and Recruitment for Graduate Studies, 508-999-8604, Fax: 508-999-8183, E-mail: graduate@umassd.edu.
Website: http://www.umassd.edu/charlton/.

University of Massachusetts Lowell, Manning School of Business, Lowell, MA 01854-2881. Offers accounting (MSA); business administration (MBA, PhD); financial management (Graduate Certificate); foundations of business (Graduate Certificate); healthcare innovation and entrepreneurship (MS); innovation and technological entrepreneurship (MS); new venture creation (Graduate Certificate); supply chain and operations management (Graduate Certificate). *Accreditation:* AACSB. Part-time and evening/weekend programs available. *Entrance requirements:* For master's, GMAT.

University of Memphis, Graduate School, Fogelman College of Business and Economics, Program in Business Administration, Memphis, TN 38152. Offers accounting (MBA, PhD); economics (MBA, PhD); executive business administration (MBA); finance (PhD); finance, insurance, and real estate (MBA, MS); international business administration (IMBA); management (MBA, MS, PhD); management information systems (MBA, MS, PhD); management science (MBA); marketing (MBA, MS); marketing and supply chain management (PhD); real estate development (MS); JD/MBA. *Accreditation:* AACSB. *Faculty:* 44 full-time (9 women), 5 part-time/adjunct (0 women). *Students:* 238 full-time (101 women), 315 part-time (113 women); includes 146 minority (80 Black or African American, non-Hispanic/Latino; 1 American Indian or Alaska Native, non-Hispanic/Latino; 46 Asian, non-Hispanic/Latino; 13 Hispanic/Latino; 2 Native Hawaiian or other Pacific Islander, non-Hispanic/Latino; 4 Two or more races, non-Hispanic/Latino), 104 international. Average age 32. 343 applicants, 62% accepted, 102 enrolled. In 2013, 140 master's, 17 doctorates awarded. *Degree requirements:* For master's, comprehensive exam; for doctorate, comprehensive exam, thesis/dissertation. *Entrance requirements:* For master's, GMAT, resume; for doctorate, GMAT, interview, minimum GPA of 3.4, resume, letter of recommendation. Additional exam requirements/recommendations for international students: Required—TOEFL (minimum score 550 paper-based). *Application deadline:* For fall admission, 8/1 for domestic students; for spring admission, 12/1 for domestic students. Application fee: $35 ($60 for international students). *Financial support:* In 2013–14, 164 students received support. Research assistantships with full tuition reimbursements available, teaching assistantships with full tuition reimbursements available, career-related internships or fieldwork, Federal Work-Study, scholarships/grants, and unspecified assistantships available. Financial award application deadline: 2/15; financial award applicants required to submit FAFSA. *Faculty research:* Competitive business strategy, finance microstructures, supply chain management innovations, health care economics, litigation risks and corporate audits. *Unit head:* Rajiv Grover, Dean, 901-678-3759, E-mail: rgrover@memphis.edu. *Application contact:* Dr. Carol V. Danehower, Associate Dean, 901-678-5402, Fax: 901-678-3579, E-mail: fcbegp@memphis.edu.
Website: http://www.memphis.edu/fcbe/grad_programs.php.

University of Michigan, Ross School of Business, Ann Arbor, MI 48109-1234. Offers accounting (M Acc); business (MBA); business administration (PhD); supply chain management (MSCM); JD/MBA; MBA/M Arch; MBA/M Eng; MBA/MA; MBA/MEM; MBA/MHSA; MBA/MM; MBA/MPP; MBA/MS; MBA/MSE; MBA/MSI; MBA/MSW; MBA/MUP; MD/MBA; MHSA/MBA. Part-time and evening/weekend programs available. *Degree requirements:* For doctorate, comprehensive exam, thesis/dissertation, oral defense of dissertation, preliminary exam. *Entrance requirements:* For master's, GMAT or GRE, completion of equivalent of four-year U.S. bachelor's degree, two letters of recommendation, essays, resume; for doctorate, GMAT or GRE. Additional exam requirements/recommendations for international students: Required—TOEFL (minimum score 600 paper-based; 100 iBT). Electronic applications accepted. Tuition and fees vary according to course level, course load, degree level, program and student level. *Faculty research:* Finance and accounting, marketing, technology and operations management, corporate strategy, management and organizations.

University of Michigan–Dearborn, College of Business, Dearborn, MI 48128-1491. Offers accounting (MBA, MS); business analytics (MS); finance (MBA, MS); human resource management (MBA); information systems (MS); international business (MBA); investment (MBA); management (MBA); management information systems (MBA); marketing (MBA); supply chain management (MBA, MS); taxation (MBA); MBA/MHSA; MBA/MSE; MBA/MSF; MBA/MSIS; MBA/MSSCM; MSF/MSA. *Accreditation:* AACSB. Part-time and evening/weekend programs available. Postbaccalaureate distance learning degree programs offered (no on-campus study). *Faculty:* 24 full-time (8 women), 5 part-time/adjunct (2 women). *Students:* 82 full-time (31 women), 323 part-time (116 women); includes 72 minority (17 Black or African American, non-Hispanic/Latino; 2 American Indian or Alaska Native, non-Hispanic/Latino; 30 Asian, non-Hispanic/Latino; 15 Hispanic/Latino; 8 Two or more races, non-Hispanic/Latino), 65 international. Average age 32. 290 applicants, 44% accepted, 99 enrolled. In 2013, 143 master's awarded. *Entrance requirements:* For master's, GMAT or GRE, pre-calculus or finite mathematics; 18 credits of accounting course work beyond introductory courses (MS in accounting). Additional exam requirements/recommendations for international students: Required—TOEFL (minimum score 560 paper-based; 84 iBT), IELTS. *Application deadline:* For fall admission, 8/1 priority date for domestic students, 5/1 priority date for international students; for winter admission, 12/1 priority date for domestic students, 9/1 priority date for international students; for spring admission, 4/1 priority date for domestic students, 1/1 priority date for international students. Applications are processed on a rolling basis. Application fee: $60. Electronic applications accepted. *Expenses:* Contact institution. *Financial support:* Career-related internships or fieldwork, Federal Work-Study, and scholarships/grants available. Support available to part-time students. Financial award application deadline: 9/1; financial award applicants required to submit FAFSA. *Faculty research:* Cultural diversity, buyer-supplier relations, error detection in data, economic evolution. *Unit head:* Dr. Raju Balakrishnan, Dean, 313-593-5248, Fax: 313-271-9835, E-mail: rajub@umich.edu. *Application contact:* Joan Doherty, Academic Advisor/Counselor, 313-593-5460, Fax: 313-271-9838, E-mail: umd-gradbusiness@umich.edu.
Website: http://www.cob.umd.umich.edu.

University of Minnesota, Twin Cities Campus, Carlson School of Management, Carlson Full-Time MBA Program, Minneapolis, MN 55455. Offers finance (MBA); information technology (MBA); management (MBA); marketing (MBA); medical industry orientation (MBA); supply chain and operations (MBA); JD/MBA; MBA/MPP; MD/MBA; MHA/MBA; Pharm D/MBA. *Accreditation:* AACSB. *Faculty:* 137 full-time (42 women), 16 part-time/adjunct (5 women). *Students:* 222 full-time (62 women); includes 30 minority (2 Black or African American, non-Hispanic/Latino; 17 Asian, non-Hispanic/Latino; 5 Hispanic/Latino; 6 Two or more races, non-Hispanic/Latino), 60 international. Average age 28. 565 applicants, 44% accepted, 113 enrolled. In 2013, 96 master's awarded. *Entrance requirements:* For master's, GMAT or GRE. Additional exam requirements/recommendations for international students: Required—TOEFL (minimum score 580 paper-based; 84 iBT), IELTS (minimum score 7), PTE. *Application deadline:* For fall admission, 4/1 for domestic students, 2/1 for international students. Application fee: $60 ($90 for international students). Electronic applications accepted. *Expenses:* Contact institution. *Financial support:* In 2013–14, 133 students received support, including 133 fellowships with full and partial tuition reimbursements available (averaging $29,445 per year); research assistantships with partial tuition reimbursements available, teaching assistantships with partial tuition reimbursements available, career-related internships or fieldwork, Federal Work-Study, institutionally sponsored loans, scholarships/grants, health care benefits, and unspecified assistantships also available. Financial award application deadline: 4/1; financial award applicants required to submit FAFSA. *Faculty research:* Finance and accounting: financial reporting, asset pricing models and corporate finance; information and decision sciences: on-line auctions, information transparency and recommender systems; marketing: psychological influences on consumer behavior, brand equity, pricing and marketing channels; operations: lean manufacturing, quality management and global supply chains; strategic management and organization: global strategy, networks, entrepreneurship and innovation, sustainability. *Unit head:* Philip J. Miller, Assistant Dean, MBA Programs and Graduate Business Career Center, 612-625-5555, Fax: 612-625-1012, E-mail: mba@umn.edu. *Application contact:* Linh Gilles, Director of Admissions and Recruiting, 612-625-5555, Fax: 612-625-1012, E-mail: ftmba@umn.edu.
Website: http://www.csom.umn.edu/MBA/full-time/.

University of Minnesota, Twin Cities Campus, Carlson School of Management, Carlson Part-Time MBA Program, Minneapolis, MN 55455. Offers finance (MBA); information technology (MBA); management (MBA); marketing (MBA); medical industry orientation (MBA); supply chain and operations (MBA). Part-time and evening/weekend programs available. *Faculty:* 137 full-time (42 women), 15 part-time/adjunct (3 women). *Students:* 1,207 part-time (393 women); includes 108 minority (21 Black or African American, non-Hispanic/Latino; 4 American Indian or Alaska Native, non-Hispanic/Latino; 72 Asian, non-Hispanic/Latino; 5 Hispanic/Latino; 1 Native Hawaiian or other Pacific Islander, non-Hispanic/Latino; 5 Two or more races, non-Hispanic/Latino), 66 international. Average age 28. 291 applicants, 86% accepted, 205 enrolled. In 2013, 372 master's awarded. *Entrance requirements:* For master's, GMAT or GRE. Additional exam requirements/recommendations for international students: Required—TOEFL (minimum score 580 paper-based; 84 iBT), IELTS (minimum score 7), PTE. *Application deadline:* For fall admission, 5/1 priority date for domestic and international students; for spring admission, 10/1 priority date for domestic and international students. Applications are processed on a rolling basis. Application fee: $60 ($90 for international students). Electronic applications accepted. *Expenses:* Contact institution. *Financial support:* Applicants required to submit FAFSA. *Faculty research:* Finance and accounting: financial reporting, asset pricing models and corporate finance; information and decision sciences: on-line auctions, information transparency and recommender systems; marketing: psychological influences on consumer behavior, brand equity, pricing and marketing channels; operations: lean manufacturing, quality management and global supply chains; strategic management and organization: global strategy, networks, entrepreneurship and innovation, sustainability. *Unit head:* Philip J. Miller, Assistant Dean, MBA Programs and Graduate Business Career Center, 612-624-2039, Fax: 612-625-1012, E-mail: mba@umn.edu. *Application contact:* Linh Gilles, Director of Admissions and Recruiting, 612-625-5555, Fax: 612-625-1012, E-mail: ptmba@umn.edu.
Website: http://www.carlsonschool.umn.edu/ptmba.

University of Missouri–St. Louis, College of Business Administration, Program in Business Administration, St. Louis, MO 63121. Offers accounting (MBA); business administration (Certificate); business intelligence (Certificate); finance (MBA); human resource management (Certificate); information systems (MBA); logistics and supply chain management (MBA, PhD, Certificate); marketing (MBA); marketing management (Certificate); operations management (MBA). *Accreditation:* AACSB. Part-time and evening/weekend programs available. *Faculty:* 30 full-time (5 women), 20 part-time/adjunct (8 women). *Students:* 114 full-time (51 women), 269 part-time (100 women); includes 43 minority (16 Black or African American, non-Hispanic/Latino; 14 Asian, non-Hispanic/Latino; 11 Hispanic/Latino; 1 Native Hawaiian or other Pacific Islander, non-Hispanic/Latino; 1 Two or more races, non-Hispanic/Latino), 56 international. Average age 31. 153 applicants, 91% accepted, 110 enrolled. In 2013, 136 master's, 7 other advanced degrees awarded. *Degree requirements:* For doctorate, thesis/dissertation. *Entrance requirements:* For master's, GMAT, 2 letters of recommendation. Additional exam requirements/recommendations for international students: Recommended—TOEFL (minimum score 550 paper-based; 79 iBT), IELTS (minimum score 6.5). *Application deadline:* For fall admission, 7/1 for domestic and international students; for spring admission, 12/1 for domestic and international students. Applications are processed on a rolling basis. Application fee: $50 ($40 for international students). Electronic applications accepted. *Expenses:* Tuition, state resident: full-time $7364; part-time $409.10 per credit hour. Tuition, nonresident: full-time $19,162; part-time

$1008.50 per credit hour. *Financial support:* In 2013–14, 14 research assistantships with full and partial tuition reimbursements (averaging $5,625 per year), 6 teaching assistantships with full and partial tuition reimbursements (averaging $9,403 per year) were awarded; career-related internships or fieldwork, Federal Work-Study, and institutionally sponsored loans also available. Support available to part-time students. Financial award application deadline: 4/1; financial award applicants required to submit FAFSA. *Faculty research:* Human resources, strategic management, marketing strategy, consumer behavior product development, advertising. *Unit head:* Francesca Ferrari, Assistant Director, 314-516-5885, Fax: 314-516-6420, E-mail: mba@umsl.edu. *Application contact:* 314-516-5458, Fax: 314-516-6996, E-mail: gradadm@umsl.edu. Website: http://mba.umsl.edu/Degree%20Programs/index.html.

The University of North Carolina at Charlotte, The Graduate School, The William States Lee College of Engineering, Department of Systems Engineering and Engineering Management, Charlotte, NC 28223-0001. Offers energy analytics (Graduate Certificate); engineering management (MSEM); engineering science (MS); infrastructure and environmental systems (PhD); Lean Six Sigma (Graduate Certificate); logistics and supply chains (Graduate Certificate); systems analytics (Graduate Certificate). Part-time and evening/weekend programs available. Postbaccalaureate distance learning degree programs offered. *Faculty:* 6 full-time (1 woman), 1 (woman) part-time/adjunct. *Students:* 17 full-time (7 women), 39 part-time (11 women); includes 12 minority (6 Black or African American, non-Hispanic/Latino; 4 Asian, non-Hispanic/Latino; 2 Hispanic/Latino), 20 international. Average age 28. 86 applicants, 65% accepted, 23 enrolled. In 2013, 8 master's awarded. *Degree requirements:* For master's, thesis or alternative, project. *Entrance requirements:* For master's, GRE or GMAT, letters of recommendation. Additional exam requirements/recommendations for international students: Required—TOEFL (minimum score 557 paper-based; 83 iBT). *Application deadline:* For fall admission, 5/1 priority date for domestic students, 5/1 for international students; for spring admission, 10/1 priority date for domestic students, 10/1 for international students. Application fee: $75. Electronic applications accepted. *Expenses:* Tuition, state resident: full-time $3522. Tuition, nonresident: full-time $16,051. *Required fees:* $2585. Tuition and fees vary according to course load and program. *Financial support:* Applicants required to submit FAFSA. *Faculty research:* Sustainable material and renewable technology; thermal analysis; large scale optimization; project risk management; supply chains; leans systems; global product innovation; quality and reliability analysis and management; productivity and project management; business forecasting, market analyses and feasibility studies. *Unit head:* Dr. Robert E. Johnson, Dean, 704-687-8242, Fax: 704-687-2352, E-mail: robejohn@.uncc.edu. *Application contact:* Kathy B. Giddings, Director of Graduate Admissions, 704-687-5503, Fax: 704-687-1668, E-mail: gradadm@uncc.edu.

The University of North Carolina at Greensboro, Graduate School, Bryan School of Business and Economics, Department of Information Systems and Operations Management, Greensboro, NC 27412-5001. Offers information systems (PhD); information technology (Certificate); information technology and management (MS); supply chain management (Certificate). *Entrance requirements:* For master's, GMAT, GRE General Test. Additional exam requirements/recommendations for international students: Required—TOEFL. Electronic applications accepted.

University of North Texas, Robert B. Toulouse School of Graduate Studies, Denton, TN 76203-5017. Offers accounting (MS, PhD); applied anthropology (MA, MS); applied behavior analysis (Certificate); applied technology and performance improvement (M Ed, MS, PhD); art education (MA, PhD); art history (MA); art museum education (Certificate); arts leadership (Certificate); audiology (Au D); behavior analysis (MS); biochemistry and molecular biology (MS, PhD); biology (MA, MS, PhD); business (PhD); business computer information systems (PhD); chemistry (MS, PhD); clinical psychology (PhD); communication studies (MA, MS); computer engineering (MS); computer science (MS); computer science and engineering (PhD); counseling (M Ed, MS, PhD), including clinical mental health counseling (MS), college and university counseling (M Ed, MS), elementary school counseling (M Ed, MS), secondary school counseling (M Ed, MS); counseling psychology (PhD); creative writing (MA); criminal justice (MS); curriculum and instruction (M Ed, PhD), including curriculum studies (PhD), early childhood studies (PhD), language and literacy studies (PhD); decision sciences (MBA); design (MA, MFA), including fashion design (MFA), innovation studies, interior design (MFA); early childhood studies (MS); economics (MS); educational leadership (M Ed, Ed D, PhD); educational psychology (MS), including family studies, gifted and talented (MS, PhD), human development, learning and cognition, research, measurement and evaluation; educational research (PhD), including gifted and talented (MS, PhD), human development and family studies, psychological aspects of sports and exercise, research, measurement and statistics; electrical engineering (MS); emergency management (MPA); engineering systems (MS); English (MA, PhD); environmental science (MS, PhD); experimental psychology (PhD); finance (MBA, MS, PhD); financial management (MPA); French (MA); health psychology and behavioral medicine (PhD); health services management (MBA); higher education (M Ed, Ed D, PhD); history (MA, MS, PhD), including European history (PhD), military history (PhD), United States history (PhD); hospitality management (MS); human resources management (MPA); information science (MS, PhD); information technologies (MBA); information technology and decision sciences (MS); interdisciplinary studies (MA, MS); international sustainable tourism (MS); jazz studies (MM); journalism (MA, MJ, Graduate Certificate), including interactive and virtual digital communication (Graduate Certificate), narrative journalism (Graduate Certificate), public relations (Graduate Certificate); kinesiology (MS); learning technologies (MS, PhD); library science (MS); local government management (MPA); logistics and supply chain management (MBA, PhD); long-term care, senior housing, and aging services (MA, MS); management science (PhD); marketing (MBA, PhD); materials science and engineering (MS, PhD); mathematics (MA, PhD); merchandising (MS); music (MA, MM Ed, PhD), including ethnomusicology (MA), music education (MM Ed, PhD), music theory (MA, PhD), musicology (MA, PhD), performance (MA); nonprofit management (MPA); operations and supply chain management (MBA); performance (MM, DMA); philosophy (MA, PhD); physics (MS, PhD); political science (MA, MS, PhD); public administration and management (PhD), including emergency management, nonprofit management, public financial management, urban management; radio, television and film (MA, MFA); recreation, event and sport management (MS); rehabilitation counseling (MS, Certificate); sociology (MA, MS, PhD); Spanish (MA); special education (M Ed, PhD), including autism intervention (PhD), emotional/behavioral disorders (PhD), mild/moderate disabilities (PhD); speech-language pathology (MA, MS); strategic management (MBA); studio art (MFA); taxation (MS); teaching (M Ed); MBA/MS; MS/MPH; MSES/MBA. Part-time and evening/weekend programs available. Postbaccalaureate distance learning degree programs offered. *Faculty:* 661 full-time (213 women), 240 part-time/adjunct (144 women). *Students:* 3,106 full-time (1,620 women), 3,543 part-time (2,221 women); includes 1,740 minority (533 Black or African American, non-Hispanic/Latino; 15 American Indian or Alaska Native, non-Hispanic/Latino; 286 Asian, non-Hispanic/Latino; 746 Hispanic/Latino; 3 Native Hawaiian or other Pacific Islander, non-Hispanic/Latino; 157 Two or more races, non-Hispanic/Latino), 1,145 international. Average age 32. 6,289 applicants, 43% accepted, 1751 enrolled. In 2013, 1,778 master's, 239 doctorates, 10 other advanced degrees awarded. Terminal master's awarded for partial completion of doctoral program. *Degree requirements:* For master's, variable foreign language requirement, comprehensive exam (for some programs), thesis (for some programs); for doctorate, variable foreign language requirement, comprehensive exam (for some programs), thesis/dissertation; for other advanced degree, variable foreign language requirement, comprehensive exam (for some programs). *Entrance requirements:* For master's and doctorate, GRE, GMAT. Additional exam requirements/recommendations for international students: Required—TOEFL (minimum score 550 paper-based; 79 iBT). *Application deadline:* For fall admission, 7/15 for domestic students, 3/15 for international students; for spring admission, 11/15 for domestic students, 9/15 for international students; for summer admission, 5/1 for domestic students. Applications are processed on a rolling basis. Application fee: $60. Electronic applications accepted. *Financial support:* Fellowships with partial tuition reimbursements, research assistantships with partial tuition reimbursements, teaching assistantships, career-related internships or fieldwork, Federal Work-Study, institutionally sponsored loans, scholarships/grants, health care benefits, and library assistantships available. Support available to part-time students. Financial award applicants required to submit FAFSA. *Unit head:* Mark Wardell, Dean, 940-565-2383, E-mail: mark.wardell@unt.edu. *Application contact:* Toulouse School of Graduate Studies, 940-565-2383, Fax: 940-565-2141, E-mail: gradsch@unt.edu. Website: http://tsgs.unt.edu/.

University of Rhode Island, Graduate School, College of Business Administration, Kingston, RI 02881. Offers accounting (MS); business administration (MBA, PhD), including finance and insurance (PhD), management (PhD), marketing (PhD), operations and supply chain management (MBA); finance (MBA); general business (MBA); management (MBA); marketing (MBA); supply chain management (MBA). *Accreditation:* AACSB. Part-time and evening/weekend programs available. *Faculty:* 43 full-time (16 women). *Students:* 103 full-time (37 women), 196 part-time (82 women); includes 42 minority (6 Black or African American, non-Hispanic/Latino; 1 American Indian or Alaska Native, non-Hispanic/Latino; 16 Asian, non-Hispanic/Latino; 13 Hispanic/Latino; 6 Two or more races, non-Hispanic/Latino), 29 international. In 2013, 119 master's, 3 doctorates awarded. *Degree requirements:* For master's, comprehensive exam (for some programs), thesis optional; for doctorate, comprehensive exam, thesis/dissertation. *Entrance requirements:* For master's, GMAT or GRE, 2 letters of recommendation, resume; for doctorate, GMAT or GRE, 3 letters of recommendation, resume. Additional exam requirements/recommendations for international students: Required—TOEFL (minimum score 575 paper-based; 91 iBT). *Application deadline:* For fall admission, 4/15 for domestic students, 2/15 for international students. Application fee: $65. Electronic applications accepted. *Expenses:* Tuition, state resident: full-time $11,532; part-time $641 per credit. Tuition, nonresident: full-time $23,606; part-time $1311 per credit. *Required fees:* $1388; $36 per credit. $35 per semester. One-time fee: $130. *Financial support:* In 2013–14, 14 teaching assistantships with full and partial tuition reimbursements (averaging $15,220 per year) were awarded. Financial award application deadline: 4/15; financial award applicants required to submit FAFSA. *Total annual research expenditures:* $66,948. *Unit head:* Dr. Mark Higgins, Dean, 401-874-4244, Fax: 401-874-4312, E-mail: markhiggins@uri.edu. *Application contact:* Lisa Lancellotta, Coordinator, MBA Programs, 401-874-4241, Fax: 401-874-4312, E-mail: mba@uri.edu. Website: http://www.cba.uri.edu/.

University of San Diego, School of Business Administration, Program in Supply Chain Management, San Diego, CA 92110-2492. Offers MS, Certificate. Postbaccalaureate distance learning degree programs offered (minimal on-campus study). *Students:* 95 part-time (26 women); includes 33 minority (4 Black or African American, non-Hispanic/Latino; 10 Asian, non-Hispanic/Latino; 17 Hispanic/Latino; 2 Two or more races, non-Hispanic/Latino), 2 international. Average age 34. In 2013, 22 master's, 23 other advanced degrees awarded. *Degree requirements:* For master's, capstone course. *Entrance requirements:* Additional exam requirements/recommendations for international students: Required—TOEFL (minimum score 580 paper-based; 92 iBT), TWE. *Application deadline:* For fall admission, 8/1 for domestic students; for spring admission, 2/1 for domestic students. Applications are processed on a rolling basis. Application fee: $80. Electronic applications accepted. *Expenses: Tuition:* Full-time $23,580; part-time $1310 per credit. *Required fees:* $350. *Financial support:* In 2013–14, 10 students received support. Scholarships/grants available. Financial award application deadline: 4/1; financial award applicants required to submit FAFSA. *Unit head:* Lauren Lukens, Director, MS Program, 619-260-7901, E-mail: msscm@sandiego.edu. *Application contact:* Monica Mahon, Associate Director of Graduate Admissions, 619-260-4524, Fax: 619-260-4158, E-mail: grads@sandiego.edu. Website: http://www.sandiego.edu/business/programs/ms-supply-chain-management/.

University of Southern California, Graduate School, Viterbi School of Engineering, Daniel J. Epstein Department of Industrial and Systems Engineering, Los Angeles, CA 90089. Offers digital supply chain management (MS); engineering management (MS); engineering technology communication (Graduate Certificate); health systems operations (Graduate Certificate); industrial and systems engineering (MS, PhD, Engr); manufacturing engineering (MS); operations research engineering (MS); optimization and supply chain management (Graduate Certificate); product development engineering (MS); safety systems and security (MS); systems architecting and engineering (MS, Graduate Certificate); systems safety and security (Graduate Certificate); transportation systems (Graduate Certificate); MS/MBA. Part-time and evening/weekend programs available. Postbaccalaureate distance learning degree programs offered (no on-campus study). Terminal master's awarded for partial completion of doctoral program. *Degree requirements:* For master's, thesis optional; for doctorate, thesis/dissertation. *Entrance requirements:* For master's and doctorate, GRE General Test. Additional exam requirements/recommendations for international students: Recommended—TOEFL. Electronic applications accepted. *Faculty research:* Health systems, music cognition and retrieval, transportation and logistics, manufacturing and automation, engineering systems design, risk and economic analysis.

The University of Tennessee at Chattanooga, Graduate School, College of Engineering and Computer Science, Department of Engineering Management, Chattanooga, TN 37403. Offers engineering management (MS); fundamentals of engineering management (Graduate Certificate); leadership and ethics (Graduate Certificate); logistics and supply chain management (Graduate Certificate); nuclear engineering (Graduate Certificate); power system protection (Graduate Certificate); power systems management (Graduate Certificate); project and value management (Graduate Certificate); quality management (Graduate Certificate); sustainable electric energy (Graduate Certificate). Postbaccalaureate distance learning degree programs offered (no on-campus study). *Faculty:* 5 full-time (1 woman). *Students:* 14 full-time (5 women), 67 part-time (14 women); includes 24 minority (13 Black or African American, non-Hispanic/Latino; 6 Asian, non-Hispanic/Latino; 4 Hispanic/Latino; 1 Two or more races, non-Hispanic/Latino), 6 international. Average age 31. 31 applicants, 45% accepted, 10 enrolled. In 2013, 31 master's, 17 other advanced degrees awarded. *Degree requirements:* For master's, thesis. *Entrance requirements:* For master's, GRE General Test, letters of recommendation; minimum undergraduate GPA of 2.5 overall or 3.0 in senior year. Additional exam requirements/recommendations for international students: Required—TOEFL (minimum score 550 paper-based; 79 iBT), IELTS (minimum score 6). *Application deadline:* For fall admission, 6/13 priority date for domestic students, 6/1 for international students; for spring admission, 10/15 priority

date for domestic students, 10/1 for international students. Applications are processed on a rolling basis. Application fee: $30 ($35 for international students). Electronic applications accepted. *Financial support:* In 2013–14, 5 research assistantships (averaging $6,528 per year), 3 teaching assistantships (averaging $6,781 per year) were awarded; career-related internships or fieldwork, scholarships/grants, and unspecified assistantships also available. Support available to part-time students. Financial award applicants required to submit FAFSA. *Faculty research:* Plant layout design, lean manufacturing, Six Sigma, value management, product development. *Unit head:* Dr. Neslihan Alp, Department Head, 423-425-4032, Fax: 423-425-5229, E-mail: neslihan-alp@utc.edu. *Application contact:* Dr. J. Randy Walker, Interim Dean of Graduate Studies, 423-425-4478, Fax: 423-425-5223, E-mail: randy-walker@utc.edu.
Website: http://www.utc.edu/Departments/engrcs/engm/index.php.

The University of Texas at Austin, Graduate School, McCombs School of Business, Department of Information, Risk, and Operations Management, Austin, TX 78712-1111. Offers information management (MBA); information systems (PhD); risk analysis and decision making (PhD); risk management (MBA); supply chain and operations management (MBA, PhD). *Degree requirements:* For doctorate, thesis/dissertation. *Entrance requirements:* For doctorate, GMAT or GRE. Electronic applications accepted. *Faculty research:* Stochastic processing and queuing, discrete nonlinear and large-scale optimization simulation, quality assurance logistics, distributed artificial intelligence, organizational modeling.

The University of Texas at Dallas, Naveen Jindal School of Management, Program in Business Administration, Richardson, TX 75080. Offers business administration (MBA, PMBA); executive business administration (EMBA); global leadership (EMBA); healthcare management for physicians (EMBA); product lifecycle and supply chain management (EMBA); project management (EMBA); real estate (MBA). *Accreditation:* AACSB. Part-time and evening/weekend programs available. Postbaccalaureate distance learning degree programs offered (no on-campus study). *Faculty:* 100 full-time (21 women), 52 part-time/adjunct (18 women). *Students:* 421 full-time (196 women), 630 part-time (398 women); includes 295 minority (45 Black or African American, non-Hispanic/Latino; 4 American Indian or Alaska Native, non-Hispanic/Latino; 151 Asian, non-Hispanic/Latino; 76 Hispanic/Latino; 19 Two or more races, non-Hispanic/Latino), 275 international. Average age 31. 940 applicants, 44% accepted, 375 enrolled. In 2013, 384 master's awarded. *Degree requirements:* For master's, thesis optional. *Entrance requirements:* For master's, GMAT, 10 years of business experience (EMBA), minimum GPA of 3.0. Additional exam requirements/recommendations for international students: Required—TOEFL (minimum score 550 paper-based). *Application deadline:* For fall admission, 7/15 for domestic students, 5/1 priority date for international students; for spring admission, 11/15 for domestic students, 9/1 priority date for international students. Applications are processed on a rolling basis. Application fee: $50 ($100 for international students). Electronic applications accepted. *Expenses:* Contact institution. *Financial support:* In 2013–14, 336 students received support. Research assistantships with partial tuition reimbursements available, teaching assistantships with partial tuition reimbursements available, career-related internships or fieldwork, Federal Work-Study, institutionally sponsored loans, scholarships/grants, and unspecified assistantships available. Support available to part-time students. Financial award application deadline: 4/30; financial award applicants required to submit FAFSA. *Faculty research:* Production scheduling, trade and finance, organizational decision-making, life/work planning. *Unit head:* Lisa Shatz, Assistant Dean, MBA Programs, 972-883-6191, E-mail: lisa.shatz@utdallas.edu. *Application contact:* Anna Walls, Enrollment Services Advisor, MBA Programs, 972-883-5951, E-mail: anna.walls@utdallas.edu.
Website: http://jindal.utdallas.edu/academic-programs/mba-programs/.

The University of Texas at Dallas, Naveen Jindal School of Management, Program in Information Systems and Operations Management, Richardson, TX 75080. Offers business analytics (MS); information technology and management (MS); supply chain management (MS). Part-time and evening/weekend programs available. *Faculty:* 14 full-time (0 women), 9 part-time/adjunct (3 women). *Students:* 668 full-time (258 women), 222 part-time (80 women); includes 78 minority (15 Black or African American, non-Hispanic/Latino; 51 Asian, non-Hispanic/Latino; 10 Hispanic/Latino; 2 Two or more races, non-Hispanic/Latino), 734 international. Average age 26. 1,622 applicants, 56% accepted, 364 enrolled. In 2013, 296 master's awarded. *Degree requirements:* For master's, thesis optional. *Entrance requirements:* For master's, GMAT. Additional exam requirements/recommendations for international students: Required—TOEFL (minimum score 550 paper-based). *Application deadline:* For fall admission, 7/15 for domestic students, 5/1 priority date for international students; for spring admission, 11/15 for domestic students, 9/1 priority date for international students. Applications are processed on a rolling basis. Application fee: $50 ($100 for international students). Electronic applications accepted. *Expenses:* Tuition, state resident: full-time $11,940; part-time $663.33 per credit hour. Tuition, nonresident: full-time $21,606; part-time $1200.33 per credit hour. *Financial support:* In 2013–14, 183 students received support, including 3 research assistantships with partial tuition reimbursements available (averaging $13,750 per year), 18 teaching assistantships with partial tuition reimbursements available (averaging $10,340 per year); career-related internships or fieldwork, Federal Work-Study, institutionally sponsored loans, scholarships/grants, and unspecified assistantships also available. Support available to part-time students. Financial award application deadline: 4/30; financial award applicants required to submit FAFSA. *Faculty research:* Technology marketing, measuring information work productivity, electronic commerce, decision support systems, data quality. *Unit head:* Dr. Srinivasan Raghunathan, Area Coordinator, Information Systems, 972-883-4377, E-mail: sraghu@utdallas.edu. *Application contact:* Dr. Milind Dawande, Area Coordinator, Supply Chain Management, 972-883-2793, E-mail: milind@utdallas.edu.
Website: http://jindal.utdallas.edu/academic-areas/information-systems-and-operations-management/.

University of Wisconsin–Madison, Graduate School, Wisconsin School of Business, Wisconsin Full-Time MBA Program, Madison, WI 53706. Offers applied security analysis (MBA); arts administration (MBA); brand and product management (MBA); corporate finance and investment banking (MBA); marketing research (MBA); operations and technology management (MBA); real estate (MBA); risk management and insurance (MBA); strategic human resource management (MBA); supply chain management (MBA). *Faculty:* 34 full-time (5 women), 30 part-time/adjunct (15 women). *Students:* 193 full-time (61 women); includes 37 minority (10 Black or African American, non-Hispanic/Latino; 14 Asian, non-Hispanic/Latino; 12 Hispanic/Latino; 1 Native Hawaiian or other Pacific Islander, non-Hispanic/Latino), 37 international. Average age 28. 460 applicants, 33% accepted, 101 enrolled. In 2013, 110 master's awarded. *Degree requirements:* For master's, thesis (for arts administration specialization). *Entrance requirements:* For master's, GMAT or GRE, bachelor's or equivalent degree, 2 years of work experience, letters of recommendation, resume. Additional exam requirements/recommendations for international students: Required—TOEFL (minimum score 600 paper-based; 100 iBT), IELTS. *Application deadline:* For fall admission, 11/5 for domestic and international students; for winter admission, 2/4 for domestic and international students; for spring admission, 4/28 for domestic students, 4/2 for international students. Applications are processed on a rolling basis. Application fee: $56. Electronic applications accepted. *Expenses:* Contact institution. *Financial support:* In 2013–14, 176 students received support, including 12 fellowships with full tuition reimbursements available (averaging $37,956 per year), 42 research assistantships with full tuition reimbursements available (averaging $28,175 per year), 43 teaching assistantships with full tuition reimbursements available (averaging $28,175 per year); scholarships/grants, health care benefits, and unspecified assistantships also available. Financial award application deadline: 4/26; financial award applicants required to submit FAFSA. *Faculty research:* Market consequences of International Financial Reporting Standards (IFRS), inter-firm relationships and strategic partnerships, application of Bayesian statistical methods and applied probability models to understanding individuals' behaviors in the context of customer relationship management (CRM) applications, liquidity provision and the structure of financial markets, strategic management of global startups. *Unit head:* Prof. Larry W. Hunter, Associate Dean of Master's Programs, 608-265-3494, Fax: 608-265-4192, E-mail: lhunter@bus.wisc.edu. *Application contact:* William H. Wait, Assistant Director of MBA Marketing and Recruiting, 608-262-4000, Fax: 608-265-4192, E-mail: wwait@bus.wisc.edu.
Website: http://www.bus.wisc.edu/mba.

University of Wisconsin–Whitewater, School of Graduate Studies, College of Business and Economics, Program in Business Administration, Whitewater, WI 53190-1790. Offers finance (MBA); human resource management (MBA); information technology management (MBA); international business (MBA); management (MBA); marketing (MBA); operations and supply chain management (MBA). *Accreditation:* AACSB. Part-time and evening/weekend programs available. Postbaccalaureate distance learning degree programs offered (no on-campus study). *Entrance requirements:* For master's, GMAT or GRE, minimum AACSB index of 1000, minimum GPA of 2.75. Additional exam requirements/recommendations for international students: Required—TOEFL (minimum score 550 paper-based; 80 iBT), IELTS (minimum score 6). Electronic applications accepted. *Faculty research:* Interface between social institutions and individual behavior, technology and innovation management, occupational mental health, workplace deviance and workplace romance.

Walden University, Graduate Programs, School of Management, Minneapolis, MN 55401. Offers accounting (MBA, MS, DBA), including accounting for the professional (MS), accounting with CPA emphasis (MS), self-designed (MS, PhD); accounting and management (MS), including accountants as strategic managers, self-designed (MS, PhD); advanced project management (Graduate Certificate); applied project management (Graduate Certificate); bridge to business administration (Post-Doctoral Certificate); bridge to management (Post-Doctoral Certificate); business administration (EMBA); business management (Graduate Certificate); communication (MS, Graduate Certificate); corporate finance (MBA); entrepreneurship (DBA); entrepreneurship and small business (MBA); finance (DBA); global supply chain management (DBA); healthcare management (MBA, DBA); human resource management (MBA, MS, Graduate Certificate), including functional human resource management (MS), general program (MS), integrating functional and strategic human resource management (MS), organizational strategy (MS); human resources management (DBA); information systems management (DBA); international business (MBA, DBA); leadership (MBA, MS, DBA), including general program (MS), human resources leadership (MS), leader development (MS), self-designed (MS, PhD); management (MS, PhD), including accounting (PhD), engineering management (PhD), finance (PhD), general program (MS), healthcare management (MS), human resource management (MS), human resources management (PhD), information systems management (PhD), leadership (MS), leadership and organizational change (PhD), marketing (MS), operations research (PhD), project management (MS), self-designed, strategy and operations (MS); marketing (MBA, DBA); project management (MBA, MS, DBA); self-designed (MBA, DBA); social impact management (DBA); technology entrepreneurship (DBA). Part-time and evening/weekend programs available. Postbaccalaureate distance learning degree programs offered (minimal on-campus study). *Faculty:* 24 full-time (9 women), 337 part-time/adjunct (127 women). *Students:* 4,369 full-time (2,379 women), 2,181 part-time (1,304 women); includes 3,669 minority (3,020 Black or African American, non-Hispanic/Latino; 22 American Indian or Alaska Native, non-Hispanic/Latino; 156 Asian, non-Hispanic/Latino; 331 Hispanic/Latino; 11 Native Hawaiian or other Pacific Islander, non-Hispanic/Latino; 129 Two or more races, non-Hispanic/Latino), 107 international. Average age 41. 2,030 applicants, 94% accepted, 1436 enrolled. In 2013, 757 master's, 128 doctorates, 32 other advanced degrees awarded. *Degree requirements:* For master's, residency (for some programs); for doctorate, thesis/dissertation (for some programs), residency. *Entrance requirements:* For master's, bachelor's degree or higher; minimum GPA of 2.5; official transcripts; goal statement (for some programs); access to computer and Internet; for doctorate, master's degree or higher; three years of related professional or academic experience (preferred); minimum GPA of 3.0; goal statement and current resume (select programs); official transcripts; access to computer and Internet; for other advanced degree, relevant work experience; access to computer and Internet. Additional exam requirements/recommendations for international students: Required—TOEFL (minimum score 550 paper-based; 79 iBT), IELTS (minimum score 6.5), Michigan English Language Assessment Battery (minimum score 82), or PTE. *Application deadline:* Applications are processed on a rolling basis. Application fee: $0. Electronic applications accepted. *Expenses: Tuition:* Full-time $11,813.55; part-time $500 per credit. *Required fees:* $618.76. *Financial support:* Fellowships, Federal Work-Study, scholarships/grants, unspecified assistantships, and family tuition reduction, active duty/veteran tuition reduction, group tuition reduction, interest-free payment plans, employee tuition reduction available. Support available to part-time students. Financial award applicants required to submit FAFSA. *Unit head:* Dr. Ward Ulmer, III, Associate Dean, 800-925-3368. *Application contact:* Jennifer Hall, Vice President of Enrollment Management, 866-4-WALDEN, E-mail: info@waldenu.edu.
Website: http://www.waldenu.edu/programs/colleges-schools/management.

Washington State University Spokane, Graduate Programs, Program in Engineering and Technology Management, Pullman, WA 99164-2785. Offers constraints management (Graduate Certificate); construction project management (Graduate Certificate); engineering and technology management (METM); facilities management (Graduate Certificate); logistics and supply chain management (Graduate Certificate); manufacturing leadership (Graduate Certificate); project management (Graduate Certificate); Six Sigma quality management (Graduate Certificate); systems engineering management (Graduate Certificate). *Degree requirements:* For master's, comprehensive exam (for some programs), thesis (for some programs), comprehensive exam or project. *Entrance requirements:* For master's, GMAT (for applicants with less than 3.0 GPA), minimum GPA of 3.0, 3 letters of reference, resume, personal statement, math through college algebra (prefer math through calculus I), experience in the engineering/technology area. Additional exam requirements/recommendations for international students: Required—TOEFL. *Expenses:* Contact institution. *Faculty research:* Operations research for decision analysis quality control and liability, analytical techniques to formulating decisions.

Washington University in St. Louis, Olin Business School, Program in Supply Chain Management, St. Louis, MO 63130-4899. Offers MS. Part-time programs available. *Faculty:* 82 full-time (18 women), 38 part-time/adjunct (8 women). *Students:* 40 full-time (20 women), 9 part-time (4 women); includes 8 minority (1 Black or African American, non-Hispanic/Latino; 6 Asian, non-Hispanic/Latino; 1 Hispanic/Latino), 32 international. Average age 27. 178 applicants, 30% accepted, 25 enrolled. In 2013, 10 master's awarded. *Entrance requirements:* For master's, GMAT or GRE. Additional exam

requirements/recommendations for international students: Required—TOEFL, IELTS. *Application deadline:* For fall admission, 10/1 for domestic and international students; for winter admission, 11/15 for domestic and international students; for spring admission, 4/1 for domestic and international students. Application fee: $100. Electronic applications accepted. *Financial support:* Applicants required to submit FAFSA. *Unit head:* Greg Hutchings, Associate Dean/Director of Specialized Master's Programs, 314-935-6380, Fax: 314-935-4464, E-mail: hutchings@wustl.edu. *Application contact:* Nikki Lemley, Associate Director, Specialized Master's Programs Admissions, 314-935-8469, Fax: 314-935-4464, E-mail: nlemley@wustl.edu.
Website: http://www.olin.wustl.edu/academicprograms/MSSCM/Pages/default.aspx.

Western Illinois University, School of Graduate Studies, College of Business and Technology, Program in Business Administration, Macomb, IL 61455-1390. Offers business administration (MBA, Certificate); supply chain management (Certificate). *Accreditation:* AACSB. Part-time programs available. *Students:* 42 full-time (23 women), 54 part-time (28 women); includes 6 minority (5 Black or African American, non-Hispanic/Latino; 1 Hispanic/Latino), 16 international. Average age 28. In 2013, 36 master's awarded. *Degree requirements:* For master's, thesis or alternative. *Entrance requirements:* For master's, GMAT. Additional exam requirements/recommendations for international students: Required—TOEFL (minimum score 550 paper-based; 80 iBT). *Application deadline:* Applications are processed on a rolling basis. Application fee: $30. Electronic applications accepted. *Financial support:* In 2013–14, 19 students received support, including 3 research assistantships with full tuition reimbursements available (averaging $7,544 per year), 16 teaching assistantships with full tuition reimbursements available (averaging $8,688 per year). Financial award applicants required to submit FAFSA. *Unit head:* Dr. John Drea, Associate Dean, 309-298-2442. *Application contact:* Dr. Nancy Parsons, Associate Provost and Director of Graduate Studies, 309-298-1806, Fax: 309-298-2345, E-mail: grad-office@wiu.edu.
Website: http://wiu.edu/cbt.

Wilfrid Laurier University, Faculty of Graduate and Postdoctoral Studies, School of Business and Economics, Department of Business, Waterloo, ON N2L 3C5, Canada. Offers accounting (PhD); finance (M Fin); financial economics (PhD); marketing (PhD); operations and supply chain management (PhD); organizational behavior and human resource management (M Sc); organizational behaviour and human resource management (PhD); supply chain management (M Sc); technology management (EMTM). *Accreditation:* AACSB. Part-time and evening/weekend programs available. *Degree requirements:* For master's, thesis optional; for doctorate, comprehensive exam, thesis/dissertation. *Entrance requirements:* For master's, GMAT, 4-year honors degree with minimum B+ average; for doctorate, GMAT, master's degree, minimum B+ average. Additional exam requirements/recommendations for international students: Required—TOEFL (minimum score 89 iBT). Electronic applications accepted. *Faculty research:* Financial economics, management and organizational behavior, operations and supply chain management.

Wright State University, School of Graduate Studies, Raj Soin College of Business, Department of Information Systems and Operations Management, Logistics and Supply Chain Management Program, Dayton, OH 45435. Offers MS.

Wright State University, School of Graduate Studies, Raj Soin College of Business, Department of Management, Dayton, OH 45435. Offers flexible business (MBA); health care management (MBA); international business (MBA); management, innovation and change (MBA); project management (MBA); supply chain management (MBA); MBA/MS. *Entrance requirements:* For master's, GMAT, minimum AACSB index of 1000. Additional exam requirements/recommendations for international students: Required—TOEFL.

Transportation Management

American Public University System, AMU/APU Graduate Programs, Charles Town, WV 25414. Offers accounting (MBA, MS); criminal justice (MA), including business administration, emergency and disaster management, general (MA, MS); educational leadership (M Ed); emergency and disaster management (MA); entrepreneurship (MBA); environmental policy and management (MS), including environmental planning, environmental sustainability, fish and wildlife management, general (MA, MS), global environmental management; finance (MBA); general (MBA); global business management (MBA); history (MA), including American history, ancient and classical history, European history, global history, public history; homeland security (MA), including business administration, counter-terrorism studies, criminal justice, cyber, emergency management and public health, intelligence studies, transportation security; homeland security resource allocation (MBA); humanities (MA); information technology (MS), including digital forensics, enterprise software development, information assurance and security, IT project management; information technology management (MBA); intelligence studies (MA), including criminal intelligence, cyber, general (MA, MS), homeland security, intelligence analysis, intelligence collection, intelligence management, intelligence operations, terrorism studies; international relations and conflict resolution (MA), including comparative and security issues, conflict resolution, international and transnational security issues, peacekeeping; legal studies (MA); management (MA), including defense management, general (MA, MS), human resource management, organizational leadership, public administration; marketing (MBA); military history (MA), including American military history, American Revolution, civil war, war since 1945, World War II; military studies (MA), including joint warfare, strategic leadership; national security studies (MA), including general (MA, MS), homeland security, regional security studies, security and intelligence analysis, terrorism studies; nonprofit management (MBA); political science (MA), including American politics and government, comparative government and development, general (MA, MS), international relations, public policy; psychology (MA), including general (MA, MS), maritime engineering management, reverse logistics management; public administration (MPA), including disaster management, environmental policy, health policy, human resources, national security, organizational management, security management; public health (MPH); reverse logistics management (MA); school counseling (M Ed); security management (MA); space studies (MS), including aerospace science, general (MA, MS), planetary science; sports and health sciences (MS); teaching (M Ed), including curriculum and instruction for elementary teachers, elementary reading, English language learners, instructional leadership, online learning, special education; transportation and logistics management (MA), including general (MA, MS), maritime engineering management, reverse logistics management. Programs offered via distance learning only. Part-time and evening/weekend programs available. Postbaccalaureate distance learning degree programs offered (no on-campus study). *Faculty:* 432 full-time (242 women), 1,722 part-time/adjunct (829 women). *Students:* 511 full-time (241 women), 10,947 part-time (4,294 women); includes 3,760 minority (2,058 Black or African American, non-Hispanic/Latino; 88 American Indian or Alaska Native, non-Hispanic/Latino; 293 Asian, non-Hispanic/Latino; 876 Hispanic/Latino; 91 Native Hawaiian or other Pacific Islander, non-Hispanic/Latino; 354 Two or more races, non-Hispanic/Latino), 134 international. Average age 36. In 2013, 3,323 master's awarded. *Degree requirements:* For master's, comprehensive exam or practicum. *Entrance requirements:* For master's, official transcript showing earned bachelor's degree from institution accredited by recognized accrediting body. Additional exam requirements/recommendations for international students: Required—TOEFL (minimum score 550 paper-based), IELTS (minimum score 6.5). *Application deadline:* Applications are processed on a rolling basis. Application fee: $0. Electronic applications accepted. *Expenses: Tuition:* Part-time $325 per semester hour. *Financial support:* Applicants required to submit FAFSA. *Faculty research:* Military history, criminal justice, management performance, national security. *Unit head:* Dr. Karan Powell, Executive Vice President and Provost, 877-468-6268, Fax: 304-724-3780. *Application contact:* Terry Grant, Vice President of Enrollment Management, 877-468-6268, Fax: 304-724-3780, E-mail: info@apus.edu.
Website: http://www.apus.edu.

California Maritime Academy, Graduate Studies, Vallejo, CA 94590. Offers transportation and engineering management (MS), including engineering management, humanitarian disaster management, transportation. Postbaccalaureate distance learning degree programs offered (no on-campus study). *Faculty:* 16 part-time/adjunct (2 women). *Students:* 40 full-time (10 women). 23 applicants, 100% accepted, 21 enrolled. In 2013, 13 master's awarded. *Degree requirements:* For master's, capstone course. *Entrance requirements:* For master's, equivalent of four-year U.S. bachelor's degree with minimum GPA of 2.5 during last two years (60 semester units or 90 quarter units) of coursework in degree program; five years of professional experience or GMAT/GRE. Additional exam requirements/recommendations for international students: Required—TOEFL (minimum score 550 paper-based). *Application deadline:* Applications are processed on a rolling basis. Application fee: $55. Electronic applications accepted. *Application contact:* Kathy Arnold, Program Coordinator, 707-654-1271, Fax: 707-654-1158, E-mail: karnold@csum.edu.
Website: http://www.csum.edu/web/industry/graduate-studies.

Embry-Riddle Aeronautical University–Worldwide, Worldwide Headquarters - Graduate Programs, Program in Business Administration and Management, Daytona Beach, FL 32114-3900. Offers air transportation management (Graduate Certificate); airport planning design and development (Graduate Certificate); aviation (MBAA); aviation enterprises in the global environment (Graduate Certificate); aviation-aerospace industrial management (Graduate Certificate); engineering management (MSEM); integrated logistics management (Graduate Certificate); leadership (MSL); logistics and supply chain management (MSLSCM); management (MSM); modeling and simulation management (Graduate Certificate); occupational safety management (MSOSM); project management (MSPM, Graduate Certificate). Part-time and evening/weekend programs available. Postbaccalaureate distance learning degree programs offered (no on-campus study). *Degree requirements:* For master's, comprehensive exam (for some programs), thesis (for some programs). *Entrance requirements:* Additional exam requirements/recommendations for international students: Recommended—TOEFL (minimum score 550 paper-based; 79 iBT). Electronic applications accepted. *Faculty research:* Healthcare operations management, humanitarian logistics, supply chain risk management, collaborative supply chain management, intersection of collaborative supply chain management and the learning organization, development of assessment tool measuring supply chain collaborative capacity, teaching effectiveness, teaching quality, management style effectiveness, aeronautics, small/medium-sized business leadership study, leadership factors, critical thinking, efficacy of ePortfolio.

Florida Institute of Technology, Graduate Programs, Extended Studies Division, Melbourne, FL 32901-6975. Offers acquisition and contract management (MS); aerospace engineering (MS); business administration (MBA, DBA); computer information systems (MS); computer science (MS); electrical engineering (MS); engineering management (MS); human resources management (MS); logistics management (MS), including humanitarian and disaster relief logistics; management (MS), including acquisition and contract management, e-business, human resources management, information systems, logistics management, management, transportation management; material acquisition management (MS); mechanical engineering (MS); operations research (MS); project management (MS), including information systems, operations research; public administration (MPA); quality management (MS); software engineering (MS); space systems (MS); space systems management (MS); supply chain management (MS); systems management (MS), including information systems, operations research; technology management (MS). Part-time and evening/weekend programs available. Postbaccalaureate distance learning degree programs offered (no on-campus study). *Faculty:* 8 full-time (1 woman), 96 part-time/adjunct (25 women). *Students:* 94 full-time (46 women), 912 part-time (397 women); includes 436 minority (290 Black or African American, non-Hispanic/Latino; 18 American Indian or Alaska Native, non-Hispanic/Latino; 38 Asian, non-Hispanic/Latino; 62 Hispanic/Latino; 2 Native Hawaiian or other Pacific Islander, non-Hispanic/Latino; 26 Two or more races, non-Hispanic/Latino), 9 international. Average age 37. 591 applicants, 44% accepted, 220 enrolled. In 2013, 522 master's awarded. *Degree requirements:* For master's, comprehensive exam (for some programs), capstone course. *Entrance requirements:* For master's, GMAT or resume showing 8 years of supervised experience, minimum GPA of 3.0, 2 letters of recommendation, resume. Additional exam requirements/recommendations for international students: Required—TOEFL (minimum score 550 paper-based; 79 iBT). *Application deadline:* For fall admission, 4/1 for international students; for spring admission, 9/30 for international students. Applications are processed on a rolling basis. Electronic applications accepted. *Expenses:* Contact institution. *Financial support:* Application deadline: 3/1; applicants required to submit FAFSA. *Unit head:* Dr. Theodore R. Richardson, III, Senior Associate Dean, 321-674-8123, Fax: 321-674-7597, E-mail: trichardson@fit.edu. *Application contact:* Carolyn Farrior, Director of Graduate Admissions, Online Learning and Off-Campus Programs, 321-674-7118, Fax: 321-674-8216, E-mail: cfarrior@fit.edu.
Website: http://es.fit.edu.

George Mason University, School of Policy, Government, and International Affairs, Program in Transportation Policy, Operations and Logistics, Arlington, VA 22201. Offers

MA, Certificate. *Faculty:* 9 full-time (5 women), 3 part-time/adjunct (0 women). *Students:* 11 full-time (1 woman), 19 part-time (4 women); includes 8 minority (4 Black or African American, non-Hispanic/Latino; 1 Asian, non-Hispanic/Latino; 2 Hispanic/Latino; 1 Two or more races, non-Hispanic/Latino), 1 international. Average age 33. 26 applicants, 81% accepted, 12 enrolled. In 2013, 8 master's awarded. *Degree requirements:* For master's, thesis or alternative. *Entrance requirements:* For master's, GRE (for students seeking merit-based scholarships), bachelor's degree with minimum GPA of 3.0, current resume, 2 letters of recommendation, expanded goals statement, 2 copies of official transcripts. Additional exam requirements/recommendations for international students: Required—TOEFL (minimum score 575 paper-based; 88 iBT), IELTS (minimum score 6.5), PTE. *Application deadline:* For fall admission, 6/1 priority date for domestic students, 5/1 priority date for international students; for spring admission, 12/1 priority date for domestic students, 11/1 priority date for international students. Applications are processed on a rolling basis. Application fee: $65 ($80 for international students). Electronic applications accepted. *Expenses:* Contact institution. *Financial support:* Career-related internships or fieldwork, Federal Work-Study, scholarships/grants, unspecified assistantships, and health care benefits (for full-time research or teaching assistantship recipients) available. Financial award application deadline: 3/1; financial award applicants required to submit FAFSA. *Unit head:* Laurie Schintler, Director, 703-993-2256, Fax: 703-993-4557, E-mail: lschintl@gmu.edu. *Application contact:* Travis Major, Director, Graduate Admissions, 703-993-1383, E-mail: tmajor@gmu.edu. Website: http://policy.gmu.edu/academic-professional-programs/masters-programs/transportation-policy-operations-logistics-tpol/.

Instituto Tecnologico de Santo Domingo, Graduate School, Area of Engineering, Santo Domingo, Dominican Republic. Offers construction administration (MS, Certificate); data telecommunications (M Eng, MS, Certificate); industrial engineering (M Eng, Certificate); industrial management (M Mgmt); information technology (Certificate); maintenance engineering (M Eng); occupational hazard prevention (M Mgmt); production management (Certificate); quantitative methods (Certificate); sanitary and environmental engineering (M Eng); structural engineering (M Eng); systems engineering and electronic data processing (Certificate); transportation (Certificate).

Iowa State University of Science and Technology, Department of Community and Regional Planning, Ames, IA 50011. Offers community and regional planning (MCRP); transportation (MS); M Arch/MCRP; MBA/MCRP; MCRP/MLA; MCRP/MPA. *Accreditation:* ACSP (one or more programs are accredited). *Degree requirements:* For master's, thesis or alternative. *Entrance requirements:* For master's, GRE General Test. Additional exam requirements/recommendations for international students: Required—TOEFL (minimum score 550 paper-based; 79 iBT), IELTS (minimum score 6.5). Electronic applications accepted. *Faculty research:* Economic development, housing, land use, geographic information systems planning in developing nations, regional and community revitalization, transportation planning in developing countries.

Iowa State University of Science and Technology, Program in Transportation, Ames, IA 50010. Offers MS. *Entrance requirements:* For master's, GMAT or GRE General Test. Additional exam requirements/recommendations for international students: Required—TOEFL (minimum score 550 paper-based; 82 iBT), IELTS (minimum score 6.5). Electronic applications accepted.

Maine Maritime Academy, Loeb-Sullivan School of International Business and Logistics, Castine, ME 04420. Offers global logistics and maritime management (MS); international logistics management (MS). Part-time programs available. *Faculty:* 6 full-time (1 woman), 2 part-time/adjunct (0 women). *Students:* 11 full-time (8 women). *Degree requirements:* For master's, capstone course. *Entrance requirements:* For master's, GMAT or GRE, letter of recommendation. Additional exam requirements/recommendations for international students: Required—TOEFL. *Application deadline:* For fall admission, 6/1 for domestic and international students; for spring admission, 3/15 for domestic and international students. Application fee: $40. Application fee is waived when completed online. *Financial support:* In 2013–14, teaching assistantships with full tuition reimbursements (averaging $6,000 per year) were awarded; career-related internships or fieldwork, Federal Work-Study, and institutionally sponsored loans also available. Support available to part-time students. Financial award application deadline: 4/15. *Unit head:* Dr. William DeWitt, Dean, 207-326-2454, Fax: 207-326-4311, E-mail: william.dewitt@mma.edu. *Application contact:* Patrick Haugen, Program Coordinator, 207-326-2212, Fax: 207-326-2411, E-mail: info.ls@mma.edu. Website: http://ibl.mainemaritime.edu.

McGill University, Faculty of Graduate and Postdoctoral Studies, Faculty of Engineering, School of Urban Planning, Montréal, QC H3A 2T5, Canada. Offers environmental planning (MUP); housing (MUP); transportation (MUP); urban design (MUP); urban planning, policy and design (PhD).

Morgan State University, School of Graduate Studies, Clarence M. Mitchell, Jr. School of Engineering, Department of Transportation, Baltimore, MD 21251. Offers MS. Part-time and evening/weekend programs available. *Degree requirements:* For master's, thesis optional, comprehensive exam or equivalent. *Entrance requirements:* For master's, minimum undergraduate GPA of 2.5. Additional exam requirements/recommendations for international students: Required—TOEFL (minimum score 550 paper-based). *Faculty research:* Distributional impacts of congestion, pricing education and training for intelligent vehicle highway systems.

Naval Postgraduate School, Departments and Academic Groups, Graduate School of Business and Public Policy, Monterey, CA 93943. Offers acquisition and contract management (MBA); business administration (EMBA, MBA); contract management (MS); defense business management (MBA); defense systems analysis (MS), including management; defense systems management (international) (MBA); financial management (MBA); information management (MBA); manpower systems analysis (MS); material logistics support management (MBA); program management (MS); resource planning and management for international defense (MBA); supply chain management (MBA); systems acquisition management (MBA); transportation management (MBA). Program only open to commissioned officers of the United States and friendly nations and selected United States federal civilian employees. *Accreditation:* AACSB; NASPAA. Part-time programs available. Postbaccalaureate distance learning degree programs offered (minimal on-campus study). *Degree requirements:* For master's, thesis (for some programs), terminal project/capstone (for some programs). *Faculty research:* U.S. and European public procurement policies for small and medium-sized enterprises, examining external validity criticisms in the choice of students as subjects in accounting experiment studies, assurance of learning in contract management education, contracting for cloud computing: opportunities and risks, NPS, Apple App Store as a business model supporting U. S. Navy requirements.

New Jersey Institute of Technology, Newark College of Engineering, Newark, NJ 07102. Offers biomedical engineering (MS, PhD); chemical engineering (MS, PhD); computer engineering (MS, PhD); electrical engineering (MS, PhD); engineering management (MS); healthcare systems management (MS); industrial engineering (MS, PhD); Internet engineering (MS); manufacturing engineering (MS); mechanical engineering (MS, PhD); occupational safety and health engineering (MS); pharmaceutical bioprocessing (MS); pharmaceutical engineering (MS); pharmaceutical systems management (MS); power and energy systems (MS); telecommunications (MS); transportation (MS, PhD). Part-time and evening/weekend programs available. *Faculty:* 133 full-time (18 women), 101 part-time/adjunct (14 women). *Students:* 823 full-time (222 women), 535 part-time (130 women); includes 361 minority (92 Black or African American, non-Hispanic/Latino; 4 American Indian or Alaska Native, non-Hispanic/Latino; 142 Asian, non-Hispanic/Latino; 123 Hispanic/Latino), 605 international. Average age 29. 2,800 applicants, 68% accepted, 523 enrolled. In 2013, 471 master's, 32 doctorates awarded. Terminal master's awarded for partial completion of doctoral program. *Degree requirements:* For master's, thesis optional; for doctorate, thesis/dissertation. *Entrance requirements:* For master's, GRE General Test; for doctorate, GRE General Test, minimum graduate GPA of 3.5. Additional exam requirements/recommendations for international students: Required—TOEFL (minimum score 550 paper-based; 79 iBT). *Application deadline:* For fall admission, 6/1 priority date for domestic students, 5/1 priority date for international students; for spring admission, 11/15 priority date for domestic and international students. Applications are processed on a rolling basis. Application fee: $65. Electronic applications accepted. *Expenses:* Tuition, state resident: full-time $17,384; part-time $945 per credit. Tuition, nonresident: full-time $25,404; part-time $1341 per credit. *Required fees:* $2396; $118 per credit. *Financial support:* Fellowships with full and partial tuition reimbursements, research assistantships with full and partial tuition reimbursements, and teaching assistantships with full and partial tuition reimbursements available. Financial award application deadline: 1/15. *Total annual research expenditures:* $16 million. *Unit head:* Dr. Basil Baltzis, Dean, 973-596-3000, E-mail: sunil.saigal@njit.edu. *Application contact:* Stephen Eck, Director of Admissions, 973-596-3300, Fax: 973-596-3461, E-mail: admissions@njit.edu. Website: http://engineering.njit.edu/.

New York University, Polytechnic School of Engineering, Department of Civil and Urban Engineering, Major in Transportation Management, New York, NY 10012-1019. Offers MS. Part-time and evening/weekend programs available. *Students:* 1 full-time (0 women), 7 part-time (1 woman); includes 3 minority (2 Asian, non-Hispanic/Latino; 1 Hispanic/Latino), 1 international. Average age 42. 12 applicants, 50% accepted, 3 enrolled. In 2013, 6 master's awarded. *Degree requirements:* For master's, comprehensive exam (for some programs), thesis (for some programs). *Entrance requirements:* Additional exam requirements/recommendations for international students: Required—TOEFL (minimum score 550 paper-based; 80 iBT); Recommended—IELTS (minimum score 6.5). *Application deadline:* For fall admission, 7/31 priority date for domestic students, 4/30 priority date for international students; for spring admission, 12/31 priority date for domestic students, 10/30 priority date for international students. Applications are processed on a rolling basis. Application fee: $75. Electronic applications accepted. *Expenses: Tuition:* Full-time $35,856; part-time $1494 per unit. *Required fees:* $1408; $64 per unit. $473 per term. Tuition and fees vary according to course load and program. *Financial support:* Fellowships, research assistantships, teaching assistantships, institutionally sponsored loans, scholarships/grants, and unspecified assistantships available. Support available to part-time students. Financial award applicants required to submit FAFSA. *Unit head:* Dr. Lawrence Chiarelli, Head, 718-260-4040, Fax: 718-260-3433, E-mail: lchiarel@poly.edu. *Application contact:* Raymond Lutzky, Director, Graduate Enrollment Management, 718-637-5984, Fax: 718-260-3624, E-mail: rlutzky@poly.edu.

North Dakota State University, College of Graduate and Interdisciplinary Studies, College of Engineering and Architecture, Department of Civil Engineering, Fargo, ND 58108. Offers civil engineering (MS, PhD); environmental engineering (MS, PhD); transportation and logistics (PhD). PhD in transportation and logistics offered jointly with Upper Great Plains Transportation Institute. Part-time programs available. Postbaccalaureate distance learning degree programs offered (minimal on-campus study). *Faculty:* 12 full-time (2 women), 1 part-time/adjunct (0 women). *Students:* 29 full-time (4 women), 19 part-time (1 woman); includes 3 minority (1 Black or African American, non-Hispanic/Latino; 1 American Indian or Alaska Native, non-Hispanic/Latino; 1 Two or more races, non-Hispanic/Latino), 27 international. Average age 29. 37 applicants, 32% accepted, 8 enrolled. In 2013, 5 master's, 2 doctorates awarded. *Degree requirements:* For master's, thesis; for doctorate, comprehensive exam, thesis/dissertation. *Entrance requirements:* Additional exam requirements/recommendations for international students: Required—TOEFL (minimum score 525 paper-based; 71 iBT). *Application deadline:* For fall admission, 2/15 priority date for domestic and international students; for spring admission, 9/15 priority date for domestic and international students. Applications are processed on a rolling basis. Application fee: $35. Electronic applications accepted. *Financial support:* Fellowships with full tuition reimbursements, research assistantships with full tuition reimbursements, teaching assistantships with full tuition reimbursements, career-related internships or fieldwork, Federal Work-Study, and institutionally sponsored loans available. Support available to part-time students. Financial award application deadline: 1/15. *Faculty research:* Wastewater, solid waste, composites, nanotechnology. *Unit head:* Dr. Eakalak Khan, Chair, 701-231-7244, Fax: 701-231-6185, E-mail: eakalak.khan@ndsu.edu. *Application contact:* Dr. Kalpana Katti, Professor and Graduate Program Coordinator, 701-231-9504, Fax: 701-231-6185, E-mail: kalpana.katti@ndsu.edu. Website: http://www.ce.ndsu.nodak.edu/.

North Dakota State University, College of Graduate and Interdisciplinary Studies, Interdisciplinary Program in Transportation and Logistics, Fargo, ND 58108. Offers managerial logistics (MML); transportation and logistics (PhD); transportation and urban systems (MS). *Students:* 37 full-time (6 women), 15 part-time (2 women); includes 7 minority (5 Black or African American, non-Hispanic/Latino; 1 Asian, non-Hispanic/Latino; 1 Two or more races, non-Hispanic/Latino), 21 international. Average age 36. 26 applicants, 62% accepted, 12 enrolled. In 2013, 5 master's, 1 doctorate awarded. *Entrance requirements:* For doctorate, 1 year of calculus, statistics and probability, minimum GPA of 3.0. Additional exam requirements/recommendations for international students: Required—TOEFL (minimum score 550 paper-based; 79 iBT). *Application deadline:* For fall admission, 5/1 priority date for domestic students. Applications are processed on a rolling basis. Application fee: $35. *Financial support:* Research assistantships with full tuition reimbursements available. *Faculty research:* Supply chain optimization, spatial analysis of transportation networks, advanced traffic analysis, transportation demand, railroad/intermodal freight. *Unit head:* Dr. Denver Tolliver, Director, 701-231-7938, Fax: 701-231-1945, E-mail: denver.tolliver@ndsu.nodak.edu. *Application contact:* Sonya Goergen, Marketing, Recruitment, and Public Relations Coordinator, 701-231-7033, Fax: 701-231-6524. Website: http://www.mountain-plains.org/education/tlprogram/.

Pontifical Catholic University of Puerto Rico, College of Business Administration, Program in Maritime Logistics and Transportation, Ponce, PR 00717-0777. Offers Professional Certificate.

San Jose State University, Graduate Studies and Research, Lucas Graduate School of Business, Program in Transportation Management, San Jose, CA 95192-0001. Offers MS. Part-time and evening/weekend programs available. Postbaccalaureate distance learning degree programs offered (minimal on-campus study). *Degree requirements:* For master's, comprehensive exam, thesis or alternative. *Entrance requirements:* For

master's, GMAT, minimum GPA of 3.0. Electronic applications accepted. *Faculty research:* Surface intermodal transportation, economics, security.

State University of New York Maritime College, Program in International Transportation Management, Throggs Neck, NY 10465-4198. Offers MS. Part-time and evening/weekend programs available. *Degree requirements:* For master's, thesis. *Entrance requirements:* For master's, minimum GPA of 2.5. Additional exam requirements/recommendations for international students: Required—TOEFL. *Faculty research:* Ports, intermodal, shipping, logistics, port tax.

Temple University, School of Environmental Design, Department of Community and Regional Planning, Ambler, PA 19002. Offers community and regional planning (MS); sustainable community planning (MS); transportation planning (MS). *Accreditation:* ACSP. Part-time and evening/weekend programs available. *Faculty:* 6 full-time (2 women), 6 part-time/adjunct (1 woman). *Students:* 12 full-time (4 women), 20 part-time (11 women); includes 5 minority (2 Black or African American, non-Hispanic/Latino; 1 Asian, non-Hispanic/Latino; 2 Hispanic/Latino), 1 international. 39 applicants, 79% accepted, 15 enrolled. In 2013, 19 master's awarded. *Entrance requirements:* For master's, GRE or GMAT, 2 letters of recommendation, minimum undergraduate GPA of 3.0, statement of goals. Additional exam requirements/recommendations for international students: Required—TOEFL (minimum score 550 paper-based; 79 iBT). *Application deadline:* For fall admission, 7/1 for domestic students, 12/15 for international students; for spring admission, 11/1 for domestic students, 8/1 for international students. Applications are processed on a rolling basis. Application fee: $60. *Financial support:* In 2013–14, 5 students received support, including 1 fellowship with full tuition reimbursement available (averaging $18,000 per year), 3 research assistantships with full tuition reimbursements available (averaging $22,700 per year); Federal Work-Study, scholarships/grants, health care benefits, and unspecified assistantships also available. Financial award application deadline: 1/15; financial award applicants required to submit FAFSA. *Faculty research:* Regional environmental planning; collaboration, management community development through sustainable food systems, storm water management and floodplain mapping, land use policy innovations, community planning for aging. *Unit head:* Dr. Deborah Howe, Chair, 267-468-8301, Fax: 267-468-8315, E-mail: deborah.howe@temple.edu. *Application contact:* Dr. Deborah Howe, Chair, 267-468-8301, Fax: 267-468-8315, E-mail: deborah.howe@temple.edu. Website: http://www.temple.edu/ambler/crp/.

Texas A&M University at Galveston, Department of Maritime Administration, Galveston, TX 77553-1675. Offers maritime administration and logistics (MMAL). Part-time and evening/weekend programs available. *Faculty:* 7 full-time (2 women), 3 part-time/adjunct (0 women). *Students:* 32 full-time (4 women), 9 part-time (2 women); includes 6 minority (2 Black or African American, non-Hispanic/Latino; 1 Asian, non-Hispanic/Latino; 2 Hispanic/Latino; 1 Two or more races, non-Hispanic/Latino). Average age 30. 25 applicants, 76% accepted, 14 enrolled. In 2013, 1 master's awarded. *Degree requirements:* For master's, thesis (for some programs). *Entrance requirements:* For master's, GMAT, statistics, microeconomics, organizational behavior, financial and managerial accounting, management information systems. Additional exam requirements/recommendations for international students: Required—TOEFL (minimum score 550 paper-based; 80 iBT), IELTS (minimum score 6). *Application deadline:* For fall admission, 6/15 for domestic students, 5/1 for international students; for spring admission, 10/15 for domestic students, 10/1 for international students. Application fee: $50 ($90 for international students). Electronic applications accepted. *Financial support:* In 2013–14, 4 students received support, including 4 teaching assistantships; scholarships/grants and unspecified assistantships also available. Financial award applicants required to submit FAFSA. *Faculty research:* International trade, inland waterways management, brokerage and chartering, organizational behavior, transportation economics, port and terminal management. *Unit head:* Dr. Joan P. Mileski, Interim Head of Maritime Administration, 409-740-4978, E-mail: mileskij@tamug.edu. *Application contact:* Nicole Kinslow, Director of Graduate Studies, 409-740-4937, Fax: 409-740-4754, E-mail: kinslown@tamug.edu. Website: http://www.tamug.edu/mara/.

Texas Southern University, School of Science and Technology, Program in Transportation, Planning and Management, Houston, TX 77004-4584. Offers MS. Part-time and evening/weekend programs available. *Faculty:* 4 full-time (2 women), 5 part-time/adjunct (1 woman). *Students:* 24 full-time (13 women), 19 part-time (10 women); includes 39 minority (21 Black or African American, non-Hispanic/Latino; 17 Asian, non-Hispanic/Latino; 1 Hispanic/Latino), 3 international. Average age 32. 25 applicants, 52% accepted, 11 enrolled. In 2013, 14 master's awarded. *Degree requirements:* For master's, comprehensive exam, thesis optional. *Entrance requirements:* For master's, GRE General Test, minimum GPA of 2.5. Additional exam requirements/recommendations for international students: Required—TOEFL. *Application deadline:* For fall admission, 7/1 for domestic and international students; for spring admission, 11/1 for domestic and international students. Applications are processed on a rolling basis. Application fee: $50 ($75 for international students). Electronic applications accepted. *Financial support:* In 2013–14, 11 research assistantships (averaging $4,946 per year) were awarded; fellowships with partial tuition reimbursements, teaching assistantships, career-related internships or fieldwork, scholarships/grants, and unspecified assistantships also available. Financial award application deadline: 5/1. *Faculty research:* Highway traffic operations, transportation and policy planning, air quality in transportation, transportation modeling. *Total annual research expenditures:* $500,000. *Unit head:* Dr. Yi Qi, Chair, 713-313-6809, E-mail: qi_yi@tsu.edu. *Application contact:* Paula Eakins, Administrative Assistant, 713-313-1841, E-mail: eakins_pl@tsu.edu. Website: http://www.cost.tsu.edu/WebPages/TransportationStudies.php.

The University of British Columbia, Sauder School of Business, Doctoral Program in Commerce and Business Administration, Vancouver, BC V6T 1Z1, Canada. Offers accounting (PhD); finance (PhD); management information systems (PhD); management science (PhD); marketing (PhD); organizational behavior (PhD); strategy and business economics (PhD); transportation and logistics (PhD); urban land economics (PhD). *Faculty:* 91 full-time (22 women). *Students:* 66 full-time (24 women). Average age 30. 418 applicants, 2% accepted, 8 enrolled. In 2013, 7 doctorates awarded. *Degree requirements:* For doctorate, comprehensive exam, thesis/dissertation. *Entrance requirements:* For doctorate, GMAT or GRE. Additional exam requirements/recommendations for international students: Required—TOEFL (minimum score 600 paper-based; 100 iBT). *Application deadline:* For fall admission, 1/31 for domestic students, 12/31 for international students. Applications are processed on a rolling basis. Application fee: $95 Canadian dollars ($153 Canadian dollars for international students). Electronic applications accepted. *Expenses:* Tuition, area resident: Full-time $8000 Canadian dollars. *Financial support:* In 2013–14, fellowships with full tuition reimbursements (averaging $17,500 per year), research assistantships with full tuition reimbursements (averaging $8,500 per year), teaching assistantships with full tuition reimbursements (averaging $17,500 per year) were awarded. Financial award application deadline: 12/31. *Unit head:* Dr. Ralph Winter, Director, 604-822-8366, Fax: 604-822-8755. *Application contact:* Elaine Cho, Administrator, PhD and M Sc Programs, 604-822-8366, Fax: 604-822-8755, E-mail: phd.program@sauder.ubc.ca. Website: http://www.sauder.ubc.ca/.

University of California, Davis, College of Engineering, Graduate Group in Transportation Technology and Policy, Davis, CA 95616. Offers MS, PhD. Terminal master's awarded for partial completion of doctoral program. *Degree requirements:* For master's, comprehensive exam (for some programs), thesis (for some programs); for doctorate, thesis/dissertation. *Entrance requirements:* For master's, GRE General Test, minimum GPA of 3.0; for doctorate, GRE General Test, minimum GPA of 3.5. Additional exam requirements/recommendations for international students: Required—TOEFL (minimum score 550 paper-based). Electronic applications accepted.

University of California, Santa Barbara, Graduate Division, College of Letters and Sciences, Division of Mathematics, Life, and Physical Sciences, Department of Geography, Santa Barbara, CA 93106-4060. Offers cognitive science (PhD); geography (MA, PhD); global studies (PhD); quantitative methods in the social sciences (PhD); technology and society (PhD); transportation (PhD); MA/PhD. *Faculty:* 21 full-time (4 women), 14 part-time/adjunct (4 women). *Students:* 66 full-time (32 women); includes 13 minority (2 Black or African American, non-Hispanic/Latino; 6 Asian, non-Hispanic/Latino; 5 Hispanic/Latino), 17 international. Average age 32. 153 applicants, 25% accepted, 16 enrolled. In 2013, 7 master's, 10 doctorates awarded. Terminal master's awarded for partial completion of doctoral program. *Degree requirements:* For master's, comprehensive exam (for some programs), thesis or alternative; for doctorate, comprehensive exam, thesis/dissertation, 1 quarter of teaching assistantship. *Entrance requirements:* For master's and doctorate, GRE (minimum combined verbal and quantitative scores of 1100 in old scoring system or 301 in new scoring system). Additional exam requirements/recommendations for international students: Required—TOEFL (minimum score 550 paper-based; 80 iBT), IELTS (minimum score 7). *Application deadline:* For fall admission, 12/15 for domestic and international students. Application fee: $80 ($100 for international students). Electronic applications accepted. *Expenses:* Tuition, state resident: part-time $5148.26 per quarter. Tuition, nonresident: part-time $10,182.26 per quarter. *Financial support:* In 2013–14, 60 students received support, including 32 fellowships with full and partial tuition reimbursements available (averaging $8,646 per year), 36 research assistantships with full and partial tuition reimbursements available (averaging $13,840 per year), 35 teaching assistantships with partial tuition reimbursements available (averaging $10,709 per year). Financial award applicants required to submit FAFSA. *Faculty research:* Earth system science; human environment relations; modeling, measurement, and computation. *Total annual research expenditures:* $3.9 million. *Unit head:* Dr. Dar Alexander Roberts, Professor/Chair, 805-880-2531, Fax: 805-893-2578, E-mail: dar@geog.ucsb.edu. *Application contact:* Karl Antonsson, Student Programs Manager, 805-456-2836, Fax: 805-893-2578, E-mail: karl@geog.ucsb.edu. Website: http://www.geog.ucsb.edu/.

The University of Tennessee, Graduate School, College of Business Administration, Program in Business Administration, Knoxville, TN 37996. Offers accounting (PhD); finance (MBA, PhD); logistics and transportation (MBA, PhD); management (PhD); marketing (MBA, PhD); operations management (MBA); professional business administration (MBA); statistics (PhD); JD/MBA; MS/MBA; Pharm D/MBA. Pharm D/MBA offered jointly with The University of Tennessee Health Science Center. *Accreditation:* AACSB. Postbaccalaureate distance learning degree programs offered. *Degree requirements:* For master's, thesis or alternative; for doctorate, thesis/dissertation. *Entrance requirements:* For master's and doctorate, GMAT, minimum GPA of 2.7. Additional exam requirements/recommendations for international students: Required—TOEFL. Electronic applications accepted. *Expenses:* Tuition, state resident: full-time $9540; part-time $531 per credit hour. Tuition, nonresident: full-time $27,728; part-time $1542 per credit hour. *Required fees:* $1404; $67 per credit hour.

University of Washington, Graduate School, Interdisciplinary Program in Global Trade, Transportation and Logistics Studies, Seattle, WA 98195. Offers Certificate.

EMBRY-RIDDLE AERONAUTICAL UNIVERSITY

College of Business–Daytona Beach

EMBRY-RIDDLE
Aeronautical University
DAYTONA BEACH, FLORIDA
COLLEGE OF BUSINESS

Programs of Study

The Embry-Riddle College of Business on the Daytona Beach campus provides graduates with two degree options for students seeking a cutting-edge management or finance education in an aviation/aerospace context. With the choice of the Master of Business Administration (M.B.A.) or the Master of Science in Aviation Finance (M.S.A.F.), the College offers students seeking a career in the aviation, airport, or aerospace industries programs designed to meet the needs of industry. Professional managers who have earned their graduate degree at Embry-Riddle Aeronautical University (ERAU) understand the imperatives of change, globalization, technological innovation, and increasingly sophisticated and demanding customers that mark the financial, strategic, and operational environments of today's airlines, airports, and aerospace firms. Both the M.B.A. and M.S.A.F. are offered as full-time residential programs. The M.S.A.F. program is also offered online. The M.B.A. curriculum combines a strong traditional business core with specializations in airport management, airline management, finance, aviation human resources, and aviation system management. The M.S.A.F. program stresses pragmatic solutions to the financial and economic problems that arise in the aviation/aerospace industry as a result of the need to finance large capital expenditures occurring in an international marketplace with changing regulations and challenging economic conditions.

Both degree programs consist of 33 credit hours. The M.B.A. consists of 21 hours of core curriculum and 12 hours of specified electives. Three hours of elective credit may be awarded for an internship, which is strongly advised for all students. The M.S.A.F. consists of a 12-hour core curriculum and 18 hours of advanced finance and economic courses with the option of a concluding internship or research project. The employer-supported Business Eagles program is open to all students and provides special access to development and placement activities. Both the M.B.A. and M.S.A.F. programs can usually be completed in sixteen to twenty-four months based on how the student progresses through the curriculum and whether an internship is taken.

Research Facilities

A collection of networked servers and PCs provide the faculty and students with the latest advances in data mining and computational facilities. Through classes, students have access to SABRE products for airline scheduling scenarios along with extensive and diverse aviation databases utilized for ongoing research projects. Students are also introduced to the latest financial modeling software. Dedicated facilities provide the opportunity to work with the Total Airspace and Airport Modeler (TAMM) and in the Radio-Frequency Identification (RFID) and Applied Aviation Simulation and Optimization labs. The multimodal transportation lab enables students to explore the viability of each transportation mode within the overall logistics and supply chain developed.

Financial Aid

Scholarships are awarded to outstanding graduate students during the admissions process. Assistantships are also available on a limited and competitive basis. Students may apply for financial aid by calling 800-943-6279 (toll-free). All graduate programs are approved for U.S. Veterans Administration education benefits.

Cost of Study

In 2014–15 tuition costs for the M.B.A. and M.S.A.F. programs are $1,280 per credit hour. The estimated cost of books and supplies is $1,400 per semester; there are also mandatory University fees estimated at $614 per semester for domestic students and $664 per semester for international students.

Living and Housing Costs

On-campus housing is available on a limited basis to graduate students on the Daytona Beach campus with an estimated cost of $4,775 per semester for room and board. Single students who share rent and utility expenses can expect off-campus room, board, and living expenses of $5,500 per semester.

Student Group

ERAU's graduate programs on the Daytona Beach campus currently enroll approximately 600 students. The students possess various cultural origins—many are from other countries, 25 percent are women, and 23 percent are members of U.S. minority groups. The graduate programs in the College of Business attract students with diverse academic backgrounds and common scholastic abilities that enrich the program. The majority of incoming students have business degrees, although all degrees are welcomed with many engineers, air science, and aviation management students from other universities continuing their air transport studies at ERAU. The average age of incoming students is 28.

Student Outcomes

In addition to contacts gained from internships with leading airlines, airports, and aerospace firms, the College of Business conducts placement activities for its graduates. Years of research and consulting have allowed the faculty to cultivate contacts within the aviation industry, and this network provides job opportunities for graduates. The Career Services Office sponsors an annual industry Career Expo, which attracts more than 100 major companies such as Boeing, Federal Express, Delta, and United Airlines. In addition, the Career Resource Center offers corporate profiles, job postings, and development information. The office also assists with resume development and interview preparation.

Location

The Daytona Beach, Florida campus is located next to the Daytona Beach International Airport, the world-famous Daytona International Speedway, and 10 minutes from Daytona's beaches. The campus is an hour's drive from Orlando and destinations such as Disney World, EPCOT, Universal Studios, SeaWorld, and other Florida attractions such as the Kennedy Space Center and St. Augustine.

The University

Since its founding in 1926, Embry-Riddle Aeronautical University has built a reputation for high-quality education within the field of aviation and has become a world leader in aerospace higher education. The University is comprised of the eastern campus in Daytona Beach, Florida; the western campus in Prescott, Arizona; and the WorldWide Campus, with off-campus programs.

Applying

A desired minimum bachelor degree cumulative GPA of 3.0 (4.0 scale) and a minimum score of 550 on the GMAT are the requirements for full admission consideration for the M.B.A. program. For the M.S.A.F. program a GPA of 3.0 (4.0 scale) and GRE General Test scores of 310 or above are required. The ability to apply test scores from either

Embry-Riddle Aeronautical University

the GMAT or GRE exam to the preferred degree program is available. Applications not meeting these qualifications may be considered for conditional admission with enhanced student oversight as an applicant matriculates into the program. Applications are accepted on a rolling basis and should be completed sixty days prior to the start of a semester for U.S. citizens, resident aliens, and international students. For international applicants the required minimum IELTS score is 6.0, or a TOEFL score of 550 or 79 on the TOFEL-IBT.

Correspondence and Information

Office of International and Graduate Admissions
Embry-Riddle Aeronautical University
600 South Clyde Morris Boulevard
Daytona Beach, Florida 32114-3900
United States
Phone: 386-226-6176 (outside the United States)
           800-388-3728 (toll-free within the United States)
Fax: 386-226-7070
E-mail: graduate.admissions@erau.edu
Website: http://www.embryriddle.edu/graduate

THE FACULTY

The College of Business (COB) faculty takes pride in bringing relevant, real-world problems, issues, and experiences into the classrooms. Faculty members give a high priority to preparing students for the leadership roles they will eventually assume. The faculty members accomplish this not only by excellence in teaching but also by advising students on research and consulting projects. Many members of the faculty serve as consultants to a variety of industries, and the diverse backgrounds of the faculty members provide a rich, multicultural experience, with an emphasis on global standards and practices.

In addition, the Embry-Riddle faculty members are the go-to references for print and broadcast journalists on questions of aviation. When the question concerns aviation business, the savvy journalist calls the experts at the Embry-Riddle College of Business. For issues such as airline mergers, acquisitions, bankruptcies, or the general state of the aviation business, members of the COB faculty have provided information to scores of journalists for countless articles and broadcasts. Such is the reputation of the faculty of the College of Business.

On the subject of aviation business, Embry-Riddle faculty members have written some of the leading textbooks in the field and worked as external experts, such as the following COB professors.

Ahmed Abdelghany, Ph.D., Assistant Professor. *Modeling Applications in the Airline Industry.*

Massoud Bazargan, Ph.D., Professor, *Airline Operations and Scheduling.*

Vedapuri Raghavan, Ph.D., Professor, Finance. *A Study of Corporate Bond Market in India: Theoretical and policy Implications, Reserve Bank of India (India's Central Bank),* DRG Report.

Dawna Rhoades, Ph.D., Professor. *Evolution of International Aviation: Phoenix Rising.*

Bijan Vasigh, Ph.D., Professor. *Introduction to Air Transport Economics, From Theory to Applications: Foundations of Airline Finance,* and *Airline Finance.*

The other faculty members of the College whom students may have as instructors in the graduate programs are:

Hari P. Adhikari, Ph.D., Assistant Professor, Finance.
Anke Arnaud, Ph.D., Associate Professor, Organizational Behavior.
Farshid Azadian, Ph.D., Assistant Professor, Logistics.
Michael Bowers, Ph.D., Professor of Entrepreneurship and Marketing

Tamilla Curtis, Ph.D., Assistant Professor, Marketing.
Jayendra Gokhale, Ph.D., Assistant Professor, Economics.
Vitaly Guzhva, Ph.D., Associate Professor, Finance.
Lee Hays, D.B.A., Assistant Professor, Management.
John Ledgerwood, CPA, MSA, Associate Professor, Accounting.
John Longshore, Ph.D., Visiting Associate Professor, Supply Chain and Logistics.
Rosemarie Reynolds, Ph.D., Associate Professor, Organizational Behavior.
Thomas Tacker, Ph.D., Professor, Economics. Co-author of *Introduction to Air Transport Economics, From Theory to Applications.*
Janet Tinoco, Ph.D., Associate Professor, Marketing and Management.
Blaise Waguespack, Ph.D., Professor, Marketing.
Michael J. Williams, Ph.D., Dean, Professor, Management Information Systems.
Chunyan Yu, Ph.D., Professor of Transport Management.
Bert Zarb, D.B.A., CPA, Professor, Accounting.
Li Zou, Ph.D., Associate Professor, Marketing.

The recently opened College of Business building on the Daytona Beach campus, part of a major infrastructure program bringing new academic and student facilities across the campus.

Students at work in the Applied Aviation Simulation Lab, which contains multiple servers to aid students in completing research projects for airlines and airports across the globe.

ACADEMIC AND PROFESSIONAL
PROGRAMS IN EDUCATION

Section 22
Education

This section contains a directory of institutions offering graduate work in education, followed by in-depth entries submitted by institutions that chose to prepare detailed program descriptions. Additional information about programs listed in the directory but not augmented by an in-depth entry may be obtained by writing directly to the dean of a graduate school or chair of a department at the address given in the directory.

For programs offering related work, see also in this book *Administration, Instruction, and Theory; Instructional Levels; Leisure Studies and Recreation; Physical Education and Kinesiology; Special Focus;* and *Subject Areas.* In other guides in this series:

Graduate Programs in the Humanities, Arts & Social Sciences
See *Psychology and Counseling (School Psychology)*
Graduate Programs in the Biological/Biomedical Sciences and Health-Related Medical Professions
See *Health-Related Professions*

CONTENTS

Program Directory
Education—General   640

Displays and Close-Ups
Adelphi University   640, 727
Manhattanville College   674, 729
Northwestern University   682, 731
University of Pennsylvania   712, 733
Vanderbilt University   721, 735

Education—General

Abilene Christian University, Graduate School, College of Education and Human Services, Abilene, TX 79699-9100. Offers M Ed, MS, MSSW, Certificate, Post-Master's Certificate. *Accreditation:* Teacher Education Accreditation Council. *Faculty:* 5 full-time (1 woman), 12 part-time/adjunct (7 women). *Students:* 156 full-time (129 women), 51 part-time (35 women); includes 61 minority (23 Black or African American, non-Hispanic/Latino; 2 American Indian or Alaska Native, non-Hispanic/Latino; 2 Asian, non-Hispanic/Latino; 25 Hispanic/Latino; 9 Two or more races, non-Hispanic/Latino), 4 international. 272 applicants, 42% accepted, 99 enrolled. In 2013, 104 master's, 5 other advanced degrees awarded. *Degree requirements:* For master's, comprehensive exam (for some programs), thesis (for some programs), practicum. *Entrance requirements:* For master's, GRE. Additional exam requirements/recommendations for international students: Required—TOEFL (minimum score 550 paper-based; 90 iBT), IELTS (minimum score 6.5), PTE. *Application deadline:* For fall admission, 8/15 priority date for domestic students; for winter admission, 10/1 priority date for domestic students; for spring admission, 12/15 priority date for domestic students; for summer admission, 4/15 for domestic students. Applications are processed on a rolling basis. Application fee: $50. Electronic applications accepted. *Expenses: Tuition:* Full-time $17,100; part-time $950 per credit hour. *Financial support:* In 2013–14, 69 students received support. Career-related internships or fieldwork and scholarships/grants available. Financial award application deadline: 4/1; financial award applicants required to submit FAFSA. *Unit head:* Dr. Donnie Snider, Dean, 325-674-2700, E-mail: dcs03b@acu.edu. *Application contact:* Corey Patterson, Director of Graduate Admission and Recruiting, 325-674-6566, Fax: 325-674-6717, E-mail: gradinfo@acu.edu.

Acacia University, American Graduate School of Education, Tempe, AZ 85284. Offers educational administration (M Ed); elementary education (MA); English as a second language (M Ed); secondary education (MA); special education (M Ed).

Acadia University, Faculty of Professional Studies, Inter-University Doctoral Program in Educational Studies, Wolfville, NS B4P 2R6, Canada. Offers PhD. Program offered jointly with Mount Saint Vincent University and St. Francis Xavier University. *Degree requirements:* For doctorate, thesis/dissertation, comprehensive research/scholarly portfolio.

Acadia University, Faculty of Professional Studies, School of Education, Wolfville, NS B4P 2R6, Canada. Offers counseling (M Ed); curriculum studies (M Ed), including cultural and media studies, learning and technology, science, math and technology; inclusive education (M Ed); leadership (M Ed). *Degree requirements:* For master's, thesis optional. *Entrance requirements:* For master's, B Ed or the equivalent, 2 years of teaching or related experience. Additional exam requirements/recommendations for international students: Required—TOEFL (minimum score 580 paper-based; 93 iBT), IELTS (minimum score 6.5).

Adams State University, The Graduate School, Department of Teacher Education, Alamosa, CO 81101. Offers education (MA); special education (MA). *Accreditation:* Teacher Education Accreditation Council. Part-time programs available. Postbaccalaureate distance learning degree programs offered. *Degree requirements:* For master's, qualifying exam. *Entrance requirements:* For master's, GRE General Test or MAT, minimum undergraduate GPA of 3.0.

Adelphi University, Ruth S. Ammon School of Education, Garden City, NY 11530-0701. Offers MA, MS, DA, Certificate. *Accreditation:* NCATE. Part-time and evening/weekend programs available. *Faculty:* 67 full-time (44 women), 129 part-time/adjunct (89 women). *Students:* 554 full-time (483 women), 294 part-time (224 women); includes 186 minority (56 Black or African American, non-Hispanic/Latino; 1 American Indian or Alaska Native, non-Hispanic/Latino; 26 Asian, non-Hispanic/Latino; 91 Hispanic/Latino; 2 Native Hawaiian or other Pacific Islander, non-Hispanic/Latino; 10 Two or more races, non-Hispanic/Latino), 56 international. Average age 27. 1,312 applicants, 44% accepted, 350 enrolled. In 2013, 423 master's, 6 doctorates, 102 other advanced degrees awarded. *Degree requirements:* For doctorate, one foreign language, comprehensive exam, thesis/dissertation. *Entrance requirements:* For master's, resume, letters of recommendation, minimum cumulative GPA of 2.75; for doctorate, GRE General Test, 3 letters of recommendation, interview. Additional exam requirements/recommendations for international students: Required—TOEFL (minimum score 550 paper-based; 80 iBT). *Application deadline:* For fall admission, 4/1 for international students; for spring admission, 11/1 for international students. Applications are processed on a rolling basis. Application fee: $50. Electronic applications accepted. *Expenses: Tuition:* Full-time $32,530; part-time $1010 per credit. *Required fees:* $1150. Tuition and fees vary according to degree level and program. *Financial support:* In 2013–14, 97 teaching assistantships with partial tuition reimbursements (averaging $7,930 per year) were awarded; career-related internships or fieldwork, Federal Work-Study, tuition waivers (full and partial), and unspecified assistantships also available. Financial award application deadline: 2/15; financial award applicants required to submit FAFSA. *Faculty research:* Multicultural and gender issues, psychometric assessment, quantitative research methods. *Unit head:* Dr. Jane Ashdown, Dean, 516-877-4065, E-mail: jashdown@adelphi.edu. *Application contact:* Christine Murphy, Director of Admissions, 516-877-3050, Fax: 516-877-3039, E-mail: graduateadmissions@adelphi.edu.
Website: http://education.adelphi.edu/.

See Display below and Close-Up on page 727.

Alabama Agricultural and Mechanical University, School of Graduate Studies, School of Education, Huntsville, AL 35811. Offers M Ed, MS, MS Ed, Ed S. *Accreditation:* NCATE. Part-time and evening/weekend programs available. *Degree requirements:* For master's, comprehensive exam. *Entrance requirements:* For master's, GRE General Test. Additional exam requirements/recommendations for international students: Required—TOEFL (minimum score 500 paper-based; 61 iBT). Electronic applications accepted. *Faculty research:* Speech defects, aging, blindness, multicultural education, learning styles.

Alabama State University, College of Education, Montgomery, AL 36101-0271. Offers M Ed, MS, Ed D, Ed S. *Accreditation:* NCATE. Part-time programs available. *Faculty:* 26 full-time (17 women), 22 part-time/adjunct (13 women). *Students:* 95 full-time (63 women), 338 part-time (256 women); includes 400 minority (392 Black or African American, non-Hispanic/Latino; 2 Asian, non-Hispanic/Latino; 5 Hispanic/Latino; 1 Two or more races, non-Hispanic/Latino). Average age 35. 183 applicants, 47% accepted, 68 enrolled. In 2013, 107 master's, 14 doctorates, 27 other advanced degrees awarded. *Degree requirements:* For master's, comprehensive exam; for Ed S, comprehensive exam, thesis. *Entrance requirements:* For master's, GRE General Test, MAT, writing competency test; for Ed S, writing competency test, GRE, MAT. Additional exam requirements/recommendations for international students: Required—TOEFL (minimum

score 500 paper-based). *Application deadline:* For fall admission, 7/15 for domestic students; for spring admission, 12/15 for domestic students. Applications are processed on a rolling basis. Application fee: $25. *Expenses:* Tuition, state resident: full-time $7958; part-time $343 per credit hour. Tuition, nonresident: full-time $14,132; part-time $686 per credit hour. *Required fees:* $446 per term. One-time fee: $1784 full-time; $892 part-time. Tuition and fees vary according to course load. *Financial support:* In 2013–14, 2 research assistantships (averaging $9,450 per year) were awarded. *Faculty research:* Whole language instruction, African-American children's literature. *Unit head:* Dr. Doris Screws, Interim Dean, 334-229-4250, E-mail: dscrews@alasu.edu. *Application contact:* Dr. William Person, Dean of Graduate Studies, 334-229-4274, Fax: 334-229-4928, E-mail: wperson@alasu.edu.
Website: http://www.alasu.edu/Education/.

Alaska Pacific University, Graduate Programs, Education Department, Program in Teaching, Anchorage, AK 99508-4672. Offers teaching (K-8) (MAT). *Degree requirements:* For master's, research project. *Entrance requirements:* For master's, GRE or MAT, PRAXIS, minimum GPA of 3.0.

Albany State University, College of Education, Albany, GA 31705-2717. Offers early childhood education (M Ed); education specialist (Ed S); educational leadership and administration (M Ed); health, physical education and recreation (M Ed); middle grades education (M Ed); school counseling (M Ed); special education (M Ed). *Accreditation:* NCATE. Part-time and evening/weekend programs available. Postbaccalaureate distance learning degree programs offered (minimal on-campus study). *Degree requirements:* For master's, comprehensive exam, internship, GACE Content Exam. *Entrance requirements:* For master's, GRE or MAT. Electronic applications accepted. *Faculty research:* GACE preparation, STEM (science, technology, engineering, and mathematics), technology education, special education, professional teacher development, health implications liberation philosophy, NET-Q, learning community, disabled or at-risk students.

Albertus Magnus College, Master of Science in Education Program, New Haven, CT 06511-1189. Offers MS Ed. *Faculty:* 3 full-time (1 woman), 9 part-time/adjunct (4 women). *Students:* 8 full-time (4 women), 15 part-time (14 women); includes 5 minority (2 Black or African American, non-Hispanic/Latino; 1 American Indian or Alaska Native, non-Hispanic/Latino; 1 Asian, non-Hispanic/Latino; 1 Hispanic/Latino). 4 applicants, 100% accepted, 4 enrolled. In 2013, 8 master's awarded. *Degree requirements:* For master's, thesis, capstone. *Entrance requirements:* For master's, bachelor's degree, official transcripts of all undergraduate work, three letters of recommendation, resume, essay, valid Connecticut Initial teacher certificate (preferred). *Application deadline:* For fall admission, 8/15 for domestic students; for spring admission, 1/15 for domestic students. Application fee: $50. *Faculty research:* Assessment, learning theory, educational leadership, differentiated instruction, multiculturalism. *Unit head:* Dr. Joan Venditto, Director, Education Programs, 203-773-8087, Fax: 203-773-4422, E-mail: jvenditto@albertus.edu. *Application contact:* Dr. Irene Rios, Dean of New Dimensions, 203-777-7100, Fax: 203-777-9906, E-mail: irios@albertus.edu.
Website: http://www.albertus.edu/masters-degrees/education/.

Albright College, Graduate Division, Reading, PA 19612-5234. Offers early childhood education (MS); elementary education (MS); English as a second language (MA); general education (MA); special education (MS). Part-time and evening/weekend programs available. *Degree requirements:* For master's, thesis. *Entrance requirements:* For master's, GRE General Test or MAT, minimum undergraduate GPA of 3.0, 2 letters of recommendation, interview. Additional exam requirements/recommendations for international students: Recommended—TOEFL (minimum score 525 paper-based). Electronic applications accepted.

Alcorn State University, School of Graduate Studies, School of Psychology and Education, Alcorn State, MS 39096-7500. Offers agricultural education (MS Ed); elementary education (MS Ed, Ed S); guidance and counseling (MS Ed); industrial education (MS Ed); secondary education (MS Ed), including health and physical education; special education (MS Ed). *Accreditation:* NCATE. *Degree requirements:* For master's, thesis optional.

Alfred University, Graduate School, Division of Education, Alfred, NY 14802-1205. Offers literacy (MS Ed). *Accreditation:* Teacher Education Accreditation Council. Part-time programs available. *Faculty:* 2 full-time (both women). *Students:* 3 full-time (all women), 4 part-time (1 woman). Average age 24. 8 applicants, 75% accepted, 5 enrolled. In 2013, 5 master's awarded. *Entrance requirements:* For master's, Liberal Arts and Sciences Test (LAST), Assessment of Teaching Skills (written) (ATS-W), Content Specialty Test (CST). Additional exam requirements/recommendations for international students: Required—TOEFL (minimum score 590 paper-based; 90 iBT), IELTS (minimum score 6.5). *Application deadline:* For fall admission, 8/1 for domestic students, 3/15 for international students; for spring admission, 12/1 for domestic students, 10/1 for international students. Applications are processed on a rolling basis. Application fee: $60. Electronic applications accepted. *Expenses: Tuition:* Full-time $38,020; part-time $810 per credit hour. *Required fees:* $950; $160 per semester. Part-time tuition and fees vary according to campus/location and program. *Financial support:* In 2013–14, 9 students received support, including 3 research assistantships with partial tuition reimbursements available (averaging $19,010 per year); tuition waivers (partial) and unspecified assistantships also available. Financial award applicants required to submit FAFSA. *Faculty research:* Literacy. *Unit head:* Dr. Ann Monroe-Baillargeon, Chair, Division of Education, 607-871-2219, E-mail: monroe@alfred.edu. *Application contact:* Sara Love, Coordinator of Graduate Admissions, 607-871-2115, Fax: 607-871-2198, E-mail: gradinquiry@alfred.edu.
Website: http://www.alfred.edu/gradschool/education/.

Alliant International University–Los Angeles, Shirley M. Hufstedler School of Education, TeachersCHOICE Preparation Programs, Alhambra, CA 91803-1360. Offers MA, Credential. Part-time programs available. *Faculty:* 10 part-time/adjunct (8 women). *Students:* 5 full-time (3 women), 7 part-time (6 women); includes 4 minority (2 Black or African American, non-Hispanic/Latino; 1 Hispanic/Latino; 1 Two or more races, non-Hispanic/Latino). Average age 35. 9 applicants, 100% accepted, 7 enrolled. In 2013, 2 master's, 35 other advanced degrees awarded. *Entrance requirements:* For master's, CBEST, CSET, interview; offer of employment as a teacher of record in a California school; minimum GPA of 2.5; 2 letters of recommendation. Additional exam requirements/recommendations for international students: Required—TOEFL (minimum score 550 paper-based). *Application deadline:* For fall admission, 8/1 priority date for domestic and international students. Application fee: $55. *Faculty research:* Multicultural and bilingual education pedagogy, teacher training pedagogy, curriculum development, instructional strategies. *Unit head:* Dr. Trudy Day, Program Director, Educational Policy and Practice, 415-955-2087, Fax: 415-955-2179, E-mail: admissions@alliant.edu. *Application contact:* Alliant International University Central Contact Center, 866-U-ALLIANT, Fax: 858-635-4555, E-mail: admissions@alliant.edu.

Alliant International University–México City, Shirley M. Hufstedler School of Education, Mexico City, Mexico. Offers teaching (MA). Part-time and evening/weekend programs available. Postbaccalaureate distance learning degree programs offered (no on-campus study). *Faculty:* 2 part-time/adjunct (both women). *Students:* 10 part-time (8 women); includes 2 minority (both Hispanic/Latino), 3 international. Average age 32. In 2013, 1 master's awarded. *Entrance requirements:* For master's, minimum GPA of 2.5, letters of recommendation. Additional exam requirements/recommendations for international students: Required—TOEFL (minimum score 550 paper-based), TWE (minimum score 5). *Application deadline:* For fall admission, 8/1 priority date for domestic and international students; for spring admission, 12/1 priority date for domestic and international students. Application fee: $55. *Financial support:* Career-related internships or fieldwork, Federal Work-Study, institutionally sponsored loans, and scholarships/grants available. Financial award application deadline: 2/15; financial award applicants required to submit FAFSA. *Unit head:* Dr. Rhonda Brinkley-Kennedy, Interim Dean, 626-270-3317, E-mail: contacto@alliantmexico.com. *Application contact:* Lesly Gutierrez Garcia, Coordinator of Admissions and Student Services, 525 5525-7651, E-mail: contacto@alliantmexico.com.
Website: http://www.alliantmexico.com/.

Alliant International University–Sacramento, Shirley M. Hufstedler School of Education, TeachersCHOICE Preparation Programs, Sacramento, CA 95833. Offers MA, Credential. *Faculty:* 1 (woman) full-time. *Students:* 5. Average age 35. *Entrance requirements:* For master's, CBEST, CSET, interview; offer of employment as a teacher of record in a California school; minimum GPA of 3.0; 2 letters of recommendation. *Application deadline:* For fall admission, 8/1 priority date for domestic and international students. Applications are processed on a rolling basis. Application fee: $45. Electronic applications accepted. *Financial support:* Application deadline: 2/1; applicants required to submit FAFSA. *Faculty research:* Innovative teacher education, educational leadership, cross-cultural education. *Unit head:* Dr. Karen Webb, Dean, 415-955-2051, Fax: 415-955-2179, E-mail: admissions@alliant.edu. *Application contact:* Alliant International University Central Contact Center, 866-U-ALLIANT, Fax: 858-635-4555, E-mail: admissions@alliant.edu.

Alliant International University–San Diego, Shirley M. Hufstedler School of Education, Teacher Education Programs, San Diego, CA 92131-1799. Offers preliminary single subject (Credential); professional clear multiple subject (Credential); professional clear single subject (Credential); teacher education (MA). Part-time and evening/weekend programs available. *Faculty:* 1 full-time (0 women), 4 part-time/adjunct (3 women). *Students:* 47 part-time (40 women). Average age 44. 55 applicants, 100% accepted, 48 enrolled. In 2013, 11 master's awarded. *Entrance requirements:* For degree, California Basic Educational Skills Test, minimum GPA of 2.5. Additional exam requirements/recommendations for international students: Required—TOEFL (minimum score 550 paper-based; 80 iBT), TWE (minimum score 5). *Application deadline:* For fall admission, 4/15 priority date for domestic and international students; for spring admission, 11/3 priority date for domestic and international students. Applications are processed on a rolling basis. Application fee: $65. Electronic applications accepted. *Financial support:* Career-related internships or fieldwork, Federal Work-Study, institutionally sponsored loans, and scholarships/grants available. Financial award application deadline: 2/15; financial award applicants required to submit FAFSA. *Faculty research:* Curriculum and instructional planning. *Unit head:* Dr. Jerold D. Miller, Program Director, 858-635-4724, Fax: 858-435-4739, E-mail: admissions@alliant.edu. *Application contact:* Alliant International University Central Contact Center, 866-U-ALLIANT, Fax: 858-635-4555, E-mail: admissions@alliant.edu.

Alliant International University–San Francisco, Shirley M. Hufstedler School of Education, Teacher Education Programs, San Francisco, CA 94133-1221. Offers auditory oral education (Certificate); CLAD (Certificate); education specialist: mild/moderate disabilities (Credential); preliminary multiple subject (Credential); preliminary single subject (Credential); professional clear multiple subject (Credential); professional clear single subject (Credential); special education (MA); teaching (MA); TESOL (Certificate). Part-time and evening/weekend programs available. *Faculty:* 6 full-time (4 women), 10 part-time/adjunct (8 women). *Students:* 16 full-time (10 women), 135 part-time (97 women); includes 22 minority (6 Black or African American, non-Hispanic/Latino; 6 Asian, non-Hispanic/Latino; 8 Hispanic/Latino; 2 Two or more races, non-Hispanic/Latino). Average age 41. 172 applicants, 94% accepted, 142 enrolled. In 2013, 11 master's, 167 other advanced degrees awarded. *Degree requirements:* For master's, thesis. *Entrance requirements:* For degree, California Basic Educational Skills Test, minimum GPA of 2.5. Additional exam requirements/recommendations for international students: Required—TOEFL (minimum score 550 paper-based), TWE (minimum score 5). *Application deadline:* For fall admission, 7/1 priority date for domestic and international students; for spring admission, 12/1 priority date for domestic and international students. Applications are processed on a rolling basis. Application fee: $55. Electronic applications accepted. *Financial support:* Career-related internships or fieldwork, Federal Work-Study, institutionally sponsored loans, and scholarships/grants available. Financial award application deadline: 2/15; financial award applicants required to submit FAFSA. *Faculty research:* Curriculum development, first year teachers, cross-cultural issues in teaching, biliteracy. *Unit head:* Dr. Debra Reeves-Gutierrez, Program Director, 415-955-2084, Fax: 415-955-2179, E-mail: admissions@alliant.edu. *Application contact:* Alliant International University Central Contact Center, 866-U-ALLIANT, Fax: 858-635-4555, E-mail: admissions@alliant.edu.
Website: http://www.alliant.edu/.

Alvernia University, Graduate Studies, Program in Education, Reading, PA 19607-1799. Offers urban education (M Ed). Part-time and evening/weekend programs available. *Degree requirements:* For master's, thesis optional. *Entrance requirements:* For master's, GRE or MAT (alumni excluded). Electronic applications accepted.

Alverno College, School of Education, Milwaukee, WI 53234-3922. Offers adaptive education (MA); administrative leadership (MA); adult education and organizational development (MA); adult educational and instructional design (MA); adult educational and instructional technology (MA); global connections in the humanities (MA); instructional leadership (MA); instructional technology for K-12 settings (MA); professional development (MA); reading education (MA); reading education with adaptive education (MA); science education (MA); teaching in alternative schools (MA). *Accreditation:* NCATE. Part-time and evening/weekend programs available. *Faculty:* 7 full-time (all women), 26 part-time/adjunct (23 women). *Students:* 48 full-time (41 women), 89 part-time (83 women); includes 41 minority (24 Black or African American, non-Hispanic/Latino; 3 Asian, non-Hispanic/Latino; 11 Hispanic/Latino; 3 Two or more races, non-Hispanic/Latino), 4 international. Average age 36. 89 applicants, 97% accepted, 59 enrolled. In 2013, 53 master's awarded. *Degree requirements:* For master's, presentation/defense of proposal, conference presentation of inquiry projects. *Entrance requirements:* For master's, bachelor's degree in related field, communication samples from work setting, 3 letters of recommendation. Additional exam requirements/recommendations for international students: Required—TOEFL. *Application deadline:* For fall admission, 7/15 priority date for domestic and international students; for spring admission, 12/15 priority date for domestic and international students. Applications are processed on a rolling basis. Application fee: $0. Electronic applications accepted. Application fee is waived when completed online. Tuition and fees vary according to program. *Financial support:* In 2013–14, 9 students received support. Federal Work-Study and scholarships/grants available. Support available to part-time students. Financial award application deadline: 4/15; financial award applicants required to submit FAFSA. *Faculty research:* Student self-assessment, self-reflection, integration of curriculum, identifying needs of students in strategic situations and designing

appropriate classroom strategies. *Unit head:* Dr. Desiree Pointer-Mace, Associate Dean, Graduate Program, 414-382-6345, Fax: 414-382-6332, E-mail: desiree.pointer-mace@alverno.edu. *Application contact:* Mary Claire Jones, Senior Graduate Admissions Counselor, 414-382-6106, Fax: 414-382-6354, E-mail: maryclaire.jones@alverno.edu.

American College of Education, Graduate Programs, Chicago, IL 60606. Offers curriculum and instruction (M Ed), including bilingual, ESL; educational leadership (M Ed); educational technology (M Ed).

American InterContinental University Online, Program in Education, Schaumburg, IL 60173. Offers curriculum and instruction (M Ed); educational assessment and evaluation (M Ed); instructional technology (M Ed); leadership of educational organizations (M Ed). Evening/weekend programs available. Postbaccalaureate distance learning degree programs offered (no on-campus study). *Entrance requirements:* Additional exam requirements/recommendations for international students: Required—TOEFL (minimum score 550 paper-based). Electronic applications accepted.

American International College, School of Graduate and Adult Education, Department of Education, Springfield, MA 01109-3189. Offers early childhood education (M Ed, CAGS); educational leadership and supervision (Ed D); elementary education (M Ed, CAGS); middle/secondary education (M Ed, CAGS); moderate disabilities (M Ed, CAGS); reading (M Ed, CAGS); school adjustment counseling (MA, CAGS); school guidance counseling (MA, CAGS); school leadership preparation (M Ed, CAGS); teaching and learning (Ed D). Evening/weekend programs available. *Faculty:* 11 full-time (9 women), 235 part-time/adjunct. *Students:* 1,530 full-time (1,219 women), 184 part-time (143 women); includes 100 minority (58 Black or African American, non-Hispanic/Latino; 3 American Indian or Alaska Native, non-Hispanic/Latino; 14 Asian, non-Hispanic/Latino; 6 Hispanic/Latino; 19 Two or more races, non-Hispanic/Latino). Average age 36. 695 applicants, 82% accepted, 508 enrolled. In 2013, 449 master's, 17 doctorates, 135 other advanced degrees awarded. Terminal master's awarded for partial completion of doctoral program. *Degree requirements:* For master's, comprehensive exam (for some programs), thesis (for some programs), practicum/culminating experience; for doctorate, comprehensive exam (for some programs), thesis/dissertation; for CAGS, practicum/culminating experience. *Entrance requirements:* For master's, graduate of accredited four-year college with minimum B-average in undergraduate course work; for doctorate, master's degree, minimum GPA of 3.0; for CAGS, M Ed or master's degree in field related to licensure from accredited institution. Additional exam requirements/recommendations for international students: Required—TOEFL or IELTS. *Application deadline:* For fall admission, 7/1 for domestic and international students; for spring admission, 12/1 for domestic and international students. Applications are processed on a rolling basis. Application fee: $50. Electronic applications accepted. *Expenses: Tuition:* Full-time $14,040; part-time $780 per credit. Tuition and fees vary according to course load, degree level and program. *Financial support:* Career-related internships or fieldwork available. Financial award applicants required to submit FAFSA. *Unit head:* Esta Sobey, Associate Dean, 413-205-3453, Fax: 413-205-3943, E-mail: esta.sobey@aic.edu. *Application contact:* Kaitlyn Rickard, Director of XCP Admissions, 413-205-3090, Fax: 413-205-3911, E-mail: kaitlyn.rickard@aic.edu.
Website: http://www.aic.edu/academics.

American Jewish University, Graduate School of Education, Program in Education, Bel Air, CA 90077-1599. Offers MA Ed. *Degree requirements:* For master's, one foreign language. *Entrance requirements:* For master's, GRE General Test, interview, minimum GPA of 3.0. Additional exam requirements/recommendations for international students: Required—TOEFL. *Faculty research:* Philosophy of education, curriculum development, teacher training.

American Jewish University, Graduate School of Education, Program in Education for Working Professionals, Bel Air, CA 90077-1599. Offers MA Ed. *Degree requirements:* For master's, comprehensive exam, internships. *Entrance requirements:* For master's, GRE General Test, interview. Additional exam requirements/recommendations for international students: Required—TOEFL.

American University, College of Arts and Sciences, Washington, DC 20016-8012. Offers addiction and addictive behavior (Certificate); anthropology (PhD); applied microeconomics (Certificate); applied statistics (Certificate); art history (MA); arts management (MA, Certificate); Asian studies (Certificate); audio production (Certificate); audio technology (MA); behavior, cognition, and neuroscience (PhD); bilingual education (MA, Certificate); biology (MA, MS); chemistry (MS); clinical psychology (PhD); computer science (MS, Certificate); creative writing (MFA); curriculum and instruction (M Ed, Certificate); economics (MA, PhD); environmental assessment (Certificate); environmental science (MS); ethics, peace, and global affairs (MA); gender analysis in economics (Certificate); health promotion management (MS); history (MA, PhD); international arts management (Certificate); international economic relations (Certificate); international economics (MA); international training and education (MA); literature (MA); mathematics (MA); North American studies (Certificate); nutrition education (MS, Certificate); philosophy (MA); professional science: biotechnology (MS); professional science: environmental assessment (MS); professional science: quantitative analysis (MS); psychobiology of healing (Certificate); psychology (MA); psychology: general (PhD); public anthropology (MA, Certificate); public sociology (Certificate); social research (Certificate); sociology (MA); Spanish: Latin American studies (MA); special education: learning disabilities (MA); statistics (MS); studio art (MFA); teaching (MAT); teaching English as a foreign language (MA); teaching: early childhood (Certificate); teaching: elementary (Certificate); teaching: ESOL (Certificate); teaching: secondary (Certificate); technology in arts management (Certificate); TESOL (MA); translation: French (Certificate); translation: Russian (Certificate); translation: Spanish (Certificate); women's, gender, and sexuality studies (Certificate). Part-time and evening/weekend programs available. Postbaccalaureate distance learning degree programs offered (no on-campus study). *Faculty:* 358 full-time (187 women), 254 part-time/adjunct (127 women). *Students:* 627 full-time (411 women), 416 part-time (300 women); includes 206 minority (91 Black or African American, non-Hispanic/Latino; 5 American Indian or Alaska Native, non-Hispanic/Latino; 32 Asian, non-Hispanic/Latino; 64 Hispanic/Latino; 1 Native Hawaiian or other Pacific Islander, non-Hispanic/Latino; 13 Two or more races, non-Hispanic/Latino), 124 international. Average age 29. 1,672 applicants, 52% accepted, 361 enrolled. In 2013, 382 master's, 38 doctorates, 33 other advanced degrees awarded. Terminal master's awarded for partial completion of doctoral program. *Degree requirements:* For master's, comprehensive exam (for some programs), thesis (for some programs); for doctorate, comprehensive exam (for some programs), thesis/dissertation. *Entrance requirements:* For master's, GRE, minimum GPA of 3.0 in last 60 credit hours, letter of recommendation, statement of purpose, resume, unofficial transcript; for doctorate, GRE, minimum GPA of 3.0 for all graduate work, letter of recommendation, statement of purpose, resume, unofficial transcript. Additional exam requirements/recommendations for international students: Required—TOEFL (minimum score 600 paper-based; 100 iBT), IELTS (minimum score 7). *Application deadline:* For fall admission, 2/1 for domestic students; for spring admission, 10/1 for domestic students. Applications are processed on a rolling basis. Application fee: $55. Electronic applications accepted. *Expenses: Tuition:* Full-time $25,920; part-time $1482 per credit hour. *Required fees:* $430. Tuition and fees vary according to course load and program. *Financial support:* Fellowships, research assistantships with full and partial tuition reimbursements, teaching assistantships with full and partial tuition reimbursements, career-related internships or fieldwork, Federal Work-Study, institutionally sponsored loans, scholarships/grants, traineeships, tuition waivers (full and partial), and unspecified assistantships available. Support available to part-time students. Financial award applicants required to submit FAFSA. *Unit head:* Dr. Peter Starr, Dean, 202-885-2446, Fax: 202-885-2429, E-mail: pstarr@american.edu. *Application contact:* Kathleen Clowery, Associate Director, Graduate Enrollment Management, 202-885-3621, Fax: 202-885-1505, E-mail: clowery@american.edu.
Website: http://www.american.edu/cas/.

The American University in Dubai, Graduate Programs, Dubai, United Arab Emirates. Offers construction management (MS); education (M Ed); finance (MBA); generalist (MBA); marketing (MBA). Part-time and evening/weekend programs available. *Degree requirements:* For master's, thesis optional. *Entrance requirements:* For master's, GMAT (for MBA); GRE (for M Ed and MS), minimum undergraduate GPA of 3.0, official transcripts, two reference forms, curriculum vitae/resume, statement of career objectives, work experience. Additional exam requirements/recommendations for international students: Required—TOEFL (minimum score 550 paper-based; 79 iBT). Electronic applications accepted.

American University of Beirut, Graduate Programs, Faculty of Arts and Sciences, Beirut, Lebanon. Offers anthropology (MA); Arab and Middle Eastern history (PhD); Arabic language and literature (MA, PhD); archaeology (MA); biology (MS); cell and molecular biology (PhD); chemistry (MS); clinical psychology (MA); computational sciences (MS); computer science (MS); economics (MA); education (MA); English language (MA); English literature (MA); environmental policy planning (MS); financial economics (MA); geology (MS); history (MA); mathematics (MA, MS); media studies (MA); Middle Eastern studies (MA); philosophy (MA); physics (MS); political studies (MA); psychology (MA); public administration (MA); sociology (MA); statistics (MA, MS); theoretical physics (PhD); transnational American studies (MA). Part-time programs available. *Faculty:* 88 full-time (22 women). *Students:* Average age 25. In 2013, 112 master's, 87 doctorates awarded. *Degree requirements:* For master's, one foreign language, comprehensive exam, thesis (for some programs); for doctorate, one foreign language, comprehensive exam, thesis/dissertation. *Entrance requirements:* For master's, GRE, letter of recommendation; for doctorate, GRE, letters of recommendation. Additional exam requirements/recommendations for international students: Required—TOEFL (minimum score 600 paper-based; 97 iBT), IELTS (minimum score 7). *Application deadline:* For fall admission, 4/30 for domestic students, 4/18 for international students; for spring admission, 11/1 for domestic and international students. Application fee: $50. *Expenses: Tuition:* Full-time $14,724; part-time $818 per credit. *Required fees:* $692; $692. Tuition and fees vary according to course load and program. *Financial support:* Research assistantships, career-related internships or fieldwork, institutionally sponsored loans, scholarships/grants, health care benefits, and unspecified assistantships available. Financial award application deadline: 2/4; financial award applicants required to submit FAFSA. *Faculty research:* Modern Middle East history; Near Eastern archaeology; Islamic history; European history; software engineering; scientific computing; data mining; the applications of cooperative learning in language teaching and teacher education; world/comparative literature; rhetoric and composition; creative writing; public management; public policy and international affairs; hydrogeology; mineralogy, petrology, and geochemistry; tectonics and structural geology; cell and molecular biology; ecology. *Unit head:* Dr. Patrick McGreevy, Dean, 961-1374374 Ext. 3800, Fax: 961-1744461, E-mail: pm07@aub.edu.lb. *Application contact:* Dr. Salim Kanaan, Director, Admissions Office, 961-1-350000 Ext. 2590, Fax: 96-1-1750775, E-mail: sk00@aub.edu.lb.
Website: http://www.aub.edu.lb/fas/.

American University of Puerto Rico, Program in Education, Bayamón, PR 00960-2037. Offers art education (M Ed); elementary education 4-6 (M Ed); elementary education K-3 (M Ed); general science education (M Ed); physical education (M Ed); special education (M Ed). *Faculty:* 17 part-time/adjunct (7 women). *Students:* 55 full-time (42 women), 105 part-time (96 women); all minorities (all Hispanic/Latino). Average age 33. 120 applicants, 99% accepted, 81 enrolled. In 2013, 52 master's awarded. *Entrance requirements:* For master's, EXADEP, GRE, or MAT, 2 letters of recommendation, minimum GPA of 2.5. *Application deadline:* For fall admission, 8/1 for domestic students; for winter admission, 10/18 for domestic students; for spring admission, 3/15 for domestic students. Applications are processed on a rolling basis. Application fee: $25. *Expenses: Tuition:* Part-time $240 per credit. Tuition and fees vary according to course load. *Unit head:* Dr. Jose A. Ramirez-Figueroa, Education and Technology Department Director/Chancellor, 787-620-2040 Ext. 2010, Fax: 787-620-2958, E-mail: jramirez@aupr.edu. *Application contact:* Keren I. Llanos-Figueroa, Information Contact, 787-620-2040 Ext. 2021, Fax: 787-785-7377, E-mail: oficnaadmisiones@aupr.edu.

Anderson University, College of Education, Anderson, SC 29621-4035. Offers M Ed. *Accreditation:* NCATE.

Anderson University, School of Education, Anderson, IN 46012-3495. Offers M Ed. *Accreditation:* NCATE.

Andrews University, School of Graduate Studies, School of Education, Berrien Springs, MI 49104. Offers MA, MAT, MS, Ed D, PhD, Ed S. *Accreditation:* NCATE. Part-time programs available. *Faculty:* 24 full-time (11 women), 1 part-time/adjunct (0 women). *Students:* 112 full-time (72 women), 75 part-time (46 women); includes 93 minority (55 Black or African American, non-Hispanic/Latino; 8 Asian, non-Hispanic/Latino; 26 Hispanic/Latino; 4 Two or more races, non-Hispanic/Latino), 59 international. Average age 41. 170 applicants, 54% accepted, 43 enrolled. In 2013, 43 master's, 14 doctorates, 11 other advanced degrees awarded. Terminal master's awarded for partial completion of doctoral program. *Degree requirements:* For doctorate, thesis/dissertation. *Entrance requirements:* For master's, GRE Subject Test. Additional exam requirements/recommendations for international students: Required—TOEFL (minimum score 550 paper-based). *Application deadline:* Applications are processed on a rolling basis. Application fee: $40. *Financial support:* Fellowships, research assistantships, teaching assistantships, career-related internships or fieldwork, Federal Work-Study, institutionally sponsored loans, and tuition waivers (partial) available. Support available to part-time students. *Unit head:* Dr. James R. Jeffery, Dean, 269-471-3464. *Application contact:* Monica Wringer, Supervisor of Graduate Admission, 800-253-2874, Fax: 269-471-6321, E-mail: graduate@andrews.edu.

Angelo State University, College of Graduate Studies, College of Education, Department of Teacher Education, San Angelo, TX 76909. Offers professional education (M Ed); special education (M Ed).

Anna Maria College, Graduate Division, Program in Education, Paxton, MA 01612. Offers early childhood education (M Ed); education (CAGS); elementary education (M Ed); English language arts (M Ed); visual arts (M Ed). Part-time and evening/weekend programs available. *Entrance requirements:* For master's, bachelor's degree in liberal arts or sciences, minimum GPA of 3.0. Additional exam requirements/recommendations for international students: Required—TOEFL (minimum score 500 paper-based). Electronic applications accepted.

Antioch University Los Angeles, Graduate Programs, Program in Education, Culver City, CA 90230. Offers MA. Evening/weekend programs available. *Entrance requirements:* Additional exam requirements/recommendations for international students: Required—TOEFL.

Antioch University Midwest, Graduate Programs, Individualized Liberal and Professional Studies Program, Yellow Springs, OH 45387-1609. Offers liberal and professional studies (MA), including counseling, creative writing, education, liberal studies, management, modern literature, psychology, visual arts. Part-time and evening/ weekend programs available. Postbaccalaureate distance learning degree programs offered (minimal on-campus study). *Degree requirements:* For master's, thesis or alternative. *Entrance requirements:* For master's, resume, goal statement, interview. Electronic applications accepted. *Expenses:* Contact institution.

Antioch University Midwest, Graduate Programs, School of Education, Yellow Springs, OH 45387-1609. Offers M Ed. *Accreditation:* NCATE. Part-time and evening/ weekend programs available. *Degree requirements:* For master's, thesis or alternative. *Entrance requirements:* For master's, resume, goal statement, interview. Electronic applications accepted. *Expenses:* Contact institution.

Antioch University New England, Graduate School, Department of Education, Keene, NH 03431-3552. Offers integrated learning (M Ed), including elementary and early childhood education, elementary education (M Ed, Certificate); teaching (M Ed, PMC), including foundations of education (M Ed), principal certification (PMC); Waldorf teacher training (M Ed, Certificate), including elementary education, foundations of education (M Ed). *Degree requirements:* For master's, thesis (for some programs), internship. *Entrance requirements:* Additional exam requirements/recommendations for international students: Required—TOEFL (minimum score 550 paper-based). Electronic applications accepted. *Expenses:* Contact institution. *Faculty research:* Classroom and school restructuring, problem-based learning, Waldorf collaborative leadership, ecological literacy.

Antioch University Santa Barbara, Program in Education/Teacher Credentialing, Santa Barbara, CA 93101-1581. Offers MA. Part-time programs available. *Entrance requirements:* Additional exam requirements/recommendations for international students: Required—TOEFL (minimum score 550 paper-based). Electronic applications accepted.

Antioch University Seattle, Graduate Programs, Program in Education, Seattle, WA 98121-1814. Offers MA. Part-time and evening/weekend programs available. *Degree requirements:* For master's, comprehensive exam (for some programs), thesis. *Entrance requirements:* For master's, WEST-B, WEST-E, current resume, transcripts of undergraduate degree and coursework (or for highest degree completed), two letters of recommendation, proof of fingerprinting and background check, moral character with fitness statement of understanding, documentation of 40 hours experience in school classroom(s), copy of WA state teaching certificate (where applicab). *Expenses:* Contact institution. *Faculty research:* Visual thinking and science education, K-8 equity and engaged pedagogy in science education, K-12 inquiry-based mathematics education, education in prisons and other institutions of confinement.

Aquinas College, School of Education, Grand Rapids, MI 49506-1799. Offers M Ed, MAT, MSE. Part-time and evening/weekend programs available. *Students:* 2 full-time (both women), 67 part-time (50 women); includes 5 minority (1 Black or African American, non-Hispanic/Latino; 2 Asian, non-Hispanic/Latino; 2 Hispanic/Latino). Average age 35. In 2013, 40 degrees awarded. *Degree requirements:* For master's, teaching project; action research. *Entrance requirements:* For master's, Michigan Basic Skills Test, minimum undergraduate GPA of 3.0, teaching certificate. Additional exam requirements/recommendations for international students: Required—TOEFL (minimum score 550 paper-based). *Application deadline:* Applications are processed on a rolling basis. Application fee: $0. *Expenses:* Contact institution. *Financial support:* Scholarships/grants available. Support available to part-time students. Financial award application deadline: 3/15. *Unit head:* Nanette Clatterbuck, Dean, 616-632-2973, Fax: 616-732-4465, E-mail: clattnan@aquinas.edu. *Application contact:* Lisa Swinehart, Administrative Assistant, 616-632-2440, E-mail: lms002@aquinas.edu. Website: http://www.aquinas.edu/education/.

Arcadia University, Graduate Studies, School of Education, Glenside, PA 19038-3295. Offers art education (M Ed); computer education (CAS); curriculum (CAS); curriculum studies (M Ed); early childhood education (M Ed, CAS), including individualized (M Ed); master teacher (M Ed), research in child development (M Ed); educational leadership (M Ed, Ed D, CAS); elementary education (M Ed, CAS); English education (MA Ed); environmental education (MA Ed, CAS); history education (MA Ed); instructional technology (M Ed); language arts (M Ed, CAS); library science (M Ed); mathematics education (M Ed, MA Ed, CAS); music education (MA Ed); psychology (MA Ed); reading (M Ed, CAS); science education (M Ed, CAS); secondary education (M Ed, CAS); special education (M Ed, Ed D, CAS); theater arts (MA Ed); written communication (MA Ed). *Accreditation:* NASAD. Part-time and evening/weekend programs available. Postbaccalaureate distance learning degree programs offered (minimal on-campus study). Electronic applications accepted. *Expenses:* Contact institution.

Argosy University, Atlanta, College of Education, Atlanta, GA 30328. Offers educational leadership (MAEd, Ed D, Ed S), including higher education administration (Ed D), K-12 education (Ed D); teaching and learning (MAEd, Ed D, Ed S), including education technology (Ed D), higher education (Ed D), K-12 education (Ed D).

Argosy University, Chicago, College of Education, Chicago, IL 60601. Offers adult education and training (MA Ed); community college executive leadership (Ed D); educational leadership (MA Ed, Ed D, Ed S), including district leadership (Ed D), higher education administration (Ed D), K-12 education (Ed D); instructional leadership (Ed D, Ed S), including higher education (Ed D), K-12 education (Ed D). Postbaccalaureate distance learning degree programs offered (minimal on-campus study).

Argosy University, Dallas, College of Education, Farmers Branch, TX 75244. Offers educational administration (MA Ed); educational leadership (Ed D); higher and postsecondary education (MA Ed); instructional leadership (MA Ed); school psychology (MA).

Argosy University, Denver, College of Education, Denver, CO 80231. Offers community college executive leadership (Ed D); educational leadership (MA Ed, Ed D), including higher education (Ed D), K-12 education (Ed D); instructional leadership (MA Ed, Ed D), including higher education administration (Ed D), K-12 education (Ed D).

Argosy University, Hawai`i, College of Education, Honolulu, HI 96813. Offers adult education and training (MAEd); educational leadership (Ed D), including higher education administration, K-12 education; instructional leadership (Ed D), including higher education, K-12 education; school psychology (MA).

Argosy University, Inland Empire, College of Education, Ontario, CA 91761. Offers community college executive leadership (Ed D); educational leadership (MA Ed, Ed D), including higher education administration (Ed D), K-12 education (Ed D); instructional leadership (MA Ed, Ed D), including higher education (Ed D), K-12 education (Ed D), multiple subject teacher preparation (MA Ed), single subject teacher preparation (MA Ed).

Argosy University, Los Angeles, College of Education, Santa Monica, CA 90045. Offers community college executive leadership (Ed D); educational leadership (MA Ed, Ed D), including higher education administration (Ed D), K-12 education (Ed D); instructional leadership (MA Ed, Ed D), including higher education (Ed D), K-12 education (Ed D), multiple subject teacher preparation (MA Ed), single subject teacher preparation (MA Ed).

Argosy University, Nashville, College of Education, Nashville, TN 37214. Offers MA Ed, Ed D, Ed S.

Argosy University, Orange County, College of Education, Orange, CA 92868. Offers community college executive leadership (Ed D); educational leadership (MA Ed, Ed D), including higher education administration (Ed D), K-12 education (Ed D); instructional leadership (MA Ed, Ed D), including education technology (Ed D), higher education (Ed D), K-12 education (Ed D), multiple subject teacher preparation (MA Ed), single subject teacher preparation (MA Ed).

Argosy University, Phoenix, College of Education, Phoenix, AZ 85021. Offers adult education and training (MA Ed); advanced educational administration (Ed D, Ed S); community college executive leadership (Ed D); educational administration (MA Ed); educational leadership (MA Ed, Ed D, Ed S), including education technology (Ed D), higher education administration (Ed D), K-12 education (Ed D); higher and postsecondary education (MA Ed); initial educational administration (Ed D, Ed S); school psychology (MA); teaching and learning (MA Ed, Ed D, Ed S), including education technology (Ed D), higher education (Ed D), K-12 education (Ed D).

Argosy University, Salt Lake City, College of Education, Draper, UT 84020. Offers educational leadership (MA Ed, Ed D).

Argosy University, San Diego, College of Education, San Diego, CA 92108. Offers community college executive leadership (Ed D); educational leadership (MA Ed, Ed D), including higher education administration (Ed D), K-12 education (Ed D); instructional leadership (MA Ed, Ed D), including higher education (Ed D), K-12 education (Ed D).

Argosy University, San Francisco Bay Area, College of Education, Alameda, CA 94501. Offers community college executive leadership (Ed D); educational leadership (MA Ed, Ed D), including education technology (Ed D), higher education administration (Ed D), K-12 education (Ed D); instructional leadership (MA Ed, Ed D), including education technology (Ed D), higher education (Ed D), K-12 education (Ed D), multiple subject teacher preparation (MA Ed), single subject teacher preparation (MA Ed).

Argosy University, Sarasota, College of Education, Sarasota, FL 34235. Offers community college executive leadership (Ed D); educational leadership (MA Ed, Ed D, Ed S), including higher education administration (Ed D), K-12 education (Ed D); school counseling (MA, Ed S); school psychology (MA); teaching and learning (MA Ed, Ed D, Ed S), including education technology (Ed D), higher education (Ed D), K-12 education (Ed D).

Argosy University, Schaumburg, College of Education, Schaumburg, IL 60173-5403. Offers community college executive leadership (Ed D); educational leadership (MA Ed, Ed D, Ed S), including district leadership (Ed D), higher education administration (Ed D), K-12 education (Ed D); instructional leadership (Ed D, Ed S), including higher education (Ed D), K-12 education (Ed D).

Argosy University, Seattle, College of Education, Seattle, WA 98121. Offers adult education and training (MA Ed); community college executive leadership (Ed D); educational leadership (MA Ed, Ed D), including higher education administration (Ed D), K-12 education (Ed D); higher and postsecondary education (MA Ed); instructional leadership (MA Ed, Ed D), including education technology (Ed D), higher education (Ed D), K-12 education (Ed D).

Argosy University, Tampa, College of Education, Tampa, FL 33607. Offers community college executive leadership (Ed D); educational leadership (MA Ed, Ed D, Ed S), including higher education administration (Ed D), K-12 education (Ed D); school counseling (MA); teaching and learning (MA Ed, Ed D, Ed S), including higher education (Ed D), K-12 education (Ed D).

Argosy University, Twin Cities, College of Education, Eagan, MN 55121. Offers advanced educational administration (Ed D, Ed S); educational leadership (MA Ed, Ed D, Ed S), including higher education administration (Ed D), K-12 education (Ed D); higher and postsecondary education (MA Ed); initial educational administration (Ed D, Ed S); instructional leadership (MA Ed, Ed D, Ed S), including education technology (Ed D), higher education (Ed D), K-12 education (Ed D).

Argosy University, Washington DC, College of Education, Arlington, VA 22209. Offers community college executive leadership (Ed D); educational leadership (MA Ed, Ed D, Ed S), including higher education administration (Ed D), K-12 education (Ed D); instructional leadership (MA Ed, Ed D, Ed S), including higher education (Ed D), K-12 education (Ed D).

Arizona State University at the Tempe campus, Mary Lou Fulton Teachers College, Phoenix, AZ 85069. Offers M Ed, MA, MC, MPE, Ed D, PhD, Graduate Certificate. Part-time and evening/weekend programs available. Postbaccalaureate distance learning degree programs offered (minimal on-campus study). *Degree requirements:* For master's, comprehensive exam (for some programs), thesis (for some programs), interactive Program of Study (iPOS) submitted before completing 50 percent of required credit hours; for doctorate, comprehensive exam, thesis/dissertation, interactive Program of Study (iPOS) submitted before completing 50 percent of required credit hours. *Entrance requirements:* For master's and doctorate, GRE General Test or GMAT, minimum GPA of 3.0 or equivalent in last 2 years of work leading to bachelor's degree. Additional exam requirements/recommendations for international students: Required—TOEFL (minimum score 80 iBT), TOEFL, IELTS, or PTE. Electronic applications accepted. *Expenses:* Contact institution.

Arkansas State University, Graduate School, College of Education and Behavioral Science, Jonesboro, AR 72467. Offers MAT, MRC, MS, MSE, Ed D, PhD, Certificate, Ed S, SCCT. *Accreditation:* NCATE. Part-time programs available. Postbaccalaureate distance learning degree programs offered (no on-campus study). *Faculty:* 52 full-time (28 women). *Students:* 147 full-time (106 women), 2,042 part-time (1,516 women); includes 413 minority (334 Black or African American, non-Hispanic/Latino; 12 American Indian or Alaska Native, non-Hispanic/Latino; 3 Asian, non-Hispanic/Latino; 31 Hispanic/Latino; 1 Native Hawaiian or other Pacific Islander, non-Hispanic/Latino; 32 Two or more races, non-Hispanic/Latino), 14 international. Average age 36. 1,767 applicants, 70% accepted, 841 enrolled. In 2013, 1,217 master's, 12 doctorates, 87 other advanced degrees awarded. *Degree requirements:* For master's and other advanced degree, comprehensive exam, thesis or alternative; for doctorate, comprehensive exam, thesis/ dissertation. *Entrance requirements:* For master's, GRE General Test or MAT, appropriate bachelor's degree, interview, letters of reference, official transcripts, immunization records; for doctorate, GRE General Test or MAT, interview, master's degree, letters of reference, official transcript, personal statement, immunization records, writing sample; for other advanced degree, GRE General Test, MAT, interview, master's degree, letters of reference, official transcript, 3 years of teaching experience, teaching license, immunization records. Additional exam requirements/ recommendations for international students: Required—TOEFL (minimum score 550

paper-based; 79 iBT), IELTS (minimum score 6), PTE (minimum score 56). *Application deadline:* Applications are processed on a rolling basis. Electronic applications accepted. *Expenses:* Tuition, state resident: full-time $4284; part-time $238 per credit hour. Tuition, nonresident: full-time $8568; part-time $476 per credit hour. *International tuition:* $9268 full-time. *Required fees:* $1098; $61 per credit hour. $25 per term. Tuition and fees vary according to course load and program. *Financial support:* In 2013–14, 55 students received support. Fellowships, teaching assistantships, career-related internships or fieldwork, scholarships/grants, and unspecified assistantships available. Financial award application deadline: 7/1; financial award applicants required to submit FAFSA. *Unit head:* Dr. Thillainatarajan Sivakumaran, Dean, 870-972-3057, Fax: 870-972-3828, E-mail: tsivkumaran@astate.edu. *Application contact:* Vickey Ring, Graduate Admissions Coordinator, 870-972-3029, Fax: 870-972-3857, E-mail: vickeyring@astate.edu.
Website: http://www.astate.edu/college/education/index.dot.

Arkansas Tech University, College of Education, Russellville, AR 72801. Offers college student personnel (MS); elementary education (M Ed); instructional improvement (M Ed); instructional technology (M Ed); physical education (M Ed); teaching (MAT). *Accreditation:* NCATE. Part-time and evening/weekend programs available. Postbaccalaureate distance learning degree programs offered (no on-campus study). *Students:* 58 full-time (39 women), 304 part-time (240 women); includes 76 minority (58 Black or African American, non-Hispanic/Latino; 3 American Indian or Alaska Native, non-Hispanic/Latino; 4 Asian, non-Hispanic/Latino; 8 Hispanic/Latino; 3 Two or more races, non-Hispanic/Latino), 2 international. Average age 32. In 2013, 130 master's awarded. *Degree requirements:* For master's, comprehensive exam, thesis optional, action research project. *Entrance requirements:* Additional exam requirements/recommendations for international students: Required—TOEFL (minimum score 550 paper-based; 79 iBT), IELTS (minimum score 6.5). *Application deadline:* For fall admission, 3/1 priority date for domestic students, 5/1 priority date for international students; for spring admission, 10/1 priority date for domestic and international students. Applications are processed on a rolling basis. Application fee: $25 ($75 for international students). Electronic applications accepted. *Expenses:* Tuition, state resident: full-time $5976; part-time $249 per credit hour. Tuition, nonresident: full-time $11,952; part-time $498 per credit hour. *Required fees:* $411 per semester. Tuition and fees vary according to course load. *Financial support:* In 2013–14, research assistantships with full tuition reimbursements (averaging $4,800 per year), teaching assistantships with full tuition reimbursements (averaging $4,800 per year) were awarded; career-related internships or fieldwork, Federal Work-Study, scholarships/grants, health care benefits, and unspecified assistantships also available. Support available to part-time students. Financial award application deadline: 4/15; financial award applicants required to submit FAFSA. *Unit head:* Dr. Sherry Field, Dean, 479-968-0418, E-mail: sfield@atu.edu. *Application contact:* Dr. Mary B. Gunter, Dean of Graduate College, 479-968-0398, Fax: 479-964-0542, E-mail: gradcollege@atu.edu.
Website: http://www.atu.edu/education/.

Arlington Baptist College, Program in Education, Arlington, TX 76012-3425. Offers curriculum and instruction (M Ed); educational leadership (M Ed). *Degree requirements:* For master's, professional portfolio; internship (for educational leadership). *Entrance requirements:* For master's, bachelor's degree from accredited college or university with minimum GPA of 3.0, minimum of 12 hours in Bible; minimum of three years' classroom teaching experience in an accredited K-12 public or private school (for educational leadership only).

Armstrong State University, School of Graduate Studies, Department of Childhood and Exceptional Student Education, Savannah, GA 31419-1997. Offers early childhood education (M Ed, MAT); reading endorsement (Certificate); special education (M Ed, MAT). *Accreditation:* NCATE. Part-time and evening/weekend programs available. Postbaccalaureate distance learning degree programs offered (minimal on-campus study). *Faculty:* 12 full-time (9 women), 4 part-time/adjunct (0 women). *Students:* 26 full-time (22 women), 208 part-time (186 women); includes 74 minority (66 Black or African American, non-Hispanic/Latino; 1 Asian, non-Hispanic/Latino; 5 Hispanic/Latino; 2 Two or more races, non-Hispanic/Latino), 1 international. Average age 33. 107 applicants, 70% accepted, 69 enrolled. In 2013, 122 master's, 64 other advanced degrees awarded. *Degree requirements:* For master's, comprehensive exam. *Entrance requirements:* For master's, GRE General Test or MAT. Additional exam requirements/recommendations for international students: Required—TOEFL (minimum score 523 paper-based). *Application deadline:* For fall admission, 6/30 priority date for domestic students, 5/1 priority date for international students; for spring admission, 11/15 priority date for domestic students, 9/15 priority date for international students; for summer admission, 4/15 priority date for domestic students, 9/15 for international students. Applications are processed on a rolling basis. Application fee: $30. Electronic applications accepted. *Expenses:* Tuition, state resident: part-time $201 per credit hour. Tuition, nonresident: part-time $745 per credit hour. *Required fees:* $310 per semester. Tuition and fees vary according to course load, campus/location and program. *Financial support:* In 2013–14, research assistantships with full tuition reimbursements (averaging $5,000 per year) were awarded; career-related internships or fieldwork, Federal Work-Study, scholarships/grants, and unspecified assistantships also available. Support available to part-time students. Financial award application deadline: 3/15; financial award applicants required to submit FAFSA. *Faculty research:* Literacy, instructional design, poetry, working with local schools. *Unit head:* Dr. John Hobe, Department Head, 912-344-2564, Fax: 912-344-3443, E-mail: john.hobe@armstrong.edu. *Application contact:* Jill Bell, Director, Graduate Enrollment Services, 912-344-2798, Fax: 912-344-3488, E-mail: graduate@armstrong.edu.
Website: http://www.armstrong.edu/Education/childhood_exceptional_education2/ceed_welcome.

Ashland University, Dwight Schar College of Education, Ashland, OH 44805-3702. Offers M Ed, Ed D. *Accreditation:* NCATE. Part-time and evening/weekend programs available. *Degree requirements:* For master's, thesis optional, capstone project; for doctorate, comprehensive exam, thesis/dissertation. *Entrance requirements:* For master's, GRE General Test or MAT, teaching certificate, minimum GPA of 2.75; for doctorate, GRE, master's degree, minimum GPA of 3.3, writing sample, letters of recommendation. Additional exam requirements/recommendations for international students: Required—TOEFL. *Faculty research:* Teacher performance, administrative performance, collaborative learning groups, talent development, environmental education.

Athabasca University, Centre for Distance Education, Athabasca, AB T9S 3A3, Canada. Offers distance education (MDE); distance education technology (Advanced Diploma). Part-time programs available. Postbaccalaureate distance learning degree programs offered (no on-campus study). *Degree requirements:* For master's, thesis optional. *Entrance requirements:* For master's, 3 or 4 year baccalaureate degree. Electronic applications accepted. *Expenses:* Contact institution. *Faculty research:* Role development, interaction, educational technology, and communities of practice in distance education; instructional design.

Athabasca University, Centre for Integrated Studies, Athabasca, AB T9S 3A3, Canada. Offers adult education (MA); community studies (MA); cultural studies (MA); educational studies (MA); global change (MA); work, organization, and leadership (MA). Part-time and evening/weekend programs available. Postbaccalaureate distance learning degree programs offered (no on-campus study). *Degree requirements:* For master's, project. *Entrance requirements:* Additional exam requirements/recommendations for international students: Required—TOEFL (minimum score 560 paper-based). Electronic applications accepted. *Faculty research:* Women's history, literature and culture studies, sustainable development, labor and education.

Auburn University, Graduate School, College of Education, Auburn University, AL 36849. Offers M Ed, MS, Ed D, PhD, Ed S, Graduate Certificate. *Accreditation:* NCATE. Part-time programs available. *Faculty:* 93 full-time (61 women), 18 part-time/adjunct (16 women). *Students:* 396 full-time (266 women), 504 part-time (321 women); includes 209 minority (190 Black or African American, non-Hispanic/Latino; 2 American Indian or Alaska Native, non-Hispanic/Latino; 9 Asian, non-Hispanic/Latino; 8 Hispanic/Latino), 20 international. Average age 33. 713 applicants, 57% accepted, 293 enrolled. In 2013, 218 master's, 48 doctorates, 37 other advanced degrees awarded. *Degree requirements:* For master's, thesis (for some programs); for doctorate, thesis/dissertation. *Entrance requirements:* For master's, doctorate, and other advanced degree, GRE General Test. Application fee: $50 ($60 for international students). Electronic applications accepted. *Expenses:* Tuition, state resident: full-time $8262; part-time $459 per credit hour. Tuition, nonresident: full-time $24,786; part-time $1377 per credit hour. Tuition and fees vary according to degree level and program. *Financial support:* Fellowships, research assistantships, teaching assistantships, career-related internships or fieldwork, and Federal Work-Study available. Support available to part-time students. Financial award application deadline: 3/15; financial award applicants required to submit FAFSA. *Faculty research:* Dropout phenomena, high school students and substance use and abuse. *Unit head:* Dr. Betty Lou Whitford, Dean, 334-844-4446. *Application contact:* Dr. George Flowers, Dean of the Graduate School, 334-844-2125.
Website: http://www.education.auburn.edu/.

Auburn University at Montgomery, School of Education, Montgomery, AL 36124-4023. Offers M Ed, Ed S. *Accreditation:* NCATE. Part-time and evening/weekend programs available. *Faculty:* 20 full-time (14 women), 3 part-time/adjunct (2 women). *Students:* 98 full-time (65 women), 220 part-time (173 women); includes 109 minority (102 Black or African American, non-Hispanic/Latino; 1 American Indian or Alaska Native, non-Hispanic/Latino; 4 Asian, non-Hispanic/Latino; 2 Hispanic/Latino), 2 international. Average age 34. In 2013, 108 master's, 14 Ed Ss awarded. *Degree requirements:* For master's and Ed S, comprehensive exam. *Entrance requirements:* For master's, GRE General Test or MAT, BS in teaching, certification; for Ed S, GRE General Test or MAT, certification. *Application deadline:* Applications are processed on a rolling basis. Electronic applications accepted. *Expenses:* Tuition, state resident: full-time $5994; part-time $333 per credit hour. Tuition, nonresident: full-time $17,982; part-time $999 per credit hour. *Financial support:* Career-related internships or fieldwork and scholarships/grants available. Support available to part-time students. Financial award application deadline: 3/1; financial award applicants required to submit FAFSA. *Unit head:* Dr. Sheila Austin, Dean, 334-244-3425, Fax: 334-244-3102, E-mail: saustin1@aum.edu. *Application contact:* Dr. Rhonda Morton, Associate Dean/Graduate Coordinator, 334-224-3287, Fax: 334-244-3978, E-mail: rmorton@aum.edu.
Website: http://www.education.aum.edu/.

Augsburg College, Program in Education, Minneapolis, MN 55454-1351. Offers MAE. *Accreditation:* NCATE. Part-time and evening/weekend programs available. *Degree requirements:* For master's, comprehensive exam, final project. *Entrance requirements:* For master's, minimum GPA of 3.0. Additional exam requirements/recommendations for international students: Required—TOEFL (minimum score 600 paper-based). Electronic applications accepted.

Augustana College, MA in Education Program, Sioux Falls, SD 57197. Offers instructional strategies (MA); reading (MA); special populations (MA); technology (MA). *Accreditation:* NCATE. Part-time and evening/weekend programs available. Postbaccalaureate distance learning degree programs offered (no on-campus study). *Faculty:* 9 full-time (6 women). *Students:* 48 part-time (40 women). Average age 33. 55 applicants, 100% accepted, 49 enrolled. In 2013, 14 master's awarded. *Degree requirements:* For master's, thesis. *Entrance requirements:* For master's, appropriate bachelor's degree, minimum GPA of 3.0, teaching certificate. Additional exam requirements/recommendations for international students: Required—TOEFL (minimum score 550 paper-based). *Application deadline:* For spring admission, 4/1 priority date for domestic and international students. Applications are processed on a rolling basis. Application fee: $50. Electronic applications accepted. *Expenses:* Contact institution. *Financial support:* Application deadline: 3/1; applicants required to submit FAFSA. *Unit head:* Dr. Sheryl Feinstein, MA in Education Program Director, 605-274-5211, E-mail: sheryl.feinstein@augie.edu. *Application contact:* Nancy Wright, Graduate Coordinator, 605-274-4043, Fax: 605-274-4450, E-mail: graduate@augie.edu.
Website: http://www.augie.edu/academics/graduate-education/master-arts-education.

Aurora University, College of Education, Aurora, IL 60506-4892. Offers curriculum and instruction (MA, Ed D); early childhood and special education (MA); education (MAT), including elementary certification; education and administration (Ed D); educational leadership (MEL); educational technology (MATL); reading instruction (MA); special education (MA). *Accreditation:* NCATE. Part-time and evening/weekend programs available. *Degree requirements:* For doctorate, comprehensive exam, thesis/dissertation. *Entrance requirements:* For master's, 2 years of teaching experience, valid teaching certificate. Additional exam requirements/recommendations for international students: Required—TOEFL (minimum score 550 paper-based). Electronic applications accepted. *Expenses:* Contact institution.

Austin College, Austin Teacher Program, Sherman, TX 75090-4400. Offers MAT. Part-time programs available. *Faculty:* 5 full-time (4 women), 1 (woman) part-time/adjunct. *Students:* 16 full-time (8 women); includes 5 minority (1 Black or African American, non-Hispanic/Latino; 1 Asian, non-Hispanic/Latino; 2 Hispanic/Latino; 1 Two or more races, non-Hispanic/Latino). *Degree requirements:* For master's, one foreign language, thesis or alternative. *Entrance requirements:* For master's, Texas Academic Skills Program Test. *Application deadline:* For fall admission, 5/1 priority date for domestic students; for spring admission, 1/15 priority date for domestic students. Applications are processed on a rolling basis. Application fee: $35. Electronic applications accepted. *Financial support:* Career-related internships or fieldwork, Federal Work-Study, scholarships/grants, and unspecified assistantships available. Support available to part-time students. Financial award application deadline: 4/1; financial award applicants required to submit FAFSA. *Application contact:* Dr. Barbara Sylvester, Director of Teaching Program, 903-813-2327, E-mail: bsylvester@austincollege.edu.
Website: http://www.austincollege.edu/.

Austin Peay State University, College of Graduate Studies, College of Education, Clarksville, TN 37044. Offers MA Ed, MAT, Ed S. *Accreditation:* NCATE. Part-time and evening/weekend programs available. Postbaccalaureate distance learning degree programs offered. *Faculty:* 15 full-time (9 women), 9 part-time/adjunct (8 women). *Students:* 76 full-time (64 women), 164 part-time (128 women); includes 33 minority (15 Black or African American, non-Hispanic/Latino; 1 American Indian or Alaska Native, non-Hispanic/Latino; 3 Asian, non-Hispanic/Latino; 6 Hispanic/Latino; 8 Two or more races, non-Hispanic/Latino). Average age 34. 61 applicants, 89% accepted, 43 enrolled. In 2013, 87 master's, 7 other advanced degrees awarded. *Degree requirements:* For

master's, comprehensive exam, thesis optional. *Entrance requirements:* For master's, GRE General Test, 3 letters of recommendation, minimum undergraduate GPA of 2.75; for Ed S, GRE General Test, master's degree, minimum graduate GPA of 3.0, 3 letters of recommendation. Additional exam requirements/recommendations for international students: Required—TOEFL (minimum score 500 paper-based). *Application deadline:* For fall admission, 8/5 priority date for domestic students. Applications are processed on a rolling basis. Application fee: $25. Electronic applications accepted. *Expenses:* Tuition, state resident: full-time $7500; part-time $375 per credit hour. Tuition, nonresident: full-time $20,800; part-time $1040 per credit hour. *Required fees:* $1284; $64.20 per credit hour. *Financial support:* In 2013–14, research assistantships with full tuition reimbursements (averaging $6,500 per year) were awarded; career-related internships or fieldwork, Federal Work-Study, institutionally sponsored loans, scholarships/grants, and unspecified assistantships also available. Support available to part-time students. Financial award application deadline: 3/1; financial award applicants required to submit FAFSA. *Unit head:* Dr. Carlette Hardin, Director, 931-221-7696, Fax: 931-221-1292, E-mail: hardinc@apsu.edu. *Application contact:* June D. Lee, Graduate Coordinator, 800-859-4723, Fax: 931-221-7641, E-mail: gradadmissions@apsu.edu. Website: http://www.apsu.edu/educ/.

Averett University, Master in Education Program, Danville, VA 24541-3692. Offers administration and supervision (M Ed); art (M Ed); biology (M Ed); chemistry (M Ed); curriculum and instruction (M Ed); early childhood (M Ed); English (M Ed); mathematics (M Ed); middle grades (M Ed); physical science (M Ed); reading specialist (M Ed); science (M Ed); special education (M Ed); special education learning disability (M Ed). Program offered on Danville Campus only. Part-time and evening/weekend programs available. *Faculty:* 4 full-time (3 women), 13 part-time/adjunct (8 women). *Students:* 43 full-time (35 women), 44 part-time (35 women); includes 7 minority (all Black or African American, non-Hispanic/Latino). *Degree requirements:* For master's, 30-credit core curriculum, minimum GPA of 3.0 throughout program, completion of degree requirements within six years from start of program. *Entrance requirements:* For master's, PRAXIS I, GRE, or MAT; writing proficiency test, minimum cumulative GPA of 3.0 over the last 60 hours of undergraduate study toward a baccalaureate degree, three letters of recommendation, Virginia teaching license (or eligibility). Additional exam requirements/recommendations for international students: Required—TOEFL (minimum score 600 paper-based; 100 iBT). *Application deadline:* Applications are processed on a rolling basis. Application fee: $100. *Expenses:* Contact institution. *Financial support:* Career-related internships or fieldwork, Federal Work-Study, and scholarships/grants available. Financial award application deadline: 4/1; financial award applicants required to submit FAFSA. *Unit head:* Wilfred Lawrence, Department Chair of Education, 434-791-5752, E-mail: priedel@averett.edu. *Application contact:* Christy Pack, Executive Director of Enrollment, 804-887-8612, E-mail: dpack@averett.edu. Website: http://www.averett.edu/adultprograms/degrees/MEDtrad.php.

Avila University, School of Education, Kansas City, MO 64145-1698. Offers English for speakers of other languages (Advanced Certificate); teaching and learning (MA); TESL (MA). Part-time and evening/weekend programs available. *Faculty:* 5 full-time (4 women), 5 part-time/adjunct (3 women). *Students:* 123 full-time (86 women), 17 part-time (13 women); includes 12 minority (6 Black or African American, non-Hispanic/Latino; 2 American Indian or Alaska Native, non-Hispanic/Latino; 1 Hispanic/Latino; 3 Two or more races, non-Hispanic/Latino), 3 international. Average age 34. 45 applicants, 64% accepted, 28 enrolled. In 2013, 46 master's awarded. *Entrance requirements:* For master's, minimum GPA of 3.0, writing sample, recommendation, interview; for Advanced Certificate, foreign language. Additional exam requirements/recommendations for international students: Required—TOEFL (minimum score 580 paper-based; 92 iBT). *Application deadline:* Applications are processed on a rolling basis. Electronic applications accepted. *Expenses:* Contact institution. *Financial support:* In 2013–14, 9 students received support, including 1 research assistantship; career-related internships or fieldwork also available. Support available to part-time students. Financial award applicants required to submit FAFSA. *Unit head:* Deana Angotti, Director of Graduate Education, 816-501-2446, Fax: 816-501-2915, E-mail: deana.angotti@avila.edu. *Application contact:* Margaret Longstreet, Office Manager, 816-501-2464, E-mail: margaret.longstreet@avila.edu.

Azusa Pacific University, School of Education, Azusa, CA 91702-7000. Offers M Ed, MA, MA Ed, Ed D, Credential. Part-time and evening/weekend programs available. *Degree requirements:* For doctorate, oral defense of dissertation, qualifying exam. *Entrance requirements:* For master's, minimum GPA of 3.0; for doctorate, GRE General Test or MAT, 5 years of experience, writing sample. Additional exam requirements/recommendations for international students: Required—TOEFL.

Baker University, School of Education, Baldwin City, KS 66006-0065. Offers MA Ed, MSSE, MSSL, MST, Ed D. Master-level programs also offered in Wichita, KS. *Accreditation:* NCATE. Part-time and evening/weekend programs available. Postbaccalaureate distance learning degree programs offered (minimal on-campus study). *Students:* 38 full-time (29 women), 436 part-time (322 women); includes 49 minority (19 Black or African American, non-Hispanic/Latino; 4 American Indian or Alaska Native, non-Hispanic/Latino; 2 Asian, non-Hispanic/Latino; 18 Hispanic/Latino; 6 Two or more races, non-Hispanic/Latino). Average age 35. In 2013, 26,021 master's, 12 doctorates awarded. *Degree requirements:* For master's, portfolio of learning; for doctorate, thesis/dissertation, portfolio of learning. *Entrance requirements:* For master's, 2 years' full-time work experience, teaching certificate; for doctorate, interview. Additional exam requirements/recommendations for international students: Required—TOEFL (minimum score 600 paper-based; 100 iBT). *Application deadline:* Applications are processed on a rolling basis. *Expenses:* Contact institution. *Financial support:* Applicants required to submit FAFSA. *Unit head:* Dr. Tes Mehring, Interim Dean of the School of Education, 913-344-1236, E-mail: tmehring@bakeru.edu. *Application contact:* Linda Reynolds, Director of Graduate Education Enrollment, 913-344-6037, E-mail: linda.reynolds@bakeru.edu. Website: http://www.bakeru.edu/soe-home.

Baldwin Wallace University, Graduate Programs, Division of Education, Berea, OH 44017-2088. Offers educational technology (MA Ed); leadership in higher education (MA Ed); literacy (MA Ed); mild/moderate educational needs (MA Ed); school leadership (MA Ed). *Accreditation:* NCATE. Part-time and evening/weekend programs available. Postbaccalaureate distance learning degree programs offered (no on-campus study). *Faculty:* 8 full-time (3 women), 15 part-time/adjunct (7 women). *Students:* 88 full-time (68 women), 85 part-time (63 women); includes 17 minority (12 Black or African American, non-Hispanic/Latino; 1 Asian, non-Hispanic/Latino; 2 Hispanic/Latino; 2 Two or more races, non-Hispanic/Latino), 1 international. Average age 31. 132 applicants, 48% accepted, 37 enrolled. In 2013, 79 master's awarded. *Degree requirements:* For master's, comprehensive exam, capstone practica or portfolio. *Entrance requirements:* For master's, bachelor's degree in field, MAT or minimum GPA of 2.75. Additional exam requirements/recommendations for international students: Required—TOEFL (minimum score 523 paper-based; 70 iBT). *Application deadline:* For fall admission, 8/15 priority date for domestic students; for spring admission, 12/15 priority date for domestic students. Applications are processed on a rolling basis. Application fee: $25. Electronic applications accepted. Application fee is waived when completed online. *Expenses:* Contact institution. *Financial support:* Career-related internships or fieldwork available.

Support available to part-time students. Financial award application deadline: 5/1; financial award applicants required to submit FAFSA. *Faculty research:* Literacy, technology and literacy, diversity in education, assessment, special education, research methodology, leadership, and organizations. *Unit head:* Dr. Karen Kaye, Chair, 440-826-2168, Fax: 440-826-3779, E-mail: kkaye@bw.edu. *Application contact:* Winifred W. Gerhardt, Director of Admission, Adult and Graduate Programs, 440-826-2222, Fax: 440-826-3830, E-mail: admission@bw.edu. Website: http://www.bw.edu/academics/mae/programs/.

Ball State University, Graduate School, Teachers College, Muncie, IN 47306-1099. Offers MA, MAE, Ed D, PhD, Ed S, Graduate Certificate. *Accreditation:* NCATE. Part-time and evening/weekend programs available. Postbaccalaureate distance learning degree programs offered (no on-campus study). *Faculty:* 85 full-time (54 women), 46 part-time/adjunct (31 women). *Students:* 566 full-time (430 women), 1,468 part-time (1,173 women); includes 185 minority (112 Black or African American, non-Hispanic/Latino; 8 American Indian or Alaska Native, non-Hispanic/Latino; 13 Asian, non-Hispanic/Latino; 34 Hispanic/Latino; 2 Native Hawaiian or other Pacific Islander, non-Hispanic/Latino; 16 Two or more races, non-Hispanic/Latino), 47 international. Average age 28. 1,602 applicants, 55% accepted, 344 enrolled. In 2013, 909 master's, 34 doctorates, 218 other advanced degrees awarded. Terminal master's awarded for partial completion of doctoral program. *Degree requirements:* For doctorate, comprehensive exam, thesis/dissertation; for other advanced degree, comprehensive exam, thesis. *Entrance requirements:* For master's, minimum undergraduate GPA of 2.75 (for most programs); for doctorate, GRE General Test, minimum graduate GPA of 3.2; for other advanced degree, GRE General Test. Additional exam requirements/recommendations for international students: Required—TOEFL (minimum score 550 paper-based), IELTS (minimum score 6.5). *Application deadline:* For fall admission, 1/1 priority date for international students. Application fee: $50. *Financial support:* In 2013–14, 194 students received support, including 130 teaching assistantships with full tuition reimbursements available (averaging $9,846 per year); research assistantships with full tuition reimbursements available, career-related internships or fieldwork, and Federal Work-Study also available. Support available to part-time students. Financial award application deadline: 3/1. *Unit head:* Dr. John E. Jacobson, Dean, 765-285-5251, Fax: 765-285-5455, E-mail: jejacobson@bsu.edu. *Application contact:* Dr. Robert Morris, Associate Provost for Research and Dean of the Graduate School, 765-285-1300, E-mail: rmorris@bsu.edu. Website: http://www.bsu.edu/teachers/.

Bank Street College of Education, Graduate School, New York, NY 10025. Offers Ed M, MS, MS Ed. *Degree requirements:* For master's, thesis. *Entrance requirements:* For master's, interview, essays. Additional exam requirements/recommendations for international students: Required—TOEFL (minimum score 600 paper-based; 100 iBT), IELTS (minimum score 7). Electronic applications accepted. *Faculty research:* Understanding developmental variations in inclusive classrooms, urban teacher education and technology, learner-centered education, improving teacher preparation.

Bard College, Master of Arts in Teaching Program, Annandale-on-Hudson, NY 12504. Offers MAT, MS/MAT. Part-time and evening/weekend programs available. *Degree requirements:* For master's, educational and disciplinary coursework and research; middle and high school teaching placements. *Entrance requirements:* For master's, resume, 3 letters of recommendation, personal statement, official transcripts. Additional exam requirements/recommendations for international students: Required—TOEFL. Electronic applications accepted.

Barry University, School of Education, Miami Shores, FL 33161-6695. Offers MS, Ed D, PhD, Certificate, Ed S. Part-time and evening/weekend programs available. Postbaccalaureate distance learning degree programs offered. *Degree requirements:* For master's, comprehensive exam; for doctorate, thesis/dissertation. *Entrance requirements:* For master's, GRE General Test or MAT, minimum GPA of 3.0; for doctorate, GRE General Test, minimum GPA of 3.25; for other advanced degree, GRE General Test, minimum GPA of 3.0. Additional exam requirements/recommendations for international students: Required—TOEFL (minimum score 550 paper-based). Electronic applications accepted.

Bayamón Central University, Graduate Programs, Program in Education, Bayamón, PR 00960-1725. Offers administration and supervision (MA Ed); commercial education (MA Ed); elementary education (K–3) (MA Ed); family counseling (Graduate Certificate); guidance and counseling (MA Ed); pre-elementary teacher (MA Ed); rehabilitation counseling (MA Ed); special education (MA Ed), including attention deficit disorder, education of the autistic, learning disabilities. Part-time and evening/weekend programs available. *Degree requirements:* For master's, comprehensive exam. *Entrance requirements:* For master's, EXADEP, bachelor's degree in education or related field.

Baylor University, Graduate School, School of Education, Waco, TX 76798. Offers MA, MPH, MS Ed, Ed D, PhD, Ed S. *Accreditation:* NCATE. Part-time programs available. Postbaccalaureate distance learning degree programs offered (minimal on-campus study). *Faculty:* 44 full-time (20 women). *Students:* 168 full-time (112 women), 65 part-time (40 women); includes 49 minority (12 Black or African American, non-Hispanic/Latino; 1 American Indian or Alaska Native, non-Hispanic/Latino; 9 Asian, non-Hispanic/Latino; 22 Hispanic/Latino; 5 Two or more races, non-Hispanic/Latino), 15 international. 248 applicants, 35% accepted, 28 enrolled. In 2013, 88 master's, 9 doctorates, 8 other advanced degrees awarded. *Degree requirements:* For master's, thesis; for doctorate, thesis/dissertation. *Entrance requirements:* Additional exam requirements/recommendations for international students: Required—TOEFL. *Application deadline:* Applications are processed on a rolling basis. Application fee: $25. Electronic applications accepted. *Expenses: Tuition:* Full-time $25,866; part-time $1437 per credit hour. *Required fees:* $2736; $152 per credit hour. Tuition and fees vary according to course load and program. *Financial support:* In 2013–14, 181 students received support, including 38 research assistantships (averaging $12,050 per year), 68 teaching assistantships (averaging $12,050 per year); career-related internships or fieldwork, Federal Work-Study, institutionally sponsored loans, scholarships/grants, and tuition waivers (partial) also available. Financial award applicants required to submit FAFSA. *Unit head:* Dr. Jon Engelhardt, Dean, 254-710-3111, Fax: 254-710-3987. *Application contact:* Julie Baker, Administrative Assistant, 254-710-3050, Fax: 254-710-3870, E-mail: julie_baker@baylor.edu. Website: http://www.baylor.edu/soe/.

Belhaven University, School of Education, Jackson, MS 39202-1789. Offers educational technology (M Ed); elementary education (M Ed, MAT); reading literacy (M Ed); secondary education (M Ed, MAT). Part-time and evening/weekend programs available. Postbaccalaureate distance learning degree programs offered (no on-campus study). *Faculty:* 7 full-time (6 women), 15 part-time/adjunct (10 women). *Students:* 1 full-time (0 women), 406 part-time (311 women); includes 254 minority (250 Black or African American, non-Hispanic/Latino; 2 Hispanic/Latino; 2 Two or more races, non-Hispanic/Latino). Average age 36. 273 applicants, 67% accepted, 162 enrolled. In 2013, 24 master's awarded. *Degree requirements:* For master's, comprehensive exam, portfolio. *Entrance requirements:* For master's, PRAXIS I and II, minimum GPA of 2.8. *Application deadline:* Applications are processed on a rolling basis. Application fee: $25. Electronic applications accepted. *Financial support:* Federal Work-Study, scholarships/grants, tuition waivers (full), and unspecified assistantships available. Support available to part-

time students. Financial award applicants required to submit FAFSA. *Unit head:* Dr. David Hand, Dean, 601-965-7020, E-mail: dhand@belhaven.edu. *Application contact:* Amanda Slaughter, Assistant Vice President for Adult and Graduate Enrollment and Student Services, 601-968-8727, Fax: 601-968-5953, E-mail: gradadmission@belhaven.edu.
Website: http://graduateed.belhaven.edu.

Bellarmine University, Annsley Frazier Thornton School of Education, Louisville, KY 40205-0671. Offers education and social change (PhD); elementary education (MA Ed, MAT); learning and behavior disorders (MA Ed, MAT); middle grades education (MA Ed, MAT); principalship (Ed S); reading and writing (MA Ed); secondary education (MAT); teacher leadership (MA Ed). *Accreditation:* NCATE. Part-time and evening/weekend programs available. *Faculty:* 13 full-time (7 women), 14 part-time/adjunct (9 women). *Students:* 60 full-time (47 women), 191 part-time (140 women); includes 35 minority (22 Black or African American, non-Hispanic/Latino; 1 American Indian or Alaska Native, non-Hispanic/Latino; 3 Asian, non-Hispanic/Latino; 5 Hispanic/Latino; 4 Two or more races, non-Hispanic/Latino). Average age 33. In 2013, 108 master's awarded. *Degree requirements:* For master's, comprehensive exam, thesis (for some programs); for doctorate, comprehensive exam, thesis/dissertation. *Entrance requirements:* For master's, GRE, baccalaureate degree from accredited institution; minimum overall GPA of 2.75, 3.0 in major; letters of recommendation; valid Kentucky provisional or professional certificate; for doctorate, GRE, minimum GPA of 3.5 in all graduate coursework; baccalaureate and master's degrees in education (MA, MS) or fields directly relevant to education; three letters of recommendation; two essays (no more than 1000 words each); interview. Additional exam requirements/recommendations for international students: Required—TOEFL (minimum score 550 paper-based; 80 iBT). *Application deadline:* Applications are processed on a rolling basis. Application fee: $25. *Expenses:* Contact institution. *Financial support:* Scholarships/grants available. Financial award applicants required to submit FAFSA. *Faculty research:* Literacy, service-learning, dispositions, educational technology, special education. *Unit head:* Dr. Robert Cooter, Dean, 502-272-8191, Fax: 502-272-8189, E-mail: rcooter@bellarmine.edu. *Application contact:* Theresa Klapheke, Administrative Director of Graduate Programs, 502-272-8271, Fax: 502-272-8002, E-mail: tklapheke@bellarmine.edu.
Website: http://www.bellarmine.edu/education/graduate.

Belmont University, College of Arts and Sciences, Nashville, TN 37212-3757. Offers education (M Ed); English (MA); special education (MA); sport administration (MSA); teaching (MAT). Part-time and evening/weekend programs available. *Faculty:* 29 full-time (21 women), 24 part-time/adjunct (12 women). *Students:* 144 full-time (97 women), 63 part-time (49 women); includes 26 minority (9 Black or African American, non-Hispanic/Latino; 1 Asian, non-Hispanic/Latino; 8 Hispanic/Latino; 8 Two or more races, non-Hispanic/Latino), 3 international. Average age 29. 201 applicants, 57% accepted, 81 enrolled. *Degree requirements:* For master's, comprehensive exam (for some programs), thesis (for some programs). *Entrance requirements:* For master's, GRE, GMAT, MAT. Additional exam requirements/recommendations for international students: Required—TOEFL. *Application deadline:* For fall admission, 8/1 for domestic students; for spring admission, 12/1 for domestic students. Applications are processed on a rolling basis. Application fee: $50. Electronic applications accepted. *Expenses:* Contact institution. *Financial support:* In 2013–14, 50 students received support. Fellowships with partial tuition reimbursements available, teaching assistantships with partial tuition reimbursements available, Federal Work-Study, institutionally sponsored loans, scholarships/grants, tuition waivers (partial), and unspecified assistantships available. Financial award application deadline: 4/15; financial award applicants required to submit FAFSA. *Unit head:* Dr. Bryce Sullivan, Dean, 615-460-6437, Fax: 615-385-5084, E-mail: bryce.sullivan@belmont.edu. *Application contact:* David Mee, Dean of Enrollment Services, 615-460-6785, Fax: 615-460-5434, E-mail: david.mee@belmont.edu.

Bemidji State University, School of Graduate Studies, Bemidji, MN 56601. Offers biology (MS); education (MS); English (MA, MS); environmental studies (MS); mathematics (MS); mathematics (elementary and middle level education) (MS); special education (M Sp Ed, MS). Part-time programs available. Postbaccalaureate distance learning degree programs offered (no on-campus study). *Faculty:* 117 full-time (53 women), 20 part-time/adjunct (15 women). *Students:* 30 full-time (17 women), 157 part-time (108 women); includes 16 minority (2 Black or African American, non-Hispanic/Latino; 4 American Indian or Alaska Native, non-Hispanic/Latino; 2 Asian, non-Hispanic/Latino; 1 Hispanic/Latino; 7 Two or more races, non-Hispanic/Latino), 1 international. Average age 35. 73 applicants, 93% accepted, 38 enrolled. In 2013, 49 master's awarded. *Degree requirements:* For master's, comprehensive exam, thesis (for some programs). *Entrance requirements:* For master's, GRE; GMAT, letters of recommendation, letters of interest. Additional exam requirements/recommendations for international students: Required—TOEFL (minimum score 550 paper-based; 80 iBT). *Application deadline:* Applications are processed on a rolling basis. Application fee: $20. Electronic applications accepted. *Expenses:* Tuition, state resident: full-time $6941; part-time $365 per credit. Tuition, nonresident: full-time $6941; part-time $365 per credit. *Required fees:* $16 per credit. Tuition and fees vary according to program and reciprocity agreements. *Financial support:* In 2013–14, 131 students received support, including 18 research assistantships with partial tuition reimbursements available (averaging $12,889 per year), 23 teaching assistantships with partial tuition reimbursements available (averaging $12,889 per year); scholarships/grants and unspecified assistantships also available. Financial award application deadline: 3/31; financial award applicants required to submit FAFSA. *Faculty research:* Human performance, sport, and health: physical education teacher education, continuum models, spiritual health, intellectual health, resiliency, health priorities; psychology: health psychology, college student drinking behavior, micro-aggressions, infant cognition, false memories, leadership assessment; biology: structure and dynamics of forest communities, aquatic and riverine ecology, interaction between animal populations and aquatic environments, cellular motility. *Unit head:* Dr. James Barta, Interim Dean of Health Sciences and Human Ecology, 218-755-3874, Fax: 218-755-2258, E-mail: jbarta@bemidjistate.edu. *Application contact:* Joan Miller, Director, School of Graduate Studies, 218-755-2027, Fax: 218-755-2258, E-mail: jmiller@bemidjistate.edu.
Website: http://www.bemidjistate.edu/academics/graduate_studies/.

Benedictine University, Graduate Programs, Program in Education, Lisle, IL 60532-0900. Offers curriculum and instruction and collaborative teaching (M Ed); elementary education (MA Ed); leadership and administration (M Ed); reading and literacy (M Ed); secondary education (MA Ed); special education (MA Ed). Part-time and evening/weekend programs available. *Students:* 6 full-time (all women), 124 part-time (106 women); includes 14 minority (8 Black or African American, non-Hispanic/Latino; 1 American Indian or Alaska Native, non-Hispanic/Latino; 2 Asian, non-Hispanic/Latino; 3 Hispanic/Latino). 21 applicants, 62% accepted, 8 enrolled. In 2013, 120 master's awarded. *Degree requirements:* For master's, comprehensive exam, thesis (for some programs). *Entrance requirements:* For master's, GRE or MAT. Additional exam requirements/recommendations for international students: Required—TOEFL (minimum score 550 paper-based). *Application deadline:* For fall admission, 9/1 for domestic students; for winter admission, 12/1 for domestic students; for spring admission, 2/15 for domestic students. Applications are processed on a rolling basis. Application fee: $40. Electronic applications accepted. *Expenses:* Contact institution. *Financial support:* Career-related internships or fieldwork and health care benefits available. Support available to part-time students. *Unit head:* MeShelda Jackson, Director, 630-829-6282, E-mail: mjackson@ben.edu. *Application contact:* Kari Gibbons, Associate Vice President, Enrollment Center, 630-829-6200, Fax: 630-829-6584, E-mail: kgibbons@ben.edu.

Bennington College, Graduate Programs, MA in Teaching a Second Language Program, Bennington, VT 05201. Offers education (MATSL); foreign language education (MATSL); French (MATSL); Spanish (MATSL). Part-time programs available. *Degree requirements:* For master's, one foreign language, 2 major projects and presentations. *Entrance requirements:* For master's, Oral Proficiency Interview (OPI). Additional exam requirements/recommendations for international students: Required—TOEFL (minimum score 577 paper-based; 91 iBT). *Expenses:* Contact institution. *Faculty research:* Acquisition, evaluation, assessment, conceptual teaching and learning, content-driven communication, applied linguistics.

Berry College, Graduate Programs, Graduate Programs in Education, Mount Berry, GA 30149-0159. Offers curriculum and instruction (M Ed, Ed S), including curriculum and instruction (Ed S); early childhood education (M Ed, MAT); educational leadership (Ed S); middle grades education and reading (M Ed, MAT), including middle grades education, reading (M Ed); secondary education (M Ed, MAT). *Accreditation:* NCATE. Part-time programs available. *Faculty:* 24 part-time/adjunct (15 women). *Students:* 12 full-time (11 women), 46 part-time (34 women); includes 7 minority (6 Black or African American, non-Hispanic/Latino; 1 Hispanic/Latino). Average age 34. In 2013, 22 master's, 45 other advanced degrees awarded. *Degree requirements:* For master's and Ed S, thesis, portfolio, oral exams. *Entrance requirements:* For master's, GRE General Test or MAT, minimum GPA of 2.5; for Ed S, M Ed from NCATE-accredited school, minimum GPA of 3.25. Additional exam requirements/recommendations for international students: Required—TOEFL (minimum score 550 paper-based). *Application deadline:* For fall admission, 7/25 for domestic students, 5/1 for international students; for spring admission, 12/1 for domestic students, 10/1 for international students. Applications are processed on a rolling basis. Application fee: $25 ($30 for international students). *Expenses:* Contact institution. *Financial support:* In 2013–14, 23 students received support, including 12 research assistantships with full tuition reimbursements available (averaging $4,174 per year); scholarships/grants, tuition waivers (partial), and unspecified assistantships also available. Support available to part-time students. Financial award application deadline: 3/1; financial award applicants required to submit FAFSA. *Unit head:* Dr. Jacqueline McDowell, Dean, Charter School of Education and Human Sciences, 706-236-1717, Fax: 706-238-5827, E-mail: jmcdowell@berry.edu. *Application contact:* Brett Kennedy, Assistant Vice President of Enrollment Management, 706-236-2215, Fax: 706-290-2178, E-mail: admissions@berry.edu.
Website: http://www.berry.edu/academics/education/graduate/.

Bethany College, Master of Arts in Teaching Program, Bethany, WV 26032. Offers MAT. Part-time programs available. *Faculty:* 4 full-time (3 women), 1 part-time/adjunct (0 women). *Students:* 28 full-time (15 women), 5 part-time (2 women); includes 1 minority (Black or African American, non-Hispanic/Latino), 1 international. Average age 27. In 2013, 8 master's awarded. *Entrance requirements:* For master's, baccalaureate degree from accredited U.S. college or university or international equivalent; minimum undergraduate GPA of 2.75. Additional exam requirements/recommendations for international students: Required—TOEFL (minimum score 500 paper-based; 90 iBT); Recommended—IELTS (minimum score 7). *Application deadline:* Applications are processed on a rolling basis. Application fee: $0. Electronic applications accepted. *Expenses: Tuition:* Full-time $8100; part-time $450 per credit. *Required fees:* $450; $25 per credit. One-time fee: $150. *Financial support:* Unspecified assistantships available. Financial award applicants required to submit FAFSA. *Unit head:* Dr. Edward Shephard, MAT Program Director, 304-829-7176, E-mail: eshephard@bethanywv.edu. *Application contact:* Mollie Cecere, Director of Enrollment Management, 304-829-7611, E-mail: mcecere@bethanywv.edu.
Website: http://www.bethanywv.edu/academics/graduate-mat/.

Bethel College, Adult and Graduate Programs, Program in Education, Mishawaka, IN 46545-5591. Offers M Ed, MAT. *Accreditation:* NCATE. Part-time programs available. *Faculty:* 10 part-time/adjunct (6 women). *Students:* 10 full-time (8 women), 41 part-time (13 women); includes 3 minority (2 Black or African American, non-Hispanic/Latino; 1 American Indian or Alaska Native, non-Hispanic/Latino). 56 applicants, 70% accepted, 25 enrolled. In 2013, 29 master's awarded. *Entrance requirements:* Additional exam requirements/recommendations for international students: Required—TOEFL (minimum score 540 paper-based). *Application deadline:* For fall admission, 5/1 for international students; for spring admission, 10/1 for international students. Application fee: $25. Electronic applications accepted. *Expenses: Required fees:* $75 per semester. Tuition and fees vary according to program. *Financial support:* Career-related internships or fieldwork available. Financial award applicants required to submit FAFSA. *Unit head:* Dr. Ralph Stutzman, Director, 574-257-3493, E-mail: stutzmr@bethelcollege.edu.

Bethel University, Graduate School, St. Paul, MN 55112-6999. Offers autism spectrum disorders (Certificate); business administration (MBA); communication (MA); counseling psychology (MA); educational leadership (Ed D); gerontology (MA); international baccalaureate education (Certificate); K-12 education (MA); literacy education (MA, Certificate); nurse educator (Certificate); nurse leader (Certificate); nurse-midwifery (MS); nursing (MS); physician assistant (MS); postsecondary teaching (Certificate); special education (MA); strategic leadership (MA); teaching (MA). Part-time and evening/weekend programs available. Postbaccalaureate distance learning degree programs offered (no on-campus study). *Faculty:* 13 full-time (7 women), 89 part-time/adjunct (43 women). *Students:* 692 full-time (457 women), 573 part-time (371 women); includes 170 minority (86 Black or African American, non-Hispanic/Latino; 1 American Indian or Alaska Native, non-Hispanic/Latino; 49 Asian, non-Hispanic/Latino; 20 Hispanic/Latino; 1 Native Hawaiian or other Pacific Islander, non-Hispanic/Latino; 13 Two or more races, non-Hispanic/Latino), 21 international. Average age 37. In 2013, 166 master's, 9 doctorates, 11 other advanced degrees awarded. *Degree requirements:* For master's, comprehensive exam (for some programs), thesis (for some programs); for doctorate, comprehensive exam, thesis/dissertation. *Entrance requirements:* Additional exam requirements/recommendations for international students: Required—TOEFL (minimum score 550 paper-based; 80 iBT). *Application deadline:* Applications are processed on a rolling basis. Electronic applications accepted. Tuition and fees vary according to course load, degree level and program. *Financial support:* Teaching assistantships, career-related internships or fieldwork, and scholarships/grants available. Support available to part-time students. Financial award applicants required to submit FAFSA. *Unit head:* Dick Crombie, Vice-President/Dean, 651-635-8000, Fax: 651-635-8004, E-mail: gs@bethel.edu. *Application contact:* Director of Admissions, 651-635-8000, Fax: 651-635-8004, E-mail: gs@bethel.edu.
Website: http://gs.bethel.edu/.

Binghamton University, State University of New York, Graduate School, School of Education, Vestal, NY 13850. Offers MAT, MS, MS Ed, Ed D, Certificate. *Accreditation:* Teacher Education Accreditation Council. Part-time and evening/weekend programs available. *Faculty:* 22 full-time (16 women), 10 part-time/adjunct (7 women). *Students:*

91 full-time (67 women), 134 part-time (112 women); includes 22 minority (9 Black or African American, non-Hispanic/Latino; 1 American Indian or Alaska Native, non-Hispanic/Latino; 7 Asian, non-Hispanic/Latino; 5 Hispanic/Latino), 7 international. Average age 32. 145 applicants, 78% accepted, 73 enrolled. In 2013, 106 master's, 3 doctorates, 6 other advanced degrees awarded. *Degree requirements:* For doctorate, thesis/dissertation. *Entrance requirements:* For master's, GRE General Test; for doctorate, GRE General Test, writing sample. Additional exam requirements/recommendations for international students: Required—TOEFL (minimum score 550 paper-based; 80 iBT). *Application deadline:* For fall admission, 2/1 priority date for domestic and international students; for spring admission, 10/15 priority date for domestic and international students. Applications are processed on a rolling basis. Application fee: $75. Electronic applications accepted. *Financial support:* In 2013–14, 28 students received support, including 2 fellowships with full tuition reimbursements available (averaging $10,000 per year), 1 teaching assistantship with full tuition reimbursement available (averaging $15,500 per year); career-related internships or fieldwork, Federal Work-Study, institutionally sponsored loans, scholarships/grants, health care benefits, tuition waivers (full and partial), and unspecified assistantships also available. Financial award application deadline: 2/15; financial award applicants required to submit FAFSA. *Unit head:* Dr. S. G. Grant, Dean, 607-777-7329, E-mail: ssgrant@binghamton.edu. *Application contact:* Kishan Zuber, Recruiting and Admissions Coordinator, 607-777-2151, Fax: 607-777-2501, E-mail: kzuber@binghamton.edu. Website: http://sehd.binghamton.edu/.

Biola University, School of Education, La Mirada, CA 90639-0001. Offers apologetics (MA Ed); curriculum and instruction (MA Ed, MAT, Certificate); early childhood (MA Ed, MAT); history and philosophy of science (MA Ed, MAT); linguistics and inter-cultural studies (MAT); linguistics and international studies (MA Ed); multiple subject (MAT); single subject (MAT); special education (MA Ed, MAT, Certificate); TESOL (MA Ed, MAT). Part-time and evening/weekend programs available. Postbaccalaureate distance learning degree programs offered (no on-campus study). *Faculty:* 14. *Students:* 51 full-time (38 women), 101 part-time (83 women); includes 47 minority (8 Black or African American, non-Hispanic/Latino; 1 American Indian or Alaska Native, non-Hispanic/Latino; 32 Asian, non-Hispanic/Latino; 6 Two or more races, non-Hispanic/Latino), 4 international. In 2013, 33 master's awarded. *Entrance requirements:* For master's, CBEST, CSET. Additional exam requirements/recommendations for international students: Required—TOEFL (minimum score 100 iBT). *Application deadline:* For fall admission, 7/1 for domestic students, 6/1 for international students; for spring admission, 12/1 for domestic students; for summer admission, 5/1 for domestic students. Applications are processed on a rolling basis. Application fee: $55. Electronic applications accepted. *Financial support:* Scholarships/grants available. Support available to part-time students. Financial award applicants required to submit FAFSA. *Faculty research:* Early childhood education, elementary education, special education, curriculum development, teacher preparation. *Unit head:* Dr. June Hetzel, Dean, 562-903-4715. *Application contact:* Graduate Admissions Office, 562-903-4752, E-mail: graduate.admissions@biola.edu. Website: http://education.biola.edu/.

Bishop's University, School of Education, Sherbrooke, QC J1M 0C8, Canada. Offers advanced studies in education (Diploma); education (M Ed, MA); teaching English as a second language (Certificate). Part-time programs available. Postbaccalaureate distance learning degree programs offered (minimal on-campus study). *Degree requirements:* For master's, thesis (for some programs). *Entrance requirements:* For master's, teaching license, 2 years of teaching experience. *Faculty research:* Integration of special needs students, multigrade classes/small schools, leadership in organizational development, second language acquisition.

Bloomsburg University of Pennsylvania, School of Graduate Studies, College of Education, Bloomsburg, PA 17815-1301. Offers M Ed, MS, Certificate. *Accreditation:* NCATE. *Faculty:* 30 full-time (16 women), 11 part-time/adjunct (7 women). *Students:* 113 full-time (91 women), 98 part-time (72 women); includes 19 minority (10 Black or African American, non-Hispanic/Latino; 1 Asian, non-Hispanic/Latino; 6 Hispanic/Latino; 2 Two or more races, non-Hispanic/Latino), 1 international. Average age 29. 186 applicants, 84% accepted, 71 enrolled. In 2013, 164 master's awarded. *Degree requirements:* For master's, thesis optional. *Entrance requirements:* For master's, minimum QPA of 3.0. Additional exam requirements/recommendations for international students: Required—TOEFL. Application fee: $35 ($60 for international students). Electronic applications accepted. *Expenses:* Tuition, state resident: full-time $7956; part-time $442 per credit. Tuition, nonresident: full-time $11,934; part-time $663 per credit. *Required fees:* $95.50 per credit. $55 per semester. Tuition and fees vary according to course load. *Financial support:* Unspecified assistantships available. *Unit head:* Dr. Tegan Kotarski, College of Education Graduate Coordinator, 570-389-3883, Fax: 570-389-5049, E-mail: tkotarsk@bloomu.edu. *Application contact:* Jennifer Richard, Administrative Assistant, 570-389-4015, Fax: 570-389-3054, E-mail: jrichard@bloomu.edu. Website: http://www.bloomu.edu/coe.

Bluffton University, Program in Education, Bluffton, OH 45817. Offers MA Ed. *Accreditation:* NCATE. Part-time programs available. *Degree requirements:* For master's, action research project, public presentation. *Entrance requirements:* Additional exam requirements/recommendations for international students: Required—TOEFL. Electronic applications accepted. *Faculty research:* Mentoring.

Boise State University, College of Education, Boise, ID 83725-0399. Offers M Ed, MA, MET, MK, MPE, MS, MS Ed, Ed D, Graduate Certificate. *Accreditation:* NCATE. Part-time programs available. *Degree requirements:* For doctorate, thesis/dissertation. *Entrance requirements:* For master's, minimum GPA of 3.0; for doctorate, GRE General Test, minimum GPA of 3.0. Electronic applications accepted.

Boston College, Lynch Graduate School of Education, Chestnut Hill, MA 02467. Offers M Ed, MA, MAT, MST, Ed D, PhD, CAES, JD/M Ed, JD/MA, M Ed/MA, MA/MA, MBA/MA. *Accreditation:* Teacher Education Accreditation Council. Part-time and evening/weekend programs available. *Faculty:* 55 full-time (33 women), 54 part-time/adjunct (35 women). *Students:* 229 full-time (172 women), 162 part-time (119 women); includes 86 minority (25 Black or African American, non-Hispanic/Latino; 2 American Indian or Alaska Native, non-Hispanic/Latino; 22 Asian, non-Hispanic/Latino; 26 Hispanic/Latino; 11 Two or more races, non-Hispanic/Latino). 1,826 applicants, 53% accepted, 391 enrolled. In 2013, 311 master's, 20 doctorates, 6 other advanced degrees awarded. Terminal master's awarded for partial completion of doctoral program. *Degree requirements:* For master's, comprehensive exam (for some programs); for doctorate, comprehensive exam, thesis/dissertation. *Entrance requirements:* For master's, letters of recommendation, transcripts, personal statement, resume; for doctorate, letters of recommendation, transcripts, writing sample, personal statement, resume. Additional exam requirements/recommendations for international students: Required—TOEFL (minimum score 100 iBT). *Application deadline:* For fall admission, 12/1 priority date for domestic and international students; for spring admission, 11/1 for domestic and international students. Application fee: $65. Electronic applications accepted. *Financial support:* Fellowships with full and partial tuition reimbursements, research assistantships with full and partial tuition reimbursements, teaching assistantships with full and partial tuition reimbursements, career-related internships or fieldwork, Federal

Work-Study, scholarships/grants, traineeships, health care benefits, tuition waivers (partial), and unspecified assistantships available. Support available to part-time students. Financial award applicants required to submit FAFSA. *Unit head:* Dr. Maureen Kenny, Dean, 617-552-4200, Fax: 617-552-0812. *Application contact:* Domenic Lomanno, Director, Graduate Admission and Financial Aid, 617-552-4214, Fax: 617-552-0398, E-mail: domenic.lomanno@bc.edu. Website: http://www.bc.edu/education/.

Boston University, School of Education, Boston, MA 02215. Offers Ed M, MAT, Ed D, CAGS. Part-time programs available. *Faculty:* 57 full-time, 39 part-time/adjunct. *Students:* 214 full-time (155 women), 340 part-time (256 women); includes 93 minority (21 Black or African American, non-Hispanic/Latino; 3 American Indian or Alaska Native, non-Hispanic/Latino; 25 Asian, non-Hispanic/Latino; 33 Hispanic/Latino; 11 Two or more races, non-Hispanic/Latino), 63 international. Average age 29. 1,270 applicants, 66% accepted, 292 enrolled. In 2013, 251 master's, 16 doctorates, 14 other advanced degrees awarded. Terminal master's awarded for partial completion of doctoral program. *Degree requirements:* For master's, thesis (for some programs); for doctorate, comprehensive exam, thesis/dissertation; for CAGS, comprehensive exam. *Entrance requirements:* For master's and CAGS, GRE General Test or MAT; for doctorate, GRE General Test. Additional exam requirements/recommendations for international students: Required—TOEFL, IELTS. *Application deadline:* For fall admission, 1/15 priority date for domestic and international students; for spring admission, 9/15 priority date for domestic and international students. Applications are processed on a rolling basis. Application fee: $70. Electronic applications accepted. *Expenses: Tuition:* Full-time $43,970; part-time $1374 per credit hour. *Required fees:* $60 per semester. Tuition and fees vary according to class time, course level and program. *Financial support:* In 2013–14, 276 students received support, including 31 fellowships with full tuition reimbursements available, 16 research assistantships, 26 teaching assistantships with partial tuition reimbursements available; career-related internships or fieldwork, Federal Work-Study, and scholarships/grants also available. Support available to part-time students. Financial award applicants required to submit FAFSA. *Faculty research:* Deaf studies, social emotional learning, civic engagement and education, STEM education, pre-college educational pipelines. *Total annual research expenditures:* $2.6 million. *Unit head:* Dr. Hardin Coleman, Dean, 617-353-3213. *Application contact:* Katherine Nelson, Director of Enrollment, 617-353-4237, Fax: 617-353-8937, E-mail: sedgrad@bu.edu. Website: http://www.bu.edu/sed.

Bowie State University, Graduate Programs, Program in Teaching, Bowie, MD 20715-9465. Offers MAT. *Accreditation:* NCATE. Part-time and evening/weekend programs available. *Entrance requirements:* For master's, PRAXIS I. Electronic applications accepted. *Expenses:* Tuition, state resident: full-time $8665. Tuition, nonresident: full-time $16,007. *Required fees:* $1927.

Bradley University, Graduate School, College of Education and Health Sciences, Peoria, IL 61625-0002. Offers MA, MSN, DPT, Certificate. *Accreditation:* NCATE. Part-time and evening/weekend programs available. *Degree requirements:* For master's, comprehensive exam, thesis optional. *Entrance requirements:* For master's, GRE General Test or MAT, letters of recommendation; for doctorate, GRE, letters of recommendation. Additional exam requirements/recommendations for international students: Required—TOEFL (minimum score 550 paper-based; 79 iBT). *Expenses: Tuition:* Full-time $14,580; part-time $810 per credit hour. Tuition and fees vary according to course load and program. *Faculty research:* Health care, professional nurse traineeship, gifted education.

Brandman University, School of Education, Irvine, CA 92618. Offers education (MA); educational leadership (MA); school counseling (MA); special education (MA); teaching (MA).

Brandon University, Faculty of Education, Brandon, MB R7A 6A9, Canada. Offers curriculum and instruction (M Ed, Diploma); educational administration (M Ed, Diploma); guidance and counseling (M Ed, Diploma); special education (M Ed, Diploma). *Degree requirements:* For master's, thesis. *Entrance requirements:* For master's, minimum GPA of 3.0, teaching certificate or equivalent. Additional exam requirements/recommendations for international students: Required—TOEFL. *Faculty research:* Comparative education, environmental studies, parent/school council.

Brenau University, Sydney O. Smith Graduate School, School of Education, Gainesville, GA 30501. Offers early childhood (Ed S); early childhood education (M Ed, MAT); middle grades (Ed S); middle grades education (M Ed, MAT); secondary education (MAT); special education (M Ed, MAT). *Accreditation:* NCATE. Part-time and evening/weekend programs available. Postbaccalaureate distance learning degree programs offered (no on-campus study). *Degree requirements:* For master's, thesis optional, comprehensive exam or applied research project, effective portfolio; for Ed S, thesis, applied research project. *Entrance requirements:* For master's, GRE, MAT, interview, minimum GPA of 3.0, 3 references, writing samples; for Ed S, GRE, MAT, master's degree, minimum GPA of 3.0, writing sample, letters of reference. Additional exam requirements/recommendations for international students: Required—TOEFL (minimum score 500 paper-based; 61 iBT); Recommended—IELTS (minimum score 5). Electronic applications accepted. *Expenses:* Contact institution.

Bridgewater State University, School of Graduate Studies, School of Education and Allied Studies, Bridgewater, MA 02325-0001. Offers M Ed, MAT, MS, CAGS. *Accreditation:* NCATE. Part-time and evening/weekend programs available. *Degree requirements:* For CAGS, comprehensive exam. *Entrance requirements:* For master's, GRE General Test or Massachusetts Test for Educator Licensure; for CAGS, master's degree. Additional exam requirements/recommendations for international students: Required—TOEFL.

Brigham Young University, Graduate Studies, David O. McKay School of Education, Provo, UT 84602. Offers M Ed, MA, MS, Ed D, PhD, Ed S. *Accreditation:* Teacher Education Accreditation Council. Part-time programs available. *Faculty:* 71 full-time (26 women), 16 part-time/adjunct (8 women). *Students:* 192 full-time (126 women), 98 part-time (46 women); includes 23 minority (2 Black or African American, non-Hispanic/Latino; 5 Asian, non-Hispanic/Latino; 11 Hispanic/Latino; 5 Native Hawaiian or other Pacific Islander, non-Hispanic/Latino), 10 international. Average age 32. 231 applicants, 45% accepted, 89 enrolled. In 2013, 65 master's, 25 doctorates, 10 other advanced degrees awarded. *Degree requirements:* For master's, comprehensive exam, thesis; for doctorate, comprehensive exam, thesis/dissertation; for Ed S, comprehensive exam (for some programs). *Entrance requirements:* For master's, GRE, MAT, LSAT, minimum GPA of 3.25, minimum 1 year of teaching experience, letters of recommendation; for doctorate, GRE, MAT, LSAT, minimum GPA of 3.0 in last 60 hours of undergraduate coursework. Additional exam requirements/recommendations for international students: Required—TOEFL (minimum score 580 paper-based; 85 iBT) or IELTS (minimum score 7). *Application deadline:* For fall admission, 1/2 for domestic and international students; for winter admission, 2/1 for domestic and international students; for spring admission, 1/15 for domestic and international students; for summer admission, 1/15 for domestic and international students. Application fee: $50. Electronic applications accepted. *Expenses: Tuition:* Full-time $6130; part-time $340 per credit hour. Tuition and fees vary according to program and student's religious affiliation. *Financial support:* In 2013–14, 197 students received support, including 6 fellowships (averaging $15,000 per year), 77

research assistantships with full and partial tuition reimbursements available (averaging $5,202 per year), 36 teaching assistantships with full and partial tuition reimbursements available (averaging $4,868 per year); career-related internships or fieldwork, institutionally sponsored loans, scholarships/grants, tuition waivers (partial), and unspecified assistantships also available. Support available to part-time students. Financial award applicants required to submit FAFSA. *Faculty research:* Reading, learning, teacher education, assessment and evaluation, speech-language pathology. *Unit head:* Dr. Mary Anne Prater, Dean, 801-422-1592, Fax: 801-422-0200, E-mail: prater@byu.edu. *Application contact:* Jay Oliver, Director, Education Student Services, 801-422-1202, Fax: 801-422-0195.
Website: http://education.byu.edu/.

Brock University, Faculty of Graduate Studies, Faculty of Education, St. Catharines, ON L2S 3A1, Canada. Offers M Ed, PhD. Part-time and evening/weekend programs available. *Degree requirements:* For master's, thesis optional; for doctorate, thesis/dissertation. *Entrance requirements:* For master's, 1 year of teaching experience, honors degree; for doctorate, master's degree. Additional exam requirements/recommendations for international students: Required—TOEFL (minimum score 550 paper-based; 80 iBT), IELTS (minimum score 6.5), TWE (minimum score 4). Electronic applications accepted. *Expenses:* Contact institution. *Faculty research:* International and comparative education, early childhood education, educational leadership, adult education.

Brooklyn College of the City University of New York, Division of Graduate Studies, School of Education, Brooklyn, NY 11210-2889. Offers MA, MAT, MS Ed, CAS. *Accreditation:* NCATE. Part-time and evening/weekend programs available. *Entrance requirements:* For master's, LAST, 2 letters of recommendation, essay, resume, state teaching certificate; for CAS, master's degree. Additional exam requirements/recommendations for international students: Required—TOEFL (minimum score 500 paper-based; 61 iBT). Electronic applications accepted.

Brown University, Graduate School, Department of Education, Providence, RI 02912. Offers teaching (MAT), including elementary education, English, history/social studies, science, secondary education; urban education policy (AM). *Degree requirements:* For master's, student teaching, portfolio. *Entrance requirements:* For master's, GRE General Test, letters of recommendation, interview. Additional exam requirements/recommendations for international students: Recommended—TOEFL.

Bucknell University, Graduate Studies, College of Arts and Sciences, Department of Education, Lewisburg, PA 17837. Offers college student personnel (MS Ed). Part-time programs available. *Degree requirements:* For master's, comprehensive exam (for some programs), thesis or alternative. *Entrance requirements:* For master's, GRE General Test, minimum GPA of 3.0. Additional exam requirements/recommendations for international students: Required—TOEFL (minimum score 600 paper-based).

Buena Vista University, School of Education, Storm Lake, IA 50588. Offers curriculum and instruction (M Ed), including effective teaching, TESL; school guidance and counseling (MS Ed). Program offered in summer only. Part-time and evening/weekend programs available. Postbaccalaureate distance learning degree programs offered (minimal on-campus study). *Degree requirements:* For master's, thesis, fieldwork/practicum, capstone portfolio. *Entrance requirements:* For master's, Analytical Writing Assessment (in-house), minimum undergraduate GPA of 2.75. Electronic applications accepted. *Faculty research:* Reading, curriculum, educational psychology, special education.

Butler University, College of Education, Indianapolis, IN 46208-3485. Offers educational administration (MS); effective teaching and leadership (MS); school counseling (MS). *Accreditation:* ACA; NCATE. Part-time and evening/weekend programs available. *Faculty:* 6 full-time (4 women), 19 part-time/adjunct (14 women). *Students:* 14 full-time (12 women), 96 part-time (71 women); includes 19 minority (13 Black or African American, non-Hispanic/Latino; 3 Asian, non-Hispanic/Latino; 2 Hispanic/Latino; 1 Two or more races, non-Hispanic/Latino), 3 international. Average age 31. 58 applicants, 79% accepted, 15 enrolled. In 2013, 51 master's awarded. *Entrance requirements:* For master's, GRE General Test, MAT, interview. *Application deadline:* For fall admission, 8/15 priority date for domestic students. Applications are processed on a rolling basis. Application fee: $35. Electronic applications accepted. *Financial support:* Institutionally sponsored loans available. Support available to part-time students. Financial award application deadline: 7/15; financial award applicants required to submit FAFSA. *Unit head:* Dr. Ena Shelley, Dean, 317-940-9752, Fax: 317-940-6481. *Application contact:* Diane Dubord, Graduate Student Services Specialist, 317-940-8100, Fax: 317-940-8250, E-mail: ddubord@butler.edu.
Website: http://www.butler.edu/academics/graduate-coe/.

Cabrini College, Graduate Studies, Radnor, PA 19087-3698. Offers accounting (M Acc); education (M Ed); leadership (MS). Part-time and evening/weekend programs available. *Faculty:* 9 full-time (7 women), 81 part-time/adjunct (64 women). *Students:* 75 full-time (53 women), 1,031 part-time (789 women); includes 135 minority (95 Black or African American, non-Hispanic/Latino; 13 Asian, non-Hispanic/Latino; 24 Hispanic/Latino; 3 Two or more races, non-Hispanic/Latino). Average age 33. 417 applicants, 73% accepted, 261 enrolled. In 2013, 717 master's awarded. *Degree requirements:* For master's, thesis optional. *Entrance requirements:* For master's, GRE and/or MAT (in some cases), bachelor's degree with minimum GPA of 3.0, one-page personal essay/statement, professional letter of recommendation. Additional exam requirements/recommendations for international students: Required—TOEFL. *Application deadline:* For fall admission, 7/29 priority date for domestic students, 7/29 for international students; for spring admission, 12/9 for domestic and international students. Applications are processed on a rolling basis. Application fee: $50. Electronic applications accepted. *Expenses: Tuition:* Part-time $595 per credit hour. *Financial support:* Career-related internships or fieldwork and unspecified assistantships available. Support available to part-time students. Financial award applicants required to submit FAFSA. *Unit head:* Dr. Jeffrey P. Gingerich, Vice Provost/Dean for Academic Affairs, 610-902-8302, Fax: 610-902-8552, E-mail: jeffrey.p.gingerich@cabrini.edu. *Application contact:* Bruce D. Bryde, Director of Enrollment and Recruiting, 610-902-8291, Fax: 610-902-8522, E-mail: bruce.d.bryde@cabrini.edu.
Website: http://cabrini.edu/graduate.

Cairn University, School of Education, Langhorne, PA 19047-2990. Offers educational leadership and administration (MS El); teacher education (MS Ed). Part-time and evening/weekend programs available. *Faculty:* 1 (woman) full-time, 2 part-time/adjunct (both women). *Students:* 6 full-time (3 women), 44 part-time (32 women); includes 20 minority (9 Black or African American, non-Hispanic/Latino; 1 American Indian or Alaska Native, non-Hispanic/Latino; 7 Asian, non-Hispanic/Latino; 2 Hispanic/Latino; 1 Native Hawaiian or other Pacific Islander, non-Hispanic/Latino), 1 international. Average age 37. 15 applicants, 73% accepted, 9 enrolled. In 2013, 28 master's awarded. *Entrance requirements:* Additional exam requirements/recommendations for international students: Required—TOEFL (minimum score 550 paper-based). *Application deadline:* Applications are processed on a rolling basis. Application fee: $25. Electronic applications accepted. *Expenses: Tuition:* Full-time $11,250; part-time $625 per credit. Tuition and fees vary according to program. *Financial support:* Scholarships/grants available. Support available to part-time students. Financial award applicants required to submit FAFSA. *Unit head:* Dr. Paula Gossard, Dean, 215-702-4264, E-mail: teacher.ed@cairn.edu. *Application contact:* Abigail Sattler, Enrollment Counselor, Graduate Education, 800-572-2472, Fax: 215-702-4248, E-mail: asattler@cairn.edu.
Website: http://www.cairn.edu/academics/education.

Caldwell University, Graduate Studies, Division of Education, Caldwell, NJ 07006-6195. Offers curriculum and instruction (MA); education (Postbaccalaureate Certificate); educational administration (MA); learning disabilities teacher-consultant (Post-Master's Certificate); literacy instruction (MA); principal (Post-Master's Certificate); reading specialist (Post-Master's Certificate); special education (MA), including special education, teaching of students with disabilities, teaching of students with disabilities and learning disabilities teacher-consultant; superintendent (Post-Master's Certificate); supervisor (Post-Master's Certificate). Part-time and evening/weekend programs available. *Faculty:* 11 full-time (7 women), 12 part-time/adjunct (6 women). *Students:* 42 full-time (31 women), 255 part-time (219 women); includes 40 minority (14 Black or African American, non-Hispanic/Latino; 5 Asian, non-Hispanic/Latino; 18 Hispanic/Latino; 1 Native Hawaiian or other Pacific Islander, non-Hispanic/Latino; 2 Two or more races, non-Hispanic/Latino). Average age 37. 140 applicants, 71% accepted, 83 enrolled. In 2013, 63 master's awarded. *Degree requirements:* For master's, comprehensive exam (for some programs). *Entrance requirements:* For master's, PRAXIS, 3 years of work experience, prior teaching certification. Additional exam requirements/recommendations for international students: Required—TOEFL (minimum score 580 paper-based). *Application deadline:* Applications are processed on a rolling basis. Application fee: $40. Electronic applications accepted. *Financial support:* Career-related internships or fieldwork available. Financial award applicants required to submit FAFSA. *Faculty research:* Curriculum and instruction, secondary education, special education, education and technology. *Unit head:* Dr. Janice Stewart, Division Associate Dean, 973-618-3626, E-mail: jstewart@caldwell.edu. *Application contact:* Vilma Mueller, Director of Graduate Studies, 973-618-3544, E-mail: graduate@caldwell.edu.

California Baptist University, Program in Education, Riverside, CA 92504-3206. Offers educational leadership for faith-based institutions (MS); educational leadership for public institutions (MS); educational technology (MS); instructional computer applications (MS); international education (MS); leadership and adult learning (MS); leadership and organizational studies (MS); reading (MS); school counseling (MS); school psychology (MS); science education (MS); special education in mild/moderate disabilities (MS); special education in moderate/severe disabilities (MS); teaching (MS); teaching and learning (MS); TESOL (teachers of English to speakers of other languages) (MS). Part-time and evening/weekend programs available. Postbaccalaureate distance learning degree programs offered (minimal on-campus study). *Faculty:* 18 full-time (9 women), 8 part-time/adjunct (5 women). *Students:* 158 full-time (127 women), 228 part-time (179 women); includes 159 minority (27 Black or African American, non-Hispanic/Latino; 4 American Indian or Alaska Native, non-Hispanic/Latino; 13 Asian, non-Hispanic/Latino; 107 Hispanic/Latino; 1 Native Hawaiian or other Pacific Islander, non-Hispanic/Latino; 7 Two or more races, non-Hispanic/Latino), 2 international. Average age 33. 298 applicants, 74% accepted, 113 enrolled. In 2013, 70 master's awarded. *Degree requirements:* For master's, comprehensive exam, project, or thesis. *Entrance requirements:* For master's, minimum undergraduate GPA of 3.0; 18 semester units of prerequisite course work in education; three recommendations; 500-word essay; interview. Additional exam requirements/recommendations for international students: Required—TOEFL (minimum score 80 iBT). *Application deadline:* For fall admission, 8/1 priority date for domestic students, 7/1 for international students; for spring admission, 12/1 priority date for domestic students, 11/1 for international students. Applications are processed on a rolling basis. Application fee: $45. Electronic applications accepted. *Expenses:* Contact institution. *Financial support:* Institutionally sponsored loans available. Financial award applicants required to submit CSS PROFILE or FAFSA. *Faculty research:* Leadership development, complexity theory, faith and learning, special education, social and philosophical contexts of education. *Unit head:* Dr. John Shoup, Dean, School of Education, 951-343-4205, Fax: 951-343-4516, E-mail: jshoup@calbaptist.edu. *Application contact:* Dr. Kathryn Norwood, Director, Master of Science Program in Education, 951-343-4760, E-mail: knorwood@calbaptist.edu.
Website: http://www.calbaptist.edu/mastersined/.

California Coast University, School of Education, Santa Ana, CA 92701. Offers administration (M Ed); curriculum and instruction (M Ed); educational administration (Ed D); educational psychology (Ed D); organizational leadership (Ed D). Postbaccalaureate distance learning degree programs offered (no on-campus study).

California Lutheran University, Graduate Studies, Graduate School of Education, Thousand Oaks, CA 91360-2787. Offers counseling and guidance (MS), including college student personnel, counseling and guidance; educational leadership (MA, Ed D), including educational leadership (K-12) (Ed D), higher education leadership (Ed D); special education (MS); teacher leadership (M Ed); teaching (M Ed). *Accreditation:* NCATE. Part-time and evening/weekend programs available. *Faculty:* 18 full-time (14 women), 28 part-time/adjunct (20 women). *Students:* 327 full-time (260 women), 96 part-time (77 women); includes 150 minority (7 Black or African American, non-Hispanic/Latino; 20 Asian, non-Hispanic/Latino; 112 Hispanic/Latino; 11 Two or more races, non-Hispanic/Latino), 1 international. Average age 33. 123 applicants, 85% accepted, 80 enrolled. In 2013, 117 master's, 9 doctorates awarded. *Entrance requirements:* For master's, GRE General Test, interview, minimum GPA of 3.0. *Application deadline:* For fall admission, 7/1 priority date for domestic students; for spring admission, 11/1 priority date for domestic students; for summer admission, 4/1 priority date for domestic students. Applications are processed on a rolling basis. Application fee: $50. *Unit head:* Dr. Robert Fraisse, Dean, 805-493-3421. *Application contact:* 805-493-3325, Fax: 805-493-3861, E-mail: clugrad@callutheran.edu.

California Polytechnic State University, San Luis Obispo, College of Science and Mathematics, School of Education, San Luis Obispo, CA 93407. Offers MA. Part-time and evening/weekend programs available. *Faculty:* 6 full-time (3 women), 8 part-time/adjunct (6 women). *Students:* 73 full-time (61 women), 4 part-time (all women); includes 27 minority (1 Black or African American, non-Hispanic/Latino; 1 Asian, non-Hispanic/Latino; 24 Hispanic/Latino; 1 Two or more races, non-Hispanic/Latino), 1 international. Average age 27. 111 applicants, 61% accepted, 55 enrolled. In 2013, 60 master's awarded. *Degree requirements:* For master's, comprehensive exam (for some programs), thesis (for some programs). *Entrance requirements:* For master's, minimum GPA of 3.0 in last 90 quarter units, letters of recommendation. Additional exam requirements/recommendations for international students: Required—TOEFL (minimum score 550 paper-based) or IELTS (minimum score 6). *Application deadline:* For fall admission, 2/1 priority date for domestic students, 11/30 for international students. Application fee: $55. *Financial support:* Fellowships, research assistantships, career-related internships or fieldwork, Federal Work-Study, and institutionally sponsored loans available. Support available to part-time students. Financial award application deadline: 3/2; financial award applicants required to submit FAFSA. *Faculty research:* Rural school counseling, partner school effectiveness, college student affairs, special education, educational leadership and administration. *Unit head:* Dr. Robert Detweiler, Interim Dean, 805-756-6585, Fax: 805-756-7430, E-mail: rdetweil@calpoly.edu. *Application contact:* Dr. James Maraviglia, Associate Vice Provost for Marketing and

Enrollment Development, 805-756-2311, Fax: 805-756-5400, E-mail: admissions@calpoly.edu. Website: http://soe.calpoly.edu/.

California State Polytechnic University, Pomona, Academic Affairs, College of Education and Integrative Studies, Pomona, CA 91768-2557. Offers MA, Ed D. Part-time programs available. *Faculty:* 38 full-time (25 women), 38 part-time/adjunct (23 women). *Students:* 39 full-time (26 women), 174 part-time (125 women); includes 106 minority (11 Black or African American, non-Hispanic/Latino; 1 American Indian or Alaska Native, non-Hispanic/Latino; 25 Asian, non-Hispanic/Latino; 64 Hispanic/Latino; 4 Native Hawaiian or other Pacific Islander, non-Hispanic/Latino; 1 Two or more races, non-Hispanic/Latino), 3 international. Average age 36. 94 applicants, 66% accepted, 25 enrolled. In 2013, 74 master's awarded. *Degree requirements:* For master's, thesis or alternative. *Application deadline:* For fall admission, 5/1 priority date for domestic students; for winter admission, 10/15 priority date for domestic students; for spring admission, 1/20 priority date for domestic students. Applications are processed on a rolling basis. Application fee: $55. Electronic applications accepted. *Expenses:* Tuition, state resident: full-time $6738. Tuition, nonresident: full-time $12,690. *Required fees:* $878; $248 per credit hour. *Financial support:* Career-related internships or fieldwork, Federal Work-Study, and institutionally sponsored loans available. Support available to part-time students. Financial award application deadline: 3/2; financial award applicants required to submit FAFSA. *Faculty research:* Cognitive style, human factors, learning-handicapped children, teaching and learning, severely handicapped children. *Unit head:* Dr. Peggy Kelly, Dean, 909-869-2307, E-mail: pkelly@csupomona.edu. *Application contact:* Dr. Dorothy MacNevin, Co-Chair, Graduate Education Department, 909-869-2311, Fax: 909-869-4822, E-mail: dmacnevin@csupomona.edu. Website: http://www.csupomona.edu/~ceis/.

California State University, Bakersfield, Division of Graduate Studies, School of Social Sciences and Education, Bakersfield, CA 93311. Offers MA, MS, MSW. *Accreditation:* NCATE. *Degree requirements:* For master's, thesis or alternative, culminating projects. *Application deadline:* Applications are processed on a rolling basis. Application fee: $55. *Unit head:* Dr. Kathleen M. Knutzen, Dean, 661-664-2210, Fax: 661-664-2016, E-mail: kknutzen@csub.edu. *Application contact:* Debbie Blowers, Assistant Director of Admissions, 661-664-3381, E-mail: dblowers@csub.edu. Website: http://www.csub.edu/sse/.

California State University, Dominguez Hills, College of Education, Carson, CA 90747-0001. Offers MA, Certificate. *Accreditation:* NCATE. Part-time and evening/weekend programs available. *Faculty:* 24 full-time (18 women), 33 part-time/adjunct (22 women). *Students:* 284 full-time (192 women), 289 part-time (210 women); includes 386 minority (96 Black or African American, non-Hispanic/Latino; 39 Asian, non-Hispanic/Latino; 231 Hispanic/Latino; 1 Native Hawaiian or other Pacific Islander, non-Hispanic/Latino; 19 Two or more races, non-Hispanic/Latino), 12 international. Average age 36. 640 applicants, 84% accepted, 221 enrolled. In 2013, 198 master's awarded. *Degree requirements:* For master's, comprehensive exam, thesis or alternative. *Entrance requirements:* For master's, minimum GPA of 2.75. Additional exam requirements/recommendations for international students: Required—TOEFL. *Application deadline:* For fall admission, 6/1 priority date for domestic students; for spring admission, 10/1 priority date for domestic students. Applications are processed on a rolling basis. Application fee: $55. *Expenses:* Tuition, state resident: full-time $6738. Tuition, nonresident: full-time $13,434. *Required fees:* $622. *Faculty research:* Science education, literacy, language acquisition, math, social adjustment. *Unit head:* Dr. Ann Chlebicki, Acting Dean, 310-243-2046, Fax: 310-243-3518, E-mail: achlebicki@csudh.edu. *Application contact:* Brandy McLelland, Director of Student Information Services and Registrar, 310-243-3645, E-mail: bmclelland@csudh.edu. Website: http://www4.csudh.edu/coe/index.

California State University, East Bay, Office of Academic Programs and Graduate Studies, College of Education and Allied Studies, Department of Teacher Education, Hayward, CA 94542-3000. Offers education (MS), including curriculum, early childhood education, educational technology leadership, reading instruction. Postbaccalaureate distance learning degree programs offered. *Degree requirements:* For master's, project or thesis. *Entrance requirements:* For master's, minimum GPA of 3.0 in field, 2.5 overall; teaching experience; baccalaureate degree; 3 letters of recommendation. Additional exam requirements/recommendations for international students: Required—TOEFL (minimum score 550 paper-based), IELTS. Electronic applications accepted. *Faculty research:* Online, pedagogy, writing, learning, teaching.

California State University, Fresno, Division of Graduate Studies, School of Education and Human Development, Fresno, CA 93740-8027. Offers MA, MS, Ed D. *Accreditation:* NCATE. Part-time and evening/weekend programs available. *Degree requirements:* For master's, thesis or alternative; for doctorate, thesis/dissertation. *Entrance requirements:* For master's, GRE General Test, MAT; for doctorate, GRE or MAT, minimum GPA of 3.2, master's degree. Additional exam requirements/recommendations for international students: Required—TOEFL. Electronic applications accepted. *Faculty research:* Adult community education, parenting, gifted and talented curriculum and instruction, peer mediation and conflict resolution.

California State University, Long Beach, Graduate Studies, College of Education, Long Beach, CA 90840. Offers MA, MS, Ed D. *Accreditation:* NCATE. Part-time and evening/weekend programs available. *Entrance requirements:* For master's, GRE General Test, minimum GPA of 2.75. Electronic applications accepted. *Faculty research:* K-16 educational reform and partnership, gender issues related to teaching and learning, urban education (poverty, diversity, language), assessment and standards-based education.

California State University, Los Angeles, Graduate Studies, Charter College of Education, Los Angeles, CA 90032-8530. Offers MA, MS, PhD. *Accreditation:* NCATE. Part-time and evening/weekend programs available. *Faculty:* 30 full-time (18 women), 47 part-time/adjunct (31 women). *Students:* 615 full-time (448 women), 648 part-time (464 women); includes 845 minority (72 Black or African American, non-Hispanic/Latino; 1 American Indian or Alaska Native, non-Hispanic/Latino; 144 Asian, non-Hispanic/Latino; 586 Hispanic/Latino; 14 Native Hawaiian or other Pacific Islander, non-Hispanic/Latino; 28 Two or more races, non-Hispanic/Latino), 62 international. Average age 33. 664 applicants, 67% accepted, 328 enrolled. In 2013, 332 master's awarded. *Degree requirements:* For doctorate, thesis/dissertation. *Entrance requirements:* For master's, minimum GPA of 2.75 in last 90 units of course work, teaching certificate; for doctorate, GRE General Test, master's degree; minimum undergraduate GPA of 3.0, graduate 3.5. Additional exam requirements/recommendations for international students: Required—TOEFL (minimum score 500 paper-based). *Application deadline:* For fall admission, 5/1 for domestic and international students. Applications are processed on a rolling basis. Application fee: $55. Electronic applications accepted. *Financial support:* Career-related internships or fieldwork and Federal Work-Study available. Support available to part-time students. Financial award application deadline: 3/1. *Unit head:* Dr. Mary Falvey, Dean, 323-343-4300, Fax: 323-343-4318, E-mail: mfalvey@calstatela.edu. *Application contact:* Dr. Larry Fritz, Dean of Graduate Studies, 323-343-3820, Fax: 323-343-5653, E-mail: lfritz@calstatela.edu. Website: http://www.calstatela.edu/academic/ccoe/index.htm.

California State University, Monterey Bay, College of Professional Studies, Institute for Advanced Studies in Education, Seaside, CA 93955-8001. Offers MA. *Accreditation:* NCATE. Part-time and evening/weekend programs available. *Degree requirements:* For master's, one foreign language, thesis, 2 years of teaching experience. *Entrance requirements:* For master's, recommendations, verification of U. S. Constitution requirement. Additional exam requirements/recommendations for international students: Required—TOEFL (minimum score 550 paper-based; 71 iBT). Electronic applications accepted. *Faculty research:* Multicultural education, linguistic diversity, behavior analysis.

California State University, Northridge, Graduate Studies, College of Education, Northridge, CA 91330. Offers MA, MA Ed, MS, Ed D. *Accreditation:* NCATE. Part-time and evening/weekend programs available. *Entrance requirements:* Additional exam requirements/recommendations for international students: Required—TOEFL. *Faculty research:* Federal teacher center support, bilingual teacher training.

California State University, Sacramento, Office of Graduate Studies, College of Education, Sacramento, CA 95819. Offers MA, MS. Part-time programs available. *Degree requirements:* For master's, thesis or alternative, writing proficiency exam. *Entrance requirements:* Additional exam requirements/recommendations for international students: Required—TOEFL. *Application deadline:* For fall admission, 3/1 for international students; for spring admission, 9/30 for international students. Applications are processed on a rolling basis. Application fee: $55. Electronic applications accepted. *Financial support:* Research assistantships, teaching assistantships, career-related internships or fieldwork, and Federal Work-Study available. Support available to part-time students. Financial award application deadline: 3/1; financial award applicants required to submit FAFSA. *Unit head:* Dr. Vanessa Sheared, Dean, 916-278-5883, E-mail: vsheared@saclink.csus.edu. *Application contact:* Jose Martinez, Graduate Admissions Supervisor, 916-278-7871, E-mail: martinj@skymail.csus.edu. Website: http://www.edweb.csus.edu.

California State University, San Bernardino, Graduate Studies, College of Education, San Bernardino, CA 92407-2397. Offers bilingual/cross-cultural education (MA); curriculum and instruction (MA); educational administration (MA); educational leadership and curriculum (Ed D); educational psychology and counseling (MA, MS), including correctional and alternative education (MA), counseling and guidance (MS), rehabilitation counseling (MA); English as a second language (MA); general education (MA); history and English for secondary teachers (MA); instructional technology (MA); reading (MA); secondary education (MA); special education and rehabilitation counseling (MA), including rehabilitation counseling, special education; teaching of science (MA); vocational and career education (MA). *Accreditation:* NCATE. Part-time and evening/weekend programs available. *Students:* 217 full-time (172 women), 353 part-time (263 women); includes 283 minority (41 Black or African American, non-Hispanic/Latino; 1 American Indian or Alaska Native, non-Hispanic/Latino; 21 Asian, non-Hispanic/Latino; 204 Hispanic/Latino; 1 Native Hawaiian or other Pacific Islander, non-Hispanic/Latino; 15 Two or more races, non-Hispanic/Latino), 35 international. Average age 34. 349 applicants, 76% accepted, 207 enrolled. In 2013, 215 master's awarded. *Degree requirements:* For master's, comprehensive exam (for some programs), thesis (for some programs), advancement to candidacy. *Entrance requirements:* For master's, minimum GPA of 3.0 in education. *Application deadline:* For fall admission, 8/31 priority date for domestic students. Application fee: $55. *Financial support:* Career-related internships or fieldwork and Federal Work-Study available. Support available to part-time students. *Faculty research:* Multicultural education, brain-based learning, science education, social studies/global education. *Unit head:* Dr. Jay Fiene, Dean, 909-537-5600, Fax: 909-537-7011, E-mail: jfiene@csusb.edu. *Application contact:* Dr. Jeffrey Thompson, Dean of Graduate Studies, 909-537-5808, E-mail: jthompso@csusb.edu.

California State University, San Marcos, School of Education, San Marcos, CA 92096-0001. Offers educational administration (MA); educational leadership (Ed D); general education (MA); literacy education (MA); special education (MA). *Accreditation:* NCATE (one or more programs are accredited). Part-time and evening/weekend programs available. *Degree requirements:* For master's, thesis. *Entrance requirements:* For master's, minimum GPA of 3.0, teaching credentials, 1 year of teaching experience. Tuition and fees vary according to program. *Faculty research:* Multicultural literature, art as knowledge, poetry and second language acquisition, restructuring K-12 education and improving the training of K-8 science teachers.

California State University, Stanislaus, College of Education, Turlock, CA 95382. Offers MA, Ed D, Graduate Certificate. *Accreditation:* NCATE. Part-time and evening/weekend programs available. *Degree requirements:* For master's, thesis. *Entrance requirements:* For master's, MAT, minimum GPA of 3.0. Additional exam requirements/recommendations for international students: Required—TOEFL (minimum score 550 paper-based).

California University of Pennsylvania, School of Graduate Studies and Research, College of Education and Human Services, California, PA 15419-1394. Offers M Ed, MAT, MS, MSW. *Accreditation:* NCATE. Part-time and evening/weekend programs available. Postbaccalaureate distance learning degree programs offered (minimal on-campus study). *Degree requirements:* For master's, comprehensive exam, thesis optional. *Entrance requirements:* For master's, PRAXIS, MAT, minimum QPA of 3.0. Additional exam requirements/recommendations for international students: Required—TOEFL (minimum score 550 paper-based; 80 iBT). Electronic applications accepted. *Faculty research:* Autism counseling, injury and education, early childhood education, National Board certification.

Calvin College, Graduate Programs in Education, Grand Rapids, MI 49546-4388. Offers curriculum and instruction (M Ed); educational leadership (M Ed); learning disabilities (M Ed); literacy (M Ed). Part-time programs available. *Faculty:* 12 full-time (5 women). *Students:* 9 full-time (7 women), 133 part-time (87 women); includes 12 minority (3 Black or African American, non-Hispanic/Latino; 3 Asian, non-Hispanic/Latino; 3 Hispanic/Latino; 3 Two or more races, non-Hispanic/Latino), 20 international. Average age 29. 15 applicants, 87% accepted, 13 enrolled. In 2013, 27 master's awarded. *Degree requirements:* For master's, thesis or seminar. *Entrance requirements:* For master's, teaching certificate. Additional exam requirements/recommendations for international students: Required—TOEFL (minimum score 550 paper-based; 80 iBT). *Application deadline:* For fall admission, 8/1 priority date for domestic students, 5/1 priority date for international students; for spring admission, 1/1 priority date for domestic students, 12/1 priority date for international students; for summer admission, 5/18 for domestic students. Applications are processed on a rolling basis. Application fee: $0. Electronic applications accepted. *Financial support:* Federal Work-Study, scholarships/grants, and tuition waivers (full and partial) available. Financial award application deadline: 4/3; financial award applicants required to submit FAFSA. *Faculty research:* Literacy, racialized gender and gendered identity, teacher learning, learning disabilities identification, leadership. *Unit head:* Dr. David Smith, Graduate Program Director, 616-526-6158, Fax: 616-526-6505, E-mail: dsmith@calvin.edu. *Application contact:* Cindi Hoekstra, Program Coordinator, 616-526-6158, Fax: 616-526-6505, E-mail: choekstr@calvin.edu. Website: http://www.calvin.edu/academic/graduate_studies.

Education—General

Cambridge College, School of Education, Cambridge, MA 02138-5304. Offers autism specialist (M Ed); autism/behavior analyst (M Ed); behavior analyst (Post-Master's Certificate); behavioral management (M Ed); early childhood teacher (M Ed); education specialist in curriculum and instruction (CAGS); educational leadership (Ed D); elementary teacher (M Ed); English as a second language (M Ed, Certificate); general science (M Ed); health education (Post-Master's Certificate); health/family and consumer sciences (M Ed); history (M Ed); individualized (M Ed); information technology literacy (M Ed); instructional technology (M Ed); interdisciplinary studies (M Ed); library teacher (M Ed); literacy education (M Ed); mathematics (M Ed); mathematics specialist (Certificate); middle school mathematics and science (M Ed); school administration (M Ed, CAGS); school guidance counselor (M Ed); school nurse education (M Ed); school social worker/school adjustment counselor (M Ed); special education administrator (CAGS); special education/moderate disabilities (M Ed); teaching skills and methodologies (M Ed). Part-time and evening/weekend programs available. Postbaccalaureate distance learning degree programs offered (minimal on-campus study). *Degree requirements:* For master's, thesis, internship/practicum (licensure program only); for doctorate, thesis/dissertation; for other advanced degree, thesis. *Entrance requirements:* For master's, interview, resume, documentation of licensure, 2 professional references; for doctorate, official transcripts, interview, resume, documentation of licensure (if any), written personal statement/essay, portfolio of scholarly and professional work, qualifying assessment, 2 professional references, health insurance, immunizations form; for other advanced degree, official transcripts, interview, resume, documentation of licensure (if any), written personal statement/essay, 2 professional references, health insurance, immunizations form. Additional exam requirements/recommendations for international students: Required—TOEFL (minimum score 550 paper-based; 79 iBT), Michigan English Language Assessment Battery (minimum score 85); Recommended—IELTS (minimum score 6). Electronic applications accepted. *Expenses:* Contact institution. *Faculty research:* Adult education, accelerated learning, mathematics education, brain compatible learning, special education and law.

Cameron University, Office of Graduate Studies, Program in Education, Lawton, OK 73505-6377. Offers M Ed. *Accreditation:* NCATE. Part-time and evening/weekend programs available. *Degree requirements:* For master's, portfolio. *Entrance requirements:* Additional exam requirements/recommendations for international students: Required—TOEFL (minimum score 550 paper-based). Electronic applications accepted. *Faculty research:* Motivation, computer learning, special education mathematics, inquiry-based learning.

Cameron University, Office of Graduate Studies, Program in Teaching, Lawton, OK 73505-6377. Offers MAT. *Accreditation:* NCATE. *Degree requirements:* For master's, portfolio. *Entrance requirements:* Additional exam requirements/recommendations for international students: Required—TOEFL (minimum score 550 paper-based). Electronic applications accepted. *Faculty research:* Teacher retention/attrition, teacher education.

Campbellsville University, School of Education, Campbellsville, KY 42718-2799. Offers curriculum and instruction (MAE); special education (MASE). *Accreditation:* NCATE. Part-time and evening/weekend programs available. Postbaccalaureate distance learning degree programs offered (minimal on-campus study). *Degree requirements:* For master's, thesis, research paper. *Entrance requirements:* For master's, GRE or PRAXIS, minimum undergraduate GPA of 2.75, teaching certificate, professional growth plan, letters of recommendation, disposition assessment, interview. Electronic applications accepted. *Faculty research:* Professional development, curriculum development, school governance, assessment, special education.

Campbell University, Graduate and Professional Programs, School of Education, Buies Creek, NC 27506. Offers administration (MSA); community counseling (MA); elementary education (M Ed); English education (M Ed); interdisciplinary studies (M Ed); mathematics education (M Ed); middle grades education (M Ed); physical education (M Ed); school counseling (M Ed); secondary education (M Ed); social science education (M Ed). *Accreditation:* NCATE. Part-time and evening/weekend programs available. *Degree requirements:* For master's, comprehensive exam. *Entrance requirements:* For master's, GRE General Test, minimum GPA of 2.7. *Faculty research:* Spiritual values and wellness issues in counseling, stress and professional burnout among counselors, thinking strategies, leadership, adaptive technology.

Canisius College, Graduate Division, School of Education and Human Services, Buffalo, NY 14208-1098. Offers MS, MS Ed, MSA, Certificate. Part-time and evening/weekend programs available. Postbaccalaureate distance learning degree programs offered (minimal on-campus study). *Faculty:* 48 full-time (28 women), 88 part-time/adjunct (47 women). *Students:* 459 full-time (313 women), 582 part-time (378 women); includes 126 minority (72 Black or African American, non-Hispanic/Latino; 3 American Indian or Alaska Native, non-Hispanic/Latino; 15 Asian, non-Hispanic/Latino; 29 Hispanic/Latino; 7 Two or more races, non-Hispanic/Latino), 33 international. Average age 29. 676 applicants, 75% accepted, 268 enrolled. In 2013, 593 master's awarded. *Degree requirements:* For master's, thesis (for some programs). *Entrance requirements:* For master's, GRE if cumulative GPA less than 2.7, transcripts, BA from accredited institution. Additional exam requirements/recommendations for international students: Required—TOEFL (minimum score 550 paper-based, 80 iBT), IELTS (minimum score 6.5), or CAEL (minimum score 70). *Application deadline:* Applications are processed on a rolling basis. Application fee: $25. Electronic applications accepted. Application fee is waived when completed online. *Expenses: Tuition:* Part-time $750 per credit hour. *Financial support:* Career-related internships or fieldwork, Federal Work-Study, scholarships/grants, tuition waivers (partial), and unspecified assistantships available. Support available to part-time students. Financial award application deadline: 4/30; financial award applicants required to submit FAFSA. *Faculty research:* Asperger's disease, autism, culturally congruent pedagogy in physical education, family as faculty, impact of trauma on adults, information processing and perceptual styles of athletes, integrating digital technologies in the classroom, long term psych-social impact on police officers, private higher education, qualities of effective coaches, reading strategies, student perceptions of online courses, teaching effectiveness, teaching methods, tutorial experiences in modern math. *Unit head:* Dr. Jeffrey R Lindauer, Dean, 716-888-3294, Fax: 716-888-3164, E-mail: lindauej@canisius.edu. *Application contact:* Julie A. Zulewski, Director of Graduate Recruitment and Admissions, 716-888-2548, Fax: 716-888-3195, E-mail: zulewskj@canisius.edu.
Website: http://www.canisius.edu/graduate/.

Capella University, School of Education, Doctoral Programs in Education, Minneapolis, MN 55402. Offers curriculum and instruction (PhD); educational leadership and management (Ed D); instructional design for online learning (PhD); K-12 studies in education (PhD); leadership for higher education (PhD); leadership in educational administration (PhD); postsecondary and adult education (PhD); professional studies in education (PhD); reading and literacy (Ed D); special education leadership (PhD); training and performance improvement (PhD).

Capella University, School of Education, Master's Programs in Education, Minneapolis, MN 55402. Offers adult education (MS); curriculum and instruction (MS); early childhood education (MS); enrollment management (MS); higher education leadership and management (MS); instructional design for online learning (MS); integrative studies (MS); K-12 studies in education (MS); leadership in educational administration (MS); reading and literacy (MS); special education teaching (MS).

Cardinal Stritch University, College of Education, Milwaukee, WI 53217-3985. Offers MA, MAT, ME, MS, Ed D, PhD. *Accreditation:* NCATE. Part-time and evening/weekend programs available. *Degree requirements:* For master's, comprehensive exam, thesis (for some programs); for doctorate, thesis/dissertation, practica/field experience. *Entrance requirements:* For doctorate, minimum GPA of 3.5 in master's coursework, portfolio, interview, letters of recommendation (3).

Caribbean University, Graduate School, Bayamón, PR 00960-0493. Offers administration and supervision (MA Ed); criminal justice (MA); curriculum and instruction (MA Ed, PhD), including elementary education (MA Ed), English education (MA Ed), history education (MA Ed), mathematics education (MA Ed), primary education (MA Ed), science education (MA Ed), Spanish education (MA Ed); educational technology in instructional systems (MA Ed); gerontology (MSN); human resources (MBA); museology, archiving and art history (MA Ed); neonatal pediatrics (MSN); physical education (MA Ed); special education (MA Ed). *Entrance requirements:* For master's, interview, minimum GPA of 2.5.

Carlow University, School of Education, Pittsburgh, PA 15213-3165. Offers art education (M Ed); early childhood education (M Ed); early childhood supervision (M Ed); education (M Ed), including art education, early childhood education, secondary education, special education. Part-time and evening/weekend programs available. Postbaccalaureate distance learning degree programs offered (no on-campus study). *Students:* 60 full-time (51 women), 59 part-time (55 women); includes 16 minority (12 Black or African American, non-Hispanic/Latino; 1 Asian, non-Hispanic/Latino; 1 Hispanic/Latino; 2 Two or more races, non-Hispanic/Latino). Average age 32. 37 applicants, 100% accepted, 26 enrolled. In 2013, 34 master's awarded. *Entrance requirements:* Additional exam requirements/recommendations for international students: Required—TOEFL (minimum score 550 paper-based). *Application deadline:* For fall admission, 6/15 priority date for domestic and international students; for spring admission, 11/15 priority date for domestic and international students. Applications are processed on a rolling basis. Application fee: $20. Electronic applications accepted. Application fee is waived when completed online. *Expenses: Tuition:* Full-time $9523; part-time $744 per credit. Tuition and fees vary according to course load, degree level and program. *Financial support:* Application deadline: 4/1; applicants required to submit FAFSA. *Unit head:* Dr. Marilyn Llewellyn, Dean, 412-578-6011, Fax: 412-578-0816, E-mail: llewellynmj@carlow.edu. *Application contact:* Jo Danhires, Administrative Assistant, Admissions, 412-578-6059, Fax: 412-578-6321, E-mail: gradstudies@carlow.edu.
Website: http://www.carlow.edu/.

Carnegie Mellon University, College of Humanities and Social Sciences, Center for Innovation in Learning, Pittsburgh, PA 15213-3891. Offers instructional science (PhD). *Faculty research:* Improvement of undergraduate education, teaching and learning at the college level.

Carroll University, Graduate Program in Education, Waukesha, WI 53186-5593. Offers education (M Ed); learning and teaching (M Ed). Part-time and evening/weekend programs available. *Degree requirements:* For master's, thesis. *Entrance requirements:* For master's, minimum undergraduate GPA of 2.5 in related field. Additional exam requirements/recommendations for international students: Required—TOEFL. Electronic applications accepted. *Faculty research:* Qualitative research methods, whole language approaches to teaching, the writing process, multicultural education, gifted/talented learners.

Carson-Newman University, Graduate Program in Education, Jefferson City, TN 37760. Offers curriculum and instruction (M Ed); educational leadership (M Ed); elementary education (MAT); school counseling (MS); secondary education (MAT); teaching English as a second language (MATESL). *Accreditation:* NCATE. Part-time and evening/weekend programs available. *Faculty:* 5 full-time (2 women), 10 part-time/adjunct (3 women). *Students:* 25 full-time (12 women), 100 part-time (70 women); includes 8 minority (4 Black or African American, non-Hispanic/Latino; 1 Asian, non-Hispanic/Latino; 1 Hispanic/Latino; 2 Two or more races, non-Hispanic/Latino), 1 international. Average age 32. In 2013, 34 master's awarded. *Degree requirements:* For master's, thesis or alternative. *Entrance requirements:* For master's, NTE, minimum GPA of 3.0 in major, 2.5 overall. *Application deadline:* For fall admission, 7/15 priority date for domestic students. Applications are processed on a rolling basis. Application fee: $25 ($50 for international students). *Expenses: Tuition:* Part-time $390 per credit hour. *Financial support:* Federal Work-Study and unspecified assistantships available. Financial award application deadline: 4/1; financial award applicants required to submit FAFSA. *Unit head:* Dr. Sharon Teets, Chair, 865-471-3461. *Application contact:* Graduate Admissions and Services Adviser, 865-471-3460, Fax: 865-471-3875.

Carthage College, Division of Teacher Education, Kenosha, WI 53140. Offers classroom guidance and counseling (M Ed); creative arts (M Ed); gifted and talented children (M Ed); language arts (M Ed); modern language (M Ed); natural sciences (M Ed); reading (M Ed, Certificate); social sciences (M Ed); teacher leadership (M Ed). Part-time and evening/weekend programs available. *Degree requirements:* For master's, thesis optional. *Entrance requirements:* For master's, MAT, minimum B average, letters of reference.

Castleton State College, Division of Graduate Studies, Department of Education, Castleton, VT 05735. Offers curriculum and instruction (MA Ed); educational leadership (MA Ed, CAGS); language arts and reading (MA Ed, CAGS); special education (MA Ed, CAGS). Part-time and evening/weekend programs available. *Degree requirements:* For master's, thesis or alternative; for CAGS, publishable paper. *Entrance requirements:* For master's, GRE General Test, MAT, interview, minimum undergraduate GPA of 3.0; for CAGS, educational research, master's degree, minimum undergraduate GPA of 3.0. *Faculty research:* Assessment, narrative.

Catawba College, Master's Program in Elementary Education, Salisbury, NC 28144-2488. Offers elementary education (M Ed). *Accreditation:* NCATE. Part-time and evening/weekend programs available. *Faculty:* 4 full-time (3 women). *Students:* 12 part-time (all women); includes 2 minority (1 Black or African American, non-Hispanic/Latino; 1 Hispanic/Latino). Average age 33. 1 applicant, 100% accepted, 1 enrolled. In 2013, 8 master's awarded. *Degree requirements:* For master's, portfolio. *Entrance requirements:* For master's, NTE, PRAXIS II, minimum undergraduate GPA of 3.0, valid teaching license, official transcripts, 3 references, essay, interview, practicing teacher. *Application deadline:* For fall admission, 7/1 for domestic students; for spring admission, 12/1 for domestic students. Applications are processed on a rolling basis. Application fee: $25. *Expenses: Tuition:* Part-time $170 per credit hour. *Financial support:* Scholarships/grants available. Financial award applicants required to submit FAFSA. *Unit head:* Dr. Rhonda L. Truitt, Chair, Department of Teacher Education, 704-637-4468, Fax: 704-637-4732, E-mail: rltruitt@catawba.edu. *Application contact:* Dr. Lou W. Kasias, Director, Graduate Program, 704-637-4462, Fax: 704-637-4732, E-mail: lakasias@catawba.edu.
Website: http://www.catawba.edu/academic/teachereducation/grad/.

The Catholic University of America, School of Arts and Sciences, Department of Education, Washington, DC 20064. Offers Catholic educational leadership and policy

studies (PhD); Catholic school leadership (MA); education (Certificate); educational psychology (PhD); secondary education (MA); special education (MA). *Accreditation:* NCATE. Part-time programs available. *Faculty:* 9 full-time (8 women), 4 part-time/ adjunct (all women). *Students:* 9 full-time (6 women), 44 part-time (37 women); includes 8 minority (3 Black or African American, non-Hispanic/Latino; 3 Hispanic/Latino; 2 Two or more races, non-Hispanic/Latino), 2 international. Average age 34. 53 applicants, 53% accepted, 17 enrolled. In 2013, 18 master's, 2 doctorates awarded. *Degree requirements:* For master's, comprehensive exam, thesis or alternative; for doctorate, comprehensive exam, thesis/dissertation; for Certificate, action research project. *Entrance requirements:* For master's and doctorate, GRE General Test or MAT, statement of purpose, official copies of academic transcripts, three letters of recommendation, interview; for Certificate, PRAXIS I, statement of purpose, official copies of academic transcripts, three letters of recommendation, interview. Additional exam requirements/recommendations for international students: Required—TOEFL (minimum score 580 paper-based). *Application deadline:* For fall admission, 8/1 priority date for domestic students, 7/15 for international students; for spring admission, 12/1 priority date for domestic students, 10/15 for international students. Applications are processed on a rolling basis. Application fee: $55. Electronic applications accepted. *Expenses: Tuition:* Full-time $38,500; part-time $1490 per credit hour. *Required fees:* $400; $1525 per credit hour. One-time fee: $425. Tuition and fees vary according to program. *Financial support:* Fellowships, research assistantships, teaching assistantships, Federal Work-Study, scholarships/grants, tuition waivers (full and partial), and unspecified assistantships available. Financial award application deadline: 2/1; financial award applicants required to submit FAFSA. *Faculty research:* Special education, early childhood education, educational psychology, Catholic school administration, leadership and policy studies, counseling, curriculum and instruction. *Total annual research expenditures:* $65,883. *Unit head:* Dr. Merylann J. Schuttloffel, Chair, 202-319-5805, Fax: 202-319-5815, E-mail: schuttloffel@cua.edu. *Application contact:* Andrew Woodall, Director of Graduate Admissions, 202-319-5057, Fax: 202-319-6533, E-mail: cua-admissions@cua.edu.
Website: http://education.cua.edu/.

Cedar Crest College, Department of Education, Allentown, PA 18104-6196. Offers M Ed. Part-time and evening/weekend programs available. *Faculty:* 4 full-time (all women), 5 part-time/adjunct (4 women). *Students:* 15 full-time (10 women), 70 part-time (62 women); includes 13 minority (4 Black or African American, non-Hispanic/Latino; 1 Asian, non-Hispanic/Latino; 6 Hispanic/Latino; 2 Two or more races, non-Hispanic/ Latino). Average age 34. In 2013, 49 master's awarded. *Entrance requirements:* Additional exam requirements/recommendations for international students: Required— TOEFL. *Application deadline:* For fall admission, 8/7 priority date for domestic and international students; for winter admission, 11/7 priority date for domestic and international students; for spring admission, 1/8 priority date for domestic and international students. Applications are processed on a rolling basis. *Expenses: Tuition:* Part-time $661 per credit. *Financial support:* In 2013–14, 60 students received support. Available to part-time students. Applicants required to submit FAFSA. *Faculty research:* Science education, reading, history of Pennsylvania, math education. *Unit head:* Dr. Jill Purdy, Graduate Program Director, 610-606-4666 Ext. 3419, E-mail: jepurdy@ cedarcrest.edu. *Application contact:* Mary Ellen Hickes, Director of School of Adult and Graduate Education, 610-606-4666, E-mail: sage@cedarcrest.edu.

Cedarville University, Graduate Programs, Cedarville, OH 45314-0601. Offers business administration (MBA); curriculum (M Ed); educational administration (M Ed); family nurse practitioner (MSN); global health ministries (MSN); instruction (M Ed); pharmacy (Pharm D). Part-time programs available. Postbaccalaureate distance learning degree programs offered (no on-campus study). *Faculty:* 23 full-time (12 women), 12 part-time/adjunct (5 women). *Students:* 119 full-time (74 women), 103 part-time (73 women); includes 16 minority (11 Black or African American, non-Hispanic/ Latino; 4 Asian, non-Hispanic/Latino; 1 Native Hawaiian or other Pacific Islander, non-Hispanic/Latino), 4 international. Average age 31. In 2013, 26 master's awarded. *Degree requirements:* For master's, thesis. *Entrance requirements:* For master's, GRE, 2 professional recommendations; for doctorate, PCAT, professional recommendation from a practicing pharmacist or current employer/supervisor, resume, essay, interview. Additional exam requirements/recommendations for international students: Required— TOEFL (minimum score 550 paper-based; 80 iBT). *Application deadline:* For fall admission, 5/1 priority date for domestic and international students; for spring admission, 11/1 priority date for domestic and international students. Applications are processed on a rolling basis. Application fee: $30. Electronic applications accepted. *Financial support:* Scholarships/grants and unspecified assistantships available. Support available to part-time students. Financial award applicants required to submit FAFSA. *Unit head:* Dr. Mark McClain, Dean of Graduate Studies, 937-766-7700, E-mail: mcclain@cedarville.edu. *Application contact:* Roscoe F. Smith, Associate Vice-President of Enrollment, 937-766-7700, Fax: 937-766-7575, E-mail: smithr@ cedarville.edu.
Website: http://www.cedarville.edu/academics/graduate/.

Centenary College, Program in Education, Hackettstown, NJ 07840-2100. Offers educational leadership (MA); instructional leadership (MA); special education (MA). *Accreditation:* Teacher Education Accreditation Council. Part-time and evening/weekend programs available. Postbaccalaureate distance learning degree programs offered (minimal on-campus study). *Degree requirements:* For master's, thesis. *Entrance requirements:* For master's, interview, minimum undergraduate GPA of 2.8.

Centenary College of Louisiana, Graduate Programs, Department of Education, Shreveport, LA 71104. Offers administration (M Ed); elementary education (MAT); secondary education (MAT); supervision of instruction (M Ed). Part-time and evening/ weekend programs available. *Degree requirements:* For master's, comprehensive exam. *Entrance requirements:* For master's, GRE General Test (M Ed), PRAXIS I and PRAXIS II (MAT), teacher certification (M Ed), minimum GPA of 2.5. *Expenses:* Contact institution. *Faculty research:* Teachers as advocates for teachers, portfolio assessment, disabled readers.

Central Connecticut State University, School of Graduate Studies, School of Education and Professional Studies, New Britain, CT 06050-4010. Offers MAT, MS, Ed D, AC, Certificate, Sixth Year Certificate. *Accreditation:* NCATE. Part-time and evening/weekend programs available. *Faculty:* 42 full-time (21 women), 52 part-time/ adjunct (33 women). *Students:* 230 full-time (175 women), 783 part-time (595 women); includes 185 minority (96 Black or African American, non-Hispanic/Latino; 1 American Indian or Alaska Native, non-Hispanic/Latino; 13 Asian, non-Hispanic/Latino; 60 Hispanic/Latino; 1 Native Hawaiian or other Pacific Islander, non-Hispanic/Latino; 14 Two or more races, non-Hispanic/Latino), 8 international. Average age 33. 530 applicants, 61% accepted, 242 enrolled. In 2013, 326 master's, 14 doctorates, 73 other advanced degrees awarded. *Degree requirements:* For master's, comprehensive exam, thesis or alternative; for doctorate, thesis/dissertation; for other advanced degree, qualifying exam. *Entrance requirements:* For master's, minimum undergraduate GPA of 2.7; for doctorate, GRE. Additional exam requirements/recommendations for international students: Required—TOEFL (minimum score 550 paper-based; 79 iBT). *Application deadline:* For fall admission, 6/1 for domestic students, 5/1 for international students; for spring admission, 11/1 for domestic and international students.

Applications are processed on a rolling basis. Application fee: $50. Electronic applications accepted. Part-time tuition and fees vary according to degree level. *Financial support:* In 2013–14, 69 students received support, including 18 research assistantships; career-related internships or fieldwork, Federal Work-Study, scholarships/grants, and unspecified assistantships also available. Support available to part-time students. Financial award application deadline: 3/1; financial award applicants required to submit FAFSA. *Unit head:* Dr. Michael Alfano, Dean, 860-832-2101, E-mail: malfano@ccsu.edu. *Application contact:* Patricia Gardner, Associate Director of Graduate Studies, 860-832-2350, Fax: 860-832-2362, E-mail: graduateadmissions@ ccsu.edu.
Website: http://www.ccsu.edu/page.cfm?p=730.

Central Methodist University, College of Graduate and Extended Studies, Fayette, MO 65248-1198. Offers clinical counseling (MS); clinical nurse leader (MSN); education (M Ed); music education (MME); nurse educator (MSN). Part-time and evening/weekend programs available. Postbaccalaureate distance learning degree programs offered (no on-campus study). *Degree requirements:* For master's, thesis. *Entrance requirements:* For master's, GRE General Test, minimum GPA of 2.75. *Application deadline:* Applications are processed on a rolling basis. Application fee: $25. Electronic applications accepted. *Expenses: Tuition:* Part-time $360 per credit hour. Part-time tuition and fees vary according to campus/location and program. *Financial support:* Tuition waivers available. Support available to part-time students. Financial award application deadline: 6/5; financial award applicants required to submit FAFSA. *Unit head:* Dr. Rita Gulstad, Provost, 660-248-6212, Fax: 660-248-6392, E-mail: rgulstad@ centralmethodist.edu. *Application contact:* Aimee Sage, Director of Graduate Admissions, 660-248-6651, Fax: 660-248-6392, E-mail: asage@centralmethodist.edu. Website: http://www.centralmethodist.edu/graduate/.

Central Michigan University, Central Michigan University Global Campus, Program in Education, Mount Pleasant, MI 48859. Offers college teaching (Graduate Certificate); community college (MA); curriculum and instruction (MA); educational technology (MA); guidance and development (MA); reading and literacy K-12 (MA); school principalship (MA), including charter school leadership; training and development (MA). *Accreditation:* Teacher Education Accreditation Council. Part-time and evening/weekend programs available. *Entrance requirements:* For master's, minimum GPA of 2.7 in major. Additional exam requirements/recommendations for international students: Required— TOEFL. *Application deadline:* Applications are processed on a rolling basis. Application fee: $50. Electronic applications accepted. *Financial support:* Scholarships/grants available. Support available to part-time students. *Unit head:* Kaleb Patrick, Director, 989-774-3144, E-mail: patri1kg@cmich.edu. *Application contact:* 877-268-4636, E-mail: cmuglobal@cmich.edu.

Central Michigan University, College of Graduate Studies, College of Education and Human Services, Mount Pleasant, MI 48859. Offers MA, MS, Ed D, Ed S, Graduate Certificate. *Accreditation:* Teacher Education Accreditation Council. Part-time and evening/weekend programs available. *Degree requirements:* For master's and other advanced degree, thesis or alternative; for doctorate, thesis/dissertation. Electronic applications accepted.

Central Washington University, Graduate Studies and Research, College of Education and Professional Studies, Department of Language, Literacy and Special Education, Ellensburg, WA 98926. Offers reading education (M Ed); special education (M Ed). Part-time programs available. *Degree requirements:* For master's, thesis or alternative. *Entrance requirements:* For master's, minimum GPA of 3.0. Additional exam requirements/recommendations for international students: Required—TOEFL (minimum score 550 paper-based; 79 iBT), IELTS (minimum score 6.5). Electronic applications accepted.

Chadron State College, School of Professional and Graduate Studies, Department of Education, Chadron, NE 69337. Offers business (MA Ed); community counseling (MA Ed); educational administration (MS Ed, Sp Ed); elementary education (MS Ed); history (MA Ed); language and literature (MA Ed); secondary administration (MS Ed); secondary education (MS Ed). *Accreditation:* NCATE. Part-time and evening/weekend programs available. Postbaccalaureate distance learning degree programs offered. *Degree requirements:* For master's, thesis optional. *Entrance requirements:* For master's, GRE General Test, GRE Writing Test, minimum GPA of 2.75 or 12 graduate hours at CSC with minimum GPA of 3.25. Additional exam requirements/ recommendations for international students: Required—TOEFL. Electronic applications accepted. *Faculty research:* Rural education, technology, mental health.

Chaminade University of Honolulu, Graduate Services, Program in Education, Honolulu, HI 96816-1578. Offers child development (M Ed); early childhood education (M Ed); educational leadership (M Ed); elementary education (MAT); instructional leadership (M Ed); Montessori education (M Ed); secondary education (MAT), including English, math, science, social studies; special education (MAT). Part-time and evening/ weekend programs available. Postbaccalaureate distance learning degree programs offered (minimal on-campus study). *Degree requirements:* For master's, thesis or alternative. *Entrance requirements:* For master's, PRAXIS (for MAT only), minimum GPA of 2.75, 3 letters of recommendation. Additional exam requirements/ recommendations for international students: Required—TOEFL (minimum score 550 paper-based). Electronic applications accepted. *Faculty research:* Peace and curriculum education.

Chapman University, College of Educational Studies, Orange, CA 92866. Offers communication sciences and disorders (MS); counseling (MA), including school counseling (MA, Credential); education (PhD), including cultural and curricular studies, disability studies, leadership studies, school psychology (PhD, Credential); educational psychology (MA); leadership development (MA); pupil personnel services (Credential), including school counseling (MA, Credential), school psychology (PhD, Credential); school psychology (Ed S); single subject (Credential); special education (MA, Credential), including mild/moderate (Credential), moderate/severe (Credential); speech language pathology (Credential); teaching (MA), including elementary education, secondary education. *Accreditation:* Teacher Education Accreditation Council. Part-time and evening/weekend programs available. *Faculty:* 29 full-time (18 women), 56 part-time/adjunct (38 women). *Students:* 251 full-time (208 women), 194 part-time (150 women); includes 185 minority (13 Black or African American, non-Hispanic/Latino; 61 Asian, non-Hispanic/Latino; 97 Hispanic/Latino; 1 Native Hawaiian or other Pacific Islander, non-Hispanic/Latino; 13 Two or more races, non-Hispanic/Latino), 7 international. Average age 29. 580 applicants, 42% accepted, 166 enrolled. In 2013, 140 master's, 10 doctorates awarded. *Entrance requirements:* Additional exam requirements/recommendations for international students: Required—TOEFL (minimum score 550 paper-based; 80 iBT). *Application deadline:* Applications are processed on a rolling basis. Application fee: $60. Electronic applications accepted. Tuition and fees vary according to program. *Financial support:* Fellowships and scholarships/grants available. Financial award application deadline: 6/30; financial award applicants required to submit FAFSA. *Unit head:* Dr. Don Cardinal, Dean, 714-997-6781, E-mail: cardinal@ chapman.edu. *Application contact:* Admissions Coordinator, 714-997-6714. Website: http://www.chapman.edu/CES/.

Education—General

Charleston Southern University, School of Education, Charleston, SC 29423-8087. Offers elementary administration and supervision (M Ed); elementary education (M Ed). *Accreditation:* NCATE. Part-time and evening/weekend programs available. *Degree requirements:* For master's, thesis optional. *Entrance requirements:* For master's, GRE or MAT. Additional exam requirements/recommendations for international students: Required—TOEFL (minimum score 550 paper-based; 79 iBT). *Expenses:* Contact institution.

Chatham University, Program in Education, Pittsburgh, PA 15232-2826. Offers early childhood education (MAT); elementary education (MAT); environmental education (K-12) (MAT); secondary art (MAT); secondary biology education (MAT); secondary chemistry education (MAT); secondary English education (MAT); secondary math education (MAT); secondary physics education (MAT); secondary social studies education (MAT); special education (MAT). *Faculty:* 1 (woman) full-time, 5 part-time/adjunct (4 women). *Students:* 19 full-time (15 women), 4 part-time (all women); includes 2 minority (1 Black or African American, non-Hispanic/Latino; 1 Asian, non-Hispanic/Latino), 2 international. Average age 28. 22 applicants, 73% accepted, 6 enrolled. In 2013, 20 master's awarded. *Degree requirements:* For master's, thesis, teaching experience. *Entrance requirements:* For master's, minimum GPA of 3.0, sample of written work, recommendation letters. Additional exam requirements/recommendations for international students: Required—TOEFL (minimum score 600 paper-based; 100 iBT), IELTS (minimum score 7), TWE. *Application deadline:* For fall admission, 4/1 priority date for domestic and international students; for spring admission, 11/1 priority date for domestic students, 10/1 priority date for international students. Applications are processed on a rolling basis. Application fee: $45. Electronic applications accepted. Application fee is waived when completed online. *Expenses: Tuition:* Full-time $14,886; part-time $827 per credit hour. One-time fee: $396 full-time. *Financial support:* Career-related internships or fieldwork available. Financial award applicants required to submit FAFSA. *Faculty research:* Gifted education, environmental education, technology in education, writing as learning, class size and achievement. *Unit head:* Dr. Edward Donovan, Director of Education Programs, 412-365-2773, E-mail: edonovan@chatham.edu. *Application contact:* Katie Noel, Assistant Director of Graduate Admission, 412-365-2758, Fax: 412-365-1609, E-mail: gradadmissions@chatham.edu.
Website: http://www.chatham.edu/mat.

Chestnut Hill College, School of Graduate Studies, Department of Education, Philadelphia, PA 19118-2693. Offers early education (M Ed, CAS), including early education, Montessori education (CAS); educational leadership (M Ed, CAS); middle education (M Ed, CAS), including elementary/middle education; reading (M Ed, CAS); secondary education (M Ed), including instructional design and e-learning; secondary education (CAS), including secondary education; special education (CAS). Part-time and evening/weekend programs available. *Faculty:* 10 full-time (7 women), 48 part-time/adjunct (34 women). *Students:* 37 full-time (32 women), 203 part-time (156 women); includes 88 minority (61 Black or African American, non-Hispanic/Latino; 1 American Indian or Alaska Native, non-Hispanic/Latino; 8 Asian, non-Hispanic/Latino; 14 Hispanic/Latino; 4 Two or more races, non-Hispanic/Latino), 2 international. Average age 33. 100 applicants, 99% accepted, 93 enrolled. In 2013, 107 master's, 82 CASs awarded. *Degree requirements:* For master's, thesis optional. *Entrance requirements:* For master's, PRAXIS I or proof of teaching certification, letters of recommendation, writing sample, 6 graduate credits with minimum B grade if undergraduate GPA less than 3.0. Additional exam requirements/recommendations for international students: Required—TOEFL (minimum score 500 paper-based), IELTS (mnimum score 6.0), or TWE (minimum score 22). *Application deadline:* For fall admission, 7/15 priority date for domestic and international students; for spring admission, 12/15 priority date for domestic and international students. Applications are processed on a rolling basis. *Expenses:* Contact institution. *Financial support:* Unspecified assistantships available. *Faculty research:* Culturally responsive pedagogy, gender issues, autism, inclusive education, mentoring and induction programs. *Unit head:* Dr. Debra Chiaradonna, Chair, 215-248-7127, Fax: 215-248-7155, E-mail: chiaradonnad@chc.edu. *Application contact:* Jayne Mashett, Director of Admissions, School of Graduate Studies, 215-248-7020, Fax: 215-248-7161, E-mail: gradadmissions@chc.edu.
Website: http://www.chc.edu/Graduate/Programs/Masters/Education/.

Cheyney University of Pennsylvania, Graduate Programs, Cheyney, PA 19319. Offers M Ed, MPA, Certificate. Part-time and evening/weekend programs available. *Degree requirements:* For master's and Certificate, thesis or alternative. *Entrance requirements:* For master's and Certificate, GRE General Test, MAT, minimum GPA of 2.75. Electronic applications accepted. *Faculty research:* Teacher motivation, critical thinking.

Chicago State University, School of Graduate and Professional Studies, College of Education, Chicago, IL 60628. Offers M Ed, MA, MAT, MS Ed, Ed D. *Accreditation:* NCATE. Part-time programs available. *Degree requirements:* For master's, thesis optional. *Entrance requirements:* For master's, minimum GPA of 2.75.

Chowan University, School of Graduate Studies, Murfreesboro, NC 27855. Offers education (M Ed). *Entrance requirements:* For master's, official transcripts, three letters of recommendation, personal statement, current teacher license. Additional exam requirements/recommendations for international students: Required—TOEFL. Electronic applications accepted.

Christian Brothers University, School of Arts, Memphis, TN 38104-5581. Offers Catholic studies (MACS); educational leadership (MSEL); teacher-leadership (M Ed); teaching (MAT). Part-time and evening/weekend programs available. *Entrance requirements:* For master's, GRE, GMAT, PRAXIS II. *Expenses:* Contact institution.

Christopher Newport University, Graduate Studies, Department of Teacher Preparation, Newport News, VA 23606-3072. Offers art (PK-12) (MAT); biology (6-12) (MAT); chemistry (6-12) (MAT); computer science (6-12) (MAT); elementary (PK-6) (MAT); English (6-12) (MAT); English as second language (PK-12) (MAT); French (PK-12) (MAT); history and social science (6-12) (MAT); mathematics (6-12) (MAT); music (PK-12) (MAT), including choral, instrumental; physics (6-12) (MAT); Spanish (PK-12) (MAT). Part-time programs available. *Faculty:* 15 full-time (7 women), 14 part-time/adjunct (13 women). *Students:* 74 full-time (64 women), 2 part-time (both women); includes 6 minority (4 Hispanic/Latino; 2 Two or more races, non-Hispanic/Latino). Average age 23. 90 applicants, 100% accepted, 67 enrolled. In 2013, 96 master's awarded. *Degree requirements:* For master's, comprehensive exam, thesis or alternative. *Entrance requirements:* For master's, PRAXIS I, minimum GPA of 3.0. Additional exam requirements/recommendations for international students: Required—TOEFL (minimum score 580 paper-based; 92 iBT). *Application deadline:* For fall admission, 4/1 for international students; for spring admission, 10/15 for domestic students, 10/1 for international students; for summer admission, 1/15 for domestic students, 3/1 for international students. Applications are processed on a rolling basis. Application fee: $50. Electronic applications accepted. *Expenses: Tuition, area resident:* Part-time $498 per credit hour. Tuition, state resident: part-time $498 per credit hour. Tuition, nonresident: part-time $899 per credit hour. *Financial support:* In 2013–14, 3 students received support, including 3 research assistantships with full tuition reimbursements available (averaging $2,000 per year); career-related internships or fieldwork, Federal Work-Study, and unspecified assistantships also available. Financial award application deadline: 3/1; financial award applicants required to submit FAFSA. *Faculty research:* Early literacy development, instructional innovations, professional teaching standards, multicultural issues, aesthetic education. *Total annual research expenditures:* $24,000. *Unit head:* Dr. Marsha Sprague, Director, 757-594-7388, Fax: 757-594-7803, E-mail: msprague@cnu.edu. *Application contact:* Lyn Sawyer, Associate Director, Graduate Admissions, 757-594-7544, Fax: 757-594-7649, E-mail: gradstdy@cnu.edu.

The Citadel, The Military College of South Carolina, Citadel Graduate College, School of Education, Charleston, SC 29409. Offers M Ed, MAE, MAT, Ed S. *Accreditation:* NCATE. Part-time and evening/weekend programs available. *Faculty:* 10 full-time (6 women), 8 part-time/adjunct (3 women). *Students:* 30 full-time (24 women), 202 part-time (145 women); includes 45 minority (41 Black or African American, non-Hispanic/Latino; 1 American Indian or Alaska Native, non-Hispanic/Latino; 2 Hispanic/Latino; 1 Two or more races, non-Hispanic/Latino). Average age 32. In 2013, 88 master's, 4 other advanced degrees awarded. *Degree requirements:* For master's and Ed S, comprehensive exam (for some programs), thesis (for some programs), internship. *Entrance requirements:* For master's, GRE (minimum score 290; 900 on old scoring system) or MAT (minimum score 396), minimum undergraduate GPA of 2.5, 2.7 for last 60 undergraduate semester hours; for Ed S, GRE (minimum score 290; 900 on old scoring system) or MAT (minimum score 396), minimum GPA of 3.5; SC State Professional Certificate with school administrator endorsement and two years in an administrative position equivalent to assistant principal or higher in education. Additional exam requirements/recommendations for international students: Required—TOEFL (minimum score 550 paper-based; 79 iBT). *Application deadline:* Applications are processed on a rolling basis. Application fee: $30. Electronic applications accepted. *Expenses: Tuition, area resident:* Part-time $525 per credit hour. Tuition, state resident: part-time $525 per credit hour. Tuition, nonresident: part-time $865 per credit hour. *Financial support:* Fellowships, career-related internships or fieldwork, health care benefits, and unspecified assistantships available. Support available to part-time students. Financial award application deadline: 7/1; financial award applicants required to submit FAFSA. *Unit head:* Dr. Tony W. Johnson, Dean, 843-953-5871, Fax: 843-953-7258, E-mail: tony.johnson@citadel.edu. *Application contact:* Dr. Robert H. McNamara, Associate Provost, The Citadel Graduate College, 843-953-5089, Fax: 843-953-7630, E-mail: cgc@citadel.edu.
Website: http://www.citadel.edu/education/.

City College of the City University of New York, Graduate School, School of Education, New York, NY 10031-9198. Offers MA, MS, AC. *Accreditation:* NCATE. Part-time and evening/weekend programs available. *Entrance requirements:* For master's, Liberal Arts and Sciences Test (LAST), Content Specialty Test (CST). Additional exam requirements/recommendations for international students: Required—TOEFL.

City University of Seattle, Graduate Division, Albright School of Education, Bellevue, WA 98005. Offers administrator certification (Certificate); curriculum and instruction (M Ed); educational leadership (Ed D); elementary education (MIT); guidance and counseling (M Ed); higher education leadership (Ed D); leadership (M Ed); leadership and school counseling (M Ed); organizational leadership (Ed D); reading and literacy (M Ed); special education (MIT); superintendent certification (Certificate). Part-time and evening/weekend programs available. Postbaccalaureate distance learning degree programs offered (no on-campus study). *Degree requirements:* For master's, comprehensive exam (for some programs), thesis (for some programs); for doctorate, comprehensive exam, thesis/dissertation. *Entrance requirements:* Additional exam requirements/recommendations for international students: Required—TOEFL (minimum score 567 paper-based; 87 iBT); Recommended—IELTS. Electronic applications accepted. *Expenses:* Contact institution.

Claremont Graduate University, Graduate Programs, School of Educational Studies, Claremont, CA 91711-6160. Offers Africana education (Certificate); education and policy (MA, PhD); higher education/student affairs (MA, PhD); human development (MA, PhD); public school administration (MA, PhD); quantitative evaluation (MA, PhD); special education (MA, PhD); teacher education (MA); teaching and learning (MA, PhD); urban leadership (PhD); MBA/PhD. PhD program offered jointly with San Diego State University. Part-time programs available. *Faculty:* 16 full-time (9 women), 1 part-time/adjunct (0 women). *Students:* 224 full-time (158 women), 221 part-time (151 women); includes 229 minority (52 Black or African American, non-Hispanic/Latino; 3 American Indian or Alaska Native, non-Hispanic/Latino; 43 Asian, non-Hispanic/Latino; 113 Hispanic/Latino; 1 Native Hawaiian or other Pacific Islander, non-Hispanic/Latino; 17 Two or more races, non-Hispanic/Latino), 15 international. Average age 39. In 2013, 51 master's, 33 doctorates, 5 other advanced degrees awarded. Terminal master's awarded for partial completion of doctoral program. *Entrance requirements:* For master's and doctorate, GRE General Test. Additional exam requirements/recommendations for international students: Required—TOEFL (minimum score 550 paper-based; 80 iBT). *Application deadline:* For fall admission, 4/1 priority date for domestic and international students. Applications are processed on a rolling basis. Application fee: $80. Electronic applications accepted. *Expenses: Tuition:* Full-time $40,560; part-time $1690 per credit. *Required fees:* $275 per semester. Tuition and fees vary according to program. *Financial support:* Fellowships, research assistantships, Federal Work-Study, institutionally sponsored loans, and scholarships/grants available. Support available to part-time students. Financial award application deadline: 2/15; financial award applicants required to submit FAFSA. *Faculty research:* Education administration, K-12 and higher education, multicultural education, education policy, diversity in higher education, faculty issues. *Unit head:* Scott Thomas, Dean, 909-621-8075, Fax: 909-621-8734, E-mail: scott.thomas@cgu.edu. *Application contact:* Julia Wendt, Director of Central Recruitment, 909-607-3689, Fax: 909-607-7285, E-mail: admiss@cgu.edu.
Website: http://www.cgu.edu/pages/267.asp.

Clarion University of Pennsylvania, Office of Transfer, Adult and Graduate Admissions, Master of Education Program, Clarion, PA 16214. Offers curriculum and instruction (M Ed); early childhood (M Ed); math education (M Ed); reading (M Ed); science education (M Ed); special education (M Ed); technology (M Ed). *Accreditation:* NCATE. Part-time programs available. Postbaccalaureate distance learning degree programs offered (no on-campus study). *Faculty:* 17 full-time (10 women). *Students:* 231 full-time (191 women), 535 part-time (448 women); includes 39 minority (12 Black or African American, non-Hispanic/Latino; 8 Asian, non-Hispanic/Latino; 11 Hispanic/Latino; 1 Native Hawaiian or other Pacific Islander, non-Hispanic/Latino; 7 Two or more races, non-Hispanic/Latino). Average age 31. 28 applicants, 75% accepted, 18 enrolled. In 2013, 99 master's awarded. *Degree requirements:* For master's, comprehensive exam, thesis, or portfolio. *Entrance requirements:* For master's, minimum QPA of 3.0. Additional exam requirements/recommendations for international students: Required—TOEFL (minimum score 550 paper-based; 80 iBT), IELTS (minimum score 7). *Application deadline:* For fall admission, 8/1 for domestic students, 4/15 for international students; for spring admission, 8/1 for domestic students, 9/15 for international students. Applications are processed on a rolling basis. Application fee: $40. Electronic applications accepted. *Expenses:* Tuition, state resident: part-time $442 per credit. Tuition, nonresident: part-time $451 per credit. *Required fees:* $142.40 per semester. One-time fee: $150 part-time. *Financial support:* In 2013–14, 8 research assistantships with full and partial tuition reimbursements (averaging $9,420 per year) were awarded;

career-related internships or fieldwork also available. Support available to part-time students. Financial award application deadline: 3/1. *Unit head:* Ray Puller, Interim Dean, 814-393-2146, Fax: 514-393-2446, E-mail: rpuller@clarion.edu. *Application contact:* Susan Staub, Assistant Director, Graduate Programs, 814-393-2337, Fax: 814-393-2722, E-mail: gradstudies@clarion.edu. Website: http://www.clarion.edu/25887/.

Clark Atlanta University, School of Education, Atlanta, GA 30314. Offers MA, MAT, Ed D, Ed S. *Accreditation:* NCATE. Part-time and evening/weekend programs available. *Faculty:* 10 full-time (4 women), 10 part-time/adjunct (7 women). *Students:* 74 full-time (55 women), 55 part-time (36 women); includes 125 minority (123 Black or African American, non-Hispanic/Latino; 1 Asian, non-Hispanic/Latino; 1 Hispanic/Latino), 1 international. Average age 33. 53 applicants, 91% accepted, 41 enrolled. In 2013, 16 master's, 14 doctorates, 1 other advanced degree awarded. *Degree requirements:* For master's, comprehensive exam; for doctorate, comprehensive exam, thesis/dissertation. *Entrance requirements:* For master's, GRE General Test, minimum undergraduate GPA of 2.6; for doctorate, GRE General Test, minimum graduate GPA of 3.0. Additional exam requirements/recommendations for international students: Required—TOEFL (minimum score 500 paper-based; 61 iBT). *Application deadline:* For fall admission, 4/1 for domestic and international students; for spring admission, 11/1 for domestic and international students. Applications are processed on a rolling basis. Application fee: $40 ($55 for international students). Electronic applications accepted. *Expenses: Tuition:* Full-time $14,616; part-time $812 per credit hour. *Required fees:* $706; $353 per semester. *Financial support:* Career-related internships or fieldwork, Federal Work-Study, scholarships/grants, and unspecified assistantships available. Support available to part-time students. Financial award application deadline: 4/30; financial award applicants required to submit FAFSA. *Unit head:* Dr. Sean Warner, Interim Dean, 404-880-8504, E-mail: swarner@cau.edu. *Application contact:* Michelle Clark-Davis, Graduate Program Admissions, 404-880-6605, E-mail: cauadmissions@cau.edu.

Clarke University, Program in Education, Dubuque, IA 52001-3198. Offers early childhood/special education (MAE); educational administration: elementary and secondary (MAE); educational media: elementary and secondary (MAE); multi-categorical resource k-12 (MAE); multidisciplinary studies (MAE); reading: elementary (MAE); technology in education (MAE). Part-time and evening/weekend programs available. Postbaccalaureate distance learning degree programs offered (minimal on-campus study). *Faculty:* 10 full-time (9 women), 1 (woman) part-time/adjunct. *Students:* 5 full-time (3 women), 27 part-time (24 women); includes 2 minority (1 Black or African American, non-Hispanic/Latino; 1 American Indian or Alaska Native, non-Hispanic/Latino). In 2013, 11 master's awarded. *Degree requirements:* For master's, comprehensive exam, thesis optional. *Entrance requirements:* For master's, GRE General Test or MAT, minimum GPA of 2.75. *Application deadline:* Applications are processed on a rolling basis. Application fee: $25. Electronic applications accepted. *Expenses: Tuition:* Part-time $660 per credit. *Required fees:* $15 per credit. *Financial support:* Career-related internships or fieldwork available. Financial award applicants required to submit FAFSA. *Unit head:* Dr. Michele Slover, Chair, 319-588-6397, Fax: 319-584-8604. *Application contact:* Kara Shroeder, Information Contact, 563-588-6354, Fax: 563-588-6789, E-mail: graduate@clarke.edu.

Clark University, Graduate School, Adam Institute for Urban Teaching and School Practice, Worcester, MA 01610-1477. Offers MAT. *Faculty:* 6 full-time (5 women), 3 part-time/adjunct (2 women). *Students:* 31 full-time (21 women), 9 part-time (all women); includes 6 minority (1 Black or African American, non-Hispanic/Latino; 1 Asian, non-Hispanic/Latino; 3 Hispanic/Latino; 1 Two or more races, non-Hispanic/Latino). Average age 24. 47 applicants, 81% accepted, 38 enrolled. In 2013, 41 master's awarded. *Degree requirements:* For master's, thesis or alternative, oral exam. *Entrance requirements:* For master's, GRE General Test, minimum GPA of 3.0, professional experience. Additional exam requirements/recommendations for international students: Required—TOEFL. *Application deadline:* For fall admission, 2/1 priority date for domestic students. Applications are processed on a rolling basis. Application fee: $50. *Expenses: Tuition:* Full-time $39,200; part-time $1225 per credit hour. *Financial support:* Fellowships with full and partial tuition reimbursements, research assistantships with full and partial tuition reimbursements, teaching assistantships with full and partial tuition reimbursements, institutionally sponsored loans, and tuition waivers (partial) available. Financial award application deadline: 5/1. *Faculty research:* Developmental learning, instructional theory, educational program management, special education, urban education. *Total annual research expenditures:* $360,000. *Unit head:* Dr. Thomas Del Prete, Director, 508-793-7197. *Application contact:* Marlene Shepard, Program Coordinator, 508-793-7715, Fax: 508-793-8864, E-mail: mshepard@clarku.edu. Website: http://www.clarku.edu/education/adam-institute/mat/index.cfm.

Clayton State University, School of Graduate Studies, College of Arts and Sciences, Program in Education, Morrow, GA 30260-0285. Offers English (MAT); mathematics (MAT). *Accreditation:* NCATE. *Entrance requirements:* For master's, GRE, GACE, 2 official copies of transcripts, 3 recommendation letters, statement of purpose. Additional exam requirements/recommendations for international students: Required—TOEFL (minimum score 550 paper-based). Electronic applications accepted.

Clemson University, Graduate School, College of Health, Education, and Human Development, Eugene T. Moore School of Education, Clemson, SC 29634. Offers administration and supervision (K-12) (M Ed, Ed S); counselor education (M Ed), including clinical mental health counseling, community mental health, school counseling (K-12); student affairs (higher education); curriculum and instruction (PhD); educational leadership (PhD), including higher education, K-12; human resource development (MHRD); literacy (M Ed); middle grades education (MAT); secondary education: math and science (MAT); special education (M Ed); teaching and learning (M Ed), including elementary education, English education, mathematics education, science education, social studies education. Part-time programs available. *Faculty:* 38 full-time (25 women), 1 (woman) part-time/adjunct. *Students:* 233 full-time (171 women), 324 part-time (199 women); includes 109 minority (83 Black or African American, non-Hispanic/Latino; 3 Asian, non-Hispanic/Latino; 14 Hispanic/Latino; 1 Native Hawaiian or other Pacific Islander, non-Hispanic/Latino; 8 Two or more races, non-Hispanic/Latino), 10 international. Average age 30. 469 applicants, 58% accepted, 190 enrolled. In 2013, 185 master's, 17 doctorates, 19 other advanced degrees awarded. *Degree requirements:* For doctorate, thesis/dissertation. *Entrance requirements:* For master's and doctorate, GRE General Test; for Ed S, GRE General Test, PRAXIS II, 1 year of teaching experience. Additional exam requirements/recommendations for international students: Required—TOEFL. *Application deadline:* Applications are processed on a rolling basis. Application fee: $70 ($80 for international students). Electronic applications accepted. *Expenses:* Contact institution. *Financial support:* In 2013–14, 147 students received support, including 17 fellowships with full and partial tuition reimbursements available (averaging $4,000 per year), 27 research assistantships with partial tuition reimbursements available (averaging $12,000 per year), 16 teaching assistantships with partial tuition reimbursements available (averaging $21,000 per year); career-related internships or fieldwork, institutionally sponsored loans, scholarships/grants, health care benefits, tuition waivers (full), and unspecified assistantships also available. Support available to part-time students. Financial award application deadline: 6/1; financial award applicants required to submit FAFSA. *Total annual research expenditures:* $5.3

million. *Unit head:* Dr. Michael J. Padilla, Director/Associate Dean, 864-656-4444, Fax: 864-656-0311, E-mail: padilla@clemson.edu. *Application contact:* Dr. David Fleming, Graduate Programs Coordinator, 864-656-1881, Fax: 864-656-0311, E-mail: dflemin@clemson.edu. Website: http://www.clemson.edu/hehd/departments/education/index.html.

Cleveland State University, College of Graduate Studies, College of Education and Human Services, Cleveland, OH 44115. Offers M Ed, MPH, PhD, Certificate, Ed S. *Accreditation:* NCATE. Part-time and evening/weekend programs available. Postbaccalaureate distance learning degree programs offered (minimal on-campus study). *Faculty:* 86 full-time (60 women), 106 part-time/adjunct (81 women). *Students:* 269 full-time (193 women), 696 part-time (533 women); includes 268 minority (214 Black or African American, non-Hispanic/Latino; 11 Asian, non-Hispanic/Latino; 29 Hispanic/Latino; 1 Native Hawaiian or other Pacific Islander, non-Hispanic/Latino; 13 Two or more races, non-Hispanic/Latino), 75 international. Average age 35. 487 applicants, 58% accepted, 243 enrolled. In 2013, 331 master's, 18 doctorates, 7 other advanced degrees awarded. *Degree requirements:* For master's, comprehensive exam (for some programs), thesis optional; for doctorate, one foreign language, comprehensive exam, thesis/dissertation; for other advanced degree, comprehensive exam (for some programs), thesis optional, internship. *Entrance requirements:* For master's, GRE General Test or MAT, minimum undergraduate GPA of 2.75, 3.0 if undergraduate degree is 6 or more years old; for doctorate, GRE General Test, master's degree, minimum graduate GPA of 3.25; for other advanced degree, GRE General Test or MAT, master's degree, minimum graduate GPA of 3.0. Additional exam requirements/recommendations for international students: Required—TOEFL (minimum score 525 paper-based; 65 iBT). *Application deadline:* For fall admission, 7/15 priority date for domestic students, 5/15 for international students; for spring admission, 12/8 priority date for domestic students, 11/1 for international students. Applications are processed on a rolling basis. Application fee: $30. Electronic applications accepted. *Expenses: Tuition,* state resident: full-time $8335; part-time $521 per credit hour. *Tuition,* nonresident: full-time $15,670; part-time $979 per credit hour. *Required fees:* $50; $25 per semester. *Financial support:* In 2013–14, 64 students received support, including 38 research assistantships with full tuition reimbursements available (averaging $6,960 per year), 2 teaching assistantships with full tuition reimbursements available (averaging $7,800 per year); career-related internships or fieldwork, Federal Work-Study, scholarships/grants, tuition waivers (partial), and unspecified assistantships also available. Support available to part-time students. Financial award application deadline: 8/1; financial award applicants required to submit FAFSA. *Faculty research:* Adult learning and development, counseling theory and practice, equity issues in education (race, ethnicity, gender, socioeconomics), health care and health education, population nursing, urban educational leadership, curriculum and instruction. *Total annual research expenditures:* $7.5 million. *Unit head:* Dr. Sajit Zachariah, Dean, 216-523-7143, Fax: 216-687-5415, E-mail: sajit.zachariah@csuohio.edu. *Application contact:* Patricia Sokolowski, Office Coordinator/Assistant to the Dean, 216-523-7143, Fax: 216-687-5415, E-mail: p.sokolowski@csuohio.edu. Website: http://www.csuohio.edu/cehs/.

Coastal Carolina University, William L. Spadoni College of Education, Conway, SC 29528-6054. Offers education (MAT); educational leadership (M Ed); learning and teaching (M Ed). *Accreditation:* NCATE. Part-time and evening/weekend programs available. *Faculty:* 14 full-time (7 women), 8 part-time/adjunct (5 women). *Students:* 82 full-time (54 women), 218 part-time (174 women); includes 37 minority (29 Black or African American, non-Hispanic/Latino; 1 American Indian or Alaska Native, non-Hispanic/Latino; 4 Hispanic/Latino; 2 Native Hawaiian or other Pacific Islander, non-Hispanic/Latino; 1 Two or more races, non-Hispanic/Latino), 1 international. Average age 33. 240 applicants, 94% accepted, 159 enrolled. In 2013, 115 master's awarded. *Degree requirements:* For master's, comprehensive exam. *Entrance requirements:* For master's, GRE, MAT, 2 letters of recommendation, evidence of teacher certification, official transcripts. Additional exam requirements/recommendations for international students: Required—TOEFL (minimum score 575 paper-based; 89 iBT). *Application deadline:* For fall admission, 7/1 priority date for domestic and international students; for spring admission, 11/1 priority date for domestic and international students; for summer admission, 5/1 priority date for domestic and international students. Applications are processed on a rolling basis. Application fee: $45. Electronic applications accepted. *Expenses: Tuition,* state resident: full-time $11,976; part-time $499 per credit hour. *Tuition,* nonresident: full-time $18,936; part-time $789 per credit hour. *Required fees:* $80; $40 per term. Tuition and fees vary according to program. *Financial support:* Fellowships, research assistantships, and unspecified assistantships available. Support available to part-time students. Financial award application deadline: 3/1; financial award applicants required to submit FAFSA. *Unit head:* Dr. Edward Jadallah, Dean, 843-349-2773, Fax: 843-349-2106, E-mail: ejadalla@coastal.edu. *Application contact:* Dr. James O. Luken, Associate Provost/Director of Graduate Studies, 843-349-2235, Fax: 843-349-6444, E-mail: joluken@coastal.edu. Website: http://www.coastal.edu/education/.

The College at Brockport, State University of New York, School of Education and Human Services, Department of Education and Human Development, Brockport, NY 14420-2997. Offers adolescence education (MS Ed), including adolescence biology education, adolescence chemistry education, adolescence earth science education, adolescence English education, adolescence mathematics education, adolescence physics education, adolescence social studies education; adolescence inclusive generalist education (MS Ed), including English, mathematics, science, social studies; bilingual education (MS Ed, AGC), including bilingual education, Spanish (AGC); childhood curriculum specialist (MS Ed); childhood literacy (MS Ed). *Accreditation:* NCATE. *Faculty:* 14 full-time (10 women), 11 part-time/adjunct (7 women). *Students:* 52 full-time (34 women), 177 part-time (138 women); includes 19 minority (5 Black or African American, non-Hispanic/Latino; 1 American Indian or Alaska Native, non-Hispanic/Latino; 2 Asian, non-Hispanic/Latino; 9 Hispanic/Latino; 2 Two or more races, non-Hispanic/Latino). 81 applicants, 81% accepted, 44 enrolled. In 2013, 71 master's, 3 AGCs awarded. *Degree requirements:* For master's, thesis or alternative. *Entrance requirements:* For master's, minimum GPA of 3.0, letters of recommendation, interview (for some programs); statement of objectives, current resume. Additional exam requirements/recommendations for international students: Required—TOEFL (minimum score 550 paper-based; 79 iBT), IELTS (minimum score 6.5). *Application deadline:* For fall admission, 3/15 priority date for domestic and international students; for spring admission, 10/15 priority date for domestic and international students; for summer admission, 3/15 priority date for domestic and international students. Application fee: $80. Electronic applications accepted. *Expenses: Tuition,* state resident: full-time $9870. *Tuition,* nonresident: full-time $18,350. *Required fees:* $1848. *Financial support:* In 2013–14, 1 fellowship with full tuition reimbursement (averaging $7,500 per year), 1 teaching assistantship with full tuition reimbursement (averaging $6,000 per year) were awarded; Federal Work-Study, scholarships/grants, and unspecified assistantships also available. Support available to part-time students. Financial award application deadline: 3/15; financial award applicants required to submit FAFSA. *Faculty research:* Educational assessment, literacy education, inclusive education, teacher preparation, qualitative methodology. *Unit head:* Dr. Don Halquist, Chairperson, 585-395-5550, Fax: 585-395-2172, E-mail: snovinge@brockport.edu. *Application contact:* Michael Harrison,

Coordinator of Certification and Graduate Advisement, 585-395-2326, Fax: 585-395-2172, E-mail: mharriso@brockport.edu.
Website: http://www.brockport.edu/ehd/.

College of Charleston, Graduate School, School of Education, Health, and Human Performance, Charleston, SC 29424-0001. Offers M Ed, MAT, Certificate. *Accreditation:* NCATE. Part-time and evening/weekend programs available. *Degree requirements:* For master's, thesis or alternative, written qualifying exam, student teaching experience (MAT). *Entrance requirements:* For master's, teaching certificate (M Ed). Additional exam requirements/recommendations for international students: Required—TOEFL (minimum score 81 iBT). Electronic applications accepted. *Faculty research:* Computer-assisted instruction, higher education, faculty development, teaching study skills to college students.

The College of Idaho, Department of Education, Caldwell, ID 83605. Offers teaching (MAT); M Div/MPPM. *Degree requirements:* For master's, thesis. *Entrance requirements:* For master's, GRE, portfolio, minimum undergraduate GPA of 3.0, interview. *Faculty research:* Discourse analysis, at-risk youth, children's literature, research design, program evaluation.

College of Mount Saint Vincent, School of Professional and Continuing Studies, Department of Teacher Education, Riverdale, NY 10471-1093. Offers instructional technology and global perspectives (Certificate); middle level education (Certificate); multicultural studies (Certificate); urban and multicultural education (MS Ed). *Accreditation:* Teacher Education Accreditation Council. Part-time programs available. *Degree requirements:* For master's, comprehensive exam. *Entrance requirements:* For master's, interview, New York teaching certificate. Additional exam requirements/recommendations for international students: Required—TOEFL.

The College of New Jersey, Graduate Studies, School of Education, Ewing, NJ 08628. Offers M Ed, MA, MAT, Certificate, Ed S. *Accreditation:* NCATE. Part-time and evening/weekend programs available. *Degree requirements:* For master's, comprehensive exam. *Entrance requirements:* For master's, GRE, minimum GPA of 3.0 in field or 2.75 overall; for other advanced degree, previous master's degree or higher. Additional exam requirements/recommendations for international students: Required—TOEFL. Electronic applications accepted.

The College of New Rochelle, Graduate School, Division of Education, New Rochelle, NY 10805-2308. Offers creative teaching and learning (MS Ed, Certificate); elementary education/early childhood education (MS Ed); literacy education (MS Ed); school administration and supervision (MS, Advanced Certificate, Advanced Diploma), including dual certification: school building leader/school district leader (MS), school building leader (MS, Advanced Certificate), school district leader (MS, Advanced Diploma); special education (MS Ed); teaching English as a second language and multilingual/multicultural education (MS Ed, Certificate), including bilingual education (Certificate), teaching English as a second language (MS Ed). Part-time and evening/weekend programs available. *Faculty:* 11 full-time (9 women), 11 part-time/adjunct (7 women). *Students:* 42 full-time (39 women), 227 part-time (207 women); includes 135 minority (85 Black or African American, non-Hispanic/Latino; 1 American Indian or Alaska Native, non-Hispanic/Latino; 6 Asian, non-Hispanic/Latino; 42 Hispanic/Latino; 1 Native Hawaiian or other Pacific Islander, non-Hispanic/Latino). Average age 30. In 2013, 120 master's awarded. *Degree requirements:* For master's, comprehensive exam (for some programs), thesis (for some programs). *Entrance requirements:* For master's, interview, minimum GPA of 3.0 in field, 2.7 overall. *Application deadline:* For fall admission, 8/1 priority date for domestic students; for spring admission, 4/6 for domestic students. Applications are processed on a rolling basis. Application fee: $35. Electronic applications accepted. *Expenses: Tuition:* Part-time $894 per credit. *Required fees:* $300 per semester. One-time fee: $200. Tuition and fees vary according to course load. *Financial support:* Career-related internships or fieldwork, Federal Work-Study, scholarships/grants, and unspecified assistantships available. Support available to part-time students. *Unit head:* Dr. Marie Ribarich, Dean, 914-654-5333, E-mail: mribarich@cnr.edu. *Application contact:* Miguel Ramos, Director of Admission for the Graduate School, 914-654-5309, E-mail: mramos@cnr.edu.

College of Saint Elizabeth, Department of Educational Leadership, Morristown, NJ 07960-6989. Offers accelerated certification for teaching (Certificate); assistive technology (Certificate); educational leadership (MA, Ed D); special education (MA). Part-time programs available. *Faculty:* 5 full-time (0 women), 21 part-time/adjunct (9 women). *Students:* 67 full-time (44 women), 146 part-time (117 women); includes 52 minority (36 Black or African American, non-Hispanic/Latino; 2 Asian, non-Hispanic/Latino; 12 Hispanic/Latino; 1 Native Hawaiian or other Pacific Islander, non-Hispanic/Latino; 1 Two or more races, non-Hispanic/Latino), 1 international. Average age 38. In 2013, 55 master's, 14 doctorates, 42 other advanced degrees awarded. *Degree requirements:* For master's, thesis or alternative; for doctorate, thesis/dissertation. *Entrance requirements:* For master's, personal written statement, interview, minimum undergraduate GPA of 3.0; for doctorate, master's degree. Additional exam requirements/recommendations for international students: Required—TOEFL. *Application deadline:* For fall admission, 6/30 priority date for domestic students; for spring admission, 11/30 for domestic students. Applications are processed on a rolling basis. Application fee: $35. Electronic applications accepted. *Expenses: Tuition:* Full-time $19,152; part-time $1064 per credit. *Financial support:* Career-related internships or fieldwork, tuition waivers (partial), and unspecified assistantships available. Support available to part-time students. Financial award application deadline: 3/15; financial award applicants required to submit FAFSA. *Faculty research:* Developmental stages for teaching and human services professionals, effectiveness of humanities core curriculum. *Unit head:* Dr. Joseph Ciccone, Associate Professor/Course of Study Coordinator, 973-290-4383, Fax: 973-290-4389, E-mail: jciccone@cse.edu. *Application contact:* Deborah S. Cobo, Associate Director for Graduate Admissions, 973-290-4194, Fax: 973-290-4710, E-mail: dscobo@cse.edu.
Website: http://www.cse.edu/academics/catalog/academic-programs/education.dot?tabID=tabMinor&divID=catalogMinor#maeducation.

College of St. Joseph, Graduate Programs, Division of Education, Rutland, VT 05701-3899. Offers elementary education (M Ed); general education (M Ed); reading (M Ed); secondary education (M Ed), including English, social studies; special education (M Ed). Part-time and evening/weekend programs available. *Degree requirements:* For master's, comprehensive exam. *Entrance requirements:* For master's, PRAXIS I, essay; two letters of reference from academic or professional sources; official transcripts of all graduate and undergraduate study. Additional exam requirements/recommendations for international students: Required—TOEFL (minimum score 550 paper-based). Electronic applications accepted. *Faculty research:* Co-teaching, Response to Intervention (RTI).

College of Saint Mary, Program in Teaching, Omaha, NE 68106. Offers MAT. Evening/weekend programs available. *Entrance requirements:* For master's, Pre-Professional Skills Tests (PPST), minimum cumulative GPA of 2.5, background check.

The College of Saint Rose, Graduate Studies, School of Education, Albany, NY 12203-1419. Offers MS, MS Ed, Certificate. *Accreditation:* NCATE. Part-time and evening/weekend programs available. *Degree requirements:* For master's, thesis or alternative. *Entrance requirements:* For master's, minimum undergraduate GPA of 3.0. Additional exam requirements/recommendations for international students: Required—TOEFL (minimum score 550 paper-based). Electronic applications accepted.

The College of St. Scholastica, Graduate Studies, Department of Education, Duluth, MN 55811-4199. Offers M Ed, MS, Certificate. *Accreditation:* Teacher Education Accreditation Council. Part-time and evening/weekend programs available. Postbaccalaureate distance learning degree programs offered (minimal on-campus study). *Faculty:* 4 full-time (2 women), 6 part-time/adjunct (5 women). *Students:* 145 full-time (108 women), 95 part-time (78 women); includes 12 minority (1 Black or African American, non-Hispanic/Latino; 2 American Indian or Alaska Native, non-Hispanic/Latino; 6 Asian, non-Hispanic/Latino; 3 Two or more races, non-Hispanic/Latino), 1 international. Average age 34. 73 applicants, 68% accepted, 41 enrolled. In 2013, 61 master's, 86 other advanced degrees awarded. *Entrance requirements:* Additional exam requirements/recommendations for international students: Required—TOEFL (minimum score 550 paper-based; 79 iBT). *Application deadline:* For fall admission, 7/15 priority date for domestic and international students; for spring admission, 11/15 for domestic and international students; for summer admission, 5/1 priority date for domestic and international students. Applications are processed on a rolling basis. Application fee: $0. Electronic applications accepted. Application fee is waived when completed online. Tuition and fees vary according to course load, program and student level. *Financial support:* In 2013–14, 10 students received support. Scholarships/grants available. Support available to part-time students. Financial award applicants required to submit FAFSA. *Unit head:* Chery Takkunen, Director, 218-723-7052, Fax: 218-723-2275. *Application contact:* Lindsay Lahti, Director of Graduate and Extended Studies Recruitment, 218-733-2240, Fax: 218-733-2275, E-mail: llahti@css.edu.
Website: http://www.css.edu/Graduate/Masters-Doctoral-and-Professional-Programs/Areas-of-Study/Graduate-Teaching-Licensure.html.

College of Staten Island of the City University of New York, Graduate Programs, School of Education, Staten Island, NY 10314-6600. Offers adolescence education (MS Ed); childhood education (MS Ed); leadership in education (Post-Master's Certificate); special education (MS Ed). *Accreditation:* NCATE. *Faculty:* 20 full-time (13 women), 20 part-time/adjunct (10 women). *Students:* 39 full-time (32 women), 436 part-time (357 women). Average age 29. 233 applicants, 68% accepted, 114 enrolled. In 2013, 172 master's, 28 other advanced degrees awarded. Application fee: $125. *Expenses:* Tuition, state resident: full-time $9240; part-time $385 per credit hour. Tuition, nonresident: full-time $17,040; part-time $710 per credit hour. *Required fees:* $428; $128 per term. *Financial support:* Applicants required to submit FAFSA. *Unit head:* Dr. Kenneth Gold, Interim Dean, 718-982-3718, Fax: 718-982-3743, E-mail: kenneth.gold@csi.cuny.edu. *Application contact:* Sasha Spence, Assistant Director for Graduate Admissions, 718-982-2019, Fax: 718-982-2500, E-mail: sasha.spence@csi.cuny.edu.
Website: http://csivc.csi.cuny.edu/education/files.

The College of William and Mary, School of Education, Williamsburg, VA 23187-8795. Offers M Ed, MA Ed, Ed D, PhD, Ed S. *Accreditation:* NCATE. Part-time and evening/weekend programs available. *Faculty:* 41 full-time (23 women), 71 part-time/adjunct (57 women). *Students:* 224 full-time (180 women), 195 part-time (152 women); includes 77 minority (43 Black or African American, non-Hispanic/Latino; 2 American Indian or Alaska Native, non-Hispanic/Latino; 8 Asian, non-Hispanic/Latino; 12 Hispanic/Latino; 12 Two or more races, non-Hispanic/Latino), 13 international. Average age 33. 542 applicants, 6% accepted, 216 enrolled. In 2013, 134 master's, 22 doctorates, 9 other advanced degrees awarded. *Degree requirements:* For master's, project; for doctorate, comprehensive exam, thesis/dissertation; for Ed S, internship. *Entrance requirements:* For master's, GRE or MAT, minimum GPA of 2.5; for doctorate, GRE or MAT, minimum GPA of 3.5; for Ed S, GRE, minimum GPA of 3.0. Additional exam requirements/recommendations for international students: Required—TOEFL, IELTS. *Application deadline:* For fall admission, 1/15 for domestic and international students; for spring admission, 10/1 for domestic and international students. Application fee: $50. Electronic applications accepted. *Expenses:* Tuition, state resident: full-time $7120; part-time $405 per credit hour. Tuition, nonresident: full-time $21,639; part-time $1050 per credit hour. *Required fees:* $4764. *Financial support:* In 2013–14, 155 students received support, including 1 fellowship with full tuition reimbursement available (averaging $20,000 per year), 97 research assistantships with full and partial tuition reimbursements available (averaging $14,717 per year); career-related internships or fieldwork, Federal Work-Study, institutionally sponsored loans, scholarships/grants, and unspecified assistantships also available. Financial award application deadline: 1/15; financial award applicants required to submit FAFSA. *Faculty research:* Writing, gifted education, curriculum and instruction, special education, leadership, faculty development, cultural diversity. *Total annual research expenditures:* $6.7 million. *Unit head:* Dr. Spencer G. Niles, Dean, 757-221-2317, E-mail: sgniles@wm.edu. *Application contact:* Dorothy Smith Osborne, Assistant Dean for Academic Programs and Student Services, 757-221-2317, Fax: 757-221-2293, E-mail: dsosbo@wm.edu.
Website: http://education.wm.edu.

Colorado Christian University, Program in Curriculum and Instruction, Lakewood, CO 80226. Offers corporate education (MACI); early childhood educator (MACI); elementary educator (MACI); instructional technology (MACI); master educator (MACI); online course developer (MACI); online teaching and learning (MACI); special education generalist (MACI). Part-time and evening/weekend programs available. *Degree requirements:* For master's, thesis optional, practicum. *Entrance requirements:* For master's, interviews, letters of recommendation. Additional exam requirements/recommendations for international students: Required—TOEFL. Electronic applications accepted. *Expenses:* Contact institution.

The Colorado College, Education Department, Colorado Springs, CO 80903-3294. Offers elementary education (MAT), including elementary school teaching; secondary education (MAT), including art teaching (K-12), English teaching, foreign language teaching, mathematics teaching, music teaching, science teaching, social studies teaching; teaching (MAT), including arts and humanities, integrated natural sciences, liberal arts, Southwest studies. *Degree requirements:* For master's, thesis, internship. Electronic applications accepted. *Faculty research:* Geology, environmental resources, urban education, educational psychology, arts integration in the classroom, literacy/early childhood.

Colorado Mesa University, Center for Teacher Education, Grand Junction, CO 81501-3122. Offers educational leadership (MAEd); English for speakers of other languages (MAEd). *Accreditation:* NCATE. Part-time programs available. Postbaccalaureate distance learning degree programs offered (minimal on-campus study). *Degree requirements:* For master's, comprehensive exam, capstone presentation. *Entrance requirements:* For master's, GRE, 2 professional letters of recommendation. Additional exam requirements/recommendations for international students: Required—TOEFL (minimum score 550 paper-based). Electronic applications accepted.

Colorado State University, Graduate School, College of Health and Human Sciences, School of Education, Fort Collins, CO 80523-1588. Offers adult education and training (M Ed); community college leadership (PhD); counseling and career development (M Ed); education and human resource studies (M Ed, PhD); educational leadership (M Ed, PhD); interdisciplinary studies (PhD); organizational performance and change (M Ed, PhD); student affairs in higher education (MS). *Accreditation:* ACA; Teacher

Education Accreditation Council. Part-time and evening/weekend programs available. *Faculty:* 19 full-time (10 women). *Students:* 84 full-time (60 women), 545 part-time (356 women); includes 115 minority (26 Black or African American, non-Hispanic/Latino; 5 American Indian or Alaska Native, non-Hispanic/Latino; 13 Asian, non-Hispanic/Latino; 56 Hispanic/Latino; 15 Two or more races, non-Hispanic/Latino), 22 international. Average age 37. 475 applicants, 38% accepted, 147 enrolled. In 2013, 1,157 master's, 43 doctorates awarded. *Degree requirements:* For master's, comprehensive exam, thesis optional; for doctorate, comprehensive exam, thesis/dissertation, minimum of 60 credits. *Entrance requirements:* For master's and doctorate, GRE, minimum GPA of 3.0. Additional exam requirements/recommendations for international students: Required—TOEFL (minimum score 550 paper-based; 80 iBT), IELTS. *Application deadline:* For fall admission, 3/1 priority date for domestic and international students; for spring admission, 9/1 for domestic and international students. Applications are processed on a rolling basis. Application fee: $50. Electronic applications accepted. *Expenses:* Tuition, state resident: full-time $9075.40; part-time $504 per credit. Tuition, nonresident: full-time $22,248; part-time $1236 per credit. *Required fees:* $1819; $60 per credit. *Financial support:* In 2013–14, 7 students received support, including 1 research assistantship with partial tuition reimbursement available (averaging $16,135 per year), 6 teaching assistantships with partial tuition reimbursements available (averaging $10,106 per year); career-related internships or fieldwork, scholarships/grants, and unspecified assistantships also available. Financial award application deadline: 3/1; financial award applicants required to submit FAFSA. *Faculty research:* Issues in STEM education, diversity and multiculturalism, teacher education leadership, distance learning and teaching. *Total annual research expenditures:* $498,539. *Unit head:* Dr. Daniel H. Robinson, Director, 970-491-6316, Fax: 970-491-1317, E-mail: dan.robinson@colostate.edu. *Application contact:* Kelli M. Clark, Academic Coordinator, 970-491-2093, Fax: 970-491-1317, E-mail: kelli.clark@colostate.edu.
Website: http://www.soe.chhs.colostate.edu/.

Colorado State University–Pueblo, College of Education, Engineering and Professional Studies, Education Program, Pueblo, CO 81001-4901. Offers art education (M Ed); foreign language education (M Ed); health and physical education (M Ed); instructional technology (M Ed); linguistically diverse education (M Ed); music education (M Ed); special education (M Ed). *Accreditation:* Teacher Education Accreditation Council. Part-time programs available. *Degree requirements:* For master's, portfolio. *Entrance requirements:* For master's, 3 recommendations, teaching license. Additional exam requirements/recommendations for international students: Required—TOEFL (minimum score 500 paper-based). Electronic applications accepted. *Faculty research:* Portfolio assessment, math education, science education.

Columbia College, Graduate Programs, Department of Education, Columbia, SC 29203-5998. Offers divergent learning (M Ed); higher education administration (M Ed). *Accreditation:* NCATE. Part-time and evening/weekend programs available. Postbaccalaureate distance learning degree programs offered. *Faculty:* 3 full-time (1 woman), 18 part-time/adjunct (10 women). *Students:* 113 full-time (96 women), 2 part-time (1 woman); includes 50 minority (46 Black or African American, non-Hispanic/Latino; 2 American Indian or Alaska Native, non-Hispanic/Latino; 2 Asian, non-Hispanic/Latino). Average age 27. 108 applicants, 81% accepted, 77 enrolled. In 2013, 106 master's awarded. *Degree requirements:* For master's, thesis. *Entrance requirements:* For master's, GRE General Test, MAT, 2 recommendations, current South Carolina teaching certificate, minimum GPA of 3.2. *Application deadline:* For fall admission, 8/22 for domestic students. Application fee: $50. *Expenses:* Contact institution. *Financial support:* Available to part-time students. Application deadline: 7/1; applicants required to submit FAFSA. *Unit head:* Dr. Chris Burkett, Chair, 803-786-3782, Fax: 803-786-3034, E-mail: chrisburkett@colacoll.edu. *Application contact:* Carolyn Emeneker, Director of Graduate School and Evening College Admissions, 803-786-3766, Fax: 803-786-3674, E-mail: emeneker@colacoll.edu.

Columbia College, Master of Arts in Teaching Program, Columbia, MO 65216-0002. Offers MAT. Part-time and evening/weekend programs available. Postbaccalaureate distance learning degree programs offered (no on-campus study). *Faculty:* 6 full-time (4 women), 8 part-time/adjunct (6 women). *Students:* 11 full-time (9 women), 75 part-time (62 women); includes 14 minority (8 Black or African American, non-Hispanic/Latino; 1 Asian, non-Hispanic/Latino; 2 Hispanic/Latino; 3 Two or more races, non-Hispanic/Latino), 2 international. Average age 36. 64 applicants, 77% accepted, 43 enrolled. In 2013, 55 master's awarded. *Entrance requirements:* For master's, 3 letters of recommendation, minimum cumulative undergraduate GPA of 3.0, resume, goal statement. Additional exam requirements/recommendations for international students: Required—TOEFL (minimum score 500 paper-based; 61 iBT). *Application deadline:* For fall admission, 8/9 priority date for domestic and international students; for spring admission, 12/27 priority date for domestic and international students. Applications are processed on a rolling basis. Application fee: $55. Electronic applications accepted. *Expenses: Tuition:* Part-time $330 per credit hour. Tuition and fees vary according to campus/location and program. *Financial support:* In 2013–14, 3 students received support. Career-related internships or fieldwork, Federal Work-Study, and scholarships/grants available. Financial award application deadline: 3/15; financial award applicants required to submit FAFSA. *Unit head:* Dr. Kristina Miller, Graduate Program Coordinator, 573-875-7590, Fax: 573-876-4493, E-mail: kmiller@ccis.edu. *Application contact:* Stephanie Johnson, Interim Director of Admissions, 573-875-7352, Fax: 573-875-7506, E-mail: sjohnson@ccis.edu.
Website: http://www.ccis.edu/graduate/academics/degrees.asp?MAT.

Columbia College Chicago, Graduate School, Department of Education, Chicago, IL 60605-1996. Offers visual arts education (MAT). Part-time and evening/weekend programs available. *Degree requirements:* For master's, thesis, student teaching experience, 100 pre-clinical hours. *Entrance requirements:* For master's, Self Assessment Essay. Additional exam requirements/recommendations for international students: Required—TOEFL (minimum score 550 paper-based). *Application deadline:* For fall admission, 1/15 priority date for domestic and international students. Applications are processed on a rolling basis. Application fee: $55 ($100 for international students). Electronic applications accepted. *Financial support:* Fellowships, career-related internships or fieldwork, Federal Work-Study, scholarships/grants, and unspecified assistantships available. Support available to part-time students. Financial award application deadline: 8/13; financial award applicants required to submit FAFSA. *Unit head:* Sheila Brady, Program Advisor, 312-369-8147, E-mail: sbrady@colum.edu. *Application contact:* Kara Leffler, Associate Director of Graduate Admissions, 312-369-7262, Fax: 312-369-8024, E-mail: kleffler@colum.edu.
Website: http://www.colum.edu/Admissions/Graduate/programs/master-of-arts-in-teaching/index.php.

Columbia International University, Columbia Graduate School, Columbia, SC 29230-3122. Offers Bible teaching (MABT); Christian higher education leadership (Ed D); Christian school educational leadership (Ed D); counseling (MACN); curriculum and instruction (M Ed), including Christian school guidance, English as a second language, learning disabilities, school technology; early childhood and elementary education (MAT); educational administration (M Ed); teaching English as a foreign language (Certificate); teaching English as a foreign language and intercultural studies (MATF). Part-time and evening/weekend programs available. *Degree requirements:* For master's, internships, professional project. *Entrance requirements:* For master's, Minnesota Multiphasic Personality Inventory, MAT, minimum GPA of 2.7. Additional exam requirements/recommendations for international students: Required—TOEFL. Electronic applications accepted.

Columbus State University, Graduate Studies, College of Education and Health Professions, Columbus, GA 31907-5645. Offers M Ed, MAT, MPA, MS, MSN, Ed D, Ed S. *Accreditation:* ACA (one or more programs are accredited); NCATE. Part-time and evening/weekend programs available. Postbaccalaureate distance learning degree programs offered (minimal on-campus study). *Faculty:* 39 full-time (23 women), 42 part-time/adjunct (35 women). *Students:* 180 full-time (124 women), 339 part-time (269 women); includes 203 minority (166 Black or African American, non-Hispanic/Latino; 2 American Indian or Alaska Native, non-Hispanic/Latino; 8 Asian, non-Hispanic/Latino; 15 Hispanic/Latino; 12 Two or more races, non-Hispanic/Latino), 3 international. Average age 34. 313 applicants, 61% accepted, 120 enrolled. In 2013, 150 master's, 4 doctorates, 40 other advanced degrees awarded. *Degree requirements:* For master's, thesis, exit exam; for doctorate, thesis/dissertation; for Ed S, thesis or alternative. *Entrance requirements:* For master's, GRE General Test, minimum undergraduate GPA of 2.75; for doctorate, GRE General Test, minimum graduate GPA of 3.5, four years of professional service; for Ed S, GRE General Test, minimum undergraduate GPA of 2.75, graduate 3.0. Additional exam requirements/recommendations for international students: Required—TOEFL (minimum score 550 paper-based; 79 iBT). *Application deadline:* For fall admission, 6/30 for domestic students, 5/1 for international students; for spring admission, 11/1 for domestic and international students; for summer admission, 3/1 for domestic and international students. Applications are processed on a rolling basis. Application fee: $40. Electronic applications accepted. *Expenses:* Tuition, state resident: full-time $4572; part-time $382 per credit hour. Tuition, nonresident: full-time $18,292; part-time $1526 per credit hour. *Required fees:* $1800; $196 per credit hour. Tuition and fees vary according to campus/location and program. *Financial support:* In 2013–14, 354 students received support, including 39 research assistantships with partial tuition reimbursements available (averaging $3,000 per year); career-related internships or fieldwork, Federal Work-Study, institutionally sponsored loans, scholarships/grants, tuition waivers (partial), and unspecified assistantships also available. Support available to part-time students. Financial award application deadline: 5/1; financial award applicants required to submit FAFSA. *Unit head:* Dr. Barbara Buckner, Dean, 706-507-8505, Fax: 706-569-3134, E-mail: buckner_barbara@columbusstate.edu. *Application contact:* Kristin Williams, Director of International and Graduate Recruitment, 706-507-8848, Fax: 706-568-5091, E-mail: williams_kristin@columbusstate.edu.
Website: http://coehp.columbusstate.edu/.

Concordia College, Program in Education, Moorhead, MN 56562. Offers world language instruction (M Ed). *Degree requirements:* For master's, thesis/seminar. *Entrance requirements:* For master's, 2 professional references, 1 personal reference.

Concordia University, College of Education, Portland, OR 97211-6099. Offers career and technical education (M Ed); curriculum and instruction (M Ed), including adolescent literacy, career and technical education, e-learning/technology education, early childhood education, English for speakers of other languages, English language development, environmental education, mathematics, methods and curriculum, reading, science, teacher leadership, the inclusive classroom; early childhood (MAT); education leadership (Ed D); educational administration (M Ed); elementary education (MAT); secondary education (MAT); special education (M Ed); teacher leadership (Ed D). Part-time programs available. Postbaccalaureate distance learning degree programs offered (no on-campus study). *Degree requirements:* For master's, comprehensive exam, work samples/portfolio. *Entrance requirements:* For master's, California Basic Educational Skills Test or PRAXIS I, minimum undergraduate GPA of 2.8, graduate 3.0; 2 letters of recommendation. Additional exam requirements/recommendations for international students: Required—TOEFL (minimum score 525 paper-based). Electronic applications accepted. *Faculty research:* Learner-centered classroom, brain-based learning, future of online learning.

Concordia University, School of Education, Irvine, CA 92612-3299. Offers curriculum and instruction (MA); education and preliminary teaching credential (M Ed); educational administration and preliminary administrative services credential (MA); educational technology (MA); school counseling with pupil personnel services credential (MA). Part-time and evening/weekend programs available. Postbaccalaureate distance learning degree programs offered (no on-campus study). *Faculty:* 15 full-time (12 women), 96 part-time/adjunct (59 women). *Students:* 885 full-time (690 women), 96 part-time (74 women); includes 282 minority (39 Black or African American, non-Hispanic/Latino; 42 Asian, non-Hispanic/Latino; 182 Hispanic/Latino; 3 Native Hawaiian or other Pacific Islander, non-Hispanic/Latino; 16 Two or more races, non-Hispanic/Latino), 1 international. Average age 39. 402 applicants, 79% accepted, 311 enrolled. In 2013, 469 master's awarded. *Degree requirements:* For master's, action research project. *Entrance requirements:* For master's, California Basic Educational Skills Test, California Subject Examinations for Teachers (M Ed and MA in educational administration and preliminary administrative services credential), official college transcript(s), signed statement of intent, two references, copy of credential. Additional exam requirements/recommendations for international students: Required—TOEFL. *Application deadline:* For fall admission, 7/15 priority date for domestic students, 6/1 for international students; for spring admission, 11/30 priority date for domestic students, 10/1 for international students. Applications are processed on a rolling basis. Application fee: $50 ($125 for international students). Electronic applications accepted. *Expenses:* Contact institution. *Financial support:* In 2013–14, 23 students received support. Scholarships/grants and unspecified assistantships available. Financial award applicants required to submit FAFSA. *Unit head:* Dr. Janice Nelson, Dean, 949-214-3334, E-mail: janice.nelson@cui.edu. *Application contact:* Patty Hunt, Admissions Coordinator, 949-214-3362, Fax: 949-214-3362, E-mail: patricia.hunt@cui.edu.

Concordia University, School of Graduate Studies, Faculty of Arts and Science, Department of Education, Montréal, QC H3G 1M8, Canada. Offers adult education (Diploma); applied linguistics (MA); child study (MA); educational studies (MA); educational technology (MA, PhD); instructional technology (Diploma); teaching English as a second language (Certificate). *Degree requirements:* For master's, one foreign language, thesis optional; for doctorate, comprehensive exam, thesis/dissertation. *Entrance requirements:* For doctorate, MA in educational technology or equivalent.

Concordia University Chicago, College of Education, Program in Teaching, River Forest, IL 60305-1499. Offers early childhood education (MAT); elementary education (MAT); secondary education (MAT). *Degree requirements:* For master's, thesis or alternative. *Entrance requirements:* For master's, minimum GPA of 2.9. Additional exam requirements/recommendations for international students: Required—TOEFL (minimum score 550 paper-based). Electronic applications accepted.

Concordia University, Nebraska, Graduate Programs in Education, Seward, NE 68434-1556. Offers M Ed, MPE, MS. *Accreditation:* NCATE. Part-time and evening/weekend programs available. *Degree requirements:* For master's, comprehensive exam, thesis or alternative. *Entrance requirements:* For master's, GRE, MAT, or NTE, minimum GPA of 3.0, BS in education or equivalent. Additional exam requirements/

recommendations for international students: Required—TOEFL. Electronic applications accepted.

Concordia University, St. Paul, College of Education and Science, St. Paul, MN 55104-5494. Offers curriculum and instruction (MA Ed), including K-12 reading; differentiated instruction (MA Ed); early childhood education (MA Ed); educational leadership (MA Ed); educational technology (MA Ed); exercise science (MA); family life education (MA); K-12 principal licensure (Ed S); K-12 reading (Certificate); special education (MA Ed, Certificate), including autism spectrum disorder (MA Ed), emotional and behavioral disorders (MA Ed), learning disabilities (MA Ed); sports management (MA); superintendent (Ed S). *Accreditation:* NCATE. Part-time and evening/weekend programs available. Postbaccalaureate distance learning degree programs offered (minimal on-campus study). *Faculty:* 12 full-time (7 women), 92 part-time/adjunct (49 women). *Students:* 915 full-time (659 women), 64 part-time (53 women); includes 99 minority (47 Black or African American, non-Hispanic/Latino; 5 American Indian or Alaska Native, non-Hispanic/Latino; 18 Asian, non-Hispanic/Latino; 15 Hispanic/Latino; 2 Native Hawaiian or other Pacific Islander, non-Hispanic/Latino; 12 Two or more races, non-Hispanic/Latino), 24 international. Average age 34. 664 applicants, 67% accepted, 411 enrolled. In 2013, 275 master's, 69 other advanced degrees awarded. *Degree requirements:* For master's, thesis (for some programs). *Entrance requirements:* For master's, official transcripts from regionally-accredited institution stating the conferral of a bachelor's degree with minimum cumulative GPA of 3.0; personal statement; professional resume; practitioner in field through work or volunteerism; resume. Additional exam requirements/recommendations for international students: Recommended—TOEFL (minimum score 547 paper-based; 78 iBT), IELTS (minimum score 6). *Application deadline:* For fall admission, 8/1 for domestic and international students; for spring admission, 12/1 for domestic and international students; for summer admission, 5/1 for domestic and international students. Applications are processed on a rolling basis. Application fee: $50. Electronic applications accepted. *Expenses: Tuition:* Full-time $6200; part-time $425 per credit. Tuition and fees vary according to degree level and program. *Financial support:* Applicants required to submit FAFSA. *Unit head:* Dr. Donald Helmstetter, Dean, 651-641-8227, Fax: 651-641-8807, E-mail: helmstetter@csp.edu. *Application contact:* Kimberly Craig, Director of Graduate and Cohort Admission, 651-603-6223, Fax: 651-603-6320, E-mail: craig@csp.edu.

Concordia University Texas, College of Education, Austin, TX 78726. Offers M Ed. Part-time and evening/weekend programs available. *Degree requirements:* For master's, thesis (for some programs), portfolio presentation.

Concordia University Wisconsin, Graduate Programs, Department of Education, Mequon, WI 53097-2402. Offers art education (MS Ed); curriculum and instruction (MS Ed); early childhood (MS Ed); educational administration (MS Ed); environmental education (MS Ed); family studies (MS Ed); reading (MS Ed); school counseling (MS Ed); special education (MS Ed). Part-time and evening/weekend programs available. Postbaccalaureate distance learning degree programs offered (minimal on-campus study). *Degree requirements:* For master's, comprehensive exam, thesis or alternative. *Entrance requirements:* For master's, minimum GPA of 3.0, teaching license. Additional exam requirements/recommendations for international students: Required—TOEFL. *Faculty research:* Motivation, developmental learning, learning styles.

Concord University, Graduate Studies, Athens, WV 24712-1000. Offers educational leadership and supervision (M Ed); geography (M Ed); health promotion (MA); reading specialist (M Ed); special education (M Ed); teaching (MAT). Part-time and evening/weekend programs available. Postbaccalaureate distance learning degree programs offered (no on-campus study). *Degree requirements:* For master's, thesis (for some programs). *Entrance requirements:* For master's, GRE or MAT, baccalaureate degree with minimum GPA of 2.5 from regionally-accredited institution; teaching license; 2 letters of recommendation; completed disposition assessment form. Electronic applications accepted.

Converse College, School of Education and Graduate Studies, Spartanburg, SC 29302-0006. Offers M Ed, M Mus, MAT, MFA, MLA, MMFT, Ed S. *Accreditation:* NASAD; NCATE. Part-time and evening/weekend programs available. *Entrance requirements:* For master's, PRAXIS II (for M Ed), minimum GPA of 2.75; for Ed S, GRE or MAT, minimum GPA of 3.0. Electronic applications accepted. *Faculty research:* Motivation, classroom management, predictors of success in classroom teaching, sex equity in public education, gifted research.

Coppin State University, Division of Graduate Studies, Division of Education, Department of Curriculum and Instruction, Program in Teaching, Baltimore, MD 21216-3698. Offers teacher education (MAT). Part-time and evening/weekend programs available. Postbaccalaureate distance learning degree programs offered. *Degree requirements:* For master's, thesis, exit portfolio. *Entrance requirements:* For master's, GRE, resume, references.

Corban University, Graduate School, Education Program, Salem, OR 97301-9392. Offers MS Ed.

Cornell University, Graduate School, Graduate Fields of Agriculture and Life Sciences, Field of Education, Ithaca, NY 14853-0001. Offers adult and extension education (MPS, MS, PhD); learning, teaching, and social policy (MPS, MS, PhD); mathematics 7-12 (MS). *Faculty:* 21 full-time (8 women). *Students:* 14 full-time (9 women); includes 2 minority (1 Asian, non-Hispanic/Latino; 1 Hispanic/Latino), 1 international. Average age 32. 20 applicants, 20% accepted, 2 enrolled. In 2013, 17 master's, 4 doctorates awarded. Terminal master's awarded for partial completion of doctoral program. *Degree requirements:* For master's, thesis (MS); for doctorate, comprehensive exam, thesis/dissertation. *Entrance requirements:* For master's and doctorate, GRE General Test, sample of written work (recommended), 2 letters of recommendation. Additional exam requirements/recommendations for international students: Required—TOEFL (minimum score 550 paper-based; 77 iBT). *Application deadline:* For fall admission, 2/15 for domestic students. Application fee: $95. Electronic applications accepted. *Financial support:* In 2013–14, 4 students received support, including 3 fellowships with full tuition reimbursements available, 1 research assistantship with full tuition reimbursement available; teaching assistantships with full tuition reimbursements available, institutionally sponsored loans, scholarships/grants, health care benefits, tuition waivers (full and partial), and unspecified assistantships also available. Financial award applicants required to submit FAFSA. *Faculty research:* Moral development and professional ethics, public issues education and community development, socio/political issues in public education, teacher education and curriculum in agricultural science and mathematics, extension research. *Unit head:* Director of Graduate Studies, 607-255-4278, Fax: 607-255-7905. *Application contact:* Graduate Field Assistant, 607-255-4278, Fax: 607-255-7905, E-mail: rh22@cornell.edu.
Website: http://www.gradschool.cornell.edu/fields.php?id-80&a-2.

Cornerstone University, Graduate Programs, Grand Rapids, MI 49525-5897. Offers business administration (MBA); education (MA Ed); management (MSM); teaching English to speakers of other languages (MA, Graduate Certificate). Programs also offered at Holland, Kalamazoo, and Troy, MI campuses. Part-time programs available. Postbaccalaureate distance learning degree programs offered. *Degree requirements:* For master's, comprehensive exam (for some programs), thesis (for some programs). *Entrance requirements:* For master's, minimum GPA of 2.5, 2 letters of reference. Additional exam requirements/recommendations for international students: Required—TOEFL (minimum score 575 paper-based). Electronic applications accepted.

Covenant College, Program in Education, Lookout Mountain, GA 30750. Offers M Ed, MAT. Part-time programs available. *Faculty:* 7 full-time (3 women), 5 part-time/adjunct (0 women). *Students:* 43 full-time (15 women), 20 part-time (16 women); includes 5 minority (2 Black or African American, non-Hispanic/Latino; 2 Asian, non-Hispanic/Latino; 1 Hispanic/Latino), 1 international. Average age 37. 27 applicants, 100% accepted, 23 enrolled. In 2013, 26 master's awarded. *Degree requirements:* For master's, comprehensive exam, special project. *Entrance requirements:* For master's, GRE General Test, 2 professional recommendations, minimum GPA of 3.0, writing sample. *Application deadline:* For fall admission, 3/31 priority date for domestic students. Applications are processed on a rolling basis. Application fee: $50. *Expenses: Tuition:* Full-time $16,050; part-time $535 per credit hour. *Required fees:* $230. *Financial support:* In 2013–14, 30 students received support. Institutionally sponsored loans, scholarships/grants, and tuition waivers (partial) available. Support available to part-time students. Financial award application deadline: 3/1; financial award applicants required to submit FAFSA. *Unit head:* Dr. Jim Drexler, Director, 706-419-1408. *Application contact:* Rebecca Dodson, Associate Director, 706-419-1406, Fax: 706-820-0672, E-mail: rdodson@covenant.edu.
Website: http://www.covenant.edu/.

Creighton University, Graduate School, College of Arts and Sciences, Department of Education, Omaha, NE 68178-0001. Offers counselor education (MS), including college student affairs, community counseling, elementary school guidance, secondary school guidance; educational leadership (MS, Ed D), including elementary school administration (MS), leadership (Ed D), secondary school administration (MS), teacher leadership (MS); special populations in education (MS); teaching (M Ed), including elementary teaching, secondary teaching. *Accreditation:* NCATE. Part-time and evening/weekend programs available. Postbaccalaureate distance learning degree programs offered (minimal on-campus study). *Faculty:* 12 full-time (6 women). *Students:* 16 full-time (14 women), 83 part-time (57 women); includes 2 minority (both Black or African American, non-Hispanic/Latino), 1 international. Average age 32. 24 applicants, 58% accepted, 11 enrolled. In 2013, 34 master's awarded. *Degree requirements:* For master's, comprehensive exam (for some programs), portfolio. *Entrance requirements:* For master's, GRE General Test, PPST, 3 letters of recommendation; writing samples, resume. Additional exam requirements/recommendations for international students: Required—TOEFL (minimum score 550 paper-based; 80 iBT). *Application deadline:* For fall admission, 7/1 priority date for domestic students, 3/1 priority date for international students; for winter admission, 12/1 for domestic students, 7/1 for international students; for spring admission, 4/1 for domestic students, 10/1 for international students; for summer admission, 3/1 for domestic and international students. Applications are processed on a rolling basis. Application fee: $50. Electronic applications accepted. *Expenses: Tuition:* Full-time $13,608; part-time $756 per credit hour. *Required fees:* $149 per semester. Tuition and fees vary according to course load, campus/location, program, reciprocity agreements and student's religious affiliation. *Financial support:* Scholarships/grants and tuition waivers (partial) available. Support available to part-time students. Financial award applicants required to submit FAFSA. *Unit head:* Dr. Debra Ponec, Chair, 402-280-2557, E-mail: dlponec@creighton.edu. *Application contact:* Valerie Mattix, Senior Program Coordinator, 402-280-2425, Fax: 402-280-2423, E-mail: valeriemattix@creighton.edu.

Cumberland University, Program in Education, Lebanon, TN 37087. Offers MAE. Part-time and evening/weekend programs available. Postbaccalaureate distance learning degree programs offered (no on-campus study). *Degree requirements:* For master's, comprehensive exam. *Entrance requirements:* For master's, GRE General Test, MAT, or NTE, 3 letters of recommendation. Additional exam requirements/recommendations for international students: Required—TOEFL (minimum score 500 paper-based).

Curry College, Graduate Studies, Program in Education, Milton, MA 02186-9984. Offers elementary education (M Ed); foundations (non-license) (M Ed); reading (M Ed, Certificate); special education (M Ed). Part-time and evening/weekend programs available. *Degree requirements:* For master's, project or thesis. *Entrance requirements:* For master's, interview, recommendations, resume, written statement. Additional exam requirements/recommendations for international students: Required—TOEFL (minimum score 550 paper-based; 80 iBT). *Expenses:* Contact institution. *Faculty research:* Classroom trauma, therapeutic writing, inclusionary practices.

Daemen College, Education Department, Amherst, NY 14226-3592. Offers adolescence education (MS); childhood education (MS); childhood special education (MS); childhood special-alternative certification (MS); early childhood special-alternative certification (MS). Part-time programs available. *Degree requirements:* For master's, thesis optional, research thesis in lieu of comprehensive exam; completion of degree within 5 years. *Entrance requirements:* For master's, 2 letters of recommendation (professional and character), proof of initial certificate of license for professional programs, resume. Additional exam requirements/recommendations for international students: Required—TOEFL (minimum score 500 paper-based; 63 iBT), IELTS (minimum score 5.5). Electronic applications accepted. *Faculty research:* Transition for students with disabilities, early childhood special education, traumatic brain injury (TBI), reading assessment.

Dakota State University, College of Education, Madison, SD 57042-1799. Offers instructional technology (MSET). *Accreditation:* NCATE. Part-time and evening/weekend programs available. Postbaccalaureate distance learning degree programs offered (minimal on-campus study). *Faculty:* 3 full-time (1 woman), 1 part-time/adjunct (0 women). *Students:* 2 full-time (0 women), 14 part-time (9 women); includes 3 minority (1 Asian, non-Hispanic/Latino; 2 Hispanic/Latino), 1 international. Average age 34. 3 applicants, 100% accepted, 3 enrolled. In 2013, 11 master's awarded. *Degree requirements:* For master's, thesis, portfolio. *Entrance requirements:* For master's, GRE General Test, demonstration of technology skills, minimum GPA of 2.7. Additional exam requirements/recommendations for international students: Required—TOEFL (minimum score 550 paper-based; 78 iBT). *Application deadline:* For fall admission, 6/15 for domestic and international students; for spring admission, 11/15 for domestic and international students. Applications are processed on a rolling basis. Application fee: $35 ($85 for international students). *Financial support:* In 2013–14, 9 students received support, including 3 fellowships with partial tuition reimbursements available (averaging $12,956 per year); research assistantships, teaching assistantships, Federal Work-Study, scholarships/grants, tuition waivers (partial), unspecified assistantships, and administrative assistantships also available. Support available to part-time students. Financial award applicants required to submit FAFSA. *Faculty research:* Educational technology evaluation, computer-supported collaborative learning, cognitive theory and visual representation of the effects of ambiguitous wireless computing on student learning and productivity. *Unit head:* Dr. Omar El-Gayar, Dean, 605-256-5799, Fax: 605-256-5093, E-mail: omar.el-gayar@dsu.edu. *Application contact:* Erin Blankespoor, Secretary, Office of Graduate Studies and Research, 605-256-5799, Fax: 605-256-5093, E-mail: erin.blankespoor@dsu.edu.
Website: http://www.dsu.edu/educate/index.aspx.

Dakota Wesleyan University, Program in Education, Mitchell, SD 57301-4398. Offers curriculum and instruction (MA Ed); educational policy and administration (MA Ed); preK-12 principal certification (MA Ed); secondary certification (MA Ed). Part-time and evening/weekend programs available. *Degree requirements:* For master's, comprehensive exam, thesis optional, electronic portfolio. *Entrance requirements:* For master's, minimum GPA of 2.7, elementary statistics course, statement of purpose, official transcripts, resume, three letters of recommendation. Additional exam requirements/recommendations for international students: Required—TOEFL (minimum score 500 paper-based), IELTS (minimum score 6.5). Electronic applications accepted. *Faculty research:* Math, political policy, technology in the classroom.

Dallas Baptist University, Dorothy M. Bush College of Education, Teaching Program, Dallas, TX 75211-9299. Offers distance learning (MAT); early childhood (MAT); elementary (MAT); English as a second language (MAT); Montessori (MAT); multisensory (MAT); secondary (MAT). Part-time and evening/weekend programs available. *Entrance requirements:* For master's, GRE General Test, minimum GPA of 3.0. Additional exam requirements/recommendations for international students: Required—TOEFL, IELTS. *Application deadline:* Applications are processed on a rolling basis. Application fee: $25. Electronic applications accepted. *Expenses: Tuition:* Full-time $13,410; part-time $745 per credit hour. *Required fees:* $300; $150 per semester. Tuition and fees vary according to degree level. *Financial support:* Federal Work-Study, institutionally sponsored loans, scholarships/grants, and tuition waivers (full and partial) available. Support available to part-time students. Financial award applicants required to submit FAFSA. *Unit head:* Dr. Carolyn Spain, Director, 214-333-5217, E-mail: graduate@dbu.edu. *Application contact:* Kit P. Montgomery, Director of Graduate Programs, 214-333-5242, Fax: 214-333-5579, E-mail: graduate@dbu.edu.
Website: http://www3.dbu.edu/graduate/mat.asp.

Defiance College, Program in Education, Defiance, OH 43512-1610. Offers adolescent and young adult licensure (MA); mild and moderate intervention specialist (MA). Part-time programs available. *Degree requirements:* For master's, thesis (for some programs). *Entrance requirements:* For master's, teaching certificate.

Delaware State University, Graduate Programs, College of Education, Health and Public Policy, Dover, DE 19901-2277. Offers MA, MS, MSW, Ed D. *Accreditation:* NCATE. Part-time and evening/weekend programs available. *Degree requirements:* For master's, comprehensive exam, thesis optional. *Entrance requirements:* For master's, GRE General Test, minimum GPA of 3.0 in major, 2.75 overall. Additional exam requirements/recommendations for international students: Required—TOEFL (minimum score 500 paper-based). Electronic applications accepted.

Delta State University, Graduate Programs, College of Education, Cleveland, MS 38733-0001. Offers M Ed, MAT, MS, Ed D, Ed S. *Accreditation:* NCATE. Part-time and evening/weekend programs available. *Faculty:* 26 full-time (16 women), 9 part-time/adjunct (4 women). *Students:* 105 full-time (70 women), 429 part-time (340 women); includes 262 minority (251 Black or African American, non-Hispanic/Latino; 7 Hispanic/Latino; 4 Two or more races, non-Hispanic/Latino), 8 international. Average age 32. 1,503 applicants, 99% accepted, 1424 enrolled. In 2013, 143 master's, 2 doctorates, 34 other advanced degrees awarded. *Degree requirements:* For master's, thesis optional; for doctorate, thesis/dissertation. *Entrance requirements:* For doctorate, GRE General Test; for Ed S, master's degree, teaching certificate. *Application deadline:* For fall admission, 8/1 priority date for domestic students; for spring admission, 12/1 priority date for domestic students. Applications are processed on a rolling basis. Application fee: $0. *Expenses:* Tuition, state resident: full-time $3006; part-time $334 per credit hour. Tuition, nonresident: full-time $3006; part-time $334 per credit hour. *Financial support:* Research assistantships, career-related internships or fieldwork, Federal Work-Study, and institutionally sponsored loans available. Support available to part-time students. Financial award application deadline: 6/1. *Unit head:* Dr. Leslie Griffin, Dean, 662-846-4400, Fax: 662-846-4402. *Application contact:* Dr. Albert Nylander, Dean of Graduate Studies, 662-846-4875, Fax: 662-846-4313, E-mail: grad-info@deltastate.edu.
Website: http://www.deltastate.edu/pages/251.asp.

DePaul University, College of Education, Chicago, IL 60614. Offers bilingual bicultural education (M Ed, MA); counseling (M Ed, MA), including clinical mental health counseling, college student development, school counseling; curriculum studies (M Ed, MA, Ed D); early childhood education (M Ed, MA, Ed D); educating adults (MA); educational leadership (M Ed, MA, Ed D), including administration and supervision (M Ed, MA), principal preparation (M Ed, MA); elementary education (MA); mathematics education (MA); mathematics for teaching (MS); middle school mathematics education (MS); reading specialist (M Ed, MA); secondary education (M Ed, MA); social and cultural foundations in education (MA); special education (M Ed, MA); world languages education (M Ed, MA). Part-time and evening/weekend programs available. Postbaccalaureate distance learning degree programs offered (no on-campus study). *Faculty:* 61 full-time (35 women), 59 part-time/adjunct (43 women). *Students:* 628 full-time (486 women), 324 part-time (243 women); includes 304 minority (144 Black or African American, non-Hispanic/Latino; 1 American Indian or Alaska Native, non-Hispanic/Latino; 38 Asian, non-Hispanic/Latino; 98 Hispanic/Latino; 23 Two or more races, non-Hispanic/Latino), 24 international. Average age 30. In 2013, 465 master's, 4 doctorates awarded. *Degree requirements:* For doctorate, thesis/dissertation. *Application deadline:* For fall admission, 8/15 for domestic students; for winter admission, 12/1 for domestic students; for spring admission, 3/1 for domestic students. Applications are processed on a rolling basis. Application fee: $40. Electronic applications accepted. Tuition and fees vary according to course level, course load and degree level. *Financial support:* Application deadline: 12/31; applicants required to submit FAFSA. *Unit head:* Dr. Paul Zionts, Dean, 773-325-7581, Fax: 773-325-7713, E-mail: pzionts@depaul.edu. *Application contact:* Farrah Dalal, Assistant Director, 773-325-2465, Fax: 773-325-2270, E-mail: fdalal@depaul.edu.
Website: http://education.depaul.edu.

DePaul University, School for New Learning, Chicago, IL 60604. Offers applied professional studies (MA); applied technology (MS); educating adults (MA). Part-time and evening/weekend programs available. *Faculty:* 16 full-time (12 women), 6 part-time/adjunct (5 women). *Students:* 24 full-time (18 women), 122 part-time (95 women); includes 93 minority (70 Black or African American, non-Hispanic/Latino; 5 Asian, non-Hispanic/Latino; 13 Hispanic/Latino; 5 Two or more races, non-Hispanic/Latino). Average age 45. In 2013, 38 master's awarded. *Degree requirements:* For master's, thesis or alternative. *Application deadline:* For fall admission, 9/1 for domestic students; for spring admission, 3/1 for domestic students. Applications are processed on a rolling basis. Electronic applications accepted. Tuition and fees vary according to course level, course load and degree level. *Financial support:* Applicants required to submit FAFSA. *Unit head:* Dr. Russ Rogers, Program Director, 312-362-8512, Fax: 312-362-8809, E-mail: rrogers@depaul.edu. *Application contact:* Sarah Hellstrom, Assistant Director, 312-362-5744, Fax: 312-362-8809, E-mail: shellstr@depaul.edu.
Website: http://snl.depaul.edu/.

DeSales University, Graduate Division, Division of Liberal Arts and Social Sciences, Program in Education, Center Valley, PA 18034-9568. Offers early childhood education Pre K-4 (M Ed); instructional technology for K-12 (M Ed); interdisciplinary (M Ed); secondary education (M Ed); special education (M Ed); teaching English to speakers of other languages (M Ed). Part-time and evening/weekend programs available. Postbaccalaureate distance learning degree programs offered (no on-campus study). *Degree requirements:* For master's, thesis project. *Entrance requirements:* Additional exam requirements/recommendations for international students: Required—TOEFL. *Application deadline:* Applications are processed on a rolling basis. Electronic applications accepted. *Expenses: Tuition:* Part-time $790 per credit. *Financial support:* Application deadline: 5/1. *Unit head:* Dr. Judith Rance-Roney, Chair, 610-282-1100 Ext. 1323, E-mail: judith.rance-roney@desales.edu. *Application contact:* Abigail Wernicki, Director of Graduate Admissions, 610-282-1100 Ext. 1768, E-mail: gradadmissions@desales.edu.

DeVry University, Graduate Programs, Pomona, CA 91768-2642. Offers M Ed, MAFM, MBA, MHRM, MISM, MNCM, MPA, MPM, MSA.

DeVry University, Graduate Programs, Miramar, FL 33027-4150. Offers M Ed, MAFM, MBA, MHRM, MISM, MNCM, MPA, MPM, MSA.

DeVry University, Graduate Programs, Orlando, FL 32839. Offers M Ed, MAFM, MBA, MHRM, MISM, MNCM, MPA, MPM, MSA.

DeVry University, Graduate Programs, Downers Grove, IL 60515. Offers accounting and financial management (MAFM); business administration (MBA); education (MS); educational technology (MS); electrical engineering (MS); human resources management (MHRM); information systems management (MISM); network and communications management (MNCM); project management (MPM); public administration (MPA).

Doane College, Program in Education, Crete, NE 68333-2430. Offers curriculum and instruction (M Ed); educational leadership (M Ed). *Accreditation:* NCATE. Part-time and evening/weekend programs available. *Students:* 125 full-time (89 women), 502 part-time (396 women); includes 25 minority (11 Black or African American, non-Hispanic/Latino; 1 American Indian or Alaska Native, non-Hispanic/Latino; 2 Asian, non-Hispanic/Latino; 9 Hispanic/Latino; 1 Native Hawaiian or other Pacific Islander, non-Hispanic/Latino; 1 Two or more races, non-Hispanic/Latino). Average age 33. In 2013, 284 master's awarded. *Degree requirements:* For master's, thesis. *Entrance requirements:* For master's, minimum GPA of 2.5. Additional exam requirements/recommendations for international students: Required—TOEFL. *Application deadline:* Applications are processed on a rolling basis. Electronic applications accepted. *Expenses:* Contact institution. *Financial support:* Applicants required to submit FAFSA. *Unit head:* Lyn C. Forester, Dean, 402-826-8604, Fax: 402-826-8278. *Application contact:* Wilma Daddario, Assistant Dean, 402-464-1223, Fax: 402-466-4228, E-mail: wdaddario@doane.edu.
Website: http://www.doane.edu/masters-degrees.

Dominican University, School of Education, River Forest, IL 60305-1099. Offers curriculum and instruction (MA Ed); early childhood education (MS); education (MAT); educational administration (MA); elementary education (MA Ed); English as a second language (MA Ed); reading (MA Ed); special education (MS). Part-time and evening/weekend programs available. Postbaccalaureate distance learning degree programs offered (no on-campus study). *Faculty:* 19 full-time (14 women), 51 part-time/adjunct (42 women). *Students:* 18 full-time (13 women), 334 part-time (274 women); includes 76 minority (26 Black or African American, non-Hispanic/Latino; 9 Asian, non-Hispanic/Latino; 41 Hispanic/Latino). Average age 32. 119 applicants, 77% accepted, 70 enrolled. In 2013, 246 master's awarded. *Entrance requirements:* For master's, Illinois Test of Basic Skills. Additional exam requirements/recommendations for international students: Required—TOEFL (minimum score 550 paper-based; 79 iBT). *Application deadline:* Applications are processed on a rolling basis. Application fee: $25. *Expenses:* Contact institution. *Financial support:* In 2013–14, 97 students received support. Career-related internships or fieldwork, scholarships/grants, and tuition waivers (partial) available. Support available to part-time students. Financial award application deadline: 8/15; financial award applicants required to submit FAFSA. *Faculty research:* Governance of private education institutions, reading and language arts, inclusion, organizational planning, leadership and vision. *Unit head:* Dr. Colleen Reardon, Dean, 718-524-6643, Fax: 708-524-6665, E-mail: creardon@dom.edu. *Application contact:* Keven Hansen, Coordinator of Recruitment and Admissions, 708-524-6921, Fax: 708-524-6665, E-mail: educate@dom.edu.
Website: http://educate.dom.edu/.

Dordt College, Program in Education, Sioux Center, IA 51250-1697. Offers M Ed. Part-time programs available. Postbaccalaureate distance learning degree programs offered (minimal on-campus study). *Degree requirements:* For master's, comprehensive exam, thesis. *Entrance requirements:* For master's, GRE or MAT. Additional exam requirements/recommendations for international students: Required—TOEFL. Electronic applications accepted.

Dowling College, Graduate Programs in Education, Oakdale, NY 11769-1999. Offers adolescence education with middle childhood extension (MS); childhood and early childhood education (MS); childhood and gifted education (MS); childhood education (1-6) (MS); computers in education (AC); early childhood education (B-2) (MS); educational administration (Ed D); educational technology leadership (MS); educational technology specialist (AC); gifted education (AC); literacy education (MS, AC), including 5-12 (MS), B-12 (MS); literacy education (MS), including B-6; school building leader (AC); school district business leader (MBA, AC); school district leader (AC); special education (MS), including autism, severe disabilities; sport management (MS). *Accreditation:* NCATE. Part-time and evening/weekend programs available. Postbaccalaureate distance learning degree programs offered (minimal on-campus study). *Faculty:* 44 full-time (24 women), 17 part-time/adjunct (8 women). *Students:* 183 full-time (124 women), 314 part-time (231 women); includes 51 minority (19 Black or African American, non-Hispanic/Latino; 1 American Indian or Alaska Native, non-Hispanic/Latino; 3 Asian, non-Hispanic/Latino; 26 Hispanic/Latino; 2 Native Hawaiian or other Pacific Islander, non-Hispanic/Latino). Average age 32. 174 applicants, 80% accepted, 82 enrolled. In 2013, 198 master's, 33 doctorates, 48 other advanced degrees awarded. *Degree requirements:* For master's and AC, comprehensive exam; for doctorate, thesis/dissertation. *Entrance requirements:* For master's, minimum GPA of 3.0; for doctorate, GRE, master's degree; for AC, teaching certificate. Additional exam requirements/recommendations for international students: Required—TOEFL (minimum score 550 paper-based). *Application deadline:* For fall admission, 9/1 priority date for domestic students; for winter admission, 1/1 priority date for domestic students; for spring admission, 2/1 priority date for domestic students. Applications are processed on a rolling basis. Application fee: $50. Electronic applications accepted. *Expenses: Tuition:* Full-time $22,731; part-time $1029 per credit. *Required fees:* $956; $956. *Financial support:* Career-related internships or fieldwork and Federal Work-Study available. Support available to part-time students. Financial award application deadline: 6/30; financial award applicants required to submit FAFSA. *Faculty research:* Natural readers, Korean styles and learning strategies, mothers of children with disabilities, computers in instruction, cultural background and organizational roadblocks to problem solving. *Unit head:* Dr. Robert Manley, Dean, 631-244-3447, E-mail: manleyr@dowling.edu. *Application contact:* Mary Boullianne, Director of Admissions, 631-244-3274, Fax: 631-244-1059, E-mail: boulliam@dowling.edu.

Education—General

Drake University, School of Education, Des Moines, IA 50311-4516. Offers MAT, MS, MSE, MST, Ed D, Ed S. Part-time and evening/weekend programs available. *Faculty:* 26 full-time (14 women), 1 part-time/adjunct (0 women). *Students:* 92 full-time (72 women), 512 part-time (372 women); includes 37 minority (13 Black or African American, non-Hispanic/Latino; 2 American Indian or Alaska Native, non-Hispanic/Latino; 4 Asian, non-Hispanic/Latino; 14 Hispanic/Latino; 4 Two or more races, non-Hispanic/Latino), 6 international. Average age 34. 150 applicants, 53% accepted, 79 enrolled. In 2013, 198 master's, 8 doctorates, 16 other advanced degrees awarded. *Degree requirements:* For master's and Ed S, comprehensive exam, internships (for some programs); for doctorate, comprehensive exam, thesis/dissertation, internships (for some programs). *Entrance requirements:* For master's, GRE General Test, MAT, or Drake Writing Assessment, resume, 2 letters of recommendation; for doctorate, GRE General Test or MAT, master's degree, 3 letters of recommendation; for Ed S, GRE General Test or MAT. Additional exam requirements/recommendations for international students: Required—TOEFL (minimum score 550 paper-based). *Application deadline:* For fall admission, 7/1 priority date for domestic students, 6/1 priority date for international students; for spring admission, 11/1 priority date for domestic students, 10/1 priority date for international students. Applications are processed on a rolling basis. Application fee: $25. Electronic applications accepted. *Expenses:* Contact institution. *Financial support:* In 2013–14, 14 research assistantships were awarded; career-related internships or fieldwork and unspecified assistantships also available. Support available to part-time students. *Faculty research:* Counseling and rehabilitation, behavioral supports, inquiry-based science methods, teacher quality enhancement. *Total annual research expenditures:* $1.5 million. *Unit head:* Dr. Janet McMahill, Dean, 515-271-3829, E-mail: janet.mcmahill@drake.edu. *Application contact:* Ann J. Martin, Graduate Coordinator, 515-271-2034, Fax: 515-271-2831, E-mail: ann.martin@drake.edu.

Drew University, Caspersen School of Graduate Studies, Program in Education, Madison, NJ 07940-1493. Offers biology (MAT); chemistry (MAT); English (MAT); French (MAT); Italian (MAT); math (MAT); physics (MAT); social studies (MAT); Spanish (MAT); theatre arts (MAT). Part-time programs available. *Degree requirements:* For master's, student teaching internship and seminar. *Entrance requirements:* For master's, transcripts, statement of purpose, three letters of recommendation. Additional exam requirements/recommendations for international students: Required—TOEFL. *Expenses:* Contact institution.

Drexel University, Goodwin College of Professional Studies, School of Education, Philadelphia, PA 19104-2875. Offers educational administration (MS); educational improvement and transformation (MS); educational leadership and management (Ed D); educational leadership development and learning technologies (PhD); global and international education (MS); higher education (MS); human resources development (MS); learning technologies (MS); mathematics, learning and teaching (MS); special education (MS); teaching, learning and curriculum (MS). Part-time and evening/weekend programs available. Postbaccalaureate distance learning degree programs offered (no on-campus study). *Degree requirements:* For doctorate, thesis/dissertation. *Entrance requirements:* For doctorate, GRE or GMAT. Additional exam requirements/recommendations for international students: Required—TOEFL, IELTS. Electronic applications accepted. Application fee is waived when completed online. *Expenses:* Contact institution. *Faculty research:* Leadership development, mathematics education, literacy, autism, educational technology.

Drury University, Graduate Programs in Education, Springfield, MO 65802. Offers elementary education (M Ed); gifted education (M Ed); human services (M Ed); instructional mathematics K-8 (M Ed); instructional technology (M Ed); middle school teaching (M Ed); secondary education (M Ed); special education (M Ed); special reading (M Ed). *Accreditation:* NCATE. Part-time and evening/weekend programs available. *Degree requirements:* For master's, thesis. *Entrance requirements:* For master's, GRE or MAT, minimum GPA of 2.75. Additional exam requirements/recommendations for international students: Required—TOEFL. Electronic applications accepted. *Faculty research:* Cultural enrichment, research skills, parental involvement relating to reading skills, reading strategies for mainstreaming children.

Duke University, Graduate School, Program in Teaching, Durham, NC 27708. Offers MAT. *Accreditation:* NCATE. *Students:* 19 full-time (11 women); includes 4 minority (1 Asian, non-Hispanic/Latino; 3 Hispanic/Latino), 1 international. 66 applicants, 44% accepted, 19 enrolled. In 2013, 14 master's awarded. *Entrance requirements:* For master's, GRE General Test. Additional exam requirements/recommendations for international students: Required—TOEFL (minimum score 577 paper-based; 90 iBT) or IELTS (minimum score 7). *Application deadline:* For fall admission, 1/31 priority date for domestic and international students. Application fee: $80. Electronic applications accepted. *Financial support:* Application deadline: 2/15. *Unit head:* Alan Teasley, Director, 919-684-4353, Fax: 919-684-4483, E-mail: alice.frederich@duke.edu. *Application contact:* Elizabeth Hutton, Director of Admissions, 919-684-3913, E-mail: grad-admissions@duke.edu.
Website: https://web.duke.edu/MAT/.

Duquesne University, School of Education, Pittsburgh, PA 15282-0001. Offers MS Ed, Ed D, PhD, Psy D, CAGS, Post-Master's Certificate. *Accreditation:* NCATE. Part-time and evening/weekend programs available. Postbaccalaureate distance learning degree programs offered (no on-campus study). *Faculty:* 52 full-time (31 women), 72 part-time/adjunct (51 women). *Students:* 556 full-time (411 women), 89 part-time (69 women); includes 105 minority (65 Black or African American, non-Hispanic/Latino; 1 American Indian or Alaska Native, non-Hispanic/Latino; 8 Asian, non-Hispanic/Latino; 18 Hispanic/Latino; 13 Two or more races, non-Hispanic/Latino), 58 international. Average age 31. 616 applicants, 47% accepted, 202 enrolled. In 2013, 228 master's, 36 doctorates, 1 other advanced degree awarded. *Degree requirements:* For master's, comprehensive exam (for some programs); for doctorate, comprehensive exam (for some programs), thesis/dissertation (for some programs); for other advanced degree, comprehensive exam (for some programs), thesis (for some programs). *Entrance requirements:* For master's, letters of recommendation, essay, personal statement, interview, bachelor's degree; for doctorate, GRE, letters of recommendation, essay, personal statement, interview, master's degree; for other advanced degree, GRE, letters of recommendation, essay, personal statement, interview, bachelor's/master's degree. Additional exam requirements/recommendations for international students: Required—TOEFL (minimum score 550 paper-based), IELTS (minimum score 7). *Application deadline:* For fall admission, 3/1 for domestic students; for spring admission, 9/1 for domestic students. Applications are processed on a rolling basis. Application fee: $0. Electronic applications accepted. Application fee is waived when completed online. *Expenses: Tuition:* Full-time $18,162; part-time $1009 per credit. *Required fees:* $1728; $96 per credit. Tuition and fees vary according to program. *Financial support:* Research assistantships, teaching assistantships with tuition reimbursements, career-related internships or fieldwork, Federal Work-Study, institutionally sponsored loans, and tuition waivers available. Support available to part-time students. *Total annual research expenditures:* $619,905. *Unit head:* Dr. Olga Welch, Dean, 412-396-6102, Fax: 412-396-5585. *Application contact:* Michael Dolinger, Director of Student and Academic Services, 412-396-6647, Fax: 412-396-5585, E-mail: dolingerm@duq.edu.
Website: http://www.duq.edu/academics/schools/education.

D'Youville College, Department of Education, Buffalo, NY 14201-1084. Offers educational leadership (Ed D); elementary education (MS Ed, Teaching Certificate); secondary education (MS Ed, Teaching Certificate); special education (MS Ed). Part-time and evening/weekend programs available. *Students:* 96 full-time (68 women), 91 part-time (60 women); includes 14 minority (9 Black or African American, non-Hispanic/Latino; 1 American Indian or Alaska Native, non-Hispanic/Latino; 4 Hispanic/Latino), 90 international. Average age 32. 383 applicants, 48% accepted, 104 enrolled. In 2013, 128 master's awarded. *Degree requirements:* For master's, one foreign language, comprehensive exam, project or thesis. *Entrance requirements:* For master's, GRE (if GPA less than 2.75), minimum GPA of 3.0. Additional exam requirements/recommendations for international students: Required—TOEFL (minimum score 500 paper-based). *Application deadline:* For fall admission, 5/1 priority date for international students; for spring admission, 9/1 priority date for international students. Applications are processed on a rolling basis. Application fee: $25. Electronic applications accepted. *Financial support:* Career-related internships or fieldwork, Federal Work-Study, institutionally sponsored loans, scholarships/grants, tuition waivers (full and partial), and unspecified assistantships available. Support available to part-time students. Financial award application deadline: 3/1; financial award applicants required to submit FAFSA. *Faculty research:* Developmental disabilities, multiculturalism, early childhood education. *Unit head:* Dr. Hilary Lochte, Chair, 716-829-8110, Fax: 716-829-7660. *Application contact:* Mark Pavone, Graduate Admissions Director, 716-829-8400, Fax: 716-829-7900, E-mail: graduateadmissions@dyc.edu.

Earlham College, Graduate Programs, Richmond, IN 47374-4095. Offers M Ed, MAT. *Entrance requirements:* For master's, GRE, PRAXIS I, PRAXIS II.

East Carolina University, Graduate School, College of Education, Greenville, NC 27858-4353. Offers MA, MA Ed, MAT, MLS, MS, MSA, Ed D, Certificate, Ed S. *Accreditation:* NCATE. Part-time and evening/weekend programs available. Postbaccalaureate distance learning degree programs offered (no on-campus study). *Degree requirements:* For master's, comprehensive exam, thesis optional; for doctorate, thesis/dissertation. *Entrance requirements:* For master's, GRE or MAT, bachelor's degree in related field, minimum GPA of 2.5; for doctorate, GRE or MAT, interview, minimum GPA of 3.5. Additional exam requirements/recommendations for international students: Required—TOEFL. *Expenses:* Tuition, state resident: full-time $4223. Tuition, nonresident: full-time $16,540. *Required fees:* $2184.

East Central University, School of Graduate Studies, Department of Education, Ada, OK 74820-6899. Offers M Ed. *Accreditation:* NCATE. Part-time and evening/weekend programs available. *Entrance requirements:* For master's, minimum GPA of 2.5. Electronic applications accepted.

Eastern Connecticut State University, School of Education and Professional Studies/Graduate Division, Willimantic, CT 06226-2295. Offers MS. *Accreditation:* NCATE. Part-time and evening/weekend programs available. *Degree requirements:* For master's, comprehensive exam, thesis optional. *Entrance requirements:* For master's, minimum GPA of 2.7. Additional exam requirements/recommendations for international students: Required—TOEFL (minimum score 550 paper-based).

Eastern Illinois University, Graduate School, College of Education and Professional Studies, Charleston, IL 61920-3099. Offers MS, MS Ed, Ed S. *Accreditation:* NCATE. Part-time and evening/weekend programs available. In 2013, 47 other advanced degrees awarded. *Degree requirements:* For Ed S, thesis. *Application deadline:* For fall admission, 3/31 priority date for domestic students. Applications are processed on a rolling basis. Application fee: $30. *Expenses: Tuition, area resident:* Part-time $283 per credit hour. Tuition, state resident: part-time $283 per credit hour. Tuition, nonresident: part-time $679 per credit hour. *Financial support:* In 2013–14, 12 research assistantships with full tuition reimbursements (averaging $8,100 per year), 13 teaching assistantships with full tuition reimbursements (averaging $8,100 per year) were awarded; career-related internships or fieldwork and Federal Work-Study also available. Support available to part-time students. *Unit head:* Dr. Diane Jackman, Dean, 217-581-2524, Fax: 217-581-2518, E-mail: dhjackman@eiu.edu. *Application contact:* Bill Elliott, Director of Graduate Admissions, 217-581-7489, Fax: 217-581-6020, E-mail: wjelliott@eiu.edu.

Eastern Kentucky University, The Graduate School, College of Education, Richmond, KY 40475-3102. Offers MA, MA Ed, MAT. *Accreditation:* NCATE. Part-time programs available. Postbaccalaureate distance learning degree programs offered (minimal on-campus study). *Entrance requirements:* For master's, GRE General Test, minimum GPA of 2.5. *Faculty research:* Dispositions to teach, technology in education, distance learning.

Eastern Mennonite University, Program in Education, Harrisonburg, VA 22802-2462. Offers MA. *Accreditation:* NCATE. Part-time programs available. *Degree requirements:* For master's, portfolio, research projects. *Entrance requirements:* For master's, 1 year of teaching experience, interview, minimum undergraduate GPA of 2.75. Additional exam requirements/recommendations for international students: Required—TOEFL (minimum score 550 paper-based). Electronic applications accepted. *Expenses:* Contact institution. *Faculty research:* Effective literacy instruction for middle school English language learners, beginning teacher's emotional experiences, constructivist learning environments, restorative discipline.

Eastern Michigan University, Graduate School, College of Education, Ypsilanti, MI 48197. Offers MA, Ed D, PhD, Graduate Certificate, Post Master's Certificate, SPA. *Accreditation:* NCATE. Part-time and evening/weekend programs available. Postbaccalaureate distance learning degree programs offered (minimal on-campus study). *Faculty:* 85 full-time (58 women). *Students:* 216 full-time (167 women), 1,053 part-time (804 women); includes 259 minority (194 Black or African American, non-Hispanic/Latino; 5 American Indian or Alaska Native, non-Hispanic/Latino; 28 Asian, non-Hispanic/Latino; 28 Hispanic/Latino; 1 Native Hawaiian or other Pacific Islander, non-Hispanic/Latino; 3 Two or more races, non-Hispanic/Latino), 26 international. Average age 34. 900 applicants, 59% accepted, 275 enrolled. In 2013, 299 master's, 14 doctorates, 573 other advanced degrees awarded. *Degree requirements:* For doctorate, thesis/dissertation. *Entrance requirements:* For master's, GRE; for doctorate, GRE General Test. Additional exam requirements/recommendations for international students: Required—TOEFL. *Application deadline:* Applications are processed on a rolling basis. Application fee: $35. *Expenses:* Tuition, state resident: full-time $12,300; part-time $466 per credit hour. Tuition, nonresident: full-time $23,159; part-time $918 per credit hour. *Required fees:* $71 per credit hour. $46 per semester. One-time fee: $100. Tuition and fees vary according to course level and degree level. *Financial support:* Fellowships, research assistantships with full tuition reimbursements, teaching assistantships with full tuition reimbursements, career-related internships or fieldwork, Federal Work-Study, institutionally sponsored loans, scholarships/grants, tuition waivers (partial), and unspecified assistantships available. Support available to part-time students. Financial award applicants required to submit FAFSA. *Unit head:* Dean, 734-487-1414, Fax: 734-484-6471. *Application contact:* Graduate Admissions, 734-487-2400, Fax: 734-487-6559, E-mail: graduate.admissions@emich.edu.
Website: http://www.emich.edu/coe/.

Eastern Nazarene College, Adult and Graduate Studies, Division of Teacher Education, Quincy, MA 02170. Offers administration (M Ed); early childhood education

(M Ed, Certificate); elementary education (M Ed, Certificate); English as a second language (Certificate); instructional enrichment and development (Certificate); middle school education (M Ed, Certificate); moderate special needs education (Certificate); principal (Certificate); program development and supervision (Certificate); secondary education (M Ed, Certificate); special education administrator (Certificate); special needs (M Ed); supervisor (Certificate); teacher of reading (M Ed, Certificate). M Ed also available through weekend program for administration, special needs, and teacher of reading only. Part-time and evening/weekend programs available. *Entrance requirements:* Additional exam requirements/recommendations for international students: Required—TOEFL (minimum score 550 paper-based).

Eastern New Mexico University, Graduate School, College of Education and Technology, Department of Educational Studies, Portales, NM 88130. Offers counseling (MA); education (M Ed), including educational administration, secondary education; school counseling (M Ed); special education (M Sp Ed), including early childhood special education, general. *Accreditation:* NCATE. Part-time and evening/weekend programs available. Postbaccalaureate distance learning degree programs offered (minimal on-campus study). *Degree requirements:* For master's, comprehensive exam, thesis optional. *Entrance requirements:* For master's, minimum GPA of 3.0, letter of recommendation, photocopy of teaching license, writing assessment, Level II teaching license (for M Ed in educational administration). Additional exam requirements/recommendations for international students: Required—TOEFL (minimum score 550 paper-based; 79 iBT), IELTS (minimum score 6). Electronic applications accepted.

Eastern Oregon University, Master of Science Program, La Grande, OR 97850-2899. Offers MS. Part-time programs available. Postbaccalaureate distance learning degree programs offered (no on-campus study). *Degree requirements:* For master's, thesis. *Entrance requirements:* For master's, GRE General Test.

Eastern University, Graduate Education Programs, St. Davids, PA 19087-3696. Offers ESL program specialist (K-12) (Certificate); general supervisor (PreK-12) (Certificate); health and physical education (K-12) (Certificate); middle level (4-8) (Certificate); multicultural education (M Ed); pre K-4 (Certificate); pre K-4 with special education (Certificate); reading (M Ed); reading specialist (K-12) (Certificate); reading supervisor (K-12) (Certificate); school health services (M Ed); school health supervisor (Certificate); school nurse (Certificate); school principalship (K-12) (Certificate); secondary biology education (7-12) (Certificate); secondary chemistry education (7-12) (Certificate); secondary communication education (7-12) (Certificate); secondary education (7-12) (Certificate); secondary English education (7-12) (Certificate); secondary math education (7-12) (Certificate); secondary social studies education (7-12) (Certificate); special education (M Ed); special education (7-12) (Certificate); special education (Pre K-8) (Certificate); special education supervisor (N-12) (Certificate); TESOL (M Ed); world language (Certificate), including French, Mandarin Chinese, Spanish. Part-time and evening/weekend programs available. Postbaccalaureate distance learning degree programs offered (no on-campus study). *Faculty:* 22 full-time (11 women), 26 part-time/adjunct (18 women). *Students:* 77 full-time (58 women), 223 part-time (149 women); includes 112 minority (81 Black or African American, non-Hispanic/Latino; 1 American Indian or Alaska Native, non-Hispanic/Latino; 9 Asian, non-Hispanic/Latino; 18 Hispanic/Latino; 1 Native Hawaiian or other Pacific Islander, non-Hispanic/Latino; 2 Two or more races, non-Hispanic/Latino), 7 international. Average age 34. 94 applicants, 100% accepted, 81 enrolled. In 2013, 120 master's awarded. *Entrance requirements:* For master's, minimum GPA of 2.5 (for M Ed); for Certificate, minimum GPA of 3.0 for certifications. Additional exam requirements/recommendations for international students: Required—TOEFL. *Application deadline:* For fall admission, 8/14 for domestic students; for spring admission, 12/20 for domestic students. Applications are processed on a rolling basis. *Application fee:* $35. Application fee is waived when completed online. *Expenses: Tuition:* Full-time $15,600; part-time $650 per credit. *Required fees:* $27.50 per semester. One-time fee: $50. Tuition and fees vary according to course load, degree level and program. *Financial support:* In 2013–14, 84 students received support, including 6 research assistantships with partial tuition reimbursements available (averaging $7,710 per year); scholarships/grants and unspecified assistantships also available. Financial award application deadline: 3/15; financial award applicants required to submit FAFSA. *Unit head:* Harry Gutelius, Associate Dean, 610-341-1729. *Application contact:* Michael Perpiglia, Associate Director of Enrollment, 610-341-5947, Fax: 484-581-1276, E-mail: mperpigl@eastern.edu. Website: http://www.eastern.edu/academics/programs/loeb-school-education-0/graduateprograms.

Eastern Washington University, Graduate Studies, College of Arts, Letters and Education, Department of Education, Cheney, WA 99004-2431. Offers adult education (M Ed); curriculum development (M Ed); early childhood education (M Ed); education (M Ed); elementary teaching (M Ed); literacy (M Ed); secondary teaching (M Ed); teaching K-8 (M Ed). Part-time programs available. *Faculty:* 29 full-time (20 women), 22 part-time/adjunct (12 women). *Students:* 43 full-time (27 women), 28 part-time (17 women); includes 10 minority (2 Black or African American, non-Hispanic/Latino; 1 American Indian or Alaska Native, non-Hispanic/Latino; 4 Asian, non-Hispanic/Latino; 3 Hispanic/Latino). Average age 38. 33 applicants, 30% accepted, 8 enrolled. In 2013, 50 master's awarded. *Degree requirements:* For master's, comprehensive exam. *Entrance requirements:* For master's, minimum GPA of 3.0. *Application deadline:* For fall admission, 4/1 priority date for domestic students; for spring admission, 1/15 for domestic students. Applications are processed on a rolling basis. *Application fee:* $50. *Financial support:* In 2013–14, 2 teaching assistantships with partial tuition reimbursements (averaging $7,000 per year) were awarded; career-related internships or fieldwork, Federal Work-Study, institutionally sponsored loans, scholarships/grants, health care benefits, tuition waivers (partial), and unspecified assistantships also available. Support available to part-time students. Financial award application deadline: 2/1; financial award applicants required to submit FAFSA. *Unit head:* Dr. Kevin Pyatt, Assistant Professor, Science and Technology, 509-359-2831, E-mail: kpyatt@ewu.edu. *Application contact:* Dr. Robin Showalter, Graduate Program Coordinator, 509-359-6492, E-mail: rshowalter@ewu.edu. Website: http://www.ewu.edu/CALE/Programs/Education.xml.

East Stroudsburg University of Pennsylvania, Graduate College, College of Education, East Stroudsburg, PA 18301-2999. Offers M Ed. Part-time and evening/weekend programs available. Postbaccalaureate distance learning degree programs offered. *Faculty:* 15 full-time (10 women), 9 part-time/adjunct (5 women). *Students:* 42 full-time (25 women), 173 part-time (127 women); includes 34 minority (12 Black or African American, non-Hispanic/Latino; 1 American Indian or Alaska Native, non-Hispanic/Latino; 1 Asian, non-Hispanic/Latino; 16 Hispanic/Latino; 1 Native Hawaiian or other Pacific Islander, non-Hispanic/Latino; 3 Two or more races, non-Hispanic/Latino), 5 international. Average age 32. 142 applicants, 67% accepted, 73 enrolled. In 2013, 120 master's awarded. *Degree requirements:* For master's, comprehensive exam, thesis (for some programs). *Entrance requirements:* Additional exam requirements/recommendations for international students: Required—TOEFL (minimum score 560 paper-based; 83 iBT) or IELTS. *Application deadline:* For fall admission, 7/31 priority date for domestic students, 6/30 priority date for international students; for spring admission, 11/30 for domestic students, 10/31 for international students. Applications are processed on a rolling basis. *Application fee:* $50. Electronic applications accepted.

Expenses: Tuition, state resident: full-time $7956; part-time $442 per credit. Tuition, nonresident: full-time $11,934; part-time $663 per credit. *Required fees:* $2129; $118 per credit. *Financial support:* Research assistantships with full and partial tuition reimbursements, career-related internships or fieldwork, Federal Work-Study, and institutionally sponsored loans available. Financial award application deadline: 3/1; financial award applicants required to submit FAFSA. *Unit head:* Dr. Pamela Kramer, Dean, 570-422-3377, Fax: 570-422-3506, E-mail: pkramer@po-box.esu.edu. *Application contact:* Kevin Quintero, Graduate Admissions Coordinator, 570-422-3536, Fax: 570-422-3711, E-mail: kquintero@esu.edu.

East Tennessee State University, School of Graduate Studies, College of Education, Johnson City, TN 37614. Offers M Ed, MA, MAT, Ed D, PhD, Ed S, Post-Master's Certificate, Postbaccalaureate Certificate. *Accreditation:* NCATE. *Faculty:* 98 full-time (57 women), 52 part-time/adjunct (31 women). *Students:* 282 full-time (190 women), 373 part-time (267 women); includes 60 minority (37 Black or African American, non-Hispanic/Latino; 5 Asian, non-Hispanic/Latino; 8 Hispanic/Latino; 10 Two or more races, non-Hispanic/Latino), 13 international. Average age 34. 499 applicants, 56% accepted, 236 enrolled. In 2013, 170 master's, 35 doctorates, 7 other advanced degrees awarded. *Entrance requirements:* Additional exam requirements/recommendations for international students: Required—TOEFL (minimum score 550 paper-based; 79 iBT). *Expenses:* Tuition, state resident: full-time $7900; part-time $395 per credit hour. Tuition, nonresident: full-time $21,960; part-time $1098 per credit hour. *Required fees:* $1345; $84 per credit hour. *Financial support:* In 2013–14, 216 students received support, including 21 fellowships with full tuition reimbursements available, 48 research assistantships with full tuition reimbursements available, 23 teaching assistantships with full tuition reimbursements available; career-related internships or fieldwork, institutionally sponsored loans, scholarships/grants, and unspecified assistantships also available. Financial award application deadline: 7/1; financial award applicants required to submit FAFSA. *Unit head:* Dr. Hal Knight, Dean, 423-439-7626, Fax: 423-439-7560, E-mail: knighth@etsu.edu. *Application contact:* School of Graduate Studies, 423-439-4221, Fax: 423-439-5624, E-mail: gradsch@etsu.edu. Website: http://www.etsu.edu/coe/.

East Texas Baptist University, Master of Education Program, Marshall, TX 75670-1498. Offers curriculum and instruction (M Ed); sports and exercise leadership (M Ed); teacher certification (M Ed). Part-time programs available. *Entrance requirements:* For master's, GRE. Additional exam requirements/recommendations for international students: Required—TOEFL (minimum score 550 paper-based; 79 iBT). Electronic applications accepted. *Expenses:* Contact institution.

Edgewood College, Program in Education, Madison, WI 53711-1997. Offers adult learning (MA Ed); bilingual teaching and learning (MA Ed); director of instruction (Certificate); director of special education and pupil services (Certificate); education (MA Ed); educational administration (MA Ed); educational leadership (Ed D); professional studies (MA Ed); program coordinator (Certificate); reading administration (MA Ed); school business administration (Certificate); school principalship K-12 (Certificate); special education (MA Ed); sustainability leadership (MA Ed); teaching and learning (MA Ed); teaching English to speakers of other languages (TESOL) (MA Ed). *Accreditation:* NCATE (one or more programs are accredited). Part-time and evening/weekend programs available. *Students:* 159 full-time (95 women), 164 part-time (121 women); includes 61 minority (19 Black or African American, non-Hispanic/Latino; 9 Asian, non-Hispanic/Latino; 25 Hispanic/Latino; 8 Two or more races, non-Hispanic/Latino), 27 international. Average age 36. In 2013, 51 master's, 22 doctorates awarded. *Degree requirements:* For master's, practicum, research project; for doctorate, comprehensive exam, thesis/dissertation. *Entrance requirements:* For master's, minimum GPA of 2.75, 2 letters of recommendation, personal statement; for doctorate, resume, letter of intent, 2 letters of recommendation, interview, writing sample. Additional exam requirements/recommendations for international students: Required—TOEFL (minimum score 525 paper-based; 72 iBT). *Application deadline:* For fall admission, 8/15 for domestic students, 5/1 for international students; for spring admission, 1/8 for domestic students, 11/1 for international students. Applications are processed on a rolling basis. *Application fee:* $30. Electronic applications accepted. *Unit head:* Dr. Timothy Slekar, Dean, E-mail: tslekar@edgewood.edu. *Application contact:* Joann Eastman, Admissions Counselor, 608-663-3250, Fax: 608-663-2214, E-mail: gps@edgewood.edu. Website: http://www.edgewood.edu/Academics/School-of-Education.

Edinboro University of Pennsylvania, School of Education, Edinboro, PA 16444. Offers M Ed, MA, MS, Certificate, Ed S. *Accreditation:* NCATE. Part-time and evening/weekend programs available. *Degree requirements:* For master's and other advanced degree, competency exam. *Entrance requirements:* For master's and other advanced degree, GRE or MAT, minimum QPA of 2.5. Electronic applications accepted.

Elizabeth City State University, School of Education and Psychology, Elizabeth City, NC 27909-7806. Offers M Ed, MSA. Part-time and evening/weekend programs available. *Faculty:* 7 full-time (4 women), 1 (woman) part-time/adjunct. *Students:* 3 full-time (2 women), 42 part-time (33 women); includes 21 minority (20 Black or African American, non-Hispanic/Latino; 1 Two or more races, non-Hispanic/Latino). Average age 37. 3 applicants, 100% accepted, 2 enrolled. In 2013, 51 master's awarded. *Degree requirements:* For master's, comprehensive exam (for some programs), thesis. *Application deadline:* For fall admission, 11/1 priority date for domestic students; for spring admission, 3/15 priority date for domestic students. Applications are processed on a rolling basis. *Application fee:* $30. Electronic applications accepted. *Expenses:* Tuition, state resident: full-time $2916; part-time $364.48 per credit. Tuition, nonresident: full-time $14,199; part-time $1774.83 per credit. *Required fees:* $2972.23; $206.58 per credit. $571.06 per semester. *Financial support:* In 2013–14, 25 students received support. Scholarships/grants and tuition waivers (partial) available. *Unit head:* Dr. Paula S. Viltz, Interim Dean, 252-335-3947, Fax: 252-335-3146. Website: http://www.ecsu.edu/academics/educationpsychology/index.cfm.

Elms College, Division of Education, Chicopee, MA 01013-2839. Offers early childhood education (MAT); education (M Ed, CAGS); elementary education (MAT); English as a second language (MAT); reading (MAT); secondary education (MAT), including biology education, English education, Spanish education; special education (MAT). Part-time and evening/weekend programs available. *Degree requirements:* For master's, thesis (for some programs). *Entrance requirements:* For master's, Massachusetts Educators Certification Test, minimum GPA of 3.0; for CAGS, master's degree in education. Additional exam requirements/recommendations for international students: Required—TOEFL.

Elon University, Program in Education, Elon, NC 27244-2010. Offers elementary education (M Ed); gifted education (M Ed); special education (M Ed). *Accreditation:* NCATE. Part-time programs available. *Faculty:* 16 full-time (13 women), 3 part-time/adjunct (2 women). *Students:* 62 part-time (53 women); includes 11 minority (5 Black or African American, non-Hispanic/Latino; 1 Asian, non-Hispanic/Latino; 5 Hispanic/Latino). Average age 33. 35 applicants, 94% accepted, 29 enrolled. *Entrance requirements:* For master's, GRE, MAT. Additional exam requirements/recommendations for international students: Required—TOEFL (minimum score 550 paper-based; 79 iBT). *Application deadline:* For winter admission, 6/1 priority date for domestic students. Applications are processed on a rolling basis. *Application fee:* $50.

Education—General

Electronic applications accepted. *Expenses:* Contact institution. *Financial support:* In 2013–14, 5 students received support. Federal Work-Study and scholarships/grants available. Support available to part-time students. Financial award application deadline: 6/1; financial award applicants required to submit FAFSA. *Faculty research:* Teaching reading to low-achieving second and third graders, pre- and post-student teaching attitudes, children's writing, whole language methodology, critical creative thinking. *Unit head:* Dr. Angela Owusu-Ansah, Director and Associate Dean of Education, 336-278-5885, Fax: 336-278-5919, E-mail: aansah@elon.edu. *Application contact:* Art Fadde, Director of Graduate Admissions, 800-334-8448 Ext. 3, Fax: 336-278-7699, E-mail: afadde@elon.edu.

Website: http://www.elon.edu/med/.

Embry-Riddle Aeronautical University–Worldwide, Worldwide Headquarters - Graduate Programs, Program in Aeronautics, Daytona Beach, FL 32114-3900. Offers aeronautical science (MAS); aviation (PhD); aviation/aerospace safety (Graduate Certificate); instructional system design (Graduate Certificate); space education (MSSE). Part-time and evening/weekend programs available. Postbaccalaureate distance learning degree programs offered (minimal on-campus study). *Degree requirements:* For master's, comprehensive exam (for some programs), thesis optional; for doctorate, comprehensive exam, thesis/dissertation. *Entrance requirements:* Additional exam requirements/recommendations for international students: Recommended—TOEFL (minimum score 550 paper-based; 79 iBT). Electronic applications accepted. *Faculty research:* Unmanned aircraft system (UAS) operations, human factors, crash investigation, reliability and hazard analysis, aviation security.

Emmanuel College, Graduate Studies, Graduate Programs in Education, Boston, MA 02115. Offers educational leadership (CAGS); elementary education (MAT); school administration (M Ed); secondary education (MAT). Part-time and evening/weekend programs available. *Faculty:* 3 full-time (all women), 10 part-time/adjunct (7 women). *Students:* 11 full-time (7 women), 22 part-time (13 women); includes 4 minority (3 Black or African American, non-Hispanic/Latino; 1 Native Hawaiian or other Pacific Islander, non-Hispanic/Latino). Average age 30. In 2013, 15 master's, 1 other advanced degree awarded. *Degree requirements:* For master's, 36 credits, including 6-credit practicum. *Entrance requirements:* For master's and CAGS, transcripts from all regionally-accredited institutions attended (showing proof of bachelor's degree completion), 2 letters of recommendation, essay, resume, interview. Additional exam requirements/recommendations for international students: Required—TOEFL (minimum score 600 paper-based; 106 iBT) or IELTS (minimum score 6.5). *Application deadline:* For fall admission, 7/31 priority date for domestic students; for spring admission, 11/30 priority date for domestic students. Applications are processed on a rolling basis. Application fee: $0. Electronic applications accepted. *Financial support:* Applicants required to submit FAFSA. *Unit head:* Sandy Robbins, Dean of Enrollment, 617-735-9700, Fax: 617-507-0434, E-mail: graduatestudies@emmanuel.edu. *Application contact:* Enrollment Counselor, 617-735-9700, Fax: 617-507-0434, E-mail: graduatestudies@emmanuel.edu.

Website: http://www.emmanuel.edu/graduate-studies-nursing/academics/education.html.

Emory & Henry College, Graduate Programs, Emory, VA 24327-0947. Offers American history (MA Ed); organizational leadership (MCOL); professional studies (M Ed); reading specialist (MA Ed). Part-time and evening/weekend programs available. *Faculty:* 7 full-time (3 women). *Students:* 11 full-time (8 women), 32 part-time (22 women); includes 1 minority (Black or African American, non-Hispanic/Latino). Average age 36. 34 applicants, 85% accepted, 28 enrolled. In 2013, 36 master's awarded. *Entrance requirements:* For master's, GRE or PRAXIS I, recommendations, writing sample. Additional exam requirements/recommendations for international students: Recommended—TOEFL. *Application deadline:* Applications are processed on a rolling basis. Application fee: $30. *Financial support:* Applicants required to submit FAFSA. *Unit head:* Dr. Jack Roper, Director of Graduate Studies, 276-944-6188, Fax: 276-944-5223, E-mail: jroper@ehc.edu. *Application contact:* Dr. Jack Roper, Director of Graduate Studies, 276-944-6188, Fax: 276-944-5223, E-mail: jroper@ehc.edu.

Emory University, Laney Graduate School, Division of Educational Studies, Atlanta, GA 30322-1100. Offers educational studies (MA, PhD); middle grades teaching (MAT); secondary teaching (MAT). *Accreditation:* NCATE. Terminal master's awarded for partial completion of doctoral program. *Degree requirements:* For master's, thesis; for doctorate, comprehensive exam, thesis/dissertation. *Entrance requirements:* For master's and doctorate, GRE General Test, minimum GPA of 3.0. Additional exam requirements/recommendations for international students: Required—TOEFL. Electronic applications accepted. *Faculty research:* Educational policy, educational measurement, urban and multicultural education, mathematics and science education, comparative education.

Emporia State University, Program in Teaching, Emporia, KS 66801-5415. Offers M Ed. Postbaccalaureate distance learning degree programs offered (no on-campus study). *Students:* 8 full-time (5 women), 35 part-time (25 women); includes 10 minority (2 Black or African American, non-Hispanic/Latino; 7 Hispanic/Latino; 1 Two or more races, non-Hispanic/Latino). 15 applicants, 73% accepted, 6 enrolled. In 2013, 7 master's awarded. *Entrance requirements:* For master's, GRE or MAT, minimum GPA of 2.5 on last 60 undergraduate hours; two personal references. *Expenses:* Tuition, area resident: Part-time $220 per credit hour. Tuition, state resident: part-time $220 per credit hour. Tuition, nonresident: part-time $685 per credit hour. *Required fees:* $73 per credit hour. *Unit head:* Dr. Paul Bland, Chair, 620-341-5777, E-mail: pbland@emporia.edu. *Application contact:* Mary Sewell, Admissions Coordinator, 800-950-GRAD, Fax: 620-341-5909, E-mail: msewell@emporia.edu.

Evangel University, Department of Education, Springfield, MO 65802. Offers educational leadership (M Ed); reading education (M Ed); secondary teaching (M Ed); teaching (MA). *Accreditation:* NCATE. Part-time and evening/weekend programs available. *Faculty:* 7 full-time (4 women), 5 part-time/adjunct (4 women). *Students:* 5 full-time (3 women), 37 part-time (28 women); includes 4 minority (3 Hispanic/Latino; 1 Two or more races, non-Hispanic/Latino). Average age 32. 17 applicants, 65% accepted, 11 enrolled. In 2013, 22 master's awarded. *Degree requirements:* For master's, comprehensive exam, thesis optional. *Entrance requirements:* For master's, PRAXIS II (preferred) or GRE. Additional exam requirements/recommendations for international students: Required—TOEFL (minimum score 550 paper-based). *Application deadline:* For fall admission, 7/15 priority date for domestic students, 8/1 for international students; for spring admission, 11/15 priority date for domestic students, 12/1 for international students. Applications are processed on a rolling basis. Application fee: $25. Electronic applications accepted. *Financial support:* In 2013–14, 13 students received support. Career-related internships or fieldwork and scholarships/grants available. Support available to part-time students. Financial award application deadline: 3/1; financial award applicants required to submit FAFSA. *Unit head:* Dr. Matt Stringer, Program Coordinator, 417-865-2815 Ext. 8563, E-mail: stringerm@evangel.edu. *Application contact:* Karen Benitez, Admissions Representative, Graduate Studies, 417-865-2811 Ext. 7227, Fax: 417-865-9599, E-mail: benitezk@evangel.edu.

Website: http://www.evangel.edu/academics/graduate-studies/graduate-programs.

The Evergreen State College, Graduate Programs, Program in Teaching, Olympia, WA 98505. Offers MIT. *Faculty:* 3 full-time (all women), 3 part-time/adjunct (2 women).

Students: 68 full-time (46 women); includes 11 minority (2 Black or African American, non-Hispanic/Latino; 1 Asian, non-Hispanic/Latino; 4 Hispanic/Latino; 4 Two or more races, non-Hispanic/Latino). Average age 30. 52 applicants, 94% accepted, 40 enrolled. In 2013, 29 master's awarded. *Degree requirements:* For master's, project, 20-week teaching internship. *Entrance requirements:* For master's, Washington Educator Skills Test-Basic, Washington Educator Skills Test-Endorsements, minimum undergraduate GPA of 3.0 for last 90 quarter hours; official transcript; resume; endorsement worksheets; 3 letters of recommendation; personal statement; essay. Additional exam requirements/recommendations for international students: Required—TOEFL (minimum score 600 paper-based; 100 iBT). *Application deadline:* For fall admission, 4/7 for domestic and international students. Application fee: $50. Electronic applications accepted. *Expenses:* Contact institution. *Financial support:* In 2013–14, 51 students received support, including 14 fellowships with partial tuition reimbursements available (averaging $723 per year); career-related internships or fieldwork, Federal Work-Study, institutionally sponsored loans, scholarships/grants, and tuition waivers (partial) also available. Financial award application deadline: 3/1; financial award applicants required to submit FAFSA. *Faculty research:* Equitable mathematics teaching and learning; pre-service and in-service teacher education; language and literacy development; literacy education; multicultural education; teaching for social justice; self-efficiency promoting democratic classrooms; transformative pedagogy and learning within a critical race framework working collaboratively in the context of schools emphasizing the cultural wealth of communities; curriculum integration, technology, qualitative research methods. *Unit head:* Dr. Sherry Walton, Director, 360-867-6753, E-mail: waltonsl@evergreen.edu. *Application contact:* Maggie Foran, Associate Director, 360-867-6559, Fax: 360-867-6575, E-mail: foranm@evergreen.edu.

Website: http://www.evergreen.edu/mit/.

Fairfield University, Graduate School of Education and Allied Professions, Fairfield, CT 06824-5195. Offers applied behavior analysis (ATC); applied psychology (MA); clinical mental health counseling (MA, CAS); early childhood studies (ATC); educational technology (MA); elementary education (MA, CAS); family studies (MA); integration of spirituality and religion in counseling (ATC); marriage and family therapy (MA); school counseling (MA, CAS); school psychology (MA, CAS); school-based marriage and family therapy (ATC); secondary education (MA); special education (MA, CAS); substance abuse counseling (ATC); teaching (Certificate); teaching and foundations (MA, CAS); TESOL, world languages, and bilingual education (MA, CAS). *Accreditation:* NCATE. Part-time and evening/weekend programs available. *Faculty:* 24 full-time (21 women), 39 part-time/adjunct (27 women). *Students:* 154 full-time (130 women), 307 part-time (248 women); includes 75 minority (14 Black or African American, non-Hispanic/Latino; 1 American Indian or Alaska Native, non-Hispanic/Latino; 10 Asian, non-Hispanic/Latino; 44 Hispanic/Latino; 6 Two or more races, non-Hispanic/Latino), 13 international. Average age 34. 263 applicants, 41% accepted, 91 enrolled. In 2013, 149 master's, 21 other advanced degrees awarded. *Degree requirements:* For master's, comprehensive exam. *Entrance requirements:* For master's, PRAXIS I (for certification programs), minimum GPA of 3.0, 2 recommendations, resume. Additional exam requirements/recommendations for international students: Required—TOEFL (minimum score 550 paper-based; 84 iBT) or IELTS (minimum score 7.5). *Application deadline:* For fall admission, 2/15 for international students; for spring admission, 10/1 for international students. Application fee: $60. Electronic applications accepted. *Expenses:* Tuition: Part-time $675 per credit hour. Tuition and fees vary according to program. *Financial support:* In 2013–14, 55 students received support. Career-related internships or fieldwork and unspecified assistantships available. Financial award applicants required to submit FAFSA. *Faculty research:* Literacy, adolescent psychology, special education, teaching development, mentoring for professional development, multicultural education. *Total annual research expenditures:* $325,000. *Unit head:* Dr. Robert D. Hannafin, Dean, 203-254-4250, Fax: 203-254-4241, E-mail: rhannafin@fairfield.edu. *Application contact:* Marianne Gumpper, Director of Graduate and Continuing Studies Admission, 203-254-4184, Fax: 203-254-4073, E-mail: gradadmis@fairfield.edu.

Website: http://www.fairfield.edu/academics/schoolscollegescenters/graduateschoolofeducationalliedprofessions/graduateprograms/.

Fairleigh Dickinson University, College at Florham, Maxwell Becton College of Arts and Sciences, Department of English, Communication and Philosophy, Program in Creative Writing and Literature for Educators, Madison, NJ 07940-1099. Offers MA.

Fairleigh Dickinson University, College at Florham, University College: Arts, Sciences, and Professional Studies, Peter Sammartino School of Education, Madison, NJ 07940-1099. Offers education for certified teachers (MA, Certificate); educational leadership (MA); instructional technology (Certificate); literacy/reading (Certificate); teaching (MAT).

Fairleigh Dickinson University, Metropolitan Campus, University College: Arts, Sciences, and Professional Studies, Peter Sammartino School of Education, Teaneck, NJ 07666-1914. Offers dyslexia specialist (Certificate); education for certified teachers (MA); educational leadership (MA); instructional technology (Certificate); learning disabilities (MA); literacy/reading (Certificate); multilingual education (MA); teacher of the handicapped (Certificate); teaching (MAT). *Accreditation:* Teacher Education Accreditation Council. Part-time programs available. *Degree requirements:* For master's, research project (MAT).

Fairmont State University, Programs in Education, Fairmont, WV 26554. Offers digital media, new literacies and learning (M Ed); education (MAT); exercise science, fitness and wellness (M Ed); online learning (M Ed); professional studies (M Ed); reading (M Ed); special education (M Ed). *Accreditation:* NCATE. Part-time and evening/weekend programs available. Postbaccalaureate distance learning degree programs offered. *Faculty:* 18 part-time/adjunct (11 women). *Students:* 75 full-time (55 women), 120 part-time (96 women); includes 11 minority (5 Black or African American, non-Hispanic/Latino; 2 American Indian or Alaska Native, non-Hispanic/Latino; 1 Asian, non-Hispanic/Latino; 1 Hispanic/Latino; 2 Two or more races, non-Hispanic/Latino), 1 international. Average age 32. 69 applicants, 86% accepted, 45 enrolled. In 2013, 82 master's awarded. *Entrance requirements:* For master's, GRE. Additional exam requirements/recommendations for international students: Required—TOEFL. *Application deadline:* For fall admission, 5/1 for domestic and international students. Applications are processed on a rolling basis. Application fee: $40. *Expenses:* Tuition, state resident: full-time $6404; part-time $349 per credit hour. Tuition, nonresident: full-time $13,694; part-time $754 per credit hour. Part-time tuition and fees vary according to course load. *Financial support:* In 2013–14, 30 students received support. *Unit head:* Dr. Carolyn Crislip-Tacy, Interim Dean, School of Education, 304-367-4143, Fax: 304-367-4599, E-mail: carolyn.crislip-tacy@fairmontstate.edu. *Application contact:* Jack Kirby, Director of Graduate Studies, 304-367-4101, E-mail: jack.kirby@fairmontstate.edu.

Website: http://www.fairmontstate.edu/graduatestudies/default.asp.

Faulkner University, College of Education, Montgomery, AL 36109-3398. Offers M Ed.

Felician College, Program in Education, Lodi, NJ 07644-2117. Offers education (MA); educational leadership (principal/supervision) (MA); educational supervision (PMC); principal (PMC); school nursing and health education (MA, Certificate). *Accreditation:* Teacher Education Accreditation Council. Part-time and evening/weekend programs available. *Students:* 10 full-time (8 women), 58 part-time (52 women); includes 23

minority (7 Black or African American, non-Hispanic/Latino; 7 Asian, non-Hispanic/Latino; 6 Hispanic/Latino; 3 Two or more races, non-Hispanic/Latino), 3 international. Average age 37. *Degree requirements:* For master's, project. *Entrance requirements:* For master's, MAT, minimum GPA of 3.0, 3 letters of recommendation. Additional exam requirements/recommendations for international students: Recommended—TOEFL (minimum score 550 paper-based). *Application deadline:* Applications are processed on a rolling basis. Application fee: $40. *Expenses: Tuition:* Part-time $945 per credit. *Required fees:* $317.50 per semester. *Financial support:* Federal Work-Study available. *Unit head:* Dr. Rosemarie Liebmann, Associate Dean, 201-559-3537, E-mail: liebmannr@felician.edu. *Application contact:* Dr. Margaret Smolin, Associate Director, Graduate Admissions, 201-559-6077, Fax: 201-559-6138, E-mail: graduate@felician.edu.

Ferris State University, College of Education and Human Services, School of Education, Big Rapids, MI 49307. Offers curriculum and instruction (M Ed), including reading, special education, subject area; educational leadership (MS); instructor (MSCTE); post-secondary administration (MSCTE); training and development (MSCTE). Part-time and evening/weekend programs available. Postbaccalaureate distance learning degree programs offered (minimal on-campus study). *Faculty:* 7 full-time (5 women), 9 part-time/adjunct (6 women). *Students:* 17 full-time (14 women), 88 part-time (53 women); includes 8 minority (3 Black or African American, non-Hispanic/Latino; 1 American Indian or Alaska Native, non-Hispanic/Latino; 1 Asian, non-Hispanic/Latino; 3 Two or more races, non-Hispanic/Latino), 12 international. Average age 35. 16 applicants, 63% accepted, 6 enrolled. In 2013, 31 master's awarded. *Degree requirements:* For master's, thesis, research paper or project. *Entrance requirements:* For master's, minimum undergraduate degree GPA of 3.0. Additional exam requirements/recommendations for international students: Required—TOEFL (minimum score 500 paper-based; 61 iBT), IELTS. *Application deadline:* For fall admission, 7/1 priority date for domestic and international students; for spring admission, 11/1 priority date for domestic and international students; for summer admission, 3/1 priority date for domestic and international students. Applications are processed on a rolling basis. Application fee: $30. Electronic applications accepted. Application fee is waived when completed online. *Financial support:* Career-related internships or fieldwork and scholarships/grants available. Support available to part-time students. Financial award applicants required to submit FAFSA. *Faculty research:* Suicide prevention, reading, women in education, special needs, administration. *Unit head:* Dr. James Powell, Director, 231-591-3512, Fax: 231-591-2043, E-mail: powelj20@ferris.edu. *Application contact:* Kimisue Worrall, Secretary, 231-591-5361, Fax: 231-591-2043. Website: http://www.ferris.edu/education/education/.

Fielding Graduate University, Graduate Programs, School of Educational Leadership for Change, Santa Barbara, CA 93105-3814. Offers collaborative educational leadership (MA), including charter school leadership, dual language; educational administration (Graduate Certificate); educational leadership and change (Ed D), including community college leadership and change. Postbaccalaureate distance learning degree programs offered (minimal on-campus study). *Faculty:* 9 full-time (6 women), 10 part-time/adjunct (6 women). *Students:* 172 full-time (121 women), 8 part-time (5 women); includes 109 minority (39 Black or African American, non-Hispanic/Latino; 19 American Indian or Alaska Native, non-Hispanic/Latino; 8 Asian, non-Hispanic/Latino; 34 Hispanic/Latino; 2 Native Hawaiian or other Pacific Islander, non-Hispanic/Latino; 7 Two or more races, non-Hispanic/Latino). Average age 48. 40 applicants, 98% accepted, 28 enrolled. In 2013, 45 doctorates awarded. *Degree requirements:* For master's, capstone research project; for doctorate, comprehensive exam, thesis/dissertation. *Entrance requirements:* For master's, BA from regionally accredited institution or equivalent with minimum GPA of 2.5; for doctorate, BA or MA from regionally accredited institution or equivalent, resume, 2 letters of recommendation, statement of purpose, reflective essay; for Graduate Certificate, BA from regionally-accredited institution or equivalent. *Application deadline:* For fall admission, 6/10 for domestic and international students; for spring admission, 11/19 for domestic and international students. Application fee: $75. Electronic applications accepted. *Expenses:* Contact institution. *Financial support:* In 2013–14, 90 students received support. Scholarships/grants, health care benefits, and tuition waivers (partial) available. Support available to part-time students. Financial award applicants required to submit FAFSA. *Unit head:* Dr. Mario R. Borunda, Dean, 805-898-2940, E-mail: mborunda@fielding.edu. *Application contact:* Admission Counselor, 800-340-1099 Ext. 4098, Fax: 805-687-9793, E-mail: elcadmissions@fielding.edu. Website: http://www.fielding.edu/programs/elc/default.aspx.

Florida Agricultural and Mechanical University, Division of Graduate Studies, Research, and Continuing Education, College of Education, Tallahassee, FL 32307-3200. Offers M Ed, MBE, MS Ed, PhD. *Accreditation:* NCATE. Part-time and evening/weekend programs available. *Degree requirements:* For master's, thesis (for some programs); for doctorate, thesis/dissertation. *Entrance requirements:* For master's, GRE General Test, minimum GPA of 3.0. Additional exam requirements/recommendations for international students: Required—TOEFL.

Florida Atlantic University, College of Education, Boca Raton, FL 33431-0991. Offers M Ed, MA, MS, Ed D, PhD, Ed S. *Accreditation:* NCATE. Part-time and evening/weekend programs available. *Faculty:* 72 full-time (42 women), 30 part-time/adjunct (19 women). *Students:* 327 full-time (249 women), 590 part-time (441 women); includes 312 minority (147 Black or African American, non-Hispanic/Latino; 2 American Indian or Alaska Native, non-Hispanic/Latino; 26 Asian, non-Hispanic/Latino; 121 Hispanic/Latino; 16 Two or more races, non-Hispanic/Latino), 18 international. Average age 34. 809 applicants, 38% accepted, 221 enrolled. In 2013, 260 master's, 23 doctorates, 25 other advanced degrees awarded. *Degree requirements:* For doctorate, comprehensive exam, thesis/dissertation; for Ed S, departmental qualifying exam. *Entrance requirements:* For master's, doctorate, and Ed S, GRE General Test. Additional exam requirements/recommendations for international students: Required—TOEFL (minimum score 500 paper-based; 61 iBT), IELTS (minimum score 6). *Application deadline:* For fall admission, 5/1 for domestic students. Applications are processed on a rolling basis. Application fee: $30. Electronic applications accepted. *Expenses:* Tuition, state resident: full-time $6660; part-time $370 per credit hour. Tuition, nonresident: full-time $18,450; part-time $1025 per credit hour. Tuition and fees vary according to course load. *Financial support:* Fellowships with partial tuition reimbursements, research assistantships with partial tuition reimbursements, teaching assistantships with partial tuition reimbursements, career-related internships or fieldwork, Federal Work-Study, and unspecified assistantships available. *Faculty research:* Marriage and family counseling, multicultural education, self-directed learning, assessment, reading. *Unit head:* Dr. Valerie J. Bristor, Dean, 561-297-3564, E-mail: bristor@fau.edu. *Application contact:* Dr. Eliah Watlington, Associate Dean, 561-296-8520, Fax: 261-297-2991, E-mail: ewatling@fau.edu. Website: http://www.coe.fau.edu/.

Florida Gulf Coast University, College of Education, Fort Myers, FL 33965-6565. Offers M Ed, MA, Ed D, Ed S. Part-time and evening/weekend programs available. Postbaccalaureate distance learning degree programs offered (minimal on-campus study). *Entrance requirements:* For master's, GRE General Test, MAT, minimum GPA of 3.0. Additional exam requirements/recommendations for international students:

Required—TOEFL (minimum score 550 paper-based). Electronic applications accepted. *Faculty research:* Inclusion, emergent literacy, pre-service and in-service teacher education, education policy.

Florida International University, College of Education, Miami, FL 33199. Offers MS, Ed D, PhD, Certificate, Ed S. *Accreditation:* NCATE. Part-time and evening/weekend programs available. *Degree requirements:* For doctorate, comprehensive exam, thesis/dissertation. *Entrance requirements:* For master's and other advanced degree, GRE General Test (for some programs); for doctorate, GRE General Test. Additional exam requirements/recommendations for international students: Required—TOEFL (minimum score 550 paper-based; 80 iBT), IELTS (minimum score 6.3). Electronic applications accepted. *Faculty research:* School improvement, cognitive processes, international development, urban education, multicultural/multilingual education.

Florida Memorial University, School of Education, Miami-Dade, FL 33054. Offers elementary education (MS); exceptional student education (MS); reading (MS). *Degree requirements:* For master's, comprehensive exam or thesis, field and clinical experiences, exit exam. *Entrance requirements:* For master's, GRE, CLAST, PRAXIS I, baccalaureate or graduate degree with minimum GPA of 3.0 in last 60 hours, 3 recommendations. Additional exam requirements/recommendations for international students: Recommended—TOEFL.

Florida Southern College, Programs in Teaching, Lakeland, FL 33801-5698. Offers M Ed, MAT. Part-time and evening/weekend programs available. *Degree requirements:* For master's, FICE General Knowledge test and professional education exam (MAT), eligibility for the Florida Professional Teacher Certificate (M Ed). *Entrance requirements:* For master's, Florida Teacher Certification exam (MAT). Additional exam requirements/recommendations for international students: Required—TOEFL (minimum score 550 paper-based).

Florida State University, The Graduate School, College of Education, Tallahassee, FL 32306. Offers MS, MST, PhD, Certificate, Ed S, JD/MS, MS/Ed S. *Accreditation:* NCATE. Part-time and evening/weekend programs available. Postbaccalaureate distance learning degree programs offered. *Faculty:* 98 full-time (56 women), 57 part-time/adjunct (41 women). *Students:* 675 full-time (435 women), 381 part-time (254 women); includes 239 minority (115 Black or African American, non-Hispanic/Latino; 5 American Indian or Alaska Native, non-Hispanic/Latino; 12 Asian, non-Hispanic/Latino; 97 Hispanic/Latino; 10 Two or more races, non-Hispanic/Latino), 208 international. Average age 31. 1,028 applicants, 57% accepted, 312 enrolled. In 2013, 331 master's, 47 doctorates, 50 other advanced degrees awarded. Terminal master's awarded for partial completion of doctoral program. *Degree requirements:* For master's and other advanced degree, comprehensive exam, thesis optional; for doctorate, comprehensive exam, thesis/dissertation, preliminary exam, prospectus defense. *Entrance requirements:* For master's, doctorate, and other advanced degree, GRE General Test, minimum GPA of 3.0. Additional exam requirements/recommendations for international students: Required—TOEFL (minimum score 550 paper-based; 80 iBT). *Application deadline:* For fall admission, 7/1 for domestic and international students; for winter admission, 11/1 for domestic and international students; for spring admission, 3/1 for domestic and international students. Applications are processed on a rolling basis. Application fee: $30. Electronic applications accepted. *Expenses:* Tuition, state resident: part-time $403.51 per credit hour. Tuition, nonresident: part-time $1004.85 per credit hour. *Required fees:* $75.81 per credit hour. One-time fee: $20 part-time. Tuition and fees vary according to course load, campus/location and student level. *Financial support:* In 2013–14, 36 students received support, including 15 fellowships with full and partial tuition reimbursements available, 226 research assistantships with full and partial tuition reimbursements available, 247 teaching assistantships with full and partial tuition reimbursements available; career-related internships or fieldwork, scholarships/grants, traineeships, health care benefits, and unspecified assistantships also available. Financial award application deadline: 1/15; financial award applicants required to submit FAFSA. *Faculty research:* Sport management and administration, educational psychology, instructional systems, teacher education, educational leadership and policy. *Total annual research expenditures:* $5.9 million. *Unit head:* Dr. Marcy P. Driscoll, Dean, 850-644-6885, Fax: 850-644-2725, E-mail: mdriscoll@fsu.edu. *Application contact:* Jennie C. Harrison, Academic Dean, 850-644-6798, Fax: 850-644-2725, E-mail: jcharrison@fsu.edu. Website: http://www.coe.fsu.edu/.

Fontbonne University, Graduate Programs, Department of Education, St. Louis, MO 63105-3098. Offers MA. *Accreditation:* NCATE. Part-time and evening/weekend programs available. Postbaccalaureate distance learning degree programs offered (minimal on-campus study). *Entrance requirements:* For master's, minimum GPA of 3.0. *Expenses: Tuition:* Full-time $11,646; part-time $647 per credit hour. *Required fees:* $324; $18 per credit hour. Tuition and fees vary according to course load and program.

Fordham University, Graduate School of Education, New York, NY 10023. Offers MAT, MS, MSE, MST, Ed D, PhD, Adv C. *Accreditation:* NCATE. Part-time and evening/weekend programs available. *Degree requirements:* For master's and Adv C, comprehensive exam (for some programs); for doctorate, thesis/dissertation. *Entrance requirements:* For master's and Adv C, minimum GPA of 3.0; for doctorate, GRE or MAT. *Expenses:* Contact institution.

Fort Hays State University, Graduate School, College of Education and Technology, Hays, KS 67601-4099. Offers MS, MSE, Ed S. *Accreditation:* NCATE. Part-time programs available. *Degree requirements:* For master's, comprehensive exam, thesis or alternative. *Entrance requirements:* Additional exam requirements/recommendations for international students: Required—TOEFL (minimum score 550 paper-based). Electronic applications accepted.

Franciscan University of Steubenville, Graduate Programs, Department of Education, Steubenville, OH 43952-1763. Offers administration (MS Ed); teaching (MS Ed). Part-time and evening/weekend programs available. *Degree requirements:* For master's, project. *Entrance requirements:* For master's, minimum undergraduate GPA of 2.5 or written exam. *Expenses:* Contact institution.

Francis Marion University, Graduate Programs, School of Education, Florence, SC 29502-0547. Offers early childhood education (M Ed); elementary education (M Ed); learning disabilities (M Ed, MAT); remedial education (M Ed); secondary education (M Ed). *Accreditation:* NCATE. Part-time programs available. *Faculty:* 17 full-time (12 women). *Students:* 5 full-time (3 women), 79 part-time (63 women); includes 33 minority (all Black or African American, non-Hispanic/Latino). Average age 34. 327 applicants, 42% accepted, 135 enrolled. In 2013, 45 master's awarded. *Degree requirements:* For master's, comprehensive exam. *Entrance requirements:* For master's, GRE General Test, MAT, NTE, or PRAXIS II. *Application deadline:* For fall admission, 3/15 priority date for domestic students; for spring admission, 10/15 priority date for domestic students. Application fee: $33. *Expenses:* Tuition, state resident: full-time $9184; part-time $459.20 per credit hour. Tuition, nonresident: full-time $18,368; part-time $918.40 per credit hour. *Required fees:* $13.50 per credit hour. $92 per semester. Tuition and fees vary according to program. *Financial support:* In 2013–14, 2 research assistantships (averaging $6,000 per year) were awarded; scholarships/grants and unspecified assistantships also available. Support available to part-time students. Financial award application deadline: 3/1; financial award applicants required to submit

FAFSA. *Faculty research:* Identification and alternate assessment of at-risk students. *Unit head:* Dr. Shirley Carr Bausmith, Dean, 843-661-1460, Fax: 843-661-4647. *Application contact:* Rannie Gamble, Administrative Manager, 843-661-1286, Fax: 843-661-4688, E-mail: rgamble@fmarion.edu.

Freed-Hardeman University, Program in Education, Henderson, TN 38340-2399. Offers curriculum and instruction (M Ed); school counseling (M Ed), including administration and supervision, special education; school leadership (Ed S). *Accreditation:* NCATE. Part-time and evening/weekend programs available. *Degree requirements:* For master's, comprehensive exam, thesis optional; for Ed S, thesis. *Entrance requirements:* For master's, GRE General Test or NTE; for Ed S, 3 years of teaching experience. Additional exam requirements/recommendations for international students: Required—TOEFL (minimum score 500 paper-based).

Fresno Pacific University, Graduate Programs, School of Education, Fresno, CA 93702-4709. Offers MA, MA Ed, Certificate. Part-time and evening/weekend programs available. *Degree requirements:* For master's, thesis (for some programs). *Entrance requirements:* For master's, interview; GMAT, GRE, MAT, or 6 units of course work with a faculty recommendation. Additional exam requirements/recommendations for international students: Required—TOEFL (minimum score 550 paper-based). *Application deadline:* For fall admission, 7/15 for domestic and international students; for spring admission, 11/15 for domestic and international students. Applications are processed on a rolling basis. Application fee: $90. Electronic applications accepted. *Expenses: Tuition:* Full-time $8910; part-time $495 per unit. *Required fees:* $270. Tuition and fees vary according to course load and program. *Financial support:* Career-related internships or fieldwork, scholarships/grants, and tuition waivers (full and partial) available. Support available to part-time students. Financial award applicants required to submit FAFSA. *Unit head:* Dr. Gary Gramenz, Dean, 559-453-5574, Fax: 559-453-7168, E-mail: gary.gramenz@fresno.edu. *Application contact:* Amanda Krum-Stovall, Director of Graduate Admissions, 559-453-2016, E-mail: amanda.krum-stovall@fresno.edu.
Website: http://www.fresno.edu/education.

Friends University, Graduate School, Wichita, KS 67213. Offers business law (MBL); Christian ministry (MACM); family therapy (MSFT); global (MBA), including accounting, business law, change management, health care leadership, management information systems, supply chain management and logistics; health care leadership (MHCL); management information systems (MMIS); operations management (MSOM); professional (MBA), including accounting, business law, change management, health care leadership, management information systems, supply chain management and logistics; teaching (MAT). Part-time and evening/weekend programs available. Postbaccalaureate distance learning degree programs offered (no on-campus study). *Faculty:* 18 full-time (8 women), 62 part-time/adjunct (28 women). *Students:* 161 full-time (111 women), 408 part-time (258 women); includes 157 minority (68 Black or African American, non-Hispanic/Latino; 7 American Indian or Alaska Native, non-Hispanic/Latino; 28 Asian, non-Hispanic/Latino; 18 Hispanic/Latino; 1 Native Hawaiian or other Pacific Islander, non-Hispanic/Latino; 35 Two or more races, non-Hispanic/Latino). Average age 36. 371 applicants, 90% accepted, 178 enrolled. In 2013, 432 master's awarded. *Degree requirements:* For master's, research project. *Entrance requirements:* For master's, bachelor's degree from accredited institution, official transcripts, interview with program director, letter(s) of recommendation. Additional exam requirements/recommendations for international students: Required—TOEFL (minimum score 560 paper-based). *Application deadline:* Applications are processed on a rolling basis. Application fee: $35 ($50 for international students). Electronic applications accepted. *Expenses: Tuition:* Part-time $631 per credit hour. Tuition and fees vary according to program. *Financial support:* In 2013–14, 30 students received support. Applicants required to submit FAFSA. *Unit head:* Dr. David Hofmeister, Dean of the Graduate School, 800-794-6945 Ext. 5858, Fax: 316-295-5040, E-mail: david_hofmeister@friends.edu. *Application contact:* Rachel Steiner, Manager, Graduate Recruiting Services, 800-794-6945, Fax: 316-295-5872, E-mail: rachel_steiner@friends.edu.
Website: http://www.friends.edu/.

Frostburg State University, Graduate School, College of Education, Frostburg, MD 21532-1099. Offers M Ed, MAT, MS. *Accreditation:* NCATE. Part-time and evening/weekend programs available. *Faculty:* 26 full-time (14 women), 19 part-time/adjunct (12 women). *Students:* 93 full-time (61 women), 259 part-time (187 women); includes 25 minority (13 Black or African American, non-Hispanic/Latino; 1 American Indian or Alaska Native, non-Hispanic/Latino; 3 Asian, non-Hispanic/Latino; 5 Hispanic/Latino; 3 Two or more races, non-Hispanic/Latino), 4 international. Average age 33. 234 applicants, 70% accepted, 145 enrolled. In 2013, 139 master's awarded. *Entrance requirements:* Additional exam requirements/recommendations for international students: Required—TOEFL. *Application deadline:* For fall admission, 7/15 priority date for domestic students. Applications are processed on a rolling basis. Application fee: $30. Electronic applications accepted. *Expenses: Tuition, area resident:* Part-time $340 per credit hour. Tuition, state resident: part-time $340 per credit hour. Tuition, nonresident: part-time $437 per credit hour. *Financial support:* In 2013–14, 29 research assistantships with full tuition reimbursements (averaging $5,000 per year) were awarded; career-related internships or fieldwork and Federal Work-Study also available. Financial award application deadline: 4/1; financial award applicants required to submit FAFSA. *Unit head:* Dr. Kenneth Witmer, Dean, 301-687-4759, E-mail: kwitmer@frostburg.edu. *Application contact:* Vickie Mazer, Director, Graduate Services, 301-687-7053, Fax: 301-687-4597, E-mail: vmmazer@frostburg.edu.

Furman University, Graduate Division, Department of Education, Greenville, SC 29613. Offers curriculum and instruction (MA); early childhood education (MA); educational leadership (Ed S); English as a second language (MA); literacy (MA); school leadership (MA); special education (MA). *Accreditation:* NCATE. Part-time programs available. Postbaccalaureate distance learning degree programs offered (minimal on-campus study). *Degree requirements:* For master's, comprehensive exam (for some programs), thesis or alternative. *Entrance requirements:* For master's, PRAXIS II. *Faculty research:* Literacy, pedagogy and practice, social justice, advanced leadership, achievement in high poverty schools.

Gallaudet University, The Graduate School, Washington, DC 20002-3625. Offers ASL/English bilingual early childhood education: birth to 5 (Certificate); audiology (Au D); clinical psychology (PhD); critical studies in the education of deaf learners (PhD); deaf and hard of hearing infants, toddlers, and their families (Certificate); deaf education (Ed S); deaf education: advanced studies (MA); deaf education: special programs (MA); deaf history (Certificate); deaf studies (MA, Certificate); educating deaf students with disabilities (Certificate); education: teacher preparation (MA), including deaf education, early childhood education and deaf education, elementary education and deaf education, secondary education and deaf education; educational neuroscience (PhD); hearing, speech and language sciences (MS, PhD); international development (MA); interpretation (MA, PhD), including combined interpreting practice and research (MA), interpreting research (MA); linguistics (MA, PhD); mental health counseling (MA); peer mentoring (Certificate); public administration (MPA); school counseling (MA); school psychology (Psy S); sign language teaching (MA); social work (MSW); speech-language pathology (MS). Part-time programs available. *Faculty:* 55 full-time (37 women). *Students:* 361 full-time (279 women), 108 part-time (73 women); includes 98 minority (39 Black or African American, non-Hispanic/Latino; 1 American Indian or Alaska Native, non-Hispanic/Latino; 12 Asian, non-Hispanic/Latino; 36 Hispanic/Latino; 1 Native Hawaiian or other Pacific Islander, non-Hispanic/Latino; 9 Two or more races, non-Hispanic/Latino), 31 international. Average age 30. 602 applicants, 49% accepted, 177 enrolled. In 2013, 140 master's, 32 doctorates, 11 other advanced degrees awarded. Terminal master's awarded for partial completion of doctoral program. *Degree requirements:* For master's, comprehensive exam (for some programs), thesis optional; for doctorate, comprehensive exam, thesis/dissertation. *Entrance requirements:* For master's and doctorate, GRE General Test or MAT, letters of recommendation, interviews, goals statement, ASL proficiency interview, written English competency. Additional exam requirements/recommendations for international students: Required—TOEFL. *Application deadline:* For fall admission, 2/15 for domestic students. Applications are processed on a rolling basis. Application fee: $75. Electronic applications accepted. *Expenses: Tuition:* Full-time $14,774; part-time $821 per credit. *Required fees:* $198 per semester. *Financial support:* In 2013–14, 325 students received support. Fellowships, research assistantships, teaching assistantships, career-related internships or fieldwork, Federal Work-Study, scholarships/grants, tuition waivers (partial), and unspecified assistantships available. Support available to part-time students. Financial award applicants required to submit FAFSA. *Faculty research:* Bimodal bilingualism development, cochlear implants, telecommunications access, cancer genetics, linguistics, visual language and visual learning, advancement of avatar and robotics translation, algal productivity and physiology in the Anacostia River. *Unit head:* Dr. Carol J. Erting, Dean, Research, Graduate School, Continuing Studies, and International Programs, 202-651-5520, Fax: 202-651-5027, E-mail: carol.erting@gallaudet.edu. *Application contact:* Wednesday Luria, Coordinator of Prospective Graduate Student Services, 202-651-5400, Fax: 202-651-5295, E-mail: graduate.school@gallaudet.edu.
Website: http://www.gallaudet.edu/x26696.xml.

Gannon University, School of Graduate Studies, College of Humanities, Education, and Social Sciences, School of Education, Erie, PA 16541-0001. Offers curriculum and instruction (M Ed); curriculum supervisor (Certificate); English as a second language (Certificate); principal certification (Certificate); reading (M Ed); reading specialist (Certificate); special education supervisor (Certificate); superintendent letter of eligibility (Certificate). Part-time and evening/weekend programs available. Postbaccalaureate distance learning degree programs offered (no on-campus study). *Faculty:* 3 full-time (all women), 16 part-time/adjunct (7 women). *Students:* 18 full-time (14 women), 151 part-time (122 women); includes 2 minority (1 Black or African American, non-Hispanic/Latino; 1 Asian, non-Hispanic/Latino), 2 international. Average age 32. 244 applicants, 52% accepted, 93 enrolled. In 2013, 102 master's, 41 Certificates awarded. *Degree requirements:* For master's, thesis (for some programs), portfolio project. *Entrance requirements:* For master's, GRE, minimum GPA of 3.0; for Certificate, GRE, master's degree (for some programs), teaching certificate, minimum GPA of 3.0, experience in field (for some programs). Additional exam requirements/recommendations for international students: Required—TOEFL (minimum score 79 iBT). *Application deadline:* Applications are processed on a rolling basis. Application fee: $25. Electronic applications accepted. *Expenses:* Contact institution. *Financial support:* In 2013–14, 3 fellowships (averaging $7,783 per year) were awarded; career-related internships or fieldwork, scholarships/grants, and unspecified assistantships also available. Financial award application deadline: 7/1; financial award applicants required to submit FAFSA. *Unit head:* Janice Whiteman, Director, 814-871-7497, E-mail: whiteman002@gannon.edu. *Application contact:* Kara Morgan, Director of Graduate Admissions, 814-871-5831, Fax: 814-871-5827, E-mail: graduate@gannon.edu.

Gardner-Webb University, Graduate School, School of Education, Boiling Springs, NC 28017. Offers curriculum and instruction (Ed D); educational leadership (Ed D); elementary education (MA); executive leadership studies (MA); middle grades education (MA); school administration (MA). *Accreditation:* NCATE. Part-time and evening/weekend programs available. *Faculty:* 12 full-time (3 women), 75 part-time/adjunct (35 women). *Students:* 486 full-time (382 women), 639 part-time (467 women); includes 358 minority (334 Black or African American, non-Hispanic/Latino; 4 American Indian or Alaska Native, non-Hispanic/Latino; 7 Asian, non-Hispanic/Latino; 13 Hispanic/Latino). Average age 36. 779 applicants, 57% accepted, 354 enrolled. In 2013, 116 master's, 10 doctorates awarded. *Degree requirements:* For master's, comprehensive exam. *Entrance requirements:* For master's, GRE General Test or NTE, PRAXIS, minimum GPA of 2.5. *Application deadline:* For fall admission, 8/1 priority date for domestic students. Applications are processed on a rolling basis. Application fee: $40. Electronic applications accepted. *Expenses: Tuition:* Full-time $7200; part-time $400 per credit hour. Tuition and fees vary according to course load and program. *Financial support:* Unspecified assistantships available. *Unit head:* Dr. Alan D. Eury, Dean, 704-406-4402, Fax: 704-406-3921, E-mail: dsimmons@gardner-webb.edu. *Application contact:* Office of Graduate Admissions, 877-498-4723, Fax: 704-406-3895, E-mail: gradinfo@gardner-webb.edu.

Geneva College, Master of Arts in Higher Education Program, Beaver Falls, PA 15010-3599. Offers campus ministry (MA); college teaching (MA); educational leadership (MA); student affairs administration (MA). Part-time and evening/weekend programs available. Postbaccalaureate distance learning degree programs offered (minimal on-campus study). *Faculty:* 4 full-time (0 women). *Students:* 29 full-time (19 women), 43 part-time (23 women); includes 4 minority (3 Black or African American, non-Hispanic/Latino; 1 Hispanic/Latino). Average age 26. 46 applicants, 100% accepted, 28 enrolled. In 2013, 23 master's awarded. *Degree requirements:* For master's, 36 hours (27 in core courses) including a capstone research project. *Entrance requirements:* For master's, minimum GPA of 3.0, writing sample, 3 letters of recommendation, essay on motivation for participation in the HED program. Additional exam requirements/recommendations for international students: Required—TOEFL. *Application deadline:* For fall admission, 9/1 priority date for domestic students; for winter admission, 1/2 priority date for domestic students; for spring admission, 3/11 priority date for domestic students. Applications are processed on a rolling basis. Electronic applications accepted. *Expenses:* Contact institution. *Financial support:* In 2013–14, 59 students received support. Unspecified assistantships available. Financial award application deadline: 8/1; financial award applicants required to submit FAFSA. *Faculty research:* Student development, learning theories, church-related higher education, assessment, organizational culture. *Unit head:* Dr. Keith Martel, Program Director, 724-847-6884, Fax: 724-847-6107, E-mail: hed@geneva.edu. *Application contact:* Jerryn S. Carson, Program Coordinator, 724-847-6510, Fax: 724-847-6696, E-mail: hed@geneva.edu.
Website: http://www.geneva.edu/page/higher_ed.

George Fox University, College of Education, Newberg, OR 97132-2697. Offers M Ed, MA, MAT, MS, Ed D, Certificate, Ed S. *Application contact:* Kipp Wilfong, Graduate Admissions Counselor, 800-631-0921, Fax: 503-554-3110, E-mail: kwilfong@georgefox.edu.

George Mason University, College of Education and Human Development, Fairfax, VA 22030. Offers M Ed, MS, PhD. *Accreditation:* NCATE. Part-time and evening/weekend programs available. Postbaccalaureate distance learning degree programs offered. *Faculty:* 126 full-time (85 women), 183 part-time/adjunct (127 women). *Students:* 487 full-time (406 women), 1,988 part-time (1,588 women); includes 562 minority (202 Black or African American, non-Hispanic/Latino; 4 American Indian or Alaska Native, non-

Hispanic/Latino; 126 Asian, non-Hispanic/Latino; 187 Hispanic/Latino; 4 Native Hawaiian or other Pacific Islander, non-Hispanic/Latino; 39 Two or more races, non-Hispanic/Latino), 37 international. Average age 34. 1,428 applicants, 70% accepted, 748 enrolled. In 2013, 897 master's, 47 doctorates awarded. *Degree requirements:* For doctorate, comprehensive exam, final project, internship. *Entrance requirements:* For master's, PRAXIS I, minimum GPA of 3.0 in last 60 hours of course work, goals statement and/or interview; for doctorate, GRE or MAT, appropriate master's degree, interview. Additional exam requirements/recommendations for international students: Required—TOEFL (minimum score 575 paper-based; 88 iBT), IELTS (minimum score 6.5), PTE. Application fee: $65 ($80 for international students). Electronic applications accepted. *Expenses:* Tuition, state resident: full-time $9350; part-time $390 per credit. Tuition, nonresident: full-time $25,754; part-time $1073 per credit. *Required fees:* $2688; $112 per credit. *Financial support:* In 2013–14, 118 students received support, including 13 fellowships (averaging $9,374 per year), 94 research assistantships with full and partial tuition reimbursements available (averaging $11,206 per year), 32 teaching assistantships with full and partial tuition reimbursements available (averaging $6,901 per year); career-related internships or fieldwork, Federal Work-Study, scholarships/grants, unspecified assistantships, and health care benefits (for full-time research or teaching assistantship recipients) also available. Support available to part-time students. Financial award application deadline: 3/1; financial award applicants required to submit FAFSA. *Faculty research:* Special education/human disabilities, mathematics/science/technology education, education leadership, school/community/agency/higher education, counseling and administration. *Total annual research expenditures:* $14.3 million. *Unit head:* Mark Ginsberg, Dean, 703-993-2004, Fax: 703-993-2001, E-mail: mginsber@gmu.edu. *Application contact:* Nicole Mariam, Graduate Admissions Coordinator, 703-993-3832, Fax: 703-993-2020, E-mail: nwhite5@gmu.edu.
Website: http://cehd.gmu.edu/.

Georgetown College, Department of Education, Georgetown, KY 40324-1696. Offers reading and writing (MA Ed); special education (MA Ed); teaching (MA Ed). *Accreditation:* NCATE. Part-time programs available. *Degree requirements:* For master's, portfolio. *Entrance requirements:* For master's, teaching certificate, minimum GPA of 2.7 or GRE General Test.

The George Washington University, Graduate School of Education and Human Development, Washington, DC 20052. Offers M Ed, MA Ed, MAT, Ed D, PhD, Certificate, Ed S, Graduate Certificate. *Accreditation:* NCATE. Part-time and evening/weekend programs available. Postbaccalaureate distance learning degree programs offered (no on-campus study). *Faculty:* 79 full-time (48 women). *Students:* 377 full-time (301 women), 1,067 part-time (819 women); includes 450 minority (293 Black or African American, non-Hispanic/Latino; 3 American Indian or Alaska Native, non-Hispanic/Latino; 60 Asian, non-Hispanic/Latino; 74 Hispanic/Latino; 4 Native Hawaiian or other Pacific Islander, non-Hispanic/Latino; 16 Two or more races, non-Hispanic/Latino), 81 international. Average age 37. 1,292 applicants, 87% accepted, 562 enrolled. In 2013, 368 master's, 67 doctorates, 177 other advanced degrees awarded. *Degree requirements:* For master's and other advanced degree, comprehensive exam; for doctorate, comprehensive exam, thesis/dissertation. *Entrance requirements:* For master's, GRE General Test or MAT, minimum GPA of 2.75; for doctorate, GRE General Test or MAT, interview, minimum GPA of 3.3; for other advanced degree, GRE General Test or MAT, minimum GPA of 3.3. *Application deadline:* For fall admission, 1/15 priority date for domestic students; for spring admission, 10/1 for domestic students. Applications are processed on a rolling basis. Application fee: $75. Electronic applications accepted. *Financial support:* In 2013–14, 279 students received support. Fellowships with tuition reimbursements available, research assistantships with tuition reimbursements available, teaching assistantships with tuition reimbursements available, career-related internships or fieldwork, Federal Work-Study, and tuition waivers (full and partial) available. Support available to part-time students. Financial award application deadline: 1/15. *Faculty research:* Policy, special education, bilingual education, counseling, human resource development. *Total annual research expenditures:* $4.6 million. *Unit head:* Dr. Michael J. Feuer, Dean, 202-994-6161, Fax: 202-994-7207, E-mail: mjfeuer@gwu.edu. *Application contact:* Sarah Lang, Director of Graduate Admissions, 202-994-1447, Fax: 202-994-7207, E-mail: slang@gwu.edu.
Website: http://gsehd.gwu.edu/.

Georgia College & State University, Graduate School, The John H. Lounsbury College of Education, Milledgeville, GA 31061. Offers M Ed, MAT, Ed S. *Accreditation:* NCATE. Part-time programs available. *Students:* 163 full-time (116 women), 120 part-time (97 women); includes 103 minority (92 Black or African American, non-Hispanic/Latino; 1 American Indian or Alaska Native, non-Hispanic/Latino; 1 Asian, non-Hispanic/Latino; 6 Hispanic/Latino; 1 Native Hawaiian or other Pacific Islander, non-Hispanic/Latino; 2 Two or more races, non-Hispanic/Latino). Average age 32. In 2013, 149 master's, 93 other advanced degrees awarded. *Degree requirements:* For master's, comprehensive exam, minimum GPA of 3.0, complete program within 4 years; for Ed S, comprehensive exam. *Entrance requirements:* For master's, on-site writing assessment, 2 professional recommendations, level 4 teaching certificate, transcript, immunization verifications; for Ed S, on-site writing assessment, master's degree, 2 years of teaching experience, 2 professional recommendations, level 5 GA teacher certification, minimum GPA of 3.25. Additional exam requirements/recommendations for international students: Recommended—TOEFL (minimum score 550 paper-based; 79 iBT). *Application deadline:* For fall admission, 7/1 priority date for domestic students; for spring admission, 11/15 priority date for domestic students. Applications are processed on a rolling basis. Application fee: $40. Electronic applications accepted. *Financial support:* In 2013–14, 11 research assistantships were awarded; career-related internships or fieldwork and unspecified assistantships also available. Support available to part-time students. Financial award application deadline: 3/1; financial award applicants required to submit FAFSA. *Application contact:* Shanda Brand, Graduate Admissions Advisor, 478-445-1383, Fax: 478-445-6582, E-mail: shanda.brand@gcsu.edu.
Website: http://www.gcsu.edu/education/graduate/index.htm.

Georgian Court University, School of Education, Lakewood, NJ 08701-2697. Offers administration and leadership (MA); education (MA). *Accreditation:* Teacher Education Accreditation Council. Part-time and evening/weekend programs available. *Faculty:* 21 full-time (14 women), 16 part-time/adjunct (12 women). *Students:* 87 full-time (78 women), 303 part-time (251 women); includes 48 minority (10 Black or African American, non-Hispanic/Latino; 1 Asian, non-Hispanic/Latino; 33 Hispanic/Latino; 4 Two or more races, non-Hispanic/Latino). In 2013, 78 master's awarded. *Degree requirements:* For master's, comprehensive exam (for some programs), thesis (for some programs). *Entrance requirements:* For master's, GRE, MAT or NTE/PRAXIS, 3 letters of recommendation. Additional exam requirements/recommendations for international students: Required—TOEFL (minimum score 550 paper-based). *Application deadline:* For fall admission, 8/1 priority date for domestic students, 4/1 for international students; for spring admission, 1/1 priority date for domestic students, 7/1 for international students. Applications are processed on a rolling basis. Application fee: $40. Electronic applications accepted. *Expenses: Tuition:* Full-time $18,912; part-time $788 per credit. *Required fees:* $906. *Financial support:* Scholarships/grants, health care benefits, and unspecified assistantships available. Financial award application deadline: 4/15; financial award applicants required to submit FAFSA. *Unit head:* Dr. Lynn DeCapua, Dean, 732-987-2729. *Application contact:* Patrick Givens, Director of Graduate Admissions, 732-987-2736, Fax: 732-987-2084, E-mail: graduateadmissions@georgian.edu.
Website: http://www.georgian.edu/education/index.htm.

Georgia Regents University, The Graduate School, College of Education, Augusta, GA 30912. Offers M Ed, MAT, Ed S. *Accreditation:* NCATE. Part-time and evening/weekend programs available. *Faculty:* 31 full-time (16 women), 28 part-time/adjunct (23 women). *Students:* 116 full-time (89 women), 104 part-time (74 women); includes 54 minority (43 Black or African American, non-Hispanic/Latino; 1 American Indian or Alaska Native, non-Hispanic/Latino; 2 Asian, non-Hispanic/Latino; 8 Hispanic/Latino), 2 international. Average age 33. 239 applicants, 82% accepted, 168 enrolled. In 2013, 72 master's, 97 other advanced degrees awarded. *Entrance requirements:* For master's, GRE, MAT, minimum GPA of 2.5. *Application deadline:* For fall admission, 7/16 priority date for domestic students. Applications are processed on a rolling basis. Application fee: $20. *Financial support:* Career-related internships or fieldwork, Federal Work-Study, institutionally sponsored loans, and unspecified assistantships available. Support available to part-time students. Financial award application deadline: 4/15; financial award applicants required to submit FAFSA. *Unit head:* Dr. Richard Harrison, Dean, 706-737-1499, Fax: 706-667-4706, E-mail: vharriso@aug.edu. *Application contact:* Andrea M. Scott, Secretary to the Dean, 706-737-1499, Fax: 706-667-4706, E-mail: ascott1@aug.edu.

Georgia Southern University, Jack N. Averitt College of Graduate Studies, College of Education, Statesboro, GA 30460. Offers M Ed, MAT, Ed D, Ed S. *Accreditation:* NCATE. Part-time and evening/weekend programs available. Postbaccalaureate distance learning degree programs offered (no on-campus study). *Faculty:* 71 full-time (43 women), 14 part-time/adjunct (8 women). *Students:* 338 full-time (260 women), 931 part-time (742 women); includes 406 minority (352 Black or African American, non-Hispanic/Latino; 4 American Indian or Alaska Native, non-Hispanic/Latino; 6 Asian, non-Hispanic/Latino; 25 Hispanic/Latino; 1 Native Hawaiian or other Pacific Islander, non-Hispanic/Latino; 18 Two or more races, non-Hispanic/Latino), 8 international. Average age 34. 374 applicants, 79% accepted, 186 enrolled. In 2013, 324 master's, 46 doctorates, 110 other advanced degrees awarded. *Degree requirements:* For master's, comprehensive exam (for some programs), portfolio or assessments; for doctorate, comprehensive exam, thesis/dissertation, exams; for Ed S, assessments. *Entrance requirements:* For master's, GRE General Test or MAT, minimum GPA of 2.5; for doctorate, GRE General Test or MAT, minimum GPA of 3.5, letters of reference, writing sample; for Ed S, GRE General Test or MAT, minimum graduate GPA of 3.25. Additional exam requirements/recommendations for international students: Required—TOEFL (minimum score 550 paper-based; 80 iBT), IELTS (minimum score 6). *Application deadline:* For fall admission, 3/1 priority date for domestic and international students; for spring admission, 10/1 priority date for domestic students, 10/1 for international students. Applications are processed on a rolling basis. Application fee: $50. Electronic applications accepted. *Expenses:* Tuition, state resident: full-time $7068; part-time $270 per semester hour. Tuition, nonresident: full-time $26,446; part-time $1077 per semester hour. *Required fees:* $2092. *Financial support:* In 2013–14, 76 students received support, including 26 research assistantships with partial tuition reimbursements available (averaging $7,200 per year), teaching assistantships with partial tuition reimbursements available (averaging $7,200 per year); career-related internships or fieldwork, Federal Work-Study, scholarships/grants, tuition waivers (partial), unspecified assistantships, and doctoral stipends also available. Support available to part-time students. Financial award application deadline: 4/15; financial award applicants required to submit FAFSA. *Faculty research:* Teacher preparation, literacy education, curriculum issues, technology-enhanced teaching and learning, school reform, assessment of teaching and learning. *Total annual research expenditures:* $97,282. *Unit head:* Dr. Thomas Koballa, Dean, 912-478-5648, Fax: 912-478-5093, E-mail: tkoballa@georgiasouthern.edu. *Application contact:* Amanda Gilliland, Coordinator of Graduate Student Recruitment, 912-478-5384, Fax: 912-478-0740, E-mail: gradadmissions@georgiasouthern.edu.
Website: http://coe.georgiasouthern.edu/.

Georgia Southwestern State University, Graduate Studies, School of Education, Americus, GA 31709-4693. Offers early childhood education (M Ed, Ed S); health and physical education (M Ed); middle grades education (M Ed, Ed S); reading (M Ed); secondary education (M Ed); special education (M Ed). *Accreditation:* NCATE. *Degree requirements:* For master's, comprehensive exam. *Entrance requirements:* For master's, GRE General Test or MAT, minimum GPA of 2.5; for Ed S, GRE General Test or MAT, minimum graduate GPA of 3.25, M Ed from accredited college or university, 3 years teaching experience. Electronic applications accepted.

Georgia State University, College of Education, Atlanta, GA 30302-3083. Offers M Ed, MAT, MS, Ed D, PhD, Ed S. *Accreditation:* NCATE. Part-time and evening/weekend programs available. Postbaccalaureate distance learning degree programs offered (minimal on-campus study). *Faculty:* 114 full-time (71 women). *Students:* 862 full-time (630 women), 514 part-time (386 women); includes 569 minority (420 Black or African American, non-Hispanic/Latino; 2 American Indian or Alaska Native, non-Hispanic/Latino; 39 Asian, non-Hispanic/Latino; 65 Hispanic/Latino; 3 Native Hawaiian or other Pacific Islander, non-Hispanic/Latino; 40 Two or more races, non-Hispanic/Latino), 44 international. Average age 32. 1,172 applicants, 36% accepted, 302 enrolled. In 2013, 551 master's, 44 doctorates, 84 other advanced degrees awarded. Terminal master's awarded for partial completion of doctoral program. *Degree requirements:* For master's, comprehensive exam (for some programs), thesis (for some programs), minimum GPA of 3.0; for doctorate, comprehensive exam, thesis/dissertation, minimum GPA of 3.5; for Ed S, thesis or alternative, minimum GPA of 3.0. *Entrance requirements:* For master's, GRE, MAT (for some programs), minimum GPA of 2.5 on all undergraduate work attempted in which letter grades were awarded; for doctorate, GRE, MAT (for some programs), minimum GPA of 3.3 on all graduate coursework for which letter grades were awarded (for PhD); for Ed S, GRE, MAT (for some programs), graduate degree from regionally-accredited college or university unless specified otherwise by the program with minimum GPA of 3.25 on all graduate coursework for which letter grades were awarded. Additional exam requirements/recommendations for international students: Required—TOEFL (minimum score 550 paper-based; 79 iBT) or IELTS (minimum score 6.5). Application fee: $50. Electronic applications accepted. *Expenses: Tuition, area resident:* Full-time $4176; part-time $348 per credit hour. Tuition, state resident: full-time $14,544; part-time $1212 per credit hour. Tuition, nonresident: full-time $14,544; part-time $1212 per credit hour. Tuition and fees vary according to course load and program. *Financial support:* In 2013–14, fellowships with full tuition reimbursements (averaging $25,000 per year), research assistantships with full and partial tuition reimbursements (averaging $4,867 per year), teaching assistantships with full and partial tuition reimbursements (averaging $4,683 per year) were awarded; career-related internships or fieldwork, Federal Work-Study, scholarships/grants, tuition waivers (partial), and unspecified assistantships also available. Support available to part-time students. *Faculty research:* Literacy: early, middle-secondary, adult and deaf/hard of hearing; teacher professional development, evaluation and urban education; STEM teacher education; health, physical activity and exercise science; school safety and counseling. *Unit head:* Dr. Paul A. Alberto, Interim Dean, 404-413-8100, Fax: 404-413-8103, E-mail: palberto@gsu.edu. *Application contact:* Nancy Keita, Director, Office of

Academic Assistance and Graduate Admissions, 404-413-8001, E-mail: nkeita@gsu.edu.
Website: http://education.gsu.edu/main/.

Goddard College, Graduate Division, Master of Arts in Education and Licensure Program, Plainfield, VT 05667-9432. Offers community education (MA); teacher licensure (MA). Part-time programs available. Postbaccalaureate distance learning degree programs offered (minimal on-campus study). *Degree requirements:* For master's, thesis. *Entrance requirements:* For master's, 3 letters of recommendation, interview. Electronic applications accepted. *Faculty research:* Democratic curriculum leadership, service learning and academic achievement, middle grades curriculum, community education.

Gonzaga University, School of Education, Spokane, WA 99258. Offers M Anesth Ed, MAA, MAC, MAP, MASPAA, MES, MIT. *Accreditation:* NCATE. Part-time and evening/weekend programs available. Postbaccalaureate distance learning degree programs offered (minimal on-campus study). *Faculty:* 29 full-time (17 women), 32 part-time/adjunct (17 women). *Students:* 134 full-time (88 women), 318 part-time (203 women); includes 39 minority (5 Black or African American, non-Hispanic/Latino; 3 American Indian or Alaska Native, non-Hispanic/Latino; 7 Asian, non-Hispanic/Latino; 15 Hispanic/Latino; 9 Two or more races, non-Hispanic/Latino), 241 international. Average age 34. 375 applicants, 66% accepted, 200 enrolled. In 2013, 221 master's awarded. *Degree requirements:* For master's, comprehensive exam. *Entrance requirements:* For master's, GRE, MAT, and/or Washington Educators Skills Test-Basic (WEST-B). Additional exam requirements/recommendations for international students: Required—TOEFL. *Application deadline:* Applications are processed on a rolling basis. Application fee: $50. Electronic applications accepted. *Expenses:* Contact institution. *Financial support:* Teaching assistantships, Federal Work-Study, and tuition waivers (full and partial) available. Support available to part-time students. Financial award application deadline: 2/1; financial award applicants required to submit FAFSA. *Unit head:* Dr. Vincent Alfonso, Dean, 509-313-3594, Fax: 509-313-5821, E-mail: alfonso@gonzaga.edu. *Application contact:* Julie McCulloh, Dean of Admissions, 509-313-6592, Fax: 509-313-5780, E-mail: mcculloh@gu.gonzaga.edu.

Gordon College, Graduate Education Program, Wenham, MA 01984-1899. Offers education (M Ed); educational leadership (Ed S); English as a second language (ESL) (Ed S); mathematics specialist (Ed S); reading (Ed S). Part-time and evening/weekend programs available. *Faculty:* 1 (woman) full-time, 45 part-time/adjunct (27 women). *Students:* 106 full-time (86 women), 281 part-time (230 women); includes 30 minority (4 Black or African American, non-Hispanic/Latino; 7 Asian, non-Hispanic/Latino; 17 Hispanic/Latino; 2 Two or more races, non-Hispanic/Latino), 5 international. In 2013, 52 master's awarded. *Degree requirements:* For master's and Ed S, action research or clinical experience (for some programs). *Entrance requirements:* For master's, GRE or MAT, references, minimum undergraduate GPA of 3.0; for Ed S, references, minimum undergraduate GPA of 3.0. Additional exam requirements/recommendations for international students: Required—TOEFL (minimum score 550 paper-based, 80 iBT) or IELTS (minimum score 6.5). *Application deadline:* Applications are processed on a rolling basis. Application fee: $50. *Expenses: Tuition:* Part-time $325 per credit. *Required fees:* $50 per term. One-time fee: $50. Tuition and fees vary according to program. *Financial support:* Applicants required to submit FAFSA. *Faculty research:* Reading, early childhood development, English language learners. *Unit head:* Dr. Janet Arndt, Director of Graduate Studies, 978-867-4355, Fax: 978-867-4663. *Application contact:* Julie Lenocker, Program Administrator, 978-867-4322, Fax: 978-867-4663, E-mail: graduate-education@gordon.edu.
Website: http://www.gordon.edu/graduate.

Goucher College, Graduate Programs in Education, Baltimore, MD 21204-2794. Offers M Ed, MAT. Part-time and evening/weekend programs available. *Faculty:* 88 part-time/adjunct (69 women). *Students:* 51 full-time (42 women), 427 part-time (328 women); includes 65 minority (54 Black or African American, non-Hispanic/Latino; 1 Asian, non-Hispanic/Latino; 7 Hispanic/Latino; 3 Two or more races, non-Hispanic/Latino), 1 international. Average age 35. 96 applicants, 86% accepted, 52 enrolled. In 2013, 93 master's awarded. *Degree requirements:* For master's, thesis (M Ed), final presentation (MAT). *Entrance requirements:* For master's, minimum GPA of 3.0. Additional exam requirements/recommendations for international students: Required—TOEFL (minimum score 560 paper-based). *Application deadline:* For fall admission, 9/1 priority date for domestic students; for spring admission, 1/15 for domestic students. Applications are processed on a rolling basis. Application fee: $60. *Financial support:* In 2013–14, 3 research assistantships with tuition reimbursements (averaging $4,500 per year) were awarded; career-related internships or fieldwork and need-based awards also available. Support available to part-time students. Financial award application deadline: 4/15; financial award applicants required to submit FAFSA. *Faculty research:* Urban education, middle school, school improvement, teacher education, at-risk student achievement. *Unit head:* Dr. Phyllis Sunshine, Director, 410-337-6047, Fax: 410-337-6394, E-mail: psunshin@goucher.edu. *Application contact:* Megan Cornett, Director of Marketing and Communications, 410-337-6200, Fax: 410-337-6085, E-mail: mcornett@goucher.edu.
Website: http://www.goucher.edu/graduate-programs/graduate-programs-in-education.

Governors State University, College of Education, Program in Education, University Park, IL 60484. Offers MA. Part-time and evening/weekend programs available. *Degree requirements:* For master's, comprehensive exam, thesis or alternative, practicum. *Entrance requirements:* For master's, minimum GPA of 2.75 in last 60 hours of undergraduate course work, 3.0 graduate. *Faculty research:* Teaching problem-solving microcomputer use in special education, science, and mathematics.

Graceland University, Gleazer School of Education, Independence, MO 64050. Offers differentiated instruction (M Ed); literacy and instruction (M Ed); management in the inclusive classroom (M Ed); mild/moderate special education (M Ed); technology integration (M Ed). *Accreditation:* NCATE. Part-time and evening/weekend programs available. Postbaccalaureate distance learning degree programs offered (no on-campus study). *Faculty:* 12 full-time (11 women), 18 part-time/adjunct (14 women). *Students:* 139 full-time (119 women), 18 part-time (14 women); includes 8 minority (3 Black or African American, non-Hispanic/Latino; 1 Asian, non-Hispanic/Latino; 4 Hispanic/Latino). Average age 36. 36 applicants, 81% accepted, 24 enrolled. In 2013, 196 master's awarded. *Degree requirements:* For master's, action research project. *Entrance requirements:* For master's, minimum GPA of 3.0, teaching certificate, current teaching contract. *Application deadline:* For fall admission, 7/15 for domestic students; for winter admission, 10/15 for domestic students; for spring admission, 1/15 priority date for domestic students. Application fee: $50. Electronic applications accepted. *Expenses: Tuition:* Part-time $450 per semester hour. Tuition and fees vary according to course load, degree level, campus/location and program. *Financial support:* Institutionally sponsored loans and scholarships/grants available. Financial award application deadline: 12/15; financial award applicants required to submit FAFSA. *Unit head:* Dr. Scott Huddleston, Dean, 641-784-5000 Ext. 4744, E-mail: huddlest@graceland.edu. *Application contact:* Cathy Porter, Program Consultant, 816-423-4716, Fax: 816-833-2990, E-mail: cgporter@graceland.edu.
Website: http://www.graceland.edu/education.

Grambling State University, School of Graduate Studies and Research, College of Education, Grambling, LA 71245. Offers M Ed, MAT, MS, Ed D, PMC. *Accreditation:* NCATE. Part-time and evening/weekend programs available. *Faculty:* 19 full-time (13 women). *Students:* 88 full-time (45 women), 167 part-time (127 women); includes 223 minority (221 Black or African American, non-Hispanic/Latino; 2 Hispanic/Latino), 9 international. Average age 35. In 2013, 84 master's, 6 doctorates, 1 other advanced degree awarded. *Degree requirements:* For master's, comprehensive exam, thesis (for some programs); for doctorate, comprehensive exam, thesis/dissertation. *Entrance requirements:* For master's, GRE; for doctorate, GRE (minimum score 1000, 500 on Verbal), master's degree, minimum GPA of 3.0 on last degree. Additional exam requirements/recommendations for international students: Required—TOEFL (minimum score 500 paper-based; 62 iBT). *Application deadline:* For fall admission, 7/1 for domestic and international students; for spring admission, 12/1 for domestic and international students; for summer admission, 5/1 for domestic and international students. Applications are processed on a rolling basis. Application fee: $20 ($30 for international students). Electronic applications accepted. *Financial support:* Research assistantships, career-related internships or fieldwork, health care benefits, tuition waivers (full), and unspecified assistantships available. Financial award application deadline: 5/31; financial award applicants required to submit FAFSA. *Unit head:* Dr. Larnell Flannagan, 318-274-3235, Fax: 318-274-2799, E-mail: flannaganl@gram.edu. *Application contact:* Katina S. Crowe-Fields, Special Assistant to Associate Vice President/Dean, 318-274-2158, Fax: 318-274-7373, E-mail: croweks@gram.edu.
Website: http://www.gram.edu/academics/majors/education/.

Grand Canyon University, College of Doctoral Studies, Phoenix, AZ 85017-1097. Offers business administration (DBA); general psychology (PhD), including cognition and instruction, industrial and organizational psychology; organizational leadership (Ed D, PhD), including behavioral health (PhD), education and effective schools (PhD), higher education (PhD), instructional leadership (PhD), organizational development (Ed D). *Degree requirements:* For doctorate, comprehensive exam, thesis/dissertation. *Entrance requirements:* For doctorate, minimum GPA of 3.4 on earned advanced degree from regionally-accredited institution; transcripts; goals statement.

Grand Canyon University, College of Education, Phoenix, AZ 85017-1097. Offers curriculum and instruction (M Ed); education administration (M Ed); elementary education (M Ed); secondary education (M Ed); special education (M Ed); teaching (MA). Part-time and evening/weekend programs available. Postbaccalaureate distance learning degree programs offered (no on-campus study). *Degree requirements:* For master's, publishable research paper (M Ed), e-portfolio. *Entrance requirements:* For master's, undergraduate degree from accredited, GCU-approved college, university, or program with minimum GPA 2.8. Additional exam requirements/recommendations for international students: Required—TOEFL (minimum score 550 paper-based; 79 iBT), IELTS (minimum score 6). Electronic applications accepted.

Grand Valley State University, College of Education, Programs in General Education, Allendale, MI 49401-9403. Offers adult and higher education (M Ed); early childhood education (M Ed); educational differentiation (M Ed); educational leadership (M Ed); educational technology integration (M Ed); elementary education (M Ed); middle level education (M Ed); school library media services (M Ed); secondary level education (M Ed); teaching English to speakers of other languages (M Ed). Part-time and evening/weekend programs available. Postbaccalaureate distance learning degree programs offered (minimal on-campus study). *Degree requirements:* For master's, thesis. *Entrance requirements:* For master's, GRE General Test or minimum GPA of 3.0. Additional exam requirements/recommendations for international students: Required—TOEFL. Electronic applications accepted. *Faculty research:* Effectiveness of technology in education, parental involvement, effective teaching, effective schools research.

Grand View University, Master of Science in Innovative Leadership Program, Des Moines, IA 50316-1599. Offers business (MS); education (MS); nursing (MS). Part-time and evening/weekend programs available. *Degree requirements:* For master's, completion of all required coursework in common core and selected track with minimum cumulative GPA of 3.0 and no more than two grades of C. *Entrance requirements:* For master's, GRE, GMAT, or essay, minimum undergraduate GPA of 3.0, professional resume, 3 letters of recommendation, interview. Additional exam requirements/recommendations for international students: Required—TOEFL (minimum score 550 paper-based). Electronic applications accepted.

Gratz College, Graduate Programs, Program in Education, Melrose Park, PA 19027. Offers MA. Part-time programs available. *Degree requirements:* For master's, one foreign language, project. *Entrance requirements:* For master's, teaching certificate.

Greensboro College, Program in Education, Greensboro, NC 27401-1875. Offers elementary education (M Ed); special education (M Ed). Part-time and evening/weekend programs available. *Degree requirements:* For master's, thesis. *Entrance requirements:* For master's, GRE, teacher license, 2 years of teaching experience, 2 letters of recommendation. Additional exam requirements/recommendations for international students: Required—TOEFL (minimum score 550 paper-based). Electronic applications accepted.

Greenville College, Program in Education, Greenville, IL 62246-0159. Offers education (MAT); elementary education (MAE); secondary education (MAE). *Degree requirements:* For master's, thesis (for some programs). *Entrance requirements:* For master's, GRE, Illinois Basic Skills Test, teacher certification. Electronic applications accepted.

Gwynedd Mercy University, Center for Lifelong Learning, Gwynedd Valley, PA 19437-0901. Offers education (MSE); educational administration (MS); management (MSM). Part-time and evening/weekend programs available. *Degree requirements:* For master's, thesis. *Entrance requirements:* For master's, minimum GPA of 3.0.

Gwynedd Mercy University, School of Education, Gwynedd Valley, PA 19437-0901. Offers educational administration (MS); master teacher (MS); reading (MS); school counseling (MS); special education (MS). Part-time and evening/weekend programs available. *Degree requirements:* For master's, thesis, internship, practicum. *Entrance requirements:* For master's, GRE or MAT; PRAXIS I, minimum GPA of 3.0. *Faculty research:* Learning and the brain, reading literacy, ethics and moral judgment, leadership, teaching and multicultural education.

Hamline University, School of Education, St. Paul, MN 55104-1284. Offers education (MA Ed, Ed D); English as a second language (MA); literacy education (MA); natural science and environmental education (MA Ed); teaching (MAT). *Accreditation:* NCATE (one or more programs are accredited). Part-time and evening/weekend programs available. Postbaccalaureate distance learning degree programs offered (no on-campus study). *Faculty:* 19 full-time (14 women), 44 part-time/adjunct (38 women). *Students:* 107 full-time (75 women), 997 part-time (744 women); includes 71 minority (23 Black or African American, non-Hispanic/Latino; 4 American Indian or Alaska Native, non-Hispanic/Latino; 17 Asian, non-Hispanic/Latino; 21 Hispanic/Latino; 6 Two or more races, non-Hispanic/Latino), 10 international. Average age 33. 395 applicants, 74% accepted, 224 enrolled. In 2013, 221 master's, 13 doctorates awarded. *Degree requirements:* For master's, foreign language (for MA in English as a second language only); thesis or capstone project; for doctorate, comprehensive exam, thesis/dissertation. *Entrance requirements:* For master's, written essay, official transcripts, 2

letters of recommendation, minimum GPA of 3.0 from bachelor's work; for doctorate, personal statement, master's degree with minimum GPA of 3.0, 3 letters of recommendation, writing sample, interview. Additional exam requirements/recommendations for international students: Required—TOEFL (minimum score 550 paper-based; 80 iBT), TOEFL (625 paper-based, 107 iBT) or IELTS (minimum 7.5) for MA in ESL. *Application deadline:* Applications are processed on a rolling basis. Application fee: $0 ($100 for international students). Electronic applications accepted. *Financial support:* Career-related internships or fieldwork, Federal Work-Study, and scholarships/grants available. Support available to part-time students. Financial award applicants required to submit FAFSA. *Faculty research:* Adult basic education, service-learning, teacher dispositions, diversity, technology. *Unit head:* Dr. Nancy Sorenson, Dean, 651-523-2600, Fax: 651-523-2489, E-mail: nsorenson01@hamline.edu. *Application contact:* Shawn Skoog, Director of Graduate Recruitment and Admission, 651-523-2900, Fax: 651-523-3058, E-mail: sskoog03@hamline.edu.
Website: http://www.hamline.edu/education.

Hampton University, Graduate College, College of Education and Continuing Studies, Hampton, VA 23668. Offers counseling (MA), including college student development, community agency counseling, pastoral counseling, school counseling; educational leadership (MA); elementary education (MA); gifted education (MA); Montessori education (MA); teaching (MT), including early childhood education, middle school education, music education, secondary education, special education. *Accreditation:* NCATE. Part-time and evening/weekend programs available. *Entrance requirements:* For master's, GRE General Test.

Hannibal-LaGrange University, Program in Education, Hannibal, MO 63401-1999. Offers literacy (MS Ed); teaching and learning (MS Ed). Part-time and evening/weekend programs available. *Degree requirements:* For master's, thesis, portfolio, documenting of program outcomes, public sharing of research. *Entrance requirements:* For master's, copy of current teaching certificate; minimum GPA of 2.75. *Faculty research:* Reading assessment, reading remediation, handwriting instruction, early childhood intervention.

Harding University, Cannon-Clary College of Education, Searcy, AR 72149-0001. Offers advanced studies in teaching and learning (M Ed); art (MSE); behavioral science (MSE); counseling (MS, Ed S); early childhood special education (M Ed, MSE); education (MSE); educational leadership (M Ed, Ed S); elementary education (M Ed); English (MSE); French (MSE); history/social science (MSE); kinesiology (MSE); math (MSE); reading (M Ed); secondary education (M Ed); Spanish (MSE); teaching (MAT); teaching English as a second language (MSE). *Accreditation:* NCATE. Part-time and evening/weekend programs available. *Faculty:* 13 full-time (5 women), 42 part-time/adjunct (24 women). *Students:* 154 full-time (119 women), 393 part-time (270 women); includes 108 minority (81 Black or African American, non-Hispanic/Latino; 5 American Indian or Alaska Native, non-Hispanic/Latino; 5 Asian, non-Hispanic/Latino; 9 Hispanic/Latino; 8 Two or more races, non-Hispanic/Latino), 15 international. Average age 36. 187 applicants, 79% accepted, 135 enrolled. In 2013, 138 master's, 17 other advanced degrees awarded. *Degree requirements:* For master's, comprehensive exam (for some programs), thesis optional, portfolio(s); for Ed S, comprehensive exam, portfolio, project. *Entrance requirements:* For master's, GRE, MAT, PRAXIS; for Ed S, MAT or GRE. Additional exam requirements/recommendations for international students: Required—TOEFL (minimum score 550 paper-based; 79 iBT). *Application deadline:* For fall admission, 8/1 for domestic and international students; for spring admission, 1/1 for domestic and international students. Applications are processed on a rolling basis. Application fee: $35. *Expenses: Tuition:* Full-time $11,574; part-time $643 per credit hour. *Required fees:* $432; $24 per credit hour. Tuition and fees vary according to course load, degree level and program. *Financial support:* In 2013–14, 36 students received support. Unspecified assistantships available. *Faculty research:* Reading, comprehension, school violence, educational technology, behavior, college choice, differentiated instruction, brain-based teaching. *Unit head:* Dr. Clara Carroll, Chair, 501-279-4501, Fax: 501-279-4083, E-mail: ccarroll@harding.edu. *Application contact:* Information Contact, 501-279-4315, E-mail: gradstudiesedu@harding.edu.
Website: http://www.harding.edu/education.

Hardin-Simmons University, Graduate School, Irvin School of Education, Abilene, TX 79698-0001. Offers M Ed, Ed D. Part-time programs available. *Faculty:* 15 full-time (7 women), 8 part-time/adjunct (4 women). *Students:* 44 full-time (28 women), 74 part-time (49 women); includes 29 minority (6 Black or African American, non-Hispanic/Latino; 2 Asian, non-Hispanic/Latino; 20 Hispanic/Latino; 1 Two or more races, non-Hispanic/Latino), 2 international. Average age 32. 53 applicants, 96% accepted, 41 enrolled. In 2013, 38 master's awarded. *Degree requirements:* For master's, comprehensive exam. *Entrance requirements:* For master's, minimum undergraduate GPA of 3.0 in major, 2.7 overall. Additional exam requirements/recommendations for international students: Required—TOEFL (minimum score 550 paper-based; 75 iBT). *Application deadline:* For fall admission, 8/15 priority date for domestic students, 4/1 for international students; for spring admission, 1/5 priority date for domestic students, 9/1 for international students. Applications are processed on a rolling basis. Application fee: $50. *Expenses: Tuition:* Full-time $13,410; part-time $745 per credit hour. *Required fees:* $325; $110 per semester. Tuition and fees vary according to program. *Financial support:* In 2013–14, 43 students received support, including 23 fellowships (averaging $1,965 per year); career-related internships or fieldwork, scholarships/grants, and coaching assistantships also available. Support available to part-time students. Financial award application deadline: 6/30; financial award applicants required to submit FAFSA. *Unit head:* Dr. Pam Williford, Dean, 325-670-1352, Fax: 325-670-5859, E-mail: pwilliford@hsutx.edu. *Application contact:* Dr. Nancy Kucinski, Dean of Graduate Studies, 325-670-1298, Fax: 325-670-1564, E-mail: gradoff@hsutx.edu.
Website: http://www.hsutx.edu/academics/irvin.

Harrison Middleton University, Graduate Program, Tempe, AZ 85282. Offers education (MA, Ed D); humanities (MA); imaginative literature (MA); interdisciplinary studies (DA); jurisprudence (MA); natural science (MA); philosophy and religion (MA); social science (MA). Part-time and evening/weekend programs available. Postbaccalaureate distance learning degree programs offered (no on-campus study). *Degree requirements:* For master's and doctorate, capstone project. *Entrance requirements:* For master's, interview; for doctorate, 2 academic letters of reference, interview, essay. Additional exam requirements/recommendations for international students: Required—TOEFL (minimum score 550 paper-based; 80 iBT). Electronic applications accepted. *Faculty research:* Japanese animation, educational leadership, war art, John Muir's wilderness.

Harvard University, Harvard Graduate School of Education, Cambridge, MA 02138. Offers Ed M, Ed D, Ed L D. Part-time programs available. *Faculty:* 68 full-time (34 women), 77 part-time/adjunct (41 women). *Students:* 857 full-time (602 women), 77 part-time (54 women); includes 292 minority (80 Black or African American, non-Hispanic/Latino; 1 American Indian or Alaska Native, non-Hispanic/Latino; 93 Asian, non-Hispanic/Latino; 78 Hispanic/Latino; 3 Native Hawaiian or other Pacific Islander, non-Hispanic/Latino; 37 Two or more races, non-Hispanic/Latino), 126 international. Average age 30. 2,652 applicants, 34% accepted, 639 enrolled. In 2013, 673 master's, 71 doctorates awarded. *Degree requirements:* For doctorate, thesis/dissertation (for some programs), capstone project in lieu of thesis (for Ed.L.D.). *Entrance requirements:* For master's, GRE General Test, statement of purpose, 3 letters of recommendation, resume, official transcripts; for doctorate, GRE General Test or GMAT (for Ed.L.D. only), statement of purpose, 3 letters of recommendation, resume, official transcripts, 2 short essay questions (for Ed.L.D. only). Additional exam requirements/recommendations for international students: Required—TOEFL (minimum score 613 paper-based; 104 iBT), TWE (minimum score 5). *Application deadline:* For fall admission, 12/2 for domestic and international students. Application fee: $85. Electronic applications accepted. *Expenses:* Contact institution. *Financial support:* In 2013–14, 628 students received support, including 121 fellowships with full and partial tuition reimbursements available (averaging $17,324 per year), 50 research assistantships (averaging $11,332 per year), 210 teaching assistantships (averaging $6,046 per year); career-related internships or fieldwork, Federal Work-Study, institutionally sponsored loans, scholarships/grants, health care benefits, tuition waivers (full and partial), and unspecified assistantships also available. Support available to part-time students. Financial award application deadline: 2/1; financial award applicants required to submit FAFSA. *Faculty research:* Learning and development, educational leadership and organizations, education policy analysis. *Total annual research expenditures:* $34.3 million. *Unit head:* James E. Ryan, Dean, 617-495-3401. *Application contact:* Information Contact, 617-495-3414, Fax: 617-496-3577, E-mail: gseadmissions@harvard.edu.
Website: http://www.gse.harvard.edu/.

Hastings College, Department of Teacher Education, Hastings, NE 68901-7696. Offers MAT. *Accreditation:* NCATE. Part-time programs available. *Degree requirements:* For master's, comprehensive exam, thesis, or oral teaching presentation; digital portfolio. *Entrance requirements:* For master's, minimum GPA of 2.5, 2 letters of reference, interview. Additional exam requirements/recommendations for international students: Required—TOEFL. Electronic applications accepted. *Faculty research:* Assessments, performance competencies.

Hebrew College, Shoolman Graduate School of Jewish Education, Newton Centre, MA 02459. Offers early childhood Jewish education (Certificate); Jewish day school education (Certificate); Jewish education (MJ Ed); Jewish family education (Certificate); Jewish special education (Certificate); Jewish youth education, informal education and camping (Certificate). Part-time and evening/weekend programs available. Postbaccalaureate distance learning degree programs offered. *Degree requirements:* For master's, one foreign language. *Entrance requirements:* For master's, GRE, interview. Additional exam requirements/recommendations for international students: Required—TOEFL.

Hebrew Union College–Jewish Institute of Religion, School of Education, New York, NY 10012-1186. Offers MARE. Part-time programs available. *Degree requirements:* For master's, one foreign language, thesis. *Entrance requirements:* For master's, GRE, minimum 2 years of college-level Hebrew.

Heidelberg University, Program in Education, Tiffin, OH 44883-2462. Offers MAE. Part-time and evening/weekend programs available. *Degree requirements:* For master's, thesis or alternative, internship, practicum. *Entrance requirements:* For master's, minimum cumulative GPA of 2.75, 3 recommendations, bachelor's degree. Additional exam requirements/recommendations for international students: Required—TOEFL (minimum score 550 paper-based).

Henderson State University, Graduate Studies, Teachers College, Arkadelphia, AR 71999-0001. Offers MAT, MS, MSE, Ed S, Graduate Certificate. *Accreditation:* NCATE. Part-time programs available. Postbaccalaureate distance learning degree programs offered (no on-campus study). *Faculty:* 21 full-time (10 women), 3 part-time/adjunct (all women). *Students:* 48 full-time (34 women), 256 part-time (187 women); includes 75 minority (59 Black or African American, non-Hispanic/Latino; 1 American Indian or Alaska Native, non-Hispanic/Latino; 8 Hispanic/Latino; 7 Two or more races, non-Hispanic/Latino), 1 international. Average age 34. 44 applicants, 100% accepted, 44 enrolled. In 2013, 93 master's, 9 other advanced degrees awarded. *Entrance requirements:* For master's, GRE General Test or MAT, minimum GPA of 2.7, teacher certification. Additional exam requirements/recommendations for international students: Required—TOEFL (minimum score 600 paper-based); Recommended—IELTS (minimum score 6.5). *Application deadline:* For fall admission, 8/1 priority date for domestic students, 6/30 priority date for international students; for spring admission, 1/1 priority date for domestic students, 11/30 priority date for international students. Applications are processed on a rolling basis. Application fee: $25 ($75 for international students). *Expenses:* Tuition, state resident: full-time $4284; part-time $238 per credit hour. Tuition, nonresident: full-time $8802; part-time $489 per credit hour. Tuition and fees vary according to course load and campus/location. *Financial support:* In 2013–14, 13 teaching assistantships with partial tuition reimbursements (averaging $4,000 per year) were awarded; scholarships/grants and unspecified assistantships also available. *Unit head:* Dr. Judy Harrison, Dean, 870-230-5358, Fax: 870-230-5455, E-mail: harrisj@hsu.edu. *Application contact:* Dr. Ken Taylor, Graduate Dean, 870-230-5126, Fax: 870-230-5479, E-mail: taylorke@hsu.edu.
Website: http://www.hsu.edu/teachers-college/.

Heritage University, Graduate Programs in Education, Toppenish, WA 98948-9599. Offers counseling (M Ed); educational administration (M Ed); professional studies (M Ed), including bilingual education/ESL, biology, English and literature, reading/literacy, special education; teaching (MIT). Part-time and evening/weekend programs available. *Degree requirements:* For master's, comprehensive exam, thesis (for some programs). *Entrance requirements:* For master's, interview, letters of recommendation, teaching certificate. Additional exam requirements/recommendations for international students: Recommended—TOEFL (minimum score 550 paper-based).

High Point University, Norcross Graduate School, High Point, NC 27262-3598. Offers business administration (MBA); educational leadership (M Ed); elementary education (M Ed); history (MA); nonprofit management (MA); secondary math (M Ed); special education (M Ed); strategic communication (MA); teaching elementary education k-6 (MAT); teaching secondary mathematics 9-12 (MAT). *Accreditation:* NCATE. Part-time and evening/weekend programs available. *Degree requirements:* For master's, comprehensive exam (for some programs), thesis (for some programs). *Entrance requirements:* For master's, GMAT (MBA), GRE, MAT, minimum GPA of 3.0. Additional exam requirements/recommendations for international students: Required—TOEFL (minimum score 550 paper-based). Electronic applications accepted.

Hodges University, Graduate Programs, Naples, FL 34119. Offers business administration (MBA); clinical mental health counseling (MS); criminal justice (MS); education (MPS); information systems management (MIS); legal studies (MS); management (MSM); public administration (MPA). Part-time and evening/weekend programs available. Postbaccalaureate distance learning degree programs offered (no on-campus study). *Faculty:* 17 full-time (5 women), 5 part-time/adjunct (3 women). *Students:* 20 full-time (13 women), 182 part-time (131 women); includes 75 minority (18 Black or African American, non-Hispanic/Latino; 1 American Indian or Alaska Native, non-Hispanic/Latino; 7 Asian, non-Hispanic/Latino; 48 Hispanic/Latino; 1 Two or more races, non-Hispanic/Latino). Average age 35. 58 applicants, 100% accepted, 58 enrolled. In 2013, 88 master's awarded. *Degree requirements:* For master's, comprehensive exam (for some programs), thesis (for some programs). *Entrance requirements:* For master's, in-house entrance exam. Additional exam requirements/recommendations for international students: Recommended—TOEFL. *Application*

deadline: Applications are processed on a rolling basis. Application fee: $50. Electronic applications accepted. *Financial support:* In 2013–14, 153 students received support. Federal Work-Study and scholarships/grants available. Financial award application deadline: 7/9; financial award applicants required to submit FAFSA. *Unit head:* Dr. Jeanette Brock, President, 239-513-1122, Fax: 239-598-6253, E-mail: jbrock@hodges.edu. *Application contact:* Christy Saunders, Director of Admissions, 239-513-1122, Fax: 239-598-6253, E-mail: csaunders@hodges.edu.

Hofstra University, School of Education, Hempstead, NY 11549. Offers MA, MS, MS Ed, Ed D, PhD, Advanced Certificate, PD. *Accreditation:* Teacher Education Accreditation Council.

Hollins University, Graduate Programs, Program in Teaching, Roanoke, VA 24020. Offers MAT. *Accreditation:* Teacher Education Accreditation Council. Part-time and evening/weekend programs available. *Degree requirements:* For master's, thesis. *Entrance requirements:* For master's, PRAXIS I, letters of recommendation, writing sample. Additional exam requirements/recommendations for international students: Required—TOEFL (minimum score 550 paper-based; 79 iBT). Electronic applications accepted. *Faculty research:* Television violence and its effect on the developing brain, phonological/phonemic awareness, technology in the classroom.

Holy Family University, Graduate School, School of Education, Philadelphia, PA 19114. Offers education (M Ed, Ed D), including early elementary education (PreK-Grade 4) (M Ed), education leadership (M Ed), educational leadership and professional studies (Ed D), general education (M Ed), middle level education (Grades 4-8) (M Ed), reading specialist (M Ed), secondary education (Grades 7-12) (M Ed), special education (M Ed), TESOL and literacy (M Ed). Part-time and evening/weekend programs available. *Faculty:* 16 full-time (11 women), 38 part-time/adjunct (19 women). *Students:* 15 full-time (11 women), 371 part-time (290 women); includes 44 minority (25 Black or African American, non-Hispanic/Latino; 5 Asian, non-Hispanic/Latino; 14 Hispanic/Latino). Average age 33. 125 applicants, 81% accepted, 80 enrolled. In 2013, 231 master's awarded. *Degree requirements:* For master's, comprehensive exam, thesis optional; for doctorate, comprehensive exam, thesis/dissertation. *Entrance requirements:* For master's, GRE or MAT (if GPA is below 3.0), interview, minimum GPA of 3.0, essay/personal statement, 2 letters of recommendation, official transcripts of all college or university work; for doctorate, GRE or MAT (taken within 5 years of application), minimum GPA of 3.5, 3 letters of recommendation, official transcripts of all college or university work, current resume, essay/personal statement, writing sample, interview. Additional exam requirements/recommendations for international students: Required—TOEFL (minimum score 550 paper-based; 79 iBT), IELTS (minimum score 6), or PTE (minimum score 54). *Application deadline:* For fall admission, 7/1 priority date for domestic and international students; for winter admission, 1/1 for domestic students; for spring admission, 11/1 priority date for domestic and international students; for summer admission, 4/1 priority date for domestic and international students. Applications are processed on a rolling basis. Application fee: $25. Electronic applications accepted. *Expenses: Tuition:* Full-time $12,060. *Required fees:* $250. Tuition and fees vary according to degree level. *Financial support:* In 2013–14, 15 students received support, including 3 research assistantships with partial tuition reimbursements available (averaging $11,127 per year). Support available to part-time students. Financial award application deadline: 2/15; financial award applicants required to submit FAFSA. *Unit head:* Dr. Kevin Zook, Dean, 267-341-3565, Fax: 215-824-2438, E-mail: kzook@holyfamily.edu. *Application contact:* Gidget Marie Montelibano, Associate Director of Graduate Admissions, 267-341-3358, Fax: 215-637-1478, E-mail: gmontelibano@holyfamily.edu.
Website: http://www.holyfamily.edu/choosing-holy-family-u/academics/school-of-education.

Holy Names University, Graduate Division, Department of Education, Oakland, CA 94619-1699. Offers educational therapy (Certificate); mild/moderate disabilities (Ed S); multiple subject teaching (Credential); single subject teaching (Credential); teaching English as a second language (TESL) (M Ed); urban education: educational therapy (M Ed); urban education: K-12 education (M Ed); urban education: special education (M Ed). Part-time programs available. *Faculty:* 4 full-time, 14 part-time/adjunct. *Students:* 25 full-time (19 women), 127 part-time (93 women); includes 74 minority (37 Black or African American, non-Hispanic/Latino; 7 Asian, non-Hispanic/Latino; 28 Hispanic/Latino; 1 Native Hawaiian or other Pacific Islander, non-Hispanic/Latino; 1 Two or more races, non-Hispanic/Latino), 2 international. Average age 35. 72 applicants, 75% accepted, 37 enrolled. In 2013, 15 master's, 22 Certificates awarded. *Degree requirements:* For master's, comprehensive exam, research paper, thesis or project. *Entrance requirements:* For master's, minimum undergraduate GPA of 2.6 overall, 3.0 in major, personal statement, two recommendations, interview. Additional exam requirements/recommendations for international students: Required—TOEFL (minimum score 550 paper-based; 79 iBT). *Application deadline:* For fall admission, 8/1 priority date for domestic students, 7/15 for international students; for spring admission, 12/1 priority date for domestic students, 12/1 for international students; for summer admission, 5/1 priority date for domestic students, 5/1 for international students. Applications are processed on a rolling basis. Application fee: $65. Electronic applications accepted. Application fee is waived when completed online. *Expenses: Tuition:* Part-time $866 per unit. *Financial support:* Career-related internships or fieldwork, Federal Work-Study, scholarships/grants, and unspecified assistantships available. Support available to part-time students. Financial award application deadline: 3/2; financial award applicants required to submit FAFSA. *Faculty research:* Cognitive development, language development, learning handicaps. *Unit head:* Dr. Kimberly Mayfiel, 510-436-1396, Fax: 510-436-1325, E-mail: mayfield@hnu.edu. *Application contact:* Graduate Admission, 800-430-1321, Fax: 510-436-1325, E-mail: graduateadmissions@hnu.edu.
Website: http://www.hnu.edu/academics/graduatePrograms/education.html.

Hood College, Graduate School, Department of Education, Frederick, MD 21701-8575. Offers curriculum and instruction (MS), including early childhood education, elementary education, elementary school science and mathematics, secondary education, special education; educational leadership (MS, Certificate); reading specialization (MS); STEM (Certificate). *Accreditation:* NCATE. Part-time and evening/weekend programs available. *Faculty:* 4 full-time (3 women), 33 part-time/adjunct (25 women). *Students:* 1 (woman) full-time, 340 part-time (282 women); includes 59 minority (31 Black or African American, non-Hispanic/Latino; 1 American Indian or Alaska Native, non-Hispanic/Latino; 10 Asian, non-Hispanic/Latino; 13 Hispanic/Latino; 4 Two or more races, non-Hispanic/Latino). Average age 33. 97 applicants, 99% accepted, 86 enrolled. In 2013, 64 master's, 40 other advanced degrees awarded. *Degree requirements:* For master's, action research project, portfolio (reading). *Entrance requirements:* For master's, minimum GPA of 2.75, teaching certification. Additional exam requirements/recommendations for international students: Required—TOEFL (minimum score 575 paper-based; 89 iBT), IELTS (minimum score 6.5). *Application deadline:* For fall admission, 7/15 priority date for domestic students, 7/15 for international students; for spring admission, 12/1 priority date for domestic students, 12/1 for international students. Applications are processed on a rolling basis. Application fee: $35. Electronic applications accepted. Application fee is waived when completed online. *Expenses: Tuition:* Part-time $405 per credit. *Required fees:* $100 per semester. *Financial support:* In 2013–14, 1 student received support. Tuition waivers (partial) and unspecified assistantships available. Financial award applicants required to submit FAFSA. *Faculty research:* Leadership, action research, brain research, learning styles. *Unit head:* Dr. Ellen Koitz, Chairperson, 301-696-3466, Fax: 301-696-3597, E-mail: koitz@hood.edu. *Application contact:* Dr. Maria Green Cowles, Dean of Graduate School, 301-696-3811, Fax: 301-696-3597, E-mail: gofurther@hood.edu.
Website: http://www.hood.edu/academics/education/index.html.

Hope International University, School of Graduate and Professional Studies, Program in Education, Fullerton, CA 92831-3138. Offers education administration (MA); elementary education (ME); secondary education (ME). Part-time and evening/weekend programs available. *Degree requirements:* For master's, comprehensive exam (for some programs), thesis. *Entrance requirements:* For master's, minimum GPA of 3.0, 2 references. Additional exam requirements/recommendations for international students: Required—TOEFL (minimum score 550 paper-based; 86 iBT); Recommended—IELTS (minimum score 6.5). Electronic applications accepted. *Expenses:* Contact institution. *Faculty research:* Distance education.

Houston Baptist University, College of Education and Behavioral Sciences, Programs in Education, Houston, TX 77074-3298. Offers bilingual education (M Ed); counselor education (M Ed); curriculum and instruction (M Ed); educational administration (M Ed); educational diagnostician (M Ed); reading education (M Ed). Part-time programs available. Postbaccalaureate distance learning degree programs offered (no on-campus study). *Entrance requirements:* For master's, GRE General Test or MAT. Additional exam requirements/recommendations for international students: Required—TOEFL (minimum score 550 paper-based).

Howard University, School of Education, Washington, DC 20059. Offers M Ed, Ed D, PhD, CAGS. *Accreditation:* NCATE. *Faculty:* 21 full-time (14 women), 18 part-time/adjunct (11 women). *Students:* 156 full-time (125 women), 124 part-time (86 women); includes 217 minority (213 Black or African American, non-Hispanic/Latino; 2 American Indian or Alaska Native, non-Hispanic/Latino; 2 Asian, non-Hispanic/Latino), 53 international. Average age 33. 132 applicants, 75% accepted, 66 enrolled. In 2013, 43 master's, 12 doctorates awarded. *Degree requirements:* For master's, comprehensive exam, expository writing exam, practicum, PRAXIS II; for doctorate, one foreign language, comprehensive exam, thesis/dissertation, expository writing exam, internship. *Entrance requirements:* For master's, PRAXIS I or GRE General Test (for curriculum and instruction students only), minimum GPA of 2.7; for doctorate, GRE General Test, minimum GPA of 3.4. Additional exam requirements/recommendations for international students: Required—TOEFL (minimum score 550 paper-based; 79 iBT). *Application deadline:* For fall admission, 2/15 priority date for domestic students; for spring admission, 11/1 for domestic students. Applications are processed on a rolling basis. Application fee: $45. Electronic applications accepted. *Financial support:* In 2013–14, 24 students received support, including 24 fellowships with full and partial tuition reimbursements available (averaging $15,000 per year); career-related internships or fieldwork, Federal Work-Study, institutionally sponsored loans, scholarships/grants, tuition waivers (full and partial), and unspecified assistantships also available. Financial award application deadline: 3/15; financial award applicants required to submit FAFSA. *Faculty research:* Policy affecting education for African-Americans; information technology use in underserved school populations; increasing literacy skills for public school students; violence intervention and prevention; successes, problems, and needs of disabled African-Americans. *Total annual research expenditures:* $2.2 million. *Unit head:* Dr. Leslie T. Fenwick, Dean, School of Education, 202-806-7340, Fax: 202-806-5302, E-mail: lfenwick@howard.edu. *Application contact:* Dr. J. Fidel Turner, Senior Associate Dean for Academic Programs and Student Affairs, 202-806-7340, Fax: 202-806-7018, E-mail: johnnie.f.turner@howard.edu.
Website: http://www.howard.edu/schooleducation/.

Humboldt State University, Academic Programs, College of Professional Studies, School of Education, Arcata, CA 95521-8299. Offers MA. Part-time and evening/weekend programs available. *Degree requirements:* For master's, thesis or alternative. *Entrance requirements:* For master's, minimum GPA of 3.0, 3 letters of recommendation. Additional exam requirements/recommendations for international students: Required—TOEFL (minimum score 500 paper-based).

Hunter College of the City University of New York, Graduate School, School of Education, New York, NY 10065-5085. Offers MA, MS, MS Ed, AC. *Accreditation:* NCATE. *Faculty:* 59 full-time (27 women), 249 part-time/adjunct (150 women). *Students:* 229 full-time (187 women), 1,544 part-time (1,217 women); includes 617 minority (169 Black or African American, non-Hispanic/Latino; 3 American Indian or Alaska Native, non-Hispanic/Latino; 155 Asian, non-Hispanic/Latino; 290 Hispanic/Latino), 34 international. Average age 30. 1,085 applicants, 52% accepted, 332 enrolled. In 2013, 816 master's, 32 other advanced degrees awarded. *Degree requirements:* For master's, thesis; for AC, portfolio review. *Entrance requirements:* For degree, minimum B average in graduate course work, teaching certificate, minimum 3 years of full-time teaching experience, interview, 2 letters of support. Additional exam requirements/recommendations for international students: Required—TOEFL. *Application deadline:* For fall admission, 4/1 for domestic students, 2/1 for international students; for spring admission, 11/1 for domestic students, 9/1 for international students. Applications are processed on a rolling basis. Application fee: $125. *Financial support:* Fellowships, career-related internships or fieldwork, Federal Work-Study, institutionally sponsored loans, and tuition waivers (full and partial) available. Support available to part-time students. *Faculty research:* Multicultural and multiracial urban education; mentoring new teachers; mathematics and science education; bilingual, bicultural, and special education. *Unit head:* Dr. David Steiner, Dean, 212-772-4622, E-mail: david.steiner@hunter.cuny.edu. *Application contact:* Milena Solo, Director for Graduate Admissions, 212-772-4482, E-mail: milena.solo@hunter.cuny.edu.
Website: http://www.hunter.cuny.edu/school-of-education/programs/graduate.

Huntington University, Graduate School, Huntington, IN 46750-1299. Offers counseling (MA), including licensed mental health counselor; education (M Ed); youth ministry leadership (MA). Part-time programs available. Postbaccalaureate distance learning degree programs offered (minimal on-campus study). *Degree requirements:* For master's, thesis. *Entrance requirements:* For master's, GRE (for counseling and education students only). Additional exam requirements/recommendations for international students: Required—TOEFL. Electronic applications accepted. *Faculty research:* Leadership, educational technology trends, evangelism, youth ministry, mental health.

Idaho State University, Office of Graduate Studies, College of Education, Pocatello, ID 83209-8059. Offers M Ed, MPE, Ed D, PhD, 5th Year Certificate, 6th Year Certificate, Ed S. *Accreditation:* NCATE. Part-time programs available. *Degree requirements:* For master's, comprehensive exam, thesis optional, oral exam, written exam; for doctorate, comprehensive exam, thesis/dissertation, written exam; for other advanced degree, comprehensive exam, oral exam, written exam, practicum or field project. *Entrance requirements:* For master's, GRE General Test or MAT, minimum undergraduate GPA of 3.0, interview, bachelor's degree or equivalent; for doctorate, GRE General Test or MAT, minimum undergraduate GPA of 3.0, 3.5 graduate; departmental interview; current curriculum vitae, computer skill competency checklist; for other advanced degree, GRE General Test, minimum graduate GPA of 3.0, master's degree, letter from

supervisor attesting to school administration potential. Additional exam requirements/recommendations for international students: Required—TOEFL (minimum score 550 paper-based; 80 iBT). Electronic applications accepted. *Faculty research:* School reform, inclusion, students at risk, teacher education standards, teaching cases, education leadership.

Illinois College, Program in Education, Jacksonville, IL 62650-2299. Offers MA Ed. *Degree requirements:* For master's, action research capstone experience. *Application deadline:* For fall admission, 5/31 priority date for domestic students. Website: http://www.ic.edu/masters.

Illinois State University, Graduate School, College of Education, Normal, IL 61790-2200. Offers MS, MS Ed, Ed D, PhD. *Accreditation:* NCATE. Part-time programs available. *Degree requirements:* For doctorate, thesis/dissertation, 2 terms of residency. *Entrance requirements:* For master's and doctorate, GRE General Test.

Indiana State University, College of Graduate and Professional Studies, College of Education, Terre Haute, IN 47809. Offers M Ed, MS, PhD, Ed S, MA/MS. *Accreditation:* NCATE. Part-time and evening/weekend programs available. *Degree requirements:* For doctorate, thesis/dissertation. *Entrance requirements:* For master's, minimum undergraduate GPA of 2.5; for doctorate, GRE General Test; for Ed S, GRE General Test, minimum graduate GPA of 3.25. Electronic applications accepted.

Indiana University Bloomington, School of Education, Bloomington, IN 47405-7000. Offers MS, Ed D, PhD, Ed S. *Accreditation:* NCATE. Part-time programs available. Postbaccalaureate distance learning degree programs offered. Terminal master's awarded for partial completion of doctoral program. *Degree requirements:* For master's, thesis optional; for doctorate, comprehensive exam, thesis/dissertation; for Ed S, comprehensive exam (for some programs), thesis (for some programs), comprehensive exam or project. *Entrance requirements:* For master's and Ed S, GRE General Test, minimum GPA of 3.0 (recommended), 3 letters of recommendation; for doctorate, GRE General Test, minimum GPA of 3.0, 3 letters of recommendation. Additional exam requirements/recommendations for international students: Required—TOEFL (minimum score 550 paper-based; 79 iBT). Electronic applications accepted.

Indiana University East, School of Education, Richmond, IN 47374-1289. Offers MS Ed. *Accreditation:* NCATE. *Entrance requirements:* For master's, 3 letters of recommendation, interview.

Indiana University Kokomo, Division of Education, Kokomo, IN 46904-9003. Offers elementary education (MS Ed). *Accreditation:* NCATE. Part-time and evening/weekend programs available. *Faculty:* 1 full-time (0 women). *Students:* 3 full-time (1 woman), 14 part-time (7 women); includes 1 minority (Asian, non-Hispanic/Latino). Average age 36. 1 applicant. *Degree requirements:* For master's, thesis optional, research project. *Entrance requirements:* For master's, GRE General Test, minimum GPA of 2.5. *Application deadline:* For fall admission, 8/1 for domestic students; for spring admission, 12/1 for domestic students. Applications are processed on a rolling basis. *Financial support:* Fellowships and minority teacher scholarships available. *Faculty research:* Reading, teaching effectiveness, portfolio, curriculum development. *Unit head:* Dr. Shirley Aamidor, Dean, 765-455-9441, E-mail: mseduc@iuk.edu. *Application contact:* Admissions Office, 765-455-9357.

Indiana University Northwest, School of Education, Gary, IN 46408-1197. Offers educational leadership (MS Ed); elementary education (MS Ed); secondary education (MS Ed). *Accreditation:* NCATE. Part-time and evening/weekend programs available. *Faculty:* 5 full-time (2 women). *Students:* 19 full-time (17 women), 119 part-time (98 women); includes 79 minority (63 Black or African American, non-Hispanic/Latino; 3 Asian, non-Hispanic/Latino; 12 Hispanic/Latino; 1 Two or more races, non-Hispanic/Latino), 1 international. Average age 37. 25 applicants, 92% accepted, 16 enrolled. In 2013, 69 master's awarded. *Entrance requirements:* For master's, GRE General Test or MAT, minimum GPA of 3.0. *Application deadline:* For fall admission, 7/15 priority date for domestic students; for spring admission, 11/15 for domestic students. *Unit head:* Dr. Stanley E. Wigle, Dean, 219-980-6989, E-mail: swigle@iun.edu. *Application contact:* Admissions Counselor, 219-980-6760, Fax: 219-980-7103. Website: http://www.iun.edu/education/degrees/masters.htm.

Indiana University of Pennsylvania, School of Graduate Studies and Research, College of Education and Educational Technology, Indiana, PA 15705. Offers M Ed, MA, MS, D Ed, PhD, Certificate. *Accreditation:* NCATE. Part-time and evening/weekend programs available. *Faculty:* 64 full-time (37 women), 8 part-time/adjunct (7 women). *Students:* 274 full-time (209 women), 476 part-time (333 women); includes 70 minority (46 Black or African American, non-Hispanic/Latino; 5 Asian, non-Hispanic/Latino; 9 Hispanic/Latino; 1 Native Hawaiian or other Pacific Islander, non-Hispanic/Latino; 9 Two or more races, non-Hispanic/Latino), 22 international. Average age 33. 895 applicants, 45% accepted, 266 enrolled. In 2013, 210 master's, 43 doctorates, 7 other advanced degrees awarded. Terminal master's awarded for partial completion of doctoral program. *Degree requirements:* For master's, thesis optional; for doctorate, comprehensive exam, thesis/dissertation. *Entrance requirements:* For master's and doctorate, 2 letters of recommendation. Additional exam requirements/recommendations for international students: Required—TOEFL (minimum score 540 paper-based; 76 iBT). *Application deadline:* Applications are processed on a rolling basis. Application fee: $50. Electronic applications accepted. *Expenses:* Tuition, state resident: full-time $3978; part-time $442 per credit. Tuition, nonresident: full-time $5967; part-time $663 per credit. *Required fees:* $2080; $115.55 per credit. $93 per semester. Tuition and fees vary according to degree level and program. *Financial support:* In 2013–14, 22 fellowships (averaging $1,314 per year), 156 research assistantships with full and partial tuition reimbursements (averaging $3,720 per year), 8 teaching assistantships with full and partial tuition reimbursements (averaging $21,420 per year) were awarded; career-related internships or fieldwork, Federal Work-Study, scholarships/grants, and unspecified assistantships also available. Support available to part-time students. Financial award application deadline: 4/15; financial award applicants required to submit FAFSA. *Unit head:* Dr. Lara Luetkehans, Dean, 724-357-2480, Fax: 724-357-5595. *Application contact:* Paula Stossel, Assistant Dean for Administration, 724-357-4511, Fax: 724-357-4862, E-mail: graduate-admissions@iup.edu. Website: http://www.iup.edu/education.

Indiana University–Purdue University Fort Wayne, College of Education and Public Policy, Fort Wayne, IN 46805-1499. Offers MPA, MPM, MS Ed, Certificate. *Accreditation:* NCATE. Part-time programs available. *Faculty:* 27 full-time (14 women), 1 part-time/adjunct (0 women). *Students:* 15 full-time (9 women), 127 part-time (93 women); includes 20 minority (8 Black or African American, non-Hispanic/Latino; 6 Asian, non-Hispanic/Latino; 5 Hispanic/Latino; 1 Two or more races, non-Hispanic/Latino), 1 international. Average age 32. 25 applicants, 96% accepted, 19 enrolled. In 2013, 90 master's, 2 Certificates awarded. *Entrance requirements:* For master's, minimum GPA of 2.5, 3 professional letters of recommendation. Additional exam requirements/recommendations for international students: Required—TOEFL (minimum score 550 paper-based; 79 iBT). *Application deadline:* For fall admission, 4/1 priority date for domestic and international students. Applications are processed on a rolling basis. Application fee: $55. *Financial support:* In 2013–14, 1 research assistantship with partial tuition reimbursement (averaging $13,322 per year), 3 teaching assistantships

with partial tuition reimbursements (averaging $13,322 per year) were awarded; scholarships/grants also available. Support available to part-time students. Financial award application deadline: 3/1; financial award applicants required to submit FAFSA. *Faculty research:* International exchange, Asian Indian ethnicity. *Total annual research expenditures:* $5,059. *Unit head:* Dr. James Burg, Interim Dean, 260-481-5406, Fax: 260-481-5408, E-mail: burgj@ipfw.edu. *Application contact:* Vicky L. Schmidt, Graduate Recorder, 260-481-6450, Fax: 260-481-5408, E-mail: schmidt@ipfw.edu. Website: http://www.ipfw.edu/cepp.

Indiana University–Purdue University Indianapolis, School of Education, Indianapolis, IN 46202-2896. Offers computer education (Certificate); curriculum and instruction (MS); early childhood (MS); educational leadership (MS, Certificate); English as a second language (Certificate); higher education and student affairs (MS); kindergarten (Certificate); language education (MS); reading (Certificate); school counseling (MS); special education (MS, Certificate). Part-time and evening/weekend programs available. *Faculty:* 41 full-time, 80 part-time/adjunct. *Students:* 113 full-time (78 women), 263 part-time (200 women); includes 88 minority (51 Black or African American, non-Hispanic/Latino; 1 American Indian or Alaska Native, non-Hispanic/Latino; 10 Asian, non-Hispanic/Latino; 19 Hispanic/Latino; 7 Two or more races, non-Hispanic/Latino), 5 international. Average age 33. 93 applicants, 54% accepted, 40 enrolled. In 2013, 179 master's awarded. *Degree requirements:* For master's, thesis optional. *Entrance requirements:* For master's, GRE General Test, minimum GPA of 3.0. Additional exam requirements/recommendations for international students: Required—TOEFL. *Application deadline:* For fall admission, 5/1 priority date for domestic students; for spring admission, 11/1 for domestic students. Application fee: $55 ($65 for international students). *Financial support:* Fellowships, research assistantships with partial tuition reimbursements, teaching assistantships, Federal Work-Study, institutionally sponsored loans, scholarships/grants, and tuition waivers (partial) available. Support available to part-time students. *Faculty research:* Teachers in the process of change, learning cycles, children's concepts of science. *Total annual research expenditures:* $614,458. *Unit head:* Dr. Pat Rogan, Executive Associate Dean, 317-274-6862, E-mail: progan@iupui.edu. *Application contact:* Donnella Dillon, Graduate Admissions Coordinator, 317-274-0645, E-mail: dmdillon@iupui.edu. Website: http://education.iupui.edu/.

Indiana University South Bend, School of Education, South Bend, IN 46634-7111. Offers counseling and human services (MS Ed); elementary and secondary education leadership (MS Ed); elementary education (MS Ed); secondary education (MS Ed); special education (MAT, MS Ed). *Accreditation:* NCATE. Part-time and evening/weekend programs available. *Faculty:* 21 full-time (11 women), 9 part-time/adjunct (3 women). *Students:* 12 full-time (8 women), 103 part-time (85 women); includes 18 minority (8 Black or African American, non-Hispanic/Latino; 1 Asian, non-Hispanic/Latino; 5 Hispanic/Latino; 4 Two or more races, non-Hispanic/Latino), 3 international. Average age 36. 24 applicants, 63% accepted, 9 enrolled. In 2013, 41 master's awarded. *Degree requirements:* For master's, thesis or alternative, exit project. *Entrance requirements:* For master's, letters of recommendation, GRE or minimum GPA of 3.0. Additional exam requirements/recommendations for international students: Required—TOEFL. *Application deadline:* For fall admission, 7/1 for domestic students; for spring admission, 11/1 for domestic students. Applications are processed on a rolling basis. Electronic applications accepted. *Financial support:* Career-related internships or fieldwork available. Support available to part-time students. Financial award application deadline: 3/1; financial award applicants required to submit FAFSA. *Faculty research:* Professional dispositions, early childhood literacy, online learning, program assessments, problem-based learning. *Unit head:* Dr. Marvin Lynn, Dean, 574-520-4339. *Application contact:* Yvonne Walker, Student Services Representative, 574-520-4185, E-mail: ydwalker@iusb.edu. Website: http://www.iusb.edu/~edud/.

Indiana University Southeast, School of Education, New Albany, IN 47150-6405. Offers counselor education (MS Ed); elementary education (MS Ed); secondary education (MS Ed). *Accreditation:* NCATE. Part-time and evening/weekend programs available. *Students:* 23 full-time (21 women), 324 part-time (248 women); includes 44 minority (34 Black or African American, non-Hispanic/Latino; 1 American Indian or Alaska Native, non-Hispanic/Latino; 1 Asian, non-Hispanic/Latino; 5 Hispanic/Latino; 3 Two or more races, non-Hispanic/Latino). Average age 33. 36 applicants, 81% accepted, 25 enrolled. In 2013, 147 master's awarded. *Entrance requirements:* For master's, minimum undergraduate GPA of 2.5, graduate 3.0. *Application deadline:* Applications are processed on a rolling basis. *Financial support:* Career-related internships or fieldwork, Federal Work-Study, and institutionally sponsored loans available. Support available to part-time students. Financial award applicants required to submit FAFSA. *Faculty research:* Learning styles, technology, constructivism, group process, innovative math strategies. *Unit head:* Dr. Gloria Murray, Dean, 812-941-2169, Fax: 812-941-2667, E-mail: soeinfo@ius.edu. *Application contact:* Admissions Counselor, 812-941-2212, Fax: 812-941-2595, E-mail: admissions@ius.edu. Website: http://www.ius.edu/education/.

Institute for Christian Studies, Graduate Programs, Toronto, ON M5T 1R4, Canada. Offers education (M Phil F, PhD); history of philosophy (M Phil F, PhD); philosophical aesthetics (M Phil F, PhD); philosophy of religion (M Phil F, PhD); political theory (M Phil F, PhD); systematic philosophy (M Phil F, PhD); theology (M Phil F, PhD); worldview studies (MWS). Part-time programs available. Postbaccalaureate distance learning degree programs offered (minimal on-campus study). *Degree requirements:* For master's, one foreign language, thesis; for doctorate, 2 foreign languages, thesis/dissertation. *Entrance requirements:* For master's and doctorate, philosophy background. Additional exam requirements/recommendations for international students: Required—TOEFL (minimum score 600 paper-based). *Faculty research:* Human rights, anthropology of self, medieval discourse, gender and body, post-modern thought; biblical hermeneutics, creational aesthetics, ecumenism, epistemology, political theory and public policy, relational psychotherapy.

Instituto Tecnologico de Santo Domingo, Graduate School, Area of Humanities and Social Sciences, Santo Domingo, Dominican Republic. Offers accounting (Certificate); adult education (Certificate); applied linguistics (MA); economics (MA); education (M Ed); educational psychology (MA, Certificate); gender and development (MA, Certificate); humanistic studies (MA); international marketing management (Certificate); international relations in the Caribbean basin (Certificate); intervention systems in family therapy (MA); linguistic and literary communication (Certificate); pedagogical support (MA); social science education (M Ed); sustainable human development (MA); terminal illness and death psychology (Certificate); youth and adult education (M Ed).

Instituto Tecnológico y de Estudios Superiores de Monterrey, Campus Central de Veracruz, Graduate Programs, Córdoba, Mexico. Offers administration (MA); administration of information technologies (MTI); computer sciences (MCC); education (MEE); educational institution administration (MAD); educational technology (MTE); electronic commerce (MCE); finance (MAF); humanistic studies (MEH); international business for Latin America (MNL); marketing (MMT); science (MCP). Part-time and evening/weekend programs available. Postbaccalaureate distance learning degree programs offered (minimal on-campus study). *Degree requirements:* For master's,

thesis (for some programs). *Entrance requirements:* For master's, PAEP College Board. Electronic applications accepted.

Instituto Tecnológico y de Estudios Superiores de Monterrey, Campus Ciudad de México, Virtual University Division, Ciudad de Mexico, Mexico. Offers administration of information technologies (MA); computer sciences (MA); education (MA, PhD); educational technology (MA); environmental engineering (MA); environmental systems (MA); humanistic studies (MA); industrial engineering (MA); international business for Latin America (MA); quality systems (MA); quality systems and productivity (MA). Part-time and evening/weekend programs available. Postbaccalaureate distance learning degree programs offered (minimal on-campus study). *Entrance requirements:* For master's and doctorate, Instituto entrance exam. Additional exam requirements/recommendations for international students: Required—TOEFL.

Instituto Tecnológico y de Estudios Superiores de Monterrey, Campus Ciudad Juárez, Program in Education, Ciudad Juárez, Mexico. Offers M Ed.

Instituto Tecnológico y de Estudios Superiores de Monterrey, Campus Ciudad Obregón, Programs in Education, Ciudad Obregón, Mexico. Offers cognitive development (ME); communications (ME); mathematics (ME).

Instituto Tecnológico y de Estudios Superiores de Monterrey, Campus Estado de México, Professional and Graduate Division, Estado de Mexico, Mexico. Offers administration of information technologies (MITA); architecture (M Arch); business administration (GMBA, MBA); computer sciences (MCS, PhD); education (M Ed); educational institution administration (MAD); educational technology and innovation (PhD); electronic commerce (MEC); environmental systems (MS); finance (MAF); humanistic studies (MHS); information sciences and knowledge management (MISKM); information systems (MS); manufacturing systems (MS); marketing (MEM); quality systems and productivity (MS); science and materials engineering (PhD); telecommunications management (MTM). Part-time programs available. Postbaccalaureate distance learning degree programs offered (minimal on-campus study). *Degree requirements:* For master's, one foreign language, thesis (for some programs); for doctorate, one foreign language, thesis/dissertation. *Entrance requirements:* For master's, E-PAEP 500, interview; for doctorate, E-PAEP 500, research proposal. Additional exam requirements/recommendations for international students: Required—TOEFL (minimum score 550 paper-based). *Faculty research:* Surface treatments by plasmas, mechanical properties, robotics, graphical computing, mechatronics security protocols.

Instituto Tecnológico y de Estudios Superiores de Monterrey, Campus Irapuato, Graduate Programs, Irapuato, Mexico. Offers administration (MBA); administration of information technology (MAIT); administration of telecommunications (MAT); architecture (M Arch); computer science (MCS); education (M Ed); educational administration (MEA); educational innovation and technology (DEIT); educational technology (MET); electronic commerce (MBA); environmental administration and planning (MEAP); environmental systems (MES); finances (MBA); humanistic studies (MHS); international management for Latin American executives (MIMLAE); library and information science (MLIS); manufacturing quality management (MMQM); marketing research (MBA).

Instituto Tecnológico y de Estudios Superiores de Monterrey, Campus Sonora Norte, Program in Education, Hermosillo, Mexico. Offers MA. *Entrance requirements:* For master's, MAT.

Inter American University of Puerto Rico, Arecibo Campus, Programs in Education, Arecibo, PR 00614-4050. Offers administration and educational supervision (MA Ed); counseling and guidance (MA Ed); curriculum and teaching (MA Ed), including biology education, English as a second language, history education, math education, Spanish; elementary education (MA Ed). *Degree requirements:* For master's, comprehensive exam, thesis optional. *Entrance requirements:* For master's, GRE, EXADEP, bachelor's degree in education or teaching license (administration and supervision) or courses in education and psychology (counseling and guidance), minimum GPA of 2.5 in last 60 credits.

Inter American University of Puerto Rico, Barranquitas Campus, Program in Education, Barranquitas, PR 00794. Offers curriculum and teaching (M Ed), including biology education, English as a second language, history education, mathematics education, Spanish; educational leadership and management (MA); elementary education (M Ed); information and library service technology (M Ed); special education (MA). *Degree requirements:* For master's, comprehensive exam, thesis optional. *Entrance requirements:* For master's, EXADEP, letter of recommendation. Electronic applications accepted.

Inter American University of Puerto Rico, Metropolitan Campus, Graduate Programs, Program in Education, San Juan, PR 00919-1293. Offers curriculum and instruction (Ed D); educational administration (Ed D); guidance and counseling (MA, Ed D); special education administration (Ed D). *Degree requirements:* For doctorate, comprehensive exam, thesis/dissertation. *Entrance requirements:* For doctorate, GRE, MAT, or EXADEP. Electronic applications accepted.

International Baptist College, Program in Education, Chandler, AZ 85286. Offers M Ed. *Degree requirements:* For master's, research paper/thesis. *Entrance requirements:* For master's, letter of recommendation.

Iona College, School of Arts and Science, Department of Education, New Rochelle, NY 10801-1890. Offers adolescence education: biology (MS Ed, MST); adolescence education: English (MS Ed, MST); adolescence education: Italian (MS Ed, MST); adolescence education: mathematics (MS Ed, MST); adolescence education: social studies (MS Ed, MST); adolescence education: Spanish (MS Ed, MST); adolescence special education 5-12 (MST); adolescence special education and literacy (MS Ed); childhood and special education (MST); childhood education (MST); early childhood and childhood (MST); educational leadership (MS Ed); literacy education: birth-grade 6 (MS Ed). *Accreditation:* NCATE. Part-time and evening/weekend programs available. *Faculty:* 11 full-time (9 women), 7 part-time/adjunct (6 women). *Students:* 34 full-time (25 women), 61 part-time (47 women); includes 5 minority (2 Asian, non-Hispanic/Latino; 3 Hispanic/Latino), 1 international. Average age 25. 27 applicants, 93% accepted, 16 enrolled. In 2013, 54 master's awarded. *Degree requirements:* For master's, thesis or alternative. *Entrance requirements:* For master's, minimum GPA of 3.0, NY State teaching certificate (for all MS Ed programs). Additional exam requirements/recommendations for international students: Required—TOEFL (minimum score 550 paper-based; 80 iBT), IELTS (minimum score 6.5). *Application deadline:* For fall admission, 8/1 priority date for domestic students, 5/1 priority date for international students; for spring admission, 1/1 priority date for domestic students, 9/1 priority date for international students. Applications are processed on a rolling basis. Application fee: $50. Electronic applications accepted. *Expenses: Tuition:* Part-time $948 per credit. *Required fees:* $235 per term. *Financial support:* In 2013–14, 84 students received support. Unspecified assistantships available. Support available to part-time students. Financial award application deadline: 4/15; financial award applicants required to submit FAFSA. *Faculty research:* Reading/writing, educational technology, administration, early literacy assessment, literacy development. *Unit head:* Margaret Smith, PhD, Chair, 914-633-2210, Fax: 914-633-2608, E-mail: msmith@iona.edu. *Application contact:* Veronica Jarek-Prinz, Director, Graduate Admissions, 914-633-2420, Fax: 914-633-2277, E-mail: vjarekprinz@iona.edu.
Website: http://www.iona.edu/Academics/School-of-Arts-Science/Departments/Education/Graduate-Programs.aspx.

Jackson State University, Graduate School, College of Education and Human Development, Jackson, MS 39217. Offers MS, MS Ed, Ed D, PhD, Ed S. *Accreditation:* NCATE. Part-time and evening/weekend programs available. Terminal master's awarded for partial completion of doctoral program. *Degree requirements:* For master's, comprehensive exam; for doctorate, comprehensive exam, thesis/dissertation. *Entrance requirements:* For master's, GRE General Test; for doctorate, MAT, teaching experience. Additional exam requirements/recommendations for international students: Required—TOEFL (minimum score 520 paper-based; 67 iBT).

Jacksonville State University, College of Graduate Studies and Continuing Education, College of Education and Professional Studies, Jacksonville, AL 36265-1602. Offers MS, MS Ed, Ed S. *Accreditation:* NCATE. Part-time and evening/weekend programs available. *Degree requirements:* For master's, comprehensive exam, thesis (for some programs). *Entrance requirements:* For master's, GRE General Test or MAT. Additional exam requirements/recommendations for international students: Required—TOEFL (minimum score 500 paper-based; 61 iBT). Electronic applications accepted.

Jacksonville University, School of Education, Jacksonville, FL 32211. Offers educational leadership (M Ed); instructional leadership and organizational development (M Ed); sport management and leadership (M Ed). Part-time and evening/weekend programs available. *Degree requirements:* For master's, comprehensive exam. *Entrance requirements:* For master's, GRE General Test, minimum GPA of 3.0. Additional exam requirements/recommendations for international students: Required—TOEFL (minimum score 550 paper-based), TWE. *Expenses:* Contact institution.

John Brown University, Graduate Education Programs, Siloam Springs, AR 72761-2121. Offers curriculum and instruction (M Ed). Part-time and evening/weekend programs available. *Faculty:* 2 full-time (both women), 5 part-time/adjunct (all women). *Students:* 16 part-time (12 women). Average age 34. 12 applicants, 100% accepted, 11 enrolled. *Entrance requirements:* For master's, GRE (minimum score of 300). Additional exam requirements/recommendations for international students: Required—TOEFL (minimum score 550 paper-based; 70 iBT). *Expenses: Tuition:* Part-time $515 per credit hour. *Financial support:* Scholarships/grants and unspecified assistantships available. *Unit head:* Dr. Gloria Gale, Associate Dean of the School of Education, E-mail: ggale@jbu.edu. *Application contact:* Christopher Greathouse, Graduate Education Representative, 866-232-4723, E-mail: grad@jbu.edu.
Website: http://www.jbu.edu/grad/education/.

John Carroll University, Graduate School, Department of Education and Allied Studies, University Heights, OH 44118-4581. Offers administration (M Ed, MA); educational and school psychology (M Ed, MA); professional teacher education (M Ed, MA); school based adolescent-young adult education (M Ed); school based early childhood education (M Ed); school based middle childhood education (M Ed); school based multi-age education (M Ed); school counseling (M Ed, MA). *Accreditation:* NCATE. Part-time and evening/weekend programs available. *Degree requirements:* For master's, comprehensive exam, research essay or thesis (MA only). *Entrance requirements:* For master's, GRE General Test or MAT, minimum GPA of 2.75. *Faculty research:* Children's literacy, diversity issues, teaching development, impact of technology.

John F. Kennedy University, School of Education and Liberal Arts, Department of Education, Pleasant Hill, CA 94523-4817. Offers MAT. Part-time and evening/weekend programs available. *Degree requirements:* For master's, thesis. *Entrance requirements:* For master's, California Basic Educational Skills Test, NTE, interview. Additional exam requirements/recommendations for international students: Required—TOEFL.

John Hancock University, Program in Education, Oakbrook Terrace, IL 60181. Offers early childhood education (MA Ed); education (MA Ed); teacher as a leader (MA Ed). *Degree requirements:* For master's, thesis or capstone.

Johns Hopkins University, School of Education, Baltimore, MD 21218. Offers M Ed, MAT, MS, Ed D, PhD, CAGS, Certificate. *Accreditation:* NCATE. Part-time and evening/weekend programs available. Postbaccalaureate distance learning degree programs offered (no on-campus study). *Faculty:* 65 full-time (42 women), 173 part-time/adjunct (112 women). *Students:* 209 full-time (143 women), 1,297 part-time (979 women); includes 479 minority (213 Black or African American, non-Hispanic/Latino; 4 American Indian or Alaska Native, non-Hispanic/Latino; 112 Asian, non-Hispanic/Latino; 92 Hispanic/Latino; 4 Native Hawaiian or other Pacific Islander, non-Hispanic/Latino; 54 Two or more races, non-Hispanic/Latino), 37 international. Average age 30. 967 applicants, 77% accepted, 457 enrolled. In 2013, 565 master's, 4 doctorates, 242 other advanced degrees awarded. *Degree requirements:* For master's, comprehensive exam (for some programs), portfolio, capstone project and/or internship; PRAXIS II (for teacher preparation programs that lead to licensure); for doctorate, comprehensive exam (for some programs), thesis/dissertation. *Entrance requirements:* For master's, GRE (for full-time programs only); PRAXIS I or equivalent (for teacher preparation programs that lead to licensure), bachelor's degree from regionally- or nationally-accredited institution, minimum GPA of 3.0 in all previous programs of study, official transcripts from all post-secondary institutions attended, essay, curriculum vitae/resume, minimum of two letters of recommendation; for doctorate, GRE (for PhD only), master's degree from regionally- or nationally-accredited institution, minimum GPA of 3.0 (for EdD only), official transcripts from all post-secondary institutions attended, three letters of recommendation, curriculum vitae/resume, personal statement; for other advanced degree, bachelor's degree from regionally- or nationally-accredited institution (master's for some programs), minimum GPA of 3.0 in all previous programs of study, official transcripts from all post-secondary institutions attended, essay, curriculum vitae/resume, minimum of two letters of recommendation. Additional exam requirements/recommendations for international students: Required—TOEFL (minimum score 600 paper-based; 100 iBT) or IELTS (minimum score 7). *Application deadline:* For fall admission, 4/1 for domestic and international students; for spring admission, 10/1 for domestic and international students; for summer admission, 2/1 for domestic and international students. Application fee: $80. Electronic applications accepted. *Financial support:* In 2013–14, 106 students received support, including 13 fellowships, 4 research assistantships, 1 teaching assistantship; Federal Work-Study and scholarships/grants also available. Support available to part-time students. Financial award application deadline: 6/1; financial award applicants required to submit FAFSA. *Faculty research:* Comprehensive school reform, use of technology in instruction, student performance in at-risk schools, dropout prevention, evidence-based decision making in education, school and public safety, literacy, college and career access of low-resourced students, neuro-education, and entrepreneurial leadership. *Total annual research expenditures:* $10.9 million. *Unit head:* Dr. David A. Andrews, Dean, 410-516-7820, Fax: 410-516-6697, E-mail: davidandrews@jhu.edu. *Application contact:* Catherine Wilson, Associate Director of Admissions, 410-516-9797, Fax: 410-516-9799, E-mail: soe.info@jhu.edu.
Website: http://education.jhu.edu.

Johnson & Wales University, MAT Program in Teacher Education, Providence, RI 02903-3703. Offers business education and secondary special education (MAT); elementary education and elementary special education (MAT); elementary education and elementary/secondary special education (MAT); elementary education and secondary special education (MAT); food service education (MAT). Part-time and evening/weekend programs available. *Entrance requirements:* For master's, MAT, minimum GPA of 2.75. Additional exam requirements/recommendations for international students: Required—TOEFL (minimum score 550 paper-based) or IELTS (recommended). *Faculty research:* Secondary education, student teaching, educational reform, evaluation procedures.

Johnson State College, Graduate Program in Education, Johnson, VT 05656. Offers applied behavior analysis (MA Ed), including applied behavior analysis; curriculum and instruction (MA Ed); literacy (MA Ed); secondary education (MA Ed); special education (MA Ed). Part-time programs available. *Faculty:* 3 full-time (1 woman), 6 part-time/adjunct (5 women). *Students:* 6 full-time (5 women), 69 part-time (52 women). Average age 28. In 2013, 44 master's awarded. *Degree requirements:* For master's, comprehensive exam, thesis or alternative. *Entrance requirements:* For master's, interview. Additional exam requirements/recommendations for international students: Required—TOEFL. *Application deadline:* For fall admission, 4/1 priority date for domestic students, 1/15 priority date for international students; for spring admission, 11/1 for domestic students, 8/15 priority date for international students. Applications are processed on a rolling basis. Electronic applications accepted. *Expenses:* Tuition, state resident: full-time $11,448; part-time $477 per credit. Tuition, nonresident: full-time $24,720; part-time $1030 per credit. Tuition and fees vary according to reciprocity agreements. *Financial support:* Unspecified assistantships available. Financial award application deadline: 3/1; financial award applicants required to submit FAFSA. *Application contact:* Catherine H. Higley, Administrative Assistant, 800-635-2356 Ext. 1244, Fax: 802-635-1248, E-mail: catherine.higley@jsc.edu.

Johnson University, Graduate and Professional Programs, Knoxville, TN 37998-1001. Offers educational technology (MA); intercultural studies (MA); leadership studies (PhD); marriage and family therapy/professional counseling (MA); New Testament (MA); school counseling (MA); teacher education (MA). *Degree requirements:* For master's, variable foreign language requirement, comprehensive exam, thesis (for some programs), internship (500 client contact hours). *Entrance requirements:* For master's, interview, minimum GPA of 3.0, 20 credits of course work in psychology, 15 credits of course work in Bible. Additional exam requirements/recommendations for international students: Required—TOEFL.

Jones International University, School of Education, Centennial, CO 80112. Offers adult education (M Ed); corporate training and knowledge management (M Ed); curriculum and instruction (M Ed), including elementary teacher licensure, secondary teacher licensure; e-learning technology and design (M Ed); educational leadership and administration (M Ed); educational leadership and administration: principal and administrator licensure (M Ed); elementary curriculum instruction and assessment (M Ed); higher education leadership and administration (M Ed); K-12 instructional technology (M Ed); K-12 instructional technology: teacher licensure (M Ed); secondary curriculum instruction and assessment (M Ed); technology and design (M Ed). Part-time and evening/weekend programs available. Postbaccalaureate distance learning degree programs offered (no on-campus study). *Entrance requirements:* For master's, minimum cumulative GPA of 2.5. Additional exam requirements/recommendations for international students: Recommended—TOEFL (minimum score 550 paper-based). Electronic applications accepted.

Kansas State University, Graduate School, College of Education, Manhattan, KS 66506. Offers MS, Ed D, PhD. *Accreditation:* NCATE. Part-time and evening/weekend programs available. Postbaccalaureate distance learning degree programs offered. *Faculty:* 43 full-time (28 women), 14 part-time/adjunct (7 women). *Students:* 202 full-time (116 women), 655 part-time (457 women); includes 135 minority (59 Black or African American, non-Hispanic/Latino; 2 American Indian or Alaska Native, non-Hispanic/Latino; 13 Asian, non-Hispanic/Latino; 47 Hispanic/Latino; 1 Native Hawaiian or other Pacific Islander, non-Hispanic/Latino; 13 Two or more races, non-Hispanic/Latino), 25 international. Average age 36. 403 applicants, 67% accepted, 199 enrolled. In 2013, 251 master's, 27 doctorates awarded. Terminal master's awarded for partial completion of doctoral program. *Degree requirements:* For master's, thesis or alternative, oral or comprehensive exam; for doctorate, thesis/dissertation, residency. *Entrance requirements:* For master's and doctorate, GRE or MAT. Additional exam requirements/recommendations for international students: Required—GRE General Test or TOEFL. *Application deadline:* For fall admission, 2/1 priority date for domestic and international students; for spring admission, 8/1 priority date for domestic and international students. Applications are processed on a rolling basis. Application fee: $50 ($75 for international students). Electronic applications accepted. *Financial support:* In 2013–14, 11 research assistantships (averaging $17,781 per year), 17 teaching assistantships with full tuition reimbursements (averaging $13,213 per year) were awarded; career-related internships or fieldwork, Federal Work-Study, institutionally sponsored loans, and scholarships/grants also available. Support available to part-time students. Financial award application deadline: 3/1; financial award applicants required to submit FAFSA. *Faculty research:* Teacher preparation, program evaluation, science education, ESL-bilingual education, rural issues in education. Total annual research expenditures: $6.8 million. *Unit head:* Dr. Debbie Mercer, Dean, 785-532-5525, Fax: 785-532-7304, E-mail: dmercer@ksu.edu. *Application contact:* Dr. Paul R. Burden, Assistant Dean, 785-532-5595, Fax: 785-532-7304, E-mail: burden@ksu.edu.
Website: http://www.coe.k-state.edu/.

Kaplan University, Davenport Campus, School of Teacher Education, Davenport, IA 52807-2095. Offers education (M Ed); secondary education (M Ed); teaching and learning (MA); teaching literacy and language: grades 6-12 (MA); teaching literacy and language: grades K-6 (MA); teaching mathematics: grades 6-8 (MA); teaching mathematics: grades 9-12 (MA); teaching mathematics: grades K-5 (MA); teaching science: grades 6-12 (MA); teaching science: grades K-6 (MA); teaching students with special needs (MA); teaching with technology (MA). Part-time and evening/weekend programs available. Postbaccalaureate distance learning degree programs offered (no on-campus study). *Entrance requirements:* Additional exam requirements/recommendations for international students: Required—TOEFL (minimum score 550 paper-based; 80 iBT).

Kean University, College of Education, Union, NJ 07083. Offers MA, MS. *Accreditation:* NCATE. Part-time programs available. *Faculty:* 59 full-time (41 women). *Students:* 191 full-time (168 women), 458 part-time (380 women); includes 201 minority (55 Black or African American, non-Hispanic/Latino; 2 American Indian or Alaska Native, non-Hispanic/Latino; 23 Asian, non-Hispanic/Latino; 114 Hispanic/Latino; 1 Native Hawaiian or other Pacific Islander, non-Hispanic/Latino; 6 Two or more races, non-Hispanic/Latino), 3 international. Average age 31. 576 applicants, 61% accepted, 232 enrolled. In 2013, 201 master's awarded. *Degree requirements:* For master's, comprehensive exam, thesis, practicum, portfolio, field experience. *Entrance requirements:* Additional exam requirements/recommendations for international students: Required—TOEFL (minimum score 550 paper-based; 79 iBT). *Application deadline:* For fall admission, 6/1 for domestic and international students; for spring admission, 12/1 for domestic and

international students. Applications are processed on a rolling basis. Application fee: $75 ($150 for international students). Electronic applications accepted. *Expenses:* Tuition, state resident: full-time $12,099; part-time $589 per credit. Tuition, nonresident: full-time $16,399; part-time $722 per credit. *Required fees:* $3050; $139 per credit. Part-time tuition and fees vary according to course level, course load, degree level and program. *Financial support:* In 2013–14, 46 research assistantships with full tuition reimbursements (averaging $3,713 per year) were awarded; unspecified assistantships also available. Financial award applicants required to submit FAFSA. *Unit head:* Dr. Susan Polirstok, Dean, 908-737-3750, Fax: 908-737-3760, E-mail: polirsts@kean.edu. *Application contact:* Ann-Marie Kay, Assistant Director of Graduate Admissions, 908-737-5922, Fax: 908-737-5925, E-mail: akay@kean.edu.
Website: http://www.kean.edu/KU/College-of-Education.

Keene State College, School of Professional and Graduate Studies, Keene, NH 03435. Offers curriculum and instruction (M Ed); education leadership (PMC); educational leadership (M Ed); safety and occupational health applied science (MS); school counselor (M Ed, PMC); special education (M Ed); teacher certification (Postbaccalaureate Certificate). *Accreditation:* NCATE. Part-time and evening/weekend programs available. *Faculty:* 8 full-time (5 women), 12 part-time/adjunct (6 women). *Students:* 39 full-time (33 women), 46 part-time (32 women); includes 8 minority (1 American Indian or Alaska Native, non-Hispanic/Latino; 2 Asian, non-Hispanic/Latino; 5 Hispanic/Latino). Average age 30. 46 applicants, 61% accepted, 13 enrolled. In 2013, 26 master's, 1 other advanced degree awarded. *Entrance requirements:* For master's, PRAXIS I, 3 references; official transcripts; minimum GPA of 2.5; interview. Additional exam requirements/recommendations for international students: Required—TOEFL (minimum score 550 paper-based; 61 iBT). *Application deadline:* For fall admission, 4/1 for domestic students; for spring admission, 12/1 for domestic students. Applications are processed on a rolling basis. Application fee: $50. Electronic applications accepted. *Expenses:* Tuition, state resident: full-time $10,410; part-time $480 per credit. Tuition, nonresident: full-time $17,795; part-time $530 per credit. *Required fees:* $2366; $94 per credit. Full-time tuition and fees vary according to course load. *Financial support:* Career-related internships or fieldwork, Federal Work-Study, institutionally sponsored loans, scholarships/grants, and unspecified assistantships available. Support available to part-time students. Financial award application deadline: 3/1; financial award applicants required to submit FAFSA. *Unit head:* Dr. Wayne Hartz, Interim Dean of Professional and Graduate Studies, 603-358-2220, E-mail: whartz@keene.edu. *Application contact:* Peggy Richmond, Director of Admissions, 603-358-2276, Fax: 603-358-2767, E-mail: admissions@keene.edu.
Website: http://www.keene.edu/gradstudies/.

Keiser University, Master of Science in Education Program, Ft. Lauderdale, FL 33309. Offers allied health teaching and leadership (MS Ed); career college administration (MS Ed); leadership (MS Ed); online teaching and learning (MS Ed); teaching and learning (MS Ed). Part-time programs available. Postbaccalaureate distance learning degree programs offered (no on-campus study).

Kennesaw State University, Leland and Clarice C. Bagwell College of Education, Kennesaw, GA 30144-5591. Offers M Ed, MAT, Ed D, Ed S. *Accreditation:* NCATE. Part-time programs available. *Students:* 188 full-time (147 women), 489 part-time (360 women); includes 170 minority (127 Black or African American, non-Hispanic/Latino; 11 Asian, non-Hispanic/Latino; 21 Hispanic/Latino; 1 Native Hawaiian or other Pacific Islander, non-Hispanic/Latino; 10 Two or more races, non-Hispanic/Latino), 4 international. Average age 36. 191 applicants, 81% accepted, 120 enrolled. In 2013, 163 master's, 10 doctorates, 43 other advanced degrees awarded. *Degree requirements:* For master's, thesis or alternative. *Entrance requirements:* For master's, GRE General Test, minimum GPA of 2.75, renewable teaching certificate. Additional exam requirements/recommendations for international students: Required—TOEFL (minimum score 550 paper-based; 80 iBT), IELTS (minimum score 6.5). *Application deadline:* For fall admission, 7/1 for domestic and international students; for spring admission, 10/1 for domestic and international students; for summer admission, 4/15 for domestic and international students. Applications are processed on a rolling basis. Application fee: $60. Electronic applications accepted. *Expenses:* Tuition, state resident: full-time $4806; part-time $267 per semester hour. Tuition, nonresident: full-time $17,298; part-time $961 per semester hour. *Required fees:* $1834; $784.50 per semester. *Financial support:* In 2013–14, 10 research assistantships with tuition reimbursements (averaging $8,000 per year) were awarded; Federal Work-Study and unspecified assistantships also available. Support available to part-time students. Financial award application deadline: 4/1; financial award applicants required to submit FAFSA. *Unit head:* Dr. Arlinda Eaton, Dean, 770-423-6117, Fax: 770-423-6567. *Application contact:* Melinda Ross, Administrative Coordinator, 770-423-6122, Fax: 770-423-6885, E-mail: ksugrad@kennesaw.edu.
Website: http://www.kennesaw.edu/education/.

Kent State University, Graduate School of Education, Health, and Human Services, Kent, OH 44242-0001. Offers M Ed, MA, MAT, MS, Au D, PhD, Ed S. *Accreditation:* NCATE. Part-time and evening/weekend programs available. Postbaccalaureate distance learning degree programs offered. *Faculty:* 200 full-time (124 women), 87 part-time/adjunct (61 women). *Students:* 919 full-time (690 women), 566 part-time (415 women); includes 184 minority (107 Black or African American, non-Hispanic/Latino; 9 American Indian or Alaska Native, non-Hispanic/Latino; 32 Asian, non-Hispanic/Latino; 13 Hispanic/Latino; 22 Native Hawaiian or other Pacific Islander, non-Hispanic/Latino; 1 Two or more races, non-Hispanic/Latino), 93 international. 1,519 applicants, 35% accepted. In 2013, 435 master's, 34 doctorates, 42 other advanced degrees awarded. *Degree requirements:* For master's, thesis (for some programs); for doctorate, comprehensive exam, thesis/dissertation. *Entrance requirements:* For doctorate and Ed S, GRE General Test. Additional exam requirements/recommendations for international students: Required—TOEFL (minimum score 550 paper-based; 80 iBT). *Application deadline:* Applications are processed on a rolling basis. Application fee: $30 ($60 for international students). Electronic applications accepted. *Financial support:* In 2013–14, 93 research assistantships with full tuition reimbursements (averaging $10,455 per year), 27 teaching assistantships (averaging $11,945 per year) were awarded; Federal Work-Study, scholarships/grants, unspecified assistantships, and 2 administrative assistantships (averaging $10,250 per year) also available. Financial award application deadline: 4/1; financial award applicants required to submit FAFSA. *Unit head:* Dr. Daniel Mahony, Dean, 330-672-2202, Fax: 330-672-3407, E-mail: dmahony@kent.edu. *Application contact:* Nancy Miller, Academic Program Coordinator, Office of Graduate Student Services, 330-672-2576, Fax: 330-672-9162, E-mail: nmiller1@kent.edu.
Website: http://www.kent.edu/ehhs/.

Kent State University at Stark, Graduate School of Education, Health and Human Services, Canton, OH 44720-7599. Offers curriculum and instruction studies (M Ed, MA).

Kutztown University of Pennsylvania, College of Education, Kutztown, PA 19530-0730. Offers M Ed, MA, MLS. *Accreditation:* NCATE. Part-time and evening/weekend programs available. *Faculty:* 28 full-time (19 women), 1 (woman) part-time/adjunct. *Students:* 156 full-time (115 women), 267 part-time (224 women); includes 40 minority (12 Black or African American, non-Hispanic/Latino; 1 American Indian or Alaska Native,

non-Hispanic/Latino; 2 Asian, non-Hispanic/Latino; 24 Hispanic/Latino; 1 Two or more races, non-Hispanic/Latino). Average age 30. 266 applicants, 60% accepted, 124 enrolled. In 2013, 140 master's awarded. *Degree requirements:* For master's, comprehensive exam. *Entrance requirements:* For master's, GRE. Additional exam requirements/recommendations for international students: Required—TOEFL (minimum score 550 paper-based; 79 iBT). *Application deadline:* For fall admission, 8/1 priority date for domestic and international students; for spring admission, 12/1 priority date for domestic and international students. Applications are processed on a rolling basis. Application fee: $35. Electronic applications accepted. *Expenses: Tuition, area resident:* Part-time $442 per credit. Tuition, state resident: part-time $442 per credit. Tuition, nonresident: part-time $663 per credit. *Required fees:* $80 per credit. *Financial support:* Career-related internships or fieldwork, Federal Work-Study, scholarships/grants, and unspecified assistantships available. Financial award application deadline: 3/1; financial award applicants required to submit FAFSA. *Unit head:* Dr. Darrell Garber, Dean, 610-683-4253, Fax: 610-683-4255, E-mail: garber@kutztown.edu. *Application contact:* Kelly Hish, Admissions Clerk, 610-683-4200, Fax: 610-683-1393, E-mail: graduate@kutztown.edu.
Website: http://www.kutztown.edu/academics/education.

LaGrange College, Graduate Programs, Department of Education, LaGrange, GA 30240-2999. Offers curriculum and instruction (M Ed, Ed S); middle grades (MAT); secondary education (MAT). Part-time and evening/weekend programs available. *Degree requirements:* For master's, comprehensive exam. *Entrance requirements:* For master's, GRE, MAT, minimum GPA of 2.5. Additional exam requirements/recommendations for international students: Required—TOEFL (minimum score 550 paper-based).

Lake Erie College, School of Education and Professional Studies, Painesville, OH 44077-3389. Offers curriculum and instruction (MS Ed); education (MS Ed); educational leadership (MS Ed); reading (MS Ed). Part-time and evening/weekend programs available. *Faculty:* 2 full-time (1 woman). *Students:* 7 part-time (4 women). Average age 27. 6 applicants, 33% accepted, 1 enrolled. In 2013, 10 master's awarded. *Degree requirements:* For master's, comprehensive exam (for some programs), thesis optional, applied research project. *Entrance requirements:* For master's, GRE General Test (minimum score of 440 verbal or 500 quantitative) or minimum GPA of 2.75; bachelor's degree from accredited 4-year institution; references; essay. Additional exam requirements/recommendations for international students: Required—TOEFL (minimum score 550 paper-based). *Application deadline:* For fall admission, 8/1 priority date for domestic students, 6/1 for international students; for spring admission, 12/15 for domestic students, 10/1 for international students. Applications are processed on a rolling basis. Application fee: $30. Electronic applications accepted. Application fee is waived when completed online. *Expenses:* Contact institution. *Financial support:* Tuition waivers and unspecified assistantships available. Financial award applicants required to submit FAFSA. *Unit head:* Prof. Dale Sheptak, Dean of the School of Education and Professional Studies, 440-375-7131, E-mail: dsheptak@lec.edu. *Application contact:* Milena Velez, Senior Admissions Counselor, 800-916-0904, Fax: 440-375-7000, E-mail: admissions@lec.edu.
Website: http://www.lec.edu/med.

Lake Forest College, Master of Arts in Teaching Program, Lake Forest, IL 60045. Offers elementary education (MAT); K-12 French (MAT); K-12 music (MAT); K-12 Spanish (MAT); K-12 visual art (MAT); secondary biology (MAT); secondary chemistry (MAT); secondary English (MAT); secondary history (MAT); secondary mathematics (MAT). *Degree requirements:* For master's, comprehensive exam, portfolio. *Entrance requirements:* For master's, GRE.

Lakehead University, Graduate Studies, Faculty of Education, Thunder Bay, ON P7B 5E1, Canada. Offers educational studies (PhD); gerontology (M Ed); women's studies (M Ed). Part-time and evening/weekend programs available. *Degree requirements:* For master's, project or thesis. *Entrance requirements:* For master's, minimum B average. Additional exam requirements/recommendations for international students: Required—TOEFL. *Faculty research:* Art education, AIDS education, language arts education, gerontology, women's studies.

Lakeland College, Graduate Studies Division, Program in Education, Sheboygan, WI 53082-0359. Offers M Ed. *Accreditation:* Teacher Education Accreditation Council. *Degree requirements:* For master's, thesis. *Expenses:* Contact institution.

Lamar University, College of Graduate Studies, College of Education and Human Development, Beaumont, TX 77710. Offers M Ed, MS, DE, Ed D, Certificate. *Accreditation:* NCATE. Part-time and evening/weekend programs available. Postbaccalaureate distance learning degree programs offered. *Degree requirements:* For master's, comprehensive exam, thesis optional; for doctorate, comprehensive exam, thesis/dissertation. *Entrance requirements:* For master's, GRE General Test, minimum GPA of 2.5; for doctorate, GRE, interview. Additional exam requirements/recommendations for international students: Required—TOEFL. *Faculty research:* School dropouts, suicide prevention in public school students, school climate and gifted performance, teacher evaluation.

Lander University, School of Education, Greenwood, SC 29649-2099. Offers elementary education (M Ed); teaching (MAT). *Accreditation:* NCATE. Part-time programs available. *Degree requirements:* For master's, comprehensive exam, thesis or alternative. *Entrance requirements:* For master's, GRE General Test. Additional exam requirements/recommendations for international students: Required—TOEFL (minimum score 550 paper-based). Electronic applications accepted.

Langston University, School of Education and Behavioral Sciences, Langston, OK 73050. Offers bilingual/multicultural (M Ed); elementary education (M Ed); English as a second language (M Ed); rehabilitation counseling (M Sc); urban education (M Ed). *Accreditation:* CORE; NCATE (one or more programs are accredited). Part-time programs available. *Degree requirements:* For master's, comprehensive exam, thesis optional. *Entrance requirements:* For master's, GRE, writing skills test, minimum GPA of 2.5, 3 letters of recommendation. Additional exam requirements/recommendations for international students: Required—TOEFL, TWE. *Faculty research:* Bilingual/multicultural education, financing post-secondary education.

La Salle University, School of Arts and Sciences, Program in Education, Philadelphia, PA 19141-1199. Offers American studies (MA); autism spectrum disorders (MA, Certificate); bilingual/bicultural studies (MA); classroom management (MA, Certificate); dual early childhood and special education (MA); dual middle-level science and math and special education secondary education (MA); education (MA); English (MA); English as a second language (Certificate); instructional coach (Certificate); instructional leadership (MA); reading specialist (MA, Certificate); secondary education (MA); special education (MA, Certificate). Part-time and evening/weekend programs available. *Faculty:* 5 full-time (4 women), 16 part-time/adjunct (10 women). *Students:* 18 full-time (13 women), 137 part-time (112 women); includes 33 minority (24 Black or African American, non-Hispanic/Latino; 9 Hispanic/Latino), 4 international. Average age 32. 47 applicants, 96% accepted, 28 enrolled. In 2013, 58 master's, 20 other advanced degrees awarded. *Degree requirements:* For master's, comprehensive exam. *Entrance requirements:* For master's and Certificate, MAT or GRE, 2 letters of recommendation. Additional exam requirements/recommendations for international students: Required—TOEFL. *Application deadline:* For fall admission, 8/15 priority date for domestic students, 7/15 for international students; for spring admission, 12/15 priority date for domestic students, 11/15 for international students; for summer admission, 4/15 priority date for domestic students, 3/15 for international students. Applications are processed on a rolling basis. Application fee: $35. Electronic applications accepted. Application fee is waived when completed online. *Expenses:* Contact institution. *Financial support:* In 2013–14, 28 students received support. Career-related internships or fieldwork, Federal Work-Study, and scholarships/grants available. Support available to part-time students. Financial award application deadline: 8/31; financial award applicants required to submit FAFSA. *Unit head:* Dr. Greer Richardson, Interim Director, 215-951-1806, Fax: 215-951-1843, E-mail: graded@lasalle.edu. *Application contact:* Paul J. Reilly, Assistant Vice President, Enrollment Services, 215-951-1946, Fax: 215-951-1462, E-mail: reilly@lasalle.edu.
Website: http://www.lasalle.edu/grad/index.php?section-education&page-index.

Lasell College, Graduate and Professional Studies in Education, Newton, MA 02466-2709. Offers elementary education (M Ed); special education (M Ed), including moderate disabilities. Part-time and evening/weekend programs available. Postbaccalaureate distance learning degree programs offered. *Faculty:* 2 full-time (both women), 5 part-time/adjunct (4 women). *Students:* 8 full-time (7 women), 23 part-time (22 women); includes 5 minority (4 Black or African American, non-Hispanic/Latino; 1 Hispanic/Latino). Average age 28. 25 applicants, 64% accepted, 15 enrolled. In 2013, 2 master's awarded. *Entrance requirements:* For master's, bachelor's degree from an accredited institution. Additional exam requirements/recommendations for international students: Required—TOEFL (minimum score 550 paper-based; 79 iBT), IELTS. *Application deadline:* For fall admission, 8/31 priority date for domestic students, 6/30 priority date for international students; for spring admission, 12/31 priority date for domestic students, 10/31 priority date for international students. Applications are processed on a rolling basis. Electronic applications accepted. *Expenses: Tuition:* Part-time $575 per credit. *Required fees:* $80 per semester. *Financial support:* Available to part-time students. Application deadline: 8/31; applicants required to submit FAFSA. *Unit head:* Dr. Joan Dolamore, Dean of Graduate and Professional Studies, 617-243-2485, Fax: 617-243-2450, E-mail: gradinfo@lasell.edu. *Application contact:* Adrienne Franciosi, Director of Graduate Admission, 617-243-2214, Fax: 617-243-2450, E-mail: gradinfo@lasell.edu.
Website: http://www.lasell.edu/Academics/Graduate-and-Professional-Studies/Master-of-Education.html.

La Sierra University, School of Education, Riverside, CA 92515. Offers MA, MAT, Ed D, Ed S. Part-time and evening/weekend programs available. Terminal master's awarded for partial completion of doctoral program. *Degree requirements:* For doctorate, thesis/dissertation; for Ed S, thesis optional. *Entrance requirements:* For master's, minimum GPA of 3.0; for doctorate, GRE General Test, GRE Subject Test, minimum GPA of 3.3; for Ed S, minimum GPA of 3.3.

Lee University, Program in Education, Cleveland, TN 37320-3450. Offers college student development (MS); curriculum and instruction (M Ed, Ed S); educational leadership (M Ed, Ed S); elementary education (MAT); higher education administration (MS); middle grades (MAT); secondary education (MAT); special education (M Ed); special education (secondary) (MAT). Part-time programs available. *Faculty:* 14 full-time (7 women), 6 part-time/adjunct (3 women). *Students:* 30 full-time (23 women), 62 part-time (37 women); includes 8 minority (3 Black or African American, non-Hispanic/Latino; 1 American Indian or Alaska Native, non-Hispanic/Latino; 2 Asian, non-Hispanic/Latino; 2 Hispanic/Latino). Average age 30. 40 applicants, 100% accepted, 30 enrolled. In 2013, 117 master's, 2 other advanced degrees awarded. *Degree requirements:* For master's, variable foreign language requirement, comprehensive exam, thesis, internship. *Entrance requirements:* For master's, MAT or GRE General Test, minimum GPA of 2.75, 3 letters of recommendation, interview, writing sample, official transcripts. Additional exam requirements/recommendations for international students: Required—TOEFL (minimum score 450 paper-based). *Application deadline:* For fall admission, 4/1 priority date for domestic and international students; for spring admission, 10/1 priority date for domestic and international students. Applications are processed on a rolling basis. Application fee: $25. *Expenses: Tuition:* Full-time $9900; part-time $550 per credit hour. *Required fees:* $35 per term. One-time fee: $25. *Financial support:* In 2013–14, 47 students received support, including 1 teaching assistantship (averaging $1,500 per year); career-related internships or fieldwork, Federal Work-Study, institutionally sponsored loans, scholarships/grants, and unspecified assistantships also available. Financial award application deadline: 3/1; financial award applicants required to submit FAFSA. *Unit head:* Dr. Gary Riggins, Director, 423-614-8193. *Application contact:* Vicki Glasscock, Graduate Admissions Director, 423-614-8059, E-mail: vglasscock@leeuniversity.edu.
Website: http://www.leeuniversity.edu/academics/graduate/education.

Lehigh University, College of Education, Bethlehem, PA 18015. Offers M Ed, MA, MS, Ed D, PhD, Certificate, Ed S, Graduate Certificate, M Ed/MA, MBA/M Ed. Part-time and evening/weekend programs available. Postbaccalaureate distance learning degree programs offered (minimal on-campus study). *Faculty:* 35 full-time (20 women), 25 part-time/adjunct (14 women). *Students:* 173 full-time (148 women), 325 part-time (205 women); includes 50 minority (17 Black or African American, non-Hispanic/Latino; 1 American Indian or Alaska Native, non-Hispanic/Latino; 10 Asian, non-Hispanic/Latino; 20 Hispanic/Latino; 1 Native Hawaiian or other Pacific Islander, non-Hispanic/Latino; 1 Two or more races, non-Hispanic/Latino), 53 international. Average age 32. 500 applicants, 50% accepted, 107 enrolled. In 2013, 179 master's, 24 doctorates awarded. Terminal master's awarded for partial completion of doctoral program. *Degree requirements:* For master's, thesis (for some programs), internship; for doctorate, comprehensive exam, thesis/dissertation, internship. *Entrance requirements:* For doctorate, GRE and/or MAT. Additional exam requirements/recommendations for international students: Required—TOEFL (minimum score 600 paper-based; 93 iBT). *Application deadline:* For fall admission, 1/1 for domestic and international students; for spring admission, 11/1 for domestic and international students; for summer admission, 5/1 for domestic and international students. Applications are processed on a rolling basis. Application fee: $65. Electronic applications accepted. *Expenses:* Contact institution. *Financial support:* In 2013–14, 122 students received support, including 5 fellowships with full and partial tuition reimbursements available (averaging $26,000 per year), 39 research assistantships with full and partial tuition reimbursements available (averaging $17,000 per year); teaching assistantships with full and partial tuition reimbursements available, career-related internships or fieldwork, Federal Work-Study, institutionally sponsored loans, scholarships/grants, tuition waivers (full and partial), and unspecified assistantships also available. Financial award application deadline: 3/1; financial award applicants required to submit FAFSA. *Faculty research:* Urban educational leadership, special education, instructional technology, school and counseling psychology, international education. *Unit head:* Dr. Gary M. Sasso, Dean, 610-758-3221, Fax: 610-758-6223, E-mail: gary.sasso@lehigh.edu. *Application contact:* Donna M. Johnson, Manager of Admissions and Recruitment, 610-758-3231, Fax: 610-758-6223, E-mail: dmj4@lehigh.edu.
Website: http://coe.lehigh.edu.

Lehman College of the City University of New York, Division of Education, Bronx, NY 10468-1589. Offers MA, MS Ed. *Accreditation:* NCATE. Part-time and evening/weekend programs available.

Le Moyne College, Department of Education, Syracuse, NY 13214. Offers adolescent education (MS Ed, MST); adolescent education/special education (MS Ed, MST); adolescent English (MST), including grades 7-12 (MS Ed, MST); adolescent English/special education (MST), including grades 7-12 (MS Ed, MST); adolescent foreign language (MST), including grades 7-12 (MS Ed, MST); adolescent history (MST), including grades 7-12 (MS Ed, MST); childhood education (MS Ed); childhood education/special education (MS Ed); elementary education (MS Ed); general education (MS Ed); inclusive childhood education (MST); literacy education (MS Ed), including birth to grade 6, grades 5-12; school building leader (MS Ed); school building leadership (CAS); school district business leader (MS Ed, CAS); school district leader (MS Ed); school district leadership (CAS); secondary education (MS Ed); special education (MS Ed); students with disabilities-generalist (MS Ed), including grades 7-12 (MS Ed, MST); teaching English to speakers of other languages (MS Ed); urban studies (MS Ed). *Accreditation:* Teacher Education Accreditation Council. Part-time and evening/weekend programs available. *Faculty:* 8 full-time (5 women), 61 part-time/adjunct (38 women). *Students:* 24 full-time (20 women), 178 part-time (133 women); includes 22 minority (12 Black or African American, non-Hispanic/Latino; 1 American Indian or Alaska Native, non-Hispanic/Latino; 3 Asian, non-Hispanic/Latino; 6 Hispanic/Latino), 1 international. Average age 31. 248 applicants, 90% accepted, 86 enrolled. In 2013, 158 master's, 37 CASs awarded. *Degree requirements:* For master's, thesis. *Entrance requirements:* For master's, GRE General Test, bachelor's degree, 2 letters of recommendation, written statement, transcripts. Additional exam requirements/recommendations for international students: Required—TOEFL (minimum score 550 paper-based; 79 iBT). *Application deadline:* For fall admission, 4/1 priority date for domestic and international students; for spring admission, 10/1 priority date for domestic and international students; for summer admission, 3/1 priority date for domestic and international students. Applications are processed on a rolling basis. Application fee: $50. *Expenses:* Contact institution. *Financial support:* In 2013–14, 26 students received support. Career-related internships or fieldwork and health care benefits available. Support available to part-time students. Financial award applicants required to submit FAFSA. *Faculty research:* Minority teachers, special education, multiculturalism, literacy, technology, media literacy learning, autism, school district organization, service-learning, higher level problem solving, teacher leadership. *Unit head:* Dr. Suzanne L. Gilmour, Chair, Department of Education/Director of Graduate Education Programs, 315-445-4376, Fax: 315-445-4744, E-mail: gilmous@lemoyne.edu. *Application contact:* Kristen P. Trapasso, Senior Director of Enrollment Management, 315-445-4265, Fax: 315-445-6092, E-mail: trapaskp@lemoyne.edu.
Website: http://www.lemoyne.edu/education.

Lenoir-Rhyne University, Graduate Programs, School of Education, Hickory, NC 28601. Offers MA. *Accreditation:* NCATE. Part-time and evening/weekend programs available. *Degree requirements:* For master's, comprehensive exam, thesis optional. *Entrance requirements:* For master's, GRE General Test or MAT, minimum undergraduate GPA of 2.7, graduate 3.0. Additional exam requirements/recommendations for international students: Required—TOEFL (minimum score 600 paper-based). Electronic applications accepted.

Lesley University, School of Education, Cambridge, MA 02138-2790. Offers arts, community, and education (M Ed); autism studies (Certificate); curriculum and instruction (M Ed, CAGS); early childhood education (M Ed); ecological teaching and learning (MS); educational studies (PhD), including adult learning, educational leadership, individually designed; elementary education (M Ed); emergent technologies for educators (Certificate); ESLArts: language learning through the arts (M Ed); high school education (M Ed); individually designed (M Ed); integrated teaching through the arts (M Ed); literacy for K-8 classroom teachers (M Ed); mathematics education (M Ed); middle school education (M Ed); moderate disabilities (M Ed); online learning (Certificate); reading (CAGS); science in education (M Ed); severe disabilities (M Ed); special needs (CAGS); specialist teacher of reading (M Ed); teacher of visual art (M Ed); technology in education (M Ed, CAGS). *Accreditation:* Teacher Education Accreditation Council. Part-time and evening/weekend programs available. Postbaccalaureate distance learning degree programs offered (no on-campus study). *Faculty:* 40 full-time (30 women), 104 part-time/adjunct (77 women). *Students:* 453 full-time (381 women), 1,672 part-time (1,435 women); includes 284 minority (139 Black or African American, non-Hispanic/Latino; 11 American Indian or Alaska Native, non-Hispanic/Latino; 38 Asian, non-Hispanic/Latino; 58 Hispanic/Latino; 5 Native Hawaiian or other Pacific Islander, non-Hispanic/Latino; 33 Two or more races, non-Hispanic/Latino), 22 international. Average age 35. In 2013, 1,137 master's, 18 doctorates, 51 other advanced degrees awarded. *Degree requirements:* For master's, practicum; for doctorate, thesis/dissertation. *Entrance requirements:* For master's, Massachusetts Tests for Educator Licensure (MTEL), transcripts, statement of purpose, recommendations; interview (for special education); for doctorate, GRE General Test, transcripts, statement of purpose, recommendations, interview, master's degree, resume; for other advanced degree, interview, master's degree. Additional exam requirements/recommendations for international students: Required—TOEFL (minimum score 550 paper-based; 80 iBT). *Application deadline:* Applications are processed on a rolling basis. Application fee: $50. Electronic applications accepted. *Expenses: Tuition:* Part-time $900 per credit. *Financial support:* In 2013–14, 15 fellowships (averaging $3,600 per year) were awarded; career-related internships or fieldwork, Federal Work-Study, scholarships/grants, tuition waivers, and unspecified assistantships also available. Financial award application deadline: 4/15; financial award applicants required to submit FAFSA. *Faculty research:* Assessment in literacy, mathematics and science; autism spectrum disorders; instructional technology and online learning; multicultural education and English language learners. *Unit head:* Dr. Jack Gillette, Dean, 617-349-8401, Fax: 617-349-8607, E-mail: jgillett@lesley.edu. *Application contact:* Martha Sheehan, Director of Admissions, 888-LESLEYU, Fax: 617-349-8313, E-mail: info@lesley.edu.
Website: http://www.lesley.edu/soe.html.

LeTourneau University, Graduate Programs, Longview, TX 75607-7001. Offers business administration (MBA); counseling (MA); education (M Ed); engineering (MS); health care administration (MS); marriage and family therapy (MA); psychology (MA); strategic leadership (MSL). Part-time programs available. Postbaccalaureate distance learning degree programs offered (no on-campus study). *Faculty:* 15 full-time (7 women), 54 part-time/adjunct (23 women). *Students:* 58 full-time (45 women), 365 part-time (287 women); includes 106 minority (51 Black or African American, non-Hispanic/Latino; 3 American Indian or Alaska Native, non-Hispanic/Latino; 1 Asian, non-Hispanic/Latino; 45 Hispanic/Latino; 6 Two or more races, non-Hispanic/Latino), 4 international. Average age 38. 263 applicants, 68% accepted, 116 enrolled. In 2013, 112 master's awarded. *Degree requirements:* For master's, thesis (for some programs). *Entrance requirements:* For master's, GRE (for engineering programs), minimum GPA of 2.8 (3.0 for counseling and engineering programs). Additional exam requirements/recommendations for international students: Required—TOEFL. *Application deadline:* For fall admission, 8/22 for domestic students, 8/29 for international students; for winter admission, 10/10 for domestic students; for spring admission, 1/2 for domestic students,

1/10 for international students; for summer admission, 5/1 for domestic and international students. Applications are processed on a rolling basis. Electronic applications accepted. Application fee is waived when completed online. *Financial support:* In 2013–14, 11 students received support, including 13 research assistantships (averaging $9,122 per year); institutionally sponsored loans and unspecified assistantships also available. Financial award applicants required to submit FAFSA. *Unit head:* Dr. Robert Hudson, Vice President and Dean of the Graduate School, 903-233-1110, E-mail: roberthudson@letu.edu. *Application contact:* Chris Fontaine, Assistant Vice President for Global Campus Admissions, 903-233-4312, E-mail: chrisfontaine@letu.edu.
Website: http://www.adults.letu.edu/.

Lewis University, College of Education, Romeoville, IL 60446. Offers advanced study in education (CAS), including general administrative, superintendent endorsement; curriculum and instruction: instructional technology (M Ed); early childhood education (MA); educational leadership (M Ed, MA); educational leadership for teaching and learning (Ed D); elementary education (MA); English as a second language (M Ed); instructional technology (M Ed); reading and literacy (M Ed, MA); secondary education (MA), including biology, chemistry, English, history, math, physics, psychology and social science; special education (MA). *Accreditation:* NCATE. Part-time and evening/weekend programs available. *Students:* 75 full-time (58 women), 362 part-time (281 women); includes 90 minority (48 Black or African American, non-Hispanic/Latino; 6 Asian, non-Hispanic/Latino; 33 Hispanic/Latino; 3 Two or more races, non-Hispanic/Latino), 6 international. *Degree requirements:* For master's, thesis optional; for doctorate, thesis/dissertation. *Entrance requirements:* For master's, departmental qualifying exam, writing exam, minimum GPA of 2.75, 3 letters of recommendation, interview. Additional exam requirements/recommendations for international students: Required—TOEFL (minimum score 550 paper-based; 80 iBT). *Application deadline:* For fall admission, 5/1 priority date for international students; for spring admission, 11/15 priority date for international students. Applications are processed on a rolling basis. Application fee: $40. Electronic applications accepted. *Financial support:* Federal Work-Study, scholarships/grants, tuition waivers (partial), and unspecified assistantships available. Financial award application deadline: 5/1; financial award applicants required to submit FAFSA. *Unit head:* Dr. Pamela Jessee, Dean, 815-836-5316, E-mail: jesseepa@lewisu.edu. *Application contact:* Linda Campbell, Graduate Admission Counselor, 815-836-5704, Fax: 815-836-5578, E-mail: campbeli@lewisu.edu.

Liberty University, School of Communication and Creative Arts, Lynchburg, VA 24515. Offers strategic communication (MA), including professional, teaching and academic. Part-time programs available. *Students:* 70 full-time (47 women), 28 part-time (19 women); includes 14 minority (10 Black or African American, non-Hispanic/Latino; 1 Asian, non-Hispanic/Latino; 3 Hispanic/Latino), 10 international. Average age 37. 158 applicants, 37% accepted, 38 enrolled. In 2013, 37 master's awarded. *Degree requirements:* For master's, thesis (for some programs). *Entrance requirements:* For master's, minimum undergraduate GPA of 3.0, faculty recommendation, written statement of purpose, writing sample. Additional exam requirements/recommendations for international students: Required—TOEFL (minimum score 600 paper-based; 100 iBT). *Application deadline:* For fall admission, 6/1 for domestic students; for spring admission, 11/1 for domestic students. Applications are processed on a rolling basis. Application fee: $50. Electronic applications accepted. *Expenses: Tuition:* Full-time $9630; part-time $535 per credit hour. *Required fees:* $175 per term. One-time fee: $50. Tuition and fees vary according to course load, degree level, campus/location and program. *Financial support:* Federal Work-Study and unspecified assistantships available. Financial award applicants required to submit FAFSA. *Unit head:* Dr. Norman Mintle, Dean, 434-582-2077, E-mail: cvkramer@liberty.edu. *Application contact:* Dr. Terry Elam, Director of Graduate Admissions, 434-582-2111, Fax: 434-582-7836, E-mail: gradadmissions@liberty.edu.
Website: http://www.liberty.edu/index.cfm?PID-8759.

Liberty University, School of Education, Lynchburg, VA 24515. Offers administration and supervision (M Ed); curriculum and instruction (Ed D, Ed S); early childhood education (M Ed); educational leadership (Ed D, Ed S); educational technology and online instruction (M Ed); elementary education (M Ed, MAT); English (M Ed); gifted education (M Ed); history (M Ed); leadership (M Ed); math specialist (M Ed); middle grades (M Ed, MAT); outdoor adventure sport (MS); reading specialist (M Ed); school counseling (M Ed); secondary education (MAT); special education (M Ed, MAT); sport management (MS), including administration, outdoor recreation, sport management, tourism; sports administration (MS); student service (M Ed); teaching and learning (M Ed); tourism (MS). *Accreditation:* NCATE. Part-time programs available. Postbaccalaureate distance learning degree programs offered (minimal on-campus study). *Students:* 2,241 full-time (1,639 women), 4,413 part-time (3,240 women); includes 2,052 minority (1,588 Black or African American, non-Hispanic/Latino; 37 American Indian or Alaska Native, non-Hispanic/Latino; 67 Asian, non-Hispanic/Latino; 173 Hispanic/Latino; 37 Native Hawaiian or other Pacific Islander, non-Hispanic/Latino; 150 Two or more races, non-Hispanic/Latino), 15 international. Average age 37. 6,185 applicants, 43% accepted, 1603 enrolled. In 2013, 1,256 master's, 117 doctorates, 470 other advanced degrees awarded. *Degree requirements:* For doctorate, comprehensive exam, thesis/dissertation. *Entrance requirements:* For master's, GRE General Test or MAT (if taken in or before 1999), 2 letters of recommendation, minimum undergraduate GPA of 3.0, curriculum vitae; for doctorate and Ed S, GRE General Test or MAT (if taken before 1999), minimum master's GPA of 3.0, 3 years of teaching experience. Additional exam requirements/recommendations for international students: Required—TOEFL (minimum score 600 paper-based; 100 iBT). *Application deadline:* For fall admission, 6/1 for domestic students; for spring admission, 11/1 for domestic students. Applications are processed on a rolling basis. Application fee: $50. Electronic applications accepted. *Expenses:* Contact institution. *Financial support:* Federal Work-Study and tuition waivers (partial) available. *Faculty research:* Self-determination, character education, bibliotherapy, learning styles, distance education. *Unit head:* Dr. Karen L. Parker, Dean, 434-582-2195, Fax: 434-582-2468, E-mail: kparker@liberty.edu. *Application contact:* Jay Bridge, Director of Graduate Admissions, 800-424-9595, Fax: 800-628-7977, E-mail: gradadmissions@liberty.edu.
Website: http://www.liberty.edu/academics/education/graduate/.

Lincoln Memorial University, Carter and Moyers School of Education, Harrogate, TN 37752-1901. Offers administration and supervision (M Ed, Ed S); counseling and guidance (M Ed); curriculum and instruction (M Ed, Ed D, Ed S); English (M Ed); executive leadership (Ed D); higher education administration (Ed D); human resource development (Ed D); leadership and administration (Ed D). Part-time and evening/weekend programs available. Postbaccalaureate distance learning degree programs offered. *Degree requirements:* For master's, comprehensive exam, thesis optional; for Ed S, comprehensive exam. *Entrance requirements:* For master's, PRAXIS, NTE, GRE, MAT, letters of recommendation; for Ed S, graduate transcripts. Additional exam requirements/recommendations for international students: Recommended—TOEFL. *Faculty research:* Brain compatible teaching and learning; poverty in Appalachia; leadership for change; ethics, moral responsibility and social justice; human and organizational learning.

Lindenwood University, Graduate Programs, School of Education, St. Charles, MO 63301-1695. Offers education (MA); educational administration (MA, Ed D, Ed S);

human performance (MS); instructional leadership (Ed D, Ed S); library media (MA); professional counseling (MA); school administration (Ed S); school counseling (MA); teaching (MA); teaching English to speakers of other languages (MA). Part-time and evening/weekend programs available. Postbaccalaureate distance learning degree programs offered (no on-campus study). *Faculty:* 50 full-time (33 women), 228 part-time/adjunct (136 women). *Students:* 454 full-time (352 women), 1,772 part-time (1,351 women); includes 637 minority (545 Black or African American, non-Hispanic/Latino; 9 American Indian or Alaska Native, non-Hispanic/Latino; 9 Asian, non-Hispanic/Latino; 42 Hispanic/Latino; 32 Two or more races, non-Hispanic/Latino), 32 international. Average age 36. 644 applicants, 71% accepted, 401 enrolled. In 2013, 564 master's, 35 doctorates, 83 other advanced degrees awarded. *Degree requirements:* For master's, thesis (for some programs), minimum GPA of 3.0; for doctorate, thesis/dissertation, minimum GPA of 3.0; for Ed S, comprehensive exam, project, minimum GPA of 3.0. *Entrance requirements:* For master's, interview, minimum GPA of 3.0, writing sample, letter of recommendation; for doctorate, GRE, minimum graduate GPA of 3.4, resume, interview, writing sample, 4 letters of recommendation; for Ed S, master's degree in education, relevant work experience. Additional exam requirements/recommendations for international students: Required—TOEFL (minimum score 550 paper-based; 80 iBT). *Application deadline:* For fall admission, 8/26 priority date for domestic and international students; for spring admission, 1/27 priority date for domestic and international students. Applications are processed on a rolling basis. Application fee: $30 ($100 for international students). Electronic applications accepted. *Expenses: Tuition:* Full-time $14,800; part-time $428 per credit hour. *Required fees:* $350. Tuition and fees vary according to course level and course load. *Financial support:* In 2013–14, 385 students received support. Career-related internships or fieldwork, Federal Work-Study, institutionally sponsored loans, scholarships/grants, tuition waivers (partial), and unspecified assistantships available. Financial award application deadline: 6/30; financial award applicants required to submit FAFSA. *Unit head:* Dr. Cynthia Bice, Dean, 636-949-4618, Fax: 636-949-4197, E-mail: cbice@lindenwood.edu. *Application contact:* Brett Barger, Dean of Evening Admissions and Extension Campuses, 636-949-4934, Fax: 636-949-4109, E-mail: adultadmissions@lindenwood.edu.

Lindenwood University–Belleville, Graduate Programs, Belleville, IL 62226. Offers business administration (MBA); communications (MA), including digital and multimedia, media management, promotions, training and development; counseling (MA); criminal justice administration (MS); education (MA); healthcare administration (MS); human resource management (MS); school administration (MA); teaching (MAT).

Lipscomb University, Program in Education, Nashville, TN 37204-3951. Offers applied behavior analysis (Certificate); collaborative professional learning (M Ed, Ed S); educational leadership (M Ed, Ed S); English language learning (M Ed, Ed S); instructional coaching (Certificate); instructional practice (M Ed); learning organizations and strategic change (Ed D); math specialty (M Ed); reading specialty (M Ed, Ed S); special education (M Ed); teaching, learning, and leading (M Ed); technology integration (M Ed); technology integration specialist (Certificate). *Accreditation:* NCATE. Part-time and evening/weekend programs available. Postbaccalaureate distance learning degree programs offered (no on-campus study). *Faculty:* 19 full-time (13 women), 28 part-time/adjunct (22 women). *Students:* 171 full-time (123 women), 509 part-time (429 women); includes 118 minority (91 Black or African American, non-Hispanic/Latino; 1 American Indian or Alaska Native, non-Hispanic/Latino; 4 Asian, non-Hispanic/Latino; 15 Hispanic/Latino; 1 Native Hawaiian or other Pacific Islander, non-Hispanic/Latino; 6 Two or more races, non-Hispanic/Latino). Average age 32. 237 applicants, 65% accepted, 150 enrolled. In 2013, 212 master's awarded. *Degree requirements:* For master's, comprehensive exam, portfolio, research project and presentation; for doctorate, practical capstone project in experiential setting. *Entrance requirements:* For master's, MAT (minimum 31) or GRE General Test (minimum 294), 2 reference letters, goals statement, writing sample, interview; for doctorate, MAT or GRE General Test, 3 reference letters, artifact of demonstrated academic excellence, written personal statements, interview. Additional exam requirements/recommendations for international students: Required—TOEFL (minimum score 570 paper-based). *Application deadline:* For fall admission, 8/29 priority date for domestic students; for spring admission, 1/15 priority date for domestic students. Applications are processed on a rolling basis. Application fee: $50 ($75 for international students). *Expenses: Tuition:* Full-time $15,570; part-time $865 per credit hour. Tuition and fees vary according to degree level and program. *Financial support:* Scholarships/grants and unspecified assistantships available. Financial award applicants required to submit FAFSA. *Faculty research:* Facilitative learning styles, leadership, student assessment, interactive multimedia inclusion, learning organizations and strategic change. *Unit head:* Dr. Deborah Boyd, Director of Graduate Studies, 615-966-6263, E-mail: deborah.boyd@lipscomb.edu. *Application contact:* Kristin Baese, Director of Enrollment and Outreach, 615-966-7628 Ext. 6081, Fax: 615-966-5173, E-mail: kristin.baese@lipscomb.edu.
Website: http://www.lipscomb.edu/education/graduate-programs.

Lock Haven University of Pennsylvania, College of Liberal Arts and Education, Lock Haven, PA 17745-2390. Offers alternative education (M Ed); educational leadership (M Ed); teaching and learning (M Ed). *Accreditation:* NCATE. Part-time and evening/weekend programs available. Postbaccalaureate distance learning degree programs offered (no on-campus study). *Degree requirements:* For master's, thesis. *Entrance requirements:* For master's, minimum undergraduate GPA of 3.0. Additional exam requirements/recommendations for international students: Required—TOEFL. *Application deadline:* Applications are processed on a rolling basis. Application fee: $25. Electronic applications accepted. *Expenses: Tuition, area resident:* Part-time $442 per credit hour. Tuition, state resident: part-time $442 per credit hour. Tuition, nonresident: part-time $663 per credit hour. *Required fees:* $208.45 per credit hour. Tuition and fees vary according to program. *Financial support:* Unspecified assistantships available. Financial award application deadline: 8/1. *Unit head:* Dr. Susan Rimby, Dean, 570-484-2137, E-mail: ser1116@lhup.edu. *Application contact:* Kelly Hibbler, Assistant to the Dean, 570-484-2147, Fax: 570-484-2734, E-mail: khibbler@lhup.edu.
Website: http://www.lhup.edu/colleges/liberal_arts_education/.

Long Island University–Brentwood Campus, School of Education, Brentwood, NY 11717. Offers childhood education (MS); early childhood education (MS); literacy (MS); mental health counseling (MS); school counseling (MS); special education (MS). Part-time and evening/weekend programs available.

Long Island University–Hudson at Westchester, Programs in Education-Teaching, Purchase, NY 10577. Offers early childhood education (MS Ed, Advanced Certificate); elementary education (MS Ed, Advanced Certificate); literacy education (MS Ed, Advanced Certificate); second language, TESOL, bilingual education (MS Ed, Advanced Certificate); special education and secondary education (MS Ed, Advanced Certificate). *Accreditation:* Teacher Education Accreditation Council. Part-time and evening/weekend programs available. *Degree requirements:* For master's, comprehensive exam.

Long Island University–LIU Brooklyn, School of Education, Brooklyn, NY 11201-8423. Offers MS, MS Ed, Certificate. *Accreditation:* Teacher Education Accreditation Council. Part-time and evening/weekend programs available. *Degree requirements:* For master's, thesis optional. *Entrance requirements:* For master's, 2 letters of recommendation. Additional exam requirements/recommendations for international students: Required—TOEFL (minimum score 500 paper-based). Electronic applications accepted.

Long Island University–LIU Post, School of Education, Brookville, NY 11548-1300. Offers MA, MS, MS Ed, Ed D, AC. *Accreditation:* Teacher Education Accreditation Council. Part-time and evening/weekend programs available. *Degree requirements:* For AC, internship. Electronic applications accepted.

Long Island University–Riverhead, Education Division, Riverhead, NY 11901. Offers applied behavior analysis (Advanced Certificate); childhood education (MS Ed), including childhood education, elementary education; literacy education (MS Ed); teaching students with disabilities (MS Ed). *Accreditation:* Teacher Education Accreditation Council. Part-time and evening/weekend programs available. *Degree requirements:* For master's, thesis (for some programs); for Advanced Certificate, comprehensive exam (for some programs). *Entrance requirements:* For master's, minimum GPA of 2.75, writing sample, letter of reference, interview, official college transcripts. Additional exam requirements/recommendations for international students: Required—TOEFL (minimum score 550 paper-based). Electronic applications accepted. Application fee is waived when completed online.

Longwood University, College of Graduate and Professional Studies, College of Education and Human Services, Farmville, VA 23909. Offers education (MS), including algebra and middle school math, counselor education, elementary and middle school math, elementary education, elementary education initial licensure, health and physical education, school librarianship, special education general curriculum, special education initial licensure; social work and communication sciences and disorders (MS). *Accreditation:* NCATE. Part-time and evening/weekend programs available. *Faculty:* 28 full-time (15 women), 9 part-time/adjunct (7 women). *Students:* 86 full-time (80 women), 187 part-time (173 women); includes 38 minority (26 Black or African American, non-Hispanic/Latino; 1 Asian, non-Hispanic/Latino; 5 Hispanic/Latino; 1 Native Hawaiian or other Pacific Islander, non-Hispanic/Latino; 5 Two or more races, non-Hispanic/Latino). 98 applicants, 89% accepted, 85 enrolled. In 2013, 132 master's awarded. *Degree requirements:* For master's, comprehensive exam (for some programs), thesis optional, professional portfolio, internship, clinical experience, or practicum. *Entrance requirements:* For master's, bachelor's degree from regionally-accredited institution, 2 recommendations, 500-word personal essay, official transcripts, minimum GPA of 2.75, valid teaching license (for some programs), passing Praxis I scores for initial teaching licensure programs. Additional exam requirements/recommendations for international students: Required—TOEFL (minimum score 570 paper-based), IELTS (minimum score 6.5). *Application deadline:* For fall admission, 5/1 priority date for domestic students; for spring admission, 10/1 priority date for domestic students; for summer admission, 2/1 priority date for domestic students. Applications are processed on a rolling basis. Application fee: $50. Electronic applications accepted. *Expenses:* Tuition, state resident: full-time $7506; part-time $327 per credit hour. Tuition, nonresident: full-time $17,100; part-time $837 per credit hour. Tuition and fees vary according to course load and campus/location. *Financial support:* Career-related internships or fieldwork and Federal Work-Study available. Financial award applicants required to submit FAFSA. *Unit head:* Dr. Peggy L. Tarpley, Chair of the Department of Education and Special Education, 434-395-2337, E-mail: tarpleypl@longwood.edu. *Application contact:* College of Graduate and Professional Studies, 434-395-2380, Fax: 434-395-2750, E-mail: graduate@longwood.edu.
Website: http://www.longwood.edu/cehs/.

Louisiana College, Graduate Programs, Pineville, LA 71359-0001. Offers teaching (MAT).

Louisiana State University and Agricultural & Mechanical College, Graduate School, College of Human Sciences and Education, Baton Rouge, LA 70803. Offers M Ed, MA, MAT, MLIS, MS, MSW, PhD, Ed S. *Accreditation:* NCATE. Part-time and evening/weekend programs available. *Students:* 530 full-time (392 women), 489 part-time (367 women); includes 268 minority (210 Black or African American, non-Hispanic/Latino; 3 American Indian or Alaska Native, non-Hispanic/Latino; 10 Asian, non-Hispanic/Latino; 27 Hispanic/Latino; 18 Two or more races, non-Hispanic/Latino), 19 international. Average age 30. 565 applicants, 70% accepted, 261 enrolled. In 2013, 333 master's, 31 doctorates, 17 other advanced degrees awarded. Terminal master's awarded for partial completion of doctoral program. *Degree requirements:* For doctorate, thesis/dissertation; for Ed S, thesis optional. *Entrance requirements:* For master's and doctorate, GRE General Test, minimum GPA of 3.0. Additional exam requirements/recommendations for international students: Required—TOEFL (minimum score 550 paper-based; 79 IBT), IELTS (minimum score 6.5), or PTE (minimum score 59). *Application deadline:* For fall admission, 1/25 priority date for domestic students, 5/15 for international students; for spring admission, 10/15 for international students. Applications are processed on a rolling basis. Application fee: $50 ($70 for international students). Electronic applications accepted. *Financial support:* In 2013–14, 698 students received support, including 25 fellowships (averaging $27,125 per year), 47 research assistantships with partial tuition reimbursements available (averaging $11,982 per year), 141 teaching assistantships with partial tuition reimbursements available (averaging $12,130 per year); career-related internships or fieldwork, Federal Work-Study, institutionally sponsored loans, health care benefits, tuition waivers (partial), and unspecified assistantships also available. Support available to part-time students. Financial award applicants required to submit FAFSA. *Faculty research:* Instructional learning, educational administration, exercise physiology, sports psychology, literacy education curriculum and instruction. *Total annual research expenditures:* $1.3 million. *Unit head:* Dr. Damon Andrew, Dean, 225-578-1252, Fax: 225-578-2267, E-mail: damonandrew@lsu.edu. *Application contact:* Dr. Renee Casbergue, Interim Associate Dean, 225-578-4701, Fax: 225-578-2267, E-mail: rcasberg@lsu.edu.
Website: http://chse.lsu.edu/.

Louisiana State University in Shreveport, College of Business, Education, and Human Development, Program in Education, Shreveport, LA 71115-2399. Offers curriculum and instruction (M Ed); educational leadership (M Ed); school counseling (M Ed). *Accreditation:* NCATE. Part-time programs available. *Students:* 1 (woman) full-time, 99 part-time (80 women); includes 26 minority (20 Black or African American, non-Hispanic/Latino; 4 Hispanic/Latino; 2 Two or more races, non-Hispanic/Latino), 1 international. Average age 37. 111 applicants, 97% accepted, 42 enrolled. In 2013, 24 master's awarded. *Degree requirements:* For master's, orally-presented project, 200-hour internship (educational leadership). *Entrance requirements:* For master's, GRE, minimum GPA of 2.5; teacher certification; recommendations and interview (for educational leadership). Additional exam requirements/recommendations for international students: Required—TOEFL (minimum score 550 paper-based; 80 iBT). *Application deadline:* For fall admission, 6/30 for domestic and international students; for spring admission, 11/30 for domestic and international students. Applications are processed on a rolling basis. Application fee: $10 ($20 for international students). *Expenses: Tuition, area resident:* Part-time $182 per credit hour. *Required fees:* $51. *Financial support:* In 2013–14, 5 research assistantships (averaging $2,150 per year) were awarded. *Unit head:* Dr. Pat Doerr, Coordinator, 318-797-5033, Fax: 318-798-4144, E-mail: pat.doerr@lsus.edu. *Application contact:* Christianne Wojcik, Director of Academic Services, 318-797-5247, Fax: 318-798-4120, E-mail: christianne.wojcik@lsus.edu.

Louisiana Tech University, Graduate School, College of Education, Ruston, LA 71272. Offers M Ed, MA, MS, Ed D, PhD. *Accreditation:* NCATE. Part-time programs available. *Degree requirements:* For doctorate, thesis/dissertation. *Entrance requirements:* For master's and doctorate, GRE General Test. *Application deadline:* For fall admission, 7/29 for domestic students; for spring admission, 2/3 for domestic students. Application fee: $20 ($30 for international students). *Financial support:* Fellowships, research assistantships, teaching assistantships, and career-related internships or fieldwork available. Financial award application deadline: 2/1. *Unit head:* Dr. Lawrence Leonard, Dean, 318-257-3712. *Application contact:* Dr. Cathy Stockton, Associate Dean of Graduate Studies, 318-257-3229, Fax: 318-257-2379, E-mail: cstock@latech.edu. Website: http://www.latech.edu/education/.

Loyola Marymount University, School of Education, Los Angeles, CA 90045. Offers MA, Ed D. *Accreditation:* NCATE. *Unit head:* Dr. Shane P. Martin, Dean, 310-338-7301, E-mail: smartin@lmu.edu. *Application contact:* Chake H. Kouyoumjian, Associate Dean of the Graduate Division, 310-338-2721, E-mail: ckouyoum@lmu.edu. Website: http://soe.lmu.edu.

Loyola University Chicago, School of Education, Chicago, IL 60660. Offers M Ed, MA, Ed D, PhD, Certificate, Ed S. *Accreditation:* NCATE. Part-time and evening/weekend programs available. Postbaccalaureate distance learning degree programs offered (minimal on-campus study). *Faculty:* 52 full-time (34 women), 100 part-time/adjunct (69 women). *Students:* 440 full-time (328 women), 249 part-time (196 women); includes 207 minority (93 Black or African American, non-Hispanic/Latino; 1 American Indian or Alaska Native, non-Hispanic/Latino; 33 Asian, non-Hispanic/Latino; 63 Hispanic/Latino; 17 Two or more races, non-Hispanic/Latino), 14 international. Average age 36. 822 applicants, 61% accepted, 255 enrolled. In 2013, 159 master's, 37 doctorates, 23 other advanced degrees awarded. *Degree requirements:* For master's, comprehensive exam (for some programs), thesis (for some programs); for doctorate, comprehensive exam, thesis/dissertation; for other advanced degree, comprehensive exam. *Entrance requirements:* For master's, minimum GPA of 3.0, 3 letters of recommendation, resume, transcripts; for doctorate, GRE, interview, minimum GPA of 3.0, 3 letters of recommendation, resume; for other advanced degree, GRE, interview, minimum GPA of 3.0, letters of recommendation, resume, transcripts. Additional exam requirements/recommendations for international students: Required—TOEFL (minimum score 550 paper-based; 79 iBT). *Application fee:* $50. Electronic applications accepted. Application fee is waived when completed online. *Expenses:* Tuition: Full-time $16,740; part-time $930 per credit. *Required fees:* $135 per semester. *Financial support:* In 2013–14, 148 fellowships with partial tuition reimbursements, 66 research assistantships with full tuition reimbursements (averaging $12,000 per year), 102 teaching assistantships (averaging $4,000 per year) were awarded; career-related internships or fieldwork, Federal Work-Study, institutionally sponsored loans, scholarships/grants, traineeships, health care benefits, tuition waivers (partial), and unspecified assistantships also available. Support available to part-time students. Financial award application deadline: 2/1; financial award applicants required to submit FAFSA. *Faculty research:* Policy studies, historical foundations, teacher education, research methodologies, comparative education. *Total annual research expenditures:* $2.1 million. *Unit head:* Dr. Michael E. Dantley, Dean, 312-915-6992, Fax: 312-915-6980, E-mail: mdantley@luc.edu. *Application contact:* Marie Rosin-Dittmar, Information Contact, 312-915-6800, E-mail: schleduc@luc.edu.
Website: http://www.luc.edu/education.

Loyola University Maryland, Graduate Programs, School of Education, Baltimore, MD 21210-2699. Offers M Ed, MA, MAT, CAS, Certificate. *Accreditation:* NCATE. Part-time and evening/weekend programs available. *Degree requirements:* For master's, thesis. *Entrance requirements:* Additional exam requirements/recommendations for international students: Required—TOEFL (minimum score 550 paper-based).

Lynchburg College, Graduate Studies, School of Education and Human Development, Lynchburg, VA 24501-3199. Offers clinical mental health counseling (M Ed); curriculum and instruction (M Ed), including instructional leadership, teacher licensure; educational leadership (M Ed); leadership studies (Ed D); reading (M Ed), including reading instruction, reading specialist; school counseling (M Ed); science education (M Ed); special education (M Ed). Part-time and evening/weekend programs available. *Faculty:* 14 full-time (9 women), 3 part-time/adjunct (1 woman). *Students:* 83 full-time (60 women), 116 part-time (89 women); includes 26 minority (18 Black or African American, non-Hispanic/Latino; 2 Asian, non-Hispanic/Latino; 4 Hispanic/Latino; 2 Two or more races, non-Hispanic/Latino), 5 international. Average age 31. In 2013, 50 master's awarded. *Degree requirements:* For master's, comprehensive exam (for some programs). *Entrance requirements:* For master's, GRE, minimum GPA of 3.0 (preferred), three letters of recommendation, official transcript (bachelor's, others as relevant), career goals statement. Additional exam requirements/recommendations for international students: Required—TOEFL (minimum score 550 paper-based; 79 iBT), IELTS (minimum score 6.5). *Application deadline:* For fall admission, 7/31 for domestic students, 6/1 for international students; for spring admission, 11/30 for domestic students, 10/15 for international students. Applications are processed on a rolling basis. Application fee: $30. Electronic applications accepted. Application fee is waived when completed online. *Financial support:* Career-related internships or fieldwork, scholarships/grants, and unspecified assistantships available. Financial award application deadline: 7/31; financial award applicants required to submit FAFSA. *Unit head:* Dr. Jan Stenette, Dean, School of Education and Human Development, 434-544-8662, Fax: 434-544-8483, E-mail: stennette@lynchburg.edu. *Application contact:* Anne Pingstock, Executive Assistant, Graduate Studies, 434-544-8383, Fax: 434-544-8483, E-mail: gradstudies@lynchburg.edu.
Website: http://www.lynchburg.edu/school-education-and-human-development.

Lyndon State College, Graduate Programs in Education, Lyndonville, VT 05851-0919. Offers education (M Ed), including curriculum and instruction, reading specialist, special education, teaching and counseling; natural sciences (MST), including science education. Part-time and evening/weekend programs available. *Degree requirements:* For master's, exam or major field project. *Entrance requirements:* Additional exam requirements/recommendations for international students: Recommended—TOEFL (minimum score 500 paper-based). *Faculty research:* Impaired reading, cognitive style, counseling relationship.

Lynn University, Donald E. and Helen L. Ross College of Education, Boca Raton, FL 33431-5598. Offers educational leadership (M Ed, Ed D); exceptional student education (M Ed). Part-time and evening/weekend programs available. *Faculty:* 2 full-time (both women), 6 part-time/adjunct (5 women). *Students:* 28 full-time (24 women), 54 part-time (28 women); includes 9 minority (8 Black or African American, non-Hispanic/Latino; 1 Hispanic/Latino), 8 international. Average age 36. 31 applicants, 97% accepted, 25 enrolled. In 2013, 29 master's, 7 doctorates awarded. *Degree requirements:* For master's, thesis (for some programs); for doctorate, thesis/dissertation, qualifying paper. *Entrance requirements:* For master's, bachelor's degree from accredited institution, minimum undergraduate GPA of 3.0, resume, 2 letters of recommendation, statement of professional goals; for doctorate, master's degree from accredited institution, minimum GPA of 3.5, resume, 2 letters of recommendation, professional practice statement, interview and presentation. Additional exam requirements/recommendations for international students: Required—TOEFL (minimum score 550 paper-based).

Application deadline: Applications are processed on a rolling basis. Application fee: $45. Electronic applications accepted. *Expenses:* Tuition: Full-time $23,760; part-time $660 per credit. *Required fees:* $300; $50 per term. Tuition and fees vary according to degree level and program. *Financial support:* Career-related internships or fieldwork, Federal Work-Study, institutionally sponsored loans, scholarships/grants, tuition waivers (partial), and unspecified assistantships available. Support available to part-time students. Financial award application deadline: 8/1; financial award applicants required to submit FAFSA. *Faculty research:* Non-traditional education, innovative curricula, multicultural education, simulation games. *Unit head:* Dr. Gregg Cox, Dean of College, 561-237-7210, E-mail: gcox@lynn.edu. *Application contact:* Steven Pruitt, Director of Graduate and Undergraduate Evening Admission, 561-237-7834, Fax: 561-237-7100, E-mail: spruitt@lynn.edu.
Website: http://www.lynn.edu/academics/colleges/education.

Madonna University, Programs in Education, Livonia, MI 48150-1173. Offers Catholic school leadership (MSA); educational leadership (MSA); learning disabilities (MAT); literacy education (MAT); teaching and learning (MAT). *Accreditation:* NCATE. Part-time and evening/weekend programs available. *Degree requirements:* For master's, thesis or alternative. Electronic applications accepted.

Maharishi University of Management, Graduate Studies, Department of Education, Fairfield, IA 52557. Offers teaching elementary education (MA); teaching secondary education (MA). *Degree requirements:* For master's, thesis or alternative. *Entrance requirements:* For master's, GRE, minimum GPA of 3.0. Additional exam requirements/recommendations for international students: Required—TOEFL. *Faculty research:* Unified field-based approach to education, moral climate, scientific study of teaching.

Malone University, Graduate Program in Education, Canton, OH 44709. Offers curriculum and instruction (MA); curriculum, instruction, and professional development (MA); educational leadership (principal license) (MA); intervention specialist (MA). Part-time and evening/weekend programs available. *Faculty:* 8 full-time (4 women), 12 part-time/adjunct (9 women). *Students:* 10 full-time (6 women), 59 part-time (44 women); includes 5 minority (2 Black or African American, non-Hispanic/Latino; 1 Hispanic/Latino; 2 Two or more races, non-Hispanic/Latino). Average age 32. In 2013, 13 master's awarded. *Degree requirements:* For master's, research project. *Entrance requirements:* For master's, minimum GPA of 3.0, teaching license. Additional exam requirements/recommendations for international students: Required—TOEFL (minimum score 550 paper-based; 79 iBT). *Application deadline:* Applications are processed on a rolling basis. *Financial support:* Tuition waivers (partial) available. Support available to part-time students. Financial award application deadline: 6/30. *Faculty research:* Educational leadership styles: Jesus as master teacher, assessment accommodations for English language learners, preparing culturally proficient teachers, using naturally occurring text in the classroom to meet the syntactic needs of students with learning disabilities, using tablet instructional technology to meet the needs of students with disabilities. *Unit head:* Dr. Moses B. Rumano, Director, 330-471-8349, Fax: 330-471-8563, E-mail: mrumano@malone.edu. *Application contact:* Dan DePasquale, Senior Recruiter, 330-471-8381, Fax: 330-471-8343, E-mail: depasquale@malone.edu. Website: http://www.malone.edu/admissions/graduate/education/.

Manchester University, Graduate Programs, Program in Education, North Manchester, IN 46962-1225. Offers M Ed. Part-time and evening/weekend programs available. Postbaccalaureate distance learning degree programs offered (minimal on-campus study). *Faculty:* 2 part-time/adjunct (1 woman). *Students:* 14 part-time (12 women). 21 applicants, 100% accepted, 14 enrolled. In 2013, 10 master's awarded. *Degree requirements:* For master's, 33 credits with minimum GPA of 3.0; culminating action research project or curriculum development project; final portfolio. *Entrance requirements:* For master's, baccalaureate degree from regionally-accredited institution; minimum cumulative undergraduate GPA of 3.0 or minimum of 9 semester hours of coursework in the M Ed with minimum B average. Additional exam requirements/recommendations for international students: Required—TOEFL (minimum score 550 paper-based; 79 iBT). *Application deadline:* Applications are processed on a rolling basis. Application fee: $25. Electronic applications accepted. Application fee is waived when completed online. *Expenses:* Contact institution. *Financial support:* Application deadline: 5/1; applicants required to submit FAFSA. *Unit head:* Dr. Michael Slavkin, Director of Teacher Education, 260-982-5056, E-mail: mlslavkin@manchester.edu. *Application contact:* Dr. Mark Huntington, Associate Dean for Academic Affairs, 260-982-5033, E-mail: mwhuntington@manchester.edu.

Manhattan College, Graduate Programs, School of Education and Health, Riverdale, NY 10471. Offers MA, MS, MS Ed, Certificate, Professional Diploma. *Accreditation:* Teacher Education Accreditation Council. Part-time and evening/weekend programs available. Postbaccalaureate distance learning degree programs offered (minimal on-campus study). *Faculty:* 11 full-time (7 women), 38 part-time/adjunct (24 women). *Students:* 94 full-time (79 women), 146 part-time (122 women). 279 applicants, 81% accepted, 157 enrolled. In 2013, 83 master's, 7 other advanced degrees awarded. *Degree requirements:* For master's and other advanced degree, thesis, internship. *Entrance requirements:* For master's and other advanced degree, minimum GPA of 3.0. Additional exam requirements/recommendations for international students: Required—TOEFL. *Application deadline:* For fall admission, 8/10 priority date for domestic students, 4/10 for international students; for spring admission, 1/7 priority date for domestic students, 8/1 for international students. Applications are processed on a rolling basis. Application fee: $60. *Expenses:* Tuition: Part-time $890 per credit. Part-time tuition and fees vary according to program. *Financial support:* In 2013–14, 6 students received support, including 1 research assistantship; scholarships/grants and tuition waivers (partial) also available. Financial award application deadline: 2/1. *Faculty research:* Leadership, assessment, professional development, school improvement. *Unit head:* Dr. Remigia Kushner, Program Director, 718-862-7473, Fax: 718-862-7816, E-mail: sbl@manhattan.edu. *Application contact:* William Bisset, Vice President for Enrollment, 718-862-7199, Fax: 718-862-8019, E-mail: william.bisset@manhattan.edu. Website: http://manhattan.edu/academics/education.

Manhattanville College, School of Education, Purchase, NY 10577-2132. Offers M Ed, MAT, MPS, Ed D. *Accreditation:* NCATE. Part-time and evening/weekend programs available. *Entrance requirements:* For master's, minimum undergraduate GPA of 3.0, 2 letters of recommendation. Additional exam requirements/recommendations for international students: Required—TOEFL (minimum score 550 paper-based). *Application deadline:* Applications are processed on a rolling basis. Application fee: $75. Electronic applications accepted. *Financial support:* Career-related internships or fieldwork, Federal Work-Study, institutionally sponsored loans, and unspecified assistantships available. Financial award application deadline: 3/1; financial award applicants required to submit FAFSA. *Unit head:* Dr. Shelley Wepner, Dean, 914-323-3153, Fax: 914-694-2386, E-mail: wepners@mville.edu. *Application contact:* Jeanine Pardey-Levine, Director of Admissions, 914-323-3208, Fax: 914-694-1732, E-mail: edschool@mville.edu.

See Display on next page and Close-Up on page 729.

Mansfield University of Pennsylvania, Graduate Studies, Department of Education and Special Education, Mansfield, PA 16933. Offers elementary education (M Ed); secondary education (MS); special education (M Ed). *Accreditation:* NCATE (one or

Education—General

more programs are accredited). Part-time and evening/weekend programs available. Postbaccalaureate distance learning degree programs offered (no on-campus study). *Degree requirements:* For master's, comprehensive exam, thesis optional. *Entrance requirements:* For master's, minimum GPA of 3.0. Additional exam requirements/recommendations for international students: Required—TOEFL (minimum score 550 paper-based). Electronic applications accepted.

Marian University, School of Education, Indianapolis, IN 46222-1997. Offers MAT. *Accreditation:* NCATE. Part-time and evening/weekend programs available. *Faculty:* 11 full-time (8 women), 19 part-time/adjunct (16 women). *Students:* 22 full-time (12 women), 327 part-time (220 women); includes 113 minority (67 Black or African American, non-Hispanic/Latino; 2 American Indian or Alaska Native, non-Hispanic/Latino; 11 Asian, non-Hispanic/Latino; 21 Hispanic/Latino; 12 Two or more races, non-Hispanic/Latino), 1 international. Average age 27. 177 applicants, 97% accepted, 158 enrolled. In 2013, 85 master's awarded. *Entrance requirements:* For master's, PRAXIS I and/or PRAXIS II. *Application deadline:* For fall admission, 2/1 priority date for domestic students. Applications are processed on a rolling basis. Application fee: $35. Electronic applications accepted. Application fee is waived when completed online. *Expenses: Tuition:* Part-time $400 per credit hour. Full-time tuition and fees vary according to degree level and program. *Financial support:* Applicants required to submit FAFSA. *Unit head:* Dr. Lindan Hill, Dean, 317-955-6089, Fax: 317-955-6448, E-mail: lhill@marian.edu. *Application contact:* Robert Kitchens, Director, Master's Bridge to Teaching Program, 317-955-6091, Fax: 317-955-6448, E-mail: rkitchens@marian.edu.

Marian University, School of Education, Fond du Lac, WI 54935-4699. Offers educational leadership (MAE, PhD); leadership studies (PhD); teacher development (MAE). PhD in leadership studies offered jointly with School of Business and Public Safety. *Accreditation:* NCATE. Part-time and evening/weekend programs available. Postbaccalaureate distance learning degree programs offered (minimal on-campus study). *Faculty:* 15 full-time (10 women), 22 part-time/adjunct (10 women). *Students:* 23 full-time (15 women), 281 part-time (197 women); includes 25 minority (13 Black or African American, non-Hispanic/Latino; 9 American Indian or Alaska Native, non-Hispanic/Latino; 2 Asian, non-Hispanic/Latino; 1 Hispanic/Latino). Average age 38. In 2013, 135 master's, 6 doctorates awarded. *Degree requirements:* For master's, exam, field-based experience project, portfolio; for doctorate, comprehensive exam, thesis/dissertation, field-based experience. *Entrance requirements:* For master's, minimum GPA of 3.0, BA in education or related field, teaching license; for doctorate, GRE, MAT, resume, 2 writing samples, interview. Additional exam requirements/recommendations for international students: Required—TOEFL (minimum score 525 paper-based; 70 iBT). *Application deadline:* Applications are processed on a rolling basis. Application fee: $50. *Expenses: Tuition:* Part-time $490 per credit hour. Tuition and fees vary according to degree level and program. *Financial support:* In 2013–14, 3 students received support. Federal Work-Study and institutionally sponsored loans available. Support available to part-time students. Financial award application deadline: 3/1; financial award applicants required to submit FAFSA. *Faculty research:* At-risk youth, multicultural issues, values in education, teaching/learning strategies. *Unit head:* Dr. Sue Stoddart, Dean, 920-923-8099, Fax: 920-923-7663, E-mail: sstoddart@marianuniversity.edu. *Application contact:* Rachel Benike, Admissions Counselor, 920-923-8118, Fax: 920-923-7154, E-mail: rlbenike43@marianuniversity.edu.
Website: http://soe.marianuniversity.edu/.

Marist College, Graduate Programs, School of Social and Behavioral Sciences, Poughkeepsie, NY 12601-1387. Offers education (M Ed, MA); mental health counseling (MA); school psychology (MA, Adv C). Part-time and evening/weekend programs available. *Degree requirements:* For master's, thesis optional. *Entrance requirements:* For master's, GRE General Test, letters of recommendation, minimum undergraduate GPA of 3.0, interview. Additional exam requirements/recommendations for international

students: Required—TOEFL (minimum score 550 paper-based; 80 iBT); Recommended—IELTS (minimum score 6.5). Electronic applications accepted. *Faculty research:* AIDS prevention, educational intervention, humanistic counseling research, aging and development, neuroimaging.

Marlboro College, Graduate and Professional Studies, Program in Teaching with Technology, Brattleboro, VT 05301. Offers MAT, Certificate. Part-time and evening/weekend programs available. Postbaccalaureate distance learning degree programs offered (minimal on-campus study). *Faculty:* 1 full-time (0 women), 10 part-time/adjunct (7 women). *Students:* 2 full-time (1 woman), 19 part-time (13 women). Average age 44. 6 applicants, 67% accepted, 2 enrolled. In 2013, 11 master's awarded. *Degree requirements:* For master's, 30 credits including capstone project. *Entrance requirements:* For master's, letter of intent, 2 letters of recommendation, transcripts. *Application deadline:* For fall admission, 7/1 priority date for domestic students; for winter admission, 11/1 priority date for domestic students; for spring admission, 3/1 priority date for domestic students. Applications are processed on a rolling basis. Application fee: $0. Electronic applications accepted. *Expenses: Tuition:* Part-time $685 per credit. Tuition and fees vary according to course load and program. *Financial support:* Applicants required to submit FAFSA. *Unit head:* Caleb Clark, Degree Chair, 802-258-9207, Fax: 802-258-9201, E-mail: cclark@marlboro.edu. *Application contact:* Matthew Livingston, Director of Graduate Admissions, 802-258-9209, Fax: 802-258-9201, E-mail: mlivingston@marlboro.edu.
Website: https://www.marlboro.edu/academics/graduate/mat.

Marquette University, Graduate School, College of Education, Milwaukee, WI 53201-1881. Offers M Ed, MA, MS, PhD, Certificate. *Accreditation:* NCATE. Part-time programs available. *Faculty:* 24 full-time (15 women), 30 part-time/adjunct (20 women). *Students:* 105 full-time (83 women), 118 part-time (77 women); includes 28 minority (10 Black or African American, non-Hispanic/Latino; 2 American Indian or Alaska Native, non-Hispanic/Latino; 4 Asian, non-Hispanic/Latino; 8 Hispanic/Latino; 4 Two or more races, non-Hispanic/Latino), 5 international. Average age 29. 296 applicants, 56% accepted, 99 enrolled. In 2013, 86 master's, 8 doctorates, 12 other advanced degrees awarded. Terminal master's awarded for partial completion of doctoral program. *Degree requirements:* For master's, comprehensive exam, thesis (for some programs); for doctorate, thesis/dissertation, qualifying exam, supporting minor. *Entrance requirements:* For master's, GRE General Test or MAT, official transcripts from all current and previous colleges/universities except Marquette, three letters of recommendation, statement of purpose; for doctorate, GRE General Test, MAT, sample of written work, official transcripts from all current and previous colleges/universities except Marquette, three letters of recommendation, statement of purpose, resume/curriculum vitae; for Certificate, GRE General Test or MAT, master's degree. Additional exam requirements/recommendations for international students: Required—TOEFL (minimum score 530 paper-based). *Application deadline:* For fall admission, 1/15 for domestic and international students. Application fee: $50. *Expenses:* Contact institution. *Financial support:* In 2013–14, 155 students received support, including 2 fellowships with full and partial tuition reimbursements available, 11 research assistantships with full tuition reimbursements available; scholarships/grants, health care benefits, tuition waivers (partial), and unspecified assistantships also available. Support available to part-time students. Financial award application deadline: 2/15. *Faculty research:* Parenting, psychology of motivation, reading assessment, socialization of educational administrators, education philosophy of Cardinal Newman. *Total annual research expenditures:* $200,057. *Unit head:* Dr. William Henk, Dean, 414-288-7376. *Application contact:* Dr. William Henk, Dean, 414-288-7376.
Website: http://www.marquette.edu/education/.

Marshall University, Academic Affairs Division, College of Education and Professional Development, Huntington, WV 25755. Offers MA, MAT, MS, Ed D, Certificate, Ed S.

Accreditation: NCATE. Part-time and evening/weekend programs available. *Faculty:* 42 full-time (20 women), 10 part-time/adjunct (7 women). *Students:* 357 full-time (262 women), 853 part-time (601 women); includes 84 minority (40 Black or African American, non-Hispanic/Latino; 2 American Indian or Alaska Native, non-Hispanic/Latino; 4 Asian, non-Hispanic/Latino; 16 Hispanic/Latino; 4 Native Hawaiian or other Pacific Islander, non-Hispanic/Latino; 18 Two or more races, non-Hispanic/Latino), 20 international. Average age 34. In 2013, 298 master's, 12 doctorates, 21 other advanced degrees awarded. *Degree requirements:* For master's, thesis optional, comprehensive or oral assessment. *Entrance requirements:* Additional exam requirements/recommendations for international students: Required—TOEFL. *Application deadline:* For fall admission, 5/1 for domestic students; for spring admission, 12/1 for domestic students. Applications are processed on a rolling basis. Application fee: $40. Electronic applications accepted. *Financial support:* Career-related internships or fieldwork, Federal Work-Study, tuition waivers (full and partial), and unspecified assistantships available. Support available to part-time students. Financial award applicants required to submit FAFSA. *Unit head:* Dr. Teresa Eagle, Dean, 304-746-8924, E-mail: thardman@marshall.edu. *Application contact:* Information Contact, 304-746-1900, Fax: 304-746-1902, E-mail: services@marshall.edu.
Website: http://www.marshall.edu/gsepd/.

Martin Luther College, Graduate Studies, New Ulm, MN 56073. Offers instruction (MS Ed); leadership (MS Ed); special education (MS Ed). Part-time programs available. Postbaccalaureate distance learning degree programs offered. *Degree requirements:* For master's, capstone project or comprehensive exam. *Entrance requirements:* For master's, undergraduate degree in education from an accredited college or university, minimum undergraduate GPA of 3.0. Electronic applications accepted.

Mary Baldwin College, Graduate Studies, Program in Teaching, Staunton, VA 24401-3610. Offers elementary education (MAT); middle grades education (MAT). *Accreditation:* Teacher Education Accreditation Council.

Marygrove College, Graduate Division, Program in the Art of Teaching, Detroit, MI 48221-2599. Offers MAT. Postbaccalaureate distance learning degree programs offered (no on-campus study). *Degree requirements:* For master's, portfolio. *Entrance requirements:* For master's, MAT, interview, minimum undergraduate GPA of 3.0, teaching certificate.

Marylhurst University, Department of Education, Marylhurst, OR 97036-0261. Offers M Ed, MA. Part-time programs available. *Degree requirements:* For master's, comprehensive exam. *Entrance requirements:* For master's, PRAXIS I or CBEST, resume, writing sample, fingerprint verification. Additional exam requirements/recommendations for international students: Required—TOEFL (minimum score 550 paper-based; 80 iBT).

Marymount University, School of Education and Human Services, Program in Education, Arlington, VA 22207-4299. Offers counselor education and supervision (Ed D); elementary education (M Ed); English as a second language (M Ed); professional studies (M Ed); secondary education (M Ed); special education: general curriculum (M Ed). *Accreditation:* NCATE. Part-time and evening/weekend programs available. *Faculty:* 8 full-time (6 women), 13 part-time/adjunct (9 women). *Students:* 76 full-time (67 women), 83 part-time (70 women); includes 30 minority (12 Black or African American, non-Hispanic/Latino; 2 American Indian or Alaska Native, non-Hispanic/Latino; 9 Asian, non-Hispanic/Latino; 6 Hispanic/Latino; 1 Two or more races, non-Hispanic/Latino), 12 international. Average age 31. 63 applicants, 95% accepted, 44 enrolled. In 2013, 88 master's awarded. *Degree requirements:* For master's, thesis or alternative; for doctorate, thesis/dissertation. *Entrance requirements:* For master's, GRE or MAT and PRAXIS I or SAT/ACT and VCLA, 2 letters of recommendation, resume, interview. Additional exam requirements/recommendations for international students: Required—TOEFL (minimum score 600 paper-based; 96 iBT), IELTS (minimum score 6.5). *Application deadline:* For fall admission, 7/1 for international students. Applications are processed on a rolling basis. Application fee: $40. Electronic applications accepted. *Expenses: Tuition:* Part-time $850 per credit. *Required fees:* $10 per credit. One-time fee: $200 part-time. Tuition and fees vary according to program. *Financial support:* In 2013–14, 41 students received support, including 4 research assistantships with full and partial tuition reimbursements available, 1 teaching assistantship with full and partial tuition reimbursement available; career-related internships or fieldwork, Federal Work-Study, scholarships/grants, and unspecified assistantships also available. Support available to part-time students. Financial award applicants required to submit FAFSA. *Unit head:* Dr. Lisa Turissini, Chair, 703-526-1668, Fax: 703-284-1631, E-mail: lisa.turissini@marymount.edu. *Application contact:* Francesca Reed, Director, Graduate Admissions, 703-284-5901, Fax: 703-527-3815, E-mail: grad.admissions@marymount.edu.
Website: http://www.marymount.edu/academics/schools/sehs/grad.aspx.

Maryville University of Saint Louis, School of Education, St. Louis, MO 63141-7299. Offers art education (MA Ed); early childhood education (MA Ed); educational leadership (Ed D); educational leadership: principal certification (MA Ed); elementary education (MA Ed); gifted education (MA Ed); higher education leadership (Ed D); literacy specialist (MA Ed); middle grades education (MA Ed); secondary teaching and inquiry (MA Ed); teacher as leader (MA Ed); teacher leadership (Ed D). *Accreditation:* NCATE. Part-time and evening/weekend programs available. *Faculty:* 10 full-time (6 women), 17 part-time/adjunct (13 women). *Students:* 21 full-time (17 women), 238 part-time (167 women); includes 64 minority (54 Black or African American, non-Hispanic/Latino; 2 Asian, non-Hispanic/Latino; 4 Hispanic/Latino; 4 Two or more races, non-Hispanic/Latino), 2 international. Average age 39. In 2013, 61 master's, 40 doctorates awarded. *Degree requirements:* For master's, thesis, project. *Entrance requirements:* For master's, minimum cumulative GPA of 3.0, 3 professional recommendations, essays, interview with program faculty; for doctorate, minimum GPA of 3.0, 3 professional recommendations, essay, interview, on-site writing sample. Additional exam requirements/recommendations for international students: Required—TOEFL (minimum score 550 paper-based). *Application deadline:* Applications are processed on a rolling basis. Application fee: $40 ($60 for international students). Electronic applications accepted. Application fee is waived when completed online. *Expenses: Tuition:* Full-time $23,812; part-time $728 per credit hour. *Required fees:* $395 per year. Tuition and fees vary according to course load, degree level and program. *Financial support:* Career-related internships or fieldwork, Federal Work-Study, tuition waivers (partial), and professional educator discounts available. Financial award application deadline: 3/1; financial award applicants required to submit FAFSA. *Faculty research:* Collaboration with public schools, pre-service program development, mathematics, diversity, literacy. *Unit head:* Dr. Cathy Bear, Dean, 314-529-9692, Fax: 314-529-9921, E-mail: cbear@maryville.edu. *Application contact:* Holly Stanwich, Graduate Admissions Coordinator, 314-529-9542, Fax: 314-529-9921, E-mail: teachered@maryville.edu.
Website: http://www.maryville.edu/ed/graduate-programs/.

Marywood University, Academic Affairs, Reap College of Education and Human Development, Department of Education, Scranton, PA 18509-1598. Offers administration and supervision of special education (MS); early childhood intervention (MS), including birth to age 9; higher education administration (MS); instructional leadership (M Ed); PreK-4 (MAT); reading education (MS); school leadership (MS); secondary/K-12 education (MAT); special education (MS). *Accreditation:* NCATE. *Entrance requirements:* Additional exam requirements/recommendations for international students: Required—TOEFL (minimum score 550 paper-based; 79 iBT). Application fee: $35. Electronic applications accepted. *Expenses: Tuition:* Part-time $775 per credit. Tuition and fees vary according to degree level. *Financial support:* Career-related internships or fieldwork, scholarships/grants, and unspecified assistantships available. Support available to part-time students. Financial award application deadline: 6/30; financial award applicants required to submit FAFSA. *Faculty research:* Catholic identity in higher education, school reading programs, teacher practice enhancement, cooperative learning, institutional and instructional leadership. *Unit head:* Dr. Patricia S. Arter, Chairperson, 570-348-6211 Ext. 2511, E-mail: psarter@marywood.edu. *Application contact:* Tammy Manka, Assistant Director of Graduate Admissions, 570-348-6211 Ext. 2322, E-mail: tmanka@marywood.edu.
Website: http://www.marywood.edu/education/.

Massachusetts College of Liberal Arts, Graduate Programs, North Adams, MA 01247-4100. Offers business (MBA); educational administration (M Ed); educational leadership (CAGS); instruction and curriculum (M Ed); instructional technology (M Ed); physical education and health (M Ed); reading (M Ed); special education (M Ed). Part-time and evening/weekend programs available. *Degree requirements:* For master's, thesis. *Entrance requirements:* For master's, writing sample.

McGill University, Faculty of Graduate and Postdoctoral Studies, Faculty of Education, Department of Integrated Studies in Education, Montréal, QC H3A 2T5, Canada. Offers culture and values in education (MA, PhD); curriculum studies (MA); educational leadership (MA, Certificate); educational studies (PhD); integrated studies in education (M Ed); second language education (MA, PhD).

McKendree University, Graduate Programs, Programs in Education, Lebanon, IL 62254-1299. Offers curriculum design and instruction (Ed D, Ed S); educational administration and leadership (MA Ed); educational studies (MA Ed); higher education administrative services (MA Ed); music education (MA Ed); reading (MA Ed); special education (MA Ed); teacher leadership (MA Ed); teaching certification (MA Ed). *Accreditation:* NCATE. Part-time and evening/weekend programs available. Postbaccalaureate distance learning degree programs offered (no on-campus study). *Entrance requirements:* For master's, official transcripts from all institutions previously attended, minimum GPA of 3.0, resume, references; for doctorate, GRE (within the past 5 years), master's degree in education and Ed S, or the equivalent, from regionally-accredited institution; official transcripts from all institutions previously attended; curriculum vitae/resume; essay/personal statement; two years of teaching/professional experience; for Ed S, GRE (within the past 5 years), master's degree in education from regionally-accredited institution of higher education; official transcripts from all institutions previously attended; curriculum vitae/resume; essay/personal statement; two years of teaching/professional experience. Additional exam requirements/recommendations for international students: Required—TOEFL. Electronic applications accepted.

McNeese State University, Doré School of Graduate Studies, Burton College of Education, Office of Student Teaching and Professional Education Services, Program in Multiple Levels Grades K-12, Lake Charles, LA 70609. Offers Postbaccalaureate Certificate. *Entrance requirements:* For degree, PRAXIS, 2 letters of recommendation, autobiography.

Medaille College, Program in Education, Buffalo, NY 14214-2695. Offers adolescent education (MS Ed); curriculum and instruction (MS Ed); education preparation (MS Ed); literacy (MS Ed); special education (MS). *Accreditation:* Teacher Education Accreditation Council. Part-time and evening/weekend programs available. *Faculty:* 12 full-time (9 women), 28 part-time/adjunct (19 women). *Students:* 159 full-time (123 women), 25 part-time (22 women); includes 8 minority (5 Black or African American, non-Hispanic/Latino; 3 Hispanic/Latino), 88 international. Average age 29. 209 applicants, 96% accepted, 61 enrolled. In 2013, 253 master's awarded. *Degree requirements:* For master's, comprehensive exam (for some programs), thesis or alternative. *Entrance requirements:* For master's, minimum undergraduate GPA of 2.7. Additional exam requirements/recommendations for international students: Required—TOEFL (minimum score 550 paper-based). *Application deadline:* For fall admission, 8/15 priority date for domestic students; for spring admission, 1/15 priority date for domestic students. Applications are processed on a rolling basis. Application fee: $35. Electronic applications accepted. *Financial support:* Federal Work-Study available. Financial award applicants required to submit FAFSA. *Faculty research:* Curriculum planning, truancy, tracking minority students, curriculum design, mentoring students. *Unit head:* Dr. Illana Lane, Dean, School of Education, 716-880-2553, E-mail: ilane@medaille.edu. *Application contact:* E-mail: sageadmissions@medaille.edu.
Website: http://www.medaille.edu.

Memorial University of Newfoundland, School of Graduate Studies, Faculty of Education, St. John's, NL A1C 5S7, Canada. Offers counseling psychology (M Ed); curriculum, teaching, and learning studies (M Ed); education (PhD); educational leadership studies (M Ed); information technology (M Ed); post-secondary studies (M Ed, Diploma), including health professional education (Diploma). Part-time programs available. *Degree requirements:* For master's, thesis optional, internship, paper folio, project; for doctorate, comprehensive exam, thesis/dissertation, thesis seminar, oral defense of thesis. *Entrance requirements:* For master's, undergraduate degree with at least 2nd class standing, 1-2 years work experience; for doctorate, minimum A average in graduate course work, MA in education, 2 years professional experience; for Diploma, 2nd class degree, 2 years of work experience with adult learners, appropriate academic qualifications and work experience in a health-related field. Electronic applications accepted. *Faculty research:* Critical thinking, literacy, cognitive studies and counseling, educational change, technology in instruction.

Mercer University, Graduate Studies, Cecil B. Day Campus, Tift College of Education (Atlanta), Macon, GA 31207-0003. Offers curriculum and instruction (PhD); early childhood education (M Ed, MAT, Ed S); educational leadership (PhD, Ed S); higher education leadership (M Ed); independent and charter school leadership (M Ed); middle grades education (M Ed, MAT); reading education (M Ed); school counseling (Ed S); secondary education (M Ed, MAT); teacher leadership (Ed S). *Accreditation:* NCATE. Part-time and evening/weekend programs available. *Faculty:* 40 full-time (20 women), 9 part-time/adjunct (4 women). *Students:* 240 full-time (197 women), 382 part-time (320 women); includes 343 minority (315 Black or African American, non-Hispanic/Latino; 4 American Indian or Alaska Native, non-Hispanic/Latino; 9 Asian, non-Hispanic/Latino; 9 Hispanic/Latino; 1 Native Hawaiian or other Pacific Islander, non-Hispanic/Latino; 5 Two or more races, non-Hispanic/Latino), 4 international. Average age 36. In 2013, 233 master's, 24 doctorates, 47 other advanced degrees awarded. *Degree requirements:* For master's and Ed S, research project; for doctorate, comprehensive exam, thesis/dissertation. *Entrance requirements:* For master's, GRE or MAT, minimum undergraduate GPA of 2.75; for doctorate, GRE; for Ed S, GRE or MAT, minimum GPA of 3.25; for EDS degrees in educational leadership and teacher leadership: 3 years of certified teaching experience. Additional exam requirements/recommendations for international students: Required—TOEFL. *Application deadline:* For fall admission, 8/1 for domestic and international students; for spring admission, 12/1 for domestic and international students; for summer admission, 5/1 for domestic and international students. Applications are processed on a rolling basis. Application fee: $25. *Expenses:*

Contact institution. *Financial support:* Federal Work-Study available. Support available to part-time students. Financial award application deadline: 5/1. *Faculty research:* Educational technology, multicultural and minority issues in education, educational leadership (P-12 and higher education), school discipline and school bullying, standards-based mathematics education. *Unit head:* Dr. Paige L. Tompkins, Interim Dean, 478-301-5397, Fax: 478-301-2280, E-mail: tompkins_pl@mercer.edu. *Application contact:* Dr. Allison Gilmore, Associate Dean for Graduate Teacher Education, 678-547-6333, Fax: 678-547-6055, E-mail: gilmore_a@mercer.edu.
Website: http://www.mercer.edu/education/.

Mercer University, Graduate Studies, Macon Campus, Tift College of Education (Macon), Macon, GA 31207-0003. Offers curriculum and instruction (PhD); education leadership (PhD), including P-12; educational leadership (Ed S); higher education (M Ed); teacher leadership (Ed S). *Accreditation:* NCATE. Part-time and evening/weekend programs available. Postbaccalaureate distance learning degree programs offered (minimal on-campus study). *Faculty:* 15 full-time (6 women), 2 part-time/adjunct (1 woman). *Students:* 39 full-time (20 women), 59 part-time (47 women); includes 41 minority (38 Black or African American, non-Hispanic/Latino; 1 Asian, non-Hispanic/Latino; 2 Hispanic/Latino), 2 international. Average age 35. In 2013, 7 master's, 18 doctorates awarded. *Degree requirements:* For master's, research project report; for doctorate, comprehensive exam, thesis/dissertation. *Entrance requirements:* For master's, GRE or MAT, minimum GPA of 2.75; for doctorate, GRE, minimum GPA of 3.5; interview; writing sample; 3 recommendations; for Ed S, GRE or MAT, minimum GPA of 3.5 (for Ed S in teacher leadership), 3.0 (for Ed S in educational leadership). Additional exam requirements/recommendations for international students: Required—TOEFL. *Application deadline:* For fall admission, 8/1 for domestic and international students; for spring admission, 12/1 for domestic and international students. Applications are processed on a rolling basis. Application fee: $35. *Expenses:* Contact institution. *Financial support:* Federal Work-Study and institutionally sponsored loans available. Support available to part-time students. Financial award application deadline: 5/1. *Faculty research:* Teacher effectiveness, specific learning disabilities, inclusion. *Unit head:* Dr. Paige L. Tompkins, Interim Dean, 478-301-5397, Fax: 478-301-2280, E-mail: tompkins_pl@mercer.edu. *Application contact:* Tracey M. Wofford, Associate Director of Admissions, 678-547-6422, Fax: 678-547-6367, E-mail: wofford_tm@mercer.edu.
Website: http://education.mercer.edu/graduate/.

Mercy College, School of Education, Dobbs Ferry, NY 10522-1189. Offers adolescence education (MS); childhood education (MS); early childhood education (MS); school building leadership (MS, Advanced Certificate); teaching English to speakers of other languages (TESOL) (MS, Advanced Certificate); teaching literacy (MS, Advanced Certificate); teaching literacy, birth-6 (MS); teaching literacy/grades 5-12 (MS). Part-time and evening/weekend programs available. Postbaccalaureate distance learning degree programs offered (no on-campus study). *Students:* 557 full-time (505 women), 905 part-time (744 women); includes 637 minority (292 Black or African American, non-Hispanic/Latino; 1 American Indian or Alaska Native, non-Hispanic/Latino; 12 Asian, non-Hispanic/Latino; 312 Hispanic/Latino; 20 Two or more races, non-Hispanic/Latino), 2 international. Average age 32. 891 applicants, 72% accepted, 461 enrolled. In 2013, 618 master's, 25 other advanced degrees awarded. *Degree requirements:* For master's, comprehensive exam (for some programs), thesis (for some programs). *Entrance requirements:* For master's, resume, undergraduate transcript. Additional exam requirements/recommendations for international students: Required—TOEFL (minimum score 600 paper-based; 100 iBT), IELTS (minimum score 8). *Application deadline:* For fall admission, 8/1 for international students. Applications are processed on a rolling basis. Application fee: $40. Electronic applications accepted. *Expenses: Tuition:* Full-time $19,344; part-time $806 per credit. *Required fees:* $580; $806 per credit. $145 per term. Tuition and fees vary according to course load, degree level and program. *Financial support:* Career-related internships or fieldwork, Federal Work-Study, scholarships/grants, and unspecified assistantships available. Support available to part-time students. Financial award applicants required to submit FAFSA. *Unit head:* Dr. Alfred S. Posamentier, Dean for the School of Education, 914-674-7350, E-mail: aposamentier@mercy.edu. *Application contact:* Allison Gurdineer, Senior Director of Admissions, 877-637-2946, Fax: 914-674-7382, E-mail: admissions@mercy.edu.
Website: https://www.mercy.edu/academics/school-of-education/.

Meredith College, John E. Weems Graduate School, School of Education, Raleigh, NC 27607-5298. Offers M Ed, MAT. *Accreditation:* NCATE. Part-time and evening/weekend programs available. *Degree requirements:* For master's, thesis optional. *Entrance requirements:* For master's, GRE General Test or MAT, minimum GPA of 2.5, teaching license, recommendations. Additional exam requirements/recommendations for international students: Required—TOEFL. Electronic applications accepted. *Expenses:* Contact institution.

Merrimack College, School of Education, North Andover, MA 01845-5800. Offers community engagement (M Ed), including community organizations, higher education, K-12 education; early childhood education (M Ed); elementary education (M Ed); English as a second language (PreK-6) (M Ed); English language learners (M Ed); general studies (M Ed); higher education (M Ed), including leadership and organizational development, student affairs; middle (M Ed); moderate disabilities (PreK-8) (M Ed); secondary (M Ed); teacher leadership (CAGS), including instructional leadership, reading specialist. Part-time and evening/weekend programs available. *Faculty:* 4 full-time (all women), 23 part-time/adjunct (15 women). *Students:* 127 full-time (104 women), 61 part-time (52 women); includes 3 minority (1 Asian, non-Hispanic/Latino; 2 Hispanic/Latino), 2 international. Average age 25. 403 applicants, 47% accepted, 138 enrolled. In 2013, 140 master's awarded. *Degree requirements:* For master's, practicum, portfolio, and state test (for licensure track); capstone (for higher education and community engagement tracks). *Entrance requirements:* For master's, MTEL (Massachusetts Tests for Educator Licensure), official transcripts from other colleges, resume, personal statement, 2 letters of recommendation, additional essay requirements for fellowships. Additional exam requirements/recommendations for international students: Required—TOEFL (minimum score 84 iBT), IELTS (minimum score 6.5). *Application deadline:* For fall admission, 8/15 for domestic and international students; for winter admission, 12/1 for domestic students, 11/15 for international students; for spring admission, 1/10 for domestic and international students; for summer admission, 5/10 for domestic and international students. Applications are processed on a rolling basis. Application fee: $0. Electronic applications accepted. Tuition and fees vary according to course load and program. *Financial support:* In 2013–14, 91 fellowships with full tuition reimbursements were awarded; career-related internships or fieldwork, scholarships/grants, and health care benefits also available. Support available to part-time students. Financial award applicants required to submit FAFSA. *Faculty research:* Expressive language, civic engagement, family life education, reading genres, the psychological process of aging. *Application contact:* Kristen English, Interim Director of Graduate Admission, 978-837-5073, E-mail: englishkr@merrimack.edu.
Website: http://www.merrimack.edu/academics/graduate/education/.

Metropolitan State University of Denver, School of Professional Studies, Denver, CO 80217-3362. Offers elementary education (MAT); special education (MAT).

Miami University, College of Education, Health and Society, Oxford, OH 45056. Offers M Ed, MA, MAT, MS, Ed D, PhD, Ed S. *Accreditation:* NCATE. *Expenses:* Tuition, state resident: full-time $12,634; part-time $526 per credit hour. Tuition, nonresident: full-time $27,892; part-time $1162 per credit hour. Part-time tuition and fees vary according to course load, campus/location and program. *Unit head:* Dr. Carine M. Feyten, Dean, 513-529-6317, E-mail: ehs@miamioh.edu. *Application contact:* Graduate Admission Coordinator, 513-529-3734, E-mail: gradschool@miamioh.edu.
Website: http://www.MiamiOH.edu/eap/.

Michigan State University, The Graduate School, College of Education, East Lansing, MI 48824. Offers MA, MS, PhD, Ed S. *Accreditation:* Teacher Education Accreditation Council. *Entrance requirements:* Additional exam requirements/recommendations for international students: Required—TOEFL. Electronic applications accepted.

MidAmerica Nazarene University, Graduate Studies in Education, Olathe, KS 66062-1899. Offers ESOL (M Ed); professional teaching (M Ed); special education (MA); technology enhanced teaching (M Ed). *Accreditation:* NCATE. Part-time and evening/weekend programs available. Postbaccalaureate distance learning degree programs offered (no on-campus study). *Degree requirements:* For master's, thesis or alternative, creative project, technology leadership practicum. *Entrance requirements:* For master's, minimum undergraduate GPA of 2.8, 2 years of teaching experience. *Expenses:* Contact institution.

Middle Tennessee State University, College of Graduate Studies, College of Education, Murfreesboro, TN 37132. Offers M Ed, PhD, Ed S. *Accreditation:* NCATE. Part-time and evening/weekend programs available. Postbaccalaureate distance learning degree programs offered. *Faculty:* 36 full-time (20 women), 29 part-time/adjunct (19 women). *Degree requirements:* For master's, comprehensive exam, thesis (for some programs); for doctorate, comprehensive exam, thesis/dissertation; for Ed S, comprehensive exam, thesis or alternative. *Entrance requirements:* For master's, doctorate, and Ed S, GRE, MAT, current teaching license or PRAXIS. Additional exam requirements/recommendations for international students: Required—TOEFL (minimum score 525 paper-based; 71 iBT) or IELTS (minimum score 6). *Application deadline:* For fall admission, 6/1 for domestic and international students. Applications are processed on a rolling basis. Application fee: $25 ($30 for international students). Electronic applications accepted. *Financial support:* In 2013–14, 21 students received support. Tuition waivers available. Support available to part-time students. Financial award application deadline: 5/1; financial award applicants required to submit FAFSA. *Unit head:* Dr. Lana Seivers, Dean, 615-898-2874, Fax: 615-898-5188, E-mail: lana.seivers@mtsu.edu. *Application contact:* Dr. Michael D. Allen, Vice Provost for Research and Dean, 615-898-2840, Fax: 615-904-8020, E-mail: michael.allen@mtsu.edu.

Midway College, Graduate Programs, Midway, KY 40347-1120. Offers education (MAT); leadership (MBA). *Degree requirements:* For master's, capstone course. *Entrance requirements:* For master's, GMAT (for MBA); GRE or PRAXIS I (for MAT), bachelor's degree; interview; minimum GPA of 3.0 (for MBA), 2.75 (for MAT); 3 years of professional work experience (for MBA). Additional exam requirements/recommendations for international students: Required—TOEFL (minimum score 550 paper-based; 80 iBT).

Midwestern State University, Graduate School, West College of Education, Wichita Falls, TX 76308. Offers M Ed, MA. Part-time and evening/weekend programs available. *Degree requirements:* For master's, comprehensive exam, thesis (for some programs). *Entrance requirements:* For master's, GRE General Test or MAT. Additional exam requirements/recommendations for international students: Required—TOEFL (minimum score 550 paper-based). *Application deadline:* For fall admission, 7/1 priority date for domestic students, 4/1 for international students; for spring admission, 11/1 priority date for domestic students, 8/1 for international students. Applications are processed on a rolling basis. Application fee: $35 ($50 for international students). Electronic applications accepted. *Expenses:* Tuition, state resident: full-time $3627; part-time $201.50 per credit hour. Tuition, nonresident: full-time $10,899; part-time $605.50 per credit hour. *Required fees:* $1357. *Financial support:* Teaching assistantships with partial tuition reimbursements, career-related internships or fieldwork, Federal Work-Study, institutionally sponsored loans, tuition waivers (partial), and unspecified assistantships available. Support available to part-time students. Financial award application deadline: 3/1; financial award applicants required to submit FAFSA. *Faculty research:* Assessment, reading education, vocabulary instruction, current role of the principal, educational research methodology. *Unit head:* Dr. Matthew Capps, Dean, 940-397-4138, Fax: 940-397-4694, E-mail: matthew.capps@mwsu.edu. *Application contact:* Dr. Matthew Capps, Dean, 940-397-4138, Fax: 940-397-4694, E-mail: matthew.capps@mwsu.edu.
Website: http://www.mwsu.edu/academics/education/.

Millersville University of Pennsylvania, College of Graduate and Professional Studies, School of Education, Millersville, PA 17551-0302. Offers M Ed, MS. *Accreditation:* NCATE. Part-time and evening/weekend programs available. *Faculty:* 74 full-time (37 women), 54 part-time/adjunct (33 women). *Students:* 105 full-time (77 women), 223 part-time (160 women); includes 26 minority (8 Black or African American, non-Hispanic/Latino; 1 American Indian or Alaska Native, non-Hispanic/Latino; 4 Asian, non-Hispanic/Latino; 12 Hispanic/Latino; 1 Two or more races, non-Hispanic/Latino), 2 international. Average age 28. 141 applicants, 80% accepted, 80 enrolled. In 2013, 139 master's awarded. *Degree requirements:* For master's, comprehensive exam (for some programs), thesis optional, graded portfolio (educational foundations). *Entrance requirements:* For master's, GRE or MAT, 3 letters of recommendation, copy of teaching certificate, official transcript, goal statement. Additional exam requirements/recommendations for international students: Required—TOEFL (minimum score 550 paper-based, 79 iBT) or IELTS (minimum score 6). *Application deadline:* For fall admission, 1/15 priority date for domestic and international students; for winter admission, 10/1 priority date for domestic and international students; for spring admission, 10/1 priority date for domestic and international students. Applications are processed on a rolling basis. Application fee: $40. Electronic applications accepted. *Expenses:* Tuition, state resident: full-time $7956; part-time $442 per credit. Tuition, nonresident: full-time $11,934; part-time $663 per credit. *Required fees:* $2196; $122 per credit. Tuition and fees vary according to course load. *Financial support:* In 2013–14, 65 students received support, including 65 research assistantships with full tuition reimbursements available (averaging $4,542 per year); institutionally sponsored loans and unspecified assistantships also available. Support available to part-time students. Financial award application deadline: 3/15; financial award applicants required to submit FAFSA. *Faculty research:* Co-teaching model for clinical experiences, professional development schools. *Unit head:* Dr. Helena Tuleya-Payne, Interim Dean, 717-872-3379, Fax: 717-872-3856, E-mail: helena.tuleya-payne@millersville.edu. *Application contact:* Dr. Victor S. DeSantis, Dean of College of Graduate and Professional Studies/Associate Provost for Civic and Community Engagement, 717-872-3099, Fax: 717-872-3453, E-mail: victor.desantis@millersville.edu.
Website: http://www.millersville.edu/education/.

Milligan College, Area of Teacher Education, Milligan College, TN 37682. Offers M Ed. *Accreditation:* NCATE. Part-time programs available. *Degree requirements:* For master's, thesis, portfolio, research project. *Entrance requirements:* For master's, MAT or GRE General Test, interview. Electronic applications accepted. *Expenses:* Contact

institution. *Faculty research:* Teacher education evaluation, professional development centers, internship, early childhood, technology.

Mills College, Graduate Studies, School of Education, Oakland, CA 94613-1000. Offers child life in hospitals (MA); early childhood education (MA); education (MA), including art education, curriculum and instruction, elementary education, English education, foreign language education, mathematics education, science education, secondary education, social studies education, teaching; educational leadership (MA, Ed D). Part-time and evening/weekend programs available. *Faculty:* 10 full-time (7 women), 13 part-time/adjunct (10 women). *Students:* 154 full-time (136 women), 54 part-time (47 women); includes 96 minority (32 Black or African American, non-Hispanic/Latino; 1 American Indian or Alaska Native, non-Hispanic/Latino; 23 Asian, non-Hispanic/Latino; 27 Hispanic/Latino; 1 Native Hawaiian or other Pacific Islander, non-Hispanic/Latino; 12 Two or more races, non-Hispanic/Latino), 2 international. Average age 25. 222 applicants, 89% accepted, 110 enrolled. In 2013, 96 master's, 38 doctorates awarded. Terminal master's awarded for partial completion of doctoral program. *Degree requirements:* For master's, comprehensive exam, thesis (for some programs); for doctorate, thesis/dissertation. *Entrance requirements:* For master's, statement of purpose, official transcript, 3 recommendations. Additional exam requirements/recommendations for international students: Required—TOEFL (minimum score 550 paper-based; 80 iBT) or IELTS (minimum score 6). *Application deadline:* For fall admission, 12/31 priority date for domestic students, 12/15 for international students; for spring admission, 11/1 priority date for domestic students, 10/1 for international students. Applications are processed on a rolling basis. Application fee: $50. Electronic applications accepted. *Expenses: Tuition:* Full-time $29,860. *Required fees:* $1134. Part-time tuition and fees vary according to course load, degree level and program. *Financial support:* In 2013–14, 130 students received support, including 130 fellowships with full and partial tuition reimbursements available (averaging $7,565 per year); career-related internships or fieldwork and scholarships/grants also available. Support available to part-time students. Financial award application deadline: 2/1; financial award applicants required to submit FAFSA. *Faculty research:* Early childhood education, teacher preparation, educational leadership. *Total annual research expenditures:* $3.5 million. *Unit head:* Dr. Katherine Schultz, Department Head, 510-430-3384, Fax: 510-430-2159, E-mail: kschultz@mills.edu. *Application contact:* Shrim Bathey, Director of Graduate Admission, 510-430-3309, Fax: 510-430-2159, E-mail: grad-admission@mills.edu.
Website: http://www.mills.edu/education.

Minnesota State University Mankato, College of Graduate Studies, College of Education, Mankato, MN 56001. Offers MAT, MS, Ed D, Certificate, SP. *Accreditation:* NCATE. Part-time and evening/weekend programs available. *Students:* 197 full-time (144 women), 516 part-time (372 women). In 2013, 46 other advanced degrees awarded. *Degree requirements:* For master's, comprehensive exam, thesis or alternative; for other advanced degree, thesis. *Entrance requirements:* For master's, GRE or MAT, minimum GPA of 3.0 during previous 2 years; for other advanced degree, minimum GPA of 3.0. Additional exam requirements/recommendations for international students: Required—TOEFL. *Application deadline:* Applications are processed on a rolling basis. Application fee: $40. Electronic applications accepted. *Financial support:* Fellowships with partial tuition reimbursements, research assistantships with full tuition reimbursements, teaching assistantships with full tuition reimbursements, career-related internships or fieldwork, Federal Work-Study, institutionally sponsored loans, and unspecified assistantships available. Support available to part-time students. Financial award application deadline: 3/15; financial award applicants required to submit FAFSA. *Faculty research:* Longitudinal studies of alternative education graduates, student achievement scores. *Unit head:* Dr. Jean Haar, Interim Dean, 507-389-5445. *Application contact:* 507-389-2321, E-mail: grad@mnsu.edu.

Minnesota State University Moorhead, Graduate Studies, College of Education and Human Services, Moorhead, MN 56563-0002. Offers counseling and student affairs (MS); curriculum and instruction (MS); educational leadership (MS, Ed S); nursing (MS); reading (MS); special education (MS); speech-language pathology (MS). *Accreditation:* NCATE. Part-time and evening/weekend programs available. *Degree requirements:* For master's, comprehensive exam, final oral exam, project or thesis. *Entrance requirements:* Additional exam requirements/recommendations for international students: Required—TOEFL. Electronic applications accepted.

Misericordia University, College of Professional Studies and Social Sciences, Program in Education, Dallas, PA 18612-1098. Offers instructional technology (MS); reading specialist (MS); special education (MS). Part-time and evening/weekend programs available. *Faculty:* 1 full-time (0 women), 12 part-time/adjunct (8 women). *Students:* 44 part-time (35 women); includes 1 minority (Hispanic/Latino). Average age 32. In 2013, 24 master's awarded. *Entrance requirements:* For master's, minimum undergraduate GPA of 3.0. Additional exam requirements/recommendations for international students: Required—TOEFL. *Application deadline:* Applications are processed on a rolling basis. Application fee: $35. Electronic applications accepted. *Expenses: Tuition:* Full-time $14,450; part-time $680 per credit. Tuition and fees vary according to degree level. *Financial support:* In 2013–14, 11 students received support. Scholarships/grants available. Support available to part-time students. Financial award application deadline: 6/30; financial award applicants required to submit FAFSA. *Unit head:* Dr. Steven Broskoske, Associate Professor, Education Department, 570-674-6761, E-mail: sbroskos@misericordia.edu. *Application contact:* David Pasquini, Assistant Director of Admissions, 570-674-8183, Fax: 570-674-6232, E-mail: dpasquin@misericordia.edu.
Website: http://www.misericordia.edu/misericordia_pg.cfm?page_id=387&subcat_id=108.

Mississippi College, Graduate School, School of Education, Clinton, MS 39058. Offers M Ed, MS, Ed D, Ed S. *Accreditation:* NCATE. Part-time and evening/weekend programs available. Postbaccalaureate distance learning degree programs offered (no on-campus study). *Degree requirements:* For master's, comprehensive exam, thesis optional. *Entrance requirements:* For master's, GRE or NTE, minimum GPA of 2.5, Class A Certificate (for some programs); for Ed S, NTE, minimum GPA of 3.0. Additional exam requirements/recommendations for international students: Recommended—TOEFL, IELTS. Electronic applications accepted.

Mississippi State University, College of Education, Mississippi State, MS 39762. Offers MAT, MS, MSIT, PhD, Ed S. *Accreditation:* NCATE. Part-time and evening/weekend programs available. Postbaccalaureate distance learning degree programs offered (minimal on-campus study). *Faculty:* 51 full-time (31 women). *Students:* 309 full-time (191 women), 459 part-time (333 women); includes 288 minority (262 Black or African American, non-Hispanic/Latino; 7 American Indian or Alaska Native, non-Hispanic/Latino; 4 Asian, non-Hispanic/Latino; 7 Hispanic/Latino; 1 Native Hawaiian or other Pacific Islander, non-Hispanic/Latino; 7 Two or more races, non-Hispanic/Latino), 10 international. Average age 34. 741 applicants, 34% accepted, 199 enrolled. In 2013, 204 master's, 25 doctorates, 18 other advanced degrees awarded. Terminal master's awarded for partial completion of doctoral program. *Degree requirements:* For master's, thesis optional, comprehensive oral or written exam; for doctorate, thesis/dissertation; for Ed S, thesis or alternative, final written or oral exam. *Entrance requirements:* For master's, doctorate, and Ed S, GRE. Additional exam requirements/recommendations

for international students: Required—TOEFL (minimum score 550 paper-based; 79 iBT); Recommended—IELTS (minimum score 6.5). *Application deadline:* For fall admission, 7/1 for domestic students, 5/1 for international students; for spring admission, 11/1 for domestic students, 9/1 for international students. Applications are processed on a rolling basis. Application fee: $60. Electronic applications accepted. *Financial support:* In 2013–14, 11 research assistantships (averaging $10,488 per year), 24 teaching assistantships (averaging $9,132 per year) were awarded; career-related internships or fieldwork, Federal Work-Study, institutionally sponsored loans, scholarships/grants, and unspecified assistantships also available. Financial award applicants required to submit FAFSA. *Faculty research:* Leadership behavior, creativity measures, early childhood education, employability of the blind, quality indicators of professional educators. *Total annual research expenditures:* $1.9 million. *Unit head:* Dr. Richard Blackbourn, Dean, 662-325-3717, Fax: 662-325-8784, E-mail: rlb277@msstate.edu. *Application contact:* Dr. Terry Jayroe, Associate Dean, 662-325-7403, Fax: 662-325-1967, E-mail: dkarriem@colled.msstate.edu.
Website: http://www.educ.msstate.edu/.

Mississippi University for Women, Graduate School, College of Education and Human Sciences, Columbus, MS 39701-9998. Offers differentiated instruction (M Ed); educational leadership (M Ed); gifted studies (M Ed); reading/literacy (M Ed); teaching (MAT). *Accreditation:* ASHA; NCATE. Part-time programs available. *Degree requirements:* For master's, comprehensive exam, thesis optional. *Entrance requirements:* For master's, GRE General Test or NTE (M Ed in gifted education or MS in speech/language pathology), MAT (M Ed in instructional management), minimum QPA of 3.0.

Mississippi Valley State University, Department of Education, Itta Bena, MS 38941-1400. Offers education (MAT); elementary education (MA). *Accreditation:* NCATE.

Missouri Baptist University, Graduate Programs, St. Louis, MO 63141-8660. Offers business administration (MBA); Christian ministries (MACM); counseling (MAC); education (MSE); education administration (MEA); educational leadership (MSE, Ed S); teaching (MAT).

Missouri Southern State University, Program in Teaching, Joplin, MO 64801-1595. Offers MAT. Program offered jointly with Missouri State University. *Accreditation:* NCATE. *Degree requirements:* For master's, research seminar.

Molloy College, Graduate Education Program, Rockville Centre, NY 11571-5002. Offers MS Ed, Advanced Certificate. *Accreditation:* NCATE. *Faculty:* 18 full-time (15 women), 7 part-time/adjunct (5 women). *Students:* 79 full-time (57 women), 175 part-time (130 women); includes 34 minority (8 Black or African American, non-Hispanic/Latino; 2 Asian, non-Hispanic/Latino; 23 Hispanic/Latino; 1 Two or more races, non-Hispanic/Latino). Average age 28. 129 applicants, 71% accepted, 85 enrolled. In 2013, 90 master's, 4 Advanced Certificates awarded. *Application deadline:* Applications are processed on a rolling basis. Application fee: $60. *Expenses: Tuition:* Full-time $16,920; part-time $940 per credit. *Required fees:* $880. *Faculty research:* Teaching English to students of other languages, learning needs of students with disabilities, diverse classrooms/multicultural education, multiple intelligences/emotional intelligences, learning styles. *Unit head:* Joanne O'Brien, Associate Dean/Director, 516-323-3116, E-mail: jobrien@molloy.edu. *Application contact:* Alina Haitz, Assistant Director of Graduate Admissions, 516-323-4008, E-mail: ahaitz@molloy.edu.

Monmouth University, The Graduate School, School of Education, West Long Branch, NJ 07764-1898. Offers applied behavioral analysis (Certificate); autism (Certificate); initial certification (MAT), including elementary level, K-12, secondary level; principal (MS Ed); principal/school administrator (MS Ed); reading specialist (MS Ed); school counseling (MS Ed); special education (MS Ed), including autism, learning disabilities teacher consultant, teacher of students with disabilities, teaching in inclusive settings; speech-language pathology (MS Ed); student affairs and college counseling (MS Ed); teaching English to speakers of other languages (TESOL) (Certificate). *Accreditation:* NCATE. Part-time and evening/weekend programs available. *Faculty:* 15 full-time (11 women), 19 part-time/adjunct (17 women). *Students:* 125 full-time (97 women), 168 part-time (146 women); includes 38 minority (12 Black or African American, non-Hispanic/Latino; 5 Asian, non-Hispanic/Latino; 16 Hispanic/Latino; 5 Two or more races, non-Hispanic/Latino). Average age 28. 176 applicants, 90% accepted, 112 enrolled. In 2013, 147 master's awarded. *Entrance requirements:* For master's, GRE within last 5 years (for MS Ed in speech-language pathology), minimum GPA of 3.0 in major; 2 letters of recommendation (for some programs), resume, personal statement or essay (depending on degree program). Additional exam requirements/recommendations for international students: Required—TOEFL (minimum score 550 paper-based; 79 iBT), IELTS (minimum score 6), Michigan English Language Assessment Battery (minimum score 77). *Application deadline:* For fall admission, 7/15 priority date for domestic students, 7/1 for international students; for spring admission, 11/15 priority date for domestic students, 11/1 for international students. Applications are processed on a rolling basis. Application fee: $50. Electronic applications accepted. *Expenses: Tuition:* Part-time $1004 per credit hour. *Required fees:* $157 per semester. *Financial support:* In 2013–14, 191 students received support, including 159 fellowships (averaging $2,786 per year), 30 research assistantships (averaging $8,755 per year); career-related internships or fieldwork, scholarships/grants, and unspecified assistantships also available. Support available to part-time students. Financial award applicants required to submit FAFSA. *Faculty research:* Multicultural literacy, science and mathematics teaching strategies, teacher as reflective practitioner, children with disabilities. *Unit head:* Dr. Jason Barr, Program Director, 732-263-5238, Fax: 732-263-5277, E-mail: jbarr@monmouth.edu. *Application contact:* Lauren Vento-Cifelli, Associate Vice President of Undergraduate and Graduate Admission, 732-571-3452, Fax: 732-263-5123, E-mail: gradadm@monmouth.edu.
Website: http://www.monmouth.edu/academics/schools/education/default.asp.

Montana State University, College of Graduate Studies, College of Education, Health, and Human Development, Department of Education, Bozeman, MT 59717. Offers adult and higher education (Ed D); curriculum and instruction (M Ed, Ed D), including professional educator (M Ed); technology education (M Ed); education (M Ed), including adult and higher education, educational leadership, school counseling; educational leadership (Ed D, Ed S). *Accreditation:* Teacher Education Accreditation Council. Part-time programs available. Postbaccalaureate distance learning degree programs offered (minimal on-campus study). *Degree requirements:* For master's, comprehensive exam; for doctorate, comprehensive exam, thesis/dissertation. *Entrance requirements:* For master's, GRE, 3 letters of reference, essays, BA transcripts; for doctorate, GRE, MAT, 3 letters of reference, essay, BA and M Ed transcripts; for Ed S, PRAXIS. Additional exam requirements/recommendations for international students: Required—TOEFL (minimum score 550 paper-based). Electronic applications accepted. *Faculty research:* Critical literacy; standards-based education; school Improvement, organizational change, leadership in rural education, leadership in Indian education; student Learning; multicultural/culturally responsive education for social justice Native American indigenous education, community-centered education teacher preparation.

Montana State University Billings, College of Education, Billings, MT 59101-0298. Offers M Ed, MS Sp Ed, Certificate. *Accreditation:* NCATE. Part-time programs available. Postbaccalaureate distance learning degree programs offered (minimal on-campus study). *Degree requirements:* For master's, thesis optional. *Entrance*

requirements: For master's, GRE General Test. *Application deadline:* For fall admission, 7/15 for international students; for spring admission, 12/1 for international students. Applications are processed on a rolling basis. Application fee: $40. *Expenses:* Tuition, state resident: full-time $2653.75; part-time $1718 per semester. Tuition, nonresident: full-time $7015; part-time $4640 per semester. *Required fees:* $2445; $444 per credit. *Financial support:* Research assistantships with partial tuition reimbursements, teaching assistantships with partial tuition reimbursements, career-related internships or fieldwork, Federal Work-Study, institutionally sponsored loans, scholarships/grants, tuition waivers (partial), and unspecified assistantships available. Support available to part-time students. Financial award application deadline: 5/1; financial award applicants required to submit FAFSA. *Faculty research:* Social studies education, science education. *Unit head:* Dr. Mary Susan Fishbaugh, Dean, 406-657-2285, Fax: 406-657-2299, E-mail: mfishbaugh@msubillings.edu. *Application contact:* David M. Sullivan, Graduate Studies Counselor, 406-657-2053, Fax: 406-657-2299, E-mail: dsullivan@msubillings.edu.
Website: http://www.msubillings.edu/coe/.

Montana State University–Northern, Graduate Programs, Havre, MT 59501-7751. Offers counselor education (M Ed); learning development (M Ed). Part-time and evening/weekend programs available. Postbaccalaureate distance learning degree programs offered (minimal on-campus study). *Degree requirements:* For master's, comprehensive exam, oral exams or thesis. *Entrance requirements:* For master's, GRE General Test or MAT, minimum GPA of 3.0. Electronic applications accepted.

Montclair State University, The Graduate School, College of Education and Human Services, Montclair, NJ 07043-1624. Offers M Ed, MA, MAT, MPH, MS, Ed D, PhD, Certificate, Post-Master's Certificate, Postbaccalaureate Certificate. *Accreditation:* NCATE. Part-time and evening/weekend programs available. *Degree requirements:* For master's, comprehensive exam (for some programs), thesis (for some programs); for doctorate, comprehensive exam, thesis/dissertation. *Entrance requirements:* For master's, GRE, GMAT, MAT, 2 letters of recommendation; for doctorate, GRE General Test, 3 letters of recommendation. Additional exam requirements/recommendations for international students: Required—TOEFL (minimum score 83 iBT) or IELTS. Electronic applications accepted. *Faculty research:* Key factors in the preparation of teachers for urban schools, factors affecting upper extremity motion patterns and injuries, implementation fidelity of instructional interventions. data-based decision-making in educational contexts, nutrition and physical activity of the aging population in the U. S.

Moravian College, Moravian College Comenius Center, Education Programs, Bethlehem, PA 18018-6650. Offers curriculum and instruction (M Ed); education (MAT). Part-time and evening/weekend programs available. *Degree requirements:* For master's, thesis. *Entrance requirements:* For master's, state teacher certification.

Morehead State University, Graduate Programs, College of Education, Morehead, KY 40351. Offers MA, MA Ed, MAT, Ed S. *Accreditation:* NCATE. Part-time and evening/weekend programs available. *Degree requirements:* For master's, comprehensive exam, thesis or alternative; for Ed S, thesis. *Entrance requirements:* For master's, GRE General Test or PRAXIS, minimum overall undergraduate GPA of 2.5; for Ed S, GRE General Test, interview, master's degree, minimum GPA of 3.5, work experience. Additional exam requirements/recommendations for international students: Required—TOEFL (minimum score 500 paper-based). Electronic applications accepted. *Faculty research:* Regional economic development, computer applications for school administrators, effectiveness of teacher interns, perceptual processes, alcoholism.

Morgan State University, School of Graduate Studies, School of Education and Urban Studies, Baltimore, MD 21251. Offers MA, MAT, MS, Ed D, PhD. Part-time programs available. *Degree requirements:* For master's, comprehensive exam; for doctorate, comprehensive exam, thesis/dissertation. *Entrance requirements:* For doctorate, GRE General Test or MAT. Additional exam requirements/recommendations for international students: Required—TOEFL (minimum score 550 paper-based). *Faculty research:* Multicultural education, cooperative learning, psychology of cognition.

Morningside College, Graduate Division, Department of Education, Sioux City, IA 51106. Offers professional educator (MAT); special education: instructional strategist I: mild/moderate elementary (K-6) (MAT); special education: instructional strategist II-mild/moderate secondary (7-12) (MAT); special education: K-12 instructional strategist II-behavior disorders/learning disabilities (MAT); special education: K-12 instructional strategist II-mental disabilities (MAT). Part-time and evening/weekend programs available. *Entrance requirements:* For master's, MAT, writing sample.

Mount Aloysius College, Program in Education, Cresson, PA 16630-1999. Offers MS. Part-time programs available.

Mount Mary University, Graduate Division, Programs in Education, Milwaukee, WI 53222-4597. Offers education (MA); professional development (MA). Part-time and evening/weekend programs available. *Faculty:* 3 full-time (all women), 3 part-time/adjunct (2 women). *Students:* 7 full-time (5 women), 28 part-time (all women); includes 6 minority (4 Black or African American, non-Hispanic/Latino; 1 Asian, non-Hispanic/Latino; 1 Hispanic/Latino), 1 international. Average age 38. 3 applicants, 100% accepted, 3 enrolled. In 2013, 16 master's awarded. *Degree requirements:* For master's, action research project. *Entrance requirements:* For master's, minimum GPA of 2.75, teaching license. Additional exam requirements/recommendations for international students: Required—TOEFL (minimum score 80 iBT) or IELTS (minimum score 6.5). *Application deadline:* For fall admission, 8/1 for domestic and international students; for spring admission, 12/1 for domestic and international students. Applications are processed on a rolling basis. Application fee: $45 ($100 for international students). Electronic applications accepted. *Expenses:* Contact institution. *Financial support:* Federal Work-Study available. Support available to part-time students. Financial award application deadline: 5/1; financial award applicants required to submit FAFSA. *Faculty research:* Staff development, writing across the curriculum, effective schools, critical thinking skills, mathematics education. *Unit head:* Dr. Deb Dosemagen, Director, 414-256-1214, E-mail: dosemagd@mtmary.edu. *Application contact:* Dr. Douglas J. Mickelson, Dean for Graduate Education, 414-256-1252, Fax: 414-256-0167, E-mail: mickelsd@mtmary.edu.
Website: http://www.mtmary.edu/majors-programs/graduate/education/index.html.

Mount Mercy University, Program in Education, Cedar Rapids, IA 52402-4797. Offers reading (MA Ed); special education (MA Ed). *Entrance requirements:* For master's, minimum cumulative GPA of 3.0, 2 letters of recommendation, resume, valid teaching license. Additional exam requirements/recommendations for international students: Required—TOEFL (minimum score 570 paper-based; 88 iBT). Electronic applications accepted.

Mount St. Joseph University, Graduate Education Program, Cincinnati, OH 45233-1670. Offers adolescent to young adult education (MA); dyslexia (Certificate); inclusive early childhood education (MA); instructional leadership (MA); middle childhood education (MA); multicultural special education (MA); Pre-K special needs (Certificate); principal licensure (MA); reading (Certificate); reading science (MA). *Accreditation:* Teacher Education Accreditation Council. Part-time and evening/weekend programs available. *Faculty:* 10 full-time (7 women), 7 part-time/adjunct (6 women). *Students:* 28 full-time (25 women), 95 part-time (76 women); includes 27 minority (19 Black or African American, non-Hispanic/Latino; 6 Hispanic/Latino; 2 Two or more races, non-Hispanic/Latino). Average age 36. 73 applicants, 44% accepted, 30 enrolled. In 2013, 69 master's awarded. *Degree requirements:* For master's, research project, student teaching, clinical and field-based experiences. *Entrance requirements:* For master's, GRE, PRAXIS II in teaching content area (math or science), 2 letters of recommendation, interview, resume. Additional exam requirements/recommendations for international students: Required—TOEFL (minimum score 560 paper-based; 83 iBT). *Application deadline:* Applications are processed on a rolling basis. Application fee: $50. Electronic applications accepted. *Expenses: Tuition:* Full-time $18,400; part-time $575 per credit hour. *Required fees:* $450; $450 per year. Part-time tuition and fees vary according to course load, degree level and program. *Financial support:* Scholarships/grants available. Financial award applicants required to submit FAFSA. *Faculty research:* Foreign and second language learning problems/reading disabilities/hyperlexia, multicultural/bilingual special education, alternative educator licensure, science education, pedagogical content knowledge. *Unit head:* Dr. Mary West, Chair, 513-244-3263, Fax: 513-244-4867, E-mail: mary_west@mail.msj.edu. *Application contact:* Mary Brigham, Assistant Director of Graduate Recruitment, 513-244-4233, Fax: 513-244-4629, E-mail: mary_brigham@mail.msj.edu.
Website: http://www.msj.edu/academics/graduate-programs/master-of-arts-initial-teacher-licensure-programs/.

Mount Saint Mary College, Division of Education, Newburgh, NY 12550-3494. Offers adolescence and special education (MS Ed); adolescence education (MS Ed); childhood and special education (MS Ed); childhood education (MS Ed); literacy (5-12) (Advanced Certificate); literacy (birth-6) (Advanced Certificate); literacy and special education (MS Ed); literacy/childhood (MS Ed); middle school (5-6) (MS Ed); middle school (7-9) (MS Ed); special education (1-6) (MS Ed); special education (7-12) (MS Ed). *Accreditation:* NCATE. Part-time and evening/weekend programs available. *Faculty:* 11 full-time (9 women), 9 part-time/adjunct (4 women). *Students:* 29 full-time (19 women), 142 part-time (117 women); includes 22 minority (5 Black or African American, non-Hispanic/Latino; 16 Hispanic/Latino; 1 Two or more races, non-Hispanic/Latino). Average age 29. 51 applicants, 65% accepted, 27 enrolled. In 2013, 72 master's awarded. *Application deadline:* Applications are processed on a rolling basis. Application fee: $45. Application fee is waived when completed online. *Expenses: Tuition:* Full-time $13,356; part-time $742 per credit. *Required fees:* $70 per semester. *Financial support:* In 2013–14, 69 students received support. Unspecified assistantships available. Financial award application deadline: 4/15; financial award applicants required to submit FAFSA. *Faculty research:* Learning and teaching styles, computers in special education, language development. *Unit head:* Dr. William Swart, Graduate Coordinator, 845-569-3149, Fax: 845-569-3535, E-mail: william.swart@msmc.edu. *Application contact:* Lisa Gallina, Director of Admissions for Graduate Programs and Adult Degree Completion, 845-569-3166, Fax: 845-569-3450, E-mail: lisa.gallina@msmc.edu.
Website: http://www.msmc.edu/Academics/Graduate_Programs/Master_of_Science_in_Education.

Mount St. Mary's College, Graduate Division, Los Angeles, CA 90049-1599. Offers business administration (MBA); counseling psychology (MS); creative writing (MFA); education (MS, Certificate); humanities (MA); nursing (MSN, Certificate); physical therapy (DPT); religious studies (MA); MFA/MA. Part-time and evening/weekend programs available. *Faculty:* 35 full-time (26 women), 112 part-time/adjunct (76 women). *Students:* 416 full-time (324 women), 233 part-time (184 women); includes 376 minority (64 Black or African American, non-Hispanic/Latino; 2 American Indian or Alaska Native, non-Hispanic/Latino; 57 Asian, non-Hispanic/Latino; 229 Hispanic/Latino; 8 Native Hawaiian or other Pacific Islander, non-Hispanic/Latino; 16 Two or more races, non-Hispanic/Latino), 4 international. Average age 33. 1,041 applicants, 22% accepted, 183 enrolled. In 2013, 168 master's, 29 doctorates awarded. *Entrance requirements:* Additional exam requirements/recommendations for international students: Required—TOEFL. *Application deadline:* Applications are processed on a rolling basis. Application fee: $50. Electronic applications accepted. *Expenses: Tuition:* Part-time $798 per unit. *Required fees:* $125 per semester. Tuition and fees vary according to program. *Financial support:* Career-related internships or fieldwork, Federal Work-Study, institutionally sponsored loans, and tuition waivers (full and partial) available. Support available to part-time students. Financial award application deadline: 3/15; financial award applicants required to submit FAFSA. *Unit head:* Dr. Linda Moody, Graduate Dean, 213-477-2800, E-mail: gradprograms@msmc.la.edu. *Application contact:* Natalie Dymchenko, Senior Graduate Admission Counselor, 213-477-2800, E-mail: gradprograms@msmc.la.edu.
Website: http://www.msmc.la.edu/admission/graduate-admission.asp.

Mount St. Mary's University, Program in Education, Emmitsburg, MD 21727-7799. Offers M Ed, MAT. *Accreditation:* NCATE. Part-time and evening/weekend programs available. *Faculty:* 6 full-time (5 women), 5 part-time/adjunct (3 women). *Students:* 27 full-time (19 women), 42 part-time (36 women); includes 7 minority (3 Black or African American, non-Hispanic/Latino; 1 Asian, non-Hispanic/Latino; 1 Hispanic/Latino; 1 Native Hawaiian or other Pacific Islander, non-Hispanic/Latino; 1 Two or more races, non-Hispanic/Latino). Average age 33. 28 applicants, 71% accepted, 20 enrolled. In 2013, 28 master's awarded. *Degree requirements:* For master's, thesis (for some programs), exit portfolio/presentation. *Entrance requirements:* For master's, PRAXIS I, PRAXIS II. Additional exam requirements/recommendations for international students: Required—TOEFL (minimum score 550 paper-based). *Application deadline:* For fall admission, 8/15 for domestic and international students. Applications are processed on a rolling basis. Application fee: $35. *Expenses:* Contact institution. *Financial support:* In 2013–14, 23 students received support. Career-related internships or fieldwork and unspecified assistantships available. Financial award applicants required to submit FAFSA. *Faculty research:* One-on-one computing initiatives, teacher decision-making, motivation to read, storytelling with English Language Learners. *Unit head:* Dr. Barbara Martin-Palmer, Dean of School of Education and Human Services, 301-447-5371, Fax: 301-447-5250, E-mail: palmer@msmary.edu. *Application contact:* Joseph Lebherz, Director, Center for Professional and Continuing Studies, 301-682-8315, Fax: 301-682-5247, E-mail: lebherz@msmary.edu.
Website: http://www.msmary.edu/School_of_education_and_human_services/graduate_programs/.

Mount Saint Vincent University, Graduate Programs, Faculty of Education, Halifax, NS B3M 2J6, Canada. Offers adult education (M Ed, MA Ed, MA-R); curriculum studies (M Ed, MA Ed, MA-R), including education of young adolescents, general studies, teaching English as a second language; educational foundations (M Ed, MA Ed, MA-R); educational psychology (M Ed, MA Ed, MA-R), including education of the blind or visually impaired (M Ed, MA Ed), education of the deaf or hard of hearing (M Ed, MA Ed), educational psychology (MA-R), human relations (M Ed, MA Ed); elementary education (M Ed, MA Ed, MA-R); literacy education (M Ed, MA Ed, MA-R); school psychology (MASP). Part-time and evening/weekend programs available. Postbaccalaureate distance learning degree programs offered (minimal on-campus study). *Degree requirements:* For master's, thesis (for some programs), practicum. *Entrance requirements:* For master's, bachelor's degree in related field. Electronic applications accepted.

Mount Vernon Nazarene University, Department of Education, Mount Vernon, OH 43050-9500. Offers education (MA Ed); professional educator's license (MA Ed). *Accreditation:* NCATE. Part-time and evening/weekend programs available. *Degree requirements:* For master's, project.

Multnomah University, Multnomah Bible College Graduate Degree Programs, Portland, OR 97220-5898. Offers counseling (MA); global development and justice (MA); teaching (MA); TESOL (MA). *Faculty:* 6 full-time (4 women), 23 part-time/adjunct (11 women). *Students:* 124 full-time (84 women), 21 part-time (12 women); includes 16 minority (4 Black or African American, non-Hispanic/Latino; 1 Asian, non-Hispanic/Latino; 7 Hispanic/Latino; 4 Two or more races, non-Hispanic/Latino), 1 international. Average age 30. 103 applicants, 94% accepted, 53 enrolled. In 2013, 49 master's awarded. *Degree requirements:* For master's, variable foreign language requirement, comprehensive exam (for some programs), thesis (for some programs). *Entrance requirements:* For master's, CBEST or WEST-B (for MAT), interview; references (4 for teaching); writing sample (for counseling). Additional exam requirements/recommendations for international students: Required—TOEFL (minimum score 550 paper-based). *Application deadline:* For fall admission, 8/1 for domestic students, 12/1 for international students; for spring admission, 12/1 for domestic and international students. Application fee: $40. *Expenses: Tuition:* Full-time $7360; part-time $460 per credit hour. *Financial support:* Career-related internships or fieldwork and scholarships/grants available. Support available to part-time students. Financial award application deadline: 7/1; financial award applicants required to submit FAFSA. *Unit head:* Dr. Rex Koivisto, Academic Dean, 503-251-6401. *Application contact:* Stephanie Pollard, Admissions Counselor, 503-251-5166, Fax: 503-254-1268, E-mail: admiss@multnomah.edu.

Murray State University, College of Education, Murray, KY 42071. Offers MA Ed, MS, Ed D, PhD, Ed S. PhD, Ed D offered jointly with University of Kentucky. *Accreditation:* NCATE. Part-time programs available.

Muskingum University, Graduate Programs in Education, New Concord, OH 43762. Offers MAE, MAT. *Accreditation:* NCATE. Part-time programs available. *Entrance requirements:* For master's, minimum GPA of 2.7, teaching license. *Faculty research:* Brain behavior relationships, school partnerships, staff development, school law, proficiency testing, multi-age groupings.

Naropa University, Graduate Programs, Program in Contemplative Education, Boulder, CO 80302-6697. Offers MA. Part-time programs available. Postbaccalaureate distance learning degree programs offered (minimal on-campus study). *Faculty:* 1 full-time (0 women), 2 part-time/adjunct (both women). *Students:* 17 part-time (16 women); includes 4 minority (3 Asian, non-Hispanic/Latino; 1 Hispanic/Latino), 1 international. Average age 41. 21 applicants, 86% accepted, 11 enrolled. In 2013, 8 master's awarded. *Degree requirements:* For master's, thesis. *Entrance requirements:* For master's, interview (by phone or in-person), 2 letters of recommendation, transcripts, resume, statement of interest. Additional exam requirements/recommendations for international students: Required—TOEFL (minimum score 600 paper-based; 80 iBT). *Application deadline:* For fall admission, 1/13 priority date for domestic students, 1/15 priority date for international students. Applications are processed on a rolling basis. Application fee: $60. Electronic applications accepted. *Expenses: Tuition:* Full-time $16,848; part-time $936 per credit. *Required fees:* $335 per semester. *Financial support:* In 2013–14, 5 students received support. Career-related internships or fieldwork, Federal Work-Study, scholarships/grants, tuition waivers (partial), and unspecified assistantships available. Support available to part-time students. Financial award application deadline: 3/1; financial award applicants required to submit FAFSA. *Unit head:* Dr. Susan Burggraf, Director, School of Natural and Social Sciences, 303-546-3524, E-mail: sburggraf@naropa.edu. *Application contact:* Office of Admissions, 303-546-3572, Fax: 303-546-3583, E-mail: admissions@naropa.edu.
Website: http://www.naropa.edu/academics/snss/grad/contemplative-education-low-residency-ma/index.php.

National Louis University, National College of Education, Chicago, IL 60603. Offers administration and supervision (M Ed, Ed D, CAS, Ed S); curriculum and instruction (M Ed, MS Ed, CAS); early childhood administration (M Ed, CAS); early childhood education (M Ed, MAT, MS Ed, CAS); education (Ed D); educational psychology/human learning and development (M Ed, MS Ed, CAS, Ed S); elementary education (MAT); interdisciplinary curriculum and instruction (M Ed); mathematics education (M Ed, MS Ed, CAS); reading and language (M Ed, MS Ed, CAS); school psychology (M Ed, Ed S); science education (M Ed, MS Ed, CAS); secondary education (MAT); special education (M Ed, MAT, CAS); technology in education (M Ed, CAS). *Accreditation:* NCATE. Part-time and evening/weekend programs available. *Degree requirements:* For doctorate, comprehensive exam, thesis/dissertation. *Entrance requirements:* For master's, MAT or GRE, minimum GPA of 3.0; for doctorate, GRE General Test, minimum GPA of 3.25, interview, resume, writing sample, 4 recommendations. Additional exam requirements/recommendations for international students: Required—TOEFL (minimum score 550 paper-based; 79 iBT).

National University, Academic Affairs, School of Education, La Jolla, CA 92037-1011. Offers applied behavior analysis (Certificate); applied school leadership (MS); autism (Certificate); best practices (Certificate); e-teaching and learning (Certificate); early childhood education (Certificate); education (MA), including best practices (M Ed, MA), e-teaching and learning (M Ed, MA), education technology, teacher leadership (M Ed, MA), teaching and learning in a global society (M Ed, MA), teaching mathematics (M Ed, MA); education with preliminary multiple or single subject (M Ed), including best practices (M Ed, MA), e-teaching and learning (M Ed, MA), educational technology (M Ed, MA), teacher leadership (M Ed, MA), teaching and learning in a global society (M Ed, MA), teaching mathematics (M Ed, MA); educational administration (MS); educational and instructional technology (MS); educational counseling (MS); educational technology (Certificate); higher education administration (MS); innovative school leadership (MS); instructional leadership (MS); juvenile justice special education (MS); reading (Certificate); school psychology (MS); special education (MS), including deaf and hard-of-hearing, mild/moderate disabilities, moderate/severe disabilities; teacher leadership (Certificate); teaching (MA), including applied behavioral analysis, autism, best practices (M Ed, MA), e-teaching and learning (M Ed, MA), early childhood education, educational technology (M Ed, MA), reading, special education, teacher leadership (M Ed, MA), teaching and learning in a global society (M Ed, MA), teaching mathematics (M Ed, MA); teaching mathematics (Certificate). Part-time and evening/weekend programs available. Postbaccalaureate distance learning degree programs offered (no on-campus study). *Faculty:* 72 full-time (43 women), 287 part-time/adjunct (170 women). *Students:* 2,433 full-time (1,744 women), 2,017 part-time (1,371 women); includes 1,834 minority (358 Black or African American, non-Hispanic/Latino; 15 American Indian or Alaska Native, non-Hispanic/Latino; 250 Asian, non-Hispanic/Latino; 1,056 Hispanic/Latino; 29 Native Hawaiian or other Pacific Islander, non-Hispanic/Latino; 126 Two or more races, non-Hispanic/Latino), 1 international. Average age 34. 1,339 applicants, 100% accepted, 1035 enrolled. In 2013, 1,662 master's awarded. *Degree requirements:* For master's, thesis (for some programs). *Entrance requirements:* For master's, interview, minimum GPA of 2.5. Additional exam requirements/recommendations for international students: Required—TOEFL (minimum score 550 paper-based; 79 iBT), IELTS (minimum score 6). *Application deadline:* Applications are

processed on a rolling basis. Application fee: $60 ($65 for international students). Electronic applications accepted. *Expenses: Tuition:* Full-time $13,824; part-time $1728 per course. One-time fee: $160. *Financial support:* Career-related internships or fieldwork, institutionally sponsored loans, scholarships/grants, and tuition waivers (partial) available. Support available to part-time students. Financial award application deadline: 6/30. *Faculty research:* Teacher education, special education, educational effectiveness, teaching abroad, school counseling. *Unit head:* School of Education, 800-628-8648, E-mail: soe@nu.edu. *Application contact:* Louis Cruz, Interim Vice President for Enrollment Services, 800-628-8648, E-mail: advisor@nu.edu.
Website: http://www.nu.edu/OurPrograms/SchoolOfEducation.html.

Nazareth College of Rochester, Graduate Studies, Department of Education, Rochester, NY 14618-3790. Offers educational technology/computer education (MS Ed); inclusive education-adolescence level (MS Ed); inclusive education-childhood level (MS Ed); inclusive education-early childhood level (MS Ed); literacy education (MS Ed); teaching English to speakers of other languages (MS Ed). *Accreditation:* Teacher Education Accreditation Council. Part-time and evening/weekend programs available. *Entrance requirements:* For master's, minimum GPA of 3.0.

Neumann University, Program in Education, Aston, PA 19014-1298. Offers MS. Part-time programs available. *Entrance requirements:* For master's, GRE, MAT, or PRAXIS. Additional exam requirements/recommendations for international students: Required—TOEFL.

New England College, Program in Education, Henniker, NH 03242-3293. Offers higher education administration (MS, Ed D); K-12 leadership (Ed D); literacy and language arts (M Ed); meeting the needs of all learners/special education (M Ed); teacher leadership/school reform (M Ed). Part-time and evening/weekend programs available.

New Jersey City University, Graduate Studies and Continuing Education, Debra Cannon Partridge Wolfe College of Education, Jersey City, NJ 07305-1597. Offers MA, MAT, Ed D. Part-time and evening/weekend programs available. *Faculty:* 57 full-time (45 women), 40 part-time/adjunct (27 women). *Students:* 173 full-time (138 women), 713 part-time (563 women); includes 421 minority (156 Black or African American, non-Hispanic/Latino; 39 Asian, non-Hispanic/Latino; 226 Hispanic/Latino), 5 international. Average age 35. In 2013, 284 master's awarded. *Entrance requirements:* Additional exam requirements/recommendations for international students: Required—TOEFL (minimum score 61 iBT). *Application deadline:* For fall admission, 8/1 for domestic students; for spring admission, 12/1 for domestic students. Application fee: $0. *Expenses: Tuition, area resident:* Part-time $527.90 per credit. Tuition, nonresident: part-time $947.75 per credit. *Financial support:* Fellowships, research assistantships, career-related internships or fieldwork, and unspecified assistantships available. *Unit head:* Dr. Allan DeFina, Dean, 201-200-2102, E-mail: adefina@njcu.edu. *Application contact:* Dr. William Bajor, Dean of Graduate Studies, 201-200-3409, Fax: 201-200-3411, E-mail: wbajor@njcu.edu.

Newman University, Master of Education Program, Wichita, KS 67213-2097. Offers building leadership (MS Ed); curriculum and instruction (MS Ed), including English as a second language, reading specialist; organizational leadership (MS Ed). *Accreditation:* NCATE. Part-time and evening/weekend programs available. Postbaccalaureate distance learning degree programs offered (no on-campus study). *Faculty:* 3 full-time (1 woman), 22 part-time/adjunct (all women). *Students:* 19 full-time (15 women), 498 part-time (407 women); includes 66 minority (19 Black or African American, non-Hispanic/Latino; 5 American Indian or Alaska Native, non-Hispanic/Latino; 10 Asian, non-Hispanic/Latino; 27 Hispanic/Latino; 1 Native Hawaiian or other Pacific Islander, non-Hispanic/Latino; 4 Two or more races, non-Hispanic/Latino). Average age 37. 67 applicants, 73% accepted, 35 enrolled. In 2013, 53 master's awarded. *Degree requirements:* For master's, thesis optional. *Entrance requirements:* For master's, 3 years' full-time teaching experience, minimum GPA of 3.0, writing sample, 2 letters of recommendation, evidence of teaching certification. Additional exam requirements/recommendations for international students: Required—TOEFL (minimum score 600 paper-based; 100 iBT). *Application deadline:* For fall admission, 8/15 priority date for domestic students, 7/15 priority date for international students; for spring admission, 1/10 priority date for domestic students, 11/15 priority date for international students. Applications are processed on a rolling basis. Application fee: $25 ($40 for international students). Electronic applications accepted. *Expenses:* Contact institution. *Financial support:* Application deadline: 8/15; applicants required to submit FAFSA. *Unit head:* Dr. Gina Marx, Director of Graduate Education, 316-942-4291 Ext. 2416, Fax: 316-942-4483, E-mail: marxg@newmanu.edu. *Application contact:* Linda Kay Sabala, Director of Graduate Admissions, 316-942-4291 Ext. 2230, Fax: 316-942-4483, E-mail: sabalal@newmanu.edu.
Website: http://www.newmanu.edu/studynu/graduate/master-science-education.

New Mexico Highlands University, Graduate Studies, School of Education, Las Vegas, NM 87701. Offers curriculum and instruction (MA); educational leadership (MA); professional counseling (MA); special education (MA), including). Part-time programs available. *Faculty:* 25 full-time (12 women), 26 part-time/adjunct (22 women). *Students:* 139 full-time (106 women), 245 part-time (180 women); includes 207 minority (10 Black or African American, non-Hispanic/Latino; 20 American Indian or Alaska Native, non-Hispanic/Latino; 3 Asian, non-Hispanic/Latino; 172 Hispanic/Latino; 1 Native Hawaiian or other Pacific Islander, non-Hispanic/Latino; 1 Two or more races, non-Hispanic/Latino), 17 international. Average age 39. 137 applicants, 99% accepted, 102 enrolled. In 2013, 112 master's awarded. *Degree requirements:* For master's, comprehensive exam, thesis or alternative. *Entrance requirements:* For master's, minimum undergraduate GPA of 3.0. Additional exam requirements/recommendations for international students: Required—TOEFL (minimum score 540 paper-based). *Application deadline:* For fall admission, 8/1 priority date for domestic students. Applications are processed on a rolling basis. Application fee: $15. *Expenses:* Tuition, state resident: full-time $4278; part-time $178 per credit hour. Tuition, nonresident: full-time $6716; part-time $281 per credit hour. One-time fee: $15. *Financial support:* Career-related internships or fieldwork, Federal Work-Study, institutionally sponsored loans, scholarships/grants, traineeships, tuition waivers (partial), and unspecified assistantships available. Support available to part-time students. Financial award application deadline: 3/1; financial award applicants required to submit FAFSA. *Faculty research:* Middle school curriculum, integrated computer applications for pre-service classroom teachers, adolescent literacy, narrative cognitive modes in New Mexico multicultural setting, math and math education. *Unit head:* Dr. Belinda Laumbach, Interim Dean, 505-454-3146, Fax: 505-454-8884, E-mail: laumbach_b@nmhu.edu. *Application contact:* Diane Trujillo, Administrative Assistant for Graduate Studies, 505-454-3266, Fax: 505-426-2117, E-mail: dtrujillo@nmhu.edu.

New Mexico State University, Graduate School, College of Education, Las Cruces, NM 88003-8001. Offers MA, MAT, Ed D, PhD, Ed S, Graduate Certificate. *Accreditation:* NCATE. Part-time and evening/weekend programs available. Postbaccalaureate distance learning degree programs offered (minimal on-campus study). *Faculty:* 66 full-time (51 women), 9 part-time/adjunct (5 women). *Students:* 319 full-time (249 women), 534 part-time (406 women); includes 482 minority (19 Black or African American, non-Hispanic/Latino; 19 American Indian or Alaska Native, non-Hispanic/Latino; 22 Asian, non-Hispanic/Latino; 406 Hispanic/Latino; 16 Two or more races, non-Hispanic/Latino), 41 international. Average age 37. 427 applicants, 48% accepted, 161 enrolled. In 2013,

169 master's, 39 doctorates, 18 other advanced degrees awarded. *Degree requirements:* For doctorate, thesis/dissertation. *Entrance requirements:* Additional exam requirements/recommendations for international students: Required—TOEFL (minimum score 550 paper-based; 79 iBT), IELTS (minimum score 6.5). *Application deadline:* Applications are processed on a rolling basis. Application fee: $40 ($50 for international students). Electronic applications accepted. *Expenses:* Tuition, state resident: full-time $5398; part-time $224.90 per credit. Tuition, nonresident: full-time $18,821; part-time $784.20 per credit. *Required fees:* $1310; $54.60 per credit. *Financial support:* In 2013–14, 250 students received support, including 6 fellowships (averaging $4,050 per year), 12 research assistantships (averaging $13,380 per year), 63 teaching assistantships (averaging $10,823 per year); career-related internships or fieldwork, Federal Work-Study, scholarships/grants, health care benefits, and unspecified assistantships also available. Support available to part-time students. Financial award application deadline: 3/1. *Faculty research:* Bilingual special education, early childhood education/Head Start, leadership in border settings, exercise physiology, school-based mental health. *Total annual research expenditures:* $401,977. *Unit head:* Dr. Michael Morehead, Dean, 575-646-3404, Fax: 575-646-6032, E-mail: mmorehea@nmsu.edu. *Application contact:* Coordinator, 575-646-2736, Fax: 575-646-7721, E-mail: gradinfo@nmsu.edu.
Website: http://education.nmsu.edu/.

New York Institute of Technology, School of Education, Old Westbury, NY 11568-8000. Offers MS, Advanced Certificate, Advanced Diploma. *Accreditation:* NCATE. Part-time and evening/weekend programs available. Postbaccalaureate distance learning degree programs offered (minimal on-campus study). *Faculty:* 12 full-time (8 women), 23 part-time/adjunct (12 women). *Students:* 25 full-time (21 women), 208 part-time (152 women); includes 71 minority (30 Black or African American, non-Hispanic/Latino; 1 American Indian or Alaska Native, non-Hispanic/Latino; 9 Asian, non-Hispanic/Latino; 27 Hispanic/Latino; 1 Native Hawaiian or other Pacific Islander, non-Hispanic/Latino; 3 Two or more races, non-Hispanic/Latino), 5 international. Average age 32. 158 applicants, 67% accepted, 71 enrolled. In 2013, 89 master's, 73 other advanced degrees awarded. *Entrance requirements:* For master's, minimum QPA of 3.0. Additional exam requirements/recommendations for international students: Required—TOEFL (minimum score 550 paper-based; 79 iBT), IELTS (minimum score 6). *Application deadline:* For fall admission, 7/1 priority date for domestic students, 6/1 for international students; for spring admission, 12/1 priority date for domestic students, 12/1 for international students. Applications are processed on a rolling basis. Application fee: $50. Electronic applications accepted. *Expenses: Tuition:* Full-time $18,900; part-time $1050 per credit. *Financial support:* Research assistantships with partial tuition reimbursements, career-related internships or fieldwork, scholarships/grants, health care benefits, tuition waivers (full and partial), and unspecified assistantships available. Support available to part-time students. Financial award applicants required to submit FAFSA. *Faculty research:* Instructional design for online instruction, integration of information and communication technologies (ICTs) and social media into learning environment, mobile learning, college and career readiness, evolving definition of new literacies and its impact on teaching and learning (twenty-first century skills). *Unit head:* Dr. Michael Uttendorfer, Dean, School of Education, 516-686-7541, Fax: 516-686-7655, E-mail: muttendo@nyit.edu. *Application contact:* Alice Dolitsky, Director, Graduate Admissions, 516-686-7520, Fax: 516-686-1116, E-mail: nyitgrad@nyit.edu.
Website: http://www.nyit.edu/education.

New York University, Steinhardt School of Culture, Education, and Human Development, New York, NY 10003. Offers MA, MFA, MM, MS, DPS, DPT, Ed D, PhD, Advanced Certificate, MA/MA, MLIS/MA, MM/Advanced Certificate. *Accreditation:* Teacher Education Accreditation Council. Part-time programs available. *Faculty:* 288 full-time (169 women), 740 part-time/adjunct (392 women). *Students:* 2,084 full-time (1,571 women), 1,259 part-time (965 women); includes 901 minority (219 Black or African American, non-Hispanic/Latino; 10 American Indian or Alaska Native, non-Hispanic/Latino; 291 Asian, non-Hispanic/Latino; 298 Hispanic/Latino; 9 Native Hawaiian or other Pacific Islander, non-Hispanic/Latino; 74 Two or more races, non-Hispanic/Latino), 680 international. Average age 30. 7,195 applicants, 41% accepted, 1192 enrolled. In 2013, 1,225 master's, 101 doctorates, 21 other advanced degrees awarded. *Degree requirements:* For master's, thesis (for some programs); for doctorate, comprehensive exam (for some programs), thesis/dissertation. *Entrance requirements:* For doctorate, GRE General Test, interview. Additional exam requirements/recommendations for international students: Required—TOEFL (minimum score 100 iBT). *Application deadline:* For fall admission, 12/1 priority date for domestic students, 12/1 for international students; for spring admission, 1/1 for domestic and international students. Applications are processed on a rolling basis. Application fee: $75. Electronic applications accepted. *Expenses:* Contact institution. *Financial support:* Fellowships with full and partial tuition reimbursements, research assistantships with full and partial tuition reimbursements, teaching assistantships with full and partial tuition reimbursements, career-related internships or fieldwork, Federal Work-Study, institutionally sponsored loans, scholarships/grants, traineeships, tuition waivers (partial), and unspecified assistantships available. Support available to part-time students. Financial award application deadline: 2/1; financial award applicants required to submit FAFSA. *Faculty research:* Equity, urban adolescents, arts in education, globalization, community and public health. *Total annual research expenditures:* $22.8 million. *Unit head:* Dr. Mary Brabeck, Dean, 212-998-5000. *Application contact:* John Myers, Director of Enrollment Management, 212-998-5030, Fax: 212-995-4328, E-mail: steinhardt.gradadmissions@nyu.edu.
Website: http://steinhardt.nyu.edu/.

Niagara University, Graduate Division of Education, Niagara Falls, NY 14109. Offers educational leadership (MS Ed, PhD, Certificate), including leadership and policy (PhD), school administration/supervision (MS Ed), school building leader (MS Ed, Certificate), school business administration (MS Ed), school district business leader (Certificate), school district leader (MS Ed, Certificate); foundations of teaching (MS Ed); foundations of teaching math, science, and technology education (MA); literacy instruction (MS Ed); mental health counseling (MS, Certificate); school counseling (MS Ed, Certificate); school psychology (MS, Certificate); teacher education (MS Ed, Certificate), including early childhood and childhood education, middle and adolescence education, special education (grades 1-12), teaching English to speakers of other languages (MS Ed). *Accreditation:* NCATE (one or more programs are accredited). Part-time and evening/weekend programs available. *Students:* 303 full-time (239 women), 240 part-time (176 women); includes 41 minority (24 Black or African American, non-Hispanic/Latino; 3 Asian, non-Hispanic/Latino; 13 Hispanic/Latino; 1 Native Hawaiian or other Pacific Islander, non-Hispanic/Latino), 161 international. Average age 31. In 2013, 262 master's, 29 other advanced degrees awarded. *Entrance requirements:* For master's, GRE General Test or MAT. Additional exam requirements/recommendations for international students: Required—TOEFL (minimum score 550 paper-based, 79 iBT) or IELTS (minimum score 6). *Application deadline:* For fall admission, 8/1 for domestic students. Applications are processed on a rolling basis. Application fee: $30. *Expenses:* Contact institution. *Financial support:* Research assistantships with full and partial tuition reimbursements, teaching assistantships with full and partial tuition reimbursements, career-related internships or fieldwork, Federal Work-Study, scholarships/grants, and unspecified assistantships available. Financial award application deadline: 4/15; financial award applicants required to submit FAFSA. *Faculty research:* Instructional supervision, appraisal and evaluation, career opportunities. *Unit head:* Dr. Debra A. Colley, Dean, 716-286-8560, Fax: 716-286-8561, E-mail: dcolley@niagara.edu. *Application contact:* Evan Pierce, Associate Director for Graduate Recruitment, 716-286-8769, Fax: 716-286-8170, E-mail: epierce@niagara.edu.
Website: http://www.niagara.edu/advance/.

Nicholls State University, Graduate Studies, College of Education, Department of Teacher Education, Thibodaux, LA 70310. Offers administration and supervision (M Ed); counselor education (M Ed); curriculum and instruction (M Ed). *Accreditation:* NCATE. Part-time and evening/weekend programs available. *Degree requirements:* For master's, comprehensive exam, portfolio. *Entrance requirements:* For master's, GRE General Test, teaching license. Electronic applications accepted.

Nipissing University, Faculty of Education, North Bay, ON P1B 8L7, Canada. Offers M Ed, Certificate. Part-time and evening/weekend programs available. *Degree requirements:* For master's, comprehensive exam (for some programs), thesis (for some programs). *Entrance requirements:* For master's, 1 year of experience, letters of recommendation, minimum undergraduate GPA of 3.0. Additional exam requirements/recommendations for international students: Required—TOEFL (minimum score 600 paper-based), IELTS (minimum score 7), TWE (minimum score 5).

Norfolk State University, School of Graduate Studies, School of Education, Norfolk, VA 23504. Offers MA, MAT. *Accreditation:* NCATE. Part-time programs available. *Students:* 111 full-time (91 women), 99 part-time (73 women); includes 180 minority (171 Black or African American, non-Hispanic/Latino; 2 Asian, non-Hispanic/Latino; 3 Hispanic/Latino; 4 Two or more races, non-Hispanic/Latino). In 2013, 104 master's awarded. *Degree requirements:* For master's, comprehensive exam. *Entrance requirements:* For master's, PRAXIS, GRE/GMAT, interview, teacher license. *Application deadline:* For fall admission, 3/1 for domestic students; for spring admission, 10/1 for domestic students. Application fee: $30. *Financial support:* Fellowships, career-related internships or fieldwork, Federal Work-Study, and unspecified assistantships available. Financial award applicants required to submit FAFSA. *Faculty research:* Urban, pre-elementary, and special education. *Unit head:* Dr. Jean Braxton, Dean, 757-823-8701, Fax: 757-823-2449, E-mail: jbraxton@nsu.edu. *Application contact:* Laurie Carpenter, Educational Support Specialist, 757-823-8015, Fax: 757-823-2849, E-mail: lcarpenter@nsu.edu.
Website: http://www.nsu.edu.

North Carolina Agricultural and Technical State University, School of Graduate Studies, School of Education, Greensboro, NC 27411. Offers MA Ed, MAT, MS. *Accreditation:* NCATE. Part-time and evening/weekend programs available. *Degree requirements:* For master's, comprehensive exam, qualifying exam. *Entrance requirements:* For master's, GRE General Test.

North Carolina Central University, School of Education, Durham, NC 27707-3129. Offers M Ed, MA, MAT, MSA. *Accreditation:* NCATE. Part-time and evening/weekend programs available. *Degree requirements:* For master's, comprehensive exam, thesis or alternative. *Entrance requirements:* For master's, minimum GPA of 3.0 in major, 2.5 overall. Additional exam requirements/recommendations for international students: Required—TOEFL.

North Carolina State University, Graduate School, College of Education, Raleigh, NC 27695. Offers M Ed, MS, MS Ed, MSA, Ed D, PhD, Certificate. *Accreditation:* NCATE. Part-time programs available. *Degree requirements:* For doctorate, thesis/dissertation. *Entrance requirements:* For master's, doctorate, and Certificate, GRE General Test or MAT, minimum GPA of 3.0 in major. Electronic applications accepted. *Faculty research:* Moral/ethical development, financial policy analysis, middle years education, adult education.

North Central College, Graduate and Continuing Studies Programs, Department of Education, Naperville, IL 60566-7063. Offers curriculum and instruction (MA Ed); leadership and administration (MA Ed). Part-time and evening/weekend programs available. *Faculty:* 11 full-time (4 women), 5 part-time/adjunct (2 women). *Students:* 6 full-time (2 women), 24 part-time (21 women); includes 1 minority (Hispanic/Latino). Average age 30. 44 applicants, 34% accepted, 14 enrolled. In 2013, 9 master's awarded. *Degree requirements:* For master's, thesis optional, clinical practicum, project. *Entrance requirements:* For master's, interview. Additional exam requirements/recommendations for international students: Required—TOEFL (minimum score 577 paper-based; 90 iBT). *Application deadline:* For fall admission, 8/15 for domestic students; for winter admission, 12/1 for domestic students; for spring admission, 2/1 for domestic students. Applications are processed on a rolling basis. Application fee: $25. *Expenses:* Contact institution. *Financial support:* Available to part-time students. *Unit head:* Dr. Maureen Kincaid, Education Department Chair, 630-637-5750, Fax: 630-637-5844, E-mail: mkincaid@noctrl.edu. *Application contact:* Wendy Kulpinski, Director of Graduate and Continuing Education Admission, 630-637-5808, Fax: 630-637-5844, E-mail: wekulpinski@noctrl.edu.

Northcentral University, Graduate Studies, Prescott Valley, AZ 86314. Offers business (MBA, DBA, PhD, Post-Master's Certificate, Postbaccalaureate Certificate); education (M Ed, Ed D, PhD, Ed S, Post-Master's Certificate, Postbaccalaureate Certificate); marriage and family therapy (MA, PhD, Post-Master's Certificate, Postbaccalaureate Certificate); psychology (MA, PhD, Post-Master's Certificate, Postbaccalaureate Certificate). Part-time and evening/weekend programs available. Postbaccalaureate distance learning degree programs offered (no on-campus study). *Faculty:* 94 full-time (58 women), 390 part-time/adjunct (164 women). *Students:* 7,902 full-time (4,776 women), 4,835 part-time (2,804 women); includes 3,752 minority (2,664 Black or African American, non-Hispanic/Latino; 82 American Indian or Alaska Native, non-Hispanic/Latino; 245 Asian, non-Hispanic/Latino; 476 Hispanic/Latino; 43 Native Hawaiian or other Pacific Islander, non-Hispanic/Latino; 242 Two or more races, non-Hispanic/Latino). Average age 44. 3,043 applicants, 69% accepted, 1734 enrolled. In 2013, 538 master's, 253 doctorates, 31 other advanced degrees awarded. *Entrance requirements:* For master's, bachelor's degree from regionally- or nationally-accredited institution, current resume or curriculum vitae, statement of intent, interview, and background check (for marriage and family therapy); for doctorate, post-baccalaureate master's degree and/or doctoral degree from nationally- or regionally-accredited academic institution; for other advanced degree, bachelor's-level or higher degree from accredited institution or university (for Post-Baccalaureate Certificate); master's and/or doctoral degree from regionally- or nationally-accredited academic institution (for Post-Master's Certificate). Additional exam requirements/recommendations for international students: Required—TOEFL (minimum score 95 iBT), IELTS (minimum score 6) or PTE (minimum score 65). *Application deadline:* Applications are processed on a rolling basis. Application fee: $0. Electronic applications accepted. *Expenses: Tuition:* Full-time $16,584; part-time $2764 per course. *Financial support:* Scholarships/grants available. *Faculty research:* Business management, curriculum and instruction, educational leadership, health psychology, organizational behavior. *Unit head:* Dr. Scott Burrus, Provost and Chief Academic Officer, 888-327-2877, Fax: 928-759-6381, E-mail: provost@ncu.edu. *Application contact:* Ken Boutelle, Vice President, Enrollment Services, 480-253-3535, E-mail: kboutelle@ncu.edu.

North Dakota State University, College of Graduate and Interdisciplinary Studies, College of Human Development and Education, School of Education, Fargo, ND 58108. Offers agricultural education (M Ed, MS), including agricultural education, agricultural extension education (MS); counseling (M Ed, MS, PhD); curriculum and instruction (M Ed, MS); education (PhD); educational leadership (M Ed, MS, Ed S); family and consumer sciences education (M Ed, MS); history education (M Ed, MS); institutional analysis (Ed D); mathematics education (M Ed, MS); music education (M Ed, MS); occupational and adult education (Ed D); science education (M Ed, MS). *Accreditation:* NCATE. Part-time and evening/weekend programs available. Postbaccalaureate distance learning degree programs offered (minimal on-campus study). *Faculty:* 25 full-time (11 women), 1 (woman) part-time/adjunct. *Students:* 110 full-time (82 women), 123 part-time (85 women); includes 14 minority (4 Black or African American, non-Hispanic/Latino; 4 American Indian or Alaska Native, non-Hispanic/Latino; 1 Native Hawaiian or other Pacific Islander, non-Hispanic/Latino; 5 Two or more races, non-Hispanic/Latino), 10 international. Average age 28. 57 applicants, 81% accepted, 42 enrolled. In 2013, 38 master's, 9 doctorates awarded. *Degree requirements:* For master's, comprehensive exam; for doctorate, thesis/dissertation; for Ed S, thesis. *Entrance requirements:* For degree, GRE General Test, master's degree, minimum GPA of 3.25. Additional exam requirements/recommendations for international students: Required—TOEFL. *Application deadline:* Applications are processed on a rolling basis. Application fee: $45 ($60 for international students). *Financial support:* Research assistantships, teaching assistantships, career-related internships or fieldwork, Federal Work-Study, institutionally sponsored loans, and tuition waivers (full) available. Financial award application deadline: 4/15. *Unit head:* Dr. William Martin, Chair, 701-231-7202, Fax: 701-231-7416, E-mail: william.martin@ndsu.edu. *Application contact:* Sonya Goergen, Marketing, Recruitment, and Public Relations Coordinator, 701-231-7033, Fax: 701-231-6524.
Website: http://www.ndsu.nodak.edu/school_of_education/.

Northeastern Illinois University, College of Graduate Studies and Research, College of Education, Chicago, IL 60625-4699. Offers MA, MAT, MS, MSI. Part-time and evening/weekend programs available. *Degree requirements:* For master's, comprehensive exam (for some programs), thesis (for some programs). *Entrance requirements:* For master's, minimum GPA of 2.75. Additional exam requirements/recommendations for international students: Required—TOEFL (minimum score 550 paper-based; 79 iBT). Electronic applications accepted. *Faculty research:* Leadership, problem-based learning strategies, school improvement, bilingual education, use of technology.

Northeastern State University, College of Education, Tahlequah, OK 74464-2399. Offers M Ed, MS, MS Ed. *Accreditation:* NCATE. Part-time and evening/weekend programs available. *Faculty:* 47 full-time (31 women), 17 part-time/adjunct (8 women). *Students:* 124 full-time (81 women), 385 part-time (269 women); includes 162 minority (17 Black or African American, non-Hispanic/Latino; 96 American Indian or Alaska Native, non-Hispanic/Latino; 4 Asian, non-Hispanic/Latino; 13 Hispanic/Latino; 32 Two or more races, non-Hispanic/Latino), 5 international. Average age 36. In 2013, 194 master's awarded. *Degree requirements:* For master's, thesis. *Entrance requirements:* For master's, GRE or MAT. Additional exam requirements/recommendations for international students: Required—TOEFL. *Application deadline:* For fall admission, 6/1 priority date for domestic students. Applications are processed on a rolling basis. Application fee: $25. Electronic applications accepted. *Expenses:* Tuition, state resident: full-time $3029; part-time $168.25 per credit hour. Tuition, nonresident: full-time $7709; part-time $428.25 per credit hour. *Required fees:* $35.90 per credit hour. *Financial support:* Teaching assistantships, career-related internships or fieldwork, and Federal Work-Study available. Financial award application deadline: 3/1. *Unit head:* Dr. Deborah Landry, Dean of the College of Education, 918-444-3700, E-mail: landryd@nsuok.edu. *Application contact:* Margie Railey, Administrative Assistant, 918-456-5511 Ext. 2093, Fax: 918-458-2061, E-mail: railey@nsouk.edu.
Website: http://academics.nsuok.edu/education/EducationHome.aspx.

Northeastern University, School of Education, Boston, MA 02115-5096. Offers curriculum, teaching, learning, and leadership (Ed D); elementary licensure (MAT); higher education administration (MAT, Ed D); Jewish education leadership (Ed D); learning and instruction (M Ed); organizational leadership studies (Ed D); secondary licensure (MAT); special education (M Ed). Part-time and evening/weekend programs available.

Northern Arizona University, Graduate College, College of Education, Flagstaff, AZ 86011. Offers M Ed, MA, Ed D, PhD, Certificate, Ed S. *Accreditation:* NCATE. Part-time and evening/weekend programs available. Postbaccalaureate distance learning degree programs offered (minimal on-campus study). *Faculty:* 109 full-time (65 women), 10 part-time/adjunct (8 women). *Students:* 605 full-time (445 women), 1,111 part-time (806 women); includes 538 minority (68 Black or African American, non-Hispanic/Latino; 92 American Indian or Alaska Native, non-Hispanic/Latino; 19 Asian, non-Hispanic/Latino; 324 Hispanic/Latino; 3 Native Hawaiian or other Pacific Islander, non-Hispanic/Latino; 32 Two or more races, non-Hispanic/Latino), 12 international. Average age 36. 625 applicants, 86% accepted, 354 enrolled. In 2013, 827 master's, 38 doctorates, 50 other advanced degrees awarded. *Degree requirements:* For master's, comprehensive exam, thesis (for some programs); for doctorate, comprehensive exam, thesis/dissertation. *Entrance requirements:* For master's, minimum GPA of 3.0; for doctorate, GRE or MAT. Additional exam requirements/recommendations for international students: Required—TOEFL (minimum score 550 paper-based; 80 iBT), IELTS (minimum score 7). *Application deadline:* Applications are processed on a rolling basis. Application fee: $65. Electronic applications accepted. *Financial support:* In 2013–14, 1 research assistantship with full tuition reimbursement (averaging $12,000 per year), 26 teaching assistantships with full tuition reimbursements (averaging $9,698 per year) were awarded; career-related internships or fieldwork, Federal Work-Study, scholarships/grants, health care benefits, tuition waivers (full and partial), and unspecified assistantships also available. Financial award applicants required to submit FAFSA. *Unit head:* Dr. Michael Sampson, Dean, 928-523-9211, Fax: 928-523-1929, E-mail: michael.sampson@nau.edu. *Application contact:* April Sandoval, Coordinator, 928-523-4348, Fax: 928-523-8950, E-mail: april.sandoval@nau.edu.
Website: http://nau.edu/coe/.

Northern Illinois University, Graduate School, College of Education, De Kalb, IL 60115-2854. Offers MS, MS Ed, Ed D, Ed S. *Accreditation:* NCATE. Part-time and evening/weekend programs available. Postbaccalaureate distance learning degree programs offered (minimal on-campus study). *Faculty:* 110 full-time (66 women), 5 part-time/adjunct (3 women). *Students:* 302 full-time (200 women), 948 part-time (670 women); includes 291 minority (166 Black or African American, non-Hispanic/Latino; 1 American Indian or Alaska Native, non-Hispanic/Latino; 28 Asian, non-Hispanic/Latino; 76 Hispanic/Latino; 20 Two or more races, non-Hispanic/Latino), 47 international. Average age 37. 377 applicants, 62% accepted, 136 enrolled. In 2013, 344 master's, 57 doctorates, 14 other advanced degrees awarded. Terminal master's awarded for partial completion of doctoral program. *Degree requirements:* For master's and Ed S, comprehensive exam, thesis optional; for doctorate, thesis/dissertation, candidacy exam, dissertation defense. *Entrance requirements:* For master's, GRE General Test or MAT, minimum GPA of 2.75; for doctorate, GRE General Test or MAT, minimum GPA of 2.75 (undergraduate), 3.2 (graduate); for Ed S, GRE General Test, master's degree; minimum undergraduate GPA of 2.75, graduate 3.2. Additional exam requirements/recommendations for international students: Required—TOEFL (minimum score 550 paper-based). *Application deadline:* For fall admission, 6/1 for domestic students, 5/1 for international students; for spring admission, 11/1 for domestic students, 10/1 for international students. Applications are processed on a rolling basis. Application fee: $40. Electronic applications accepted. *Financial support:* In 2013–14, 5 research assistantships with full tuition reimbursements were awarded; fellowships with full tuition reimbursements, teaching assistantships with full tuition reimbursements, career-related internships or fieldwork, Federal Work-Study, scholarships/grants, tuition waivers (full), and staff assistantships also available. Support available to part-time students. Financial award applicants required to submit FAFSA. *Unit head:* Dr. La Vonne I. Neal, Dean, 815-753-1949, Fax: 851-753-2100. *Application contact:* Graduate School Office, 815-753-0395, E-mail: gradsch@niu.edu.
Website: http://www.cedu.niu.edu/.

Northern Kentucky University, Office of Graduate Programs, College of Education and Human Services, Highland Heights, KY 41099. Offers MA, MAT, MS, MSW, Ed D, Certificate, Ed S. *Accreditation:* NCATE. Part-time and evening/weekend programs available. *Faculty:* 43 full-time (26 women), 20 part-time/adjunct (12 women). *Students:* 238 full-time (199 women), 278 part-time (219 women); includes 49 minority (30 Black or African American, non-Hispanic/Latino; 5 Asian, non-Hispanic/Latino; 9 Hispanic/Latino; 2 Native Hawaiian or other Pacific Islander, non-Hispanic/Latino; 3 Two or more races, non-Hispanic/Latino), 2 international. Average age 33. 300 applicants, 56% accepted, 149 enrolled. In 2013, 152 master's, 13 doctorates, 3 other advanced degrees awarded. *Degree requirements:* For master's, comprehensive exam (for some programs), thesis (for some programs). *Entrance requirements:* For master's, GRE. Additional exam requirements/recommendations for international students: Required—TOEFL (minimum score 550 paper-based; 79 iBT); Recommended—IELTS (minimum score 6.5). *Application deadline:* For fall admission, 6/1 for international students; for spring admission, 10/1 for international students. Application fee: $40. Electronic applications accepted. *Expenses:* Tuition, state resident: full-time $4446; part-time $494 per credit hour. Tuition, nonresident: full-time $6885; part-time $765 per credit hour. *Required fees:* $72 per semester. One-time fee: $125.50. Part-time tuition and fees vary according to course load, degree level, program and reciprocity agreements. *Financial support:* In 2013–14, 107 students received support. Unspecified assistantships available. Financial award applicants required to submit FAFSA. *Unit head:* Dr. Paul Wirtz, Dean, 859-572-5229, Fax: 859-572-6623, E-mail: wasicskom1@nku.edu. *Application contact:* Dr. Christian Gamm, Director of Graduate Programs, 859-572-6364, Fax: 859-572-6670, E-mail: gammc1@nku.edu.
Website: http://www.nku.edu/~education/.

Northern Michigan University, College of Graduate Studies, College of Health Sciences and Professional Studies, School of Education, Leadership and Public Service, Marquette, MI 49855-5301. Offers administration and supervision (MAE, Ed S); elementary education (MAE); instruction (MAE); learning disabilities (MAE); public administration (MPA), including criminal justice administration, healthcare administration, human resource administration, public management, state and local government; reading education (MAE, Ed S), including literacy leadership (Ed S), reading (MAE), reading specialist (MAE); school guidance counseling (MAE); science education (MS); secondary education (MAE). *Accreditation:* Teacher Education Accreditation Council. Part-time programs available. Postbaccalaureate distance learning degree programs offered (no on-campus study). *Faculty:* 12 full-time (7 women), 3 part-time/adjunct (1 woman). *Students:* 25 full-time (16 women), 170 part-time (130 women); includes 12 minority (2 Black or African American, non-Hispanic/Latino; 5 American Indian or Alaska Native, non-Hispanic/Latino; 4 Hispanic/Latino; 1 Two or more races, non-Hispanic/Latino), 1 international. Average age 33. 39 applicants, 95% accepted, 35 enrolled. In 2013, 48 master's, 5 other advanced degrees awarded. *Degree requirements:* For master's, thesis (for some programs). *Entrance requirements:* For master's, minimum GPA of 3.0. Additional exam requirements/recommendations for international students: Required—TOEFL (minimum score 550 paper-based; 79 iBT), IELTS (minimum score 6.5). *Application deadline:* For fall admission, 7/1 priority date for domestic students; for winter admission, 11/15 for domestic students; for spring admission, 3/17 for domestic students. Applications are processed on a rolling basis. Application fee: $50. *Expenses:* Tuition, state resident: part-time $427 per credit. Tuition, nonresident: part-time $614.50 per credit. *Required fees:* $325 per semester. Tuition and fees vary according to course load and program. *Financial support:* In 2013–14, 2 research assistantships were awarded; career-related internships or fieldwork, Federal Work-Study, institutionally sponsored loans, and unspecified assistantships also available. Support available to part-time students. Financial award application deadline: 3/1. *Unit head:* Dr. Joseph Lubig, Associate Dean, School of Education, Leadership, and Public Service, 906-227-2780, Fax: 906-227-2764, E-mail: jlubig@nmu.edu. *Application contact:* Nancy E. Carter, Certification Counselor and Graduate Programs Coordinator, 906-227-1625, Fax: 906-227-2764, E-mail: ncarter@nmu.edu.
Website: http://www.nmu.edu/education/.

Northern State University, MS Ed Program in Educational Studies, Aberdeen, SD 57401-7198. Offers MS Ed. Part-time programs available. Postbaccalaureate distance learning degree programs offered (minimal on-campus study). *Faculty:* 59 full-time (26 women), 6 part-time/adjunct (2 women). *Students:* 5 full-time (4 women), 7 part-time (4 women). Average age 25. 11 applicants, 36% accepted, 5 enrolled. In 2013, 12 master's awarded. *Degree requirements:* For master's, comprehensive exam, thesis optional. *Entrance requirements:* For master's, minimum GPA of 2.75. Additional exam requirements/recommendations for international students: Required—TOEFL (minimum score 550 paper-based; 78 iBT), IELTS (minimum score 6). *Application deadline:* Applications are processed on a rolling basis. Application fee: $35. Electronic applications accepted. *Expenses:* Tuition, state resident: full-time $3634. Tuition, nonresident: full-time $7690. One-time fee: $35 full-time. Part-time tuition and fees vary according to course load, degree level, campus/location and reciprocity agreements. *Financial support:* In 2013–14, 3 teaching assistantships (averaging $6,478 per year) were awarded; career-related internships or fieldwork, Federal Work-Study, institutionally sponsored loans, scholarships/grants, and unspecified assistantships also available. Support available to part-time students. Financial award application deadline: 3/1; financial award applicants required to submit FAFSA. *Unit head:* Dr. Constance Geier, Dean of Education, 605-626-2558, Fax: 605-626-7190, E-mail: connie.geier@northern.edu. *Application contact:* Tammy K. Griffith, Program Assistant, 605-626-2558, Fax: 605-626-7190, E-mail: tammy.griffith@northern.edu.

North Greenville University, T. Walter Brashier Graduate School, Greer, SC 29651. Offers Christian ministry (MCM, D Min); education (M Ed, MAT); financial planning (MBA); human resources (MBA). Part-time and evening/weekend programs available. Postbaccalaureate distance learning degree programs offered (no on-campus study). *Faculty:* 10 full-time (2 women), 8 part-time/adjunct (1 woman). *Students:* 164 full-time (52 women), 186 part-time (52 women); includes 45 minority (35 Black or African American, non-Hispanic/Latino; 2 American Indian or Alaska Native, non-Hispanic/Latino; 8 Hispanic/Latino). Average age 38. 200 applicants, 90% accepted, 130 enrolled. In 2013, 71 master's, 3 doctorates awarded. *Degree requirements:* For master's,

Education—General

comprehensive exam (for some programs), thesis or alternative, capstone course. *Entrance requirements:* For master's, minimum GPA of 2.25 overall, 2.5 in major; for doctorate, MAT. Additional exam requirements/recommendations for international students: Required—TOEFL (minimum score 550 paper-based). *Application deadline:* For fall admission, 8/1 for domestic students, 6/1 for international students; for winter admission, 1/1 for domestic students, 10/1 for international students; for spring admission, 3/1 for domestic students, 1/1 for international students. Applications are processed on a rolling basis. Application fee: $30. Electronic applications accepted. *Expenses: Tuition:* Part-time $425 per hour. *Financial support:* In 2013–14, 112 students received support, including 1 research assistantship (averaging $2,000 per year); Federal Work-Study, institutionally sponsored loans, scholarships/grants, tuition waivers (partial), and unspecified assistantships also available. Support available to part-time students. Financial award applicants required to submit FAFSA. *Faculty research:* Organizational behavior, church growth, homiletics, human resources, business strategy. *Unit head:* Dr. Joseph Samuel Isgett, Jr., Vice President for Graduate Studies, 864-877-3052, Fax: 864-877-1653, E-mail: sisgett@ngu.edu. *Application contact:* Tawana P. Scott, Dean of Graduate Academic Services, 864-877-1598, Fax: 864-877-1653, E-mail: tscott@ngu.edu.
Website: http://www.ngu.edu/gradschool.php.

North Park University, School of Education, Chicago, IL 60625-4895. Offers MA. *Degree requirements:* For master's, thesis. *Entrance requirements:* For master's, GRE General Test. *Faculty research:* Teacher leadership, research design, teacher education.

Northwest Christian University, School of Education and Counseling, Eugene, OR 97401-3745. Offers clinical mental health counseling (MA); curriculum and instructional technology (M Ed); education (M Ed); school counseling (MA). Part-time and evening/weekend programs available. *Entrance requirements:* For master's, MAT, interview, minimum GPA of 3.0. Electronic applications accepted.

Northwest Oklahoma State University, School of Professional Studies, Alva, OK 73717-2799. Offers adult education management and administration (M Ed); counseling psychology (MCP); curriculum and instruction (M Ed); educational leadership (M Ed); elementary education (M Ed); reading specialist (M Ed); school counseling (M Ed); secondary education (M Ed). *Accreditation:* NCATE (one or more programs are accredited). Part-time programs available. *Degree requirements:* For master's, comprehensive exam (for some programs), thesis optional, portfolio. *Entrance requirements:* For master's, GRE General Test or MAT, minimum GPA of 2.75.

Northwestern State University of Louisiana, Graduate Studies and Research, College of Education and Human Development, Natchitoches, LA 71497. Offers M Ed, MA, MAT, Ed S. *Accreditation:* NCATE. *Degree requirements:* For master's, comprehensive exam, thesis (for some programs); for Ed S, comprehensive exam, thesis. *Entrance requirements:* For master's, GRE General Test, GRE Subject Test, minimum undergraduate GPA of 2.5; for Ed S, GRE General Test. Additional exam requirements/recommendations for international students: Required—TOEFL. Electronic applications accepted. *Faculty research:* Teacher-parent-child-friendly physical activities for young children, Net generation and social media, positive emotion and multimedia learning, the effects of Web-based mathematics resources on the motivation and achievement of high school students with learning disabilities, educational leadership.

Northwestern University, The Graduate School, School of Education and Social Policy, Evanston, IL 60208. Offers education (MS), including elementary teaching, secondary teaching, teacher leadership; human development and social policy (PhD); learning and organizational change (MS); learning sciences (MA, PhD). MA and PhD admissions and degrees offered through The Graduate School. Part-time and evening/weekend programs available. *Degree requirements:* For doctorate, comprehensive exam, thesis/dissertation. *Entrance requirements:* For master's and doctorate, GRE General Test. Electronic applications accepted. *Expenses:* Contact institution. *Faculty research:* Technology, curriculum design, welfare, education reform, learning.
See Display below and Close-Up on page 731.

Northwest Missouri State University, Graduate School, College of Education and Human Services, Maryville, MO 64468-6001. Offers MS, MS Ed, Certificate, Ed S. *Accreditation:* NCATE. Part-time programs available. *Degree requirements:* For master's, comprehensive exam; for other advanced degree, comprehensive exam, thesis. *Entrance requirements:* For master's, GRE General Test, writing sample; for other advanced degree, minimum graduate GPA of 3.25. Additional exam requirements/recommendations for international students: Required—TOEFL (minimum score 550 paper-based). Electronic applications accepted. *Faculty research:* Great books of educational administration.

Northwest Nazarene University, Graduate Studies, Program in Teacher Education, Nampa, ID 83686-5897. Offers curriculum and instruction (M Ed); educational leadership (M Ed, Ed D, Ed S); exceptional child (M Ed); reading education (M Ed). *Accreditation:* ACA (one or more programs are accredited); NCATE. Part-time programs available. Postbaccalaureate distance learning degree programs offered (no on-campus study). *Faculty:* 6 full-time (5 women), 29 part-time/adjunct (16 women). *Students:* 101 full-time (66 women), 98 part-time (74 women); includes 14 minority (1 Asian, non-Hispanic/Latino; 10 Hispanic/Latino; 3 Two or more races, non-Hispanic/Latino), 12 international. Average age 38. In 2013, 60 master's, 28 doctorates, 14 other advanced degrees awarded. *Degree requirements:* For master's, comprehensive exam (for some programs), action research project; for doctorate, thesis/dissertation; for Ed S, comprehensive exam (for some programs). *Entrance requirements:* For master's, minimum undergraduate GPA of 2.8 overall or 3.0 during final 30 semester credits, undergraduate degree; for doctorate, Ed S or equivalent; for Ed S, EDS - MEd required. Additional exam requirements/recommendations for international students: Recommended—TOEFL (minimum score 80 iBT). *Application deadline:* For fall admission, 9/1 for domestic students. Applications are processed on a rolling basis. Application fee: $50. *Expenses: Tuition:* Part-time $565 per credit. *Financial support:* In 2013–14, research assistantships (averaging $5,000 per year) were awarded. *Faculty research:* Action research, cooperative learning, accountability, institutional accreditation. *Unit head:* Dr. Paula Kellerer, Chair, 208-467-8729, Fax: 208-467-8562. *Application contact:* Lynette Kingsmore, Admissions Counselor, 208-467-8107, Fax: 208-467-8786, E-mail: lkingsmore@nnu.edu.
Website: http://www.nnu.edu/graded/.

Northwest University, School of Education, Kirkland, WA 98033. Offers education (M Ed); teaching (MIT). Part-time and evening/weekend programs available. *Faculty:* 5 full-time (2 women), 7 part-time/adjunct (5 women). *Students:* 22 full-time (16 women), 5 part-time (all women); includes 5 minority (1 Black or African American, non-Hispanic/Latino; 1 American Indian or Alaska Native, non-Hispanic/Latino; 2 Asian, non-Hispanic/Latino; 1 Hispanic/Latino). 56 applicants, 63% accepted, 26 enrolled. In 2013, 41 master's awarded. *Degree requirements:* For master's, action research project. *Entrance requirements:* For master's, Washington Educator Skills Test-Basic (WEST-B)/Washington Educator Skills Test-Endorsements (WEST-E), minimum GPA of 3.3. Additional exam requirements/recommendations for international students: Recommended—TOEFL. *Application deadline:* For fall admission, 4/1 priority date for domestic students. Application fee: $75. Electronic applications accepted. *Expenses:* Contact institution. *Financial support:* Federal Work-Study, health care benefits, and tuition waivers (full and partial) available. *Unit head:* Dr. Ron Jacobson, Dean, 425-889-5304, E-mail: ron.jacobson@northwestu.edu. *Application contact:* Aaron Oosterwyk,

---

NORTHWESTERN UNIVERSITY
School of Education and Social Policy

Northwestern University's School of Education and Social Policy offers programs leading to the M.S., M.A., and Ph.D. degrees. The following programs are offered:

- Education (M.S.), with concentrations in public and private school teaching, and advanced teaching

- Higher Education (M.S.)

- Learning and Organizational Change (M.S.)

- Learning Sciences (M.A. and Ph.D.)

- Human Development and Social Policy (Ph.D.).

For more information, please contact:

School of Education and Social Policy
Northwestern University
2120 Campus Drive
Evanston, Illinois 60208-2610
http://www.sesp.northwestern.edu

Director of Graduate and Professional Studies Enrollment, 425-889-7792, Fax: 425-803-3059, E-mail: aaron.oosterwyk@northwestu.edu.
Website: http://www.northwestu.edu/education/.

Notre Dame de Namur University, Division of Academic Affairs, School of Education and Leadership, Program in Education, Belmont, CA 94002-1908. Offers curriculum and instruction (MA); disciplinary studies (MA); educational technology (MA); multiple subject teaching credential (Certificate); single subject teaching credential (Certificate). Part-time and evening/weekend programs available. *Degree requirements:* For master's, thesis (for some programs). *Entrance requirements:* For master's, CBEST, CSET, valid teaching credential or substantial teaching experience. Additional exam requirements/recommendations for international students: Required—TOEFL (minimum score 550 paper-based; 79 iBT). Electronic applications accepted.

Notre Dame of Maryland University, Graduate Studies, Program in Teaching, Baltimore, MD 21210-2476. Offers MA. *Accreditation:* NCATE. *Entrance requirements:* For master's, Watson-Glaser Critical Thinking Appraisal, writing test, grammar test, interview. Additional exam requirements/recommendations for international students: Required—TOEFL (minimum score 500 paper-based; 61 iBT). Electronic applications accepted.

Nova Southeastern University, Abraham S. Fischler School of Education, North Miami Beach, FL 33162. Offers education (MS, Ed D, Ed S); instructional design and diversity education (MS); instructional technology and distance education (MS); speech language pathology (MS, SLPD); teaching and learning (MA). Part-time and evening/weekend programs available. Postbaccalaureate distance learning degree programs offered. *Faculty:* 120 full-time (73 women), 279 part-time/adjunct (208 women). *Students:* 2,970 full-time (2,377 women), 3,619 part-time (2,946 women); includes 3,896 minority (2,352 Black or African American, non-Hispanic/Latino; 21 American Indian or Alaska Native, non-Hispanic/Latino; 90 Asian, non-Hispanic/Latino; 1,348 Hispanic/Latino; 6 Native Hawaiian or other Pacific Islander, non-Hispanic/Latino; 79 Two or more races, non-Hispanic/Latino), 39 international. Average age 40. 2,794 applicants, 53% accepted, 968 enrolled. In 2013, 1,103 master's, 426 doctorates, 349 other advanced degrees awarded. *Degree requirements:* For master's, practicum, internship; for doctorate, thesis/dissertation; for Ed S, thesis, practicum, internship. *Entrance requirements:* For master's, MAT or GRE (for some programs), CLAST, PRAXIS I, CBEST, General Knowledge Test, teaching certification, minimum GPA of 2.5, verification of teaching, BS; for doctorate, MAT or GRE, master's degree, minimum cumulative GPA of 3.0; for Ed S, MAT or GRE, master's degree, teaching certificate; minimum GPA of 3.0. Additional exam requirements/recommendations for international students: Recommended—TOEFL (minimum score 550 paper-based; 80 iBT), IELTS (minimum score 6). *Application deadline:* Applications are processed on a rolling basis. Application fee: $50. Electronic applications accepted. *Financial support:* In 2013–14, 68 students received support. Career-related internships or fieldwork and Federal Work-Study available. Support available to part-time students. Financial award application deadline: 4/15; financial award applicants required to submit FAFSA. *Faculty research:* Instructional technology and distance education, educational leadership, speech language pathology, quality of life. *Total annual research expenditures:* $1.8 million. *Unit head:* Dr. H. Wells Singleton, Provost/Dean, 954-262-8730, Fax: 954-262-3894, E-mail: singlew@nova.edu. *Application contact:* Dr. Timothy Shields, Dean of Student Affairs, 800-986-3223 Ext. 8500, E-mail: shieldsd@nova.edu.
Website: http://www.fischlerschool.nova.edu/.

Oakland City University, School of Education, Oakland City, IN 47660-1099. Offers educational leadership (Ed D); teaching (MA). *Accreditation:* NCATE. Terminal master's awarded for partial completion of doctoral program. *Degree requirements:* For master's, thesis; for doctorate, comprehensive exam, thesis/dissertation. *Entrance requirements:* For master's, MAT, minimum GPA of 3.0, interview, resume, letters of recommendation; for doctorate, MAT, GRE, minimum GPA of 3.2, interview, resume, letters of recommendation. *Expenses:* Contact institution. *Faculty research:* Assessment, cultural diversity, teacher education, education leadership.

Oakland University, Graduate Study and Lifelong Learning, School of Education and Human Services, Rochester, MI 48309-4401. Offers M Ed, MA, MAT, MTD, PhD, Certificate, Ed S. *Accreditation:* Teacher Education Accreditation Council. Part-time and evening/weekend programs available. *Faculty:* 52 full-time (34 women), 50 part-time/adjunct (36 women). *Students:* 412 full-time (356 women), 833 part-time (658 women); includes 184 minority (128 Black or African American, non-Hispanic/Latino; 7 American Indian or Alaska Native, non-Hispanic/Latino; 23 Asian, non-Hispanic/Latino; 19 Hispanic/Latino; 7 Two or more races, non-Hispanic/Latino), 13 international. Average age 34. 747 applicants, 50% accepted, 350 enrolled. In 2013, 443 master's, 13 doctorates, 139 other advanced degrees awarded. *Degree requirements:* For doctorate, thesis/dissertation. *Entrance requirements:* For master's and doctorate, minimum GPA of 3.0 for unconditional admission. Additional exam requirements/recommendations for international students: Required—TOEFL (minimum score 550 paper-based). *Application deadline:* Applications are processed on a rolling basis. Application fee: $35. Electronic applications accepted. *Financial support:* Career-related internships or fieldwork, Federal Work-Study, institutionally sponsored loans, and tuition waivers (full) available. Financial award application deadline: 3/1; financial award applicants required to submit FAFSA. *Unit head:* Dr. Mary L. Otto, Dean, 248-370-3050, Fax: 248-370-4202, E-mail: otto@oakland.edu. *Application contact:* Christina J. Grabowski, Associate Director of Graduate Study and Lifelong Learning, 248-370-3167, Fax: 248-370-4114, E-mail: grabowsk@oakland.edu.

Occidental College, Graduate Studies, Department of Education, Los Angeles, CA 90041-3314. Offers elementary education (MAT), including liberal studies; secondary education (MAT), including English and comparative literary studies, history, life science, mathematics, physical science, social science, Spanish. Part-time programs available. *Degree requirements:* For master's, comprehensive exam, synthesis paper. *Entrance requirements:* For master's, GRE General Test, minimum GPA of 3.0. Additional exam requirements/recommendations for international students: Required—TOEFL (minimum score 625 paper-based). *Expenses:* Contact institution. *Faculty research:* Preparing teacher-leaders, curriculum development.

Ohio Dominican University, Graduate Programs, Division of Education, Columbus, OH 43219-2099. Offers curriculum and instruction (M Ed); educational leadership (M Ed); teaching English to speakers of other languages (MA). *Accreditation:* NCATE. Part-time and evening/weekend programs available. Postbaccalaureate distance learning degree programs offered. *Degree requirements:* For master's, thesis or alternative. *Entrance requirements:* For master's, minimum undergraduate GPA of 3.0, teaching certificate, teaching experience, 3 letters of recommendation. Additional exam requirements/recommendations for international students: Required—TOEFL (minimum score 550 paper-based), IELTS (minimum score 6.5).

The Ohio State University, Graduate School, College of Education and Human Ecology, Columbus, OH 43210. Offers M Ed, MA, MS, PhD, Ed S. *Accreditation:* NCATE. *Faculty:* 138. *Students:* 765 full-time (557 women), 232 part-time (165 women); includes 157 minority (74 Black or African American, non-Hispanic/Latino; 1 American Indian or Alaska Native, non-Hispanic/Latino; 23 Asian, non-Hispanic/Latino; 46 Hispanic/Latino; 13 Two or more races, non-Hispanic/Latino), 187 international. Average age 30. In 2013, 480 master's, 76 doctorates, 5 other advanced degrees awarded. Terminal master's awarded for partial completion of doctoral program. *Degree requirements:* For master's, comprehensive exam (for some programs), thesis optional; for doctorate, comprehensive exam, thesis/dissertation. *Entrance requirements:* For master's and doctorate, GRE or GMAT. Additional exam requirements/recommendations for international students: Required—TOEFL (minimum score 550 paper-based; 79 iBT), Michigan English Language Assessment Battery (minimum score 82). *Application deadline:* For fall admission, 12/1 for domestic and international students; for winter admission, 12/1 for domestic students, 11/1 for international students; for spring admission, 12/1 for domestic students, 11/1 for international students. Applications are processed on a rolling basis. Application fee: $60 ($70 for international students). Electronic applications accepted. *Financial support:* Fellowships with tuition reimbursements, research assistantships with tuition reimbursements, teaching assistantships with tuition reimbursements, career-related internships or fieldwork, Federal Work-Study, institutionally sponsored loans, scholarships/grants, traineeships, health care benefits, and unspecified assistantships available. Support available to part-time students. *Faculty research:* Math and science education; teaching professional development; issues related to urban education; health, well-being, and sports; literacy education. *Total annual research expenditures:* $19 million. *Unit head:* Cheryl Achterberg, Dean, 614-292-2461, Fax: 614-292-8052, E-mail: achterberg.1@osu.edu. *Application contact:* Graduate Admissions, 614-292-9444, Fax: 614-292-3895, E-mail: gradadmissions@osu.edu.
Website: http://ehe.osu.edu/.

The Ohio State University at Lima, Graduate Programs, Lima, OH 45804. Offers early childhood education (M Ed); education (MA); middle childhood education (M Ed); social work (MSW). Part-time programs available. *Faculty:* 37. *Students:* 8 full-time (6 women), 8 part-time (7 women). Average age 31. Terminal master's awarded for partial completion of doctoral program. *Degree requirements:* For master's, comprehensive exam (for some programs), thesis (for some programs). *Entrance requirements:* For master's, GRE, minimum GPA of 3.0. Additional exam requirements/recommendations for international students: Required—TOEFL (minimum score 550 paper-based, 79 iBT), IELTS (minimum score 7), or Michigan English Language Assessment Battery (minimum score 82). *Application deadline:* For fall admission, 6/1 for domestic and international students; for spring admission, 10/15 for domestic and international students. Applications are processed on a rolling basis. Application fee: $60 ($70 for international students). Electronic applications accepted. *Financial support:* Application deadline: 2/15. *Unit head:* Dr. Gregory Rose, Interim Dean and Director, 419-995-8481, E-mail: rose.9@osu.edu. *Application contact:* Graduate Admissions, 614-292-9444, Fax: 614-292-3895, E-mail: gradadmissions@osu.edu.

The Ohio State University at Marion, Graduate Programs, Marion, OH 43302-5695. Offers early childhood education (pre-K to grade 3) (M Ed); education - teaching and learning (MA); middle childhood education (grades 4-9) (M Ed). Part-time programs available. *Faculty:* 38. *Students:* 17 full-time (13 women); includes 1 minority (Asian, non-Hispanic/Latino). Average age 27. *Degree requirements:* For master's, comprehensive exam (for some programs), thesis (for some programs). *Entrance requirements:* For master's, GRE, minimum undergraduate GPA of 3.0. Additional exam requirements/recommendations for international students: Required—TOEFL (minimum score 550 paper-based, 79 iBT), IELTS (minimum score 7) or Michigan English Language Assessment Battery (minimum score 82). *Application deadline:* For fall admission, 6/1 for domestic students, 6/1 priority date for international students; for spring admission, 10/15 for domestic students, 10/15 priority date for international students. Applications are processed on a rolling basis. Application fee: $60 ($70 for international students). Electronic applications accepted. *Financial support:* Application deadline: 2/15; applicants required to submit FAFSA. *Unit head:* Dr. Gregory S. Rose, Dean/Director, 740-725-6218, E-mail: rose.9@osu.edu. *Application contact:* Graduate Admissions, 614-292-9444, Fax: 614-292-3895, E-mail: gradadmissions@osu.edu.

The Ohio State University–Mansfield Campus, Graduate Programs, Mansfield, OH 44906-1599. Offers early childhood education (M Ed); education (MA); middle childhood education (M Ed); social work (MSW). Part-time programs available. *Faculty:* 40. *Students:* 18 full-time (17 women), 30 part-time (29 women). Average age 31. *Degree requirements:* For master's, comprehensive exam (for some programs), thesis (for some programs). *Entrance requirements:* For master's, GRE, minimum GPA of 3.0. Additional exam requirements/recommendations for international students: Required—TOEFL (minimum 550 paper-based, 79 iBT), IELTS (minimum score 7) or Michigan English Language Assessment Battery (minimum score 82). *Application deadline:* For fall admission, 6/1 for domestic and international students; for spring admission, 10/15 for domestic and international students. Applications are processed on a rolling basis. Application fee: $60 ($70 for international students). Electronic applications accepted. *Financial support:* Teaching assistantships with full tuition reimbursements, Federal Work-Study, and scholarships/grants available. Support available to part-time students. Financial award application deadline: 2/15. *Unit head:* Dr. Stephen M. Gavazzi, Dean and Director, 419-755-4221, Fax: 419-755-4241, E-mail: gavazzi.1@osu.edu. *Application contact:* Graduate Admissions, 614-292-9444, Fax: 614-292-3895, E-mail: gradadmissions@osu.edu.

The Ohio State University–Newark Campus, Graduate Programs, Newark, OH 43055-1797. Offers early/middle childhood education (M Ed); education - teaching and learning (MA); social work (MSW). Part-time programs available. *Faculty:* 53. *Students:* 10 full-time (9 women), 27 part-time (24 women); includes 3 minority (1 Black or African American, non-Hispanic/Latino; 2 Hispanic/Latino). Average age 35. Terminal master's awarded for partial completion of doctoral program. *Degree requirements:* For master's, comprehensive exam (for some programs), thesis (for some programs). *Entrance requirements:* For master's, GRE, minimum GPA of 3.0. Additional exam requirements/recommendations for international students: Required—TOEFL (minimum score 550 paper-based; 79 iBT), IELTS (minimum score 7), or Michigan English Language Assessment Battery (minimum score 82). *Application deadline:* For fall admission, 6/1 for domestic and international students; for spring admission, 10/15 for domestic students, 2/1 for international students. Applications are processed on a rolling basis. Application fee: $60 ($70 for international students). Electronic applications accepted. *Financial support:* Application deadline: 2/15. *Unit head:* Dr. William L. MacDonald, Dean/Director, 740-366-9333 Ext. 330, E-mail: macdonald.24@osu.edu. *Application contact:* Graduate Admissions, 614-292-9444, Fax: 614-292-3985, E-mail: gradadmissions@osu.edu.

Ohio University, Graduate College, Gladys W. and David H. Patton College of Education and Human Services, Athens, OH 45701-2979. Offers M Ed, MS, MSA, Ed D, PhD. *Accreditation:* NCATE. Part-time and evening/weekend programs available. *Degree requirements:* For master's, comprehensive exam (for some programs), thesis or alternative; for doctorate, comprehensive exam, thesis/dissertation. *Entrance requirements:* For master's, GRE General Test or MAT; for doctorate, GRE General Test, MAT, master's degree. Additional exam requirements/recommendations for international students: Required—TOEFL (minimum score 550 paper-based; 80 iBT) or IELTS (minimum score 6.5). Electronic applications accepted. *Faculty research:* School improvement, partnerships, literacy, rural education.

Education—General

Ohio Valley University, School of Graduate Education, Vienna, WV 26105-8000. Offers curriculum and instruction (M Ed). Postbaccalaureate distance learning degree programs offered. *Faculty:* 2 full-time (both women), 2 part-time/adjunct (both women). *Students:* 10 full-time (4 women), 30 part-time (18 women). *Entrance requirements:* For master's, 2 letters of recommendation, official transcripts from all previous institutions, essay. Application fee: $30. *Unit head:* Dr. Toni DeVore, Chair, 304-865-6149, E-mail: toni.devore@ovu.edu. *Application contact:* Brad Wilson, Coordinator of Recruiting and Retention, 304-865-6177, E-mail: brad.wilson@ovu.edu.
Website: http://www.ovu.edu/academics/education/school-of-graduate-education.html.

Oklahoma City University, Petree College of Arts and Sciences, Programs in Education, Oklahoma City, OK 73106-1402. Offers applied behavioral studies (M Ed); early childhood education (M Ed), including Montessori education; elementary education (M Ed), including Montessori education. Part-time and evening/weekend programs available. *Students:* 35 full-time (20 women), 9 part-time (7 women); includes 17 minority (12 Black or African American, non-Hispanic/Latino; 1 American Indian or Alaska Native, non-Hispanic/Latino; 1 Asian, non-Hispanic/Latino; 3 Two or more races, non-Hispanic/Latino), 6 international. Average age 32. 49 applicants, 61% accepted, 20 enrolled. In 2013, 24 master's awarded. *Entrance requirements:* For master's, bachelor's degree from accredited institution, minimum GPA of 3.0, essay, recommendation letters. Additional exam requirements/recommendations for international students: Required—TOEFL (minimum score 550 paper-based; 80 iBT). *Application deadline:* Applications are processed on a rolling basis. Application fee: $50. Electronic applications accepted. *Expenses: Tuition:* Full-time $16,848; part-time $936 per credit hour. Tuition and fees vary according to course load, degree level and program. *Financial support:* Career-related internships or fieldwork, Federal Work-Study, institutionally sponsored loans, scholarships/grants, and tuition waivers available. Support available to part-time students. Financial award application deadline: 6/1; financial award applicants required to submit FAFSA. *Faculty research:* Adult literacy, cognition, reading strategies. *Unit head:* Dr. Lois Lawler-Brown, Chair, 405-208-5374, Fax: 405-208-6012, E-mail: llbrown@okcu.edu. *Application contact:* Heidi Puckett, Director of Graduate Admissions, 800-633-7242, Fax: 405-208-5916, E-mail: gadmissions@okcu.edu.
Website: http://www.okcu.edu/petree/education/graduate.aspx.

Oklahoma State University, College of Education, Stillwater, OK 74078. Offers MS, Ed D, PhD, Ed S. *Accreditation:* NCATE. Part-time programs available. Postbaccalaureate distance learning degree programs offered. *Faculty:* 95 full-time (63 women), 83 part-time/adjunct (49 women). *Students:* 280 full-time (190 women), 589 part-time (386 women); includes 186 minority (37 Black or African American, non-Hispanic/Latino; 41 American Indian or Alaska Native, non-Hispanic/Latino; 12 Asian, non-Hispanic/Latino; 49 Hispanic/Latino; 47 Two or more races, non-Hispanic/Latino), 30 international. Average age 36. 513 applicants, 40% accepted, 163 enrolled. In 2013, 162 master's, 57 doctorates awarded. *Degree requirements:* For master's, thesis or alternative; for doctorate, comprehensive exam, thesis/dissertation. *Entrance requirements:* For master's and doctorate, GRE or GMAT. Additional exam requirements/recommendations for international students: Required—TOEFL (minimum score 550 paper-based; 79 iBT). *Application deadline:* For fall admission, 3/1 priority date for international students; for spring admission, 8/1 priority date for international students. Applications are processed on a rolling basis. Application fee: $40 ($75 for international students). Electronic applications accepted. *Expenses: Tuition:* state resident: full-time $4272; part-time $178 per credit hour. Tuition, nonresident: full-time $17,472; part-time $709 per credit hour. *Required fees:* $2413.20; $100.55 per credit hour. One-time fee: $50 full-time. Part-time tuition and fees vary according to course load and campus/location. *Financial support:* In 2013–14, 48 research assistantships (averaging $9,698 per year), 75 teaching assistantships (averaging $9,085 per year) were awarded; career-related internships or fieldwork, Federal Work-Study, scholarships/grants, health care benefits, tuition waivers (partial), and unspecified assistantships also available. Support available to part-time students. Financial award application deadline: 3/1; financial award applicants required to submit FAFSA. *Unit head:* Dr. Pamela Carroll, Dean, 405-744-3373, Fax: 405-744-6399.
Website: http://education.okstate.edu/.

Old Dominion University, Darden College of Education, Norfolk, VA 23529. Offers MS, MS Ed, PhD, Ed S. Part-time and evening/weekend programs available. Postbaccalaureate distance learning degree programs offered (no on-campus study). *Faculty:* 94 full-time (55 women), 62 part-time/adjunct (40 women). *Students:* 649 full-time (526 women), 764 part-time (543 women); includes 323 minority (214 Black or African American, non-Hispanic/Latino; 1 American Indian or Alaska Native, non-Hispanic/Latino; 12 Asian, non-Hispanic/Latino; 63 Hispanic/Latino; 3 Native Hawaiian or other Pacific Islander, non-Hispanic/Latino; 30 Two or more races, non-Hispanic/Latino), 18 international. Average age 33. 1,125 applicants, 72% accepted. In 2013, 493 master's, 41 doctorates, 24 other advanced degrees awarded. *Degree requirements:* For master's, thesis (for some programs), exam; for doctorate, comprehensive exam, thesis/dissertation; for Ed S, comprehensive exam. *Entrance requirements:* For doctorate, GRE General Test, master's degree, minimum GPA of 3.25; for Ed S, GRE General Test or MAT. Additional exam requirements/recommendations for international students: Required—TOEFL (minimum score 550 paper-based). *Application deadline:* For fall admission, 6/1 priority date for domestic and international students; for spring admission, 11/1 priority date for domestic and international students. Applications are processed on a rolling basis. Application fee: $50. Electronic applications accepted. *Expenses: Tuition:* state resident: full-time $9888; part-time $412 per credit. Tuition, nonresident: full-time $25,152; part-time $1048 per credit. *Required fees:* $59 per semester. One-time fee: $50. *Financial support:* In 2013–14, 141 students received support, including 4 fellowships with full and partial tuition reimbursements available (averaging $15,000 per year), 60 research assistantships with full and partial tuition reimbursements available (averaging $15,000 per year), 72 teaching assistantships with full and partial tuition reimbursements available (averaging $15,000 per year); career-related internships or fieldwork, Federal Work-Study, institutionally sponsored loans, scholarships/grants, tuition waivers (partial), and unspecified assistantships also available. Support available to part-time students. Financial award application deadline: 2/15; financial award applicants required to submit CSS PROFILE or FAFSA. *Faculty research:* Effective urban teaching practices, curriculum theory, clinical practices, special education, instructional technology. *Total annual research expenditures:* $8.1 million. *Unit head:* Dr. Linda Irwin-DeVitis, Dean, 757-683-3938, Fax: 757-683-5083, E-mail: ldevitis@odu.edu. *Application contact:* Nechell Bonds, Director of Admissions, 757-683-3685, Fax: 757-683-3255, E-mail: gradadmit@odu.edu.
Website: http://education.odu.edu/.

Olivet College, Program in Education, Olivet, MI 49076-9701. Offers MAT. *Degree requirements:* For master's, portfolio. *Entrance requirements:* For master's, current K-12 teacher certification. Electronic applications accepted.

Olivet Nazarene University, Graduate School, Division of Education, Bourbonnais, IL 60914. Offers curriculum and instruction (MAE); elementary education (MAT); library information specialist (MAE); reading specialist (MAE); school leadership (MAE); secondary education (MAT). *Accreditation:* NCATE. Evening/weekend programs available. *Degree requirements:* For master's, thesis or alternative.

Oral Roberts University, School of Education, Tulsa, OK 74171. Offers Christian school administration (K-12) (MA Ed, Ed D); Christian school curriculum development (MA Ed); college and higher education administration (Ed D); public school administration (K-12) (MA Ed, Ed D); public school teaching (MA Ed). *Accreditation:* NCATE. Part-time programs available. Postbaccalaureate distance learning degree programs offered (minimal on-campus study). *Degree requirements:* For master's, comprehensive exam, thesis optional; for doctorate, comprehensive exam, thesis/dissertation. *Entrance requirements:* For master's, GRE General Test or MAT, minimum GPA of 3.0; for doctorate, minimum GPA of 3.0. Additional exam requirements/recommendations for international students: Required—TOEFL (minimum score 500 paper-based). *Expenses:* Contact institution. *Faculty research:* Teacher effectiveness, college success in high achieving African-Americans, professional development practices.

Oregon State University, College of Education, Program in Education, Corvallis, OR 97331. Offers Ed M, MAIS, MS, Ed D, PhD. Part-time programs available. Postbaccalaureate distance learning degree programs offered (no on-campus study). *Faculty:* 9 full-time (5 women), 5 part-time/adjunct (2 women). *Students:* 3 full-time (0 women), 96 part-time (62 women); includes 28 minority (7 Black or African American, non-Hispanic/Latino; 3 American Indian or Alaska Native, non-Hispanic/Latino; 6 Asian, non-Hispanic/Latino; 9 Hispanic/Latino; 3 Two or more races, non-Hispanic/Latino). Average age 44. 46 applicants, 48% accepted, 18 enrolled. In 2013, 20 master's, 14 doctorates awarded. Terminal master's awarded for partial completion of doctoral program. *Median time to degree:* Of those who began their doctoral program in fall 2005, 45% received their degree in 8 years or less. *Degree requirements:* For master's, variable foreign language requirement, thesis (for some programs); for doctorate, variable foreign language requirement, thesis/dissertation. *Entrance requirements:* Additional exam requirements/recommendations for international students: Required—TOEFL (minimum score 575 paper-based). *Application deadline:* For fall admission, 3/1 for domestic students. Application fee: $60. *Expenses:* Tuition, state resident: full-time $11,664; part-time $432 per credit hour. Tuition, nonresident: full-time $19,197; part-time $711 per credit hour. *Required fees:* $1446; $443 per quarter. One-time fee: $300. Tuition and fees vary according to course load and program. *Financial support:* Fellowships, research assistantships, teaching assistantships, career-related internships or fieldwork, Federal Work-Study, and institutionally sponsored loans available. Support available to part-time students. Financial award application deadline: 2/1. *Faculty research:* School administration, educational foundations, research methodology, education policy development, higher education administration. *Unit head:* Dr. Larry Flick, Dean, 541-737-3664, E-mail: larry.flick@oregonstate.edu. *Application contact:* Dr. Randy Bell, Associate Dean for Academic Affairs, 541-737-6387, Fax: 541-737-3313, E-mail: randy.bell@oregonstate.edu.

Oregon State University–Cascades, Program in Education, Bend, OR 97701. Offers MAT.

Ottawa University, Graduate Studies-Arizona, Program in Education, Ottawa, KS 66067-3399. Offers community college counseling (MA); curriculum and instruction (MA); early childhood (MA); education intervention (MA); education leadership (MA); education technology (MA); Montessori early childhood education (MA); Montessori elementary education (MA); professional development (MA); school guidance counseling (MA); special education - cross categorical (MA). Programs offered in Mesa, Phoenix, Tempe and West Valley, AZ. *Accreditation:* NCATE. Part-time programs available. *Degree requirements:* For master's, thesis or alternative. *Entrance requirements:* For master's, minimum undergraduate GPA of 3.0, copy of current state certification or teaching license. Additional exam requirements/recommendations for international students: Required—TOEFL (minimum score 550 paper-based). Electronic applications accepted. *Expenses:* Contact institution.

Otterbein University, Department of Education, Westerville, OH 43081. Offers MAE, MAT. *Accreditation:* NCATE. *Degree requirements:* For master's, capstone project. *Entrance requirements:* For master's, 2 reference forms, essay, interview. Additional exam requirements/recommendations for international students: Required—TOEFL (minimum score 550 paper-based; 79 iBT). *Faculty research:* Computer technology middle level education, assessment, teacher leadership, multicultural education.

Our Lady of Holy Cross College, Program in Education and Counseling, New Orleans, LA 70131-7399. Offers administration and supervision (M Ed); curriculum and instruction (M Ed); marriage and family counseling (MA); school counseling (M Ed, MA). *Accreditation:* ACA; NCATE. Part-time and evening/weekend programs available. *Degree requirements:* For master's, thesis. *Entrance requirements:* For master's, GRE General Test, minimum GPA of 2.7.

Our Lady of the Lake University of San Antonio, School of Professional Studies, San Antonio, TX 78207-4689. Offers communication and learning disorders (MA); curriculum and instruction (M Ed), including bilingual education, early childhood education, English as a second language, integrated math teaching, integrated science teaching, reading specialist; early elementary education (M Ed); generic special education (M Ed), including elementary education; human sciences (MA); intermediate education (M Ed), including math/science education, professional studies; learning resources specialist (M Ed); nursing (MSN), including nurse administration, nurse education; principal (M Ed); psychology (MS, Psy D), including counseling psychology, marriage and family therapy (MS), school psychology (MS); school counseling (M Ed); secondary education (M Ed). Part-time and evening/weekend programs available. Postbaccalaureate distance learning degree programs offered (minimal on-campus study). *Faculty:* 26 full-time (20 women), 14 part-time/adjunct (10 women). *Students:* 252 full-time (229 women), 107 part-time (95 women); includes 233 minority (33 Black or African American, non-Hispanic/Latino; 1 American Indian or Alaska Native, non-Hispanic/Latino; 6 Asian, non-Hispanic/Latino; 193 Hispanic/Latino), 1 international. Average age 34. 608 applicants, 25% accepted, 103 enrolled. In 2013, 75 master's, 10 doctorates awarded. *Degree requirements:* For master's, comprehensive exam; for doctorate, thesis/dissertation, internship, qualifying exam. *Entrance requirements:* For master's, GRE General Test or MAT; for doctorate, GRE General Test or MAT, interview. Additional exam requirements/recommendations for international students: Required—TOEFL. *Application deadline:* For fall admission, 4/1 priority date for domestic and international students; for spring admission, 11/1 priority date for domestic and international students; for summer admission, 2/1 priority date for domestic students, 2/12 priority date for international students. Applications are processed on a rolling basis. Application fee: $25 ($50 for international students). Electronic applications accepted. *Expenses: Tuition:* Full-time $9120; part-time $760 per credit. *Required fees:* $698; $334 per trimester. Tuition and fees vary according to course load, degree level, campus/location and program. *Financial support:* Research assistantships, teaching assistantships, career-related internships or fieldwork, Federal Work-Study, institutionally sponsored loans, scholarships/grants, and tuition waivers (partial) available. Support available to part-time students. Financial award application deadline: 4/15. *Faculty research:* Culturally and linguistically diverse persons within various professional contexts, research, service-learning, student-centeredness, clinical experiences. *Unit head:* Dr. Marcheta Evans, Dean, 210-431-4140, E-mail: sps@

ollusa.edu. *Application contact:* Graduate Admission, 210-431-3961 Ext. 2314, Fax: 210-431-4013, E-mail: gradadm@lake.ollusa.edu.
Website: http://www.ollusa.edu/s/1190/ollu.aspx?sid=1190&gid=1&pgid=975.

Pace University, School of Education, New York, NY 10038. Offers adolescent education (MST); childhood education (MST); early childhood development, learning and intervention (MST); educational leadership (MS Ed); educational technology studies (MS); inclusive adolescent education (MST); literacy (MS Ed); school business management (Certificate); special education (MS Ed). *Accreditation:* NCATE. Part-time and evening/weekend programs available. *Students:* 186 full-time (154 women), 441 part-time (315 women); includes 209 minority (89 Black or African American, non-Hispanic/Latino; 2 American Indian or Alaska Native, non-Hispanic/Latino; 30 Asian, non-Hispanic/Latino; 74 Hispanic/Latino; 1 Native Hawaiian or other Pacific Islander, non-Hispanic/Latino; 13 Two or more races, non-Hispanic/Latino), 7 international. Average age 29. 207 applicants, 71% accepted, 105 enrolled. In 2013, 296 master's, 25 other advanced degrees awarded. *Degree requirements:* For master's, internship. *Entrance requirements:* For master's, interview, teaching certificate. Additional exam requirements/recommendations for international students: Required—TOEFL. *Application deadline:* For fall admission, 8/1 priority date for domestic students, 6/1 for international students; for spring admission, 12/1 priority date for domestic students, 10/1 for international students. Applications are processed on a rolling basis. Application fee: $70. Electronic applications accepted. *Expenses:* Contact institution. *Financial support:* Research assistantships, career-related internships or fieldwork, and Federal Work-Study available. Support available to part-time students. Financial award applicants required to submit FAFSA. *Faculty research:* Teacher education, technology in education, STEM, literacy education, special education. *Total annual research expenditures:* $1.3 million. *Unit head:* Dr. Andrea M. Spencer, Dean, School of Education, 914-773-3341, E-mail: aspencer@pace.edu. *Application contact:* Susan Ford-Goldschein, Director of Graduate Admissions, 212-346-1660, Fax: 212-346-1585, E-mail: gradnyc@pace.edu.
Website: http://www.pace.edu/school-of-education.

Pacific Lutheran University, Graduate Programs and Continuing Education, School of Education and Kinesiology, Tacoma, WA 98447. Offers MAE. *Accreditation:* NCATE. Part-time and evening/weekend programs available. *Faculty:* 9 full-time (5 women), 8 part-time/adjunct (2 women). *Students:* 49 full-time (35 women), 30 part-time (23 women); includes 18 minority (5 Black or African American, non-Hispanic/Latino; 5 Asian, non-Hispanic/Latino; 4 Hispanic/Latino; 4 Two or more races, non-Hispanic/Latino), 1 international. Average age 34. 91 applicants, 78% accepted, 52 enrolled. In 2013, 35 master's awarded. *Degree requirements:* For master's, comprehensive exam, thesis optional. *Entrance requirements:* For master's, WEST B or WEST B exemption, interview. Additional exam requirements/recommendations for international students: Required—TOEFL (minimum score 550 paper-based; 88 iBT). *Application deadline:* For fall admission, 11/20 priority date for domestic and international students; for winter admission, 1/15 priority date for domestic and international students; for spring admission, 3/7 priority date for domestic and international students. Applications are processed on a rolling basis. Application fee: $40. Electronic applications accepted. *Expenses:* Contact institution. *Financial support:* In 2013–14, 13 students received support. Fellowships, Federal Work-Study, scholarships/grants, and unspecified assistantships available. Financial award application deadline: 3/1; financial award applicants required to submit FAFSA. *Unit head:* Dr. Frank Kline, Dean, 253-535-7272, E-mail: klinefm@plu.edu. *Application contact:* Rachel Christopherson, Director of Graduate Admission, 253-535-8570, Fax: 253-536-5136, E-mail: gradadmission@plu.edu.

Pacific Union College, Education Department, Angwin, CA 94508-9707. Offers education (M Ed); elementary teaching (MAT); secondary teaching (MAT). Part-time programs available. *Faculty:* 3 full-time (1 woman), 3 part-time/adjunct (all women). *Students:* 3 full-time (2 women), 11 part-time (7 women); includes 4 minority (1 Black or African American, non-Hispanic/Latino; 2 Asian, non-Hispanic/Latino; 1 Hispanic/Latino). Average age 35. In 2013, 2 master's awarded. *Degree requirements:* For master's, thesis, action research project, field experiences. *Entrance requirements:* For master's, GRE (for M Ed), two interviews, teaching credential, letters of recommendation, essay. *Application deadline:* Applications are processed on a rolling basis. Application fee: $0. *Expenses: Tuition:* Full-time $26,550; part-time $770 per quarter hour. *Required fees:* $930. Full-time tuition and fees vary according to course load and student's religious affiliation. Part-time tuition and fees vary according to class time and student's religious affiliation. *Financial support:* In 2013–14, 2 students received support. Scholarships/grants available. Support available to part-time students. *Faculty research:* Choice theory. *Unit head:* Prof. Thomas Lee, Chair, 707-965-6646, Fax: 707-965-6645, E-mail: tdlee@puc.edu. *Application contact:* Marsha Crow, Assistant Chair/Accreditation and Certification Specialist/Credential Analyst, 707-965-6643, Fax: 707-965-6645, E-mail: mcrow@puc.edu.
Website: http://www.puc.edu/academics/departments/education/.

Pacific University, College of Education, Forest Grove, OR 97116-1797. Offers early childhood education (MAT); education (MAE); elementary education (MAT); high school education (MAT); middle school education (MAT); special education (MAT); visual function in learning (M Ed). *Accreditation:* NCATE. Part-time and evening/weekend programs available. *Degree requirements:* For master's, research project. *Entrance requirements:* For master's, California Basic Educational Skills Test, PRAXIS II, minimum undergraduate GPA of 2.75, 3.0 graduate. Additional exam requirements/recommendations for international students: Required—TOEFL. Electronic applications accepted. *Expenses:* Contact institution. *Faculty research:* Defining a culturally competent classroom, technology in the k-12 classroom, Socratic seminars, social studies education.

Palm Beach Atlantic University, School of Education and Behavioral Studies, West Palm Beach, FL 33416-4708. Offers counseling psychology (MS), including addictions/mental health, general counseling, marriage and family therapy, mental health counseling, school guidance counseling. Part-time and evening/weekend programs available. *Faculty:* 9 full-time (3 women), 12 part-time/adjunct (4 women). *Students:* 272 full-time (225 women), 65 part-time (57 women); includes 152 minority (81 Black or African American, non-Hispanic/Latino; 3 Asian, non-Hispanic/Latino; 55 Hispanic/Latino; 1 Native Hawaiian or other Pacific Islander, non-Hispanic/Latino; 12 Two or more races, non-Hispanic/Latino), 10 international. Average age 35. 110 applicants, 87% accepted, 87 enrolled. In 2013, 112 master's awarded. *Entrance requirements:* For master's, GRE or MAT and MMPI-2, minimum GPA of 3.0. Additional exam requirements/recommendations for international students: Required—TOEFL (minimum score 550 paper-based; 79 iBT). *Application deadline:* For fall admission, 7/15 priority date for domestic students; for spring admission, 11/15 priority date for domestic students. Applications are processed on a rolling basis. Application fee: $45. Electronic applications accepted. *Expenses: Tuition:* Part-time $495 per credit hour. *Required fees:* $495 per credit hour. Part-time tuition and fees vary according to course load and program. *Financial support:* Application deadline: 5/1; applicants required to submit FAFSA. *Unit head:* Dr. Gene Sale, Program Director, 561-803-2352. *Application contact:* Graduate Admissions, 888-468-6722, E-mail: grad@pba.edu.
Website: http://www.pba.edu/graduate-counseling-program.

Park University, School of Graduate and Professional Studies, Kansas City, MO 54105. Offers adult education (M Ed); business and government leadership (Graduate Certificate); business, government, and global society (MPA); communication and leadership (MA); creative and life writing (Graduate Certificate); disaster and emergency management (MPA, Graduate Certificate); educational leadership (M Ed); finance (MBA, Graduate Certificate); general business (MBA); global business (Graduate Certificate); healthcare administration (MHA); healthcare services management and leadership (Graduate Certificate); international business (MBA); language and literacy (M Ed), including English for speakers of other languages, special reading teacher/literacy coach; leadership of international healthcare organizations (Graduate Certificate); management information systems (MBA, Graduate Certificate); music performance (ADP, Graduate Certificate), including cello (MM, ADP), piano (MM, ADP), viola (MM, ADP), violin (MM, ADP); nonprofit and community services management (MPA); nonprofit leadership (Graduate Certificate); performance (MM), including cello (MM, ADP), piano (MM, ADP), viola (MM, ADP), violin (MM, ADP); public management (MPA); social work (MSW); teacher leadership (M Ed), including curriculum and assessment, instructional leader. Part-time and evening/weekend programs available. Postbaccalaureate distance learning degree programs offered (no on-campus study). *Students:* 862 full-time (482 women); includes 55 minority (30 Black or African American, non-Hispanic/Latino; 2 American Indian or Alaska Native, non-Hispanic/Latino; 4 Asian, non-Hispanic/Latino; 14 Hispanic/Latino; 5 Two or more races, non-Hispanic/Latino), 141 international. Average age 34. 497 applicants, 62% accepted, 119 enrolled. In 2013, 281 master's, 14 other advanced degrees awarded. *Degree requirements:* For master's, comprehensive exam (for some programs), thesis (for some programs), internship (for some programs); exam (for some programs). *Entrance requirements:* For master's, GRE or GMAT (for some programs), teacher certification (for some M Ed programs), letters of recommendation, essay, resume (for some programs). Additional exam requirements/recommendations for international students: Required—TOEFL (minimum score 550 paper-based; 79 iBT), IELTS (minimum score 6). *Application deadline:* For fall admission, 8/1 priority date for domestic students, 7/15 priority date for international students; for spring admission, 1/1 priority date for domestic students, 11/1 priority date for international students. Applications are processed on a rolling basis. Application fee: $50 ($100 for international students). Electronic applications accepted. *Financial support:* In 2013–14, 2 research assistantships with full tuition reimbursements (averaging $15,760 per year) were awarded. Financial award applicants required to submit FAFSA. *Unit head:* Dr. Laurie Dipadova-Stocks, Dean of Graduate and Professional Studies, 816-559-5624, Fax: 816-472-1173, E-mail: ldipadovastocks@park.edu. *Application contact:* Judith Appollis, Director of Graduate Admissions and Internationalization, School of Graduate and Professional Studies, 816-559-5627, Fax: 816-472-1173, E-mail: gradschool@park.edu.
Website: http://www.park.edu/grad.

Penn State Harrisburg, Graduate School, School of Behavioral Sciences and Education, Middletown, PA 17057-4898. Offers applied behavior analysis (MA); applied clinical psychology (MA); applied psychological research (MA); community psychology and social change (MA); health education (M Ed); literacy education (M Ed); teaching and curriculum (M Ed, Certificate); training and development (M Ed). Part-time and evening/weekend programs available. *Financial support:* Career-related internships or fieldwork available. *Unit head:* Dr. Mukund S. Kulkarni, Chancellor, 717-948-6105, Fax: 717-948-6452, E-mail: msk5@psu.edu. *Application contact:* Robert W. Coffman, Jr., Director of Enrollment Management, Admissions, 717-948-6250, Fax: 717-948-6325, E-mail: ric1@psu.edu.
Website: http://harrisburg.psu.edu/behavioral-sciences-and-education/.

Penn State University Park, Graduate School, College of Education, State College, PA 16802. Offers M Ed, MA, MPS, MS, D Ed, PhD, Certificate. *Accreditation:* NCATE. Part-time and evening/weekend programs available. *Students:* 523 full-time (357 women), 244 part-time (152 women); includes 137 minority (57 Black or African American, non-Hispanic/Latino; 4 American Indian or Alaska Native, non-Hispanic/Latino; 33 Asian, non-Hispanic/Latino; 30 Hispanic/Latino; 1 Native Hawaiian or other Pacific Islander, non-Hispanic/Latino; 12 Two or more races, non-Hispanic/Latino), 171 international. Average age 34. 630 applicants, 52% accepted, 170 enrolled. In 2013, 146 master's, 72 doctorates awarded. *Entrance requirements:* Additional exam requirements/recommendations for international students: Required—TOEFL (minimum score 550 paper-based; 80 iBT). *Application deadline:* Applications are processed on a rolling basis. Application fee: $65. Electronic applications accepted. *Financial support:* Fellowships, research assistantships, teaching assistantships, career-related internships or fieldwork, Federal Work-Study, and unspecified assistantships available. Support available to part-time students. Financial award application deadline: 2/15; financial award applicants required to submit FAFSA. *Unit head:* Dr. David H. Monk, Dean, 814-865-2523, Fax: 814-865-0555, E-mail: dhm6@psu.edu. *Application contact:* Cynthia E. Nicosia, Director, Graduate Enrollment Services, 814-865-1834, Fax: 814-863-4627, E-mail: cey1@psu.edu.
Website: http://www.ed.psu.edu/educ/.

Pepperdine University, Graduate School of Education and Psychology, Division of Education, MA Program in Education, Malibu, CA 90263. Offers MA. Part-time and evening/weekend programs available. Postbaccalaureate distance learning degree programs offered (minimal on-campus study). *Students:* 107 full-time (87 women), 35 part-time (24 women); includes 56 minority (19 Black or African American, non-Hispanic/Latino; 1 American Indian or Alaska Native, non-Hispanic/Latino; 12 Asian, non-Hispanic/Latino; 20 Hispanic/Latino; 4 Native Hawaiian or other Pacific Islander, non-Hispanic/Latino), 15 international. *Entrance requirements:* For master's, two professional recommendations, one-to-two page statement of educational purpose. Additional exam requirements/recommendations for international students: Required—TOEFL. *Application deadline:* For fall admission, 6/1 priority date for domestic students; for spring admission, 10/1 priority date for domestic students. Applications are processed on a rolling basis. Application fee: $55. Tuition and fees vary according to program. *Financial support:* Career-related internships or fieldwork, institutionally sponsored loans, scholarships/grants, traineeships, and unspecified assistantships available. Support available to part-time students. Financial award application deadline: 7/1; financial award applicants required to submit FAFSA. *Unit head:* Dr. Nancy Harding, Director, Teacher Education, 310-568-5600, E-mail: nancy.harding@pepperdine.edu. *Application contact:* Jennifer Agatep, Admissions Manager, Education, 310-258-2849, E-mail: jennifer.agatep@pepperdine.edu.
Website: http://gsep.pepperdine.edu/masters-education/.

Peru State College, Graduate Programs, Program in Education, Peru, NE 68421. Offers curriculum and instruction (MS Ed). *Accreditation:* NCATE. Part-time programs available. *Faculty:* 5 full-time (2 women), 5 part-time/adjunct (4 women). *Students:* 211 full-time (166 women), 158 part-time (118 women); includes 20 minority (9 Black or African American, non-Hispanic/Latino; 3 Asian, non-Hispanic/Latino; 8 Hispanic/Latino). In 2013, 52 master's awarded. *Degree requirements:* For master's, comprehensive exam (for some programs), thesis optional. *Application deadline:* Applications are processed on a rolling basis. Application fee: $0. *Unit head:* Dr. Greg Seay, Dean of Graduate Programs, 402-872-2283, Fax: 402-872-2413, E-mail: gseay@peru.edu. *Application contact:* Emily Volker, Program Coordinator, 402-872-2282, Fax: 402-872-2413, E-mail: evolker@peru.edu.

Education—General

Piedmont College, School of Education, Demorest, GA 30535-0010. Offers art education (MAT); early childhood education (MA, MAT); instructional technology (MAT); middle grades education (MA, MAT); music education (MAT); secondary education (MA, MAT); special education (MA, MAT); teacher leadership (Ed S). Part-time and evening/weekend programs available. *Students:* 312 full-time (242 women), 694 part-time (563 women); includes 153 minority (103 Black or African American, non-Hispanic/Latino; 3 American Indian or Alaska Native, non-Hispanic/Latino; 17 Asian, non-Hispanic/Latino; 19 Hispanic/Latino; 11 Two or more races, non-Hispanic/Latino), 1 international. Average age 37. 165 applicants, 72% accepted, 118 enrolled. In 2013, 333 master's, 15 doctorates, 457 other advanced degrees awarded. *Degree requirements:* For master's, thesis, field experience in the classroom teaching; for doctorate, thesis/dissertation. *Entrance requirements:* For master's, GRE General Test, MAT, minimum undergraduate GPA of 2.5; for Ed S, minimum graduate GPA of 3.5, valid teaching certificate. Additional exam requirements/recommendations for international students: Required—TOEFL (minimum score 550 paper-based). *Application deadline:* For fall admission, 7/15 for domestic students; for spring admission, 12/1 for domestic students. Applications are processed on a rolling basis. Electronic applications accepted. *Expenses: Tuition:* Full-time $7992; part-time $444 per credit hour. *Financial support:* Career-related internships or fieldwork, Federal Work-Study, and unspecified assistantships available. Support available to part-time students. Financial award applicants required to submit FAFSA. *Unit head:* Dr. Don Gnecco, Dean, 706-778-3000 Ext. 1201, Fax: 706-776-9608, E-mail: dgnecco@piedmont.edu. *Application contact:* Kathleen Anderson, Director of Graduate Enrollment Management, 706-778-8500 Ext. 1181, Fax: 706-778-0150, E-mail: kanderson@piedmont.edu.

Pittsburg State University, Graduate School, College of Education, Pittsburg, KS 66762. Offers MAT, MS, Ed S. *Accreditation:* NCATE. *Degree requirements:* For master's, thesis or alternative.

Plymouth State University, College of Graduate Studies, Graduate Studies in Education, Certificate of Advanced Graduate Studies Programs, Plymouth, NH 03264-1595. Offers clinical mental health counseling (CAGS); educational leadership (CAGS); higher education (CAGS); school psychology (CAGS). Part-time and evening/weekend programs available.

Point Loma Nazarene University, School of Education, Program in Teaching, San Diego, CA 92106-2899. Offers education specialist (MAT). Part-time and evening/weekend programs available. *Students:* 110 full-time (81 women), 188 part-time (143 women); includes 115 minority (14 Black or African American, non-Hispanic/Latino; 2 American Indian or Alaska Native, non-Hispanic/Latino; 10 Asian, non-Hispanic/Latino; 78 Hispanic/Latino; 1 Native Hawaiian or other Pacific Islander, non-Hispanic/Latino; 10 Two or more races, non-Hispanic/Latino). Average age 30. 117 applicants, 63% accepted, 65 enrolled. In 2013, 40 master's awarded. *Entrance requirements:* For master's, CBEST, letters of recommendation, essay, interview. *Application deadline:* For fall admission, 8/4 priority date for domestic students; for spring admission, 12/8 priority date for domestic students; for summer admission, 4/13 priority date for domestic students. Applications are processed on a rolling basis. Application fee: $50. Electronic applications accepted. *Expenses: Tuition:* Full-time $6900; part-time $567 per credit hour. *Financial support:* Applicants required to submit FAFSA. *Unit head:* Jill Hamilton Bunch, Associate Dean, Bakersfield Regional Center, 661-321-3483, E-mail: jillhamilton-bunch@pointloma.edu. *Application contact:* Laura Leinweber, Director of Graduate Admission, 866-692-4723, E-mail: lauraleinweber@pointloma.edu.
Website: http://www.pointloma.edu/discover/graduate-school-san-diego/san-diego-graduate-programs-masters-degree-san-diego/education/master-arts-teaching.

Point Park University, School of Arts and Sciences, Department of Education, Pittsburgh, PA 15222-1984. Offers curriculum and instruction (MA); educational administration (MA); special education (M Ed); teaching and leadership (M Ed). Part-time and evening/weekend programs available. *Degree requirements:* For master's, comprehensive exam (for some programs), thesis or alternative. *Entrance requirements:* For master's, minimum GPA of 3.0, resume, 2 letters of recommendation. Additional exam requirements/recommendations for international students: Required—TOEFL. Electronic applications accepted.

Pontifical Catholic University of Puerto Rico, College of Education, Ponce, PR 00717-0777. Offers M Ed, MA Ed, MRE, PhD. Part-time and evening/weekend programs available. *Degree requirements:* For master's, comprehensive exam, thesis (for some programs). *Entrance requirements:* For master's, GRE General Test, 2 letters of recommendation, interview, minimum GPA of 2.75; for doctorate, EXADEP, GRE or MAT, 3 letters of recommendation. *Faculty research:* Teaching English as a second language, learning styles, leadership styles.

Portland State University, Graduate Studies, School of Education, Portland, OR 97207-0751. Offers M Ed, MA, MAT, MS, MST, Ed D. *Accreditation:* NCATE. Part-time and evening/weekend programs available. *Faculty:* 59 full-time (37 women), 116 part-time/adjunct (81 women). *Students:* 451 full-time (336 women), 672 part-time (470 women); includes 217 minority (28 Black or African American, non-Hispanic/Latino; 10 American Indian or Alaska Native, non-Hispanic/Latino; 42 Asian, non-Hispanic/Latino; 96 Hispanic/Latino; 4 Native Hawaiian or other Pacific Islander, non-Hispanic/Latino; 37 Two or more races, non-Hispanic/Latino), 23 international. Average age 37. 747 applicants, 48% accepted, 325 enrolled. In 2013, 485 master's, 18 doctorates awarded. *Degree requirements:* For doctorate, thesis/dissertation. *Entrance requirements:* For master's, minimum GPA of 3.0 in upper-division course work or 2.75 overall. Additional exam requirements/recommendations for international students: Required—TOEFL (minimum score 550 paper-based). *Application deadline:* For fall admission, 4/1 for domestic and international students; for winter admission, 9/1 for domestic and international students; for spring admission, 11/1 for domestic and international students. Application fee: $50. *Expenses:* Tuition, state resident: full-time $9207; part-time $341 per credit. Tuition, nonresident: full-time $14,391; part-time $533 per credit. *Required fees:* $1263; $22 per credit. $98 per quarter. One-time fee: $150. Tuition and fees vary according to program. *Financial support:* In 2013–14, 2 research assistantships with full and partial tuition reimbursements (averaging $6,310 per year), 2 teaching assistantships with full and partial tuition reimbursements (averaging $7,755 per year) were awarded; career-related internships or fieldwork, Federal Work-Study, institutionally sponsored loans, scholarships/grants, and unspecified assistantships also available. Support available to part-time students. Financial award application deadline: 3/1; financial award applicants required to submit FAFSA. *Total annual research expenditures:* $2.3 million. *Unit head:* Dr. Randy Hitz, Dean, 503-725-4697, Fax: 503-725-5399, E-mail: hitz@pdx.edu. *Application contact:* Information Contact, 503-725-4619, Fax: 503-725-5599, E-mail: gseinfo@pdx.edu.
Website: http://www.ed.pdx.edu/.

Post University, Program in Education, Waterbury, CT 06723-2540. Offers education (M Ed); higher education administration (M Ed); instructional design and technology (M Ed); online teaching (M Ed); teaching and learning (M Ed); TESOL (teaching English to speakers of other languages) (M Ed). Postbaccalaureate distance learning degree programs offered.

Prairie View A&M University, College of Education, Prairie View, TX 77446-0519. Offers M Ed, MA, MS, MS Ed, PhD. *Accreditation:* NCATE. Part-time and evening/weekend programs available. Postbaccalaureate distance learning degree programs offered (no on-campus study). *Faculty:* 36 full-time (16 women), 20 part-time/adjunct (14 women). *Students:* 226 full-time (166 women), 507 part-time (401 women); includes 687 minority (646 Black or African American, non-Hispanic/Latino; 7 Asian, non-Hispanic/Latino; 30 Hispanic/Latino; 4 Two or more races, non-Hispanic/Latino), 6 international. Average age 35. 434 applicants, 53% accepted, 166 enrolled. In 2013, 231 master's, 3 doctorates awarded. *Degree requirements:* For master's, thesis optional, minimum GPA of 3.0; for doctorate, comprehensive exam, thesis/dissertation. *Entrance requirements:* For master's, 3 letters of reference, minimum undergraduate GPA of 2.5; for doctorate, GRE General Test, 3 letters of reference, minimum undergraduate GPA of 3.0, essay. Additional exam requirements/recommendations for international students: Required—TOEFL (minimum score 550 paper-based). *Application deadline:* For fall admission, 7/1 priority date for domestic students, 7/1 for international students; for spring admission, 11/1 priority date for domestic students, 11/1 for international students. Applications are processed on a rolling basis. Application fee: $50. Electronic applications accepted. *Expenses:* Tuition, state resident: full-time $3776; part-time $209.77 per credit hour. Tuition, nonresident: full-time $10,183; part-time $565.77 per credit hour. *Required fees:* $2037; $446.50 per credit hour. *Financial support:* In 2013–14, 1,050 students received support, including 7 research assistantships with tuition reimbursements available (averaging $24,000 per year); fellowships with tuition reimbursements available, teaching assistantships, career-related internships or fieldwork, institutionally sponsored loans, scholarships/grants, and unspecified assistantships also available. Support available to part-time students. Financial award application deadline: 4/1; financial award applicants required to submit FAFSA. *Faculty research:* Mentoring, assessment, humanistic education, diversity, literacy education, recruitment, student retention, school collaboration, leadership skills, structural equations. *Unit head:* Dr. Lucian Yates, Dean, 936-261-3600, Fax: 936-261-2911, E-mail: luyates@pvamu.edu. *Application contact:* Head.

Prescott College, Graduate Programs, Program in Education, Prescott, AZ 86301. Offers early childhood education (MA); early childhood special education (MA); education (MA); elementary education (MA); environmental education leadership and administration (MA); equine-assisted learning (MA); school guidance counseling (MA); secondary education (MA); special education: learning disabilities (MA); special education: mental retardation (MA); special education: serious emotional disabilities (MA); student-directed independent study (MA); sustainability education (PhD). Part-time programs available. Postbaccalaureate distance learning degree programs offered (minimal on-campus study). *Degree requirements:* For master's, thesis, fieldwork or internship, practicum; for doctorate, thesis/dissertation. *Entrance requirements:* For master's, 2 letters of recommendation, resume; for doctorate, 3 letters of recommendation, resume, official transcripts, personal statement, program proposal. Additional exam requirements/recommendations for international students: Required—TOEFL (minimum score 500 paper-based). Electronic applications accepted.

Purdue University, Graduate School, College of Education, West Lafayette, IN 47907. Offers MS, MS Ed, PhD, Ed S. *Accreditation:* NCATE. Part-time and evening/weekend programs available. *Faculty:* 54 full-time (39 women), 42 part-time/adjunct (35 women). *Students:* 187 full-time (126 women), 316 part-time (222 women); includes 85 minority (29 Black or African American, non-Hispanic/Latino; 3 American Indian or Alaska Native, non-Hispanic/Latino; 18 Asian, non-Hispanic/Latino; 27 Hispanic/Latino; 1 Native Hawaiian or other Pacific Islander, non-Hispanic/Latino; 7 Two or more races, non-Hispanic/Latino), 73 international. Average age 36. 320 applicants, 55% accepted, 104 enrolled. In 2013, 86 master's, 41 doctorates awarded. *Degree requirements:* For master's, thesis optional; for doctorate, thesis/dissertation, oral and written exams; for Ed S, oral presentation, project. *Entrance requirements:* For master's, GRE General Test (if undergraduate GPA is below 3.0), minimum undergraduate GPA of 3.0 or equivalent; for doctorate, GRE General Test (minimum combined verbal and quantitative score of 1000, 300 for new scoring), minimum undergraduate GPA of 3.0 or equivalent; master's degree with minimum GPA of 3.0 or equivalent; for Ed S, GRE General Test (minimum combined verbal and quantitative score of 1000, 300 for new scoring), minimum undergraduate GPA of 3.0 or equivalent; master's degree. Additional exam requirements/recommendations for international students: Required—TOEFL (minimum score 550 paper-based; 77 iBT); Recommended—TWE. *Application deadline:* For fall admission, 12/15 for domestic students, 3/1 for international students; for spring admission, 9/15 for domestic students, 8/1 for international students. Application fee: $60 ($75 for international students). Electronic applications accepted. *Financial support:* Fellowships with full tuition reimbursements, research assistantships with full tuition reimbursements, teaching assistantships with full tuition reimbursements, career-related internships or fieldwork, and tuition waivers (full) available. Support available to part-time students. Financial award application deadline: 3/1; financial award applicants required to submit FAFSA. *Unit head:* Maryann J.T. Santos de Barona, Dean, 765-494-2336, E-mail: msdb@purdue.edu. *Application contact:* Graduate School Admissions, 765-494-2600, Fax: 765-494-0136, E-mail: gradinfo@purdue.edu.
Website: http://www.education.purdue.edu/.

Purdue University Calumet, Graduate Studies Office, School of Education, Hammond, IN 46323-2094. Offers counseling (MS Ed), including human services, mental health counseling, school counseling; educational administration (MS Ed); instructional technology (MS Ed); special education (MS Ed). *Accreditation:* NCATE. *Entrance requirements:* Additional exam requirements/recommendations for international students: Required—TOEFL.

Purdue University North Central, Program in Education, Westville, IN 46391-9542. Offers elementary education (MS Ed). *Accreditation:* NCATE. Part-time and evening/weekend programs available. *Degree requirements:* For master's, one foreign language. *Entrance requirements:* For master's, GRE, minimum GPA of 3.0. Electronic applications accepted. *Faculty research:* Diversity, integration.

Queens College of the City University of New York, Division of Graduate Studies, Division of Education, Flushing, NY 11367-1597. Offers MA, MS Ed, AC. *Accreditation:* NCATE. Part-time and evening/weekend programs available. *Degree requirements:* For master's, research project; for AC, thesis optional. *Entrance requirements:* For master's, minimum GPA of 3.0. Additional exam requirements/recommendations for international students: Required—TOEFL.

Queen's University at Kingston, School of Graduate Studies, Faculty of Education, Kingston, ON K7L 3N6, Canada. Offers M Ed, PhD. Part-time programs available. *Degree requirements:* For master's, thesis optional; for doctorate, comprehensive exam, thesis/dissertation. *Entrance requirements:* Additional exam requirements/recommendations for international students: Required—TOEFL (minimum score 580 paper-based); Recommended—TWE (minimum score 4). *Faculty research:* Literacy, assessment and evaluation, special needs, mathematics, science and technology education.

Queens University of Charlotte, Wayland H. Cato, Jr. School of Education, Charlotte, NC 28274-0002. Offers education in literacy (M Ed); elementary education (MAT); school administration (MSA). *Accreditation:* NCATE. Part-time and evening/weekend programs available. *Degree requirements:* For master's, comprehensive exam. *Entrance requirements:* For master's, GRE General Test. *Expenses:* Contact institution.

Quincy University, Program in Education, Quincy, IL 62301-2699. Offers curriculum and instruction (MS Ed), including bilingual/English as a second language; leadership (MS Ed); reading education (MS Ed); special education (MS Ed); teacher leader (MS Ed). Part-time and evening/weekend programs available. Postbaccalaureate distance learning degree programs offered (minimal on-campus study). *Students:* 62 full-time (39 women), 97 part-time (68 women); includes 43 minority (29 Black or African American, non-Hispanic/Latino; 1 American Indian or Alaska Native, non-Hispanic/Latino; 4 Asian, non-Hispanic/Latino; 9 Hispanic/Latino). In 2013, 105 master's awarded. *Degree requirements:* For master's, comprehensive exam (for some programs), thesis optional. *Entrance requirements:* For master's, MAT or GRE. Additional exam requirements/recommendations for international students: Required—TOEFL (minimum score 550 paper-based; 79 iBT). *Application deadline:* Applications are processed on a rolling basis. Application fee: $25. Electronic applications accepted. *Expenses: Tuition:* Full-time $9600; part-time $400 per semester hour. *Required fees:* $720; $30 per semester hour. Tuition and fees vary according to course load and program. *Financial support:* Applicants required to submit FAFSA. *Unit head:* Dr. Kristen R. Anguiano, Director, 217-228-5432 Ext. 3119, E-mail: anguikr@quincy.edu. *Application contact:* Office of Admissions, 217-228-5210, Fax: 217-228-5479, E-mail: admissions@quincy.edu.
Website: http://www.quincy.edu/academics/graduate-programs/education.

Quinnipiac University, School of Education, Hamden, CT 06518-1940. Offers MAT, MS, Diploma. *Accreditation:* NCATE. Part-time and evening/weekend programs available. Postbaccalaureate distance learning degree programs offered (no on-campus study). *Faculty:* 18 full-time (10 women), 55 part-time/adjunct (29 women). *Students:* 99 full-time (90 women), 77 part-time (51 women); includes 13 minority (3 Black or African American, non-Hispanic/Latino; 1 American Indian or Alaska Native, non-Hispanic/Latino; 9 Hispanic/Latino). 133 applicants, 93% accepted, 120 enrolled. In 2013, 142 master's, 25 other advanced degrees awarded. *Entrance requirements:* For master's, PRAXIS I, minimum GPA of 2.67, interview. *Application deadline:* For fall admission, 4/1 priority date for domestic students. Applications are processed on a rolling basis. Application fee: $45. Electronic applications accepted. *Expenses: Tuition:* Part-time $920 per credit. *Required fees:* $37 per credit. *Financial support:* Career-related internships or fieldwork, Federal Work-Study, tuition waivers (full and partial), and unspecified assistantships available. Support available to part-time students. Financial award application deadline: 6/1; financial award applicants required to submit FAFSA. *Faculty research:* Equity and excellence in education, school leadership. *Application contact:* Office of Graduate Admissions, 800-462-1944, Fax: 203-582-3443, E-mail: graduate@quinnipiac.edu.
Website: http://www.quinnipiac.edu/gradeducation.

Radford University, College of Graduate and Professional Studies, College of Education and Human Development, Radford, VA 24142. Offers MS, Certificate. *Accreditation:* NCATE. Part-time and evening/weekend programs available. *Faculty:* 24 full-time (16 women), 18 part-time/adjunct (12 women). *Students:* 156 full-time (123 women), 177 part-time (123 women); includes 24 minority (13 Black or African American, non-Hispanic/Latino; 2 Asian, non-Hispanic/Latino; 4 Hispanic/Latino; 5 Two or more races, non-Hispanic/Latino), 2 international. Average age 31. 157 applicants, 94% accepted, 116 enrolled. In 2013, 163 master's, 5 other advanced degrees awarded. *Degree requirements:* For master's, comprehensive exam, thesis optional. *Entrance requirements:* For master's, GRE or MAT, minimum GPA of 3.0; 2-3 letters of reference; essay/personal statement, current teaching license or teaching experience; resume; official transcripts. Additional exam requirements/recommendations for international students: Required—TOEFL (minimum score 550 paper-based; 79 iBT). *Application deadline:* For fall admission, 2/15 priority date for domestic students, 12/1 for international students; for spring admission, 7/1 for international students. Applications are processed on a rolling basis. Application fee: $50. Electronic applications accepted. *Expenses:* Tuition, state resident: full-time $6800; part-time $283 per credit hour. Tuition, nonresident: full-time $15,610; part-time $627 per credit hour. *Required fees:* $2944; $123 per credit hour. Tuition and fees vary according to program. *Financial support:* In 2013–14, 48 students received support, including 38 research assistantships (averaging $7,342 per year), 3 teaching assistantships with partial tuition reimbursements available (averaging $11,000 per year); career-related internships or fieldwork, Federal Work-Study, institutionally sponsored loans, scholarships/grants, and unspecified assistantships also available. Financial award application deadline: 3/1; financial award applicants required to submit FAFSA. *Unit head:* Dr. Patricia Shoemaker, Dean, 540-831-5439, Fax: 540-831-6682, E-mail: pshoemak@radford.edu. *Application contact:* Rebecca Conner, Director, Graduate Enrollment, 540-831-6296, Fax: 540-831-6061, E-mail: gradcollege@radford.edu.
Website: http://www.radford.edu/content/cehd/home.html.

Randolph College, Programs in Education, Lynchburg, VA 24503. Offers curriculum and instruction (MAT); special education-learning disabilities (M Ed, MAT). *Accreditation:* Teacher Education Accreditation Council. *Entrance requirements:* For master's, minimum GPA of 3.0 in prerequisite education coursework, 2.7 in major or field of interest (MAT); teaching license (M Ed); 2 recommendations; interview.

Regent University, Graduate School, School of Education, Virginia Beach, VA 23464-9800. Offers adult education (Ed D, PhD); advanced educational leadership (Ed D, PhD); career switcher with licensure (M Ed), including alternative licensure; character education (Ed D, PhD); Christian education leadership (Ed D); Christian school administration (M Ed); curriculum and instruction (M Ed); distance education (Ed D, PhD); educational leadership (M Ed); educational leadership - special education (Ed S); educational psychology (Ed D); elementary education (M Ed); higher education (Ed D, PhD); higher education leadership and management (Ed D); K-12 school leadership (Ed D, PhD); leadership in mathematics education (M Ed); reading specialist (M Ed); special education (M Ed, Ed D, PhD); student affairs (M Ed); TESOL (M Ed), including adult education, PreK-12. *Accreditation:* Teacher Education Accreditation Council. Part-time and evening/weekend programs available. Postbaccalaureate distance learning degree programs offered (minimal on-campus study). *Faculty:* 25 full-time (12 women), 50 part-time/adjunct (31 women). *Students:* 100 full-time (78 women), 754 part-time (614 women); includes 225 minority (191 Black or African American, non-Hispanic/Latino; 1 American Indian or Alaska Native, non-Hispanic/Latino; 7 Asian, non-Hispanic/Latino; 26 Hispanic/Latino), 16 international. Average age 39. 487 applicants, 63% accepted, 233 enrolled. In 2013, 202 master's, 19 doctorates awarded. *Degree requirements:* For master's, thesis or alternative; for doctorate, comprehensive exam, thesis/dissertation. *Entrance requirements:* For master's, MAT, minimum undergraduate GPA of 2.75, writing sample, resume, recommendations, interview; for doctorate, GRE, writing sample, 3 years of relevant professional experience, master's-level paper, copies of published work, resume, transcripts, interview, recommendations. Additional exam requirements/recommendations for international students: Required—TOEFL (minimum score 577 paper-based). *Application deadline:* For fall admission, 4/1 priority date for domestic students; for spring admission, 10/15 priority date for domestic students. Applications are processed on a rolling basis. Application fee: $50. Electronic applications accepted. Tuition and fees vary according to course load and degree level. *Financial support:* Fellowships, career-related internships or fieldwork, scholarships/grants, tuition waivers (full and partial), and unspecified assistantships available. Support available to part-time students. Financial award application deadline: 4/1;

financial award applicants required to submit FAFSA. *Faculty research:* Character development and discipline for children, education leadership development, diversity in schools, classroom management, technology in education settings. *Unit head:* Dr. Alan Arroyo, Dean, 757-352-4261, Fax: 757-352-4318, E-mail: alanarr@regent.edu. *Application contact:* Matthew Chadwick, Director of Enrollment Support Services, 800-373-5504, Fax: 757-352-4381, E-mail: admissions@regent.edu.
Website: http://www.regent.edu/education/.

Regis College, Department of Education, Weston, MA 02493. Offers elementary teacher (MAT); higher education leadership (Ed D); reading (MAT); special education (MAT). Part-time and evening/weekend programs available. *Degree requirements:* For master's, thesis. *Entrance requirements:* For master's, GRE or MAT. Additional exam requirements/recommendations for international students: Required—TOEFL. Electronic applications accepted. *Faculty research:* Reflective teaching, gender-based education, integrated teaching.

Regis University, College for Professional Studies, School of Education, Education Division, Denver, CO 80221-1099. Offers adult learning, training, and development (M Ed, Certificate); autism education (Certificate); curriculum, instruction, and assessment (M Ed); educational leadership (M Ed); gifted and talented education (M Ed); gifted/talented education (Certificate); initial licensure (M Ed); instructional technology (M Ed, Certificate); literacy (Certificate); reading (M Ed); school executive leadership (Certificate); space studies (M Ed). Program also offered in Henderson and Las Vegas (Summerlin), NV. *Accreditation:* Teacher Education Accreditation Council. Part-time and evening/weekend programs available. Postbaccalaureate distance learning degree programs offered (no on-campus study). *Degree requirements:* For master's, thesis. *Entrance requirements:* For master's, resume, minimum GPA of 2.75, criminal background check. Additional exam requirements/recommendations for international students: Required—TOEFL, TWE (minimum score 5). *Application deadline:* For fall admission, 7/23 priority date for domestic students; for winter admission, 9/17 priority date for domestic students; for spring admission, 12/3 priority date for domestic students. Applications are processed on a rolling basis. Application fee: $75. Electronic applications accepted. *Expenses:* Contact institution. *Financial support:* Federal Work-Study and scholarships/grants available. *Faculty research:* Issues of equity in the middle school classroom, professional learning communities, school reform, sociolinguistic and discursive obstacles to student integration, inclusive language arts curriculum. *Unit head:* Dr. Janna L. Oakes, Dean, 303-458-4302. *Application contact:* Information Contact, 303-458-4300, Fax: 303-964-5274, E-mail: masters@regis.edu.

Regis University, Regis College, Denver, CO 80221-1099. Offers biomedical sciences (MS); education (MA). *Accreditation:* Teacher Education Accreditation Council. Part-time programs available. *Faculty:* 11 full-time (8 women), 24 part-time/adjunct (23 women). *Students:* 41 full-time (24 women), 52 part-time (47 women); includes 14 minority (2 Black or African American, non-Hispanic/Latino; 3 Asian, non-Hispanic/Latino; 9 Hispanic/Latino). Average age 38. 195 applicants, 100% accepted, 165 enrolled. In 2013, 36 master's awarded. *Degree requirements:* For master's, thesis (for some programs), capstone presentation. *Entrance requirements:* For master's, official transcript reflecting baccalaureate degree awarded from U.S.-based regionally-accredited college or university. Additional exam requirements/recommendations for international students: Required—TOEFL (minimum score 550 paper-based; 82 iBT). *Application deadline:* For fall admission, 4/15 priority date for domestic students, 7/1 priority date for international students; for spring admission, 12/15 priority date for domestic students. Applications are processed on a rolling basis. Application fee: $75. Electronic applications accepted. *Expenses:* Contact institution. *Financial support:* In 2013–14, 2 students received support. Federal Work-Study and scholarships/grants available. Financial award application deadline: 4/15; financial award applicants required to submit FAFSA. *Unit head:* Dr. Stephen Doty, Interim Academic Dean, 303-458-4040. *Application contact:* Sarah Engel, Director of Admissions, 303-458-4900, Fax: 303-964-5534, E-mail: regisadm@regis.edu.
Website: http://www.regis.edu/RC.aspx.

Reinhardt University, Program in Early Childhood Education, Waleska, GA 30183-2981. Offers M Ed, MAT. Part-time and evening/weekend programs available. Postbaccalaureate distance learning degree programs offered. *Degree requirements:* For master's, comprehensive exam. *Entrance requirements:* For master's, GACE, background check. Additional exam requirements/recommendations for international students: Required—TOEFL. Electronic applications accepted.

Rhode Island College, School of Graduate Studies, Feinstein School of Education and Human Development, Program in Education, Providence, RI 02908-1991. Offers PhD. Program offered jointly with University of Rhode Island. *Accreditation:* NCATE. Part-time and evening/weekend programs available. *Faculty:* 7 part-time/adjunct (5 women). *Students:* 58 part-time (41 women); includes 4 minority (1 Black or African American, non-Hispanic/Latino; 2 Asian, non-Hispanic/Latino; 1 Hispanic/Latino). Average age 41. In 2013, 8 doctorates awarded. *Degree requirements:* For doctorate, comprehensive exam, thesis/dissertation. *Entrance requirements:* For doctorate, GRE, two official transcripts from all colleges and universities attended, 3 letters of recommendation, personal statement, professional resume. Additional exam requirements/recommendations for international students: Recommended—TOEFL (minimum score 550 paper-based; 79 iBT). *Application deadline:* For fall admission, 1/29 for domestic students. Applications are processed on a rolling basis. Application fee: $65. *Expenses:* Tuition, state resident: full-time $8928; part-time $372 per credit hour. Tuition, nonresident: full-time $17,376; part-time $724 per credit hour. *Required fees:* $602; $22 per credit. $72 per term. *Financial support:* Health care benefits available. Support available to part-time students. Financial award application deadline: 5/15; financial award applicants required to submit FAFSA. *Unit head:* Dr. Janet Johnson, Co-Director, 401-456-8701. *Application contact:* Graduate Studies, 401-456-8700.
Website: http://www.ric.edu/feinsteinschooleducationhumandevelopment/jointPHD.php.

Rice University, Graduate Programs, Programs in Education Certification, Houston, TX 77251-1892. Offers MAT. *Entrance requirements:* For master's, GRE General Test, minimum GPA of 3.0. Additional exam requirements/recommendations for international students: Required—TOEFL (minimum score 600 paper-based; 90 iBT). Electronic applications accepted. *Faculty research:* Assessment, integration of math and science.

The Richard Stockton College of New Jersey, School of Graduate and Continuing Studies, Program in Education, Galloway, NJ 08205-9441. Offers MA. *Accreditation:* Teacher Education Accreditation Council. Part-time and evening/weekend programs available. *Faculty:* 6 full-time (5 women), 10 part-time/adjunct (7 women). *Students:* 7 full-time (6 women), 162 part-time (138 women); includes 27 minority (5 Black or African American, non-Hispanic/Latino; 1 Asian, non-Hispanic/Latino; 18 Hispanic/Latino; 3 Two or more races, non-Hispanic/Latino), 1 international. Average age 36. 99 applicants, 83% accepted, 55 enrolled. In 2013, 37 master's awarded. *Degree requirements:* For master's, comprehensive exam (for some programs), project. *Entrance requirements:* For master's, GRE, MAT, minimum GPA of 2.75, teaching certificate. *Application deadline:* For fall admission, 7/1 for domestic students; for spring admission, 12/1 for domestic students. Applications are processed on a rolling basis. Application fee: $50. Electronic applications accepted. *Expenses: Tuition, area resident:* Part-time $559 per credit. Tuition, state resident: part-time $559 per credit. Tuition, nonresident: part-time

$861 per credit. *Required fees:* $168.23 per credit. $75 per semester. Tuition and fees vary according to course load and degree level. *Financial support:* In 2013–14, 7 students received support, including 2 fellowships, 10 research assistantships with partial tuition reimbursements available; career-related internships or fieldwork, Federal Work-Study, scholarships/grants, and unspecified assistantships also available. Support available to part-time students. Financial award application deadline: 3/1; financial award applicants required to submit FAFSA. *Faculty research:* Curriculum instruction, math, science, special education, language arts, literacy. *Unit head:* Dr. Kim LeBak, Program Director, 609-626-3640, E-mail: gradschool@stockton.edu. *Application contact:* Tara Williams, Assistant Director of Graduate Enrollment Management, 609-626-3640, Fax: 609-626-6050, E-mail: gradschool@stockton.edu.

Rider University, Department of Graduate Education, Leadership and Counseling, Lawrenceville, NJ 08648-3001. Offers counseling services (MA, Certificate, Ed S), including counseling services (MA, Ed S), director of school counseling (Certificate), school counseling services (Certificate); curriculum, instruction and supervision (MA, Certificate), including curriculum, instruction and supervision (MA), supervisor (Certificate); educational administration (MA, Certificate), including educational administration (MA), principal (Certificate), school administrator (Certificate); organizational leadership (MA); reading/language arts (MA, Certificate), including reading specialist (Certificate), reading/language arts (MA); school psychology (Certificate, Ed S); special education (MA, Certificate), including alternative route in special education (Certificate), special education (MA), teacher of students with disabilities (Certificate), teacher of the handicapped (Certificate); teacher certification (Certificate), including business education, elementary education, English as a second language, English education, mathematics education, preschool to grade 3, science education, social studies education, world languages; teaching (MA). *Accreditation:* NCATE. Part-time and evening/weekend programs available. *Degree requirements:* For master's, comprehensive exam (for some programs), thesis or alternative, internship, portfolios; for other advanced degree, internship, professional portfolio. *Entrance requirements:* For master's, GRE (counseling, school psychology), MAT, interview, resume, letters of recommendation; for other advanced degree, PRAXIS. Additional exam requirements/recommendations for international students: Required—TOEFL (minimum score 550 paper-based). Electronic applications accepted. *Faculty research:* Gifted students, self-esteem, hope and mental health, conflicts in group work, cultural diversity and counseling assessment of special needs in children.

Rivier University, School of Graduate Studies, Department of Education, Nashua, NH 03060. Offers curriculum and instruction (M Ed); early childhood education (M Ed); educational administration (M Ed); educational studies (M Ed); elementary education (M Ed); elementary education and general special education (M Ed); emotional and behavioral disorders (M Ed); general social education (M Ed); leadership and learning (Ed D, CAGS); learning disabilities (M Ed); learning disabilities and reading (M Ed); mental health counseling (MA); reading (M Ed); school counseling (M Ed). Part-time and evening/weekend programs available. *Degree requirements:* For master's, comprehensive exam (for some programs), internships. *Entrance requirements:* For master's, GRE General Test or MAT.

Robert Morris University, Graduate Studies, School of Education and Social Sciences, Moon Township, PA 15108-1189. Offers business education (MS); education (Postbaccalaureate Certificate); instructional leadership (MS), including education, sport management; instructional management and leadership (PhD). *Accreditation:* Teacher Education Accreditation Council. Part-time and evening/weekend programs available. Postbaccalaureate distance learning degree programs offered (no on-campus study). *Faculty:* 20 full-time (9 women), 6 part-time/adjunct (3 women). *Students:* 203 part-time (127 women); includes 20 minority (11 Black or African American, non-Hispanic/Latino; 3 Asian, non-Hispanic/Latino; 2 Hispanic/Latino; 4 Two or more races, non-Hispanic/Latino), 4 international. Average age 26. 126 applicants, 44% accepted, 43 enrolled. In 2013, 102 master's, 6 doctorates awarded. *Degree requirements:* For doctorate, thesis/dissertation. *Entrance requirements:* Additional exam requirements/recommendations for international students: Required—TOEFL (minimum score 550 paper-based; 79 iBT). *Application deadline:* For fall admission, 7/1 priority date for domestic and international students; for spring admission, 11/1 priority date for domestic and international students. Applications are processed on a rolling basis. Application fee: $35. Electronic applications accepted. *Expenses:* Contact institution. *Unit head:* Dr. Mary Ann Rafoth, Dean, 412-397-3488, Fax: 412-397-2524, E-mail: rafoth@rmu.edu. *Application contact:* Assistant Dean, Graduate Admissions, 412-397-5200, Fax: 412-397-5915, E-mail: graduateadmissions@rmu.edu.
Website: http://www.rmu.edu/web/cms/schools/sess/.

Roberts Wesleyan College, Department of Teacher Education, Rochester, NY 14624-1997. Offers adolescence education (M Ed); childhood and special education (M Ed); literacy education (M Ed); special education online (M Ed). Part-time and evening/weekend programs available. *Faculty:* 10 full-time (7 women), 12 part-time/adjunct (6 women). *Students:* 37 full-time (29 women), 10 part-time (6 women); includes 16 minority (15 Black or African American, non-Hispanic/Latino; 1 Hispanic/Latino). Average age 33. 72 applicants, 63% accepted, 34 enrolled. In 2013, 20 master's awarded. *Degree requirements:* For master's, thesis. *Application deadline:* For fall admission, 6/1 for domestic and international students; for spring admission, 11/1 for domestic and international students; for summer admission, 3/1 for domestic and international students. Applications are processed on a rolling basis. Electronic applications accepted. Application fee is waived when completed online. *Expenses: Tuition:* Full-time $12,816; part-time $712 per credit hour. One-time fee: $300. Tuition and fees vary according to course load and program. *Financial support:* In 2013–14, 7 students received support. Career-related internships or fieldwork available. Financial award application deadline: 9/1; financial award applicants required to submit FAFSA. *Unit head:* Dr. Sharon Harris-Ewing, Chair, 585-594-6935, E-mail: harrisewing_sharon@roberts.edu. *Application contact:* Paul Ziegler, Director of Marketing and Recruitment for Teacher Education, 585-594-6146, Fax: 585-594-6108, E-mail: ziegler_paul@roberts.edu.
Website: https://www.roberts.edu/department-of-teacher-education.aspx.

Rockford University, Graduate Studies, Department of Education, Rockford, IL 61108-2393. Offers early childhood education (MAT); elementary education (MAT); instructional strategies (MAT); reading (MAT); secondary education (MAT); special education (MAT). Part-time and evening/weekend programs available. *Degree requirements:* For master's, thesis optional, professional portfolio (for instructional strategies program). *Entrance requirements:* For master's, GRE General Test, basic skills test (for students seeking certification), 3 letters of recommendation. Additional exam requirements/recommendations for international students: Required—TOEFL (minimum score 550 paper-based; 79 iBT). Electronic applications accepted.

Rockhurst University, School of Graduate and Professional Studies, Program in Education, Kansas City, MO 64110-2561. Offers M Ed. *Accreditation:* Teacher Education Accreditation Council. Part-time and evening/weekend programs available. *Faculty:* 6 full-time (5 women), 17 part-time/adjunct (16 women). *Students:* 37 full-time (25 women), 95 part-time (62 women); includes 28 minority (16 Black or African American, non-Hispanic/Latino; 2 Asian, non-Hispanic/Latino; 8 Hispanic/Latino; 2 Two or more races, non-Hispanic/Latino). Average age 30. 75 applicants, 67% accepted, 39 enrolled. In 2013, 47 master's awarded. *Entrance requirements:* For master's, minimum GPA of 2.5, 2 letters of recommendation. Additional exam requirements/recommendations for international students: Required—TOEFL (minimum score 550 paper-based; 79 iBT). *Application deadline:* Applications are processed on a rolling basis. Application fee: $25. Electronic applications accepted. Application fee is waived when completed online. *Expenses:* Contact institution. *Financial support:* Applicants required to submit FAFSA. *Faculty research:* English language learners, urban literacy, online discussions, character education, teaching K-12 students about math and literacy. *Unit head:* Mary Pat Shelledy, Chair, 816-501-3538, E-mail: marypat.shelledy@rockhurst.edu. *Application contact:* Cheryl Hooper, Director of Graduate Recruitment and Admission, 816-501-4097, Fax: 816-501-4241, E-mail: cheryl.hooper@rockhurst.edu.
Website: http://www.rockhurst.edu/academic/education/index.asp.

Roger Williams University, Feinstein College of Arts and Sciences, Bristol, RI 02809. Offers clinical psychology (MA); education (MAT); forensic psychology (MA); literacy (MA). Part-time and evening/weekend programs available. Postbaccalaureate distance learning degree programs offered (minimal on-campus study). *Faculty:* 6 full-time (1 woman). *Students:* 38 full-time (31 women), 1 part-time (0 women); includes 5 minority (1 Black or African American, non-Hispanic/Latino; 1 Asian, non-Hispanic/Latino; 2 Hispanic/Latino; 1 Two or more races, non-Hispanic/Latino), 2 international. Average age 24. 109 applicants, 56% accepted, 18 enrolled. In 2013, 36 master's awarded. *Degree requirements:* For master's, thesis optional, internship. *Entrance requirements:* For master's, GRE, 3 letters of recommendation. Additional exam requirements/recommendations for international students: Required—TOEFL (minimum score 85 iBT), IELTS. *Application deadline:* Applications are processed on a rolling basis. Application fee: $50. Electronic applications accepted. *Expenses:* Contact institution. *Financial support:* In 2013–14, 39 students received support, including 5 research assistantships (averaging $5,000 per year). Financial award application deadline: 6/15; financial award applicants required to submit FAFSA. *Unit head:* Robert Eisinger, Dean, 401-254-3149, E-mail: reisinger@rwu.edu. *Application contact:* Jamie Grenon, Director of Graduate Admissions, 401-254-6000, Fax: 401-254-3557, E-mail: gradadmit@rwu.edu.
Website: http://www.rwu.edu/academics/schools/fcas/.

Roger Williams University, School of Education, Bristol, RI 02809. Offers MA, MAT. Part-time and evening/weekend programs available. *Faculty:* 5 full-time (4 women), 8 part-time/adjunct (7 women). *Students:* 11 full-time (10 women), 62 part-time (54 women); includes 3 minority (1 Black or African American, non-Hispanic/Latino; 1 Asian, non-Hispanic/Latino; 1 Hispanic/Latino). Average age 33. 19 applicants, 63% accepted, 8 enrolled. In 2013, 16 master's awarded. *Entrance requirements:* For master's, resume, 3 letters of recommendation. Additional exam requirements/recommendations for international students: Recommended—TOEFL (minimum score 85 iBT), IELTS. *Application deadline:* Applications are processed on a rolling basis. Application fee: $50. Electronic applications accepted. *Expenses:* Contact institution. *Financial support:* In 2013–14, 19 students received support. Application deadline: 6/15; applicants required to submit FAFSA. *Unit head:* Dr. Rachel McCormack, Program Director, 401-254-3019, Fax: 401-254-3710, E-mail: rmccormack@rwu.edu. *Application contact:* Jamie Grenon, Director of Graduate Admission, 401-254-6000, Fax: 401-254-3557, E-mail: gradadmit@rwu.edu.
Website: http://www.rwu.edu/academics/schools/sed/.

Rollins College, Hamilton Holt School, Graduate Studies in Education, Winter Park, FL 32789. Offers elementary education (M Ed, MAT). Part-time and evening/weekend programs available. *Faculty:* 6 full-time (3 women), 5 part-time/adjunct (2 women). *Students:* 12 full-time (6 women), 20 part-time (15 women); includes 7 minority (3 Black or African American, non-Hispanic/Latino; 1 Asian, non-Hispanic/Latino; 3 Hispanic/Latino), 2 international. Average age 32. 4 applicants, 100% accepted, 4 enrolled. In 2013, 8 master's awarded. *Degree requirements:* For master's, comprehensive exam, Professional Education Test (PED) and Subject Area Examination (SAE) of the Florida Teacher Certification Examinations (FTCE), successful review of the Expanded Teacher Education Portfolio (ETEP), successful completion of all required coursework. *Entrance requirements:* For master's, General Knowledge Test of the Florida Teacher Certification Examination (FTCE), official transcripts, letter(s) of recommendation, essay. Additional exam requirements/recommendations for international students: Required—TOEFL (minimum score 550 paper-based; 80 iBT). *Application deadline:* For fall admission, 8/11 for domestic students; for spring admission, 12/10 for domestic students. Applications are processed on a rolling basis. Application fee: $50. *Expenses:* Contact institution. *Financial support:* In 2013–14, 13 students received support. Federal Work-Study, scholarships/grants, and unspecified assistantships available. Support available to part-time students. Financial award applicants required to submit FAFSA. *Unit head:* Dr. J. Scott Hewit, Faculty Director, 407-646-2300, E-mail: shewit@rollins.edu. *Application contact:* 407-646-1568, Fax: 407-975-6430.
Website: http://www.rollins.edu/holt/graduate/gse.html.

Roosevelt University, Graduate Division, College of Education, Chicago, IL 60605. Offers MA, Ed D. *Accreditation:* ACA; NCATE. Part-time and evening/weekend programs available. *Degree requirements:* For doctorate, thesis/dissertation. *Entrance requirements:* For doctorate, GRE or MAT.

Rosemont College, Schools of Graduate and Professional Studies, Graduate Education PreK-4 Program, Rosemont, PA 19010-1699. Offers elementary certification (MA); PreK-4 (MA). Part-time and evening/weekend programs available. *Degree requirements:* For master's, thesis optional. *Entrance requirements:* For master's, minimum college GPA of 3.0, 3 letters of recommendation. Additional exam requirements/recommendations for international students: Required—TOEFL. Electronic applications accepted. Application fee is waived when completed online.

Rowan University, Graduate School, College of Education, Glassboro, NJ 08028-1701. Offers M Ed, MA, MST, Ed D, CAGS, CGS, Certificate, Ed S, Postbaccalaureate Certificate. *Accreditation:* NCATE. Part-time and evening/weekend programs available. *Faculty:* 62 full-time (43 women), 41 part-time/adjunct (30 women). *Students:* 156 full-time (118 women), 758 part-time (570 women); includes 184 minority (113 Black or African American, non-Hispanic/Latino; 3 American Indian or Alaska Native, non-Hispanic/Latino; 14 Asian, non-Hispanic/Latino; 50 Hispanic/Latino; 4 Two or more races, non-Hispanic/Latino), 3 international. Average age 35. 371 applicants, 94% accepted, 237 enrolled. In 2013, 222 master's, 17 doctorates, 40 other advanced degrees awarded. *Degree requirements:* For master's, comprehensive exam, thesis; for doctorate, thesis/dissertation. *Entrance requirements:* For master's, GRE General Test, PRAXIS I, PRAXIS II; for doctorate, GRE, master's degree. Additional exam requirements/recommendations for international students: Required—TOEFL. *Application deadline:* Applications are processed on a rolling basis. Application fee: $65. Electronic applications accepted. *Expenses: Tuition, area resident:* Part-time $638 per credit. Tuition, state resident: full-time $5742. *Required fees:* $142 per credit. Tuition and fees vary according to course level and program. *Financial support:* Career-related internships or fieldwork, Federal Work-Study, scholarships/grants, health care benefits, and unspecified assistantships available. Support available to part-time students. *Unit head:* Dr. Horacio Sosa, Dean, College of Graduate and Continuing Education, 856-256-4747, Fax: 856-256-5638, E-mail: sosa@rowan.edu. *Application contact:* Admissions

and Enrollment Services, 856-256-5145, Fax: 856-256-5637, E-mail: cgceadmissions@rowan.edu.

Rutgers, The State University of New Jersey, New Brunswick, Graduate School of Education, New Brunswick, NJ 08901. Offers Ed M, Ed D, PhD. *Accreditation:* Teacher Education Accreditation Council. Part-time and evening/weekend programs available. Terminal master's awarded for partial completion of doctoral program. *Degree requirements:* For master's, comprehensive exam (for some programs); for doctorate, thesis/dissertation. *Entrance requirements:* For master's and doctorate, GRE General Test. Additional exam requirements/recommendations for international students: Required—TOEFL (minimum score 575 paper-based; 83 iBT). Electronic applications accepted.

Sacred Heart University, Graduate Programs, Isabelle Farrington College of Education, Fairfield, CT 06825-1000. Offers administration (CAS); educational technology (MAT); elementary education (MAT); leadership/literacy (CAS), including literacy; reading (CAS); secondary education (MAT); teaching (CAS). Part-time and evening/weekend programs available. *Faculty:* 23 full-time (13 women), 32 part-time/adjunct (14 women). *Students:* 210 full-time (155 women), 603 part-time (451 women); includes 86 minority (38 Black or African American, non-Hispanic/Latino; 1 American Indian or Alaska Native, non-Hispanic/Latino; 6 Asian, non-Hispanic/Latino; 35 Hispanic/Latino; 6 Two or more races, non-Hispanic/Latino). Average age 35. 278 applicants, 95% accepted, 227 enrolled. In 2013, 262 master's, 72 other advanced degrees awarded. *Degree requirements:* For master's, comprehensive exam (for some programs), thesis (for some programs). *Entrance requirements:* For master's, PRAXIS (teacher certification/MAT), minimum GPA of 2.75; for CAS, PRAXIS I, minimum GPA of 2.75. Additional exam requirements/recommendations for international students: Required—PTE; Recommended—TOEFL (minimum score 570 paper-based; 80 iBT), IELTS (minimum score 6.5). *Application deadline:* Applications are processed on a rolling basis. Application fee: $60. Electronic applications accepted. *Expenses:* Contact institution. *Financial support:* Teaching assistantships with partial tuition reimbursements, career-related internships or fieldwork, institutionally sponsored loans, traineeships, tuition waivers (partial), and unspecified assistantships available. Support available to part-time students. Financial award applicants required to submit FAFSA. *Faculty research:* Reading education, learning theory, teacher preparation, education of underachievers. *Unit head:* Dr. Jim Carl, Dean, 203-396-8454, Fax: 203-365-7513, E-mail: carlj@sacredheart.edu. *Application contact:* Kathy Dilks, Executive Director of Graduate Admissions, 203-365-7619, Fax: 203-365-4732, E-mail: gradstudies@sacredheart.edu.
Website: http://www.sacredheart.edu/academics/isabellefarringtoncollegeofeducation/.

Sage Graduate School, Esteves School of Education, Troy, NY 12180-4115. Offers MAT, MS, MS Ed, Ed D, Post Master's Certificate. *Accreditation:* NCATE. Part-time and evening/weekend programs available. *Faculty:* 10 full-time (5 women), 33 part-time/adjunct (25 women). *Students:* 81 full-time (73 women), 265 part-time (209 women); includes 52 minority (13 Black or African American, non-Hispanic/Latino; 3 American Indian or Alaska Native, non-Hispanic/Latino; 6 Asian, non-Hispanic/Latino; 22 Hispanic/Latino; 2 Native Hawaiian or other Pacific Islander, non-Hispanic/Latino; 6 Two or more races, non-Hispanic/Latino). Average age 29. 381 applicants, 52% accepted, 116 enrolled. In 2013, 186 master's, 11 doctorates, 9 other advanced degrees awarded. *Entrance requirements:* Additional exam requirements/recommendations for international students: Required—TOEFL (minimum score 550 paper-based). *Application deadline:* Applications are processed on a rolling basis. Application fee: $40. *Expenses:* Tuition: Full-time $11,880; part-time $660 per credit hour. *Financial support:* Fellowships, research assistantships, Federal Work-Study, scholarships/grants, tuition waivers (partial), and unspecified assistantships available. Support available to part-time students. Financial award application deadline: 3/1; financial award applicants required to submit FAFSA. *Faculty research:* Literacy development in at-risk children, effective behavior strategies for class instruction. *Unit head:* Dr. Lori Quigley, Dean, Esteves School of Education, 518-244-2326, Fax: 518-244-4571, E-mail: l.quigley@sage.edu. *Application contact:* Wendy D. Diefendorf, Director of Graduate and Adult Admission, 518-244-2443, Fax: 518-244-6880, E-mail: diefew@sage.edu.

Saginaw Valley State University, College of Education, University Center, MI 48710. Offers M Ed, MA, MAT, Ed S. *Accreditation:* NCATE. Part-time and evening/weekend programs available. Postbaccalaureate distance learning degree programs offered (minimal on-campus study). *Faculty:* 64 full-time (45 women), 28 part-time/adjunct (19 women). *Students:* 36 full-time (28 women), 533 part-time (399 women); includes 28 minority (15 Black or African American, non-Hispanic/Latino; 4 American Indian or Alaska Native, non-Hispanic/Latino; 8 Hispanic/Latino; 1 Two or more races, non-Hispanic/Latino), 14 international. Average age 35. 123 applicants, 91% accepted, 72 enrolled. In 2013, 234 master's, 19 other advanced degrees awarded. *Entrance requirements:* For master's, minimum GPA of 3.0, teaching certificate. Additional exam requirements/recommendations for international students: Required—TOEFL (minimum score 550 paper-based; 79 iBT). *Application deadline:* For fall admission, 7/15 for international students; for winter admission, 11/15 for international students; for spring admission, 4/15 for international students. Applications are processed on a rolling basis. Application fee: $30 ($80 for international students). Electronic applications accepted. *Expenses:* Tuition, state resident: full-time $8933; part-time $496.30 per credit hour. Tuition, nonresident: full-time $16,806; part-time $933.65 per credit hour. *Required fees:* $263; $14.60 per credit hour. Tuition and fees vary according to degree level. *Financial support:* Federal Work-Study and scholarships/grants available. Support available to part-time students. Financial award applicants required to submit FAFSA. *Unit head:* Dr. Mary Harmon, Dean, 989-964-7107, Fax: 989-964-4563, E-mail: coeconnect@svsu.edu. *Application contact:* Jenna Briggs, Director, Graduate and International Admissions, 989-964-6096, Fax: 989-964-2788, E-mail: gradadm@svsu.edu.
Website: http://www.svsu.edu/coe.

St. Ambrose University, College of Education and Health Sciences, Program in Education, Davenport, IA 52803-2898. Offers special education (M Ed); teaching (M Ed). *Accreditation:* Teacher Education Accreditation Council. Part-time and evening/weekend programs available. Postbaccalaureate distance learning degree programs offered (no on-campus study). *Degree requirements:* For master's, comprehensive exam. *Entrance requirements:* For master's, GRE General Test or MAT, minimum GPA of 2.75. Additional exam requirements/recommendations for international students: Required—TOEFL. Electronic applications accepted. *Faculty research:* Disabilities and postsecondary career avenues, self-determination.

St. Bonaventure University, School of Graduate Studies, School of Education, St. Bonaventure, NY 14778-2284. Offers MS Ed, Adv C. *Accreditation:* NCATE. Part-time and evening/weekend programs available. *Faculty:* 16 full-time (10 women), 10 part-time/adjunct (7 women). *Students:* 110 full-time (92 women), 80 part-time (63 women); includes 7 minority (3 Black or African American, non-Hispanic/Latino; 1 American Indian or Alaska Native, non-Hispanic/Latino; 1 Hispanic/Latino; 2 Two or more races, non-Hispanic/Latino), 1 international. Average age 28. 115 applicants, 93% accepted, 59 enrolled. In 2013, 128 master's, 18 Adv Cs awarded. *Degree requirements:* For master's and Adv C, comprehensive exam, thesis optional, student teaching, electronic portfolio, internship, practicum. *Entrance requirements:* For master's, undergraduate degree in teachable content area; minimum GPA of 3.0, interview, writing sample, two

letters of recommendation, teaching or counseling certification, 3 years of K-12 school experience; for Adv C, teaching or counseling certification, master's degree, interview, references (ability to do graduate work, success as a teacher), writing sample, minimum undergraduate GPA of 3.0, two letters of recommendation, transcripts, 3 years of K-12 school experience, minimum GPA of 3.0. Additional exam requirements/recommendations for international students: Required—TOEFL (minimum score 550 paper-based; 79 iBT). *Application deadline:* For fall admission, 6/15 priority date for domestic students, 2/1 priority date for international students; for spring admission, 11/15 priority date for domestic students, 7/1 priority date for international students. Applications are processed on a rolling basis. Application fee: $0. Electronic applications accepted. *Financial support:* In 2013–14, 12 research assistantships with full and partial tuition reimbursements were awarded; career-related internships or fieldwork, Federal Work-Study, scholarships/grants, health care benefits, tuition waivers (partial), and unspecified assistantships also available. Support available to part-time students. Financial award application deadline: 4/15; financial award applicants required to submit FAFSA. *Unit head:* Dr. Joseph E. Zimmer, Dean, 716-375-2388, Fax: 716-375-2360, E-mail: jezimmer@sbu.edu. *Application contact:* Bruce Campbell, Director of Graduate Admissions, 716-375-2429, Fax: 716-375-4015, E-mail: gradsch@sbu.edu.

St. Catherine University, Graduate Programs, Program in Education–Curriculum and Instruction, St. Paul, MN 55105. Offers MA. Part-time and evening/weekend programs available. Postbaccalaureate distance learning degree programs offered (minimal on-campus study). *Degree requirements:* For master's, thesis. *Entrance requirements:* For master's, current teaching license, classroom experience, minimum GPA of 3.0. Additional exam requirements/recommendations for international students: Required—Michigan English Language Assessment Battery or TOEFL (minimum score 600 paper-based; 100 iBT). *Expenses:* Contact institution.

St. Catherine University, Graduate Programs, Program in Education - Initial Licensure, St. Paul, MN 55105. Offers MA. Part-time and evening/weekend programs available.

St. Cloud State University, School of Graduate Studies, School of Education, St. Cloud, MN 56301-4498. Offers MS, Ed D. *Accreditation:* NCATE. Part-time and evening/weekend programs available. Postbaccalaureate distance learning degree programs offered (no on-campus study). *Degree requirements:* For master's, comprehensive exam (for some programs), thesis or alternative; for doctorate, comprehensive exam, thesis/dissertation. *Entrance requirements:* For master's, GRE General Test (for some programs), minimum GPA of 2.75; for doctorate, GRE. Additional exam requirements/recommendations for international students: Required—Michigan English Language Assessment Battery; Recommended—TOEFL (minimum score 550 paper-based), IELTS (minimum score 6.5).

Saint Francis University, Graduate Education Program, Loretto, PA 15940-0600. Offers education (M Ed); leadership (M Ed); reading (M Ed). Part-time programs available. *Faculty:* 16 part-time/adjunct (8 women). *Students:* 5 full-time (4 women), 93 part-time (68 women); includes 1 minority (Black or African American, non-Hispanic/Latino). Average age 28. 15 applicants, 100% accepted, 15 enrolled. In 2013, 45 master's awarded. *Degree requirements:* For master's, comprehensive exam, thesis optional. *Entrance requirements:* For master's, GRE or MAT (if undergraduate GPA less than 3.0). Additional exam requirements/recommendations for international students: Required—TOEFL (minimum score 550 paper-based; 75 iBT), IELTS (minimum score 6.5), International Test of English Proficiency (minimum score 4). *Application deadline:* Applications are processed on a rolling basis. Application fee: $30. *Expenses:* Contact institution. *Financial support:* Applicants required to submit FAFSA. *Unit head:* Dr. Janette D. Kelly, Director, 814-472-3068, Fax: 814-472-3864, E-mail: jkelly@francis.edu. *Application contact:* Sherri L. Toth, Coordinator, 814-472-3058, Fax: 814-472-3864, E-mail: stoth@francis.edu.
Website: http://www.francis.edu/master-of-education/.

St. Francis Xavier University, Graduate Studies, Graduate Studies in Education, Antigonish, NS B2G 2W5, Canada. Offers curriculum and instruction (M Ed); educational administration and leadership (M Ed). Part-time programs available. Postbaccalaureate distance learning degree programs offered (minimal on-campus study). *Degree requirements:* For master's, thesis. *Entrance requirements:* For master's, minimum undergraduate B average, 2 years of teaching experience. *Faculty research:* Inclusive education, qualitative research.

St. John Fisher College, Ralph C. Wilson Jr. School of Education, Rochester, NY 14618-3597. Offers MS, MS Ed, Ed D, Certificate. *Accreditation:* NCATE. Part-time and evening/weekend programs available. *Faculty:* 20 full-time (13 women), 19 part-time/adjunct (15 women). *Students:* 154 full-time (108 women), 134 part-time (100 women); includes 84 minority (51 Black or African American, non-Hispanic/Latino; 4 Asian, non-Hispanic/Latino; 23 Hispanic/Latino; 2 Native Hawaiian or other Pacific Islander, non-Hispanic/Latino; 4 Two or more races, non-Hispanic/Latino), 1 international. Average age 34. 239 applicants, 64% accepted, 149 enrolled. In 2013, 96 master's, 46 doctorates awarded. *Degree requirements:* For doctorate, thesis/dissertation. *Entrance requirements:* For master's and doctorate, 2 letters of recommendation, current resume. Additional exam requirements/recommendations for international students: Required—TOEFL (minimum score 575 paper-based; 80 iBT). *Application deadline:* Applications are processed on a rolling basis. Application fee: $30. Electronic applications accepted. *Expenses:* Tuition: Part-time $795 per credit hour. *Required fees:* $10 per credit hour. Tuition and fees vary according to course load, degree level and program. *Financial support:* In 2013–14, 50 students received support. Scholarships/grants available. Financial award applicants required to submit FAFSA. *Unit head:* Dr. Michael Wischnowski, Interim Dean, 585-385-7361, E-mail: mwischnowski@sjfc.edu. *Application contact:* Jose Perales, Director of Graduate Admissions, 585-385-8067, E-mail: jperales@sjfc.edu.

St. John's University, The School of Education, Queens, NY 11439. Offers MS Ed, Ed D, PhD, Adv C, Certificate. *Accreditation:* Teacher Education Accreditation Council. Part-time and evening/weekend programs available. Postbaccalaureate distance learning degree programs offered (no on-campus study). *Faculty:* 50 full-time (31 women), 88 part-time/adjunct (47 women). *Students:* 304 full-time (250 women), 1,158 part-time (856 women); includes 510 minority (217 Black or African American, non-Hispanic/Latino; 1 American Indian or Alaska Native, non-Hispanic/Latino; 68 Asian, non-Hispanic/Latino; 210 Hispanic/Latino; 1 Native Hawaiian or other Pacific Islander, non-Hispanic/Latino; 13 Two or more races, non-Hispanic/Latino), 77 international. Average age 32. 887 applicants, 92% accepted, 451 enrolled. In 2013, 427 master's, 44 doctorates, 43 other advanced degrees awarded. *Degree requirements:* For master's, comprehensive exam (for some programs), thesis (for some programs); residency; for doctorate, comprehensive exam, thesis/dissertation. *Entrance requirements:* For master's, 2 letters of recommendation, official transcript, minimum GPA of 3.0, personal statement, resume; for doctorate, GRE General Test, MAT (for PhD in literacy), interview, writing sample, 2 years of teaching experience, resume (for PhD in literacy only), personal statement, minimum master's GPA of 3.2; for other advanced degree, 2 letters of recommendation, master's degree from accredited college or university. Additional exam requirements/recommendations for international students: Required—TOEFL (minimum score 600 paper-based; 100 iBT), IELTS (minimum score 5.5). *Application deadline:* For fall admission, 4/1 priority date for domestic students, 5/1 priority date for international students; for spring admission, 11/1 priority date for

domestic and international students. Applications are processed on a rolling basis. Application fee: $70. Electronic applications accepted. *Expenses: Tuition:* Full-time $19,800; part-time $1100 per credit. *Required fees:* $170 per semester. *Financial support:* In 2013–14, 96 fellowships with full and partial tuition reimbursements (averaging $20,078 per year), 9 research assistantships with full and partial tuition reimbursements (averaging $14,333 per year), 1 teaching assistantship with full and partial tuition reimbursement (averaging $24,000 per year) were awarded; career-related internships or fieldwork, scholarships/grants, and unspecified assistantships also available. Support available to part-time students. Financial award application deadline: 3/1; financial award applicants required to submit FAFSA. *Faculty research:* Results of school partnerships, effective means of working with recent immigrant populations, results of graduates who participated in programs leading to alternative certification routes, resolution of issues surrounding middle schools, identifying means of supporting children at both ends of the academic continuum. *Unit head:* Dr. Michael Sampson, Dean, 718-990-1305. *Application contact:* Dr. Kelly K. Ronayne, Associate Dean for Graduate Admissions, 718-990-2304, Fax: 718-990-2343, E-mail: graded@stjohns.edu.
Website: http://www.stjohns.edu/academics/schools-and-colleges/school-education.

St. Joseph's College, New York, Graduate Programs, Program in Education, Brooklyn, NY 11205-3688. Offers infant/toddler early childhood special education (MA); literacy and cognition (MA); special education (MA), including severe and multiple disabilities.

Saint Joseph's College of Maine, Master of Science in Education Program, Standish, ME 04084. Offers adult education and training (MS Ed); Catholic school leadership (MS Ed); health care educator (MS Ed); school educator (MS Ed). Program available by correspondence. Part-time programs available. Postbaccalaureate distance learning degree programs offered (minimal on-campus study). Electronic applications accepted.

Saint Joseph's University, College of Arts and Sciences, Department of Education, Philadelphia, PA 19131-1395. Offers curriculum supervisor (Certificate); educational leadership (MS, Ed D); elementary education (MS, Certificate); elementary/middle school education (Certificate); instructional technology (MS, Certificate); principal certification (Certificate); professional education (MS); reading specialist (MS, Certificate); reading supervisor (Certificate); secondary education (MS, Certificate); special education (MS, Certificate); superintendent's letter of eligibility (Certificate); supervisor of special education (Certificate). Part-time and evening/weekend programs available. Postbaccalaureate distance learning degree programs offered (no on-campus study). *Faculty:* 32 full-time (25 women), 75 part-time/adjunct (53 women). *Students:* 91 full-time (81 women), 858 part-time (656 women); includes 133 minority (96 Black or African American, non-Hispanic/Latino; 3 American Indian or Alaska Native, non-Hispanic/Latino; 9 Asian, non-Hispanic/Latino; 20 Hispanic/Latino; 5 Native Hawaiian or other Pacific Islander, non-Hispanic/Latino), 16 international. Average age 31. 359 applicants, 77% accepted, 203 enrolled. In 2013, 363 master's, 9 doctorates, 1 other advanced degree awarded. *Entrance requirements:* For master's, 2 letters of recommendation, minimum GPA of 3.0, official transcripts, personal statement; for doctorate, GRE, master's degree from accredited institution, minimum graduate GPA of 3.5, computer competence, commitment to participate in cohort, interview with program director. Additional exam requirements/recommendations for international students: Required—TOEFL (minimum score 550 paper-based; 79 iBT), IELTS (minimum score 6.5). *Application deadline:* For fall admission, 7/15 priority date for domestic students, 4/15 for international students; for winter admission, 11/15 for domestic students, 1/15 for international students; for spring admission, 11/15 priority date for domestic students, 10/15 for international students. Applications are processed on a rolling basis. Application fee: $35. Electronic applications accepted. *Expenses:* Contact institution. *Financial support:* Unspecified assistantships available. Financial award applicants required to submit FAFSA. *Faculty research:* Factors predicting early mathematics skills for low income children, early child care and development, preschool quality. *Total annual research expenditures:* $229,264. *Unit head:* Dr. John Vacca, Associate Dean, Education, 610-660-3131, E-mail: gradstudies@sju.edu. *Application contact:* Elisabeth Woodward, Director of Marketing and Admissions, Graduate Arts and Sciences, 610-660-3131, Fax: 610-660-3230, E-mail: gradstudies@sju.edu.
Website: http://sju.edu/int/academics/cas/grad/education/index.html.

St. Lawrence University, Department of Education, Canton, NY 13617-1455. Offers counseling and human development (M Ed, MS, CAS), including mental health counseling (MS), school counseling (M Ed, CAS); educational leadership (M Ed, CAS), including combined school building leadership/school district leadership (CAS), educational leadership (M Ed), school building leadership (M Ed), school district leadership (CAS); general studies in education (M Ed). *Accreditation:* Teacher Education Accreditation Council. Part-time and evening/weekend programs available. *Degree requirements:* For master's, thesis optional. *Entrance requirements:* For master's, GRE General Test. *Faculty research:* Defense mechanisms, conflict negotiations and mediation, teacher education policy.

Saint Leo University, Graduate Studies in Education, Saint Leo, FL 33574-6665. Offers educational leadership (M Ed); exceptional student education (M Ed); instructional design (MS); instructional leadership (M Ed); reading (M Ed). Part-time and evening/weekend programs available. Postbaccalaureate distance learning degree programs offered (minimal on-campus study). *Faculty:* 10 full-time (8 women), 31 part-time/adjunct (23 women). *Students:* 680 full-time (554 women), 4 part-time (all women); includes 83 minority (51 Black or African American, non-Hispanic/Latino; 2 Asian, non-Hispanic/Latino; 27 Hispanic/Latino; 3 Two or more races, non-Hispanic/Latino), 4 international. Average age 36. In 2013, 295 master's awarded. *Degree requirements:* For master's, comprehensive exam, appropriate State of Florida certification tests. *Entrance requirements:* For master's, GRE (minimum score of 1000) or MAT (minimum score of 410) if undergraduate GPA for last 60 hours of coursework was below 3.0 (for M Ed), bachelor's degree with minimum GPA of 3.0 for last 60 hours of coursework from regionally-accredited college or university, 2 recommendations, resume, statement of professional goals, copy of valid teaching certificate (for M Ed). Additional exam requirements/recommendations for international students: Required—TOEFL (minimum score 550 paper-based; 80 iBT). *Application deadline:* For fall admission, 7/1 priority date for domestic students, 7/1 for international students; for winter admission, 7/1 for international students; for spring admission, 11/1 priority date for domestic students. Applications are processed on a rolling basis. Application fee: $80. Electronic applications accepted. *Expenses:* Contact institution. *Financial support:* In 2013–14, 618 students received support. Career-related internships or fieldwork, Federal Work-Study, scholarships/grants, and health care benefits available. Financial award application deadline: 3/1; financial award applicants required to submit FAFSA. *Faculty research:* The role of the school leader in data analysis of student achievement, teacher recruitment, teacher effectiveness. *Unit head:* Dr. Sharyn Disabato, Director of Graduate Education, 352-588-8309, Fax: 352-588-8861, E-mail: med@saintleo.edu. *Application contact:* Joshua Stagner, Director of Graduate Admission, 800-707-8846, Fax: 352-588-7873, E-mail: grad.admissions@saintleo.edu.
Website: http://www.saintleo.edu/admissions/graduate.aspx.

Saint Louis University, Graduate Education, College of Education and Public Service, Department of Educational Studies, St. Louis, MO 63103-2097. Offers curriculum and instruction (MA, Ed D, PhD); educational foundations (MA, Ed D, PhD); special education (MA); teaching (MAT). *Accreditation:* NCATE. Part-time programs available. *Degree requirements:* For master's, comprehensive exam; for doctorate, comprehensive exam, thesis/dissertation, preliminary oral and written exams. *Entrance requirements:* For master's, GRE General Test or MAT, letters of recommendation, resume; for doctorate, GRE General Test, letters of recommendation, resumé, goal statement, transcripts. Additional exam requirements/recommendations for international students: Required—TOEFL (minimum score 525 paper-based). Electronic applications accepted. *Faculty research:* Teacher preparation, multicultural issues, children with special needs, qualitative research in education, inclusion.

Saint Martin's University, Office of Graduate Studies, College of Education, Lacey, WA 98503. Offers administration (M Ed); English as a second language (M Ed); guidance and counseling (M Ed); reading (M Ed); special education (M Ed); teaching (MIT). *Accreditation:* Teacher Education Accreditation Council. Part-time and evening/weekend programs available. *Faculty:* 10 full-time (6 women), 15 part-time/adjunct (12 women). *Students:* 57 full-time (35 women), 52 part-time (38 women); includes 20 minority (7 Black or African American, non-Hispanic/Latino; 1 American Indian or Alaska Native, non-Hispanic/Latino; 2 Asian, non-Hispanic/Latino; 6 Hispanic/Latino; 1 Native Hawaiian or other Pacific Islander, non-Hispanic/Latino; 3 Two or more races, non-Hispanic/Latino). Average age 35. 63 applicants, 25% accepted, 13 enrolled. In 2013, 12 master's awarded. *Degree requirements:* For master's, comprehensive exam (for some programs), thesis or alternative, project or comprehensives. *Entrance requirements:* For master's, GRE General Test or MAT, three letters of recommendations; curriculum vitae. Additional exam requirements/recommendations for international students: Required—TOEFL (minimum score 550 paper-based; 79 iBT); Recommended—IELTS (minimum score 6.5). *Application deadline:* For fall admission, 4/1 priority date for domestic and international students; for spring admission, 11/1 priority date for domestic and international students. Applications are processed on a rolling basis. Application fee: $50. Electronic applications accepted. *Expenses: Tuition:* Part-time $990 per credit hour. Tuition and fees vary according to course level and program. *Financial support:* Career-related internships or fieldwork, Federal Work-Study, institutionally sponsored loans, and unspecified assistantships available. Support available to part-time students. Financial award application deadline: 3/1; financial award applicants required to submit FAFSA. *Faculty research:* Reader's theatre and reader/writer workshops, curriculum and assessment integration, gender and equity, classroom evaluations, organizational leadership. *Unit head:* Dr. Joyce Westgard, Dean, College of Education and Professional Psychology, 360-438-4509, Fax: 360-438-4486, E-mail: westgard@stmartin.edu. *Application contact:* Marie C. Boisvert, Administrative Assistant, 360-412-6145, E-mail: gradstudies@stmartin.edu.
Website: http://www.stmartin.edu/gradstudies.

Saint Mary's College of California, Kalmanovitz School of Education, Moraga, CA 94575. Offers M Ed, MA, MAT, Ed D. Part-time and evening/weekend programs available. *Degree requirements:* For master's, thesis or alternative; for doctorate, thesis/dissertation. *Entrance requirements:* For master's, interview, minimum GPA of 3.0; for doctorate, GRE or MAT, interview, MA, minimum GPA of 3.0. *Expenses:* Contact institution. *Faculty research:* Teacher effectiveness, school-based management, multicultural teaching, language and literacy development.

St. Mary's College of Maryland, Department of Educational Studies, St. Mary's City, MD 20686-3001. Offers MAT. *Faculty:* 6 full-time (5 women), 3 part-time/adjunct (2 women). *Students:* 26 full-time (20 women); includes 3 minority (2 Black or African American, non-Hispanic/Latino; 1 Asian, non-Hispanic/Latino). Average age 23. 45 applicants, 80% accepted, 26 enrolled. In 2013, 29 master's awarded. *Degree requirements:* For master's, internship, electronic portfolio, research projects, PRAXIS II. *Entrance requirements:* For master's, SAT, ACT, GRE or PRAXIS I, 2 letters of recommendation, minimum GPA of 3.0. Additional exam requirements/recommendations for international students: Required—TOEFL. *Application deadline:* For fall admission, 10/1 for domestic students; for spring admission, 1/31 priority date for domestic and international students. Applications are processed on a rolling basis. Application fee: $50. *Financial support:* In 2013–14, 8 students received support. Application deadline: 4/1; applicants required to submit FAFSA. *Faculty research:* Supporting English language learners across the curriculum, supporting women and minorities in math and science, instructional technology, multicultural young adult literature, educating teachers to be advocates for equity and social justice. *Unit head:* Dr. Angela Johnson, Director of Teacher Education, 240-895-2018, E-mail: mat@smcm.edu.
Website: http://www.smcm.edu/educationstudies/.

St. Mary's University, Graduate School, Department of Teacher Education, San Antonio, TX 78228-8507. Offers Catholic principalship (Certificate); Catholic school leadership (MA, Certificate), including Catholic school administrators (Certificate), Catholic school leadership (MA), Catholic school teachers (Certificate); educational leadership (MA, Certificate), including educational leadership (MA), principalship (mid-management) (Certificate); reading (MA). Part-time and evening/weekend programs available. *Degree requirements:* For master's, comprehensive exam. *Entrance requirements:* For master's, GRE General Test. Additional exam requirements/recommendations for international students: Required—TOEFL (minimum score 550 paper-based; 80 iBT). Electronic applications accepted.

Saint Mary's University of Minnesota, Schools of Graduate and Professional Programs, Graduate School of Education, Education Program, Winona, MN 55987-1399. Offers culturally responsive teaching (Certificate); education (MA); gifted and talented instruction (Certificate). *Unit head:* Lynn Albee, Director, 612-728-5179, Fax: 612-728-5128, E-mail: lgalbe02@smumn.edu. *Application contact:* Russell Kreager, Director of Admissions for Graduate and Professional Programs, 612-728-5207, Fax: 612-728-5121, E-mail: rkreager@smumn.edu.
Website: http://www.smumn.edu/graduate-home/areas-of-study/graduate-school-of-education/ma-in-education.

Saint Mary's University of Minnesota, Schools of Graduate and Professional Programs, Graduate School of Education, Education-Wisconsin Program, Winona, MN 55987-1399. Offers MA. *Unit head:* Dr. Lynda Sullivan, Director, 877-442-4020, E-mail: lsulliva@smumn.edu. *Application contact:* Russell Kreager, Director of Admissions for Graduate and Professional Programs, 612-728-5207, Fax: 612-728-5121, E-mail: rkreager@smumn.edu.
Website: http://www.smumn.edu/graduate-home/areas-of-study/graduate-school-of-education/ma-in-education-wisconsin.

Saint Mary's University of Minnesota, Schools of Graduate and Professional Programs, Graduate School of Education, Teaching and Learning Program, Winona, MN 55987-1399. Offers M Ed. *Unit head:* Suzanne Peterson, Director, 952-891-3792, E-mail: speterso@smumn.edu. *Application contact:* Jana Korder, Director of Admissions for Graduate and Professional Programs, 507-457-6615, E-mail: jkorder@smumn.edu.
Website: http://www.smumn.edu/graduate-home/areas-of-study/graduate-school-of-education/med-in-teaching-learning.

Saint Michael's College, Graduate Programs, Program in Education, Colchester, VT 05439. Offers administration (M Ed, CAGS); arts in education (CAGS); curriculum and instruction (M Ed, CAGS); information technology (CAGS); reading (M Ed); special

education (M Ed, CAGS); technology (M Ed). Part-time and evening/weekend programs available. *Degree requirements:* For master's, thesis. *Entrance requirements:* For master's, minimum GPA of 3.0. Electronic applications accepted. *Faculty research:* Integrative curriculum, moral and spiritual dimensions of education, learning styles, multiple intelligences, integrating technology into the curriculum.

Saint Peter's University, Graduate Programs in Education, Jersey City, NJ 07306-5997. Offers director of school counseling services (Certificate); educational leadership (MA Ed, Ed D); higher education (Ed D); middle school mathematics (Certificate); professional/associate counselor (Certificate); reading (MA Ed); school business administrator (Certificate); school counseling (MA, Certificate); special education (MA Ed, Certificate), including applied behavioral analysis (MA Ed), literacy (MA Ed), teacher of students with disabilities (Certificate); teaching (MA Ed, Certificate), including 6-8 middle school education, K-12 secondary education, K-5 elementary education. *Accreditation:* Teacher Education Accreditation Council. Part-time and evening/weekend programs available. *Degree requirements:* For master's, comprehensive exam; for doctorate, comprehensive exam, thesis/dissertation. *Entrance requirements:* For master's and doctorate, GRE or MAT. Additional exam requirements/recommendations for international students: Required—TOEFL. Electronic applications accepted.

St. Thomas Aquinas College, Division of Teacher Education, Sparkill, NY 10976. Offers adolescence education (MST); childhood and special education (MST); childhood education (MST); educational leadership (MS Ed); reading (MS Ed, PMC); special education (MS Ed, PMC); teaching (MS Ed), including elementary education, middle school education, secondary education. *Accreditation:* NCATE. Part-time and evening/weekend programs available. *Degree requirements:* For master's, comprehensive exam, comprehensive professional portfolio; for PMC, action research project. *Entrance requirements:* For master's, New York State Qualifying Exam, GRE General Test or minimum GPA of 3.0, teaching certificate; for PMC, GRE General Test or minimum GPA of 3.0. Electronic applications accepted. *Faculty research:* Computer applications in education, adolescent special education students, literacy development, inclusive practices for special education students.

St. Thomas University, School of Leadership Studies, Institute for Education, Miami Gardens, FL 33054-6459. Offers earth/space science (Certificate); educational administration (MS, Certificate); educational leadership (Ed D); elementary education (MS); ESOL (Certificate); gifted education (Certificate); instructional technology (MS, Certificate); professional/studies (Certificate); reading (MS, Certificate); special education (MS). Part-time and evening/weekend programs available. *Degree requirements:* For master's, comprehensive exam; for doctorate, comprehensive exam, thesis/dissertation. *Entrance requirements:* For master's, interview, minimum GPA of 3.0 or GRE; for doctorate, GRE or MAT. Additional exam requirements/recommendations for international students: Required—TOEFL (minimum score 550 paper-based; 79 iBT). Electronic applications accepted.

Saint Vincent College, Program in Education, Latrobe, PA 15650-2690. Offers curriculum and instruction (MS); educational media and technology (MS); environmental education (MS); school administration and supervision (MS); special education (MS). Part-time and evening/weekend programs available. *Degree requirements:* For master's, comprehensive exam. *Entrance requirements:* For master's, GRE (if undergraduate GPA less than 3.0). Additional exam requirements/recommendations for international students: Required—TOEFL (minimum score 550 paper-based). *Faculty research:* Assessment and instructional technology.

Saint Xavier University, Graduate Studies, School of Education, Chicago, IL 60655-3105. Offers counseling (MA); curriculum and instruction (MA); early childhood education (MA); educational administration (MA); elementary education (MA); individualized studies (MA), including educational technology, English as a second language (ESL), ISTEM (integrative science, technology, engineering, and math), science education; music education (MA); reading (MA); secondary education (MA); Spanish education (MA); special education (MA); teaching and leadership (MA). *Accreditation:* NCATE. Part-time and evening/weekend programs available. *Degree requirements:* For master's, thesis or project. *Entrance requirements:* For master's, minimum GPA of 3.0. *Expenses:* Contact institution.

Salem College, Department of Education, Winston-Salem, NC 27101. Offers art education (MAT); elementary education (M Ed, MAT); language and literacy (M Ed); middle school education (MAT); school counseling (M Ed); second language studies (MAT); secondary education (MAT); special education (M Ed, MAT). *Accreditation:* NCATE. Part-time and evening/weekend programs available. Postbaccalaureate distance learning degree programs offered (minimal on-campus study). *Degree requirements:* For master's, practicum (MAT), project (M Ed), oral and written comprehensive exams. *Entrance requirements:* For master's, minimum GPA of 2.5. *Faculty research:* Content area reading strategies, literacy development, brain compatible instruction.

Salem International University, School of Education, Salem, WV 26426-0500. Offers curriculum and instruction (M Ed); educational leadership (M Ed). Part-time and evening/weekend programs available. Postbaccalaureate distance learning degree programs offered. *Degree requirements:* For master's, comprehensive exam (for some programs), thesis (for some programs). *Entrance requirements:* For master's, GRE, MAT, NTE, 3 letters of recommendation. Additional exam requirements/recommendations for international students: Required—TOEFL (minimum score 550 paper-based). Electronic applications accepted. *Expenses:* Contact institution. *Faculty research:* Improved classroom effectiveness.

Salisbury University, Department of Education Specialties, Salisbury, MD 21801-6837. Offers curriculum and instruction (M Ed), including curriculum and instruction, post secondary track; educational leadership (M Ed); reading specialist (M Ed); secondary education (MAT). *Accreditation:* NCATE. Part-time programs available. *Degree requirements:* For master's, comprehensive exam (for some programs), thesis optional. *Application deadline:* For fall admission, 3/3 for domestic students; for spring admission, 10/1 for domestic students. *Expenses: Tuition, area resident:* Part-time $342 per credit hour. Tuition, state resident: part-time $342 per credit hour. Tuition, nonresident: part-time $631 per credit hour. *Required fees:* $76 per credit hour. Tuition and fees vary according to program. *Financial support:* Application deadline: 3/1.

Samford University, Orlean Bullard Beeson School of Education, Birmingham, AL 35229. Offers early childhood/elementary education (MS Ed); educational leadership (MS Ed, Ed D); gifted education (MS Ed); instructional leadership (MS Ed, Ed S); secondary collaboration (MS Ed); M Div/MS Ed. *Accreditation:* NCATE. Part-time and evening/weekend programs available. *Faculty:* 10 full-time (5 women), 16 part-time/adjunct (15 women). *Students:* 40 full-time (25 women), 210 part-time (156 women); includes 39 minority (33 Black or African American, non-Hispanic/Latino; 3 American Indian or Alaska Native, non-Hispanic/Latino; 2 Asian, non-Hispanic/Latino; 1 Hispanic/Latino), 4 international. Average age 38. 81 applicants, 89% accepted, 70 enrolled. In 2013, 94 master's, 21 doctorates, 16 other advanced degrees awarded. *Degree requirements:* For master's and Ed S, comprehensive exam; for doctorate, comprehensive exam, thesis/dissertation. *Entrance requirements:* For master's, GRE (minimum score of 295) or MAT (minimum score of 396); waived if previously completed a graduate degree, writing sample, statement of purpose, 3 letters of recommendation, 2 original copies of all transcripts, minimum GPA of 2.75, teaching certificate; for doctorate, minimum GPA of 3.7, professional resume, writing sample, 3 letters of recommendation, 1 original copy of all transcripts; for Ed S, master's degree, teaching certificate, minimum GPA of 3.25, 3 letters of recommendation, 2 original copies of all transcripts, writing sample, statement of purpose. Additional exam requirements/recommendations for international students: Required—TOEFL (minimum score 90 iBT), IELTS (minimum score 7). *Application deadline:* For fall admission, 7/30 for domestic and international students; for winter admission, 4/5 for domestic students; for spring admission, 12/5 for domestic and international students; for summer admission, 4/18 for domestic and international students. Applications are processed on a rolling basis. Application fee: $35. Electronic applications accepted. *Expenses: Tuition:* Full-time $11,552; part-time $722 per credit. *Required fees:* $500; $250 per term. *Financial support:* In 2013–14, 162 students received support. Research assistantships, career-related internships or fieldwork, Federal Work-Study, scholarships/grants, and tuition waivers (partial) available. Support available to part-time students. Financial award applicants required to submit FAFSA. *Faculty research:* Research on gifted/high ability students (K-12), school law, the characteristics of beginning teachers, the nature of school reform, school culture, quality improvement in education, K-12 student achievement, reading research, classroom management, reading intervention, schema theory. *Unit head:* Dr. Maurice Persall, Chair, Department of Educational Leadership, 205-726-2019, E-mail: jmpersal@samford.edu. *Application contact:* Brooke Gilreath Karr, Graduate Admissions Coordinator, 205-729-2783, Fax: 205-726-4233, E-mail: kbgilrea@samford.edu.
Website: http://www.samford.edu/education/.

Sam Houston State University, College of Education and Applied Science, Huntsville, TX 77341. Offers M Ed, MA, MLS, Ed D, PhD. *Accreditation:* NCATE. Part-time and evening/weekend programs available. Postbaccalaureate distance learning degree programs offered (no on-campus study). *Faculty:* 79 full-time (56 women), 2 part-time/adjunct (1 woman). *Students:* 321 full-time (259 women), 1,066 part-time (901 women); includes 553 minority (236 Black or African American, non-Hispanic/Latino; 4 American Indian or Alaska Native, non-Hispanic/Latino; 17 Asian, non-Hispanic/Latino; 266 Hispanic/Latino; 30 Two or more races, non-Hispanic/Latino), 44 international. Average age 35. 738 applicants, 94% accepted, 335 enrolled. In 2013, 405 master's, 37 doctorates awarded. *Degree requirements:* For master's, comprehensive exam (for some programs), thesis optional, portfolio; for doctorate, comprehensive exam (for some programs), thesis/dissertation. *Entrance requirements:* For master's and doctorate, GRE General Test. Additional exam requirements/recommendations for international students: Required—TOEFL (minimum score 550 paper-based; 79 iBT), IELTS (minimum score 6.5). *Application deadline:* For fall admission, 8/1 for domestic students, 6/25 for international students; for spring admission, 12/1 for domestic students, 11/12 for international students. Applications are processed on a rolling basis. Application fee: $45 ($75 for international students). Electronic applications accepted. *Financial support:* In 2013–14, 17 research assistantships (averaging $11,999 per year), 7 teaching assistantships (averaging $9,765 per year) were awarded; career-related internships or fieldwork, Federal Work-Study, institutionally sponsored loans, scholarships/grants, tuition waivers (partial), and unspecified assistantships also available. Support available to part-time students. Financial award application deadline: 5/31; financial award applicants required to submit FAFSA. *Unit head:* Dr. A. Jerry Bruce, Interim Dean, 936-294-1101, Fax: 936-294-1102, E-mail: psy_ajb@shsu.edu. *Application contact:* -.
Website: http://www.shsu.edu/~edu_www.

San Diego State University, Graduate and Research Affairs, College of Education, San Diego, CA 92182. Offers MA, MS, Ed D, PhD. *Accreditation:* NCATE. Part-time and evening/weekend programs available. *Degree requirements:* For master's, thesis optional; for doctorate, thesis/dissertation. *Entrance requirements:* For master's, GRE General Test, letters of reference; for doctorate, GRE General Test, 3 letters of reference, resumé. Additional exam requirements/recommendations for international students: Required—TOEFL. Electronic applications accepted. *Faculty research:* Special education, rehabilitation counseling, educational psychology.

San Francisco State University, Division of Graduate Studies, College of Education, San Francisco, CA 94132-1722. Offers MA, MS, Ed D, PhD, AC, Certificate, Credential. *Accreditation:* NCATE. *Unit head:* Dr. Elizabeth Kean, Interim Dean, 415-338-2687, Fax: 415-338-7019, E-mail: bkean@sfsu.edu. *Application contact:* Victoria Narkewicz, Executive Assistant, 415-338-2687, Fax: 415-338-7019, E-mail: toria@sfsu.edu.
Website: http://coe.sfsu.edu/.

San Jose State University, Graduate Studies and Research, Connie L. Lurie College of Education, San Jose, CA 95192-0001. Offers MA, Certificate. *Accreditation:* NCATE. Evening/weekend programs available. Electronic applications accepted.

Santa Clara University, School of Education and Counseling Psychology, Santa Clara, CA 95053. Offers alternative and correctional education (Certificate); counseling (MA); counseling psychology (MA); educational administration (MA); interdisciplinary education (MA); teaching (MA). Part-time and evening/weekend programs available. *Faculty:* 56 full-time (21 women), 41 part-time/adjunct (23 women). *Students:* 232 full-time (192 women), 329 part-time (262 women); includes 162 minority (14 Black or African American, non-Hispanic/Latino; 1 American Indian or Alaska Native, non-Hispanic/Latino; 59 Asian, non-Hispanic/Latino; 75 Hispanic/Latino; 2 Native Hawaiian or other Pacific Islander, non-Hispanic/Latino; 11 Two or more races, non-Hispanic/Latino), 21 international. Average age 31. 322 applicants, 77% accepted, 178 enrolled. In 2013, 176 master's, 36 other advanced degrees awarded. *Degree requirements:* For master's, comprehensive exam (for some programs), thesis (for some programs); for Certificate, comprehensive exam. *Entrance requirements:* For master's, GRE or MAT, transcript, letters of recommendation, essay. Additional exam requirements/recommendations for international students: Required—TOEFL. *Application deadline:* For fall admission, 6/15 for domestic and international students; for winter admission, 10/15 for domestic and international students; for spring admission, 1/31 for domestic and international students. Applications are processed on a rolling basis. Application fee: $50. Electronic applications accepted. *Expenses:* Contact institution. *Financial support:* In 2013–14, 281 students received support. Fellowships, research assistantships, Federal Work-Study, institutionally sponsored loans, and scholarships/grants available. Support available to part-time students. Financial award application deadline: 5/15; financial award applicants required to submit FAFSA. *Faculty research:* Cognitive behavioral therapies and positive psychology, multicultural counseling and Latino mental health. *Unit head:* Nicholas Ladany, Dean, 408-554-4455, Fax: 408-554-5038, E-mail: nladany@scu.edu. *Application contact:* Kelly Pjesky, Admissions Director, 408-554-7884, Fax: 408-554-4367, E-mail: kpjesky@scu.edu.
Website: http://www.scu.edu/ecppm/.

Sarah Lawrence College, Graduate Studies, Program in Art of Teaching, Bronxville, NY 10708-5999. Offers MS Ed. Part-time programs available. *Faculty:* 8 part-time/adjunct (7 women). *Students:* 15 full-time (12 women), 2 part-time (both women); includes 10 minority (3 Black or African American, non-Hispanic/Latino; 4 Hispanic/Latino; 3 Two or more races, non-Hispanic/Latino). In 2013, 14 master's awarded. *Degree requirements:* For master's, thesis, fieldwork, oral presentation. *Entrance requirements:* For master's, minimum B average in undergraduate coursework. Additional exam requirements/recommendations for international students: Required—

TOEFL (minimum score 600 paper-based). *Application deadline:* For fall admission, 3/1 priority date for domestic and international students. Applications are processed on a rolling basis. Application fee: $60. Electronic applications accepted. *Expenses:* Contact institution. *Financial support:* In 2013–14, 17 students received support, including 12 fellowships (averaging $13,395 per year); career-related internships or fieldwork, scholarships/grants, and unspecified assistantships also available. Support available to part-time students. Financial award application deadline: 3/1; financial award applicants required to submit FAFSA. *Unit head:* Sara Wilford, Director, 914-395-2371, E-mail: swilford@sarahlawrence.edu. *Application contact:* Emanual Lomax, Director of Graduate Admissions, 914-395-2371, E-mail: elomax@sarahlawrence.edu.
Website: https://www.slc.edu/teaching/.

Schreiner University, Department of Education, Kerrville, TX 78028-5697. Offers education (M Ed); principal (Certificate). Part-time and evening/weekend programs available. Postbaccalaureate distance learning degree programs offered (minimal on-campus study). *Faculty:* 3 full-time (2 women), 1 (woman) part-time/adjunct. *Students:* 40 full-time (30 women), 5 part-time (4 women); includes 15 minority (1 Black or African American, non-Hispanic/Latino; 13 Hispanic/Latino; 1 Two or more races, non-Hispanic/Latino). Average age 35. 29 applicants, 93% accepted, 25 enrolled. In 2013, 29 master's, 11 Certificates awarded. *Entrance requirements:* For master's, GRE (waived if undergraduate cumulative GPA is 3.0 or above), 3 references; transcripts; interview. Additional exam requirements/recommendations for international students: Required—TOEFL. *Application deadline:* For fall admission, 8/1 priority date for domestic students, 8/1 for international students; for spring admission, 12/1 priority date for domestic students, 12/1 for international students; for summer admission, 5/1 priority date for domestic students, 5/1 for international students. Applications are processed on a rolling basis. Application fee: $25. Electronic applications accepted. *Expenses: Tuition:* Full-time $17,604; part-time $489 per credit hour. Tuition and fees vary according to course load and program. *Financial support:* In 2013–14, 42 students received support. Scholarships/grants available. Financial award application deadline: 8/1; financial award applicants required to submit FAFSA. *Unit head:* Dr. Neva Cramer, Director, Teacher Education, 830-792-7266, Fax: 830-792-7382, E-mail: nvcramer@schreiner.edu. *Application contact:* Caroline Randall, Director of Admission, 830-792-7224, Fax: 830-792-7226, E-mail: gradadmissions@schreiner.edu.
Website: http://www.schreiner.edu/academics/graduate/index.html.

Seattle University, College of Education, Seattle, WA 98122-1090. Offers M Ed, MA, MIT, Ed D, Certificate, Ed S, Post-Master's Certificate. *Accreditation:* NCATE. Part-time and evening/weekend programs available. *Faculty:* 33 full-time (19 women), 14 part-time/adjunct (7 women). *Students:* 192 full-time (150 women), 343 part-time (246 women); includes 161 minority (30 Black or African American, non-Hispanic/Latino; 5 American Indian or Alaska Native, non-Hispanic/Latino; 50 Asian, non-Hispanic/Latino; 44 Hispanic/Latino; 2 Native Hawaiian or other Pacific Islander, non-Hispanic/Latino; 30 Two or more races, non-Hispanic/Latino), 10 international. Average age 32. 477 applicants, 45% accepted, 122 enrolled. In 2013, 189 master's, 13 doctorates, 24 other advanced degrees awarded. *Degree requirements:* For master's and other advanced degree, comprehensive exam; for doctorate, comprehensive exam, thesis/dissertation. *Entrance requirements:* For doctorate, GRE General Test, MAT, interview, MA, minimum GPA of 3.5, 3 years of related experience. Additional exam requirements/recommendations for international students: Required—TOEFL. *Application deadline:* Applications are processed on a rolling basis. Application fee: $55. Electronic applications accepted. *Expenses:* Contact institution. *Financial support:* In 2013–14, 67 students received support. Career-related internships or fieldwork, Federal Work-Study, scholarships/grants, and unspecified assistantships available. Support available to part-time students. Financial award applicants required to submit FAFSA. *Faculty research:* Service-learning, learning and technology, assessment models of professional education, alternative delivery systems. *Unit head:* Dr. Deanna Sands, Dean, 206-296-5758, E-mail: sandsd@seattleu.edu. *Application contact:* Janet Shandley, Director of Graduate Admissions, 206-296-5900, Fax: 206-298-5656, E-mail: grad_admissions@seattleu.edu.
Website: http://www.seattleu.edu/soe/.

Seton Hall University, College of Education and Human Services, South Orange, NJ 07079-2697. Offers MA, MS, Ed D, Exec Ed D, PhD, Ed S, Professional Diploma. *Accreditation:* NCATE. Part-time and evening/weekend programs available. *Degree requirements:* For master's, comprehensive exam (for some programs), internship; for doctorate, comprehensive exam, thesis/dissertation, internship. *Entrance requirements:* For master's, GRE or MAT, PRAXIS, letters of recommendation, interview, personal statement, curriculum vitae, transcript; for doctorate, GRE, interview, letters of recommendation, personal statement, curriculum vitae, transcript; for other advanced degree, GRE or MAT, PRAXIS, interview, letters of recommendation, personal statement, curriculum vitae, transcript. Electronic applications accepted. *Faculty research:* Information technology and classrooms, adult development including career family systems, therapy effectiveness, management systems, principal effectiveness.

Seton Hill University, Program in Inclusive Education, Greensburg, PA 15601. Offers MA. Part-time and evening/weekend programs available. Postbaccalaureate distance learning degree programs offered (no on-campus study). *Faculty:* 4 full-time (all women), 6 part-time/adjunct (4 women). *Students:* 2 full-time (1 woman), 7 part-time (all women). Average age 27. 7 applicants, 29% accepted, 1 enrolled. In 2013, 1 master's awarded. *Entrance requirements:* For master's, 3 letters of recommendation, transcripts, letter of intent, resume. Additional exam requirements/recommendations for international students: Required—TOEFL (minimum score 600 paper-based; 100 iBT), IELTS (minimum score 6.5). *Application deadline:* Applications are processed on a rolling basis. Application fee: $0. Electronic applications accepted. *Expenses: Tuition:* Full-time $14,220; part-time $790 per credit. *Required fees:* $700; $34 per credit. $50 per semester. *Financial support:* Scholarships/grants and tuition discounts available. Financial award application deadline: 7/15. *Faculty research:* Autism, integrating technology into instruction. *Unit head:* Jennifer Suppo, Director, 724-830-1032, E-mail: jsuppo@setonhill.edu. *Application contact:* Laurel Komarny, Program Counselor, 724-838-4209, E-mail: lkomarny@setonhill.edu.
Website: http://www.setonhill.edu/academics/gradaute_programs/inclusive_education.

Shawnee State University, Program in Curriculum and Instruction, Portsmouth, OH 45662-4344. Offers M Ed. *Accreditation:* NCATE.

Shenandoah University, School of Education and Human Development, Winchester, VA 22601-5195. Offers MS, MSE, D Ed, D Prof, Certificate. *Accreditation:* Teacher Education Accreditation Council. Part-time and evening/weekend programs available. Postbaccalaureate distance learning degree programs offered (minimal on-campus study). *Faculty:* 12 full-time (8 women), 63 part-time/adjunct (46 women). *Students:* 35 full-time (20 women), 394 part-time (294 women); includes 50 minority (22 Black or African American, non-Hispanic/Latino; 3 American Indian or Alaska Native, non-Hispanic/Latino; 12 Asian, non-Hispanic/Latino; 13 Hispanic/Latino), 14 international. Average age 37. 201 applicants, 91% accepted, 149 enrolled. In 2013, 92 master's, 1 doctorate, 31 other advanced degrees awarded. *Degree requirements:* For master's, comprehensive exam (for some programs), thesis (for some programs), internship; for doctorate, comprehensive exam, thesis/dissertation; for Certificate, full-time teaching in area for 1 year. *Entrance requirements:* For master's, minimum GPA of 3.0 or satisfactory GRE, 3 letters of recommendation, valid teaching license, writing sample; for doctorate, minimum graduate GPA of 3.5, 3 years of teaching experience, 3 letters of recommendation, writing samples, interview, resume; for Certificate, minimum undergraduate GPA of 3.0, essay, 3 letters of recommendation. Additional exam requirements/recommendations for international students: Required—TOEFL (minimum score 550 paper-based; 79 iBT), IELTS (minimum score 6.5). *Application deadline:* For fall admission, 5/1 for domestic and international students; for spring admission, 10/15 for domestic and international students; for summer admission, 2/15 for domestic and international students. Application fee: $30. Electronic applications accepted. *Expenses: Tuition:* Full-time $19,176; part-time $799 per credit. *Required fees:* $365 per term. Tuition and fees vary according to course level, course load and program. *Financial support:* In 2013–14, 6 students received support. Career-related internships or fieldwork and scholarships/grants available. Support available to part-time students. Financial award application deadline: 3/15; financial award applicants required to submit FAFSA. *Unit head:* Dr. Calvin Allen, Dean and Associate Vice President, 540-665-4587, Fax: 540-665-4644, E-mail: callen@su.edu. *Application contact:* Andrew Woodall, Executive Director of Recruitment and Admissions, 540-665-4581, Fax: 540-665-4627, E-mail: admit@su.edu.
Website: http://www.education.su.edu.

Shippensburg University of Pennsylvania, School of Graduate Studies, College of Education and Human Services, Shippensburg, PA 17257-2299. Offers M Ed, MAT, MS, MSW, Certificate. *Accreditation:* NCATE. Part-time and evening/weekend programs available. *Faculty:* 50 full-time (28 women), 9 part-time/adjunct (7 women). *Students:* 140 full-time (112 women), 254 part-time (195 women); includes 44 minority (24 Black or African American, non-Hispanic/Latino; 1 American Indian or Alaska Native, non-Hispanic/Latino; 4 Asian, non-Hispanic/Latino; 6 Hispanic/Latino; 9 Two or more races, non-Hispanic/Latino), 4 international. Average age 29. 325 applicants, 62% accepted, 143 enrolled. In 2013, 198 master's awarded. *Entrance requirements:* Additional exam requirements/recommendations for international students: Required—TOEFL (minimum score 580 paper-based); Recommended—IELTS (minimum score 6). *Application deadline:* For fall admission, 4/30 for international students; for spring admission, 9/30 for international students. Applications are processed on a rolling basis. Application fee: $45. Electronic applications accepted. *Expenses: Tuition, area resident:* Part-time $442 per credit. Tuition, state resident: part-time $442 per credit. Tuition, nonresident: part-time $663 per credit. *Required fees:* $127 per credit. *Financial support:* In 2013–14, 75 research assistantships with full tuition reimbursements (averaging $5,000 per year) were awarded; career-related internships or fieldwork, scholarships/grants, unspecified assistantships, and resident hall director and student payroll positions also available. Support available to part-time students. Financial award application deadline: 3/1; financial award applicants required to submit FAFSA. *Unit head:* Dr. James R. Johnson, Dean, 717-477-1373, Fax: 717-477-4012, E-mail: jrjohnson@ship.edu. *Application contact:* Jeremy R. Goshorn, Assistant Dean of Graduate Admissions, 717-477-1231, Fax: 717-477-4016, E-mail: jrgoshorn@ship.edu.
Website: http://www.ship.edu/COEHS/.

Siena Heights University, Graduate College, Adrian, MI 49221-1796. Offers clinical mental health counseling (MA); education leadership (Specialist); leadership (MA), including health care, higher education leadership, organizational; teacher education (MA), including early childhood, early childhood: Montessori-based, education leadership: principal, elementary education, K-12 reading, leadership: higher education, secondary education, K-12 reading, special education, K-12 cognitive impairment, special education, K-12 learning disabled. Part-time and evening/weekend programs available. *Faculty:* 37. *Students:* 9 full-time (7 women), 251 part-time (179 women). In 2013, 32 master's awarded. *Degree requirements:* For master's, thesis, presentation. *Entrance requirements:* For master's, minimum GPA of 3.0, current resume, essay, all post-secondary transcripts, 3 letters of reference, conviction disclosure form; copy of teaching certificate (for some education programs); for Specialist, master's degree, minimum GPA of 3.0, current resume, essay, all post-secondary transcripts, 3 letters of reference, conviction disclosure form; copy of teaching certificate (for some education programs). *Application deadline:* Applications are processed on a rolling basis. Application fee: $50. *Expenses: Tuition:* Part-time $535 per semester hour. *Required fees:* $130 per semester. *Financial support:* Career-related internships or fieldwork, Federal Work-Study, and resident assistantships available. Financial award application deadline: 9/1; financial award applicants required to submit FAFSA. *Unit head:* Dr. Linda S. Pettit, Dean, Graduate College, 517-264-7661, Fax: 517-264-7714, E-mail: lpettit@sienahts.edu.
Website: http://www.sienaheights.edu.

Sierra Nevada College, Teacher Education Program, Incline Village, NV 89451. Offers advanced teaching and leadership (M Ed); elementary education (MAT); secondary education (MAT). Part-time and evening/weekend programs available. Postbaccalaureate distance learning degree programs offered (minimal on-campus study). *Degree requirements:* For master's, comprehensive exam, thesis, PRAXIS I and II. *Entrance requirements:* For master's, 2 letters of recommendation, minimum GPA of 3.0. Electronic applications accepted.

Silver Lake College of the Holy Family, Division of Graduate Studies, Program in Education, Manitowoc, WI 54220-9319. Offers administrative leadership (MA Ed); teacher leadership (MA Ed). Part-time and evening/weekend programs available. Postbaccalaureate distance learning degree programs offered (no on-campus study). *Faculty:* 1 (woman) full-time, 9 part-time/adjunct (5 women). *Students:* 1 (woman) full-time, 74 part-time (53 women); includes 5 minority (4 Black or African American, non-Hispanic/Latino; 1 Asian, non-Hispanic/Latino). Average age 40. 42 applicants, 98% accepted, 14 enrolled. In 2013, 13 master's awarded. *Degree requirements:* For master's, comprehensive exam, thesis or alternative, public presentation of culminating project. *Entrance requirements:* For master's, minimum undergraduate GPA of 3.0, writing sample, 3 letters of recommendation. Additional exam requirements/recommendations for international students: Required—TOEFL. *Application deadline:* For fall admission, 8/1 for domestic and international students; for spring admission, 12/1 for domestic and international students. Applications are processed on a rolling basis. Application fee: $0. Electronic applications accepted. *Expenses: Tuition:* Part-time $500 per credit. *Financial support:* Scholarships/grants available. Support available to part-time students. Financial award application deadline: 6/30; financial award applicants required to submit FAFSA. *Unit head:* Sr. Marcolette Madden, Director, 800-236-4752 Ext. 375, Fax: 920-684-7082, E-mail: marcolette.madden@sl.edu. *Application contact:* Jamie Grant, Director of Admissions, 920-686-6206, Fax: 920-686-6322, E-mail: jamie.grant@sl.edu.
Website: https://www.sl.edu/adult-education/academics/graduate-program/master-of-arts-in-education/.

Simmons College, School of Social Work, Boston, MA 02115. Offers assistive technology (MS Ed, Ed S); behavior analysis (MS, PhD, Ed S); education (MA, CAGS); language and literacy (MS Ed, Ed S); social work (MSW, PhD); special education (MS Ed), including moderate disabilities, severe disabilities; teaching (MAT), including elementary education, general education, high school education; teaching English as a second language (MA, CAGS); urban leadership (MSW); MSW/MBA. *Accreditation:* CSWE (one or more programs are accredited). Part-time programs available.

Postbaccalaureate distance learning degree programs offered (no on-campus study). *Students:* 519 full-time (454 women), 703 part-time (604 women); includes 192 minority (61 Black or African American, non-Hispanic/Latino; 1 American Indian or Alaska Native, non-Hispanic/Latino; 35 Asian, non-Hispanic/Latino; 71 Hispanic/Latino; 2 Native Hawaiian or other Pacific Islander, non-Hispanic/Latino; 22 Two or more races, non-Hispanic/Latino), 16 international. 952 applicants, 66% accepted, 353 enrolled. In 2013, 159 master's, 2 doctorates awarded. Terminal master's awarded for partial completion of doctoral program. *Degree requirements:* For master's, thesis (for some programs); for doctorate, comprehensive exam (for some programs), thesis/dissertation (for some programs). *Entrance requirements:* For master's, GRE, MAT, MTEL (for different programs); for doctorate, GRE, BCBA Analyst Exam. Additional exam requirements/recommendations for international students: Required—TOEFL (minimum score 600 paper-based; 100 iBT). *Application deadline:* Applications are processed on a rolling basis. Application fee: $45. Electronic applications accepted. *Financial support:* Teaching assistantships and scholarships/grants available. *Unit head:* Dr. Stefan Krug, Dean, 617-521-3924. *Application contact:* Carlos D. Frontado, Director of Admissions, 617-521-3920, Fax: 617-521-3980, E-mail: ssw@simmons.edu.
Website: http://www.simmons.edu/ssw/.

Simon Fraser University, Office of Graduate Studies, Faculty of Education, Burnaby, BC V5A 1S6, Canada. Offers M Ed, M Sc, MA, Ed D, PhD, Graduate Diploma. *Students:* 759 full-time (556 women), 459 part-time (398 women). 699 applicants, 62% accepted, 346 enrolled. In 2013, 279 master's, 30 doctorates, 85 other advanced degrees awarded. *Degree requirements:* For doctorate, thesis/dissertation. *Entrance requirements:* Additional exam requirements/recommendations for international students: Recommended—TOEFL (minimum score 580 paper-based; 93 iBT), IELTS (minimum score 7), TWE (minimum score 5). Application fee: $90 ($125 for international students). Electronic applications accepted. *Expenses: Tuition, area resident:* Full-time $5084 Canadian dollars. *Required fees:* $840 Canadian dollars. *Financial support:* In 2013–14, 57 students received support, including 48 fellowships (averaging $6,250 per year), teaching assistantships (averaging $5,608 per year); research assistantships, career-related internships or fieldwork, and scholarships/grants also available. Support available to part-time students. *Unit head:* Dr. Robin Bryan, Graduate Chair, 778-782-4858. *Application contact:* Lilian Yuen Walker, Administrative Assistant, 778-782-9488, Fax: 778-782-4320, E-mail: gse-sec@sfu.ca.
Website: http://www.sfu.ca/education.html.

Simpson College, Department of Education, Indianola, IA 50125-1297. Offers secondary education (MAT). *Degree requirements:* For master's, PRAXIS II, electronic portfolio. *Entrance requirements:* For master's, bachelor's degree; minimum cumulative GPA of 2.75, 3.0 in major; 3 letters of recommendation.

Simpson University, School of Education, Redding, CA 96003-8606. Offers education (MA), including curriculum, education leadership; education and preliminary administrative services credential (MA); education and preliminary teaching credential (MA); teaching (MA). Part-time and evening/weekend programs available. *Faculty:* 5 full-time (2 women), 16 part-time/adjunct (7 women). *Students:* 45 full-time (27 women), 84 part-time (59 women); includes 24 minority (4 Black or African American, non-Hispanic/Latino; 2 American Indian or Alaska Native, non-Hispanic/Latino; 13 Asian, non-Hispanic/Latino; 4 Hispanic/Latino; 1 Native Hawaiian or other Pacific Islander, non-Hispanic/Latino). Average age 36. 54 applicants, 67% accepted, 29 enrolled. In 2013, 29 master's awarded. *Degree requirements:* For master's, thesis optional. *Entrance requirements:* For master's, GRE. Additional exam requirements/recommendations for international students: Required—TOEFL (minimum score 550 paper-based). *Application deadline:* Applications are processed on a rolling basis. Application fee: $25. Electronic applications accepted. Tuition and fees vary according to program. *Financial support:* Scholarships/grants available. Financial award applicants required to submit FAFSA. *Unit head:* Dr. Glee Brooks, Dean of Education, 530-226-4188, Fax: 530-226-4872, E-mail: gbrooks@simpsonu.edu. *Application contact:* Kimberly Snow, Assistant Director of Graduate Admissions, 530-226-4633, E-mail: ksnow@simpsonu.edu.

Sinte Gleska University, Graduate Education Program, Mission, SD 57555. Offers elementary education (M Ed). Part-time and evening/weekend programs available. *Degree requirements:* For master's, thesis. *Entrance requirements:* For master's, 2 years of experience in elementary education, minimum GPA of 2.5, South Dakota elementary education certification. *Faculty research:* American Indian graduate education, teaching of Native American students.

Slippery Rock University of Pennsylvania, Graduate Studies (Recruitment), College of Education, Slippery Rock, PA 16057-1383. Offers M Ed, MA, MS. *Accreditation:* NCATE. Part-time and evening/weekend programs available. Postbaccalaureate distance learning degree programs offered. *Faculty:* 34 full-time (17 women). *Students:* 188 full-time (139 women), 216 part-time (183 women); includes 20 minority (12 Black or African American, non-Hispanic/Latino; 1 American Indian or Alaska Native, non-Hispanic/Latino; 2 Asian, non-Hispanic/Latino; 4 Hispanic/Latino; 1 Two or more races, non-Hispanic/Latino), 2 international. Average age 28. 450 applicants, 75% accepted, 212 enrolled. In 2013, 202 master's awarded. *Degree requirements:* For master's, comprehensive exam (for some programs), thesis (for some programs), internship (depending on program). *Entrance requirements:* For master's, GRE General Test, MAT, minimum GPA of 2.75 (depending on program). Additional exam requirements/recommendations for international students: Required—TOEFL (minimum score 550 paper-based; 80 iBT). *Application deadline:* For fall admission, 3/1 priority date for domestic students, 5/1 priority date for international students; for spring admission, 10/1 priority date for domestic students, 9/1 priority date for international students. Applications are processed on a rolling basis. Application fee: $25 ($30 for international students). Electronic applications accepted. *Expenses:* Tuition, state resident: full-time $7956; part-time $442 per credit. Tuition, nonresident: full-time $11,934; part-time $663 per credit. *Required fees:* $2896; $148 per credit. Tuition and fees vary according to degree level and program. *Financial support:* Career-related internships or fieldwork, Federal Work-Study, institutionally sponsored loans, scholarships/grants, tuition waivers (partial), and unspecified assistantships available. Support available to part-time students. Financial award application deadline: 5/1; financial award applicants required to submit FAFSA. *Unit head:* Dr. Keith Dils, Dean, 724-738-2007, Fax: 724-738-2880, E-mail: keith.dils@sru.edu. *Application contact:* Brandi Weber-Mortimer, Director of Graduate Admissions, 724-738-2051, Fax: 724-738-2146, E-mail: graduate.admissions@sru.edu.

Smith College, Graduate and Special Programs, Department of Education and Child Study, Northampton, MA 01063. Offers education of the deaf (MED); elementary education (MAT); middle school education (MAT); secondary education (MAT), including biological sciences education, chemistry education, English education, French education, geology education, government education, history education, mathematics education, physics education, Spanish education. Part-time programs available. *Faculty:* 6 full-time (4 women), 3 part-time/adjunct (2 women). *Students:* 23 full-time (20 women), 6 part-time (all women); includes 1 minority (Asian, non-Hispanic/Latino), 2 international. Average age 30. 58 applicants, 76% accepted, 31 enrolled. In 2013, 35 master's awarded. *Entrance requirements:* Additional exam requirements/recommendations for international students: Required—TOEFL (minimum score 595 paper-based; 97 iBT). *Application deadline:* For fall admission, 4/1 for domestic students, 1/15 for international students; for spring admission, 12/1 for domestic students. Application fee: $60. *Expenses: Tuition:* Full-time $32,160; part-time $1340 per credit. *Financial support:* In 2013–14, 26 students received support, including 6 fellowships with full tuition reimbursements available; career-related internships or fieldwork, institutionally sponsored loans, and scholarships/grants also available. Support available to part-time students. Financial award application deadline: 1/15; financial award applicants required to submit CSS PROFILE or FAFSA. *Unit head:* Susan Etheredge, Chair, 413-585-3256, Fax: 413-585-3268, E-mail: sethered@smith.edu. *Application contact:* Ruth Morgan, Administrative Assistant, 413-585-3050, Fax: 413-585-3054, E-mail: gradstdy@smith.edu.

Sonoma State University, School of Education, Rohnert Park, CA 94928. Offers curriculum, teaching, and learning (MA); early childhood education (MA); education (Ed D); educational administration (MA); multiple subject (Credential); reading and literacy (MA); single subject (Credential); special education (MA, Credential). *Accreditation:* NCATE. Part-time and evening/weekend programs available. *Faculty:* 11 full-time (9 women), 1 (woman) part-time/adjunct. *Students:* 162 full-time (119 women), 165 part-time (125 women); includes 61 minority (4 Black or African American, non-Hispanic/Latino; 1 American Indian or Alaska Native, non-Hispanic/Latino; 12 Asian, non-Hispanic/Latino; 29 Hispanic/Latino; 1 Native Hawaiian or other Pacific Islander, non-Hispanic/Latino; 14 Two or more races, non-Hispanic/Latino), 1 international. Average age 33. 314 applicants, 82% accepted, 75 enrolled. In 2013, 41 master's, 287 other advanced degrees awarded. *Degree requirements:* For master's, thesis or alternative. *Entrance requirements:* For master's, minimum GPA of 2.5. Additional exam requirements/recommendations for international students: Required—TOEFL (minimum score 500 paper-based). Application fee: $55. *Expenses:* Tuition, state resident: full-time $8500. Tuition, nonresident: full-time $12,964. *Required fees:* $1762. *Financial support:* In 2013–14, 1 research assistantship (averaging $1,876 per year) was awarded; fellowships, career-related internships or fieldwork, and Federal Work-Study also available. Support available to part-time students. Financial award application deadline: 3/2; financial award applicants required to submit FAFSA. *Unit head:* Dr. Carlos Ayala, Dean, 707-664-4412, E-mail: carlos.ayala@sonoma.edu. *Application contact:* Dr. Jennifer Mahdavi, Coordinator of Graduate Studies, 707-664-3311, E-mail: jennifer.mahdavi@sonoma.edu.
Website: http://www.sonoma.edu/education/.

South Carolina State University, School of Graduate and Professional Studies, Department of Education, Orangeburg, SC 29117-0001. Offers early childhood and special education (M Ed); early childhood education (MAT); elementary education (M Ed, MAT); general science (MAT); mathematics (MAT); secondary education (M Ed), including biology education, business education, counselor education, English education, home economics education, industrial education, mathematics education, science education, social studies education; special education (M Ed), including emotionally handicapped, learning disabilities, mentally handicapped. *Accreditation:* NCATE. Part-time and evening/weekend programs available. *Faculty:* 9 full-time (3 women), 4 part-time/adjunct (3 women). *Students:* 32 full-time (26 women), 33 part-time (26 women); includes 63 minority (61 Black or African American, non-Hispanic/Latino; 2 Asian, non-Hispanic/Latino). Average age 31. 21 applicants, 100% accepted, 21 enrolled. In 2013, 15 master's awarded. *Degree requirements:* For master's, thesis optional, departmental qualifying exam. *Entrance requirements:* For master's, GRE General Test, NTE, interview, teaching certificate. *Application deadline:* For fall admission, 6/15 priority date for domestic students, 6/15 for international students; for spring admission, 11/1 for domestic and international students. Applications are processed on a rolling basis. Application fee: $25. Electronic applications accepted. *Expenses:* Tuition, state resident: full-time $8906; part-time $543 per credit hour. Tuition, nonresident: full-time $18,040; part-time $1051 per credit hour. *Financial support:* Fellowships, career-related internships or fieldwork, Federal Work-Study, and institutionally sponsored loans available. Financial award application deadline: 6/1. *Faculty research:* Critical thinking, child abuse, stress, test-taking skills, conflict resolution, mainstreaming. *Unit head:* Dr. Margaret Evelyn Fields, Interim Chair, 803-536-7098, Fax: 803-516-4568, E-mail: efields@scsu.edu. *Application contact:* Curtis Foskey, Coordinator of Graduate Studies, 803-536-8419, Fax: 803-536-8812, E-mail: cfoskey@scsu.edu.

South Dakota State University, Graduate School, College of Education and Human Sciences, Brookings, SD 57007. Offers M Ed, MFCS, MS, PhD. *Degree requirements:* For master's, thesis, oral exam. *Entrance requirements:* Additional exam requirements/recommendations for international students: Required—TOEFL.

Southeastern Louisiana University, College of Education, Hammond, LA 70402. Offers M Ed, MAT, Ed D. *Accreditation:* NCATE. Part-time programs available. *Faculty:* 26 full-time (17 women), 1 part-time/adjunct (0 women). *Students:* 44 full-time (42 women), 460 part-time (373 women); includes 134 minority (103 Black or African American, non-Hispanic/Latino; 1 American Indian or Alaska Native, non-Hispanic/Latino; 4 Asian, non-Hispanic/Latino; 20 Hispanic/Latino; 6 Two or more races, non-Hispanic/Latino). Average age 36. 146 applicants, 66% accepted, 96 enrolled. In 2013, 163 master's awarded. *Degree requirements:* For master's, comprehensive exam (for some programs), thesis optional; for doctorate, thesis/dissertation. *Entrance requirements:* For doctorate, GRE (minimum combined score for verbal and quantitative sections of 900), master's degree from an accredited university; minimum GPA of 3.0 on the last 60 undergraduate hours, 3.25 on all graduate-level course work. Additional exam requirements/recommendations for international students: Required—TOEFL (minimum score 500 paper-based; 61 iBT), IELTS (minimum score 5.5). *Application deadline:* For fall admission, 7/15 priority date for domestic students, 6/1 priority date for international students; for spring admission, 12/1 priority date for domestic students, 10/1 priority date for international students. Applications are processed on a rolling basis. Application fee: $20 ($30 for international students). Electronic applications accepted. *Expenses:* Tuition, state resident: full-time $5047. Tuition, nonresident: full-time $17,066. *Required fees:* $1213. Tuition and fees vary according to degree level. *Financial support:* Career-related internships or fieldwork, Federal Work-Study, institutionally sponsored loans, scholarships/grants, and unspecified assistantships available. Support available to part-time students. Financial award application deadline: 5/1; financial award applicants required to submit FAFSA. *Total annual research expenditures:* $48,796. *Unit head:* Dr. Shirley Jacob, Interim Dean, 985-549-2217, Fax: 985-549-2070, E-mail: sjacob@selu.edu. *Application contact:* Sandra Meyers, Graduate Admissions Analyst, 985-549-5620, Fax: 985-549-5632, E-mail: admissions@selu.edu.
Website: http://www.selu.edu/acad_research/colleges/edu_hd/index.html.

Southeastern Oklahoma State University, School of Education, Durant, OK 74701-0609. Offers math specialist (M Ed); reading specialist (M Ed); school administration (M Ed); school counseling (M Ed). *Accreditation:* NCATE. Part-time and evening/weekend programs available. *Degree requirements:* For master's, comprehensive exam, thesis optional, portfolio (M Ed). *Entrance requirements:* For master's, GRE General Test (for school counseling), minimum GPA of 3.0 in last 60 hours or 2.75 overall. Additional exam requirements/recommendations for international students: Required—TOEFL (minimum score 550 paper-based; 79 iBT). Electronic applications accepted.

Education—General

Southeastern University, College of Education, Lakeland, FL 33801-6099. Offers educational leadership (M Ed); elementary education (M Ed); teaching and learning (M Ed).

Southern Adventist University, School of Education and Psychology, Collegedale, TN 37315-0370. Offers clinical mental health counseling (MS); inclusive education (MS Ed); instructional leadership (MS Ed); literacy education (MS Ed); outdoor teacher education (MS Ed); school counseling (MS). *Accreditation:* NCATE. Part-time and evening/weekend programs available. *Degree requirements:* For master's, comprehensive exam (for some programs), thesis optional, position paper (MS), portfolio (MS Ed in outdoor teacher education). *Entrance requirements:* For master's, interview (MS); 9 semester hours of upper-division course work in psychology or related field, including 1 course in psychology research or statistics; 9 semester hours of education (MS Ed). Additional exam requirements/recommendations for international students: Required—TOEFL (minimum score 600 paper-based; 100 iBT). Electronic applications accepted.

Southern Arkansas University–Magnolia, Graduate Programs, Magnolia, AR 71753. Offers agriculture (MS); business administration (MBA); computer and information sciences (MS); education (M Ed), including counseling and development, curriculum and instruction, educational administration and supervision, elementary education, reading, secondary education, TESOL; kinesiology (M Ed); library media and information specialist (M Ed); mental health and clinical counseling (MS); public administration (MPA); school counseling (M Ed); teaching (MAT). *Accreditation:* NCATE. Part-time and evening/weekend programs available. Postbaccalaureate distance learning degree programs offered. *Faculty:* 34 full-time (15 women), 8 part-time/adjunct (5 women). *Students:* 48 full-time (22 women), 269 part-time (167 women); includes 85 minority (78 Black or African American, non-Hispanic/Latino; 2 Asian, non-Hispanic/Latino; 2 Hispanic/Latino; 1 Native Hawaiian or other Pacific Islander, non-Hispanic/Latino; 2 Two or more races, non-Hispanic/Latino), 5 international. Average age 33. 149 applicants, 73% accepted, 109 enrolled. In 2013, 149 master's awarded. *Degree requirements:* For master's, comprehensive exam (for some programs), thesis optional. *Entrance requirements:* For master's, GRE, MAT or GMAT, minimum GPA of 2.5. Additional exam requirements/recommendations for international students: Required—TOEFL, IELTS. *Application deadline:* For fall admission, 7/10 for domestic and international students; for winter admission, 12/1 for domestic and international students; for spring admission, 12/1 for domestic and international students; for summer admission, 4/1 for domestic students. Applications are processed on a rolling basis. Application fee: $25 ($50 for international students). Electronic applications accepted. *Expenses:* Tuition, state resident: part-time $254 per credit hour. Tuition, nonresident: part-time $370 per credit hour. *Required fees:* $136 per credit hour. $259 per semester. Tuition and fees vary according to course load and program. *Financial support:* Career-related internships or fieldwork, Federal Work-Study, scholarships/grants, tuition waivers (full), and unspecified assistantships available. Financial award applicants required to submit FAFSA. *Faculty research:* Alternative certification for teachers, supervision of instruction, instructional leadership, counseling. *Unit head:* Dr. Kim Bloss, Dean, School of Graduate Studies, 870-235-4150, Fax: 870-235-5227, E-mail: kkbloss@saumag.edu. *Application contact:* Shrijana Malaka, Admissions Specialist, 870-235-4150, Fax: 870-235-5227, E-mail: smalakar@saumag.edu.
Website: http://www.saumag.edu/graduate.

Southern Connecticut State University, School of Graduate Studies, School of Education, New Haven, CT 06515-1355. Offers MLS, MS, MS Ed, Ed D, Diploma, JD/MLS, MLS/MA, MLS/MS. *Accreditation:* NCATE. Part-time programs available. *Degree requirements:* For doctorate, comprehensive exam, thesis/dissertation. *Entrance requirements:* For degree, master's degree. Electronic applications accepted.

Southern Illinois University Carbondale, Graduate School, College of Education and Human Services, Carbondale, IL 62901-4701. Offers MPH, MS, MS Ed, MSW, PhD, JD/MSW. *Accreditation:* NCATE. Part-time programs available. *Faculty:* 175 full-time (74 women), 25 part-time/adjunct (6 women). *Students:* 526 full-time (342 women), 499 part-time (319 women); includes 202 minority (153 Black or African American, non-Hispanic/Latino; 5 American Indian or Alaska Native, non-Hispanic/Latino; 17 Asian, non-Hispanic/Latino; 27 Hispanic/Latino), 98 international. Average age 34. 606 applicants, 40% accepted, 201 enrolled. In 2013, 315 master's, 78 doctorates awarded. Terminal master's awarded for partial completion of doctoral program. *Degree requirements:* For doctorate, thesis/dissertation. *Entrance requirements:* For master's, minimum GPA of 2.7. Additional exam requirements/recommendations for international students: Required—TOEFL. Application fee: $50. *Financial support:* In 2013–14, 306 students received support, including 8 fellowships, 115 research assistantships, 166 teaching assistantships; career-related internships or fieldwork, Federal Work-Study, institutionally sponsored loans, traineeships, tuition waivers (full), and unspecified assistantships also available. Support available to part-time students. *Faculty research:* Safety education, community health, curriculum development, gifted, effective schools. *Unit head:* Dr. Keith Wilson, Dean, 618-453-2415, E-mail: kbwilson@siu.edu. *Application contact:* Supervisor, Admissions, 618-453-2415.
Website: http://web.coehs.siu.edu/.

Southern Illinois University Edwardsville, Graduate School, School of Education, Edwardsville, IL 62026. Offers MA, MAT, MS, MS Ed, Ed D, Ed S, Post-Master's Certificate, Postbaccalaureate Certificate, SD. *Accreditation:* NCATE. Part-time programs available. *Faculty:* 81 full-time (45 women). *Students:* 173 full-time (131 women), 432 part-time (296 women); includes 105 minority (68 Black or African American, non-Hispanic/Latino; 1 American Indian or Alaska Native, non-Hispanic/Latino; 6 Asian, non-Hispanic/Latino; 14 Hispanic/Latino; 1 Native Hawaiian or other Pacific Islander, non-Hispanic/Latino; 15 Two or more races, non-Hispanic/Latino), 10 international. 488 applicants, 48% accepted. In 2013, 287 master's, 14 doctorates, 25 other advanced degrees awarded. *Degree requirements:* For master's, comprehensive exam (for some programs), thesis (for some programs), final exam, portfolio. *Entrance requirements:* For master's, GRE. Additional exam requirements/recommendations for international students: Required—TOEFL (minimum score 550 paper-based, 79 iBT), IELTS (minimum score 6.5), Michigan Test of English Language Proficiency or PTE. *Application deadline:* For fall admission, 7/18 for domestic students, 6/1 for international students; for spring admission, 12/12 for domestic students, 10/1 for international students; for summer admission, 4/24 for domestic students, 3/1 for international students. Applications are processed on a rolling basis. Application fee: $30. Electronic applications accepted. *Expenses:* Tuition, state resident: full-time $3551. Tuition, nonresident: full-time $8378. *Financial support:* In 2013–14, 108 students received support, including 3 fellowships with full tuition reimbursements available (averaging $8,370 per year), 30 research assistantships with full tuition reimbursements available (averaging $9,585 per year), 75 teaching assistantships with full tuition reimbursements available (averaging $9,585 per year); institutionally sponsored loans, scholarships/grants, and unspecified assistantships also available. Financial award application deadline: 3/1; financial award applicants required to submit FAFSA. *Unit head:* Dr. Bette Bergeron, Dean, 618-650-3350, E-mail: bberger@siue.edu. *Application contact:* Melissa K. Mace, Assistant Director of Graduate and International Recruitment, 618-650-2756, Fax: 618-650-3618, E-mail: mmace@siue.edu.
Website: http://www.siue.edu/education.

Southern Methodist University, Annette Caldwell Simmons School of Education and Human Development, Department of Teaching and Learning, Dallas, TX 75275. Offers bilingual/ESL education (MBE); education (M Ed, PhD); gifted education (MBE); reading and writing (M Ed); special education (M Ed). Part-time and evening/weekend programs available. Terminal master's awarded for partial completion of doctoral program. *Degree requirements:* For master's, comprehensive exam, minimum GPA of 3.0; for doctorate, thesis/dissertation, qualifying exams, major area paper, evidence of teaching competency, dissemination of research (e.g., conference presentation), professional portfolio. *Entrance requirements:* For master's, minimum GPA of 3.0 or GRE, 3 letters of recommendation; for doctorate, GRE, minimum GPA of 3.3, 3 years of full-time teaching, 3 letters of recommendation, interview. Additional exam requirements/recommendations for international students: Required—TOEFL. Electronic applications accepted. *Faculty research:* Reading intervention, mathematics intervention, bilingual education, new literacies.

Southern New Hampshire University, School of Education, Manchester, NH 03106-1045. Offers business education (M Ed); child development (M Ed); curriculum and instruction (M Ed), including education leadership, reading, special education, technology integration; education (M Ed); educational leadership (M Ed, Ed D); educational studies (M Ed); elementary education (M Ed); English (MAT); English for speakers of other languages (M Ed); reading and writing specialist (M Ed); school business administration (Certificate); secondary education (M Ed); special education (M Ed); technology integration specialist (M Ed). Part-time and evening/weekend programs available. Postbaccalaureate distance learning degree programs offered (no on-campus study). *Degree requirements:* For master's, comprehensive exam (for some programs), thesis or alternative. *Entrance requirements:* For master's, PRAXIS I, minimum GPA of 2.75. Additional exam requirements/recommendations for international students: Required—TOEFL (minimum score 550 paper-based). Electronic applications accepted. *Expenses:* Contact institution.

Southern Oregon University, Graduate Studies, School of Education, Ashland, OR 97520. Offers elementary education (MA Ed, MS Ed), including classroom teacher, early childhood, handicapped learner, reading, supervision; secondary education (MA Ed, MS Ed), including classroom teacher, handicapped learner, reading, supervision; teaching (MAT). Postbaccalaureate distance learning degree programs offered (minimal on-campus study). *Faculty:* 23 full-time (16 women), 21 part-time/adjunct (20 women). *Students:* 92 full-time (68 women), 118 part-time (88 women); includes 19 minority (1 Black or African American, non-Hispanic/Latino; 1 American Indian or Alaska Native, non-Hispanic/Latino; 2 Asian, non-Hispanic/Latino; 10 Hispanic/Latino; 5 Two or more races, non-Hispanic/Latino), 5 international. Average age 36. 22 applicants, 59% accepted, 12 enrolled. In 2013, 127 master's awarded. *Degree requirements:* For master's, thesis optional. *Entrance requirements:* For master's, GRE General Test, minimum cumulative GPA of 3.0 in the last 90 quarter credits (60 semester credits) of undergraduate coursework. Additional exam requirements/recommendations for international students: Required—TOEFL (minimum score 540 paper-based; 76 iBT), IELTS (minimum score 6), ELPT (minimum score 964) or ELS (minimum score 112). *Application deadline:* For fall admission, 7/31 priority date for domestic and international students; for winter admission, 11/15 priority date for domestic and international students; for spring admission, 1/7 priority date for domestic and international students. Applications are processed on a rolling basis. Application fee: $50. Electronic applications accepted. *Expenses:* Tuition, state resident: full-time $13,635; part-time $378.72 per credit hour. Tuition, nonresident: full-time $17,042; part-time $473.40 per credit hour. *Required fees:* $408 per quarter. *Financial support:* Research assistantships with partial tuition reimbursements, career-related internships or fieldwork, institutionally sponsored loans, scholarships/grants, and unspecified assistantships available. *Unit head:* Dr. Gerry McCain, Graduate Program Coordinator, 541-552-6934, E-mail: mccaing@sou.edu. *Application contact:* Kelly Moutsatson, Director of Admissions, 541-552-6411, Fax: 541-552-8403, E-mail: admissions@sou.edu.
Website: http://www.sou.edu/education/.

Southern University and Agricultural and Mechanical College, Graduate School, College of Education, Baton Rouge, LA 70813. Offers M Ed, MA, MS, PhD. *Accreditation:* NCATE. *Degree requirements:* For master's, comprehensive exam, thesis optional. *Entrance requirements:* For master's and doctorate, GRE General Test. Additional exam requirements/recommendations for international students: Required—TOEFL (minimum score 525 paper-based).

Southern Utah University, Program in Education, Cedar City, UT 84720-2498. Offers M Ed, Certificate. *Accreditation:* Teacher Education Accreditation Council. Part-time programs available. *Students:* 30 full-time (20 women), 355 part-time (245 women); includes 14 minority (2 Black or African American, non-Hispanic/Latino; 3 American Indian or Alaska Native, non-Hispanic/Latino; 2 Asian, non-Hispanic/Latino; 7 Hispanic/Latino). Average age 37. 65 applicants, 85% accepted, 10 enrolled. In 2013, 186 master's, 17 Certificates awarded. *Entrance requirements:* For master's, GRE (if GPA is less than 3.25). Additional exam requirements/recommendations for international students: Required—TOEFL (minimum score 550 paper-based, 79 iBT) or IELTS (minimum score 6). *Application deadline:* For fall admission, 7/15 for domestic and international students; for spring admission, 11/15 for domestic and international students; for summer admission, 4/15 for domestic and international students. Applications are processed on a rolling basis. Application fee: $60 ($65 for international students). Electronic applications accepted. *Expenses:* Contact institution. *Financial support:* Tuition waivers (partial) available. *Unit head:* Dr. Thomas Cunningham, Program Director, 435-865-8242, Fax: 435-865-8485, E-mail: cunningham@suu.edu. *Application contact:* Sandy Ward, Program Specialist, 435-865-8759, Fax: 435-865-8485, E-mail: ward_s@suu.edu.
Website: http://www.suu.edu/ed/.

Southern Wesleyan University, Program in Education, Central, SC 29630-1020. Offers M Ed. Program also offered at Greenville, S. C. site. *Accreditation:* NCATE. Evening/weekend programs available. *Entrance requirements:* For master's, GRE General Test or MAT, 1 year teaching experience, minimum undergraduate GPA of 3.0, teacher certification. Additional exam requirements/recommendations for international students: Required—TOEFL (minimum score 500 paper-based).

Southwest Baptist University, Program in Education, Bolivar, MO 65613-2597. Offers education (MS); educational administration (MS, Ed S). Part-time programs available. *Degree requirements:* For master's, comprehensive exam, thesis optional, 6-hour residency; for Ed S, comprehensive exam, 5-hour residency. *Entrance requirements:* For master's, GRE or PRAXIS II, interviews, minimum GPA of 2.75; for Ed S, master's degree. Additional exam requirements/recommendations for international students: Required—TOEFL (minimum score 550 paper-based). *Faculty research:* At-risk programs, principal retention, mentoring beginning principals.

Southwestern Adventist University, Education Department, Keene, TX 76059. Offers curriculum and instruction with reading emphasis (M Ed); educational leadership (M Ed). Part-time and evening/weekend programs available. *Degree requirements:* For master's, thesis or alternative, professional paper. *Entrance requirements:* For master's, GRE General Test.

Southwestern Assemblies of God University, Thomas F. Harrison School of Graduate Studies, Program in Education, Waxahachie, TX 75165-5735. Offers Christian school administration (MS); curriculum development (MS); early education administration (M Ed); middle and secondary education (M Ed). *Degree requirements:* For master's, comprehensive written and oral exams. *Entrance requirements:* For master's, GRE General Test, minimum GPA of 2.5. Electronic applications accepted.

Southwestern College, Education Programs, Winfield, KS 67156-2499. Offers curriculum and instruction (M Ed); education (Ed D); special education (M Ed); teaching (MA). *Accreditation:* NCATE. Part-time and evening/weekend programs available. Postbaccalaureate distance learning degree programs offered (minimal on-campus study). *Faculty:* 5 full-time (4 women), 22 part-time/adjunct (17 women). *Students:* 9 full-time (7 women), 145 part-time (105 women); includes 22 minority (6 Black or African American, non-Hispanic/Latino; 1 American Indian or Alaska Native, non-Hispanic/Latino; 1 Asian, non-Hispanic/Latino; 8 Hispanic/Latino; 6 Two or more races, non-Hispanic/Latino), 4 international. Average age 39. 127 applicants, 79% accepted, 68 enrolled. In 2013, 96 master's awarded. Terminal master's awarded for partial completion of doctoral program. *Degree requirements:* For master's, practicum, portfolio; for doctorate, thesis/dissertation, professional portfolio. *Entrance requirements:* For master's, baccalaureate degree, minimum GPA of 2.5, valid teaching certificate (for special education); for doctorate, baccalaureate degree with minimum GPA of 3.25, current teaching experience, and GRE; or master's degree with minimum GPA of 3.5. Additional exam requirements/recommendations for international students: Required—TOEFL (minimum score 550 paper-based). *Application deadline:* For fall admission, 8/1 for domestic students; for spring admission, 12/1 for domestic students. Applications are processed on a rolling basis. Application fee: $0. Electronic applications accepted. *Expenses:* Contact institution. *Financial support:* In 2013–14, 4 students received support. Federal Work-Study, tuition waivers (partial), and unspecified assistantships available. Financial award application deadline: 4/1; financial award applicants required to submit FAFSA. *Unit head:* Dr. Cameron Carlson, Dean of Education, 800-846-1543 Ext. 6115, Fax: 620-229-6341, E-mail: cameron.carlson@sckans.edu. *Application contact:* Marla Sexson, Vice President for Enrollment Management, 620-229-6364, Fax: 620-229-6344, E-mail: marla.sexson@sckans.edu.
Website: http://www.sckans.edu/graduate/education-med/.

Southwestern Oklahoma State University, College of Professional and Graduate Studies, School of Behavioral Sciences and Education, Weatherford, OK 73096-3098. Offers community counseling (M Ed); early childhood education (M Ed); educational administration (M Ed); elementary education (M Ed); health sciences and microbiology (M Ed); kinesiology (M Ed); parks and recreation management (M Ed); school counseling (M Ed); school psychology (MS); school psychometry (M Ed); secondary education (M Ed); special education (M Ed). *Accreditation:* NCATE. Part-time and evening/weekend programs available. Postbaccalaureate distance learning degree programs offered (minimal on-campus study). *Degree requirements:* For master's, exam. *Entrance requirements:* For master's, GRE General Test or minimum undergraduate GPA of 3.0. Additional exam requirements/recommendations for international students: Required—TOEFL.

Southwest Minnesota State University, Department of Education, Marshall, MN 56258. Offers ESL (MS); math (MS); reading (MS); special education (MS), including developmental disabilities, early childhood education, emotional behavioral disorders, learning disabilities; teaching, learning and leadership (MS). Part-time and evening/weekend programs available. Postbaccalaureate distance learning degree programs offered (no on-campus study). *Entrance requirements:* Additional exam requirements/recommendations for international students: Required—TOEFL or IELTS; Recommended—TOEFL (minimum score 550 paper-based; 80 iBT), IELTS.

Spalding University, Graduate Studies, College of Education, Louisville, KY 40203-2188. Offers M Ed, MA, MA Ed, MAT, Ed D. *Accreditation:* NCATE. Part-time and evening/weekend programs available. *Faculty:* 15 full-time (13 women), 6 part-time/adjunct (4 women). *Students:* 139 full-time (97 women), 69 part-time (51 women); includes 84 minority (81 Black or African American, non-Hispanic/Latino; 1 Hispanic/Latino; 2 Two or more races, non-Hispanic/Latino), 5 international. Average age 37. 105 applicants, 53% accepted, 43 enrolled. In 2013, 87 master's, 16 doctorates awarded. *Degree requirements:* For master's, portfolio, final project, clinical experience; for doctorate, comprehensive exam, thesis/dissertation. *Entrance requirements:* For master's and doctorate, GRE General Test or MAT, interview, resume, recommendations. Additional exam requirements/recommendations for international students: Required—TOEFL (minimum score 535 paper-based). *Application deadline:* Applications are processed on a rolling basis. Application fee: $30. Electronic applications accepted. *Expenses: Tuition:* Full-time $21,450. *Required fees:* $810. Tuition and fees vary according to course load, degree level, program and student level. *Financial support:* Scholarships/grants, traineeships, and unspecified assistantships available. Financial award application deadline: 3/30; financial award applicants required to submit FAFSA. *Faculty research:* School leadership, assessment of student learning, classroom management. *Unit head:* Dr. Beverly Keepers, Dean, 502-873-4268, E-mail: bkeepers@spalding.edu. *Application contact:* Bonnie Caughron, Admissions Office, 502-873-4262, E-mail: bcaughron@spalding.edu.

Spring Arbor University, School of Education, Spring Arbor, MI 49283-9799. Offers education (MAE); reading (MAR); special education (MSE). *Accreditation:* Teacher Education Accreditation Council. Part-time and evening/weekend programs available. Postbaccalaureate distance learning degree programs offered (minimal on-campus study). *Faculty:* 6 full-time (5 women), 13 part-time/adjunct (8 women). *Students:* 49 full-time (44 women), 175 part-time (141 women); includes 13 minority (10 Black or African American, non-Hispanic/Latino; 1 Asian, non-Hispanic/Latino; 2 Hispanic/Latino). Average age 36. In 2013, 54 master's awarded. *Degree requirements:* For master's, thesis. *Entrance requirements:* For master's, official transcripts from all institutions attended, including evidence of an earned bachelor's degree from regionally-accredited college or university with minimum cumulative GPA of 3.0 for the last two years of the bachelor's degree; two professional letters of recommendation. Additional exam requirements/recommendations for international students: Required—TOEFL (minimum score 600 paper-based). *Application deadline:* For fall admission, 9/1 priority date for domestic students; for winter admission, 2/1 priority date for domestic students; for spring admission, 2/1 priority date for domestic students. Applications are processed on a rolling basis. Application fee: $40. Electronic applications accepted. *Financial support:* Applicants required to submit FAFSA. *Unit head:* Dr. Linda Sherrill, Dean, 517-750-1200 Ext. 1562, Fax: 517-750-6629, E-mail: lsherril@arbor.edu. *Application contact:* James R. Weidman, Coordinator of Graduate Recruitment, 517-750-6523, Fax: 517-750-6629, E-mail: jimw@arbor.edu.
Website: http://www.arbor.edu/academics/school-of-education/.

Springfield College, Graduate Programs, Program in Education, Springfield, MA 01109-3797. Offers counseling and secondary education (M Ed, MS); early childhood education (M Ed, MS); education (M Ed, MS); educational administration (M Ed, MS); educational studies (M Ed, MS); elementary education (M Ed, MS); secondary education (M Ed, MS); special education (M Ed, MS). Part-time and evening/weekend programs available. *Faculty:* 6 full-time. *Students:* 47 full-time. 45 applicants, 87% accepted, 35 enrolled. In 2013, 15 master's awarded. *Entrance requirements:*

Additional exam requirements/recommendations for international students: Required—TOEFL (minimum score 550 paper-based); Recommended—IELTS (minimum score 6). *Application deadline:* For fall admission, 1/15 for domestic and international students; for winter admission, 11/1 for domestic and international students; for spring admission, 11/1 for domestic and international students. Applications are processed on a rolling basis. Application fee: $50. Electronic applications accepted. *Expenses: Tuition:* Full-time $13,620; part-time $908 per credit. *Financial support:* Fellowships with partial tuition reimbursements, teaching assistantships with partial tuition reimbursements, career-related internships or fieldwork, Federal Work-Study, institutionally sponsored loans, and unspecified assistantships available. Financial award application deadline: 3/1; financial award applicants required to submit FAFSA. *Unit head:* Jennifer Johnston, Program Coordinator, 413-748-3348, E-mail: jjohnston@springfieldcollege.edu. *Application contact:* Evelyn Cohen, Associate Director of Graduate Admissions, 413-748-3479, Fax: 413-748-3694, E-mail: ecohen@springfieldcollege.edu.

Spring Hill College, Graduate Programs, Program in Education, Mobile, AL 36608-1791. Offers early childhood education (MAT, MS Ed); educational theory (MS Ed); elementary education (MAT, MS Ed); secondary education (MAT, MS Ed). Part-time programs available. *Faculty:* 3 full-time (all women). *Students:* 2 full-time (both women), 17 part-time (14 women); includes 2 minority (both Black or African American, non-Hispanic/Latino). Average age 32. In 2013, 7 master's awarded. *Degree requirements:* For master's, comprehensive exam, completion of program within 6 calendar years of entrance into graduate studies at Spring Hill; documentation of course field assignments (MS) or completion of internship (MAT). *Entrance requirements:* For master's, GRE, MAT, or PRAXIS (varies by program), bachelor's degree with minimum undergraduate GPA of 3.0; class B certificate (MS) or minimum number of hours in specific fields (MAT). Additional exam requirements/recommendations for international students: Required—TOEFL (minimum score 550 paper-based; 80 iBT), IELTS (minimum score 6.5), CPE or CAE (minimum score C), Michigan English Language Assessment Battery (minimum score 90). *Application deadline:* For fall admission, 8/1 priority date for domestic and international students; for spring admission, 12/1 priority date for domestic and international students. Applications are processed on a rolling basis. Application fee: $25 ($35 for international students). Electronic applications accepted. *Expenses:* Contact institution. *Financial support:* Applicants required to submit FAFSA. *Unit head:* Dr. Lori P. Aultman, Chair of Teacher Education, 251-380-3473, Fax: 251-460-2184, E-mail: laultman@shc.edu. *Application contact:* Donna B. Tarasavage, Associate Director, Academic Affairs, 251-380-3067, Fax: 251-460-2182, E-mail: dtarasavage@shc.edu.
Website: http://www.shc.edu/page/teacher-education.

Stanford University, School of Education, Stanford, CA 94305-9991. Offers MA, MAE, PhD, MA/JD, MA/MBA, MPP/MA. *Accreditation:* NCATE. *Degree requirements:* For doctorate, thesis/dissertation. *Entrance requirements:* For master's and doctorate, GRE General Test. Electronic applications accepted. *Expenses: Tuition:* Full-time $42,690; part-time $949 per credit. *Required fees:* $185.

State University of New York at Fredonia, Graduate Studies, College of Education, Fredonia, NY 14063-1136. Offers educational administration (CAS); elementary education (MS Ed); literacy (MS Ed); secondary education (MS Ed); teaching English to speakers of other languages (MS Ed). *Accreditation:* NCATE. Part-time and evening/weekend programs available. *Degree requirements:* For master's, thesis optional; for CAS, thesis or alternative. *Expenses:* Tuition, state resident: full-time $7398; part-time $411 per credit hour. Tuition, nonresident: full-time $13,770; part-time $765 per credit hour. *Required fees:* $1143.90; $63.55 per credit hour. Tuition and fees vary according to course load.

State University of New York at New Paltz, Graduate School, School of Education, New Paltz, NY 12561. Offers MAT, MPS, MS Ed, MST, AC, CAS. *Accreditation:* NCATE. Part-time and evening/weekend programs available. *Faculty:* 37 full-time (28 women), 53 part-time/adjunct (42 women). *Students:* 183 full-time (137 women), 310 part-time (236 women); includes 76 minority (10 Black or African American, non-Hispanic/Latino; 8 Asian, non-Hispanic/Latino; 52 Hispanic/Latino; 6 Two or more races, non-Hispanic/Latino), 1 international. Average age 30. 292 applicants, 86% accepted, 166 enrolled. In 2013, 248 master's, 46 other advanced degrees awarded. *Degree requirements:* For master's, comprehensive exam (for some programs), portfolio; for other advanced degree, internship. *Entrance requirements:* For master's, GRE, MAT, minimum GPA of 3.0, New York State Teaching Certificate; for other advanced degree, minimum GPA of 3.0. Additional exam requirements/recommendations for international students: Required—TOEFL (minimum score 550 paper-based; 80 iBT), IELTS (minimum score 6.5). *Application deadline:* For fall admission, 3/1 priority date for domestic and international students; for spring admission, 10/1 priority date for domestic and international students. Applications are processed on a rolling basis. Application fee: $50. Electronic applications accepted. *Expenses: Tuition,* state resident: full-time $9870; part-time $411 per credit. Tuition, nonresident: full-time $18,350; part-time $765 per credit. *Required fees:* $1213. Tuition and fees vary according to program. *Financial support:* Application deadline: 8/1. *Faculty research:* Kindergarten readiness, translation learning experiences, assessment in mathematics education, long and short term outcomes of delayed school entry, parental involvement in children's education. *Unit head:* Dr. Michael Rosenberg, Dean, 845-257-2800, E-mail: schoolofed@newpaltz.edu. *Application contact:* Caroline Murphy, Graduate Admissions Advisor, 845-257-3285, Fax: 845-257-3284, E-mail: gradschool@newpaltz.edu.
Website: http://www.newpaltz.edu/schoolofed/.

State University of New York at Oswego, Graduate Studies, School of Education, Oswego, NY 13126. Offers MAT, MS, MS Ed, MST, CAS, MS/CAS. *Accreditation:* NCATE. Part-time programs available. *Degree requirements:* For master's, comprehensive exam (for some programs), thesis optional. *Entrance requirements:* For degree, GRE General Test, interview, MA or MS, minimum GPA of 3.0. Additional exam requirements/recommendations for international students: Required—TOEFL (minimum score 560 paper-based).

State University of New York College at Cortland, Graduate Studies, School of Education, Cortland, NY 13045. Offers childhood/early child education (MS Ed, MST); educational leadership (CAS); literacy education (MS Ed); teaching students with disabilities (MS Ed). *Accreditation:* NCATE. Part-time and evening/weekend programs available. *Entrance requirements:* Additional exam requirements/recommendations for international students: Required—TOEFL. *Expenses:* Tuition, state resident: full-time $9870; part-time $411 per credit hour. Tuition, nonresident: full-time $18,350; part-time $765 per credit hour. *Required fees:* $1458; $65 per credit hour.

State University of New York College at Geneseo, Graduate Studies, School of Education, Geneseo, NY 14454-1401. Offers adolescence education (MS Ed); childhood multicultural education (1-6) (MS Ed); early childhood education (MS Ed); literacy (MS Ed). *Accreditation:* NCATE. Part-time and evening/weekend programs available. *Faculty:* 20 full-time (12 women), 1 (woman) part-time/adjunct. *Students:* 52 full-time (43 women), 68 part-time (56 women); includes 4 minority (1 Asian, non-Hispanic/Latino; 3 Hispanic/Latino), 1 international. Average age 25. 55 applicants, 100% accepted, 35 enrolled. In 2013, 88 master's awarded. *Degree requirements:* For master's, thesis optional. *Application deadline:* For fall admission, 3/1 priority date for domestic students; for spring admission, 10/1 for domestic students. Application fee:

$50. *Expenses:* Tuition, state resident: full-time $8790; part-time $411 per credit hour. Tuition, nonresident: full-time $18,350; part-time $765 per credit hour. *Required fees:* $795; $32.90 per credit hour. *Financial support:* In 2013–14, 6 students received support. Scholarships/grants, health care benefits, tuition waivers (full), and unspecified assistantships available. Support available to part-time students. Financial award application deadline: 4/1; financial award applicants required to submit FAFSA. *Unit head:* Dr. Anjoo Sikka, Dean of School of Education, 585-245-5151, Fax: 585-245-5220, E-mail: sikka@geneseo.edu. *Application contact:* Tracy Peterson, Director of Student Success, 585-245-5443, Fax: 585-245-5220, E-mail: peterson@geneseo.edu.

State University of New York College at Oneonta, Graduate Education, Division of Education, Oneonta, NY 13820-4015. Offers educational psychology and counseling (MS Ed, CAS), including school counselor K-12; educational technology specialist (MS Ed); elementary education and reading (MS Ed), including childhood education, literacy education; secondary education (MS Ed), including adolescence education; special education (MS Ed), including adolescence, childhood. *Accreditation:* NCATE. Part-time and evening/weekend programs available. *Entrance requirements:* For master's, GRE General Test.

State University of New York Empire State College, School for Graduate Studies, Programs in Education, Saratoga Springs, NY 12866-4391. Offers adult learning (MA); learning and emerging technologies (MA); teaching (MAT); teaching and learning (M Ed). Postbaccalaureate distance learning degree programs offered.

Stephen F. Austin State University, Graduate School, College of Education, Nacogdoches, TX 75962. Offers M Ed, MA, MS, Ed D. *Accreditation:* NCATE. Part-time and evening/weekend programs available. *Degree requirements:* For master's, comprehensive exam; for doctorate, thesis/dissertation. *Entrance requirements:* For master's, GRE General Test; for doctorate, GRE General Test, interview, writing sample. Additional exam requirements/recommendations for international students: Required—TOEFL.

Stetson University, College of Arts and Sciences, Division of Education, DeLand, FL 32723. Offers M Ed, MS, Ed S. *Accreditation:* NCATE (one or more programs are accredited). Part-time and evening/weekend programs available. *Faculty:* 12 full-time (10 women), 4 part-time/adjunct (3 women). *Students:* 126 full-time (105 women), 24 part-time (18 women); includes 36 minority (11 Black or African American, non-Hispanic/Latino; 1 American Indian or Alaska Native, non-Hispanic/Latino; 22 Hispanic/Latino; 2 Two or more races, non-Hispanic/Latino), 2 international. Average age 31. 79 applicants, 81% accepted, 58 enrolled. In 2013, 83 master's awarded. *Entrance requirements:* For master's, GRE or MAT; for Ed S, GRE General Test or MAT. *Application deadline:* For fall admission, 8/1 priority date for domestic students; for spring admission, 1/1 priority date for domestic students; for summer admission, 5/1 priority date for domestic students. Applications are processed on a rolling basis. Application fee: $50. Electronic applications accepted. *Financial support:* Career-related internships or fieldwork, institutionally sponsored loans, scholarships/grants, and tuition waivers (partial) available. Support available to part-time students. *Faculty research:* Values, cultural diversity, cooperative learning, reading. *Unit head:* Dr. Karen Ryan, Dean, 386-822-7515. *Application contact:* Jamie Vanderlip, Assistant Director of Graduate Admissions, 386-822-7100, Fax: 386-822-7112, E-mail: jlszarol@stetson.edu.

Strayer University, Graduate Studies, Washington, DC 20005-2603. Offers accounting (MS); acquisition (MBA); business administration (MBA); communications technology (MS); educational management (M Ed); finance (MBA); health services administration (MHSA); hospitality and tourism management (MBA); human resource management (MBA); information systems (MS), including computer security management, decision support system management, enterprise resource management, network management, software engineering management, systems development management; management (MBA); management information systems (MS); marketing (MBA); professional accounting (MS), including accounting information systems, controllership, taxation; public administration (MPA); supply chain management (MBA); technology in education (M Ed). Programs also offered at campus locations in Birmingham, AL; Chamblee, GA; Cobb County, GA; Morrow, GA; White Marsh, MD; Charleston, SC; Columbia, SC; Greensboro, NC; Greenville, SC; Lexington, KY; Louisville, KY; Nashville, TN; North Raleigh, NC; Washington, DC. Part-time and evening/weekend programs available. Postbaccalaureate distance learning degree programs offered (minimal on-campus study). *Degree requirements:* For master's, thesis. *Entrance requirements:* For master's, GMAT, GRE General Test, bachelor's degree from an accredited college or university, minimum undergraduate GPA of 2.75. Electronic applications accepted.

Sul Ross State University, Rio Grande College of Sul Ross State University, Alpine, TX 79832. Offers business administration (MBA); teacher education (M Ed), including bilingual education, counseling, educational diagnostics, elementary education, general education, reading, school administration, secondary education. Part-time and evening/weekend programs available. Postbaccalaureate distance learning degree programs offered (no on-campus study). *Degree requirements:* For master's, comprehensive exam, thesis optional, minimum GPA of 3.0. *Entrance requirements:* For master's, GMAT or GRE General Test, minimum GPA of 2.5 in last 60 hours of undergraduate work. Additional exam requirements/recommendations for international students: Required—TOEFL.

Sul Ross State University, School of Professional Studies, Department of Teacher Education, Alpine, TX 79832. Offers counseling (M Ed); educational diagnostics (M Ed); reading specialist (M Ed, Certificate), including master reading teacher (Certificate), Texas reading specialist (M Ed); school administration (M Ed). Part-time and evening/weekend programs available. *Degree requirements:* For master's, thesis optional. *Entrance requirements:* For master's, GMAT or GRE General Test, minimum GPA of 2.5 in last 60 hours of undergraduate work. *Faculty research:* Critical thinking skills, adolescent eating disorders, reading-based study skills, cross-cultural adaptations, educational leadership.

Sweet Briar College, Department of Education, Sweet Briar, VA 24595. Offers M Ed, MAT. Part-time programs available. *Degree requirements:* For master's, comprehensive exam (for some programs), thesis. *Entrance requirements:* For master's, PRAXIS I and II; Virginia Communication and Literacy Assessment, Virginia Reading Assessment (MAT); GRE (M Ed), current teaching license (M Ed). Additional exam requirements/recommendations for international students: Required—TOEFL (minimum score 550 paper-based; 79 iBT), IELTS (minimum score 6.5). Electronic applications accepted. *Faculty research:* Differentiation of K-12 student achievement, mentoring and teacher retention, teaching science by inquiry.

Syracuse University, School of Education, Syracuse, NY 13244. Offers M Mus, MS, Ed D, PhD, CAS, Ed D/PhD. *Accreditation:* NCATE. Part-time programs available. *Students:* 346 full-time (252 women), 233 part-time (166 women); includes 113 minority (55 Black or African American, non-Hispanic/Latino; 6 American Indian or Alaska Native, non-Hispanic/Latino; 12 Asian, non-Hispanic/Latino; 25 Hispanic/Latino; 3 Native Hawaiian or other Pacific Islander, non-Hispanic/Latino; 12 Two or more races, non-Hispanic/Latino), 61 international. Average age 30. 533 applicants, 64% accepted, 135 enrolled. In 2013, 178 master's, 20 doctorates, 22 other advanced degrees awarded. *Degree requirements:* For master's, thesis or alternative; for doctorate, comprehensive exam, thesis/dissertation; for CAS, thesis. *Entrance requirements:* For master's, GRE

(for some programs); for doctorate and CAS, GRE. Additional exam requirements/recommendations for international students: Required—TOEFL (minimum score 100 iBT). *Application deadline:* For fall admission, 1/15 priority date for domestic and international students; for spring admission, 10/15 priority date for domestic and international students. Applications are processed on a rolling basis. Application fee: $75. Electronic applications accepted. *Financial support:* Fellowships with full tuition reimbursements, research assistantships with full and partial tuition reimbursements, teaching assistantships with full and partial tuition reimbursements, career-related internships or fieldwork, institutionally sponsored loans, scholarships/grants, health care benefits, tuition waivers (partial), and unspecified assistantships available. Financial award application deadline: 1/1; financial award applicants required to submit FAFSA. *Faculty research:* Teaching and curriculum, reading and language arts, literacy, inclusive education, communication sciences and disorders. *Application contact:* Laurie Deyo, Graduate Recruiter, School of Education, 315-443-2505, E-mail: e-gradrcrt@syr.edu.
Website: http://soeweb.syr.edu/.

Tarleton State University, College of Graduate Studies, College of Education, Stephenville, TX 76402. Offers M Ed, Ed D, Certificate. Part-time and evening/weekend programs available. Postbaccalaureate distance learning degree programs offered (minimal on-campus study). *Faculty:* 33 full-time (21 women), 21 part-time/adjunct (12 women). *Students:* 98 full-time (76 women), 475 part-time (360 women); includes 154 minority (62 Black or African American, non-Hispanic/Latino; 7 American Indian or Alaska Native, non-Hispanic/Latino; 5 Asian, non-Hispanic/Latino; 63 Hispanic/Latino; 17 Two or more races, non-Hispanic/Latino), 1 international. Average age 36. 171 applicants, 86% accepted, 119 enrolled. In 2013, 190 master's, 11 doctorates awarded. *Degree requirements:* For master's, comprehensive exam, thesis (for some programs); for doctorate, thesis/dissertation. *Entrance requirements:* For master's, GRE General Test, minimum GPA of 3.0; for doctorate, GRE, 4 letters of reference, leadership portfolio. Additional exam requirements/recommendations for international students: Required—TOEFL (minimum score 550 paper-based; 80 iBT). *Application deadline:* For fall admission, 8/15 priority date for domestic students; for spring admission, 1/7 for domestic students. Applications are processed on a rolling basis. Application fee: $30 ($130 for international students). Electronic applications accepted. *Expenses:* Tuition, state resident: full-time $3312; part-time $184 per credit hour. Tuition, nonresident: full-time $9144; part-time $508 per credit hour. *Required fees:* $1916. Tuition and fees vary according to course load and campus/location. *Financial support:* Research assistantships, teaching assistantships with partial tuition reimbursements, career-related internships or fieldwork, Federal Work-Study, institutionally sponsored loans, and tuition waivers (partial) available. Support available to part-time students. Financial award application deadline: 5/1; financial award applicants required to submit FAFSA. *Unit head:* Dr. Jill Burk, Dean, 254-968-9089, Fax: 254-968-9525, E-mail: burk@tarleton.edu. *Application contact:* Information Contact, 254-968-9104, Fax: 254-968-9670, E-mail: gradoffice@tarleton.edu.
Website: http://www.tarleton.edu/COEWEB/coe/.

Teachers College, Columbia University, Graduate Faculty of Education, New York, NY 10027-6696. Offers Ed M, MA, MS, Ed D, Ed DCT, PhD, Certificate. *Accreditation:* NCATE. Part-time and evening/weekend programs available. *Faculty:* 216 full-time, 151 part-time/adjunct. *Students:* 1,693 full-time (1,287 women), 3,276 part-time (2,497 women); includes 1,633 minority (464 Black or African American, non-Hispanic/Latino; 558 Asian, non-Hispanic/Latino; 443 Hispanic/Latino; 11 Native Hawaiian or other Pacific Islander, non-Hispanic/Latino; 157 Two or more races, non-Hispanic/Latino), 842 international. Average age 30. 5,824 applicants, 55% accepted, 1394 enrolled. In 2013, 1,968 master's, 217 doctorates awarded. *Degree requirements:* For doctorate, comprehensive exam, thesis/dissertation. Application fee: $65. Electronic applications accepted. *Financial support:* Fellowships, research assistantships, teaching assistantships, career-related internships or fieldwork, Federal Work-Study, institutionally sponsored loans, traineeships, tuition waivers (full and partial), and unspecified assistantships available. Support available to part-time students. Financial award application deadline: 2/1. *Faculty research:* Education and the economy, postsecondary governance and finance, career success, dropout prevention evaluation, education across the lifespan. *Unit head:* Susan Furhman, President, 212-678-3050. *Application contact:* Thomas P. Rock, Director of Admissions, 212-678-3083, Fax: 212-678-4171, E-mail: rock@tc.edu.
Website: http://www.tc.columbia.edu/.

Temple University, College of Education, Philadelphia, PA 19122-6096. Offers Ed M, MS Ed, Ed D, PhD, Ed S. *Accreditation:* Teacher Education Accreditation Council. Part-time and evening/weekend programs available. *Faculty:* 62 full-time (39 women), 134 part-time/adjunct (0 women). *Students:* 256 full-time (196 women), 379 part-time (241 women); includes 145 minority (98 Black or African American, non-Hispanic/Latino; 2 American Indian or Alaska Native, non-Hispanic/Latino; 10 Asian, non-Hispanic/Latino; 25 Hispanic/Latino; 10 Two or more races, non-Hispanic/Latino), 39 international. 643 applicants, 49% accepted, 191 enrolled. In 2013, 285 master's, 46 doctorates awarded. *Degree requirements:* For doctorate, thesis/dissertation. *Entrance requirements:* Additional exam requirements/recommendations for international students: Required—TOEFL. *Application deadline:* For fall admission, 4/1 for domestic students, 1/1 for international students; for spring admission, 10/1 for domestic students, 7/3 for international students. Applications are processed on a rolling basis. Application fee: $60. Electronic applications accepted. *Financial support:* In 2013–14, 4 research assistantships with full tuition reimbursements (averaging $20,333 per year), 5 teaching assistantships with full tuition reimbursements (averaging $17,046 per year) were awarded; career-related internships or fieldwork, Federal Work-Study, scholarships/grants, health care benefits, and unspecified assistantships also available. Financial award application deadline: 1/15; financial award applicants required to submit FAFSA. *Faculty research:* Curriculum development, instruction, technology, learning, educational achievement. *Unit head:* Dr. Gregory Anderson, Dean, 215-204-8017, Fax: 215-204-5622, E-mail: coedean@temple.edu. *Application contact:* Felicia Neuber, Enrollment Management, 215-204-2011, E-mail: educate@temple.edu.
Website: http://www.temple.edu/education/.

Tennessee State University, The School of Graduate Studies and Research, College of Education, Nashville, TN 37209-1561. Offers M Ed, MA Ed, MS, Ed D, PhD, Ed S. *Accreditation:* NCATE. Part-time and evening/weekend programs available. *Students:* 146 full-time (104 women), 400 part-time (282 women); includes 354 minority (345 Black or African American, non-Hispanic/Latino; 2 American Indian or Alaska Native, non-Hispanic/Latino; 3 Asian, non-Hispanic/Latino; 4 Hispanic/Latino), 12 international. Average age 35. *Degree requirements:* For doctorate, thesis/dissertation. *Entrance requirements:* For doctorate, minimum GPA of 3.25. *Application deadline:* Applications are processed on a rolling basis. Application fee: $25. *Financial support:* Fellowships, research assistantships, teaching assistantships, career-related internships or fieldwork, and institutionally sponsored loans available. Support available to part-time students. Financial award application deadline: 5/1; financial award applicants required to submit FAFSA. *Faculty research:* Class size, biobehavioral research, equity, dropout rate, K–12 teachers: first 5 years of employment. *Unit head:* Dr. Kimberly King-Jupiter, Dean, 615-963-5446, E-mail: kkingjup@tnstate.edu. *Application contact:* Deborah Chisom, Director

of Graduate Admissions, 615-963-5962, Fax: 615-963-5963, E-mail: dchiscom@tnstate.edu.
Website: http://www.tnstate.edu/coe/.

Tennessee Technological University, College of Graduate Studies, College of Education, Cookeville, TN 38505. Offers M Ed, MA, PhD, Ed S. *Accreditation:* NCATE. Part-time and evening/weekend programs available. *Faculty:* 58 full-time (16 women). *Students:* 174 full-time (121 women), 324 part-time (236 women); includes 53 minority (38 Black or African American, non-Hispanic/Latino; 1 American Indian or Alaska Native, non-Hispanic/Latino; 3 Asian, non-Hispanic/Latino; 5 Hispanic/Latino; 6 Two or more races, non-Hispanic/Latino), 9 international. Average age 27. 266 applicants, 68% accepted, 122 enrolled. In 2013, 145 master's, 1 doctorate, 64 other advanced degrees awarded. *Degree requirements:* For master's and Ed S, comprehensive exam, thesis or alternative; for doctorate, comprehensive exam, thesis/dissertation. *Entrance requirements:* For master's, GRE or MAT; for doctorate, GRE; for Ed S, MAT or GRE. Additional exam requirements/recommendations for international students: Required—TOEFL (minimum score 527 paper-based; 71 iBT), IELTS (minimum score 5.5), PTE (minimum score 48), or TOEIC (Test of English as an International Communication). *Application deadline:* For fall admission, 8/1 for domestic students, 5/1 for international students; for spring admission, 12/1 for domestic students, 10/1 for international students. Applications are processed on a rolling basis. Application fee: $35 ($40 for international students). Electronic applications accepted. *Expenses:* Tuition, state resident: full-time $9347; part-time $465 per credit hour. Tuition, nonresident: full-time $23,635; part-time $1152 per credit hour. *Financial support:* In 2013–14, 42 fellowships (averaging $8,000 per year), 33 research assistantships (averaging $4,000 per year), 26 teaching assistantships (averaging $4,000 per year) were awarded; career-related internships or fieldwork also available. Support available to part-time students. Financial award application deadline: 4/1. *Faculty research:* Teacher evaluation. *Unit head:* Dr. Matthew R. Smith, Dean, 931-372-3124, Fax: 931-372-6319, E-mail: mrsmith@tntech.edu. *Application contact:* Shelia K. Kendrick, Coordinator of Graduate Studies, 931-372-3808, Fax: 931-372-3497, E-mail: skendrick@tntech.edu.

Tennessee Temple University, Graduate Studies in Education, Chattanooga, TN 37404. Offers M Ed. Part-time programs available. *Degree requirements:* For master's, comprehensive exam, thesis or alternative. *Entrance requirements:* For master's, GRE, minimum GPA of 3.0.

Tennessee Wesleyan College, Department of Education, Athens, TN 37303. Offers curriculum leadership (MS). Evening/weekend programs available. *Degree requirements:* For master's, internship.

Texas A&M International University, Office of Graduate Studies and Research, College of Education, Laredo, TX 78041-1900. Offers MS, MS Ed. Part-time and evening/weekend programs available. *Faculty:* 7 full-time (4 women), 4 part-time/adjunct (2 women). *Students:* 26 full-time (22 women), 243 part-time (184 women); includes 258 minority (2 Black or African American, non-Hispanic/Latino; 1 Asian, non-Hispanic/Latino; 255 Hispanic/Latino), 2 international. Average age 33. 128 applicants, 78% accepted, 76 enrolled. In 2013, 100 master's awarded. *Degree requirements:* For master's, thesis (for some programs). *Entrance requirements:* For master's, GRE General Test. Additional exam requirements/recommendations for international students: Required—TOEFL (minimum score 550 paper-based; 79 iBT). *Application deadline:* For fall admission, 4/30 priority date for domestic students, 4/30 for international students; for spring admission, 11/30 for domestic students, 10/1 for international students. Applications are processed on a rolling basis. Application fee: $35 ($50 for international students). *Expenses:* Tuition, state resident: full-time $5184. *International tuition:* $11,556 full-time. *Financial support:* In 2013–14, 7 students received support, including 4 fellowships, 3 research assistantships; Federal Work-Study and institutionally sponsored loans also available. Support available to part-time students. Financial award application deadline: 4/1; financial award applicants required to submit FAFSA. *Unit head:* Dr. Catheryn Weitman, Dean, 956-326-2420, E-mail: catheryn.weitman@tamiu.edu. *Application contact:* Suzanne Hansen-Alford, Director of Graduate Recruiting, 956-326-3023, Fax: 956-326-3021, E-mail: graduateschool@tamiu.edu.
Website: http://www.tamiu.edu/coedu/.

Texas A&M University, College of Education and Human Development, College Station, TX 77843. Offers M Ed, MS, Ed D, PhD. Part-time and evening/weekend programs available. Postbaccalaureate distance learning degree programs offered (no on-campus study). *Faculty:* 151. *Students:* 585 full-time (403 women), 730 part-time (530 women); includes 418 minority (150 Black or African American, non-Hispanic/Latino; 36 Asian, non-Hispanic/Latino; 214 Hispanic/Latino; 18 Two or more races, non-Hispanic/Latino), 187 international. Average age 33. 676 applicants, 62% accepted, 289 enrolled. In 2013, 315 master's, 106 doctorates awarded. *Degree requirements:* For doctorate, thesis/dissertation. *Entrance requirements:* For master's and doctorate, GRE General Test. Additional exam requirements/recommendations for international students: Required—TOEFL. Application fee: $50 ($75 for international students). Electronic applications accepted. *Expenses:* Tuition, state resident: full-time $4078; part-time $226.55 per credit hour. Tuition, nonresident: full-time $10,450; part-time $580.55 per credit hour. *Required fees:* $2328; $278.50 per credit hour. $642.45 per semester. *Financial support:* In 2013–14, fellowships with partial tuition reimbursements (averaging $12,000 per year), research assistantships with partial tuition reimbursements (averaging $10,000 per year), teaching assistantships with partial tuition reimbursements (averaging $10,000 per year) were awarded; career-related internships or fieldwork, Federal Work-Study, institutionally sponsored loans, scholarships/grants, tuition waivers (partial), and unspecified assistantships also available. Financial award applicants required to submit FAFSA. *Unit head:* Dr. Doug Palmer, Dean, 979-862-6649, E-mail: dpalmer@tamu.edu. *Application contact:* Dr. Becky Carr, Assistant Dean for Administrative Services, 979-862-1342, Fax: 979-845-6129, E-mail: bcarr@tamu.edu.
Website: http://education.tamu.edu/.

Texas A&M University–Commerce, Graduate School, College of Education and Human Services, Commerce, TX 75429-3011. Offers M Ed, MA, MS, MSW, Ed D, PhD. Part-time programs available. Terminal master's awarded for partial completion of doctoral program. *Degree requirements:* For master's, comprehensive exam; for doctorate, thesis/dissertation, departmental qualifying exam. *Entrance requirements:* For master's and doctorate, GRE General Test. Electronic applications accepted. *Expenses:* Tuition, state resident: full-time $3630; part-time $2420 per year. Tuition, nonresident: full-time $9948; part-time $6632.16 per year. *Required fees:* $1006 per year. Tuition and fees vary according to course load. *Faculty research:* Reading, early childhood, deviance, migration, physical fitness.

Texas A&M University–Corpus Christi, Graduate Studies and Research, College of Education, Corpus Christi, TX 78412-5503. Offers counseling (MS, PhD), including counseling (MS), counselor education (PhD); curriculum and instruction (MS, Ed D); early childhood education (MS); educational administration (MS); educational leadership (Ed D); educational technology (MS); elementary education (MS); kinesiology (MS); reading (MS); secondary education (MS); special education (MS). Part-time and evening/weekend programs available. *Degree requirements:* For master's, comprehensive exam, thesis (for some programs); for doctorate, comprehensive exam, thesis/dissertation. *Entrance requirements:* For master's, GRE General Test. Additional exam requirements/recommendations for international students: Required—TOEFL. Electronic applications accepted.

Texas A&M University–Kingsville, College of Graduate Studies, College of Education, Kingsville, TX 78363. Offers M Ed, MA, MS, Ed D, PhD. Part-time and evening/weekend programs available. *Faculty:* 23 full-time (13 women), 8 part-time/adjunct (2 women). *Students:* 129 full-time (91 women), 324 part-time (241 women); includes 346 minority (16 Black or African American, non-Hispanic/Latino; 1 American Indian or Alaska Native, non-Hispanic/Latino; 1 Asian, non-Hispanic/Latino; 325 Hispanic/Latino; 1 Native Hawaiian or other Pacific Islander, non-Hispanic/Latino; 2 Two or more races, non-Hispanic/Latino), 25 international. Average age 35. 153 applicants, 97% accepted, 103 enrolled. In 2013, 97 master's, 18 doctorates awarded. *Degree requirements:* For master's, comprehensive exam; for doctorate, one foreign language, comprehensive exam, thesis/dissertation. *Entrance requirements:* For master's, GRE General Test, minimum GPA of 3.0; for doctorate, GRE General Test, MAT, minimum GPA of 3.25. *Application deadline:* For fall admission, 6/1 for domestic students; for spring admission, 11/15 for domestic students. Applications are processed on a rolling basis. Application fee: $35 ($50 for international students). *Financial support:* Fellowships, teaching assistantships, Federal Work-Study, institutionally sponsored loans, scholarships/grants, and tuition waivers (partial) available. Support available to part-time students. Financial award application deadline: 5/15. *Faculty research:* Rural schools, facilities planning, linguistics. *Unit head:* Dr. Fred Litton, Dean, 361-593-2801. *Application contact:* Dr. Alberto M. Olivares, Dean, College of Graduate Studies, 361-593-2808, Fax: 361-593-3412, E-mail: a-olivares@tamuk.edu.

Texas A&M University–Texarkana, Graduate Studies and Research, College of Education and Liberal Arts, Texarkana, TX 75505-5518. Offers adult education (MS); curriculum and instruction (M Ed); education (MS); educational administration (M Ed); English (MA); instructional technology (MS); interdisciplinary studies (MA, MS); special education (MS). Part-time and evening/weekend programs available. *Degree requirements:* For master's, comprehensive exam (for some programs), thesis optional. *Entrance requirements:* For master's, minimum GPA of 2.5 on last 60 hours of bachelor's degree. Additional exam requirements/recommendations for international students: Required—TOEFL. Electronic applications accepted.

Texas Christian University, College of Education, Fort Worth, TX 76129. Offers M Ed, Ed D, PhD, Certificate, MBA/Ed D. Part-time and evening/weekend programs available. *Faculty:* 26 full-time (20 women), 2 part-time/adjunct (1 woman). *Students:* 60 full-time (54 women), 120 part-time (85 women); includes 44 minority (16 Black or African American, non-Hispanic/Latino; 7 Asian, non-Hispanic/Latino; 18 Hispanic/Latino; 3 Two or more races, non-Hispanic/Latino), 7 international. Average age 31. 112 applicants, 75% accepted, 60 enrolled. In 2013, 65 master's, 11 doctorates awarded. *Degree requirements:* For master's, paper/thesis; for doctorate, comprehensive exam, thesis/dissertation. *Entrance requirements:* For master's, GRE (for counseling and educational leadership only); for doctorate, GRE or MAT. Additional exam requirements/recommendations for international students: Required—TOEFL (minimum score 550 paper-based; 80 iBT). *Application deadline:* For fall admission, 11/16 for domestic and international students; for spring admission, 3/1 for domestic and international students. Application fee: $60. Electronic applications accepted. *Expenses: Tuition:* Part-time $1270 per credit hour. Tuition and fees vary according to course load and program. *Financial support:* In 2013–14, 46 teaching assistantships with full tuition reimbursements were awarded; career-related internships or fieldwork, scholarships/grants, and unspecified assistantships also available. Financial award application deadline: 3/1; financial award applicants required to submit FAFSA. *Unit head:* Dr. Jan Lacina, Associate Dean, 817-257-6786, E-mail: j.lacina@tcu.edu. *Application contact:* Lori L Kimball, Administrative Program Specialist, 817-257-7661, E-mail: l.kimball@tcu.edu.
Website: http://www.coe.tcu.edu/graduate-students-graduate-programs.asp.

Texas Southern University, College of Education, Houston, TX 77004-4584. Offers M Ed, MS, Ed D. Part-time and evening/weekend programs available. *Faculty:* 22 full-time (10 women), 21 part-time/adjunct (18 women). *Students:* 147 full-time (105 women), 205 part-time (160 women); includes 337 minority (324 Black or African American, non-Hispanic/Latino; 2 Asian, non-Hispanic/Latino; 11 Hispanic/Latino), 4 international. Average age 36. 172 applicants, 50% accepted, 70 enrolled. In 2013, 56 master's, 9 doctorates awarded. *Degree requirements:* For master's, comprehensive exam; for doctorate, comprehensive exam, thesis/dissertation. *Entrance requirements:* For master's, GRE General Test, minimum GPA of 2.5; for doctorate, GRE General Test or MAT, master's degree, minimum B+ average. Additional exam requirements/recommendations for international students: Required—TOEFL. *Application deadline:* For fall admission, 7/1 for domestic and international students; for spring admission, 11/1 for domestic and international students. Applications are processed on a rolling basis. Application fee: $50 ($75 for international students). Electronic applications accepted. *Financial support:* Fellowships, research assistantships, teaching assistantships, scholarships/grants, and unspecified assistantships available. Support available to part-time students. Financial award application deadline: 5/1. *Unit head:* Dr. Lillian Poats, Dean, 713-313-7978, E-mail: poats_lb@tsu.edu. *Application contact:* Dr. Gregory Maddox, Dean of the Graduate School, 713-313-7011 Ext. 4410, Fax: 713-639-1876, E-mail: maddox_gh@tsu.edu.
Website: http://www.tsu.edu/academics/colleges__schools/college_of_education/.

Texas State University, Graduate School, College of Education, San Marcos, TX 78666. Offers M Ed, MA, MS, MSRLS, PhD, SSP. Part-time and evening/weekend programs available. *Faculty:* 110 full-time (65 women), 29 part-time/adjunct (22 women). *Students:* 565 full-time (446 women), 647 part-time (490 women); includes 417 minority (98 Black or African American, non-Hispanic/Latino; 6 American Indian or Alaska Native, non-Hispanic/Latino; 26 Asian, non-Hispanic/Latino; 266 Hispanic/Latino; 21 Two or more races, non-Hispanic/Latino), 21 international. Average age 32. 832 applicants, 60% accepted, 308 enrolled. In 2013, 439 master's, 24 doctorates awarded. *Degree requirements:* For master's, comprehensive exam, thesis (for some programs). *Entrance requirements:* For master's, GRE (for some programs), Deadlines for applications vary by programs. Additional exam requirements/recommendations for international students: Required—TOEFL (minimum score 550 paper-based; 78 iBT). *Application deadline:* For fall admission, 6/15 priority date for domestic students, 6/1 for international students; for spring admission, 10/15 priority date for domestic students, 10/1 for international students. Applications are processed on a rolling basis. Application fee: $40 ($90 for international students). Electronic applications accepted. *Expenses:* Tuition, state resident: full-time $6663; part-time $278 per credit hour. Tuition, nonresident: full-time $15,159; part-time $632 per credit hour. *Required fees:* $1872; $54 per credit hour. $306 per term. Tuition and fees vary according to course load. *Financial support:* In 2013–14, 653 students received support, including 122 research assistantships (averaging $13,706 per year), 86 teaching assistantships (averaging $14,847 per year); fellowships, career-related internships or fieldwork, Federal Work-Study, and institutionally sponsored loans also available. Support available to part-time students. Financial award application deadline: 4/1; financial award applicants required to submit FAFSA. *Faculty research:* Developmental education research, novice teacher induction, college and career initiative, link P-16 pipeline, teacher quality, family literacy.

Education—General

Total annual research expenditures: $3.3 million. *Unit head:* Dr. Stan Carpenter, Dean, 512-245-2150, Fax: 512-245-3158, E-mail: sc33@txstate.edu. *Application contact:* Dr. Andrea Golato, Dean of Graduate School, 512-245-2581, Fax: 512-245-8365, E-mail: gradcollege@txstate.edu.
Website: http://www.education.txstate.edu/.

Texas Tech University, Graduate School, College of Education, Lubbock, TX 79409-1071. Offers M Ed, MS, Ed D, PhD. *Accreditation:* NCATE. Part-time programs available. *Faculty:* 74 full-time (42 women). *Students:* 269 full-time (211 women), 743 part-time (553 women); includes 293 minority (86 Black or African American, non-Hispanic/Latino; 5 American Indian or Alaska Native, non-Hispanic/Latino; 12 Asian, non-Hispanic/Latino; 172 Hispanic/Latino; 18 Two or more races, non-Hispanic/Latino), 68 international. Average age 36. 563 applicants, 70% accepted, 265 enrolled. In 2013, 215 master's, 52 doctorates awarded. *Degree requirements:* For master's, thesis or alternative; for doctorate, thesis/dissertation. *Entrance requirements:* For master's and doctorate, GRE General Test. Additional exam requirements/recommendations for international students: Required—TOEFL (minimum score 550 paper-based; 79 iBT). *Application deadline:* For fall admission, 6/1 priority date for domestic students, 1/15 priority date for international students; for spring admission, 9/1 priority date for domestic students, 6/15 priority date for international students. Applications are processed on a rolling basis. Application fee: $60. Electronic applications accepted. *Expenses:* Contact institution. *Financial support:* In 2013–14, 333 students received support, including 319 fellowships (averaging $2,776 per year), 53 research assistantships (averaging $4,729 per year), 14 teaching assistantships (averaging $4,592 per year); career-related internships or fieldwork, Federal Work-Study, institutionally sponsored loans, scholarships/grants, traineeships, health care benefits, and unspecified assistantships also available. Support available to part-time students. Financial award application deadline: 2/15; financial award applicants required to submit FAFSA. *Faculty research:* Multicultural foundations of education, teacher education, psychological processes of teaching and learning, teaching populations with special needs, institutional technology. *Total annual research expenditures:* $3 million. *Unit head:* Dr. Scott Ridley, Dean, 806-834-1431, Fax: 806-742-2179, E-mail: scott.ridley@ttu.edu. *Application contact:* Ashley Penner, Coordinator, 806-834-7568, Fax: 806-742-2179, E-mail: ashley.penner@ttu.edu.
Website: http://www.educ.ttu.edu/.

Texas Wesleyan University, Graduate Programs, Programs in Education, Fort Worth, TX 76105-1536. Offers education (M Ed, Ed D); marriage and family therapy (MSMFT); professional counseling (MA); school counseling (MS). Part-time and evening/weekend programs available. Postbaccalaureate distance learning degree programs offered (no on-campus study). *Entrance requirements:* For master's, GRE General Test, minimum GPA of 3.0 in final 60 hours of undergraduate course work, interview. *Faculty research:* Teacher effectiveness, bilingual education, analytic teaching.

Texas Woman's University, Graduate School, College of Professional Education, Denton, TX 76201. Offers M Ed, MA, MAT, MLS, MS, Ed D, PhD. Part-time and evening/weekend programs available. *Faculty:* 58 full-time (48 women), 66 part-time/adjunct (53 women). *Students:* 268 full-time (249 women), 952 part-time (881 women); includes 443 minority (206 Black or African American, non-Hispanic/Latino; 14 American Indian or Alaska Native, non-Hispanic/Latino; 29 Asian, non-Hispanic/Latino; 194 Hispanic/Latino), 24 international. Average age 36. 429 applicants, 61% accepted, 206 enrolled. In 2013, 367 master's, 17 doctorates awarded. Terminal master's awarded for partial completion of doctoral program. *Degree requirements:* For master's, comprehensive exam (for some programs), thesis (for some programs); for doctorate, comprehensive exam, thesis/dissertation. *Entrance requirements:* For master's and doctorate, minimum GPA of 3.0. Additional exam requirements/recommendations for international students: Required—TOEFL (minimum score 550 paper-based; 79 iBT). *Application deadline:* For fall admission, 7/1 priority date for domestic students, 3/1 for international students; for spring admission, 12/1 priority date for domestic students, 7/1 for international students. Applications are processed on a rolling basis. Application fee: $50 ($75 for international students). Electronic applications accepted. *Expenses:* Tuition, state resident: full-time $4182; part-time $233.32 per credit hour. Tuition, nonresident: full-time $10,716; part-time $595.32 per credit hour. *Financial support:* In 2013–14, 332 students received support, including 40 research assistantships (averaging $12,164 per year), 8 teaching assistantships (averaging $12,164 per year); career-related internships or fieldwork, Federal Work-Study, institutionally sponsored loans, scholarships/grants, traineeships, health care benefits, and unspecified assistantships also available. Support available to part-time students. Financial award application deadline: 3/1; financial award applicants required to submit FAFSA. *Total annual research expenditures:* $254,752. *Unit head:* Dr. Jerry Whitworth, Interim Dean, 940-898-2202, Fax: 940-898-2209, E-mail: cope@twu.edu. *Application contact:* Dr. Samuel Wheeler, Assistant Director of Admissions, 940-898-3188, Fax: 940-898-3081, E-mail: wheelersr@twu.edu.
Website: http://www.twu.edu/college-professional-education/.

Thomas More College, Program in Teaching, Crestview Hills, KY 41017-3495. Offers MAT. *Faculty:* 3 full-time (all women), 3 part-time/adjunct (2 women). *Students:* 17 part-time (11 women); includes 1 minority (Hispanic/Latino). Average age 34. 18 applicants, 61% accepted, 7 enrolled. In 2013, 22 master's awarded. *Degree requirements:* For master's, comprehensive exam. *Entrance requirements:* For master's, GRE (minimum scores: verbal 450, quantitative 490, and analytical 4.0) or PPST (minimum scores: math 174, reading 176, and writing 174), minimum undergraduate content GPA of 2.75, interview. Additional exam requirements/recommendations for international students: Required—TOEFL (minimum score 600 paper-based; 100 iBT). *Application deadline:* For fall admission, 5/1 for domestic students. Applications are processed on a rolling basis. Application fee: $0. Electronic applications accepted. *Expenses: Tuition:* Full-time $13,807; part-time $460 per credit hour. Tuition and fees vary according to program. *Financial support:* In 2013–14, 6 students received support. Federal Work-Study, institutionally sponsored loans, and scholarships/grants available. Financial award application deadline: 3/15; financial award applicants required to submit FAFSA. *Unit head:* Joyce Fortney Hamberg, PhD, Director, 859-344-3338, Fax: 859-344-3345, E-mail: hamberj@thomasmore.edu.

Thomas University, Department of Education, Thomasville, GA 31792-7499. Offers M Ed. Part-time programs available. *Entrance requirements:* For master's, resume, 3 academic/professional references. Additional exam requirements/recommendations for international students: Required—TOEFL (minimum score 600 paper-based). Electronic applications accepted.

Thompson Rivers University, Program in Education, Kamloops, BC V2C 0C8, Canada. Offers M Ed. Part-time programs available. *Entrance requirements:* For master's, 2 letters of reference, minimum GPA of 3.0 in final 2 years of undergraduate degree.

Touro College, Graduate School of Education, New York, NY 10010. Offers education and special education (MS); education biology (MS); instructional technology (MS); mathematics education (MS); school leadership (MS); teaching English to speakers of other languages (MS); teaching literacy (MS). Part-time and evening/weekend programs available. Postbaccalaureate distance learning degree programs offered (no on-campus study). *Faculty:* 75 full-time, 131 part-time/adjunct. *Students:* 327 full-time (272 women),

2,454 part-time (2,103 women); includes 840 minority (333 Black or African American, non-Hispanic/Latino; 4 American Indian or Alaska Native, non-Hispanic/Latino; 139 Asian, non-Hispanic/Latino; 334 Hispanic/Latino; 8 Native Hawaiian or other Pacific Islander, non-Hispanic/Latino; 22 Two or more races, non-Hispanic/Latino), 4 international. 1,422 applicants, 50% accepted, 675 enrolled. In 2013, 6 master's awarded. *Entrance requirements:* Additional exam requirements/recommendations for international students: Required—TOEFL (minimum score 83 iBT), IELTS (minimum score 6.5). *Application deadline:* For fall admission, 8/26 for domestic students, 7/15 for international students; for spring admission, 12/31 for domestic students, 12/15 for international students. Applications are processed on a rolling basis. Application fee: $50. *Financial support:* Federal Work-Study available. Financial award applicants required to submit FAFSA. *Faculty research:* Equity assistance, language development, scholar communications, Latin American studies and cultural sensitivity, behavior management techniques and strategies in special education. *Unit head:* Dr. LaMar Miller, Dean, 212-463-0400 Ext. 5561, Fax: 212-462-4889, E-mail: lpmiller@touro.edu. *Application contact:* Natalie Arroyo, Admissions, 212-463-0400.

Touro University, Graduate Programs, Vallejo, CA 94592. Offers education (MA); medical health sciences (MS); osteopathic medicine (DO); pharmacy (Pharm D); public health (MPH). *Accreditation:* AOsA; ARC-PA. Part-time and evening/weekend programs available. *Faculty:* 103 full-time (54 women), 57 part-time/adjunct (33 women). *Students:* 1,390 full-time (841 women), 27 part-time (20 women). *Degree requirements:* For master's, comprehensive exam, thesis; for doctorate, comprehensive exam. *Entrance requirements:* For doctorate, BS/BA. *Application deadline:* For fall admission, 3/15 for domestic students; for winter admission, 12/1 for domestic students. Applications are processed on a rolling basis. Application fee: $100. Electronic applications accepted. *Financial support:* Fellowships, research assistantships, teaching assistantships, Federal Work-Study, and scholarships/grants available. Support available to part-time students. Financial award applicants required to submit FAFSA. *Faculty research:* Cancer, heart disease. *Application contact:* Steve Davis, Director of Admissions, 707-638-5270, Fax: 707-638-5250, E-mail: steven.davis@tu.edu.

Towson University, Program in Teaching, Towson, MD 21252-0001. Offers MAT. *Students:* 107 full-time (72 women), 90 part-time (59 women); includes 35 minority (20 Black or African American, non-Hispanic/Latino; 3 American Indian or Alaska Native, non-Hispanic/Latino; 7 Asian, non-Hispanic/Latino; 3 Hispanic/Latino; 2 Two or more races, non-Hispanic/Latino), 4 international. *Entrance requirements:* For master's, ACT, GRE, PRAXIS I or SAT, 2 letters of reference, resume, minimum GPA of 3.0, essay. *Application deadline:* For fall admission, 6/15 for domestic and international students; for spring admission, 10/15 for domestic and international students. Applications are processed on a rolling basis. Application fee: $45. Electronic applications accepted. *Financial support:* Application deadline: 4/1. *Unit head:* Judith Reber, Graduate Program Director, 410-704-4935, E-mail: jreber@towson.edu. *Application contact:* Alicia Arkell-Kleis, Information Contact, 410-704-6004, E-mail: grads@towson.edu.
Website: http://grad.towson.edu/program/master/educ-mat/.

Trevecca Nazarene University, Graduate Education Program, Nashville, TN 37210-2877. Offers curriculum, assessment, and instruction K-12 (M Ed); educational leadership (M Ed); English language learners (PreK-12) (M Ed); leadership and professional practice (Ed D); library and information science (MLI Sc); teacher leader (M Ed); teaching (MAE, MAT), including teaching 7-12 (MAT), teaching K-6 (MAT); visual impairments special education (M Ed). *Accreditation:* NCATE. Part-time and evening/weekend programs available. Postbaccalaureate distance learning degree programs offered. *Faculty:* 19 full-time (17 women), 14 part-time/adjunct (5 women). *Students:* 186 full-time (137 women), 134 part-time (94 women); includes 93 minority (87 Black or African American, non-Hispanic/Latino; 1 American Indian or Alaska Native, non-Hispanic/Latino; 2 Asian, non-Hispanic/Latino; 1 Hispanic/Latino; 1 Native Hawaiian or other Pacific Islander, non-Hispanic/Latino; 1 Two or more races, non-Hispanic/Latino), 2 international. In 2013, 201 master's, 40 doctorates awarded. *Degree requirements:* For master's, comprehensive exam, exit assessment/e-portfolio; for doctorate, thesis/dissertation, proposal study, symposium presentation. *Entrance requirements:* For master's, GRE with minimum score of 378 or MAT with minimum score of 290, ACT with minimum score of 22 or SAT with minimum score of 1020 (for MAT programs only); PRAXIS (for MAT and MAE programs), minimum GPA of 2.7, official transcript from regionally accredited institution, 3+ years successful teaching experience (Teacher Leader and Education Leadership majors), technology pre-assessment written requirements (some majors); for doctorate, GRE or MAT, minimum GPA of 3.4, official transcript from regionally-accredited institution, resume, writing sample, interview, reference forms. Additional exam requirements/recommendations for international students: Required—TOEFL (minimum score 550 paper-based). *Application deadline:* Applications are processed on a rolling basis. *Expenses:* Contact institution. *Financial support:* Applicants required to submit FAFSA. *Unit head:* Dr. Suzie Harris, Dean, School of Education/Director of Graduate Education Programs, 615-248-1201, Fax: 615-248-1597, E-mail: admissions_ged@trevecca.edu. *Application contact:* 615-248-1529, E-mail: cll@trevecca.edu.
Website: http://www.trevecca.edu/academics/schools-colleges/education/.

Trident University International, College of Education, Cypress, CA 90630. Offers MA Ed, PhD. Part-time and evening/weekend programs available. Postbaccalaureate distance learning degree programs offered (no on-campus study). *Degree requirements:* For doctorate, comprehensive exam, thesis/dissertation, defense of dissertation. *Entrance requirements:* For master's, minimum GPA of 2.5 (students with GPA 3.0 or greater may transfer up to 30% of graduate level credits); for doctorate, minimum GPA of 3.4, curriculum vitae, course work in research methods or statistics. Additional exam requirements/recommendations for international students: Required—TOEFL (minimum score 525 paper-based). Electronic applications accepted.

Trinity International University, Trinity Graduate School, Deerfield, IL 60015-1284. Offers bioethics (MA); communication and culture (MA); counseling psychology (MA); instructional leadership (M Ed); teaching (MA). Part-time and evening/weekend programs available. Postbaccalaureate distance learning degree programs offered (minimal on-campus study). *Degree requirements:* For master's, comprehensive exam. *Entrance requirements:* For master's, GRE General Test or MAT, minimum undergraduate GPA of 3.0. Additional exam requirements/recommendations for international students: Required—TOEFL (minimum score 580 paper-based), TWE (minimum score 4). Electronic applications accepted.

Trinity University, Department of Education, San Antonio, TX 78212-7200. Offers school administration (M Ed); school psychology (MA); teacher education (MAT). *Accreditation:* NCATE. Part-time and evening/weekend programs available. *Entrance requirements:* For master's, GRE General Test, minimum GPA of 3.0, interview.

Trinity Washington University, School of Education, Washington, DC 20017-1094. Offers clinical mental health counseling (MA); early childhood education (MAT); educating for change (M Ed); educational administration (MSA); elementary education (MAT); reading (M Ed); school counseling (MA); secondary education (MAT), including English, social studies; special education (MAT). *Accreditation:* NCATE. Part-time and evening/weekend programs available. *Degree requirements:* For master's, thesis (for some programs), capstone project(s). *Entrance requirements:* For master's, PRAXIS I, minimum GPA of 2.8. Additional exam requirements/recommendations for international

students: Required—TOEFL (minimum score 550 paper-based). *Application deadline:* For fall admission, 4/1 priority date for domestic students; for winter admission, 11/1 priority date for domestic students; for spring admission, 11/1 priority date for domestic students. Applications are processed on a rolling basis. Application fee: $40. *Expenses: Tuition:* Part-time $715 per credit. *Financial support:* Career-related internships or fieldwork, health care benefits, and unspecified assistantships available. Support available to part-time students. Financial award application deadline: 4/1; financial award applicants required to submit FAFSA. *Faculty research:* Technology, literacy, special education, organizations, inclusion models. *Unit head:* Dr. Janet Stocks, Dean, 202-884-9380, Fax: 202-884-9506, E-mail: stocksj@trinitydc.edu. *Application contact:* Erika Davis, Director of Admissions for School of Education, 202-884-9400, Fax: 202-884-9229, E-mail: daviser@trinitydc.edu.
Website: http://www.trinitydc.edu/education/.

Troy University, Graduate School, College of Arts and Sciences, Program in Public Administration, Troy, AL 36082. Offers education (MPA); environmental management (MPA); government contracting (MPA); health care administration (MPA); justice administration (MPA); national security affairs (MPA); nonprofit management (MPA); public human resources management (MPA); public management (MPA). *Accreditation:* NASPAA. Part-time and evening/weekend programs available. Postbaccalaureate distance learning degree programs offered (no on-campus study). *Faculty:* 15 full-time (9 women), 7 part-time/adjunct (4 women). *Students:* 95 full-time (62 women), 307 part-time (204 women); includes 231 minority (195 Black or African American, non-Hispanic/Latino; 3 American Indian or Alaska Native, non-Hispanic/Latino; 5 Asian, non-Hispanic/Latino; 15 Hispanic/Latino; 13 Two or more races, non-Hispanic/Latino). Average age 32. 172 applicants, 87% accepted, 107 enrolled. In 2013, 159 master's awarded. *Degree requirements:* For master's, capstone course with minimum B grade, minimum GPA of 3.0, admission to candidacy. *Entrance requirements:* For master's, GRE (minimum score of 850 on old exam or 294 on new exam), MAT (minimum score of 400) or GMAT (minimum score of 490), bachelor's degree; minimum undergraduate GPA of 2.5 or 3.0 on last 30 semester hours, letter of recommendation; essay. Additional exam requirements/recommendations for international students: Required—TOEFL (minimum score 523 paper-based; 70 iBT), IELTS (minimum score 6). *Application deadline:* Applications are processed on a rolling basis. Application fee: $50. Electronic applications accepted. *Expenses:* Tuition, state resident: full-time $6084; part-time $338 per credit hour. Tuition, nonresident: full-time $12,168; part-time $676 per credit hour. *Required fees:* $630; $35 per credit hour. $50 per semester. *Financial support:* Available to part-time students. Applicants required to submit FAFSA. *Unit head:* Dr. Sam Shelton, Chairman, 334-670-3754, Fax: 334-670-5647, E-mail: ssheltonl@troy.edu. *Application contact:* Brenda K. Campbell, Director of Graduate Admissions, 334-670-3178, Fax: 334-670-3733, E-mail: bcamp@troy.edu.

Troy University, Graduate School, College of Education, Troy, AL 36082. Offers M Ed, MS, Ed S. *Accreditation:* NCATE. Part-time and evening/weekend programs available. *Faculty:* 525 full-time (476 women), 51 part-time/adjunct (21 women). *Students:* 532 full-time (434 women), 1,063 part-time (873 women); includes 934 minority (810 Black or African American, non-Hispanic/Latino; 5 American Indian or Alaska Native, non-Hispanic/Latino; 8 Asian, non-Hispanic/Latino; 81 Hispanic/Latino; 30 Two or more races, non-Hispanic/Latino). Average age 33. 598 applicants, 82% accepted, 269 enrolled. In 2013, 538 master's, 19 other advanced degrees awarded. *Degree requirements:* For master's, comprehensive exam, thesis. *Entrance requirements:* For master's, GRE (minimum score of 850 on old exam or 290 on new exam), GMAT (minimum score of 380), or MAT (minimum score of 385), bachelor's degree; minimum undergraduate GPA of 2.5 or 3.0 on last 30 semester hours, letter of recommendation; for Ed S, GRE (minimum score of 850 on old exam or 290 on new exam), GMAT (minimum score of 380), or MAT (minimum score of 385), Alabama Class A certificate or equivalent, minimum graduate GPA of 3.0. Additional exam requirements/recommendations for international students: Required—TOEFL (minimum score 523 paper-based; 70 iBT), IELTS (minimum score 6). *Application deadline:* For fall admission, 6/1 for international students; for spring admission, 10/15 for international students. Applications are processed on a rolling basis. Application fee: $50. Electronic applications accepted. *Expenses:* Tuition, state resident: full-time $6084; part-time $338 per credit hour. Tuition, nonresident: full-time $12,168; part-time $676 per credit hour. *Required fees:* $630; $35 per credit hour. $50 per semester. *Financial support:* Career-related internships or fieldwork available. Support available to part-time students. Financial award applicants required to submit FAFSA. *Unit head:* Dr. Kathryn Hildebrand, Dean, 334-670-3365, Fax: 334-670-3474, E-mail: khildebrand@troy.edu. *Application contact:* Brenda K. Campbell, Director of Graduate Admissions, 334-670-3178, Fax: 334-670-3733, E-mail: bcamp@troy.edu.

Truman State University, Graduate School, School of Health Sciences and Education, Program in Education, Kirksville, MO 63501-4221. Offers MAE. *Accreditation:* NCATE. *Degree requirements:* For master's, comprehensive exam, thesis or alternative. *Entrance requirements:* For master's, GRE, minimum GPA of 2.75. Additional exam requirements/recommendations for international students: Required—TOEFL (minimum score 550 paper-based). Electronic applications accepted.

Tufts University, Graduate School of Arts and Sciences, Department of Education, Medford, MA 02155. Offers art education (MAT); education (MA, MAT, MS, PhD), including educational studies (MA), elementary education (MAT), middle and secondary education (MA, MAT), museum education (MA), secondary education (MA), STEM education (MS, PhD); school psychology (MA, Ed S). *Faculty:* 13 full-time, 9 part-time/adjunct. *Students:* 140 full-time (119 women); includes 33 minority (5 Black or African American, non-Hispanic/Latino; 1 American Indian or Alaska Native, non-Hispanic/Latino; 8 Asian, non-Hispanic/Latino; 11 Hispanic/Latino; 8 Two or more races, non-Hispanic/Latino), 5 international. Average age 27. 227 applicants, 60% accepted, 66 enrolled. In 2013, 121 master's, 11 other advanced degrees awarded. *Degree requirements:* For doctorate, thesis/dissertation. *Entrance requirements:* For master's and doctorate, GRE General Test. Additional exam requirements/recommendations for international students: Required—TOEFL (minimum score 550 paper-based; 80 iBT), IELTS (minimum score 6.5). *Application deadline:* For fall admission, 1/2 for domestic and international students; for spring admission, 10/15 for domestic students, 9/15 for international students. Applications are processed on a rolling basis. Application fee: $75. Electronic applications accepted. *Financial support:* Teaching assistantships with full and partial tuition reimbursements, Federal Work-Study, scholarships/grants, and tuition waivers (partial) available. Support available to part-time students. Financial award application deadline: 1/2. *Unit head:* David Hammer, Chair, 617-627-3244. *Application contact:* Patricia Romeo, Department Administrator, 617-627-3244.
Website: http://www.ase.tufts.edu/education/.

Tusculum College, Graduate School, Program in Education, Greeneville, TN 37743-9997. Offers adult education (MA Ed); K–12 (MA Ed). Evening/weekend programs available. *Degree requirements:* For master's, thesis or alternative. *Entrance requirements:* For master's, 3 years of work experience, minimum GPA of 2.75.

Union College, Graduate Programs, Department of Education, Barbourville, KY 40906-1499. Offers elementary education (MA); health and physical education (MA); middle grades (MA); music education (MA); principalship (MA); reading specialist (MA); secondary education (MA); special education (MA). *Degree requirements:* For master's, thesis optional. *Entrance requirements:* For master's, GRE General Test, NTE.

Union Graduate College, School of Education, Schenectady, NY 12308-3107. Offers biology (MAT); chemistry (MAT); Chinese (MAT); earth science (MAT); English (MA, MAT); English and history (MA); French (MAT); general science (MAT); German (MAT); history (MA); Latin (MAT); life sciences (MS); mathematics (MAT); mathematics and computer technology (MS); mentoring and teacher leadership (AC); middle childhood extension (AC); national board certification and teacher leadership (AC); physical sciences (MS); physics (MAT); social studies (MAT); Spanish (MAT); technology (MAT). *Accreditation:* Teacher Education Accreditation Council. *Faculty:* 3 full-time (1 woman), 56 part-time/adjunct (34 women). *Students:* 32 full-time (16 women), 27 part-time (22 women); includes 15 minority (1 Black or African American, non-Hispanic/Latino; 4 Asian, non-Hispanic/Latino; 6 Hispanic/Latino; 4 Two or more races, non-Hispanic/Latino), 1 international. Average age 32. In 2013, 25 master's, 11 other advanced degrees awarded. *Degree requirements:* For master's, thesis or project. *Entrance requirements:* For master's, minimum GPA of 3.0, letters of recommendation. Additional exam requirements/recommendations for international students: Required—TOEFL (minimum score 550 paper-based). *Application deadline:* Applications are processed on a rolling basis. Application fee: $60. Electronic applications accepted. *Expenses:* Contact institution. *Financial support:* Career-related internships or fieldwork, Federal Work-Study, scholarships/grants, health care benefits, and tuition waivers (partial) available. Support available to part-time students. Financial award applicants required to submit FAFSA. *Faculty research:* Transformative learning, science education, National Board Certification, teacher leadership, teacher quality. *Unit head:* Dr. Lynn Gelzheiser, Dean, 518-631-9870, Fax: 518-631-9901. *Application contact:* Nicki Foley, Assistant, 518-631-9871, Fax: 518-631-9903, E-mail: foleyn@uniongraduatecollege.edu.

Union Institute & University, Doctor of Education Program, Cincinnati, OH 45206-1925. Offers educational leadership (Ed D); higher education (Ed D). M Ed offered online and in Vermont and Florida, Ed S in Florida; Ed D program is offered online with limited residency in Ohio. Postbaccalaureate distance learning degree programs offered (minimal on-campus study). *Degree requirements:* For doctorate, comprehensive exam, thesis/dissertation, electronic portfolio. *Entrance requirements:* For doctorate, master's degree from regionally-accredited institution, letters of recommendation, essay. *Faculty research:* Adult education, higher education, social responsibility in education, educational technology.

Union University, School of Education, Jackson, TN 38305-3697. Offers education (M Ed, MA Ed); education administration generalist (Ed S); educational leadership (Ed D); educational supervision (Ed S); higher education (Ed D). M Ed also available at Germantown campus. *Accreditation:* NCATE. Part-time and evening/weekend programs available. *Degree requirements:* For master's, thesis (for some programs), capstone research course; for doctorate, comprehensive exam, thesis/dissertation; for Ed S, thesis or alternative. *Entrance requirements:* For master's, MAT, PRAXIS II or GRE, minimum GPA of 3.0, teaching license, writing sample; for doctorate, GRE, minimum graduate GPA of 3.2, writing sample; for Ed S, PRAXIS II, minimum graduate GPA of 3.2, writing sample. *Faculty research:* Mathematics education, direct instruction, language disorders and special education, brain compatible learning, empathy and school leadership.

United States University, School of Education, Cypress, CA 90630. Offers administration (MA Ed); early childhood education (MA Ed); general (MA Ed); higher education administration (MA Ed); Spanish language education (MA Ed); special education (MA Ed). *Degree requirements:* For master's, portfolio. *Entrance requirements:* For master's, minimum undergraduate GPA of 2.5. Additional exam requirements/recommendations for international students: Required—TOEFL (minimum score 500 paper-based; 61 iBT).

Universidad Autonoma de Guadalajara, Graduate Programs, Guadalajara, Mexico. Offers administrative law and justice (LL M); advertising and corporate communications (MA); architecture (M Arch); business (MBA); computational science (MCC); education (Ed M, Ed D); English-Spanish translation (MA); entrepreneurship and management (MBA); integrated management of digital animation (MA); international business (MIB); international corporate law (LL M); internet technologies (MS); manufacturing systems (MMS); occupational health (MS); philosophy (MA, PhD); power electronics (MS); quality systems (MQS); renewable energy (MS); social evaluation of projects (MBA); strategic market research (MBA); tax law (MA); teaching mathematics (MA).

Universidad de las Americas, A.C., Program in Education, Mexico City, Mexico. Offers M Ed. *Entrance requirements:* For master's, 2 years of professional experience; undergraduate degree in early childhood education, human communication, psychology, science of education, special education or related fields.

Universidad de las Américas Puebla, Division of Graduate Studies, School of Social Sciences, Program in Education, Puebla, Mexico. Offers MA. Part-time and evening/weekend programs available. *Degree requirements:* For master's, one foreign language, thesis. *Faculty research:* Curriculum development, curriculum evaluation, instructional technology, critical thinking.

Universidad del Turabo, Graduate Programs, Programs in Education, Gurabo, PR 00778-3030. Offers administration of school libraries (M Ed, Certificate); athletic training (MPHE); coaching (MPHE); curriculum and instruction and appropriate environment (D Ed); curriculum and teaching (M Ed); educational administration (M Ed); educational leadership (D Ed); guidance counseling (M Ed); library service and information technology (M Ed); special education (M Ed); teaching at primary level (M Ed); teaching English as a second language (M Ed); teaching of fine arts (M Ed); wellness (MPHE). Part-time and evening/weekend programs available. *Entrance requirements:* For master's, GRE, EXADEP, interview.

Universidad Metropolitana, School of Education, San Juan, PR 00928-1150. Offers administration and supervision (M Ed); curriculum and teaching (M Ed); educational administration and supervision (M Ed); managing recreation and sports services (M Ed); pre-school centers administration (M Ed); special education (M Ed); teaching of physical education (M Ed), including teaching of adult physical education, teaching of elementary physical education, teaching of secondary physical education. Part-time and evening/weekend programs available. *Degree requirements:* For master's, thesis or alternative. Electronic applications accepted.

Université de Moncton, Faculty of Education, Graduate Studies in Education, Moncton, NB E1A 3E9, Canada. Offers educational psychology (M Ed, MA Ed); guidance (M Ed, MA Ed); school administration (M Ed, MA Ed); teaching (M Ed, MA Ed). Part-time programs available. *Degree requirements:* For master's, proficiency in English and French. *Entrance requirements:* For master's, minimum GPA of 3.0. *Faculty research:* Guidance, ethnolinguistic vitality, children's rights, ecological education, entrepreneurship.

Université de Montréal, Faculty of Education, Montréal, QC H3C 3J7, Canada. Offers M Ed, MA, PhD, DESS. Part-time and evening/weekend programs available. *Degree requirements:* For doctorate, thesis/dissertation, general exam. Electronic applications accepted.

Education—General

Université de Saint-Boniface, Department of Education, Saint-Boniface, MB R2H 0H7, Canada. Offers M Ed.

Université de Sherbrooke, Faculty of Education, Sherbrooke, QC J1K 2R1, Canada. Offers M Ed, MA, Diploma. Part-time and evening/weekend programs available. *Degree requirements:* For master's, thesis. *Faculty research:* Career education, teaching, professional instruction.

Université du Québec à Chicoutimi, Graduate Programs, Program in Education, Chicoutimi, QC G7H 2B1, Canada. Offers M Ed, MA, PhD. PhD offered jointly with Université du Québec à Rimouski, Université du Québec à Trois-Rivières, Université du Québec en Outaouais, Université du Québec en Abitibi-Témiscamingue. and Université du Québec à Montréal. Part-time programs available. *Degree requirements:* For doctorate, thesis/dissertation. *Entrance requirements:* For master's, appropriate bachelor's degree, proficiency in French; for doctorate, appropriate master's degree, proficiency in French.

Université du Québec à Montréal, Graduate Programs, Program in Education, Montréal, QC H3C 3P8, Canada. Offers education (M Ed, MA, PhD); education of the environmental sciences (Diploma). PhD offered jointly with Université du Québec à Chicoutimi, Université du Québec à Rimouski, Université du Québec à Trois-Rivières, Université du Québec en Outaouais, and Université du Québec en Abitibi-Témiscamingue. Part-time programs available. *Degree requirements:* For master's, thesis (for some programs); for doctorate, thesis/dissertation. *Entrance requirements:* For master's and Diploma, appropriate bachelor's degree or equivalent, proficiency in French; for doctorate, appropriate master's degree or equivalent, proficiency in French.

Université du Québec à Rimouski, Graduate Programs, Program in Education, Rimouski, QC G5L 3A1, Canada. Offers M Ed, MA, PhD, Diploma. M Ed and MA offered jointly with Université du Québec en Outaouais and Université du Québec en Abitibi-Témiscamingue; PhD with Université du Québec à Chicoutimi, Université du Québec à Trois-Rivières, Université du Québec en Outaouais, and Université du Québec en Abitibi-Témiscamingue. Part-time programs available. *Degree requirements:* For master's, thesis optional; for doctorate, thesis/dissertation. *Entrance requirements:* For master's, appropriate bachelor's degree, proficiency in French; for doctorate, appropriate master's degree, proficiency in French.

Université du Québec à Trois-Rivières, Graduate Programs, Program in Education, Trois-Rivières, QC G9A 5H7, Canada. Offers M Ed, PhD. Part-time programs available. *Degree requirements:* For master's, research report. *Entrance requirements:* For master's, appropriate bachelor's degree, proficiency in French.

Université du Québec en Abitibi-Témiscamingue, Graduate Programs, Program in Education, Rouyn-Noranda, QC J9X 5E4, Canada. Offers M Ed, MA, PhD, DESS. M Ed and MA offered jointly with Université du Québec à Rimouski and Université du Québec en Outaouais; PhD with Université du Québec à Chicoutimi, Université du Québec à Rimouski, Université du Québec à Trois-Rivières, Université du Québec en Outaouais, and Université du Québec à Montréal. Part-time programs available. *Degree requirements:* For master's, thesis optional; for doctorate, thesis/dissertation. *Entrance requirements:* For master's, appropriate bachelor's degree, proficiency in French; for doctorate, appropriate master's degree, proficiency in French.

Université du Québec en Outaouais, Graduate Programs, Program in Education, Gatineau, QC J8X 3X7, Canada. Offers M Ed, MA, PhD, DESS, Diploma. Part-time programs available. *Degree requirements:* For master's, thesis optional; for doctorate, thesis/dissertation. *Entrance requirements:* For master's, appropriate bachelor's degree, proficiency in French; for doctorate, appropriate master's degree, proficiency in French.

Université Laval, Faculty of Education, Québec, QC G1K 7P4, Canada. Offers MA, PhD, Diploma. Part-time programs available. *Degree requirements:* For doctorate, comprehensive exam, thesis/dissertation. Electronic applications accepted.

Université Sainte-Anne, Program in Education, Church Point, NS B0W 1M0, Canada. Offers M Ed. Part-time programs available.

University at Albany, State University of New York, School of Education, Albany, NY 12222-0001. Offers MA, MS, Ed D, PhD, Psy D, CAS. *Accreditation:* Teacher Education Accreditation Council. Part-time and evening/weekend programs available. *Degree requirements:* For doctorate, thesis/dissertation. *Entrance requirements:* For doctorate, GRE General Test. Additional exam requirements/recommendations for international students: Required—TOEFL (minimum score 550 paper-based). Electronic applications accepted.

University at Buffalo, the State University of New York, Graduate School, Graduate School of Education, Buffalo, NY 14260. Offers Ed M, MA, MLS, MS, Ed D, PhD, Advanced Certificate, Certificate, Certificate/Ed M. *Accreditation:* Teacher Education Accreditation Council. Part-time programs available. Postbaccalaureate distance learning degree programs offered (no on-campus study). *Faculty:* 75 full-time (51 women), 128 part-time/adjunct (106 women). *Students:* 562 full-time (428 women), 712 part-time (520 women); includes 134 minority (73 Black or African American, non-Hispanic/Latino; 10 American Indian or Alaska Native, non-Hispanic/Latino; 27 Asian, non-Hispanic/Latino; 24 Hispanic/Latino), 130 international. Average age 31. 1,191 applicants, 74% accepted, 518 enrolled. In 2013, 432 master's, 46 doctorates, 74 other advanced degrees awarded. Terminal master's awarded for partial completion of doctoral program. *Degree requirements:* For master's, comprehensive exam; for doctorate, thesis/dissertation. *Entrance requirements:* For master's, GRE General Test; for doctorate, GRE, MAT. Additional exam requirements/recommendations for international students: Required—TOEFL (minimum score 79 iBT). *Application deadline:* Applications are processed on a rolling basis. Application fee: $50. Electronic applications accepted. *Financial support:* In 2013–14, 108 fellowships (averaging $8,191 per year), 64 research assistantships with tuition reimbursements (averaging $10,540 per year) were awarded; teaching assistantships, career-related internships or fieldwork, Federal Work-Study, institutionally sponsored loans, and unspecified assistantships also available. Financial award applicants required to submit FAFSA. *Faculty research:* Early childhood mathematics education, finance and management of higher education, curricular policy, practice and reform, student behavior in small classes, psychological measurement and assessment. *Total annual research expenditures:* $1.3 million. *Unit head:* Dr. Jaekyung Lee, Dean, 716-645-6640, Fax: 716-645-2479, E-mail: gse-info@buffalo.edu. *Application contact:* Dr. Radhika Suresh, Assistant Dean for Enrollment Management, 716-645-2110, Fax: 716-645-7937, E-mail: gse-info@buffalo.edu.
Website: http://www.gse.buffalo.edu/.

The University of Akron, Graduate School, College of Education, Akron, OH 44325. Offers MA, MS, PhD. *Accreditation:* NCATE. Part-time programs available. *Faculty:* 49 full-time (37 women), 166 part-time/adjunct (107 women). *Students:* 457 full-time (275 women), 625 part-time (480 women); includes 173 minority (131 Black or African American, non-Hispanic/Latino; 14 Asian, non-Hispanic/Latino; 15 Hispanic/Latino; 1 Native Hawaiian or other Pacific Islander, non-Hispanic/Latino; 12 Two or more races, non-Hispanic/Latino), 51 international. Average age 33. 553 applicants, 58% accepted, 316 enrolled. In 2013, 353 master's, 20 doctorates awarded. Terminal master's awarded for partial completion of doctoral program. *Degree requirements:* For master's, comprehensive exam, thesis optional; for doctorate, one foreign language, comprehensive exam, thesis/dissertation, written and oral exams. *Entrance requirements:* For master's, letters of recommendation, resume, statement of purpose; for doctorate, GRE or MAT, minimum GPA of 3.25, writing sample, interview, letters of recommendation, curriculum vitae/resume, statement of purpose indicating nature of interest in the program and future career goals. Additional exam requirements/recommendations for international students: Required—TOEFL (minimum score 550 paper-based; 79 iBT). *Application deadline:* For fall admission, 12/1 for domestic students, 3/1 for international students; for spring admission, 10/15 for domestic and international students. Applications are processed on a rolling basis. Application fee: $40 ($60 for international students). Electronic applications accepted. *Expenses:* Tuition, state resident: full-time $7430; part-time $412.80 per credit hour. Tuition, nonresident: full-time $12,722; part-time $706.80 per credit hour. *Required fees:* $53 per credit hour. $12 per semester. Tuition and fees vary according to course load and program. *Financial support:* In 2013–14, 22 research assistantships with full tuition reimbursements, 112 teaching assistantships with full tuition reimbursements were awarded. *Faculty research:* History, philosophy of education, ethnographic research in education, case study methodology in education, multiple linear regression. *Total annual research expenditures:* $2.2 million. *Unit head:* Dr. Susan Clark, Interim Dean, 330-972-7780, E-mail: sclark1@uakron.edu.
Website: http://www.uakron.edu/education/.

The University of Alabama at Birmingham, School of Education, Birmingham, AL 35294. Offers MA, MA Ed, Ed D, PhD, Ed S. *Accreditation:* NCATE. Part-time and evening/weekend programs available. *Degree requirements:* For master's, thesis optional; for doctorate, thesis/dissertation; for Ed S, comprehensive exam, thesis optional. *Entrance requirements:* For master's, GRE General Test, MAT, or NTE, minimum GPA of 3.0; for doctorate, GRE General Test, MAT, minimum GPA of 3.25; for Ed S, GRE General Test, MAT, minimum GPA of 3.0, master's degree. Electronic applications accepted.

University of Alaska Anchorage, College of Education, Anchorage, AK 99508. Offers M Ed, Certificate. *Accreditation:* NCATE. Part-time programs available. *Degree requirements:* For master's, comprehensive exam, thesis or alternative, portfolio. *Entrance requirements:* For master's, interview, minimum GPA of 3.0. Additional exam requirements/recommendations for international students: Required—TOEFL (minimum score 550 paper-based).

University of Alaska Fairbanks, School of Education, Fairbanks, AK 99775. Offers counseling (M Ed), including counseling; education (M Ed, Graduate Certificate), including cross-cultural education (M Ed), curriculum and instruction (M Ed), education (M Ed), elementary education (M Ed), language and literacy (M Ed), reading (M Ed), secondary education (M Ed), special education (M Ed); guidance and counseling (M Ed). *Accreditation:* NCATE. Postbaccalaureate distance learning degree programs offered. *Faculty:* 23 full-time (14 women), 1 part-time/adjunct (0 women). *Students:* 59 full-time (45 women), 116 part-time (85 women); includes 24 minority (2 Black or African American, non-Hispanic/Latino; 10 American Indian or Alaska Native, non-Hispanic/Latino; 7 Hispanic/Latino; 1 Native Hawaiian or other Pacific Islander, non-Hispanic/Latino; 4 Two or more races, non-Hispanic/Latino), 2 international. Average age 35. 77 applicants, 62% accepted, 40 enrolled. In 2013, 56 master's, 32 other advanced degrees awarded. *Degree requirements:* For master's, comprehensive exam, thesis or alternative, student teaching. *Entrance requirements:* For master's, GRE General Test, PRAXIS I, PRAXIS II, writing sample, evidence of technology competence, criminal background check. Additional exam requirements/recommendations for international students: Required—TOEFL (minimum score 550 paper-based; 80 iBT). *Application deadline:* For fall admission, 3/1 for domestic and international students; for spring admission, 10/15 for domestic students, 9/1 for international students. Application fee: $60. Electronic applications accepted. *Expenses:* Tuition, state resident: full-time $7254; part-time $403 per credit. Tuition, nonresident: full-time $14,814; part-time $823 per credit. Tuition and fees vary according to course level, course load and reciprocity agreements. *Financial support:* In 2013–14, 4 teaching assistantships with tuition reimbursements (averaging $10,932 per year) were awarded; fellowships with tuition reimbursements, research assistantships with tuition reimbursements, career-related internships or fieldwork, Federal Work-Study, scholarships/grants, health care benefits, and unspecified assistantships also available. Support available to part-time students. Financial award application deadline: 2/15; financial award applicants required to submit FAFSA. *Faculty research:* Native ways of knowing, classroom research in methods of literacy instruction, multiple intelligence theory, geometry concept development, mathematics and science curriculum development. *Total annual research expenditures:* $244,000. *Unit head:* Allan Morotti, Dean, 907-474-7341, Fax: 907-474-5451, E-mail: uaf-soe-school@alaska.edu. *Application contact:* Libby Eddy, Registrar and Director of Admissions, 907-474-7500, Fax: 907-474-7097, E-mail: admissions@uaf.edu.
Website: https://sites.google.com/a/alaska.edu/soe-home/.

University of Alaska Southeast, Graduate Programs, Program in Education, Juneau, AK 99801. Offers early childhood education (M Ed, MAT); educational technology (M Ed); elementary education (MAT); reading (M Ed); secondary education (MAT). *Accreditation:* NCATE. Part-time and evening/weekend programs available. Postbaccalaureate distance learning degree programs offered (minimal on-campus study). *Degree requirements:* For master's, comprehensive exam or project, portfolio. *Entrance requirements:* For master's, PRAXIS, minimum GPA of 3.0, writing sample, letters of recommendation. Electronic applications accepted. *Faculty research:* Applied classroom research, culturally responsive practices, action research, teaching effectiveness.

The University of Arizona, College of Education, Tucson, AZ 85721. Offers M Ed, MA, MS, Ed D, PhD, Ed S. Part-time programs available. Postbaccalaureate distance learning degree programs offered (no on-campus study). *Faculty:* 51 full-time (33 women), 2 part-time/adjunct (both women). *Students:* 460 full-time (338 women), 280 part-time (195 women); includes 235 minority (32 Black or African American, non-Hispanic/Latino; 9 American Indian or Alaska Native, non-Hispanic/Latino; 9 Asian, non-Hispanic/Latino; 124 Hispanic/Latino; 1 Native Hawaiian or other Pacific Islander, non-Hispanic/Latino; 60 Two or more races, non-Hispanic/Latino), 41 international. Average age 36. 516 applicants, 57% accepted, 175 enrolled. In 2013, 187 master's, 30 doctorates awarded. Terminal master's awarded for partial completion of doctoral program. *Degree requirements:* For master's, comprehensive exam, thesis (for some programs); for doctorate, comprehensive exam, thesis/dissertation. *Entrance requirements:* For doctorate, GRE. Additional exam requirements/recommendations for international students: Required—TOEFL (minimum score 550 paper-based; 79 iBT). *Application deadline:* For fall admission, 2/1 priority date for domestic and international students; for spring admission, 10/1 priority date for domestic students, 9/1 priority date for international students. Applications are processed on a rolling basis. Application fee: $75. Electronic applications accepted. *Expenses:* Tuition, state resident: full-time $11,526. Tuition, nonresident: full-time $27,398. *Financial support:* In 2013–14, 40 research assistantships with full tuition reimbursements (averaging $17,222 per year), 41 teaching assistantships with full tuition reimbursements (averaging $16,275 per year) were awarded; career-related internships or fieldwork, Federal Work-Study, institutionally sponsored loans, scholarships/grants, health care benefits, tuition waivers (full and partial), and unspecified assistantships also available. Support available to part-

time students. Financial award application deadline: 3/1. *Faculty research:* Teacher effectiveness, pupil achievement, learning skills, program evaluation, instructional method effects. *Total annual research expenditures:* $5.3 million. *Unit head:* Dr. Ronald Marx, Dean, 520-621-1081, Fax: 520-621-9271, E-mail: ronmarx@email.arizona.edu. *Application contact:* General Information Contact, 520-621-3471, Fax: 520-621-4101, E-mail: gradadm@grad.arizona.edu.
Website: http://www.coe.arizona.edu.

University of Arkansas, Graduate School, College of Education and Health Professions, Fayetteville, AR 72701-1201. Offers M Ed, MAT, MAT, MS, MSN, Ed D, PhD, Ed S. *Accreditation:* NCATE. *Degree requirements:* For doctorate, thesis/dissertation. Electronic applications accepted.

University of Arkansas at Little Rock, Graduate School, College of Education, Little Rock, AR 72204-1099. Offers M Ed, MA, Ed D, Ed S, Graduate Certificate. *Accreditation:* CORE; NCATE (one or more programs are accredited). Part-time and evening/weekend programs available. *Degree requirements:* For doctorate, comprehensive exam, oral defense of dissertation, residency; for other advanced degree, comprehensive exam. *Entrance requirements:* For master's, minimum GPA of 2.75; for doctorate, GRE General Test or MAT, minimum graduate GPA of 3.0, teaching certificate, work experience; for other advanced degree, GRE General Test or MAT, teaching certificate. *Expenses:* Tuition, state resident: full-time $5690; part-time $284.50 per credit hour. Tuition, nonresident: full-time $13,030; part-time $651.50 per credit hour. *Required fees:* $1121; $672 per term. One-time fee: $40 full-time.

University of Arkansas at Monticello, School of Education, Monticello, AR 71656. Offers education (M Ed, MAT); educational leadership (M Ed). *Accreditation:* NCATE. Part-time and evening/weekend programs available. Postbaccalaureate distance learning degree programs offered (minimal on-campus study). *Degree requirements:* For master's, comprehensive exam. *Entrance requirements:* For master's, minimum GPA of 3.0. Additional exam requirements/recommendations for international students: Required—TOEFL (minimum score 550 paper-based). Electronic applications accepted.

University of Arkansas at Pine Bluff, School of Education, Pine Bluff, AR 71601-2799. Offers early childhood education (M Ed); secondary education (M Ed), including English education, mathematics education, physical education, science education, social studies education; teaching (MAT). *Accreditation:* NCATE. Part-time and evening/weekend programs available. *Degree requirements:* For master's, comprehensive exam. *Entrance requirements:* For master's, GRE, minimum GPA of 2.75, NTE or Standard Arkansas Teaching Certificate. *Faculty research:* Teacher certification, accreditation, assessment, standards, portfolio development, rehabilitation, technology.

University of Bridgeport, School of Education, Department of Education, Bridgeport, CT 06604. Offers education (MS); educational management (Ed D, Diploma), including intermediate administrator or supervisor (Diploma), leadership (Ed D); elementary education (MS, Diploma), including early childhood education, elementary education; middle school education (MS); music education (MS); remedial reading and language arts (Diploma); secondary education (MS, Diploma), including computer specialist (Diploma), international education (Diploma), reading specialist, secondary education. Part-time and evening/weekend programs available. *Faculty:* 12 full-time (5 women), 108 part-time/adjunct (60 women). *Students:* 155 full-time (108 women), 139 part-time (98 women); includes 48 minority (22 Black or African American, non-Hispanic/Latino; 9 Asian, non-Hispanic/Latino; 15 Hispanic/Latino; 2 Two or more races, non-Hispanic/Latino), 2 international. Average age 30. 306 applicants, 55% accepted, 107 enrolled. In 2013, 153 master's, 16 other advanced degrees awarded. *Degree requirements:* For master's, final exam, final project, or thesis; for doctorate, comprehensive exam, thesis/dissertation; for Diploma, thesis or alternative, final project. *Entrance requirements:* For master's, minimum undergraduate QPA of 2.67; for doctorate, GRE, MAT; for Diploma, GRE General Test or MAT, minimum graduate QPA of 3.0. Additional exam requirements/recommendations for international students: Recommended—TOEFL (minimum score 550 paper-based; 80 iBT), IELTS (minimum score 6.5). *Application deadline:* For fall admission, 8/1 priority date for domestic and international students; for spring admission, 12/1 priority date for domestic and international students. Applications are processed on a rolling basis. Application fee: $50. Electronic applications accepted. *Expenses:* Contact institution. *Financial support:* In 2013–14, 120 students received support. Fellowships, research assistantships, teaching assistantships, career-related internships or fieldwork, Federal Work-Study, and institutionally sponsored loans available. Support available to part-time students. Financial award application deadline: 6/1; financial award applicants required to submit FAFSA. *Faculty research:* Self-concept, internship assessment, stress and situational development, follow-up of graduation, trend analysis. *Unit head:* Dr. Allen P. Cook, Dean, 203-576-4192, Fax: 203-576-4200, E-mail: acook@bridgeport.edu. *Application contact:* Leanne Proctor, Director of Graduate Admissions, 203-576-4552, Fax: 203-576-4941, E-mail: admit@bridgeport.edu.

The University of British Columbia, Faculty of Education, Vancouver, BC V6T1Z4, Canada. Offers M Ed, M Sc, MA, MET, MHK, Ed D, PhD, Diploma. Part-time and evening/weekend programs available. Postbaccalaureate distance learning degree programs offered (no on-campus study). Terminal master's awarded for partial completion of doctoral program. *Degree requirements:* For master's, thesis (for some programs); for doctorate, comprehensive exam, thesis/dissertation. *Entrance requirements:* Additional exam requirements/recommendations for international students: Required—TOEFL. Electronic applications accepted. *Expenses:* Contact institution. *Faculty research:* Curriculum and pedagogy; school counseling psychology; educational administration; human kinetics; language and literacy education.

University of California, Berkeley, Graduate Division, School of Education, Berkeley, CA 94720-1500. Offers MA, PhD, MA/Credential, PhD/Credential, PhD/MA. Terminal master's awarded for partial completion of doctoral program. *Degree requirements:* For master's, exam or thesis; for doctorate, thesis/dissertation, oral qualifying exam (PhD). *Entrance requirements:* For master's and doctorate, GRE General Test, minimum undergraduate GPA of 3.0 during last 2 years, 3 letters of recommendation. *Faculty research:* Cognition and development; language, literacy and culture.

University of California, Berkeley, UC Berkeley Extension, Certificate Programs in Education, Berkeley, CA 94720-1500. Offers college admissions and career planning (Certificate); teaching English as a second language (Certificate).

University of California, Davis, Graduate Studies, Graduate Group in Education, Davis, CA 95616. Offers education (MA, Ed D); instructional studies (PhD); psychological studies (PhD); sociocultural studies (PhD). Ed D offered jointly with California State University, Fresno. Terminal master's awarded for partial completion of doctoral program. *Degree requirements:* For master's, comprehensive exam (for some programs), thesis (for some programs); for doctorate, thesis/dissertation. *Entrance requirements:* For master's and doctorate, GRE. Additional exam requirements/recommendations for international students: Required—TOEFL (minimum score 550 paper-based). Electronic applications accepted. *Faculty research:* Language and literacy, mathematics education, science education, teacher development, school psychology.

University of California, Irvine, Department of Education, Irvine, CA 92697. Offers educational administration (Ed D); educational administration and leadership (Ed D); elementary and secondary education (MAT). Part-time and evening/weekend programs available. *Students:* 254 full-time (194 women), 4 part-time (3 women); includes 125 minority (1 Black or African American, non-Hispanic/Latino; 69 Asian, non-Hispanic/Latino; 41 Hispanic/Latino; 2 Native Hawaiian or other Pacific Islander, non-Hispanic/Latino; 12 Two or more races, non-Hispanic/Latino), 11 international. Average age 28. 506 applicants, 70% accepted, 200 enrolled. In 2013, 133 master's, 17 doctorates awarded. *Degree requirements:* For doctorate, thesis/dissertation. *Entrance requirements:* For master's, GRE, minimum GPA of 3.0; for doctorate, GRE General Test, minimum GPA of 3.0. Additional exam requirements/recommendations for international students: Required—TOEFL (minimum score 550 paper-based). *Application deadline:* For fall admission, 1/2 priority date for domestic students, 1/2 for international students. Application fee: $80 ($100 for international students). Electronic applications accepted. *Financial support:* Fellowships, research assistantships with full tuition reimbursements, institutionally sponsored loans, traineeships, health care benefits, and unspecified assistantships available. Financial award application deadline: 3/1; financial award applicants required to submit FAFSA. *Faculty research:* Education technology, learning theory, social theory, cultural diversity, postmodernism. *Unit head:* Deborah L. Vandell, Dean, 949-824-8026, Fax: 949-824-3968, E-mail: dvandell@uci.edu. *Application contact:* Judi Conroy, Director of Student Services, 949-824-7465, Fax: 949-824-9103, E-mail: jconroy@uci.edu.
Website: http://www.gse.uci.edu/.

University of California, Los Angeles, Graduate Division, Graduate School of Education and Information Studies, Department of Education, Los Angeles, CA 90095. Offers M Ed, MA, Ed D, PhD. Evening/weekend programs available. *Degree requirements:* For master's, comprehensive exam; for doctorate, thesis/dissertation, oral and written qualifying exams. *Entrance requirements:* For master's, GRE General Test, minimum GPA of 3.0; for doctorate, GRE General Test, minimum undergraduate GPA of 3.0. Additional exam requirements/recommendations for international students: Required—TOEFL (minimum score 560 paper-based; 87 iBT). Electronic applications accepted.

University of California, Riverside, Graduate Division, Graduate School of Education, Riverside, CA 92521-0102. Offers autism (M Ed); diversity and equity (M Ed); education specialist (Credential); education, society and culture (MA, PhD); educational psychology (MA, PhD); general education (M Ed); higher education administration and policy (M Ed, PhD); multiple subject (Credential); reading (M Ed); school psychology (PhD); single subject (Credential); special education (M Ed, MA, PhD); TESOL (M Ed). *Faculty:* 22 full-time (11 women), 14 part-time/adjunct (10 women). *Students:* 218 full-time (148 women); includes 95 minority (10 Black or African American, non-Hispanic/Latino; 30 Asian, non-Hispanic/Latino; 49 Hispanic/Latino; 6 Two or more races, non-Hispanic/Latino), 12 international. Average age 31. 236 applicants, 66% accepted, 78 enrolled. In 2013, 66 master's, 13 doctorates, 86 other advanced degrees awarded. Terminal master's awarded for partial completion of doctoral program. *Degree requirements:* For master's, thesis optional, comprehensive exams or thesis (MA), case study or analytical report (M Ed); for doctorate, thesis/dissertation, written and oral qualifying exams, college teaching practicum. *Entrance requirements:* For master's, GRE General Test (for MA); CBEST and CSET (for M Ed in general education only), UCR Extension TESOL certificate (for M Ed with TESOL emphasis only); for doctorate, GRE General Test, writing sample; for Credential, CBEST, CSET. Additional exam requirements/recommendations for international students: Required—TOEFL (minimum score 550 paper-based; 80 iBT), IELTS (minimum score 7). *Application deadline:* For fall admission, 9/1 for domestic students, 5/1 for international students; for winter admission, 11/15 for domestic students, 7/1 for international students; for spring admission, 3/1 for domestic students, 10/1 for international students. Applications are processed on a rolling basis. Application fee: $80 ($100 for international students). Electronic applications accepted. *Financial support:* In 2013–14, 58 students received support, including 31 fellowships with full tuition reimbursements available, 11 research assistantships with full tuition reimbursements available (averaging $14,691 per year), 5 teaching assistantships with full tuition reimbursements available (averaging $17,655 per year); career-related internships or fieldwork, Federal Work-Study, institutionally sponsored loans, scholarships/grants, and unspecified assistantships also available. Financial award application deadline: 1/5. *Faculty research:* Responsiveness to intervention, faculty core, response to intervention of English language learners, advanced modeling techniques, study on social capital, trust, and motivation. *Total annual research expenditures:* $1.9 million. *Unit head:* Prof. Douglas Mitchell, Interim Dean and Professor, 951-827-5802, Fax: 951-827-3942, E-mail: douglas.mitchell@ucr.edu. *Application contact:* Prof. Michael Orosco, Assistant Professor and Graduate Advisor of Admissions, 951-827-6362, Fax: 951-827-3291, E-mail: edgrad@ucr.edu.
Website: http://www.education.ucr.edu/.

University of California, San Diego, Office of Graduate Studies, Program in Education Studies, La Jolla, CA 92093. Offers education (M Ed); educational leadership (Ed D); teaching and learning (M Ed, MA, Ed D), including bilingual education (M Ed), curriculum design (MA). Ed D offered jointly with California State University, San Marcos. *Students:* 66 full-time (46 women), 66 part-time (54 women); includes 66 minority (11 Black or African American, non-Hispanic/Latino; 6 American Indian or Alaska Native, non-Hispanic/Latino; 29 Asian, non-Hispanic/Latino; 20 Hispanic/Latino), 1 international. 91 applicants, 87% accepted, 64 enrolled. In 2013, 78 master's, 15 doctorates awarded. *Degree requirements:* For master's, thesis (for some programs), student teaching; for doctorate, thesis/dissertation. *Entrance requirements:* For master's, GRE General Test; CBEST and appropriate CSET exam (for select tracks), current teaching or educational assignment (for select tracks); for doctorate, GRE General Test, current teaching or educational assignment (for select tracks). Additional exam requirements/recommendations for international students: Required—TOEFL, IELTS. *Application deadline:* For fall admission, 2/4 for domestic students; for winter admission, 8/1 for domestic students; for summer admission, 2/4 for domestic students. Application fee: $80 ($100 for international students). Electronic applications accepted. *Expenses:* Tuition, state resident: full-time $11,220; part-time $1870 per quarter. Tuition, nonresident: full-time $26,322; part-time $4387 per quarter. *Required fees:* $519.50 per quarter. Part-time tuition and fees vary according to course load and program. *Financial support:* Fellowships and scholarships/grants available. Financial award applicants required to submit FAFSA. *Faculty research:* Language, culture and literacy development of deaf/hard of hearing children; equity issues in education; educational reform; evaluation, assessment, and research methodologies; distributed learning. *Unit head:* Alan J. Daly, Chair, 858-822-6472, E-mail: ajdaly@ucsd.edu. *Application contact:* Giselle Van Luit, Graduate Coordinator, 858-534-2958, E-mail: edsinfo@ucsd.edu.

University of California, Santa Barbara, Graduate Division, Gevirtz Graduate School of Education, Santa Barbara, CA 93106-9490. Offers counseling, clinical and school psychology (M Ed, MA, PhD, Credential), including clinical psychology (PhD), counseling psychology (MA, PhD), school psychology (M Ed, PhD), school psychology: pupil personnel services (Credential); education (M Ed, MA, PhD, Credential), including multiple subject teaching (Credential), single subject teaching (Credential), special education (Credential), teaching (M Ed); MA/PhD. *Accreditation:* APA (one or more programs are accredited). *Faculty:* 40 full-time (24 women), 2 part-time/adjunct (0 women). *Students:* 328 full-time (251 women); includes 91 minority (10 Black or African

American, non-Hispanic/Latino; 1 American Indian or Alaska Native, non-Hispanic/ Latino; 27 Asian, non-Hispanic/Latino; 52 Hispanic/Latino; 1 Native Hawaiian or other Pacific Islander, non-Hispanic/Latino), 28 international. Average age 31. 569 applicants, 35% accepted, 116 enrolled. In 2013, 120 master's, 41 doctorates, 76 other advanced degrees awarded. Terminal master's awarded for partial completion of doctoral program. *Degree requirements:* For master's, comprehensive exam (for some programs), thesis (for some programs); for doctorate, comprehensive exam (for some programs), thesis/dissertation. *Entrance requirements:* For master's and doctorate, GRE; for Credential, GRE or MAT, CSET, CBEST. Additional exam requirements/ recommendations for international students: Required—TOEFL (minimum score 550 paper-based; 80 iBT), IELTS (minimum score 7). *Application deadline:* Applications are processed on a rolling basis. Application fee: $80 ($100 for international students). Electronic applications accepted. *Expenses:* Tuition, state resident: part-time $5148.26 per quarter. Tuition, nonresident: part-time $10,182.26 per quarter. *Financial support:* In 2013–14, 245 students received support, including 380 fellowships with partial tuition reimbursements available (averaging $6,364 per year), 69 research assistantships with full and partial tuition reimbursements available (averaging $5,233 per year), 153 teaching assistantships with partial tuition reimbursements available (averaging $3,220 per year); career-related internships or fieldwork also available. Financial award applicants required to submit FAFSA. *Faculty research:* Needs of diverse students, school accountability and leadership, school violence, language learning and literacy, science/math education. *Total annual research expenditures:* $3.9 million. *Unit head:* Amy Meredith, Student and Academic Affairs Manager, 805-893-2137, Fax: 805-893-2588, E-mail: amyh@education.ucsb.edu. *Application contact:* Martiza Fuljencio, Student Affairs Officer, 805-893-2137, Fax: 805-893-2588, E-mail: maritza@ education.ucsb.edu.
Website: http://www.education.ucsb.edu/.

University of California, Santa Cruz, Division of Graduate Studies, Division of Social Sciences, Department of Education, Santa Cruz, CA 95064. Offers MA, PhD. Terminal master's awarded for partial completion of doctoral program. *Degree requirements:* For master's, thesis; for doctorate, thesis/dissertation. *Entrance requirements:* Additional exam requirements/recommendations for international students: Required—TOEFL (minimum score 550 paper-based; 83 iBT); Recommended—IELTS (minimum score 8). Electronic applications accepted. *Faculty research:* Bilingual/multicultural education, special education, curriculum and instruction, child development, gaps in the learning opportunities of underserved students, discovery of more effective practices.

University of Central Arkansas, Graduate School, College of Education, Conway, AR 72035-0001. Offers MAT, MS, MSE, Ed S, Graduate Certificate, PMC. *Accreditation:* NCATE. Part-time and evening/weekend programs available. Postbaccalaureate distance learning degree programs offered (minimal on-campus study). Terminal master's awarded for partial completion of doctoral program. *Degree requirements:* For master's, comprehensive exam, thesis optional, portfolio. *Entrance requirements:* For master's, GRE General Test, minimum GPA of 2.7. Additional exam requirements/ recommendations for international students: Required—TOEFL (minimum score 550 paper-based; 80 iBT). Electronic applications accepted.

University of Central Arkansas, Graduate School, College of Education, Department of Teaching and Learning, Graduate Program in Teaching, Conway, AR 72035-0001. Offers MAT. Part-time programs available. Postbaccalaureate distance learning degree programs offered (minimal on-campus study). *Degree requirements:* For master's, comprehensive exam, thesis optional. *Entrance requirements:* For master's, GRE General Test, minimum GPA of 2.7. Additional exam requirements/recommendations for international students: Required—TOEFL (minimum score 550 paper-based). Electronic applications accepted.

University of Central Arkansas, Graduate School, College of Education, Department of Teaching and Learning, Program in Advanced Studies of Teaching and Learning, Conway, AR 72035-0001. Offers MSE. Evening/weekend programs available. Postbaccalaureate distance learning degree programs offered (minimal on-campus study). *Entrance requirements:* For master's, GRE General Test, minimum GPA of 2.7. Additional exam requirements/recommendations for international students: Required—TOEFL (minimum score 550 paper-based). Electronic applications accepted.

University of Central Missouri, The Graduate School, Warrensburg, MO 6409. Offers accountancy (MA); accounting (MBA); applied mathematics (MS); aviation safety (MA); biology (MS); business administration (MBA); career and technical education leadership (MS); college student personnel administration (MS); communication (MA); computer science (MS); counseling (MS); criminal justice (MS); educational leadership (Ed D); educational technology (MS); elementary and early childhood education (MSE); English (MA); environmental studies (MA); finance (MBA); history (MA); human services/ educational technology (Ed S); human services/learning resources (Ed S); human services/professional counseling (Ed S); industrial hygiene (MS); industrial management (MS); information systems (MBA); information technology (MS); kinesiology (MS); library science and information services (MS); literacy education (MSE); marketing (MBA); mathematics (MS); music (MA); occupational safety management (MS); psychology (MS); rural family nursing (MS); school administration (MSE); social gerontology (MS); sociology (MA); special education (MSE); speech language pathology (MS); superintendency (Ed S); teaching (MAT); teaching English as a second language (MA); technology (MS); technology management (PhD); theatre (MA). Part-time programs available. *Faculty:* 233. *Students:* 890 full-time (396 women), 1,486 part-time (1,001 women); includes 192 minority (97 Black or African American, non-Hispanic/Latino; 9 American Indian or Alaska Native, non-Hispanic/Latino; 32 Asian, non-Hispanic/Latino; 40 Hispanic/Latino; 3 Native Hawaiian or other Pacific Islander, non-Hispanic/Latino; 11 Two or more races, non-Hispanic/Latino), 539 international. Average age 31. 1,953 applicants, 75% accepted. In 2013, 719 master's, 58 other advanced degrees awarded. *Degree requirements:* For master's and Ed S, comprehensive exam (for some programs), thesis (for some programs). *Entrance requirements:* Additional exam requirements/recommendations for international students: Required—TOEFL (minimum score 550 paper-based; 79 iBT). *Application deadline:* For fall admission, 6/1 for domestic students; for spring admission, 10/1 for domestic and international students. Applications are processed on a rolling basis. Application fee: $30 ($75 for international students). Electronic applications accepted. *Expenses:* Tuition, state resident: full-time $7326; part-time $276.25 per credit hour. Tuition, nonresident: full-time $13,956; part-time $552.50 per credit hour. *Required fees:* $29 per credit hour. *Financial support:* In 2013–14, 118 students received support, including 271 research assistantships with full and partial tuition reimbursements available (averaging $7,500 per year), 109 teaching assistantships with full and partial tuition reimbursements available (averaging $7,500 per year); career-related internships or fieldwork, Federal Work-Study, scholarships/ grants, and administrative and laboratory assistantships also available. Support available to part-time students. Financial award application deadline: 3/1; financial award applicants required to submit FAFSA. *Unit head:* Dr. Joseph Vaughn, Assistant Provost for Research/Dean, 660-543-4092, Fax: 660-543-4778, E-mail: vaughn@ ucmo.edu. *Application contact:* Brittany Lawrence, Graduate Student Services Coordinator, 660-543-4621, Fax: 660-543-4778, E-mail: gradinfo@ucmo.edu.
Website: http://www.ucmo.edu/graduate/.

University of Central Oklahoma, The Jackson College of Graduate Studies, College of Education and Professional Studies, Edmond, OK 73034-5209. Offers M Ed, MA, MS. *Accreditation:* NCATE. Part-time programs available. *Faculty:* 51 full-time (31 women), 67 part-time/adjunct (40 women). *Students:* 342 full-time (275 women), 735 part-time (592 women); includes 278 minority (126 Black or African American, non-Hispanic/ Latino; 34 American Indian or Alaska Native, non-Hispanic/Latino; 16 Asian, non-Hispanic/Latino; 54 Hispanic/Latino; 1 Native Hawaiian or other Pacific Islander, non-Hispanic/Latino; 47 Two or more races, non-Hispanic/Latino), 93 international. Average age 33. 490 applicants, 87% accepted, 273 enrolled. In 2013, 374 master's awarded. *Degree requirements:* For master's, comprehensive exam (for some programs), thesis (for some programs). *Entrance requirements:* For master's, GRE. Additional exam requirements/recommendations for international students: Required—TOEFL (minimum score 550 paper-based; 79 iBT), IELTS (minimum score 6.5). *Application deadline:* For fall admission, 7/1 for international students; for spring admission, 11/1 for international students. Applications are processed on a rolling basis. Application fee: $50. Electronic applications accepted. *Expenses:* Tuition, state resident: full-time $4137; part-time $206.85 per credit hour. Tuition, nonresident: full-time $10,359; part-time $517.95 per credit hour. *Required fees:* $481. Tuition and fees vary according to course load and program. *Financial support:* In 2013–14, 228 students received support, including 34 research assistantships with partial tuition reimbursements available (averaging $4,304 per year), 6 teaching assistantships with tuition reimbursements available (averaging $7,493 per year); career-related internships or fieldwork, scholarships/grants, tuition waivers (partial), and unspecified assistantships also available. Financial award application deadline: 3/31; financial award applicants required to submit FAFSA. *Unit head:* Dr. James Machell, Dean, 405-974-5701, Fax: 405-974-3851. *Application contact:* Dr. Richard Bernard, Dean, Jackson College of Graduate Studies, 405-974-3493, Fax: 405-974-3852, E-mail: gradcoll@uco.edu.
Website: http://www.uco.edu/ceps/.

University of Cincinnati, Graduate School, College of Education, Criminal Justice, and Human Services, Cincinnati, OH 45221. Offers M Ed, MA, MS, Ed D, PhD, CAGS, Certificate, Ed S. *Accreditation:* NCATE. Part-time programs available. Postbaccalaureate distance learning degree programs offered (no on-campus study). *Degree requirements:* For master's, comprehensive exam (for some programs), thesis (for some programs); for doctorate, comprehensive exam, thesis/dissertation. *Entrance requirements:* For master's and doctorate, GRE. Additional exam requirements/ recommendations for international students: Required—TOEFL (minimum score 550 paper-based), OEPT 3. Electronic applications accepted. *Faculty research:* Alcohol and drug prevention, family-based prevention, criminal justice, literacy, urban education.

University of Colorado Boulder, Graduate School, School of Education, Boulder, CO 80309. Offers MA, PhD. *Accreditation:* NCATE. *Faculty:* 31 full-time (15 women). *Students:* 154 full-time (104 women), 178 part-time (149 women); includes 102 minority (10 Black or African American, non-Hispanic/Latino; 2 American Indian or Alaska Native, non-Hispanic/Latino; 7 Asian, non-Hispanic/Latino; 73 Hispanic/Latino; 3 Native Hawaiian or other Pacific Islander, non-Hispanic/Latino; 7 Two or more races, non-Hispanic/Latino), 7 international. Average age 34. 246 applicants, 51% accepted, 66 enrolled. In 2013, 148 master's, 13 doctorates awarded. Terminal master's awarded for partial completion of doctoral program. *Degree requirements:* For master's, comprehensive exam, thesis or alternative; for doctorate, one foreign language, comprehensive exam, thesis/dissertation. *Entrance requirements:* For master's, GRE General Test or MAT, minimum undergraduate GPA of 2.75; for doctorate, GRE General Test. *Application deadline:* For fall admission, 2/1 for domestic students, 12/1 for international students; for spring admission, 9/1 for domestic and international students. Application fee: $50 ($60 for international students). Electronic applications accepted. *Financial support:* In 2013–14, 414 students received support, including 47 fellowships (averaging $3,334 per year), 79 research assistantships with full and partial tuition reimbursements available (averaging $28,144 per year), 49 teaching assistantships with full and partial tuition reimbursements available (averaging $15,687 per year); institutionally sponsored loans, scholarships/grants, health care benefits, and unspecified assistantships also available. Financial award applicants required to submit FAFSA. *Faculty research:* Teacher education, classroom instruction, minority education, educational reform, bilingual/bicultural education. *Total annual research expenditures:* $8 million.
Website: http://www.colorado.edu/education/.

University of Colorado Colorado Springs, College of Education, Colorado Springs, CO 80933-7150. Offers counseling and human services (MA); curriculum and instruction (MA); educational administration (MA); educational leadership (MA, PhD); special education (MA). *Accreditation:* ACA; NCATE. Part-time and evening/weekend programs available. Postbaccalaureate distance learning degree programs offered (minimal on-campus study). *Faculty:* 25 full-time (17 women), 39 part-time/adjunct (29 women). *Students:* 220 full-time (146 women), 237 part-time (163 women); includes 86 minority (18 Black or African American, non-Hispanic/Latino; 3 American Indian or Alaska Native, non-Hispanic/Latino; 11 Asian, non-Hispanic/Latino; 46 Hispanic/Latino; 8 Two or more races, non-Hispanic/Latino), 16 international. Average age 35. 182 applicants, 88% accepted, 118 enrolled. In 2013, 140 master's, 8 doctorates awarded. *Degree requirements:* For master's, comprehensive exam, thesis or alternative, microcomputer proficiency; for doctorate, comprehensive exam, thesis/dissertation, research lab. *Entrance requirements:* For master's, GRE General Test. Additional exam requirements/ recommendations for international students: Recommended—TOEFL. *Application deadline:* For fall admission, 2/28 priority date for domestic students, 2/28 for international students; for spring admission, 10/15 for domestic and international students. Applications are processed on a rolling basis. Application fee: $60 ($75 for international students). *Expenses:* Tuition, state resident: full-time $8882; part-time $1622 per course. Tuition, nonresident: full-time $17,435; part-time $3048 per course. One-time fee: $100. Tuition and fees vary according to course load, degree level, campus/location and program. *Financial support:* In 2013–14, 23 students received support, including 23 fellowships (averaging $1,577 per year); career-related internships or fieldwork, Federal Work-Study, and scholarships/grants also available. Support available to part-time students. Financial award application deadline: 3/1; financial award applicants required to submit FAFSA. *Faculty research:* Linguistically diverse education (LDE), educational policy, evidence-based reading and writing instruction, relational and social aggression, positive behavior supports (PBS), inclusive schooling, K-12 education policy. *Total annual research expenditures:* $136,574. *Unit head:* Dr. Mary Snyder, Dean, 719-255-3701, Fax: 719-262-4133, E-mail: msnyder3@uccs.edu. *Application contact:* Juliane Field, Director, 719-255-4526, Fax: 719-255-4110, E-mail: jfield@uccs.edu.
Website: http://www.uccs.edu/coe.

University of Colorado Denver, School of Education and Human Development, Denver, CO 80204. Offers MA, MS Ed, Ed D, PhD, Ed S. *Accreditation:* NCATE. Part-time and evening/weekend programs available. Postbaccalaureate distance learning degree programs offered (no on-campus study). *Faculty:* 57 full-time (38 women), 88 part-time/adjunct (62 women). *Students:* 947 full-time (756 women), 427 part-time (352 women); includes 192 minority (27 Black or African American, non-Hispanic/Latino; 4 American Indian or Alaska Native, non-Hispanic/Latino; 30 Asian, non-Hispanic/Latino; 112 Hispanic/Latino; 19 Two or more races, non-Hispanic/Latino), 31 international.

Average age 33. 616 applicants, 69% accepted, 316 enrolled. In 2013, 441 master's, 20 doctorates, 25 other advanced degrees awarded. *Degree requirements:* For master's and Ed S, comprehensive exam (for some programs); for doctorate, comprehensive exam, thesis/dissertation. *Entrance requirements:* Additional exam requirements/recommendations for international students: Required—TOEFL (minimum score 537 paper-based; 75 iBT); Recommended—IELTS (minimum score 6.5). Application fee: $50 ($75 for international students). Electronic applications accepted. *Expenses:* Contact institution. *Financial support:* In 2013–14, 101 students received support. Fellowships, research assistantships, teaching assistantships, Federal Work-Study, institutionally sponsored loans, scholarships/grants, and traineeships available. Financial award application deadline: 4/1; financial award applicants required to submit FAFSA. *Faculty research:* Educational equity: race, class, culture, power and privilege; analytic approaches to educational program effectiveness and measuring student learning; early childhood special education/early intervention policies; recruiting and retention of African-American teachers; secondary and postsecondary institutions; accountability systems to improve public education. *Total annual research expenditures:* $5.3 million. *Unit head:* Rebecca Kantor, Dean, 303-315-6343, E-mail: rebecca.kantor@ucdenver.edu. *Application contact:* Student Services Center, 303-315-6300, Fax: 303-315-6311, E-mail: education@ucdenver.edu.
Website: http://www.ucdenver.edu/academics/colleges/SchoolOfEducation/Pages/home.aspx.

University of Connecticut, Graduate School, Neag School of Education, Storrs, CT 06269. Offers MA, DPT, Ed D, PhD, Post-Master's Certificate. *Accreditation:* NCATE. Terminal master's awarded for partial completion of doctoral program. *Degree requirements:* For master's, comprehensive exam, thesis or alternative; for doctorate, thesis/dissertation. *Entrance requirements:* For doctorate, GRE General Test. Additional exam requirements/recommendations for international students: Required—TOEFL (minimum score 550 paper-based). Electronic applications accepted.

University of Delaware, College of Education and Human Development, School of Education, Newark, DE 19716. Offers education (PhD); educational leadership (Ed D); higher education (M Ed); instruction (MI); reading (M Ed); school leadership (M Ed); school psychology (MA, Ed S); teaching English as a second language (TESL) (MA). *Accreditation:* NCATE. Part-time and evening/weekend programs available. Terminal master's awarded for partial completion of doctoral program. *Degree requirements:* For master's, comprehensive exam (for some programs), thesis (for some programs); for doctorate, comprehensive exam (for some programs), thesis/dissertation. *Entrance requirements:* For master's and doctorate, GRE, 3 letters of recommendation. Additional exam requirements/recommendations for international students: Required—TOEFL (minimum score 600 paper-based). Electronic applications accepted. *Faculty research:* Teacher education; curriculum theory and development; community based education models, educational leadership.

University of Denver, Morgridge College of Education, Denver, CO 80208. Offers child, family and school psychology (MA, PhD, Ed S); counseling psychology (MA, PhD); curriculum and instruction (MA, Ed D, PhD); curriculum instruction and teaching (Certificate); early childhood special education (MA); educational leadership and policy studies (MA, Ed D, PhD, Certificate); higher education (MA, Ed D, PhD); law librarianship (Certificate); library and information science (MLIS); research methods and statistics (MA, PhD). *Accreditation:* ALA; APA (one or more programs are accredited). Part-time and evening/weekend programs available. Postbaccalaureate distance learning degree programs offered (no on-campus study). *Faculty:* 35 full-time (21 women), 63 part-time/adjunct (43 women). *Students:* 435 full-time (332 women), 414 part-time (297 women); includes 194 minority (45 Black or African American, non-Hispanic/Latino; 9 American Indian or Alaska Native, non-Hispanic/Latino; 16 Asian, non-Hispanic/Latino; 96 Hispanic/Latino; 2 Native Hawaiian or other Pacific Islander, non-Hispanic/Latino; 26 Two or more races, non-Hispanic/Latino), 14 international. Average age 32. 672 applicants, 61% accepted, 193 enrolled. In 2013, 248 master's, 30 doctorates, 130 other advanced degrees awarded. Terminal master's awarded for partial completion of doctoral program. *Degree requirements:* For master's, comprehensive exam; for doctorate, 2 foreign languages, comprehensive exam, thesis/dissertation. *Entrance requirements:* For master's and doctorate, GRE General Test or GMAT. Additional exam requirements/recommendations for international students: Required—TOEFL (minimum score 550 paper-based; 80 iBT). *Application deadline:* Applications are processed on a rolling basis. Application fee: $65. Electronic applications accepted. *Financial support:* In 2013–14, 706 students received support, including 54 research assistantships with full and partial tuition reimbursements available (averaging $15,599 per year), 77 teaching assistantships with full and partial tuition reimbursements available (averaging $12,804 per year); career-related internships or fieldwork, Federal Work-Study, institutionally sponsored loans, scholarships/grants, and unspecified assistantships also available. Support available to part-time students. Financial award application deadline: 2/15; financial award applicants required to submit FAFSA. *Faculty research:* Principal and teacher preparation, development and assessments, gifted education, service-learning, early childhood, mathematics education, access to higher education. *Total annual research expenditures:* $6.3 million. *Unit head:* Dr. Karen Riley, Interim Dean, 303-871-3665, E-mail: karen.riley@du.edu. *Application contact:* Jodi Dye, Assistant Director of Admissions, 303-871-2510, E-mail: jodi.dye@du.edu.
Website: http://morgridge.du.edu/.

University of Detroit Mercy, College of Liberal Arts and Education, Department of Education, Detroit, MI 48221. Offers curriculum and instruction (MA); educational administration (MA); special education (MA), including emotionally impaired, learning disabilities. Part-time and evening/weekend programs available.

The University of Findlay, Office of Graduate Admissions, Findlay, OH 45840-3653. Offers athletic training (MAT); business (MBA), including health care management, hospitality management, organizational leadership, public management; education (MA Ed), including administration, children's literature, early childhood, human resource development, reading, science, special education, technology; environmental, safety and health management (MSEM); health informatics (MS); occupational therapy (MOT); pharmacy (Pharm D); physical therapy (DPT); physician assistant (MPA); rhetoric and writing (MA); teaching English to speakers of other languages (TESOL) and bilingual education (MA). Part-time and evening/weekend programs available. Postbaccalaureate distance learning degree programs offered (no on-campus study). *Faculty:* 209 full-time (98 women), 69 part-time/adjunct (38 women). *Students:* 551 full-time (332 women), 457 part-time (276 women); includes 77 minority (37 Black or African American, non-Hispanic/Latino; 1 American Indian or Alaska Native, non-Hispanic/Latino; 15 Asian, non-Hispanic/Latino; 23 Hispanic/Latino; 1 Native Hawaiian or other Pacific Islander, non-Hispanic/Latino), 135 international. Average age 28. 637 applicants, 66% accepted, 241 enrolled. In 2013, 267 master's, 91 doctorates awarded. *Degree requirements:* For master's, thesis, cumulative project, capstone project. *Entrance requirements:* For master's, GRE/GMAT, bachelor's degree from accredited institution, minimum undergraduate GPA of 2.5 in last 64 hours of course work; for doctorate, GRE, minimum cumulative GPA of 3.0. Additional exam requirements/recommendations for international students: Required—TOEFL (minimum score 80 iBT). *Application deadline:* Applications are processed on a rolling basis. Application fee: $25. Electronic

applications accepted. *Expenses: Required fees:* $146 per semester. Tuition and fees vary according to degree level and program. *Financial support:* In 2013–14, 11 research assistantships with full and partial tuition reimbursements (averaging $4,000 per year), 10 teaching assistantships with full and partial tuition reimbursements (averaging $3,600 per year) were awarded; career-related internships or fieldwork, Federal Work-Study, health care benefits, and unspecified assistantships also available. Financial award application deadline: 4/1; financial award applicants required to submit FAFSA. *Unit head:* Christopher M. Harris, Director of Admissions, 419-434-4347, E-mail: harrisc1@findlay.edu. *Application contact:* Emily Ickes, Graduate Admissions Counselor, 419-434-6933, Fax: 419-434-4898, E-mail: ickese@findlay.edu.
Website: http://www.findlay.edu/admissions/graduate/Pages/default.aspx.

University of Florida, Graduate School, College of Education, Gainesville, FL 32611. Offers M Ed, MAE, Ed D, PhD, Ed S, PhD/JD. *Accreditation:* NCATE. Part-time and evening/weekend programs available. Postbaccalaureate distance learning degree programs offered (minimal on-campus study). Terminal master's awarded for partial completion of doctoral program. *Degree requirements:* For master's, comprehensive exam (for some programs), thesis (for some programs); for doctorate, comprehensive exam (for some programs), thesis/dissertation (for some programs), capstone project (for professional practice). *Entrance requirements:* For master's and doctorate, GRE General Test, minimum GPA of 3.0; for Ed S, GRE General Test. Additional exam requirements/recommendations for international students: Required—TOEFL (minimum score 550 paper-based; 80 iBT), IELTS (minimum score 6). Electronic applications accepted. *Expenses:* Tuition, state resident: full-time $12,640. Tuition, nonresident: full-time $30,000. *Faculty research:* Early childhood, child and adolescents, diverse learners, race/ethnicity issues, teacher education, professional development, language and literacy development, policy development.

University of Georgia, College of Education, Athens, GA 30602. Offers M Ed, MA, MA Ed, MAT, MM Ed, MS, Ed D, PhD, Ed S. *Accreditation:* NCATE. *Degree requirements:* For doctorate, thesis/dissertation. *Entrance requirements:* For doctorate, GRE General Test. Electronic applications accepted.

University of Great Falls, Graduate Studies, Program in Education, Great Falls, MT 59405. Offers M Ed. Part-time and evening/weekend programs available. *Degree requirements:* For master's, thesis, extensive portfolio. *Entrance requirements:* For master's, GRE General Test or MAT, 3 letters of recommendation, BA or BS from accredited college, teacher certification, interview. Additional exam requirements/recommendations for international students: Required—TOEFL (minimum score 500 paper-based). Electronic applications accepted. *Faculty research:* Native American attitudinal research.

University of Guam, Office of Graduate Studies, School of Education, Mangilao, GU 96923. Offers M Ed, MA. *Accreditation:* NCATE. Part-time programs available. *Degree requirements:* For master's, comprehensive oral and written exams. *Entrance requirements:* For master's, GRE General Test. Additional exam requirements/recommendations for international students: Required—TOEFL. *Faculty research:* Multicultural issues, computerized student advising.

University of Hartford, College of Education, Nursing, and Health Professions, West Hartford, CT 06117-1599. Offers M Ed, MS, MSN, MSPT, DPT, Ed D, CAGS, Sixth Year Certificate. *Accreditation:* NCATE. Part-time and evening/weekend programs available. *Degree requirements:* For doctorate, thesis/dissertation; for other advanced degree, comprehensive exam or research project. *Entrance requirements:* For doctorate, MAT. Additional exam requirements/recommendations for international students: Required—TOEFL (minimum score 550 paper-based). Electronic applications accepted. *Expenses:* Contact institution.

University of Hawaii at Hilo, Program in Education, Hilo, HI 96720-4091. Offers M Ed. Part-time and evening/weekend programs available. *Faculty:* 5 full-time (all women). *Students:* 20 part-time (16 women); includes 14 minority (7 Asian, non-Hispanic/Latino; 1 Hispanic/Latino; 3 Native Hawaiian or other Pacific Islander, non-Hispanic/Latino; 3 Two or more races, non-Hispanic/Latino). Average age 38. 1 applicant. In 2013, 23 master's awarded. *Entrance requirements:* Additional exam requirements/recommendations for international students: Required—TOEFL, IELTS. *Application deadline:* For fall admission, 2/1 priority date for domestic students, 1/1 priority date for international students; for spring admission, 10/15 priority date for domestic students, 10/1 priority date for international students. Application fee: $50. Electronic applications accepted. *Expenses:* Tuition, state resident: full-time $4668. Tuition, nonresident: full-time $10,704. Tuition and fees vary according to course load and program. *Financial support:* Application deadline: 3/1; applicants required to submit FAFSA. *Unit head:* Jan Zulich, Program Chair, 808-932-7102, E-mail: jzulich@hawaii.edu. *Application contact:* UH Hilo Admissions Office, 808-932-7446, Fax: 808-932-7459, E-mail: uhhadm@hawaii.edu.
Website: http://hilo.hawaii.edu/depts/education/MEdProgram.php.

University of Hawaii at Hilo, Program in Teaching, Hilo, HI 96720-4091. Offers MA. *Faculty:* 6 full-time (all women). *Students:* 29 full-time (21 women); includes 21 minority (1 American Indian or Alaska Native, non-Hispanic/Latino; 6 Asian, non-Hispanic/Latino; 3 Hispanic/Latino; 1 Native Hawaiian or other Pacific Islander, non-Hispanic/Latino; 10 Two or more races, non-Hispanic/Latino). Average age 30. 41 applicants, 71% accepted, 29 enrolled. *Entrance requirements:* Additional exam requirements/recommendations for international students: Required—TOEFL, IELTS. *Application deadline:* For fall admission, 2/1 priority date for domestic students. Application fee: $50. Electronic applications accepted. *Expenses:* Tuition, state resident: full-time $4668. Tuition, nonresident: full-time $10,704. Tuition and fees vary according to course load and program. *Financial support:* Application deadline: 3/1; applicants required to submit FAFSA. *Unit head:* Jan Zulich, Program Chair, 808-932-7102, Fax: 808-932-7098, E-mail: jzulich@hawaii.edu. *Application contact:* UH Hilo Admissions Office, 808-932-7446, Fax: 808-932-7459, E-mail: uhhadm@hawaii.edu.
Website: http://hilo.hawaii.edu/depts/education/.

University of Hawaii at Manoa, Graduate Division, College of Education, Honolulu, HI 96822. Offers M Ed, M Ed T, MS, Ed D, PhD, Graduate Certificate. *Accreditation:* NCATE. Part-time and evening/weekend programs available. *Entrance requirements:* Additional exam requirements/recommendations for international students: Required—TOEFL or IELTS.

University of Houston, College of Education, Houston, TX 77204. Offers M Ed, Ed D, PhD. *Accreditation:* NCATE. Part-time programs available. *Degree requirements:* For master's, comprehensive exam or thesis; for doctorate, comprehensive exam, thesis/dissertation. *Entrance requirements:* For master's, GRE General Test, transcripts, 3 letters of recommendation, curriculum vita, goal statement; for doctorate, GRE General Test, transcripts, 3 letters of recommendation, curriculum vita, goal statement, writing sample, interview. Additional exam requirements/recommendations for international students: Required—TOEFL (minimum score 550 paper-based). Electronic applications accepted.

University of Houston–Clear Lake, School of Education, Houston, TX 77058-1002. Offers MS, Ed D. *Accreditation:* NCATE. Part-time and evening/weekend programs available. *Degree requirements:* For master's, thesis optional; for doctorate, comprehensive exam, thesis/dissertation. *Entrance requirements:* For master's, GRE or

minimum GPA of 3.0 in last 60 hours; for doctorate, GRE, master's degree, letters of reference. Additional exam requirements/recommendations for international students: Required—TOEFL (minimum score 550 paper-based). Electronic applications accepted.

University of Houston–Victoria, School of Education and Human Development, Victoria, TX 77901-4450. Offers administration and supervision (M Ed); adult and higher education (M Ed); counseling (M Ed); curriculum and instruction (M Ed); special education (M Ed). Part-time and evening/weekend programs available. Postbaccalaureate distance learning degree programs offered (minimal on-campus study). *Faculty:* 22 full-time (19 women). *Students:* 56 full-time (52 women), 325 part-time (274 women); includes 211 minority (113 Black or African American, non-Hispanic/Latino; 2 American Indian or Alaska Native, non-Hispanic/Latino; 16 Asian, non-Hispanic/Latino; 68 Hispanic/Latino; 12 Two or more races, non-Hispanic/Latino), 3 international. *Degree requirements:* For master's, comprehensive exam, project or thesis. *Entrance requirements:* For master's, GRE General Test. Additional exam requirements/recommendations for international students: Required—TOEFL. *Application deadline:* For fall admission, 6/1 for international students; for spring admission, 10/1 for international students. Applications are processed on a rolling basis. Application fee: $0. Electronic applications accepted. *Expenses:* Tuition, state resident: full-time $4534; part-time $251 per credit hour. Tuition, nonresident: full-time $10,906; part-time $606 per contact hour. *Required fees:* $68 per semester hour. Tuition and fees vary according to course load. *Financial support:* In 2013–14, research assistantships with partial tuition reimbursements (averaging $2,000 per year), teaching assistantships with partial tuition reimbursements (averaging $2,000 per year) were awarded; Federal Work-Study, scholarships/grants, and unspecified assistantships also available. Support available to part-time students. Financial award application deadline: 4/15; financial award applicants required to submit FAFSA. *Faculty research:* Reading and language arts education, evaluation and diagnosis of special children's abilities. *Unit head:* Freddie W. Litton, Dean, 361-570-4260, Fax: 361-580-5580. *Application contact:* Sandy Hybner, Senior Recruitment Coordinator, 361-570-4252, Fax: 361-580-5580, E-mail: hybners@uhv.edu.
Website: http://www.uhv.edu/edu/.

University of Idaho, College of Graduate Studies, College of Education, Moscow, ID 83844-3080. Offers M Ed, MS, MSAT, DAT, Ed D, PhD, Ed S. *Accreditation:* NCATE. *Faculty:* 52 full-time, 14 part-time/adjunct. *Students:* 141 full-time (85 women), 331 part-time (212 women). Average age 39. In 2013, 151 master's, 40 doctorates, 39 other advanced degrees awarded. *Degree requirements:* For doctorate, thesis/dissertation. *Entrance requirements:* For master's, minimum GPA of 2.8; for doctorate, minimum undergraduate GPA of 2.8, 3.0 graduate. Additional exam requirements/recommendations for international students: Required—TOEFL (minimum score 550 paper-based). *Application deadline:* For fall admission, 8/1 for domestic students; for spring admission, 12/15 for domestic students. Applications are processed on a rolling basis. Application fee: $60. Electronic applications accepted. *Expenses:* Tuition, state resident: full-time $5596; part-time $363 per credit hour. Tuition, nonresident: full-time $18,672; part-time $1089 per credit hour. *Financial support:* Teaching assistantships and Federal Work-Study available. Support available to part-time students. Financial award applicants required to submit FAFSA. *Faculty research:* Technology integration, curricular development for cooperative environments, increasing science literacy, best practices for online pedagogy. *Unit head:* Dr. Corinne Mantle-Bromley, Dean, 208-885-6772, E-mail: coe@uidaho.edu. *Application contact:* Stephanie Thomas, Graduate Recruitment Coordinator, 208-885-4001, Fax: 208-885-4406, E-mail: gadms@uidaho.edu.
Website: http://www.uidaho.edu/ed/.

University of Illinois at Chicago, Graduate College, College of Education, Chicago, IL 60607-7128. Offers M Ed, Ed D, PhD. Part-time and evening/weekend programs available. *Faculty:* 53 full-time (32 women), 23 part-time/adjunct (18 women). *Students:* 258 full-time (190 women), 424 part-time (313 women); includes 279 minority (125 Black or African American, non-Hispanic/Latino; 36 Asian, non-Hispanic/Latino; 105 Hispanic/Latino; 13 Two or more races, non-Hispanic/Latino), 25 international. Average age 33. 422 applicants, 54% accepted, 180 enrolled. In 2013, 199 master's, 40 doctorates awarded. Terminal master's awarded for partial completion of doctoral program. *Degree requirements:* For doctorate, thesis/dissertation. *Entrance requirements:* For master's, minimum GPA of 2.75; for doctorate, GRE General Test, minimum GPA of 2.75. Additional exam requirements/recommendations for international students: Required—TOEFL. *Application deadline:* For fall admission, 1/9 for domestic and international students; for spring admission, 10/1 for domestic and international students. Applications are processed on a rolling basis. Application fee: $40 ($50 for international students). Electronic applications accepted. *Expenses:* Tuition, state resident: full-time $11,066; part-time $3689 per term. Tuition, nonresident: full-time $23,064; part-time $7688 per term. *Required fees:* $3004; $1190 per term. Tuition and fees vary according to course level and program. *Financial support:* In 2013–14, 118 students received support, including 5 fellowships with full tuition reimbursements available; research assistantships with full tuition reimbursements available, teaching assistantships with full tuition reimbursements available, career-related internships or fieldwork, Federal Work-Study, institutionally sponsored loans, traineeships, tuition waivers (full), and unspecified assistantships also available. Support available to part-time students. Financial award application deadline: 3/1; financial award applicants required to submit FAFSA. *Faculty research:* Teaching and learning, program design, school and classroom organization with emphasis on urban settings. *Unit head:* Prof. Alfred Tatum, Interim Dean, 312-996-5641, E-mail: atatum1@uic.edu. *Application contact:* Receptionist, 312-413-2550, E-mail: gradcoll@uic.edu.
Website: http://education.uic.edu/.

University of Illinois at Springfield, Graduate Programs, College of Education and Human Services, Springfield, IL 62703-5407. Offers MA, CAS, Graduate Certificate. Part-time and evening/weekend programs available. Postbaccalaureate distance learning degree programs offered (no on-campus study). *Faculty:* 18 full-time (10 women), 15 part-time/adjunct (9 women). *Students:* 78 full-time (65 women), 268 part-time (208 women); includes 63 minority (47 Black or African American, non-Hispanic/Latino; 2 American Indian or Alaska Native, non-Hispanic/Latino; 1 Asian, non-Hispanic/Latino; 7 Hispanic/Latino; 6 Two or more races, non-Hispanic/Latino), 1 international. Average age 34. 171 applicants, 40% accepted, 63 enrolled. In 2013, 134 master's, 9 other advanced degrees awarded. *Entrance requirements:* Additional exam requirements/recommendations for international students: Required—TOEFL (minimum score 500 paper-based; 61 iBT). Application fee: $60 ($75 for international students). Electronic applications accepted. *Expenses:* Tuition, state resident: full-time $7440. Tuition, nonresident: full-time $15,744. *Required fees:* $2985.60. *Financial support:* In 2013–14, fellowships with full tuition reimbursements (averaging $9,900 per year), research assistantships with full tuition reimbursements (averaging $9,550 per year), teaching assistantships with full tuition reimbursements (averaging $9,700 per year) were awarded; career-related internships or fieldwork, Federal Work-Study, scholarships/grants, health care benefits, and unspecified assistantships also available. Support available to part-time students. Financial award application deadline: 11/15; financial award applicants required to submit FAFSA. *Unit head:* Dr. Hanfu Mi, Dean, 217-206-6784, Fax: 217-206-6775, E-mail: hmi2@uis.edu. *Application contact:* Dr. Lynn Pardie, Office of Graduate Studies, 800-252-8533, Fax: 217-206-7623, E-mail: lpard1@uis.edu.

University of Illinois at Urbana–Champaign, Graduate College, College of Education, Champaign, IL 61820. Offers Ed M, MA, MS, Ed D, PhD, CAS, MBA/M Ed. Part-time programs available. Postbaccalaureate distance learning degree programs offered (no on-campus study). *Students:* 800. Application fee: $75 ($90 for international students). *Unit head:* Mary A. Kalantzis, Dean, 217-333-0960, Fax: 217-333-5847, E-mail: kalantzi@illinois.edu. *Application contact:* Gregory S. Harman, Admissions Support Staff, 217-244-4637.
Website: http://education.illinois.edu/.

University of Indianapolis, Graduate Programs, School of Education, Indianapolis, IN 46227-3697. Offers art education (MAT); biology (MAT); chemistry (MAT); curriculum and instruction (MA); earth sciences (MAT); education (MA, MAT); educational leadership (MA); elementary education (MA); English (MAT); French (MAT); math (MAT); physical education (MAT); physics (MAT); secondary education (MA), including art education, education, English education, social studies education; social studies (MAT); Spanish (MAT). *Accreditation:* NCATE. Part-time and evening/weekend programs available. *Faculty:* 5 full-time (4 women), 2 part-time/adjunct (1 woman). *Students:* 19 full-time (9 women), 54 part-time (27 women); includes 13 minority (5 Black or African American, non-Hispanic/Latino; 1 Asian, non-Hispanic/Latino; 5 Hispanic/Latino; 2 Two or more races, non-Hispanic/Latino), 1 international. Average age 32. In 2013, 52 master's awarded. *Entrance requirements:* For master's, GRE Subject Test, PRAXIS I, minimum GPA of 2.5, 3 letters of recommendation, interview. Additional exam requirements/recommendations for international students: Required—TOEFL (minimum score 550 paper-based). *Application deadline:* Applications are processed on a rolling basis. Application fee: $50. *Expenses: Tuition:* Full-time $5436; part-time $810 per credit hour. *Financial support:* Federal Work-Study available. Financial award application deadline: 5/1; financial award applicants required to submit FAFSA. *Faculty research:* Assessment of teacher education, perceptions of prospective teachers by parents. *Unit head:* Dr. Kathy Moran, Dean, 317-788-3285, Fax: 317-788-3300, E-mail: kmoran@uindy.edu. *Application contact:* Jeni Kirby, Administrative Assistant, Teacher Education, 317-788-2113, E-mail: kirbyj@uindy.edu.
Website: http://education.uindy.edu/.

The University of Iowa, Graduate College, College of Education, Iowa City, IA 52242-1316. Offers MA, MAT, MM, PhD, Ed S. *Degree requirements:* For master's and Ed S, exam; for doctorate, comprehensive exam, thesis/dissertation. *Entrance requirements:* For master's, doctorate, and Ed S, GRE General Test, minimum GPA of 3.0. Additional exam requirements/recommendations for international students: Required—TOEFL (minimum score 550 paper-based; 81 iBT). Electronic applications accepted. *Faculty research:* Computer-assisted instrumentation, testing and measurement, instructional design.

University of Jamestown, Program in Education, Jamestown, ND 58405. Offers curriculum and instruction (M Ed). *Degree requirements:* For master's, thesis or project. *Expenses: Tuition:* Full-time $24,600; part-time $425 per credit. *Required fees:* $180. Tuition and fees vary according to degree level.

The University of Kansas, Graduate Studies, School of Education, Lawrence, KS 66045-3101. Offers MA, MS, MS Ed, Ed D, PhD, Ed S. *Accreditation:* NCATE. Part-time programs available. *Faculty:* 119. *Students:* 519 full-time (336 women), 328 part-time (245 women); includes 110 minority (31 Black or African American, non-Hispanic/Latino; 13 American Indian or Alaska Native, non-Hispanic/Latino; 24 Asian, non-Hispanic/Latino; 27 Hispanic/Latino; 15 Two or more races, non-Hispanic/Latino), 113 international. Average age 32. 641 applicants, 60% accepted, 225 enrolled. In 2013, 241 master's, 78 doctorates, 9 other advanced degrees awarded. *Degree requirements:* For doctorate, thesis/dissertation. *Entrance requirements:* For master's and Ed S, minimum GPA of 3.0; for doctorate, GRE General Test. Additional exam requirements/recommendations for international students: Required—TOEFL. Application fee: $55 ($65 for international students). Electronic applications accepted. *Financial support:* Fellowships, research assistantships with partial tuition reimbursements, teaching assistantships with full and partial tuition reimbursements, career-related internships or fieldwork, scholarships/grants, and unspecified assistantships available. Financial award application deadline: 2/1. *Unit head:* Dr. Rick J. Ginsberg, Dean, 785-864-3726, E-mail: ginsberg@ku.edu. *Application contact:* Kim Huggett, Graduate Admissions Coordinator, 785-864-4510, E-mail: khuggett@ku.edu.
Website: http://www.soe.ku.edu/.

University of Kentucky, Graduate School, College of Education, Lexington, KY 40506-0032. Offers M Ed, MA Ed, MRC, MS, MS Ed, Ed D, PhD, Ed S. *Accreditation:* NCATE. Part-time and evening/weekend programs available. Terminal master's awarded for partial completion of doctoral program. *Degree requirements:* For master's and Ed S, comprehensive exam; for doctorate, comprehensive exam, thesis/dissertation. *Entrance requirements:* For master's, GRE General Test, minimum undergraduate GPA of 2.75; for doctorate, GRE General Test, minimum graduate GPA of 3.0; for Ed S, GRE General Test. Additional exam requirements/recommendations for international students: Required—TOEFL (minimum score 550 paper-based). Electronic applications accepted.

University of La Verne, College of Education and Organizational Leadership, Credential Program in Teacher Education, La Verne, CA 91750-4443. Offers multiple subject (Credential); single subject (Credential); teaching (Credential). *Accreditation:* NCATE. Part-time programs available. *Faculty:* 7 full-time (4 women), 1 (woman) part-time/adjunct. *Students:* 41 full-time (26 women), 92 part-time (69 women); includes 63 minority (2 Black or African American, non-Hispanic/Latino; 1 American Indian or Alaska Native, non-Hispanic/Latino; 3 Asian, non-Hispanic/Latino; 56 Hispanic/Latino; 1 Two or more races, non-Hispanic/Latino). Average age 29. *Entrance requirements:* For degree, California Basic Educational Skills Test, minimum GPA of 3.0, interview, writing sample. Additional exam requirements/recommendations for international students: Required—TOEFL (minimum score 550 paper-based). *Application deadline:* Applications are processed on a rolling basis. Application fee: $50. *Expenses:* Contact institution. *Financial support:* Institutionally sponsored loans, scholarships/grants, and unspecified assistantships available. Financial award application deadline: 3/2; financial award applicants required to submit FAFSA. *Unit head:* Dr. Anita Flemington, Chairperson, 909-593-3511 Ext. 4623, E-mail: aflemington@laverne.edu. *Application contact:* Christy Ranells, Program and Admission Specialist, 909-448-4644, Fax: 909-392-2744, E-mail: cranells@laverne.edu.
Website: http://laverne.edu/education/.

University of La Verne, College of Education and Organizational Leadership, Master's Program in Education, La Verne, CA 91750-4443. Offers advanced teaching skills (M Ed); education (special emphasis) (M Ed); educational leadership (M Ed); reading (M Ed). *Accreditation:* NCATE. Part-time programs available. *Faculty:* 7 full-time (4 women), 1 (woman) part-time/adjunct. *Students:* 42 full-time (34 women), 114 part-time (88 women); includes 71 minority (4 Black or African American, non-Hispanic/Latino; 7 Asian, non-Hispanic/Latino; 54 Hispanic/Latino; 6 Two or more races, non-Hispanic/Latino), 3 international. Average age 31. In 2013, 87 master's awarded. *Degree requirements:* For master's, thesis optional. *Entrance requirements:* For master's, California Basic Educational Skills Test, interview, writing sample, minimum GPA of 3.0,

3 letters of recommendation. Additional exam requirements/recommendations for international students: Required—TOEFL (minimum score 550 paper-based). *Application deadline:* Applications are processed on a rolling basis. Application fee: $50. *Expenses:* Contact institution. *Financial support:* Institutionally sponsored loans and unspecified assistantships available. Financial award application deadline: 3/2; financial award applicants required to submit FAFSA. *Unit head:* Lynn Stanton-Riggs, Chair, 909-448-4625, E-mail: lstanton-riggs@laverne.edu. *Application contact:* Christy Ranells, Program and Admission Specialist, 909-448-4644, Fax: 909-392-2744, E-mail: cranells@laverne.edu.
Website: http://www.laverne.edu/education/.

University of La Verne, Regional and Online Campuses, Graduate Credential Program in Education, California Statewide Campus, La Verne, CA 91750-4443. Offers administration services (preliminary) (Credential); education specialist: mild/moderate (Credential); multiple subject teaching (Credential); pupil personnel services: school counseling (Credential); single subject teaching (Credential). *Accreditation:* NCATE. Part-time programs available. *Faculty:* 10 full-time (7 women), 1 (woman) part-time/adjunct. *Students:* 128 full-time (92 women), 49 part-time (43 women); includes 58 minority (6 Black or African American, non-Hispanic/Latino; 1 American Indian or Alaska Native, non-Hispanic/Latino; 3 Asian, non-Hispanic/Latino; 44 Hispanic/Latino; 4 Two or more races, non-Hispanic/Latino). Average age 32. In 2013, 24 Credentials awarded. *Entrance requirements:* For degree, California Basic Educational Skills Test, minimum undergraduate GPA of 2.75, 3 letters of recommendation, interview. *Application deadline:* Applications are processed on a rolling basis. Application fee: $50. *Expenses:* Contact institution. *Financial support:* Institutionally sponsored loans available. Financial award application deadline: 3/2; financial award applicants required to submit FAFSA. *Unit head:* Pam Bergovoy, Assistant Dean, Regional and Online Campuses/Director, Center for Educators, 909-448-4953, E-mail: pbergovoy@laverne.edu.
Website: http://www.laverne.edu/locations.

University of La Verne, Regional and Online Campuses, Graduate Programs, Central Coast/Vandenberg Air Force Base Campuses, La Verne, CA 91750-4443. Offers business administration for experienced professionals (MBA), including health services management, information technology; education (special emphasis) (M Ed); educational counseling (MS); educational leadership (M Ed); multiple subject (elementary) (Credential); preliminary administrative services (Credential); pupil personnel services (Credential); single subject (secondary) (Credential). Part-time programs available. *Faculty:* 11 part-time/adjunct (2 women). *Students:* 17 full-time (7 women), 34 part-time (22 women); includes 15 minority (1 Black or African American, non-Hispanic/Latino; 1 American Indian or Alaska Native, non-Hispanic/Latino; 1 Asian, non-Hispanic/Latino; 10 Hispanic/Latino; 2 Two or more races, non-Hispanic/Latino). Average age 38. In 2013, 25 master's awarded. *Application deadline:* Applications are processed on a rolling basis. Application fee: $50. *Expenses:* Contact institution. *Financial support:* Institutionally sponsored loans available. Financial award application deadline: 3/2; financial award applicants required to submit FAFSA. *Unit head:* Kitt Vincent, Director, Central Coast Campus, 805-788-6202, Fax: 805-788-6201, E-mail: kvincent@laverne.edu. *Application contact:* Gene Teal, Admissions, 805-788-6205, Fax: 805-788-6201, E-mail: eteal@laverne.edu.
Website: http://www.laverne.edu/locations.

University of La Verne, Regional and Online Campuses, Master's Programs in Education, California Statewide Campus, La Verne, CA 91750-4443. Offers administration services (preliminary) (Credential); education specialist: mild/moderate (Credential); educational counseling (MS); educational leadership (M Ed); multiple subject teaching (Credential); pupil personnel services: school counseling (Credential); single subject teaching (Credential); special education studies (MS); special emphasis (M Ed). *Accreditation:* NCATE. *Faculty:* 6 full-time (2 women), 23 part-time/adjunct (16 women). *Students:* 109 full-time (88 women), 63 part-time (53 women); includes 94 minority (8 Black or African American, non-Hispanic/Latino; 6 Asian, non-Hispanic/Latino; 76 Hispanic/Latino; 4 Two or more races, non-Hispanic/Latino). Average age 33. In 2013, 76 master's awarded. *Entrance requirements:* For master's, California Basic Educational Skills Test, 3 letters of recommendation, teaching credential. *Application deadline:* Applications are processed on a rolling basis. Application fee: $50. *Expenses:* Contact institution. *Financial support:* Fellowships and institutionally sponsored loans available. Financial award application deadline: 3/2; financial award applicants required to submit FAFSA. *Unit head:* Pam Bergovoy, Assistant Dean, Regional and Online Campuses/Director, Center for Educators, 909-448-4953, E-mail: pbergovoy@laverne.edu.
Website: http://www.laverne.edu/locations.

University of Lethbridge, School of Graduate Studies, Lethbridge, AB T1K 3M4, Canada. Offers accounting (MScM); addictions counseling (M Sc); agricultural biotechnology (M Sc); agricultural studies (M Sc, MA); anthropology (MA); archaeology (M Sc, MA); art (MA, MFA); biochemistry (M Sc); biological sciences (M Sc); biomolecular science (PhD); biosystems and biodiversity (PhD); Canadian studies (MA); chemistry (M Sc); computer science (M Sc); computer science and geographical information science (M Sc); counseling (MC); counseling psychology (M Ed); dramatic arts (MA); earth, space, and physical science (PhD); economics (MA); education (MA); educational leadership (M Ed); English (MA); environmental science (M Sc); evolution and behavior (PhD); exercise science (M Sc); finance (MScM); French (MA); French/German (MA); French/Spanish (MA); general education (M Ed); general management (MScM); geography (M Sc, MA); German (MA); health sciences (M Sc); human resource management and labour relations (MScM); individualized multidisciplinary (M Sc, MA); information systems (MScM); international management (MScM); kinesiology (M Sc, MA); marketing (MScM); mathematics (M Sc); modern languages (MA); music (M Mus, MA); Native American studies (MA); neuroscience (M Sc, PhD); new media (MA, MFA); nursing (M Sc); philosophy (MA); physics (M Sc); policy and strategy (MScM); political science (MA); psychology (M Sc, MA); religious studies (MA); sociology (MA); theatre and dramatic arts (MFA); theoretical and computational science (PhD); urban and regional studies (MA); women and gender studies (MA). Part-time and evening/weekend programs available. *Degree requirements:* For doctorate, comprehensive exam, thesis/dissertation. *Entrance requirements:* For master's, GMAT (for M Sc in management), bachelor's degree in related field, minimum GPA of 3.0 during previous 20 graded semester courses, 2 years teaching or related experience (M Ed); for doctorate, master's degree, minimum graduate GPA of 3.5. Additional exam requirements/recommendations for international students: Required—TOEFL. Application fee: $60 Canadian dollars. *Financial support:* Fellowships, research assistantships, teaching assistantships, scholarships/grants, health care benefits, and unspecified assistantships available. *Faculty research:* Movement and brain plasticity, gibberellin physiology, photosynthesis, carbon cycling, molecular properties of main-group ring components. *Application contact:* School of Graduate Studies, 403-329-2793, Fax: 403-332-5239, E-mail: sgsinquiries@uleth.ca.
Website: http://www.uleth.ca/graduatestudies/.

University of Louisiana at Lafayette, College of Education, Lafayette, LA 70504. Offers M Ed, Ed D. *Accreditation:* NCATE. Part-time programs available. *Degree requirements:* For master's, thesis or alternative. *Entrance requirements:* For master's, GRE General Test, teaching certificate. Additional exam requirements/

recommendations for international students: Required—TOEFL (minimum score 550 paper-based). Electronic applications accepted.

University of Louisville, Graduate School, College of Education and Human Development, Louisville, KY 40292-0001. Offers M Ed, MA, MAT, MS, Ed D, PhD, Ed S. *Accreditation:* NCATE. Part-time and evening/weekend programs available. Postbaccalaureate distance learning degree programs offered. *Students:* 449 full-time (316 women), 608 part-time (420 women); includes 195 minority (130 Black or African American, non-Hispanic/Latino; 3 American Indian or Alaska Native, non-Hispanic/Latino; 14 Asian, non-Hispanic/Latino; 33 Hispanic/Latino; 1 Native Hawaiian or other Pacific Islander, non-Hispanic/Latino; 14 Two or more races, non-Hispanic/Latino), 39 international. Average age 32. 682 applicants, 61% accepted, 307 enrolled. In 2013, 208 master's, 12 doctorates, 6 other advanced degrees awarded. Terminal master's awarded for partial completion of doctoral program. *Entrance requirements:* For master's, doctorate, and Ed S, GRE General Test. Additional exam requirements/recommendations for international students: Required—TOEFL (minimum score 560 paper-based; 83 iBT). *Application deadline:* For fall admission, 5/1 priority date for international students; for spring admission, 11/1 priority date for international students; for summer admission, 4/1 priority date for international students. Application fee: $60. Electronic applications accepted. *Expenses:* Tuition, state resident: full-time $10,788; part-time $599 per credit hour. Tuition, nonresident: full-time $22,446; part-time $1247 per credit hour. *Required fees:* $196. Tuition and fees vary according to program and reciprocity agreements. *Financial support:* Fellowships with full tuition reimbursements, research assistantships with full tuition reimbursements, teaching assistantships with full tuition reimbursements, career-related internships or fieldwork, Federal Work-Study, scholarships/grants, and health care benefits available. Financial award application deadline: 6/1; financial award applicants required to submit FAFSA. *Faculty research:* Mathematics and science education, early childhood development, literacy acquisition and development, culturally-responsive education, health promotion, sports administration, exercise physiology, prevention science, counseling psychology, mental health counseling, school counseling, college student personnel, art therapy, educational leadership, school reform, evaluation, P-12 and higher education administration, organizational development, instructional technology development. *Total annual research expenditures:* $6.4 million. *Unit head:* Dr. Elisabeth A. Larson, Interim Dean, 502-852-6044, Fax: 502-852-1464, E-mail: ann.larson@louisville.edu. *Application contact:* Libby Leggett, Executive Director, Graduate Admissions, 502-852-3101, Fax: 502-852-6536, E-mail: gradadm@louisville.edu.
Website: http://www.louisville.edu/education.

University of Maine, Graduate School, College of Education and Human Development, Orono, ME 04469. Offers M Ed, MA, MAT, MS, Ed D, PhD, CAS, CGS. *Accreditation:* NCATE. Part-time and evening/weekend programs available. *Faculty:* 44 full-time (22 women), 35 part-time/adjunct (24 women). *Students:* 187 full-time (125 women), 232 part-time (175 women); includes 20 minority (8 Black or African American, non-Hispanic/Latino; 5 American Indian or Alaska Native, non-Hispanic/Latino; 3 Asian, non-Hispanic/Latino; 3 Hispanic/Latino; 1 Two or more races, non-Hispanic/Latino), 9 international. Average age 37. 182 applicants, 63% accepted, 89 enrolled. In 2013, 108 master's, 5 doctorates, 23 other advanced degrees awarded. *Degree requirements:* For master's, thesis (for some programs); for doctorate, comprehensive exam, thesis/dissertation. *Entrance requirements:* For master's, GRE General Test, MAT; for doctorate, GRE General Test; for other advanced degree, MA, M Ed, or MS. Additional exam requirements/recommendations for international students: Required—TOEFL. *Application deadline:* For fall admission, 1/15 priority date for domestic students. Applications are processed on a rolling basis. Application fee: $65. Electronic applications accepted. *Expenses:* Tuition, state resident: full-time $7524. Tuition, nonresident: full-time $23,112. *Required fees:* $1970. *Financial support:* In 2013–14, 85 students received support, including 1 fellowship, 18 teaching assistantships with full tuition reimbursements available (averaging $14,600 per year); career-related internships or fieldwork, Federal Work-Study, institutionally sponsored loans, and unspecified assistantships also available. Support available to part-time students. Financial award application deadline: 3/1. *Unit head:* Dr. William Nichols, Dean, 207-581-2441, Fax: 207-581-2423. *Application contact:* Scott G. Delcourt, Associate Dean of the Graduate School, 207-581-3291, Fax: 207-581-3232, E-mail: graduate@maine.edu.
Website: http://umaine.edu/edhd/.

University of Maine at Farmington, Program in Education, Farmington, ME 04938-1990. Offers early childhood education (MS Ed); educational leadership (MS Ed). *Accreditation:* NCATE. Part-time and evening/weekend programs available. Postbaccalaureate distance learning degree programs offered (minimal on-campus study). *Faculty:* 10 full-time (9 women), 4 part-time/adjunct (2 women). *Students:* 43 full-time (38 women); includes 2 minority (1 American Indian or Alaska Native, non-Hispanic/Latino; 1 Hispanic/Latino). *Degree requirements:* For master's, capstone project (for educational leadership). *Entrance requirements:* For master's, baccalaureate degree from accredited institution, valid teaching certificate or professional experience in education, professional employment by school district or other educational institution, minimum of two years' experience in professional education. *Application deadline:* Applications are processed on a rolling basis. Application fee: $60. *Expenses:* Tuition, state resident: full-time $4930; part-time $379 per credit. Tuition, nonresident: full-time $7150; part-time $550 per credit. *Required fees:* $84 per semester. One-time fee: $100. *Faculty research:* School improvement strategies, technology integration. *Application contact:* Graduate Studies, 207-778-7502, Fax: 207-778-8134, E-mail: umfmasters@maine.edu.
Website: http://www2.umf.maine.edu/gradstudies/.

The University of Manchester, School of Education, Manchester, United Kingdom. Offers counseling (D Couns); counseling psychology (D Couns); education (M Phil, Ed D, PhD); educational and child psychology (Ed D); educational psychology (Ed D).

University of Manitoba, Faculty of Graduate Studies, College Universitaire de Saint Boniface, Education Program–Saint-Boniface, Winnipeg, MB R3T 2N2, Canada. Offers M Ed.

University of Manitoba, Faculty of Graduate Studies, Faculty of Education, Winnipeg, MB R3T 2N2, Canada. Offers M Ed, PhD. *Degree requirements:* For master's, thesis or alternative.

University of Mary, School of Education and Behavioral Sciences, Department of Education, Bismarck, ND 58504-9652. Offers college teaching (M Ed); curriculum, instruction and assessment (M Ed); early childhood education (M Ed); early childhood special education (M Ed); elementary administration (M Ed); emotional disorders (M Ed); learning disabilities (M Ed); reading (M Ed); secondary administration (M Ed); special education strategist (M Ed). Part-time programs available. *Degree requirements:* For master's, portfolio or thesis. *Entrance requirements:* For master's, interview, letters of reference, minimum GPA of 2.5. Additional exam requirements/recommendations for international students: Required—TOEFL (minimum score 500 paper-based; 71 iBT). Electronic applications accepted. *Faculty research:* Innovative pedagogy in higher education, technology in education, content standards, children of poverty, children with diverse learning needs.

Education—General

University of Mary Hardin-Baylor, Graduate Studies in Education, Belton, TX 76513. Offers administration of intervention programs (M Ed); curriculum and instruction (M Ed); educational administration (M Ed, Ed D), including higher education (Ed D), leadership in nursing education (Ed D), P-12 (Ed D). Part-time and evening/weekend programs available. *Faculty:* 13 full-time (10 women), 6 part-time/adjunct (2 women). *Students:* 46 full-time (33 women), 61 part-time (40 women); includes 35 minority (15 Black or African American, non-Hispanic/Latino; 1 American Indian or Alaska Native, non-Hispanic/Latino; 19 Hispanic/Latino), 1 international. Average age 38. 72 applicants, 88% accepted, 47 enrolled. In 2013, 13 master's, 30 doctorates awarded. *Degree requirements:* For master's, comprehensive exam; for doctorate, thesis/dissertation. *Entrance requirements:* For master's, minimum GPA of 3.0, interview; for doctorate, minimum GPA of 3.5, interview, essay, resume, employment verification, employer letter of support, 3 letters of recommendation. Additional exam requirements/recommendations for international students: Required—TOEFL (minimum score 550 paper-based; 80 iBT), IELTS (minimum score 6). *Application deadline:* For fall admission, 6/1 for domestic students, 6/15 priority date for international students; for spring admission, 11/1 for domestic students, 10/15 priority date for international students. Applications are processed on a rolling basis. Application fee: $35 ($135 for international students). Electronic applications accepted. *Expenses: Tuition:* Full-time $14,130; part-time $785 per credit hour. *Required fees:* $1350; $75 per credit hour. $50 per term. *Financial support:* Federal Work-Study and scholarships (for some active duty military personnel only) available. Support available to part-time students. Financial award application deadline: 6/1; financial award applicants required to submit FAFSA. *Unit head:* Dr. Marlene Zipperlen, Dean, College of Education/Director, Doctor of Education Program, 254-295-4572, Fax: 254-295-4480, E-mail: mzipperlen@umhb.edu. *Application contact:* Melissa Ford, Director of Graduate Admissions, 254-295-4020, Fax: 254-295-5038, E-mail: mford@umhb.edu.
Website: http://graduate.umhb.edu/education/.

University of Maryland, Baltimore County, Graduate School, College of Arts, Humanities and Social Sciences, Department of Education, Baltimore, MD 21250. Offers distance education (Postbaccalaureate Certificate); education (MAE), including K-8 mathematics instructional leadership, K-8 science education, K-8 STEM education, secondary mathematics education, secondary science education, secondary STEM education; instructional systems development (MA, Graduate Certificate), including distance education (Graduate Certificate), instructional design for e-learning (Graduate Certificate), instructional systems development, instructional technology (Graduate Certificate); mathematics education (Postbaccalaureate Certificate); mathematics instructional leadership (K-8) (Postbaccalaureate Certificate); teaching (MAT), including early childhood education, elementary education, secondary education; teaching English to speakers of other languages (MA, Postbaccalaureate Certificate). *Accreditation:* NCATE. Part-time and evening/weekend programs available. Postbaccalaureate distance learning degree programs offered (no on-campus study). *Faculty:* 21 full-time (15 women), 25 part-time/adjunct (19 women). *Students:* 85 full-time (64 women), 387 part-time (293 women); includes 110 minority (70 Black or African American, non-Hispanic/Latino; 1 American Indian or Alaska Native, non-Hispanic/Latino; 14 Asian, non-Hispanic/Latino; 17 Hispanic/Latino; 1 Native Hawaiian or other Pacific Islander, non-Hispanic/Latino; 7 Two or more races, non-Hispanic/Latino), 9 international. Average age 34. 90 applicants, 94% accepted, 80 enrolled. In 2013, 100 master's awarded. *Degree requirements:* For master's, comprehensive exam (for some programs), thesis (for some programs). *Entrance requirements:* For master's, GRE General Test, GRE Subject Test (MA in TESOL), PRAXIS I (MAT), PRAXIS II (MAE), minimum GPA of 3.0. Additional exam requirements/recommendations for international students: Required—TOEFL. *Application deadline:* For fall admission, 6/1 for domestic students; for spring admission, 11/1 for domestic students. Applications are processed on a rolling basis. Application fee: $50. Electronic applications accepted. One-time fee: $200 full-time. *Financial support:* In 2013–14, 12 students received support, including teaching assistantships with full tuition reimbursements available (averaging $12,000 per year); fellowships, career-related internships or fieldwork, Federal Work-Study, scholarships/grants, tuition waivers (partial), and unspecified assistantships also available. Financial award application deadline: 3/1. *Faculty research:* Teacher leadership; STEM education; ESOL/bilingual education; early childhood education; language, literacy and culture. *Total annual research expenditures:* $1.3 million. *Unit head:* Dr. Eugene Schaffer, Department Chair, 410-455-2466, Fax: 410-455-3986, E-mail: schaffer@umbc.edu. *Application contact:* Dr. Susan M. Blunck, Graduate Program Director, 410-455-2869, Fax: 410-455-3986, E-mail: blunck@umbc.edu.
Website: http://www.umbc.edu/education/.

University of Maryland, College Park, Academic Affairs, College of Education, College Park, MD 20742. Offers M Ed, MA, Ed D, PhD, AGSC, CAGS. *Accreditation:* NCATE. Part-time and evening/weekend programs available. Postbaccalaureate distance learning degree programs offered. *Faculty:* 196 full-time (141 women), 55 part-time/adjunct (45 women). *Students:* 632 full-time (472 women), 311 part-time (242 women); includes 295 minority (118 Black or African American, non-Hispanic/Latino; 1 American Indian or Alaska Native, non-Hispanic/Latino; 83 Asian, non-Hispanic/Latino; 59 Hispanic/Latino; 2 Native Hawaiian or other Pacific Islander, non-Hispanic/Latino; 32 Two or more races, non-Hispanic/Latino), 108 international. 1,267 applicants, 30% accepted, 235 enrolled. In 2013, 303 master's, 102 doctorates awarded. *Degree requirements:* For doctorate, thesis/dissertation. *Entrance requirements:* For master's, GRE General Test or MAT, minimum GPA of 3.0. *Application deadline:* For fall admission, 3/1 for domestic students, 2/1 for international students; for spring admission, 9/1 for domestic students, 6/1 for international students. Applications are processed on a rolling basis. Application fee: $75. Electronic applications accepted. *Expenses:* Tuition, state resident: full-time $10,314; part-time $573 per credit hour. Tuition, nonresident: full-time $22,248; part-time $1236 per credit. *Required fees:* $1446; $403.15 per semester. Tuition and fees vary according to program. *Financial support:* In 2013–14, 51 fellowships with full and partial tuition reimbursements (averaging $23,735 per year), 14 research assistantships (averaging $17,887 per year), 224 teaching assistantships (averaging $17,171 per year) were awarded; career-related internships or fieldwork, Federal Work-Study, and scholarships/grants also available. Support available to part-time students. Financial award applicants required to submit FAFSA. *Total annual research expenditures:* $11.2 million. *Unit head:* Dr. Donna L. Wiseman, Dean, 301-405-2336, Fax: 301-314-9890, E-mail: dlwise@umd.edu. *Application contact:* Dr. Charles A Caramello, Dean of Graduate School, 301-405-0358, Fax: 301-314-9305, E-mail: ccaramel@umd.edu.

University of Maryland Eastern Shore, Graduate Programs, Department of Education, Program in Teaching, Princess Anne, MD 21853-1299. Offers MAT. Program offered jointly with Salisbury University. *Accreditation:* NCATE. *Degree requirements:* For master's, comprehensive exam, internship, seminar paper, PRAXIS II. *Entrance requirements:* For master's, PRAXIS I, interview, minimum GPA of 3.0, writing sample. Additional exam requirements/recommendations for international students: Required—TOEFL (minimum score 80 iBT). Electronic applications accepted.

University of Maryland University College, Graduate School of Management and Technology, Master of Arts in Teaching Program, Adelphi, MD 20783. Offers MAT. Part-time and evening/weekend programs available. *Students:* 6 full-time (all women), 117 part-time (78 women); includes 26 minority (12 Black or African American, non-Hispanic/Latino; 1 American Indian or Alaska Native, non-Hispanic/Latino; 4 Asian, non-Hispanic/Latino; 4 Hispanic/Latino; 5 Two or more races, non-Hispanic/Latino). Average age 34. 75 applicants, 100% accepted, 28 enrolled. In 2013, 38 master's awarded. *Degree requirements:* For master's, comprehensive exam, thesis or alternative. *Application deadline:* Applications are processed on a rolling basis. Application fee: $50. Electronic applications accepted. *Financial support:* Application deadline: 6/1; applicants required to submit FAFSA. *Unit head:* Dr. Virginia Pilato, Chair, Education Department, 240-684-2400, Fax: 240-684-2401, E-mail: virginia.pilato@umuc.edu. *Application contact:* Coordinator, Graduate Admissions, 800-888-8682, Fax: 240-684-2151, E-mail: newgrad@umuc.edu.
Website: http://www.umuc.edu/programs/grad/mat/mat.shtml.

University of Maryland University College, Graduate School of Management and Technology, Program in Education, Adelphi, MD 20783. Offers M Ed. Part-time and evening/weekend programs available. Postbaccalaureate distance learning degree programs offered (no on-campus study). *Students:* 2 full-time (both women), 211 part-time (169 women); includes 77 minority (53 Black or African American, non-Hispanic/Latino; 13 Asian, non-Hispanic/Latino; 6 Hispanic/Latino; 5 Two or more races, non-Hispanic/Latino), 7 international. Average age 35. 99 applicants, 100% accepted, 47 enrolled. In 2013, 54 master's awarded. *Degree requirements:* For master's, thesis or alternative. *Application deadline:* Applications are processed on a rolling basis. Application fee: $50. Electronic applications accepted. *Financial support:* Federal Work-Study and scholarships/grants available. Support available to part-time students. Financial award application deadline: 6/1; financial award applicants required to submit FAFSA. *Unit head:* Dr. Katherine Woodward, Director, 240-684-2400, Fax: 240-684-2401, E-mail: katherine.woodward@umuc.edu. *Application contact:* Coordinator, Graduate Admissions, 800-888-8682, Fax: 240-684-2151, E-mail: newgrad@umuc.edu.

University of Mary Washington, College of Education, Fredericksburg, VA 22401. Offers education (M Ed); elementary education (MS). Part-time and evening/weekend programs available. *Faculty:* 18 full-time (16 women), 30 part-time/adjunct (23 women). *Students:* 42 full-time (37 women), 212 part-time (180 women); includes 22 minority (3 Black or African American, non-Hispanic/Latino; 4 Asian, non-Hispanic/Latino; 6 Hispanic/Latino; 9 Two or more races, non-Hispanic/Latino). Average age 31. 238 applicants, 61% accepted, 86 enrolled. In 2013, 132 master's awarded. *Degree requirements:* For master's, one foreign language, comprehensive exam (for some programs). *Entrance requirements:* For master's, PRAXIS I or Virginia Department of Education accepted equivalent. Additional exam requirements/recommendations for international students: Required—TOEFL (minimum score 570 paper-based; 88 iBT), IELTS (minimum score 6.5). *Application deadline:* For fall admission, 4/15 for domestic and international students; for spring admission, 9/15 for domestic and international students. Applications are processed on a rolling basis. Application fee: $50. Electronic applications accepted. Application fee is waived when completed online. *Expenses: Tuition, area resident:* Part-time $444 per credit hour. Tuition, state resident: part-time $444 per credit hour. Tuition, nonresident: part-time $883 per credit hour. *Required fees:* $30 per semester. *Financial support:* In 2013–14, 20 students received support, including 3 fellowships with partial tuition reimbursements available (averaging $9,000 per year); research assistantships, teaching assistantships, and scholarships/grants also available. Financial award application deadline: 4/25; financial award applicants required to submit FAFSA. *Unit head:* Dr. Mary L. Gendernalik-Cooper, Dean, 540-654-1290. *Application contact:* Dre N. Anthes, Director of Graduate Admissions, 540-286-8030, Fax: 540-286-8085, E-mail: aanthes@umw.edu.
Website: http://www.umw.edu/education/.

University of Massachusetts Amherst, Graduate School, College of Education, Amherst, MA 01003. Offers M Ed, Ed D, PhD, Ed S. *Accreditation:* NCATE. Part-time programs available. Postbaccalaureate distance learning degree programs offered (minimal on-campus study). *Faculty:* 95 full-time (55 women). *Students:* 387 full-time (267 women), 270 part-time (199 women); includes 117 minority (42 Black or African American, non-Hispanic/Latino; 4 American Indian or Alaska Native, non-Hispanic/Latino; 11 Asian, non-Hispanic/Latino; 48 Hispanic/Latino; 12 Two or more races, non-Hispanic/Latino), 100 international. Average age 34. 847 applicants, 49% accepted, 210 enrolled. In 2013, 191 master's, 34 doctorates, 24 other advanced degrees awarded. Terminal master's awarded for partial completion of doctoral program. *Degree requirements:* For doctorate, comprehensive exam, thesis/dissertation. *Entrance requirements:* Additional exam requirements/recommendations for international students: Required—TOEFL (minimum score 550 paper-based; 80 iBT), IELTS (minimum score 6.5). *Application deadline:* For fall admission, 1/15 for domestic and international students. Applications are processed on a rolling basis. Application fee: $75. Electronic applications accepted. *Financial support:* Fellowships with full and partial tuition reimbursements, research assistantships with full and partial tuition reimbursements, teaching assistantships with full and partial tuition reimbursements, career-related internships or fieldwork, Federal Work-Study, scholarships/grants, traineeships, health care benefits, tuition waivers (full and partial), and unspecified assistantships available. Support available to part-time students. Financial award application deadline: 1/15. *Unit head:* Dr. Christine B. McCormick, Dean, 413-545-2705, Fax: 413-545-4240. *Application contact:* Lindsay DeSantis, Supervisor of Admissions, 413-545-0722, Fax: 413-577-0010, E-mail: gradadm@grad.umass.edu.
Website: http://www.umass.edu/education/.

University of Massachusetts Boston, Office of Graduate Studies, Graduate College of Education, Boston, MA 02125-3393. Offers M Ed, MA, Ed D, CAGS, Certificate. Part-time and evening/weekend programs available. *Degree requirements:* For master's, comprehensive exam; for doctorate, comprehensive exam, thesis/dissertation. *Entrance requirements:* For master's, GRE General Test or MAT; for doctorate, GRE General Test or MAT, minimum GPA of 2.75; for other advanced degree, minimum GPA of 2.75. *Faculty research:* Effects of ethnicity on applied psychology and education, enhancing equity and excellence in public schools, diversity and change in higher education, improving the functioning of individuals with disabilities.

University of Massachusetts Dartmouth, Graduate School, College of Arts and Sciences, School of Education, North Dartmouth, MA 02747-2300. Offers Ed D, PhD, Postbaccalaureate Certificate. Part-time programs available. *Faculty:* 11 full-time (4 women), 10 part-time/adjunct (5 women). *Students:* 18 full-time (6 women), 178 part-time (117 women); includes 21 minority (7 Black or African American, non-Hispanic/Latino; 1 American Indian or Alaska Native, non-Hispanic/Latino; 6 Hispanic/Latino; 7 Two or more races, non-Hispanic/Latino), 2 international. Average age 36. 103 applicants, 94% accepted, 74 enrolled. In 2013, 1 doctorate, 13 other advanced degrees awarded. Terminal master's awarded for partial completion of doctoral program. *Degree requirements:* For doctorate, comprehensive exam, thesis/dissertation. *Entrance requirements:* For doctorate, GRE, statement of purpose (minimum of 300 words), resume, 3 letters of recommendation, official transcripts, scholarly writing sample for Educational Leadership (minimum of 10 pages); for Postbaccalaureate Certificate, MTEL (Massachusetts Tests for Educator Licensure), statement of purpose (minimum of 300 words), resume, 2 letters of recommendation, official transcripts. Additional exam requirements/recommendations for international students: Required—TOEFL (minimum score 533 paper-based; 72 iBT). *Application deadline:* For fall admission, 3/31 for domestic students, 2/28 for international students; for spring admission, 11/15 for

domestic students, 10/15 for international students. Applications are processed on a rolling basis. Application fee: $60. Electronic applications accepted. *Expenses:* Tuition, state resident: full-time $2071; part-time $86.29 per credit. Tuition, nonresident: full-time $8099; part-time $337.46 per credit. Tuition and fees vary according to course load and reciprocity agreements. *Financial support:* In 2013–14, 2 fellowships with full tuition reimbursements (averaging $9,885 per year), 2 research assistantships with full tuition reimbursements (averaging $21,500 per year), 4 teaching assistantships with full tuition reimbursements (averaging $16,000 per year) were awarded; Federal Work-Study and unspecified assistantships also available. Support available to part-time students. Financial award application deadline: 3/1; financial award applicants required to submit FAFSA. *Faculty research:* Role of metacognition in advanced mathematical thinking, education reform, reading/special education, higher education policy, curricular theory, qualitative methods. *Total annual research expenditures:* $1.9 million. *Unit head:* Dr. Jeannette Riley, Interim Dean, College of Arts and Sciences, 508-999-8279, Fax: 508-999-9125, E-mail: j1riley@umassd.edu. *Application contact:* Steven Briggs, Director of Marketing and Recruitment for Graduate Studies, 508-999-8604, Fax: 508-999-8183, E-mail: graduate@umassd.edu.
Website: http://www.umassd.edu/cas/schoolofeducation.

University of Massachusetts Lowell, Graduate School of Education, Lowell, MA 01854-2881. Offers administration, planning, and policy (CAGS); curriculum and instruction (M Ed, CAGS); educational administration (M Ed); language arts and literacy (Ed D); leadership in schooling (Ed D); math and science education (Ed D); reading and language (M Ed, CAGS). *Accreditation:* NCATE. Part-time and evening/weekend programs available. Postbaccalaureate distance learning degree programs offered (no on-campus study). Terminal master's awarded for partial completion of doctoral program. *Degree requirements:* For doctorate, thesis/dissertation. *Entrance requirements:* For master's, doctorate, and CAGS, GRE General Test. Additional exam requirements/recommendations for international students: Required—TOEFL. Electronic applications accepted.

University of Memphis, Graduate School, College of Education, Memphis, TN 38152. Offers M Ed, MAT, MS, Ed D, PhD, Graduate Certificate. *Accreditation:* NCATE. Part-time and evening/weekend programs available. *Faculty:* 91 full-time (43 women), 34 part-time/adjunct (22 women). *Students:* 290 full-time (211 women), 651 part-time (499 women); includes 362 minority (313 Black or African American, non-Hispanic/Latino; 6 American Indian or Alaska Native, non-Hispanic/Latino; 9 Asian, non-Hispanic/Latino; 15 Hispanic/Latino; 19 Two or more races, non-Hispanic/Latino), 24 international. Average age 34. 472 applicants, 68% accepted, 91 enrolled. In 2013, 230 master's, 37 doctorates, 17 other advanced degrees awarded. Terminal master's awarded for partial completion of doctoral program. *Degree requirements:* For master's, comprehensive exam; for doctorate, comprehensive exam, thesis/dissertation. *Entrance requirements:* For master's, GRE General Test or MAT; for doctorate, GRE General Test. *Application deadline:* Applications are processed on a rolling basis. Application fee: $35 ($60 for international students). *Financial support:* In 2013–14, 921 students received support. Research assistantships with full tuition reimbursements available, teaching assistantships with full tuition reimbursements available, career-related internships or fieldwork, Federal Work-Study, scholarships/grants, tuition waivers (partial), and unspecified assistantships available. Financial award application deadline: 2/15; financial award applicants required to submit FAFSA. *Faculty research:* Urban school effectiveness, literacy development, teacher effectiveness, exercise physiology, crisis counseling. *Total annual research expenditures:* $3.3 million. *Unit head:* Dr. Donald J. Wagner, Dean, 901-678-4265, Fax: 901-678-4778, E-mail: djwagner@memphis.edu. *Application contact:* Dr. Ernest A. Rakow, Associate Dean of Administration and Graduate Programs, 901-678-2363, Fax: 901-678-4778, E-mail: erakow@memphis.edu.
Website: http://www.memphis.edu/coe.

University of Miami, Graduate School, School of Education and Human Development, Coral Gables, FL 33124. Offers MS Ed, Ed D, PhD, Certificate, Ed S. *Faculty:* 72 full-time (37 women), 51 part-time/adjunct (31 women). *Students:* 219 full-time (149 women), 112 part-time (81 women); includes 153 minority (45 Black or African American, non-Hispanic/Latino; 6 Asian, non-Hispanic/Latino; 90 Hispanic/Latino; 2 Native Hawaiian or other Pacific Islander, non-Hispanic/Latino; 10 Two or more races, non-Hispanic/Latino), 31 international. Average age 26. 484 applicants, 25% accepted, 119 enrolled. In 2013, 95 master's, 6 doctorates awarded. Terminal master's awarded for partial completion of doctoral program. *Degree requirements:* For master's, comprehensive exam (for some programs), thesis optional, electronic portfolio, special project, personal growth experience; for doctorate, thesis/dissertation, qualifying exam, portfolio. *Entrance requirements:* For master's and doctorate, GRE General Test. Additional exam requirements/recommendations for international students: Required—TOEFL (minimum score 550 paper-based; 80 iBT); Recommended—IELTS (minimum score 6.5). *Application deadline:* For fall admission, 10/1 for international students. Application fee: $65. Electronic applications accepted. *Financial support:* In 2013–14, 253 students received support, including 3 fellowships with full tuition reimbursements available (averaging $25,200 per year), 47 research assistantships with full and partial tuition reimbursements available (averaging $18,900 per year), 14 teaching assistantships with full and partial tuition reimbursements available (averaging $18,900 per year); career-related internships or fieldwork, institutionally sponsored loans, scholarships/grants, traineeships, health care benefits, tuition waivers (full and partial), and unspecified assistantships also available. Support available to part-time students. Financial award application deadline: 3/1; financial award applicants required to submit FAFSA. *Faculty research:* Social skills and learning disabilities, planning for mainstreamed pupils, alcohol and drug abuse, restructuring education for all learners. *Total annual research expenditures:* $3.4 million. *Unit head:* Dr. Walter Secada, Senior Associate Dean, 305-284-2102, Fax: 305-284-9395, E-mail: wsecada@miami.edu. *Application contact:* Lois Heffernan, Graduate Admissions Coordinator, 305-284-2167, Fax: 305-284-9395, E-mail: lheffernan@miami.edu.
Website: http://www.education.miami.edu.

University of Michigan, Horace H. Rackham School of Graduate Studies, Combined Program in Education and Psychology, Ann Arbor, MI 48109. Offers PhD. *Accreditation:* Teacher Education Accreditation Council. *Faculty:* 17 part-time/adjunct (9 women). *Students:* 38 full-time (27 women); includes 18 minority (9 Black or African American, non-Hispanic/Latino; 2 Asian, non-Hispanic/Latino; 3 Hispanic/Latino; 4 Two or more races, non-Hispanic/Latino), 7 international. Average age 28. 90 applicants, 13% accepted, 8 enrolled. In 2013, 5 doctorates awarded. *Degree requirements:* For doctorate, thesis/dissertation, independent research project, preliminary exam, oral defense of dissertation. *Entrance requirements:* For doctorate, GRE General Test with Analytical Writing Test. Additional exam requirements/recommendations for international students: Required—TOEFL (minimum score 600 paper-based; 100 iBT). *Application deadline:* For fall admission, 12/1 for domestic and international students. Application fee: $65 ($75 for international students). Electronic applications accepted. Tuition and fees vary according to course level, course load, degree level, program and student level. *Financial support:* In 2013–14, 37 students received support, including 61 fellowships with full tuition reimbursements available (averaging $27,644 per year), 10 research assistantships with full tuition reimbursements available (averaging $31,621 per year), 25 teaching assistantships with full tuition reimbursements available (averaging $30,389 per year); institutionally sponsored loans, scholarships/grants, traineeships, tuition waivers (full and partial), and unspecified assistantships also available. Financial award application deadline: 12/1. *Faculty research:* Human development in context of schools, families, communities; cognitive and learning sciences; motivation and self-regulated learning; culture, ethnicity, social and class influences on learning and motivation. *Unit head:* Dr. Robert J. Jagers, Director, 734-647-0626, Fax: 734-615-2164, E-mail: rjagers@umich.edu. *Application contact:* Janie Knieper, Administrative Specialist, 734-763-0680, Fax: 734-615-2164, E-mail: cpep@umich.edu.
Website: http://www.soe.umich.edu/academics/doctoral_programs/ep/.

University of Michigan, School of Education, Ann Arbor, MI 48109-1259. Offers MA, MS, PhD, MA/Certification, MBA/MA, MPP/MA, PhD/MA. *Accreditation:* Teacher Education Accreditation Council. *Faculty:* 48 full-time (28 women). *Students:* 387 full-time (269 women), 68 part-time (51 women); includes 132 minority (43 Black or African American, non-Hispanic/Latino; 4 American Indian or Alaska Native, non-Hispanic/Latino; 28 Asian, non-Hispanic/Latino; 41 Hispanic/Latino; 16 Two or more races, non-Hispanic/Latino), 49 international. 948 applicants, 42% accepted, 177 enrolled. In 2013, 185 master's, 33 doctorates awarded. Terminal master's awarded for partial completion of doctoral program. *Degree requirements:* For master's, thesis optional; for doctorate, comprehensive exam, thesis/dissertation. *Entrance requirements:* For master's and doctorate, GRE General Test. Additional exam requirements/recommendations for international students: Required—TOEFL (minimum score 560 paper-based). *Application deadline:* For fall admission, 12/1 priority date for domestic students, 12/1 for international students. Application fee: $65 ($75 for international students). Electronic applications accepted. Tuition and fees vary according to course level, course load, degree level, program and student level. *Financial support:* In 2013–14, 349 students received support, including 1,222 fellowships (averaging $5,500 per year), 160 research assistantships with full tuition reimbursements available (averaging $19,000 per year), 87 teaching assistantships with full tuition reimbursements available (averaging $19,000 per year); career-related internships or fieldwork, Federal Work-Study, institutionally sponsored loans, scholarships/grants, health care benefits, tuition waivers, and unspecified assistantships also available. Support available to part-time students. Financial award application deadline: 12/1; financial award applicants required to submit FAFSA. *Faculty research:* Teaching, learning, policy, leadership, technology. *Total annual research expenditures:* $22 million. *Unit head:* Dr. Deborah Loewenberg Ball, Dean, 734-615-4415, Fax: 734-764-3473, E-mail: dball@umich.edu. *Application contact:* Jessica Mason, Admissions and Student Affairs Assistant, 734-615-1528, Fax: 734-647-9158, E-mail: soe.student.affairs@umich.edu.
Website: http://www.soe.umich.edu/.

University of Michigan–Dearborn, College of Education, Health, and Human Services, Doctoral Program in Education, Dearborn, MI 48126. Offers curriculum and practice (Ed D); educational leadership (Ed D); metropolitan education (Ed D). Part-time and evening/weekend programs available. *Faculty:* 7 full-time (5 women), 2 part-time/adjunct (0 women). *Students:* 4 full-time (all women), 35 part-time (27 women); includes 15 minority (11 Black or African American, non-Hispanic/Latino; 1 Asian, non-Hispanic/Latino; 3 Hispanic/Latino). Average age 40. 26 applicants, 42% accepted, 7 enrolled. *Degree requirements:* For doctorate, comprehensive exam, thesis/dissertation. *Entrance requirements:* For doctorate, GRE (taken within the last 5 years), master's degree with minimum GPA of 3.3, 3 letters of recommendation (1 from faculty), 3 years' professional and/or teaching experience. Additional exam requirements/recommendations for international students: Required—TOEFL (minimum score 560 paper-based; 84 iBT). *Application deadline:* For fall admission, 3/1 for domestic and international students. Application fee: $60. Electronic applications accepted. *Expenses:* Tuition, state resident: full-time $11,838; part-time $686 per credit hour. Tuition, nonresident: full-time $20,926; part-time $1206 per credit hour. *Required fees:* $760; $286 per semester. Tuition and fees vary according to course load and program. *Financial support:* Scholarships/grants available. Financial award application deadline: 2/1; financial award applicants required to submit FAFSA. *Faculty research:* Educational leadership, metropolitan education, curriculum and practice, educational psychology, special education, assessment. *Unit head:* Dr. Bonnie M. Beyer, Coordinator, 313-593-5583, E-mail: beyer@umd.umich.edu. *Application contact:* Elizabeth Morden, Program Assistant, 313-583-6333, Fax: 313-593-4748, E-mail: emorden@umich.edu.
Website: http://cehhs.umd.umich.edu/cehhs_edd/.

University of Michigan–Dearborn, College of Education, Health, and Human Services, Master of Arts in Teaching Program, Dearborn, MI 48126-2638. Offers MAT. *Accreditation:* Teacher Education Accreditation Council. Part-time and evening/weekend programs available. Postbaccalaureate distance learning degree programs offered (minimal on-campus study). *Faculty:* 4 full-time (3 women), 6 part-time/adjunct (4 women). *Students:* 9 full-time (5 women), 6 part-time (5 women); includes 2 minority (1 Black or African American, non-Hispanic/Latino; 1 Asian, non-Hispanic/Latino). Average age 35. 4 applicants, 75% accepted, 3 enrolled. In 2013, 12 master's awarded. *Entrance requirements:* For master's, Michigan Test for Teacher Certification (Basic Skills Test and Subject Area Test in teaching), minimum cumulative GPA of 3.0, interview, 3 letters of recommendation, statement of purpose. Additional exam requirements/recommendations for international students: Required—TOEFL (minimum score 560 paper-based; 84 iBT). *Application deadline:* For fall admission, 8/1 priority date for domestic students, 5/1 priority date for international students; for winter admission, 12/1 priority date for domestic students, 9/1 priority date for international students; for spring admission, 4/1 priority date for domestic students, 1/1 priority date for international students. Applications are processed on a rolling basis. Application fee: $60. Electronic applications accepted. *Expenses:* Tuition, state resident: full-time $11,838; part-time $686 per credit hour. Tuition, nonresident: full-time $20,926; part-time $1206 per credit hour. *Required fees:* $760; $286 per semester. Tuition and fees vary according to course load and program. *Financial support:* Career-related internships or fieldwork and scholarships/grants available. Support available to part-time students. Financial award application deadline: 4/1; financial award applicants required to submit FAFSA. *Unit head:* Dr. Paul R. Fossum, Coordinator, 313-593-0982, Fax: 313-593-9961, E-mail: pfossum@umich.edu. *Application contact:* Judy Garfield, Customer Service Assistant, 313-593-5090, Fax: 313-593-4748, E-mail: jlgarfie@umd.umich.edu.
Website: http://cehhs.umd.umich.edu/cehhs_mat/.

University of Michigan–Flint, School of Education and Human Services, Flint, MI 48502-1950. Offers early childhood education (MA); education (MA, Ed D), including education (MA), educational leadership (Ed D), elementary education with teaching certification (MA), literacy (K-12) (MA), technology in education (MA); education specialist (Ed S), including curriculum and instruction, education leadership; secondary education (MA); special education (MA). Part-time programs available. *Faculty:* 9 full-time (6 women), 12 part-time/adjunct (7 women). *Students:* 31 full-time (20 women), 206 part-time (153 women); includes 35 minority (31 Black or African American, non-Hispanic/Latino; 1 American Indian or Alaska Native, non-Hispanic/Latino; 1 Asian, non-Hispanic/Latino; 2 Hispanic/Latino), 1 international. Average age 36. 135 applicants, 80% accepted, 91 enrolled. In 2013, 99 master's awarded. *Entrance requirements:* For master's, BS with minimum GPA of 3.0. Additional exam requirements/recommendations for international students: Required—TOEFL (minimum score 560 paper-based; 84 iBT), IELTS (minimum score 6.5). *Application deadline:* For fall

admission, 8/1 priority date for domestic students, 5/1 priority date for international students; for winter admission, 11/15 priority date for domestic students, 9/1 priority date for international students; for spring admission, 3/15 priority date for domestic students, 1/1 priority date for international students. Application fee: $55. Electronic applications accepted. *Expenses:* Contact institution. *Financial support:* Federal Work-Study, scholarships/grants, and unspecified assistantships available. Support available to part-time students. Financial award application deadline: 3/1; financial award applicants required to submit FAFSA. *Unit head:* Dr. Bob Barnett, Interim Dean, 810-766-6878, Fax: 810-766-6891, E-mail: rbarnett@umflint.edu. *Application contact:* Bradley T. Maki, Director of Graduate Admissions, 810-762-3171, Fax: 810-766-6789, E-mail: bmaki@umflint.edu.
Website: http://www.umflint.edu/sehs/.

University of Minnesota, Duluth, Graduate School, College of Education and Human Service Professions, Department of Education, Duluth, MN 55812-2496. Offers Ed D. Part-time and evening/weekend programs available. *Degree requirements:* For doctorate, comprehensive exam. *Entrance requirements:* For doctorate, GRE, MA (preferred) minimum GPA of 3.0, 3 letters of recommendation, 3 work samples. Additional exam requirements/recommendations for international students: Required—TOEFL (minimum score 550 paper-based).

University of Minnesota, Twin Cities Campus, Graduate School, College of Education and Human Development, Minneapolis, MN 55455-0213. Offers M Ed, MA, MSW, Ed D, PhD, Certificate, Ed S. *Accreditation:* NCATE. Part-time programs available. *Faculty:* 180 full-time (95 women). *Students:* 1,430 full-time (1,019 women), 806 part-time (554 women); includes 363 minority (126 Black or African American, non-Hispanic/Latino; 25 American Indian or Alaska Native, non-Hispanic/Latino; 136 Asian, non-Hispanic/Latino; 75 Hispanic/Latino; 1 Native Hawaiian or other Pacific Islander, non-Hispanic/Latino), 207 international. Average age 33. 2,094 applicants, 57% accepted, 851 enrolled. In 2013, 1,102 master's, 155 doctorates, 169 other advanced degrees awarded. Application fee: $75 ($95 for international students). *Financial support:* In 2013–14, 100 fellowships (averaging $8,109 per year), 9 research assistantships with full tuition reimbursements (averaging $13,588 per year), 16 teaching assistantships with full tuition reimbursements (averaging $8,852 per year) were awarded; scholarships/grants and tuition waivers (partial) also available. Financial award applicants required to submit FAFSA. *Faculty research:* Learning technologies, literacy, violence prevention, exercise science and movement, assessment and accountability, aging, science and mathematics education, curriculum-based measurement and student assessment. *Total annual research expenditures:* $42.4 million. *Unit head:* Dr. Jean K. Quam, Dean, 612-626-9252, Fax: 612-626-7496, E-mail: jquam@umn.edu. *Application contact:* Dr. Jennifer Engler, Assistant Dean for Student Services, 612-626-2887, Fax: 612-626-7496, E-mail: engle009@umn.edu.
Website: http://www.cehd.umn.edu.

University of Mississippi, Graduate School, School of Education, Oxford, MS 38677. Offers M Ed, MA, Ed D, PhD, Ed S, Specialist. *Accreditation:* NCATE. *Faculty:* 55 full-time (35 women), 34 part-time/adjunct (28 women). *Students:* 225 full-time (182 women), 375 part-time (283 women); includes 203 minority (176 Black or African American, non-Hispanic/Latino; 3 American Indian or Alaska Native, non-Hispanic/Latino; 1 Asian, non-Hispanic/Latino; 12 Hispanic/Latino; 11 Two or more races, non-Hispanic/Latino), 7 international. In 2013, 226 master's, 10 doctorates, 30 other advanced degrees awarded. *Degree requirements:* For doctorate, thesis/dissertation. *Entrance requirements:* For master's, GRE General Test, minimum GPA of 3.0; for doctorate, GRE General Test. Additional exam requirements/recommendations for international students: Required—TOEFL. *Application deadline:* For fall admission, 4/1 for domestic students; for spring admission, 10/1 for domestic students. Applications are processed on a rolling basis. Application fee: $40. Electronic applications accepted. *Financial support:* Scholarships/grants available. Financial award application deadline: 3/1; financial award applicants required to submit FAFSA. *Unit head:* Dr. David Rock, Interim Dean, 662-915-7063, Fax: 662-915-7249, E-mail: soe@olemiss.edu. *Application contact:* Dr. Christy M. Wyandt, Associate Dean, 662-915-7474, Fax: 662-915-7577, E-mail: cwyandt@olemiss.edu.

University of Missouri, Graduate School, College of Education, Columbia, MO 65211. Offers M Ed, MA, Ed D, PhD, Ed S. Part-time and evening/weekend programs available. *Faculty:* 93 full-time (56 women), 14 part-time/adjunct (10 women). *Students:* 610 full-time (421 women), 914 part-time (625 women); includes 167 minority (82 Black or African American, non-Hispanic/Latino; 1 American Indian or Alaska Native, non-Hispanic/Latino; 15 Asian, non-Hispanic/Latino; 45 Hispanic/Latino; 24 Two or more races, non-Hispanic/Latino), 95 international. Average age 34. 1,039 applicants, 57% accepted, 493 enrolled. In 2013, 464 master's, 117 doctorates, 89 other advanced degrees awarded. Terminal master's awarded for partial completion of doctoral program. *Degree requirements:* For master's, variable foreign language requirement, thesis (for some programs); for doctorate, variable foreign language requirement, comprehensive exam (for some programs), thesis/dissertation. *Entrance requirements:* For master's, minimum GPA of 3.0; for doctorate, GRE General Test. *Application deadline:* Applications are processed on a rolling basis. Application fee: $55 ($75 for international students). *Financial support:* Fellowships, research assistantships, teaching assistantships, institutionally sponsored loans, scholarships/grants, traineeships, health care benefits, and unspecified assistantships available. Support available to part-time students. *Unit head:* Dr. Rose Porter, Interim Dean, 573-882-8524, E-mail: porterr@missouri.edu. *Application contact:* Adrienne Vaughn, Recruitment Coordinator, 573-884-3811, E-mail: alvhcd@mizzou.edu.
Website: http://education.missouri.edu/.

University of Missouri–Kansas City, School of Education, Kansas City, MO 64110-2499. Offers administration (Ed D); counseling and guidance (MA, Ed S), including mental health counseling (Ed S), school counseling (Ed S); counseling psychology (PhD); curriculum and instruction (MA, Ed S), including language and literacy (Ed S); education (PhD), including higher education administration, PK-12 education administration; educational administration (MA, Ed S), including advanced principal (Ed S), beginning principal (Ed S), district-level administration (Ed S); reading education (MA, Ed S); special education (MA). PhD in education offered through the School of Graduate Studies. *Accreditation:* NCATE. Part-time and evening/weekend programs available. *Faculty:* 44 full-time (34 women), 60 part-time/adjunct (45 women). *Students:* 206 full-time (145 women), 394 part-time (291 women); includes 154 minority (99 Black or African American, non-Hispanic/Latino; 13 Asian, non-Hispanic/Latino; 30 Hispanic/Latino; 1 Native Hawaiian or other Pacific Islander, non-Hispanic/Latino; 11 Two or more races, non-Hispanic/Latino), 16 international. Average age 32. 401 applicants, 48% accepted, 188 enrolled. In 2013, 156 master's, 9 doctorates, 24 other advanced degrees awarded. *Degree requirements:* For doctorate, thesis/dissertation, internship, practicum. *Entrance requirements:* For master's, GRE, minimum GPA of 2.75, 2 letters of reference, written statement of purpose; for doctorate, GRE, minimum GPA of 3.0; for Ed S, minimum GPA of 3.0. Additional exam requirements/recommendations for international students: Required—TOEFL (minimum score 550 paper-based; 80 iBT). *Application deadline:* For fall admission, 4/1 priority date for domestic and international students; for spring admission, 11/1 priority date for domestic and international students. Applications are processed on a rolling basis. Application fee: $45 ($50 for international students). *Expenses:* Tuition, state resident: full-time $6073; part-time $337.40 per credit hour. Tuition, nonresident: full-time $15,680; part-time $871.10 per credit hour. *Required fees:* $97.59 per credit hour. Full-time tuition and fees vary according to program. *Financial support:* In 2013–14, 12 research assistantships with partial tuition reimbursements (averaging $11,140 per year) were awarded; career-related internships or fieldwork, Federal Work-Study, institutionally sponsored loans, and tuition waivers (full and partial) also available. Support available to part-time students. Financial award application deadline: 3/1; financial award applicants required to submit FAFSA. *Faculty research:* Urban education, inquiry-based field study, theories of counseling and psychotherapy, school literacy, educational technology. *Unit head:* Dr. Wanda Blanchett, Dean, 816-235-2234, Fax: 816-235-5270, E-mail: education@umkc.edu. *Application contact:* Erica Hernandez-Scott, Student Recruiter, 816-235-1295, Fax: 816-235-5270, E-mail: hernandeze@umkc.edu.
Website: http://education.umkc.edu.

University of Missouri–St. Louis, College of Education, St. Louis, MO 63121. Offers M Ed, Ed D, PhD, Certificate, Ed S. *Accreditation:* NCATE. Part-time and evening/weekend programs available. *Faculty:* 64 full-time (34 women), 80 part-time/adjunct (48 women). *Students:* 201 full-time (162 women), 1,117 part-time (830 women); includes 384 minority (296 Black or African American, non-Hispanic/Latino; 6 American Indian or Alaska Native, non-Hispanic/Latino; 30 Asian, non-Hispanic/Latino; 38 Hispanic/Latino; 14 Two or more races, non-Hispanic/Latino), 37 international. Average age 34. 463 applicants, 86% accepted, 257 enrolled. In 2013, 336 master's, 24 doctorates, 49 other advanced degrees awarded. *Degree requirements:* For master's, comprehensive exam, thesis optional; for doctorate, thesis/dissertation. *Entrance requirements:* For doctorate, GRE General Test, 3 letters of recommendation. Additional exam requirements/recommendations for international students: Recommended—TOEFL (minimum score 550 paper-based; 79 iBT), IELTS (minimum score 6.5). *Application deadline:* For fall admission, 7/1 priority date for domestic and international students; for spring admission, 12/1 priority date for domestic and international students. Applications are processed on a rolling basis. Application fee: $50 ($40 for international students). Electronic applications accepted. *Expenses:* Tuition, state resident: full-time $7364; part-time $409.10 per credit hour. Tuition, nonresident: full-time $19,162; part-time $1008.50 per credit hour. *Financial support:* In 2013–14, 30 research assistantships with full and partial tuition reimbursements (averaging $11,565 per year), 13 teaching assistantships with full and partial tuition reimbursements (averaging $12,400 per year) were awarded. Financial award application deadline: 4/1; financial award applicants required to submit FAFSA. *Faculty research:* Remedial reading, literacy, educational policy and research, science education. *Unit head:* Dr. Kathleen Haywood, Director of Graduate Studies, 314-516-5483, Fax: 314-516-5227, E-mail: kathleen_haywood@umsl.edu. *Application contact:* 314-516-5458, Fax: 314-516-6996, E-mail: gradadm@umsl.edu.
Website: http://coe.umsl.edu/.

University of Mobile, Graduate Programs, Program in Education, Mobile, AL 36613. Offers MA. Part-time programs available. *Faculty:* 6 full-time (5 women), 4 part-time/adjunct (3 women). *Students:* 5 full-time (all women), 40 part-time (39 women); includes 34 minority (32 Black or African American, non-Hispanic/Latino; 1 American Indian or Alaska Native, non-Hispanic/Latino; 1 Asian, non-Hispanic/Latino). Average age 35. 10 applicants, 100% accepted, 8 enrolled. In 2013, 21 master's awarded. *Degree requirements:* For master's, comprehensive exam, thesis optional. *Entrance requirements:* For master's, GRE, Alabama teaching certificate. Additional exam requirements/recommendations for international students: Required—TOEFL (minimum score 550 paper-based; 80 iBT). *Application deadline:* For fall admission, 8/3 for domestic students; for spring admission, 12/23 for domestic students. Applications are processed on a rolling basis. Application fee: $40 ($50 for international students). *Financial support:* Application deadline: 8/1. *Faculty research:* Retention, writing across the curriculum. *Unit head:* Dr. Peter Kingsford, Dean, School of Education, 251-442-2355, Fax: 251-442-2523, E-mail: pkingsford@umobile.edu. *Application contact:* Danielle M. Riley, Administrative Assistant to Dean of Graduate Programs, 251-442-2270, Fax: 251-442-2523, E-mail: driley@umobile.edu.
Website: http://www.umobile.edu/Academics/AcademicAreas/SchoolofEducation/MasterofArtsinEducation.aspx.

The University of Montana, Graduate School, College of Visual and Performing Arts, School of Art, Missoula, MT 59812-0002. Offers fine arts (MA, MFA), including art (MA), art history (MA), ceramics (MFA), integrated arts and education (MA), media arts (MFA), painting and drawing (MFA), photography (MFA), printmaking (MFA), sculpture (MFA). *Accreditation:* NASAD (one or more programs are accredited). *Degree requirements:* For master's, thesis exhibit. *Entrance requirements:* For master's, GRE General Test, portfolio.

The University of Montana, Graduate School, College of Visual and Performing Arts, School of Theatre and Dance, Missoula, MT 59812-0002. Offers fine arts (MA, MFA), including acting (MFA), design/technology (MFA), directing (MFA), drama (MA), integrated arts and education (MA), media arts (MFA). *Accreditation:* NAST (one or more programs are accredited). *Degree requirements:* For master's, thesis or alternative. *Entrance requirements:* For master's, GRE General Test, audition, portfolio, production notebook.

The University of Montana, Graduate School, Phyllis J. Washington College of Education and Human Sciences, Missoula, MT 59812-0002. Offers M Ed, MA, MS, Ed D, Ed S. *Accreditation:* NCATE. Part-time programs available. *Degree requirements:* For Ed S, thesis. *Entrance requirements:* For master's, GRE General Test, minimum GPA of 3.0; for Ed S, GRE General Test. Additional exam requirements/recommendations for international students: Required—TOEFL. *Faculty research:* Cooperative learning, administrative styles.

University of Montevallo, College of Education, Montevallo, AL 35115. Offers M Ed, Ed S. *Accreditation:* NCATE. Part-time and evening/weekend programs available. *Students:* 109 full-time (85 women), 206 part-time (155 women); includes 79 minority (72 Black or African American, non-Hispanic/Latino; 1 American Indian or Alaska Native, non-Hispanic/Latino; 2 Hispanic/Latino; 4 Two or more races, non-Hispanic/Latino). In 2013, 116 master's, 33 Ed Ss awarded. *Degree requirements:* For master's, comprehensive exam. *Entrance requirements:* For master's, GRE General Test, MAT, minimum undergraduate GPA of 2.5. Additional exam requirements/recommendations for international students: Required—TOEFL (minimum score 550 paper-based). *Application deadline:* For fall admission, 7/15 for domestic students; for spring admission, 11/15 for domestic students. Application fee: $25. *Financial support:* Federal Work-Study, scholarships/grants, and unspecified assistantships available. *Unit head:* Dr. Anna E. McEwan, Dean, 205-665-6360, E-mail: mcewanae@montevallo.edu. *Application contact:* Kevin Thornthwaite, Director, Graduate Admissions and Records, 205-665-6350, E-mail: graduate@montevallo.edu.
Website: http://www.montevallo.edu/education/college-of-education/.

University of Nebraska at Kearney, Graduate Programs, College of Education, Kearney, NE 68849-0001. Offers MA Ed, MS Ed, Ed S. *Accreditation:* NCATE. Part-time and evening/weekend programs available. Postbaccalaureate distance learning degree programs offered. *Degree requirements:* For master's, thesis optional. *Entrance requirements:* Additional exam requirements/recommendations for international

students: Required—TOEFL (minimum score 550 paper-based; 79 iBT). Electronic applications accepted.

University of Nebraska at Omaha, Graduate Studies, College of Education, Omaha, NE 68182. Offers MA, MS, Ed D, PhD, Certificate, Ed S. *Accreditation:* NCATE. Part-time and evening/weekend programs available. *Faculty:* 62 full-time (37 women). *Students:* 185 full-time (123 women), 625 part-time (491 women); includes 88 minority (20 Black or African American, non-Hispanic/Latino; 2 American Indian or Alaska Native, non-Hispanic/Latino; 11 Asian, non-Hispanic/Latino; 34 Hispanic/Latino; 21 Two or more races, non-Hispanic/Latino), 12 international. Average age 33. 402 applicants, 40% accepted, 100 enrolled. In 2013, 210 master's, 12 doctorates, 2 other advanced degrees awarded. *Degree requirements:* For master's, comprehensive exam (for some programs), thesis (for some programs); for doctorate, comprehensive exam, thesis/dissertation. *Entrance requirements:* Additional exam requirements/recommendations for international students: Required—TOEFL, IELTS, PTE. *Application deadline:* Applications are processed on a rolling basis. Application fee: $45. Electronic applications accepted. *Financial support:* In 2013–14, 46 students received support, including 31 research assistantships with tuition reimbursements available, 15 teaching assistantships with tuition reimbursements available; fellowships, career-related internships or fieldwork, Federal Work-Study, institutionally sponsored loans, scholarships/grants, tuition waivers (full), and unspecified assistantships also available. Support available to part-time students. Financial award application deadline: 3/1; financial award applicants required to submit FAFSA. *Unit head:* Dr. Nancy Edick, Dean, 402-554-2719.

University of Nevada, Las Vegas, Graduate College, College of Education, Las Vegas, NV 89154-3001. Offers M Ed, MS, Ed D, PhD, Advanced Certificate, Certificate, Ed S, PhD/JD. Part-time and evening/weekend programs available. *Faculty:* 85 full-time (43 women), 67 part-time/adjunct (45 women). *Students:* 463 full-time (342 women), 457 part-time (334 women); includes 292 minority (79 Black or African American, non-Hispanic/Latino; 2 American Indian or Alaska Native, non-Hispanic/Latino; 52 Asian, non-Hispanic/Latino; 90 Hispanic/Latino; 6 Native Hawaiian or other Pacific Islander, non-Hispanic/Latino; 63 Two or more races, non-Hispanic/Latino), 32 international. Average age 34. 392 applicants, 86% accepted, 288 enrolled. In 2013, 331 master's, 53 doctorates, 12 other advanced degrees awarded. *Degree requirements:* For master's, comprehensive exam (for some programs), thesis optional; for doctorate, comprehensive exam, thesis/dissertation. *Entrance requirements:* Additional exam requirements/recommendations for international students: Required—TOEFL (minimum score 550 paper-based; 80 iBT), IELTS (minimum score 7). *Application deadline:* For fall admission, 5/1 for international students; for spring admission, 10/1 for international students. Application fee: $60 ($95 for international students). Electronic applications accepted. *Expenses:* Tuition, state resident: full-time $4752; part-time $264 per credit. Tuition, nonresident: full-time $18,662; part-time $554.50 per credit. *International tuition:* $18,952 full-time. *Required fees:* $532; $12 per credit. $266 per semester. One-time fee: $35. Tuition and fees vary according to course load and program. *Financial support:* In 2013–14, 118 students received support, including 84 research assistantships with partial tuition reimbursements available (averaging $10,200 per year), 34 teaching assistantships with partial tuition reimbursements available (averaging $12,317 per year); institutionally sponsored loans, scholarships/grants, health care benefits, and unspecified assistantships also available. Financial award application deadline: 3/1. *Faculty research:* Technology integration in general and special education, assessment of behavioral and emotional disorders, teacher quality and student achievement, evidence-based practices in special education (autism and emotional and behavioral disorders), math and science education. *Total annual research expenditures:* $1.2 million. *Unit head:* Dr. Kim Metcalf, Dean, 702-895-3375, Fax: 702-895-4068, E-mail: kim.matcalf@unlv.edu. *Application contact:* Graduate College Admissions Evaluator, 702-895-3320, Fax: 702-895-4180, E-mail: gradcollege@unlv.edu. Website: http://education.unlv.edu/.

University of Nevada, Reno, Graduate School, College of Education, Reno, NV 89557. Offers M Ed, MA, MS, Ed D, PhD, Ed S. *Accreditation:* NCATE. Terminal master's awarded for partial completion of doctoral program. *Degree requirements:* For master's, thesis optional; for doctorate, thesis/dissertation. *Entrance requirements:* For master's, GRE, minimum GPA of 2.75; for doctorate, GRE, minimum GPA of 3.0. Additional exam requirements/recommendations for international students: Required—TOEFL (minimum score 500 paper-based; 61 iBT), IELTS (minimum score 6). Electronic applications accepted.

University of New Brunswick Fredericton, School of Graduate Studies, Faculty of Education, Fredericton, NB E3B 5A3, Canada. Offers M Ed, PhD. Part-time programs available. Postbaccalaureate distance learning degree programs offered. *Faculty:* 31 full-time (17 women), 14 part-time/adjunct (9 women). *Students:* 75 full-time (55 women), 359 part-time (259 women). In 2013, 225 master's, 4 doctorates awarded. *Degree requirements:* For master's, variable foreign language requirement, thesis optional; for doctorate, variable foreign language requirement, comprehensive exam, thesis/dissertation. *Entrance requirements:* For master's, minimum GPA of 3.0. Additional exam requirements/recommendations for international students: Required—TOEFL (minimum score 650 paper-based); Recommended—TWE (minimum score 5.5). *Application deadline:* For fall admission, 8/31 priority date for domestic students, 1/31 priority date for international students; for winter admission, 1/31 priority date for domestic and international students; for spring admission, 1/31 for domestic students, 1/31 priority date for international students. Application fee: $50 Canadian dollars. Electronic applications accepted. *Financial support:* In 2013–14, 51 research assistantships, 30 teaching assistantships were awarded; fellowships and tuition waivers also available. *Faculty research:* Adult education, educational administration and leadership, counseling, exceptional learners, critical studies. *Unit head:* Dr. David Wagner, Associate Dean, 506-447-3294, Fax: 506-453-3569, E-mail: dwagner@unb.ca. *Application contact:* Carolyn King, Graduate Secretary, 506-458-7147, Fax: 506-453-3569, E-mail: kingc@unb.ca. Website: http://go.unb.ca/gradprograms.

University of New England, College of Arts and Sciences, Program in Education, Biddeford, ME 04005-9526. Offers advanced educational leadership (CAGS); career and technical education (MS Ed, CAGS); curriculum and instruction strategies (CAGS); curriculum and instruction strategy (MS Ed); educational leadership (MS Ed, CAGS); inclusion education (MS Ed); leadership, ethics and change (CAGS); literacy K-12 (MS Ed, CAGS); teaching methodologies (MS Ed). Part-time and evening/weekend programs available. Postbaccalaureate distance learning degree programs offered (no on-campus study). *Faculty:* 5 full-time (4 women), 17 part-time/adjunct (9 women). *Students:* 295 full-time (228 women), 233 part-time (175 women); includes 26 minority (19 Black or African American, non-Hispanic/Latino; 2 American Indian or Alaska Native, non-Hispanic/Latino; 2 Asian, non-Hispanic/Latino; 2 Hispanic/Latino; 1 Two or more races, non-Hispanic/Latino). Average age 37. 289 applicants, 84% accepted, 189 enrolled. In 2013, 257 master's, 106 CAGSs awarded. *Degree requirements:* For master's, collaborative action research project, integrative seminar portfolio. *Entrance requirements:* For master's, teaching certificate, 2 years of teaching experience. *Application deadline:* For fall admission, 9/15 for domestic students; for spring admission, 1/15 for domestic students. Applications are processed on a rolling basis.

Application fee: $40. Electronic applications accepted. *Financial support:* Application deadline: 5/1; applicants required to submit FAFSA. *Faculty research:* Distance learning, effective teaching, transition planning, adult learning. *Unit head:* Paulette St. Ours, Associate Dean, College of Arts and Sciences, 207-602-2400, E-mail: pstours@une.edu. *Application contact:* Dr. Cynthia Forrest, Vice President for Student Affairs, 207-221-4225, Fax: 207-523-1925, E-mail: gradadmissions@une.edu. Website: http://www.une.edu/cas/education/msonline.cfm.

University of New Hampshire, Graduate School, College of Liberal Arts, Department of Education, Durham, NH 03824. Offers counseling (M Ed); early childhood education (M Ed, Postbaccalaureate Certificate), including early childhood education, special needs (M Ed); education (PhD); educational administration (Ed S, Postbaccalaureate Certificate); elementary education (M Ed); secondary education (M Ed, MAT); special education (M Ed, Postbaccalaureate Certificate); teacher leadership (M Ed, Postbaccalaureate Certificate). *Accreditation:* Teacher Education Accreditation Council. Part-time programs available. *Faculty:* 22 full-time (13 women). *Students:* 131 full-time (102 women), 172 part-time (116 women); includes 20 minority (3 Black or African American, non-Hispanic/Latino; 4 Asian, non-Hispanic/Latino; 8 Hispanic/Latino; 5 Two or more races, non-Hispanic/Latino), 4 international. Average age 29. 158 applicants, 78% accepted, 88 enrolled. In 2013, 184 master's, 7 doctorates, 12 other advanced degrees awarded. *Degree requirements:* For doctorate, thesis/dissertation. *Entrance requirements:* For master's, doctorate, and other advanced degree, GRE General Test. Additional exam requirements/recommendations for international students: Required—TOEFL (minimum score 550 paper-based; 80 iBT). *Application deadline:* For fall admission, 4/1 priority date for domestic students, 4/1 for international students; for spring admission, 12/1 priority date for domestic students. Applications are processed on a rolling basis. Application fee: $65. Electronic applications accepted. *Expenses:* Tuition, state resident: full-time $13,500; part-time $750 per credit hour. Tuition, nonresident: full-time $26,200; part-time $1100 per credit hour. *Required fees:* $1741; $435.25 per term. Tuition and fees vary according to course level, course load, campus/location and program. *Financial support:* In 2013–14, 33 students received support, including 1 research assistantship, 15 teaching assistantships; fellowships, career-related internships or fieldwork, Federal Work-Study, scholarships/grants, and tuition waivers (full and partial) also available. Support available to part-time students. Financial award application deadline: 2/15. *Unit head:* Dr. Mike Middleton, Chairperson, 603-862-7054, E-mail: education.department@unh.edu. *Application contact:* Lisa Wilder, Administrative Assistant, 603-862-2381, E-mail: education.department@unh.edu. Website: http://www.unh.edu/education/.

University of New Hampshire, Graduate School Manchester Campus, Manchester, NH 03101. Offers business administration (MBA); counseling (M Ed); education (M Ed, MAT); educational administration and supervision (M Ed, Ed S); information technology (MS); management of technology (MS); public administration (MPA); public health (MPH, Certificate); social work (MSW); software systems engineering (Certificate). Part-time and evening/weekend programs available. *Students:* 2 full-time (0 women), 5 part-time (0 women), 2 international. Average age 38. 6 applicants, 17% accepted, 1 enrolled. In 2013, 1 master's awarded. *Degree requirements:* For master's, thesis or alternative. *Entrance requirements:* Additional exam requirements/recommendations for international students: Required—TOEFL (minimum score 550 paper-based; 80 iBT). *Application deadline:* For fall admission, 6/1 for domestic students, 4/1 for international students; for spring admission, 12/1 for domestic students. Applications are processed on a rolling basis. Application fee: $65. Electronic applications accepted. *Expenses:* Tuition, state resident: full-time $13,500; part-time $750 per credit hour. Tuition, nonresident: full-time $26,200; part-time $1100 per credit hour. *Required fees:* $1741; $435.25 per term. Tuition and fees vary according to course level, course load, campus/location and program. *Financial support:* Fellowships, research assistantships, teaching assistantships, Federal Work-Study, scholarships/grants, health care benefits, and unspecified assistantships available. Support available to part-time students. Financial award application deadline: 3/1; financial award applicants required to submit FAFSA. *Unit head:* Candice Brown, Director, 603-641-4313, E-mail: unhm.gradcenter@unh.edu. *Application contact:* Graduate Admissions Office, 603-862-3000, Fax: 603-862-0275, E-mail: grad.school@unh.edu. Website: http://www.gradschool.unh.edu/manchester/.

University of New Haven, Graduate School, College of Arts and Sciences, Programs in Education, West Haven, CT 06516-1916. Offers professional education (MS); teacher certification (MS). Part-time and evening/weekend programs available. *Students:* 111 full-time (77 women), 44 part-time (30 women); includes 20 minority (7 Black or African American, non-Hispanic/Latino; 1 American Indian or Alaska Native, non-Hispanic/Latino; 2 Asian, non-Hispanic/Latino; 7 Hispanic/Latino; 1 Native Hawaiian or other Pacific Islander, non-Hispanic/Latino; 2 Two or more races, non-Hispanic/Latino), 4 international. 160 applicants, 79% accepted, 95 enrolled. In 2013, 107 master's awarded. *Degree requirements:* For master's, comprehensive exam (for some programs), field experience. *Entrance requirements:* For master's, PRAXIS I. Additional exam requirements/recommendations for international students: Required—TOEFL (minimum score 80 iBT), IELTS, PTE (minimum score 53). *Application deadline:* For fall admission, 5/31 for international students; for winter admission, 10/15 for international students; for spring admission, 1/15 for international students. Applications are processed on a rolling basis. Application fee: $75. Electronic applications accepted. Application fee is waived when completed online. *Expenses: Tuition:* Full-time $21,600; part-time $800 per credit hour. *Required fees:* $45 per trimester. *Financial support:* Research assistantships with partial tuition reimbursements, teaching assistantships with partial tuition reimbursements, career-related internships or fieldwork, Federal Work-Study, scholarships/grants, and unspecified assistantships available. Support available to part-time students. Financial award applicants required to submit FAFSA. *Unit head:* Dr. Nancy S. Niemi, Chair, 203-932-7466, E-mail: nniemi@newhaven.edu. *Application contact:* Eloise Gormley, Director of Graduate Admissions, 203-932-7440, E-mail: gradinfo@newhaven.edu. Website: http://www.newhaven.edu/4601/Education/.

University of New Mexico, Graduate School, College of Education, Albuquerque, NM 87131-2039. Offers MA, MS, Ed D, PhD, Ed S, Graduate Certificate. *Accreditation:* NCATE. Part-time and evening/weekend programs available. Postbaccalaureate distance learning degree programs offered (minimal on-campus study). *Faculty:* 119 full-time (79 women), 33 part-time/adjunct (14 women). *Students:* 498 full-time (345 women), 669 part-time (508 women); includes 508 minority (38 Black or African American, non-Hispanic/Latino; 66 American Indian or Alaska Native, non-Hispanic/Latino; 28 Asian, non-Hispanic/Latino; 354 Hispanic/Latino; 4 Native Hawaiian or other Pacific Islander, non-Hispanic/Latino; 18 Two or more races, non-Hispanic/Latino), 67 international. 530 applicants, 55% accepted, 240 enrolled. In 2013, 345 master's, 37 doctorates, 19 other advanced degrees awarded. *Degree requirements:* For master's, comprehensive exam (for some programs), thesis (for some programs); for doctorate, variable foreign language requirement, comprehensive exam, thesis/dissertation. *Entrance requirements:* Additional exam requirements/recommendations for international students: Required—TOEFL (minimum score 550 paper-based), IELTS (minimum score 7). *Application deadline:* For fall admission, 3/1 for international students; for spring admission, 8/1 for international students. Application fee: $50. Electronic applications accepted. *Financial support:* Career-related internships or

fieldwork, Federal Work-Study, scholarships/grants, health care benefits, and unspecified assistantships available. Support available to part-time students. Financial award application deadline: 3/1; financial award applicants required to submit FAFSA. *Faculty research:* Best practices in pedagogy, quantitative analysis and assessment, socio-cultural issues, educational leadership, health and wellness across the lifespan. *Unit head:* Dr. Richard Howell, Dean, 505-277-2231, Fax: 505-277-8427, E-mail: rhowell@unm.edu. *Application contact:* Academic Graduate Coordinator, 505-277-3190, E-mail: coeac@unm.edu.
Website: http://coe.unm.edu/.

University of New Orleans, Graduate School, College of Education and Human Development, New Orleans, LA 70148. Offers M Ed, MAT, PhD. *Accreditation:* NCATE. Part-time programs available. Postbaccalaureate distance learning degree programs offered. *Degree requirements:* For master's, comprehensive exam, thesis optional; for doctorate, comprehensive exam, thesis/dissertation. *Entrance requirements:* For master's and doctorate, GRE General Test. Additional exam requirements/recommendations for international students: Required—TOEFL (minimum score 550 paper-based; 79 iBT). Electronic applications accepted. *Faculty research:* Special education and habilitation, educational administration, exercise physiology, wellness, effective school instruction.

University of North Alabama, College of Education, Florence, AL 35632-0001. Offers MA, MA Ed, MS, Ed S. *Accreditation:* NCATE. Part-time and evening/weekend programs available. *Faculty:* 20 full-time (14 women). *Students:* 99 full-time (68 women), 237 part-time (181 women); includes 35 minority (24 Black or African American, non-Hispanic/Latino; 5 American Indian or Alaska Native, non-Hispanic/Latino; 2 Hispanic/Latino; 4 Two or more races, non-Hispanic/Latino), 9 international. Average age 33. 315 applicants, 83% accepted, 157 enrolled. In 2013, 97 master's, 4 other advanced degrees awarded. *Degree requirements:* For master's, comprehensive exam. *Entrance requirements:* For master's, GRE, MAT, PRAXIS II, or NTE, minimum GPA of 2.5, Alabama Class B Certificate or equivalent, teaching experience. Additional exam requirements/recommendations for international students: Required—TOEFL (minimum score 550 paper-based; 79 iBT), IELTS (minimum score 6). *Application deadline:* For fall admission, 7/1 priority date for domestic students, 7/1 for international students; for spring admission, 12/1 for domestic and international students. Applications are processed on a rolling basis. Application fee: $25 ($50 for international students). Electronic applications accepted. *Expenses:* Tuition, state resident: full-time $4968; part-time $3312 per year. Tuition, nonresident: full-time $9936; part-time $6624 per year. *Required fees:* $970; $60.33 per credit. $362 per semester. *Financial support:* Federal Work-Study available. Support available to part-time students. Financial award application deadline: 4/1; financial award applicants required to submit FAFSA. *Unit head:* Dr. Donna Jacobs, Dean, 256-765-4252, Fax: 256-765-4664, E-mail: dpjacobs@una.edu. *Application contact:* Russ Darracott, Graduate Admissions Counselor, 256-765-4447, E-mail: erdarracott@una.edu.
Website: http://www.una.edu/education/.

The University of North Carolina at Chapel Hill, Graduate School, School of Education, Chapel Hill, NC 27514-3500. Offers M Ed, MA, MAT, MSA, Ed D, PhD. *Accreditation:* NCATE. Part-time programs available. *Degree requirements:* For master's, comprehensive exam, thesis (for some programs); for doctorate, comprehensive exam, thesis/dissertation. *Entrance requirements:* For master's and doctorate, GRE General Test, minimum GPA of 3.0 during last 2 years of undergraduate course work. Additional exam requirements/recommendations for international students: Required—TOEFL (minimum score 550 paper-based). Electronic applications accepted. *Faculty research:* Curriculum development; school success and intervention; professional development, recruitment and retention; service-learning; evaluation.

The University of North Carolina at Greensboro, Graduate School, School of Education, Greensboro, NC 27412-5001. Offers M Ed, MLIS, MS, MSA, Ed D, PhD, Certificate, Ed S, PMC, MS/Ed S, MS/PhD. *Accreditation:* NCATE. Part-time and evening/weekend programs available. *Degree requirements:* For doctorate, thesis/dissertation. *Entrance requirements:* For master's, doctorate, and other advanced degree, GRE General Test. Additional exam requirements/recommendations for international students: Required—TOEFL. Electronic applications accepted. *Faculty research:* Effects of homogeneous grouping, women in higher education, assessment of student achievement.

The University of North Carolina at Pembroke, Graduate Studies, School of Education, Pembroke, NC 28372-1510. Offers counseling (MA Ed), including clinical mental health counseling, professional school counseling; elementary education (MA Ed); health, physical education, and recreation (MA), including physical education; middle grades education (MA Ed, MAT); reading education (MA Ed); school administration (MSA). *Accreditation:* NCATE. Part-time and evening/weekend programs available. *Degree requirements:* For master's, comprehensive exam (for some programs), thesis optional. *Entrance requirements:* For master's, GRE General Test or MAT, minimum GPA of 3.0 in major, 2.5 overall. Additional exam requirements/recommendations for international students: Required—TOEFL.

The University of North Carolina Wilmington, Watson College of Education, Wilmington, NC 28403-3297. Offers M Ed, MA, MAT, MS, MSA, Ed D. *Accreditation:* NCATE. Part-time and evening/weekend programs available. *Faculty:* 48 full-time (32 women). *Students:* 123 full-time (97 women), 241 part-time (179 women); includes 66 minority (49 Black or African American, non-Hispanic/Latino; 3 American Indian or Alaska Native, non-Hispanic/Latino; 7 Hispanic/Latino; 7 Two or more races, non-Hispanic/Latino), 5 international. Average age 33. 129 applicants, 95% accepted, 94 enrolled. In 2013, 77 master's, 4 doctorates awarded. *Degree requirements:* For master's, comprehensive exam, thesis (for some programs); for doctorate, comprehensive exam, thesis/dissertation. *Entrance requirements:* For master's, GRE General Test, MAT, minimum B average in upper-division undergraduate course work. Additional exam requirements/recommendations for international students: Required—TOEFL (minimum score 550 paper-based; 79 iBT), IELTS (minimum score 6.5). *Application deadline:* For fall admission, 6/1 for domestic students. Applications are processed on a rolling basis. Application fee: $60. *Expenses:* Tuition, state resident: full-time $4163. Tuition, nonresident: full-time $16,098. *Financial support:* In 2013–14, 19 teaching assistantships with full and partial tuition reimbursements (averaging $14,000 per year) were awarded; career-related internships or fieldwork, Federal Work-Study, and unspecified assistantships also available. Support available to part-time students. Financial award application deadline: 3/15. *Unit head:* Dr. Kenneth Teitelbaum, Dean, 910-962-3354, E-mail: teitelbaumk@uncw.edu. *Application contact:* Dr. Ron Vetter, Dean, Graduate School, 910-962-3224, E-mail: vetterr@uncw.edu.
Website: http://www.uncw.edu/ed/index.html.

University of North Dakota, Graduate School, College of Education and Human Development, Grand Forks, ND 58202. Offers M Ed, MA, MS, MSW, Ed D, PhD, Specialist. *Accreditation:* NCATE. Part-time and evening/weekend programs available. Postbaccalaureate distance learning degree programs offered (minimal on-campus study). *Degree requirements:* For master's, comprehensive exam, thesis or alternative; for doctorate, comprehensive exam, thesis/dissertation; for Specialist, comprehensive exam (for some programs), thesis (for some programs). *Entrance requirements:* For master's, GRE General Test, MAT, GRE Subject Test, minimum GPA of 3.0; for doctorate, GRE Subject Test, minimum GPA of 3.5. Additional exam requirements/recommendations for international students: Required—TOEFL (minimum score 550 paper-based; 79 iBT), IELTS (minimum score 6.5). Electronic applications accepted.

University of Northern British Columbia, Office of Graduate Studies, Prince George, BC V2N 4Z9, Canada. Offers business administration (Diploma); community health science (M Sc); disability management (MA); education (M Ed); first nations studies (MA); gender studies (MA); history (MA); interdisciplinary studies (MA); international studies (MA); mathematical, computer and physical sciences (M Sc); natural resources and environmental studies (M Sc, MA, MNRES, PhD); political science (MA); psychology (M Sc, PhD); social work (MSW). Part-time and evening/weekend programs available. Postbaccalaureate distance learning degree programs offered (no on-campus study). *Degree requirements:* For master's, thesis; for doctorate, thesis/dissertation. *Entrance requirements:* For master's, GRE, minimum B average in undergraduate course work; for doctorate, candidacy exam, minimum A average in graduate course work.

University of Northern Colorado, Graduate School, College of Education and Behavioral Sciences, Greeley, CO 80639. Offers MA, MAT, MS, Ed D, PhD, Ed S. *Accreditation:* NCATE. Part-time programs available. Postbaccalaureate distance learning degree programs offered. *Degree requirements:* For master's, comprehensive exam, thesis optional; for doctorate, comprehensive exam, thesis/dissertation; for Ed S, comprehensive exam, thesis. *Entrance requirements:* For doctorate, GRE General Test.

University of Northern Iowa, Graduate College, College of Education, Cedar Falls, IA 50614. Offers MA, MAE, MS, Ed D, Ed S. Part-time and evening/weekend programs available. *Students:* 200 full-time (140 women), 367 part-time (266 women); includes 46 minority (31 Black or African American, non-Hispanic/Latino; 7 Asian, non-Hispanic/Latino; 7 Hispanic/Latino; 1 Two or more races, non-Hispanic/Latino), 33 international. 375 applicants, 57% accepted, 141 enrolled. In 2013, 167 master's, 26 doctorates, 13 other advanced degrees awarded. *Degree requirements:* For Ed S, thesis or alternative. *Entrance requirements:* For master's, minimum GPA of 3.0; for doctorate, GRE, master's degree, minimum GPA of 3.5; for Ed S, GRE General Test, GRE Subject Test. Additional exam requirements/recommendations for international students: Required—TOEFL (minimum score 500 paper-based; 61 iBT). *Application deadline:* For fall admission, 8/1 priority date for domestic students. Applications are processed on a rolling basis. Application fee: $50 ($70 for international students). Electronic applications accepted. *Financial support:* Career-related internships or fieldwork, Federal Work-Study, institutionally sponsored loans, scholarships/grants, and tuition waivers (full and partial) available. Support available to part-time students. Financial award application deadline: 2/1. *Unit head:* Dr. Dwight Watson, Dean, 319-273-2717, Fax: 319-273-2607, E-mail: dwight.watson@uni.edu. *Application contact:* Laurie S. Russell, Record Analyst, 319-273-2623, Fax: 319-273-2885, E-mail: laurie.russell@uni.edu.
Website: http://www.uni.edu/coe/.

University of North Florida, College of Education and Human Services, Jacksonville, FL 32224. Offers M Ed, Ed D. *Accreditation:* NCATE. Part-time and evening/weekend programs available. *Faculty:* 52 full-time (32 women), 8 part-time/adjunct (6 women). *Students:* 115 full-time (92 women), 321 part-time (236 women); includes 120 minority (80 Black or African American, non-Hispanic/Latino; 1 American Indian or Alaska Native, non-Hispanic/Latino; 7 Asian, non-Hispanic/Latino; 22 Hispanic/Latino; 1 Native Hawaiian or other Pacific Islander, non-Hispanic/Latino; 9 Two or more races, non-Hispanic/Latino), 9 international. Average age 35. 239 applicants, 62% accepted, 106 enrolled. In 2013, 133 master's, 12 doctorates awarded. Terminal master's awarded for partial completion of doctoral program. *Degree requirements:* For doctorate, thesis/dissertation. *Entrance requirements:* For master's, GRE General Test, minimum GPA of 3.0 in last 60 hours, interview, 3 letters of recommendation; for doctorate, GRE General Test, master's degree, interview, writing sample, 3 letters of recommendation. Additional exam requirements/recommendations for international students: Required—TOEFL (minimum score 500 paper-based). *Application deadline:* For fall admission, 7/1 priority date for domestic students, 5/1 for international students; for spring admission, 11/1 priority date for domestic students, 10/1 for international students. Application fee: $30. Electronic applications accepted. *Expenses:* Tuition, state resident: full-time $9794; part-time $408.10 per credit hour. Tuition, nonresident: full-time $22,383; part-time $932.61 per credit hour. *Required fees:* $2020; $84.20 per credit hour. Tuition and fees vary according to course load and program. *Financial support:* In 2013–14, 86 students received support, including 12 research assistantships (averaging $3,327 per year); teaching assistantships, career-related internships or fieldwork, Federal Work-Study, scholarships/grants, and tuition waivers (partial) also available. Support available to part-time students. Financial award application deadline: 4/1; financial award applicants required to submit FAFSA. *Faculty research:* Effective instruction, technology education, exceptional student education, multiculturalism. *Total annual research expenditures:* $990,257. *Unit head:* Dr. Larry Daniel, Dean, 904-620-2520, E-mail: ldaniel@unf.edu. *Application contact:* Dr. John Kemppainen, Director, Office of Student Services, 904-620-2530, Fax: 904-620-1135, E-mail: jkemppai@unf.edu.
Website: http://www.unf.edu/coehs/.

University of North Georgia, School of Education, Dahlonega, GA 30597. Offers art education (MAT); early childhood education (M Ed); English education (MAT); history education (MAT); math education (MAT); middle grades education (M Ed, MAT); physical education (MS); school leadership (Ed S); secondary education (M Ed), including English education, history education, mathematics education, physical education; teacher education (MAT). *Accreditation:* NCATE. Part-time and evening/weekend programs available. Postbaccalaureate distance learning degree programs offered (no on-campus study). *Degree requirements:* For master's, comprehensive exam, thesis optional. *Entrance requirements:* For master's, GRE or MAT, GACE, minimum GPA of 2.75; for Ed S, GRE General Test or MAT, 3 years of teaching experience, master's degree, minimum graduate GPA of 3.25, leadership position in the school. Additional exam requirements/recommendations for international students: Required—TOEFL (minimum score 550 paper-based; 79 iBT), IELTS (minimum score 6.5). Electronic applications accepted. *Faculty research:* Identification of professional development school structures supporting P-12 student achievement, impact of diverse field placement settings in teacher belief development among preservice teachers, use of inquiry methodology in social studies teaching with English language learners, use of instructional differentiation in the middle grades classroom, effects of international school placements on preservice teacher beliefs and attitudes.

University of North Texas, Robert B. Toulouse School of Graduate Studies, Denton, TX 76203-5017. Offers accounting (MS, PhD); applied anthropology (MA, MS); applied behavior analysis (Certificate); applied technology and performance improvement (M Ed, MS, PhD); art education (MA, PhD); art history (MA); art museum education (Certificate); arts leadership (Certificate); audiology (Au D); behavior analysis (MS); biochemistry and molecular biology (MS, PhD); biology (MA, MS, PhD); business (PhD); business computer information systems (PhD); chemistry (MS, PhD); clinical psychology (PhD); communication studies (MA, MS); computer engineering (MS); computer science (MS); computer science and engineering (PhD); counseling (M Ed, MS, PhD), including clinical mental health counseling (MS), college and university counseling (M Ed, MS), elementary school counseling (M Ed, MS), secondary school counseling (M Ed, MS); counseling psychology (PhD); creative writing (MA); criminal justice (MS); curriculum

and instruction (M Ed, PhD), including curriculum studies (PhD), early childhood studies (PhD), language and literacy studies (PhD); decision sciences (MBA); design (MA, MFA), including fashion design (MFA), innovation studies, interior design (MFA); early childhood studies (MS); economics (MS); educational leadership (M Ed, Ed D, PhD); educational psychology (MS), including family studies, gifted and talented (MS, PhD); human development, learning and cognition, research, measurement and evaluation; educational research (PhD), including gifted and talented (MS, PhD), human development and family studies, psychological aspects of sports and exercise, research, measurement and statistics; electrical engineering (MS); emergency management (MPA); engineering systems (MS); English (MA, PhD); environmental science (MS, PhD); experimental psychology (PhD); finance (MBA, MS, PhD); financial management (MPA); French (MA); health psychology and behavioral medicine (PhD); health services management (MBA); higher education (M Ed, Ed D, PhD); history (MA, MS, PhD), including European history (PhD), military history (PhD), United States history (PhD); hospitality management (MS); human resources management (MPA); information science (MS, PhD); information technologies (MBA); information technology and decision sciences (MS); interdisciplinary studies (MA, MS); international sustainable tourism (MS); jazz studies (MM); journalism (MA, MJ, Graduate Certificate), including interactive and virtual digital communication (Graduate Certificate), narrative journalism (Graduate Certificate), public relations (Graduate Certificate); kinesiology (MS); learning technologies (MS, PhD); library science (MS); local government management (MPA); logistics and supply chain management (MBA, PhD); long-term care, senior housing, and aging services (MA, MS); management science (PhD); marketing (MBA, PhD); materials science and engineering (MS, PhD); mathematics (MA, PhD); merchandising (MS); music (MA, MM Ed, PhD), including ethnomusicology (MA), music education (MM Ed, PhD), music theory (MA, PhD), musicology (MA, PhD), performance (MA); nonprofit management (MPA); operations and supply chain management (MBA); performance (MM, DMA); philosophy (MA, PhD); physics (MS, PhD); political science (MA, MS, PhD); public administration and management (PhD), including emergency management, nonprofit management, public financial management, urban management; radio, television and film (MA, MFA); recreation, event and sport management (MS); rehabilitation counseling (MS, Certificate); sociology (MA, MS, PhD); Spanish (MA); special education (M Ed, PhD), including autism intervention (PhD), emotional/behavioral disorders (PhD), mild/moderate disabilities (PhD); speech-language pathology (MA, MS); strategic management (MBA); studio art (MFA); taxation (MS); teaching (M Ed); MBA/MS; MS/MPH; MSES/MBA. Part-time and evening/weekend programs available. Postbaccalaureate distance learning degree programs offered. *Faculty:* 661 full-time (213 women), 240 part-time/adjunct (144 women). *Students:* 3,106 full-time (1,620 women), 3,543 part-time (2,221 women); includes 1,740 minority (533 Black or African American, non-Hispanic/Latino; 15 American Indian or Alaska Native, non-Hispanic/Latino; 286 Asian, non-Hispanic/Latino; 746 Hispanic/Latino; 3 Native Hawaiian or other Pacific Islander, non-Hispanic/Latino; 157 Two or more races, non-Hispanic/Latino), 1,145 international. Average age 32. 6,289 applicants, 43% accepted, 1751 enrolled. In 2013, 1,778 master's, 239 doctorates, 10 other advanced degrees awarded. Terminal master's awarded for partial completion of doctoral program. *Degree requirements:* For master's, variable foreign language requirement, comprehensive exam (for some programs), thesis (for some programs); for doctorate, variable foreign language requirement, comprehensive exam (for some programs), thesis/dissertation; for other advanced degree, variable foreign language requirement, comprehensive exam (for some programs). *Entrance requirements:* For master's and doctorate, GRE, GMAT. Additional exam requirements/recommendations for international students: Required—TOEFL (minimum score 550 paper-based; 79 iBT). *Application deadline:* For fall admission, 7/15 for domestic students, 3/15 for international students; for spring admission, 11/15 for domestic students, 9/15 for international students; for summer admission, 5/1 for domestic students. Applications are processed on a rolling basis. Application fee: $60. Electronic applications accepted. *Financial support:* Fellowships with partial tuition reimbursements, research assistantships with partial tuition reimbursements, teaching assistantships, career-related internships or fieldwork, Federal Work-Study, institutionally sponsored loans, scholarships/grants, health care benefits, and library assistantships available. Support available to part-time students. Financial award applicants required to submit FAFSA. *Unit head:* Mark Wardell, Dean, 940-565-2383, E-mail: mark.wardell@unt.edu. *Application contact:* Toulouse School of Graduate Studies, 940-565-2383, Fax: 940-565-2141, E-mail: gradsch@unt.edu. Website: http://tsgs.unt.edu/.

University of Northwestern–St. Paul, Program in Education, St. Paul, MN 55113-1598. Offers MA Ed. Part-time and evening/weekend programs available. Postbaccalaureate distance learning degree programs offered (no on-campus study). *Expenses: Tuition:* Full-time $8820; part-time $490 per credit. Website: http://www.unwsp.edu/web/grad-studies/master-of-arts-in-education.

University of Notre Dame, Graduate School, College of Arts and Letters, Division of Social Science, Institute for Educational Initiatives, Notre Dame, IN 46556. Offers M Ed, MA. Enrollment restricted to participants in the Alliance for Catholic Education (ACE) program. *Entrance requirements:* For master's, GRE General Test, acceptance into the Alliance for Catholic Education program. Electronic applications accepted. *Faculty research:* Effective teaching, motivation, social and ethical development, literacy.

University of Oklahoma, Jeannine Rainbolt College of Education, Norman, OK 73019. Offers M Ed, Ed D, PhD, Graduate Certificate. *Accreditation:* NCATE. Part-time and evening/weekend programs available. *Faculty:* 76 full-time (47 women), 5 part-time/adjunct (3 women). *Students:* 332 full-time (221 women), 474 part-time (343 women); includes 202 minority (73 Black or African American, non-Hispanic/Latino; 47 American Indian or Alaska Native, non-Hispanic/Latino; 12 Asian, non-Hispanic/Latino; 35 Hispanic/Latino; 1 Native Hawaiian or other Pacific Islander, non-Hispanic/Latino; 34 Two or more races, non-Hispanic/Latino), 31 international. Average age 33. 424 applicants, 63% accepted, 222 enrolled. In 2013, 150 master's, 36 doctorates, 4 other advanced degrees awarded. Terminal master's awarded for partial completion of doctoral program. *Degree requirements:* For master's, comprehensive exam (for some programs), thesis (for some programs); for doctorate, comprehensive exam, thesis/dissertation (for some programs). *Entrance requirements:* Additional exam requirements/recommendations for international students: Required—TOEFL (minimum score 79 iBT). *Application deadline:* For fall admission, 6/1 for domestic students, 3/1 for international students; for spring admission, 11/1 for domestic students, 9/1 for international students. Application fee: $50 ($100 for international students). Electronic applications accepted. *Expenses:* Tuition, state resident: full-time $4205; part-time $175.20 per credit hour. Tuition, nonresident: full-time $16,205; part-time $675.20 per credit hour. *Required fees:* $2745; $103.85 per credit hour. $126.50 per semester. *Financial support:* In 2013–14, 483 students received support, including 3 fellowships with full tuition reimbursements available (averaging $5,000 per year), 66 research assistantships with partial tuition reimbursements available (averaging $14,015 per year), 18 teaching assistantships with partial tuition reimbursements available (averaging $10,576 per year); career-related internships or fieldwork, Federal Work-Study, scholarships/grants, health care benefits, and unspecified assistantships also available. Support available to part-time students. Financial award application deadline: 6/1; financial award applicants required to submit FAFSA. *Total annual research

expenditures: $10.3 million. *Unit head:* Dr. Gregg Garn, Dean, 405-325-1081, Fax: 405-325-7390, E-mail: garn@ou.edu. *Application contact:* Dr. Sherry Cox, Assistant Dean, 405-325-2238, Fax: 405-325-7620, E-mail: scox@ou.edu. Website: http://www.ou.edu/education/.

University of Oregon, Graduate School, College of Education, Eugene, OR 97403. Offers M Ed, MA, MS, D Ed, PhD. Part-time programs available. Terminal master's awarded for partial completion of doctoral program. *Degree requirements:* For master's, exam, paper, or project; for doctorate, comprehensive exam, thesis/dissertation. *Entrance requirements:* Additional exam requirements/recommendations for international students: Required—TOEFL. *Faculty research:* Basic and applied research in teaching, learning and habilitation in all settings, schooling effectiveness.

University of Ottawa, Faculty of Graduate and Postdoctoral Studies, Faculty of Education, Ottawa, ON K1N 6N5, Canada. Offers M Ed, MA Ed, PhD, Certificate. Postbaccalaureate distance learning degree programs offered (minimal on-campus study). *Degree requirements:* For master's, thesis or alternative; for doctorate, comprehensive exam, thesis/dissertation, seminar. *Entrance requirements:* For master's, honors degree or equivalent, minimum B average; for doctorate, master's degree, minimum B+ average. Electronic applications accepted. *Faculty research:* Teaching, learning and evaluation; second language education; organizational studies in education; society, culture and literacies; educational counseling.

University of Pennsylvania, Graduate School of Education, Philadelphia, PA 19104. Offers M Phil, MS Ed, Ed D, PhD, Certificate, DMD/MS Ed. *Faculty:* 66 full-time (26 women), 42 part-time/adjunct (21 women). *Students:* 1,129 full-time (811 women), 231 part-time (163 women); includes 385 minority (173 Black or African American, non-Hispanic/Latino; 5 American Indian or Alaska Native, non-Hispanic/Latino; 91 Asian, non-Hispanic/Latino; 74 Hispanic/Latino; 42 Two or more races, non-Hispanic/Latino), 301 international. 2,763 applicants, 48% accepted, 817 enrolled. In 2013, 582 master's, 92 doctorates awarded. Terminal master's awarded for partial completion of doctoral program. *Degree requirements:* For master's, exam; for doctorate, thesis/dissertation, exam. *Entrance requirements:* For master's, GRE. *Application deadline:* For fall admission, 12/15 priority date for domestic students. Applications are processed on a rolling basis. Application fee: $70. Electronic applications accepted. *Expenses:* Contact institution. *Financial support:* In 2013–14, 101 students received support. Fellowships, research assistantships, teaching assistantships, institutionally sponsored loans, scholarships/grants, traineeships, health care benefits, and unspecified assistantships available. Financial award application deadline: 12/15. *Unit head:* Dr. Andrew Porter, Dean, 215-898-7014. *Application contact:* 215-898-6415, Fax: 215-746-6884, E-mail: admissions@gse.upenn.edu. Website: http://www.gse.upenn.edu.

See Display on next page and Close-Up on page 733.

University of Pennsylvania, Graduate School of Education, Division of Teaching, Learning, and Leadership, Program in Teaching, Learning, and Teacher Education, Philadelphia, PA 19104. Offers Ed D, PhD. *Students:* 44 full-time (28 women), 12 part-time (10 women); includes 13 minority (4 Black or African American, non-Hispanic/Latino; 1 American Indian or Alaska Native, non-Hispanic/Latino; 4 Asian, non-Hispanic/Latino; 3 Hispanic/Latino; 1 Two or more races, non-Hispanic/Latino), 7 international. 102 applicants, 31% accepted, 17 enrolled. In 2013, 5 doctorates awarded. *Unit head:* Dr. Andrew Porter, Dean, 215-898-7014. *Application contact:* 215-746-2566, E-mail: edwardsv@gse.upenn.edu. Website: http://www.gse.upenn.edu/tll.

University of Phoenix–Austin Campus, College of Education, Austin, TX 78759. Offers curriculum and instruction (MA Ed).

University of Phoenix–Bay Area Campus, College of Education, San Jose, CA 95134-1805. Offers administration and supervision (MA Ed); adult education and training (MA Ed); early childhood education (MA Ed); education (Ed S); educational leadership (Ed D); elementary teacher education (MA Ed); higher education administration (PhD); secondary teacher education (MA Ed); special education (MA Ed); teacher leadership (MA Ed). Evening/weekend programs available. Postbaccalaureate distance learning degree programs offered (no on-campus study). *Degree requirements:* For master's, thesis (for some programs). *Entrance requirements:* For master's, minimum undergraduate GPA of 2.5, 3 years of work experience. Additional exam requirements/recommendations for international students: Required—TOEFL (minimum score 550 paper-based; 79 iBT). Electronic applications accepted.

University of Phoenix–Central Massachusetts Campus, College of Education, Westborough, MA 01581-3906. Offers MA Ed. Evening/weekend programs available. *Degree requirements:* For master's, thesis (for some programs). *Entrance requirements:* For master's, minimum undergraduate GPA of 2.5, 3 years of work experience. Additional exam requirements/recommendations for international students: Required—TOEFL (minimum score 550 paper-based; 79 iBT). Electronic applications accepted.

University of Phoenix–Central Valley Campus, College of Education, Fresno, CA 93720-1562. Offers curriculum and instruction (MA Ed); curriculum and instruction-computer education (MA Ed); elementary teacher education (MA Ed); secondary teacher education (MA Ed).

University of Phoenix–Chattanooga Campus, College of Education, Chattanooga, TN 37421-3707. Offers administration and supervision (MA Ed); curriculum and instruction (MA Ed); elementary teacher education (MA Ed); secondary teacher education (MA Ed).

University of Phoenix–Dallas Campus, College of Education, Dallas, TX 75251. Offers curriculum and instruction (MA Ed).

University of Phoenix–Denver Campus, College of Education, Lone Tree, CO 80124-5453. Offers administration and supervision (MAEd); curriculum instruction (MAEd); elementary teacher education (MAEd); school counseling (MSC); secondary teacher education (MAEd). Evening/weekend programs available. *Degree requirements:* For master's, thesis (for some programs). *Entrance requirements:* For master's, minimum undergraduate GPA of 2.5, 3 years work experience. Additional exam requirements/recommendations for international students: Required—TOEFL (minimum score 550 paper-based; 79 iBT). Electronic applications accepted.

University of Phoenix–Hawaii Campus, College of Education, Honolulu, HI 96813-4317. Offers administration and supervision (MA Ed); curriculum and instruction (MA Ed); elementary education (MA Ed); secondary education (MA Ed); special education (MA Ed); teacher education for elementary licensure (MA Ed). Evening/weekend programs available. *Degree requirements:* For master's, thesis (for some programs). *Entrance requirements:* For master's, minimum undergraduate GPA of 2.5, 3 years of work experience. Additional exam requirements/recommendations for international students: Required—TOEFL (minimum score 550 paper-based; 79 iBT). Electronic applications accepted.

University of Phoenix–Houston Campus, College of Education, Houston, TX 77079-2004. Offers curriculum and instruction (MA Ed).

University of Phoenix–Idaho Campus, College of Education, Meridian, ID 83642-5114. Offers administration and supervision (MA Ed); curriculum and instruction

Education—General

(MA Ed); elementary teacher education (MA Ed); secondary teacher education (MA Ed). Evening/weekend programs available. *Degree requirements:* For master's, thesis (for some programs). *Entrance requirements:* For master's, minimum undergraduate GPA of 2.5, 3 years of work experience. Additional exam requirements/recommendations for international students: Required—TOEFL (minimum score 550 paper-based). Electronic applications accepted.

University of Phoenix–Indianapolis Campus, College of Education, Indianapolis, IN 46250-932. Offers elementary teacher education (MA Ed); secondary teacher education (MA Ed).

University of Phoenix–Kansas City Campus, College of Education, Kansas City, MO 64131. Offers administration and supervision (MA Ed). Postbaccalaureate distance learning degree programs offered.

University of Phoenix–Las Vegas Campus, College of Education, Las Vegas, NV 89135. Offers administration and supervision (MA Ed); curriculum and instruction (MA Ed); school counseling (MSC); teacher education-elementary licensure (MA Ed). Evening/weekend programs available. *Degree requirements:* For master's, thesis (for some programs). *Entrance requirements:* For master's, minimum undergraduate GPA of 2.5, 3 years of work experience. Additional exam requirements/recommendations for international students: Required—TOEFL (minimum score 550 paper-based; 79 iBT). Electronic applications accepted.

University of Phoenix–Louisiana Campus, College of Education, Metairie, LA 70001-2082. Offers curriculum and instruction (MA Ed); early childhood education (MA Ed). Postbaccalaureate distance learning degree programs offered. *Degree requirements:* For master's, thesis. *Entrance requirements:* For master's, minimum undergraduate GPA of 2.5, 3 years work experience. Additional exam requirements/recommendations for international students: Required—TOEFL (minimum score 550 paper-based; 79 iBT).

University of Phoenix–Madison Campus, College of Education, Madison, WI 53718-2416. Offers education (Ed S); educational leadership (Ed D); educational leadership: curriculum and instruction (Ed D); higher education administration (PhD).

University of Phoenix–Memphis Campus, College of Education, Cordova, TN 38018. Offers administration and supervision (MA Ed); curriculum and instruction (MA Ed); elementary teacher education (MA Ed); secondary teacher education (MA Ed).

University of Phoenix–Nashville Campus, College of Education, Nashville, TN 37214-5048. Offers administration and supervision (MA Ed); curriculum and instruction (MA Ed); elementary teacher education (MA Ed); secondary teacher education (MA Ed). Evening/weekend programs available. *Degree requirements:* For master's, thesis (for some programs). *Entrance requirements:* For master's, minimum undergraduate GPA of 2.5, 3 years work experience. Additional exam requirements/recommendations for international students: Required—TOEFL (minimum score 500 paper-based; 79 iBT). Electronic applications accepted.

University of Phoenix–New Mexico Campus, College of Education, Albuquerque, NM 87113-1570. Offers administration and supervision (MAEd); curriculum and instruction (MAEd); elementary teacher education (MAEd); school counseling (MSC); secondary teacher education (MAEd). Evening/weekend programs available. *Degree requirements:* For master's, thesis (for some programs). *Entrance requirements:* For master's, minimum undergraduate GPA of 2.5, 3 years of work experience. Additional exam requirements/recommendations for international students: Required—TOEFL (minimum score 550 paper-based; 79 iBT). Electronic applications accepted.

University of Phoenix–North Florida Campus, College of Education, Jacksonville, FL 32216-0959. Offers administration and supervision (MA Ed); curriculum and instruction (MA Ed), including computer education, mathematics education; early childhood education (MA Ed); elementary teacher education (MA Ed); secondary teacher

education (MA Ed). Evening/weekend programs available. *Degree requirements:* For master's, thesis (for some programs). *Entrance requirements:* For master's, 3 years of work experience, minimum undergraduate GPA of 2.5. Additional exam requirements/recommendations for international students: Required—TOEFL (minimum score 550 paper-based; 49 iBT). Electronic applications accepted.

University of Phoenix–Omaha Campus, College of Education, Omaha, NE 68154-5240. Offers administration and supervision (MA Ed); curriculum and instruction (MA Ed), including adult education, computer education, curriculum and instruction, English and language arts education, English as a second language, mathematics education; elementary teacher education (MA Ed); secondary teacher education (MA Ed); special education (MA Ed).

University of Phoenix–Online Campus, College of Education, Phoenix, AZ 85034-7209. Offers administration and supervision (MAEd, Certificate); adult education and training (MAEd); curriculum and instruction (MAEd), including computer education, curriculum and instruction, English as a second language, language arts, mathematics, reading; early childhood education (MAEd); educational studies (MAEd); elementary teacher education (MAEd), including early childhood, elementary teacher education, high school middle level, middle level; principal licensure (Certificate); secondary teacher education (MAEd); special education (MAEd, Certificate); teacher education (MAEd), including middle level generalist; teacher education middle level mathematics (MAEd), including middle level mathematics; teacher education middle level science (MAEd), including middle level science; teacher education secondary mathematics (MAEd); teacher education secondary science (MAEd); teacher leadership (MAEd); teachers of English learners (Certificate); transition to teaching (Certificate), including elementary education, secondary education. *Accreditation:* Teacher Education Accreditation Council. Evening/weekend programs available. Postbaccalaureate distance learning degree programs offered. *Entrance requirements:* Additional exam requirements/recommendations for international students: Required—TOEFL, TOEIC (Test of English as an International Communication), Berlitz Online English Proficiency Exam, PTE, or IELTS. Electronic applications accepted. *Expenses:* Contact institution.

University of Phoenix–Oregon Campus, College of Education, Tigard, OR 97223. Offers curriculum and instruction (MA Ed); early childhood education (MA Ed); elementary education (MA Ed), including early childhood specialization, middle level specialization; secondary education (MA Ed). Evening/weekend programs available. *Degree requirements:* For master's, thesis (for some programs). *Entrance requirements:* For master's, minimum undergraduate GPA of 2.5, 3 years work experience. Additional exam requirements/recommendations for international students: Required—TOEFL (minimum score 550 paper-based; 79 iBT). Electronic applications accepted.

University of Phoenix–Phoenix Campus, College of Education, Tempe, AZ 85282-2371. Offers administration and supervision (MA Ed); adult education and training (MA Ed); curriculum and instruction reading (MA Ed); early childhood education (MA Ed); education studies (MA Ed); elementary teacher education (MA Ed); secondary teacher education (MA Ed); special education (MA Ed); teacher leadership (MA Ed). Evening/weekend programs available. Postbaccalaureate distance learning degree programs offered. *Entrance requirements:* Additional exam requirements/recommendations for international students: Required—TOEFL, TOEIC (Test of English as an International Communication), Berlitz Online English Proficiency Exam, PTE, or IELTS. Electronic applications accepted. *Expenses:* Contact institution.

University of Phoenix–Puerto Rico Campus, College of Education, Guaynabo, PR 00968. Offers administration and supervision (MA Ed); early childhood education (MA Ed); school counselor (MSC). Evening/weekend programs available. *Degree requirements:* For master's, thesis (for some programs). *Entrance requirements:* For master's, minimum undergraduate GPA of 2.5, 3 years work experience. Additional

exam requirements/recommendations for international students: Required—TOEFL (minimum score 550 paper-based; 79 iBT). Electronic applications accepted.

University of Phoenix–Richmond-Virginia Beach Campus, College of Education, Glen Allen, VA 23060. Offers administration and supervision (MA Ed); curriculum and instruction (MA Ed).

University of Phoenix–Sacramento Valley Campus, College of Education, Sacramento, CA 95833-3632. Offers adult education (MA Ed); curriculum instruction (MA Ed); elementary teacher education (MA Ed); secondary teacher education (MA Ed); teacher education (Certificate). Evening/weekend programs available. *Degree requirements:* For master's, thesis (for some programs). *Entrance requirements:* For master's, 3 years of work experience, minimum undergraduate GPA of 2.5. Additional exam requirements/recommendations for international students: Required—TOEFL (minimum score 550 paper-based; 79 iBT). Electronic applications accepted.

University of Phoenix–San Diego Campus, College of Education, San Diego, CA 92123. Offers curriculum and instruction (MA Ed), including computer education, curriculum and instruction, English as a second language; elementary teacher education (MA Ed); secondary teacher education (MA Ed). Evening/weekend programs available. *Degree requirements:* For master's, thesis (for some programs). *Entrance requirements:* For master's, 3 years of work experience, minimum undergraduate GPA of 3.0. Additional exam requirements/recommendations for international students: Required—TOEFL (minimum score 550 paper-based; 79 iBT). Electronic applications accepted.

University of Phoenix–Southern Arizona Campus, College of Education, Tucson, AZ 85711. Offers administration and supervision (MA Ed); adult education and training (MA Ed); curriculum instruction (MA Ed); educational counseling (MA Ed); elementary teacher education (MA Ed); school counseling (MSC); secondary teacher education (MA Ed); special education (MA Ed, Certificate). Evening/weekend programs available. *Degree requirements:* For master's, thesis (for some programs). *Entrance requirements:* For master's, minimum undergraduate GPA of 2.5, 3 years of work experience. Additional exam requirements/recommendations for international students: Required—TOEFL (minimum score 550 paper-based; 79 iBT). Electronic applications accepted.

University of Phoenix–Southern California Campus, College of Education, Costa Mesa, CA 92626. Offers administration and supervision (MA Ed, Certificate); adult education and training (MA Ed); educational studies (MA Ed); elementary teacher education (MA Ed); secondary teacher education (MA Ed); teacher leadership (MA Ed); teachers of English learners (Certificate). Evening/weekend programs available. Postbaccalaureate distance learning degree programs offered. *Entrance requirements:* Additional exam requirements/recommendations for international students: Required—TOEFL, TOEIC (Test of English as an International Communication), Berlitz Online English Proficiency Exam, PTE, or IELTS. Electronic applications accepted. *Expenses:* Contact institution.

University of Phoenix–Southern Colorado Campus, College of Education, Colorado Springs, CO 80903. Offers administration and supervision (MA Ed); curriculum and instruction (MA Ed); elementary teacher education (MA Ed); principal licensure certification (Certificate); school counseling (MSC); secondary teacher education (MA Ed). Evening/weekend programs available. *Degree requirements:* For master's, thesis (for some programs). *Entrance requirements:* For master's, minimum undergraduate GPA of 2.5, 3 years of work experience. Additional exam requirements/recommendations for international students: Required—TOEFL (minimum score 550 paper-based; 79 iBT). Electronic applications accepted.

University of Phoenix–South Florida Campus, College of Education, Miramar, FL 33030. Offers administration and supervision (MA Ed); curriculum and instruction (MA Ed), including computer education, curriculum and instruction, mathematics education; early childhood education (MA Ed); elementary teacher education (MA Ed); secondary teacher education (MA Ed). Evening/weekend programs available. *Degree requirements:* For master's, thesis (for some programs). *Entrance requirements:* For master's, 3 years of work experience, minimum undergraduate GPA of 2.5. Additional exam requirements/recommendations for international students: Required—TOEFL (minimum score 550 paper-based; 79 iBT). Electronic applications accepted.

University of Phoenix–Springfield Campus, College of Education, Springfield, MO 65804-7211. Offers administration and supervision (MA Ed); curriculum and instruction (MA Ed), including computer education, curriculum and instruction, English and language arts education, English as a second language, mathematics education; English and language arts education (MA Ed).

University of Phoenix–Utah Campus, College of Education, Salt Lake City, UT 84123-4617. Offers administration and supervision (MA Ed); curriculum and instruction (MA Ed); elementary teacher education (MA Ed); school counseling (MSC); secondary teacher education (MA Ed); special education (MA Ed). Evening/weekend programs available. *Degree requirements:* For master's, thesis (for some programs). *Entrance requirements:* For master's, minimum undergraduate GPA of 2.5, 3 years work experience. Additional exam requirements/recommendations for international students: Required—TOEFL (minimum score 550 paper-based; 79 iBT). Electronic applications accepted.

University of Phoenix–Washington D.C. Campus, College of Education, Washington, DC 20001. Offers administration and supervision (MA Ed); adult education and training (MA Ed); computer education (MA Ed); curriculum and instruction (MA Ed, Ed D); early childhood education (MA Ed); education (Ed S); educational leadership (Ed D); educational technology (Ed D); elementary teacher education (MA Ed); English and language arts education (MA Ed); English as a second language (MA Ed); higher education administration (PhD); mathematics education (MA Ed); secondary teacher education (MA Ed); special education (MA Ed); teacher leadership (MA Ed).

University of Phoenix–West Florida Campus, College of Education, Temple Terrace, FL 33637. Offers administration and supervision (MA Ed); curriculum and instruction (MA Ed), including computer education, curriculum and instruction, mathematics education; curriculum and technology (MA Ed); early childhood education (MA Ed); elementary teacher education (MA Ed); secondary teacher education (MA Ed). Evening/weekend programs available. *Degree requirements:* For master's, thesis (for some programs). *Entrance requirements:* For master's, 3 years of work experience, minimum undergraduate GPA of 2.5. Additional exam requirements/recommendations for international students: Required—TOEFL (minimum score 550 paper-based; 79 iBT).

University of Pittsburgh, School of Education, Pittsburgh, PA 15260. Offers M Ed, MA, MAT, MS, Ed D, PhD. Part-time and evening/weekend programs available. Postbaccalaureate distance learning degree programs offered (minimal on-campus study). *Faculty:* 86 full-time (49 women), 135 part-time/adjunct (88 women). *Students:* 462 full-time (347 women), 455 part-time (342 women); includes 114 minority (43 Black or African American, non-Hispanic/Latino; 23 Asian, non-Hispanic/Latino; 33 Hispanic/Latino; 15 Two or more races, non-Hispanic/Latino), 105 international. Average age 32. 754 applicants, 69% accepted, 317 enrolled. In 2013, 355 master's, 47 doctorates awarded. Terminal master's awarded for partial completion of doctoral program. *Degree requirements:* For master's, comprehensive exam, thesis (for some programs); for doctorate, comprehensive exam, thesis/dissertation. *Entrance requirements:* For doctorate, GRE. Additional exam requirements/recommendations for international students: Required—TOEFL (minimum score 550 paper-based; 80 iBT). *Application deadline:* For fall admission, 2/1 priority date for domestic students, 2/1 for international students; for spring admission, 11/15 priority date for domestic students, 7/1 for international students. Applications are processed on a rolling basis. Application fee: $50. Electronic applications accepted. *Expenses:* Tuition, state resident: full-time $19,964; part-time $807 per credit. Tuition, nonresident: full-time $32,686; part-time $1337 per credit. *Required fees:* $740; $200. Tuition and fees vary according to program. *Financial support:* In 2013–14, 20 fellowships with full and partial tuition reimbursements (averaging $19,219 per year), 60 research assistantships with full and partial tuition reimbursements (averaging $16,950 per year), 54 teaching assistantships with full and partial tuition reimbursements (averaging $16,950 per year) were awarded; career-related internships or fieldwork, Federal Work-Study, institutionally sponsored loans, scholarships/grants, traineeships, tuition waivers (partial), and unspecified assistantships also available. Support available to part-time students. Financial award applicants required to submit FAFSA. *Total annual research expenditures:* $15.3 million. *Unit head:* Dr. Alan Lesgold, Dean, 412-648-1773, Fax: 412-648-1825, E-mail: al@pitt.edu. *Application contact:* Maggie Sikora, Director of Admissions, 412-648-7056, Fax: 412-648-1899, E-mail: soeinfo@pitt.edu.
Website: http://www.education.pitt.edu/.

University of Portland, School of Education, Portland, OR 97203-5798. Offers education (MA, MAT); educational leadership (M Ed); English for speakers of other languages (M Ed); initial administrator licensure (M Ed); neuroeducation (Ed D); organizational leadership and development (Ed D); reading (M Ed); special education (M Ed). M Ed also available through the Graduate Outreach Program for teachers residing in the Oregon and Washington state areas. *Accreditation:* NCATE. Part-time and evening/weekend programs available. *Faculty:* 17 full-time (10 women), 12 part-time/adjunct (4 women). *Students:* 47 full-time (29 women), 214 part-time (155 women); includes 25 minority (1 Black or African American, non-Hispanic/Latino; 1 American Indian or Alaska Native, non-Hispanic/Latino; 8 Asian, non-Hispanic/Latino; 6 Hispanic/Latino; 6 Native Hawaiian or other Pacific Islander, non-Hispanic/Latino; 3 Two or more races, non-Hispanic/Latino), 63 international. Average age 32. In 2013, 96 master's awarded. *Entrance requirements:* For master's, minimum GPA of 3.0, teaching certificate, letters of recommendation, resume, statement of goals, official transcripts. Additional exam requirements/recommendations for international students: Required—TOEFL (minimum score 550 paper-based; 80 iBT), IELTS (minimum score 7). *Application deadline:* For fall admission, 7/15 priority date for domestic and international students; for spring admission, 12/15 priority date for domestic and international students. Applications are processed on a rolling basis. Application fee: $50. *Expenses: Tuition:* Part-time $1025 per credit hour. Tuition and fees vary according to program. *Financial support:* Federal Work-Study and scholarships/grants available. Support available to part-time students. Financial award application deadline: 3/1; financial award applicants required to submit FAFSA. *Faculty research:* Multicultural education, supervision/leadership. *Unit head:* Dr. Bruce Weitzel, Associate Dean, 503-943-7135, E-mail: soed@up.edu. *Application contact:* Dr. Matt Baasten, Assistant to the Provost and Dean of the Graduate School, 503-943-7107, Fax: 503-943-7315, E-mail: baasten@up.edu.
Website: http://education.up.edu/default.aspx?cid-4318&pid-5590.

University of Prince Edward Island, Faculty of Education, Charlottetown, PE C1A 4P3, Canada. Offers leadership and learning (M Ed). Part-time programs available. *Degree requirements:* For master's, thesis. *Entrance requirements:* For master's, 2 years of professional experience, bachelor of education, professional certificate. Additional exam requirements/recommendations for international students: Required—TOEFL (minimum score 550 paper-based; 80 iBT), Canadian Academic English Language Assessment, Michigan English Language Assessment Battery, Canadian Test of English for Scholars and Trainees. *Faculty research:* Distance learning, aboriginal communities and education leadership development, international development, immersion language learning.

University of Puerto Rico, Río Piedras Campus, College of Education, San Juan, PR 00931-3300. Offers M Ed, MS, Ed D. *Accreditation:* NCATE. Part-time programs available. *Degree requirements:* For master's, thesis; for doctorate, thesis/dissertation, internship. *Entrance requirements:* For master's, GRE or PAEG, minimum GPA of 3.0, letter of recommendation; for doctorate, GRE or PAEG, master's degree, minimum GPA of 3.0, letter of recommendation (2), interview. *Faculty research:* Curriculum, math teaching.

University of Puget Sound, Graduate Studies, School of Education, Tacoma, WA 98416. Offers M Ed, MAT. *Degree requirements:* For master's, capstone course. *Entrance requirements:* For master's, GRE General Test, WEST-B, and WEST-E (for some programs), minimum baccalaureate GPA of 3.0. Additional exam requirements/recommendations for international students: Required—TOEFL (minimum score 550 paper-based; 90 iBT). Electronic applications accepted. *Expenses:* Contact institution. *Faculty research:* Suicide prevention, mathematics education, professional development, social studies education, gender studies.

University of Redlands, School of Education, Redlands, CA 92373-0999. Offers MA, Ed D, Certificate. Part-time and evening/weekend programs available. *Entrance requirements:* For master's, minimum undergraduate GPA of 3.0, 2 letters of recommendation. Additional exam requirements/recommendations for international students: Required—TOEFL (minimum score 550 paper-based). *Expenses:* Contact institution.

University of Regina, Faculty of Graduate Studies and Research, Faculty of Education, Regina, SK S4S 0A2, Canada. Offers M Ed, MA Ed, MHRD, PhD, Master's Certificate. Part-time programs available. *Faculty:* 42 full-time (23 women), 18 part-time/adjunct (10 women). *Students:* 88 full-time (70 women), 254 part-time (188 women). 176 applicants, 65% accepted. In 2013, 112 master's, 7 doctorates, 1 other advanced degree awarded. *Degree requirements:* For master's, thesis (for some programs), practicum, project, or thesis; for doctorate, thesis/dissertation. *Entrance requirements:* For master's, 4-year B Ed or equivalent, two years of teaching or other relevant professional experience. Additional exam requirements/recommendations for international students: Required—TOEFL (minimum score 580 paper-based; 80 iBT), IELTS (minimum score 6.5). *Application deadline:* For fall admission, 2/15 for domestic and international students; for winter admission, 10/15 for domestic and international students; for spring admission, 2/15 for domestic and international students. Application fee: $100. Electronic applications accepted. *Expenses: Tuition, area resident:* Full-time $4338 Canadian dollars. *International tuition:* $7338 Canadian dollars full-time. *Required fees:* $449.25 Canadian dollars. *Financial support:* In 2013–14, 14 fellowships (averaging $6,286 per year), 4 research assistantships (averaging $5,875 per year), 10 teaching assistantships (averaging $2,413 per year) were awarded; career-related internships or fieldwork and scholarships/grants also available. Financial award application deadline: 6/15. *Faculty research:* Curriculum and instruction, educational administration, educational psychology, human resource development, adult education. *Unit head:* Dr. Ken Montgomery, Associate Dean, Research and Graduate Programs in Education, 306-585-5031, Fax: 306-585-5387, E-mail: ken.montgomery@uregina.ca. *Application*

contact: Tania Gates, Graduate Program Coordinator, 306-585-4506, Fax: 306-585-5387, E-mail: edgrad@uregina.ca.
Website: http://www.uregina.ca/education.

University of Rhode Island, Graduate School, College of Human Science and Services, School of Education, Kingston, RI 02881. Offers adult education (MA); education (PhD); elementary education (MA); music education (MM); reading education (MA); secondary education (MA); special education (MA); MS/PhD. *Accreditation:* NCATE. Part-time and evening/weekend programs available. *Faculty:* 16 full-time (9 women). *Students:* 64 full-time (48 women), 91 part-time (68 women); includes 17 minority (8 Black or African American, non-Hispanic/Latino; 2 American Indian or Alaska Native, non-Hispanic/Latino; 2 Asian, non-Hispanic/Latino; 3 Hispanic/Latino; 2 Two or more races, non-Hispanic/Latino), 6 international. In 2013, 47 master's, 11 doctorates awarded. *Degree requirements:* For master's, comprehensive exam (for some programs), thesis optional; for doctorate, comprehensive exam, thesis/dissertation. *Entrance requirements:* For master's, 2 letters of recommendation; interview (for special education applicants); for doctorate, GRE, 3 letters of recommendation, resume. Additional exam requirements/recommendations for international students: Required—TOEFL (minimum score 600 paper-based; 100 iBT). *Application deadline:* For fall admission, 1/31 for domestic and international students. Application fee: $65. Electronic applications accepted. *Expenses:* Tuition, state resident: full-time $11,532; part-time $641 per credit. Tuition, nonresident: full-time $23,606; part-time $1311 per credit. *Required fees:* $1388; $36 per credit. $35 per semester. One-time fee: $130. *Financial support:* In 2013–14, 2 research assistantships with full and partial tuition reimbursements (averaging $11,883 per year), 4 teaching assistantships with full and partial tuition reimbursements (averaging $8,488 per year) were awarded; career-related internships or fieldwork also available. Financial award application deadline: 1/31; financial award applicants required to submit FAFSA. *Total annual research expenditures:* $1.1 million. *Unit head:* Dr. David Byrd, Director, 401-874-5484, Fax: 401-874-5471, E-mail: dbyrd@uri.edu. *Application contact:* Graduate Admissions, 401-874-2872, E-mail: gradadm@etal.uri.edu.
Website: http://www.uri.edu/hss/education/.

University of Rio Grande, Graduate School, Rio Grande, OH 45674. Offers classroom teaching (M Ed), including fine arts, learning disabilities, mathematics, reading education. *Accreditation:* NCATE. Part-time and evening/weekend programs available. *Degree requirements:* For master's, final research project, portfolio. *Entrance requirements:* For master's, minimum GPA of 2.7 in major, 2.5 overall. Additional exam requirements/recommendations for international students: Required—TOEFL. *Faculty research:* Interagency collaboration, reading and mathematics, learning styles, college access, literacy.

University of Rochester, Margaret Warner Graduate School of Education and Human Development, Rochester, NY 14627. Offers MS, Ed D, PhD. *Accreditation:* ACA (one or more programs are accredited); NCATE. Part-time and evening/weekend programs available. Terminal master's awarded for partial completion of doctoral program. *Degree requirements:* For master's, thesis (for some programs); for doctorate, thesis/dissertation, qualifying exam. *Expenses: Tuition:* Full-time $44,580; part-time $1394 per credit hour. *Required fees:* $492.

University of St. Francis, College of Education, Joliet, IL 60435-6169. Offers educational leadership (MS, Ed D); elementary education (M Ed); higher education (MS); reading (MS); secondary education (M Ed), including English education, math education, science education, social studies education, visual arts education; special education (M Ed); teaching and learning (MS). *Accreditation:* NCATE. Part-time and evening/weekend programs available. Postbaccalaureate distance learning degree programs offered (no on-campus study). *Faculty:* 10 full-time (8 women), 34 part-time/adjunct (25 women). *Students:* 14 full-time (13 women), 250 part-time (183 women); includes 34 minority (20 Black or African American, non-Hispanic/Latino; 1 American Indian or Alaska Native, non-Hispanic/Latino; 13 Hispanic/Latino), 1 international. Average age 36. 133 applicants, 62% accepted, 71 enrolled. In 2013, 147 master's awarded. *Degree requirements:* For doctorate, thesis/dissertation. *Entrance requirements:* For doctorate, master's degree, IL Type 75 or Principal's endorsement, interview, minimum undergraduate GPA of 3.0, professional portfolio, letter of recommendation. Additional exam requirements/recommendations for international students: Required—TOEFL (minimum score 550 paper-based; 79 iBT), IELTS (minimum score 6.5). *Application deadline:* Applications are processed on a rolling basis. Application fee: $30. Electronic applications accepted. Application fee is waived when completed online. *Expenses:* Contact institution. *Financial support:* In 2013–14, 10 students received support. Scholarships/grants, tuition waivers (partial), and unspecified assistantships available. Support available to part-time students. Financial award applicants required to submit FAFSA. *Unit head:* Dr. John Gambro, Dean, 815-740-3829, Fax: 815-740-2264, E-mail: jgambro@stfrancis.edu. *Application contact:* Sandra Sloka, Director of Admissions for Graduate and Degree Completion Programs, 800-735-7500, Fax: 815-740-3431, E-mail: ssloka@stfrancis.edu.
Website: http://www.stfrancis.edu/academics/college-of-education/.

University of Saint Francis, Graduate School, Department of Education, Fort Wayne, IN 46808-3994. Offers 21st century interventions (Post Master's Certificate); special education (MS Ed), including intense intervention, mild intervention, special education. *Accreditation:* NCATE. Part-time and evening/weekend programs available. Postbaccalaureate distance learning degree programs offered (no on-campus study). *Faculty:* 2. *Students:* 3 full-time (1 woman), 14 part-time (13 women); includes 1 minority (Black or African American, non-Hispanic/Latino). Average age 31. 4 applicants, 100% accepted, 4 enrolled. In 2013, 6 master's awarded. *Degree requirements:* For master's, comprehensive exam. *Entrance requirements:* For master's, GRE or MAT if undergraduate GPA is less than 3.0, minimum undergraduate GPA of 2.8; standard teaching license and/or bachelor's degree from regionally-accredited institution (or CASA scores if no license). *Application deadline:* For fall admission, 7/1 priority date for domestic students; for spring admission, 11/1 priority date for domestic students. Applications are processed on a rolling basis. Application fee: $20. Application fee is waived when completed online. *Financial support:* Federal Work-Study, scholarships/grants, and unspecified assistantships available. Support available to part-time students. Financial award application deadline: 3/10; financial award applicants required to submit FAFSA. *Unit head:* Maureen McCon, Licensing Officer/Unit Assessment System (UAS) Coordinator, 260-399-7700 Ext. 8415, Fax: 260-399-8170, E-mail: mmccon@sf.edu. *Application contact:* James Cashdollar, Admissions Counselor, 260-399-7700 Ext. 6302, Fax: 260-399-8152, E-mail: jcashdollar@sf.edu.
Website: http://www.sf.edu/sf/education.

University of Saint Joseph, Department of Education, West Hartford, CT 06117-2700. Offers education (MA); special education (MA). Part-time and evening/weekend programs available. *Degree requirements:* For master's, comprehensive exam, thesis or alternative. *Entrance requirements:* For master's, 2 letters of recommendation. Electronic applications accepted. Application fee is waived when completed online.

University of Saint Mary, Graduate Programs, Program in Education, Leavenworth, KS 66048-5082. Offers MA. *Accreditation:* NCATE. Part-time and evening/weekend programs available. Postbaccalaureate distance learning degree programs offered (no on-campus study). *Students:* 40 full-time (27 women), 5 part-time (all women); includes 3 minority (1 Asian, non-Hispanic/Latino; 2 Hispanic/Latino). *Degree requirements:* For master's, thesis, oral presentation. *Entrance requirements:* For master's, minimum undergraduate GPA of 2.75, bachelor's degree from accredited college, interview, official transcripts, two letters of recommendation, essay. *Application deadline:* Applications are processed on a rolling basis. Application fee: $25. *Expenses: Tuition:* Part-time $550 per credit hour. *Faculty research:* Curriculum and instruction. *Unit head:* Dr. Gwen Landever, Chair, 913-319-3009, E-mail: landever59@stmary.edu. *Application contact:* Dr. Ron Logan, Graduate Dean, 913-345-8288, Fax: 913-345-2802, E-mail: loganr@stmary.edu.

University of Saint Mary, Graduate Programs, Program in Teaching, Leavenworth, KS 66048-5082. Offers MAT. Part-time and evening/weekend programs available. *Degree requirements:* For master's, thesis. *Entrance requirements:* For master's, minimum undergraduate GPA of 2.75. *Expenses: Tuition:* Part-time $550 per credit hour.

University of St. Thomas, Graduate Studies, School of Education, St. Paul, MN 55105-1096. Offers MA, Ed D, Certificate, Ed S. Part-time and evening/weekend programs available. *Entrance requirements:* For master's, minimum GPA of 3.0 or MAT. Additional exam requirements/recommendations for international students: Required—TOEFL (minimum score 550 paper-based; 80 iBT). *Application deadline:* For fall admission, 6/1 priority date for domestic students; for spring admission, 11/1 priority date for domestic students. Applications are processed on a rolling basis. Application fee: $50. *Expenses:* Contact institution. *Financial support:* Fellowships, research assistantships, career-related internships or fieldwork, institutionally sponsored loans, and scholarships/grants available. Support available to part-time students. Financial award applicants required to submit FAFSA. *Unit head:* Dr. Mark Salisbury, Dean, 651-962-4435, Fax: 651-962-4169, E-mail: marksalisbury@stthomas.edu. *Application contact:* Dr. Mark Salisbury, Dean, 651-962-4435, Fax: 651-962-4169, E-mail: marksalisbury@stthomas.edu.

University of St. Thomas, School of Education, Houston, TX 77006-4696. Offers all level education (M Ed); bilingual/dual language (M Ed); Catholic school teaching (M Ed); Catholic/private school leadership (M Ed); counselor education (M Ed); curriculum and instruction (M Ed); educational leadership (M Ed); elementary teaching (M Ed); English as a second language (M Ed); exceptionality/educational diagnostician (M Ed); exceptionality/special education (M Ed); generalist (M Ed); reading (M Ed); secondary teaching (M Ed). *Accreditation:* Teacher Education Accreditation Council. Part-time and evening/weekend programs available. Postbaccalaureate distance learning degree programs offered (no on-campus study). *Faculty:* 40 full-time (26 women), 43 part-time/adjunct (31 women). *Students:* 27 full-time (20 women), 1,091 part-time (981 women); includes 691 minority (247 Black or African American, non-Hispanic/Latino; 1 American Indian or Alaska Native, non-Hispanic/Latino; 44 Asian, non-Hispanic/Latino; 379 Hispanic/Latino; 2 Native Hawaiian or other Pacific Islander, non-Hispanic/Latino; 18 Two or more races, non-Hispanic/Latino), 28 international. Average age 36. 858 applicants, 83% accepted, 458 enrolled. In 2013, 454 master's awarded. *Degree requirements:* For master's, thesis, field experience. *Entrance requirements:* For master's, GRE or MAT if GPA is below 3.0, bachelor's degree; minimum GPA of 2.75 in bachelor's degree or last 60 credit hours; official transcripts from all institutions; goal statement of 250-300 words; 1 reference. Additional exam requirements/recommendations for international students: Required—TOEFL. *Application deadline:* Applications are processed on a rolling basis. Application fee: $35. Electronic applications accepted. *Expenses:* Contact institution. *Financial support:* In 2013–14, 41 students received support. Federal Work-Study, scholarships/grants, and state work-study, institutional employment available. Support available to part-time students. Financial award application deadline: 4/15; financial award applicants required to submit FAFSA. *Faculty research:* Leadership, diversity, personality traits, second language acquisition. *Unit head:* Dr. Robert LeBlanc, Dean, 713-525-3540, Fax: 713-525-3871, E-mail: education@stthom.edu. *Application contact:* Rita Paredes, Administrative Assistant, 713-525-3442, Fax: 713-525-3871, E-mail: rparede@stthom.edu.
Website: http://www.stthom.edu/Academics/School_of_Education/Index.aqf.

University of San Diego, School of Leadership and Education Sciences, San Diego, CA 92110-2492. Offers M Ed, MA, MAT, PhD, Certificate. *Accreditation:* NCATE. Part-time and evening/weekend programs available. *Faculty:* 31 full-time (18 women), 96 part-time/adjunct (72 women). *Students:* 319 full-time (259 women), 269 part-time (200 women); includes 220 minority (29 Black or African American, non-Hispanic/Latino; 2 American Indian or Alaska Native, non-Hispanic/Latino; 38 Asian, non-Hispanic/Latino; 112 Hispanic/Latino; 5 Native Hawaiian or other Pacific Islander, non-Hispanic/Latino; 34 Two or more races, non-Hispanic/Latino), 39 international. Average age 30. In 2013, 220 master's, 13 doctorates awarded. *Degree requirements:* For master's, international experience; for doctorate, comprehensive exam (for some programs), thesis/dissertation (for some programs), international experience. *Entrance requirements:* For doctorate, GRE General Test, master's degree. Additional exam requirements/recommendations for international students: Required—TOEFL (minimum score 580 paper-based; 83 iBT), TWE. Application fee: $45. *Expenses: Tuition:* Full-time $23,580; part-time $1310 per credit. *Required fees:* $350. *Financial support:* In 2013–14, 364 students received support. Career-related internships or fieldwork, Federal Work-Study, institutionally sponsored loans, unspecified assistantships, and stipends available. Support available to part-time students. Financial award application deadline: 4/1; financial award applicants required to submit FAFSA. *Unit head:* Dr. Paula A. Cordeiro, Dean, 619-260-4540, Fax: 619-260-6835, E-mail: cordeiro@sandiego.edu. *Application contact:* Monica Mahon, Associate Director of Graduate Admissions, 619-260-4524, Fax: 619-260-4158, E-mail: grads@sandiego.edu.
Website: http://www.sandiego.edu/soles/.

University of San Francisco, School of Education, San Francisco, CA 94117-1080. Offers MA, Ed D. Part-time and evening/weekend programs available. *Faculty:* 26 full-time (17 women), 109 part-time/adjunct (70 women). *Students:* 772 full-time (594 women), 198 part-time (143 women); includes 409 minority (63 Black or African American, non-Hispanic/Latino; 2 American Indian or Alaska Native, non-Hispanic/Latino; 102 Asian, non-Hispanic/Latino; 192 Hispanic/Latino; 4 Native Hawaiian or other Pacific Islander, non-Hispanic/Latino; 46 Two or more races, non-Hispanic/Latino), 47 international. Average age 32. 917 applicants, 82% accepted, 385 enrolled. In 2013, 413 master's, 32 doctorates awarded. *Degree requirements:* For doctorate, thesis/dissertation. *Entrance requirements:* For master's, CBEST, CSET, and/or CSET Writing Skills (depending on program); for doctorate, GRE or MAT. Additional exam requirements/recommendations for international students: Required—TOEFL (minimum score 580 paper-based; 92 iBT), IELTS (minimum score 7), PTE (minimum score 62). *Application deadline:* For fall admission, 5/1 priority date for domestic and international students; for spring admission, 10/1 priority date for domestic and international students. Applications are processed on a rolling basis. Application fee: $55 ($65 for international students). Electronic applications accepted. *Expenses: Tuition:* Full-time $21,150; part-time $1175 per unit. Tuition and fees vary according to course load, campus/location and program. *Financial support:* In 2013–14, 111 students received support. Fellowships, research assistantships, and teaching assistantships available. Financial award application deadline: 3/2; financial award applicants required to submit FAFSA. *Unit head:* Dr. Kevin Kumashiro, Dean, 415-422-6525. *Application contact:* Amy Fogliani, Associate Director of Graduate Outreach, 415-422-5467, E-mail: schoolofeducation@usfca.edu.

University of Saskatchewan, College of Graduate Studies and Research, College of Education, Saskatoon, SK S7N 5A2, Canada. Offers M Ed, MC Ed, PhD, Diploma. Part-time programs available. *Degree requirements:* For master's, thesis (for some programs); for doctorate, comprehensive exam (for some programs), thesis/dissertation. *Entrance requirements:* Additional exam requirements/recommendations for international students: Required—TOEFL (minimum score 80 iBT); Recommended—IELTS (minimum score 6.5). Electronic applications accepted. *Expenses: Tuition, area resident:* Full-time $3585 Canadian dollars; part-time $585 Canadian dollars per course. Tuition, nonresident: part-time $877 Canadian dollars per course. *International tuition:* $5377 Canadian dollars full-time. *Required fees:* $889.51 Canadian dollars.

The University of Scranton, College of Graduate and Continuing Education, Department of Education, Scranton, PA 18510. Offers curriculum and instruction (MA, MS); early childhood education (MS); educational administration (MS); reading education (MS); secondary education (MS). *Accreditation:* NCATE. Part-time and evening/weekend programs available. Postbaccalaureate distance learning degree programs offered (no on-campus study). *Faculty:* 17 full-time (11 women), 47 part-time/adjunct (18 women). *Students:* 169 full-time (106 women), 175 part-time (116 women); includes 45 minority (21 Black or African American, non-Hispanic/Latino; 1 American Indian or Alaska Native, non-Hispanic/Latino; 4 Asian, non-Hispanic/Latino; 18 Hispanic/Latino; 1 Two or more races, non-Hispanic/Latino), 2 international. Average age 28. 91 applicants, 92% accepted. In 2013, 291 master's awarded. *Degree requirements:* For master's, comprehensive exam, thesis (for some programs), capstone experience. *Entrance requirements:* For master's, minimum GPA of 3.0. Additional exam requirements/recommendations for international students: Required—TOEFL (minimum score 500 paper-based), IELTS (minimum score 6). *Application deadline:* Applications are processed on a rolling basis. Application fee: $0. *Financial support:* In 2013–14, 14 students received support, including 14 teaching assistantships with full and partial tuition reimbursements available (averaging $4,400 per year); fellowships, career-related internships or fieldwork, Federal Work-Study, and unspecified assistantships also available. Support available to part-time students. Financial award application deadline: 3/1. *Faculty research:* Meta-analysis as a research tool, family involvement in school activities, effect of curriculum integration on student learning and attitude, the effects of inclusion on students, development of emotional intelligence of young children. *Unit head:* Dr. Art Chambers, Chair, 570-941-4668, Fax: 570-941-5515, E-mail: lchambersa2@scranton.edu. *Application contact:* Joseph M. Roback, Director of Admissions, 570-941-4385, Fax: 570-941-5928, E-mail: robackj2@scranton.edu. Website: http://matrix.scranton.edu/academics/pcps/education/.

University of Sioux Falls, Fredrikson School of Education, Sioux Falls, SD 57105-1699. Offers educational administration (Ed S), including principal leadership, superintendent and district leadership; leadership in reading (M Ed); leadership in schools (M Ed); leadership in technology (M Ed); teaching (M Ed). Admission in summer only. *Accreditation:* NCATE. Part-time and evening/weekend programs available. *Degree requirements:* For master's, comprehensive exam (for some programs), research application project; for Ed S, comprehensive exam, portfolio. *Entrance requirements:* For master's, minimum GPA of 3.0, 1 year of teaching experience; for Ed S, minimum 3 years of teaching experience, minimum cumulative GPA of 3.5, 1 year of administrative experience. Additional exam requirements/recommendations for international students: Required—TOEFL. *Faculty research:* Reading, literacy, leadership.

University of South Africa, College of Human Sciences, Pretoria, South Africa. Offers adult education (M Ed); African languages (MA, PhD); African politics (MA, PhD); Afrikaans (MA, PhD); ancient history (MA, PhD); ancient Near Eastern studies (MA, PhD); anthropology (MA, PhD); applied linguistics (MA, PhD); Arabic (MA, PhD); archaeology (MA); art history (MA); Biblical archaeology (MA); Biblical studies (M Th, D Th, PhD); Christian spirituality (M Th, D Th); church history (M Th, D Th); classical studies (MA, PhD); clinical psychology (MA); communication (MA, PhD); comparative education (M Ed, Ed D); consulting psychology (D Admin, D Com, PhD); curriculum studies (M Ed, Ed D); development studies (M Admin, MA, D Admin, PhD); didactics (M Ed, Ed D); education (M Tech); education management (M Ed, Ed D); educational psychology (M Ed); English (MA); environmental education (M Ed); French (MA, PhD); German (MA, PhD); Greek (MA); guidance and counseling (M Ed); health studies (MA, PhD), including health sciences education (MA), health services management (MA), medical and surgical nursing science (critical care general) (MA), midwifery and neonatal nursing science (MA), trauma and emergency care (MA); history (MA, PhD); history of education (Ed D); inclusive education (M Ed, Ed D); information and communications technology policy and regulation (MA); information science (MA, MIS, PhD); international politics (MA, PhD); Islamic studies (MA, PhD); Italian (MA, PhD); Judaica (MA, PhD); linguistics (MA, PhD); mathematical education (M Ed); mathematics education (MA); missiology (M Th, D Th); modern Hebrew (MA, PhD); musicology (MA, MMus, D Mus, PhD); natural science education (M Ed); New Testament (M Th, D Th); Old Testament (D Th); pastoral therapy (M Th, D Th); philosophy (MA); philosophy of education (M Ed, Ed D); politics (MA, PhD); Portuguese (MA, PhD); practical theology (M Th, D Th); psychology (MA, MS, PhD); psychology of education (M Ed, Ed D); public health (MA); religious studies (MA, D Th, PhD); Romance languages (MA); Russian (MA, PhD); Semitic languages (MA, PhD); social behavior studies in HIV/AIDS (MA); social science (mental health) (MA); social science in development studies (MA); social science in psychology (MA); social science in social work (MA); social science in sociology (MA); social work (MSW, DSW, PhD); socio-education (M Ed, Ed D); sociolinguistics (MA); sociology (MA, PhD); Spanish (MA, PhD); systematic theology (M Th, D Th); TESOL (teaching English to speakers of other languages) (MA); theological ethics (M Th, D Th); theory of literature (MA, PhD); urban ministries (D Th); urban ministry (M Th).

University of South Alabama, Graduate School, College of Education, Mobile, AL 36688-0002. Offers M Ed, MS, PhD, Ed S. *Accreditation:* NCATE. Part-time programs available. *Faculty:* 39 full-time (20 women), 6 part-time/adjunct (4 women). *Students:* 251 full-time (184 women), 150 part-time (124 women); includes 86 minority (67 Black or African American, non-Hispanic/Latino; 1 American Indian or Alaska Native, non-Hispanic/Latino; 2 Asian, non-Hispanic/Latino; 7 Hispanic/Latino; 1 Native Hawaiian or other Pacific Islander, non-Hispanic/Latino; 8 Two or more races, non-Hispanic/Latino), 7 international. 186 applicants, 58% accepted, 96 enrolled. In 2013, 137 master's, 4 doctorates awarded. *Degree requirements:* For master's, comprehensive exam; for doctorate, comprehensive exam, thesis/dissertation. *Entrance requirements:* For master's, GRE General Test or MAT. Additional exam requirements/recommendations for international students: Required—TOEFL. *Application deadline:* For fall admission, 7/15 priority date for domestic students, 6/15 priority date for international students; for spring admission, 12/1 priority date for domestic students, 11/1 priority date for international students. Applications are processed on a rolling basis. Application fee: $35. *Expenses:* Tuition, state resident: full-time $8976; part-time $374 per credit hour. Tuition, nonresident: full-time $17,952; part-time $748 per credit hour. *Financial support:* In 2013–14, 23 research assistantships, 10 teaching assistantships were awarded; career-related internships or fieldwork also available. Support available to part-time students. Financial award application deadline: 4/1. *Unit head:* Dr. Richard Hayes, Dean, 251-380-2738. *Application contact:* Dr. Abigail Baxter, Director of Graduate Studies, 251-380-2738, Fax: 251-380-2748, E-mail: abaxter@southalabama.edu. Website: http://www.southalabama.edu/coe.

University of South Carolina, The Graduate School, College of Education, Columbia, SC 29208. Offers IMA, M Ed, MAT, MS, MT, Ed D, PhD, Certificate, Ed S. *Accreditation:* NCATE. Part-time and evening/weekend programs available. Postbaccalaureate distance learning degree programs offered (minimal on-campus study). *Degree requirements:* For master's, comprehensive exam, thesis (for some programs), foreign language (MA); for doctorate, one foreign language, comprehensive exam, thesis/dissertation. *Entrance requirements:* For master's, GRE General Test or MAT, official transcripts, letters of recommendation, letter of intent; for doctorate, GRE General Test or MAT/qualifying exams, letters of recommendation, letters of intent, interview. Electronic applications accepted. *Faculty research:* Inquiry learning, assessment of student learning, equity issues in education, multicultural education, cultural diversity.

University of South Carolina Upstate, Graduate Programs, Spartanburg, SC 29303-4999. Offers early childhood education (M Ed); elementary education (M Ed); informatics (MS); special education: visual impairment (M Ed). *Accreditation:* NCATE. Part-time and evening/weekend programs available. *Faculty:* 8 full-time (6 women), 5 part-time/adjunct (4 women). *Students:* 10 full-time (4 women), 13 part-time (11 women); includes 8 minority (6 Black or African American, non-Hispanic/Latino; 2 Two or more races, non-Hispanic/Latino). Average age 33. In 2013, 11 master's awarded. *Degree requirements:* For master's, professional portfolio. *Entrance requirements:* For master's, GRE General Test or MAT, interview, minimum undergraduate GPA of 2.5, teaching certificate, 2 letters of recommendation. *Application deadline:* Applications are processed on a rolling basis. Application fee: $40. *Expenses:* Tuition, state resident: full-time $11,272; part-time $470 per semester hour. Tuition, nonresident: full-time $24,196; part-time $1008 per semester hour. Tuition and fees vary according to course load and program. *Financial support:* Institutionally sponsored loans and institutional work-study available. Financial award application deadline: 7/15; financial award applicants required to submit FAFSA. *Faculty research:* Promoting university diversity awareness, rough and tumble play, social justice education, American Indian literatures and cultures, diversity and multicultural education, science teaching strategy. *Unit head:* Dr. Tina Herzberg, Director of Graduate Programs, 864-503-5572, Fax: 864-503-5573, E-mail: rstevens@uscupstate.edu. *Application contact:* Donette Stewart, Associate Vice Chancellor for Enrollment Services, 864-503-5280, E-mail: dstewart@uscupstate.edu. Website: http://www.uscupstate.edu/graduate/.

The University of South Dakota, Graduate School, School of Education, Vermillion, SD 57069-2390. Offers MA, MS, Ed D, PhD, Ed S. *Accreditation:* NCATE. Part-time and evening/weekend programs available. Postbaccalaureate distance learning degree programs offered (no on-campus study). *Degree requirements:* For master's and Ed S, comprehensive exam, thesis or alternative; for doctorate, comprehensive exam, thesis/dissertation. *Entrance requirements:* For master's and doctorate, GRE General Test or Miller Analogies Test, minimum GPA of 2.7. Additional exam requirements/recommendations for international students: Required—TOEFL (minimum score 550 paper-based; 79 iBT). Electronic applications accepted.

University of Southern California, Graduate School, Rossier School of Education, Los Angeles, CA 90089. Offers MAT, ME, MMFT, Ed D, PhD. *Degree requirements:* For master's, thesis optional; for doctorate, thesis/dissertation. *Entrance requirements:* For master's and doctorate, GRE. Additional exam requirements/recommendations for international students: Required—TOEFL (minimum score 100 iBT). Electronic applications accepted. *Faculty research:* Data-driven decision-making in K-12 schools and districts; examination of college and university leadership and management in U. S. and Asia; studies in facilitating student learning; organizational change and the role of leaders; leadership, diversity, learning and accountability.

University of Southern Indiana, Graduate Studies, College of Science, Engineering, and Education, Department of Teacher Education, Evansville, IN 47712-3590. Offers elementary education (MS); secondary education (MS). *Accreditation:* NCATE. Part-time and evening/weekend programs available. *Faculty:* 8 full-time (7 women), 3 part-time/adjunct (1 woman). *Students:* 2 full-time (both women), 83 part-time (71 women); includes 2 minority (1 Black or African American, non-Hispanic/Latino; 1 Two or more races, non-Hispanic/Latino), 8 international. Average age 33. 25 applicants, 76% accepted, 16 enrolled. In 2013, 44 master's awarded. *Entrance requirements:* For master's, GRE General Test, NTE or PRAXIS II, minimum GPA of 3.0, teaching license. Additional exam requirements/recommendations for international students: Required—TOEFL (minimum score 550 paper-based; 79 iBT), IELTS (minimum score 6). *Application deadline:* For fall admission, 7/1 priority date for domestic students, 1/1 priority date for international students. Applications are processed on a rolling basis. Application fee: $40. Electronic applications accepted. *Expenses:* Tuition, state resident: full-time $5567; part-time $309 per credit hour. Tuition, nonresident: full-time $10,977; part-time $610 per credit. *Required fees:* $23 per semester. *Financial support:* In 2013–14, 12 students received support. Federal Work-Study, scholarships/grants, tuition waivers (full and partial), and unspecified assistantships available. Financial award application deadline: 3/1; financial award applicants required to submit FAFSA. *Unit head:* Dr. Vella Goebel, Director, 812-461-5306, E-mail: vgoebel@usi.edu. *Application contact:* Dr. Mayola Rowser, Interim Director, Graduate Studies, 812-465-7016, Fax: 812-464-1956, E-mail: mrowser@usi.edu.

University of Southern Maine, College of Management and Human Service, School of Education and Human Development, Gorham, ME 04038. Offers MS, MS Ed, Psy D, CAS, CGS, Certificate. *Accreditation:* Teacher Education Accreditation Council. Part-time and evening/weekend programs available. Postbaccalaureate distance learning degree programs offered (minimal on-campus study). *Faculty:* 29 full-time (17 women), 19 part-time/adjunct (14 women). *Students:* 160 full-time (119 women), 377 part-time (297 women); includes 21 minority (3 Black or African American, non-Hispanic/Latino; 7 American Indian or Alaska Native, non-Hispanic/Latino; 3 Asian, non-Hispanic/Latino; 4 Hispanic/Latino; 1 Native Hawaiian or other Pacific Islander, non-Hispanic/Latino; 3 Two or more races, non-Hispanic/Latino), 1 international. Average age 36. 292 applicants, 74% accepted, 159 enrolled. In 2013, 194 master's, 5 doctorates, 76 other advanced degrees awarded. Terminal master's awarded for partial completion of doctoral program. *Degree requirements:* For master's, comprehensive exam (for some programs), thesis or alternative; for doctorate, thesis/dissertation; for other advanced degree, thesis or alternative. *Entrance requirements:* For master's, GRE General Test or MAT, PRAXIS (for extended teacher education), proof of teacher certification; for doctorate, GRE; for other advanced degree, master's degree. Additional exam requirements/recommendations for international students: Required—TOEFL (minimum score 550 paper-based; 79 iBT). Application fee: $65. Electronic applications accepted. *Expenses:* Tuition, state resident: part-time $380 per credit. Tuition, nonresident: part-time $1026 per credit. Part-time tuition and fees vary according to program. *Financial support:* Research assistantships, career-related internships or fieldwork, Federal Work-Study, institutionally sponsored loans, scholarships/grants, and unspecified assistantships available. Support available to part-time students. Financial award application deadline: 3/1; financial award applicants required to submit FAFSA. *Faculty research:* Teacher development, library technology outreach, literacy through literature, college-bound, multicultural education, school psychology, education policy and evaluation. *Application contact:* Mary Sloan, Assistant Dean of Graduate Studies and Director of Graduate Admissions, 207-780-4386, E-mail: gradstudies@usm.maine.edu. Website: http://www.usm.maine.edu/sehd/.

Education—General

University of Southern Mississippi, Graduate School, College of Education and Psychology, Hattiesburg, MS 39406-0001. Offers M Ed, MA, MAT, MLIS, MS, Ed D, PhD, Ed S, Graduate Certificate. *Accreditation:* NCATE. Part-time programs available. *Faculty:* 98 full-time (51 women), 13 part-time/adjunct (4 women). *Students:* 255 full-time (195 women), 522 part-time (399 women); includes 181 minority (139 Black or African American, non-Hispanic/Latino; 5 Asian, non-Hispanic/Latino; 14 Hispanic/Latino; 23 Two or more races, non-Hispanic/Latino), 20 international. Average age 35. 412 applicants, 45% accepted, 145 enrolled. In 2013, 174 master's, 76 doctorates, 29 other advanced degrees awarded. Terminal master's awarded for partial completion of doctoral program. *Degree requirements:* For master's, comprehensive exam, thesis (for some programs); for doctorate, comprehensive exam, thesis/dissertation; for other advanced degree, comprehensive exam, thesis. *Entrance requirements:* For master's, GRE General Test, MAT, minimum GPA of 2.75 on last 60 hours; for doctorate, GRE General Test, minimum GPA of 3.5; for other advanced degree, GRE General Test. Additional exam requirements/recommendations for international students: Required—TOEFL, IELTS. *Application deadline:* For fall admission, 3/1 priority date for domestic students, 3/1 for international students; for spring admission, 11/1 priority date for domestic students, 11/1 for international students. Applications are processed on a rolling basis. Application fee: $50. Electronic applications accepted. *Financial support:* In 2013–14, 80 research assistantships with full tuition reimbursements (averaging $9,586 per year), 53 teaching assistantships with full tuition reimbursements (averaging $7,775 per year) were awarded; career-related internships or fieldwork, Federal Work-Study, institutionally sponsored loans, scholarships/grants, health care benefits, and unspecified assistantships also available. Financial award application deadline: 3/15; financial award applicants required to submit FAFSA. *Faculty research:* Reading, sleep, animal cognition. *Unit head:* Dr. Ann P. Blackwell, Dean, 601-266-4568, Fax: 601-266-4175. *Application contact:* Shonna Breland, Manager of Graduate Admissions, 601-266-6563, Fax: 601-266-5138.
Website: http://www.usm.edu/graduateschool/table.php.

University of South Florida, College of Education, Tampa, FL 33620-9951. Offers M Ed, MA, MAT, Ed D, PhD, Ed S. *Accreditation:* NCATE. Part-time and evening/weekend programs available. Postbaccalaureate distance learning degree programs offered (no on-campus study). *Degree requirements:* For master's, comprehensive exam, thesis (for some programs), project (for some programs); for doctorate, comprehensive exam, thesis/dissertation, philosophies of inquiry; multiple research methods. *Entrance requirements:* For master's, GRE General Test, minimum GPA of 3.5 in last 60 hours of course work; for doctorate, GRE General Test, minimum GPA of 3.5; for Ed S, GRE General Test. Additional exam requirements/recommendations for international students: Required—TOEFL (minimum score 550 paper-based). Electronic applications accepted. *Faculty research:* Scholarship of teaching and learning, educator preparation, diversity issues as they relate to PK-20 education, urban education.

University of South Florida–St. Petersburg Campus, College of Education, St. Petersburg, FL 33701. Offers educational leadership development (M Ed); elementary education (MA), including math/science; English education (MA); middle grades STEM education (MS); reading education (MA). Part-time programs available. *Degree requirements:* For master's, comprehensive exam, practicum, internship, comprehensive portfolio. *Entrance requirements:* For master's, State of Florida General Knowledge Test (GKT), Florida Teaching Certificate (for non-initial certification programs), letters of recommendation. Additional exam requirements/recommendations for international students: Required—TOEFL (minimum score 550 paper-based; 79 iBT); Recommended—IELTS. Electronic applications accepted.

University of South Florida Sarasota-Manatee, College of Education, Sarasota, FL 34243. Offers education (MA); educational leadership (M Ed), including curriculum leadership, K-12, non-public/charter school leadership; English education (MA); teaching K-6 with ESOL endorsement (MAT). Part-time and evening/weekend programs available. *Faculty:* 7 full-time (all women), 5 part-time/adjunct (3 women). *Students:* 11 full-time (9 women), 43 part-time (33 women); includes 6 minority (2 Black or African American, non-Hispanic/Latino; 2 Hispanic/Latino; 1 Native Hawaiian or other Pacific Islander, non-Hispanic/Latino; 1 Two or more races, non-Hispanic/Latino). Average age 33. 46 applicants, 39% accepted, 15 enrolled. In 2013, 33 master's awarded. *Degree requirements:* For master's, comprehensive exam (for some programs). *Entrance requirements:* For master's, GRE (within last 5 years) or minimum GPA of 3.0, letters of recommendation. Additional exam requirements/recommendations for international students: Required—TOEFL (minimum score 550 paper-based; 79 iBT), IELTS (minimum score 6.5). *Application deadline:* For fall admission, 3/1 priority date for domestic students, 3/1 for international students; for spring admission, 10/1 priority date for domestic students, 10/1 for international students. Applications are processed on a rolling basis. Application fee: $30. Electronic applications accepted. *Expenses:* Tuition, state resident: full-time $10,029; part-time $418 per credit. Tuition, nonresident: full-time $20,727; part-time $863 per credit. *Required fees:* $10; $5. Tuition and fees vary according to program. *Financial support:* In 2013–14, 10 students received support. Career-related internships or fieldwork, institutionally sponsored loans, scholarships/grants, health care benefits, and unspecified assistantships available. Support available to part-time students. Financial award application deadline: 3/1; financial award applicants required to submit FAFSA. *Faculty research:* Child development, student achievement, inter-generational studies, equitable implementation of educational policy, linguistics and its applications. *Unit head:* Dr. Terry A. Osborn, Dean, 941-359-4531, Fax: 941-359-4778, E-mail: terryosborn@sar.usf.edu. *Application contact:* Andy Telatovich, Director, Admissions, 941-359-4330, Fax: 941-359-4585, E-mail: atelatovich@sar.usf.edu.
Website: http://usfsm.edu/college-of-education/.

The University of Tampa, Program in Teaching, Tampa, FL 33606-1490. Offers curricula and instructional leadership (M Ed); teaching (M Ed). Part-time and evening/weekend programs available. *Faculty:* 7 full-time (4 women), 6 part-time/adjunct (5 women). *Students:* 34 full-time (26 women), 47 part-time (32 women); includes 27 minority (11 Black or African American, non-Hispanic/Latino; 1 Asian, non-Hispanic/Latino; 11 Hispanic/Latino; 4 Two or more races, non-Hispanic/Latino), 3 international. Average age 32. 115 applicants, 54% accepted, 32 enrolled. In 2013, 9 master's awarded. *Entrance requirements:* For master's, Florida Teacher Certification Exam, PRAXIS, GRE, or GMAT, bachelor's degree in education or professional teaching certificate. Additional exam requirements/recommendations for international students: Required—TOEFL (minimum score 577 paper-based; 90 iBT), IELTS (minimum score 7). *Application deadline:* For fall admission, 5/1 for domestic students. Applications are processed on a rolling basis. Application fee: $40. Electronic applications accepted. *Expenses: Tuition:* Full-time $8928; part-time $558 per credit hour. *Required fees:* $80; $80 $40 per term. Tuition and fees vary according to program. *Financial support:* In 2013–14, 24 students received support. Scholarships/grants available. Financial award applicants required to submit FAFSA. *Faculty research:* Diversity in the classroom, technology integration, assessment methodologies, complex and ill-structured problem solving, and communities of practice. *Unit head:* Dr. Johnathan McKeown, Director, Education Master's Program, 813-257-6306, E-mail: jmckeown@ut.edu. *Application contact:* Brent Benner, Director of Admissions, 813-257-3642, E-mail: bbenner@ut.edu.
Website: http://www.ut.edu/graduate.

The University of Tennessee, Graduate School, College of Education, Health and Human Sciences, Knoxville, TN 37996. Offers MPH, MS, Ed D, PhD, Ed S, MS/MPH. *Accreditation:* NCATE. Part-time and evening/weekend programs available. Postbaccalaureate distance learning degree programs offered (no on-campus study). Terminal master's awarded for partial completion of doctoral program. *Degree requirements:* For master's and Ed S, thesis optional; for doctorate, thesis/dissertation. *Entrance requirements:* For master's, minimum GPA of 2.7; for doctorate and Ed S, GRE General Test, minimum GPA of 2.7. Additional exam requirements/recommendations for international students: Required—TOEFL. Electronic applications accepted. *Expenses:* Tuition, state resident: full-time $9540; part-time $531 per credit hour. Tuition, nonresident: full-time $27,728; part-time $1542 per credit hour. *Required fees:* $1404; $67 per credit hour.

The University of Tennessee at Chattanooga, Graduate School, College of Health, Education and Professional Studies, School of Education, Chattanooga, TN 37403. Offers counseling (M Ed), including community counseling, school counseling; education (M Ed, Post-Master's Certificate), including elementary education (M Ed), school leadership, secondary education (M Ed), special education (M Ed); educational specialist (Ed S), including educational technology, school psychology; learning and leadership (Ed D), including educational leadership. *Accreditation:* ACA; NCATE. Part-time and evening/weekend programs available. Postbaccalaureate distance learning degree programs offered (no on-campus study). *Faculty:* 24 full-time (17 women), 6 part-time/adjunct (4 women). *Students:* 107 full-time (86 women), 263 part-time (192 women); includes 71 minority (46 Black or African American, non-Hispanic/Latino; 2 American Indian or Alaska Native, non-Hispanic/Latino; 5 Asian, non-Hispanic/Latino; 11 Hispanic/Latino; 7 Two or more races, non-Hispanic/Latino), 2 international. Average age 34. 121 applicants, 83% accepted, 67 enrolled. In 2013, 125 master's, 10 doctorates, 3 other advanced degrees awarded. *Degree requirements:* For master's, comprehensive exam, thesis optional, culminating experience; for doctorate, comprehensive exam, thesis/dissertation; for other advanced degree, internship. *Entrance requirements:* For master's, GRE General Test, PPST 1, teaching certificate; for doctorate, GRE General Test, master's degree, two years of practical work experience in organizational environment; for other advanced degree, GRE General Test, letters of reference. Additional exam requirements/recommendations for international students: Required—TOEFL (minimum score 550 paper-based; 79 iBT), IELTS (minimum score 6). *Application deadline:* For fall admission, 6/13 for domestic students, 6/1 for international students; for spring admission, 10/15 for domestic students, 10/1 for international students. Applications are processed on a rolling basis. Application fee: $30 ($35 for international students). Electronic applications accepted. *Financial support:* In 2013–14, 20 research assistantships with tuition reimbursements (averaging $6,340 per year), 4 teaching assistantships with tuition reimbursements (averaging $7,234 per year) were awarded; career-related internships or fieldwork, institutionally sponsored loans, scholarships/grants, and unspecified assistantships also available. Support available to part-time students. Financial award applicants required to submit FAFSA. *Faculty research:* School counseling, community counseling, elementary and secondary education, school leadership and administration. *Total annual research expenditures:* $967,880. *Unit head:* Dr. Linda Johnston, Director, 423-425-4122, Fax: 423-425-5380, E-mail: linda-johnston@utc.edu. *Application contact:* Dr. J. Randy Walker, Interim Dean of Graduate Studies, 423-425-4478, Fax: 423-425-5223, E-mail: randy-walker@utc.edu.
Website: http://www.utc.edu/school-education/abouttheschool/gradprograms.php.

The University of Tennessee at Martin, Graduate Programs, College of Education, Health and Behavioral Sciences, Martin, TN 38238-1000. Offers MS Ed. *Accreditation:* NCATE. Part-time programs available. *Faculty:* 45. *Students:* 39 full-time (31 women), 178 part-time (134 women); includes 28 minority (26 Black or African American, non-Hispanic/Latino; 2 Two or more races, non-Hispanic/Latino). 123 applicants, 59% accepted, 54 enrolled. In 2013, 57 master's awarded. *Degree requirements:* For master's, comprehensive exam. *Entrance requirements:* For master's, GRE General Test, minimum GPA of 2.5. Additional exam requirements/recommendations for international students: Required—TOEFL (minimum score 525 paper-based; 71 iBT). *Application deadline:* For fall admission, 7/29 priority date for domestic and international students; for spring admission, 12/12 priority date for domestic and international students. Applications are processed on a rolling basis. Application fee: $30 ($130 for international students). Electronic applications accepted. *Financial support:* In 2013–14, 10 students received support, including 2 research assistantships with full tuition reimbursements available (averaging $7,540 per year), 8 teaching assistantships with full tuition reimbursements available (averaging $7,597 per year); scholarships/grants and unspecified assistantships also available. Support available to part-time students. Financial award application deadline: 1/15; financial award applicants required to submit FAFSA. *Faculty research:* Environmental education, self-concept, science education, attention deficit disorder, special education. *Unit head:* Dr. Gail Stephens, Interim Dean, 731-881-7127, Fax: 731-881-7975, E-mail: gstephe6@utm.edu. *Application contact:* Jolene L. Cunningham, Student Services Specialist, 731-881-7012, Fax: 731-881-7499, E-mail: jcunningham@utm.edu.
Website: http://www.utm.edu/departments/cehbs/.

The University of Texas at Arlington, Graduate School, College of Education and Health Professions, Arlington, TX 76019. Offers M Ed, MS, PhD.

The University of Texas at Arlington, Graduate School, Department of Curriculum and Instruction, Arlington, TX 76019. Offers curriculum and instruction (M Ed); teaching (with certification) (M Ed T). *Accreditation:* NCATE. Part-time and evening/weekend programs available. Postbaccalaureate distance learning degree programs offered (no on-campus study). *Degree requirements:* For master's, comprehensive exam (for some programs), comprehensive activity, research project. *Entrance requirements:* For master's, GRE General Test, minimum undergraduate GPA of 3.0 in last 60 hours of course work, writing sample, 3 letters of recommendation. Additional exam requirements/recommendations for international students: Required—TOEFL (minimum score 550 paper-based). Electronic applications accepted.

The University of Texas at Austin, Graduate School, College of Education, Austin, TX 78712-1111. Offers M Ed, MA, MS, Ed D, PhD. Part-time programs available. *Entrance requirements:* For master's and doctorate, GRE General Test. Electronic applications accepted.

The University of Texas at Brownsville, Graduate Studies, College of Education, Brownsville, TX 78520-4991. Offers bilingual education (M Ed); counseling and guidance (M Ed); curriculum and instruction (M Ed); early childhood education (M Ed); educational leadership (M Ed); educational technology (M Ed); exercise science (MS); special education (M Ed). Part-time and evening/weekend programs available. Postbaccalaureate distance learning degree programs offered (no on-campus study). *Faculty:* 51 full-time (28 women). *Students:* 60 full-time (43 women), 496 part-time (363 women); includes 467 minority (4 Black or African American, non-Hispanic/Latino; 1 American Indian or Alaska Native, non-Hispanic/Latino; 10 Asian, non-Hispanic/Latino; 451 Hispanic/Latino; 1 Native Hawaiian or other Pacific Islander, non-Hispanic/Latino), 12 international. 161 applicants, 67% accepted, 81 enrolled. In 2013, 142 master's awarded. *Degree requirements:* For master's, comprehensive exam (for some programs), thesis optional, electronic portfolio. *Entrance requirements:* For master's,

GRE General Test, curriculum vitae or resume, teaching certificate. Additional exam requirements/recommendations for international students: Required—TOEFL (minimum score 550 paper-based; 77 iBT). *Application deadline:* For fall admission, 7/1 priority date for domestic students, 7/1 for international students; for spring admission, 12/1 priority date for domestic students, 12/1 for international students. Applications are processed on a rolling basis. Application fee: $30. Electronic applications accepted. *Expenses:* Tuition, state resident: full-time $3444; part-time $1148 per semester. Tuition, nonresident: full-time $9816. *Required fees:* $1018; $221 per credit hour. $401 per semester. *Financial support:* In 2013–14, 136 students received support, including 6 research assistantships (averaging $10,000 per year); career-related internships or fieldwork, Federal Work-Study, scholarships/grants, tuition waivers (partial), and unspecified assistantships also available. Support available to part-time students. Financial award application deadline: 3/1; financial award applicants required to submit FAFSA. *Unit head:* Dr. Miguel Angel Escotet, Dean, 956-882-7220, Fax: 956-882-7431, E-mail: miguel.escotet@utb.edu. *Application contact:* Mari E. Stevens, Graduate Studies Specialist, 956-882-6587, Fax: 956-882-7279, E-mail: mari.stevens@utb.edu. Website: http://www.utb.edu/vpaa/coe/Pages/default.aspx.

The University of Texas at El Paso, Graduate School, College of Education, El Paso, TX 79968-0001. Offers M Ed, MA, Ed D, PhD. Part-time and evening/weekend programs available. Postbaccalaureate distance learning degree programs offered. *Degree requirements:* For master's, thesis optional; for doctorate, thesis/dissertation. *Entrance requirements:* For master's, minimum GPA of 3.0, letter of intent, resume, letters of recommendation, copy of teaching certificate, district service record; for doctorate, GRE, resume, letters of recommendation, scholarly paper. Additional exam requirements/recommendations for international students: Required—TOEFL; Recommended—IELTS. Electronic applications accepted.

The University of Texas of the Permian Basin, Office of Graduate Studies, School of Education, Odessa, TX 79762-0001. Offers MA. *Accreditation:* NCATE. *Entrance requirements:* For master's, GRE General Test. Additional exam requirements/recommendations for international students: Required—TOEFL (minimum score 550 paper-based).

The University of Texas–Pan American, College of Education, Edinburg, TX 78539. Offers M Ed, MA, MS, Ed D, PhD. Ed D offered jointly with The University of Texas at Austin. Part-time and evening/weekend programs available. *Degree requirements:* For master's, thesis optional. *Entrance requirements:* For master's, GRE General Test. *Expenses:* Tuition, state resident: full-time $5986; part-time $333 per credit hour. Tuition, nonresident: full-time $12,358; part-time $687 per credit hour. *Required fees:* $782. Tuition and fees vary according to program. *Faculty research:* Literacy development, bilingual education, brain mapping.

University of the Cumberlands, Graduate Programs in Education, Williamsburg, KY 40769-1372. Offers all grades (P-12) (M Ed); business and marketing (MA Ed, MAT); counselor education and supervision (Ed D); director of pupil personnel (Certificate); director of special education (Certificate); educational administration and supervision (Ed S); educational leadership (Ed D); elementary education (MA Ed, MAT); instructional leadership - principalship (MA Ed); instructional leadership - school principal (Certificate); middle school education (MA Ed, MAT); reading and writing (MA Ed); school counseling (MA Ed); school superintendent (Certificate); secondary education (MA Ed, MAT); special education (MAT); supervisor of instruction (Certificate); teacher leader (MA Ed). Part-time and evening/weekend programs available. Postbaccalaureate distance learning degree programs offered. *Degree requirements:* For master's, comprehensive exam. Electronic applications accepted.

University of the District of Columbia, College of Arts and Sciences, Department of Education, Washington, DC 20008-1175. Offers early childhood education (MA); special education (MA). *Accreditation:* NCATE. Part-time programs available. *Degree requirements:* For master's, comprehensive exam, research paper. *Entrance requirements:* For master's, GRE General Test, writing proficiency exam. *Expenses:* Tuition, area resident: Full-time $7883.28; part-time $437.96 per credit hour. Tuition, state resident: full-time $8923.14. Tuition, nonresident: full-time $15,163; part-time $842.40 per credit hour. *Required fees:* $620; $30 per credit hour.

University of the Incarnate Word, Extended Academic Programs, Program in Education, San Antonio, TX 78209-6397. Offers M Ed. Part-time and evening/weekend programs available. Postbaccalaureate distance learning degree programs offered (minimal on-campus study). *Faculty:* 1 (woman) full-time, 4 part-time/adjunct (1 woman). *Students:* 24 part-time (13 women); includes 17 minority (4 Black or African American, non-Hispanic/Latino; 1 Asian, non-Hispanic/Latino; 12 Hispanic/Latino). Average age 38. 10 applicants, 100% accepted, 9 enrolled. In 2013, 5 master's awarded. *Entrance requirements:* For master's, GRE, baccalaureate degree with minimum GPA of 2.5. Additional exam requirements/recommendations for international students: Required—TOEFL (minimum score 560 paper-based; 83 iBT). *Application deadline:* Applications are processed on a rolling basis. Electronic applications accepted. *Expenses:* Tuition: Part-time $815 per credit hour. *Required fees:* $86 per credit hour. One-time fee: $40 part-time. Tuition and fees vary according to degree level and program. *Financial support:* Applicants required to submit FAFSA. *Unit head:* Dr. Cyndi Porter, Vice President, 877-603-1130, E-mail: porter@uiwtx.edu. *Application contact:* Julie Weber, Director of Marketing and Recruitment, 210-832-2100, Fax: 210-829-2756, E-mail: eapadmission@uiwtx.edu.
Website: http://online.uiw.edu/academics/graduate-degrees/master-of-education-in-teacher-leadership.

University of the Incarnate Word, School of Graduate Studies and Research, Dreeben School of Education, Program in Teaching, San Antonio, TX 78209-6397. Offers all-level teaching (MAT); elementary teaching (MAT); secondary teaching (MAT). Part-time and evening/weekend programs available. *Faculty:* 17 full-time (9 women), 6 part-time/adjunct (all women). *Students:* 1 full-time (0 women), 45 part-time (40 women); includes 28 minority (1 Black or African American, non-Hispanic/Latino; 26 Hispanic/Latino; 1 Two or more races, non-Hispanic/Latino). Average age 26. 17 applicants, 88% accepted, 8 enrolled. In 2013, 6 master's awarded. *Degree requirements:* For master's, internship. *Entrance requirements:* For master's, GRE, Texas Higher Education Assessment test (THEA), interview. Additional exam requirements/recommendations for international students: Required—TOEFL (minimum score 560 paper-based; 83 iBT). *Application deadline:* Applications are processed on a rolling basis. Application fee: $20. Electronic applications accepted. *Expenses:* Tuition: Part-time $815 per credit hour. *Required fees:* $86 per credit hour. One-time fee: $40 part-time. Tuition and fees vary according to degree level and program. *Financial support:* Federal Work-Study and scholarships/grants available. Financial award applicants required to submit FAFSA. *Unit head:* Dr. Elda Martinez, Director of Teacher Education, 210-832-3297, Fax: 210-829-3134, E-mail: eemartin@uiwtx.edu. *Application contact:* Andrea Cyterski-Acosta, Dean of Enrollment, 210-829-6005, Fax: 210-829-3921, E-mail: admis@uiwtx.edu.
Website: http://www.uiw.edu/education/graduate.html.

University of the Incarnate Word, School of Graduate Studies and Research, Dreeben School of Education, Programs in Education, San Antonio, TX 78209-6397. Offers adult education (M Ed, MA); cross-cultural education (M Ed, MA); early childhood literacy (M Ed, MA); general education (M Ed, MA); higher education (PhD); instructional technology (M Ed, MA); international education and entrepreneurship (PhD); kinesiology (M Ed, MA); literacy (M Ed, MA); organizational leadership (PhD); organizational learning and learning (M Ed, MA); reading (M Ed, MA); special education (M Ed, MA); teacher leadership (M Ed, MA). Part-time and evening/weekend programs available. *Faculty:* 17 full-time (9 women), 6 part-time/adjunct (all women). *Students:* 23 full-time (13 women), 187 part-time (122 women); includes 114 minority (24 Black or African American, non-Hispanic/Latino; 1 American Indian or Alaska Native, non-Hispanic/Latino; 3 Asian, non-Hispanic/Latino; 85 Hispanic/Latino; 1 Two or more races, non-Hispanic/Latino), 30 international. Average age 41. 52 applicants, 67% accepted, 25 enrolled. In 2013, 12 master's, 14 doctorates awarded. *Degree requirements:* For master's, capstone; for doctorate, thesis/dissertation, qualifying exam. *Entrance requirements:* For master's, baccalaureate degree; minimum foundation GPA of 2.5; interview; for doctorate, master's degree; interview; supervised writing sample. Additional exam requirements/recommendations for international students: Required—TOEFL (minimum score 560 paper-based; 83 iBT). *Application deadline:* Applications are processed on a rolling basis. Application fee: $20. Electronic applications accepted. *Expenses:* Tuition: Part-time $815 per credit hour. *Required fees:* $86 per credit hour. One-time fee: $40 part-time. Tuition and fees vary according to degree level and program. *Financial support:* In 2013–14, 5 research assistantships were awarded; Federal Work-Study and scholarships/grants also available. Financial award applicants required to submit FAFSA. *Unit head:* Dr. Denise Staudt, Dean, Dreeben School of Education, 210-829-2762, E-mail: staudt@uiwtx.edu. *Application contact:* Andrea Cyterski-Acosta, Dean of Enrollment, 210-829-6005, Fax: 210-829-3921, E-mail: admis@uiwtx.edu.
Website: http://www.uiw.edu/education/index.htm.

University of the Pacific, Gladys L. Benerd School of Education, Stockton, CA 95211-0197. Offers M Ed, MA, Ed D, Ed S. *Accreditation:* NCATE. *Faculty:* 17 full-time (11 women), 3 part-time/adjunct (2 women). *Students:* 140 full-time (97 women), 214 part-time (154 women); includes 126 minority (31 Black or African American, non-Hispanic/Latino; 2 American Indian or Alaska Native, non-Hispanic/Latino; 29 Asian, non-Hispanic/Latino; 50 Hispanic/Latino; 1 Native Hawaiian or other Pacific Islander, non-Hispanic/Latino; 13 Two or more races, non-Hispanic/Latino), 27 international. Average age 32. 186 applicants, 76% accepted, 98 enrolled. In 2013, 141 master's, 23 doctorates awarded. *Degree requirements:* For doctorate, thesis/dissertation. *Entrance requirements:* For master's, GRE General Test; for doctorate, GRE General Test, GRE Subject Test. Additional exam requirements/recommendations for international students: Required—TOEFL (minimum score 475 paper-based). *Application deadline:* For fall admission, 3/1 priority date for domestic students; for spring admission, 10/15 for domestic students. Applications are processed on a rolling basis. Application fee: $75. *Financial support:* In 2013–14, 8 teaching assistantships were awarded; institutionally sponsored loans also available. Support available to part-time students. Financial award application deadline: 3/1; financial award applicants required to submit FAFSA. *Unit head:* Dr. Lynn Beck, Dean, 209-946-2683, E-mail: lbeck@pacific.edu. *Application contact:* Office of Graduate Admissions, 209-946-2344.

University of the Sacred Heart, Graduate Programs, Department of Education, San Juan, PR 00914-0383. Offers early childhood education (M Ed); information technology and multimedia (Certificate); instruction systems and education technology (M Ed), including English, information technology and multimedia, instructional design, mathematics, Spanish. Part-time and evening/weekend programs available. *Degree requirements:* For master's, thesis. *Entrance requirements:* For master's, EXADEP, minimum undergraduate GPA of 2.75, interview.

University of the Southwest, Graduate Programs, Hobbs, NM 88240-9129. Offers business administration (MBA); curriculum and instruction (MSE); curriculum and instruction: bilingual (MSE); curriculum and instruction: TESOL (MSE); early childhood education (MSE); educational administration (MSE); mental health counseling (MSE); school counseling (MSE); special education (MSE); sports management (MBA). Part-time and evening/weekend programs available. Postbaccalaureate distance learning degree programs offered (no on-campus study). *Degree requirements:* For master's, comprehensive exam, thesis (for some programs). *Entrance requirements:* Additional exam requirements/recommendations for international students: Recommended—TOEFL. Electronic applications accepted.

University of the Virgin Islands, Graduate Programs, Division of Education, Saint Thomas, VI 00802-9990. Offers MAE. Part-time and evening/weekend programs available. *Degree requirements:* For master's, comprehensive exam, thesis or alternative. *Entrance requirements:* For master's, minimum GPA of 2.5, BA degree from accredited institution. Additional exam requirements/recommendations for international students: Required—TOEFL (minimum score 550 paper-based). *Faculty research:* Student self-concept and sense of futility.

The University of Toledo, College of Graduate Studies, Judith Herb College of Education, Toledo, OH 43606-3390. Offers MAE, ME, MES, MME, DE, PhD, Certificate, Ed S. *Accreditation:* NCATE. Part-time and evening/weekend programs available. *Faculty:* 99. *Students:* 77 full-time (48 women), 327 part-time (248 women); includes 65 minority (50 Black or African American, non-Hispanic/Latino; 1 Asian, non-Hispanic/Latino; 12 Hispanic/Latino; 2 Two or more races, non-Hispanic/Latino), 24 international. Average age 36. 126 applicants, 76% accepted, 70 enrolled. In 2013, 143 master's, 9 doctorates awarded. Terminal master's awarded for partial completion of doctoral program. *Degree requirements:* For master's, thesis; for doctorate, comprehensive exam (for some programs), thesis/dissertation (for some programs); for other advanced degree, thesis optional. *Entrance requirements:* For master's and other advanced degree, minimum cumulative GPA of 2.7 for all previous academic work, letters of recommendation, statement of purpose, transcripts from all prior institutions attended; for doctorate, GRE, minimum cumulative GPA of 2.7 for all previous academic work, 3.0 for occupational therapy and physical therapy; letters of recommendation; statement of purpose; transcripts from all prior institutions attended. Additional exam requirements/recommendations for international students: Required—TOEFL (minimum score 550 paper-based; 80 iBT). *Application deadline:* For fall admission, 1/15 priority date for domestic and international students. Applications are processed on a rolling basis. Application fee: $45 ($75 for international students). Electronic applications accepted. *Financial support:* In 2013–14, 7 research assistantships with full and partial tuition reimbursements (averaging $11,571 per year), 16 teaching assistantships with full and partial tuition reimbursements (averaging $8,025 per year) were awarded; career-related internships or fieldwork, Federal Work-Study, institutionally sponsored loans, scholarships/grants, tuition waivers (full and partial), unspecified assistantships, and administrative assistantships also available. Support available to part-time students. *Unit head:* Dr. Penny Poplin-Gosetti, Dean, 419-530-5402, E-mail: beverly.schmoll@utoledo.edu. *Application contact:* Graduate School Office, 419-530-4723, Fax: 419-530-4724, E-mail: grdsch@utnet.utoledo.edu.
Website: http://www.utoledo.edu/eduhshs/.

University of Toronto, School of Graduate Studies, Ontario Institute for Studies in Education, Toronto, ON M5S 1A1, Canada. Offers M Ed, MA, MT, Ed D, PhD. Part-time and evening/weekend programs available. *Degree requirements:* For master's, thesis (for some programs); for doctorate, thesis/dissertation. *Entrance requirements:* For master's, minimum B average in final year, 1 year of professional experience in field

(MA, M Ed); for doctorate, minimum B+ average, professional experience in education or a relevant field (Ed D). Additional exam requirements/recommendations for international students: Required—TOEFL (minimum score 580 paper-based; 93 iBT), TWE (minimum score 5). *Expenses:* Contact institution.

The University of Tulsa, Graduate School, College of Arts and Sciences, Program in Educational Studies, Tulsa, OK 74104-3189. Offers MA. Part-time programs available. *Faculty:* 5 full-time (2 women). *Students:* 15 full-time (8 women), 1 part-time (0 women); includes 4 minority (2 Black or African American, non-Hispanic/Latino; 1 American Indian or Alaska Native, non-Hispanic/Latino; 1 Hispanic/Latino), 5 international. Average age 25. 3 applicants, 100% accepted, 2 enrolled. In 2013, 9 master's awarded. *Entrance requirements:* For master's, GRE. Additional exam requirements/recommendations for international students: Required—TOEFL (minimum score 90 iBT). *Application deadline:* Applications are processed on a rolling basis. Application fee: $40. Electronic applications accepted. *Expenses: Tuition:* Full-time $19,566; part-time $1087 per credit hour. *Required fees:* $1690; $5 per credit hour. $160 per semester. Tuition and fees vary according to course load. *Financial support:* In 2013–14, 3 students received support, including 3 teaching assistantships (averaging $12,766 per year); career-related internships or fieldwork, institutionally sponsored loans, scholarships/grants, health care benefits, tuition waivers, and unspecified assistantships also available. Support available to part-time students. Financial award application deadline: 2/1. *Faculty research:* Language, discourse, and development; educational foundations. *Unit head:* Dr. Diane Beals, Chair, 918-631-2045, Fax: 918-631-3033, E-mail: diane-beals@utulsa.edu. *Application contact:* Dr. Avi Mintz, Advisor, 918-631-2919, Fax: 918-631-3033, E-mail: avi-mintz@utulsa.edu.
Website: http://www.utulsa.edu/academics/colleges/henry-kendall-college-of-arts-and-sciences/Departments-and-Schools/DepartmentOfEducationalStudies.aspx.

The University of Tulsa, Graduate School, College of Arts and Sciences, School of Urban Education, Tulsa, OK 74104-3189. Offers education (M Ed, MA), including education (MA), elementary education (M Ed), secondary education (M Ed); mathematics and science education (MSMSE); teaching arts (MTA), including art, biology, English, history, mathematics. *Accreditation:* Teacher Education Accreditation Council. Part-time programs available. *Faculty:* 7 full-time (3 women). *Students:* 7 full-time (2 women), 8 part-time (4 women); includes 1 minority (Black or African American, non-Hispanic/Latino), 2 international. Average age 30. 11 applicants, 91% accepted, 8 enrolled. In 2013, 11 master's awarded. *Degree requirements:* For master's, thesis optional. *Entrance requirements:* For master's, GRE General Test. Additional exam requirements/recommendations for international students: Required—TOEFL (minimum score 577 paper-based; 91 iBT), IELTS (minimum score 6.5). *Application deadline:* For fall admission, 2/1 priority date for domestic students. Applications are processed on a rolling basis. Application fee: $40. Electronic applications accepted. *Expenses: Tuition:* Full-time $19,566; part-time $1087 per credit hour. *Required fees:* $1690; $5 per credit hour. $160 per semester. Tuition and fees vary according to course load. *Financial support:* In 2013–14, 10 students received support, including 1 research assistantship with full and partial tuition reimbursement available (averaging $12,766 per year), 9 teaching assistantships with full and partial tuition reimbursements available (averaging $10,543 per year); fellowships with full and partial tuition reimbursements available, career-related internships or fieldwork, Federal Work-Study, scholarships/grants, health care benefits, tuition waivers (full and partial), and unspecified assistantships also available. Support available to part-time students. Financial award application deadline: 2/1; financial award applicants required to submit FAFSA. *Faculty research:* Elementary/secondary certification; math/science education; educational foundations; language, discourse, and development. *Total annual research expenditures:* $137,161. *Unit head:* Dr. Kalpana Misra, Dean, 918-631-2541, Fax: 918-631-3721, E-mail: kalpana-misra@utulsa.edu. *Application contact:* Dr. David Brown, Advisor, 918-631-2719, Fax: 918-631-2133, E-mail: david-brown@utulsa.edu.
Website: http://www.cas.utulsa.edu/education/.

University of Utah, Graduate School, College of Education, Salt Lake City, UT 84112. Offers M Ed, M Stat, MA, MS, Ed D, PhD, MPA/PhD. *Accreditation:* Teacher Education Accreditation Council. *Faculty:* 50 full-time (29 women), 42 part-time/adjunct (35 women). *Students:* 253 full-time (189 women), 227 part-time (143 women); includes 111 minority (14 Black or African American, non-Hispanic/Latino; 3 American Indian or Alaska Native, non-Hispanic/Latino; 15 Asian, non-Hispanic/Latino; 63 Hispanic/Latino; 4 Native Hawaiian or other Pacific Islander, non-Hispanic/Latino; 12 Two or more races, non-Hispanic/Latino), 16 international. Average age 34. 422 applicants, 46% accepted, 155 enrolled. In 2013, 138 master's, 23 doctorates awarded. *Degree requirements:* For master's, variable foreign language requirement, comprehensive exam (for some programs), thesis (for some programs); for doctorate, variable foreign language requirement, comprehensive exam (for some programs), thesis/dissertation. *Entrance requirements:* For master's and doctorate, minimum GPA of 3.0. Additional exam requirements/recommendations for international students: Required—TOEFL. *Application deadline:* For fall admission, 2/15 for domestic and international students; for spring admission, 11/1 for domestic and international students. Application fee: $55 ($65 for international students). Electronic applications accepted. *Expenses:* Contact institution. *Financial support:* Fellowships with full and partial tuition reimbursements, research assistantships with full and partial tuition reimbursements, teaching assistantships with full and partial tuition reimbursements, career-related internships or fieldwork, Federal Work-Study, institutionally sponsored loans, scholarships/grants, health care benefits, tuition waivers (full), and unspecified assistantships available. Support available to part-time students. Financial award application deadline: 2/1; financial award applicants required to submit FAFSA. *Faculty research:* Leadership, autism, reading instruction, mental retardation, diagnosis. *Total annual research expenditures:* $508,705. *Unit head:* Maria E. Franquiz, Dean, 801-581-8221, E-mail: maria.franquiz@utah.edu. *Application contact:* Julie Gerstner, Executive Secretary, Dean's Office, 801-581-5791, E-mail: julie.gerstner@utah.edu.
Website: http://education.utah.edu/.

University of Vermont, Graduate College, College of Education and Social Services, Burlington, VT 05405. Offers M Ed, MAT, MS, MSW, Ed D, PhD. *Accreditation:* NCATE. Part-time programs available. *Students:* 348 (250 women); includes 38 minority (11 Black or African American, non-Hispanic/Latino; 3 American Indian or Alaska Native, non-Hispanic/Latino; 3 Asian, non-Hispanic/Latino; 17 Hispanic/Latino; 4 Two or more races, non-Hispanic/Latino), 5 international. 541 applicants, 50% accepted, 114 enrolled. In 2013, 181 master's, 11 doctorates awarded. *Degree requirements:* For doctorate, thesis/dissertation. *Entrance requirements:* Additional exam requirements/recommendations for international students: Required—TOEFL (minimum score 550 paper-based; 80 iBT). Application fee: $65. Electronic applications accepted. *Financial support:* Fellowships, research assistantships, teaching assistantships, career-related internships or fieldwork, and Federal Work-Study available. *Unit head:* Dr. Fayneese Miller, Dean, 802-656-3424.

University of Victoria, Faculty of Graduate Studies, Faculty of Education, Victoria, BC V8W 2Y2, Canada. Offers M Ed, M Sc, MA, PhD.

University of Virginia, Curry School of Education, Charlottesville, VA 22903. Offers M Ed, MT, Ed D, PhD, Ed S, MBA/M Ed, MPP/PhD. *Accreditation:* Teacher Education Accreditation Council. *Faculty:* 100 full-time (58 women), 5 part-time/adjunct (3 women). *Students:* 713 full-time (566 women), 135 part-time (89 women); includes 135 minority (46 Black or African American, non-Hispanic/Latino; 1 American Indian or Alaska Native, non-Hispanic/Latino; 39 Asian, non-Hispanic/Latino; 31 Hispanic/Latino; 18 Two or more races, non-Hispanic/Latino), 26 international. Average age 27. 1,053 applicants, 38% accepted, 213 enrolled. In 2013, 401 master's, 59 doctorates, 60 other advanced degrees awarded. *Degree requirements:* For master's, comprehensive exam (for some programs), thesis (for some programs); for doctorate, comprehensive exam (for some programs), thesis/dissertation. *Entrance requirements:* For master's, doctorate, and Ed S, GRE General Test, letters of recommendation. Additional exam requirements/recommendations for international students: Required—TOEFL (minimum score 600 paper-based; 90 iBT), IELTS (minimum score 7). *Application deadline:* Applications are processed on a rolling basis. Application fee: $60. Electronic applications accepted. *Expenses:* Tuition, state resident: part-time $334 per credit hour. Tuition, nonresident: part-time $1224 per credit hour. *Financial support:* Fellowships, research assistantships, teaching assistantships, and Federal Work-Study available. Financial award application deadline: 1/5; financial award applicants required to submit FAFSA. *Unit head:* Robert C. Pianta, Dean, 434-924-3334, E-mail: pianta@virginia.edu. *Application contact:* Office of Admissions and Student Services, 434-924-0742, E-mail: curry-admissions@virginia.edu.
Website: http://curry.edschool.virginia.edu/.

University of Washington, Graduate School, College of Education, Seattle, WA 98195. Offers curriculum and instruction (M Ed, Ed D, PhD), including educational technology, general curriculum (Ed D, PhD), language, literacy, and culture, mathematics education, multicultural education, reading and language arts education (Ed D), science education, social studies education, teaching and curriculum (M Ed); educational leadership and policy studies (M Ed, Ed D, PhD), including administration (Ed D), educational policy, organization, and leadership (M Ed, PhD), higher education, leadership for learning (Ed D), social and cultural foundations of education (M Ed, PhD); educational psychology (M Ed, PhD), including educational psychology (PhD), human development and cognition (M Ed), learning sciences, measurement, statistics and research design (M Ed), school psychology (M Ed); instructional leadership (M Ed); intercollegiate athletic leadership (M Ed); special education (M Ed, Ed D, PhD), including early childhood special education (M Ed), emotional and behavioral disabilities (M Ed), learning disabilities (M Ed), low-incidence disabilities (M Ed), severe disabilities (M Ed), special education (Ed D, PhD); teacher education (MIT). *Accreditation:* APA. Part-time and evening/weekend programs available. *Degree requirements:* For master's, thesis optional; for doctorate, thesis/dissertation. *Entrance requirements:* For master's and doctorate, GRE General Test, minimum GPA of 3.0. Additional exam requirements/recommendations for international students: Required—TOEFL. Electronic applications accepted. *Faculty research:* School restructuring/effective schools, special education interventions, literacy and writing, technology, school partnerships, teacher preparation.

University of Washington, Bothell, Program in Education, Bothell, WA 98011-8246. Offers education (M Ed); leadership development for educators (M Ed); secondary/middle level endorsement (M Ed). Part-time and evening/weekend programs available. *Degree requirements:* For master's, thesis. *Entrance requirements:* Additional exam requirements/recommendations for international students: Required—TOEFL. Electronic applications accepted. *Faculty research:* Multicultural education in citizenship education, intercultural education, knowledge and practice in the principalship, educational public policy, national board certification for teachers, teacher learning in literacy, technology and its impact on teaching and learning of mathematics, reading assessments, professional development in literacy education and mobility, digital media, education and class.

University of Washington, Tacoma, Graduate Programs, Program in Education, Tacoma, WA 98402-3100. Offers education (M Ed); educational administration (principal or program administrator certification) (M Ed); elementary education teacher certification (M Ed); elementary education/special education teacher certification (M Ed); secondary science or math teacher certification (M Ed). Part-time and evening/weekend programs available. *Degree requirements:* For master's, culminating project. *Entrance requirements:* For master's, WEST-B, WEST-E (teacher certification programs only), official sealed transcript from every college/university attended, personal goal statement, letters of recommendation, copy of valid teaching certificate. Additional exam requirements/recommendations for international students: Required—TOEFL (minimum score 580 paper-based; 92 iBT). Electronic applications accepted. *Faculty research:* Global learning communities for English/Chinese languages, evaluation of mathematics and reading intervention programs, response to intervention, school-wide behavioral and emotional support, mathematics education and culturally responsive mathematics education.

The University of West Alabama, School of Graduate Studies, College of Education, Livingston, AL 35470. Offers M Ed, MAT, MSCE, Ed S. *Accreditation:* NCATE. Part-time and evening/weekend programs available. Postbaccalaureate distance learning degree programs offered (no on-campus study). *Faculty:* 54 full-time (26 women), 73 part-time/adjunct (48 women). *Students:* 2,194 full-time (1,884 women), 234 part-time (182 women); includes 1,386 minority (1,336 Black or African American, non-Hispanic/Latino; 17 American Indian or Alaska Native, non-Hispanic/Latino; 4 Asian, non-Hispanic/Latino; 14 Hispanic/Latino; 15 Two or more races, non-Hispanic/Latino), 5 international. Average age 31. 840 applicants, 97% accepted, 519 enrolled. In 2013, 660 master's, 205 other advanced degrees awarded. *Degree requirements:* For master's, comprehensive exam, thesis optional. *Entrance requirements:* For master's, GRE General Test, MAT, minimum GPA of 2.75. Additional exam requirements/recommendations for international students: Required—TOEFL (minimum score 500 paper-based; 61 iBT). *Application deadline:* For fall admission, 8/12 priority date for domestic students; for spring admission, 3/24 for domestic students. Applications are processed on a rolling basis. Application fee: $25 ($50 for international students). Electronic applications accepted. Tuition and fees vary according to course load. *Financial support:* In 2013–14, 50 students received support, including 25 teaching assistantships (averaging $5,267 per year); career-related internships or fieldwork, Federal Work-Study, scholarships/grants, and unspecified assistantships also available. Support available to part-time students. Financial award application deadline: 3/1; financial award applicants required to submit FAFSA. *Unit head:* Dr. Kathy Chandler, Dean of Graduate Studies, 205-652-3421, Fax: 205-652-3706, E-mail: kchandler@uwa.edu.
Website: http://www.uwa.edu/coe/.

The University of Western Ontario, Faculty of Graduate Studies, Social Sciences Division, Faculty of Education, London, ON N6A 5B8, Canada. Offers M Ed. Part-time programs available. *Entrance requirements:* For master's, minimum B average.

University of West Florida, College of Professional Studies, Ed D Programs, Specialization in Curriculum and Instruction: Teacher Education, Pensacola, FL 32514-5750. Offers Ed D. Part-time and evening/weekend programs available. *Degree requirements:* For doctorate, comprehensive exam, thesis/dissertation. *Entrance requirements:* For doctorate, GRE, MAT, or GMAT, letter of intent; writing sample; three letters of recommendation; two completed disposition assessment forms; written statement of goals; interview with admissions committee. Additional exam requirements/

recommendations for international students: Required—TOEFL (minimum score 550 paper-based).

University of West Georgia, College of Education, Carrollton, GA 30118. Offers M Ed, MAT, Ed D, Ed S. *Accreditation:* NCATE. Part-time and evening/weekend programs available. Postbaccalaureate distance learning degree programs offered (minimal on-campus study). *Faculty:* 49 full-time (31 women), 6 part-time/adjunct (5 women). *Students:* 404 full-time (322 women), 855 part-time (700 women); includes 481 minority (403 Black or African American, non-Hispanic/Latino; 1 American Indian or Alaska Native, non-Hispanic/Latino; 10 Asian, non-Hispanic/Latino; 27 Hispanic/Latino; 21 Native Hawaiian or other Pacific Islander, non-Hispanic/Latino; 19 Two or more races, non-Hispanic/Latino), 8 international. Average age 34. 612 applicants, 78% accepted, 236 enrolled. In 2013, 234 master's, 11 doctorates, 147 other advanced degrees awarded. *Degree requirements:* For master's and Ed S, comprehensive exam; for doctorate, comprehensive exam, thesis/dissertation. *Entrance requirements:* Additional exam requirements/recommendations for international students: Required—TOEFL (minimum score 523 paper-based; 69 iBT); Recommended—IELTS (minimum score 6). *Application deadline:* For fall admission, 7/21 for domestic students, 6/1 for international students; for spring admission, 11/30 for domestic students, 10/15 for international students. Applications are processed on a rolling basis. Application fee: $40. Electronic applications accepted. *Expenses:* Tuition, state resident: full-time $4600; part-time $192 per semester hour. Tuition, nonresident: full-time $17,880; part-time $745 per semester hour. *Required fees:* $1858; $46.34 per semester hour. $512 per semester. Tuition and fees vary according to course load, degree level, campus/location and program. *Financial support:* In 2013–14, 40 students received support, including 9 research assistantships with full tuition reimbursements available (averaging $3,000 per year); career-related internships or fieldwork, scholarships/grants, and unspecified assistantships also available. Support available to part-time students. Financial award application deadline: 4/1; financial award applicants required to submit FAFSA. *Faculty research:* Distance education, technology integration, collaboration, e-books for children, instructional design, early childhood education, social justice. *Total annual research expenditures:* $1.3 million. *Unit head:* Dr. Diane Hoff, Dean, 678-839-6570, Fax: 678-839-6098, E-mail: dhoff@westga.edu. *Application contact:* Deanna Richards, Coordinator, Graduate Studies, 678-839-5946, E-mail: drichard@westga.edu.
Website: http://coe.westga.edu/.

University of Windsor, Faculty of Graduate Studies, Faculty of Education, Windsor, ON N9B 3P4, Canada. Offers education (M Ed); educational studies (PhD). Part-time and evening/weekend programs available. *Degree requirements:* For master's, thesis or alternative; for doctorate, comprehensive exam, thesis/dissertation. *Entrance requirements:* For master's, minimum B average, teaching certificate; for doctorate, M Ed or MA in education, minimum A average, evidence of research competencies. Additional exam requirements/recommendations for international students: Required—TOEFL (minimum score 600 paper-based). Electronic applications accepted. *Faculty research:* School structures, teacher morale, cognitive deficits, new technologies in art education, internal and external factors that affect learning and teaching.

University of Wisconsin–Eau Claire, College of Education and Human Sciences, Eau Claire, WI 54702-4004. Offers ME-PD, MS, MSE, MST. *Faculty:* 19 full-time (13 women), 2 part-time/adjunct (both women). *Students:* 38 full-time (35 women), 25 part-time (21 women); includes 3 minority (1 Black or African American, non-Hispanic/Latino; 1 Hispanic/Latino; 1 Two or more races, non-Hispanic/Latino), 1 international. Average age 28. 168 applicants, 14% accepted, 21 enrolled. In 2013, 37 master's awarded. *Degree requirements:* For master's, comprehensive exam. *Entrance requirements:* For master's, GRE (MAT, MST, MSE, MS); pre-professional skills test (MAT), minimum undergraduate GPA of 2.75 or 3.0 in the last half of undergraduate work. Additional exam requirements/recommendations for international students: Required—TOEFL (minimum score 79 iBT). *Application deadline:* For fall admission, 7/1 priority date for domestic students, 6/1 priority date for international students; for spring admission, 12/1 priority date for domestic students, 11/1 priority date for international students. Applications are processed on a rolling basis. Application fee: $56. Electronic applications accepted. *Expenses:* Tuition, state resident: full-time $7640; part-time $424.47 per credit. Tuition, nonresident: full-time $16,771; part-time $931.74 per credit. *Required fees:* $1146; $63.65 per credit. *Financial support:* In 2013–14, 11 students received support. Application deadline: 3/1; applicants required to submit FAFSA. *Unit head:* Dr. Gail Scukanec, Dean, 715-836-3264, Fax: 715-836-3245, E-mail: scukangp@uwec.edu. *Application contact:* Nancy Amdahl, Graduate Dean Assistant, 715-836-2721, Fax: 715-836-2902, E-mail: graduate@uwec.edu.
Website: http://www.uwec.edu/coehs.

University of Wisconsin–Green Bay, Graduate Studies, Program in Applied Leadership for Teaching and Learning, Green Bay, WI 54311-7001. Offers MS Ed. Part-time and evening/weekend programs available. *Faculty:* 4 full-time (2 women), 5 part-time/adjunct (4 women). *Students:* 1 (woman) full-time, 30 part-time (21 women); includes 4 minority (all Two or more races, non-Hispanic/Latino). Average age 38. 9 applicants, 22% accepted, 1 enrolled. In 2013, 4 master's awarded. *Degree requirements:* For master's, thesis or alternative. *Entrance requirements:* For master's, minimum GPA of 3.0. *Application deadline:* For fall admission, 8/1 for domestic students; for spring admission, 11/1 for domestic students. Applications are processed on a rolling basis. Application fee: $56. Electronic applications accepted. *Expenses:* Tuition, state resident: full-time $7640; part-time $424 per credit. Tuition, nonresident: full-time $16,772; part-time $932 per credit. *Required fees:* $1378. Full-time tuition and fees vary according to course load and reciprocity agreements. *Financial support:* Application deadline: 7/15. *Faculty research:* Curriculum design, assessment. *Unit head:* Dr. Tim Kaufman, Director, 920-465-2964, E-mail: kaufmant@uwgb.edu. *Application contact:* Mary Valitchka, Graduate Studies Coordinator, 920-465-2123, Fax: 920-465-2043, E-mail: valitchm@uwgb.edu.
Website: http://www.uwgb.edu/graduate/.

University of Wisconsin–La Crosse, Graduate Studies, College of Liberal Studies, Department of Educational Studies, Master of Education-Professional Development Learning Community Program, La Crosse, WI 54601-3742. Offers ME-PD. Part-time and evening/weekend programs available. Postbaccalaureate distance learning degree programs offered (minimal on-campus study). *Students:* 27 part-time (24 women); includes 1 minority (Asian, non-Hispanic/Latino). Average age 30. 21 applicants, 100% accepted, 21 enrolled. In 2013, 56 master's awarded. *Degree requirements:* For master's, professional development plan and classroom action research. *Entrance requirements:* Additional exam requirements/recommendations for international students: Required—TOEFL (minimum score 550 paper-based; 79 iBT). *Application deadline:* Applications are processed on a rolling basis. Electronic applications accepted. *Financial support:* Federal Work-Study, scholarships/grants, and health care benefits available. Support available to part-time students. Financial award application deadline: 3/15; financial award applicants required to submit FAFSA. *Faculty research:* Impact of learning community on student learning, constructivism in education, transformational learning, education of children who are homeless or at risk for homelessness. *Unit head:* Dr. Patricia A. Markos, Director, 608-785-5087, Fax: 608-785-6560, E-mail: lc@uwlax.edu. *Application contact:* Corey Sjoquist, Director of Admissions, 608-785-8939, E-mail: admissions@uwlax.edu.
Website: http://www.masterteacherscommunity.org.

University of Wisconsin–Madison, Graduate School, School of Education, Madison, WI 53706-1380. Offers MA, MFA, MS, PhD, Certificate. *Faculty:* 146 full-time (73 women). *Students:* 805 full-time (561 women), 286 part-time (189 women). In 2013, 216 master's, 72 doctorates awarded. *Degree requirements:* For doctorate, thesis/dissertation. *Entrance requirements:* Additional exam requirements/recommendations for international students: Required—TOEFL (minimum score 580 paper-based; 92 iBT), IELTS (minimum score 7). Application fee: $56. *Expenses:* Tuition, state resident: full-time $10,728; part-time $790 per credit. Tuition, nonresident: full-time $24,054; part-time $1623 per credit. *Required fees:* $1130; $119 per credit. *Financial support:* In 2013–14, 51 fellowships with full tuition reimbursements, 18 research assistantships with full tuition reimbursements, 214 teaching assistantships with full tuition reimbursements were awarded; Federal Work-Study, scholarships/grants, traineeships, health care benefits, unspecified assistantships, and project assistantships also available. *Total annual research expenditures:* $28.5 million. *Unit head:* Dr. Julie K. Underwood, Dean, 608-262-1763. *Application contact:* 608-262-2433, Fax: 608-262-5134, E-mail: gradadmiss@mail.bascom.wisc.edu.
Website: http://www.education.wisc.edu.

University of Wisconsin–Milwaukee, Graduate School, School of Education, Milwaukee, WI 53201. Offers MS, PhD, Certificate, Ed S. Part-time programs available. *Faculty:* 61 full-time (40 women), 2 part-time/adjunct (1 woman). *Students:* 277 full-time (209 women), 341 part-time (247 women); includes 158 minority (76 Black or African American, non-Hispanic/Latino; 4 American Indian or Alaska Native, non-Hispanic/Latino; 15 Asian, non-Hispanic/Latino; 20 Hispanic/Latino; 43 Two or more races, non-Hispanic/Latino), 17 international. Average age 34. 469 applicants, 59% accepted, 141 enrolled. In 2013, 181 master's, 16 doctorates, 10 other advanced degrees awarded. *Degree requirements:* For doctorate, thesis/dissertation. *Entrance requirements:* For doctorate, GRE General Test. *Application deadline:* For fall admission, 1/1 priority date for domestic students; for spring admission, 9/1 for domestic students. Applications are processed on a rolling basis. Application fee: $56 ($96 for international students). Electronic applications accepted. *Financial support:* In 2013–14, 7 teaching assistantships were awarded; fellowships, career-related internships or fieldwork, Federal Work-Study, health care benefits, unspecified assistantships, and project assistantships also available. Support available to part-time students. Financial award application deadline: 4/15; financial award applicants required to submit FAFSA. *Total annual research expenditures:* $1.8 million. *Unit head:* Carol Colbeck, Dean, 414-229-4181, E-mail: colbeck@uwm.edu. *Application contact:* General Information Contact, 414-229-4982, Fax: 414-229-6967, E-mail: gradschool@uwm.edu.
Website: http://www.uwm.edu/SOE/.

University of Wisconsin–Oshkosh, Graduate Studies, College of Education and Human Services, Oshkosh, WI 54901. Offers MS, MSE. Part-time and evening/weekend programs available. *Degree requirements:* For master's, comprehensive exam (for some programs), thesis or alternative, field report, PPST, PRAXIS II. *Entrance requirements:* For master's, PPST, PRAXIS II, teaching license, letters of recommendation, interview. Additional exam requirements/recommendations for international students: Required—TOEFL (minimum score 550 paper-based; 79 iBT). Electronic applications accepted.

University of Wisconsin–Platteville, School of Graduate Studies, College of Liberal Arts and Education, School of Education, Platteville, WI 53818-3099. Offers adult education (MSE); elementary education (MSE); English education (MSE); middle school education (MSE); secondary education (MSE). *Accreditation:* NCATE. Part-time programs available. *Faculty:* 5 full-time (3 women), 13 part-time/adjunct (7 women). *Students:* 90 full-time (70 women), 30 part-time (16 women); includes 25 minority (21 Black or African American, non-Hispanic/Latino; 1 American Indian or Alaska Native, non-Hispanic/Latino; 2 Asian, non-Hispanic/Latino; 1 Hispanic/Latino), 3 international. 45 applicants, 96% accepted, 38 enrolled. In 2013, 82 master's awarded. *Degree requirements:* For master's, comprehensive exam, thesis or alternative. *Entrance requirements:* Additional exam requirements/recommendations for international students: Required—TOEFL (minimum score 500 paper-based; 61 iBT), IELTS (minimum score 6). *Application deadline:* For fall admission, 7/1 priority date for domestic students; for spring admission, 11/1 for domestic students. Applications are processed on a rolling basis. Application fee: $56. Electronic applications accepted. *Financial support:* Research assistantships with partial tuition reimbursements, career-related internships or fieldwork, Federal Work-Study, institutionally sponsored loans, scholarships/grants, and unspecified assistantships available. Support available to part-time students. Financial award applicants required to submit FAFSA. *Unit head:* Dr. Karen Stinson, Director, 608-342-1131, Fax: 608-342-1133, E-mail: stinsonk@uwplatt.edu. *Application contact:* Dee Dunbar, School of Graduate Studies, 608-342-1322, Fax: 608-342-1389, E-mail: dunbard@uwplatt.edu.
Website: http://www.uwplatt.edu/.

University of Wisconsin–River Falls, Outreach and Graduate Studies, College of Education and Professional Studies, Department of Teacher Education, River Falls, WI 54022. Offers elementary education (MSE); professional development shared inquiry communities (MSE); reading (MSE). Part-time programs available. *Degree requirements:* For master's, comprehensive exam, thesis or alternative. *Entrance requirements:* For master's, minimum GPA of 2.75. Additional exam requirements/recommendations for international students: Required—TOEFL (minimum score 500 paper-based; 65 iBT), IELTS (minimum score 5.5). Electronic applications accepted.

University of Wisconsin–Stevens Point, College of Professional Studies, School of Education, Stevens Point, WI 54481-3897. Offers education—general/reading (MSE); education—general/special (MSE); educational administration (MSE); elementary education (MSE); guidance and counseling (MSE). Part-time programs available. *Degree requirements:* For master's, comprehensive exam, thesis or alternative. *Entrance requirements:* For master's, teacher certification, minimum undergraduate GPA of 3.0, 2 years of teaching experience, letters of recommendation. Additional exam requirements/recommendations for international students: Required—TOEFL (minimum score 523 paper-based). *Faculty research:* Gifted education, early childhood special education, curriculum and instruction, standards-based education.

University of Wisconsin–Stout, Graduate School, School of Education, Menomonie, WI 54751. Offers MS, MS Ed, Ed S. *Accreditation:* NCATE. Part-time programs available. Postbaccalaureate distance learning degree programs offered (no on-campus study). *Degree requirements:* For master's and Ed S, thesis. *Entrance requirements:* For degree, minimum GPA of 3.25. Additional exam requirements/recommendations for international students: Required—TOEFL (minimum score 500 paper-based; 61 iBT). Electronic applications accepted.

University of Wisconsin–Superior, Graduate Division, Department of Teacher Education, Superior, WI 54880-4500. Offers instruction (MSE); special education (MSE), including emotional/behavior disabilities, learning disabilities; teaching reading (MSE). Part-time and evening/weekend programs available. Postbaccalaureate distance learning degree programs offered (minimal on-campus study). *Faculty:* 7 full-time (6 women). *Students:* 21 full-time (15 women), 3 part-time (all women); includes 1 minority

(Asian, non-Hispanic/Latino). Average age 34. 10 applicants, 50% accepted, 3 enrolled. In 2013, 17 master's awarded. *Degree requirements:* For master's, research project. *Entrance requirements:* For master's, minimum GPA of 2.75, teaching certificate. *Application deadline:* For fall admission, 4/1 priority date for domestic students; for spring admission, 10/15 priority date for domestic students. Applications are processed on a rolling basis. Application fee: $45. Electronic applications accepted. *Expenses:* Tuition, state resident: full-time $4526; part-time $649.24 per credit. Tuition, nonresident: full-time $9091; part-time $1156.51 per credit. *Financial support:* Career-related internships or fieldwork, Federal Work-Study, institutionally sponsored loans, scholarships/grants, and tuition waivers (partial) available. Support available to part-time students. Financial award application deadline: 4/15; financial award applicants required to submit FAFSA. *Faculty research:* Science teaching. *Unit head:* Terri Kronzer, Chairperson, 715-394-8506, E-mail: tkronzer@uwsuper.edu. *Application contact:* Suzie Finckler, Student Status Examiner, 715-394-8295, Fax: 715-394-8371, E-mail: gradstudy@uwsuper.edu.

University of Wisconsin–Whitewater, School of Graduate Studies, College of Education and Professional Studies, Whitewater, WI 53190-1790. Offers MS, MS Ed, MSE. *Accreditation:* NCATE. Part-time and evening/weekend programs available. Postbaccalaureate distance learning degree programs offered (no on-campus study). *Entrance requirements:* Additional exam requirements/recommendations for international students: Required—TOEFL (minimum score 550 paper-based). Electronic applications accepted.

Upper Iowa University, Master of Education Program, Fayette, IA 52142-1857. Offers M Ed.

Urbana University, College of Education and Sports Studies, Urbana, OH 43078-2091. Offers classroom education (M Ed). Part-time and evening/weekend programs available. *Degree requirements:* For master's, comprehensive oral exam, capstone research project. *Entrance requirements:* For master's, minimum GPA of 2.7, teaching license. Additional exam requirements/recommendations for international students: Required—TOEFL (minimum score 550 paper-based). *Faculty research:* Best professional practices, reading/special education, classroom management, teaching models, school finance.

Ursuline College, School of Graduate Studies, Program for Advanced Study in Education (PASE), Pepper Pike, OH 44124-4398. Offers MA. Part-time programs available. *Faculty:* 2 part-time/adjunct (1 woman). *Students:* 1 (woman) part-time; minority (Black or African American, non-Hispanic/Latino). Average age 58. 8 applicants, 88% accepted, 1 enrolled. In 2013, 7 master's awarded. *Degree requirements:* For master's, comprehensive exam (for some programs), thesis (for some programs). *Entrance requirements:* Additional exam requirements/recommendations for international students: Required—TOEFL (minimum score 500 paper-based). *Application deadline:* Applications are processed on a rolling basis. Application fee: $25. Electronic applications accepted. *Expenses: Tuition:* Full-time $16,920; part-time $940 per credit. *Required fees:* $270. *Financial support:* Applicants required to submit FAFSA. *Unit head:* Joseph LaGuardia, Assistant Director, 440-646-6046, Fax: 440-684-8328, E-mail: jlaguardia@ursuline.edu. *Application contact:* Stephanie Pratt, Graduate Admission Coordinator, 440-646-8119, Fax: 440-684-6138, E-mail: graduateadmissions@ursuline.edu.

Ursuline College, School of Graduate Studies, Program in Education, Pepper Pike, OH 44124-4398. Offers art education (MA); early childhood education (MA); language arts education (MA); life science education (MA); math education (MA); middle school education (MA); social studies education (MA); special education (MA). *Accreditation:* NCATE. *Faculty:* 4 full-time (all women), 7 part-time/adjunct (5 women). *Students:* 18 full-time (16 women), 7 part-time (all women); includes 8 minority (4 Black or African American, non-Hispanic/Latino; 2 Asian, non-Hispanic/Latino; 2 Hispanic/Latino). Average age 34. 1 applicant, 100% accepted, 1 enrolled. In 2013, 25 master's awarded. *Degree requirements:* For master's, comprehensive exam. *Entrance requirements:* For master's, minimum undergraduate GPA of 3.0. Additional exam requirements/recommendations for international students: Required—TOEFL (minimum score 500 paper-based). *Application deadline:* For fall admission, 8/1 priority date for domestic students. Applications are processed on a rolling basis. Application fee: $25. *Expenses:* Contact institution. *Financial support:* In 2013–14, 1 student received support. Federal Work-Study available. Financial award application deadline: 3/1. *Unit head:* Dr. Edna West, Director, Master's Apprentice Program, 440-646-6134, Fax: 440-646-8328, E-mail: ewest@ursuline.edu. *Application contact:* Stephanie Pratt, Graduate Admission Coordinator, 440-646-8119, Fax: 440-684-6138, E-mail: graduateadmissions@ursuline.edu.

Utah State University, School of Graduate Studies, Emma Eccles Jones College of Education and Human Services, Logan, UT 84322. Offers M Ed, MA, MFHD, MRC, MS, Au D, Ed D, PhD, Ed S. *Accreditation:* Teacher Education Accreditation Council. Part-time and evening/weekend programs available. Postbaccalaureate distance learning degree programs offered (no on-campus study). *Degree requirements:* For doctorate, comprehensive exam, thesis/dissertation. *Entrance requirements:* For master's, GRE General Test, minimum GPA of 3.0; for doctorate, GRE General Test, master's degree; for Ed S, GRE General Test, GRE Subject Test. Additional exam requirements/recommendations for international students: Required—TOEFL (minimum score 550 paper-based). *Faculty research:* Literacy instruction, design and delivery of instruction, children at-risk and their families, hearing assessment and management, language and literacy development.

Utah Valley University, Program in Education, Orem, UT 84058-5999. Offers educational technology (M Ed); elementary mathematics (M Ed); English as a second language (M Ed); models of instruction (M Ed). *Accreditation:* Teacher Education Accreditation Council. Part-time programs available. *Faculty:* 4 full-time (2 women). *Students:* 107 part-time (76 women); includes 2 minority (1 Asian, non-Hispanic/Latino; 1 Hispanic/Latino). Average age 33. *Degree requirements:* For master's, project. *Entrance requirements:* For master's, GRE, 3 letters of recommendation, interview. Additional exam requirements/recommendations for international students: Required—TOEFL (minimum score 83 iBT). *Application deadline:* For fall admission, 3/31 for domestic and international students. Application fee: $45 ($100 for international students). Electronic applications accepted. *Expenses:* Tuition, state resident: full-time $8520; part-time $355 per credit. Tuition, nonresident: full-time $21,232; part-time $885 per credit. *Required fees:* $700; $350 per semester. Tuition and fees vary according to program. *Financial support:* Application deadline: 5/1; applicants required to submit FAFSA. *Unit head:* Parker Fewson, Dean, School of Education, 801-863-8006. *Application contact:* Mary Sowder, Coordinator of Graduate Studies, 801-863-6723.

Utica College, Teacher Education Programs, Utica, NY 13502-4892. Offers MS, MS Ed, CAS. *Accreditation:* Teacher Education Accreditation Council. *Faculty:* 10 full-time (7 women). *Students:* 17 full-time (12 women), 55 part-time (33 women); includes 4 minority (1 Black or African American, non-Hispanic/Latino; 2 Hispanic/Latino; 1 Two or more races, non-Hispanic/Latino). Average age 28. In 2013, 45 master's awarded. *Degree requirements:* For master's, comprehensive exam or thesis. *Entrance requirements:* For master's, CST, LAST, minimum GPA of 3.0. Additional exam requirements/recommendations for international students: Required—TOEFL (minimum score 525 paper-based). *Application deadline:* Applications are processed on a rolling basis. Application fee: $50. Electronic applications accepted. *Expenses:* Contact institution. *Financial support:* Career-related internships or fieldwork, scholarships/grants, tuition waivers (partial), and unspecified assistantships available. Support available to part-time students. Financial award application deadline: 3/15; financial award applicants required to submit FAFSA. *Unit head:* Dr. Patrice Hallock, Director, Institute for Excellence in Education, 315-792-3162, E-mail: phallock@utica.edu. *Application contact:* John D. Rowe, Director of Graduate Admissions, 315-792-3824, Fax: 315-792-3003, E-mail: jrowe@utica.edu.

Valley City State University, Online Master of Education Program, Valley City, ND 58072. Offers elementary education (M Ed); English education (M Ed); library and information technologies (M Ed); teaching and technology (M Ed); teaching English language learners (ELL) (M Ed); technology education (M Ed). *Accreditation:* NCATE. Part-time and evening/weekend programs available. Postbaccalaureate distance learning degree programs offered (no on-campus study). *Faculty:* 21 full-time (14 women), 7 part-time/adjunct (all women). *Students:* 2 full-time (both women), 151 part-time (102 women); includes 10 minority (1 Black or African American, non-Hispanic/Latino; 3 Asian, non-Hispanic/Latino; 2 Hispanic/Latino; 4 Two or more races, non-Hispanic/Latino), 1 international. Average age 34. 27 applicants, 93% accepted, 21 enrolled. In 2013, 45 master's awarded. *Degree requirements:* For master's, action research report, comprehensive portfolio. *Entrance requirements:* For master's, GRE, MAT, PRAXIS II or National Teaching Board for Professional Standards (if GPA is less than 3.0). Additional exam requirements/recommendations for international students: Required—TOEFL (minimum score 525 paper-based; 71 iBT); Recommended—IELTS (minimum score 5.5). *Application deadline:* For fall admission, 7/19 priority date for domestic and international students; for spring admission, 12/13 priority date for domestic and international students; for summer admission, 5/9 priority date for domestic and international students. Applications are processed on a rolling basis. Application fee: $35. Electronic applications accepted. *Expenses:* Contact institution. *Financial support:* In 2013–14, 24 students received support. Scholarships/grants and tuition waivers (full and partial) available. Financial award application deadline: 5/15; financial award applicants required to submit FAFSA. *Faculty research:* Academically at-risk students in higher education, communication pedagogy and technology, gender communication, computer-mediated communication, creativity in music, STEM education in K-12. *Total annual research expenditures:* $26,000. *Unit head:* Dr. Gary Thompson, Dean, 701-845-7197, E-mail: gary.thompson@vcsu.edu. *Application contact:* Misty Lindgren, Graduate Studies, 701-845-7303, Fax: 701-845-7190, E-mail: misty.lindgren@vcsu.edu.
Website: http://www.vcsu.edu/graduate.

Valparaiso University, Graduate School, Department of Education, Valparaiso, IN 46383. Offers initial licensure (M Ed); instructional leadership (M Ed); teaching and learning (M Ed); M Ed/Ed S. *Accreditation:* NCATE. Part-time and evening/weekend programs available. Postbaccalaureate distance learning degree programs offered (minimal on-campus study). *Faculty:* 13 part-time/adjunct (11 women). *Students:* 48 full-time (36 women), 18 part-time (17 women); includes 10 minority (4 Asian, non-Hispanic/Latino; 4 Hispanic/Latino; 2 Two or more races, non-Hispanic/Latino), 5 international. Average age 27. In 2013, 20 master's awarded. *Entrance requirements:* For master's, GRE General Test, minimum GPA of 3.0. Additional exam requirements/recommendations for international students: Required—TOEFL (minimum score 550 paper-based; 80 iBT), IELTS (minimum score 6). *Application deadline:* Applications are processed on a rolling basis. Application fee: $30 ($50 for international students). Electronic applications accepted. *Expenses: Tuition:* Full-time $10,350; part-time $575 per credit hour. *Required fees:* $378; $101 per term. Tuition and fees vary according to course load and program. *Financial support:* Traineeships and unspecified assistantships available. Support available to part-time students. Financial award applicants required to submit FAFSA. *Unit head:* Dr. Jon Kilpinen, Acting Chair, Department of Education, 219-464-5314, Fax: 219-464-6720. *Application contact:* Jessica Choquette, Graduate Admissions Specialist, 219-464-5313, Fax: 219-464-5381, E-mail: jessica.choquette@valpo.edu.
Website: http://www.valpo.edu/education/.

Vanderbilt University, Graduate School, Program in Learning, Teaching and Diversity, Nashville, TN 37240-1001. Offers MS, PhD. *Faculty:* 15 full-time (6 women), 2 part-time/adjunct (1 woman). *Students:* 42 full-time (27 women), 2 part-time (1 woman); includes 8 minority (3 Black or African American, non-Hispanic/Latino; 2 Asian, non-Hispanic/Latino; 1 Hispanic/Latino; 2 Two or more races, non-Hispanic/Latino), 3 international. Average age 32. 133 applicants, 5% accepted, 6 enrolled. In 2013, 10 doctorates awarded. *Degree requirements:* For doctorate, comprehensive exam, thesis/dissertation. *Entrance requirements:* For doctorate, GRE General Test. Additional exam requirements/recommendations for international students: Required—TOEFL (minimum score 570 paper-based; 88 iBT). *Application deadline:* For fall admission, 12/31 for domestic and international students. Electronic applications accepted. *Financial support:* Fellowships with full and partial tuition reimbursements, research assistantships with full tuition reimbursements, teaching assistantships with full tuition reimbursements, Federal Work-Study, institutionally sponsored loans, scholarships/grants, traineeships, and health care benefits available. Financial award application deadline: 1/15; financial award applicants required to submit CSS PROFILE or FAFSA. *Faculty research:* New pedagogies for math, science, and language; the support of English language learners; the uses of new technology and media in the classroom; middle school mathematics and the institutional setting of teaching. *Unit head:* Dr. Clifford Hofwolt, Director of Graduate Studies, 615-322-8227, Fax: 615-322-8014, E-mail: clifford.hofwolt@vanderbilt.edu. *Application contact:* Angela Saylor, Administrative Assistant, 615-322-8092, Fax: 615-322-8014, E-mail: angela.saylor@vanderbilt.edu.
Website: http://peabody.vanderbilt.edu/departments/tl/index.php.

Vanderbilt University, Peabody College, Nashville, TN 37240-1001. Offers M Ed, MPP, Ed D. *Accreditation:* APA (one or more programs are accredited); NCATE. Part-time programs available. *Faculty:* 146 full-time (86 women), 69 part-time/adjunct (42 women). *Students:* 505 full-time (396 women), 164 part-time (113 women); includes 114 minority (56 Black or African American, non-Hispanic/Latino; 19 Asian, non-Hispanic/Latino; 28 Hispanic/Latino; 1 Native Hawaiian or other Pacific Islander, non-Hispanic/Latino; 10 Two or more races, non-Hispanic/Latino), 43 international. Average age 26. 1,063 applicants, 65% accepted, 319 enrolled. In 2013, 272 master's, 24 doctorates awarded. *Degree requirements:* For master's, comprehensive exam, thesis optional; for doctorate, thesis/dissertation, qualifying examinations, residency. *Entrance requirements:* For master's, GRE General Test, MAT; for doctorate, GRE General Test. Additional exam requirements/recommendations for international students: Required—TOEFL (minimum score 550 paper-based; 80 iBT). *Application deadline:* For fall admission, 12/31 priority date for domestic and international students; for spring admission, 11/1 priority date for domestic and international students. Applications are processed on a rolling basis. Application fee: $0. Electronic applications accepted. *Expenses:* Contact institution. *Financial support:* In 2013–14, 460 students received support, including 5 fellowships with full and partial tuition reimbursements available, 142 research assistantships with full and partial tuition reimbursements available, 54 teaching assistantships with full and partial tuition reimbursements available; career-related internships or fieldwork, Federal Work-Study, institutionally sponsored loans,

scholarships/grants, traineeships, tuition waivers (partial), and unspecified assistantships also available. Support available to part-time students. Financial award application deadline: 1/15; financial award applicants required to submit FAFSA. *Unit head:* Dr. Camilla P. Benbow, Dean, 615-322-8407, Fax: 615-322-8501, E-mail: camilla.benbow@vanderbilt.edu. *Application contact:* Kimberly Tanner, Director of Graduate and Professional Admissions, 615-332-8410, Fax: 615-343-3474, E-mail: kim.tanner@vanderbilt.edu.
Website: http://peabody.vanderbilt.edu/.

See Display below and Close-Up on page 735.

Vanguard University of Southern California, Graduate Programs in Education, Costa Mesa, CA 92626-9601. Offers MA. Evening/weekend programs available. *Degree requirements:* For master's, thesis or alternative. *Entrance requirements:* For master's, California Basic Educational Skills Test, California Subject Examinations for Teachers, minimum GPA of 3.0. Additional exam requirements/recommendations for international students: Required—TOEFL (minimum score 550 paper-based; 79 iBT). Electronic applications accepted. *Expenses:* Contact institution. *Faculty research:* Reading, educational administration.

Villanova University, Graduate School of Liberal Arts and Sciences, Department of Education and Counseling, Villanova, PA 19085-1699. Offers clinical mental health counseling (MS), including counseling and human relations; education plus teacher certification (MA); elementary school counseling (MS), including counseling and human relations; graduate education (MA); secondary school counseling (MS), including counseling and human relations; teacher leadership (MA). Part-time and evening/weekend programs available. *Students:* 66 full-time (51 women), 29 part-time (17 women); includes 14 minority (6 Black or African American, non-Hispanic/Latino; 2 Asian, non-Hispanic/Latino; 3 Hispanic/Latino; 3 Two or more races, non-Hispanic/Latino), 3 international. Average age 30. 85 applicants, 80% accepted, 39 enrolled. In 2013, 61 master's awarded. *Degree requirements:* For master's, comprehensive exam. *Entrance requirements:* For master's, GRE or MAT, minimum GPA of 3.0, statement of goals, 3 letters of recommendation or valid teacher certification for Education. Additional exam requirements/recommendations for international students: Required—TOEFL or IELTS. *Application deadline:* For fall admission, 3/1 priority date for domestic students, 5/1 for international students; for spring admission, 11/15 priority date for domestic students, 10/15 for international students; for summer admission, 5/1 for domestic students. Applications are processed on a rolling basis. Application fee: $50. Electronic applications accepted. *Financial support:* Research assistantships, teaching assistantships, scholarships/grants, and unspecified assistantships available. Financial award applicants required to submit FAFSA. *Unit head:* Dr. Edward Fierros, Chairperson, 610-519-4625. *Application contact:* Dean, Graduate School of Liberal Arts and Sciences.
Website: http://www.education.villanova.edu/.

Virginia Commonwealth University, Graduate School, School of Education, Richmond, VA 23284-9005. Offers M Ed, MS, MSAT, MT, Ed D, PhD, Certificate. *Accreditation:* NCATE. Part-time programs available. *Degree requirements:* For doctorate, thesis/dissertation. *Entrance requirements:* For master's, GRE General Test or MAT; for doctorate, GRE (PhD only), MAT (EdD only), interview, master's degree. Additional exam requirements/recommendations for international students: Required—TOEFL (minimum score 600 paper-based; 100 iBT); Recommended—IELTS (minimum score 6.5). Electronic applications accepted.

Virginia Polytechnic Institute and State University, VT Online, Blacksburg, VA 24061. Offers advanced transportation systems (Certificate); aerospace engineering (MS); agricultural and life sciences (MSLFS); business information systems (Graduate Certificate); career and technical education (MS); civil engineering (MS); computer engineering (M Eng, MS); decision support systems (Graduate Certificate); eLearning leadership (MA); electrical engineering (M Eng, MS); engineering administration (MEA); environmental engineering (Certificate); environmental politics and policy (Graduate Certificate); environmental sciences and engineering (MS); foundations of political analysis (Graduate Certificate); health product risk management (Graduate Certificate); industrial and systems engineering (MS); information policy and society (Graduate Certificate); information security (Graduate Certificate); information technology (MIT); instructional technology (MA); integrative STEM education (MA Ed); liberal arts (Graduate Certificate); life sciences: health product risk management (MS); natural resources (MNR, Graduate Certificate); networking (Graduate Certificate); nonprofit and nongovernmental organization management (Graduate Certificate); ocean engineering (MS); political science (MA); security studies (Graduate Certificate); software development (Graduate Certificate). *Expenses:* Tuition, state resident: full-time $11,185; part-time $621.50 per credit hour. Tuition, nonresident: full-time $22,146; part-time $1230.25 per credit hour. *Required fees:* $2442; $449.25 per semester. Tuition and fees vary according to course load, campus/location and program.

Virginia State University, School of Graduate Studies, Research, and Outreach, School of Liberal Arts and Education, Petersburg, VA 23806-0001. Offers M Ed, MA, MS, CAGS. *Accreditation:* NCATE. Part-time and evening/weekend programs available.

Viterbo University, Graduate Programs in Education, La Crosse, WI 54601-4797. Offers MAE. Weekend courses available in summer. *Accreditation:* NCATE. Part-time and evening/weekend programs available. *Faculty:* 1 (woman) full-time, 75 part-time/adjunct (51 women). *Students:* 49 full-time (30 women), 85 part-time (56 women); includes 1 minority (Hispanic/Latino). Average age 33. In 2013, 233 master's awarded. *Degree requirements:* For master's, comprehensive exam, thesis, 30 credits of course work. *Entrance requirements:* For master's, transcripts, teaching license, written narrative. Application fee: $50. Electronic applications accepted. *Expenses: Tuition:* Full-time $7140; part-time $444 per credit hour. *Required fees:* $100. *Unit head:* Dr. Barbara Gayle, Dean of Graduate Studies, 608-796-3080, E-mail: bmgayle@viterbo.edu. *Application contact:* Susan Hughes, Program Specialist and Graduate Student Advisor, 608-796-3394, E-mail: srhughes@viterbo.edu.

Wagner College, Division of Graduate Studies, Department of Education, Staten Island, NY 10301-4495. Offers childhood education/special education (MS Ed); early childhood education/special education (birth-grade 2) (MS Ed); educational leadership (MS Ed, Certificate), including educational leadership (Certificate), school building leader (MS Ed); literacy (B-6) (MS Ed); secondary education/special education (MS Ed), including language arts, languages other than English, mathematics and technology, science and technology, social studies. *Accreditation:* NCATE. Part-time and evening/weekend programs available. *Degree requirements:* For master's, thesis (for some programs). *Entrance requirements:* For master's, minimum GPA of 3.0. Electronic applications accepted. *Expenses: Tuition:* Full-time $17,496; part-time $972 per credit. Tuition and fees vary according to course load.

Wake Forest University, Graduate School of Arts and Sciences, Department of Education, Winston-Salem, NC 27109. Offers secondary education (MA Ed). *Accreditation:* ACA; NCATE. *Faculty:* 6 full-time (2 women). *Students:* 20 full-time (12 women); includes 2 minority (1 Black or African American, non-Hispanic/Latino; 1 Asian, non-Hispanic/Latino). Average age 24. 35 applicants, 69% accepted, 20 enrolled. In 2013, 14 master's awarded. *Degree requirements:* For master's, thesis optional. *Entrance requirements:* For master's, GRE General Test. Additional exam requirements/recommendations for international students: Required—TOEFL (minimum score 550 paper-based). *Application deadline:* For fall admission, 1/15 for domestic students, 1/15 priority date for international students. Application fee: $75. Electronic applications accepted. *Expenses:* Contact institution. *Financial support:* In 2013–14, 20 students

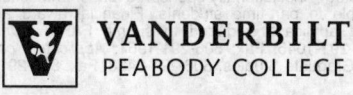

received support, including 20 fellowships with full tuition reimbursements available (averaging $48,000 per year); teaching assistantships with full tuition reimbursements available, scholarships/grants, and tuition waivers (full) also available. Financial award application deadline: 2/15. *Faculty research:* Teaching and learning. *Unit head:* Dr. Woodrow Hood, Chair, 336-758-5348, Fax: 336-758-4591, E-mail: hoodwb@wfu.edu. *Application contact:* Dr. Leah McCoy, Program Director, 336-758-5498, Fax: 336-758-4591, E-mail: mccoy@wfu.edu.
Website: http://college.wfu.edu/education/graduate-program/overview-of-graduate-programs/.

Walden University, Graduate Programs, Richard W. Riley College of Education and Leadership, Minneapolis, MN 55401. *Accreditation:* NCATE. Part-time and evening/weekend programs available. Postbaccalaureate distance learning degree programs offered (minimal on-campus study). *Faculty:* 23 full-time (15 women), 830 part-time/adjunct (569 women). *Students:* 8,671 full-time (7,197 women), 2,122 part-time (1,735 women); includes 4,734 minority (3,802 Black or African American, non-Hispanic/Latino; 50 American Indian or Alaska Native, non-Hispanic/Latino; 136 Asian, non-Hispanic/Latino; 539 Hispanic/Latino; 35 Native Hawaiian or other Pacific Islander, non-Hispanic/Latino; 172 Two or more races, non-Hispanic/Latino), 73 international. Average age 40. 2,646 applicants, 96% accepted, 2074 enrolled. In 2013, 2,214 master's, 354 doctorates, 479 other advanced degrees awarded. *Degree requirements:* For doctorate, thesis/dissertation (for some programs), residency; for other advanced degree, residency (for some programs). *Entrance requirements:* For master's, bachelor's degree or higher; minimum GPA of 2.5; official transcripts; goal statement (for some programs); access to computer and Internet; for doctorate, master's degree or higher; three years of related professional or academic experience (preferred); minimum GPA of 3.0; goal statement and current resume (select programs); official transcripts; access to computer and Internet; for other advanced degree, relevant work experience; access to computer and Internet. Additional exam requirements/recommendations for international students: Required—TOEFL (minimum score 550 paper-based; 79 iBT), IELTS (minimum score 6.5), Michigan English Language Assessment Battery (minimum score 82), or PTE. *Application deadline:* Applications are processed on a rolling basis. Application fee: $0. Electronic applications accepted. *Expenses: Tuition:* Full-time $11,813.55; part-time $500 per credit. *Required fees:* $618.76. *Financial support:* In 2013–14, 1 fellowship was awarded; Federal Work-Study, scholarships/grants, unspecified assistantships, and family tuition reduction, active duty/veteran tuition reduction, group tuition reduction, interest-free payment plans, employee tuition reduction also available. Support available to part-time students. Financial award applicants required to submit FAFSA. *Unit head:* Dr. Kate Steffens, Dean, 800-925-3368. *Application contact:* Jennifer Hall, Vice President of Enrollment Management, 866-4-WALDEN, E-mail: info@waldenu.edu.
Website: http://www.waldenu.edu/colleges-schools/riley-college-of-education/.

Walla Walla University, Graduate School, School of Education and Psychology, College Place, WA 99324-1198. Offers counseling psychology (MA); curriculum and instruction (M Ed, MA, MAT); educational leadership (M Ed, MA, MAT); literacy instruction (M Ed, MA, MAT); students at risk (M Ed, MA, MAT); teaching (MAT). Part-time programs available. *Entrance requirements:* For master's, GRE General Test, minimum GPA of 2.75. Additional exam requirements/recommendations for international students: Required—TOEFL (minimum score 550 paper-based; 79 iBT). Electronic applications accepted. *Faculty research:* Admissions/retention, instructional psychology, moral development, teaching of reading.

Walsh University, Graduate Studies, Program in Education, North Canton, OH 44720-3396. Offers 21st-century technologies (MA Ed); leadership (MA Ed); reading literacy (MA Ed); traditional program (MA Ed). *Accreditation:* NCATE. Part-time and evening/weekend programs available. *Faculty:* 6 full-time (3 women), 10 part-time/adjunct (all women). *Students:* 13 full-time (10 women), 18 part-time (14 women), 1 international. Average age 32. 16 applicants, 100% accepted, 6 enrolled. In 2013, 46 master's awarded. *Degree requirements:* For master's, comprehensive exam (for some programs), thesis optional, action research project or comprehensive exam. *Entrance requirements:* For master's, MAT (minimum score 396) or GRE (minimum scores: verbal 145, quantitative 146, combined 291, writing 3.0), interview, minimum GPA of 3.0, writing sample, 3 recommendation forms, notarized affidavit of good moral character. Additional exam requirements/recommendations for international students: Required—TOEFL (minimum score 500 paper-based; 61 iBT). *Application deadline:* For fall admission, 7/15 priority date for domestic students. Applications are processed on a rolling basis. Application fee: $25. Electronic applications accepted. *Expenses: Tuition:* Full-time $10,890; part-time $605 per credit hour. *Required fees:* $100; $100. *Financial support:* In 2013–14, 41 students received support, including 3 research assistantships with partial tuition reimbursements available (averaging $12,355 per year), 5 teaching assistantships (averaging $4,734 per year); scholarships/grants, tuition waivers (partial), and unspecified assistantships also available. Support available to part-time students. Financial award application deadline: 12/31; financial award applicants required to submit FAFSA. *Faculty research:* Technology in education, strategies for working with children with special needs, reading literacy, whole brain teaching, hybrid learning, online teaching, global learning. *Unit head:* Dr. Gary Jacobs, Director, 330-490-7336, Fax: 330-490-7326, E-mail: gjacobs@walsh.edu. *Application contact:* Audra Dice, Graduate and Transfer Admissions Counselor, 330-490-7181, Fax: 330-244-4680, E-mail: adice@walsh.edu.

Warner Pacific College, Graduate Programs, Portland, OR 97215-4099. Offers Biblical and theological studies (MA); Biblical studies (M Rel); education (M Ed); management and organizational leadership (MS); not-for-profit leadership (MSM); pastoral ministries (M Rel); religion and ethics (M Rel); teaching (MAT); theology (M Rel). Part-time programs available. *Faculty:* 20 part-time/adjunct (6 women). *Students:* 57 full-time (26 women), 4 part-time (2 women); includes 5 minority (4 Black or African American, non-Hispanic/Latino; 1 Asian, non-Hispanic/Latino). *Degree requirements:* For master's, thesis or alternative, presentation of defense. *Entrance requirements:* For master's, interview, minimum GPA of 2.5, letters of recommendation. *Application deadline:* Applications are processed on a rolling basis. *Expenses: Tuition:* Part-time $630 per credit hour. *Financial support:* Application deadline: 7/1; applicants required to submit FAFSA. *Faculty research:* New Testament studies, nineteenth-century Wesleyan theology, preaching and church growth, Christian ethics. *Unit head:* Dr. Andrea P. Cook, President, 503-517-1045, Fax: 503-517-1350. *Application contact:* Dr. John Fazio, Professor, 503-517-1043, Fax: 503-517-1350, E-mail: jfazio@warnerpacific.edu.

Warner University, School of Education, Lake Wales, FL 33859. Offers MAEd. Part-time and evening/weekend programs available. *Degree requirements:* For master's, thesis, accomplished practices portfolio. *Entrance requirements:* For master's, minimum GPA of 3.0 in last 60 hours of undergraduate coursework; 2 letters of recommendation. Additional exam requirements/recommendations for international students: Required—TOEFL (minimum score 550 paper-based). Electronic applications accepted.

Washburn University, College of Arts and Sciences, Department of Education, Topeka, KS 66621. Offers curriculum and instruction (M Ed); educational leadership (M Ed); reading (M Ed); special education (M Ed). *Accreditation:* NCATE. Part-time programs available. *Faculty:* 7 full-time (5 women). *Students:* 32 part-time (21 women). Average age 33. In 2013, 9 master's awarded. *Degree requirements:* For master's, comprehensive exam, thesis or alternative, portfolio, comprehensive paper, or action research project. *Entrance requirements:* For master's, department exam, GRE General Test, or MAT, minimum GPA of 3.0 in graduate coursework or last 60 hours of undergraduate coursework. Additional exam requirements/recommendations for international students: Required—TOEFL (minimum score 80 iBT). *Application deadline:* For fall admission, 8/1 for domestic and international students; for spring admission, 11/1 for domestic and international students. Applications are processed on a rolling basis. *Expenses:* Tuition, state resident: full-time $5850; part-time $325 per credit hour. Tuition, nonresident: full-time $11,916; part-time $662 per credit hour. *Required fees:* $86; $43 per semester. Tuition and fees vary according to program. *Financial support:* Federal Work-Study, institutionally sponsored loans, and scholarships/grants available. Support available to part-time students. Financial award applicants required to submit FAFSA. *Faculty research:* Reading/literature/literacy, foundations, special education, diversity, teaching and technology. *Unit head:* Dr. Donna Lalonde, Interim Chairperson, 785-670-1943, Fax: 785-670-1046, E-mail: donna.lalonde@washburn.edu. *Application contact:* Tara Porter, Licensure Officer, 785-670-1434, Fax: 785-670-1046, E-mail: tara.porter@washburn.edu.
Website: http://www.washburn.edu/academics/college-schools/arts-sciences/departments/education.

Washington State University, Graduate School, College of Education, Pullman, WA 99164. Offers Ed M, MA, MIT, Ed D, PhD. *Degree requirements:* For master's, comprehensive exam (for some programs), thesis (for some programs), oral and written exams; for doctorate, comprehensive exam, thesis/dissertation, oral and written exams, internship. *Entrance requirements:* For master's, GRE General Test, minimum GPA of 3.0, 3 letters of recommendation, transcripts showing all college or university course work, statement of professional objectives, current curriculum vitae/resume; for doctorate, GRE General Test or MAT, minimum GPA of 3.0, 3 letters of recommendation, transcripts showing all college or university course work, statement of professional objectives, current curriculum vitae/resume. Additional exam requirements/recommendations for international students: Required—TOEFL (minimum score 550 paper-based; 80 iBT). Electronic applications accepted.

Washington State University Spokane, Graduate Programs, Education Department, Spokane, WA 99210. Offers curriculum and instruction (Ed M); educational leadership (Ed M, MA); principal (Certificate); program administrator (Certificate); superintendent (Certificate); teaching (MIT), including elementary, secondary. *Degree requirements:* For master's, comprehensive exam (for some programs), thesis (for some programs). *Entrance requirements:* For master's, GRE or GMAT, minimum GPA of 3.0, 3 letters of recommendation, resume. Additional exam requirements/recommendations for international students: Required—TOEFL (minimum score 550 paper-based).

Washington State University Tri-Cities, Graduate Programs, Program in Education, Richland, WA 99352-1671. Offers educational leadership (Ed M, Ed D); literacy (Ed M); secondary certification (Ed M); teaching (MIT). Part-time programs available. *Degree requirements:* For master's, comprehensive exam, thesis or alternative; for doctorate, comprehensive exam, thesis/dissertation. *Entrance requirements:* For master's, GRE, minimum GPA of 3.0, Working with Youth form, Character and Fitness form, 3 letters of recommendation. Additional exam requirements/recommendations for international students: Required—TOEFL. Electronic applications accepted. *Faculty research:* Multicultural counseling, socio-cultural influences in schools, diverse learners, teacher education, K-12 educational leadership.

Washington State University Vancouver, Graduate Programs, College of Education, Vancouver, WA 98686. Offers Ed M, MIT, Ed D. Part-time programs available. *Degree requirements:* For master's, comprehensive exam, thesis (for some programs); for doctorate, comprehensive exam, thesis/dissertation. *Entrance requirements:* For master's, WEST-B, PRAXIS II (for MIT), minimum GPA of 3.0, 3 letters of recommendation. Additional exam requirements/recommendations for international students: Required—TOEFL (minimum score 550 paper-based). *Faculty research:* Language literacy and culture, developing learning community, developing teacher-mentors.

Washington University in St. Louis, Graduate School of Arts and Sciences, Department of Education, St. Louis, MO 63130-4899. Offers educational research (PhD); elementary education (MA Ed); secondary education (MAT). *Students:* 20 full-time (17 women); includes 3 minority (all Black or African American, non-Hispanic/Latino), 1 international. 55 applicants, 44% accepted, 9 enrolled. In 2013, 9 master's, 1 doctorate awarded. *Degree requirements:* For master's, thesis or alternative; for doctorate, thesis/dissertation. *Entrance requirements:* For master's, GRE General Test; for doctorate, GRE General Test. Additional exam requirements/recommendations for international students: Required—TOEFL. *Application deadline:* For fall admission, 1/1 for domestic students. Application fee: $45. Electronic applications accepted. *Financial support:* Fellowships, teaching assistantships, and tuition waivers (full and partial) available. Financial award application deadline: 1/15. *Faculty research:* Teacher education, educational studies, urban education, policy studies, science and math education, literacy studies. *Unit head:* Dr. Cindy Brantmeier, Chair, 314-935-6791.
Website: http://education.wustl.edu/.

Wayland Baptist University, Graduate Programs, Program in Education, Plainview, TX 79072-6998. Offers education administration (M Ed); education diagnostics (M Ed); education literacy (M Ed); elementary certification (M Ed); English (M Ed); English as a second language (M Ed); higher education administration (M Ed); human resources (M Ed); instructional leadership (M Ed); instructional technology (M Ed); science education (M Ed); secondary certification (M Ed); social studies (M Ed); special education (M Ed). Part-time and evening/weekend programs available. Postbaccalaureate distance learning degree programs offered (no on-campus study). *Faculty:* 33 full-time (17 women), 28 part-time/adjunct (17 women). *Students:* 22 full-time (15 women), 316 part-time (189 women); includes 130 minority (48 Black or African American, non-Hispanic/Latino; 3 American Indian or Alaska Native, non-Hispanic/Latino; 71 Hispanic/Latino; 1 Native Hawaiian or other Pacific Islander, non-Hispanic/Latino; 7 Two or more races, non-Hispanic/Latino). Average age 39. 80 applicants, 96% accepted, 44 enrolled. In 2013, 170 master's awarded. *Degree requirements:* For master's, comprehensive exam, capstone course. *Entrance requirements:* For master's, GRE, GMAT or MAT. Additional exam requirements/recommendations for international students: Required—TOEFL (minimum score 500 paper-based; 61 iBT). *Application deadline:* Applications are processed on a rolling basis. Application fee: $50. Electronic applications accepted. *Expenses: Tuition:* Full-time $8190; part-time $455 per credit hour. *Required fees:* $970; $455 per credit hour. $485 per semester. *Financial support:* Federal Work-Study, institutionally sponsored loans, and scholarships/grants available. Support available to part-time students. Financial award application deadline: 5/1; financial award applicants required to submit FAFSA. *Unit head:* Dr. Jim Todd, Chairman, 806-291-1045, Fax: 806-291-1951. *Application contact:* Amanda Stanton, Coordinator of Graduate Studies, 806-291-3423, Fax: 806-291-1950, E-mail: stanton@wbu.edu.

Waynesburg University, Graduate and Professional Studies, Canonsburg, PA 15370. Offers business (MBA), including energy management, finance, health systems, human resources, leadership, market development; counseling (MA), including addictions counseling, clinical mental health; education (M Ed, MAT), including autism (M Ed), curriculum and instruction (M Ed), educational leadership (M Ed), online teaching

(M Ed); nursing (MSN), including administration, education, informatics; nursing practice (DNP); special education (M Ed); technology (M Ed); MSN/MBA. *Accreditation:* AACN. Part-time and evening/weekend programs available. *Faculty:* 11 full-time (5 women), 136 part-time/adjunct (80 women). *Students:* 146 full-time (99 women), 419 part-time (268 women). In 2013, 290 master's, 7 doctorates awarded. *Degree requirements:* For doctorate, thesis/dissertation. *Entrance requirements:* Additional exam requirements/recommendations for international students: Required—TOEFL. *Application deadline:* For fall admission, 8/1 priority date for domestic students. Applications are processed on a rolling basis. Electronic applications accepted. *Financial support:* Available to part-time students. Application deadline: 5/1. *Unit head:* David Mariner, Dean, 724-743-4420, Fax: 724-743-4425, E-mail: dmariner@waynesburg.edu. *Application contact:* Dr. Michael Bednarski, Director of Enrollment, 724-743-4420, Fax: 724-743-4425, E-mail: mbednars@waynesburg.edu.
Website: http://www.waynesburg.edu/.

Wayne State College, School of Education and Counseling, Wayne, NE 68787. Offers MSE, Ed S. *Accreditation:* NCATE. Part-time and evening/weekend programs available. *Degree requirements:* For master's, comprehensive exam, thesis (for some programs). *Entrance requirements:* For master's, GRE General Test, minimum cumulative GPA of 3.0; for Ed S, GRE General Test, minimum GPA of 3.2 in all program coursework. Additional exam requirements/recommendations for international students: Required—TOEFL (minimum score 550 paper-based).

Wayne State University, College of Education, Detroit, MI 48202. Offers M Ed, MA, MAT, Ed D, PhD, Certificate, Ed S, M Ed/MA. Part-time and evening/weekend programs available. Postbaccalaureate distance learning degree programs offered. *Students:* 595 full-time (457 women), 947 part-time (709 women); includes 575 minority (468 Black or African American, non-Hispanic/Latino; 8 American Indian or Alaska Native, non-Hispanic/Latino; 28 Asian, non-Hispanic/Latino; 42 Hispanic/Latino; 2 Native Hawaiian or other Pacific Islander, non-Hispanic/Latino; 27 Two or more races, non-Hispanic/Latino), 50 international. Average age 36. 768 applicants, 39% accepted, 201 enrolled. In 2013, 317 master's, 44 doctorates, 84 other advanced degrees awarded. Terminal master's awarded for partial completion of doctoral program. *Degree requirements:* For master's, thesis (for some programs); for doctorate, thesis/dissertation, written exam. *Entrance requirements:* For master's, eligibility for state provisional teaching certificate; satisfactory background in area of specialization; baccalaureate degree with minimum upper-division GPA of 2.75; for doctorate, minimum undergraduate GPA of 3.0, master's 3.5; 3 years of teaching experience (for some programs); for other advanced degree, master's degree from accredited institution; minimum undergraduate upper-division GPA of 2.6, 3.4 master's; fulfillment of special requirements in area of concentration; three years' teaching experience (excluding instructional technology). Additional exam requirements/recommendations for international students: Required—TOEFL (minimum score 550 paper-based; 79 iBT), TWE (minimum score 5.5), Michigan English Language Assessment Battery (minimum score 85); Recommended—IELTS (minimum score 6.5). *Application deadline:* For fall admission, 6/1 priority date for domestic students, 5/1 for international students; for winter admission, 10/1 priority date for domestic students, 9/1 priority date for international students; for spring admission, 2/1 priority date for domestic students, 1/1 priority date for international students. Applications are processed on a rolling basis. Application fee: $0. Electronic applications accepted. *Expenses:* Tuition, state resident: part-time $554.15 per credit. Tuition, nonresident: part-time $1200.35 per credit. *Required fees:* $42.15 per credit. $268.30 per semester. Tuition and fees vary according to course load and program. *Financial support:* In 2013–14, 238 students received support, including 8 fellowships with tuition reimbursements available (averaging $14,458 per year), 12 research assistantships (averaging $16,901 per year); teaching assistantships with tuition reimbursements available, career-related internships or fieldwork, Federal Work-Study, scholarships/grants, health care benefits, and unspecified assistantships also available. Support available to part-time students. Financial award application deadline: 3/31; financial award applicants required to submit FAFSA. *Faculty research:* Alternative routes to teacher certification; innovations in science, mathematics and technology education; literacy; K-12 school reform, including special education and self-determination for special populations; adult workplace learning. *Total annual research expenditures:* $1.1 million. *Unit head:* Dr. Carolyn Shields, Dean, 313-577-1620, Fax: 313-577-3606, E-mail: cshields@wayne.edu. *Application contact:* Janice Green, Assistant Dean, 313-577-1605, E-mail: jwgreen@wayne.edu.
Website: http://coe.wayne.edu/.

Weber State University, Jerry and Vickie Moyes College of Education, Ogden, UT 84408-1001. Offers M Ed, MSAT. *Accreditation:* NCATE. Part-time and evening/weekend programs available. *Faculty:* 22 full-time (14 women), 3 part-time/adjunct (1 woman). *Students:* 45 full-time (27 women), 147 part-time (111 women); includes 6 minority (2 American Indian or Alaska Native, non-Hispanic/Latino; 4 Hispanic/Latino), 6 international. Average age 34. 93 applicants, 82% accepted, 64 enrolled. In 2013, 52 master's awarded. *Degree requirements:* For master's, project presentation and exam. *Entrance requirements:* For master's, MAT or GRE. Additional exam requirements/recommendations for international students: Required—TOEFL (minimum score 550 paper-based). *Application deadline:* For fall admission, 5/1 priority date for domestic students; for spring admission, 11/1 priority date for domestic students. Applications are processed on a rolling basis. Application fee: $60 ($90 for international students). *Expenses:* Tuition, state resident: full-time $7118; part-time $253 per credit hour. Tuition, nonresident: full-time $12,480; part-time $634 per credit hour. *Required fees:* $34.33; $34.33 per credit hour. $257 per semester. Full-time tuition and fees vary according to course load. *Financial support:* In 2013–14, 35 students received support. Institutionally sponsored loans, scholarships/grants, tuition waivers (full and partial), and unspecified assistantships available. Support available to part-time students. Financial award application deadline: 4/1; financial award applicants required to submit FAFSA. *Unit head:* Dr. Jack Rasmussen, Dean, 801-626-6273, Fax: 801-626-7427, E-mail: jrasmussen@weber.edu. *Application contact:* Dr. Claudia Eliason, Director, 801-626-7719, Fax: 801-626-7427, E-mail: eeliason@weber.edu.
Website: http://www.weber.edu/education/.

Webster University, School of Education, St. Louis, MO 63119-3194. Offers MA, MAT, Ed S. *Accreditation:* NCATE. Part-time programs available. Postbaccalaureate distance learning degree programs offered (no on-campus study). *Degree requirements:* For master's, thesis (for some programs). *Entrance requirements:* For master's, minimum GPA of 2.5. Additional exam requirements/recommendations for international students: Required—TOEFL. *Expenses: Tuition:* Full-time $11,610; part-time $645 per credit hour. Tuition and fees vary according to campus/location and program.

Wesleyan College, Department of Education, Macon, GA 31210-4462. Offers early childhood education (MA). Part-time programs available. *Degree requirements:* For master's, thesis or alternative, practicum, professional portfolio. *Entrance requirements:* For master's, GRE or MAT, interview, teaching certificate, 3 letters of recommendation. Additional exam requirements/recommendations for international students: Required—TOEFL. *Faculty research:* Neuroscience, gender bias in science and mathematics.

Wesley College, Education Program, Dover, DE 19901-3875. Offers M Ed, MA Ed, MAT. *Accreditation:* NCATE. Part-time and evening/weekend programs available. *Degree requirements:* For master's, thesis optional. *Entrance requirements:* For

master's, GRE. *Faculty research:* Learning styles, community-higher education partnerships, curriculum models, science learning and teaching, literacy development in early elementary.

West Chester University of Pennsylvania, College of Education, West Chester, PA 19383. Offers M Ed, MS, Certificate, Teaching Certificate. *Accreditation:* NCATE. Part-time and evening/weekend programs available. Postbaccalaureate distance learning degree programs offered (no on-campus study). *Faculty:* 37 full-time (27 women), 13 part-time/adjunct (8 women). *Students:* 156 full-time (130 women), 409 part-time (357 women); includes 59 minority (32 Black or African American, non-Hispanic/Latino; 3 American Indian or Alaska Native, non-Hispanic/Latino; 4 Asian, non-Hispanic/Latino; 13 Hispanic/Latino; 7 Two or more races, non-Hispanic/Latino), 4 international. Average age 29. 324 applicants, 84% accepted, 159 enrolled. In 2013, 212 master's, 10 other advanced degrees awarded. *Degree requirements:* For master's, comprehensive exam (for some programs), thesis (for some programs). *Entrance requirements:* Additional exam requirements/recommendations for international students: Required—TOEFL (minimum score 550 paper-based; 80 iBT). *Application deadline:* For fall admission, 4/15 priority date for domestic students, 3/15 for international students; for spring admission, 10/15 priority date for domestic students, 9/1 for international students. Applications are processed on a rolling basis. Application fee: $45. Electronic applications accepted. *Expenses:* Tuition, state resident: full-time $7956; part-time $442 per credit. Tuition, nonresident: full-time $11,934; part-time $663 per credit. *Required fees:* $2134.20; $106.24 per credit. Tuition and fees vary according to campus/location and program. *Financial support:* Unspecified assistantships available. Support available to part-time students. Financial award application deadline: 2/15; financial award applicants required to submit FAFSA. *Unit head:* Dr. Kenneth D. Witmer, Jr., Dean, 610-436-2321, Fax: 610-436-3102, E-mail: kcrouse@wcupa.edu. *Application contact:* Office of Graduate Studies, 610-436-2943, Fax: 610-436-2763, E-mail: gradstudy@wcupa.edu.
Website: http://www.wcupa.edu/_academics/sch_sed/.

Western Carolina University, Graduate School, College of Education and Allied Professions, Cullowhee, NC 28723. Offers M Ed, MA, MA Ed, MAT, MS, MSA, Ed D, Ed S, PMC. *Accreditation:* NCATE. Part-time and evening/weekend programs available. Postbaccalaureate distance learning degree programs offered. *Degree requirements:* For master's, comprehensive exam, thesis; for doctorate, comprehensive exam, thesis/dissertation. *Entrance requirements:* For master's, GRE, appropriate undergraduate degree with minimum GPA of 3.0, 3 recommendations, writing sample, resume, interview; for doctorate, GRE General Test, minimum graduate GPA of 3.5, appropriate master's degree; for other advanced degree, GRE General Test, minimum graduate GPA of 3.5, work experience, appropriate master's degree. Additional exam requirements/recommendations for international students: Required—TOEFL (minimum score 550 paper-based; 79 iBT). *Faculty research:* Evolutionary psychology, marital and family development, program evaluation, rural education, special education, educational leadership, employee recruitment/retention.

Western Connecticut State University, Division of Graduate Studies, School of Professional Studies, Department of Education and Educational Psychology, Danbury, CT 06810-6885. Offers community counseling (MS); counselor education (MS), including guidance and counseling; curriculum (MS); English education (MS); instructional leadership (Ed D); instructional technology (MS); mathematics education (MS); reading (MS); school counseling (MS); secondary education (MAT), including biology, mathematics; special education (MS). *Accreditation:* NCATE. Part-time programs available. *Degree requirements:* For master's, thesis or alternative, completion of program in 6 years. *Entrance requirements:* For master's, MAT (if GPA is below 2.8), valid teaching certificate, letters of reference; for doctorate, GRE or MAT, resume, three recommendations (one in a supervisory capacity in an educational setting), satisfactory interview with WCSU representatives from the EdD Admissions Committee. Additional exam requirements/recommendations for international students: Recommended—TOEFL (minimum score 550 paper-based; 79 iBT), IELTS (minimum score 6). *Expenses:* Contact institution. *Faculty research:* Cultural diversity in teacher and counselor education programs, African-American educational leaders, urban education and equity.

Western Governors University, Teachers College, Salt Lake City, UT 84107. Offers curriculum and instruction (MS); educational leadership (MS); educational studies (MA); educational studies (5-12) (MA), including mathematics; elementary education (K-8) (MAT, Postbaccalaureate Certificate); elementary education (PreK-8) (MAT); English language learning (K-12) (MA); instructional design (MAT); learning and technology (M Ed, MA); management and innovation (M Ed); mathematics (5-12) (MAT, Postbaccalaureate Certificate); mathematics (5-9) (MAT, Postbaccalaureate Certificate); mathematics education (5-12) (MA); mathematics education (5-9) (MA); mathematics education (K-6) (MA); measurement and evaluation (M Ed); science (5-12) (Postbaccalaureate Certificate); science (5-9) (MAT, Postbaccalaureate Certificate); science education (5-12) (MA), including biology, chemistry, geology, physics; science education (5-9) (MA); social science (5-12) (MAT, Postbaccalaureate Certificate); special education (MAT, MS). *Accreditation:* NCATE. Evening/weekend programs available. Postbaccalaureate distance learning degree programs offered (no on-campus study). *Degree requirements:* For master's, capstone project. *Entrance requirements:* For master's and Postbaccalaureate Certificate, Readiness Assessment, transcripts. Additional exam requirements/recommendations for international students: Required—TOEFL (minimum score 450 paper-based; 80 iBT). Electronic applications accepted. *Expenses:* Contact institution.

Western Illinois University, School of Graduate Studies, College of Education and Human Services, Macomb, IL 61455-1390. Offers MA, MS, MS Ed, Ed D, Certificate, Ed S. *Accreditation:* NCATE. Part-time and evening/weekend programs available. Postbaccalaureate distance learning degree programs offered (no on-campus study). *Students:* 268 full-time (153 women), 623 part-time (424 women); includes 103 minority (47 Black or African American, non-Hispanic/Latino; 2 American Indian or Alaska Native, non-Hispanic/Latino; 12 Asian, non-Hispanic/Latino; 35 Hispanic/Latino; 7 Two or more races, non-Hispanic/Latino), 25 international. Average age 31. In 2013, 336 master's, 3 doctorates, 34 other advanced degrees awarded. *Degree requirements:* For master's, comprehensive exam (for some programs), thesis or alternative; for doctorate, comprehensive exam, thesis/dissertation, electronic portfolio. *Entrance requirements:* For master's, GRE and MAT (for selected programs); for doctorate, GRE. Additional exam requirements/recommendations for international students: Required—TOEFL. *Application deadline:* Applications are processed on a rolling basis. Application fee: $30. Electronic applications accepted. *Financial support:* In 2013–14, 157 students received support, including 127 research assistantships with full tuition reimbursements available (averaging $7,544 per year), 30 teaching assistantships with full tuition reimbursements available (averaging $8,688 per year). Financial award applicants required to submit FAFSA. *Unit head:* Dr. Sterling Saddler, Dean, 309-298-1690. *Application contact:* Dr. Nancy Parsons, Associate Provost and Director of Graduate Studies, 309-298-1806, Fax: 309-298-2345, E-mail: grad-office@wiu.edu.
Website: http://wiu.edu/coehs.

Western Michigan University, Graduate College, College of Education and Human Development, Kalamazoo, MI 49008. Offers MA, MS, Ed D, PhD, Ed S, Graduate Certificate. *Accreditation:* NCATE. Part-time programs available. *Degree requirements:*

Education—General

For doctorate, thesis/dissertation; for other advanced degree, thesis, oral exams. *Entrance requirements:* For doctorate and other advanced degree, GRE General Test.

Western New Mexico University, Graduate Division, School of Education, Silver City, NM 88062-0680. Offers bilingual education (MAT); counseling (MA); educational leadership (MA); elementary education (MAT); reading (MAT); school psychology (MA); secondary education (MAT); special education (MAT); TESOL (teaching English to speakers of other languages) (MAT). *Accreditation:* NCATE. *Degree requirements:* For master's, comprehensive exam. *Entrance requirements:* For master's, GRE General Test, GRE Subject Test, minimum GPA of 3.2 in last 64 hours of undergraduate study. Additional exam requirements/recommendations for international students: Required—TOEFL (minimum score 550 paper-based). Electronic applications accepted.

Western Oregon University, Graduate Programs, College of Education, Monmouth, OR 97361-1394. Offers MAT, MS, MS Ed. *Accreditation:* NCATE. Part-time and evening/weekend programs available. Postbaccalaureate distance learning degree programs offered (minimal on-campus study). *Degree requirements:* For master's, comprehensive exam (for some programs), thesis optional, written exam. *Entrance requirements:* For master's, minimum GPA of 3.0. Additional exam requirements/recommendations for international students: Required—TOEFL (minimum score 550 paper-based; 79 iBT), IELTS (minimum score 6.5). *Faculty research:* Effectiveness of work, sample methodology, documentation of learning gains, appropriateness of advanced proficiency.

Western State Colorado University, Graduate Programs in Education, Gunnison, CO 81231. Offers education administrator leadership (MA); reading leadership (MA); teacher leadership (MA). Postbaccalaureate distance learning degree programs offered (minimal on-campus study). *Degree requirements:* For master's, capstone.

Western Washington University, Graduate School, Woodring College of Education, Bellingham, WA 98225-5996. Offers M Ed, MA, MIT. *Accreditation:* NCATE. Part-time programs available. Postbaccalaureate distance learning degree programs offered (minimal on-campus study). *Degree requirements:* For master's, comprehensive exam, thesis optional. *Entrance requirements:* For master's, GRE General Test or MAT, minimum GPA of 3.0 in last 60 semester hours or last 90 quarter hours. Additional exam requirements/recommendations for international students: Required—TOEFL (minimum score 567 paper-based). Electronic applications accepted.

Westfield State University, Division of Graduate and Continuing Education, Department of Education, Westfield, MA 01086. Offers early childhood education (M Ed); elementary education (M Ed); occupational education (M Ed, CAGS); reading (M Ed); school administration (M Ed, CAGS); secondary education (M Ed); special education (M Ed); technology for educators (M Ed). *Accreditation:* NCATE. Part-time and evening/weekend programs available. *Degree requirements:* For master's, comprehensive exam; for CAGS, research-based field internship. *Entrance requirements:* For master's, GRE General Test or MAT, minimum undergraduate GPA of 2.7; for CAGS, master's degree. *Faculty research:* Collaborative teacher education, developmental early childhood education.

West Liberty University, College of Education, West Liberty, WV 26074. Offers MA Ed. *Accreditation:* NCATE. *Degree requirements:* For master's, capstone experience. *Entrance requirements:* For master's, GRE or MAT, minimum GPA of 2.5, teaching license, interview. Electronic applications accepted. *Expenses:* Tuition, state resident: part-time $375 per hour. Tuition, nonresident: part-time $584 per hour. *Unit head:* Dr. Keely Camden, Dean, 304-336-8247, E-mail: kcamden@westliberty.edu. Website: http://westliberty.edu/education/.

Westminster College, Programs in Education, New Wilmington, PA 16172-0001. Offers administration (M Ed, Certificate); reading (M Ed, Certificate); school counseling (M Ed, Certificate). Part-time and evening/weekend programs available. *Degree requirements:* For master's, comprehensive exam, portfolio. *Entrance requirements:* For master's, GRE or MAT, minimum GPA of 3.0.

Westminster College, School of Education, Salt Lake City, UT 84105-3697. Offers community leadership (MACL); education (M Ed); teaching (MAT). *Accreditation:* Teacher Education Accreditation Council. Part-time and evening/weekend programs available. *Faculty:* 14 full-time (12 women), 25 part-time/adjunct (16 women). *Students:* 110 full-time (87 women), 71 part-time (55 women); includes 16 minority (2 Black or African American, non-Hispanic/Latino; 2 Asian, non-Hispanic/Latino; 12 Hispanic/Latino), 2 international. Average age 33. 150 applicants, 69% accepted, 85 enrolled. In 2013, 96 degrees awarded. *Degree requirements:* For master's, project or thesis. *Entrance requirements:* For master's, personal resume, 2 letters of recommendation, minimum GPA of 3.0, copy of current teaching certificate, statement of purpose, official transcript. Additional exam requirements/recommendations for international students: Required—TOEFL (minimum score 600 paper-based; 100 iBT), IELTS (minimum score 7.5). *Application deadline:* For fall admission, 8/1 for domestic students, 6/1 for international students; for spring admission, 1/1 for domestic students; for summer admission, 5/1 for domestic students. Application fee: $50. Electronic applications accepted. *Expenses:* Contact institution. *Financial support:* In 2013–14, 10 students received support. Career-related internships or fieldwork, unspecified assistantships, and tuition reimbursements, tuition remission available. Support available to part-time students. Financial award applicants required to submit FAFSA. *Faculty research:* Early childhood literacy, English as a second language instruction, special education, instruction in teacher education, e-portfolios as assessment tools, funds of knowledge. *Unit head:* Robert Shaw, Dean, School of Education, 801-832-2470, Fax: 801-832-3105. *Application contact:* Dr. John Baworowsky, Vice President of Enrollment Management, 801-832-2200, Fax: 801-832-3101, E-mail: admission@westminstercollege.edu. Website: http://www.westminstercollege.edu/med.

West Texas A&M University, College of Education and Social Sciences, Department of Education, Canyon, TX 79016-0001. Offers clinical mental health (MA); curriculum and instruction (M Ed); educational diagnostician (M Ed); educational leadership (M Ed); instructional design and technology (M Ed); reading education (M Ed); school counseling (M Ed); special education (M Ed); teaching (MAT). Part-time and evening/weekend programs available. Postbaccalaureate distance learning degree programs offered (minimal on-campus study). *Degree requirements:* For master's, comprehensive exam, thesis optional. *Entrance requirements:* For master's, GRE General Test. Additional exam requirements/recommendations for international students: Required—TOEFL (minimum score 550 paper-based). Electronic applications accepted. *Faculty research:* Modified internship for novice teachers, effective instructional strategies, cognitive-relational group, community college, recruitment/retention.

West Virginia University, College of Human Resources and Education, Morgantown, WV 26506. Offers MA, MS, Au D, Ed D, PhD. *Accreditation:* NCATE. Part-time and evening/weekend programs available. Postbaccalaureate distance learning degree programs offered (no on-campus study). *Degree requirements:* For master's, content exams; for doctorate, comprehensive exam, thesis/dissertation. *Entrance requirements:* Additional exam requirements/recommendations for international students: Required—TOEFL. Electronic applications accepted. *Faculty research:* Internet training and integration for teachers, rural education, teacher preparation, organization of schools, evaluation of personnel.

West Virginia Wesleyan College, Department of Education, Buckhannon, WV 26201. Offers M Ed. *Accreditation:* NCATE.

Wheaton College, Graduate School, Department of Education, Wheaton, IL 60187-5593. Offers elementary education (MAT); secondary education (MAT). *Accreditation:* NCATE. *Degree requirements:* For master's, thesis or alternative. *Entrance requirements:* For master's, GRE General Test or MAT. Additional exam requirements/recommendations for international students: Required—TOEFL (minimum score 550 paper-based; 80 iBT), IELTS (minimum score 6.5). Electronic applications accepted.

Wheelock College, Graduate Programs, Boston, MA 02215-4176. Offers MS, MSW. *Accreditation:* NCATE (one or more programs are accredited). Part-time and evening/weekend programs available. Postbaccalaureate distance learning degree programs offered (minimal on-campus study). *Entrance requirements:* For master's, interview. Additional exam requirements/recommendations for international students: Required—TOEFL (minimum score 550 paper-based). *Faculty research:* Teacher development and leadership, national standards science education, high academic achievement for students of color, cultural influences on development, media literacy.

Whittier College, Graduate Programs, Department of Education and Child Development, Whittier, CA 90608-0634. Offers educational administration (MA Ed); elementary education (MA Ed); secondary education (MA Ed). Part-time and evening/weekend programs available. *Degree requirements:* For master's, thesis. *Entrance requirements:* For master's, GRE General Test, MAT, minimum GPA of 3.5, academic writing sample.

Whitworth University, School of Education, Graduate Studies in Education, Spokane, WA 99251-0001. Offers administration (M Ed); counseling (M Ed), including school counselors, social agency/church setting; elementary education (M Ed); gifted and talented (MAT); secondary education (M Ed); special education (MAT); teaching (MIT). *Accreditation:* NCATE. Part-time and evening/weekend programs available. *Degree requirements:* For master's, comprehensive exam, thesis (for some programs). *Entrance requirements:* For master's, GRE General Test, MAT. Additional exam requirements/recommendations for international students: Required—TOEFL. *Faculty research:* Rural program development, mainstreaming, special needs learners.

Wichita State University, Graduate School, College of Education, Wichita, KS 67260. Offers M Ed, MAT, Ed D, Ed S. *Accreditation:* NCATE. Part-time and evening/weekend programs available. *Unit head:* Dr. Shirley Lefever-Davis, Interim Dean, 316-978-3301, Fax: 316-978-3302, E-mail: shirley.lefever-davis@wichita.edu. *Application contact:* Jordan Oleson, Admissions Coordinator, 316-978-3095, Fax: 316-978-3253, E-mail: jordan.oleson@wichita.edu. Website: http://www.wichita.edu/education.

Widener University, School of Human Service Professions, Center for Education, Chester, PA 19013-5792. Offers adult education (M Ed); counseling in higher education (M Ed); counselor education (M Ed); early childhood education (M Ed); educational foundations (M Ed); educational leadership (M Ed); educational psychology (M Ed); elementary education (M Ed); English and language arts (M Ed); health education (M Ed); higher education leadership (Ed D); home and school visitor (M Ed); human sexuality (M Ed, PhD); mathematics education (M Ed); middle school education (M Ed); principalship (M Ed); reading and language arts (Ed D); reading education (M Ed); school administration (Ed D); science education (M Ed); social studies education (M Ed); special education (M Ed); technology education (M Ed). *Accreditation:* NCATE. Part-time and evening/weekend programs available. *Faculty:* 34 full-time (22 women), 37 part-time/adjunct (14 women). *Students:* 64 full-time (44 women), 209 part-time (146 women); includes 49 minority (39 Black or African American, non-Hispanic/Latino; 1 American Indian or Alaska Native, non-Hispanic/Latino; 4 Asian, non-Hispanic/Latino; 4 Hispanic/Latino; 1 Two or more races, non-Hispanic/Latino), 8 international. Average age 39. 139 applicants, 88% accepted. In 2013, 168 master's, 31 doctorates awarded. Terminal master's awarded for partial completion of doctoral program. *Degree requirements:* For doctorate, thesis/dissertation. *Entrance requirements:* For master's, minimum GPA of 2.5; for doctorate, GRE or MAT, minimum GPA of 2.0 (undergraduate), 3.5 (graduate). *Application deadline:* Applications are processed on a rolling basis. Application fee: $25 ($300 for international students). Electronic applications accepted. *Expenses:* Contact institution. *Financial support:* Career-related internships or fieldwork, tuition waivers (full and partial), and unspecified assistantships available. Support available to part-time students. Financial award application deadline: 5/1. *Faculty research:* Reading and cognition, adult education, technology education, educational leadership, special education. *Unit head:* Dr. Michael W. LeDoux, Associate Dean, 610-499-4294, Fax: 610-499-4623, E-mail: mwledoux@widener.edu. *Application contact:* Dr. Roberta Nolan, Director of Graduate Admissions, 610-499-4125, E-mail: rdnolan@widener.edu.

Wilkes University, College of Graduate and Professional Studies, School of Education, Wilkes-Barre, PA 18766-0002. Offers art and science of teaching (MS Ed); classroom technology (MS Ed); early childhood literacy (MS Ed); educational development and strategies (MS Ed); educational leadership (MS Ed); educational technology (Ed D); higher education administration (Ed D); instructional media (MS Ed); instructional technology (MS Ed); international school leadership (MS Ed); K-12 administration (Ed D); middle level education (MS Ed); online teaching (MS Ed); reading (MS Ed); school business leadership (MS Ed); secondary education (MS Ed), including biology, chemistry, English, history, mathematics; special education (MS Ed); teaching English as a second language (MS Ed); twenty-first century teaching and learning (MS Ed). Part-time and evening/weekend programs available. Postbaccalaureate distance learning degree programs offered (minimal on-campus study). *Students:* 46 full-time (37 women), 1,410 part-time (1,039 women); includes 67 minority (12 Black or African American, non-Hispanic/Latino; 2 American Indian or Alaska Native, non-Hispanic/Latino; 11 Asian, non-Hispanic/Latino; 28 Hispanic/Latino; 1 Native Hawaiian or other Pacific Islander, non-Hispanic/Latino; 13 Two or more races, non-Hispanic/Latino), 6 international. Average age 34. In 2013, 852 master's, 10 doctorates awarded. *Entrance requirements:* Additional exam requirements/recommendations for international students: Required—TOEFL (minimum score 550 paper-based; 79 iBT). *Application deadline:* Applications are processed on a rolling basis. Application fee: $45. Electronic applications accepted. *Expenses:* Contact institution. *Financial support:* Federal Work-Study and unspecified assistantships available. Financial award application deadline: 3/1; financial award applicants required to submit FAFSA. *Unit head:* Dr. Rhonda Waskiewicz, Interim Dean, Education, 570-408-4332, Fax: 570-408-7872, E-mail: rhonda.waskiewicz@wilkes.edu. *Application contact:* Joanne Thomas, Interim Director of Graduate Education, 570-408-4234, Fax: 570-408-7846, E-mail: joanne.thomas1@wilkes.edu. Website: http://www.wilkes.edu/pages/383.asp.

Willamette University, Graduate School of Education, Salem, OR 97301-3931. Offers environmental literacy (M Ed); reading (M Ed); special education (M Ed); teaching (MAT). *Accreditation:* NCATE. Evening/weekend programs available. *Degree requirements:* For master's, leadership project (action research). *Entrance requirements:* For master's, California Basic Educational Skills Test, Multiple Subject Assessment for Teachers, PRAXIS, minimum GPA of 3.0, classroom experience, 2 letters of reference. Additional exam requirements/recommendations for international

students: Recommended—TOEFL. Electronic applications accepted. *Expenses:* Contact institution. *Faculty research:* Educational leadership, multicultural education, middle school education, clinical supervision, educational technology.

William Carey University, School of Education, Hattiesburg, MS 39401-5499. Offers art education (M Ed); art of teaching (M Ed); elementary education (M Ed, Ed S); English education (M Ed); gifted education (M Ed); history and social science (M Ed); mild/moderate disabilities (M Ed); secondary education (M Ed). *Accreditation:* NCATE. Part-time programs available. *Degree requirements:* For master's, comprehensive exam. *Entrance requirements:* For master's, GRE, MAT, minimum GPA of 2.5, Class A teacher's license. Additional exam requirements/recommendations for international students: Required—TOEFL (minimum score 550 paper-based).

William Howard Taft University, Graduate Programs, The Boyer Graduate School of Education, Santa Ana, CA 92704. Offers M Ed.

William Paterson University of New Jersey, College of Education, Wayne, NJ 07470-8420. Offers curriculum and learning (M Ed); educational leadership (M Ed); reading (M Ed); special education and counseling services (M Ed), including counseling services, special education; teaching (MAT). *Accreditation:* NCATE. Part-time and evening/weekend programs available. Postbaccalaureate distance learning degree programs offered. *Faculty:* 33 full-time (8 women), 32 part-time/adjunct (9 women). *Students:* 118 full-time (92 women), 519 part-time (431 women); includes 134 minority (35 Black or African American, non-Hispanic/Latino; 1 American Indian or Alaska Native, non-Hispanic/Latino; 6 Asian, non-Hispanic/Latino; 86 Hispanic/Latino; 6 Two or more races, non-Hispanic/Latino). Average age 34. 439 applicants, 74% accepted, 240 enrolled. In 2013, 144 master's awarded. *Degree requirements:* For master's, comprehensive exam, thesis (for some programs), exit interview (for some programs), practicum/internship. *Entrance requirements:* For master's, GRE/MAT, minimum GPA of 2.75, teaching certificate. Additional exam requirements/recommendations for international students: Required—TOEFL (minimum score 550 paper-based; 79 iBT), IELTS (minimum score 6). *Application deadline:* For fall admission, 6/1 for domestic students, 5/1 for international students; for spring admission, 11/1 for domestic students, 10/1 for international students. Applications are processed on a rolling basis. Application fee: $50. Electronic applications accepted. *Financial support:* Research assistantships with full tuition reimbursements, career-related internships or fieldwork, Federal Work-Study, and unspecified assistantships available. Support available to part-time students. Financial award application deadline: 4/1; financial award applicants required to submit FAFSA. *Faculty research:* IPads in the classroom, characteristics of effective elementary teachers in language arts and mathematics, gender issues in science, after-school programs, middle class parents' roles and gentrifying school districts. *Unit head:* Dr. Candace Burns, Dean, 973-720-2137, Fax: 973-720-2955, E-mail: burnsc@wpunj.edu. *Application contact:* Liana Fornarotto, Assistant Director, Graduate Admissions, 973-720-3578, Fax: 973-720-2035, E-mail: fornarottol@wpunj.edu.
Website: http://www.wpunj.edu/coe.

Wilmington College, Department of Education, Wilmington, OH 45177. Offers reading (M Ed); special education (M Ed). Part-time programs available. *Degree requirements:* For master's, comprehensive exam. *Entrance requirements:* For master's, GRE or MAT, minimum GPA of 3.0, 2 letters of recommendation. Additional exam requirements/recommendations for international students: Required—TOEFL. *Faculty research:* Reading instruction, special education practices, conflict resolution in the schools, models of higher education for teachers.

Wilmington University, College of Education, New Castle, DE 19720-6491. Offers applied technology in education (M Ed); career and technical education (M Ed); educational leadership (Ed D); elementary and secondary school counseling (M Ed); elementary studies (M Ed); ESOL literacy (M Ed); higher education leadership (Ed D); instruction: gifted and talented (M Ed); instruction: teacher of reading (M Ed); instruction: teaching and learning (M Ed); organizational leadership (Ed D); school leadership (M Ed); secondary education (MAT); special education (M Ed). *Accreditation:* NCATE. Part-time and evening/weekend programs available. *Entrance requirements:* For master's, 2 letters of recommendation, interview. Additional exam requirements/recommendations for international students: Required—TOEFL (minimum score 500 paper-based). Electronic applications accepted.

Wilson College, Program in Education, Chambersburg, PA 17201-1285. Offers M Ed. Evening/weekend programs available. *Degree requirements:* For master's, project. *Entrance requirements:* For master's, PRAXIS, minimum undergraduate cumulative GPA of 3.0, 2 letters of recommendation, current certification for eligibility to teach in grades K-12, resume, personal interview. Electronic applications accepted.

Wingate University, Thayer School of Education, Wingate, NC 28174-0159. Offers community college leadership (Ed D); educational leadership (MA Ed, Ed D); elementary education (MA Ed, MAT); health and physical education (MA Ed); sport administration (MA Ed). *Accreditation:* NCATE. Part-time and evening/weekend programs available. *Degree requirements:* For master's, portfolio. *Entrance requirements:* For master's, GRE General Test or MAT, teaching certificate (MA Ed).

Winona State University, College of Education, Department of Education, Winona, MN 55987. Offers MS. *Accreditation:* NCATE. Part-time and evening/weekend programs available. *Degree requirements:* For master's, comprehensive exam, thesis (for some programs). *Entrance requirements:* For master's, minimum GPA of 2.75/teaching license.

Winthrop University, College of Education, Rock Hill, SC 29733. Offers M Ed, MAT, MS. *Accreditation:* NCATE. Part-time programs available. *Entrance requirements:* Additional exam requirements/recommendations for international students: Required—TOEFL (minimum paper-based score of 520, iBT 68) or IELTS (minimum score of 6). Electronic applications accepted.

Wittenberg University, Graduate Program, Springfield, OH 45501-0720. Offers education (MA). *Accreditation:* NCATE.

Worcester State University, Graduate Studies, Department of Education, Worcester, MA 01602-2597. Offers early childhood education (M Ed); education (M Ed); elementary education (M Ed); English as a second language (M Ed); health education (M Ed); leadership and administration (M Ed, CAGS, Postbaccalaureate Certificate); middle school education (M Ed, Postbaccalaureate Certificate); moderate special needs (M Ed, Postbaccalaureate Certificate); reading (M Ed, CAGS, Postbaccalaureate Certificate); school psychology (CAGS); secondary education (M Ed). Part-time and evening/weekend programs available. *Faculty:* 14 full-time (11 women), 22 part-time/adjunct (10 women). *Students:* 30 full-time (25 women), 238 part-time (174 women); includes 17 minority (3 Black or African American, non-Hispanic/Latino; 1 American Indian or Alaska Native, non-Hispanic/Latino; 3 Asian, non-Hispanic/Latino; 9 Hispanic/Latino; 1 Two or more races, non-Hispanic/Latino), 1 international. Average age 34. 251 applicants, 72% accepted, 44 enrolled. In 2013, 49 master's, 179 CAGSs awarded. *Degree requirements:* For master's, comprehensive exam (for some programs), thesis optional. *Entrance requirements:* For master's, GRE General Test, MAT or GMAT, teaching certificate. Additional exam requirements/recommendations for international students: Required—TOEFL (minimum score 500 paper-based; 61 iBT). *Application deadline:* For fall admission, 6/15 for domestic and international students; for spring admission, 4/1 for domestic and international students. Applications are processed on a rolling basis. Application fee: $40. Electronic applications accepted. *Expenses: Tuition, area resident:* Part-time $150 per credit. Tuition, state resident: part-time $150 per credit. Tuition, nonresident: part-time $150 per credit. *Required fees:* $114.50 per credit. *Financial support:* In 2013–14, 5 students received support, including 5 research assistantships with full tuition reimbursements available (averaging $4,800 per year); career-related internships or fieldwork, scholarships/grants, and unspecified assistantships also available. Financial award application deadline: 3/1; financial award applicants required to submit FAFSA. *Unit head:* Dr. Carol Donnelly, Coordinator, 508-929-8667, Fax: 508-929-8164, E-mail: cdonnelly@worcester.edu. *Application contact:* Sara Grady, Assistant Dean of Graduate and Continuing Education, 508-929-8787, Fax: 508-929-8100, E-mail: sara.grady@worcester.edu.

Wright State University, School of Graduate Studies, College of Education and Human Services, Dayton, OH 45435. Offers M Ed, MA, MRC, MS, MST, Ed S. *Accreditation:* NCATE. Part-time and evening/weekend programs available. *Degree requirements:* For Ed S, thesis. *Entrance requirements:* For master's, GRE General Test, MAT, PRAXIS II; for Ed S, GRE General Test, MAT. Additional exam requirements/recommendations for international students: Required—TOEFL.

Xavier University, College of Social Sciences, Health and Education, School of Education, Cincinnati, OH 45207. Offers M Ed, MA, MS. *Accreditation:* Teacher Education Accreditation Council. *Faculty:* 34 full-time (18 women), 65 part-time/adjunct (36 women). *Students:* 201 full-time (144 women), 349 part-time (265 women); includes 80 minority (46 Black or African American, non-Hispanic/Latino; 12 Asian, non-Hispanic/Latino; 14 Hispanic/Latino; 1 Native Hawaiian or other Pacific Islander, non-Hispanic/Latino; 7 Two or more races, non-Hispanic/Latino), 9 international. Average age 32. 129 applicants, 97% accepted, 94 enrolled. In 2013, 257 master's awarded. *Entrance requirements:* Additional exam requirements/recommendations for international students: Required—TOEFL (minimum score 550 paper-based; 79 iBT). *Application deadline:* Applications are processed on a rolling basis. Application fee: $35. Electronic applications accepted. *Expenses: Tuition:* Part-time $594 per credit hour. *Required fees:* $3 per semester. *Financial support:* In 2013–14, 393 students received support. Applicants required to submit FAFSA. *Faculty research:* Early childhood literacy, service-learning, family resiliency/special needs families, technology integration, leadership theory, Montessori methodology. *Unit head:* Dr. Dennis Long, Associate Dean of Social Sciences, Health, and Education, 513-745-3521, Fax: 513-745-1052, E-mail: longd3@xavier.edu. *Application contact:* Roger Bosse, Graduate Services Director, 513-745-3357, Fax: 513-745-1048, E-mail: bosse@xavier.edu.
Website: http://www.xavier.edu/education/.

Xavier University of Louisiana, Graduate School, Programs in Education, New Orleans, LA 70125-1098. Offers curriculum and instruction (MA); education administration and supervision (MA); guidance and counseling (MA). *Accreditation:* NCATE. Part-time and evening/weekend programs available. *Degree requirements:* For master's, comprehensive exam, thesis or alternative. *Entrance requirements:* For master's, GRE General Test, MAT, minimum GPA of 2.5. Additional exam requirements/recommendations for international students: Required—TOEFL.

York College of Pennsylvania, Department of Education, York, PA 17405-7199. Offers educational leadership (M Ed); reading specialist (M Ed). Part-time and evening/weekend programs available. *Faculty:* 3 full-time (2 women), 8 part-time/adjunct (5 women). *Students:* 43 part-time (34 women); includes 1 minority (Hispanic/Latino). Average age 31. 15 applicants, 67% accepted, 7 enrolled. In 2013, 15 master's awarded. *Degree requirements:* For master's, comprehensive exam, thesis optional, portfolio. *Entrance requirements:* For master's, GRE, MAT or PRAXIS, letters of recommendation, portfolio. *Application deadline:* For fall admission, 7/15 priority date for domestic students; for spring admission, 11/15 priority date for domestic students; for summer admission, 4/15 priority date for domestic students. Applications are processed on a rolling basis. Application fee: $0. Electronic applications accepted. *Expenses: Tuition:* Full-time $12,870; part-time $715 per credit. *Required fees:* $1660; $360 per semester. Tuition and fees vary according to degree level. *Faculty research:* Mentoring, principal development, principal retention. *Unit head:* Dr. Philip Monteith, Director, 717-815-6406, E-mail: med@ycp.edu. *Application contact:* Irene Z. Altland, Administrative Assistant, 717-815-6406, Fax: 717-849-1629, E-mail: med@ycp.edu.
Website: http://www.ycp.edu/academics/academic-departments/education/.

York University, Faculty of Graduate Studies, Faculty of Education, Toronto, ON M3J 1P3, Canada. Offers M Ed, PhD. Part-time programs available. *Degree requirements:* For master's, thesis or alternative; for doctorate, comprehensive exam, thesis/dissertation. Electronic applications accepted.

Youngstown State University, Graduate School, Beeghly College of Education, Youngstown, OH 44555-0001. Offers MS Ed, Ed D. *Accreditation:* NCATE. Part-time and evening/weekend programs available. *Degree requirements:* For master's, comprehensive exam; for doctorate, comprehensive exam, thesis/dissertation. *Entrance requirements:* For master's, minimum GPA of 2.7; for doctorate, GRE General Test, GRE Subject Test, interview, minimum GPA of 3.5. Additional exam requirements/recommendations for international students: Required—TOEFL. *Faculty research:* Euthanasia, psychometrics, ethical issues, community relations, educational law.

ADELPHI UNIVERSITY
Ruth S. Ammon School of Education

Programs of Study

The Ruth S. Ammon School of Education at Adelphi University offers a comprehensive array of graduate programs in three departments: curriculum and instruction, communication sciences and disorders, and exercise science, health studies, physical education, and sport management. Dedicated faculty members, mentoring programs, flexible scheduling, a convenient off-campus center in Manhattan, extensive partnerships with community school districts and healthcare institutions, and a professional development initiative help candidates achieve their academic and professional goals.

The Department of Curriculum and Instruction offers in-service and precertification degree programs in the Master of Arts and Post-Master's Certificate in Early Childhood Education; the Master of Science and Post-Master's Certificate in Early Childhood Special Education; the Master of Arts in Childhood Education; the Master of Science and Post-Master's Certificate in Childhood Special Education; the Master of Science in Bilingual Childhood Special Education; the Master of Arts in Adolescent Education (science, English, mathematics, and social studies); the Master of Science in Adolescent Special Education; the Master of Science in Literacy; the Master of Arts in Art Education; the Master of Arts and Post-Master's Certificate in TESOL; the Master of Arts and Post-Master's Certificate in Educational Leadership; the Master of Arts and Post-Master's Certificate in Educational Technology; the Post-Master's Certificate in Bilingual Education for Certified Teachers; and the Post-Master's Certificate in Bilingual Certification Extension for School Social Work.

The Department of Exercise Science, Health Studies, Physical Education and Sport Management offers the Master of Science in Exercise Science; the Master of Science in Sport Management; the Master of Arts in Health Education; the Master of Arts and Graduate Certificate in Physical Education; and the Master of Arts and Post-Master's Certificate in Community Health Promotion.

The Department of Communication Sciences and Disorders offers the Master of Science in Speech-Language Pathology; the Master of Science in TSSLD; the Post-Master's Certificate in Bilingual Education for TSSLD-Certified Teachers; the Doctor of Philosophy in Speech-Language Pathology; and the Doctor of Audiology.

The Ruth S. Ammon School of Education prepares teachers to make a difference. Many of the distinguished faculty members are leaders in their fields. They share their passion for teaching in an environment that fosters creativity and excellence. Students have the opportunity to collaborate on faculty research and presentations at national and international conferences. Adelphi students engage in meaningful partnerships with local schools and service organizations. Through established mentoring programs, students learn from master teachers and clinical experts who set the standards for best practices in teaching. Students get invaluable firsthand experience with mentors and clinicians in community-based service programs.

Research Facilities

The University's primary research holdings are at Swirbul Library and include 603,000 volumes (including bound periodicals and government publications); 786,000 items in microformats; 35,000 audiovisual items; and online access to more than 80,000 e-book titles, 76,000 electronic journal titles, and 265 research databases.

Research, laboratory and clinical programs and facilities are offered in all departments of the Ruth S. Ammon School of Education. The Hy Weinberg Center, dedicated to research in communication disorders and clinical and therapeutic services, is equipped with state-of-the-art clinical audiometric instrumentation, as well as speech and hearing laboratories for the objective measurement of important parameters of speech and voice. Research conducted in the Human Performance Laboratory is showcased at the Annual Student Research Symposium. Its facilities include a multiple 12-lead ECG/exercise stress system, hydrostatic weighing, pulmonary-function testing, Cybex isokinetic muscle testing, an adult fitness and cardiopulmonary rehabilitation program, DEXA, and POLAR Heart Rate Training Center. The Center for Literacy and Learning offers a practicum in assessing and addressing literacy needs, and the new Alice Brown Early Learning Center provides field experience in child development and early childhood curriculum.

Value

Earning an Adelphi degree means joining a growing network of more than 90,000 alumni. For the eighth straight year, Adelphi was designated a Best Buy by the *Fiske Guide to Colleges*, one of only twenty private universities nationwide to earn that distinction. *The Princeton Review* also named Adelphi a Best College in the Northeast and *Forbes* magazine named Adelphi a Top College. According to payscale.com's 2013 College Education ROI rankings, Adelphi ranks in the top 15 percent of colleges and universities nationwide for return on investment. The numbers speak for themselves—91 percent of Adelphi undergraduates receive financial aid or scholarships.

Financial Aid

Adelphi University offers financial aid counseling, federal and state aid programs, and scholarship and fellowship programs that include a limited number of graduate assistantships. Programs include the Federal Direct Stafford Loan; Federal Work-Study Program; Adelphi's Pathways to Teaching, scholarships for students seeking teacher certification in secondary mathematics and science that are funded by a grant from the U.S. Department of Education; Project BEST: Bilingual Educators in Science Technology for qualified bilingual candidates seeking a career in science education; Science Education Advancement (SEA), a program for graduate science education students; the New York State Tuition Assistance Program (TAP); New York State Scholarship Programs; Vietnam and Persian Gulf Veterans Tuition Awards; and Regents Professional Opportunity Scholarships. Students with outstanding undergraduate or graduate records in education can apply for paid graduate internships in adolescent education.

Cost of Study

For the 2014–15 academic year, the tuition rate is $1,105 per credit for all education programs except communication sciences and disorders, which has a tuition rate of $1,125 per credit. University fees range from $330 to $575 per semester.

Living and Housing Costs

Living and housing costs vary considerably depending on personal circumstances. Most graduate students in the Ammon School of Education attend on a part-time basis and live off campus in established households. Information on residence hall fees can be found online at adelphi.edu.

Adelphi University

Location

Located in Garden City, New York, just 23 miles from Manhattan, where students can take advantage of numerous cultural and internship opportunities, Adelphi's 75-acre suburban campus is known for the beauty of its landscape and architecture. The campus is a short walk from the Long Island Rail Road and is convenient to New York's major airports and several major highways. Off-campus centers are located in Manhattan, the Hudson Valley, and Suffolk County.

The University

Founded in 1896, Adelphi is a fully accredited, private university with nearly 8,000 undergraduate, graduate, and returning-adult students in the arts and sciences, business, clinical psychology, education, nursing, and social work. A visionary in the field of education, the Ammon School seeks to meet the personal needs and professional goals of its students through community partnerships and programs in education, communication disorders, and health sciences.

Applying

Candidates must possess a bachelor's degree from an accredited college or university and present evidence of their academic accomplishment. Admission is competitive, and requirements for specific programs in the Ruth S. Ammon School of Education vary considerably. Applications and admission requirements for specific programs can be found online at admissions.adelphi.edu/onlineapp.php.

Correspondence and Information

800-ADELPHI (toll-free)
education.adelphi.edu

THE FACULTY

Full-time faculty members in the Ammon School of Education number more than 60 individuals in three departments. Prospective students should visit the website at academics.adelphi.edu/bulletin-index.php or education.adelphi.edu/our-faculty for complete faculty member information, including credentials and specific research projects.

Faculty members in the Department of Communication Sciences and Disorders specialize in research pertinent to assessing and developing intervention strategies for speech, language, and hearing disorders.

Faculty members in the Department of Curriculum and Instruction specialize in research pertaining to adolescent, childhood, and early childhood education; art education; bilingual/TESOL education; educational leadership; and special education.

Faculty members in the Department of Exercise Science, Health Studies, Physical Education, and Sport Management specialize in research pertinent to human nutrition, stress reduction, and physical activity for a diverse population in school settings, the community, and the workplace.

Students in the Ruth S. Ammon School of Education take advantage of authentic academic and field experiences and become change agents through research, collaboration, and leadership.

The Ruth S. Ammon School of Education provides educational opportunities for professional growth at the bachelor's, master's, and doctoral levels.

MANHATTANVILLE COLLEGE
School of Education

Programs of Study

The School of Education at Manhattanville College offers programs to prepare graduates for careers in education at all levels, from teaching to leadership and administration. Undergraduates often earn a double major in education and another liberal arts concentration, while the graduate program is geared to students interested in becoming teachers, often after having had other careers, and to classroom teachers who want to extend their teaching certifications or update their knowledge base. All programs are registered with and approved by the New York State Education Department. The School of Education is accredited by the National Council for Accreditation of Teacher Education (NCATE).

Manhattanville offers a graduate-level accelerated teacher certification program, Jump Start, which is especially popular with adults who are changing careers. Jump Start is also open to those eligible to complete a post-master's certification program. Cohorts begin twice a year, in fall and spring. Jump Start students are eligible to be in their own classrooms by September of the following year as well-prepared, fully paid teachers with full benefits while they finish the additional requirements for the master's degree. The program is usually available for dual certification with special education in the areas of childhood education, mathematics, biology, chemistry, social studies, and English, and for single certifications in physics, Spanish, visual arts, TESOL, and physical education.

Manhattanville offers three master's programs, the Master of Arts in Teaching (M.A.T.), the Master of Professional Studies (M.P.S.), and the Master in Educational Studies (M.Ed.), as well as a Doctor of Education (Ed.D.) degree in educational leadership. In addition, Manhattanville offers classes in more than sixty areas of concentration leading to eighteen different New York State certifications. Manhattanville also offers post-master's certifications, certificates of advanced study, and a professional diploma.

The Master of Arts in Teaching degree program is intended for graduates with few or no prior courses in education. On completion of the program, the candidate is eligible for New York State certification as a teacher of childhood (grades 1–6), early childhood (birth–grade 2), early childhood and childhood (birth–grade 6), biology (grades 5–12), chemistry (grades 5–12), English (grades 5–12), French (grades 7–12), Italian (grades 7–12), Latin (grades 7–12), mathematics (grades 5–12), music (all grades), physical education and sports pedagogy (all grades), physics (grades 7–12), social studies (grades 5–12), Spanish (grades 7–12), or visual arts (all grades). Most M.A.T. programs range from 36 to 39 credits. The program in childhood/early childhood is 49 credits. All M.A.T. programs include one semester of full-time student teaching or supervised fieldwork.

The Master of Professional Studies degree includes programs in educational leadership (SBL), literacy, special education, or teaching English to speakers of another language (all grades or adult and international settings). There are also dual-certification programs in childhood, secondary, or middle child/adolescence literacy and special education. On completion of the program, the candidate is eligible for either initial or professional certification. The classification is determined by the credentials presented at the time of matriculation into the selected program. M.P.S. programs require from 36 to 47 credits, depending on the program and the area in which certification is sought.

The Doctor of Education (Ed.D.) degree program in Educational Leadership is designed to meet the needs of midcareer professionals who have leadership experience in public or private schools, community programs, governmental agencies, or nongovernmental organizations with major education initiatives. This program builds on Manhattanville's educational leadership master's and professional diploma certification programs for building-level and/or district-level leadership.

The certification programs offer students who already hold a functionally related master's degree an opportunity to complete a program of 27 to 30 credits that makes them eligible for certification in a specific field and level of education. Manhattanville also offers a 15-credit Teacher Leader program for those interested in serving as leaders in their schools.

In addition there are several advanced certificate programs in the areas of bilingual education (childhood/Spanish), health and wellness, administration of physical education, athletics and sport pedagogy, and education for sustainability.

Research Facilities

Manhattanville's teaching library ranks among the foremost undergraduate teaching libraries in the country. The Manhattanville library provides a wide range of subscription databases, electronic journals, and electronic books to support teaching and learning at every level. The Educational Resource Center in the library building has curriculum materials to assist preservice and new teachers. Reference service is available both in person during the day and evening hours, and online at any time from anywhere in the world. Students and faculty members may also text questions to a librarian. A library mobile app delivers services to users on the go.

Manhattanville College supports instruction in French, Spanish, Russian, Italian, German, Chinese, Japanese, Hindi, Marathi, modern Hebrew, and English as a second language. The College provides tutoring in every academic subject, customized services for students with special needs, audiovisual facilities, and a leading Information Literacy instruction program. The library building is open 24 hours, 7 days a week through most of the fall and spring semesters, and it has computer labs, quiet study areas, group-study rooms, and a café where students and faculty members can meet informally. The Manhattanville College Library has a dedicated Education Librarian who works with the faculty members and undergraduate, graduate, and doctoral students to assist in any way with their research needs.

Manhattanville, which was named one of the top 100 wired colleges in the U.S., has state-of-the-art computers, computer labs, and campus networking for student use and instruction.

Financial Aid

Family Educational Loans are available to graduate students. A deferred payment plan is also available. There are a limited number of graduate assistantships, for which matriculated students work 200 hours to earn the cost of 6 credit hours. A maximum of three assistantships per student are possible, and courses must be taken concurrently with the assistantship. For further information, prospective students should contact the Office of Financial Aid, Reid Hall, Purchase, New York 10577 (telephone: 914-323-5357).

Cost of Study

Tuition was $895 per credit for 2013–14. There is a semester registration fee of $60 and there are some course fees.

Living and Housing Costs

Most School of Education graduate students live and work in their own homes and communities throughout Westchester and the surrounding counties. For campus housing information, students should call Residence Life at 914-323-5217.

Student Group

There are approximately 900 students in the School of Education at Manhattanville College. Fifty-five percent are career changers. Their average age is 30.

Manhattanville College

Location

Manhattanville's campus, 100 acres of suburban countryside, is located in New York's Westchester County, just minutes from White Plains to the west and Greenwich, Connecticut, to the east. It is 30 miles from Manhattan. The campus is accessible via public transportation.

The College

Manhattanville College is a coeducational, independent liberal arts college whose mission is to educate ethically and socially responsible leaders for the global community. Founded in 1841, the College has 1,600 undergraduate students and almost 1,200 graduate students. Of the graduate students, 820 are enrolled in the School of Education. Manhattanville offers bachelor's, master's, and doctoral degrees in more than fifty academic concentrations in the arts and sciences. Its curriculum nurtures intellectual curiosity and independent thinking.

Applying

Applications are reviewed on a continuing basis. Applicants are encouraged to apply at least sixty days in advance of the semester for which matriculation is sought (fall, spring, summer I, or summer II). Application requirements are the submission of a completed application form, a fee of $70, two recommendations, a two- to three-page typewritten essay on the applicant's background and philosophy of education, and official transcripts of all previous college work (both undergraduate and graduate). Limited study as a nonmatriculated student is permitted.

Correspondence and Information

Jeanine Pardey-Levine
Director of Graduate Enrollment Management
School of Education
Manhattanville College
2900 Purchase Street
Purchase, New York 10577
Phone: 914-323-5142 (Admissions)
Fax: 914-694-1732
E-mail: edschool@mville.edu
Website: http://www.mville.edu/graduate/academics/education.html

THE FACULTY

School of Education Administration

Shelley B. Wepner, Professor and Dean; Ed.D., Pennsylvania.
Joan Gujarati, Associate Dean of Accreditation and Technology; Ed.D., Columbia Teachers College.
Anita Nordal, Assistant Dean for Outreach; Ed.M., Columbia Teachers College.
Jody Green, Assistant Dean for Graduate Advising; M.S.Ed., Fordham.
Danielle Wachter, Assistant to the Dean; B.S., LIU, Southampton.
Mikki Shaw, Director of Jump Start; Ed.D., Columbia Teachers College.
Jeanine Pardey-Levine, Director of Graduate Enrollment Management; M.M., Hartford.
Gail Robinson, Director of Field Placement, Certification, and Community Outreach; M.S., CUNY, Hunter.
Renee Gargano, Coordinator of Applied Research and Fieldwork, Doctoral Program; Ed.M., Boston University.

Curriculum and Instruction

Barbara Allen-Lyall, Instructor; M.Ed., Lesley.
Victoria Fantozzi, Assistant Professor and Department Chair; Ph.D., Virginia
JoAnne Ferrara, Associate Professor and Associate Dean for Undergraduate Admissions and Advising; Ed.D., Nova Southeastern.

Frederick Heckendorn III, Assistant Professor of Secondary/ Social Studies Education; Ed.D., Hofstra.
Sherie McClam, Assistant Professor; Ph.D., Colorado at Boulder.
Lynn Huber, Assistant Professor; Ph.D., Fordham.
Dennis Debay; Ph.D., Boston College.

Early Childhood

Victoria Fantozzi, Assistant Professor for Early Childhood and Childhood, Ph.D., Virginia.
Patricia Vardin, Associate Professor and Department Chair; Ed.D., Columbia Teachers College.

Educational Leadership and Special Subjects

Yiping Wan, Professor; and Coordinator of the Doctoral Program Ph.D., Texas at Austin.
Lenora Boehlert, Assistant Professor, Educational Leadership; Ed.D., Vanderbilt.
Stephen Caldas, Professor for the Doctoral Program; Ph.D., LSU.
Kenneth Mitchell, Associate Professor for the Doctoral Program; Ed.D., Fordham.
Robert Monson, Visiting Associate Professor for the Doctoral Program; Ph.D., St. Louis.
Rhonda Clements, Professor and Program Director of Physical Education and Sports Pedagogy; Ed.D., Columbia Teachers College.
Diane Gomez, Associate Professor of ESL/Foreign Language and Department Chair; Ph.D., Fordham.
Laurence Krute, Associate Professor of ESL/Foreign Language and Associate Dean of Graduate Advising; Ph.D., Columbia.

Literacy

Katherine Cunningham, Assistant Professor; Ed.D., Columbia Teachers College.
Kristin Rainville, Assistant Professor and Department Chair; Ed.D., Columbia Teachers College.
Courtney Ryan Kelly, Associate Professor; Ph.D., Ohio State.

Special Education

Vance Austin, Associate Professor and Department Chair; Ph.D., Fordham.
Ellis I. Barowsky, Professor; Ph.D., CUNY Graduate Center.
Nikki Josephs, Ph.D., Georgia State.
Micheline S. Malow, Associate Professor and Associate Department Chair; Ph.D., CUNY Graduate Center.

NORTHWESTERN UNIVERSITY
School of Education and Social Policy

Programs of Study

Northwestern University's School of Education and Social Policy offers programs leading to the M.S., M.A., and Ph.D. degrees. There are four program areas: Education (M.S.), Higher Education (M.S.), Learning and Organizational Change (M.S.), Learning Sciences (M.A. and Ph.D.), and Human Development and Social Policy (Ph.D.).

The Learning Sciences M.A. and Ph.D. programs are dedicated to the preparation of researchers, developers, and practitioners qualified to advance the scientific understanding and practice of teaching and learning. Both programs in the learning sciences are interdisciplinary, offering a synthesis of computational, educational, and social science research; linguistics; computer science; anthropology; and cognitive science.

The Human Development and Social Policy Ph.D. program prepares students to bridge human development, social science, and social policy. Graduates of this program assume positions as professors, researchers, and policy makers who can bring multidisciplinary knowledge about human development to affect policy.

Concentrations in the M.S. in Education program include public and private school teaching, advanced teaching, and higher education administration. Students enrolled full-time typically complete the program in twelve months, provided they matriculate with no course deficiencies; opportunities for part-time study toward a master's degree are also available.

Research Facilities

Northwestern's research libraries contain more than 5.6 million volumes, 4.64 million microfilm units, and 137,446 current periodical and serial publications. Research and teaching activities are supported by a state-of-the-art multimedia computing network with full Internet access. The School is actively involved with the Institute for Policy Research, a University-wide research center that promotes interdisciplinary urban policy research and training. Specialized research and service resources within the School include the Center for Talent Development, a nationally prominent center that identifies and provides programming for academically talented youth, their parents, and the professionals who work with them. The Tarry Center for Collaborative Teaching and Learning provides state-of-the-art facilities for innovative teaching with technology.

Financial Aid

Several forms of aid are available, including fellowships and scholarships. In addition, there are teaching assistantships awarded to doctoral students who work with the School's undergraduate programs. Special opportunities for research assistantships and other employment also exist within the School's and the University's many research centers. Arrangements for loans are also possible.

Cost of Study

Tuition for full-time study in the M.S. in Education program in 2014–15 is $47,010; part-time enrollment tuition is $3,132 per course. Tuition for full-time study in the M.S. in Higher Education program in 2014–15 is $53,625; part-time enrollment tuition is $3,575 per course. Tuition for full-time study in the M.S. in Learning and Organizational Change program is $63,105; part-time enrollment is $4,207 per course. Tuition for full-time study (three courses per quarter) in pursuit of the M.A. or Ph.D. in 2014–15 is $60,160 for the academic year or $15,040 per quarter.

Living and Housing Costs

The University operates a residence in Evanston for the use of graduate students. For those Northwestern students interested in securing off-campus housing near the University, information and assistance are also available.

Student Group

Graduate study occurs within the context of individualized instruction, and enrollments are selective. Currently, 181 students are enrolled in master's programs, and 44 are enrolled in Ph.D. programs. Since an interdisciplinary perspective is valued, students with preparation in a wide range of disciplinary areas are encouraged to apply.

Student Outcomes

Graduates teach and conduct research in academic and nonacademic settings; occupy strategic policy positions in government, corporations, and institutions; and assume positions of responsibility in a wide range of service organizations. Potential professional settings for learning sciences graduates include University research and teaching as well as business, industry, or school system-based careers studying, designing, and/or implementing learning environments. Graduates of the Ph.D. in Human Development and Social Policy program assume positions as teachers, researchers, or policy makers who can bring multidisciplinary knowledge about human development directly to bear upon policy. Graduates of the Learning Sciences M.A. program are practitioners in the vanguard of teaching and learning systems development and instructional resource development. Most students in the M.S. in Education and Higher Education programs gain on-site experience through supervised internships for future careers as professional educators and administrators.

Location

The campus is located on Lake Michigan, 12 miles north of Chicago. The beautiful lakefront campus offers a rich cultural environment through a wealth of theatrical, musical, and athletic events. The extensive cultural resources of Chicago are readily accessible via public transportation.

The University and The School

Established in 1851, Northwestern has grown to become one of the most distinguished private universities in the country. The School of Education and Social Policy has developed from its origins as a department of pedagogy by continually broadening its scope to encompass those educative, learning, and socializing experiences that take place throughout the life span in families, schools, communities, and the workplace.

Applying

Applications for admission are reviewed and acted upon as they are received. Students should consult program brochures for specific application deadlines. Applicants planning to seek financial aid must meet early submission deadlines.

Correspondence and Information

School of Education and Social Policy
Northwestern University
2120 Campus Drive
Evanston, Illinois 60208-2610
Phone: 847-491-3790 (Office of Student Affairs)
847-467-1458 (M.S. in Education)
847-491-4620 (M.S. in Higher Education)
847-491-4329 (Human Development and Social Policy Ph.D.)
847-491-7376 (Learning and Organizational Change M.S.)
847-491-7494 (Learning Sciences M.A.)
847-491-7494 (Learning Sciences Ph.D.)
Website: http://www.sesp.northwestern.edu

THE FACULTY AND THEIR RESEARCH

Emma Adam, Ph.D., Minnesota. Parent, child, and adolescent stress and emotion; attachment; health policy.

Lindsay Chase-Lansdale, Ph.D., Michigan. Child and adolescent development, family functioning, public policy, multidisciplinary research, poverty and welfare reform, family structure, risk and resilience.

Cynthia Coburn, Ph.D., Stanford. Relationship between instruction policy and teachers' classroom practices in urban schools.

Jeannette Colyvas, Ph.D., Stanford. Organizations and entrepreneurship; comparing public, private, and nonprofit forms of organizing; the study of networks.

Mesmin Destin, Ph.D., Michigan. Academic motivation and achievement, small classroom-based interventions to improve school outcomes for low-income and minority youth.

Timothy Dohrer, Ph.D., Penn State. Curriculum and instruction.

Matthew Easterday, Ph.D., Carnegie Mellon. Human-computer interaction, constructionism, computer-based modeling.

David Figlio, Ph.D., Wisconsin–Madison. Accountability policy, economics of education, teacher quality, teacher labor markets, anti-poverty policy, intergenerational transmission of human capital, evaluation design.

Kenneth D. Forbus, Ph.D., MIT. Qualitative physics, cognitive simulation of analogy, intelligence tutoring systems and learning environments for science and engineering.

Wendi Gardner, Ph.D., Ohio State. Centrality of social inclusion to the self.

Dedre Gentner, Ph.D., Berkeley. Learning, reasoning, and conceptual change in adults and children; mental models; acquisition of meaning.

Elizabeth Gerber, Ph.D., Stanford. Design and innovation work practices.

Northwestern University

Jonathan Guryan, Ph.D., MIT. Racial inequality, economics of education.

Claudia Haase, Ph.D., Jena (Germany). Emotion, motivation, life span development, aging, well-being, physical health, career success, relationship satisfaction, statistical methods.

Romana Hasnain-Wynia, Ph.D., Brandeis. Equity in health care, reducing disparities in health care, quality of care for diverse populations, health policy.

Larry Hedges, Ph.D., Stanford. Statistical methods for research in education, social sciences, and policy studies; social distribution of test scores.

Susan Hespos, Ph.D., Emory. Object representation, number and spatial relationships.

Barton J. Hirsch, Ph.D., Oregon. Community psychology, social networks, ecology of adolescent development, after-school programs.

Michael Horn, Ph.D., Tufts. Design of educational technology, learning in museums, computer programming, tangible interaction.

Simone Ispa-Landa, Ph.D., Harvard. Qualitative methods, race and ethnic rlations, social identity, American family, intersectionality theory, micro-macro links.

Kirabo Jackson, Ph.D., Harvard. Economics of education, labor economics, public finance, applied econometrics, development.

Kemi Jona, Ph.D., Northwestern. Online learning, virtual schools, online laboratory science course design, corporate e-learning strategy and design.

John Kretzmann, Ph.D., Northwestern. Sociology, community development, asset building in communities.

Eva Lam, Ph.D., Berkeley. Second language and literacy development, digital literacy and learning, language and identity, language socialization, globalization and English learning, multilingualism and cultural diversity in education.

Carol D. Lee, Ph.D., Chicago. Cultural contexts affecting learning broadly and literacy specifically, teacher preparation and development, classroom discourse, urban education.

Dan A. Lewis, Ph.D., California, Santa Cruz. Policy analysis, urban social problems, community organization, urban school reform.

Gregory Light, Ph.D., London. Student learning in higher and professional education, faculty development, faculty concepts and approaches to teaching, variation theory.

Regina Logan, Ph.D., Northwestern. Teaching and learning processes, adulthood and aging, gender studies.

Jelani Mandara, Ph.D., California, Riverside. Effects of parenting, fathers, and other home factors on child and adolescent academic and social development, achievement gap, and person-centered research methods.

Dan P. McAdams, Ph.D., Harvard. Personality development, identity and life stories, intimacy, adult development, narrative psychology, modernity and the self, autobiographical memory, psychological biography.

Thomas McDade, Ph.D., Emory. Human biology, biocultural perspectives on health and human development, medical anthropology and global health, ecological immunology, stress, health disparities.

Steven McGee, Ph.D., Northwestern. Science education, urban education reform, high school transformation, assessment, educational testing, science curriculum development.

Douglas L. Medin, Ph.D., South Dakota. Learning, reasoning, and conceptual change in adults and children; mental models; acquisition of meaning; culture and education.

Paula M. Olszewski-Kubilius, Ph.D., Northwestern. Gifted education, child development, minority gifted child development, accelerated educational programs, needs of special populations of gifted children.

Penelope L. Peterson, Ph.D., Stanford. Learning and teaching in schools and classrooms, particularly in mathematics and literacy; teacher learning in reform contexts; relations among educational research, policy, and practice.

Deborah Puntenney, Ph.D, Northwestern. Community development.

David Rapp, Ph.D., SUNY at Stony Brook. Experimental psychology, comprehension of texts, psychology of learning, multimedia learning, visualization and learning tools.

Brian J. Reiser, Ph.D., Yale. Intelligent tutoring systems, interactive learning environments for science and technology, scientific inquiry skills.

Christopher K. Riesbeck, Ph.D., Stanford. Natural language and analyzers, case-based reasoners, intelligent computational media.

James E. Rosenbaum, Ph.D., Harvard. Adolescent and adult development, poverty and housing, welfare reform, high school to work transition.

Diane Schanzenbach, Ph.D., Princeton. Early childhood education, accountability policy, economics of education, obesity, anti-poverty policy, education and health.

Heather Schoenfeld, Ph.D., Northwestern. Law and society, race and inequality, crime and punishment, historical and comparative methods.

Kimberly Scott, Ph.D., Ohio State. Organizational effectiveness and change, organizational learning, job satisfaction.

Lilah Shapiro, Ph.D., Chicago. Sociology, social psychology, identity, life story and narrative, ethnicity, religion, assimilation and immigration, diaspora experiences, family dynamics.

Bruce Sherin, Ph.D., Berkeley. Science education, instructional technology, external representations in science and mathematical learning.

Miriam Sherin, Ph.D., Berkeley. Mathematics teaching and learning, teacher cognition, teacher education.

Ryan Smerek, Ph.D., Michigan. Organizational learning, leadership, job satisfaction, organizational culture, open-book finance.

Bruce D. Spencer, Ph.D., Yale. Social and educational measurement, statistics for policy analysis, demography, decision theory.

James P. Spillane, Ph.D., Michigan State. Educational policy, intergovernmental relations, school reform, relations between policy and local practice.

Reed Stevens, Ph.D., Berkeley. Curriculum design, learning in atypical settings, design of learning tools.

Linda Teplin, Ph.D., Northwestern. Epidemiologic studies of psychiatric disorders, juvenile justice, drug abuse, public health policy, HIV/AIDS risk behaviors, correlates of violence.

Lois Trautvetter, Ph.D., Michigan. Higher education, gender issues and females in science.

David H. Uttal, Ph.D., Michigan. Mental representation, cognitive development, spatial cognition, early symbolization.

Laurie Wakschlag, Ph.D., Chicago. Behavioral sciences.

Ellen Wartella, Ph.D., Minnesota. Effects of media on children and adolescents, impact of food marketing on childhood obesity.

Sandra R. Waxman, Ph.D., Pennsylvania. Language and conceptual development, early cognitive development, language and thought.

Uri Wilensky, Ph.D., MIT. Science and mathematics learning and technology, connected learning, constructionism, computer-based modeling, agent-based modeling, complex systems and education.

Michael Wolf, Ph.D., Illinois. Adult literacy, patient education, medication and safety adherence.

UNIVERSITY OF PENNSYLVANIA
Graduate School of Education

Programs of Study

The Graduate School of Education at the University of Pennsylvania (Penn GSE) strives to be the most intellectually exciting place in education in the world. The smallest school among the top 5 nationally ranked graduate schools of education boasts eight academic divisions, over thirty programs, and thirty-two in-house research centers and initiatives. No other education school enjoys a university environment as supportive of practical knowledge-building as the Ivy League's University of Pennsylvania.

Penn GSE, one of the nation's premier research education schools, is notably entrepreneurial, launching innovative degree programs for practicing professionals, unique partnerships with local educators, and the first-ever business plan competition devoted exclusively to educational products and programs. Students are both learners and agents of change within the university and the surrounding Philadelphia neighborhoods.

Executive, full- and part-time programs leading to the Ph.D., Ed.D., M.S.Ed., M.S. and M.Phil.Ed. degrees are offered.

Research Facilities

Research centers at Penn GSE bring faculty members and students together to study the various intersections of education and society. This research includes international studies of cross-cultural and comparative education. The centers include the Center for Research and Evaluation in Social Policy, the Center for Minority Serving Institutions, the Study of Race and Equity in Education, the Center for Urban Ethnography, the Consortium for Policy Research in Education, the National Center on Adult Literacy, and the Penn Child Research Center. A full list is available online at http://www.gse.upenn.edu/research-centers.

Financial Aid

Penn GSE is committed to making graduate education affordable, and offers generous scholarships, fellowships, and assistantships to many of its students. Students view a Penn graduate degree as an investment in their future and finance their graduate education through a combination of institutional funding, federal aid, private educational loans, and other sources. Graduate assistantships, scholarships, fellowships, and research assistantships are awarded by the School based on academic merit. Financial aid for Penn GSE students is available through the School, private sources, and from the state and federal governments through loans and work-study jobs.

Cost of Study

The most current tuition rates can be found online at http://www.gse.upenn.edu/admissions_financial/tuition.

Living and Housing Costs

University graduate housing is available on campus for single students as well as married students and their families. On-campus housing ranges from $815 per month for a single room to $1,565 per month for an apartment. Off-campus apartment rents in University City range upward from $937 per month.

Student Group

Penn GSE students range from recent college graduates to career changers and experienced practitioners. The approximately 600 students beginning course work in 2013 made up a broad demographic spectrum, representing forty states; international students comprised 25 percent of the class, representing twenty-one countries. The age ranges for 2013–14 were as follows: master's students, 20–56; Ph.D. students, 22–32; and Ed.D. students, 25–62.

Student Outcomes

Penn GSE graduates pursue careers in a variety of fields, including schools, government agencies, universities, think tanks, foundations, and corporations. In these fields, they work in positions that include superintendents, principals, teachers, counselors, university professors, policy analysts, researchers, foundation officers, psychologists, and higher education administrators.

Location

Penn GSE's location in a major metropolitan area enhances the quality of its programs, research, and student life. Philadelphia is a thriving mix of ethnic neighborhoods, historic colonial streets, and contemporary architecture. With close to 100 institutions of higher learning, the city is a magnet for students from around the world. The city's cultural and recreational life includes a world-class orchestra and opera, dozens of museums, four professional sports teams, art galleries, secondhand bookstores, jazz clubs, an Italian market, and a renowned international film festival. The city is conveniently located in the metropolitan northeastern United States, within 2 hours of Baltimore, New York, and Washington, D.C.

The School

Penn GSE, one of the best graduate schools of education in the United States, is one of only three Ivy League schools of education. The School is noted for excellence in educational research in the areas of policy, evaluation, sociocultural foundations, and urban education.

University of Pennsylvania

Penn GSE is deeply committed to the city of Philadelphia through both research and practice. Students, faculty, and staff are involved in hundreds of initiatives throughout the Greater Philadelphia area, ranging from high-quality after-school programs, to research that sparks national conversations, to the development of an acclaimed public school partnership with the School District of Philadelphia.

Applying

To apply and learn more about application deadlines, prospective students can visit http://www.gse.upenn.edu/admissions_financial/howtoapply.

THE FACULTY

For a full list of all Penn GSE faculty members, including associated faculty members, students should visit http://www.gse.upenn.edu/directory/fac_div.

Correspondence and Information

Admissions Office
Graduate School of Education
University of Pennsylvania
3700 Walnut Street
Philadelphia, Pennsylvania 19104-6216
Phone: 215-898-6415
E-mail: admissions@gse.upenn.edu
Website: http://www.gse.upenn.edu

VANDERBILT UNIVERSITY
Peabody College

VANDERBILT UNIVERSITY ♦ Peabody College

Programs of Study

Vanderbilt University's Peabody College of Education and Human Development offers programs leading to the Master of Education (M.Ed.), Master of Public Policy (M.P.P.), and Doctor of Education (Ed.D.) degrees. The Vanderbilt Graduate School, through Peabody departments, offers the Doctor of Philosophy (Ph.D.) degree. Peabody is committed to preparing students to become research scholars or innovative practitioners in the field of education and human development. Students may attend full- or part-time. Weekend courses are offered in several programs for working professionals who want to earn an advanced degree.

Students may pursue the Master of Education (M.Ed.) in child studies; clinical psychological assessment; community development and action; elementary education; English language learners; higher education administration (including specializations in administration, student life, and service learning); human development counseling (with specializations in school and community counseling); independent school leadership; international education policy and management; leadership and organizational performance; learning, diversity, and urban studies; learning and instruction (including specializations in teaching and learning; digital literacies; language, culture, and international studies; science and mathematics; or an individualized program); quantitative methods; reading education; secondary education; and special education (including specializations in applied behavior analysis, early childhood, high-incidence disabilities, and low-incidence disabilities). A Master of Public Policy is available in education policy. Vanderbilt also offers a joint M.P.P./J.D. program.

Students interested in doctoral study may enroll in educational leadership and policy (Ed.D.); educational neuroscience (Ph.D); higher education leadership and policy (Ed.D.); community research and action (Ph.D.); leadership and policy studies (Ph.D., with specializations in educational leadership and policy, higher education leadership and policy, and international education policy and management); learning, teaching, and diversity (Ph.D., with specializations in development, learning, and diversity; language, literacy, and culture; mathematics and science; and science and learning environment design); psychological sciences (Ph.D., with specializations in clinical science, cognitive science, developmental science, and quantitative methods and evaluation); and special education (Ph.D., with specializations in early childhood, high-incidence disabilities, and severe disabilities).

Peabody's teacher education and advanced certification programs are approved by the National Council for Accreditation of Teacher Education (NCATE). Programs in psychology and counseling are accredited by the American Psychological Association and the Council on Accreditation of Counseling and Related Educational Programs (CACREP), respectively.

Research Opportunities

In addition to the Vanderbilt University Library System, which has more than 2.6 million volumes, excellent research facilities and opportunities to conduct research are available through the Vanderbilt Kennedy Center for Research on Human Development, the Peabody Research Institute, the Susan Gray School, the National Center on School Choice, the National Center on Performance Initiatives, and the Center for Community Studies. The many local field sites available for research include hospitals, Metropolitan Nashville Public Schools, private schools, rehabilitation centers, schools for people with disabilities, government agencies, corporations, and nonprofit organizations.

Financial Aid

More than 65 percent of new students at Peabody receive financial aid. The College sponsors several substantial scholarship programs with offerings that range from partial to full tuition. In addition, assistantships, traineeships, loans, and part-time employment are available. Awards are made annually, and every attempt is made to meet a student's financial need. Application for financial aid does not affect the admission decision.

Cost of Study

Tuition for study at Peabody College for the 2014–15 academic year is $1,421 per semester credit hour for the M.Ed., M.P.P., and Ed.D. programs, and $1,782 per semester credit hour for programs offered through the Graduate School.

Living and Housing Costs

Vanderbilt's location in Nashville offers students the advantage of a wide range of living choices. Costs for housing, food, and other living expenses are moderate when compared with other metropolitan areas nationwide.

Student Group

Vanderbilt has a diverse student body of about 12,000. Peabody has an enrollment of approximately 1,800 students, of whom about 700 are graduate students. Women make up about 65 percent of Peabody's graduate students, while students from underrepresented groups make up about 20 percent. Students have a broad range of academic backgrounds and include recent graduates of baccalaureate programs as well as men and women who have many years of professional experience. The median age of current students is 27.

Student Outcomes

Graduates who earn a master's or doctoral degree from Peabody are prepared to work for educational, corporate, government, and service organizations in a variety of roles. More than 10,000 alumni are practicing teachers, more than 175 are school superintendents, and more than 50 are current or former college or university presidents.

Location

Nashville, the capital of Tennessee, is a cosmopolitan city with a metropolitan area population of 1.23 million. Vanderbilt University is one of more than a dozen institutions of higher learning located in Nashville and the surrounding area, leading Nashville to be called the "Athens of the South."

Nashville offers residents and visitors much in the way of music, art, and recreation. More than 100 local venues provide a wide variety of music, while classical and contemporary music is performed by the Nashville Symphony Orchestra and the Nashville Chamber Orchestra. The Tennessee Performing Arts Center (TPAC) is home to two theater companies, a ballet company, and an opera company. Vanderbilt's own Great Performances series frequently brings the best in chamber music, new music, theater, and all forms of dance to the Vanderbilt campus. Outstanding exhibitions of fine art can be seen at the Frist Center for the Visual Arts and at Cheekwood Botanical Garden and Museum of Art. There are more than 6,000 acres of public parks in the city, and the surrounding region of rolling hills and lakes is dotted with state parks and recreation areas.

Nashville has been named one of the 15 best U.S. cities for work and family by *Fortune* magazine, was ranked as the most popular U.S. city for corporate relocations by *Expansion Management* magazine, and was named by *Forbes* magazine as one of the 25 cities most likely to have the country's highest job growth over the coming five years. More information on Nashville can be found online at http://www.vanderbilt.edu/nashville.

The University and The College

Vanderbilt University, founded in 1873, is a private nondenominational institution with a strong tradition of graduate and professional education. Peabody, recognized for more than a century as one of the nation's foremost independent colleges of education, merged with Vanderbilt University in 1979. The College is currently ranked the number two graduate school of education in the nation by *U.S. News & World Report*. Peabody seeks to create knowledge through research, to prepare leaders, to support practitioners, and to strengthen communities at all levels.

Vanderbilt University

Applying

Admission to professional degree programs is based on an evaluation of the applicant's potential for academic success and professional service, with consideration given to transcripts of previous course work, GRE General Test or MAT scores, letters of reference, and a letter outlining personal goals. Additional supporting credentials, such as a sample of the applicant's scholarly writing or a personal interview, may also be required.

The application fee is waived for applicants who apply online at http://peabody.vanderbilt.edu/degrees-programs/admissions_and_programs.php. A nonrefundable $40 fee must accompany each paper application. Applicants who apply after the deadline should know that admission and financial assistance depend upon the availability of space and funds in the department in which they seek to study. Deadlines are December 1 for the Ph.D. and Ed.D. programs and December 31 for the M.Ed. and M.P.P. programs.

Correspondence and Information

Graduate Admissions
Peabody College of Vanderbilt University
Peabody Station, Box 227
Nashville, Tennessee 37203
United States
Phone: 615-322-8410
Fax: 615-322-4029
E-mail: peabody.admissions@vanderbilt.edu
Website: http://peabody.vanderbilt.edu

THE FACULTY

Department of Human and Organizational Development
Sandra Barnes, Professor; Ph.D., Georgia State.
Kimberly D. Bess, Assistant Professor; Ph.D., Vanderbilt.
Victoria J. Davis, Clinical Assistant Professor; Ed.D., Vanderbilt.
James C. Fraser, Associate Professor; Ph.D., Georgia State.
Gina Frieden, Assistant Professor of the Practice; Ph.D., Memphis State.
Susan K. Friedman, Lecturer; M.B.A., Arizona State.
Leigh Gilchrist, Assistant Professor of the Practice; Ed.D., Vanderbilt.
Brian Griffith, Assistant Clinical Professor; Ph.D., South Carolina.
Craig Anne Heflinger, Professor; Ph.D., Vanderbilt.
Velma McBride Murry, Professor; Ph.D., Missouri–Columbia.
Maury Nation, Associate Professor; Ph.D., South Carolina.
Allison Patton McGuire, Lecturer; Ph.D., Vanderbilt.
Douglas Perkins, Professor; Ph.D., NYU.
Sharon Shields, Professor of the Practice; Ph.D., George Peabody.
Marybeth Shinn, Professor; Ph.D., Michigan.
Heather Smith, Assistant Professor of the Practice; Ph.D., Central Florida.
Paul Speer, Professor; Ph.D., Missouri–Kansas City.
Sarah V. Suiter, Assistant Professor of the Practice; Ph.D., Vanderbilt.
William L. Turner, Professor; Ph.D., Virginia Tech.
Andrew Van Schaack, Assistant Professor of the Practice; Ph.D., Utah State.

Department of Leadership, Policy, and Organizations
Robert Dale Ballou, Associate Professor; Ph.D., Yale.
Angela Boatman, Assistant Professor; Ed.D, Harvard.
John Braxton, Professor; D.Ed., Penn State.
Mark D. Cannon, Associate Professor; Ph.D., Harvard.
Xiu Cravens, Assistant Professor of the Practice; Ph.D., Vanderbilt.
Robert L. Crowson, Professor; Ph.D., Chicago.
Corbette Doyle, Lecturer; M.B.A., Vanderbilt.
William R. Doyle, Assistant Professor; Ph.D., Stanford.
Mimi Engel, Assistant Professor; Ph.D., Northwestern.
Brent Evans, Assistant Professor; Ph.D., Stanford.
Stella M. Flores, Associate Professor; Ed.D., Harvard.
Ellen Goldring, Professor; Ph.D., Chicago.
Gary T. Henry, Professor; Ph.D., Wisconsin.
Stephen P. Heyneman, Professor; Ph.D., Chicago.
David Laird, Assistant Professor of the Practice; Ed.D., Vanderbilt.
Catherine Gavin Loss, Assistant Professor of the Practice; Ph.D., Virginia.
Christopher P. Loss, Assistant Professor; Ph.D., Virginia.
Joseph Murphy, Professor; Ph.D., Ohio State.
Christine Quinn Trank, Associate Professor of the Practice; Ph.D, Iowa.
Dayle Savage, Assistant Professor of the Practice; Ed.D., Vanderbilt.
Claire Smrekar, Associate Professor; Ph.D., Stanford.
Matthew Springer, Assistant Professor; Ph.D., Vanderbilt.
Deborah Tobey, Lecturer; Ed.D., Vanderbilt.

Department of Psychology and Human Development
Camilla P. Benbow, Professor; Ed.D., Johns Hopkins.
Sun-Joo Cho, Assistant Professor; Ph.D., Georgia.
David A. Cole, Professor; Ph.D., Houston.
Bruce E. Compas, Professor; Ph.D., UCLA.
Elizabeth May Dykens, Professor; Ph.D., Kansas.
Judy Garber, Associate Professor; Ph.D., Minnesota, Twin Cities.
Daniel T. Levin, Associate Professor; Ph.D., Cornell.
David Lubinski, Professor; Ph.D., Minnesota.

Joseph McLaughlin, Associate Professor; Ph.D., Vanderbilt.
Amy Needham, Professor; Ph.D., Illinois.
Laura R. Novick, Associate Professor; Ph.D., Stanford.
Gavin Price, Assistant Professor; Ph.D., Jyväskylä (Finland).
John R. Rieser, Professor; Ph.D., Minnesota, Twin Cities.
Bethany Rittle-Johnson, Associate Professor; Ph.D., Carnegie Mellon.
Joseph Lee Rodgers III, Professor; Ph.D., North Carolina.
Megan M. Saylor, Associate Professor; Ph.D., Oregon.
Craig A. Smith, Associate Professor; Ph.D., Stanford.
James Steiger, Professor; Ph.D., Purdue.
Georgene Troseth, Associate Professor; Ph.D., Illinois at Urbana-Champaign.
Leigh Wadsworth, Senior Lecturer; Ph.D., Arizona State.
Tedra Ann Walden, Professor; Ph.D., Florida.
Bahr Weiss, Associate Professor; Ph.D., North Carolina at Chapel Hill.

Department of Special Education
Erin Barton, Assistant Professor; Ph.D., Vanderbilt.
Andrea Capizzi, Assistant Professor of the Practice; Ph.D., Vanderbilt.
Donald Compton, Professor; Ph.D., Northwestern.
Laurie Cutting, Professor; Ph.D., Northwestern.
Alex da Fonte, Assistant Professor; M.S., Purdue.
Donna Y. Ford, Professor; Ph.D., Cleveland State.
Douglas Fuchs, Professor; Ph.D., Minnesota.
Lynn Fuchs, Professor; Ph.D., Minnesota.
Deborah D. Hatton, Associate Professor; Ph.D., North Carolina.
Mary Louise Hemmeter, Professor; Ph.D., Vanderbilt.
Robert Hodapp, Professor; Ph.D., Boston University.
Ann Kaiser, Professor; Ph.D., Kansas.
Victoria Knight, Assistant Professor; Ph.D., North Carolina.
Joseph Lambert, Assistant Professor of the Practice; Ph.D., Utah State.
Christopher Lemons, Assistant Professor; Ph.D., Vanderbilt.
Blair Lloyd, Assistant Professor; Ph.D., Vanderbilt.
Kim Paulsen, Professor of the Practice; Ed.D., Nevada, Las Vegas.
Naomi Tyler, Associate Professor of the Practice; Ph.D., New Mexico State.
Joseph H. Wehby, Associate Professor; Ph.D., Vanderbilt.
Paul J. Yoder, Professor; Ph.D., North Carolina.

Department of Teaching and Learning
Paul A. Cobb, Professor; Ph.D., Georgia.
Douglas Clark, Associate Professor; Ph.D., Berkeley.
David Dickinson, Professor; Ed.D., Harvard.
Dale C. Farran, Professor; Ph.D., Bryn Mawr.
Kathy A. Ganske, Professor of the Practice; Ph.D., Virginia.
Melissa Sommerfield Gresalfi, Associate Professor; Ph.D., Stanford.
Andrew L. Hofstetler, Assistant Professor of the Practice; Ph.D., Illinois.
Clifford A. Hofwolt, Associate Professor; Ed.D., Northern Colorado.
Ilana Horn, Associate Professor; Ph.D., Berkeley.
Robert T. Jimenez, Professor; Ph.D., Illinois at Urbana-Champaign.
Kevin Leander, Associate Professor; Ph.D., Illinois.
Richard Lehrer, Professor; Ph.D., Chicago.
Ann M. Neely, Associate Professor of the Practice; Ed.D., Georgia.
Amy Palmeri, Assistant Professor of the Practice; Ph.D., Indiana Bloomington.
Lisa Pray, Professor of the Practice; Ph.D., Arizona State.
Deborah W. Rowe, Associate Professor; Ph.D., Indiana.
Leona Schauble, Professor; Ph.D., Columbia.
Pratim Sengupta, Assistant Professor; Ph.D., Northwestern.
Barbara Stengel, Professor of the Practice; Ph.D., Pittsburgh.

The Faye and Joe Wyatt Center for Education.

Section 23
Administration, Instruction, and Theory

This section contains a directory of institutions offering graduate work in administration, instruction, and theory. Additional information about programs listed in the directory but not augmented by an in-depth entry may be obtained by writing directly to the dean of a graduate school or chair of a department at the address given in the directory.

For programs offering related work, see also in this book *Education, Instructional Levels, Leisure Studies and Recreation, Physical Education and Kinesiology, Special Focus*, and *Subject Areas*. In other guides in this series:

Graduate Programs in the Humanities, Arts & Social Sciences
See *Psychology and Counseling (School Psychology)*
Graduate Programs in the Biological/Biomedical Sciences and Health-Related Medical Professions
See *Health-Related Professions*

CONTENTS

Program Directories

Curriculum and Instruction 738
Distance Education Development 777
Educational Leadership and Administration 781
Educational Measurement and Evaluation 861
Educational Media/Instructional Technology 871
Educational Policy 906
Educational Psychology 912
Foundations and Philosophy of Education 925
International and Comparative Education 933
Student Affairs 937

Display and Close-Up

See:

Syracuse University—Library and Information Studies 1583, 1599

Curriculum and Instruction

Abilene Christian University, Graduate School, College of Education and Human Services, Graduate Studies in Education, Curriculum and Instruction Program, Abilene, TX 79699-9100. Offers M Ed. Part-time programs available. Postbaccalaureate distance learning degree programs offered (no on-campus study). *Students:* 2 full-time (both women), 4 part-time (all women); includes 1 minority (Black or African American, non-Hispanic/Latino). 6 applicants, 17% accepted. In 2013, 21 master's awarded. *Degree requirements:* For master's, capstone. *Entrance requirements:* Additional exam requirements/recommendations for international students: Required—TOEFL (minimum score 550 paper-based; 90 iBT), IELTS (minimum score 6.5), PTE. *Application deadline:* For fall admission, 8/15 priority date for domestic students; for winter admission, 10/1 priority date for domestic students; for spring admission, 12/15 priority date for domestic students; for summer admission, 4/15 for domestic students. Applications are processed on a rolling basis. Application fee: $50. Electronic applications accepted. *Expenses:* Contact institution. *Financial support:* Career-related internships or fieldwork and Federal Work-Study available. Support available to part-time students. Financial award application deadline: 4/1; financial award applicants required to submit FAFSA. *Unit head:* Dr. Lloyd Goldsmith, Graduate Director, 325-674-2946, Fax: 325-674-2123, E-mail: lloyd.goldsmith@acu.edu. *Application contact:* Corey Patterson, Director of Graduate Admission and Recruiting, 325-674-6566, Fax: 325-674-6717, E-mail: gradinfo@acu.edu.

Acadia University, Faculty of Professional Studies, School of Education, Program in Curriculum Studies, Wolfville, NS B4P 2R6, Canada. Offers cultural and media studies (M Ed); learning and technology (M Ed); science, math and technology (M Ed). Part-time programs available. *Degree requirements:* For master's, thesis optional. *Entrance requirements:* For master's, B Ed or the equivalent, minimum B average in undergraduate course work, 2 years of teaching experience. Additional exam requirements/recommendations for international students: Required—TOEFL (minimum score 580 paper-based; 93 iBT), IELTS (minimum score 6.5). *Faculty research:* Literacy development, postmodern philosophy and curriculum theory, historiography, philosophy of education, learning and technology.

American College of Education, Graduate Programs, Chicago, IL 60606. Offers curriculum and instruction (M Ed), including bilingual, ESL; educational leadership (M Ed); educational technology (M Ed).

American InterContinental University Online, Program in Education, Schaumburg, IL 60173. Offers curriculum and instruction (M Ed); educational assessment and evaluation (M Ed); instructional technology (M Ed); leadership of educational organizations (M Ed). Evening/weekend programs available. Postbaccalaureate distance learning degree programs offered (no on-campus study). *Entrance requirements:* Additional exam requirements/recommendations for international students: Required—TOEFL (minimum score 550 paper-based). Electronic applications accepted.

American Public University System, AMU/APU Graduate Programs, Charles Town, WV 25414. Offers accounting (MBA, MS); criminal justice (MA), including business administration, emergency and disaster management, general (MA, MS); educational leadership (M Ed); emergency and disaster management (MA); entrepreneurship (MBA); environmental policy and management (MS), including environmental planning, environmental sustainability, fish and wildlife management, general (MA, MS), global environmental management; finance (MBA); general (MBA); global business management (MBA); history (MA), including American history, ancient and classical history, European history, global history, public history; homeland security (MA), including business administration, counter-terrorism studies, criminal justice, cyber, emergency management and public health, intelligence studies, transportation security; homeland security resource allocation (MBA); humanities (MA); information technology (MS), including digital forensics, enterprise software development, information assurance and security, IT project management; information technology management (MBA); intelligence studies (MA), including criminal intelligence, cyber, general (MA, MS), homeland security, intelligence analysis, intelligence collection, intelligence management, intelligence operations, terrorism studies; international relations and conflict resolution (MA), including comparative and security issues, conflict resolution, international and transnational security issues, peacekeeping; legal studies (MA); management (MA), including defense management, general (MA, MS), human resource management, organizational leadership, public administration; marketing (MBA); military history (MA), including American military history, American Revolution, civil war, war since 1945, World War II; military studies (MA), including joint warfare, strategic leadership; national security studies (MA), including general (MA, MS), homeland security, regional security studies, security and intelligence analysis, terrorism studies; nonprofit management (MBA); political science (MA), including American politics and government, comparative government and development, general (MA, MS), international relations, public policy; psychology (MA), including general (MA, MS), maritime engineering management, reverse logistics management; public administration (MPA), including disaster management, environmental policy, health policy, human resources, national security, organizational management, security management; public health (MPH); reverse logistics management (MA); school counseling (M Ed); security management (MA); space studies (MS), including aerospace science, general (MA, MS), planetary science; sports and health sciences (MS); teaching (M Ed), including curriculum and instruction for elementary teachers, elementary reading, English language learners, instructional leadership, online learning, special education; transportation and logistics management (MA), including general (MA, MS), maritime engineering management, reverse logistics management. Programs offered via distance learning only. Part-time and evening/weekend programs available. Postbaccalaureate distance learning degree programs offered (no on-campus study). *Faculty:* 432 full-time (242 women), 1,722 part-time/adjunct (829 women). *Students:* 511 full-time (241 women), 10,947 part-time (4,294 women); includes 3,760 minority (2,058 Black or African American, non-Hispanic/Latino; 88 American Indian or Alaska Native, non-Hispanic/Latino; 293 Asian, non-Hispanic/Latino; 876 Hispanic/Latino; 91 Native Hawaiian or other Pacific Islander, non-Hispanic/Latino; 354 Two or more races, non-Hispanic/Latino), 134 international. Average age 36. In 2013, 3,323 master's awarded. *Degree requirements:* For master's, comprehensive exam or practicum. *Entrance requirements:* For master's, official transcript showing earned bachelor's degree from institution accredited by recognized accrediting body. Additional exam requirements/recommendations for international students: Required—TOEFL (minimum score 550 paper-based), IELTS (minimum score 6.5). *Application deadline:* Applications are processed on a rolling basis. Application fee: $0. Electronic applications accepted. *Expenses: Tuition:* Part-time $325 per semester hour. *Financial support:* Applicants required to submit FAFSA. *Faculty research:* Military history, criminal justice, management performance, national security. *Unit head:* Dr. Karan Powell, Executive Vice President and Provost, 877-468-6268, Fax: 304-724-3780. *Application contact:* Terry Grant, Vice President of Enrollment Management, 877-468-6268, Fax: 304-724-3780, E-mail: info@apus.edu.
Website: http://www.apus.edu.

American University, College of Arts and Sciences, Washington, DC 20016-8012. Offers addiction and addictive behavior (Certificate); anthropology (PhD); applied microeconomics (Certificate); applied statistics (Certificate); art history (MA); arts management (MA, Certificate); Asian studies (Certificate); audio production (Certificate); audio technology (MA); behavior, cognition, and neuroscience (PhD); bilingual education (MA, Certificate); biology (MA, MS); chemistry (MS); clinical psychology (PhD); computer science (MS, Certificate); creative writing (MFA); curriculum and instruction (M Ed, Certificate); economics (MA, PhD); environmental assessment (Certificate); environmental science (MS); ethics, peace, and global affairs (MA); gender analysis in economics (Certificate); health promotion management (MS); history (MA, PhD); international arts management (Certificate); international economic relations (Certificate); international economics (MA); international training and education (MA); literature (MA); mathematics (MA); North American studies (Certificate); nutrition education (MS, Certificate); philosophy (MA); professional science: biotechnology (MS); professional science: environmental assessment (MS); professional science: quantitative analysis (MS); psychobiology of healing (Certificate); psychology (MA); psychology: general (PhD); public anthropology (MA, Certificate); public sociology (Certificate); social research (Certificate); sociology (MA); Spanish: Latin American studies (MA); special education: learning disabilities (MA); statistics (MS); studio art (MFA); teaching (MAT); teaching English as a foreign language (MA); teaching: early childhood (Certificate); teaching: elementary (Certificate); teaching: ESOL (Certificate); teaching: secondary (Certificate); technology in arts management (Certificate); TESOL (MA); translation: French (Certificate); translation: Russian (Certificate); translation: Spanish (Certificate); women's, gender, and sexuality studies (Certificate). Part-time and evening/weekend programs available. Postbaccalaureate distance learning degree programs offered (no on-campus study). *Faculty:* 358 full-time (187 women), 254 part-time/adjunct (127 women). *Students:* 627 full-time (411 women), 416 part-time (300 women); includes 206 minority (91 Black or African American, non-Hispanic/Latino; 5 American Indian or Alaska Native, non-Hispanic/Latino; 32 Asian, non-Hispanic/Latino; 64 Hispanic/Latino; 1 Native Hawaiian or other Pacific Islander, non-Hispanic/Latino; 13 Two or more races, non-Hispanic/Latino), 124 international. Average age 29. 1,672 applicants, 52% accepted, 361 enrolled. In 2013, 382 master's, 38 doctorates, 33 other advanced degrees awarded. Terminal master's awarded for partial completion of doctoral program. *Degree requirements:* For master's, comprehensive exam (for some programs), thesis (for some programs); for doctorate, comprehensive exam (for some programs), thesis/dissertation. *Entrance requirements:* For master's, GRE, minimum GPA of 3.0 in last 60 credit hours, letter of recommendation, statement of purpose, resume, unofficial transcript; for doctorate, GRE, minimum GPA of 3.0 for all graduate work, letter of recommendation, statement of purpose, resume, unofficial transcript. Additional exam requirements/recommendations for international students: Required—TOEFL (minimum score 600 paper-based; 100 iBT), IELTS (minimum score 7). *Application deadline:* For fall admission, 2/1 for domestic students; for spring admission, 10/1 for domestic students. Applications are processed on a rolling basis. Application fee: $55. Electronic applications accepted. *Expenses: Tuition:* Full-time $25,920; part-time $1482 per credit hour. *Required fees:* $430. Tuition and fees vary according to course load and program. *Financial support:* Fellowships, research assistantships with full and partial tuition reimbursements, teaching assistantships with full and partial tuition reimbursements, career-related internships or fieldwork, Federal Work-Study, institutionally sponsored loans, scholarships/grants, traineeships, tuition waivers (full and partial), and unspecified assistantships available. Support available to part-time students. Financial award applicants required to submit FAFSA. *Unit head:* Dr. Peter Starr, Dean, 202-885-2446, Fax: 202-885-2429, E-mail: pstarr@american.edu. *Application contact:* Kathleen Clowery, Associate Director, Graduate Enrollment Management, 202-885-3621, Fax: 202-885-1505, E-mail: clowery@american.edu.
Website: http://www.american.edu/cas/.

Andrews University, School of Graduate Studies, School of Education, Department of Teaching, Learning, and Curriculum, Program in Curriculum and Instruction, Berrien Springs, MI 49104. Offers MA, Ed D, PhD, Ed S. *Faculty:* 5 full-time (1 woman). *Students:* 11 full-time (8 women), 24 part-time (20 women); includes 10 minority (9 Black or African American, non-Hispanic/Latino; 1 Asian, non-Hispanic/Latino), 13 international. Average age 47. 16 applicants, 31% accepted, 3 enrolled. In 2013, 4 master's, 1 doctorate, 1 other advanced degree awarded. *Degree requirements:* For master's, thesis optional; for doctorate, thesis/dissertation. *Entrance requirements:* For master's, GRE Subject Test. Additional exam requirements/recommendations for international students: Required—TOEFL (minimum score 550 paper-based). *Application deadline:* Applications are processed on a rolling basis. Application fee: $40. *Financial support:* Fellowships, research assistantships, teaching assistantships, career-related internships or fieldwork, Federal Work-Study, institutionally sponsored loans, and tuition waivers (partial) available. Support available to part-time students. *Unit head:* Dr. Larry D. Burton, Coordinator, 269-971-6674. *Application contact:* Monica Wringer, Supervisor of Graduate Admission, 800-253-2874, Fax: 269-471-6321, E-mail: graduate@andrews.edu.

Angelo State University, College of Graduate Studies, College of Education, Department of Curriculum and Instruction, Program in Curriculum and Instruction, San Angelo, TX 76909. Offers MA. Part-time and evening/weekend programs available. *Degree requirements:* For master's, comprehensive exam. *Entrance requirements:* Additional exam requirements/recommendations for international students: Required—TOEFL or IELTS. Electronic applications accepted.

Appalachian State University, Cratis D. Williams Graduate School, Department of Curriculum and Instruction, Boone, NC 28608. Offers curriculum specialist (MA); educational media (MA); elementary education (MA); middle grades education (MA), including language arts, mathematics, science, social studies. *Accreditation:* NCATE. Part-time and evening/weekend programs available. Postbaccalaureate distance learning degree programs offered (no on-campus study). *Degree requirements:* For master's, comprehensive exam, thesis or alternative. *Entrance requirements:* For master's, GRE General Test or MAT, 3 letters of recommendation. Additional exam requirements/recommendations for international students: Required—TOEFL (minimum score 570 paper-based; 79 iBT), IELTS (minimum score 6.5). Electronic applications accepted. *Faculty research:* Media literacy, elementary teaching, curriculum development, online learning environments.

Arcadia University, Graduate Studies, School of Education, Glenside, PA 19038-3295. Offers art education (M Ed); computer education (CAS); curriculum (CAS); curriculum studies (M Ed); early childhood education (M Ed, CAS), including individualized (M Ed), master teacher (M Ed), research in child development (M Ed); educational leadership

(M Ed, Ed D, CAS); elementary education (M Ed, CAS); English education (MA Ed); environmental education (MA Ed, CAS); history education (MA Ed); instructional technology (M Ed); language arts (M Ed, CAS); library science (M Ed); mathematics education (M Ed, MA Ed, CAS); music education (MA Ed); psychology (MA Ed); reading (M Ed, CAS); science education (M Ed, CAS); secondary education (M Ed, CAS); special education (M Ed, Ed D, CAS); theater arts (MA Ed); written communication (MA Ed). *Accreditation:* NASAD. Part-time and evening/weekend programs available. Postbaccalaureate distance learning degree programs offered (minimal on-campus study). Electronic applications accepted. *Expenses:* Contact institution.

Arizona State University at the Tempe campus, Mary Lou Fulton Teachers College, Program in Curriculum and Instruction, Phoenix, AZ 85069. Offers curriculum and instruction (M Ed, MA, PhD); elementary education (M Ed); physical education (MPE); secondary education (M Ed). Part-time and evening/weekend programs available. Postbaccalaureate distance learning degree programs offered (minimal on-campus study). Terminal master's awarded for partial completion of doctoral program. *Degree requirements:* For master's, thesis or alternative, applied project, interactive Program of Study (iPOS) submitted before completing 50 percent of required credit hours; for doctorate, comprehensive exam, thesis/dissertation, interactive Program of Study (iPOS) submitted before completing 50 percent of required credit hours. *Entrance requirements:* For master's, GRE or GMAT (for some programs), minimum GPA of 3.0 or equivalent in last 2 years of work leading to bachelor's degree, 3 letters of recommendation, personal statement describing research and career goals, curriculum vitae or resume, IVP fingerprint clearance card (for those seeking Arizona certification); for doctorate, GRE or GMAT (depending on program), minimum GPA of 3.0 or equivalent in last 2 years of work leading to bachelor's degree, 3 letters of recommendation, personal statement describing research and career goals, curriculum vitae or resume. Additional exam requirements/recommendations for international students: Required—TOEFL, IELTS, or PTE. Electronic applications accepted. *Expenses:* Contact institution. *Faculty research:* Early childhood, media and computers, elementary education, secondary education, English education, bilingual education, language and literacy, science education, engineering education, exercise and wellness education.

Arkansas Tech University, College of Education, Russellville, AR 72801. Offers college student personnel (MS); elementary education (M Ed); instructional improvement (M Ed); instructional technology (M Ed); physical education (M Ed); teaching (MAT). *Accreditation:* NCATE. Part-time and evening/weekend programs available. Postbaccalaureate distance learning degree programs offered (no on-campus study). *Students:* 58 full-time (39 women), 304 part-time (240 women); includes 76 minority (58 Black or African American, non-Hispanic/Latino; 3 American Indian or Alaska Native, non-Hispanic/Latino; 4 Asian, non-Hispanic/Latino; 8 Hispanic/Latino; 3 Two or more races, non-Hispanic/Latino), 2 international. Average age 32. In 2013, 130 master's awarded. *Degree requirements:* For master's, comprehensive exam, thesis optional, action research project. *Entrance requirements:* Additional exam requirements/recommendations for international students: Required—TOEFL (minimum score 550 paper-based; 79 iBT), IELTS (minimum score 6.5). *Application deadline:* For fall admission, 3/1 priority date for domestic students, 5/1 priority date for international students; for spring admission, 10/1 priority date for domestic and international students. Applications are processed on a rolling basis. Application fee: $25 ($75 for international students). Electronic applications accepted. *Expenses:* Tuition, state resident: full-time $5976; part-time $249 per credit hour. Tuition, nonresident: full-time $11,952; part-time $498 per credit hour. Required fees: $411 per semester. Tuition and fees vary according to course load. *Financial support:* In 2013–14, research assistantships with full tuition reimbursements (averaging $4,800 per year), teaching assistantships with full tuition reimbursements (averaging $4,800 per year) were awarded; career-related internships or fieldwork, Federal Work-Study, scholarships/grants, health care benefits, and unspecified assistantships also available. Support available to part-time students. Financial award application deadline: 4/15; financial award applicants required to submit FAFSA. *Unit head:* Dr. Sherry Field, Dean, 479-968-0418, E-mail: sfield@atu.edu. *Application contact:* Dr. Mary B. Gunter, Dean of Graduate College, 479-968-0398, Fax: 479-964-0542, E-mail: gradcollege@atu.edu. Website: http://www.atu.edu/education/.

Arlington Baptist College, Program in Education, Arlington, TX 76012-3425. Offers curriculum and instruction (M Ed); educational leadership (M Ed). *Degree requirements:* For master's, professional portfolio; internship (for educational leadership). *Entrance requirements:* For master's, bachelor's degree from accredited college or university with minimum GPA of 3.0, minimum of 12 hours in Bible; minimum of three years' classroom teaching experience in an accredited K-12 public or private school (for educational leadeship only).

Armstrong State University, School of Graduate Studies, Department of Adolescent and Adult Education, Savannah, GA 31419-1997. Offers adolescent and adult education (Certificate); adult education and community leadership (M Ed); curriculum and instruction (M Ed); secondary education (MAT). Part-time and evening/weekend programs available. Postbaccalaureate distance learning degree programs offered (minimal on-campus study). *Faculty:* 10 full-time (8 women), 2 part-time/adjunct (1 woman). *Students:* 35 full-time (29 women), 80 part-time (57 women); includes 34 minority (31 Black or African American, non-Hispanic/Latino; 1 Asian, non-Hispanic/Latino; 2 Hispanic/Latino). Average age 34. 61 applicants, 79% accepted, 43 enrolled. In 2013, 59 master's awarded. *Degree requirements:* For master's, comprehensive exam (for some programs), thesis (for some programs). *Entrance requirements:* For master's, GRE, MAT, minimum GPA of 2.5 and disposition statement (for MAT), 3.0 and clear certification (for M Ed). Additional exam requirements/recommendations for international students: Required—TOEFL (minimum score 523 paper-based). *Application deadline:* For fall admission, 6/30 priority date for domestic students, 5/1 priority date for international students; for spring admission, 11/15 priority date for domestic students, 9/15 priority date for international students; for summer admission, 4/15 priority date for domestic students, 9/15 for international students. Applications are processed on a rolling basis. Application fee: $30. Electronic applications accepted. *Expenses:* Tuition, state resident: part-time $201 per credit hour. Tuition, nonresident: part-time $745 per credit hour. Required fees: $310 per semester. Tuition and fees vary according to course load, campus/location and program. *Financial support:* In 2013–14, research assistantships with full tuition reimbursements (averaging $5,000 per year) were awarded; career-related internships or fieldwork, Federal Work-Study, scholarships/grants, and unspecified assistantships also available. Support available to part-time students. Financial award application deadline: 3/15; financial award applicants required to submit FAFSA. *Faculty research:* Women's issues, education pedagogy, reading, heat of body metabolism, geographic education. *Unit head:* Dr. Patrick Thomas, Interim Department Head, 912-344-2562, Fax: 912-344-3496, E-mail: patrick.thomas@armstrong.edu. *Application contact:* Jill Bell, Director, Graduate Enrollment Services, 912-344-2798, Fax: 912-344-3488, E-mail: graduate@armstrong.edu. Website: http://www.armstrong.edu/Education/adolescent_adult_education2/aaed_welcome.

Ashland University, Dwight Schar College of Education, Department of Educational Administration, Ashland, OH 44805-3702. Offers curriculum specialist (M Ed);

principalship (M Ed); pupil services (M Ed). Part-time programs available. *Degree requirements:* For master's, thesis or alternative, internship. *Entrance requirements:* For master's, teaching certificate or license, bachelor's degree, minimum cumulative GPA of 2.75. Additional exam requirements/recommendations for international students: Required—TOEFL. Electronic applications accepted. *Faculty research:* Gender and religious considerations in employment, Interstate School Leaders Licensure Consortium (ISLLC) standards, adjunct faculty training, politics of school finance, ethnicity and employment.

Auburn University, Graduate School, College of Education, Department of Educational Foundations, Leadership, and Technology, Auburn University, AL 36849. Offers adult education (M Ed, MS, Ed D); curriculum and instruction (M Ed, MS, Ed D, Ed S); curriculum supervision (M Ed, MS, Ed D, Ed S); educational psychology (PhD); higher education administration (M Ed, MS, Ed D, Ed S); media instructional design (MS); media specialist (M Ed); school administration (M Ed, MS, Ed D, Ed S). *Accreditation:* NCATE. Part-time programs available. *Faculty:* 25 full-time (15 women), 6 part-time/adjunct (5 women). *Students:* 104 full-time (65 women), 250 part-time (140 women); includes 98 minority (90 Black or African American, non-Hispanic/Latino; 1 American Indian or Alaska Native, non-Hispanic/Latino; 4 Asian, non-Hispanic/Latino; 3 Hispanic/Latino), 14 international. Average age 36. 188 applicants, 66% accepted, 76 enrolled. In 2013, 51 master's, 22 doctorates, 10 other advanced degrees awarded. *Degree requirements:* For master's, thesis (for some programs); for doctorate, thesis/dissertation; for Ed S, field project. *Entrance requirements:* For master's, doctorate, and Ed S, GRE General Test. *Application deadline:* For fall admission, 7/7 for domestic students; for spring admission, 11/24 for domestic students. Applications are processed on a rolling basis. Application fee: $50 ($60 for international students). Electronic applications accepted. *Expenses:* Tuition, state resident: full-time $8262; part-time $459 per credit hour. Tuition, nonresident: full-time $24,786; part-time $1377 per credit hour. Tuition and fees vary according to degree level and program. *Financial support:* Teaching assistantships and Federal Work-Study available. Support available to part-time students. Financial award application deadline: 3/15; financial award applicants required to submit FAFSA. *Unit head:* Dr. Sherida Downer, Head, 334-844-4460. *Application contact:* Dr. George Flowers, Dean of the Graduate School, 334-844-4700. Website: http://www.education.auburn.edu/academic_departments/eflt/.

Aurora University, College of Education, Aurora, IL 60506-4892. Offers curriculum and instruction (MA, Ed D); early childhood and special education (MA); education (MAT), including elementary certification; education and administration (Ed D); educational leadership (MEL); educational technology (MATL); reading instruction (MA); special education (MA). *Accreditation:* NCATE. Part-time and evening/weekend programs available. *Degree requirements:* For doctorate, comprehensive exam, thesis/dissertation. *Entrance requirements:* For master's, 2 years of teaching experience, valid teaching certificate. Additional exam requirements/recommendations for international students: Required—TOEFL (minimum score 550 paper-based). Electronic applications accepted. *Expenses:* Contact institution.

Austin Peay State University, College of Graduate Studies, College of Education, Department of Educational Specialties, Clarksville, TN 37044. Offers administration and supervision (Ed S); curriculum and instruction (MA Ed); education leadership (MA Ed); elementary education (Ed S); secondary education (Ed S); special education (MA Ed). Part-time and evening/weekend programs available. Postbaccalaureate distance learning degree programs offered. *Faculty:* 8 full-time (5 women), 4 part-time/adjunct (3 women). *Students:* 6 full-time (5 women), 87 part-time (73 women); includes 10 minority (5 Black or African American, non-Hispanic/Latino; 1 American Indian or Alaska Native, non-Hispanic/Latino; 1 Asian, non-Hispanic/Latino; 1 Hispanic/Latino; 2 Two or more races, non-Hispanic/Latino). Average age 35. 11 applicants, 82% accepted, 6 enrolled. In 2013, 37 master's, 6 Ed Ss awarded. *Degree requirements:* For master's, comprehensive exam, thesis optional. *Entrance requirements:* For master's, GRE General Test, 3 letters of recommendation, minimum undergraduate GPA of 2.75. Additional exam requirements/recommendations for international students: Required—TOEFL (minimum score 500 paper-based). *Application deadline:* For fall admission, 8/5 priority date for domestic students. Applications are processed on a rolling basis. Application fee: $25. Electronic applications accepted. *Expenses:* Tuition, state resident: full-time $7500; part-time $375 per credit hour. Tuition, nonresident: full-time $20,800; part-time $1040 per credit hour. Required fees: $1284; $64.20 per credit hour. *Financial support:* Career-related internships or fieldwork, Federal Work-Study, institutionally sponsored loans, scholarships/grants, and unspecified assistantships available. Support available to part-time students. Financial award application deadline: 3/1; financial award applicants required to submit FAFSA. *Unit head:* Dr. Moniqueka Gold, Chair, 931-221-7696, Fax: 931-221-1292, E-mail: goldm@apsu.edu. *Application contact:* June D. Lee, Graduate Coordinator, 800-859-4723, Fax: 931-221-7641, E-mail: gradadmissions@apsu.edu.

Austin Peay State University, College of Graduate Studies, College of Education, Department of Teaching and Learning, Clarksville, TN 37044. Offers elementary education K-6 (MAT); reading (MA Ed); secondary education 7-12 (MAT); special education K-12 (MAT). Part-time and evening/weekend programs available. Postbaccalaureate distance learning degree programs offered. *Faculty:* 7 full-time (4 women), 5 part-time/adjunct (all women). *Students:* 70 full-time (59 women), 77 part-time (55 women); includes 23 minority (10 Black or African American, non-Hispanic/Latino; 2 Asian, non-Hispanic/Latino; 5 Hispanic/Latino; 6 Two or more races, non-Hispanic/Latino). Average age 33. 50 applicants, 90% accepted, 37 enrolled. In 2013, 60 master's awarded. *Degree requirements:* For master's, comprehensive exam, thesis optional. *Entrance requirements:* For master's, GRE General Test, 3 letters of recommendation, minimum undergraduate GPA of 2.75. Additional exam requirements/recommendations for international students: Required—TOEFL (minimum score 500 paper-based). *Application deadline:* For fall admission, 8/5 priority date for domestic students. Applications are processed on a rolling basis. Application fee: $25. Electronic applications accepted. *Expenses:* Tuition, state resident: full-time $7500; part-time $375 per credit hour. Tuition, nonresident: full-time $20,800; part-time $1040 per credit hour. Required fees: $1284; $64.20 per credit hour. *Financial support:* Career-related internships or fieldwork, Federal Work-Study, institutionally sponsored loans, scholarships/grants, and unspecified assistantships available. Support available to part-time students. Financial award application deadline: 3/1; financial award applicants required to submit FAFSA. *Unit head:* Dr. Rebecca McMahan, Chair, 931-221-7513, Fax: 931-221-1292, E-mail: mcmahanb@apsu.edu. *Application contact:* June D. Lee, Graduate Coordinator, 800-859-4723, Fax: 931-221-7641, E-mail: gradadmissions@apsu.edu.

Averett University, Master in Education Program, Danville, VA 24541-3692. Offers administration and supervision (M Ed); art (M Ed); biology (M Ed); chemistry (M Ed); curriculum and instruction (M Ed); early childhood (M Ed); English (M Ed); mathematics (M Ed); middle grades (M Ed); physical science (M Ed); reading specialist (M Ed); science (M Ed); special education (M Ed); special education learning disability (M Ed). Program offered on Danville Campus only. Part-time and evening/weekend programs available. *Faculty:* 4 full-time (3 women), 13 part-time/adjunct (8 women). *Students:* 43 full-time (35 women), 44 part-time (35 women); includes 7 minority (all Black or African American, non-Hispanic/Latino). *Degree requirements:* For master's, 30-credit core

curriculum, minimum GPA of 3.0 throughout program, completion of degree requirements within six years from start of program. *Entrance requirements:* For master's, PRAXIS I, GRE, or MAT; writing proficiency test, minimum cumulative GPA of 3.0 over the last 60 hours of undergraduate study toward a baccalaureate degree, three letters of recommendation, Virginia teaching license (or eligibility). Additional exam requirements/recommendations for international students: Required—TOEFL (minimum score 600 paper-based; 100 iBT). *Application deadline:* Applications are processed on a rolling basis. Application fee: $100. *Expenses:* Contact institution. *Financial support:* Career-related internships or fieldwork, Federal Work-Study, and scholarships/grants available. Financial award application deadline: 4/1; financial award applicants required to submit FAFSA. *Unit head:* Wilfred Lawrence, Department Chair of Education, 434-791-5752, E-mail: priedel@averett.edu. *Application contact:* Christy Pack, Executive Director of Enrollment, 804-887-8612, E-mail: dpack@averett.edu.
Website: http://www.averett.edu/adultprograms/degrees/MEDtrad.php.

Azusa Pacific University, School of Education, Department of Foundations and Transdisciplinary Studies, Program in Curriculum and Instruction in Multicultural Contexts, Azusa, CA 91702-7000. Offers MA Ed. *Accreditation:* NCATE. Part-time and evening/weekend programs available. *Degree requirements:* For master's, core exams, oral presentation. *Entrance requirements:* For master's, 12 units of course work in education, minimum GPA of 3.0. *Faculty research:* Diversity in teacher education programs, teacher morale, student perception of school, case study instruction.

Azusa Pacific University, School of Education, Department of Foundations and Transdisciplinary Studies, Program in Teaching, Azusa, CA 91702-7000. Offers MA Ed.

Ball State University, Graduate School, Teachers College, Department of Educational Studies, Program in Curriculum, Muncie, IN 47306-1099. Offers MAE, Ed S. *Accreditation:* NCATE. *Students:* 2 full-time (1 woman), 43 part-time (33 women); includes 2 minority (both Black or African American, non-Hispanic/Latino). Average age 36. 17 applicants, 82% accepted, 3 enrolled. In 2013, 50 master's awarded. *Degree requirements:* For Ed S, thesis. *Entrance requirements:* For degree, GRE General Test, interview. Application fee: $50. *Financial support:* In 2013–14, 2 students received support. Application deadline: 3/1. *Unit head:* Dr. Jayne Beilke, Head, 785-285-5460, Fax: 785-285-5489, E-mail: jbeilke@bsu.edu. *Application contact:* Dr. Robert Morris, Associate Provost for Research and Dean of the Graduate School, 765-285-1300, E-mail: rmorris@bsu.edu.
Website: http://www.bsu.edu/teachers/departments/edstudies/.

Baptist Bible College of Pennsylvania, Graduate Studies, Clarks Summit, PA 18411-1297. Offers Bible (MA); counseling (MA, MS); curriculum and instruction (M Ed); educational administration (M Ed); intercultural studies (MA); literature (MA); missions (MA); organizational leadership (MA); reading specialist (M Ed); secondary English/communications (M Ed); social entrepreneurship (MA); worldview studies (MA). MA in missions program available only for Association of Baptists for World Evangelism missionary personnel. Part-time and evening/weekend programs available. Postbaccalaureate distance learning degree programs offered (no on-campus study). *Entrance requirements:* Additional exam requirements/recommendations for international students: Required—TOEFL (minimum score 500 paper-based).

Barry University, School of Education, Program in Curriculum and Instruction, Miami Shores, FL 33161-6695. Offers accomplished teacher (Ed S); culture, language and literacy (TESOL) (PhD); curriculum evaluation and research (PhD); early childhood (Ed S); early childhood education (PhD); elementary (Ed S); elementary education (PhD); ESOL (Ed S); gifted (Ed S); Montessori (Ed S); PKP/elementary (Ed S); reading (Ed S); reading, language and cognition (PhD). *Entrance requirements:* For doctorate, GRE, minimum GPA of 3.25.

Baylor University, Graduate School, School of Education, Department of Curriculum and Instruction, Waco, TX 76798. Offers MA, MS Ed, Ed D, PhD. *Accreditation:* NCATE. Part-time programs available. *Faculty:* 13 full-time (8 women). *Students:* 32 full-time (27 women), 20 part-time (12 women); includes 8 minority (1 Black or African American, non-Hispanic/Latino; 3 Asian, non-Hispanic/Latino; 4 Hispanic/Latino), 4 international. Average age 30. 32 applicants, 81% accepted, 22 enrolled. In 2013, 14 master's, 7 doctorates awarded. *Degree requirements:* For master's, comprehensive exam, thesis optional; for doctorate, comprehensive exam, thesis/dissertation. *Entrance requirements:* For master's and doctorate, GRE General Test (including Analytic Writing). Additional exam requirements/recommendations for international students: Required—TOEFL (minimum score 550 paper-based) or IELTS (minimum score 6.5). *Application deadline:* For fall admission, 3/15 priority date for domestic and international students; for spring admission, 10/15 priority date for domestic and international students. Applications are processed on a rolling basis. Application fee: $25. *Expenses: Tuition:* Full-time $25,866; part-time $1437 per credit hour. *Required fees:* $2736; $152 per credit hour. Tuition and fees vary according to course load and program. *Financial support:* In 2013–14, 48 students received support, including 8 research assistantships (averaging $17,500 per year), 6 teaching assistantships (averaging $6,600 per year); Federal Work-Study, institutionally sponsored loans, scholarships/grants, health care benefits, and unspecified assistantships also available. Support available to part-time students. Financial award application deadline: 3/15. *Faculty research:* Curriculum and pedagogy, elementary education, English language arts education, literacy and reading education, mathematics education, qualitative research, science education, social foundations and cultural studies, social studies education, secondary education, teacher education, technology education. *Unit head:* Dr. Trena Wilkerson, Graduate Program Director, 254-710-6162, Fax: 254-710-3160, E-mail: trena_wilkerson@baylor.edu. *Application contact:* Carol Stukenbroeker, Administrative Assistant, 254-710-2410, Fax: 254-710-3160, E-mail: carol_stukenbroeker@baylor.edu.
Website: http://www.baylor.edu/soe/ci/.

Belmont University, College of Arts and Sciences, Nashville, TN 37212-3757. Offers education (M Ed); English (MA); special education (MA); sport administration (MSA); teaching (MAT). Part-time and evening/weekend programs available. *Faculty:* 29 full-time (21 women), 24 part-time/adjunct (12 women). *Students:* 144 full-time (97 women), 63 part-time (49 women); includes 26 minority (9 Black or African American, non-Hispanic/Latino; 1 Asian, non-Hispanic/Latino; 8 Hispanic/Latino; 8 Two or more races, non-Hispanic/Latino), 3 international. Average age 29. 201 applicants, 57% accepted, 81 enrolled. *Degree requirements:* For master's, comprehensive exam (for some programs), thesis (for some programs). *Entrance requirements:* For master's, GRE, GMAT, MAT. Additional exam requirements/recommendations for international students: Required—TOEFL. *Application deadline:* For fall admission, 8/1 for domestic students; for spring admission, 12/1 for domestic students. Applications are processed on a rolling basis. Application fee: $50. Electronic applications accepted. *Expenses:* Contact institution. *Financial support:* In 2013–14, 50 students received support. Fellowships with partial tuition reimbursements available, teaching assistantships with partial tuition reimbursements available, Federal Work-Study, institutionally sponsored loans, scholarships/grants, tuition waivers (partial), and unspecified assistantships available. Financial award application deadline: 4/15; financial award applicants required to submit FAFSA. *Unit head:* Dr. Bryce Sullivan, Dean, 615-460-6437, Fax: 615-385-5084, E-mail: bryce.sullivan@belmont.edu. *Application contact:* David Mee, Dean of Enrollment Services, 615-460-6785, Fax: 615-460-5434, E-mail: david.mee@belmont.edu.

Benedictine University, Graduate Programs, Program in Education, Lisle, IL 60532-0900. Offers curriculum and instruction and collaborative teaching (M Ed); elementary education (MA Ed); leadership and administration (M Ed); reading and literacy (M Ed); secondary education (MA Ed); special education (MA Ed). Part-time and evening/weekend programs available. *Students:* 6 full-time (all women), 124 part-time (106 women); includes 14 minority (8 Black or African American, non-Hispanic/Latino; 1 American Indian or Alaska Native, non-Hispanic/Latino; 2 Asian, non-Hispanic/Latino; 3 Hispanic/Latino). 21 applicants, 62% accepted, 8 enrolled. In 2013, 120 master's awarded. *Degree requirements:* For master's, comprehensive exam, thesis (for some programs). *Entrance requirements:* For master's, GRE or MAT. Additional exam requirements/recommendations for international students: Required—TOEFL (minimum score 550 paper-based). *Application deadline:* For fall admission, 9/1 for domestic students; for winter admission, 12/1 for domestic students; for spring admission, 2/15 for domestic students. Applications are processed on a rolling basis. Application fee: $40. Electronic applications accepted. *Expenses:* Contact institution. *Financial support:* Career-related internships or fieldwork and health care benefits available. Support available to part-time students. *Unit head:* MeShelda Jackson, Director, 630-829-6282, E-mail: mjackson@ben.edu. *Application contact:* Kari Gibbons, Associate Vice President, Enrollment Center, 630-829-6200, Fax: 630-829-6584, E-mail: kgibbons@ben.edu.

Berry College, Graduate Programs, Graduate Programs in Education, Program in Curriculum and Instruction, Mount Berry, GA 30149-0159. Offers Ed S. *Accreditation:* NCATE. *Faculty:* 6 part-time/adjunct (2 women). *Students:* 3 full-time (all women), 2 part-time (1 woman). Average age 29. *Degree requirements:* For Ed S, thesis, portfolio, oral exams. *Entrance requirements:* For degree, M Ed from NCATE-accredited school, minimum GPA of 3.25. Additional exam requirements/recommendations for international students: Required—TOEFL (minimum score 550 paper-based). *Application deadline:* For fall admission, 7/25 for domestic students, 5/1 for international students; for spring admission, 12/1 for domestic students, 10/1 for international students. Applications are processed on a rolling basis. Application fee: $25 ($30 for international students). Electronic applications accepted. *Expenses:* Contact institution. *Financial support:* In 2013–14, 5 students received support, including 3 research assistantships with full tuition reimbursements available (averaging $4,889 per year); scholarships/grants also available. Support available to part-time students. Financial award application deadline: 3/1; financial award applicants required to submit FAFSA. *Unit head:* Dr. Jacqueline McDowell, Dean, 706-236-1717, Fax: 706-238-5827, E-mail: jmcdowell@berry.edu. *Application contact:* Brett Kennedy, Assistant Vice President of Enrollment Management, 706-236-2215, Fax: 706-290-2178, E-mail: admissions@berry.edu.
Website: http://www.berry.edu/academics/education/graduate/.

Biola University, School of Education, La Mirada, CA 90639-0001. Offers apologetics (MA Ed); curriculum and instruction (MA Ed, MAT, Certificate); early childhood (MA Ed, MAT); history and philosophy of science (MA Ed, MAT); linguistics and inter-cultural studies (MAT); linguistics and international studies (MA Ed); multiple subject (MAT); single subject (MAT); special education (MA Ed, MAT, Certificate); TESOL (MA Ed, MAT). Part-time and evening/weekend programs available. Postbaccalaureate distance learning degree programs offered (no on-campus study). *Faculty:* 14. *Students:* 51 full-time (38 women), 101 part-time (83 women); includes 47 minority (8 Black or African American, non-Hispanic/Latino; 1 American Indian or Alaska Native, non-Hispanic/Latino; 32 Asian, non-Hispanic/Latino; 6 Two or more races, non-Hispanic/Latino), 4 international. In 2013, 33 master's awarded. *Entrance requirements:* For master's, CBEST, CSET. Additional exam requirements/recommendations for international students: Required—TOEFL (minimum score 100 iBT). *Application deadline:* For fall admission, 7/1 for domestic students, 6/1 for international students; for spring admission, 12/1 for domestic students; for summer admission, 5/1 for domestic students. Applications are processed on a rolling basis. Application fee: $55. Electronic applications accepted. *Financial support:* Scholarships/grants available. Support available to part-time students. Financial award applicants required to submit FAFSA. *Faculty research:* Early childhood education, elementary education, special education, curriculum development, teacher preparation. *Unit head:* Dr. June Hetzel, Dean, 562-903-4715. *Application contact:* Graduate Admissions Office, 562-903-4752, E-mail: graduate.admissions@biola.edu.
Website: http://education.biola.edu/.

Black Hills State University, Graduate Studies, Program in Curriculum and Instruction, Spearfish, SD 57799. Offers MS. Part-time programs available. *Faculty:* 14 full-time (9 women), 2 part-time/adjunct (both women). *Students:* 3 full-time (all women), 103 part-time (89 women); includes 2 minority (1 Black or African American, non-Hispanic/Latino; 1 American Indian or Alaska Native, non-Hispanic/Latino). Average age 38. 74 applicants, 97% accepted, 48 enrolled. In 2013, 24 master's awarded. *Entrance requirements:* Additional exam requirements/recommendations for international students: Required—TOEFL (minimum score 500 paper-based; 60 iBT). *Application deadline:* Applications are processed on a rolling basis. Application fee: $35. *Expenses:* Tuition, state resident: full-time $3718; part-time $201.85 per credit hour. Tuition, nonresident: full-time $7686; part-time $427.30 per credit hour. Tuition and fees vary according to course load, program and reciprocity agreements. *Unit head:* Dr. Faye LaDuke Pelster, Coordinator, 605-642-6627, Fax: 605-642-6032, E-mail: faye.laduke@bhsu.edu. *Application contact:* 605-642-6627, Fax: 605-642-6032, E-mail: faye.laduke@bhsu.edu.

Bloomsburg University of Pennsylvania, School of Graduate Studies, College of Education, Department of Educational Studies and Secondary Education, Program in Curriculum and Instruction, Bloomsburg, PA 17815-1301. Offers M Ed, Certificate. *Accreditation:* NCATE. *Faculty:* 10 full-time (4 women), 3 part-time/adjunct (1 woman). *Students:* 35 full-time (25 women), 13 part-time (7 women); includes 2 minority (both Hispanic/Latino). Average age 32. 36 applicants, 89% accepted, 15 enrolled. In 2013, 41 master's awarded. *Degree requirements:* For master's, thesis. *Entrance requirements:* For master's, MAT, GRE, or PRAXIS, minimum QPA of 3.0, interview. Additional exam requirements/recommendations for international students: Required—TOEFL (minimum score 550 paper-based; 79 iBT). *Application deadline:* Applications are processed on a rolling basis. Application fee: $35 ($60 for international students). Electronic applications accepted. *Expenses:* Tuition, state resident: full-time $7956; part-time $442 per credit. Tuition, nonresident: full-time $11,934; part-time $663 per credit. *Required fees:* $95.50 per credit. $55 per semester. Tuition and fees vary according to course load. *Financial support:* Unspecified assistantships available. *Unit head:* Dr. Tegan Kotarski, College of Education Graduate Coordinator, 570-389-3883, Fax: 570-389-5049, E-mail: tkotarsk@bloomu.edu. *Application contact:* Jennifer Richard, Administrative Assistant, 570-389-4015, Fax: 570-389-3054, E-mail: jrichard@bloomu.edu.
Website: http://www.bloomu.edu/gradschool/curriculum-instruction.

Bob Jones University, Graduate Programs, Greenville, SC 29614. Offers accountancy (MS); Bible (MA); Bible translation (MA); Biblical studies (Certificate); broadcast management (MS); business administration (MBA); church history (MA, PhD); church ministries (MA); church music (MM); cinema and video production (MA); counseling (MS); curriculum and instruction (Ed D); divinity (M Div); dramatic production (MA); educational leadership (MS, Ed D, Ed S); elementary education (M Ed, MAT); English

(M Ed, MA, MAT); fine arts (MA); graphic design (MA); history (M Ed, MA); illustration (MA); interpretative speech (MA); mathematics (M Ed, MAT); medical missions (Certificate); ministry (MM, D Min); multi-categorical special education (M Ed, MAT); music (M Ed); New Testament interpretation (PhD); Old Testament interpretation (PhD); orchestral instrument performance (MM); organ performance (MM); pastoral studies (MA); personnel services (MS, Ed S); piano pedagogy (MM); piano performance (MM); platform arts (MA); radio and television broadcasting (MS); rhetoric and public address (MA); secondary education (M Ed); studio art (MA); teaching Bible (MA); theology (MA, PhD); voice performance (MM); youth ministries (MA); M Div/MM.

Boise State University, College of Education, Department of Curriculum, Instruction and Foundational Studies, Boise, ID 83725-0399. Offers curriculum and instruction (Ed D); education, curriculum and instruction (MA); educational leadership (M Ed). *Accreditation:* NCATE. Part-time programs available. *Degree requirements:* For master's, thesis optional. *Entrance requirements:* For master's, minimum GPA of 3.0. Electronic applications accepted.

Boston College, Lynch Graduate School of Education, Program in Curriculum and Instruction, Chestnut Hill, MA 02467-3800. Offers M Ed, PhD, CAES, JD/M Ed. Part-time and evening/weekend programs available. *Students:* 51 full-time (38 women), 11 part-time (10 women). 196 applicants, 50% accepted, 62 enrolled. In 2013, 37 master's, 8 doctorates, 1 other advanced degree awarded. Terminal master's awarded for partial completion of doctoral program. *Degree requirements:* For master's and CAES, comprehensive exam; for doctorate, comprehensive exam, thesis/dissertation. *Entrance requirements:* For master's and CAES, GRE General Test or MAT; for doctorate, GRE General Test. Additional exam requirements/recommendations for international students: Required—TOEFL (minimum score 550 paper-based; 100 iBT). *Application deadline:* For fall admission, 12/1 priority date for domestic and international students; for spring admission, 11/1 for domestic and international students. Application fee: $65. Electronic applications accepted. *Financial support:* Fellowships with full and partial tuition reimbursements, research assistantships with full and partial tuition reimbursements, teaching assistantships with full and partial tuition reimbursements, career-related internships or fieldwork, Federal Work-Study, scholarships/grants, traineeships, health care benefits, tuition waivers (full and partial), and unspecified assistantships available. Support available to part-time students. Financial award applicants required to submit FAFSA. *Faculty research:* Literacy, bilingualism, urban education, technology and education, diversity and social justice in education. *Unit head:* Dr. Alec Peck, Chairperson, 617-552-4214, Fax: 617-552-0398. *Application contact:* Domenic Lomanno, Director, Graduate Admission and Financial Aid, 617-552-4214, Fax: 617-552-0398, E-mail: lomanno@bc.edu.
Website: http://www.bc.edu/schools/lsoe/academics/departments/teseci/graduate/curriculum.html.

Bowling Green State University, Graduate College, College of Education and Human Development, School of Education and Intervention Services, Teaching and Learning Division, Program in Curriculum and Teaching, Bowling Green, OH 43403. Offers curriculum (M Ed); master teaching (M Ed). Part-time and evening/weekend programs available. *Degree requirements:* For master's, thesis or alternative. *Entrance requirements:* For master's, GRE General Test or PRAXIS. Additional exam requirements/recommendations for international students: Required—TOEFL. Electronic applications accepted. *Faculty research:* Cognitive development in cultural context, sociocultural and activity theory, philosophy in education, performance assessment.

Bradley University, Graduate School, College of Education and Health Sciences, Department of Curriculum and Instruction, Peoria, IL 61625-0002. Offers MA, Certificate. *Accreditation:* NCATE. Part-time and evening/weekend programs available. *Degree requirements:* For master's, comprehensive exam, thesis optional. *Entrance requirements:* For master's, GRE General Test or MAT, 2 letters of recommendation. Additional exam requirements/recommendations for international students: Required—TOEFL (minimum score 550 paper-based; 79 iBT). *Expenses: Tuition:* Full-time $14,580; part-time $810 per credit hour. Tuition and fees vary according to course load and program.

Brandon University, Faculty of Education, Brandon, MB R7A 6A9, Canada. Offers curriculum and instruction (M Ed, Diploma); educational administration (M Ed, Diploma); guidance and counseling (M Ed, Diploma); special education (M Ed, Diploma). *Degree requirements:* For master's, thesis. *Entrance requirements:* For master's, minimum GPA of 3.0, teaching certificate or equivalent. Additional exam requirements/recommendations for international students: Required—TOEFL. *Faculty research:* Comparative education, environmental studies, parent/school council.

Brescia University, Program in Curriculum and Instruction, Owensboro, KY 42301-3023. Offers MSCI. Part-time and evening/weekend programs available. *Degree requirements:* For master's, action research project, portfolio. *Entrance requirements:* For master's, PRAXIS II, interview, minimum GPA of 2.5. Electronic applications accepted.

Buena Vista University, School of Education, Storm Lake, IA 50588. Offers curriculum and instruction (M Ed), including effective teaching, TESL; school guidance and counseling (MS Ed). Program offered in summer only. Part-time and evening/weekend programs available. Postbaccalaureate distance learning degree programs offered (minimal on-campus study). *Degree requirements:* For master's, thesis, fieldwork/practicum, capstone portfolio. *Entrance requirements:* For master's, Analytical Writing Assessment (in-house), minimum undergraduate GPA of 2.75. Electronic applications accepted. *Faculty research:* Reading, curriculum, educational psychology, special education.

Caldwell University, Graduate Studies, Division of Education, Caldwell, NJ 07006-6195. Offers curriculum and instruction (MA); education (Postbaccalaureate Certificate); educational administration (MA); learning disabilities teacher-consultant (Post-Master's Certificate); literacy instruction (MA); principal (Post-Master's Certificate); reading specialist (Post-Master's Certificate); special education (MA), including special education, teaching of students with disabilities, teaching of students with disabilities and learning disabilities teacher-consultant; superintendent (Post-Master's Certificate); supervisor (Post-Master's Certificate). Part-time and evening/weekend programs available. *Faculty:* 11 full-time (7 women), 12 part-time/adjunct (6 women). *Students:* 42 full-time (31 women), 255 part-time (219 women); includes 40 minority (14 Black or African American, non-Hispanic/Latino; 5 Asian, non-Hispanic/Latino; 18 Hispanic/Latino; 1 Native Hawaiian or other Pacific Islander, non-Hispanic/Latino; 2 Two or more races, non-Hispanic/Latino). Average age 37. 140 applicants, 71% accepted, 83 enrolled. In 2013, 63 master's awarded. *Degree requirements:* For master's, comprehensive exam (for some programs). *Entrance requirements:* For master's, PRAXIS, 3 years of work experience, prior teaching certification. Additional exam requirements/recommendations for international students: Required—TOEFL (minimum score 580 paper-based). *Application deadline:* Applications are processed on a rolling basis. Application fee: $40. Electronic applications accepted. *Financial support:* Career-related internships or fieldwork available. Financial award applicants required to submit FAFSA. *Faculty research:* Curriculum and instruction, secondary education, special education, education and technology. *Unit head:* Dr. Janice Stewart, Division Associate Dean, 973-618-3626, E-mail: jstewart@caldwell.edu. *Application contact:* Vilma Mueller, Director of Graduate Studies, 973-618-3544, E-mail: graduate@caldwell.edu.

California Baptist University, Program in Education, Riverside, CA 92504-3206. Offers educational leadership for faith-based institutions (MS); educational leadership for public institutions (MS); educational technology (MS); instructional computer applications (MS); international education (MS); leadership and adult learning (MS); leadership and organizational studies (MS); reading (MS); school counseling (MS); school psychology (MS); science education (MS); special education in mild/moderate disabilities (MS); special education in moderate/severe disabilities (MS); teaching (MS); teaching and learning (MS); TESOL (teachers of English to speakers of other languages) (MS). Part-time and evening/weekend programs available. Postbaccalaureate distance learning degree programs offered (minimal on-campus study). *Faculty:* 18 full-time (9 women), 8 part-time/adjunct (5 women). *Students:* 158 full-time (127 women), 228 part-time (179 women); includes 159 minority (27 Black or African American, non-Hispanic/Latino; 4 American Indian or Alaska Native, non-Hispanic/Latino; 13 Asian, non-Hispanic/Latino; 107 Hispanic/Latino; 1 Native Hawaiian or other Pacific Islander, non-Hispanic/Latino; 7 Two or more races, non-Hispanic/Latino), 2 international. Average age 33. 298 applicants, 74% accepted, 113 enrolled. In 2013, 70 master's awarded. *Degree requirements:* For master's, comprehensive exam, project, or thesis. *Entrance requirements:* For master's, minimum undergraduate GPA of 3.0; 18 semester units of prerequisite course work in education; three recommendations; 500-word essay; interview. Additional exam requirements/recommendations for international students: Required—TOEFL (minimum score 80 iBT). *Application deadline:* For fall admission, 8/1 priority date for domestic students, 7/1 for international students; for spring admission, 12/1 priority date for domestic students, 11/1 for international students. Applications are processed on a rolling basis. Application fee: $45. Electronic applications accepted. *Expenses:* Contact institution. *Financial support:* Institutionally sponsored loans available. Financial award applicants required to submit CSS PROFILE or FAFSA. *Faculty research:* Leadership development, complexity theory, faith and learning, special education, social and philosophical contexts of education. *Unit head:* Dr. John Shoup, Dean, School of Education, 951-343-4205, Fax: 951-343-4516, E-mail: jshoup@calbaptist.edu. *Application contact:* Dr. Kathryn Norwood, Director, Master of Science Program in Education, 951-343-4760, E-mail: knorwood@calbaptist.edu.
Website: http://www.calbaptist.edu/mastersined/.

California Coast University, School of Education, Santa Ana, CA 92701. Offers administration (M Ed); curriculum and instruction (M Ed); educational administration (Ed D); educational psychology (Ed D); organizational leadership (Ed D). Postbaccalaureate distance learning degree programs offered (no on-campus study).

California State Polytechnic University, Pomona, Academic Affairs, College of Education and Integrative Studies, Master's Programs in Education, Pomona, CA 91768-2557. Offers curriculum and instruction (MA); educational leadership (MA); educational multimedia (MA); special education (MA). *Students:* 39 full-time (26 women), 140 part-time (96 women); includes 91 minority (9 Black or African American, non-Hispanic/Latino; 1 American Indian or Alaska Native, non-Hispanic/Latino; 24 Asian, non-Hispanic/Latino; 53 Hispanic/Latino; 3 Native Hawaiian or other Pacific Islander, non-Hispanic/Latino; 1 Two or more races, non-Hispanic/Latino), 3 international. Average age 35. 64 applicants, 64% accepted, 25 enrolled. In 2013, 74 master's awarded. Application fee: $55. *Expenses:* Tuition, state resident: full-time $6738. Tuition, nonresident: full-time $12,690. *Required fees:* $878; $248 per credit hour. *Unit head:* Dr. Peggy Kelly, Dean, 909-869-2307, E-mail: pkelly@csupomona.edu. *Application contact:* Dr. Dorothy MacNevin, Co-Chair, Graduate Education Department, 909-869-2311, Fax: 909-869-4822, E-mail: dmacnevin@csupomona.edu.

California State University, Bakersfield, Division of Graduate Studies, Extended University Programs, Bakersfield, CA 93311. Offers administration (MS); curriculum and instruction (MA Ed). *Accreditation:* AACSB. Postbaccalaureate distance learning degree programs offered. *Degree requirements:* For master's, capstone course. *Entrance requirements:* For master's, resume, 3 letters of reference. Additional exam requirements/recommendations for international students: Required—TOEFL (minimum score 550 paper-based). Application fee: $75. *Unit head:* Rhonda Dawson, Director, 661-654-3489, Fax: 661-664-2447, E-mail: rdawson@csub.edu. *Application contact:* Debbie Blowers, Assistant Director of Admissions, 661-664-3381, E-mail: dblowers@csub.edu.
Website: http://www.csub.edu/regional/index.html.

California State University, Chico, Office of Graduate Studies, College of Communication and Education, School of Education, Option in Curriculum and Instruction, Chico, CA 95929-0722. Offers MA. *Degree requirements:* For master's, comprehensive exam, thesis or project. *Entrance requirements:* Additional exam requirements/recommendations for international students: Required—TOEFL (minimum score 550 paper-based; 80 iBT), IELTS (minimum score 6.5), PTE (minimum score 59). Electronic applications accepted.

California State University, Dominguez Hills, College of Education, Division of Graduate Education, Program in Curriculum and Instruction, Carson, CA 90747-0001. Offers MA. Part-time and evening/weekend programs available. *Faculty:* 3 full-time (2 women). *Students:* 39 full-time (28 women), 68 part-time (46 women); includes 76 minority (22 Black or African American, non-Hispanic/Latino; 3 Asian, non-Hispanic/Latino; 46 Hispanic/Latino; 5 Two or more races, non-Hispanic/Latino), 2 international. Average age 31. 54 applicants, 96% accepted, 45 enrolled. In 2013, 25 master's awarded. *Degree requirements:* For master's, comprehensive exam. *Entrance requirements:* For master's, minimum GPA of 2.75. Additional exam requirements/recommendations for international students: Required—TOEFL. *Application deadline:* For fall admission, 6/1 for domestic students. Applications are processed on a rolling basis. Application fee: $55. *Expenses:* Tuition, state resident: full-time $6738. Tuition, nonresident: full-time $13,434. *Required fees:* $622. *Faculty research:* Cooperative learning, student engagement. *Unit head:* Dr. Leena Furtado, Professor, 310-243-2743, E-mail: lfurtado@csudh.edu. *Application contact:* Admissions Office, 310-243-3530.
Website: http://www4.csudh.edu/coe/programs/grad-prgs/curriculum/index.

California State University, Fresno, Division of Graduate Studies, School of Education and Human Development, Department of Curriculum and Instruction, Fresno, CA 93740-8027. Offers education (MA), including curriculum and instruction. *Accreditation:* NCATE. Part-time and evening/weekend programs available. *Degree requirements:* For master's, thesis or alternative. *Entrance requirements:* For master's, GRE General Test, MAT, minimum GPA of 2.75. Additional exam requirements/recommendations for international students: Required—TOEFL. Electronic applications accepted. *Faculty research:* Teacher excellence, teacher quality improvement, online assessment.

California State University, Northridge, Graduate Studies, College of Education, Department of Elementary Education, Northridge, CA 91330. Offers curriculum and instruction (MA); language and literacy (MA); multilingual/multicultural education (MA); teaching and learning (MA). *Accreditation:* NCATE. Part-time and evening/weekend programs available. *Degree requirements:* For master's, comprehensive exam. *Entrance requirements:* For master's, GRE General Test or minimum GPA of 3.0. Additional exam requirements/recommendations for international students: Required—TOEFL.

Curriculum and Instruction

California State University, Sacramento, Office of Graduate Studies, College of Education, Department of Teacher Education, Sacramento, CA 95819. Offers behavioral sciences (MA), including gender equity studies; curriculum and instruction (MA); educational technology (MA); language and literacy (MA). Part-time programs available. *Entrance requirements:* Additional exam requirements/recommendations for international students: Required—TOEFL. *Application deadline:* For fall admission, 3/1 for domestic and international students; for spring admission, 9/15 for domestic students, 9/30 for international students. Applications are processed on a rolling basis. Application fee: $55. Electronic applications accepted. *Financial support:* Teaching assistantships, career-related internships or fieldwork, and Federal Work-Study available. Support available to part-time students. Financial award application deadline: 3/1; financial award applicants required to submit FAFSA. *Faculty research:* Technology integration and psychological implications for teaching and learning; inquiry-based research and learning in science and technology; uncovering the process of everyday creativity in teachers and other leaders; universal design as a foundation for inclusion; bullying, cyber-bullying and impact on school success; diversity, social justice in adult/ vocational education. *Unit head:* Dr. Rita Johnson, Chair, 916-278-4356, E-mail: rjohnson@csus.edu. *Application contact:* Jose Martinez, Graduate Admissions Supervisor, 916-278-7871, E-mail: martinj@skymail.csus.edu. Website: http://www.edweb.csus.edu/edte.

California State University, San Bernardino, Graduate Studies, College of Education, Program in Curriculum and Instruction, San Bernardino, CA 92407-2397. Offers MA. *Students:* 7 full-time (5 women), 10 part-time (5 women); includes 9 minority (8 Hispanic/ Latino; 1 Two or more races, non-Hispanic/Latino). Average age 30. 12 applicants, 67% accepted, 6 enrolled. In 2013, 16 master's awarded. *Degree requirements:* For master's, comprehensive exam (for some programs), thesis (for some programs). Application fee: $55. *Unit head:* Dr. Jay Fiene, Dean, 909-537-5600, Fax: 909-537-7510, E-mail: jfiene@ csusb.edu. *Application contact:* Dr. Jeffrey Thompson, Dean of Graduate Studies, 909-537-5058, E-mail: skamusik@csusb.edu.

California State University, Stanislaus, College of Education, Program in Education (MA), Turlock, CA 95382. Offers curriculum and instruction (MA), including education technology, elementary education, multilingual education, physical education, reading, secondary education, special education; school administration (MA); school counseling (MA). Part-time and evening/weekend programs available. *Degree requirements:* For master's, comprehensive exam (for some programs), thesis (for some programs). *Entrance requirements:* For master's, MAT, GRE, or CBEST (varies by concentration), 3 letters of recommendation, personal statement. Additional exam requirements/ recommendations for international students: Required—TOEFL (minimum score 550 paper-based). Electronic applications accepted. *Faculty research:* Children's perspectives on historical events, method elementary schools dual language education, K-12 reading programs.

Calvin College, Graduate Programs in Education, Grand Rapids, MI 49546-4388. Offers curriculum and instruction (M Ed); educational leadership (M Ed); learning disabilities (M Ed); literacy (M Ed). Part-time programs available. *Faculty:* 12 full-time (5 women). *Students:* 9 full-time (7 women), 133 part-time (87 women); includes 12 minority (3 Black or African American, non-Hispanic/Latino; 3 Asian, non-Hispanic/ Latino; 3 Hispanic/Latino; 3 Two or more races, non-Hispanic/Latino), 20 international. Average age 29. 15 applicants, 87% accepted, 13 enrolled. In 2013, 27 master's awarded. *Degree requirements:* For master's, thesis or seminar. *Entrance requirements:* For master's, teaching certificate. Additional exam requirements/recommendations for international students: Required—TOEFL (minimum score 550 paper-based; 80 iBT). *Application deadline:* For fall admission, 8/1 priority date for domestic students, 5/1 priority date for international students; for spring admission, 1/1 priority date for domestic students, 12/1 priority date for international students; for summer admission, 5/18 for domestic students. Applications are processed on a rolling basis. Application fee: $0. Electronic applications accepted. *Financial support:* Federal Work-Study, scholarships/ grants, and tuition waivers (full and partial) available. Financial award application deadline: 4/3; financial award applicants required to submit FAFSA. *Faculty research:* Literacy, racialized gender and gendered identity, teacher learning, learning disabilities identification, leadership. *Unit head:* Dr. David Smith, Graduate Program Director, 616-526-6158, Fax: 616-526-6505, E-mail: dsmith@calvin.edu. *Application contact:* Cindi Hoekstra, Program Coordinator, 616-526-6158, Fax: 616-526-6505, E-mail: choekstr@ calvin.edu. Website: http://www.calvin.edu/academic/graduate_studies.

Cambridge College, School of Education, Cambridge, MA 02138-5304. Offers autism specialist (M Ed); autism/behavior analyst (M Ed); behavior analyst (Post-Master's Certificate); behavioral management (M Ed); early childhood teacher (M Ed); education specialist in curriculum and instruction (CAGS); educational leadership (Ed D); elementary teacher (M Ed); English as a second language (M Ed, Certificate); general science (M Ed); health education (Post-Master's Certificate); health/family and consumer sciences (M Ed); history (M Ed); individualized (M Ed); information technology literacy (M Ed); instructional technology (M Ed); interdisciplinary studies (M Ed); library teacher (M Ed); literacy education (M Ed); mathematics (M Ed); mathematics specialist (Certificate); middle school mathematics and science (M Ed); school administration (M Ed, CAGS); school guidance counselor (M Ed); school nurse education (M Ed); school social worker/school adjustment counselor (M Ed); special education administrator (CAGS); special education/moderate disabilities (M Ed); teaching skills and methodologies (M Ed). Part-time and evening/weekend programs available. Postbaccalaureate distance learning degree programs offered (minimal on-campus study). *Degree requirements:* For master's, thesis, internship/practicum (licensure program only); for doctorate, thesis/dissertation; for other advanced degree, thesis. *Entrance requirements:* For master's, interview, resume, documentation of licensure, 2 professional references; for doctorate, official transcripts, interview, resume, documentation of licensure (if any), written personal statement/essay, portfolio of scholarly and professional work, qualifying assessment, 2 professional references, health insurance, immunizations form; for other advanced degree, official transcripts, interview, resume, documentation of licensure (if any), written personal statement/ essay, 2 professional references, health insurance, immunizations form. Additional exam requirements/recommendations for international students: Required—TOEFL (minimum score 550 paper-based; 79 iBT), Michigan English Language Assessment Battery (minimum score 85); Recommended—IELTS (minimum score 6). Electronic applications accepted. *Expenses:* Contact institution. *Faculty research:* Adult education, accelerated learning, mathematics education, brain compatible learning, special education and law.

Campbellsville University, School of Education, Campbellsville, KY 42718-2799. Offers curriculum and instruction (MAE); special education (MASE). *Accreditation:* NCATE. Part-time and evening/weekend programs available. Postbaccalaureate distance learning degree programs offered (minimal on-campus study). *Degree requirements:* For master's, thesis, research paper. *Entrance requirements:* For master's, GRE or PRAXIS, minimum undergraduate GPA of 2.75, teaching certificate, professional growth plan, letters of recommendation, disposition assessment, interview. Electronic applications accepted. *Faculty research:* Professional development, curriculum development, school governance, assessment, special education.

Capella University, School of Education, Doctoral Programs in Education, Minneapolis, MN 55402. Offers curriculum and instruction (PhD); educational leadership and management (Ed D); instructional design for online learning (PhD); K-12 studies in education (PhD); leadership for higher education (PhD); leadership in educational administration (PhD); postsecondary and adult education (PhD); professional studies in education (PhD); reading and literacy (Ed D); special education leadership (PhD); training and performance improvement (PhD).

Capella University, School of Education, Master's Programs in Education, Minneapolis, MN 55402. Offers adult education (MS); curriculum and instruction (MS); early childhood education (MS); enrollment management (MS); higher education leadership and management (MS); instructional design for online learning (MS); integrative studies (MS); K-12 studies in education (MS); leadership in educational administration (MS); reading and literacy (MS); special education teaching (MS).

Caribbean University, Graduate School, Bayamón, PR 00960-0493. Offers administration and supervision (MA Ed); criminal justice (MA); curriculum and instruction (MA Ed, PhD), including elementary education (MA Ed), English education (MA Ed), history education (MA Ed), mathematics education (MA Ed), primary education (MA Ed), science education (MA Ed), Spanish education (MA Ed); educational technology in instructional systems (MA Ed); gerontology (MSN); human resources (MBA); museology, archiving and art history (MA Ed); neonatal pediatrics (MSN); physical education (MA Ed); special education (MA Ed). *Entrance requirements:* For master's, interview, minimum GPA of 2.5.

Carson-Newman University, Graduate Program in Education, Jefferson City, TN 37760. Offers curriculum and instruction (M Ed); educational leadership (M Ed); elementary education (MAT); school counseling (MS); secondary education (MAT); teaching English as a second language (MATESL). *Accreditation:* NCATE. Part-time and evening/weekend programs available. *Faculty:* 5 full-time (2 women), 10 part-time/ adjunct (3 women). *Students:* 25 full-time (12 women), 100 part-time (70 women); includes 8 minority (4 Black or African American, non-Hispanic/Latino; 1 Asian, non-Hispanic/Latino; 1 Hispanic/Latino; 2 Two or more races, non-Hispanic/Latino), 1 international. Average age 32. In 2013, 34 master's awarded. *Degree requirements:* For master's, thesis or alternative. *Entrance requirements:* For master's, NTE, minimum GPA of 3.0 in major, 2.5 overall. *Application deadline:* For fall admission, 7/15 priority date for domestic students. Applications are processed on a rolling basis. Application fee: $25 ($50 for international students). *Expenses: Tuition:* Part-time $390 per credit hour. *Financial support:* Federal Work-Study and unspecified assistantships available. Financial award application deadline: 4/1; financial award applicants required to submit FAFSA. *Unit head:* Dr. Sharon Teets, Chair, 865-471-3461. *Application contact:* Graduate Admissions and Services Adviser, 865-471-3460, Fax: 865-471-3875.

Castleton State College, Division of Graduate Studies, Department of Education, Program in Curriculum and Instruction, Castleton, VT 05735. Offers MA Ed. Part-time and evening/weekend programs available. *Degree requirements:* For master's, thesis or alternative. *Entrance requirements:* For master's, GRE General Test, MAT, interview, minimum undergraduate GPA of 3.0.

Cedarville University, Graduate Programs, Cedarville, OH 45314-0601. Offers business administration (MBA); curriculum (M Ed); educational administration (M Ed); family nurse practitioner (MSN); global health ministries (MSN); instruction (M Ed); pharmacy (Pharm D). Part-time programs available. Postbaccalaureate distance learning degree programs offered (no on-campus study). *Faculty:* 23 full-time (12 women), 12 part-time/adjunct (5 women). *Students:* 119 full-time (74 women), 103 part-time (73 women); includes 16 minority (11 Black or African American, non-Hispanic/ Latino; 4 Asian, non-Hispanic/Latino; 1 Native Hawaiian or other Pacific Islander, non-Hispanic/Latino), 4 international. Average age 31. In 2013, 26 master's awarded. *Degree requirements:* For master's, thesis. *Entrance requirements:* For master's, GRE, 2 professional recommendations; for doctorate, PCAT, professional recommendation from a practicing pharmacist or current employer/supervisor, resume, essay, interview. Additional exam requirements/recommendations for international students: Required— TOEFL (minimum score 550 paper-based; 80 iBT). *Application deadline:* For fall admission, 5/1 priority date for domestic and international students; for spring admission, 11/1 priority date for domestic and international students. Applications are processed on a rolling basis. Application fee: $30. Electronic applications accepted. *Financial support:* Scholarships/grants and unspecified assistantships available. Support available to part-time students. Financial award applicants required to submit FAFSA. *Unit head:* Dr. Mark McClain, Dean of Graduate Studies, 937-766-7700, E-mail: mcclain@cedarville.edu. *Application contact:* Roscoe F. Smith, Associate Vice-President of Enrollment, 937-766-7700, Fax: 937-766-7575, E-mail: smithr@ cedarville.edu. Website: http://www.cedarville.edu/academics/graduate/.

Centenary College of Louisiana, Graduate Programs, Department of Education, Shreveport, LA 71104. Offers administration (M Ed); elementary education (MAT); secondary education (MAT); supervision of instruction (M Ed). Part-time and evening/ weekend programs available. *Degree requirements:* For master's, comprehensive exam. *Entrance requirements:* For master's, GRE General Test (M Ed), PRAXIS I and PRAXIS II (MAT), teacher certification (M Ed), minimum GPA of 2.5. *Expenses:* Contact institution. *Faculty research:* Teachers as advocates for teachers, portfolio assessment, disabled readers.

Central Michigan University, Central Michigan University Global Campus, Program in Education, Mount Pleasant, MI 48859. Offers college teaching (Graduate Certificate); community college (MA); curriculum and instruction (MA); educational technology (MA); guidance and development (MA); reading and literacy K-12 (MA); school principalship (MA), including charter school leadership; training and development (MA). *Accreditation:* Teacher Education Accreditation Council. Part-time and evening/weekend programs available. *Entrance requirements:* For master's, minimum GPA of 2.7 in major. Additional exam requirements/recommendations for international students: Required— TOEFL. *Application deadline:* Applications are processed on a rolling basis. Application fee: $50. Electronic applications accepted. *Financial support:* Scholarships/grants available. Support available to part-time students. *Unit head:* Kaleb Patrick, Director, 989-774-3144, E-mail: patri1kg@cmich.edu. *Application contact:* 877-268-4636, E-mail: cmuglobal@cmich.edu.

Central Michigan University, College of Graduate Studies, College of Education and Human Services, Department of Educational Leadership, Mount Pleasant, MI 48859. Offers educational leadership (Ed D), including educational technology (Ed D, Ed S), higher education leadership, K-12 curriculum, K-12 leadership; general educational administration (Ed S), including administrative leadership K-12, educational technology (Ed D, Ed S), higher education administration, instructional leadership K-12; school principalship (MA), including charter school leadership, site-based leadership; student affairs administration (MA); teacher leadership (MA). Part-time and evening/weekend programs available. *Degree requirements:* For master's and Ed S, thesis or alternative; for doctorate, thesis/dissertation. *Entrance requirements:* For doctorate, GRE or MAT, master's degree, minimum GPA of 3.5, 3 years of professional education experience. Electronic applications accepted. *Faculty research:* Elementary administration,

secondary administration, student achievement, in-service training, internships in administration.

Central Washington University, Graduate Studies and Research, College of Education and Professional Studies, Department of Educational Foundations and Curriculum, Program in Master Teacher, Ellensburg, WA 98926. Offers M Ed. Part-time programs available. *Degree requirements:* For master's, comprehensive exam (for some programs), thesis or alternative. *Entrance requirements:* For master's, minimum GPA of 3.0, 1 year of contracted teaching experience. Additional exam requirements/recommendations for international students: Required—TOEFL (minimum score 550 paper-based; 79 iBT), IELTS (minimum score 6.5). Electronic applications accepted.

Chapman University, College of Educational Studies, Orange, CA 92866. Offers communication sciences and disorders (MS); counseling (MA), including school counseling (MA, Credential); education (PhD), including cultural and curricular studies, disability studies, leadership studies, school psychology (PhD, Credential); educational psychology (MA); leadership development (MA); pupil personnel services (Credential), including school counseling (MA, Credential), school psychology (PhD, Credential); school psychology (Ed S); single subject (Credential); special education (MA, Credential), including mild/moderate (Credential), moderate/severe (Credential); speech language pathology (Credential); teaching (MA), including elementary education, secondary education. *Accreditation:* Teacher Education Accreditation Council. Part-time and evening/weekend programs available. *Faculty:* 29 full-time (18 women), 56 part-time/adjunct (38 women). *Students:* 251 full-time (208 women), 194 part-time (150 women); includes 185 minority (13 Black or African American, non-Hispanic/Latino; 61 Asian, non-Hispanic/Latino; 97 Hispanic/Latino; 1 Native Hawaiian or other Pacific Islander, non-Hispanic/Latino; 13 Two or more races, non-Hispanic/Latino), 7 international. Average age 29. 580 applicants, 42% accepted, 166 enrolled. In 2013, 140 master's, 10 doctorates awarded. *Entrance requirements:* Additional exam requirements/recommendations for international students: Required—TOEFL (minimum score 550 paper-based; 80 iBT). *Application deadline:* Applications are processed on a rolling basis. Application fee: $60. Electronic applications accepted. Tuition and fees vary according to program. *Financial support:* Fellowships and scholarships/grants available. Financial award application deadline: 6/30; financial award applicants required to submit FAFSA. *Unit head:* Dr. Don Cardinal, Dean, 714-997-6781, E-mail: cardinal@chapman.edu. *Application contact:* Admissions Coordinator, 714-997-6714.
Website: http://www.chapman.edu/CES/.

City University of Seattle, Graduate Division, Albright School of Education, Bellevue, WA 98005. Offers administrator certification (Certificate); curriculum and instruction (M Ed); educational leadership (Ed D); elementary education (MIT); guidance and counseling (M Ed); higher education leadership (Ed D); leadership (M Ed); leadership and school counseling (M Ed); organizational leadership (Ed D); reading and literacy (M Ed); special education (MIT); superintendent certification (Certificate). Part-time and evening/weekend programs available. Postbaccalaureate distance learning degree programs offered (no on-campus study). *Degree requirements:* For master's, comprehensive exam (for some programs), thesis (for some programs); for doctorate, comprehensive exam, thesis/dissertation. *Entrance requirements:* Additional exam requirements/recommendations for international students: Required—TOEFL (minimum score 567 paper-based; 87 iBT); Recommended—IELTS. Electronic applications accepted. *Expenses:* Contact institution.

Clarion University of Pennsylvania, Office of Transfer, Adult and Graduate Admissions, Master of Education Program, Clarion, PA 16214. Offers curriculum and instruction (M Ed); early childhood (M Ed); math education (M Ed); reading (M Ed); science education (M Ed); special education (M Ed); technology (M Ed). *Accreditation:* NCATE. Part-time programs available. Postbaccalaureate distance learning degree programs offered (no on-campus study). *Faculty:* 17 full-time (10 women). *Students:* 231 full-time (191 women), 535 part-time (448 women); includes 39 minority (12 Black or African American, non-Hispanic/Latino; 8 Asian, non-Hispanic/Latino; 11 Hispanic/Latino; 1 Native Hawaiian or other Pacific Islander, non-Hispanic/Latino; 7 Two or more races, non-Hispanic/Latino). Average age 31. 28 applicants, 75% accepted, 18 enrolled. In 2013, 99 master's awarded. *Degree requirements:* For master's, comprehensive exam, thesis, or portfolio. *Entrance requirements:* For master's, minimum QPA of 3.0. Additional exam requirements/recommendations for international students: Required—TOEFL (minimum score 550 paper-based; 80 iBT), IELTS (minimum score 7). *Application deadline:* For fall admission, 8/1 for domestic students, 4/15 for international students; for spring admission, 8/1 for domestic students, 9/15 for international students. Applications are processed on a rolling basis. Application fee: $40. Electronic applications accepted. *Expenses:* Tuition, state resident: part-time $442 per credit. Tuition, nonresident: part-time $451 per credit. *Required fees:* $142.40 per semester. One-time fee: $150 part-time. *Financial support:* In 2013–14, 8 research assistantships with full and partial tuition reimbursements (averaging $9,420 per year) were awarded; career-related internships or fieldwork also available. Support available to part-time students. Financial award application deadline: 3/1. *Unit head:* Ray Puller, Interim Dean, 814-393-2146, Fax: 514-393-2446, E-mail: rpuller@clarion.edu. *Application contact:* Susan Staub, Assistant Director, Graduate Programs, 814-393-2337, Fax: 814-393-2722, E-mail: gradstudies@clarion.edu.
Website: http://www.clarion.edu/25887/.

Clark Atlanta University, School of Education, Department of Curriculum, Atlanta, GA 30314. Offers special education general curriculum (MA); teaching math and science (MAT). Part-time programs available. *Faculty:* 2 full-time (1 woman), 1 (woman) part-time/adjunct. *Students:* 9 full-time (8 women), 3 part-time (1 woman); includes 11 minority (all Black or African American, non-Hispanic/Latino). Average age 28. 8 applicants, 88% accepted, 7 enrolled. In 2013, 4 master's awarded. *Degree requirements:* For master's, one foreign language, comprehensive exam. *Entrance requirements:* For master's, GRE General Test, minimum undergraduate GPA of 2.6. Additional exam requirements/recommendations for international students: Required—TOEFL (minimum score 500 paper-based; 61 iBT). *Application deadline:* For fall admission, 4/1 for domestic and international students; for spring admission, 11/1 for domestic and international students. Applications are processed on a rolling basis. Application fee: $40 ($55 for international students). *Expenses: Tuition:* Full-time $14,616; part-time $812 per credit hour. *Required fees:* $706; $353 per semester. *Financial support:* Career-related internships or fieldwork, Federal Work-Study, scholarships/grants, and unspecified assistantships available. Support available to part-time students. Financial award application deadline: 4/30; financial award applicants required to submit FAFSA. *Unit head:* Dr. Doris Terrell, Chairperson, 404-880-6336, E-mail: dterrell@cau.edu. *Application contact:* Michelle Clark-Davis, Graduate Program Admissions, 404-880-6605, E-mail: cauadmissions@cau.edu.
Website: http://www.cau.edu/School_of_Education_curriculum_dept.aspx.

Clemson University, Graduate School, College of Health, Education, and Human Development, Eugene T. Moore School of Education, Program in Curriculum and Instruction, Clemson, SC 29634. Offers PhD. *Accreditation:* NCATE. Part-time and evening/weekend programs available. *Students:* 24 full-time (14 women), 17 part-time (12 women); includes 3 minority (all Black or African American, non-Hispanic/Latino), 5 international. Average age 37. 21 applicants, 52% accepted, 5 enrolled. In 2013, 4 doctorates awarded. *Degree requirements:* For doctorate, comprehensive exam, thesis/dissertation. *Entrance requirements:* For doctorate, GRE General Test, teaching certificate; 3 years of teaching experience. Additional exam requirements/recommendations for international students: Required—TOEFL; Recommended—IELTS. *Application deadline:* For fall admission, 3/1 for domestic and international students; for spring admission, 10/1 for domestic and international students. Applications are processed on a rolling basis. Application fee: $70 ($80 for international students). Electronic applications accepted. *Expenses:* Contact institution. *Financial support:* In 2013–14, 28 students received support, including 3 fellowships with full and partial tuition reimbursements available (averaging $5,000 per year), 6 research assistantships with partial tuition reimbursements available (averaging $12,118 per year), 11 teaching assistantships with partial tuition reimbursements available (averaging $22,636 per year); institutionally sponsored loans, health care benefits, and unspecified assistantships also available. Financial award application deadline: 3/1; financial award applicants required to submit FAFSA. *Faculty research:* Elementary and early childhood education, secondary education (English, math, social studies, and science), special education, reading and literacy. *Unit head:* Dr. Michael J. Padilla, Director/Associate Dean, 864-656-4444, Fax: 864-656-0311, E-mail: padilla@clemson.edu. *Application contact:* Dr. David Fleming, Graduate Coordinator, 864-656-1881, Fax: 864-656-0311, E-mail: dflemin@clemson.edu.
Website: http://www.grad.clemson.edu/programs/Curriculum-Instruction/.

The College at Brockport, State University of New York, School of Education and Human Services, Department of Education and Human Development, Program in Childhood Curriculum Specialist, Brockport, NY 14420-2997. Offers MS Ed. *Accreditation:* NCATE. Part-time programs available. *Students:* 1 (woman) full-time, 18 part-time (13 women); includes 3 minority (1 Asian, non-Hispanic/Latino; 1 Hispanic/Latino; 1 Two or more races, non-Hispanic/Latino). 1 applicant, 100% accepted. In 2013, 11 master's awarded. *Degree requirements:* For master's, thesis or alternative. *Entrance requirements:* For master's, minimum GPA of 3.0, letters of recommendation; statement of objectives; current resume. Additional exam requirements/recommendations for international students: Required—TOEFL (minimum score 550 paper-based; 79 iBT), IELTS (minimum score 6.5). *Application deadline:* For fall admission, 3/15 priority date for domestic and international students; for spring admission, 10/15 priority date for domestic and international students. Application fee: $80. Electronic applications accepted. *Expenses:* Tuition, state resident: full-time $9870. Tuition, nonresident: full-time $18,350. *Required fees:* $1848. *Financial support:* Federal Work-Study, scholarships/grants, and unspecified assistantships available. Support available to part-time students. Financial award application deadline: 3/15; financial award applicants required to submit FAFSA. *Unit head:* Dr. Don Halquist, Chairperson, 585-395-5550, Fax: 585-395-2172, E-mail: snovinge@brockport.edu. *Application contact:* Michael Harrison, Coordinator of Certification and Graduate Advisement, 585-395-2326, Fax: 585-395-2172, E-mail: mharriso@brockport.edu.
Website: http://www.brockport.edu/ehd.

The College of Idaho, Department of Education, Caldwell, ID 83605. Offers teaching (MAT); M Div/MPPM. *Degree requirements:* For master's, thesis. *Entrance requirements:* For master's, GRE, portfolio, minimum undergraduate GPA of 3.0, interview. *Faculty research:* Discourse analysis, at-risk youth, children's literature, research design, program evaluation.

The College of Saint Rose, Graduate Studies, School of Education, Department of Teacher Education, Albany, NY 12203-1419. Offers adolescence education (MS Ed); childhood education (MS Ed); curriculum and instruction (MS Ed); early childhood education (MS Ed). Part-time and evening/weekend programs available. *Entrance requirements:* For master's, minimum undergraduate GPA of 3.0. Additional exam requirements/recommendations for international students: Required—TOEFL (minimum score 550 paper-based). Electronic applications accepted.

The College of William and Mary, School of Education, Program in Curriculum and Instruction, Williamsburg, VA 23187-8795. Offers elementary education (MA Ed); gifted education (MA Ed); literacy leadership (MA Ed); math specialist (MA Ed); secondary education (MA Ed), including English education, mathematics education, modern foreign languages education, science education, social studies education; special education (MA Ed), including collaborating master educator, general curriculum. *Accreditation:* NCATE. Part-time programs available. *Faculty:* 15 full-time (10 women), 44 part-time/adjunct (38 women). *Students:* 66 full-time (55 women), 27 part-time (26 women); includes 17 minority (4 Black or African American, non-Hispanic/Latino; 1 American Indian or Alaska Native, non-Hispanic/Latino; 3 Asian, non-Hispanic/Latino; 5 Hispanic/Latino; 4 Two or more races, non-Hispanic/Latino). Average age 28. 179 applicants, 72% accepted, 92 enrolled. In 2013, 76 master's awarded. *Degree requirements:* For master's, project. *Entrance requirements:* For master's, GRE or MAT, minimum GPA of 2.5. Additional exam requirements/recommendations for international students: Required—TOEFL, IELTS. *Application deadline:* For fall admission, 1/15 for domestic and international students; for spring admission, 10/1 for domestic and international students. Application fee: $50. Electronic applications accepted. *Expenses:* Tuition, state resident: full-time $7120; part-time $405 per credit hour. Tuition, nonresident: full-time $21,639; part-time $1050 per credit hour. *Required fees:* $4764. *Financial support:* In 2013–14, 49 students received support, including 6 research assistantships with full and partial tuition reimbursements available (averaging $8,269 per year); career-related internships or fieldwork, Federal Work-Study, institutionally sponsored loans, scholarships/grants, and unspecified assistantships also available. Financial award application deadline: 1/15; financial award applicants required to submit FAFSA. *Faculty research:* National Council of Teachers of Mathematics standards, counseling, self-concept and self-esteem, special education, curriculum development. *Unit head:* Dr. Mark Hofer, Area Coordinator, 757-221-1713, E-mail: mjhofe@wm.edu. *Application contact:* Dorothy Smith Osborne, Assistant Dean for Academic Programs and Student Services, 757-221-2317, Fax: 757-221-2293, E-mail: dsosbo@wm.edu.
Website: http://education.wm.edu.

The College of William and Mary, School of Education, Program in Education Policy, Planning, and Leadership, Williamsburg, VA 23187-8795. Offers curriculum and educational technology (Ed D, PhD); curriculum leadership (Ed D, PhD); educational leadership (M Ed), including higher education administration (M Ed, Ed D, PhD), K-12 administration and supervision; educational policy, planning, and leadership (Ed D, PhD), including general education administration, gifted education administration, higher education administration (M Ed, Ed D, PhD). *Accreditation:* NCATE. Part-time and evening/weekend programs available. *Faculty:* 10 full-time (5 women), 17 part-time/adjunct (13 women). *Students:* 64 full-time (52 women), 145 part-time (106 women); includes 46 minority (33 Black or African American, non-Hispanic/Latino; 3 Asian, non-Hispanic/Latino; 4 Hispanic/Latino; 6 Two or more races, non-Hispanic/Latino), 9 international. Average age 38. 133 applicants, 74% accepted, 72 enrolled. In 2013, 24 master's, 17 doctorates awarded. *Degree requirements:* For doctorate, comprehensive exam, thesis/dissertation. *Entrance requirements:* For master's, GRE or MAT, minimum GPA of 2.5; for doctorate, GRE or MAT, minimum GPA of 3.0. Additional exam requirements/recommendations for international students: Required—TOEFL, IELTS. *Application deadline:* For fall admission, 1/15 for domestic and international students. Application fee: $50. Electronic applications accepted. *Expenses:* Tuition, state resident: full-time $7120; part-time $405 per credit hour. Tuition, nonresident: full-time

$21,639; part-time $1050 per credit hour. *Required fees:* $4764. *Financial support:* In 2013–14, 58 students received support, including 1 fellowship (averaging $20,000 per year), 51 research assistantships with full and partial tuition reimbursements available (averaging $16,551 per year); career-related internships or fieldwork, Federal Work-Study, institutionally sponsored loans, scholarships/grants, and unspecified assistantships also available. Support available to part-time students. Financial award application deadline: 1/15; financial award applicants required to submit FAFSA. *Faculty research:* Higher education policy, faculty incentives, history of adversity, resilience, leadership. *Unit head:* Dr. James Stronge, Area Coordinator, 757-221-2339, E-mail: jhstro@wm.edu. *Application contact:* Dorothy Smith Osborne, Assistant Dean for Academic Programs and Student Services, 757-221-2317, Fax: 757-221-2293, E-mail: dsosbo@wm.edu.
Website: http://education.wm.edu.

Colorado Christian University, Program in Curriculum and Instruction, Lakewood, CO 80226. Offers corporate education (MACI); early childhood educator (MACI); elementary educator (MACI); instructional technology (MACI); master educator (MACI); online course developer (MACI); online teaching and learning (MACI); special education generalist (MACI). Part-time and evening/weekend programs available. *Degree requirements:* For master's, thesis optional, practicum. *Entrance requirements:* For master's, interviews, letters of recommendation. Additional exam requirements/recommendations for international students: Required—TOEFL. Electronic applications accepted. *Expenses:* Contact institution.

Columbia International University, Columbia Graduate School, Columbia, SC 29230-3122. Offers Bible teaching (MABT); Christian higher education leadership (Ed D); Christian school educational leadership (Ed D); counseling (MACN); curriculum and instruction (M Ed), including Christian school guidance, English as a second language, learning disabilities, school technology; early childhood and elementary education (MAT); educational administration (M Ed); teaching English as a foreign language (Certificate); teaching English as a foreign language and intercultural studies (MATF). Part-time and evening/weekend programs available. *Degree requirements:* For master's, internships, professional project. *Entrance requirements:* For master's, Minnesota Multiphasic Personality Inventory, MAT, minimum GPA of 2.7. Additional exam requirements/recommendations for international students: Required—TOEFL. Electronic applications accepted.

Columbus State University, Graduate Studies, College of Education and Health Professions, Department of Counseling, Foundations, and Leadership, Columbus, GA 31907-5645. Offers community counseling (MS); curriculum and leadership (Ed D); educational leadership (M Ed, Ed S); higher education (M Ed); school counseling (M Ed, Ed S). *Accreditation:* ACA; NCATE. Part-time and evening/weekend programs available. Postbaccalaureate distance learning degree programs offered (minimal on-campus study). *Faculty:* 13 full-time (5 women), 11 part-time/adjunct (7 women). *Students:* 94 full-time (64 women), 120 part-time (96 women); includes 95 minority (78 Black or African American, non-Hispanic/Latino; 1 American Indian or Alaska Native, non-Hispanic/Latino; 2 Asian, non-Hispanic/Latino; 9 Hispanic/Latino; 5 Two or more races, non-Hispanic/Latino). Average age 35. 139 applicants, 58% accepted, 49 enrolled. In 2013, 44 master's, 4 doctorates, 14 other advanced degrees awarded. *Degree requirements:* For master's, thesis, exit exam; for doctorate, comprehensive exam, thesis/dissertation; for Ed S, thesis or alternative. *Entrance requirements:* For master's, GRE General Test, minimum undergraduate GPA of 2.75; for doctorate, GRE General Test, minimum graduate GPA of 3.5, four years of professional service; for Ed S, GRE General Test, minimum undergraduate GPA of 2.75, graduate 3.0. Additional exam requirements/recommendations for international students: Required—TOEFL (minimum score 550 paper-based; 79 iBT). *Application deadline:* For fall admission, 6/30 for domestic and international students; for spring admission, 11/1 for domestic and international students; for summer admission, 3/1 for domestic and international students. Applications are processed on a rolling basis. Application fee: $40. Electronic applications accepted. *Expenses:* Tuition, state resident: full-time $4572; part-time $382 per credit hour. Tuition, nonresident: full-time $18,292; part-time $1526 per credit hour. *Required fees:* $1800; $196 per credit hour. Tuition and fees vary according to campus/location and program. *Financial support:* In 2013–14, 143 students received support, including 9 research assistantships with partial tuition reimbursements available (averaging $3,000 per year); career-related internships or fieldwork, Federal Work-Study, institutionally sponsored loans, scholarships/grants, tuition waivers (partial), and unspecified assistantships also available. Support available to part-time students. Financial award application deadline: 5/1; financial award applicants required to submit FAFSA. *Unit head:* Dr. Michael L. Baltimore, Department Chair, 706-569-3013, Fax: 706-569-3134, E-mail: baltimore_michael@columbusstate.edu. *Application contact:* Kristin Williams, Director of International and Graduate Recruitment, 706-507-8848, Fax: 706-568-5091, E-mail: williams_kristin@columbusstate.edu.
Website: http://cfl.columbusstate.edu/.

Concordia University, College of Education, Portland, OR 97211-6099. Offers career and technical education (M Ed); curriculum and instruction (M Ed), including adolescent literacy, career and technical education, e-learning/technology education, early childhood education, English for speakers of other languages, English language development, environmental education, mathematics, methods and curriculum, reading, science, teacher leadership, the inclusive classroom; early childhood (MAT); education leadership (Ed D); educational administration (M Ed); elementary education (MAT); secondary education (MAT); special education (M Ed); teacher leadership (Ed D). Part-time programs available. Postbaccalaureate distance learning degree programs offered (no on-campus study). *Degree requirements:* For master's, comprehensive exam, work samples/portfolio. *Entrance requirements:* For master's, California Basic Educational Skills Test or PRAXIS I, minimum undergraduate GPA of 2.8, graduate 3.0; 2 letters of recommendation. Additional exam requirements/recommendations for international students: Required—TOEFL (minimum score 525 paper-based). Electronic applications accepted. *Faculty research:* Learner-centered classroom, brain-based learning, future of online learning.

Concordia University, School of Education, Irvine, CA 92612-3299. Offers curriculum and instruction (MA); education and preliminary teaching credential (M Ed); educational administration and preliminary administrative services credential (MA); educational technology (MA); school counseling with pupil personnel services credential (MA). Part-time and evening/weekend programs available. Postbaccalaureate distance learning degree programs offered (no on-campus study). *Faculty:* 15 full-time (12 women), 96 part-time/adjunct (59 women). *Students:* 885 full-time (690 women), 96 part-time (74 women); includes 282 minority (39 Black or African American, non-Hispanic/Latino; 42 Asian, non-Hispanic/Latino; 182 Hispanic/Latino; 3 Native Hawaiian or other Pacific Islander, non-Hispanic/Latino; 16 Two or more races, non-Hispanic/Latino), 1 international. Average age 39. 402 applicants, 79% accepted, 311 enrolled. In 2013, 469 master's awarded. *Degree requirements:* For master's, action research project. *Entrance requirements:* For master's, California Basic Educational Skills Test, California Subject Examinations for Teachers (M Ed and MA in educational administration and preliminary administrative services credential), official college transcript(s), signed statement of intent, two references, copy of credential. Additional exam requirements/recommendations for international students: Required—TOEFL. *Application deadline:* For fall admission, 7/15 priority date for domestic students, 6/1 for international students; for spring admission, 11/30 priority date for domestic students, 10/1 for international students. Applications are processed on a rolling basis. Application fee: $50 ($125 for international students). Electronic applications accepted. *Expenses:* Contact institution. *Financial support:* In 2013–14, 23 students received support. Scholarships/grants and unspecified assistantships available. Financial award applicants required to submit FAFSA. *Unit head:* Dr. Janice Nelson, Dean, 949-214-3334, E-mail: janice.nelson@cui.edu. *Application contact:* Patty Hunt, Admissions Coordinator, 949-214-3362, Fax: 949-214-3362, E-mail: patricia.hunt@cui.edu.

Concordia University Ann Arbor, Graduate Programs, Ann Arbor, MI 48105-2797. Offers curriculum and instruction (MS); educational leadership (MS); organizational leadership and administration (MS). Part-time and evening/weekend programs available. *Degree requirements:* For master's, thesis. *Entrance requirements:* Additional exam requirements/recommendations for international students: Required—TOEFL (minimum score 80 iBT); Recommended—IELTS (minimum score 6.5). Electronic applications accepted.

Concordia University Chicago, College of Education, Program in Curriculum and Instruction, River Forest, IL 60305-1499. Offers MA. MA offered jointly with the Chicago Consortium of Colleges and Universities. *Accreditation:* NCATE. Part-time and evening/weekend programs available. *Degree requirements:* For master's, comprehensive exam, thesis. *Entrance requirements:* For master's, minimum GPA of 2.9. Additional exam requirements/recommendations for international students: Required—TOEFL (minimum score 550 paper-based). Electronic applications accepted. *Faculty research:* School discipline, school improvement, leadership.

Concordia University, St. Paul, College of Education and Science, St. Paul, MN 55104-5494. Offers curriculum and instruction (MA Ed), including K-12 reading; differentiated instruction (MA Ed); early childhood education (MA Ed); educational leadership (MA Ed); educational technology (MA Ed); exercise science (MA); family life education (MA); K-12 principal licensure (Ed S); K-12 reading (Certificate); special education (MA Ed, Certificate), including autism spectrum disorder (MA Ed), emotional and behavioral disorders (MA Ed), learning disabilities (MA Ed); sports management (MA); superintendent (Ed S). *Accreditation:* NCATE. Part-time and evening/weekend programs available. Postbaccalaureate distance learning degree programs offered (minimal on-campus study). *Faculty:* 12 full-time (7 women), 92 part-time/adjunct (49 women). *Students:* 915 full-time (659 women), 64 part-time (53 women); includes 99 minority (47 Black or African American, non-Hispanic/Latino; 5 American Indian or Alaska Native, non-Hispanic/Latino; 18 Asian, non-Hispanic/Latino; 15 Hispanic/Latino; 2 Native Hawaiian or other Pacific Islander, non-Hispanic/Latino; 12 Two or more races, non-Hispanic/Latino), 24 international. Average age 34. 664 applicants, 67% accepted, 411 enrolled. In 2013, 275 master's, 69 other advanced degrees awarded. *Degree requirements:* For master's, thesis (for some programs). *Entrance requirements:* For master's, official transcripts from regionally-accredited institution stating the conferral of a bachelor's degree with minimum cumulative GPA of 3.0; personal statement; professional resume; practitioner in field through work or volunteerism; resume. Additional exam requirements/recommendations for international students: Recommended—TOEFL (minimum score 547 paper-based; 78 iBT), IELTS (minimum score 6). *Application deadline:* For fall admission, 8/1 for domestic and international students; for spring admission, 12/1 for domestic and international students; for summer admission, 5/1 for domestic and international students. Applications are processed on a rolling basis. Application fee: $50. Electronic applications accepted. *Expenses: Tuition:* Full-time $6200; part-time $425 per credit. Tuition and fees vary according to degree level and program. *Financial support:* Applicants required to submit FAFSA. *Unit head:* Dr. Donald Helmstetter, Dean, 651-641-8227, Fax: 651-641-8807, E-mail: helmstetter@csp.edu. *Application contact:* Kimberly Craig, Director of Graduate and Cohort Admission, 651-603-6223, Fax: 651-603-6320, E-mail: craig@csp.edu.

Concordia University Wisconsin, Graduate Programs, Department of Education, Program in Curriculum and Instruction, Mequon, WI 53097-2402. Offers MS Ed. Postbaccalaureate distance learning degree programs offered (minimal on-campus study). *Degree requirements:* For master's, comprehensive exam, thesis or alternative. *Entrance requirements:* For master's, minimum GPA of 3.0, teaching license. Additional exam requirements/recommendations for international students: Required—TOEFL.

Coppin State University, Division of Graduate Studies, Division of Education, Department of Curriculum and Instruction, Program in Curriculum and Instruction, Baltimore, MD 21216-3698. Offers M Ed. Part-time and evening/weekend programs available. Postbaccalaureate distance learning degree programs offered. *Degree requirements:* For master's, thesis. *Entrance requirements:* For master's, GRE or MAT, minimum GPA of 3.0, teacher certification.

Cornell University, Graduate School, Graduate Fields of Agriculture and Life Sciences, Field of Education, Ithaca, NY 14853-0001. Offers adult and extension education (MPS, MS, PhD); learning, teaching, and social policy (MPS, MS, PhD); mathematics 7-12 (MS). *Faculty:* 21 full-time (8 women). *Students:* 14 full-time (9 women); includes 2 minority (1 Asian, non-Hispanic/Latino; 1 Hispanic/Latino), 1 international. Average age 32. 20 applicants, 20% accepted, 2 enrolled. In 2013, 17 master's, 4 doctorates awarded. Terminal master's awarded for partial completion of doctoral program. *Degree requirements:* For master's, thesis (MS); for doctorate, comprehensive exam, thesis/dissertation. *Entrance requirements:* For master's and doctorate, GRE General Test, sample of written work (recommended), 2 letters of recommendation. Additional exam requirements/recommendations for international students: Required—TOEFL (minimum score 550 paper-based; 77 iBT). *Application deadline:* For fall admission, 2/15 for domestic students. Application fee: $95. Electronic applications accepted. *Financial support:* In 2013–14, 4 students received support, including 3 fellowships with full tuition reimbursements available, 1 research assistantship with full tuition reimbursement available; teaching assistantships with full tuition reimbursements available, institutionally sponsored loans, scholarships/grants, health care benefits, tuition waivers (full and partial), and unspecified assistantships also available. Financial award applicants required to submit FAFSA. *Faculty research:* Moral development and professional ethics, public issues education and community development, socio/political issues in public education, teacher education and curriculum in agricultural science and mathematics, extension research. *Unit head:* Director of Graduate Studies, 607-255-4278, Fax: 607-255-7905. *Application contact:* Graduate Field Assistant, 607-255-4278, Fax: 607-255-7905, E-mail: rh22@cornell.edu.
Website: http://www.gradschool.cornell.edu/fields.php?id-80&a-2.

Dakota Wesleyan University, Program in Education, Mitchell, SD 57301-4398. Offers curriculum and instruction (MA Ed); educational policy and administration (MA Ed); preK-12 principal certification (MA Ed); secondary certification (MA Ed). Part-time and evening/weekend programs available. *Degree requirements:* For master's, comprehensive exam, thesis optional, electronic portfolio. *Entrance requirements:* For master's, minimum GPA of 2.7, elementary statistics course, statement of purpose, official transcripts, resume, three letters of recommendation. Additional exam requirements/recommendations for international students: Required—TOEFL (minimum score 500 paper-based), IELTS (minimum score 6.5). Electronic applications accepted. *Faculty research:* Math, political policy, technology in the classroom.

Dallas Baptist University, Dorothy M. Bush College of Education, Program in Curriculum and Instruction, Dallas, TX 75211-9299. Offers M Ed. Part-time and evening/weekend programs available. *Entrance requirements:* For master's, GRE General Test, minimum GPA of 3.0. Additional exam requirements/recommendations for international students: Required—TOEFL, IELTS. Application fee: $25. *Expenses: Tuition:* Full-time $13,410; part-time $745 per credit hour. *Required fees:* $300; $150 per semester. Tuition and fees vary according to degree level. *Financial support:* Federal Work-Study, institutionally sponsored loans, scholarships/grants, and tuition waivers (full and partial) available. Support available to part-time students. Financial award applicants required to submit FAFSA. *Unit head:* Dr. Deborah H. Tribble, Director, 214-333-5201, E-mail: graduate@dbu.edu. *Application contact:* Kit P. Montgomery, Director of Graduate Programs, 214-333-5242, Fax: 214-333-5579, E-mail: graduate@dbu.edu.
Website: http://www3.dbu.edu/graduate/curriculum_instruction.asp.

Delaware State University, Graduate Programs, College of Education, Health and Public Policy, Program in Curriculum and Instruction, Dover, DE 19901-2277. Offers MA. Part-time and evening/weekend programs available. *Degree requirements:* For master's, comprehensive exam, thesis optional. *Entrance requirements:* For master's, GRE General Test, minimum GPA of 3.0 in major, 2.75 overall. Additional exam requirements/recommendations for international students: Required—TOEFL (minimum score 550 paper-based). Electronic applications accepted.

Delaware Valley College, Program in Educational Leadership, Doylestown, PA 18901-2697. Offers instruction, curriculum and technology (MS); school administration and leadership (MS). Part-time and evening/weekend programs available. *Entrance requirements:* For master's, minimum undergraduate GPA of 3.0.

DePaul University, College of Education, Chicago, IL 60614. Offers bilingual bicultural education (M Ed, MA); counseling (M Ed, MA), including clinical mental health counseling, college student development, school counseling; curriculum studies (M Ed, MA, Ed D); early childhood education (M Ed, MA, Ed D); educating adults (MA); educational leadership (M Ed, MA, Ed D), including administration and supervision (M Ed, MA), principal preparation (M Ed, MA); elementary education (MA); mathematics education (MA); mathematics for teaching (MS); middle school mathematics education (MS); reading specialist (M Ed, MA); secondary education (M Ed); social and cultural foundations in education (MA); special education (M Ed, MA); world languages education (M Ed, MA). Part-time and evening/weekend programs available. Postbaccalaureate distance learning degree programs offered (no on-campus study). *Faculty:* 61 full-time (35 women), 59 part-time/adjunct (43 women). *Students:* 628 full-time (486 women), 324 part-time (243 women); includes 304 minority (144 Black or African American, non-Hispanic/Latino; 1 American Indian or Alaska Native, non-Hispanic/Latino; 38 Asian, non-Hispanic/Latino; 98 Hispanic/Latino; 23 Two or more races, non-Hispanic/Latino), 24 international. Average age 30. In 2013, 465 master's, 4 doctorates awarded. *Degree requirements:* For doctorate, thesis/dissertation. *Application deadline:* For fall admission, 8/15 for domestic students; for winter admission, 12/1 for domestic students; for spring admission, 3/1 for domestic students. Applications are processed on a rolling basis. Application fee: $40. Electronic applications accepted. Tuition and fees vary according to course level, course load and degree level. *Financial support:* Application deadline: 12/31; applicants required to submit FAFSA. *Unit head:* Dr. Paul Zionts, Dean, 773-325-7581, Fax: 773-325-7713, E-mail: pzionts@depaul.edu. *Application contact:* Farrah Dalal, Assistant Director, 773-325-2465, Fax: 773-325-2270, E-mail: fdalal@depaul.edu.
Website: http://education.depaul.edu.

Doane College, Program in Education, Crete, NE 68333-2430. Offers curriculum and instruction (M Ed); educational leadership (M Ed). *Accreditation:* NCATE. Part-time and evening/weekend programs available. *Students:* 125 full-time (89 women), 502 part-time (396 women); includes 25 minority (11 Black or African American, non-Hispanic/Latino; 1 American Indian or Alaska Native, non-Hispanic/Latino; 2 Asian, non-Hispanic/Latino; 9 Hispanic/Latino; 1 Native Hawaiian or other Pacific Islander, non-Hispanic/Latino; 1 Two or more races, non-Hispanic/Latino). Average age 33. In 2013, 284 master's awarded. *Degree requirements:* For master's, thesis. *Entrance requirements:* For master's, minimum GPA of 2.5. Additional exam requirements/recommendations for international students: Required—TOEFL. *Application deadline:* Applications are processed on a rolling basis. Electronic applications accepted. *Expenses:* Contact institution. *Financial support:* Applicants required to submit FAFSA. *Unit head:* Lyn C. Forester, Dean, 402-826-8604, Fax: 402-826-8278. *Application contact:* Wilma Daddario, Assistant Dean, 402-464-1223, Fax: 402-466-4228, E-mail: wdaddario@doane.edu.
Website: http://www.doane.edu/masters-degrees.

Dominican University, School of Education, River Forest, IL 60305-1099. Offers curriculum and instruction (MA Ed); early childhood education (MS); education (MAT); educational administration (MA); elementary education (MA Ed); English as a second language (MA Ed); reading (MA Ed); special education (MS). Part-time and evening/weekend programs available. Postbaccalaureate distance learning degree programs offered (no on-campus study). *Faculty:* 19 full-time (14 women), 51 part-time/adjunct (42 women). *Students:* 18 full-time (13 women), 334 part-time (274 women); includes 76 minority (26 Black or African American, non-Hispanic/Latino; 9 Asian, non-Hispanic/Latino; 41 Hispanic/Latino). Average age 32. 119 applicants, 77% accepted, 70 enrolled. In 2013, 246 master's awarded. *Entrance requirements:* For master's, Illinois Test of Basic Skills. Additional exam requirements/recommendations for international students: Required—TOEFL (minimum score 550 paper-based; 79 iBT). *Application deadline:* Applications are processed on a rolling basis. Application fee: $25. *Expenses:* Contact institution. *Financial support:* In 2013–14, 97 students received support. Career-related internships or fieldwork, scholarships/grants, and tuition waivers (partial) available. Support available to part-time students. Financial award application deadline: 8/15; financial award applicants required to submit FAFSA. *Faculty research:* Governance of private education institutions, reading and language arts, inclusion, organizational planning, leadership and vision. *Unit head:* Dr. Colleen Reardon, Dean, 718-524-6643, Fax: 708-524-6665, E-mail: creardon@dom.edu. *Application contact:* Keven Hansen, Coordinator of Recruitment and Admissions, 708-524-6921, Fax: 708-524-6665, E-mail: educate@dom.edu.
Website: http://educate.dom.edu/.

Drexel University, Goodwin College of Professional Studies, School of Education, Philadelphia, PA 19104-2875. Offers educational administration (MS); educational improvement and transformation (MS); educational leadership and management (Ed D); educational leadership development and learning technologies (PhD); global and international education (MS); higher education (MS); human resources development (MS); learning technologies (MS); mathematics, learning and teaching (MS); special education (MS); teaching, learning and curriculum (MS). Part-time and evening/weekend programs available. Postbaccalaureate distance learning degree programs offered (no on-campus study). *Degree requirements:* For doctorate, thesis/dissertation. *Entrance requirements:* For doctorate, GRE or GMAT. Additional exam requirements/recommendations for international students: Required—TOEFL, IELTS. Electronic applications accepted. Application fee is waived when completed online. *Expenses:* Contact institution. *Faculty research:* Leadership development, mathematics education, literacy, autism, educational technology.

Duquesne University, School of Education, Department of Foundations and Leadership, Program in School Administration and Supervision, Pittsburgh, PA 15282-0001. Offers curriculum and instruction (Post-Master's Certificate); school administration K-12 (MS Ed, Post-Master's Certificate); school supervision (MS Ed). Part-time and evening/weekend programs available. *Faculty:* 2 full-time (both women). *Students:* 33 full-time (29 women), 11 part-time (8 women); includes 3 minority (1 Black or African American, non-Hispanic/Latino; 1 Asian, non-Hispanic/Latino; 1 Hispanic/Latino). Average age 34. 37 applicants, 59% accepted, 22 enrolled. In 2013, 19 master's awarded. *Degree requirements:* For master's, thesis optional. *Entrance requirements:* For master's and Post-Master's Certificate, bachelor's degree. Additional exam requirements/recommendations for international students: Required—TOEFL (minimum score 550 paper-based), IELTS (minimum score 7). *Application deadline:* For fall admission, 9/1 for domestic students; for spring admission, 1/1 for domestic students. Applications are processed on a rolling basis. Application fee: $0. Electronic applications accepted. Application fee is waived when completed online. *Expenses: Tuition:* Full-time $18,162; part-time $1009 per credit. *Required fees:* $1728; $96 per credit. Tuition and fees vary according to program. *Financial support:* Research assistantships available. Support available to part-time students. *Unit head:* Dr. Fran Serenka, Associate Professor and Director, 412-396-5274, Fax: 412-396-1274, E-mail: serenkaf@duq.edu. *Application contact:* Michael Dolinger, Director of Student and Academic Services, 412-396-6647, Fax: 412-396-5585, E-mail: dolingerm@duq.edu.
Website: http://www.duq.edu/academics/schools/education/graduate-programs-education/school-admin-and-supervision.

East Carolina University, Graduate School, College of Education, Department of Curriculum and Instruction, Greenville, NC 27858-4353. Offers assistive technology (Certificate); autism (Certificate); deaf/blindness (Certificate); elementary education (MA Ed); English education (MA Ed); history (MA Ed); middle grade education (MA Ed); reading education (MA Ed); special education (MA Ed); teaching (MAT). Part-time programs available. Postbaccalaureate distance learning degree programs offered. *Degree requirements:* For master's, comprehensive exam, thesis optional. *Entrance requirements:* For master's, GRE General Test or MAT, interview, bachelor's degree in related field, minimum GPA of 2.5, teaching license. Additional exam requirements/recommendations for international students: Required—TOEFL. *Expenses:* Tuition, state resident: full-time $4223. Tuition, nonresident: full-time $16,540. *Required fees:* $2184.

Eastern Kentucky University, The Graduate School, College of Education, Department of Curriculum and Instruction, Richmond, KY 40475-3102. Offers elementary education (MA Ed), including early elementary education, reading; library science (MA Ed); music education (MA Ed); secondary and higher education (MA Ed), including secondary education; teaching (MAT). *Accreditation:* NCATE. Part-time programs available. *Degree requirements:* For master's, portfolio is part of exam. *Entrance requirements:* For master's, GRE General Test, PRAXIS II (KY), minimum GPA of 2.5. *Faculty research:* Technology in education, reading instruction, e-portfolios, induction to teacher education, dispositions of teachers.

Eastern Michigan University, Graduate School, College of Education, Department of Teacher Education, Program in Curriculum and Instruction, Ypsilanti, MI 48197. Offers MA. *Students:* 1 full-time (0 women), 28 part-time (23 women); includes 6 minority (5 Black or African American, non-Hispanic/Latino; 1 Hispanic/Latino), 1 international. Average age 32. 9 applicants, 89% accepted, 4 enrolled. In 2013, 20 master's awarded. *Expenses:* Tuition, state resident: full-time $12,300; part-time $466 per credit hour. Tuition, nonresident: full-time $23,159; part-time $918 per credit hour. *Required fees:* $71 per credit hour. $46 per semester. One-time fee: $100. Tuition and fees vary according to course level and degree level. *Unit head:* Dr. Martha Kinney-Sedgwick, Interim Department Head, 734-487-3260, Fax: 734-487-2101, E-mail: mkinneys@emich.edu. *Application contact:* Dr. Virginia Harder, Graduate Coordinator/Advisor, 734-487-2729, Fax: 734-487-2101, E-mail: vharder1@emich.edu.

Eastern Michigan University, Graduate School, College of Education, Department of Teacher Education, Programs in K–12 Education, Ypsilanti, MI 48197. Offers curriculum and instruction (MA); elementary education (MA); K-12 education (MA); middle school education (MA); secondary school education (MA). *Accreditation:* NCATE. Part-time and evening/weekend programs available. Postbaccalaureate distance learning degree programs offered (minimal on-campus study). *Students:* 11 full-time (4 women), 46 part-time (31 women); includes 8 minority (4 Black or African American, non-Hispanic/Latino; 1 American Indian or Alaska Native, non-Hispanic/Latino; 3 Hispanic/Latino). Average age 36. 41 applicants, 78% accepted, 20 enrolled. In 2013, 5 master's awarded. *Entrance requirements:* For master's, GRE. Additional exam requirements/recommendations for international students: Required—TOEFL. *Application deadline:* Applications are processed on a rolling basis. Application fee: $35. *Expenses:* Tuition, state resident: full-time $12,300; part-time $466 per credit hour. Tuition, nonresident: full-time $23,159; part-time $918 per credit hour. *Required fees:* $71 per credit hour. $46 per semester. One-time fee: $100. Tuition and fees vary according to course level and degree level. *Financial support:* Fellowships, research assistantships with full tuition reimbursements, teaching assistantships with full tuition reimbursements, career-related internships or fieldwork, Federal Work-Study, institutionally sponsored loans, scholarships/grants, tuition waivers (partial), and unspecified assistantships available. Support available to part-time students. Financial award applicants required to submit FAFSA. *Unit head:* Dr. Martha Kinney-Sedgwick, Interim Department Head, 734-487-3260, Fax: 734-487-2101, E-mail: mkinneys@emich.edu. *Application contact:* Dr. Ethan Lowenstein, Coordinator, 734-487-3260, Fax: 734-487-2101, E-mail: elowste@emich.edu.

Eastern New Mexico University, Graduate School, College of Education and Technology, Department of Curriculum and Instruction, Portales, NM 88130. Offers bilingual education (M Ed); educational technology (M Ed); elementary education (M Ed); English as a second language (M Ed); pedagogy and learning (M Ed); professional technical education (M Ed); reading/literacy (M Ed). Part-time programs available. Postbaccalaureate distance learning degree programs offered (minimal on-campus study). *Degree requirements:* For master's, comprehensive exam, thesis optional. *Entrance requirements:* For master's, minimum GPA of 3.0, photocopy of teaching license, writing assessment, letter of recommendation. Additional exam requirements/recommendations for international students: Required—TOEFL (minimum score 550 paper-based; 79 iBT), IELTS (minimum score 6). Electronic applications accepted.

Eastern Washington University, Graduate Studies, College of Arts, Letters and Education, Department of Education, Program in Curriculum Development, Cheney, WA 99004-2431. Offers M Ed. *Students:* 6 part-time (3 women); includes 2 minority (1 American Indian or Alaska Native, non-Hispanic/Latino; 1 Hispanic/Latino). Average age 34. 3 applicants, 67% accepted, 2 enrolled. In 2013, 9 master's awarded. *Degree requirements:* For master's, comprehensive exam. *Entrance requirements:* For master's, minimum GPA of 3.0. *Application deadline:* For fall admission, 4/1 priority date for domestic students; for spring admission, 1/15 for domestic students. Applications are processed on a rolling basis. Application fee: $50. *Financial support:* In 2013–14, teaching assistantships with partial tuition reimbursements (averaging $7,000 per year) were awarded; career-related internships or fieldwork, Federal Work-Study,

institutionally sponsored loans, scholarships/grants, health care benefits, tuition waivers (partial), and unspecified assistantships also available. Support available to part-time students. Financial award application deadline: 2/1. *Unit head:* Robin Showalter, Program Coordinator, 509-359-6492, E-mail: rshowalter@mail.ewu.edu. *Application contact:* Dr. Kevin Pyatt, Graduate Program Coordinator, 509-359-6091, E-mail: kpyatt@ewu.edu.

East Tennessee State University, School of Graduate Studies, College of Education, Department of Curriculum and Instruction, Johnson City, TN 37614. Offers educational media and educational technology (M Ed), including educational communications and technology, school library media; elementary education (M Ed); reading (MA), including reading education, storytelling; school library professional (Post-Master's Certificate); secondary education (M Ed), including classroom technology, secondary education (M Ed, MAT); storytelling (Postbaccalaureate Certificate); teacher education with multiple levels (MAT), including elementary education, middle grades education, secondary education (M Ed, MAT). *Accreditation:* NCATE. Part-time and evening/weekend programs available. Postbaccalaureate distance learning degree programs offered (no on-campus study). *Faculty:* 25 full-time (18 women), 12 part-time/adjunct (8 women). *Students:* 66 full-time (50 women), 97 part-time (85 women); includes 5 minority (3 Black or African American, non-Hispanic/Latino; 2 Two or more races, non-Hispanic/Latino), 2 international. Average age 31. 144 applicants, 57% accepted, 70 enrolled. In 2013, 83 master's, 5 other advanced degrees awarded. *Degree requirements:* For master's, comprehensive exam, thesis optional, student teaching, practicum; for other advanced degree, field work (school library); culminating experience (storytelling). *Entrance requirements:* For master's, GRE, SAT, ACT, PRAXIS, minimum GPA of 3.0; for other advanced degree, master's degree, TN teaching license (for school library professional Post-Master's Certificate); three letters of recommendation (for storytelling Postbaccalaureate Certificate). Additional exam requirements/recommendations for international students: Required—TOEFL (minimum score 550 paper-based; 79 iBT). *Application deadline:* For fall admission, 6/1 for domestic students, 4/30 for international students; for spring admission, 11/1 for domestic students, 4/30 for international students. Application fee: $35 ($45 for international students). Electronic applications accepted. *Expenses:* Tuition, state resident: full-time $7900; part-time $395 per credit hour. Tuition, nonresident: full-time $21,960; part-time $1098 per credit hour. *Required fees:* $1345; $84 per credit hour. *Financial support:* In 2013–14, 43 students received support, including 6 research assistantships with full tuition reimbursements available (averaging $6,000 per year), 10 teaching assistantships with full tuition reimbursements available (averaging $6,000 per year); career-related internships or fieldwork, institutionally sponsored loans, scholarships/grants, and unspecified assistantships also available. Financial award application deadline: 7/1; financial award applicants required to submit FAFSA. *Faculty research:* Critical thinking; curriculum development in reading, math, and science education; cultural diversity; cognitive processes; effective teaching strategies. *Unit head:* Dr. Rhona Hurwitz, Chair, 423-439-7598, Fax: 423-439-8362, E-mail: hurwitz@etsu.edu. *Application contact:* Fiona Goodyear, Graduate Specialist, 423-439-6148, Fax: 423-439-5624, E-mail: goodyear@etsu.edu.
Website: http://www.etsu.edu/coe/cuai/.

East Texas Baptist University, Master of Education Program, Marshall, TX 75670-1498. Offers curriculum and instruction (M Ed); sports and exercise leadership (M Ed); teacher certification (M Ed). Part-time programs available. *Entrance requirements:* For master's, GRE. Additional exam requirements/recommendations for international students: Required—TOEFL (minimum score 550 paper-based; 79 iBT). Electronic applications accepted. *Expenses:* Contact institution.

Emporia State University, Program in Curriculum and Instruction, Emporia, KS 66801-5415. Offers curriculum leadership (MS); effective practitioner (MS); national board certification (MS). *Accreditation:* NCATE. Part-time programs available. *Faculty:* 7 full-time (1 woman), 2 part-time/adjunct (0 women). *Students:* 12 full-time (11 women), 99 part-time (80 women); includes 9 minority (4 Black or African American, non-Hispanic/Latino; 4 Hispanic/Latino; 1 Two or more races, non-Hispanic/Latino). 43 applicants, 86% accepted, 27 enrolled. In 2013, 42 master's awarded. *Degree requirements:* For master's, comprehensive exam or thesis, practicum. *Entrance requirements:* For master's, GRE or MAT, appropriate bachelor's degree, teacher certification, 1 year of teaching experience, letters of recommendation. *Application deadline:* For fall admission, 8/15 priority date for domestic students. Applications are processed on a rolling basis. Application fee: $30 ($75 for international students). Electronic applications accepted. *Expenses: Tuition, area resident:* Part-time $220 per credit hour. Tuition, state resident: part-time $220 per credit hour. Tuition, nonresident: part-time $685 per credit hour. *Required fees:* $73 per credit hour. *Financial support:* In 2013–14, 1 research assistantship with full tuition reimbursement (averaging $7,200 per year) was awarded; career-related internships or fieldwork, Federal Work-Study, institutionally sponsored loans, health care benefits, and unspecified assistantships also available. Financial award application deadline: 3/15; financial award applicants required to submit FAFSA. *Unit head:* Dr. Paul Bland, Chair, 620-341-5777, E-mail: pbland@emporia.edu. *Application contact:* Mary Sewell, Admissions Coordinator, 800-950-GRAD, Fax: 620-341-5909, E-mail: msewell@emporia.edu.
Website: http://www.emporia.edu/sleme/graduate-programs/ci.html.

Fairleigh Dickinson University, Metropolitan Campus, University College: Arts, Sciences, and Professional Studies, Peter Sammartino School of Education, Program in Teaching, Teaneck, NJ 07666-1914. Offers MAT.

Ferris State University, College of Education and Human Services, School of Education, Big Rapids, MI 49307. Offers curriculum and instruction (M Ed), including reading, special education, subject area; educational leadership (MS); instructor (MSCTE); post-secondary administration (MSCTE); training and development (MSCTE). Part-time and evening/weekend programs available. Postbaccalaureate distance learning degree programs offered (minimal on-campus study). *Faculty:* 7 full-time (5 women), 9 part-time/adjunct (6 women). *Students:* 17 full-time (14 women), 88 part-time (53 women); includes 8 minority (3 Black or African American, non-Hispanic/Latino; 1 American Indian or Alaska Native, non-Hispanic/Latino; 1 Asian, non-Hispanic/Latino; 3 Two or more races, non-Hispanic/Latino), 12 international. Average age 35. 16 applicants, 63% accepted, 6 enrolled. In 2013, 31 master's awarded. *Degree requirements:* For master's, thesis, research paper or project. *Entrance requirements:* For master's, minimum undergraduate degree GPA of 3.0. Additional exam requirements/recommendations for international students: Required—TOEFL (minimum score 500 paper-based; 61 iBT), IELTS. *Application deadline:* For fall admission, 7/1 priority date for domestic and international students; for spring admission, 11/1 priority date for domestic and international students; for summer admission, 3/1 priority date for domestic and international students. Applications are processed on a rolling basis. Application fee: $30. Electronic applications accepted. Application fee is waived when completed online. *Financial support:* Career-related internships or fieldwork and scholarships/grants available. Support available to part-time students. Financial award applicants required to submit FAFSA. *Faculty research:* Suicide prevention, reading, women in education, special needs, administration. *Unit head:* Dr. James Powell, Director, 231-591-3512, Fax: 231-591-2043, E-mail: powelj20@ferris.edu. *Application contact:* Kimisue Worrall, Secretary, 231-591-5361, Fax: 231-591-2043.
Website: http://www.ferris.edu/education/education/.

Fitchburg State University, Division of Graduate and Continuing Education, Program in Curriculum and Teaching, Fitchburg, MA 01420-2697. Offers M Ed. Part-time and evening/weekend programs available. *Entrance requirements:* Additional exam requirements/recommendations for international students: Required—TOEFL (minimum score 550 paper-based; 79 iBT). Electronic applications accepted.

Florida Atlantic University, College of Education, Department of Curriculum, Culture, and Educational Inquiry, Boca Raton, FL 33431-0991. Offers curriculum and instruction (M Ed, PhD, Ed S); early childhood education (M Ed); multicultural education (M Ed); TESOL and bilingual education (MA). Part-time and evening/weekend programs available. *Faculty:* 9 full-time (8 women), 3 part-time/adjunct (all women). *Students:* 17 full-time (14 women), 119 part-time (93 women); includes 41 minority (18 Black or African American, non-Hispanic/Latino; 4 Asian, non-Hispanic/Latino; 18 Hispanic/Latino; 1 Two or more races, non-Hispanic/Latino), 5 international. Average age 36. 49 applicants, 39% accepted, 13 enrolled. In 2013, 31 master's, 2 other advanced degrees awarded. *Entrance requirements:* Additional exam requirements/recommendations for international students: Required—TOEFL (minimum score 500 paper-based; 61 iBT), IELTS (minimum score 6). *Application deadline:* For fall admission, 7/1 for domestic students, 2/15 for international students; for spring admission, 11/1 for domestic students, 7/15 for international students. Application fee: $30. *Expenses:* Tuition, state resident: full-time $6660; part-time $370 per credit hour. Tuition, nonresident: full-time $18,450; part-time $1025 per credit hour. Tuition and fees vary according to course load. *Faculty research:* Multicultural education, early intervention strategies, family literacy, religious diversity in schools, early childhood curriculum. *Unit head:* Dr. Emery Hyslop-Margison, Interim Chair, 561-297-3965, E-mail: ehyslopmargison@fau.edu. *Application contact:* Dr. Eliah Watlington, Associate Dean, 561-296-8520, Fax: 261-297-2991, E-mail: ewatling@fau.edu.
Website: http://www.coe.fau.edu/academicdepartments/ccei/.

Florida Atlantic University, College of Education, Department of Teaching and Learning, Boca Raton, FL 33431-0991. Offers curriculum and instruction (M Ed), including art, biology, chemistry, English, French, German, mathematics, music, physics, Pre-K and primary education, reading, social sciences, Spanish; elementary education (M Ed); environmental education (M Ed); reading education (M Ed); social foundations of education (M Ed), including educational psychology, educational technology, multilingual education. *Accreditation:* NCATE. Part-time and evening/weekend programs available. *Faculty:* 16 full-time (12 women), 1 (woman) part-time/adjunct. *Students:* 56 full-time (46 women), 96 part-time (78 women); includes 39 minority (10 Black or African American, non-Hispanic/Latino; 6 Asian, non-Hispanic/Latino; 20 Hispanic/Latino; 3 Two or more races, non-Hispanic/Latino), 4 international. Average age 32. 101 applicants, 54% accepted, 42 enrolled. In 2013, 64 master's awarded. *Entrance requirements:* For master's, GRE General Test, minimum GPA of 3.0 in last 2 years of undergraduate course work. Additional exam requirements/recommendations for international students: Required—TOEFL (minimum score 500 paper-based; 61 iBT), IELTS (minimum score 6). *Application deadline:* For fall admission, 7/1 for domestic students, 2/15 for international students; for spring admission, 11/1 for domestic students, 7/15 for international students. Applications are processed on a rolling basis. Application fee: $30. *Expenses:* Tuition, state resident: full-time $6660; part-time $370 per credit hour. Tuition, nonresident: full-time $18,450; part-time $1025 per credit hour. Tuition and fees vary according to course load. *Financial support:* Fellowships with partial tuition reimbursements, research assistantships with partial tuition reimbursements, teaching assistantships with partial tuition reimbursements, career-related internships or fieldwork, scholarships/grants, and unspecified assistantships available. *Faculty research:* Technology, teaching English to speakers of other languages, math teaching, electronic portfolio assessment, global perspectives through social studies. *Unit head:* Dr. Barbara Ridener, Chairperson, 561-297-3588. *Application contact:* Dr. Eliah Watlington, Associate Dean, 561-296-8520, Fax: 261-297-2991, E-mail: ewatling@fau.edu.
Website: http://www.coe.fau.edu/academicdepartments/tl/.

Florida Gulf Coast University, College of Education, Program in Curriculum and Instruction, Fort Myers, FL 33965-6565. Offers curriculum and instruction (Ed D, Ed S); educational technology (M Ed, MA); English education (M Ed). Part-time and evening/weekend programs available. Postbaccalaureate distance learning degree programs offered (minimal on-campus study). *Degree requirements:* For master's, final project or portfolio. *Entrance requirements:* For master's, GRE General Test, MAT, minimum undergraduate GPA of 3.0 in last 2 years. Additional exam requirements/recommendations for international students: Required—TOEFL (minimum score 550 paper-based). Electronic applications accepted. *Faculty research:* Internet in schools, technology in pre-service and in-service teacher training.

Florida International University, College of Education, Department of Teaching and Learning, Miami, FL 33199. Offers art education (MA, MS); curriculum and instruction (MS, Ed D, PhD, Ed S), including curriculum development (MS), elementary education (MS), English education (MS), learning technologies (MS), mathematics education (MS), modern language education (MS), physical education (MS), science education (MS), social studies education (MS), special education (MS); early childhood education (MS); exceptional student education (Ed D); foreign language education (MS), including foreign language education, teaching English to speakers of other languages (TESOL); international/intercultural education (MS); language, literacy and culture (PhD); mathematics, science, and learning technologies (PhD); physical education (MS), including sport and fitness; reading education (MS). Part-time and evening/weekend programs available. *Degree requirements:* For doctorate, comprehensive exam, thesis/dissertation. *Entrance requirements:* For master's, GRE General Test, Florida General Knowledge Test or Florida College Level Academic Skills Test; for doctorate and Ed S, GRE General Test. Additional exam requirements/recommendations for international students: Required—TOEFL (minimum score 550 paper-based; 80 iBT), IELTS (minimum score 6.3). Electronic applications accepted.

Florida State University, The Graduate School, College of Education, School of Teacher Education, Tallahassee, FL 32306. Offers curriculum and instruction (MS, MST, PhD, Ed S), including early childhood education (MS, PhD, Ed S), elementary education (MS, PhD, Ed S), English education (MS, PhD, Ed S), English teaching (MST), exceptional student education (MST), foreign and second language education (MS, PhD, Ed S), foreign and second language teaching (MST), math education (MS, PhD, Ed S), math teaching (MST), reading education and language arts (MS, PhD, Ed S), science education (MS, PhD, Ed S), social science education (MS, PhD, Ed S), social science teaching (MST), special education (MS, PhD, Ed S), special education studies (MST), visual disabilities (MS, Ed S). Part-time programs available. *Faculty:* 30 full-time (20 women), 22 part-time/adjunct (18 women). *Students:* 183 full-time (151 women), 92 part-time (80 women); includes 47 minority (20 Black or African American, non-Hispanic/Latino; 3 American Indian or Alaska Native, non-Hispanic/Latino; 1 Asian, non-Hispanic/Latino; 20 Hispanic/Latino; 3 Two or more races, non-Hispanic/Latino), 61 international. Average age 30. 199 applicants, 79% accepted, 86 enrolled. In 2013, 119 master's, 9 doctorates, 4 other advanced degrees awarded. *Degree requirements:* For

master's and Ed S, comprehensive exam, thesis optional; for doctorate, comprehensive exam, thesis/dissertation, preliminary exam, prospectus defense. *Entrance requirements:* For master's, doctorate, and Ed S, GRE General Test, minimum GPA of 3.0. Additional exam requirements/recommendations for international students: Required—TOEFL (minimum score 550 paper-based; 80 iBT). *Application deadline:* For fall admission, 7/1 for domestic and international students; for winter admission, 10/1 for domestic students, 11/1 for international students; for spring admission, 3/1 for domestic and international students. Applications are processed on a rolling basis. Application fee: $30. Electronic applications accepted. *Expenses:* Tuition, state resident: part-time $403.51 per credit hour. Tuition, nonresident: part-time $1004.85 per credit hour. *Required fees:* $75.81 per credit hour. One-time fee: $20 part-time. Tuition and fees vary according to course load, campus/location and student level. *Financial support:* In 2013–14, 113 students received support, including 55 research assistantships with full and partial tuition reimbursements available, 18 teaching assistantships with full and partial tuition reimbursements available; fellowships with full and partial tuition reimbursements available, career-related internships or fieldwork, scholarships/grants, health care benefits, and unspecified assistantships also available. Financial award application deadline: 1/15; financial award applicants required to submit FAFSA. *Faculty research:* Effective intervention and assessment strategies to improve reading skills; literacy teaching and learning through technology; understanding of student sense-making through instructions, especially STEM learning for all students; international education and consequences of globalization; support professional teacher development and adoption of effective/transformative practices. *Total annual research expenditures:* $1.3 million. *Unit head:* Dr. Sherry Southerland, Chair, 850-644-4880, Fax: 850-644-7736, E-mail: ssoutherland@admin.fsu.edu. *Application contact:* Dawn Matthews, Academic Support Assistant, 850-644-2122, Fax: 850-644-7736, E-mail: dmatthews@fsu.edu.
Website: http://www.coe.fsu.edu/STE.

Fordham University, Graduate School of Education, Division of Curriculum and Teaching, New York, NY 10023. Offers adult education (MS, MSE); bilingual teacher education (MSE); curriculum and teaching (MSE); early childhood education (MSE); elementary education (MST); language, literacy, and learning (PhD); reading education (MSE, Adv C); secondary education (MAT, MSE); special education (MSE, Adv C); teaching English as a second language (MSE). *Accreditation:* NCATE. *Degree requirements:* For doctorate, thesis/dissertation; for Adv C, thesis. *Entrance requirements:* For doctorate, MAT, GRE General Test.

Framingham State University, Continuing Education, Program in Curriculum and Instructional Technology, Framingham, MA 01701-9101. Offers M Ed. Postbaccalaureate distance learning degree programs offered.

Franciscan University of Steubenville, Graduate Programs, Department of Education, Steubenville, OH 43952-1763. Offers administration (MS Ed); teaching (MS Ed). Part-time and evening/weekend programs available. *Degree requirements:* For master's, project. *Entrance requirements:* For master's, minimum undergraduate GPA of 2.5 or written exam. *Expenses:* Contact institution.

Franklin Pierce University, Graduate Studies, Rindge, NH 03461-0060. Offers curriculum and instruction (M Ed); emerging network technologies (Graduate Certificate); energy and sustainability studies (MBA); health administration (MBA, Graduate Certificate); human resource management (MBA, Graduate Certificate); information technology (MBA); information technology management (MS); leadership (MBA, DA); nursing (MS); physical therapy (DPT); physician assistant studies (MPAS); special education (M Ed); sports management (MBA). *Accreditation:* APTA. Part-time programs available. Postbaccalaureate distance learning degree programs offered (no on-campus study). *Degree requirements:* For master's, concentrated original research projects; student teaching; fieldwork and/or internship; leadership project; PRAXIS I and II (for M Ed); for doctorate, concentrated original research projects, clinical fieldwork and/or internship, leadership project. *Entrance requirements:* For master's, minimum GPA of 2.5, 3 letters of recommendation, competencies in accounting, economics, statistics, and computer skills through life experience or undergraduate coursework (for MBA); certification/e-portfolio, minimum C grade in all education courses (for M Ed); license to practice as RN (for MS in nursing); for doctorate, GRE, BA/BS, 3 letters of recommendation, personal mission statement, interview, writing sample, minimum cumulative GPA of 2.8, master's degree (for DA); 80 hours of observation/work in PT settings, completion of anatomy, chemistry, physics, and statistics, minimum GPA of 3.0 (for DPT). Additional exam requirements/recommendations for international students: Required—TOEFL (minimum score 550 paper-based; 61 iBT). Electronic applications accepted. *Faculty research:* Evidence-based practice in sports physical therapy, human resource management in economic crisis, leadership in nursing, innovation in sports facility management, differentiated learning and understanding by design.

Freed-Hardeman University, Program in Education, Henderson, TN 38340-2399. Offers curriculum and instruction (M Ed); school counseling (M Ed), including administration and supervision, special education; school leadership (Ed S). *Accreditation:* NCATE. Part-time and evening/weekend programs available. *Degree requirements:* For master's, comprehensive exam, thesis optional; for Ed S, thesis. *Entrance requirements:* For master's, GRE General Test or NTE; for Ed S, 3 years of teaching experience. Additional exam requirements/recommendations for international students: Required—TOEFL (minimum score 500 paper-based).

Fresno Pacific University, Graduate Programs, School of Education, Division of Foundations, Curriculum and Teaching, Program in Curriculum and Teaching, Fresno, CA 93702-4709. Offers MA. Part-time and evening/weekend programs available. Postbaccalaureate distance learning degree programs offered (no on-campus study). *Students:* 2 full-time (both women), 49 part-time (43 women); includes 24 minority (3 Black or African American, non-Hispanic/Latino; 2 American Indian or Alaska Native, non-Hispanic/Latino; 1 Asian, non-Hispanic/Latino; 17 Hispanic/Latino; 1 Two or more races, non-Hispanic/Latino). Average age 36. In 2013, 21 master's awarded. *Degree requirements:* For master's, thesis or alternative. *Entrance requirements:* For master's, interview, statement of intent, three references, official transcript, BA/BS, minimum GPA of 2.75. Additional exam requirements/recommendations for international students: Required—TOEFL (minimum score 550 paper-based). *Application deadline:* For fall admission, 7/15 for domestic and international students; for spring admission, 11/15 for domestic and international students. Applications are processed on a rolling basis. Application fee: $90. Electronic applications accepted. *Expenses:* Tuition: Full-time $8910; part-time $495 per unit. *Required fees:* $270. Tuition and fees vary according to course load and program. *Financial support:* Scholarships/grants and tuition waivers (full and partial) available. Support available to part-time students. Financial award applicants required to submit FAFSA. *Unit head:* Jeanne Janzen, EdD, Director, 559-453-5550, Fax: 559-453-2001, E-mail: jjanzen@fresno.edu. *Application contact:* Amanda Krum-Stovall, Director of Graduate Admissions, 559-453-2016, E-mail: amanda.krum-stovall@fresno.edu.
Website: http://grad.fresno.edu/programs/master-arts-curriculum-teaching.

Frostburg State University, Graduate School, College of Education, Department of Educational Professions, Program in Curriculum and Instruction, Frostburg, MD 21532-1099. Offers educational technology (M Ed); elementary education (M Ed); secondary education (M Ed). Part-time and evening/weekend programs available. *Degree*

requirements: For master's, thesis or alternative. *Entrance requirements:* For master's, teaching certificate. Additional exam requirements/recommendations for international students: Required—TOEFL. Electronic applications accepted. *Expenses: Tuition, area resident:* Part-time $340 per credit hour. Tuition, state resident: part-time $340 per credit hour. Tuition, nonresident: part-time $437 per credit hour.

Furman University, Graduate Division, Department of Education, Greenville, SC 29613. Offers curriculum and instruction (MA); early childhood education (MA); educational leadership (Ed S); English as a second language (MA); literacy (MA); school leadership (MA); special education (MA). *Accreditation:* NCATE. Part-time programs available. Postbaccalaureate distance learning degree programs offered (minimal on-campus study). *Degree requirements:* For master's, comprehensive exam (for some programs), thesis or alternative. *Entrance requirements:* For master's, PRAXIS II. *Faculty research:* Literacy, pedagogy and practice, social justice, advanced leadership, achievement in high poverty schools.

Gannon University, School of Graduate Studies, College of Humanities, Education, and Social Sciences, School of Education, Program in Curriculum and Instruction, Erie, PA 16541-0001. Offers M Ed. Part-time and evening/weekend programs available. Postbaccalaureate distance learning degree programs offered (no on-campus study). *Students:* 15 full-time (11 women), 103 part-time (81 women), 2 international. Average age 31. 83 applicants, 88% accepted, 57 enrolled. In 2013, 89 master's awarded. *Degree requirements:* For master's, thesis or alternative, portfolio project. *Entrance requirements:* For master's, GRE, minimum GPA of 3.0, teacher certification. Additional exam requirements/recommendations for international students: Required—TOEFL (minimum score 79 iBT). *Application deadline:* Applications are processed on a rolling basis. Application fee: $25. Electronic applications accepted. *Expenses:* Contact institution. *Financial support:* Scholarships/grants available. Financial award application deadline: 7/1; financial award applicants required to submit FAFSA. *Unit head:* Janice Whiteman, Director, 814-871-7497, E-mail: whiteman002@gannon.edu. *Application contact:* Kara Morgan, Director of Graduate Admissions, 814-871-5831, Fax: 814-871-5827, E-mail: graduate@gannon.edu.

Gannon University, School of Graduate Studies, College of Humanities, Education, and Social Sciences, School of Education, Program in Curriculum Supervisor, Erie, PA 16541-0001. Offers Certificate. Part-time and evening/weekend programs available. Postbaccalaureate distance learning degree programs offered. *Students:* 3 part-time (all women). Average age 31. 3 applicants, 100% accepted, 1 enrolled. *Degree requirements:* For Certificate, internship. *Entrance requirements:* Additional exam requirements/recommendations for international students: Required—TOEFL (minimum score 79 iBT). *Application deadline:* Applications are processed on a rolling basis. Application fee: $25. Electronic applications accepted. *Expenses:* Contact institution. *Financial support:* Application deadline: 7/1; applicants required to submit FAFSA. *Unit head:* Dr. Kathleen Kingston, Director, 814-871-5626, E-mail: kingston002@gannon.edu. *Application contact:* Kara Morgan, Director of Graduate Admissions, 814-871-5831, Fax: 814-871-5827, E-mail: graduate@gannon.edu.

Gardner-Webb University, Graduate School, School of Education, Program in Curriculum and Instruction, Boiling Springs, NC 28017. Offers Ed D. *Students:* 1 (woman) full-time, 132 part-time (114 women); includes 40 minority (38 Black or African American, non-Hispanic/Latino; 1 Asian, non-Hispanic/Latino; 1 Hispanic/Latino). Average age 38. 157 applicants, 48% accepted, 66 enrolled. In 2013, 3 doctorates awarded. *Expenses: Tuition:* Full-time $7200; part-time $400 per credit hour. Tuition and fees vary according to course load and program. *Unit head:* Dr. Alan D. Eury, Chair, 704-406-4402, Fax: 704-406-3921, E-mail: dsimmons@gardner-webb.edu. *Application contact:* Office of Graduate Admissions, 877-498-4723, Fax: 704-406-3895, E-mail: gradinfo@gardner-webb.edu.

George Fox University, College of Education, Educational Foundations and Leadership Program, Newberg, OR 97132-2697. Offers continuing administrator license (Certificate); curriculum and instruction (M Ed); educational leadership (M Ed, Ed D); ESOL (Certificate); higher education (M Ed); initial administrator license (Certificate); instructional leadership (Ed S); library media (M Ed, Certificate); literacy (M Ed); reading (M Ed); secondary education (M Ed). *Accreditation:* NCATE. Part-time and evening/weekend programs available. Postbaccalaureate distance learning degree programs offered (minimal on-campus study). *Faculty:* 7 full-time (3 women), 5 part-time/adjunct (4 women). *Students:* 194 part-time (128 women); includes 15 minority (1 Black or African American, non-Hispanic/Latino; 1 American Indian or Alaska Native, non-Hispanic/Latino; 3 Asian, non-Hispanic/Latino; 6 Hispanic/Latino; 1 Native Hawaiian or other Pacific Islander, non-Hispanic/Latino; 3 Two or more races, non-Hispanic/Latino), 2 international. Average age 42. 46 applicants, 85% accepted, 39 enrolled. In 2013, 15 master's, 16 doctorates, 106 Certificates awarded. *Degree requirements:* For master's, thesis (for some programs); for doctorate, comprehensive exam, thesis/dissertation, project. *Entrance requirements:* For master's, minimum undergraduate GPA of 3.0 during previous 2 years of course work, resume, 3 professional recommendations on university forms, official transcripts; for doctorate, GRE, master's degree with minimum GPA of 3.25, 3 years of relevant professional experience, interview, personal essay, scholarly work, 3 professional recommendations on university forms along with 3 written letters of recommendation, official transcripts. Additional exam requirements/recommendations for international students: Required—TOEFL (minimum score 577 paper-based; 90 iBT). *Application deadline:* For fall admission, 7/15 for domestic and international students; for winter admission, 11/1 for domestic and international students; for spring admission, 4/1 for domestic and international students. Applications are processed on a rolling basis. Application fee: $40. Electronic applications accepted. *Expenses:* Contact institution. *Financial support:* Career-related internships or fieldwork available. Financial award applicants required to submit FAFSA. *Unit head:* Dr. Scot Headley, Professor/Chair, 503-554-2836, E-mail: sheadley@georgefox.edu. *Application contact:* Kipp Wilfong, Graduate Admissions Counselor, 800-631-0921, Fax: 503-554-3110, E-mail: kwilfong@georgefox.edu.
Website: http://www.georgefox.edu/education/index.html.

George Mason University, College of Education and Human Development, Programs in Curriculum and Instruction, Fairfax, VA 22030. Offers M Ed. *Faculty:* 45 full-time (36 women), 120 part-time/adjunct (101 women). *Students:* 239 full-time (201 women), 729 part-time (589 women); includes 210 minority (52 Black or African American, non-Hispanic/Latino; 63 Asian, non-Hispanic/Latino; 79 Hispanic/Latino; 3 Native Hawaiian or other Pacific Islander, non-Hispanic/Latino; 13 Two or more races, non-Hispanic/Latino), 14 international. Average age 31. 535 applicants, 78% accepted, 336 enrolled. In 2013, 386 master's awarded. *Degree requirements:* For master's, comprehensive exam, thesis (for some programs). *Entrance requirements:* For master's, PRAXIS I, PRAXIS II, Virginia Communication and Literacy Assessment Test (VCLA), minimum GPA of 3.0 in last 60 hours, licensed as teacher or educational administrator, 3 recommendation letters, interview. Additional exam requirements/recommendations for international students: Required—TOEFL (minimum score 575 paper-based; 88 iBT), IELTS (minimum score 6.5), PTE. *Application deadline:* Applications are processed on a rolling basis. Application fee: $65 ($80 for international students). Electronic applications accepted. *Expenses:* Tuition, state resident: full-time $9350; part-time $390 per credit. Tuition, nonresident: full-time $25,754; part-time $1073 per credit. *Required fees:* $2688; $112 per credit. *Financial support:* In 2013–14, 5 students received support,

including 1 fellowship (averaging $2,000 per year), 1 research assistantship with full and partial tuition reimbursement available (averaging $5,528 per year), 3 teaching assistantships with full and partial tuition reimbursements available (averaging $13,781 per year); career-related internships or fieldwork, Federal Work-Study, scholarships/grants, unspecified assistantships, and health care benefits (for full-time research or teaching assistantship recipients) also available. Support available to part-time students. Financial award application deadline: 3/1; financial award applicants required to submit FAFSA. *Faculty research:* Achievement gaps and superintendent decisions, constructivist view of classroom teaching, cost of cheating, creating a critical literacy milieu in kindergarten. *Unit head:* Elizabeth Sturtevant, Professor and Division Director of Literacy, 703-993-2052, Fax: 703-993-2013, E-mail: esturtev@gmu.edu. *Application contact:* Allison Parsons, Program Coordinator for Literacy, 703-993-5257, Fax: 703-993-2013, E-mail: award12@gmu.edu.
Website: http://gse.gmu.edu/div_lt/.

The George Washington University, Graduate School of Education and Human Development, Department of Curriculum and Pedagogy, Program in Curriculum and Instruction, Washington, DC 20052. Offers MA Ed, Ed D, Ed S. *Accreditation:* NCATE. Evening/weekend programs available. *Students:* 19 full-time (13 women), 38 part-time (30 women); includes 13 minority (6 Black or African American, non-Hispanic/Latino; 4 Asian, non-Hispanic/Latino; 3 Hispanic/Latino), 6 international. Average age 35. 48 applicants, 83% accepted, 10 enrolled. In 2013, 8 master's, 3 doctorates, 1 other advanced degree awarded. *Degree requirements:* For master's and Ed S, comprehensive exam; for doctorate, comprehensive exam, thesis/dissertation. *Entrance requirements:* For master's, GRE General Test or MAT, minimum GPA of 2.75, resume; for doctorate and Ed S, GRE General Test or MAT, interview, minimum GPA of 3.3. *Application deadline:* For fall admission, 1/15 priority date for domestic students; for spring admission, 10/1 for domestic students. Applications are processed on a rolling basis. Application fee: $75. *Financial support:* In 2013–14, 25 students received support. Fellowships, research assistantships, career-related internships or fieldwork, Federal Work-Study, and tuition waivers (partial) available. Financial award application deadline: 1/15; financial award applicants required to submit FAFSA. *Faculty research:* Cognitive skills-teaching, metacognitive strategies, adult basic literacy. *Unit head:* Dr. Sharon Lynch, Faculty Coordinator, 202-994-6174, E-mail: slynch@gwu.edu. *Application contact:* Sarah Lang, Director of Graduate Admissions, 202-994-1447, Fax: 202-994-7207, E-mail: slang@gwu.edu.

Georgia College & State University, Graduate School, The John H. Lounsbury College of Education, Program in Curriculum and Instruction, Milledgeville, GA 31061. Offers Ed S. *Students:* 8 part-time (all women); includes 5 minority (4 Black or African American, non-Hispanic/Latino; 1 Hispanic/Latino). Average age 35. *Entrance requirements:* For degree, on site writing assessment, minimum GPA of 3.25, level 5 certification, 2 years of teaching experience. Additional exam requirements/recommendations for international students: Recommended—TOEFL (minimum score 550 paper-based; 79 iBT). *Application deadline:* For fall admission, 7/1 for domestic students; for spring admission, 11/15 for domestic students. Application fee: $40. *Financial support:* Applicants required to submit FAFSA. *Application contact:* Shanda Brand, Graduate Admissions Advisor, 478-445-1383, Fax: 478-445-6582, E-mail: shanda.brand@gcsu.edu.

Georgia Regents University, The Graduate School, College of Education, Program in Curriculum/Instruction, Augusta, GA 30912. Offers M Ed. *Faculty:* 1 full-time (0 women), 4 part-time/adjunct (all women). *Students:* 59 full-time (51 women), 102 part-time (88 women); includes 53 minority (46 Black or African American, non-Hispanic/Latino; 1 Asian, non-Hispanic/Latino; 5 Hispanic/Latino; 1 Two or more races, non-Hispanic/Latino). Average age 33. 29 applicants, 86% accepted, 20 enrolled. In 2013, 28 master's awarded. *Degree requirements:* For master's, thesis, portfolio. *Entrance requirements:* For master's, GRE, MAT, minimum GPA of 2.5. Application fee: $20. *Financial support:* Career-related internships or fieldwork, Federal Work-Study, institutionally sponsored loans, and unspecified assistantships available. Support available to part-time students. Financial award application deadline: 4/15; financial award applicants required to submit FAFSA. *Unit head:* Dr. J. Gordon Eisenman, Chair, 706-737-1496, Fax: 706-667-4706, E-mail: geisenman@aug.edu. *Application contact:* Andrea M. Scott, Secretary to the Dean, 706-737-1499, Fax: 706-667-4706, E-mail: ascott1@aug.edu.

Georgia Southern University, Jack N. Averitt College of Graduate Studies, College of Education, Department of Curriculum, Foundations, and Reading, Program in Curriculum Studies, Statesboro, GA 30460. Offers Ed D. Part-time programs available. *Students:* 18 full-time (14 women), 144 part-time (111 women); includes 49 minority (39 Black or African American, non-Hispanic/Latino; 1 American Indian or Alaska Native, non-Hispanic/Latino; 2 Asian, non-Hispanic/Latino; 3 Hispanic/Latino; 4 Two or more races, non-Hispanic/Latino), 2 international. Average age 42. 2 applicants, 100% accepted, 1 enrolled. In 2013, 21 doctorates awarded. *Degree requirements:* For doctorate, thesis/dissertation, exams. *Entrance requirements:* For doctorate, GRE or MAT, letters of reference, minimum GPA of 3.5, writing sample. Additional exam requirements/recommendations for international students: Required—TOEFL (minimum score 550 paper-based; 80 iBT), IELTS (minimum score 6). Application fee: $50. Electronic applications accepted. *Expenses:* Tuition, state resident: full-time $7068; part-time $270 per semester hour. Tuition, nonresident: full-time $26,446; part-time $1077 per semester hour. *Required fees:* $2092. *Financial support:* In 2013–14, 5 students received support, including research assistantships with partial tuition reimbursements available (averaging $9,500 per year), teaching assistantships with partial tuition reimbursements available (averaging $9,500 per year); career-related internships or fieldwork, Federal Work-Study, scholarships/grants, and unspecified assistantships also available. Support available to part-time students. Financial award application deadline: 4/15; financial award applicants required to submit FAFSA. *Faculty research:* Curriculum theory, cultural studies, narrative research, postmodern theory, critical race theory, international education, feminism, media literacy, documentary studies, posthuman condition, social and cultural foundations of education, democracy and education. *Unit head:* Dr. Daniel Chapman, Program Coordinator, 912-478-5715, E-mail: dechapman@georgiasouthern.edu. *Application contact:* Amanda Gilliland, Coordinator for Graduate Student Recruitment, 912-478-5384, Fax: 912-478-0740, E-mail: gradadmissions@georgiasouthern.edu.
Website: http://coe.georgiasouthern.edu/cs/.

Georgia Southern University, Jack N. Averitt College of Graduate Studies, College of Education, Department of Teaching and Learning, Program in Curriculum and Instruction - Accomplished Teaching, Statesboro, GA 30460. Offers M Ed. Part-time programs available. Postbaccalaureate distance learning degree programs offered (no on-campus study). *Students:* 30 full-time (26 women), 124 part-time (101 women); includes 38 minority (32 Black or African American, non-Hispanic/Latino; 1 American Indian or Alaska Native, non-Hispanic/Latino; 3 Hispanic/Latino; 2 Two or more races, non-Hispanic/Latino). Average age 30. 49 applicants, 94% accepted, 30 enrolled. In 2013, 11 master's awarded. *Entrance requirements:* For master's, current Georgia teaching certificate. Additional exam requirements/recommendations for international students: Required—IELTS (minimum score 6). *Expenses:* Tuition, state resident: full-time $7068; part-time $270 per semester hour. Tuition, nonresident: full-time $26,446; part-time $1077 per semester hour. *Required fees:* $2092. *Faculty research:* Teacher preparation, curriculum design, assessment for improved student outcomes, reflective practices of infield teachers, diversity responsive methods in instruction. *Unit head:* Dr. Kymberly Drawdy, Chair, 912-478-5041, E-mail: kharris@georgiasouthern.edu. *Application contact:* Amanda Gilliland, Coordinator for Graduate Student Recruitment, 912-478-5384, Fax: 912-478-0740, E-mail: gradschool@georgiasouthern.edu.

Grambling State University, School of Graduate Studies and Research, College of Education, Department of Curriculum and Instruction, Grambling, LA 71245. Offers curriculum and instruction (MS); special education (M Ed). Part-time programs available. *Faculty:* 6 full-time (5 women). *Students:* 14 full-time (11 women), 48 part-time (43 women); includes 59 minority (58 Black or African American, non-Hispanic/Latino; 1 Hispanic/Latino), 2 international. Average age 35. In 2013, 29 master's awarded. *Degree requirements:* For master's, comprehensive exam, thesis (for some programs). *Entrance requirements:* Additional exam requirements/recommendations for international students: Required—TOEFL (minimum score 500 paper-based; 62 iBT). *Application deadline:* For fall admission, 7/1 for domestic and international students; for spring admission, 12/1 for domestic and international students; for summer admission, 5/1 for domestic and international students. *Financial support:* Application deadline: 5/31; applicants required to submit FAFSA. *Unit head:* Dr. Patricia P. Johnson, Interim Department Head, 318-274-2251, Fax: 318-274-3213, E-mail: johnsonp@gram.edu. *Application contact:* Katina S. Crowe-Fields, Special Assistant to Associate Vice President/Dean, 318-274-2158, Fax: 318-274-7373, E-mail: croweks@gram.edu.
Website: http://www.gram.edu/academics/majors/education/departments/instruction/.

Grambling State University, School of Graduate Studies and Research, College of Education, Department of Educational Leadership, Grambling, LA 71245. Offers developmental education (MS, Ed D, PMC), including curriculum and instructional design (Ed D), English (MS), guidance and counseling (MS), higher education administration and management (Ed D), mathematics (MS), reading (MS), science (MS), student development and personnel services (Ed D); educational leadership (M Ed). Part-time and evening/weekend programs available. *Faculty:* 10 full-time (7 women). *Students:* 19 full-time (13 women), 89 part-time (70 women); includes 83 minority (82 Black or African American, non-Hispanic/Latino; 1 Hispanic/Latino), 6 international. Average age 40. In 2013, 13 master's, 6 doctorates, 1 other advanced degree awarded. *Degree requirements:* For master's, comprehensive exam, thesis (for some programs); for doctorate, comprehensive exam, thesis/dissertation. *Entrance requirements:* For master's, GRE, minimum GPA of 2.5 on last degree; for doctorate, GRE (minimum score 1000, 500 on Verbal), master's degree, minimum GPA of 3.0 on last degree. Additional exam requirements/recommendations for international students: Required—TOEFL (minimum score 500 paper-based; 62 iBT). *Application deadline:* For fall admission, 7/1 for domestic and international students; for spring admission, 12/1 for domestic and international students; for summer admission, 5/1 for domestic and international students. Applications are processed on a rolling basis. Application fee: $20 ($30 for international students). Electronic applications accepted. *Financial support:* Research assistantships, health care benefits, tuition waivers (full), and unspecified assistantships available. Financial award application deadline: 5/31; financial award applicants required to submit FAFSA. *Unit head:* Dr. Olatunde Ogunyemi, Department Head, 318-274-2549, Fax: 318-274-6249, E-mail: ogunyemio@gram.edu. *Application contact:* Brenda Cooper, Administrative Assistant III, 318-274-2238, Fax: 318-274-6249, E-mail: cooper@gram.edu.
Website: http://www.gram.edu/academics/majors/education/departments/leadership/.

Grand Canyon University, College of Education, Phoenix, AZ 85017-1097. Offers curriculum and instruction (M Ed); education administration (M Ed); elementary education (M Ed); secondary education (M Ed); special education (M Ed); teaching (MA). Part-time and evening/weekend programs available. Postbaccalaureate distance learning degree programs offered (no on-campus study). *Degree requirements:* For master's, publishable research paper (M Ed), e-portfolio. *Entrance requirements:* For master's, undergraduate degree from accredited, GCU-approved college, university, or program with minimum GPA 2.8. Additional exam requirements/recommendations for international students: Required—TOEFL (minimum score 550 paper-based; 79 iBT), IELTS (minimum score 6). Electronic applications accepted.

Grand Valley State University, College of Education, Program in Instruction and Curriculum, Allendale, MI 49401-9403. Offers M Ed.

Harvard University, Harvard Graduate School of Education, Master's Programs in Education, Cambridge, MA 02138. Offers arts in education (Ed M); education policy and management (Ed M); higher education (Ed M); human development and psychology (Ed M); international education policy (Ed M); language and literacy (Ed M); learning and teaching (Ed M); mind, brain, and education (Ed M); prevention science and practice (Ed M); school leadership (Ed M); special studies (Ed M); teacher education (Ed M); technology, innovation, and education (Ed M). Part-time programs available. *Faculty:* 68 full-time (34 women), 77 part-time/adjunct (41 women). *Students:* 557 full-time (410 women), 69 part-time (50 women); includes 179 minority (34 Black or African American, non-Hispanic/Latino; 1 American Indian or Alaska Native, non-Hispanic/Latino; 62 Asian, non-Hispanic/Latino; 52 Hispanic/Latino; 2 Native Hawaiian or other Pacific Islander, non-Hispanic/Latino; 28 Two or more races, non-Hispanic/Latino), 100 international. Average age 28. 1,756 applicants, 47% accepted, 589 enrolled. In 2013, 673 master's awarded. *Entrance requirements:* For master's, GRE General Test, statement of purpose, 3 letters of recommendation, resume, official transcripts. Additional exam requirements/recommendations for international students: Required—TOEFL (minimum score 613 paper-based; 104 iBT), TWE (minimum score 5). *Application deadline:* For fall admission, 1/3 for domestic and international students. Application fee: $85. Electronic applications accepted. *Expenses:* Contact institution. *Financial support:* In 2013–14, 375 students received support, including 12 fellowships with full and partial tuition reimbursements available (averaging $13,925 per year), 2 research assistantships (averaging $2,174 per year); career-related internships or fieldwork, Federal Work-Study, institutionally sponsored loans, scholarships/grants, health care benefits, tuition waivers (full and partial), and unspecified assistantships also available. Support available to part-time students. Financial award application deadline: 2/1; financial award applicants required to submit FAFSA. *Faculty research:* Learning and development, educational leadership and organizations, education policy analysis. *Total annual research expenditures:* $34.3 million. *Unit head:* Jennifer L. Petrallia, Assistant Dean, 617-495-8445. *Application contact:* Information Contact, 617-495-3414, Fax: 617-496-3577, E-mail: gseadmissions@harvard.edu.
Website: http://www.gse.harvard.edu/.

Henderson State University, Graduate Studies, Teachers College, Department of Advanced Instructional Studies, Arkadelphia, AR 71999-0001. Offers early childhood (P-4) (MSE); education (MAT); English as a second language (Graduate Certificate); instructional facilitator (Graduate Certificate); middle school (MSE); reading (MSE); special education (MSE). *Accreditation:* NCATE. Part-time programs available. *Faculty:* 7 full-time (3 women), 2 part-time/adjunct (both women). *Students:* 1 (woman) full-time, 99 part-time (88 women); includes 20 minority (13 Black or African American, non-Hispanic/Latino; 1 American Indian or Alaska Native, non-Hispanic/Latino; 5 Hispanic/Latino; 1 Two or more races, non-Hispanic/Latino), 1 international. Average age 36. 7 applicants, 100% accepted, 7 enrolled. In 2013, 45 master's awarded. *Entrance requirements:* For master's, GRE General Test or MAT, minimum GPA of 2.7, teacher

certification. Additional exam requirements/recommendations for international students: Required—TOEFL (minimum score 600 paper-based); Recommended—IELTS (minimum score 6.5). *Application deadline:* For fall admission, 8/1 priority date for domestic students, 6/30 priority date for international students; for spring admission, 1/1 priority date for domestic students, 11/30 priority date for international students. Applications are processed on a rolling basis. Application fee: $25 ($75 for international students). *Expenses:* Tuition, state resident: full-time $4284; part-time $238 per credit hour. Tuition, nonresident: full-time $8802; part-time $489 per credit hour. Tuition and fees vary according to course load and campus/location. *Financial support:* In 2013–14, 1 teaching assistantship with partial tuition reimbursement (averaging $4,000 per year) was awarded; scholarships/grants and unspecified assistantships also available. *Unit head:* Dr. Gary Smithey, Chairperson, 870-230-5361, Fax: 870-230-5455, E-mail: smitheg@hsu.edu. *Application contact:* Dr. Ken Taylor, Graduate Dean, 870-230-5126, Fax: 870-230-5479, E-mail: taylorke@hsu.edu.

Hood College, Graduate School, Department of Education, Frederick, MD 21701-8575. Offers curriculum and instruction (MS), including early childhood education, elementary education, elementary school science and mathematics, secondary education, special education; educational leadership (MS, Certificate); reading specialization (MS); STEM (Certificate). *Accreditation:* NCATE. Part-time and evening/weekend programs available. *Faculty:* 4 full-time (3 women), 33 part-time/adjunct (25 women). *Students:* 1 (woman) full-time, 340 part-time (282 women); includes 59 minority (31 Black or African American, non-Hispanic/Latino; 1 American Indian or Alaska Native, non-Hispanic/Latino; 10 Asian, non-Hispanic/Latino; 13 Hispanic/Latino; 4 Two or more races, non-Hispanic/Latino). Average age 33. 97 applicants, 99% accepted, 86 enrolled. In 2013, 64 master's, 40 other advanced degrees awarded. *Degree requirements:* For master's, action research project, portfolio (reading). *Entrance requirements:* For master's, minimum GPA of 2.75, teaching certification. Additional exam requirements/recommendations for international students: Required—TOEFL (minimum score 575 paper-based; 89 iBT), IELTS (minimum score 6.5). *Application deadline:* For fall admission, 7/15 priority date for domestic students, 7/15 for international students; for spring admission, 12/1 priority date for domestic students, 12/1 for international students. Applications are processed on a rolling basis. Application fee: $35. Electronic applications accepted. Application fee is waived when completed online. *Expenses: Tuition:* Part-time $405 per credit. *Required fees:* $100 per semester. *Financial support:* In 2013–14, 1 student received support. Tuition waivers (partial) and unspecified assistantships available. Financial award applicants required to submit FAFSA. *Faculty research:* Leadership, action research, brain research, learning styles. *Unit head:* Dr. Ellen Koitz, Chairperson, 301-696-3466, Fax: 301-696-3597, E-mail: koitz@hood.edu. *Application contact:* Dr. Maria Green Cowles, Dean of Graduate School, 301-696-3811, Fax: 301-696-3597, E-mail: gofurther@hood.edu.
Website: http://www.hood.edu/academics/education/index.html.

Houston Baptist University, College of Education and Behavioral Sciences, Programs in Education, Houston, TX 77074-3298. Offers bilingual education (M Ed); counselor education (M Ed); curriculum and instruction (M Ed); educational administration (M Ed); educational diagnostician (M Ed); reading education (M Ed). Part-time programs available. Postbaccalaureate distance learning degree programs offered (no on-campus study). *Entrance requirements:* For master's, GRE General Test or MAT. Additional exam requirements/recommendations for international students: Required—TOEFL (minimum score 550 paper-based).

Idaho State University, Office of Graduate Studies, College of Education, Department of Educational Foundations, Pocatello, ID 83209-8059. Offers child and family studies (M Ed); curriculum leadership (M Ed); education (M Ed); educational administration (M Ed); educational foundations (5th Year Certificate); elementary education (M Ed), including K-12 education, literacy, secondary education. Part-time programs available. *Degree requirements:* For master's, comprehensive exam, thesis optional, oral exam, written exam; for 5th Year Certificate, comprehensive exam, thesis (for some programs), oral exam, written exam. *Entrance requirements:* For master's, GRE General Test or MAT, minimum undergraduate GPA of 3.0; for 5th Year Certificate, GRE General Test, minimum undergraduate GPA of 3.0, master's degree. Additional exam requirements/recommendations for international students: Required—TOEFL (minimum score 550 paper-based; 80 iBT). Electronic applications accepted. *Faculty research:* Child and families studies; business education; special education; math, science, and technology education.

Illinois State University, Graduate School, College of Education, Department of Curriculum and Instruction, Normal, IL 61790-2200. Offers curriculum and instruction (MS, MS Ed, Ed D); educational policies (Ed D); postsecondary education (Ed D); reading (MS Ed); supervision (Ed D). *Accreditation:* NCATE. *Degree requirements:* For master's, variable foreign language requirement, thesis or alternative; for doctorate, variable foreign language requirement, thesis/dissertation, 2 terms of residency, internship. *Entrance requirements:* For master's, GRE General Test, minimum GPA of 3.0 in last 60 hours of course work; for doctorate, GRE General Test. *Faculty research:* In-service and pre-service teacher education for teachers of English language learners; teachers for all children: developing a model for alternative, bilingual elementary certification for paraprofessionals in Illinois; Illinois Geographic Alliance, Connections Project.

Indiana State University, College of Graduate and Professional Studies, College of Education, Department of Curriculum, Instruction, and Media Technology, Terre Haute, IN 47809. Offers curriculum and instruction (M Ed, PhD); educational technology (MS). *Accreditation:* NCATE. *Degree requirements:* For doctorate, thesis/dissertation. *Entrance requirements:* For doctorate, GRE General Test. Electronic applications accepted. *Faculty research:* Discipline FERPA reading, teacher strengths and needs.

Indiana University Bloomington, School of Education, Department of Curriculum and Instruction, Bloomington, IN 47405-7000. Offers art education (MS, Ed D, PhD); curriculum studies (Ed D, PhD); elementary education (MS, Ed D, PhD, Ed S); mathematics education (MS, Ed D, PhD); science education (MS, Ed D, PhD); secondary education (MS, Ed D, PhD); social studies education (MS, PhD); special education (PhD, Ed S). *Accreditation:* NCATE. Part-time and evening/weekend programs available. Terminal master's awarded for partial completion of doctoral program. *Degree requirements:* For doctorate, thesis/dissertation; for Ed S, comprehensive exam or project. *Entrance requirements:* For master's, doctorate, and Ed S, GRE General Test. Electronic applications accepted.

Indiana University of Pennsylvania, School of Graduate Studies and Research, College of Education and Educational Technology, Department of Professional Studies in Education, Program in Curriculum and Instruction, Indiana, PA 15705-1087. Offers D Ed. *Accreditation:* NCATE. Part-time and evening/weekend programs available. *Faculty:* 19 full-time (12 women), 1 part-time/adjunct (0 women). *Students:* 16 full-time (12 women), 104 part-time (81 women); includes 9 minority (6 Black or African American, non-Hispanic/Latino; 1 Asian, non-Hispanic/Latino; 1 Hispanic/Latino; 1 Two or more races, non-Hispanic/Latino), 8 international. Average age 39. 61 applicants, 67% accepted, 32 enrolled. In 2013, 13 doctorates awarded. *Degree requirements:* For doctorate, one foreign language, comprehensive exam, thesis/dissertation. *Entrance requirements:* For doctorate, 2 letters of recommendation; recorded five-minute, research-based presentation; 1.5 hour online writing task. Additional exam

requirements/recommendations for international students: Required—TOEFL (minimum score 540 paper-based). *Application deadline:* Applications are processed on a rolling basis. Application fee: $50. Electronic applications accepted. *Expenses:* Tuition, state resident: full-time $3978; part-time $442 per credit. Tuition, nonresident: full-time $5967; part-time $663 per credit. *Required fees:* $2080; $115.55 per credit. $93 per semester. Tuition and fees vary according to degree level and program. *Financial support:* In 2013–14, 3 fellowships with full tuition reimbursements (averaging $2,402 per year), 29 research assistantships with full and partial tuition reimbursements (averaging $3,511 per year), 4 teaching assistantships with partial tuition reimbursements (averaging $22,848 per year) were awarded; career-related internships or fieldwork, Federal Work-Study, scholarships/grants, and unspecified assistantships also available. Support available to part-time students. Financial award application deadline: 4/15; financial award applicants required to submit FAFSA. *Unit head:* Dr. Mary R. Jalongo, Graduate Coordinator, 724-357-2417, E-mail: mjalongo@iup.edu. *Application contact:* Paula Stossel, Assistant Dean for Administration, 724-357-4511, E-mail: graduate-admissions@iup.edu.
Website: http://www.iup.edu/grad/CandI/default.aspx.

Indiana University–Purdue University Indianapolis, School of Education, Indianapolis, IN 46202-2896. Offers computer education (Certificate); curriculum and instruction (MS); early childhood (MS); educational leadership (MS, Certificate); English as a second language (Certificate); higher education and student affairs (MS); kindergarten (Certificate); language education (MS); reading (Certificate); school counseling (MS); special education (MS, Certificate). Part-time and evening/weekend programs available. *Faculty:* 41 full-time, 80 part-time/adjunct. *Students:* 113 full-time (78 women), 263 part-time (200 women); includes 88 minority (51 Black or African American, non-Hispanic/Latino; 1 American Indian or Alaska Native, non-Hispanic/Latino; 10 Asian, non-Hispanic/Latino; 19 Hispanic/Latino; 7 Two or more races, non-Hispanic/Latino), 5 international. Average age 33. 93 applicants, 54% accepted, 40 enrolled. In 2013, 179 master's awarded. *Degree requirements:* For master's, thesis optional. *Entrance requirements:* For master's, GRE General Test, minimum GPA of 3.0. Additional exam requirements/recommendations for international students: Required—TOEFL. *Application deadline:* For fall admission, 5/1 priority date for domestic students; for spring admission, 11/1 for domestic students. Application fee: $55 ($65 for international students). *Financial support:* Fellowships, research assistantships with partial tuition reimbursements, teaching assistantships, Federal Work-Study, institutionally sponsored loans, scholarships/grants, and tuition waivers (partial) available. Support available to part-time students. *Faculty research:* Teachers in the process of change, learning cycles, children's concepts of science. *Total annual research expenditures:* $614,458. *Unit head:* Dr. Pat Rogan, Executive Associate Dean, 317-274-6862, E-mail: progan@iupui.edu. *Application contact:* Donnella Dillon, Graduate Admissions Coordinator, 317-274-0645, E-mail: dmdillon@iupui.edu.
Website: http://education.iupui.edu/.

Inter American University of Puerto Rico, Arecibo Campus, Programs in Education, Arecibo, PR 00614-4050. Offers administration and educational supervision (MA Ed); counseling and guidance (MA Ed); curriculum and teaching (MA Ed), including biology education, English as a second language, history education, math education, Spanish; elementary education (MA Ed). *Degree requirements:* For master's, comprehensive exam, thesis optional. *Entrance requirements:* For master's, GRE, EXADEP, bachelor's degree in education or teaching license (administration and supervision) or courses in education and psychology (counseling and guidance), minimum GPA of 2.5 in last 60 credits.

Inter American University of Puerto Rico, Barranquitas Campus, Program in Education, Barranquitas, PR 00794. Offers curriculum and teaching (M Ed), including biology education, English as a second language, history education, mathematics education, Spanish; educational leadership and management (MA); elementary education (M Ed); information and library service technology (M Ed); special education (MA). *Degree requirements:* For master's, comprehensive exam, thesis optional. *Entrance requirements:* For master's, EXADEP, letter of recommendation. Electronic applications accepted.

Inter American University of Puerto Rico, Metropolitan Campus, Graduate Programs, Program in Education, San Juan, PR 00919-1293. Offers curriculum and instruction (Ed D); educational administration (Ed D); guidance and counseling (MA, Ed D); special education administration (Ed D). *Degree requirements:* For doctorate, comprehensive exam, thesis/dissertation. *Entrance requirements:* For doctorate, GRE, MAT, or EXADEP. Electronic applications accepted.

Inter American University of Puerto Rico, San Germán Campus, Graduate Studies Center, Program in Curriculum and Instruction, San Germán, PR 00683-5008. Offers Ed D. Part-time and evening/weekend programs available. *Faculty:* 9 full-time (6 women), 13 part-time/adjunct (7 women). *Students:* 35 full-time (30 women), 73 part-time (60 women); includes 107 minority (all Black or African American, non-Hispanic/Latino). Average age 43. 14 applicants, 86% accepted, 12 enrolled. In 2013, 10 doctorates awarded. *Expenses: Tuition:* Full-time $2424; part-time $202 per credit hour. *Required fees:* $260 per semester. Tuition and fees vary according to course level, course load, degree level and program. *Unit head:* Dr. Elba T. Irizarry, Director of Graduate Studies Center, 787-264-1912 Ext. 7357, Fax: 787-892-6350, E-mail: elbat@sg.inter.edu. *Application contact:* Dr. Mari Valentin, Program Coordinator, 787-264-1912 Ext. 7358, E-mail: mari_valentin@intersg.edu.

Iowa State University of Science and Technology, Department of Curriculum and Instruction, Ames, IA 50011. Offers curriculum and instructional technology (M Ed, MS, PhD); elementary education (M Ed, MS); historical, philosophical, and comparative studies in education (M Ed, MS); special education (M Ed, MS, PhD). *Degree requirements:* For master's, thesis or alternative; for doctorate, thesis/dissertation. *Entrance requirements:* For master's and doctorate, GRE General Test. Additional exam requirements/recommendations for international students: Required—TOEFL (minimum score 560 paper-based; 83 iBT), IELTS (minimum score 6.5). Electronic applications accepted.

John Brown University, Graduate Education Programs, Siloam Springs, AR 72761-2121. Offers curriculum and instruction (M Ed). Part-time and evening/weekend programs available. *Faculty:* 2 full-time (both women), 5 part-time/adjunct (all women). *Students:* 16 part-time (12 women). Average age 34. 12 applicants, 100% accepted, 11 enrolled. *Entrance requirements:* For master's, GRE (minimum score of 300). Additional exam requirements/recommendations for international students: Required—TOEFL (minimum score 550 paper-based; 70 iBT). *Expenses: Tuition:* Part-time $515 per credit hour. *Financial support:* Scholarships/grants and unspecified assistantships available. *Unit head:* Dr. Gloria Gale, Associate Dean of the School of Education, E-mail: ggale@jbu.edu. *Application contact:* Christopher Greathouse, Graduate Education Representative, 866-232-4723, E-mail: grad@jbu.edu.
Website: http://www.jbu.edu/grad/education/.

Johnson State College, Graduate Program in Education, Johnson, VT 05656. Offers applied behavior analysis (MA Ed), including applied behavior analysis; curriculum and instruction (MA Ed); literacy (MA Ed); secondary education (MA Ed); special education (MA Ed). Part-time programs available. *Faculty:* 3 full-time (1 woman), 6 part-time/

adjunct (5 women). *Students:* 6 full-time (5 women), 69 part-time (52 women). Average age 28. In 2013, 44 master's awarded. *Degree requirements:* For master's, comprehensive exam, thesis or alternative. *Entrance requirements:* For master's, interview. Additional exam requirements/recommendations for international students: Required—TOEFL. *Application deadline:* For fall admission, 4/1 priority date for domestic students, 1/15 priority date for international students; for spring admission, 11/1 for domestic students, 8/15 priority date for international students. Applications are processed on a rolling basis. Electronic applications accepted. *Expenses:* Tuition, state resident: full-time $11,448; part-time $477 per credit. Tuition, nonresident: full-time $24,720; part-time $1030 per credit. Tuition and fees vary according to reciprocity agreements. *Financial support:* Unspecified assistantships available. Financial award application deadline: 3/1; financial award applicants required to submit FAFSA. *Application contact:* Catherine H. Higley, Administrative Assistant, 800-635-2356 Ext. 1244, Fax: 802-635-1248, E-mail: catherine.higley@jsc.edu.

Jones International University, School of Education, Centennial, CO 80112. Offers adult education (M Ed); corporate training and knowledge management (M Ed); curriculum and instruction (M Ed), including elementary teacher licensure, secondary teacher licensure; e-learning technology and design (M Ed); educational leadership and administration (M Ed); educational leadership and administration: principal and administrator licensure (M Ed); elementary curriculum instruction and assessment (M Ed); higher education leadership and administration (M Ed); K-12 instructional technology (M Ed); K-12 instructional technology: teacher licensure (M Ed); secondary curriculum instruction and assessment (M Ed); technology and design (M Ed). Part-time and evening/weekend programs available. Postbaccalaureate distance learning degree programs offered (no on-campus study). *Entrance requirements:* For master's, minimum cumulative GPA of 2.5. Additional exam requirements/recommendations for international students: Recommended—TOEFL (minimum score 550 paper-based). Electronic applications accepted.

Kansas State University, Graduate School, College of Education, Department of Curriculum and Instruction, Manhattan, KS 66506. Offers career and technical education (Ed D, PhD); curriculum studies (Ed D, PhD); digital teaching and learning (MS); educational computing, design and online learning (MS); educational technology (Ed D, PhD); elementary/middle level curriculum and instruction (MS); English as a second language (MS); language/diversity education (Ed D, PhD); literacy education (Ed D, PhD); mathematics education (Ed D, PhD); middle level/secondary curriculum and instruction (MS); reading and language arts (MS); reading specialist endorsement (MS); science education (Ed D, PhD); social science education (Ed D, PhD); teacher education (Ed D, PhD); teacher leader/school improvement (MS, Ed D). *Accreditation:* NCATE. Part-time programs available. Postbaccalaureate distance learning degree programs offered (minimal on-campus study). *Faculty:* 18 full-time (13 women), 7 part-time/adjunct (4 women). *Students:* 39 full-time (23 women), 122 part-time (94 women); includes 19 minority (3 Black or African American, non-Hispanic/Latino; 2 Asian, non-Hispanic/Latino; 12 Hispanic/Latino; 2 Two or more races, non-Hispanic/Latino), 12 international. Average age 36. 80 applicants, 50% accepted, 34 enrolled. In 2013, 40 master's, 13 doctorates awarded. *Degree requirements:* For master's, comprehensive exam, portfolio, project, report or thesis; for doctorate, comprehensive exam, thesis/dissertation, preliminary exam. *Entrance requirements:* For master's, minimum GPA of 3.0, letters of recommendation; for doctorate, GRE, minimum GPA of 3.0, letters of recommendation, evidence of scholarly writing. Additional exam requirements/recommendations for international students: Required—TOEFL (minimum score 550 paper-based; 80 iBT). *Application deadline:* For fall admission, 3/1 priority date for domestic students, 2/1 priority date for international students; for spring admission, 10/1 priority date for domestic students, 8/1 priority date for international students. Applications are processed on a rolling basis. Application fee: $50 ($75 for international students). Electronic applications accepted. *Financial support:* In 2013–14, 1 research assistantship (averaging $16,900 per year), 8 teaching assistantships (averaging $12,466 per year) were awarded; career-related internships or fieldwork, institutionally sponsored loans, and scholarships/grants also available. Support available to part-time students. Financial award application deadline: 3/1; financial award applicants required to submit FAFSA. *Faculty research:* Literacy and technology, critical race theory and diversity, achievement gaps, school improvement, teacher education. *Total annual research expenditures:* $543,677. *Unit head:* Dr. Todd Goodson, Chair, 785-532-5904, Fax: 785-532-7304, E-mail: tgoodson@ksu.edu. *Application contact:* Dona Deam, Application Contact, 785-532-5595, Fax: 785-532-7304, E-mail: ddeam@ksu.edu.
Website: http://www.coe.k-state.edu/departments/edci/.

Kean University, College of Education, Program in Early Childhood Education, Union, NJ 07083. Offers administration in early childhood and family studies (MA); advanced curriculum and teaching (MA); classroom instruction (MA), including preschool-third grade; education for family living (MA). *Accreditation:* NCATE. Part-time programs available. *Faculty:* 22 full-time (12 women). *Students:* 3 full-time (2 women), 30 part-time (all women); includes 14 minority (4 Black or African American, non-Hispanic/Latino; 4 Asian, non-Hispanic/Latino; 6 Hispanic/Latino), 1 international. Average age 31. 29 applicants, 79% accepted, 15 enrolled. In 2013, 15 master's awarded. *Degree requirements:* For master's, portfolio. *Entrance requirements:* For master's, GRE General Test, PRAXIS Early Childhood Content Knowledge (for some programs), minimum GPA of 3.0, 2 letters of recommendation, teacher certification (for some programs), personal statement, official transcripts, resume. Additional exam requirements/recommendations for international students: Required—TOEFL (minimum score 550 paper-based; 79 iBT). *Application deadline:* For fall admission, 6/1 for domestic and international students; for spring admission, 12/1 for domestic and international students. Applications are processed on a rolling basis. Application fee: $75 ($150 for international students). Electronic applications accepted. *Expenses:* Tuition, state resident: full-time $12,099; part-time $589 per credit. Tuition, nonresident: full-time $16,399; part-time $722 per credit. *Required fees:* $3050; $139 per credit. Part-time tuition and fees vary according to course level, course load, degree level and program. *Financial support:* In 2013–14, research assistantships with full tuition reimbursements (averaging $3,713 per year) were awarded; unspecified assistantships also available. Financial award applicants required to submit FAFSA. *Unit head:* Dr. Polly Ashelman, Program Coordinator, 908-737-3785, E-mail: pashelma@kean.edu. *Application contact:* Ann-Marie Kay, Assistant Director of Graduate Admissions, 908-737-5922, Fax: 908-737-5925, E-mail: akay@kean.edu.
Website: http://grad.kean.edu/masters-programs/administration-early-childhood-family-studies.

Kean University, College of Education, Program in Instruction and Curriculum, Union, NJ 07083. Offers bilingual/bicultural education (MA); classroom instruction (MA); earth science (MA); mathematics/science/computer education (MA); teaching (MA); teaching English as a second language (MA); world languages (Spanish) (MA). *Accreditation:* NCATE. Part-time programs available. *Faculty:* 22 full-time (12 women). *Students:* 16 full-time (10 women), 100 part-time (72 women); includes 57 minority (8 Black or African American, non-Hispanic/Latino; 3 Asian, non-Hispanic/Latino; 45 Hispanic/Latino; 1 Two or more races, non-Hispanic/Latino). Average age 35. 56 applicants, 100% accepted, 38 enrolled. In 2013, 42 master's awarded. *Degree requirements:* For master's, comprehensive exam, thesis (for some programs), two-semester advanced seminar. *Entrance requirements:* For master's, GRE General Test or MAT, PRAXIS, minimum GPA of 3.0, personal statement, professional resume/curriculum vitae, commitment to working with children, certification (for some programs). Additional exam requirements/recommendations for international students: Required—TOEFL (minimum score 550 paper-based; 79 iBT). *Application deadline:* For fall admission, 6/1 for domestic and international students; for spring admission, 12/1 for domestic and international students. Applications are processed on a rolling basis. Application fee: $75 ($150 for international students). Electronic applications accepted. *Expenses:* Tuition, state resident: full-time $12,099; part-time $589 per credit. Tuition, nonresident: full-time $16,399; part-time $722 per credit. *Required fees:* $3050; $139 per credit. Part-time tuition and fees vary according to course level, course load, degree level and program. *Financial support:* In 2013–14, 6 research assistantships with full tuition reimbursements (averaging $3,713 per year) were awarded; unspecified assistantships also available. Financial award applicants required to submit FAFSA. *Unit head:* Dr. Gail Verdi, Program Coordinator, 908-737-3908, E-mail: gverdi@kean.edu. *Application contact:* Ann-Marie Kay, Assistant Director for Graduate Admissions, 908-737-5922, Fax: 908-737-5925, E-mail: akay@kean.edu.
Website: http://grad.kean.edu/masters-programs/bilingualbicultural-education-instruction-and-curriculum.

Keene State College, School of Professional and Graduate Studies, Keene, NH 03435. Offers curriculum and instruction (M Ed); education leadership (PMC); educational leadership (M Ed); safety and occupational health applied science (MS); school counselor (M Ed, PMC); special education (M Ed); teacher certification (Postbaccalaureate Certificate). *Accreditation:* NCATE. Part-time and evening/weekend programs available. *Faculty:* 8 full-time (5 women), 12 part-time/adjunct (6 women). *Students:* 39 full-time (33 women), 46 part-time (32 women); includes 8 minority (1 American Indian or Alaska Native, non-Hispanic/Latino; 2 Asian, non-Hispanic/Latino; 5 Hispanic/Latino). Average age 30. 46 applicants, 61% accepted, 13 enrolled. In 2013, 26 master's, 1 other advanced degree awarded. *Entrance requirements:* For master's, PRAXIS I, 3 references; official transcripts; minimum GPA of 2.5; interview. Additional exam requirements/recommendations for international students: Required—TOEFL (minimum score 550 paper-based; 61 iBT). *Application deadline:* For fall admission, 4/1 for domestic students; for spring admission, 12/1 for domestic students. Applications are processed on a rolling basis. Application fee: $50. Electronic applications accepted. *Expenses:* Tuition, state resident: full-time $10,410; part-time $480 per credit. Tuition, nonresident: full-time $17,795; part-time $530 per credit. *Required fees:* $2366; $94 per credit. Full-time tuition and fees vary according to course load. *Financial support:* Career-related internships or fieldwork, Federal Work-Study, institutionally sponsored loans, scholarships/grants, and unspecified assistantships available. Support available to part-time students. Financial award application deadline: 3/1; financial award applicants required to submit FAFSA. *Unit head:* Dr. Wayne Hartz, Interim Dean of Professional and Graduate Studies, 603-358-2220, E-mail: whartz@keene.edu. *Application contact:* Peggy Richmond, Director of Admissions, 603-358-2276, Fax: 603-358-2767, E-mail: admissions@keene.edu.
Website: http://www.keene.edu/gradstudies/.

Kent State University, Graduate School of Education, Health, and Human Services, School of Teaching, Learning and Curriculum Studies, Program in Curriculum and Instruction, Kent, OH 44242-0001. Offers M Ed, PhD, Ed S. *Accreditation:* NCATE. Part-time and evening/weekend programs available. *Faculty:* 25 full-time (17 women), 2 part-time/adjunct (both women). *Students:* 78 full-time (56 women), 48 part-time (37 women); includes 14 minority (6 Black or African American, non-Hispanic/Latino; 1 American Indian or Alaska Native, non-Hispanic/Latino; 6 Asian, non-Hispanic/Latino; 1 Hispanic/Latino), 14 international. 66 applicants, 23% accepted. In 2013, 16 master's, 11 doctorates, 1 other advanced degree awarded. *Degree requirements:* For doctorate, comprehensive exam, thesis/dissertation. *Entrance requirements:* For master's, 2 letters of reference, goals statement; for doctorate, GRE General Test, 2 letters of reference, goals statement, writing sample, resume; for Ed S, GRE General Test, 2 letters of reference, goals statement. Additional exam requirements/recommendations for international students: Required—TOEFL (minimum score 550 paper-based; 80 iBT). *Application deadline:* Applications are processed on a rolling basis. Application fee: $30 ($60 for international students). Electronic applications accepted. *Financial support:* In 2013–14, 19 research assistantships with full tuition reimbursements (averaging $12,563 per year), 4 teaching assistantships with full tuition reimbursements (averaging $13,500 per year) were awarded; Federal Work-Study, scholarships/grants, and unspecified assistantships also available. Financial award application deadline: 4/1; financial award applicants required to submit FAFSA. *Faculty research:* Gender equity issues in teaching, learning math and science, teaching as inquiry artistry, curriculum studies for democratic humanism. *Unit head:* Dr. James Henderson, Coordinator, 330-672-0631, E-mail: jhenders@kent.edu. *Application contact:* Nancy Miller, Academic Program Director, Office of Graduate Student Services, 330-672-2576, Fax: 330-672-9162, E-mail: ogs@kent.edu.

Kent State University at Stark, Graduate School of Education, Health and Human Services, Canton, OH 44720-7599. Offers curriculum and instruction studies (M Ed, MA).

Kutztown University of Pennsylvania, College of Education, Program in Secondary Education, Kutztown, PA 19530-0730. Offers biology (M Ed); curriculum and instruction (M Ed); English (M Ed); mathematics (M Ed); social studies (M Ed). *Accreditation:* NCATE. Part-time and evening/weekend programs available. *Faculty:* 6 full-time (2 women). *Students:* 34 full-time (17 women), 46 part-time (34 women); includes 4 minority (1 Asian, non-Hispanic/Latino; 3 Hispanic/Latino). Average age 31. 50 applicants, 70% accepted, 26 enrolled. In 2013, 31 master's awarded. *Degree requirements:* For master's, comprehensive exam, thesis optional. *Entrance requirements:* For master's, GRE General Test. Additional exam requirements/recommendations for international students: Required—TOEFL (minimum score 550 paper-based; 79 iBT). *Application deadline:* For fall admission, 8/1 priority date for domestic and international students; for spring admission, 12/1 priority date for domestic and international students. Applications are processed on a rolling basis. Application fee: $35. Electronic applications accepted. *Expenses: Tuition, area resident:* Part-time $442 per credit. Tuition, state resident: part-time $442 per credit. Tuition, nonresident: part-time $663 per credit. *Required fees:* $80 per credit. *Financial support:* Career-related internships or fieldwork, Federal Work-Study, scholarships/grants, and unspecified assistantships available. Financial award application deadline: 3/1; financial award applicants required to submit FAFSA. *Unit head:* Dr. Theresa Stahler, Chairperson, 610-683-4259, Fax: 610-683-1338, E-mail: stahler@kutztown.edu. *Application contact:* Kelly Hish, Admissions Clerk, 610-683-4200, Fax: 610-683-1393, E-mail: graduate@kutztown.edu.

LaGrange College, Graduate Programs, Department of Education, LaGrange, GA 30240-2999. Offers curriculum and instruction (M Ed, Ed S); middle grades (MAT); secondary education (MAT). Part-time and evening/weekend programs available. *Degree requirements:* For master's, comprehensive exam. *Entrance requirements:* For master's, GRE, MAT, minimum GPA of 2.5. Additional exam requirements/recommendations for international students: Required—TOEFL (minimum score 550 paper-based).

Lake Erie College, School of Education and Professional Studies, Painesville, OH 44077-3389. Offers curriculum and instruction (MS Ed); education (MS Ed); educational leadership (MS Ed); reading (MS Ed). Part-time and evening/weekend programs available. *Faculty:* 2 full-time (1 woman). *Students:* 7 part-time (4 women). Average age 27. 6 applicants, 33% accepted, 1 enrolled. In 2013, 10 master's awarded. *Degree requirements:* For master's, comprehensive exam (for some programs), thesis optional, applied research project. *Entrance requirements:* For master's, GRE General Test (minimum score of 440 verbal or 500 quantitative) or minimum GPA of 2.75; bachelor's degree from accredited 4-year institution; references; essay. Additional exam requirements/recommendations for international students: Required—TOEFL (minimum score 550 paper-based). *Application deadline:* For fall admission, 8/1 priority date for domestic students, 6/1 for international students; for spring admission, 12/15 for domestic students, 10/1 for international students. Applications are processed on a rolling basis. Application fee: $30. Electronic applications accepted. Application fee is waived when completed online. *Expenses:* Contact institution. *Financial support:* Tuition waivers and unspecified assistantships available. Financial award applicants required to submit FAFSA. *Unit head:* Prof. Dale Sheptak, Dean of the School of Education and Professional Studies, 440-375-7131, E-mail: dsheptak@lec.edu. *Application contact:* Milena Velez, Senior Admissions Counselor, 800-916-0904, Fax: 440-375-7000, E-mail: admissions@lec.edu.
Website: http://www.lec.edu/med.

Lander University, School of Education, Greenwood, SC 29649-2099. Offers elementary education (M Ed); teaching (MAT). *Accreditation:* NCATE. Part-time programs available. *Degree requirements:* For master's, comprehensive exam, thesis or alternative. *Entrance requirements:* For master's, GRE General Test. Additional exam requirements/recommendations for international students: Required—TOEFL (minimum score 550 paper-based). Electronic applications accepted.

La Sierra University, School of Education, Department of Curriculum and Instruction, Riverside, CA 92515. Offers curriculum and instruction (MA, Ed D, Ed S); teaching (MAT). Part-time and evening/weekend programs available. *Degree requirements:* For doctorate, thesis/dissertation; for Ed S, thesis optional. *Entrance requirements:* For master's, minimum GPA of 3.0; for doctorate, GRE General Test, GRE Subject Test, minimum GPA of 3.3; for Ed S, minimum GPA of 3.3. *Faculty research:* New teacher success, politics of knowledge, computer-assisted instruction, diversity issues.

Lee University, Program in Education, Cleveland, TN 37320-3450. Offers college student development (MS); curriculum and instruction (M Ed, Ed S); educational leadership (M Ed, Ed S); elementary education (MAT); higher education administration (MS); middle grades (MAT); secondary education (MAT); special education (M Ed); special education (secondary) (MAT). Part-time programs available. *Faculty:* 14 full-time (7 women), 6 part-time/adjunct (3 women). *Students:* 30 full-time (23 women), 62 part-time (37 women); includes 8 minority (3 Black or African American, non-Hispanic/Latino; 1 American Indian or Alaska Native, non-Hispanic/Latino; 2 Asian, non-Hispanic/Latino; 2 Hispanic/Latino). Average age 30. 40 applicants, 100% accepted, 30 enrolled. In 2013, 117 master's, 2 other advanced degrees awarded. *Degree requirements:* For master's, variable foreign language requirement, comprehensive exam, thesis, internship. *Entrance requirements:* For master's, MAT or GRE General Test, minimum GPA of 2.75, 3 letters of recommendation, interview, writing sample, official transcripts. Additional exam requirements/recommendations for international students: Required—TOEFL (minimum score 450 paper-based). *Application deadline:* For fall admission, 4/1 priority date for domestic and international students; for spring admission, 10/1 priority date for domestic and international students. Applications are processed on a rolling basis. Application fee: $25. *Expenses: Tuition:* Full-time $9900; part-time $550 per credit hour. *Required fees:* $35 per term. One-time fee: $25. *Financial support:* In 2013–14, 47 students received support, including 1 teaching assistantship (averaging $1,500 per year); career-related internships or fieldwork, Federal Work-Study, institutionally sponsored loans, scholarships/grants, and unspecified assistantships also available. Financial award application deadline: 3/1; financial award applicants required to submit FAFSA. *Unit head:* Dr. Gary Riggins, Director, 423-614-8193. *Application contact:* Vicki Glasscock, Graduate Admissions Director, 423-614-8059, E-mail: vglasscock@leeuniversity.edu.
Website: http://www.leeuniversity.edu/academics/graduate/education.

Lehigh University, College of Education, Program in Educational Leadership, Bethlehem, PA 18015. Offers educational leadership (M Ed, Ed D); K-12 principal (Certificate); superintendent of schools (Certificate); supervisor of curriculum and instruction (Certificate); supervisor of pupil services (Certificate); supervisor of special education (Certificate); MBA/M Ed. Part-time and evening/weekend programs available. Postbaccalaureate distance learning degree programs offered (minimal on-campus study). *Faculty:* 7 full-time (2 women), 7 part-time/adjunct (2 women). *Students:* 7 full-time (6 women), 114 part-time (54 women); includes 14 minority (8 Black or African American, non-Hispanic/Latino; 1 American Indian or Alaska Native, non-Hispanic/Latino; 5 Hispanic/Latino), 11 international. Average age 36. 66 applicants, 76% accepted, 17 enrolled. In 2013, 45 master's, 15 doctorates awarded. *Degree requirements:* For doctorate, comprehensive exam, thesis/dissertation. *Entrance requirements:* For master's and Certificate, minimum undergraduate GPA of 3.0; for doctorate, GRE General Test or MAT, minimum graduate GPA of 3.6, 2 letters of recommendation, essay, transcript. Additional exam requirements/recommendations for international students: Required—TOEFL (minimum score 600 paper-based; 93 iBT). *Application deadline:* For fall admission, 1/15 for domestic and international students; for spring admission, 11/1 for domestic and international students. Applications are processed on a rolling basis. Application fee: $65. Electronic applications accepted. *Financial support:* In 2013–14, 1 student received support. Fellowships with full and partial tuition reimbursements available, research assistantships with full and partial tuition reimbursements available, teaching assistantships with full and partial tuition reimbursements available, career-related internships or fieldwork, Federal Work-Study, institutionally sponsored loans, scholarships/grants, tuition waivers (full and partial), and unspecified assistantships available. Financial award application deadline: 1/31; financial award applicants required to submit FAFSA. *Faculty research:* School finance and law, supervision of instruction, middle-level education, organizational change, leadership preparation and development, international school leadership, urban school leadership, comparative education, social justice. *Unit head:* Dr. Floyd D. Beachum, Director, 610-758-5955, Fax: 610-758-3227, E-mail: fdb209@lehigh.edu. *Application contact:* Donna M. Johnson, Manager, Graduate Programs Admissions, 610-758-3231, Fax: 610-758-6223, E-mail: dmj4@lehigh.edu.
Website: http://coe.lehigh.edu/academics/disciplines/edl.

Lesley University, School of Education, Cambridge, MA 02138-2790. Offers arts, community, and education (M Ed); autism studies (Certificate); curriculum and instruction (M Ed, CAGS); early childhood education (M Ed); ecological teaching and learning (MS); educational studies (PhD), including adult learning, educational leadership, individually designed; elementary education (M Ed); emergent technologies for educators (Certificate); ESLArts: language learning through the arts (M Ed); high school education (M Ed); individually designed (M Ed); integrated teaching through the arts (M Ed); literacy for K-8 classroom teachers (M Ed); mathematics education (M Ed); middle school education (M Ed); moderate disabilities (M Ed); online learning (Certificate); reading (CAGS); science in education (M Ed); severe disabilities (M Ed); special needs (CAGS); specialist teacher of reading (M Ed); teacher of visual art (M Ed); technology in education (M Ed, CAGS). *Accreditation:* Teacher Education Accreditation Council. Part-time and evening/weekend programs available. Postbaccalaureate distance learning degree programs offered (no on-campus study). *Faculty:* 40 full-time (30 women), 104 part-time/adjunct (77 women). *Students:* 453 full-time (381 women), 1,672 part-time (1,435 women); includes 284 minority (139 Black or African American, non-Hispanic/Latino; 11 American Indian or Alaska Native, non-Hispanic/Latino; 38 Asian, non-Hispanic/Latino; 58 Hispanic/Latino; 5 Native Hawaiian or other Pacific Islander, non-Hispanic/Latino; 33 Two or more races, non-Hispanic/Latino), 22 international. Average age 35. In 2013, 1,137 master's, 18 doctorates, 51 other advanced degrees awarded. *Degree requirements:* For master's, practicum; for doctorate, thesis/dissertation. *Entrance requirements:* For master's, Massachusetts Tests for Educator Licensure (MTEL), transcripts, statement of purpose, recommendations; interview (for special education); for doctorate, GRE General Test, transcripts, statement of purpose, recommendations, interview, master's degree, resume; for other advanced degree, interview, master's degree. Additional exam requirements/recommendations for international students: Required—TOEFL (minimum score 550 paper-based; 80 iBT). *Application deadline:* Applications are processed on a rolling basis. Application fee: $50. Electronic applications accepted. *Expenses: Tuition:* Part-time $900 per credit. *Financial support:* In 2013–14, 15 fellowships (averaging $3,600 per year) were awarded; career-related internships or fieldwork, Federal Work-Study, scholarships/grants, tuition waivers, and unspecified assistantships also available. Financial award application deadline: 4/15; financial award applicants required to submit FAFSA. *Faculty research:* Assessment in literacy, mathematics and science; autism spectrum disorders; instructional technology and online learning; multicultural education and English language learners. *Unit head:* Dr. Jack Gillette, Dean, 617-349-8401, Fax: 617-349-8607, E-mail: jgillett@lesley.edu. *Application contact:* Martha Sheehan, Director of Admissions, 888-LESLEYU, Fax: 617-349-8313, E-mail: info@lesley.edu.
Website: http://www.lesley.edu/soe.html.

Lewis & Clark College, Graduate School of Education and Counseling, Department of Teacher Education, Program in Curriculum and Instruction, Portland, OR 97219-7899. Offers M Ed. Part-time and evening/weekend programs available. *Entrance requirements:* For master's, minimum GPA of 2.75. Additional exam requirements/recommendations for international students: Required—TOEFL (minimum score 575 paper-based). Electronic applications accepted.

Liberty University, School of Education, Lynchburg, VA 24515. Offers administration and supervision (M Ed); curriculum and instruction (Ed D, Ed S); early childhood education (M Ed); educational leadership (Ed D, Ed S); educational technology and online instruction (M Ed); elementary education (M Ed, MAT); English (M Ed); gifted education (M Ed); history (M Ed); leadership (M Ed); math specialist (M Ed); middle grades (M Ed, MAT); outdoor adventure sport (MS); reading specialist (M Ed); school counseling (M Ed); secondary education (MAT); special education (M Ed, MAT); sport management (MS), including administration, outdoor recreation, sport management, tourism; sports administration (MS); student service (M Ed); teaching and learning (M Ed); tourism (MS). *Accreditation:* NCATE. Part-time programs available. Postbaccalaureate distance learning degree programs offered (minimal on-campus study). *Students:* 2,241 full-time (1,639 women), 4,413 part-time (3,240 women); includes 2,052 minority (1,588 Black or African American, non-Hispanic/Latino; 37 American Indian or Alaska Native, non-Hispanic/Latino; 67 Asian, non-Hispanic/Latino; 173 Hispanic/Latino; 37 Native Hawaiian or other Pacific Islander, non-Hispanic/Latino; 150 Two or more races, non-Hispanic/Latino), 15 international. Average age 37. 6,185 applicants, 43% accepted, 1603 enrolled. In 2013, 1,256 master's, 117 doctorates, 470 other advanced degrees awarded. *Degree requirements:* For doctorate, comprehensive exam, thesis/dissertation. *Entrance requirements:* For master's, GRE General Test or MAT (if taken in or before 1999), 2 letters of recommendation, minimum undergraduate GPA of 3.0, curriculum vitae; for doctorate and Ed S, GRE General Test or MAT (if taken before 1999), minimum master's GPA of 3.0, 3 years of teaching experience. Additional exam requirements/recommendations for international students: Required—TOEFL (minimum score 600 paper-based; 100 iBT). *Application deadline:* For fall admission, 6/1 for domestic students; for spring admission, 11/1 for domestic students. Applications are processed on a rolling basis. Application fee: $50. Electronic applications accepted. *Expenses:* Contact institution. *Financial support:* Federal Work-Study and tuition waivers (partial) available. *Faculty research:* Self-determination, character education, bibliotherapy, learning styles, distance education. *Unit head:* Dr. Karen L. Parker, Dean, 434-582-2195, Fax: 434-582-2468, E-mail: kparker@liberty.edu. *Application contact:* Jay Bridge, Director of Graduate Admissions, 800-424-9595, Fax: 800-628-7977, E-mail: gradadmissions@liberty.edu.
Website: http://www.liberty.edu/academics/education/graduate/.

Lincoln Memorial University, Carter and Moyers School of Education, Harrogate, TN 37752-1901. Offers administration and supervision (M Ed, Ed S); counseling and guidance (M Ed); curriculum and instruction (M Ed, Ed D, Ed S); English (M Ed); executive leadership (Ed D); higher education administration (Ed D); human resource development (Ed D); leadership and administration (Ed D). Part-time and evening/weekend programs available. Postbaccalaureate distance learning degree programs offered. *Degree requirements:* For master's, comprehensive exam, thesis optional; for Ed S, comprehensive exam. *Entrance requirements:* For master's, PRAXIS, NTE, GRE, MAT, letters of recommendation; for Ed S, graduate transcripts. Additional exam requirements/recommendations for international students: Recommended—TOEFL. *Faculty research:* Brain compatible teaching and learning; poverty in Appalachia; leadership for change; ethics, moral responsibility and social justice; human and organizational learning.

Louisiana State University in Shreveport, College of Business, Education, and Human Development, Program in Education, Shreveport, LA 71115-2399. Offers curriculum and instruction (M Ed); educational leadership (M Ed); school counseling (M Ed). *Accreditation:* NCATE. Part-time programs available. *Students:* 1 (woman) full-time, 99 part-time (80 women); includes 26 minority (20 Black or African American, non-Hispanic/Latino; 4 Hispanic/Latino; 2 Two or more races, non-Hispanic/Latino), 1 international. Average age 37. 111 applicants, 97% accepted, 42 enrolled. In 2013, 24 master's awarded. *Degree requirements:* For master's, orally-presented project, 200-hour internship (educational leadership). *Entrance requirements:* For master's, GRE, minimum GPA of 2.5; teacher certification; recommendations and interview (for educational leadership). Additional exam requirements/recommendations for international students: Required—TOEFL (minimum score 550 paper-based; 80 iBT). *Application deadline:* For fall admission, 6/30 for domestic and international students; for spring admission, 11/30 for domestic and international students. Applications are processed on a rolling basis. Application fee: $10 ($20 for international students). *Expenses: Tuition, area resident:* Part-time $182 per credit hour. *Required fees:* $51. *Financial support:* In 2013–14, 5 research assistantships (averaging $2,150 per year) were awarded. *Unit head:* Dr. Pat Doerr, Coordinator, 318-797-5033, Fax: 318-798-4144, E-mail: pat.doerr@lsus.edu. *Application contact:* Christianne Wojcik, Director of Academic Services, 318-797-5247, Fax: 318-798-4120, E-mail: christianne.wojcik@lsus.edu.

Curriculum and Instruction

Louisiana Tech University, Graduate School, College of Education, Department of Curriculum, Instruction and Leadership, Ruston, LA 71272. Offers curriculum and instruction (M Ed, Ed D), including adult education (M Ed), early childhood (M Ed), English education (M Ed), mathematics education (M Ed), science education (M Ed), social studies education (M Ed), special education (M Ed); educational leadership (M Ed, Ed D). *Accreditation:* NCATE. Part-time programs available. *Degree requirements:* For doctorate, thesis/dissertation. *Entrance requirements:* For master's and doctorate, GRE General Test. *Application deadline:* For fall admission, 7/29 for domestic students; for spring admission, 2/3 for domestic students. Application fee: $20 ($30 for international students). *Financial support:* Fellowships, research assistantships, and teaching assistantships available. Financial award application deadline: 2/1. *Unit head:* Dr. Pauline Leonard, Head, 318-257-4609, Fax: 318-257-2379. *Application contact:* Dr. John Harrison, Associate Dean of Graduate Studies, 318-257-3229, Fax: 318-257-2379, E-mail: johnharrison@latech.edu.
Website: http://www.latech.edu/education/cil/.

Lourdes University, Graduate School, Sylvania, OH 43560-2898. Offers business (MBA); leadership (M Ed); nurse anesthesia (MSN); nurse educator (MSN); nurse leader (MSN); organizational leadership (MOL); reading (M Ed); teaching and curriculum (M Ed); theology (MA). Evening/weekend programs available. *Entrance requirements:* Additional exam requirements/recommendations for international students: Required—TOEFL. *Application deadline:* For fall admission, 6/15 priority date for domestic students; for spring admission, 11/1 priority date for domestic students. Application fee: $25. *Application contact:* Melissa Bergfeld, Administrative Assistant, 419-824-3517, Fax: 419-824-3510, E-mail: mbergfeld2@lourdes.edu.
Website: http://www.lourdes.edu/gradschool.aspx.

Loyola University Chicago, School of Education, Program in Curriculum and Instruction, Chicago, IL 60660. Offers M Ed, Ed D. Part-time and evening/weekend programs available. *Faculty:* 23 full-time (16 women), 49 part-time/adjunct (42 women). *Students:* 68. Average age 35. 34 applicants, 56% accepted, 13 enrolled. In 2013, 6 master's, 6 doctorates awarded. Terminal master's awarded for partial completion of doctoral program. *Degree requirements:* For master's, comprehensive exam; for doctorate, comprehensive exam, thesis/dissertation. *Entrance requirements:* For master's, 3 references, minimum GPA of 3.0, resume; for doctorate, GRE, 3 references, interview, minimum GPA of 3.0, resume. Additional exam requirements/recommendations for international students: Required—TOEFL (minimum score 550 paper-based; 79 iBT). *Application deadline:* For fall admission, 2/15 for domestic and international students; for spring admission, 11/1 for domestic and international students. Applications are processed on a rolling basis. Application fee: $50. Electronic applications accepted. Application fee is waived when completed online. *Expenses: Tuition:* Full-time $16,740; part-time $930 per credit. *Required fees:* $135 per semester. *Financial support:* In 2013–14, research assistantships with full tuition reimbursements (averaging $12,000 per year), 6 teaching assistantships with full tuition reimbursements (averaging $12,000 per year) were awarded; fellowships with partial tuition reimbursements, institutionally sponsored loans, scholarships/grants, tuition waivers (partial), and unspecified assistantships also available. Support available to part-time students. Financial award application deadline: 2/1; financial award applicants required to submit FAFSA. *Faculty research:* School improvement, technology, change, reading. *Unit head:* Dr. Ann Marie Ryan, Director, 312-915-6232, E-mail: aryan3@luc.edu. *Application contact:* Marie Rosin-Dittmar, Information Contact, 312-915-6800, E-mail: schleduc@luc.edu.

Loyola University Maryland, Graduate Programs, School of Education, Program in Curriculum and Instruction, Baltimore, MD 21210-2699. Offers M Ed, MA, CAS. Part-time programs available. *Degree requirements:* For master's, thesis. *Entrance requirements:* For master's, essay, transcripts, resume. Additional exam requirements/recommendations for international students: Required—TOEFL (minimum score 550 paper-based). Electronic applications accepted.

Lynchburg College, Graduate Studies, School of Education and Human Development, M Ed Program in Curriculum and Instruction, Lynchburg, VA 24501-3199. Offers instructional leadership (M Ed); teacher licensure (M Ed). Part-time and evening/weekend programs available. *Faculty:* 7 full-time (4 women). *Students:* 7 full-time (5 women), 8 part-time (6 women); includes 2 minority (1 Black or African American, non-Hispanic/Latino; 1 Asian, non-Hispanic/Latino). Average age 29. In 2013, 3 master's awarded. *Degree requirements:* For master's, National Board Certification portfolio or comprehensive exam. *Entrance requirements:* For master's, GRE, minimum GPA of 3.0 (preferred), official transcripts (bachelor's, others as relevant), three letters of recommendation, career goals statement. Additional exam requirements/recommendations for international students: Required—TOEFL (minimum score 550 paper-based; 79 iBT), IELTS (minimum score 6.5). *Application deadline:* For fall admission, 7/31 for domestic students, 6/1 for international students; for spring admission, 11/30 for domestic students, 10/15 for international students. Applications are processed on a rolling basis. Application fee: $30. Electronic applications accepted. Application fee is waived when completed online. *Financial support:* Fellowships, research assistantships, Federal Work-Study, scholarships/grants, health care benefits, and unspecified assistantships available. Support available to part-time students. Financial award application deadline: 7/31; financial award applicants required to submit FAFSA. *Unit head:* Dr. John Walker, Associate Professor/Program Director, Curriculum and Instruction, 434-544-8032, Fax: 434-544-8483, E-mail: walker.jc@lynchburg.edu. *Application contact:* Anne Pingstock, Executive Assistant, Graduate Studies, 434-544-8383, Fax: 434-544-8483, E-mail: gradstudies@lynchburg.edu.
Website: http://www.lynchburg.edu/master-education-curriculum-and-instruction.

Lyndon State College, Graduate Programs in Education, Department of Education, Lyndonville, VT 05851-0919. Offers curriculum and instruction (M Ed); reading specialist (M Ed); special education (M Ed); teaching and counseling (M Ed). Part-time and evening/weekend programs available. *Degree requirements:* For master's, exam or major field project. *Entrance requirements:* Additional exam requirements/recommendations for international students: Recommended—TOEFL (minimum score 500 paper-based).

Malone University, Graduate Program in Education, Canton, OH 44709. Offers curriculum and instruction (MA); curriculum, instruction, and professional development (MA); educational leadership (principal license) (MA); intervention specialist (MA). Part-time and evening/weekend programs available. *Faculty:* 8 full-time (4 women), 12 part-time/adjunct (9 women). *Students:* 10 full-time (6 women), 59 part-time (44 women); includes 5 minority (2 Black or African American, non-Hispanic/Latino; 1 Hispanic/Latino; 2 Two or more races, non-Hispanic/Latino). Average age 32. In 2013, 13 master's awarded. *Degree requirements:* For master's, research project. *Entrance requirements:* For master's, minimum GPA of 3.0, teaching license. Additional exam requirements/recommendations for international students: Required—TOEFL (minimum score 550 paper-based; 79 iBT). *Application deadline:* Applications are processed on a rolling basis. *Financial support:* Tuition waivers (partial) available. Support available to part-time students. Financial award application deadline: 6/30. *Faculty research:* Educational leadership styles: Jesus as master teacher, assessment accommodations for English language learners, preparing culturally proficient teachers, using naturally occurring text in the classroom to meet the syntactic needs of students with learning disabilities, using tablet instructional technology to meet the needs of students with disabilities. *Unit head:* Dr. Moses B. Rumano, Director, 330-471-8349, Fax: 330-471-8563, E-mail: mrumano@malone.edu. *Application contact:* Dan DePasquale, Senior Recruiter, 330-471-8381, Fax: 330-471-8343, E-mail: depasquale@malone.edu.
Website: http://www.malone.edu/admissions/graduate/education/.

Marquette University, Graduate School, College of Education, Department of Educational Policy and Leadership, Milwaukee, WI 53201-1881. Offers college student personnel administration (M Ed); curriculum and instruction (MA); education (MA); educational administration (M Ed); educational policy and foundations (MA); elementary education (Certificate); literacy (MA); principal (Certificate); reading specialist (Certificate); reading teacher (Certificate); secondary education (Certificate); superintendent (Certificate). Part-time and evening/weekend programs available. *Faculty:* 15 full-time (10 women), 3 part-time/adjunct (2 women). *Students:* 39 full-time (31 women), 107 part-time (70 women); includes 19 minority (7 Black or African American, non-Hispanic/Latino; 2 American Indian or Alaska Native, non-Hispanic/Latino; 3 Asian, non-Hispanic/Latino; 6 Hispanic/Latino; 1 Two or more races, non-Hispanic/Latino), 2 international. Average age 30. 144 applicants, 74% accepted, 67 enrolled. In 2013, 48 master's, 4 doctorates, 12 other advanced degrees awarded. Terminal master's awarded for partial completion of doctoral program. *Degree requirements:* For master's, comprehensive exam, thesis (for some programs); for doctorate, thesis/dissertation, qualifying exam, supporting minor. *Entrance requirements:* For master's, GRE General Test or MAT, official transcripts from all current and previous colleges/universities except Marquette, three letters of recommendation, statement of purpose; for doctorate, GRE General Test, MAT, sample of written work, official transcripts from all current and previous colleges/universities except Marquette, three letters of recommendation, statement of purpose, resume/curriculum vitae; for Certificate, GRE General Test or MAT, master's degree. Additional exam requirements/recommendations for international students: Required—TOEFL (minimum score 530 paper-based). *Application deadline:* For fall admission, 1/15 for domestic and international students. Application fee: $50. *Expenses:* Contact institution. *Financial support:* In 2013–14, 130 students received support, including 1 fellowship with full tuition reimbursement available (averaging $18,780 per year), 5 research assistantships with full tuition reimbursements available (averaging $13,404 per year); health care benefits, tuition waivers (partial), and unspecified assistantships also available. Support available to part-time students. Financial award application deadline: 2/15. *Faculty research:* Leadership; social justice in education; development of lifelong learners; race, class, and schooling in historical perspective; urban teacher education. *Unit head:* Dr. Ellen Eckman, Chair, 414-288-1561, E-mail: ellen.eckman@marquette.edu. *Application contact:* Dr. Sharon Chubbuck, Associate Professor, 414-288-5895.

Martin Luther College, Graduate Studies, New Ulm, MN 56073. Offers instruction (MS Ed); leadership (MS Ed); special education (MS Ed). Part-time programs available. Postbaccalaureate distance learning degree programs offered. *Degree requirements:* For master's, capstone project or comprehensive exam. *Entrance requirements:* For master's, undergraduate degree in education from an accredited college or university, minimum undergraduate GPA of 3.0. Electronic applications accepted.

Massachusetts College of Liberal Arts, Graduate Programs, North Adams, MA 01247-4100. Offers business (MBA); educational administration (M Ed); educational leadership (CAGS); instruction and curriculum (M Ed); instructional technology (M Ed); physical education and health (M Ed); reading (M Ed); special education (M Ed). Part-time and evening/weekend programs available. *Degree requirements:* For master's, thesis. *Entrance requirements:* For master's, writing sample.

McDaniel College, Graduate and Professional Studies, Program in Curriculum and Instruction, Westminster, MD 21157-4390. Offers MS. *Degree requirements:* For master's, comprehensive exam (for some programs), thesis optional. *Entrance requirements:* For master's, letter of reference. Additional exam requirements/recommendations for international students: Required—TOEFL.

McGill University, Faculty of Graduate and Postdoctoral Studies, Faculty of Education, Department of Integrated Studies in Education, Montréal, QC H3A 2T5, Canada. Offers culture and values in education (MA, PhD); curriculum studies (MA); educational leadership (MA, Certificate); educational studies (PhD); integrated studies in education (M Ed); second language education (MA, PhD).

McKendree University, Graduate Programs, Programs in Education, Lebanon, IL 62254-1299. Offers curriculum design and instruction (Ed D, Ed S); educational administration and leadership (MA Ed); educational studies (MA Ed); higher education administrative services (MA Ed); music education (MA Ed); reading (MA Ed); special education (MA Ed); teacher leadership (MA Ed); teaching certification (MA Ed). *Accreditation:* NCATE. Part-time and evening/weekend programs available. Postbaccalaureate distance learning degree programs offered (no on-campus study). *Entrance requirements:* For master's, official transcripts from all institutions previously attended, minimum GPA of 3.0, resume, references; for doctorate, GRE (within the past 5 years), master's degree in education and Ed S, or the equivalent, from regionally-accredited institution; official transcripts from all institutions previously attended; curriculum vitae/resume; essay/personal statement; two years of teaching/professional experience; for Ed S, GRE (within the past 5 years), master's degree in education from regionally-accredited institution of higher education; official transcripts from all institutions previously attended; curriculum vitae/resume; essay/personal statement; two years of teaching/professional experience. Additional exam requirements/recommendations for international students: Required—TOEFL. Electronic applications accepted.

McNeese State University, Doré School of Graduate Studies, Burton College of Education, Office of Graduate Education Programs, Program in Curriculum and Instruction, Lake Charles, LA 70609. Offers early childhood education (M Ed); elementary education (M Ed); reading (M Ed); secondary education (M Ed). Evening/weekend programs available. *Entrance requirements:* For master's, GRE, teaching certificate.

Medaille College, Program in Education, Buffalo, NY 14214-2695. Offers adolescent education (MS Ed); curriculum and instruction (MS Ed); education preparation (MS Ed); literacy (MS Ed); special education (MS). *Accreditation:* Teacher Education Accreditation Council. Part-time and evening/weekend programs available. *Faculty:* 12 full-time (9 women), 28 part-time/adjunct (19 women). *Students:* 159 full-time (123 women), 25 part-time (22 women); includes 8 minority (5 Black or African American, non-Hispanic/Latino; 3 Hispanic/Latino), 88 international. Average age 29. 209 applicants, 96% accepted, 61 enrolled. In 2013, 253 master's awarded. *Degree requirements:* For master's, comprehensive exam (for some programs), thesis or alternative. *Entrance requirements:* For master's, minimum undergraduate GPA of 2.7. Additional exam requirements/recommendations for international students: Required—TOEFL (minimum score 550 paper-based). *Application deadline:* For fall admission, 8/15 priority date for domestic students; for spring admission, 1/15 priority date for domestic students. Applications are processed on a rolling basis. Application fee: $35. Electronic applications accepted. *Financial support:* Federal Work-Study available. Financial award applicants required to submit FAFSA. *Faculty research:* Curriculum

planning, truancy, tracking minority students, curriculum design, mentoring students. *Unit head:* Dr. Illana Lane, Dean, School of Education, 716-880-2553, E-mail: ilane@medaille.edu. *Application contact:* E-mail: sageadmissions@medaille.edu.
Website: http://www.medaille.edu.

Memorial University of Newfoundland, School of Graduate Studies, Faculty of Education, St. John's, NL A1C 5S7, Canada. Offers counseling psychology (M Ed); curriculum, teaching, and learning studies (M Ed); education (PhD); educational leadership studies (M Ed); information technology (M Ed); post-secondary studies (M Ed, Diploma), including health professional education (Diploma). Part-time programs available. *Degree requirements:* For master's, thesis optional, internship, paper folio, project; for doctorate, comprehensive exam, thesis/dissertation, thesis seminar, oral defense of thesis. *Entrance requirements:* For master's, undergraduate degree with at least 2nd class standing, 1-2 years work experience; for doctorate, minimum A average in graduate course work, MA in education, 2 years professional experience; for Diploma, 2nd class degree, 2 years of work experience with adult learners, appropriate academic qualifications and work experience in a health-related field. Electronic applications accepted. *Faculty research:* Critical thinking, literacy, cognitive studies and counseling, educational change, technology in instruction.

Mercer University, Graduate Studies, Cecil B. Day Campus, Tift College of Education (Atlanta), Macon, GA 31207-0003. Offers curriculum and instruction (PhD); early childhood education (M Ed, MAT, Ed S); educational leadership (PhD, Ed S); higher education leadership (M Ed); independent and charter school leadership (M Ed); middle grades education (M Ed, MAT); reading education (M Ed); school counseling (Ed S); secondary education (M Ed, MAT); teacher leadership (Ed S). *Accreditation:* NCATE. Part-time and evening/weekend programs available. *Faculty:* 40 full-time (20 women), 9 part-time/adjunct (4 women). *Students:* 240 full-time (197 women), 382 part-time (320 women); includes 343 minority (315 Black or African American, non-Hispanic/Latino; 4 American Indian or Alaska Native, non-Hispanic/Latino; 9 Asian, non-Hispanic/Latino; 9 Hispanic/Latino; 1 Native Hawaiian or other Pacific Islander, non-Hispanic/Latino; 5 Two or more races, non-Hispanic/Latino), 4 international. Average age 36. In 2013, 233 master's, 24 doctorates, 47 other advanced degrees awarded. *Degree requirements:* For master's and Ed S, research project; for doctorate, comprehensive exam, thesis/dissertation. *Entrance requirements:* For master's, GRE or MAT, minimum undergraduate GPA of 2.75; for doctorate, GRE; for Ed S, GRE or MAT, minimum GPA of 3.25; for EDS degrees in educational leadership and teacher leadership: 3 years of certified teaching experience. Additional exam requirements/recommendations for international students: Required—TOEFL. *Application deadline:* For fall admission, 8/1 for domestic and international students; for spring admission, 12/1 for domestic and international students; for summer admission, 5/1 for domestic and international students. Applications are processed on a rolling basis. Application fee: $25. *Expenses:* Contact institution. *Financial support:* Federal Work-Study available. Support available to part-time students. Financial award application deadline: 5/1. *Faculty research:* Educational technology, multicultural and minority issues in education, educational leadership (P-12 and higher education), school discipline and school bullying, standards-based mathematics education. *Unit head:* Dr. Paige L. Tompkins, Interim Dean, 478-301-5397, Fax: 478-301-2280, E-mail: tompkins_pl@mercer.edu. *Application contact:* Dr. Allison Gilmore, Associate Dean for Graduate Teacher Education, 678-547-6333, Fax: 678-547-6055, E-mail: gilmore_a@mercer.edu.
Website: http://www.mercer.edu/education/.

Mercer University, Graduate Studies, Macon Campus, Tift College of Education (Macon), Macon, GA 31207-0003. Offers curriculum and instruction (PhD); education leadership (PhD), including P-12; educational leadership (Ed S); higher education (M Ed); teacher leadership (Ed S). *Accreditation:* NCATE. Part-time and evening/weekend programs available. Postbaccalaureate distance learning degree programs offered (minimal on-campus study). *Faculty:* 15 full-time (6 women), 2 part-time/adjunct (1 woman). *Students:* 39 full-time (20 women), 59 part-time (47 women); includes 41 minority (38 Black or African American, non-Hispanic/Latino; 1 Asian, non-Hispanic/Latino; 2 Hispanic/Latino), 2 international. Average age 35. In 2013, 7 master's, 18 doctorates awarded. *Degree requirements:* For master's, research project report; for doctorate, comprehensive exam, thesis/dissertation. *Entrance requirements:* For master's, GRE or MAT, minimum GPA of 2.75; for doctorate, GRE, minimum GPA of 3.5; interview; writing sample; 3 recommendations; for Ed S, GRE or MAT, minimum GPA of 3.5 (for Ed S in teacher leadership), 3.0 (for Ed S in educational leadership). Additional exam requirements/recommendations for international students: Required—TOEFL. *Application deadline:* For fall admission, 8/1 for domestic and international students; for spring admission, 12/1 for domestic and international students. Applications are processed on a rolling basis. Application fee: $35. *Expenses:* Contact institution. *Financial support:* Federal Work-Study and institutionally sponsored loans available. Support available to part-time students. Financial award application deadline: 5/1. *Faculty research:* Teacher effectiveness, specific learning disabilities, inclusion. *Unit head:* Dr. Paige L. Tompkins, Interim Dean, 478-301-5397, Fax: 478-301-2280, E-mail: tompkins_pl@mercer.edu. *Application contact:* Tracey M. Wofford, Associate Director of Admissions, 678-547-6422, Fax: 678-547-6367, E-mail: wofford_tm@mercer.edu.
Website: http://education.mercer.edu/graduate/.

Messiah College, Program in Education, Mechanicsburg, PA 17055. Offers curriculum and instruction (M Ed); special education (M Ed); teaching English to speakers of other languages (M Ed). Part-time programs available. Postbaccalaureate distance learning degree programs offered (no on-campus study). Electronic applications accepted. *Expenses: Tuition:* Part-time $595 per credit hour. *Required fees:* $30 per course. *Faculty research:* Socio-cultural perspectives on education, TESOL, autism, special education.

Michigan State University, The Graduate School, College of Education, Department of Teacher Education, East Lansing, MI 48824. Offers curriculum, instruction and teacher education (PhD, Ed S); teaching and curriculum (MA). *Entrance requirements:* Additional exam requirements/recommendations for international students: Required—TOEFL. Electronic applications accepted.

Middle Tennessee State University, College of Graduate Studies, College of Education, Department of Educational Leadership, Program in Curriculum and Instruction, Murfreesboro, TN 37132. Offers curriculum and instruction (M Ed, Ed S); English as a second language (M Ed, Ed S); secondary education (M Ed); technology and curriculum design (Ed S). *Accreditation:* NCATE. Part-time and evening/weekend programs available. Postbaccalaureate distance learning degree programs offered. *Faculty:* 22 full-time (11 women), 22 part-time/adjunct (12 women). *Degree requirements:* For master's, comprehensive exam; for Ed S, comprehensive exam, thesis or alternative. *Entrance requirements:* For master's and Ed S, GRE, MAT or PRAXIS. Additional exam requirements/recommendations for international students: Required—TOEFL (minimum score 525 paper-based; 71 iBT) or IELTS (minimum score 6). *Application deadline:* For fall admission, 6/1 for domestic and international students. Applications are processed on a rolling basis. Application fee: $25 ($30 for international students). Electronic applications accepted. *Financial support:* Tuition waivers available. Support available to part-time students. Financial award application deadline: 5/1. *Unit head:* Dr. James Huffman, Chair, 615-898-2331, Fax: 615-898-2859, E-mail: jim.huffman@mtsu.edu. *Application contact:* Dr. Michael D. Allen, Vice Provost for Research and Dean, 615-898-2840, Fax: 615-904-8020, E-mail: michael.allen@mtsu.edu.

Midwestern State University, Graduate School, West College of Education, Program in Curriculum and Instruction, Wichita Falls, TX 76308. Offers M Ed. Part-time and evening/weekend programs available. *Degree requirements:* For master's, comprehensive exam. *Entrance requirements:* For master's, GRE General Test, MAT, or GMAT. Additional exam requirements/recommendations for international students: Required—TOEFL (minimum score 550 paper-based). *Application deadline:* For fall admission, 7/1 priority date for domestic students, 4/1 for international students; for spring admission, 11/1 priority date for domestic students, 8/1 for international students. Applications are processed on a rolling basis. Application fee: $35 ($50 for international students). Electronic applications accepted. *Expenses:* Tuition, state resident: full-time $3627; part-time $201.50 per credit hour. Tuition, nonresident: full-time $10,899; part-time $605.50 per credit hour. *Required fees:* $1357. *Financial support:* Teaching assistantships with partial tuition reimbursements, career-related internships or fieldwork, Federal Work-Study, institutionally sponsored loans, scholarships/grants, tuition waivers (partial), and unspecified assistantships available. Support available to part-time students. Financial award application deadline: 3/1; financial award applicants required to submit FAFSA. *Faculty research:* Role of the twenty-first century principal, instructional effectiveness, motivation, curriculum theory, educational research methodology. *Unit head:* Dr. Pamela Whitehouse, Graduate Coordinator, 940-397-4139, Fax: 940-397-4672, E-mail: pamela.whitehouse@mwsu.edu. *Application contact:* Dr. Pamela Whitehouse, Graduate Coordinator, 940-397-4139, Fax: 940-397-4672, E-mail: pamela.whitehouse@mwsu.edu.
Website: http://www.mwsu.edu/academics/education/.

Mills College, Graduate Studies, School of Education, Oakland, CA 94613-1000. Offers child life in hospitals (MA); early childhood education (MA); education (MA), including art education, curriculum and instruction, elementary education, English education, foreign language education, mathematics education, science education, secondary education, social studies education, teaching; educational leadership (MA, Ed D). Part-time and evening/weekend programs available. *Faculty:* 10 full-time (7 women), 13 part-time/adjunct (10 women). *Students:* 154 full-time (136 women), 54 part-time (47 women); includes 96 minority (32 Black or African American, non-Hispanic/Latino; 1 American Indian or Alaska Native, non-Hispanic/Latino; 23 Asian, non-Hispanic/Latino; 27 Hispanic/Latino; 1 Native Hawaiian or other Pacific Islander, non-Hispanic/Latino; 12 Two or more races, non-Hispanic/Latino), 2 international. Average age 25. 222 applicants, 89% accepted, 110 enrolled. In 2013, 96 master's, 38 doctorates awarded. Terminal master's awarded for partial completion of doctoral program. *Degree requirements:* For master's, comprehensive exam, thesis (for some programs); for doctorate, thesis/dissertation. *Entrance requirements:* For master's, statement of purpose, official transcript, 3 recommendations. Additional exam requirements/recommendations for international students: Required—TOEFL (minimum score 550 paper-based; 80 iBT) or IELTS (minimum score 6). *Application deadline:* For fall admission, 12/31 priority date for domestic students, 12/15 for international students; for spring admission, 11/1 priority date for domestic students, 10/1 for international students. Applications are processed on a rolling basis. Application fee: $50. Electronic applications accepted. *Expenses: Tuition:* Full-time $29,860. *Required fees:* $1134. Part-time tuition and fees vary according to course load, degree level and program. *Financial support:* In 2013–14, 130 students received support, including 130 fellowships with full and partial tuition reimbursements available (averaging $7,565 per year); career-related internships or fieldwork and scholarships/grants also available. Support available to part-time students. Financial award application deadline: 2/1; financial award applicants required to submit FAFSA. *Faculty research:* Early childhood education, teacher preparation, educational leadership. *Total annual research expenditures:* $3.5 million. *Unit head:* Dr. Katherine Schultz, Department Head, 510-430-3384, Fax: 510-430-2159, E-mail: kschultz@mills.edu. *Application contact:* Shrim Bathey, Director of Graduate Admission, 510-430-3309, Fax: 510-430-2159, E-mail: grad-admission@mills.edu.
Website: http://www.mills.edu/education.

Minnesota State University Mankato, College of Graduate Studies, College of Education, Department of Educational Studies: K–12 and Secondary Programs, Mankato, MN 56001. Offers curriculum and instruction (SP); educational technology (MS); library media education (MS, Certificate); teacher licensure (MAT); teaching and learning (MS, Certificate). *Accreditation:* NCATE. *Students:* 53 full-time (35 women), 107 part-time (73 women). *Degree requirements:* For master's, comprehensive exam, thesis or alternative; for other advanced degree, comprehensive exam, thesis. *Entrance requirements:* For master's, GRE General Test or MAT, minimum GPA of 3.0 during previous 2 years; for other advanced degree, GRE, minimum GPA of 3.0. Additional exam requirements/recommendations for international students: Required—TOEFL. *Application deadline:* For fall admission, 7/1 priority date for domestic students, 5/1 for international students; for spring admission, 11/1 for domestic students, 10/1 for international students. Applications are processed on a rolling basis. Application fee: $40. Electronic applications accepted. *Financial support:* Application deadline: 3/15. *Unit head:* Dr. Kitty Foord, Chairperson, 507-389-1965. *Application contact:* 507-389-2321, E-mail: grad@mnsu.edu.
Website: http://ed.mnsu.edu/ksp/.

Minnesota State University Moorhead, Graduate Studies, College of Education and Human Services, Program in Curriculum and Instruction, Moorhead, MN 56563-0002. Offers MS. *Accreditation:* NCATE. Part-time programs available. *Degree requirements:* For master's, comprehensive exam, final oral exam, project or thesis. *Entrance requirements:* For master's, MAT, bachelor's degree in education, minimum GPA of 2.75, one year teaching experience. Additional exam requirements/recommendations for international students: Required—TOEFL (minimum score 550 paper-based). Electronic applications accepted.

Misericordia University, College of Professional Studies and Social Sciences, Program in Education, Dallas, PA 18612-1098. Offers instructional technology (MS); reading specialist (MS); special education (MS). Part-time and evening/weekend programs available. *Faculty:* 1 full-time (0 women), 12 part-time/adjunct (8 women). *Students:* 44 part-time (35 women); includes 1 minority (Hispanic/Latino). Average age 32. In 2013, 24 master's awarded. *Entrance requirements:* For master's, minimum undergraduate GPA of 3.0. Additional exam requirements/recommendations for international students: Required—TOEFL. *Application deadline:* Applications are processed on a rolling basis. Application fee: $35. Electronic applications accepted. *Expenses: Tuition:* Full-time $14,450; part-time $680 per credit. Tuition and fees vary according to degree level. *Financial support:* In 2013–14, 11 students received support. Scholarships/grants available. Support available to part-time students. Financial award application deadline: 6/30; financial award applicants required to submit FAFSA. *Unit head:* Dr. Steven Broskoske, Associate Professor, Education Department, 570-674-6761, E-mail: sbroskos@misericordia.edu. *Application contact:* David Pasquini, Assistant Director of Admissions, 570-674-8183, Fax: 570-674-6232, E-mail: dpasquin@misericordia.edu.
Website: http://www.misericordia.edu/misericordia_pg.cfm?page_id=387&subcat_id=108.

Curriculum and Instruction

Mississippi College, Graduate School, School of Education, Department of Teacher Education and Leadership, Clinton, MS 39058. Offers art (M Ed); biological science (M Ed); business education (M Ed); computer science (M Ed); dyslexia therapy (M Ed); educational leadership (M Ed, Ed D, Ed S); elementary education (M Ed, Ed S); English (M Ed); higher education administration (MS); mathematics (M Ed); secondary education (M Ed); social studies (history) (M Ed); teaching arts (M Ed). Part-time programs available. Postbaccalaureate distance learning degree programs offered (no on-campus study). *Degree requirements:* For master's, comprehensive exam, thesis optional. *Entrance requirements:* For master's, NTE. Additional exam requirements/ recommendations for international students: Recommended—TOEFL, IELTS. Electronic applications accepted.

Mississippi State University, College of Education, Department of Curriculum, Instruction and Special Education, Mississippi State, MS 39762. Offers curriculum and instruction (PhD), including early childhood education (MS, PhD), elementary education (PhD, Ed S), general curriculum and instruction, reading education, secondary education (PhD, Ed S), special education (PhD, Ed S); education (Ed S), including elementary education (PhD, Ed S), secondary education (PhD, Ed S), special education (PhD, Ed S); elementary education (MS), including early childhood education (MS, PhD), general elementary education, middle level education; middle level alternate route (MAT); secondary education (MS); secondary teacher alternate route (MAT); special education (MS). *Accreditation:* NCATE. Part-time and evening/weekend programs available. *Faculty:* 11 full-time (9 women). *Students:* 58 full-time (40 women), 143 part-time (100 women); includes 62 minority (56 Black or African American, non-Hispanic/ Latino; 2 American Indian or Alaska Native, non-Hispanic/Latino; 3 Hispanic/Latino; 1 Two or more races, non-Hispanic/Latino). Average age 33. 181 applicants, 32% accepted, 52 enrolled. In 2013, 44 master's, 1 doctorate, 7 other advanced degrees awarded. *Degree requirements:* For master's, comprehensive exam; for doctorate, thesis/dissertation; for Ed S, comprehensive exam, thesis or alternative. *Entrance requirements:* For master's, GRE, minimum GPA of 2.75 in junior and senior year, eligibility for initial teacher certification; for doctorate, GRE, minimum GPA of 3.4 on previous graduate work; for Ed S, GRE, minimum GPA of 3.2 on master's degree. Additional exam requirements/recommendations for international students: Required—TOEFL (minimum score 550 paper-based; 79 iBT); Recommended—IELTS (minimum score 6.5). *Application deadline:* For fall admission, 3/1 priority date for domestic students, 5/1 for international students; for spring admission, 9/1 priority date for domestic students, 9/1 for international students. Applications are processed on a rolling basis. Application fee: $60. Electronic applications accepted. *Financial support:* In 2013–14, 7 research assistantships with full and partial tuition reimbursements (averaging $9,623 per year), 2 teaching assistantships (averaging $11,382 per year) were awarded; Federal Work-Study, institutionally sponsored loans, scholarships/ grants, and unspecified assistantships also available. Financial award application deadline: 4/1; financial award applicants required to submit FAFSA. *Faculty research:* Early childhood education, reading, rural schools, multicultural education, use of technology in instruction. *Unit head:* Dr. Devon Brenner, Professor and Interim Head, 662-325-7119, Fax: 662-325-7857, E-mail: devon@ra.msstate.edu. *Application contact:* Dr. Dana Franz, Graduate Coordinator, 662-325-3703, Fax: 662-325-7857, E-mail: tstevonson@colled.msstate.edu.
Website: http://www.cise.msstate.edu/.

Mississippi University for Women, Graduate School, College of Education and Human Sciences, Columbus, MS 39701-9998. Offers differentiated instruction (M Ed); educational leadership (M Ed); gifted studies (M Ed); reading/literacy (M Ed); teaching (MAT). *Accreditation:* ASHA; NCATE. Part-time programs available. *Degree requirements:* For master's, comprehensive exam, thesis optional. *Entrance requirements:* For master's, GRE General Test or NTE (M Ed in gifted education or MS in speech/language pathology), MAT (M Ed in instructional management), minimum QPA of 3.0.

Montana State University, College of Graduate Studies, College of Education, Health, and Human Development, Department of Education, Bozeman, MT 59717. Offers adult and higher education (Ed D); curriculum and instruction (M Ed, Ed D), including professional educator (M Ed), technology education (M Ed); education (M Ed), including adult and higher education, educational leadership, school counseling; educational leadership (Ed D, Ed S). *Accreditation:* Teacher Education Accreditation Council. Part-time programs available. Postbaccalaureate distance learning degree programs offered (minimal on-campus study). *Degree requirements:* For master's, comprehensive exam; for doctorate, comprehensive exam, thesis/dissertation. *Entrance requirements:* For master's, GRE, 3 letters of reference, essays, BA transcripts; for doctorate, GRE, MAT, 3 letters of reference, essay, BA and M Ed transcripts; for Ed S, PRAXIS. Additional exam requirements/recommendations for international students: Required—TOEFL (minimum score 550 paper-based). Electronic applications accepted. *Faculty research:* Critical literacy; standards-based education; school Improvement, organizational change, leadership in rural education, leadership in Indian education; student Learning; multicultural/culturally responsive education for social justice Native American indigenous education, community-centered education teacher preparation.

Montana State University Billings, College of Education, Department of Educational Theory and Practice, Option in General Curriculum, Billings, MT 59101-0298. Offers M Ed. *Accreditation:* NCATE. Part-time programs available. *Degree requirements:* For master's, thesis or professional paper and/or field experience. *Entrance requirements:* For master's, GRE General Test or MAT, minimum GPA of 3.0 (undergraduate), 3.25 (graduate). *Application deadline:* Applications are processed on a rolling basis. Application fee: $40. *Expenses:* Tuition, state resident: full-time $2653.75; part-time $1718 per semester. Tuition, nonresident: full-time $7015; part-time $4640 per semester. *Required fees:* $2445; $444 per credit. *Financial support:* Teaching assistantships, career-related internships or fieldwork, Federal Work-Study, institutionally sponsored loans, scholarships/grants, tuition waivers (partial), and unspecified assistantships available. Support available to part-time students. Financial award application deadline: 5/1. *Faculty research:* Social studies education, science education. *Unit head:* Dr. Tony Hecimovic, Professor, 406-657-2210, Fax: 406-657-2807, E-mail: thecimovic@msubillings.edu. *Application contact:* David M. Sullivan, Graduate Studies Counselor, 406-657-2053, Fax: 406-657-2299, E-mail: dsullivan@msubillings.edu.

Montclair State University, The Graduate School, College of Education and Human Services, Department of Educational Foundations, Montclair, NJ 07043-1624. Offers educational foundations (Certificate); pedagogy and philosophy (Ed D). Part-time and evening/weekend programs available. *Entrance requirements:* For doctorate, GRE General Test, 3 years of classroom teaching experience, interview, writing sample. Additional exam requirements/recommendations for international students: Required—TOEFL (minimum score 83 iBT) or IELTS. Electronic applications accepted. *Faculty research:* Pragmatism and education: theoretical and practical, history of education, children and philosophy, academic development, developing theory and practice - transforming K-12 school pedagogy.

Montclair State University, The Graduate School, College of Education and Human Services, Department of Secondary and Special Education, Program in Teaching in Subject Area, Montclair, NJ 07043-1624. Offers art (MAT); biology (MAT); chemistry (MAT); earth science (MAT); English (MAT); French (MAT); health and physical education (MAT); health education (MAT); mathematics (MAT); music (MAT); physical education (MAT); physical science (MAT); social studies (MAT); Spanish (MAT); teacher of English as a second language (MAT). *Degree requirements:* For master's, comprehensive exam, thesis or alternative. *Entrance requirements:* For master's, GRE General Test, interview, 2 letters of recommendation. Additional exam requirements/ recommendations for international students: Required—TOEFL (minimum score 83 iBT), IELTS (minimum score 6.5). Electronic applications accepted.

Moravian College, Moravian College Comenius Center, Education Programs, Bethlehem, PA 18018-6650. Offers curriculum and instruction (M Ed); education (MAT). Part-time and evening/weekend programs available. *Degree requirements:* For master's, thesis. *Entrance requirements:* For master's, state teacher certification.

Morehead State University, Graduate Programs, College of Education, Department of Curriculum and Instruction, Morehead, KY 40351. Offers curriculum and instruction (Ed S); elementary education (MA Ed), including elementary education, international education, middle school education, reading; secondary education (MA Ed); special education (MA Ed); teaching (MAT). Part-time and evening/weekend programs available. *Degree requirements:* For master's, comprehensive exam, thesis optional; for Ed S, thesis, oral exam. *Entrance requirements:* For master's, GRE General Test, minimum GPA of 2.75, teaching certificate; for Ed S, GRE General Test, interview, master's degree, minimum GPA of 3.5, work experience. Additional exam requirements/ recommendations for international students: Required—TOEFL (minimum score 500 paper-based). Electronic applications accepted. *Faculty research:* Communicative competence of learning-disabled students, teaching social studies in elementary schools, ungraded primary school organization, study skills.

Morehead State University, Graduate Programs, College of Education, Department of Foundational and Graduate Studies in Education, Morehead, KY 40351. Offers adult and higher education (MA, Ed S); certified professional counselor (Ed S); counseling P-12 (MA); curriculum and instruction (Ed S); educational technology (MA Ed); instructional leadership (Ed S); school administration (MA); school counseling (Ed S); teacher leader business and marketing content (MA Ed); teacher leader business and marketing technology (MA Ed); teacher leader educational technology (MA Ed); teacher leader English (MA Ed); teacher leader gifted education (MA Ed); teacher leader IECE certification (MA Ed); teacher leader interdisciplinary education P-5 (MA Ed); teacher leader middle grades (MA Ed); teacher leader non IECE certification (MA Ed); teacher leader reading/writing - non-certification (MA Ed); teacher leader reading/writing certification (MA Ed); teacher leader school communication - certification (MA Ed); teacher leader school communication - non-certification (MA Ed); teacher leader social studies (MA Ed); teacher leader special education (MA Ed). *Accreditation:* NCATE. Part-time and evening/weekend programs available. *Degree requirements:* For master's, thesis optional, oral and/or written comprehensive exams; for Ed S, thesis, oral exam. *Entrance requirements:* For master's, GRE General Test, minimum overall undergraduate GPA of 2.5; for Ed S, GRE General Test, interview, master's degree, minimum GPA of 3.5, work experience. Additional exam requirements/ recommendations for international students: Required—TOEFL (minimum score 500 paper-based). Electronic applications accepted. *Faculty research:* Character education, school accountability, computer applications for school administrators.

Mount Saint Vincent University, Graduate Programs, Faculty of Education, Program in Curriculum Studies, Halifax, NS B3M 2J6, Canada. Offers education of young adolescents (M Ed, MA Ed, MA-R); general studies (M Ed, MA Ed, MA-R); teaching English as a second language (M Ed, MA Ed, MA-R). Part-time and evening/weekend programs available. Postbaccalaureate distance learning degree programs offered (minimal on-campus study). *Degree requirements:* For master's, thesis (for some programs). *Entrance requirements:* For master's, bachelor's degree in related field, minimum B average, 1 year of teaching experience. Electronic applications accepted. *Faculty research:* Science education, cultural studies, international education, curriculum development.

National Louis University, National College of Education, Chicago, IL 60603. Offers administration and supervision (M Ed, Ed D, CAS, Ed S); curriculum and instruction (M Ed, MS Ed, CAS); early childhood administration (M Ed, CAS); early childhood education (M Ed, MAT, MS Ed, CAS); education (Ed D); educational psychology/human learning and development (M Ed, MS Ed, CAS, Ed S); elementary education (MAT); interdisciplinary curriculum and instruction (M Ed); mathematics education (M Ed, MS Ed, CAS); reading and language (M Ed, MS Ed, CAS); school psychology (M Ed, Ed S); science education (M Ed, MS Ed, CAS); secondary education (MAT); special education (M Ed, MAT, CAS); technology in education (M Ed, CAS). *Accreditation:* NCATE. Part-time and evening/weekend programs available. *Degree requirements:* For doctorate, comprehensive exam, thesis/dissertation. *Entrance requirements:* For master's, MAT or GRE, minimum GPA of 3.0; for doctorate, GRE General Test, minimum GPA of 3.25, interview, resume, writing sample, 4 recommendations. Additional exam requirements/recommendations for international students: Required—TOEFL (minimum score 550 paper-based; 79 iBT).

Newman University, Master of Education Program, Wichita, KS 67213-2097. Offers building leadership (MS Ed); curriculum and instruction (MS Ed), including English as a second language, reading specialist; organizational leadership (MS Ed). *Accreditation:* NCATE. Part-time and evening/weekend programs available. Postbaccalaureate distance learning degree programs offered (no on-campus study). *Faculty:* 3 full-time (1 woman), 22 part-time/adjunct (all women). *Students:* 19 full-time (15 women), 498 part-time (407 women); includes 66 minority (19 Black or African American, non-Hispanic/ Latino; 5 American Indian or Alaska Native, non-Hispanic/Latino; 10 Asian, non-Hispanic/Latino; 27 Hispanic/Latino; 1 Native Hawaiian or other Pacific Islander, non-Hispanic/Latino; 4 Two or more races, non-Hispanic/Latino). Average age 37. 67 applicants, 73% accepted, 35 enrolled. In 2013, 53 master's awarded. *Degree requirements:* For master's, thesis optional. *Entrance requirements:* For master's, 3 years' full-time teaching experience, minimum GPA of 3.0, writing sample, 2 letters of recommendation, evidence of teaching certification. Additional exam requirements/ recommendations for international students: Required—TOEFL (minimum score 600 paper-based; 100 iBT). *Application deadline:* For fall admission, 8/15 priority date for domestic students, 7/15 priority date for international students; for spring admission, 1/ 10 priority date for domestic students, 11/15 priority date for international students. Applications are processed on a rolling basis. Application fee: $25 ($40 for international students). Electronic applications accepted. *Expenses:* Contact institution. *Financial support:* Application deadline: 8/15; applicants required to submit FAFSA. *Unit head:* Dr. Gina Marx, Director of Graduate Education, 316-942-4291 Ext. 2416, Fax: 316-942-4483, E-mail: marxg@newmanu.edu. *Application contact:* Linda Kay Sabala, Director of Graduate Admissions, 316-942-4291 Ext. 2230, Fax: 316-942-4483, E-mail: sabalal@newmanu.edu.
Website: http://www.newmanu.edu/studynu/graduate/master-science-education.

New Mexico Highlands University, Graduate Studies, School of Education, Las Vegas, NM 87701. Offers curriculum and instruction (MA); educational leadership (MA); professional counseling (MA); special education (MA), including). Part-time programs available. *Faculty:* 25 full-time (12 women), 26 part-time/adjunct (22 women). *Students:* 139 full-time (106 women), 245 part-time (180 women); includes 207 minority (10 Black

or African American, non-Hispanic/Latino; 20 American Indian or Alaska Native, non-Hispanic/Latino; 3 Asian, non-Hispanic/Latino; 172 Hispanic/Latino; 1 Native Hawaiian or other Pacific Islander, non-Hispanic/Latino; 1 Two or more races, non-Hispanic/Latino), 17 international. Average age 39. 137 applicants, 99% accepted, 102 enrolled. In 2013, 112 master's awarded. *Degree requirements:* For master's, comprehensive exam, thesis or alternative. *Entrance requirements:* For master's, minimum undergraduate GPA of 3.0. Additional exam requirements/recommendations for international students: Required—TOEFL (minimum score 540 paper-based). *Application deadline:* For fall admission, 8/1 priority date for domestic students. Applications are processed on a rolling basis. Application fee: $15. *Expenses:* Tuition, state resident: full-time $4278; part-time $178 per credit hour. Tuition, nonresident: full-time $6716; part-time $281 per credit hour. One-time fee: $15. *Financial support:* Career-related internships or fieldwork, Federal Work-Study, institutionally sponsored loans, scholarships/grants, traineeships, tuition waivers (partial), and unspecified assistantships available. Support available to part-time students. Financial award application deadline: 3/1; financial award applicants required to submit FAFSA. *Faculty research:* Middle school curriculum, integrated computer applications for pre-service classroom teachers, adolescent literacy, narrative cognitive modes in New Mexico multicultural setting, math and math education. *Unit head:* Dr. Belinda Laumbach, Interim Dean, 505-454-3146, Fax: 505-454-8884, E-mail: laumbach_b@nmhu.edu. *Application contact:* Diane Trujillo, Administrative Assistant for Graduate Studies, 505-454-3266, Fax: 505-426-2117, E-mail: dtrujillo@nmhu.edu.

New Mexico State University, Graduate School, College of Education, Department of Curriculum and Instruction, Las Cruces, NM 88003-8001. Offers curriculum and instruction (MAT, Ed D, PhD); general education (MA). *Accreditation:* NCATE. Part-time and evening/weekend programs available. Postbaccalaureate distance learning degree programs offered (no on-campus study). *Faculty:* 29 full-time (20 women), 7 part-time/adjunct (4 women). *Students:* 152 full-time (110 women), 290 part-time (228 women); includes 237 minority (16 Black or African American, non-Hispanic/Latino; 6 American Indian or Alaska Native, non-Hispanic/Latino; 13 Asian, non-Hispanic/Latino; 197 Hispanic/Latino; 5 Two or more races, non-Hispanic/Latino), 32 international. Average age 37. 153 applicants, 72% accepted, 83 enrolled. In 2013, 85 master's, 17 doctorates awarded. *Degree requirements:* For master's, thesis optional; for doctorate, comprehensive exam, thesis/dissertation. *Entrance requirements:* For master's, minimum cumulative GPA of 3.0; for doctorate, portfolio. Additional exam requirements/recommendations for international students: Required—TOEFL (minimum score 550 paper-based; 79 iBT), IELTS (minimum score 6.5). *Application deadline:* For fall admission, 12/15 priority date for domestic and international students; for spring admission, 11/1 for domestic students. Applications are processed on a rolling basis. Application fee: $40 ($50 for international students). *Expenses:* Tuition, state resident: full-time $5398; part-time $224.90 per credit. Tuition, nonresident: full-time $18,821; part-time $784.20 per credit. *Required fees:* $1310; $54.60 per credit. *Financial support:* In 2013–14, 103 students received support, including 1 research assistantship (averaging $16,261 per year), 19 teaching assistantships (averaging $15,132 per year); career-related internships or fieldwork, Federal Work-Study, scholarships/grants, health care benefits, and unspecified assistantships also available. Support available to part-time students. Financial award application deadline: 3/1. *Faculty research:* Bilingual and English as a second language education, critical pedagogy/multicultural education, learning design and technology, early childhood education, language literacy and culture. *Total annual research expenditures:* $11,339. *Unit head:* Dr. David Rutledge, Associate Department Head for Graduate Studies, 575-646-5411, Fax: 575-646-5436, E-mail: rutledge@nmsu.edu. *Application contact:* Felicia Rios, Coordinator/Administrative Assistant, Graduate Programs, 575-646-5821, Fax: 575-646-5436, E-mail: candi_grad@nmsu.edu.
Website: http://ci.education.nmsu.edu.

Nicholls State University, Graduate Studies, College of Education, Department of Teacher Education, Thibodaux, LA 70310. Offers administration and supervision (M Ed); counselor education (M Ed); curriculum and instruction (M Ed). *Accreditation:* NCATE. Part-time and evening/weekend programs available. *Degree requirements:* For master's, comprehensive exam, portfolio. *Entrance requirements:* For master's, GRE General Test, teaching license. Electronic applications accepted.

North Carolina Central University, School of Education, Department of Curriculum, Instruction and Professional Studies, Durham, NC 27707-3129. Offers curriculum and instruction (MA), including elementary education, middle grades education. *Accreditation:* NCATE. Part-time and evening/weekend programs available. *Degree requirements:* For master's, comprehensive exam, thesis or alternative. *Entrance requirements:* For master's, minimum GPA of 3.0 in major, 2.5 overall. Additional exam requirements/recommendations for international students: Required—TOEFL. *Faculty research:* Simulation of decision-making behavior of school boards.

North Carolina State University, Graduate School, College of Education, Department of Curriculum and Instruction, Program in Curriculum and Instruction, Raleigh, NC 27695. Offers M Ed, MS, PhD. *Accreditation:* NCATE. *Degree requirements:* For master's, thesis (for some programs); for doctorate, thesis/dissertation. *Entrance requirements:* For master's, GRE General Test or MAT, minimum GPA of 3.0 in major; for doctorate, GRE General Test, minimum GPA of 3.0 in major. Electronic applications accepted. *Faculty research:* Curriculum development, teacher development, intervention for exceptional children, literacy development.

North Central College, Graduate and Continuing Studies Programs, Department of Education, Naperville, IL 60566-7063. Offers curriculum and instruction (MA Ed); leadership and administration (MA Ed). Part-time and evening/weekend programs available. *Faculty:* 11 full-time (4 women), 5 part-time/adjunct (2 women). *Students:* 6 full-time (2 women), 24 part-time (21 women); includes 1 minority (Hispanic/Latino). Average age 30. 44 applicants, 34% accepted, 14 enrolled. In 2013, 9 master's awarded. *Degree requirements:* For master's, thesis optional, clinical practicum, project. *Entrance requirements:* For master's, interview. Additional exam requirements/recommendations for international students: Required—TOEFL (minimum score 577 paper-based; 90 iBT). *Application deadline:* For fall admission, 8/15 for domestic students; for winter admission, 12/1 for domestic students; for spring admission, 2/1 for domestic students. Applications are processed on a rolling basis. Application fee: $25. *Expenses:* Contact institution. *Financial support:* Available to part-time students. *Unit head:* Dr. Maureen Kincaid, Education Department Chair, 630-637-5750, Fax: 630-637-5844, E-mail: mkincaid@noctrl.edu. *Application contact:* Wendy Kulpinski, Director of Graduate and Continuing Education Admission, 630-637-5808, Fax: 630-637-5844, E-mail: wekulpinski@noctrl.edu.

North Dakota State University, College of Graduate and Interdisciplinary Studies, College of Human Development and Education, School of Education, Program in Curriculum and Instruction, Fargo, ND 58108. Offers M Ed, MS. *Students:* 41 full-time (31 women), 66 part-time (50 women); includes 6 minority (1 Black or African American, non-Hispanic/Latino; 2 American Indian or Alaska Native, non-Hispanic/Latino; 1 Native Hawaiian or other Pacific Islander, non-Hispanic/Latino; 2 Two or more races, non-Hispanic/Latino), 8 international. Average age 40. 41 applicants, 76% accepted, 28 enrolled. In 2013, 6 master's awarded. *Degree requirements:* For master's, comprehensive exam, thesis (for some programs). *Entrance requirements:* For master's,

Cooperative English Test, GRE General Test, MAT. Additional exam requirements/recommendations for international students: Required—TOEFL. *Application deadline:* For fall admission, 5/1 for domestic students. Applications are processed on a rolling basis. Application fee: $35. *Financial support:* Teaching assistantships, career-related internships or fieldwork, Federal Work-Study, institutionally sponsored loans, and tuition waivers (full) available. Financial award application deadline: 4/15. *Unit head:* Dr. William Martin, Chair, 701-231-7202, Fax: 701-231-7416, E-mail: william.martin@ndsu.edu. *Application contact:* Dr. Justin Wageman, Associate Professor, 701-231-7108, Fax: 701-231-9685, E-mail: justin.wageman@ndsu.edu.

Northeastern University, School of Education, Boston, MA 02115-5096. Offers curriculum, teaching, learning, and leadership (Ed D); elementary licensure (MAT); higher education administration (MAT, Ed D); Jewish education leadership (Ed D); learning and instruction (M Ed); organizational leadership studies (Ed D); secondary licensure (MAT); special education (M Ed). Part-time and evening/weekend programs available.

Northern Illinois University, Graduate School, College of Education, Department of Special and Early Education, De Kalb, IL 60115-2854. Offers curriculum and instruction (MS Ed, Ed D), including curriculum leadership (Ed D), elementary education (Ed D), secondary education (Ed D); early childhood education (MS Ed); elementary education (MS Ed); special education (MS Ed). Part-time and evening/weekend programs available. *Faculty:* 22 full-time (14 women), 2 part-time/adjunct (both women). *Students:* 52 full-time (41 women), 168 part-time (137 women); includes 29 minority (11 Black or African American, non-Hispanic/Latino; 7 Asian, non-Hispanic/Latino; 6 Hispanic/Latino; 5 Two or more races, non-Hispanic/Latino), 3 international. Average age 36. 38 applicants, 63% accepted, 18 enrolled. In 2013, 59 master's, 15 doctorates awarded. *Degree requirements:* For master's, comprehensive exam, thesis optional; for doctorate, thesis/dissertation, candidacy exam, dissertation defense. *Entrance requirements:* For master's, GRE General Test or MAT, minimum undergraduate GPA of 2.75; for doctorate, GRE General Test or MAT, minimum undergraduate GPA of 2.75, graduate 3.2. Additional exam requirements/recommendations for international students: Required—TOEFL (minimum score 550 paper-based). *Application deadline:* For fall admission, 6/1 for domestic students, 5/1 for international students; for spring admission, 11/1 for domestic students, 10/1 for international students. Applications are processed on a rolling basis. Application fee: $40. Electronic applications accepted. *Financial support:* In 2013–14, 24 research assistantships with full tuition reimbursements were awarded; fellowships with full tuition reimbursements, teaching assistantships with full tuition reimbursements, career-related internships or fieldwork, Federal Work-Study, scholarships/grants, tuition waivers (full), and unspecified assistantships also available. Support available to part-time students. Financial award applicants required to submit FAFSA. *Faculty research:* Teacher certification, stress reduction during student teaching, teaching history, portfolios in student teaching. *Unit head:* Dr. Barbara Schwartz-Bechet, Interim Chair, 815-753-1619, E-mail: seed@niu.edu. *Application contact:* Gail Myers, Clerk, Graduate Advising, 815-753-0381, E-mail: gmyers@niu.edu.
Website: http://www.cedu.niu.edu/seed/.

Northern Michigan University, College of Graduate Studies, College of Health Sciences and Professional Studies, School of Education, Leadership and Public Service, Marquette, MI 49855-5301. Offers administration and supervision (MAE, Ed S); elementary education (MAE); instruction (MAE); learning disabilities (MAE); public administration (MPA), including criminal justice administration, healthcare administration, human resource administration, public management, state and local government; reading education (MAE, Ed S), including literacy leadership (Ed S), reading (MAE), reading specialist (MAE); school guidance counseling (MAE); science education (MS); secondary education (MAE). *Accreditation:* Teacher Education Accreditation Council. Part-time programs available. Postbaccalaureate distance learning degree programs offered (no on-campus study). *Faculty:* 12 full-time (7 women), 3 part-time/adjunct (1 woman). *Students:* 25 full-time (16 women), 170 part-time (130 women); includes 12 minority (2 Black or African American, non-Hispanic/Latino; 5 American Indian or Alaska Native, non-Hispanic/Latino; 4 Hispanic/Latino; 1 Two or more races, non-Hispanic/Latino), 1 international. Average age 33. 39 applicants, 95% accepted, 35 enrolled. In 2013, 48 master's, 5 other advanced degrees awarded. *Degree requirements:* For master's, thesis (for some programs). *Entrance requirements:* For master's, minimum GPA of 3.0. Additional exam requirements/recommendations for international students: Required—TOEFL (minimum score 550 paper-based; 79 iBT), IELTS (minimum score 6.5). *Application deadline:* For fall admission, 7/1 priority date for domestic students; for winter admission, 11/15 for domestic students; for spring admission, 3/17 for domestic students. Applications are processed on a rolling basis. Application fee: $50. *Expenses:* Tuition, state resident: part-time $427 per credit. Tuition, nonresident: part-time $614.50 per credit. *Required fees:* $325 per semester. Tuition and fees vary according to course load and program. *Financial support:* In 2013–14, 2 research assistantships were awarded; career-related internships or fieldwork, Federal Work-Study, institutionally sponsored loans, and unspecified assistantships also available. Support available to part-time students. Financial award application deadline: 3/1. *Unit head:* Dr. Joseph Lubig, Associate Dean, School of Education, Leadership, and Public Service, 906-227-2780, Fax: 906-227-2764, E-mail: jlubig@nmu.edu. *Application contact:* Nancy E. Carter, Certification Counselor and Graduate Programs Coordinator, 906-227-1625, Fax: 906-227-2764, E-mail: ncarter@nmu.edu.
Website: http://www.nmu.edu/education/.

Northern State University, MS Ed Program in Teaching and Learning, Aberdeen, SD 57401-7198. Offers MS Ed. *Accreditation:* NCATE. Part-time and evening/weekend programs available. Postbaccalaureate distance learning degree programs offered. *Faculty:* 7 full-time (6 women), 4 part-time/adjunct (1 woman). *Students:* 10 full-time (9 women), 87 part-time (76 women); includes 3 minority (1 American Indian or Alaska Native, non-Hispanic/Latino; 1 Asian, non-Hispanic/Latino; 1 Hispanic/Latino). Average age 25. 7 applicants, 57% accepted, 4 enrolled. In 2013, 21 master's awarded. *Degree requirements:* For master's, comprehensive exam, thesis optional. *Entrance requirements:* For master's, minimum GPA of 2.75. Additional exam requirements/recommendations for international students: Required—TOEFL (minimum score 550 paper-based; 78 iBT), IELTS (minimum score 6). *Application deadline:* For fall admission, 8/15 for domestic and international students; for spring admission, 12/15 for domestic and international students. Applications are processed on a rolling basis. Application fee: $35. Electronic applications accepted. *Expenses:* Tuition, state resident: full-time $3634. Tuition, nonresident: full-time $7690. One-time fee: $35 full-time. Part-time tuition and fees vary according to course load, degree level, campus/location and reciprocity agreements. *Financial support:* In 2013–14, 2 students received support, including 2 teaching assistantships with partial tuition reimbursements available (averaging $6,478 per year); career-related internships or fieldwork, Federal Work-Study, institutionally sponsored loans, scholarships/grants, and unspecified assistantships also available. Support available to part-time students. Financial award application deadline: 3/1; financial award applicants required to submit FAFSA. *Unit head:* Dr. Constance Geier, Dean of Education, 605-626-2558, Fax: 605-626-7190, E-mail: connie.geier@northern.edu. *Application contact:* Tammy K. Griffith, Program Assistant, 605-626-2558, Fax: 605-626-7190, E-mail: tammy.griffith@northern.edu.

Curriculum and Instruction

Northwest Christian University, School of Education and Counseling, Eugene, OR 97401-3745. Offers clinical mental health counseling (MA); curriculum and instructional technology (M Ed); education (M Ed); school counseling (MA). Part-time and evening/weekend programs available. *Entrance requirements:* For master's, MAT, interview, minimum GPA of 3.0. Electronic applications accepted.

Northwestern Oklahoma State University, School of Professional Studies, Program in Curriculum and Instruction, Alva, OK 73717-2799. Offers M Ed. Part-time programs available. *Degree requirements:* For master's, thesis optional, portfolio. *Entrance requirements:* For master's, GRE General Test or MAT, minimum GPA of 2.75.

Northwestern State University of Louisiana, Graduate Studies and Research, College of Education and Human Development, Program in Curriculum and Instruction, Natchitoches, LA 71497. Offers M Ed. *Entrance requirements:* Additional exam requirements/recommendations for international students: Required—TOEFL. Electronic applications accepted.

Northwest Nazarene University, Graduate Studies, Program in Teacher Education, Nampa, ID 83686-5897. Offers curriculum and instruction (M Ed); educational leadership (M Ed, Ed D, Ed S); exceptional child (M Ed); reading education (M Ed). *Accreditation:* ACA (one or more programs are accredited); NCATE. Part-time programs available. Postbaccalaureate distance learning degree programs offered (no on-campus study). *Faculty:* 6 full-time (5 women), 29 part-time/adjunct (16 women). *Students:* 101 full-time (66 women), 98 part-time (74 women); includes 14 minority (1 Asian, non-Hispanic/Latino; 10 Hispanic/Latino; 3 Two or more races, non-Hispanic/Latino), 12 international. Average age 38. In 2013, 60 master's, 28 doctorates, 14 other advanced degrees awarded. *Degree requirements:* For master's, comprehensive exam (for some programs), action research project; for doctorate, thesis/dissertation; for Ed S, comprehensive exam (for some programs). *Entrance requirements:* For master's, minimum undergraduate GPA of 2.8 overall or 3.0 during final 30 semester credits, undergraduate degree; for doctorate, Ed S or equivalent; for Ed S, EDS - MEd required. Additional exam requirements/recommendations for international students: Recommended—TOEFL (minimum score 80 iBT). *Application deadline:* For fall admission, 9/1 for domestic students. Applications are processed on a rolling basis. Application fee: $50. *Expenses: Tuition:* Part-time $565 per credit. *Financial support:* In 2013–14, research assistantships (averaging $5,000 per year) were awarded. *Faculty research:* Action research, cooperative learning, accountability, institutional accreditation. *Unit head:* Dr. Paula Kellerer, Chair, 208-467-8729, Fax: 208-467-8562. *Application contact:* Lynette Kingsmore, Admissions Counselor, 208-467-8107, Fax: 208-467-8786, E-mail: lkingsmore@nnu.edu.
Website: http://www.nnu.edu/graded/.

Notre Dame de Namur University, Division of Academic Affairs, School of Education and Leadership, Program in Education, Belmont, CA 94002-1908. Offers curriculum and instruction (MA); disciplinary studies (MA); educational technology (MA); multiple subject teaching credential (Certificate); single subject teaching credential (Certificate). Part-time and evening/weekend programs available. *Degree requirements:* For master's, thesis (for some programs). *Entrance requirements:* For master's, CBEST, CSET, valid teaching credential or substantial teaching experience. Additional exam requirements/recommendations for international students: Required—TOEFL (minimum score 550 paper-based; 79 iBT). Electronic applications accepted.

Ohio Dominican University, Graduate Programs, Division of Education, Columbus, OH 43219-2099. Offers curriculum and instruction (M Ed); educational leadership (M Ed); teaching English to speakers of other languages (MA). *Accreditation:* NCATE. Part-time and evening/weekend programs available. Postbaccalaureate distance learning degree programs offered. *Degree requirements:* For master's, thesis or alternative. *Entrance requirements:* For master's, minimum undergraduate GPA of 3.0, teaching certificate, teaching experience, 3 letters of recommendation. Additional exam requirements/recommendations for international students: Required—TOEFL (minimum score 550 paper-based), IELTS (minimum score 6.5).

Ohio University, Graduate College, Gladys W. and David H. Patton College of Education and Human Services, Department of Teacher Education, Athens, OH 45701-2979. Offers adolescent to young adult education (M Ed); curriculum and instruction (M Ed, PhD); early childhood/special education (M Ed); intervention specialist/mild-moderate needs (M Ed); intervention specialist/moderate-intensive needs (M Ed); mathematics education (PhD); middle childhood education (M Ed); reading education (M Ed); social studies education (PhD). Part-time and evening/weekend programs available. *Degree requirements:* For master's, thesis or alternative; for doctorate, comprehensive exam, thesis/dissertation. *Entrance requirements:* For master's, GRE General Test or MAT (if GPA is below 2.9); for doctorate, GRE General Test, minimum GPA of 3.4, work experience. Additional exam requirements/recommendations for international students: Required—TOEFL (minimum score 550 paper-based; 80 iBT) or IELTS (minimum score 6.5). Electronic applications accepted. *Faculty research:* Cognition literacy, character education, teacher's education reform, disabilities.

Ohio Valley University, School of Graduate Education, Vienna, WV 26105-8000. Offers curriculum and instruction (M Ed). Postbaccalaureate distance learning degree programs offered. *Faculty:* 2 full-time (both women), 2 part-time/adjunct (both women). *Students:* 10 full-time (4 women), 30 part-time (18 women). *Entrance requirements:* For master's, 2 letters of recommendation, official transcripts from all previous institutions, essay. Application fee: $30. *Unit head:* Dr. Toni DeVore, Chair, 304-865-6149, E-mail: toni.devore@ovu.edu. *Application contact:* Brad Wilson, Coordinator of Recruiting and Retention, 304-865-6177, E-mail: brad.wilson@ovu.edu.
Website: http://www.ovu.edu/academics/education/school-of-graduate-education.html.

Oklahoma State University, College of Education, School of Teaching and Curriculum Leadership, Stillwater, OK 74078. Offers MS, PhD. Part-time programs available. *Faculty:* 31 full-time (30 women), 38 part-time/adjunct (33 women). *Students:* 63 full-time (51 women), 191 part-time (139 women); includes 49 minority (11 Black or African American, non-Hispanic/Latino; 11 American Indian or Alaska Native, non-Hispanic/Latino; 3 Asian, non-Hispanic/Latino; 10 Hispanic/Latino; 14 Two or more races, non-Hispanic/Latino), 6 international. Average age 38. 85 applicants, 58% accepted, 41 enrolled. In 2013, 50 master's, 15 doctorates awarded. *Degree requirements:* For master's, thesis or alternative; for doctorate, comprehensive exam, thesis/dissertation. *Entrance requirements:* For master's and doctorate, GRE or GMAT. Additional exam requirements/recommendations for international students: Required—TOEFL (minimum score 550 paper-based; 79 iBT). *Application deadline:* For fall admission, 3/1 priority date for international students; for spring admission, 8/1 priority date for international students. Applications are processed on a rolling basis. Application fee: $40 ($75 for international students). Electronic applications accepted. *Expenses: Tuition,* state resident: full-time $4272; part-time $178 per credit hour. Tuition, nonresident: full-time $17,472; part-time $709 per credit hour. *Required fees:* $2413.20; $100.55 per credit hour. One-time fee: $50 full-time. Part-time tuition and fees vary according to course load and campus/location. *Financial support:* In 2013–14, 11 research assistantships (averaging $10,591 per year), 11 teaching assistantships (averaging $8,652 per year) were awarded; career-related internships or fieldwork, Federal Work-Study, scholarships/grants, health care benefits, tuition waivers (partial), and unspecified assistantships also available. Support available to part-time students. Financial award

application deadline: 3/1; financial award applicants required to submit FAFSA. *Unit head:* Dr. Pamela U. Brown, Head, 405-744-9214, Fax: 405-744-6290, E-mail: pamela.u.brown@okstate.edu.
Website: http://education.okstate.edu/stcl.

Old Dominion University, Darden College of Education, Doctoral Program in Curriculum and Instruction, Norfolk, VA 23529. Offers PhD. Part-time and evening/weekend programs available. *Faculty:* 19 full-time (13 women). *Students:* 12 full-time (8 women), 11 part-time (9 women); includes 3 minority (2 Black or African American, non-Hispanic/Latino; 1 Hispanic/Latino). Average age 39. 19 applicants, 53% accepted, 8 enrolled. In 2013, 5 doctorates awarded. *Degree requirements:* For doctorate, comprehensive exam, thesis/dissertation. *Entrance requirements:* For doctorate, GRE, letters of recommendation; minimum undergraduate GPA of 2.8, graduate 3.2. Additional exam requirements/recommendations for international students: Required—TOEFL (minimum score 600 paper-based). *Application deadline:* For fall admission, 3/15 priority date for domestic and international students; for spring admission, 11/15 for domestic and international students. Applications are processed on a rolling basis. Application fee: $50. Electronic applications accepted. *Expenses: Tuition,* state resident: full-time $9888; part-time $412 per credit. Tuition, nonresident: full-time $25,152; part-time $1048 per credit. *Required fees:* $59 per semester. One-time fee: $50. *Financial support:* In 2013–14, fellowships with full tuition reimbursements (averaging $15,000 per year), 4 teaching assistantships with full tuition reimbursements (averaging $15,000 per year) were awarded. Financial award application deadline: 4/15. *Faculty research:* Curriculum change, language arts, library science, multicultural education, foundations in education. *Unit head:* Dr. Richard Overbaugh, Graduate Program Director, 757-683-3284, Fax: 757-683-5862, E-mail: roverbau@odu.edu. *Application contact:* William Heffelfinger, Director of Graduate Admissions, 757-683-5554, Fax: 757-683-3255, E-mail: gradadmit@odu.edu.
Website: http://education.odu.edu/eci/ciphd/.

Old Dominion University, Darden College of Education, Program in Physical Education, Curriculum and Instruction Emphasis, Norfolk, VA 23529. Offers MS Ed. Part-time and evening/weekend programs available. *Faculty:* 2 full-time (1 woman), 1 (woman) part-time/adjunct. *Students:* 1 full-time (0 women), 5 part-time (3 women), 1 international. Average age 29. 6 applicants, 83% accepted, 1 enrolled. In 2013, 5 master's awarded. *Degree requirements:* For master's, comprehensive exam (for some programs), thesis or alternative, internship, research project. *Entrance requirements:* For master's, GRE, PRAXIS I (for licensure only), minimum GPA of 2.8 overall, 3.0 in major. Additional exam requirements/recommendations for international students: Required—TOEFL (minimum score 500 paper-based). *Application deadline:* For fall admission, 3/1 priority date for domestic students; for spring admission, 11/1 for domestic students. Application fee: $50. Electronic applications accepted. *Expenses: Tuition,* state resident: full-time $9888; part-time $412 per credit. Tuition, nonresident: full-time $25,152; part-time $1048 per credit. *Required fees:* $59 per semester. One-time fee: $50. *Financial support:* In 2013–14, 1 teaching assistantship with partial tuition reimbursement (averaging $9,000 per year) was awarded; unspecified assistantships also available. Financial award application deadline: 4/15. *Faculty research:* Motor development, motivation and learning in physical education, curriculum and instruction. *Unit head:* Dr. Lynn Ridinger, Graduate Program Director, 757-683-4995, E-mail: lridinge@odu.edu. *Application contact:* William Heffelfinger, Director of Graduate Admissions, 757-683-5554, Fax: 757-683-3255, E-mail: gradadmit@odu.edu.
Website: http://education.odu.edu/esper/academics/degrees/hpe/hpe.shtml.

Olivet Nazarene University, Graduate School, Division of Education, Program in Curriculum and Instruction, Bourbonnais, IL 60914. Offers MAE. Evening/weekend programs available. *Degree requirements:* For master's, thesis or alternative.

Oral Roberts University, School of Education, Tulsa, OK 74171. Offers Christian school administration (K-12) (MA Ed, Ed D); Christian school curriculum development (MA Ed); college and higher education administration (Ed D); public school administration (K-12) (MA Ed, Ed D); public school teaching (MA Ed). *Accreditation:* NCATE. Part-time programs available. Postbaccalaureate distance learning degree programs offered (minimal on-campus study). *Degree requirements:* For master's, comprehensive exam, thesis optional; for doctorate, comprehensive exam, thesis/dissertation. *Entrance requirements:* For master's, GRE General Test or MAT, minimum GPA of 3.0; for doctorate, minimum GPA of 3.0. Additional exam requirements/recommendations for international students: Required—TOEFL (minimum score 500 paper-based). *Expenses:* Contact institution. *Faculty research:* Teacher effectiveness, college success in high achieving African-Americans, professional development practices.

Ottawa University, Graduate Studies-Arizona, Program in Education, Ottawa, KS 66067-3399. Offers community college counseling (MA); curriculum and instruction (MA); early childhood (MA); education intervention (MA); education leadership (MA); education technology (MA); Montessori early childhood education (MA); Montessori elementary education (MA); professional development (MA); school guidance counseling (MA); special education - cross categorical (MA). Programs offered in Mesa, Phoenix, Tempe and West Valley, AZ. *Accreditation:* NCATE. Part-time programs available. *Degree requirements:* For master's, thesis or alternative. *Entrance requirements:* For master's, minimum undergraduate GPA of 3.0, copy of current state certification or teaching license. Additional exam requirements/recommendations for international students: Required—TOEFL (minimum score 550 paper-based). Electronic applications accepted. *Expenses:* Contact institution.

Our Lady of Holy Cross College, Program in Education and Counseling, New Orleans, LA 70131-7399. Offers administration and supervision (M Ed); curriculum and instruction (M Ed); marriage and family counseling (MA); school counseling (M Ed, MA). *Accreditation:* ACA; NCATE. Part-time and evening/weekend programs available. *Degree requirements:* For master's, thesis. *Entrance requirements:* For master's, GRE General Test, minimum GPA of 2.7.

Our Lady of the Lake University of San Antonio, School of Professional Studies, Program in Curriculum and Instruction, San Antonio, TX 78207-4689. Offers bilingual education (M Ed); early childhood education (M Ed); English as a second language (M Ed); integrated math teaching (M Ed); integrated science teaching (M Ed); reading specialist (M Ed). Part-time and evening/weekend programs available. *Faculty:* 6 full-time (4 women), 3 part-time/adjunct (all women). *Students:* 4 full-time (all women), 84 part-time (72 women); includes 52 minority (2 Black or African American, non-Hispanic/Latino; 2 Asian, non-Hispanic/Latino; 48 Hispanic/Latino). Average age 40. 9 applicants, 56% accepted, 1 enrolled. In 2013, 8 master's awarded. *Degree requirements:* For master's, comprehensive exam. *Entrance requirements:* For master's, GRE General Test or MAT. Additional exam requirements/recommendations for international students: Required—TOEFL. *Application deadline:* For fall admission, 4/1 priority date for domestic and international students; for spring admission, 11/1 priority date for domestic and international students; for summer admission, 2/1 priority date for domestic students, 4/1 priority date for international students. Applications are processed on a rolling basis. Application fee: $25 ($50 for international students). Electronic applications accepted. *Expenses: Tuition:* Full-time $9120; part-time $760 per credit. *Required fees:* $698; $334 per trimester. Tuition and fees vary according to course load, degree level, campus/location and program. *Financial support:* Research assistantships, teaching

assistantships, career-related internships or fieldwork, Federal Work-Study, institutionally sponsored loans, scholarships/grants, and tuition waivers (partial) available. Support available to part-time students. Financial award application deadline: 4/1. *Faculty research:* Professional educator to understand and meet the comprehensive needs of a diverse student population, life-long learners, innovative practices. *Unit head:* Dr. Jerrie Jackson, 210-434-6711 Ext. 2698, E-mail: jjackson@lake.ollusa.edu. *Application contact:* Graduate Admission, 210-431-3961, Fax: 210-431-4013, E-mail: gradadm@lake.ollusa.edu.
Website: http://www.ollusa.edu/s/1190/ollu-3-column-noads.aspx?sid=1190&gid=1&pgid=4173.

Pacific Lutheran University, Graduate Programs and Continuing Education, School of Education and Kinesiology, Program in Initial Teaching Certification, Tacoma, WA 98447. Offers MAE. *Accreditation:* NCATE. *Faculty:* 9 full-time (5 women), 8 part-time/adjunct (2 women). *Students:* 47 full-time (33 women), 24 part-time (18 women); includes 18 minority (5 Black or African American, non-Hispanic/Latino; 5 Asian, non-Hispanic/Latino; 4 Hispanic/Latino; 4 Two or more races, non-Hispanic/Latino), 1 international. Average age 29. 79 applicants, 77% accepted, 45 enrolled. In 2013, 25 master's awarded. *Degree requirements:* For master's, comprehensive exam, thesis optional. *Entrance requirements:* For master's, WEST-B or WEST-B Exemption (or CBEST and/or PRAXIS for out-of-state applicants), interview. Additional exam requirements/recommendations for international students: Required—TOEFL (minimum score 550 paper-based; 88 iBT), ACTFL. *Application deadline:* For fall admission, 11/20 priority date for domestic and international students; for winter admission, 1/15 priority date for domestic and international students; for spring admission, 3/7 priority date for domestic and international students. Applications are processed on a rolling basis. Application fee: $40. Electronic applications accepted. *Expenses:* Contact institution. *Financial support:* In 2013–14, 8 students received support, including 10 fellowships (averaging $3,000 per year); Federal Work-Study and scholarships/grants also available. Financial award application deadline: 3/1; financial award applicants required to submit FAFSA. *Unit head:* Dr. Michael Hillis, Graduate Director, 253-535-7272, Fax: 253-535-7184, E-mail: educ@plu.edu. *Application contact:* Bree Van Horn, Assistant Director of Admission and Advising, 253-535-7276, Fax: 253-536-5136, E-mail: educ@plu.edu.

Park University, School of Graduate and Professional Studies, Kansas City, MO 54105. Offers adult education (M Ed); business and government leadership (Graduate Certificate); business, government, and global society (MPA); communication and leadership (MA); creative and life writing (Graduate Certificate); disaster and emergency management (MPA, Graduate Certificate); educational leadership (M Ed); finance (MBA, Graduate Certificate); general business (MBA); global business (Graduate Certificate); healthcare administration (MHA); healthcare services management and leadership (Graduate Certificate); international business (MBA); language and literacy (M Ed), including English for speakers of other languages, special reading teacher/literacy coach; leadership of international healthcare organizations (Graduate Certificate); management information systems (MBA, Graduate Certificate); music performance (ADP, Graduate Certificate), including cello (MM, ADP), piano (MM, ADP), viola (MM, ADP), violin (MM, ADP); nonprofit and community services management (MPA); nonprofit leadership (Graduate Certificate); performance (MM), including cello (MM, ADP), piano (MM, ADP), viola (MM, ADP), violin (MM, ADP); public management (MPA); social work (MSW); teacher leadership (M Ed), including curriculum and assessment, instructional leader. Part-time and evening/weekend programs available. Postbaccalaureate distance learning degree programs offered (no on-campus study). *Students:* 862 full-time (482 women); includes 55 minority (30 Black or African American, non-Hispanic/Latino; 2 American Indian or Alaska Native, non-Hispanic/Latino; 4 Asian, non-Hispanic/Latino; 14 Hispanic/Latino; 5 Two or more races, non-Hispanic/Latino), 141 international. Average age 34. 497 applicants, 62% accepted, 119 enrolled. In 2013, 281 master's, 14 other advanced degrees awarded. *Degree requirements:* For master's, comprehensive exam (for some programs), thesis (for some programs), internship (for some programs); exam (for some programs). *Entrance requirements:* For master's, GRE or GMAT (for some programs), teacher certification (for some M Ed programs), letters of recommendation, essay, resume (for some programs). Additional exam requirements/recommendations for international students: Required—TOEFL (minimum score 550 paper-based; 79 iBT), IELTS (minimum score 6). *Application deadline:* For fall admission, 8/1 priority date for domestic students, 7/15 priority date for international students; for spring admission, 1/1 priority date for domestic students, 11/1 priority date for international students. Applications are processed on a rolling basis. Application fee: $50 ($100 for international students). Electronic applications accepted. *Financial support:* In 2013–14, 2 research assistantships with full tuition reimbursements (averaging $15,760 per year) were awarded. Financial award applicants required to submit FAFSA. *Unit head:* Dr. Laurie Dipadova-Stocks, Dean of Graduate and Professional Studies, 816-559-5624, Fax: 816-472-1173, E-mail: ldipadovastocks@park.edu. *Application contact:* Judith Appollis, Director of Graduate Admissions and Internationalization, School of Graduate and Professional Studies, 816-559-5627, Fax: 816-472-1173, E-mail: gradschool@park.edu.
Website: http://www.park.edu/grad.

Penn State Harrisburg, Graduate School, School of Behavioral Sciences and Education, Middletown, PA 17057-4898. Offers applied behavior analysis (MA); applied clinical psychology (MA); applied psychological research (MA); community psychology and social change (MA); health education (M Ed); literacy education (M Ed); teaching and curriculum (M Ed, Certificate); training and development (M Ed). Part-time and evening/weekend programs available. *Financial support:* Career-related internships or fieldwork available. *Unit head:* Dr. Mukund S. Kulkarni, Chancellor, 717-948-6105, Fax: 717-948-6452, E-mail: msk5@psu.edu. *Application contact:* Robert W. Coffman, Jr., Director of Enrollment Management, Admissions, 717-948-6250, Fax: 717-948-6325, E-mail: ric1@psu.edu.
Website: http://harrisburg.psu.edu/behavioral-sciences-and-education/.

Penn State University Park, Graduate School, College of Education, Department of Curriculum and Instruction, State College, PA 16802. Offers M Ed, MS, PhD, Certificate. *Accreditation:* NCATE. *Unit head:* Dr. David H. Monk, Dean, 814-865-2523, Fax: 814-865-0555, E-mail: dhm6@psu.edu. *Application contact:* Cynthia E. Nicosia, Director, Graduate Enrollment Services, 814-865-1834, Fax: 814-863-4627, E-mail: cey1@psu.edu.
Website: http://www.ed.psu.edu/educ/c-and-i/Home/.

Peru State College, Graduate Programs, Program in Education, Peru, NE 68421. Offers curriculum and instruction (MS Ed). *Accreditation:* NCATE. Part-time programs available. *Faculty:* 5 full-time (2 women), 5 part-time/adjunct (4 women). *Students:* 211 full-time (166 women), 158 part-time (118 women); includes 20 minority (9 Black or African American, non-Hispanic/Latino; 3 Asian, non-Hispanic/Latino; 8 Hispanic/Latino). In 2013, 52 master's awarded. *Degree requirements:* For master's, comprehensive exam (for some programs), thesis optional. *Application deadline:* Applications are processed on a rolling basis. Application fee: $0. *Unit head:* Dr. Greg Seay, Dean of Graduate Programs, 402-872-2283, Fax: 402-872-2413, E-mail: gseay@peru.edu. *Application contact:* Emily Volker, Program Coordinator, 402-872-2282, Fax: 402-872-2413, E-mail: evolker@peru.edu.

Plymouth State University, College of Graduate Studies, Graduate Studies in Education, Program in Secondary Education, Plymouth, NH 03264-1595. Offers curriculum and instruction (M Ed); language education (M Ed); library media (M Ed); physical education (M Ed); social studies education (M Ed); special education (M Ed). Part-time and evening/weekend programs available. *Entrance requirements:* For master's, MAT.

Point Park University, School of Arts and Sciences, Department of Education, Pittsburgh, PA 15222-1984. Offers curriculum and instruction (MA); educational administration (MA); special education (M Ed); teaching and leadership (M Ed). Part-time and evening/weekend programs available. *Degree requirements:* For master's, comprehensive exam (for some programs), thesis or alternative. *Entrance requirements:* For master's, minimum GPA of 3.0, resume, 2 letters of recommendation. Additional exam requirements/recommendations for international students: Required—TOEFL. Electronic applications accepted.

Pontifical Catholic University of Puerto Rico, College of Education, Doctoral Program in Curriculum and Instruction, Ponce, PR 00717-0777. Offers PhD. *Degree requirements:* For doctorate, thesis/dissertation. *Entrance requirements:* For doctorate, EXADEP, GRE General Test or MAT, 3 letters of recommendation.

Pontifical Catholic University of Puerto Rico, College of Education, Master's Program in Curriculum and Instruction, Ponce, PR 00717-0777. Offers M Ed. *Degree requirements:* For master's, comprehensive exam, thesis (for some programs). *Entrance requirements:* For master's, GRE, 2 letters of recommendation, interview, minimum GPA of 2.75.

Portland State University, Graduate Studies, School of Education, Department of Curriculum and Instruction, Portland, OR 97207-0751. Offers early childhood education (MA, MS); education (M Ed, MA, MS); educational leadership: curriculum and instruction (Ed D); educational media/school librarianship (MA, MS); elementary education (M Ed, MAT, MST); reading (MA, MS); secondary education (M Ed, MAT, MST). *Accreditation:* NCATE. Part-time programs available. *Faculty:* 22 full-time (15 women), 28 part-time/adjunct (20 women). *Students:* 29 full-time (23 women), 162 part-time (123 women); includes 26 minority (3 Black or African American, non-Hispanic/Latino; 6 Asian, non-Hispanic/Latino; 13 Hispanic/Latino; 4 Two or more races, non-Hispanic/Latino), 6 international. Average age 36. 145 applicants, 69% accepted, 93 enrolled. In 2013, 257 master's, 5 doctorates awarded. *Degree requirements:* For master's, comprehensive exam, thesis or alternative; for doctorate, thesis/dissertation. *Entrance requirements:* For master's, California Basic Educational Skills Test, minimum GPA of 3.0 in upper-division course work or 2.75 overall. Additional exam requirements/recommendations for international students: Required—TOEFL (minimum score 550 paper-based). *Application deadline:* For fall admission, 4/1 for domestic and international students; for winter admission, 9/1 for domestic and international students; for spring admission, 11/1 for domestic and international students. Applications are processed on a rolling basis. Application fee: $50. *Expenses:* Tuition, state resident: full-time $9207; part-time $341 per credit. Tuition, nonresident: full-time $14,391; part-time $533 per credit. *Required fees:* $1263; $22 per credit. $98 per quarter. One-time fee: $150. Tuition and fees vary according to program. *Financial support:* In 2013–14, 1 research assistantship with full tuition reimbursement (averaging $6,248 per year), 2 teaching assistantships with full tuition reimbursements (averaging $7,755 per year) were awarded; career-related internships or fieldwork, Federal Work-Study, and institutionally sponsored loans also available. Support available to part-time students. Financial award application deadline: 3/1; financial award applicants required to submit FAFSA. *Faculty research:* Early literacy, characteristics of successful teachers of at-risk students, participation of women/minorities in technology courses, selection of cooperating teachers. *Total annual research expenditures:* $1 million. *Unit head:* Christine Chaille, Head, 503-725-4753, Fax: 203-725-8475, E-mail: chaillec@pdx.edu. *Application contact:* Jake Fernandez, Department Assistant, 503-725-4756, Fax: 503-725-8475, E-mail: jifern@pdx.edu.
Website: http://www.ed.pdx.edu/ci/.

Prairie View A&M University, College of Education, Department of Curriculum and Instruction, Prairie View, TX 77446-0519. Offers curriculum and instruction (M Ed, MS Ed); special education (M Ed, MS Ed). *Accreditation:* NCATE. Part-time and evening/weekend programs available. *Faculty:* 7 full-time (5 women), 5 part-time/adjunct (all women). *Students:* 15 full-time (12 women), 43 part-time (35 women); includes 53 minority (51 Black or African American, non-Hispanic/Latino; 1 Asian, non-Hispanic/Latino; 1 Hispanic/Latino). Average age 36. 57 applicants, 100% accepted, 21 enrolled. In 2013, 13 master's awarded. *Degree requirements:* For master's, thesis optional. *Entrance requirements:* For master's, GRE, minimum GPA of 2.5, 3 references. *Application deadline:* For fall admission, 7/1 priority date for domestic students, 7/1 for international students; for winter admission, 3/1 priority date for domestic students, 3/1 for international students; for spring admission, 11/1 priority date for domestic students, 11/1 for international students. Applications are processed on a rolling basis. Application fee: $50. Electronic applications accepted. *Expenses:* Tuition, state resident: full-time $3776; part-time $209.77 per credit hour. Tuition, nonresident: full-time $10,183; part-time $565.77 per credit hour. *Required fees:* $2037; $446.50 per credit hour. *Financial support:* In 2013–14, 1 research assistantship with tuition reimbursement (averaging $18,000 per year) was awarded; fellowships with tuition reimbursements, teaching assistantships, career-related internships or fieldwork, institutionally sponsored loans, scholarships/grants, health care benefits, tuition waivers (full and partial), and unspecified assistantships also available. Support available to part-time students. Financial award application deadline: 4/1. *Faculty research:* Metacognitive strategies, emotionally disturbed, language arts, teachers recruit, diversity, recruitment, retention, school collaboration. *Total annual research expenditures:* $25,000. *Unit head:* Dr. Edward Mason, Head, 936-261-3403, Fax: 936-261-3419, E-mail: elmason@pvamu.edu. *Application contact:* Head.

Purdue University, Graduate School, College of Education, Department of Curriculum and Instruction, West Lafayette, IN 47907. Offers agricultural and extension education (PhD, Ed S); agriculture and extension education (MS, MS Ed); art education (PhD); curriculum studies (MS Ed, PhD, Ed S); educational technology (MS Ed, PhD, Ed S); elementary education (MS Ed); family and consumer sciences education (MS Ed, PhD, Ed S); foreign language education (MS Ed, PhD, Ed S); industrial technology (PhD, Ed S); language arts (MS Ed, PhD, Ed S); literacy (MS Ed, PhD, Ed S); mathematics/science education (MS, MS Ed, PhD, Ed S); social studies (MS Ed, PhD); social studies education (Ed S); vocational/industrial education (MS Ed, PhD, Ed S); vocational/technical education (MS Ed, PhD, Ed S). *Accreditation:* NCATE. Part-time and evening/weekend programs available. *Faculty:* 29 full-time (19 women), 33 part-time/adjunct (29 women). *Students:* 85 full-time (53 women), 271 part-time (195 women); includes 62 minority (19 Black or African American, non-Hispanic/Latino; 3 American Indian or Alaska Native, non-Hispanic/Latino; 13 Asian, non-Hispanic/Latino; 22 Hispanic/Latino; 1 Native Hawaiian or other Pacific Islander, non-Hispanic/Latino; 4 Two or more races, non-Hispanic/Latino), 41 international. Average age 36. 155 applicants, 71% accepted, 71 enrolled. In 2013, 60 master's, 20 doctorates awarded. *Degree requirements:* For master's, thesis optional; for doctorate, thesis/dissertation, oral and written exams; for Ed S, oral presentation, project. *Entrance requirements:* For master's, GRE General Test (if undergraduate GPA is below 3.0), minimum undergraduate GPA of 3.0 or equivalent; for doctorate, GRE General Test (minimum combined verbal and

quantitative score of 1000, 300 for new scoring), minimum undergraduate GPA of 3.0 or equivalent; master's degree with minimum GPA of 3.0 or equivalent; for Ed S, GRE General Test (minimum combined verbal and quantitative score of 1000, 300 for new scoring), minimum undergraduate GPA of 3.0 or equivalent; master's degree. Additional exam requirements/recommendations for international students: Required—TOEFL (minimum score 550 paper-based; 77 iBT). *Application deadline:* For fall admission, 12/15 for domestic students, 3/1 for international students; for spring admission, 9/15 for domestic students, 8/1 for international students. Application fee: $60 ($75 for international students). Electronic applications accepted. *Financial support:* Fellowships with full tuition reimbursements, research assistantships with full tuition reimbursements, teaching assistantships with full tuition reimbursements, career-related internships or fieldwork, and tuition waivers (full) available. Support available to part-time students. Financial award application deadline: 3/1; financial award applicants required to submit FAFSA. *Faculty research:* Literacy acquisition and development, teacher beliefs and knowledge, recruitment and retention of underrepresented students, economic education, literacy discourse. *Unit head:* Dr. Phillip J. VanFossen, Head, 765-494-7935, Fax: 765-496-1622, E-mail: vanfoss@purdue.edu. *Application contact:* Cindy Blankenship, Graduate Contact, 765-494-2345, Fax: 765-494-5832, E-mail: prater0@purdue.edu.
Website: http://www.edci.purdue.edu/.

Quincy University, Program in Education, Quincy, IL 62301-2699. Offers curriculum and instruction (MS Ed), including bilingual/English as a second language; leadership (MS Ed); reading education (MS Ed); special education (MS Ed); teacher leader (MS Ed). Part-time and evening/weekend programs available. Postbaccalaureate distance learning degree programs offered (minimal on-campus study). *Students:* 62 full-time (39 women), 97 part-time (68 women); includes 43 minority (29 Black or African American, non-Hispanic/Latino; 1 American Indian or Alaska Native, non-Hispanic/Latino; 4 Asian, non-Hispanic/Latino; 9 Hispanic/Latino). In 2013, 105 master's awarded. *Degree requirements:* For master's, comprehensive exam (for some programs), thesis optional. *Entrance requirements:* For master's, MAT or GRE. Additional exam requirements/recommendations for international students: Required—TOEFL (minimum score 550 paper-based; 79 iBT). *Application deadline:* Applications are processed on a rolling basis. Application fee: $25. Electronic applications accepted. *Expenses: Tuition:* Full-time $9600; part-time $400 per semester hour. *Required fees:* $720; $30 per semester hour. Tuition and fees vary according to course load and program. *Financial support:* Applicants required to submit FAFSA. *Unit head:* Dr. Kristen R. Anguiano, Director, 217-228-5432 Ext. 3119, E-mail: anguikr@quincy.edu. *Application contact:* Office of Admissions, 217-228-5210, Fax: 217-228-5479, E-mail: admissions@quincy.edu.
Website: http://www.quincy.edu/academics/graduate-programs/education.

Radford University, College of Graduate and Professional Studies, College of Education and Human Development, School of Teacher Education and Leadership, Program in Education, Radford, VA 24142. Offers curriculum and instruction (MS); early childhood education (MS); educational technology (MS); math education content area studies (MS). *Accreditation:* NCATE. Part-time and evening/weekend programs available. *Faculty:* 6 full-time (4 women), 2 part-time/adjunct (1 woman). *Students:* 68 full-time (53 women), 30 part-time (20 women); includes 6 minority (3 Black or African American, non-Hispanic/Latino; 1 Asian, non-Hispanic/Latino; 1 Hispanic/Latino; 1 Two or more races, non-Hispanic/Latino). Average age 28. 38 applicants, 100% accepted, 28 enrolled. In 2013, 42 master's awarded. *Degree requirements:* For master's, comprehensive exam. *Entrance requirements:* For master's, GRE, minimum GPA of 3.0, 2 letters of professional reference, personal statement, resume, official transcripts. Additional exam requirements/recommendations for international students: Required—TOEFL (minimum score 550 paper-based; 79 iBT). *Application deadline:* For fall admission, 2/15 priority date for domestic students, 12/1 for international students; for spring admission, 7/1 for international students. Applications are processed on a rolling basis. Application fee: $50. Electronic applications accepted. *Expenses:* Tuition, state resident: full-time $6800; part-time $283 per credit hour. Tuition, nonresident: full-time $15,610; part-time $627 per credit hour. *Required fees:* $2944; $123 per credit hour. Tuition and fees vary according to program. *Financial support:* In 2013–14, 24 students received support, including 19 research assistantships (averaging $7,105 per year); career-related internships or fieldwork, Federal Work-Study, institutionally sponsored loans, scholarships/grants, and unspecified assistantships also available. Financial award application deadline: 3/1; financial award applicants required to submit FAFSA. *Faculty research:* Pedagogy of mathematics education. *Unit head:* Dr. Kristan Morrison, Coordinator, 540-831-7120, Fax: 540-831-5059, E-mail: kmorrison12@radford.edu. *Application contact:* Rebecca Conner, Director, Graduate Enrollment, 540-831-6296, Fax: 540-831-6061, E-mail: gradcollege@radford.edu.
Website: http://www.radford.edu/content/cehd/home/departments/STEL/programs/education-master.html.

Randolph College, Programs in Education, Lynchburg, VA 24503. Offers curriculum and instruction (MAT); special education-learning disabilities (M Ed, MAT). *Accreditation:* Teacher Education Accreditation Council. *Entrance requirements:* For master's, minimum GPA of 3.0 in prerequisite education coursework, 2.7 in major or field of interest (MAT); teaching license (M Ed); 2 recommendations; interview.

Regent University, Graduate School, School of Education, Virginia Beach, VA 23464-9800. Offers adult education (Ed D, PhD); advanced educational leadership (Ed D, PhD); career switcher with licensure (M Ed), including alternative licensure; character education (Ed D, PhD); Christian education leadership (Ed D); Christian school administration (M Ed); curriculum and instruction (M Ed); distance education (Ed D, PhD); educational leadership (M Ed); educational leadership - special education (Ed S); educational psychology (Ed D); elementary education (M Ed); higher education (Ed D, PhD); higher education leadership and management (Ed D); K-12 school leadership (Ed D, PhD); leadership in mathematics education (M Ed); reading specialist (M Ed); special education (M Ed, Ed D, PhD); student affairs (M Ed); TESOL (M Ed), including adult education, PreK-12. *Accreditation:* Teacher Education Accreditation Council. Part-time and evening/weekend programs available. Postbaccalaureate distance learning degree programs offered (minimal on-campus study). *Faculty:* 25 full-time (12 women), 50 part-time/adjunct (31 women). *Students:* 100 full-time (78 women), 754 part-time (614 women); includes 225 minority (191 Black or African American, non-Hispanic/Latino; 1 American Indian or Alaska Native, non-Hispanic/Latino; 7 Asian, non-Hispanic/Latino; 26 Hispanic/Latino), 16 international. Average age 39. 487 applicants, 63% accepted, 233 enrolled. In 2013, 202 master's, 19 doctorates awarded. *Degree requirements:* For master's, thesis or alternative; for doctorate, comprehensive exam, thesis/dissertation. *Entrance requirements:* For master's, MAT, minimum undergraduate GPA of 2.75, writing sample, resume, recommendations, interview; for doctorate, GRE, writing sample, 3 years of relevant professional experience, master's-level paper, copies of published work, resume, transcripts, interview, recommendations. Additional exam requirements/recommendations for international students: Required—TOEFL (minimum score 577 paper-based). *Application deadline:* For fall admission, 4/1 priority date for domestic students; for spring admission, 10/15 priority date for domestic students. Applications are processed on a rolling basis. Application fee: $50. Electronic applications accepted. Tuition and fees vary according to course load and degree level. *Financial support:* Fellowships, career-related internships or fieldwork, scholarships/grants, tuition waivers (full and partial), and unspecified assistantships available. Support available to part-time students. Financial award application deadline: 4/1; financial award applicants required to submit FAFSA. *Faculty research:* Character development and discipline for children, education leadership development, diversity in schools, classroom management, technology in education settings. *Unit head:* Dr. Alan Arroyo, Dean, 757-352-4261, Fax: 757-352-4318, E-mail: alanarr@regent.edu. *Application contact:* Matthew Chadwick, Director of Enrollment Support Services, 800-373-5504, Fax: 757-352-4381, E-mail: admissions@regent.edu.
Website: http://www.regent.edu/education/.

Regis University, College for Professional Studies, School of Education, Education Division, Denver, CO 80221-1099. Offers adult learning, training, and development (M Ed, Certificate); autism education (Certificate); curriculum, instruction, and assessment (M Ed); educational leadership (M Ed); gifted and talented education (M Ed); gifted/talented education (Certificate); initial licensure (M Ed); instructional technology (M Ed, Certificate); literacy (Certificate); reading (M Ed); school executive leadership (Certificate); space studies (M Ed). Program also offered in Henderson and Las Vegas (Summerlin), NV. *Accreditation:* Teacher Education Accreditation Council. Part-time and evening/weekend programs available. Postbaccalaureate distance learning degree programs offered (no on-campus study). *Degree requirements:* For master's, thesis. *Entrance requirements:* For master's, resume, minimum GPA of 2.75, criminal background check. Additional exam requirements/recommendations for international students: Required—TOEFL, TWE (minimum score 5). *Application deadline:* For fall admission, 7/23 priority date for domestic students; for winter admission, 9/17 priority date for domestic students; for spring admission, 12/3 priority date for domestic students. Applications are processed on a rolling basis. Application fee: $75. Electronic applications accepted. *Expenses:* Contact institution. *Financial support:* Federal Work-Study and scholarships/grants available. *Faculty research:* Issues of equity in the middle school classroom, professional learning communities, school reform, sociolinguistic and discursive obstacles to student integration, inclusive language arts curriculum. *Unit head:* Dr. Janna L. Oakes, Dean, 303-458-4302. *Application contact:* Information Contact, 303-458-4300, Fax: 303-964-5274, E-mail: masters@regis.edu.

Rider University, Department of Graduate Education, Leadership and Counseling, Program in Curriculum, Instruction and Supervision, Lawrenceville, NJ 08648-3001. Offers curriculum, instruction and supervision (MA); supervisor (Certificate). *Accreditation:* NCATE. Part-time and evening/weekend programs available. *Degree requirements:* For master's, comprehensive exam, practicum project. *Entrance requirements:* For master's, interview, 2 letters of recommendation from current supervisors, resume. Additional exam requirements/recommendations for international students: Required—TOEFL (minimum score 550 paper-based). Electronic applications accepted. *Faculty research:* Curriculum change, curriculum development, teacher evaluation.

Rivier University, School of Graduate Studies, Department of Education, Nashua, NH 03060. Offers curriculum and instruction (M Ed); early childhood education (M Ed); educational administration (M Ed); educational studies (M Ed); elementary education (M Ed); elementary education and general special education (M Ed); emotional and behavioral disorders (M Ed); general social education (M Ed); leadership and learning (Ed D, CAGS); learning disabilities (M Ed); learning disabilities and reading (M Ed); mental health counseling (MA); reading (M Ed); school counseling (M Ed). Part-time and evening/weekend programs available. *Degree requirements:* For master's, comprehensive exam (for some programs), internships. *Entrance requirements:* For master's, GRE General Test or MAT.

St. Catherine University, Graduate Programs, Program in Education–Curriculum and Instruction, St. Paul, MN 55105. Offers MA. Part-time and evening/weekend programs available. Postbaccalaureate distance learning degree programs offered (minimal on-campus study). *Degree requirements:* For master's, thesis. *Entrance requirements:* For master's, current teaching license, classroom experience, minimum GPA of 3.0. Additional exam requirements/recommendations for international students: Required—Michigan English Language Assessment Battery or TOEFL (minimum score 600 paper-based; 100 iBT). *Expenses:* Contact institution.

St. Cloud State University, School of Graduate Studies, School of Education, Department of Teacher Development, St. Cloud, MN 56301-4498. Offers curriculum and instruction (MS). *Degree requirements:* For master's, thesis or alternative. *Entrance requirements:* For master's, GRE General Test, minimum GPA of 2.75. Additional exam requirements/recommendations for international students: Required—Michigan English Language Assessment Battery; Recommended—TOEFL (minimum score 550 paper-based), IELTS (minimum score 6.5). Electronic applications accepted.

St. Francis Xavier University, Graduate Studies, Graduate Studies in Education, Antigonish, NS B2G 2W5, Canada. Offers curriculum and instruction (M Ed); educational administration and leadership (M Ed). Part-time programs available. Postbaccalaureate distance learning degree programs offered (minimal on-campus study). *Degree requirements:* For master's, thesis. *Entrance requirements:* For master's, minimum undergraduate B average, 2 years of teaching experience. *Faculty research:* Inclusive education, qualitative research.

Saint Joseph's University, College of Arts and Sciences, Department of Education, Philadelphia, PA 19131-1395. Offers curriculum supervisor (Certificate); educational leadership (MS, Ed D); elementary education (MS, Certificate); elementary/middle school education (Certificate); instructional technology (MS, Certificate); principal certification (Certificate); professional education (MS); reading specialist (MS, Certificate); reading supervisor (Certificate); secondary education (MS, Certificate); special education (MS, Certificate); superintendent's letter of eligibility (Certificate); supervisor of special education (Certificate). Part-time and evening/weekend programs available. Postbaccalaureate distance learning degree programs offered (no on-campus study). *Faculty:* 32 full-time (25 women), 75 part-time/adjunct (53 women). *Students:* 91 full-time (81 women), 858 part-time (656 women); includes 133 minority (96 Black or African American, non-Hispanic/Latino; 3 American Indian or Alaska Native, non-Hispanic/Latino; 9 Asian, non-Hispanic/Latino; 20 Hispanic/Latino; 5 Native Hawaiian or other Pacific Islander, non-Hispanic/Latino), 16 international. Average age 31. 359 applicants, 77% accepted, 203 enrolled. In 2013, 363 master's, 9 doctorates, 1 other advanced degree awarded. *Entrance requirements:* For master's, 2 letters of recommendation, minimum GPA of 3.0, official transcripts, personal statement; for doctorate, GRE, master's degree from accredited institution, minimum graduate GPA of 3.5, computer competence, commitment to participate in cohort, interview with program director. Additional exam requirements/recommendations for international students: Required—TOEFL (minimum score 550 paper-based; 79 iBT), IELTS (minimum score 6.5). *Application deadline:* For fall admission, 7/15 priority date for domestic students, 4/15 for international students; for winter admission, 11/15 for domestic students, 1/15 for international students; for spring admission, 11/15 priority date for domestic students, 10/15 for international students. Applications are processed on a rolling basis. Application fee: $35. Electronic applications accepted. *Expenses:* Contact institution. *Financial support:* Unspecified assistantships available. Financial award applicants required to submit FAFSA. *Faculty research:* Factors predicting early mathematics skills for low income children, early child care and development, preschool quality. *Total*

annual research expenditures: $229,264. *Unit head:* Dr. John Vacca, Associate Dean, Education, 610-660-3131, E-mail: gradstudies@sju.edu. *Application contact:* Elisabeth Woodward, Director of Marketing and Admissions, Graduate Arts and Sciences, 610-660-3131, Fax: 610-660-3230, E-mail: gradstudies@sju.edu.
Website: http://sju.edu/int/academics/cas/grad/education/index.html.

Saint Leo University, Graduate Studies in Education, Saint Leo, FL 33574-6665. Offers educational leadership (M Ed); exceptional student education (M Ed); instructional design (MS); instructional leadership (M Ed); reading (M Ed). Part-time and evening/weekend programs available. Postbaccalaureate distance learning degree programs offered (minimal on-campus study). *Faculty:* 10 full-time (8 women), 31 part-time/adjunct (23 women). *Students:* 680 full-time (554 women), 4 part-time (all women); includes 83 minority (51 Black or African American, non-Hispanic/Latino; 2 Asian, non-Hispanic/Latino; 27 Hispanic/Latino; 3 Two or more races, non-Hispanic/Latino), 4 international. Average age 36. In 2013, 295 master's awarded. *Degree requirements:* For master's, comprehensive exam, appropriate State of Florida certification tests. *Entrance requirements:* For master's, GRE (minimum score of 1000) or MAT (minimum score of 410) if undergraduate GPA for last 60 hours of coursework was below 3.0 (for M Ed), bachelor's degree with minimum GPA of 3.0 for last 60 hours of coursework from regionally-accredited college or university, 2 recommendations, résumé, statement of professional goals, copy of valid teaching certificate (for M Ed). Additional exam requirements/recommendations for international students: Required—TOEFL (minimum score 550 paper-based; 80 iBT). *Application deadline:* For fall admission, 7/1 priority date for domestic students, 7/1 for international students; for winter admission, 7/1 for international students; for spring admission, 11/1 priority date for domestic students. Applications are processed on a rolling basis. Application fee: $80. Electronic applications accepted. *Expenses:* Contact institution. *Financial support:* In 2013–14, 618 students received support. Career-related internships or fieldwork, Federal Work-Study, scholarships/grants, and health care benefits available. Financial award application deadline: 3/1; financial award applicants required to submit FAFSA. *Faculty research:* The role of the school leader in data analysis of student achievement, teacher recruitment, teacher effectiveness. *Unit head:* Dr. Sharyn Disabato, Director of Graduate Education, 352-588-8309, Fax: 352-588-8861, E-mail: med@saintleo.edu. *Application contact:* Joshua Stagner, Director of Graduate Admission, 800-707-8846, Fax: 352-588-7873, E-mail: grad.admissions@saintleo.edu.
Website: http://www.saintleo.edu/admissions/graduate.aspx.

Saint Louis University, Graduate Education, College of Education and Public Service, Department of Educational Studies, St. Louis, MO 63103-2097. Offers curriculum and instruction (MA, Ed D, PhD); educational foundations (MA, Ed D, PhD); special education (MA); teaching (MAT). *Accreditation:* NCATE. Part-time programs available. *Degree requirements:* For master's, comprehensive exam; for doctorate, comprehensive exam, thesis/dissertation, preliminary oral and written exams. *Entrance requirements:* For master's, GRE General Test or MAT, letters of recommendation, resume; for doctorate, GRE General Test, letters of recommendation, resumé, goal statement, transcripts. Additional exam requirements/recommendations for international students: Required—TOEFL (minimum score 525 paper-based). Electronic applications accepted. *Faculty research:* Teacher preparation, multicultural issues, children with special needs, qualitative research in education, inclusion.

Saint Mary's College of California, Kalmanovitz School of Education, Program in Early Childhood Education, Moraga, CA 94575. Offers curriculum and instruction (MA); supervision and leadership (MA). Part-time and evening/weekend programs available. *Degree requirements:* For master's, thesis or alternative. *Entrance requirements:* For master's, interview, minimum GPA of 3.0.

Saint Mary's College of California, Kalmanovitz School of Education, Program in Instruction, Moraga, CA 94575. Offers M Ed.

Saint Michael's College, Graduate Programs, Program in Education, Colchester, VT 05439. Offers administration (M Ed, CAGS); arts in education (CAGS); curriculum and instruction (M Ed, CAGS); information technology (CAGS); reading (M Ed); special education (M Ed, CAGS); technology (M Ed). Part-time and evening/weekend programs available. *Degree requirements:* For master's, thesis. *Entrance requirements:* For master's, minimum GPA of 3.0. Electronic applications accepted. *Faculty research:* Integrative curriculum, moral and spiritual dimensions of education, learning styles, multiple intelligences, integrating technology into the curriculum.

Saint Vincent College, Program in Education, Latrobe, PA 15650-2690. Offers curriculum and instruction (MS); educational media and technology (MS); environmental education (MS); school administration and supervision (MS); special education (MS). Part-time and evening/weekend programs available. *Degree requirements:* For master's, comprehensive exam. *Entrance requirements:* For master's, GRE (if undergraduate GPA less than 3.0). Additional exam requirements/recommendations for international students: Required—TOEFL (minimum score 550 paper-based). *Faculty research:* Assessment and instructional technology.

Saint Xavier University, Graduate Studies, School of Education, Chicago, IL 60655-3105. Offers counseling (MA); curriculum and instruction (MA); early childhood education (MA); educational administration (MA); elementary education (MA); individualized studies (MA), including educational technology, English as a second language (ESL), ISTEM (integrative science, technology, engineering, and math), science education; music education (MA); reading (MA); secondary education (MA); Spanish education (MA); special education (MA); teaching and leadership (MA). *Accreditation:* NCATE. Part-time and evening/weekend programs available. *Degree requirements:* For master's, thesis or project. *Entrance requirements:* For master's, minimum GPA of 3.0. *Expenses:* Contact institution.

Salem International University, School of Education, Salem, WV 26426-0500. Offers curriculum and instruction (M Ed); educational leadership (M Ed). Part-time and evening/weekend programs available. Postbaccalaureate distance learning degree programs offered. *Degree requirements:* For master's, comprehensive exam (for some programs), thesis (for some programs). *Entrance requirements:* For master's, GRE, MAT, NTE, 3 letters of recommendation. Additional exam requirements/recommendations for international students: Required—TOEFL (minimum score 550 paper-based). Electronic applications accepted. *Expenses:* Contact institution. *Faculty research:* Improved classroom effectiveness.

Salisbury University, Department of Education Specialties, Program in Curriculum and Instruction, Salisbury, MD 21801-6837. Offers curriculum and instruction (M Ed); post secondary track (M Ed). Part-time and evening/weekend programs available. *Faculty:* 7 full-time (6 women), 3 part-time/adjunct (all women). *Students:* 14 full-time (5 women), 73 part-time (53 women); includes 15 minority (9 Black or African American, non-Hispanic/Latino; 4 Hispanic/Latino; 2 Two or more races, non-Hispanic/Latino), 2 international. Average age 29. 40 applicants, 53% accepted, 21 enrolled. In 2013, 33 master's awarded. *Entrance requirements:* For master's, 2 letters of recommendation, current license or licensure eligible. Additional exam requirements/recommendations for international students: Required—TOEFL (minimum score 550 paper-based; 79 iBT), IELTS (minimum score 6.5). *Application deadline:* For fall admission, 4/1 for domestic and international students; for spring admission, 10/1 for domestic and international students. Applications are processed on a rolling basis. Application fee: $50. Electronic applications accepted. *Expenses: Tuition, area resident:* Part-time $342 per credit hour. Tuition, state resident: part-time $342 per credit hour. Tuition, nonresident: part-time $631 per credit hour. *Required fees:* $76 per credit hour. Tuition and fees vary according to program. *Financial support:* In 2013–14, 17 teaching assistantships with full tuition reimbursements (averaging $5,000 per year) were awarded; career-related internships or fieldwork, institutionally sponsored loans, scholarships/grants, and unspecified assistantships also available. Support available to part-time students. Financial award application deadline: 3/1; financial award applicants required to submit FAFSA. *Faculty research:* School improvements, educational technology, leadership, professional development schools, literacy. *Unit head:* Dr. Nancy Michelson, Chair of Department of Education Specialties, 410-548-2430, E-mail: nlmichelson@salisbury.edu. *Application contact:* Claire Williams, Program Management Specialist, 410-543-6281, E-mail: clwilliams@salisbury.edu.

Sam Houston State University, College of Education and Applied Science, Department of Curriculum and Instruction, Huntsville, TX 77341. Offers curriculum and instruction (M Ed, MA); instructional technology (M Ed). *Accreditation:* NCATE. Part-time and evening/weekend programs available. *Faculty:* 19 full-time (13 women). *Students:* 53 full-time (39 women), 251 part-time (194 women); includes 124 minority (62 Black or African American, non-Hispanic/Latino; 1 American Indian or Alaska Native, non-Hispanic/Latino; 4 Asian, non-Hispanic/Latino; 47 Hispanic/Latino; 10 Two or more races, non-Hispanic/Latino), 4 international. Average age 32. 201 applicants, 94% accepted, 89 enrolled. In 2013, 114 master's awarded. *Degree requirements:* For master's, comprehensive exam, thesis optional. *Entrance requirements:* For master's, GRE General Test. Additional exam requirements/recommendations for international students: Required—TOEFL (minimum score 550 paper-based; 79 iBT), IELTS (minimum score 6.5). *Application deadline:* For fall admission, 8/1 for domestic students, 6/25 for international students; for spring admission, 12/1 for domestic students, 11/12 for international students. Applications are processed on a rolling basis. Application fee: $45 ($75 for international students). Electronic applications accepted. *Financial support:* In 2013–14, 3 research assistantships (averaging $9,542 per year) were awarded; career-related internships or fieldwork, Federal Work-Study, institutionally sponsored loans, scholarships/grants, tuition waivers (partial), and unspecified assistantships also available. Support available to part-time students. Financial award application deadline: 5/31; financial award applicants required to submit FAFSA. *Unit head:* Dr. Daphne Johnson, Chair, 936-294-3875, Fax: 936-294-1056, E-mail: edu_dxe@shsu.edu. *Application contact:* Molly Doughtie, Advisor, 936-294-1105, E-mail: edu_mej@shsu.edu.
Website: http://www.shsu.edu/~cai_www/.

San Diego State University, Graduate and Research Affairs, College of Education, School of Teacher Education, Program in Elementary Curriculum and Instruction, San Diego, CA 92182. Offers MA. *Accreditation:* NCATE. Evening/weekend programs available. *Entrance requirements:* For master's, GRE General Test, letters of reference. Additional exam requirements/recommendations for international students: Required—TOEFL. Electronic applications accepted.

San Diego State University, Graduate and Research Affairs, College of Education, School of Teacher Education, Program in Secondary Curriculum and Instruction, San Diego, CA 92182. Offers MA. *Accreditation:* NCATE. *Entrance requirements:* For master's, GRE General Test, letters of reference. Additional exam requirements/recommendations for international students: Required—TOEFL. Electronic applications accepted.

San Jose State University, Graduate Studies and Research, Connie L. Lurie College of Education, Department of Elementary Education, San Jose, CA 95192-0001. Offers curriculum and instruction (MA); reading (Certificate). *Accreditation:* NCATE. *Degree requirements:* For master's, thesis or alternative. Electronic applications accepted.

Seattle Pacific University, Master of Education in Curriculum and Instruction Program, Seattle, WA 98119-1997. Offers reading/language arts education (M Ed). *Accreditation:* NCATE. Part-time and evening/weekend programs available. *Students:* 1 (woman) full-time, 14 part-time (12 women); includes 6 minority (3 Asian, non-Hispanic/Latino; 2 Hispanic/Latino; 1 Two or more races, non-Hispanic/Latino). Average age 36. In 2013, 35 master's awarded. *Degree requirements:* For master's, comprehensive exam. *Entrance requirements:* For master's, GRE General Test or MAT, copy of teaching certificate, official transcript(s), resume, personal statement, two letters of recommendation. Additional exam requirements/recommendations for international students: Required—TOEFL (minimum score 550 paper-based). *Application deadline:* For fall admission, 8/15 priority date for domestic students, 7/1 for international students; for winter admission, 11/15 for domestic students; for spring admission, 2/15 priority date for domestic students, 3/1 for international students; for summer admission, 5/15 for domestic students. Applications are processed on a rolling basis. Application fee: $50. Electronic applications accepted. *Expenses:* Contact institution. *Financial support:* Applicants required to submit FAFSA. *Faculty research:* Educational technology, classroom environments, character education. *Unit head:* Dr. Tracy Williams, Chair, 206-281-2293, E-mail: williamst@spu.edu. *Application contact:* The Graduate Center, 206-281-2091.

Shawnee State University, Program in Curriculum and Instruction, Portsmouth, OH 45662-4344. Offers M Ed. *Accreditation:* NCATE.

Shaw University, Department of Education, Raleigh, NC 27601-2399. Offers curriculum and instruction (MS). Part-time and evening/weekend programs available. *Faculty:* 1 (woman) full-time, 1 (woman) part-time/adjunct. *Students:* 1 (woman) full-time, 20 part-time (18 women); includes 15 minority (13 Black or African American, non-Hispanic/Latino; 2 Hispanic/Latino). Average age 36. 9 applicants, 100% accepted, 7 enrolled. In 2013, 4 master's awarded. *Degree requirements:* For master's, comprehensive exam, thesis, practicum/internship, PRAXIS II. *Entrance requirements:* For master's, GRE General Test, letters of recommendation. Additional exam requirements/recommendations for international students: Required—TOEFL (minimum score 500 paper-based). *Application deadline:* For fall admission, 4/1 priority date for domestic students, 1/30 priority date for international students; for spring admission, 10/31 priority date for domestic students, 8/30 priority date for international students. Applications are processed on a rolling basis. Application fee: $50. Electronic applications accepted. *Expenses: Tuition:* Full-time $10,404; part-time $578 per semester hour. *Required fees:* $2784. *Financial support:* In 2013–14, 1 student received support. Career-related internships or fieldwork, Federal Work-Study, scholarships/grants, and tuition waivers (full) available. Support available to part-time students. Financial award applicants required to submit FAFSA. *Faculty research:* Multicultural education, instructional technology. *Unit head:* Dr. Paula Moten-Tolson, Chairperson, 919-546-8544, Fax: 919-546-8531, E-mail: pmoten@shawu.edu. *Application contact:* Dr. Juanita Linton, Coordinator of Graduate Education, 919-278-2661, Fax: 919-546-8531, E-mail: jlinton@shawu.edu.

Shepherd University, Program in Curriculum and Instruction, Shepherdstown, WV 25443. Offers MA. *Accreditation:* NCATE.

Shippensburg University of Pennsylvania, School of Graduate Studies, College of Education and Human Services, Department of Teacher Education, Shippensburg, PA 17257-2299. Offers curriculum and instruction (M Ed), including biology, early childhood

education, elementary education, geography/earth science, history, mathematics, middle level education, modern languages; reading (M Ed). *Accreditation:* NCATE. Part-time and evening/weekend programs available. *Faculty:* 13 full-time (9 women), 2 part-time/adjunct (both women). *Students:* 6 full-time (all women), 72 part-time (61 women); includes 5 minority (1 Black or African American, non-Hispanic/Latino; 1 Asian, non-Hispanic/Latino; 2 Hispanic/Latino; 1 Two or more races, non-Hispanic/Latino), 1 international. Average age 30. 55 applicants, 60% accepted, 24 enrolled. In 2013, 63 master's awarded. *Degree requirements:* For master's, comprehensive exam (for some programs), thesis optional, practicum or internship; capstone seminar (for some programs). *Entrance requirements:* For master's, MAT or GRE (if GPA less than 2.75), interview, 3 letters of reference, questionnaire of teaching background and future goals. Additional exam requirements/recommendations for international students: Required—TOEFL (minimum score 580 paper-based); Recommended—IELTS (minimum score 6). *Application deadline:* For fall admission, 4/1 priority date for domestic students, 4/30 for international students; for spring admission, 9/1 priority date for domestic students, 9/30 for international students. Applications are processed on a rolling basis. Application fee: $45. Electronic applications accepted. *Expenses: Tuition, area resident:* Part-time $442 per credit. Tuition, state resident: part-time $442 per credit. Tuition, nonresident: part-time $663 per credit. *Required fees:* $127 per credit. *Financial support:* In 2013–14, 4 research assistantships with full tuition reimbursements (averaging $5,000 per year) were awarded; career-related internships or fieldwork, scholarships/grants, unspecified assistantships, and resident hall director and student payroll positions also available. Support available to part-time students. Financial award application deadline: 3/1; financial award applicants required to submit FAFSA. *Unit head:* Dr. Christine A. Royce, Chairperson, 717-477-1688, Fax: 717-477-4046, E-mail: caroyc@ship.edu. *Application contact:* Jeremy R. Goshorn, Assistant Dean of Graduate Admissions, 717-477-1231, Fax: 717-477-4016, E-mail: jrgoshorn@ship.edu.
Website: http://www.ship.edu/teacher/.

Shorter University, Professional Studies, Rome, GA 30165. Offers accountancy (MAC); business administration (MBA); curriculum and instruction (M Ed); leadership (MA). Evening/weekend programs available. *Degree requirements:* For master's, project. *Entrance requirements:* For master's, minimum undergraduate GPA of 2.75 in last 60 hours, 3 years of work experience. Additional exam requirements/recommendations for international students: Required—TOEFL (minimum score 550 paper-based; 79 iBT). *Faculty research:* Systems design, leadership, pedagogy using technology.

Simon Fraser University, Office of Graduate Studies, Faculty of Education, Programs in Curriculum and Instruction, Burnaby, BC V5A 1S6, Canada. Offers curriculum and instruction (M Ed); curriculum and instruction foundations (M Ed, MA); curriculum theory and implementation (PhD); educational practice (M Ed); philosophy of education (PhD). *Degree requirements:* For master's, comprehensive exam (for some programs), thesis (for some programs); for doctorate, comprehensive exam, thesis/dissertation. *Entrance requirements:* For master's, minimum GPA of 3.0 (on scale of 4.33) or 3.33 based on the last 60 credits of undergraduate courses; for doctorate, minimum GPA of 3.5 (on scale of 4.33). Additional exam requirements/recommendations for international students: Recommended—TOEFL (minimum score 580 paper-based; 93 iBT), IELTS (minimum score 7), TWE (minimum score 5). Electronic applications accepted. *Expenses: Tuition, area resident:* Full-time $5084 Canadian dollars. *Required fees:* $840 Canadian dollars. *Faculty research:* Philosophy of education, applied and comparative epistemology, ethics and moral education, critical multicultural practices.

Simpson University, School of Education, Redding, CA 96003-8606. Offers education (MA), including curriculum, education leadership; education and preliminary administrative services credential (MA); education and preliminary teaching credential (MA); teaching (MA). Part-time and evening/weekend programs available. *Faculty:* 5 full-time (2 women), 16 part-time/adjunct (7 women). *Students:* 45 full-time (27 women), 84 part-time (59 women); includes 24 minority (4 Black or African American, non-Hispanic/Latino; 2 American Indian or Alaska Native, non-Hispanic/Latino; 13 Asian, non-Hispanic/Latino; 4 Hispanic/Latino; 1 Native Hawaiian or other Pacific Islander, non-Hispanic/Latino). Average age 36. 54 applicants, 67% accepted, 29 enrolled. In 2013, 29 master's awarded. *Degree requirements:* For master's, thesis optional. *Entrance requirements:* For master's, GRE. Additional exam requirements/recommendations for international students: Required—TOEFL (minimum score 550 paper-based). *Application deadline:* Applications are processed on a rolling basis. Application fee: $25. Electronic applications accepted. Tuition and fees vary according to program. *Financial support:* Scholarships/grants available. Financial award applicants required to submit FAFSA. *Unit head:* Dr. Glee Brooks, Dean of Education, 530-226-4188, Fax: 530-226-4872, E-mail: gbrooks@simpsonu.edu. *Application contact:* Kimberly Snow, Assistant Director of Graduate Admissions, 530-226-4633, E-mail: ksnow@simpsonu.edu.

Sonoma State University, School of Education, Rohnert Park, CA 94928. Offers curriculum, teaching, and learning (MA); early childhood education (MA); education (Ed D); educational administration (MA); multiple subject (Credential); reading and literacy (MA); single subject (Credential); special education (MA, Credential). *Accreditation:* NCATE. Part-time and evening/weekend programs available. *Faculty:* 11 full-time (9 women), 1 (woman) part-time/adjunct. *Students:* 162 full-time (119 women), 165 part-time (125 women); includes 61 minority (4 Black or African American, non-Hispanic/Latino; 1 American Indian or Alaska Native, non-Hispanic/Latino; 12 Asian, non-Hispanic/Latino; 29 Hispanic/Latino; 1 Native Hawaiian or other Pacific Islander, non-Hispanic/Latino; 14 Two or more races, non-Hispanic/Latino), 1 international. Average age 33. 314 applicants, 82% accepted, 75 enrolled. In 2013, 41 master's, 287 other advanced degrees awarded. *Degree requirements:* For master's, thesis or alternative. *Entrance requirements:* For master's, minimum GPA of 2.5. Additional exam requirements/recommendations for international students: Required—TOEFL (minimum score 500 paper-based). Application fee: $55. *Expenses:* Tuition, state resident: full-time $8500. Tuition, nonresident: full-time $12,964. *Required fees:* $1762. *Financial support:* In 2013–14, 1 research assistantship (averaging $1,876 per year) was awarded; fellowships, career-related internships or fieldwork, and Federal Work-Study also available. Support available to part-time students. Financial award application deadline: 3/2; financial award applicants required to submit FAFSA. *Unit head:* Dr. Carlos Ayala, Dean, 707-664-4412, E-mail: carlos.ayala@sonoma.edu. *Application contact:* Dr. Jennifer Mahdavi, Coordinator of Graduate Studies, 707-664-3311, E-mail: jennifer.mahdavi@sonoma.edu.
Website: http://www.sonoma.edu/education/.

South Dakota State University, Graduate School, College of Education and Human Sciences, Department of Educational Leadership, Brookings, SD 57007. Offers curriculum and instruction (M Ed); educational administration (M Ed). Part-time and evening/weekend programs available. Postbaccalaureate distance learning degree programs offered (minimal on-campus study). *Degree requirements:* For master's, portfolio, oral exam. *Entrance requirements:* For master's, minimum GPA of 2.75. Additional exam requirements/recommendations for international students: Required—TOEFL (minimum score 550 paper-based; 80 iBT). *Faculty research:* Inclusion school climate, K-12 reform and restructuring, rural development, ESL, leadership.

Southeastern Louisiana University, College of Education, Department of Teaching and Learning, Hammond, LA 70402. Offers curriculum and instruction (M Ed);

elementary education (MAT); special education (M Ed); special education: early interventionist (MAT). *Accreditation:* NCATE. Part-time and evening/weekend programs available. *Faculty:* 11 full-time (9 women). *Students:* 40 full-time (38 women), 191 part-time (165 women); includes 55 minority (35 Black or African American, non-Hispanic/Latino; 1 American Indian or Alaska Native, non-Hispanic/Latino; 4 Asian, non-Hispanic/Latino; 13 Hispanic/Latino; 2 Two or more races, non-Hispanic/Latino), 2 international. Average age 34. 35 applicants, 66% accepted, 20 enrolled. In 2013, 50 master's awarded. *Degree requirements:* For master's, comprehensive exam (for some programs), thesis (for some programs), action research project, oral defense of research project, portfolio, teaching certificate, minimum cumulative GPA of 3.0. *Entrance requirements:* For master's, GRE (verbal and quantitative), PRAXIS (MAT). Additional exam requirements/recommendations for international students: Required—TOEFL (minimum score 500 paper-based; 61 iBT). *Application deadline:* For fall admission, 7/15 priority date for domestic students, 6/1 priority date for international students; for spring admission, 12/1 priority date for domestic students, 10/1 priority date for international students. Applications are processed on a rolling basis. Application fee: $20 ($30 for international students). Electronic applications accepted. *Expenses:* Tuition, state resident: full-time $5047. Tuition, nonresident: full-time $17,066. *Required fees:* $1213. Tuition and fees vary according to degree level. *Financial support:* Career-related internships or fieldwork, Federal Work-Study, institutionally sponsored loans, scholarships/grants, and unspecified assistantships available. Support available to part-time students. Financial award application deadline: 5/1; financial award applicants required to submit FAFSA. *Faculty research:* ESL, dyslexia, pre-service teachers, inclusion, early childhood education. *Total annual research expenditures:* $45,104. *Unit head:* Dr. Cynthia Elliott, Interim Department Head, 985-549-2221, Fax: 985-549-5009, E-mail: celliott@selu.edu. *Application contact:* Sandra Meyers, Graduate Admissions Analyst, 985-549-5620, Fax: 985-549-5632, E-mail: admissions@selu.edu.
Website: http://www.selu.edu/acad_research/depts/teach_lrn/index.html.

Southern Arkansas University–Magnolia, Graduate Programs, Magnolia, AR 71753. Offers agriculture (MS); business administration (MBA); computer and information sciences (MS); education (M Ed), including counseling and development, curriculum and instruction, educational administration and supervision, elementary education, reading, secondary education, TESOL; kinesiology (M Ed); library media and information specialist (M Ed); mental health and clinical counseling (MS); public administration (MPA); school counseling (M Ed); teaching (MAT). *Accreditation:* NCATE. Part-time and evening/weekend programs available. Postbaccalaureate distance learning degree programs offered. *Faculty:* 34 full-time (15 women), 8 part-time/adjunct (5 women). *Students:* 48 full-time (22 women), 269 part-time (167 women); includes 85 minority (78 Black or African American, non-Hispanic/Latino; 2 Asian, non-Hispanic/Latino; 2 Hispanic/Latino; 1 Native Hawaiian or other Pacific Islander, non-Hispanic/Latino; 2 Two or more races, non-Hispanic/Latino), 5 international. Average age 33. 149 applicants, 73% accepted, 109 enrolled. In 2013, 149 master's awarded. *Degree requirements:* For master's, comprehensive exam (for some programs), thesis optional. *Entrance requirements:* For master's, GRE, MAT or GMAT, minimum GPA of 2.5. Additional exam requirements/recommendations for international students: Required—TOEFL, IELTS. *Application deadline:* For fall admission, 7/10 for domestic and international students; for winter admission, 12/1 for domestic and international students; for spring admission, 12/1 for domestic and international students; for summer admission, 4/1 for domestic students. Applications are processed on a rolling basis. Application fee: $25 ($50 for international students). Electronic applications accepted. *Expenses:* Tuition, state resident: part-time $254 per credit hour. Tuition, nonresident: part-time $370 per credit hour. *Required fees:* $136 per credit hour. $259 per semester. Tuition and fees vary according to course load and program. *Financial support:* Career-related internships or fieldwork, Federal Work-Study, scholarships/grants, tuition waivers (full), and unspecified assistantships available. Financial award applicants required to submit FAFSA. *Faculty research:* Alternative certification for teachers, supervision of instruction, instructional leadership, counseling. *Unit head:* Dr. Kim Bloss, Dean, School of Graduate Studies, 870-235-4150, Fax: 870-235-5227, E-mail: kkbloss@saumag.edu. *Application contact:* Shrijana Malaka, Admissions Specialist, 870-235-4150, Fax: 870-235-5227, E-mail: smalakar@saumag.edu.
Website: http://www.saumag.edu/graduate.

Southern Illinois University Carbondale, Graduate School, College of Education and Human Services, Department of Curriculum and Instruction, Carbondale, IL 62901-4701. Offers MS Ed, PhD. *Accreditation:* NCATE. Part-time programs available. *Faculty:* 42 full-time (23 women). *Students:* 74 full-time (36 women), 98 part-time (78 women); includes 19 minority (13 Black or African American, non-Hispanic/Latino; 2 Asian, non-Hispanic/Latino; 4 Hispanic/Latino), 43 international. 63 applicants, 38% accepted, 18 enrolled. In 2013, 59 master's, 7 doctorates awarded. *Degree requirements:* For doctorate, variable foreign language requirement, thesis/dissertation. *Entrance requirements:* For master's, minimum GPA of 2.7; for doctorate, GRE or MAT, minimum GPA of 3.25. Additional exam requirements/recommendations for international students: Required—TOEFL. *Application deadline:* Applications are processed on a rolling basis. Application fee: $50. *Financial support:* In 2013–14, 4 fellowships with full tuition reimbursements, 10 research assistantships with full tuition reimbursements, 45 teaching assistantships with full tuition reimbursements were awarded; career-related internships or fieldwork, Federal Work-Study, institutionally sponsored loans, and tuition waivers (full) also available. Support available to part-time students. *Faculty research:* Early childhood, science/environmental education, teacher education, instructional development/technology, reading. *Total annual research expenditures:* $3 million. *Unit head:* Dr. John McIntyre, Chair, 618-536-2441, E-mail: johnm@siu.edu. *Application contact:* Debbie Blair, Administrative Clerk, 618-453-4267, Fax: 618-453-4244, E-mail: dkblair@siu.edu.

Southern Illinois University Edwardsville, Graduate School, School of Education, Department of Curriculum and Instruction, Program in Curriculum and Instruction, Edwardsville, IL 62026. Offers MS Ed. *Accreditation:* NCATE. Part-time and evening/weekend programs available. *Faculty:* 17 full-time (11 women). *Students:* 4 full-time (2 women), 46 part-time (37 women); includes 8 minority (5 Black or African American, non-Hispanic/Latino; 1 Asian, non-Hispanic/Latino; 1 Hispanic/Latino; 1 Native Hawaiian or other Pacific Islander, non-Hispanic/Latino), 1 international. 9 applicants, 100% accepted. In 2013, 53 master's awarded. *Degree requirements:* For master's, thesis (for some programs), final exam/paper. *Entrance requirements:* For master's, teaching certificate. Additional exam requirements/recommendations for international students: Required—TOEFL (minimum score 550 paper-based, 79 iBT), IELTS (minimum score 6.5), Michigan Test of English Language Proficiency or PTE. *Application deadline:* For fall admission, 7/18 for domestic students, 6/1 for international students; for spring admission, 12/12 for domestic students, 10/1 for international students; for summer admission, 4/24 for domestic students, 3/1 for international students. Applications are processed on a rolling basis. Application fee: $30. Electronic applications accepted. *Expenses:* Tuition, state resident: full-time $3551. Tuition, nonresident: full-time $8378. *Financial support:* In 2013–14, 4 students received support, including 1 fellowship (averaging $8,370 per year), 1 research assistantship (averaging $9,585 per year), 2 teaching assistantships (averaging $9,585 per year); institutionally sponsored loans, scholarships/grants, and unspecified assistantships also available. Financial award application deadline: 3/1; financial award applicants required to submit FAFSA. *Unit*

head: Dr. Susan Breck, Director, 618-650-3444, E-mail: sbreck@siue.edu. *Application contact:* Melissa K. Mace, Assistant Director of Graduate and International Recruitment, 618-650-2756, Fax: 618-650-3618, E-mail: mmace@siue.edu.
Website: http://www.siue.edu/education/ci/.

Southern New Hampshire University, School of Education, Manchester, NH 03106-1045. Offers business education (M Ed); child development (M Ed); curriculum and instruction (M Ed), including education leadership, reading, special education, technology integration; education (M Ed); educational leadership (M Ed, Ed D); educational studies (M Ed); elementary education (M Ed); English (MAT); English for speakers of other languages (M Ed); reading and writing specialist (M Ed); school business administration (Certificate); secondary education (M Ed); special education (M Ed); technology integration specialist (M Ed). Part-time and evening/weekend programs available. Postbaccalaureate distance learning degree programs offered (no on-campus study). *Degree requirements:* For master's, comprehensive exam (for some programs), thesis or alternative. *Entrance requirements:* For master's, PRAXIS I, minimum GPA of 2.75. Additional exam requirements/recommendations for international students: Required—TOEFL (minimum score 550 paper-based). Electronic applications accepted. *Expenses:* Contact institution.

Southwestern Adventist University, Education Department, Keene, TX 76059. Offers curriculum and instruction with reading emphasis (M Ed); educational leadership (M Ed). Part-time and evening/weekend programs available. *Degree requirements:* For master's, thesis or alternative, professional paper. *Entrance requirements:* For master's, GRE General Test.

Southwestern Assemblies of God University, Thomas F. Harrison School of Graduate Studies, Program in Education, Waxahachie, TX 75165-5735. Offers Christian school administration (MS); curriculum development (MS); early education administration (M Ed); middle and secondary education (M Ed). *Degree requirements:* For master's, comprehensive written and oral exams. *Entrance requirements:* For master's, GRE General Test, minimum GPA of 2.5. Electronic applications accepted.

Southwestern College, Education Programs, Winfield, KS 67156-2499. Offers curriculum and instruction (M Ed); education (Ed D); special education (M Ed); teaching (MA). *Accreditation:* NCATE. Part-time and evening/weekend programs available. Postbaccalaureate distance learning degree programs offered (minimal on-campus study). *Faculty:* 5 full-time (4 women), 22 part-time/adjunct (17 women). *Students:* 9 full-time (7 women), 145 part-time (105 women); includes 22 minority (6 Black or African American, non-Hispanic/Latino; 1 American Indian or Alaska Native, non-Hispanic/Latino; 1 Asian, non-Hispanic/Latino; 8 Hispanic/Latino; 6 Two or more races, non-Hispanic/Latino), 4 international. Average age 39. 127 applicants, 79% accepted, 68 enrolled. In 2013, 96 master's awarded. Terminal master's awarded for partial completion of doctoral program. *Degree requirements:* For master's, practicum, portfolio; for doctorate, thesis/dissertation, professional portfolio. *Entrance requirements:* For master's, baccalaureate degree, minimum GPA of 2.5, valid teaching certificate (for special education); for doctorate, baccalaureate degree with minimum GPA of 3.25, current teaching experience, and GRE; or master's degree with minimum GPA of 3.5. Additional exam requirements/recommendations for international students: Required—TOEFL (minimum score 550 paper-based). *Application deadline:* For fall admission, 8/1 for domestic students; for spring admission, 12/1 for domestic students. Applications are processed on a rolling basis. Application fee: $0. Electronic applications accepted. *Expenses:* Contact institution. *Financial support:* In 2013–14, 4 students received support. Federal Work-Study, tuition waivers (partial), and unspecified assistantships available. Financial award application deadline: 4/1; financial award applicants required to submit FAFSA. *Unit head:* Dr. Cameron Carlson, Dean of Education, 800-846-1543 Ext. 6115, Fax: 620-229-6341, E-mail: cameron.carlson@sckans.edu. *Application contact:* Marla Sexson, Vice President for Enrollment Management, 620-229-6364, Fax: 620-229-6344, E-mail: marla.sexson@sckans.edu.
Website: http://www.sckans.edu/graduate/education-med/.

Stanford University, School of Education, Program in Curriculum and Teacher Education, Stanford, CA 94305-9991. Offers MA. *Degree requirements:* For master's, thesis (for some programs). *Entrance requirements:* For master's, GRE General Test. Electronic applications accepted. *Expenses: Tuition:* Full-time $42,690; part-time $949 per credit. *Required fees:* $185.

State University of New York at Plattsburgh, Division of Education, Health, and Human Services, Program in Teacher Education: Teaching and Learning, Plattsburgh, NY 12901-2681. Offers MS Ed. Part-time and evening/weekend programs available. *Students:* 8 full-time (7 women), 20 part-time (16 women). Average age 31. *Entrance requirements:* For master's, minimum GPA of 2.5. Additional exam requirements/recommendations for international students: Required—TOEFL. *Application deadline:* For fall admission, 2/15 priority date for domestic students; for spring admission, 10/15 priority date for domestic students. Applications are processed on a rolling basis. Application fee: $75. *Financial support:* Application deadline: 4/15; applicants required to submit FAFSA. *Unit head:* Dr. Heidi Schnackenberg, Coordinator, 518-564-5143, E-mail: schnachl@plattsburgh.edu. *Application contact:* Betsy Kane, Director, Graduate Admissions, 518-564-4723, Fax: 518-564-4722, E-mail: bkane002@plattsburgh.edu.

State University of New York College at Potsdam, School of Education and Professional Studies, Program in Curriculum and Instruction, Potsdam, NY 13676. Offers childhood education (MST); curriculum and instruction (MS Ed). *Accreditation:* NCATE. Postbaccalaureate distance learning degree programs offered (minimal on-campus study). *Degree requirements:* For master's, thesis (for some programs). *Entrance requirements:* For master's, minimum GPA of 2.75 in last 60 credit hours of undergraduate study. Additional exam requirements/recommendations for international students: Required—TOEFL (minimum score 550 paper-based; 80 iBT), IELTS (minimum score 6). Electronic applications accepted.

Stephens College, Division of Graduate and Continuing Studies, Program in Curriculum and Instruction, Columbia, MO 65215-0002. Offers M Ed. Part-time programs available. Postbaccalaureate distance learning degree programs offered (minimal on-campus study). *Entrance requirements:* For master's, minimum GPA of 3.5 in last 60 hours. Additional exam requirements/recommendations for international students: Required—TOEFL.

Stetson University, College of Arts and Sciences, Division of Education, Department of Teacher Education, Program in Curriculum and Instruction, DeLand, FL 32723. Offers Ed S. *Faculty:* 7 full-time (5 women). *Students:* 3 full-time (all women), 5 part-time (2 women); includes 3 minority (all Black or African American, non-Hispanic/Latino). Average age 36. 5 applicants, 100% accepted, 4 enrolled. *Entrance requirements:* Additional exam requirements/recommendations for international students: Required—TOEFL, IELTS. *Application deadline:* For fall admission, 8/1 priority date for domestic students; for spring admission, 1/1 priority date for domestic students; for summer admission, 5/1 priority date for domestic students. Applications are processed on a rolling basis. Application fee: $50. Electronic applications accepted. *Unit head:* Dr. Glen Epley, Interim Director, 386-822-7075. *Application contact:* Jamie Vanderlip, Assistant Director of Graduate Admissions, 386-822-7100, Fax: 386-822-7112, E-mail: jlszarol@stetson.edu.

Syracuse University, School of Education, Program in Instructional Design, Development, and Evaluation, Syracuse, NY 13244. Offers MS, PhD, CAS. Part-time programs available. *Students:* 35 full-time (23 women), 13 part-time (6 women); includes 6 minority (4 Black or African American, non-Hispanic/Latino; 1 American Indian or Alaska Native, non-Hispanic/Latino; 1 Asian, non-Hispanic/Latino), 18 international. Average age 34. 27 applicants, 59% accepted, 8 enrolled. In 2013, 10 master's, 7 doctorates awarded. *Degree requirements:* For master's, thesis or alternative; for doctorate, comprehensive exam, thesis/dissertation. *Entrance requirements:* For doctorate, GRE, interview, master's degree; for CAS, GRE (recommended), interview. Additional exam requirements/recommendations for international students: Required—TOEFL (minimum score 100 iBT). *Application deadline:* For fall admission, 1/15 priority date for domestic and international students; for spring admission, 10/15 priority date for domestic and international students. Applications are processed on a rolling basis. Application fee: $75. Electronic applications accepted. *Financial support:* Fellowships with full tuition reimbursements, research assistantships with full and partial tuition reimbursements, and teaching assistantships with full and partial tuition reimbursements available. Financial award application deadline: 1/1; financial award applicants required to submit FAFSA. *Faculty research:* Cultural pluralism and instructional design, corrections training, aging and learning, the University and social change, investigative evaluation. *Unit head:* Dr. Tiffany A. Koszalka, Chair, 315-443-3703, E-mail: takoszal@syr.edu. *Application contact:* Laurie Deyo, Graduate Recruiter, School of Education, 315-443-2505, E-mail: e-gradrcrt@syr.edu.
Website: http://soeweb.syr.edu/idde/instrucdesign.html.

Syracuse University, School of Education, Program in Teaching and Curriculum, Syracuse, NY 13244. Offers MS, PhD. Part-time programs available. *Students:* 23 full-time (18 women), 19 part-time (15 women); includes 3 minority (all Black or African American, non-Hispanic/Latino), 10 international. Average age 40. 29 applicants, 55% accepted, 10 enrolled. In 2013, 11 master's, 2 doctorates awarded. *Degree requirements:* For master's, thesis or alternative; for doctorate, comprehensive exam, thesis/dissertation. *Entrance requirements:* For doctorate, GRE, writing sample; master's degree; interview (recommended); resume. Additional exam requirements/recommendations for international students: Required—TOEFL (minimum score 100 iBT). *Application deadline:* For fall admission, 1/15 priority date for domestic and international students; for spring admission, 10/15 priority date for domestic and international students. Applications are processed on a rolling basis. Application fee: $75. Electronic applications accepted. *Financial support:* Fellowships with full tuition reimbursements, teaching assistantships with full and partial tuition reimbursements, and tuition waivers available. Financial award application deadline: 1/1. *Unit head:* Dr. Benjamin Dotger, 315-443-9659, E-mail: bdotger@syr.edu. *Application contact:* Laurie Deyo, Graduate Recruiter, School of Education, 315-443-2505, E-mail: e-gradrcrt@syr.edu.
Website: http://soeweb.syr.edu/.

Tarleton State University, College of Graduate Studies, College of Education, Department of Curriculum and Instruction, Stephenville, TX 76402. Offers M Ed. Part-time and evening/weekend programs available. *Faculty:* 11 full-time (10 women), 1 (woman) part-time/adjunct. *Students:* 9 full-time (8 women), 117 part-time (102 women); includes 32 minority (14 Black or African American, non-Hispanic/Latino; 2 American Indian or Alaska Native, non-Hispanic/Latino; 2 Asian, non-Hispanic/Latino; 12 Hispanic/Latino; 2 Two or more races, non-Hispanic/Latino). Average age 37. 42 applicants, 90% accepted, 32 enrolled. In 2013, 28 master's awarded. *Degree requirements:* For master's, comprehensive exam. *Entrance requirements:* For master's, GRE General Test, minimum GPA of 3.0. Additional exam requirements/recommendations for international students: Required—TOEFL (minimum score 550 paper-based; 80 iBT). *Application deadline:* For fall admission, 8/15 priority date for domestic students; for spring admission, 1/7 for domestic students. Applications are processed on a rolling basis. Application fee: $30 ($130 for international students). Electronic applications accepted. *Expenses:* Tuition, state resident: full-time $3312; part-time $184 per credit hour. Tuition, nonresident: full-time $9144; part-time $508 per credit hour. *Required fees:* $1916. Tuition and fees vary according to course load and campus/location. *Financial support:* Research assistantships, teaching assistantships, career-related internships or fieldwork, Federal Work-Study, and institutionally sponsored loans available. Support available to part-time students. Financial award application deadline: 5/1; financial award applicants required to submit FAFSA. *Unit head:* Dr. Ann Calahan, Head, 254-968-9933, Fax: 254-968-9947, E-mail: acalahan@tarleton.edu. *Application contact:* Information Contact, 254-968-9104, Fax: 254-968-9670, E-mail: gradoffice@tarleton.edu.
Website: http://www.tarleton.edu/COEWEB/teachered.

Teachers College, Columbia University, Graduate Faculty of Education, Department of Curriculum and Teaching, Program in Curriculum and Teaching, New York, NY 10027. Offers Ed M, MA, Ed D. *Faculty:* 6 full-time, 2 part-time/adjunct. *Students:* 63 full-time (55 women), 122 part-time (110 women); includes 65 minority (18 Black or African American, non-Hispanic/Latino; 21 Asian, non-Hispanic/Latino; 17 Hispanic/Latino; 1 Native Hawaiian or other Pacific Islander, non-Hispanic/Latino; 8 Two or more races, non-Hispanic/Latino), 20 international. Average age 34. 115 applicants, 64% accepted, 39 enrolled. In 2013, 44 master's, 7 doctorates awarded. *Degree requirements:* For master's, project; for doctorate, comprehensive exam, thesis/dissertation. *Entrance requirements:* For master's, resume and proof of initial New York state teacher certification (formerly provisional) or certification from another state, or proof of accredited teacher preparation/student program completion; minimum undergraduate GPA of 3.0 (for MA); for doctorate, GRE General Test or MAT, writing sample. Additional exam requirements/recommendations for international students: Required—TOEFL. *Application deadline:* For fall admission, 1/2 priority date for domestic students. Application fee: $65. *Financial support:* Career-related internships or fieldwork, Federal Work-Study, institutionally sponsored loans, and tuition waivers (full and partial) available. Support available to part-time students. Financial award application deadline: 2/1. *Faculty research:* Teacher education, reading education, curriculum development. *Unit head:* Prof. Marjorie Siegel, Chair, 212-678-3765, Fax: 212-678-3237, E-mail: ms399@columbia.edu. *Application contact:* Peter Shon, Assistant Director of Admission, 212-678-3305, Fax: 212-678-4171, E-mail: shon@exchange.tc.columbia.edu.
Website: http://www.tc.edu/c&t/.

Temple University, College of Health Professions and Social Work, Department of Kinesiology, Philadelphia, PA 19122. Offers athletic training (MS, PhD); behavioral sciences (Ed M); curriculum and instruction (MS); integrated exercise physiology (PhD); integrative exercise physiology (MS); kinesiology (MS); psychology of movement (MS); somatic sciences (PhD). Part-time programs available. *Faculty:* 15 full-time (7 women). *Students:* 49 full-time (30 women), 8 part-time (5 women); includes 6 minority (2 Black or African American, non-Hispanic/Latino; 1 Asian, non-Hispanic/Latino; 2 Hispanic/Latino; 1 Two or more races, non-Hispanic/Latino), 6 international. 100 applicants, 33% accepted, 18 enrolled. In 2013, 15 master's, 6 doctorates awarded. Terminal master's awarded for partial completion of doctoral program. *Degree requirements:* For master's, thesis, final project; for doctorate, comprehensive exam, thesis/dissertation. *Entrance requirements:* For master's, GRE General Test or MAT, minimum undergraduate GPA of 3.0, 3 letters of reference, statement of goals, interview, resume; for doctorate, GRE

General Test, minimum undergraduate GPA of 3.0, 3 letters of reference, statement of goals, interview, resume. Additional exam requirements/recommendations for international students: Required—TOEFL (minimum score 550 paper-based; 79 iBT). *Application deadline:* For fall admission, 1/15 for domestic students, 12/15 for international students; for spring admission, 10/1 for domestic students, 8/1 for international students. Applications are processed on a rolling basis. Application fee: $60. Electronic applications accepted. *Financial support:* In 2013–14, 4 research assistantships with full and partial tuition reimbursements (averaging $16,459 per year), 24 teaching assistantships with full and partial tuition reimbursements (averaging $15,966 per year) were awarded; fellowships, career-related internships or fieldwork, Federal Work-Study, scholarships/grants, tuition waivers, and unspecified assistantships also available. Financial award application deadline: 1/15. *Faculty research:* Exercise physiology, athletic training, motor neuroscience, exercise and sports psychology. *Total annual research expenditures:* $318,204. *Unit head:* Dr. John Jeka, Department Chair, 214-204-4405, Fax: 215-204-4414, E-mail: jjeka@temple.edu. *Application contact:* Megan P. Mannal DiMarco, 215-204-7503, E-mail: megan.dimarco@temple.edu.
Website: http://chpsw.temple.edu/kinesiology/home.

Tennessee State University, The School of Graduate Studies and Research, College of Education, Department of Teaching and Learning, Program in Curriculum and Instruction, Nashville, TN 37209-1561. Offers M Ed, Ed D. *Accreditation:* NCATE. *Degree requirements:* For master's, thesis optional; for doctorate, thesis/dissertation. *Entrance requirements:* For master's, GRE General Test or MAT, minimum GPA of 2.5; for doctorate, GRE General Test or MAT, minimum GPA of 3.25. Additional exam requirements/recommendations for international students: Required—TOEFL.

Tennessee Technological University, College of Graduate Studies, College of Education, Department of Curriculum and Instruction, Program in Curriculum, Cookeville, TN 38505. Offers MA, Ed S. *Accreditation:* NCATE. Part-time and evening/weekend programs available. *Faculty:* 2 full-time (1 woman). *Students:* 27 full-time (22 women), 57 part-time (50 women); includes 3 minority (2 Black or African American, non-Hispanic/Latino; 1 Hispanic/Latino), 5 international. Average age 27. 44 applicants, 57% accepted, 20 enrolled. In 2013, 28 master's, 13 other advanced degrees awarded. *Degree requirements:* For master's and Ed S, comprehensive exam, thesis or alternative. *Entrance requirements:* For master's and Ed S, MAT or GRE. Additional exam requirements/recommendations for international students: Required—TOEFL (minimum score 527 paper-based; 71 iBT), IELTS (minimum score 5.5), PTE (minimum score 48), or TOEIC (Test of English as an International Communication). *Application deadline:* For fall admission, 8/1 for domestic students, 5/1 for international students; for spring admission, 12/1 for domestic students, 10/1 for international students. Applications are processed on a rolling basis. Application fee: $35 ($40 for international students). Electronic applications accepted. *Expenses:* Tuition, state resident: full-time $9347; part-time $465 per credit hour. Tuition, nonresident: full-time $23,635; part-time $1152 per credit hour. *Financial support:* In 2013–14, 2 fellowships (averaging $8,000 per year), research assistantships (averaging $4,000 per year), 1 teaching assistantship (averaging $4,000 per year) were awarded. Financial award application deadline: 4/1. *Unit head:* Dr. Jeremy Wendt, Interim Chairperson, 931-372-3181, Fax: 931-372-6270, E-mail: jwendt@tntech.edu. *Application contact:* Shelia K. Kendrick, Coordinator of Graduate Studies, 931-372-3808, Fax: 931-372-3497, E-mail: skendrick@tntech.edu.

Tennessee Temple University, Graduate Studies in Education, Program in Instructional Effectiveness, Chattanooga, TN 37404-3587. Offers M Ed. *Degree requirements:* For master's, comprehensive exam, thesis or alternative. *Entrance requirements:* For master's, GRE, minimum cumulative undergraduate GPA of 3.0, 3 references.

Tennessee Wesleyan College, Department of Education, Athens, TN 37303. Offers curriculum leadership (MS). Evening/weekend programs available. *Degree requirements:* For master's, internship.

Texas A&M International University, Office of Graduate Studies and Research, College of Education, Department of Curriculum and Pedagogy, Laredo, TX 78041-1900. Offers MS. *Faculty:* 9 full-time (7 women), 1 (woman) part-time/adjunct. *Students:* 4 full-time (3 women), 56 part-time (46 women); includes 56 minority (all Hispanic/Latino), 1 international. Average age 33. 30 applicants, 80% accepted, 18 enrolled. In 2013, 13 master's awarded. *Degree requirements:* For master's, comprehensive exam. *Entrance requirements:* Additional exam requirements/recommendations for international students: Required—TOEFL (minimum score 550 paper-based; 79 iBT). *Application deadline:* For fall admission, 4/30 priority date for domestic students, 4/30 for international students; for spring admission, 11/30 for domestic students, 10/1 for international students. Applications are processed on a rolling basis. Application fee: $35 ($50 for international students). *Expenses:* Tuition, state resident: full-time $5184. *International tuition:* $11,556 full-time. *Financial support:* In 2013–14, 1 student received support, including 5 research assistantships; Federal Work-Study, scholarships/grants, and unspecified assistantships also available. Financial award application deadline: 4/1. *Unit head:* Dr. Diana Linn, Chair, 956-326-2677, E-mail: dlinn@tamiu.edu. *Application contact:* Suzanne Hansen-Alford, Director of Graduate Recruiting, 956-326-3023, E-mail: graduateschool@tamiu.edu.
Website: http://www.tamiu.edu/coedu/dept_cirr_ist.shtml.

Texas A&M University, College of Education and Human Development, Department of Teaching, Learning, and Culture, College Station, TX 77843. Offers curriculum and instruction (M Ed, MS, Ed D, PhD). Part-time programs available. *Faculty:* 39. *Students:* 122 full-time (91 women), 269 part-time (213 women); includes 101 minority (45 Black or African American, non-Hispanic/Latino; 6 Asian, non-Hispanic/Latino; 44 Hispanic/Latino; 6 Two or more races, non-Hispanic/Latino), 56 international. Average age 33. 121 applicants, 79% accepted, 64 enrolled. In 2013, 116 master's, 35 doctorates awarded. *Degree requirements:* For master's, comprehensive exam, thesis (for some programs); for doctorate, comprehensive exam, thesis/dissertation. *Entrance requirements:* For master's, GRE General Test, minimum GPA of 3.0; for doctorate, GRE General Test, 3 years of teaching experience. Additional exam requirements/recommendations for international students: Required—TOEFL (minimum score 550 paper-based). *Application deadline:* For fall admission, 1/15 priority date for domestic and international students; for spring admission, 9/15 priority date for domestic and international students. Applications are processed on a rolling basis. Application fee: $50 ($75 for international students). Electronic applications accepted. *Expenses:* Tuition, state resident: full-time $4078; part-time $226.55 per credit hour. Tuition, nonresident: full-time $10,450; part-time $580.55 per credit hour. *Required fees:* $2328; $278.50 per credit hour. $642.45 per semester. *Financial support:* In 2013–14, fellowships with partial tuition reimbursements (averaging $3,000 per year), teaching assistantships with partial tuition reimbursements (averaging $7,200 per year) were awarded; research assistantships with partial tuition reimbursements, career-related internships or fieldwork, Federal Work-Study, institutionally sponsored loans, scholarships/grants, tuition waivers (partial), and unspecified assistantships also available. Support available to part-time students. Financial award application deadline: 4/1; financial award applicants required to submit FAFSA. *Unit head:* Dr. Yeping Li, Head, 979-845-8384, Fax: 979-845-9663, E-mail: yepingli@tamu.edu. *Application contact:* Clarissa Gonzalez, Academic Advisor II, 979-845-8384, Fax: 979-845-9663, E-mail: cgonzalea@tamu.edu.
Website: http://tlac.tamu.edu.

Texas A&M University–Corpus Christi, Graduate Studies and Research, College of Education, Program in Curriculum and Instruction, Corpus Christi, TX 78412-5503. Offers MS, Ed D. Part-time and evening/weekend programs available. *Degree requirements:* For master's, comprehensive exam, thesis (for some programs). *Entrance requirements:* For master's, GRE General Test. Additional exam requirements/recommendations for international students: Required—TOEFL. Electronic applications accepted.

Texas A&M University–Texarkana, Graduate Studies and Research, College of Education and Liberal Arts, Texarkana, TX 75505-5518. Offers adult education (MS); curriculum and instruction (M Ed); education (MS); educational administration (M Ed); English (MA); instructional technology (MS); interdisciplinary studies (MA, MS); special education (MS). Part-time and evening/weekend programs available. *Degree requirements:* For master's, comprehensive exam (for some programs), thesis optional. *Entrance requirements:* For master's, minimum GPA of 2.5 on last 60 hours of bachelor's degree. Additional exam requirements/recommendations for international students: Required—TOEFL. Electronic applications accepted.

Texas Christian University, College of Education, Program in Curriculum Studies, Fort Worth, TX 76129-0002. Offers M Ed, PhD. Part-time and evening/weekend programs available. *Students:* 7 full-time (6 women), 4 part-time (all women); includes 3 minority (2 Black or African American, non-Hispanic/Latino; 1 Hispanic/Latino), 2 international. Average age 31. 5 applicants, 100% accepted, 4 enrolled. In 2013, 6 master's awarded. *Degree requirements:* For master's, comprehensive exam, thesis; for doctorate, comprehensive exam, thesis/dissertation. *Entrance requirements:* For doctorate, GRE. Additional exam requirements/recommendations for international students: Required—TOEFL (minimum score 550 paper-based; 80 iBT). *Application deadline:* For fall admission, 11/16 for domestic and international students; for winter admission, 2/1 for domestic and international students; for spring admission, 3/1 for domestic and international students. Application fee: $60. Electronic applications accepted. *Expenses: Tuition:* Part-time $1270 per credit hour. Tuition and fees vary according to course load and program. *Financial support:* Teaching assistantships with full tuition reimbursements, career-related internships or fieldwork, scholarships/grants, and unspecified assistantships available. Financial award application deadline: 2/1; financial award applicants required to submit FAFSA. *Unit head:* Dr. Jan Lacina, Associate Dean, 817-257-6786, E-mail: j.lacina@tcu.edu. *Application contact:* Lori Kimball, Administrative Program Specialist, 817-257-7661, E-mail: l.kimball@tcu.edu.
Website: http://www.coe.tcu.edu/graduate-students-phd-curriculum-studies.asp.

Texas Southern University, College of Education, Area of Curriculum and Instruction, Houston, TX 77004-4584. Offers bilingual education (M Ed); curriculum and instruction (Ed D); secondary education (M Ed). Part-time and evening/weekend programs available. *Faculty:* 2 full-time (1 woman), 8 part-time/adjunct (all women). *Students:* 18 full-time (17 women), 38 part-time (32 women); includes 55 minority (53 Black or African American, non-Hispanic/Latino; 2 Hispanic/Latino), 1 international. Average age 36. 27 applicants, 22% accepted, 5 enrolled. In 2013, 7 master's, 2 doctorates awarded. *Degree requirements:* For master's, comprehensive exam; for doctorate, comprehensive exam, thesis/dissertation. *Entrance requirements:* For master's, GRE General Test, minimum GPA of 2.5; for doctorate, GRE General Test or MAT, master's degree, minimum B+ average. Additional exam requirements/recommendations for international students: Required—TOEFL. *Application deadline:* For fall admission, 7/1 for domestic and international students; for spring admission, 11/1 for domestic and international students. Applications are processed on a rolling basis. Application fee: $50 ($75 for international students). Electronic applications accepted. *Financial support:* Fellowships, teaching assistantships, scholarships/grants, and unspecified assistantships available. Support available to part-time students. Financial award application deadline: 5/1. *Unit head:* Dr. Ingrid Haynes-Mays, Interim Chair, 713-313-7179, Fax: 713-313-7496, E-mail: haynesmaysi@tsu.edu. *Application contact:* Dr. Gregory Maddox, Dean of the Graduate School, 713-313-7011 Ext. 4410, Fax: 713-639-1876, E-mail: maddox_gh@tsu.edu.
Website: http://www.tsu.edu/academics/colleges__schools/College_of_Education/Departments/default.php.

Texas Tech University, Graduate School, College of Education, Department of Curriculum and Instruction, Lubbock, TX 79409-1071. Offers bilingual education (M Ed); curriculum and instruction (M Ed, PhD); elementary education (M Ed); language/literacy education (M Ed); multidisciplinary science (MS); secondary education (M Ed). *Accreditation:* NCATE. Part-time programs available. Postbaccalaureate distance learning degree programs offered (minimal on-campus study). *Faculty:* 27 full-time (21 women). *Students:* 49 full-time (40 women), 194 part-time (149 women); includes 74 minority (13 Black or African American, non-Hispanic/Latino; 6 Asian, non-Hispanic/Latino; 50 Hispanic/Latino; 5 Two or more races, non-Hispanic/Latino), 20 international. Average age 38. 105 applicants, 66% accepted, 46 enrolled. In 2013, 48 master's, 14 doctorates awarded. *Degree requirements:* For master's, comprehensive exam (for some programs), thesis optional; for doctorate, comprehensive exam, thesis/dissertation. *Entrance requirements:* For master's, bachelor's degree; resume; letter of intent; academic writing sample; 2 letters of recommendation; for doctorate, GRE, master's degree; resume; letter of intent; academic writing sample; 3 letters of recommendation. Additional exam requirements/recommendations for international students: Required—TOEFL (minimum score 550 paper-based; 79 iBT). *Application deadline:* For fall admission, 6/1 priority date for domestic students, 1/15 priority date for international students; for spring admission, 9/1 priority date for domestic students, 6/15 priority date for international students. Applications are processed on a rolling basis. Application fee: $60. Electronic applications accepted. *Expenses:* Tuition, state resident: full-time $6062; part-time $252.57 per credit hour. Tuition, nonresident: full-time $14,558; part-time $606.57 per credit hour. *Required fees:* $2655; $35 per credit hour. $907.50 per semester. Tuition and fees vary according to course load. *Financial support:* In 2013–14, 94 students received support, including 89 fellowships (averaging $2,276 per year), 14 research assistantships (averaging $5,226 per year), 6 teaching assistantships (averaging $4,517 per year); career-related internships or fieldwork, Federal Work-Study, institutionally sponsored loans, scholarships/grants, traineeships, health care benefits, and unspecified assistantships also available. Support available to part-time students. Financial award application deadline: 2/1; financial award applicants required to submit FAFSA. *Faculty research:* Teacher education, curriculum studies, bilingual education, science and math education, language and literacy education. *Total annual research expenditures:* $413,968. *Unit head:* Dr. Margaret Ann Price, Department Chair, Curriculum and Instruction, 806-834-4347, E-mail: peggie.price@ttu.edu. *Application contact:* Stephenie A. Jones, Administrative Assistant, 806-834-2751, Fax: 806-742-2179, E-mail: stephenie.a.jones@ttu.edu.
Website: http://www.educ.ttu.edu.

Texas Woman's University, Graduate School, College of Professional Education, Department of Teacher Education, Denton, TX 76201. Offers administration (M Ed, MA); special education (M Ed, MA, PhD), including educational diagnostician (M Ed, MA); teaching, learning, and curriculum (M Ed). Part-time programs available. *Faculty:* 16 full-

time (13 women), 37 part-time/adjunct (29 women). *Students:* 15 full-time (all women), 135 part-time (120 women); includes 56 minority (26 Black or African American, non-Hispanic/Latino; 4 American Indian or Alaska Native, non-Hispanic/Latino; 1 Asian, non-Hispanic/Latino; 25 Hispanic/Latino), 3 international. Average age 37. 29 applicants, 69% accepted, 17 enrolled. In 2013, 51 master's, 1 doctorate awarded. Terminal master's awarded for partial completion of doctoral program. *Degree requirements:* For master's, comprehensive exam, thesis, professional paper (M Ed); for doctorate, comprehensive exam, thesis/dissertation. *Entrance requirements:* For master's, minimum GPA of 3.0 on last 60 undergraduate hours, 2 letters of reference, resume, copy of certifications, teacher service record, statement of intent; for doctorate, GRE General Test, minimum GPA of 3.0, 3 letters of reference, resume, copy of certifications, teacher service record, statement of intent. Additional exam requirements/recommendations for international students: Required—TOEFL (minimum score 550 paper-based; 79 iBT). *Application deadline:* For fall admission, 7/1 priority date for domestic students, 3/1 for international students; for spring admission, 11/1 priority date for domestic students, 7/1 for international students. Applications are processed on a rolling basis. Application fee: $50 ($75 for international students). Electronic applications accepted. *Expenses:* Tuition, state resident: full-time $4182; part-time $233.32 per credit hour. Tuition, nonresident: full-time $10,716; part-time $595.32 per credit hour. *Financial support:* In 2013–14, 42 students received support, including 8 research assistantships (averaging $12,942 per year); career-related internships or fieldwork, Federal Work-Study, institutionally sponsored loans, scholarships/grants, traineeships, health care benefits, and unspecified assistantships also available. Support available to part-time students. Financial award application deadline: 3/1; financial award applicants required to submit FAFSA. *Faculty research:* Language and literacy, classroom management, learning disabilities, staff and professional development, leadership preparation practice. *Unit head:* Dr. Jane Pemberton, Chair, 940-898-2271, Fax: 940-898-2270, E-mail: teachereducation@twu.edu. *Application contact:* Dr. Samuel Wheeler, Assistant Director of Admissions, 940-898-3188, Fax: 940-898-3081, E-mail: wheelersr@twu.edu.
Website: http://www.twu.edu/teacher-education/.

Trevecca Nazarene University, Graduate Education Program, Nashville, TN 37210-2877. Offers curriculum, assessment, and instruction K-12 (M Ed); educational leadership (M Ed); English language learners (PreK-12) (M Ed); leadership and professional practice (Ed D); library and information science (MLI Sc); teacher leader (M Ed); teaching (MAE, MAT), including teaching 7-12 (MAT), teaching K-6 (MAT); visual impairments special education (M Ed). *Accreditation:* NCATE. Part-time and evening/weekend programs available. Postbaccalaureate distance learning degree programs offered. *Faculty:* 19 full-time (17 women), 14 part-time/adjunct (5 women). *Students:* 186 full-time (137 women), 134 part-time (94 women); includes 93 minority (87 Black or African American, non-Hispanic/Latino; 1 American Indian or Alaska Native, non-Hispanic/Latino; 2 Asian, non-Hispanic/Latino; 1 Hispanic/Latino; 1 Native Hawaiian or other Pacific Islander, non-Hispanic/Latino; 1 Two or more races, non-Hispanic/Latino), 2 international. In 2013, 201 master's, 40 doctorates awarded. *Degree requirements:* For master's, comprehensive exam, exit assessment/e-portfolio; for doctorate, thesis/dissertation, proposal study, symposium presentation. *Entrance requirements:* For master's, GRE with minimum score of 378 or MAT with minimum score of 290, ACT with minimum score of 22 or SAT with minimum score of 1020 (for MAT programs only); PRAXIS (for MAT and MAE programs), minimum GPA of 2.7, official transcript from regionally accredited institution, 3+ years successful teaching experience (Teacher Leader and Education Leadership majors), technology pre-assessment written requirements (some majors); for doctorate, GRE or MAT, minimum GPA of 3.4, official transcript from regionally-accredited institution, resume, writing sample, interview, reference forms. Additional exam requirements/recommendations for international students: Required—TOEFL (minimum score 550 paper-based). *Application deadline:* Applications are processed on a rolling basis. *Expenses:* Contact institution. *Financial support:* Applicants required to submit FAFSA. *Unit head:* Dr. Suzie Harris, Dean, School of Education/Director of Graduate Education Programs, 615-248-1201, Fax: 615-248-1597, E-mail: admissions_ged@trevecca.edu. *Application contact:* 615-248-1529, E-mail: cll@trevecca.edu.
Website: http://www.trevecca.edu/academics/schools-colleges/education/.

Trinity Washington University, School of Education, Washington, DC 20017-1094. Offers clinical mental health counseling (MA); early childhood education (MAT); educating for change (M Ed); educational administration (MSA); elementary education (MAT); reading (M Ed); school counseling (MA); secondary education (MAT), including English, social studies; special education (MAT). *Accreditation:* NCATE. Part-time and evening/weekend programs available. *Degree requirements:* For master's, thesis (for some programs), capstone project(s). *Entrance requirements:* For master's, PRAXIS I, minimum GPA of 2.8. Additional exam requirements/recommendations for international students: Required—TOEFL (minimum score 550 paper-based). *Application deadline:* For fall admission, 4/1 priority date for domestic students; for winter admission, 11/1 priority date for domestic students; for spring admission, 11/1 priority date for domestic students. Applications are processed on a rolling basis. Application fee: $40. *Expenses: Tuition:* Part-time $715 per credit. *Financial support:* Career-related internships or fieldwork, health care benefits, and unspecified assistantships available. Support available to part-time students. Financial award application deadline: 4/1; financial award applicants required to submit FAFSA. *Faculty research:* Technology, literacy, special education, organizations, inclusion models. *Unit head:* Dr. Janet Stocks, Dean, 202-884-9380, Fax: 202-884-9506, E-mail: stocksj@trinitydc.edu. *Application contact:* Erika Davis, Director of Admissions for School of Education, 202-884-9400, Fax: 202-884-9229, E-mail: daviser@trinitydc.edu.
Website: http://www.trinitydc.edu/education/.

Universidad Adventista de las Antillas, EGECED Department, Mayagüez, PR 00681-0118. Offers curriculum and instruction (M Ed); health education (M Ed); medical surgical nursing (MN); school administration and supervision (M Ed). *Degree requirements:* For master's, comprehensive exam (for some programs), thesis (for some programs). *Entrance requirements:* For master's, EXADEP or GRE General Test, recommendations. Application fee: $175. Electronic applications accepted. *Expenses: Tuition:* Full-time $2400; part-time $200 per credit. *Required fees:* $235 per semester. One-time fee: $30. Tuition and fees vary according to course load. *Financial support:* Fellowships and Federal Work-Study available. *Unit head:* Director, 787-834-9595 Ext. 2282, Fax: 787-834-9595. *Application contact:* Prof. Yolanda Ferrer, Director of Admission, 787-834-9595 Ext. 2261, Fax: 787-834-9597, E-mail: admissions@uaa.edu.
Website: http://www.uaa.edu.

Universidad del Turabo, Graduate Programs, Programs in Education, Program in Curriculum and Instruction and Appropriate Environment, Gurabo, PR 00778-3030. Offers D Ed.

Universidad del Turabo, Graduate Programs, Programs in Education, Program in Curriculum and Teaching, Gurabo, PR 00778-3030. Offers M Ed. *Entrance requirements:* For master's, EXADEP, GRE, interview.

Universidad Metropolitana, School of Education, Program in Curriculum and Teaching, San Juan, PR 00928-1150. Offers M Ed. Part-time and evening/weekend programs available. *Degree requirements:* For master's, thesis or alternative. *Entrance requirements:* For master's, EXADEP, interview.

Université de Montréal, Faculty of Education, Department of Didactics, Montréal, QC H3C 3J7, Canada. Offers M Ed, MA, PhD, DESS. Terminal master's awarded for partial completion of doctoral program. *Degree requirements:* For master's, thesis (for some programs); for doctorate, thesis/dissertation, general exam. Electronic applications accepted. *Faculty research:* Teaching of French as a first or second language, teaching of science and technology, teaching of mathematics, teaching of arts.

Université Laval, Faculty of Education, Department of Teaching and Learning Studies, Programs in Didactics, Québec, QC G1K 7P4, Canada. Offers MA, PhD. Terminal master's awarded for partial completion of doctoral program. *Degree requirements:* For master's, thesis (for some programs); for doctorate, comprehensive exam, thesis/dissertation. *Entrance requirements:* For master's and doctorate, English exam (comprehension of written English), knowledge of French. Electronic applications accepted.

University at Albany, State University of New York, School of Education, Department of Educational Theory and Practice, Albany, NY 12222-0001. Offers curriculum and instruction (MS, Ed D, CAS); curriculum planning and development (MA); educational communications (MS, CAS). Evening/weekend programs available. *Degree requirements:* For doctorate, one foreign language, thesis/dissertation. *Entrance requirements:* For doctorate, GRE General Test. Additional exam requirements/recommendations for international students: Required—TOEFL (minimum score 550 paper-based). Electronic applications accepted.

University at Buffalo, the State University of New York, Graduate School, Graduate School of Education, Department of Learning and Instruction, Buffalo, NY 14260. Offers biology education (Ed M, Certificate); chemistry education (Ed M, Certificate); childhood education (Ed M); childhood education with bilingual extension (Ed M); curriculum, instruction and the science of learning (PhD); early childhood education (Ed M); early childhood education with bilingual extension (birth-grade 2) (Ed M); earth science education (Ed M, Certificate); education studies (Ed M); educational technology and new literacies (Certificate); elementary education (Ed D); English education (Ed M, Certificate); English for speakers of other languages (Ed M); foreign and second language education (PhD); French education (Ed M, Certificate); German education (Ed M, Certificate); gifted education (Certificate); Latin education (Ed M, Certificate); literacy specialist (Ed M); literacy teaching and learning (Certificate); mathematics education (Ed M, Certificate); music education (Ed M, Certificate); physics education (Ed M, Certificate); science and the public (Ed M); social studies education (Ed M, Certificate); Spanish education (Ed M, Certificate); special education (PhD); teaching English to speakers of other languages (Ed M). Part-time and evening/weekend programs available. Postbaccalaureate distance learning degree programs offered (no on-campus study). *Faculty:* 31 full-time (23 women), 64 part-time/adjunct (53 women). *Students:* 275 full-time (215 women), 293 part-time (205 women); includes 35 minority (16 Black or African American, non-Hispanic/Latino; 5 American Indian or Alaska Native, non-Hispanic/Latino; 11 Asian, non-Hispanic/Latino; 3 Hispanic/Latino), 97 international. Average age 30. 544 applicants, 81% accepted, 246 enrolled. In 2013, 222 master's, 17 doctorates, 35 other advanced degrees awarded. *Degree requirements:* For master's, comprehensive exam; for doctorate, thesis/dissertation, research analysis exam, research experience component. *Entrance requirements:* For master's, content test in science and math, letters of reference; for doctorate, GRE General Test or MAT, interview, writing sample, letters of recommendation. Additional exam requirements/recommendations for international students: Required—TOEFL (minimum score 600 paper-based; 96 iBT). *Application deadline:* For fall admission, 2/1 priority date for domestic and international students; for spring admission, 11/15 priority date for domestic students, 10/1 for international students. Applications are processed on a rolling basis. Application fee: $50. Electronic applications accepted. *Financial support:* In 2013–14, 50 fellowships (averaging $8,589 per year), 31 research assistantships with tuition reimbursements (averaging $11,406 per year) were awarded; teaching assistantships, career-related internships or fieldwork, Federal Work-Study, institutionally sponsored loans, scholarships/grants, tuition waivers, and unspecified assistantships also available. Financial award application deadline: 2/28; financial award applicants required to submit FAFSA. *Faculty research:* Science assessment, foreign language teaching and learning, early learning, new literacies, gender and education. *Total annual research expenditures:* $1.7 million. *Unit head:* Dr. Suzanne Miller, Chair, 716-645-2455, Fax: 716-645-3161, E-mail: smiller@buffalo.edu. *Application contact:* Cathy Dimino, Admissions Assistant, 716-645-2110, Fax: 716-645-7937, E-mail: cadimino@buffalo.edu.
Website: http://gse.buffalo.edu/lai.

The University of Alabama at Birmingham, School of Education, Program in Curriculum Education, Birmingham, AL 35294. Offers Ed S. *Degree requirements:* For Ed S, comprehensive exam, thesis optional. *Entrance requirements:* For degree, GRE General Test, MAT, minimum GPA of 3.0, master's degree.

University of Alaska Fairbanks, School of Education, Program in Education, Fairbanks, AK 99775. Offers curriculum and instruction (M Ed); education (M Ed, Graduate Certificate); elementary education (M Ed); language and literacy (M Ed); reading (M Ed); secondary education (M Ed); special education (M Ed). *Faculty:* 23 full-time (14 women), 1 part-time/adjunct (0 women). *Students:* 37 full-time (26 women), 78 part-time (54 women); includes 15 minority (6 American Indian or Alaska Native, non-Hispanic/Latino; 6 Hispanic/Latino; 3 Two or more races, non-Hispanic/Latino), 2 international. Average age 34. 37 applicants, 68% accepted, 19 enrolled. In 2013, 39 master's, 28 other advanced degrees awarded. *Degree requirements:* For master's, comprehensive exam, thesis, oral defense. *Entrance requirements:* Additional exam requirements/recommendations for international students: Required—TOEFL (minimum score 550 paper-based; 80 iBT). *Application deadline:* For fall admission, 5/1 for domestic students, 3/1 for international students; for spring admission, 10/15 for domestic students, 8/1 for international students. Applications are processed on a rolling basis. Application fee: $60. Electronic applications accepted. *Expenses:* Tuition, state resident: full-time $7254; part-time $403 per credit. Tuition, nonresident: full-time $14,814; part-time $823 per credit. Tuition and fees vary according to course level, course load and reciprocity agreements. *Financial support:* In 2013–14, 1 teaching assistantship with tuition reimbursement (averaging $11,011 per year) was awarded; fellowships with tuition reimbursements, research assistantships with tuition reimbursements, career-related internships or fieldwork, Federal Work-Study, scholarships/grants, health care benefits, and unspecified assistantships also available. Support available to part-time students. Financial award application deadline: 6/1; financial award applicants required to submit FAFSA. *Unit head:* Allan Morotti, Interim Dean, 907-474-7341, Fax: 907-474-5451, E-mail: uaf-soe-school@alaska.edu. *Application contact:* Libby Eddy, Director of Admissions, 907-474-7500, Fax: 907-474-7097, E-mail: admissions@uaf.edu.
Website: https://sites.google.com/a/alaska.edu/soe-graduate/.

University of Arkansas, Graduate School, College of Education and Health Professions, Department of Curriculum and Instruction, Program in Curriculum and Instruction, Fayetteville, AR 72701-1201. Offers PhD. Part-time programs available.

Degree requirements: For doctorate, thesis/dissertation. *Entrance requirements:* For doctorate, GRE General Test. Electronic applications accepted.

The University of British Columbia, Faculty of Education, Centre for Cross-Faculty Inquiry in Education, Vancouver, BC V6T 1Z1, Canada. Offers curriculum and instruction (M Ed, MA, PhD); early childhood education (M Ed, MA). Part-time and evening/weekend programs available. *Students:* 81 full-time, 43 part-time. 58 applicants, 72% accepted, 27 enrolled. Terminal master's awarded for partial completion of doctoral program. *Degree requirements:* For master's, thesis (MA); for doctorate, thesis/dissertation. *Entrance requirements:* Additional exam requirements/recommendations for international students: Required—TOEFL (minimum score 567 paper-based). *Application deadline:* For fall admission, 1/1 for domestic and international students. Application fee: $90 Canadian dollars ($150 Canadian dollars for international students). Electronic applications accepted. *Expenses:* Tuition, area resident: Full-time $8000 Canadian dollars. *Financial support:* In 2013–14, 20 students received support. Fellowships with tuition reimbursements available, research assistantships with tuition reimbursements available, teaching assistantships with tuition reimbursements available, institutionally sponsored loans, scholarships/grants, and tuition waivers (full and partial) available.

The University of British Columbia, Faculty of Education, Department of Curriculum and Pedagogy, Vancouver, BC V6T 1Z4, Canada. Offers art education (M Ed, MA); business education (MA); curriculum studies (M Ed, MA, PhD); home economics education (M Ed, MA); math education (M Ed, MA); music education (M Ed, MA); physical education (M Ed, MA); science education (M Ed, MA); social studies education (M Ed, MA); technology studies education (M Ed, MA). Part-time programs available. Postbaccalaureate distance learning degree programs offered (no on-campus study). *Faculty:* 32 full-time (14 women), 1 (woman) part-time/adjunct. *Students:* 163 full-time, 134 part-time, 42 international. Average age 40. 160 applicants, 75% accepted, 97 enrolled. In 2013, 68 master's, 7 doctorates awarded. *Degree requirements:* For master's, thesis (MA); for doctorate, comprehensive exam, thesis/dissertation. *Entrance requirements:* Additional exam requirements/recommendations for international students: Required—TOEFL (minimum score 580 paper-based; 92 iBT), IELTS (minimum score 6.5). *Application deadline:* For fall admission, 12/1 for domestic and international students; for spring admission, 10/1 for domestic students, 9/1 for international students. Application fee: $90 Canadian dollars ($150 Canadian dollars for international students). Electronic applications accepted. *Expenses:* Contact institution. *Financial support:* In 2013–14, 10 fellowships with partial tuition reimbursements (averaging $16,000 per year), 11 research assistantships with partial tuition reimbursements (averaging $14,000 per year), 27 teaching assistantships with partial tuition reimbursements (averaging $14,000 per year) were awarded; tuition waivers (partial) also available. *Faculty research:* School subjects, teaching and learning. *Unit head:* Dr. Peter Grimmett, Head, 604-822-5422, Fax: 604-822-4714, E-mail: anna.ip@ubc.ca. *Application contact:* Basia Zurek, Graduate Programs Assistant, 604-822-5367, Fax: 604-822-4714, E-mail: edcp.grad@ubc.ca. Website: http://www.edcp.educ.ubc.ca/.

University of Calgary, Faculty of Graduate Studies, Werklund School of Education, Graduate Division of Educational Research, Calgary, AB T2N 1N4, Canada. Offers adult learning (M Ed, MA, Ed D, PhD); curriculum and learning (M Ed, MA, Ed D, PhD); educational leadership (M Ed, MA, Ed D, PhD); languages and diversity (M Ed, MA, Ed D, PhD); learning sciences (M Ed, MA, Ed D, PhD). Ed D in educational leadership offered via distance delivery. Part-time and evening/weekend programs available. Postbaccalaureate distance learning degree programs offered (minimal on-campus study). *Degree requirements:* For master's, thesis (for some programs); for doctorate, thesis/dissertation, candidacy exam. *Entrance requirements:* For master's, minimum GPA of 3.0, 3 letters of reference; for doctorate, minimum GPA of 3.5, 3 letters of reference. Additional exam requirements/recommendations for international students: Required—TOEFL, IELTS. Electronic applications accepted. *Faculty research:* Curriculum, leadership, technology, contexts, gifted, second language teaching, work place and adult learning.

University of California, Davis, Graduate Studies, Graduate Group in Education, Davis, CA 95616. Offers education (MA, Ed D); instructional studies (PhD); psychological studies (PhD); sociocultural studies (PhD). Ed D offered jointly with California State University, Fresno. Terminal master's awarded for partial completion of doctoral program. *Degree requirements:* For master's, comprehensive exam (for some programs), thesis (for some programs); for doctorate, thesis/dissertation. *Entrance requirements:* For master's and doctorate, GRE. Additional exam requirements/recommendations for international students: Required—TOEFL (minimum score 550 paper-based). Electronic applications accepted. *Faculty research:* Language and literacy, mathematics education, science education, teacher development, school psychology.

University of California, San Diego, Office of Graduate Studies, Program in Education Studies, La Jolla, CA 92093. Offers education (M Ed); educational leadership (Ed D); teaching and learning (M Ed, MA, Ed D), including bilingual education (M Ed); curriculum design (MA). Ed D offered jointly with California State University, San Marcos. *Students:* 66 full-time (46 women), 66 part-time (54 women); includes 66 minority (11 Black or African American, non-Hispanic/Latino; 6 American Indian or Alaska Native, non-Hispanic/Latino; 29 Asian, non-Hispanic/Latino; 20 Hispanic/Latino), 1 international. 91 applicants, 87% accepted, 64 enrolled. In 2013, 78 master's, 15 doctorates awarded. *Degree requirements:* For master's, thesis (for some programs), student teaching; for doctorate, thesis/dissertation. *Entrance requirements:* For master's, GRE General Test; CBEST and appropriate CSET exam (for select tracks), current teaching or educational assignment (for select tracks); for doctorate, GRE General Test, current teaching or educational assignment (for select tracks). Additional exam requirements/recommendations for international students: Required—TOEFL, IELTS. *Application deadline:* For fall admission, 2/4 for domestic students; for winter admission, 8/1 for domestic students; for summer admission, 2/4 for domestic students. Application fee: $80 ($100 for international students). Electronic applications accepted. *Expenses:* Tuition, state resident: full-time $11,220; part-time $1870 per quarter. Tuition, nonresident: full-time $26,322; part-time $4387 per quarter. *Required fees:* $519.50 per quarter. Part-time tuition and fees vary according to course load and program. *Financial support:* Fellowships and scholarships/grants available. Financial award applicants required to submit FAFSA. *Faculty research:* Language, culture and literacy development of deaf/hard of hearing children; equity issues in education; educational reform; evaluation, assessment, and research methodologies; distributed learning. *Unit head:* Alan J. Daly, Chair, 858-822-6472, E-mail: ajdaly@ucsd.edu. *Application contact:* Giselle Van Luit, Graduate Coordinator, 858-534-2958, E-mail: edsinfo@ucsd.edu.

University of Central Arkansas, Graduate School, College of Education, Department of Leadership Studies, Conway, AR 72035-0001. Offers college student personnel (MS); district-level administration (PMC); educational leadership - district level (Ed S); instructional technology (MS); library media and information technology (MS); school counseling (MS); school leadership (MS); school-based leadership adult education program administration (PMC); school-based leadership building administration (PMC); school-based leadership curriculum administration (PMC); school-based leadership

gifted and talented program administration (PMC); school-based leadership special education program administration (PMC). *Accreditation:* NCATE. Part-time and evening/weekend programs available. Postbaccalaureate distance learning degree programs offered (minimal on-campus study). *Degree requirements:* For master's and other advanced degree, comprehensive exam. *Entrance requirements:* For master's, GRE. Additional exam requirements/recommendations for international students: Required—TOEFL (minimum score 80 iBT). Electronic applications accepted. *Expenses:* Contact institution.

University of Cincinnati, Graduate School, College of Education, Criminal Justice, and Human Services, Division of Teacher Education, Program in Curriculum and Instruction, Cincinnati, OH 45221. Offers M Ed, Ed D. *Accreditation:* NCATE. Part-time programs available. *Degree requirements:* For master's, thesis; for doctorate, thesis/dissertation. *Entrance requirements:* For master's, GRE General Test; for doctorate, GRE General Test, GRE Subject Test. Additional exam requirements/recommendations for international students: Required—TOEFL (minimum score 550 paper-based), TWE (minimum score 4.5), OEPT. Electronic applications accepted.

University of Colorado Boulder, Graduate School, School of Education, Division of Instruction and Curriculum, Boulder, CO 80309. Offers MA, PhD. *Accreditation:* NCATE. *Students:* 58 full-time (38 women), 36 part-time (31 women); includes 16 minority (1 Black or African American, non-Hispanic/Latino; 1 American Indian or Alaska Native, non-Hispanic/Latino; 1 Asian, non-Hispanic/Latino; 8 Hispanic/Latino; 1 Native Hawaiian or other Pacific Islander, non-Hispanic/Latino; 4 Two or more races, non-Hispanic/Latino). Average age 31. 103 applicants, 64% accepted, 28 enrolled. In 2013, 40 master's, 5 doctorates awarded. Terminal master's awarded for partial completion of doctoral program. *Degree requirements:* For master's, comprehensive exam, thesis or alternative; for doctorate, one foreign language, comprehensive exam, thesis/dissertation. *Entrance requirements:* For master's, GRE General Test or MAT, minimum undergraduate GPA of 2.75; for doctorate, GRE General Test. *Application deadline:* For fall admission, 2/1 for domestic students, 12/1 for international students; for spring admission, 9/1 for domestic and international students. Application fee: $50 ($60 for international students). Electronic applications accepted. *Financial support:* In 2013–14, 119 students received support, including 32 fellowships (averaging $2,388 per year), 22 research assistantships with full and partial tuition reimbursements available (averaging $25,903 per year), 20 teaching assistantships with full and partial tuition reimbursements available (averaging $16,442 per year); institutionally sponsored loans, scholarships/grants, health care benefits, and unspecified assistantships also available. Financial award applicants required to submit FAFSA. Website: http://www.colorado.edu/education/.

University of Colorado Colorado Springs, College of Education, Colorado Springs, CO 80933-7150. Offers counseling and human services (MA); curriculum and instruction (MA); educational administration (MA); educational leadership (MA, PhD); special education (MA). *Accreditation:* ACA; NCATE. Part-time and evening/weekend programs available. Postbaccalaureate distance learning degree programs offered (minimal on-campus study). *Faculty:* 25 full-time (17 women), 39 part-time/adjunct (29 women). *Students:* 220 full-time (146 women), 237 part-time (163 women); includes 86 minority (18 Black or African American, non-Hispanic/Latino; 3 American Indian or Alaska Native, non-Hispanic/Latino; 11 Asian, non-Hispanic/Latino; 46 Hispanic/Latino; 8 Two or more races, non-Hispanic/Latino), 16 international. Average age 35. 182 applicants, 88% accepted, 118 enrolled. In 2013, 140 master's, 8 doctorates awarded. *Degree requirements:* For master's, comprehensive exam, thesis or alternative, microcomputer proficiency; for doctorate, comprehensive exam, thesis/dissertation, research lab. *Entrance requirements:* For master's, GRE General Test. Additional exam requirements/recommendations for international students: Recommended—TOEFL. *Application deadline:* For fall admission, 2/28 priority date for domestic students, 2/28 for international students; for spring admission, 10/15 for domestic and international students. Applications are processed on a rolling basis. Application fee: $60 ($75 for international students). *Expenses:* Tuition, state resident: full-time $8882; part-time $1622 per course. Tuition, nonresident: full-time $17,435; part-time $3048 per course. One-time fee: $100. Tuition and fees vary according to course load, degree level, campus/location and program. *Financial support:* In 2013–14, 23 students received support, including 23 fellowships (averaging $1,577 per year); career-related internships or fieldwork, Federal Work-Study, and scholarships/grants also available. Support available to part-time students. Financial award application deadline: 3/1; financial award applicants required to submit FAFSA. *Faculty research:* Linguistically diverse education (LDE), educational policy, evidence-based reading and writing instruction, relational and social aggression, positive behavior supports (PBS), inclusive schooling, K-12 education policy. *Total annual research expenditures:* $136,574. *Unit head:* Dr. Mary Snyder, Dean, 719-255-3701, Fax: 719-262-4133, E-mail: msnyder3@uccs.edu. *Application contact:* Juliane Field, Director, 719-255-4526, Fax: 719-255-4110, E-mail: jfield@uccs.edu. Website: http://www.uccs.edu/coe.

University of Delaware, College of Education and Human Development, School of Education, Newark, DE 19716. Offers education (PhD); educational leadership (Ed D); higher education (M Ed); instruction (MI); reading (M Ed); school leadership (M Ed); school psychology (MA, Ed S); teaching English as a second language (TESL) (MA). *Accreditation:* NCATE. Part-time and evening/weekend programs available. Terminal master's awarded for partial completion of doctoral program. *Degree requirements:* For master's, comprehensive exam (for some programs), thesis (for some programs); for doctorate, comprehensive exam (for some programs), thesis/dissertation. *Entrance requirements:* For master's and doctorate, GRE, 3 letters of recommendation. Additional exam requirements/recommendations for international students: Required—TOEFL (minimum score 600 paper-based). Electronic applications accepted. *Faculty research:* Teacher education; curriculum theory and development; community based education models, educational leadership.

University of Denver, Morgridge College of Education, Denver, CO 80208. Offers child, family and school psychology (MA, PhD, Ed S); counseling psychology (MA, PhD); curriculum and instruction (MA, Ed D, PhD); curriculum instruction and teaching (Certificate); early childhood special education (MA); educational leadership and policy studies (MA, Ed D, PhD, Certificate); higher education (MA, Ed D, PhD); law librarianship (Certificate); library and information science (MLIS); research methods and statistics (MA, PhD). *Accreditation:* ALA; APA (one or more programs are accredited). Part-time and evening/weekend programs available. Postbaccalaureate distance learning degree programs offered (no on-campus study). *Faculty:* 35 full-time (21 women), 63 part-time/adjunct (43 women). *Students:* 435 full-time (332 women), 414 part-time (297 women); includes 194 minority (45 Black or African American, non-Hispanic/Latino; 9 American Indian or Alaska Native, non-Hispanic/Latino; 16 Asian, non-Hispanic/Latino; 96 Hispanic/Latino; 2 Native Hawaiian or other Pacific Islander, non-Hispanic/Latino; 26 Two or more races, non-Hispanic/Latino), 14 international. Average age 32. 672 applicants, 61% accepted, 193 enrolled. In 2013, 248 master's, 30 doctorates, 130 other advanced degrees awarded. Terminal master's awarded for partial completion of doctoral program. *Degree requirements:* For master's, comprehensive exam; for doctorate, 2 foreign languages, comprehensive exam, thesis/dissertation. *Entrance requirements:* For master's and doctorate, GRE General Test or

GMAT. Additional exam requirements/recommendations for international students: Required—TOEFL (minimum score 550 paper-based; 80 iBT). *Application deadline:* Applications are processed on a rolling basis. Application fee: $65. Electronic applications accepted. *Financial support:* In 2013–14, 706 students received support, including 54 research assistantships with full and partial tuition reimbursements available (averaging $15,599 per year), 77 teaching assistantships with full and partial tuition reimbursements available (averaging $12,804 per year); career-related internships or fieldwork, Federal Work-Study, institutionally sponsored loans, scholarships/grants, and unspecified assistantships also available. Support available to part-time students. Financial award application deadline: 2/15; financial award applicants required to submit FAFSA. *Faculty research:* Principal and teacher preparation, development and assessments, gifted education, service-learning, early childhood, mathematics education, access to higher education. *Total annual research expenditures:* $6.3 million. *Unit head:* Dr. Karen Riley, Interim Dean, 303-871-3665, E-mail: karen.riley@du.edu. *Application contact:* Jodi Dye, Assistant Director of Admissions, 303-871-2510, E-mail: jodi.dye@du.edu.
Website: http://morgridge.du.edu/.

University of Detroit Mercy, College of Liberal Arts and Education, Department of Education, Program in Curriculum and Instruction, Detroit, MI 48221. Offers MA. Part-time and evening/weekend programs available. *Degree requirements:* For master's, thesis or alternative. *Entrance requirements:* For master's, minimum GPA of 2.75. *Faculty research:* Integrative curriculum planning, curriculum planning for ethical and character education.

University of Florida, Graduate School, College of Education, School of Teaching and Learning, Gainesville, FL 32611. Offers curriculum and instruction (M Ed, MAE, Ed D, PhD, Ed S), including bilingual/ESOL specialization; elementary education (M Ed, MAE); English education (M Ed, MAE); mathematics education (M Ed, MAE); reading education (M Ed, MAE); science education (M Ed, MAE); social studies education (M Ed, MAE). *Accreditation:* NCATE. Part-time and evening/weekend programs available. Postbaccalaureate distance learning degree programs offered (no on-campus study). *Faculty:* 24 full-time (17 women), 12 part-time/adjunct (7 women). *Students:* 201 full-time (162 women), 325 part-time (255 women); includes 124 minority (36 Black or African American, non-Hispanic/Latino; 4 American Indian or Alaska Native, non-Hispanic/Latino; 10 Asian, non-Hispanic/Latino; 74 Hispanic/Latino), 47 international. Average age 34. 220 applicants, 55% accepted, 64 enrolled. In 2013, 215 master's, 15 doctorates, 14 other advanced degrees awarded. Terminal master's awarded for partial completion of doctoral program. *Degree requirements:* For master's, comprehensive exam (for some programs), thesis (for some programs); for doctorate, comprehensive exam (for some programs), thesis/dissertation (for some programs). *Entrance requirements:* For master's and doctorate, GRE General Test, minimum GPA of 3.0; for Ed S, GRE General Test. Additional exam requirements/recommendations for international students: Required—TOEFL (minimum score 550 paper-based; 80 iBT), IELTS (minimum score 6). *Application deadline:* For fall admission, 2/15 for domestic students, 12/1 for international students; for spring admission, 9/15 for domestic students, 3/1 for international students. Applications are processed on a rolling basis. Application fee: $30. Electronic applications accepted. *Expenses:* Tuition, state resident: full-time $12,640. Tuition, nonresident: full-time $30,000. *Financial support:* In 2013–14, 52 students received support, including 3 fellowships (averaging $2,365 per year), 20 research assistantships (averaging $11,715 per year), 58 teaching assistantships (averaging $8,410 per year); career-related internships or fieldwork and unspecified assistantships also available. Financial award applicants required to submit FAFSA. *Faculty research:* Early childhood, child and adolescents, diverse learners, race/ethnicity issues, teacher education, professional development, language and literacy development, policy development. *Unit head:* Elizabeth Bondy, PhD, Interim Director and Professor, 352-273-4242, Fax: 352-392-9193, E-mail: bondy@coe.ufl.edu. *Application contact:* Sevan Terzian, Graduate Coordinator, 352-273-4216, Fax: 352-392-9193, E-mail: sterzian@coe.ufl.edu.
Website: http://education.ufl.edu/school-teaching-learning/.

University of Hawaii at Manoa, Graduate Division, College of Education, Department of Curriculum Studies, Honolulu, HI 96822. Offers curriculum studies (M Ed); early childhood education (M Ed). Part-time programs available. *Degree requirements:* For master's, thesis optional. *Entrance requirements:* Additional exam requirements/recommendations for international students: Required—TOEFL (minimum score 500 paper-based; 61 iBT), IELTS (minimum score 5).

University of Hawaii at Manoa, Graduate Division, College of Education, PhD in Education Program, Honolulu, HI 96822. Offers curriculum and instruction (PhD); educational administration (PhD); educational foundations (PhD); educational policy studies (PhD); educational technology (PhD); exceptionalities (PhD); kinesiology (PhD). Part-time and evening/weekend programs available. *Degree requirements:* For doctorate, thesis/dissertation. *Entrance requirements:* For doctorate, GRE General Test, sample of written work. Additional exam requirements/recommendations for international students: Required—TOEFL (minimum score 600 paper-based; 100 iBT), IELTS (minimum score 7).

University of Houston, College of Education, Department of Curriculum and Instruction, Houston, TX 77204. Offers administration and supervision (M Ed); curriculum and instruction (M Ed, Ed D); professional leadership (Ed D). *Accreditation:* NCATE. Part-time and evening/weekend programs available. *Degree requirements:* For master's, comprehensive exam, thesis optional; for doctorate, comprehensive exam, thesis/dissertation. *Entrance requirements:* For master's and doctorate, GRE, minimum cumulative undergraduate GPA of 2.6, 3 letters of recommendation, resume/vita, goal statement. Additional exam requirements/recommendations for international students: Required—TOEFL (minimum score 550 paper-based; 79 iBT). Electronic applications accepted. *Faculty research:* Teaching-learning process, instructional technology in schools, teacher education, classroom management, at-risk students.

University of Houston–Clear Lake, School of Education, Program in Curriculum and Instruction, Houston, TX 77058-1002. Offers curriculum and instruction (MS); early childhood education (MS); reading (MS); school library and information science (MS). Part-time and evening/weekend programs available. *Degree requirements:* For master's, thesis (for some programs). *Entrance requirements:* For master's, GRE or minimum GPA of 3.0 in last 60 hours. Additional exam requirements/recommendations for international students: Required—TOEFL (minimum score 550 paper-based). Electronic applications accepted.

University of Houston–Downtown, College of Public Service, Department of Urban Education, Houston, TX 77002. Offers curriculum and instruction (MAT); elementary (EC-6) generalist certification (MAT); elementary/middle school (4-8) generalist certification (MAT); secondary education certification (MAT). Part-time and evening/weekend programs available. Postbaccalaureate distance learning degree programs offered. *Faculty:* 7 full-time (3 women). *Students:* 4 full-time (3 women), 28 part-time (19 women); includes 22 minority (14 Black or African American, non-Hispanic/Latino; 1 Asian, non-Hispanic/Latino; 6 Hispanic/Latino; 1 Two or more races, non-Hispanic/Latino). Average age 36. 31 applicants, 87% accepted, 27 enrolled. In 2013, 10 master's awarded. *Degree requirements:* For master's, capstone course with completed project, position paper, grant proposal, empirical study, curriculum development/revision, or advanced technology project presented at annual Graduate Project Exhibition. *Entrance requirements:* For master's, GRE, personal statement, 3 recommendation forms. Additional exam requirements/recommendations for international students: Required—TOEFL (minimum score 550 paper-based; 80 iBT). *Application deadline:* For fall admission, 7/15 for domestic and international students; for spring admission, 11/15 for domestic and international students. Application fee: $35 ($60 for international students). Electronic applications accepted. *Expenses:* Tuition, state resident: full-time $4212; part-time $234 per credit hour. Tuition, nonresident: full-time $9684; part-time $538 per credit hour. *Required fees:* $1074. Tuition and fees vary according to program. *Financial support:* Scholarships/grants available. Financial award applicants required to submit FAFSA. *Unit head:* Dr. Viola Garcia, Department Chair, 713-221-8165, Fax: 713-226-5294, E-mail: garciav@uhd.edu. *Application contact:* Ceshia Love, Assistant Director of Graduate Admissions, 713-221-8093, Fax: 713-223-7408, E-mail: gradadmissions@uhd.edu.
Website: http://www.uhd.edu/academic/colleges/publicservice/urbaned/.

University of Houston–Victoria, School of Education and Human Development, Victoria, TX 77901-4450. Offers administration and supervision (M Ed); adult and higher education (M Ed); counseling (M Ed); curriculum and instruction (M Ed); special education (M Ed). Part-time and evening/weekend programs available. Postbaccalaureate distance learning degree programs offered (minimal on-campus study). *Faculty:* 22 full-time (19 women). *Students:* 56 full-time (52 women), 325 part-time (274 women); includes 211 minority (113 Black or African American, non-Hispanic/Latino; 2 American Indian or Alaska Native, non-Hispanic/Latino; 16 Asian, non-Hispanic/Latino; 68 Hispanic/Latino; 12 Two or more races, non-Hispanic/Latino), 3 international. *Degree requirements:* For master's, comprehensive exam, project or thesis. *Entrance requirements:* For master's, GRE General Test. Additional exam requirements/recommendations for international students: Required—TOEFL. *Application deadline:* For fall admission, 6/1 for international students; for spring admission, 10/1 for international students. Applications are processed on a rolling basis. Application fee: $0. Electronic applications accepted. *Expenses:* Tuition, state resident: full-time $4534; part-time $251 per credit hour. Tuition, nonresident: full-time $10,906; part-time $606 per contact hour. *Required fees:* $68 per semester hour. Tuition and fees vary according to course load. *Financial support:* In 2013–14, research assistantships with partial tuition reimbursements (averaging $2,000 per year), teaching assistantships with partial tuition reimbursements (averaging $2,000 per year) were awarded; Federal Work-Study, scholarships/grants, and unspecified assistantships also available. Support available to part-time students. Financial award application deadline: 4/15; financial award applicants required to submit FAFSA. *Faculty research:* Reading and language arts education, evaluation and diagnosis of special children's abilities. *Unit head:* Freddie W. Litton, Dean, 361-570-4260, Fax: 361-580-5580. *Application contact:* Sandy Hybner, Senior Recruitment Coordinator, 361-570-4252, Fax: 361-580-5580, E-mail: hybners@uhv.edu.
Website: http://www.uhv.edu/edu/.

University of Idaho, College of Graduate Studies, College of Education, Department of Curriculum and Instruction, Moscow, ID 83844-3082. Offers curriculum and instruction (M Ed, Ed S); industrial technology education (M Ed). *Faculty:* 24 full-time, 2 part-time/adjunct. *Students:* 10 full-time, 44 part-time. Average age 39. In 2013, 51 master's awarded. *Entrance requirements:* For master's, minimum GPA of 2.8. Additional exam requirements/recommendations for international students: Required—TOEFL (minimum score 550 paper-based). *Application deadline:* For fall admission, 8/1 for domestic students; for spring admission, 12/15 for domestic students. Applications are processed on a rolling basis. Application fee: $60. Electronic applications accepted. *Expenses:* Tuition, state resident: full-time $5596; part-time $363 per credit hour. Tuition, nonresident: full-time $18,672; part-time $1089 per credit hour. *Financial support:* Research assistantships and teaching assistantships available. Financial award applicants required to submit FAFSA. *Unit head:* Dr. Paul H. Gathercoal, Chair, 208-885-6587. *Application contact:* Stephanie Thomas, Graduate Recruitment Coordinator, 208-885-4001, Fax: 208-885-4406, E-mail: gadms@uidaho.edu.
Website: http://www.uidaho.edu/ed/ci.

University of Illinois at Chicago, Graduate College, College of Education, Department of Curriculum and Instruction, Chicago, IL 60607-7128. Offers curriculum studies (PhD); educational studies (M Ed); elementary education (M Ed); instructional leadership (M Ed); literacy, language and culture (M Ed, PhD); science education (M Ed); secondary education (M Ed). Part-time and evening/weekend programs available. *Faculty:* 20 full-time (10 women), 10 part-time/adjunct (8 women). *Students:* 124 full-time (89 women), 155 part-time (117 women); includes 117 minority (51 Black or African American, non-Hispanic/Latino; 19 Asian, non-Hispanic/Latino; 43 Hispanic/Latino; 4 Two or more races, non-Hispanic/Latino), 11 international. Average age 32. 154 applicants, 70% accepted, 74 enrolled. In 2013, 108 master's, 16 doctorates awarded. *Degree requirements:* For doctorate, thesis/dissertation. *Entrance requirements:* For master's, minimum GPA of 2.75; for doctorate, GRE General Test, minimum GPA of 2.75. Additional exam requirements/recommendations for international students: Required—TOEFL. *Application deadline:* For fall admission, 1/9 for domestic and international students; for spring admission, 10/1 for domestic and international students. Applications are processed on a rolling basis. Application fee: $40 ($50 for international students). Electronic applications accepted. *Expenses:* Tuition, state resident: full-time $11,066; part-time $3689 per term. Tuition, nonresident: full-time $23,064; part-time $7688 per term. *Required fees:* $3004; $1190 per term. Tuition and fees vary according to course level and program. *Financial support:* In 2013–14, 101 students received support, including 4 fellowships with full tuition reimbursements available; research assistantships with full tuition reimbursements available, teaching assistantships with full tuition reimbursements available, career-related internships or fieldwork, Federal Work-Study, institutionally sponsored loans, traineeships, tuition waivers (full), and unspecified assistantships also available. Support available to part-time students. Financial award application deadline: 3/1; financial award applicants required to submit FAFSA. *Faculty research:* Curriculum theory, curriculum development, research on teaching, curriculum and context, reading/literacy. *Total annual research expenditures:* $70,000. *Unit head:* Prof. Alfred Tatum, Associate Professor/Director/Chair, 312-413-3883, Fax: 312-996-8134, E-mail: atatum1@uic.edu.
Website: http://education.uic.edu.

University of Illinois at Urbana–Champaign, Graduate College, College of Education, Department of Curriculum and Instruction, Champaign, IL 61820. Offers curriculum and instruction (Ed M, MA, MS, Ed D, PhD, CAS); early childhood education (Ed M); elementary education (Ed M); secondary education (Ed M). Part-time programs available. Postbaccalaureate distance learning degree programs offered (no on-campus study). *Students:* 140 (105 women). Application fee: $75 ($90 for international students). *Unit head:* Fouad Abd El Khalick, Head, 217-244-1221, Fax: 217-244-4572, E-mail: fouad@illinois.edu. *Application contact:* Myranda Lyons, Office Support Associate, 217-244-8286, Fax: 217-244-4572, E-mail: mjlyons@illinois.edu.
Website: http://education.illinois.edu/ci.

University of Indianapolis, Graduate Programs, School of Education, Indianapolis, IN 46227-3697. Offers art education (MAT); biology (MAT); chemistry (MAT); curriculum and instruction (MA); earth sciences (MAT); education (MA, MAT); educational

leadership (MA); elementary education (MA); English (MAT); French (MAT); math (MAT); physical education (MAT); physics (MAT); secondary education (MA), including art education, education, English education, social studies education; social studies (MAT); Spanish (MAT). *Accreditation:* NCATE. Part-time and evening/weekend programs available. *Faculty:* 5 full-time (4 women), 2 part-time/adjunct (1 woman). *Students:* 19 full-time (9 women), 54 part-time (27 women); includes 13 minority (5 Black or African American, non-Hispanic/Latino; 1 Asian, non-Hispanic/Latino; 5 Hispanic/Latino; 2 Two or more races, non-Hispanic/Latino), 1 international. Average age 32. In 2013, 52 master's awarded. *Entrance requirements:* For master's, GRE Subject Test, PRAXIS I, minimum GPA of 2.5, 3 letters of recommendation, interview. Additional exam requirements/recommendations for international students: Required—TOEFL (minimum score 550 paper-based). *Application deadline:* Applications are processed on a rolling basis. Application fee: $50. *Expenses: Tuition:* Full-time $5436; part-time $810 per credit hour. *Financial support:* Federal Work-Study available. Financial award application deadline: 5/1; financial award applicants required to submit FAFSA. *Faculty research:* Assessment of teacher education, perceptions of prospective teachers by parents. *Unit head:* Dr. Kathy Moran, Dean, 317-788-3285, Fax: 317-788-3300, E-mail: kmoran@uindy.edu. *Application contact:* Jeni Kirby, Administrative Assistant, Teacher Education, 317-788-2113, E-mail: kirbyj@uindy.edu.
Website: http://education.uindy.edu/.

University of Jamestown, Program in Education, Jamestown, ND 58405. Offers curriculum and instruction (M Ed). *Degree requirements:* For master's, thesis or project. *Expenses: Tuition:* Full-time $24,600; part-time $425 per credit. *Required fees:* $180. Tuition and fees vary according to degree level.

The University of Kansas, Graduate Studies, School of Education, Department of Curriculum and Teaching, Lawrence, KS 66045-3101. Offers curriculum and instruction (MA, MS Ed, Ed D, PhD). Part-time and evening/weekend programs available. *Faculty:* 32. *Students:* 97 full-time (67 women), 90 part-time (77 women); includes 18 minority (1 Black or African American, non-Hispanic/Latino; 1 American Indian or Alaska Native, non-Hispanic/Latino; 9 Asian, non-Hispanic/Latino; 6 Hispanic/Latino; 1 Two or more races, non-Hispanic/Latino), 30 international. Average age 34. 100 applicants, 64% accepted, 36 enrolled. In 2013, 97 master's, 16 doctorates awarded. *Degree requirements:* For master's, comprehensive exam (for some programs), thesis optional; for doctorate, comprehensive exam, thesis/dissertation. *Entrance requirements:* For master's, minimum GPA of 3.0; for doctorate, GRE General Test, minimum graduate GPA of 3.5. Additional exam requirements/recommendations for international students: Required—TOEFL (minimum score 590 paper-based; 96 iBT), IELTS (minimum score 7). *Application deadline:* For fall admission, 3/15 priority date for domestic and international students; for spring admission, 10/15 priority date for domestic and international students. Applications are processed on a rolling basis. Application fee: $55 ($65 for international students). Electronic applications accepted. *Financial support:* Fellowships, research assistantships with full and partial tuition reimbursements, teaching assistantships with full and partial tuition reimbursements, Federal Work-Study, scholarships/grants, and unspecified assistantships available. Financial award application deadline: 3/15; financial award applicants required to submit FAFSA. *Faculty research:* Community-based field experiences in teacher education, vocabulary and narrative development of primary students, narrative inquiry, engaging students in critical thinking by using technology in the classroom, argumentation and evaluation intervention in science education. *Unit head:* Dr. Steven Hugh White, Associate Professor and Chair, 785-864-4435, Fax: 785-864-5207, E-mail: s-white@ku.edu. *Application contact:* Susan M. McGee, Graduate Admissions Coordinator, 785-864-4437, Fax: 785-864-5207, E-mail: smmcgee@ku.edu.
Website: http://ct.soe.ku.edu/.

University of Kentucky, Graduate School, College of Education, Department of Curriculum and Instruction, Lexington, KY 40506-0032. Offers curriculum and instruction (Ed D); elementary education (MA Ed); instructional system design (MS Ed); literacy (MA Ed); middle school education (MA Ed, MS Ed); secondary education (MA Ed, MS Ed). *Accreditation:* NCATE. *Degree requirements:* For master's, comprehensive exam, thesis optional; for doctorate, comprehensive exam, thesis/dissertation. *Entrance requirements:* For master's, GRE General Test, minimum undergraduate GPA of 2.75; for doctorate, GRE General Test, minimum graduate GPA of 3.0. Additional exam requirements/recommendations for international students: Required—TOEFL (minimum score 550 paper-based). Electronic applications accepted. *Faculty research:* Educational reform, multicultural education, classroom instructional practices, performance based assessment, primary school programs.

University of Louisiana at Lafayette, College of Education, Graduate Studies and Research in Education, Program in Curriculum and Instruction, Lafayette, LA 70504. Offers M Ed. *Accreditation:* NCATE. *Degree requirements:* For master's, thesis or alternative. *Entrance requirements:* For master's, GRE General Test, teaching certificate. Additional exam requirements/recommendations for international students: Required—TOEFL (minimum score 550 paper-based). Electronic applications accepted.

University of Louisiana at Monroe, Graduate School, College of Arts, Education, and Sciences, School of Education, Program in Curriculum and Instruction, Monroe, LA 71209-0001. Offers art education (M Ed); biology education (M Ed); chemistry education (M Ed); curriculum and instruction (Ed D); early childhood education (M Ed); earth science education (M Ed); educational leadership (M Ed); elementary education (1-5) (M Ed); English as a second language (M Ed); English education (M Ed); family and consumer education (M Ed); French education (M Ed); history education (M Ed); math education (M Ed); middle school education (M Ed); music education (M Ed); reading education (K-12) (M Ed); Spanish education (M Ed); special education - academically gifted (M Ed); special education - early intervention (M Ed); special education - educational diagnostician (M Ed); special education - mild/moderate disabilities (M Ed); speech education (M Ed). *Accreditation:* NCATE. *Degree requirements:* For master's, comprehensive exam (for some programs), thesis; for doctorate, thesis/dissertation, internships. *Entrance requirements:* For master's, GRE General Test; for doctorate, GRE General Test, minimum undergraduate GPA of 2.75, graduate 3.25. Additional exam requirements/recommendations for international students: Required—TOEFL (minimum score 500 paper-based; 61 iBT). *Application deadline:* For fall admission, 8/24 priority date for domestic students, 7/1 for international students; for winter admission, 12/14 priority date for domestic students; for spring admission, 1/19 for domestic students, 11/1 for international students. Applications are processed on a rolling basis. Application fee: $20 ($30 for international students). Electronic applications accepted. *Expenses:* Tuition, state resident: full-time $6607. Tuition, nonresident: full-time $17,179. Full-time tuition and fees vary according to program. *Financial support:* Research assistantships, career-related internships or fieldwork, Federal Work-Study, and unspecified assistantships available. Financial award application deadline: 4/1; financial award applicants required to submit FAFSA. *Unit head:* Dr. Dorothy Schween, Director, 318-342-1268, Fax: 318-342-3131, E-mail: schween@ulm.edu. *Application contact:* Dr. Dorothy Schween, Director, 318-342-1268, Fax: 318-342-3131, E-mail: schween@ulm.edu.

University of Louisville, Graduate School, College of Education and Human Development, Department of Teaching and Learning, Louisville, KY 40292-0001. Offers art education (MAT); curriculum and instruction (PhD); early elementary education (MAT); instructional technology (M Ed); interdisciplinary early childhood education (MAT); middle school education (MAT); music education (MAT); secondary education (MAT); special education (MAT); teacher leadership (M Ed). Part-time and evening/weekend programs available. *Students:* 137 full-time (93 women), 208 part-time (131 women); includes 44 minority (25 Black or African American, non-Hispanic/Latino; 1 American Indian or Alaska Native, non-Hispanic/Latino; 3 Asian, non-Hispanic/Latino; 12 Hispanic/Latino; 3 Two or more races, non-Hispanic/Latino), 2 international. Average age 32. 150 applicants, 51% accepted, 54 enrolled. In 2013, 127 master's, 5 doctorates awarded. *Degree requirements:* For doctorate, comprehensive exam, thesis/dissertation. *Entrance requirements:* For master's, GRE General Test, PRAXIS II (for some programs); for doctorate, GRE General Test. Additional exam requirements/recommendations for international students: Required—TOEFL (minimum score 560 paper-based; 83 iBT). *Application deadline:* For fall admission, 5/1 priority date for international students; for spring admission, 11/1 priority date for international students; for summer admission, 4/1 priority date for international students. Application fee: $60. Electronic applications accepted. *Expenses:* Tuition, state resident: full-time $10,788; part-time $599 per credit hour. Tuition, nonresident: full-time $22,446; part-time $1247 per credit hour. *Required fees:* $196. Tuition and fees vary according to program and reciprocity agreements. *Financial support:* Fellowships, research assistantships, teaching assistantships, career-related internships or fieldwork, Federal Work-Study, scholarships/grants, and unspecified assistantships available. Financial award application deadline: 6/1; financial award applicants required to submit FAFSA. *Faculty research:* Mathematics teacher education and ongoing professional development in pedagogy and content knowledge; development of literacy, including early literacy in science and mathematics and literacy development for English language learners; immersive visualizations for promoting STEM education from nanoscience to cosmic scales; evidence-based practices for students with disabilities; urban education, including teacher response to intervention systems in schools and cross-cultural competence. *Unit head:* Dr. Ann E. Larson, Acting Chair, 502-852-6431, Fax: 502-852-1497, E-mail: ann@louisville.edu. *Application contact:* Libby Leggett, Director, Graduate Admissions, 502-852-3101, Fax: 502-852-6536, E-mail: gradadm@louisville.edu.
Website: http://louisville.edu/delphi.

University of Manitoba, Faculty of Graduate Studies, Faculty of Education, Department of Curriculum, Teaching and Learning, Winnipeg, MB R3T 2N2, Canada. Offers language and literacy (M Ed); second language education (M Ed); studies in curriculum, teaching and learning (M Ed). *Degree requirements:* For master's, thesis or alternative.

University of Mary, School of Education and Behavioral Sciences, Department of Education, Bismarck, ND 58504-9652. Offers college teaching (M Ed); curriculum, instruction and assessment (M Ed); early childhood education (M Ed); early childhood special education (M Ed); elementary administration (M Ed); emotional disorders (M Ed); learning disabilities (M Ed); reading (M Ed); secondary administration (M Ed); special education strategist (M Ed). Part-time programs available. *Degree requirements:* For master's, portfolio or thesis. *Entrance requirements:* For master's, interview, letters of reference, minimum GPA of 2.5. Additional exam requirements/recommendations for international students: Required—TOEFL (minimum score 500 paper-based; 71 iBT). Electronic applications accepted. *Faculty research:* Innovative pedagogy in higher education, technology in education, content standards, children of poverty, children with diverse learning needs.

University of Mary Hardin-Baylor, Graduate Studies in Education, Belton, TX 76513. Offers administration of intervention programs (M Ed); curriculum and instruction (M Ed); educational administration (M Ed, Ed D), including higher education (Ed D), leadership in nursing education (Ed D), P-12 (Ed D). Part-time and evening/weekend programs available. *Faculty:* 13 full-time (10 women), 6 part-time/adjunct (2 women). *Students:* 46 full-time (33 women), 61 part-time (40 women); includes 35 minority (15 Black or African American, non-Hispanic/Latino; 1 American Indian or Alaska Native, non-Hispanic/Latino; 19 Hispanic/Latino), 1 international. Average age 38. 72 applicants, 88% accepted, 47 enrolled. In 2013, 13 master's, 30 doctorates awarded. *Degree requirements:* For master's, comprehensive exam; for doctorate, thesis/dissertation. *Entrance requirements:* For master's, minimum GPA of 3.0, interview; for doctorate, minimum GPA of 3.5, interview, essay, resume, employment verification, employer letter of support, 3 letters of recommendation. Additional exam requirements/recommendations for international students: Required—TOEFL (minimum score 550 paper-based; 80 iBT), IELTS (minimum score 6). *Application deadline:* For fall admission, 6/1 for domestic students, 6/15 priority date for international students; for spring admission, 11/1 for domestic students, 10/15 priority date for international students. Applications are processed on a rolling basis. Application fee: $35 ($135 for international students). Electronic applications accepted. *Expenses: Tuition:* Full-time $14,130; part-time $785 per credit hour. *Required fees:* $1350; $75 per credit hour. $50 per term. *Financial support:* Federal Work-Study and scholarships (for some active duty military personnel only) available. Support available to part-time students. Financial award application deadline: 6/1; financial award applicants required to submit FAFSA. *Unit head:* Dr. Marlene Zipperlen, Dean, College of Education/Director, Doctor of Education Program, 254-295-4572, Fax: 254-295-4480, E-mail: mzipperlen@umhb.edu. *Application contact:* Melissa Ford, Director of Graduate Admissions, 254-295-4020, Fax: 254-295-5038, E-mail: mford@umhb.edu.
Website: http://graduate.umhb.edu/education/.

University of Maryland, College Park, Academic Affairs, College of Education, Department of Teaching, Learning, Policy and Leadership, College Park, MD 20742. Offers reading (M Ed, MA, PhD, CAGS); secondary education (M Ed, MA, Ed D, PhD, CAGS); teaching English to speakers of other languages (M Ed). *Accreditation:* NCATE. Part-time and evening/weekend programs available. Postbaccalaureate distance learning degree programs offered (no on-campus study). *Faculty:* 63 full-time (43 women), 20 part-time/adjunct (13 women). *Students:* 283 full-time (209 women), 188 part-time (151 women); includes 158 minority (58 Black or African American, non-Hispanic/Latino; 53 Asian, non-Hispanic/Latino; 23 Hispanic/Latino; 1 Native Hawaiian or other Pacific Islander, non-Hispanic/Latino; 23 Two or more races, non-Hispanic/Latino), 52 international. 482 applicants, 44% accepted, 126 enrolled. In 2013, 211 master's, 42 doctorates awarded. *Degree requirements:* For master's, comprehensive exam, seminar paper; for doctorate, comprehensive exam, thesis/dissertation, published paper, oral exam. *Entrance requirements:* For master's, GRE General Test or MAT, minimum GPA of 3.0, 3 letters of recommendation; for doctorate, GRE General Test or MAT, minimum undergraduate GPA of 3.0, graduate 3.5; 3 letters of recommendation. *Application deadline:* For fall admission, 2/1 priority date for domestic students, 9/1 priority date for international students; for spring admission, 9/1 for domestic students, 8/1 for international students. Applications are processed on a rolling basis. Application fee: $75. Electronic applications accepted. *Expenses:* Tuition, state resident: full-time $10,314; part-time $573 per credit hour. Tuition, nonresident: full-time $22,248; part-time $1236 per credit. *Required fees:* $1446; $403.15 per semester. Tuition and fees vary according to program. *Financial support:* In 2013–14, 11 fellowships with full and partial tuition reimbursements (averaging $22,271 per year), 7 research assistantships with tuition reimbursements (averaging $18,573 per year), 85 teaching assistantships with tuition reimbursements (averaging $17,609 per year) were awarded; Federal Work-Study and scholarships/grants also available. Support available to part-time students. Financial award applicants required to submit FAFSA. *Faculty research:* Teacher

preparation, curriculum study, in-service education. *Total annual research expenditures:* $3.9 million. *Unit head:* Francine Hultgren, Interim Chair, 301-405-3117, E-mail: fh@umd.edu. *Application contact:* Dr. Charles A. Caramello, Dean of Graduate School, 301-405-0358, Fax: 301-314-9305, E-mail: ccaramel@umd.edu.

University of Massachusetts Boston, Office of Graduate Studies, Graduate College of Education, Program in Instructional Design, Boston, MA 02125-3393. Offers M Ed. Part-time and evening/weekend programs available. *Degree requirements:* For master's, comprehensive exam, thesis optional, practicum. *Entrance requirements:* For master's, MAT, minimum GPA of 2.75. *Faculty research:* Distance education, adult education.

University of Massachusetts Lowell, Graduate School of Education, Lowell, MA 01854-2881. Offers administration, planning, and policy (CAGS); curriculum and instruction (M Ed, CAGS); educational administration (M Ed); language arts and literacy (Ed D); leadership in schooling (Ed D); math and science education (Ed D); reading and language (M Ed, CAGS). *Accreditation:* NCATE. Part-time and evening/weekend programs available. Postbaccalaureate distance learning degree programs offered (no on-campus study). Terminal master's awarded for partial completion of doctoral program. *Degree requirements:* For doctorate, thesis/dissertation. *Entrance requirements:* For master's, doctorate, and CAGS, GRE General Test. Additional exam requirements/recommendations for international students: Required—TOEFL. Electronic applications accepted.

University of Memphis, Graduate School, College of Education, Department of Instruction and Curriculum Leadership, Memphis, TN 38152. Offers early childhood education (MAT, MS, Ed D); elementary education (MAT); instruction and curriculum (MS, Ed D); instruction design and technology (MS, Ed D); middle grades education (MAT); reading (MS, Ed D); secondary education (MAT); special education (MAT, MS, Ed D). *Accreditation:* NCATE (one or more programs are accredited). Part-time programs available. *Faculty:* 30 full-time (18 women), 16 part-time/adjunct (10 women). *Students:* 55 full-time (44 women), 370 part-time (300 women); includes 169 minority (153 Black or African American, non-Hispanic/Latino; 5 American Indian or Alaska Native, non-Hispanic/Latino; 1 Asian, non-Hispanic/Latino; 6 Hispanic/Latino; 4 Two or more races, non-Hispanic/Latino), 7 international. Average age 35. 181 applicants, 84% accepted, 21 enrolled. In 2013, 137 master's, 10 doctorates awarded. Terminal master's awarded for partial completion of doctoral program. *Degree requirements:* For master's, comprehensive exam, thesis or alternative; for doctorate, comprehensive exam, thesis/dissertation. *Entrance requirements:* For master's, GRE General Test, minimum GPA of 2.5; for doctorate, GRE General Test, GRE Subject Test, 2 years of teaching experience. *Application deadline:* For fall admission, 8/1 for domestic students; for spring admission, 12/1 for domestic students. Applications are processed on a rolling basis. Application fee: $35 ($60 for international students). Electronic applications accepted. *Financial support:* In 2013–14, 635 students received support. Research assistantships with full tuition reimbursements available, teaching assistantships with full tuition reimbursements available, career-related internships or fieldwork, Federal Work-Study, institutionally sponsored loans, scholarships/grants, traineeships, and unspecified assistantships available. Support available to part-time students. Financial award application deadline: 2/15; financial award applicants required to submit FAFSA. *Faculty research:* Effective urban teachers, preparation and retention of urban teachers, technology utilization in schools, field-based teacher preparation programs, effective use of online instruction. *Unit head:* Dr. Sandra Cooley-Nichols, Interim Chair, 901-678-2365. *Application contact:* Dr. Sally Blake, Director of Graduate Studies, 901-678-4861.
Website: http://www.memphis.edu/icl/.

University of Michigan–Dearborn, College of Education, Health, and Human Services, Doctoral Program in Education, Dearborn, MI 48126. Offers curriculum and practice (Ed D); educational leadership (Ed D); metropolitan education (Ed D). Part-time and evening/weekend programs available. *Faculty:* 7 full-time (5 women), 2 part-time/adjunct (0 women). *Students:* 4 full-time (all women), 35 part-time (27 women); includes 15 minority (11 Black or African American, non-Hispanic/Latino; 1 Asian, non-Hispanic/Latino; 3 Hispanic/Latino). Average age 40. 26 applicants, 42% accepted, 7 enrolled. *Degree requirements:* For doctorate, comprehensive exam, thesis/dissertation. *Entrance requirements:* For doctorate, GRE (taken within the last 5 years), master's degree with minimum GPA of 3.3, 3 letters of recommendation (1 from faculty), 3 years' professional and/or teaching experience. Additional exam requirements/recommendations for international students: Required—TOEFL (minimum score 560 paper-based; 84 iBT). *Application deadline:* For fall admission, 3/1 for domestic and international students. Application fee: $60. Electronic applications accepted. *Expenses:* Tuition, state resident: full-time $11,838; part-time $686 per credit hour. Tuition, nonresident: full-time $20,926; part-time $1206 per credit hour. *Required fees:* $760; $286 per semester. Tuition and fees vary according to course load and program. *Financial support:* Scholarships/grants available. Financial award application deadline: 2/1; financial award applicants required to submit FAFSA. *Faculty research:* Educational leadership, metropolitan education, curriculum and practice, educational psychology, special education, assessment. *Unit head:* Dr. Bonnie M. Beyer, Coordinator, 313-593-5583, E-mail: beyer@umd.umich.edu. *Application contact:* Elizabeth Morden, Program Assistant, 313-583-6333, Fax: 313-593-4748, E-mail: emorden@umich.edu.
Website: http://cehhs.umd.umich.edu/cehhs_edd/.

University of Michigan–Flint, School of Education and Human Services, Flint, MI 48502-1950. Offers early childhood education (MA); education (MA, Ed D), including education (MA), educational leadership (Ed D), elementary education with teaching certification (MA), literacy (K-12) (MA), technology in education (MA); education specialist (Ed S), including curriculum and instruction, education leadership; secondary education (MA); special education (MA). Part-time programs available. *Faculty:* 9 full-time (6 women), 12 part-time/adjunct (7 women). *Students:* 31 full-time (20 women), 206 part-time (153 women); includes 35 minority (31 Black or African American, non-Hispanic/Latino; 1 American Indian or Alaska Native, non-Hispanic/Latino; 1 Asian, non-Hispanic/Latino; 2 Hispanic/Latino), 1 international. Average age 36. 135 applicants, 80% accepted, 91 enrolled. In 2013, 99 master's awarded. *Entrance requirements:* For master's, BS with minimum GPA of 3.0. Additional exam requirements/recommendations for international students: Required—TOEFL (minimum score 560 paper-based; 84 iBT), IELTS (minimum score 6.5). *Application deadline:* For fall admission, 8/1 priority date for domestic students, 5/1 priority date for international students; for winter admission, 11/15 priority date for domestic students, 9/1 priority date for international students; for spring admission, 3/15 priority date for domestic students, 1/1 priority date for international students. Application fee: $55. Electronic applications accepted. *Expenses:* Contact institution. *Financial support:* Federal Work-Study, scholarships/grants, and unspecified assistantships available. Support available to part-time students. Financial award application deadline: 3/1; financial award applicants required to submit FAFSA. *Unit head:* Dr. Bob Barnett, Interim Dean, 810-766-6878, Fax: 810-766-6891, E-mail: rbarnett@umflint.edu. *Application contact:* Bradley T. Maki, Director of Graduate Admissions, 810-762-3171, Fax: 810-766-6789, E-mail: bmaki@umflint.edu.
Website: http://www.umflint.edu/sehs/.

University of Minnesota, Twin Cities Campus, Graduate School, College of Education and Human Development, Department of Curriculum and Instruction, Minneapolis, MN 55455-0213. Offers art education (M Ed, MA, PhD); children's literature (M Ed, MA, PhD); curriculum and instruction (MA, PhD); early childhood education (M Ed, PhD); elementary education (M Ed, MA, PhD); English education (MA, PhD); environmental education (M Ed); family education (M Ed, MA, Ed D, PhD); instructional systems and technology (M Ed, MA, PhD); language arts (MA, PhD); language immersion education (Certificate); literacy education (MA); mathematics education (MA, PhD); reading education (MA, PhD); science education (MA, PhD); second languages and cultures education (MA, PhD); social studies education (MA, PhD); teaching (M Ed), including Chinese, earth science, elementary special education, English, English as a second language, French, German, Hebrew, Japanese, life sciences, mathematics, middle school science, science, second languages and cultures, social studies, Spanish; technology enhanced learning (Certificate); writing education (M Ed, MA, PhD). *Faculty:* 29 full-time (16 women). *Students:* 425 full-time (301 women), 220 part-time (153 women); includes 85 minority (21 Black or African American, non-Hispanic/Latino; 6 American Indian or Alaska Native, non-Hispanic/Latino; 42 Asian, non-Hispanic/Latino; 16 Hispanic/Latino), 50 international. Average age 32. 551 applicants, 68% accepted, 340 enrolled. In 2013, 618 master's, 33 doctorates, 6 other advanced degrees awarded. Application fee: $75 ($95 for international students). *Financial support:* In 2013–14, 25 fellowships (averaging $28,500 per year), 23 research assistantships with full tuition reimbursements (averaging $8,082 per year), 81 teaching assistantships with full tuition reimbursements (averaging $9,974 per year) were awarded. *Faculty research:* Teaching and learning; quality of education; influence of cultural, linguistic, social, political, technological and economic factors on teaching, learning and educational research; relationship between educational practice and a democratic and just society. *Total annual research expenditures:* $272,048. *Unit head:* Dr. Nina Asher, Chair, 612-624-4772, Fax: 612-624-1357, E-mail: nasher@umn.edu. *Application contact:* Dr. Jennifer Engler, Assistant Dean, 612-626-2887, Fax: 612-626-7496, E-mail: engle009@umn.edu.
Website: http://www.cehd.umn.edu/ci.

University of Mississippi, Graduate School, School of Education, Department of Teacher Education, Oxford, MS 38677. Offers curriculum and instruction (MA); elementary education (M Ed, Ed D, Ed S); literacy education (M Ed); secondary education (M Ed, PhD, Ed S); special education (M Ed, PhD, Ed S). *Accreditation:* NCATE. *Faculty:* 42 full-time (29 women), 25 part-time/adjunct (22 women). *Students:* 70 full-time (59 women), 194 part-time (156 women); includes 67 minority (60 Black or African American, non-Hispanic/Latino; 1 Asian, non-Hispanic/Latino; 4 Hispanic/Latino; 2 Two or more races, non-Hispanic/Latino), 1 international. In 2013, 122 master's, 1 doctorate awarded. *Degree requirements:* For master's, thesis (for some programs); for doctorate, one foreign language, thesis/dissertation. *Entrance requirements:* For master's, GRE General Test, minimum GPA of 3.0; for doctorate, GRE General Test. Additional exam requirements/recommendations for international students: Required—TOEFL. *Application deadline:* For fall admission, 7/1 for domestic students; for spring admission, 10/1 for domestic students. Applications are processed on a rolling basis. Application fee: $40. *Financial support:* Scholarships/grants available. Financial award application deadline: 3/1; financial award applicants required to submit FAFSA. *Unit head:* Dr. Susan McClelland, Interim Chair, 662-915-7350. *Application contact:* Dr. Christy M. Wyandt, Associate Dean, 662-915-7474, Fax: 662-915-7577, E-mail: cwyandt@olemiss.edu.
Website: http://education.olemiss.edu/dco/teacher_education.html.

University of Missouri, Graduate School, College of Education, Department of Educational, School, and Counseling Psychology, Columbia, MO 65211. Offers counseling psychology (M Ed, MA, PhD, Ed S); educational psychology (M Ed, MA, PhD, Ed S); learning and instruction (M Ed); school psychology (M Ed, MA, PhD, Ed S). *Accreditation:* APA (one or more programs are accredited). Part-time programs available. *Faculty:* 25 full-time (13 women), 4 part-time/adjunct (2 women). *Students:* 191 full-time (125 women), 143 part-time (80 women); includes 72 minority (38 Black or African American, non-Hispanic/Latino; 5 Asian, non-Hispanic/Latino; 21 Hispanic/Latino; 8 Two or more races, non-Hispanic/Latino), 35 international. Average age 29. 354 applicants, 38% accepted, 116 enrolled. In 2013, 59 master's, 16 doctorates, 13 other advanced degrees awarded. *Degree requirements:* For doctorate, thesis/dissertation. *Entrance requirements:* For master's, doctorate, and Ed S, GRE General Test, minimum GPA of 3.0. Additional exam requirements/recommendations for international students: Required—TOEFL (minimum score 580 paper-based; 92 iBT). *Application deadline:* For fall admission, 12/1 priority date for domestic and international students. Applications are processed on a rolling basis. Application fee: $55 ($75 for international students). Electronic applications accepted. *Financial support:* Fellowships, research assistantships, teaching assistantships, institutionally sponsored loans, traineeships, health care benefits, and unspecified assistantships available. Support available to part-time students. *Faculty research:* Out-of-school learning, social cognitive career theory, black psychology and the intersectionality of social identities, test session behavior. *Unit head:* Dr. Matthew Martens, Division Executive Director, 573-882-9434, E-mail: martensmp@missouri.edu. *Application contact:* Latoya Luther, Senior Secretary, 573-882-7732, E-mail: lutherl@missouri.edu.
Website: http://education.missouri.edu/ESCP/.

University of Missouri, Graduate School, College of Education, Department of Learning, Teaching and Curriculum, Columbia, MO 65211. Offers agricultural education (M Ed, PhD, Ed S); art education (M Ed, PhD, Ed S); business and office education (M Ed, PhD, Ed S); early childhood education (M Ed, PhD, Ed S); elementary education (M Ed, PhD, Ed S); English education (M Ed, PhD, Ed S); foreign language education (M Ed, PhD, Ed S); health education and promotion (M Ed, PhD); learning and instruction (M Ed); marketing education (M Ed, PhD, Ed S); mathematics education (M Ed, PhD, Ed S); music education (M Ed, PhD, Ed S); reading education (M Ed, PhD, Ed S); science education (M Ed, PhD, Ed S); social studies education (M Ed, PhD, Ed S); vocational education (M Ed, PhD, Ed S). Part-time programs available. *Faculty:* 26 full-time (16 women), 3 part-time/adjunct (2 women). *Students:* 186 full-time (143 women), 197 part-time (172 women); includes 19 minority (4 Black or African American, non-Hispanic/Latino; 4 Asian, non-Hispanic/Latino; 6 Hispanic/Latino; 5 Two or more races, non-Hispanic/Latino), 25 international. Average age 31. 288 applicants, 65% accepted, 160 enrolled. In 2013, 202 master's, 18 doctorates, 7 other advanced degrees awarded. Terminal master's awarded for partial completion of doctoral program. *Degree requirements:* For doctorate, thesis/dissertation. *Entrance requirements:* For master's and Ed S, GRE General Test or MAT, minimum GPA of 3.0; for doctorate, GRE General Test, minimum GPA of 3.0. Additional exam requirements/recommendations for international students: Required—TOEFL (minimum score 600 paper-based; 100 iBT). *Application deadline:* For fall admission, 12/1 priority date for domestic and international students. Applications are processed on a rolling basis. Application fee: $55 ($75 for international students). Electronic applications accepted. *Financial support:* Fellowships, research assistantships, teaching assistantships, institutionally sponsored loans, traineeships, health care benefits, and unspecified assistantships available. Support available to part-time students. *Faculty research:* Curriculum development and research, teacher education, art education, business and marketing, early childhood education, English education, literacy/reading education, mathematics education, music education, science education, social studies education. *Unit head:* Dr. James Tarr,

Associate Division Director, 573-882-4034, E-mail: tarrj@missouri.edu. *Application contact:* Fran Colley, Academic Advisor, 573-882-6462, E-mail: colleyf@missouri.edu.
Website: http://education.missouri.edu/LTC/.

University of Missouri, Graduate School, College of Education, Department of Special Education, Columbia, MO 65211. Offers administration and supervision of special education (PhD); behavior disorders (M Ed, PhD); curriculum development of exceptional students (M Ed, PhD); early childhood special education (M Ed, PhD); general special education (M Ed, MA, PhD); learning and instruction (M Ed); learning disabilities (M Ed, PhD); mental retardation (M Ed, PhD). Part-time and evening/weekend programs available. Postbaccalaureate distance learning degree programs offered (no on-campus study). *Faculty:* 11 full-time (8 women), 1 (woman) part-time/adjunct. *Students:* 21 full-time (19 women), 43 part-time (37 women); includes 4 minority (2 Black or African American, non-Hispanic/Latino; 1 Hispanic/Latino; 1 Two or more races, non-Hispanic/Latino), 2 international. Average age 32. 42 applicants, 64% accepted, 23 enrolled. In 2013, 28 master's, 6 doctorates awarded. *Degree requirements:* For master's, comprehensive exam, thesis or alternative; for doctorate, comprehensive exam, thesis/dissertation. *Entrance requirements:* For master's and doctorate, GRE General Test, letters of recommendation. Additional exam requirements/recommendations for international students: Required—TOEFL (minimum score 500 paper-based; 61 iBT). *Application deadline:* For fall admission, 1/15 priority date for domestic and international students; for winter admission, 11/1 priority date for domestic and international students; for spring admission, 4/1 priority date for domestic and international students. Application fee: $55 ($75 for international students). Electronic applications accepted. *Financial support:* Fellowships with full and partial tuition reimbursements, research assistantships with full and partial tuition reimbursements, teaching assistantships with full and partial tuition reimbursements, career-related internships or fieldwork, scholarships/grants, health care benefits, and unspecified assistantships available. *Faculty research:* Positive behavior support, applied behavior analysis, attention deficit disorder, pre-linguistic development, school discipline. *Total annual research expenditures:* $1.4 million. *Unit head:* Dr. Mike Pullis, Department Chair, 573-882-8192, E-mail: pullism@missouri.edu. *Application contact:* Recruitment Coordinator, 573-884-3742, E-mail: mucoesped@missouri.edu.
Website: http://education.missouri.edu/SPED/.

University of Missouri–Kansas City, School of Education, Kansas City, MO 64110-2499. Offers administration (Ed D); counseling and guidance (MA, Ed S), including mental health counseling (Ed S), school counseling (Ed S); counseling psychology (PhD); curriculum and instruction (MA, Ed S), including language and literacy (Ed S); education (PhD), including higher education administration, PK-12 education administration; educational administration (MA, Ed S), including advanced principal (Ed S), beginning principal (Ed S), district-level administration (Ed S); reading education (MA, Ed S); special education (MA). PhD in education offered through the School of Graduate Studies. *Accreditation:* NCATE. Part-time and evening/weekend programs available. *Faculty:* 44 full-time (34 women), 60 part-time/adjunct (45 women). *Students:* 206 full-time (145 women), 394 part-time (291 women); includes 154 minority (99 Black or African American, non-Hispanic/Latino; 13 Asian, non-Hispanic/Latino; 30 Hispanic/Latino; 1 Native Hawaiian or other Pacific Islander, non-Hispanic/Latino; 11 Two or more races, non-Hispanic/Latino), 16 international. Average age 32. 401 applicants, 48% accepted, 188 enrolled. In 2013, 156 master's, 9 doctorates, 24 other advanced degrees awarded. *Degree requirements:* For doctorate, thesis/dissertation, internship, practicum. *Entrance requirements:* For master's, GRE, minimum GPA of 2.75, 2 letters of reference, written statement of purpose; for doctorate, GRE, minimum GPA of 3.0; for Ed S, minimum GPA of 3.0. Additional exam requirements/recommendations for international students: Required—TOEFL (minimum score 550 paper-based; 80 iBT). *Application deadline:* For fall admission, 4/1 priority date for domestic and international students; for spring admission, 11/1 priority date for domestic and international students. Applications are processed on a rolling basis. Application fee: $45 ($50 for international students). *Expenses:* Tuition, state resident: full-time $6073; part-time $337.40 per credit hour. Tuition, nonresident: full-time $15,680; part-time $871.10 per credit hour. *Required fees:* $97.59 per credit hour. Full-time tuition and fees vary according to program. *Financial support:* In 2013–14, 12 research assistantships with partial tuition reimbursements (averaging $11,140 per year) were awarded; career-related internships or fieldwork, Federal Work-Study, institutionally sponsored loans, and tuition waivers (full and partial) also available. Support available to part-time students. Financial award application deadline: 3/1; financial award applicants required to submit FAFSA. *Faculty research:* Urban education, inquiry-based field study, theories of counseling and psychotherapy, school literacy, educational technology. *Unit head:* Dr. Wanda Blanchett, Dean, 816-235-2234, Fax: 816-235-5270, E-mail: education@umkc.edu. *Application contact:* Erica Hernandez-Scott, Student Recruiter, 816-235-1295, Fax: 816-235-5270, E-mail: hernandeze@umkc.edu.
Website: http://education.umkc.edu.

University of Missouri–St. Louis, College of Education, Division of Teaching and Learning, St. Louis, MO 63121. Offers autism studies (Certificate); elementary education (M Ed), including early childhood, general, reading; secondary education (M Ed), including curriculum and instruction, general, middle level education, reading, teaching English to speakers of other languages (TESOL); secondary school teaching (Certificate); special education (M Ed), including autism and developmental disabilities, cross-categorical disabilities, early childhood; teaching English to speakers of other languages (Certificate). Part-time and evening/weekend programs available. *Faculty:* 20 full-time (11 women), 1 (woman) part-time/adjunct. *Students:* 42 full-time (33 women), 578 part-time (442 women); includes 152 minority (101 Black or African American, non-Hispanic/Latino; 1 American Indian or Alaska Native, non-Hispanic/Latino; 20 Asian, non-Hispanic/Latino; 23 Hispanic/Latino; 7 Two or more races, non-Hispanic/Latino), 19 international. Average age 29. 245 applicants, 97% accepted, 166 enrolled. In 2013, 219 master's, 14 Certificates awarded. *Degree requirements:* For master's, comprehensive exam. *Entrance requirements:* Additional exam requirements/recommendations for international students: Recommended—TOEFL (minimum score 550 paper-based; 79 iBT), IELTS (minimum score 6.5). *Application deadline:* For fall admission, 7/1 priority date for domestic and international students; for spring admission, 12/1 priority date for domestic and international students. Application fee: $50 ($40 for international students). Electronic applications accepted. *Expenses:* Tuition, state resident: full-time $7364; part-time $409.10 per credit hour. Tuition, nonresident: full-time $19,162; part-time $1008.50 per credit hour. *Financial support:* Application deadline: 4/1; applicants required to submit FAFSA. *Unit head:* Dr. Patricia Kopetz, Chair, 314-516-5791. *Application contact:* 314-516-5458, Fax: 314-516-6996, E-mail: gadadm@umsl.edu.
Website: http://coe.umsl.edu/web/divisions/teach-learn/index.html.

The University of Montana, Graduate School, Phyllis J. Washington College of Education and Human Sciences, Department of Curriculum and Instruction, Missoula, MT 59812-0002. Offers M Ed, Ed D. Part-time programs available. *Degree requirements:* For doctorate, thesis/dissertation. *Entrance requirements:* For master's, GRE General Test. Additional exam requirements/recommendations for international students: Required—TOEFL.

University of Nebraska at Kearney, Graduate Programs, College of Education, Department of Teacher Education, Kearney, NE 68849-0001. Offers curriculum and instruction (MA Ed), including early childhood education, elementary education, English as a second language, instructional effectiveness, reading/special education, secondary education; instructional technology (MS Ed), including information technology, instructional technology, school librarian; reading PK-12 (MA Ed); special education (MA Ed), including advanced practitioner, gifted, mild/moderate. Part-time and evening/weekend programs available. *Degree requirements:* For master's, comprehensive exam, thesis optional. *Entrance requirements:* For master's, portfolio or GRE. Additional exam requirements/recommendations for international students: Required—TOEFL (minimum score 550 paper-based). Electronic applications accepted.

University of Nebraska–Lincoln, Graduate College, College of Education and Human Sciences, Department of Teaching, Learning and Teacher Education, Lincoln, NE 68588. Offers adult and continuing education (MA); educational studies (Ed D, PhD), including special education (Ed D); teaching, learning and teacher education (M Ed, MA, MST, Ed D, PhD); vocational and adult education (M Ed, MA). *Accreditation:* NCATE. *Degree requirements:* For master's, thesis optional. *Entrance requirements:* Additional exam requirements/recommendations for international students: Required—TOEFL (minimum score 550 paper-based). Electronic applications accepted. *Faculty research:* Teacher education, instructional leadership, literacy education, technology, improvement of school curriculum.

University of Nebraska–Lincoln, Graduate College, College of Education and Human Sciences, Interdepartmental Area of Administration, Curriculum and Instruction, Lincoln, NE 68588. Offers Ed D, PhD, JD/PhD. *Accreditation:* NCATE. Postbaccalaureate distance learning degree programs offered. *Degree requirements:* For doctorate, comprehensive exam, thesis/dissertation. *Entrance requirements:* For doctorate, GRE, curriculum vitae. Additional exam requirements/recommendations for international students: Required—TOEFL (minimum score 550 paper-based). Electronic applications accepted.

University of Nevada, Las Vegas, Graduate College, College of Education, Department of Teaching and Learning, Las Vegas, NV 89154-3005. Offers curriculum and instruction (M Ed, MS, Ed D, PhD, Ed S), including teacher education (PhD). Part-time and evening/weekend programs available. *Faculty:* 24 full-time (10 women), 7 part-time/adjunct (6 women). *Students:* 246 full-time (162 women), 194 part-time (128 women); includes 131 minority (36 Black or African American, non-Hispanic/Latino; 1 American Indian or Alaska Native, non-Hispanic/Latino; 32 Asian, non-Hispanic/Latino; 27 Hispanic/Latino; 1 Native Hawaiian or other Pacific Islander, non-Hispanic/Latino; 34 Two or more races, non-Hispanic/Latino), 16 international. Average age 34. 185 applicants, 95% accepted, 160 enrolled. In 2013, 156 master's, 5 doctorates awarded. *Degree requirements:* For master's, comprehensive exam (for some programs), thesis (for some programs); for doctorate, comprehensive exam, thesis/dissertation, defense of dissertation, article for publication (curriculum and instruction); for Ed S, comprehensive exam, oral presentation of special project or professional paper. *Entrance requirements:* For doctorate and Ed S, GRE General Test. Additional exam requirements/recommendations for international students: Required—TOEFL (minimum score 550 paper-based; 80 iBT), IELTS (minimum score 7). *Application deadline:* For fall admission, 6/1 for domestic students, 5/1 for international students; for spring admission, 11/1 for domestic students, 10/1 for international students. Application fee: $60 ($95 for international students). Electronic applications accepted. *Expenses:* Tuition, state resident: full-time $4752; part-time $264 per credit. Tuition, nonresident: full-time $18,662; part-time $554.50 per credit. *International tuition:* $18,952 full-time. *Required fees:* $532; $12 per credit. $266 per semester. One-time fee: $35. Tuition and fees vary according to course load and program. *Financial support:* In 2013–14, 35 students received support, including 18 research assistantships with partial tuition reimbursements available (averaging $9,847 per year), 17 teaching assistantships with partial tuition reimbursements available (averaging $13,471 per year); institutionally sponsored loans, scholarships/grants, health care benefits, and unspecified assistantships also available. Financial award application deadline: 3/1. *Faculty research:* Content area and critical literacy, education in content areas, teacher education, STEM education, technology education. *Total annual research expenditures:* $669,806. *Unit head:* Dr. Randall Boone, Chair/Professor, 702-895-3331, Fax: 702-895-4898, E-mail: randall.boone@unlv.edu. *Application contact:* Graduate College Admissions Evaluator, 702-895-3320, Fax: 702-895-4180, E-mail: gradcollege@unlv.edu.
Website: http://tl.unlv.edu/.

University of Nevada, Reno, Graduate School, College of Education, Department of Curriculum, Teaching and Learning, Program in Curriculum and Instruction, Reno, NV 89557. Offers PhD. *Degree requirements:* For doctorate, thesis/dissertation. *Entrance requirements:* For doctorate, GRE General Test, minimum GPA of 3.0. Additional exam requirements/recommendations for international students: Required—TOEFL (minimum score 500 paper-based; 61 iBT), IELTS (minimum score 6). Electronic applications accepted. *Faculty research:* Education, development, pedagogy.

University of Nevada, Reno, Graduate School, College of Education, Department of Curriculum, Teaching and Learning, Program in Curriculum, Teaching and Learning, Reno, NV 89557. Offers Ed D, PhD. *Degree requirements:* For doctorate, comprehensive exam, thesis/dissertation. *Entrance requirements:* For doctorate, GRE General Test, minimum GPA of 3.0. Additional exam requirements/recommendations for international students: Required—TOEFL (minimum score 500 paper-based; 61 iBT), IELTS (minimum score 6). Electronic applications accepted. *Faculty research:* Education, trends, pedagogy.

University of New England, College of Arts and Sciences, Program in Education, Biddeford, ME 04005-9526. Offers advanced educational leadership (CAGS); career and technical education (MS Ed, CAGS); curriculum and instruction strategies (CAGS); curriculum and instruction strategy (MS Ed); educational leadership (MS Ed, CAGS); inclusion education (MS Ed); leadership, ethics and change (CAGS); literacy K-12 (MS Ed, CAGS); teaching methodologies (MS Ed). Part-time and evening/weekend programs available. Postbaccalaureate distance learning degree programs offered (no on-campus study). *Faculty:* 5 full-time (4 women), 17 part-time/adjunct (9 women). *Students:* 295 full-time (228 women), 233 part-time (175 women); includes 26 minority (19 Black or African American, non-Hispanic/Latino; 2 American Indian or Alaska Native, non-Hispanic/Latino; 2 Asian, non-Hispanic/Latino; 2 Hispanic/Latino; 1 Two or more races, non-Hispanic/Latino). Average age 37. 289 applicants, 84% accepted, 189 enrolled. In 2013, 257 master's, 106 CAGSs awarded. *Degree requirements:* For master's, collaborative action research project, integrative seminar portfolio. *Entrance requirements:* For master's, teaching certificate, 2 years of teaching experience. *Application deadline:* For fall admission, 9/15 for domestic students; for spring admission, 1/15 for domestic students. Applications are processed on a rolling basis. Application fee: $40. Electronic applications accepted. *Financial support:* Application deadline: 5/1; applicants required to submit FAFSA. *Faculty research:* Distance learning, effective teaching, transition planning, adult learning. *Unit head:* Paulette St. Ours, Associate Dean, College of Arts and Sciences, 207-602-2400, E-mail: pstours@une.edu. *Application contact:* Dr. Cynthia Forrest, Vice President for Student Affairs, 207-221-4225, Fax: 207-523-1925, E-mail: gradadmissions@une.edu.
Website: http://www.une.edu/cas/education/msonline.cfm.

University of New Mexico, Graduate School, College of Education, Department of Teacher Education, Educational Leadership and Policy, Program in Curriculum and Instruction, Albuquerque, NM 87131-2039. Offers Ed S. *Students:* 1 (woman) full-time; minority (Hispanic/Latino). Average age 29. 2 applicants. *Unit head:* Dr. Rosalita Mitchell, Department Chair, 505-277-9611, Fax: 505-277-0455, E-mail: ted@unm.edu. *Application contact:* Sarah Valles, Department Administrator, 505-277-0504, Fax: 505-277-0455, E-mail: ted@unm.edu.

University of New Orleans, Graduate School, College of Education and Human Development, Department of Curriculum and Instruction, New Orleans, LA 70148. Offers M Ed, PhD. *Accreditation:* NCATE. Evening/weekend programs available. *Degree requirements:* For doctorate, variable foreign language requirement, thesis/dissertation. *Entrance requirements:* For master's, GRE General Test; for doctorate, GRE General Test, GRE Subject Test. Additional exam requirements/recommendations for international students: Required—TOEFL (minimum score 550 paper-based; 79 iBT). Electronic applications accepted.

The University of North Carolina at Chapel Hill, Graduate School, School of Education, Program in Education, Chapel Hill, NC 27599. Offers culture, curriculum and change (MA, PhD); early childhood, intervention and literacy (MA, PhD); educational psychology, measurement and evaluation (MA, PhD). *Accreditation:* NCATE. *Degree requirements:* For master's, thesis; for doctorate, comprehensive exam, thesis/dissertation. *Entrance requirements:* For master's, GRE General Test, minimum GPA of 3.0 during last 2 years of undergraduates course work; for doctorate, GRE General Test, minimum GPA of 3.0 during last 2 years of undergraduate course work. Additional exam requirements/recommendations for international students: Required—TOEFL (minimum score 550 paper-based). Electronic applications accepted.

The University of North Carolina at Charlotte, The Graduate School, College of Education, Department of Educational Leadership, Charlotte, NC 28223-0001. Offers curriculum and supervision (M Ed); educational leadership (Ed D); instructional systems technology (M Ed); school administration (MSA, Post-Master's Certificate). Part-time and evening/weekend programs available. *Faculty:* 24 full-time (13 women), 7 part-time/adjunct (5 women). *Students:* 28 full-time (20 women), 225 part-time (141 women); includes 65 minority (55 Black or African American, non-Hispanic/Latino; 3 Asian, non-Hispanic/Latino; 4 Hispanic/Latino; 3 Two or more races, non-Hispanic/Latino), 1 international. Average age 37. 71 applicants, 92% accepted, 59 enrolled. In 2013, 48 master's, 6 doctorates, 16 other advanced degrees awarded. *Degree requirements:* For master's, thesis. *Entrance requirements:* For master's and doctorate, GRE or MAT. Additional exam requirements/recommendations for international students: Required—TOEFL (minimum score 550 paper-based; 83 iBT). *Application deadline:* For fall admission, 5/1 priority date for domestic students, 5/1 for international students; for spring admission, 10/1 priority date for domestic students, 10/1 for international students. Applications are processed on a rolling basis. Application fee: $75. Electronic applications accepted. *Expenses:* Tuition, state resident: full-time $3522. Tuition, nonresident: full-time $16,051. *Required fees:* $2585. Tuition and fees vary according to course load and program. *Financial support:* In 2013–14, 7 students received support, including 6 research assistantships (averaging $8,163 per year); career-related internships or fieldwork, institutionally sponsored loans, scholarships/grants, unspecified assistantships, and administrative assistantships also available. Support available to part-time students. Financial award application deadline: 4/1; financial award applicants required to submit FAFSA. *Faculty research:* Educational leadership theory and practice, instructional systems technology, educational research methodology, curriculum and supervision in the schools, school law and finance. *Total annual research expenditures:* $1.2 million. *Unit head:* Dr. Jim Bird, Interim Chair, 704-687-1821, Fax: 704-687-3493, E-mail: jjbird@uncc.edu. *Application contact:* Kathy B. Giddings, Director of Graduate Admissions, 704-687-5503, Fax: 704-687-1668, E-mail: gradadm@uncc.edu.
Website: http://education.uncc.edu/eart.

The University of North Carolina at Charlotte, The Graduate School, College of Education, Department of Middle, Secondary and K-12 Education, Charlotte, NC 28223-0001. Offers curriculum and instruction (PhD); English education (MA); mathematics education (MA); middle grades education (MAT); secondary education (MAT); teaching English as a second language (M Ed). *Faculty:* 19 full-time (11 women), 7 part-time/adjunct (3 women). *Students:* 16 full-time (14 women), 30 part-time (24 women); includes 8 minority (6 Black or African American, non-Hispanic/Latino; 1 Hispanic/Latino; 1 Two or more races, non-Hispanic/Latino). Average age 32. 23 applicants, 87% accepted, 19 enrolled. In 2013, 21 master's awarded. *Degree requirements:* For master's, thesis. *Entrance requirements:* For master's, GRE or MAT. Additional exam requirements/recommendations for international students: Required—TOEFL (minimum score 557 paper-based; 83 iBT). *Application deadline:* For fall admission, 5/1 priority date for domestic students, 5/1 for international students; for spring admission, 10/1 priority date for domestic students, 10/1 for international students. Applications are processed on a rolling basis. Application fee: $75. Electronic applications accepted. *Expenses:* Tuition, state resident: full-time $3522. Tuition, nonresident: full-time $16,051. *Required fees:* $2585. Tuition and fees vary according to course load and program. *Financial support:* In 2013–14, 6 students received support, including 1 fellowship (averaging $50,000 per year), 3 research assistantships (averaging $5,400 per year), 2 teaching assistantships (averaging $9,500 per year); career-related internships or fieldwork, institutionally sponsored loans, scholarships/grants, and unspecified assistantships also available. Support available to part-time students. Financial award application deadline: 4/1; financial award applicants required to submit FAFSA. *Total annual research expenditures:* $98,589. *Unit head:* Dr. Warren DiBiase, Chair, 704-687-8881, Fax: 704-687-6430, E-mail: wjdibias@uncc.edu. *Application contact:* Kathy B. Giddings, Director of Graduate Admissions, 704-687-5503, Fax: 704-687-1668, E-mail: gradadm@uncc.edu.
Website: http://education.uncc.edu/mdsk.

The University of North Carolina at Greensboro, Graduate School, School of Education, Department of Curriculum and Instruction, Greensboro, NC 27412-5001. Offers college teaching and adult learning (Certificate); curriculum and instruction (M Ed), including chemistry education, elementary education, English as a second language, French education, instructional technology, mathematics education, middle grades education, reading education, science education, social studies education, Spanish education; curriculum and teaching (PhD), including higher education, teacher education and development; English as a second language (Certificate); higher education (M Ed); supervision (M Ed). *Accreditation:* NCATE. Part-time programs available. *Degree requirements:* For doctorate, thesis/dissertation. *Entrance requirements:* For master's and doctorate, GRE General Test. Additional exam requirements/recommendations for international students: Required—TOEFL. Electronic applications accepted. *Faculty research:* Community college literacy program, middle school mathematics/computer mathematics.

The University of North Carolina at Greensboro, Graduate School, School of Education, Department of Educational Leadership and Cultural Foundations, Greensboro, NC 27412-5001. Offers curriculum and teaching (PhD), including cultural studies; educational leadership (Ed D, Ed S); school administration (MSA). *Accreditation:* NCATE. *Degree requirements:* For doctorate, thesis/dissertation.

Entrance requirements: For master's, doctorate, and Ed S, GRE General Test. Additional exam requirements/recommendations for international students: Required—TOEFL. Electronic applications accepted.

University of Northern Iowa, Graduate College, College of Education, Department of Curriculum and Instruction, Ed D Program in Curriculum and Instruction, Cedar Falls, IA 50614. Offers Ed D. Part-time and evening/weekend programs available. *Students:* 4 full-time (3 women), 16 part-time (11 women); includes 1 minority (Black or African American, non-Hispanic/Latino), 3 international. 5 applicants, 40% accepted, 1 enrolled. In 2013, 7 doctorates awarded. *Degree requirements:* For doctorate, thesis/dissertation. *Entrance requirements:* For doctorate, GRE, minimum GPA of 3.0, master's degree. Additional exam requirements/recommendations for international students: Required—TOEFL (minimum score 500 paper-based; 61 iBT). *Application deadline:* For fall admission, 8/1 priority date for domestic students. Applications are processed on a rolling basis. Application fee: $50 ($70 for international students). *Financial support:* Career-related internships or fieldwork, Federal Work-Study, and tuition waivers (full and partial) available. Support available to part-time students. Financial award application deadline: 2/1. *Unit head:* Dr. Linda Fitzgerald, Coordinator, 319-273-2214, Fax: 319-273-5886, E-mail: linda.fitzgerald@uni.edu. *Application contact:* Laurie S. Russell, Record Analyst, 319-273-2623, Fax: 319-273-2885, E-mail: laurie.russell@uni.edu.
Website: http://www.uni.edu/coe/graduate/doctorates/edd-curriculum-and-instruction.

University of North Texas, Robert B. Toulouse School of Graduate Studies, Denton, TN 76203-5017. Offers accounting (MS, PhD); applied anthropology (MA, MS); applied behavior analysis (Certificate); applied technology and performance improvement (M Ed, MS, PhD); art education (MA, PhD); art history (MA); art museum education (Certificate); arts leadership (Certificate); audiology (Au D); behavior analysis (MS); biochemistry and molecular biology (MS, PhD); biology (MA, MS, PhD); business (PhD); business computer information systems (PhD); chemistry (MS, PhD); clinical psychology (PhD); communication studies (MA, MS); computer engineering (MS); computer science (MS); computer science and engineering (PhD); counseling (M Ed, MS, PhD), including clinical mental health counseling (MS), college and university counseling (M Ed, MS), elementary school counseling (M Ed, MS), secondary school counseling (M Ed, MS); counseling psychology (PhD); creative writing (MA); criminal justice (MS); curriculum and instruction (M Ed, PhD), including curriculum studies (PhD), early childhood studies (PhD), language and literacy studies (PhD); decision sciences (MBA); design (MA, MFA), including fashion design (MFA), innovation studies, interior design (MFA); early childhood studies (MS); economics (MS); educational leadership (M Ed, Ed D, PhD); educational psychology (MS), including family studies, gifted and talented (MS, PhD); human development, learning and cognition, research, measurement and evaluation; educational research (PhD), including gifted and talented (MS, PhD), human development and family studies, psychological aspects of sports and exercise, research, measurement and statistics; electrical engineering (MS); emergency management (MPA); engineering systems (MS); English (MA, PhD); environmental science (MS, PhD); experimental psychology (PhD); finance (MBA, MS, PhD); financial management (MPA); French (MA); health psychology and behavioral medicine (PhD); health services management (MBA); higher education (M Ed, Ed D, PhD); history (MA, MS, PhD), including European history (PhD), military history (PhD), United States history (PhD); hospitality management (MS); human resources management (MPA); information science (MS, PhD); information technologies (MBA); information technology and decision sciences (MS); interdisciplinary studies (MA, MS); international sustainable tourism (MS); jazz studies (MM); journalism (MA, MJ, Graduate Certificate), including interactive and virtual digital communication (Graduate Certificate), narrative journalism (Graduate Certificate), public relations (Graduate Certificate); kinesiology (MS); learning technologies (MS, PhD); library science (MS); local government management (MPA); logistics and supply chain management (MBA, PhD); long-term care, senior housing, and aging services (MA, MS); management science (PhD); marketing (MBA, PhD); materials science and engineering (MS, PhD); mathematics (MA, PhD); merchandising (MS); music (MA, MM Ed, PhD), including ethnomusicology (MA), music education (MM Ed, PhD), music theory (MA, PhD), musicology (MA, PhD), performance (MA); nonprofit management (MPA); operations and supply chain management (MBA); performance (MM, DMA); philosophy (MA, PhD); physics (MS, PhD); political science (MA, MS, PhD); public administration and management (PhD), including emergency management, nonprofit management, public financial management, urban management; radio, television and film (MA, MFA); recreation, event and sport management (MS); rehabilitation counseling (MS, Certificate); sociology (MA, MS, PhD); Spanish (MA); special education (M Ed, PhD), including autism intervention (PhD), emotional/behavioral disorders (PhD), mild/moderate disabilities (PhD); speech-language pathology (MA, MS); strategic management (MBA); studio art (MFA); taxation (MS); teaching (M Ed); MBA/MS; MS/MPH; MSES/MBA. Part-time and evening/weekend programs available. Postbaccalaureate distance learning degree programs offered. *Faculty:* 661 full-time (213 women), 240 part-time/adjunct (144 women). *Students:* 3,106 full-time (1,620 women), 3,543 part-time (2,221 women); includes 1,740 minority (533 Black or African American, non-Hispanic/Latino; 15 American Indian or Alaska Native, non-Hispanic/Latino; 286 Asian, non-Hispanic/Latino; 746 Hispanic/Latino; 3 Native Hawaiian or other Pacific Islander, non-Hispanic/Latino; 157 Two or more races, non-Hispanic/Latino), 1,145 international. Average age 32. 6,289 applicants, 43% accepted, 1751 enrolled. In 2013, 1,778 master's, 239 doctorates, 10 other advanced degrees awarded. Terminal master's awarded for partial completion of doctoral program. *Degree requirements:* For master's, variable foreign language requirement, comprehensive exam (for some programs), thesis (for some programs); for doctorate, variable foreign language requirement, comprehensive exam (for some programs), thesis/dissertation; for other advanced degree, variable foreign language requirement, comprehensive exam (for some programs). *Entrance requirements:* For master's and doctorate, GRE, GMAT. Additional exam requirements/recommendations for international students: Required—TOEFL (minimum score 550 paper-based; 79 iBT). *Application deadline:* For fall admission, 7/15 for domestic students, 3/15 for international students; for spring admission, 11/15 for domestic students, 9/15 for international students; for summer admission, 5/1 for domestic students. Applications are processed on a rolling basis. Application fee: $60. Electronic applications accepted. *Financial support:* Fellowships with partial tuition reimbursements, research assistantships with partial tuition reimbursements, teaching assistantships, career-related internships or fieldwork, Federal Work-Study, institutionally sponsored loans, scholarships/grants, health care benefits, and library assistantships available. Support available to part-time students. Financial award applicants required to submit FAFSA. *Unit head:* Mark Wardell, Dean, 940-565-2383, E-mail: mark.wardell@unt.edu. *Application contact:* Toulouse School of Graduate Studies, 940-565-2383, Fax: 940-565-2141, E-mail: gradsch@unt.edu.
Website: http://tsgs.unt.edu/.

University of Oklahoma, Jeannine Rainbolt College of Education, Department of Educational Leadership and Policy Studies, Program in Educational Administration, Curriculum and Supervision, Norman, OK 73019. Offers M Ed, Ed D, PhD. *Accreditation:* NCATE. Part-time and evening/weekend programs available. *Students:* 28 full-time (19 women), 178 part-time (126 women); includes 36 minority (13 Black or African American, non-Hispanic/Latino; 11 American Indian or Alaska Native, non-Hispanic/Latino; 2 Asian, non-Hispanic/Latino; 6 Hispanic/Latino; 4 Two or more races,

non-Hispanic/Latino), 1 international. Average age 36. 95 applicants, 85% accepted, 70 enrolled. In 2013, 28 master's, 8 doctorates awarded. Terminal master's awarded for partial completion of doctoral program. *Degree requirements:* For master's, thesis optional, comprehensive portfolio; for doctorate, variable foreign language requirement, thesis/dissertation, residency. *Entrance requirements:* For master's, bachelor's degree in education; minimum GPA of 3.0 in last 60 undergraduate hours; for doctorate, GRE, professional biography; career statement; 2 writing samples. Additional exam requirements/recommendations for international students: Required—TOEFL (minimum score 79 iBT). *Application deadline:* For fall admission, 4/15 for domestic and international students; for spring admission, 10/15 for domestic and international students. Applications are processed on a rolling basis. Application fee: $50 ($100 for international students). Electronic applications accepted. *Expenses:* Tuition, state resident: full-time $4205; part-time $175.20 per credit hour. Tuition, nonresident: full-time $16,205; part-time $675.20 per credit hour. *Required fees:* $2745; $103.85 per credit hour. $126.50 per semester. *Financial support:* In 2013–14, 89 students received support. Unspecified assistantships available. Financial award application deadline: 6/1; financial award applicants required to submit FAFSA. *Faculty research:* Moral-ethical leadership, Indian education, school-collective trust, school finance, diversity issues. *Unit head:* Dr. David Tan, Chair, 405-325-5986, Fax: 405-325-2403, E-mail: dtan@ou.edu. *Application contact:* Geri Evans, Graduate Programs Representative, 405-325-5978, Fax: 405-325-2403, E-mail: gevans@ou.edu.
Website: http://www.ou.edu/education/elps.

University of Oklahoma, Jeannine Rainbolt College of Education, Department of Instructional Leadership and Academic Curriculum, Norman, OK 73072. Offers communication, culture and pedagogy for Hispanic populations in educational settings (Graduate Certificate); instructional leadership and academic curriculum (M Ed, PhD), including bilingual education (PhD), early childhood education, elementary education, English education, instructional leadership, mathematics education, reading education, science education, science, technology, engineering and mathematics education (M Ed), secondary education, social studies education, teacher education (M Ed), world language education (M Ed). *Accreditation:* NCATE. Part-time and evening/weekend programs available. Postbaccalaureate distance learning degree programs offered (no on-campus study). *Faculty:* 22 full-time (15 women), 1 (woman) part-time/adjunct. *Students:* 64 full-time (49 women), 103 part-time (81 women); includes 33 minority (8 Black or African American, non-Hispanic/Latino; 9 American Indian or Alaska Native, non-Hispanic/Latino; 5 Asian, non-Hispanic/Latino; 4 Hispanic/Latino; 1 Native Hawaiian or other Pacific Islander, non-Hispanic/Latino; 6 Two or more races, non-Hispanic/Latino), 10 international. Average age 34. 50 applicants, 84% accepted, 36 enrolled. In 2013, 26 master's, 11 doctorates awarded. Terminal master's awarded for partial completion of doctoral program. *Degree requirements:* For master's, comprehensive exam (for some programs), thesis (for some programs); for doctorate, comprehensive exam, thesis/dissertation. *Entrance requirements:* For master's, essay; for doctorate, GRE, 3 recommendation letters; autobiography, statement of objectives; essay on chosen major; transcripts; writing sample. Additional exam requirements/recommendations for international students: Required—TOEFL (minimum score 79 iBT). *Application deadline:* For fall admission, 4/30 for domestic and international students; for spring admission, 10/31 for domestic and international students; for summer admission, 3/15 for domestic and international students. Applications are processed on a rolling basis. Application fee: $50 ($100 for international students). Electronic applications accepted. *Expenses:* Tuition, state resident: full-time $4205; part-time $175.20 per credit hour. Tuition, nonresident: full-time $16,205; part-time $675.20 per credit hour. *Required fees:* $2745; $103.85 per credit hour. $126.50 per semester. *Financial support:* In 2013–14, 98 students received support, including 10 research assistantships with partial tuition reimbursements available (averaging $10,671 per year), 7 teaching assistantships with partial tuition reimbursements available (averaging $10,753 per year); Federal Work-Study, institutionally sponsored loans, scholarships/grants, and unspecified assistantships also available. Support available to part-time students. Financial award application deadline: 6/1; financial award applicants required to submit FAFSA. *Total annual research expenditures:* $1 million. *Unit head:* Dr. Stacy Reeder, Chair/Graduate Liaison, 405-325-1498, Fax: 405-325-4061, E-mail: reeder@ou.edu. *Application contact:* Lynn Crussel, Graduate Programs Officer, 405-325-1498, Fax: 405-325-4061, E-mail: lcrussel@ou.edu.
Website: http://education.ou.edu/departments/ilac.

University of Phoenix–Austin Campus, College of Education, Austin, TX 78759. Offers curriculum and instruction (MA Ed).

University of Phoenix–Central Valley Campus, College of Education, Fresno, CA 93720-1562. Offers curriculum and instruction (MA Ed); curriculum and instruction-computer education (MA Ed); elementary teacher education (MA Ed); secondary teacher education (MA Ed).

University of Phoenix–Chattanooga Campus, College of Education, Chattanooga, TN 37421-3707. Offers administration and supervision (MA Ed); curriculum and instruction (MA Ed); elementary teacher education (MA Ed); secondary teacher education (MA Ed).

University of Phoenix–Dallas Campus, College of Education, Dallas, TX 75251. Offers curriculum and instruction (MA Ed).

University of Phoenix–Denver Campus, College of Education, Lone Tree, CO 80124-5453. Offers administration and supervision (MAEd); curriculum instruction (MAEd); elementary teacher education (MAEd); school counseling (MSC); secondary teacher education (MAEd). Evening/weekend programs available. *Degree requirements:* For master's, thesis (for some programs). *Entrance requirements:* For master's, minimum undergraduate GPA of 2.5, 3 years work experience. Additional exam requirements/recommendations for international students: Required—TOEFL (minimum score 550 paper-based; 79 iBT). Electronic applications accepted.

University of Phoenix–Hawaii Campus, College of Education, Honolulu, HI 96813-4317. Offers administration and supervision (MA Ed); curriculum and instruction (MA Ed); elementary education (MA Ed); secondary education (MA Ed); special education (MA Ed); teacher education for elementary licensure (MA Ed). Evening/weekend programs available. *Degree requirements:* For master's, thesis (for some programs). *Entrance requirements:* For master's, minimum undergraduate GPA of 2.5, 3 years of work experience. Additional exam requirements/recommendations for international students: Required—TOEFL (minimum score 550 paper-based; 79 iBT). Electronic applications accepted.

University of Phoenix–Houston Campus, College of Education, Houston, TX 77079-2004. Offers curriculum and instruction (MA Ed).

University of Phoenix–Idaho Campus, College of Education, Meridian, ID 83642-5114. Offers administration and supervision (MA Ed); curriculum and instruction (MA Ed); elementary teacher education (MA Ed); secondary teacher education (MA Ed). Evening/weekend programs available. *Degree requirements:* For master's, thesis (for some programs). *Entrance requirements:* For master's, minimum undergraduate GPA of 2.5, 3 years of work experience. Additional exam requirements/recommendations for international students: Required—TOEFL (minimum score 550 paper-based). Electronic applications accepted.

University of Phoenix–Las Vegas Campus, College of Education, Las Vegas, NV 89135. Offers administration and supervision (MA Ed); curriculum and instruction (MA Ed); school counseling (MSC); teacher education-elementary licensure (MA Ed). Evening/weekend programs available. *Degree requirements:* For master's, thesis (for some programs). *Entrance requirements:* For master's, minimum undergraduate GPA of 2.5, 3 years of work experience. Additional exam requirements/recommendations for international students: Required—TOEFL (minimum score 550 paper-based; 79 iBT). Electronic applications accepted.

University of Phoenix–Louisiana Campus, College of Education, Metairie, LA 70001-2082. Offers curriculum and instruction (MA Ed); early childhood education (MA Ed). Postbaccalaureate distance learning degree programs offered. *Degree requirements:* For master's, thesis. *Entrance requirements:* For master's, minimum undergraduate GPA of 2.5, 3 years work experience. Additional exam requirements/recommendations for international students: Required—TOEFL (minimum score 550 paper-based; 79 iBT).

University of Phoenix–Madison Campus, College of Education, Madison, WI 53718-2416. Offers education (Ed S); educational leadership (Ed D); educational leadership: curriculum and instruction (Ed D); higher education administration (PhD).

University of Phoenix–Memphis Campus, College of Education, Cordova, TN 38018. Offers administration and supervision (MA Ed); curriculum and instruction (MA Ed); elementary teacher education (MA Ed); secondary teacher education (MA Ed).

University of Phoenix–Nashville Campus, College of Education, Nashville, TN 37214-5048. Offers administration and supervision (MA Ed); curriculum and instruction (MA Ed); elementary teacher education (MA Ed); secondary teacher education (MA Ed). Evening/weekend programs available. *Degree requirements:* For master's, thesis (for some programs). *Entrance requirements:* For master's, minimum undergraduate GPA of 2.5, 3 years work experience. Additional exam requirements/recommendations for international students: Required—TOEFL (minimum score 500 paper-based; 79 iBT). Electronic applications accepted.

University of Phoenix–New Mexico Campus, College of Education, Albuquerque, NM 87113-1570. Offers administration and supervision (MAEd); curriculum and instruction (MAEd); elementary teacher education (MAEd); school counseling (MSC); secondary teacher education (MAEd). Evening/weekend programs available. *Degree requirements:* For master's, thesis (for some programs). *Entrance requirements:* For master's, minimum undergraduate GPA of 2.5, 3 years of work experience. Additional exam requirements/recommendations for international students: Required—TOEFL (minimum score 550 paper-based; 79 iBT). Electronic applications accepted.

University of Phoenix–North Florida Campus, College of Education, Jacksonville, FL 32216-0959. Offers administration and supervision (MA Ed); curriculum and instruction (MA Ed), including computer education, mathematics education; early childhood education (MA Ed); elementary teacher education (MA Ed); secondary teacher education (MA Ed). Evening/weekend programs available. *Degree requirements:* For master's, thesis (for some programs). *Entrance requirements:* For master's, 3 years of work experience, minimum undergraduate GPA of 2.5. Additional exam requirements/recommendations for international students: Required—TOEFL (minimum score 550 paper-based; 49 iBT). Electronic applications accepted.

University of Phoenix–Omaha Campus, College of Education, Omaha, NE 68154-5240. Offers administration and supervision (MA Ed); curriculum and instruction (MA Ed), including adult education, computer education, curriculum and instruction, English and language arts education, English as a second language, mathematics education; elementary teacher education (MA Ed); secondary teacher education (MA Ed); special education (MA Ed).

University of Phoenix–Online Campus, College of Education, Phoenix, AZ 85034-7209. Offers administration and supervision (MAEd, Certificate); adult education and training (MAEd); curriculum and instruction (MAEd), including computer education, curriculum and instruction, English as a second language, language arts, mathematics, reading; early childhood education (MAEd); educational studies (MAEd); elementary teacher education (MAEd), including early childhood, elementary teacher education, high school middle level, middle level; principal licensure (Certificate); secondary teacher education (MAEd); special education (MAEd, Certificate); teacher education (MAEd), including middle level generalist; teacher education middle level mathematics (MAEd), including middle level mathematics; teacher education middle level science (MAEd), including middle level science; teacher education secondary mathematics (MAEd); teacher education secondary science (MAEd); teacher leadership (MAEd); teachers of English learners (Certificate); transition to teaching (Certificate), including elementary education, secondary education. *Accreditation:* Teacher Education Accreditation Council. Evening/weekend programs available. Postbaccalaureate distance learning degree programs offered. *Entrance requirements:* Additional exam requirements/recommendations for international students: Required—TOEFL, TOEIC (Test of English as an International Communication), Berlitz Online English Proficiency Exam, PTE, or IELTS. Electronic applications accepted. *Expenses:* Contact institution.

University of Phoenix–Online Campus, School of Advanced Studies, Phoenix, AZ 85034-7209. Offers business administration (DBA); education (Ed S); educational leadership (Ed D), including curriculum and instruction, education technology, educational leadership; health administration (DHA); higher education administration (PhD); industrial/organizational psychology (PhD); nursing (PhD); organizational leadership (DM), including information systems and technology, organizational leadership. Evening/weekend programs available. Postbaccalaureate distance learning degree programs offered. *Degree requirements:* For doctorate, thesis/dissertation. *Entrance requirements:* Additional exam requirements/recommendations for international students: Required—TOEFL, TOEIC (Test of English as an International Communication), Berlitz Online English Proficiency Exam, PTE, or IELTS. Electronic applications accepted. *Expenses:* Contact institution.

University of Phoenix–Oregon Campus, College of Education, Tigard, OR 97223. Offers curriculum and instruction (MA Ed); early childhood education (MA Ed); elementary education (MA Ed), including early childhood specialization, middle level specialization; secondary education (MA Ed). Evening/weekend programs available. *Degree requirements:* For master's, thesis (for some programs). *Entrance requirements:* For master's, minimum undergraduate GPA of 2.5, 3 years work experience. Additional exam requirements/recommendations for international students: Required—TOEFL (minimum score 550 paper-based; 79 iBT). Electronic applications accepted.

University of Phoenix–Phoenix Campus, College of Education, Tempe, AZ 85282-2371. Offers administration and supervision (MA Ed); adult education and training (MA Ed); curriculum and instruction reading (MA Ed); early childhood education (MA Ed); education studies (MA Ed); elementary teacher education (MA Ed); secondary teacher education (MA Ed); special education (MA Ed); teacher leadership (MA Ed). Evening/weekend programs available. Postbaccalaureate distance learning degree programs offered. *Entrance requirements:* Additional exam requirements/recommendations for international students: Required—TOEFL, TOEIC (Test of English as an International Communication), Berlitz Online English Proficiency Exam, PTE, or IELTS. Electronic applications accepted. *Expenses:* Contact institution.

University of Phoenix–Richmond-Virginia Beach Campus, College of Education, Glen Allen, VA 23060. Offers administration and supervision (MA Ed); curriculum and instruction (MA Ed).

University of Phoenix–Sacramento Valley Campus, College of Education, Sacramento, CA 95833-3632. Offers adult education (MA Ed); curriculum instruction (MA Ed); elementary teacher education (MA Ed); secondary teacher education (MA Ed); teacher education (Certificate). Evening/weekend programs available. *Degree requirements:* For master's, thesis (for some programs). *Entrance requirements:* For master's, 3 years of work experience, minimum undergraduate GPA of 2.5. Additional exam requirements/recommendations for international students: Required—TOEFL (minimum score 550 paper-based; 79 iBT). Electronic applications accepted.

University of Phoenix–San Antonio Campus, College of Education, San Antonio, TX 78230. Offers curriculum and instruction (MA Ed).

University of Phoenix–San Diego Campus, College of Education, San Diego, CA 92123. Offers curriculum and instruction (MA Ed), including computer education, curriculum and instruction, English as a second language; elementary teacher education (MA Ed); secondary teacher education (MA Ed). Evening/weekend programs available. *Degree requirements:* For master's, thesis (for some programs). *Entrance requirements:* For master's, 3 years of work experience, minimum undergraduate GPA of 3.0. Additional exam requirements/recommendations for international students: Required—TOEFL (minimum score 550 paper-based; 79 iBT). Electronic applications accepted.

University of Phoenix–Southern Arizona Campus, College of Education, Tucson, AZ 85711. Offers administration and supervision (MA Ed); adult education and training (MA Ed); curriculum instruction (MA Ed); educational counseling (MA Ed); elementary teacher education (MA Ed); school counseling (MSC); secondary teacher education (MA Ed); special education (MA Ed, Certificate). Evening/weekend programs available. *Degree requirements:* For master's, thesis (for some programs). *Entrance requirements:* For master's, minimum undergraduate GPA of 2.5, 3 years of work experience. Additional exam requirements/recommendations for international students: Required—TOEFL (minimum score 550 paper-based; 79 iBT). Electronic applications accepted.

University of Phoenix–Southern Colorado Campus, College of Education, Colorado Springs, CO 80903. Offers administration and supervision (MA Ed); curriculum and instruction (MA Ed); elementary teacher education (MA Ed); principal licensure certification (Certificate); school counseling (MSC); secondary teacher education (MA Ed). Evening/weekend programs available. *Degree requirements:* For master's, thesis (for some programs). *Entrance requirements:* For master's, minimum undergraduate GPA of 2.5, 3 years of work experience. Additional exam requirements/recommendations for international students: Required—TOEFL (minimum score 550 paper-based; 79 iBT). Electronic applications accepted.

University of Phoenix–South Florida Campus, College of Education, Miramar, FL 33030. Offers administration and supervision (MA Ed); curriculum and instruction (MA Ed), including computer education, curriculum and instruction, mathematics education; early childhood education (MA Ed); elementary teacher education (MA Ed); secondary teacher education (MA Ed). Evening/weekend programs available. *Degree requirements:* For master's, thesis (for some programs). *Entrance requirements:* For master's, 3 years of work experience, minimum undergraduate GPA of 2.5. Additional exam requirements/recommendations for international students: Required—TOEFL (minimum score 550 paper-based; 79 iBT). Electronic applications accepted.

University of Phoenix–Springfield Campus, College of Education, Springfield, MO 65804-7211. Offers administration and supervision (MA Ed); curriculum and instruction (MA Ed), including computer education, curriculum and instruction, English and language arts education, English as a second language, mathematics education; English and language arts education (MA Ed).

University of Phoenix–Utah Campus, College of Education, Salt Lake City, UT 84123-4617. Offers administration and supervision (MA Ed); curriculum and instruction (MA Ed); elementary teacher education (MA Ed); school counseling (MSC); secondary teacher education (MA Ed); special education (MA Ed). Evening/weekend programs available. *Degree requirements:* For master's, thesis (for some programs). *Entrance requirements:* For master's, minimum undergraduate GPA of 2.5, 3 years work experience. Additional exam requirements/recommendations for international students: Required—TOEFL (minimum score 550 paper-based; 79 iBT). Electronic applications accepted.

University of Phoenix–Washington D.C. Campus, College of Education, Washington, DC 20001. Offers administration and supervision (MA Ed); adult education and training (MA Ed); computer education (MA Ed); curriculum and instruction (MA Ed, Ed D); early childhood education (MA Ed); education (Ed S); educational leadership (Ed D); educational technology (Ed D); elementary teacher education (MA Ed); English and language arts education (MA Ed); English as a second language (MA Ed); higher education administration (PhD); mathematics education (MA Ed); secondary teacher education (MA Ed); special education (MA Ed); teacher leadership (MA Ed).

University of Phoenix–West Florida Campus, College of Education, Temple Terrace, FL 33637. Offers administration and supervision (MA Ed); curriculum and instruction (MA Ed), including computer education, curriculum and instruction, mathematics education; curriculum and technology (MA Ed); early childhood education (MA Ed); elementary teacher education (MA Ed); secondary teacher education (MA Ed). Evening/weekend programs available. *Degree requirements:* For master's, thesis (for some programs). *Entrance requirements:* For master's, 3 years of work experience, minimum undergraduate GPA of 2.5. Additional exam requirements/recommendations for international students: Required—TOEFL (minimum score 550 paper-based; 79 iBT).

University of Puerto Rico, Río Piedras Campus, College of Education, Program in Curriculum and Teaching, San Juan, PR 00931-3300. Offers biology education (M Ed); chemistry education (M Ed); curriculum and teaching (Ed D); history education (M Ed); mathematics education (M Ed); physics education (M Ed); Spanish education (M Ed). Part-time programs available. *Degree requirements:* For master's, thesis; for doctorate, thesis/dissertation, internship. *Entrance requirements:* For master's, PAEG or GRE, minimum GPA of 3.0, letter of recommendation; for doctorate, GRE or PAEG, master's degree, minimum GPA of 3.0, letter of recommendation (2), interview. *Faculty research:* Curriculum, math teaching.

University of Regina, Faculty of Graduate Studies and Research, Faculty of Education, Department of Curriculum and Instruction, Regina, SK S4S 0A2, Canada. Offers M Ed. Part-time programs available. *Faculty:* 42 full-time (23 women), 18 part-time/adjunct (10 women). *Students:* 16 full-time (13 women), 138 part-time (109 women). 95 applicants, 80% accepted. In 2013, 50 master's awarded. *Degree requirements:* For master's, thesis (for some programs), practicum, project, or thesis. *Entrance requirements:* For master's, bachelor's degree in education, 2 years of teaching experience or other relevant professional experience. Additional exam requirements/recommendations for international students: Required—TOEFL (minimum score 580 paper-based; 80 iBT), IELTS (minimum score 6.5). *Application deadline:* For fall admission, 2/15 for domestic and international students; for winter admission, 10/15 for domestic and international students; for spring admission, 2/15 for domestic students. Application fee: $100. Electronic applications accepted. *Expenses: Tuition, area resident:* Full-time $4338

Canadian dollars. *International tuition:* $7338 Canadian dollars full-time. *Required fees:* $449.25 Canadian dollars. *Financial support:* In 2013–14, 2 fellowships (averaging $6,000 per year), 2 teaching assistantships (averaging $2,356 per year) were awarded; research assistantships and scholarships/grants also available. Financial award application deadline: 6/15. *Faculty research:* Writing process and pedagogy: the Saskatchewan Writing Project; second language reading, writing, and spoken acquisition; assessing experiential learning; multicultural and anti-racist relations issues in curriculum; social media and open education. *Unit head:* Dr. Ken Montgomery, Associate Dean, Research and Graduate Programs in Education, 306-585-5031, Fax: 306-585-5387, E-mail: ken.montgomery@uregina.ca. *Application contact:* Tania Gates, Graduate Program Coordinator, 306-585-4506, Fax: 306-585-5387, E-mail: edgrad@uregina.ca.

University of Rochester, Eastman School of Music, Program in Music Theory Pedagogy, Rochester, NY 14627. Offers MA. *Expenses: Tuition:* Full-time $44,580; part-time $1394 per credit hour. *Required fees:* $492.

University of Rochester, Margaret Warner Graduate School of Education and Human Development, Doctoral Programs in Education, Rochester, NY 14627. Offers counseling (Ed D); educational administration (Ed D); educational policy and theory (PhD); higher education (PhD); human development in educational context (PhD); teaching, curriculum, and change (PhD). *Expenses: Tuition:* Full-time $44,580; part-time $1394 per credit hour. *Required fees:* $492.

University of Rochester, Margaret Warner Graduate School of Education and Human Development, Master's Program in Teaching and Curriculum, Rochester, NY 14627. Offers MS. *Expenses: Tuition:* Full-time $44,580; part-time $1394 per credit hour. *Required fees:* $492.

University of St. Francis, College of Education, Joliet, IL 60435-6169. Offers educational leadership (MS, Ed D); elementary education (M Ed); higher education (MS); reading (MS); secondary education (M Ed), including English education, math education, science education, social studies education, visual arts education; special education (M Ed); teaching and learning (MS). *Accreditation:* NCATE. Part-time and evening/weekend programs available. Postbaccalaureate distance learning degree programs offered (no on-campus study). *Faculty:* 10 full-time (8 women), 34 part-time/adjunct (25 women). *Students:* 14 full-time (13 women), 250 part-time (183 women); includes 34 minority (20 Black or African American, non-Hispanic/Latino; 1 American Indian or Alaska Native, non-Hispanic/Latino; 13 Hispanic/Latino), 1 international. Average age 36. 133 applicants, 62% accepted, 71 enrolled. In 2013, 147 master's awarded. *Degree requirements:* For doctorate, thesis/dissertation. *Entrance requirements:* For doctorate, master's degree, IL Type 75 or Principal's endorsement, interview, minimum undergraduate GPA of 3.0, professional portfolio, letter of recommendation. Additional exam requirements/recommendations for international students: Required—TOEFL (minimum score 550 paper-based; 79 iBT), IELTS (minimum score 6.5). *Application deadline:* Applications are processed on a rolling basis. Application fee: $30. Electronic applications accepted. Application fee is waived when completed online. *Expenses:* Contact institution. *Financial support:* In 2013–14, 10 students received support. Scholarships/grants, tuition waivers (partial), and unspecified assistantships available. Support available to part-time students. Financial award applicants required to submit FAFSA. *Unit head:* Dr. John Gambro, Dean, 815-740-3829, Fax: 815-740-2264, E-mail: jgambro@stfrancis.edu. *Application contact:* Sandra Sloka, Director of Admissions for Graduate and Degree Completion Programs, 800-735-7500, Fax: 815-740-3431, E-mail: ssloka@stfrancis.edu. Website: http://www.stfrancis.edu/academics/college-of-education/.

University of St. Thomas, Graduate Studies, School of Education, Department of Teacher Education, St. Paul, MN 55105-1096. Offers curriculum and instruction (MA), including elementary, individualized, K-12, secondary; elementary education (MA); English as a second language (MA); math education (Certificate); multicultural education (Certificate); reading (MA, Certificate), including elementary (MA), K-12 (MA). *Accreditation:* NCATE. Part-time and evening/weekend programs available. *Entrance requirements:* For master's, minimum GPA of 3.0 or MAT. Additional exam requirements/recommendations for international students: Required—TOEFL (minimum score 550 paper-based; 80 iBT). *Application deadline:* For fall admission, 6/1 for domestic students; for spring admission, 11/1 for domestic students. Applications are processed on a rolling basis. Application fee: $50. *Financial support:* Fellowships, research assistantships, institutionally sponsored loans, and scholarships/grants available. Support available to part-time students. Financial award applicants required to submit FAFSA. *Unit head:* Dr. Jan L. H. Frank, Chair, 651-962-4446, Fax: 651-962-4169, E-mail: jlhfrank@stthomas.edu. *Application contact:* Rosemary R. Barreto, Department Assistant, 651-962-4420, Fax: 651-962-4169, E-mail: barr7879@stthomas.edu.

University of St. Thomas, School of Education, Houston, TX 77006-4696. Offers all level education (M Ed); bilingual/dual language (M Ed); Catholic school teaching (M Ed); Catholic/private school leadership (M Ed); counselor education (M Ed); curriculum and instruction (M Ed); educational leadership (M Ed); elementary teaching (M Ed); English as a second language (M Ed); exceptionality/educational diagnostician (M Ed); exceptionality/special education (M Ed); generalist (M Ed); reading (M Ed); secondary teaching (M Ed). *Accreditation:* Teacher Education Accreditation Council. Part-time and evening/weekend programs available. Postbaccalaureate distance learning degree programs offered (no on-campus study). *Faculty:* 40 full-time (26 women), 43 part-time/adjunct (31 women). *Students:* 27 full-time (20 women), 1,091 part-time (981 women); includes 691 minority (247 Black or African American, non-Hispanic/Latino; 1 American Indian or Alaska Native, non-Hispanic/Latino; 44 Asian, non-Hispanic/Latino; 379 Hispanic/Latino; 2 Native Hawaiian or other Pacific Islander, non-Hispanic/Latino; 18 Two or more races, non-Hispanic/Latino), 28 international. Average age 36. 858 applicants, 83% accepted, 458 enrolled. In 2013, 454 master's awarded. *Degree requirements:* For master's, thesis, field experience. *Entrance requirements:* For master's, GRE or MAT if GPA is below 3.0, bachelor's degree; minimum GPA of 2.75 in bachelor's degree or last 60 credit hours; official transcripts from all institutions; goal statement of 250-300 words; 1 reference. Additional exam requirements/recommendations for international students: Required—TOEFL. *Application deadline:* Applications are processed on a rolling basis. Application fee: $35. Electronic applications accepted. *Expenses:* Contact institution. *Financial support:* In 2013–14, 41 students received support. Federal Work-Study, scholarships/grants, and state work-study, institutional employment available. Support available to part-time students. Financial award application deadline: 4/15; financial award applicants required to submit FAFSA. *Faculty research:* Leadership, diversity, personality traits, second language acquisition. *Unit head:* Dr. Robert LeBlanc, Dean, 713-525-3540, Fax: 713-525-3871, E-mail: education@stthom.edu. *Application contact:* Rita Paredes, Administrative Assistant, 713-525-3442, Fax: 713-525-3871, E-mail: rparede@stthom.edu. Website: http://www.stthom.edu/Academics/School_of_Education/Index.aqf.

University of San Diego, School of Leadership and Education Sciences, Department of Learning and Teaching, San Diego, CA 92110-2492. Offers curriculum and instruction (M Ed); special education (M Ed); special education with deaf and hard of hearing (M Ed); teaching (MAT); TESOL, literacy and culture (M Ed). Part-time and evening/weekend programs available. *Faculty:* 10 full-time (6 women), 46 part-time/adjunct (38

women). *Students:* 132 full-time (100 women), 52 part-time (43 women); includes 141 minority (1 Black or African American, non-Hispanic/Latino; 16 American Indian or Alaska Native, non-Hispanic/Latino; 30 Asian, non-Hispanic/Latino; 79 Hispanic/Latino; 1 Native Hawaiian or other Pacific Islander, non-Hispanic/Latino; 14 Two or more races, non-Hispanic/Latino), 4 international. Average age 29. 253 applicants, 85% accepted, 108 enrolled. In 2013, 94 master's awarded. *Degree requirements:* For master's, thesis (for some programs), international experience. *Entrance requirements:* For master's, California Basic Educational Skills Test, minimum GPA of 3.0. Additional exam requirements/recommendations for international students: Required—TOEFL (minimum score 580 paper-based; 83 iBT), TWE. *Application deadline:* For fall admission, 3/1 priority date for domestic and international students; for spring admission, 10/15 priority date for domestic and international students. Applications are processed on a rolling basis. Application fee: $45. Electronic applications accepted. *Expenses: Tuition:* Full-time $23,580; part-time $1310 per credit. *Required fees:* $350. *Financial support:* In 2013–14, 52 students received support. Career-related internships or fieldwork, Federal Work-Study, institutionally sponsored loans, and stipends available. Support available to part-time students. Financial award application deadline: 4/1; financial award applicants required to submit FAFSA. *Faculty research:* Action research methodology, cultural studies, instructional theories and practices, second language acquisition, school reform. *Unit head:* Dr. Heather Lattimer, Director, 619-260-7616, Fax: 619-260-8159, E-mail: hlattimer@sandiego.edu. *Application contact:* Monica Mahon, Associate Director of Graduate Admissions, 619-260-4524, Fax: 619-260-4158, E-mail: grads@sandiego.edu.
Website: http://www.sandiego.edu/soles/departments/learning-and-teaching/.

University of San Francisco, School of Education, Department of Learning and Instruction, San Francisco, CA 94117-1080. Offers digital technologies for teaching and learning (MA); learning and instruction (MA, Ed D); special education (MA, Ed D); teaching reading (MA). Part-time and evening/weekend programs available. *Faculty:* 7 full-time (4 women), 6 part-time/adjunct (4 women). *Students:* 76 full-time (59 women), 40 part-time (26 women); includes 35 minority (5 Black or African American, non-Hispanic/Latino; 2 American Indian or Alaska Native, non-Hispanic/Latino; 9 Asian, non-Hispanic/Latino; 16 Hispanic/Latino; 3 Two or more races, non-Hispanic/Latino), 5 international. Average age 39. 73 applicants, 86% accepted, 40 enrolled. In 2013, 14 master's, 7 doctorates awarded. *Degree requirements:* For doctorate, thesis/dissertation. *Application deadline:* For fall admission, 3/1 priority date for domestic and international students; for spring admission, 11/1 priority date for domestic and international students. Applications are processed on a rolling basis. Application fee: $55 ($65 for international students). Electronic applications accepted. *Expenses: Tuition:* Full-time $21,150; part-time $1175 per unit. Tuition and fees vary according to course load, campus/location and program. *Financial support:* In 2013–14, 14 students received support. Fellowships, research assistantships, and teaching assistantships available. Financial award application deadline: 3/2; financial award applicants required to submit FAFSA. *Unit head:* Dr. Patricia Busk, Chair, 415-422-6289. *Application contact:* Amy Fogliani, Associate Director of Graduate Outreach, 415-422-5467, E-mail: schoolofeducation@usfca.edu.

University of Saskatchewan, College of Graduate Studies and Research, College of Education, Department of Curriculum Studies, Saskatoon, SK S7N 5A2, Canada. Offers M Ed, PhD, Diploma. Part-time programs available. *Degree requirements:* For master's, thesis (for some programs); for doctorate, comprehensive exam (for some programs), thesis/dissertation. *Entrance requirements:* For master's, MAT. Additional exam requirements/recommendations for international students: Required—TOEFL (minimum score 80 iBT); Recommended—IELTS (minimum score 6.5). Electronic applications accepted. *Expenses: Tuition, area resident:* Full-time $3585 Canadian dollars; part-time $585 Canadian dollars per course. Tuition, nonresident: part-time $877 Canadian dollars per course. *International tuition:* $5377 Canadian dollars full-time. *Required fees:* $889.51 Canadian dollars.

The University of Scranton, College of Graduate and Continuing Education, Department of Education, Program in Curriculum and Instruction, Scranton, PA 18510. Offers MA, MS. Part-time and evening/weekend programs available. Postbaccalaureate distance learning degree programs offered (no on-campus study). *Students:* 57 full-time (37 women), 66 part-time (62 women); includes 11 minority (5 Black or African American, non-Hispanic/Latino; 1 Asian, non-Hispanic/Latino; 5 Hispanic/Latino), 1 international. Average age 32. 19 applicants, 95% accepted. In 2013, 120 master's awarded. *Degree requirements:* For master's, comprehensive exam, thesis (for some programs), capstone experience. *Entrance requirements:* For master's, minimum GPA of 3.0. Additional exam requirements/recommendations for international students: Required—TOEFL (minimum score 500 paper-based), IELTS (minimum score 6). *Application deadline:* Applications are processed on a rolling basis. Application fee: $0. *Financial support:* Federal Work-Study and unspecified assistantships available. Financial award application deadline: 3/1. *Unit head:* Dr. Art Chambers, Director, 570-941-4668, Fax: 570-941-5515, E-mail: chambersa2@scranton.edu. *Application contact:* Joseph M. Roback, Director of Admissions, 570-941-4385, Fax: 570-941-5928, E-mail: robackj2@scranton.edu.

University of South Africa, College of Human Sciences, Pretoria, South Africa. Offers adult education (M Ed); African languages (MA, PhD); African politics (MA, PhD); Afrikaans (MA, PhD); ancient history (MA, PhD); ancient Near Eastern studies (MA, PhD); anthropology (MA, PhD); applied linguistics (MA); Arabic (MA, PhD); archaeology (MA); art history (MA); Biblical archaeology (MA); Biblical studies (M Th, D Th, PhD); Christian spirituality (M Th, D Th); church history (M Th, D Th); classical studies (MA, PhD); clinical psychology (MA); communication (MA, PhD); comparative education (M Ed, Ed D); consulting psychology (D Admin, D Com, PhD); curriculum studies (M Ed, Ed D); development studies (M Admin, MA, D Admin, PhD); didactics (M Ed, Ed D); education (M Tech); education management (M Ed, Ed D); educational psychology (M Ed); English (MA); environmental education (M Ed); French (MA, PhD); German (MA, PhD); Greek (MA); guidance and counseling (M Ed); health studies (MA, PhD), including health sciences education (MA), health services management (MA), medical and surgical nursing science (critical care general) (MA), midwifery and neonatal nursing science (MA), trauma and emergency care (MA); history (MA, PhD); history of education (Ed D); inclusive education (M Ed, Ed D); information and communications technology policy and regulation (MA); information science (MA, MIS, PhD); international politics (MA, PhD); Islamic studies (MA, PhD); Italian (MA, PhD); Judaica (MA, PhD); linguistics (MA, PhD); mathematical education (M Ed); mathematics education (MA); missiology (M Th, D Th); modern Hebrew (MA, PhD); musicology (MA, MMus, D Mus, PhD); natural science education (M Ed); New Testament (M Th, D Th); Old Testament (D Th); pastoral therapy (M Th, D Th); philosophy (MA); philosophy of education (M Ed, Ed D); politics (MA, PhD); Portuguese (MA, PhD); practical theology (M Th, D Th); psychology (MA, MS, PhD); psychology of education (M Ed, Ed D); public health (MA); religious studies (MA, D Th, PhD); Romance languages (MA); Russian (MA, PhD); Semitic languages (MA, PhD); social behavior studies in HIV/AIDS (MA); social science (mental health) (MA); social science in development studies (MA); social science in psychology (MA); social science in social work (MA); social science in sociology (MA); social work (MSW, DSW, PhD); socio-education (M Ed, Ed D); sociolinguistics (MA); sociology (MA, PhD); Spanish (MA, PhD); systematic theology (M Th, D Th); TESOL (teaching English to speakers of other languages) (MA); theological ethics (M Th, D Th); theory of literature (MA, PhD); urban ministries (D Th); urban ministry (M Th).

University of South Carolina, The Graduate School, College of Education, Department of Instruction and Teacher Education, Program in Curriculum and Instruction, Columbia, SC 29208. Offers Ed D. This degree cuts across two departments and represents 6 different concentrations. *Accreditation:* NCATE. Part-time and evening/weekend programs available. *Degree requirements:* For doctorate, comprehensive exam, thesis/dissertation. *Entrance requirements:* For doctorate, GRE General Test or MAT, interview, resume, letter of intent, letters of reference. Electronic applications accepted. *Faculty research:* Teacher education, historian recording project, curriculum development in international areas, human sexuality.

The University of South Dakota, Graduate School, School of Education, Division of Curriculum and Instruction, Vermillion, SD 57069-2390. Offers curriculum and instruction (Ed D, Ed S); elementary education (MA); secondary education (MA); special education (MA); technology for education and training (MS). *Accreditation:* NCATE. Part-time programs available. Postbaccalaureate distance learning degree programs offered. *Degree requirements:* For master's and Ed S, comprehensive exam, thesis or alternative; for doctorate, comprehensive exam, thesis/dissertation. *Entrance requirements:* For master's, doctorate, and Ed S, GRE General Test, MAT, minimum GPA of 2.7. Additional exam requirements/recommendations for international students: Required—TOEFL (minimum score 550 paper-based; 79 iBT). Electronic applications accepted.

University of Southern Mississippi, Graduate School, College of Education and Psychology, Department of Curriculum, Instruction, and Special Education, Hattiesburg, MS 39406-0001. Offers elementary education (M Ed, PhD, Ed S); instructional technology (MS, PhD); secondary education (MAT); special education (M Ed, PhD, Ed S). Part-time programs available. *Faculty:* 23 full-time (17 women), 3 part-time/adjunct (2 women). *Students:* 20 full-time (19 women), 59 part-time (49 women); includes 18 minority (14 Black or African American, non-Hispanic/Latino; 3 Hispanic/Latino; 1 Two or more races, non-Hispanic/Latino). Average age 36. 21 applicants, 95% accepted, 17 enrolled. In 2013, 22 master's, 3 doctorates, 13 other advanced degrees awarded. *Degree requirements:* For master's and Ed S, comprehensive exam, thesis (for some programs); for doctorate, comprehensive exam, thesis/dissertation. *Entrance requirements:* For master's, GRE General Test, MAT, minimum GPA of 3.0; for doctorate, GRE General Test, minimum GPA of 3.5; for Ed S, GRE General Test, MAT, minimum GPA of 3.25. Additional exam requirements/recommendations for international students: Required—TOEFL, IELTS. *Application deadline:* For fall admission, 3/1 priority date for domestic students, 3/1 for international students; for spring admission, 1/10 priority date for domestic and international students. Applications are processed on a rolling basis. Application fee: $50. *Financial support:* In 2013–14, 9 research assistantships with tuition reimbursements (averaging $18,316 per year), 2 teaching assistantships with full tuition reimbursements (averaging $8,500 per year) were awarded; Federal Work-Study, institutionally sponsored loans, scholarships/grants, health care benefits, tuition waivers (partial), and unspecified assistantships also available. Financial award application deadline: 3/15; financial award applicants required to submit FAFSA. *Faculty research:* Mathematical problem solving, integrative curriculum, writing process, teacher education models. *Total annual research expenditures:* $100,000. *Unit head:* Dr. Ravic P. Ringlaben, Chair, 601-266-4547, Fax: 601-266-4175. *Application contact:* David Daves, Director of Graduate Studies, 601-266-6005, Fax: 601-266-4548.
Website: http://www.usm.edu/graduateschool/table.php.

University of South Florida, College of Education, Department of Secondary Education, Tampa, FL 33620-9951. Offers English education (M Ed, MA, MAT, PhD); foreign language education/ESOL (M Ed, MA, MAT); instructional technology (M Ed, PhD, Ed S); mathematics education (M Ed, MA, MAT, PhD, Ed S); science education (M Ed, MA, MAT, PhD); second language acquisition/instructional technology (PhD); secondary education (M Ed, PhD); secondary education/TESOL (M Ed); social science education (M Ed, MA, MAT); teaching and learning in the content area (PhD). *Accreditation:* NCATE. Part-time and evening/weekend programs available. *Degree requirements:* For master's, variable foreign language requirement, comprehensive exam, project (for some programs); for doctorate, variable foreign language requirement, comprehensive exam, thesis/dissertation, philosophies of inquiry; multiple research methods. *Entrance requirements:* For master's, GRE General Test or General Knowledge Test, minimum GPA of 3.0; for doctorate, GRE General Test, minimum GPA of 3.5; for Ed S, GRE General Test. Additional exam requirements/recommendations for international students: Required—TOEFL (minimum score 550 paper-based; 79 iBT). Electronic applications accepted. *Faculty research:* English language learners/multicultural, social science education, mathematics education, science education, instructional technology.

University of South Florida Sarasota-Manatee, College of Education, Sarasota, FL 34243. Offers education (MA); educational leadership (M Ed), including curriculum leadership, K-12, non-public/charter school leadership; English education (MA); teaching K-6 with ESOL endorsement (MAT). Part-time and evening/weekend programs available. *Faculty:* 7 full-time (all women), 5 part-time/adjunct (3 women). *Students:* 11 full-time (9 women), 43 part-time (33 women); includes 6 minority (2 Black or African American, non-Hispanic/Latino; 2 Hispanic/Latino; 1 Native Hawaiian or other Pacific Islander, non-Hispanic/Latino; 1 Two or more races, non-Hispanic/Latino). Average age 33. 46 applicants, 39% accepted, 15 enrolled. In 2013, 33 master's awarded. *Degree requirements:* For master's, comprehensive exam (for some programs). *Entrance requirements:* For master's, GRE (within last 5 years) or minimum GPA of 3.0, letters of recommendation. Additional exam requirements/recommendations for international students: Required—TOEFL (minimum score 550 paper-based; 79 iBT), IELTS (minimum score 6.5). *Application deadline:* For fall admission, 3/1 priority date for domestic students, 3/1 for international students; for spring admission, 10/1 priority date for domestic students, 10/1 for international students. Applications are processed on a rolling basis. Application fee: $30. Electronic applications accepted. *Expenses:* Tuition, state resident: full-time $10,029; part-time $418 per credit. Tuition, nonresident: full-time $20,727; part-time $863 per credit. *Required fees:* $10; $5. Tuition and fees vary according to program. *Financial support:* In 2013–14, 10 students received support. Career-related internships or fieldwork, institutionally sponsored loans, scholarships/grants, health care benefits, and unspecified assistantships available. Support available to part-time students. Financial award application deadline: 3/1; financial award applicants required to submit FAFSA. *Faculty research:* Child development, student achievement, inter-generational studies, equitable implementation of educational policy, linguistics and its applications. *Unit head:* Dr. Terry A. Osborn, Dean, 941-359-4531, Fax: 941-359-4778, E-mail: terryosborn@sar.usf.edu. *Application contact:* Andy Telatovich, Director, Admissions, 941-359-4330, Fax: 941-359-4585, E-mail: atelatovich@sar.usf.edu.
Website: http://usfsm.edu/college-of-education/.

The University of Tampa, Program in Teaching, Tampa, FL 33606-1490. Offers curricula and instructional leadership (M Ed); teaching (M Ed). Part-time and evening/weekend programs available. *Faculty:* 7 full-time (4 women), 6 part-time/adjunct (5 women). *Students:* 34 full-time (26 women), 47 part-time (32 women); includes 27

minority (11 Black or African American, non-Hispanic/Latino; 1 Asian, non-Hispanic/Latino; 11 Hispanic/Latino; 4 Two or more races, non-Hispanic/Latino), 3 international. Average age 32. 115 applicants, 54% accepted, 32 enrolled. In 2013, 9 master's awarded. *Entrance requirements:* For master's, Florida Teacher Certification Exam, PRAXIS, GRE, or GMAT, bachelor's degree in education or professional teaching certificate. Additional exam requirements/recommendations for international students: Required—TOEFL (minimum score 577 paper-based; 90 iBT), IELTS (minimum score 7). *Application deadline:* For fall admission, 5/1 for domestic students. Applications are processed on a rolling basis. Application fee: $40. Electronic applications accepted. *Expenses: Tuition:* Full-time $8928; part-time $558 per credit hour. *Required fees:* $80; $80 $40 per term. Tuition and fees vary according to program. *Financial support:* In 2013–14, 24 students received support. Scholarships/grants available. Financial award applicants required to submit FAFSA. *Faculty research:* Diversity in the classroom, technology integration, assessment methodologies, complex and ill-structured problem solving, and communities of practice. *Unit head:* Dr. Johnathan McKeown, Director, Education Master's Program, 813-257-6306, E-mail: jmckeown@ut.edu. *Application contact:* Brent Benner, Director of Admissions, 813-257-3642, E-mail: bbenner@ut.edu. Website: http://www.ut.edu/graduate.

The University of Tennessee, Graduate School, College of Education, Health and Human Sciences, Program in Education, Knoxville, TN 37996. Offers art education (MS); counseling education (PhD); cultural studies in education (PhD); curriculum (MS, Ed S); curriculum, educational research and evaluation (Ed D, PhD); early childhood education (PhD); early childhood special education (MS); education of deaf and hard of hearing (MS); educational administration and policy studies (Ed D, PhD); educational administration and supervision (Ed S); educational psychology (Ed D, PhD); elementary education (MS, Ed S); elementary teaching (MS); English education (MS, Ed S); exercise science (PhD); foreign language/ESL education (MS, Ed S); instructional technology (MS, Ed D, PhD, Ed S); literacy, language and ESL education (PhD); literacy, language education, and ESL education (Ed D); mathematics education (MS, Ed S); modified and comprehensive special education (MS); reading education (MS, Ed S); school counseling (Ed S); school psychology (PhD, Ed S); science education (MS, Ed S); secondary teaching (MS); social foundations (MS); social science education (MS, Ed S); socio-cultural foundations of sports and education (PhD); special education (Ed S); teacher education (Ed D, PhD). *Accreditation:* NCATE. Part-time and evening/weekend programs available. *Degree requirements:* For master's and Ed S, thesis optional; for doctorate, variable foreign language requirement, thesis/dissertation. *Entrance requirements:* For master's, minimum GPA of 2.7; for doctorate and Ed S, GRE General Test, minimum GPA of 2.7. Additional exam requirements/recommendations for international students: Required—TOEFL. Electronic applications accepted. *Expenses:* Tuition, state resident: full-time $9540; part-time $531 per credit hour. Tuition, nonresident: full-time $27,728; part-time $1542 per credit hour. *Required fees:* $1404; $67 per credit hour.

The University of Tennessee at Martin, Graduate Programs, College of Education, Health and Behavioral Sciences, Program in Teaching, Martin, TN 38238-1000. Offers curriculum and instruction (MS Ed), including 7-12, K-6; initial licensure (MS Ed), including elementary, secondary; initial licensure K-12 (MS Ed), including physical education, special education; interdisciplinary (MS Ed). Part-time programs available. *Students:* 20 full-time (14 women), 88 part-time (65 women); includes 9 minority (8 Black or African American, non-Hispanic/Latino; 1 Two or more races, non-Hispanic/Latino). 78 applicants, 64% accepted, 33 enrolled. In 2013, 32 master's awarded. *Degree requirements:* For master's, comprehensive exam. *Entrance requirements:* For master's, GRE General Test, minimum GPA of 2.5. Additional exam requirements/recommendations for international students: Required—TOEFL (minimum score 525 paper-based; 71 iBT). *Application deadline:* For fall admission, 7/29 priority date for domestic students, 7/29 for international students; for spring admission, 12/12 priority date for domestic students, 12/12 for international students. Applications are processed on a rolling basis. Application fee: $30 ($130 for international students). Electronic applications accepted. *Financial support:* Research assistantships with full tuition reimbursements, teaching assistantships with full tuition reimbursements, career-related internships or fieldwork, scholarships/grants, and unspecified assistantships available. Financial award application deadline: 3/1. *Faculty research:* Special education, science/math/technology, school reform, reading. *Unit head:* Dr. Gail Stephens, Interim Dean, 731-881-7127, Fax: 731-881-7975, E-mail: gstephe6@utm.edu. *Application contact:* Jolene L. Cunningham, Student Services Specialist, 731-881-7012, Fax: 731-881-7499, E-mail: jcunningham@utm.edu.

The University of Texas at Arlington, Graduate School, Department of Curriculum and Instruction, Arlington, TX 76019. Offers curriculum and instruction (M Ed); teaching (with certification) (M Ed T). *Accreditation:* NCATE. Part-time and evening/weekend programs available. Postbaccalaureate distance learning degree programs offered (no on-campus study). *Degree requirements:* For master's, comprehensive exam (for some programs), comprehensive activity, research project. *Entrance requirements:* For master's, GRE General Test, minimum undergraduate GPA of 3.0 in last 60 hours of course work, writing sample, 3 letters of recommendation. Additional exam requirements/recommendations for international students: Required—TOEFL (minimum score 550 paper-based). Electronic applications accepted.

The University of Texas at Austin, Graduate School, College of Education, Department of Curriculum and Instruction, Austin, TX 78712-1111. Offers bilingual/bicultural education (M Ed, MA, PhD); cultural studies in education (M Ed, MA, PhD); early childhood education (M Ed, MA, PhD); language and literacy studies (M Ed, PhD); learning technologies (M Ed, MA, PhD); physical education (M Ed, MA, PhD). Terminal master's awarded for partial completion of doctoral program. *Degree requirements:* For doctorate, thesis/dissertation. *Entrance requirements:* For master's and doctorate, GRE General Test. Electronic applications accepted.

The University of Texas at Brownsville, Graduate Studies, College of Education, Brownsville, TX 78520-4991. Offers bilingual education (M Ed); counseling and guidance (M Ed); curriculum and instruction (M Ed); early childhood education (M Ed); educational leadership (M Ed); educational technology (M Ed); exercise science (MS); special education (M Ed). Part-time and evening/weekend programs available. Postbaccalaureate distance learning degree programs offered (no on-campus study). *Faculty:* 51 full-time (28 women). *Students:* 60 full-time (43 women), 496 part-time (363 women); includes 467 minority (4 Black or African American, non-Hispanic/Latino; 1 American Indian or Alaska Native, non-Hispanic/Latino; 10 Asian, non-Hispanic/Latino; 451 Hispanic/Latino; 1 Native Hawaiian or other Pacific Islander, non-Hispanic/Latino), 12 international. 161 applicants, 67% accepted, 81 enrolled. In 2013, 142 master's awarded. *Degree requirements:* For master's, comprehensive exam (for some programs), thesis optional, electronic portfolio. *Entrance requirements:* For master's, GRE General Test, curriculum vitae or resume, teaching certificate. Additional exam requirements/recommendations for international students: Required—TOEFL (minimum score 550 paper-based; 77 iBT). *Application deadline:* For fall admission, 7/1 priority date for domestic students, 7/1 for international students; for spring admission, 12/1 priority date for domestic students, 12/1 for international students. Applications are processed on a rolling basis. Application fee: $30. Electronic applications accepted. *Expenses:* Tuition, state resident: full-time $3444; part-time $1148 per semester. Tuition, nonresident: full-time $9816. *Required fees:* $1018; $221 per credit hour. $401 per semester. *Financial support:* In 2013–14, 136 students received support, including 6 research assistantships (averaging $10,000 per year); career-related internships or fieldwork, Federal Work-Study, scholarships/grants, tuition waivers (partial), and unspecified assistantships also available. Support available to part-time students. Financial award application deadline: 3/1; financial award applicants required to submit FAFSA. *Unit head:* Dr. Miguel Angel Escotet, Dean, 956-882-7220, Fax: 956-882-7431, E-mail: miguel.escotet@utb.edu. *Application contact:* Mari E. Stevens, Graduate Studies Specialist, 956-882-6587, Fax: 956-882-7279, E-mail: mari.stevens@utb.edu. Website: http://www.utb.edu/vpaa/coe/Pages/default.aspx.

The University of Texas at El Paso, Graduate School, College of Education, Department of Teacher Education, El Paso, TX 79968-0001. Offers education (MA); instruction (M Ed); reading education (M Ed); teaching, learning, and culture (PhD). Part-time and evening/weekend programs available. *Degree requirements:* For master's, thesis optional. *Entrance requirements:* For master's, GRE General Test, minimum GPA of 3.0. Additional exam requirements/recommendations for international students: Required—TOEFL. Electronic applications accepted.

The University of Texas at San Antonio, College of Education and Human Development, Department of Interdisciplinary Learning and Teaching, San Antonio, TX 78249-0617. Offers education (MA), including curriculum and instruction, early childhood and elementary education, instructional technology, reading and literacy, special education; interdisciplinary learning and teaching (PhD). Part-time and evening/weekend programs available. *Faculty:* 22 full-time (16 women), 1 (woman) part-time/adjunct. *Students:* 109 full-time (80 women), 272 part-time (221 women); includes 209 minority (24 Black or African American, non-Hispanic/Latino; 3 American Indian or Alaska Native, non-Hispanic/Latino; 12 Asian, non-Hispanic/Latino; 166 Hispanic/Latino; 4 Two or more races, non-Hispanic/Latino), 40 international. Average age 33. 178 applicants, 87% accepted, 80 enrolled. In 2013, 136 master's, 7 doctorates awarded. *Degree requirements:* For master's, comprehensive exam, thesis optional, 36 hours of course work without thesis (33 with thesis); for doctorate, comprehensive exam, thesis/dissertation, minimum of 60 semester credit hours. *Entrance requirements:* For master's, bachelor's degree with minimum GPA of 3.0 in last 60 hours of coursework; 18 hours of undergraduate coursework in education or related field; for doctorate, GRE, transcripts from all colleges and universities attended, professional vitae demonstrating experience in work environment where education was primary professional emphasis, 3 letters of recommendation, statement of purpose, minimum GPA of 3.5. Additional exam requirements/recommendations for international students: Required—TOEFL (minimum score 550 paper-based; 79 iBT), IELTS (minimum score 6.5). *Application deadline:* For fall admission, 7/1 for domestic students, 4/1 for international students; for spring admission, 11/1 for domestic students, 9/1 for international students. Applications are processed on a rolling basis. Application fee: $45 ($80 for international students). Electronic applications accepted. *Expenses:* Tuition, state resident: full-time $4671. Tuition, nonresident: full-time $8708. *International tuition:* $17,415 full-time. *Required fees:* $1924.60. Tuition and fees vary according to course load and degree level. *Financial support:* In 2013–14, 7 fellowships with partial tuition reimbursements (averaging $27,000 per year) were awarded; career-related internships or fieldwork, Federal Work-Study, and scholarships/grants also available. Support available to part-time students. *Faculty research:* Explorations of science, learning and teaching, family involvement in early childhood, culturally-responsive literacy instruction in diverse settings, STEM education, autism spectrum disorder. *Total annual research expenditures:* $5.9 million. *Unit head:* Dr. Maria R. Cortez, Department Chair, 210-458-5969, Fax: 210-458-7281, E-mail: mari.cortez@utsa.edu. *Application contact:* Erin Doran, Student Development Specialist, 210-458-7443, Fax: 210-458-7281, E-mail: erin.doran@utsa.edu.
Website: http://education.utsa.edu/interdisciplinary_learning_and_teaching/.

University of the Pacific, Gladys L. Benerd School of Education, Department of Curriculum and Instruction, Stockton, CA 95211-0197. Offers curriculum and instruction (M Ed, MA, Ed D); education (M Ed); special education (MA). *Accreditation:* NCATE. *Faculty:* 10 full-time (6 women), 3 part-time/adjunct (2 women). *Students:* 87 full-time (65 women), 139 part-time (103 women); includes 74 minority (18 Black or African American, non-Hispanic/Latino; 1 American Indian or Alaska Native, non-Hispanic/Latino; 18 Asian, non-Hispanic/Latino; 32 Hispanic/Latino; 1 Native Hawaiian or other Pacific Islander, non-Hispanic/Latino; 4 Two or more races, non-Hispanic/Latino), 23 international. Average age 30. 108 applicants, 81% accepted, 65 enrolled. In 2013, 111 master's, 5 doctorates awarded. *Degree requirements:* For master's, thesis (for some programs). *Entrance requirements:* For master's, GRE General Test. Additional exam requirements/recommendations for international students: Required—TOEFL (minimum score 475 paper-based). *Application deadline:* For fall admission, 3/1 priority date for domestic students; for spring admission, 10/1 priority date for domestic students. Applications are processed on a rolling basis. Application fee: $75. *Financial support:* In 2013–14, 7 teaching assistantships were awarded. Financial award application deadline: 3/1; financial award applicants required to submit FAFSA. *Unit head:* Dr. Marilyn Draheim, Chairperson, 209-946-2685, E-mail: mdraheim@pacific.edu. *Application contact:* Office of Graduate Admissions, 209-946-2344.

University of the Southwest, Graduate Programs, Hobbs, NM 88240-9129. Offers business administration (MBA); curriculum and instruction (MSE); curriculum and instruction: bilingual (MSE); curriculum and instruction: TESOL (MSE); early childhood education (MSE); educational administration (MSE); mental health counseling (MSE); school counseling (MSE); special education (MSE); sports management (MBA). Part-time and evening/weekend programs available. Postbaccalaureate distance learning degree programs offered (no on-campus study). *Degree requirements:* For master's, comprehensive exam, thesis (for some programs). *Entrance requirements:* Additional exam requirements/recommendations for international students: Recommended—TOEFL. Electronic applications accepted.

The University of Toledo, College of Graduate Studies, Judith Herb College of Education, Department of Curriculum and Instruction, Toledo, OH 43606-3390. Offers art education (ME); career and technical education (ME); career-technical education (Ed S); curriculum and instruction (ME, PhD, Ed S); early childhood education (PhD, Ed S); education and biology (MES); education and chemistry (MES); education and economics (MAE); education and English (MAE); education and French (MAE); education and geography (MAE); education and geology (MES); education and German (MAE); education and history (MAE); education and mathematics (MAE, MES); education and physics (MES); education and political science (MAE); education and sociology (MAE); education and Spanish (MAE); educational media (PhD); educational technology (ME); educational technology: virtual educator (Certificate); elementary education (PhD); English as a second language (MAE); gifted and talented (PhD); middle childhood education licensure (ME); music education (MME); secondary education (PhD); secondary education licensure (ME); special education (PhD, Ed S). *Accreditation:* NCATE. Part-time and evening/weekend programs available. *Faculty:* 41. *Students:* 53 full-time (30 women), 154 part-time (111 women); includes 21 minority (16 Black or African American, non-Hispanic/Latino; 4 Hispanic/Latino; 1 Two or more races, non-Hispanic/Latino), 21 international. Average age 34. 82 applicants, 79% accepted, 47 enrolled. In 2013, 80 master's, 5 doctorates awarded. *Degree requirements:* For

master's, comprehensive exam, thesis or alternative; for doctorate, comprehensive exam, thesis/dissertation; for other advanced degree, thesis optional. *Entrance requirements:* For master's, doctorate, and other advanced degree, minimum cumulative GPA of 2.7 for all previous academic work, letters of recommendation. Additional exam requirements/recommendations for international students: Required—TOEFL (minimum score 550 paper-based; 80 iBT). *Application deadline:* For fall admission, 1/15 priority date for domestic and international students. Applications are processed on a rolling basis. Application fee: $45 ($75 for international students). Electronic applications accepted. *Financial support:* In 2013–14, 5 research assistantships with full and partial tuition reimbursements (averaging $13,200 per year), 11 teaching assistantships with full and partial tuition reimbursements (averaging $8,809 per year) were awarded; career-related internships or fieldwork, Federal Work-Study, institutionally sponsored loans, scholarships/grants, tuition waivers (full and partial), unspecified assistantships, and administrative assistantships also available. Support available to part-time students. *Unit head:* Dr. Joan Kaderavek, Chair, 419-530-5373, E-mail: eigh.chiarelott@utoledo.edu. *Application contact:* Graduate School Office, 419-530-4723, Fax: 419-530-4724, E-mail: grdsch@utnet.utoledo.edu.
Website: http://www.utoledo.edu/eduhshs/.

University of Vermont, Graduate College, College of Education and Social Services, Department of Education, Program in Curriculum and Instruction, Burlington, VT 05405. Offers M Ed, MAT. *Accreditation:* NCATE. *Students:* 99 (74 women); includes 2 minority (1 American Indian or Alaska Native, non-Hispanic/Latino; 1 Hispanic/Latino), 1 international. 103 applicants, 50% accepted, 12 enrolled. In 2013, 72 master's awarded. *Entrance requirements:* For master's, GRE (for M Ed), resume (for M Ed and MAT). Additional exam requirements/recommendations for international students: Required—TOEFL (minimum score 550 paper-based; 80 iBT). *Application deadline:* For fall admission, 3/15 priority date for domestic students, 3/15 for international students. Applications are processed on a rolling basis. Application fee: $65. Electronic applications accepted. *Financial support:* Fellowships, teaching assistantships, and career-related internships or fieldwork available. Financial award application deadline: 3/1. *Unit head:* Dr. Maureen Neumann, Chairperson, 802-656-3356. *Application contact:* Prof. Maureen Neumann, M Ed Coordinator, 802-656-1410.

University of Victoria, Faculty of Graduate Studies, Faculty of Education, Department of Curriculum and Instruction, Victoria, BC V8W 2Y2, Canada. Offers art education (M Ed, PhD); curriculum studies (M Ed, MA, PhD); early childhood education (M Ed, PhD); educational studies (PhD); language and literacy (M Ed, MA, PhD); mathematics (M Ed, MA, PhD); music education (M Ed, MA, PhD); science (M Ed, MA, PhD); social studies (M Ed, MA); social, cultural and foundational studies (MA, PhD); technology and environmental education (PhD). Part-time programs available. *Degree requirements:* For master's, thesis, project (M Ed); for doctorate, comprehensive exam, thesis/dissertation. *Entrance requirements:* For master's, minimum B average. Additional exam requirements/recommendations for international students: Required—TOEFL (minimum score 575 paper-based), IELTS (minimum score 7). Electronic applications accepted. *Faculty research:* Elementary and secondary English, language arts, curriculum theory and practice, educational media and technology, educational administration and leadership, history and philosophy of education.

University of Virginia, Curry School of Education, Department of Curriculum, Instruction, and Special Education, Program in Curriculum and Instruction, Charlottesville, VA 22903. Offers curriculum and instruction (M Ed, Ed S); elementary education (M Ed, Ed D); English (M Ed, Ed D); foreign language (M Ed); mathematics (M Ed, Ed D); reading (M Ed, Ed D, Ed S); science (Ed D); social studies (M Ed). *Students:* 42 full-time (30 women), 37 part-time (32 women); includes 4 minority (1 Black or African American, non-Hispanic/Latino; 2 Hispanic/Latino; 1 Two or more races, non-Hispanic/Latino), 1 international. Average age 31. 76 applicants, 74% accepted, 39 enrolled. In 2013, 84 master's, 3 doctorates, 23 other advanced degrees awarded. *Degree requirements:* For master's, comprehensive exam (for some programs); for doctorate, comprehensive exam, thesis/dissertation; for Ed S, comprehensive exam. *Entrance requirements:* For master's, doctorate, and Ed S, GRE General Test, 2 letters of recommendation. Additional exam requirements/recommendations for international students: Required—TOEFL (minimum score 600 paper-based; 90 iBT), IELTS (minimum score 7). *Application deadline:* Applications are processed on a rolling basis. Application fee: $60. Electronic applications accepted. *Expenses:* Tuition, state resident: part-time $334 per credit hour. Tuition, nonresident: part-time $1224 per credit hour. *Financial support:* Fellowships with tuition reimbursements, research assistantships with tuition reimbursements, and teaching assistantships with tuition reimbursements available. Financial award application deadline: 1/5; financial award applicants required to submit FAFSA. *Unit head:* Stephanie van Hover, Chair, 434-924-0841, E-mail: sdv2w@virginia.edu. *Application contact:* Karen Dwier, Information Contact, 434-924-0831, E-mail: kgd9g@virginia.edu.
Website: http://curry.virginia.edu/academics/areas-of-study/curriculum-teaching-learning.

University of Virginia, Curry School of Education, Program in Education, Charlottesville, VA 22903. Offers administration and supervision (PhD); applied developmental science (PhD); counselor education (PhD); curriculum and instruction (PhD); early childhood special education (MT); education evaluation (PhD); educational psychology (PhD); educational research (PhD); elementary education (MT); English education (MT, PhD); foreign language education (MT); higher education (PhD); instructional technology (PhD); kinesiology (MT, PhD); math education (PhD); reading education (PhD); research, statistics and evaluation (PhD); school psychology (PhD); science education (PhD); social studies education (MT, PhD); special education (PhD); world languages education (MT). *Students:* 474 full-time (379 women), 35 part-time (19 women); includes 89 minority (30 Black or African American, non-Hispanic/Latino; 1 American Indian or Alaska Native, non-Hispanic/Latino; 26 Asian, non-Hispanic/Latino; 19 Hispanic/Latino; 13 Two or more races, non-Hispanic/Latino), 21 international. Average age 26. 312 applicants, 49% accepted, 80 enrolled. In 2013, 137 master's, 38 doctorates awarded. *Degree requirements:* For master's, comprehensive exam (for some programs), field project; for doctorate, comprehensive exam, thesis/dissertation. *Entrance requirements:* For doctorate, GRE General Test. Additional exam requirements/recommendations for international students: Required—TOEFL (minimum score 600 paper-based; 90 iBT), IELTS (minimum score 7). *Application deadline:* Applications are processed on a rolling basis. Application fee: $60. Electronic applications accepted. *Expenses:* Tuition, state resident: part-time $334 per credit hour. Tuition, nonresident: part-time $1224 per credit hour. *Financial support:* Fellowships, research assistantships, and teaching assistantships available. Financial award application deadline: 1/5; financial award applicants required to submit FAFSA. *Unit head:* Robert C. Pianta, Dean, 434-924-3334, E-mail: pianta@virginia.edu. *Application contact:* Office of Admissions and Student Services, 434-924-0742, E-mail: curry-admissions@virginia.edu.
Website: http://curry.virginia.edu/teacher-education.

University of Washington, Graduate School, College of Education, Seattle, WA 98195. Offers curriculum and instruction (M Ed, Ed D, PhD), including educational technology, general curriculum (Ed D, PhD), language, literacy, and culture, mathematics education, multicultural education, reading and language arts education (Ed D), science education, social studies education, teaching and curriculum (M Ed); educational leadership and policy studies (M Ed, Ed D, PhD), including administration (Ed D), educational policy, organization, and leadership (M Ed, PhD), higher education, leadership for learning (Ed D), social and cultural foundations of education (M Ed, PhD); educational psychology (M Ed, PhD), including educational psychology (PhD), human development and cognition (M Ed), learning sciences, measurement, statistics and research design (M Ed), school psychology (M Ed); instructional leadership (M Ed); intercollegiate athletic leadership (M Ed); special education (M Ed, Ed D, PhD), including early childhood special education (M Ed), emotional and behavioral disabilities (M Ed), learning disabilities (M Ed), low-incidence disabilities (M Ed), severe disabilities (M Ed), special education (Ed D, PhD); teacher education (MIT). *Accreditation:* APA. Part-time and evening/weekend programs available. *Degree requirements:* For master's, thesis optional; for doctorate, thesis/dissertation. *Entrance requirements:* For master's and doctorate, GRE General Test, minimum GPA of 3.0. Additional exam requirements/recommendations for international students: Required—TOEFL. Electronic applications accepted. *Faculty research:* School restructuring/effective schools, special education interventions, literacy and writing, technology, school partnerships, teacher preparation.

The University of West Alabama, School of Graduate Studies, College of Education, Departments of Instructional Leadership and Support/Curriculum and Instruction, Livinston, AL 35470. Offers continuing education (MSCE), including college student development, continuing education, counseling and psychology, family counseling, guidance and counseling; early childhood education (M Ed, Ed S), including early childhood development (Ed S), early childhood education (M Ed); education administration (M Ed); elementary education (M Ed, Ed S); instructional leadership (M Ed, Ed S), including instructional leadership, teacher leader (Ed S); library media (M Ed, Ed S); physical education and athletic training (M Ed, MAT), including physical education; school counseling (M Ed, Ed S), including counseling (Ed S), school counseling; secondary education (M Ed, MAT), including biology (MAT), English language arts (MAT), history (MAT), mathematics (MAT), physical education, science (MAT), secondary education (M Ed), social science (MAT); special education (M Ed, Ed S), including collaborative special education 6-12 (Ed S), collaborative special education K-6 (Ed S), special education (M Ed). *Accreditation:* NCATE. Part-time and evening/weekend programs available. Postbaccalaureate distance learning degree programs offered (no on-campus study). *Faculty:* 54 full-time (26 women), 73 part-time/adjunct (48 women). *Students:* 2,194 full-time (1,884 women), 234 part-time (182 women); includes 1,386 minority (1,336 Black or African American, non-Hispanic/Latino; 17 American Indian or Alaska Native, non-Hispanic/Latino; 4 Asian, non-Hispanic/Latino; 14 Hispanic/Latino; 15 Two or more races, non-Hispanic/Latino), 5 international. Average age 31. 840 applicants, 97% accepted, 519 enrolled. In 2013, 660 master's, 205 other advanced degrees awarded. *Degree requirements:* For master's, comprehensive exam, thesis optional. *Entrance requirements:* For master's, GRE General Test, MAT, minimum GPA of 2.75. Additional exam requirements/recommendations for international students: Required—TOEFL (minimum score 500 paper-based; 61 iBT). *Application deadline:* For fall admission, 8/12 priority date for domestic students; for spring admission, 3/24 for domestic students. Applications are processed on a rolling basis. Application fee: $25 ($50 for international students). Electronic applications accepted. Tuition and fees vary according to course load. *Financial support:* In 2013–14, 50 students received support, including 25 teaching assistantships (averaging $5,267 per year); career-related internships or fieldwork, Federal Work-Study, scholarships/grants, and unspecified assistantships also available. Support available to part-time students. Financial award application deadline: 3/1; financial award applicants required to submit FAFSA. *Unit head:* Dr. Reenay Rogers, Chair of Instructional Leadership and Support, 205-652-5423, Fax: 205-652-3706, E-mail: rrogers@uwa.edu. *Application contact:* Dr. Kathy Chandler, Dean of Graduate Studies, 205-652-3421, Fax: 205-652-3670, E-mail: kchandler@uwa.edu.

The University of Western Ontario, Faculty of Graduate Studies, Social Sciences Division, Faculty of Education, Program in Educational Studies, London, ON N6A 5B8, Canada. Offers curriculum studies (M Ed); educational policy studies (M Ed); educational psychology/special education (M Ed). Part-time programs available. *Faculty research:* Reflective practice, gender and schooling, feminist pedagogy, narrative inquiry, second language, multiculturalism in Canada, education and law.

University of West Florida, College of Professional Studies, Department of Applied Science, Technology and Administration, Pensacola, FL 32514-5750. Offers career and technical education (M Ed); curriculum and instruction (Ed S); curriculum and instruction: instructional technology (Ed D); educational leadership (M Ed), including education and training management; instructional technology (M Ed), including educational leadership, instructional technology. *Entrance requirements:* For master's, GRE, GMAT, or MAT, letter of intent, names of references. Additional exam requirements/recommendations for international students: Required—TOEFL (minimum score 550 paper-based). Electronic applications accepted.

University of West Florida, College of Professional Studies, Department of Research and Advanced Studies, Program in Curriculum and Instruction: Specialist in Education, Pensacola, FL 32514-5750. Offers Ed S. *Accreditation:* NCATE. Evening/weekend programs available. *Entrance requirements:* Additional exam requirements/recommendations for international students: Required—TOEFL (minimum score 550 paper-based).

University of West Florida, College of Professional Studies, School of Education, Program in Curriculum and Instruction, Pensacola, FL 32514-5750. Offers curriculum and instruction: special education (M Ed); elementary education (M Ed); primary education (M Ed). Part-time and evening/weekend programs available. *Entrance requirements:* For master's, GRE (minimum score 450 verbal) or MAT (minimum score 396) if bachelor's GPA less than 3.0, state teaching certification; letter of intent; two professional references. Additional exam requirements/recommendations for international students: Required—TOEFL (minimum score 550 paper-based).

University of Wisconsin–Madison, Graduate School, School of Education, Department of Curriculum and Instruction, Madison, WI 53706-1380. Offers art education (MA); curriculum and instruction (MS, PhD); education and mathematics (MA); French education (MA); German education (MA); music education (MS); science education (MS); Spanish education (MA). *Accreditation:* NASM (one or more programs are accredited). *Degree requirements:* For doctorate, thesis/dissertation. Application fee: $56. *Expenses:* Tuition, state resident: full-time $10,728; part-time $790 per credit. Tuition, nonresident: full-time $24,054; part-time $1623 per credit. *Required fees:* $1130; $119 per credit. *Financial support:* Project assistantships available. *Unit head:* Dr. Beth Graue, Chair, 608-263-4600, E-mail: graue@education.wisc.edu. *Application contact:* 608-262-2433, Fax: 608-262-5134, E-mail: gradadmiss@mail.bascom.wisc.edu.
Website: http://www.education.wisc.edu/ci.

University of Wisconsin–Milwaukee, Graduate School, School of Education, Department of Curriculum and Instruction, Milwaukee, WI 53201-0413. Offers curriculum planning and instruction improvement (MS); early childhood education (MS); elementary education (MS); junior high/middle school education (MS); reading education (MS); secondary education (MS); teaching in an urban setting (MS). Part-time programs available. *Faculty:* 18 full-time (13 women). *Students:* 17 full-time (10 women),

46 part-time (42 women); includes 15 minority (7 Black or African American, non-Hispanic/Latino; 1 Asian, non-Hispanic/Latino; 7 Two or more races, non-Hispanic/Latino), 1 international. Average age 32. 35 applicants, 69% accepted, 11 enrolled. In 2013, 31 master's awarded. *Degree requirements:* For master's, thesis or alternative. *Entrance requirements:* Additional exam requirements/recommendations for international students: Required—TOEFL (minimum score 550 paper-based; 79 iBT), IELTS (minimum score 6.5). *Application deadline:* For fall admission, 1/1 priority date for domestic students; for spring admission, 9/1 for domestic students. Applications are processed on a rolling basis. Application fee: $56 ($96 for international students). Electronic applications accepted. *Financial support:* In 2013–14, 1 fellowship was awarded; research assistantships, teaching assistantships, career-related internships or fieldwork, health care benefits, unspecified assistantships, and project assistantships also available. Support available to part-time students. Financial award application deadline: 4/15; financial award applicants required to submit FAFSA. *Unit head:* Raquel Oxford, Department Chair, 414-229-4884, Fax: 414-229-5571, E-mail: roxford@uwm.edu. *Application contact:* General Information Contact, 414-229-4982, Fax: 414-229-6967, E-mail: gradschool@uwm.edu.
Website: http://www.uwm.edu/SOE/.

University of Wisconsin–Milwaukee, Graduate School, School of Education, Urban Education Doctoral Program, Milwaukee, WI 53201-0413. Offers adult, continuing and higher education leadership (PhD); curriculum and instruction (PhD); educational administration (PhD); exceptional education (PhD); multicultural studies (PhD); social foundations of education (PhD). *Students:* 51 full-time (37 women), 40 part-time (25 women); includes 32 minority (16 Black or African American, non-Hispanic/Latino; 1 American Indian or Alaska Native, non-Hispanic/Latino; 3 Asian, non-Hispanic/Latino; 5 Hispanic/Latino; 7 Two or more races, non-Hispanic/Latino), 3 international. Average age 41. 25 applicants, 44% accepted, 4 enrolled. In 2013, 11 doctorates awarded. *Degree requirements:* For doctorate, comprehensive exam, thesis/dissertation. *Entrance requirements:* For doctorate, GRE General Test, minimum undergraduate GPA of 2.85, graduate 3.5. Additional exam requirements/recommendations for international students: Required—TOEFL (minimum score 550 paper-based; 79 iBT), IELTS (minimum score 6.5). *Application deadline:* For fall admission, 1/1 priority date for domestic students; for spring admission, 9/1 for domestic students. Applications are processed on a rolling basis. Application fee: $56 ($96 for international students). Electronic applications accepted. *Financial support:* In 2013–14, 11 fellowships, 1 teaching assistantship were awarded; research assistantships, career-related internships or fieldwork, health care benefits, unspecified assistantships, and project assistantships also available. Support available to part-time students. Financial award application deadline: 4/15; financial award applicants required to submit FAFSA. *Unit head:* Raji Swaminathan, Representative, 414-229-6740, Fax: 414-229-2920, E-mail: swaminar@uwm.edu. *Application contact:* General Information Contact, 414-229-4982, Fax: 414-229-6967, E-mail: gradschool@uwm.edu.
Website: http://www4.uwm.edu/soe/academics/urban_ed/.

University of Wisconsin–Oshkosh, Graduate Studies, College of Education and Human Services, Department of Curriculum and Instruction, Oshkosh, WI 54901. Offers MSE. Part-time and evening/weekend programs available. *Degree requirements:* For master's, thesis or alternative, seminar paper. *Entrance requirements:* For master's, teaching license, letters of recommendation. Additional exam requirements/recommendations for international students: Required—TOEFL (minimum score 550 paper-based; 79 iBT). Electronic applications accepted. *Faculty research:* Early childhood, middle school teaching, literacy, elementary teaching, bilingual education.

University of Wisconsin–Superior, Graduate Division, Department of Teacher Education, Program in Instruction, Superior, WI 54880-4500. Offers MSE. Part-time and evening/weekend programs available. *Faculty:* 3 full-time (2 women). *Students:* 5 full-time (4 women). Average age 34. 4 applicants. In 2013, 3 master's awarded. *Degree requirements:* For master's, comprehensive exam, thesis or alternative, research project. *Entrance requirements:* For master's, minimum GPA of 2.75, teaching certificate. *Application deadline:* For fall admission, 4/1 priority date for domestic students; for spring admission, 10/15 priority date for domestic students. Applications are processed on a rolling basis. Application fee: $56. Electronic applications accepted. *Expenses:* Tuition, state resident: full-time $4526; part-time $649.24 per credit. Tuition, nonresident: full-time $9091; part-time $1156.51 per credit. *Financial support:* Career-related internships or fieldwork, Federal Work-Study, institutionally sponsored loans, scholarships/grants, and tuition waivers (partial) available. Support available to part-time students. Financial award application deadline: 4/15; financial award applicants required to submit FAFSA. *Unit head:* Dr. Suzanne Griffith, Coordinator, 715-394-8316, E-mail: sgriffit@uwsuper.edu. *Application contact:* Suzie Finckler, Student Status Examiner, 715-394-8295, Fax: 715-394-8371, E-mail: gradstudy@uwsuper.edu.
Website: http://www.uwsuper.edu/.

University of Wisconsin–Whitewater, School of Graduate Studies, College of Education and Professional Studies, Department of Curriculum and Instruction, Whitewater, WI 53190-1790. Offers professional development (MS), including bilingual education, challenging advanced learners, curriculum and instruction, educational leadership, health, human performance and recreation, health, physical education and coaching, information technologies and libraries, reading. *Accreditation:* NCATE. Part-time and evening/weekend programs available. Postbaccalaureate distance learning degree programs offered. *Degree requirements:* For master's, thesis or integrated project. *Entrance requirements:* Additional exam requirements/recommendations for international students: Required—TOEFL (minimum score 550 paper-based; 80 iBT), IELTS (minimum score 6). Electronic applications accepted. *Faculty research:* Hybrid of exercise physiology and psychology; gender equity; education, pedagogy, and technology; comprehensive school health education.

University of Wyoming, College of Education, Programs in Curriculum and Instruction, Laramie, WY 82071. Offers MA, Ed D, PhD. Part-time programs available. Postbaccalaureate distance learning degree programs offered. Terminal master's awarded for partial completion of doctoral program. *Degree requirements:* For master's, comprehensive exam, thesis; for doctorate, comprehensive exam, thesis/dissertation. *Entrance requirements:* For master's, minimum GPA of 3.0, 3 letters of reference, writing samples; for doctorate, accredited master's degree, 3 letters of reference, 3 years of teaching experience, writing sample. Additional exam requirements/recommendations for international students: Required—TOEFL (minimum score 525 paper-based). *Faculty research:* Teaching and learning teacher education, multi-cultural education, early childhood, discipline-specific pedagogy.

Utah State University, School of Graduate Studies, Emma Eccles Jones College of Education and Human Services, Doctoral Program in Education, Logan, UT 84322. Offers business information systems (Ed D, PhD); curriculum and instruction (Ed D, PhD); research and evaluation (PhD). *Degree requirements:* For doctorate, comprehensive exam, thesis/dissertation. *Entrance requirements:* For doctorate, GRE General Test, minimum GPA of 3.0, master's degree. Additional exam requirements/recommendations for international students: Required—TOEFL. Electronic applications accepted. *Faculty research:* Language and literacy development, math and science education, instructional technology, hearing problems/deafness, domestic violence and animal abuse.

Virginia Polytechnic Institute and State University, Graduate School, College of Liberal Arts and Human Sciences, Blacksburg, VA 24061. Offers career and technical education (MS Ed, Ed D, PhD, Ed S); communication (MA); counselor education (MA Ed, Ed D, PhD, Ed S); creative writing (MFA); curriculum and instruction (MA Ed, Ed D, PhD, Ed S); educational leadership and policy studies (MA Ed, Ed D, PhD, Ed S); educational research and evaluation (PhD); English (MA); foreign languages, cultures, and literatures (MA); higher education and student affairs (MA Ed); history (MA); human development (MS, PhD); material culture and public humanities (MA); philosophy (MA); political science (MA); rhetoric and writing (PhD); science and technology studies (MS, PhD); social, political, ethical, and cultural thought (PhD); sociology (MS, PhD); theater arts (MFA). *Faculty:* 410 full-time (211 women), 6 part-time/adjunct (5 women). *Students:* 688 full-time (464 women), 576 part-time (372 women); includes 243 minority (144 Black or African American, non-Hispanic/Latino; 3 American Indian or Alaska Native, non-Hispanic/Latino; 29 Asian, non-Hispanic/Latino; 48 Hispanic/Latino; 1 Native Hawaiian or other Pacific Islander, non-Hispanic/Latino; 18 Two or more races, non-Hispanic/Latino), 84 international. Average age 34. 1,054 applicants, 48% accepted, 374 enrolled. In 2013, 314 master's, 74 doctorates, 14 other advanced degrees awarded. *Degree requirements:* For master's, comprehensive exam (for some programs), thesis (for some programs); for doctorate, comprehensive exam (for some programs), thesis/dissertation (for some programs). *Entrance requirements:* For master's and doctorate, GRE/GMAT (may vary by department). Additional exam requirements/recommendations for international students: Required—TOEFL (minimum score 550 paper-based). *Application deadline:* For fall admission, 8/1 for domestic students, 4/1 for international students; for spring admission, 1/1 for domestic students, 9/1 for international students. Applications are processed on a rolling basis. Application fee: $75. Electronic applications accepted. *Expenses:* Tuition, state resident: full-time $11,185; part-time $621.50 per credit hour. Tuition, nonresident: full-time $22,146; part-time $1230.25 per credit hour. *Required fees:* $2442; $449.25 per semester. Tuition and fees vary according to course load, campus/location and program. *Financial support:* In 2013–14, 19 research assistantships with full tuition reimbursements (averaging $17,115 per year), 205 teaching assistantships with full tuition reimbursements (averaging $14,433 per year) were awarded. Financial award application deadline: 3/1; financial award applicants required to submit FAFSA. *Total annual research expenditures:* $6.8 million. *Unit head:* Joan Hirt, Interim Dean, 540-231-6779, Fax: 540-231-7157, E-mail: jbhirt@vt.edu. *Application contact:* Melissa Elliott, Executive Assistant, 540-231-6779, Fax: 540-231-7157, E-mail: elliott1@vt.edu.
Website: http://www.clahs.vt.edu/.

Walden University, Graduate Programs, Richard W. Riley College of Education and Leadership, Minneapolis, MN 55401. *Accreditation:* NCATE. Part-time and evening/weekend programs available. Postbaccalaureate distance learning degree programs offered (minimal on-campus study). *Faculty:* 23 full-time (15 women), 830 part-time/adjunct (569 women). *Students:* 8,671 full-time (7,197 women), 2,122 part-time (1,735 women); includes 4,734 minority (3,802 Black or African American, non-Hispanic/Latino; 50 American Indian or Alaska Native, non-Hispanic/Latino; 136 Asian, non-Hispanic/Latino; 539 Hispanic/Latino; 35 Native Hawaiian or other Pacific Islander, non-Hispanic/Latino; 172 Two or more races, non-Hispanic/Latino), 73 international. Average age 40. 2,646 applicants, 96% accepted, 2074 enrolled. In 2013, 2,214 master's, 354 doctorates, 479 other advanced degrees awarded. *Degree requirements:* For doctorate, thesis/dissertation (for some programs), residency; for other advanced degree, residency (for some programs). *Entrance requirements:* For master's, bachelor's degree or higher; minimum GPA of 2.5; official transcripts; goal statement (for some programs); access to computer and Internet; for doctorate, master's degree or higher; three years of related professional or academic experience (preferred); minimum GPA of 3.0; goal statement and current resume (select programs); official transcripts; access to computer and Internet; for other advanced degree, relevant work experience; access to computer and Internet. Additional exam requirements/recommendations for international students: Required—TOEFL (minimum score 550 paper-based; 79 iBT), IELTS (minimum score 6.5), Michigan English Language Assessment Battery (minimum score 82), or PTE. *Application deadline:* Applications are processed on a rolling basis. Application fee: $0. Electronic applications accepted. *Expenses:* *Tuition:* Full-time $11,813.55; part-time $500 per credit. *Required fees:* $618.76. *Financial support:* In 2013–14, 1 fellowship was awarded; Federal Work-Study, scholarships/grants, unspecified assistantships, and family tuition reduction, active duty/veteran tuition reduction, group tuition reduction, interest-free payment plans, employee tuition reduction also available. Support available to part-time students. Financial award applicants required to submit FAFSA. *Unit head:* Dr. Kate Steffens, Dean, 800-925-3368. *Application contact:* Jennifer Hall, Vice President of Enrollment Management, 866-4-WALDEN, E-mail: info@waldenu.edu.
Website: http://www.waldenu.edu/colleges-schools/riley-college-of-education/.

Walla Walla University, Graduate School, School of Education and Psychology, College Place, WA 99324-1198. Offers counseling psychology (MA); curriculum and instruction (M Ed, MA, MAT); educational leadership (M Ed, MA, MAT); literacy instruction (M Ed, MA, MAT); students at risk (M Ed, MA, MAT); teaching (MAT). Part-time programs available. *Entrance requirements:* For master's, GRE General Test, minimum GPA of 2.75. Additional exam requirements/recommendations for international students: Required—TOEFL (minimum score 550 paper-based; 79 iBT). Electronic applications accepted. *Faculty research:* Admissions/retention, instructional psychology, moral development, teaching of reading.

Washburn University, College of Arts and Sciences, Department of Education, Topeka, KS 66621. Offers curriculum and instruction (M Ed); educational leadership (M Ed); reading (M Ed); special education (M Ed). *Accreditation:* NCATE. Part-time programs available. *Faculty:* 7 full-time (5 women). *Students:* 32 part-time (21 women). Average age 33. In 2013, 9 master's awarded. *Degree requirements:* For master's, comprehensive exam, thesis or alternative, portfolio, comprehensive paper, or action research project. *Entrance requirements:* For master's, department exam, GRE General Test, or MAT, minimum GPA of 3.0 in graduate coursework or last 60 hours of undergraduate coursework. Additional exam requirements/recommendations for international students: Required—TOEFL (minimum score 80 iBT). *Application deadline:* For fall admission, 8/1 for domestic and international students; for spring admission, 11/1 for domestic and international students. Applications are processed on a rolling basis. *Expenses:* Tuition, state resident: full-time $5850; part-time $325 per credit hour. Tuition, nonresident: full-time $11,916; part-time $662 per credit hour. *Required fees:* $86; $43 per semester. Tuition and fees vary according to program. *Financial support:* Federal Work-Study, institutionally sponsored loans, and scholarships/grants available. Support available to part-time students. Financial award applicants required to submit FAFSA. *Faculty research:* Reading/literature/literacy, foundations, special education, diversity, teaching and technology. *Unit head:* Dr. Donna Lalonde, Interim Chairperson, 785-670-1943, Fax: 785-670-1046, E-mail: donna.lalonde@washburn.edu. *Application contact:* Tara Porter, Licensure Officer, 785-670-1434, Fax: 785-670-1046, E-mail: tara.porter@washburn.edu.
Website: http://www.washburn.edu/academics/college-schools/arts-sciences/departments/education.

Washington State University, Graduate School, College of Education, Department of Teaching and Learning, Program in Curriculum and Instruction, Pullman, WA 99164. Offers Ed M, MA. *Degree requirements:* For master's, comprehensive exam (for some

programs), thesis (for some programs), written or oral exam. *Entrance requirements:* For master's, minimum GPA of 3.0, letters of recommendation, transcripts, resume/ curriculum vitae, personal statement. Additional exam requirements/recommendations for international students: Required—TOEFL (minimum score 550 paper-based; 80 iBT). Electronic applications accepted. *Faculty research:* Second language acquisition, ethnographic approaches to language-minority education programs and language policies in public schools, language and education in culturally and linguistically diverse settings using ethnographic and sociolinguistic perspectives.

Washington State University Spokane, Graduate Programs, Education Department, Spokane, WA 99210. Offers curriculum and instruction (Ed M); educational leadership (Ed M, MA); principal (Certificate); program administrator (Certificate); superintendent (Certificate); teaching (MIT), including elementary, secondary. *Degree requirements:* For master's, comprehensive exam (for some programs), thesis (for some programs). *Entrance requirements:* For master's, GRE or GMAT, minimum GPA of 3.0, 3 letters of recommendation, resume. Additional exam requirements/recommendations for international students: Required—TOEFL (minimum score 550 paper-based).

Waynesburg University, Graduate and Professional Studies, Canonsburg, PA 15370. Offers business (MBA), including energy management, finance, health systems, human resources, leadership, market development; counseling (MA), including addictions counseling, clinical mental health; education (M Ed, MAT), including autism (M Ed), curriculum and instruction (M Ed), educational leadership (M Ed), online teaching (M Ed); nursing (MSN), including administration, education, informatics; nursing practice (DNP); special education (M Ed); technology (M Ed); MSN/MBA. *Accreditation:* AACN. Part-time and evening/weekend programs available. *Faculty:* 11 full-time (5 women), 136 part-time/adjunct (80 women). *Students:* 146 full-time (99 women), 419 part-time (268 women). In 2013, 290 master's, 7 doctorates awarded. *Degree requirements:* For doctorate, thesis/dissertation. *Entrance requirements:* Additional exam requirements/ recommendations for international students: Required—TOEFL. *Application deadline:* For fall admission, 8/1 priority date for domestic students. Applications are processed on a rolling basis. Electronic applications accepted. *Financial support:* Available to part-time students. Application deadline: 5/1. *Unit head:* David Mariner, Dean, 724-743-4420, Fax: 724-743-4425, E-mail: dmariner@waynesburg.edu. *Application contact:* Dr. Michael Bednarski, Director of Enrollment, 724-743-4420, Fax: 724-743-4425, E-mail: mbednars@waynesburg.edu.
Website: http://www.waynesburg.edu/.

Wayne State College, School of Education and Counseling, Department of Educational Foundations and Leadership, Program in Curriculum and Instruction, Wayne, NE 68787. Offers alternative education (MSE); business and information technology education (MSE); communication arts education (MSE); early childhood education (MSE); elementary education (MSE); English as a second language (MSE); English education (MSE); family and consumer sciences education (MSE); industrial technology and vocational education (MSE); learning communities (MSE); mathematics education (MSE); music education (MSE); science education (MSE); social science education (MSE). *Accreditation:* NCATE. Part-time and evening/weekend programs available. *Degree requirements:* For master's, comprehensive exam, thesis optional. *Entrance requirements:* For master's, GRE General Test. Additional exam requirements/ recommendations for international students: Required—TOEFL (minimum score 550 paper-based).

Wayne State University, College of Education, Division of Administrative and Organizational Studies, Detroit, MI 48202. Offers college and university teaching (Certificate); educational administration and supervision (Ed S); educational leadership (M Ed); educational leadership and policy studies (Ed D, PhD); educational technology (Certificate); instructional technology (M Ed, Ed D, PhD, Ed S); online teaching (Certificate); secondary curriculum and instruction (Ed S); special education administration (Ed S). Part-time programs available. Postbaccalaureate distance learning degree programs offered. *Students:* 96 full-time (68 women), 207 part-time (137 women); includes 133 minority (115 Black or African American, non-Hispanic/Latino; 4 American Indian or Alaska Native, non-Hispanic/Latino; 2 Asian, non-Hispanic/Latino; 8 Hispanic/Latino; 4 Two or more races, non-Hispanic/Latino), 14 international. Average age 39. 127 applicants, 50% accepted, 42 enrolled. In 2013, 47 master's, 15 doctorates, 41 other advanced degrees awarded. *Degree requirements:* For doctorate, thesis/ dissertation. *Entrance requirements:* For master's, baccalaureate degree from accredited U.S. institution or equivalent from college or university of government-recognized standing; minimum undergraduate GPA of 2.75 in upper-division coursework; for doctorate, GRE or MAT, interview; autobiography or curriculum vitae; references; master's degree; minimum undergraduate GPA of 3.0, graduate 3.75; 3 years of relevant experience; foundational course work; for other advanced degree, master's degree from accredited institution, minimum upper-division GPA of 2.6 or 3.4 master's, fulfillment of the special requirements of the area of concentration, 3 years of teaching experience (except for instructional technology). Additional exam requirements/recommendations for international students: Required—TOEFL (minimum score 550 paper-based; 79 iBT), Michigan English Language Assessment Battery (minimum score 85); Recommended—IELTS (minimum score 6.5), TWE (minimum score 5.5). *Application deadline:* For fall admission, 6/1 priority date for domestic students, 5/1 priority date for international students; for winter admission, 10/1 priority date for domestic students, 9/1 priority date for international students; for spring admission, 2/1 priority date for domestic students, 1/1 priority date for international students. Applications are processed on a rolling basis. Application fee: $0. Electronic applications accepted. *Expenses:* Tuition, state resident: part-time $554.15 per credit. Tuition, nonresident: part-time $1200.35 per credit. *Required fees:* $42.15 per credit. $268.30 per semester. Tuition and fees vary according to course load and program. *Financial support:* In 2013–14, 48 students received support, including 3 fellowships with tuition reimbursements available (averaging $15,541 per year), 4 research assistantships with tuition reimbursements available (averaging $16,508 per year); career-related internships or fieldwork, Federal Work-Study, scholarships/grants, health care benefits, and unspecified assistantships also available. Support available to part-time students. Financial award application deadline: 3/31; financial award applicants required to submit FAFSA. *Faculty research:* Total quality management, participatory management, administering educational technology, school improvement, principalship. *Total annual research expenditures:* $6,888. *Unit head:* Dr. William Hill, Assistant Dean, 313-577-9316, E-mail: william_e_hill@wayne.edu. *Application contact:* Janice Green, Assistant Dean, 313-577-1605, E-mail: jwgreen@wayne.edu.
Website: http://coe.wayne.edu/aos/index.php.

Wayne State University, College of Education, Division of Teacher Education, Detroit, MI 48202. Offers art education (M Ed), including art therapy; autism spectrum disorders (Certificate); bilingual/bicultural education (M Ed, Certificate); career and technical education (M Ed, Certificate); cognitive impairment (Certificate); curriculum and instruction (Ed D, PhD, Ed S), including art education (PhD), bilingual education (Ed D, Ed S), bilingual-bicultural education (PhD), career and technical education (MAT, Ed D, PhD, Ed S), early childhood education (MAT, Ed D, PhD, Ed S), elementary education, English as a second language (MAT, Ed D, Ed S), English education (MAT, Ed D, PhD, Ed S), foreign language education (MAT, PhD), K-12 curriculum, mathematics education (MAT, Ed D, PhD, Ed S), science education (MAT, Ed D, PhD, Ed S), secondary education, social studies education (MAT, Ed S), social studies education: secondary (Ed D, PhD); early childhood education (M Ed, Certificate); elementary education (M Ed, MAT), including children's literature (MAT), early childhood education (MAT, Ed D, PhD, Ed S), general elementary education (MAT); elementary or secondary education (MAT), including bilingual/bicultural education, English as a second language (MAT, Ed D, Ed S), mathematics education (MAT, Ed D, PhD, Ed S), science education (MAT, Ed D, PhD, Ed S), social studies education (MAT, Ed S); emotionally impaired (Certificate); English as a second language (Certificate); English education (M Ed), including secondary; foreign language education (M Ed); K-12 reading specialist (Certificate); learning disabilities (Certificate); mathematics education (M Ed), including secondary; reading (M Ed, Ed S); reading, language and literature (Ed D); science education (M Ed), including secondary; secondary education (MAT), including art education (K-12), career and technical education (MAT, Ed D, PhD, Ed S), English education (MAT, Ed D, PhD, Ed S), foreign language education (MAT, PhD), kinesiology; social studies education (M Ed), including secondary; special education (M Ed, MAT, Ed D, PhD, Ed S); visual arts education (Certificate). Part-time programs available. *Faculty:* 36 full-time (25 women), 55 part-time/adjunct (43 women). *Students:* 218 full-time (163 women), 448 part-time (344 women); includes 218 minority (177 Black or African American, non-Hispanic/Latino; 2 American Indian or Alaska Native, non-Hispanic/ Latino; 11 Asian, non-Hispanic/Latino; 19 Hispanic/Latino; 1 Native Hawaiian or other Pacific Islander, non-Hispanic/Latino; 8 Two or more races, non-Hispanic/Latino), 10 international. Average age 37. 258 applicants, 30% accepted, 52 enrolled. In 2013, 183 master's, 10 doctorates, 35 other advanced degrees awarded. *Degree requirements:* For master's, thesis, essay or project (for some M Ed programs), professional field experience (for MAT programs); for doctorate, thesis/dissertation. *Entrance requirements:* For master's, Michigan Basic Skills Test (MA in teaching), admission to the graduate school, verification of participation in group work with children and Michigan State Police Criminal Background check; for doctorate, minimum undergraduate GPA of 3.0, graduate 3.5; interview, curriculum vitae; references. Additional exam requirements/recommendations for international students: Required—TOEFL (minimum score 550 paper-based; 79 iBT), TWE (minimum score 5.5), Michigan English Language Assessment Battery (minimum score 85); Recommended—IELTS (minimum score 6.5). *Application deadline:* For fall admission, 6/1 priority date for domestic students, 5/1 priority date for international students; for winter admission, 10/1 priority date for domestic students, 9/1 priority date for international students; for spring admission, 2/1 priority date for domestic students, 1/1 priority date for international students. Applications are processed on a rolling basis. Application fee: $0. Electronic applications accepted. *Expenses:* Tuition, state resident: part-time $554.15 per credit. Tuition, nonresident: part-time $1200.35 per credit. *Required fees:* $42.15 per credit. $268.30 per semester. Tuition and fees vary according to course load and program. *Financial support:* In 2013–14, 83 students received support, including 1 fellowship (averaging $16,842 per year), 1 research assistantship with tuition reimbursement available (averaging $21,229 per year); career-related internships or fieldwork, Federal Work-Study, scholarships/grants, health care benefits, and unspecified assistantships also available. Support available to part-time students. Financial award application deadline: 3/31; financial award applicants required to submit FAFSA. *Faculty research:* Improving students' skill achievement in mathematics; improving elementary children's understanding of informational text; teachers' use of their pedagogical and mathematical knowledge in the interactive work of teaching; the intersection of identity construction in teaching and learning; identifying effective methods of literacy instruction and assessments for bilingual students in elementary language arts classrooms. *Total annual research expenditures:* $368,105. *Unit head:* Dr. Kathleen Crawford-McKinney, Assistant Dean, 313-577-0122. *Application contact:* Janice Green, Assistant Dean, 313-577-1605, E-mail: jwgreen@wayne.edu.
Website: http://coe.wayne.edu/ted/index.php.

Weber State University, Jerry and Vickie Moyes College of Education, Program in Curriculum and Instruction, Ogden, UT 84408-1001. Offers M Ed. *Accreditation:* NCATE. Part-time and evening/weekend programs available. *Faculty:* 17 full-time (11 women). *Students:* 14 full-time (10 women), 146 part-time (110 women); includes 4 minority (2 American Indian or Alaska Native, non-Hispanic/Latino; 2 Hispanic/Latino), 3 international. Average age 37. 60 applicants, 97% accepted, 50 enrolled. In 2013, 38 master's awarded. *Degree requirements:* For master's, thesis or alternative, project presentation and exam. *Entrance requirements:* For master's, MAT or GRE, minimum GPA of 3.0 in last 90 credits. Additional exam requirements/recommendations for international students: Required—TOEFL (minimum score 550 paper-based). *Application deadline:* For fall admission, 5/1 priority date for domestic students; for spring admission, 11/1 priority date for domestic students. Applications are processed on a rolling basis. Application fee: $60 ($90 for international students). *Expenses:* Tuition, state resident: full-time $7118; part-time $253 per credit hour. Tuition, nonresident: full-time $12,480; part-time $634 per credit hour. *Required fees:* $34.33; $34.33 per credit hour. $257 per semester. Full-time tuition and fees vary according to course load. *Financial support:* In 2013–14, 17 students received support. Institutionally sponsored loans, scholarships/grants, tuition waivers (full), and unspecified assistantships available. Support available to part-time students. Financial award application deadline: 4/1; financial award applicants required to submit FAFSA. *Faculty research:* Special needs, best practices in education literacy, metacognition. *Unit head:* Dr. Peggy Saunders, Director, 801-626-7673, Fax: 801-626-7427, E-mail: psaunders@weber.edu. *Application contact:* Dr. Peggy Saunders, Director, 801-626-7673, Fax: 801-626-7427, E-mail: psaunders@weber.edu.
Website: http://www.weber.edu/education/.

Western Connecticut State University, Division of Graduate Studies, School of Professional Studies, Department of Education and Educational Psychology, Curriculum Option, Danbury, CT 06810-6885. Offers MS. Part-time programs available. *Degree requirements:* For master's, thesis or alternative, thesis research project or 3 extra classes and comprehensive exam, completion of program in 6 years. *Entrance requirements:* For master's, minimum GPA of 2.8 or MAT, teaching certificate in elementary or secondary education. Additional exam requirements/recommendations for international students: Recommended—TOEFL (minimum score 550 paper-based; 79 iBT), IELTS (minimum score 6). *Faculty research:* Teaching various methods of instruction that include class discussions, lectures, independent projects, cooperative learning, experiential learning and field studies, recitals, demonstrations, shows, group projects, and technology-enhanced instruction.

Western New England University, College of Arts and Sciences, Program in Curriculum and Instruction, Springfield, MA 01119. Offers M Ed. Part-time and evening/ weekend programs available. Postbaccalaureate distance learning degree programs offered. *Faculty:* 3 full-time (2 women). *Students:* 25 part-time (17 women); includes 2 minority (1 Black or African American, non-Hispanic/Latino; 1 Asian, non-Hispanic/ Latino). Average age 34. 5 applicants. In 2013, 21 master's awarded. *Entrance requirements:* For master's, initial license for elementary teaching, two letters of recommendation, official transcript, resume, personal statement. Additional exam requirements/recommendations for international students: Required—TOEFL. *Application deadline:* Applications are processed on a rolling basis. Application fee: $30. Electronic applications accepted. Tuition and fees vary according to program. *Financial support:* Application deadline: 4/15; applicants required to submit FAFSA. *Unit head:*

Dr. Saeed Ghahramani, Dean, 413-782-1218, Fax: 413-796-2118, E-mail: sghahram@wne.edu. *Application contact:* Matthew Fox, Director of Recruiting and Marketing for Adult Learners, 413-782-1517, Fax: 413-782-1779, E-mail: study@wne.edu. Website: http://www1.wne.edu/artsandsciences/index.cfm?selection-doc.1672.

West Texas A&M University, College of Education and Social Sciences, Department of Education, Program in Curriculum and Instruction, Canyon, TX 79016-0001. Offers M Ed. Part-time and evening/weekend programs available. Postbaccalaureate distance learning degree programs offered. *Degree requirements:* For master's, comprehensive exam, thesis optional. *Entrance requirements:* For master's, GRE General Test, 18 semester hours of education course work. Additional exam requirements/recommendations for international students: Required—TOEFL (minimum score 550 paper-based). Electronic applications accepted.

West Virginia University, College of Human Resources and Education, Department of Curriculum and Instruction/Literacy Studies, Morgantown, WV 26506. Offers curriculum and instruction (Ed D); elementary education (MA); reading (MA); secondary education (MA), including higher education curriculum and teaching, secondary education; special education (Ed D), including special education. *Accreditation:* NCATE. Part-time and evening/weekend programs available. *Degree requirements:* For doctorate, comprehensive exam, thesis/dissertation. *Entrance requirements:* For master's, minimum GPA of 2.75; for doctorate, GRE General Test or MAT, 3 letters of recommendation, curriculum vitae. Additional exam requirements/recommendations for international students: Required—TOEFL. *Faculty research:* Teacher education, curriculum development, educational technology, curriculum assessment.

Wichita State University, Graduate School, College of Education, Department of Curriculum and Instruction, Wichita, KS 67260. Offers curriculum and instruction (M Ed); special education (M Ed), including adaptive, early childhood unified (M Ed, MAT), functional, gifted; teaching (MAT), including curriculum and instruction, early childhood unified (M Ed, MAT). *Accreditation:* NCATE. Part-time and evening/weekend programs available. *Entrance requirements:* For master's, MAT, minimum GPA of 2.75. *Unit head:* Dr. Janice Ewing, Chairperson, 316-978-3322, E-mail: janice.ewing@wichita.edu. *Application contact:* Jordan Oleson, Admission Coordinator, 316-978-3095, Fax: 316-978-3253, E-mail: jordan.oleson@wichita.edu.

Wilkes University, College of Graduate and Professional Studies, School of Education, Wilkes-Barre, PA 18766-0002. Offers art and science of teaching (MS Ed); classroom technology (MS Ed); early childhood literacy (MS Ed); educational development and strategies (MS Ed); educational leadership (MS Ed); educational technology (Ed D); higher education administration (Ed D); instructional media (MS Ed); instructional technology (MS Ed); international school leadership (MS Ed); K-12 administration (Ed D); middle level education (MS Ed); online teaching (MS Ed); reading (MS Ed); school business leadership (MS Ed); secondary education (MS Ed), including biology, chemistry, English, history, mathematics; special education (MS Ed); teaching English as a second language (MS Ed); twenty-first century teaching and learning (MS Ed). Part-time and evening/weekend programs available. Postbaccalaureate distance learning degree programs offered (minimal on-campus study). *Students:* 46 full-time (37 women), 1,410 part-time (1,039 women); includes 67 minority (12 Black or African American, non-Hispanic/Latino; 2 American Indian or Alaska Native, non-Hispanic/Latino; 11 Asian, non-Hispanic/Latino; 28 Hispanic/Latino; 1 Native Hawaiian or other Pacific Islander, non-Hispanic/Latino; 13 Two or more races, non-Hispanic/Latino), 6 international. Average age 34. In 2013, 852 master's, 10 doctorates awarded. *Entrance requirements:* Additional exam requirements/recommendations for international students: Required—TOEFL (minimum score 550 paper-based; 79 iBT). *Application deadline:* Applications are processed on a rolling basis. Application fee: $45. Electronic applications accepted. *Expenses:* Contact institution. *Financial support:* Federal Work-Study and unspecified assistantships available. Financial award application deadline: 3/1; financial award applicants required to submit FAFSA. *Unit head:* Dr. Rhonda Waskiewicz, Interim Dean, Education, 570-408-4332, Fax: 570-408-7872, E-mail: rhonda.waskiewicz@wilkes.edu. *Application contact:* Joanne Thomas, Interim Director

of Graduate Education, 570-408-4234, Fax: 570-408-7846, E-mail: joanne.thomas1@wilkes.edu.
Website: http://www.wilkes.edu/pages/383.asp.

William Woods University, Graduate and Adult Studies, Fulton, MO 65251-1098. Offers administration (M Ed, Ed S); athletic/activities administration (M Ed); curriculum and instruction (M Ed, Ed S); educational leadership (Ed D); equestrian education (M Ed); health management (MBA); human resources (MBA); leadership (MBA); marketing, advertising, and public relations (MBA); teaching and technology (M Ed). Part-time and evening/weekend programs available. *Faculty:* 231 part-time/adjunct (87 women). *Students:* 418 full-time (276 women), 716 part-time (433 women); includes 51 minority (34 Black or African American, non-Hispanic/Latino; 4 American Indian or Alaska Native, non-Hispanic/Latino; 5 Asian, non-Hispanic/Latino; 3 Hispanic/Latino; 5 Two or more races, non-Hispanic/Latino), 4 international. Average age 35. In 2013, 507 master's, 8 doctorates, 143 other advanced degrees awarded. *Degree requirements:* For master's, capstone course (MBA), action research (M Ed); for Ed S, field experience. *Entrance requirements:* Additional exam requirements/recommendations for international students: Required—TOEFL (minimum score 550 paper-based). *Application deadline:* Applications are processed on a rolling basis. Application fee: $0. Electronic applications accepted. *Expenses:* Contact institution. *Financial support:* Institutionally sponsored loans available. Financial award applicants required to submit FAFSA. *Unit head:* Dr. Michael Westerfield, Vice President and Dean of the Graduate College, 573-592-4383, Fax: 573-592-1164. *Application contact:* Jessica Brush, Director of Operations, 573-592-4227, Fax: 573-592-1164, E-mail: jessica.brush@williamwoods.ede.
Website: http://www.williamwoods.edu/evening_programs/index.asp.

Wright State University, School of Graduate Studies, College of Education and Human Services, Department of Educational Leadership, Program in Advanced Educational Leadership, Dayton, OH 45435. Offers advanced curriculum and instruction (Ed S); higher education-adult education (Ed S); superintendent (Ed S). *Accreditation:* NCATE. *Degree requirements:* For Ed S, thesis. *Entrance requirements:* For degree, GRE General Test, MAT. Additional exam requirements/recommendations for international students: Required—TOEFL.

Wright State University, School of Graduate Studies, College of Education and Human Services, Department of Educational Leadership, Programs in Educational Leadership, Dayton, OH 45435. Offers curriculum and instruction: teacher leader (MA); educational administrative specialist: teacher leader (M Ed); educational administrative specialist: vocational education administration (M Ed, MA); student affairs in higher education-administration (M Ed, MA). *Accreditation:* NCATE. *Degree requirements:* For master's, thesis (for some programs). *Entrance requirements:* For master's, GRE General Test, MAT. Additional exam requirements/recommendations for international students: Required—TOEFL.

Xavier University of Louisiana, Graduate School, Programs in Education, New Orleans, LA 70125-1098. Offers curriculum and instruction (MA); education administration and supervision (MA); guidance and counseling (MA). *Accreditation:* NCATE. Part-time and evening/weekend programs available. *Degree requirements:* For master's, comprehensive exam, thesis or alternative. *Entrance requirements:* For master's, GRE General Test, MAT, minimum GPA of 2.5. Additional exam requirements/recommendations for international students: Required—TOEFL.

Youngstown State University, Graduate School, Beeghly College of Education, Department of Teacher Education, Youngstown, OH 44555-0001. Offers adolescent/young adult education (MS Ed); content area concentration (MS Ed); early childhood education (MS Ed); educational technology (MS Ed); literacy (MS Ed); middle childhood education (MS Ed); special education (MS Ed), including gifted and talented education, special education. *Accreditation:* NCATE. Part-time and evening/weekend programs available. *Degree requirements:* For master's, comprehensive exam. *Entrance requirements:* For master's, GRE, MAT, or teaching certificate; minimum GPA of 2.7. Additional exam requirements/recommendations for international students: Required—TOEFL. *Faculty research:* Multicultural literacy, hands-on mathematics teaching, integrated instruction, reading comprehension, emergent curriculum.

Distance Education Development

American Public University System, AMU/APU Graduate Programs, Charles Town, WV 25414. Offers accounting (MBA, MS); criminal justice (MA), including business administration, emergency and disaster management, general (MA, MS); educational leadership (M Ed); emergency and disaster management (MA); entrepreneurship (MBA); environmental policy and management (MS), including environmental planning, environmental sustainability, fish and wildlife management, general (MA, MS), global environmental management; finance (MBA); general (MBA); global business management (MBA); history (MA), including American history, ancient and classical history, European history, global history, public history; homeland security (MA), including business administration, counter-terrorism studies, criminal justice, cyber, emergency management and public health, intelligence studies, transportation security; homeland security resource allocation (MBA); humanities (MA); information technology (MS), including digital forensics, enterprise software development, information assurance and security, IT project management; information technology management (MBA); intelligence studies (MA), including criminal intelligence, cyber, general (MA, MS), homeland security, intelligence analysis, intelligence collection, intelligence management, intelligence operations, terrorism studies; international relations and conflict resolution (MA), including comparative and security issues, conflict resolution, international and transnational security issues, peacekeeping; legal studies (MA); management (MA), including defense management, general (MA, MS), human resource management, organizational leadership, public administration; marketing (MBA); military history (MA), including American military history, American Revolution, civil war, war since 1945, World War II; military studies (MA), including joint warfare, strategic leadership; national security studies (MA), including general (MA, MS), homeland security, regional security studies, security and intelligence analysis, terrorism studies; nonprofit management (MBA); political science (MA), including American politics and government, comparative government and development, general (MA, MS), international relations, public policy; psychology (MA), including general (MA, MS), maritime engineering management, reverse logistics management; public administration (MPA), including disaster management, environmental policy, health policy, human resources, national security, organizational management, security management; public health (MPH); reverse logistics management (MA); school counseling (M Ed); security management (MA); space studies (MS), including aerospace science, general (MA, MS), planetary science; sports and health sciences (MS); teaching (M Ed), including

curriculum and instruction for elementary teachers, elementary reading, English language learners, instructional leadership, online learning, special education; transportation and logistics management (MA), including general (MA, MS), maritime engineering management, reverse logistics management. Programs offered via distance learning only. Part-time and evening/weekend programs available. Postbaccalaureate distance learning degree programs offered (no on-campus study). *Faculty:* 432 full-time (242 women), 1,722 part-time/adjunct (829 women). *Students:* 511 full-time (241 women), 10,947 part-time (4,294 women); includes 3,760 minority (2,058 Black or African American, non-Hispanic/Latino; 88 American Indian or Alaska Native, non-Hispanic/Latino; 293 Asian, non-Hispanic/Latino; 876 Hispanic/Latino; 91 Native Hawaiian or other Pacific Islander, non-Hispanic/Latino; 354 Two or more races, non-Hispanic/Latino), 134 international. Average age 36. In 2013, 3,323 master's awarded. *Degree requirements:* For master's, comprehensive exam or practicum. *Entrance requirements:* For master's, official transcript showing earned bachelor's degree from institution accredited by recognized accrediting body. Additional exam requirements/recommendations for international students: Required—TOEFL (minimum score 550 paper-based), IELTS (minimum score 6.5). *Application deadline:* Applications are processed on a rolling basis. Application fee: $0. Electronic applications accepted. *Expenses:* Tuition: Part-time $325 per semester hour. *Financial support:* Applicants required to submit FAFSA. *Faculty research:* Military history, criminal justice, management performance, national security. *Unit head:* Dr. Karan Powell, Executive Vice President and Provost, 877-468-6268, Fax: 304-724-3780. *Application contact:* Terry Grant, Vice President of Enrollment Management, 877-468-6268, Fax: 304-724-3780, E-mail: info@apus.edu.
Website: http://www.apus.edu.

Athabasca University, Centre for Distance Education, Athabasca, AB T9S 3A3, Canada. Offers distance education (MDE); distance education technology (Advanced Diploma). Part-time programs available. Postbaccalaureate distance learning degree programs offered (no on-campus study). *Degree requirements:* For master's, thesis optional. *Entrance requirements:* For master's, 3 or 4 year baccalaureate degree. Electronic applications accepted. *Expenses:* Contact institution. *Faculty research:* Role development, interaction, educational technology, and communities of practice in distance education; instructional design.

Distance Education Development

Barry University, School of Education, Graduate Certificate Programs, Miami Shores, FL 33161-6695. Offers advanced teaching and learning with technology (Certificate); distance education (Certificate); higher education technology integration (Certificate); human resources: not for profit and religious organizations (Certificate); K-12 technology integration (Certificate).

Brandeis University, Rabb School of Continuing Studies, Division of Graduate Professional Studies, Master of Science in Online Instructional Design and Technology Program, Waltham, MA 02454-9110. Offers MS. Part-time programs available. Postbaccalaureate distance learning degree programs offered (no on-campus study). *Faculty:* 2 full-time (1 woman), 33 part-time/adjunct (10 women). *Students:* Average age 35. *Entrance requirements:* For master's, four-year bachelor's degree from regionally-accredited U.S. institution or equivalent; official transcript(s) from every college or university attended; resume or curriculum vitae; statement of goals; letter of recommendation. Additional exam requirements/recommendations for international students: Required—TOEFL (minimum scores: 600 paper-based, 100 iBT), IELTS (7), or PTE. *Application deadline:* For fall admission, 7/15 priority date for domestic and international students; for spring admission, 11/15 priority date for domestic and international students; for summer admission, 3/15 priority date for domestic and international students. Applications are processed on a rolling basis. Electronic applications accepted. *Unit head:* Brian Salerno, Chair, 781-736-3443, Fax: 781-736-3420, E-mail: bsalerno@brandeis.edu. *Application contact:* Frances Stearns, Associate Director of Admissions and Student Services, 781-736-8785, Fax: 781-736-3420, E-mail: fstearns@brandeis.edu.
Website: http://www.brandeis.edu/gps.

Capella University, School of Education, Doctoral Programs in Education, Minneapolis, MN 55402. Offers curriculum and instruction (PhD); educational leadership and management (Ed D); instructional design for online learning (PhD); K-12 studies in education (PhD); leadership for higher education (PhD); leadership in educational administration (PhD); postsecondary and adult education (PhD); professional studies in education (PhD); reading and literacy (Ed D); special education leadership (PhD); training and performance improvement (PhD).

Capella University, School of Education, Master's Programs in Education, Minneapolis, MN 55402. Offers adult education (MS); curriculum and instruction (MS); early childhood education (MS); enrollment management (MS); higher education leadership and management (MS); instructional design for online learning (MS); integrative studies (MS); K-12 studies in education (MS); leadership in educational administration (MS); reading and literacy (MS); special education teaching (MS).

Chestnut Hill College, School of Graduate Studies, Program in Instructional Technology, Philadelphia, PA 19118-2693. Offers instructional design and e-learning (MS); instructional technology specialist (MS, CAS). Part-time and evening/weekend programs available. *Faculty:* 1 full-time (0 women), 4 part-time/adjunct (0 women). *Students:* 4 full-time (3 women), 8 part-time (4 women), 5 international. Average age 33. 3 applicants, 100% accepted. In 2013, 7 master's, 1 other advanced degree awarded. *Degree requirements:* For master's, special project/internship. *Entrance requirements:* For master's, GRE General Test or MAT, letters of recommendation, writing sample. Additional exam requirements/recommendations for international students: Required—TOEFL (minimum score 500 paper-based), IELTS (mnimum score 6.0), or TWE (minimum score 22). *Application deadline:* For fall admission, 7/1 for domestic and international students; for spring admission, 11/1 for domestic and international students; for summer admission, 4/1 for domestic students. Applications are processed on a rolling basis. *Expenses:* Contact institution. *Financial support:* Unspecified assistantships available. *Faculty research:* Instructional design, learning management systems and related technologies, video as a teaching and learning tool, Web 2.0 technologies and virtual worlds as a learning tool, utilization of laptops and iPads in the classroom. *Unit head:* Dr. Yefim Kats, Coordinator, 215-248-7008, Fax: 215-248-7155, E-mail: katsy@chc.edu. *Application contact:* Jayne Mashett, Director of Admissions, School of Graduate Studies, 215-248-7020, Fax: 215-248-7161, E-mail: gradadmissions@chc.edu.
Website: http://www.chc.edu/Graduate/Programs/Masters/Instructional_Technology/.

Colorado Christian University, Program in Curriculum and Instruction, Lakewood, CO 80226. Offers corporate education (MACI); early childhood educator (MACI); elementary educator (MACI); instructional technology (MACI); master educator (MACI); online course developer (MACI); online teaching and learning (MACI); special education generalist (MACI). Part-time and evening/weekend programs available. *Degree requirements:* For master's, thesis optional, practicum. *Entrance requirements:* For master's, interviews, letters of recommendation. Additional exam requirements/recommendations for international students: Required—TOEFL. Electronic applications accepted. *Expenses:* Contact institution.

Dallas Baptist University, Dorothy M. Bush College of Education, Teaching Program, Dallas, TX 75211-9299. Offers distance learning (MAT); early childhood (MAT); elementary (MAT); English as a second language (MAT); Montessori (MAT); multisensory (MAT); secondary (MAT). Part-time and evening/weekend programs available. *Entrance requirements:* For master's, GRE General Test, minimum GPA of 3.0. Additional exam requirements/recommendations for international students: Required—TOEFL, IELTS. *Application deadline:* Applications are processed on a rolling basis. Application fee: $25. Electronic applications accepted. *Expenses: Tuition:* Full-time $13,410; part-time $745 per credit hour. *Required fees:* $300; $150 per semester. Tuition and fees vary according to degree level. *Financial support:* Federal Work-Study, institutionally sponsored loans, scholarships/grants, and tuition waivers (full and partial) available. Support available to part-time students. Financial award applicants required to submit FAFSA. *Unit head:* Dr. Carolyn Spain, Director, 214-333-5217, E-mail: graduate@dbu.edu. *Application contact:* Kit P. Montgomery, Director of Graduate Programs, 214-333-5242, Fax: 214-333-5579, E-mail: graduate@dbu.edu.
Website: http://www3.dbu.edu/graduate/mat.asp.

East Carolina University, Graduate School, College of Education, Department of Mathematics, Science, and Instructional Technology Education, Greenville, NC 27858-4353. Offers computer-based instruction (Certificate); distance learning and administration (Certificate); instructional technology (MA Ed, MS); mathematics (MA Ed); performance improvement (Certificate); science education (MA, MA Ed); special endorsement in computer education (Certificate). Part-time and evening/weekend programs available. *Degree requirements:* For master's, comprehensive exam, thesis optional. *Entrance requirements:* For master's, GRE General Test or MAT, interview, minimum GPA of 2.5, bachelor's degree in related field, teaching license (MA Ed). Additional exam requirements/recommendations for international students: Required—TOEFL. *Expenses:* Tuition, state resident: full-time $4223. Tuition, nonresident: full-time $16,540. *Required fees:* $2184.

Endicott College, Van Loan School of Graduate and Professional Studies, Program in Integrative Education, Beverly, MA 01915-2096. Offers M Ed. Program offered in conjunction with The Institute for Educational Studies (TIES). Part-time and evening/weekend programs available. Postbaccalaureate distance learning degree programs offered (no on-campus study). *Degree requirements:* For master's, thesis. *Entrance requirements:* Additional exam requirements/recommendations for international students: Required—TOEFL. *Application deadline:* Applications are processed on a rolling basis. Application fee: $50. *Expenses:* Contact institution. *Financial support:* Tuition waivers (partial) available. Financial award applicants required to submit FAFSA. *Unit head:* Dr. Enid E. Larsen, Assistant Dean of Academic Programs, 978-232-2198, Fax: 978-232-3000, E-mail: elarsen@endicott.edu. *Application contact:* Dr. Phil Snow Gang, Academic Dean, 406-387-5107, Fax: 413-778-9644, E-mail: ties@endicott.edu.
Website: http://www.endicott.edu/VanLoan/Graduate-Studies/Master-Education/Integrative-Education.aspx.

Fairmont State University, Programs in Education, Fairmont, WV 26554. Offers digital media, new literacies and learning (M Ed); education (MAT); exercise science, fitness and wellness (M Ed); online learning (M Ed); professional studies (M Ed); reading (M Ed); special education (M Ed). *Accreditation:* NCATE. Part-time and evening/weekend programs available. Postbaccalaureate distance learning degree programs offered. *Faculty:* 18 part-time/adjunct (11 women). *Students:* 75 full-time (55 women), 120 part-time (96 women); includes 11 minority (5 Black or African American, non-Hispanic/Latino; 2 American Indian or Alaska Native, non-Hispanic/Latino; 1 Asian, non-Hispanic/Latino; 1 Hispanic/Latino; 2 Two or more races, non-Hispanic/Latino), 1 international. Average age 32. 69 applicants, 86% accepted, 45 enrolled. In 2013, 82 master's awarded. *Entrance requirements:* For master's, GRE. Additional exam requirements/recommendations for international students: Required—TOEFL. *Application deadline:* For fall admission, 5/1 for domestic and international students. Applications are processed on a rolling basis. Application fee: $40. *Expenses:* Tuition, state resident: full-time $6404; part-time $349 per credit hour. Tuition, nonresident: full-time $13,694; part-time $754 per credit hour. Part-time tuition and fees vary according to course load. *Financial support:* In 2013–14, 30 students received support. *Unit head:* Dr. Carolyn Crislip-Tacy, Interim Dean, School of Education, 304-367-4143, Fax: 304-367-4599, E-mail: carolyn.crislip-tacy@fairmontstate.edu. *Application contact:* Jack Kirby, Director of Graduate Studies, 304-367-4101, E-mail: jack.kirby@fairmontstate.edu.
Website: http://www.fairmontstate.edu/graduatestudies/default.asp.

The George Washington University, Graduate School of Education and Human Development, Department of Educational Leadership, Program in E-Learning, Washington, DC 20052. Offers Graduate Certificate. *Students:* 12 part-time (7 women); includes 3 minority (1 Black or African American, non-Hispanic/Latino; 1 Asian, non-Hispanic/Latino; 1 Hispanic/Latino). Average age 46. 6 applicants, 100% accepted, 4 enrolled. In 2013, 2 Graduate Certificates awarded. *Unit head:* Virginia Roach, Chair, 202-994-3094, E-mail: vroach@gwu.edu. *Application contact:* Sarah Lang, Director of Graduate Admissions, 202-994-1447, Fax: 202-994-7207, E-mail: slang@gwu.edu.
Website: http://gsehd.gwu.edu/e-learning-certificate.

Jones International University, School of Education, Centennial, CO 80112. Offers adult education (M Ed); corporate training and knowledge management (M Ed); curriculum and instruction (M Ed), including elementary teacher licensure, secondary teacher licensure; e-learning technology and design (M Ed); educational leadership and administration (M Ed); educational leadership and administration: principal and administrator licensure (M Ed); elementary curriculum instruction and assessment (M Ed); higher education leadership and administration (M Ed); K-12 instructional technology (M Ed); K-12 instructional technology: teacher licensure (M Ed); secondary curriculum instruction and assessment (M Ed); technology and design (M Ed). Part-time and evening/weekend programs available. Postbaccalaureate distance learning degree programs offered (no on-campus study). *Entrance requirements:* For master's, minimum cumulative GPA of 2.5. Additional exam requirements/recommendations for international students: Recommended—TOEFL (minimum score 550 paper-based). Electronic applications accepted.

Keiser University, Master of Science in Education Program, Ft. Lauderdale, FL 33309. Offers allied health teaching and leadership (MS Ed); career college administration (MS Ed); leadership (MS Ed); online teaching and learning (MS Ed); teaching and learning (MS Ed). Part-time programs available. Postbaccalaureate distance learning degree programs offered (no on-campus study).

Lesley University, School of Education, Cambridge, MA 02138-2790. Offers arts, community, and education (M Ed); autism studies (Certificate); curriculum and instruction (M Ed, CAGS); early childhood education (M Ed); ecological teaching and learning (MS); educational studies (PhD), including adult learning, educational leadership, individually designed; elementary education (M Ed); emergent technologies for educators (Certificate); ESLArts: language learning through the arts (M Ed); high school education (M Ed); individually designed (M Ed); integrated teaching through the arts (M Ed); literacy for K-8 classroom teachers (M Ed); mathematics education (M Ed); middle school education (M Ed); moderate disabilities (M Ed); online learning (Certificate); reading (CAGS); science in education (M Ed); severe disabilities (M Ed); special needs (CAGS); specialist teacher of reading (M Ed); teacher of visual art (M Ed); technology in education (M Ed, CAGS). *Accreditation:* Teacher Education Accreditation Council. Part-time and evening/weekend programs available. Postbaccalaureate distance learning degree programs offered (no on-campus study). *Faculty:* 40 full-time (30 women), 104 part-time/adjunct (77 women). *Students:* 453 full-time (381 women), 1,672 part-time (1,435 women); includes 284 minority (139 Black or African American, non-Hispanic/Latino; 11 American Indian or Alaska Native, non-Hispanic/Latino; 38 Asian, non-Hispanic/Latino; 58 Hispanic/Latino; 5 Native Hawaiian or other Pacific Islander, non-Hispanic/Latino; 33 Two or more races, non-Hispanic/Latino), 22 international. Average age 35. In 2013, 1,137 master's, 18 doctorates, 51 other advanced degrees awarded. *Degree requirements:* For master's, practicum; for doctorate, thesis/dissertation. *Entrance requirements:* For master's, Massachusetts Tests for Educator Licensure (MTEL), transcripts, statement of purpose, recommendations; interview (for special education); for doctorate, GRE General Test, transcripts, statement of purpose, recommendations, interview, master's degree, resume; for other advanced degree, interview, master's degree. Additional exam requirements/recommendations for international students: Required—TOEFL (minimum score 550 paper-based; 80 iBT). *Application deadline:* Applications are processed on a rolling basis. Application fee: $50. Electronic applications accepted. *Expenses: Tuition:* Part-time $900 per credit. *Financial support:* In 2013–14, 15 fellowships (averaging $3,600 per year) were awarded; career-related internships or fieldwork, Federal Work-Study, scholarships/grants, tuition waivers, and unspecified assistantships also available. Financial award application deadline: 4/15; financial award applicants required to submit FAFSA. *Faculty research:* Assessment in literacy, mathematics and science; autism spectrum disorders; instructional technology and online learning; multicultural education and English language learners. *Unit head:* Dr. Jack Gillette, Dean, 617-349-8401, Fax: 617-349-8607, E-mail: jgillett@lesley.edu. *Application contact:* Martha Sheehan, Director of Admissions, 888-LESLEYU, Fax: 617-349-8313, E-mail: info@lesley.edu.
Website: http://www.lesley.edu/soe.html.

Liberty University, School of Education, Lynchburg, VA 24515. Offers administration and supervision (M Ed); curriculum and instruction (Ed D, Ed S); early childhood education (M Ed); educational leadership (Ed D, Ed S); educational technology and online instruction (M Ed); elementary education (M Ed, MAT); English (M Ed); gifted education (M Ed); history (M Ed); leadership (M Ed); math specialist (M Ed); middle

grades (M Ed, MAT); outdoor adventure sport (MS); reading specialist (M Ed); school counseling (M Ed); secondary education (MAT); special education (M Ed, MAT); sport management (MS), including administration, outdoor recreation, sport management, tourism; sports administration (MS); student service (M Ed); teaching and learning (M Ed); tourism (MS). *Accreditation:* NCATE. Part-time programs available. Postbaccalaureate distance learning degree programs offered (minimal on-campus study). *Students:* 2,241 full-time (1,639 women), 4,413 part-time (3,240 women); includes 2,052 minority (1,588 Black or African American, non-Hispanic/Latino; 37 American Indian or Alaska Native, non-Hispanic/Latino; 67 Asian, non-Hispanic/Latino; 173 Hispanic/Latino; 37 Native Hawaiian or other Pacific Islander, non-Hispanic/Latino; 150 Two or more races, non-Hispanic/Latino), 15 international. Average age 37. 6,185 applicants, 43% accepted, 1603 enrolled. In 2013, 1,256 master's, 117 doctorates, 470 other advanced degrees awarded. *Degree requirements:* For doctorate, comprehensive exam, thesis/dissertation. *Entrance requirements:* For master's, GRE General Test or MAT (if taken in or before 1999), 2 letters of recommendation, minimum undergraduate GPA of 3.0, curriculum vitae; for doctorate and Ed S, GRE General Test or MAT (if taken before 1999), minimum master's GPA of 3.0, 3 years of teaching experience. Additional exam requirements/recommendations for international students: Required—TOEFL (minimum score 600 paper-based; 100 iBT). *Application deadline:* For fall admission, 6/1 for domestic students; for spring admission, 11/1 for domestic students. Applications are processed on a rolling basis. Application fee: $50. Electronic applications accepted. *Expenses:* Contact institution. *Financial support:* Federal Work-Study and tuition waivers (partial) available. *Faculty research:* Self-determination, character education, bibliotherapy, learning styles, distance education. *Unit head:* Dr. Karen L. Parker, Dean, 434-582-2195, Fax: 434-582-2468, E-mail: kparker@liberty.edu. *Application contact:* Jay Bridge, Director of Graduate Admissions, 800-424-9595, Fax: 800-628-7977, E-mail: gradadmissions@liberty.edu.
Website: http://www.liberty.edu/academics/education/graduate/.

National University, Academic Affairs, School of Education, La Jolla, CA 92037-1011. Offers applied behavior analysis (Certificate); applied school leadership (MS); autism (Certificate); best practices (Certificate); e-teaching and learning (Certificate); early childhood education (Certificate); education (MA), including best practices (M Ed, MA), e-teaching and learning (M Ed, MA), education technology, teacher leadership (M Ed, MA), teaching and learning in a global society (M Ed, MA), teaching mathematics (M Ed, MA); education with preliminary multiple or single subject (M Ed), including best practices (M Ed, MA), e-teaching and learning (M Ed, MA), educational technology (M Ed, MA), teacher leadership (M Ed, MA), teaching and learning in a global society (M Ed, MA), teaching mathematics (M Ed, MA); educational administration (MS); educational and instructional technology (MS); educational counseling (MS); educational technology (Certificate); higher education administration (MS); innovative school leadership (MS); instructional leadership (MS); juvenile justice special education (MS); reading (Certificate); school psychology (MS); special education (MS), including deaf and hard-of-hearing, mild/moderate disabilities, moderate/severe disabilities; teacher leadership (Certificate); teaching (MA), including applied behavioral analysis, autism, best practices (M Ed, MA), e-teaching and learning (M Ed, MA), early childhood education, educational technology (M Ed, MA), reading, special education, teacher leadership (M Ed, MA), teaching and learning in a global society (M Ed, MA), teaching mathematics (M Ed, MA); teaching mathematics (Certificate). Part-time and evening/weekend programs available. Postbaccalaureate distance learning degree programs offered (no on-campus study). *Faculty:* 72 full-time (43 women), 287 part-time/adjunct (170 women). *Students:* 2,433 full-time (1,744 women), 2,017 part-time (1,371 women); includes 1,834 minority (358 Black or African American, non-Hispanic/Latino; 15 American Indian or Alaska Native, non-Hispanic/Latino; 250 Asian, non-Hispanic/Latino; 1,056 Hispanic/Latino; 29 Native Hawaiian or other Pacific Islander, non-Hispanic/Latino; 126 Two or more races, non-Hispanic/Latino), 1 international. Average age 34. 1,339 applicants, 100% accepted, 1035 enrolled. In 2013, 1,662 master's awarded. *Degree requirements:* For master's, thesis (for some programs). *Entrance requirements:* For master's, interview, minimum GPA of 2.5. Additional exam requirements/recommendations for international students: Required—TOEFL (minimum score 550 paper-based; 79 iBT), IELTS (minimum score 6). *Application deadline:* Applications are processed on a rolling basis. Application fee: $60 ($65 for international students). Electronic applications accepted. *Expenses: Tuition:* Full-time $13,824; part-time $1728 per course. One-time fee: $160. *Financial support:* Career-related internships or fieldwork, institutionally sponsored loans, scholarships/grants, and tuition waivers (partial) available. Support available to part-time students. Financial award application deadline: 6/30. *Faculty research:* Teacher education, special education, educational effectiveness, teaching abroad, school counseling. *Unit head:* School of Education, 800-628-8648, E-mail: soe@nu.edu. *Application contact:* Louis Cruz, Interim Vice President for Enrollment Services, 800-628-8648, E-mail: advisor@nu.edu.
Website: http://www.nu.edu/OurPrograms/SchoolOfEducation.html.

New Mexico State University, Graduate School, College of Education, Online Teaching and Learning Program, Las Cruces, NM 88003-8001. Offers Graduate Certificate. *Students:* 5 full-time (4 women), 18 part-time (15 women); includes 7 minority (1 American Indian or Alaska Native, non-Hispanic/Latino; 5 Hispanic/Latino; 1 Two or more races, non-Hispanic/Latino), 1 international. Average age 45. 4 applicants, 75% accepted, 1 enrolled. In 2013, 8 Graduate Certificates awarded. *Degree requirements:* For Graduate Certificate, thesis optional, practicum. *Entrance requirements:* Additional exam requirements/recommendations for international students: Required—TOEFL (minimum score 550 paper-based; 79 iBT), IELTS (minimum score 6.5). Application fee: $40 ($50 for international students). *Expenses:* Tuition, state resident: full-time $5398; part-time $224.90 per credit. Tuition, nonresident: full-time $18,821; part-time $784.20 per credit. *Required fees:* $1310; $54.60 per credit. *Financial support:* In 2013–14, 3 students received support, including 2 research assistantships (averaging $13,790 per year); Federal Work-Study, health care benefits, and unspecified assistantships also available. *Unit head:* Susie Bussman, Director of Instructional Innovation and Quality, 575-646-1650, E-mail: suceppib@nmsu.edu. *Application contact:* Coordinator, 575-646-2736, Fax: 575-646-7721, E-mail: gradinfo@nmsu.edu.
Website: http://otl.nmsu.edu/.

New York Institute of Technology, School of Education, Department of Instructional Technology, Old Westbury, NY 11568-8000. Offers computers in education (Advanced Certificate); distance learning (Advanced Certificate); emerging technologies for training (Advanced Certificate); instructional design for global e-learning (Advanced Certificate); instructional technology (MS); virtual education (Advanced Certificate). Part-time and evening/weekend programs available. Postbaccalaureate distance learning degree programs offered (minimal on-campus study). *Faculty:* 6 full-time (3 women), 38 part-time/adjunct (20 women). *Students:* 10 full-time (8 women), 111 part-time (74 women); includes 30 minority (12 Black or African American, non-Hispanic/Latino; 4 Asian, non-Hispanic/Latino; 13 Hispanic/Latino; 1 Two or more races, non-Hispanic/Latino), 3 international. Average age 32. 58 applicants, 76% accepted, 31 enrolled. In 2013, 67 master's, 1 other advanced degree awarded. *Degree requirements:* For master's, thesis. *Entrance requirements:* For master's, minimum QPA of 3.0; for Advanced Certificate, master's degree, minimum GPA of 3.0, 3 years of teaching experience, New York teaching certificate, 2 letters of recommendation. Additional exam requirements/recommendations for international students: Required—TOEFL (minimum score 550 paper-based; 79 iBT), IELTS (minimum score 6). *Application deadline:* For fall admission, 7/1 priority date for domestic students, 6/1 for international students; for spring admission, 12/1 priority date for domestic students, 12/1 for international students. Applications are processed on a rolling basis. Application fee: $50. Electronic applications accepted. *Expenses: Tuition:* Full-time $18,900; part-time $1050 per credit. *Financial support:* Research assistantships with partial tuition reimbursements, career-related internships or fieldwork, scholarships/grants, health care benefits, tuition waivers (full and partial), and unspecified assistantships available. Support available to part-time students. Financial award applicants required to submit FAFSA. *Faculty research:* Integration of information and communication technologies (ICTs) and social media into learning environments, urban K-12 teachers' effective use of technology to enhance student achievement, instructional design for online instruction, STEM education for K-12 teachers, collaborative and performance-based approaches to pedagogy and technology integration in the K-12 classroom, online learning in higher education. *Unit head:* Dr. Sarah McPherson, Department Chairperson, 516-686-1053, Fax: 516-686-7655, E-mail: smcphers@nyit.edu. *Application contact:* Alice Dolitsky, Director, Graduate Admissions, 516-686-7520, Fax: 516-686-1116, E-mail: nyitgrad@nyit.edu.
Website: http://www.nyit.edu/education/instructional_technology.

Nova Southeastern University, Abraham S. Fischler School of Education, North Miami Beach, FL 33162. Offers education (MS, Ed D, Ed S); instructional design and diversity education (MS); instructional technology and distance education (MS); speech language pathology (MS, SLPD); teaching and learning (MA). Part-time and evening/weekend programs available. Postbaccalaureate distance learning degree programs offered. *Faculty:* 120 full-time (73 women), 279 part-time/adjunct (208 women). *Students:* 2,970 full-time (2,377 women), 3,619 part-time (2,946 women); includes 3,896 minority (2,352 Black or African American, non-Hispanic/Latino; 21 American Indian or Alaska Native, non-Hispanic/Latino; 90 Asian, non-Hispanic/Latino; 1,348 Hispanic/Latino; 6 Native Hawaiian or other Pacific Islander, non-Hispanic/Latino; 79 Two or more races, non-Hispanic/Latino), 39 international. Average age 40. 2,794 applicants, 53% accepted, 968 enrolled. In 2013, 1,103 master's, 426 doctorates, 349 other advanced degrees awarded. *Degree requirements:* For master's, practicum, internship; for doctorate, thesis/dissertation; for Ed S, thesis, practicum, internship. *Entrance requirements:* For master's, MAT or GRE (for some programs), CLAST, PRAXIS I, CBEST, General Knowledge Test, teaching certification, minimum GPA of 2.5, verification of teaching, BS; for doctorate, MAT or GRE, master's degree, minimum cumulative GPA of 3.0; for Ed S, MAT or GRE, master's degree, teaching certificate; minimum GPA of 3.0. Additional exam requirements/recommendations for international students: Recommended—TOEFL (minimum score 550 paper-based; 80 iBT), IELTS (minimum score 6). *Application deadline:* Applications are processed on a rolling basis. Application fee: $50. Electronic applications accepted. *Financial support:* In 2013–14, 68 students received support. Career-related internships or fieldwork and Federal Work-Study available. Support available to part-time students. Financial award application deadline: 4/15; financial award applicants required to submit FAFSA. *Faculty research:* Instructional technology and distance education, educational leadership, speech language pathology, quality of life. *Total annual research expenditures:* $1.8 million. *Unit head:* Dr. H. Wells Singleton, Provost/Dean, 954-262-8730, Fax: 954-262-3894, E-mail: singlew@nova.edu. *Application contact:* Dr. Timothy Shields, Dean of Student Affairs, 800-986-3223 Ext. 8500, E-mail: shieldsd@nova.edu.
Website: http://www.fischlerschool.nova.edu/.

Oklahoma State University, Graduate College, Stillwater, OK 74078. Offers aerospace security (Graduate Certificate); bioenergy and sustainable technology (Graduate Certificate); bioinformatics (Graduate Certificate); business data mining (Graduate Certificate); business sustainability (Graduate Certificate); engineering and technology management (Graduate Certificate); entrepreneurship (Graduate Certificate); environmental science (MS); global issues (Graduate Certificate); grassland management (Graduate Certificate); information assurance (Graduate Certificate); interdisciplinary sciences (MS); interdisciplinary toxicology (Graduate Certificate); international studies (MS); non-profit management (Graduate Certificate); online teaching (Graduate Certificate); photonics (PhD); plant science (PhD); teaching English to speakers of other languages (Graduate Certificate); telecommunications management (MS). Programs are interdisciplinary. *Faculty:* 4 full-time (2 women), 2 part-time/adjunct (1 woman). *Students:* 74 full-time (58 women), 147 part-time (74 women); includes 44 minority (12 Black or African American, non-Hispanic/Latino; 8 American Indian or Alaska Native, non-Hispanic/Latino; 10 Asian, non-Hispanic/Latino; 6 Hispanic/Latino; 8 Two or more races, non-Hispanic/Latino), 43 international. Average age 32. 495 applicants, 70% accepted, 75 enrolled. In 2013, 55 master's, 11 doctorates awarded. *Degree requirements:* For master's, thesis (for some programs); for doctorate, comprehensive exam, thesis/dissertation. *Entrance requirements:* For master's and doctorate, GRE or GMAT. Additional exam requirements/recommendations for international students: Required—TOEFL (minimum score 550 paper-based; 79 iBT). *Application deadline:* For fall admission, 3/1 priority date for international students; for spring admission, 8/1 priority date for international students. Applications are processed on a rolling basis. Application fee: $40 ($75 for international students). Electronic applications accepted. *Expenses:* Tuition, state resident: full-time $4272; part-time $178 per credit hour. Tuition, nonresident: full-time $17,472; part-time $709 per credit hour. *Required fees:* $2413.20; $100.55 per credit hour. One-time fee: $50 full-time. Part-time tuition and fees vary according to course load and campus/location. *Financial support:* Career-related internships or fieldwork, Federal Work-Study, scholarships/grants, health care benefits, tuition waivers (partial), and unspecified assistantships available. Support available to part-time students. Financial award application deadline: 3/1; financial award applicants required to submit FAFSA. *Unit head:* Dr. Sheryl Tucker, Dean, 405-744-7099, Fax: 405-744-0355, E-mail: grad-i@okstate.edu. *Application contact:* Dr. Susan Mathew, Coordinator of Admissions, 405-744-6368, Fax: 405-744-0355, E-mail: grad-i@okstate.edu.
Website: http://gradcollege.okstate.edu/.

Post University, Program in Education, Waterbury, CT 06723-2540. Offers education (M Ed); higher education administration (M Ed); instructional design and technology (M Ed); online teaching (M Ed); teaching and learning (M Ed); TESOL (teaching English to speakers of other languages) (M Ed). Postbaccalaureate distance learning degree programs offered.

Regent University, Graduate School, School of Education, Virginia Beach, VA 23464-9800. Offers adult education (Ed D, PhD); advanced educational leadership (Ed D, PhD); career switcher with licensure (M Ed), including alternative licensure; character education (Ed D, PhD); Christian education leadership (Ed D); Christian school administration (M Ed); curriculum and instruction (M Ed); distance education (Ed D, PhD); educational leadership (M Ed); educational leadership - special education (Ed S); educational psychology (Ed D); elementary education (M Ed); higher education (Ed D, PhD); higher education leadership and management (Ed D); K-12 school leadership (Ed D, PhD); leadership in mathematics education (M Ed); reading specialist (M Ed); special education (M Ed, Ed D, PhD); student affairs (M Ed); TESOL (M Ed), including adult education, PreK-12. *Accreditation:* Teacher Education Accreditation Council. Part-time and evening/weekend programs available. Postbaccalaureate distance learning degree programs offered (minimal on-campus study). *Faculty:* 25 full-time (12 women),

50 part-time/adjunct (31 women). *Students:* 100 full-time (78 women), 754 part-time (614 women); includes 225 minority (191 Black or African American, non-Hispanic/Latino; 1 American Indian or Alaska Native, non-Hispanic/Latino; 7 Asian, non-Hispanic/Latino; 26 Hispanic/Latino), 16 international. Average age 39. 487 applicants, 63% accepted, 233 enrolled. In 2013, 202 master's, 19 doctorates awarded. *Degree requirements:* For master's, thesis or alternative; for doctorate, comprehensive exam, thesis/dissertation. *Entrance requirements:* For master's, MAT, minimum undergraduate GPA of 2.75, writing sample, resume, recommendations, interview; for doctorate, GRE, writing sample, 3 years of relevant professional experience, master's-level paper, copies of published work, resume, transcripts, interview, recommendations. Additional exam requirements/recommendations for international students: Required—TOEFL (minimum score 577 paper-based). *Application deadline:* For fall admission, 4/1 priority date for domestic students; for spring admission, 10/15 priority date for domestic students. Applications are processed on a rolling basis. Application fee: $50. Electronic applications accepted. Tuition and fees vary according to course load and degree level. *Financial support:* Fellowships, career-related internships or fieldwork, scholarships/grants, tuition waivers (full and partial), and unspecified assistantships available. Support available to part-time students. Financial award application deadline: 4/1; financial award applicants required to submit FAFSA. *Faculty research:* Character development and discipline for children, education leadership development, diversity in schools, classroom management, technology in education settings. *Unit head:* Dr. Alan Arroyo, Dean, 757-352-4261, Fax: 757-352-4318, E-mail: alanarr@regent.edu. *Application contact:* Matthew Chadwick, Director of Enrollment Support Services, 800-373-5504, Fax: 757-352-4381, E-mail: admissions@regent.edu.
Website: http://www.regent.edu/education/.

Saginaw Valley State University, College of Education, Program in E-Learning, University Center, MI 48710. Offers MA. Part-time and evening/weekend programs available. *Students:* 2 full-time (both women), 2 part-time (1 woman); includes 1 minority (American Indian or Alaska Native, non-Hispanic/Latino), 1 international. Average age 41. 2 applicants. In 2013, 4 master's awarded. *Degree requirements:* For master's, capstone course or thesis. *Entrance requirements:* For master's, minimum GPA of 3.0. Additional exam requirements/recommendations for international students: Required—TOEFL (minimum score 550 paper-based; 79 iBT). *Application deadline:* For fall admission, 7/15 for international students; for winter admission, 11/15 for international students; for spring admission, 4/15 for international students. Application fee: $30 ($80 for international students). *Expenses:* Tuition, state resident: full-time $8933; part-time $496.30 per credit hour. Tuition, nonresident: full-time $16,806; part-time $933.65 per credit hour. *Required fees:* $263; $14.60 per credit hour. Tuition and fees vary according to degree level. *Financial support:* Federal Work-Study and scholarships/grants available. Support available to part-time students. *Unit head:* Dr. Mary Harmon, Dean, 989-964-7107, Fax: 989-964-4563, E-mail: coeconnect@svsu.edu. *Application contact:* Jenna Briggs, Director, Graduate and International Admissions, 989-964-6096, Fax: 989-964-2788, E-mail: gradadm@svsu.edu.

Télé-université, Graduate Programs, Québec, QC G1K 9H5, Canada. Offers computer science (PhD); corporate finance (MS); distance learning (MS). Part-time programs available.

Thomas Edison State College, Heavin School of Arts and Sciences, Program in Online Learning and Teaching, Trenton, NJ 08608-1176. Offers Graduate Certificate. Part-time programs available. Postbaccalaureate distance learning degree programs offered (no on-campus study). *Entrance requirements:* Additional exam requirements/recommendations for international students: Required—TOEFL (minimum score 550 paper-based; 79 iBT). Electronic applications accepted.

University of Colorado Denver, School of Education and Human Development, Information and Learning Technologies Program, Denver, CO 80217-3364. Offers e-learning design and implementation (MA); instructional design and adult learning (MA); K-12 teaching (MA). Part-time and evening/weekend programs available. Postbaccalaureate distance learning degree programs offered (no on-campus study). *Students:* 60 full-time (49 women), 59 part-time (43 women); includes 16 minority (2 Black or African American, non-Hispanic/Latino; 3 Asian, non-Hispanic/Latino; 10 Hispanic/Latino; 1 Two or more races, non-Hispanic/Latino), 1 international. Average age 38. 32 applicants, 88% accepted, 23 enrolled. In 2013, 47 master's awarded. *Degree requirements:* For master's, comprehensive exam (for some programs), comprehensive exam or online portfolio; 30 credit hours. *Entrance requirements:* For master's, GRE or MAT (if GPA is below 2.75), resume, statement of intent, three letters of recommendation. Additional exam requirements/recommendations for international students: Required—TOEFL (minimum score 537 paper-based; 75 iBT); Recommended—IELTS (minimum score 6.5). *Application deadline:* For fall admission, 5/15 for domestic students, 5/1 for international students; for spring admission, 11/15 for domestic students, 11/1 for international students. Application fee: $50 ($75 for international students). *Expenses:* Contact institution. *Financial support:* In 2013–14, 2 students received support. Fellowships, research assistantships, teaching assistantships, Federal Work-Study, institutionally sponsored loans, scholarships/grants, and traineeships available. Financial award application deadline: 4/1; financial award applicants required to submit FAFSA. *Faculty research:* Technology for educational management, instructional design foundations, e-Learning, educational design. *Unit head:* Brent Wilson, Professor, 303-315-4963, E-mail: brent.wilson@ucdenver.edu. *Application contact:* Hans Broers, Academic Advisor, 303-315-6351, Fax: 303-315-6311, E-mail: hans.broers@ucdenver.edu.
Website: http://www.ucdenver.edu/academics/colleges/SchoolOfEducation/Academics/MASTERS/ILT/Pages/default.aspx.

University of Maryland, Baltimore County, Graduate School, College of Arts, Humanities and Social Sciences, Department of Education, Program in Instructional Systems Development, Halethorpe, MD 21227. Offers distance education (Graduate Certificate); instructional design for e-learning (Graduate Certificate); instructional systems development (MA, Graduate Certificate); instructional technology (Graduate Certificate). Part-time and evening/weekend programs available. Postbaccalaureate distance learning degree programs offered (no on-campus study). *Faculty:* 2 full-time (0 women), 13 part-time/adjunct (6 women). *Students:* 4 full-time (3 women), 155 part-time (118 women); includes 61 minority (48 Black or African American, non-Hispanic/Latino; 3 Asian, non-Hispanic/Latino; 4 Hispanic/Latino; 1 Native Hawaiian or other Pacific Islander, non-Hispanic/Latino; 5 Two or more races, non-Hispanic/Latino), 2 international. Average age 37. 88 applicants, 91% accepted, 60 enrolled. In 2013, 28 master's, 57 other advanced degrees awarded. *Degree requirements:* For master's, comprehensive exam (for some programs), portfolio (for some programs). *Entrance requirements:* Additional exam requirements/recommendations for international students: Required—TOEFL (minimum score 550 paper-based; 80 iBT). *Application deadline:* For fall admission, 6/1 priority date for domestic students, 1/1 priority date for international students; for spring admission, 11/1 priority date for domestic students, 6/1 for international students; for summer admission, 3/1 priority date for domestic students. Applications are processed on a rolling basis. Application fee: $50. Electronic applications accepted. One-time fee: $200 full-time. *Financial support:* Applicants required to submit FAFSA. *Faculty research:* E-learning, distance education, instructional design. *Unit head:* Dr. Greg Williams, Graduate Program Director, 443-543-5447, Fax: 443-543-5096, E-mail: gregw@umbc.edu. *Application contact:* Renee Eisenhuth, Graduate Program Coordinator, 443-543-5446, Fax: 443-543-5096, E-mail: reisen@umbc.edu.
Website: http://www.umbc.edu/isd.

University of Maryland University College, Graduate School of Management and Technology, Program in Distance Education, Adelphi, MD 20783. Offers MDE, Certificate. Part-time and evening/weekend programs available. Postbaccalaureate distance learning degree programs offered (no on-campus study). *Students:* 3 full-time (2 women), 175 part-time (128 women); includes 79 minority (65 Black or African American, non-Hispanic/Latino; 2 Asian, non-Hispanic/Latino; 9 Hispanic/Latino; 3 Two or more races, non-Hispanic/Latino), 26 international. Average age 41. 92 applicants, 100% accepted, 41 enrolled. In 2013, 22 master's, 35 other advanced degrees awarded. *Degree requirements:* For master's, thesis or alternative. *Application deadline:* Applications are processed on a rolling basis. Application fee: $50. Electronic applications accepted. *Financial support:* Federal Work-Study and scholarships/grants available. Support available to part-time students. Financial award application deadline: 6/1; financial award applicants required to submit FAFSA. *Unit head:* Dr. Stella Porto, Director, 240-684-2400, Fax: 240-684-2401, E-mail: stella.porto@umuc.edu. *Application contact:* Coordinator, Graduate Admissions, 800-888-8682, Fax: 240-684-2151, E-mail: newgrad@umuc.edu.
Website: http://www.umuc.edu/grad/mde/mde.shtml.

University of South Florida, University College/Distance Education, Tampa, FL 33620-9951. *Unit head:* Kathy Barnes, Interdisciplinary Programs Coordinator, 813-974-8031, Fax: 813-974-7061, E-mail: barnesk@usf.edu. *Application contact:* Karen Tylinski, Metro Initiatives, 813-974-9943, Fax: 813-974-7061, E-mail: ktylinsk@usf.edu.
Website: http://uc.usf.edu/.

Virginia Polytechnic Institute and State University, VT Online, Blacksburg, VA 24061. Offers advanced transportation systems (Certificate); aerospace engineering (MS); agricultural and life sciences (MSLFS); business information systems (Graduate Certificate); career and technical education (MS); civil engineering (MS); computer engineering (M Eng, MS); decision support systems (Graduate Certificate); eLearning leadership (MA); electrical engineering (M Eng, MS); engineering administration (MEA); environmental engineering (Certificate); environmental politics and policy (Graduate Certificate); environmental sciences and engineering (MS); foundations of political analysis (Graduate Certificate); health product risk management (Graduate Certificate); industrial and systems engineering (MS); information policy and society (Graduate Certificate); information security (Graduate Certificate); information technology (MIT); instructional technology (MA); integrative STEM education (MA Ed); liberal arts (Graduate Certificate); life sciences: health product risk management (MS); natural resources (MNR, Graduate Certificate); networking (Graduate Certificate); nonprofit and nongovernmental organization management (Graduate Certificate); ocean engineering (MS); political science (MA); security studies (Graduate Certificate); software development (Graduate Certificate). *Expenses:* Tuition, state resident: full-time $11,185; part-time $621.50 per credit hour. Tuition, nonresident: full-time $22,146; part-time $1230.25 per credit hour. *Required fees:* $2442; $449.25 per semester. Tuition and fees vary according to course load, campus/location and program.

Walden University, Graduate Programs, Richard W. Riley College of Education and Leadership, Minneapolis, MN 55401. *Accreditation:* NCATE. Part-time and evening/weekend programs available. Postbaccalaureate distance learning degree programs offered (minimal on-campus study). *Faculty:* 23 full-time (15 women), 830 part-time/adjunct (569 women). *Students:* 8,671 full-time (7,197 women), 2,122 part-time (1,735 women); includes 4,734 minority (3,802 Black or African American, non-Hispanic/Latino; 50 American Indian or Alaska Native, non-Hispanic/Latino; 136 Asian, non-Hispanic/Latino; 539 Hispanic/Latino; 35 Native Hawaiian or other Pacific Islander, non-Hispanic/Latino; 172 Two or more races, non-Hispanic/Latino), 73 international. Average age 40. 2,646 applicants, 96% accepted, 2074 enrolled. In 2013, 2,214 master's, 354 doctorates, 479 other advanced degrees awarded. *Degree requirements:* For doctorate, thesis/dissertation (for some programs), residency; for other advanced degree, residency (for some programs). *Entrance requirements:* For master's, bachelor's degree or higher; minimum GPA of 2.5; official transcripts; goal statement (for some programs); access to computer and Internet; for doctorate, master's degree or higher; three years of related professional or academic experience (preferred); minimum GPA of 3.0; goal statement and current resume (select programs); official transcripts; access to computer and Internet; for other advanced degree, relevant work experience; access to computer and Internet. Additional exam requirements/recommendations for international students: Required—TOEFL (minimum score 550 paper-based; 79 iBT), IELTS (minimum score 6.5), Michigan English Language Assessment Battery (minimum score 82), or PTE. *Application deadline:* Applications are processed on a rolling basis. Application fee: $0. Electronic applications accepted. *Expenses:* Tuition: Full-time $11,813.55; part-time $500 per credit. *Required fees:* $618.76. *Financial support:* In 2013–14, 1 fellowship was awarded; Federal Work-Study, scholarships/grants, unspecified assistantships, and family tuition reduction, active duty/veteran tuition reduction, group tuition reduction, interest-free payment plans, employee tuition reduction also available. Support available to part-time students. Financial award applicants required to submit FAFSA. *Unit head:* Dr. Kate Steffens, Dean, 800-925-3368. *Application contact:* Jennifer Hall, Vice President of Enrollment Management, 866-4-WALDEN, E-mail: info@waldenu.edu.
Website: http://www.waldenu.edu/colleges-schools/riley-college-of-education/.

Waynesburg University, Graduate and Professional Studies, Canonsburg, PA 15370. Offers business (MBA), including energy management, finance, health systems, human resources, leadership, market development; counseling (MA), including addictions counseling, clinical mental health; education (M Ed, MAT), including autism (M Ed), curriculum and instruction (M Ed), educational leadership (M Ed), online teaching (M Ed); nursing (MSN), including administration, education, informatics; nursing practice (DNP); special education (M Ed); technology (M Ed); MSN/MBA. *Accreditation:* AACN. Part-time and evening/weekend programs available. *Faculty:* 11 full-time (5 women), 136 part-time/adjunct (80 women). *Students:* 146 full-time (99 women), 419 part-time (268 women). In 2013, 290 master's, 7 doctorates awarded. *Degree requirements:* For doctorate, thesis/dissertation. *Entrance requirements:* Additional exam requirements/recommendations for international students: Required—TOEFL. *Application deadline:* For fall admission, 8/1 priority date for domestic students. Applications are processed on a rolling basis. Electronic applications accepted. *Financial support:* Available to part-time students. Application deadline: 5/1. *Unit head:* David Mariner, Dean, 724-743-4420, Fax: 724-743-4425, E-mail: dmariner@waynesburg.edu. *Application contact:* Dr. Michael Bednarski, Director of Enrollment, 724-743-4420, Fax: 724-743-4425, E-mail: mbednars@waynesburg.edu.
Website: http://www.waynesburg.edu/.

Wayne State University, College of Education, Division of Administrative and Organizational Studies, Detroit, MI 48202. Offers college and university teaching (Certificate); educational administration and supervision (Ed S); educational leadership (M Ed); educational leadership and policy studies (Ed D, PhD); educational technology (Certificate); instructional technology (M Ed, Ed D, PhD, Ed S); online teaching (Certificate); secondary curriculum and instruction (Ed S); special education administration (Ed S). Part-time programs available. Postbaccalaureate distance

learning degree programs offered. *Students:* 96 full-time (68 women), 207 part-time (137 women); includes 133 minority (115 Black or African American, non-Hispanic/Latino; 4 American Indian or Alaska Native, non-Hispanic/Latino; 2 Asian, non-Hispanic/Latino; 8 Hispanic/Latino; 4 Two or more races, non-Hispanic/Latino), 14 international. Average age 39. 127 applicants, 50% accepted, 42 enrolled. In 2013, 47 master's, 15 doctorates, 41 other advanced degrees awarded. *Degree requirements:* For doctorate, thesis/dissertation. *Entrance requirements:* For master's, baccalaureate degree from accredited U.S. institution or equivalent from college or university of government-recognized standing; minimum undergraduate GPA of 2.75 in upper-division coursework; for doctorate, GRE or MAT, interview; autobiography or curriculum vitae; references; master's degree; minimum undergraduate GPA of 3.0, graduate 3.75; 3 years of relevant experience; foundational course work; for other advanced degree, master's degree from accredited institution, minimum upper-division GPA of 2.6 or 3.4 master's, fulfillment of the special requirements of the area of concentration, 3 years of teaching experience (except for instructional technology). Additional exam requirements/recommendations for international students: Required—TOEFL (minimum score 550 paper-based; 79 iBT), Michigan English Language Assessment Battery (minimum score 85); Recommended—IELTS (minimum score 6.5), TWE (minimum score 5.5). *Application deadline:* For fall admission, 6/1 priority date for domestic students, 5/1 priority date for international students; for winter admission, 10/1 priority date for domestic students, 9/1 priority date for international students; for spring admission, 2/1 priority date for domestic students, 1/1 priority date for international students. Applications are processed on a rolling basis. Application fee: $0. Electronic applications accepted. *Expenses:* Tuition, state resident: part-time $554.15 per credit. Tuition, nonresident: part-time $1200.35 per credit. *Required fees:* $42.15 per credit. $268.30 per semester. Tuition and fees vary according to course load and program. *Financial support:* In 2013–14, 48 students received support, including 3 fellowships with tuition reimbursements available (averaging $15,541 per year), 4 research assistantships with tuition reimbursements available (averaging $16,508 per year); career-related internships or fieldwork, Federal Work-Study, scholarships/grants, health care benefits, and unspecified assistantships also available. Support available to part-time students. Financial award application deadline: 3/31; financial award applicants required to submit FAFSA. *Faculty research:* Total quality management, participatory management, administering educational technology, school improvement, principalship. *Total annual research expenditures:* $6,888. *Unit head:* Dr. William Hill, Assistant Dean, 313-577-9316, E-mail: william_e_hill@wayne.edu. *Application contact:* Janice Green, Assistant Dean, 313-577-1605, E-mail: jwgreen@wayne.edu.
Website: http://coe.wayne.edu/aos/index.php.

Western Illinois University, School of Graduate Studies, College of Education and Human Services, Department of Instructional Design and Technology, Macomb, IL 61455-1390. Offers distance learning (Certificate); educational technology specialist (Certificate); graphic applications (Certificate); instructional design and technology (MS); multimedia (Certificate); technology integration in education (Certificate); training development (Certificate). Part-time programs available. Postbaccalaureate distance learning degree programs offered (no on-campus study). *Students:* 28 full-time (11 women), 80 part-time (50 women); includes 17 minority (9 Black or African American, non-Hispanic/Latino; 1 American Indian or Alaska Native, non-Hispanic/Latino; 3 Asian, non-Hispanic/Latino; 3 Hispanic/Latino; 1 Two or more races, non-Hispanic/Latino), 8 international. Average age 35. In 2013, 23 master's, 7 other advanced degrees awarded. *Degree requirements:* For master's, thesis or alternative. *Entrance requirements:* Additional exam requirements/recommendations for international students: Required—TOEFL (minimum score 550 paper-based; 80 iBT). *Application deadline:* Applications are processed on a rolling basis. Application fee: $30. Electronic applications accepted. *Financial support:* In 2013–14, 12 students received support, including 5 research assistantships with full tuition reimbursements available (averaging $7,544 per year), 7 teaching assistantships with full tuition reimbursements available (averaging $8,688 per year). Financial award applicants required to submit FAFSA. *Unit head:* Dr. Hoyet Hemphill, Chairperson, 309-298-1952. *Application contact:* Dr. Nancy Parsons, Associate Provost and Director of Graduate Studies, 309-298-1806, Fax: 309-298-2345, E-mail: grad-office@wiu.edu.
Website: http://wiu.edu/idt.

Wilkes University, College of Graduate and Professional Studies, School of Education, Wilkes-Barre, PA 18766-0002. Offers art and science of teaching (MS Ed); classroom technology (MS Ed); early childhood literacy (MS Ed); educational development and strategies (MS Ed); educational leadership (MS Ed); educational technology (Ed D); higher education administration (Ed D); instructional media (MS Ed); instructional technology (MS Ed); international school leadership (MS Ed); K-12 administration (Ed D); middle level education (MS Ed); online teaching (MS Ed); reading (MS Ed); school business leadership (MS Ed); secondary education (MS Ed), including biology, chemistry, English, history, mathematics; special education (MS Ed); teaching English as a second language (MS Ed); twenty-first century teaching and learning (MS Ed). Part-time and evening/weekend programs available. Postbaccalaureate distance learning degree programs offered (minimal on-campus study). *Students:* 46 full-time (37 women), 1,410 part-time (1,039 women); includes 67 minority (12 Black or African American, non-Hispanic/Latino; 2 American Indian or Alaska Native, non-Hispanic/Latino; 11 Asian, non-Hispanic/Latino; 28 Hispanic/Latino; 1 Native Hawaiian or other Pacific Islander, non-Hispanic/Latino; 13 Two or more races, non-Hispanic/Latino), 6 international. Average age 34. In 2013, 852 master's, 10 doctorates awarded. *Entrance requirements:* Additional exam requirements/recommendations for international students: Required—TOEFL (minimum score 550 paper-based; 79 iBT). *Application deadline:* Applications are processed on a rolling basis. Application fee: $45. Electronic applications accepted. *Expenses:* Contact institution. *Financial support:* Federal Work-Study and unspecified assistantships available. Financial award application deadline: 3/1; financial award applicants required to submit FAFSA. *Unit head:* Dr. Rhonda Waskiewicz, Interim Dean, Education, 570-408-4332, Fax: 570-408-7872, E-mail: rhonda.waskiewicz@wilkes.edu. *Application contact:* Joanne Thomas, Interim Director of Graduate Education, 570-408-4234, Fax: 570-408-7846, E-mail: joanne.thomas1@wilkes.edu.
Website: http://www.wilkes.edu/pages/383.asp.

Educational Leadership and Administration

Abilene Christian University, Graduate School, College of Education and Human Services, Graduate Studies in Education, Leadership of Learning Program, Abilene, TX 79699-9100. Offers leadership of digital learning (M Ed, Certificate), including digital learning (M Ed), leadership of learning (Certificate); leadership of learning (M Ed), including conflict resolution, principalship. Part-time programs available. Postbaccalaureate distance learning degree programs offered (no on-campus study). *Students:* 28 full-time (24 women), 18 part-time (13 women); includes 14 minority (5 Black or African American, non-Hispanic/Latino; 1 American Indian or Alaska Native, non-Hispanic/Latino; 1 Asian, non-Hispanic/Latino; 7 Hispanic/Latino). 23 applicants, 83% accepted, 19 enrolled. In 2013, 34 master's awarded. *Degree requirements:* For master's, comprehensive exam, practicum. *Entrance requirements:* Additional exam requirements/recommendations for international students: Required—TOEFL (minimum score 550 paper-based; 90 iBT), IELTS (minimum score 6.5), PTE. *Application deadline:* For fall admission, 8/15 priority date for domestic students; for winter admission, 10/1 priority date for domestic students; for spring admission, 12/15 priority date for domestic students; for summer admission, 4/15 for domestic students. Applications are processed on a rolling basis. Application fee: $50. Electronic applications accepted. *Expenses:* Contact institution. *Financial support:* In 2013–14, 13 students received support. Application deadline: 4/1; applicants required to submit FAFSA. *Unit head:* Dr. Lloyd Goldsmith, Graduate Director, 325-674-2946, Fax: 325-674-2123, E-mail: lloyd.goldsmith@acu.edu. *Application contact:* Corey Patterson, Director of Graduate Admission and Recruiting, 325-674-6566, Fax: 325-674-6717, E-mail: gradinfo@acu.edu.

Abilene Christian University, Graduate School, College of Education and Human Services, Graduate Studies in Education, Superintendent Certification Program, Abilene, TX 79699-9100. Offers Post-Master's Certificate. Part-time programs available. Postbaccalaureate distance learning degree programs offered (no on-campus study). *Students:* 6 part-time (1 woman); includes 2 minority (both Black or African American, non-Hispanic/Latino). 7 applicants, 100% accepted, 6 enrolled. In 2013, 5 Post-Master's Certificates awarded. *Entrance requirements:* Additional exam requirements/recommendations for international students: Required—TOEFL (minimum score 550 paper-based; 90 iBT), IELTS (minimum score 6.5), PTE. *Application deadline:* For fall admission, 8/15 priority date for domestic students; for winter admission, 10/1 for domestic students; for spring admission, 11/15 priority date for domestic students; for summer admission, 4/15 for domestic students. Applications are processed on a rolling basis. Application fee: $50. Electronic applications accepted. *Expenses: Tuition:* Full-time $17,100; part-time $950 per credit hour. *Financial support:* In 2013–14, 6 students received support. Application deadline: 4/1; applicants required to submit FAFSA. *Unit head:* Dr. Bruce Scott, Graduate Director, 325-674-2974, Fax: 325-674-2123, E-mail: bruce.scott@acu.edu. *Application contact:* Corey Patterson, Director of Graduate Admission and Recruiting, 325-674-6566, Fax: 325-674-6717, E-mail: gradinfo@acu.edu.

Acacia University, American Graduate School of Education, Tempe, AZ 85284. Offers educational administration (M Ed); elementary education (MA); English as a second language (M Ed); secondary education (MA); special education (M Ed).

Acadia University, Faculty of Professional Studies, School of Education, Program in Leadership, Wolfville, NS B4P 2R6, Canada. Offers M Ed. Part-time programs available. *Degree requirements:* For master's, thesis optional. *Entrance requirements:* For master's, B Ed or the equivalent, 2 years teaching or related experience. Additional exam requirements/recommendations for international students: Required—TOEFL (minimum score 580 paper-based; 93 iBT), IELTS (minimum score 6.5). *Faculty research:* Organizational theory and structural change, professionalism, sexuality education.

Adelphi University, Ruth S. Ammon School of Education, Program in Educational Leadership and Technology, Garden City, NY 11530-0701. Offers MA, Certificate. *Students:* 8 full-time (7 women), 8 part-time (7 women); includes 1 minority (Black or African American, non-Hispanic/Latino). Average age 39. In 2013, 4 other advanced degrees awarded. *Entrance requirements:* For master's, 2 letters of recommendation, resume, letter attesting to teaching experience (3 years full-time K-12). Additional exam requirements/recommendations for international students: Required—TOEFL (minimum score 550 paper-based; 80 iBT). *Application deadline:* For fall admission, 8/15 priority date for domestic students, 4/1 for international students; for spring admission, 1/15 priority date for domestic students, 11/1 for international students. Applications are processed on a rolling basis. Application fee: $50. Electronic applications accepted. *Expenses: Tuition:* Full-time $32,530; part-time $1010 per credit. *Required fees:* $1150. Tuition and fees vary according to degree level and program. *Financial support:* Research assistantships, career-related internships or fieldwork, Federal Work-Study, tuition waivers, and unspecified assistantships available. Financial award application deadline: 2/15; financial award applicants required to submit FAFSA. *Faculty research:* Technology methodology focusing on in-service and pre-service curriculum. *Unit head:* Dr. Devin Thornburg, Director, 516-877-4026, E-mail: thornburg@adelphi.edu. *Application contact:* Christine Murphy, Director of Admissions, 516-877-3050, Fax: 516-877-3039, E-mail: graduateadmissions@adelphi.edu.

Alabama Agricultural and Mechanical University, School of Graduate Studies, School of Education, Area in Secondary Education, Huntsville, AL 35811. Offers education (M Ed, Ed S); higher administration (MS). *Accreditation:* NCATE. Evening/weekend programs available. *Degree requirements:* For master's, comprehensive exam; for Ed S, thesis. *Entrance requirements:* For master's, GRE General Test. Additional exam requirements/recommendations for international students: Required—TOEFL (minimum score 500 paper-based; 61 iBT). Electronic applications accepted. *Faculty research:* World peace through education, computer-assisted instruction.

Alabama State University, College of Education, Department of Instructional Support Programs, Montgomery, AL 36101-0271. Offers counselor education (M Ed, MS, Ed S), including general counseling (MS, Ed S), school counseling (M Ed, Ed S); educational administration (M Ed, Ed D, Ed S), including educational administration (Ed S), educational leadership, policy and law (Ed D), instructional leadership (M Ed); library education media (M Ed, Ed S). Part-time programs available. *Faculty:* 8 full-time (4 women), 14 part-time/adjunct (8 women). *Students:* 57 full-time (41 women), 175 part-time (126 women); includes 209 minority (203 Black or African American, non-Hispanic/Latino; 2 Asian, non-Hispanic/Latino; 4 Hispanic/Latino). Average age 39. 86 applicants, 48% accepted, 34 enrolled. In 2013, 28 master's, 14 doctorates, 7 other advanced degrees awarded. *Degree requirements:* For master's, comprehensive exam; for Ed S, comprehensive exam, thesis. *Entrance requirements:* For master's and Ed S, GRE General Test, MAT, writing competency test. Additional exam requirements/recommendations for international students: Required—TOEFL (minimum score 500 paper-based). *Application deadline:* For fall admission, 7/15 for domestic students; for

spring admission, 12/15 for domestic students. Applications are processed on a rolling basis. Application fee: $10. *Expenses:* Tuition, state resident: full-time $7958; part-time $343 per credit hour. Tuition, nonresident: full-time $14,132; part-time $686 per credit hour. *Required fees:* $446 per term. One-time fee: $1784 full-time; $892 part-time. Tuition and fees vary according to course load. *Financial support:* In 2013–14, research assistantships (averaging $9,450 per year) were awarded. *Unit head:* Dr. Necoal Driver, Chair, 334-229-6882, Fax: 334-229-6904, E-mail: ndriver@alasu.edu. *Application contact:* Dr. Doris Screws, Dean of Graduate Studies, 334-229-4274, Fax: 334-229-4928, E-mail: dscrews@alasu.edu.
Website: http://www.alasu.edu/academics/colleges—departments/college-of-education/instructional-support-programs/index.aspx.

Albany State University, College of Education, Albany, GA 31705-2717. Offers early childhood education (M Ed); education specialist (Ed S); educational leadership and administration (M Ed); health, physical education and recreation (M Ed); middle grades education (M Ed); school counseling (M Ed); special education (M Ed). *Accreditation:* NCATE. Part-time and evening/weekend programs available. Postbaccalaureate distance learning degree programs offered (minimal on-campus study). *Degree requirements:* For master's, comprehensive exam, internship, GACE Content Exam. *Entrance requirements:* For master's, GRE or MAT. Electronic applications accepted. *Faculty research:* GACE preparation, STEM (science, technology, engineering, and mathematics), technology education, special education, professional teacher development, health implications liberation philosophy, NET-Q, learning community, disabled or at-risk students.

Alliant International University–San Diego, Shirley M. Hufstedler School of Education, Educational Leadership Programs, San Diego, CA 92131-1799. Offers educational administration (MA); educational leadership and management (K-12) (Ed D); higher education (Ed D, Certificate); preliminary administrative services (Credential). Part-time programs available. *Faculty:* 4 full-time (2 women), 3 part-time/adjunct (2 women). *Students:* 8 full-time (3 women), 25 part-time (14 women); includes 15 minority (6 Black or African American, non-Hispanic/Latino; 4 Asian, non-Hispanic/Latino; 5 Hispanic/Latino), 4 international. Average age 43. 21 applicants, 71% accepted, 11 enrolled. In 2013, 1 master's, 3 doctorates awarded. *Degree requirements:* For doctorate, comprehensive exam, thesis/dissertation. *Entrance requirements:* For master's, minimum GPA of 2.5, letters of recommendation; for doctorate, minimum GPA of 3.0, letters of recommendation. Additional exam requirements/recommendations for international students: Required—TOEFL (minimum score 550 paper-based; 80 iBT), TWE (minimum score 5). *Application deadline:* For fall admission, 4/15 priority date for domestic and international students; for spring admission, 11/3 priority date for domestic and international students; for summer admission, 2/15 for domestic and international students. Applications are processed on a rolling basis. Application fee: $65. Electronic applications accepted. *Financial support:* Federal Work-Study, institutionally sponsored loans, and scholarships/grants available. Financial award application deadline: 2/15; financial award applicants required to submit FAFSA. *Faculty research:* Global education, women and international educational opportunities. *Unit head:* Dr. Trudy Day, Program Director, Educational Policy and Practice Programs, 415-955-2102, Fax: 415-955-2179, E-mail: admissions@alliant.edu. *Application contact:* Alliant International University Central Contact Center, 866-U-ALLIANT, Fax: 858-635-4555, E-mail: admissions@alliant.edu.

Alliant International University–San Francisco, Shirley M. Hufstedler School of Education, Educational Leadership Programs, San Francisco, CA 94133-1221. Offers community college administration (Ed D); educational administration (MA); educational leadership and management (K-12) (Ed D); higher education (Ed D); preliminary administrative services (Credential). Part-time programs available. *Faculty:* 5 full-time (2 women), 2 part-time/adjunct (both women). *Students:* 1 (woman) full-time, 5 part-time (1 woman); includes 4 minority (1 Asian, non-Hispanic/Latino; 2 Hispanic/Latino; 1 Two or more races, non-Hispanic/Latino), 1 international. Average age 45. In 2013, 1 doctorate awarded. *Degree requirements:* For doctorate, comprehensive exam, thesis/dissertation. *Entrance requirements:* For master's and doctorate, minimum GPA of 3.0, letters of recommendation. Additional exam requirements/recommendations for international students: Required—TOEFL (minimum score 550 paper-based; 80 iBT), TWE (minimum score 5). *Application deadline:* For fall admission, 7/1 priority date for domestic and international students; for spring admission, 12/1 priority date for domestic and international students. Applications are processed on a rolling basis. Application fee: $65. Electronic applications accepted. *Financial support:* Federal Work-Study, institutionally sponsored loans, and scholarships/grants available. Financial award application deadline: 2/15; financial award applicants required to submit FAFSA. *Faculty research:* Leadership in higher education, community colleges. *Unit head:* Dr. Ed Shenk, Educational Policy and Practice Director, 415-955-2193, Fax: 415-955-2179, E-mail: admissions@alliant.edu. *Application contact:* Alliant International University Central Contact Center, 866-U-ALLIANT, Fax: 858-635-4555; E-mail: admissions@alliant.edu.
Website: http://www.alliant.edu/gsoe/.

Alverno College, School of Education, Milwaukee, WI 53234-3922. Offers adaptive education (MA); administrative leadership (MA); adult education and organizational development (MA); adult educational and instructional design (MA); adult educational and instructional technology (MA); global connections in the humanities (MA); instructional leadership (MA); instructional technology for K-12 settings (MA); professional development (MA); reading education (MA); reading education with adaptive education (MA); science education (MA); teaching in alternative schools (MA). *Accreditation:* NCATE. Part-time and evening/weekend programs available. *Faculty:* 7 full-time (all women), 26 part-time/adjunct (23 women). *Students:* 48 full-time (41 women), 89 part-time (83 women); includes 41 minority (24 Black or African American, non-Hispanic/Latino; 3 Asian, non-Hispanic/Latino; 11 Hispanic/Latino; 3 Two or more races, non-Hispanic/Latino), 4 international. Average age 36. 89 applicants, 97% accepted, 59 enrolled. In 2013, 53 master's awarded. *Degree requirements:* For master's, presentation/defense of proposal, conference presentation of inquiry projects. *Entrance requirements:* For master's, bachelor's degree in related field, communication samples from work setting, 3 letters of recommendation. Additional exam requirements/recommendations for international students: Required—TOEFL. *Application deadline:* For fall admission, 7/15 priority date for domestic and international students; for spring admission, 12/15 priority date for domestic and international students. Applications are processed on a rolling basis. Application fee: $0. Electronic applications accepted. Application fee is waived when completed online. Tuition and fees vary according to program. *Financial support:* In 2013–14, 9 students received support. Federal Work-Study and scholarships/grants available. Support available to part-time students. Financial award application deadline: 4/15; financial award applicants required to submit FAFSA. *Faculty research:* Student self-assessment, self-reflection, integration of curriculum, identifying needs of students in strategic situations and designing appropriate classroom strategies. *Unit head:* Dr. Desiree Pointer-Mace, Associate Dean, Graduate Program, 414-382-6345, Fax: 414-382-6332, E-mail: desiree.pointer-mace@alverno.edu. *Application contact:* Mary Claire Jones, Senior Graduate Admissions Counselor, 414-382-6106, Fax: 414-382-6354, E-mail: maryclaire.jones@alverno.edu.

American College of Education, Graduate Programs, Chicago, IL 60606. Offers curriculum and instruction (M Ed), including bilingual, ESL; educational leadership (M Ed); educational technology (M Ed).

American InterContinental University Online, Program in Education, Schaumburg, IL 60173. Offers curriculum and instruction (M Ed); educational assessment and evaluation (M Ed); instructional technology (M Ed); leadership of educational organizations (M Ed). Evening/weekend programs available. Postbaccalaureate distance learning degree programs offered (no on-campus study). *Entrance requirements:* Additional exam requirements/recommendations for international students: Required—TOEFL (minimum score 550 paper-based). Electronic applications accepted.

American International College, School of Graduate and Adult Education, Department of Education, Springfield, MA 01109-3189. Offers early childhood education (M Ed, CAGS); educational leadership and supervision (Ed D); elementary education (M Ed, CAGS); middle/secondary education (M Ed, CAGS); moderate disabilities (M Ed, CAGS); reading (M Ed, CAGS); school adjustment counseling (MA, CAGS); school guidance counseling (MA, CAGS); school leadership preparation (M Ed, CAGS); teaching and learning (Ed D). Evening/weekend programs available. *Faculty:* 11 full-time (9 women), 235 part-time/adjunct. *Students:* 1,530 full-time (1,219 women), 184 part-time (143 women); includes 100 minority (58 Black or African American, non-Hispanic/Latino; 3 American Indian or Alaska Native, non-Hispanic/Latino; 14 Asian, non-Hispanic/Latino; 6 Hispanic/Latino; 19 Two or more races, non-Hispanic/Latino). Average age 36. 695 applicants, 82% accepted, 508 enrolled. In 2013, 449 master's, 17 doctorates, 135 other advanced degrees awarded. Terminal master's awarded for partial completion of doctoral program. *Degree requirements:* For master's, comprehensive exam (for some programs), thesis (for some programs), practicum/culminating experience; for doctorate, comprehensive exam (for some programs), thesis/dissertation; for CAGS, practicum/culminating experience. *Entrance requirements:* For master's, graduate of accredited four-year college with minimum B-average in undergraduate course work; for doctorate, master's degree, minimum GPA of 3.0; for CAGS, M Ed or master's degree in field related to licensure from accredited institution. Additional exam requirements/recommendations for international students: Required—TOEFL or IELTS. *Application deadline:* For fall admission, 7/1 for domestic and international students; for spring admission, 12/1 for domestic and international students. Applications are processed on a rolling basis. Application fee: $50. Electronic applications accepted. *Expenses: Tuition:* Full-time $14,040; part-time $780 per credit. Tuition and fees vary according to course load, degree level and program. *Financial support:* Career-related internships or fieldwork available. Financial award applicants required to submit FAFSA. *Unit head:* Esta Sobey, Associate Dean, 413-205-3453, Fax: 413-205-3943, E-mail: esta.sobey@aic.edu. *Application contact:* Kaitlyn Rickard, Director of XCP Admissions, 413-205-3090, Fax: 413-205-3911, E-mail: kaitlyn.rickard@aic.edu.
Website: http://www.aic.edu/academics.

American Public University System, AMU/APU Graduate Programs, Charles Town, WV 25414. Offers accounting (MBA, MS); criminal justice (MA), including business administration, emergency and disaster management, general (MA, MS); educational leadership (M Ed); emergency and disaster management (MA); entrepreneurship (MBA); environmental policy and management (MS), including environmental planning, environmental sustainability, fish and wildlife management, general (MA, MS), global environmental management; finance (MBA); general (MBA); global business management (MBA); history (MA), including American history, ancient and classical history, European history, global history, public history; homeland security (MA), including business administration, counter-terrorism studies, criminal justice, cyber, emergency management and public health, intelligence studies, transportation security; homeland security resource allocation (MBA); humanities (MA); information technology (MS), including digital forensics, enterprise software development, information assurance and security, IT project management; information technology management (MBA); intelligence studies (MA), including criminal intelligence, cyber, general (MA, MS), homeland security, intelligence analysis, intelligence collection, intelligence management, intelligence operations, terrorism studies; international relations and conflict resolution (MA), including comparative and security issues, conflict resolution, international and transnational security issues, peacekeeping; legal studies (MA); management (MA), including defense management, general (MA, MS), human resource management, organizational leadership, public administration; marketing (MBA); military history (MA), including American military history, American Revolution, civil war, war since 1945, World War II; military studies (MA), including joint warfare, strategic leadership; national security studies (MA), including general (MA, MS), homeland security, regional security studies, security and intelligence analysis, terrorism studies; nonprofit management (MBA); political science (MA), including American politics and government, comparative government and development, general (MA, MS), international relations, public policy; psychology (MA), including general (MA, MS), maritime engineering management, reverse logistics management; public administration (MPA), including disaster management, environmental policy, health policy, human resources, national security, organizational management, security management; public health (MPH); reverse logistics management (MA); school counseling (M Ed); security management (MA); space studies (MS), including aerospace science, general (MA, MS), planetary science; sports and health sciences (MS); teaching (M Ed), including curriculum and instruction for elementary teachers, elementary reading, English language learners, instructional leadership, online learning, special education; transportation and logistics management (MA), including general (MA, MS), maritime engineering management, reverse logistics management. Programs offered via distance learning only. Part-time and evening/weekend programs available. Postbaccalaureate distance learning degree programs offered (no on-campus study). *Faculty:* 432 full-time (242 women), 1,722 part-time/adjunct (829 women). *Students:* 511 full-time (241 women), 10,947 part-time (4,294 women); includes 3,760 minority (2,058 Black or African American, non-Hispanic/Latino; 88 American Indian or Alaska Native, non-Hispanic/Latino; 293 Asian, non-Hispanic/Latino; 876 Hispanic/Latino; 91 Native Hawaiian or other Pacific Islander, non-Hispanic/Latino; 354 Two or more races, non-Hispanic/Latino), 134 international. Average age 36. In 2013, 3,323 master's awarded. *Degree requirements:* For master's, comprehensive exam or practicum. *Entrance requirements:* For master's, official transcript showing earned bachelor's degree from institution accredited by recognized accrediting body. Additional exam requirements/recommendations for international students: Required—TOEFL (minimum score 550 paper-based), IELTS (minimum score 6.5). *Application deadline:* Applications are processed on a rolling basis. Application fee: $0. Electronic applications accepted. *Expenses: Tuition:* Part-time $325 per semester hour. *Financial support:* Applicants required to submit FAFSA. *Faculty research:* Military history, criminal justice, management performance, national security. *Unit head:* Dr. Karan Powell, Executive Vice President and Provost, 877-468-6268, Fax: 304-724-3780. *Application contact:* Terry Grant, Vice President of Enrollment Management, 877-468-6268, Fax: 304-724-3780, E-mail: info@apus.edu.
Website: http://www.apus.edu.

Andrews University, School of Graduate Studies, School of Education, Department of Leadership and Educational Administration, Program in Educational Administration and Leadership, Berrien Springs, MI 49104. Offers MA, Ed D, PhD, Ed S. *Faculty:* 4 full-time

(0 women). *Students:* 1 full-time (0 women), 39 part-time (23 women); includes 21 minority (15 Black or African American, non-Hispanic/Latino; 4 Hispanic/Latino; 2 Two or more races, non-Hispanic/Latino), 5 international. Average age 40. 6 applicants, 83% accepted, 1 enrolled. In 2013, 8 master's, 2 doctorates awarded. *Degree requirements:* For master's, thesis or alternative; for doctorate, thesis/dissertation. *Entrance requirements:* For master's and doctorate, GRE Subject Test. Additional exam requirements/recommendations for international students: Required—TOEFL (minimum score 550 paper-based). *Application deadline:* Applications are processed on a rolling basis. Application fee: $40. *Financial support:* Research assistantships available. *Unit head:* Dr. Robson Marinho, Coordinator, 269-471-3487. *Application contact:* Monica Wringer, Supervisor of Graduate Admission, 800-253-2874, Fax: 269-471-6321, E-mail: graduate@andrews.edu.

Andrews University, School of Graduate Studies, School of Education, Department of Leadership and Educational Administration, Program in Leadership, Berrien Springs, MI 49104. Offers MA, Ed D, PhD, Ed S. *Students:* 1 (woman) full-time, 84 part-time (34 women); includes 20 minority (11 Black or African American, non-Hispanic/Latino; 3 Asian, non-Hispanic/Latino; 6 Hispanic/Latino), 20 international. Average age 42. 51 applicants, 41% accepted, 12 enrolled. In 2013, 3 master's, 11 doctorates awarded. *Entrance requirements:* For master's, GRE. Additional exam requirements/recommendations for international students: Required—TOEFL (minimum score 550 paper-based). Application fee: $40. *Unit head:* Dr. Robson Marinho, Chair, 269-471-6580. *Application contact:* Monica Wringer, Supervisor of Graduate Admission, 800-253-2874, Fax: 269-471-6321, E-mail: graduate@andrews.edu.

Angelo State University, College of Graduate Studies, College of Education, Department of Curriculum and Instruction, Program in School Administration, San Angelo, TX 76909. Offers principal (Certificate); school administration (M Ed); superintendent (Certificate). Part-time and evening/weekend programs available. *Degree requirements:* For master's, comprehensive exam. *Entrance requirements:* Additional exam requirements/recommendations for international students: Required—TOEFL or IELTS. Electronic applications accepted.

Antioch University New England, Graduate School, Department of Education, Experienced Educators Program, Keene, NH 03431-3552. Offers foundations of education (M Ed), including applied behavioral analysis, autism spectrum disorders, educating for sustainability, next-generation learning using technology, problem-based learning using critical skills, teacher leadership; principal certification (PMC). *Degree requirements:* For master's, thesis, practicum. *Entrance requirements:* For master's, previous course work and work experience in education. Additional exam requirements/recommendations for international students: Required—TOEFL (minimum score 550 paper-based). Electronic applications accepted. *Expenses:* Contact institution. *Faculty research:* Classroom action research, school restructuring, problem-based learning, brain-based learning.

Appalachian State University, Cratis D. Williams Graduate School, Department of Leadership and Educational Studies, Boone, NC 28608. Offers educational administration (Ed S); educational media (MA); higher education (MA, Ed S); library science (MLS); school administration (MSA). Part-time and evening/weekend programs available. Postbaccalaureate distance learning degree programs offered (no on-campus study). *Degree requirements:* For master's and Ed S, comprehensive exam, thesis optional. *Entrance requirements:* For master's and Ed S, GRE or MAT, 3 letters of recommendation. Additional exam requirements/recommendations for international students: Required—TOEFL (minimum score 570 paper-based; 79 iBT), IELTS (minimum score 6.5). Electronic applications accepted. *Faculty research:* Brain, learning and meditation; leadership of teaching and learning.

Appalachian State University, Cratis D. Williams Graduate School, Program in Educational Leadership, Boone, NC 28608. Offers licensure (superintendent) (Ed D). *Accreditation:* NCATE. Part-time programs available. Postbaccalaureate distance learning degree programs offered (no on-campus study). *Degree requirements:* For doctorate, comprehensive exam, thesis/dissertation. *Entrance requirements:* For doctorate, GRE General Test, 4 letters of recommendation. Additional exam requirements/recommendations for international students: Required—TOEFL (minimum score 570 paper-based; 79 iBT) or IELTS (minimum score 6.5). Electronic applications accepted. *Faculty research:* Sustainability of organizations, cultural pedagogy.

Arcadia University, Graduate Studies, School of Education, Glenside, PA 19038-3295. Offers art education (M Ed); computer education (CAS); curriculum (CAS); curriculum studies (M Ed); early childhood education (M Ed, CAS), including individualized (M Ed), master teacher (M Ed), research in child development (M Ed); educational leadership (M Ed, Ed D, CAS); elementary education (M Ed, CAS); English education (MA Ed); environmental education (MA Ed, CAS); history education (MA Ed); instructional technology (M Ed); language arts (M Ed, CAS); library science (M Ed); mathematics education (M Ed, MA Ed, CAS); music education (MA Ed); psychology (MA Ed); reading (M Ed, CAS); science education (M Ed, CAS); secondary education (M Ed, CAS); special education (M Ed, Ed D, CAS); theater arts (MA Ed); written communication (MA Ed). *Accreditation:* NASAD. Part-time and evening/weekend programs available. Postbaccalaureate distance learning degree programs offered (minimal on-campus study). Electronic applications accepted. *Expenses:* Contact institution.

Argosy University, Atlanta, College of Education, Atlanta, GA 30328. Offers educational leadership (MAEd, Ed D, Ed S), including higher education administration (Ed D), K-12 education (Ed D); teaching and learning (MAEd, Ed S), including education technology (Ed D), higher education (Ed D), K-12 education (Ed D).

Argosy University, Chicago, College of Education, Chicago, IL 60601. Offers adult education and training (MA Ed); community college executive leadership (Ed D); educational leadership (MA Ed, Ed D, Ed S), including district leadership (Ed D), higher education administration (Ed D), K-12 education (Ed D); instructional leadership (Ed D, Ed S), including higher education (Ed D), K-12 education (Ed D). Postbaccalaureate distance learning degree programs offered (minimal on-campus study).

Argosy University, Dallas, College of Education, Farmers Branch, TX 75244. Offers educational administration (MA Ed); educational leadership (Ed D); higher and postsecondary education (MA Ed); instructional leadership (MA Ed); school psychology (MA).

Argosy University, Denver, College of Education, Denver, CO 80231. Offers community college executive leadership (Ed D); educational leadership (MA Ed, Ed D), including higher education (Ed D), K-12 education (Ed D); instructional leadership (MA Ed, Ed D), including higher education administration (Ed D), K-12 education (Ed D).

Argosy University, Hawai`i, College of Education, Honolulu, HI 96813. Offers adult education and training (MAEd); educational leadership (Ed D), including higher education administration, K-12 education; instructional leadership (Ed D), including higher education, K-12 education; school psychology (MA).

Argosy University, Inland Empire, College of Education, Ontario, CA 91761. Offers community college executive leadership (Ed D); educational leadership (MA Ed, Ed D), including higher education administration (Ed D), K-12 education (Ed D); instructional leadership (MA Ed, Ed D), including higher education (Ed D), K-12 education (Ed D), multiple subject teacher preparation (MA Ed), single subject teacher preparation (MA Ed).

Argosy University, Los Angeles, College of Education, Santa Monica, CA 90045. Offers community college executive leadership (Ed D); educational leadership (MA Ed, Ed D), including higher education administration (Ed D), K-12 education (Ed D); instructional leadership (MA Ed, Ed D), including higher education (Ed D), K-12 education (Ed D), multiple subject teacher preparation (MA Ed), single subject teacher preparation (MA Ed).

Argosy University, Nashville, College of Education, Program in Educational Leadership, Nashville, TN 37214. Offers educational leadership (MA Ed, Ed S); higher education administration (Ed D); K-12 education (Ed D).

Argosy University, Nashville, College of Education, Program in Instructional Leadership, Nashville, TN 37214. Offers education technology (Ed D); higher education administration (Ed D); instructional leadership (MA Ed, Ed S); K-12 education (Ed D).

Argosy University, Orange County, College of Education, Orange, CA 92868. Offers community college executive leadership (Ed D); educational leadership (MA Ed, Ed D), including higher education administration (Ed D), K-12 education (Ed D); instructional leadership (MA Ed, Ed D), including education technology (Ed D), higher education (Ed D), K-12 education (Ed D), multiple subject teacher preparation (MA Ed), single subject teacher preparation (MA Ed).

Argosy University, Phoenix, College of Education, Phoenix, AZ 85021. Offers adult education and training (MA Ed); advanced educational administration (Ed D, Ed S); community college executive leadership (Ed D); educational administration (MA Ed); educational leadership (MA Ed, Ed D, Ed S), including education technology (Ed D), higher education administration (Ed D), K-12 education (Ed D); higher and postsecondary education (MA Ed); initial educational administration (Ed D, Ed S); school psychology (MA); teaching and learning (MA Ed, Ed D, Ed S), including education technology (Ed D), higher education (Ed D), K-12 education (Ed D).

Argosy University, Salt Lake City, College of Education, Draper, UT 84020. Offers educational leadership (MA Ed, Ed D).

Argosy University, San Diego, College of Education, San Diego, CA 92108. Offers community college executive leadership (Ed D); educational leadership (MA Ed, Ed D), including higher education administration (Ed D), K-12 education (Ed D); instructional leadership (MA Ed, Ed D), including higher education (Ed D), K-12 education (Ed D).

Argosy University, San Francisco Bay Area, College of Education, Alameda, CA 94501. Offers community college executive leadership (Ed D); educational leadership (MA Ed, Ed D), including education technology (Ed D), higher education administration (Ed D), K-12 education (Ed D); instructional leadership (MA Ed, Ed D), including education technology (Ed D), higher education (Ed D), K-12 education (Ed D), multiple subject teacher preparation (MA Ed), single subject teacher preparation (MA Ed).

Argosy University, Sarasota, College of Education, Sarasota, FL 34235. Offers community college executive leadership (Ed D); educational leadership (MA Ed, Ed D, Ed S), including higher education administration (Ed D), K-12 education (Ed D); school counseling (MA, Ed S); school psychology (MA); teaching and learning (MA Ed, Ed D, Ed S), including education technology (Ed D), higher education (Ed D), K-12 education (Ed D).

Argosy University, Schaumburg, College of Education, Schaumburg, IL 60173-5403. Offers community college executive leadership (Ed D); educational leadership (MA Ed, Ed D, Ed S), including district leadership (Ed D), higher education administration (Ed D), K-12 education (Ed D); instructional leadership (Ed D, Ed S), including higher education (Ed D), K-12 education (Ed D).

Argosy University, Seattle, College of Education, Seattle, WA 98121. Offers adult education and training (MA Ed); community college executive leadership (Ed D); educational leadership (MA Ed, Ed D), including higher education administration (Ed D), K-12 education (Ed D); higher and postsecondary education (MA Ed); instructional leadership (MA Ed, Ed D), including education technology (Ed D), higher education (Ed D), K-12 education (Ed D).

Argosy University, Tampa, College of Education, Tampa, FL 33607. Offers community college executive leadership (Ed D); educational leadership (MA Ed, Ed D, Ed S), including higher education administration (Ed D), K-12 education (Ed D); school counseling (MA); teaching and learning (MA Ed, Ed D, Ed S), including higher education (Ed D), K-12 education (Ed D).

Argosy University, Twin Cities, College of Education, Eagan, MN 55121. Offers advanced educational administration (Ed D, Ed S); educational leadership (MA Ed, Ed D, Ed S), including higher education administration (Ed D), K-12 education (Ed D); higher and postsecondary education (MA Ed); initial educational administration (Ed D, Ed S); instructional leadership (MA Ed, Ed D, Ed S), including education technology (Ed D), higher education (Ed D), K-12 education (Ed D).

Argosy University, Washington DC, College of Education, Arlington, VA 22209. Offers community college executive leadership (Ed D); educational leadership (MA Ed, Ed D, Ed S), including higher education administration (Ed D), K-12 education (Ed D); instructional leadership (MA Ed, Ed D, Ed S), including higher education (Ed D), K-12 education (Ed D).

Arizona State University at the Tempe campus, Mary Lou Fulton Teachers College, Program in Educational Administration and Supervision, Phoenix, AZ 85069. Offers educational administration and supervision (M Ed); leadership and innovation (Ed D). Part-time and evening/weekend programs available. Postbaccalaureate distance learning degree programs offered (minimal on-campus study). Terminal master's awarded for partial completion of doctoral program. *Degree requirements:* For master's, thesis or alternative, written portfolio, internship, interactive Program of Study (iPOS) submitted before completing 50 percent of required credit hours; for doctorate, thesis/dissertation, interactive Program of Study (iPOS) submitted before completing 50 percent of required credit hours. *Entrance requirements:* For master's, minimum GPA of 3.0 or equivalent in last 2 years of work leading to bachelor's degree, 1 year of teaching experience, 3 letters of recommendation, personal statement, writing sample, curriculum vitae or resume; for doctorate, master's degree in education or related field, resume, personal statement, writing samples based on short writing prompts, 3 letters of recommendation. Additional exam requirements/recommendations for international students: Required—TOEFL, IELTS, or PTE. Electronic applications accepted.

Arizona State University at the Tempe campus, Mary Lou Fulton Teachers College, Program in Educational Leadership and Policy Studies, Phoenix, AZ 85069. Offers PhD. Fall admission only. *Degree requirements:* For doctorate, comprehensive exam, thesis/dissertation, interactive Program of Study (iPOS) submitted before completing 50 percent of required credit hours. *Entrance requirements:* For doctorate, GRE, minimum GPA of 3.0 or equivalent in last 2 years of work leading to bachelor's degree, 3 letters of recommendation, personal statement, writing sample, curriculum vitae or resume. Additional exam requirements/recommendations for international students: Required—TOEFL (minimum score 80 iBT), TOEFL, IELTS, or PTE. Electronic applications accepted. *Expenses:* Contact institution. *Faculty research:* Education policy analysis, school finance and quantitative methods, school improvement in ethnically, linguistically

and economically diverse communities, parent/teacher engagement, school choice, accountability polices, school finance litigation, school segregation.

Arkansas State University, Graduate School, College of Education and Behavioral Science, School of Teacher Education and Leadership, Jonesboro, AR 72467. Offers community college administration (SCCT); curriculum and instruction (MSE); early childhood education (MAT, MSE); early childhood services (MS); educational leadership (MSE, Ed D, PhD, Ed S); educational theory and practice (MSE); middle level education (MAT, MSE); reading (MSE, Ed S); special education - gifted, talented, and creative (MSE); special education - instructional specialist grades 4-12 (MSE); special education - instructional specialist grades P-4 (MSE). *Accreditation:* NCATE. Part-time programs available. Postbaccalaureate distance learning degree programs offered. *Faculty:* 28 full-time (16 women). *Students:* 77 full-time (68 women), 1,934 part-time (1,449 women); includes 361 minority (290 Black or African American, non-Hispanic/Latino; 11 American Indian or Alaska Native, non-Hispanic/Latino; 3 Asian, non-Hispanic/Latino; 26 Hispanic/Latino; 1 Native Hawaiian or other Pacific Islander, non-Hispanic/Latino; 30 Two or more races, non-Hispanic/Latino), 5 international. Average age 36. 1,627 applicants, 71% accepted, 770 enrolled. In 2013, 1,182 master's, 12 doctorates, 76 other advanced degrees awarded. *Degree requirements:* For master's, comprehensive exam, thesis or alternative; for doctorate, comprehensive exam, thesis/dissertation; for other advanced degree, comprehensive exam. *Entrance requirements:* For master's, GRE General Test or MAT, appropriate bachelor's degree, official transcripts, immunization records, letters of reference, interview; for doctorate, GRE General Test or MAT, interview, master's degree, letters of reference, official transcript, personal statement, writing sample, immunization records; for other advanced degree, GRE General Test or MAT, interview, master's degree, official transcript, immunization records, letters of reference, 3 years of teaching experience, teaching license. Additional exam requirements/recommendations for international students: Required—TOEFL (minimum score 550 paper-based; 79 iBT), IELTS (minimum score 6), PTE (minimum score 56). *Application deadline:* For fall admission, 7/1 for domestic and international students; for spring admission, 11/15 for domestic students, 11/14 for international students. Applications are processed on a rolling basis. Electronic applications accepted. *Expenses:* Tuition, state resident: full-time $4284; part-time $238 per credit hour. Tuition, nonresident: full-time $8568; part-time $476 per credit hour. *International tuition:* $9268 full-time. *Required fees:* $1098; $61 per credit hour. $25 per term. Tuition and fees vary according to course load and program. *Financial support:* In 2013–14, 20 students received support. Fellowships, teaching assistantships, career-related internships or fieldwork, scholarships/grants, and unspecified assistantships available. Financial award application deadline: 7/1; financial award applicants required to submit FAFSA. *Unit head:* Dr. Annette Hux, Interim Chair, 870-972-3059, Fax: 870-972-3344, E-mail: ahux@astate.edu. *Application contact:* Vickey Ring, Graduate Admissions Coordinator, 870-972-3029, Fax: 870-972-3857, E-mail: vickeyring@astate.edu.
Website: http://www.astate.edu/college/education/departments/school-of-teacher-education-and-leadership/index.dot.

Arkansas Tech University, Center for Leadership and Learning, Russellville, AR 72801. Offers educational leadership (M Ed, Ed S); school counseling and leadership (M Ed); teaching, learning and leadership (M Ed). Part-time and evening/weekend programs available. *Students:* 144 part-time (117 women); includes 17 minority (8 Black or African American, non-Hispanic/Latino; 1 Asian, non-Hispanic/Latino; 4 Hispanic/Latino; 4 Two or more races, non-Hispanic/Latino). Average age 35. In 2013, 20 master's, 5 Ed Ss awarded. *Degree requirements:* For master's, comprehensive exam (for some programs), thesis (for some programs), project, internship, portfolio. *Entrance requirements:* For master's, PRAXIS; for Ed S, teaching and administrative licenses. Additional exam requirements/recommendations for international students: Required—TOEFL (minimum score 550 paper-based; 79 iBT), IELTS (minimum score 6.5). *Application deadline:* For fall admission, 3/1 priority date for domestic students, 5/1 priority date for international students; for spring admission, 10/1 priority date for domestic and international students. Applications are processed on a rolling basis. Application fee: $25 ($75 for international students). Electronic applications accepted. *Expenses:* Tuition, state resident: full-time $5976; part-time $249 per credit hour. Tuition, nonresident: full-time $11,952; part-time $498 per credit hour. *Required fees:* $411 per semester. Tuition and fees vary according to course load. *Financial support:* In 2013–14, research assistantships with full tuition reimbursements (averaging $4,800 per year), teaching assistantships with full tuition reimbursements (averaging $4,800 per year) were awarded; career-related internships or fieldwork, Federal Work-Study, scholarships/grants, health care benefits, and unspecified assistantships also available. Support available to part-time students. Financial award application deadline: 4/15; financial award applicants required to submit FAFSA. *Unit head:* Dr. Mona Chadwick, Head, Center for Leadership and Learning, 479-498-6022, Fax: 479-498-6075, E-mail: cll@atu.edu. *Application contact:* Dr. Mary B. Gunter, Dean of Graduate College, 479-968-0398, Fax: 479-964-0542, E-mail: gradcollege@atu.edu.
Website: http://www.atu.edu/cll/.

Arlington Baptist College, Program in Education, Arlington, TX 76012-3425. Offers curriculum and instruction (M Ed); educational leadership (M Ed). *Degree requirements:* For master's, professional portfolio; internship (for educational leadership). *Entrance requirements:* For master's, bachelor's degree from accredited college or university with minimum GPA of 3.0, minimum of 12 hours in Bible; minimum of three years' classroom teaching experience in an accredited K-12 public or private school (for educational leadeship only).

Asbury University, School of Graduate and Professional Studies, Wilmore, KY 40390-1198. Offers biology: alternative certificate (MA Ed); chemistry: alternative certificate (MA Ed); English (MA Ed); English as a second language (MA Ed); ESL (MA Ed); French (MA Ed); Latin: alternative certificate (MA Ed); mathematics: alternative certificate (MA Ed); reading/writing endorsement (MA Ed); social studies (MA Ed); social work (MSW), including child and family services; Spanish (MA Ed); special education (MA Ed); special education: alternative certificate (MA Ed); teacher as leader endorsement (MA Ed). *Accreditation:* NCATE. Part-time programs available. *Degree requirements:* For master's, action research project, portfolio. *Entrance requirements:* For master's, PRAXIS/NTE, minimum GPA of 2.75, letters of recommendation. Additional exam requirements/recommendations for international students: Required—TOEFL (minimum score 550 paper-based). Electronic applications accepted.

Ashland University, Dwight Schar College of Education, Department of Educational Administration, Ashland, OH 44805-3702. Offers curriculum specialist (M Ed); principalship (M Ed); pupil services (M Ed). Part-time programs available. *Degree requirements:* For master's, thesis or alternative, internship. *Entrance requirements:* For master's, teaching certificate or license, bachelor's degree, minimum cumulative GPA of 2.75. Additional exam requirements/recommendations for international students: Required—TOEFL. Electronic applications accepted. *Faculty research:* Gender and religious considerations in employment, Interstate School Leaders Licensure Consortium (ISLLC) standards, adjunct faculty training, politics of school finance, ethnicity and employment.

Ashland University, Dwight Schar College of Education, Department of Educational Foundations, Ashland, OH 44805-3702. Offers teacher leader (M Ed). Part-time and evening/weekend programs available. *Degree requirements:* For master's, inquiry seminar, internship, or thesis. *Entrance requirements:* For master's, teaching certificate or license, bachelor's degree, minimum cumulative GPA of 2.75. Additional exam requirements/recommendations for international students: Required—TOEFL. Electronic applications accepted. *Faculty research:* Character education, teacher reflection, religion and education, professional education, environmental education.

Ashland University, Dwight Schar College of Education, Doctoral Program in Educational Leadership Studies, Ashland, OH 44805-3702. Offers Ed D. Part-time and evening/weekend programs available. *Degree requirements:* For doctorate, comprehensive exam, thesis/dissertation. *Entrance requirements:* For doctorate, GRE, master's degree, minimum GPA of 3.3, writing sample, letters of recommendation. Additional exam requirements/recommendations for international students: Required—TOEFL. Electronic applications accepted. *Expenses:* Contact institution. *Faculty research:* School funding, charter schools, administrative jobs, continuous improvement, marginalized groups, school finance, minority superintendent trends, teacher salaries, minority recruiting, women's issues.

Auburn University, Graduate School, College of Education, Department of Educational Foundations, Leadership, and Technology, Auburn University, AL 36849. Offers adult education (M Ed, MS, Ed D); curriculum and instruction (M Ed, MS, Ed D, Ed S); curriculum supervision (M Ed, MS, Ed D, Ed S); educational psychology (PhD); higher education administration (M Ed, MS, Ed D, Ed S); media instructional design (MS); media specialist (M Ed); school administration (M Ed, MS, Ed D, Ed S). *Accreditation:* NCATE. Part-time programs available. *Faculty:* 25 full-time (15 women), 6 part-time/adjunct (5 women). *Students:* 104 full-time (65 women), 250 part-time (140 women); includes 98 minority (90 Black or African American, non-Hispanic/Latino; 1 American Indian or Alaska Native, non-Hispanic/Latino; 4 Asian, non-Hispanic/Latino; 3 Hispanic/Latino), 14 international. Average age 36. 188 applicants, 66% accepted, 76 enrolled. In 2013, 51 master's, 22 doctorates, 10 other advanced degrees awarded. *Degree requirements:* For master's, thesis (for some programs); for doctorate, thesis/dissertation; for Ed S, field project. *Entrance requirements:* For master's, doctorate, and Ed S, GRE General Test. *Application deadline:* For fall admission, 7/7 for domestic students; for spring admission, 11/24 for domestic students. Applications are processed on a rolling basis. Application fee: $50 ($60 for international students). Electronic applications accepted. *Expenses:* Tuition, state resident: full-time $8262; part-time $459 per credit hour. Tuition, nonresident: full-time $24,786; part-time $1377 per credit hour. Tuition and fees vary according to degree level and program. *Financial support:* Teaching assistantships and Federal Work-Study available. Support available to part-time students. Financial award application deadline: 3/15; financial award applicants required to submit FAFSA. *Unit head:* Dr. Sherida Downer, Head, 334-844-4460. *Application contact:* Dr. George Flowers, Dean of the Graduate School, 334-844-4700.
Website: http://www.education.auburn.edu/academic_departments/eflt/.

Auburn University at Montgomery, School of Education, Department of Counselor, Leadership, and Special Education, Montgomery, AL 36124-4023. Offers counseling education (M Ed, Ed S), including counseling and development (Ed S), school counseling (Ed S); early childhood special education (M Ed); instructional leadership (Ed S); special education (Ed S); special education/collaborative teacher (M Ed). *Accreditation:* ACA; NCATE. Part-time and evening/weekend programs available. *Faculty:* 6 full-time (5 women), 2 part-time/adjunct (1 woman). *Students:* 15 full-time (11 women), 55 part-time (42 women); includes 32 minority (31 Black or African American, non-Hispanic/Latino; 1 Hispanic/Latino). Average age 33. In 2013, 22 master's awarded. *Degree requirements:* For master's and Ed S, comprehensive exam. *Entrance requirements:* For master's, GRE General Test or MAT, certification, BS in teaching; for Ed S, GRE General Test or MAT, certification. *Application deadline:* Applications are processed on a rolling basis. Electronic applications accepted. *Expenses:* Tuition, state resident: full-time $5994; part-time $333 per credit hour. Tuition, nonresident: full-time $17,982; part-time $999 per credit hour. *Financial support:* Career-related internships or fieldwork and scholarships/grants available. Support available to part-time students. Financial award application deadline: 3/1; financial award applicants required to submit FAFSA. *Unit head:* Dr. Sheila Austin, Dean, 334-244-3425, Fax: 334-244-3102, E-mail: saustin1@aum.edu. *Application contact:* Dr. Rhonda Morton, Associate Dean/Graduate Coordinator, 334-244-3287, Fax: 334-244-3978, E-mail: rmorton@aum.edu.
Website: http://www.aum.edu/Education.

Aurora University, College of Education, Aurora, IL 60506-4892. Offers curriculum and instruction (MA, Ed D); early childhood and special education (MA); education (MAT), including elementary certification; education and administration (Ed D); educational leadership (MEL); educational technology (MATL); reading instruction (MA); special education (MA). *Accreditation:* NCATE. Part-time and evening/weekend programs available. *Degree requirements:* For doctorate, comprehensive exam, thesis/dissertation. *Entrance requirements:* For master's, 2 years of teaching experience, valid teaching certificate. Additional exam requirements/recommendations for international students: Required—TOEFL (minimum score 550 paper-based). Electronic applications accepted. *Expenses:* Contact institution.

Austin Peay State University, College of Graduate Studies, College of Education, Department of Educational Specialties, Clarksville, TN 37044. Offers administration and supervision (Ed S); curriculum and instruction (MA Ed); education leadership (MA Ed); elementary education (Ed S); secondary education (Ed S); special education (MA Ed). Part-time and evening/weekend programs available. Postbaccalaureate distance learning degree programs offered. *Faculty:* 8 full-time (5 women), 4 part-time/adjunct (3 women). *Students:* 6 full-time (5 women), 87 part-time (73 women); includes 10 minority (5 Black or African American, non-Hispanic/Latino; 1 American Indian or Alaska Native, non-Hispanic/Latino; 1 Asian, non-Hispanic/Latino; 1 Hispanic/Latino; 2 Two or more races, non-Hispanic/Latino). Average age 35. 11 applicants, 82% accepted, 6 enrolled. In 2013, 37 master's, 6 Ed Ss awarded. *Degree requirements:* For master's, comprehensive exam, thesis optional. *Entrance requirements:* For master's, GRE General Test, 3 letters of recommendation, minimum undergraduate GPA of 2.75. Additional exam requirements/recommendations for international students: Required—TOEFL (minimum score 500 paper-based). *Application deadline:* For fall admission, 8/5 priority date for domestic students. Applications are processed on a rolling basis. Application fee: $25. Electronic applications accepted. *Expenses:* Tuition, state resident: full-time $7500; part-time $375 per credit hour. Tuition, nonresident: full-time $20,800; part-time $1040 per credit hour. *Required fees:* $1284; $64.20 per credit hour. *Financial support:* Career-related internships or fieldwork, Federal Work-Study, institutionally sponsored loans, scholarships/grants, and unspecified assistantships available. Support available to part-time students. Financial award application deadline: 3/1; financial award applicants required to submit FAFSA. *Unit head:* Dr. Moniqueka Gold, Chair, 931-221-7696, Fax: 931-221-1292, E-mail: goldm@apsu.edu. *Application contact:* June D. Lee, Graduate Coordinator, 800-859-4723, Fax: 931-221-7641, E-mail: gradadmissions@apsu.edu.

Averett University, Master in Education Program, Danville, VA 24541-3692. Offers administration and supervision (M Ed); art (M Ed); biology (M Ed); chemistry (M Ed); curriculum and instruction (M Ed); early childhood (M Ed); English (M Ed); mathematics (M Ed); middle grades (M Ed); physical science (M Ed); reading specialist (M Ed); science (M Ed); special education (M Ed); special education learning disability (M Ed). Program offered on Danville Campus only. Part-time and evening/weekend programs

available. *Faculty:* 4 full-time (3 women), 13 part-time/adjunct (8 women). *Students:* 43 full-time (35 women), 44 part-time (35 women); includes 7 minority (all Black or African American, non-Hispanic/Latino). *Degree requirements:* For master's, 30-credit core curriculum, minimum GPA of 3.0 throughout program, completion of degree requirements within six years from start of program. *Entrance requirements:* For master's, PRAXIS I, GRE, or MAT; writing proficiency test, minimum cumulative GPA of 3.0 over the last 60 hours of undergraduate study toward a baccalaureate degree, three letters of recommendation, Virginia teaching license (or eligibility). Additional exam requirements/recommendations for international students: Required—TOEFL (minimum score 600 paper-based; 100 iBT). *Application deadline:* Applications are processed on a rolling basis. Application fee: $100. *Expenses:* Contact institution. *Financial support:* Career-related internships or fieldwork, Federal Work-Study, and scholarships/grants available. Financial award application deadline: 4/1; financial award applicants required to submit FAFSA. *Unit head:* Wilfred Lawrence, Department Chair of Education, 434-791-5752, E-mail: priedel@averett.edu. *Application contact:* Christy Pack, Executive Director of Enrollment, 804-887-8612, E-mail: dpack@averett.edu.
Website: http://www.averett.edu/adultprograms/degrees/MEDtrad.php.

Azusa Pacific University, School of Behavioral and Applied Sciences, Department of Doctoral Higher Education, Program in Higher Education Leadership, Azusa, CA 91702-7000. Offers Ed D.

Azusa Pacific University, School of Education, Program in School Administration, Azusa, CA 91702-7000. Offers MA. Part-time and evening/weekend programs available. *Degree requirements:* For master's, comprehensive exam or thesis, core exams, oral presentation. *Entrance requirements:* For master's, 12 units of course work in education, minimum GPA of 3.0. *Faculty research:* Instructional supervision, outcome-based education, technology and online searching, teacher preparation.

Baldwin Wallace University, Graduate Programs, Division of Education, Leadership in Higher Education Program, Berea, OH 44017-2088. Offers MA Ed. Part-time and evening/weekend programs available. *Faculty:* 2 full-time (1 woman), 4 part-time/adjunct (1 woman). *Students:* 24 full-time (21 women), 3 part-time (all women); includes 5 minority (3 Black or African American, non-Hispanic/Latino; 1 Asian, non-Hispanic/Latino; 1 Two or more races, non-Hispanic/Latino). Average age 29. 52 applicants, 23% accepted, 11 enrolled. In 2013, 11 master's awarded. *Degree requirements:* For master's, comprehensive exam (for some programs), capstone project, portfolio. *Entrance requirements:* For master's, bachelor's degree, MAT or minimum GPA of 2.75. Additional exam requirements/recommendations for international students: Required—TOEFL (minimum score 523 paper-based; 70 iBT). *Application deadline:* For fall admission, 8/15 for domestic students; for spring admission, 12/15 for domestic students. Applications are processed on a rolling basis. Application fee: $25. Electronic applications accepted. Application fee is waived when completed online. Tuition and fees vary according to program. *Financial support:* Paid internships for full-time students available. Financial award application deadline: 5/1; financial award applicants required to submit FAFSA. *Faculty research:* Program development in higher education, leadership styles, the psychology of leadership and learning in higher education. *Unit head:* Dr. Ken Schneck, Director, 440-826-8062, Fax: 440-826-3779, E-mail: kschneck@bw.edu. *Application contact:* Lydia Avery, Associate Director of Admission, Adult and Graduate Programs, 440-826-2222, Fax: 440-826-3830, E-mail: admission@bw.edu.
Website: http://www.bw.edu/academics/mae/hedleader.

Baldwin Wallace University, Graduate Programs, Division of Education, Specialization in School Leadership, Berea, OH 44017-2088. Offers MA Ed. Part-time and evening/weekend programs available. Postbaccalaureate distance learning degree programs offered (no on-campus study). *Faculty:* 2 full-time (0 women), 7 part-time/adjunct (2 women). *Students:* 14 full-time (5 women), 17 part-time (6 women); includes 2 minority (both Black or African American, non-Hispanic/Latino). Average age 31. 9 applicants, 78% accepted, 2 enrolled. In 2013, 7 master's awarded. *Degree requirements:* For master's, comprehensive exam, 2-semester internship. *Entrance requirements:* For master's, bachelor's degree in field, MAT or minimum GPA of 2.75. Additional exam requirements/recommendations for international students: Required—TOEFL (minimum score 523 paper-based; 70 iBT). *Application deadline:* For fall admission, 8/15 priority date for domestic students; for spring admission, 12/15 priority date for domestic students. Applications are processed on a rolling basis. Application fee: $25. Electronic applications accepted. Application fee is waived when completed online. *Expenses:* Contact institution. *Financial support:* Career-related internships or fieldwork available. Support available to part-time students. Financial award application deadline: 5/1; financial award applicants required to submit FAFSA. *Faculty research:* Leadership styles, instructional strategies, formative assessment. *Unit head:* Dr. Karen Kaye, Chair, 440-826-2168, Fax: 440-826-3779, E-mail: kkaye@bw.edu. *Application contact:* Winifred W. Gerhardt, Director of Admission, Adult and Graduate Programs, 440-826-2222, Fax: 440-826-3830, E-mail: admission@bw.edu.
Website: http://www.bw.edu/academics/mae/leader/.

Ball State University, Graduate School, Teachers College, Department of Educational Leadership, Program in Educational Administration, Muncie, IN 47306-1099. Offers MAE, Ed D. *Accreditation:* NCATE. *Students:* 38 full-time (20 women), 266 part-time (130 women); includes 28 minority (23 Black or African American, non-Hispanic/Latino; 1 Asian, non-Hispanic/Latino; 3 Hispanic/Latino; 1 Two or more races, non-Hispanic/Latino). Average age 29. 71 applicants, 66% accepted, 30 enrolled. In 2013, 205 master's, 4 doctorates awarded. *Degree requirements:* For doctorate, thesis/dissertation. *Entrance requirements:* For doctorate, GRE General Test, interview, minimum graduate GPA of 3.2. Application fee: $50. *Financial support:* In 2013–14, 1 student received support. Application deadline: 3/1. *Unit head:* Dr. Joseph McKinney, Head, 765-285-8495, E-mail: jmckinne@bsu.edu. *Application contact:* Dr. Janet Sauer, Academic Advisement Recruiter, School of Extended Education, 765-285-1599, E-mail: jssauer@bsu.edu.

Ball State University, Graduate School, Teachers College, Department of Educational Leadership, Program in School Superintendency, Muncie, IN 47306-1099. Offers Ed S. *Accreditation:* NCATE. *Students:* 8 part-time (4 women); includes 1 minority (Black or African American, non-Hispanic/Latino). Average age 38. 13 applicants, 38% accepted, 1 enrolled. In 2013, 15 Ed Ss awarded. *Degree requirements:* For Ed S, thesis. *Entrance requirements:* For degree, GRE General Test, interview. Application fee: $50. *Financial support:* Application deadline: 3/1. *Unit head:* Dr. Joseph McKinney, Chairperson, Educational Leadership, 765-285-8495, Fax: 765-285-2166, E-mail: jmckinne@bsu.edu. *Application contact:* Dr. William Sharp, Professor, Educational Leadership, 765-285-8488, E-mail: bsharp@bsu.edu.

Ball State University, Graduate School, Teachers College, Department of Educational Studies, Program in Executive Development, Muncie, IN 47306-1099. Offers MA. *Students:* 10 full-time (7 women), 30 part-time (22 women); includes 8 minority (7 Black or African American, non-Hispanic/Latino; 1 Two or more races, non-Hispanic/Latino). Average age 31. 19 applicants, 79% accepted, 8 enrolled. In 2013, 14 master's awarded. Application fee: $50. *Financial support:* In 2013–14, 1 student received support. Application deadline: 3/1. *Unit head:* Dr. Jayne Beilke, Director, 765-285-5460, Fax: 765-285-5489, E-mail: jbeilke@bsu.edu. *Application contact:* Dr. Robert Morris,

Associate Provost for Research and Dean of the Graduate School, 765-285-1300, E-mail: rmorris@bsu.edu.

Ball State University, Graduate School, Teachers College, Department of Educational Studies, Program in Student Affairs Administration in Higher Education, Muncie, IN 47306-1099. Offers MA. *Accreditation:* NCATE. *Students:* 40 full-time (25 women); includes 7 minority (4 Black or African American, non-Hispanic/Latino; 1 Asian, non-Hispanic/Latino; 1 Hispanic/Latino; 1 Native Hawaiian or other Pacific Islander, non-Hispanic/Latino). Average age 22. 216 applicants, 15% accepted, 29 enrolled. In 2013, 32 master's awarded. *Entrance requirements:* For master's, GRE General Test, interview. Application fee: $50. *Financial support:* In 2013–14, 41 students received support, including 40 research assistantships with full tuition reimbursements available (averaging $15,978 per year), 10 teaching assistantships with full tuition reimbursements available (averaging $10,771 per year). Financial award application deadline: 3/1. *Unit head:* Dr. Jayne Beilke, Director, 765-285-5460, Fax: 765-285-2464, E-mail: jbeilke@bsu.edu. *Application contact:* Dr. Roger Wessel, Professor of Higher Education, 765-285-5486, E-mail: rwessel@bsu.edu.
Website: http://www.bsu.edu/teachers/departments/edstudies/.

Bank Street College of Education, Graduate School, Programs in Educational Leadership, New York, NY 10025. Offers early childhood leadership (MS Ed); educational leadership (MS Ed); leadership for educational change (Ed M, MS Ed); leadership in community-based learning (MS Ed); leadership in mathematics education (MS Ed); leadership in museum education (MS Ed); leadership in the arts: creative writing (MS Ed); leadership in the arts: visual arts (MS Ed). *Degree requirements:* For master's, thesis. *Entrance requirements:* For master's, interview, essays, minimum of 2 years experience as a classroom teacher. Additional exam requirements/recommendations for international students: Required—TOEFL (minimum score 600 paper-based; 100 iBT), IELTS (minimum score 7). Electronic applications accepted. *Faculty research:* Leadership in urban schools, leadership in small schools, mathematics in elementary schools, professional development in early childhood, leadership in arts education, leadership in special education, museum leadership, community-based leadership.

Baptist Bible College of Pennsylvania, Graduate Studies, Clarks Summit, PA 18411-1297. Offers Bible (MA); counseling (MA, MS); curriculum and instruction (M Ed); educational administration (M Ed); intercultural studies (MA); literature (MA); missions (MA); organizational leadership (MA); reading specialist (M Ed); secondary English/communications (M Ed); social entrepreneurship (MA); worldview studies (MA). MA in missions program available only for Association of Baptists for World Evangelism missionary personnel. Part-time and evening/weekend programs available. Postbaccalaureate distance learning degree programs offered (no on-campus study). *Entrance requirements:* Additional exam requirements/recommendations for international students: Required—TOEFL (minimum score 500 paper-based).

Barry University, School of Education, Program in Educational Leadership, Miami Shores, FL 33161-6695. Offers MS, Ed D, Certificate, Ed S. Part-time and evening/weekend programs available. *Degree requirements:* For master's and other advanced degree, comprehensive exam. *Entrance requirements:* For master's, GRE General Test or MAT, minimum GPA of 3.0; for other advanced degree, GRE General Test, minimum GPA of 3.0. Electronic applications accepted.

Barry University, School of Education, Program in Higher Education Administration, Miami Shores, FL 33161-6695. Offers MS. Part-time and evening/weekend programs available. *Degree requirements:* For master's, comprehensive exam. *Entrance requirements:* For master's, GRE General Test or MAT, minimum GPA of 3.0. Electronic applications accepted.

Barry University, School of Education, Program in Leadership and Education, Miami Shores, FL 33161-6695. Offers educational technology (PhD); exceptional student education (PhD); higher education administration (PhD); human resource development (PhD); leadership (PhD). Part-time and evening/weekend programs available. *Degree requirements:* For doctorate, thesis/dissertation. *Entrance requirements:* For doctorate, GRE General Test, minimum GPA of 3.25. Electronic applications accepted.

Baruch College of the City University of New York, School of Public Affairs, Program in Educational Leadership, New York, NY 10010-5585. Offers educational leadership (MS Ed); school building leadership (Advanced Certificate); school district leadership (Advanced Certificate). Part-time and evening/weekend programs available. *Degree requirements:* For master's, internship. *Entrance requirements:* For master's, GRE or master's degree. Additional exam requirements/recommendations for international students: Required—TOEFL. Electronic applications accepted. *Faculty research:* School administration, program development, school leadership, violence in schools, school leadership development, school reform, school discipline policy, program development.

Baruch College of the City University of New York, School of Public Affairs, Program in Higher Education Administration, New York, NY 10010-5585. Offers MS Ed. Part-time and evening/weekend programs available. *Entrance requirements:* For master's, GRE General Test. Additional exam requirements/recommendations for international students: Required—TOEFL. Electronic applications accepted. *Expenses:* Contact institution.

Bayamón Central University, Graduate Programs, Program in Education, Bayamón, PR 00960-1725. Offers administration and supervision (MA Ed); commercial education (MA Ed); elementary education (K–3) (MA Ed); family counseling (Graduate Certificate); guidance and counseling (MA Ed); pre-elementary teacher (MA Ed); rehabilitation counseling (MA Ed); special education (MA Ed), including attention deficit disorder, education of the autistic, learning disabilities. Part-time and evening/weekend programs available. *Degree requirements:* For master's, comprehensive exam. *Entrance requirements:* For master's, EXADEP, bachelor's degree in education or related field.

Baylor University, Graduate School, School of Education, Department of Educational Administration, Waco, TX 76798. Offers MS Ed, Ed S. *Accreditation:* NCATE. *Students:* 27 full-time (21 women), 9 part-time (4 women); includes 7 minority (1 Black or African American, non-Hispanic/Latino; 1 Asian, non-Hispanic/Latino; 5 Hispanic/Latino). 90 applicants, 44% accepted. In 2013, 19 master's awarded. *Entrance requirements:* For master's, GRE General Test. *Application deadline:* Applications are processed on a rolling basis. Application fee: $25. *Expenses:* Tuition: Full-time $25,866; part-time $1437 per credit hour. *Required fees:* $2736; $152 per credit hour. Tuition and fees vary according to course load and program. *Financial support:* In 2013–14, 20 students received support, including 2 research assistantships; teaching assistantships, Federal Work-Study, institutionally sponsored loans, and scholarships/grants also available. *Unit head:* Dr. Robert Cloud, Graduate Program Director, 254-710-6110, Fax: 254-710-3265, E-mail: robert_cloud@baylor.edu. *Application contact:* Julie Baker, Administrative Assistant, 254-710-3050, Fax: 254-710-3870, E-mail: julie_l_baker@baylor.edu.
Website: https://www.baylor.edu/soe/eda/.

Bay Path College, Program in Higher Education Administration, Longmeadow, MA 01106-2292. Offers enrollment management (MS); general administration (MS); institutional advancement (MS); online teaching and program administration (MS). Part-time programs available. Postbaccalaureate distance learning degree programs offered (no on-campus study). *Students:* 3 full-time (2 women), 44 part-time (36 women);

includes 8 minority (5 Black or African American, non-Hispanic/Latino; 1 Asian, non-Hispanic/Latino; 1 Hispanic/Latino; 1 Two or more races, non-Hispanic/Latino). Average age 37. 37 applicants, 81% accepted, 21 enrolled. In 2013, 16 master's awarded. *Degree requirements:* For master's, 8 core courses (24 credits) and 4 elective courses (12 credits) for a total of 36 credits. *Application deadline:* Applications are processed on a rolling basis. Application fee: $45. Electronic applications accepted. Application fee is waived when completed online. *Financial support:* In 2013–14, 9 students received support. Scholarships/grants available. Financial award applicants required to submit FAFSA. *Unit head:* Dr. Lauren Way, Program Director, 413-565-1193. *Application contact:* Lisa Adams, Director of Graduate Admissions, 413-565-1317, Fax: 413-565-1250, E-mail: ladams@baypath.edu.
Website: http://graduate.baypath.edu/Graduate-Programs/Programs-Online/MS-Programs/Higher-Education-Administration.

Bellarmine University, Annsley Frazier Thornton School of Education, Louisville, KY 40205-0671. Offers education and social change (PhD); elementary education (MA Ed, MAT); learning and behavior disorders (MA Ed, MAT); middle grades education (MA Ed, MAT); principalship (Ed S); reading and writing (MA Ed); secondary education (MAT); teacher leadership (MA Ed). *Accreditation:* NCATE. Part-time and evening/weekend programs available. *Faculty:* 13 full-time (7 women), 14 part-time/adjunct (9 women). *Students:* 60 full-time (47 women), 191 part-time (140 women); includes 35 minority (22 Black or African American, non-Hispanic/Latino; 1 American Indian or Alaska Native, non-Hispanic/Latino; 3 Asian, non-Hispanic/Latino; 5 Hispanic/Latino; 4 Two or more races, non-Hispanic/Latino). Average age 33. In 2013, 108 master's awarded. *Degree requirements:* For master's, comprehensive exam, thesis (for some programs); for doctorate, comprehensive exam, thesis/dissertation. *Entrance requirements:* For master's, GRE, baccalaureate degree from accredited institution; minimum overall GPA of 2.75, 3.0 in major; letters of recommendation; valid Kentucky provisional or professional certificate; for doctorate, GRE, minimum GPA of 3.5 in all graduate coursework; baccalaureate and master's degrees in education (MA, MS) or fields directly relevant to education; three letters of recommendation; two essays (no more than 1000 words each); interview. Additional exam requirements/recommendations for international students: Required—TOEFL (minimum score 550 paper-based; 80 iBT). *Application deadline:* Applications are processed on a rolling basis. Application fee: $25. *Expenses:* Contact institution. *Financial support:* Scholarships/grants available. Financial award applicants required to submit FAFSA. *Faculty research:* Literacy, service-learning, dispositions, educational technology, special education. *Unit head:* Dr. Robert Cooter, Dean, 502-272-8191, Fax: 502-272-8189, E-mail: rcooter@bellarmine.edu. *Application contact:* Theresa Klapheke, Administrative Director of Graduate Programs, 502-272-8271, Fax: 502-272-8002, E-mail: tklapheke@bellarmine.edu.
Website: http://www.bellarmine.edu/education/graduate.

Benedictine College, Master of Arts in Education Program, Atchison, KS 66002-1499. Offers M Ed. *Faculty:* 3 full-time (2 women), 1 (woman) part-time/adjunct. *Students:* 3 full-time (all women). 6 applicants, 100% accepted, 6 enrolled. In 2013, 3 master's awarded. *Entrance requirements:* For master's, minimum GPA of 3.0 in last two years (60 hours) of college course work from accredited institutions, official transcripts, bachelor's degree, teacher certification/licensure, resume, essay. *Application deadline:* For fall admission, 8/15 for domestic students. Applications are processed on a rolling basis. *Faculty research:* Teacher leadership, special education issues, diversity in schools, Catholic social leadership, professional development. *Unit head:* Dr. Cheryl Reding, Director, 913-360-7384, E-mail: creding@benedictine.edu. *Application contact:* Donna Bonnel, Administrative Assistant, 913-367-5340 Ext. 2524, Fax: 913-367-5462, E-mail: emba@benedictine.edu.

Benedictine College, Master of Arts Program in School Leadership, Atchison, KS 66002-1499. Offers MA. *Accreditation:* NCATE. Part-time and evening/weekend programs available. *Faculty:* 3 full-time (2 women), 1 (woman) part-time/adjunct. *Students:* 18 full-time (10 women). 9 applicants, 100% accepted, 9 enrolled. In 2013, 6 master's awarded. *Degree requirements:* For master's, comprehensive exam, practicum. *Entrance requirements:* For master's, minimum GPA of 3.0. *Application deadline:* For fall admission, 8/15 priority date for domestic students; for spring admission, 5/15 priority date for domestic students. Applications are processed on a rolling basis. Application fee: $35. *Expenses:* Contact institution. *Financial support:* Scholarships/grants available. Support available to part-time students. Financial award applicants required to submit FAFSA. *Faculty research:* Teacher leadership, special education issues, diversity in schools, Catholic school leadership, professional development. *Unit head:* Dr. Cheryl Reding, Director, 913-360-7384, E-mail: creding@benedictine.edu. *Application contact:* Donna Bonnel, Administrative Assistant, 913-360-7589, Fax: 913-360-7301, E-mail: emba@benedictine.edu.
Website: http://www.benedictine.edu/masl.

Benedictine University, Graduate Programs, Program in Education, Lisle, IL 60532-0900. Offers curriculum and instruction and collaborative teaching (M Ed); elementary education (MA Ed); leadership and administration (M Ed); reading and literacy (M Ed); secondary education (MA Ed); special education (MA Ed). Part-time and evening/weekend programs available. *Students:* 6 full-time (all women), 124 part-time (106 women); includes 14 minority (8 Black or African American, non-Hispanic/Latino; 1 American Indian or Alaska Native, non-Hispanic/Latino; 2 Asian, non-Hispanic/Latino; 3 Hispanic/Latino). 21 applicants, 62% accepted, 8 enrolled. In 2013, 120 master's awarded. *Degree requirements:* For master's, comprehensive exam, thesis (for some programs). *Entrance requirements:* For master's, GRE or MAT. Additional exam requirements/recommendations for international students: Required—TOEFL (minimum score 550 paper-based). *Application deadline:* For fall admission, 9/1 for domestic students; for winter admission, 12/1 for domestic students; for spring admission, 2/15 for domestic students. Applications are processed on a rolling basis. Application fee: $40. Electronic applications accepted. *Expenses:* Contact institution. *Financial support:* Career-related internships or fieldwork and health care benefits available. Support available to part-time students. *Unit head:* MeShelda Jackson, Director, 630-829-6282, E-mail: mjackson@ben.edu. *Application contact:* Kari Gibbons, Associate Vice President, Enrollment Center, 630-829-6200, Fax: 630-829-6584, E-mail: kgibbons@ben.edu.

Benedictine University, Graduate Programs, Program in Higher Education and Organizational Change, Lisle, IL 60532-0900. Offers Ed D. *Students:* 43 full-time (30 women), 47 part-time (30 women); includes 26 minority (18 Black or African American, non-Hispanic/Latino; 2 Asian, non-Hispanic/Latino; 6 Hispanic/Latino). 32 applicants, 94% accepted, 26 enrolled. In 2013, 9 doctorates awarded. Application fee: $40. *Expenses: Tuition:* Part-time $590 per credit hour. *Unit head:* Dr. Sunil Chand, Director, 630-829-1930, E-mail: schand@ben.edu. *Application contact:* Kari Gibbons, Associate Vice President, Enrollment Center, 630-829-6200, Fax: 630-829-6584, E-mail: kgibbons@ben.edu.

Berry College, Graduate Programs, Graduate Programs in Education, Program in Educational Leadership, Mount Berry, GA 30149-0159. Offers Ed S. *Faculty:* 2 part-time/adjunct (1 woman). *Students:* 18 part-time (14 women); includes 6 minority (all Black or African American, non-Hispanic/Latino). Average age 40. In 2013, 45 Ed Ss awarded. *Degree requirements:* For Ed S, thesis, portfolio, oral exams. *Entrance requirements:* For degree, M Ed from NCATE-accredited school, minimum GPA of 3.25. Additional exam requirements/recommendations for international students: Required—TOEFL (minimum score 550 paper-based). *Application deadline:* For fall admission, 7/25 for domestic students, 5/1 for international students; for spring admission, 12/1 for domestic students, 10/1 for international students. Applications are processed on a rolling basis. Application fee: $25 ($30 for international students). Electronic applications accepted. *Expenses: Tuition:* Full-time $9900; part-time $550 per credit hour. *Required fees:* $150. Tuition and fees vary according to program. *Financial support:* In 2013–14, 2 students received support. Research assistantships available. Support available to part-time students. Financial award application deadline: 3/1; financial award applicants required to submit FAFSA. *Unit head:* Dr. Jacqueline McDowell, Dean, Charter School of Education and Human Sciences, 706-236-1717, Fax: 706-238-5827, E-mail: jmcdowell@berry.edu. *Application contact:* Brett Kennedy, Assistant Vice President of Enrollment Management, 706-236-2215, Fax: 706-290-2178, E-mail: admissions@berry.edu.
Website: http://www.berry.edu/academics/education/graduate/.

Bethel University, Graduate Programs, McKenzie, TN 38201. Offers administration and supervision (MA Ed); business administration (MBA); conflict resolution (MA); physician assistant studies (MS). Part-time and evening/weekend programs available. *Degree requirements:* For master's, thesis (for some programs). *Entrance requirements:* For master's, GRE General Test or MAT, minimum undergraduate GPA of 2.5.

Bethel University, Graduate School, St. Paul, MN 55112-6999. Offers autism spectrum disorders (Certificate); business administration (MBA); communication (MA); counseling psychology (MA); educational leadership (Ed D); gerontology (MA); international baccalaureate education (Certificate); K-12 education (MA); literacy education (MA, Certificate); nurse educator (Certificate); nurse leader (Certificate); nurse-midwifery (MS); nursing (MS); physician assistant (MS); postsecondary teaching (Certificate); special education (MA); strategic leadership (MA); teaching (MA). Part-time and evening/weekend programs available. Postbaccalaureate distance learning degree programs offered (no on-campus study). *Faculty:* 13 full-time (7 women), 89 part-time/adjunct (43 women). *Students:* 692 full-time (457 women), 573 part-time (371 women); includes 170 minority (86 Black or African American, non-Hispanic/Latino; 1 American Indian or Alaska Native, non-Hispanic/Latino; 49 Asian, non-Hispanic/Latino; 20 Hispanic/Latino; 1 Native Hawaiian or other Pacific Islander, non-Hispanic/Latino; 13 Two or more races, non-Hispanic/Latino), 21 international. Average age 37. In 2013, 166 master's, 9 doctorates, 11 other advanced degrees awarded. *Degree requirements:* For master's, comprehensive exam (for some programs), thesis (for some programs); for doctorate, comprehensive exam, thesis/dissertation. *Entrance requirements:* Additional exam requirements/recommendations for international students: Required—TOEFL (minimum score 550 paper-based; 80 iBT). *Application deadline:* Applications are processed on a rolling basis. Electronic applications accepted. Tuition and fees vary according to course load, degree level and program. *Financial support:* Teaching assistantships, career-related internships or fieldwork, and scholarships/grants available. Support available to part-time students. Financial award applicants required to submit FAFSA. *Unit head:* Dick Crombie, Vice-President/Dean, 651-635-8000, Fax: 651-635-8004, E-mail: gs@bethel.edu. *Application contact:* Director of Admissions, 651-635-8000, Fax: 651-635-8004, E-mail: gs@bethel.edu.
Website: http://gs.bethel.edu/.

Binghamton University, State University of New York, Graduate School, College of Community and Public Affairs, Department of Student Affairs Administration, Vestal, NY 13850. Offers MS. *Faculty:* 3 full-time (2 women), 1 part-time/adjunct (0 women). *Students:* 37 full-time (26 women), 11 part-time (6 women); includes 7 minority (1 Black or African American, non-Hispanic/Latino; 1 Asian, non-Hispanic/Latino; 5 Hispanic/Latino). Average age 27. 32 applicants, 94% accepted, 19 enrolled. In 2013, 17 master's awarded. Application fee: $75. *Financial support:* In 2013–14, 32 students received support. Career-related internships or fieldwork, Federal Work-Study, institutionally sponsored loans, scholarships/grants, health care benefits, and unspecified assistantships available. Financial award application deadline: 2/15; financial award applicants required to submit FAFSA. *Unit head:* Dr. Mary Ann Swain, Chair, 607-777-9219, E-mail: mswain@binghamton.edu. *Application contact:* Kishan Zuber, Recruiting and Admissions Coordinator, 607-777-2151, Fax: 607-777-2501, E-mail: kzuber@binghamton.edu.
Website: http://www2.binghamton.edu/ccpa/student-affairs-administration/.

Binghamton University, State University of New York, Graduate School, School of Education, Program in Educational Theory and Practice, Vestal, NY 13850. Offers educational leadership (Certificate); educational studies (MS); educational theory and practice (Ed D). MS program also offered for working teachers in Greater New Orleans. *Students:* 6 full-time (5 women), 83 part-time (67 women); includes 12 minority (7 Black or African American, non-Hispanic/Latino; 1 American Indian or Alaska Native, non-Hispanic/Latino; 2 Asian, non-Hispanic/Latino; 2 Hispanic/Latino), 6 international. Average age 42. 36 applicants, 50% accepted, 12 enrolled. In 2013, 16 master's, 3 doctorates, 6 other advanced degrees awarded. *Degree requirements:* For doctorate, thesis/dissertation. *Entrance requirements:* For doctorate, GRE General Test, writing sample. Additional exam requirements/recommendations for international students: Required—TOEFL (minimum score 550 paper-based; 80 iBT). *Application deadline:* For fall admission, 2/1 priority date for domestic and international students. Applications are processed on a rolling basis. Application fee: $75. Electronic applications accepted. *Financial support:* In 2013–14, 11 students received support, including 1 fellowship with full tuition reimbursement available (averaging $15,500 per year), 1 teaching assistantship with full tuition reimbursement available (averaging $15,500 per year); career-related internships or fieldwork, Federal Work-Study, institutionally sponsored loans, scholarships/grants, health care benefits, tuition waivers (full), and unspecified assistantships also available. Financial award application deadline: 2/15; financial award applicants required to submit FAFSA. *Unit head:* Dr. S. G. Grant, Dean of The Graduate School of Education, 607-777-6041, E-mail: jcarpent@binghamton.edu. *Application contact:* Kishan Zuber, Recruiting and Admissions Coordinator, 607-777-2151, Fax: 607-777-2501, E-mail: kzuber@binghamton.edu.
Website: http://www2.binghamton.edu/gse/doctoral-program/index.html.

Bob Jones University, Graduate Programs, Greenville, SC 29614. Offers accountancy (MS); Bible (MA); Bible translation (MA); Biblical studies (Certificate); broadcast management (MS); business administration (MBA); church history (MA, PhD); church ministries (MA); church music (MM); cinema and video production (MA); counseling (MS); curriculum and instruction (Ed D); divinity (M Div); dramatic production (MA); educational leadership (MS, Ed D, Ed S); elementary education (M Ed, MAT); English (M Ed, MA, MAT); fine arts (MA); graphic design (MA); history (M Ed, MA); illustration (MA); interpretative speech (MA); mathematics (M Ed, MAT); medical missions (Certificate); ministry (MM, D Min); multi-categorical special education (M Ed, MAT); music (M Ed); New Testament interpretation (PhD); Old Testament interpretation (PhD); orchestral instrument performance (MM); organ performance (MM); pastoral studies (MA); personnel services (MS, Ed S); piano pedagogy (MM); piano performance (MM); platform arts (MA); radio and television broadcasting (MS); rhetoric and public address (MA); secondary education (M Ed); studio art (MA); teaching Bible (MA); theology (MA, PhD); voice performance (MM); youth ministries (MA); M Div/MM.

Boise State University, College of Education, Department of Curriculum, Instruction and Foundational Studies, Boise, ID 83725-0399. Offers curriculum and instruction (Ed D); education, curriculum and instruction (MA); educational leadership (M Ed). *Accreditation:* NCATE. Part-time programs available. *Degree requirements:* For master's, thesis optional. *Entrance requirements:* For master's, minimum GPA of 3.0. Electronic applications accepted.

Boston College, Lynch Graduate School of Education, Program in Educational Leadership, Chestnut Hill, MA 02467-3800. Offers M Ed, Ed D, CAES, JD/M Ed. Part-time and evening/weekend programs available. *Students:* 7 full-time (3 women), 4 part-time (2 women). 41 applicants, 56% accepted, 11 enrolled. In 2013, 9 master's, 4 CAESs awarded. *Degree requirements:* For master's and CAES, comprehensive exam. *Entrance requirements:* For master's and CAES, GRE General Test or MAT; for doctorate, GRE General Test. Additional exam requirements/recommendations for international students: Required—TOEFL (minimum score 100 iBT). *Application deadline:* For fall admission, 12/1 priority date for domestic and international students; for spring admission, 11/1 for domestic and international students. Application fee: $65. Electronic applications accepted. *Financial support:* Fellowships with full and partial tuition reimbursements, research assistantships with full and partial tuition reimbursements, teaching assistantships with full and partial tuition reimbursements, career-related internships or fieldwork, Federal Work-Study, scholarships/grants, traineeships, health care benefits, tuition waivers (full and partial), and unspecified assistantships available. Support available to part-time students. Financial award applicants required to submit FAFSA. *Faculty research:* Politics of urban education, principalship, urban Catholic schools, educational leadership, educational law and policy. *Unit head:* Dr. Ana M. Martinez-Aleman, Chairperson, 617-552-4214, Fax: 617-552-0398. *Application contact:* Domenic Lomanno, Director, Graduate Admission and Financial Aid, 617-552-4214, Fax: 617-552-0398, E-mail: lomanno@bc.edu.

Bowie State University, Graduate Programs, Program in Educational Leadership/Executive Fellows, Bowie, MD 20715-9465. Offers Ed D. Part-time and evening/weekend programs available. *Degree requirements:* For doctorate, comprehensive exam, thesis/dissertation. Electronic applications accepted. *Expenses:* Tuition, state resident: full-time $8665. Tuition, nonresident: full-time $16,007. *Required fees:* $1927.

Bowie State University, Graduate Programs, Program in Elementary and Secondary School Administration, Bowie, MD 20715-9465. Offers M Ed. Part-time and evening/weekend programs available. *Degree requirements:* For master's, comprehensive exam. *Entrance requirements:* For master's, copy of Advance Teaching Certificate, 3 years teaching experience, letter of recommendation from current supervisor. Electronic applications accepted. *Expenses:* Tuition, state resident: full-time $8665. Tuition, nonresident: full-time $16,007. *Required fees:* $1927.

Bowie State University, Graduate Programs, Program in School Administration and Supervision, Bowie, MD 20715-9465. Offers M Ed. Part-time and evening/weekend programs available. *Degree requirements:* For master's, comprehensive exam, thesis optional, research paper. *Entrance requirements:* For master's, minimum undergraduate GPA of 3.0, 3 years of teaching experience, teaching certificate. *Expenses:* Tuition, state resident: full-time $8665. Tuition, nonresident: full-time $16,007. *Required fees:* $1927.

Bowling Green State University, Graduate College, College of Education and Human Development, School of Leadership and Policy Studies, Program in Educational Administration and Supervision, Bowling Green, OH 43403. Offers educational administration and supervision (M Ed, Ed S); leadership studies (Ed D). *Accreditation:* NCATE. Part-time and evening/weekend programs available. *Degree requirements:* For master's, thesis or alternative; for doctorate, comprehensive exam, thesis/dissertation; for Ed S, thesis or alternative, field experience or internship. *Entrance requirements:* For master's, doctorate, and Ed S, GRE General Test. Additional exam requirements/recommendations for international students: Required—TOEFL. Electronic applications accepted. *Faculty research:* Professional development for school leaders, organizational development, school finance, legal challenges to school decision making, administering urban schools.

Bowling Green State University, Graduate College, College of Education and Human Development, School of Leadership and Policy Studies, Program in Higher Education Administration, Bowling Green, OH 43403. Offers PhD. *Accreditation:* NCATE. Part-time programs available. *Degree requirements:* For doctorate, comprehensive exam, thesis/dissertation. *Entrance requirements:* For doctorate, GRE General Test. Additional exam requirements/recommendations for international students: Required—TOEFL. Electronic applications accepted. *Faculty research:* Adult learners, legal issues, intellectual development.

Bradley University, Graduate School, College of Education and Health Sciences, Department of Educational Leadership and Human Development, Peoria, IL 61625-0002. Offers human development counseling (MA), including community and agency counseling, school counseling; leadership in educational administration (MA); leadership in human service administration (MA). *Accreditation:* ACA; NCATE. Part-time and evening/weekend programs available. *Degree requirements:* For master's, comprehensive exam, thesis optional. *Entrance requirements:* For master's, GRE General Test or MAT, interview, 3 letters of recommendation. Additional exam requirements/recommendations for international students: Required—TOEFL (minimum score 550 paper-based; 79 iBT). *Expenses:* Tuition: Full-time $14,580; part-time $810 per credit hour. Tuition and fees vary according to course load and program.

Brandman University, School of Education, Irvine, CA 92618. Offers education (MA); educational leadership (MA); school counseling (MA); special education (MA); teaching (MA).

Brandon University, Faculty of Education, Brandon, MB R7A 6A9, Canada. Offers curriculum and instruction (M Ed, Diploma); educational administration (M Ed, Diploma); guidance and counseling (M Ed, Diploma); special education (M Ed, Diploma). *Degree requirements:* For master's, thesis. *Entrance requirements:* For master's, minimum GPA of 3.0, teaching certificate or equivalent. Additional exam requirements/recommendations for international students: Required—TOEFL. *Faculty research:* Comparative education, environmental studies, parent/school council.

Bridgewater State University, School of Graduate Studies, School of Education and Allied Studies, Department of Secondary Education and Professional Programs, Program in Educational Leadership, Bridgewater, MA 02325-0001. Offers M Ed, CAGS. *Accreditation:* NCATE. Part-time and evening/weekend programs available. *Degree requirements:* For master's and CAGS, comprehensive exam. *Entrance requirements:* For master's, GRE General Test or Massachusetts Test for Educator Licensure, work experience; for CAGS, master's degree.

Brigham Young University, Graduate Studies, David O. McKay School of Education, Department of Educational Leadership and Foundations, Provo, UT 84602. Offers M Ed, Ed D. Part-time and evening/weekend programs available. *Faculty:* 10 full-time (2 women), 2 part-time/adjunct (0 women). *Students:* 7 full-time (5 women), 67 part-time (25 women); includes 5 minority (1 Asian, non-Hispanic/Latino; 2 Hispanic/Latino; 2 Native Hawaiian or other Pacific Islander, non-Hispanic/Latino), 5 international. Average age 37. 55 applicants, 51% accepted, 26 enrolled. In 2013, 25 master's, 5 doctorates

awarded. *Degree requirements:* For master's, comprehensive exam, thesis or alternative; for doctorate, comprehensive exam, thesis/dissertation. *Entrance requirements:* For master's, GRE, MAT, LSAT, GMAT; for doctorate, GRE, LSAT, GMAT. Additional exam requirements/recommendations for international students: Required—TOEFL (minimum score 580 paper-based; 85 iBT). *Application deadline:* For fall and spring admission, 2/15 for domestic and international students; for summer admission, 3/1 for domestic and international students. Application fee: $50. Electronic applications accepted. *Expenses:* Tuition: Full-time $6130; part-time $340 per credit hour. Tuition and fees vary according to program and student's religious affiliation. *Financial support:* In 2013–14, research assistantships (averaging $950 per year) were awarded. Financial award application deadline: 9/1. *Faculty research:* Mentoring, pre-service training of administrators, policy development, cross-cultural studies of educational leadership. *Unit head:* Dr. Sterling Clint Hilton, Chair, 801-422-4291, Fax: 801-422-0196, E-mail: edlfsec@byu.edu. *Application contact:* Bonnie Bennett, Department Secretary, 801-422-3813, Fax: 801-422-0196, E-mail: bonnie_bennett@byu.edu.
Website: http://education.byu.edu/edlf/.

Brooklyn College of the City University of New York, Division of Graduate Studies, School of Education, Program in Educational Leadership, Brooklyn, NY 11210-2889. Offers MS Ed. Part-time and evening/weekend programs available. *Entrance requirements:* For master's, 2 supervisory letters of recommendation, essay, resume, teaching certificate, interview, supplemental application. Additional exam requirements/recommendations for international students: Required—TOEFL (minimum score 500 paper-based; 61 iBT). Electronic applications accepted.

Buffalo State College, State University of New York, The Graduate School, Faculty of Applied Science and Education, Department of Elementary Education and Reading, Program in Educational Leadership, Buffalo, NY 14222-1095. Offers CAS. *Accreditation:* NCATE. Part-time and evening/weekend programs available. *Degree requirements:* For CAS, internship. *Entrance requirements:* For degree, master's degree, New York teaching certificate, 3 years of teaching experience. Additional exam requirements/recommendations for international students: Required—TOEFL (minimum score 550 paper-based).

Butler University, College of Education, Indianapolis, IN 46208-3485. Offers educational administration (MS); effective teaching and leadership (MS); school counseling (MS). *Accreditation:* ACA; NCATE. Part-time and evening/weekend programs available. *Faculty:* 6 full-time (4 women), 19 part-time/adjunct (14 women). *Students:* 14 full-time (12 women), 96 part-time (71 women); includes 19 minority (13 Black or African American, non-Hispanic/Latino; 3 Asian, non-Hispanic/Latino; 2 Hispanic/Latino; 1 Two or more races, non-Hispanic/Latino), 3 international. Average age 31. 58 applicants, 79% accepted, 15 enrolled. In 2013, 51 master's awarded. *Entrance requirements:* For master's, GRE General Test, MAT, interview. *Application deadline:* For fall admission, 8/15 priority date for domestic students. Applications are processed on a rolling basis. Application fee: $35. Electronic applications accepted. *Financial support:* Institutionally sponsored loans available. Support available to part-time students. Financial award application deadline: 7/15; financial award applicants required to submit FAFSA. *Unit head:* Dr. Ena Shelley, Dean, 317-940-9752, Fax: 317-940-6481. *Application contact:* Diane Dubord, Graduate Student Services Specialist, 317-940-8100, Fax: 317-940-8250, E-mail: ddubord@butler.edu.
Website: http://www.butler.edu/academics/graduate-coe/.

Cairn University, School of Education, Langhorne, PA 19047-2990. Offers educational leadership and administration (MS El); teacher education (MS Ed). Part-time and evening/weekend programs available. *Faculty:* 1 (woman) full-time, 2 part-time/adjunct (both women). *Students:* 6 full-time (3 women), 44 part-time (32 women); includes 20 minority (9 Black or African American, non-Hispanic/Latino; 1 American Indian or Alaska Native, non-Hispanic/Latino; 7 Asian, non-Hispanic/Latino; 2 Hispanic/Latino; 1 Native Hawaiian or other Pacific Islander, non-Hispanic/Latino), 1 international. Average age 37. 15 applicants, 73% accepted, 9 enrolled. In 2013, 28 master's awarded. *Entrance requirements:* Additional exam requirements/recommendations for international students: Required—TOEFL (minimum score 550 paper-based). *Application deadline:* Applications are processed on a rolling basis. Application fee: $25. Electronic applications accepted. *Expenses:* Tuition: Full-time $11,250; part-time $625 per credit. Tuition and fees vary according to program. *Financial support:* Scholarships/grants available. Support available to part-time students. Financial award applicants required to submit FAFSA. *Unit head:* Dr. Paula Gossard, Dean, 215-702-4264, E-mail: teacher.ed@cairn.edu. *Application contact:* Abigail Sattler, Enrollment Counselor, Graduate Education, 800-572-2472, Fax: 215-702-4248, E-mail: asattler@cairn.edu.
Website: http://www.cairn.edu/academics/education.

Caldwell University, Graduate Studies, Division of Education, Caldwell, NJ 07006-6195. Offers curriculum and instruction (MA); education (Postbaccalaureate Certificate); educational administration (MA); learning disabilities teacher-consultant (Post-Master's Certificate); literacy instruction (MA); principal (Post-Master's Certificate); reading specialist (Post-Master's Certificate); special education (MA), including special education, teaching of students with disabilities, teaching of students with disabilities and learning disabilities teacher-consultant; superintendent (Post-Master's Certificate); supervisor (Post-Master's Certificate). Part-time and evening/weekend programs available. *Faculty:* 11 full-time (7 women), 12 part-time/adjunct (6 women). *Students:* 42 full-time (31 women), 255 part-time (219 women); includes 40 minority (14 Black or African American, non-Hispanic/Latino; 5 Asian, non-Hispanic/Latino; 18 Hispanic/Latino; 1 Native Hawaiian or other Pacific Islander, non-Hispanic/Latino; 2 Two or more races, non-Hispanic/Latino). Average age 37. 140 applicants, 71% accepted, 83 enrolled. In 2013, 63 master's awarded. *Degree requirements:* For master's, comprehensive exam (for some programs). *Entrance requirements:* For master's, PRAXIS, 3 years of work experience, prior teaching certification. Additional exam requirements/recommendations for international students: Required—TOEFL (minimum score 580 paper-based). *Application deadline:* Applications are processed on a rolling basis. Application fee: $40. Electronic applications accepted. *Financial support:* Career-related internships or fieldwork available. Financial award applicants required to submit FAFSA. *Faculty research:* Curriculum and instruction, secondary education, special education, education and technology. *Unit head:* Dr. Janice Stewart, Division Associate Dean, 973-618-3626, E-mail: jstewart@caldwell.edu. *Application contact:* Vilma Mueller, Director of Graduate Studies, 973-618-3544, E-mail: graduate@caldwell.edu.

California Baptist University, Program in Education, Riverside, CA 92504-3206. Offers educational leadership for faith-based institutions (MS); educational leadership for public institutions (MS); educational technology (MS); instructional computer applications (MS); international education (MS); leadership and adult learning (MS); leadership and organizational studies (MS); reading (MS); school counseling (MS); school psychology (MS); science education (MS); special education in mild/moderate disabilities (MS); special education in moderate/severe disabilities (MS); teaching (MS); teaching and learning (MS); TESOL (teachers of English to speakers of other languages) (MS). Part-time and evening/weekend programs available. Postbaccalaureate distance learning degree programs offered (minimal on-campus study). *Faculty:* 18 full-time (9 women), 8 part-time/adjunct (5 women). *Students:* 158 full-time (127 women), 228 part-time (179 women); includes 159 minority (27 Black or

African American, non-Hispanic/Latino; 4 American Indian or Alaska Native, non-Hispanic/Latino; 13 Asian, non-Hispanic/Latino; 107 Hispanic/Latino; 1 Native Hawaiian or other Pacific Islander, non-Hispanic/Latino; 7 Two or more races, non-Hispanic/Latino), 2 international. Average age 33. 298 applicants, 74% accepted, 113 enrolled. In 2013, 70 master's awarded. *Degree requirements:* For master's, comprehensive exam, project, or thesis. *Entrance requirements:* For master's, minimum undergraduate GPA of 3.0; 18 semester units of prerequisite course work in education; three recommendations; 500-word essay; interview. Additional exam requirements/recommendations for international students: Required—TOEFL (minimum score 80 iBT). *Application deadline:* For fall admission, 8/1 priority date for domestic students, 7/1 for international students; for spring admission, 12/1 priority date for domestic students, 11/1 for international students. Applications are processed on a rolling basis. Application fee: $45. Electronic applications accepted. *Expenses:* Contact institution. *Financial support:* Institutionally sponsored loans available. Financial award applicants required to submit CSS PROFILE or FAFSA. *Faculty research:* Leadership development, complexity theory, faith and learning, special education, social and philosophical contexts of education. *Unit head:* Dr. John Shoup, Dean, School of Education, 951-343-4205, Fax: 951-343-4516, E-mail: jshoup@calbaptist.edu. *Application contact:* Dr. Kathryn Norwood, Director, Master of Science Program in Education, 951-343-4760, E-mail: knorwood@calbaptist.edu.
Website: http://www.calbaptist.edu/mastersined/.

California Baptist University, Program in Leadership and Adult Learning, Riverside, CA 92504-3206. Offers MA. Part-time and evening/weekend programs available. *Degree requirements:* For master's, professional training or leadership tactics. *Entrance requirements:* For master's, minimum undergraduate GPA of 2.75, bachelor's degree transcripts, three recommendations, essay, resume. Additional exam requirements/recommendations for international students: Required—TOEFL (minimum score 80 iBT). *Application deadline:* For fall admission, 8/1 priority date for domestic students, 7/1 for international students; for spring admission, 12/1 priority date for domestic students, 11/1 for international students. Applications are processed on a rolling basis. Application fee: $45. Electronic applications accepted. *Expenses:* Contact institution. *Financial support:* Applicants required to submit CSS PROFILE or FAFSA. *Unit head:* Dr. John Shoup, Dean, School of Education, 951-343-4205, E-mail: jshoup@calbaptist.edu. *Application contact:* Fax: 877-228-8877.
Website: http://www.calbaptist.edu/explore-cbu/schools-colleges/school-education/programs/graduate/master-arts-leadership-and-adult-learning/.

California Coast University, School of Education, Santa Ana, CA 92701. Offers administration (M Ed); curriculum and instruction (M Ed); educational administration (Ed D); educational psychology (Ed D); organizational leadership (Ed D). Postbaccalaureate distance learning degree programs offered (no on-campus study).

California Lutheran University, Graduate Studies, Graduate School of Education, Thousand Oaks, CA 91360-2787. Offers counseling and guidance (MS), including college student personnel, counseling and guidance; educational leadership (MA, Ed D), including educational leadership (K-12) (Ed D), higher education leadership (Ed D); special education (MS); teacher leadership (M Ed); teaching (M Ed). *Accreditation:* NCATE. Part-time and evening/weekend programs available. *Faculty:* 18 full-time (14 women), 28 part-time/adjunct (20 women). *Students:* 327 full-time (260 women), 96 part-time (77 women); includes 150 minority (7 Black or African American, non-Hispanic/Latino; 20 Asian, non-Hispanic/Latino; 112 Hispanic/Latino; 11 Two or more races, non-Hispanic/Latino), 1 international. Average age 33. 123 applicants, 85% accepted, 80 enrolled. In 2013, 117 master's, 9 doctorates awarded. *Entrance requirements:* For master's, GRE General Test, interview, minimum GPA of 3.0. *Application deadline:* For fall admission, 7/1 priority date for domestic students; for spring admission, 11/1 priority date for domestic students; for summer admission, 4/1 priority date for domestic students. Applications are processed on a rolling basis. Application fee: $50. *Unit head:* Dr. Robert Fraisse, Dean, 805-493-3421. *Application contact:* 805-493-3325, Fax: 805-493-3861, E-mail: clugrad@callutheran.edu.

California State Polytechnic University, Pomona, Academic Affairs, College of Education and Integrative Studies, Ed D Program in Educational Leadership, Pomona, CA 91768-2557. Offers Ed D. *Students:* 34 part-time (29 women); includes 15 minority (2 Black or African American, non-Hispanic/Latino; 1 Asian, non-Hispanic/Latino; 11 Hispanic/Latino; 1 Native Hawaiian or other Pacific Islander, non-Hispanic/Latino). Average age 40. 30 applicants, 70% accepted, 18 enrolled. Application fee: $55. *Expenses:* Tuition, state resident: full-time $6738. Tuition, nonresident: full-time $12,690. *Required fees:* $878; $248 per credit hour. *Unit head:* Dr. Peggy Kelly, Dean, 909-869-2307, E-mail: pkelly@csupomona.edu. *Application contact:* Dr. Dorothy MacNevin, Co-Chair, Graduate Education Department, 909-869-2311, Fax: 909-869-4822, E-mail: dmacnevin@csupomona.edu.
Website: http://www.csupomona.edu/~doctoralstudies/.

California State Polytechnic University, Pomona, Academic Affairs, College of Education and Integrative Studies, Master's Programs in Education, Pomona, CA 91768-2557. Offers curriculum and instruction (MA); educational leadership (MA); educational multimedia (MA); special education (MA). *Students:* 39 full-time (26 women), 140 part-time (96 women); includes 91 minority (9 Black or African American, non-Hispanic/Latino; 1 American Indian or Alaska Native, non-Hispanic/Latino; 24 Asian, non-Hispanic/Latino; 53 Hispanic/Latino; 3 Native Hawaiian or other Pacific Islander, non-Hispanic/Latino; 1 Two or more races, non-Hispanic/Latino), 3 international. Average age 35. 64 applicants, 64% accepted, 25 enrolled. In 2013, 74 master's awarded. Application fee: $55. *Expenses:* Tuition, state resident: full-time $6738. Tuition, nonresident: full-time $12,690. *Required fees:* $878; $248 per credit hour. *Unit head:* Dr. Peggy Kelly, Dean, 909-869-2307, E-mail: pkelly@csupomona.edu. *Application contact:* Dr. Dorothy MacNevin, Co-Chair, Graduate Education Department, 909-869-2311, Fax: 909-869-4822, E-mail: dmacnevin@csupomona.edu.

California State University, Bakersfield, Division of Graduate Studies, School of Social Sciences and Education, Program in Educational Administration, Bakersfield, CA 93311. Offers MA. *Degree requirements:* For master's, thesis or alternative, project or culminating exam. *Application deadline:* Applications are processed on a rolling basis. Application fee: $55. *Unit head:* Dr. Louis Wildman, Graduate Coordinator, 661-664-3047, Fax: 661-664-2278, E-mail: lwildman@csub.edu. *Application contact:* Debbie Blowers, Assistant Director of Admissions, 661-664-3381, E-mail: dblowers@csub.edu.
Website: http://www.csub.edu/sse/departments/advancededucationalstudies/education_administration/index.html.

California State University, Chico, Office of Graduate Studies, College of Communication and Education, School of Education, Option in Educational Leadership Administration, Chico, CA 95929-0722. Offers MA. *Accreditation:* NCATE. *Degree requirements:* For master's, comprehensive exam, thesis or project. *Entrance requirements:* Additional exam requirements/recommendations for international students: Required—TOEFL (minimum score 550 paper-based; 80 iBT), IELTS (minimum score 6.5). Electronic applications accepted.

California State University, Dominguez Hills, College of Education, Division of Graduate Education, Program in School Leadership, Carson, CA 90747-0001. Offers MA. Part-time and evening/weekend programs available. *Faculty:* 2 full-time (1 woman), 7 part-time/adjunct (3 women). *Students:* 145 full-time (84 women), 19 part-time (10 women); includes 113 minority (30 Black or African American, non-Hispanic/Latino; 13 Asian, non-Hispanic/Latino; 63 Hispanic/Latino; 7 Two or more races, non-Hispanic/Latino), 1 international. Average age 38. 164 applicants, 97% accepted, 133 enrolled. In 2013, 65 master's awarded. *Degree requirements:* For master's, comprehensive exam. *Entrance requirements:* For master's, minimum GPA of 2.75. *Application deadline:* For fall admission, 6/1 for domestic students. Applications are processed on a rolling basis. Application fee: $55. *Expenses:* Tuition, state resident: full-time $6738. Tuition, nonresident: full-time $13,434. *Required fees:* $622. *Faculty research:* Educational leadership, teacher retention, accountability, decision-making. *Unit head:* Dr. Ann Chlebicki, Executive Director, 310-243-3510, E-mail: achlebicki@csudh.edu. *Application contact:* Admissions Office, 310-243-3530.
Website: http://www4.csudh.edu/coe/programs/grad-prgs/slp/index.

California State University, East Bay, Office of Academic Programs and Graduate Studies, College of Education and Allied Studies, Department of Educational Leadership, Hayward, CA 94542-3000. Offers educational leadership (MS, Ed D); urban teaching leadership (MS). *Accreditation:* NCATE. Part-time and evening/weekend programs available. Postbaccalaureate distance learning degree programs offered. *Degree requirements:* For master's, comprehensive exam, project or thesis; for doctorate, thesis/dissertation. *Entrance requirements:* For master's, CBEST, teaching or services credential and experience; minimum GPA of 3.0; for doctorate, GRE, MA with minimum GPA of 3.0; PK-12 leadership position; portfolio of work samples; employer/district support agreement. Additional exam requirements/recommendations for international students: Required—TOEFL (minimum score 550 paper-based). Electronic applications accepted.

California State University, Fresno, Division of Graduate Studies, School of Education and Human Development, Department of Educational Research and Administration, Fresno, CA 93740-8027. Offers education (MA), including administration and supervision. *Accreditation:* NCATE. Part-time and evening/weekend programs available. *Degree requirements:* For master's, thesis or alternative. *Entrance requirements:* For master's, GRE General Test, MAT, minimum GPA of 2.75. Additional exam requirements/recommendations for international students: Required—TOEFL. Electronic applications accepted. *Faculty research:* Substance abuse on youth education.

California State University, Fresno, Division of Graduate Studies, School of Education and Human Development, Doctoral Program in Educational Leadership, Fresno, CA 93740-8027. Offers Ed D. Part-time programs available. *Degree requirements:* For doctorate, thesis/dissertation. *Entrance requirements:* For doctorate, GRE or MAT, minimum GPA of 3.2, master's degree. Additional exam requirements/recommendations for international students: Required—TOEFL. Electronic applications accepted. *Faculty research:* Minority special education leadership, literacy, ethics of leadership, organizational planning, language development.

California State University, Fullerton, Graduate Studies, College of Education, Department of Educational Leadership, Fullerton, CA 92834-9480. Offers community college educational leadership (Ed D); educational administration (MS); higher education (MS); pre K-12 educational leadership (Ed D). *Accreditation:* NCATE. Part-time programs available. *Students:* 2 full-time (0 women), 230 part-time (147 women); includes 133 minority (26 Black or African American, non-Hispanic/Latino; 33 Asian, non-Hispanic/Latino; 67 Hispanic/Latino; 7 Two or more races, non-Hispanic/Latino), 12 international. Average age 36. 192 applicants, 48% accepted, 84 enrolled. In 2013, 52 master's, 26 doctorates awarded. *Degree requirements:* For master's, thesis or alternative, project. *Entrance requirements:* For master's, minimum GPA of 2.5. Application fee: $55. *Financial support:* Career-related internships or fieldwork, Federal Work-Study, institutionally sponsored loans, and scholarships/grants available. Support available to part-time students. Financial award application deadline: 3/1; financial award applicants required to submit FAFSA. *Faculty research:* Creation of a substance abuse prevention training and demonstration program. *Unit head:* Jennifer Goldstein, Head, 657-278-3963. *Application contact:* Admissions/Applications, 657-278-2371.

California State University, Long Beach, Graduate Studies, College of Education, Department of Advanced Studies in Education and Counseling, Program in Educational Administration, Long Beach, CA 90840. Offers MA, Ed D. *Degree requirements:* For master's, comprehensive exam, project or thesis. *Entrance requirements:* For master's, GRE General Test, minimum GPA of 2.75. Electronic applications accepted.

California State University, Northridge, Graduate Studies, College of Education, Department of Educational Leadership and Policy Studies, Northridge, CA 91330. Offers education (MA); educational administration (MA); educational leadership (Ed D). *Accreditation:* NCATE. Part-time and evening/weekend programs available. *Entrance requirements:* For master's, 2 letters of recommendation. Additional exam requirements/recommendations for international students: Required—TOEFL. *Faculty research:* Bilingual educational training.

California State University, Sacramento, Office of Graduate Studies, College of Education, Department of Educational Leadership and Policy Studies, Sacramento, CA 95819. Offers educational leadership (MA), including PreK-12; higher education leadership (MA), including community college leadership, student services. Part-time programs available. *Degree requirements:* For master's, thesis or project; writing proficiency exam. *Entrance requirements:* For master's, minimum GPA of 2.5. Additional exam requirements/recommendations for international students: Required—TOEFL. *Application deadline:* For fall admission, 3/1 for domestic and international students; for spring admission, 9/30 for international students. Applications are processed on a rolling basis. Application fee: $55. Electronic applications accepted. *Financial support:* Career-related internships or fieldwork and Federal Work-Study available. Support available to part-time students. Financial award application deadline: 3/1; financial award applicants required to submit FAFSA. *Unit head:* Dr. Francisco Reveles, Chair, 916-278-5388, Fax: 916-278-4608, E-mail: revelesf@csus.edu. *Application contact:* Jose Martinez, Graduate Admissions Supervisor, 916-278-7871, E-mail: martinj@skymail.csus.edu.
Website: http://www.edweb.csus.edu/edlp.

California State University, San Bernardino, Graduate Studies, College of Education, Program in Educational Administration, San Bernardino, CA 92407-2397. Offers MA. Part-time and evening/weekend programs available. *Students:* 28 full-time (17 women), 27 part-time (20 women); includes 19 minority (2 Black or African American, non-Hispanic/Latino; 16 Hispanic/Latino; 1 Two or more races, non-Hispanic/Latino). Average age 38. 34 applicants, 85% accepted, 23 enrolled. In 2013, 52 master's awarded. *Degree requirements:* For master's, thesis or alternative. *Entrance requirements:* For master's, minimum GPA of 3.0 in education. *Application deadline:* For fall admission, 8/31 priority date for domestic students. Application fee: $55. *Financial support:* Career-related internships or fieldwork available. Support available to part-time students. *Unit head:* Dr. Thelma Moore-Steward, Interim Department Chair, 909-537-5646, Fax: 909-537-7510, E-mail: msteward@csusb.edu. *Application contact:* Dr. Jeffrey Thompson, Dean of Graduate Studies, 909-537-5058, E-mail: jthompso@csusb.edu.

California State University, San Bernardino, Graduate Studies, College of Education, Program in Educational Leadership and Curriculum, San Bernardino, CA 92407-2397. Offers Ed D. *Students:* 1 (woman) full-time, 53 part-time (37 women); includes 110

minority (88 Black or African American, non-Hispanic/Latino; 3 Asian, non-Hispanic/Latino; 18 Hispanic/Latino; 1 Two or more races, non-Hispanic/Latino), 1 international. Average age 38. 18 applicants, 83% accepted, 14 enrolled. *Unit head:* Dr. Jay Feine, Dean, 909-537-7621, E-mail: jfiene@csusb.edu. *Application contact:* Dr. Jeffrey Thompson, Dean of Graduate Studies, 909-537-5058, E-mail: jthompso@csusb.edu.

California State University, San Marcos, School of Education, San Marcos, CA 92096-0001. Offers educational administration (MA); educational leadership (Ed D); general education (MA); literacy education (MA); special education (MA). *Accreditation:* NCATE (one or more programs are accredited). Part-time and evening/weekend programs available. *Degree requirements:* For master's, thesis. *Entrance requirements:* For master's, minimum GPA of 3.0, teaching credentials, 1 year of teaching experience. Tuition and fees vary according to program. *Faculty research:* Multicultural literature, art as knowledge, poetry and second language acquisition, restructuring K–12 education and improving the training of K–8 science teachers.

California State University, Stanislaus, College of Education, Program in Education (MA), Turlock, CA 95382. Offers curriculum and instruction (MA), including education technology, elementary education, multilingual education, physical education, reading, secondary education, special education; school administration (MA); school counseling (MA). Part-time and evening/weekend programs available. *Degree requirements:* For master's, comprehensive exam (for some programs), thesis (for some programs). *Entrance requirements:* For master's, MAT, GRE, or CBEST (varies by concentration), 3 letters of recommendation, personal statement. Additional exam requirements/recommendations for international students: Required—TOEFL (minimum score 550 paper-based). Electronic applications accepted. *Faculty research:* Children's perspectives on historical events, method elementary schools dual language education, K-12 reading programs.

California State University, Stanislaus, College of Education, Programs in Educational Leadership (Ed D), Turlock, CA 95382. Offers community college leadership (Ed D); P-12 leadership (Ed D). Part-time and evening/weekend programs available. *Degree requirements:* For doctorate, thesis/dissertation. *Entrance requirements:* For doctorate, GRE, minimum GPA of 3.0, 3 letters of reference, interview, personal statement. Additional exam requirements/recommendations for international students: Required—TOEFL (minimum score 550 paper-based). Electronic applications accepted.

California University of Pennsylvania, School of Graduate Studies and Research, College of Education and Human Services, Program in School Administration, California, PA 15419-1394. Offers M Ed. *Accreditation:* NCATE. Part-time and evening/weekend programs available. *Degree requirements:* For master's, comprehensive exam, thesis optional. *Entrance requirements:* For master's, MAT, interview, minimum GPA of 3.0, teaching certificate, 2 years of teaching experience. Additional exam requirements/recommendations for international students: Required—TOEFL (minimum score 550 paper-based; 80 iBT). Electronic applications accepted. *Faculty research:* Educational leadership, peer coaching, online education-effective teaching strategies, instruction strategies, school law.

Calumet College of Saint Joseph, Program in Leadership in Teaching, Whiting, IN 46394-2195. Offers MS Ed.

Calvin College, Graduate Programs in Education, Grand Rapids, MI 49546-4388. Offers curriculum and instruction (M Ed); educational leadership (M Ed); learning disabilities (M Ed); literacy (M Ed). Part-time programs available. *Faculty:* 12 full-time (5 women). *Students:* 9 full-time (7 women), 133 part-time (87 women); includes 12 minority (3 Black or African American, non-Hispanic/Latino; 3 Asian, non-Hispanic/Latino; 3 Hispanic/Latino; 3 Two or more races, non-Hispanic/Latino), 20 international. Average age 29. 15 applicants, 87% accepted, 13 enrolled. In 2013, 27 master's awarded. *Degree requirements:* For master's, thesis or seminar. *Entrance requirements:* For master's, teaching certificate. Additional exam requirements/recommendations for international students: Required—TOEFL (minimum score 550 paper-based; 80 iBT). *Application deadline:* For fall admission, 8/1 priority date for domestic students, 5/1 priority date for international students; for spring admission, 1/1 priority date for domestic students, 12/1 priority date for international students; for summer admission, 5/18 for domestic students. Applications are processed on a rolling basis. Application fee: $0. Electronic applications accepted. *Financial support:* Federal Work-Study, scholarships/grants, and tuition waivers (full and partial) available. Financial award application deadline: 4/3; financial award applicants required to submit FAFSA. *Faculty research:* Literacy, racialized gender and gendered identity, teacher learning, learning disabilities identification, leadership. *Unit head:* Dr. David Smith, Graduate Program Director, 616-526-6158, Fax: 616-526-6505, E-mail: dsmith@calvin.edu. *Application contact:* Cindi Hoekstra, Program Coordinator, 616-526-6158, Fax: 616-526-6505, E-mail: choekstr@calvin.edu.
Website: http://www.calvin.edu/academic/graduate_studies.

Cambridge College, School of Education, Cambridge, MA 02138-5304. Offers autism specialist (M Ed); autism/behavior analyst (M Ed); behavior analyst (Post-Master's Certificate); behavioral management (M Ed); early childhood teacher (M Ed); education specialist in curriculum and instruction (CAGS); educational leadership (Ed D); elementary teacher (M Ed); English as a second language (M Ed, Certificate); general science (M Ed); health education (Post-Master's Certificate); health/family and consumer sciences (M Ed); history (M Ed); individualized (M Ed); information technology literacy (M Ed); instructional technology (M Ed); interdisciplinary studies (M Ed); library teacher (M Ed); literacy education (M Ed); mathematics (M Ed); mathematics specialist (Certificate); middle school mathematics and science (M Ed); school administration (M Ed, CAGS); school guidance counselor (M Ed); school nurse education (M Ed); school social worker/school adjustment counselor (M Ed); special education administrator (CAGS); special education/moderate disabilities (M Ed); teaching skills and methodologies (M Ed). Part-time and evening/weekend programs available. Postbaccalaureate distance learning degree programs offered (minimal on-campus study). *Degree requirements:* For master's, thesis, internship/practicum (licensure program only); for doctorate, thesis/dissertation; for other advanced degree, thesis. *Entrance requirements:* For master's, interview, resume, documentation of licensure, 2 professional references; for doctorate, official transcripts, interview, resume, documentation of licensure (if any), written personal statement/essay, portfolio of scholarly and professional work, qualifying assessment, 2 professional references, health insurance, immunizations form; for other advanced degree, official transcripts, interview, resume, documentation of licensure (if any), written personal statement/essay, 2 professional references, health insurance, immunizations form. Additional exam requirements/recommendations for international students: Required—TOEFL (minimum score 550 paper-based; 79 iBT), Michigan English Language Assessment Battery (minimum score 85); Recommended—IELTS (minimum score 6). Electronic applications accepted. *Expenses:* Contact institution. *Faculty research:* Adult education, accelerated learning, mathematics education, brain compatible learning, special education and law.

Cameron University, Office of Graduate Studies, Program in Educational Leadership, Lawton, OK 73505-6377. Offers MS. Part-time and evening/weekend programs available. *Degree requirements:* For master's, portfolio.

Campbell University, Graduate and Professional Programs, School of Education, Buies Creek, NC 27506. Offers administration (MSA); community counseling (MA); elementary education (M Ed); English education (M Ed); interdisciplinary studies (M Ed); mathematics education (M Ed); middle grades education (M Ed); physical education (M Ed); school counseling (M Ed); secondary education (M Ed); social science education (M Ed). *Accreditation:* NCATE. Part-time and evening/weekend programs available. *Degree requirements:* For master's, comprehensive exam. *Entrance requirements:* For master's, GRE General Test, minimum GPA of 2.7. *Faculty research:* Spiritual values and wellness issues in counseling, stress and professional burnout among counselors, thinking strategies, leadership, adaptive technology.

Canisius College, Graduate Division, School of Education and Human Services, Department of Graduate Education and Leadership, Buffalo, NY 14208-1098. Offers business and marketing education (MS Ed); college student personnel (MS Ed); deaf education (MS Ed); deaf/adolescent education, grades 7-12 (MS Ed); deaf/childhood education, grades 1-6 (MS Ed); differentiated instruction (MS Ed); education administration (MS); educational administration (MS Ed); educational technologies (Certificate); gifted education extension (Certificate); literacy (MS Ed); reading (Certificate); school building leadership (MS Ed, Certificate); school district leadership (Certificate); teacher leader (Certificate); TESOL (MS Ed). *Accreditation:* NCATE. Part-time and evening/weekend programs available. Postbaccalaureate distance learning degree programs offered (minimal on-campus study). *Faculty:* 6 full-time (5 women), 33 part-time/adjunct (20 women). *Students:* 134 full-time (106 women), 267 part-time (213 women); includes 36 minority (22 Black or African American, non-Hispanic/Latino; 1 American Indian or Alaska Native, non-Hispanic/Latino; 3 Asian, non-Hispanic/Latino; 8 Hispanic/Latino; 2 Two or more races, non-Hispanic/Latino), 2 international. Average age 30. 282 applicants, 80% accepted, 120 enrolled. In 2013, 178 master's awarded. *Entrance requirements:* For master's, GRE if cumulative GPA less than 2.7, transcripts, two letters of recommendation. Additional exam requirements/recommendations for international students: Required—TOEFL (minimum score 550 paper-based, 80 iBT), IELTS (minimum score 6.5), or CAEL (minimum score 70). *Application deadline:* Applications are processed on a rolling basis. Application fee: $25. Electronic applications accepted. Application fee is waived when completed online. *Expenses:* Tuition: Part-time $750 per credit hour. *Financial support:* Career-related internships or fieldwork, Federal Work-Study, scholarships/grants, tuition waivers (partial), and unspecified assistantships available. Support available to part-time students. Financial award application deadline: 4/30; financial award applicants required to submit FAFSA. *Faculty research:* Asperger's disease, autism, private higher education, reading strategies. *Unit head:* Dr. Rosemary K. Murray, Chair/Associate Professor of Graduate Education and Leadership, 716-888-3723, E-mail: murray1@canisius.edu. *Application contact:* Julie A. Zulewski, Director of Graduate Admissions, 716-888-2548, Fax: 716-888-3195, E-mail: zulewskj@canisius.edu.
Website: http://www.canisius.edu/graduate/.

Capella University, School of Education, Doctoral Programs in Education, Minneapolis, MN 55402. Offers curriculum and instruction (PhD); educational leadership and management (Ed D); instructional design for online learning (PhD); K-12 studies in education (PhD); leadership for higher education (PhD); leadership in educational administration (PhD); postsecondary and adult education (PhD); professional studies in education (PhD); reading and literacy (Ed D); special education leadership (PhD); training and performance improvement (PhD).

Capella University, School of Education, Master's Programs in Education, Minneapolis, MN 55402. Offers adult education (MS); curriculum and instruction (MS); early childhood education (MS); enrollment management (MS); higher education leadership and management (MS); instructional design for online learning (MS); integrative studies (MS); K-12 studies in education (MS); leadership in educational administration (MS); reading and literacy (MS); special education teaching (MS).

Cardinal Stritch University, College of Education, Department of Education, Milwaukee, WI 53217-3985. Offers education (ME); educational leadership (MS); leadership for the advancement of learning and service (Ed D, PhD); teaching (MAT); urban education (MA). *Accreditation:* NCATE. Evening/weekend programs available. *Degree requirements:* For master's, comprehensive exam, thesis (for some programs), research project, faculty recommendation; for doctorate, thesis/dissertation, practica, field experience. *Entrance requirements:* For master's, letters of recommendation (3), minimum GPA of 3.0; for doctorate, minimum GPA of 3.5 in master's coursework, letters of recommendation (3).

Caribbean University, Graduate School, Bayamón, PR 00960-0493. Offers administration and supervision (MA Ed); criminal justice (MA); curriculum and instruction (MA Ed, PhD), including elementary education (MA Ed), English education (MA Ed), history education (MA Ed), mathematics education (MA Ed), primary education (MA Ed), science education (MA Ed), Spanish education (MA Ed); educational technology in instructional systems (MA Ed); gerontology (MSN); human resources (MBA); museology, archiving and art history (MA Ed); neonatal pediatrics (MSN); physical education (MA Ed); special education (MA Ed). *Entrance requirements:* For master's, interview, minimum GPA of 2.5.

Carson-Newman University, Graduate Program in Education, Jefferson City, TN 37760. Offers curriculum and instruction (M Ed); educational leadership (M Ed); elementary education (MAT); school counseling (MS); secondary education (MAT); teaching English as a second language (MATESL). *Accreditation:* NCATE. Part-time and evening/weekend programs available. *Faculty:* 5 full-time (2 women), 10 part-time/adjunct (3 women). *Students:* 25 full-time (12 women), 100 part-time (70 women); includes 8 minority (4 Black or African American, non-Hispanic/Latino; 1 Asian, non-Hispanic/Latino; 1 Hispanic/Latino; 2 Two or more races, non-Hispanic/Latino), 1 international. Average age 32. In 2013, 34 master's awarded. *Degree requirements:* For master's, thesis or alternative. *Entrance requirements:* For master's, NTE, minimum GPA of 3.0 in major, 2.5 overall. *Application deadline:* For fall admission, 7/15 priority date for domestic students. Applications are processed on a rolling basis. Application fee: $25 ($50 for international students). *Expenses:* Tuition: Part-time $390 per credit hour. *Financial support:* Federal Work-Study and unspecified assistantships available. Financial award application deadline: 4/1; financial award applicants required to submit FAFSA. *Unit head:* Dr. Sharon Teets, Chair, 865-471-3461. *Application contact:* Graduate Admissions and Services Adviser, 865-471-3460, Fax: 865-471-3875.

Carthage College, Division of Teacher Education, Kenosha, WI 53140. Offers classroom guidance and counseling (M Ed); creative arts (M Ed); gifted and talented children (M Ed); language arts (M Ed); modern language (M Ed); natural sciences (M Ed); reading (M Ed, Certificate); social sciences (M Ed); teacher leadership (M Ed). Part-time and evening/weekend programs available. *Degree requirements:* For master's, thesis optional. *Entrance requirements:* For master's, MAT, minimum B average, letters of reference.

Castleton State College, Division of Graduate Studies, Department of Education, Program in Educational Leadership, Castleton, VT 05735. Offers MA Ed, CAGS. Part-time and evening/weekend programs available. *Degree requirements:* For master's, thesis or alternative; for CAGS, publishable paper. *Entrance requirements:* For master's,

GRE General Test, MAT, interview, minimum undergraduate GPA of 3.0; for CAGS, educational research, master's degree, minimum undergraduate GPA of 3.0.

The Catholic University of America, School of Arts and Sciences, Department of Education, Washington, DC 20064. Offers Catholic educational leadership and policy studies (PhD); Catholic school leadership (MA); education (Certificate); educational psychology (PhD); secondary education (MA); special education (MA). *Accreditation:* NCATE. Part-time programs available. *Faculty:* 9 full-time (8 women), 4 part-time/adjunct (all women). *Students:* 9 full-time (6 women), 44 part-time (37 women); includes 8 minority (3 Black or African American, non-Hispanic/Latino; 3 Hispanic/Latino; 2 Two or more races, non-Hispanic/Latino), 2 international. Average age 34. 53 applicants, 53% accepted, 17 enrolled. In 2013, 18 master's, 2 doctorates awarded. *Degree requirements:* For master's, comprehensive exam, thesis or alternative; for doctorate, comprehensive exam, thesis/dissertation; for Certificate, action research project. *Entrance requirements:* For master's and doctorate, GRE General Test or MAT, statement of purpose, official copies of academic transcripts, three letters of recommendation, interview; for Certificate, PRAXIS I, statement of purpose, official copies of academic transcripts, three letters of recommendation, interview. Additional exam requirements/recommendations for international students: Required—TOEFL (minimum score 580 paper-based). *Application deadline:* For fall admission, 8/1 priority date for domestic students, 7/15 for international students; for spring admission, 12/1 priority date for domestic students, 10/15 for international students. Applications are processed on a rolling basis. Application fee: $55. Electronic applications accepted. *Expenses: Tuition:* Full-time $38,500; part-time $1490 per credit hour. *Required fees:* $400; $1525 per credit hour. One-time fee: $425. Tuition and fees vary according to program. *Financial support:* Fellowships, research assistantships, teaching assistantships, Federal Work-Study, scholarships/grants, tuition waivers (full and partial), and unspecified assistantships available. Financial award application deadline: 2/1; financial award applicants required to submit FAFSA. *Faculty research:* Special education, early childhood education, educational psychology, Catholic school administration, leadership and policy studies, counseling, curriculum and instruction. *Total annual research expenditures:* $65,883. *Unit head:* Dr. Merylann J. Schuttloffel, Chair, 202-319-5805, Fax: 202-319-5815, E-mail: schuttloffel@cua.edu. *Application contact:* Andrew Woodall, Director of Graduate Admissions, 202-319-5057, Fax: 202-319-6533, E-mail: cua-admissions@cua.edu.
Website: http://education.cua.edu/.

Cedarville University, Graduate Programs, Cedarville, OH 45314-0601. Offers business administration (MBA); curriculum (M Ed); educational administration (M Ed); family nurse practitioner (MSN); global health ministries (MSN); instruction (M Ed); pharmacy (Pharm D). Part-time programs available. Postbaccalaureate distance learning degree programs offered (no on-campus study). *Faculty:* 23 full-time (12 women), 12 part-time/adjunct (5 women). *Students:* 119 full-time (74 women), 103 part-time (73 women); includes 16 minority (11 Black or African American, non-Hispanic/Latino; 4 Asian, non-Hispanic/Latino; 1 Native Hawaiian or other Pacific Islander, non-Hispanic/Latino), 4 international. Average age 31. In 2013, 26 master's awarded. *Degree requirements:* For master's, thesis. *Entrance requirements:* For master's, GRE, 2 professional recommendations; for doctorate, PCAT, professional recommendation from a practicing pharmacist or current employer/supervisor, resume, essay, interview. Additional exam requirements/recommendations for international students: Required—TOEFL (minimum score 550 paper-based; 80 iBT). *Application deadline:* For fall admission, 5/1 priority date for domestic and international students; for spring admission, 11/1 priority date for domestic and international students. Applications are processed on a rolling basis. Application fee: $30. Electronic applications accepted. *Financial support:* Scholarships/grants and unspecified assistantships available. Support available to part-time students. Financial award applicants required to submit FAFSA. *Unit head:* Dr. Mark McClain, Dean of Graduate Studies, 937-766-7700, E-mail: mcclain@cedarville.edu. *Application contact:* Roscoe F. Smith, Associate Vice-President of Enrollment, 937-766-7700, Fax: 937-766-7575, E-mail: smithr@cedarville.edu.
Website: http://www.cedarville.edu/academics/graduate/.

Centenary College, Program in Education, Hackettstown, NJ 07840-2100. Offers educational leadership (MA); instructional leadership (MA); special education (MA). *Accreditation:* Teacher Education Accreditation Council. Part-time and evening/weekend programs available. Postbaccalaureate distance learning degree programs offered (minimal on-campus study). *Degree requirements:* For master's, thesis. *Entrance requirements:* For master's, interview, minimum undergraduate GPA of 2.8.

Centenary College of Louisiana, Graduate Programs, Department of Education, Shreveport, LA 71104. Offers administration (M Ed); elementary education (MAT); secondary education (MAT); supervision of instruction (M Ed). Part-time and evening/weekend programs available. *Degree requirements:* For master's, comprehensive exam. *Entrance requirements:* For master's, GRE General Test (M Ed), PRAXIS I and PRAXIS II (MAT), teacher certification (M Ed), minimum GPA of 2.5. *Expenses:* Contact institution. *Faculty research:* Teachers as advocates for teachers, portfolio assessment, disabled readers.

Central Connecticut State University, School of Graduate Studies, School of Education and Professional Studies, Department of Educational Leadership, Program in Educational Leadership, New Britain, CT 06050-4010. Offers MS, Ed D, AC, Sixth Year Certificate. Part-time and evening/weekend programs available. *Students:* 3 full-time (1 woman), 225 part-time (145 women); includes 37 minority (18 Black or African American, non-Hispanic/Latino; 3 Asian, non-Hispanic/Latino; 14 Hispanic/Latino; 1 Native Hawaiian or other Pacific Islander, non-Hispanic/Latino; 1 Two or more races, non-Hispanic/Latino). Average age 40. 130 applicants, 71% accepted, 67 enrolled. In 2013, 89 master's, 14 doctorates, 47 other advanced degrees awarded. *Degree requirements:* For master's, thesis or alternative; for doctorate, thesis/dissertation or alternative; for other advanced degree, thesis or alternative, qualifying exam. *Entrance requirements:* For master's, minimum undergraduate GPA of 2.7; for doctorate, GRE, master's degree, essay, interview, resume, letters of recommendation; for other advanced degree, master's degree, minimum undergraduate GPA of 3.0, essay, portfolio, letters of recommendation. Additional exam requirements/recommendations for international students: Required—TOEFL (minimum score 550 paper-based; 79 iBT). *Application deadline:* For fall admission, 6/1 for domestic students, 5/1 for international students; for spring admission, 11/1 for domestic and international students. Applications are processed on a rolling basis. Application fee: $50. Electronic applications accepted. Part-time tuition and fees vary according to degree level. *Unit head:* Dr. Ellen Retelle, Chair, 860-832-2130, E-mail: retelleelm@ccsu.edu. *Application contact:* Patricia Gardner, Associate Director of Graduate Studies, 860-832-2350, Fax: 860-832-2362, E-mail: graduateadmissions@ccsu.edu.

Central Michigan University, Central Michigan University Global Campus, Program in Education, Mount Pleasant, MI 48859. Offers college teaching (Graduate Certificate); community college (MA); curriculum and instruction (MA); educational technology (MA); guidance and development (MA); reading and literacy K-12 (MA); school principalship (MA), including charter school leadership; training and development (MA). *Accreditation:* Teacher Education Accreditation Council. Part-time and evening/weekend programs available. *Entrance requirements:* For master's, minimum GPA of 2.7 in major. Additional exam requirements/recommendations for international students: Required—TOEFL. *Application deadline:* Applications are processed on a rolling basis. Application fee: $50. Electronic applications accepted. *Financial support:* Scholarships/grants available. Support available to part-time students. *Unit head:* Kaleb Patrick, Director, 989-774-3144, E-mail: patri1kg@cmich.edu. *Application contact:* 877-268-4636, E-mail: cmuglobal@cmich.edu.

Central Michigan University, Central Michigan University Global Campus, Program in Educational Leadership, Mount Pleasant, MI 48859. Offers educational administration (Ed S); educational administration and community leadership (Ed D). Part-time and evening/weekend programs available. *Entrance requirements:* Additional exam requirements/recommendations for international students: Required—TOEFL. *Application deadline:* Applications are processed on a rolling basis. Application fee: $50. Electronic applications accepted. *Financial support:* Scholarships/grants available. Support available to part-time students. *Unit head:* Patrick Graham, Coordinator, New Program and Cohort Enrollment Support, 989-774-1661, E-mail: graha1pm@cmich.edu. *Application contact:* 877-268-4636, E-mail: cmuglobal@cmich.edu.

Central Michigan University, College of Graduate Studies, College of Education and Human Services, Department of Educational Leadership, Mount Pleasant, MI 48859. Offers educational leadership (Ed D), including educational technology (Ed D, Ed S), higher education leadership, K-12 curriculum, K-12 leadership; general educational administration (Ed S), including administrative leadership K-12, educational technology (Ed D, Ed S), higher education administration, instructional leadership K-12; school principalship (MA), including charter school leadership, site-based leadership; student affairs administration (MA); teacher leadership (MA). Part-time and evening/weekend programs available. *Degree requirements:* For master's and Ed S, thesis or alternative; for doctorate, thesis/dissertation. *Entrance requirements:* For doctorate, GRE or MAT, master's degree, minimum GPA of 3.5, 3 years of professional education experience. Electronic applications accepted. *Faculty research:* Elementary administration, secondary administration, student achievement, in-service training, internships in administration.

Central Washington University, Graduate Studies and Research, College of Education and Professional Studies, Department of Advanced Programs, Ellensburg, WA 98926. Offers higher education (M Ed); school administration (M Ed); school instructional leadership (M Ed). Part-time programs available. *Degree requirements:* For master's, comprehensive exam, thesis or alternative. *Entrance requirements:* Additional exam requirements/recommendations for international students: Required—TOEFL (minimum score 550 paper-based), IELTS (minimum score 6.5). Electronic applications accepted.

Chadron State College, School of Professional and Graduate Studies, Department of Education, Chadron, NE 69337. Offers business (MA Ed); community counseling (MA Ed); educational administration (MS Ed, Sp Ed); elementary education (MS Ed); history (MA Ed); language and literature (MA Ed); secondary administration (MS Ed); secondary education (MS Ed). *Accreditation:* NCATE. Part-time and evening/weekend programs available. Postbaccalaureate distance learning degree programs offered. *Degree requirements:* For master's, thesis optional. *Entrance requirements:* For master's, GRE General Test, GRE Writing Test, minimum GPA of 2.75 or 12 graduate hours at CSC with minimum GPA of 3.25. Additional exam requirements/recommendations for international students: Required—TOEFL. Electronic applications accepted. *Faculty research:* Rural education, technology, mental health.

Chaminade University of Honolulu, Graduate Services, Program in Education, Honolulu, HI 96816-1578. Offers child development (M Ed); early childhood education (M Ed); educational leadership (M Ed); elementary education (MAT); instructional leadership (M Ed); Montessori education (M Ed); secondary education (MAT), including English, math, science, social studies; special education (MAT). Part-time and evening/weekend programs available. Postbaccalaureate distance learning degree programs offered (minimal on-campus study). *Degree requirements:* For master's, thesis or alternative. *Entrance requirements:* For master's, PRAXIS (for MAT only), minimum GPA of 2.75, 3 letters of recommendation. Additional exam requirements/recommendations for international students: Required—TOEFL (minimum score 550 paper-based). Electronic applications accepted. *Faculty research:* Peace and curriculum education.

Chapman University, College of Educational Studies, Orange, CA 92866. Offers communication sciences and disorders (MS); counseling (MA), including school counseling (MA, Credential); education (PhD), including cultural and curricular studies, disability studies, leadership studies, school psychology (PhD, Credential); educational psychology (MA); leadership development (MA); pupil personnel services (Credential), including school counseling (MA, Credential), school psychology (PhD, Credential); school psychology (Ed S); single subject (Credential); special education (MA, Credential), including mild/moderate (Credential), moderate/severe (Credential); speech language pathology (Credential); teaching (MA), including elementary education, secondary education. *Accreditation:* Teacher Education Accreditation Council. Part-time and evening/weekend programs available. *Faculty:* 29 full-time (18 women), 56 part-time/adjunct (38 women). *Students:* 251 full-time (208 women), 194 part-time (150 women); includes 185 minority (13 Black or African American, non-Hispanic/Latino; 61 Asian, non-Hispanic/Latino; 97 Hispanic/Latino; 1 Native Hawaiian or other Pacific Islander, non-Hispanic/Latino; 13 Two or more races, non-Hispanic/Latino), 7 international. Average age 29. 580 applicants, 42% accepted, 166 enrolled. In 2013, 140 master's, 10 doctorates awarded. *Entrance requirements:* Additional exam requirements/recommendations for international students: Required—TOEFL (minimum score 550 paper-based; 80 iBT). *Application deadline:* Applications are processed on a rolling basis. Application fee: $60. Electronic applications accepted. Tuition and fees vary according to program. *Financial support:* Fellowships and scholarships/grants available. Financial award application deadline: 6/30; financial award applicants required to submit FAFSA. *Unit head:* Dr. Don Cardinal, Dean, 714-997-6781, E-mail: cardinal@chapman.edu. *Application contact:* Admissions Coordinator, 714-997-6714.
Website: http://www.chapman.edu/CES/.

Charleston Southern University, School of Education, Charleston, SC 29423-8087. Offers elementary administration and supervision (M Ed); elementary education (M Ed). *Accreditation:* NCATE. Part-time and evening/weekend programs available. *Degree requirements:* For master's, thesis optional. *Entrance requirements:* For master's, GRE or MAT. Additional exam requirements/recommendations for international students: Required—TOEFL (minimum score 550 paper-based; 79 iBT). *Expenses:* Contact institution.

Chestnut Hill College, School of Graduate Studies, Department of Education, Program in Educational Leadership, Philadelphia, PA 19118-2693. Offers M Ed, CAS. Part-time and evening/weekend programs available. *Faculty:* 10 full-time (7 women), 48 part-time/adjunct (34 women). *Students:* 7 part-time (4 women); includes 3 minority (all Black or African American, non-Hispanic/Latino), 1 international. Average age 33. In 2013, 7 master's awarded. *Degree requirements:* For master's, thesis optional. *Entrance requirements:* For master's, PRAXIS I or proof of teaching certification, letters of recommendation, writing sample, 6 graduate credits with minimum B grade if undergraduate GPA less than 3.0. Additional exam requirements/recommendations for

international students: Required—TOEFL (minimum score 500 paper-based), IELTS (mnimum score 6.0), or TWE (minimum score 22). *Application deadline:* For fall admission, 7/1 for domestic and international students; for spring admission, 11/1 for domestic and international students; for summer admission, 4/1 for domestic and international students. Applications are processed on a rolling basis. *Expenses:* Contact institution. *Financial support:* Unspecified assistantships available. *Faculty research:* Mentoring and induction program. *Unit head:* Dr. Debra Chiaradonna, Chair, Education Department, 215-248-7127, Fax: 215-248-7155, E-mail: chiaradonnad@chc.edu. *Application contact:* Jayne Mashett, Director of Admissions, School of Graduate Studies, 215-248-7020, Fax: 215-248-7161, E-mail: gradadmissions@chc.edu.
Website: http://www.chc.edu/Graduate/Programs/Masters/Education/.

Cheyney University of Pennsylvania, Graduate Programs, Principal Certification Program (K-12), Cheyney, PA 19319. Offers Certificate. Program also offered on campus of West Chester University of Pennsylvania. *Entrance requirements:* For degree, five years of professional school experience.

Cheyney University of Pennsylvania, Graduate Programs, Program in Educational Leadership, Cheyney, PA 19319. Offers M Ed, Certificate. Part-time and evening/weekend programs available. *Degree requirements:* For master's, thesis or alternative; for Certificate, internship. *Entrance requirements:* For master's, minimum GPA of 3.0, writing sample. Electronic applications accepted. *Faculty research:* Teacher motivation, critical thinking.

Chicago State University, School of Graduate and Professional Studies, College of Education, Department of Educational Leadership, Curriculum and Foundations, Program in Educational Leadership, Chicago, IL 60628. Offers educational leadership (Ed D); general administration (MA); higher education administration (MA). *Accreditation:* NCATE. *Degree requirements:* For master's, comprehensive exam, thesis optional. *Entrance requirements:* For master's, minimum GPA of 2.75.

Christian Brothers University, School of Arts, Memphis, TN 38104-5581. Offers Catholic studies (MACS); educational leadership (MSEL); teacher-leadership (M Ed); teaching (MAT). Part-time and evening/weekend programs available. *Entrance requirements:* For master's, GRE, GMAT, PRAXIS II. *Expenses:* Contact institution.

The Citadel, The Military College of South Carolina, Citadel Graduate College, School of Education, Program in Educational Administration, Charleston, SC 29409. Offers elementary/secondary school administration and supervision (M Ed); school superintendency (Ed S). *Accreditation:* NCATE. Part-time and evening/weekend programs available. *Faculty:* 10 full-time (6 women), 8 part-time/adjunct (3 women). *Students:* 65 part-time (42 women); includes 19 minority (17 Black or African American, non-Hispanic/Latino; 1 American Indian or Alaska Native, non-Hispanic/Latino; 1 Hispanic/Latino). Average age 36. In 2013, 26 master's awarded. *Degree requirements:* For master's and Ed S, comprehensive exam, internship. *Entrance requirements:* For master's, GRE (minimum score 290; 900 on old scoring system) or MAT (minimum score 396), minimum undergraduate GPA of 2.5, valid South Carolina teaching certificate, one year of teaching experience; for Ed S, GRE (minimum score 900) or MAT (minimum score 396), minimum GPA of 3.5; South Carolina State Certificate in school administration or administrative position equivalent to assistant principal or higher in education; valid South Carolina teaching certificate; three years' teaching experience. Additional exam requirements/recommendations for international students: Required—TOEFL (minimum score 550 paper-based). *Application deadline:* Applications are processed on a rolling basis. Application fee: $30. Electronic applications accepted. *Expenses: Tuition, area resident:* Part-time $525 per credit hour. Tuition, state resident: part-time $525 per credit hour. Tuition, nonresident: part-time $865 per credit hour. *Financial support:* Career-related internships or fieldwork, health care benefits, and unspecified assistantships available. Support available to part-time students. Financial award application deadline: 7/1; financial award applicants required to submit FAFSA. *Unit head:* Dr. Mary Lou Yeatts, Coordinator, 843-953-5201, Fax: 843-953-7258, E-mail: marylou.yeatts@citadel.edu. *Application contact:* Dr. Robert H. McNamara, Associate Provost, The Citadel Graduate College, 843-953-5089, Fax: 843-953-7630, E-mail: cgc@citadel.edu.
Website: http://www.citadel.edu/education/educational-leadership.html.

City College of the City University of New York, Graduate School, School of Education, Department of Leadership and Special Education, New York, NY 10031-9198. Offers bilingual special education (MS Ed); educational leadership (MS, AC); teacher of students with disabilities in childhood education (MS Ed); teacher of students with disabilities in middle childhood education (MS Ed). *Degree requirements:* For master's, thesis, research paper. *Entrance requirements:* For master's, Liberal Arts and Sciences Test (LAST), Content Specialty Test (CST), interview; minimum GPA of 3.0 in major, 2.5 overall. Additional exam requirements/recommendations for international students: Required—TOEFL. *Faculty research:* Dynamics of organizational change, impact of laws on educational policy, leadership development in schools.

City University of Seattle, Graduate Division, Albright School of Education, Bellevue, WA 98005. Offers administrator certification (Certificate); curriculum and instruction (M Ed); educational leadership (Ed D); elementary education (MIT); guidance and counseling (M Ed); higher education leadership (Ed D); leadership (M Ed); leadership and school counseling (M Ed); organizational leadership (Ed D); reading and literacy (M Ed); special education (MIT); superintendent certification (Certificate). Part-time and evening/weekend programs available. Postbaccalaureate distance learning degree programs offered (no on-campus study). *Degree requirements:* For master's, comprehensive exam (for some programs), thesis (for some programs); for doctorate, comprehensive exam, thesis/dissertation. *Entrance requirements:* Additional exam requirements/recommendations for international students: Required—TOEFL (minimum score 567 paper-based; 87 iBT); Recommended—IELTS. Electronic applications accepted. *Expenses:* Contact institution.

City University of Seattle, Graduate Division, Division of Doctoral Studies, Bellevue, WA 98005. Offers leadership (Ed D). Postbaccalaureate distance learning degree programs offered (minimal on-campus study).

Claremont Graduate University, Graduate Programs, School of Educational Studies, Claremont, CA 91711-6160. Offers Africana education (Certificate); education and policy (MA, PhD); higher education/student affairs (MA, PhD); human development (MA, PhD); public school administration (MA, PhD); quantitative evaluation (MA, PhD); special education (MA, PhD); teacher education (MA); teaching and learning (MA, PhD); urban leadership (PhD); MBA/PhD. PhD program offered jointly with San Diego State University. Part-time programs available. *Faculty:* 16 full-time (9 women), 1 part-time/adjunct (0 women). *Students:* 224 full-time (158 women), 221 part-time (151 women); includes 229 minority (52 Black or African American, non-Hispanic/Latino; 3 American Indian or Alaska Native, non-Hispanic/Latino; 43 Asian, non-Hispanic/Latino; 113 Hispanic/Latino; 1 Native Hawaiian or other Pacific Islander, non-Hispanic/Latino; 17 Two or more races, non-Hispanic/Latino), 15 international. Average age 39. In 2013, 51 master's, 33 doctorates, 5 other advanced degrees awarded. Terminal master's awarded for partial completion of doctoral program. *Entrance requirements:* For master's and doctorate, GRE General Test. Additional exam requirements/recommendations for international students: Required—TOEFL (minimum score 550 paper-based; 80 iBT). *Application deadline:* For fall admission, 4/1 priority date for domestic and international students. Applications are processed on a rolling basis. Application fee: $80. Electronic applications accepted. *Expenses: Tuition:* Full-time $40,560; part-time $1690 per credit. *Required fees:* $275 per semester. Tuition and fees vary according to program. *Financial support:* Fellowships, research assistantships, Federal Work-Study, institutionally sponsored loans, and scholarships/grants available. Support available to part-time students. Financial award application deadline: 2/15; financial award applicants required to submit FAFSA. *Faculty research:* Education administration, K-12 and higher education, multicultural education, education policy, diversity in higher education, faculty issues. *Unit head:* Scott Thomas, Dean, 909-621-8075, Fax: 909-621-8734, E-mail: scott.thomas@cgu.edu. *Application contact:* Julia Wendt, Director of Central Recruitment, 909-607-3689, Fax: 909-607-7285, E-mail: admiss@cgu.edu.
Website: http://www.cgu.edu/pages/267.asp.

Clark Atlanta University, School of Education, Department of Educational Leadership, Atlanta, GA 30314. Offers MA, Ed D, Ed S. Part-time and evening/weekend programs available. *Faculty:* 4 full-time (2 women), 5 part-time/adjunct (4 women). *Students:* 32 full-time (19 women), 47 part-time (30 women); includes 76 minority (74 Black or African American, non-Hispanic/Latino; 1 Asian, non-Hispanic/Latino; 1 Hispanic/Latino), 1 international. Average age 37. 22 applicants, 86% accepted, 17 enrolled. In 2013, 2 master's, 14 doctorates, 1 other advanced degree awarded. *Degree requirements:* For master's and Ed S, comprehensive exam; for doctorate, comprehensive exam, thesis/dissertation. *Entrance requirements:* For master's, GRE General Test, minimum undergraduate GPA of 2.6; for doctorate and Ed S, GRE General Test, minimum graduate GPA of 3.0. Additional exam requirements/recommendations for international students: Required—TOEFL (minimum score 500 paper-based; 61 iBT). *Application deadline:* For fall admission, 4/1 for domestic and international students; for spring admission, 11/1 for domestic and international students. Applications are processed on a rolling basis. Application fee: $40 ($55 for international students). Electronic applications accepted. *Expenses: Tuition:* Full-time $14,616; part-time $812 per credit hour. *Required fees:* $706; $353 per semester. *Financial support:* Career-related internships or fieldwork, Federal Work-Study, scholarships/grants, and unspecified assistantships available. Support available to part-time students. Financial award application deadline: 4/30; financial award applicants required to submit FAFSA. *Unit head:* Dr. Moses Norman, Chairperson, 404-880-8495, E-mail: mnorman@cau.edu. *Application contact:* Michelle Clark-Davis, Graduate Program Admissions, 404-880-6605, E-mail: cauadmissions@cau.edu.

Clarke University, Program in Education, Dubuque, IA 52001-3198. Offers early childhood/special education (MAE); educational administration: elementary and secondary (MAE); educational media: elementary and secondary (MAE); multi-categorical resource k-12 (MAE); multidisciplinary studies (MAE); reading: elementary (MAE); technology in education (MAE). Part-time and evening/weekend programs available. Postbaccalaureate distance learning degree programs offered (minimal on-campus study). *Faculty:* 10 full-time (9 women), 1 (woman) part-time/adjunct. *Students:* 5 full-time (3 women), 27 part-time (24 women); includes 2 minority (1 Black or African American, non-Hispanic/Latino; 1 American Indian or Alaska Native, non-Hispanic/Latino). In 2013, 11 master's awarded. *Degree requirements:* For master's, comprehensive exam, thesis optional. *Entrance requirements:* For master's, GRE General Test or MAT, minimum GPA of 2.75. *Application deadline:* Applications are processed on a rolling basis. Application fee: $25. Electronic applications accepted. *Expenses: Tuition:* Part-time $660 per credit. *Required fees:* $15 per credit. *Financial support:* Career-related internships or fieldwork available. Financial award applicants required to submit FAFSA. *Unit head:* Dr. Michele Slover, Chair, 319-588-6397, Fax: 319-584-8604. *Application contact:* Kara Shroeder, Information Contact, 563-588-6354, Fax: 563-588-6789, E-mail: graduate@clarke.edu.

Clearwater Christian College, Graduate Studies in Education, Clearwater, FL 33759-4595. Offers M Ed. Part-time programs available. Postbaccalaureate distance learning degree programs offered (no on-campus study). *Degree requirements:* For master's, thesis or practicum. *Entrance requirements:* For master's, GRE, 3 years teaching experience. Additional exam requirements/recommendations for international students: Required—TOEFL (minimum score 600 paper-based). Electronic applications accepted. *Faculty research:* Bullying in school, supervision, administration, creating learning environments.

Clemson University, Graduate School, College of Health, Education, and Human Development, Eugene T. Moore School of Education, Program in Administration and Supervision (K-12), Clemson, SC 29634. Offers M Ed, Ed S. Part-time and evening/weekend programs available. *Students:* 2 full-time (0 women), 61 part-time (44 women); includes 5 minority (3 Black or African American, non-Hispanic/Latino; 2 Two or more races, non-Hispanic/Latino). Average age 34. 24 applicants, 88% accepted, 20 enrolled. In 2013, 20 master's, 19 Ed Ss awarded. *Degree requirements:* For master's and Ed S, comprehensive exam. *Entrance requirements:* For master's, GRE General Test or MAT, 1 year of teaching experience; for Ed S, GRE General Test, 1 year of teaching experience. Additional exam requirements/recommendations for international students: Required—TOEFL; Recommended—IELTS. *Application deadline:* For fall admission, 3/1 for domestic and international students; for spring admission, 10/1 for domestic and international students. Applications are processed on a rolling basis. Application fee: $70 ($80 for international students). Electronic applications accepted. *Financial support:* In 2013–14, 1 student received support. Research assistantships with partial tuition reimbursements available, institutionally sponsored loans, health care benefits, and unspecified assistantships available. Financial award application deadline: 6/1; financial award applicants required to submit FAFSA. *Faculty research:* School finance, educational assessment and accountability policies, politics of education, school improvement, complex organizations, school law. *Unit head:* Dr. Michael J. Padilla, Director/Associate Dean, 864-656-4444, Fax: 864-656-0311, E-mail: padilla@clemson.edu. *Application contact:* Dr. David Fleming, Graduate Coordinator, 864-656-1881, Fax: 864-656-0311, E-mail: dflemin@clemson.edu.
Website: http://www.clemson.edu/hehd/departments/education/academics/graduate/MEd-AS/.

Clemson University, Graduate School, College of Health, Education, and Human Development, Eugene T. Moore School of Education, Program in Educational Leadership, Clemson, SC 29634. Offers higher education (PhD); K-12 (PhD). *Accreditation:* NCATE. Part-time and evening/weekend programs available. *Students:* 26 full-time (13 women), 76 part-time (46 women); includes 28 minority (25 Black or African American, non-Hispanic/Latino; 2 Hispanic/Latino; 1 Two or more races, non-Hispanic/Latino), 2 international. Average age 37. 26 applicants, 54% accepted, 13 enrolled. In 2013, 13 doctorates awarded. *Degree requirements:* For doctorate, comprehensive exam, thesis/dissertation, preliminary exam. *Entrance requirements:* For doctorate, GRE General Test, master's degree in related field. Additional exam requirements/recommendations for international students: Required—TOEFL; Recommended—IELTS. *Application deadline:* For fall admission, 3/1 for domestic and international students; for spring admission, 10/1 for domestic and international students. Application fee: $70 ($80 for international students). Electronic applications accepted. *Financial support:* In 2013–14, 19 students received support, including 2 fellowships with full and partial tuition reimbursements available (averaging $5,000 per

year), 12 research assistantships with partial tuition reimbursements available (averaging $14,221 per year); teaching assistantships with partial tuition reimbursements available, institutionally sponsored loans, health care benefits, and unspecified assistantships also available. Financial award application deadline: 6/1; financial award applicants required to submit FAFSA. *Faculty research:* Higher education leadership, P-12 educational leadership. *Unit head:* Dr. Michael J. Padilla, Director/Associate Dean, 864-656-4444, Fax: 864-656-0311, E-mail: padilla@clemson.edu. *Application contact:* Dr. David Fleming, Graduate Coordinator, 864-656-1881, Fax: 864-656-0311, E-mail: dflemin@clemson.edu.

Cleveland State University, College of Graduate Studies, College of Education and Human Services, Department of Counseling, Administration, Supervision and Adult Learning (CASAL), Cleveland, OH 44115. Offers adult learning and development (M Ed); chemical dependency counseling (Certificate); clinical mental health counseling (M Ed); early childhood mental health counseling (Certificate); educational administration and supervision (M Ed); organizational leadership (M Ed); school administration (Ed S); school counseling (M Ed). *Accreditation:* ACA (one or more programs are accredited). Part-time and evening/weekend programs available. *Faculty:* 15 full-time (8 women), 19 part-time/adjunct (10 women). *Students:* 79 full-time (61 women), 237 part-time (188 women); includes 101 minority (86 Black or African American, non-Hispanic/Latino; 3 Asian, non-Hispanic/Latino; 11 Hispanic/Latino; 1 Two or more races, non-Hispanic/Latino), 8 international. Average age 36. 131 applicants, 69% accepted, 49 enrolled. In 2013, 99 master's, 7 Certificates awarded. *Degree requirements:* For master's, comprehensive exam (for some programs), thesis optional, internship. *Entrance requirements:* For master's, GRE General Test or MAT, letter of recommendation and minimum GPA of 2.75 (for counseling); 2 letters of recommendation and interviews (for organizational leadership). Additional exam requirements/recommendations for international students: Required—TOEFL (minimum score 525 paper-based), IELTS (minimum score 6). *Application deadline:* For fall admission, 6/21 for domestic students, 5/15 for international students; for spring admission, 8/31 for domestic students, 11/1 for international students. Application fee: $30. Electronic applications accepted. *Expenses:* Tuition, state resident: full-time $8335; part-time $521 per credit hour. Tuition, nonresident: full-time $15,670; part-time $979 per credit hour. *Required fees:* $50; $25 per semester. *Financial support:* In 2013–14, 19 students received support, including 10 research assistantships with full and partial tuition reimbursements available (averaging $11,882 per year), 5 teaching assistantships with full and partial tuition reimbursements available (averaging $11,882 per year); scholarships/grants and unspecified assistantships also available. Support available to part-time students. *Faculty research:* Education law, career development, bullying, psychopharmacology, counseling and spirituality. *Total annual research expenditures:* $225,821. *Unit head:* Dr. Ann L. Bauer, Chairperson, 216-687-4582, Fax: 216-687-5378, E-mail: a.l.bauer@csuohio.edu. *Application contact:* Deborah L. Brown, Interim Assistant Director, Graduate Admissions, 216-523-7572, Fax: 216-687-5400, E-mail: d.l.brown@csuohio.edu.
Website: http://www.csuohio.edu/cehs/departments/CASAL/casal_dept.html.

Cleveland State University, College of Graduate Studies, College of Education and Human Services, Program in Urban Education, Specialization in School Administration, Cleveland, OH 44115. Offers PhD. Part-time programs available. *Faculty:* 4 full-time (0 women). *Students:* 2 full-time (both women), 7 part-time (3 women); includes 5 minority (4 Black or African American, non-Hispanic/Latino; 1 Asian, non-Hispanic/Latino). Average age 42. 10 applicants, 40% accepted. In 2013, 2 doctorates awarded. *Degree requirements:* For doctorate, one foreign language, comprehensive exam, thesis/dissertation. *Entrance requirements:* For doctorate, General GRE Test (minimum score of 297 for combined Verbal and Quantitative exams, 4.0 preferred for Analytical Writing), minimum graduate GPA of 3.25, curriculum vitae or resume, personal statement, 2 letters of recommendation. Additional exam requirements/recommendations for international students: Required—TOEFL (minimum score 525 paper-based), IELTS (minimum score 6). *Expenses:* Tuition, state resident: full-time $8335; part-time $521 per credit hour. Tuition, nonresident: full-time $15,670; part-time $979 per credit hour. *Required fees:* $50; $25 per semester. *Financial support:* In 2013–14, 1 student received support, including 1 teaching assistantship with full tuition reimbursement available (averaging $5,900 per year); tuition waivers also available. Support available to part-time students. Financial award application deadline: 4/1; financial award applicants required to submit FAFSA. *Faculty research:* Theory and practice of management and leadership in educational, government, human resource development, and social service settings. *Unit head:* Dr. Graham Stead, Director, Doctoral Studies, 216-687-3828, E-mail: g.b.stead@csuohio.edu. *Application contact:* Rita M. Grabowski, Administrative Coordinator, 216-687-4697, Fax: 216-875-9697, E-mail: r.grabowski@csuohio.edu.
Website: http://www.csuohio.edu/cehs/departments/DOC/sas_doc.html.

Coastal Carolina University, William L. Spadoni College of Education, Conway, SC 29528-6054. Offers education (MAT); educational leadership (M Ed); learning and teaching (M Ed). *Accreditation:* NCATE. Part-time and evening/weekend programs available. *Faculty:* 14 full-time (7 women), 8 part-time/adjunct (5 women). *Students:* 82 full-time (54 women), 218 part-time (174 women); includes 37 minority (29 Black or African American, non-Hispanic/Latino; 1 American Indian or Alaska Native, non-Hispanic/Latino; 4 Hispanic/Latino; 2 Native Hawaiian or other Pacific Islander, non-Hispanic/Latino; 1 Two or more races, non-Hispanic/Latino), 1 international. Average age 33. 240 applicants, 94% accepted, 159 enrolled. In 2013, 115 master's awarded. *Degree requirements:* For master's, comprehensive exam. *Entrance requirements:* For master's, GRE, MAT, 2 letters of recommendation, evidence of teacher certification, official transcripts. Additional exam requirements/recommendations for international students: Required—TOEFL (minimum score 575 paper-based; 89 iBT). *Application deadline:* For fall admission, 7/1 priority date for domestic and international students; for spring admission, 11/1 priority date for domestic and international students; for summer admission, 5/1 priority date for domestic and international students. Applications are processed on a rolling basis. Application fee: $45. Electronic applications accepted. *Expenses:* Tuition, state resident: full-time $11,976; part-time $499 per credit hour. Tuition, nonresident: full-time $18,936; part-time $789 per credit hour. *Required fees:* $80; $40 per term. Tuition and fees vary according to program. *Financial support:* Fellowships, research assistantships, and unspecified assistantships available. Support available to part-time students. Financial award application deadline: 3/1; financial award applicants required to submit FAFSA. *Unit head:* Dr. Edward Jadallah, Dean, 843-349-2773, Fax: 843-349-2106, E-mail: ejadalla@coastal.edu. *Application contact:* Dr. James O. Luken, Associate Provost/Director of Graduate Studies, 843-349-2235, Fax: 843-349-6444, E-mail: joluken@coastal.edu.
Website: http://www.coastal.edu/education/.

The College at Brockport, State University of New York, School of Education and Human Services, Department of Counselor Education, Brockport, NY 14420-2997. Offers college counseling (MS Ed, CAS); mental health counseling (MS, CAS); school counseling (MS Ed, CAS); school counselor supervision (CAS). *Accreditation:* ACA (one or more programs are accredited). Part-time programs available. *Faculty:* 6 full-time (4 women), 5 part-time/adjunct (4 women). *Students:* 26 full-time (22 women), 62 part-time (48 women); includes 19 minority (11 Black or African American, non-Hispanic/Latino; 1 American Indian or Alaska Native, non-Hispanic/Latino; 1 Asian, non-Hispanic/Latino; 4

Hispanic/Latino; 2 Two or more races, non-Hispanic/Latino). 73 applicants, 30% accepted, 15 enrolled. In 2013, 20 master's, 7 other advanced degrees awarded. *Degree requirements:* For master's, thesis, internship. *Entrance requirements:* For master's, group interview, letters of recommendation, written objectives; for CAS, master's degree, New York state school counselor certificate. Additional exam requirements/recommendations for international students: Required—TOEFL (minimum score 550 paper-based; 79 iBT), IELTS (minimum score 6.5). *Application deadline:* For fall admission, 2/1 priority date for domestic and international students; for spring admission, 9/1 priority date for domestic and international students; for summer admission, 2/1 priority date for domestic and international students. Application fee: $80. Electronic applications accepted. *Expenses:* Tuition, state resident: full-time $9870. Tuition, nonresident: full-time $18,350. *Required fees:* $1848. *Financial support:* In 2013–14, 1 fellowship with full tuition reimbursement (averaging $7,500 per year), 1 teaching assistantship with full tuition reimbursement (averaging $6,000 per year) were awarded; Federal Work-Study, scholarships/grants, and unspecified assistantships also available. Support available to part-time students. Financial award application deadline: 3/15; financial award applicants required to submit FAFSA. *Faculty research:* Gender and diversity issues; counseling outcomes; spirituality; school, college and mental health counseling; obesity. *Unit head:* Dr. Thomas Hernandez, Chair, 585-395-2258, Fax: 585-395-2366, E-mail: thernandez@brockport.edu. *Application contact:* Danielle A. Welch, Graduate Admissions Counselor, 585-395-5465, Fax: 585-395-2515.
Website: http://www.brockport.edu/edc/.

The College at Brockport, State University of New York, School of Education and Human Services, Department of Educational Administration, Brockport, NY 14420-2997. Offers school building leader/school district leader (CAS); school district business leader (CAS). Part-time programs available. *Faculty:* 3 full-time (1 woman), 4 part-time/adjunct (1 woman). *Students:* 1 full-time (0 women), 114 part-time (59 women); includes 8 minority (7 Black or African American, non-Hispanic/Latino; 1 Hispanic/Latino). 27 applicants, 96% accepted, 21 enrolled. In 2013, 57 CASs awarded. *Degree requirements:* For CAS, thesis or alternative, internship. *Entrance requirements:* For degree, minimum GPA of 3.0. Additional exam requirements/recommendations for international students: Required—TOEFL (minimum score 550 paper-based; 79 iBT), IELTS (minimum score 6.5). *Application deadline:* For fall admission, 4/15 priority date for domestic and international students; for spring admission, 11/15 priority date for domestic and international students. Application fee: $80. Electronic applications accepted. *Expenses:* Tuition, state resident: full-time $9870. Tuition, nonresident: full-time $18,350. *Required fees:* $1848. *Financial support:* Federal Work-Study, scholarships/grants, and unspecified assistantships available. Support available to part-time students. Financial award application deadline: 3/15; financial award applicants required to submit FAFSA. *Faculty research:* Superintendency, budgeting, school business administration, leadership, special education administration. *Unit head:* Carol Godsave, Chairperson, 585-395-5512, Fax: 585-395-2172, E-mail: cgodsave@brockport.edu. *Application contact:* Danielle A. Welch, Graduate Admissions Counselor, 585-395-2525, Fax: 585-395-2515.
Website: http://www.brockport.edu/edadmin/.

The College of New Jersey, Graduate Studies, School of Education, Department of Educational Administration and Secondary Education, Program in Educational Leadership, Ewing, NJ 08628. Offers M Ed, Certificate. Part-time and evening/weekend programs available. *Degree requirements:* For master's, comprehensive exam. *Entrance requirements:* For master's, GRE, minimum GPA of 3.0 in field or 2.75 overall; for Certificate, previous master's degree or higher. Additional exam requirements/recommendations for international students: Required—TOEFL. Electronic applications accepted.

The College of New Rochelle, Graduate School, Division of Education, Program in School Administration and Supervision, New Rochelle, NY 10805-2308. Offers dual certification: school building leader/school district leader (MS); school building leader (MS, Advanced Certificate); school district leader (MS, Advanced Diploma). *Degree requirements:* For master's, internship. *Entrance requirements:* For master's, interview, minimum GPA of 3.0 in field, 2.7 overall, minimum 3 years teaching or education administration experience. *Expenses: Tuition:* Part-time $894 per credit. *Required fees:* $300 per semester. One-time fee: $200. Tuition and fees vary according to course load. *Faculty research:* Training administrators in Eastern Europe, leadership.

College of Saint Elizabeth, Department of Educational Leadership, Morristown, NJ 07960-6989. Offers accelerated certification for teaching (Certificate); assistive technology (Certificate); educational leadership (MA, Ed D); special education (MA). Part-time programs available. *Faculty:* 5 full-time (0 women), 21 part-time/adjunct (9 women). *Students:* 67 full-time (44 women), 146 part-time (117 women); includes 52 minority (36 Black or African American, non-Hispanic/Latino; 2 Asian, non-Hispanic/Latino; 12 Hispanic/Latino; 1 Native Hawaiian or other Pacific Islander, non-Hispanic/Latino; 1 Two or more races, non-Hispanic/Latino), 1 international. Average age 38. In 2013, 55 master's, 14 doctorates, 42 other advanced degrees awarded. *Degree requirements:* For master's, thesis or alternative; for doctorate, thesis/dissertation. *Entrance requirements:* For master's, personal written statement, interview, minimum undergraduate GPA of 3.0; for doctorate, master's degree. Additional exam requirements/recommendations for international students: Required—TOEFL. *Application deadline:* For fall admission, 6/30 priority date for domestic students; for spring admission, 11/30 for domestic students. Applications are processed on a rolling basis. Application fee: $35. Electronic applications accepted. *Expenses: Tuition:* Full-time $19,152; part-time $1064 per credit. *Financial support:* Career-related internships or fieldwork, tuition waivers (partial), and unspecified assistantships available. Support available to part-time students. Financial award application deadline: 3/15; financial award applicants required to submit FAFSA. *Faculty research:* Developmental stages for teaching and human services professionals, effectiveness of humanities core curriculum. *Unit head:* Dr. Joseph Ciccone, Associate Professor/Course of Study Coordinator, 973-290-4383, Fax: 973-290-4389, E-mail: jciccone@cse.edu. *Application contact:* Deborah S. Cobo, Associate Director for Graduate Admissions, 973-290-4194, Fax: 973-290-4710, E-mail: dscobo@cse.edu.
Website: http://www.cse.edu/academics/catalog/academic-programs/education.dot?tabID=tabMinor&divID=catalogMinor#maeducation.

College of Saint Mary, Program in Education, Omaha, NE 68106. Offers assessment leadership (MSE); English as a second language (MSE). Part-time programs available. *Entrance requirements:* For master's, technology competency test or equivalent, minimum cumulative GPA of 3.0, teaching certificate, 2 letters of reference, resume.

The College of Saint Rose, Graduate Studies, School of Education, Program in Educational Leadership, Albany, NY 12203-1419. Offers educational leadership (MS Ed); school building leader (Certificate); school district business leader (Certificate); school district leader (Certificate). Part-time and evening/weekend programs available. *Degree requirements:* For master's, comprehensive exam or thesis. *Entrance requirements:* For master's, minimum undergraduate GPA of 3.0, timed writing sample, interview, permanent certification or 3 years teaching experience. Additional exam requirements/recommendations for international students: Required—TOEFL (minimum score 550 paper-based). Electronic applications accepted.

The College of Saint Rose, Graduate Studies, School of Education, Program in Higher Education Leadership and Administration, Albany, NY 12203-1419. Offers MS Ed. Evening/weekend programs available. *Degree requirements:* For master's, capstone seminar. *Entrance requirements:* For master's, resume, one letter of recommendation.

College of Staten Island of the City University of New York, Graduate Programs, School of Education, Program in Leadership in Education, Staten Island, NY 10314-6600. Offers Post-Master's Certificate. Part-time and evening/weekend programs available. *Faculty:* 1 (woman) full-time, 1 (woman) part-time/adjunct. *Students:* 26. Average age 37. 17 applicants, 82% accepted, 11 enrolled. In 2013, 14 Post-Master's Certificates awarded. *Degree requirements:* For Post-Master's Certificate, thesis. *Entrance requirements:* For degree, master's degree with minimum GPA of 3.0, in-person interview, three professional recommendations, evidence of four year's teaching experience. Additional exam requirements/recommendations for international students: Required—TOEFL (minimum score 550 paper-based; 79 iBT), IELTS (minimum score 6.5). *Application deadline:* For fall admission, 5/1 for domestic and international students. Application fee: $125. Electronic applications accepted. *Expenses:* Tuition, state resident: full-time $9240; part-time $385 per credit hour. Tuition, nonresident: full-time $17,040; part-time $710 per credit hour. *Required fees:* $428; $128 per term. *Financial support:* Career-related internships or fieldwork, Federal Work-Study, and scholarships/grants available. Support available to part-time students. Financial award applicants required to submit FAFSA. *Unit head:* Dr. Ruth Silverberg, Graduate Program Coordinator, 718-982-3726, Fax: 718-982-3743, E-mail: ruth.silverberg@csi.cuny.edu. *Application contact:* Sasha Spence, Assistant Director for Graduate Admissions, 718-982-2019, Fax: 718-982-2500, E-mail: sasha.spence@csi.cuny.edu. Website: http://csivc.csi.cuny.edu/education/files.

The College of William and Mary, School of Education, Program in Curriculum and Instruction, Williamsburg, VA 23187-8795. Offers elementary education (MA Ed); gifted education (MA Ed); literacy leadership (MA Ed); math specialist (MA Ed); secondary education (MA Ed), including English education, mathematics education, modern foreign languages education, science education, social studies education; special education (MA Ed), including collaborating master educator, general curriculum. *Accreditation:* NCATE. Part-time programs available. *Faculty:* 15 full-time (10 women), 44 part-time/adjunct (38 women). *Students:* 66 full-time (55 women), 27 part-time (26 women); includes 17 minority (4 Black or African American, non-Hispanic/Latino; 1 American Indian or Alaska Native, non-Hispanic/Latino; 3 Asian, non-Hispanic/Latino; 5 Hispanic/Latino; 4 Two or more races, non-Hispanic/Latino). Average age 28. 179 applicants, 72% accepted, 92 enrolled. In 2013, 76 master's awarded. *Degree requirements:* For master's, project. *Entrance requirements:* For master's, GRE or MAT, minimum GPA of 2.5. Additional exam requirements/recommendations for international students: Required—TOEFL, IELTS. *Application deadline:* For fall admission, 1/15 for domestic and international students; for spring admission, 10/1 for domestic and international students. Application fee: $50. Electronic applications accepted. *Expenses:* Tuition, state resident: full-time $7120; part-time $405 per credit hour. Tuition, nonresident: full-time $21,639; part-time $1050 per credit hour. *Required fees:* $4764. *Financial support:* In 2013–14, 49 students received support, including 6 research assistantships with full and partial tuition reimbursements available (averaging $8,269 per year); career-related internships or fieldwork, Federal Work-Study, institutionally sponsored loans, scholarships/grants, and unspecified assistantships also available. Financial award application deadline: 1/15; financial award applicants required to submit FAFSA. *Faculty research:* National Council of Teachers of Mathematics standards, counseling, self-concept and self-esteem, special education, curriculum development. *Unit head:* Dr. Mark Hofer, Area Coordinator, 757-221-1713, E-mail: mjhofe@wm.edu. *Application contact:* Dorothy Smith Osborne, Assistant Dean for Academic Programs and Student Services, 757-221-2317, Fax: 757-221-2293, E-mail: dsosbo@wm.edu. Website: http://education.wm.edu.

The College of William and Mary, School of Education, Program in Education Policy, Planning, and Leadership, Williamsburg, VA 23187-8795. Offers curriculum and educational technology (Ed D, PhD); curriculum leadership (Ed D, PhD); educational leadership (M Ed), including higher education administration (M Ed, Ed D, PhD), K-12 administration and supervision; educational policy, planning, and leadership (Ed D, PhD), including general education administration, gifted education administration, higher education administration (M Ed, Ed D, PhD). *Accreditation:* NCATE. Part-time and evening/weekend programs available. *Faculty:* 10 full-time (5 women), 17 part-time/adjunct (13 women). *Students:* 64 full-time (52 women), 145 part-time (106 women); includes 46 minority (33 Black or African American, non-Hispanic/Latino; 3 Asian, non-Hispanic/Latino; 4 Hispanic/Latino; 6 Two or more races, non-Hispanic/Latino; 9 international. Average age 38. 133 applicants, 74% accepted, 72 enrolled. In 2013, 24 master's, 17 doctorates awarded. *Degree requirements:* For doctorate, comprehensive exam, thesis/dissertation. *Entrance requirements:* For master's, GRE or MAT, minimum GPA of 2.5; for doctorate, GRE or MAT, minimum GPA of 3.0. Additional exam requirements/recommendations for international students: Required—TOEFL, IELTS. *Application deadline:* For fall admission, 1/15 for domestic and international students. Application fee: $50. Electronic applications accepted. *Expenses:* Tuition, state resident: full-time $7120; part-time $405 per credit hour. Tuition, nonresident: full-time $21,639; part-time $1050 per credit hour. *Required fees:* $4764. *Financial support:* In 2013–14, 58 students received support, including 1 fellowship (averaging $20,000 per year), 51 research assistantships with full and partial tuition reimbursements available (averaging $16,551 per year); career-related internships or fieldwork, Federal Work-Study, institutionally sponsored loans, scholarships/grants, and unspecified assistantships also available. Support available to part-time students. Financial award application deadline: 1/15; financial award applicants required to submit FAFSA. *Faculty research:* Higher education policy, faculty incentives, history of adversity, resilience, leadership. *Unit head:* Dr. James Stronge, Area Coordinator, 757-221-2339, E-mail: jhstro@wm.edu. *Application contact:* Dorothy Smith Osborne, Assistant Dean for Academic Programs and Student Services, 757-221-2317, Fax: 757-221-2293, E-mail: dsosbo@wm.edu. Website: http://education.wm.edu.

Colorado Mesa University, Center for Teacher Education, Grand Junction, CO 81501-3122. Offers educational leadership (MAEd); English for speakers of other languages (MAEd). *Accreditation:* NCATE. Part-time programs available. Postbaccalaureate distance learning degree programs offered (minimal on-campus study). *Degree requirements:* For master's, comprehensive exam, capstone presentation. *Entrance requirements:* For master's, GRE, 2 professional letters of recommendation. Additional exam requirements/recommendations for international students: Required—TOEFL (minimum score 550 paper-based). Electronic applications accepted.

Colorado State University, Graduate School, College of Health and Human Sciences, School of Education, Fort Collins, CO 80523-1588. Offers adult education and training (M Ed); community college leadership (PhD); counseling and career development (M Ed); education and human resource studies (M Ed, PhD); educational leadership (M Ed, PhD); interdisciplinary studies (PhD); organizational performance and change (M Ed, PhD); student affairs in higher education (MS). *Accreditation:* ACA; Teacher Education Accreditation Council. Part-time and evening/weekend programs available. *Faculty:* 19 full-time (10 women). *Students:* 84 full-time (60 women), 545 part-time (356

women); includes 115 minority (26 Black or African American, non-Hispanic/Latino; 5 American Indian or Alaska Native, non-Hispanic/Latino; 13 Asian, non-Hispanic/Latino; 56 Hispanic/Latino; 15 Two or more races, non-Hispanic/Latino), 22 international. Average age 37. 475 applicants, 38% accepted, 147 enrolled. In 2013, 1,157 master's, 43 doctorates awarded. *Degree requirements:* For master's, comprehensive exam, thesis optional; for doctorate, comprehensive exam, thesis/dissertation, minimum of 60 credits. *Entrance requirements:* For master's and doctorate, GRE, minimum GPA of 3.0. Additional exam requirements/recommendations for international students: Required—TOEFL (minimum score 550 paper-based; 80 iBT), IELTS. *Application deadline:* For fall admission, 3/1 priority date for domestic and international students; for spring admission, 9/1 for domestic and international students. Applications are processed on a rolling basis. Application fee: $50. Electronic applications accepted. *Expenses:* Tuition, state resident: full-time $9075.40; part-time $504 per credit. Tuition, nonresident: full-time $22,248; part-time $1236 per credit. *Required fees:* $1819; $60 per credit. *Financial support:* In 2013–14, 7 students received support, including 1 research assistantship with partial tuition reimbursement available (averaging $16,135 per year), 6 teaching assistantships with partial tuition reimbursements available (averaging $10,106 per year); career-related internships or fieldwork, scholarships/grants, and unspecified assistantships also available. Financial award application deadline: 3/1; financial award applicants required to submit FAFSA. *Faculty research:* Issues in STEM education, diversity and multiculturalism, teacher education leadership, distance learning and teaching. *Total annual research expenditures:* $498,539. *Unit head:* Dr. Daniel H. Robinson, Director, 970-491-6316, Fax: 970-491-1317, E-mail: dan.robinson@colostate.edu. *Application contact:* Kelli M. Clark, Academic Coordinator, 970-491-2093, Fax: 970-491-1317, E-mail: kelli.clark@colostate.edu. Website: http://www.soe.chhs.colostate.edu/.

Columbia College, Graduate Programs, Department of Education, Columbia, SC 29203-5998. Offers divergent learning (M Ed); higher education administration (M Ed). *Accreditation:* NCATE. Part-time and evening/weekend programs available. Postbaccalaureate distance learning degree programs offered. *Faculty:* 3 full-time (1 woman), 18 part-time/adjunct (10 women). *Students:* 113 full-time (96 women), 2 part-time (1 woman); includes 50 minority (46 Black or African American, non-Hispanic/Latino; 2 American Indian or Alaska Native, non-Hispanic/Latino; 2 Asian, non-Hispanic/Latino). Average age 27. 108 applicants, 81% accepted, 77 enrolled. In 2013, 106 master's awarded. *Degree requirements:* For master's, thesis. *Entrance requirements:* For master's, GRE General Test, MAT, 2 recommendations, current South Carolina teaching certificate, minimum GPA of 3.2. *Application deadline:* For fall admission, 8/22 for domestic students. Application fee: $50. *Expenses:* Contact institution. *Financial support:* Available to part-time students. Application deadline: 7/1; applicants required to submit FAFSA. *Unit head:* Dr. Chris Burkett, Chair, 803-786-3782, Fax: 803-786-3034, E-mail: chrisburkett@colacoll.edu. *Application contact:* Carolyn Emeneker, Director of Graduate School and Evening College Admissions, 803-786-3766, Fax: 803-786-3674, E-mail: emeneker@colacoll.edu.

Columbia College, Master of Education in Educational Leadership Program, Columbia, MO 65216-0002. Offers M Ed. Part-time and evening/weekend programs available. Postbaccalaureate distance learning degree programs offered (no on-campus study). *Faculty:* 5 full-time (3 women), 5 part-time/adjunct (2 women). *Students:* 1 (woman) full-time, 3 part-time (all women). Average age 39. 4 applicants, 100% accepted, 4 enrolled. *Entrance requirements:* Additional exam requirements/recommendations for international students: Required—TOEFL (minimum score 550 paper-based; 61 iBT). *Application deadline:* For fall admission, 8/9 priority date for domestic and international students; for spring admission, 12/27 priority date for domestic and international students. Applications are processed on a rolling basis. Application fee: $55. Electronic applications accepted. *Expenses:* Tuition: Part-time $330 per credit hour. Tuition and fees vary according to campus/location and program. *Financial support:* Federal Work-Study and scholarships/grants available. Financial award application deadline: 3/1; financial award applicants required to submit FAFSA. *Unit head:* Teresa VanDover, M Ed Coordinator, 573-875-7794, E-mail: tmvandover@ccis.edu. *Application contact:* Stephanie Johnson, Interim Director of Admissions, 573-875-7352, Fax: 573-875-7506, E-mail: sjohnson@ccis.edu.

Columbia International University, Columbia Graduate School, Columbia, SC 29230-3122. Offers Bible teaching (MABT); Christian higher education leadership (Ed D); Christian school educational leadership (Ed D); counseling (MACN); curriculum and instruction (M Ed), including Christian school guidance, English as a second language, learning disabilities, school technology; early childhood and elementary education (MAT); educational administration (M Ed); teaching English as a foreign language (Certificate); teaching English as a foreign language and intercultural studies (MATF). Part-time and evening/weekend programs available. *Degree requirements:* For master's, internships, professional project. *Entrance requirements:* For master's, Minnesota Multiphasic Personality Inventory, MAT, minimum GPA of 2.7. Additional exam requirements/recommendations for international students: Required—TOEFL. Electronic applications accepted.

Columbus State University, Graduate Studies, College of Education and Health Professions, Department of Counseling, Foundations, and Leadership, Columbus, GA 31907-5645. Offers community counseling (MS); curriculum and leadership (Ed D); educational leadership (M Ed, Ed S); higher education (M Ed); school counseling (M Ed, Ed S). *Accreditation:* ACA; NCATE. Part-time and evening/weekend programs available. Postbaccalaureate distance learning degree programs offered (minimal on-campus study). *Faculty:* 13 full-time (5 women), 11 part-time/adjunct (7 women). *Students:* 94 full-time (64 women), 120 part-time (96 women); includes 95 minority (78 Black or African American, non-Hispanic/Latino; 1 American Indian or Alaska Native, non-Hispanic/Latino; 2 Asian, non-Hispanic/Latino; 9 Hispanic/Latino; 5 Two or more races, non-Hispanic/Latino). Average age 35. 139 applicants, 58% accepted, 49 enrolled. In 2013, 44 master's, 4 doctorates, 14 other advanced degrees awarded. *Degree requirements:* For master's, thesis, exit exam; for doctorate, comprehensive exam, thesis/dissertation; for Ed S, thesis or alternative. *Entrance requirements:* For master's, GRE General Test, minimum undergraduate GPA of 2.75; for doctorate, GRE General Test, minimum graduate GPA of 3.5, four years of professional service; for Ed S, GRE General Test, minimum undergraduate GPA of 2.75, graduate 3.0. Additional exam requirements/recommendations for international students: Required—TOEFL (minimum score 550 paper-based; 79 iBT). *Application deadline:* For fall admission, 6/30 for domestic and international students; for spring admission, 11/1 for domestic and international students; for summer admission, 3/1 for domestic and international students. Applications are processed on a rolling basis. Application fee: $40. Electronic applications accepted. *Expenses:* Tuition, state resident: full-time $4572; part-time $382 per credit hour. Tuition, nonresident: full-time $18,292; part-time $1526 per credit hour. *Required fees:* $1800; $196 per credit hour. Tuition and fees vary according to campus/location and program. *Financial support:* In 2013–14, 143 students received support, including 9 research assistantships with partial tuition reimbursements available (averaging $3,000 per year); career-related internships or fieldwork, Federal Work-Study, institutionally sponsored loans, scholarships/grants, tuition waivers (partial), and unspecified assistantships also available. Support available to part-time students. Financial award application deadline: 5/1; financial award applicants required to submit FAFSA. *Unit head:* Dr. Michael L. Baltimore, Department Chair, 706-569-3013, Fax:

706-569-3134, E-mail: baltimore_michael@columbusstate.edu. *Application contact:* Kristin Williams, Director of International and Graduate Recruitment, 706-507-8848, Fax: 706-568-5091, E-mail: williams_kristin@columbusstate.edu.
Website: http://cfl.columbusstate.edu/.

Columbus State University, Graduate Studies, College of Education and Health Professions, Department of Teacher Education, Columbus, GA 31907-5645. Offers accomplished teaching (M Ed); early childhood education (M Ed, MAT, Ed S); middle grades education (M Ed, MAT, Ed S); school library media (M Ed, MAT); secondary education (M Ed, MAT, Ed S), including English/language arts (M Ed, Ed S), general science (M Ed), mathematics (M Ed, Ed S), science (Ed S), social science (M Ed, Ed S); special education (M Ed, MAT, Ed S), including general curriculum (M Ed, MAT); teacher leadership (M Ed). *Accreditation:* NCATE. Part-time and evening/weekend programs available. Postbaccalaureate distance learning degree programs offered (minimal on-campus study). *Faculty:* 17 full-time (12 women), 31 part-time/adjunct (28 women). *Students:* 59 full-time (48 women), 190 part-time (150 women); includes 85 minority (68 Black or African American, non-Hispanic/Latino; 1 American Indian or Alaska Native, non-Hispanic/Latino; 6 Asian, non-Hispanic/Latino; 4 Hispanic/Latino; 6 Two or more races, non-Hispanic/Latino), 2 international. Average age 34. 132 applicants, 58% accepted, 50 enrolled. In 2013, 86 master's, 26 other advanced degrees awarded. *Degree requirements:* For master's, thesis, exit exam; for Ed S, thesis or alternative. *Entrance requirements:* For master's, GRE General Test, minimum undergraduate GPA of 2.75; for Ed S, GRE General Test, minimum undergraduate GPA of 2.75, graduate 3.0. Additional exam requirements/recommendations for international students: Required—TOEFL (minimum score 550 paper-based; 79 iBT). *Application deadline:* For fall admission, 6/30 for domestic students, 5/1 for international students; for spring admission, 11/1 for domestic and international students; for summer admission, 3/1 for domestic and international students. Applications are processed on a rolling basis. Application fee: $40. Electronic applications accepted. *Expenses:* Tuition, state resident: full-time $4572; part-time $382 per credit hour. Tuition, nonresident: full-time $18,292; part-time $1526 per credit hour. *Required fees:* $1800; $196 per credit hour. Tuition and fees vary according to campus/location and program. *Financial support:* In 2013–14, 173 students received support, including 12 research assistantships with partial tuition reimbursements available (averaging $3,000 per year); career-related internships or fieldwork, Federal Work-Study, institutionally sponsored loans, scholarships/grants, tuition waivers (partial), and unspecified assistantships also available. Support available to part-time students. Financial award application deadline: 5/1; financial award applicants required to submit FAFSA. *Unit head:* Dr. Deirdre Greer, Department Chair, 706-507-8034, Fax: 706-568-3134, E-mail: greer_deirdre@columbusstate.edu. *Application contact:* Kristin Williams, Director of International and Graduate Recruitment, 706-507-8848, Fax: 706-568-5091, E-mail: williams_kristin@columbusstate.edu.
Website: http://te.columbusstate.edu/.

Concordia University, College of Education, Portland, OR 97211-6099. Offers career and technical education (M Ed); curriculum and instruction (M Ed), including adolescent literacy, career and technical education, e-learning/technology education, early childhood education, English for speakers of other languages, English language development, environmental education, mathematics, methods and curriculum, reading, science, teacher leadership, the inclusive classroom; early childhood (MAT); education leadership (Ed D); educational administration (M Ed); elementary education (MAT); secondary education (MAT); special education (M Ed); teacher leadership (Ed D). Part-time programs available. Postbaccalaureate distance learning degree programs offered (no on-campus study). *Degree requirements:* For master's, comprehensive exam, work samples/portfolio. *Entrance requirements:* For master's, California Basic Educational Skills Test or PRAXIS I, minimum undergraduate GPA of 2.8, graduate 3.0; 2 letters of recommendation. Additional exam requirements/recommendations for international students: Required—TOEFL (minimum score 525 paper-based). Electronic applications accepted. *Faculty research:* Learner-centered classroom, brain-based learning, future of online learning.

Concordia University, School of Education, Irvine, CA 92612-3299. Offers curriculum and instruction (MA); education and preliminary teaching credential (M Ed); educational administration and preliminary administrative services credential (MA); educational technology (MA); school counseling with pupil personnel services credential (MA). Part-time and evening/weekend programs available. Postbaccalaureate distance learning degree programs offered (no on-campus study). *Faculty:* 15 full-time (12 women), 96 part-time/adjunct (59 women). *Students:* 885 full-time (690 women), 96 part-time (74 women); includes 282 minority (39 Black or African American, non-Hispanic/Latino; 42 Asian, non-Hispanic/Latino; 182 Hispanic/Latino; 3 Native Hawaiian or other Pacific Islander, non-Hispanic/Latino; 16 Two or more races, non-Hispanic/Latino), 1 international. Average age 39. 402 applicants, 79% accepted, 311 enrolled. In 2013, 469 master's awarded. *Degree requirements:* For master's, action research project. *Entrance requirements:* For master's, California Basic Educational Skills Test, California Subject Examinations for Teachers (M Ed and MA in educational administration and preliminary administrative services credential), official college transcript(s), signed statement of intent, two references, copy of credential. Additional exam requirements/recommendations for international students: Required—TOEFL. *Application deadline:* For fall admission, 7/15 priority date for domestic students, 6/1 for international students; for spring admission, 11/30 priority date for domestic students, 10/1 for international students. Applications are processed on a rolling basis. Application fee: $50 ($125 for international students). Electronic applications accepted. *Expenses:* Contact institution. *Financial support:* In 2013–14, 23 students received support. Scholarships/grants and unspecified assistantships available. Financial award applicants required to submit FAFSA. *Unit head:* Dr. Janice Nelson, Dean, 949-214-3334, E-mail: janice.nelson@cui.edu. *Application contact:* Patty Hunt, Admissions Coordinator, 949-214-3362, Fax: 949-214-3362, E-mail: patricia.hunt@cui.edu.

Concordia University Ann Arbor, Graduate Programs, Ann Arbor, MI 48105-2797. Offers curriculum and instruction (MS); educational leadership (MS); organizational leadership and administration (MS). Part-time and evening/weekend programs available. *Degree requirements:* For master's, thesis. *Entrance requirements:* Additional exam requirements/recommendations for international students: Required—TOEFL (minimum score 80 iBT); Recommended—IELTS (minimum score 6.5). Electronic applications accepted.

Concordia University Chicago, College of Education, Program in School Leadership, River Forest, IL 60305-1499. Offers MA, Ed D, CAS. MA offered jointly with the Chicago Consortium of Colleges and Universities. *Accreditation:* NCATE. Part-time and evening/weekend programs available. *Degree requirements:* For master's, comprehensive exam, thesis optional; for CAS, thesis, final project. *Entrance requirements:* For master's, minimum GPA of 2.9; for CAS, master's degree. Additional exam requirements/recommendations for international students: Required—TOEFL (minimum score 550 paper-based). Electronic applications accepted. *Faculty research:* Effectiveness of urban Lutheran schools in impacting children's faith development, effectiveness of centers for urban ministries in supporting urban ministry and teaching science.

Concordia University, Nebraska, Graduate Programs in Education, Program in Educational Administration, Seward, NE 68434-1556. Offers elementary and secondary education (M Ed); elementary education (M Ed); secondary education (M Ed). *Accreditation:* NCATE. Part-time programs available. *Degree requirements:* For master's, thesis or alternative. *Entrance requirements:* For master's, GRE, MAT, or NTE, BS in education or equivalent, minimum GPA of 3.0.

Concordia University, St. Paul, College of Education and Science, St. Paul, MN 55104-5494. Offers curriculum and instruction (MA Ed), including K-12 reading; differentiated instruction (MA Ed); early childhood education (MA Ed); educational leadership (MA Ed); educational technology (MA Ed); exercise science (MA); family life education (MA); K-12 principal licensure (Ed S); K-12 reading (Certificate); special education (MA Ed, Certificate), including autism spectrum disorder (MA Ed), emotional and behavioral disorders (MA Ed), learning disabilities (MA Ed); sports management (MA); superintendent (Ed S). *Accreditation:* NCATE. Part-time and evening/weekend programs available. Postbaccalaureate distance learning degree programs offered (minimal on-campus study). *Faculty:* 12 full-time (7 women), 92 part-time/adjunct (49 women). *Students:* 915 full-time (659 women), 64 part-time (53 women); includes 99 minority (47 Black or African American, non-Hispanic/Latino; 5 American Indian or Alaska Native, non-Hispanic/Latino; 18 Asian, non-Hispanic/Latino; 15 Hispanic/Latino; 2 Native Hawaiian or other Pacific Islander, non-Hispanic/Latino; 12 Two or more races, non-Hispanic/Latino), 24 international. Average age 34. 664 applicants, 67% accepted, 411 enrolled. In 2013, 275 master's, 69 other advanced degrees awarded. *Degree requirements:* For master's, thesis (for some programs). *Entrance requirements:* For master's, official transcripts from regionally-accredited institution stating the conferral of a bachelor's degree with minimum cumulative GPA of 3.0; personal statement; professional resume; practitioner in field through work or volunteerism; resume. Additional exam requirements/recommendations for international students: Recommended—TOEFL (minimum score 547 paper-based; 78 iBT), IELTS (minimum score 6). *Application deadline:* For fall admission, 8/1 for domestic and international students; for spring admission, 12/1 for domestic and international students; for summer admission, 5/1 for domestic and international students. Applications are processed on a rolling basis. Application fee: $50. Electronic applications accepted. *Expenses: Tuition:* Full-time $6200; part-time $425 per credit. Tuition and fees vary according to degree level and program. *Financial support:* Applicants required to submit FAFSA. *Unit head:* Dr. Donald Helmstetter, Dean, 651-641-8227, Fax: 651-641-8807, E-mail: helmstetter@csp.edu. *Application contact:* Kimberly Craig, Director of Graduate and Cohort Admission, 651-603-6223, Fax: 651-603-6320, E-mail: craig@csp.edu.

Concordia University Wisconsin, Graduate Programs, Department of Education, Program in Educational Administration, Mequon, WI 53097-2402. Offers MS Ed. Part-time and evening/weekend programs available. Postbaccalaureate distance learning degree programs offered (minimal on-campus study). *Degree requirements:* For master's, comprehensive exam, thesis or alternative. *Entrance requirements:* For master's, minimum GPA of 3.0. Additional exam requirements/recommendations for international students: Required—TOEFL.

Concord University, Graduate Studies, Athens, WV 24712-1000. Offers educational leadership and supervision (M Ed); geography (M Ed); health promotion (MA); reading specialist (M Ed); special education (M Ed); teaching (MAT). Part-time and evening/weekend programs available. Postbaccalaureate distance learning degree programs offered (no on-campus study). *Degree requirements:* For master's, thesis (for some programs). *Entrance requirements:* For master's, GRE or MAT, baccalaureate degree with minimum GPA of 2.5 from regionally-accredited institution; teaching license; 2 letters of recommendation; completed disposition assessment form. Electronic applications accepted.

Converse College, School of Education and Graduate Studies, Education Specialist Program, Spartanburg, SC 29302-0006. Offers administration and leadership (Ed S); administration and supervision (Ed S); literacy (Ed S). *Accreditation:* AAMFT/COAMFTE. Part-time programs available. *Entrance requirements:* For degree, GRE or MAT (marriage and family therapy), minimum GPA of 3.0. Electronic applications accepted.

Converse College, School of Education and Graduate Studies, Program in Leadership, Spartanburg, SC 29302-0006. Offers administration and supervision (M Ed). *Degree requirements:* For master's, capstone paper. *Entrance requirements:* For master's, NTE, minimum GPA of 2.75, nomination by school district, 3 recommendations. Electronic applications accepted.

Creighton University, Graduate School, College of Arts and Sciences, Department of Education, Program in Educational Leadership, Omaha, NE 68178-0001. Offers elementary school administration (MS); leadership (Ed D); secondary school administration (MS); teacher leadership (MS). Part-time and evening/weekend programs available. Postbaccalaureate distance learning degree programs offered (no on-campus study). *Faculty:* 12 full-time (6 women). *Students:* 24 part-time (15 women). Average age 31. 16 applicants, 56% accepted, 7 enrolled. In 2013, 13 master's awarded. *Degree requirements:* For master's, portfolio. *Entrance requirements:* For master's, 2 writing samples, 3 letters of recommendation. Additional exam requirements/recommendations for international students: Required—TOEFL (minimum score 550 paper-based; 80 iBT). *Application deadline:* For fall admission, 7/1 for domestic students, 3/1 for international students; for winter admission, 10/1 for domestic students, 5/1 for international students; for spring admission, 3/1 for domestic students, 10/1 for international students. Applications are processed on a rolling basis. Application fee: $50. Electronic applications accepted. *Expenses: Tuition:* Full-time $13,608; part-time $756 per credit hour. *Required fees:* $149 per semester. Tuition and fees vary according to course load, campus/location, program, reciprocity agreements and student's religious affiliation. *Financial support:* Scholarships/grants and tuition waivers (partial) available. Support available to part-time students. Financial award application deadline: 5/1; financial award applicants required to submit FAFSA. *Unit head:* Dr. Timothy J. Cook, Professor of Education, 402-280-2561, E-mail: timcook@creighton.edu. *Application contact:* Valerie Mattix, Senior Program Coordinator, 402-280-2425, Fax: 402-280-2423, E-mail: valeriemattix@creighton.edu.

Creighton University, Graduate School, Interdisciplinary EdD Program in Leadership, Omaha, NE 68178-0001. Offers Ed D. Part-time programs available. Postbaccalaureate distance learning degree programs offered (minimal on-campus study). *Faculty:* 5 full-time (4 women), 23 part-time/adjunct (12 women). *Students:* 101 full-time (43 women), 172 part-time (72 women); includes 60 minority (40 Black or African American, non-Hispanic/Latino; 4 American Indian or Alaska Native, non-Hispanic/Latino; 9 Asian, non-Hispanic/Latino; 7 Hispanic/Latino), 2 international. Average age 41. 52 applicants, 81% accepted, 35 enrolled. In 2013, 5 doctorates awarded. *Degree requirements:* For doctorate, thesis/dissertation. *Entrance requirements:* For doctorate, master's or equivalent professional degree, current resume, official transcripts, three recommendations. Additional exam requirements/recommendations for international students: Required—TOEFL (minimum score 550 paper-based; 80 iBT). *Application deadline:* For fall admission, 6/15 priority date for domestic students, 6/15 for international students; for winter admission, 10/15 for domestic and international students; for spring admission, 3/15 priority date for domestic students, 3/15 for international students; for summer admission, 3/1 for domestic and international

students. Applications are processed on a rolling basis. Application fee: $50. Electronic applications accepted. *Expenses: Tuition:* Full-time $13,608; part-time $756 per credit hour. *Required fees:* $149 per semester. Tuition and fees vary according to course load, campus/location, program, reciprocity agreements and student's religious affiliation. *Financial support:* In 2013–14, 8 students received support. Scholarships/grants available. Financial award application deadline: 5/1; financial award applicants required to submit FAFSA. *Unit head:* Dr. Isabelle D. Cherney, Director, 402-280-1228, E-mail: cherneyi@creighton.edu. *Application contact:* Chris Karasek, Program Manager, 402-280-2392, Fax: 402-280-2423, E-mail: chriskarasek@creighton.edu.
Website: https://www.creighton.edu/gradschool/edd/home/.

Dakota Wesleyan University, Program in Education, Mitchell, SD 57301-4398. Offers curriculum and instruction (MA Ed); educational policy and administration (MA Ed); preK-12 principal certification (MA Ed); secondary certification (MA Ed). Part-time and evening/weekend programs available. *Degree requirements:* For master's, comprehensive exam, thesis optional, electronic portfolio. *Entrance requirements:* For master's, minimum GPA of 2.7, elementary statistics course, statement of purpose, official transcripts, resume, three letters of recommendation. Additional exam requirements/recommendations for international students: Required—TOEFL (minimum score 500 paper-based), IELTS (minimum score 6.5). Electronic applications accepted. *Faculty research:* Math, political policy, technology in the classroom.

Dallas Baptist University, Dorothy M. Bush College of Education, Program in Educational Leadership, Dallas, TX 75211-9299. Offers M Ed. Part-time and evening/weekend programs available. *Entrance requirements:* For master's, GRE General Test, minimum GPA of 3.0. Additional exam requirements/recommendations for international students: Required—TOEFL, IELTS. *Application deadline:* Applications are processed on a rolling basis. Application fee: $25. Electronic applications accepted. *Expenses: Tuition:* Full-time $13,410; part-time $745 per credit hour. *Required fees:* $300; $150 per semester. Tuition and fees vary according to degree level. *Financial support:* Federal Work-Study, institutionally sponsored loans, scholarships/grants, and tuition waivers (full and partial) available. Support available to part-time students. Financial award applicants required to submit FAFSA. *Faculty research:* Emerging literacy, self-directed schools. *Unit head:* Dr. Tam Jones, Director, 214-333-6841, Fax: 214-333-5551, E-mail: graduate@dbu.edu. *Application contact:* Kit P. Montgomery, Director of Graduate Programs, 214-333-5242, Fax: 214-333-5579, E-mail: graduate@dbu.edu.
Website: http://www3.dbu.edu/graduate/education.asp.

Dallas Theological Seminary, Graduate Programs, Dallas, TX 75204-6499. Offers adult education (Th M); apologetics (Th M); Bible backgrounds (Th M); Bible translation (Th M); Biblical and theological studies (Certificate); biblical counseling (MA); biblical exegesis and linguistics (MA); biblical exposition (PhD); biblical studies (MA); Biblical theology (Th M); children's education (Th M); Christian education (MA, D Min); Christian leadership (MA); cross-cultural ministries (MA); educational administration (Th M); educational leadership (Th M); evangelism and discipleship (Th M); exposition of Biblical books (Th M); family life education (Th M); general studies (Th M); Hebrew and cognate studies (Th M); hermeneutics (Th M); historical theology (Th M); homiletics (Th M); intercultural ministries (Th M); Jesus studies (Th M); leadership studies (Th M); media and communication (MA); media arts (Th M); ministry (D Min); ministry with women (Th M); New Testament studies (Th M, PhD); Old Testament studies (Th M, PhD); parachurch ministries (Th M); pastoral care and counseling (Th M); pastoral theology and practice (Th M); philosophy (Th M); sacred theology (STM); spiritual formation (Th M); systematic theology (Th M); teaching in Christian institutions (Th M); theological studies (PhD); urban ministries (Th M); worship studies (Th M); youth education (Th M). *Accreditation:* ATS (one or more programs are accredited). Part-time programs available. Postbaccalaureate distance learning degree programs offered (no on-campus study). *Faculty:* 66 full-time (4 women), 35 part-time/adjunct (8 women). *Students:* 901 full-time (252 women), 1,210 part-time (432 women); includes 552 minority (232 Black or African American, non-Hispanic/Latino; 5 American Indian or Alaska Native, non-Hispanic/Latino; 172 Asian, non-Hispanic/Latino; 104 Hispanic/Latino; 4 Native Hawaiian or other Pacific Islander, non-Hispanic/Latino; 35 Two or more races, non-Hispanic/Latino), 258 international. Average age 36. 978 applicants, 89% accepted, 607 enrolled. In 2013, 358 master's, 27 doctorates, 34 other advanced degrees awarded. *Degree requirements:* For master's, variable foreign language requirement, thesis (for some programs); for doctorate, 2 foreign languages, thesis/dissertation. *Entrance requirements:* For master's, GRE or MAT (if minimum undergraduate cumulative GPA is below 2.5 or undergraduate degree is unaccredited). Additional exam requirements/recommendations for international students: Required—TOEFL (minimum score 575 paper-based; 85 iBT), TWE. *Application deadline:* For fall admission, 7/1 for domestic students, 1/1 for international students; for winter admission, 11/1 for domestic students; for spring admission, 11/1 for domestic students. Applications are processed on a rolling basis. Application fee: $50. Electronic applications accepted. *Financial support:* In 2013–14, 1,042 students received support. Career-related internships or fieldwork, scholarships/grants, and tuition waivers (full and partial) available. Financial award application deadline: 2/28. *Unit head:* Dr. Mark L. Bailey, President, 214-887-5004, Fax: 214-887-5532. *Application contact:* Greg Hatteberg, Director of Admissions and Student Advising, 214-887-5040, Fax: 214-841-3664, E-mail: admissions@dts.edu.

Delaware State University, Graduate Programs, College of Education, Health and Public Policy, Program in Educational Leadership, Dover, DE 19901-2277. Offers MA, Ed D. *Entrance requirements:* Additional exam requirements/recommendations for international students: Required—TOEFL (minimum score 550 paper-based).

Delaware Valley College, Program in Educational Leadership, Doylestown, PA 18901-2697. Offers instruction, curriculum and technology (MS); school administration and leadership (MS). Part-time and evening/weekend programs available. *Entrance requirements:* For master's, minimum undergraduate GPA of 3.0.

Delta State University, Graduate Programs, College of Education, Thad Cochran Center for Rural School Leadership and Research, Program in Professional Studies, Cleveland, MS 38733-0001. Offers counselor education (Ed D); educational leadership (Ed D); elementary education (Ed D); higher education (Ed D). Part-time and evening/weekend programs available. *Students:* 3 full-time (all women), 90 part-time (58 women); includes 31 minority (all Black or African American, non-Hispanic/Latino), 1 international. Average age 38. 44 applicants, 95% accepted, 28 enrolled. In 2013, 2 doctorates awarded. *Degree requirements:* For doctorate, thesis/dissertation. *Entrance requirements:* For doctorate, GRE General Test. *Application deadline:* For fall admission, 8/1 priority date for domestic students; for spring admission, 12/1 priority date for domestic students. Applications are processed on a rolling basis. Application fee: $0. *Expenses:* Tuition, state resident: full-time $3006; part-time $334 per credit hour. Tuition, nonresident: full-time $3006; part-time $334 per credit hour. *Financial support:* Research assistantships, career-related internships or fieldwork, Federal Work-Study, and institutionally sponsored loans available. Support available to part-time students. Financial award application deadline: 6/1. *Unit head:* Dr. Dan McFall, Interim Chair, 662-846-4395, Fax: 662-846-4402. *Application contact:* Dr. Albert Nylander, Dean of Graduate Studies, 662-846-4875, Fax: 662-846-4313, E-mail: grad-info@deltastate.edu.

Delta State University, Graduate Programs, College of Education, Thad Cochran Center for Rural School Leadership and Research, Programs in Educational Administration and Supervision, Cleveland, MS 38733-0001. Offers M Ed, Ed S. *Accreditation:* NCATE. Part-time and evening/weekend programs available. *Faculty:* 2 full-time (1 woman), 3 part-time/adjunct (1 woman). *Students:* 4 full-time (3 women), 79 part-time (58 women); includes 58 minority (all Black or African American, non-Hispanic/Latino). Average age 38. 33 applicants, 85% accepted, 22 enrolled. In 2013, 12 master's, 21 Ed Ss awarded. *Degree requirements:* For master's, thesis optional. *Entrance requirements:* For master's, GRE General Test or MAT; for Ed S, master's degree, teaching certificate. *Application deadline:* For fall admission, 8/1 priority date for domestic students; for spring admission, 12/1 priority date for domestic students. Applications are processed on a rolling basis. Application fee: $0. *Expenses:* Tuition, state resident: full-time $3006; part-time $334 per credit hour. Tuition, nonresident: full-time $3006; part-time $334 per credit hour. *Financial support:* Research assistantships, career-related internships or fieldwork, Federal Work-Study, and institutionally sponsored loans available. Support available to part-time students. Financial award application deadline: 6/1. *Unit head:* Dr. Dan McFall, Interim Chair, 662-846-4395, Fax: 662-846-4402. *Application contact:* Dr. Albert Nylander, Dean of Graduate Studies, 662-846-4875, Fax: 662-846-4313, E-mail: grad-info@deltastate.edu.

DePaul University, College of Education, Chicago, IL 60614. Offers bilingual bicultural education (M Ed, MA); counseling (M Ed, MA), including clinical mental health counseling, college student development, school counseling; curriculum studies (M Ed, MA, Ed D); early childhood education (M Ed, MA, Ed D); educating adults (MA); educational leadership (M Ed, MA, Ed D), including administration and supervision (M Ed, MA), principal preparation (M Ed, MA); elementary education (MA); mathematics education (MA); mathematics for teaching (MS); middle school mathematics education (MS); reading specialist (M Ed, MA); secondary education (M Ed); social and cultural foundations in education (MA); special education (M Ed, MA); world languages education (M Ed, MA). Part-time and evening/weekend programs available. Postbaccalaureate distance learning degree programs offered (no on-campus study). *Faculty:* 61 full-time (35 women), 59 part-time/adjunct (43 women). *Students:* 628 full-time (486 women), 324 part-time (243 women); includes 304 minority (144 Black or African American, non-Hispanic/Latino; 1 American Indian or Alaska Native, non-Hispanic/Latino; 38 Asian, non-Hispanic/Latino; 98 Hispanic/Latino; 23 Two or more races, non-Hispanic/Latino), 24 international. Average age 30. In 2013, 465 master's, 4 doctorates awarded. *Degree requirements:* For doctorate, thesis/dissertation. *Application deadline:* For fall admission, 8/15 for domestic students; for winter admission, 12/1 for domestic students; for spring admission, 3/1 for domestic students. Applications are processed on a rolling basis. Application fee: $40. Electronic applications accepted. Tuition and fees vary according to course level, course load and degree level. *Financial support:* Application deadline: 12/31; applicants required to submit FAFSA. *Unit head:* Dr. Paul Zionts, Dean, 773-325-7581, Fax: 773-325-7713, E-mail: pzionts@depaul.edu. *Application contact:* Farrah Dalal, Assistant Director, 773-325-2465, Fax: 773-325-2270, E-mail: fdalal@depaul.edu.
Website: http://education.depaul.edu.

Doane College, Program in Education, Crete, NE 68333-2430. Offers curriculum and instruction (M Ed); educational leadership (M Ed). *Accreditation:* NCATE. Part-time and evening/weekend programs available. *Students:* 125 full-time (89 women), 502 part-time (396 women); includes 25 minority (11 Black or African American, non-Hispanic/Latino; 1 American Indian or Alaska Native, non-Hispanic/Latino; 2 Asian, non-Hispanic/Latino; 9 Hispanic/Latino; 1 Native Hawaiian or other Pacific Islander, non-Hispanic/Latino; 1 Two or more races, non-Hispanic/Latino). Average age 33. In 2013, 284 master's awarded. *Degree requirements:* For master's, thesis. *Entrance requirements:* For master's, minimum GPA of 2.5. Additional exam requirements/recommendations for international students: Required—TOEFL. *Application deadline:* Applications are processed on a rolling basis. Electronic applications accepted. *Expenses:* Contact institution. *Financial support:* Applicants required to submit FAFSA. *Unit head:* Lyn C. Forester, Dean, 402-826-8604, Fax: 402-826-8278. *Application contact:* Wilma Daddario, Assistant Dean, 402-464-1223, Fax: 402-466-4228, E-mail: wdaddario@doane.edu.
Website: http://www.doane.edu/masters-degrees.

Dominican University, School of Education, River Forest, IL 60305-1099. Offers curriculum and instruction (MA Ed); early childhood education (MS); education (MAT); educational administration (MA); elementary education (MA Ed); English as a second language (MA Ed); reading (MA Ed); special education (MS). Part-time and evening/weekend programs available. Postbaccalaureate distance learning degree programs offered (no on-campus study). *Faculty:* 19 full-time (14 women), 51 part-time/adjunct (42 women). *Students:* 18 full-time (13 women), 334 part-time (274 women); includes 76 minority (26 Black or African American, non-Hispanic/Latino; 9 Asian, non-Hispanic/Latino; 41 Hispanic/Latino). Average age 32. 119 applicants, 77% accepted, 70 enrolled. In 2013, 246 master's awarded. *Entrance requirements:* For master's, Illinois Test of Basic Skills. Additional exam requirements/recommendations for international students: Required—TOEFL (minimum score 550 paper-based; 79 iBT). *Application deadline:* Applications are processed on a rolling basis. Application fee: $25. *Expenses:* Contact institution. *Financial support:* In 2013–14, 97 students received support. Career-related internships or fieldwork, scholarships/grants, and tuition waivers (partial) available. Support available to part-time students. Financial award application deadline: 8/15; financial award applicants required to submit FAFSA. *Faculty research:* Governance of private education institutions, reading and language arts, inclusion, organizational planning, leadership and vision. *Unit head:* Dr. Colleen Reardon, Dean, 718-524-6643, Fax: 708-524-6665, E-mail: creardon@dom.edu. *Application contact:* Kevin Hansen, Coordinator of Recruitment and Admissions, 708-524-6921, Fax: 708-524-6665, E-mail: educate@dom.edu.
Website: http://educate.dom.edu/.

Dowling College, Graduate Programs in Education, Oakdale, NY 11769-1999. Offers adolescence education with middle childhood extension (MS); childhood and early childhood education (MS); childhood and gifted education (MS); childhood education (1-6) (MS); computers in education (AC); early childhood education (B-2) (MS); educational administration (Ed D); educational technology leadership (MS); educational technology specialist (AC); gifted education (AC); literacy education (MS, AC), including 5-12 (MS), B-12 (MS); literacy education (MS), including B-6; school building leader (AC); school district business leader (MBA, AC); school district leader (AC); special education (MS), including autism, severe disabilities; sport management (MS). *Accreditation:* NCATE. Part-time and evening/weekend programs available. Postbaccalaureate distance learning degree programs offered (minimal on-campus study). *Faculty:* 44 full-time (24 women), 17 part-time/adjunct (8 women). *Students:* 183 full-time (124 women), 314 part-time (231 women); includes 51 minority (19 Black or African American, non-Hispanic/Latino; 1 American Indian or Alaska Native, non-Hispanic/Latino; 3 Asian, non-Hispanic/Latino; 26 Hispanic/Latino; 2 Native Hawaiian or other Pacific Islander, non-Hispanic/Latino). Average age 32. 174 applicants, 80% accepted, 82 enrolled. In 2013, 198 master's, 33 doctorates, 48 other advanced degrees awarded. *Degree requirements:* For master's and AC, comprehensive exam; for doctorate, thesis/dissertation. *Entrance requirements:* For master's, minimum GPA of 3.0; for doctorate, GRE, master's degree; for AC, teaching certificate. Additional exam requirements/recommendations for international students: Required—TOEFL (minimum score 550 paper-based). *Application deadline:* For fall admission, 9/1 priority date for domestic students; for

winter admission, 1/1 priority date for domestic students; for spring admission, 2/1 priority date for domestic students. Applications are processed on a rolling basis. Application fee: $50. Electronic applications accepted. *Expenses: Tuition:* Full-time $22,731; part-time $1029 per credit. *Required fees:* $956; $956. *Financial support:* Career-related internships or fieldwork and Federal Work-Study available. Support available to part-time students. Financial award application deadline: 6/30; financial award applicants required to submit FAFSA. *Faculty research:* Natural readers, Korean styles and learning strategies, mothers of children with disabilities, computers in instruction, cultural background and organizational roadblocks to problem solving. *Unit head:* Dr. Robert Manley, Dean, 631-244-3447, E-mail: manleyr@dowling.edu. *Application contact:* Mary Boullianne, Director of Admissions, 631-244-3274, Fax: 631-244-1059, E-mail: boulliam@dowling.edu.

Dowling College, School of Business, Oakdale, NY 11769. Offers aviation management (MBA, Certificate); corporate finance (MBA, Certificate); health care management (MBA); human resource management (Certificate); information systems management (MBA); management and leadership (MBA); marketing (Certificate); project management (Certificate); public management (MBA); school district business leader (MBA); sport, event and entertainment management (Certificate); JD/MBA. Part-time and evening/weekend programs available. Postbaccalaureate distance learning degree programs offered (minimal on-campus study). *Faculty:* 7 full-time (2 women), 43 part-time/adjunct (7 women). *Students:* 183 full-time (79 women), 299 part-time (142 women); includes 137 minority (84 Black or African American, non-Hispanic/Latino; 14 Asian, non-Hispanic/Latino; 20 Hispanic/Latino; 19 Native Hawaiian or other Pacific Islander, non-Hispanic/Latino). Average age 32. 360 applicants, 58% accepted, 127 enrolled. In 2013, 235 master's, 15 other advanced degrees awarded. *Degree requirements:* For master's, comprehensive exam, thesis optional. *Entrance requirements:* For master's, minimum GPA of 2.8, 2 letters of recommendation, courses or seminar in accounting and finance, resume. Additional exam requirements/recommendations for international students: Required—TOEFL (minimum score 550 paper-based). *Application deadline:* For fall admission, 9/1 priority date for domestic students; for winter admission, 1/1 priority date for domestic students; for spring admission, 2/1 priority date for domestic students. Applications are processed on a rolling basis. Application fee: $50. Electronic applications accepted. *Expenses: Tuition:* Full-time $22,731; part-time $1029 per credit. *Required fees:* $956; $956. *Financial support:* Career-related internships or fieldwork and Federal Work-Study available. Support available to part-time students. Financial award application deadline: 6/30; financial award applicants required to submit FAFSA. *Faculty research:* International finance, computer applications, labor relations, executive development. *Unit head:* Dr. Elana Zolfo, Dean, 631-244-3266, Fax: 631-244-1018, E-mail: zolfoe@dowling.edu. *Application contact:* Mary Boullianne, Dean of Admissions, 631-244-3274, Fax: 631-244-1059, E-mail: boulliam@dowling.edu.

Drexel University, Goodwin College of Professional Studies, School of Education, Philadelphia, PA 19104-2875. Offers educational administration (MS); educational improvement and transformation (MS); educational leadership and management (Ed D); educational leadership development and learning technologies (PhD); global and international education (MS); higher education (MS); human resources development (MS); learning technologies (MS); mathematics, learning and teaching (MS); special education (MS); teaching, learning and curriculum (MS). Part-time and evening/weekend programs available. Postbaccalaureate distance learning degree programs offered (no on-campus study). *Degree requirements:* For doctorate, thesis/dissertation. *Entrance requirements:* For doctorate, GRE or GMAT. Additional exam requirements/recommendations for international students: Required—TOEFL, IELTS. Electronic applications accepted. Application fee is waived when completed online. *Expenses:* Contact institution. *Faculty research:* Leadership development, mathematics education, literacy, autism, educational technology.

Duquesne University, School of Education, Department of Foundations and Leadership, Professional Doctorate in Educational Leadership Program (ProDEL), Pittsburgh, PA 15282-0001. Offers Ed D. Part-time and evening/weekend programs available. *Faculty:* 7 full-time (3 women). *Students:* 55 full-time (32 women); includes 15 minority (14 Black or African American, non-Hispanic/Latino; 1 Two or more races, non-Hispanic/Latino), 6 international. Average age 43. 43 applicants, 49% accepted, 20 enrolled. In 2013, 2 doctorates awarded. *Degree requirements:* For doctorate, thesis/dissertation. *Entrance requirements:* For doctorate, GRE, letters of recommendation, essay, interview, master's degree. Additional exam requirements/recommendations for international students: Required—TOEFL (minimum score 550 paper-based), IELTS (minimum score 7). *Application deadline:* For fall admission, 3/1 for domestic students. Electronic applications accepted. *Expenses: Tuition:* Full-time $18,162; part-time $1009 per credit. *Required fees:* $1728; $96 per credit. Tuition and fees vary according to program. *Unit head:* Dr. Rick McCown, Professor and Chair, 412-396-5568, Fax: 412-396-6017, E-mail: mccown@duq.edu. *Application contact:* Michael Dolinger, Director of Student and Academic Services, 412-396-6647, Fax: 412-396-5585, E-mail: dolingerm@duq.edu. Website: http://www.duq.edu/academics/schools/education/graduate-programs-education/educational-leadership.

Duquesne University, School of Education, Department of Foundations and Leadership, Program in School Administration and Supervision, Pittsburgh, PA 15282-0001. Offers curriculum and instruction (Post-Master's Certificate); school administration K-12 (MS Ed, Post-Master's Certificate); school supervision (MS Ed). Part-time and evening/weekend programs available. *Faculty:* 2 full-time (both women). *Students:* 33 full-time (29 women), 11 part-time (8 women); includes 3 minority (1 Black or African American, non-Hispanic/Latino; 1 Asian, non-Hispanic/Latino; 1 Hispanic/Latino). Average age 34. 37 applicants, 59% accepted, 22 enrolled. In 2013, 19 master's awarded. *Degree requirements:* For master's, thesis optional. *Entrance requirements:* For master's and Post-Master's Certificate, bachelor's degree. Additional exam requirements/recommendations for international students: Required—TOEFL (minimum score 550 paper-based), IELTS (minimum score 7). *Application deadline:* For fall admission, 9/1 for domestic students; for spring admission, 1/1 for domestic students. Applications are processed on a rolling basis. Application fee: $0. Electronic applications accepted. Application fee is waived when completed online. *Expenses: Tuition:* Full-time $18,162; part-time $1009 per credit. *Required fees:* $1728; $96 per credit. Tuition and fees vary according to program. *Financial support:* Research assistantships available. Support available to part-time students. *Unit head:* Dr. Fran Serenka, Associate Professor and Director, 412-396-5274, Fax: 412-396-1274, E-mail: serenkaf@duq.edu. *Application contact:* Michael Dolinger, Director of Student and Academic Services, 412-396-6647, Fax: 412-396-5585, E-mail: dolingerm@duq.edu. Website: http://www.duq.edu/academics/schools/education/graduate-programs-education/school-admin-and-supervision.

D'Youville College, Department of Education, Buffalo, NY 14201-1084. Offers educational leadership (Ed D); elementary education (MS Ed, Teaching Certificate); secondary education (MS Ed, Teaching Certificate); special education (MS Ed). Part-time and evening/weekend programs available. *Students:* 96 full-time (68 women), 91 part-time (60 women); includes 14 minority (9 Black or African American, non-Hispanic/Latino; 1 American Indian or Alaska Native, non-Hispanic/Latino; 4 Hispanic/Latino), 90

international. Average age 32. 383 applicants, 48% accepted, 104 enrolled. In 2013, 128 master's awarded. *Degree requirements:* For master's, one foreign language, comprehensive exam, project or thesis. *Entrance requirements:* For master's, GRE (if GPA less than 2.75), minimum GPA of 3.0. Additional exam requirements/recommendations for international students: Required—TOEFL (minimum score 500 paper-based). *Application deadline:* For fall admission, 5/1 priority date for international students; for spring admission, 9/1 priority date for international students. Applications are processed on a rolling basis. Application fee: $25. Electronic applications accepted. *Financial support:* Career-related internships or fieldwork, Federal Work-Study, institutionally sponsored loans, scholarships/grants, tuition waivers (full and partial), and unspecified assistantships available. Support available to part-time students. Financial award application deadline: 3/1; financial award applicants required to submit FAFSA. *Faculty research:* Developmental disabilities, multiculturalism, early childhood education. *Unit head:* Dr. Hilary Lochte, Chair, 716-829-8110, Fax: 716-829-7660. *Application contact:* Mark Pavone, Graduate Admissions Director, 716-829-8400, Fax: 716-829-7900, E-mail: graduateadmissions@dyc.edu.

East Carolina University, Graduate School, College of Education, Department of Educational Leadership, Greenville, NC 27858-4353. Offers educational administration and supervision (Ed S); educational leadership (Ed D); school administration (MSA). *Accreditation:* NCATE. Part-time and evening/weekend programs available. Postbaccalaureate distance learning degree programs offered (minimal on-campus study). *Degree requirements:* For master's, comprehensive exam, thesis optional; for doctorate, thesis/dissertation. *Entrance requirements:* For master's, GRE General Test or MAT, interview, minimum GPA of 2.5, bachelor's degree in related field, teaching license (MA Ed); for doctorate, GRE or MAT, interview, minimum GPA of 3.5. Additional exam requirements/recommendations for international students: Required—TOEFL. *Expenses:* Tuition, state resident: full-time $4223. Tuition, nonresident: full-time $16,540. *Required fees:* $2184.

East Carolina University, Graduate School, College of Education, Department of Higher, Adult, and Counselor Education, Greenville, NC 27858-4353. Offers adult education (MA Ed); counselor education (MS); higher education administration (Ed D). *Accreditation:* NCATE. Part-time and evening/weekend programs available. *Degree requirements:* For master's, comprehensive exam, thesis optional. *Entrance requirements:* For master's, GRE General Test or MAT, interview, minimum GPA of 2.5, bachelor's degree in related field, teaching license (MA Ed). Additional exam requirements/recommendations for international students: Required—TOEFL. *Expenses:* Tuition, state resident: full-time $4223. Tuition, nonresident: full-time $16,540. *Required fees:* $2184.

Eastern Illinois University, Graduate School, College of Education and Professional Studies, Department of Educational Leadership, Charleston, IL 61920-3099. Offers MS Ed, Ed S. *Accreditation:* NCATE. Part-time and evening/weekend programs available. *Degree requirements:* For master's, fieldwork; for Ed S, thesis. *Expenses: Tuition, area resident:* Part-time $283 per credit hour. Tuition, state resident: part-time $283 per credit hour. Tuition, nonresident: part-time $679 per credit hour.

Eastern Kentucky University, The Graduate School, College of Education, Department of Counseling and Educational Leadership, Richmond, KY 40475-3102. Offers human services (MA); instructional leadership (MA Ed); mental health counseling (MA); school counseling (MA Ed). *Accreditation:* ACA (one or more programs are accredited); NCATE. Part-time programs available. Postbaccalaureate distance learning degree programs offered. *Entrance requirements:* For master's, GRE General Test, minimum GPA of 2.5.

Eastern Michigan University, Graduate School, College of Education, Department of Leadership and Counseling, Programs in Educational Leadership, Ypsilanti, MI 48197. Offers community college leadership (Graduate Certificate); educational leadership (MA, Ed D, SPA); higher education/general administration (MA); higher education/student affairs (MA); K-12 administration (MA); K-12 basic administration (Post Master's Certificate). Part-time and evening/weekend programs available. Postbaccalaureate distance learning degree programs offered (no on-campus study). *Students:* 50 full-time (31 women), 397 part-time (252 women); includes 124 minority (93 Black or African American, non-Hispanic/Latino; 2 American Indian or Alaska Native, non-Hispanic/Latino; 7 Asian, non-Hispanic/Latino; 15 Hispanic/Latino; 1 Native Hawaiian or other Pacific Islander, non-Hispanic/Latino; 6 Two or more races, non-Hispanic/Latino), 6 international. Average age 37. 261 applicants, 79% accepted, 136 enrolled. In 2013, 80 master's, 11 doctorates, 40 other advanced degrees awarded. *Degree requirements:* For master's, portfolio. *Entrance requirements:* For doctorate, GRE. Additional exam requirements/recommendations for international students: Required—TOEFL. *Application deadline:* For winter admission, 2/1 for domestic and international students. Applications are processed on a rolling basis. Application fee: $35. *Expenses:* Tuition, state resident: full-time $12,300; part-time $466 per credit hour. Tuition, nonresident: full-time $23,159; part-time $918 per credit hour. *Required fees:* $71 per credit hour. $46 per semester. One-time fee: $100. Tuition and fees vary according to course level and degree level. *Financial support:* Fellowships, research assistantships with full tuition reimbursements, teaching assistantships with full tuition reimbursements, career-related internships or fieldwork, Federal Work-Study, institutionally sponsored loans, scholarships/grants, tuition waivers (partial), and unspecified assistantships available. Support available to part-time students. *Unit head:* Dr. Jaclynn Tracy, Department Head, 734-487-0255, Fax: 734-487-4608, E-mail: jtracy@emich.edu. *Application contact:* Dr. Ella Burton, Coordinator of Advising for Programs in Educational Leadership, 734-487-0255, Fax: 734-487-4608, E-mail: eburton1@emich.edu.

Eastern Michigan University, Graduate School, College of Education, Department of Special Education, Programs in Special Education, Ypsilanti, MI 48197. Offers administration and supervision (SPA); curriculum development (SPA); special education (MA). *Accreditation:* NCATE. Part-time and evening/weekend programs available. Postbaccalaureate distance learning degree programs offered (minimal on-campus study). *Students:* 1 (woman) full-time, 41 part-time (34 women); includes 5 minority (4 Black or African American, non-Hispanic/Latino; 1 Hispanic/Latino). Average age 42. 20 applicants, 75% accepted, 6 enrolled. In 2013, 5 master's, 6 other advanced degrees awarded. *Entrance requirements:* For master's, GRE General Test. Additional exam requirements/recommendations for international students: Required—TOEFL. *Application deadline:* Applications are processed on a rolling basis. Application fee: $35. *Expenses:* Tuition, state resident: full-time $12,300; part-time $466 per credit hour. Tuition, nonresident: full-time $23,159; part-time $918 per credit hour. *Required fees:* $71 per credit hour. $46 per semester. One-time fee: $100. Tuition and fees vary according to course level and degree level. *Financial support:* Fellowships, research assistantships with full tuition reimbursements, teaching assistantships with full tuition reimbursements, career-related internships or fieldwork, Federal Work-Study, institutionally sponsored loans, scholarships/grants, tuition waivers (partial), and unspecified assistantships available. Support available to part-time students. Financial award applicants required to submit FAFSA. *Unit head:* Dr. Janet Fisher, Interim Department Head, 734-487-2716, Fax: 734-487-2473, E-mail: jfisher3@emich.edu. *Application contact:* Dr. Steven Camron, Advisor, 734-487-3300, Fax: 734-487-2473, E-mail: scamron@emich.edu.

Eastern Nazarene College, Adult and Graduate Studies, Division of Teacher Education, Quincy, MA 02170. Offers administration (M Ed); early childhood education (M Ed, Certificate); elementary education (M Ed, Certificate); English as a second language (Certificate); instructional enrichment and development (Certificate); middle school education (M Ed, Certificate); moderate special needs education (Certificate); principal (Certificate); program development and supervision (Certificate); secondary education (M Ed, Certificate); special education administrator (Certificate); special needs (M Ed); supervisor (Certificate); teacher of reading (M Ed, Certificate). M Ed also available through weekend program for administration, special needs, and teacher of reading only. Part-time and evening/weekend programs available. *Entrance requirements:* Additional exam requirements/recommendations for international students: Required—TOEFL (minimum score 550 paper-based).

Eastern New Mexico University, Graduate School, College of Education and Technology, Department of Educational Studies, Portales, NM 88130. Offers counseling (MA); education (M Ed), including educational administration, secondary education; school counseling (M Ed); special education (M Sp Ed), including early childhood special education, general. *Accreditation:* NCATE. Part-time and evening/weekend programs available. Postbaccalaureate distance learning degree programs offered (minimal on-campus study). *Degree requirements:* For master's, comprehensive exam, thesis optional. *Entrance requirements:* For master's, minimum GPA of 3.0, letter of recommendation, photocopy of teaching license, writing assessment, Level II teaching license (for M Ed in educational administration). Additional exam requirements/recommendations for international students: Required—TOEFL (minimum score 550 paper-based; 79 iBT), IELTS (minimum score 6). Electronic applications accepted.

Eastern University, Graduate Education Programs, St. Davids, PA 19087-3696. Offers ESL program specialist (K-12) (Certificate); general supervisor (PreK-12) (Certificate); health and physical education (K-12) (Certificate); middle level (4-8) (Certificate); multicultural education (M Ed); pre K-4 (Certificate); pre K-4 with special education (Certificate); reading (M Ed); reading specialist (K-12) (Certificate); reading supervisor (K-12) (Certificate); school health services (M Ed); school health supervisor (Certificate); school nurse (Certificate); school principalship (K-12) (Certificate); secondary biology education (7-12) (Certificate); secondary chemistry education (7-12) (Certificate); secondary communication education (7-12) (Certificate); secondary education (7-12) (Certificate); secondary English education (7-12) (Certificate); secondary math education (7-12) (Certificate); secondary social studies education (7-12) (Certificate); special education (M Ed); special education (7-12) (Certificate); special education (Pre K-8) (Certificate); special education supervisor (N-12) (Certificate); TESOL (M Ed); world language (Certificate), including French, Mandarin Chinese, Spanish. Part-time and evening/weekend programs available. Postbaccalaureate distance learning degree programs offered (no on-campus study). *Faculty:* 22 full-time (11 women), 26 part-time/adjunct (18 women). *Students:* 77 full-time (58 women), 223 part-time (149 women); includes 112 minority (81 Black or African American, non-Hispanic/Latino; 1 American Indian or Alaska Native, non-Hispanic/Latino; 9 Asian, non-Hispanic/Latino; 18 Hispanic/Latino; 1 Native Hawaiian or other Pacific Islander, non-Hispanic/Latino; 2 Two or more races, non-Hispanic/Latino), 7 international. Average age 34. 94 applicants, 100% accepted, 81 enrolled. In 2013, 120 master's awarded. *Entrance requirements:* For master's, minimum GPA of 2.5 (for M Ed); for Certificate, minimum GPA of 3.0 for certifications. Additional exam requirements/recommendations for international students: Required—TOEFL. *Application deadline:* For fall admission, 8/14 for domestic students; for spring admission, 12/20 for domestic students. Applications are processed on a rolling basis. Application fee: $35. Application fee is waived when completed online. *Expenses: Tuition:* Full-time $15,600; part-time $650 per credit. *Required fees:* $27.50 per semester. One-time fee: $50. Tuition and fees vary according to course load, degree level and program. *Financial support:* In 2013–14, 84 students received support, including 6 research assistantships with partial tuition reimbursements available (averaging $7,710 per year); scholarships/grants and unspecified assistantships also available. Financial award application deadline: 3/15; financial award applicants required to submit FAFSA. *Unit head:* Harry Gutelius, Associate Dean, 610-341-1729. *Application contact:* Michael Perpiglia, Associate Director of Enrollment, 610-341-5947, Fax: 484-581-1276, E-mail: mperpigl@eastern.edu.
Website: http://www.eastern.edu/academics/programs/loeb-school-education-0/graduateprograms.

East Tennessee State University, School of Graduate Studies, College of Education, Department of Educational Leadership and Policy Analysis, Johnson City, TN 37614. Offers administration endorsement (Ed S); administrative endorsement (Ed D); classroom leadership (Ed D); counselor leadership (Ed S); postsecondary and private sector leadership (Ed D); school administration and leadership (M Ed); school leadership (Ed D); school system leadership (Ed S); student personnel leadership (M Ed); teacher leadership (M Ed, Ed S). *Accreditation:* NCATE. Part-time programs available. Postbaccalaureate distance learning degree programs offered. *Faculty:* 12 full-time (6 women), 8 part-time/adjunct (5 women). *Students:* 17 full-time (15 women), 217 part-time (134 women); includes 38 minority (26 Black or African American, non-Hispanic/Latino; 4 Asian, non-Hispanic/Latino; 4 Hispanic/Latino; 4 Two or more races, non-Hispanic/Latino). Average age 41. 101 applicants, 50% accepted, 45 enrolled. In 2013, 4 master's, 33 doctorates, 2 other advanced degrees awarded. *Degree requirements:* For master's, comprehensive exam, portfolio development and presentation, performance assessment; for doctorate, comprehensive exam, thesis/dissertation, residency, internship; for Ed S, comprehensive exam, field experience; internship (for counselor leadership concentration). *Entrance requirements:* For master's, writing assessment, minimum GPA of 2.75, professional resume, teaching certificate and experience, interview; for doctorate, GRE General Test, writing assessment, professional resume, teaching certificate (except for post secondary and private sector leadership concentration), interview, four letters of recommendation; for Ed S, writing assessment, professional resume, teaching certificate (for counselor leadership concentration). Additional exam requirements/recommendations for international students: Required—TOEFL (minimum score 550 paper-based; 79 iBT). *Application deadline:* For fall admission, 5/1 for domestic students, 4/30 for international students; for spring admission, 10/1 for domestic students, 9/30 for international students. Application fee: $35 ($45 for international students). Electronic applications accepted. *Expenses:* Tuition, state resident: full-time $7900; part-time $395 per credit hour. Tuition, nonresident: full-time $21,960; part-time $1098 per credit hour. *Required fees:* $1345; $84 per credit hour. *Financial support:* In 2013–14, 13 students received support, including 7 fellowships with full tuition reimbursements available (averaging $9,800 per year), research assistantships with full tuition reimbursements available (averaging $6,000 per year), 1 teaching assistantship with full tuition reimbursement available (averaging $6,000 per year); career-related internships or fieldwork, institutionally sponsored loans, scholarships/grants, and unspecified assistantships also available. Financial award application deadline: 7/1; financial award applicants required to submit FAFSA. *Faculty research:* Assessment and evaluation; examining school leadership, management, and accountability systems that limit learning; college and university enrollment and retention issues. *Unit head:* Dr. Pam Scott, Chair, 423-439-4430, Fax: 423-439-7636, E-mail: scottp@etsu.edu. *Application contact:* Cindy Hill, Graduate Specialist, 423-439-6590, Fax: 423-439-5624, E-mail: hillcc@etsu.edu.

Edgewood College, Program in Education, Madison, WI 53711-1997. Offers adult learning (MA Ed); bilingual teaching and learning (MA Ed); director of instruction (Certificate); director of special education and pupil services (Certificate); education (MA Ed); educational administration (MA Ed); educational leadership (Ed D); professional studies (MA Ed); program coordinator (Certificate); reading administration (MA Ed); school business administration (Certificate); school principalship K-12 (Certificate); special education (MA Ed); sustainability leadership (MA Ed); teaching and learning (MA Ed); teaching English to speakers of other languages (TESOL) (MA Ed). *Accreditation:* NCATE (one or more programs are accredited). Part-time and evening/weekend programs available. *Students:* 159 full-time (95 women), 164 part-time (121 women); includes 61 minority (19 Black or African American, non-Hispanic/Latino; 9 Asian, non-Hispanic/Latino; 25 Hispanic/Latino; 8 Two or more races, non-Hispanic/Latino), 27 international. Average age 36. In 2013, 51 master's, 22 doctorates awarded. *Degree requirements:* For master's, practicum, research project; for doctorate, comprehensive exam, thesis/dissertation. *Entrance requirements:* For master's, minimum GPA of 2.75, 2 letters of recommendation, personal statement; for doctorate, resume, letter of intent, 2 letters of recommendation, interview, writing sample. Additional exam requirements/recommendations for international students: Required—TOEFL (minimum score 525 paper-based; 72 iBT). *Application deadline:* For fall admission, 8/15 for domestic students, 5/1 for international students; for spring admission, 1/8 for domestic students, 11/1 for international students. Applications are processed on a rolling basis. Application fee: $30. Electronic applications accepted. *Unit head:* Dr. Timothy Slekar, Dean, E-mail: tslekar@edgewood.edu. *Application contact:* Joann Eastman, Admissions Counselor, 608-663-3250, Fax: 608-663-2214, E-mail: gps@edgewood.edu.
Website: http://www.edgewood.edu/Academics/School-of-Education.

Edinboro University of Pennsylvania, School of Education, Department of Professional Studies, Edinboro, PA 16444. Offers counseling (MA); educational leadership (M Ed); educational psychology (M Ed); reading (M Ed); school psychology (MS, Ed S). Part-time and evening/weekend programs available. *Degree requirements:* For master's, thesis or alternative, competency exam; for Ed S, thesis or alternative. *Entrance requirements:* For master's and Ed S, GRE or MAT, minimum QPA of 2.5. Electronic applications accepted.

Elizabeth City State University, School of Education and Psychology, Master of School Administration Program, Elizabeth City, NC 27909-7806. Offers MSA. Part-time and evening/weekend programs available. *Faculty:* 3 full-time (1 woman). *Students:* 1 full-time (0 women), 30 part-time (23 women); includes 15 minority (all Black or African American, non-Hispanic/Latino). Average age 38. 2 applicants, 100% accepted, 2 enrolled. In 2013, 44 master's awarded. *Degree requirements:* For master's, thesis or alternative, electronic portfolio. *Entrance requirements:* For master's, MAT, GRE, minimum GPA of 3.0, 3 years of teaching experience, 3 letters of recommendation, two official transcripts from all undergraduate/graduate schools attended, teacher license, 3-4 page statement of purpose. Additional exam requirements/recommendations for international students: Required—TOEFL (minimum score 550 paper-based, 80 iBT) or IELTS (minimum score 6.5). *Application deadline:* For fall admission, 7/15 priority date for domestic students, 7/15 for international students; for spring admission, 11/15 priority date for domestic students, 11/15 for international students; for summer admission, 3/15 priority date for domestic and international students. Applications are processed on a rolling basis. Application fee: $30. Electronic applications accepted. *Expenses:* Tuition, state resident: full-time $2916; part-time $364.48 per credit. Tuition, nonresident: full-time $14,199; part-time $1774.83 per credit. *Required fees:* $2972.23; $206.58 per credit. $571.06 per semester. *Financial support:* In 2013–14, 25 students received support. Scholarships/grants and health care benefits available. Financial award application deadline: 6/30; financial award applicants required to submit FAFSA. *Faculty research:* Mentoring, assessment, professional learning communities, common core standards, Interstate School Leaders Licensure Consortium (ISLLC), differentiating instruction. *Unit head:* Dr. Saundra S. Copeland, Coordinator, 252-335-3337, Fax: 252-335-3554, E-mail: sscopeland@mail.ecsu.edu. *Application contact:* Dr. Paula S. Viltz, Interim Dean, School of Education & Psychology and Graduate Education, 252-335-3297, Fax: 252-335-3146, E-mail: psviltz@mail.ecsu.edu.
Website: http://www.ecsu.edu/academics/graduate/schooladmin/index.cfm.

Elmhurst College, Graduate Programs, Program in Teacher Leadership, Elmhurst, IL 60126-3296. Offers M Ed. Part-time and evening/weekend programs available. *Faculty:* 1 (woman) full-time, 1 (woman) part-time/adjunct. *Students:* 12 part-time (11 women). Average age 30. 8 applicants, 75% accepted, 5 enrolled. In 2013, 4 master's awarded. *Entrance requirements:* For master's, 3 recommendations, resume, statement of purpose. Additional exam requirements/recommendations for international students: Required—TOEFL (minimum score 550 paper-based; 79 iBT). *Application deadline:* Applications are processed on a rolling basis. Application fee: $0. Electronic applications accepted. *Expenses:* Contact institution. *Financial support:* In 2013–14, 1 student received support. Federal Work-Study and scholarships/grants available. Support available to part-time students. Financial award application deadline: 6/1; financial award applicants required to submit FAFSA. *Application contact:* Timothy J. Panfil, Director of Enrollment Management, School for Professional Studies, 630-617-3300 Ext. 3256, Fax: 630-617-6471, E-mail: panfilt@elmhurst.edu.

Emmanuel College, Graduate Studies, Graduate Programs in Education, Boston, MA 02115. Offers educational leadership (CAGS); elementary education (MAT); school administration (M Ed); secondary education (MAT). Part-time and evening/weekend programs available. *Faculty:* 3 full-time (all women), 10 part-time/adjunct (7 women). *Students:* 11 full-time (7 women), 22 part-time (13 women); includes 4 minority (3 Black or African American, non-Hispanic/Latino; 1 Native Hawaiian or other Pacific Islander, non-Hispanic/Latino). Average age 30. In 2013, 15 master's, 1 other advanced degree awarded. *Degree requirements:* For master's, 36 credits, including 6-credit practicum. *Entrance requirements:* For master's and CAGS, transcripts from all regionally-accredited institutions attended (showing proof of bachelor's degree completion), 2 letters of recommendation, essay, resume, interview. Additional exam requirements/recommendations for international students: Required—TOEFL (minimum score 600 paper-based; 106 iBT) or IELTS (minimum score 6.5). *Application deadline:* For fall admission, 7/31 priority date for domestic students; for spring admission, 11/30 priority date for domestic students. Applications are processed on a rolling basis. Application fee: $0. Electronic applications accepted. *Financial support:* Applicants required to submit FAFSA. *Unit head:* Sandy Robbins, Dean of Enrollment, 617-735-9700, Fax: 617-507-0434, E-mail: graduatestudies@emmanuel.edu. *Application contact:* Enrollment Counselor, 617-735-9700, Fax: 617-507-0434, E-mail: graduatestudies@emmanuel.edu.
Website: http://www.emmanuel.edu/graduate-studies-nursing/academics/education.html.

Emporia State University, Program in Curriculum and Instruction, Emporia, KS 66801-5415. Offers curriculum leadership (MS); effective practitioner (MS); national board certification (MS). *Accreditation:* NCATE. Part-time programs available. *Faculty:* 7 full-time (1 woman), 2 part-time/adjunct (0 women). *Students:* 12 full-time (11 women), 99 part-time (80 women); includes 9 minority (4 Black or African American, non-Hispanic/Latino; 4 Hispanic/Latino; 1 Two or more races, non-Hispanic/Latino). 43 applicants,

86% accepted, 27 enrolled. In 2013, 42 master's awarded. *Degree requirements:* For master's, comprehensive exam or thesis, practicum. *Entrance requirements:* For master's, GRE or MAT, appropriate bachelor's degree, teacher certification, 1 year of teaching experience, letters of recommendation. *Application deadline:* For fall admission, 8/15 priority date for domestic students. Applications are processed on a rolling basis. Application fee: $30 ($75 for international students). Electronic applications accepted. *Expenses: Tuition, area resident:* Part-time $220 per credit hour. Tuition, state resident: part-time $220 per credit hour. Tuition, nonresident: part-time $685 per credit hour. *Required fees:* $73 per credit hour. *Financial support:* In 2013–14, 1 research assistantship with full tuition reimbursement (averaging $7,200 per year) was awarded; career-related internships or fieldwork, Federal Work-Study, institutionally sponsored loans, health care benefits, and unspecified assistantships also available. Financial award application deadline: 3/15; financial award applicants required to submit FAFSA. *Unit head:* Dr. Paul Bland, Chair, 620-341-5777, E-mail: pbland@emporia.edu. *Application contact:* Mary Sewell, Admissions Coordinator, 800-950-GRAD, Fax: 620-341-5909, E-mail: msewell@emporia.edu.
Website: http://www.emporia.edu/sleme/graduate-programs/ci.html.

Emporia State University, Program in Educational Administration, Emporia, KS 66801-5415. Offers elementary administration (MS); elementary/secondary administration (MS); secondary administration (MS). *Accreditation:* NCATE. Part-time programs available. *Faculty:* 7 full-time (1 woman), 2 part-time/adjunct (0 women). *Students:* 24 full-time (11 women), 98 part-time (35 women); includes 16 minority (2 Black or African American, non-Hispanic/Latino; 1 American Indian or Alaska Native, non-Hispanic/Latino; 1 Asian, non-Hispanic/Latino; 11 Hispanic/Latino; 1 Two or more races, non-Hispanic/Latino). 27 applicants, 78% accepted, 15 enrolled. In 2013, 57 master's awarded. *Degree requirements:* For master's, comprehensive exam or thesis, practicum. *Entrance requirements:* For master's, GRE or MAT, appropriate bachelor's degree, letters of recommendation, teacher certification, 1 year of teaching experience. *Application deadline:* For fall admission, 8/15 priority date for domestic students. Applications are processed on a rolling basis. Application fee: $30 ($75 for international students). Electronic applications accepted. *Expenses: Tuition, area resident:* Part-time $220 per credit hour. Tuition, state resident: part-time $220 per credit hour. Tuition, nonresident: part-time $685 per credit hour. *Required fees:* $73 per credit hour. *Financial support:* Career-related internships or fieldwork, Federal Work-Study, institutionally sponsored loans, health care benefits, and unspecified assistantships available. Financial award application deadline: 3/15; financial award applicants required to submit FAFSA. *Unit head:* Dr. Paul Bland, Chair, 620-341-5777, E-mail: pbland@emporia.edu. *Application contact:* Mary Sewell, Admissions Coordinator, 800-950-GRAD, Fax: 620-341-5909, E-mail: msewell@emporia.edu.

Emporia State University, Program in Instructional Leadership, Emporia, KS 66801-5415. Offers MS. Part-time and evening/weekend programs available. *Students:* 9 part-time (7 women). In 2013, 2 master's awarded. *Degree requirements:* For master's, comprehensive exam. *Entrance requirements:* For master's, GRE or MAT, minimum GPA of 2.5 on last 60 undergraduate hours; official transcripts; essay; two personal references; copy of teaching certificate. *Expenses: Tuition, area resident:* Part-time $220 per credit hour. Tuition, state resident: part-time $220 per credit hour. Tuition, nonresident: part-time $685 per credit hour. *Required fees:* $73 per credit hour. *Unit head:* Dr. Paul Bland, Chair, 620-341-5777, E-mail: pbland@emporia.edu. *Application contact:* Mary Sewell, Admissions Coordinator, 800-950-GRAD, Fax: 620-341-5909, E-mail: msewell@emporia.edu.

Endicott College, Van Loan School of Graduate and Professional Studies, Program in Educational Leadership, Beverly, MA 01915-2096. Offers Ed D. *Faculty:* 3 full-time (1 woman), 6 part-time/adjunct (3 women). *Students:* 10 part-time (5 women). Average age 44. 6 applicants, 83% accepted, 4 enrolled. *Degree requirements:* For doctorate, comprehensive exam, thesis/dissertation, apprenticeship. *Entrance requirements:* For doctorate, GRE or MAT, official transcripts, three letters of recommendation, personal statement, resume or curriculum vitae, writing sample, interview. Additional exam requirements/recommendations for international students: Required—TOEFL. *Application deadline:* For fall admission, 6/1 for domestic students. *Unit head:* Dr. Jo Ann Gammel, Associate Professor/Director, 978-998-7753, Fax: 978-232-3000, E-mail: jgammel@endicott.edu. *Application contact:* Dr. Mary Huegel, Vice President and Dean of the School of Graduate and Professional Studies, 978-232-2084, Fax: 978-232-3000, E-mail: mhuegel@endicott.edu.
Website: http://www.endicott.edu/GradProf/GPSGrad/GPSGradEdD.aspx.

Evangel University, Department of Education, Springfield, MO 65802. Offers educational leadership (M Ed); reading education (M Ed); secondary teaching (M Ed); teaching (MA). *Accreditation:* NCATE. Part-time and evening/weekend programs available. *Faculty:* 7 full-time (4 women), 5 part-time/adjunct (4 women). *Students:* 5 full-time (3 women), 37 part-time (28 women); includes 4 minority (3 Hispanic/Latino; 1 Two or more races, non-Hispanic/Latino). Average age 32. 17 applicants, 65% accepted, 11 enrolled. In 2013, 22 master's awarded. *Degree requirements:* For master's, comprehensive exam, thesis optional. *Entrance requirements:* For master's, PRAXIS II (preferred) or GRE. Additional exam requirements/recommendations for international students: Required—TOEFL (minimum score 550 paper-based). *Application deadline:* For fall admission, 7/15 priority date for domestic students, 8/1 for international students; for spring admission, 11/15 priority date for domestic students, 12/1 for international students. Applications are processed on a rolling basis. Application fee: $25. Electronic applications accepted. *Financial support:* In 2013–14, 13 students received support. Career-related internships or fieldwork and scholarships/grants available. Support available to part-time students. Financial award application deadline: 3/1; financial award applicants required to submit FAFSA. *Unit head:* Dr. Matt Stringer, Program Coordinator, 417-865-2815 Ext. 8563, E-mail: stringerm@evangel.edu. *Application contact:* Karen Benitez, Admissions Representative, Graduate Studies, 417-865-2811 Ext. 7227, Fax: 417-865-9599, E-mail: benitezk@evangel.edu.
Website: http://www.evangel.edu/academics/graduate-studies/graduate-programs.

Fairleigh Dickinson University, College at Florham, University College: Arts, Sciences, and Professional Studies, Peter Sammartino School of Education, Program in Educational Leadership, Madison, NJ 07940-1099. Offers MA.

Fairleigh Dickinson University, Metropolitan Campus, University College: Arts, Sciences, and Professional Studies, Peter Sammartino School of Education, Program in Educational Leadership, Teaneck, NJ 07666-1914. Offers MA.

Fayetteville State University, Graduate School, Programs in Educational Leadership and School Administration, Fayetteville, NC 28301-4298. Offers educational leadership (Ed D); school administration (MSA). *Accreditation:* NCATE (one or more programs are accredited). Part-time and evening/weekend programs available. *Faculty:* 7 full-time (4 women), 2 part-time/adjunct (1 woman). *Students:* 48 full-time (32 women), 43 part-time (29 women); includes 68 minority (58 Black or African American, non-Hispanic/Latino; 2 American Indian or Alaska Native, non-Hispanic/Latino; 1 Asian, non-Hispanic/Latino; 5 Hispanic/Latino; 2 Two or more races, non-Hispanic/Latino). Average age 42. 39 applicants, 100% accepted, 39 enrolled. In 2013, 14 master's, 7 doctorates awarded. *Degree requirements:* For master's, internship, written and oral exams. *Entrance requirements:* For master's, GRE or MAT, minimum GPA of 2.5. *Application deadline:* For fall admission, 4/1 for domestic students. Applications are processed on a rolling basis. Application fee: $40. Electronic applications accepted. *Faculty research:* First-generation college students and academic successes, educational law and higher education, educational policy and K-12/higher education. *Total annual research expenditures:* $20,000. *Unit head:* Dr. Miriam Chitiga, Interim Chairperson, 910-672-1731, E-mail: mchitiga@uncfsu.edu. *Application contact:* Katrina Hoffman, Graduate Admission Officer, 910-672-1374, Fax: 910-672-1470, E-mail: khoffma1@uncfsu.edu.

Felician College, Program in Education, Lodi, NJ 07644-2117. Offers education (MA); educational leadership (principal/supervision) (MA); educational supervision (PMC); principal (PMC); school nursing and health education (MA, Certificate). *Accreditation:* Teacher Education Accreditation Council. Part-time and evening/weekend programs available. *Students:* 10 full-time (8 women), 58 part-time (52 women); includes 23 minority (7 Black or African American, non-Hispanic/Latino; 7 Asian, non-Hispanic/Latino; 6 Hispanic/Latino; 3 Two or more races, non-Hispanic/Latino), 3 international. Average age 37. *Degree requirements:* For master's, project. *Entrance requirements:* For master's, MAT, minimum GPA of 3.0, 3 letters of recommendation. Additional exam requirements/recommendations for international students: Recommended—TOEFL (minimum score 550 paper-based). *Application deadline:* Applications are processed on a rolling basis. Application fee: $40. *Expenses: Tuition:* Part-time $945 per credit. *Required fees:* $317.50 per semester. *Financial support:* Federal Work-Study available. *Unit head:* Dr. Rosemarie Liebmann, Associate Dean, 201-559-3537, E-mail: liebmannr@felician.edu. *Application contact:* Dr. Margaret Smolin, Associate Director, Graduate Admissions, 201-559-6077, Fax: 201-559-6138, E-mail: graduate@felician.edu.

Ferris State University, College of Education and Human Services, School of Education, Big Rapids, MI 49307. Offers curriculum and instruction (M Ed), including reading, special education, subject area; educational leadership (MS); instructor (MSCTE); post-secondary administration (MSCTE); training and development (MSCTE). Part-time and evening/weekend programs available. Postbaccalaureate distance learning degree programs offered (minimal on-campus study). *Faculty:* 7 full-time (5 women), 9 part-time/adjunct (6 women). *Students:* 17 full-time (14 women), 88 part-time (53 women); includes 8 minority (3 Black or African American, non-Hispanic/Latino; 1 American Indian or Alaska Native, non-Hispanic/Latino; 1 Asian, non-Hispanic/Latino; 3 Two or more races, non-Hispanic/Latino), 12 international. Average age 35. 16 applicants, 63% accepted, 6 enrolled. In 2013, 31 master's awarded. *Degree requirements:* For master's, thesis, research paper or project. *Entrance requirements:* For master's, minimum undergraduate degree GPA of 3.0. Additional exam requirements/recommendations for international students: Required—TOEFL (minimum score 500 paper-based; 61 iBT), IELTS. *Application deadline:* For fall admission, 7/1 priority date for domestic and international students; for spring admission, 11/1 priority date for domestic and international students; for summer admission, 3/1 priority date for domestic and international students. Applications are processed on a rolling basis. Application fee: $30. Electronic applications accepted. Application fee is waived when completed online. *Financial support:* Career-related internships or fieldwork and scholarships/grants available. Support available to part-time students. Financial award applicants required to submit FAFSA. *Faculty research:* Suicide prevention, reading, women in education, special needs, administration. *Unit head:* Dr. James Powell, Director, 231-591-3512, Fax: 231-591-2043, E-mail: powelj20@ferris.edu. *Application contact:* Kimisue Worrall, Secretary, 231-591-5361, Fax: 231-591-2043.
Website: http://www.ferris.edu/education/education/.

Ferris State University, Extended and International Operations, Big Rapids, MI 49307. Offers community college leadership (Ed D). Evening/weekend programs available. Postbaccalaureate distance learning degree programs offered (minimal on-campus study). *Faculty:* 26 part-time/adjunct (16 women). *Students:* 59 full-time (31 women); includes 14 minority (10 Black or African American, non-Hispanic/Latino; 2 Asian, non-Hispanic/Latino; 1 Hispanic/Latino; 1 Two or more races, non-Hispanic/Latino). Average age 44. 40 applicants, 85% accepted, 29 enrolled. In 2013, 5 doctorates awarded. *Degree requirements:* For doctorate, thesis/dissertation, e-portfolio demonstrating completion of program outcomes. *Entrance requirements:* For doctorate, master's degree with minimum GPA of 3.25, fierce commitment to the mission of community colleges, essay, writing samples. *Application deadline:* For fall admission, 12/15 for domestic and international students; for winter admission, 1/27 for domestic and international students; for spring admission, 4/18 for domestic and international students. Applications are processed on a rolling basis. Application fee: $30. Electronic applications accepted. Application fee is waived when completed online. *Expenses:* Contact institution. *Financial support:* In 2013–14, 10 students received support. Applicants required to submit FAFSA. *Unit head:* Dr. Roberta Teahen, Director, 231-591-3805, E-mail: robertateahen@ferris.edu. *Application contact:* Andrea Wirgau, Assistant Director, 231-591-2710, Fax: 231-591-3539, E-mail: andreawirgau@ferris.edu.

Fielding Graduate University, Graduate Programs, School of Educational Leadership for Change, Santa Barbara, CA 93105-3814. Offers collaborative educational leadership (MA), including charter school leadership, dual language; educational administration (Graduate Certificate); educational leadership and change (Ed D), including community college leadership and change. Postbaccalaureate distance learning degree programs offered (minimal on-campus study). *Faculty:* 9 full-time (6 women), 10 part-time/adjunct (6 women). *Students:* 172 full-time (121 women), 8 part-time (5 women); includes 109 minority (39 Black or African American, non-Hispanic/Latino; 19 American Indian or Alaska Native, non-Hispanic/Latino; 8 Asian, non-Hispanic/Latino; 34 Hispanic/Latino; 2 Native Hawaiian or other Pacific Islander, non-Hispanic/Latino; 7 Two or more races, non-Hispanic/Latino). Average age 48. 40 applicants, 98% accepted, 28 enrolled. In 2013, 45 doctorates awarded. *Degree requirements:* For master's, capstone research project; for doctorate, comprehensive exam, thesis/dissertation. *Entrance requirements:* For master's, BA from regionally accredited institution or equivalent with minimum GPA of 2.5; for doctorate, BA or MA from regionally accredited institution or equivalent, resume, 2 letters of recommendation, statement of purpose, reflective essay; for Graduate Certificate, BA from regionally-accredited institution or equivalent. *Application deadline:* For fall admission, 6/10 for domestic and international students; for spring admission, 11/19 for domestic and international students. Application fee: $75. Electronic applications accepted. *Expenses:* Contact institution. *Financial support:* In 2013–14, 90 students received support. Scholarships/grants, health care benefits, and tuition waivers (partial) available. Support available to part-time students. Financial award applicants required to submit FAFSA. *Unit head:* Dr. Mario R. Borunda, Dean, 805-898-2940, E-mail: mborunda@fielding.edu. *Application contact:* Admission Counselor, 800-340-1099 Ext. 4098, Fax: 805-687-9793, E-mail: elcadmissions@fielding.edu.
Website: http://www.fielding.edu/programs/elc/default.aspx.

Fitchburg State University, Division of Graduate and Continuing Education, Program in Educational Leadership and Management, Fitchburg, MA 01420-2697. Offers educational leadership and management (M Ed, CAGS); educational technology (Certificate); school principal (M Ed, CAGS); supervisor/director (M Ed, CAGS); technology leader (M Ed, CAGS). *Accreditation:* NCATE. Part-time and evening/weekend programs available. *Entrance requirements:* Additional exam requirements/

recommendations for international students: Required—TOEFL (minimum score 550 paper-based; 79 iBT). Electronic applications accepted.

Florida Agricultural and Mechanical University, Division of Graduate Studies, Research, and Continuing Education, College of Education, Department of Educational Leadership and Human Services, Tallahassee, FL 32307-3200. Offers administration and supervision (M Ed, MS Ed, PhD); adult education (M Ed, MS Ed); educational leadership (PhD); guidance and counseling (M Ed, MS Ed). *Accreditation:* NCATE. *Degree requirements:* For master's, thesis (for some programs); for doctorate, thesis/dissertation. *Entrance requirements:* For master's, GRE General Test, minimum GPA of 3.0. Additional exam requirements/recommendations for international students: Required—TOEFL.

Florida Atlantic University, College of Education, Department of Educational Leadership and Research Methodology, Boca Raton, FL 33431-0991. Offers adult and community education (M Ed, PhD, Ed S); educational leadership (M Ed, PhD, Ed S); higher education (M Ed, PhD); K-12 school leadership (M Ed, PhD, Ed S). *Accreditation:* NCATE. Part-time and evening/weekend programs available. Postbaccalaureate distance learning degree programs offered (minimal on-campus study). *Faculty:* 19 full-time (9 women), 16 part-time/adjunct (7 women). *Students:* 97 full-time (72 women), 227 part-time (150 women); includes 140 minority (83 Black or African American, non-Hispanic/Latino; 8 Asian, non-Hispanic/Latino; 41 Hispanic/Latino; 8 Two or more races, non-Hispanic/Latino), 2 international. Average age 37. 180 applicants, 50% accepted, 74 enrolled. In 2013, 80 master's, 11 doctorates, 19 other advanced degrees awarded. *Degree requirements:* For doctorate, comprehensive exam, thesis/dissertation, departmental qualifying exam; for Ed S, departmental qualifying exam. *Entrance requirements:* For master's, GRE General Test, minimum GPA of 3.0 during previous 2 years; for doctorate, GRE General Test, minimum GPA of 3.5; for Ed S, GRE General Test. Additional exam requirements/recommendations for international students: Required—TOEFL (minimum score 500 paper-based; 61 iBT), IELTS (minimum score 6). *Application deadline:* For fall admission, 7/1 for domestic students, 2/15 for international students; for spring admission, 9/15 for domestic students, 7/15 for international students. Applications are processed on a rolling basis. Application fee: $30. Electronic applications accepted. *Expenses:* Tuition, state resident: full-time $6660; part-time $370 per credit hour. Tuition, nonresident: full-time $18,450; part-time $1025 per credit hour. Tuition and fees vary according to course load. *Financial support:* Fellowships, research assistantships, teaching assistantships, career-related internships or fieldwork, and tuition waivers (partial) available. *Faculty research:* Self-directed learning, school reform issues, legal issues, mentoring, school leadership. *Unit head:* Dr. Robert E. Shockley, Chair, 561-297-3550, Fax: 561-297-3618, E-mail: shockley@fau.edu. *Application contact:* Kathy DuBois, Senior Secretary, 561-297-3550, Fax: 561-297-3618, E-mail: edleadership@fau.edu.
Website: http://www.coe.fau.edu/academicdepartments/el/.

Florida Gulf Coast University, College of Education, Program in Educational Leadership, Fort Myers, FL 33965-6565. Offers M Ed, MA, Ed D, Ed S. Part-time and evening/weekend programs available. *Degree requirements:* For master's, thesis or alternative, learning and professional portfolios. *Entrance requirements:* For master's, GRE General Test, MAT, minimum GPA of 3.0. Additional exam requirements/recommendations for international students: Required—TOEFL (minimum score 550 paper-based). Electronic applications accepted. *Faculty research:* Inclusion, technology in teaching, curriculum development in educational leadership, education policy and law.

Florida International University, College of Education, Department of Leadership and Professional Studies, Miami, FL 33199. Offers adult education and human resource development (MS, Ed D); counseling (MS), including rehabilitation counseling, school counseling; counselor education (MS), including clinical mental health counseling; educational administration and supervision (Ed D); educational leadership (MS, Certificate, Ed S); higher education (Ed D); higher education administration (MS); recreation and sport management (MS), including recreation and sport management, recreational therapy; school psychology (Ed S); urban education (MS), including instruction in urban settings, learning technologies, multicultural/bilingual, multicultural/TESOL, urban education. Part-time and evening/weekend programs available. *Degree requirements:* For doctorate, thesis/dissertation. *Entrance requirements:* For master's, minimum GPA of 3.0; for doctorate and other advanced degree, GRE General Test. Additional exam requirements/recommendations for international students: Required—TOEFL (minimum score 550 paper-based; 80 iBT), IELTS (minimum score 6.3). Electronic applications accepted.

Florida State University, The Graduate School, College of Education, Department of Educational Leadership and Policy Studies, Program in Educational Leadership and Policy, Tallahassee, FL 32306. Offers education policy and evaluation (MS, PhD); educational leadership/administration (MS, PhD, Certificate, Ed S). Part-time and evening/weekend programs available. *Faculty:* 15 full-time (12 women). *Students:* 25 full-time (16 women), 97 part-time (63 women); includes 47 minority (23 Black or African American, non-Hispanic/Latino; 2 Asian, non-Hispanic/Latino; 21 Hispanic/Latino; 1 Two or more races, non-Hispanic/Latino), 6 international. Average age 36. 72 applicants, 56% accepted, 25 enrolled. In 2013, 24 master's, 4 doctorates, 16 other advanced degrees awarded. Terminal master's awarded for partial completion of doctoral program. *Degree requirements:* For master's and other advanced degree, comprehensive exam, thesis optional; for doctorate, comprehensive exam, thesis/dissertation. *Entrance requirements:* For master's, GRE General Test, minimum GPA of 3.0; for doctorate and other advanced degree, GRE General Test, minimum graduate GPA of 3.0. Additional exam requirements/recommendations for international students: Required—TOEFL (minimum score 550 paper-based; 80 iBT). *Application deadline:* For fall admission, 7/1 for domestic and international students; for winter admission, 11/1 for domestic and international students; for spring admission, 3/1 for domestic and international students. Application fee: $30. Electronic applications accepted. *Expenses:* Tuition, state resident: part-time $403.51 per credit hour. Tuition, nonresident: part-time $1004.85 per credit hour. *Required fees:* $75.81 per credit hour. One-time fee: $20 part-time. Tuition and fees vary according to course load, campus/location and student level. *Financial support:* Fellowships with full and partial tuition reimbursements, research assistantships with full and partial tuition reimbursements, teaching assistantships with full and partial tuition reimbursements, career-related internships or fieldwork, scholarships/grants, health care benefits, and unspecified assistantships available. Financial award application deadline: 1/15; financial award applicants required to submit FAFSA. *Faculty research:* Issues in higher education law; diversity, equity, and social justice; educational issues in Western and non-Western countries. *Unit head:* Dr. Stacey Rutledge, Program Coordinator, 850-644-8163, Fax: 850-644-1258, E-mail: sarutledge@fsu.edu. *Application contact:* Linda J. Lyons, Academic Support Assistant, 850-644-7077, Fax: 850-644-1258, E-mail: ljlyons@fsu.edu.
Website: http://www.coe.fsu.edu/Current-Students/Departments/Educational-Leadership-and-Policy-Studies-ELPS/Current-Students/Degree-Programs.

Fordham University, Graduate School of Education, Division of Educational Leadership, Administration and Policy, New York, NY 10023. Offers administration and supervision (MSE, Adv C); administration and supervision for church leaders (PhD); educational administration and supervision (Ed D, PhD); human resource program administration (MS). *Accreditation:* NCATE. *Degree requirements:* For doctorate, thesis/dissertation. *Entrance requirements:* For doctorate, MAT, GRE General Test.

Fort Hays State University, Graduate School, College of Education and Technology, Department of Educational Administration and Counseling, Program in Educational Administration, Hays, KS 67601-4099. Offers MS, Ed S. *Accreditation:* NCATE. *Degree requirements:* For master's and Ed S, comprehensive exam, thesis or alternative. *Entrance requirements:* For master's, GRE General Test or MAT. Additional exam requirements/recommendations for international students: Required—TOEFL (minimum score 550 paper-based). Electronic applications accepted. *Faculty research:* Guide to negotiations, nutrition program for disadvantaged, accountability, student insurance practices, student liability.

Fort Lewis College, Program in Teacher Leadership, Durango, CO 81301-3999. Offers MA, Certificate. *Degree requirements:* For master's, culminating research project. *Entrance requirements:* For master's and Certificate, baccalaureate degree from regionally-accredited college or university; minimum cumulative undergraduate and graduate GPA of 3.0; one year of full-time teaching experience in P-12 schools.

Framingham State University, Continuing Education, Program in Educational Leadership, Framingham, MA 01701-9101. Offers MA. Part-time and evening/weekend programs available. *Entrance requirements:* For master's, MAT.

Franciscan University of Steubenville, Graduate Programs, Department of Education, Steubenville, OH 43952-1763. Offers administration (MS Ed); teaching (MS Ed). Part-time and evening/weekend programs available. *Degree requirements:* For master's, project. *Entrance requirements:* For master's, minimum undergraduate GPA of 2.5 or written exam. *Expenses:* Contact institution.

Freed-Hardeman University, Program in Education, Henderson, TN 38340-2399. Offers curriculum and instruction (M Ed); school counseling (M Ed), including administration and supervision, special education; school leadership (Ed S). *Accreditation:* NCATE. Part-time and evening/weekend programs available. *Degree requirements:* For master's, comprehensive exam, thesis optional; for Ed S, thesis. *Entrance requirements:* For master's, GRE General Test or NTE; for Ed S, 3 years of teaching experience. Additional exam requirements/recommendations for international students: Required—TOEFL (minimum score 500 paper-based).

Fresno Pacific University, Graduate Programs, School of Education, Division of Administration, Fresno, CA 93702-4709. Offers MA. Part-time and evening/weekend programs available. *Faculty:* 1 full-time. *Students:* 2 full-time (both women), 20 part-time (13 women); includes 12 minority (2 Black or African American, non-Hispanic/Latino; 1 American Indian or Alaska Native, non-Hispanic/Latino; 9 Hispanic/Latino). Average age 40. In 2013, 16 master's awarded. *Degree requirements:* For master's, thesis or alternative, 4 practica. *Entrance requirements:* Additional exam requirements/recommendations for international students: Required—TOEFL (minimum score 550 paper-based). *Application deadline:* For fall admission, 7/15 for domestic and international students; for spring admission, 11/15 for domestic students, 1/15 for international students. Applications are processed on a rolling basis. Application fee: $90. Electronic applications accepted. *Expenses: Tuition:* Full-time $8910; part-time $495 per unit. *Required fees:* $270. Tuition and fees vary according to course load and program. *Financial support:* Career-related internships or fieldwork, scholarships/grants, and tuition waivers (full and partial) available. Support available to part-time students. Financial award applicants required to submit FAFSA. *Unit head:* Brendta Friesen, Program Director, 559-453-2203, Fax: 559-453-2001, E-mail: brendta.friesen@fresno.edu. *Application contact:* Amanda Krum-Strovall, Director of Graduate Admissions, 559-453-2016, E-mail: amanda.krum-stovall@fresno.edu.
Website: http://grad.fresno.edu/programs/master-arts-degree-education-administrative-services-emphasis.

Frostburg State University, Graduate School, College of Education, Department of Educational Professions, Program in Educational Administration and Supervision, Frostburg, MD 21532-1099. Offers elementary (M Ed); secondary (M Ed). Part-time and evening/weekend programs available. *Degree requirements:* For master's, thesis or alternative. *Entrance requirements:* For master's, teaching certificate. Additional exam requirements/recommendations for international students: Required—TOEFL. Electronic applications accepted. *Expenses: Tuition, area resident:* Part-time $340 per credit hour. Tuition, state resident: part-time $340 per credit hour. Tuition, nonresident: part-time $437 per credit hour. *Faculty research:* Practicum experience in schools.

Furman University, Graduate Division, Department of Education, Greenville, SC 29613. Offers curriculum and instruction (MA); early childhood education (MA); educational leadership (Ed S); English as a second language (MA); literacy (MA); school leadership (MA); special education (MA). *Accreditation:* NCATE. Part-time programs available. Postbaccalaureate distance learning degree programs offered (minimal on-campus study). *Degree requirements:* For master's, comprehensive exam (for some programs), thesis or alternative. *Entrance requirements:* For master's, PRAXIS II. *Faculty research:* Literacy, pedagogy and practice, social justice, advanced leadership, achievement in high poverty schools.

Gannon University, School of Graduate Studies, College of Humanities, Education, and Social Sciences, School of Education, Program in Principal Certification, Erie, PA 16541-0001. Offers Certificate. Part-time and evening/weekend programs available. *Students:* 19 part-time (13 women); includes 1 minority (Black or African American, non-Hispanic/Latino). Average age 36. 28 applicants, 96% accepted, 21 enrolled. In 2013, 28 Certificates awarded. *Degree requirements:* For Certificate, internship, portfolio. *Entrance requirements:* For degree, master's degree, minimum GPA of 3.0, educational certification, 2 years of teaching experience. Additional exam requirements/recommendations for international students: Required—TOEFL (minimum score 79 iBT). *Application deadline:* Applications are processed on a rolling basis. Application fee: $25. Electronic applications accepted. *Expenses:* Contact institution. *Financial support:* Scholarships/grants available. Financial award application deadline: 7/1; financial award applicants required to submit FAFSA. *Unit head:* Dr. Kathleen Kingston, Director, 814-871-5626, E-mail: kingston002@gannon.edu. *Application contact:* Kara Morgan, Director of Graduate Admissions, 814-871-5831, Fax: 814-871-5827, E-mail: graduate@gannon.edu.

Gannon University, School of Graduate Studies, College of Humanities, Education, and Social Sciences, School of Education, Program in Superintendent Letter of Eligibility Certification, Erie, PA 16541-0001. Offers Certificate. Part-time and evening/weekend programs available. *Students:* 1 (woman) part-time. Average age 45. 4 applicants, 75% accepted. In 2013, 13 Certificates awarded. *Degree requirements:* For Certificate, thesis or alternative, superintendent internship, portfolio. *Entrance requirements:* For degree, master's degree; minimum GPA of 3.0; 6 years of educational experience, 3 under administrative or supervisory certificate; letters of recommendation. Additional exam requirements/recommendations for international students: Required—TOEFL (minimum score 79 iBT). *Application deadline:* Applications are processed on a rolling basis. Application fee: $25. Electronic applications accepted. *Expenses:* Contact institution. *Financial support:* Scholarships/grants available. Financial award application deadline: 7/1; financial award applicants required to submit FAFSA. *Unit head:* Dr. Kathleen Kingston, Director, 814-871-5626, E-mail: kingston002@gannon.edu. *Application*

contact: Kara Morgan, Director of Graduate Admission, 814-871-5831, Fax: 814-871-5827, E-mail: graduate@gannon.edu.

Gannon University, School of Graduate Studies, College of Humanities, Education, and Social Sciences, School of Humanities, Program in Organizational Learning and Leadership, Erie, PA 16541-0001. Offers PhD. Part-time and evening/weekend programs available. *Students:* 5 full-time (2 women), 56 part-time (39 women); includes 2 minority (both Black or African American, non-Hispanic/Latino). Average age 42. 16 applicants, 81% accepted, 9 enrolled. In 2013, 6 doctorates awarded. *Degree requirements:* For doctorate, thesis/dissertation. *Entrance requirements:* For doctorate, GRE, minimum graduate GPA of 3.5, 2 years of post-baccalaureate work experience, letters of recommendation, statement of purpose. Additional exam requirements/recommendations for international students: Required—TOEFL (minimum score 79 iBT). *Application deadline:* For spring admission, 2/1 for domestic students. Applications are processed on a rolling basis. Application fee: $50. Electronic applications accepted. *Expenses: Tuition:* Full-time $15,930; part-time $885 per credit. *Required fees:* $430; $18 per credit. Tuition and fees vary according to course load, degree level and program. *Financial support:* Scholarships/grants and unspecified assistantships available. Financial award applicants required to submit FAFSA. *Unit head:* Dr. Gail Latta, Director, 814-871-5792, E-mail: latta001@gannon.edu. *Application contact:* Kara Morgan, Director of Graduate Admissions, 814-871-5831, Fax: 814-871-5827, E-mail: graduate@gannon.edu.

Gardner-Webb University, Graduate School, School of Education, Program in Educational Leadership, Boiling Springs, NC 28017. Offers Ed D. *Students:* 1 (woman) full-time, 113 part-time (69 women); includes 35 minority (32 Black or African American, non-Hispanic/Latino; 1 American Indian or Alaska Native, non-Hispanic/Latino; 2 Asian, non-Hispanic/Latino). Average age 39. 113 applicants, 24% accepted, 27 enrolled. In 2013, 7 doctorates awarded. *Expenses: Tuition:* Full-time $7200; part-time $400 per credit hour. Tuition and fees vary according to course load and program. *Unit head:* Dr. Alan D. Eury, Chair, 704-406-4402, Fax: 704-406-3921, E-mail: dsimmons@gardner-webb.edu. *Application contact:* Office of Graduate Admissions, 877-498-4723, Fax: 704-406-3895, E-mail: gradinfo@gardner-webb.edu.

Gardner-Webb University, Graduate School, School of Education, Program in Executive Leadership Studies, Boiling Springs, NC 28017. Offers MA. *Students:* 295 full-time (201 women), 209 part-time (137 women); includes 166 minority (156 Black or African American, non-Hispanic/Latino; 1 American Indian or Alaska Native, non-Hispanic/Latino; 3 Asian, non-Hispanic/Latino; 6 Hispanic/Latino). Average age 35. 279 applicants, 72% accepted, 166 enrolled. *Expenses: Tuition:* Full-time $7200; part-time $400 per credit hour. Tuition and fees vary according to course load and program. *Unit head:* Dr. Alan D. Eury, Dean, 704-406-4402, Fax: 704-406-3921, E-mail: dsimmons@gardner-webb.edu. *Application contact:* Office of Graduate Admissions, 877-498-4723, Fax: 704-406-3895, E-mail: gradinfo@gardner-webb.edu.

Gardner-Webb University, Graduate School, School of Education, Program in School Administration, Boiling Springs, NC 28017. Offers MA. *Accreditation:* NCATE. Part-time and evening/weekend programs available. *Students:* 2 full-time (both women), 135 part-time (103 women); includes 68 minority (65 Black or African American, non-Hispanic/Latino; 1 American Indian or Alaska Native, non-Hispanic/Latino; 2 Hispanic/Latino). Average age 39. 120 applicants, 73% accepted, 68 enrolled. In 2013, 80 master's awarded. *Degree requirements:* For master's, comprehensive exam. *Entrance requirements:* For master's, GRE General Test or NTE, PRAXIS, minimum GPA of 2.5. *Application deadline:* For fall admission, 8/1 priority date for domestic students. Applications are processed on a rolling basis. Application fee: $40. Electronic applications accepted. *Expenses: Tuition:* Full-time $7200; part-time $400 per credit hour. Tuition and fees vary according to course load and program. *Financial support:* Unspecified assistantships available. *Unit head:* Dr. Alan D. Eury, Dean of the School of Education, 704-406-4402. *Application contact:* Office of Graduate Admissions, 877-498-4723, Fax: 704-406-3895, E-mail: gradinfo@gardner-webb.edu.

Geneva College, Master of Arts in Higher Education Program, Beaver Falls, PA 15010-3599. Offers campus ministry (MA); college teaching (MA); educational leadership (MA); student affairs administration (MA). Part-time and evening/weekend programs available. Postbaccalaureate distance learning degree programs offered (minimal on-campus study). *Faculty:* 4 full-time (0 women). *Students:* 29 full-time (19 women), 43 part-time (23 women); includes 4 minority (3 Black or African American, non-Hispanic/Latino; 1 Hispanic/Latino). Average age 26. 46 applicants, 100% accepted, 28 enrolled. In 2013, 23 master's awarded. *Degree requirements:* For master's, 36 hours (27 in core courses) including a capstone research project. *Entrance requirements:* For master's, minimum GPA of 3.0, writing sample, 3 letters of recommendation, essay on motivation for participation in the HED program. Additional exam requirements/recommendations for international students: Required—TOEFL. *Application deadline:* For fall admission, 9/1 priority date for domestic students; for winter admission, 1/2 priority date for domestic students; for spring admission, 3/11 priority date for domestic students. Applications are processed on a rolling basis. Electronic applications accepted. *Expenses:* Contact institution. *Financial support:* In 2013–14, 59 students received support. Unspecified assistantships available. Financial award application deadline: 8/1; financial award applicants required to submit FAFSA. *Faculty research:* Student development, learning theories, church-related higher education, assessment, organizational culture. *Unit head:* Dr. Keith Martel, Program Director, 724-847-6884, Fax: 724-847-6107, E-mail: hed@geneva.edu. *Application contact:* Jerryn S. Carson, Program Coordinator, 724-847-6510, Fax: 724-847-6696, E-mail: hed@geneva.edu.
Website: http://www.geneva.edu/page/higher_ed.

George Fox University, College of Education, Educational Foundations and Leadership Program, Newberg, OR 97132-2697. Offers continuing administrator license (Certificate); curriculum and instruction (M Ed); educational leadership (M Ed, Ed D); ESOL (Certificate); higher education (M Ed); initial administrator license (Certificate); instructional leadership (Ed S); library media (M Ed, Certificate); literacy (M Ed); reading (M Ed); secondary education (M Ed). *Accreditation:* NCATE. Part-time and evening/weekend programs available. Postbaccalaureate distance learning degree programs offered (minimal on-campus study). *Faculty:* 7 full-time (3 women), 5 part-time/adjunct (4 women). *Students:* 194 part-time (128 women); includes 15 minority (1 Black or African American, non-Hispanic/Latino; 1 American Indian or Alaska Native, non-Hispanic/Latino; 3 Asian, non-Hispanic/Latino; 6 Hispanic/Latino; 1 Native Hawaiian or other Pacific Islander, non-Hispanic/Latino; 3 Two or more races, non-Hispanic/Latino), 2 international. Average age 42. 46 applicants, 85% accepted, 39 enrolled. In 2013, 15 master's, 16 doctorates, 106 Certificates awarded. *Degree requirements:* For master's, thesis (for some programs); for doctorate, comprehensive exam, thesis/dissertation, project. *Entrance requirements:* For master's, minimum undergraduate GPA of 3.0 during previous 2 years of course work, resume, 3 professional recommendations on university forms, official transcripts; for doctorate, GRE, master's degree with minimum GPA of 3.25, 3 years of relevant professional experience, interview, personal essay, scholarly work, 3 professional recommendations on university forms along with 3 written letters of recommendation, official transcripts. Additional exam requirements/recommendations for international students: Required—TOEFL (minimum score 577 paper-based; 90 iBT). *Application deadline:* For fall admission, 7/15 for domestic and international students; for winter admission, 11/1 for domestic and international students; for spring admission, 4/1 for domestic and international students. Applications are processed on a rolling basis. Application fee: $40. Electronic applications accepted. *Expenses:* Contact institution. *Financial support:* Career-related internships or fieldwork available. Financial award applicants required to submit FAFSA. *Unit head:* Dr. Scot Headley, Professor/Chair, 503-554-2836, E-mail: sheadley@georgefox.edu. *Application contact:* Kipp Wilfong, Graduate Admissions Counselor, 800-631-0921, Fax: 503-554-3110, E-mail: kwilfong@georgefox.edu.
Website: http://www.georgefox.edu/education/index.html.

George Mason University, College of Education and Human Development, Program in Education Leadership, Fairfax, VA 22030. Offers M Ed. *Accreditation:* NCATE. *Faculty:* 8 full-time (4 women), 13 part-time/adjunct (5 women). *Students:* 2 full-time (1 woman), 265 part-time (204 women); includes 51 minority (17 Black or African American, non-Hispanic/Latino; 12 Asian, non-Hispanic/Latino; 17 Hispanic/Latino; 1 Native Hawaiian or other Pacific Islander, non-Hispanic/Latino; 4 Two or more races, non-Hispanic/Latino). Average age 37. 125 applicants, 79% accepted, 82 enrolled. In 2013, 124 master's awarded. *Entrance requirements:* For master's, bachelor's degree from regionally-accredited institution with minimum GPA of 3.0 overall or in last 60 credit hours; 2 official transcripts; expanded goals statement; 3 letters of recommendation; 3 years of documented teaching experience. Additional exam requirements/recommendations for international students: Required—TOEFL (minimum score 575 paper-based; 88 iBT), IELTS (minimum score 6.5), PTE. *Application deadline:* For fall admission, 4/1 priority date for domestic students; for spring admission, 11/1 for domestic students. Applications are processed on a rolling basis. Application fee: $65 ($80 for international students). Electronic applications accepted. *Expenses:* Tuition, state resident: full-time $9350; part-time $390 per credit. Tuition, nonresident: full-time $25,754; part-time $1073 per credit. *Required fees:* $2688; $112 per credit. *Financial support:* Career-related internships or fieldwork, Federal Work-Study, scholarships/grants, unspecified assistantships, and health care benefits (for full-time research or teaching assistantship recipients) available. Financial award application deadline: 3/1; financial award applicants required to submit FAFSA. *Faculty research:* Understanding of the complexities of change in schools, communities, and organizations; education law; foundations of education leadership, history and leadership. *Unit head:* Anne Marie Balzano, Academic Program Coordinator, 703-993-5699, Fax: 703-993-2013, E-mail: alohse@gmu.edu. *Application contact:* Farnoosh Shahrokhi, Outreach and Administrative Coordinator, 703-993-2009, Fax: 703-993-3643, E-mail: fshahrok@gmu.edu.
Website: http://gse.gmu.edu/programs/edleadership/.

George Mason University, College of Humanities and Social Sciences, Interdisciplinary Studies Program, Fairfax, VA 22030. Offers community college teaching (MAIS); computational social science (MAIS); energy and sustainability (MAIS); film and video studies (MAIS); folklore studies (MAIS); higher education administration (MAIS); neuroethics (MAIS); religion, culture and values (MAIS); social entrepreneurship (MAIS); war and military in society (MAIS); women and gender studies (MAIS). *Faculty:* 10 full-time (3 women), 7 part-time/adjunct (3 women). *Students:* 31 full-time (17 women), 79 part-time (50 women); includes 30 minority (17 Black or African American, non-Hispanic/Latino; 4 Asian, non-Hispanic/Latino; 6 Hispanic/Latino; 3 Two or more races, non-Hispanic/Latino), 3 international. Average age 33. 78 applicants, 59% accepted, 25 enrolled. In 2013, 32 master's awarded. *Degree requirements:* For master's, project or thesis. *Entrance requirements:* For master's, 3 letters of recommendation; writing sample; official transcript; resume. Additional exam requirements/recommendations for international students: Required—TOEFL (minimum score 570 paper-based; 88 iBT), IELTS (minimum score 6.5), PTE. *Application deadline:* For fall admission, 3/1 priority date for domestic students; for spring admission, 10/15 for domestic students. Application fee: $65 ($80 for international students). Electronic applications accepted. *Expenses:* Tuition, state resident: full-time $9350; part-time $390 per credit. Tuition, nonresident: full-time $25,754; part-time $1073 per credit. *Required fees:* $2688; $112 per credit. *Financial support:* In 2013–14, 8 students received support, including 3 research assistantships with full and partial tuition reimbursements available (averaging $10,238 per year), 5 teaching assistantships with full and partial tuition reimbursements available (averaging $7,655 per year); career-related internships or fieldwork, Federal Work-Study, scholarships/grants, unspecified assistantships, and health care benefits (for full-time research or teaching assistantship recipients) also available. Support available to part-time students. Financial award application deadline: 3/1; financial award applicants required to submit FAFSA. *Faculty research:* Combined English and folklore, religious and cultural studies (Christianity and Muslim society). *Unit head:* Jan Arminio, Interim Director, 703-993-2064, Fax: 703-993-2307, E-mail: jarminio@gmu.edu. *Application contact:* Becky Durham, Administrative Coordinator, 703-993-8762, Fax: 703-993-5585, E-mail: rdurham4@gmu.edu.
Website: http://mais.gmu.edu.

The George Washington University, Graduate School of Education and Human Development, Department of Educational Leadership, Program in Educational Administration and Policy Studies, Washington, DC 20052. Offers education policy (Ed D); educational administration (Ed D). Educational administration program offered at Newport News and Alexandria, VA. *Accreditation:* NCATE. *Students:* 6 full-time (4 women), 146 part-time (106 women); includes 48 minority (35 Black or African American, non-Hispanic/Latino; 7 Asian, non-Hispanic/Latino; 5 Hispanic/Latino; 1 Native Hawaiian or other Pacific Islander, non-Hispanic/Latino), 3 international. Average age 40. 31 applicants, 48% accepted, 4 enrolled. In 2013, 14 doctorates awarded. *Degree requirements:* For doctorate, comprehensive exam, thesis/dissertation. *Entrance requirements:* For doctorate, GRE General Test or MAT, interview, minimum GPA of 3.3. *Application deadline:* For fall admission, 1/15 priority date for domestic students; for spring admission, 10/1 for domestic students. Applications are processed on a rolling basis. Application fee: $75. *Financial support:* In 2013–14, 9 students received support. Fellowships, research assistantships, teaching assistantships, career-related internships or fieldwork, Federal Work-Study, and tuition waivers (partial) available. Financial award application deadline: 1/15; financial award applicants required to submit FAFSA. *Unit head:* Prof. Yas Nakib, Program Coordinator, 202-994-8816, E-mail: nakib@gwu.edu. *Application contact:* Sarah Lang, Director, Admissions and Marketing, 202-994-1447, Fax: 202-994-7207, E-mail: slang@gwu.edu.

The George Washington University, Graduate School of Education and Human Development, Department of Educational Leadership, Program in Educational Leadership and Administration, Washington, DC 20052. Offers MA Ed, Certificate, Ed S. Programs offered at Newport News and Alexandria, VA. *Accreditation:* NCATE. Evening/weekend programs available. *Students:* 13 full-time (11 women), 148 part-time (112 women); includes 58 minority (47 Black or African American, non-Hispanic/Latino; 1 American Indian or Alaska Native, non-Hispanic/Latino; 2 Asian, non-Hispanic/Latino; 5 Hispanic/Latino; 1 Native Hawaiian or other Pacific Islander, non-Hispanic/Latino; 2 Two or more races, non-Hispanic/Latino), 4 international. Average age 38. 151 applicants, 99% accepted, 113 enrolled. In 2013, 37 master's, 38 Certificates awarded. *Degree requirements:* For master's, comprehensive exam. *Entrance requirements:* For master's, GRE General Test or MAT, interview, minimum GPA of 2.75. *Application deadline:* For fall admission, 1/15 priority date for domestic students; for spring admission, 10/1 for domestic students. Applications are processed on a rolling basis. Application fee: $75. *Financial support:* Fellowships, teaching assistantships, career-

related internships or fieldwork, and Federal Work-Study available. Financial award application deadline: 1/15; financial award applicants required to submit FAFSA. *Faculty research:* Organizational learning. *Unit head:* Dr. Linda K. Lemasters, Director, 757-269-2218, E-mail: lindal@gwu.edu. *Application contact:* Sarah Lang, Director of Graduate Admissions, 202-994-1447, Fax: 202-994-7207, E-mail: slang@gwu.edu.

The George Washington University, Graduate School of Education and Human Development, Department of Educational Leadership, Program in Higher Education Administration, Washington, DC 20052. Offers MA Ed, Ed D, Ed S. *Accreditation:* NCATE. *Students:* 24 full-time (20 women), 91 part-time (61 women); includes 35 minority (19 Black or African American, non-Hispanic/Latino; 7 Asian, non-Hispanic/Latino; 8 Hispanic/Latino; 1 Two or more races, non-Hispanic/Latino), 1 international. Average age 33. 141 applicants, 71% accepted, 7 enrolled. In 2013, 29 master's, 14 doctorates, 1 other advanced degree awarded. *Degree requirements:* For master's and Ed S, comprehensive exam; for doctorate, comprehensive exam, thesis/dissertation. *Entrance requirements:* For master's, GRE General Test or MAT, minimum GPA of 2.75; for doctorate, GRE General Test or MAT, interview, minimum GPA of 3.3; for Ed S, GRE General Test or MAT, minimum GPA of 3.3. *Application deadline:* For fall admission, 1/15 priority date for domestic students; for spring admission, 10/1 for domestic students. Applications are processed on a rolling basis. Application fee: $75. *Financial support:* In 2013–14, 17 students received support. Fellowships, research assistantships, career-related internships or fieldwork, Federal Work-Study, and tuition waivers (partial) available. Financial award application deadline: 1/15; financial award applicants required to submit FAFSA. *Faculty research:* Technology in higher education administration. *Unit head:* Virginia Roach, Chair, 202-994-3094, E-mail: vroach@gwu.edu. *Application contact:* Sarah Lang, Director of Graduate Admissions, 202-994-1447, Fax: 202-994-7207, E-mail: slang@gwu.edu.

The George Washington University, Graduate School of Education and Human Development, Department of Educational Leadership, Program in Leadership in Educational Technology, Washington, DC 20052. Offers Graduate Certificate. *Students:* 4 part-time (2 women); includes 1 minority (Black or African American, non-Hispanic/Latino). Average age 32. 2 applicants, 100% accepted, 2 enrolled. In 2013, 3 Graduate Certificates awarded. *Unit head:* Virginia Roach, Chair, 202-994-3094, E-mail: vroach@gwu.edu. *Application contact:* Sarah Lang, Director of Graduate Admissions, 202-994-1447, Fax: 202-994-7207, E-mail: slang@gwu.edu.
Website: http://gsehd.gwu.edu/programs/etl/certificate/let.

Georgia College & State University, Graduate School, The John H. Lounsbury College of Education, Program in Educational Leadership, Milledgeville, GA 31061. Offers Ed S. *Accreditation:* NCATE. Part-time and evening/weekend programs available. *Students:* 64 full-time (46 women), 2 part-time (0 women); includes 30 minority (29 Black or African American, non-Hispanic/Latino; 1 Two or more races, non-Hispanic/Latino). Average age 38. In 2013, 45 Ed Ss awarded. *Entrance requirements:* Additional exam requirements/recommendations for international students: Required—TOEFL (minimum score 550 paper-based; 79 iBT). *Application deadline:* For fall admission, 7/1 priority date for domestic students; for spring admission, 11/15 priority date for domestic students. Application fee: $40. Electronic applications accepted. *Application contact:* Shanda Brand, Graduate Admission Advisor, 478-445-1383.

Georgian Court University, School of Arts and Sciences, Lakewood, NJ 08701-2697. Offers applied behavior analysis (MA); Catholic school leadership (Certificate); clinical mental health counseling (MA); holistic health studies (MA, Certificate); homeland security (MS); parish administration (Certificate); pastoral ministry (Certificate); professional counseling (Certificate); religious education (Certificate); school psychology (MA, Certificate); theology (MA, Certificate). Part-time and evening/weekend programs available. *Faculty:* 20 full-time (9 women), 9 part-time/adjunct (6 women). *Students:* 94 full-time (82 women), 134 part-time (117 women); includes 43 minority (13 Black or African American, non-Hispanic/Latino; 2 Asian, non-Hispanic/Latino; 25 Hispanic/Latino; 3 Two or more races, non-Hispanic/Latino), 1 international. In 2013, 60 master's awarded. *Degree requirements:* For master's, comprehensive exam (for some programs), thesis (for some programs). *Entrance requirements:* For master's, GRE, MAT, or NTE/PRAXIS, 3 letters of recommendation. Additional exam requirements/recommendations for international students: Required—TOEFL (minimum score 550 paper-based). *Application deadline:* For fall admission, 8/1 priority date for domestic students, 4/1 for international students; for spring admission, 1/1 priority date for domestic students, 7/1 for international students. Applications are processed on a rolling basis. Application fee: $40. Electronic applications accepted. *Expenses: Tuition:* Full-time $18,912; part-time $788 per credit. *Required fees:* $906. *Financial support:* Scholarships/grants, health care benefits, and unspecified assistantships available. Financial award application deadline: 4/15; financial award applicants required to submit FAFSA. *Unit head:* Dr. Rita Kipp, Dean, 732-987-2493, Fax: 732-987-2007. *Application contact:* Patrick Givens, Director of Graduate Admissions, 732-987-2736, Fax: 732-987-2084, E-mail: graduateadmissions@georgian.edu.
Website: http://www.georgian.edu/arts_sciences/index.htm.

Georgian Court University, School of Education, Lakewood, NJ 08701-2697. Offers administration and leadership (MA); education (MA). *Accreditation:* Teacher Education Accreditation Council. Part-time and evening/weekend programs available. *Faculty:* 21 full-time (14 women), 16 part-time/adjunct (12 women). *Students:* 87 full-time (78 women), 303 part-time (251 women); includes 48 minority (10 Black or African American, non-Hispanic/Latino; 1 Asian, non-Hispanic/Latino; 33 Hispanic/Latino; 4 Two or more races, non-Hispanic/Latino). In 2013, 78 master's awarded. *Degree requirements:* For master's, comprehensive exam (for some programs), thesis (for some programs). *Entrance requirements:* For master's, GRE, MAT or NTE/PRAXIS, 3 letters of recommendation. Additional exam requirements/recommendations for international students: Required—TOEFL (minimum score 550 paper-based). *Application deadline:* For fall admission, 8/1 priority date for domestic students, 4/1 for international students; for spring admission, 1/1 priority date for domestic students, 7/1 for international students. Applications are processed on a rolling basis. Application fee: $40. Electronic applications accepted. *Expenses: Tuition:* Full-time $18,912; part-time $788 per credit. *Required fees:* $906. *Financial support:* Scholarships/grants, health care benefits, and unspecified assistantships available. Financial award application deadline: 4/15; financial award applicants required to submit FAFSA. *Unit head:* Dr. Lynn DeCapua, Dean, 732-987-2729. *Application contact:* Patrick Givens, Director of Graduate Admissions, 732-987-2736, Fax: 732-987-2084, E-mail: graduateadmissions@georgian.edu.
Website: http://www.georgian.edu/education/index.htm.

Georgia Regents University, The Graduate School, College of Education, Program in Educational Leadership, Augusta, GA 30912. Offers M Ed, Ed S. *Accreditation:* NCATE. Part-time and evening/weekend programs available. *Faculty:* 10 full-time (3 women), 5 part-time/adjunct (3 women). *Students:* 24 full-time (16 women), 11 part-time (10 women); includes 9 minority (7 Black or African American, non-Hispanic/Latino; 1 Hispanic/Latino; 1 Two or more races, non-Hispanic/Latino). Average age 36. 36 applicants, 42% accepted, 12 enrolled. In 2013, 21 master's, 47 Ed Ss awarded. *Degree requirements:* For master's, comprehensive exam; for Ed S, comprehensive exam, thesis. *Entrance requirements:* For master's, GRE, MAT, minimum GPA of 2.5; for Ed S, GRE, MAT. *Application deadline:* For fall admission, 8/1 priority date for domestic students. Applications are processed on a rolling basis. Application fee: $20. *Financial support:* In 2013–14, 2 students received support. Career-related internships or fieldwork, Federal Work-Study, institutionally sponsored loans, and unspecified assistantships available. Support available to part-time students. Financial award application deadline: 4/15; financial award applicants required to submit FAFSA. *Faculty research:* Restructuring schools, financing education, student transition. *Unit head:* Dr. Charles Jackson, Chair, 706-737-1497, Fax: 706-667-4706, E-mail: cjackson@aug.edu. *Application contact:* Andrea M. Scott, Secretary to the Dean, 706-737-1499, Fax: 706-667-4706, E-mail: ascott1@aug.edu.

Georgia Southern University, Jack N. Averitt College of Graduate Studies, College of Education, Department of Leadership, Technology, and Human Development, Program in Educational Administration, Statesboro, GA 30460. Offers Ed D. Part-time and evening/weekend programs available. *Students:* 3 full-time (all women), 109 part-time (72 women); includes 55 minority (50 Black or African American, non-Hispanic/Latino; 4 Hispanic/Latino; 1 Two or more races, non-Hispanic/Latino), 1 international. Average age 41. 8 applicants, 50% accepted, 2 enrolled. In 2013, 25 doctorates awarded. *Degree requirements:* For doctorate, thesis/dissertation, exams. *Entrance requirements:* For doctorate, GRE General Test or MAT, minimum GPA of 3.5, letters of reference, resume. Additional exam requirements/recommendations for international students: Required—TOEFL (minimum score 550 paper-based; 80 iBT), IELTS (minimum score 6). *Application deadline:* For fall admission, 3/1 for domestic students, 3/1 priority date for international students; for spring admission, 11/1 for domestic students, 10/1 for international students. Applications are processed on a rolling basis. Application fee: $50. Electronic applications accepted. *Expenses:* Tuition, state resident: full-time $7068; part-time $270 per semester hour. Tuition, nonresident: full-time $26,446; part-time $1077 per semester hour. *Required fees:* $2092. *Financial support:* In 2013–14, 3 students received support, including fellowships with partial tuition reimbursements available (averaging $9,500 per year), research assistantships with partial tuition reimbursements available (averaging $9,500 per year), teaching assistantships with partial tuition reimbursements available (averaging $9,500 per year); Federal Work-Study, scholarships/grants, tuition waivers (partial), and unspecified assistantships also available. Support available to part-time students. Financial award application deadline: 4/15; financial award applicants required to submit FAFSA. *Faculty research:* National and local policies regarding school renewal, student achievement, and university leadership; roles and responsibilities of the assistant principal/deputy head teacher in the U.S., U.K. and China; development of an instrument to measure student dispositions; the impact of cultural context on leadership practices and behaviors; technology leadership preparation. *Unit head:* Dr. Devon Jensen, Program Coordinator, 912-478-5307, Fax: 912-478-7140, E-mail: devonjensen@georgiasouthern.edu. *Application contact:* Amanda Gilliland, Coordinator for Graduate Student Recruitment, 912-478-5384, Fax: 912-478-0740, E-mail: gradadmissions@georgiasouthern.edu.
Website: http://coe.georgiasouthern.edu/edld/m-ed/.

Georgia Southern University, Jack N. Averitt College of Graduate Studies, College of Education, Department of Leadership, Technology, and Human Development, Program in Educational Leadership, Statesboro, GA 30460. Offers M Ed, Ed D, Ed S. *Accreditation:* NCATE. Part-time and evening/weekend programs available. *Students:* 10 full-time (4 women), 53 part-time (38 women); includes 19 minority (18 Black or African American, non-Hispanic/Latino; 1 Hispanic/Latino). Average age 38. 45 applicants, 76% accepted, 14 enrolled. In 2013, 18 master's, 19 other advanced degrees awarded. *Degree requirements:* For master's, comprehensive exam, transition point assessments; for Ed S, transition point assessments. *Entrance requirements:* For master's, GRE General Test or MAT, minimum GPA of 2.5, 3 years of teaching experience; for Ed S, GRE General Test or MAT, minimum graduate GPA of 3.25. Additional exam requirements/recommendations for international students: Required—TOEFL (minimum score 550 paper-based; 80 iBT), IELTS (minimum score 6). *Application deadline:* For fall admission, 3/1 priority date for domestic and international students; for spring admission, 10/1 priority date for domestic students, 10/1 for international students. Applications are processed on a rolling basis. Application fee: $50. Electronic applications accepted. *Expenses:* Tuition, state resident: full-time $7068; part-time $270 per semester hour. Tuition, nonresident: full-time $26,446; part-time $1077 per semester hour. *Required fees:* $2092. *Financial support:* In 2013–14, 2 students received support, including research assistantships with partial tuition reimbursements available (averaging $7,200 per year), teaching assistantships with partial tuition reimbursements available (averaging $7,200 per year); career-related internships or fieldwork, Federal Work-Study, scholarships/grants, tuition waivers (partial), and unspecified assistantships also available. Support available to part-time students. Financial award application deadline: 4/15; financial award applicants required to submit FAFSA. *Faculty research:* Principalship, performance-based leadership preparation, instructional technology for school leaders, dispositions of educational leaders, school/system-wide support services, student-oriented support services, universal vs. cultural contextuality of international educational leadership characteristics and behaviors. *Unit head:* Dr. Teri Melton, Program Coordinator, 912-478-0510, Fax: 912-478-7104, E-mail: tamelton@georgiasouthern.edu. *Application contact:* Amanda Gilliland, Coordinator for Graduate Student Recruitment, 912-478-5384, Fax: 912-478-0740, E-mail: gradadmissions@georgiasouthern.edu.
Website: http://cogs.georgiasouthern.edu/admission/GraduatePrograms/coe_mededleader.php.

Georgia State University, College of Education, Department of Educational Policy Studies, Program in Educational Leadership, Atlanta, GA 30302-3083. Offers educational leadership (M Ed, Ed D, Ed S); urban teacher leadership (M Ed). *Accreditation:* NCATE. Part-time programs available. *Students:* Average age 0. *Degree requirements:* For master's, comprehensive exam, thesis or alternative, 36 semester hours; for doctorate, comprehensive exam, thesis/dissertation, 54 semester hours (for EdD); 69 semester hours (for PhD); for Ed S, thesis, 30 semester hours of coursework. *Entrance requirements:* For master's, GRE; for doctorate and Ed S, GRE, MAT. Additional exam requirements/recommendations for international students: Required—TOEFL (minimum score 550 paper-based; 79 iBT) or IELTS (minimum score 6.5). *Application deadline:* For fall admission, 5/1 for domestic and international students; for winter admission, 2/1 for domestic students; for spring admission, 10/1 for domestic and international students. Applications are processed on a rolling basis. Application fee: $50. Electronic applications accepted. *Expenses: Tuition, area resident:* Full-time $4176; part-time $348 per credit hour. Tuition, state resident: full-time $14,544; part-time $1212 per credit hour. Tuition, nonresident: full-time $14,544; part-time $1212 per credit hour. Tuition and fees vary according to course load and program. *Financial support:* In 2013–14, research assistantships with full tuition reimbursements (averaging $6,000 per year) were awarded; fellowships, teaching assistantships with full tuition reimbursements, career-related internships or fieldwork, scholarships/grants, health care benefits, tuition waivers, and unspecified assistantships also available. Support available to part-time students. Financial award application deadline: 3/15. *Faculty research:* Practices with diverse populations, leadership and success, the cohort model of instruction, technology in the schools, instructional supervision and academic coaching. *Unit head:* Dr. Jami Berry, Clinical Assistant Professor, 404-413-8030, Fax: 404-413-8003, E-mail: jberry2@gsu.edu. *Application contact:* Aishah Cowan,

Educational Leadership and Administration

Administrative Academic Specialist, 404-413-8273, Fax: 404-413-8033, E-mail: acowan@gsu.edu. Website: http://education.gsu.edu/eps/4580.html.

Golden Gate Baptist Theological Seminary, Graduate and Professional Programs, Mill Valley, CA 94941-3197. Offers divinity (M Div); early childhood education (Certificate); education leadership (MAEL, Diploma); ministry (D Min); theological studies (MTS); theology (Th M); youth ministry (Certificate). *Accreditation:* ACIPE; ATS (one or more programs are accredited). Part-time and evening/weekend programs available. *Degree requirements:* For master's, thesis (for some programs); for doctorate, 2 foreign languages, thesis/dissertation. *Entrance requirements:* For doctorate, MAT. Additional exam requirements/recommendations for international students: Required—TOEFL (minimum score 550 paper-based). Electronic applications accepted.

Gonzaga University, School of Education, Program in Administration and Curriculum, Spokane, WA 99258. Offers MAA. *Accreditation:* NCATE. Part-time programs available. *Faculty:* 6 full-time (3 women), 11 part-time/adjunct (5 women). *Students:* 25 full-time (10 women), 189 part-time (124 women); includes 1 minority (American Indian or Alaska Native, non-Hispanic/Latino), 198 international. Average age 39. 143 applicants, 73% accepted, 98 enrolled. In 2013, 94 master's awarded. *Degree requirements:* For master's, comprehensive exam. *Entrance requirements:* For master's, GRE General Test or MAT, minimum B average in undergraduate course work. Additional exam requirements/recommendations for international students: Required—TOEFL. *Application deadline:* For fall admission, 7/20 priority date for domestic students; for spring admission, 11/1 for domestic students. Applications are processed on a rolling basis. Application fee: $50. Electronic applications accepted. *Expenses:* Contact institution. *Financial support:* Teaching assistantships available. Support available to part-time students. Financial award application deadline: 2/1; financial award applicants required to submit FAFSA. *Unit head:* Dr. Albert Fein, Department Chair and Program Director, 509-328-4220 Ext. 3654. *Application contact:* Julie McCulloh, Dean of Admissions, 509-313-6592, Fax: 509-313-5780, E-mail: mcculloh@gu.gonzaga.edu.

Gonzaga University, School of Professional Studies, Program in Leadership Studies, Spokane, WA 99258. Offers PhD. Part-time and evening/weekend programs available. *Faculty:* 4 full-time (2 women), 1 part-time/adjunct (0 women). *Students:* 6 full-time (3 women), 75 part-time (42 women); includes 10 minority (3 Black or African American, non-Hispanic/Latino; 1 American Indian or Alaska Native, non-Hispanic/Latino; 1 Asian, non-Hispanic/Latino; 3 Hispanic/Latino; 1 Native Hawaiian or other Pacific Islander, non-Hispanic/Latino; 1 Two or more races, non-Hispanic/Latino), 8 international. Average age 44. 20 applicants, 95% accepted, 6 enrolled. In 2013, 16 doctorates awarded. *Degree requirements:* For doctorate, thesis/dissertation. *Entrance requirements:* For doctorate, MAT and/or GRE. *Application deadline:* For fall admission, 7/16 for domestic students; for spring admission, 11/16 for domestic students; for summer admission, 3/16 for domestic students. Application fee: $50. Electronic applications accepted. *Expenses:* Contact institution. *Financial support:* Application deadline: 2/1; applicants required to submit FAFSA. *Unit head:* Dr. JoAnn Danelo Barbour, Department Chair, 509-313-3630, E-mail: barbourj@gonzaga.edu. *Application contact:* Julie McCulloh, Dean of Admissions, 509-313-6592, Fax: 509-313-5780, E-mail: mcculloh@gu.gonzaga.edu.

Gordon College, Graduate Education Program, Wenham, MA 01984-1899. Offers education (M Ed); educational leadership (Ed S); English as a second language (ESL) (Ed S); mathematics specialist (Ed S); reading (Ed S). Part-time and evening/weekend programs available. *Faculty:* 1 (woman) full-time, 45 part-time/adjunct (27 women). *Students:* 106 full-time (86 women), 281 part-time (230 women); includes 30 minority (4 Black or African American, non-Hispanic/Latino; 7 Asian, non-Hispanic/Latino; 17 Hispanic/Latino; 2 Two or more races, non-Hispanic/Latino), 5 international. In 2013, 52 master's awarded. *Degree requirements:* For master's and Ed S, action research or clinical experience (for some programs). *Entrance requirements:* For master's, GRE or MAT, references, minimum undergraduate GPA of 3.0; for Ed S, references, minimum undergraduate GPA of 3.0. Additional exam requirements/recommendations for international students: Required—TOEFL (minimum score 550 paper-based, 80 iBT) or IELTS (minimum score 6.5). *Application deadline:* Applications are processed on a rolling basis. Application fee: $50. *Expenses: Tuition:* Part-time $325 per credit. *Required fees:* $50 per term. One-time fee: $50. Tuition and fees vary according to program. *Financial support:* Applicants required to submit FAFSA. *Faculty research:* Reading, early childhood development, English language learners. *Unit head:* Dr. Janet Arndt, Director of Graduate Studies, 978-867-4355, Fax: 978-867-4663. *Application contact:* Julie Lenocker, Program Administrator, 978-867-4322, Fax: 978-867-4663, E-mail: graduate-education@gordon.edu. Website: http://www.gordon.edu/graduate.

Governors State University, College of Education, Program in Educational Administration and Supervision, University Park, IL 60484. Offers MA. Part-time and evening/weekend programs available. *Degree requirements:* For master's, comprehensive exam, practicum. *Entrance requirements:* For master's, minimum GPA of 2.75 in last 60 hours of undergraduate course work, 3.0 graduate.

Graceland University, Gleazer School of Education, Independence, MO 64050. Offers differentiated instruction (M Ed); literacy and instruction (M Ed); management in the inclusive classroom (M Ed); mild/moderate special education (M Ed); technology integration (M Ed). *Accreditation:* NCATE. Part-time and evening/weekend programs available. Postbaccalaureate distance learning degree programs offered (no on-campus study). *Faculty:* 12 full-time (11 women), 18 part-time/adjunct (14 women). *Students:* 139 full-time (119 women), 18 part-time (14 women); includes 8 minority (3 Black or African American, non-Hispanic/Latino; 1 Asian, non-Hispanic/Latino; 4 Hispanic/Latino). Average age 36. 36 applicants, 81% accepted, 24 enrolled. In 2013, 196 master's awarded. *Degree requirements:* For master's, action research project. *Entrance requirements:* For master's, minimum GPA of 3.0, teaching certificate, current teaching contract. *Application deadline:* For fall admission, 7/15 for domestic students; for winter admission, 10/15 for domestic students; for spring admission, 1/15 priority date for domestic students. Application fee: $50. Electronic applications accepted. *Expenses: Tuition:* Part-time $450 per semester hour. Tuition and fees vary according to course load, degree level, campus/location and program. *Financial support:* Institutionally sponsored loans and scholarships/grants available. Financial award application deadline: 12/15; financial award applicants required to submit FAFSA. *Unit head:* Dr. Scott Huddleston, Dean, 641-784-5000 Ext. 4744, E-mail: huddlest@graceland.edu. *Application contact:* Cathy Porter, Program Consultant, 816-423-4716, Fax: 816-833-2990, E-mail: cgporter@graceland.edu. Website: http://www.graceland.edu/education.

Grambling State University, School of Graduate Studies and Research, College of Education, Department of Educational Leadership, Grambling, LA 71245. Offers developmental education (MS, Ed D, PMC), including curriculum and instructional design (Ed D), English (MS), guidance and counseling (MS), higher education administration and management (Ed D), mathematics (MS), reading (MS), science (MS), student development and personnel services (Ed D); educational leadership (M Ed). Part-time and evening/weekend programs available. *Faculty:* 10 full-time (7 women). *Students:* 19 full-time (13 women), 89 part-time (70 women); includes 83 minority (82 Black or African American, non-Hispanic/Latino; 1 Hispanic/Latino), 6 international. Average age 40. In 2013, 13 master's, 6 doctorates, 1 other advanced

degree awarded. *Degree requirements:* For master's, comprehensive exam, thesis (for some programs); for doctorate, comprehensive exam, thesis/dissertation. *Entrance requirements:* For master's, GRE, minimum GPA of 2.5 on last degree; for doctorate, GRE (minimum score 1000, 500 on Verbal), master's degree, minimum GPA of 3.0 on last degree. Additional exam requirements/recommendations for international students: Required—TOEFL (minimum score 500 paper-based; 62 iBT). *Application deadline:* For fall admission, 7/1 for domestic and international students; for spring admission, 12/1 for domestic and international students; for summer admission, 5/1 for domestic and international students. Applications are processed on a rolling basis. Application fee: $20 ($30 for international students). Electronic applications accepted. *Financial support:* Research assistantships, health care benefits, tuition waivers (full), and unspecified assistantships available. Financial award application deadline: 5/31; financial award applicants required to submit FAFSA. *Unit head:* Dr. Olatunde Ogunyemi, Department Head, 318-274-2549, Fax: 318-274-6249, E-mail: ogunyemio@gram.edu. *Application contact:* Brenda Cooper, Administrative Assistant III, 318-274-2238, Fax: 318-274-6249, E-mail: cooper@gram.edu. Website: http://www.gram.edu/academics/majors/education/departments/leadership/.

Grand Canyon University, College of Doctoral Studies, Phoenix, AZ 85017-1097. Offers business administration (DBA); general psychology (PhD), including cognition and instruction, industrial and organizational psychology; organizational leadership (Ed D, PhD), including behavioral health (PhD), education and effective schools (PhD), higher education (PhD), instructional leadership (PhD), organizational development (Ed D). *Degree requirements:* For doctorate, comprehensive exam, thesis/dissertation. *Entrance requirements:* For doctorate, minimum GPA of 3.4 on earned advanced degree from regionally-accredited institution; transcripts; goals statement.

Grand Canyon University, College of Education, Phoenix, AZ 85017-1097. Offers curriculum and instruction (M Ed); education administration (M Ed); elementary education (M Ed); secondary education (M Ed); special education (M Ed); teaching (MA). Part-time and evening/weekend programs available. Postbaccalaureate distance learning degree programs offered (no on-campus study). *Degree requirements:* For master's, publishable research paper (M Ed), e-portfolio. *Entrance requirements:* For master's, undergraduate degree from accredited, GCU-approved college, university, or program with minimum GPA 2.8. Additional exam requirements/recommendations for international students: Required—TOEFL (minimum score 550 paper-based; 79 iBT), IELTS (minimum score 6). Electronic applications accepted.

Grand Valley State University, College of Education, Program in Educational Leadership, Allendale, MI 49401-9403. Offers M Ed.

Grand Valley State University, College of Education, Program in Leadership, Allendale, MI 49401-9403. Offers Ed S. *Entrance requirements:* For degree, GRE, master's degree with minimum GPA of 3.0, resume, 3 recommendations. Electronic applications accepted.

Grand Valley State University, College of Education, Programs in General Education, Allendale, MI 49401-9403. Offers adult and higher education (M Ed); early childhood education (M Ed); educational differentiation (M Ed); educational leadership (M Ed); educational technology integration (M Ed); elementary education (M Ed); middle level education (M Ed); school library media services (M Ed); secondary level education (M Ed); teaching English to speakers of other languages (M Ed). Part-time and evening/weekend programs available. Postbaccalaureate distance learning degree programs offered (minimal on-campus study). *Degree requirements:* For master's, thesis. *Entrance requirements:* For master's, GRE General Test or minimum GPA of 3.0. Additional exam requirements/recommendations for international students: Required—TOEFL. Electronic applications accepted. *Faculty research:* Effectiveness of technology in education, parental involvement, effective teaching, effective schools research.

Gwynedd Mercy University, Center for Lifelong Learning, Gwynedd Valley, PA 19437-0901. Offers education (MSE); educational administration (MS); management (MSM). Part-time and evening/weekend programs available. *Degree requirements:* For master's, thesis. *Entrance requirements:* For master's, minimum GPA of 3.0.

Gwynedd Mercy University, School of Education, Gwynedd Valley, PA 19437-0901. Offers educational administration (MS); master teacher (MS); reading (MS); school counseling (MS); special education (MS). Part-time and evening/weekend programs available. *Degree requirements:* For master's, thesis, internship, practicum. *Entrance requirements:* For master's, GRE or MAT; PRAXIS I, minimum GPA of 3.0. *Faculty research:* Learning and the brain, reading literacy, ethics and moral judgment, leadership, teaching and multicultural education.

Hampton University, Graduate College, College of Education and Continuing Studies, Hampton, VA 23668. Offers counseling (MA), including college student development, community agency counseling, pastoral counseling, school counseling; educational leadership (MA); elementary education (MA); gifted education (MA); Montessori education (MA); teaching (MT), including early childhood education, middle school education, music education, secondary education, special education. *Accreditation:* NCATE. Part-time and evening/weekend programs available. *Entrance requirements:* For master's, GRE General Test.

Hampton University, Hampton U Online, Hampton, VA 23668. Offers business administration (PhD); educational management (PhD); health administration (MHA); nursing (MSN, PhD).

Harding University, Cannon-Clary College of Education, Searcy, AR 72149-0001. Offers advanced studies in teaching and learning (M Ed); art (MSE); behavioral science (MSE); counseling (MS, Ed S); early childhood special education (M Ed, MSE); education (MSE); educational leadership (M Ed, Ed S); elementary education (M Ed); English (MSE); French (MSE); history/social science (MSE); kinesiology (MSE); math (MSE); reading (M Ed); secondary education (M Ed); Spanish (MSE); teaching (MAT); teaching English as a second language (MSE). *Accreditation:* NCATE. Part-time and evening/weekend programs available. *Faculty:* 13 full-time (5 women), 42 part-time/adjunct (24 women). *Students:* 154 full-time (119 women), 393 part-time (270 women); includes 108 minority (81 Black or African American, non-Hispanic/Latino; 5 American Indian or Alaska Native, non-Hispanic/Latino; 5 Asian, non-Hispanic/Latino; 9 Hispanic/Latino; 8 Two or more races, non-Hispanic/Latino), 15 international. Average age 36. 187 applicants, 79% accepted, 135 enrolled. In 2013, 138 master's, 17 other advanced degrees awarded. *Degree requirements:* For master's, comprehensive exam (for some programs), thesis optional, portfolio(s); for Ed S, comprehensive exam, portfolio, project. *Entrance requirements:* For master's, GRE, MAT, PRAXIS; for Ed S, MAT or GRE. Additional exam requirements/recommendations for international students: Required—TOEFL (minimum score 550 paper-based; 79 iBT). *Application deadline:* For fall admission, 8/1 for domestic and international students; for spring admission, 1/1 for domestic and international students. Applications are processed on a rolling basis. Application fee: $35. *Expenses: Tuition:* Full-time $11,574; part-time $643 per credit hour. *Required fees:* $432; $24 per credit hour. Tuition and fees vary according to course load, degree level and program. *Financial support:* In 2013–14, 36 students received support. Unspecified assistantships available. *Faculty research:* Reading, comprehension, school violence, educational technology, behavior, college choice, differentiated instruction, brain-based teaching. *Unit head:* Dr. Clara Carroll, Chair, 501-

279-4501, Fax: 501-279-4083, E-mail: ccarroll@harding.edu. *Application contact:* Information Contact, 501-279-4315, E-mail: gradstudiesedu@harding.edu.
Website: http://www.harding.edu/education.

Hardin-Simmons University, Graduate School, Irvin School of Education, Program in Education Leadership, Abilene, TX 79698-0001. Offers Ed D. Part-time programs available. *Faculty:* 3 full-time (0 women), 1 part-time/adjunct (0 women). *Students:* 16 part-time (12 women), 1 international. Average age 37. 11 applicants, 100% accepted, 6 enrolled. *Application deadline:* For fall admission, 7/15 priority date for domestic students, 4/1 for international students; for spring admission, 1/5 priority date for domestic students, 8/1 for international students. Applications are processed on a rolling basis. Application fee: $50. *Expenses: Tuition:* Full-time $13,410; part-time $745 per credit hour. *Required fees:* $325; $110 per semester. Tuition and fees vary according to program. *Financial support:* In 2013–14, 2 students received support, including 1 fellowship (averaging $2,400 per year); scholarships/grants also available. Support available to part-time students. Financial award application deadline: 6/30; financial award applicants required to submit FAFSA. *Unit head:* Dr. Pam Williford, Dean, 325-670-1352, Fax: 325-670-5859, E-mail: pwilliford@hsutx.edu. *Application contact:* Dr. Nancy Kucinski, Dean of Graduate Studies, 325-670-1298, Fax: 325-670-1564, E-mail: gradoff@hsutx.edu.
Website: http://www.hsutx.edu/doctorateinleadership.

Harvard University, Harvard Graduate School of Education, Doctoral Program in Education, Cambridge, MA 02138. Offers culture, communities and education (Ed D); education policy, leadership and instructional practice (Ed D); higher education (Ed D); human development and education (Ed D); quantitative policy analysis in education (Ed D). *Faculty:* 68 full-time (34 women), 77 part-time/adjunct (41 women). *Students:* 221 full-time (148 women), 8 part-time (4 women); includes 70 minority (28 Black or African American, non-Hispanic/Latino; 22 Asian, non-Hispanic/Latino; 14 Hispanic/Latino; 1 Native Hawaiian or other Pacific Islander, non-Hispanic/Latino; 5 Two or more races, non-Hispanic/Latino), 26 international. Average age 34. 472 applicants, 8% accepted, 25 enrolled. In 2013, 50 doctorates awarded. Terminal master's awarded for partial completion of doctoral program. *Degree requirements:* For doctorate, thesis/dissertation. *Entrance requirements:* For doctorate, GRE General Test, statement of purpose, 3 letters of recommendation, resume, official transcripts. Additional exam requirements/recommendations for international students: Required—TOEFL (minimum score 613 paper-based; 104 iBT), TWE (minimum score 5). *Application deadline:* For fall admission, 12/2 for domestic and international students. Application fee: $85. Electronic applications accepted. *Expenses:* Contact institution. *Financial support:* In 2013–14, 168 students received support, including 66 fellowships with full and partial tuition reimbursements available (averaging $15,034 per year), 48 research assistantships (averaging $11,714 per year), 190 teaching assistantships (averaging $6,097 per year); career-related internships or fieldwork, Federal Work-Study, institutionally sponsored loans, scholarships/grants, health care benefits, tuition waivers (full and partial), and unspecified assistantships also available. Support available to part-time students. Financial award application deadline: 2/1; financial award applicants required to submit FAFSA. *Faculty research:* Learning and development, educational leadership and organizations, education policy analysis. *Total annual research expenditures:* $34.3 million. *Unit head:* Dr. Barbara Selmo, Assistant Dean, 617-496-4406. *Application contact:* Information Contact, 617-495-3414, Fax: 617-496-3577, E-mail: gseadmissions@harvard.edu.
Website: http://gse.harvard.edu/.

Harvard University, Harvard Graduate School of Education, Doctor of Education Leadership (Ed.L.D.) Program, Cambridge, MA 02138. Offers Ed L D. *Faculty:* 68 full-time (34 women), 77 part-time/adjunct (41 women). *Students:* 79 full-time (44 women); includes 43 minority (18 Black or African American, non-Hispanic/Latino; 9 Asian, non-Hispanic/Latino; 12 Hispanic/Latino; 4 Two or more races, non-Hispanic/Latino). Average age 34. 424 applicants, 6% accepted, 25 enrolled. In 2013, 21 doctorates awarded. *Degree requirements:* For doctorate, thesis/dissertation, capstone project. *Entrance requirements:* For doctorate, GRE or GMAT, statement of purpose, 3 letters of recommendation, resume, official transcripts, 2 short essay questions. Additional exam requirements/recommendations for international students: Required—TOEFL (minimum score 613 paper-based; 104 iBT), TWE (minimum score 5). *Application deadline:* For fall admission, 12/13 for domestic and international students. Application fee: $85. Electronic applications accepted. *Expenses: Tuition:* Full-time $38,888. *Required fees:* $958. Tuition and fees vary according to campus/location, program and student level. *Financial support:* In 2013–14, 75 students received support, including 43 fellowships (averaging $21,788 per year), 20 teaching assistantships (averaging $5,537 per year); career-related internships or fieldwork, Federal Work-Study, institutionally sponsored loans, scholarships/grants, health care benefits, tuition waivers, and unspecified assistantships also available. Financial award application deadline: 2/1; financial award applicants required to submit FAFSA. *Faculty research:* System level leadership in education. *Total annual research expenditures:* $34.3 million. *Unit head:* Dr. Julie Vultaggio, Assistant Dean, Doctor of Education Leadership Program, 617-496-3572. *Application contact:* Information Contact, 617-495-3414, Fax: 617-496-3577, E-mail: gseadmissions@harvard.edu.
Website: http://www.gse.harvard.edu/academics/doctorate/edld/index.html.

Harvard University, Harvard Graduate School of Education, Master's Programs in Education, Cambridge, MA 02138. Offers arts in education (Ed M); education policy and management (Ed M); higher education (Ed M); human development and psychology (Ed M); international education policy (Ed M); language and literacy (Ed M); learning and teaching (Ed M); mind, brain, and education (Ed M); prevention science and practice (Ed M); school leadership (Ed M); special studies (Ed M); teacher education (Ed M); technology, innovation, and education (Ed M). Part-time programs available. *Faculty:* 68 full-time (34 women), 77 part-time/adjunct (41 women). *Students:* 557 full-time (410 women), 69 part-time (50 women); includes 179 minority (34 Black or African American, non-Hispanic/Latino; 1 American Indian or Alaska Native, non-Hispanic/Latino; 62 Asian, non-Hispanic/Latino; 52 Hispanic/Latino; 2 Native Hawaiian or other Pacific Islander, non-Hispanic/Latino; 28 Two or more races, non-Hispanic/Latino), 100 international. Average age 28. 1,756 applicants, 47% accepted, 589 enrolled. In 2013, 673 master's awarded. *Entrance requirements:* For master's, GRE General Test, statement of purpose, 3 letters of recommendation, resume, official transcripts. Additional exam requirements/recommendations for international students: Required—TOEFL (minimum score 613 paper-based; 104 iBT), TWE (minimum score 5). *Application deadline:* For fall admission, 1/3 for domestic and international students. Application fee: $85. Electronic applications accepted. *Expenses:* Contact institution. *Financial support:* In 2013–14, 375 students received support, including 12 fellowships with full and partial tuition reimbursements available (averaging $13,925 per year), 2 research assistantships (averaging $2,174 per year); career-related internships or fieldwork, Federal Work-Study, institutionally sponsored loans, scholarships/grants, health care benefits, tuition waivers (full and partial), and unspecified assistantships also available. Support available to part-time students. Financial award application deadline: 2/1; financial award applicants required to submit FAFSA. *Faculty research:* Learning and development, educational leadership and organizations, education policy analysis. *Total annual research expenditures:* $34.3 million. *Unit head:* Jennifer L. Petrallia, Assistant Dean, 617-495-8445. *Application contact:* Information Contact, 617-495-3414, Fax: 617-496-3577, E-mail: gseadmissions@harvard.edu.
Website: http://www.gse.harvard.edu/.

Henderson State University, Graduate Studies, Teachers College, Department of Educational Leadership, Arkadelphia, AR 71999-0001. Offers MSE, Ed S, Graduate Certificate. Part-time programs available. Postbaccalaureate distance learning degree programs offered (no on-campus study). *Faculty:* 5 full-time (3 women). *Students:* 50 part-time (28 women); includes 7 minority (all Black or African American, non-Hispanic/Latino). Average age 38. 2 applicants, 100% accepted, 2 enrolled. In 2013, 4 master's, 9 other advanced degrees awarded. *Entrance requirements:* For master's, GRE or MAT, minimum GPA of 2.7, teacher's licensure. Additional exam requirements/recommendations for international students: Required—TOEFL (minimum score 600 paper-based); Recommended—IELTS (minimum score 6.5). *Application deadline:* For fall admission, 8/1 priority date for domestic students, 6/30 priority date for international students; for spring admission, 1/1 priority date for domestic students, 11/30 priority date for international students. Applications are processed on a rolling basis. Application fee: $25 ($75 for international students). *Expenses:* Tuition, state resident: full-time $4284; part-time $238 per credit hour. Tuition, nonresident: full-time $8802; part-time $489 per credit hour. Tuition and fees vary according to course load and campus/location. *Financial support:* In 2013–14, 1 teaching assistantship with partial tuition reimbursement (averaging $4,000 per year) was awarded; scholarships/grants and unspecified assistantships also available. *Unit head:* Dr. Pat Weaver, Coordinator, 870-230-5351, E-mail: weaverp@hsu.edu. *Application contact:* Dr. Ken Taylor, Graduate Dean, 870-230-5126, Fax: 870-230-5479, E-mail: taylorke@hsu.edu.

Heritage University, Graduate Programs in Education, Program in Educational Administration, Toppenish, WA 98948-9599. Offers M Ed. Part-time and evening/weekend programs available. *Degree requirements:* For master's, comprehensive exam, thesis optional, special project. *Entrance requirements:* For master's, valid teaching certificate, 3 years of teaching experience, interview, letters of recommendation.

High Point University, Norcross Graduate School, High Point, NC 27262-3598. Offers business administration (MBA); educational leadership (M Ed); elementary education (M Ed); history (MA); nonprofit management (MA); secondary math (M Ed); special education (M Ed); strategic communication (MA); teaching elementary education k-6 (MAT); teaching secondary mathematics 9-12 (MAT). *Accreditation:* NCATE. Part-time and evening/weekend programs available. *Degree requirements:* For master's, comprehensive exam (for some programs), thesis (for some programs). *Entrance requirements:* For master's, GMAT (MBA), GRE, MAT, minimum GPA of 3.0. Additional exam requirements/recommendations for international students: Required—TOEFL (minimum score 550 paper-based). Electronic applications accepted.

Hofstra University, School of Education, Programs in Educational Policy and Leadership, Hempstead, NY 11549. Offers educational and policy leadership (MS Ed, Ed D), including K-12 (MS Ed), K-12/higher education (Ed D); educational policy and leadership (Advanced Certificate), including school district business leader; foundations of education (MA, Advanced Certificate); higher education leadership and policy studies (MS Ed).

Holy Family University, Graduate School, School of Education, Doctor of Education Programs, Philadelphia, PA 19114. Offers educational leadership and professional studies (Ed D). *Degree requirements:* For doctorate, thesis/dissertation. *Expenses: Tuition:* Full-time $12,060. *Required fees:* $250. Tuition and fees vary according to degree level. *Unit head:* Dr. Elizabeth Jones, Director, 267-341-3313, E-mail: ejones1760@holyfamily.edu. *Application contact:* Gidget Marie Montelibano, Associate Director of Graduate Admissions, 267-341-3358, Fax: 215-637-1478, E-mail: gmontelibano@holyfamily.edu.

Holy Family University, Graduate School, School of Education, Master of Education Programs, Philadelphia, PA 19114. Offers early elementary education (PreK-Grade 4) (M Ed); education leadership (M Ed); general education (M Ed); middle level education (Grades 4-8) (M Ed); reading specialist (M Ed); secondary education (Grades 7-12) (M Ed); special education (M Ed); TESOL and literacy (M Ed). *Expenses: Tuition:* Full-time $12,060. *Required fees:* $250. Tuition and fees vary according to degree level. *Unit head:* Dr. Leonard Soroka, Dean, 267-341-3565, Fax: 215-824-2438, E-mail: lsoroka@holyfamily.edu. *Application contact:* Gidget Marie Montelibano, Associate Director of Graduate Admissions, 267-341-3358, Fax: 215-637-1478, E-mail: gmontelibano@holyfamily.edu.

Hood College, Graduate School, Department of Education, Frederick, MD 21701-8575. Offers curriculum and instruction (MS), including early childhood education, elementary education, elementary school science and mathematics, secondary education, special education; educational leadership (MS, Certificate); reading specialization (MS); STEM (Certificate). *Accreditation:* NCATE. Part-time and evening/weekend programs available. *Faculty:* 4 full-time (3 women), 33 part-time/adjunct (25 women). *Students:* 1 (woman) full-time, 340 part-time (282 women); includes 59 minority (31 Black or African American, non-Hispanic/Latino; 1 American Indian or Alaska Native, non-Hispanic/Latino; 10 Asian, non-Hispanic/Latino; 13 Hispanic/Latino; 4 Two or more races, non-Hispanic/Latino). Average age 33. 97 applicants, 99% accepted, 86 enrolled. In 2013, 64 master's, 40 other advanced degrees awarded. *Degree requirements:* For master's, action research project, portfolio (reading). *Entrance requirements:* For master's, minimum GPA of 2.75, teaching certification. Additional exam requirements/recommendations for international students: Required—TOEFL (minimum score 575 paper-based; 89 iBT), IELTS (minimum score 6.5). *Application deadline:* For fall admission, 7/15 priority date for domestic students, 7/15 for international students; for spring admission, 12/1 priority date for domestic students, 12/1 for international students. Applications are processed on a rolling basis. Application fee: $35. Electronic applications accepted. Application fee is waived when completed online. *Expenses: Tuition:* Part-time $405 per credit. *Required fees:* $100 per semester. *Financial support:* In 2013–14, 1 student received support. Tuition waivers (partial) and unspecified assistantships available. Financial award applicants required to submit FAFSA. *Faculty research:* Leadership, action research, brain research, learning styles. *Unit head:* Dr. Ellen Koitz, Chairperson, 301-696-3466, Fax: 301-696-3597, E-mail: koitz@hood.edu. *Application contact:* Dr. Maria Green Cowles, Dean of Graduate School, 301-696-3811, Fax: 301-696-3597, E-mail: gofurther@hood.edu.
Website: http://www.hood.edu/academics/education/index.html.

Hope International University, School of Graduate and Professional Studies, Program in Education, Fullerton, CA 92831-3138. Offers education administration (MA); elementary education (ME); secondary education (ME). Part-time and evening/weekend programs available. *Degree requirements:* For master's, comprehensive exam (for some programs), thesis. *Entrance requirements:* For master's, minimum GPA of 3.0, 2 references. Additional exam requirements/recommendations for international students: Required—TOEFL (minimum score 550 paper-based; 86 iBT); Recommended—IELTS (minimum score 6.5). Electronic applications accepted. *Expenses:* Contact institution. *Faculty research:* Distance education.

Houston Baptist University, College of Education and Behavioral Sciences, Programs in Education, Houston, TX 77074-3298. Offers bilingual education (M Ed); counselor

education (M Ed); curriculum and instruction (M Ed); educational administration (M Ed); educational diagnostician (M Ed); reading education (M Ed). Part-time programs available. Postbaccalaureate distance learning degree programs offered (no on-campus study). *Entrance requirements:* For master's, GRE General Test or MAT. Additional exam requirements/recommendations for international students: Required—TOEFL (minimum score 550 paper-based).

Howard Payne University, Program in Instructional Leadership, Brownwood, TX 76801-2715. Offers M Ed. Part-time and evening/weekend programs available. Postbaccalaureate distance learning degree programs offered (no on-campus study). *Faculty:* 1 full-time (0 women), 2 part-time/adjunct (1 woman). *Students:* 9 full-time (4 women), 4 part-time (3 women); includes 4 minority (all Hispanic/Latino). Average age 36. 8 applicants, 100% accepted, 7 enrolled. In 2013, 1 master's awarded. *Degree requirements:* For master's, comprehensive exam (for some programs), thesis or alternative. *Entrance requirements:* For master's, undergraduate degree, valid teaching certificate. Additional exam requirements/recommendations for international students: Required—TOEFL (minimum score 79 iBT). *Application deadline:* For fall admission, 7/1 for domestic students; for spring admission, 12/1 for domestic students. Applications are processed on a rolling basis. Application fee: $0. Electronic applications accepted. *Expenses: Tuition:* Full-time $8820; part-time $490 per credit hour. *Financial support:* Application deadline: 3/15; applicants required to submit FAFSA. *Unit head:* Dr. Joe Robinson, Director of Instructional Leadership Graduate Program/Professor of Education, 325-649-8205, E-mail: jrobinson@hputx.edu. *Application contact:* Susan Sharp, Administrative Assistant, School of Education/Certification Officer, 325-649-8144, E-mail: ssharp@hputx.edu.
Website: http://www.hputx.edu/academics/schools/school-of-education/school-of-education-graduate-program/.

Howard University, School of Education, Department of Educational Leadership and Policy Studies, Washington, DC 20059. Offers educational administration (Ed D); educational administration and supervision (M Ed, CAGS). Part-time programs available. *Faculty:* 5 full-time (2 women), 7 part-time/adjunct (2 women). *Students:* 33 full-time (26 women), 53 part-time (33 women); includes 72 minority (71 Black or African American, non-Hispanic/Latino; 1 American Indian or Alaska Native, non-Hispanic/Latino), 10 international. Average age 40. 54 applicants, 70% accepted, 10 enrolled. In 2013, 4 master's, 4 doctorates awarded. *Degree requirements:* For master's, comprehensive exam, School Leaders Licensure Assessment, practicum; for doctorate, comprehensive exam, thesis/dissertation, internship; for CAGS, thesis. *Entrance requirements:* For master's, minimum GPA of 2.7; for doctorate, minimum GPA of 3.0. Additional exam requirements/recommendations for international students: Required—TOEFL (minimum score 550 paper-based; 79 iBT). *Application deadline:* For fall admission, 4/15 priority date for domestic students, 4/1 for international students; for spring admission, 11/15 for domestic students. Applications are processed on a rolling basis. Application fee: $45. Electronic applications accepted. *Financial support:* In 2013–14, 4 students received support, including 4 fellowships with full and partial tuition reimbursements available (averaging $15,000 per year); career-related internships or fieldwork, Federal Work-Study, institutionally sponsored loans, scholarships/grants, tuition waivers (full and partial), and unspecified assistantships also available. Financial award application deadline: 3/15; financial award applicants required to submit FAFSA. *Unit head:* Dr. Dawn G. Williams, Chair, Department of Educational Administration and Policy, 202-806-7342, Fax: 202-806-5310, E-mail: dgwilliams@howard.edu. *Application contact:* Naomi Black, Administrative Assistant, Department of Educational Administration and Policy, 202-806-7342, Fax: 202-806-5310, E-mail: nblack@howard.edu.
Website: http://www.howard.edu/schooleducation/departments/elps/ELPS_Overview.html.

Hunter College of the City University of New York, Graduate School, School of Education, Department of Curriculum and Teaching, Program in Educational Supervision and Administration, New York, NY 10065-5085. Offers AC. *Faculty:* 3 full-time (2 women), 9 part-time/adjunct (6 women). *Students:* 1 (woman) full-time, 108 part-time (65 women); includes 26 minority (8 Black or African American, non-Hispanic/Latino; 4 Asian, non-Hispanic/Latino; 14 Hispanic/Latino), 1 international. Average age 34. 65 applicants, 63% accepted, 36 enrolled. In 2013, 22 ACs awarded. *Degree requirements:* For AC, portfolio review. *Entrance requirements:* For degree, minimum B average in graduate course work, teaching certificate, minimum 3 years of full-time teaching experience, interview, 2 letters of support. Additional exam requirements/recommendations for international students: Required—TOEFL. *Application deadline:* For fall admission, 4/1 for domestic students, 2/1 for international students; for spring admission, 11/1 for domestic students, 9/1 for international students. Applications are processed on a rolling basis. Application fee: $125. *Financial support:* Federal Work-Study and tuition waivers (partial) available. Support available to part-time students. *Faculty research:* Supervision of instruction, theory in action, human relations and leadership. *Unit head:* Dr. Marcia Knoll, Coordinator, 212-772-4761, E-mail: mknoll@hunter.cuny.edu. *Application contact:* Milena Solo, Director for Graduate Admissions, 212-772-4482, E-mail: admissions@hunter.cuny.edu.
Website: http://www.hunter.cuny.edu/school-of-education/programs/graduate/administration-supervision.

Idaho State University, Office of Graduate Studies, College of Education, Department of Educational Foundations, Pocatello, ID 83209-8059. Offers child and family studies (M Ed); curriculum leadership (M Ed); education (M Ed); educational administration (M Ed); educational foundations (5th Year Certificate); elementary education (M Ed), including K-12 education, literacy, secondary education. Part-time programs available. *Degree requirements:* For master's, comprehensive exam, thesis optional, oral exam, written exam; for 5th Year Certificate, comprehensive exam, thesis (for some programs), oral exam, written exam. *Entrance requirements:* For master's, GRE General Test or MAT, minimum undergraduate GPA of 3.0; for 5th Year Certificate, GRE General Test, minimum undergraduate GPA of 3.0, master's degree. Additional exam requirements/recommendations for international students: Required—TOEFL (minimum score 550 paper-based; 80 iBT). Electronic applications accepted. *Faculty research:* Child and families studies; business education; special education; math, science, and technology education.

Idaho State University, Office of Graduate Studies, College of Education, Department of Educational Leadership and Instructional Design, Pocatello, ID 83209-8059. Offers educational administration (M Ed, 6th Year Certificate, Ed S); educational leadership (Ed D), including education training and development, educational administration, educational technology, higher education administration; educational leadership and instructional design (PhD); instructional technology (M Ed). Part-time programs available. *Degree requirements:* For master's, comprehensive exam, thesis optional, internship, oral exam or deferred thesis; for doctorate, comprehensive exam, thesis/dissertation, written exam; for other advanced degree, comprehensive exam, thesis (for some programs), written and oral exam. *Entrance requirements:* For master's, MAT, bachelor's degree, minimum GPA of 3.0, 1 year of training experience; for doctorate, GRE General Test or MAT, minimum GPA of 3.0 (undergraduate), 3.5 (graduate); departmental interview; for other advanced degree, GRE General Test, minimum GPA of 3.0, master's degree. Additional exam requirements/recommendations for international students: Required—TOEFL (minimum score 550 paper-based; 80 iBT). Electronic applications accepted. *Faculty research:* Educational leadership, gender issues in education and sport, staff development.

Illinois State University, Graduate School, College of Education, Department of Educational Administration and Foundations, Normal, IL 61790-2200. Offers college student personnel administration (MS); educational administration (MS, MS Ed, Ed D, PhD). *Accreditation:* NCATE. *Degree requirements:* For doctorate, variable foreign language requirement, thesis/dissertation, 2 terms of residency. *Entrance requirements:* For master's, GRE General Test, minimum GPA of 2.6 in last 60 hours of course work; for doctorate, GRE General Test, master's degree or equivalent, minimum GPA of 3.5. *Faculty research:* Illinois Principals Association, special populations professional development and technical assistance project, Illinois state action for education leadership project.

Immaculata University, College of Graduate Studies, Program in Educational Leadership and Administration, Immaculata, PA 19345. Offers educational leadership and administration (MA, Ed D); elementary education (Certificate); school principal (Certificate); school superintendent (Certificate); secondary education (Certificate); special education (Certificate). Part-time and evening/weekend programs available. *Degree requirements:* For master's, comprehensive exam, thesis optional; for doctorate, comprehensive exam, thesis/dissertation. *Entrance requirements:* For master's, GRE or MAT, minimum GPA of 3.0; for doctorate, GRE General Test or MAT, minimum GPA of 3.5. Additional exam requirements/recommendations for international students: Required—TOEFL. Electronic applications accepted. *Faculty research:* Cooperative learning, school-based management, whole language, performance assessment.

Indiana State University, College of Graduate and Professional Studies, College of Education, Department of Educational Leadership, Administration, and Foundations, Terre Haute, IN 47809. Offers educational administration (PhD); leadership in higher education (PhD); school administration (Ed S); school administration and supervision (M Ed); student affairs in higher education (MS). *Accreditation:* NCATE. Part-time and evening/weekend programs available. Terminal master's awarded for partial completion of doctoral program. *Degree requirements:* For master's, thesis; for doctorate, thesis/dissertation. *Entrance requirements:* For master's, GRE General Test, minimum undergraduate GPA of 2.5; for doctorate, GRE General Test, minimum undergraduate GPA of 3.5; for Ed S, GRE General Test, minimum graduate GPA of 3.25. Electronic applications accepted.

Indiana University Bloomington, School of Education, Department of Educational Leadership and Policy Studies, Bloomington, IN 47405-7000. Offers education policy studies (PhD); educational leadership (MS, Ed D, Ed S); higher education (MS, Ed D, PhD); history and philosophy of education (MS); history of education (PhD); international and comparative education (MS, PhD); philosophy of education (PhD); student affairs administration (MS). *Accreditation:* NCATE. Part-time and evening/weekend programs available. *Degree requirements:* For master's, thesis optional; for doctorate, comprehensive exam, thesis/dissertation; for Ed S, comprehensive exam or project. *Entrance requirements:* For master's, doctorate, and Ed S, GRE General Test. Additional exam requirements/recommendations for international students: Required—TOEFL (minimum score 79 iBT). Electronic applications accepted. *Faculty research:* Student engagement at higher education institutions in the nation, Reading First professional development initiative, state finance policy on financial access to higher education, school reform, special needs studies.

Indiana University Northwest, School of Education, Gary, IN 46408-1197. Offers educational leadership (MS Ed); elementary education (MS Ed); secondary education (MS Ed). *Accreditation:* NCATE. Part-time and evening/weekend programs available. *Faculty:* 5 full-time (2 women). *Students:* 19 full-time (17 women), 119 part-time (98 women); includes 79 minority (63 Black or African American, non-Hispanic/Latino; 3 Asian, non-Hispanic/Latino; 12 Hispanic/Latino; 1 Two or more races, non-Hispanic/Latino), 1 international. Average age 37. 25 applicants, 92% accepted, 16 enrolled. In 2013, 69 master's awarded. *Entrance requirements:* For master's, GRE General Test or MAT, minimum GPA of 3.0. *Application deadline:* For fall admission, 7/15 priority date for domestic students; for spring admission, 11/15 for domestic students. *Unit head:* Dr. Stanley E. Wigle, Dean, 219-980-6989, E-mail: swigle@iun.edu. *Application contact:* Admissions Counselor, 219-980-6760, Fax: 219-980-7103.
Website: http://www.iun.edu/education/degrees/masters.htm.

Indiana University of Pennsylvania, School of Graduate Studies and Research, College of Education and Educational Technology, Department of Professional Studies in Education, Certification Program for Principal, Indiana, PA 15705-1087. Offers Certificate. Part-time and evening/weekend programs available. *Faculty:* 19 full-time (12 women), 1 part-time/adjunct (0 women). *Students:* 1 full-time (0 women), 27 part-time (11 women). Average age 35. 35 applicants, 77% accepted, 22 enrolled. *Entrance requirements:* For degree, 2 letters of recommendation. Additional exam requirements/recommendations for international students: Required—TOEFL (minimum score 540 paper-based). *Application deadline:* For fall admission, 7/1 priority date for domestic students; for spring admission, 11/1 for domestic students. Applications are processed on a rolling basis. Application fee: $50. Electronic applications accepted. *Expenses:* Tuition, state resident: full-time $3978; part-time $442 per credit. Tuition, nonresident: full-time $5967; part-time $663 per credit. *Required fees:* $2080; $115.55 per credit. $93 per semester. Tuition and fees vary according to degree level and program. *Financial support:* Career-related internships or fieldwork, Federal Work-Study, and scholarships/grants available. Support available to part-time students. Financial award application deadline: 4/15; financial award applicants required to submit FAFSA. *Unit head:* Dr. Cathy Kauffman, Graduate Coordinator, 724-357-3928, E-mail: ckaufman@iup.edu. *Application contact:* Paula Stossel, Assistant Dean for Administration, 724-357-4511, E-mail: graduate-admissions@iup.edu.
Website: http://www.iup.edu/pse/programs/principalcert/default.aspx.

Indiana University of Pennsylvania, School of Graduate Studies and Research, College of Education and Educational Technology, Department of Professional Studies in Education, Doctoral Program in Administration and Leadership Studies, Indiana, PA 15705-1087. Offers D Ed. Program also offered jointly with East Stroudsburg University of Pennsylvania. Part-time and evening/weekend programs available. *Faculty:* 19 full-time (12 women), 1 part-time/adjunct (0 women). *Students:* 4 full-time (0 women), 55 part-time (28 women); includes 10 minority (5 Black or African American, non-Hispanic/Latino; 1 Hispanic/Latino; 1 Native Hawaiian or other Pacific Islander, non-Hispanic/Latino; 3 Two or more races, non-Hispanic/Latino). Average age 41. 5 applicants. In 2013, 16 doctorates awarded. *Degree requirements:* For doctorate, one foreign language, comprehensive exam, thesis/dissertation, written exam. *Entrance requirements:* For doctorate, 2 letters of recommendation, interview. *Application deadline:* Applications are processed on a rolling basis. Application fee: $50. Electronic applications accepted. *Expenses:* Tuition, state resident: full-time $3978; part-time $442 per credit. Tuition, nonresident: full-time $5967; part-time $663 per credit. *Required fees:* $2080; $115.55 per credit. $93 per semester. Tuition and fees vary according to degree level and program. *Financial support:* In 2013–14, 11 fellowships with full tuition reimbursements (averaging $545 per year), 3 research assistantships with full and partial tuition reimbursements (averaging $5,153 per year) were awarded; teaching assistantships, career-related internships or fieldwork, Federal Work-Study,

scholarships/grants, and unspecified assistantships also available. Support available to part-time students. Financial award application deadline: 4/15; financial award applicants required to submit FAFSA. *Unit head:* Dr. Robert Millward, Graduate Coordinator, 724-357-5593, E-mail: robert.millward@iup.edu. *Application contact:* Paula Stossel, Assistant Dean for Administration, 724-357-4511, E-mail: graduate-admissions@iup.edu.
Website: http://www.iup.edu/upper.aspx?id-92694.

Indiana University of Pennsylvania, School of Graduate Studies and Research, College of Humanities and Social Sciences, Department of Sociology, Program in Administration and Leadership Studies, Indiana, PA 15705-1087. Offers PhD. Part-time and evening/weekend programs available. *Faculty:* 13 full-time (7 women). *Students:* 3 full-time (2 women), 100 part-time (52 women); includes 10 minority (7 Black or African American, non-Hispanic/Latino; 1 Asian, non-Hispanic/Latino; 2 Hispanic/Latino), 1 international. Average age 43. 54 applicants, 31% accepted, 16 enrolled. In 2013, 14 doctorates awarded. *Degree requirements:* For doctorate, comprehensive exam, thesis/dissertation. *Entrance requirements:* For doctorate, GRE, resume, writing sample, 3 letters of recommendation. Additional exam requirements/recommendations for international students: Required—TOEFL (minimum score 540 paper-based). *Application deadline:* For fall admission, 2/15 priority date for domestic students. Applications are processed on a rolling basis. Application fee: $50. Electronic applications accepted. *Expenses:* Tuition, state resident: full-time $3978; part-time $442 per credit. Tuition, nonresident: full-time $5967; part-time $663 per credit. *Required fees:* $2080; $115.55 per credit. $93 per semester. Tuition and fees vary according to degree level and program. *Financial support:* In 2013–14, 5 fellowships with full tuition reimbursements (averaging $1,202 per year), 8 research assistantships with full and partial tuition reimbursements (averaging $4,244 per year), 2 teaching assistantships with partial tuition reimbursements (averaging $22,848 per year) were awarded; career-related internships or fieldwork, Federal Work-Study, scholarships/grants, and unspecified assistantships also available. Support available to part-time students. Financial award application deadline: 4/15; financial award applicants required to submit FAFSA. *Unit head:* Dr. John Anderson, Graduate Coordinator, 724-357-1291, E-mail: janderson@iup.edu. *Application contact:* Paula Stossel, Assistant Dean, 724-357-2222, Fax: 724-357-4862, E-mail: graduate-admissions@iup.edu.
Website: http://www.iup.edu/grad/ALS/default.aspx.

Indiana University–Purdue University Fort Wayne, College of Education and Public Policy, Department of Professional Studies, Fort Wayne, IN 46805-1499. Offers counselor education (MS Ed); couple and family counseling (MS Ed); educational leadership (MS Ed); school counseling (MS Ed); special education (MS Ed, Certificate). Part-time programs available. *Faculty:* 7 full-time (6 women). *Students:* 5 full-time (2 women), 100 part-time (80 women); includes 11 minority (8 Black or African American, non-Hispanic/Latino; 1 Asian, non-Hispanic/Latino; 2 Hispanic/Latino), 1 international. Average age 32. 14 applicants, 100% accepted, 9 enrolled. In 2013, 57 master's awarded. *Degree requirements:* For master's, comprehensive exam, practicum, internship, portfolio. *Entrance requirements:* For master's, minimum GPA of 2.5, three professional letters of recommendation. Additional exam requirements/recommendations for international students: Required—TOEFL (minimum score 550 paper-based; 79 iBT). *Application deadline:* For fall admission, 4/1 priority date for domestic and international students. Applications are processed on a rolling basis. Application fee: $55. *Financial support:* In 2013–14, 1 research assistantship with partial tuition reimbursement (averaging $13,322 per year), 1 teaching assistantship with partial tuition reimbursement (averaging $13,322 per year) were awarded; scholarships/grants also available. Support available to part-time students. Financial award application deadline: 3/1; financial award applicants required to submit FAFSA. *Faculty research:* Perceptions of children and early adolescents at-risk. *Unit head:* Dr. Jane Leatherman, Acting Chair, 260-481-5742, Fax: 260-481-5408, E-mail: leatherj@ipfw.edu. *Application contact:* Vicky L. Schmidt, Graduate Recorder, 260-481-6450, Fax: 260-481-5408, E-mail: schmidt@ipfw.edu.
Website: http://new.ipfw.edu/education.

Indiana University–Purdue University Indianapolis, School of Education, Indianapolis, IN 46202-2896. Offers computer education (Certificate); curriculum and instruction (MS); early childhood (MS); educational leadership (MS, Certificate); English as a second language (Certificate); higher education and student affairs (MS); kindergarten (Certificate); language education (MS); reading (Certificate); school counseling (MS); special education (MS, Certificate). Part-time and evening/weekend programs available. *Faculty:* 41 full-time, 80 part-time/adjunct. *Students:* 113 full-time (78 women), 263 part-time (200 women); includes 88 minority (51 Black or African American, non-Hispanic/Latino; 1 American Indian or Alaska Native, non-Hispanic/Latino; 10 Asian, non-Hispanic/Latino; 19 Hispanic/Latino; 7 Two or more races, non-Hispanic/Latino), 5 international. Average age 33. 93 applicants, 54% accepted, 40 enrolled. In 2013, 179 master's awarded. *Degree requirements:* For master's, thesis optional. *Entrance requirements:* For master's, GRE General Test, minimum GPA of 3.0. Additional exam requirements/recommendations for international students: Required—TOEFL. *Application deadline:* For fall admission, 5/1 priority date for domestic students; for spring admission, 11/1 for domestic students. Application fee: $55 ($65 for international students). *Financial support:* Fellowships, research assistantships with partial tuition reimbursements, teaching assistantships, Federal Work-Study, institutionally sponsored loans, scholarships/grants, and tuition waivers (partial) available. Support available to part-time students. *Faculty research:* Teachers in the process of change, learning cycles, children's concepts of science. *Total annual research expenditures:* $614,458. *Unit head:* Dr. Pat Rogan, Executive Associate Dean, 317-274-6862, E-mail: progan@iupui.edu. *Application contact:* Donnella Dillon, Graduate Admissions Coordinator, 317-274-0645, E-mail: dmdillon@iupui.edu.
Website: http://education.iupui.edu/.

Indiana Wesleyan University, College of Adult and Professional Studies, School of Educational Leadership, Marion, IN 46953. Offers M Ed, Ed S. *Accreditation:* NCATE. Part-time and evening/weekend programs available. Postbaccalaureate distance learning degree programs offered (no on-campus study). *Degree requirements:* For master's, portfolio. *Entrance requirements:* For master's, minimum GPA of 2.75, teaching experience, teaching license. Additional exam requirements/recommendations for international students: Required—TOEFL (minimum score 550 paper-based). Electronic applications accepted. *Expenses: Tuition:* Full-time $8712; part-time $484 per credit hour. *Required fees:* $1673; $105 per credit hour. Tuition and fees vary according to course load, degree level, campus/location and program. *Faculty research:* Mentoring, performance-based assessments, faith integration, integration of technology, program assessment.

Instituto Tecnologico de Santo Domingo, Graduate School, Area of Humanities and Social Sciences, Santo Domingo, Dominican Republic. Offers accounting (Certificate); adult education (Certificate); applied linguistics (MA); economics (MA); education (M Ed); educational psychology (MA, Certificate); gender and development (MA, Certificate); humanistic studies (MA); international marketing management (Certificate); international relations in the Caribbean basin (Certificate); intervention systems in family therapy (MA); linguistic and literary communication (Certificate); pedagogical support (MA); social science education (M Ed); sustainable human development (MA); terminal illness and death psychology (Certificate); youth and adult education (M Ed).

Instituto Tecnológico y de Estudios Superiores de Monterrey, Campus Central de Veracruz, Graduate Programs, Córdoba, Mexico. Offers administration (MA); administration of information technologies (MTI); computer sciences (MCC); education (MEE); educational institution administration (MAD); educational technology (MTE); electronic commerce (MCE); finance (MAF); humanistic studies (MEH); international business for Latin America (MNL); marketing (MMT); science (MCP). Part-time and evening/weekend programs available. Postbaccalaureate distance learning degree programs offered (minimal on-campus study). *Degree requirements:* For master's, thesis (for some programs). *Entrance requirements:* For master's, PAEP College Board. Electronic applications accepted.

Instituto Tecnológico y de Estudios Superiores de Monterrey, Campus Ciudad Juárez, Program in Educational Administration, Ciudad Juárez, Mexico. Offers MEA.

Instituto Tecnológico y de Estudios Superiores de Monterrey, Campus Estado de México, Professional and Graduate Division, Estado de Mexico, Mexico. Offers administration of information technologies (MITA); architecture (M Arch); business administration (GMBA, MBA); computer sciences (MCS, PhD); education (M Ed); educational institution administration (MAD); educational technology and innovation (PhD); electronic commerce (MEC); environmental systems (MS); finance (MAF); humanistic studies (MHS); information sciences and knowledge management (MISKM); information systems (MS); manufacturing systems (MS); marketing (MEM); quality systems and productivity (MS); science and materials engineering (PhD); telecommunications management (MTM). Part-time programs available. Postbaccalaureate distance learning degree programs offered (minimal on-campus study). *Degree requirements:* For master's, one foreign language, thesis (for some programs); for doctorate, one foreign language, thesis/dissertation. *Entrance requirements:* For master's, E-PAEP 500, interview; for doctorate, E-PAEP 500, research proposal. Additional exam requirements/recommendations for international students: Required—TOEFL (minimum score 550 paper-based). *Faculty research:* Surface treatments by plasmas, mechanical properties, robotics, graphical computing, mechatronics security protocols.

Instituto Tecnológico y de Estudios Superiores de Monterrey, Campus Irapuato, Graduate Programs, Irapuato, Mexico. Offers administration (MBA); administration of information technology (MAIT); administration of telecommunications (MAT); architecture (M Arch); computer science (MCS); education (M Ed); educational administration (MEA); educational innovation and technology (DEIT); educational technology (MET); electronic commerce (MBA); environmental administration and planning (MEAP); environmental systems (MES); finances (MBA); humanistic studies (MHS); international management for Latin American executives (MIMLAE); library and information science (MLIS); manufacturing quality management (MMQM); marketing research (MBA).

Inter American University of Puerto Rico, Aguadilla Campus, Graduate School, Aguadilla, PR 00605. Offers accounting (MBA); counseling psychology specializing in family (MS); criminal justice (MA); educative management and leadership (MA); elementary education (M Ed); finance (MBA); human resources (MBA); industrial management (MBA); management information systems (MBA); marketing (MBA). Part-time and evening/weekend programs available. *Degree requirements:* For master's, comprehensive exam. *Entrance requirements:* For master's, EXADEP, 2 letters of recommendation, minimum GPA of 2.5. Electronic applications accepted.

Inter American University of Puerto Rico, Arecibo Campus, Programs in Education, Arecibo, PR 00614-4050. Offers administration and educational supervision (MA Ed); counseling and guidance (MA Ed); curriculum and teaching (MA Ed), including biology education, English as a second language, history education, math education, Spanish; elementary education (MA Ed). *Degree requirements:* For master's, comprehensive exam, thesis optional. *Entrance requirements:* For master's, GRE, EXADEP, bachelor's degree in education or teaching license (administration and supervision) or courses in education and psychology (counseling and guidance), minimum GPA of 2.5 in last 60 credits.

Inter American University of Puerto Rico, Barranquitas Campus, Program in Education, Barranquitas, PR 00794. Offers curriculum and teaching (M Ed), including biology education, English as a second language, history education, mathematics education, Spanish; educational leadership and management (MA); elementary education (M Ed); information and library service technology (M Ed); special education (MA). *Degree requirements:* For master's, comprehensive exam, thesis optional. *Entrance requirements:* For master's, EXADEP, letter of recommendation. Electronic applications accepted.

Inter American University of Puerto Rico, Metropolitan Campus, Graduate Programs, Program in Education, San Juan, PR 00919-1293. Offers curriculum and instruction (Ed D); educational administration (Ed D); guidance and counseling (MA, Ed D); special education administration (Ed D). *Degree requirements:* For doctorate, comprehensive exam, thesis/dissertation. *Entrance requirements:* For doctorate, GRE, MAT, or EXADEP. Electronic applications accepted.

Iona College, School of Arts and Science, Department of Education, New Rochelle, NY 10801-1890. Offers adolescence education: biology (MS Ed, MST); adolescence education: English (MS Ed, MST); adolescence education: Italian (MS Ed, MST); adolescence education: mathematics (MS Ed, MST); adolescence education: social studies (MS Ed, MST); adolescence education: Spanish (MS Ed, MST); adolescence special education 5-12 (MST); adolescence special education and literacy (MS Ed); childhood and special education (MST); childhood education (MST); early childhood and childhood (MST); educational leadership (MS Ed); literacy education: birth-grade 6 (MS Ed). *Accreditation:* NCATE. Part-time and evening/weekend programs available. *Faculty:* 11 full-time (9 women), 7 part-time/adjunct (6 women). *Students:* 34 full-time (25 women), 61 part-time (47 women); includes 5 minority (2 Asian, non-Hispanic/Latino; 3 Hispanic/Latino), 1 international. Average age 25. 27 applicants, 93% accepted, 16 enrolled. In 2013, 54 master's awarded. *Degree requirements:* For master's, thesis or alternative. *Entrance requirements:* For master's, minimum GPA of 3.0, NY State teaching certificate (for all MS Ed programs). Additional exam requirements/recommendations for international students: Required—TOEFL (minimum score 550 paper-based; 80 iBT), IELTS (minimum score 6.5). *Application deadline:* For fall admission, 8/1 priority date for domestic students, 5/1 priority date for international students; for spring admission, 1/1 priority date for domestic students, 9/1 priority date for international students. Applications are processed on a rolling basis. Application fee: $50. Electronic applications accepted. *Expenses: Tuition:* Part-time $948 per credit. *Required fees:* $235 per term. *Financial support:* In 2013–14, 84 students received support. Unspecified assistantships available. Support available to part-time students. Financial award application deadline: 4/15; financial award applicants required to submit FAFSA. *Faculty research:* Reading/writing, educational technology, administration, early literacy assessment, literacy development. *Unit head:* Margaret Smith, PhD, Chair, 914-633-2210, Fax: 914-633-2608, E-mail: msmith@iona.edu. *Application contact:* Veronica

Jarek-Prinz, Director, Graduate Admissions, 914-633-2420, Fax: 914-633-2277, E-mail: vjarekprinz@iona.edu.
Website: http://www.iona.edu/Academics/School-of-Arts-Science/Departments/Education/Graduate-Programs.aspx.

Iowa State University of Science and Technology, Department of Educational Leadership and Policy Studies, Ames, IA 50011. Offers counselor education (M Ed, MS); educational administration (M Ed, MS); educational leadership (PhD); higher education (M Ed, MS); organizational learning and human resource development (M Ed, MS); research and evaluation (MS); student affairs (MS). *Degree requirements:* For master's, thesis or alternative; for doctorate, thesis/dissertation. *Entrance requirements:* For master's and doctorate, GRE General Test. Additional exam requirements/recommendations for international students: Required—TOEFL (minimum score 560 paper-based; 83 iBT), IELTS (minimum score 6.5). Electronic applications accepted.

Jackson State University, Graduate School, College of Education and Human Development, Department of Educational Leadership, Jackson, MS 39217. Offers education administration (Ed S); educational administration (MS Ed, PhD); secondary education (MS Ed, Ed S), including educational technology (MS Ed). *Accreditation:* NCATE. Part-time and evening/weekend programs available. *Degree requirements:* For master's, comprehensive exam, thesis or alternative; for doctorate, comprehensive exam, thesis/dissertation; for Ed S, comprehensive exam, thesis. *Entrance requirements:* For master's, GRE General Test; for doctorate, MAT, GRE, teaching experience. Additional exam requirements/recommendations for international students: Required—TOEFL (minimum score 520 paper-based; 67 iBT).

Jacksonville State University, College of Graduate Studies and Continuing Education, College of Education and Professional Studies, Program in Educational Administration, Jacksonville, AL 36265-1602. Offers MS Ed, Ed S. *Accreditation:* NCATE. Part-time and evening/weekend programs available. *Degree requirements:* For master's, comprehensive exam, thesis (for some programs). *Entrance requirements:* For master's, GRE General Test or MAT. Additional exam requirements/recommendations for international students: Required—TOEFL (minimum score 61 iBT). Electronic applications accepted.

Jacksonville University, School of Education, Jacksonville, FL 32211. Offers educational leadership (M Ed); instructional leadership and organizational development (M Ed); sport management and leadership (M Ed). Part-time and evening/weekend programs available. *Degree requirements:* For master's, comprehensive exam. *Entrance requirements:* For master's, GRE General Test, minimum GPA of 3.0. Additional exam requirements/recommendations for international students: Required—TOEFL (minimum score 550 paper-based), TWE. *Expenses:* Contact institution.

James Madison University, The Graduate School, College of Education, Adult Education Department, Program in Educational Leadership, Harrisonburg, VA 22807. Offers M Ed. *Accreditation:* NCATE. Part-time and evening/weekend programs available. *Students:* 1 part-time (0 women). Average age 27. *Entrance requirements:* For master's, GRE General Test. Additional exam requirements/recommendations for international students: Required—TOEFL. *Application deadline:* For fall admission, 5/1 priority date for domestic students; for spring admission, 9/1 priority date for domestic students. Applications are processed on a rolling basis. Application fee: $55. Electronic applications accepted. *Financial support:* Federal Work-Study available. Financial award application deadline: 3/1; financial award applicants required to submit FAFSA. *Unit head:* Dr. Diane Foucar-Szocki, Academic Unit Head, 540-568-6794. *Application contact:* Lynette M. Bible, Director of Graduate Admissions, 540-568-6395, Fax: 540-568-7860, E-mail: biblelm@jmu.edu.

John Brown University, Graduate Business Programs, Siloam Springs, AR 72761-2121. Offers global continuous improvement (MBA); higher education leadership (MS); international community development leadership (MS); leadership and ethics (MBA, MS). *Accreditation:* ACBSP. Part-time and evening/weekend programs available. Postbaccalaureate distance learning degree programs offered (minimal on-campus study). *Faculty:* 6 full-time (1 woman), 29 part-time/adjunct (8 women). *Students:* 23 full-time (13 women), 210 part-time (102 women); includes 41 minority (14 Black or African American, non-Hispanic/Latino; 5 American Indian or Alaska Native, non-Hispanic/Latino; 3 Asian, non-Hispanic/Latino; 11 Hispanic/Latino; 8 Two or more races, non-Hispanic/Latino), 3 international. Average age 34. 121 applicants, 98% accepted, 99 enrolled. *Entrance requirements:* For master's, MAT, GMAT or GRE if undergraduate GPA is less than 3.0, recommendation forms from three people, 200-word essay describing professional plans and reason for seeking acceptance. Additional exam requirements/recommendations for international students: Required—TOEFL (minimum score 550 paper-based; 70 iBT). *Application deadline:* Applications are processed on a rolling basis. Application fee: $35 ($100 for international students). Electronic applications accepted. *Expenses: Tuition:* Part-time $515 per credit hour. *Financial support:* Fellowships with full tuition reimbursements, scholarships/grants, and unspecified assistantships available. Financial award applicants required to submit FAFSA. *Unit head:* Dr. Joe Walenciak, Program Director, 479-524-7431, E-mail: jwalenci@jbu.edu. *Application contact:* Brent Young, Graduate Business Representative, 479-524-7450, E-mail: byoung@jbu.edu.
Website: http://www.jbu.edu/grad/business/.

John Carroll University, Graduate School, Department of Education and Allied Studies, Program in Administration, University Heights, OH 44118-4581. Offers M Ed, MA. *Accreditation:* NCATE. Part-time and evening/weekend programs available. *Degree requirements:* For master's, comprehensive exam, research essay or thesis (MA only). *Entrance requirements:* For master's, GRE General Test or MAT, minimum GPA of 2.75, interview, teachers license, 2 years experience. Electronic applications accepted.

John Hancock University, Program in Education, Oakbrook Terrace, IL 60181. Offers early childhood education (MA Ed); education (MA Ed); teacher as a leader (MA Ed). *Degree requirements:* For master's, thesis or capstone.

Johns Hopkins University, School of Education, Certificate Programs in Education, Baltimore, MD 21218-2699. Offers advanced methods for differentiated instruction and inclusive education (Certificate); applied behavior analysis (Certificate); counseling (CAGS); data-based decision making and organizational improvement (Certificate); early intervention/preschool special education specialist (Certificate); education leadership for independent schools (Certificate); education of students with autism and other pervasive developmental disorders (Certificate); evidence-based teaching in the health professions (Certificate); gifted education (Certificate); K-8 mathematics lead-teacher (Certificate); K-8 STEM education lead-teacher (Certificate); leadership for school, family, and community collaboration (Certificate); leadership in technology integration (Certificate); mental health counseling (Certificate); mind, brain, and teaching (Certificate); school administration and supervision (Certificate); urban education (Certificate). Part-time and evening/weekend programs available. Postbaccalaureate distance learning degree programs offered (no on-campus study). *Students:* 7 full-time (4 women), 216 part-time (169 women); includes 66 minority (35 Black or African American, non-Hispanic/Latino; 17 Asian, non-Hispanic/Latino; 6 Hispanic/Latino; 8 Two or more races, non-Hispanic/Latino), 6 international. Average age 35. 257 applicants, 81% accepted, 62 enrolled. In 2013, 202 CAGSs awarded. *Entrance requirements:* For degree, bachelor's degree from regionally- or nationally-accredited institution (master's for some programs), minimum GPA of 3.0 in all previous programs of study, official transcripts from all post-secondary institutions attended, essay, curriculum vitae/resume, minimum of two letters of recommendation. Additional exam requirements/recommendations for international students: Required—TOEFL (minimum score 600 paper-based; 100 iBT) or IELTS (minimum score 7). *Application deadline:* For fall admission, 4/1 for domestic students; for spring admission, 10/1 for domestic students; for summer admission, 2/1 for domestic students. Application fee: $80. Electronic applications accepted. *Financial support:* Application deadline: 6/1; applicants required to submit FAFSA. *Unit head:* Dr. David A. Andrews, Dean, 410-516-7820, Fax: 410-516-6697, E-mail: davidandrews@jhu.edu. *Application contact:* Catherine Wilson, Associate Director of Admissions, 410-516-9797, Fax: 410-516-9799, E-mail: soe.info@jhu.edu.

Johns Hopkins University, School of Education, Doctoral Programs in Education, Baltimore, MD 21218-2699. Offers Ed D, PhD. Part-time and evening/weekend programs available. Postbaccalaureate distance learning degree programs offered (no on-campus study). *Students:* 19 full-time (16 women), 80 part-time (53 women); includes 33 minority (18 Black or African American, non-Hispanic/Latino; 4 Asian, non-Hispanic/Latino; 8 Hispanic/Latino; 3 Two or more races, non-Hispanic/Latino), 3 international. Average age 38. 202 applicants, 38% accepted, 58 enrolled. In 2013, 4 doctorates awarded. *Degree requirements:* For doctorate, comprehensive exam (for some programs), thesis/dissertation. *Entrance requirements:* For doctorate, GRE (for PhD students only), master's degree from regionally- or nationally-accredited institution, minimum GPA of 3.0 (for EdD only), official transcripts from all post-secondary institutions attended, three letters of recommendation, curriculum vitae/resume, personal statement. Additional exam requirements/recommendations for international students: Required—TOEFL (minimum score 600 paper-based; 100 iBT) or IELTS (minimum score 7). Application fee: $80. Electronic applications accepted. *Financial support:* In 2013–14, 13 fellowships, 4 research assistantships, 1 teaching assistantship were awarded. Financial award application deadline: 6/1; financial award applicants required to submit FAFSA. *Unit head:* Dr. David A. Andrews, Dean, 410-516-7820, Fax: 410-516-6697, E-mail: davidandrews@jhu.edu. *Application contact:* Catherine Wilson, Associate Director of Admissions, 410-516-9797, Fax: 410-516-9799, E-mail: soe.info@jhu.edu.

Johns Hopkins University, School of Education, Master's Programs in Education, Baltimore, MD 21218-2699. Offers counseling (MS), including mental health counseling, school counseling; education (MS), including educational studies, gifted education, reading, school administration and supervision, technology for educators; elementary education (MAT); health professions (M Ed); intelligence analysis (MS); management (MS); secondary education (MAT); special education (MS), including early childhood special education, general special education studies, mild to moderate disabilities, severe disabilities. Part-time and evening/weekend programs available. Postbaccalaureate distance learning degree programs offered (no on-campus study). *Students:* 183 full-time (123 women), 1,001 part-time (757 women); includes 380 minority (160 Black or African American, non-Hispanic/Latino; 4 American Indian or Alaska Native, non-Hispanic/Latino; 91 Asian, non-Hispanic/Latino; 78 Hispanic/Latino; 4 Native Hawaiian or other Pacific Islander, non-Hispanic/Latino; 43 Two or more races, non-Hispanic/Latino), 28 international. Average age 28. 508 applicants, 90% accepted, 337 enrolled. In 2013, 565 degrees awarded. *Degree requirements:* For master's, comprehensive exam (for some programs), portfolio, capstone project and/or internship; PRAXIS II (for teacher preparation programs that lead to licensure). *Entrance requirements:* For master's, GRE (for full-time programs only); PRAXIS I or equivalent (for teacher preparation programs that lead to licensure), bachelor's degree from regionally- or nationally-accredited institution, minimum GPA of 3.0 in all previous programs of study, official transcripts from all post-secondary institutions attended, essay, curriculum vitae/resume, minimum of two letters of recommendation. Additional exam requirements/recommendations for international students: Required—TOEFL (minimum score 600 paper-based; 100 iBT) or IELTS (minimum score 7). *Application deadline:* For fall admission, 4/1 for domestic and international students; for spring admission, 10/1 for domestic and international students; for summer admission, 2/1 for domestic and international students. Application fee: $80. Electronic applications accepted. *Financial support:* Application deadline: 6/1; applicants required to submit FAFSA. *Unit head:* Dr. David A. Andrews, Dean, 410-516-7820, Fax: 410-516-6697, E-mail: davidandrews@jhu.edu. *Application contact:* Catherine Wilson, Associate Director of Admissions, 410-516-9797, Fax: 410-516-9799, E-mail: soe.info@jhu.edu.

Johnson & Wales University, Graduate School, Ed D Program in Educational Leadership, Providence, RI 02903-3703. Offers Ed D. Part-time programs available. *Degree requirements:* For doctorate, thesis/dissertation. *Entrance requirements:* For doctorate, MAT, minimum GPA of 3.25; master's degree in appropriate field from accredited institution. Additional exam requirements/recommendations for international students: Required—TOEFL (minimum score 550 paper-based); Recommended—IELTS, TWE. *Faculty research:* Site-based management, collaborative learning, technology and education, K-16 education.

Jones International University, School of Education, Centennial, CO 80112. Offers adult education (M Ed); corporate training and knowledge management (M Ed); curriculum and instruction (M Ed), including elementary teacher licensure, secondary teacher licensure; e-learning technology and design (M Ed); educational leadership and administration (M Ed); educational leadership and administration: principal and administrator licensure (M Ed); elementary curriculum instruction and assessment (M Ed); higher education leadership and administration (M Ed); K-12 instructional technology (M Ed); K-12 instructional technology: teacher licensure (M Ed); secondary curriculum instruction and assessment (M Ed); technology and design (M Ed). Part-time and evening/weekend programs available. Postbaccalaureate distance learning degree programs offered (no on-campus study). *Entrance requirements:* For master's, minimum cumulative GPA of 2.5. Additional exam requirements/recommendations for international students: Recommended—TOEFL (minimum score 550 paper-based). Electronic applications accepted.

Kansas State University, Graduate School, College of Education, Department of Curriculum and Instruction, Manhattan, KS 66506. Offers career and technical education (Ed D, PhD); curriculum studies (Ed D, PhD); digital teaching and learning (MS); educational computing, design and online learning (MS); educational technology (Ed D, PhD); elementary/middle level curriculum and instruction (MS); English as a second language (MS); language/diversity education (Ed D, PhD); literacy education (Ed D, PhD); mathematics education (Ed D, PhD); middle level/secondary curriculum and instruction (MS); reading and language arts (MS); reading specialist endorsement (MS); science education (Ed D, PhD); social science education (Ed D, PhD); teacher education (Ed D, PhD); teacher leader/school improvement (MS, Ed D). *Accreditation:* NCATE. Part-time programs available. Postbaccalaureate distance learning degree programs offered (minimal on-campus study). *Faculty:* 18 full-time (13 women), 7 part-time/adjunct (4 women). *Students:* 39 full-time (23 women), 122 part-time (94 women); includes 19 minority (3 Black or African American, non-Hispanic/Latino; 2 Asian, non-Hispanic/Latino; 12 Hispanic/Latino; 2 Two or more races, non-Hispanic/Latino), 12 international. Average age 36. 80 applicants, 50% accepted, 34 enrolled. In 2013, 40 master's, 13 doctorates awarded. *Degree requirements:* For master's, comprehensive exam, portfolio, project, report or thesis; for doctorate, comprehensive exam, thesis/

dissertation, preliminary exam. *Entrance requirements:* For master's, minimum GPA of 3.0, letters of recommendation; for doctorate, GRE, minimum GPA of 3.0, letters of recommendation, evidence of scholarly writing. Additional exam requirements/recommendations for international students: Required—TOEFL (minimum score 550 paper-based; 80 iBT). *Application deadline:* For fall admission, 3/1 priority date for domestic students, 2/1 priority date for international students; for spring admission, 10/1 priority date for domestic students, 8/1 priority date for international students. Applications are processed on a rolling basis. Application fee: $50 ($75 for international students). Electronic applications accepted. *Financial support:* In 2013–14, 1 research assistantship (averaging $16,900 per year), 8 teaching assistantships (averaging $12,466 per year) were awarded; career-related internships or fieldwork, institutionally sponsored loans, and scholarships/grants also available. Support available to part-time students. Financial award application deadline: 3/1; financial award applicants required to submit FAFSA. *Faculty research:* Literacy and technology, critical race theory and diversity, achievement gaps, school improvement, teacher education. *Total annual research expenditures:* $543,677. *Unit head:* Dr. Todd Goodson, Chair, 785-532-5904, Fax: 785-532-7304, E-mail: tgoodson@ksu.edu. *Application contact:* Dona Deam, Application Contact, 785-532-5595, Fax: 785-532-7304, E-mail: ddeam@ksu.edu.
Website: http://www.coe.k-state.edu/departments/edci/.

Kansas State University, Graduate School, College of Education, Department of Educational Leadership, Manhattan, KS 66506. Offers adult, occupational and continuing education (MS, Ed D, PhD); educational leadership (MS, Ed D). *Accreditation:* NCATE. *Faculty:* 11 full-time (6 women), 3 part-time/adjunct (2 women). *Students:* 46 full-time (13 women), 206 part-time (106 women); includes 33 minority (14 Black or African American, non-Hispanic/Latino; 2 Asian, non-Hispanic/Latino; 12 Hispanic/Latino; 5 Two or more races, non-Hispanic/Latino), 4 international. Average age 39. 76 applicants, 72% accepted, 48 enrolled. In 2013, 94 master's, 7 doctorates awarded. *Degree requirements:* For master's, comprehensive exam; for doctorate, comprehensive exam, thesis/dissertation. *Entrance requirements:* For master's, minimum undergraduate GPA of 3.0; for doctorate, GRE General Test, minimum GPA of 3.0 in last 60 hours. Additional exam requirements/recommendations for international students: Required—TOEFL. *Application deadline:* For fall admission, 2/1 priority date for domestic and international students; for spring admission, 8/1 priority date for domestic and international students. Applications are processed on a rolling basis. Application fee: $50 ($75 for international students). Electronic applications accepted. *Financial support:* Career-related internships or fieldwork, institutionally sponsored loans, and scholarships/grants available. Support available to part-time students. Financial award application deadline: 3/1; financial award applicants required to submit FAFSA. *Faculty research:* Educational law, school finance, school facilities, organizational leadership, adult learning, distance learning/education. *Total annual research expenditures:* $7,569. *Unit head:* David C. Thompson, Head, 785-532-5535, Fax: 785-532-7304, E-mail: thomsond@ksu.edu. *Application contact:* Dona Deam, Applications Contact, 785-532-5595, Fax: 785-532-7304, E-mail: ddeam@ksu.edu.
Website: http://www.coe.k-state.edu/departments/edlea/index.html.

Kaplan University, Davenport Campus, School of Higher Education Studies, Davenport, IA 52807-2095. Offers college administration and leadership (MS); college teaching and learning (MS); student services (MS). Part-time and evening/weekend programs available. Postbaccalaureate distance learning degree programs offered (no on-campus study). *Entrance requirements:* Additional exam requirements/recommendations for international students: Required—TOEFL (minimum score 550 paper-based; 80 iBT).

Kean University, Nathan Weiss Graduate College, Program in Educational Administration, Union, NJ 07083. Offers school business administration (MA); supervisors and principals (MA); supervisors, principals and school business administrators (MA). *Accreditation:* NCATE. Part-time programs available. *Faculty:* 7 full-time (4 women). *Students:* 4 full-time (2 women), 148 part-time (89 women); includes 46 minority (24 Black or African American, non-Hispanic/Latino; 4 Asian, non-Hispanic/Latino; 18 Hispanic/Latino), 1 international. Average age 36. 99 applicants, 99% accepted, 59 enrolled. In 2013, 49 master's awarded. *Degree requirements:* For master's, comprehensive exam (for some programs), portfolio, field experience, research component, internship, teaching experience. *Entrance requirements:* For master's, GRE General Test or MAT, minimum GPA of 3.0; New Jersey or out-of-state Standard Instructional or Educational Services Certificate; one year of experience under the appropriate certificate; official transcripts from all institutions attended; two letters of recommendation; personal statement; professional resume/curriculum vitae. Additional exam requirements/recommendations for international students: Required—TOEFL (minimum score 550 paper-based; 79 iBT). *Application deadline:* For fall admission, 6/1 for domestic and international students; for spring admission, 12/1 for domestic and international students. Applications are processed on a rolling basis. Application fee: $75 ($150 for international students). Electronic applications accepted. *Expenses:* Tuition, state resident: full-time $12,099; part-time $589 per credit. Tuition, nonresident: full-time $16,399; part-time $722 per credit. *Required fees:* $3050; $139 per credit. Part-time tuition and fees vary according to course level, course load, degree level and program. *Financial support:* In 2013–14, research assistantships with full tuition reimbursements (averaging $3,713 per year) were awarded; unspecified assistantships also available. Financial award applicants required to submit FAFSA. *Unit head:* Dr. Leila Sadeghi, Program Coordinator, 908-737-5977, E-mail: lsadeghi@kean.edu. *Application contact:* Ann-Marie Kay, Assistant Director of Graduate Admissions, 908-737-5922, Fax: 908-737-5925, E-mail: akay@kean.edu.
Website: http://grad.kean.edu/edleadership.

Kean University, Nathan Weiss Graduate College, Program in Educational Leadership, Union, NJ 07083. Offers Ed D. Part-time programs available. *Faculty:* 7 full-time (4 women). *Students:* 1 full-time (0 women), 58 part-time (43 women); includes 43 minority (37 Black or African American, non-Hispanic/Latino; 6 Hispanic/Latino), 1 international. Average age 42. 13 applicants, 92% accepted, 9 enrolled. In 2013, 4 doctorates awarded. *Degree requirements:* For doctorate, comprehensive exam, thesis/dissertation. *Entrance requirements:* For doctorate, GRE or MAT, master's degree from accredited college or university, minimum GPA of 3.0 in last degree attained, substantial experience working in education or family support agencies, 2 letters of recommendation, personal interview, transcripts, leadership portfolio, resume, letter of endorsement from superintendent or agency director. Additional exam requirements/recommendations for international students: Required—TOEFL (minimum score 550 paper-based; 79 iBT). *Application deadline:* For fall admission, 6/1 for domestic and international students; for spring admission, 12/1 for domestic and international students. Applications are processed on a rolling basis. Application fee: $75 ($150 for international students). Electronic applications accepted. *Expenses:* Contact institution. *Financial support:* In 2013–14, research assistantships with full tuition reimbursements (averaging $3,713 per year) were awarded; unspecified assistantships also available. Financial award applicants required to submit FAFSA. *Unit head:* Dr. Kathleen Callahan, Program Director, 908-737-5974, E-mail: kcallaha@kean.edu. *Application contact:* Reenat Hasan, Admissions Counselor, 908-737-5923, Fax: 908-737-5925, E-mail: hasanr@kean.edu.
Website: http://grad.kean.edu/edleadership/edd.

Keene State College, School of Professional and Graduate Studies, Keene, NH 03435. Offers curriculum and instruction (M Ed); education leadership (PMC); educational leadership (M Ed); safety and occupational health applied science (MS); school counselor (M Ed, PMC); special education (M Ed); teacher certification (Postbaccalaureate Certificate). *Accreditation:* NCATE. Part-time and evening/weekend programs available. *Faculty:* 8 full-time (5 women), 12 part-time/adjunct (6 women). *Students:* 39 full-time (33 women), 46 part-time (32 women); includes 8 minority (1 American Indian or Alaska Native, non-Hispanic/Latino; 2 Asian, non-Hispanic/Latino; 5 Hispanic/Latino). Average age 30. 46 applicants, 61% accepted, 13 enrolled. In 2013, 26 master's, 1 other advanced degree awarded. *Entrance requirements:* For master's, PRAXIS I, 3 references; official transcripts; minimum GPA of 2.5; interview. Additional exam requirements/recommendations for international students: Required—TOEFL (minimum score 550 paper-based; 61 iBT). *Application deadline:* For fall admission, 4/1 for domestic students; for spring admission, 12/1 for domestic students. Applications are processed on a rolling basis. Application fee: $50. Electronic applications accepted. *Expenses:* Tuition, state resident: full-time $10,410; part-time $480 per credit. Tuition, nonresident: full-time $17,795; part-time $530 per credit. *Required fees:* $2366; $94 per credit. Full-time tuition and fees vary according to course load. *Financial support:* Career-related internships or fieldwork, Federal Work-Study, institutionally sponsored loans, scholarships/grants, and unspecified assistantships available. Support available to part-time students. Financial award application deadline: 3/1; financial award applicants required to submit FAFSA. *Unit head:* Dr. Wayne Hartz, Interim Dean of Professional and Graduate Studies, 603-358-2220, E-mail: whartz@keene.edu. *Application contact:* Peggy Richmond, Director of Admissions, 603-358-2276, Fax: 603-358-2767, E-mail: admissions@keene.edu.
Website: http://www.keene.edu/gradstudies/.

Keiser University, EdS in Educational Leadership Program, Ft. Lauderdale, FL 33309. Offers Ed S.

Keiser University, Joint MS Ed/MBA Program, Ft. Lauderdale, FL 33309. Offers MS Ed/MBA.

Keiser University, Master of Science in Education Program, Ft. Lauderdale, FL 33309. Offers allied health teaching and leadership (MS Ed); career college administration (MS Ed); leadership (MS Ed); online teaching and learning (MS Ed); teaching and learning (MS Ed). Part-time programs available. Postbaccalaureate distance learning degree programs offered (no on-campus study).

Keiser University, PhD in Educational Leadership Program, Ft. Lauderdale, FL 33309. Offers PhD.

Kennesaw State University, Leland and Clarice C. Bagwell College of Education, Program in Graduate Education, Kennesaw, GA 30144-5591. Offers educational leadership (M Ed); educational leadership technology (M Ed); elementary and early childhood education (M Ed); instructional technology (M Ed); middle grades education (M Ed); reading (M Ed); secondary education (M Ed); special education (M Ed); teaching English to speakers of other languages (M Ed). *Accreditation:* NCATE. Part-time programs available. *Students:* 65 full-time (60 women), 229 part-time (158 women); includes 66 minority (46 Black or African American, non-Hispanic/Latino; 6 Asian, non-Hispanic/Latino; 9 Hispanic/Latino; 5 Two or more races, non-Hispanic/Latino), 1 international. Average age 34. 56 applicants, 86% accepted, 43 enrolled. In 2013, 109 master's awarded. *Degree requirements:* For master's, thesis or alternative. *Entrance requirements:* For master's, GRE General Test, T-4 state certification, minimum GPA of 2.75. Additional exam requirements/recommendations for international students: Required—TOEFL (minimum score 550 paper-based; 80 iBT), IELTS (minimum score 6.5). *Application deadline:* For fall admission, 7/1 for domestic and international students; for spring admission, 10/1 for domestic and international students; for summer admission, 4/15 for domestic and international students. Applications are processed on a rolling basis. Application fee: $60. Electronic applications accepted. *Expenses:* Tuition, state resident: full-time $4806; part-time $267 per semester hour. Tuition, nonresident: full-time $17,298; part-time $961 per semester hour. *Required fees:* $1834; $784.50 per semester. *Financial support:* In 2013–14, 10 research assistantships with tuition reimbursements (averaging $8,000 per year) were awarded; Federal Work-Study and unspecified assistantships also available. Support available to part-time students. Financial award application deadline: 4/1; financial award applicants required to submit FAFSA. *Unit head:* Melinda Ross, Administrative Coordinator for Graduate Programs in Education, 770-423-6043, E-mail: graded@kennesaw.edu. *Application contact:* Melinda Ross, Admissions Counselor, 770-423-6043, Fax: 770-423-6885, E-mail: ksugrad@kennesaw.edu.
Website: http://www.kennesaw.edu/education/grad/.

Kennesaw State University, Leland and Clarice C. Bagwell College of Education, Program in Leadership for Learning, Kennesaw, GA 30144-5591. Offers Ed D, Ed S. Part-time and evening/weekend programs available. *Students:* 41 full-time (28 women), 95 part-time (54 women); includes 76 minority (67 Black or African American, non-Hispanic/Latino; 1 Asian, non-Hispanic/Latino; 5 Hispanic/Latino; 3 Two or more races, non-Hispanic/Latino). Average age 39. 107 applicants, 81% accepted, 62 enrolled. In 2013, 10 doctorates, 43 other advanced degrees awarded. *Degree requirements:* For doctorate, thesis/dissertation. *Entrance requirements:* For doctorate, GRE General Test, minimum graduate GPA of 3.0, resume. Additional exam requirements/recommendations for international students: Required—TOEFL (minimum score 550 paper-based; 80 iBT), IELTS (minimum score 6). *Application deadline:* For fall admission, 6/1 for domestic and international students; for spring admission, 9/1 for domestic and international students; for summer admission, 4/14 for domestic students, 4/15 for international students. Application fee: $60. Electronic applications accepted. *Expenses:* Tuition, state resident: full-time $4806; part-time $267 per semester hour. Tuition, nonresident: full-time $17,298; part-time $961 per semester hour. *Required fees:* $1834; $784.50 per semester. *Financial support:* In 2013–14, 2 research assistantships with tuition reimbursements (averaging $8,000 per year) were awarded; unspecified assistantships also available. Financial award application deadline: 4/1; financial award applicants required to submit FAFSA. *Unit head:* Dr. Corrie Davis, Director of EdD and EdS Programs, 770-423-6481, E-mail: graded@kennesaw.edu. *Application contact:* Melinda Ross, Administrative Coordinator, 770-423-6122, Fax: 770-423-6885, E-mail: ksugrad@kennesaw.edu.

Kent State University, Graduate School of Education, Health, and Human Services, School of Foundations, Leadership and Administration, Program in K-12 Leadership, Kent, OH 44242-0001. Offers M Ed, PhD, Ed S. *Faculty:* 1 full-time (0 women), 3 part-time/adjunct (1 woman). *Students:* 16 full-time (9 women), 26 part-time (17 women); includes 3 minority (1 Black or African American, non-Hispanic/Latino; 1 American Indian or Alaska Native, non-Hispanic/Latino; 1 Asian, non-Hispanic/Latino), 2 international. 49 applicants, 31% accepted. In 2013, 14 master's, 3 other advanced degrees awarded. *Degree requirements:* For master's, thesis optional; for doctorate, comprehensive exam, thesis/dissertation. *Entrance requirements:* For master's, GRE if GPA is below 3.0, 2 letters of reference, goals statement; for doctorate, GRE, minimum master's-level GPA of 3.5, interview, resume, 2 letters of reference, goals statement; for Ed S, GRE. Additional exam requirements/recommendations for international students: Required—TOEFL (minimum score 550 paper-based; 80 iBT). *Application deadline:* Applications are processed on a rolling basis. Application fee: $30 ($60 for international

students). Electronic applications accepted. *Financial support:* In 2013–14, 1 research assistantship (averaging $12,000 per year), 1 teaching assistantship (averaging $12,000 per year) were awarded; Federal Work-Study, scholarships/grants, health care benefits, and unspecified assistantships also available. *Unit head:* Christa Boske, Coordinator, 330-672-0656, E-mail: cboske@kent.edu. *Application contact:* Nancy Miller, Academic Program Director, Office of Graduate Student Services, 330-672-2576, Fax: 330-672-9162, E-mail: ogs@kent.edu.

Kutztown University of Pennsylvania, College of Education, Program in Student Affairs in Higher Education, Kutztown, PA 19530-0730. Offers M Ed. *Accreditation:* NCATE. Part-time and evening/weekend programs available. *Faculty:* 2 full-time (both women). *Students:* 26 full-time (21 women), 15 part-time (12 women); includes 6 minority (4 Black or African American, non-Hispanic/Latino; 2 Hispanic/Latino). Average age 29. 23 applicants, 65% accepted, 12 enrolled. In 2013, 7 master's awarded. *Degree requirements:* For master's, comprehensive exam. *Entrance requirements:* For master's, GRE General Test, interview. Additional exam requirements/recommendations for international students: Required—TOEFL (minimum score 550 paper-based; 79 iBT). *Application deadline:* For fall admission, 3/1 for domestic and international students; for spring admission, 10/1 for domestic and international students. Application fee: $35. Electronic applications accepted. *Expenses: Tuition, area resident:* Part-time $442 per credit. Tuition, state resident: part-time $442 per credit. Tuition, nonresident: part-time $663 per credit. *Required fees:* $80 per credit. *Financial support:* Career-related internships or fieldwork, Federal Work-Study, scholarships/grants, and unspecified assistantships available. Financial award application deadline: 3/1; financial award applicants required to submit FAFSA. *Unit head:* Dr. Margaret Herrick, Chairperson, 610-683-4225, Fax: 610-683-1585, E-mail: herrick@kutztown.edu. *Application contact:* Kelly Hish, Admissions Clerk, 610-683-4200, Fax: 610-683-1393, E-mail: graduate@kutztown.edu.

Lake Erie College, School of Education and Professional Studies, Painesville, OH 44077-3389. Offers curriculum and instruction (MS Ed); education (MS Ed); educational leadership (MS Ed); reading (MS Ed). Part-time and evening/weekend programs available. *Faculty:* 2 full-time (1 woman). *Students:* 7 part-time (4 women). Average age 27. 6 applicants, 33% accepted, 1 enrolled. In 2013, 10 master's awarded. *Degree requirements:* For master's, comprehensive exam (for some programs), thesis optional, applied research project. *Entrance requirements:* For master's, GRE General Test (minimum score of 440 verbal or 500 quantitative) or minimum GPA of 2.75; bachelor's degree from accredited 4-year institution; references; essay. Additional exam requirements/recommendations for international students: Required—TOEFL (minimum score 550 paper-based). *Application deadline:* For fall admission, 8/1 priority date for domestic students, 6/1 for international students; for spring admission, 12/15 for domestic students, 10/1 for international students. Applications are processed on a rolling basis. Application fee: $30. Electronic applications accepted. Application fee is waived when completed online. *Expenses:* Contact institution. *Financial support:* Tuition waivers and unspecified assistantships available. Financial award applicants required to submit FAFSA. *Unit head:* Prof. Dale Sheptak, Dean of the School of Education and Professional Studies, 440-375-7131, E-mail: dsheptak@lec.edu. *Application contact:* Milena Velez, Senior Admissions Counselor, 800-916-0904, Fax: 440-375-7000, E-mail: admissions@lec.edu.
Website: http://www.lec.edu/med.

Lamar University, College of Graduate Studies, College of Education and Human Development, Department of Educational Leadership, Beaumont, TX 77710. Offers counseling and development (M Ed, Certificate); education administration (M Ed); educational leadership (DE); principal (Certificate); school superintendent (Certificate); supervision (M Ed); technology application (Certificate). Part-time and evening/weekend programs available. Terminal master's awarded for partial completion of doctoral program. *Degree requirements:* For master's, comprehensive exam, thesis optional; for doctorate, thesis/dissertation. *Entrance requirements:* For master's, GRE General Test, minimum GPA of 2.5; for doctorate, GRE. Additional exam requirements/recommendations for international students: Required—TOEFL. *Faculty research:* School dropouts, suicide prevention in public school students, school climate and gifted performance, teacher evaluation.

La Salle University, School of Arts and Sciences, Program in Education, Philadelphia, PA 19141-1199. Offers American studies (MA); autism spectrum disorders (MA, Certificate); bilingual/bicultural studies (MA); classroom management (MA, Certificate); dual early childhood and special education (MA); dual middle-level science and math and special education secondary education (MA); education (MA); English (MA); English as a second language (Certificate); instructional coach (Certificate); instructional leadership (MA); reading specialist (MA, Certificate); secondary education (MA); special education (MA, Certificate). Part-time and evening/weekend programs available. *Faculty:* 5 full-time (4 women), 16 part-time/adjunct (10 women). *Students:* 18 full-time (13 women), 137 part-time (112 women); includes 33 minority (24 Black or African American, non-Hispanic/Latino; 9 Hispanic/Latino), 4 international. Average age 32. 47 applicants, 96% accepted, 28 enrolled. In 2013, 58 master's, 20 other advanced degrees awarded. *Degree requirements:* For master's, comprehensive exam. *Entrance requirements:* For master's and Certificate, MAT or GRE, 2 letters of recommendation. Additional exam requirements/recommendations for international students: Required—TOEFL. *Application deadline:* For fall admission, 8/15 priority date for domestic students, 7/15 for international students; for spring admission, 12/15 priority date for domestic students, 11/15 for international students; for summer admission, 4/15 priority date for domestic students, 3/15 for international students. Applications are processed on a rolling basis. Application fee: $35. Electronic applications accepted. Application fee is waived when completed online. *Expenses:* Contact institution. *Financial support:* In 2013–14, 28 students received support. Career-related internships or fieldwork, Federal Work-Study, and scholarships/grants available. Support available to part-time students. Financial award application deadline: 8/31; financial award applicants required to submit FAFSA. *Unit head:* Dr. Greer Richardson, Interim Director, 215-951-1806, Fax: 215-951-1843, E-mail: graded@lasalle.edu. *Application contact:* Paul J. Reilly, Assistant Vice President, Enrollment Services, 215-951-1946, Fax: 215-951-1462, E-mail: reilly@lasalle.edu.
Website: http://www.lasalle.edu/grad/index.php?section-education&page-index.

La Sierra University, School of Education, Department of Administration and Leadership, Riverside, CA 92515. Offers MA, Ed D, Ed S. Part-time and evening/weekend programs available. Terminal master's awarded for partial completion of doctoral program. *Degree requirements:* For master's, thesis optional; for doctorate, thesis/dissertation, fieldwork, qualifying exam; for Ed S, thesis optional, fieldwork. *Entrance requirements:* For master's, minimum GPA of 3.0; for doctorate, GRE General Test, GRE Subject Test, minimum GPA of 3.3, Ed S; for Ed S, master's degree, minimum GPA of 3.3.

Lebanon Valley College, Program in Business Administration, Annville, PA 17003-1400. Offers business administration (MBA); healthcare management (MBA); school leadership (MBA). *Accreditation:* ACBSP. Part-time and evening/weekend programs available. *Faculty:* 3 full-time (0 women), 16 part-time/adjunct (2 women). *Students:* 14 full-time (6 women), 156 part-time (82 women); includes 12 minority (4 Black or African American, non-Hispanic/Latino; 1 American Indian or Alaska Native, non-Hispanic/Latino; 4 Asian, non-Hispanic/Latino; 3 Hispanic/Latino). Average age 38. In 2013, 48 master's awarded. *Entrance requirements:* For master's, 3 years of work experience. *Application deadline:* Applications are processed on a rolling basis. Application fee: $30. Electronic applications accepted. *Expenses:* Contact institution. *Financial support:* Application deadline: 5/1; applicants required to submit FAFSA. *Unit head:* Brenda Adams, Director of the MBA Program, 717-867-6335, Fax: 717-867-6018, E-mail: badams@lvc.edu. *Application contact:* Susan Greenawalt, Graduate Studies and Continuing Education Assistant/Records Coordinator, 717-867-6213, Fax: 717-867-6018, E-mail: greenawa@lvc.edu.
Website: http://www.lvc.edu/mba.

Lee University, Program in Education, Cleveland, TN 37320-3450. Offers college student development (MS); curriculum and instruction (M Ed, Ed S); educational leadership (M Ed, Ed S); elementary education (MAT); higher education administration (MS); middle grades (MAT); secondary education (MAT); special education (M Ed); special education (secondary) (MAT). Part-time programs available. *Faculty:* 14 full-time (7 women), 6 part-time/adjunct (3 women). *Students:* 30 full-time (23 women), 62 part-time (37 women); includes 8 minority (3 Black or African American, non-Hispanic/Latino; 1 American Indian or Alaska Native, non-Hispanic/Latino; 2 Asian, non-Hispanic/Latino; 2 Hispanic/Latino). Average age 30. 40 applicants, 100% accepted, 30 enrolled. In 2013, 117 master's, 2 other advanced degrees awarded. *Degree requirements:* For master's, variable foreign language requirement, comprehensive exam, thesis, internship. *Entrance requirements:* For master's, MAT or GRE General Test, minimum GPA of 2.75, 3 letters of recommendation, interview, writing sample, official transcripts. Additional exam requirements/recommendations for international students: Required—TOEFL (minimum score 450 paper-based). *Application deadline:* For fall admission, 4/1 priority date for domestic and international students; for spring admission, 10/1 priority date for domestic and international students. Applications are processed on a rolling basis. Application fee: $25. *Expenses: Tuition:* Full-time $9900; part-time $550 per credit hour. *Required fees:* $35 per term. One-time fee: $25. *Financial support:* In 2013–14, 47 students received support, including 1 teaching assistantship (averaging $1,500 per year); career-related internships or fieldwork, Federal Work-Study, institutionally sponsored loans, scholarships/grants, and unspecified assistantships also available. Financial award application deadline: 3/1; financial award applicants required to submit FAFSA. *Unit head:* Dr. Gary Riggins, Director, 423-614-8193. *Application contact:* Vicki Glasscock, Graduate Admissions Director, 423-614-8059, E-mail: vglasscock@leeuniversity.edu.
Website: http://www.leeuniversity.edu/academics/graduate/education.

Lehigh University, College of Education, Program in Educational Leadership, Bethlehem, PA 18015. Offers educational leadership (M Ed, Ed D); K-12 principal (Certificate); superintendent of schools (Certificate); supervisor of curriculum and instruction (Certificate); supervisor of pupil services (Certificate); supervisor of special education (Certificate); MBA/M Ed. Part-time and evening/weekend programs available. Postbaccalaureate distance learning degree programs offered (minimal on-campus study). *Faculty:* 7 full-time (2 women), 7 part-time/adjunct (2 women). *Students:* 7 full-time (6 women), 114 part-time (54 women); includes 14 minority (8 Black or African American, non-Hispanic/Latino; 1 American Indian or Alaska Native, non-Hispanic/Latino; 5 Hispanic/Latino), 11 international. Average age 36. 66 applicants, 76% accepted, 17 enrolled. In 2013, 45 master's, 15 doctorates awarded. *Degree requirements:* For doctorate, comprehensive exam, thesis/dissertation. *Entrance requirements:* For master's and Certificate, minimum undergraduate GPA of 3.0; for doctorate, GRE General Test or MAT, minimum graduate GPA of 3.6, 2 letters of recommendation, essay, transcript. Additional exam requirements/recommendations for international students: Required—TOEFL (minimum score 600 paper-based; 93 iBT). *Application deadline:* For fall admission, 1/15 for domestic and international students; for spring admission, 11/1 for domestic and international students. Applications are processed on a rolling basis. Application fee: $65. Electronic applications accepted. *Financial support:* In 2013–14, 1 student received support. Fellowships with full and partial tuition reimbursements available, research assistantships with full and partial tuition reimbursements available, teaching assistantships with full and partial tuition reimbursements available, career-related internships or fieldwork, Federal Work-Study, institutionally sponsored loans, scholarships/grants, tuition waivers (full and partial), and unspecified assistantships available. Financial award application deadline: 1/31; financial award applicants required to submit FAFSA. *Faculty research:* School finance and law, supervision of instruction, middle-level education, organizational change, leadership preparation and development, international school leadership, urban school leadership, comparative education, social justice. *Unit head:* Dr. Floyd D. Beachum, Director, 610-758-5955, Fax: 610-758-3227, E-mail: fdb209@lehigh.edu. *Application contact:* Donna M. Johnson, Manager, Graduate Programs Admissions, 610-758-3231, Fax: 610-758-6223, E-mail: dmj4@lehigh.edu.
Website: http://coe.lehigh.edu/academics/disciplines/edl.

Le Moyne College, Department of Education, Syracuse, NY 13214. Offers adolescent education (MS Ed, MST); adolescent education/special education (MS Ed, MST); adolescent English (MST), including grades 7-12 (MS Ed, MST); adolescent English/special education (MST), including grades 7-12 (MS Ed, MST); adolescent foreign language (MST), including grades 7-12 (MS Ed, MST); adolescent history (MST), including grades 7-12 (MS Ed, MST); childhood education (MS Ed); childhood education/special education (MS Ed); elementary education (MS Ed); general education (MS Ed); inclusive childhood education (MST); literacy education (MS Ed), including birth to grade 6, grades 5-12; school building leader (MS Ed); school building leadership (CAS); school district business leader (MS Ed, CAS); school district leader (MS Ed); school district leadership (CAS); secondary education (MS Ed); special education (MS Ed); students with disabilities-generalist (MS Ed), including grades 7-12 (MS Ed, MST); teaching English to speakers of other languages (MS Ed); urban studies (MS Ed). *Accreditation:* Teacher Education Accreditation Council. Part-time and evening/weekend programs available. *Faculty:* 8 full-time (5 women), 61 part-time/adjunct (38 women). *Students:* 24 full-time (20 women), 178 part-time (133 women); includes 22 minority (12 Black or African American, non-Hispanic/Latino; 1 American Indian or Alaska Native, non-Hispanic/Latino; 3 Asian, non-Hispanic/Latino; 6 Hispanic/Latino), 1 international. Average age 31. 248 applicants, 90% accepted, 86 enrolled. In 2013, 158 master's, 37 CASs awarded. *Degree requirements:* For master's, thesis. *Entrance requirements:* For master's, GRE General Test, bachelor's degree, 2 letters of recommendation, written statement, transcripts. Additional exam requirements/recommendations for international students: Required—TOEFL (minimum score 550 paper-based; 79 iBT). *Application deadline:* For fall admission, 4/1 priority date for domestic and international students; for spring admission, 10/1 priority date for domestic and international students; for summer admission, 3/1 priority date for domestic and international students. Applications are processed on a rolling basis. Application fee: $50. *Expenses:* Contact institution. *Financial support:* In 2013–14, 26 students received support. Career-related internships or fieldwork and health care benefits available. Support available to part-time students. Financial award applicants required to submit FAFSA. *Faculty research:* Minority teachers, special education, multiculturalism, literacy, technology, media literacy learning, autism, school district organization, service-learning, higher level problem solving, teacher leadership. *Unit head:* Dr. Suzanne L. Gilmour, Chair, Department of Education/Director of Graduate Education Programs, 315-445-4376, Fax: 315-445-

4744, E-mail: gilmous@lemoyne.edu. *Application contact:* Kristen P. Trapasso, Senior Director of Enrollment Management, 315-445-4265, Fax: 315-445-6092, E-mail: trapaskp@lemoyne.edu.
Website: http://www.lemoyne.edu/education.

Lesley University, School of Education, Cambridge, MA 02138-2790. Offers arts, community, and education (M Ed); autism studies (Certificate); curriculum and instruction (M Ed, CAGS); early childhood education (M Ed); ecological teaching and learning (MS); educational studies (PhD), including adult learning, educational leadership, individually designed; elementary education (M Ed); emergent technologies for educators (Certificate); ESLArts: language learning through the arts (M Ed); high school education (M Ed); individually designed (M Ed); integrated teaching through the arts (M Ed); literacy for K-8 classroom teachers (M Ed); mathematics education (M Ed); middle school education (M Ed); moderate disabilities (M Ed); online learning (Certificate); reading (CAGS); science in education (M Ed); severe disabilities (M Ed); special needs (CAGS); specialist teacher of reading (M Ed); teacher of visual art (M Ed); technology in education (M Ed, CAGS). *Accreditation:* Teacher Education Accreditation Council. Part-time and evening/weekend programs available. Postbaccalaureate distance learning degree programs offered (no on-campus study). *Faculty:* 40 full-time (30 women), 104 part-time/adjunct (77 women). *Students:* 453 full-time (381 women), 1,672 part-time (1,435 women); includes 284 minority (139 Black or African American, non-Hispanic/Latino; 11 American Indian or Alaska Native, non-Hispanic/Latino; 38 Asian, non-Hispanic/Latino; 58 Hispanic/Latino; 5 Native Hawaiian or other Pacific Islander, non-Hispanic/Latino; 33 Two or more races, non-Hispanic/Latino), 22 international. Average age 35. In 2013, 1,137 master's, 18 doctorates, 51 other advanced degrees awarded. *Degree requirements:* For master's, practicum; for doctorate, thesis/dissertation. *Entrance requirements:* For master's, Massachusetts Tests for Educator Licensure (MTEL), transcripts, statement of purpose, recommendations; interview (for special education); for doctorate, GRE General Test, transcripts, statement of purpose, recommendations, interview, master's degree, resume; for other advanced degree, interview, master's degree. Additional exam requirements/recommendations for international students: Required—TOEFL (minimum score 550 paper-based; 80 iBT). *Application deadline:* Applications are processed on a rolling basis. Application fee: $50. Electronic applications accepted. *Expenses: Tuition:* Part-time $900 per credit. *Financial support:* In 2013–14, 15 fellowships (averaging $3,600 per year) were awarded; career-related internships or fieldwork, Federal Work-Study, scholarships/grants, tuition waivers, and unspecified assistantships also available. Financial award application deadline: 4/15; financial award applicants required to submit FAFSA. *Faculty research:* Assessment in literacy, mathematics and science; autism spectrum disorders; instructional technology and online learning; multicultural education and English language learners. *Unit head:* Dr. Jack Gillette, Dean, 617-349-8401, Fax: 617-349-8607, E-mail: jgillett@lesley.edu. *Application contact:* Martha Sheehan, Director of Admissions, 888-LESLEYU, Fax: 617-349-8313, E-mail: info@lesley.edu.
Website: http://www.lesley.edu/soe.html.

Lewis & Clark College, Graduate School of Education and Counseling, Department of Educational Leadership, Program in Educational Leadership, Portland, OR 97219-7899. Offers educational leadership (Ed D, Ed S). Part-time and evening/weekend programs available. *Degree requirements:* For doctorate, thesis/dissertation. *Entrance requirements:* For doctorate, master's degree plus minimum of 14 degree-applicable, post-master's semester credits; minimum undergraduate GPA of 2.75. Additional exam requirements/recommendations for international students: Required—TOEFL (minimum score 575 paper-based). Electronic applications accepted.

Lewis University, College of Education, Program in Educational Leadership, Romeoville, IL 60446. Offers M Ed, MA. Part-time and evening/weekend programs available. *Students:* 7 full-time (4 women), 38 part-time (28 women); includes 12 minority (8 Black or African American, non-Hispanic/Latino; 1 Asian, non-Hispanic/Latino; 3 Hispanic/Latino). Average age 34. *Entrance requirements:* For master's, departmental qualifying exams, writing exam, minimum GPA of 2.75, 2 letters of recommendation, interview. Additional exam requirements/recommendations for international students: Required—TOEFL (minimum score 550 paper-based; 80 iBT). *Application deadline:* For fall admission, 5/1 priority date for international students; for spring admission, 11/15 priority date for international students. Application fee: $40. *Financial support:* Federal Work-Study, scholarships/grants, and unspecified assistantships available. Financial award application deadline: 5/1; financial award applicants required to submit FAFSA. *Unit head:* Dr. Jane Petrek, Director, 815-838-0500 Ext. 5039, Fax: 815-836-5879, E-mail: petrekja@lewisu.edu. *Application contact:* Linda Campbell, Graduate Admission Counselor, 815-836-5704, Fax: 815-836-5578, E-mail: campbeli@lewisu.edu.

Lewis University, College of Education, Program in Educational Leadership for Teaching and Learning, Romeoville, IL 60446. Offers Ed D. *Students:* 7 full-time (4 women), 38 part-time (28 women); includes 12 minority (8 Black or African American, non-Hispanic/Latino; 1 Asian, non-Hispanic/Latino; 3 Hispanic/Latino). Average age 34. *Degree requirements:* For doctorate, thesis/dissertation. *Entrance requirements:* For doctorate, GRE, letters of recommendation, personal statement, academic and scholarly work. Additional exam requirements/recommendations for international students: Required—TOEFL (minimum score 550 paper-based; 80 iBT). Application fee: $40. *Financial support:* Application deadline: 5/1; applicants required to submit FAFSA. *Unit head:* Dr. Lauren Hoffman, Program Director, 815-838-0500 Ext. 5501, E-mail: hoffmala@lewisu.edu. *Application contact:* Office of Graduate and Adult Admission, 815-836-5610, E-mail: grad@lewisu.edu.

Liberty University, School of Education, Lynchburg, VA 24515. Offers administration and supervision (M Ed); curriculum and instruction (Ed D, Ed S); early childhood education (M Ed); educational leadership (Ed D, Ed S); educational technology and online instruction (M Ed); elementary education (M Ed, MAT); English (M Ed); gifted education (M Ed); history (M Ed); leadership (M Ed); math specialist (M Ed); middle grades (M Ed, MAT); outdoor adventure sport (MS); reading specialist (M Ed); school counseling (M Ed); secondary education (MAT); special education (M Ed, MAT); sport management (MS), including administration, outdoor recreation, sport management, tourism; sports administration (MS); student service (M Ed); teaching and learning (M Ed); tourism (MS). *Accreditation:* NCATE. Part-time programs available. Postbaccalaureate distance learning degree programs offered (minimal on-campus study). *Students:* 2,241 full-time (1,639 women), 4,413 part-time (3,240 women); includes 2,052 minority (1,588 Black or African American, non-Hispanic/Latino; 37 American Indian or Alaska Native, non-Hispanic/Latino; 67 Asian, non-Hispanic/Latino; 173 Hispanic/Latino; 37 Native Hawaiian or other Pacific Islander, non-Hispanic/Latino; 150 Two or more races, non-Hispanic/Latino), 15 international. Average age 37. 6,185 applicants, 43% accepted, 1603 enrolled. In 2013, 1,256 master's, 117 doctorates, 470 other advanced degrees awarded. *Degree requirements:* For doctorate, comprehensive exam, thesis/dissertation. *Entrance requirements:* For master's, GRE General Test or MAT (if taken in or before 1999), 2 letters of recommendation, minimum undergraduate GPA of 3.0, curriculum vitae; for doctorate and Ed S, GRE General Test or MAT (if taken before 1999), minimum master's GPA of 3.0, 3 years of teaching experience. Additional exam requirements/recommendations for international students: Required—TOEFL (minimum score 600 paper-based; 100 iBT). *Application deadline:* For fall admission, 6/1 for domestic students; for spring admission, 11/1 for domestic students. Applications are processed on a rolling basis. Application fee: $50. Electronic applications accepted. *Expenses:* Contact institution. *Financial support:* Federal Work-Study and tuition waivers (partial) available. *Faculty research:* Self-determination, character education, bibliotherapy, learning styles, distance education. *Unit head:* Dr. Karen L. Parker, Dean, 434-582-2195, Fax: 434-582-2468, E-mail: kparker@liberty.edu. *Application contact:* Jay Bridge, Director of Graduate Admissions, 800-424-9595, Fax: 800-628-7977, E-mail: gradadmissions@liberty.edu.
Website: http://www.liberty.edu/academics/education/graduate/.

Lincoln Memorial University, Carter and Moyers School of Education, Harrogate, TN 37752-1901. Offers administration and supervision (M Ed, Ed S); counseling and guidance (M Ed); curriculum and instruction (M Ed, Ed D, Ed S); English (M Ed); executive leadership (Ed D); higher education administration (Ed D); human resource development (Ed D); leadership and administration (Ed D). Part-time and evening/weekend programs available. Postbaccalaureate distance learning degree programs offered. *Degree requirements:* For master's, comprehensive exam, thesis optional; for Ed S, comprehensive exam. *Entrance requirements:* For master's, PRAXIS, NTE, GRE, MAT, letters of recommendation; for Ed S, graduate transcripts. Additional exam requirements/recommendations for international students: Recommended—TOEFL. *Faculty research:* Brain compatible teaching and learning; poverty in Appalachia; leadership for change; ethics, moral responsibility and social justice; human and organizational learning.

Lincoln University, Graduate Programs, Philadelphia, PA 19104. Offers early childhood education (M Ed); educational leadership (M Ed); human resources (MSA), including finance, human resources management; human services (MHS); reading (MSR). Evening/weekend programs available. *Faculty:* 10 full-time (4 women), 34 part-time/adjunct (19 women). *Students:* 224 full-time (145 women), 115 part-time (74 women); includes 328 minority (311 Black or African American, non-Hispanic/Latino; 17 Hispanic/Latino). Average age 40. 237 applicants, 65% accepted, 64 enrolled. In 2013, 155 master's awarded. *Degree requirements:* For master's, thesis. *Entrance requirements:* For master's, working as full-time, paid staff member in the human services field, at least one year of paid experience in this field, and undergraduate degree in human services or a related field from an accredited institution (for MHS). *Application deadline:* For fall admission, 6/1 priority date for domestic and international students. Applications are processed on a rolling basis. Application fee: $50. *Expenses:* Tuition, state resident: full-time $10,106; part-time $567 per hour. Tuition, nonresident: full-time $17,636; part-time $949 per hour. *Financial support:* Application deadline: 8/1. *Unit head:* Dr. Cheryl Gooch, Dean, School of Humanities and Graduate Studies, 484-365-7664, E-mail: cgooch@lincoln.edu. *Application contact:* Jernice Lea, Director of Graduate Admissions, 215-590-8233, Fax: 215-387-3859, E-mail: jlea@lincoln.edu.
Website: http://www.lincoln.edu/academicaffairs/uc.html.

Lincoln University, Graduate Studies, Jefferson City, MO 65101. Offers business administration (MBA), including accounting, entrepreneurship, management, public administration and policy; educational leadership (Ed S), including elementary leadership, secondary leadership, superintendency; guidance and counseling (M Ed), including community/agency counseling, elementary school, secondary school; history (MA); school administration and supervision (M Ed), including elementary school administration, secondary school administration, special education administration; school teaching (M Ed), including elementary school teaching, secondary school teaching; sociology (MA); sociology/criminal justice (MA). Part-time and evening/weekend programs available. Postbaccalaureate distance learning degree programs offered (minimal on-campus study). *Students:* 42 full-time (29 women), 109 part-time (66 women); includes 51 minority (37 Black or African American, non-Hispanic/Latino; 10 American Indian or Alaska Native, non-Hispanic/Latino; 1 Asian, non-Hispanic/Latino; 2 Hispanic/Latino; 1 Two or more races, non-Hispanic/Latino), 10 international. Average age 33. 84 applicants, 76% accepted, 51 enrolled. In 2013, 73 master's, 6 other advanced degrees awarded. *Degree requirements:* For master's and Ed S, comprehensive exam, thesis optional. *Entrance requirements:* For master's and Ed S, GRE, MAT or GMAT, minimum GPA of 2.75 in major, 2.5 overall; 3 letters of recommendation; minimum C average in English composition; personal statement of purpose. Additional exam requirements/recommendations for international students: Required—TOEFL (minimum score 500 paper-based; 61 iBT). *Application deadline:* For fall admission, 8/1 priority date for domestic and international students; for spring admission, 12/1 priority date for domestic and international students; for summer admission, 5/1 priority date for domestic and international students. Applications are processed on a rolling basis. Application fee: $30. *Expenses:* Tuition, state resident: full-time $6840; part-time $285 per credit hour. Tuition, nonresident: full-time $12,720; part-time $530 per credit hour. *Required fees:* $587; $587 per year. Tuition and fees vary according to course load. *Financial support:* Federal Work-Study and scholarships/grants available. Support available to part-time students. Financial award application deadline: 3/1; financial award applicants required to submit FAFSA. *Unit head:* Dr. Linda S. Bickel, Dean, 573-681-5247, Fax: 573-681-5106, E-mail: gradschool@lincolnu.edu. *Application contact:* Irasema Steck, Administrative Assistant, 573-681-5247, Fax: 573-681-5106, E-mail: gradschool@lincolnu.edu.
Website: http://www.lincolnu.edu/web/graduate-studies/graduate-studies.

Lindenwood University, Graduate Programs, School of Education, St. Charles, MO 63301-1695. Offers education (MA); educational administration (MA, Ed D, Ed S); human performance (MS); instructional leadership (Ed D, Ed S); library media (MA); professional counseling (MA); school administration (Ed S); school counseling (MA); teaching (MA); teaching English to speakers of other languages (MA). Part-time and evening/weekend programs available. Postbaccalaureate distance learning degree programs offered (no on-campus study). *Faculty:* 50 full-time (33 women), 228 part-time/adjunct (136 women). *Students:* 454 full-time (352 women), 1,772 part-time (1,351 women); includes 637 minority (545 Black or African American, non-Hispanic/Latino; 9 American Indian or Alaska Native, non-Hispanic/Latino; 9 Asian, non-Hispanic/Latino; 42 Hispanic/Latino; 32 Two or more races, non-Hispanic/Latino), 32 international. Average age 36. 644 applicants, 71% accepted, 401 enrolled. In 2013, 564 master's, 35 doctorates, 83 other advanced degrees awarded. *Degree requirements:* For master's, thesis (for some programs), minimum GPA of 3.0; for doctorate, thesis/dissertation, minimum GPA of 3.0; for Ed S, comprehensive exam, project, minimum GPA of 3.0. *Entrance requirements:* For master's, interview, minimum GPA of 3.0, writing sample, letter of recommendation; for doctorate, GRE, minimum graduate GPA of 3.4, resume, interview, writing sample, 4 letters of recommendation; for Ed S, master's degree in education, relevant work experience. Additional exam requirements/recommendations for international students: Required—TOEFL (minimum score 550 paper-based; 80 iBT). *Application deadline:* For fall admission, 8/26 priority date for domestic and international students; for spring admission, 1/27 priority date for domestic and international students. Applications are processed on a rolling basis. Application fee: $30 ($100 for international students). Electronic applications accepted. *Expenses: Tuition:* Full-time $14,800; part-time $428 per credit hour. *Required fees:* $350. Tuition and fees vary according to course level and course load. *Financial support:* In 2013–14, 385 students received support. Career-related internships or fieldwork, Federal Work-Study, institutionally sponsored loans, scholarships/grants, tuition waivers (partial), and unspecified

assistantships available. Financial award application deadline: 6/30; financial award applicants required to submit FAFSA. *Unit head:* Dr. Cynthia Bice, Dean, 636-949-4618, Fax: 636-949-4197, E-mail: cbice@lindenwood.edu. *Application contact:* Brett Barger, Dean of Evening Admissions and Extension Campuses, 636-949-4934, Fax: 636-949-4109, E-mail: adultadmissions@lindenwood.edu.

Lindenwood University–Belleville, Graduate Programs, Belleville, IL 62226. Offers business administration (MBA); communications (MA), including digital and multimedia, media management, promotions, training and development; counseling (MA); criminal justice administration (MS); education (MA); healthcare administration (MS); human resource management (MS); school administration (MA); teaching (MAT).

Lipscomb University, Program in Education, Nashville, TN 37204-3951. Offers applied behavior analysis (Certificate); collaborative professional learning (M Ed, Ed S); educational leadership (M Ed, Ed S); English language learning (M Ed, Ed S); instructional coaching (Certificate); instructional practice (M Ed); learning organizations and strategic change (Ed D); math specialty (M Ed); reading specialty (M Ed, Ed S); special education (M Ed); teaching, learning, and leading (M Ed); technology integration (M Ed); technology integration specialist (Certificate). *Accreditation:* NCATE. Part-time and evening/weekend programs available. Postbaccalaureate distance learning degree programs offered (no on-campus study). *Faculty:* 19 full-time (13 women), 28 part-time/adjunct (22 women). *Students:* 171 full-time (123 women), 509 part-time (429 women); includes 118 minority (91 Black or African American, non-Hispanic/Latino; 1 American Indian or Alaska Native, non-Hispanic/Latino; 4 Asian, non-Hispanic/Latino; 15 Hispanic/Latino; 1 Native Hawaiian or other Pacific Islander, non-Hispanic/Latino; 6 Two or more races, non-Hispanic/Latino). Average age 32. 237 applicants, 65% accepted, 150 enrolled. In 2013, 212 master's awarded. *Degree requirements:* For master's, comprehensive exam, portfolio, research project and presentation; for doctorate, practical capstone project in experiential setting. *Entrance requirements:* For master's, MAT (minimum 31) or GRE General Test (minimum 294), 2 reference letters, goals statement, writing sample, interview; for doctorate, MAT or GRE General Test, 3 reference letters, artifact of demonstrated academic excellence, written personal statements, interview. Additional exam requirements/recommendations for international students: Required—TOEFL (minimum score 570 paper-based). *Application deadline:* For fall admission, 8/29 priority date for domestic students; for spring admission, 1/15 priority date for domestic students. Applications are processed on a rolling basis. Application fee: $50 ($75 for international students). *Expenses: Tuition:* Full-time $15,570; part-time $865 per credit hour. Tuition and fees vary according to degree level and program. *Financial support:* Scholarships/grants and unspecified assistantships available. Financial award applicants required to submit FAFSA. *Faculty research:* Facilitative learning styles, leadership, student assessment, interactive multimedia inclusion, learning organizations and strategic change. *Unit head:* Dr. Deborah Boyd, Director of Graduate Studies, 615-966-6263, E-mail: deborah.boyd@lipscomb.edu. *Application contact:* Kristin Baese, Director of Enrollment and Outreach, 615-966-7628 Ext. 6081, Fax: 615-966-5173, E-mail: kristin.baese@lipscomb.edu.
Website: http://www.lipscomb.edu/education/graduate-programs.

Lock Haven University of Pennsylvania, College of Liberal Arts and Education, Lock Haven, PA 17745-2390. Offers alternative education (M Ed); educational leadership (M Ed); teaching and learning (M Ed). *Accreditation:* NCATE. Part-time and evening/weekend programs available. Postbaccalaureate distance learning degree programs offered (no on-campus study). *Degree requirements:* For master's, thesis. *Entrance requirements:* For master's, minimum undergraduate GPA of 3.0. Additional exam requirements/recommendations for international students: Required—TOEFL. *Application deadline:* Applications are processed on a rolling basis. Application fee: $25. Electronic applications accepted. *Expenses: Tuition, area resident:* Part-time $442 per credit hour. Tuition, state resident: part-time $442 per credit hour. Tuition, nonresident: part-time $663 per credit hour. *Required fees:* $208.45 per credit hour. Tuition and fees vary according to program. *Financial support:* Unspecified assistantships available. Financial award application deadline: 8/1. *Unit head:* Dr. Susan Rimby, Dean, 570-484-2137, E-mail: ser1116@lhup.edu. *Application contact:* Kelly Hibbler, Assistant to the Dean, 570-484-2147, Fax: 570-484-2734, E-mail: khibbler@lhup.edu.
Website: http://www.lhup.edu/colleges/liberal_arts_education/.

Long Island University–Hudson at Rockland, Graduate School, Program in Educational Leadership, Orangeburg, NY 10962. Offers MS Ed, Advanced Certificate. Part-time programs available. *Entrance requirements:* For master's, college transcripts, two letters of recommendation, resume.

Long Island University–LIU Brooklyn, School of Education, Department of Human Development and Leadership, Program in Leadership and Policy, Brooklyn, NY 11201-8423. Offers MS. *Degree requirements:* For master's, thesis optional. *Entrance requirements:* For master's, 2 letters of recommendation. Additional exam requirements/recommendations for international students: Required—TOEFL (minimum score 500 paper-based).

Long Island University–LIU Post, School of Education, Department of Educational Leadership and Administration, Brookville, NY 11548-1300. Offers school administration and supervision (MS Ed); school building leader (AC); school district business leader (AC); school district leader (AC). Part-time and evening/weekend programs available. *Degree requirements:* For master's, comprehensive exam or research project, internship; for AC, internship. *Entrance requirements:* For master's, minimum GPA of 3.0, 3 years of teaching experience. Electronic applications accepted. *Faculty research:* Leadership administration, computers in decision making, curricular innovation and school business administration.

Long Island University–LIU Post, School of Education, Program in Interdisciplinary Educational Studies, Brookville, NY 11548-1300. Offers educational leadership (Ed D); teaching and learning (Ed D). Part-time programs available. *Degree requirements:* For doctorate, comprehensive exam, thesis/dissertation, portfolio. *Entrance requirements:* For doctorate, master's degree in education or a related field, 3 letters of recommendation, writing sample, curriculum vitae/resume. Additional exam requirements/recommendations for international students: Required—TOEFL (minimum score 600 paper-based).

Loras College, Graduate Division, Program in Educational Leadership, Dubuque, IA 52004-0178. Offers MA. Part-time and evening/weekend programs available. *Degree requirements:* For master's, comprehensive exam, thesis optional. *Entrance requirements:* For master's, minimum cumulative undergraduate GPA of 3.0.

Louisiana State University and Agricultural & Mechanical College, Graduate School, College of Human Sciences and Education, Department of Educational Theory, Policy and Practice, Baton Rouge, LA 70803. Offers counseling (M Ed, MA, Ed S); educational administration (M Ed, MA, PhD, Ed S); educational technology (MA); elementary education (M Ed, MAT); higher education (PhD); research methodology (PhD); secondary education (M Ed, MAT). PhD programs offered jointly with Louisiana State University in Shreveport. *Accreditation:* ACA (one or more programs are accredited); NCATE. Part-time and evening/weekend programs available. *Faculty:* 39 full-time (22 women). *Students:* 185 full-time (136 women), 177 part-time (140 women); includes 110 minority (90 Black or African American, non-Hispanic/Latino; 1 American Indian or Alaska Native, non-Hispanic/Latino; 5 Asian, non-Hispanic/Latino; 9 Hispanic/Latino; 5 Two or more races, non-Hispanic/Latino), 5 international. Average age 31. 167 applicants, 66% accepted, 76 enrolled. In 2013, 134 master's, 23 doctorates, 17 other advanced degrees awarded. Terminal master's awarded for partial completion of doctoral program. *Degree requirements:* For doctorate, thesis/dissertation; for Ed S, thesis optional. *Entrance requirements:* For master's and doctorate, GRE General Test, minimum GPA of 3.0. Additional exam requirements/recommendations for international students: Required—TOEFL (minimum score 550 paper-based; 79 IBT), IELTS (minimum score 6.5), or PTE (minimum score 59). *Application deadline:* For fall admission, 1/25 priority date for domestic students, 5/15 for international students; for spring admission, 10/15 for international students. Applications are processed on a rolling basis. Application fee: $50 ($70 for international students). Electronic applications accepted. *Financial support:* In 2013–14, 253 students received support, including 5 fellowships (averaging $32,204 per year), 27 research assistantships with full and partial tuition reimbursements available (averaging $10,199 per year), 68 teaching assistantships with full and partial tuition reimbursements available (averaging $12,316 per year); career-related internships or fieldwork, Federal Work-Study, institutionally sponsored loans, health care benefits, and unspecified assistantships also available. Support available to part-time students. Financial award applicants required to submit FAFSA. *Faculty research:* Literary, curriculum studies, science education, K-12 leadership, higher education. *Total annual research expenditures:* $735,835. *Unit head:* Dr. Earl Cheek, Jr., Chair, 225-578-1258, Fax: 225-578-2267, E-mail: echeek@lsu.edu. *Application contact:* Dr. Kristin Gansle, Graduate Coordinator, 225-578-6780, Fax: 225-578-2267, E-mail: kgansle@lsu.edu.

Louisiana State University in Shreveport, College of Business, Education, and Human Development, Program in Education, Shreveport, LA 71115-2399. Offers curriculum and instruction (M Ed); educational leadership (M Ed); school counseling (M Ed). *Accreditation:* NCATE. Part-time programs available. *Students:* 1 (woman) full-time, 99 part-time (80 women); includes 26 minority (20 Black or African American, non-Hispanic/Latino; 4 Hispanic/Latino; 2 Two or more races, non-Hispanic/Latino), 1 international. Average age 37. 111 applicants, 97% accepted, 42 enrolled. In 2013, 24 master's awarded. *Degree requirements:* For master's, orally-presented project, 200-hour internship (educational leadership). *Entrance requirements:* For master's, GRE, minimum GPA of 2.5; teacher certification; recommendations and interview (for educational leadership). Additional exam requirements/recommendations for international students: Required—TOEFL (minimum score 550 paper-based; 80 iBT). *Application deadline:* For fall admission, 6/30 for domestic and international students; for spring admission, 11/30 for domestic and international students. Applications are processed on a rolling basis. Application fee: $10 ($20 for international students). *Expenses: Tuition, area resident:* Part-time $182 per credit hour. *Required fees:* $51. *Financial support:* In 2013–14, 5 research assistantships (averaging $2,150 per year) were awarded. *Unit head:* Dr. Pat Doerr, Coordinator, 318-797-5033, Fax: 318-798-4144, E-mail: pat.doerr@lsus.edu. *Application contact:* Christianne Wojcik, Director of Academic Services, 318-797-5247, Fax: 318-798-4120, E-mail: christianne.wojcik@lsus.edu.

Louisiana Tech University, Graduate School, College of Education, Department of Curriculum, Instruction and Leadership, Ruston, LA 71272. Offers curriculum and instruction (M Ed, Ed D), including adult education (M Ed), early childhood (M Ed), English education (M Ed), mathematics education (M Ed), science education (M Ed), social studies education (M Ed), special education (M Ed); educational leadership (M Ed, Ed D). *Accreditation:* NCATE. Part-time programs available. *Degree requirements:* For doctorate, thesis/dissertation. *Entrance requirements:* For master's and doctorate, GRE General Test. *Application deadline:* For fall admission, 7/29 for domestic students; for spring admission, 2/3 for domestic students. Application fee: $20 ($30 for international students). *Financial support:* Fellowships, research assistantships, and teaching assistantships available. Financial award application deadline: 2/1. *Unit head:* Dr. Pauline Leonard, Head, 318-257-4609, Fax: 318-257-2379. *Application contact:* Dr. John Harrison, Associate Dean of Graduate Studies, 318-257-3229, Fax: 318-257-2379, E-mail: johnharrison@latech.edu.
Website: http://www.latech.edu/education/cil/.

Lourdes University, Graduate School, Sylvania, OH 43560-2898. Offers business (MBA); leadership (M Ed); nurse anesthesia (MSN); nurse educator (MSN); nurse leader (MSN); organizational leadership (MOL); reading (M Ed); teaching and curriculum (M Ed); theology (MA). Evening/weekend programs available. *Entrance requirements:* Additional exam requirements/recommendations for international students: Required—TOEFL. *Application deadline:* For fall admission, 6/15 priority date for domestic students; for spring admission, 11/1 priority date for domestic students. Application fee: $25. *Application contact:* Melissa Bergfeld, Administrative Assistant, 419-824-3517, Fax: 419-824-3510, E-mail: mbergfeld2@lourdes.edu.
Website: http://www.lourdes.edu/gradschool.aspx.

Loyola Marymount University, School of Education, Department of Educational Leadership, Doctorate in Educational Leadership for Social Justice Program, Los Angeles, CA 90045. Offers Ed D. Part-time programs available. *Faculty:* 10 full-time (7 women), 7 part-time/adjunct (3 women). *Students:* 18 full-time (9 women), 42 part-time (23 women); includes 40 minority (10 Black or African American, non-Hispanic/Latino; 5 Asian, non-Hispanic/Latino; 23 Hispanic/Latino; 2 Two or more races, non-Hispanic/Latino), 1 international. Average age 37. 51 applicants, 43% accepted, 17 enrolled. In 2013, 13 doctorates awarded. *Degree requirements:* For doctorate, thesis/dissertation. *Entrance requirements:* For doctorate, GRE, interview, resume, 3 letters of recommendation. Additional exam requirements/recommendations for international students: Required—TOEFL (minimum score 600 paper-based; 100 iBT). *Application deadline:* For fall admission, 1/25 for domestic students. Application fee: $50. Electronic applications accepted. Application fee is waived when completed online. *Financial support:* In 2013–14, 52 students received support, including 4 research assistantships (averaging $2,100 per year); institutionally sponsored loans, scholarships/grants, and unspecified assistantships also available. Support available to part-time students. Financial award application deadline: 6/30; financial award applicants required to submit FAFSA. *Total annual research expenditures:* $531,433. *Unit head:* Dr. Shane P. Martin, Dean, 310-338-7301, E-mail: smartin@lmu.edu. *Application contact:* Chake H. Kouyoumjian, Associate Dean of Graduate Studies, 310-338-2721, E-mail: ckouyoum@lmu.edu.
Website: http://soe.lmu.edu/admissions/programs/edd/.

Loyola Marymount University, School of Education, Department of Educational Leadership, Program in Catholic School Administration, Los Angeles, CA 90045. Offers MA. Part-time programs available. *Faculty:* 10 full-time (7 women), 7 part-time/adjunct (3 women). *Students:* 14 full-time (11 women), 42 part-time (28 women); includes 19 minority (1 Black or African American, non-Hispanic/Latino; 3 Asian, non-Hispanic/Latino; 15 Hispanic/Latino), 2 international. Average age 37. 33 applicants, 85% accepted, 26 enrolled. *Degree requirements:* For master's, comprehensive exam. *Entrance requirements:* For master's, CBEST, CSET, 2 letters of recommendation, full-time employment in the Archdiocese of Los Angeles. Additional exam requirements/recommendations for international students: Required—TOEFL (minimum score 600 paper-based; 100 iBT). *Application deadline:* For fall admission, 6/15 for domestic students; for spring admission, 11/15 for domestic students. Application fee: $50.

Electronic applications accepted. *Financial support:* In 2013–14, 56 students received support. Institutionally sponsored loans, scholarships/grants, and unspecified assistantships available. Financial award application deadline: 6/30; financial award applicants required to submit FAFSA. *Total annual research expenditures:* $531,433. *Unit head:* Dr. Franca Dell'Olio, Program Director, 310-258-8737, E-mail: fdellolio@lmu.edu. *Application contact:* Chake H. Kouyoumjian, Associate Dean of the Graduate Division, 310-338-2721, E-mail: ckouyoum@lmu.edu.
Website: http://soe.lmu.edu/admissions/programs/schooladministration/maincatholicschooladministration/.

Loyola Marymount University, School of Education, Department of Educational Leadership, Program in School Administration, Los Angeles, CA 90045. Offers MA. Part-time and evening/weekend programs available. *Faculty:* 10 full-time (7 women), 7 part-time/adjunct (3 women). *Students:* 15 full-time (10 women), 1 part-time (0 women); includes 9 minority (8 Hispanic/Latino; 1 Two or more races, non-Hispanic/Latino). Average age 32. 6 applicants, 83% accepted, 5 enrolled. In 2013, 6 master's awarded. *Degree requirements:* For master's, comprehensive exam. *Entrance requirements:* For master's, CBEST, 2 letters of recommendation. Additional exam requirements/recommendations for international students: Required—TOEFL (minimum score 600 paper-based; 100 iBT). *Application deadline:* For fall admission, 5/1 for domestic students; for spring admission, 11/1 for domestic students. Application fee: $50. Electronic applications accepted. *Financial support:* In 2013–14, 16 students received support. Scholarships/grants and unspecified assistantships available. Support available to part-time students. Financial award application deadline: 6/30; financial award applicants required to submit FAFSA. *Total annual research expenditures:* $399,200. *Unit head:* Dr. Franca Dell'Olio, Program Director, 310-258-8737, E-mail: fdellolio@lmu.edu. *Application contact:* Chake H. Kouyoumjian, Associate Dean of Graduate Studies, 310-338-2721, E-mail: ckouyoum@lmu.edu.
Website: http://soe.lmu.edu/admissions/programs/schooladministration/.

Loyola University Chicago, School of Education, Program in Administration and Supervision, Chicago, IL 60660. Offers M Ed, Ed D, Certificate. Part-time and evening/weekend programs available. *Faculty:* 3 full-time (all women), 11 part-time/adjunct (6 women). *Students:* 87. Average age 35. 37 applicants, 57% accepted, 20 enrolled. In 2013, 9 doctorates awarded. *Degree requirements:* For master's, comprehensive exam; for doctorate, comprehensive exam, thesis/dissertation. *Entrance requirements:* For master's, minimum GPA of 3.0, letters of recommendation, resume, transcripts; for doctorate, GRE General Test, interview, minimum GPA of 3.0, letters of recommendation, resume. Additional exam requirements/recommendations for international students: Required—TOEFL (minimum score 550 paper-based; 79 iBT). *Application deadline:* For fall admission, 2/15 for domestic and international students; for spring admission, 11/1 for domestic and international students. Applications are processed on a rolling basis. Application fee: $50. Electronic applications accepted. Application fee is waived when completed online. *Expenses: Tuition:* Full-time $16,740; part-time $930 per credit. *Required fees:* $135 per semester. *Financial support:* In 2013–14, 38 fellowships were awarded; research assistantships with full tuition reimbursements, teaching assistantships with full tuition reimbursements, career-related internships or fieldwork, institutionally sponsored loans, scholarships/grants, tuition waivers, and unspecified assistantships also available. Support available to part-time students. Financial award application deadline: 2/1; financial award applicants required to submit FAFSA. *Faculty research:* Leadership, school law, school administration, supervision, ethics. *Unit head:* Dr. Janis Fine, Director, 312-915-7022, Fax: 312-915-6980, E-mail: jfine@luc.edu. *Application contact:* Marie Rosin-Dittmar, Information Contact, 312-915-6800, E-mail: schleduc@luc.edu.

Loyola University Maryland, Graduate Programs, School of Education, Program in Educational Leadership, Baltimore, MD 21210-2699. Offers M Ed, MA, CAS, Certificate. Part-time programs available. *Degree requirements:* For master's, thesis. *Entrance requirements:* For master's, transcripts, essay, resume. Additional exam requirements/recommendations for international students: Required—TOEFL (minimum score 550 paper-based). Electronic applications accepted.

Lynchburg College, Graduate Studies, School of Education and Human Development, EdD Program in Leadership Studies, Lynchburg, VA 24501-3199. Offers Ed D. Evening/weekend programs available. *Faculty:* 6 full-time (4 women), 3 part-time/adjunct (2 women). *Students:* 3 full-time (2 women), 42 part-time (24 women); includes 8 minority (7 Black or African American, non-Hispanic/Latino; 1 Asian, non-Hispanic/Latino), 1 international. Average age 41. *Degree requirements:* For doctorate, comprehensive exam, thesis/dissertation. *Entrance requirements:* For doctorate, GRE or GMAT, current resume or curriculum vitae, career goals statement, master's degree, official transcripts (bachelor's, master's, others of relevance), master's-level research course, three letters of recommendation, evidence of strong writing skills. Additional exam requirements/recommendations for international students: Required—TOEFL (minimum score 550 paper-based; 79 iBT), IELTS (minimum score 6.5). *Application deadline:* For fall admission, 7/31 for domestic students, 6/1 for international students; for spring admission, 11/30 for domestic students, 10/15 for international students. Applications are processed on a rolling basis. Application fee: $30. Electronic applications accepted. Application fee is waived when completed online. *Financial support:* Application deadline: 7/31; applicants required to submit FAFSA. *Unit head:* Dr. Roger Jones, Program Director, 434-544-8444, Fax: 434-544-8483, E-mail: jones@lynchburg.edu. *Application contact:* Anne Pingstock, Executive Assistant, 434-544-8383, Fax: 434-544-8483, E-mail: gradstudies@lynchburg.edu.
Website: http://www.lynchburg.edu/edd-leadership-studies/doctor-education-leadership-studies.

Lynchburg College, Graduate Studies, School of Education and Human Development, M Ed Program in Educational Leadership, Lynchburg, VA 24501-3199. Offers M Ed. Part-time and evening/weekend programs available. *Faculty:* 3 full-time (1 woman). *Students:* 11 full-time (4 women), 32 part-time (13 women); includes 4 minority (all Black or African American, non-Hispanic/Latino). Average age 31. In 2013, 11 master's awarded. *Degree requirements:* For master's, internship; ISLLC exam or comprehensive exam. *Entrance requirements:* For master's, GRE, minimum GPA of 3.0 (preferred), official transcripts (bachelor's, others as relevant), three letters of recommendation, career goals statement. Additional exam requirements/recommendations for international students: Required—TOEFL (minimum score 550 paper-based; 79 iBT), IELTS (minimum score 6.5). *Application deadline:* For fall admission, 7/31 for domestic students, 6/1 for international students; for spring admission, 11/30 for domestic students, 10/5 for international students. Applications are processed on a rolling basis. Application fee: $30. Electronic applications accepted. Application fee is waived when completed online. *Financial support:* Fellowships, research assistantships, career-related internships or fieldwork, Federal Work-Study, scholarships/grants, health care benefits, and unspecified assistantships available. Support available to part-time students. Financial award application deadline: 7/31; financial award applicants required to submit FAFSA. *Unit head:* Dr. Roger Jones, Professor/Director, Leadership Studies, 434-544-8444, E-mail: jones@lynchburg.edu. *Application contact:* Anne Pingstock, Executive Assistant, Graduate Studies, 434-544-8383, Fax: 434-544-8483, E-mail: gradstudies@lynchburg.edu.
Website: http://www.lynchburg.edu/master-education-educational-leadership.

Lynn University, Donald E. and Helen L. Ross College of Education, Boca Raton, FL 33431-5598. Offers educational leadership (M Ed, Ed D); exceptional student education (M Ed). Part-time and evening/weekend programs available. *Faculty:* 2 full-time (both women), 6 part-time/adjunct (5 women). *Students:* 28 full-time (24 women), 54 part-time (28 women); includes 9 minority (8 Black or African American, non-Hispanic/Latino; 1 Hispanic/Latino), 8 international. Average age 36. 31 applicants, 97% accepted, 25 enrolled. In 2013, 29 master's, 7 doctorates awarded. *Degree requirements:* For master's, thesis (for some programs); for doctorate, thesis/dissertation, qualifying paper. *Entrance requirements:* For master's, bachelor's degree from accredited institution, minimum undergraduate GPA of 3.0, resume, 2 letters of recommendation, statement of professional goals; for doctorate, master's degree from accredited institution, minimum GPA of 3.5, resume, 2 letters of recommendation, professional practice statement, interview and presentation. Additional exam requirements/recommendations for international students: Required—TOEFL (minimum score 550 paper-based). *Application deadline:* Applications are processed on a rolling basis. Application fee: $45. Electronic applications accepted. *Expenses: Tuition:* Full-time $23,760; part-time $660 per credit. *Required fees:* $300; $50 per term. Tuition and fees vary according to degree level and program. *Financial support:* Career-related internships or fieldwork, Federal Work-Study, institutionally sponsored loans, scholarships/grants, tuition waivers (partial), and unspecified assistantships available. Support available to part-time students. Financial award application deadline: 8/1; financial award applicants required to submit FAFSA. *Faculty research:* Non-traditional education, innovative curricula, multicultural education, simulation games. *Unit head:* Dr. Gregg Cox, Dean of College, 561-237-7210, E-mail: gcox@lynn.edu. *Application contact:* Steven Pruitt, Director of Graduate and Undergraduate Evening Admission, 561-237-7834, Fax: 561-237-7100, E-mail: spruitt@lynn.edu.
Website: http://www.lynn.edu/academics/colleges/education.

Madonna University, Programs in Education, Livonia, MI 48150-1173. Offers Catholic school leadership (MSA); educational leadership (MSA); learning disabilities (MAT); literacy education (MAT); teaching and learning (MAT). *Accreditation:* NCATE. Part-time and evening/weekend programs available. *Degree requirements:* For master's, thesis or alternative. Electronic applications accepted.

Malone University, Graduate Program in Education, Canton, OH 44709. Offers curriculum and instruction (MA); curriculum, instruction, and professional development (MA); educational leadership (principal license) (MA); intervention specialist (MA). Part-time and evening/weekend programs available. *Faculty:* 8 full-time (4 women), 12 part-time/adjunct (9 women). *Students:* 10 full-time (6 women), 59 part-time (44 women); includes 5 minority (2 Black or African American, non-Hispanic/Latino; 1 Hispanic/Latino; 2 Two or more races, non-Hispanic/Latino). Average age 32. In 2013, 13 master's awarded. *Degree requirements:* For master's, research project. *Entrance requirements:* For master's, minimum GPA of 3.0, teaching license. Additional exam requirements/recommendations for international students: Required—TOEFL (minimum score 550 paper-based; 79 iBT). *Application deadline:* Applications are processed on a rolling basis. *Financial support:* Tuition waivers (partial) available. Support available to part-time students. Financial award application deadline: 6/30. *Faculty research:* Educational leadership styles: Jesus as master teacher, assessment accommodations for English language learners, preparing culturally proficient teachers, using naturally occurring text in the classroom to meet the syntactic needs of students with learning disabilities, using tablet instructional technology to meet the needs of students with disabilities. *Unit head:* Dr. Moses B. Rumano, Director, 330-471-8349, Fax: 330-471-8563, E-mail: mrumano@malone.edu. *Application contact:* Dan DePasquale, Senior Recruiter, 330-471-8381, Fax: 330-471-8343, E-mail: depasquale@malone.edu.
Website: http://www.malone.edu/admissions/graduate/education/.

Manhattan College, Graduate Programs, School of Education and Health, Program in School Building Leadership, Riverdale, NY 10471. Offers MA, Professional Diploma. Part-time and evening/weekend programs available. Postbaccalaureate distance learning degree programs offered (minimal on-campus study). *Faculty:* 1 (woman) full-time, 6 part-time/adjunct (3 women). *Students:* 23 part-time (16 women); includes 7 minority (4 Black or African American, non-Hispanic/Latino; 3 Hispanic/Latino). 70 applicants, 50% accepted, 23 enrolled. In 2013, 4 master's, 3 other advanced degrees awarded. *Degree requirements:* For master's, thesis, internship; for Professional Diploma, internship. *Entrance requirements:* For master's, minimum GPA of 3.0, 3 years of teaching, professional recommendation; for Professional Diploma, minimum GPA of 3.0. Additional exam requirements/recommendations for international students: Required—TOEFL. *Application deadline:* For fall admission, 8/1 priority date for domestic students, 4/1 priority date for international students; for spring admission, 1/1 priority date for domestic students, 9/1 priority date for international students. Applications are processed on a rolling basis. Application fee: $60. *Expenses:* Contact institution. *Financial support:* In 2013–14, 6 students received support. Scholarships/grants available. *Faculty research:* Distance learning and teacher efficacy, leadership and student achievement, professional development and student achievement, leadership development, professional development for teachers. *Unit head:* Dr. Remigia Kushner, Program Director, 718-862-7473, Fax: 718-862-7816, E-mail: sr.remigia.kushner@manhattan.edu. *Application contact:* William Bisset, Vice President for Enrollment, 718-862-7199, Fax: 718-862-8019, E-mail: william.bisset@manhattan.edu.
Website: http://manhattan.edu/academics/education/school-building-leadership.

Manhattanville College, School of Education, Program in Educational Leadership, Purchase, NY 10577-2132. Offers MPS, Ed D. Part-time and evening/weekend programs available. *Degree requirements:* For doctorate, thesis/dissertation. *Entrance requirements:* For master's, minimum undergraduate GPA of 3.0, 2 letters of recommendation. Additional exam requirements/recommendations for international students: Required—TOEFL. Electronic applications accepted.

Marian University, School of Education, Fond du Lac, WI 54935-4699. Offers educational leadership (MAE, PhD); leadership studies (PhD); teacher development (MAE). PhD in leadership studies offered jointly with School of Business and Public Safety. *Accreditation:* NCATE. Part-time and evening/weekend programs available. Postbaccalaureate distance learning degree programs offered (minimal on-campus study). *Faculty:* 15 full-time (10 women), 22 part-time/adjunct (10 women). *Students:* 23 full-time (15 women), 281 part-time (197 women); includes 25 minority (13 Black or African American, non-Hispanic/Latino; 9 American Indian or Alaska Native, non-Hispanic/Latino; 2 Asian, non-Hispanic/Latino; 1 Hispanic/Latino). Average age 38. In 2013, 135 master's, 6 doctorates awarded. *Degree requirements:* For master's, exam, field-based experience project, portfolio; for doctorate, comprehensive exam, thesis/dissertation, field-based experience. *Entrance requirements:* For master's, minimum GPA of 3.0, BA in education or related field, teaching license; for doctorate, GRE, MAT, resume, 2 writing samples, interview. Additional exam requirements/recommendations for international students: Required—TOEFL (minimum score 525 paper-based; 70 iBT). *Application deadline:* Applications are processed on a rolling basis. Application fee: $50. *Expenses: Tuition:* Part-time $490 per credit hour. Tuition and fees vary according to degree level and program. *Financial support:* In 2013–14, 3 students received support. Federal Work-Study and institutionally sponsored loans available. Support available to part-time students. Financial award application deadline: 3/1; financial award applicants

required to submit FAFSA. *Faculty research:* At-risk youth, multicultural issues, values in education, teaching/learning strategies. *Unit head:* Dr. Sue Stoddart, Dean, 920-923-8099, Fax: 920-923-7663, E-mail: sstoddart@marianuniversity.edu. *Application contact:* Rachel Benike, Admissions Counselor, 920-923-8118, Fax: 920-923-7154, E-mail: rlbenike43@marianuniversity.edu.
Website: http://soe.marianuniversity.edu/.

Marquette University, Graduate School, College of Education, Department of Educational Policy and Leadership, Milwaukee, WI 53201-1881. Offers college student personnel administration (M Ed); curriculum and instruction (MA); education (MA); educational administration (M Ed); educational policy and foundations (MA); elementary education (Certificate); literacy (MA); principal (Certificate); reading specialist (Certificate); reading teacher (Certificate); secondary education (Certificate); superintendent (Certificate). Part-time and evening/weekend programs available. *Faculty:* 15 full-time (10 women), 3 part-time/adjunct (2 women). *Students:* 39 full-time (31 women), 107 part-time (70 women); includes 19 minority (7 Black or African American, non-Hispanic/Latino; 2 American Indian or Alaska Native, non-Hispanic/Latino; 3 Asian, non-Hispanic/Latino; 6 Hispanic/Latino; 1 Two or more races, non-Hispanic/Latino), 2 international. Average age 30. 144 applicants, 74% accepted, 67 enrolled. In 2013, 48 master's, 4 doctorates, 12 other advanced degrees awarded. Terminal master's awarded for partial completion of doctoral program. *Degree requirements:* For master's, comprehensive exam, thesis (for some programs); for doctorate, thesis/dissertation, qualifying exam, supporting minor. *Entrance requirements:* For master's, GRE General Test or MAT, official transcripts from all current and previous colleges/universities except Marquette, three letters of recommendation, statement of purpose; for doctorate, GRE General Test, MAT, sample of written work, official transcripts from all current and previous colleges/universities except Marquette, three letters of recommendation, statement of purpose, resume/curriculum vitae; for Certificate, GRE General Test or MAT, master's degree. Additional exam requirements/recommendations for international students: Required—TOEFL (minimum score 530 paper-based). *Application deadline:* For fall admission, 1/15 for domestic and international students. Application fee: $50. *Expenses:* Contact institution. *Financial support:* In 2013–14, 130 students received support, including 1 fellowship with full tuition reimbursement available (averaging $18,780 per year), 5 research assistantships with full tuition reimbursements available (averaging $13,404 per year); health care benefits, tuition waivers (partial), and unspecified assistantships also available. Support available to part-time students. Financial award application deadline: 2/15. *Faculty research:* Leadership; social justice in education; development of lifelong learners; race, class, and schooling in historical perspective; urban teacher education. *Unit head:* Dr. Ellen Eckman, Chair, 414-288-1561, E-mail: ellen.eckman@marquette.edu. *Application contact:* Dr. Sharon Chubbuck, Associate Professor, 414-288-5895.

Marshall University, Academic Affairs Division, College of Education and Professional Development, Program in Leadership Studies, Huntington, WV 25755. Offers MA, MS, Ed D, Certificate, Ed S. Part-time and evening/weekend programs available. *Students:* 59 full-time (25 women), 329 part-time (176 women); includes 39 minority (14 Black or African American, non-Hispanic/Latino; 1 American Indian or Alaska Native, non-Hispanic/Latino; 3 Asian, non-Hispanic/Latino; 9 Hispanic/Latino; 4 Native Hawaiian or other Pacific Islander, non-Hispanic/Latino; 8 Two or more races, non-Hispanic/Latino). Average age 40. In 2013, 48 master's, 12 doctorates, 11 other advanced degrees awarded. *Degree requirements:* For master's, thesis optional, comprehensive or oral assessment. *Entrance requirements:* For master's, GRE General Test or MAT. Application fee: $40. *Financial support:* Career-related internships or fieldwork, Federal Work-Study, tuition waivers (full), and unspecified assistantships available. Support available to part-time students. Financial award applicants required to submit FAFSA. *Unit head:* Dr. Michael Cunningham, Program Director, 800-642-9842 Ext. 61912, E-mail: mcunningham@marshall.edu. *Application contact:* Information Contact, 304-746-1900, Fax: 304-746-1902, E-mail: services@marshall.edu.

Martin Luther College, Graduate Studies, New Ulm, MN 56073. Offers instruction (MS Ed); leadership (MS Ed); special education (MS Ed). Part-time programs available. Postbaccalaureate distance learning degree programs offered. *Degree requirements:* For master's, capstone project or comprehensive exam. *Entrance requirements:* For master's, undergraduate degree in education from an accredited college or university, minimum undergraduate GPA of 3.0. Electronic applications accepted.

Marygrove College, Graduate Division, Program in Educational Leadership, Detroit, MI 48221-2599. Offers MA. Part-time and evening/weekend programs available. *Degree requirements:* For master's, research project. *Entrance requirements:* For master's, MAT, interview, minimum undergraduate GPA of 3.0.

Marymount University, School of Education and Human Services, Program in Administration and Supervision, Arlington, VA 22207-4299. Offers M Ed, Certificate. Part-time and evening/weekend programs available. Postbaccalaureate distance learning degree programs offered (minimal on-campus study). *Faculty:* 1 (woman) full-time, 2 part-time/adjunct (1 woman). *Students:* 27 part-time (15 women); includes 6 minority (1 Black or African American, non-Hispanic/Latino; 1 Asian, non-Hispanic/Latino; 3 Hispanic/Latino; 1 Native Hawaiian or other Pacific Islander, non-Hispanic/Latino), 1 international. Average age 39. In 2013, 13 master's, 1 Certificate awarded. *Degree requirements:* For master's, thesis or alternative. *Entrance requirements:* For master's, GRE General Test or MAT, 3 letters of recommendation, interview, resume; for Certificate, 3 letters of recommendation, interview, resume, essay. Additional exam requirements/recommendations for international students: Required—TOEFL (minimum score 600 paper-based; 96 iBT), IELTS (minimum score 6.5). *Application deadline:* For fall admission, 5/1 priority date for domestic students. Applications are processed on a rolling basis. Application fee: $40. Electronic applications accepted. *Expenses: Tuition:* Part-time $850 per credit. *Required fees:* $10 per credit. One-time fee: $200 part-time. Tuition and fees vary according to program. *Financial support:* In 2013–14, 1 student received support. Research assistantships with full and partial tuition reimbursements available, career-related internships or fieldwork, Federal Work-Study, scholarships/grants, and unspecified assistantships available. Support available to part-time students. Financial award applicants required to submit FAFSA. *Unit head:* Sr. Patricia Earl, Coordinator, 703-284-1517, Fax: 703-284-1631, E-mail: patricia.earl@marymount.edu. *Application contact:* Francesca Reed, Director, Graduate Admissions, 703-284-5901, Fax: 703-527-3815, E-mail: grad.admissions@marymount.edu.
Website: http://www.marymount.edu/academics/programs/edAdmin.

Maryville University of Saint Louis, School of Education, St. Louis, MO 63141-7299. Offers art education (MA Ed); early childhood education (MA Ed); educational leadership (Ed D); educational leadership: principal certification (MA Ed); elementary education (MA Ed); gifted education (MA Ed); higher education leadership (Ed D); literacy specialist (MA Ed); middle grades education (MA Ed); secondary teaching and inquiry (MA Ed); teacher as leader (MA Ed); teacher leadership (Ed D). *Accreditation:* NCATE. Part-time and evening/weekend programs available. *Faculty:* 10 full-time (6 women), 17 part-time/adjunct (13 women). *Students:* 21 full-time (17 women), 238 part-time (167 women); includes 64 minority (54 Black or African American, non-Hispanic/Latino; 2 Asian, non-Hispanic/Latino; 4 Hispanic/Latino; 4 Two or more races, non-Hispanic/Latino), 2 international. Average age 39. In 2013, 61 master's, 40 doctorates awarded. *Degree requirements:* For master's, thesis, project. *Entrance requirements:* For master's, minimum cumulative GPA of 3.0, 3 professional recommendations, essays, interview with program faculty; for doctorate, minimum GPA of 3.0, 3 professional recommendations, essay, interview, on-site writing sample. Additional exam requirements/recommendations for international students: Required—TOEFL (minimum score 550 paper-based). *Application deadline:* Applications are processed on a rolling basis. Application fee: $40 ($60 for international students). Electronic applications accepted. Application fee is waived when completed online. *Expenses: Tuition:* Full-time $23,812; part-time $728 per credit hour. *Required fees:* $395 per year. Tuition and fees vary according to course load, degree level and program. *Financial support:* Career-related internships or fieldwork, Federal Work-Study, tuition waivers (partial), and professional educator discounts available. Financial award application deadline: 3/1; financial award applicants required to submit FAFSA. *Faculty research:* Collaboration with public schools, pre-service program development, mathematics, diversity, literacy. *Unit head:* Dr. Cathy Bear, Dean, 314-529-9692, Fax: 314-529-9921, E-mail: cbear@maryville.edu. *Application contact:* Holly Stanwich, Graduate Admissions Coordinator, 314-529-9542, Fax: 314-529-9921, E-mail: teachered@maryville.edu.
Website: http://www.maryville.edu/ed/graduate-programs/.

Marywood University, Academic Affairs, Reap College of Education and Human Development, Department of Education, Program in Higher Education Administration, Scranton, PA 18509-1598. Offers MS. Part-time and evening/weekend programs available. *Entrance requirements:* Additional exam requirements/recommendations for international students: Required—TOEFL (minimum score 550 paper-based; 79 iBT). *Application deadline:* For fall admission, 4/1 priority date for domestic students, 3/31 priority date for international students; for spring admission, 11/1 priority date for domestic students, 8/31 priority date for international students. Applications are processed on a rolling basis. Application fee: $30. Electronic applications accepted. *Expenses: Tuition:* Part-time $775 per credit. Tuition and fees vary according to degree level. *Financial support:* Research assistantships with tuition reimbursements, career-related internships or fieldwork, scholarships/grants, and unspecified assistantships available. Support available to part-time students. Financial award application deadline: 6/30; financial award applicants required to submit FAFSA. *Faculty research:* Integrated thematic instruction. *Unit head:* Dr. Patricia S. Arter, Chairperson, 570-348-6211 Ext. 2511, E-mail: psarter@marywood.edu. *Application contact:* Tammy Manka, Assistant Director of Graduate Admissions, 570-348-6211 Ext. 2322, E-mail: tmanka@marywood.edu.
Website: http://www.marywood.edu/education/graduate-programs/ms_higher_education_administration.html.

Marywood University, Academic Affairs, Reap College of Education and Human Development, Department of Education, Program in Instructional Leadership, Scranton, PA 18509-1598. Offers M Ed. *Application deadline:* For fall admission, 4/1 for domestic students, 3/31 for international students; for spring admission, 11/1 for domestic students, 8/31 for international students. Applications are processed on a rolling basis. Electronic applications accepted. *Expenses: Tuition:* Part-time $775 per credit. Tuition and fees vary according to degree level. *Financial support:* Career-related internships or fieldwork, scholarships/grants, and unspecified assistantships available. Support available to part-time students. Financial award application deadline: 6/30. *Unit head:* Dr. Patricia S. Arter, Chairperson, 570-348-6211 Ext. 2511, E-mail: psarter@marywood.edu. *Application contact:* Tammy Manka, Assistant Director of Graduate Admissions, 570-348-6211 Ext. 2322, E-mail: tmanka@marywood.edu.
Website: http://www.marywood.edu/education/graduate-programs/med-instructional-leadership.html.

Marywood University, Academic Affairs, Reap College of Education and Human Development, Department of Education, Program in School Leadership with Principal Certification, Scranton, PA 18509-1598. Offers MS. *Accreditation:* NCATE. *Entrance requirements:* Additional exam requirements/recommendations for international students: Required—TOEFL (minimum score 550 paper-based; 79 iBT). *Application deadline:* For fall admission, 4/1 priority date for domestic students, 3/31 priority date for international students; for spring admission, 11/1 priority date for domestic students, 8/31 priority date for international students. Applications are processed on a rolling basis. Application fee: $35. Electronic applications accepted. *Expenses: Tuition:* Part-time $775 per credit. Tuition and fees vary according to degree level. *Financial support:* Career-related internships or fieldwork, scholarships/grants, and unspecified assistantships available. Support available to part-time students. Financial award application deadline: 6/30; financial award applicants required to submit FAFSA. *Faculty research:* School board leadership and development, site-based decision-making, educational administration. *Unit head:* Dr. Patricia S. Arter, Chairperson, 570-348-6211 Ext. 2511, E-mail: psarter@marywood.edu. *Application contact:* Tammy Manka, Assistant Director of Graduate Admissions, 570-348-6211 Ext. 2322, E-mail: tmanka@marywood.edu.
Website: http://www.marywood.edu/education/graduate-programs/ms-principal.html.

Marywood University, Academic Affairs, Reap College of Education and Human Development, Doctoral Program in Human Development, Emphasis in Educational Administration, Scranton, PA 18509-1598. Offers PhD. *Entrance requirements:* Additional exam requirements/recommendations for international students: Required—TOEFL (minimum score 550 paper-based; 79 iBT). *Application deadline:* For fall admission, 1/30 priority date for domestic and international students. Application fee: $35. Electronic applications accepted. *Expenses:* Contact institution. *Financial support:* Career-related internships or fieldwork, scholarships/grants, and unspecified assistantships available. Support available to part-time students. Financial award application deadline: 6/30; financial award applicants required to submit FAFSA. *Unit head:* Dr. Joseph Polizzi, Coordinator, 570-348-6279, E-mail: japolizzi@marywood.edu. *Application contact:* Tammy Manka, Assistant Director of Graduate Admissions, 570-348-6211 Ext. 2322, E-mail: tmanka@marywood.edu.
Website: http://www.marywood.edu/phd/specializations.html.

Marywood University, Academic Affairs, Reap College of Education and Human Development, Doctoral Program in Human Development, Emphasis in Higher Education Administration, Scranton, PA 18509-1598. Offers PhD. *Entrance requirements:* Additional exam requirements/recommendations for international students: Required—TOEFL (minimum score 550 paper-based; 79 iBT). *Application deadline:* For fall admission, 1/30 for domestic and international students. Application fee: $35. Electronic applications accepted. *Expenses:* Contact institution. *Financial support:* Career-related internships or fieldwork, scholarships/grants, and unspecified assistantships available. Support available to part-time students. Financial award application deadline: 6/30; financial award applicants required to submit FAFSA. *Unit head:* Dr. Tonya Nicole Saddler, Coordinator, 570-348-6270, E-mail: saddlert@marywood.edu. *Application contact:* Tammy Manka, Assistant Director of Graduate Admissions, 570-348-6211 Ext. 2322, E-mail: tmanka@marywood.edu.
Website: http://www.marywood.edu/phd/specializations.html.

Marywood University, Academic Affairs, Reap College of Education and Human Development, Doctoral Program in Human Development, Emphasis in Instructional Leadership, Scranton, PA 18509-1598. Offers PhD. *Entrance requirements:* Additional exam requirements/recommendations for international students: Required—TOEFL

(minimum score 550 paper-based; 79 iBT). *Application deadline:* For fall admission, 1/30 priority date for domestic and international students. Application fee: $35. Electronic applications accepted. *Expenses:* Contact institution. *Financial support:* Career-related internships or fieldwork, scholarships/grants, and unspecified assistantships available. Support available to part-time students. Financial award application deadline: 6/30; financial award applicants required to submit FAFSA. *Unit head:* Sr. Kathryn Clauss, Coordinator, 570-348-6279, E-mail: kclauss@marywood.edu. *Application contact:* Tammy Manka, Assistant Director of Graduate Admissions, 570-348-6211 Ext. 2322, E-mail: tmanka@marywood.edu.
Website: http://www.marywood.edu/phd/specializations.html.

Massachusetts College of Liberal Arts, Graduate Programs, North Adams, MA 01247-4100. Offers business (MBA); educational administration (M Ed); educational leadership (CAGS); instruction and curriculum (M Ed); instructional technology (M Ed); physical education and health (M Ed); reading (M Ed); special education (M Ed). Part-time and evening/weekend programs available. *Degree requirements:* For master's, thesis. *Entrance requirements:* For master's, writing sample.

McDaniel College, Graduate and Professional Studies, Program in Educational Administration, Westminster, MD 21157-4390. Offers MS. Part-time and evening/weekend programs available. *Degree requirements:* For master's, comprehensive exam (for some programs), thesis optional, portfolio. *Entrance requirements:* For master's, GRE General Test, MAT, or NTE/PRAXIS I. Additional exam requirements/recommendations for international students: Required—TOEFL.

McGill University, Faculty of Graduate and Postdoctoral Studies, Faculty of Education, Department of Integrated Studies in Education, Montréal, QC H3A 2T5, Canada. Offers culture and values in education (MA, PhD); curriculum studies (MA); educational leadership (MA, Certificate); educational studies (PhD); integrated studies in education (M Ed); second language education (MA, PhD).

McKendree University, Graduate Programs, Programs in Education, Lebanon, IL 62254-1299. Offers curriculum design and instruction (Ed D, Ed S); educational administration and leadership (MA Ed); educational studies (MA Ed); higher education administrative services (MA Ed); music education (MA Ed); reading (MA Ed); special education (MA Ed); teacher leadership (MA Ed); teaching certification (MA Ed). *Accreditation:* NCATE. Part-time and evening/weekend programs available. Postbaccalaureate distance learning degree programs offered (no on-campus study). *Entrance requirements:* For master's, official transcripts from all institutions previously attended, minimum GPA of 3.0, resume, references; for doctorate, GRE (within the past 5 years), master's degree in education and Ed S, or the equivalent, from regionally-accredited institution; official transcripts from all institutions previously attended; curriculum vitae/resume; essay/personal statement; two years of teaching/professional experience; for Ed S, GRE (within the past 5 years), master's degree in education from regionally-accredited institution of higher education; official transcripts from all institutions previously attended; curriculum vitae/resume; essay/personal statement; two years of teaching/professional experience. Additional exam requirements/recommendations for international students: Required—TOEFL. Electronic applications accepted.

McNeese State University, Doré School of Graduate Studies, Burton College of Education, Office of Graduate Education Programs, Program in Educational Leadership, Lake Charles, LA 70609. Offers educational leadership (M Ed, Ed S); educational technology (Ed S). Evening/weekend programs available. *Degree requirements:* For Ed S, comprehensive exam. *Entrance requirements:* For master's, GRE, teaching certificate, 3 years of full-time teaching experience; for Ed S, teaching certificate, 3 years of teaching experience, 1 year of administration or supervision experience, master's degree with 12 semester hours in education.

Memorial University of Newfoundland, School of Graduate Studies, Faculty of Education, St. John's, NL A1C 5S7, Canada. Offers counseling psychology (M Ed); curriculum, teaching, and learning studies (M Ed); education (PhD); educational leadership studies (M Ed); information technology (M Ed); post-secondary studies (M Ed, Diploma), including health professional education (Diploma). Part-time programs available. *Degree requirements:* For master's, thesis optional, internship, paper folio, project; for doctorate, comprehensive exam, thesis/dissertation, thesis seminar, oral defense of thesis. *Entrance requirements:* For master's, undergraduate degree with at least 2nd class standing, 1-2 years work experience; for doctorate, minimum A average in graduate course work, MA in education, 2 years professional experience; for Diploma, 2nd class degree, 2 years of work experience with adult learners, appropriate academic qualifications and work experience in a health-related field. Electronic applications accepted. *Faculty research:* Critical thinking, literacy, cognitive studies and counseling, educational change, technology in instruction.

Mercer University, Graduate Studies, Cecil B. Day Campus, Tift College of Education (Atlanta), Macon, GA 31207-0003. Offers curriculum and instruction (PhD); early childhood education (M Ed, MAT, Ed S); educational leadership (PhD, Ed S); higher education leadership (M Ed); independent and charter school leadership (M Ed); middle grades education (M Ed, MAT); reading education (M Ed); school counseling (Ed S); secondary education (M Ed, MAT); teacher leadership (Ed S). *Accreditation:* NCATE. Part-time and evening/weekend programs available. *Faculty:* 40 full-time (20 women), 9 part-time/adjunct (4 women). *Students:* 240 full-time (197 women), 382 part-time (320 women); includes 343 minority (315 Black or African American, non-Hispanic/Latino; 4 American Indian or Alaska Native, non-Hispanic/Latino; 9 Asian, non-Hispanic/Latino; 9 Hispanic/Latino; 1 Native Hawaiian or other Pacific Islander, non-Hispanic/Latino; 5 Two or more races, non-Hispanic/Latino), 4 international. Average age 36. In 2013, 233 master's, 24 doctorates, 47 other advanced degrees awarded. *Degree requirements:* For master's and Ed S, research project; for doctorate, comprehensive exam, thesis/dissertation. *Entrance requirements:* For master's, GRE or MAT, minimum undergraduate GPA of 2.75; for doctorate, GRE; for Ed S, GRE or MAT, minimum GPA of 3.25; for EDS degrees in educational leadership and teacher leadership: 3 years of certified teaching experience. Additional exam requirements/recommendations for international students: Required—TOEFL. *Application deadline:* For fall admission, 8/1 for domestic and international students; for spring admission, 12/1 for domestic and international students; for summer admission, 5/1 for domestic and international students. Applications are processed on a rolling basis. Application fee: $25. *Expenses:* Contact institution. *Financial support:* Federal Work-Study available. Support available to part-time students. Financial award application deadline: 5/1. *Faculty research:* Educational technology, multicultural and minority issues in education, educational leadership (P-12 and higher education), school discipline and school bullying, standards-based mathematics education. *Unit head:* Dr. Paige L. Tompkins, Interim Dean, 478-301-5397, Fax: 478-301-2280, E-mail: tompkins_pl@mercer.edu. *Application contact:* Dr. Allison Gilmore, Associate Dean for Graduate Teacher Education, 678-547-6333, Fax: 678-547-6055, E-mail: gilmore_a@mercer.edu.
Website: http://www.mercer.edu/education/.

Mercer University, Graduate Studies, Macon Campus, Tift College of Education (Macon), Macon, GA 31207-0003. Offers curriculum and instruction (PhD); education leadership (PhD), including P-12; educational leadership (Ed S); higher education (M Ed); teacher leadership (Ed S). *Accreditation:* NCATE. Part-time and evening/

weekend programs available. Postbaccalaureate distance learning degree programs offered (minimal on-campus study). *Faculty:* 15 full-time (6 women), 2 part-time/adjunct (1 woman). *Students:* 39 full-time (20 women), 59 part-time (47 women); includes 41 minority (38 Black or African American, non-Hispanic/Latino; 1 Asian, non-Hispanic/Latino; 2 Hispanic/Latino), 2 international. Average age 35. In 2013, 7 master's, 18 doctorates awarded. *Degree requirements:* For master's, research project report; for doctorate, comprehensive exam, thesis/dissertation. *Entrance requirements:* For master's, GRE or MAT, minimum GPA of 2.75; for doctorate, GRE, minimum GPA of 3.5; interview; writing sample; 3 recommendations; for Ed S, GRE or MAT, minimum GPA of 3.5 (for Ed S in teacher leadership), 3.0 (for Ed S in educational leadership). Additional exam requirements/recommendations for international students: Required—TOEFL. *Application deadline:* For fall admission, 8/1 for domestic and international students; for spring admission, 12/1 for domestic and international students. Applications are processed on a rolling basis. Application fee: $35. *Expenses:* Contact institution. *Financial support:* Federal Work-Study and institutionally sponsored loans available. Support available to part-time students. Financial award application deadline: 5/1. *Faculty research:* Teacher effectiveness, specific learning disabilities, inclusion. *Unit head:* Dr. Paige L. Tompkins, Interim Dean, 478-301-5397, Fax: 478-301-2280, E-mail: tompkins_pl@mercer.edu. *Application contact:* Tracey M. Wofford, Associate Director of Admissions, 678-547-6422, Fax: 678-547-6367, E-mail: wofford_tm@mercer.edu. Website: http://education.mercer.edu/graduate/.

Mercy College, School of Education, Advanced Certificate Program in School Building Leadership, Dobbs Ferry, NY 10522-1189. Offers Advanced Certificate. Part-time and evening/weekend programs available. *Students:* 2 full-time (both women), 16 part-time (12 women); includes 6 minority (all Black or African American, non-Hispanic/Latino). Average age 37. 12 applicants, 67% accepted, 7 enrolled. In 2013, 2 Advanced Certificates awarded. *Degree requirements:* For Advanced Certificate, thesis or alternative, capstone. *Entrance requirements:* For degree, initial or professional teaching certification; interview with program director or faculty advisor; two years of teaching or specialty area experience; resume; master's degree from accredited institution. Additional exam requirements/recommendations for international students: Required—TOEFL (minimum score 600 paper-based; 100 iBT), IELTS (minimum score 8). *Application deadline:* For fall admission, 8/1 for international students. Applications are processed on a rolling basis. Application fee: $40. Electronic applications accepted. *Expenses: Tuition:* Full-time $19,344; part-time $806 per credit. *Required fees:* $580; $806 per credit. $145 per term. Tuition and fees vary according to course load, degree level and program. *Financial support:* In 2013–14, 10 students received support. Career-related internships or fieldwork, Federal Work-Study, scholarships/grants, and unspecified assistantships available. Support available to part-time students. Financial award applicants required to submit FAFSA. *Faculty research:* School law, leadership, supervision. *Unit head:* Dr. Andrew Peiser, Chairperson, 914-674-7489, Fax: 914-674-7352, E-mail: apeiser@mercy.edu. *Application contact:* Mary Ellen Hoffman, Director, Graduate Education Programs, 914-674-7334, E-mail: mhoffman@mercy.edu.

Mercy College, School of Education, Program in School Building Leadership, Dobbs Ferry, NY 10522-1189. Offers MS. Part-time and evening/weekend programs available. Postbaccalaureate distance learning degree programs offered (minimal on-campus study). *Students:* 33 full-time (25 women), 178 part-time (121 women); includes 96 minority (48 Black or African American, non-Hispanic/Latino; 1 Asian, non-Hispanic/Latino; 42 Hispanic/Latino; 5 Two or more races, non-Hispanic/Latino). Average age 32. 166 applicants, 81% accepted, 103 enrolled. In 2013, 78 master's awarded. *Degree requirements:* For master's, comprehensive exam (for some programs), thesis (for some programs). *Entrance requirements:* For master's, resume, interview, undergraduate transcript. Additional exam requirements/recommendations for international students: Required—TOEFL (minimum score 600 paper-based; 100 iBT), IELTS (minimum score 8). *Application deadline:* For fall admission, 8/1 for international students. Applications are processed on a rolling basis. Application fee: $40. Electronic applications accepted. *Expenses: Tuition:* Full-time $19,344; part-time $806 per credit. *Required fees:* $580; $806 per credit. $145 per term. Tuition and fees vary according to course load, degree level and program. *Financial support:* Career-related internships or fieldwork, Federal Work-Study, scholarships/grants, and unspecified assistantships available. Support available to part-time students. Financial award applicants required to submit FAFSA. *Unit head:* Dr. Alfred S. Posamentier, Dean for the School of Education, 914-674-7350, E-mail: aposamentier@mercy.edu. *Application contact:* Allison Gurdineer, Senior Director of Admissions, 877-637-2946, Fax: 914-674-7382, E-mail: admissions@mercy.edu.
Website: https://www.mercy.edu/academics/school-of-education/department-of-school-building-leadership/.

Mercyhurst University, Graduate Studies, Program in Organizational Leadership, Erie, PA 16546. Offers accounting (MS); entrepreneurship (MS); higher education administration (MS); human resources (MS); nonprofit management (MS); organizational leadership (Certificate); sports leadership (MS). Part-time and evening/weekend programs available. *Degree requirements:* For master's, thesis. *Entrance requirements:* For master's, GRE General Test or MAT, interview, resume, essay, three professional references, transcripts. Additional exam requirements/recommendations for international students: Required—TOEFL. Electronic applications accepted. *Faculty research:* Leadership training, organizational communication, leadership pedagogy.

Mercyhurst University, Graduate Studies, Program in Special Education, Erie, PA 16546. Offers bilingual/bicultural special education (MS); educational leadership (Certificate); special education (MS). Part-time and evening/weekend programs available. *Degree requirements:* For master's, thesis optional. *Entrance requirements:* For master's, GRE or PRAXIS I, interview, resume, essay, three professional references, transcripts. Additional exam requirements/recommendations for international students: Required—TOEFL. Electronic applications accepted. *Faculty research:* College-age learning disabled program, teacher preparation/collaboration, applied behavior analysis, special education policy issues.

Merrimack College, School of Education, North Andover, MA 01845-5800. Offers community engagement (M Ed), including community organizations, higher education, K-12 education; early childhood education (M Ed); elementary education (M Ed); English as a second language (PreK-6) (M Ed); English language learners (M Ed); general studies (M Ed); higher education (M Ed), including leadership and organizational development, student affairs; middle (M Ed); moderate disabilities (PreK-8) (M Ed); secondary (M Ed); teacher leadership (CAGS), including instructional leadership, reading specialist. Part-time and evening/weekend programs available. *Faculty:* 4 full-time (all women), 23 part-time/adjunct (15 women). *Students:* 127 full-time (104 women), 61 part-time (52 women); includes 3 minority (1 Asian, non-Hispanic/Latino; 2 Hispanic/Latino), 2 international. Average age 25. 403 applicants, 47% accepted, 138 enrolled. In 2013, 140 master's awarded. *Degree requirements:* For master's, practicum, portfolio, and state test (for licensure track); capstone (for higher education and community engagement tracks). *Entrance requirements:* For master's, MTEL (Massachusetts Tests for Educator Licensure), official transcripts from other colleges, resume, personal statement, 2 letters of recommendation, additional essay requirements for fellowships. Additional exam requirements/recommendations for international students: Required—TOEFL (minimum score 84 iBT), IELTS (minimum

score 6.5). *Application deadline:* For fall admission, 8/15 for domestic and international students; for winter admission, 12/1 for domestic students, 11/15 for international students; for spring admission, 1/10 for domestic and international students; for summer admission, 5/10 for domestic and international students. Applications are processed on a rolling basis. Application fee: $0. Electronic applications accepted. Tuition and fees vary according to course load and program. *Financial support:* In 2013–14, 91 fellowships with full tuition reimbursements were awarded; career-related internships or fieldwork, scholarships/grants, and health care benefits also available. Support available to part-time students. Financial award applicants required to submit FAFSA. *Faculty research:* Expressive language, civic engagement, family life education, reading genres, the psychological process of aging. *Application contact:* Kristen English, Interim Director of Graduate Admission, 978-837-5073, E-mail: englishkr@merrimack.edu.
Website: http://www.merrimack.edu/academics/graduate/education/.

Miami University, College of Education, Health and Society, Department of Educational Leadership, Oxford, OH 45056. Offers educational administration (Ed D, PhD); school leadership (M Ed); student affairs in higher education (MS, PhD). *Accreditation:* NCATE. Part-time and evening/weekend programs available. *Students:* 99 full-time (65 women), 90 part-time (61 women); includes 44 minority (29 Black or African American, non-Hispanic/Latino; 2 Asian, non-Hispanic/Latino; 9 Hispanic/Latino; 4 Two or more races, non-Hispanic/Latino), 8 international. Average age 34. In 2013, 82 master's, 10 doctorates awarded. *Entrance requirements:* Additional exam requirements/recommendations for international students: Required—TOEFL (minimum score 550 paper-based). Application fee: $50. Electronic applications accepted. *Expenses:* Tuition, state resident: full-time $12,634; part-time $526 per credit hour. Tuition, nonresident: full-time $27,892; part-time $1162 per credit hour. Part-time tuition and fees vary according to course load, campus/location and program. *Financial support:* Research assistantships with full and partial tuition reimbursements, teaching assistantships with partial tuition reimbursements, career-related internships or fieldwork, Federal Work-Study, scholarships/grants, health care benefits, tuition waivers (partial), and unspecified assistantships available. Financial award application deadline: 2/15; financial award applicants required to submit FAFSA. *Unit head:* Dr. Kathleen Knight Abowitz, Chair, 513-529-6825, E-mail: knightk2@miamioh.edu. *Application contact:* Dr. Thomas Poetter, Professor and Director of Graduate Studies, 513-529-6853, E-mail: poettets@miamioh.edu.
Website: http://www.MiamiOH.edu/EDL.

Michigan State University, The Graduate School, College of Education, Department of Educational Administration, East Lansing, MI 48824. Offers higher, adult and lifelong education (MA, PhD); K–12 educational administration (MA, PhD, Ed S); student affairs administration (MA). Part-time programs available. *Entrance requirements:* Additional exam requirements/recommendations for international students: Required—TOEFL. Electronic applications accepted.

Middle Tennessee State University, College of Graduate Studies, College of Education, Department of Educational Leadership, Program in Administration and Supervision, Murfreesboro, TN 37132. Offers M Ed, Ed S. Part-time and evening/weekend programs available. Postbaccalaureate distance learning degree programs offered. *Faculty:* 22 full-time (11 women), 22 part-time/adjunct (12 women). *Students:* 38 full-time (26 women), 114 part-time (94 women). 107 applicants, 82% accepted. In 2013, 120 master's, 92 Ed Ss awarded. *Degree requirements:* For master's, comprehensive exam; for Ed S, comprehensive exam, thesis or alternative. *Entrance requirements:* For master's and Ed S, GRE, MAT or current teaching license. Additional exam requirements/recommendations for international students: Required—TOEFL (minimum score 525 paper-based; 71 iBT) or IELTS (minimum score 6). *Application deadline:* For fall admission, 6/1 for domestic and international students. Applications are processed on a rolling basis. Application fee: $25 ($30 for international students). Electronic applications accepted. *Financial support:* Tuition waivers available. Support available to part-time students. Financial award application deadline: 5/1. *Unit head:* Dr. James Huffman, Chair, 615-898-2331, Fax: 615-898-2859, E-mail: jim.huffman@mtsu.edu. *Application contact:* Dr. Michael D. Allen, Vice Provost for Research and Dean, 615-898-2840, Fax: 615-904-8020, E-mail: michael.allen@mtsu.edu.

Midwestern State University, Graduate School, West College of Education, Programs in Educational Leadership and Technology, Wichita Falls, TX 76308. Offers bilingual education/English language learners (M Ed); educational leadership (M Ed); educational technology (M Ed). Part-time and evening/weekend programs available. *Degree requirements:* For master's, comprehensive exam. *Entrance requirements:* For master's, GRE General Test or MAT. Additional exam requirements/recommendations for international students: Required—TOEFL (minimum score 550 paper-based). *Application deadline:* For fall admission, 7/1 priority date for domestic students, 4/1 for international students; for spring admission, 11/1 priority date for domestic students, 8/1 for international students. Applications are processed on a rolling basis. Application fee: $35 ($50 for international students). Electronic applications accepted. *Expenses:* Tuition, state resident: full-time $3627; part-time $201.50 per credit hour. Tuition, nonresident: full-time $10,899; part-time $605.50 per credit hour. *Required fees:* $1357. *Financial support:* Career-related internships or fieldwork, Federal Work-Study, institutionally sponsored loans, scholarships/grants, tuition waivers (partial), and unspecified assistantships available. Support available to part-time students. Financial award application deadline: 3/1; financial award applicants required to submit FAFSA. *Faculty research:* Role of the principal in the twenty-first century, culturally proficient leadership, human diversity, immigration, teacher collaboration. *Unit head:* Dr. Pamela Whitehouse, Graduate Coordinator, 940-397-4139, Fax: 940-397-4694, E-mail: pamela.whitehouse@mwsu.edu. *Application contact:* Dr. Pamela Whitehouse, Graduate Coordinator, 940-397-4139, Fax: 940-397-4694, E-mail: pamela.whitehouse@mwsu.edu.
Website: http://www.mwsu.edu/academics/education/.

Mills College, Graduate Studies, MBA/MA Program in Educational Leadership, Oakland, CA 94613-1000. Offers MBA/MA. Program offered jointly between School of Education and Lorry I. Lokey Graduate School of Business. *Faculty:* 12 full-time (10 women), 11 part-time/adjunct (8 women). *Students:* 18 full-time (11 women), 3 part-time (all women); includes 11 minority (3 Black or African American, non-Hispanic/Latino; 2 Asian, non-Hispanic/Latino; 4 Hispanic/Latino; 2 Two or more races, non-Hispanic/Latino), 1 international. Average age 30. 8 applicants, 75% accepted, 5 enrolled. *Entrance requirements:* Additional exam requirements/recommendations for international students: Required—TOEFL (minimum score 550 paper-based; 80 iBT) or IELTS (minimum score 6). *Application deadline:* For fall admission, 2/1 priority date for domestic students, 12/15 priority date for international students. Applications are processed on a rolling basis. Application fee: $50. *Expenses: Tuition:* Full-time $29,860. *Required fees:* $1134. Part-time tuition and fees vary according to course load, degree level and program. *Financial support:* In 2013–14, 16 students received support, including 16 fellowships (averaging $9,438 per year). Financial award application deadline: 2/1; financial award applicants required to submit FAFSA. *Unit head:* Dr. Deborah Merril-Sands, Dean of the Graduate School of Business, 510-430-3345, Fax: 510-430-2159, E-mail: dmerrillsands@mills.edu. *Application contact:* Shrim Bathey, Director of Graduate Admission, 510-430-3309, Fax: 510-430-2159, E-mail: grad-admission@mills.edu.
Website: http://www.mills.edu/MBAMAEdLdrshp.

Mills College, Graduate Studies, School of Education, Oakland, CA 94613-1000. Offers child life in hospitals (MA); early childhood education (MA); education (MA), including art education, curriculum and instruction, elementary education, English education, foreign language education, mathematics education, science education, secondary education, social studies education, teaching; educational leadership (MA, Ed D). Part-time and evening/weekend programs available. *Faculty:* 10 full-time (7 women), 13 part-time/adjunct (10 women). *Students:* 154 full-time (136 women), 54 part-time (47 women); includes 96 minority (32 Black or African American, non-Hispanic/Latino; 1 American Indian or Alaska Native, non-Hispanic/Latino; 23 Asian, non-Hispanic/Latino; 27 Hispanic/Latino; 1 Native Hawaiian or other Pacific Islander, non-Hispanic/Latino; 12 Two or more races, non-Hispanic/Latino), 2 international. Average age 25. 222 applicants, 89% accepted, 110 enrolled. In 2013, 96 master's, 38 doctorates awarded. Terminal master's awarded for partial completion of doctoral program. *Degree requirements:* For master's, comprehensive exam, thesis (for some programs); for doctorate, thesis/dissertation. *Entrance requirements:* For master's, statement of purpose, official transcript, 3 recommendations. Additional exam requirements/recommendations for international students: Required—TOEFL (minimum score 550 paper-based; 80 iBT) or IELTS (minimum score 6). *Application deadline:* For fall admission, 12/31 priority date for domestic students, 12/15 for international students; for spring admission, 11/1 priority date for domestic students, 10/1 for international students. Applications are processed on a rolling basis. Application fee: $50. Electronic applications accepted. *Expenses: Tuition:* Full-time $29,860. *Required fees:* $1134. Part-time tuition and fees vary according to course load, degree level and program. *Financial support:* In 2013–14, 130 students received support, including 130 fellowships with full and partial tuition reimbursements available (averaging $7,565 per year); career-related internships or fieldwork and scholarships/grants also available. Support available to part-time students. Financial award application deadline: 2/1; financial award applicants required to submit FAFSA. *Faculty research:* Early childhood education, teacher preparation, educational leadership. *Total annual research expenditures:* $3.5 million. *Unit head:* Dr. Katherine Schultz, Department Head, 510-430-3384, Fax: 510-430-2159, E-mail: kschultz@mills.edu. *Application contact:* Shrim Bathey, Director of Graduate Admission, 510-430-3309, Fax: 510-430-2159, E-mail: grad-admission@mills.edu.
Website: http://www.mills.edu/education.

Minnesota State University Mankato, College of Graduate Studies, College of Education, Department of Educational Leadership, Program in Experiential Education, Mankato, MN 56001. Offers MS. *Accreditation:* NCATE. Part-time and evening/weekend programs available. *Students:* 22 full-time (11 women), 16 part-time (6 women). *Degree requirements:* For master's, thesis or alternative. *Entrance requirements:* For master's, minimum GPA of 3.0 during previous 2 years. Additional exam requirements/recommendations for international students: Required—TOEFL. *Application deadline:* For fall admission, 7/1 priority date for domestic students; for spring admission, 11/1 for domestic students. Applications are processed on a rolling basis. Application fee: $40. Electronic applications accepted. *Financial support:* Research assistantships with full tuition reimbursements, teaching assistantships with full tuition reimbursements, career-related internships or fieldwork, Federal Work-Study, and unspecified assistantships available. Support available to part-time students. Financial award application deadline: 3/15; financial award applicants required to submit FAFSA. *Unit head:* Dr. Jasper Hunt, Graduate Coordinator, 507-389-1116. *Application contact:* 507-389-2321, E-mail: grad@mnsu.edu.

Minnesota State University Moorhead, Graduate Studies, College of Education and Human Services, Program in Educational Leadership, Moorhead, MN 56563-0002. Offers MS, Ed S. MS, Ed S offered jointly with North Dakota State University. *Accreditation:* NCATE. Part-time programs available. *Degree requirements:* For master's, comprehensive exam, final oral exam, project or thesis. *Entrance requirements:* For master's, 2 letters of recommendation, minimum GPA of 3.0. Additional exam requirements/recommendations for international students: Required—TOEFL (minimum score 550 paper-based). Electronic applications accepted.

Mississippi College, Graduate School, School of Education, Department of Teacher Education and Leadership, Clinton, MS 39058. Offers art (M Ed); biological science (M Ed); business education (M Ed); computer science (M Ed); dyslexia therapy (M Ed); educational leadership (M Ed, Ed D, Ed S); elementary education (M Ed, Ed S); English (M Ed); higher education administration (MS); mathematics (M Ed); secondary education (M Ed); social studies (history) (M Ed); teaching arts (M Ed). Part-time programs available. Postbaccalaureate distance learning degree programs offered (no on-campus study). *Degree requirements:* For master's, comprehensive exam, thesis optional. *Entrance requirements:* For master's, NTE. Additional exam requirements/recommendations for international students: Recommended—TOEFL, IELTS. Electronic applications accepted.

Mississippi College, Graduate School, School of Education, Program in Higher Education Administration, Clinton, MS 39058. Offers MS. Part-time programs available. Postbaccalaureate distance learning degree programs offered (no on-campus study). *Degree requirements:* For master's, comprehensive exam, thesis optional. *Entrance requirements:* For master's, GRE or GMAT, minimum GPA of 3.0. Additional exam requirements/recommendations for international students: Recommended—TOEFL, IELTS.

Mississippi State University, College of Education, Department of Leadership and Foundations, Mississippi State, MS 39762. Offers community college education (MAT); community college leadership (PhD); education (Ed S), including school administration; elementary, middle and secondary education administration (PhD); school administration (MS); workforce education leadership (MS). MS in workforce educational leadership held jointly with Alcorn State University. *Faculty:* 9 full-time (3 women). *Students:* 50 full-time (26 women), 156 part-time (100 women); includes 104 minority (99 Black or African American, non-Hispanic/Latino; 1 American Indian or Alaska Native, non-Hispanic/Latino; 1 Asian, non-Hispanic/Latino; 1 Hispanic/Latino; 1 Native Hawaiian or other Pacific Islander, non-Hispanic/Latino; 1 Two or more races, non-Hispanic/Latino). Average age 39. 121 applicants, 32% accepted, 33 enrolled. In 2013, 47 master's, 15 doctorates, 7 other advanced degrees awarded. *Degree requirements:* For master's and Ed S, comprehensive exam, thesis; for doctorate, comprehensive exam, thesis/dissertation. *Entrance requirements:* For master's, GRE, minimum GPA of 2.75 in junior and senior courses; for doctorate, GRE, minimum GPA of 3.4 on previous graduate work; for Ed S, GRE, minimum GPA of 3.2, master's degree. Additional exam requirements/recommendations for international students: Required—TOEFL (minimum score 550 paper-based; 79 iBT); Recommended—IELTS (minimum score 6.5). *Application deadline:* For fall admission, 7/1 for domestic students, 5/1 for international students; for spring admission, 11/1 for domestic students, 9/1 for international students. Application fee: $60. *Financial support:* In 2013–14, 3 research assistantships with full tuition reimbursements (averaging $12,400 per year), 1 teaching assistantship with full tuition reimbursement (averaging $10,194 per year) were awarded; Federal Work-Study, institutionally sponsored loans, and unspecified assistantships also available. Financial

award application deadline: 4/1; financial award applicants required to submit FAFSA. *Unit head:* Dr. David Morse, Interim Department Head and Professor, 662-325-0969, Fax: 662-325-0975, E-mail: dmorse@colled.msstate.edu. Website: http://www.leadershipandfoundations.msstate.edu/.

Mississippi University for Women, Graduate School, College of Education and Human Sciences, Columbus, MS 39701-9998. Offers differentiated instruction (M Ed); educational leadership (M Ed); gifted studies (M Ed); reading/literacy (M Ed); teaching (MAT). *Accreditation:* ASHA; NCATE. Part-time programs available. *Degree requirements:* For master's, comprehensive exam, thesis optional. *Entrance requirements:* For master's, GRE General Test or NTE (M Ed in gifted education or MS in speech/language pathology), MAT (M Ed in instructional management), minimum QPA of 3.0.

Missouri Baptist University, Graduate Programs, St. Louis, MO 63141-8660. Offers business administration (MBA); Christian ministries (MACM); counseling (MAC); education (MSE); education administration (MEA); educational leadership (MSE, Ed S); teaching (MAT).

Missouri State University, Graduate College, College of Education, Department of Counseling, Leadership, and Special Education, Program in Educational Administration, Springfield, MO 65897. Offers educational administration (MS Ed, Ed S); elementary education (MS Ed); elementary principal (Ed S); secondary education (MS Ed); secondary principal (Ed S); superintendent (Ed S). Part-time and evening/weekend programs available. *Students:* 30 full-time (22 women), 88 part-time (56 women); includes 7 minority (1 Black or African American, non-Hispanic/Latino; 1 American Indian or Alaska Native, non-Hispanic/Latino; 3 Hispanic/Latino; 2 Two or more races, non-Hispanic/Latino), 2 international. Average age 35. 49 applicants, 100% accepted, 44 enrolled. In 2013, 57 master's, 16 Ed Ss awarded. *Degree requirements:* For master's and Ed S, comprehensive exam, thesis or alternative. *Entrance requirements:* For master's, minimum GPA of 2.75; for Ed S, GRE General Test, MAT, minimum GPA of 2.75. Additional exam requirements/recommendations for international students: Required—TOEFL (minimum score 550 paper-based; 79 iBT). *Application deadline:* For fall admission, 7/20 priority date for domestic students, 5/1 for international students; for spring admission, 12/20 priority date for domestic students, 9/1 for international students. Applications are processed on a rolling basis. Application fee: $35 ($50 for international students). Electronic applications accepted. *Expenses:* Tuition, state resident: full-time $4500; part-time $250 per credit hour. Tuition, nonresident: full-time $9018; part-time $501 per credit hour. *Required fees:* $361 per semester. Tuition and fees vary according to course level, course load and program. *Financial support:* Career-related internships or fieldwork, Federal Work-Study, institutionally sponsored loans, scholarships/grants, and unspecified assistantships available. Financial award application deadline: 3/31; financial award applicants required to submit FAFSA. *Unit head:* Dr. Kim Finch, Program Coordinator, 417-836-5192, Fax: 417-836-4918, E-mail: kimfinch@missouristate.edu. *Application contact:* Misty Stewart, Coordinator of Admissions and Recruitment, 417-836-6079, Fax: 417-836-6200, E-mail: mistystewart@missouristate.edu. Website: http://education.missouristate.edu/edadmin/.

Monmouth University, The Graduate School, School of Education, West Long Branch, NJ 07764-1898. Offers applied behavioral analysis (Certificate); autism (Certificate); initial certification (MAT), including elementary level, K-12, secondary level; principal (MS Ed); principal/school administrator (MS Ed); reading specialist (MS Ed); school counseling (MS Ed); special education (MS Ed), including autism, learning disabilities teacher consultant, teacher of students with disabilities, teaching in inclusive settings; speech-language pathology (MS Ed); student affairs and college counseling (MS Ed); teaching English to speakers of other languages (TESOL) (Certificate). *Accreditation:* NCATE. Part-time and evening/weekend programs available. *Faculty:* 15 full-time (11 women), 19 part-time/adjunct (17 women). *Students:* 125 full-time (97 women), 168 part-time (146 women); includes 38 minority (12 Black or African American, non-Hispanic/Latino; 5 Asian, non-Hispanic/Latino; 16 Hispanic/Latino; 5 Two or more races, non-Hispanic/Latino). Average age 28. 176 applicants, 90% accepted, 112 enrolled. In 2013, 147 master's awarded. *Entrance requirements:* For master's, GRE within last 5 years (for MS Ed in speech-language pathology), minimum GPA of 3.0 in major; 2 letters of recommendation (for some programs), resume, personal statement or essay (depending on degree program). Additional exam requirements/recommendations for international students: Required—TOEFL (minimum score 550 paper-based; 79 iBT), IELTS (minimum score 6), Michigan English Language Assessment Battery (minimum score 77). *Application deadline:* For fall admission, 7/15 priority date for domestic students, 7/1 for international students; for spring admission, 11/15 priority date for domestic students, 11/1 for international students. Applications are processed on a rolling basis. Application fee: $50. Electronic applications accepted. *Expenses: Tuition:* Part-time $1004 per credit hour. *Required fees:* $157 per semester. *Financial support:* In 2013–14, 191 students received support, including 159 fellowships (averaging $2,786 per year), 30 research assistantships (averaging $8,755 per year); career-related internships or fieldwork, scholarships/grants, and unspecified assistantships also available. Support available to part-time students. Financial award applicants required to submit FAFSA. *Faculty research:* Multicultural literacy, science and mathematics teaching strategies, teacher as reflective practitioner, children with disabilities. *Unit head:* Dr. Jason Barr, Program Director, 732-263-5238, Fax: 732-263-5277, E-mail: jbarr@monmouth.edu. *Application contact:* Lauren Vento-Cifelli, Associate Vice President of Undergraduate and Graduate Admission, 732-571-3452, Fax: 732-263-5123, E-mail: gradadm@monmouth.edu. Website: http://www.monmouth.edu/academics/schools/education/default.asp.

Montana State University, College of Graduate Studies, College of Education, Health, and Human Development, Department of Education, Bozeman, MT 59717. Offers adult and higher education (Ed D); curriculum and instruction (M Ed, Ed D), including professional educator (M Ed), technology education (M Ed); education (M Ed), including adult and higher education, educational leadership, school counseling; educational leadership (Ed D, Ed S). *Accreditation:* Teacher Education Accreditation Council. Part-time programs available. Postbaccalaureate distance learning degree programs offered (minimal on-campus study). *Degree requirements:* For master's, comprehensive exam; for doctorate, comprehensive exam, thesis/dissertation. *Entrance requirements:* For master's, GRE, 3 letters of reference, essays, BA transcripts; for doctorate, GRE, MAT, 3 letters of reference, essay, BA and M Ed transcripts; for Ed S, PRAXIS. Additional exam requirements/recommendations for international students: Required—TOEFL (minimum score 550 paper-based). Electronic applications accepted. *Faculty research:* Critical literacy; standards-based education; school Improvement, organizational change, leadership in rural education, leadership in Indian education; student Learning; multicultural/culturally responsive education for social justice Native American indigenous education, community-centered education teacher preparation.

Montclair State University, The Graduate School, College of Education and Human Services, Department of Counseling and Educational Leadership, Program in Educational Leadership, Montclair, NJ 07043-1624. Offers MA. Part-time and evening/weekend programs available. *Degree requirements:* For master's, comprehensive exam, thesis or alternative. *Entrance requirements:* For master's, GRE General Test, interview, 2 letters of recommendation. Additional exam requirements/recommendations for international students: Required—TOEFL (minimum score 83 iBT), IELTS (minimum score 6.5). Electronic applications accepted.

Montclair State University, The Graduate School, College of Education and Human Services, Doctoral Program in Teacher Education and Teacher Development, Montclair, NJ 07043-1624. Offers Ed D. Part-time and evening/weekend programs available. *Degree requirements:* For doctorate, comprehensive exam (for some programs), thesis/dissertation. *Entrance requirements:* For doctorate, GRE General Test, interview, 3 letters of recommendation, essay. Additional exam requirements/recommendations for international students: Required—TOEFL (minimum score 83 iBT), IELTS (minimum score 6.5). Electronic applications accepted.

Morehead State University, Graduate Programs, College of Education, Department of Foundational and Graduate Studies in Education, Morehead, KY 40351. Offers adult and higher education (MA, Ed S); certified professional counselor (Ed S); counseling P-12 (MA); curriculum and instruction (Ed S); educational technology (MA Ed); instructional leadership (Ed S); school administration (MA); school counseling (Ed S); teacher leader business and marketing content (MA Ed); teacher leader business and marketing technology (MA Ed); teacher leader educational technology (MA Ed); teacher leader English (MA Ed); teacher leader gifted education (MA Ed); teacher leader IECE certification (MA Ed); teacher leader interdisciplinary education P-5 (MA Ed); teacher leader middle grades (MA Ed); teacher leader non IECE certification (MA Ed); teacher leader reading/writing - non-certification (MA Ed); teacher leader reading/writing certification (MA Ed); teacher leader school communication - certification (MA Ed); teacher leader school communication - non-certification (MA Ed); teacher leader social studies (MA Ed); teacher leader special education (MA Ed). *Accreditation:* NCATE. Part-time and evening/weekend programs available. *Degree requirements:* For master's, thesis optional, oral and/or written comprehensive exams; for Ed S, thesis, oral exam. *Entrance requirements:* For master's, GRE General Test, minimum overall undergraduate GPA of 2.5; for Ed S, GRE General Test, interview, master's degree, minimum GPA of 3.5, work experience. Additional exam requirements/recommendations for international students: Required—TOEFL (minimum score 500 paper-based). Electronic applications accepted. *Faculty research:* Character education, school accountability, computer applications for school administrators.

Morgan State University, School of Graduate Studies, School of Education and Urban Studies, Department of Advanced Studies, Leadership and Policy, Program in Community College Leadership, Baltimore, MD 21251. Offers Ed D. *Accreditation:* NCATE. Part-time and evening/weekend programs available. *Degree requirements:* For doctorate, comprehensive exam, thesis/dissertation. *Entrance requirements:* For doctorate, GRE General Test or MAT. Additional exam requirements/recommendations for international students: Required—TOEFL (minimum score 550 paper-based). *Faculty research:* Multicultural education, cooperative learning, psychology of cognition.

Morgan State University, School of Graduate Studies, School of Education and Urban Studies, Department of Advanced Studies, Leadership and Policy, Program in Educational Administration and Supervision, Baltimore, MD 21251. Offers urban educational leadership (Ed D). *Accreditation:* NCATE. Part-time and evening/weekend programs available. *Faculty research:* Multicultural education, cooperative learning, psychology of cognition.

Morgan State University, School of Graduate Studies, School of Education and Urban Studies, Department of Advanced Studies, Leadership and Policy, Program in Higher Education Administration, Baltimore, MD 21251. Offers higher education (PhD); higher education administration (MA). *Degree requirements:* For doctorate, comprehensive exam, thesis/dissertation. *Entrance requirements:* For doctorate, GRE General Test or MAT, minimum GPA of 3.0.

Mount St. Joseph University, Graduate Education Program, Cincinnati, OH 45233-1670. Offers adolescent to young adult education (MA); dyslexia (Certificate); inclusive early childhood education (MA); instructional leadership (MA); middle childhood education (MA); multicultural special education (MA); Pre-K special needs (Certificate); principal licensure (MA); reading (Certificate); reading science (MA). *Accreditation:* Teacher Education Accreditation Council. Part-time and evening/weekend programs available. *Faculty:* 10 full-time (7 women), 7 part-time/adjunct (6 women). *Students:* 28 full-time (25 women), 95 part-time (76 women); includes 27 minority (19 Black or African American, non-Hispanic/Latino; 6 Hispanic/Latino; 2 Two or more races, non-Hispanic/Latino). Average age 36. 73 applicants, 44% accepted, 30 enrolled. In 2013, 69 master's awarded. *Degree requirements:* For master's, research project, student teaching, clinical and field-based experiences. *Entrance requirements:* For master's, GRE, PRAXIS II in teaching content area (math or science), 2 letters of recommendation, interview, resume. Additional exam requirements/recommendations for international students: Required—TOEFL (minimum score 560 paper-based; 83 iBT). *Application deadline:* Applications are processed on a rolling basis. Application fee: $50. Electronic applications accepted. *Expenses: Tuition:* Full-time $18,400; part-time $575 per credit hour. *Required fees:* $450; $450 per year. Part-time tuition and fees vary according to course load, degree level and program. *Financial support:* Scholarships/grants available. Financial award applicants required to submit FAFSA. *Faculty research:* Foreign and second language learning problems/reading disabilities/hyperlexia, multicultural/bilingual special education, alternative educator licensure, science education, pedagogical content knowledge. *Unit head:* Dr. Mary West, Chair, 513-244-3263, Fax: 513-244-4867, E-mail: mary_west@mail.msj.edu. *Application contact:* Mary Brigham, Assistant Director of Graduate Recruitment, 513-244-4233, Fax: 513-244-4629, E-mail: mary_brigham@mail.msj.edu. Website: http://www.msj.edu/academics/graduate-programs/master-of-arts-initial-teacher-licensure-programs/.

Murray State University, College of Education, Department of Educational Studies, Leadership and Counseling, Program in School Administration, Murray, KY 42071. Offers MA Ed, Ed S. *Accreditation:* NCATE. Part-time programs available. *Degree requirements:* For master's and Ed S, comprehensive exam. *Entrance requirements:* For degree, GRE General Test. Additional exam requirements/recommendations for international students: Required—TOEFL.

National Louis University, National College of Education, Chicago, IL 60603. Offers administration and supervision (M Ed, Ed D, CAS, Ed S); curriculum and instruction (M Ed, MS Ed, CAS); early childhood administration (M Ed, CAS); early childhood education (M Ed, MAT, MS Ed, CAS); education (Ed D); educational psychology/human learning and development (M Ed, MS Ed, CAS, Ed S); elementary education (MAT); interdisciplinary curriculum and instruction (M Ed); mathematics education (M Ed, MS Ed, CAS); reading and language (M Ed, MS Ed, CAS); school psychology (M Ed, Ed S); science education (M Ed, MS Ed, CAS); secondary education (MAT); special education (M Ed, MAT, CAS); technology in education (M Ed, CAS). *Accreditation:* NCATE. Part-time and evening/weekend programs available. *Degree requirements:* For doctorate, comprehensive exam, thesis/dissertation. *Entrance requirements:* For master's, MAT or GRE, minimum GPA of 3.0; for doctorate, GRE General Test, minimum GPA of 3.25, interview, resume, writing sample, 4 recommendations. Additional exam requirements/recommendations for international students: Required—TOEFL (minimum score 550 paper-based; 79 iBT).

Educational Leadership and Administration

National University, Academic Affairs, School of Education, La Jolla, CA 92037-1011. Offers applied behavior analysis (Certificate); applied school leadership (MS); autism (Certificate); best practices (Certificate); e-teaching and learning (Certificate); early childhood education (Certificate); education (MA), including best practices (M Ed, MA), e-teaching and learning (M Ed, MA), education technology, teacher leadership (M Ed, MA), teaching and learning in a global society (M Ed, MA), teaching mathematics (M Ed, MA); education with preliminary multiple or single subject (M Ed), including best practices (M Ed, MA), e-teaching and learning (M Ed, MA), educational technology (M Ed, MA), teacher leadership (M Ed, MA), teaching and learning in a global society (M Ed, MA), teaching mathematics (M Ed, MA); educational administration (MS); educational and instructional technology (MS); educational counseling (MS); educational technology (Certificate); higher education administration (MS); innovative school leadership (MS); instructional leadership (MS); juvenile justice special education (MS); reading (Certificate); school psychology (MS); special education (MS), including deaf and hard-of-hearing, mild/moderate disabilities, moderate/severe disabilities; teacher leadership (Certificate); teaching (MA), including applied behavioral analysis, autism, best practices (M Ed, MA), e-teaching and learning (M Ed, MA), early childhood education, educational technology (M Ed, MA), reading, special education, teacher leadership (M Ed, MA), teaching and learning in a global society (M Ed, MA), teaching mathematics (M Ed, MA); teaching mathematics (Certificate). Part-time and evening/weekend programs available. Postbaccalaureate distance learning degree programs offered (no on-campus study). *Faculty:* 72 full-time (43 women), 287 part-time/adjunct (170 women). *Students:* 2,433 full-time (1,744 women), 2,017 part-time (1,371 women); includes 1,834 minority (358 Black or African American, non-Hispanic/Latino; 15 American Indian or Alaska Native, non-Hispanic/Latino; 250 Asian, non-Hispanic/Latino; 1,056 Hispanic/Latino; 29 Native Hawaiian or other Pacific Islander, non-Hispanic/Latino; 126 Two or more races, non-Hispanic/Latino; 1 international. Average age 34. 1,339 applicants, 100% accepted, 1035 enrolled. In 2013, 1,662 master's awarded. *Degree requirements:* For master's, thesis (for some programs). *Entrance requirements:* For master's, interview, minimum GPA of 2.5. Additional exam requirements/recommendations for international students: Required—TOEFL (minimum score 550 paper-based; 79 iBT), IELTS (minimum score 6). *Application deadline:* Applications are processed on a rolling basis. Application fee: $60 ($65 for international students). Electronic applications accepted. *Expenses: Tuition:* Full-time $13,824; part-time $1728 per course. One-time fee: $160. *Financial support:* Career-related internships or fieldwork, institutionally sponsored loans, scholarships/grants, and tuition waivers (partial) available. Support available to part-time students. Financial award application deadline: 6/30. *Faculty research:* Teacher education, special education, educational effectiveness, teaching abroad, school counseling. *Unit head:* School of Education, 800-628-8648, E-mail: soe@nu.edu. *Application contact:* Louis Cruz, Interim Vice President for Enrollment Services, 800-628-8648, E-mail: advisor@nu.edu.
Website: http://www.nu.edu/OurPrograms/SchoolOfEducation.html.

Neumann University, Program in Educational Leadership, Aston, PA 19014-1298. Offers Ed D. *Degree requirements:* For doctorate, comprehensive exam, thesis/dissertation. *Entrance requirements:* For doctorate, PRAXIS, GRE. *Expenses:* Contact institution.

New England College, Program in Education, Henniker, NH 03242-3293. Offers higher education administration (MS, Ed D); K-12 leadership (Ed D); literacy and language arts (M Ed); meeting the needs of all learners/special education (M Ed); teacher leadership/school reform (M Ed). Part-time and evening/weekend programs available.

New Jersey City University, Graduate Studies and Continuing Education, Debra Cannon Partridge Wolfe College of Education, Department of Educational Leadership, Jersey City, NJ 07305-1597. Offers basics and urban studies (MA); bilingual/bicultural education and English as a second language (MA); educational administration and supervision (MA). Part-time and evening/weekend programs available. *Faculty:* 9 full-time (7 women), 7 part-time/adjunct (4 women). *Students:* 25 full-time (17 women), 206 part-time (155 women); includes 121 minority (17 Black or African American, non-Hispanic/Latino; 7 Asian, non-Hispanic/Latino; 97 Hispanic/Latino), 2 international. Average age 37. In 2013, 71 master's awarded. *Entrance requirements:* Additional exam requirements/recommendations for international students: Required—TOEFL (minimum score 61 iBT). *Application deadline:* For fall admission, 8/1 priority date for domestic students; for spring admission, 12/1 for domestic students. Applications are processed on a rolling basis. Application fee: $0. *Expenses: Tuition,* area resident: Part-time $527.90 per credit. Tuition, nonresident: part-time $947.75 per credit. *Financial support:* Fellowships, teaching assistantships, career-related internships or fieldwork, and unspecified assistantships available. *Unit head:* Dr. Catherine Rogers, Chairperson, 201-200-3012, E-mail: cshevey@njcu.edu. *Application contact:* Dr. William Bajor, Dean of Graduate Studies, 201-200-3409, Fax: 201-200-3411, E-mail: wbajor@njcu.edu.

Newman Theological College, Religious Education Programs, Edmonton, AB T6V 1H3, Canada. Offers Catholic school administration (CCSA); religious education (MRE, GDRE). Part-time programs available. Postbaccalaureate distance learning degree programs offered (no on-campus study). *Degree requirements:* For master's, thesis or alternative. *Entrance requirements:* For master's, 2 years of successful teaching experience, graduate diploma in religious education; for other advanced degree, bachelor's degree in education, teaching certificate. Additional exam requirements/recommendations for international students: Required—TOEFL (minimum score 560 paper-based; 86 iBT), IELTS (minimum score 6.5), TWE (minimum score 5).

Newman University, Master of Education Program, Wichita, KS 67213-2097. Offers building leadership (MS Ed); curriculum and instruction (MS Ed), including English as a second language, reading specialist; organizational leadership (MS Ed). *Accreditation:* NCATE. Part-time and evening/weekend programs available. Postbaccalaureate distance learning degree programs offered (no on-campus study). *Faculty:* 3 full-time (1 woman), 22 part-time/adjunct (all women). *Students:* 19 full-time (15 women), 498 part-time (407 women); includes 66 minority (19 Black or African American, non-Hispanic/Latino; 5 American Indian or Alaska Native, non-Hispanic/Latino; 10 Asian, non-Hispanic/Latino; 27 Hispanic/Latino; 1 Native Hawaiian or other Pacific Islander, non-Hispanic/Latino; 4 Two or more races, non-Hispanic/Latino). Average age 37. 67 applicants, 73% accepted, 35 enrolled. In 2013, 53 master's awarded. *Degree requirements:* For master's, thesis optional. *Entrance requirements:* For master's, 3 years' full-time teaching experience, minimum GPA of 3.0, writing sample, 2 letters of recommendation, evidence of teaching certification. Additional exam requirements/recommendations for international students: Required—TOEFL (minimum score 600 paper-based; 100 iBT). *Application deadline:* For fall admission, 8/15 priority date for domestic students, 7/15 priority date for international students; for spring admission, 1/10 priority date for domestic students, 11/15 priority date for international students. Applications are processed on a rolling basis. Application fee: $25 ($40 for international students). Electronic applications accepted. *Expenses:* Contact institution. *Financial support:* Application deadline: 8/15; applicants required to submit FAFSA. *Unit head:* Dr. Gina Marx, Director of Graduate Education, 316-942-4291 Ext. 2416, Fax: 316-942-4483, E-mail: marxg@newmanu.edu. *Application contact:* Linda Kay Sabala, Director of Graduate Admissions, 316-942-4291 Ext. 2230, Fax: 316-942-4483, E-mail: sabalal@newmanu.edu.
Website: http://www.newmanu.edu/studynu/graduate/master-science-education.

New Mexico Highlands University, Graduate Studies, School of Education, Las Vegas, NM 87701. Offers curriculum and instruction (MA); educational leadership (MA); professional counseling (MA); special education (MA), including). Part-time programs available. *Faculty:* 25 full-time (12 women), 26 part-time/adjunct (22 women). *Students:* 139 full-time (106 women), 245 part-time (180 women); includes 207 minority (10 Black or African American, non-Hispanic/Latino; 20 American Indian or Alaska Native, non-Hispanic/Latino; 3 Asian, non-Hispanic/Latino; 172 Hispanic/Latino; 1 Native Hawaiian or other Pacific Islander, non-Hispanic/Latino; 1 Two or more races, non-Hispanic/Latino); 17 international. Average age 39. 137 applicants, 99% accepted, 102 enrolled. In 2013, 112 master's awarded. *Degree requirements:* For master's, comprehensive exam, thesis or alternative. *Entrance requirements:* For master's, minimum undergraduate GPA of 3.0. Additional exam requirements/recommendations for international students: Required—TOEFL (minimum score 540 paper-based). *Application deadline:* For fall admission, 8/1 priority date for domestic students. Applications are processed on a rolling basis. Application fee: $15. *Expenses: Tuition,* state resident: full-time $4278; part-time $178 per credit hour. Tuition, nonresident: full-time $6716; part-time $281 per credit hour. One-time fee: $15. *Financial support:* Career-related internships or fieldwork, Federal Work-Study, institutionally sponsored loans, scholarships/grants, traineeships, tuition waivers (partial), and unspecified assistantships available. Support available to part-time students. Financial award application deadline: 3/1; financial award applicants required to submit FAFSA. *Faculty research:* Middle school curriculum, integrated computer applications for pre-service classroom teachers, adolescent literacy, narrative cognitive modes in New Mexico multicultural setting, math and math education. *Unit head:* Dr. Belinda Laumbach, Interim Dean, 505-454-3146, Fax: 505-454-8884, E-mail: laumbach_b@nmhu.edu. *Application contact:* Diane Trujillo, Administrative Assistant for Graduate Studies, 505-454-3266, Fax: 505-426-2117, E-mail: dtrujillo@nmhu.edu.

New Mexico State University, Graduate School, College of Education, Department of Educational Management and Development, Las Cruces, NM 88003-8001. Offers educational administration (MA, Ed D, PhD). *Accreditation:* NCATE. Part-time and evening/weekend programs available. Postbaccalaureate distance learning degree programs offered (minimal on-campus study). *Faculty:* 8 full-time (6 women). *Students:* 10 full-time (8 women), 154 part-time (107 women); includes 112 minority (1 Black or African American, non-Hispanic/Latino; 9 American Indian or Alaska Native, non-Hispanic/Latino; 2 Asian, non-Hispanic/Latino; 96 Hispanic/Latino; 4 Two or more races, non-Hispanic/Latino), 2 international. Average age 41. 47 applicants, 53% accepted, 20 enrolled. In 2013, 21 master's, 14 doctorates awarded. *Degree requirements:* For master's, variable foreign language requirement, comprehensive exam, thesis optional, internship; for doctorate, variable foreign language requirement, comprehensive exam, thesis/dissertation, internship. *Entrance requirements:* For master's, minimum GPA of 3.0, PK-12 educational administration, current teaching license, minimum 3 years of teaching in PK-12 sector; for doctorate, minimum GPA of 3.0, master's degree. Additional exam requirements/recommendations for international students: Required—TOEFL (minimum score 550 paper-based; 79 iBT), IELTS (minimum score 6.5). *Application deadline:* For fall admission, 7/15 for domestic and international students; for spring admission, 12/1 for domestic and international students. Application fee: $40 ($50 for international students). Electronic applications accepted. *Expenses:* Tuition, state resident: full-time $5398; part-time $224.90 per credit. Tuition, nonresident: full-time $18,821; part-time $784.20 per credit. Required fees: $1310; $54.60 per credit. *Financial support:* In 2013–14, 22 students received support, including 2 research assistantships (averaging $18,547 per year), 3 teaching assistantships (averaging $11,110 per year); Federal Work-Study, health care benefits, and unspecified assistantships also available. *Faculty research:* Leadership in PK-12 and postsecondary education, community college administration, program evaluation, leadership for social justice, educational change. Total annual research expenditures: $1,449. *Unit head:* Dr. Mary Prentice, Academic Department Head, 575-646-2962, Fax: 575-646-4767, E-mail: mprentic@nmsu.edu. *Application contact:* Jeanette Jones, Programs Coordinator/Recruiting Contact, 575-646-5927, Fax: 575-646-4767, E-mail: jjjones@nmsu.edu.
Website: http://emd.education.nmsu.edu.

New York Institute of Technology, School of Education, Department of Educational Leadership, Old Westbury, NY 11568-8000. Offers school leadership and technology (Advanced Diploma). Part-time and evening/weekend programs available. *Faculty:* 11 part-time/adjunct (7 women). *Students:* 13 part-time (11 women); includes 3 minority (all Black or African American, non-Hispanic/Latino). Average age 37. 8 applicants, 100% accepted, 6 enrolled. In 2013, 14 Advanced Diplomas awarded. *Degree requirements:* For Advanced Diploma, internship. *Entrance requirements:* For degree, 3 years of full-time teaching experience, permanent teacher certification in New York state. Additional exam requirements/recommendations for international students: Required—TOEFL (minimum score 550 paper-based; 79 iBT), IELTS (minimum score 6). *Application deadline:* For fall admission, 7/1 for domestic students, 6/1 for international students; for spring admission, 12/1 for domestic and international students. Application fee: $50. *Expenses: Tuition:* Full-time $18,900; part-time $1050 per credit. *Financial support:* Career-related internships or fieldwork, scholarships/grants, health care benefits, tuition waivers, and unspecified assistantships available. Support available to part-time students. Financial award applicants required to submit FAFSA. *Unit head:* Dr. Sarah McPherson, Dean, 516-686-1053, Fax: 516-686-7655, E-mail: smcphers@nyit.edu. *Application contact:* Alice Dolitsky, Director, Graduate Admissions, 516-686-7520, Fax: 516-686-1116, E-mail: nyitgrad@nyit.edu.
Website: http://www.nyit.edu/education/leadership.

New York University, Steinhardt School of Culture, Education, and Human Development, Department of Administration, Leadership, and Technology, Program in Educational Leadership, New York, NY 10003. Offers educational leadership (Ed D, PhD); educational leadership, politics and advocacy (MA); school building leader (MA); school district leader (Advanced Certificate). Part-time and evening/weekend programs available. *Faculty:* 5 full-time (2 women). *Students:* 34 full-time (26 women), 60 part-time (43 women); includes 47 minority (16 Black or African American, non-Hispanic/Latino; 9 Asian, non-Hispanic/Latino; 15 Hispanic/Latino; 7 Two or more races, non-Hispanic/Latino), 7 international. Average age 36. 159 applicants, 52% accepted, 31 enrolled. In 2013, 38 master's, 4 doctorates, 2 other advanced degrees awarded. *Degree requirements:* For master's, thesis (for some programs); for doctorate, thesis/dissertation. *Entrance requirements:* For doctorate, GRE General Test, interview; for Advanced Certificate, master's degree. Additional exam requirements/recommendations for international students: Required—TOEFL (minimum score 100 iBT). *Application deadline:* For fall admission, 12/1 priority date for domestic and international students; for spring admission, 10/1 for domestic and international students. Applications are processed on a rolling basis. Application fee: $75. Electronic applications accepted. *Expenses: Tuition:* Full-time $35,856; part-time $1494 per unit. Required fees: $1408; $64 per unit. $473 per term. Tuition and fees vary according to course load and program. *Financial support:* Fellowships with full and partial tuition reimbursements, teaching assistantships with partial tuition reimbursements, career-related internships or

fieldwork, Federal Work-Study, institutionally sponsored loans, scholarships/grants, tuition waivers (partial), and unspecified assistantships available. Support available to part-time students. Financial award application deadline: 2/1; financial award applicants required to submit FAFSA. *Faculty research:* Schools and communities; critical theories of race, class and gender; school restructuring; educational reform; social organization of schools, educational advocacy. *Unit head:* Prof. Terry Astuto, Director, 212-998-5520, Fax: 212-995-4041, E-mail: terry.astuto@nyu.edu. *Application contact:* 212-998-5030, Fax: 212-995-4328, E-mail: steinhardt.gradadmissions@nyu.edu.
Website: http://steinhardt.nyu.edu/alt/edleadership.

Niagara University, Graduate Division of Education, Concentration in Educational Leadership, Niagara Falls, NY 14109. Offers leadership and policy (PhD); school administration/supervision (MS Ed); school building leader (MS Ed, Certificate); school business administration (MS Ed); school district business leader (Certificate); school district leader (MS Ed, Certificate). Part-time and evening/weekend programs available. Postbaccalaureate distance learning degree programs offered (no on-campus study). *Students:* 38 full-time (23 women), 82 part-time (51 women); includes 12 minority (9 Black or African American, non-Hispanic/Latino; 1 Asian, non-Hispanic/Latino; 2 Hispanic/Latino), 44 international. Average age 39. In 2013, 48 master's, 8 other advanced degrees awarded. *Entrance requirements:* For master's, GRE General Test or MAT; for Certificate, GRE General Test and GRE Subject Test or MAT. Additional exam requirements/recommendations for international students: Required—TOEFL (minimum score 550 paper-based, 79 iBT) or IELTS (minimum score 6). *Application deadline:* For fall admission, 8/1 for domestic students. Applications are processed on a rolling basis. Application fee: $30. *Expenses:* Contact institution. *Financial support:* In 2013–14, 1 research assistantship with full and partial tuition reimbursement was awarded; teaching assistantships with full and partial tuition reimbursements, career-related internships or fieldwork, Federal Work-Study, scholarships/grants, and unspecified assistantships also available. Support available to part-time students. Financial award application deadline: 4/15. *Unit head:* Dr. Kristine Augustyniak, Chair, 716-286-8548, E-mail: kma@niagara.edu. *Application contact:* Dr. Debra A. Colley, Dean of Education, 716-286-8560, Fax: 716-286-8561, E-mail: dcolley@niagara.edu.
Website: http://www.niagara.edu/educational-leadership-online.

Nicholls State University, Graduate Studies, College of Education, Department of Teacher Education, Thibodaux, LA 70310. Offers administration and supervision (M Ed); counselor education (M Ed); curriculum and instruction (M Ed). *Accreditation:* NCATE. Part-time and evening/weekend programs available. *Degree requirements:* For master's, comprehensive exam, portfolio. *Entrance requirements:* For master's, GRE General Test, teaching license. Electronic applications accepted.

Norfolk State University, School of Graduate Studies, School of Education, Department of Secondary Education and School Leadership, Norfolk, VA 23504. Offers principal preparation (MA); secondary education (MAT); urban education/administration (MA), including teaching. *Accreditation:* NCATE. Part-time programs available. *Faculty:* 3 full-time, 1 part-time/adjunct. *Students:* 89 full-time (71 women), 73 part-time (49 women); includes 143 minority (137 Black or African American, non-Hispanic/Latino; 1 Asian, non-Hispanic/Latino; 3 Hispanic/Latino; 2 Two or more races, non-Hispanic/Latino), 2 international. Average age 32. In 2013, 94 master's awarded. *Entrance requirements:* For master's, GRE General Test, PRAXIS I, minimum GPA of 3.0 in major, 2.5 overall. Additional exam requirements/recommendations for international students: Required—TOEFL (minimum score 500 paper-based). *Application deadline:* For fall admission, 3/1 for domestic and international students; for spring admission, 10/1 for domestic and international students. Application fee: $30. *Financial support:* Fellowships and career-related internships or fieldwork available. *Unit head:* Dr. Margaret Knight, Acting Head, 757-823-8715, Fax: 757-823-8757, E-mail: mknight@nsu.edu. *Application contact:* Karen Fauntleroy, Education Specialist, 757-823-8178, Fax: 757-823-8757, E-mail: kfauntleroy@nsu.edu.

North American University, Program in Educational Leadership, Houston, TX 77038. Offers M Ed.

North Carolina Agricultural and Technical State University, School of Graduate Studies, School of Education, Department of Human Development and Services, Greensboro, NC 27411. Offers adult education (MS); counseling (MS); school administration (MS). *Accreditation:* ACA. Part-time and evening/weekend programs available. *Degree requirements:* For master's, comprehensive exam, thesis, qualifying exam. *Entrance requirements:* For master's, GRE General Test, minimum GPA of 3.0.

North Carolina Central University, School of Education, Program in School Administration, Durham, NC 27707-3129. Offers MSA.

North Carolina State University, Graduate School, College of Education, Department of Adult and Higher Education, Program in Higher Education Administration, Raleigh, NC 27695. Offers M Ed, MS, Ed D. *Degree requirements:* For master's, thesis (for some programs); for doctorate, thesis/dissertation. *Entrance requirements:* For master's and doctorate, GRE General Test or MAT, minimum GPA of 3.0 in major. Electronic applications accepted.

North Carolina State University, Graduate School, College of Education, Department of Educational Leadership and Policy Studies, Program in Educational Administration and Supervision, Raleigh, NC 27695. Offers Ed D. *Degree requirements:* For doctorate, thesis/dissertation. *Entrance requirements:* For doctorate, GRE General Test or MAT, minimum GPA of 3.0, interview, sample of work. Electronic applications accepted.

North Carolina State University, Graduate School, College of Education, Department of Educational Leadership and Policy Studies, Program in School Administration, Raleigh, NC 27695. Offers MSA. *Degree requirements:* For master's, comprehensive exam, thesis optional. *Entrance requirements:* For master's, GRE General Test or MAT, minimum GPA of 3.0 in major, 3 years of teaching experience. Electronic applications accepted. *Faculty research:* State and national policy, educational evaluation, cohort preparation programs.

North Central College, Graduate and Continuing Studies Programs, Department of Education, Naperville, IL 60566-7063. Offers curriculum and instruction (MA Ed); leadership and administration (MA Ed). Part-time and evening/weekend programs available. *Faculty:* 11 full-time (4 women), 5 part-time/adjunct (2 women). *Students:* 6 full-time (2 women), 24 part-time (21 women); includes 1 minority (Hispanic/Latino). Average age 30. 44 applicants, 34% accepted, 14 enrolled. In 2013, 9 master's awarded. *Degree requirements:* For master's, thesis optional, clinical practicum, project. *Entrance requirements:* For master's, interview. Additional exam requirements/recommendations for international students: Required—TOEFL (minimum score 577 paper-based; 90 iBT). *Application deadline:* For fall admission, 8/15 for domestic students; for winter admission, 12/1 for domestic students; for spring admission, 2/1 for domestic students. Applications are processed on a rolling basis. Application fee: $25. *Expenses:* Contact institution. *Financial support:* Available to part-time students. *Unit head:* Dr. Maureen Kincaid, Education Department Chair, 630-637-5750, Fax: 630-637-5844, E-mail: mkincaid@noctrl.edu. *Application contact:* Wendy Kulpinski, Director of Graduate and Continuing Education Admission, 630-637-5808, Fax: 630-637-5844, E-mail: wekulpinski@noctrl.edu.

North Central College, Graduate and Continuing Studies Programs, Program in Leadership Studies, Naperville, IL 60566-7063. Offers higher education leadership (MLD); professional leadership (MLD); social entrepreneurship (MLD); sports leadership (MLD). Part-time and evening/weekend programs available. *Faculty:* 9 full-time (1 woman), 16 part-time/adjunct (9 women). *Students:* 42 full-time (24 women), 24 part-time (8 women); includes 16 minority (10 Black or African American, non-Hispanic/Latino; 6 Hispanic/Latino), 4 international. Average age 28. 104 applicants, 51% accepted, 23 enrolled. In 2013, 36 master's awarded. *Degree requirements:* For master's, thesis optional, project. *Entrance requirements:* For master's, interview. Additional exam requirements/recommendations for international students: Required—TOEFL (minimum score 570 paper-based; 90 iBT). *Application deadline:* For fall admission, 8/15 for domestic students; for winter admission, 12/1 for domestic students; for spring admission, 2/1 for domestic students. Applications are processed on a rolling basis. Application fee: $25. *Expenses:* Contact institution. *Financial support:* In 2013–14, 1 student received support. Scholarships/grants available. Support available to part-time students. *Unit head:* Dr. Thomas Cavenagh, Program Coordinator, Leadership Studies, 630-637-5285. *Application contact:* Wendy Kulpinski, Director of Graduate and Continuing Education Admission, 630-637-5808, Fax: 630-637-5844, E-mail: wekulpinski@noctrl.edu.

North Dakota State University, College of Graduate and Interdisciplinary Studies, College of Human Development and Education, School of Education, Program in Educational Leadership, Fargo, ND 58108. Offers M Ed, MS, Ed S. MS and Ed S offered jointly with Minnesota State University Moorhead. *Accreditation:* NCATE. Part-time and evening/weekend programs available. Postbaccalaureate distance learning degree programs offered (minimal on-campus study). *Students:* 15 full-time (5 women), 34 part-time (15 women); includes 3 minority (2 Black or African American, non-Hispanic/Latino; 1 American Indian or Alaska Native, non-Hispanic/Latino), 1 international. Average age 35. 9 applicants, 89% accepted, 8 enrolled. In 2013, 13 master's awarded. *Entrance requirements:* For degree, GRE General Test, master's degree, minimum GPA of 3.25. Additional exam requirements/recommendations for international students: Required—TOEFL. *Application deadline:* Applications are processed on a rolling basis. Application fee: $35. *Financial support:* In 2013–14, 1 teaching assistantship with full tuition reimbursement (averaging $800 per year) was awarded; career-related internships or fieldwork, Federal Work-Study, institutionally sponsored loans, and tuition waivers (full) also available. Financial award application deadline: 4/15. *Faculty research:* Organizational change and development, goal setting and systematic planning, beginning teacher assistance. *Unit head:* Dr. Ann Clapper, Chair, 701-231-7202, Fax: 701-231-7205, E-mail: ann.clapper@ndsu.edu. *Application contact:* Vicki Ihry, Administrative Assistant, 701-231-9732, Fax: 701-231-7205, E-mail: vicki.ihry@ndsu.edu.
Website: http://www.ndsu.nodak.edu/ed_lead/.

Northeastern Illinois University, College of Graduate Studies and Research, College of Education, Program in Human Resource Development, Chicago, IL 60625-4699. Offers educational leadership (MA); human resource development (MA). Part-time and evening/weekend programs available. *Degree requirements:* For master's, comprehensive papers. *Entrance requirements:* For master's, minimum GPA of 2.75, BA in human resource development. Additional exam requirements/recommendations for international students: Required—TOEFL (minimum score 550 paper-based; 79 iBT). Electronic applications accepted. *Faculty research:* Analogics, development of expertise, case-based instruction, action science organizational development, theoretical model building.

Northeastern Illinois University, College of Graduate Studies and Research, College of Education, Program in School Leadership, Chicago, IL 60625-4699. Offers educational administration and supervision (MA), including chief school business official, community college administration. Part-time and evening/weekend programs available. *Degree requirements:* For master's, comprehensive exam, practicum. *Entrance requirements:* For master's, 2 years of teaching experience, minimum GPA of 2.75. Additional exam requirements/recommendations for international students: Required—TOEFL (minimum score 550 paper-based; 79 iBT). Electronic applications accepted. *Faculty research:* Student motivation, leadership, teacher expectation, educational partnerships, community/school relations.

Northeastern State University, College of Education, Department of Educational Foundations and Leadership, Program in Higher Education Leadership, Tahlequah, OK 74464-2399. Offers MS. *Faculty:* 14 full-time (10 women), 7 part-time/adjunct (2 women). *Students:* 13 full-time (6 women), 31 part-time (21 women); includes 23 minority (5 Black or African American, non-Hispanic/Latino; 15 American Indian or Alaska Native, non-Hispanic/Latino; 2 Hispanic/Latino; 1 Two or more races, non-Hispanic/Latino). Average age 37. In 2013, 2 master's awarded. *Degree requirements:* For master's, thesis. *Entrance requirements:* For master's, MAT or GRE. Additional exam requirements/recommendations for international students: Required—TOEFL. *Application deadline:* For fall admission, 6/1 priority date for domestic students. Applications are processed on a rolling basis. Application fee: $25. Electronic applications accepted. *Expenses:* Tuition, state resident: full-time $3029; part-time $168.25 per credit hour. Tuition, nonresident: full-time $7709; part-time $428.25 per credit hour. *Required fees:* $35.90 per credit hour. *Financial support:* Application deadline: 3/1. *Unit head:* Dr. Susan Frusher, Head, 918-449-6000 Ext. 3714, E-mail: frusher@nsuok.edu. *Application contact:* Margie Railey, Administrative Assistant, 918-456-5511 Ext. 2093, Fax: 918-458-2061, E-mail: railey@nsuok.edu.
Website: http://academics.nsuok.edu/education/DegreePrograms/GraduatePrograms/HigherEducationLeadership.aspx.

Northeastern State University, College of Education, Department of Educational Foundations and Leadership, Program in School Administration, Tahlequah, OK 74464-2399. Offers M Ed. Part-time and evening/weekend programs available. *Faculty:* 14 full-time (10 women), 7 part-time/adjunct (2 women). *Students:* 16 full-time (4 women), 101 part-time (34 women); includes 35 minority (2 Black or African American, non-Hispanic/Latino; 25 American Indian or Alaska Native, non-Hispanic/Latino; 2 Asian, non-Hispanic/Latino; 6 Two or more races, non-Hispanic/Latino). Average age 37. In 2013, 16 master's awarded. *Degree requirements:* For master's, thesis. *Entrance requirements:* For master's, MAT or GRE, minimum GPA of 3.0. Additional exam requirements/recommendations for international students: Required—TOEFL. *Application deadline:* For fall admission, 6/1 priority date for domestic students. Applications are processed on a rolling basis. Application fee: $25. Electronic applications accepted. *Expenses:* Tuition, state resident: full-time $3029; part-time $168.25 per credit hour. Tuition, nonresident: full-time $7709; part-time $428.25 per credit hour. *Required fees:* $35.90 per credit hour. *Financial support:* Teaching assistantships and Federal Work-Study available. Financial award application deadline: 3/1. *Unit head:* Dr. Jim Ferrell, Assistant Professor, 918-444-3722, E-mail: ferrellj@nsuok.edu. *Application contact:* Margie Railey, Administrative Assistant, 918-456-5511 Ext. 2093, Fax: 918-458-2061, E-mail: railey@nsuok.edu.
Website: http://academics.nsuok.edu/education/DegreePrograms/GraduatePrograms/SchoolAdministration.aspx.

Northeastern University, School of Education, Boston, MA 02115-5096. Offers curriculum, teaching, learning, and leadership (Ed D); elementary licensure (MAT);

higher education administration (MAT, Ed D); Jewish education leadership (Ed D); learning and instruction (M Ed); organizational leadership studies (Ed D); secondary licensure (MAT); special education (M Ed). Part-time and evening/weekend programs available.

Northern Arizona University, Graduate College, College of Education, Department of Educational Leadership, Flagstaff, AZ 86011. Offers community college/higher education (M Ed); educational foundations (M Ed); educational leadership (M Ed, Ed D); principal (Certificate); principal K-12 (M Ed); school leadership K-12 (M Ed); superintendent (Certificate). Part-time programs available. *Faculty:* 22 full-time (9 women). *Students:* 159 full-time (103 women), 528 part-time (331 women); includes 199 minority (36 Black or African American, non-Hispanic/Latino; 20 American Indian or Alaska Native, non-Hispanic/Latino; 11 Asian, non-Hispanic/Latino; 115 Hispanic/Latino; 1 Native Hawaiian or other Pacific Islander, non-Hispanic/Latino; 16 Two or more races, non-Hispanic/Latino). Average age 38. 211 applicants, 97% accepted, 148 enrolled. In 2013, 269 master's, 20 doctorates, 47 Certificates awarded. *Degree requirements:* For master's, comprehensive exam, thesis (for some programs); for doctorate, comprehensive exam, thesis/dissertation. *Entrance requirements:* For master's, minimum GPA of 3.0; for doctorate, GRE or MAT, minimum GPA of 3.5. Additional exam requirements/recommendations for international students: Required—TOEFL (minimum score 550 paper-based; 80 iBT), IELTS (minimum score 7). *Application deadline:* For fall admission, 3/1 priority date for international students; for spring admission, 9/15 priority date for international students. Applications are processed on a rolling basis. Application fee: $65. Electronic applications accepted. *Financial support:* In 2013–14, 1 research assistantship with full tuition reimbursement (averaging $12,000 per year) was awarded. Financial award applicants required to submit FAFSA. *Unit head:* Dr. Michael Schwanenberger, Chair, 928-523-4212, Fax: 928-523-1929, E-mail: michael.schwanenberger@nau.edu. *Application contact:* Jennifer Offutt, Administrative Assistant, 928-523-5098, Fax: 928-523-1929, E-mail: jennifer.offutt@nau.edu.
Website: http://nau.edu/coe/ed-leadership/.

Northern Illinois University, Graduate School, College of Education, Department of Leadership, Educational Psychology and Foundations, De Kalb, IL 60115-2854. Offers educational administration (MS Ed, Ed D, Ed S); educational psychology (MS Ed, Ed D); foundations of education (MS Ed); school business management (MS Ed). Part-time and evening/weekend programs available. Postbaccalaureate distance learning degree programs offered (minimal on-campus study). *Faculty:* 23 full-time (12 women). *Students:* 7 full-time (4 women), 221 part-time (125 women); includes 36 minority (17 Black or African American, non-Hispanic/Latino; 18 Hispanic/Latino; 1 Two or more races, non-Hispanic/Latino), 2 international. Average age 40. 52 applicants, 71% accepted, 15 enrolled. In 2013, 76 master's, 14 doctorates, 18 other advanced degrees awarded. *Degree requirements:* For master's, comprehensive exam, thesis optional; for doctorate, thesis/dissertation, candidacy exam, dissertation defense. *Entrance requirements:* For master's, minimum undergraduate GPA of 2.75; for doctorate, GRE General Test, minimum undergraduate GPA of 2.75, 3.2 graduate; for Ed S, GRE General Test, minimum GPA of 2.75 (undergraduate), 3.2 (graduate). Additional exam requirements/recommendations for international students: Required—TOEFL (minimum score 550 paper-based). *Application deadline:* For fall admission, 6/1 for domestic students, 5/1 for international students; for spring admission, 11/1 for domestic students, 10/1 for international students. Applications are processed on a rolling basis. Application fee: $40. Electronic applications accepted. *Financial support:* In 2013–14, 2 research assistantships with full tuition reimbursements were awarded; fellowships with full tuition reimbursements, teaching assistantships with full tuition reimbursements, career-related internships or fieldwork, Federal Work-Study, scholarships/grants, tuition waivers (full), and staff assistantships also available. Support available to part-time students. Financial award applicants required to submit FAFSA. *Faculty research:* Interpersonal forgiveness, learner-centered education, psychedelic studies, senior theory, professional growth. *Unit head:* Dr. Patrick A. Roberts, Acting Chair, 815-753-4404, E-mail: lepf@niu.edu. *Application contact:* Graduate School Office, 815-753-0395, E-mail: gradsch@niu.edu.
Website: http://cedu.niu.edu/LEPF/.

Northern Illinois University, Graduate School, College of Education, Department of Special and Early Education, De Kalb, IL 60115-2854. Offers curriculum and instruction (MS Ed, Ed D), including curriculum leadership (Ed D), elementary education (Ed D), secondary education (Ed D); early childhood education (MS Ed); elementary education (MS Ed); special education (MS Ed). Part-time and evening/weekend programs available. *Faculty:* 22 full-time (14 women), 2 part-time/adjunct (both women). *Students:* 52 full-time (41 women), 168 part-time (137 women); includes 29 minority (11 Black or African American, non-Hispanic/Latino; 7 Asian, non-Hispanic/Latino; 6 Hispanic/Latino; 5 Two or more races, non-Hispanic/Latino), 3 international. Average age 36. 38 applicants, 63% accepted, 18 enrolled. In 2013, 59 master's, 15 doctorates awarded. *Degree requirements:* For master's, comprehensive exam, thesis optional; for doctorate, thesis/dissertation, candidacy exam, dissertation defense. *Entrance requirements:* For master's, GRE General Test or MAT, minimum undergraduate GPA of 2.75; for doctorate, GRE General Test or MAT, minimum undergraduate GPA of 2.75, graduate 3.2. Additional exam requirements/recommendations for international students: Required—TOEFL (minimum score 550 paper-based). *Application deadline:* For fall admission, 6/1 for domestic students, 5/1 for international students; for spring admission, 11/1 for domestic students, 10/1 for international students. Applications are processed on a rolling basis. Application fee: $40. Electronic applications accepted. *Financial support:* In 2013–14, 24 research assistantships with full tuition reimbursements were awarded; fellowships with full tuition reimbursements, teaching assistantships with full tuition reimbursements, career-related internships or fieldwork, Federal Work-Study, scholarships/grants, tuition waivers (full), and unspecified assistantships also available. Support available to part-time students. Financial award applicants required to submit FAFSA. *Faculty research:* Teacher certification, stress reduction during student teaching, teaching history, portfolios in student teaching. *Unit head:* Dr. Barbara Schwartz-Bechet, Interim Chair, 815-753-1619, E-mail: seed@niu.edu. *Application contact:* Gail Myers, Clerk, Graduate Advising, 815-753-0381, E-mail: gmyers@niu.edu.
Website: http://www.cedu.niu.edu/seed/.

Northern Kentucky University, Office of Graduate Programs, College of Education and Human Services, Doctor of Education in Educational Leadership Program, Highland Heights, KY 41099. Offers Ed D. Part-time and evening/weekend programs available. *Faculty:* 5 full-time (2 women), 1 part-time/adjunct (0 women). *Students:* 39 full-time (25 women), 21 part-time (15 women); includes 8 minority (6 Black or African American, non-Hispanic/Latino; 1 Asian, non-Hispanic/Latino; 1 Two or more races, non-Hispanic/Latino). Average age 44. 35 applicants, 51% accepted, 13 enrolled. In 2013, 13 doctorates awarded. *Entrance requirements:* For doctorate, curriculum vitae, 500-word leadership situation account, 3 letters of recommendation, 5 professional references, interview. Additional exam requirements/recommendations for international students: Required—TOEFL (minimum score 550 paper-based; 79 iBT); Recommended—IELTS (minimum score 6.5). *Application deadline:* For fall admission, 2/1 priority date for domestic students, 6/1 for international students. Application fee: $50. Electronic applications accepted. *Expenses:* Tuition, state resident: full-time $4446; part-time $494 per credit hour. Tuition, nonresident: full-time $6885; part-time $765 per credit hour. *Required fees:* $72 per semester. One-time fee: $125.50. Part-time tuition and fees vary according to course load, degree level, program and reciprocity agreements. *Financial support:* In 2013–14, 7 students received support. Application deadline: 5/1; applicants required to submit FAFSA. *Faculty research:* Educator dispositions, civic engagement and service-learning in education, school leadership, technology in education, professional development. *Unit head:* James W. Koschoreck, Program Director, 859-572-6039, E-mail: koschorecj1@nku.edu. *Application contact:* Dr. Christian Gamm, Director of Graduate Programs, 859-572-6364, Fax: 859-572-6670, E-mail: gammc1@nku.edu.
Website: http://coehs.nku.edu/gradprograms/edd.html.

Northern Kentucky University, Office of Graduate Programs, College of Education and Human Services, Education Program: Teacher as a Leader, Highland Heights, KY 41099. Offers MA, Certificate. Part-time and evening/weekend programs available. Postbaccalaureate distance learning degree programs offered (no on-campus study). *Faculty:* 9 full-time (7 women), 1 (woman) part-time/adjunct. *Students:* 6 full-time (5 women), 145 part-time (117 women); includes 8 minority (2 Asian, non-Hispanic/Latino; 6 Hispanic/Latino). Average age 31. 66 applicants, 59% accepted, 31 enrolled. In 2013, 63 master's awarded. *Degree requirements:* For master's, thesis optional, portfolio. *Entrance requirements:* For master's, GRE, teacher certification, bachelor's degree in appropriate subject area, minimum GPA of 2.5, 3 letters of recommendation, 1 year of teaching experience, statement of personal goals. Additional exam requirements/recommendations for international students: Required—TOEFL (minimum score 550 paper-based; 79 iBT); Recommended—IELTS (minimum score 6.5). *Application deadline:* For fall admission, 6/1 for domestic students, 6/1 priority date for international students; for spring admission, 11/1 for domestic students, 10/1 priority date for international students. Application fee: $40. Electronic applications accepted. *Expenses:* Tuition, state resident: full-time $4446; part-time $494 per credit hour. Tuition, nonresident: full-time $6885; part-time $765 per credit hour. *Required fees:* $72 per semester. One-time fee: $125.50. Part-time tuition and fees vary according to course load, degree level, program and reciprocity agreements. *Financial support:* In 2013–14, 40 students received support. Scholarships/grants and unspecified assistantships available. *Faculty research:* Teaching with technology, middle school education, children with disabilities, teaching in the content areas, diversifying faculty. *Unit head:* Dr. Shawn Faulkner, Chair for Teacher Education, 859-572-1910, Fax: 859-572-6096, E-mail: faulkners1@nku.edu. *Application contact:* Beth McCubbin, Academic Coordinator, 859-572-5237, Fax: 859-572-1384, E-mail: mccubine2@nku.edu.
Website: http://coehs.nku.edu/gradprograms/maed.html.

Northern Kentucky University, Office of Graduate Programs, College of Education and Human Services, Education Specialist in Educational Leadership Program, Highland Heights, KY 41099. Offers Ed S. *Faculty:* 3 full-time (2 women), 2 part-time/adjunct (1 woman). *Students:* 31 part-time (23 women); includes 1 minority (Hispanic/Latino). Average age 36. 9 applicants, 11% accepted, 1 enrolled. *Degree requirements:* For Ed S, capstone. *Entrance requirements:* For degree, minimum master's GPA of 3.5, three letters of recommendation,three essays, professional folio, interview. *Application deadline:* For fall admission, 7/1 priority date for domestic students, 6/1 priority date for international students; for spring admission, 10/1 priority date for international students; for summer admission, 5/1 for domestic students. Application fee: $50. *Expenses:* Tuition, state resident: full-time $4446; part-time $494 per credit hour. Tuition, nonresident: full-time $6885; part-time $765 per credit hour. *Required fees:* $72 per semester. One-time fee: $125.50. Part-time tuition and fees vary according to course load, degree level, program and reciprocity agreements. *Financial support:* In 2013–14, 5 students received support. *Unit head:* Dr. Rosa Weaver, Program Director, 859-572-5536, Fax: 859-572-6623, E-mail: weaverro@nku.edu. *Application contact:* Dr. Christian Gamm, Director of Graduate Programs, 859-572-6934, Fax: 859-572-6670, E-mail: gammc1@nku.edu.

Northern Kentucky University, Office of Graduate Programs, College of Education and Human Services, Program in Instructional Leadership, Highland Heights, KY 41099. Offers MA. Part-time and evening/weekend programs available. Postbaccalaureate distance learning degree programs offered (no on-campus study). *Faculty:* 3 full-time (2 women). *Students:* 1 (woman) part-time. Average age 44. In 2013, 21 master's awarded. *Degree requirements:* For master's, comprehensive exam, portfolio. *Entrance requirements:* For master's, GRE, teaching certificate, 3 letters of recommendation, 3 years of teaching experience, letter of introduction and interest, 3 essays, interview. Additional exam requirements/recommendations for international students: Required—TOEFL (minimum score 550 paper-based; 79 iBT); Recommended—IELTS (minimum score 6.5). *Application deadline:* For fall admission, 7/1 for domestic students, 6/1 for international students; for spring admission, 12/1 priority date for domestic students, 10/1 for international students. Applications are processed on a rolling basis. Application fee: $40. Electronic applications accepted. *Expenses:* Tuition, state resident: full-time $4446; part-time $494 per credit hour. Tuition, nonresident: full-time $6885; part-time $765 per credit hour. *Required fees:* $72 per semester. One-time fee: $125.50. Part-time tuition and fees vary according to course load, degree level, program and reciprocity agreements. *Financial support:* Unspecified assistantships available. Financial award applicants required to submit FAFSA. *Faculty research:* Ethics, law, redesign of principal preparation, principal preparation for low-achieving poverty schools. *Unit head:* Dr. Rosa Weaver, Program Coordinator, 859-572-5536, Fax: 859-572-6592, E-mail: weaverro@nku.edu. *Application contact:* Dr. Christian Gamm, Director of Graduate Programs, 859-572-6364, Fax: 859-572-6670, E-mail: gammc1@nku.edu.
Website: http://coehs.nku.edu/gradprograms/educationalleadership/edspecialist.html.

Northern Michigan University, College of Graduate Studies, College of Health Sciences and Professional Studies, School of Education, Leadership and Public Service, Marquette, MI 49855-5301. Offers administration and supervision (MAE, Ed S); elementary education (MAE); instruction (MAE); learning disabilities (MAE); public administration (MPA), including criminal justice administration, healthcare administration, human resource administration, public management, state and local government; reading education (MAE, Ed S), including literacy leadership (Ed S), reading (MAE), reading specialist (MAE); school guidance counseling (MAE); science education (MS); secondary education (MAE). *Accreditation:* Teacher Education Accreditation Council. Part-time programs available. Postbaccalaureate distance learning degree programs offered (no on-campus study). *Faculty:* 12 full-time (7 women), 3 part-time/adjunct (1 woman). *Students:* 25 full-time (16 women), 170 part-time (130 women); includes 12 minority (2 Black or African American, non-Hispanic/Latino; 5 American Indian or Alaska Native, non-Hispanic/Latino; 4 Hispanic/Latino; 1 Two or more races, non-Hispanic/Latino), 1 international. Average age 33. 39 applicants, 95% accepted, 35 enrolled. In 2013, 48 master's, 5 other advanced degrees awarded. *Degree requirements:* For master's, thesis (for some programs). *Entrance requirements:* For master's, minimum GPA of 3.0. Additional exam requirements/recommendations for international students: Required—TOEFL (minimum score 550 paper-based; 79 iBT), IELTS (minimum score 6.5). *Application deadline:* For fall admission, 7/1 priority date for domestic students; for winter admission, 11/15 for domestic students; for spring admission, 3/17 for domestic students. Applications are processed on a rolling basis. Application fee: $50. *Expenses:* Tuition, state resident: part-time $427 per credit. Tuition, nonresident: part-time $614.50 per credit. *Required*

fees: $325 per semester. Tuition and fees vary according to course load and program. *Financial support:* In 2013–14, 2 research assistantships were awarded; career-related internships or fieldwork, Federal Work-Study, institutionally sponsored loans, and unspecified assistantships also available. Support available to part-time students. Financial award application deadline: 3/1. *Unit head:* Dr. Joseph Lubig, Associate Dean, School of Education, Leadership, and Public Service, 906-227-2780, Fax: 906-227-2764, E-mail: jlubig@nmu.edu. *Application contact:* Nancy E. Carter, Certification Counselor and Graduate Programs Coordinator, 906-227-1625, Fax: 906-227-2764, E-mail: ncarter@nmu.edu.
Website: http://www.nmu.edu/education/.

Northern State University, MS Ed Program in Leadership and Administration, Aberdeen, SD 57401-7198. Offers MS Ed. *Accreditation:* NCATE. Part-time and evening/weekend programs available. Postbaccalaureate distance learning degree programs offered. *Faculty:* 3 full-time (1 woman), 4 part-time/adjunct (1 woman). *Students:* 3 full-time (1 woman), 15 part-time (3 women). Average age 32. 4 applicants, 100% accepted, 4 enrolled. In 2013, 22 master's awarded. *Degree requirements:* For master's, comprehensive exam, thesis optional. *Entrance requirements:* For master's, minimum GPA of 2.75. Additional exam requirements/recommendations for international students: Required—TOEFL (minimum score 550 paper-based; 78 iBT), IELTS (minimum score 6). *Application deadline:* For fall admission, 8/15 for domestic and international students; for spring admission, 12/15 for domestic and international students. Applications are processed on a rolling basis. Application fee: $35. Electronic applications accepted. *Expenses:* Tuition, state resident: full-time $3634. Tuition, nonresident: full-time $7690. One-time fee: $35 full-time. Part-time tuition and fees vary according to course load, degree level, campus/location and reciprocity agreements. *Financial support:* In 2013–14, 2 teaching assistantships with partial tuition reimbursements (averaging $6,478 per year) were awarded; career-related internships or fieldwork, Federal Work-Study, institutionally sponsored loans, scholarships/grants, and unspecified assistantships also available. Support available to part-time students. Financial award application deadline: 3/1; financial award applicants required to submit FAFSA. *Unit head:* Dr. Constance Geier, Dean of Education, 605-626-2558, Fax: 605-626-7190, E-mail: connie.geier@northern.edu. *Application contact:* Tammy K. Griffith, Program Assistant, 605-626-2558, Fax: 605-626-7190, E-mail: tammy.griffith@northern.edu.

Northwestern Oklahoma State University, School of Professional Studies, Program in Educational Leadership, Alva, OK 73717-2799. Offers M Ed. Part-time programs available. *Degree requirements:* For master's, thesis optional, portfolio. *Entrance requirements:* For master's, GRE General Test or MAT, minimum GPA of 2.75.

Northwestern State University of Louisiana, Graduate Studies and Research, College of Education and Human Development, Programs in Educational Leadership and Instruction, Natchitoches, LA 71497. Offers counseling (Ed S); educational leadership (M Ed, Ed S); educational technology (Ed S); elementary teaching (Ed S); reading (Ed S); secondary teaching (Ed S); special education (Ed S). *Accreditation:* NASAD. *Degree requirements:* For master's, comprehensive exam, thesis (for some programs). *Entrance requirements:* For master's and Ed S, GRE General Test. Additional exam requirements/recommendations for international students: Required—TOEFL. Electronic applications accepted.

Northwestern University, The Graduate School, School of Education and Social Policy, Education and Social Policy Program, Evanston, IL 60035. Offers elementary teaching (MS); secondary teaching (MS); teacher leadership (MS). Part-time and evening/weekend programs available. *Degree requirements:* For master's, research project. *Entrance requirements:* For master's, GRE General Test, Illinois State Board of Education Basic Skills Exam (secondary and elementary), bachelor's degree. Additional exam requirements/recommendations for international students: Recommended—TOEFL. Electronic applications accepted. *Faculty research:* Cultural context and literacy, philosophy of education and interpretive discussion, productivity, enhancing research and teaching, motivation, new and junior faculty issues, professional development for K-12 teachers to improve math and science teaching, female/underrepresented students/faculty in STEM disciplines.

Northwest Missouri State University, Graduate School, College of Education and Human Services, Department of Professional Education, Program in Educational Leadership, Maryville, MO 64468-6001. Offers educational leadership: elementary (MS Ed); educational leadership: K-12 (MS Ed); educational leadership: secondary (MS Ed); elementary principalship (Ed S); secondary principalship (Ed S); superintendency (Ed S). *Accreditation:* NCATE. Part-time programs available. *Degree requirements:* For master's, comprehensive exam; for Ed S, comprehensive exam, thesis. *Entrance requirements:* For master's, GRE General Test, minimum undergraduate GPA of 2.75, teaching certificate, writing sample; for Ed S, minimum graduate GPA of 3.25. Additional exam requirements/recommendations for international students: Required—TOEFL (minimum score 550 paper-based).

Northwest Nazarene University, Graduate Studies, Program in Teacher Education, Nampa, ID 83686-5897. Offers curriculum and instruction (M Ed); educational leadership (M Ed, Ed D, Ed S); exceptional child (M Ed); reading education (M Ed). *Accreditation:* ACA (one or more programs are accredited); NCATE. Part-time programs available. Postbaccalaureate distance learning degree programs offered (no on-campus study). *Faculty:* 6 full-time (5 women), 29 part-time/adjunct (16 women). *Students:* 101 full-time (66 women), 98 part-time (74 women); includes 14 minority (1 Asian, non-Hispanic/Latino; 10 Hispanic/Latino; 3 Two or more races, non-Hispanic/Latino), 12 international. Average age 38. In 2013, 60 master's, 28 doctorates, 14 other advanced degrees awarded. *Degree requirements:* For master's, comprehensive exam (for some programs), action research project; for doctorate, thesis/dissertation; for Ed S, comprehensive exam (for some programs). *Entrance requirements:* For master's, minimum undergraduate GPA of 2.8 overall or 3.0 during final 30 semester credits, undergraduate degree; for doctorate, Ed S or equivalent; for Ed S, EDS - MEd required. Additional exam requirements/recommendations for international students: Recommended—TOEFL (minimum score 80 iBT). *Application deadline:* For fall admission, 9/1 for domestic students. Applications are processed on a rolling basis. Application fee: $50. *Expenses: Tuition:* Part-time $565 per credit. *Financial support:* In 2013–14, research assistantships (averaging $5,000 per year) were awarded. *Faculty research:* Action research, cooperative learning, accountability, institutional accreditation. *Unit head:* Dr. Paula Kellerer, Chair, 208-467-8729, Fax: 208-467-8562. *Application contact:* Lynette Kingsmore, Admissions Counselor, 208-467-8107, Fax: 208-467-8786, E-mail: lkingsmore@nnu.edu.
Website: http://www.nnu.edu/graded/.

Notre Dame de Namur University, Division of Academic Affairs, School of Education and Leadership, Program in School Administration, Belmont, CA 94002-1908. Offers administrative services credential (Certificate); school administration (MA). Part-time and evening/weekend programs available. *Degree requirements:* For master's, thesis optional, capstone course. *Entrance requirements:* For master's, interview, valid teaching credential, minimum 1 year of classroom teaching experience. Additional exam requirements/recommendations for international students: Required—TOEFL (minimum score 550 paper-based; 79 iBT). Electronic applications accepted.

Notre Dame of Maryland University, Graduate Studies, Leadership in Teaching Program, Baltimore, MD 21210-2476. Offers MA. *Entrance requirements:* For master's, interview, 1 year of teaching experience, minimum GPA of 3.0. Additional exam requirements/recommendations for international students: Required—TOEFL (minimum score 500 paper-based; 61 iBT). Electronic applications accepted.

Notre Dame of Maryland University, Graduate Studies, Program in Instructional Leadership for Changing Populations, Baltimore, MD 21210-2476. Offers PhD. *Entrance requirements:* Additional exam requirements/recommendations for international students: Required—TOEFL (minimum score 500 paper-based; 61 iBT).

Oakland City University, School of Education, Oakland City, IN 47660-1099. Offers educational leadership (Ed D); teaching (MA). *Accreditation:* NCATE. Terminal master's awarded for partial completion of doctoral program. *Degree requirements:* For master's, thesis; for doctorate, comprehensive exam, thesis/dissertation. *Entrance requirements:* For master's, MAT, minimum GPA of 3.0, interview, resume, letters of recommendation; for doctorate, MAT, GRE, minimum GPA of 3.2, interview, resume, letters of recommendation. *Expenses:* Contact institution. *Faculty research:* Assessment, cultural diversity, teacher education, education leadership.

Oakland University, Graduate Study and Lifelong Learning, School of Education and Human Services, Department of Educational Leadership, Rochester, MI 48309-4401. Offers educational leadership (M Ed, PhD); higher education (Certificate); higher education administration (Certificate); school administration (Ed S). *Faculty:* 11 full-time (all women), 4 part-time/adjunct (2 women). *Students:* 22 full-time (15 women), 216 part-time (143 women); includes 43 minority (37 Black or African American, non-Hispanic/Latino; 1 American Indian or Alaska Native, non-Hispanic/Latino; 1 Asian, non-Hispanic/Latino; 4 Hispanic/Latino), 1 international. Average age 39. 149 applicants, 90% accepted, 118 enrolled. In 2013, 27 master's, 138 other advanced degrees awarded. *Entrance requirements:* Additional exam requirements/recommendations for international students: Required—TOEFL (minimum score 550 paper-based). *Application deadline:* For fall admission, 7/15 for domestic students, 5/1 priority date for international students; for winter admission, 9/1 priority date for international students. Application fee: $0. *Financial support:* Federal Work-Study, institutionally sponsored loans, and tuition waivers (full) available. Financial award application deadline: 3/1; financial award applicants required to submit FAFSA. *Faculty research:* Grizzlies Response: Awareness and suicide prevention at Oakland University. *Total annual research expenditures:* $56,687. *Unit head:* Dr. William G. Keane, Chair, 248-370-3070, Fax: 248-370-4605. *Application contact:* Christina J. Grabowski, Associate Director of Graduate Study and Lifelong Learning, 248-370-3167, Fax: 248-370-4114, E-mail: grabowsk@oakland.edu.

Oakland University, Graduate Study and Lifelong Learning, School of Education and Human Services, Department of Teacher Development and Educational Studies, Rochester, MI 48309-4401. Offers education studies (M Ed); secondary education (MAT). *Faculty:* 6 full-time (3 women), 17 part-time/adjunct (11 women). *Students:* 85 full-time (71 women), 151 part-time (99 women); includes 42 minority (24 Black or African American, non-Hispanic/Latino; 2 American Indian or Alaska Native, non-Hispanic/Latino; 9 Asian, non-Hispanic/Latino; 7 Hispanic/Latino), 3 international. Average age 30. 175 applicants, 47% accepted, 76 enrolled. In 2013, 69 master's awarded. *Entrance requirements:* For master's, minimum GPA of 3.0 for unconditional admission. *Application deadline:* For fall admission, 3/1 for domestic students. Application fee: $35. Electronic applications accepted. *Financial support:* Federal Work-Study, institutionally sponsored loans, and tuition waivers (full) available. Financial award application deadline: 3/1; financial award applicants required to submit FAFSA. *Total annual research expenditures:* $182,162. *Unit head:* Dr. Dyanne M. Tracy, Chair, 248-370-3064, Fax: 248-370-4605, E-mail: dtracy@oakland.edu. *Application contact:* Christina J. Grabowski, Associate Director of Graduate Study and Lifelong Learning, 248-370-3167, Fax: 248-370-4114, E-mail: grabowsk@oakland.edu.

Oglala Lakota College, Graduate Studies, Program in Educational Administration, Kyle, SD 57752-0490. Offers MA. Part-time and evening/weekend programs available. *Entrance requirements:* For master's, minimum GPA of 2.5.

Ohio Dominican University, Graduate Programs, Division of Education, Columbus, OH 43219-2099. Offers curriculum and instruction (M Ed); educational leadership (M Ed); teaching English to speakers of other languages (MA). *Accreditation:* NCATE. Part-time and evening/weekend programs available. Postbaccalaureate distance learning degree programs offered. *Degree requirements:* For master's, thesis or alternative. *Entrance requirements:* For master's, minimum undergraduate GPA of 3.0, teaching certificate, teaching experience, 3 letters of recommendation. Additional exam requirements/recommendations for international students: Required—TOEFL (minimum score 550 paper-based), IELTS (minimum score 6.5).

The Ohio State University, Graduate School, College of Education and Human Ecology, Department of Educational Studies, Columbus, OH 43210. Offers M Ed, MA, PhD, Ed S. *Accreditation:* NCATE. Part-time programs available. *Faculty:* 32. *Students:* 325 full-time (223 women), 135 part-time (84 women); includes 92 minority (47 Black or African American, non-Hispanic/Latino; 1 American Indian or Alaska Native, non-Hispanic/Latino; 7 Asian, non-Hispanic/Latino; 27 Hispanic/Latino; 10 Two or more races, non-Hispanic/Latino), 37 international. Average age 31. In 2013, 128 master's, 31 doctorates, 5 other advanced degrees awarded. *Degree requirements:* For master's, thesis optional; for doctorate, thesis/dissertation. *Entrance requirements:* For master's and doctorate, GRE General Test. Additional exam requirements/recommendations for international students: Required—TOEFL (minimum score 550 paper-based; 79 iBT), Michigan English Language Assessment Battery (minimum score 82); Recommended—IELTS (minimum score 7). *Application deadline:* For fall admission, 12/1 priority date for domestic and international students; for winter admission, 12/1 for domestic students, 11/1 for international students; for spring admission, 11/1 priority date for domestic and international students. Applications are processed on a rolling basis. Application fee: $60 ($70 for international students). Electronic applications accepted. *Financial support:* Fellowships with tuition reimbursements, research assistantships with tuition reimbursements, teaching assistantships with tuition reimbursements, Federal Work-Study, institutionally sponsored loans, and unspecified assistantships available. Support available to part-time students. *Unit head:* Eric Anderman, Chair, 614-688-3484, E-mail: anderman.1@osu.edu. *Application contact:* Deb Zabloudil, Director of Graduate Student Services, 614-688-4007, E-mail: zabloudil.1@osu.edu.
Website: http://ehe.osu.edu/educational-studies/.

Ohio University, Graduate College, Gladys W. and David H. Patton College of Education and Human Services, Department of Educational Studies, Athens, OH 45701-2979. Offers computer education and technology (M Ed); cultural studies (M Ed); educational administration (M Ed, Ed D); educational research and evaluation (M Ed, PhD); instructional technology (PhD). Part-time and evening/weekend programs available. Postbaccalaureate distance learning degree programs offered (minimal on-campus study). *Degree requirements:* For master's, thesis or alternative; for doctorate, comprehensive exam, thesis/dissertation. *Entrance requirements:* For master's, GRE General Test (if GPA less than 2.9); for doctorate, GRE General Test, GRE Subject Test, minimum GPA of 2.9, work experience, 3 letters of reference, autobiography. Additional exam requirements/recommendations for international students: Required—

Educational Leadership and Administration

TOEFL (minimum score 550 paper-based; 80 iBT) or IELTS (minimum score 6.5). Electronic applications accepted. *Faculty research:* Race, class and gender; computer programs; development and organization theory; evaluation/development of instruments, leadership.

Oklahoma State University, College of Education, School of Teaching and Curriculum Leadership, Stillwater, OK 74078. Offers MS, PhD. Part-time programs available. *Faculty:* 31 full-time (30 women), 38 part-time/adjunct (33 women). *Students:* 63 full-time (51 women), 191 part-time (139 women); includes 49 minority (11 Black or African American, non-Hispanic/Latino; 11 American Indian or Alaska Native, non-Hispanic/Latino; 3 Asian, non-Hispanic/Latino; 10 Hispanic/Latino; 14 Two or more races, non-Hispanic/Latino), 6 international. Average age 38. 85 applicants, 58% accepted, 41 enrolled. In 2013, 50 master's, 15 doctorates awarded. *Degree requirements:* For master's, thesis or alternative; for doctorate, comprehensive exam, thesis/dissertation. *Entrance requirements:* For master's and doctorate, GRE or GMAT. Additional exam requirements/recommendations for international students: Required—TOEFL (minimum score 550 paper-based; 79 iBT). *Application deadline:* For fall admission, 3/1 priority date for international students; for spring admission, 8/1 priority date for international students. Applications are processed on a rolling basis. Application fee: $40 ($75 for international students). Electronic applications accepted. *Expenses:* Tuition, state resident: full-time $4272; part-time $178 per credit hour. Tuition, nonresident: full-time $17,472; part-time $709 per credit hour. *Required fees:* $2413.20; $100.55 per credit hour. One-time fee: $50 full-time. Part-time tuition and fees vary according to course load and campus/location. *Financial support:* In 2013–14, 11 research assistantships (averaging $10,591 per year), 11 teaching assistantships (averaging $8,652 per year) were awarded; career-related internships or fieldwork, Federal Work-Study, scholarships/grants, health care benefits, tuition waivers (partial), and unspecified assistantships also available. Support available to part-time students. Financial award application deadline: 3/1; financial award applicants required to submit FAFSA. *Unit head:* Dr. Pamela U. Brown, Head, 405-744-9214, Fax: 405-744-6290, E-mail: pamela.u.brown@okstate.edu.
Website: http://education.okstate.edu/stcl.

Old Dominion University, Darden College of Education, Programs in Educational Leadership and Administration, Norfolk, VA 23529. Offers educational leadership (PhD, Ed S); educational training (MS Ed); principal preparation (MS Ed). *Accreditation:* NCATE. Part-time and evening/weekend programs available. Postbaccalaureate distance learning degree programs offered (minimal on-campus study). *Faculty:* 4 full-time (1 woman), 11 part-time/adjunct (2 women). *Students:* 20 full-time (13 women), 164 part-time (110 women); includes 51 minority (44 Black or African American, non-Hispanic/Latino; 1 Asian, non-Hispanic/Latino; 5 Hispanic/Latino; 1 Two or more races, non-Hispanic/Latino), 1 international. Average age 37. 79 applicants, 97% accepted, 51 enrolled. In 2013, 22 master's, 19 other advanced degrees awarded. *Degree requirements:* For master's and Ed S, comprehensive exam, thesis optional, internship, portfolio, school leadership licensure assessment; for doctorate, comprehensive exam, thesis/dissertation. *Entrance requirements:* For master's, GRE General Test or MAT, minimum GPA of 3.0 in major, letter of recommendation; for doctorate, GRE, minimum graduate GPA of 3.5, 3 letters of recommendation; for Ed S, GRE General Test or MAT, minimum GPA of 3.0 in major, 2 letters of recommendation. Additional exam requirements/recommendations for international students: Required—TOEFL (minimum score 550 paper-based). *Application deadline:* For fall admission, 6/1 priority date for domestic students, 2/15 priority date for international students; for winter admission, 10/1 priority date for international students; for spring admission, 11/1 priority date for domestic students, 2/1 priority date for international students. Applications are processed on a rolling basis. Application fee: $50. Electronic applications accepted. *Expenses:* Tuition, state resident: full-time $9888; part-time $412 per credit. Tuition, nonresident: full-time $25,152; part-time $1048 per credit. *Required fees:* $59 per semester. One-time fee: $50. *Financial support:* In 2013–14, 48 students received support, including 1 fellowship with tuition reimbursement available (averaging $15,000 per year), 3 teaching assistantships with tuition reimbursements available (averaging $15,000 per year); career-related internships or fieldwork, scholarships/grants, and tuition waivers (partial) also available. Support available to part-time students. Financial award application deadline: 2/15; financial award applicants required to submit FAFSA. *Faculty research:* Principal and leadership preparation, supervision, policy studies, finance, teacher quality. *Total annual research expenditures:* $500,000. *Unit head:* Dr. Karen Sanzo, Graduate Program Director, 757-683-6698, Fax: 757-683-4413, E-mail: ksanzo@odu.edu. *Application contact:* William Heffelfinger, Director of Graduate Admissions, 757-683-5554, Fax: 757-683-3255, E-mail: gradadmit@odu.edu.
Website: http://education.odu.edu/efl/academics/educational/.

Old Dominion University, Darden College of Education, Programs in Higher Education, Norfolk, VA 23529. Offers educational leadership (MS Ed, Ed S), including higher education. Part-time programs available. *Faculty:* 3 full-time (0 women), 8 part-time/adjunct (2 women). *Students:* 31 full-time (25 women), 14 part-time (9 women); includes 18 minority (14 Black or African American, non-Hispanic/Latino; 3 Hispanic/Latino; 1 Two or more races, non-Hispanic/Latino). Average age 29. 59 applicants, 64% accepted, 18 enrolled. In 2013, 25 master's, 2 Ed Ss awarded. *Degree requirements:* For master's, comprehensive exam. *Entrance requirements:* For master's, GRE, minimum undergraduate GPA of 2.8; for Ed S, GRE, 2 letters of reference, minimum GPA of 3.5, master's degree. Additional exam requirements/recommendations for international students: Required—TOEFL. *Application deadline:* For fall admission, 3/1 priority date for domestic and international students; for winter admission, 10/1 for domestic and international students; for spring admission, 3/1 for domestic and international students. Applications are processed on a rolling basis. Application fee: $50. Electronic applications accepted. *Expenses:* Tuition, state resident: full-time $9888; part-time $412 per credit. Tuition, nonresident: full-time $25,152; part-time $1048 per credit. *Required fees:* $59 per semester. One-time fee: $50. *Financial support:* Research assistantships with partial tuition reimbursements, career-related internships or fieldwork, scholarships/grants, and unspecified assistantships available. *Faculty research:* Law leadership, student development, research administration, international higher education administration. *Unit head:* Dr. Chris Glass, Graduate Program Director, 757-683-4118, E-mail: hied@odu.edu. *Application contact:* William Heffelfinger, Director of Graduate Admissions, 757-683-5554, Fax: 757-683-3255, E-mail: gradadmit@odu.edu.
Website: http://education.odu.edu/efl/academics/highered/msed/msed_international_2.shtml.

Olivet Nazarene University, Graduate School, Division of Education, Program in School Leadership, Bourbonnais, IL 60914. Offers MAE.

Oral Roberts University, School of Education, Tulsa, OK 74171. Offers Christian school administration (K-12) (MA Ed, Ed D); Christian school curriculum development (MA Ed); college and higher education administration (Ed D); public school administration (K-12) (MA Ed, Ed D); public school teaching (MA Ed). *Accreditation:* NCATE. Part-time programs available. Postbaccalaureate distance learning degree programs offered (minimal on-campus study). *Degree requirements:* For master's, comprehensive exam, thesis optional; for doctorate, comprehensive exam, thesis/dissertation. *Entrance requirements:* For master's, GRE General Test or MAT, minimum

GPA of 3.0; for doctorate, minimum GPA of 3.0. Additional exam requirements/recommendations for international students: Required—TOEFL (minimum score 500 paper-based). *Expenses:* Contact institution. *Faculty research:* Teacher effectiveness, college success in high achieving African-Americans, professional development practices.

Oregon State University, College of Education, Program in Adult Education, Corvallis, OR 97331. Offers Ed M, MAIS. *Accreditation:* NCATE. Part-time programs available. *Faculty:* 4 full-time (all women), 1 (woman) part-time/adjunct. *Students:* 1 full-time (0 women), 23 part-time (16 women); includes 6 minority (1 Black or African American, non-Hispanic/Latino; 1 Asian, non-Hispanic/Latino; 2 Hispanic/Latino; 2 Two or more races, non-Hispanic/Latino). Average age 41. 29 applicants, 48% accepted, 13 enrolled. In 2013, 12 master's awarded. *Degree requirements:* For master's, thesis or alternative. *Entrance requirements:* For master's, minimum GPA of 3.0 in last 90 hours. Additional exam requirements/recommendations for international students: Required—TOEFL (minimum score 575 paper-based). *Application deadline:* For fall admission, 3/31 for domestic students. Applications are processed on a rolling basis. Application fee: $60. *Expenses:* Tuition, state resident: full-time $11,664; part-time $432 per credit hour. Tuition, nonresident: full-time $19,197; part-time $711 per credit hour. *Required fees:* $1446; $443 per quarter. One-time fee: $300. Tuition and fees vary according to course load and program. *Financial support:* Research assistantships, teaching assistantships, career-related internships or fieldwork, Federal Work-Study, and institutionally sponsored loans available. Support available to part-time students. Financial award application deadline: 2/1. *Faculty research:* Adult training and developmental psychology, cross-cultural communication, leadership development and human relations, adult literacy. *Unit head:* Dr. Larry Flick, Dean, 541-737-3664, E-mail: larry.flick@oregonstate.edu. *Application contact:* Shelley Dubkin-Lee, Adult Education Advisor, 541-737-5963, E-mail: shelley.dubkin-lee@oregonstate.edu.
Website: http://education.oregonstate.edu/adult-education-masters-degree-program.

Ottawa University, Graduate Studies-Arizona, Program in Education, Ottawa, KS 66067-3399. Offers community college counseling (MA); curriculum and instruction (MA); early childhood (MA); education intervention (MA); education leadership (MA); education technology (MA); Montessori early childhood education (MA); Montessori elementary education (MA); professional development (MA); school guidance counseling (MA); special education - cross categorical (MA). Programs offered in Mesa, Phoenix, Tempe and West Valley, AZ. *Accreditation:* NCATE. Part-time programs available. *Degree requirements:* For master's, thesis or alternative. *Entrance requirements:* For master's, minimum undergraduate GPA of 3.0, copy of current state certification or teaching license. Additional exam requirements/recommendations for international students: Required—TOEFL (minimum score 550 paper-based). Electronic applications accepted. *Expenses:* Contact institution.

Our Lady of Holy Cross College, Program in Education and Counseling, New Orleans, LA 70131-7399. Offers administration and supervision (M Ed); curriculum and instruction (M Ed); marriage and family counseling (MA); school counseling (M Ed, MA). *Accreditation:* ACA; NCATE. Part-time and evening/weekend programs available. *Degree requirements:* For master's, thesis. *Entrance requirements:* For master's, GRE General Test, minimum GPA of 2.7.

Our Lady of the Lake University of San Antonio, School of Professional Studies, Program in Principal, San Antonio, TX 78207-4689. Offers M Ed. Part-time and evening/weekend programs available. *Faculty:* 6 full-time (4 women), 3 part-time/adjunct (all women). *Students:* 1 applicant, 100% accepted. In 2013, 1 master's awarded. *Degree requirements:* For master's, comprehensive exam, thesis optional, exam, internship. *Entrance requirements:* For master's, GRE General Test or MAT. Additional exam requirements/recommendations for international students: Required—TOEFL. *Application deadline:* For fall admission, 4/1 priority date for domestic and international students; for spring admission, 11/1 priority date for domestic and international students; for summer admission, 2/1 priority date for domestic and international students. Applications are processed on a rolling basis. Application fee: $25 ($50 for international students). Electronic applications accepted. *Expenses:* Tuition: full-time $9120; part-time $760 per credit. *Required fees:* $698; $334 per trimester. Tuition and fees vary according to course load, degree level, campus/location and program. *Financial support:* Research assistantships, teaching assistantships, career-related internships or fieldwork, Federal Work-Study, institutionally sponsored loans, scholarships/grants, and tuition waivers (partial) available. Support available to part-time students. Financial award application deadline: 4/15. *Faculty research:* Professional educator to understand and meet the comprehensive needs of a diverse student population, life-long learners, innovative practices. *Unit head:* Dr. Jerrie Jackson, Head, 210-434-6711 Ext. 2698, E-mail: jjackson@lake.ollusa.edu. *Application contact:* Graduate Admission, 210-431-3961, Fax: 210-431-4013, E-mail: gradadm@lake.ollusa.edu.
Website: http://www.ollusa.edu/s/1190/ollu-3-column-noads.aspx?sid=1190&gid=1&pgid=3855.

Pace University, School of Education, New York, NY 10038. Offers adolescent education (MST); childhood education (MST); early childhood development, learning and intervention (MST); educational leadership (MS Ed); educational technology studies (MS); inclusive adolescent education (MST); literacy (MS Ed); school business management (Certificate); special education (MS Ed). *Accreditation:* NCATE. Part-time and evening/weekend programs available. *Students:* 186 full-time (154 women), 441 part-time (315 women); includes 209 minority (89 Black or African American, non-Hispanic/Latino; 2 American Indian or Alaska Native, non-Hispanic/Latino; 30 Asian, non-Hispanic/Latino; 74 Hispanic/Latino; 1 Native Hawaiian or other Pacific Islander, non-Hispanic/Latino; 13 Two or more races, non-Hispanic/Latino), 7 international. Average age 29. 207 applicants, 71% accepted, 105 enrolled. In 2013, 296 master's, 25 other advanced degrees awarded. *Degree requirements:* For master's, internship. *Entrance requirements:* For master's, interview, teaching certificate. Additional exam requirements/recommendations for international students: Required—TOEFL. *Application deadline:* For fall admission, 8/1 priority date for domestic students, 6/1 for international students; for spring admission, 12/1 priority date for domestic students, 10/1 for international students. Applications are processed on a rolling basis. Application fee: $70. Electronic applications accepted. *Expenses:* Contact institution. *Financial support:* Research assistantships, career-related internships or fieldwork, and Federal Work-Study available. Support available to part-time students. Financial award applicants required to submit FAFSA. *Faculty research:* Teacher education, technology in education, STEM, literacy education, special education. *Total annual research expenditures:* $1.3 million. *Unit head:* Dr. Andrea M. Spencer, Dean, School of Education, 914-773-3341, E-mail: aspencer@pace.edu. *Application contact:* Susan Ford-Goldschein, Director of Graduate Admissions, 212-346-1660, Fax: 212-346-1585, E-mail: gradnyc@pace.edu.
Website: http://www.pace.edu/school-of-education.

Pacific Lutheran University, Graduate Programs and Continuing Education, School of Education and Kinesiology, Program for Principal Certification, Tacoma, WA 98447. Offers MAE. Part-time and evening/weekend programs available. *Faculty:* 9 full-time (5 women), 8 part-time/adjunct (2 women). *Students:* 3 part-time (2 women). Average age 37. 10 applicants, 90% accepted, 6 enrolled. In 2013, 1 master's awarded. *Degree requirements:* For master's, culminating portfolio and internship. *Entrance requirements:*

For master's, teaching certificate with three years of experience. Additional exam requirements/recommendations for international students: Required—TOEFL (minimum score 550 paper-based; 88 iBT). *Application deadline:* For fall admission, 11/20 priority date for domestic and international students; for winter admission, 1/15 priority date for domestic and international students; for spring admission, 3/7 priority date for domestic and international students. Applications are processed on a rolling basis. Application fee: $40. Electronic applications accepted. *Expenses: Tuition:* Full-time $18,560; part-time $1160. Tuition and fees vary according to program and student level. *Financial support:* In 2013–14, 2 students received support. Scholarships/grants available. Financial award application deadline: 3/1; financial award applicants required to submit FAFSA. *Unit head:* Dr. Frank Kline, Dean, 253-535-7272, E-mail: klinefm@plu.edu. *Application contact:* Bree Van Horn, Assistant Director of Admission and Advising, 253-535-7276, Fax: 253-536-5136, E-mail: educ@plu.edu.

Pacific Lutheran University, Graduate Programs and Continuing Education, School of Education and Kinesiology, Program in Educational Leadership, Tacoma, WA 98447. Offers MAE. *Accreditation:* NCATE. Part-time and evening/weekend programs available. *Faculty:* 9 full-time (5 women), 8 part-time/adjunct (2 women). *Students:* 2 full-time (both women), 3 part-time (all women). Average age 36. 2 applicants, 50% accepted, 1 enrolled. In 2013, 1 master's awarded. *Degree requirements:* For master's, comprehensive exam, thesis or alternative, portfolio, internship. *Entrance requirements:* For master's, interview, teaching certificate, three years of teaching experience. Additional exam requirements/recommendations for international students: Required—TOEFL (minimum score 550 paper-based; 88 iBT). *Application deadline:* For fall admission, 11/20 priority date for domestic and international students; for winter admission, 1/15 priority date for domestic and international students; for spring admission, 3/7 priority date for domestic and international students. Applications are processed on a rolling basis. Application fee: $40. Electronic applications accepted. *Expenses: Tuition:* Full-time $18,560; part-time $1160. Tuition and fees vary according to program and student level. *Financial support:* In 2013–14, 3 students received support. Scholarships/grants available. Financial award application deadline: 3/1; financial award applicants required to submit FAFSA. *Unit head:* Dr. Frank Kline, Dean, 253-535-7272, Fax: 253-535-7184, E-mail: educ@plu.edu. *Application contact:* Bree Van Horn, Assistant Director of Admission and Advising, 253-535-7276, Fax: 253-536-5136, E-mail: educ@plu.edu.

Park University, School of Graduate and Professional Studies, Kansas City, MO 54105. Offers adult education (M Ed); business and government leadership (Graduate Certificate); business, government, and global society (MPA); communication and leadership (MA); creative and life writing (Graduate Certificate); disaster and emergency management (MPA, Graduate Certificate); educational leadership (M Ed); finance (MBA, Graduate Certificate); general business (MBA); global business (Graduate Certificate); healthcare administration (MHA); healthcare services management and leadership (Graduate Certificate); international business (MBA); language and literacy (M Ed), including English for speakers of other languages, special reading teacher/literacy coach; leadership of international healthcare organizations (Graduate Certificate); management information systems (MBA, Graduate Certificate); music performance (ADP, Graduate Certificate), including cello (MM, ADP), piano (MM, ADP), viola (MM, ADP), violin (MM, ADP); nonprofit and community services management (MPA); nonprofit leadership (Graduate Certificate); performance (MM), including cello (MM, ADP), piano (MM, ADP), viola (MM, ADP), violin (MM, ADP); public management (MPA); social work (MSW); teacher leadership (M Ed), including curriculum and assessment, instructional leader. Part-time and evening/weekend programs available. Postbaccalaureate distance learning degree programs offered (no on-campus study). *Students:* 862 full-time (482 women); includes 55 minority (30 Black or African American, non-Hispanic/Latino; 2 American Indian or Alaska Native, non-Hispanic/Latino; 4 Asian, non-Hispanic/Latino; 14 Hispanic/Latino; 5 Two or more races, non-Hispanic/Latino), 141 international. Average age 34. 497 applicants, 62% accepted, 119 enrolled. In 2013, 281 master's, 14 other advanced degrees awarded. *Degree requirements:* For master's, comprehensive exam (for some programs), thesis (for some programs), internship (for some programs); exam (for some programs). *Entrance requirements:* For master's, GRE or GMAT (for some programs), teacher certification (for some M Ed programs), letters of recommendation, essay, resume (for some programs). Additional exam requirements/recommendations for international students: Required—TOEFL (minimum score 550 paper-based; 79 iBT), IELTS (minimum score 6). *Application deadline:* For fall admission, 8/1 priority date for domestic students, 7/15 priority date for international students; for spring admission, 1/1 priority date for domestic students, 11/1 priority date for international students. Applications are processed on a rolling basis. Application fee: $50 ($100 for international students). Electronic applications accepted. *Financial support:* In 2013–14, 2 research assistantships with full tuition reimbursements (averaging $15,760 per year) were awarded. Financial award applicants required to submit FAFSA. *Unit head:* Dr. Laurie Dipadova-Stocks, Dean of Graduate and Professional Studies, 816-559-5624, Fax: 816-472-1173, E-mail: ldipadovastocks@park.edu. *Application contact:* Judith Appollis, Director of Graduate Admissions and Internationalization, School of Graduate and Professional Studies, 816-559-5627, Fax: 816-472-1173, E-mail: gradschool@park.edu.
Website: http://www.park.edu/grad.

Penn State University Park, Graduate School, College of Education, Department of Education Policy Studies, State College, PA 16802. Offers college student affairs (M Ed); educational leadership (M Ed, D Ed, PhD, Certificate); educational theory and policy (MA, PhD); higher education (M Ed, D Ed, PhD). *Accreditation:* NCATE. *Unit head:* Dr. David H. Monk, Dean, 814-865-2523, Fax: 814-865-0555, E-mail: dhm6@psu.edu. *Application contact:* Cynthia E. Nicosia, Director, Graduate Enrollment Services, 814-865-1834, Fax: 814-863-4627, E-mail: cey1@psu.edu.
Website: http://www.ed.psu.edu/educ/eps/.

Pepperdine University, Graduate School of Education and Psychology, Division of Education, Ed D Program in Educational Leadership, Administration, and Policy, Malibu, CA 90263. Offers Ed D. Part-time and evening/weekend programs available. *Students:* 1 (woman) full-time, 73 part-time (59 women); includes 36 minority (20 Black or African American, non-Hispanic/Latino; 2 American Indian or Alaska Native, non-Hispanic/Latino; 4 Asian, non-Hispanic/Latino; 10 Hispanic/Latino), 1 international. In 2013, 18 doctorates awarded. *Degree requirements:* For doctorate, thesis/dissertation. *Entrance requirements:* For doctorate, MAT, GRE (verbal and quantitative sections), or GMAT, 1,000- to 2,000-word statement of educational purpose, three recommendations, personal interviews, on-site writing sample. Additional exam requirements/recommendations for international students: Required—TOEFL. *Application deadline:* For fall admission, 5/2 priority date for domestic students. Applications are processed on a rolling basis. Application fee: $55. *Expenses:* Contact institution. *Financial support:* Application deadline: 7/1; applicants required to submit FAFSA. *Unit head:* Dr. Linda Purrington, Director, 310-258-2568, E-mail: linda.purrington@pepperdine.edu. *Application contact:* Jennifer Agatep, Admissions Manager, Education, 310-258-2849, E-mail: jennifer.agatep@pepperdine.edu.
Website: http://gsep.pepperdine.edu/doctorate-educational-leadership-administration-policy/.

Pepperdine University, Graduate School of Education and Psychology, Division of Education, Ed D Program in Organizational Leadership, Malibu, CA 90263. Offers Ed D. Part-time and evening/weekend programs available. *Students:* 112 full-time (65 women), 164 part-time (101 women); includes 115 minority (54 Black or African American, non-Hispanic/Latino; 3 American Indian or Alaska Native, non-Hispanic/Latino; 26 Asian, non-Hispanic/Latino; 30 Hispanic/Latino; 2 Native Hawaiian or other Pacific Islander, non-Hispanic/Latino), 16 international. 121 applicants, 84% accepted, 58 enrolled. In 2013, 30 doctorates awarded. *Degree requirements:* For doctorate, thesis/dissertation. *Entrance requirements:* For doctorate, GMAT or GRE General Test, MAT, 1,000- to 2,000-word statement of educational purpose, three recommendations, personal interviews, on-site writing sample. Additional exam requirements/recommendations for international students: Required—TOEFL. *Application deadline:* For fall admission, 7/1 for domestic students. Applications are processed on a rolling basis. Application fee: $55. *Expenses:* Contact institution. *Financial support:* Research assistantships, teaching assistantships, institutionally sponsored loans, and scholarships/grants available. Support available to part-time students. Financial award application deadline: 7/1; financial award applicants required to submit FAFSA. *Unit head:* Christie Dailo, Program Administrator, 310-568-5612, E-mail: christie.dailo@pepperdine.edu. *Application contact:* Jennifer Agatep, Admissions Manager, Education, 310-258-2849, E-mail: jennifer.agatep@pepperdine.edu.

Pepperdine University, Graduate School of Education and Psychology, Division of Education, MS Program in Administration and Preliminary Administrative Services Credential, Malibu, CA 90263. Offers MS. *Students:* 14 full-time (7 women); includes 7 minority (1 Black or African American, non-Hispanic/Latino; 1 Asian, non-Hispanic/Latino; 5 Hispanic/Latino). *Entrance requirements:* For master's, GRE General Test, CBEST, two recommendation forms; signed Principal's Consent form indicating support of principal or supervising administrator under whom the administrative field work will be accomplished; one- to two-page statement of educational purpose. Additional exam requirements/recommendations for international students: Required—TOEFL. *Application deadline:* For fall admission, 7/1 for domestic students. Applications are processed on a rolling basis. Application fee: $45. Tuition and fees vary according to program. *Financial support:* Research assistantships and teaching assistantships available. Financial award application deadline: 7/1. *Unit head:* Dr. Linda Purrington, Director, 310-258-2500, E-mail: linda.purrington@pepperdine.edu. *Application contact:* Jennifer Agatep, Admissions Manager, Education, 310-258-2849, E-mail: jennifer.agatep@pepperdine.edu.
Website: http://gsep.pepperdine.edu/masters-educational-leadership-administration/.

Piedmont College, School of Education, Demorest, GA 30535-0010. Offers art education (MAT); early childhood education (MA, MAT); instructional technology (MAT); middle grades education (MA, MAT); music education (MAT); secondary education (MA, MAT); special education (MA, MAT); teacher leadership (Ed S). Part-time and evening/weekend programs available. *Students:* 312 full-time (242 women), 694 part-time (563 women); includes 153 minority (103 Black or African American, non-Hispanic/Latino; 3 American Indian or Alaska Native, non-Hispanic/Latino; 17 Asian, non-Hispanic/Latino; 19 Hispanic/Latino; 11 Two or more races, non-Hispanic/Latino), 1 international. Average age 37. 165 applicants, 72% accepted, 118 enrolled. In 2013, 333 master's, 15 doctorates, 457 other advanced degrees awarded. *Degree requirements:* For master's, thesis, field experience in the classroom teaching; for doctorate, thesis/dissertation. *Entrance requirements:* For master's, GRE General Test, MAT, minimum undergraduate GPA of 2.5; for Ed S, minimum graduate GPA of 3.5, valid teaching certificate. Additional exam requirements/recommendations for international students: Required—TOEFL (minimum score 550 paper-based). *Application deadline:* For fall admission, 7/15 for domestic students; for spring admission, 12/1 for domestic students. Applications are processed on a rolling basis. Electronic applications accepted. *Expenses: Tuition:* Full-time $7992; part-time $444 per credit hour. *Financial support:* Career-related internships or fieldwork, Federal Work-Study, and unspecified assistantships available. Support available to part-time students. Financial award applicants required to submit FAFSA. *Unit head:* Dr. Don Gnecco, Dean, 706-778-3000 Ext. 1201, Fax: 706-776-9608, E-mail: dgnecco@piedmont.edu. *Application contact:* Kathleen Anderson, Director of Graduate Enrollment Management, 706-778-8500 Ext. 1181, Fax: 706-778-0150, E-mail: kanderson@piedmont.edu.

Pittsburg State University, Graduate School, College of Education, Department of Special Services and Leadership Studies, Program in Educational Leadership, Pittsburg, KS 66762. Offers MS.

Pittsburg State University, Graduate School, College of Education, Department of Special Services and Leadership Studies, Program in General School Administration, Pittsburg, KS 66762. Offers Ed S.

Plymouth State University, College of Graduate Studies, Graduate Studies in Education, Certificate of Advanced Graduate Studies Programs, Plymouth, NH 03264-1595. Offers clinical mental health counseling (CAGS); educational leadership (CAGS); higher education (CAGS); school psychology (CAGS). Part-time and evening/weekend programs available.

Plymouth State University, College of Graduate Studies, Graduate Studies in Education, Program in Educational Leadership, Plymouth, NH 03264-1595. Offers M Ed. *Accreditation:* NCATE. Part-time and evening/weekend programs available. *Degree requirements:* For master's, thesis optional, PRAXIS. *Entrance requirements:* For master's, MAT, minimum GPA of 3.0.

Point Loma Nazarene University, School of Education, Program in Education, San Diego, CA 92106-2899. Offers counseling and guidance (MA); educational leadership (MA); teaching and learning (MA). Part-time and evening/weekend programs available. *Students:* 26 full-time (24 women), 126 part-time (92 women); includes 68 minority (11 Black or African American, non-Hispanic/Latino; 2 American Indian or Alaska Native, non-Hispanic/Latino; 8 Asian, non-Hispanic/Latino; 42 Hispanic/Latino; 4 Native Hawaiian or other Pacific Islander, non-Hispanic/Latino; 1 Two or more races, non-Hispanic/Latino). Average age 50. 65 applicants, 71% accepted, 41 enrolled. In 2013, 103 master's awarded. *Entrance requirements:* For master's, interview, letters of recommendation, essay. Additional exam requirements/recommendations for international students: Required—TOEFL. *Application deadline:* For fall admission, 8/4 priority date for domestic students; for spring admission, 12/8 priority date for domestic students; for summer admission, 4/12 priority date for domestic students. Applications are processed on a rolling basis. Application fee: $50. Electronic applications accepted. *Expenses: Tuition:* Full-time $6900; part-time $567 per credit hour. *Financial support:* Applicants required to submit FAFSA. *Unit head:* Dr. Deborah Erickson, Dean of the School of Education, 619-849-2332, Fax: 619-849-2579, E-mail: deberickson@pointloma.edu. *Application contact:* Laura Leinweber, Director of Graduate Admission, 866-693-4723, E-mail: lauraleinweber@pointloma.edu.
Website: http://www.pointloma.edu/discover/graduate-school-san-diego/san-diego-graduate-programs-masters-degree-san-diego/education/master-arts-education.

Point Park University, School of Arts and Sciences, Department of Education, Pittsburgh, PA 15222-1984. Offers curriculum and instruction (MA); educational administration (MA); special education (M Ed); teaching and leadership (M Ed). Part-time and evening/weekend programs available. *Degree requirements:* For master's,

comprehensive exam (for some programs), thesis or alternative. *Entrance requirements:* For master's, minimum GPA of 3.0, resume, 2 letters of recommendation. Additional exam requirements/recommendations for international students: Required—TOEFL. Electronic applications accepted.

Pontifical Catholic University of Puerto Rico, College of Education, Program in Educational Leadership and Administration, Ponce, PR 00717-0777. Offers PhD.

Portland State University, Graduate Studies, School of Education, Department of Educational Policy, Foundations, and Administrative Studies, Portland, OR 97207-0751. Offers educational leadership (MA, MS, Ed D); postsecondary, adult and continuing education (Ed D). *Accreditation:* NCATE. Part-time and evening/weekend programs available. *Faculty:* 14 full-time (9 women), 9 part-time/adjunct (5 women). *Students:* 231 full-time (154 women), 382 part-time (256 women); includes 139 minority (22 Black or African American, non-Hispanic/Latino; 8 American Indian or Alaska Native, non-Hispanic/Latino; 24 Asian, non-Hispanic/Latino; 59 Hispanic/Latino; 3 Native Hawaiian or other Pacific Islander, non-Hispanic/Latino; 23 Two or more races, non-Hispanic/Latino), 11 international. Average age 38. 210 applicants, 60% accepted, 125 enrolled. In 2013, 79 master's, 13 doctorates awarded. *Degree requirements:* For master's, thesis or alternative, written exam or research project; for doctorate, comprehensive exam, thesis/dissertation. *Entrance requirements:* For master's, California Basic Educational Skills Test, minimum GPA of 3.0 in upper-division course work or 2.75 overall; for doctorate, GRE General Test or MAT. Additional exam requirements/recommendations for international students: Required—TOEFL (minimum score 550 paper-based). *Application deadline:* For fall admission, 4/1 for domestic and international students; for winter admission, 9/1 for domestic and international students; for spring admission, 11/1 for domestic and international students. Applications are processed on a rolling basis. Application fee: $50. *Expenses:* Tuition, state resident: full-time $9207; part-time $341 per credit. Tuition, nonresident: full-time $14,391; part-time $533 per credit. *Required fees:* $1263; $22 per credit. $98 per quarter. One-time fee: $150. Tuition and fees vary according to program. *Financial support:* Career-related internships or fieldwork, Federal Work-Study, and institutionally sponsored loans available. Support available to part-time students. Financial award application deadline: 3/1; financial award applicants required to submit FAFSA. *Faculty research:* Leadership development and research, principals and urban schools, accelerated schools, cooperative learning, family involvement in schools. *Total annual research expenditures:* $43,200. *Unit head:* Candyce Reynolds, Chair, 503-725-4657, Fax: 503-725-8475, E-mail: reynoldsc@pdx.edu. *Application contact:* Mindy Friend, Department Assistant, 503-725-4716, Fax: 503-725-8475, E-mail: mfriend@pdx.edu.
Website: http://www.ed.pdx.edu/epfa/.

Post University, Program in Education, Waterbury, CT 06723-2540. Offers education (M Ed); higher education administration (M Ed); instructional design and technology (M Ed); online teaching (M Ed); teaching and learning (M Ed); TESOL (teaching English to speakers of other languages) (M Ed). Postbaccalaureate distance learning degree programs offered.

Prairie View A&M University, College of Education, Department of Educational Leadership and Counseling, Prairie View, TX 77446-0519. Offers counseling (MA, MS Ed); educational administration (M Ed, MS Ed); educational leadership (PhD). *Accreditation:* NCATE. Part-time and evening/weekend programs available. *Faculty:* 28 full-time (10 women), 13 part-time/adjunct (9 women). *Students:* 193 full-time (144 women), 450 part-time (359 women); includes 607 minority (571 Black or African American, non-Hispanic/Latino; 6 Asian, non-Hispanic/Latino; 26 Hispanic/Latino; 4 Two or more races, non-Hispanic/Latino), 5 international. Average age 34. 337 applicants, 55% accepted, 125 enrolled. In 2013, 197 master's, 5 doctorates awarded. *Degree requirements:* For master's, thesis optional; for doctorate, comprehensive exam, thesis/dissertation. *Entrance requirements:* For master's, GRE General Test, 3 letters of reference, minimum undergraduate GPA of 2.5; for doctorate, GRE General Test, 3 letters of reference. Additional exam requirements/recommendations for international students: Required—TOEFL (minimum score 550 paper-based). *Application deadline:* For fall admission, 7/1 priority date for domestic students, 7/1 for international students; for spring admission, 11/1 priority date for domestic students, 11/1 for international students. Applications are processed on a rolling basis. Application fee: $50. Electronic applications accepted. *Expenses:* Tuition, state resident: full-time $3776; part-time $209.77 per credit hour. Tuition, nonresident: full-time $10,183; part-time $565.77 per credit hour. *Required fees:* $2037; $446.50 per credit hour. *Financial support:* In 2013–14, 600 students received support. Career-related internships or fieldwork available. Support available to part-time students. Financial award application deadline: 4/1; financial award applicants required to submit FAFSA. *Faculty research:* Mentoring, personality assessment, holistic/humanistic education. *Unit head:* Dr. Pamela Barber-Freeman, Interim Head, 936-261-3530, Fax: 936-261-3617, E-mail: ptfreeman@pvamu.edu. *Application contact:* Head.

Prescott College, Graduate Programs, Program in Education, Prescott, AZ 86301. Offers early childhood education (MA); early childhood special education (MA); education (MA); elementary education (MA); environmental education leadership and administration (MA); equine-assisted learning (MA); school guidance counseling (MA); secondary education (MA); special education: learning disabilities (MA); special education: mental retardation (MA); special education: serious emotional disabilities (MA); student-directed independent study (MA); sustainability education (PhD). Part-time programs available. Postbaccalaureate distance learning degree programs offered (minimal on-campus study). *Degree requirements:* For master's, thesis, fieldwork or internship, practicum; for doctorate, thesis/dissertation. *Entrance requirements:* For master's, 2 letters of recommendation, resume; for doctorate, 3 letters of recommendation, resume, official transcripts, personal statement, program proposal. Additional exam requirements/recommendations for international students: Required—TOEFL (minimum score 500 paper-based). Electronic applications accepted.

Providence College, Programs in Administration, Providence, RI 02918. Offers elementary administration (M Ed); secondary administration (M Ed). Part-time and evening/weekend programs available. *Faculty:* 14 part-time/adjunct (6 women). *Students:* 5 full-time (1 woman), 50 part-time (31 women). Average age 37. 9 applicants, 100% accepted, 8 enrolled. In 2013, 33 master's awarded. *Degree requirements:* For master's, comprehensive exam, portfolio. *Entrance requirements:* For master's, GRE General Test. Additional exam requirements/recommendations for international students: Required—TOEFL (minimum score 550 paper-based; 80 iBT). *Application deadline:* For fall admission, 8/1 priority date for domestic and international students; for spring admission, 12/1 priority date for domestic and international students. Applications are processed on a rolling basis. Application fee: $55. *Expenses: Tuition:* Part-time $432 per credit. *Required fees:* $432 per credit. *Financial support:* Career-related internships or fieldwork, institutionally sponsored loans, and unspecified assistantships available. Support available to part-time students. Financial award application deadline: 8/1; financial award applicants required to submit FAFSA. *Unit head:* Francis J. Leary, Director, 401-865-2881, E-mail: fleary@providence.edu. *Application contact:* Rev. Mark D. Nowel, Dean of Undergraduate and Graduate Studies, 401-865-2649, Fax: 401-865-1496, E-mail: mnowel@providence.edu.
Website: http://www.providence.edu/professional-studies/graduate-degrees/Pages/master-education-administration.aspx.

Purdue University, Graduate School, College of Education, Department of Educational Studies, West Lafayette, IN 47907. Offers administration (MS Ed, PhD, Ed S); counseling and development (MS Ed, PhD); education of the gifted (MS Ed); educational psychology (MS Ed, PhD); foundations of education (MS Ed, PhD); higher education administration (MS Ed, PhD); special education (MS Ed, PhD). *Accreditation:* ACA (one or more programs are accredited); NCATE (one or more programs are accredited). Part-time and evening/weekend programs available. *Faculty:* 21 full-time (17 women), 7 part-time/adjunct (4 women). *Students:* 102 full-time (73 women), 45 part-time (27 women); includes 23 minority (10 Black or African American, non-Hispanic/Latino; 5 Asian, non-Hispanic/Latino; 5 Hispanic/Latino; 3 Two or more races, non-Hispanic/Latino), 32 international. Average age 35. 165 applicants, 40% accepted, 33 enrolled. In 2013, 26 master's, 21 doctorates awarded. *Degree requirements:* For master's, thesis optional; for doctorate, thesis/dissertation, oral and written exams; for Ed S, oral presentation, project. *Entrance requirements:* For master's, GRE General Test (except for special education if undergraduate GPA is higher than a 3.0), minimum undergraduate GPA of 3.0; for doctorate and Ed S, GRE General Test (minimum combined score of 1000, 300 for new scoring), minimum undergraduate GPA of 3.0. Additional exam requirements/recommendations for international students: Required—TOEFL (minimum score 550 paper-based; 77 iBT), TWE (minimum score 5). *Application deadline:* Applications are processed on a rolling basis. Application fee: $60 ($75 for international students). Electronic applications accepted. *Financial support:* Fellowships with full tuition reimbursements, research assistantships with full tuition reimbursements, teaching assistantships with full tuition reimbursements, career-related internships or fieldwork, and tuition waivers (full) available. Support available to part-time students. Financial award application deadline: 3/1; financial award applicants required to submit FAFSA. *Faculty research:* Motivation, learning disabilities, school learning, group processes, cognitive development. *Unit head:* Dr. Ala Samrapungavan, Head, 765-494-9170, Fax: 765-496-1228, E-mail: ala@purdue.edu. *Application contact:* Cindy Blankenship, Graduate Contact, 765-494-2345, Fax: 765-494-5832, E-mail: prater0@purdue.edu.
Website: http://www.edst.purdue.edu/.

Purdue University Calumet, Graduate Studies Office, School of Education, Program in Educational Administration, Hammond, IN 46323-2094. Offers MS Ed. *Entrance requirements:* Additional exam requirements/recommendations for international students: Required—TOEFL.

Queens College of the City University of New York, Division of Graduate Studies, Division of Education, Department of Educational and Community Programs, Program in Educational Leadership, Flushing, NY 11367-1597. Offers AC. Part-time programs available. *Degree requirements:* For AC, thesis optional, internship. *Entrance requirements:* For degree, master's degree or equivalent. Additional exam requirements/recommendations for international students: Required—TOEFL.

Queens University of Charlotte, Wayland H. Cato, Jr. School of Education, Charlotte, NC 28274-0002. Offers education in literacy (M Ed); elementary education (MAT); school administration (MSA). *Accreditation:* NCATE. Part-time and evening/weekend programs available. *Degree requirements:* For master's, comprehensive exam. *Entrance requirements:* For master's, GRE General Test. *Expenses:* Contact institution.

Quincy University, Program in Education, Quincy, IL 62301-2699. Offers curriculum and instruction (MS Ed), including bilingual/English as a second language; leadership (MS Ed); reading education (MS Ed); special education (MS Ed); teacher leader (MS Ed). Part-time and evening/weekend programs available. Postbaccalaureate distance learning degree programs offered (minimal on-campus study). *Students:* 62 full-time (39 women), 97 part-time (68 women); includes 43 minority (29 Black or African American, non-Hispanic/Latino; 1 American Indian or Alaska Native, non-Hispanic/Latino; 4 Asian, non-Hispanic/Latino; 9 Hispanic/Latino). In 2013, 105 master's awarded. *Degree requirements:* For master's, comprehensive exam (for some programs), thesis optional. *Entrance requirements:* For master's, MAT or GRE. Additional exam requirements/recommendations for international students: Required—TOEFL (minimum score 550 paper-based; 79 iBT). *Application deadline:* Applications are processed on a rolling basis. Application fee: $25. Electronic applications accepted. *Expenses: Tuition:* Full-time $9600; part-time $400 per semester hour. *Required fees:* $720; $30 per semester hour. Tuition and fees vary according to course load and program. *Financial support:* Applicants required to submit FAFSA. *Unit head:* Dr. Kristen R. Anguiano, Director, 217-228-5432 Ext. 3119, E-mail: anguikr@quincy.edu. *Application contact:* Office of Admissions, 217-228-5210, Fax: 217-228-5479, E-mail: admissions@quincy.edu.
Website: http://www.quincy.edu/academics/graduate-programs/education.

Quinnipiac University, School of Education, Program in Educational Leadership, Hamden, CT 06518-1940. Offers Diploma. Part-time and evening/weekend programs available. *Faculty:* 6 part-time/adjunct (1 woman). *Students:* 41 part-time (27 women); includes 6 minority (1 Black or African American, non-Hispanic/Latino; 5 Hispanic/Latino). 17 applicants, 94% accepted, 15 enrolled. In 2013, 27 Diplomas awarded. *Entrance requirements:* For degree, 3 years of experience in pre K-12 setting, interview, 3 credits in special education course. *Application deadline:* For fall admission, 7/30 priority date for domestic students; for spring admission, 12/15 priority date for domestic students; for summer admission, 5/30 priority date for domestic students. Applications are processed on a rolling basis. Application fee: $45. Electronic applications accepted. *Expenses:* Contact institution. *Financial support:* Federal Work-Study and unspecified assistantships available. Support available to part-time students. Financial award application deadline: 6/1; financial award applicants required to submit FAFSA. *Faculty research:* Leadership and teacher quality, leadership and student achievement. *Unit head:* Gary Alger, Program Director, E-mail: gary.alger@quinnipiac.edu. *Application contact:* Office of Graduate Admissions, 800-462-1944, Fax: 203-582-3443, E-mail: graduate@quinnipiac.edu.
Website: http://www.quinnipiac.edu/edleadership.

Quinnipiac University, School of Education, Program in Teacher Leadership, Hamden, CT 06518-1940. Offers MS. Part-time and evening/weekend programs available. Postbaccalaureate distance learning degree programs offered (no on-campus study). *Faculty:* 4 full-time (3 women), 3 part-time/adjunct (1 woman). *Students:* 32 part-time (21 women); includes 1 minority (Black or African American, non-Hispanic/Latino). 16 applicants, 94% accepted, 15 enrolled. In 2013, 30 master's awarded. *Degree requirements:* For master's, capstone experience. *Application deadline:* For fall admission, 8/15 for domestic students; for spring admission, 1/15 for domestic students. Applications are processed on a rolling basis. Application fee: $45. Electronic applications accepted. *Expenses: Tuition:* Part-time $920 per credit. *Required fees:* $37 per credit. *Financial support:* Federal Work-Study and unspecified assistantships available. Support available to part-time students. Financial award application deadline: 6/1; financial award applicants required to submit FAFSA. *Faculty research:* Leadership and school climate, distributed leadership, teacher retention. *Unit head:* Gary Alger, Director, E-mail: gary.alger@quinnipiac.edu. *Application contact:* Quinnipiac University Online Admissions Office, 800-462-1944, E-mail: quonlineadmissions@quinnipiac.edu.
Website: http://www.quinnipiac.edu/qu-online/academics/degree-programs/ms-in-teacher-leadership.

Radford University, College of Graduate and Professional Studies, College of Education and Human Development, School of Teacher Education and Leadership, Program in Educational Leadership, Radford, VA 24142. Offers MS, Certificate. *Accreditation:* NCATE. Part-time and evening/weekend programs available. *Faculty:* 2 full-time (1 woman), 5 part-time/adjunct (0 women). *Students:* 1 (woman) full-time, 80 part-time (46 women); includes 4 minority (2 Black or African American, non-Hispanic/Latino; 1 Hispanic/Latino; 1 Two or more races, non-Hispanic/Latino). Average age 38. 40 applicants, 98% accepted, 37 enrolled. In 2013, 27 master's, 1 other advanced degree awarded. *Degree requirements:* For master's, comprehensive exam. *Entrance requirements:* For master's, GRE or MAT, minimum GPA of 2.75, 3 years of K-12 classroom experience, writing sample, 3 letters of reference, resume, official transcripts. Additional exam requirements/recommendations for international students: Required—TOEFL (minimum score 550 paper-based; 79 iBT). *Application deadline:* For fall admission, 2/15 priority date for domestic students, 12/1 for international students; for spring admission, 7/1 for international students. Applications are processed on a rolling basis. Application fee: $50. Electronic applications accepted. *Expenses:* Tuition, state resident: full-time $6800; part-time $283 per credit hour. Tuition, nonresident: full-time $15,610; part-time $627 per credit hour. *Required fees:* $2944; $123 per credit hour. Tuition and fees vary according to program. *Financial support:* In 2013–14, 1 student received support. Career-related internships or fieldwork, Federal Work-Study, institutionally sponsored loans, scholarships/grants, and unspecified assistantships available. Financial award application deadline: 3/1; financial award applicants required to submit FAFSA. *Unit head:* Dr. Brad Bizzell, Coordinator, 540-831-5140, Fax: 540-831-5059, E-mail: bbizzell@radford.edu. *Application contact:* Rebecca Conner, Director, Graduate Enrollment, 540-831-6296, Fax: 540-831-6061, E-mail: gradcollege@radford.edu.
Website: http://www.radford.edu/content/cehd/home/departments/STEL/programs/education-leadership.html.

Ramapo College of New Jersey, Master of Arts in Educational Leadership Program, Mahwah, NJ 07430-1680. Offers MA. Part-time and evening/weekend programs available. *Faculty:* 1 full-time (0 women), 4 part-time/adjunct (0 women). *Students:* 19 full-time (15 women), 14 part-time (4 women); includes 4 minority (1 Black or African American, non-Hispanic/Latino; 1 Asian, non-Hispanic/Latino; 2 Hispanic/Latino). Average age 30. In 2013, 7 master's awarded. *Degree requirements:* For master's, thesis. *Entrance requirements:* For master's, PRAXIS, official transcript; personal statement; 2 letters of recommendation; resume; state-issued teaching certificate. Additional exam requirements/recommendations for international students: Required—TOEFL (minimum score 550 paper-based; 79 iBT). *Application deadline:* For fall admission, 9/1 for domestic and international students; for spring admission, 1/30 for domestic and international students. Applications are processed on a rolling basis. Application fee: $60. Electronic applications accepted. *Expenses: Tuition, area resident:* Part-time $582.45 per credit. Tuition, nonresident: part-time $748.70 per credit. *Required fees:* $127.05 per credit. *Unit head:* Dr. Brian P. Chinni, Assistant Professor, 201-684-7613, E-mail: bchinni@ramapo.edu. *Application contact:* Karen A. Viviani, Secretarial Assistant, 201-684-7638, E-mail: kdroubi@ramapo.edu.
Website: http://www.ramapo.edu/mael/.

Regent University, Graduate School, School of Education, Virginia Beach, VA 23464-9800. Offers adult education (Ed D, PhD); advanced educational leadership (Ed D, PhD); career switcher with licensure (M Ed), including alternative licensure; character education (Ed D, PhD); Christian education leadership (Ed D); Christian school administration (M Ed); curriculum and instruction (M Ed); distance education (Ed D, PhD); educational leadership (M Ed); educational leadership - special education (Ed S); educational psychology (Ed D); elementary education (M Ed); higher education (Ed D, PhD); higher education leadership and management (Ed D); K-12 school leadership (Ed D, PhD); leadership in mathematics education (M Ed); reading specialist (M Ed); special education (M Ed, Ed D, PhD); student affairs (M Ed); TESOL (M Ed), including adult education, PreK-12. *Accreditation:* Teacher Education Accreditation Council. Part-time and evening/weekend programs available. Postbaccalaureate distance learning degree programs offered (minimal on-campus study). *Faculty:* 25 full-time (12 women), 50 part-time/adjunct (31 women). *Students:* 100 full-time (78 women), 754 part-time (614 women); includes 225 minority (191 Black or African American, non-Hispanic/Latino; 1 American Indian or Alaska Native, non-Hispanic/Latino; 7 Asian, non-Hispanic/Latino; 26 Hispanic/Latino), 16 international. Average age 39. 487 applicants, 63% accepted, 233 enrolled. In 2013, 202 master's, 19 doctorates awarded. *Degree requirements:* For master's, thesis or alternative; for doctorate, comprehensive exam, thesis/dissertation. *Entrance requirements:* For master's, MAT, minimum undergraduate GPA of 2.75, writing sample, resume, recommendations, interview; for doctorate, GRE, writing sample, 3 years of relevant professional experience, master's-level paper, copies of published work, resume, transcripts, interview, recommendations. Additional exam requirements/recommendations for international students: Required—TOEFL (minimum score 577 paper-based). *Application deadline:* For fall admission, 4/1 priority date for domestic students; for spring admission, 10/15 priority date for domestic students. Applications are processed on a rolling basis. Application fee: $50. Electronic applications accepted. Tuition and fees vary according to course load and degree level. *Financial support:* Fellowships, career-related internships or fieldwork, scholarships/grants, tuition waivers (full and partial), and unspecified assistantships available. Support available to part-time students. Financial award application deadline: 4/1; financial award applicants required to submit FAFSA. *Faculty research:* Character development and discipline for children, education leadership development, diversity in schools, classroom management, technology in education settings. *Unit head:* Dr. Alan Arroyo, Dean, 757-352-4261, Fax: 757-352-4318, E-mail: alanarr@regent.edu. *Application contact:* Matthew Chadwick, Director of Enrollment Support Services, 800-373-5504, Fax: 757-352-4381, E-mail: admissions@regent.edu.
Website: http://www.regent.edu/education/.

Regis College, Department of Education, Weston, MA 02493. Offers elementary teacher (MAT); higher education leadership (Ed D); reading (MAT); special education (MAT). Part-time and evening/weekend programs available. *Degree requirements:* For master's, thesis. *Entrance requirements:* For master's, GRE or MAT. Additional exam requirements/recommendations for international students: Required—TOEFL. Electronic applications accepted. *Faculty research:* Reflective teaching, gender-based education, integrated teaching.

Regis University, College for Professional Studies, School of Education, Education Division, Denver, CO 80221-1099. Offers adult learning, training, and development (M Ed, Certificate); autism education (Certificate); curriculum, instruction, and assessment (M Ed); educational leadership (M Ed); gifted and talented education (M Ed); gifted/talented education (Certificate); initial licensure (M Ed); instructional technology (M Ed, Certificate); literacy (Certificate); reading (M Ed); school executive leadership (Certificate); space studies (M Ed). Program also offered in Henderson and Las Vegas (Summerlin), NV. *Accreditation:* Teacher Education Accreditation Council. Part-time and evening/weekend programs available. Postbaccalaureate distance learning degree programs offered (no on-campus study). *Degree requirements:* For master's, thesis. *Entrance requirements:* For master's, resume, minimum GPA of 2.75, criminal background check. Additional exam requirements/recommendations for international students: Required—TOEFL, TWE (minimum score 5). *Application*

deadline: For fall admission, 7/23 priority date for domestic students; for winter admission, 9/17 priority date for domestic students; for spring admission, 12/3 priority date for domestic students. Applications are processed on a rolling basis. Application fee: $75. Electronic applications accepted. *Expenses:* Contact institution. *Financial support:* Federal Work-Study and scholarships/grants available. *Faculty research:* Issues of equity in the middle school classroom, professional learning communities, school reform, sociolinguistic and discursive obstacles to student integration, inclusive language arts curriculum. *Unit head:* Dr. Janna L. Oakes, Dean, 303-458-4302. *Application contact:* Information Contact, 303-458-4300, Fax: 303-964-5274, E-mail: masters@regis.edu.

Rhode Island College, School of Graduate Studies, Feinstein School of Education and Human Development, Department of Counseling, Educational Leadership, and School Psychology, Providence, RI 02908-1991. Offers advanced counseling (CGS); agency counseling (MA); co-occurring disorders (MA, CGS); educational leadership (M Ed); mental health counseling (CAGS); school counseling (MA); school psychology (CAGS); teacher leadership (CGS). *Accreditation:* NCATE. Part-time and evening/weekend programs available. *Faculty:* 10 full-time (6 women), 8 part-time/adjunct (7 women). *Students:* 38 full-time (32 women), 133 part-time (99 women); includes 18 minority (7 Black or African American, non-Hispanic/Latino; 2 Asian, non-Hispanic/Latino; 8 Hispanic/Latino; 1 Two or more races, non-Hispanic/Latino), 1 international. Average age 34. In 2013, 50 master's, 23 other advanced degrees awarded. *Degree requirements:* For master's and other advanced degree, comprehensive exam (for some programs), thesis (for some programs). *Entrance requirements:* For master's, GRE General Test or MAT, undergraduate transcripts; minimum undergraduate GPA of 3.0; for other advanced degree, GRE or MAT (for most programs), undergraduate transcripts; minimum undergraduate GPA of 3.0; 3 letters of recommendation; current resume. Additional exam requirements/recommendations for international students: Recommended—TOEFL (minimum score 550 paper-based; 79 iBT). *Application deadline:* For fall admission, 3/1 for domestic students; for spring admission, 11/1 for domestic students. Applications are processed on a rolling basis. Application fee: $50. *Expenses:* Tuition, state resident: full-time $8928; part-time $372 per credit hour. Tuition, nonresident: full-time $17,376; part-time $724 per credit hour. *Required fees:* $602; $22 per credit. $72 per term. *Financial support:* In 2013–14, 4 teaching assistantships with full tuition reimbursements (averaging $2,250 per year) were awarded; career-related internships or fieldwork, Federal Work-Study, scholarships/grants, health care benefits, and unspecified assistantships also available. Support available to part-time students. Financial award application deadline: 5/15; financial award applicants required to submit FAFSA. *Unit head:* Dr. Kalina Brabeck, Chair, 401-456-8023. *Application contact:* Graduate Studies, 401-456-8700.
Website: http://www.ric.edu/counselingEducationalLeadershipSchoolPsychology/index.php.

The Richard Stockton College of New Jersey, School of Graduate and Continuing Studies, Program in Educational Leadership, Galloway, NJ 08205-9441. Offers MA. Part-time and evening/weekend programs available. *Faculty:* 2 full-time (0 women), 1 part-time/adjunct (0 women). *Students:* 19 part-time (13 women); includes 2 minority (both Black or African American, non-Hispanic/Latino). Average age 37. 7 applicants, 71% accepted, 4 enrolled. In 2013, 4 master's awarded. *Degree requirements:* For master's, thesis, final project, internship. *Entrance requirements:* For master's, MAT, GRE, teaching certificate. *Application deadline:* For fall admission, 7/1 for domestic students; for spring admission, 12/1 for domestic students. *Expenses: Tuition, area resident:* Part-time $559 per credit. Tuition, state resident: part-time $559 per credit. Tuition, nonresident: part-time $861 per credit. *Required fees:* $168.23 per credit. $75 per semester. Tuition and fees vary according to course load and degree level. *Financial support:* Fellowships, research assistantships with partial tuition reimbursements, scholarships/grants, and unspecified assistantships available. Support available to part-time students. Financial award application deadline: 3/1; financial award applicants required to submit FAFSA. *Unit head:* Dr. Ron Tinsley, Program Director, 609-626-3640, E-mail: gradschool@stockton.edu. *Application contact:* Tara Williams, Assistant Director of Graduate Enrollment Management, 609-626-3640, Fax: 609-626-6050, E-mail: gradschool@stockton.edu.
Website: http://www.stockton.edu/grad.

Rider University, Department of Graduate Education, Leadership, and Counseling, Program in Curriculum, Instruction and Supervision, Lawrenceville, NJ 08648-3001. Offers curriculum, instruction and supervision (MA); supervisor (Certificate). *Accreditation:* NCATE. Part-time and evening/weekend programs available. *Degree requirements:* For master's, comprehensive exam, practicum project. *Entrance requirements:* For master's, interview, 2 letters of recommendation from current supervisors, resume. Additional exam requirements/recommendations for international students: Required—TOEFL (minimum score 550 paper-based). Electronic applications accepted. *Faculty research:* Curriculum change, curriculum development, teacher evaluation.

Rider University, Department of Graduate Education, Leadership, and Counseling, Program in Educational Administration, Lawrenceville, NJ 08648-3001. Offers educational administration (MA); principal (Certificate); school administrator (Certificate). *Accreditation:* NCATE. Part-time and evening/weekend programs available. *Degree requirements:* For master's, comprehensive exam, research project. *Entrance requirements:* For master's, interview, resume, 2 letters of recommendation. Additional exam requirements/recommendations for international students: Required—TOEFL (minimum score 550 paper-based). Electronic applications accepted. *Faculty research:* National/state standards, urban education, administrative leadership, financing public education, community school linkages.

Rivier University, School of Graduate Studies, Department of Education, Nashua, NH 03060. Offers curriculum and instruction (M Ed); early childhood education (M Ed); educational administration (M Ed); educational studies (M Ed); elementary education (M Ed); elementary education and general special education (M Ed); emotional and behavioral disorders (M Ed); general social education (M Ed); leadership and learning (Ed D, CAGS); learning disabilities (M Ed); learning disabilities and reading (M Ed); mental health counseling (MA); reading (M Ed); school counseling (M Ed). Part-time and evening/weekend programs available. *Degree requirements:* For master's, comprehensive exam (for some programs), internships. *Entrance requirements:* For master's, GRE General Test or MAT.

Robert Morris University, Graduate Studies, School of Education and Social Sciences, Moon Township, PA 15108-1189. Offers business education (MS); education (Postbaccalaureate Certificate); instructional leadership (MS), including education, sport management; instructional management and leadership (PhD). *Accreditation:* Teacher Education Accreditation Council. Part-time and evening/weekend programs available. Postbaccalaureate distance learning degree programs offered (no on-campus study). *Faculty:* 20 full-time (9 women), 6 part-time/adjunct (3 women). *Students:* 203 part-time (127 women); includes 20 minority (11 Black or African American, non-Hispanic/Latino; 3 Asian, non-Hispanic/Latino; 2 Hispanic/Latino; 4 Two or more races, non-Hispanic/Latino), 4 international. Average age 26. 126 applicants, 44% accepted, 43 enrolled. In 2013, 102 master's, 6 doctorates awarded. *Degree requirements:* For doctorate, thesis/dissertation. *Entrance requirements:* Additional exam requirements/recommendations

for international students: Required—TOEFL (minimum score 550 paper-based; 79 iBT). *Application deadline:* For fall admission, 7/1 priority date for domestic and international students; for spring admission, 11/1 priority date for domestic and international students. Applications are processed on a rolling basis. Application fee: $35. Electronic applications accepted. *Expenses:* Contact institution. *Unit head:* Dr. Mary Ann Rafoth, Dean, 412-397-3488, Fax: 412-397-2524, E-mail: rafoth@rmu.edu. *Application contact:* Assistant Dean, Graduate Admissions, 412-397-5200, Fax: 412-397-5915, E-mail: graduateadmissions@rmu.edu.
Website: http://www.rmu.edu/web/cms/schools/sess/.

Robert Morris University Illinois, Morris Graduate School of Management, Chicago, IL 60605. Offers accounting (MBA); accounting/finance (MBA); business analytics (MIS); design and media (MM); educational technology (MM); health care administration (MM); higher education administration (MM); human resource management (MBA); information security (MIS); information systems (MIS); law enforcement administration (MM); management (MBA); management/finance (MBA); management/human resource management (MBA); mobile computing (MIS); sports administration (MM). Part-time and evening/weekend programs available. *Faculty:* 12 full-time (5 women), 18 part-time/adjunct (4 women). *Students:* 240 full-time (128 women), 195 part-time (127 women); includes 242 minority (147 Black or African American, non-Hispanic/Latino; 2 American Indian or Alaska Native, non-Hispanic/Latino; 24 Asian, non-Hispanic/Latino; 63 Hispanic/Latino; 1 Native Hawaiian or other Pacific Islander, non-Hispanic/Latino; 5 Two or more races, non-Hispanic/Latino), 26 international. Average age 33. 210 applicants, 63% accepted, 116 enrolled. In 2013, 278 master's awarded. *Entrance requirements:* For master's, official transcripts, two letters of recommendation. Additional exam requirements/recommendations for international students: Required—TOEFL (minimum score 550 paper-based). *Application deadline:* Applications are processed on a rolling basis. Application fee: $20 ($100 for international students). Electronic applications accepted. *Expenses: Tuition:* Full-time $14,400; part-time $2400 per course. *Financial support:* In 2013–14, 488 students received support. Federal Work-Study and scholarships/grants available. Support available to part-time students. Financial award applicants required to submit FAFSA. *Unit head:* Kayed Akkawi, Dean for Morris Graduate School of Management, 312-935-6050, Fax: 312-935-6020, E-mail: kakkawi@robertmorris.edu. *Application contact:* Fernando Villeda, Dean of Graduate Enrollment, 312-935-6050, Fax: 312-935-6020, E-mail: fvilleda@robertmorris.edu.

Rocky Mountain College, Program in Educational Leadership, Billings, MT 59102-1796. Offers M Ed. Electronic applications accepted. *Expenses:* Contact institution.

Roosevelt University, Graduate Division, College of Education, Program in Teacher Leadership (LEAD), Chicago, IL 60605. Offers MA.

Rowan University, Graduate School, College of Education, Department of Educational Leadership, Program in Educational Leadership, Glassboro, NJ 08028-1701. Offers Ed D, CAGS. *Accreditation:* NCATE. Part-time and evening/weekend programs available. *Faculty:* 5 full-time (3 women), 9 part-time/adjunct (7 women). *Students:* 1 (woman) full-time, 229 part-time (142 women); includes 73 minority (54 Black or African American, non-Hispanic/Latino; 1 American Indian or Alaska Native, non-Hispanic/Latino; 3 Asian, non-Hispanic/Latino; 14 Hispanic/Latino; 1 Two or more races, non-Hispanic/Latino). Average age 42. 110 applicants, 89% accepted, 74 enrolled. In 2013, 17 doctorates awarded. *Degree requirements:* For doctorate, thesis/dissertation. *Entrance requirements:* For doctorate, GMAT or GRE General Test, master's degree. Additional exam requirements/recommendations for international students: Required—TOEFL. *Application deadline:* For fall admission, 6/1 for domestic and international students. Applications are processed on a rolling basis. Application fee: $65. Electronic applications accepted. *Expenses: Tuition, area resident:* Part-time $638 per credit. Tuition, state resident: full-time $5742. *Required fees:* $142 per credit. Tuition and fees vary according to course level and program. *Financial support:* Career-related internships or fieldwork, scholarships/grants, health care benefits, and unspecified assistantships available. Support available to part-time students. *Unit head:* Dr. Horacio Sosa, Dean, College of Graduate and Continuing Education, 856-256-4747, Fax: 856-256-5638, E-mail: sosa@rowan.edu. *Application contact:* Admissions and Enrollment Services, 856-256-5145, Fax: 856-256-5637.

Rowan University, Graduate School, College of Education, Department of Special Educational Services/Instruction, Program in Higher Education Administration, Glassboro, NJ 08028-1701. Offers MA. *Accreditation:* NCATE. Part-time and evening/weekend programs available. *Faculty:* 4 full-time (2 women), 3 part-time/adjunct (1 woman). *Students:* 22 full-time (17 women), 12 part-time (10 women); includes 8 minority (4 Black or African American, non-Hispanic/Latino; 2 Asian, non-Hispanic/Latino; 2 Hispanic/Latino), 2 international. Average age 28. 30 applicants, 97% accepted, 15 enrolled. In 2013, 13 master's awarded. *Degree requirements:* For master's, comprehensive exam, thesis. *Entrance requirements:* For master's, GRE General Test, minimum GPA of 2.8, 2 years of teaching experience. Additional exam requirements/recommendations for international students: Required—TOEFL. *Application deadline:* For fall admission, 6/1 for domestic students; for spring admission, 12/1 for domestic students; for summer admission, 2/15 for domestic students. Applications are processed on a rolling basis. Application fee: $65. Electronic applications accepted. *Expenses: Tuition, area resident:* Part-time $638 per credit. Tuition, state resident: full-time $5742. *Required fees:* $142 per credit. Tuition and fees vary according to course level and program. *Financial support:* Career-related internships or fieldwork, scholarships/grants, health care benefits, and unspecified assistantships available. Support available to part-time students. *Unit head:* Dr. Horacio Sosa, Dean, College of Graduate and Continuing Education, 856-256-4747, Fax: 856-256-5638, E-mail: sosa@rowan.edu. *Application contact:* Admissions and Enrollment Services, 856-256-5435, Fax: 856-256-5637, E-mail: cgceadmissions@rowan.edu.

Rowan University, Graduate School, College of Education, Department of Special Educational Services/Instruction, Program in School Administration, Glassboro, NJ 08028-1701. Offers MA. *Faculty:* 2 full-time (both women), 2 part-time/adjunct (both women). *Students:* 114 part-time (72 women); includes 29 minority (20 Black or African American, non-Hispanic/Latino; 1 American Indian or Alaska Native, non-Hispanic/Latino; 1 Asian, non-Hispanic/Latino; 7 Hispanic/Latino). Average age 35. 3 applicants, 100% accepted. In 2013, 42 master's awarded. Application fee: $65. *Expenses: Tuition, area resident:* Part-time $638 per credit. Tuition, state resident: full-time $5742. *Required fees:* $142 per credit. Tuition and fees vary according to course level and program. *Unit head:* Dr. Horacio Sosa, Dean, College of Graduate and Continuing Education, 856-256-4747, Fax: 856-256-5638, E-mail: sosa@rowan.edu. *Application contact:* Admissions and Enrollment Services, 856-256-5145, Fax: 856-256-5637, E-mail: cgceadmissions@rowan.edu.

Rowan University, Graduate School, College of Education, Department of Special Educational Services/Instruction, Program in Supervisor Certification, Glassboro, NJ 08028-1701. Offers CAGS. *Faculty:* 1 (woman) full-time, 1 part-time/adjunct (0 women). *Students:* 25 part-time (20 women); includes 1 minority (Asian, non-Hispanic/Latino). Average age 38. 3 applicants, 67% accepted. In 2013, 5 CAGSs awarded. Application fee: $65. *Expenses: Tuition, area resident:* Part-time $638 per credit. Tuition, state resident: full-time $5742. *Required fees:* $142 per credit. Tuition and fees vary according to course level and program. *Unit head:* Dr. Horacio Sosa, Dean, College of Graduate and Continuing Education, 856-256-4747, Fax: 856-256-5638, E-mail: sosa@rowan.edu. *Application contact:* Admissions and Enrollment Services, 856-256-5145, Fax: 856-256-5637, E-mail: cgceadmissions@rowan.edu.

Rowan University, Graduate School, College of Education, Department of Teacher Education, Program in Teacher Leadership, Glassboro, NJ 08028-1701. Offers M Ed. Part-time and evening/weekend programs available. *Faculty:* 5 full-time (4 women). *Students:* 6 full-time (4 women), 33 part-time (23 women); includes 7 minority (4 Black or African American, non-Hispanic/Latino; 3 Hispanic/Latino). Average age 32. 15 applicants, 100% accepted, 13 enrolled. In 2013, 27 master's awarded. *Degree requirements:* For master's, thesis. *Entrance requirements:* For master's, GRE General Test, minimum GPA of 2.8, 1 year of teaching experience. Additional exam requirements/recommendations for international students: Required—TOEFL. *Application deadline:* Applications are processed on a rolling basis. Application fee: $65. Electronic applications accepted. *Expenses: Tuition, area resident:* Part-time $638 per credit. Tuition, state resident: full-time $5742. *Required fees:* $142 per credit. Tuition and fees vary according to course level and program. *Financial support:* Career-related internships or fieldwork, scholarships/grants, health care benefits, and unspecified assistantships available. *Unit head:* Dr. Horacio Sosa, Dean, College of Graduate and Continuing Education, 856-256-4747, Fax: 856-256-5638, E-mail: sosa@rowan.edu. *Application contact:* Admissions and Enrollment Services, 856-256-5435, Fax: 856-256-5637, E-mail: cgceadmissions@rowan.edu.

Rutgers, The State University of New Jersey, Camden, Graduate School of Arts and Sciences, Department of Public Policy and Administration, Camden, NJ 08102. Offers education policy and leadership (MPA); international public service and development (MPA); public management (MPA); JD/MPA; MPA/MA. *Accreditation:* NASPAA. Part-time and evening/weekend programs available. *Degree requirements:* For master's, directed study, research workshop, 42 credits. *Entrance requirements:* For master's, GRE General Test, GMAT or LSAT, 3 letters of recommendation; resume. Additional exam requirements/recommendations for international students: Required—TOEFL (minimum score 550 paper-based), IELTS. Electronic applications accepted. *Faculty research:* Nonprofit management, county and municipal administration, health and human services, government communication, administrative law, educational finance.

Rutgers, The State University of New Jersey, New Brunswick, Graduate School of Education, Department of Educational Theory, Policy and Administration, Programs in Educational Administration and Supervision, Piscataway, NJ 08854-8097. Offers Ed M, Ed D. Part-time and evening/weekend programs available. *Degree requirements:* For doctorate, thesis/dissertation, qualifying exam. *Entrance requirements:* For master's, GRE General Test, minimum GPA of 3.0; for doctorate, GRE General Test, minimum GPA of 3.0, master's degree in educational administration. Additional exam requirements/recommendations for international students: Required—TOEFL. Electronic applications accepted. *Faculty research:* Leadership of education, finance, law, schools as organizations.

Sacred Heart University, Graduate Programs, Isabelle Farrington College of Education, Department of Teacher Education, Fairfield, CT 06825-1000. Offers administration (CAS); advanced educational studies for teachers (CAS); educational technology (Certificate); teaching (MAT); TESOL (MAT); Web development (Certificate). *Faculty:* 14 full-time (7 women), 15 part-time/adjunct (8 women). *Students:* 210 full-time (155 women), 517 part-time (376 women); includes 78 minority (36 Black or African American, non-Hispanic/Latino; 1 American Indian or Alaska Native, non-Hispanic/Latino; 5 Asian, non-Hispanic/Latino; 31 Hispanic/Latino; 5 Two or more races, non-Hispanic/Latino). Average age 34. 90 applicants, 90% accepted, 75 enrolled. In 2013, 262 master's, 60 other advanced degrees awarded. *Entrance requirements:* For master's, bachelor's degree, copy of official teaching certificate, background check. Additional exam requirements/recommendations for international students: Required—PTE; Recommended—TOEFL (minimum score 570 paper-based; 80 iBT), IELTS (minimum score 6.5). *Application deadline:* Applications are processed on a rolling basis. Application fee: $60. Electronic applications accepted. *Expenses: Tuition:* Full-time $22,775; part-time $617 per credit. *Financial support:* Applicants required to submit FAFSA. *Unit head:* Dr. Jim Carl, Dean, 203-371-7800, Fax: 203-365-7513, E-mail: carlj@sacredheart.edu. *Application contact:* Kathy Dilks, Executive Director of Graduate Admissions, 203-365-7619, Fax: 203-365-4732, E-mail: gradstudies@sacredheart.edu.
Website: http://www.sacredheart.edu/academics/isabellefarringtoncollegeofeducation/.

Sage Graduate School, Esteves School of Education, Program in Educational Leadership, Troy, NY 12180-4115. Offers Ed D. Part-time programs available. *Faculty:* 10 full-time (5 women), 7 part-time/adjunct (4 women). *Students:* 57 part-time (30 women); includes 16 minority (6 Black or African American, non-Hispanic/Latino; 1 American Indian or Alaska Native, non-Hispanic/Latino; 2 Asian, non-Hispanic/Latino; 7 Hispanic/Latino). Average age 45. 95 applicants, 47% accepted, 31 enrolled. In 2013, 11 doctorates awarded. *Degree requirements:* For doctorate, comprehensive exam. *Entrance requirements:* For doctorate, minimum GPA of 3.5, 60 graduate credits from an accredited institution, 3 references addressing leadership skill potential, writing sample, personal interview. Additional exam requirements/recommendations for international students: Required—TOEFL (minimum score 550 paper-based). *Application deadline:* Applications are processed on a rolling basis. Application fee: $40. *Expenses: Tuition:* Full-time $11,880; part-time $660 per credit hour. *Financial support:* Fellowships, research assistantships, Federal Work-Study, scholarships/grants, and unspecified assistantships available. Support available to part-time students. *Unit head:* Dr. Lori Quigley, Dean, Esteves School of Education, 518-244-2326, Fax: 518-244-4571, E-mail: l.quigley@sage.edu. *Application contact:* Dr. Robert Bradley, Chair, Educational Leadership, 518-244-4588, Fax: 518-266-1391, E-mail: bradlr2@sage.edu.

Saginaw Valley State University, College of Education, Program in Educational Leadership, University Center, MI 48710. Offers chief business officers (M Ed); education leadership (Ed S); educational administration and supervision (M Ed); educational leadership (M Ed); principalship (M Ed); superintendency (M Ed). *Accreditation:* NCATE. Part-time and evening/weekend programs available. Postbaccalaureate distance learning degree programs offered (minimal on-campus study). *Students:* 10 full-time (7 women), 147 part-time (71 women); includes 9 minority (4 Black or African American, non-Hispanic/Latino; 1 American Indian or Alaska Native, non-Hispanic/Latino; 3 Hispanic/Latino; 1 Two or more races, non-Hispanic/Latino), 3 international. Average age 36. 54 applicants, 91% accepted, 34 enrolled. In 2013, 52 master's, 19 Ed Ss awarded. *Degree requirements:* For master's, capstone course. *Entrance requirements:* For master's, minimum GPA of 3.0, teaching certificate; for Ed S, master's degree with minimum GPA of 3.3. Additional exam requirements/recommendations for international students: Required—TOEFL (minimum score 550 paper-based; 79 iBT). *Application deadline:* For fall admission, 7/15 for international students; for winter admission, 11/15 for international students; for spring admission, 4/15 for international students. Applications are processed on a rolling basis. Application fee: $30 ($80 for international students). Electronic applications accepted. *Expenses:* Tuition, state resident: full-time $8933; part-time $496.30 per credit hour. Tuition, nonresident: full-time $16,806; part-time $933.65 per credit hour. *Required fees:* $263; $14.60 per credit hour. Tuition and fees vary according to degree level. *Financial support:* Federal Work-Study and scholarships/grants available. Support available to part-time students. Financial award applicants required to submit FAFSA. *Unit head:* Dr. Mary Harmon, Dean, 989-964-7107, Fax: 989-964-4563, E-mail: coeconnect@

svsu.edu. *Application contact:* Jenna Briggs, Director, Graduate and International Admissions, 989-964-6096, Fax: 989-964-2788, E-mail: gradadm@svsu.edu.

St. Ambrose University, College of Education and Health Sciences, Program in Educational Administration, Davenport, IA 52803-2898. Offers MEA. Part-time and evening/weekend programs available. *Entrance requirements:* Additional exam requirements/recommendations for international students: Required—TOEFL. Electronic applications accepted.

St. Bonaventure University, School of Graduate Studies, School of Education, Program in Educational Leadership, St. Bonaventure, NY 14778-2284. Offers educational leadership (MS Ed); school building leader (Adv C); school district leader (Adv C). Hybrid format offered in Olean and Buffalo Center (Hamburg, NY). Part-time and evening/weekend programs available. Postbaccalaureate distance learning degree programs offered (minimal on-campus study). *Faculty:* 3 full-time (2 women). *Students:* 3 full-time (2 women), 27 part-time (20 women); includes 2 minority (both Black or African American, non-Hispanic/Latino). Average age 38. 22 applicants, 95% accepted, 5 enrolled. In 2013, 9 master's, 15 Adv Cs awarded. *Degree requirements:* For master's, comprehensive exam, thesis optional, practicum, internship, electronic portfolio; for Adv C, comprehensive exam, practicum, internship, electronic portfolio. *Entrance requirements:* For master's, teaching or counseling certification, 3 years of K-12 school experience, minimum GPA of 3.0, two letters of recommendation (at least one from a principal or superintendent), interview, writing sample; for Adv C, teaching or counseling certification, 3 years of K-12 school experience, minimum GPA of 3.0, references (ability to do graduate work, success as a teacher/counselor), interview, writing sample. Additional exam requirements/recommendations for international students: Required—TOEFL (minimum score 550 paper-based; 79 iBT). *Application deadline:* For fall admission, 6/15 priority date for domestic students, 2/1 priority date for international students; for spring admission, 11/1 for domestic students. Applications are processed on a rolling basis. Application fee: $0. Electronic applications accepted. *Financial support:* In 2013–14, 1 research assistantship was awarded; Federal Work-Study, scholarships/grants, health care benefits, tuition waivers (partial), and unspecified assistantships also available. Support available to part-time students. Financial award application deadline: 4/15; financial award applicants required to submit FAFSA. *Unit head:* Dr. Darlene McDonough, Director, 716-375-4026, Fax: 716-375-2360, E-mail: dmcdonou@sbu.edu. *Application contact:* Bruce Campbell, Director of Graduate Admissions, 716-375-2429, Fax: 716-375-4015, E-mail: gradsch@sbu.edu. Website: http://www.sbu.edu/academics/schools/education/graduate-degrees-certificates/msed-in-educational-leadership.

St. Cloud State University, School of Graduate Studies, School of Education, Department of Educational Leadership and Higher Education, Program in Higher Education Administration, St. Cloud, MN 56301-4498. Offers MS, Ed D.

St. Cloud State University, School of Graduate Studies, School of Health and Human Services, Department of Counseling and Community Psychology, Program in Educational Administration and Leadership, St. Cloud, MN 56301-4498. Offers MS. Part-time programs available. *Degree requirements:* For master's, comprehensive exam (for some programs), thesis or alternative. *Entrance requirements:* For master's, GRE General Test, minimum GPA of 2.75. Additional exam requirements/recommendations for international students: Required—Michigan English Language Assessment Battery; Recommended—TOEFL (minimum score 550 paper-based), IELTS (minimum score 6.5). Electronic applications accepted.

Saint Francis University, Graduate Education Program, Loretto, PA 15940-0600. Offers education (M Ed); leadership (M Ed); reading (M Ed). Part-time programs available. *Faculty:* 16 part-time/adjunct (8 women). *Students:* 5 full-time (4 women), 93 part-time (68 women); includes 1 minority (Black or African American, non-Hispanic/Latino). Average age 28. 15 applicants, 100% accepted, 15 enrolled. In 2013, 45 master's awarded. *Degree requirements:* For master's, comprehensive exam, thesis optional. *Entrance requirements:* For master's, GRE or MAT (if undergraduate GPA less than 3.0). Additional exam requirements/recommendations for international students: Required—TOEFL (minimum score 550 paper-based; 75 iBT), IELTS (minimum score 6.5), International Test of English Proficiency (minimum score 4). *Application deadline:* Applications are processed on a rolling basis. Application fee: $30. *Expenses:* Contact institution. *Financial support:* Applicants required to submit FAFSA. *Unit head:* Dr. Janette D. Kelly, Director, 814-472-3068, Fax: 814-472-3864, E-mail: jkelly@francis.edu. *Application contact:* Sherri L. Toth, Coordinator, 814-472-3058, Fax: 814-472-3864, E-mail: stoth@francis.edu.
Website: http://www.francis.edu/master-of-education/.

St. Francis Xavier University, Graduate Studies, Graduate Studies in Education, Antigonish, NS B2G 2W5, Canada. Offers curriculum and instruction (M Ed); educational administration and leadership (M Ed). Part-time programs available. Postbaccalaureate distance learning degree programs offered (minimal on-campus study). *Degree requirements:* For master's, thesis. *Entrance requirements:* For master's, minimum undergraduate B average, 2 years of teaching experience. *Faculty research:* Inclusive education, qualitative research.

St. John Fisher College, Ralph C. Wilson Jr. School of Education, Educational Leadership Program, Rochester, NY 14618-3597. Offers MS Ed. Part-time and evening/weekend programs available. *Faculty:* 1 (woman) full-time, 5 part-time/adjunct (4 women). *Students:* 26 part-time (20 women); includes 6 minority (3 Black or African American, non-Hispanic/Latino; 1 Hispanic/Latino; 2 Two or more races, non-Hispanic/Latino). Average age 35. 19 applicants, 79% accepted, 13 enrolled. In 2013, 15 master's awarded. *Degree requirements:* For master's, capstone project, internship. *Entrance requirements:* For master's, teacher certification, minimum 2 years of teaching experience, 2 letters of recommendation, current resume. Additional exam requirements/recommendations for international students: Required—TOEFL (minimum score 575 paper-based; 80 iBT). *Application deadline:* Applications are processed on a rolling basis. Application fee: $30. Electronic applications accepted. *Expenses: Tuition:* Part-time $795 per credit hour. *Required fees:* $10 per credit hour. Tuition and fees vary according to course load, degree level and program. *Financial support:* In 2013–14, 2 students received support. Scholarships/grants available. Financial award applicants required to submit FAFSA. *Faculty research:* Urban school leadership, assessment, effective school leadership. *Unit head:* Dr. Diane Reed, Director, 585-385-7257, E-mail: wstroud@sjfc.edu. *Application contact:* Jose Perales, Director of Graduate Admissions, 585-385-8067, E-mail: jperales@sjfc.edu.

St. John Fisher College, Ralph C. Wilson Jr. School of Education, Executive Leadership Program, Rochester, NY 14618-3597. Offers Ed D. Evening/weekend programs available. *Faculty:* 10 full-time (6 women), 5 part-time/adjunct (3 women). *Students:* 82 full-time (53 women), 34 part-time (20 women); includes 59 minority (40 Black or African American, non-Hispanic/Latino; 1 Asian, non-Hispanic/Latino; 15 Hispanic/Latino; 2 Native Hawaiian or other Pacific Islander, non-Hispanic/Latino; 1 Two or more races, non-Hispanic/Latino). Average age 46. 97 applicants, 80% accepted, 61 enrolled. In 2013, 46 doctorates awarded. *Degree requirements:* For doctorate, comprehensive exam, thesis/dissertation, field experiences. *Entrance requirements:* For doctorate, 3 professional writing samples, 2 letters of reference, interview, minimum 3 years' management experience, master's degree. Additional exam requirements/

recommendations for international students: Required—TOEFL (minimum score 575 paper-based; 80 iBT). *Application deadline:* For fall admission, 3/1 for domestic and international students. Applications are processed on a rolling basis. Electronic applications accepted. *Expenses: Tuition:* Part-time $795 per credit hour. *Required fees:* $10 per credit hour. Tuition and fees vary according to course load, degree level and program. *Financial support:* In 2013–14, 10 students received support. Scholarships/grants available. Financial award applicants required to submit FAFSA. *Faculty research:* Leadership, organizational development. *Unit head:* Dr. Jeannine Dingus-Eason, Program Director, 585-385-8002, E-mail: jdingus@sjfc.edu. *Application contact:* Jose Perales, Director of Graduate Admissions, 585-385-8067, E-mail: jperales@sjfc.edu.
Website: http://www.sjfc.edu/academics/education/departments/edd/index.dot.

St. John's University, The School of Education, Division of Administrative and Instructional Leadership, Instructional Leadership Program, Queens, NY 11439. Offers Ed D, Adv C. Part-time and evening/weekend programs available. *Students:* 10 full-time (8 women), 105 part-time (72 women); includes 35 minority (22 Black or African American, non-Hispanic/Latino; 4 Asian, non-Hispanic/Latino; 9 Hispanic/Latino), 5 international. Average age 42. 57 applicants, 89% accepted, 30 enrolled. In 2013, 22 doctorates, 6 Adv Cs awarded. *Degree requirements:* For doctorate, comprehensive exam, thesis/dissertation. *Entrance requirements:* For doctorate, GRE General Test, interview, minimum GPA of 3.2, 2 letters of recommendation, resume, writing samples, master's degree in education or related field; for Adv C, official transcript, minimum GPA of 3.0, 2 letters of recommendation, master's degree in education or related field. Additional exam requirements/recommendations for international students: Required—TOEFL (minimum score 600 paper-based; 100 iBT), IELTS (minimum score 5.5). *Application deadline:* For fall admission, 8/17 for domestic students, 5/1 priority date for international students; for spring admission, 1/5 for domestic students, 11/1 priority date for international students. Applications are processed on a rolling basis. Application fee: $70. Electronic applications accepted. *Expenses: Tuition:* Full-time $19,800; part-time $1100 per credit. *Required fees:* $170 per semester. *Financial support:* Fellowships, research assistantships, career-related internships or fieldwork, and scholarships/grants available. Support available to part-time students. Financial award application deadline: 3/1; financial award applicants required to submit FAFSA. *Faculty research:* Mathematics learning disabilities and difficulties with students identified as learning disabled or students who are English Language Learners, identification of mathematical giftedness in students who are English Language Learners, effects of parental participation and parenting behaviors on the science and mathematics academic achievement of school-age students, analysis of major theoretical perspectives in curriculum design and implementation. *Unit head:* Dr. Rene Parmar, Chair, 718-990-5915, E-mail: parmarr@stjohns.edu. *Application contact:* Dr. Kelly K. Ronayne, Associate Dean of Graduate Admissions, 718-990-2304, Fax: 718-990-2343, E-mail: graded@stjohns.edu.

St. John's University, The School of Education, Division of Administrative and Instructional Leadership, Program in Educational Administration and Supervision, Queens, NY 11439. Offers administration and supervision (Ed D). Part-time and evening/weekend programs available. Postbaccalaureate distance learning degree programs offered. *Students:* 1 (woman) full-time, 95 part-time (64 women); includes 22 minority (14 Black or African American, non-Hispanic/Latino; 1 Asian, non-Hispanic/Latino; 7 Hispanic/Latino), 1 international. Average age 41. 47 applicants, 85% accepted, 15 enrolled. In 2013, 18 doctorates, 1 Adv C awarded. *Degree requirements:* For doctorate, thesis/dissertation, clinical residency. *Entrance requirements:* For doctorate, GRE General Test, interview, minimum GPA of 3.0, 2 letters of recommendation, resume, writing samples, minimum 3 years of professional experience. Additional exam requirements/recommendations for international students: Required—TOEFL (minimum score 600 paper-based; 100 iBT), IELTS (minimum score 5.5). *Application deadline:* For fall admission, 8/17 for domestic students, 5/1 priority date for international students; for spring admission, 1/5 for domestic students, 11/1 priority date for international students. Applications are processed on a rolling basis. Application fee: $70. Electronic applications accepted. *Expenses: Tuition:* Full-time $19,800; part-time $1100 per credit. *Required fees:* $170 per semester. *Financial support:* Research assistantships and career-related internships or fieldwork available. Support available to part-time students. Financial award application deadline: 3/1; financial award applicants required to submit FAFSA. *Faculty research:* School administrators' accountability in response to New York State and federal regulations and reforms, including merit pay, decision-making in technology within the framework of instructional design; budgetary and expenditure decision-making among school district administrators in response to fiscal restraints, compliance, and changing demographics; twenty-first century technological tools in today's schools; teacher decision-making models based on decision theory. *Unit head:* Dr. Rene Parmar, Chair, 718-990-5915, E-mail: parmarr@stjohns.edu. *Application contact:* Dr. Kelly K. Ronayne, Associate Dean of Graduate Admissions, 718-990-2304, Fax: 718-990-2343, E-mail: graded@stjohns.edu.

St. John's University, The School of Education, Division of Administrative and Instructional Leadership, Program in School Building Leadership, Queens, NY 11439. Offers MS Ed, Adv C. Part-time and evening/weekend programs available. Postbaccalaureate distance learning degree programs offered. *Students:* 10 full-time (6 women), 162 part-time (111 women); includes 53 minority (26 Black or African American, non-Hispanic/Latino; 3 Asian, non-Hispanic/Latino; 24 Hispanic/Latino), 6 international. Average age 38. 91 applicants, 96% accepted, 63 enrolled. In 2013, 63 master's, 12 Adv Cs awarded. *Degree requirements:* For master's and Adv C, comprehensive exam, internship. *Entrance requirements:* For master's, official transcript with minimum GPA of 3.0, minimum 3 years of successful teaching experience, New York State Permanent Teaching Certification, bachelor's degree; for Adv C, minimum GPA of 3.5, minimum 3 years of successful teaching experience, New York State Permanent Teaching Certification, essay, 2 letters of reference, transcripts. Additional exam requirements/recommendations for international students: Required—TOEFL (minimum score 600 paper-based; 100 iBT), IELTS (minimum score 5.5). *Application deadline:* For fall admission, 8/17 for domestic students, 5/1 priority date for international students; for spring admission, 1/5 for domestic students, 11/1 priority date for international students. Applications are processed on a rolling basis. Application fee: $70. Electronic applications accepted. *Expenses: Tuition:* Full-time $19,800; part-time $1100 per credit. *Required fees:* $170 per semester. *Financial support:* Research assistantships, career-related internships or fieldwork, and scholarships/grants available. Support available to part-time students. Financial award application deadline: 3/1; financial award applicants required to submit FAFSA. *Faculty research:* Analysis of non-public school graduate student outcomes in programs and certification, Catholic school parents' perceptions of school and after school programs, issues in school business leadership from a financial management perspective. *Unit head:* Dr. Rene Parmar, Chair, 718-990-5915, E-mail: parmarr@stjohns.edu. *Application contact:* Dr. Kelly K. Ronayne, Associate Dean for Graduate Admissions, 718-990-2304, Fax: 718-990-2343, E-mail: graded@stjohns.edu.

St. John's University, The School of Education, Division of Administrative and Instructional Leadership, Program in School District Leadership, Queens, NY 11439. Offers Adv C. Part-time and evening/weekend programs available. Postbaccalaureate

distance learning degree programs offered. *Students:* 3 part-time (1 woman); includes 1 minority (Black or African American, non-Hispanic/Latino), 1 international. Average age 48. 4 applicants, 100% accepted, 2 enrolled. In 2013, 4 Adv Cs awarded. *Degree requirements:* For Adv C, comprehensive exam. *Entrance requirements:* For degree, minimum GPA of 3.0, minimum 3 years of successful teaching experience, New York State Permanent Teaching Certification, bachelor's degree. Additional exam requirements/recommendations for international students: Required—TOEFL (minimum score 600 paper-based; 100 iBT), IELTS (minimum score 5.5). *Application deadline:* For fall admission, 8/17 for domestic students, 5/1 priority date for international students; for spring admission, 1/5 for domestic students, 11/1 priority date for international students. Applications are processed on a rolling basis. Application fee: $70. Electronic applications accepted. *Expenses: Tuition:* Full-time $19,800; part-time $1100 per credit. *Required fees:* $170 per semester. *Financial support:* Research assistantships and career-related internships or fieldwork available. Support available to part-time students. Financial award application deadline: 3/1; financial award applicants required to submit FAFSA. *Faculty research:* Analysis of school district finances related to resource allocation and decision-making, responsiveness of districts to New York State proposition 13 (property tax caps), implementation of technology planning for the twenty-first century at the school district level. *Unit head:* Dr. Rene Parmar, Chair, 718-990-5915, E-mail: parmarr@stjohns.edu. *Application contact:* Dr. Kelly K. Ronayne, Associate Dean of Graduate Admissions, 718-990-2304, Fax: 718-990-2343, E-mail: graded@stjohns.edu.

Saint Joseph's College of Maine, Master of Science in Education Program, Standish, ME 04084. Offers adult education and training (MS Ed); Catholic school leadership (MS Ed); health care educator (MS Ed); school educator (MS Ed). Program available by correspondence. Part-time programs available. Postbaccalaureate distance learning degree programs offered (minimal on-campus study). Electronic applications accepted.

Saint Joseph's University, College of Arts and Sciences, Department of Education, Philadelphia, PA 19131-1395. Offers curriculum supervisor (Certificate); educational leadership (MS, Ed D); elementary education (MS, Certificate); elementary/middle school education (Certificate); instructional technology (MS, Certificate); principal certification (Certificate); professional education (MS); reading specialist (MS, Certificate); reading supervisor (Certificate); secondary education (MS, Certificate); special education (MS, Certificate); superintendent's letter of eligibility (Certificate); supervisor of special education (Certificate). Part-time and evening/weekend programs available. Postbaccalaureate distance learning degree programs offered (no on-campus study). *Faculty:* 32 full-time (25 women), 75 part-time/adjunct (53 women). *Students:* 91 full-time (81 women), 858 part-time (656 women); includes 133 minority (96 Black or African American, non-Hispanic/Latino; 3 American Indian or Alaska Native, non-Hispanic/Latino; 9 Asian, non-Hispanic/Latino; 20 Hispanic/Latino; 5 Native Hawaiian or other Pacific Islander, non-Hispanic/Latino), 16 international. Average age 31. 359 applicants, 77% accepted, 203 enrolled. In 2013, 363 master's, 9 doctorates, 1 other advanced degree awarded. *Entrance requirements:* For master's, 2 letters of recommendation, minimum GPA of 3.0, official transcripts, personal statement; for doctorate, GRE, master's degree from accredited institution, minimum graduate GPA of 3.5, computer competence, commitment to participate in cohort, interview with program director. Additional exam requirements/recommendations for international students: Required—TOEFL (minimum score 550 paper-based; 79 iBT), IELTS (minimum score 6.5). *Application deadline:* For fall admission, 7/15 priority date for domestic students, 4/15 for international students; for winter admission, 11/15 for domestic students, 1/15 for international students; for spring admission, 11/15 priority date for domestic students, 10/15 for international students. Applications are processed on a rolling basis. Application fee: $35. Electronic applications accepted. *Expenses:* Contact institution. *Financial support:* Unspecified assistantships available. Financial award applicants required to submit FAFSA. *Faculty research:* Factors predicting early mathematics skills for low income children, early child care and development, preschool quality. *Total annual research expenditures:* $229,264. *Unit head:* Dr. John Vacca, Associate Dean, Education, 610-660-3131, E-mail: gradstudies@sju.edu. *Application contact:* Elisabeth Woodward, Director of Marketing and Admissions, Graduate Arts and Sciences, 610-660-3131, Fax: 610-660-3230, E-mail: gradstudies@sju.edu. Website: http://sju.edu/int/academics/cas/grad/education/index.html.

St. Lawrence University, Department of Education, Program in Educational Leadership, Canton, NY 13617-1455. Offers combined school building leadership/school district leadership (CAS); educational leadership (M Ed); school building leadership (M Ed); school district leadership (CAS). Part-time and evening/weekend programs available. *Entrance requirements:* For master's, GRE General Test. *Faculty research:* Leadership.

Saint Leo University, Graduate Studies in Education, Saint Leo, FL 33574-6665. Offers educational leadership (M Ed); exceptional student education (M Ed); instructional design (MS); instructional leadership (M Ed); reading (M Ed). Part-time and evening/weekend programs available. Postbaccalaureate distance learning degree programs offered (minimal on-campus study). *Faculty:* 10 full-time (8 women), 31 part-time/adjunct (23 women). *Students:* 680 full-time (554 women), 4 part-time (all women); includes 83 minority (51 Black or African American, non-Hispanic/Latino; 2 Asian, non-Hispanic/Latino; 27 Hispanic/Latino; 3 Two or more races, non-Hispanic/Latino), 4 international. Average age 36. In 2013, 295 master's awarded. *Degree requirements:* For master's, comprehensive exam, appropriate State of Florida certification tests. *Entrance requirements:* For master's, GRE (minimum score of 1000) or MAT (minimum score of 410) if undergraduate GPA for last 60 hours of coursework was below 3.0 (for M Ed), bachelor's degree with minimum GPA of 3.0 for last 60 hours of coursework from regionally-accredited college or university, 2 recommendations, resume, statement of professional goals, copy of valid teaching certificate (for M Ed). Additional exam requirements/recommendations for international students: Required—TOEFL (minimum score 550 paper-based; 80 iBT). *Application deadline:* For fall admission, 7/1 priority date for domestic students, 7/1 for international students; for winter admission, 7/1 for international students; for spring admission, 11/1 priority date for domestic students. Applications are processed on a rolling basis. Application fee: $80. Electronic applications accepted. *Expenses:* Contact institution. *Financial support:* In 2013–14, 618 students received support. Career-related internships or fieldwork, Federal Work-Study, scholarships/grants, and health care benefits available. Financial award application deadline: 3/1; financial award applicants required to submit FAFSA. *Faculty research:* The role of the school leader in data analysis of student achievement, teacher recruitment, teacher effectiveness. *Unit head:* Dr. Sharyn Disabato, Director of Graduate Education, 352-588-8309, Fax: 352-588-8861, E-mail: med@saintleo.edu. *Application contact:* Joshua Stagner, Director of Graduate Admission, 800-707-8846, Fax: 352-588-7873, E-mail: grad.admissions@saintleo.edu. Website: http://www.saintleo.edu/admissions/graduate.aspx.

Saint Louis University, Graduate Education, College of Education and Public Service and Graduate Education, Department of Educational Leadership and Higher Education, St. Louis, MO 63103-2097. Offers Catholic school leadership (MA); educational administration (MA, Ed D, PhD, Ed S); higher education (MA, Ed D, PhD); student personnel administration (MA). *Accreditation:* NCATE. Part-time programs available. *Degree requirements:* For master's, comprehensive written and oral exam; for

doctorate, comprehensive exam, thesis/dissertation, preliminary oral and written exams. *Entrance requirements:* For master's, GRE General Test, MAT, LSAT, GMAT or MCAT, letters of recommendation, resume; for doctorate and Ed S, GRE General Test, LSAT, GMAT or MCAT, letters of recommendation, resumé, goal statement, transcripts. Additional exam requirements/recommendations for international students: Required—TOEFL (minimum score 525 paper-based). Electronic applications accepted. *Faculty research:* Superintendent of schools, school finance, school facilities, student personal administration, building leadership.

Saint Martin's University, Office of Graduate Studies, College of Education, Lacey, WA 98503. Offers administration (M Ed); English as a second language (M Ed); guidance and counseling (M Ed); reading (M Ed); special education (M Ed); teaching (MIT). *Accreditation:* Teacher Education Accreditation Council. Part-time and evening/weekend programs available. *Faculty:* 10 full-time (6 women), 15 part-time/adjunct (12 women). *Students:* 57 full-time (35 women), 52 part-time (38 women); includes 20 minority (7 Black or African American, non-Hispanic/Latino; 1 American Indian or Alaska Native, non-Hispanic/Latino; 2 Asian, non-Hispanic/Latino; 6 Hispanic/Latino; 1 Native Hawaiian or other Pacific Islander, non-Hispanic/Latino; 3 Two or more races, non-Hispanic/Latino). Average age 35. 63 applicants, 25% accepted, 13 enrolled. In 2013, 12 master's awarded. *Degree requirements:* For master's, comprehensive exam (for some programs), thesis or alternative, project or comprehensives. *Entrance requirements:* For master's, GRE General Test or MAT, three letters of recommendations; curriculum vitae. Additional exam requirements/recommendations for international students: Required—TOEFL (minimum score 550 paper-based; 79 iBT); Recommended—IELTS (minimum score 6.5). *Application deadline:* For fall admission, 4/1 priority date for domestic and international students; for spring admission, 11/1 priority date for domestic and international students. Applications are processed on a rolling basis. Application fee: $50. Electronic applications accepted. *Expenses: Tuition:* Part-time $990 per credit hour. Tuition and fees vary according to course level and program. *Financial support:* Career-related internships or fieldwork, Federal Work-Study, institutionally sponsored loans, and unspecified assistantships available. Support available to part-time students. Financial award application deadline: 3/1; financial award applicants required to submit FAFSA. *Faculty research:* Reader's theatre and reader/writer workshops, curriculum and assessment integration, gender and equity, classroom evaluations, organizational leadership. *Unit head:* Dr. Joyce Westgard, Dean, College of Education and Professional Psychology, 360-438-4509, Fax: 360-438-4486, E-mail: westgard@stmartin.edu. *Application contact:* Marie C. Boisvert, Administrative Assistant, 360-412-6145, E-mail: gradstudies@stmartin.edu. Website: http://www.stmartin.edu/gradstudies.

Saint Mary's College of California, Kalmanovitz School of Education, Program in Early Childhood Education, Moraga, CA 94575. Offers curriculum and instruction (MA); supervision and leadership (MA). Part-time and evening/weekend programs available. *Degree requirements:* For master's, thesis or alternative. *Entrance requirements:* For master's, interview, minimum GPA of 3.0.

Saint Mary's College of California, Kalmanovitz School of Education, Program in Educational Leadership, Moraga, CA 94575. Offers M Ed, MA, Ed D. Part-time and evening/weekend programs available. *Degree requirements:* For master's, thesis or alternative; for doctorate, thesis/dissertation. *Entrance requirements:* For master's, interview, minimum GPA of 3.0, teaching credential; for doctorate, GRE or MAT, interview, MA, minimum GPA of 3.0. *Faculty research:* Building communities, programs in educational leadership, alignment of curriculum to standards.

Saint Mary's College of California, Kalmanovitz School of Education, Teaching Leadership Program, Moraga, CA 94575. Offers MA.

St. Mary's University, Graduate School, Department of Teacher Education, Program in Catholic School Leadership, San Antonio, TX 78228-8507. Offers Catholic school administrators (Certificate); Catholic school leadership (MA); Catholic school teachers (Certificate). Part-time and evening/weekend programs available. Postbaccalaureate distance learning degree programs offered (minimal on-campus study). *Degree requirements:* For master's, comprehensive exam. *Entrance requirements:* For master's, GRE General Test. Additional exam requirements/recommendations for international students: Required—TOEFL (minimum score 550 paper-based; 80 iBT). Electronic applications accepted.

St. Mary's University, Graduate School, Department of Teacher Education, Program in Educational Leadership, San Antonio, TX 78228-8507. Offers educational leadership (MA); principalship (mid-management) (Certificate). Part-time programs available. *Degree requirements:* For master's, comprehensive exam. *Entrance requirements:* For master's, GRE. Additional exam requirements/recommendations for international students: Required—TOEFL (minimum score 550 paper-based; 80 iBT). Electronic applications accepted.

Saint Mary's University of Minnesota, Schools of Graduate and Professional Programs, Graduate School of Education, Educational Administration Program, Winona, MN 55987-1399. Offers educational administration (Certificate, Ed S), including director of special education, K-12 principal, superintendent. *Unit head:* Dr. William Bjorum, Director, 612-728-5126, Fax: 612-728-5121, E-mail: wbjorum@smumn.edu. *Application contact:* Russell Kreager, Director of Admissions for Graduate and Professional Programs, 612-728-5207, Fax: 612-728-5121, E-mail: rkreager@smumn.edu. Website: http://www.smumn.edu/graduate-home/areas-of-study/graduate-school-of-education/eds-in-educational-administration-director-of-special-education-k-12-pr.

Saint Mary's University of Minnesota, Schools of Graduate and Professional Programs, Graduate School of Education, Educational Leadership Program, Winona, MN 55987-1399. Offers MA, Ed D. *Unit head:* Dr. Nelson Updaw, Director, 612-728-5191, Fax: 612-728-5121, E-mail: nupdaw@smumn.edu. *Application contact:* Russell Kreager, Director of Admissions for Graduate and Professional Programs, 612-728-5207, Fax: 612-728-5121, E-mail: rkreager@smumn.edu. Website: http://www.smumn.edu/graduate-home/areas-of-study/graduate-school-of-education/edd-in-leadership.

Saint Mary's University of Minnesota, Schools of Graduate and Professional Programs, Graduate School of Education, Institute for LaSallian Studies, Winona, MN 55987-1399. Offers LaSallian leadership (MA); LaSallian studies (MA). *Unit head:* Dr. Roxanne Eubank, Director, 612-728-5217, E-mail: reubank@smumn.edu. *Application contact:* Russell Kreager, Director of Admissions for Graduate and Professional Programs, 612-728-5207, Fax: 612-728-5121, E-mail: rkreager@smumn.edu. Website: http://www.smumn.edu/graduate-home/areas-of-study/graduate-school-of-education/ma-in-lasallian-studies.

Saint Michael's College, Graduate Programs, Program in Education, Colchester, VT 05439. Offers administration (M Ed, CAGS); arts in education (CAGS); curriculum and instruction (M Ed, CAGS); information technology (CAGS); reading (M Ed); special education (M Ed, CAGS); technology (M Ed). Part-time and evening/weekend programs available. *Degree requirements:* For master's, thesis. *Entrance requirements:* For master's, minimum GPA of 3.0. Electronic applications accepted. *Faculty research:* Integrative curriculum, moral and spiritual dimensions of education, learning styles, multiple intelligences, integrating technology into the curriculum.

Saint Peter's University, Graduate Programs in Education, Program in Educational Leadership, Jersey City, NJ 07306-5997. Offers MA Ed, Ed D. Part-time and evening/weekend programs available. *Degree requirements:* For master's, comprehensive exam; for doctorate, comprehensive exam, thesis/dissertation. *Entrance requirements:* For master's and doctorate, GRE or MAT. Additional exam requirements/recommendations for international students: Required—TOEFL. Electronic applications accepted.

St. Thomas Aquinas College, Division of Teacher Education, Sparkill, NY 10976. Offers adolescence education (MST); childhood and special education (MST); childhood education (MST); educational leadership (MS Ed); reading (MS Ed, PMC); special education (MS Ed, PMC); teaching (MS Ed), including elementary education, middle school education, secondary education. *Accreditation:* NCATE. Part-time and evening/weekend programs available. *Degree requirements:* For master's, comprehensive exam, comprehensive professional portfolio; for PMC, action research project. *Entrance requirements:* For master's, New York State Qualifying Exam, GRE General Test or minimum GPA of 3.0, teaching certificate; for PMC, GRE General Test or minimum GPA of 3.0. Electronic applications accepted. *Faculty research:* Computer applications in education, adolescent special education students, literacy development, inclusive practices for special education students.

St. Thomas University, School of Leadership Studies, Institute for Education, Miami Gardens, FL 33054-6459. Offers earth/space science (Certificate); educational administration (MS, Certificate); educational leadership (Ed D); elementary education (MS); ESOL (Certificate); gifted education (Certificate); instructional technology (MS, Certificate); professional/studies (Certificate); reading (MS, Certificate); special education (MS). Part-time and evening/weekend programs available. *Degree requirements:* For master's, comprehensive exam; for doctorate, comprehensive exam, thesis/dissertation. *Entrance requirements:* For master's, interview, minimum GPA of 3.0 or GRE; for doctorate, GRE or MAT. Additional exam requirements/recommendations for international students: Required—TOEFL (minimum score 550 paper-based; 79 iBT). Electronic applications accepted.

Saint Vincent College, Program in Education, Latrobe, PA 15650-2690. Offers curriculum and instruction (MS); educational media and technology (MS); environmental education (MS); school administration and supervision (MS); special education (MS). Part-time and evening/weekend programs available. *Degree requirements:* For master's, comprehensive exam. *Entrance requirements:* For master's, GRE (if undergraduate GPA less than 3.0). Additional exam requirements/recommendations for international students: Required—TOEFL (minimum score 550 paper-based). *Faculty research:* Assessment and instructional technology.

Saint Xavier University, Graduate Studies, School of Education, Chicago, IL 60655-3105. Offers counseling (MA); curriculum and instruction (MA); early childhood education (MA); educational administration (MA); elementary education (MA); individualized studies (MA), including educational technology, English as a second language (ESL), ISTEM (integrative science, technology, engineering, and math), science education; music education (MA); reading (MA); secondary education (MA); Spanish education (MA); special education (MA); teaching and leadership (MA). *Accreditation:* NCATE. Part-time and evening/weekend programs available. *Degree requirements:* For master's, thesis or project. *Entrance requirements:* For master's, minimum GPA of 3.0. *Expenses:* Contact institution.

Salem International University, School of Education, Salem, WV 26426-0500. Offers curriculum and instruction (M Ed); educational leadership (M Ed). Part-time and evening/weekend programs available. Postbaccalaureate distance learning degree programs offered. *Degree requirements:* For master's, comprehensive exam (for some programs), thesis (for some programs). *Entrance requirements:* For master's, GRE, MAT, NTE, 3 letters of recommendation. Additional exam requirements/recommendations for international students: Required—TOEFL (minimum score 550 paper-based). Electronic applications accepted. *Expenses:* Contact institution. *Faculty research:* Improved classroom effectiveness.

Salem State University, School of Graduate Studies, Program in Higher Education in Student Affairs, Salem, MA 01970-5353. Offers M Ed. Part-time and evening/weekend programs available. *Students:* 21 full-time (16 women), 39 part-time (25 women); includes 21 minority (9 Black or African American, non-Hispanic/Latino; 3 Asian, non-Hispanic/Latino; 8 Hispanic/Latino; 1 Two or more races, non-Hispanic/Latino). 39 applicants, 92% accepted, 22 enrolled. In 2013, 4 degrees awarded. *Entrance requirements:* For master's, GRE or MAT. Additional exam requirements/recommendations for international students: Required—TOEFL (minimum score 550 paper-based; 80 iBT) or IELTS (minimum score 5.5). *Application deadline:* For fall admission, 5/1 for domestic students. Application fee: $50. *Financial support:* Career-related internships or fieldwork, Federal Work-Study, scholarships/grants, and unspecified assistantships available. Support available to part-time students. Financial award application deadline: 5/1; financial award applicants required to submit FAFSA. *Application contact:* Dr. Lee A. Brossoit, Assistant Dean of Graduate Admissions, 978-542-6675, Fax: 978-542-7215, E-mail: lbrossoit@salemstate.edu. Website: http://www.salemstate.edu/academics/schools/12569.php.

Salisbury University, Department of Education Specialties, Program in Educational Leadership, Salisbury, MD 21801-6837. Offers M Ed. Part-time and evening/weekend programs available. *Faculty:* 3 full-time (0 women), 2 part-time/adjunct (0 women). *Students:* 1 full-time (0 women), 35 part-time (26 women); includes 4 minority (all Black or African American, non-Hispanic/Latino), 1 international. Average age 31. 11 applicants, 73% accepted, 8 enrolled. In 2013, 21 master's awarded. *Degree requirements:* For master's, comprehensive exam. *Entrance requirements:* For master's, 2 recommendations, evidence of minimum 2 years of teaching performance, minimum undergraduate GPA of 3.0, interview. Additional exam requirements/recommendations for international students: Required—TOEFL (minimum score 550 paper-based; 79 iBT), IELTS (minimum score 6.5). *Application deadline:* For fall admission, 4/1 for domestic and international students; for spring admission, 10/1 for domestic and international students; for summer admission, 4/1 for domestic and international students. Applications are processed on a rolling basis. Application fee: $50. Electronic applications accepted. *Expenses: Tuition, area resident:* Part-time $342 per credit hour. Tuition, state resident: part-time $342 per credit hour. Tuition, nonresident: part-time $631 per credit hour. *Required fees:* $76 per credit hour. Tuition and fees vary according to program. *Financial support:* Career-related internships or fieldwork, institutionally sponsored loans, and unspecified assistantships available. Support available to part-time students. Financial award application deadline: 3/1; financial award applicants required to submit FAFSA. *Faculty research:* Writing, literacy and diversity, professional development schools, mentoring and co-teaching, technology in education. *Unit head:* Dr. Gwen Beegle, Director of M Ed Programs, 410-543-6393, E-mail: gpbeegle@salisbury.edu. *Application contact:* Claire Williams, Program Management Specialist, 410-543-6281, E-mail: clwilliams@salisbury.edu. Website: http://www.salisbury.edu/educationspecialties/med-edld.html.

Samford University, Orlean Bullard Beeson School of Education, Birmingham, AL 35229. Offers early childhood/elementary education (MS Ed); educational leadership (MS Ed, Ed D); gifted education (MS Ed); instructional leadership (MS Ed, Ed S);

secondary collaboration (MS Ed); M Div/MS Ed. *Accreditation:* NCATE. Part-time and evening/weekend programs available. *Faculty:* 10 full-time (5 women), 16 part-time/adjunct (15 women). *Students:* 40 full-time (25 women), 210 part-time (156 women); includes 39 minority (33 Black or African American, non-Hispanic/Latino; 3 American Indian or Alaska Native, non-Hispanic/Latino; 2 Asian, non-Hispanic/Latino; 1 Hispanic/Latino), 4 international. Average age 38. 81 applicants, 89% accepted, 70 enrolled. In 2013, 94 master's, 21 doctorates, 16 other advanced degrees awarded. *Degree requirements:* For master's and Ed S, comprehensive exam; for doctorate, comprehensive exam, thesis/dissertation. *Entrance requirements:* For master's, GRE (minimum score of 295) or MAT (minimum score of 396); waived if previously completed a graduate degree, writing sample, statement of purpose, 3 letters of recommendation, 2 original copies of all transcripts, minimum GPA of 2.75, teaching certificate; for doctorate, minimum GPA of 3.7, professional resume, writing sample, 3 letters of recommendation, 1 original copy of all transcripts; for Ed S, master's degree, teaching certificate, minimum GPA of 3.25, 3 letters of recommendation, 2 original copies of all transcripts, writing sample, statement of purpose. Additional exam requirements/recommendations for international students: Required—TOEFL (minimum score 90 iBT), IELTS (minimum score 7). *Application deadline:* For fall admission, 7/30 for domestic and international students; for winter admission, 4/5 for domestic students; for spring admission, 12/5 for domestic and international students; for summer admission, 4/18 for domestic and international students. Applications are processed on a rolling basis. Application fee: $35. Electronic applications accepted. *Expenses: Tuition:* Full-time $11,552; part-time $722 per credit. *Required fees:* $500; $250 per term. *Financial support:* In 2013–14, 162 students received support. Research assistantships, career-related internships or fieldwork, Federal Work-Study, scholarships/grants, and tuition waivers (partial) available. Support available to part-time students. Financial award applicants required to submit FAFSA. *Faculty research:* Research on gifted/high ability students (K-12), school law, the characteristics of beginning teachers, the nature of school reform, school culture, quality improvement in education, K-12 student achievement, reading research, classroom management, reading intervention, schema theory. *Unit head:* Dr. Maurice Persall, Chair, Department of Educational Leadership, 205-726-2019, E-mail: jmpersal@samford.edu. *Application contact:* Brooke Gilreath Karr, Graduate Admissions Coordinator, 205-729-2783, Fax: 205-726-4233, E-mail: kbgilrea@samford.edu. Website: http://www.samford.edu/education/.

Sam Houston State University, College of Education and Applied Science, Department of Educational Leadership and Counseling, Huntsville, TX 77341. Offers administration (M Ed); clinical mental health counseling (MA); counselor education (PhD); developmental education administration (Ed D); educational leadership (Ed D); higher education administration (MA); instructional leadership (M Ed, MA); school counseling (M Ed). Part-time and evening/weekend programs available. Postbaccalaureate distance learning degree programs offered (no on-campus study). *Faculty:* 29 full-time (16 women). *Students:* 220 full-time (178 women), 463 part-time (374 women); includes 265 minority (128 Black or African American, non-Hispanic/Latino; 3 American Indian or Alaska Native, non-Hispanic/Latino; 6 Asian, non-Hispanic/Latino; 115 Hispanic/Latino; 13 Two or more races, non-Hispanic/Latino), 24 international. Average age 35. 294 applicants, 96% accepted, 130 enrolled. In 2013, 166 master's, 32 doctorates awarded. *Degree requirements:* For master's, comprehensive exam, thesis (for some programs); for doctorate, comprehensive exam, thesis/dissertation. *Entrance requirements:* For master's, GRE General Test. Additional exam requirements/recommendations for international students: Required—TOEFL (minimum score 550 paper-based; 79 iBT). *Application deadline:* For fall admission, 8/1 for domestic students, 6/25 for international students; for spring admission, 12/1 for domestic students, 11/12 for international students. Applications are processed on a rolling basis. Application fee: $45 ($75 for international students). Electronic applications accepted. *Financial support:* In 2013–14, 7 research assistantships (averaging $9,335 per year), 3 teaching assistantships (averaging $6,183 per year) were awarded; career-related internships or fieldwork, Federal Work-Study, institutionally sponsored loans, scholarships/grants, tuition waivers (partial), and unspecified assistantships also available. Support available to part-time students. Financial award application deadline: 5/31; financial award applicants required to submit FAFSA. *Unit head:* Dr. Stacey Edmonson, Chair, 936-294-1752, Fax: 936-294-3886, E-mail: edu_sle01@shsu.edu. *Application contact:* Dr. Barbara Polnick, Advisor, 936-294-3859, E-mail: bpolnick@shsu.edu. Website: http://www.shsu.edu/~edu_elc/.

San Diego State University, Graduate and Research Affairs, College of Education, Department of Administration, Rehabilitation and Post-Secondary Education, San Diego, CA 92182. Offers educational leadership in post-secondary education (MA); rehabilitation counseling (MS), including deafness. Evening/weekend programs available. Postbaccalaureate distance learning degree programs offered. *Degree requirements:* For master's, comprehensive exam (for some programs), thesis (for some programs). *Entrance requirements:* For master's, GRE General Test, letters of reference. Additional exam requirements/recommendations for international students: Required—TOEFL. Electronic applications accepted. *Faculty research:* Rehabilitation in cultural diversity, distance learning technology.

San Diego State University, Graduate and Research Affairs, College of Education, Department of Educational Leadership, San Diego, CA 92182. Offers MA. *Accreditation:* NCATE. Evening/weekend programs available. *Entrance requirements:* For master's, GRE General Test, letters of reference. Additional exam requirements/recommendations for international students: Required—TOEFL. Electronic applications accepted.

San Francisco State University, Division of Graduate Studies, College of Education, Department of Equity, Leadership Studies, and Instructional Technologies, Program in Educational Administration, San Francisco, CA 94132-1722. Offers administrative services (Credential); educational administration (MA). *Accreditation:* NCATE. *Application deadline:* Applications are processed on a rolling basis. *Unit head:* Dr. David Hemphill, Interim Chair, 415-338-1653, E-mail: hemphill@sfsu.edu. *Application contact:* Dr. Andrew Dubin, Graduate Coordinator, 415-338-1300, E-mail: adubin@sfsu.edu. Website: http://coe.sfsu.edu/elsit.

San Francisco State University, Division of Graduate Studies, College of Education, Program in Educational Leadership, San Francisco, CA 94132-1722. Offers Ed D. *Unit head:* Dr. Robert Gabriner, Director, 415-405-4103, E-mail: gabriner@sfsu.edu. *Application contact:* Dr. Norena Norton Badway, Graduate Coordinator, 415-405-4103, E-mail: nbadway@sfsu.edu. Website: http://www.sfsu.edu/~edd/.

San Jose State University, Graduate Studies and Research, Connie L. Lurie College of Education, Department of Educational Leadership, San Jose, CA 95192-0001. Offers educational administration (K-12) (MA); higher education administration (MA). *Accreditation:* NCATE. *Degree requirements:* For master's, thesis or alternative. Electronic applications accepted.

Santa Clara University, School of Education and Counseling Psychology, Santa Clara, CA 95053. Offers alternative and correctional education (Certificate); counseling (MA); counseling psychology (MA); educational administration (MA); interdisciplinary

education (MA); teaching (MA). Part-time and evening/weekend programs available. *Faculty:* 56 full-time (21 women), 41 part-time/adjunct (23 women). *Students:* 232 full-time (192 women), 329 part-time (262 women); includes 162 minority (14 Black or African American, non-Hispanic/Latino; 1 American Indian or Alaska Native, non-Hispanic/Latino; 59 Asian, non-Hispanic/Latino; 75 Hispanic/Latino; 2 Native Hawaiian or other Pacific Islander, non-Hispanic/Latino; 11 Two or more races, non-Hispanic/Latino), 21 international. Average age 31. 322 applicants, 77% accepted, 178 enrolled. In 2013, 176 master's, 36 other advanced degrees awarded. *Degree requirements:* For master's, comprehensive exam (for some programs), thesis (for some programs); for Certificate, comprehensive exam. *Entrance requirements:* For master's, GRE or MAT, transcript, letters of recommendation, essay. Additional exam requirements/recommendations for international students: Required—TOEFL. *Application deadline:* For fall admission, 6/15 for domestic and international students; for winter admission, 10/15 for domestic and international students; for spring admission, 1/31 for domestic and international students. Applications are processed on a rolling basis. Application fee: $50. Electronic applications accepted. *Expenses:* Contact institution. *Financial support:* In 2013–14, 281 students received support. Fellowships, research assistantships, Federal Work-Study, institutionally sponsored loans, and scholarships/grants available. Support available to part-time students. Financial award application deadline: 5/15; financial award applicants required to submit FAFSA. *Faculty research:* Cognitive behavioral therapies and positive psychology, multicultural counseling and Latino mental health. *Unit head:* Nicholas Ladany, Dean, 408-554-4455, Fax: 408-554-5038, E-mail: nladany@scu.edu. *Application contact:* Kelly Pjesky, Admissions Director, 408-554-7884, Fax: 408-554-4367, E-mail: kpjesky@scu.edu.
Website: http://www.scu.edu/ecppm/.

Schreiner University, Department of Education, Kerrville, TX 78028-5697. Offers education (M Ed); principal (Certificate). Part-time and evening/weekend programs available. Postbaccalaureate distance learning degree programs offered (minimal on-campus study). *Faculty:* 3 full-time (2 women), 1 (woman) part-time/adjunct. *Students:* 40 full-time (30 women), 5 part-time (4 women); includes 15 minority (1 Black or African American, non-Hispanic/Latino; 13 Hispanic/Latino; 1 Two or more races, non-Hispanic/Latino). Average age 35. 29 applicants, 93% accepted, 25 enrolled. In 2013, 29 master's, 11 Certificates awarded. *Entrance requirements:* For master's, GRE (waived if undergraduate cumulative GPA is 3.0 or above), 3 references; transcripts; interview. Additional exam requirements/recommendations for international students: Required—TOEFL. *Application deadline:* For fall admission, 8/1 priority date for domestic students, 8/1 for international students; for spring admission, 12/1 priority date for domestic students, 12/1 for international students; for summer admission, 5/1 priority date for domestic students, 5/1 for international students. Applications are processed on a rolling basis. Application fee: $25. Electronic applications accepted. *Expenses: Tuition:* Full-time $17,604; part-time $489 per credit hour. Tuition and fees vary according to course load and program. *Financial support:* In 2013–14, 42 students received support. Scholarships/grants available. Financial award application deadline: 8/1; financial award applicants required to submit FAFSA. *Unit head:* Dr. Neva Cramer, Director, Teacher Education, 830-792-7266, Fax: 830-792-7382, E-mail: nvcramer@schreiner.edu. *Application contact:* Caroline Randall, Director of Admission, 830-792-7224, Fax: 830-792-7226, E-mail: gradadmissions@schreiner.edu.
Website: http://www.schreiner.edu/academics/graduate/index.html.

Seattle Pacific University, Master of Education in Educational Leadership Program, Seattle, WA 98119-1997. Offers educational leadership (M Ed, Ed D); principal (Certificate); program administrator (Certificate); superintendent (Certificate). *Accreditation:* NCATE. Part-time and evening/weekend programs available. *Students:* 11 full-time (7 women), 138 part-time (97 women); includes 13 minority (4 Black or African American, non-Hispanic/Latino; 1 American Indian or Alaska Native, non-Hispanic/Latino; 4 Asian, non-Hispanic/Latino; 2 Hispanic/Latino; 2 Two or more races, non-Hispanic/Latino), 11 international. Average age 38. 84 applicants, 68% accepted, 56 enrolled. In 2013, 2 master's, 10 doctorates awarded. *Degree requirements:* For master's, comprehensive exam; for doctorate, comprehensive exam, thesis/dissertation. *Entrance requirements:* For master's, GRE (minimum combined verbal and quantitative score of 950) or MAT (minimum 385 scaled score), or minimum undergraduate GPA of 3.0 cumulative or in last 45 credits of completed undergraduate coursework, copy of teaching certificate, official transcript(s) from each college/university attended, resume, personal statement (1-2 pages); for doctorate, GRE General Test or MAT, minimum GPA of 3.0, formal interview. *Application deadline:* For fall admission, 8/15 priority date for domestic students; for winter admission, 11/15 for domestic students; for spring admission, 2/15 priority date for domestic students; for summer admission, 5/15 for domestic students. Applications are processed on a rolling basis. Application fee: $50. Electronic applications accepted. *Financial support:* Career-related internships or fieldwork available. Financial award applicants required to submit FAFSA. *Unit head:* Dr. William Prenevost, Chair, 206-281-2370, Fax: 206-281-2756, E-mail: prenew@spu.edu. *Application contact:* The Graduate Center, 206-281-2091.
Website: http://spu.edu/academics/school-of-education/graduate-programs/educational-leadership-programs.

Seattle University, College of Education, Program in Educational Administration, Seattle, WA 98122-1090. Offers M Ed, MA, Certificate, Ed S. *Accreditation:* NCATE. Part-time and evening/weekend programs available. *Faculty:* 3 full-time (0 women), 2 part-time/adjunct (1 woman). *Students:* 1 (woman) full-time, 47 part-time (27 women); includes 13 minority (3 Black or African American, non-Hispanic/Latino; 5 Asian, non-Hispanic/Latino; 3 Hispanic/Latino; 1 Native Hawaiian or other Pacific Islander, non-Hispanic/Latino; 1 Two or more races, non-Hispanic/Latino), 1 international. Average age 37. 15 applicants, 73% accepted, 9 enrolled. In 2013, 6 master's, 5 other advanced degrees awarded. *Degree requirements:* For master's and other advanced degree, comprehensive exam. *Entrance requirements:* For master's, GRE, MAT, or minimum GPA of 3.0; interview; 1 year of related experience. Additional exam requirements/recommendations for international students: Required—TOEFL. *Application deadline:* For fall admission, 8/20 priority date for domestic students; for winter admission, 11/20 for domestic students; for spring admission, 2/20 for domestic students. Applications are processed on a rolling basis. Application fee: $55. *Financial support:* In 2013–14, 11 students received support. Career-related internships or fieldwork and Federal Work-Study available. Support available to part-time students. Financial award applicants required to submit FAFSA. *Unit head:* Dr. Michael Silver, Director, 206-296-5798, E-mail: silverm@seattleu.edu. *Application contact:* Janet Shandley, Associate Dean of Graduate Admissions, 206-296-5900, Fax: 206-298-5656, E-mail: grad_admissions@seattleu.edu.
Website: http://www.seattleu.edu/coe/edadmin/default.aspx?id=8202.

Seattle University, College of Education, Program in Educational Leadership, Seattle, WA 98122-1090. Offers Ed D. *Accreditation:* NCATE. Part-time and evening/weekend programs available. *Faculty:* 5 full-time (2 women), 1 part-time/adjunct (0 women). *Students:* 9 full-time (4 women), 59 part-time (37 women); includes 24 minority (12 Black or African American, non-Hispanic/Latino; 3 American Indian or Alaska Native, non-Hispanic/Latino; 3 Asian, non-Hispanic/Latino; 4 Hispanic/Latino; 2 Two or more races, non-Hispanic/Latino). Average age 44. 2 applicants, 100% accepted, 2 enrolled. In 2013, 13 doctorates awarded. *Degree requirements:* For doctorate, comprehensive exam, thesis/dissertation. *Entrance requirements:* For doctorate, GRE General Test, MAT, interview, MA, minimum GPA of 3.5, 3 years of related experience. Additional exam requirements/recommendations for international students: Required—TOEFL. *Application deadline:* For fall admission, 4/1 for domestic students. Application fee: $55. *Expenses:* Contact institution. *Financial support:* In 2013–14, 10 students received support. Career-related internships or fieldwork and Federal Work-Study available. Support available to part-time students. Financial award applicants required to submit FAFSA. *Unit head:* Dr. Laurie Stevahn, Chair, 206-296-5750, E-mail: stevahnl@seattleu.edu. *Application contact:* Janet Shandley, Associate Dean of Graduate Admissions, 206-296-5900, Fax: 206-298-5656, E-mail: grad_admissions@seattleu.edu.
Website: https://www.seattleu.edu/coe/edlr/.

Seattle University, College of Education, Program in Student Development Administration, Seattle, WA 98122-1090. Offers M Ed, MA. Part-time and evening/weekend programs available. *Faculty:* 5 full-time (3 women), 1 part-time/adjunct (0 women). *Students:* 32 full-time (25 women), 30 part-time (22 women); includes 25 minority (4 Black or African American, non-Hispanic/Latino; 9 Asian, non-Hispanic/Latino; 6 Hispanic/Latino; 6 Two or more races, non-Hispanic/Latino), 1 international. Average age 25. 108 applicants, 48% accepted, 24 enrolled. In 2013, 36 master's awarded. *Degree requirements:* For master's, comprehensive exam. *Entrance requirements:* For master's, GRE, MAT, or minimum GPA of 3.0, two recommendations, resume, self-assessment form, autobiography. Additional exam requirements/recommendations for international students: Required—TOEFL. *Application deadline:* For fall admission, 1/15 priority date for domestic students; for winter admission, 11/20 for domestic students; for spring admission, 2/20 for domestic students. Applications are processed on a rolling basis. Application fee: $55. *Financial support:* In 2013–14, 7 students received support. Career-related internships or fieldwork, Federal Work-Study, and unspecified assistantships available. Support available to part-time students. Financial award applicants required to submit FAFSA. *Unit head:* Dr. Jeremy Stringer, Coordinator, 206-296-6170, E-mail: stringer@seattleu.edu. *Application contact:* Janet Shandley, Associate Dean of Graduate Admissions, 206-296-5900, Fax: 206-298-5656, E-mail: grad_admissions@seattleu.edu.
Website: https://www.seattleu.edu/coe/sda/.

Seton Hall University, College of Education and Human Services, Department of Education Leadership, Management and Policy, Program in Higher Education Administration, South Orange, NJ 07079-2697. Offers Ed D, PhD. *Accreditation:* NCATE. Part-time and evening/weekend programs available. *Faculty:* 12 full-time (4 women), 1 part-time/adjunct (0 women). *Students:* 20 full-time (12 women), 73 part-time (45 women); includes 24 minority (15 Black or African American, non-Hispanic/Latino; 9 Hispanic/Latino), 9 international. Average age 41. 26 applicants, 81% accepted, 16 enrolled. In 2013, 7 degrees awarded. *Degree requirements:* For doctorate, comprehensive exam, thesis/dissertation, internship. *Entrance requirements:* For doctorate, GRE or MAT, interview, minimum GPA of 3.5. Additional exam requirements/recommendations for international students: Required—TOEFL. *Application deadline:* For fall admission, 2/1 priority date for domestic students; for spring admission, 10/1 for domestic students. Applications are processed on a rolling basis. Application fee: $75. *Financial support:* In 2013–14, 7 research assistantships with tuition reimbursements (averaging $5,000 per year) were awarded. Financial award application deadline: 2/1. *Unit head:* Dr. Michael Osnato, Chair, 973-275-2446, E-mail: osnatomi@shu.edu. *Application contact:* Diana Minakakis, Associate Dean, 973-275-2824, Fax: 973-275-2187, E-mail: diana.minakakis@shu.edu.
Website: http://www.shu.edu/academics/education/edd-higher-ed/index.cfm.

Seton Hall University, College of Education and Human Services, Department of Education Leadership, Management and Policy, Program in K–12 Leadership, Management and Policy, South Orange, NJ 07079-2697. Offers Ed D, Exec Ed D, Ed S. Part-time and evening/weekend programs available. *Faculty:* 12 full-time (4 women), 1 part-time/adjunct (0 women). *Students:* 36 full-time (21 women), 232 part-time (145 women); includes 60 minority (41 Black or African American, non-Hispanic/Latino; 4 Asian, non-Hispanic/Latino; 15 Hispanic/Latino), 2 international. Average age 43. 40 applicants, 78% accepted, 20 enrolled. In 2013, 21 doctorates, 10 other advanced degrees awarded. *Degree requirements:* For doctorate, comprehensive exam, thesis/dissertation. *Entrance requirements:* For doctorate, MAT or GRE, interview. *Application deadline:* For fall admission, 2/1 for domestic students; for spring admission, 12/1 for domestic students. Applications are processed on a rolling basis. Application fee: $75. *Financial support:* In 2013–14, 2 research assistantships with full tuition reimbursements (averaging $4,500 per year) were awarded; unspecified assistantships also available. Financial award application deadline: 2/1. *Unit head:* Dr. Michael Osnato, Chair, 973-275-2446, E-mail: osnatomi@shu.edu. *Application contact:* Dr. Jan Furman, Director, 973-761-9397.
Website: http://www.shu.edu/academics/education/edd-k-12-administration/index.cfm.

Shasta Bible College, Program in School and Church Administration, Redding, CA 96002. Offers MS. Part-time and evening/weekend programs available. *Degree requirements:* For master's, comprehensive exam (for some programs), thesis or alternative. *Entrance requirements:* For master's, cumulative GPA of 3.0, 9 semester hours of education or psychology courses. Additional exam requirements/recommendations for international students: Required—TOEFL (minimum score 550 paper-based).

Shippensburg University of Pennsylvania, School of Graduate Studies, College of Education and Human Services, Department of Educational Leadership and Special Education, Shippensburg, PA 17257-2299. Offers school administration principal K-12 (M Ed); special education (M Ed), including behavior disorders, comprehensive, learning disabilities, mental retardation/development disabilities. *Accreditation:* NCATE. Part-time and evening/weekend programs available. *Faculty:* 10 full-time (4 women), 1 (woman) part-time/adjunct. *Students:* 8 full-time (all women), 70 part-time (48 women); includes 1 minority (Two or more races, non-Hispanic/Latino), 3 international. Average age 30. 63 applicants, 68% accepted, 29 enrolled. In 2013, 53 master's awarded. *Degree requirements:* For master's, candidacy, thesis, or practicum. *Entrance requirements:* For master's, instructional or educational specialist certificate; 3 letters of reference; 2 years of successful teaching experience; interview and GRE or MAT (if GPA is less than 2.75); statement of purpose; writing sample; personal goals statement and resume. Additional exam requirements/recommendations for international students: Required—TOEFL (minimum score 580 paper-based); Recommended—IELTS (minimum score 6). *Application deadline:* For fall admission, 2/1 for domestic students, 4/30 for international students; for spring admission, 7/1 for domestic students, 9/30 for international students. Applications are processed on a rolling basis. Application fee: $45. Electronic applications accepted. *Expenses: Tuition, area resident:* Part-time $442 per credit. Tuition, state resident: part-time $442 per credit. Tuition, nonresident: part-time $663 per credit. *Required fees:* $127 per credit. *Financial support:* In 2013–14, 1 research assistantship with full tuition reimbursement (averaging $5,000 per year) was awarded; career-related internships or fieldwork, scholarships/grants, unspecified assistantships, and resident hall director and student payroll positions also available. Support available to part-time students. Financial award application deadline: 3/1; financial award applicants required to submit FAFSA. *Unit head:* Dr. Christopher L. Schwilk, Chairperson, 717-477-1591, Fax: 717-477-4026, E-mail: clschwi@ship.edu.

Application contact: Jeremy R. Goshorn, Assistant Dean of Graduate Admissions, 717-477-1231, Fax: 717-477-4016, E-mail: jrgoshorn@ship.edu.
Website: http://www.ship.edu/else/.

Siena Heights University, Graduate College, Adrian, MI 49221-1796. Offers clinical mental health counseling (MA); education leadership (Specialist); leadership (MA), including health care, higher education leadership, organizational; teacher education (MA), including early childhood, early childhood: Montessori-based, education leadership: principal, elementary education, K-12 reading, leadership: higher education, secondary education, K-12 reading, special education, K-12 cognitive impairment, special education, K-12 learning disabled. Part-time and evening/weekend programs available. *Faculty:* 37. *Students:* 9 full-time (7 women), 251 part-time (179 women). In 2013, 32 master's awarded. *Degree requirements:* For master's, thesis, presentation. *Entrance requirements:* For master's, minimum GPA of 3.0, current resume, essay, all post-secondary transcripts, 3 letters of reference, conviction disclosure form; copy of teaching certificate (for some education programs); for Specialist, master's degree, minimum GPA of 3.0, current resume, essay, all post-secondary transcripts, 3 letters of reference, conviction disclosure form; copy of teaching certificate (for some education programs). *Application deadline:* Applications are processed on a rolling basis. Application fee: $50. *Expenses: Tuition:* Part-time $535 per semester hour. *Required fees:* $130 per semester. *Financial support:* Career-related internships or fieldwork, Federal Work-Study, and resident assistantships available. Financial award application deadline: 9/1; financial award applicants required to submit FAFSA. *Unit head:* Dr. Linda S. Pettit, Dean, Graduate College, 517-264-7661, Fax: 517-264-7714, E-mail: lpettit@sienahts.edu.
Website: http://www.sienaheights.edu.

Sierra Nevada College, Teacher Education Program, Incline Village, NV 89451. Offers advanced teaching and leadership (M Ed); elementary education (MAT); secondary education (MAT). Part-time and evening/weekend programs available. Postbaccalaureate distance learning degree programs offered (minimal on-campus study). *Degree requirements:* For master's, comprehensive exam, thesis, PRAXIS I and II. *Entrance requirements:* For master's, 2 letters of recommendation, minimum GPA of 3.0. Electronic applications accepted.

Silver Lake College of the Holy Family, Division of Graduate Studies, Program in Education, Manitowoc, WI 54220-9319. Offers administrative leadership (MA Ed); teacher leadership (MA Ed). Part-time and evening/weekend programs available. Postbaccalaureate distance learning degree programs offered (no on-campus study). *Faculty:* 1 (woman) full-time, 9 part-time/adjunct (5 women). *Students:* 1 (woman) full-time, 74 part-time (53 women); includes 5 minority (4 Black or African American, non-Hispanic/Latino; 1 Asian, non-Hispanic/Latino). Average age 40. 42 applicants, 98% accepted, 14 enrolled. In 2013, 13 master's awarded. *Degree requirements:* For master's, comprehensive exam, thesis or alternative, public presentation of culminating project. *Entrance requirements:* For master's, minimum undergraduate GPA of 3.0, writing sample, 3 letters of recommendation. Additional exam requirements/recommendations for international students: Required—TOEFL. *Application deadline:* For fall admission, 8/1 for domestic and international students; for spring admission, 12/1 for domestic and international students. Applications are processed on a rolling basis. Application fee: $0. Electronic applications accepted. *Expenses: Tuition:* Part-time $500 per credit. *Financial support:* Scholarships/grants available. Support available to part-time students. Financial award application deadline: 6/30; financial award applicants required to submit FAFSA. *Unit head:* Sr. Marcolette Madden, Director, 800-236-4752 Ext. 375, Fax: 920-684-7082, E-mail: marcolette.madden@sl.edu. *Application contact:* Jamie Grant, Director of Admissions, 920-686-6206, Fax: 920-686-6322, E-mail: jamie.grant@sl.edu.
Website: https://www.sl.edu/adult-education/academics/graduate-program/master-of-arts-in-education/.

Simon Fraser University, Office of Graduate Studies, Faculty of Education, Program in Educational Leadership, Burnaby, BC V5A 1S6, Canada. Offers M Ed, MA, Ed D. Part-time and evening/weekend programs available. *Degree requirements:* For master's, comprehensive exam (for some programs), thesis (for some programs); for doctorate, comprehensive exam, thesis/dissertation. *Entrance requirements:* For master's, minimum GPA of 3.0 (on scale of 4.33), or 3.33 based on last 60 credits of undergraduate courses; for doctorate, minimum GPA of 3.5 (on scale of 4.33). Additional exam requirements/recommendations for international students: Recommended—TOEFL (minimum score 580 paper-based; 93 iBT), IELTS (minimum score 7), TWE (minimum score 5). Electronic applications accepted. *Expenses: Tuition, area resident:* Full-time $5084 Canadian dollars. *Required fees:* $840 Canadian dollars. *Faculty research:* Language learning, assessment and accountability policy, intersections between student affairs and services, recruitment and retention, indigenous peoples, student success in post-secondary education.

Simpson University, School of Education, Redding, CA 96003-8606. Offers education (MA), including curriculum, education leadership; education and preliminary administrative services credential (MA); education and preliminary teaching credential (MA); teaching (MA). Part-time and evening/weekend programs available. *Faculty:* 5 full-time (2 women), 16 part-time/adjunct (7 women). *Students:* 45 full-time (27 women), 84 part-time (59 women); includes 24 minority (4 Black or African American, non-Hispanic/Latino; 2 American Indian or Alaska Native, non-Hispanic/Latino; 13 Asian, non-Hispanic/Latino; 4 Hispanic/Latino; 1 Native Hawaiian or other Pacific Islander, non-Hispanic/Latino). Average age 36. 54 applicants, 67% accepted, 29 enrolled. In 2013, 29 master's awarded. *Degree requirements:* For master's, thesis optional. *Entrance requirements:* For master's, GRE. Additional exam requirements/recommendations for international students: Required—TOEFL (minimum score 550 paper-based). *Application deadline:* Applications are processed on a rolling basis. Application fee: $25. Electronic applications accepted. Tuition and fees vary according to program. *Financial support:* Scholarships/grants available. Financial award applicants required to submit FAFSA. *Unit head:* Dr. Glee Brooks, Dean of Education, 530-226-4188, Fax: 530-226-4872, E-mail: gbrooks@simpsonu.edu. *Application contact:* Kimberly Snow, Assistant Director of Graduate Admissions, 530-226-4633, E-mail: ksnow@simpsonu.edu.

Slippery Rock University of Pennsylvania, Graduate Studies (Recruitment), College of Education, Department of Secondary Education/Foundations of Education, Slippery Rock, PA 16057-1383. Offers educational leadership (M Ed); secondary education (M Ed), including English, math/science, social studies/history. *Accreditation:* NCATE. Part-time and evening/weekend programs available. *Faculty:* 12 full-time (5 women). *Students:* 48 full-time (24 women), 10 part-time (6 women). Average age 27. 50 applicants, 84% accepted, 29 enrolled. In 2013, 28 master's awarded. *Degree requirements:* For master's, comprehensive exam, thesis (for some programs). *Entrance requirements:* For master's, GRE General Test, MAT, minimum GPA of 2.8 or 3.0 (depending on program); copy of teaching certification and two letters of recommendation (for some programs). Additional exam requirements/recommendations for international students: Required—TOEFL (minimum score 550 paper-based; 80 iBT). *Application deadline:* For fall admission, 3/1 priority date for domestic students, 5/1 priority date for international students; for spring admission, 10/1 priority date for domestic students, 9/1 priority date for international students. Applications are processed on a rolling basis. Application fee: $25 ($30 for international students). Electronic applications accepted. *Expenses:* Tuition, state resident: full-time $7956; part-time $442 per credit. Tuition, nonresident: full-time $11,934; part-time $663 per credit. *Required fees:* $2896; $148 per credit. Tuition and fees vary according to degree level and program. *Financial support:* Career-related internships or fieldwork, Federal Work-Study, institutionally sponsored loans, scholarships/grants, tuition waivers (partial), and unspecified assistantships available. Support available to part-time students. Financial award application deadline: 5/1; financial award applicants required to submit FAFSA. *Unit head:* Dr. Jeffrey Lehman, Graduate Coordinator, 724-738-2311, Fax: 724-738-4987, E-mail: jeffrey.lehman@sru.edu. *Application contact:* Brandi Weber-Mortimer, Interim Director of Graduate Studies, 724-738-2051, Fax: 724-738-2146, E-mail: graduate.admissions@sru.edu.

Slippery Rock University of Pennsylvania, Graduate Studies (Recruitment), College of Education, Department of Special Education, Slippery Rock, PA 16057-1383. Offers autism (M Ed); birth to grade 8 (M Ed); grade 7 to grade 12 (M Ed); master teacher (M Ed); supervision (M Ed). *Accreditation:* NCATE. Part-time and evening/weekend programs available. Postbaccalaureate distance learning degree programs offered (no on-campus study). *Faculty:* 8 full-time (4 women). *Students:* 31 full-time (28 women), 154 part-time (130 women); includes 5 minority (2 Black or African American, non-Hispanic/Latino; 2 Asian, non-Hispanic/Latino; 1 Hispanic/Latino). Average age 29. 187 applicants, 90% accepted, 107 enrolled. In 2013, 81 master's awarded. *Degree requirements:* For master's, thesis optional. *Entrance requirements:* For master's, GRE General Test, MAT, minimum GPA of 3.0, official transcripts, teaching certification. Additional exam requirements/recommendations for international students: Required—TOEFL (minimum score 550 paper-based; 80 iBT). *Application deadline:* For fall admission, 3/1 priority date for domestic students, 5/1 priority date for international students; for spring admission, 10/1 priority date for domestic students, 9/1 priority date for international students. Applications are processed on a rolling basis. Application fee: $25 ($30 for international students). Electronic applications accepted. *Expenses:* Tuition, state resident: full-time $7956; part-time $442 per credit. Tuition, nonresident: full-time $11,934; part-time $663 per credit. *Required fees:* $2896; $148 per credit. Tuition and fees vary according to degree level and program. *Financial support:* Career-related internships or fieldwork, Federal Work-Study, institutionally sponsored loans, scholarships/grants, tuition waivers (partial), and unspecified assistantships available. Support available to part-time students. Financial award application deadline: 5/1; financial award applicants required to submit FAFSA. *Unit head:* Dr. Robert Isherwood, Graduate Coordinator, 724-738-2453, Fax: 724-738-4395, E-mail: robert.isherwood@sru.edu. *Application contact:* Brandi Weber-Mortimer, Director of Graduate Admissions, 724-738-2051, Fax: 724-738-2146, E-mail: graduate.admissions@sru.edu.

Sonoma State University, School of Education, Rohnert Park, CA 94928. Offers curriculum, teaching, and learning (MA); early childhood education (MA); education (Ed D); educational administration (MA); multiple subject (Credential); reading and literacy (MA); single subject (Credential); special education (MA, Credential). *Accreditation:* NCATE. Part-time and evening/weekend programs available. *Faculty:* 11 full-time (9 women), 1 (woman) part-time/adjunct. *Students:* 162 full-time (119 women), 165 part-time (125 women); includes 61 minority (4 Black or African American, non-Hispanic/Latino; 1 American Indian or Alaska Native, non-Hispanic/Latino; 12 Asian, non-Hispanic/Latino; 29 Hispanic/Latino; 1 Native Hawaiian or other Pacific Islander, non-Hispanic/Latino; 14 Two or more races, non-Hispanic/Latino), 1 international. Average age 33. 314 applicants, 82% accepted, 75 enrolled. In 2013, 41 master's, 287 other advanced degrees awarded. *Degree requirements:* For master's, thesis or alternative. *Entrance requirements:* For master's, minimum GPA of 2.5. Additional exam requirements/recommendations for international students: Required—TOEFL (minimum score 500 paper-based). Application fee: $55. *Expenses:* Tuition, state resident: full-time $8500. Tuition, nonresident: full-time $12,964. *Required fees:* $1762. *Financial support:* In 2013–14, 1 research assistantship (averaging $1,876 per year) was awarded; fellowships, career-related internships or fieldwork, and Federal Work-Study also available. Support available to part-time students. Financial award application deadline: 3/2; financial award applicants required to submit FAFSA. *Unit head:* Dr. Carlos Ayala, Dean, 707-664-4412, E-mail: carlos.ayala@sonoma.edu. *Application contact:* Dr. Jennifer Mahdavi, Coordinator of Graduate Studies, 707-664-3311, E-mail: jennifer.mahdavi@sonoma.edu.
Website: http://www.sonoma.edu/education/.

South Dakota State University, Graduate School, College of Education and Human Sciences, Department of Educational Leadership, Brookings, SD 57007. Offers curriculum and instruction (M Ed); educational administration (M Ed). Part-time and evening/weekend programs available. Postbaccalaureate distance learning degree programs offered (minimal on-campus study). *Degree requirements:* For master's, portfolio, oral exam. *Entrance requirements:* For master's, minimum GPA of 2.75. Additional exam requirements/recommendations for international students: Required—TOEFL (minimum score 550 paper-based; 80 iBT). *Faculty research:* Inclusion school climate, K-12 reform and restructuring, rural development, ESL, leadership.

Southeastern Louisiana University, College of Education, Department of Educational Leadership and Technology, Hammond, LA 70402. Offers educational leadership (M Ed, Ed D); educational technology leadership (M Ed). Part-time and evening/weekend programs available. *Faculty:* 14 full-time (7 women), 1 part-time/adjunct (0 women). *Students:* 4 full-time (all women), 269 part-time (208 women); includes 78 minority (67 Black or African American, non-Hispanic/Latino; 7 Hispanic/Latino; 4 Two or more races, non-Hispanic/Latino), 1 international. Average age 37. 55 applicants, 87% accepted, 30 enrolled. In 2013, 94 master's, 4 doctorates awarded. *Degree requirements:* For master's, comprehensive exam; for doctorate, comprehensive exam, thesis/dissertation. *Entrance requirements:* For master's, GRE (verbal and quantitative); for doctorate, GRE, master's degree with minimum GPA of 3.25, 3.0 on the last 60 undergraduate hours. Additional exam requirements/recommendations for international students: Required—TOEFL (minimum score 500 paper-based; 61 iBT). *Application deadline:* For fall admission, 7/15 priority date for domestic students, 6/1 priority date for international students; for spring admission, 12/1 priority date for domestic students, 10/1 priority date for international students. Applications are processed on a rolling basis. Application fee: $20 ($30 for international students). Electronic applications accepted. *Expenses:* Tuition, state resident: full-time $5047. Tuition, nonresident: full-time $17,066. *Required fees:* $1213. Tuition and fees vary according to degree level. *Financial support:* Career-related internships or fieldwork, Federal Work-Study, institutionally sponsored loans, scholarships/grants, and unspecified assistantships available. Support available to part-time students. Financial award application deadline: 5/1; financial award applicants required to submit FAFSA. *Faculty research:* Technology leadership in schools, techno stress for educational leaders, dispositions of effective leaders. *Total annual research expenditures:* $3,692. *Unit head:* Dr. Jeffrey Oescher, Interim Department Head, 985-549-5713, Fax: 985-549-5712, E-mail: jeffrey.oescher@selu.edu. *Application contact:* Sandra Meyers, Graduate Admissions Analyst, 985-549-2066, Fax: 985-549-5632, E-mail: admissions@selu.edu.
Website: http://www.selu.edu/acad_research/depts/edlt.

Southeastern Oklahoma State University, School of Education, Durant, OK 74701-0609. Offers math specialist (M Ed); reading specialist (M Ed); school administration (M Ed); school counseling (M Ed). *Accreditation:* NCATE. Part-time and evening/

weekend programs available. *Degree requirements:* For master's, comprehensive exam, thesis optional, portfolio (M Ed). *Entrance requirements:* For master's, GRE General Test (for school counseling), minimum GPA of 3.0 in last 60 hours or 2.75 overall. Additional exam requirements/recommendations for international students: Required—TOEFL (minimum score 550 paper-based; 79 iBT). Electronic applications accepted.

Southeastern University, College of Education, Lakeland, FL 33801-6099. Offers educational leadership (M Ed); elementary education (M Ed); teaching and learning (M Ed).

Southeast Missouri State University, School of Graduate Studies, Department of Educational Leadership and Counseling, Program in Educational Administration, Cape Girardeau, MO 63701-4799. Offers educational administration (Ed S); educational leadership development (Ed S); elementary administration and supervision (MA); higher education administration (MA); school administration (MA); secondary administration and supervision (MA); teacher leadership (MA). *Accreditation:* NCATE. Part-time and evening/weekend programs available. *Faculty:* 6 full-time (3 women), 4 part-time/adjunct (1 woman). *Students:* 48 full-time (27 women), 181 part-time (118 women); includes 18 minority (11 Black or African American, non-Hispanic/Latino; 1 American Indian or Alaska Native, non-Hispanic/Latino; 2 Asian, non-Hispanic/Latino; 3 Hispanic/Latino; 1 Two or more races, non-Hispanic/Latino), 2 international. Average age 34. 83 applicants, 100% accepted, 83 enrolled. In 2013, 88 master's, 28 other advanced degrees awarded. *Degree requirements:* For master's and Ed S, comprehensive exam, thesis or alternative, paper. *Entrance requirements:* For master's, minimum undergraduate GPA of 2.75, valid teacher certification; for Ed S, minimum graduate GPA of 3.5; master's degree; valid teaching certificate. Additional exam requirements/recommendations for international students: Required—TOEFL (minimum score 550 paper-based; 79 iBT), IELTS (minimum score 6), PTE (minimum score 53). *Application deadline:* For fall admission, 8/1 for domestic students, 6/1 for international students; for spring admission, 11/21 for domestic students, 10/1 for international students; for summer admission, 5/15 for domestic students. Applications are processed on a rolling basis. Application fee: $30 ($40 for international students). Electronic applications accepted. *Expenses:* Tuition, state resident: full-time $5139; part-time $285.50 per credit hour. Tuition, nonresident: full-time $9099; part-time $505.50 per credit hour. *Financial support:* In 2013–14, 25 students received support. Career-related internships or fieldwork, Federal Work-Study, scholarships/grants, traineeships, tuition waivers (full), and unspecified assistantships available. Financial award application deadline: 6/30; financial award applicants required to submit FAFSA. *Faculty research:* Learning and the technology push, administration and student success, ethics of leaders. *Unit head:* Dr. Ruth Ann Williams, Professor/Interim Chair, Department of Educational Leadership and Counseling, 573-651-2417, E-mail: raroberts@semo.edu. *Application contact:* Alisa Aleen McFerron, Assistant Director of Admissions for Operations, 573-651-5937, E-mail: amcferron@semo.edu.
Website: http://www4.semo.edu/edadmin/admin.

Southern Adventist University, School of Education and Psychology, Collegedale, TN 37315-0370. Offers clinical mental health counseling (MS); inclusive education (MS Ed); instructional leadership (MS Ed); literacy education (MS Ed); outdoor teacher education (MS Ed); school counseling (MS). *Accreditation:* NCATE. Part-time and evening/weekend programs available. *Degree requirements:* For master's, comprehensive exam (for some programs), thesis optional, position paper (MS), portfolio (MS Ed in outdoor teacher education). *Entrance requirements:* For master's, interview (MS); 9 semester hours of upper-division course work in psychology or related field, including 1 course in psychology research or statistics; 9 semester hours of education (MS Ed). Additional exam requirements/recommendations for international students: Required—TOEFL (minimum score 600 paper-based; 100 iBT). Electronic applications accepted.

Southern Arkansas University–Magnolia, Graduate Programs, Magnolia, AR 71753. Offers agriculture (MS); business administration (MBA); computer and information sciences (MS); education (M Ed), including counseling and development, curriculum and instruction, educational administration and supervision, elementary education, reading, secondary education, TESOL; kinesiology (M Ed); library media and information specialist (M Ed); mental health and clinical counseling (MS); public administration (MPA); school counseling (M Ed); teaching (MAT). *Accreditation:* NCATE. Part-time and evening/weekend programs available. Postbaccalaureate distance learning degree programs offered. *Faculty:* 34 full-time (15 women), 8 part-time/adjunct (5 women). *Students:* 48 full-time (22 women), 269 part-time (167 women); includes 85 minority (78 Black or African American, non-Hispanic/Latino; 2 Asian, non-Hispanic/Latino; 2 Hispanic/Latino; 1 Native Hawaiian or other Pacific Islander, non-Hispanic/Latino; 2 Two or more races, non-Hispanic/Latino), 5 international. Average age 33. 149 applicants, 73% accepted, 109 enrolled. In 2013, 149 master's awarded. *Degree requirements:* For master's, comprehensive exam (for some programs), thesis optional. *Entrance requirements:* For master's, GRE, MAT or GMAT, minimum GPA of 2.5. Additional exam requirements/recommendations for international students: Required—TOEFL, IELTS. *Application deadline:* For fall admission, 7/10 for domestic and international students; for winter admission, 12/1 for domestic and international students; for spring admission, 12/1 for domestic and international students; for summer admission, 4/1 for domestic students. Applications are processed on a rolling basis. Application fee: $25 ($50 for international students). Electronic applications accepted. *Expenses:* Tuition, state resident: part-time $254 per credit hour. Tuition, nonresident: part-time $370 per credit hour. *Required fees:* $136 per credit hour. $259 per semester. Tuition and fees vary according to course load and program. *Financial support:* Career-related internships or fieldwork, Federal Work-Study, scholarships/grants, tuition waivers (full), and unspecified assistantships available. Financial award applicants required to submit FAFSA. *Faculty research:* Alternative certification for teachers, supervision of instruction, instructional leadership, counseling. *Unit head:* Dr. Kim Bloss, Dean, School of Graduate Studies, 870-235-4150, Fax: 870-235-5227, E-mail: kkbloss@saumag.edu. *Application contact:* Shrijana Malaka, Admissions Specialist, 870-235-4150, Fax: 870-235-5227, E-mail: smalakar@saumag.edu.
Website: http://www.saumag.edu/graduate.

Southern Connecticut State University, School of Graduate Studies, School of Education, Department of Educational Leadership, New Haven, CT 06515-1355. Offers educational foundations (Diploma), including foundational studies; educational leadership (Ed D, Diploma); research, statistics, and measurement (MS). Part-time and evening/weekend programs available. *Entrance requirements:* For degree, master's degree, minimum GPA of 3.0, writing sample. Electronic applications accepted.

Southern Illinois University Carbondale, Graduate School, College of Education and Human Services, Department of Educational Administration and Higher Education, Program in Educational Administration, Carbondale, IL 62901-4701. Offers MS Ed, PhD. PhD offered jointly with Southeast Missouri State University. *Accreditation:* NCATE. Part-time programs available. *Faculty:* 9 full-time (3 women). *Students:* 8 full-time (6 women), 74 part-time (38 women); includes 18 minority (15 Black or African American, non-Hispanic/Latino; 1 American Indian or Alaska Native, non-Hispanic/Latino; 1 Asian, non-Hispanic/Latino; 1 Hispanic/Latino), 2 international. 19 applicants, 42% accepted, 5 enrolled. In 2013, 6 master's, 3 doctorates awarded. *Degree requirements:* For master's, thesis or alternative; for doctorate, thesis/dissertation. *Entrance requirements:* For master's, GRE General Test, MAT, minimum GPA of 2.7; for doctorate, GRE General Test, MAT, minimum GPA of 3.5. Additional exam requirements/recommendations for international students: Required—TOEFL. *Application deadline:* For fall admission, 5/15 for domestic students; for spring admission, 9/15 for domestic students. Applications are processed on a rolling basis. Application fee: $50. *Financial support:* In 2013–14, 7 students received support, including 1 research assistantship with full tuition reimbursement available, 3 teaching assistantships with full tuition reimbursements available; fellowships with full tuition reimbursements available, career-related internships or fieldwork, Federal Work-Study, institutionally sponsored loans, and tuition waivers (full) also available. Support available to part-time students. Financial award application deadline: 4/1. *Faculty research:* School principalship, history and philosophy of education, supervision. *Unit head:* Dr. Keith Wilson, Chair, 618-536-4434, Fax: 618-453-4338, E-mail: kbwilson@siu.edu. *Application contact:* Pam Battaglia, Admissions Secretary, 618-536-4434, Fax: 618-453-4338, E-mail: pbatta@siu.edu.

Southern Illinois University Edwardsville, Graduate School, School of Education, Department of Educational Leadership, Program in Educational Administration, Edwardsville, IL 62026. Offers MS Ed, Ed S. *Accreditation:* NCATE. Part-time and evening/weekend programs available. *Students:* 3 full-time (2 women), 141 part-time (85 women); includes 26 minority (20 Black or African American, non-Hispanic/Latino; 2 Hispanic/Latino; 4 Two or more races, non-Hispanic/Latino). 7 applicants, 100% accepted. In 2013, 59 master's, 12 Ed Ss awarded. *Degree requirements:* For master's, thesis or alternative, portfolio. *Entrance requirements:* Additional exam requirements/recommendations for international students: Required—TOEFL (minimum score 550 paper-based, 79 iBT), IELTS (minimum score 6.5), Michigan Test of English Language Proficiency or PTE. *Application deadline:* For fall admission, 7/18 for domestic students, 6/1 for international students; for spring admission, 12/12 for domestic students, 10/1 for international students; for summer admission, 4/24 for domestic students, 3/1 for international students. Applications are processed on a rolling basis. Application fee: $30. Electronic applications accepted. *Expenses:* Tuition, state resident: full-time $3551. Tuition, nonresident: full-time $8378. *Financial support:* Fellowships with tuition reimbursements, research assistantships with full tuition reimbursements, teaching assistantships with tuition reimbursements, institutionally sponsored loans, scholarships/grants, and unspecified assistantships available. Financial award application deadline: 3/1; financial award applicants required to submit FAFSA. *Unit head:* Dr. Allison Reeves, Program Director, 618-650-3297, E-mail: alireev@siue.edu. *Application contact:* Melissa K. Mace, Assistant Director of Graduate and International Recruitment, 618-650-2756, Fax: 618-650-3618, E-mail: mmace@siue.edu.
Website: http://www.siue.edu/education/edld/.

Southern Illinois University Edwardsville, Graduate School, School of Education, Department of Educational Leadership, Program in Educational Leadership, Edwardsville, IL 62026. Offers Ed D. Part-time and evening/weekend programs available. *Students:* 18 part-time (11 women); includes 3 minority (all Black or African American, non-Hispanic/Latino). In 2013, 14 doctorates awarded. *Degree requirements:* For doctorate, thesis/dissertation or alternative, project. *Entrance requirements:* For doctorate, GRE. Additional exam requirements/recommendations for international students: Required—TOEFL (minimum score 550 paper-based, 79 iBT), IELTS (minimum score 6.5), Michigan Test of English Language Proficiency or PTE. *Application deadline:* For fall admission, 4/1 for domestic and international students; for spring admission, 12/7 for domestic students, 10/1 for international students. Application fee: $30. Electronic applications accepted. *Expenses:* Tuition, state resident: full-time $3551. Tuition, nonresident: full-time $8378. *Financial support:* Institutionally sponsored loans, scholarships/grants, and unspecified assistantships available. Financial award application deadline: 3/1; financial award applicants required to submit FAFSA. *Unit head:* Dr. Allison Reeves, Program Director, 618-650-3297, E-mail: alireev@siue.edu. *Application contact:* Melissa K. Mace, Assistant Director of Graduate and International Recruitment, 618-650-2756, Fax: 618-650-3618, E-mail: mmace@siue.edu.
Website: http://www.siue.edu/education/edld/.

Southern New Hampshire University, School of Education, Manchester, NH 03106-1045. Offers business education (M Ed); child development (M Ed); curriculum and instruction (M Ed), including education leadership, reading, special education, technology integration; education (M Ed); educational leadership (M Ed, Ed D); educational studies (M Ed); elementary education (M Ed); English (MAT); English for speakers of other languages (M Ed); reading and writing specialist (M Ed); school business administration (Certificate); secondary education (M Ed); special education (M Ed); technology integration specialist (M Ed). Part-time and evening/weekend programs available. Postbaccalaureate distance learning degree programs offered (no on-campus study). *Degree requirements:* For master's, comprehensive exam (for some programs), thesis or alternative. *Entrance requirements:* For master's, PRAXIS I, minimum GPA of 2.75. Additional exam requirements/recommendations for international students: Required—TOEFL (minimum score 550 paper-based). Electronic applications accepted. *Expenses:* Contact institution.

Southern Oregon University, Graduate Studies, School of Education, Ashland, OR 97520. Offers elementary education (MA Ed, MS Ed), including classroom teacher, early childhood, handicapped learner, reading, supervision; secondary education (MA Ed, MS Ed), including classroom teacher, handicapped learner, reading, supervision; teaching (MAT). Postbaccalaureate distance learning degree programs offered (minimal on-campus study). *Faculty:* 23 full-time (16 women), 21 part-time/adjunct (20 women). *Students:* 92 full-time (68 women), 118 part-time (88 women); includes 19 minority (1 Black or African American, non-Hispanic/Latino; 1 American Indian or Alaska Native, non-Hispanic/Latino; 2 Asian, non-Hispanic/Latino; 10 Hispanic/Latino; 5 Two or more races, non-Hispanic/Latino), 5 international. Average age 36. 22 applicants, 59% accepted, 12 enrolled. In 2013, 127 master's awarded. *Degree requirements:* For master's, thesis optional. *Entrance requirements:* For master's, GRE General Test, minimum cumulative GPA of 3.0 in the last 90 quarter credits (60 semester credits) of undergraduate coursework. Additional exam requirements/recommendations for international students: Required—TOEFL (minimum score 540 paper-based; 76 iBT), IELTS (minimum score 6), ELPT (minimum score 964) or ELS (minimum score 112). *Application deadline:* For fall admission, 7/31 priority date for domestic and international students; for winter admission, 11/15 priority date for domestic and international students; for spring admission, 1/7 priority date for domestic and international students. Applications are processed on a rolling basis. Application fee: $50. Electronic applications accepted. *Expenses:* Tuition, state resident: full-time $13,635; part-time $378.72 per credit hour. Tuition, nonresident: full-time $17,042; part-time $473.40 per credit hour. *Required fees:* $408 per quarter. *Financial support:* Research assistantships with partial tuition reimbursements, career-related internships or fieldwork, institutionally sponsored loans, scholarships/grants, and unspecified assistantships available. *Unit head:* Dr. Gerry McCain, Graduate Program Coordinator, 541-552-6934, E-mail: mccaing@sou.edu. *Application contact:* Kelly Moutsatson, Director of Admissions, 541-552-6411, Fax: 541-552-8403, E-mail: admissions@sou.edu.
Website: http://www.sou.edu/education/.

Southern University and Agricultural and Mechanical College, Graduate School, College of Education, Department of Behavioral Studies and Educational Leadership, Program in Administration and Supervision, Baton Rouge, LA 70813. Offers M Ed.

Southern University and Agricultural and Mechanical College, Graduate School, College of Education, Department of Behavioral Studies and Educational Leadership, Program in Educational Leadership, Baton Rouge, LA 70813. Offers M Ed. *Entrance requirements:* For master's, GRE General Test.

Southwest Baptist University, Program in Education, Bolivar, MO 65613-2597. Offers education (MS); educational administration (MS, Ed S). Part-time programs available. *Degree requirements:* For master's, comprehensive exam, thesis optional, 6-hour residency; for Ed S, comprehensive exam, 5-hour residency. *Entrance requirements:* For master's, GRE or PRAXIS II, interviews, minimum GPA of 2.75; for Ed S, master's degree. Additional exam requirements/recommendations for international students: Required—TOEFL (minimum score 550 paper-based). *Faculty research:* At-risk programs, principal retention, mentoring beginning principals.

Southwestern Adventist University, Education Department, Keene, TX 76059. Offers curriculum and instruction with reading emphasis (M Ed); educational leadership (M Ed). Part-time and evening/weekend programs available. *Degree requirements:* For master's, thesis or alternative, professional paper. *Entrance requirements:* For master's, GRE General Test.

Southwestern Assemblies of God University, Thomas F. Harrison School of Graduate Studies, Program in Education, Waxahachie, TX 75165-5735. Offers Christian school administration (MS); curriculum development (MS); early education administration (M Ed); middle and secondary education (M Ed). *Degree requirements:* For master's, comprehensive written and oral exams. *Entrance requirements:* For master's, GRE General Test, minimum GPA of 2.5. Electronic applications accepted.

Southwestern Oklahoma State University, College of Professional and Graduate Studies, School of Behavioral Sciences and Education, Specialization in Educational Administration, Weatherford, OK 73096-3098. Offers M Ed. M Ed distance learning degree program offered to Oklahoma residents only. *Accreditation:* NCATE. Part-time and evening/weekend programs available. Postbaccalaureate distance learning degree programs offered (minimal on-campus study). *Degree requirements:* For master's, exam. *Entrance requirements:* For master's, GRE General Test or minimum undergraduate GPA of 3.0, portfolio. Additional exam requirements/recommendations for international students: Required—TOEFL.

Southwest Minnesota State University, Department of Education, Marshall, MN 56258. Offers ESL (MS); math (MS); reading (MS); special education (MS), including developmental disabilities, early childhood education, emotional behavioral disorders, learning disabilities; teaching, learning and leadership (MS). Part-time and evening/weekend programs available. Postbaccalaureate distance learning degree programs offered (no on-campus study). *Entrance requirements:* Additional exam requirements/recommendations for international students: Required—TOEFL or IELTS; Recommended—TOEFL (minimum score 550 paper-based; 80 iBT), IELTS.

Spalding University, Graduate Studies, College of Education, Program in Leadership Education, Louisville, KY 40203-2188. Offers M Ed, Ed D. *Accreditation:* NCATE. Part-time and evening/weekend programs available. *Faculty:* 3 full-time (2 women). *Students:* 47 full-time (34 women), 33 part-time (22 women); includes 41 minority (40 Black or African American, non-Hispanic/Latino; 1 Hispanic/Latino), 5 international. Average age 40. 28 applicants, 68% accepted, 13 enrolled. In 2013, 6 master's, 16 doctorates awarded. *Degree requirements:* For doctorate, comprehensive exam, thesis/dissertation. *Entrance requirements:* For master's, GRE or MAT, interview, letters of recommendations, resume; for doctorate, GRE General Test or MAT, interview, letters of recommendations, resume. Additional exam requirements/recommendations for international students: Required—TOEFL (minimum score 535 paper-based). *Application deadline:* Applications are processed on a rolling basis. Electronic applications accepted. *Expenses: Tuition:* Full-time $21,450. *Required fees:* $810. Tuition and fees vary according to course load, degree level, program and student level. *Financial support:* Scholarships/grants and unspecified assistantships available. Financial award application deadline: 3/30; financial award applicants required to submit FAFSA. *Faculty research:* Leadership of schools, achievement gap, women in leadership. *Unit head:* Dr. Beverly Keepers, Dean, 502-873-4268, E-mail: bkeepers@spalding.edu. *Application contact:* Dr. Rita Greer, Director, 502-873-4265, E-mail: rgreer@spalding.edu.

Spalding University, Graduate Studies, College of Education, Programs in Education, Louisville, KY 40203-2188. Offers art teacher education (MAT); business teacher education (MAT); elementary school education (MAT); foreign language (MAT); general education (MA Ed); high school education (MAT); middle school education (MAT); school administration (MA Ed); secondary education (MAT); special education (learning and behavioral disorders) (MAT); student guidance counselor (MA); teacher education and professional development (MAT). *Accreditation:* NCATE. Part-time and evening/weekend programs available. *Faculty:* 12 full-time (11 women), 6 part-time/adjunct (4 women). *Students:* 92 full-time (63 women), 36 part-time (29 women); includes 43 minority (41 Black or African American, non-Hispanic/Latino; 2 Two or more races, non-Hispanic/Latino). Average age 35. 77 applicants, 48% accepted, 30 enrolled. In 2013, 81 master's awarded. *Degree requirements:* For master's, portfolio, final project, clinical experience. *Entrance requirements:* For master's, GRE General Test or MAT, interview, letters of recommendation, resume. Additional exam requirements/recommendations for international students: Required—TOEFL (minimum score 535 paper-based). *Application deadline:* Applications are processed on a rolling basis. Application fee: $30. Electronic applications accepted. *Expenses: Tuition:* Full-time $21,450. *Required fees:* $810. Tuition and fees vary according to course load, degree level, program and student level. *Financial support:* Scholarships/grants, traineeships, and unspecified assistantships available. Financial award application deadline: 3/30; financial award applicants required to submit FAFSA. *Faculty research:* Instructional technology, achievement gap, classroom management, assessment. *Unit head:* Dr. Beverly Keepers, Dean, 502-588-7121, Fax: 502-585-7123, E-mail: bkeepers@spalding.edu. *Application contact:* Bonnie Caughron, Administrative Assistant, College of Education, 502-873-4262, E-mail: bcaughron@spalding.edu.

Springfield College, Graduate Programs, Program in Education, Springfield, MA 01109-3797. Offers counseling and secondary education (M Ed, MS); early childhood education (M Ed, MS); education (M Ed, MS); educational administration (M Ed, MS); educational studies (M Ed, MS); elementary education (M Ed, MS); secondary education (M Ed, MS); special education (M Ed, MS). Part-time and evening/weekend programs available. *Faculty:* 6 full-time. *Students:* 47 full-time. 45 applicants, 87% accepted, 35 enrolled. In 2013, 15 master's awarded. *Entrance requirements:* Additional exam requirements/recommendations for international students: Required—TOEFL (minimum score 550 paper-based); Recommended—IELTS (minimum score 6). *Application deadline:* For fall admission, 1/15 for domestic and international students; for winter admission, 11/1 for domestic and international students; for spring admission, 11/1 for domestic and international students. Applications are processed on a rolling basis. Application fee: $50. Electronic applications accepted. *Expenses: Tuition:* Full-time $13,620; part-time $908 per credit. *Financial support:* Fellowships with partial tuition

reimbursements, teaching assistantships with partial tuition reimbursements, career-related internships or fieldwork, Federal Work-Study, institutionally sponsored loans, and unspecified assistantships available. Financial award application deadline: 3/1; financial award applicants required to submit FAFSA. *Unit head:* Jennifer Johnston, Program Coordinator, 413-748-3348, E-mail: jjohnston@springfieldcollege.edu. *Application contact:* Evelyn Cohen, Associate Director of Graduate Admissions, 413-748-3479, Fax: 413-748-3694, E-mail: ecohen@springfieldcollege.edu.

Stanford University, School of Education, Program in Policy, Organization, and Leadership Studies, Stanford, CA 94305-9991. Offers MA, MA/MBA. *Degree requirements:* For master's, thesis (for some programs). *Entrance requirements:* For master's, GRE General Test. Electronic applications accepted. *Expenses: Tuition:* Full-time $42,690; part-time $949 per credit. *Required fees:* $185.

State University of New York at Fredonia, Graduate Studies, College of Education, Program in Educational Administration, Fredonia, NY 14063-1136. Offers CAS. Part-time and evening/weekend programs available. *Degree requirements:* For CAS, thesis or alternative. *Expenses:* Tuition, state resident: full-time $7398; part-time $411 per credit hour. Tuition, nonresident: full-time $13,770; part-time $765 per credit hour. *Required fees:* $1143.90; $63.55 per credit hour. Tuition and fees vary according to course load.

State University of New York at New Paltz, Graduate School, School of Education, Department of Educational Administration, New Paltz, NY 12561. Offers educational leadership (MS Ed); school building leader (CAS); school district business leader (CAS); school district leader (CAS). Part-time and evening/weekend programs available. *Faculty:* 2 full-time (0 women), 12 part-time/adjunct (7 women). *Students:* 5 full-time (1 woman), 69 part-time (39 women); includes 14 minority (4 Black or African American, non-Hispanic/Latino; 1 Asian, non-Hispanic/Latino; 8 Hispanic/Latino; 1 Two or more races, non-Hispanic/Latino). Average age 40. 33 applicants, 97% accepted, 23 enrolled. In 2013, 3 master's, 46 CASs awarded. *Degree requirements:* For CAS, internship. *Entrance requirements:* For master's, GRE General Test or MAT, minimum GPA of 3.0, New York state teaching certificate; for CAS, minimum GPA of 3.0, proof of 3 years' teaching experience, New York state teaching certificate. Additional exam requirements/recommendations for international students: Required—TOEFL (minimum score 550 paper-based; 80 iBT), IELTS (minimum score 6.5). *Application deadline:* For fall admission, 5/15 priority date for domestic and international students; for spring admission, 11/15 priority date for domestic and international students. Applications are processed on a rolling basis. Application fee: $50. Electronic applications accepted. *Expenses:* Tuition, state resident: full-time $9870; part-time $411 per credit. Tuition, nonresident: full-time $18,350; part-time $765 per credit. *Required fees:* $1213. Tuition and fees vary according to program. *Financial support:* Application deadline: 8/1. *Faculty research:* Time management of administrators, social justice, women in educational leadership, diversity in educational leadership, superintendency. *Unit head:* Dr. Karen Bell, Program Director, 845-257-2810, E-mail: edadmin@newpaltz.edu. *Application contact:* Caroline Murphy, Graduate Admissions Advisor, 845-257-3285, Fax: 845-257-3284, E-mail: gradschool@newpaltz.edu. Website: http://www.newpaltz.edu/edadmin/.

State University of New York at Oswego, Graduate Studies, School of Education, Department of Educational Administration, Oswego, NY 13126. Offers educational administration and supervision (CAS); school building leadership (CAS). Part-time programs available. *Degree requirements:* For CAS, comprehensive exam, internship. *Entrance requirements:* For degree, interview, MA or MS, minimum GPA of 3.0, teaching certificate. Additional exam requirements/recommendations for international students: Required—TOEFL (minimum score 560 paper-based). *Faculty research:* Professional growth and development, leadership, governance, strategic planning, shared decision making.

State University of New York at Plattsburgh, Division of Education, Health, and Human Services, Program in Educational Leadership, Plattsburgh, NY 12901-2681. Offers CAS. Part-time and evening/weekend programs available. *Students:* 21 part-time (13 women). Average age 40. *Entrance requirements:* Additional exam requirements/recommendations for international students: Required—TOEFL. *Application deadline:* For fall admission, 2/15 priority date for domestic students; for spring admission, 10/15 priority date for domestic students. Applications are processed on a rolling basis. Application fee: $75. *Financial support:* Federal Work-Study available. Support available to part-time students. Financial award application deadline: 4/15; financial award applicants required to submit FAFSA. *Unit head:* Michael Johnson, Coordinator, 518-792-5425 Ext. 105, E-mail: johnsomj@plattsburgh.edu. *Application contact:* Betsy Kane, Director, Graduate Admissions, 518-564-4723, Fax: 518-564-4722, E-mail: bkane002@plattsburgh.edu.

State University of New York College at Cortland, Graduate Studies, School of Education, Program in Educational Leadership, Cortland, NY 13045. Offers school building leader (CAS); school building leader and school district leader (CAS); school district business leader (CAS); school district leader (CAS). Part-time and evening/weekend programs available. *Degree requirements:* For CAS, one foreign language. *Entrance requirements:* For degree, MS in education, permanent New York teaching certificate. Additional exam requirements/recommendations for international students: Required—TOEFL. *Expenses:* Tuition, state resident: full-time $9870; part-time $411 per credit hour. Tuition, nonresident: full-time $18,350; part-time $765 per credit hour. *Required fees:* $1458; $65 per credit hour.

Stephen F. Austin State University, Graduate School, College of Education, Department of Secondary Education and Educational Leadership, Nacogdoches, TX 75962. Offers educational leadership (Ed D); secondary education (M Ed). *Accreditation:* NCATE. *Degree requirements:* For master's, comprehensive exam; for doctorate, thesis/dissertation. *Entrance requirements:* For master's, GRE General Test; for doctorate, GRE General Test, interview, writing sample. Additional exam requirements/recommendations for international students: Required—TOEFL. Electronic applications accepted.

Stetson University, College of Arts and Sciences, Division of Education, Department of Teacher Education, Program in Educational Leadership, DeLand, FL 32723. Offers M Ed. *Accreditation:* NCATE. Evening/weekend programs available. *Faculty:* 7 full-time (5 women). *Students:* 40 full-time (27 women), 2 part-time (1 woman); includes 11 minority (4 Black or African American, non-Hispanic/Latino; 5 Hispanic/Latino; 2 Two or more races, non-Hispanic/Latino). Average age 33. 28 applicants, 93% accepted, 24 enrolled. In 2013, 38 master's awarded. *Degree requirements:* For master's, comprehensive exam. *Entrance requirements:* For master's, GRE or MAT. Additional exam requirements/recommendations for international students: Required—TOEFL (minimum score 90 iBT), IELTS (minimum score 7). *Application deadline:* For fall admission, 8/1 priority date for domestic students; for spring admission, 1/1 priority date for domestic students; for summer admission, 5/1 priority date for domestic students. Applications are processed on a rolling basis. Application fee: $50. Electronic applications accepted. *Financial support:* Career-related internships or fieldwork available. *Unit head:* Dr. Glen Epley, Interim Director, 386-822-7075. *Application contact:* Jamie Vanderlip, Assistant Director of Graduate Admissions, 386-822-7100, Fax: 386-822-7112, E-mail: jlszarol@stetson.edu.

Educational Leadership and Administration

Stony Brook University, State University of New York, School of Professional Development, Stony Brook, NY 11794. Offers biology (MAT); chemistry (MAT); coaching (Graduate Certificate); earth science (MAT); educational computing (Graduate Certificate); educational leadership (Advanced Certificate); English (MAT); environmental management (Graduate Certificate); French (MAT); German (MAT); higher education administration (MA, Certificate); human resource management (MS, Graduate Certificate); industrial management (Graduate Certificate); information systems management (Graduate Certificate); Italian (MAT); liberal studies (MA); mathematics (MAT); operations research (Graduate Certificate); physics (MAT); school district business leadership (Advanced Certificate); social science and the professions (MPS), including environmental management, human resource management; social studies (MAT); Spanish (MAT). Part-time and evening/weekend programs available. Postbaccalaureate distance learning degree programs offered. *Faculty:* 2 full-time (1 woman), 70 part-time/adjunct (30 women). *Students:* 241 full-time (135 women), 954 part-time (673 women); includes 209 minority (65 Black or African American, non-Hispanic/Latino; 2 American Indian or Alaska Native, non-Hispanic/Latino; 32 Asian, non-Hispanic/Latino; 104 Hispanic/Latino; 6 Two or more races, non-Hispanic/Latino), 7 international. Average age 28. 353 applicants, 92% accepted, 248 enrolled. In 2013, 312 master's, 131 other advanced degrees awarded. *Degree requirements:* For master's, one foreign language, thesis or alternative. *Application deadline:* For fall admission, 1/15 for domestic students; for spring admission, 10/1 for domestic students. Applications are processed on a rolling basis. Application fee: $100. *Expenses:* Tuition, state resident: full-time $9870; part-time $411 per credit. Tuition, nonresident: full-time $18,350; part-time $765 per credit. *Financial support:* Fellowships, research assistantships, teaching assistantships, and career-related internships or fieldwork available. Support available to part-time students. *Unit head:* Dr. Thomas Sexton, Interim Dean, 631-632-7181, Fax: 631-632-9046, E-mail: thomas.sexton@stonybrook.edu. *Application contact:* 631-632-7050 Ext. 1, E-mail: spd@stonybrook.edu.
Website: http://www.stonybrook.edu/spd/.

Sul Ross State University, Rio Grande College of Sul Ross State University, Alpine, TX 79832. Offers business administration (MBA); teacher education (M Ed), including bilingual education, counseling, educational diagnostics, elementary education, general education, reading, school administration, secondary education. Part-time and evening/weekend programs available. Postbaccalaureate distance learning degree programs offered (no on-campus study). *Degree requirements:* For master's, comprehensive exam, thesis optional, minimum GPA of 3.0. *Entrance requirements:* For master's, GMAT or GRE General Test, minimum GPA of 2.5 in last 60 hours of undergraduate work. Additional exam requirements/recommendations for international students: Required—TOEFL.

Sul Ross State University, School of Professional Studies, Department of Teacher Education, Program in School Administration, Alpine, TX 79832. Offers M Ed. Part-time and evening/weekend programs available. *Degree requirements:* For master's, thesis optional. *Entrance requirements:* For master's, GMAT or GRE General Test, minimum GPA of 2.5 in last 60 hours of undergraduate work.

Syracuse University, School of Education, Program in Educational Leadership, Syracuse, NY 13244. Offers MS, Ed D, CAS. Part-time programs available. *Students:* 5 full-time (3 women), 81 part-time (59 women); includes 13 minority (8 Black or African American, non-Hispanic/Latino; 2 Asian, non-Hispanic/Latino; 1 Hispanic/Latino; 2 Two or more races, non-Hispanic/Latino). Average age 41. 24 applicants, 42% accepted, 3 enrolled. In 2013, 1 master's, 7 other advanced degrees awarded. *Degree requirements:* For master's, thesis or alternative; for doctorate, comprehensive exam, thesis/dissertation; for CAS, thesis. *Entrance requirements:* For doctorate, GRE, master's degree, writing sample, resume; for CAS, master's degree, minimum three years of teaching experience, resume. Additional exam requirements/recommendations for international students: Required—TOEFL (minimum score 100 iBT). *Application deadline:* For fall admission, 2/1 priority date for domestic and international students; for spring admission, 10/15 priority date for domestic and international students. Applications are processed on a rolling basis. Application fee: $75. Electronic applications accepted. *Financial support:* Fellowships with full tuition reimbursements, research assistantships with full and partial tuition reimbursements, and teaching assistantships with full and partial tuition reimbursements available. Financial award application deadline: 1/1; financial award applicants required to submit FAFSA. *Unit head:* Dr. Joseph Shedd, Program Coordinator, 315-443-1468, E-mail: jbshedd@syr.edu. *Application contact:* Laurie Deyo, Graduate Recruiter, School of Education, 315-443-2505, E-mail: e-gradrcrt@syr.edu.
Website: http://soe.syr.edu/academic/teaching_and_leadership/graduate/CAS/educational_leadership/default.aspx.

Syracuse University, School of Education, Program in School District Business Leadership, Syracuse, NY 13244. Offers CAS. Part-time programs available. *Students:* 1 applicant. *Degree requirements:* For CAS, thesis or alternative, internship. *Entrance requirements:* For degree, master's degree, resume. Additional exam requirements/recommendations for international students: Required—TOEFL (minimum score 100 iBT). *Application deadline:* For fall admission, 1/15 priority date for domestic and international students. Applications are processed on a rolling basis. Electronic applications accepted. *Unit head:* Dr. Joseph Shedd, Co-Coordinator, 315-443-2685, E-mail: jbshedd@syr.edu. *Application contact:* Laurie Deyo, Graduate Recruiter, School of Education, 315-443-2505, E-mail: e-gradrcrt@syr.edu.
Website: http://soeweb.syr.edu/academic/teaching_and_leadership/graduate/CAS/school_district_business_leadership/default.aspx.

Tarleton State University, College of Graduate Studies, College of Education, Department of Educational Leadership and Policy Studies, Stephenville, TX 76402. Offers educational administration (M Ed); educational leadership (Ed D, Certificate). Part-time and evening/weekend programs available. Postbaccalaureate distance learning degree programs offered (minimal on-campus study). *Faculty:* 9 full-time (3 women), 5 part-time/adjunct (3 women). *Students:* 28 full-time (27 women), 162 part-time (103 women); includes 46 minority (23 Black or African American, non-Hispanic/Latino; 5 American Indian or Alaska Native, non-Hispanic/Latino; 1 Asian, non-Hispanic/Latino; 14 Hispanic/Latino; 3 Two or more races, non-Hispanic/Latino). Average age 39. 27 applicants, 89% accepted, 21 enrolled. In 2013, 58 master's, 8 doctorates awarded. *Degree requirements:* For master's, comprehensive exam, thesis optional; for doctorate, thesis/dissertation. *Entrance requirements:* For master's, GRE General Test, minimum GPA of 3.0; for doctorate, GRE, 4 letters of reference, leadership portfolio. Additional exam requirements/recommendations for international students: Required—TOEFL (minimum score 550 paper-based; 80 iBT). *Application deadline:* For fall admission, 8/15 priority date for domestic students; for spring admission, 1/7 for domestic students. Applications are processed on a rolling basis. Application fee: $30 ($130 for international students). Electronic applications accepted. *Expenses:* Tuition, state resident: full-time $3312; part-time $184 per credit hour. Tuition, nonresident: full-time $9144; part-time $508 per credit hour. *Required fees:* $1916. Tuition and fees vary according to course load and campus/location. *Financial support:* Teaching assistantships, career-related internships or fieldwork, Federal Work-Study, and institutionally sponsored loans available. Support available to part-time students. Financial award application deadline: 5/1; financial award applicants required to submit FAFSA. *Unit head:* Dr. Mark Littleton,

Interim Department Head, 254-968-9804, Fax: 254-968-9979, E-mail: mlittleton@tarleton.edu. *Application contact:* Information Contact, 254-968-9104, Fax: 254-968-9670, E-mail: gradoffice@tarleton.edu.
Website: http://www.tarleton.edu/COEWEB/edlps.

Tarleton State University, College of Graduate Studies, College of Education, Department of Psychology and Counseling, Stephenville, TX 76402. Offers counseling and psychology (M Ed), including counseling, counseling psychology, educational psychology; educational administration (M Ed); secondary education (Certificate); special education (Certificate). Part-time and evening/weekend programs available. Postbaccalaureate distance learning degree programs offered (minimal on-campus study). *Faculty:* 8 full-time (6 women), 14 part-time/adjunct (7 women). *Students:* 60 full-time (48 women), 183 part-time (157 women); includes 63 minority (21 Black or African American, non-Hispanic/Latino; 3 Asian, non-Hispanic/Latino; 30 Hispanic/Latino; 9 Two or more races, non-Hispanic/Latino). Average age 34. 78 applicants, 81% accepted, 47 enrolled. In 2013, 76 master's awarded. *Degree requirements:* For master's, comprehensive exam, thesis optional. *Entrance requirements:* For master's, GRE General Test, minimum GPA of 3.0. Additional exam requirements/recommendations for international students: Required—TOEFL (minimum score 550 paper-based; 80 iBT). *Application deadline:* For fall admission, 8/15 priority date for domestic students; for spring admission, 1/7 for domestic students. Applications are processed on a rolling basis. Application fee: $30 ($130 for international students). Electronic applications accepted. *Expenses:* Tuition, state resident: full-time $3312; part-time $184 per credit hour. Tuition, nonresident: full-time $9144; part-time $508 per credit hour. *Required fees:* $1916. Tuition and fees vary according to course load and campus/location. *Financial support:* Research assistantships, teaching assistantships, career-related internships or fieldwork, Federal Work-Study, institutionally sponsored loans, and tuition waivers (partial) available. Support available to part-time students. Financial award application deadline: 5/1; financial award applicants required to submit FAFSA. *Unit head:* Dr. Bob Newby, Department Head, 254-968-9813, Fax: 254-968-1991, E-mail: newby@tarleton.edu. *Application contact:* Information Contact, 254-968-9104, Fax: 254-968-9670, E-mail: gradoffice@tarleton.edu.
Website: http://www.tarleton.edu/COEWEB/pc/.

Teachers College, Columbia University, Graduate Faculty of Education, Department of Organization and Leadership, New York, NY 10027-6696. Offers adult education guided intensive study (Ed D); adult learning and leadership (Ed M, MA, Ed D); higher education (Ed M, MA, Ed D); inquiry in education leadership (Ed D); nurse executive (MA, Ed D), including administration studies (MA), nurse executive (Ed D), professorial studies (MA); social and organizational psychology (MA), including change leadership, social-organizational psychology. Part-time and evening/weekend programs available. *Faculty:* 27 full-time, 25 part-time/adjunct. *Students:* 287 full-time (183 women), 490 part-time (322 women); includes 292 minority (112 Black or African American, non-Hispanic/Latino; 74 Asian, non-Hispanic/Latino; 84 Hispanic/Latino; 22 Two or more races, non-Hispanic/Latino), 81 international. Average age 33. 526 applicants, 57% accepted, 132 enrolled. In 2013, 356 master's, 25 doctorates awarded. *Degree requirements:* For doctorate, thesis/dissertation. Application fee: $65. *Financial support:* Fellowships, research assistantships, career-related internships or fieldwork, Federal Work-Study, institutionally sponsored loans, and tuition waivers (full and partial) available. Support available to part-time students. Financial award application deadline: 2/1. *Unit head:* Prof. Anna Neumann, Chair, 212-678-3258, Fax: 212-678-3036, E-mail: an350@columbia.edu. *Application contact:* Debbie Lesperance, Assistant Director of Admission, 212-678-3710, Fax: 212-678-4171.

Temple University, College of Education, Department of Psychological Studies in Education, Department of Educational Leadership and Policy Studies, Philadelphia, PA 19122-6096. Offers educational leadership (Ed D), including higher education, K-12. Part-time and evening/weekend programs available. *Faculty:* 7 full-time (3 women). *Students:* 10 full-time (7 women), 66 part-time (42 women); includes 20 minority (15 Black or African American, non-Hispanic/Latino; 1 American Indian or Alaska Native, non-Hispanic/Latino; 1 Asian, non-Hispanic/Latino; 3 Hispanic/Latino), 24 international. 58 applicants, 69% accepted, 24 enrolled. In 2013, 6 master's awarded. Terminal master's awarded for partial completion of doctoral program. *Degree requirements:* For master's, comprehensive exam, thesis or alternative, internship; for doctorate, thesis/dissertation, preliminary exam. *Entrance requirements:* For master's, GRE General Test or MAT, minimum undergraduate GPA of 3.0, 2 letters of recommendation, goal statement, resume; for doctorate, GRE General Test or MAT, minimum undergraduate GPA of 3.0, 3 letters of recommendation, goal statement, resume. Additional exam requirements/recommendations for international students: Required—TOEFL (minimum score 550 paper-based; 79 iBT). *Application deadline:* For fall admission, 1/5 for domestic students, 10/7 for international students; for spring admission, 11/1 for domestic students, 11/3 for international students. Application fee: $60. Electronic applications accepted. *Financial support:* In 2013–14, 2 students received support, including 1 research assistantship with full tuition reimbursement available (averaging $20,333 per year), 1 teaching assistantship with full tuition reimbursement available (averaging $17,046 per year); career-related internships or fieldwork, Federal Work-Study, scholarships/grants, health care benefits, and unspecified assistantships also available. Financial award application deadline: 1/15; financial award applicants required to submit FAFSA. *Faculty research:* School leadership, educational policy, educational accountability, democratic leadership, equity and access. *Unit head:* Dr. Joan Shapiro, Professor, 215-204-6645, E-mail: joan.shapiro@temple.edu. *Application contact:* Felicia Neuber, Enrollment Management, 215-204-8011, E-mail: educate@temple.edu.
Website: http://education.temple.edu/leadership.

Tennessee State University, The School of Graduate Studies and Research, College of Education, Department of Educational Administration, Nashville, TN 37209-1561. Offers administration and supervision (M Ed, Ed D, Ed S). *Accreditation:* NCATE. *Entrance requirements:* For master's, GRE General Test, GRE Subject Test, minimum GPA of 2.5; for doctorate, GRE General Test, MAT, interview, minimum GPA of 3.25, work experience.

Tennessee Technological University, College of Graduate Studies, College of Education, Department of Curriculum and Instruction, Program in Instructional Leadership, Cookeville, TN 38505. Offers MA, Ed S. *Accreditation:* NCATE. Part-time and evening/weekend programs available. *Faculty:* 9 full-time (3 women). *Students:* 4 full-time (2 women), 45 part-time (23 women); includes 13 minority (12 Black or African American, non-Hispanic/Latino; 1 Hispanic/Latino). Average age 27. 29 applicants, 59% accepted, 8 enrolled. In 2013, 8 master's, 28 other advanced degrees awarded. *Degree requirements:* For master's and Ed S, comprehensive exam, thesis or alternative. *Entrance requirements:* For master's and Ed S, MAT or GRE. Additional exam requirements/recommendations for international students: Required—TOEFL (minimum score 527 paper-based; 71 iBT), IELTS (minimum score 5.5), PTE (minimum score 48), or TOEIC (Test of English as an International Communication). *Application deadline:* For fall admission, 8/1 for domestic students, 5/1 for international students; for spring admission, 12/1 for domestic students, 10/1 for international students. Applications are processed on a rolling basis. Application fee: $35 ($40 for international students). Electronic applications accepted. *Expenses:* Tuition, state resident: full-time $9347; part-time $465 per credit hour. Tuition, nonresident: full-time $23,635; part-time $1152

per credit hour. *Financial support:* In 2013–14, 33 fellowships (averaging $8,000 per year), 11 research assistantships (averaging $4,000 per year), 7 teaching assistantships (averaging $4,000 per year) were awarded; career-related internships or fieldwork also available. Financial award application deadline: 4/1. *Faculty research:* School board member training, community school education. *Unit head:* Dr. Jeremy Wendt, Interim Chairperson, 931-372-3181, Fax: 931-372-6270, E-mail: jwendt@tntech.edu. *Application contact:* Shelia K. Kendrick, Coordinator of Graduate Studies, 931-372-3808, Fax: 931-372-3497, E-mail: skendrick@tntech.edu.

Tennessee Temple University, Graduate Studies in Education, Program in Educational Leadership, Chattanooga, TN 37404-3587. Offers M Ed. *Degree requirements:* For master's, comprehensive exam, thesis or alternative. *Entrance requirements:* For master's, GRE, minimum cumulative undergraduate GPA of 3.0, 3 references.

Tennessee Wesleyan College, Department of Education, Athens, TN 37303. Offers curriculum leadership (MS). Evening/weekend programs available. *Degree requirements:* For master's, internship.

Texas A&M International University, Office of Graduate Studies and Research, College of Education, Department of Professional Programs, Laredo, TX 78041-1900. Offers educational administration (MS Ed); generic special education (MS Ed); school counseling (MS). *Faculty:* 7 full-time (4 women), 4 part-time/adjunct (2 women). *Students:* 19 full-time (18 women), 137 part-time (104 women); includes 150 minority (2 Black or African American, non-Hispanic/Latino; 148 Hispanic/Latino), 1 international. Average age 33. 61 applicants, 75% accepted, 42 enrolled. In 2013, 87 master's awarded. *Entrance requirements:* Additional exam requirements/recommendations for international students: Required—TOEFL (minimum score 550 paper-based; 79 iBT). *Application deadline:* For fall admission, 4/30 priority date for domestic students, 4/30 for international students; for spring admission, 11/30 priority date for domestic students, 10/1 for international students. Application fee: $35 ($50 for international students). *Expenses:* Tuition, state resident: full-time $5184. *International tuition:* $11,556 full-time. *Financial support:* In 2013–14, 5 students received support, including 1 teaching assistantship; fellowships, research assistantships, Federal Work-Study, scholarships/grants, and unspecified assistantships also available. Financial award application deadline: 4/1. *Unit head:* Dr. Randel Brown, Chair, 956-326-2679, E-mail: brown@tamiu.edu. *Application contact:* Suzanne H. Alford, Director of Admissions, 956-326-3023, E-mail: graduateschool@tamiu.edu.
Website: http://www.tamiu.edu/coedu/DOPPPrograms.shtml.

Texas A&M University, College of Education and Human Development, Department of Educational Administration and Human Resource Development, College Station, TX 77843. Offers educational administration (M Ed, MS, Ed D, PhD); educational human resource development (MS, PhD). Part-time programs available. *Faculty:* 33. *Students:* 109 full-time (77 women), 247 part-time (155 women); includes 139 minority (55 Black or African American, non-Hispanic/Latino; 11 Asian, non-Hispanic/Latino; 71 Hispanic/Latino; 2 Two or more races, non-Hispanic/Latino), 39 international. Average age 38. 139 applicants, 55% accepted, 63 enrolled. In 2013, 88 master's, 33 doctorates awarded. *Degree requirements:* For master's, thesis optional; for doctorate, thesis/dissertation. *Entrance requirements:* For master's, GRE General Test, writing exam, interview, professional experience; for doctorate, GRE General Test, writing exam, interview/presentation, professional experience. Additional exam requirements/recommendations for international students: Required—TOEFL. *Application deadline:* For fall admission, 12/1 for domestic and international students; for spring admission, 8/15 for domestic and international students. Application fee: $50 ($75 for international students). Electronic applications accepted. *Expenses:* Tuition, state resident: full-time $4078; part-time $226.55 per credit hour. Tuition, nonresident: full-time $10,450; part-time $580.55 per credit hour. *Required fees:* $2328; $278.50 per credit hour. $642.45 per semester. *Financial support:* In 2013–14, fellowships (averaging $20,000 per year), research assistantships (averaging $12,000 per year) were awarded; career-related internships or fieldwork and institutionally sponsored loans also available. Support available to part-time students. Financial award application deadline: 3/1; financial award applicants required to submit FAFSA. *Faculty research:* Higher education administration, public school administration, student affairs. *Unit head:* Dr. Fred M. Nafukho, Head, 979-862-3395, Fax: 979-862-4347, E-mail: fnafukho@tamu.edu. *Application contact:* Joyce Nelson, Director of Academic Advising, 979-847-9098, Fax: 979-862-4347, E-mail: jnelson@tamu.edu.
Website: http://eahr.tamu.edu.

Texas A&M University–Commerce, Graduate School, College of Education and Human Services, Department of Educational Leadership, Commerce, TX 75429-3011. Offers educational administration (M Ed, Ed D); educational technology (M Ed, MS); higher education (MS, Ed D); training and development (MS). Part-time programs available. Terminal master's awarded for partial completion of doctoral program. *Degree requirements:* For master's, comprehensive exam, thesis (for some programs); for doctorate, thesis/dissertation, departmental qualifying exam. *Entrance requirements:* For master's, GRE General Test; for doctorate, GRE General Test, writing skills exam, interview. Electronic applications accepted. *Expenses:* Tuition, state resident: full-time $3630; part-time $2420 per year. Tuition, nonresident: full-time $9948; part-time $6632.16 per year. *Required fees:* $1006 per year. Tuition and fees vary according to course load. *Faculty research:* Property tax reform, politics of education, administrative stress.

Texas A&M University–Corpus Christi, Graduate Studies and Research, College of Education, Program in Educational Administration, Corpus Christi, TX 78412-5503. Offers MS. Part-time and evening/weekend programs available. *Degree requirements:* For master's, comprehensive exam, thesis (for some programs). *Entrance requirements:* For master's, GRE General Test. Additional exam requirements/recommendations for international students: Required—TOEFL. Electronic applications accepted.

Texas A&M University–Corpus Christi, Graduate Studies and Research, College of Education, Program in Educational Leadership, Corpus Christi, TX 78412-5503. Offers Ed D. Program offered jointly with Texas A&M University–Kingsville. Part-time and evening/weekend programs available. *Degree requirements:* For doctorate, comprehensive exam, thesis/dissertation. *Entrance requirements:* Additional exam requirements/recommendations for international students: Required—TOEFL. Electronic applications accepted.

Texas A&M University–Kingsville, College of Graduate Studies, College of Education, Department of Education, Program in Higher Education Administration Leadership, Kingsville, TX 78363. Offers PhD. Program offered jointly with Texas A&M University. *Faculty:* 10 full-time (8 women), 9 part-time/adjunct (5 women). *Students:* 19 full-time (11 women), 58 part-time (40 women); includes 57 minority (2 Black or African American, non-Hispanic/Latino; 1 Asian, non-Hispanic/Latino; 54 Hispanic/Latino). Average age 42. 5 applicants, 80% accepted, 1 enrolled. In 2013, 11 doctorates awarded. *Degree requirements:* For doctorate, one foreign language, comprehensive exam, thesis/dissertation. *Entrance requirements:* For doctorate, GRE General Test, MAT, minimum GPA of 3.25. *Application deadline:* For fall admission, 6/1 for domestic students; for spring admission, 11/15 for domestic students. Applications are processed on a rolling basis. Application fee: $35 ($50 for international students). *Financial support:* Application deadline: 5/15. *Unit head:* Dr. Travis Polk, Chair, 361-593-3204. *Application contact:* Dr. Alberto M. Olivares, Dean, College of Graduate Studies, 361-593-2808, Fax: 361-593-3412, E-mail: a-olivares@tamuk.edu.

Texas A&M University–Kingsville, College of Graduate Studies, College of Education, Department of Education, Program in School Administration, Kingsville, TX 78363. Offers MA, MS, Ed D. Ed D offered jointly with Texas A&M University–Corpus Christi. Part-time and evening/weekend programs available. *Faculty:* 10 full-time (8 women), 9 part-time/adjunct (5 women). *Students:* 8 full-time (4 women), 54 part-time (34 women); includes 48 minority (5 Black or African American, non-Hispanic/Latino; 43 Hispanic/Latino). Average age 33. 21 applicants, 95% accepted, 12 enrolled. In 2013, 24 master's awarded. *Degree requirements:* For master's, comprehensive exam, mini-thesis; for doctorate, one foreign language, comprehensive exam, thesis/dissertation. *Entrance requirements:* For master's, GRE General Test, MAT, minimum GPA of 3.0; for doctorate, GRE General Test, MAT, minimum GPA of 3.25. *Application deadline:* For fall admission, 6/1 for domestic students; for spring admission, 11/15 for domestic students. Applications are processed on a rolling basis. Application fee: $35 ($50 for international students). *Financial support:* Application deadline: 5/15. *Faculty research:* Funding sources in public education. *Unit head:* Dr. Ronald McKenzie, Director, 361-593-3203, E-mail: kfrfm00@tamuk.edu. *Application contact:* Dr. Alberto M. Olivares, Dean, College of Graduate Studies, 361-593-2808, Fax: 361-593-3412, E-mail: a-olivares@tamuk.edu.

Texas A&M University–San Antonio, Department of Leadership and Counseling, San Antonio, TX 78224. Offers counseling and guidance (MA); educational leadership (MA). Part-time and evening/weekend programs available. *Degree requirements:* For master's, comprehensive exam, thesis or alternative. *Entrance requirements:* For master's, MAT. Additional exam requirements/recommendations for international students: Required—TOEFL (minimum score 550 paper-based; 80 iBT), IELTS (minimum score 6). Electronic applications accepted.

Texas A&M University–Texarkana, Graduate Studies and Research, College of Education and Liberal Arts, Texarkana, TX 75505-5518. Offers adult education (MS); curriculum and instruction (M Ed); education (MS); educational administration (M Ed); English (MA); instructional technology (MS); interdisciplinary studies (MA, MS); special education (MS). Part-time and evening/weekend programs available. *Degree requirements:* For master's, comprehensive exam (for some programs), thesis optional. *Entrance requirements:* For master's, minimum GPA of 2.5 on last 60 hours of bachelor's degree. Additional exam requirements/recommendations for international students: Required—TOEFL. Electronic applications accepted.

Texas Christian University, College of Education, Doctorate of Educational Leadership in Higher Education Program, Fort Worth, TX 76129-0002. Offers Ed D. Part-time and evening/weekend programs available. *Students:* 1 full-time (0 women), 14 part-time (7 women); includes 4 minority (1 Black or African American, non-Hispanic/Latino; 1 Asian, non-Hispanic/Latino; 2 Hispanic/Latino). Average age 37. 12 applicants, 83% accepted, 6 enrolled. *Degree requirements:* For doctorate, comprehensive exam, thesis/dissertation, field-based experience, dissertation/capstone experience. *Entrance requirements:* For doctorate, GRE or MAT. Additional exam requirements/recommendations for international students: Required—TOEFL (minimum score 550 paper-based; 80 iBT). *Application deadline:* For winter admission, 2/1 for domestic and international students. Electronic applications accepted. *Expenses: Tuition:* Part-time $1270 per credit hour. Tuition and fees vary according to course load and program. *Financial support:* Teaching assistantships with full tuition reimbursements, career-related internships or fieldwork, scholarships/grants, and unspecified assistantships available. Financial award application deadline: 2/1; financial award applicants required to submit FAFSA. *Unit head:* Dr. Jan Lacina, Associate Dean, 817-257-6786, E-mail: j.lacina@tcu.edu. *Application contact:* Lori Kimball, Administrative Program Specialist, 817-257-7661, E-mail: l.kimball@tcu.edu.
Website: http://www.coe.tcu.edu/graduate-students-graduate-programs.asp.

Texas Christian University, College of Education, Ed D in Educational Leadership Program, Fort Worth, TX 76129-0002. Offers educational leadership (Ed D); higher education (Ed D). Part-time and evening/weekend programs available. *Students:* 3 full-time (all women), 18 part-time (10 women); includes 5 minority (2 Black or African American, non-Hispanic/Latino; 1 Asian, non-Hispanic/Latino; 2 Hispanic/Latino), 1 international. Average age 36. 8 applicants, 75% accepted, 4 enrolled. In 2013, 10 doctorates awarded. *Degree requirements:* For doctorate, comprehensive exam, thesis/dissertation. *Entrance requirements:* For doctorate, GRE or MAT. Additional exam requirements/recommendations for international students: Required—TOEFL (minimum score 550 paper-based; 80 iBT). *Application deadline:* For winter admission, 2/1 for domestic and international students. Application fee: $60. Electronic applications accepted. *Expenses: Tuition:* Part-time $1270 per credit hour. Tuition and fees vary according to course load and program. *Financial support:* Teaching assistantships with full tuition reimbursements, career-related internships or fieldwork, scholarships/grants, and unspecified assistantships available. Financial award application deadline: 2/1; financial award applicants required to submit FAFSA. *Unit head:* Dr. Jan Lacina, Associate Dean, 817-257-6786, E-mail: j.lacina@tcu.edu. *Application contact:* Lori Kimball, Administrative Program Specialist, 817-257-7661, E-mail: l.kimball@tcu.edu.
Website: http://www.coe.tcu.edu/graduate-students-graduate-programs.asp.

Texas Christian University, College of Education, Master of Education in Educational Leadership Program, Fort Worth, TX 76129-0002. Offers educational leadership (M Ed); principal (Certificate). Part-time and evening/weekend programs available. *Students:* 3 full-time (2 women), 29 part-time (15 women); includes 9 minority (5 Black or African American, non-Hispanic/Latino; 1 Asian, non-Hispanic/Latino; 2 Hispanic/Latino; 1 Two or more races, non-Hispanic/Latino), 2 international. Average age 31. 22 applicants, 91% accepted, 16 enrolled. In 2013, 21 master's awarded. *Entrance requirements:* For master's, GRE or MAT. Additional exam requirements/recommendations for international students: Required—TOEFL (minimum score 550 paper-based; 80 iBT). *Application deadline:* For fall admission, 11/16 for domestic and international students; for spring admission, 3/1 for domestic and international students. Application fee: $60. Electronic applications accepted. *Expenses: Tuition:* Part-time $1270 per credit hour. Tuition and fees vary according to course load and program. *Financial support:* Teaching assistantships with full tuition reimbursements, career-related internships or fieldwork, scholarships/grants, and unspecified assistantships available. Financial award application deadline: 3/1; financial award applicants required to submit FAFSA. *Unit head:* Dr. Jan Lacina, Associate Dean, 817-257-6786, E-mail: j.lacina@tcu.edu. *Application contact:* Lori Kimball, Administrative Program Specialist, 817-257-7661, E-mail: l.kimball@tcu.edu.
Website: http://www.coe.tcu.edu/graduate-students-graduate-programs.asp.

Texas Christian University, Neeley School of Business at TCU, MBA/Ed D in Educational Leadership Joint Program, Fort Worth, TX 76129-0002. Offers MBA/Ed D. Part-time and evening/weekend programs available. *Entrance requirements:* Additional exam requirements/recommendations for international students: Required—TOEFL (minimum score 550 paper-based; 80 iBT). *Application deadline:* For fall admission, 2/1 for domestic and international students. Application fee: $60. *Expenses: Tuition:* Part-time $1270 per credit hour. Tuition and fees vary according to course load and program. *Financial support:* Teaching assistantships with full tuition reimbursements, career-related internships or fieldwork, scholarships/grants, and unspecified assistantships

available. Support available to part-time students. Financial award application deadline: 3/1; financial award applicants required to submit FAFSA. *Unit head:* Dr. Jan Lacina, Associate Dean, 817-257-6786, E-mail: j.lacina@tcu.edu. *Application contact:* Lori Kimball, Administrative Program Specialist, 817-257-7661, E-mail: l.kimball@tcu.edu.
Website: http://www.neeley.tcu.edu/Academics/MBA_Ed_D_Degree/MBA_Ed_D__Degree.aspx.

Texas Southern University, College of Education, Department of Educational Administration and Foundation, Houston, TX 77004-4584. Offers educational administration (M Ed, Ed D). Part-time and evening/weekend programs available. *Faculty:* 12 full-time (5 women), 5 part-time/adjunct (4 women). *Students:* 46 full-time (30 women), 56 part-time (37 women); includes 98 minority (96 Black or African American, non-Hispanic/Latino; 1 Asian, non-Hispanic/Latino; 1 Hispanic/Latino), 1 international. Average age 39. 45 applicants, 64% accepted, 23 enrolled. In 2013, 8 master's, 4 doctorates awarded. *Degree requirements:* For master's, comprehensive exam; for doctorate, comprehensive exam, thesis/dissertation. *Entrance requirements:* For master's, GRE General Test, minimum GPA of 2.5; for doctorate, GRE General Test or MAT, master's degree, minimum B+ average. Additional exam requirements/recommendations for international students: Required—TOEFL. *Application deadline:* For fall admission, 7/1 for domestic and international students; for spring admission, 11/1 for domestic and international students. Applications are processed on a rolling basis. Application fee: $50 ($75 for international students). Electronic applications accepted. *Financial support:* Fellowships, research assistantships, teaching assistantships, scholarships/grants, and unspecified assistantships available. Support available to part-time students. Financial award application deadline: 5/1. *Unit head:* Dr. Danita Bailey-Perry, Interim Chair, 713-313-4418, E-mail: bailey_dm@tsu.edu. *Application contact:* Dr. Gregory Maddox, Dean of the Graduate School, 713-313-7011 Ext. 4410, Fax: 713-639-1876, E-mail: maddox_gh@tsu.edu.
Website: http://www.tsu.edu/academics/colleges__schools/College_of_Education/Departments/default.php.

Texas State University, Graduate School, College of Education, Department of Counseling, Leadership, Adult Education, and School Psychology, Program in Educational Leadership and School Improvement, San Marcos, TX 78666. Offers education leadership (M Ed, MA); school improvement (PhD). Part-time and evening/weekend programs available. *Faculty:* 11 full-time (3 women). *Students:* 14 full-time (9 women), 149 part-time (108 women); includes 69 minority (11 Black or African American, non-Hispanic/Latino; 1 American Indian or Alaska Native, non-Hispanic/Latino; 1 Asian, non-Hispanic/Latino; 55 Hispanic/Latino; 1 Two or more races, non-Hispanic/Latino). Average age 38. 101 applicants, 50% accepted, 31 enrolled. In 2013, 46 master's, 8 doctorates awarded. *Degree requirements:* For master's, comprehensive exam, thesis (for some programs). *Entrance requirements:* For master's, GRE General Test (recommended), minimum GPA of 2.75 in last 60 hours of course work; for doctorate, GRE General Test (recommended), master's degree with minimum GPA of 3.5 in all related course work. Additional exam requirements/recommendations for international students: Required—TOEFL (minimum score 550 paper-based; 78 iBT), IELTS (minimum score 6.5). *Application deadline:* For fall admission, 6/15 for domestic students, 6/1 for international students. Applications are processed on a rolling basis. Application fee: $40 ($90 for international students). Electronic applications accepted. *Expenses:* Tuition, state resident: full-time $6663; part-time $278 per credit hour. Tuition, nonresident: full-time $15,159; part-time $632 per credit hour. *Required fees:* $1872; $54 per credit hour. $306 per term. Tuition and fees vary according to course load. *Financial support:* In 2013–14, 49 students received support, including 2 research assistantships (averaging $23,950 per year), 7 teaching assistantships (averaging $22,711 per year); career-related internships or fieldwork, Federal Work-Study, and institutionally sponsored loans also available. Support available to part-time students. Financial award application deadline: 4/1; financial award applicants required to submit FAFSA. *Faculty research:* Superintendency, middle management, supervision, junior college. *Unit head:* Dr. Trae Stewart, Graduate Advisor, 512-245-9909, E-mail: traestewart@txstate.edu. *Application contact:* Dr. Andrea Golato, Dean of Graduate School, 512-245-2581, Fax: 512-245-8365, E-mail: gradcollege@txstate.edu.
Website: http://www.txstate.edu/clas/Educational-Leadership.html.

Texas Tech University, Graduate School, College of Education, Department of Educational Psychology and Leadership, Lubbock, TX 79409-1071. Offers counselor education (M Ed, PhD); educational leadership (M Ed, Ed D); educational psychology (M Ed, PhD); higher education (M Ed, Ed D); higher education research (PhD); instructional technology (M Ed, Ed D); special education (M Ed, Ed D, PhD). *Accreditation:* ACA; NCATE. Part-time and evening/weekend programs available. Postbaccalaureate distance learning degree programs offered (minimal on-campus study). *Faculty:* 42 full-time (20 women). *Students:* 220 full-time (171 women), 549 part-time (404 women); includes 219 minority (73 Black or African American, non-Hispanic/Latino; 5 American Indian or Alaska Native, non-Hispanic/Latino; 6 Asian, non-Hispanic/Latino; 122 Hispanic/Latino; 13 Two or more races, non-Hispanic/Latino), 48 international. Average age 36. 437 applicants, 72% accepted, 215 enrolled. In 2013, 137 master's, 38 doctorates awarded. Terminal master's awarded for partial completion of doctoral program. *Degree requirements:* For master's, comprehensive exam, thesis optional; for doctorate, comprehensive exam, thesis/dissertation. *Entrance requirements:* For master's, GRE (for some programs); for doctorate, GRE. Additional exam requirements/recommendations for international students: Required—TOEFL (minimum score 550 paper-based; 79 iBT). *Application deadline:* For fall admission, 6/1 priority date for domestic students, 1/15 priority date for international students; for spring admission, 9/1 priority date for domestic students, 6/15 priority date for international students. Applications are processed on a rolling basis. Application fee: $60. Electronic applications accepted. *Expenses:* Tuition, state resident: full-time $6062; part-time $252.57 per credit hour. Tuition, nonresident: full-time $14,558; part-time $606.57 per credit hour. *Required fees:* $2655; $35 per credit hour. $907.50 per semester. Tuition and fees vary according to course load. *Financial support:* In 2013–14, 188 students received support, including 179 fellowships (averaging $2,580 per year), 39 research assistantships (averaging $4,550 per year), 8 teaching assistantships (averaging $4,647 per year); scholarships/grants and unspecified assistantships also available. Support available to part-time students. Financial award application deadline: 1/3; financial award applicants required to submit FAFSA. *Faculty research:* Cognitive, motivational, and developmental processes in learning; counseling education; instructional technology; generic special education and sensory impairment; community college administration; K-12 school administration. *Total annual research expenditures:* $708,063. *Unit head:* Dr. Fred Hartmeister, Chair, 806-834-0248, Fax: 806-742-2179, E-mail: fred.hartmeister@ttu.edu. *Application contact:* Pam Smith, Admissions Advisor, 806-834-2969, Fax: 806-742-2179, E-mail: pam.smith@ttu.edu.
Website: http://www.educ.ttu.edu/.

Texas Woman's University, Graduate School, College of Professional Education, Department of Teacher Education, Denton, TX 76201. Offers administration (M Ed, MA); special education (M Ed, MA, PhD), including educational diagnostician (M Ed, MA); teaching, learning, and curriculum (M Ed). Part-time programs available. *Faculty:* 16 full-time (13 women), 37 part-time/adjunct (29 women). *Students:* 15 full-time (all women), 135 part-time (120 women); includes 56 minority (26 Black or African American, non-Hispanic/Latino; 4 American Indian or Alaska Native, non-Hispanic/Latino; 1 Asian, non-Hispanic/Latino; 25 Hispanic/Latino), 3 international. Average age 37. 29 applicants, 69% accepted, 17 enrolled. In 2013, 51 master's, 1 doctorate awarded. Terminal master's awarded for partial completion of doctoral program. *Degree requirements:* For master's, comprehensive exam, thesis, professional paper (M Ed); for doctorate, comprehensive exam, thesis/dissertation. *Entrance requirements:* For master's, minimum GPA of 3.0 on last 60 undergraduate hours, 2 letters of reference, resume, copy of certifications, teacher service record, statement of intent; for doctorate, GRE General Test, minimum GPA of 3.0, 3 letters of reference, resume, copy of certifications, teacher service record, statement of intent. Additional exam requirements/recommendations for international students: Required—TOEFL (minimum score 550 paper-based; 79 iBT). *Application deadline:* For fall admission, 7/1 priority date for domestic students, 3/1 for international students; for spring admission, 11/1 priority date for domestic students, 7/1 for international students. Applications are processed on a rolling basis. Application fee: $50 ($75 for international students). Electronic applications accepted. *Expenses:* Tuition, state resident: full-time $4182; part-time $233.32 per credit hour. Tuition, nonresident: full-time $10,716; part-time $595.32 per credit hour. *Financial support:* In 2013–14, 42 students received support, including 8 research assistantships (averaging $12,942 per year); career-related internships or fieldwork, Federal Work-Study, institutionally sponsored loans, scholarships/grants, traineeships, health care benefits, and unspecified assistantships also available. Support available to part-time students. Financial award application deadline: 3/1; financial award applicants required to submit FAFSA. *Faculty research:* Language and literacy, classroom management, learning disabilities, staff and professional development, leadership preparation practice. *Unit head:* Dr. Jane Pemberton, Chair, 940-898-2271, Fax: 940-898-2270, E-mail: teachereducation@twu.edu. *Application contact:* Dr. Samuel Wheeler, Assistant Director of Admissions, 940-898-3188, Fax: 940-898-3081, E-mail: wheelersr@twu.edu.
Website: http://www.twu.edu/teacher-education/.

Thomas Edison State College, Heavin School of Arts and Sciences, Program in Educational Leadership, Trenton, NJ 08608-1176. Offers MAEL. Part-time programs available. Postbaccalaureate distance learning degree programs offered (no on-campus study). *Degree requirements:* For master's, field-based practicum, professional portfolio development. *Entrance requirements:* For master's, at least 3 years of teaching experience; valid teacher's certification; letter of recommendation from a building-level administrator; school setting and on-site mentor available to conduct site-based fieldwork and inquiry projects successfully for each course; statement of goals and objectives. Additional exam requirements/recommendations for international students: Required—TOEFL (minimum score 550 paper-based; 79 iBT). Electronic applications accepted.

Touro College, Graduate School of Education, New York, NY 10010. Offers education and special education (MS); education biology (MS); instructional technology (MS); mathematics education (MS); school leadership (MS); teaching English to speakers of other languages (MS); teaching literacy (MS). Part-time and evening/weekend programs available. Postbaccalaureate distance learning degree programs offered (no on-campus study). *Faculty:* 75 full-time, 131 part-time/adjunct. *Students:* 327 full-time (272 women), 2,454 part-time (2,103 women); includes 840 minority (333 Black or African American, non-Hispanic/Latino; 4 American Indian or Alaska Native, non-Hispanic/Latino; 139 Asian, non-Hispanic/Latino; 334 Hispanic/Latino; 8 Native Hawaiian or other Pacific Islander, non-Hispanic/Latino; 22 Two or more races, non-Hispanic/Latino), 4 international. 1,422 applicants, 50% accepted, 675 enrolled. In 2013, 6 master's awarded. *Entrance requirements:* Additional exam requirements/recommendations for international students: Required—TOEFL (minimum score 83 iBT), IELTS (minimum score 6.5). *Application deadline:* For fall admission, 8/26 for domestic students, 7/15 for international students; for spring admission, 12/31 for domestic students, 12/15 for international students. Applications are processed on a rolling basis. Application fee: $50. *Financial support:* Federal Work-Study available. Financial award applicants required to submit FAFSA. *Faculty research:* Equity assistance, language development, scholar communications, Latin American studies and cultural sensitivity, behavior management techniques and strategies in special education. *Unit head:* Dr. LaMar Miller, Dean, 212-463-0400 Ext. 5561, Fax: 212-462-4889, E-mail: lpmiller@touro.edu. *Application contact:* Natalie Arroyo, Admissions, 212-463-0400.

Trevecca Nazarene University, Graduate Education Program, Nashville, TN 37210-2877. Offers curriculum, assessment, and instruction K-12 (M Ed); educational leadership (M Ed); English language learners (PreK-12) (M Ed); leadership and professional practice (Ed D); library and information science (MLI Sc); teacher leader (M Ed); teaching (MAE, MAT), including teaching 7-12 (MAT), teaching K-6 (MAT); visual impairments special education (M Ed). *Accreditation:* NCATE. Part-time and evening/weekend programs available. Postbaccalaureate distance learning degree programs offered. *Faculty:* 19 full-time (17 women), 14 part-time/adjunct (5 women). *Students:* 186 full-time (137 women), 134 part-time (94 women); includes 93 minority (87 Black or African American, non-Hispanic/Latino; 1 American Indian or Alaska Native, non-Hispanic/Latino; 2 Asian, non-Hispanic/Latino; 1 Hispanic/Latino; 1 Native Hawaiian or other Pacific Islander, non-Hispanic/Latino; 1 Two or more races, non-Hispanic/Latino), 2 international. In 2013, 201 master's, 40 doctorates awarded. *Degree requirements:* For master's, comprehensive exam, exit assessment/e-portfolio; for doctorate, thesis/dissertation, proposal study, symposium presentation. *Entrance requirements:* For master's, GRE with minimum score of 378 or MAT with minimum score of 290, ACT with minimum score of 22 or SAT with minimum score of 1020 (for MAT programs only); PRAXIS (for MAT and MAE programs), minimum GPA of 2.7, official transcript from regionally accredited institution, 3+ years successful teaching experience (Teacher Leader and Education Leadership majors), technology pre-assessment written requirements (some majors); for doctorate, GRE or MAT, minimum GPA of 3.4, official transcript from regionally-accredited institution, resume, writing sample, interview, reference forms. Additional exam requirements/recommendations for international students: Required—TOEFL (minimum score 550 paper-based). *Application deadline:* Applications are processed on a rolling basis. *Expenses:* Contact institution. *Financial support:* Applicants required to submit FAFSA. *Unit head:* Dr. Suzie Harris, Dean, School of Education/Director of Graduate Education Programs, 615-248-1201, Fax: 615-248-1597, E-mail: admissions_ged@trevecca.edu. *Application contact:* 615-248-1529, E-mail: cll@trevecca.edu.
Website: http://www.trevecca.edu/academics/schools-colleges/education/.

Trident University International, College of Education, Program in Educational Leadership, Cypress, CA 90630. Offers e-learning leadership (MA Ed, PhD); educational leadership (MA Ed); higher education leadership (PhD); K-12 leadership (PhD). Part-time and evening/weekend programs available. Postbaccalaureate distance learning degree programs offered (no on-campus study). *Degree requirements:* For doctorate, comprehensive exam, thesis/dissertation, defense of dissertation. *Entrance requirements:* For master's, minimum GPA of 2.5 (students with GPA 3.0 or greater may transfer up to 30% of graduate level credits); for doctorate, minimum GPA of 3.4, course work in research methods or statistics. Additional exam requirements/recommendations for international students: Required—TOEFL. Electronic applications accepted.

Trinity Baptist College, Graduate Programs, Jacksonville, FL 32221. Offers educational leadership (M Ed); ministry (MA); special education (M Ed).

Postbaccalaureate distance learning degree programs offered. *Entrance requirements:* For master's, GRE (for M Ed), 2 letters of recommendation; minimum GPA of 2.5 (for M Min), 3.0 (for M Ed); computer proficiency.

Trinity International University, Trinity Graduate School, Deerfield, IL 60015-1284. Offers bioethics (MA); communication and culture (MA); counseling psychology (MA); instructional leadership (M Ed); teaching (MA). Part-time and evening/weekend programs available. Postbaccalaureate distance learning degree programs offered (minimal on-campus study). *Degree requirements:* For master's, comprehensive exam. *Entrance requirements:* For master's, GRE General Test or MAT, minimum undergraduate GPA of 3.0. Additional exam requirements/recommendations for international students: Required—TOEFL (minimum score 580 paper-based), TWE (minimum score 4). Electronic applications accepted.

Trinity University, Department of Education, Program in School Administration, San Antonio, TX 78212-7200. Offers M Ed. *Accreditation:* NCATE. Part-time and evening/weekend programs available. *Entrance requirements:* For master's, GRE General Test, interview, minimum GPA of 3.0.

Trinity Washington University, School of Education, Washington, DC 20017-1094. Offers clinical mental health counseling (MA); early childhood education (MAT); educating for change (M Ed); educational administration (MSA); elementary education (MAT); reading (M Ed); school counseling (MA); secondary education (MAT), including English, social studies; special education (MAT). *Accreditation:* NCATE. Part-time and evening/weekend programs available. *Degree requirements:* For master's, thesis (for some programs), capstone project(s). *Entrance requirements:* For master's, PRAXIS I, minimum GPA of 2.8. Additional exam requirements/recommendations for international students: Required—TOEFL (minimum score 550 paper-based). *Application deadline:* For fall admission, 4/1 priority date for domestic students; for winter admission, 11/1 priority date for domestic students; for spring admission, 11/1 priority date for domestic students. Applications are processed on a rolling basis. Application fee: $40. *Expenses: Tuition:* Part-time $715 per credit. *Financial support:* Career-related internships or fieldwork, health care benefits, and unspecified assistantships available. Support available to part-time students. Financial award application deadline: 4/1; financial award applicants required to submit FAFSA. *Faculty research:* Technology, literacy, special education, organizations, inclusion models. *Unit head:* Dr. Janet Stocks, Dean, 202-884-9380, Fax: 202-884-9506, E-mail: stocksj@trinitydc.edu. *Application contact:* Erika Davis, Director of Admissions for School of Education, 202-884-9400, Fax: 202-884-9229, E-mail: daviser@trinitydc.edu. Website: http://www.trinitydc.edu/education/.

Trinity Western University, School of Graduate Studies, Program in Leadership, Langley, BC V2Y 1Y1, Canada. Offers business (MA, Certificate); Christian ministry (MA); education (MA, Certificate); healthcare (MA, Certificate); non-profit (MA, Certificate). Postbaccalaureate distance learning degree programs offered (minimal on-campus study). *Degree requirements:* For master's, major project. *Entrance requirements:* For master's, minimum GPA of 2.7. Additional exam requirements/recommendations for international students: Required—TOEFL (minimum score 620 paper-based; 105 iBT). Electronic applications accepted. *Expenses:* Contact institution. *Faculty research:* Servant leadership.

Troy University, Graduate School, College of Education, Program in Educational Administration/Leadership, Troy, AL 36082. Offers MS, Ed S. *Accreditation:* NCATE. Part-time and evening/weekend programs available. *Faculty:* 7 full-time (2 women), 7 part-time/adjunct (3 women). *Students:* 34 full-time (18 women), 36 part-time (23 women); includes 23 minority (21 Black or African American, non-Hispanic/Latino; 1 Hispanic/Latino; 1 Two or more races, non-Hispanic/Latino). Average age 36. 59 applicants, 51% accepted, 9 enrolled. In 2013, 23 master's, 14 other advanced degrees awarded. *Degree requirements:* For master's, comprehensive exam, thesis, internship. *Entrance requirements:* For master's, GRE (minimum score of 850 on old exam or 290 on new exam), GMAT (minimum score of 380), or MAT (minimum score of 385), bachelor's degree; minimum undergraduate GPA of 2.5 or 3.0 on last 30 semester hours, letter of recommendation; 3 years of teaching experience; for Ed S, GRE (minimum score of 850 on old exam or 290 on new exam), GMAT (minimum score of 380), or MAT (minimum score of 380), master's degree. Additional exam requirements/recommendations for international students: Required—TOEFL (minimum score 523 paper-based; 70 iBT), IELTS (minimum score 6). *Application deadline:* Applications are processed on a rolling basis. Application fee: $50. Electronic applications accepted. *Expenses:* Tuition, state resident: full-time $6084; part-time $338 per credit hour. Tuition, nonresident: full-time $12,168; part-time $676 per credit hour. *Required fees:* $630; $35 per credit hour. $50 per semester. *Financial support:* Available to part-time students. Applicants required to submit FAFSA. *Unit head:* Dr. Jan Oliver, Associate Professor, 334-670-3444, Fax: 334-670-3474, E-mail: oliverj@troy.edu. *Application contact:* Jessida McConnell, Graduate Admissions, 334-448-5106, Fax: 334-448-5299, E-mail: jcmcconnell@troy.edu.

Troy University, Graduate School, College of Education, Program in Postsecondary Education, Troy, AL 36082. Offers adult education (M Ed); biology (M Ed); criminal justice (M Ed); English (M Ed); foundations of education (M Ed); general science (M Ed); higher education administration (M Ed); history (M Ed); instructional technology (M Ed); mathematics (M Ed); music industry (M Ed); physical fitness (M Ed); political science (M Ed); public administration (M Ed); social science (M Ed); teaching English (M Ed). *Accreditation:* NCATE. Part-time and evening/weekend programs available. *Faculty:* 30 full-time (11 women), 8 part-time/adjunct (1 woman). *Students:* 17 full-time (13 women), 106 part-time (84 women); includes 55 minority (45 Black or African American, non-Hispanic/Latino; 3 Asian, non-Hispanic/Latino; 2 Hispanic/Latino; 5 Two or more races, non-Hispanic/Latino). Average age 34. 109 applicants, 83% accepted, 5 enrolled. In 2013, 130 master's awarded. *Degree requirements:* For master's, comprehensive exam (for some programs), thesis (for some programs), thesis or comprehensive exam. *Entrance requirements:* For master's, GRE (minimum score of 850 on old exam or 290 on new exam), GMAT (minimum score of 380), or MAT (minimum score of 385), bachelor's degree; minimum undergraduate GPA of 2.5 or 3.0 on last 30 semester hours, letter of recommendation. Additional exam requirements/recommendations for international students: Required—TOEFL (minimum score 523 paper-based; 70 iBT), IELTS (minimum score 6). *Application deadline:* Applications are processed on a rolling basis. Application fee: $50. Electronic applications accepted. *Expenses:* Tuition, state resident: full-time $6084; part-time $338 per credit hour. Tuition, nonresident: full-time $12,168; part-time $676 per credit hour. *Required fees:* $630; $35 per credit hour. $50 per semester. *Financial support:* Available to part-time students. Applicants required to submit FAFSA. *Unit head:* Dr. Jan Oliver, Associate Professor, 334-670-3444, Fax: 334-670-3474, E-mail: oliver@troy.edu. *Application contact:* Brenda K. Campbell, Director of Graduate Admissions, 334-670-3178, Fax: 334-670-3733, E-mail: bcamp@troy.edu.

Union College, Graduate Programs, Department of Education, Barbourville, KY 40906-1499. Offers elementary education (MA); health and physical education (MA); middle grades (MA); music education (MA); principalship (MA); reading specialist (MA); secondary education (MA); special education (MA). *Degree requirements:* For master's, thesis optional. *Entrance requirements:* For master's, GRE General Test, NTE.

Union College, Graduate Programs, Educational Leadership Program, Barbourville, KY 40906-1499. Offers principalship (MA).

Union Graduate College, School of Education, Schenectady, NY 12308-3107. Offers biology (MAT); chemistry (MAT); Chinese (MAT); earth science (MAT); English (MA, MAT); English and history (MA); French (MAT); general science (MAT); German (MAT); history (MA); Latin (MAT); life sciences (MS); mathematics (MAT); mathematics and computer technology (MS); mentoring and teacher leadership (AC); middle childhood extension (AC); national board certification and teacher leadership (AC); physical sciences (MS); physics (MAT); social studies (MAT); Spanish (MAT); technology (MAT). *Accreditation:* Teacher Education Accreditation Council. *Faculty:* 3 full-time (1 woman), 56 part-time/adjunct (34 women). *Students:* 32 full-time (16 women), 27 part-time (22 women); includes 15 minority (1 Black or African American, non-Hispanic/Latino; 4 Asian, non-Hispanic/Latino; 6 Hispanic/Latino; 4 Two or more races, non-Hispanic/Latino), 1 international. Average age 32. In 2013, 25 master's, 11 other advanced degrees awarded. *Degree requirements:* For master's, thesis or project. *Entrance requirements:* For master's, minimum GPA of 3.0, letters of recommendation. Additional exam requirements/recommendations for international students: Required—TOEFL (minimum score 550 paper-based). *Application deadline:* Applications are processed on a rolling basis. Application fee: $60. Electronic applications accepted. *Expenses:* Contact institution. *Financial support:* Career-related internships or fieldwork, Federal Work-Study, scholarships/grants, health care benefits, and tuition waivers (partial) available. Support available to part-time students. Financial award applicants required to submit FAFSA. *Faculty research:* Transformative learning, science education, National Board Certification, teacher leadership, teacher quality. *Unit head:* Dr. Lynn Gelzheiser, Dean, 518-631-9870, Fax: 518-631-9901. *Application contact:* Nicki Foley, Assistant, 518-631-9871, Fax: 518-631-9903, E-mail: foleyn@uniongraduatecollege.edu.

Union Institute & University, Doctor of Education Program, Cincinnati, OH 45206-1925. Offers educational leadership (Ed D); higher education (Ed D). M Ed offered online and in Vermont and Florida, Ed S in Florida; Ed D program is offered online with limited residency in Ohio. Postbaccalaureate distance learning degree programs offered (minimal on-campus study). *Degree requirements:* For doctorate, comprehensive exam, thesis/dissertation, electronic portfolio. *Entrance requirements:* For doctorate, master's degree from regionally-accredited institution, letters of recommendation, essay. *Faculty research:* Adult education, higher education, social responsibility in education, educational technology.

Union University, School of Education, Jackson, TN 38305-3697. Offers education (M Ed, MA Ed); education administration generalist (Ed S); educational leadership (Ed D); educational supervision (Ed S); higher education (Ed D). M Ed also available at Germantown campus. *Accreditation:* NCATE. Part-time and evening/weekend programs available. *Degree requirements:* For master's, thesis (for some programs), capstone research course; for doctorate, comprehensive exam, thesis/dissertation; for Ed S, thesis or alternative. *Entrance requirements:* For master's, MAT, PRAXIS II or GRE, minimum GPA of 3.0, teaching license, writing sample; for doctorate, GRE, minimum graduate GPA of 3.2, writing sample; for Ed S, PRAXIS II, minimum graduate GPA of 3.2, writing sample. *Faculty research:* Mathematics education, direct instruction, language disorders and special education, brain compatible learning, empathy and school leadership.

United States University, School of Education, Cypress, CA 90630. Offers administration (MA Ed); early childhood education (MA Ed); general (MA Ed); higher education administration (MA Ed); Spanish language education (MA Ed); special education (MA Ed). *Degree requirements:* For master's, portfolio. *Entrance requirements:* For master's, minimum undergraduate GPA of 2.5. Additional exam requirements/recommendations for international students: Required—TOEFL (minimum score 500 paper-based; 61 iBT).

Universidad Adventista de las Antillas, EGECED Department, Mayagüez, PR 00681-0118. Offers curriculum and instruction (M Ed); health education (M Ed); medical surgical nursing (MN); school administration and supervision (M Ed). *Degree requirements:* For master's, comprehensive exam (for some programs), thesis (for some programs). *Entrance requirements:* For master's, EXADEP or GRE General Test, recommendations. Application fee: $175. Electronic applications accepted. *Expenses: Tuition:* Full-time $2400; part-time $200 per credit. *Required fees:* $235 per semester. One-time fee: $30. Tuition and fees vary according to course load. *Financial support:* Fellowships and Federal Work-Study available. *Unit head:* Director, 787-834-9595 Ext. 2282, Fax: 787-834-9595. *Application contact:* Prof. Yolanda Ferrer, Director of Admission, 787-834-9595 Ext. 2261, Fax: 787-834-9597, E-mail: admissions@uaa.edu. Website: http://www.uaa.edu.

Universidad del Turabo, Graduate Programs, Programs in Education, Program in Administration of School Libraries, Gurabo, PR 00778-3030. Offers M Ed, Certificate.

Universidad del Turabo, Graduate Programs, Programs in Education, Program in Educational Administration, Gurabo, PR 00778-3030. Offers M Ed. *Entrance requirements:* For master's, GRE, EXADEP, interview.

Universidad del Turabo, Graduate Programs, Programs in Education, Program in Educational Leadership, Gurabo, PR 00778-3030. Offers D Ed.

Universidad Iberoamericana, Graduate School, Santo Domingo D.N., Dominican Republic. Offers business administration (MBA, PMBA); constitutional law (LL M); dentistry (DMD); educational management (MA); integrated marketing communication (MA); psychopedagogical intervention (M Ed); real estate law (LL M); strategic management of human talent (MM).

Universidad Metropolitana, School of Education, Program in Educational Administration and Supervision, San Juan, PR 00928-1150. Offers M Ed. Part-time programs available. *Degree requirements:* For master's, thesis or alternative. *Entrance requirements:* For master's, EXADEP, interview. Electronic applications accepted.

Universidad Metropolitana, School of Education, Program in Pre-School Centers Administration, San Juan, PR 00928-1150. Offers M Ed. Part-time programs available. *Degree requirements:* For master's, thesis or alternative. *Entrance requirements:* For master's, EXADEP, interview. Electronic applications accepted.

Université de Moncton, Faculty of Education, Graduate Studies in Education, Moncton, NB E1A 3E9, Canada. Offers educational psychology (M Ed, MA Ed); guidance (M Ed, MA Ed); school administration (M Ed, MA Ed); teaching (M Ed, MA Ed). Part-time programs available. *Degree requirements:* For master's, proficiency in English and French. *Entrance requirements:* For master's, minimum GPA of 3.0. *Faculty research:* Guidance, ethnolinguistic vitality, children's rights, ecological education, entrepreneurship.

Université de Montréal, Faculty of Education, Department of Administration and Foundations of Education, Montréal, QC H3C 3J7, Canada. Offers M Ed, MA, PhD, DESS. Part-time programs available. *Degree requirements:* For master's, thesis; for doctorate, thesis/dissertation, general exam. *Entrance requirements:* For master's and DESS, bachelor's degree in related field with minimum B average; for doctorate, master's degree in related field with minimum B average. Electronic applications accepted. *Faculty research:* Pluriethnicity, formative education, comparative education, diagnostic evaluation.

Educational Leadership and Administration

Université de Sherbrooke, Faculty of Education, Program in School Administration, Sherbrooke, QC J1K 2R1, Canada. Offers M Ed. Part-time and evening/weekend programs available. *Degree requirements:* For master's, thesis.

Université du Québec à Trois-Rivières, Graduate Programs, Program in Educational Administration, Trois-Rivières, QC G9A 5H7, Canada. Offers DESS.

Université Laval, Faculty of Education, Department of Foundations and Interventions in Education, Programs in Educational Administration and Evaluation, Québec, QC G1K 7P4, Canada. Offers MA, PhD. Terminal master's awarded for partial completion of doctoral program. *Degree requirements:* For master's, thesis (for some programs); for doctorate, comprehensive exam, thesis/dissertation. *Entrance requirements:* For master's and doctorate, English exam (comprehension of written English), knowledge of French and English. Electronic applications accepted.

Université Laval, Faculty of Education, Department of Foundations and Interventions in Education, Programs in Educational Practice, Québec, QC G1K 7P4, Canada. Offers educational pedagogy (Diploma); pedagogy management and development (Diploma); school adaptation (Diploma). Part-time programs available. *Entrance requirements:* For degree, English exam (comprehension of written English), knowledge of French and English. Electronic applications accepted.

University at Albany, State University of New York, School of Education, Department of Educational Administration and Policy Studies, Albany, NY 12222-0001. Offers MS, PhD, CAS. Evening/weekend programs available. *Degree requirements:* For doctorate, one foreign language, thesis/dissertation. *Entrance requirements:* For doctorate, GRE General Test, GRE Subject Test. Additional exam requirements/recommendations for international students: Required—TOEFL (minimum score 550 paper-based). Electronic applications accepted.

University at Buffalo, the State University of New York, Graduate School, Graduate School of Education, Department of Educational Leadership and Policy, Buffalo, NY 14260. Offers education studies (Ed M); educational administration (Ed M, Ed D, PhD); educational culture, policy and society (PhD); higher education administration (Ed M, PhD); school building leadership (Certificate); school business and human resource administration (Certificate); school district business leadership (Certificate); school district leadership (Certificate). Part-time and evening/weekend programs available. *Faculty:* 13 full-time (7 women), 8 part-time/adjunct (all women). *Students:* 65 full-time (40 women), 139 part-time (83 women); includes 40 minority (24 Black or African American, non-Hispanic/Latino; 6 Asian, non-Hispanic/Latino; 10 Hispanic/Latino), 15 international. Average age 35. 159 applicants, 71% accepted, 65 enrolled. In 2013, 44 master's, 14 doctorates, 19 other advanced degrees awarded. *Degree requirements:* For master's, comprehensive exam (for some programs), thesis optional; for doctorate, comprehensive exam, thesis/dissertation. *Entrance requirements:* For master's, interview, letters of reference; for doctorate, GRE General Test or MAT, writing sample, letters of reference. Additional exam requirements/recommendations for international students: Required—TOEFL (minimum score 550 paper-based; 79 iBT). *Application deadline:* For fall admission, 2/1 priority date for domestic students, 2/1 for international students; for spring admission, 11/15 priority date for domestic students, 10/1 for international students. Applications are processed on a rolling basis. Application fee: $50. Electronic applications accepted. *Financial support:* In 2013–14, 20 fellowships (averaging $6,639 per year), 6 research assistantships with tuition reimbursements (averaging $10,500 per year) were awarded; career-related internships or fieldwork, Federal Work-Study, institutionally sponsored loans, scholarships/grants, health care benefits, tuition waivers, and unspecified assistantships also available. Financial award application deadline: 3/15; financial award applicants required to submit FAFSA. *Faculty research:* College access and choice, school leadership preparation and practice, public policy, curriculum and pedagogy, comparative and international education. *Total annual research expenditures:* $455,347. *Unit head:* Dr. Janina C. Brutt-Griffler, Chair, 716-645-2471, Fax: 716-645-2481, E-mail: bruttg@buffalo.edu. *Application contact:* Ryan Taugrin, Admission and Student Services Coordinator, 716-645-2110, Fax: 716-645-7937, E-mail: ryantaug@buffalo.edu.
Website: http://gse.buffalo.edu/elp.

The University of Akron, Graduate School, College of Education, Department of Educational Foundations and Leadership, Program in Higher Education Administration, Akron, OH 44325. Offers MA, MS. *Accreditation:* NCATE. *Students:* 39 full-time (27 women), 17 part-time (14 women); includes 10 minority (8 Black or African American, non-Hispanic/Latino; 1 Hispanic/Latino; 1 Two or more races, non-Hispanic/Latino), 7 international. Average age 28. 42 applicants, 86% accepted, 19 enrolled. In 2013, 22 master's awarded. *Degree requirements:* For master's, comprehensive exam. *Entrance requirements:* For master's, GRE, minimum GPA of 2.75, declaration of intent that includes statement of professional goals and reasons for choosing the field of higher education administration and The University of Akron. Additional exam requirements/recommendations for international students: Required—TOEFL (minimum score 550 paper-based; 79 iBT). *Application deadline:* Applications are processed on a rolling basis. Application fee: $40 ($60 for international students). Electronic applications accepted. *Expenses:* Tuition, state resident: full-time $7430; part-time $412.80 per credit hour. Tuition, nonresident: full-time $12,722; part-time $706.80 per credit hour. *Required fees:* $53 per credit hour. $12 per semester. Tuition and fees vary according to course load and program. *Financial support:* Fellowships, research assistantships, and teaching assistantships available. *Unit head:* Dr. Sharon Kruse, Coordinator, 330-972-8177, E-mail: skruse@uakron.edu.

The University of Akron, Graduate School, College of Education, Department of Educational Foundations and Leadership, Program in Principalship, Akron, OH 44325. Offers MA, MS. *Students:* 1 (woman) full-time, 46 part-time (27 women); includes 2 minority (both Black or African American, non-Hispanic/Latino). Average age 34. 16 applicants, 81% accepted, 11 enrolled. In 2013, 25 master's awarded. *Degree requirements:* For master's, portfolio assessment. *Entrance requirements:* For master's, minimum GPA of 2.75, valid Ohio teacher license. Additional exam requirements/recommendations for international students: Required—TOEFL (minimum score 550 paper-based; 79 iBT). *Application deadline:* Applications are processed on a rolling basis. Application fee: $40 ($60 for international students). Electronic applications accepted. *Expenses:* Tuition, state resident: full-time $7430; part-time $412.80 per credit hour. Tuition, nonresident: full-time $12,722; part-time $706.80 per credit hour. *Required fees:* $53 per credit hour. $12 per semester. Tuition and fees vary according to course load and program. *Unit head:* Dr. Sharon Kruse, Coordinator, 330-972-7773, E-mail: skruse@uakron.edu.

The University of Alabama, Graduate School, College of Education, Department of Educational Leadership, Policy, and Technology Studies, Educational Administration Program, Tuscaloosa, AL 35487. Offers Ed D, PhD. Evening/weekend programs available. *Students:* 4 full-time (2 women), 43 part-time (26 women); includes 12 minority (10 Black or African American, non-Hispanic/Latino; 2 American Indian or Alaska Native, non-Hispanic/Latino), 2 international. Average age 43. 5 applicants, 20% accepted. In 2013, 14 doctorates awarded. *Degree requirements:* For doctorate, comprehensive exam, thesis/dissertation. *Entrance requirements:* For doctorate, MAT, GRE, master's degree in field. *Application deadline:* For fall admission, 10/31 priority date for domestic students, 9/1 priority date for international students; for winter admission, 2/1 for domestic and international students; for spring admission, 4/1 priority date for domestic and international students. Applications are processed on a rolling basis. Application fee: $50 ($60 for international students). Electronic applications accepted. *Expenses:* Tuition, state resident: full-time $9450. Tuition, nonresident: full-time $23,950. *Financial support:* In 2013–14, 2 research assistantships with tuition reimbursements (averaging $11,900 per year) were awarded; health care benefits and unspecified assistantships also available. Financial award application deadline: 4/1. *Unit head:* Dr. David R. Dagley, Professor of Educational Leadership, 205-348-5159, Fax: 205-348-2161, E-mail: ddagley@bamaed.ua.edu. *Application contact:* Dr. Kathy S. Wetzel, Assistant Dean for Student Services, 205-348-1154, Fax: 205-348-0080, E-mail: kwetzel@bamaed.ua.edu.
Website: http://www.elpts.ua.edu.

The University of Alabama, Graduate School, College of Education, Department of Educational Leadership, Policy, and Technology Studies, Educational Leadership Program, Tuscaloosa, AL 35487. Offers MA, Ed S. Part-time and evening/weekend programs available. *Faculty:* 24 full-time (12 women), 2 part-time/adjunct (1 woman). *Students:* 4 full-time (1 woman), 80 part-time (45 women); includes 15 minority (12 Black or African American, non-Hispanic/Latino; 1 American Indian or Alaska Native, non-Hispanic/Latino; 1 Asian, non-Hispanic/Latino; 1 Hispanic/Latino). Average age 38. 38 applicants, 68% accepted, 25 enrolled. In 2013, 29 master's, 9 other advanced degrees awarded. *Degree requirements:* For master's, comprehensive exam, internship. *Entrance requirements:* For master's, MAT, GRE, 3 years of teaching experience, teaching certification, interview, portfolio. Additional exam requirements/recommendations for international students: Required—TOEFL. *Application deadline:* For fall admission, 9/1 priority date for domestic and international students; for winter admission, 2/1 priority date for domestic and international students; for spring admission, 4/1 priority date for domestic and international students. Application fee: $50 ($60 for international students). Electronic applications accepted. *Expenses:* Tuition, state resident: full-time $9450. Tuition, nonresident: full-time $23,950. *Financial support:* In 2013–14, 2 research assistantships with full tuition reimbursements (averaging $11,900 per year) were awarded. *Faculty research:* Instructional supervision, school effectiveness, organizational theory, politics of education, educational law. *Unit head:* Dr. Bob Johnson, Professor, 205-348-6417, Fax: 205-348-2161, E-mail: bjohnson@bamaed.ua.edu. *Application contact:* Dr. Kathy S. Wetzel, Assistant Dean for Student Services, 205-348-1154, Fax: 205-348-0080, E-mail: kwetzel@bamaed.ua.edu.

The University of Alabama, Graduate School, College of Education, Department of Educational Leadership, Policy, and Technology Studies, Higher Education Administration Program, Tuscaloosa, AL 35487. Offers MA, Ed D, PhD. Evening/weekend programs available. *Students:* 46 full-time (22 women), 114 part-time (61 women); includes 33 minority (23 Black or African American, non-Hispanic/Latino; 1 American Indian or Alaska Native, non-Hispanic/Latino; 1 Asian, non-Hispanic/Latino; 4 Hispanic/Latino; 4 Two or more races, non-Hispanic/Latino), 1 international. Average age 38. 73 applicants, 63% accepted, 27 enrolled. In 2013, 11 master's, 12 doctorates awarded. Terminal master's awarded for partial completion of doctoral program. *Degree requirements:* For master's, comprehensive exam; for doctorate, comprehensive exam, thesis/dissertation. *Entrance requirements:* For master's, GRE, MAT or GMAT; for doctorate, GRE or MAT. Additional exam requirements/recommendations for international students: Required—TOEFL. *Application deadline:* For fall admission, 2/15 for domestic and international students. Application fee: $50 ($60 for international students). Electronic applications accepted. *Expenses:* Tuition, state resident: full-time $9450. Tuition, nonresident: full-time $23,950. *Financial support:* In 2013–14, 5 students received support, including 2 research assistantships with full tuition reimbursements available (averaging $11,900 per year); career-related internships or fieldwork, scholarships/grants, and unspecified assistantships also available. *Faculty research:* College teaching and learning, faculty-administration relations, community colleges, organizational change, student affairs. *Unit head:* Dr. Nathaniel Bray, Coordinator and Associate Professor, 205-348-1159, Fax: 205-348-2161, E-mail: nbray@bamaed.ua.edu. *Application contact:* Donna Smith, Administrative Assistant, 205-348-6871, Fax: 205-348-2161, E-mail: dbsmith@bamaed.ua.edu.

The University of Alabama, Graduate School, College of Education, Department of Educational Leadership, Policy, and Technology Studies, Instructional Leadership Program, Tuscaloosa, AL 35487. Offers Ed D, PhD. Evening/weekend programs available. *Students:* 61 full-time (48 women), 139 part-time (115 women); includes 49 minority (42 Black or African American, non-Hispanic/Latino; 2 American Indian or Alaska Native, non-Hispanic/Latino; 1 Hispanic/Latino; 1 Native Hawaiian or other Pacific Islander, non-Hispanic/Latino; 3 Two or more races, non-Hispanic/Latino), 2 international. Average age 43. 32 applicants, 69% accepted, 16 enrolled. In 2013, 21 doctorates awarded. *Degree requirements:* For doctorate, comprehensive exam, thesis/dissertation. *Entrance requirements:* For doctorate, GRE, MAT, master's degree. *Application deadline:* For fall admission, 9/1 for domestic and international students; for winter admission, 2/1 for domestic and international students; for spring admission, 4/1 for domestic and international students. Applications are processed on a rolling basis. Application fee: $50 ($60 for international students). Electronic applications accepted. *Expenses:* Tuition, state resident: full-time $9450. Tuition, nonresident: full-time $23,950. *Financial support:* In 2013–14, 2 research assistantships with tuition reimbursements (averaging $11,900 per year), 2 teaching assistantships with tuition reimbursements (averaging $11,900 per year) were awarded; health care benefits and unspecified assistantships also available. *Unit head:* Dr. John Petrovic, Professor in Foundations of Education, 205-348-0465, Fax: 205-348-2161, E-mail: petrovic@bamaed.ua.edu. *Application contact:* Dr. Kathy S. Wetzel, Assistant Dean for Student Services, 205-348-1154, Fax: 205-348-0080, E-mail: kwetzel@bamaed.ua.edu.
Website: http://www.elpts.ua.edu.

The University of Alabama at Birmingham, School of Education, Program in Educational Leadership, Birmingham, AL 35294. Offers MA Ed, Ed D, PhD, Ed S. Ed D, PhD offered jointly with The University of Alabama (Tuscaloosa). *Accreditation:* NCATE. Part-time programs available. *Degree requirements:* For master's, thesis optional; for doctorate, thesis/dissertation; for Ed S, comprehensive exam, thesis optional. *Entrance requirements:* For master's, GRE General Test, MAT, or NTE, minimum GPA of 3.0; for doctorate, GRE General Test, MAT, minimum GPA of 3.25; for Ed S, GRE General Test, MAT, minimum GPA of 3.0, master's degree. Electronic applications accepted.

University of Alaska Anchorage, College of Education, Program in Educational Leadership, Anchorage, AK 99508. Offers educational leadership (M Ed); principal licensure (Certificate); superintendent (Certificate). Part-time programs available. *Entrance requirements:* For master's, GRE or MAT, interview, minimum GPA of 3.0. Additional exam requirements/recommendations for international students: Required—TOEFL (minimum score 550 paper-based).

University of Alberta, Faculty of Graduate Studies and Research, Department of Educational Policy Studies, Edmonton, AB T6G 2E1, Canada. Offers adult education (M Ed, Ed D, PhD); educational administration and leadership (M Ed, Ed D, PhD, Postgraduate Diploma); First Nations education (M Ed, Ed D, PhD); theoretical, cultural and international studies in education (M Ed, Ed D, PhD). *Degree requirements:* For master's, thesis (for some programs); for doctorate, thesis/dissertation. *Entrance*

requirements: For master's, minimum GPA of 6.5 on a 9.0 scale; for doctorate, minimum GPA of 7.5 on a 9.0 scale. Additional exam requirements/recommendations for international students: Required—TOEFL (minimum score 580 paper-based). Electronic applications accepted.

The University of Arizona, College of Education, Department of Educational Policy Studies and Practice, Program of Educational Leadership, Tucson, AZ 85721. Offers M Ed, Ed D, Ed S. Part-time programs available. *Faculty:* 10 full-time (5 women). *Students:* 25 full-time (15 women), 58 part-time (32 women); includes 29 minority (8 Black or African American, non-Hispanic/Latino; 1 American Indian or Alaska Native, non-Hispanic/Latino; 17 Hispanic/Latino; 3 Two or more races, non-Hispanic/Latino), 1 international. Average age 41. 44 applicants, 70% accepted, 14 enrolled. In 2013, 21 master's, 5 doctorates awarded. *Degree requirements:* For master's and Ed S, capstone experience; for doctorate, comprehensive exam, thesis/dissertation. *Entrance requirements:* For master's, leadership experience; for doctorate, GRE General Test, minimum GPA of 3.5, 3 letters of recommendation, curriculum vitae, writing sample. Additional exam requirements/recommendations for international students: Required— TOEFL (minimum score 550 paper-based; 79 iBT). *Application deadline:* For fall admission, 3/1 for domestic students, 12/1 for international students. Applications are processed on a rolling basis. Application fee: $75. Electronic applications accepted. *Expenses:* Tuition, state resident: full-time $11,526. Tuition, nonresident: full-time $27,398. *Financial support:* In 2013–14, 7 research assistantships with partial tuition reimbursements (averaging $15,794 per year), 4 teaching assistantships with partial tuition reimbursements (averaging $9,253 per year) were awarded; career-related internships or fieldwork, scholarships/grants, health care benefits, and unspecified assistantships also available. *Faculty research:* School governance, higher order thinking, restructuring schools, bilingual education policy, authority in education. *Total annual research expenditures:* $406,708. *Unit head:* Dr. Gary Rhoades, Professor and Department Head, 520-621-7313, Fax: 520-621-1875, E-mail: grhoades@email.arizona.edu. *Application contact:* Margo Sallet, Graduate Program Coordinator, 520-621-7313, Fax: 520-621-1875, E-mail: msallet@email.arizona.edu.
Website: http://grad.arizona.edu/live/programs/description/51.

The University of Arizona, College of Science, Department of Mathematics, Program in Middle School Mathematics Teaching Leadership, Tucson, AZ 85721. Offers MA. Part-time programs available. *Students:* 18 full-time (14 women), 8 part-time (all women); includes 13 minority (1 Asian, non-Hispanic/Latino; 8 Hispanic/Latino; 1 Native Hawaiian or other Pacific Islander, non-Hispanic/Latino; 3 Two or more races, non-Hispanic/Latino). Average age 44. In 2013, 12 master's awarded. *Degree requirements:* For master's, thesis, internships, colloquium, business courses. *Entrance requirements:* For master's, GRE, minimum GPA of 3.0, statement of purpose. Additional exam requirements/recommendations for international students: Required—TOEFL (minimum score 550 paper-based). Application fee: $75. *Expenses:* Tuition, state resident: full-time $11,526. Tuition, nonresident: full-time $27,398. *Financial support:* Research assistantships, teaching assistantships, career-related internships or fieldwork, Federal Work-Study, scholarships/grants, health care benefits, and unspecified assistantships available. *Faculty research:* Algebra, coding theory, graph theory, combinatorics, probability. *Unit head:* William McCallum, Head, 520-621-2068, E-mail: stovall@math.arizona.edu. *Application contact:* Teresa Stoval, 520-626-6145, E-mail: stovall@math.arizona.edu.
Website: http://math.arizona.edu/.

University of Arkansas, Graduate School, College of Education and Health Professions, Department of Curriculum and Instruction, Program in Educational Leadership, Fayetteville, AR 72701-1201. Offers M Ed, Ed D, Ed S. *Accreditation:* NCATE. Part-time and evening/weekend programs available. *Degree requirements:* For doctorate, thesis/dissertation. *Entrance requirements:* For master's, GRE General Test, MAT or minimum GPA of 3.0; for doctorate, GRE General Test or MAT. Electronic applications accepted.

University of Arkansas at Little Rock, Graduate School, College of Education, Department of Educational Leadership, Program in Educational Administration, Little Rock, AR 72204-1099. Offers educational administration (M Ed, Ed S); educational administration and supervision (Ed D). Part-time and evening/weekend programs available. *Degree requirements:* For master's, comprehensive exam; for doctorate, comprehensive exam, oral defense of dissertation, residency; for Ed S, comprehensive exam, professional project. *Entrance requirements:* For master's, GRE General Test or MAT, 4 years of work experience (minimum 3 in teaching), interview, minimum GPA of 2.75, teaching certificate; for doctorate, GRE General Test or MAT, 4 years of work experience, minimum graduate GPA of 3.0, teaching certificate; for Ed S, GRE General Test or MAT, 4 years of work experience, minimum GPA of 2.75, teaching certificate. *Expenses:* Tuition, state resident: full-time $5690; part-time $284.50 per credit hour. Tuition, nonresident: full-time $13,030; part-time $651.50 per credit hour. *Required fees:* $1121; $672 per term. One-time fee: $40 full-time.

University of Arkansas at Little Rock, Graduate School, College of Education, Department of Educational Leadership, Program in Higher Education Administration, Little Rock, AR 72204-1099. Offers Ed D. *Degree requirements:* For doctorate, comprehensive exam, oral defense of dissertation, residency. *Entrance requirements:* For doctorate, GRE General Test or MAT, interview, minimum graduate GPA of 3.0, teaching certificate, work experience. *Expenses:* Tuition, state resident: full-time $5690; part-time $284.50 per credit hour. Tuition, nonresident: full-time $13,030; part-time $651.50 per credit hour. *Required fees:* $1121; $672 per term. One-time fee: $40 full-time.

University of Arkansas at Monticello, School of Education, Monticello, AR 71656. Offers education (M Ed, MAT); educational leadership (M Ed). *Accreditation:* NCATE. Part-time and evening/weekend programs available. Postbaccalaureate distance learning degree programs offered (minimal on-campus study). *Degree requirements:* For master's, comprehensive exam. *Entrance requirements:* For master's, minimum GPA of 3.0. Additional exam requirements/recommendations for international students: Required—TOEFL (minimum score 550 paper-based). Electronic applications accepted.

University of Bridgeport, School of Education, Department of Education, Bridgeport, CT 06604. Offers education (MS); educational management (Ed D, Diploma), including intermediate administrator or supervisor (Diploma), leadership (Ed D); elementary education (MS, Diploma), including early childhood education, elementary education; middle school education (MS); music education (MS); remedial reading and language arts (Diploma); secondary education (MS, Diploma), including computer specialist (Diploma), international education (Diploma), reading specialist, secondary education. Part-time and evening/weekend programs available. *Faculty:* 12 full-time (5 women), 108 part-time/adjunct (60 women). *Students:* 155 full-time (108 women), 139 part-time (98 women); includes 48 minority (22 Black or African American, non-Hispanic/Latino; 9 Asian, non-Hispanic/Latino; 15 Hispanic/Latino; 2 Two or more races, non-Hispanic/Latino), 2 international. Average age 30. 306 applicants, 55% accepted, 107 enrolled. In 2013, 153 master's, 16 other advanced degrees awarded. *Degree requirements:* For master's, final exam, final project, or thesis; for doctorate, comprehensive exam, thesis/dissertation; for Diploma, thesis or alternative, final project. *Entrance requirements:* For master's, minimum undergraduate QPA of 2.67; for doctorate, GRE, MAT; for Diploma, GRE General Test or MAT, minimum graduate QPA of 3.0. Additional exam

requirements/recommendations for international students: Recommended—TOEFL (minimum score 550 paper-based; 80 iBT), IELTS (minimum score 6.5). *Application deadline:* For fall admission, 8/1 priority date for domestic and international students; for spring admission, 12/1 priority date for domestic and international students. Applications are processed on a rolling basis. Application fee: $50. Electronic applications accepted. *Expenses:* Contact institution. *Financial support:* In 2013–14, 120 students received support. Fellowships, research assistantships, teaching assistantships, career-related internships or fieldwork, Federal Work-Study, and institutionally sponsored loans available. Support available to part-time students. Financial award application deadline: 6/1; financial award applicants required to submit FAFSA. *Faculty research:* Self-concept, internship assessment, stress and situational development, follow-up of graduation, trend analysis. *Unit head:* Dr. Allen P. Cook, Dean, 203-576-4192, Fax: 203-576-4200, E-mail: acook@bridgeport.edu. *Application contact:* Leanne Proctor, Director of Graduate Admissions, 203-576-4552, Fax: 203-576-4941, E-mail: admit@bridgeport.edu.

University of Bridgeport, School of Education, Department of Educational Leadership, Bridgeport, CT 06604. Offers intermediate administrator or supervisor (Diploma); leadership (Ed D). *Faculty:* 2 full-time (0 women), 4 part-time/adjunct (2 women). *Students:* 28 full-time (21 women), 87 part-time (58 women); includes 22 minority (12 Black or African American, non-Hispanic/Latino; 1 Asian, non-Hispanic/Latino; 7 Hispanic/Latino; 2 Two or more races, non-Hispanic/Latino), 5 international. Average age 39. 63 applicants, 63% accepted, 22 enrolled. In 2013, 7 doctorates, 25 Diplomas awarded. *Degree requirements:* For doctorate, comprehensive exam, thesis/dissertation; for Diploma, thesis or alternative, final project. *Entrance requirements:* For doctorate, GRE, MAT; for Diploma, GRE General Test or MAT, minimum graduate QPA of 3.0. Additional exam requirements/recommendations for international students: Recommended—TOEFL (minimum score 550 paper-based; 80 iBT), IELTS (minimum score 6.5). *Application deadline:* For fall admission, 8/1 priority date for domestic and international students; for spring admission, 12/1 priority date for domestic and international students. Applications are processed on a rolling basis. Application fee: $50. Electronic applications accepted. *Expenses:* Contact institution. *Financial support:* In 2013–14, 20 students received support. Fellowships, research assistantships, teaching assistantships, career-related internships or fieldwork, Federal Work-Study, and institutionally sponsored loans available. Support available to part-time students. Financial award application deadline: 6/1; financial award applicants required to submit FAFSA. *Unit head:* Dr. Thomas W. Christ, Chairman, 203-576-4028, Fax: 203-576-4102, E-mail: tchrist@bridgeport.edu. *Application contact:* Leanne Proctor, Director of Graduate Admissions, 203-576-4552, Fax: 203-576-4941, E-mail: admit@bridgeport.edu.

The University of British Columbia, Faculty of Education, Department of Educational Studies, Vancouver, BC V6T 1Z1, Canada. Offers adult education (M Ed, MA); adult learning and global change (M Ed); educational administration (M Ed, MA); educational leadership and policy (Ed D); educational studies (PhD); higher education (M Ed, MA); society, culture and politics in education (M Ed, MA). Part-time and evening/weekend programs available. Terminal master's awarded for partial completion of doctoral program. *Degree requirements:* For master's, thesis; for doctorate, comprehensive exam, thesis/dissertation, master's thesis. *Entrance requirements:* For master's, minimum B+ average, 4-year undergraduate degree, field-related experience; for doctorate, minimum B+ average, 4-year undergraduate degree, master's degree, field-related experience. Additional exam requirements/recommendations for international students: Required—TOEFL (minimum score 600 paper-based; 100 iBT) or IELTS (minimum score 6.5). Electronic applications accepted. *Expenses:* Tuition, area resident: Full-time $8000 Canadian dollars. *Faculty research:* Educational leadership educational administration adult education politics in education, global change and adult learning.

University of Calgary, Faculty of Graduate Studies, Werklund School of Education, Graduate Division of Educational Research, Calgary, AB T2N 1N4, Canada. Offers adult learning (M Ed, MA, Ed D, PhD); curriculum and learning (M Ed, MA, Ed D, PhD); educational leadership (M Ed, MA, Ed D, PhD); languages and diversity (M Ed, MA, Ed D, PhD); learning sciences (M Ed, MA, Ed D, PhD). Ed D in educational leadership offered via distance delivery. Part-time and evening/weekend programs available. Postbaccalaureate distance learning degree programs offered (minimal on-campus study). *Degree requirements:* For master's, thesis (for some programs); for doctorate, thesis/dissertation, candidacy exam. *Entrance requirements:* For master's, minimum GPA of 3.0, 3 letters of reference; for doctorate, minimum GPA of 3.5, 3 letters of reference. Additional exam requirements/recommendations for international students: Required—TOEFL, IELTS. Electronic applications accepted. *Faculty research:* Curriculum, leadership, technology, contexts, gifted, second language teaching, work place and adult learning.

University of California, Irvine, Department of Education, Irvine, CA 92697. Offers educational administration (Ed D); educational administration and leadership (Ed D); elementary and secondary education (MAT). Part-time and evening/weekend programs available. *Students:* 254 full-time (194 women), 4 part-time (3 women); includes 125 minority (1 Black or African American, non-Hispanic/Latino; 69 Asian, non-Hispanic/Latino; 41 Hispanic/Latino; 2 Native Hawaiian or other Pacific Islander, non-Hispanic/Latino; 12 Two or more races, non-Hispanic/Latino), 11 international. Average age 28. 506 applicants, 70% accepted, 200 enrolled. In 2013, 133 master's, 17 doctorates awarded. *Degree requirements:* For doctorate, thesis/dissertation. *Entrance requirements:* For master's, GRE, minimum GPA of 3.0; for doctorate, GRE General Test, minimum GPA of 3.0. Additional exam requirements/recommendations for international students: Required—TOEFL (minimum score 550 paper-based). *Application deadline:* For fall admission, 1/2 priority date for domestic students, 1/2 for international students. Application fee: $80 ($100 for international students). Electronic applications accepted. *Financial support:* Fellowships, research assistantships with full tuition reimbursements, institutionally sponsored loans, traineeships, health care benefits, and unspecified assistantships available. Financial award application deadline: 3/1; financial award applicants required to submit FAFSA. *Faculty research:* Education technology, learning theory, social theory, cultural diversity, postmodernism. *Unit head:* Deborah L. Vandell, Dean, 949-824-8026, Fax: 949-824-3968, E-mail: dvandell@uci.edu. *Application contact:* Judi Conroy, Director of Student Services, 949-824-7465, Fax: 949-824-9103, E-mail: jconroy@uci.edu.
Website: http://www.gse.uci.edu/.

University of California, Los Angeles, Graduate Division, Graduate School of Education and Information Studies, Program in Educational Leadership, Los Angeles, CA 90095. Offers Ed D. Evening/weekend programs available. *Degree requirements:* For doctorate, thesis/dissertation, oral and written qualifying exams. *Entrance requirements:* For doctorate, GRE General Test, minimum undergraduate GPA of 3.0, resume. Electronic applications accepted.

University of California, Riverside, Graduate Division, Graduate School of Education, Riverside, CA 92521-0102. Offers autism (M Ed); diversity and equity (M Ed); education specialist (Credential); education, society and culture (MA, PhD); educational psychology (MA, PhD); general education (M Ed); higher education administration and policy (M Ed, PhD); multiple subject (Credential); reading (M Ed); school psychology

(PhD); single subject (Credential); special education (M Ed, MA, PhD); TESOL (M Ed). *Faculty:* 22 full-time (11 women), 14 part-time/adjunct (10 women). *Students:* 218 full-time (148 women); includes 95 minority (10 Black or African American, non-Hispanic/Latino; 30 Asian, non-Hispanic/Latino; 49 Hispanic/Latino; 6 Two or more races, non-Hispanic/Latino), 12 international. Average age 31. 236 applicants, 66% accepted, 78 enrolled. In 2013, 66 master's, 13 doctorates, 86 other advanced degrees awarded. Terminal master's awarded for partial completion of doctoral program. *Degree requirements:* For master's, thesis optional, comprehensive exams or thesis (MA), case study or analytical report (M Ed); for doctorate, thesis/dissertation, written and oral qualifying exams, college teaching practicum. *Entrance requirements:* For master's, GRE General Test (for MA); CBEST and CSET (for M Ed in general education only), UCR Extension TESOL certificate (for M Ed with TESOL emphasis only); for doctorate, GRE General Test, writing sample; for Credential, CBEST, CSET. Additional exam requirements/recommendations for international students: Required—TOEFL (minimum score 550 paper-based; 80 iBT), IELTS (minimum score 7). *Application deadline:* For fall admission, 9/1 for domestic students, 5/1 for international students; for winter admission, 11/15 for domestic students, 7/1 for international students; for spring admission, 3/1 for domestic students, 10/1 for international students. Applications are processed on a rolling basis. Application fee: $80 ($100 for international students). Electronic applications accepted. *Financial support:* In 2013–14, 58 students received support, including 31 fellowships with full tuition reimbursements available, 11 research assistantships with full tuition reimbursements available (averaging $14,691 per year), 5 teaching assistantships with full tuition reimbursements available (averaging $17,655 per year); career-related internships or fieldwork, Federal Work-Study, institutionally sponsored loans, scholarships/grants, and unspecified assistantships also available. Financial award application deadline: 1/5. *Faculty research:* Responsiveness to intervention, faculty core, response to intervention of English language learners, advanced modeling techniques, study on social capital, trust, and motivation. *Total annual research expenditures:* $1.9 million. *Unit head:* Prof. Douglas Mitchell, Interim Dean and Professor, 951-827-5802, Fax: 951-827-3942, E-mail: douglas.mitchell@ucr.edu. *Application contact:* Prof. Michael Orosco, Assistant Professor and Graduate Advisor of Admissions, 951-827-6362, Fax: 951-827-3291, E-mail: edgrad@ucr.edu. Website: http://www.education.ucr.edu/.

University of California, San Diego, Office of Graduate Studies, Program in Education Studies, La Jolla, CA 92093. Offers education (M Ed); educational leadership (Ed D); teaching and learning (M Ed, MA, Ed D), including bilingual education (M Ed), curriculum design (MA). Ed D offered jointly with California State University, San Marcos. *Students:* 66 full-time (46 women), 66 part-time (54 women); includes 66 minority (11 Black or African American, non-Hispanic/Latino; 6 American Indian or Alaska Native, non-Hispanic/Latino; 29 Asian, non-Hispanic/Latino; 20 Hispanic/Latino), 1 international. 91 applicants, 87% accepted, 64 enrolled. In 2013, 78 master's, 15 doctorates awarded. *Degree requirements:* For master's, thesis (for some programs), student teaching; for doctorate, thesis/dissertation. *Entrance requirements:* For master's, GRE General Test; CBEST and appropriate CSET exam (for select tracks), current teaching or educational assignment (for select tracks); for doctorate, GRE General Test, current teaching or educational assignment (for select tracks). Additional exam requirements/recommendations for international students: Required—TOEFL, IELTS. *Application deadline:* For fall admission, 2/4 for domestic students; for winter admission, 8/1 for domestic students; for summer admission, 2/4 for domestic students. Application fee: $80 ($100 for international students). Electronic applications accepted. *Expenses:* Tuition, state resident: full-time $11,220; part-time $1870 per quarter. Tuition, nonresident: full-time $26,322; part-time $4387 per quarter. *Required fees:* $519.50 per quarter. Part-time tuition and fees vary according to course load and program. *Financial support:* Fellowships and scholarships/grants available. Financial award applicants required to submit FAFSA. *Faculty research:* Language, culture and literacy development of deaf/hard of hearing children; equity issues in education; educational reform; evaluation, assessment, and research methodologies; distributed learning. *Unit head:* Alan J. Daly, Chair, 858-822-6472, E-mail: ajdaly@ucsd.edu. *Application contact:* Giselle Van Luit, Graduate Coordinator, 858-534-2958, E-mail: edsinfo@ucsd.edu.

University of Central Arkansas, Graduate School, College of Education, Department of Leadership Studies, Conway, AR 72035-0001. Offers college student personnel (MS); district-level administration (PMC); educational leadership - district level (Ed S); instructional technology (MS); library media and information technology (MS); school counseling (MS); school leadership (MS); school-based leadership adult education program administration (PMC); school-based leadership building administration (PMC); school-based leadership curriculum administration (PMC); school-based leadership gifted and talented program administration (PMC); school-based leadership special education program administration (PMC). *Accreditation:* NCATE. Part-time and evening/weekend programs available. Postbaccalaureate distance learning degree programs offered (minimal on-campus study). *Degree requirements:* For master's and other advanced degree, comprehensive exam. *Entrance requirements:* For master's, GRE. Additional exam requirements/recommendations for international students: Required—TOEFL (minimum score 80 iBT). Electronic applications accepted. *Expenses:* Contact institution.

University of Central Florida, College of Education and Human Performance, Department of Educational and Human Sciences, Program in Educational Leadership, Orlando, FL 32816. Offers educational leadership (MA, Ed D), including community college education (MA), higher education (Ed D), student personnel (MA). Part-time and evening/weekend programs available. *Students:* 108 full-time (79 women), 259 part-time (180 women); includes 105 minority (43 Black or African American, non-Hispanic/Latino; 1 American Indian or Alaska Native, non-Hispanic/Latino; 8 Asian, non-Hispanic/Latino; 49 Hispanic/Latino; 4 Two or more races, non-Hispanic/Latino), 1 international. Average age 33. 218 applicants, 82% accepted, 117 enrolled. In 2013, 42 master's, 22 doctorates awarded. *Degree requirements:* For master's, thesis or alternative; for doctorate, thesis/dissertation, candidacy exam. *Entrance requirements:* For master's, GRE General Test; for doctorate, GRE General Test, GRE Subject Test, minimum GPA of 3.0, resume. Additional exam requirements/recommendations for international students: Required—TOEFL. *Application deadline:* For fall admission, 2/20 priority date for domestic students; for spring admission, 9/20 priority date for domestic students. Application fee: $30. Electronic applications accepted. *Financial support:* In 2013–14, 14 students received support, including 2 fellowships with partial tuition reimbursements available (averaging $2,800 per year), 12 research assistantships with partial tuition reimbursements available (averaging $6,700 per year), 1 teaching assistantship with partial tuition reimbursement available (averaging $6,600 per year); career-related internships or fieldwork, Federal Work-Study, institutionally sponsored loans, tuition waivers (partial), and unspecified assistantships also available. Financial award application deadline: 3/1; financial award applicants required to submit FAFSA. *Unit head:* Dr. Kenneth Murray, Program Coordinator, 407-832-1468, E-mail: kenneth.murray@ucf.edu. *Application contact:* Barbara Rodriguez Lamas, Director, Admissions and Student Services, 407-823-2766, Fax: 407-823-6442, E-mail: gradadmissions@ucf.edu.
Website: http://education.ucf.edu/departments.cfm.

University of Central Florida, College of Education and Human Performance, School of Teaching, Learning, and Leadership, Program in Mathematics Education, Orlando, FL 32816. Offers teacher education (MAT), including mathematics education, middle school mathematics; teacher leadership (M Ed). *Accreditation:* NCATE. Part-time and evening/weekend programs available. *Students:* 3 full-time (1 woman), 35 part-time (22 women); includes 12 minority (2 Black or African American, non-Hispanic/Latino; 3 Asian, non-Hispanic/Latino; 7 Hispanic/Latino). Average age 24. 11 applicants, 64% accepted, 3 enrolled. In 2013, 23 master's awarded. *Entrance requirements:* For master's, GRE General Test. Additional exam requirements/recommendations for international students: Required—TOEFL. *Application deadline:* For fall admission, 7/15 for domestic students; for spring admission, 12/1 for domestic students. Application fee: $30. Electronic applications accepted. *Financial support:* In 2013–14, 1 student received support. Fellowships, research assistantships, teaching assistantships, career-related internships or fieldwork, Federal Work-Study, institutionally sponsored loans, tuition waivers (partial), and unspecified assistantships available. Financial award application deadline: 3/1; financial award applicants required to submit FAFSA. *Unit head:* Dr. Erhan Seluk Haciomeroglu, Program Coordinator, 407-823-4336, E-mail: erhan.haciomeroglu@ucf.edu. *Application contact:* Barbara Rodriguez Lamas, Director, Admissions and Student Support, 407-823-2766, Fax: 407-823-6442, E-mail: gradadmissions@ucf.edu.

University of Central Florida, College of Education and Human Performance, School of Teaching, Learning, and Leadership, Teacher Leadership and Educational Leadership Program, Orlando, FL 32816. Offers teacher leadership (M Ed). *Students:* 8 full-time (5 women), 56 part-time (47 women); includes 5 minority (2 Black or African American, non-Hispanic/Latino; 1 Asian, non-Hispanic/Latino; 1 Hispanic/Latino; 1 Two or more races, non-Hispanic/Latino). Average age 31. 27 applicants, 85% accepted, 18 enrolled. In 2013, 16 master's awarded. Application fee: $30. Electronic applications accepted. *Financial support:* In 2013–14, 1 student received support, including 1 research assistantship with partial tuition reimbursement available (averaging $7,200 per year). *Unit head:* Dr. Gillian Eriksson, Program Coordinator, 407-823-6493, E-mail: gillian.eriksson@ucf.edu. *Application contact:* Barbara Rodriguez Lamas, Director, Admissions and Student Services, 407-823-2766, Fax: 407-823-6442, E-mail: gradadmissions@ucf.edu.
Website: http://education.ucf.edu/departments.cfm.

University of Central Missouri, The Graduate School, Warrensburg, MO 6409. Offers accountancy (MA); accounting (MBA); applied mathematics (MS); aviation safety (MA); biology (MS); business administration (MBA); career and technical education leadership (MS); college student personnel administration (MS); communication (MA); computer science (MS); counseling (MS); criminal justice (MS); educational leadership (Ed D); educational technology (MS); elementary and early childhood education (MSE); English (MA); environmental studies (MA); finance (MBA); history (MA); human services/educational technology (Ed S); human services/learning resources (Ed S); human services/professional counseling (Ed S); industrial hygiene (MS); industrial management (MS); information systems (MBA); information technology (MS); kinesiology (MS); library science and information services (MS); literacy education (MSE); marketing (MBA); mathematics (MS); music (MA); occupational safety management (MS); psychology (MS); rural family nursing (MS); school administration (MSE); social gerontology (MS); sociology (MA); special education (MSE); speech language pathology (MS); superintendency (Ed S); teaching (MAT); teaching English as a second language (MA); technology (MS); technology management (PhD); theatre (MA). Part-time programs available. *Faculty:* 233. *Students:* 890 full-time (396 women), 1,486 part-time (1,001 women); includes 192 minority (97 Black or African American, non-Hispanic/Latino; 9 American Indian or Alaska Native, non-Hispanic/Latino; 32 Asian, non-Hispanic/Latino; 40 Hispanic/Latino; 3 Native Hawaiian or other Pacific Islander, non-Hispanic/Latino; 11 Two or more races, non-Hispanic/Latino), 539 international. Average age 31. 1,953 applicants, 75% accepted. In 2013, 719 master's, 58 other advanced degrees awarded. *Degree requirements:* For master's and Ed S, comprehensive exam (for some programs), thesis (for some programs). *Entrance requirements:* Additional exam requirements/recommendations for international students: Required—TOEFL (minimum score 550 paper-based; 79 iBT). *Application deadline:* For fall admission, 6/1 for domestic students; for spring admission, 10/1 for domestic and international students. Applications are processed on a rolling basis. Application fee: $30 ($75 for international students). Electronic applications accepted. *Expenses:* Tuition, state resident: full-time $7326; part-time $276.25 per credit hour. Tuition, nonresident: full-time $13,956; part-time $552.50 per credit hour. *Required fees:* $29 per credit hour. *Financial support:* In 2013–14, 118 students received support, including 271 research assistantships with full and partial tuition reimbursements available (averaging $7,500 per year), 109 teaching assistantships with full and partial tuition reimbursements available (averaging $7,500 per year); career-related internships or fieldwork, Federal Work-Study, scholarships/grants, and administrative and laboratory assistantships also available. Support available to part-time students. Financial award application deadline: 3/1; financial award applicants required to submit FAFSA. *Unit head:* Dr. Joseph Vaughn, Assistant Provost for Research/Dean, 660-543-4092, Fax: 660-543-4778, E-mail: vaughn@ucmo.edu. *Application contact:* Brittany Lawrence, Graduate Student Services Coordinator, 660-543-4621, Fax: 660-543-4778, E-mail: gradinfo@ucmo.edu.
Website: http://www.ucmo.edu/graduate/.

University of Central Oklahoma, The Jackson College of Graduate Studies, College of Education and Professional Studies, Department of Advanced Professional and Special Services, Edmond, OK 73034-5209. Offers educational leadership (M Ed); library media education (M Ed); reading (M Ed); school counseling (M Ed); special education (M Ed), including mild/moderate disabilities, severe-profound/multiple disabilities, special education; speech-language pathology (MS). Part-time programs available. *Faculty:* 14 full-time (9 women), 16 part-time/adjunct (8 women). *Students:* 87 full-time (80 women), 298 part-time (251 women); includes 77 minority (32 Black or African American, non-Hispanic/Latino; 10 American Indian or Alaska Native, non-Hispanic/Latino; 2 Asian, non-Hispanic/Latino; 15 Hispanic/Latino; 18 Two or more races, non-Hispanic/Latino), 9 international. Average age 34. 147 applicants, 94% accepted, 89 enrolled. In 2013, 163 master's awarded. *Degree requirements:* For master's, comprehensive exam (for some programs), thesis (for some programs). *Entrance requirements:* For master's, GRE. Additional exam requirements/recommendations for international students: Required—TOEFL (minimum score 550 paper-based; 79 iBT), IELTS (minimum score 6.5). *Application deadline:* For fall admission, 7/1 for international students; for spring admission, 7/1 for international students. Applications are processed on a rolling basis. Application fee: $50. Electronic applications accepted. *Expenses:* Tuition, state resident: full-time $4137; part-time $206.85 per credit hour. Tuition, nonresident: full-time $10,359; part-time $517.95 per credit hour. *Required fees:* $481. Tuition and fees vary according to course load and program. *Financial support:* In 2013–14, 93 students received support, including 4 research assistantships with partial tuition reimbursements available (averaging $8,133 per year); teaching assistantships with partial tuition reimbursements available, career-related internships or fieldwork, scholarships/grants, tuition waivers (partial), and unspecified assistantships also available. Financial award application deadline: 3/31; financial award applicants required to submit FAFSA. *Faculty research:* Intellectual freedom, fair use copyright, technology integration, young adult literature, distance learning. *Unit head:* Dr. Patsy Couts, Chair, 405-974-3888, Fax: 405-

974-3857, E-mail: pcouts@uco.edu. *Application contact:* Dr. Richard Bernard, Dean, Graduate College, 405-974-3493, Fax: 405-974-3852, E-mail: gradcoll@uco.edu.
Website: http://www.uco.edu/ceps/dept/apss/.

University of Cincinnati, Graduate School, College of Education, Criminal Justice, and Human Services, Division of Educational Studies, Program in Educational Leadership, Cincinnati, OH 45221. Offers M Ed, Ed S. *Accreditation:* NCATE. Part-time programs available. Postbaccalaureate distance learning degree programs offered. *Degree requirements:* For master's, thesis or alternative. *Entrance requirements:* For master's, GRE General Test, 3 letters of reference, resume, minimum GPA of 2.8; for Ed S, references, interview. Additional exam requirements/recommendations for international students: Required—TOEFL (minimum score 550 paper-based). Electronic applications accepted.

University of Cincinnati, Graduate School, College of Education, Criminal Justice, and Human Services, Division of Educational Studies, Program in Urban Educational Leadership, Cincinnati, OH 45221. Offers Ed D. *Degree requirements:* For doctorate, thesis/dissertation. *Entrance requirements:* For doctorate, GRE General Test, GRE Subject Test. Additional exam requirements/recommendations for international students: Required—TOEFL (minimum score 550 paper-based), OEPT.

University of Colorado Colorado Springs, College of Education, Colorado Springs, CO 80933-7150. Offers counseling and human services (MA); curriculum and instruction (MA); educational administration (MA); educational leadership (MA, PhD); special education (MA). *Accreditation:* ACA; NCATE. Part-time and evening/weekend programs available. Postbaccalaureate distance learning degree programs offered (minimal on-campus study). *Faculty:* 25 full-time (17 women), 39 part-time/adjunct (29 women). *Students:* 220 full-time (146 women), 237 part-time (163 women); includes 86 minority (18 Black or African American, non-Hispanic/Latino; 3 American Indian or Alaska Native, non-Hispanic/Latino; 11 Asian, non-Hispanic/Latino; 46 Hispanic/Latino; 8 Two or more races, non-Hispanic/Latino), 16 international. Average age 35. 182 applicants, 88% accepted, 118 enrolled. In 2013, 140 master's, 8 doctorates awarded. *Degree requirements:* For master's, comprehensive exam, thesis or alternative, microcomputer proficiency; for doctorate, comprehensive exam, thesis/dissertation, research lab. *Entrance requirements:* For master's, GRE General Test. Additional exam requirements/recommendations for international students: Recommended—TOEFL. *Application deadline:* For fall admission, 2/28 priority date for domestic students, 2/28 for international students; for spring admission, 10/15 for domestic and international students. Applications are processed on a rolling basis. Application fee: $60 ($75 for international students). *Expenses:* Tuition, state resident: full-time $8882; part-time $1622 per course. Tuition, nonresident: full-time $17,435; part-time $3048 per course. One-time fee: $100. Tuition and fees vary according to course load, degree level, campus/location and program. *Financial support:* In 2013–14, 23 students received support, including 23 fellowships (averaging $1,577 per year); career-related internships or fieldwork, Federal Work-Study, and scholarships/grants also available. Support available to part-time students. Financial award application deadline: 3/1; financial award applicants required to submit FAFSA. *Faculty research:* Linguistically diverse education (LDE), educational policy, evidence-based reading and writing instruction, relational and social aggression, positive behavior supports (PBS), inclusive schooling, K-12 education policy. *Total annual research expenditures:* $136,574. *Unit head:* Dr. Mary Snyder, Dean, 719-255-3701, Fax: 719-262-4133, E-mail: msnyder3@uccs.edu. *Application contact:* Juliane Field, Director, 719-255-4526, Fax: 719-255-4110, E-mail: jfield@uccs.edu.
Website: http://www.uccs.edu/coe.

University of Colorado Denver, School of Education and Human Development, Administrative Leadership and Policy Studies Program, Denver, CO 80217. Offers MA, Ed S. *Accreditation:* NCATE. Part-time and evening/weekend programs available. *Students:* 137 full-time (98 women), 11 part-time (10 women); includes 21 minority (5 Black or African American, non-Hispanic/Latino; 1 American Indian or Alaska Native, non-Hispanic/Latino; 1 Asian, non-Hispanic/Latino; 11 Hispanic/Latino; 3 Two or more races, non-Hispanic/Latino), 1 international. Average age 36. 72 applicants, 85% accepted, 55 enrolled. In 2013, 11 master's, 15 other advanced degrees awarded. *Degree requirements:* For master's, comprehensive exam, 9 credit hours beyond the 32 required for principal-administrator licensure; for Ed S, comprehensive exam, 9 credit hours beyond the 32 required for principal-administrator licensure (for those already holding MA). *Entrance requirements:* For master's and Ed S, GRE or MAT (if GPA is below 2.75), minimum GPA of 2.75, interview, 3 letters of recommendation, resume. Additional exam requirements/recommendations for international students: Required—TOEFL (minimum score 525 paper-based; 71 iBT); Recommended—IELTS (minimum score 6.3). *Application deadline:* For fall admission, 5/15 for domestic students, 5/1 for international students; for spring admission, 10/1 for domestic students, 9/15 for international students. Application fee: $50 ($75 for international students). Electronic applications accepted. *Expenses:* Contact institution. *Financial support:* In 2013–14, 2 students received support. Fellowships, research assistantships, teaching assistantships, Federal Work-Study, institutionally sponsored loans, scholarships/grants, and traineeships available. Financial award application deadline: 4/1; financial award applicants required to submit FAFSA. *Faculty research:* Learning cultures, teaching and learning in educational administration. *Unit head:* Connie Fulmer, Professor, 303-315-4962, E-mail: connie.fulmer@ucdenver.edu. *Application contact:* Rebecca Schell, Academic Advisor, 303-315-4978, E-mail: rebecca.schell@ucdenver.edu.
Website: http://www.ucdenver.edu/academics/colleges/SchoolOfEducation/Academics/MASTERS/PrincipalandSchoolLeadership/Pages/AdministrativeLeadership.aspx.

University of Colorado Denver, School of Education and Human Development, Program in Educational Leadership and Innovation, Denver, CO 80217-3364. Offers educational studies and research (PhD), including administrative leadership and policy, early childhood special education, math education, research, assessment and evaluation, science education, urban ecologies. Part-time and evening/weekend programs available. *Students:* 16 full-time (12 women), 12 part-time (9 women); includes 6 minority (2 Black or African American, non-Hispanic/Latino; 3 Asian, non-Hispanic/Latino; 1 Hispanic/Latino), 1 international. Average age 39. 16 applicants, 31% accepted, 4 enrolled. In 2013, 10 doctorates awarded. *Degree requirements:* For doctorate, comprehensive exam, thesis/dissertation, 75 credit hours (for PhD). *Entrance requirements:* For doctorate, GRE or equivalent, resume or curriculum vitae, letters of recommendation, master's degree or equivalent, completion of basic or advanced statistics course with minimum B grade. Additional exam requirements/recommendations for international students: Required—TOEFL (minimum score 537 paper-based; 75 iBT); Recommended—IELTS (minimum score 6.5). *Application deadline:* For fall admission, 5/1 priority date for domestic students, 4/15 priority date for international students. Applications are processed on a rolling basis. Application fee: $50 ($75 for international students). Electronic applications accepted. *Expenses:* Contact institution. *Financial support:* In 2013–14, 19 students received support. Fellowships, research assistantships, teaching assistantships, Federal Work-Study, institutionally sponsored loans, scholarships/grants, and traineeships available. Financial award application deadline: 4/1; financial award applicants required to submit FAFSA. *Faculty research:* Administrative leadership and policy studies, early childhood education, research in diversity, paraprofessionals in education, urban schools lab. *Unit head:* Dr. Deanna Sands, Associate Dean, Research and Professional Development, 303-315-4931, E-mail: deanna.sands@ucdenver.edu. *Application contact:* Student Services Center, 303-315-6300, Fax: 303-315-6311, E-mail: education@ucdenver.edu.
Website: http://www.ucdenver.edu/academics/colleges/SchoolOfEducation/Academics/Doctorate/Pages/PhD.aspx.

University of Colorado Denver, School of Education and Human Development, Program in Leadership for Educational Equity, Denver, CO 80217. Offers executive leadership (Ed D); instructional leadership (Ed D). *Students:* 28 full-time (20 women), 8 part-time (7 women); includes 10 minority (3 Black or African American, non-Hispanic/Latino; 2 Asian, non-Hispanic/Latino; 5 Hispanic/Latino). Average age 41. In 2013, 10 doctorates awarded. *Degree requirements:* For doctorate, thesis/dissertation, 69 credit hours, including 24 credits in dissertation and independent study. *Entrance requirements:* For doctorate, GRE General Test, resume with minimum of 5 years experience in an educational background, 2-3 professional artifacts illuminating leadership experiences, three professional letters of recommendation, master's degree with recommended minimum GPA of 3.2. Additional exam requirements/recommendations for international students: Required—TOEFL (minimum score 550 paper-based; 80 iBT); Recommended—IELTS (minimum score 6.8). *Application deadline:* For fall admission, 5/1 for domestic students, 4/15 priority date for international students; for spring admission, 10/1 for international students. Applications are processed on a rolling basis. Application fee: $50 ($75 for international students). *Financial support:* In 2013–14, 6 students received support. Fellowships, research assistantships, teaching assistantships, Federal Work-Study, institutionally sponsored loans, scholarships/grants, and traineeships available. Financial award application deadline: 4/1; financial award applicants required to submit FAFSA. *Unit head:* Dr. Shelley Zion, Executive Director of the Center for Continuing Professional Education, 303-315-4920, E-mail: shelley.zion@ucdenver.edu. *Application contact:* Student Services Center, 303-315-6300, Fax: 303-315-6311, E-mail: education@ucdenver.edu.
Website: http://www.ucdenver.edu/academics/colleges/SchoolOfEducation/Academics/Doctorate/Pages/EdD.aspx.

University of Connecticut, Graduate School, Neag School of Education, Department of Educational Leadership, Field of Educational Administration, Storrs, CT 06269. Offers Ed D, PhD, Post-Master's Certificate. *Accreditation:* NCATE. *Degree requirements:* For doctorate, thesis/dissertation. *Entrance requirements:* For doctorate, GRE General Test. Additional exam requirements/recommendations for international students: Required—TOEFL (minimum score 550 paper-based). Electronic applications accepted.

University of Dayton, Department of Counselor Education and Human Services, Dayton, OH 45469-1300. Offers clinical mental health counseling (MS Ed); college student personnel (MS Ed); higher education administration (MS Ed); human services (MS Ed); school counseling (MS Ed); school psychology (MS Ed, Ed S). *Accreditation:* ACA; NCATE. Part-time and evening/weekend programs available. *Faculty:* 11 full-time (7 women), 46 part-time/adjunct (31 women). *Students:* 212 full-time (170 women), 151 part-time (118 women); includes 73 minority (61 Black or African American, non-Hispanic/Latino; 1 Asian, non-Hispanic/Latino; 8 Hispanic/Latino; 3 Two or more races, non-Hispanic/Latino), 4 international. Average age 32. 295 applicants, 47% accepted, 103 enrolled. In 2013, 147 master's, 5 Ed Ss awarded. *Degree requirements:* For master's, comprehensive exam (for some programs), thesis (for some programs), exit exam. *Entrance requirements:* For master's, MAT or GRE (if GPA less than 2.75), interview, writing sample. Additional exam requirements/recommendations for international students: Required—TOEFL (minimum score 550 paper-based; 80 iBT). *Application deadline:* For fall admission, 4/10 for domestic students, 4/10 priority date for international students; for winter admission, 9/10 for domestic students, 7/1 for international students; for spring admission, 9/10 for domestic students, 9/10 priority date for international students. Application fee: $0 ($50 for international students). Electronic applications accepted. *Expenses: Tuition:* Full-time $10,296; part-time $858 per credit hour. *Required fees:* $50; $25. *Financial support:* In 2013–14, 10 research assistantships with full tuition reimbursements (averaging $8,720 per year) were awarded; career-related internships or fieldwork, institutionally sponsored loans, health care benefits, and unspecified assistantships also available. Financial award application deadline: 3/1; financial award applicants required to submit FAFSA. *Faculty research:* Mindfulness, forgiveness in relationships, positive psychology in couples counseling, traumatic brain injury responses, college student development. *Unit head:* Dr. Molly Schaller, Chairperson, 937-229-3644, Fax: 937-229-1055, E-mail: mschaller1@udayton.edu. *Application contact:* Kathleen Brown, Administrative Assistant, 937-229-3644, Fax: 937-229-1055, E-mail: kbrown1@udayton.edu.
Website: http://www.udayton.edu/education/edc/index.php.

University of Dayton, Department of Teacher Education, Dayton, OH 45469-1300. Offers adolescence to young adult education (MS Ed); early childhood education (MS Ed); early childhood leadership and advocacy (MS Ed); interdisciplinary education studies (MS Ed); intervention specialist education, mild/moderate (MS Ed); literacy (MS Ed); middle childhood education (MS Ed); multi-age education (MS Ed); music education (MS Ed); teacher as leader (MS Ed); technology enhanced learning (MS Ed). Part-time and evening/weekend programs available. Postbaccalaureate distance learning degree programs offered (no on-campus study). *Faculty:* 19 full-time (13 women), 21 part-time/adjunct (18 women). *Students:* 69 full-time (57 women), 86 part-time (75 women); includes 16 minority (10 Black or African American, non-Hispanic/Latino; 2 Asian, non-Hispanic/Latino; 4 Hispanic/Latino), 10 international. Average age 31. 140 applicants, 54% accepted, 39 enrolled. In 2013, 93 master's awarded. *Degree requirements:* For master's, variable foreign language requirement, comprehensive exam (for some programs), thesis. *Entrance requirements:* For master's, GRE or MAT, minimum GPA of 2.75. Additional exam requirements/recommendations for international students: Required—TOEFL (minimum score 550 paper-based; 80 iBT), IELTS (minimum score 6.5). *Application deadline:* For fall admission, 3/1 for domestic students, 5/1 for international students; for winter admission, 7/1 for international students; for spring admission, 11/1 for international students. Applications are processed on a rolling basis. Application fee: $0 ($50 for international students). Electronic applications accepted. *Expenses:* Contact institution. *Financial support:* In 2013–14, 61 students received support, including 5 research assistantships with full tuition reimbursements available (averaging $8,720 per year), 3 teaching assistantships with full tuition reimbursements available (averaging $8,720 per year); career-related internships or fieldwork, institutionally sponsored loans, scholarships/grants, traineeships, health care benefits, and unspecified assistantships also available. Support available to part-time students. Financial award application deadline: 3/1; financial award applicants required to submit FAFSA. *Faculty research:* Diversity, literacy, art representation by young children, preservice teacher preparation. *Unit head:* Dr. Connie L. Bowman, Chair, 937-229-3305, E-mail: cbowman1@udayton.edu. *Application contact:* Gina Seiter, Graduate Program Advisor, 937-229-3103, E-mail: gseiter1@udayton.edu.

University of Dayton, Doctoral Program in Educational Leadership, Dayton, OH 45469-1300. Offers PhD. Evening/weekend programs available. *Faculty:* 9 full-time (4 women). *Students:* 36 full-time (19 women); includes 1 minority (Black or African American, non-Hispanic/Latino), 1 international. Average age 42. 21 applicants, 24% accepted, 4 enrolled. In 2013, 10 doctorates awarded. *Degree requirements:* For doctorate,

comprehensive exam, thesis/dissertation. *Entrance requirements:* For doctorate, GRE, administration experience, minimum GPA of 3.25 in master's degree program. Additional exam requirements/recommendations for international students: Required—TOEFL (minimum score 550 paper-based; 80 iBT). *Application deadline:* For fall admission, 5/1 priority date for international students; for winter admission, 7/1 for international students; for spring admission, 11/1 priority date for international students. Applications are processed on a rolling basis. Application fee: $0 ($50 for international students). Electronic applications accepted. *Expenses: Tuition:* Full-time $10,296; part-time $858 per credit hour. *Required fees:* $50; $25. *Financial support:* In 2013–14, 6 research assistantships with full tuition reimbursements (averaging $12,600 per year) were awarded; institutionally sponsored loans, health care benefits, and unspecified assistantships also available. Financial award application deadline: 3/1; financial award applicants required to submit FAFSA. *Faculty research:* Education law, school finance, faculty development, K-12 administration, higher education administration. *Unit head:* Dr. Charles J. Russo, Interim Director, 937-229-3722, Fax: 937-229-4824, E-mail: crusso1@udayton.edu. *Application contact:* Nancy Crouchley, Administrative Assistant, 937-229-4003, Fax: 937-229-4729, E-mail: ncrouchley1@udayton.edu.
Website: http://www.udayton.edu/education/phd/.

University of Dayton, Educational Leadership Program, Dayton, OH 45469-1300. Offers MS Ed, Ed S. Part-time and evening/weekend programs available. Postbaccalaureate distance learning degree programs offered (no on-campus study). *Faculty:* 8 full-time (3 women), 12 part-time/adjunct (4 women). *Students:* 140 full-time (104 women), 213 part-time (146 women); includes 28 minority (21 Black or African American, non-Hispanic/Latino; 1 American Indian or Alaska Native, non-Hispanic/Latino; 2 Asian, non-Hispanic/Latino; 4 Hispanic/Latino), 59 international. Average age 33. 73 applicants, 59% accepted, 24 enrolled. In 2013, 119 master's, 2 Ed Ss awarded. *Degree requirements:* For master's, comprehensive exam (for some programs), thesis or alternative. *Entrance requirements:* For master's, MAT or GRE if undergraduate GPA is below 2.75, minimum GPA of 2.75. Additional exam requirements/recommendations for international students: Required—TOEFL (minimum score 550 paper-based; 80 iBT). *Application deadline:* For fall admission, 1/20 for domestic students, 5/1 for international students; for winter admission, 10/10 for domestic students, 10/1 for international students; for spring admission, 1/14 for domestic students, 11/1 for international students. Applications are processed on a rolling basis. Application fee: $0 ($50 for international students). Electronic applications accepted. *Expenses: Tuition:* Full-time $10,296; part-time $858 per credit hour. *Required fees:* $50; $25. *Financial support:* In 2013–14, 1 research assistantship with full tuition reimbursement (averaging $17,165 per year) was awarded; institutionally sponsored loans, health care benefits, and unspecified assistantships also available. Financial award application deadline: 3/1; financial award applicants required to submit FAFSA. *Faculty research:* Administrator perceptions toward the Ohio Teach Evaluation System, qualitative study of undergraduate students who engage in community service, qualitative study of urban girls in elementary schools. *Unit head:* Dr. David D. Dolph, Chair, 937-229-3737, Fax: 937-229-3392, E-mail: ddolph1@udayton.edu. *Application contact:* Janice Keivel, Administrative Associate, 937-229-3738, Fax: 937-229-3392, E-mail: jkeivel1@udayton.edu.
Website: http://www.udayton.edu/education/edl.

University of Delaware, College of Education and Human Development, School of Education, Newark, DE 19716. Offers education (PhD); educational leadership (Ed D); higher education (M Ed); instruction (MI); reading (M Ed); school leadership (M Ed); school psychology (MA, Ed S); teaching English as a second language (TESL) (MA). *Accreditation:* NCATE. Part-time and evening/weekend programs available. Terminal master's awarded for partial completion of doctoral program. *Degree requirements:* For master's, comprehensive exam (for some programs), thesis (for some programs); for doctorate, comprehensive exam (for some programs), thesis/dissertation. *Entrance requirements:* For master's and doctorate, GRE, 3 letters of recommendation. Additional exam requirements/recommendations for international students: Required—TOEFL (minimum score 600 paper-based). Electronic applications accepted. *Faculty research:* Teacher education; curriculum theory and development; community based education models, educational leadership.

University of Denver, Morgridge College of Education, Denver, CO 80208. Offers child, family and school psychology (MA, PhD, Ed S); counseling psychology (MA, PhD); curriculum and instruction (MA, Ed D, PhD); curriculum instruction and teaching (Certificate); early childhood special education (MA); educational leadership and policy studies (MA, Ed D, PhD, Certificate); higher education (MA, Ed D, PhD); law librarianship (Certificate); library and information science (MLIS); research methods and statistics (MA, PhD). *Accreditation:* ALA; APA (one or more programs are accredited). Part-time and evening/weekend programs available. Postbaccalaureate distance learning degree programs offered (no on-campus study). *Faculty:* 35 full-time (21 women), 63 part-time/adjunct (43 women). *Students:* 435 full-time (332 women), 414 part-time (297 women); includes 194 minority (45 Black or African American, non-Hispanic/Latino; 9 American Indian or Alaska Native, non-Hispanic/Latino; 16 Asian, non-Hispanic/Latino; 96 Hispanic/Latino; 2 Native Hawaiian or other Pacific Islander, non-Hispanic/Latino; 26 Two or more races, non-Hispanic/Latino), 14 international. Average age 32. 672 applicants, 61% accepted, 193 enrolled. In 2013, 248 master's, 30 doctorates, 130 other advanced degrees awarded. Terminal master's awarded for partial completion of doctoral program. *Degree requirements:* For master's, comprehensive exam; for doctorate, 2 foreign languages, comprehensive exam, thesis/dissertation. *Entrance requirements:* For master's and doctorate, GRE General Test or GMAT. Additional exam requirements/recommendations for international students: Required—TOEFL (minimum score 550 paper-based; 80 iBT). *Application deadline:* Applications are processed on a rolling basis. Application fee: $65. Electronic applications accepted. *Financial support:* In 2013–14, 706 students received support, including 54 research assistantships with full and partial tuition reimbursements available (averaging $15,599 per year), 77 teaching assistantships with full and partial tuition reimbursements available (averaging $12,804 per year); career-related internships or fieldwork, Federal Work-Study, institutionally sponsored loans, scholarships/grants, and unspecified assistantships also available. Support available to part-time students. Financial award application deadline: 2/15; financial award applicants required to submit FAFSA. *Faculty research:* Principal and teacher preparation, development and assessments, gifted education, service-learning, early childhood, mathematics education, access to higher education. *Total annual research expenditures:* $6.3 million. *Unit head:* Dr. Karen Riley, Interim Dean, 303-871-3665, E-mail: karen.riley@du.edu. *Application contact:* Jodi Dye, Assistant Director of Admissions, 303-871-2510, E-mail: jodi.dye@du.edu.
Website: http://morgridge.du.edu/.

University of Detroit Mercy, College of Liberal Arts and Education, Department of Education, Program in Educational Administration, Detroit, MI 48221. Offers MA. *Degree requirements:* For master's, thesis or alternative. *Entrance requirements:* For master's, minimum GPA of 2.75.

The University of Findlay, Office of Graduate Admissions, Findlay, OH 45840-3653. Offers athletic training (MAT); business (MBA), including health care management, hospitality management, organizational leadership, public management; education (MA Ed), including administration, children's literature, early childhood, human resource development, reading, science, special education, technology; environmental, safety and health management (MSEM); health informatics (MS); occupational therapy (MOT); pharmacy (Pharm D); physical therapy (DPT); physician assistant (MPA); rhetoric and writing (MA); teaching English to speakers of other languages (TESOL) and bilingual education (MA). Part-time and evening/weekend programs available. Postbaccalaureate distance learning degree programs offered (no on-campus study). *Faculty:* 209 full-time (98 women), 69 part-time/adjunct (38 women). *Students:* 551 full-time (332 women), 457 part-time (276 women); includes 77 minority (37 Black or African American, non-Hispanic/Latino; 1 American Indian or Alaska Native, non-Hispanic/Latino; 15 Asian, non-Hispanic/Latino; 23 Hispanic/Latino; 1 Native Hawaiian or other Pacific Islander, non-Hispanic/Latino), 135 international. Average age 28. 637 applicants, 66% accepted, 241 enrolled. In 2013, 267 master's, 91 doctorates awarded. *Degree requirements:* For master's, thesis, cumulative project, capstone project. *Entrance requirements:* For master's, GRE/GMAT, bachelor's degree from accredited institution, minimum undergraduate GPA of 2.5 in last 64 hours of course work; for doctorate, GRE, minimum cumulative GPA of 3.0. Additional exam requirements/recommendations for international students: Required—TOEFL (minimum score 80 iBT). *Application deadline:* Applications are processed on a rolling basis. Application fee: $25. Electronic applications accepted. *Expenses: Required fees:* $146 per semester. Tuition and fees vary according to degree level and program. *Financial support:* In 2013–14, 11 research assistantships with full and partial tuition reimbursements (averaging $4,000 per year), 10 teaching assistantships with full and partial tuition reimbursements (averaging $3,600 per year) were awarded; career-related internships or fieldwork, Federal Work-Study, health care benefits, and unspecified assistantships also available. Financial award application deadline: 4/1; financial award applicants required to submit FAFSA. *Unit head:* Christopher M. Harris, Director of Admissions, 419-434-4347, E-mail: harrisc1@findlay.edu. *Application contact:* Emily Ickes, Graduate Admissions Counselor, 419-434-6933, Fax: 419-434-4898, E-mail: ickese@findlay.edu.
Website: http://www.findlay.edu/admissions/graduate/Pages/default.aspx.

University of Florida, Graduate School, College of Education, School of Human Development and Organizational Studies in Education, Gainesville, FL 32611. Offers counseling and counselor education (Ed D, PhD), including counseling and counselor education, marriage and family counseling, mental health counseling, school counseling and guidance; educational leadership (M Ed, MAE, Ed D, PhD, Ed S), including educational leadership (Ed D, PhD), educational policy (Ed D, PhD); higher education administration (Ed D, PhD, Ed S), including education policy (Ed D), educational policy (Ed D, PhD), higher education administration (Ed D, PhD); marriage and family counseling (M Ed, MAE, Ed S); mental health counseling (M Ed, MAE, Ed S); research and evaluation methodology (M Ed, MAE, Ed D, PhD, Ed S); school counseling and guidance (M Ed, MAE, Ed S); student personnel in higher education (M Ed, MAE, Ed S). *Accreditation:* ACA (one or more programs are accredited); NCATE. Part-time programs available. Postbaccalaureate distance learning degree programs offered. *Faculty:* 20 full-time (11 women), 4 part-time/adjunct (1 woman). *Students:* 291 full-time (232 women), 212 part-time (157 women); includes 145 minority (71 Black or African American, non-Hispanic/Latino; 3 American Indian or Alaska Native, non-Hispanic/Latino; 11 Asian, non-Hispanic/Latino; 60 Hispanic/Latino), 38 international. Average age 31. 271 applicants, 42% accepted, 75 enrolled. In 2013, 71 master's, 31 doctorates, 62 other advanced degrees awarded. Terminal master's awarded for partial completion of doctoral program. *Degree requirements:* For master's, thesis optional; for doctorate, comprehensive exam, thesis/dissertation. *Entrance requirements:* For master's and doctorate, GRE General Test, minimum GPA of 3.0 (undergraduate), 3.5 (graduate); for Ed S, GRE General Test. Additional exam requirements/recommendations for international students: Required—TOEFL (minimum score 550 paper-based; 80 iBT), IELTS (minimum score 6). *Application deadline:* Applications are processed on a rolling basis. Application fee: $30. Electronic applications accepted. *Expenses:* Tuition, state resident: full-time $12,640. Tuition, nonresident: full-time $30,000. *Financial support:* In 2013–14, 85 students received support, including 6 fellowships (averaging $12,190 per year), 48 research assistantships (averaging $15,155 per year), 50 teaching assistantships (averaging $9,080 per year); career-related internships or fieldwork and unspecified assistantships also available. Financial award applicants required to submit FAFSA. *Unit head:* Glenn E. Good, PhD, Dean and Professor, 352-273-4135, Fax: 352-846-2697, E-mail: ggood@ufl.edu. *Application contact:* Thomasenia L. Adams, PhD, Professor and Associate Dean, 352-273-4119, Fax: 352-846-2697, E-mail: tla@coe.ufl.edu.
Website: http://education.ufl.edu/hdose/.

University of Georgia, College of Education, Department of Lifelong Education, Administration and Policy, Athens, GA 30602. Offers adult education (M Ed, Ed D, PhD, Ed S); educational administration and policy (M Ed, PhD, Ed S); educational leadership (Ed D); human resource and organizational design (M Ed). *Accreditation:* NCATE. *Entrance requirements:* For master's and Ed S, GRE General Test or MAT; for doctorate, GRE General Test. Electronic applications accepted.

University of Guam, Office of Graduate Studies, School of Education, Program in Administration and Supervision, Mangilao, GU 96923. Offers M Ed. *Degree requirements:* For master's, comprehensive oral and written exams, special project or thesis. *Entrance requirements:* For master's, GRE General Test. Additional exam requirements/recommendations for international students: Required—TOEFL.

University of Hartford, College of Education, Nursing, and Health Professions, Doctoral Program in Educational Leadership, West Hartford, CT 06117-1599. Offers Ed D. *Accreditation:* NCATE. Part-time and evening/weekend programs available. *Degree requirements:* For doctorate, thesis/dissertation. *Entrance requirements:* For doctorate, MAT, 3 letters of recommendation, writing samples, interview, resume, letter of support from employer. *Expenses:* Contact institution.

University of Hartford, College of Education, Nursing, and Health Professions, Program in Educational Leadership, West Hartford, CT 06117-1599. Offers administration and supervision (CAGS). *Accreditation:* NCATE. Part-time and evening/weekend programs available. *Degree requirements:* For CAGS, comprehensive exam or research project. *Entrance requirements:* For degree, GRE General Test or MAT, interview. Additional exam requirements/recommendations for international students: Required—TOEFL (minimum score 550 paper-based). Electronic applications accepted.

University of Hawaii at Manoa, Graduate Division, College of Education, Department of Educational Administration, Honolulu, HI 96822. Offers M Ed. Part-time programs available. *Degree requirements:* For master's, thesis optional. *Entrance requirements:* Additional exam requirements/recommendations for international students: Required—TOEFL (minimum score 600 paper-based; 100 iBT), IELTS (minimum score 7). *Faculty research:* Leadership, educational policy, organizational processes, finance.

University of Hawaii at Manoa, Graduate Division, College of Education, Ed D in Professional Practice Program, Honolulu, HI 96822. Offers Ed D. *Entrance requirements:* Additional exam requirements/recommendations for international students: Required—TOEFL (minimum score 600 paper-based; 100 iBT).

University of Hawaii at Manoa, Graduate Division, College of Education, PhD in Education Program, Honolulu, HI 96822. Offers curriculum and instruction (PhD);

educational administration (PhD); educational foundations (PhD); educational policy studies (PhD); educational technology (PhD); exceptionalities (PhD); kinesiology (PhD). Part-time and evening/weekend programs available. *Degree requirements:* For doctorate, thesis/dissertation. *Entrance requirements:* For doctorate, GRE General Test, sample of written work. Additional exam requirements/recommendations for international students: Required—TOEFL (minimum score 600 paper-based; 100 iBT), IELTS (minimum score 7).

University of Houston, College of Education, Department of Curriculum and Instruction, Houston, TX 77204. Offers administration and supervision (M Ed); curriculum and instruction (M Ed, Ed D); professional leadership (Ed D). *Accreditation:* NCATE. Part-time and evening/weekend programs available. *Degree requirements:* For master's, comprehensive exam, thesis optional; for doctorate, comprehensive exam, thesis/dissertation. *Entrance requirements:* For master's and doctorate, GRE, minimum cumulative undergraduate GPA of 2.6, 3 letters of recommendation, resume/vita, goal statement. Additional exam requirements/recommendations for international students: Required—TOEFL (minimum score 550 paper-based; 79 iBT). Electronic applications accepted. *Faculty research:* Teaching-learning process, instructional technology in schools, teacher education, classroom management, at-risk students.

University of Houston, College of Education, Department of Educational Leadership and Cultural Studies, Houston, TX 77204. Offers administration and supervision (M Ed, Ed D); higher education (M Ed); historical, social, and cultural foundations of education (M Ed). *Accreditation:* NCATE. Part-time and evening/weekend programs available. *Degree requirements:* For master's, comprehensive exam or thesis; for doctorate, comprehensive exam, thesis/dissertation. *Entrance requirements:* For master's, GRE General Test, minimum cumulative GPA of 2.6, 3 letters of recommendation, resume/vitae, goal statement; for doctorate, GRE General Test, minimum cumulative GPA of 2.6, 3 letters of recommendation, resume/vitae, goal statement, writing sample, interview. Additional exam requirements/recommendations for international students: Required—TOEFL (minimum score 550 paper-based; 79 iBT). Electronic applications accepted. *Faculty research:* Change, supervision, multiculturalism, evaluation, policy.

University of Houston, College of Education, Department of Educational Psychology, Houston, TX 77204. Offers administration and supervision - higher education (M Ed); counseling (M Ed); counseling psychology (PhD); educational psychology (M Ed); school psychology (PhD); school psychology and individual differences (PhD); special education (M Ed). *Accreditation:* NCATE. Part-time and evening/weekend programs available. Postbaccalaureate distance learning degree programs offered (no on-campus study). *Degree requirements:* For master's, comprehensive exam or thesis; for doctorate, comprehensive exam, thesis/dissertation. *Entrance requirements:* For master's, GRE, transcripts, 3 letters of recommendation, curriculum vita, goal statement; for doctorate, GRE, transcripts, 3 letters of recommendation, curriculum vita, goal statement, writing sample, interview. Additional exam requirements/recommendations for international students: Required—TOEFL (minimum score 550 paper-based; 79 iBT), IELTS (minimum score 6.5). Electronic applications accepted. *Faculty research:* Evidence-based assessment and intervention, multicultural issues in psychology, social and cultural context of learning, systemic barriers to college, motivational aspects of self-regulated learning.

University of Houston–Clear Lake, School of Education, Program in Educational Leadership, Houston, TX 77058-1002. Offers educational leadership (Ed D); educational management (MS). *Degree requirements:* For master's, thesis optional; for doctorate, comprehensive exam, thesis/dissertation.

University of Houston–Victoria, School of Education and Human Development, Victoria, TX 77901-4450. Offers administration and supervision (M Ed); adult and higher education (M Ed); counseling (M Ed); curriculum and instruction (M Ed); special education (M Ed). Part-time and evening/weekend programs available. Postbaccalaureate distance learning degree programs offered (minimal on-campus study). *Faculty:* 22 full-time (19 women). *Students:* 56 full-time (52 women), 325 part-time (274 women); includes 211 minority (113 Black or African American, non-Hispanic/Latino; 2 American Indian or Alaska Native, non-Hispanic/Latino; 16 Asian, non-Hispanic/Latino; 68 Hispanic/Latino; 12 Two or more races, non-Hispanic/Latino), 3 international. *Degree requirements:* For master's, comprehensive exam, project or thesis. *Entrance requirements:* For master's, GRE General Test. Additional exam requirements/recommendations for international students: Required—TOEFL. *Application deadline:* For fall admission, 6/1 for international students; for spring admission, 10/1 for international students. Applications are processed on a rolling basis. Application fee: $0. Electronic applications accepted. *Expenses:* Tuition, state resident: full-time $4534; part-time $251 per credit hour. Tuition, nonresident: full-time $10,906; part-time $606 per contact hour. *Required fees:* $68 per semester hour. Tuition and fees vary according to course load. *Financial support:* In 2013–14, research assistantships with partial tuition reimbursements (averaging $2,000 per year), teaching assistantships with partial tuition reimbursements (averaging $2,000 per year) were awarded; Federal Work-Study, scholarships/grants, and unspecified assistantships also available. Support available to part-time students. Financial award application deadline: 4/15; financial award applicants required to submit FAFSA. *Faculty research:* Reading and language arts education, evaluation and diagnosis of special children's abilities. *Unit head:* Freddie W. Litton, Dean, 361-570-4260, Fax: 361-580-5580. *Application contact:* Sandy Hybner, Senior Recruitment Coordinator, 361-570-4252, Fax: 361-580-5580, E-mail: hybners@uhv.edu.
Website: http://www.uhv.edu/edu/.

University of Idaho, College of Graduate Studies, College of Education, Department of Leadership and Counseling, Boise, ID 83844-2282. Offers adult/organizational learning and leadership (MS, Ed S); educational leadership (M Ed, Ed S); rehabilitation counseling and human services (M Ed, MS); school counseling (M Ed, MS); special education (M Ed). *Faculty:* 13 full-time, 11 part-time/adjunct. *Students:* 58 full-time (39 women), 200 part-time (121 women). Average age 39. In 2013, 83 master's, 38 other advanced degrees awarded. *Entrance requirements:* Additional exam requirements/recommendations for international students: Required—TOEFL (minimum score 550 paper-based). *Application deadline:* Applications are processed on a rolling basis. Application fee: $60. Electronic applications accepted. *Expenses:* Tuition, state resident: full-time $5596; part-time $363 per credit hour. Tuition, nonresident: full-time $18,672; part-time $1089 per credit hour. *Financial support:* Applicants required to submit FAFSA. *Unit head:* Dr. Jeffrey Brooks, Chair, 208-364-4047, E-mail: mweitz@uidaho.edu. *Application contact:* Stephanie Thomas, Graduate Recruitment Coordinator, 208-885-4001, Fax: 208-885-4406, E-mail: gadms@uidaho.edu.
Website: http://www.uidaho.edu/ed/leadershipcounseling.

University of Illinois at Chicago, Graduate College, College of Education, Department of Curriculum and Instruction, Chicago, IL 60607-7128. Offers curriculum studies (PhD); educational studies (M Ed); elementary education (M Ed); instructional leadership (M Ed); literacy, language and culture (M Ed, PhD); science education (M Ed); secondary education (M Ed). Part-time and evening/weekend programs available. *Faculty:* 20 full-time (10 women), 10 part-time/adjunct (8 women). *Students:* 124 full-time (89 women), 155 part-time (117 women); includes 117 minority (51 Black or African American, non-Hispanic/Latino; 19 Asian, non-Hispanic/Latino; 43 Hispanic/Latino; 4 Two or more races, non-Hispanic/Latino), 11 international. Average age 32. 154

applicants, 70% accepted, 74 enrolled. In 2013, 108 master's, 16 doctorates awarded. *Degree requirements:* For doctorate, thesis/dissertation. *Entrance requirements:* For master's, minimum GPA of 2.75; for doctorate, GRE General Test, minimum GPA of 2.75. Additional exam requirements/recommendations for international students: Required—TOEFL. *Application deadline:* For fall admission, 1/9 for domestic and international students; for spring admission, 10/1 for domestic and international students. Applications are processed on a rolling basis. Application fee: $40 ($50 for international students). Electronic applications accepted. *Expenses:* Tuition, state resident: full-time $11,066; part-time $3689 per term. Tuition, nonresident: full-time $23,064; part-time $7688 per term. *Required fees:* $3004; $1190 per term. Tuition and fees vary according to course level and program. *Financial support:* In 2013–14, 101 students received support, including 4 fellowships with full tuition reimbursements available; research assistantships with full tuition reimbursements available, teaching assistantships with full tuition reimbursements available, career-related internships or fieldwork, Federal Work-Study, institutionally sponsored loans, traineeships, tuition waivers (full), and unspecified assistantships also available. Support available to part-time students. Financial award application deadline: 3/1; financial award applicants required to submit FAFSA. *Faculty research:* Curriculum theory, curriculum development, research on teaching, curriculum and context, reading/literacy. *Total annual research expenditures:* $70,000. *Unit head:* Prof. Alfred Tatum, Associate Professor/Director/Chair, 312-413-3883, Fax: 312-996-8134, E-mail: atatum1@uic.edu.
Website: http://education.uic.edu.

University of Illinois at Chicago, Graduate College, College of Education, Department of Educational Policy Studies, Chicago, IL 60607-7128. Offers policy studies (M Ed); policy studies in urban education (PhD); urban education leadership (Ed D). *Faculty:* 12 full-time (6 women). *Students:* 45 full-time (33 women), 103 part-time (69 women); includes 78 minority (38 Black or African American, non-Hispanic/Latino; 4 Asian, non-Hispanic/Latino; 31 Hispanic/Latino; 5 Two or more races, non-Hispanic/Latino), 2 international. Average age 36. 71 applicants, 44% accepted, 22 enrolled. In 2013, 14 master's, 16 doctorates awarded. *Expenses:* Tuition, state resident: full-time $11,066; part-time $3689 per term. Tuition, nonresident: full-time $23,064; part-time $7688 per term. *Required fees:* $3004; $1190 per term. Tuition and fees vary according to course level and program. *Total annual research expenditures:* $290,000. *Unit head:* Prof. David Mayrowetz, Chair, 312-996-3326, E-mail: dmayro@uic.edu. *Application contact:* Receptionist, 312-413-2550, E-mail: gradcoll@uic.edu.
Website: http://education.uic.edu.

University of Illinois at Springfield, Graduate Programs, College of Education and Human Services, Department of Educational Leadership, Springfield, IL 62703-5407. Offers chief school business official endorsement (CAS); educational leadership (MA, CAS); English as a second language (Graduate Certificate); legal aspects of education (Graduate Certificate); school superintendent endorsement (CAS); teacher leadership (MA). Part-time and evening/weekend programs available. Postbaccalaureate distance learning degree programs offered (no on-campus study). *Faculty:* 7 full-time (2 women), 13 part-time/adjunct (8 women). *Students:* 7 full-time (all women), 139 part-time (95 women); includes 14 minority (11 Black or African American, non-Hispanic/Latino; 1 American Indian or Alaska Native, non-Hispanic/Latino; 1 Hispanic/Latino; 1 Two or more races, non-Hispanic/Latino). Average age 35. 47 applicants, 53% accepted, 24 enrolled. In 2013, 62 master's, 8 other advanced degrees awarded. *Degree requirements:* For master's, project or thesis, capstone course (for teacher leadership option). *Entrance requirements:* For master's, minimum undergraduate GPA of 3.0. Additional exam requirements/recommendations for international students: Required—TOEFL (minimum score 500 paper-based; 61 iBT). *Application deadline:* Applications are processed on a rolling basis. Application fee: $60 ($75 for international students). Electronic applications accepted. *Expenses:* Tuition, state resident: full-time $7440. Tuition, nonresident: full-time $15,744. *Required fees:* $2985.60. *Financial support:* In 2013–14, fellowships with full tuition reimbursements (averaging $9,900 per year), research assistantships with full tuition reimbursements (averaging $9,550 per year), teaching assistantships with full tuition reimbursements (averaging $9,700 per year) were awarded; career-related internships or fieldwork, Federal Work-Study, scholarships/grants, health care benefits, and unspecified assistantships also available. Support available to part-time students. Financial award application deadline: 11/15; financial award applicants required to submit FAFSA. *Unit head:* Dr. Scott Day, Program Administrator, 217-206-7520, Fax: 217-206-6775, E-mail: day.scott@uis.edu. *Application contact:* Dr. Lynn Pardie, Office of Graduate Studies, 800-252-8533, Fax: 217-206-7623, E-mail: lpard1@uis.edu.
Website: http://www.uis.edu/edl/.

University of Illinois at Urbana–Champaign, Graduate College, College of Education, Department of Education Policy, Organization, and Leadership, Champaign, IL 61820. Offers educational organization and leadership (Ed M, MS, Ed D, PhD, CAS); educational policy studies (Ed M, MA, PhD); human resource education (Ed M, MS, Ed D, PhD, CAS). Part-time programs available. Postbaccalaureate distance learning degree programs offered (no on-campus study). *Students:* 518 (342 women). Application fee: $75 ($90 for international students). *Unit head:* James Anderson, Head, 217-333-2446, Fax: 217-244-5632, E-mail: janders@illinois.edu. *Application contact:* Rebecca Grady, Office Support Specialist, 217-265-5404, Fax: 217-244-5632, E-mail: rgrady@illinois.edu.
Website: http://education.illinois.edu/epol.

University of Indianapolis, Graduate Programs, School of Education, Indianapolis, IN 46227-3697. Offers art education (MAT); biology (MAT); chemistry (MAT); curriculum and instruction (MA); earth sciences (MAT); education (MA, MAT); educational leadership (MA); elementary education (MA); English (MAT); French (MAT); math (MAT); physical education (MAT); physics (MAT); secondary education (MA), including art education, education, English education, social studies education; social studies (MAT); Spanish (MAT). *Accreditation:* NCATE. Part-time and evening/weekend programs available. *Faculty:* 5 full-time (4 women), 2 part-time/adjunct (1 woman). *Students:* 19 full-time (9 women), 54 part-time (27 women); includes 13 minority (5 Black or African American, non-Hispanic/Latino; 1 Asian, non-Hispanic/Latino; 5 Hispanic/Latino; 2 Two or more races, non-Hispanic/Latino), 1 international. Average age 32. In 2013, 52 master's awarded. *Entrance requirements:* For master's, GRE Subject Test, PRAXIS I, minimum GPA of 2.5, 3 letters of recommendation, interview. Additional exam requirements/recommendations for international students: Required—TOEFL (minimum score 550 paper-based). *Application deadline:* Applications are processed on a rolling basis. Application fee: $50. *Expenses:* Tuition: Full-time $5436; part-time $810 per credit hour. *Financial support:* Federal Work-Study available. Financial award application deadline: 5/1; financial award applicants required to submit FAFSA. *Faculty research:* Assessment of teacher education, perceptions of prospective teachers by parents. *Unit head:* Dr. Kathy Moran, Dean, 317-788-3285, Fax: 317-788-3300, E-mail: kmoran@uindy.edu. *Application contact:* Jeni Kirby, Administrative Assistant, Teacher Education, 317-788-2113, E-mail: kirbyj@uindy.edu.
Website: http://education.uindy.edu/.

The University of Iowa, Graduate College, College of Education, Department of Educational Policy and Leadership Studies, Program in Educational Leadership, Iowa City, IA 52242-1316. Offers MA, PhD, Ed S. *Degree requirements:* For master's and

Ed S, exam; for doctorate, comprehensive exam, thesis/dissertation. *Entrance requirements:* For master's, doctorate, and Ed S, GRE General Test, minimum GPA of 3.0. Additional exam requirements/recommendations for international students: Required—TOEFL (minimum score 550 paper-based; 81 iBT). Electronic applications accepted.

The University of Kansas, Graduate Studies, School of Education, Department of Educational Leadership and Policy Studies, Education Leadership and Policy Program, Lawrence, KS 66045-3101. Offers educational administration (Ed D, PhD); foundations (PhD); higher education (Ed D, PhD); policy studies (PhD). Part-time and evening/weekend programs available. *Faculty:* 15. *Students:* 106 full-time (63 women), 46 part-time (19 women); includes 32 minority (10 Black or African American, non-Hispanic/Latino; 4 American Indian or Alaska Native, non-Hispanic/Latino; 6 Asian, non-Hispanic/Latino; 7 Hispanic/Latino; 5 Two or more races, non-Hispanic/Latino), 27 international. Average age 37. 63 applicants, 71% accepted, 32 enrolled. In 2013, 31 doctorates awarded. *Degree requirements:* For doctorate, comprehensive exam, thesis/dissertation. *Entrance requirements:* For doctorate, GRE General Test, minimum graduate GPA of 3.5. Additional exam requirements/recommendations for international students: Required—TOEFL (minimum score 570 paper-based; 80 iBT). *Application deadline:* For fall admission, 7/1 for domestic and international students; for spring admission, 11/1 for domestic and international students. Applications are processed on a rolling basis. Application fee: $55 ($65 for international students). Electronic applications accepted. *Financial support:* Fellowships, research assistantships with full and partial tuition reimbursements, teaching assistantships with full and partial tuition reimbursements, scholarships/grants, and unspecified assistantships available. Financial award application deadline: 3/15. *Faculty research:* Historical and philosophical issues in education, education policy and leadership, higher education faculty, research on college students, education technology. *Unit head:* Dr. Susan Twombly, Chair, 785-864-9721, Fax: 785-864-4697, E-mail: stwombly@ku.edu. *Application contact:* Denise Brubaker, Admissions Coordinator, 785-864-7973, Fax: 785-864-4697, E-mail: brubaker@ku.edu.
Website: http://elps.soe.ku.edu/.

The University of Kansas, Graduate Studies, School of Education, Department of Educational Leadership and Policy Studies, Program in Educational Administration, Lawrence, KS 66045-3101. Offers MS Ed, Ed D, PhD. Program begins in Summer semester only. Part-time and evening/weekend programs available. *Faculty:* 15. *Students:* 2 full-time (1 woman), 17 part-time (12 women); includes 1 minority (Black or African American, non-Hispanic/Latino), 2 international. Average age 29. 19 applicants, 79% accepted, 12 enrolled. In 2013, 5 master's awarded. *Degree requirements:* For master's, comprehensive exam; for doctorate, comprehensive exam, thesis/dissertation. *Entrance requirements:* For master's, minimum GPA of 3.0; for doctorate, GRE General Test, minimum graduate GPA of 3.5. Additional exam requirements/recommendations for international students: Required—TOEFL (minimum score 570 paper-based; 80 iBT). Application fee: $55 ($65 for international students). Electronic applications accepted. *Financial support:* Application deadline: 3/1. *Faculty research:* Policy studies, law, personnel, leadership, organizational studies. *Unit head:* Dr. Susan Twombly, Chair, 785-864-9721, Fax: 785-864-4697, E-mail: stwombly@ku.edu. *Application contact:* Denise Brubaker, Admissions Coordinator, 785-864-7973, Fax: 785-864-4697, E-mail: brubaker@ku.edu.
Website: http://elps.soe.ku.edu/academics/edadmin/mse.

University of Kentucky, Graduate School, College of Education, Department of Educational Leadership Studies, Lexington, KY 40506-0032. Offers administration and supervision (Ed S); educational leadership (M Ed, Ed D, PhD, Ed S); educational sciences (PhD); instruction and administration (Ed D); school administration (M Ed); school technology leadership (M Ed, PhD, Ed S); teacher leadership (M Ed, Ed S). *Degree requirements:* For master's and Ed S, comprehensive exam; for doctorate, comprehensive exam, thesis/dissertation. *Entrance requirements:* For master's, GRE General Test, minimum undergraduate GPA of 2.75; for doctorate, GRE General Test, minimum graduate GPA of 3.0. Additional exam requirements/recommendations for international students: Required—TOEFL (minimum score 550 paper-based). Electronic applications accepted. *Faculty research:* School governance, teacher empowerment, planned change, systemic reform, issues of equity and fairness.

University of La Verne, College of Education and Organizational Leadership, Doctoral Program in Organizational Leadership, La Verne, CA 91750-4443. Offers Ed D. Part-time programs available. *Faculty:* 10 part-time/adjunct (5 women). *Students:* 125 full-time (83 women), 68 part-time (46 women); includes 73 minority (23 Black or African American, non-Hispanic/Latino; 1 American Indian or Alaska Native, non-Hispanic/Latino; 4 Asian, non-Hispanic/Latino; 45 Hispanic/Latino), 1 international. Average age 45. In 2013, 62 doctorates awarded. *Degree requirements:* For doctorate, thesis/dissertation. *Entrance requirements:* For doctorate, GRE or MAT, minimum graduate GPA of 3.0, resume or curriculum vitae, 2 endorsement forms. Additional exam requirements/recommendations for international students: Required—TOEFL (minimum score 550 paper-based). *Application deadline:* Applications are processed on a rolling basis. Application fee: $75. *Expenses:* Contact institution. *Financial support:* Institutionally sponsored loans available. Financial award application deadline: 3/2; financial award applicants required to submit FAFSA. *Unit head:* Dr. Laura Hyatt, Chairperson, 909-448-4583, E-mail: lhyatt@laverne.edu. *Application contact:* Christy Ranells, Program and Admission Specialist, 909-448-4644, Fax: 909-392-2744, E-mail: cranells@laverne.edu.
Website: http://laverne.edu/education/.

University of La Verne, College of Education and Organizational Leadership, Master's Program in Education, La Verne, CA 91750-4443. Offers advanced teaching skills (M Ed); education (special emphasis) (M Ed); educational leadership (M Ed); reading (M Ed). *Accreditation:* NCATE. Part-time programs available. *Faculty:* 7 full-time (4 women), 1 (woman) part-time/adjunct. *Students:* 42 full-time (34 women), 114 part-time (88 women); includes 71 minority (4 Black or African American, non-Hispanic/Latino; 7 Asian, non-Hispanic/Latino; 54 Hispanic/Latino; 6 Two or more races, non-Hispanic/Latino), 3 international. Average age 31. In 2013, 87 master's awarded. *Degree requirements:* For master's, thesis optional. *Entrance requirements:* For master's, California Basic Educational Skills Test, interview, writing sample, minimum GPA of 3.0, 3 letters of recommendation. Additional exam requirements/recommendations for international students: Required—TOEFL (minimum score 550 paper-based). *Application deadline:* Applications are processed on a rolling basis. Application fee: $50. *Expenses:* Contact institution. *Financial support:* Institutionally sponsored loans and unspecified assistantships available. Financial award application deadline: 3/2; financial award applicants required to submit FAFSA. *Unit head:* Lynn Stanton-Riggs, Chair, 909-448-4625, E-mail: lstanton-riggs@laverne.edu. *Application contact:* Christy Ranells, Program and Admission Specialist, 909-448-4644, Fax: 909-392-2744, E-mail: cranells@laverne.edu.
Website: http://www.laverne.edu/education/.

University of La Verne, College of Education and Organizational Leadership, Program in Educational Management, La Verne, CA 91750-4443. Offers preliminary administrative services (Credential); professional administrative services (Credential). *Entrance requirements:* Additional exam requirements/recommendations for international students: Required—TOEFL (minimum score 550 paper-based). *Application deadline:* Applications are processed on a rolling basis. Application fee: $50. *Expenses:* Contact institution. *Financial support:* Institutionally sponsored loans available. Financial award application deadline: 3/2; financial award applicants required to submit FAFSA.
Website: http://laverne.edu/education/.

University of La Verne, Regional and Online Campuses, Graduate Credential Program in Education, California Statewide Campus, La Verne, CA 91750-4443. Offers administration services (preliminary) (Credential); education specialist: mild/moderate (Credential); multiple subject teaching (Credential); pupil personnel services: school counseling (Credential); single subject teaching (Credential). *Accreditation:* NCATE. Part-time programs available. *Faculty:* 10 full-time (7 women), 1 (woman) part-time/adjunct. *Students:* 128 full-time (92 women), 49 part-time (43 women); includes 58 minority (6 Black or African American, non-Hispanic/Latino; 1 American Indian or Alaska Native, non-Hispanic/Latino; 3 Asian, non-Hispanic/Latino; 44 Hispanic/Latino; 4 Two or more races, non-Hispanic/Latino). Average age 32. In 2013, 24 Credentials awarded. *Entrance requirements:* For degree, California Basic Educational Skills Test, minimum undergraduate GPA of 2.75, 3 letters of recommendation, interview. *Application deadline:* Applications are processed on a rolling basis. Application fee: $50. *Expenses:* Contact institution. *Financial support:* Institutionally sponsored loans available. Financial award application deadline: 3/2; financial award applicants required to submit FAFSA. *Unit head:* Pam Bergovoy, Assistant Dean, Regional and Online Campuses/Director, Center for Educators, 909-448-4953, E-mail: pbergovoy@laverne.edu.
Website: http://www.laverne.edu/locations.

University of La Verne, Regional and Online Campuses, Graduate Programs, Central Coast/Vandenberg Air Force Base Campuses, La Verne, CA 91750-4443. Offers business administration for experienced professionals (MBA), including health services management, information technology; education (special emphasis) (M Ed); educational counseling (MS); educational leadership (M Ed); multiple subject (elementary) (Credential); preliminary administrative services (Credential); pupil personnel services (Credential); single subject (secondary) (Credential). Part-time programs available. *Faculty:* 11 part-time/adjunct (2 women). *Students:* 17 full-time (7 women), 34 part-time (22 women); includes 15 minority (1 Black or African American, non-Hispanic/Latino; 1 American Indian or Alaska Native, non-Hispanic/Latino; 1 Asian, non-Hispanic/Latino; 10 Hispanic/Latino; 2 Two or more races, non-Hispanic/Latino). Average age 38. In 2013, 25 master's awarded. *Application deadline:* Applications are processed on a rolling basis. Application fee: $50. *Expenses:* Contact institution. *Financial support:* Institutionally sponsored loans available. Financial award application deadline: 3/2; financial award applicants required to submit FAFSA. *Unit head:* Kitt Vincent, Director, Central Coast Campus, 805-788-6202, Fax: 805-788-6201, E-mail: kvincent@laverne.edu. *Application contact:* Gene Teal, Admissions, 805-788-6205, Fax: 805-788-6201, E-mail: eteal@laverne.edu.
Website: http://www.laverne.edu/locations.

University of La Verne, Regional and Online Campuses, Graduate Programs, High Desert Campus, Victorville, CA 92392. Offers business administration for experienced professionals (MBA); educational counseling (MS); educational leadership (M Ed); multiple subject (elementary) (Credential); preliminary administrative services (Credential); pupil personnel services (Credential); single subject (secondary) (Credential). *Faculty:* 3 part-time/adjunct (0 women). *Students:* 10 full-time (6 women), 17 part-time (12 women); includes 14 minority (3 Black or African American, non-Hispanic/Latino; 3 Asian, non-Hispanic/Latino; 6 Hispanic/Latino; 1 Native Hawaiian or other Pacific Islander, non-Hispanic/Latino; 1 Two or more races, non-Hispanic/Latino). Average age 38. In 2013, 6 master's awarded. *Application deadline:* Applications are processed on a rolling basis. Application fee: $50. *Expenses:* Contact institution. *Financial support:* Application deadline: 3/2; applicants required to submit FAFSA. *Unit head:* Juli Roberts, Regional Campus Director, 760-955-6448, Fax: 760-843-9505, E-mail: jroberts@laverne.edu. *Application contact:* Donald Parker, Associate Director of Admissions, 760-955-6477, E-mail: dparker@laverne.edu.
Website: http://www.laverne.edu/locations/victorville/.

University of La Verne, Regional and Online Campuses, Graduate Programs, Kern County Campus, Bakersfield, CA 93301. Offers business administration for experienced professionals (MBA-EP); education (special emphasis) (M Ed); educational counseling (MS); educational leadership (M Ed); health administration (MHA); leadership and management (MS); mild/moderate education specialist preliminary (Credential); multiple subject (elementary) (Credential); organizational leadership (Ed D); preliminary administrative services (Credential); single subject (secondary) (Credential); special education studies (MS). Part-time and evening/weekend programs available. *Faculty:* 2 part-time/adjunct (1 woman). *Students:* 1 (woman) full-time, 5 part-time (3 women); includes 4 minority (3 Hispanic/Latino; 1 Two or more races, non-Hispanic/Latino). Average age 36. In 2013, 4 master's awarded. *Application deadline:* Applications are processed on a rolling basis. Application fee: $50. *Expenses:* Contact institution. *Financial support:* Institutionally sponsored loans available. Financial award application deadline: 3/2; financial award applicants required to submit FAFSA. *Unit head:* Nora Dominguez, Regional Campus Director, 661-861-6802, E-mail: ndominguez@laverne.edu. *Application contact:* Regina Benavides, Associate Director of Admissions, 661-861-6807, E-mail: rbenavides@laverne.edu.
Website: http://laverne.edu/locations/bakersfield/.

University of La Verne, Regional and Online Campuses, Graduate Programs, Orange County Campus, Irvine, CA 92606. Offers business administration for experienced professionals (MBA); educational counseling (MS); educational leadership (M Ed); health administration (MHA); leadership and management (MS); preliminary administrative services (Credential); pupil personnel services (Credential). Part-time programs available. *Faculty:* 3 full-time (all women), 12 part-time/adjunct (3 women). *Students:* 38 full-time (21 women), 78 part-time (36 women); includes 69 minority (7 Black or African American, non-Hispanic/Latino; 1 American Indian or Alaska Native, non-Hispanic/Latino; 19 Asian, non-Hispanic/Latino; 40 Hispanic/Latino; 1 Native Hawaiian or other Pacific Islander, non-Hispanic/Latino; 1 Two or more races, non-Hispanic/Latino). Average age 37. In 2013, 30 master's awarded. *Application deadline:* Applications are processed on a rolling basis. Application fee: $50. *Expenses:* Contact institution. *Financial support:* Institutionally sponsored loans available. Financial award application deadline: 3/2; financial award applicants required to submit FAFSA. *Unit head:* Pam Bergovoy, Director, Center for Educators, 909-448-4953, E-mail: pbergovoy@laverne.edu. *Application contact:* Alison Rodriguez-Balles, Associate Director of Admissions, 714-505-6943, E-mail: arodriguez2@laverne.edu.
Website: http://laverne.edu/locations/irvine/.

University of La Verne, Regional and Online Campuses, Graduate Programs, San Fernando Valley Campus, Burbank, CA 91505. Offers business administration for experienced professionals (MBA-EP); educational counseling (MS); educational leadership (M Ed); leadership and management (MS); preliminary administrative services (Credential); pupil personnel services (Credential). Part-time and evening/weekend programs available. *Faculty:* 2 full-time (1 woman), 12 part-time/adjunct (5 women). *Students:* 46 full-time (20 women), 128 part-time (76 women); includes 121 minority (29 Black or African American, non-Hispanic/Latino; 19 Asian, non-Hispanic/

Latino; 66 Hispanic/Latino; 1 Native Hawaiian or other Pacific Islander, non-Hispanic/Latino; 6 Two or more races, non-Hispanic/Latino). Average age 38. In 2013, 79 master's awarded. *Application deadline:* Applications are processed on a rolling basis. Application fee: $50. *Expenses:* Contact institution. *Financial support:* Institutionally sponsored loans available. Financial award application deadline: 3/2; financial award applicants required to submit FAFSA. *Unit head:* Dr. Nelly Kazman, Senior Executive Director, 818-295-6502, E-mail: nkazman@laverne.edu. *Application contact:* Debi Hrboka, Associate Director of Admissions, 818-295-6508, E-mail: dhrboka@laverne.edu.
Website: http://laverne.edu/locations/burbank/.

University of La Verne, Regional and Online Campuses, Graduate Programs, Ventura County/Point Mugu Naval Air Station Campuses, Oxnard, CA 93036. Offers business administration for experienced professionals (MS); educational counseling (MS); educational leadership (M Ed); leadership and management (MS); multiple subject (elementary) (Credential); pupil personnel services (Credential); single subject (secondary) (Credential). Part-time and evening/weekend programs available. *Faculty:* 12 part-time/adjunct (2 women). *Students:* 34 full-time (13 women), 37 part-time (20 women); includes 39 minority (3 Black or African American, non-Hispanic/Latino; 2 American Indian or Alaska Native, non-Hispanic/Latino; 3 Asian, non-Hispanic/Latino; 29 Hispanic/Latino; 2 Two or more races, non-Hispanic/Latino). Average age 38. In 2013, 31 master's awarded. Application fee: $50. *Expenses:* Contact institution. *Financial support:* Institutionally sponsored loans available. Financial award application deadline: 3/2; financial award applicants required to submit FAFSA. *Unit head:* Jamie Dempsey, Director, Point Mugu, 661-986-6902, E-mail: jdempsey@laverne.edu. *Application contact:* Kevin Laack, Regional Campus Director, Ventura, 805-981-6022, E-mail: klaack@laverne.edu.
Website: http://laverne.edu/locations/oxnard/.

University of La Verne, Regional and Online Campuses, Master's Programs in Education, California Statewide Campus, La Verne, CA 91750-4443. Offers administration services (preliminary) (Credential); education specialist: mild/moderate (Credential); educational counseling (MS); educational leadership (M Ed); multiple subject teaching (Credential); pupil personnel services: school counseling (Credential); single subject teaching (Credential); special education studies (MS); special emphasis (M Ed). *Accreditation:* NCATE. *Faculty:* 6 full-time (2 women), 23 part-time/adjunct (16 women). *Students:* 109 full-time (88 women), 63 part-time (53 women); includes 94 minority (8 Black or African American, non-Hispanic/Latino; 6 Asian, non-Hispanic/Latino; 76 Hispanic/Latino; 4 Two or more races, non-Hispanic/Latino). Average age 33. In 2013, 76 master's awarded. *Entrance requirements:* For master's, California Basic Educational Skills Test, 3 letters of recommendation, teaching credential. *Application deadline:* Applications are processed on a rolling basis. Application fee: $50. *Expenses:* Contact institution. *Financial support:* Fellowships and institutionally sponsored loans available. Financial award application deadline: 3/2; financial award applicants required to submit FAFSA. *Unit head:* Pam Bergovoy, Assistant Dean, Regional and Online Campuses/Director, Center for Educators, 909-448-4953, E-mail: pbergovoy@laverne.edu.
Website: http://www.laverne.edu/locations.

University of Lethbridge, School of Graduate Studies, Lethbridge, AB T1K 3M4, Canada. Offers accounting (MScM); addictions counseling (M Sc); agricultural biotechnology (M Sc); agricultural studies (M Sc, MA); anthropology (MA); archaeology (M Sc, MA); art (MA, MFA); biochemistry (M Sc); biological sciences (M Sc); biomolecular science (PhD); biosystems and biodiversity (PhD); Canadian studies (MA); chemistry (M Sc); computer science (M Sc); computer science and geographical information science (M Sc); counseling (MC); counseling psychology (M Ed); dramatic arts (MA); earth, space, and physical science (PhD); economics (MA); education (MA); educational leadership (M Ed); English (MA); environmental science (M Sc); evolution and behavior (PhD); exercise science (M Sc); finance (MScM); French (MA); French/German (MA); French/Spanish (MA); general education (M Ed); general management (MScM); geography (M Sc, MA); German (MA); health sciences (M Sc); human resource management and labour relations (MScM); individualized multidisciplinary (M Sc, MA); information systems (MScM); international management (MScM); kinesiology (M Sc, MA); marketing (MScM); mathematics (M Sc); modern languages (MA); music (M Mus, MA); Native American studies (MA); neuroscience (M Sc, PhD); new media (MA, MFA); nursing (M Sc); philosophy (MA); physics (M Sc); policy and strategy (MScM); political science (MA); psychology (M Sc, MA); religious studies (MA); sociology (MA); theatre and dramatic arts (MFA); theoretical and computational science (PhD); urban and regional studies (MA); women and gender studies (MA). Part-time and evening/weekend programs available. *Degree requirements:* For doctorate, comprehensive exam, thesis/dissertation. *Entrance requirements:* For master's, GMAT (for M Sc in management), bachelor's degree in related field, minimum GPA of 3.0 during previous 20 graded semester courses, 2 years teaching or related experience (M Ed); for doctorate, master's degree, minimum graduate GPA of 3.5. Additional exam requirements/recommendations for international students: Required—TOEFL. Application fee: $60 Canadian dollars. *Financial support:* Fellowships, research assistantships, teaching assistantships, scholarships/grants, health care benefits, and unspecified assistantships available. *Faculty research:* Movement and brain plasticity, gibberellin physiology, photosynthesis, carbon cycling, molecular properties of main-group ring components. *Application contact:* School of Graduate Studies, 403-329-2793, Fax: 403-332-5239, E-mail: sgsinquiries@uleth.ca.
Website: http://www.uleth.ca/graduatestudies/.

University of Louisiana at Lafayette, College of Education, Graduate Studies and Research in Education, Program in Administration and Supervision, Lafayette, LA 70504. Offers M Ed. *Degree requirements:* For master's, thesis or alternative. *Entrance requirements:* For master's, GRE General Test, teaching certificate. Additional exam requirements/recommendations for international students: Required—TOEFL (minimum score 550 paper-based). Electronic applications accepted.

University of Louisiana at Lafayette, College of Education, Graduate Studies and Research in Education, Program in Educational Leadership, Lafayette, LA 70504. Offers M Ed, Ed D. *Entrance requirements:* Additional exam requirements/recommendations for international students: Required—TOEFL (minimum score 550 paper-based).

University of Louisiana at Monroe, Graduate School, College of Arts, Education, and Sciences, School of Education, Program in Curriculum and Instruction, Monroe, LA 71209-0001. Offers art education (M Ed); biology education (M Ed); chemistry education (M Ed); curriculum and instruction (Ed D); early childhood education (M Ed); earth science education (M Ed); educational leadership (M Ed); elementary education (1-5) (M Ed); English as a second language (M Ed); English education (M Ed); family and consumer education (M Ed); French education (M Ed); history education (M Ed); math education (M Ed); middle school education (M Ed); music education (M Ed); reading education (K-12) (M Ed); Spanish education (M Ed); special education - academically gifted (M Ed); special education - early intervention (M Ed); special education - educational diagnostician (M Ed); special education - mild/moderate disabilities (M Ed); speech education (M Ed). *Accreditation:* NCATE. *Degree requirements:* For master's, comprehensive exam (for some programs), thesis; for doctorate, thesis/dissertation, internships. *Entrance requirements:* For master's, GRE General Test; for doctorate,

GRE General Test, minimum undergraduate GPA of 2.75, graduate 3.25. Additional exam requirements/recommendations for international students: Required—TOEFL (minimum score 500 paper-based; 61 iBT). *Application deadline:* For fall admission, 8/24 priority date for domestic students, 7/1 for international students; for winter admission, 12/14 priority date for domestic students; for spring admission, 1/19 for domestic students, 11/1 for international students. Applications are processed on a rolling basis. Application fee: $20 ($30 for international students). Electronic applications accepted. *Expenses:* Tuition, state resident: full-time $6607. Tuition, nonresident: full-time $17,179. Full-time tuition and fees vary according to program. *Financial support:* Research assistantships, career-related internships or fieldwork, Federal Work-Study, and unspecified assistantships available. Financial award application deadline: 4/1; financial award applicants required to submit FAFSA. *Unit head:* Dr. Dorothy Schween, Director, 318-342-1268, Fax: 318-342-3131, E-mail: schween@ulm.edu. *Application contact:* Dr. Dorothy Schween, Director, 318-342-1268, Fax: 318-342-3131, E-mail: schween@ulm.edu.

University of Louisville, Graduate School, College of Education and Human Development, Department of Leadership, Foundations and Human Resource Education, Louisville, KY 40292-0001. Offers educational leadership and organizational development (Ed D, PhD); higher education (MA); human resource education (MS); P-12 educational administration (M Ed, Ed S). *Accreditation:* NCATE. Part-time and evening/weekend programs available. Postbaccalaureate distance learning degree programs offered. *Students:* 68 full-time (44 women), 319 part-time (227 women); includes 80 minority (61 Black or African American, non-Hispanic/Latino; 5 Asian, non-Hispanic/Latino; 9 Hispanic/Latino; 1 Native Hawaiian or other Pacific Islander, non-Hispanic/Latino; 4 Two or more races, non-Hispanic/Latino), 27 international. Average age 36. 219 applicants, 76% accepted, 136 enrolled. In 2013, 19 master's, 5 doctorates, 4 other advanced degrees awarded. *Degree requirements:* For doctorate, comprehensive exam, thesis/dissertation. *Entrance requirements:* For master's, doctorate, and Ed S, GRE General Test. Additional exam requirements/recommendations for international students: Required—TOEFL (minimum score 560 paper-based; 83 iBT). *Application deadline:* For fall admission, 5/1 priority date for international students; for winter admission, 11/1 priority date for international students; for summer admission, 1/1 priority date for international students. Applications are processed on a rolling basis. Application fee: $60. Electronic applications accepted. *Expenses:* Tuition, state resident: full-time $10,788; part-time $599 per credit hour. Tuition, nonresident: full-time $22,446; part-time $1247 per credit hour. *Required fees:* $196. Tuition and fees vary according to program and reciprocity agreements. *Financial support:* Fellowships, research assistantships, teaching assistantships, career-related internships or fieldwork, Federal Work-Study, scholarships/grants, health care benefits, and unspecified assistantships available. Financial award application deadline: 6/1; financial award applicants required to submit FAFSA. *Faculty research:* Evaluation of methods and programs to improve elementary and secondary education; research on organizational and human resource development; student access, retention and success in post-secondary education; educational policy analysis; multivariate quantitative research methods. *Unit head:* Dr. Gaetane Jean-Marie, Chair, 502-852-0634, Fax: 502-852-1164, E-mail: g0jean01@louisville.edu. *Application contact:* Libby Leggett, Director, Graduate Admissions, 502-852-3101, Fax: 502-852-6536, E-mail: gradadm@louisville.edu.
Website: http://www.louisville.edu/education/departments/elfh.

University of Louisville, Graduate School, College of Education and Human Development, Department of Teaching and Learning, Louisville, KY 40292-0001. Offers art education (MAT); curriculum and instruction (PhD); early elementary education (MAT); instructional technology (M Ed); interdisciplinary early childhood education (MAT); middle school education (MAT); music education (MAT); secondary education (MAT); special education (MAT); teacher leadership (M Ed). Part-time and evening/weekend programs available. *Students:* 137 full-time (93 women), 208 part-time (131 women); includes 44 minority (25 Black or African American, non-Hispanic/Latino; 1 American Indian or Alaska Native, non-Hispanic/Latino; 3 Asian, non-Hispanic/Latino; 12 Hispanic/Latino; 3 Two or more races, non-Hispanic/Latino), 2 international. Average age 32. 150 applicants, 51% accepted, 54 enrolled. In 2013, 127 master's, 5 doctorates awarded. *Degree requirements:* For doctorate, comprehensive exam, thesis/dissertation. *Entrance requirements:* For master's, GRE General Test, PRAXIS II (for some programs); for doctorate, GRE General Test. Additional exam requirements/recommendations for international students: Required—TOEFL (minimum score 560 paper-based; 83 iBT). *Application deadline:* For fall admission, 5/1 priority date for international students; for spring admission, 11/1 priority date for international students; for summer admission, 4/1 priority date for international students. Application fee: $60. Electronic applications accepted. *Expenses:* Tuition, state resident: full-time $10,788; part-time $599 per credit hour. Tuition, nonresident: full-time $22,446; part-time $1247 per credit hour. *Required fees:* $196. Tuition and fees vary according to program and reciprocity agreements. *Financial support:* Fellowships, research assistantships, teaching assistantships, career-related internships or fieldwork, Federal Work-Study, scholarships/grants, and unspecified assistantships available. Financial award application deadline: 6/1; financial award applicants required to submit FAFSA. *Faculty research:* Mathematics teacher education and ongoing professional development in pedagogy and content knowledge; development of literacy, including early literacy in science and mathematics and literacy development for English language learners; immersive visualizations for promoting STEM education from nanoscience to cosmic scales; evidence-based practices for students with disabilities; urban education, including teacher response to intervention systems in schools and cross-cultural competence. *Unit head:* Dr. Ann E. Larson, Acting Chair, 502-852-6431, Fax: 502-852-1497, E-mail: ann@louisville.edu. *Application contact:* Libby Leggett, Director, Graduate Admissions, 502-852-3101, Fax: 502-852-6536, E-mail: gradadm@louisville.edu.
Website: http://louisville.edu/delphi.

University of Maine, Graduate School, College of Education and Human Development, Department of Educational Leadership, Higher Education, and Human Development, Orono, ME 04469. Offers educational leadership (M Ed, Ed D, CAS); higher education (M Ed, MA, MS, Ed D, PhD, CAS); human development (MS). Part-time programs available. *Students:* 56 full-time (21 women), 73 part-time (41 women); includes 7 minority (2 Black or African American, non-Hispanic/Latino; 1 American Indian or Alaska Native, non-Hispanic/Latino; 2 Asian, non-Hispanic/Latino; 2 Hispanic/Latino), 4 international. Average age 39. 64 applicants, 63% accepted, 27 enrolled. In 2013, 20 master's, 6 other advanced degrees awarded. *Degree requirements:* For master's, thesis (for some programs); for doctorate, comprehensive exam, thesis/dissertation. *Entrance requirements:* For master's, GRE General Test, MAT; for doctorate, GRE. Additional exam requirements/recommendations for international students: Required—TOEFL. *Application deadline:* For fall admission, 2/1 priority date for domestic students. Applications are processed on a rolling basis. Application fee: $65. Electronic applications accepted. *Expenses:* Tuition, state resident: full-time $7524. Tuition, nonresident: full-time $23,112. *Required fees:* $1970. *Financial support:* In 2013–14, 26 students received support, including 1 research assistantship (averaging $18,000 per year), 3 teaching assistantships (averaging $14,600 per year); career-related internships or fieldwork, Federal Work-Study, institutionally sponsored loans, tuition waivers (full and partial), and unspecified assistantships also available. Financial award application

deadline: 3/1. *Faculty research:* Leadership formation, school organization, collective efficacy and collaborative climate of high schools, change process in high schools, principalship; equity policy; gender and education; doctoral student development, retention, and attrition; faculty development and socialization; sexuality education and curriculum development; family/domestic violence; friendship/kin relationships; early childhood education; support for families with members with disabilities. *Unit head:* Dr. Janet Spector, Coordinator, 207-581-3162, Fax: 207-581-3120. *Application contact:* Scott G. Delcourt, Associate Dean of the Graduate School, 207-581-3291, Fax: 207-581-3232, E-mail: graduate@maine.edu.
Website: http://www.umaine.edu/edhd/.

University of Maine at Farmington, Program in Education, Farmington, ME 04938-1990. Offers early childhood education (MS Ed); educational leadership (MS Ed). *Accreditation:* NCATE. Part-time and evening/weekend programs available. Postbaccalaureate distance learning degree programs offered (minimal on-campus study). *Faculty:* 10 full-time (9 women), 4 part-time/adjunct (2 women). *Students:* 43 full-time (38 women); includes 2 minority (1 American Indian or Alaska Native, non-Hispanic/Latino; 1 Hispanic/Latino). *Degree requirements:* For master's, capstone project (for educational leadership). *Entrance requirements:* For master's, baccalaureate degree from accredited institution, valid teaching certificate or professional experience in education, professional employment by school district or other educational institution, minimum of two years' experience in professional education. *Application deadline:* Applications are processed on a rolling basis. Application fee: $60. *Expenses:* Tuition, state resident: full-time $4930; part-time $379 per credit. Tuition, nonresident: full-time $7150; part-time $550 per credit. *Required fees:* $84 per semester. One-time fee: $100. *Faculty research:* School improvement strategies, technology integration. *Application contact:* Graduate Studies, 207-778-7502, Fax: 207-778-8134, E-mail: umfmasters@maine.edu.
Website: http://www2.umf.maine.edu/gradstudies/.

University of Manitoba, Faculty of Graduate Studies, Faculty of Education, Department of Educational Administration, Foundations and Psychology, Winnipeg, MB R3T 2N2, Canada. Offers adult and post-secondary education (M Ed); educational administration (M Ed); guidance and counseling (M Ed); inclusive special education (M Ed); social foundations of education (M Ed). *Degree requirements:* For master's, thesis or alternative.

University of Mary, School of Education and Behavioral Sciences, Department of Education, Bismarck, ND 58504-9652. Offers college teaching (M Ed); curriculum, instruction and assessment (M Ed); early childhood education (M Ed); early childhood special education (M Ed); elementary administration (M Ed); emotional disorders (M Ed); learning disabilities (M Ed); reading (M Ed); secondary administration (M Ed); special education strategist (M Ed). Part-time programs available. *Degree requirements:* For master's, portfolio or thesis. *Entrance requirements:* For master's, interview, letters of reference, minimum GPA of 2.5. Additional exam requirements/recommendations for international students: Required—TOEFL (minimum score 500 paper-based; 71 iBT). Electronic applications accepted. *Faculty research:* Innovative pedagogy in higher education, technology in education, content standards, children of poverty, children with diverse learning needs.

University of Mary Hardin-Baylor, Graduate Studies in Education, Belton, TX 76513. Offers administration of intervention programs (M Ed); curriculum and instruction (M Ed); educational administration (M Ed, Ed D), including higher education (Ed D), leadership in nursing education (Ed D), P-12 (Ed D). Part-time and evening/weekend programs available. *Faculty:* 13 full-time (10 women), 6 part-time/adjunct (2 women). *Students:* 46 full-time (33 women), 61 part-time (40 women); includes 35 minority (15 Black or African American, non-Hispanic/Latino; 1 American Indian or Alaska Native, non-Hispanic/Latino; 19 Hispanic/Latino), 1 international. Average age 38. 72 applicants, 88% accepted, 47 enrolled. In 2013, 13 master's, 30 doctorates awarded. *Degree requirements:* For master's, comprehensive exam; for doctorate, thesis/dissertation. *Entrance requirements:* For master's, minimum GPA of 3.0, interview; for doctorate, minimum GPA of 3.5, interview, essay, resume, employment verification, employer letter of support, 3 letters of recommendation. Additional exam requirements/recommendations for international students: Required—TOEFL (minimum score 550 paper-based; 80 iBT), IELTS (minimum score 6). *Application deadline:* For fall admission, 6/1 for domestic students, 6/15 priority date for international students; for spring admission, 11/1 for domestic students, 10/15 priority date for international students. Applications are processed on a rolling basis. Application fee: $35 ($135 for international students). Electronic applications accepted. *Expenses: Tuition:* Full-time $14,130; part-time $785 per credit hour. *Required fees:* $1350; $75 per credit hour. $50 per term. *Financial support:* Federal Work-Study and scholarships (for some active duty military personnel only) available. Support available to part-time students. Financial award application deadline: 6/1; financial award applicants required to submit FAFSA. *Unit head:* Dr. Marlene Zipperlen, Dean, College of Education/Director, Doctor of Education Program, 254-295-4572, Fax: 254-295-4480, E-mail: mzipperlen@umhb.edu. *Application contact:* Melissa Ford, Director of Graduate Admissions, 254-295-4020, Fax: 254-295-5038, E-mail: mford@umhb.edu.
Website: http://graduate.umhb.edu/education/.

University of Maryland, College Park, Academic Affairs, College of Education, Department of Counseling, Higher Education and Special Education, College Park, MD 20742. Offers college student personnel (M Ed, MA); college student personnel administration (PhD); community counseling (CAGS); community/career counseling (M Ed, MA); counseling and personnel services (M Ed, MA, PhD), including art therapy (M Ed), college student personnel (M Ed), counseling and personnel services (PhD), counseling psychology (M Ed), mental health counseling (M Ed), school counseling (M Ed); counseling psychology (PhD); counselor education (PhD); rehabilitation counseling (M Ed, MA, AGSC); school counseling (M Ed, MA); school psychology (M Ed, MA, PhD). *Accreditation:* ACA (one or more programs are accredited); APA (one or more programs are accredited); NCATE. Part-time and evening/weekend programs available. Postbaccalaureate distance learning degree programs offered (no on-campus study). *Faculty:* 63 full-time (43 women), 9 part-time/adjunct (8 women). *Students:* 244 full-time (189 women), 76 part-time (54 women); includes 96 minority (40 Black or African American, non-Hispanic/Latino; 1 American Indian or Alaska Native, non-Hispanic/Latino; 23 Asian, non-Hispanic/Latino; 26 Hispanic/Latino; 6 Two or more races, non-Hispanic/Latino), 34 international. 623 applicants, 21% accepted, 83 enrolled. In 2013, 64 master's, 41 doctorates awarded. *Degree requirements:* For master's, thesis (for some programs); for doctorate, thesis/dissertation. *Entrance requirements:* For master's, GRE General Test or MAT, minimum GPA of 3.0, 3 letters of recommendation; for doctorate, GRE General Test or MAT, minimum GPA of 3.5, 3 letters of recommendation. Additional exam requirements/recommendations for international students: Required—TOEFL. *Application deadline:* For fall admission, 12/1 for domestic students, 12/15 for international students; for spring admission, 12/1 for domestic students, 6/1 for international students. Applications are processed on a rolling basis. Application fee: $75. Electronic applications accepted. *Expenses:* Tuition, state resident: full-time $10,314; part-time $573 per credit hour. Tuition, nonresident: full-time $22,248; part-time $1236 per credit. *Required fees:* $1446; $403.15 per semester. Tuition and fees vary according to program. *Financial support:* In 2013–14, 31 fellowships with full and partial tuition reimbursements (averaging $21,772 per year), 7 research assistantships with tuition reimbursements (averaging $17,202 per year), 100 teaching assistantships with tuition reimbursements (averaging $16,637 per year) were awarded; career-related internships or fieldwork, Federal Work-Study, and scholarships/grants also available. Support available to part-time students. Financial award applicants required to submit FAFSA. *Faculty research:* Educational psychology, counseling, health. *Total annual research expenditures:* $3.2 million. *Unit head:* Dennis Kivlighan, Chair, 301-405-2858, E-mail: dennisk@umd.edu. *Application contact:* Dr. Charles A. Caramello, Dean of Graduate School, 301-405-0358, Fax: 301-314-9305, E-mail: ccaramel@umd.edu.

University of Maryland, College Park, Academic Affairs, College of Education, Department of Education Policy and Leadership, College Park, MD 20742. Offers curriculum and educational communications (M Ed, MA, Ed D, PhD); social foundations of education (M Ed, MA, Ed D, PhD, CAGS). *Accreditation:* NCATE. Part-time and evening/weekend programs available. Postbaccalaureate distance learning degree programs offered (minimal on-campus study). *Students:* 1 (woman) full-time. In 2013, 1 doctorate awarded. *Degree requirements:* For master's, thesis or alternative, internship and/or field experience; for doctorate, comprehensive exam, thesis/dissertation, practicum or internship. *Entrance requirements:* For master's, GRE General Test or MAT, minimum GPA of 3.0, scholarly writing sample, 3 letters of recommendation; for doctorate, GRE General Test or MAT, scholarly writing sample; minimum undergraduate GPA of 3.0, graduate 3.5. *Application deadline:* For fall admission, 2/1 for domestic students, 9/1 for international students. *Expenses:* Tuition, state resident: full-time $10,314; part-time $573 per credit hour. Tuition, nonresident: full-time $22,248; part-time $1236 per credit. *Required fees:* $1446; $403.15 per semester. Tuition and fees vary according to program. *Financial support:* Career-related internships or fieldwork, Federal Work-Study, and scholarships/grants available. Support available to part-time students. Financial award applicants required to submit FAFSA. *Faculty research:* Educational technology, adult and higher education. *Unit head:* Francine Hultgren, Chair, 301-405-3117, E-mail: fh@umd.edu. *Application contact:* Dr. Charles A. Caramello, Dean of Graduate School, 301-405-0358, Fax: 301-314-9305, E-mail: ccaramel@umd.edu.

University of Maryland Eastern Shore, Graduate Programs, Department of Education, Program in Education Leadership, Princess Anne, MD 21853-1299. Offers Ed D. Evening/weekend programs available. *Degree requirements:* For doctorate, comprehensive exam, thesis/dissertation, internship. *Entrance requirements:* For doctorate, interview, writing sample, state certification in a standard area, 3 years of recent teaching or successful professional experience in K-12 school setting. Additional exam requirements/recommendations for international students: Required—TOEFL (minimum score 80 iBT). Electronic applications accepted.

University of Massachusetts Amherst, Graduate School, College of Education, Program in Education, Amherst, MA 01003. Offers bilingual/English as a second language/multicultural education (M Ed, Ed S); child study and early education (M Ed); children, families and schools (Ed D, Ed S); early childhood and elementary teacher education (M Ed); educational leadership (M Ed); educational policy and leadership (Ed D); higher education (M Ed); international education (M Ed); language, literacy and culture (Ed D); learning, media and technology (M Ed, Ed S); mathematics, science, and learning technologies (Ed D); psychometric methods, educational statistics and research methods (Ed D); reading and writing (M Ed); school counselor education (M Ed, Ed S); school psychology (Ed S); science education (Ed S); secondary teacher education (M Ed); social justice education (M Ed, Ed D, Ed S); special education (M Ed, Ed D, Ed S); teacher education and school improvement (Ed D, Ed S). *Accreditation:* NCATE. Part-time programs available. Postbaccalaureate distance learning degree programs offered (minimal on-campus study). *Faculty:* 95 full-time (55 women). *Students:* 357 full-time (240 women), 264 part-time (194 women); includes 114 minority (41 Black or African American, non-Hispanic/Latino; 4 American Indian or Alaska Native, non-Hispanic/Latino; 10 Asian, non-Hispanic/Latino; 47 Hispanic/Latino; 12 Two or more races, non-Hispanic/Latino), 100 international. Average age 34. 761 applicants, 51% accepted, 200 enrolled. In 2013, 186 master's, 31 doctorates, 22 other advanced degrees awarded. Terminal master's awarded for partial completion of doctoral program. *Degree requirements:* For doctorate, comprehensive exam, thesis/dissertation. *Entrance requirements:* Additional exam requirements/recommendations for international students: Required—TOEFL (minimum score 550 paper-based; 80 iBT), IELTS (minimum score 6.5). *Application deadline:* For fall admission, 1/15 for domestic and international students. Applications are processed on a rolling basis. Application fee: $75. Electronic applications accepted. *Financial support:* Fellowships with full and partial tuition reimbursements, research assistantships with full and partial tuition reimbursements, teaching assistantships with full and partial tuition reimbursements, career-related internships or fieldwork, Federal Work-Study, scholarships/grants, traineeships, health care benefits, tuition waivers (full and partial), and unspecified assistantships available. Support available to part-time students. Financial award application deadline: 1/15; financial award applicants required to submit FAFSA. *Unit head:* Dr. Linda L. Griffin, Graduate Program Director, 413-545-6984, Fax: 413-545-1523. *Application contact:* Lindsay DeSantis, Supervisor of Admissions, 413-545-0722, Fax: 413-577-0010, E-mail: gradadm@grad.umass.edu.
Website: http://www.umass.edu/education/.

University of Massachusetts Boston, Office of Graduate Studies, Graduate College of Education, School Organization, Curriculum and Instruction Department, Program in Educational Administration, Boston, MA 02125-3393. Offers M Ed, CAGS. Part-time and evening/weekend programs available. *Degree requirements:* For master's, comprehensive exam, practicum; for CAGS, comprehensive exam. *Entrance requirements:* For master's, GRE General Test or MAT, 2 years of teaching experience, minimum GPA of 2.75; for CAGS, minimum GPA of 2.75. *Faculty research:* Power in the classroom, teacher leadership, professional development schools.

University of Massachusetts Boston, Office of Graduate Studies, Graduate College of Education, School Organization, Curriculum and Instruction Department, Program in Education, Track in Higher Education Administration, Boston, MA 02125-3393. Offers Ed D. Part-time and evening/weekend programs available. *Degree requirements:* For doctorate, comprehensive exam, thesis/dissertation. *Entrance requirements:* For doctorate, GRE General Test or MAT, minimum GPA of 2.75. *Faculty research:* Women, higher education and professionalization, school reform, urban classroom, higher education policy.

University of Massachusetts Boston, Office of Graduate Studies, Graduate College of Education, School Organization, Curriculum and Instruction Department, Program in Education, Track in Urban School Leadership, Boston, MA 02125-3393. Offers Ed D. Part-time and evening/weekend programs available. *Degree requirements:* For doctorate, comprehensive exam, thesis/dissertation. *Entrance requirements:* For doctorate, GRE General Test or MAT, minimum GPA of 2.75. *Faculty research:* School reform, race and culture in schools, race and higher education, language, literacy and writing.

University of Massachusetts Dartmouth, Graduate School, College of Arts and Sciences, School of Education, Program in Educational Leadership, North Dartmouth, MA 02747-2300. Offers Ed D, PhD. Part-time programs available. *Faculty:* 4 full-time (0

women). *Students:* 37 part-time (19 women); includes 6 minority (4 Black or African American, non-Hispanic/Latino; 1 American Indian or Alaska Native, non-Hispanic/Latino; 1 Two or more races, non-Hispanic/Latino). Average age 38. 25 applicants, 96% accepted, 14 enrolled. *Degree requirements:* For doctorate, comprehensive exam, thesis/dissertation. *Entrance requirements:* For doctorate, GRE or GMAT, statement of purpose (minimum of 300 words), resume, 3 letters of recommendation, official transcripts, scholarly writing sample (minimum of 10 pages). Additional exam requirements/recommendations for international students: Required—TOEFL (minimum score 600 paper-based). *Application deadline:* For fall admission, 3/31 priority date for domestic students, 2/28 priority date for international students. Applications are processed on a rolling basis. Application fee: $60. Electronic applications accepted. *Expenses:* Tuition, state resident: full-time $2071; part-time $86.29 per credit. Tuition, nonresident: full-time $8099; part-time $337.46 per credit. Tuition and fees vary according to course load and reciprocity agreements. *Financial support:* In 2013–14, 1 fellowship with full tuition reimbursement (averaging $17,000 per year) was awarded; Federal Work-Study and unspecified assistantships also available. Support available to part-time students. Financial award application deadline: 3/1; financial award applicants required to submit FAFSA. *Faculty research:* Curricular theory, higher education policy, gaming policy, qualitative methods, critical theory. *Total annual research expenditures:* $166,000. *Unit head:* Joao Paraskeva, Graduate Program Director, 508-910-6697, Fax: 508-910-9058, E-mail: jparaskeva@umassd.edu. *Application contact:* Steven Briggs, Director of Marketing and Recruitment for Graduate Studies, 508-999-8604, Fax: 508-999-8183, E-mail: graduate@umassd.edu.
Website: http://www.umassd.edu/educationalleadership/.

University of Massachusetts Lowell, Graduate School of Education, Lowell, MA 01854-2881. Offers administration, planning, and policy (CAGS); curriculum and instruction (M Ed, CAGS); educational administration (M Ed); language arts and literacy (Ed D); leadership in schooling (Ed D); math and science education (Ed D); reading and language (M Ed, CAGS). *Accreditation:* NCATE. Part-time and evening/weekend programs available. Postbaccalaureate distance learning degree programs offered (no on-campus study). Terminal master's awarded for partial completion of doctoral program. *Degree requirements:* For doctorate, thesis/dissertation. *Entrance requirements:* For master's, doctorate, and CAGS, GRE General Test. Additional exam requirements/recommendations for international students: Required—TOEFL. Electronic applications accepted.

University of Memphis, Graduate School, College of Education, Department of Leadership, Memphis, TN 38152. Offers adult education (Ed D); educational leadership (Ed D); higher education (Ed D); leadership (MS); policy studies (Ed D); school administration and supervision (MS). *Accreditation:* NCATE. Part-time and evening/weekend programs available. Postbaccalaureate distance learning degree programs offered (minimal on-campus study). *Faculty:* 12 full-time (4 women), 2 part-time/adjunct (0 women). *Students:* 12 full-time (8 women), 138 part-time (87 women); includes 86 minority (79 Black or African American, non-Hispanic/Latino; 1 Asian, non-Hispanic/Latino; 1 Hispanic/Latino; 5 Two or more races, non-Hispanic/Latino), 1 international. Average age 40. 65 applicants, 66% accepted, 10 enrolled. In 2013, 12 master's, 13 doctorates awarded. *Degree requirements:* For master's, comprehensive exam, thesis optional; for doctorate, comprehensive exam, thesis/dissertation. *Entrance requirements:* For master's and doctorate, GRE. *Application deadline:* For fall admission, 4/1 for domestic students; for spring admission, 10/1 for domestic students. Application fee: $35 ($60 for international students). Electronic applications accepted. *Financial support:* In 2013–14, 70 students received support. Research assistantships with full tuition reimbursements available, teaching assistantships, Federal Work-Study, scholarships/grants, and unspecified assistantships available. Financial award application deadline: 2/15; financial award applicants required to submit FAFSA. *Faculty research:* School improvement, social justice, online learning, adult learning, diversity. *Unit head:* Katrina Mayer, Interim Chair, 901-678-2466, E-mail: kmeyer@memphis.edu. *Application contact:* Larry McNeal, Professor, School Administration and Supervision Programs, 901-678-2369, E-mail: lmcneal1@memphis.edu.
Website: http://www.memphis.edu/lead.

University of Michigan–Dearborn, College of Education, Health, and Human Services, Doctoral Program in Education, Dearborn, MI 48126. Offers curriculum and practice (Ed D); educational leadership (Ed D); metropolitan education (Ed D). Part-time and evening/weekend programs available. *Faculty:* 7 full-time (5 women), 2 part-time/adjunct (0 women). *Students:* 4 full-time (all women), 35 part-time (27 women); includes 15 minority (11 Black or African American, non-Hispanic/Latino; 1 Asian, non-Hispanic/Latino; 3 Hispanic/Latino). Average age 40. 26 applicants, 42% accepted, 7 enrolled. *Degree requirements:* For doctorate, comprehensive exam, thesis/dissertation. *Entrance requirements:* For doctorate, GRE (taken within the last 5 years), master's degree with minimum GPA of 3.3, 3 letters of recommendation (1 from faculty), 3 years' professional and/or teaching experience. Additional exam requirements/recommendations for international students: Required—TOEFL (minimum score 560 paper-based; 84 iBT). *Application deadline:* For fall admission, 3/1 for domestic and international students. Application fee: $60. Electronic applications accepted. *Expenses:* Tuition, state resident: full-time $11,838; part-time $686 per credit hour. Tuition, nonresident: full-time $20,926; part-time $1206 per credit hour. *Required fees:* $760; $286 per semester. Tuition and fees vary according to course load and program. *Financial support:* Scholarships/grants available. Financial award application deadline: 2/1; financial award applicants required to submit FAFSA. *Faculty research:* Educational leadership, metropolitan education, curriculum and practice, educational psychology, special education, assessment. *Unit head:* Dr. Bonnie M. Beyer, Coordinator, 313-593-5583, E-mail: beyer@umd.umich.edu. *Application contact:* Elizabeth Morden, Program Assistant, 313-583-6333, Fax: 313-593-4748, E-mail: emorden@umich.edu.
Website: http://cehhs.umd.umich.edu/cehhs_edd/.

University of Michigan–Dearborn, College of Education, Health, and Human Services, Program in Educational Leadership, Dearborn, MI 48126. Offers MA. Part-time and evening/weekend programs available. Postbaccalaureate distance learning degree programs offered (minimal on-campus study). *Faculty:* 2 full-time (both women), 2 part-time/adjunct (0 women). *Students:* 1 full-time (0 women), 31 part-time (9 women); includes 5 minority (3 Black or African American, non-Hispanic/Latino; 2 Asian, non-Hispanic/Latino). Average age 32. 10 applicants, 80% accepted, 6 enrolled. In 2013, 8 master's awarded. *Entrance requirements:* For master's, minimum GPA of 3.0; official transcripts of all undergraduate/graduate work completed; 3 recommendation forms and letters on letterhead; statement of purpose/personal statement; teaching certificate. Additional exam requirements/recommendations for international students: Required—TOEFL (minimum score 560 paper-based; 84 iBT). *Application deadline:* For fall admission, 8/1 priority date for domestic students, 5/1 for international students; for winter admission, 12/1 priority date for domestic students, 9/1 for international students; for spring admission, 4/1 priority date for domestic students, 1/1 for international students. Applications are processed on a rolling basis. Application fee: $60. Electronic applications accepted. *Expenses:* Tuition, state resident: full-time $11,838; part-time $686 per credit hour. Tuition, nonresident: full-time $20,926; part-time $1206 per credit hour. *Required fees:* $760; $286 per semester. Tuition and fees vary according to course load and program. *Financial support:* Scholarships/grants available. Financial award applicants required to submit FAFSA. *Unit head:* Dr. Bonnie M. Beyer, Professor/

Program Coordinator, 313-593-5583, Fax: 313-593-4748, E-mail: beyere@umd.umich.edu. *Application contact:* Elizabeth Morden, Customer Service Assistant, 313-583-6333, Fax: 313-593-4748, E-mail: emorden@umd.umich.edu.
Website: http://cehhs.umd.umich.edu/cehhs_mael/.

University of Michigan–Flint, Graduate Programs, Program in Public Administration, Flint, MI 48502-1950. Offers administration of non-profit agencies (MPA); criminal justice administration (MPA); educational administration (MPA); healthcare administration (MPA). Part-time programs available. *Faculty:* 6 full-time (2 women), 12 part-time/adjunct (4 women). *Students:* 16 full-time (6 women), 112 part-time (74 women); includes 34 minority (24 Black or African American, non-Hispanic/Latino; 1 American Indian or Alaska Native, non-Hispanic/Latino; 1 Asian, non-Hispanic/Latino; 5 Hispanic/Latino; 3 Two or more races, non-Hispanic/Latino), 4 international. Average age 33. 75 applicants, 65% accepted, 44 enrolled. In 2013, 59 master's awarded. *Degree requirements:* For master's, thesis or alternative, internship. *Entrance requirements:* For master's, minimum GPA of 3.0, 1 course each in American government, microeconomics and statistics. Additional exam requirements/recommendations for international students: Required—TOEFL (minimum score 560 paper-based; 84 iBT), IELTS (minimum score 6.5). *Application deadline:* For fall admission, 8/1 for domestic students, 5/1 for international students; for winter admission, 11/15 for domestic students, 9/1 for international students; for spring admission, 3/15 for domestic students, 1/1 for international students; for summer admission, 5/15 for domestic students. Applications are processed on a rolling basis. Application fee: $55. Electronic applications accepted. *Expenses:* Contact institution. *Financial support:* Career-related internships or fieldwork, Federal Work-Study, and scholarships/grants available. Support available to part-time students. Financial award application deadline: 3/1; financial award applicants required to submit FAFSA. *Unit head:* Dr. Kathryn Schellenberg, Director, 810-762-3340, E-mail: kathsch@umflint.edu. *Application contact:* Bradley T. Maki, Director of Graduate Admissions, 810-762-3171, Fax: 810-766-6789, E-mail: bmaki@umflint.edu.
Website: http://www.umflint.edu/graduateprograms/public-administration-mpa.

University of Michigan–Flint, School of Education and Human Services, Flint, MI 48502-1950. Offers early childhood education (MA); education (MA, Ed D), including education (MA), educational leadership (Ed D), elementary education with teaching certification (MA), literacy (K-12) (MA), technology in education (MA); education specialist (Ed S), including curriculum and instruction, education leadership; secondary education (MA); special education (MA). Part-time programs available. *Faculty:* 9 full-time (6 women), 12 part-time/adjunct (7 women). *Students:* 31 full-time (20 women), 206 part-time (153 women); includes 35 minority (31 Black or African American, non-Hispanic/Latino; 1 American Indian or Alaska Native, non-Hispanic/Latino; 1 Asian, non-Hispanic/Latino; 2 Hispanic/Latino), 1 international. Average age 36. 135 applicants, 80% accepted, 91 enrolled. In 2013, 99 master's awarded. *Entrance requirements:* For master's, BS with minimum GPA of 3.0. Additional exam requirements/recommendations for international students: Required—TOEFL (minimum score 560 paper-based; 84 iBT), IELTS (minimum score 6.5). *Application deadline:* For fall admission, 8/1 priority date for domestic students, 5/1 priority date for international students; for winter admission, 11/15 priority date for domestic students, 9/1 priority date for international students; for spring admission, 3/15 priority date for domestic students, 1/1 priority date for international students. Application fee: $55. Electronic applications accepted. *Expenses:* Contact institution. *Financial support:* Federal Work-Study, scholarships/grants, and unspecified assistantships available. Support available to part-time students. Financial award application deadline: 3/1; financial award applicants required to submit FAFSA. *Unit head:* Dr. Bob Barnett, Interim Dean, 810-766-6878, Fax: 810-766-6891, E-mail: rbarnett@umflint.edu. *Application contact:* Bradley T. Maki, Director of Graduate Admissions, 810-762-3171, Fax: 810-766-6789, E-mail: bmaki@umflint.edu.
Website: http://www.umflint.edu/sehs/.

University of Minnesota, Twin Cities Campus, Graduate School, College of Education and Human Development, Department of Organizational Leadership, Policy and Development, Program in Educational Administration, Minneapolis, MN 55455-0213. Offers MA, Ed D, PhD. *Students:* 41 full-time (22 women), 102 part-time (59 women); includes 19 minority (11 Black or African American, non-Hispanic/Latino; 5 Asian, non-Hispanic/Latino; 3 Hispanic/Latino), 8 international. Average age 37. 179 applicants, 60% accepted, 72 enrolled. In 2013, 4 master's, 10 doctorates awarded. Application fee: $75 ($95 for international students). *Unit head:* Dr. Rebecca Ropers-Huilman, Chair, 612-624-1006, Fax: 612-624-3377, E-mail: ropers@umn.edu. *Application contact:* Dr. Jennifer Engler, Assistant Dean, 612-626-2887, Fax: 612-626-7496, E-mail: engle009@umn.edu.
Website: http://www.cehd.umn.edu/EdPA/EdAd/.

University of Mississippi, Graduate School, School of Education, Department of Leadership and Counselor Education, Oxford, MS 38677. Offers counselor education (M Ed, PhD); educational leadership (M Ed, PhD, Ed S); higher education/student personnel (MA, PhD); play therapy (Ed S). *Accreditation:* ACA; NCATE. *Faculty:* 13 full-time (6 women), 9 part-time/adjunct (6 women). *Students:* 155 full-time (123 women), 181 part-time (127 women); includes 136 minority (116 Black or African American, non-Hispanic/Latino; 3 American Indian or Alaska Native, non-Hispanic/Latino; 8 Hispanic/Latino; 9 Two or more races, non-Hispanic/Latino), 6 international. In 2013, 104 master's, 9 doctorates awarded. *Degree requirements:* For doctorate, thesis/dissertation. *Entrance requirements:* For master's, GRE General Test, minimum GPA of 3.0; for doctorate, GRE General Test. Additional exam requirements/recommendations for international students: Required—TOEFL. *Application deadline:* For fall admission, 4/1 for domestic students; for spring admission, 10/1 for domestic students. Applications are processed on a rolling basis. Application fee: $40. Electronic applications accepted. *Financial support:* Scholarships/grants available. Financial award application deadline: 3/1; financial award applicants required to submit FAFSA. *Unit head:* Dr. Timothy Letzring, Chair, 662-915-7069, Fax: 662-915-7230. *Application contact:* Dr. Christy M. Wyandt, Associate Dean, 662-915-7474, Fax: 662-915-7577, E-mail: cwyandt@olemiss.edu.
Website: http://education.olemiss.edu/dco/leadership_counselor_education.html.

University of Missouri, Graduate School, College of Education, Department of Educational Leadership and Policy Analysis, Columbia, MO 65211. Offers education administration (M Ed, MA, Ed D, PhD, Ed S); higher and adult education (M Ed, MA, Ed D, PhD, Ed S). Part-time programs available. *Faculty:* 15 full-time (8 women), 5 part-time/adjunct (4 women). *Students:* 118 full-time (67 women), 273 part-time (158 women); includes 52 minority (30 Black or African American, non-Hispanic/Latino; 1 American Indian or Alaska Native, non-Hispanic/Latino; 4 Asian, non-Hispanic/Latino; 10 Hispanic/Latino; 7 Two or more races, non-Hispanic/Latino), 18 international. Average age 37. 233 applicants, 62% accepted, 120 enrolled. In 2013, 35 master's, 70 doctorates, 31 other advanced degrees awarded. *Degree requirements:* For doctorate, variable foreign language requirement, comprehensive exam (for some programs), thesis/dissertation. *Entrance requirements:* For master's, doctorate, and Ed S, minimum GPA of 3.0. Additional exam requirements/recommendations for international students: Required—TOEFL (minimum score 500 paper-based; 61 iBT), IELTS (minimum score 5.5). *Application deadline:* For fall admission, 1/15 priority date for domestic and

international students; for winter admission, 9/15 priority date for domestic and international students; for spring admission, 10/15 for domestic students. Applications are processed on a rolling basis. Application fee: $55 ($75 for international students). Electronic applications accepted. *Financial support:* Fellowships with full tuition reimbursements, research assistantships with full tuition reimbursements, teaching assistantships with full tuition reimbursements, institutionally sponsored loans, scholarships/grants, health care benefits, and unspecified assistantships available. *Faculty research:* Administrative communication and behavior, middle schools leadership, administration of special education. *Unit head:* Dr. Jeni Hart, Associate Division Director, 573-882-4225, E-mail: hartjl@missouri.edu. *Application contact:* Betty Kissane, Office Support Assistant IV, 573-882-8221, E-mail: kissaneb@missouri.edu. Website: http://elpa.missouri.edu/.

University of Missouri–Kansas City, School of Education, Kansas City, MO 64110-2499. Offers administration (Ed D); counseling and guidance (MA, Ed S), including mental health counseling (Ed S), school counseling (Ed S); counseling psychology (PhD); curriculum and instruction (MA, Ed S), including language and literacy (Ed S); education (PhD), including higher education administration, PK-12 education administration; educational administration (MA, Ed S), including advanced principal (Ed S), beginning principal (Ed S), district-level administration (Ed S); reading education (MA, Ed S); special education (MA). PhD in education offered through the School of Graduate Studies. *Accreditation:* NCATE. Part-time and evening/weekend programs available. *Faculty:* 44 full-time (34 women), 60 part-time/adjunct (45 women). *Students:* 206 full-time (145 women), 394 part-time (291 women); includes 154 minority (99 Black or African American, non-Hispanic/Latino; 13 Asian, non-Hispanic/Latino; 30 Hispanic/Latino; 1 Native Hawaiian or other Pacific Islander, non-Hispanic/Latino; 11 Two or more races, non-Hispanic/Latino), 16 international. Average age 32. 401 applicants, 48% accepted, 188 enrolled. In 2013, 156 master's, 9 doctorates, 24 other advanced degrees awarded. *Degree requirements:* For doctorate, thesis/dissertation, internship, practicum. *Entrance requirements:* For master's, GRE, minimum GPA of 2.75, 2 letters of reference, written statement of purpose; for doctorate, GRE, minimum GPA of 3.0; for Ed S, minimum GPA of 3.0. Additional exam requirements/recommendations for international students: Required—TOEFL (minimum score 550 paper-based; 80 iBT). *Application deadline:* For fall admission, 4/1 priority date for domestic and international students; for spring admission, 11/1 priority date for domestic and international students. Applications are processed on a rolling basis. Application fee: $45 ($50 for international students). *Expenses:* Tuition, state resident: full-time $6073; part-time $337.40 per credit hour. Tuition, nonresident: full-time $15,680; part-time $871.10 per credit hour. *Required fees:* $97.59 per credit hour. Full-time tuition and fees vary according to program. *Financial support:* In 2013–14, 12 research assistantships with partial tuition reimbursements (averaging $11,140 per year) were awarded; career-related internships or fieldwork, Federal Work-Study, institutionally sponsored loans, and tuition waivers (full and partial) also available. Support available to part-time students. Financial award application deadline: 3/1; financial award applicants required to submit FAFSA. *Faculty research:* Urban education, inquiry-based field study, theories of counseling and psychotherapy, school literacy, educational technology. *Unit head:* Dr. Wanda Blanchett, Dean, 816-235-2234, Fax: 816-235-5270, E-mail: education@umkc.edu. *Application contact:* Erica Hernandez-Scott, Student Recruiter, 816-235-1295, Fax: 816-235-5270, E-mail: hernandeze@umkc.edu. Website: http://education.umkc.edu.

University of Missouri–St. Louis, College of Education, Division of Educational Leadership and Policy Studies, St. Louis, MO 63121. Offers adult and higher education (M Ed), including adult education, higher education; educational administration (M Ed, Ed S), including community education (M Ed), elementary education (M Ed), secondary education (M Ed); institutional research (Certificate). *Accreditation:* NCATE. Part-time and evening/weekend programs available. *Faculty:* 13 full-time (8 women), 5 part-time/adjunct (2 women). *Students:* 17 full-time (13 women), 154 part-time (114 women); includes 77 minority (75 Black or African American, non-Hispanic/Latino; 1 Asian, non-Hispanic/Latino; 1 Hispanic/Latino), 7 international. Average age 35. 120 applicants, 68% accepted, 40 enrolled. In 2013, 63 master's, 28 Certificates awarded. *Degree requirements:* For master's, comprehensive exam (for some programs); for other advanced degree, comprehensive exam (for some programs), thesis or alternative. *Entrance requirements:* Additional exam requirements/recommendations for international students: Recommended—TOEFL (minimum score 550 paper-based; 79 iBT), IELTS (minimum score 6.5). *Application deadline:* For fall admission, 7/1 priority date for domestic and international students; for spring admission, 12/1 priority date for domestic and international students. Applications are processed on a rolling basis. Application fee: $50 ($40 for international students). Electronic applications accepted. *Expenses:* Tuition, state resident: full-time $7364; part-time $409.10 per credit hour. Tuition, nonresident: full-time $19,162; part-time $1008.50 per credit hour. *Financial support:* In 2013–14, 1 research assistantship with full and partial tuition reimbursement (averaging $12,000 per year), teaching assistantships with full and partial tuition reimbursements (averaging $8,470 per year) were awarded. Financial award application deadline: 4/1; financial award applicants required to submit FAFSA. *Faculty research:* Educational policy research; philosophy of education; higher, adult, and vocational education; school initiatives, change, and reform. *Unit head:* Dr. E. Kathleen Sullivan Brown, Chair, 514-516-5944. *Application contact:* 314-516-5458, Fax: 314-516-6996, E-mail: gradadm@umsl.edu. Website: http://coe.umsl.edu/web/divisions/elaps/index.html.

University of Missouri–St. Louis, College of Education, Interdisciplinary Doctoral Programs, St. Louis, MO 63121. Offers adult and higher education (Ed D); counseling (PhD); counselor education (Ed D); educational administration (Ed D); educational leadership and policy studies (PhD); educational psychology (PhD); teaching-learning processes (Ed D, PhD). *Faculty:* 72 full-time (33 women). *Students:* 58 full-time (46 women), 240 part-time (154 women); includes 106 minority (86 Black or African American, non-Hispanic/Latino; 4 American Indian or Alaska Native, non-Hispanic/Latino; 6 Asian, non-Hispanic/Latino; 8 Hispanic/Latino; 2 Two or more races, non-Hispanic/Latino), 9 international. Average age 42. 67 applicants, 58% accepted, 24 enrolled. In 2013, 24 doctorates awarded. *Degree requirements:* For doctorate, thesis/dissertation. *Entrance requirements:* For doctorate, GRE General Test, 3 letters of recommendation; personal interview. Additional exam requirements/recommendations for international students: Recommended—TOEFL (minimum score 550 paper-based; 79 iBT), IELTS (minimum score 6.5). *Application deadline:* For fall admission, 3/1 for domestic and international students; for spring admission, 10/1 for domestic and international students. Application fee: $50 ($40 for international students). Electronic applications accepted. *Expenses:* Tuition, state resident: full-time $7364; part-time $409.10 per credit hour. Tuition, nonresident: full-time $19,162; part-time $1008.50 per credit hour. *Financial support:* In 2013–14, 13 research assistantships (averaging $12,240 per year), 9 teaching assistantships (averaging $12,240 per year) were awarded. Financial award application deadline: 4/1; financial award applicants required to submit FAFSA. *Faculty research:* Higher education law and policy, gender and higher education, student retention, lifelong learning orientation, school counselor's role in violence prevention. *Unit head:* Dr. Kathleen Haywood, Director of Graduate Studies, 314-516-5483, Fax: 314-516-5227, E-mail: kathleen_haywood@umsl.edu. *Application contact:* 314-516-5458, Fax: 314-516-6996, E-mail: gradadm@umsl.edu.

The University of Montana, Graduate School, Phyllis J. Washington College of Education and Human Sciences, Department of Educational Leadership and Counseling, Program in Educational Leadership, Missoula, MT 59812-0002. Offers M Ed, Ed D, Ed S. *Degree requirements:* For doctorate, thesis/dissertation; for Ed S, thesis. *Entrance requirements:* For master's and Ed S, GRE General Test. Additional exam requirements/recommendations for international students: Required—TOEFL.

University of Montevallo, College of Education, Program in Educational Administration, Montevallo, AL 35115. Offers M Ed, Ed S. *Accreditation:* NCATE. Part-time and evening/weekend programs available. *Students:* 3 full-time (all women), 63 part-time (50 women); includes 31 minority (30 Black or African American, non-Hispanic/Latino; 1 Two or more races, non-Hispanic/Latino). In 2013, 20 master's, 33 Ed Ss awarded. *Degree requirements:* For master's and Ed S, comprehensive exam. *Entrance requirements:* For master's, GRE General Test or MAT. Additional exam requirements/recommendations for international students: Required—TOEFL (minimum score 550 paper-based). *Application deadline:* For fall admission, 7/15 for domestic students; for spring admission, 11/15 for domestic students. Application fee: $25. *Financial support:* Federal Work-Study, scholarships/grants, and unspecified assistantships available. *Unit head:* Dr. Anna E. McEwan, Dean of Education, 205-665-6360, E-mail: mcewanae@montevallo.edu. *Application contact:* Kevin Thornthwaite, Director, Graduate Admissions and Records, 205-665-6350, E-mail: graduate@montevallo.edu. Website: http://www.montevallo.edu/education/college-of-education/traditional-masters-degrees/leadership/.

University of Mount Union, Program in Educational Leadership, Alliance, OH 44601-3993. Offers MA. Part-time programs available. Postbaccalaureate distance learning degree programs offered (minimal on-campus study). *Faculty:* 1 (woman) full-time. *Students:* 29 part-time (22 women); includes 1 minority (Two or more races, non-Hispanic/Latino). 35 applicants, 57% accepted, 14 enrolled. *Entrance requirements:* For master's, MAT and/or GRE General Test, two recommendations, official transcript from each college or university previously attended, curriculum vitae or resume, personal statement. Additional exam requirements/recommendations for international students: Required—TOEFL (minimum score 100 iBT). *Application deadline:* For fall admission, 8/15 for domestic and international students. Applications are processed on a rolling basis. Application fee: $30. Electronic applications accepted. *Expenses: Tuition:* Full-time $26,280; part-time $520 per credit hour. *Required fees:* $485; $80 per semester. Tuition and fees vary according to program. *Financial support:* Applicants required to submit FAFSA. *Unit head:* Dr. Thomas Gannon, Director, 800-992-6682. *Application contact:* Jessie Canavan, Director of Admissions, 330-823-2579, E-mail: canavajl@mountunion.edu. Website: http://www.mountunion.edu/mael.

University of Nebraska at Kearney, Graduate Programs, College of Education, Department of Educational Administration, Kearney, NE 68849-0001. Offers curriculum supervisor of academic area (MA Ed); school principalship 7-12 (MA Ed); school principalship PK-8 (MA Ed); school superintendent (Ed S); supervisor of special education (MA Ed). *Accreditation:* NCATE. Part-time and evening/weekend programs available. *Degree requirements:* For master's, thesis optional; for Ed S, thesis. *Entrance requirements:* For master's, letters of recommendation, resume, letter of interest. Additional exam requirements/recommendations for international students: Required—TOEFL (minimum score 550 paper-based). Electronic applications accepted. *Faculty research:* Leadership and organizational behavior.

University of Nebraska at Omaha, Graduate Studies, College of Education, Department of Educational Administration and Supervision, Omaha, NE 68182. Offers educational administration and supervision (Ed D); educational leadership (MS, Ed S). *Accreditation:* NCATE. Part-time and evening/weekend programs available. *Faculty:* 6 full-time (2 women). *Students:* 6 full-time (4 women), 106 part-time (68 women); includes 16 minority (7 Black or African American, non-Hispanic/Latino; 2 Asian, non-Hispanic/Latino; 4 Hispanic/Latino; 3 Two or more races, non-Hispanic/Latino), 2 international. Average age 37. 39 applicants, 59% accepted, 18 enrolled. In 2013, 29 master's, 12 doctorates, 2 other advanced degrees awarded. *Degree requirements:* For master's, comprehensive exam, thesis (for some programs); for doctorate, comprehensive exam, thesis/dissertation; for Ed S, comprehensive exam, thesis. *Entrance requirements:* For master's, minimum GPA of 3.0, transcripts, resume, copy of teaching certificate, 3 letters of recommendation, statement of purpose; for doctorate, GRE General Test, resume, 3 samples of research/written work, 3 letters of recommendation, statement of purpose, transcripts. Additional exam requirements/recommendations for international students: Required—TOEFL, IELTS, PTE. *Application deadline:* For fall admission, 6/1 priority date for domestic students; for spring admission, 10/1 priority date for domestic students; for summer admission, 2/1 for domestic students. Applications are processed on a rolling basis. Application fee: $45. Electronic applications accepted. *Financial support:* In 2013–14, 5 students received support, including 4 research assistantships with tuition reimbursements available, 1 teaching assistantship with tuition reimbursement available; Federal Work-Study, institutionally sponsored loans, scholarships/grants, tuition waivers (partial), and unspecified assistantships also available. Support available to part-time students. Financial award application deadline: 3/1. *Application contact:* Dr. Kay Keiser, Graduate Program Chair, 402-554-2721, E-mail: graduate@unomaha.edu.

University of Nebraska–Lincoln, Graduate College, College of Education and Human Sciences, Department of Educational Administration, Lincoln, NE 68588. Offers M Ed, MA, Ed D, Certificate. Ed D offered jointly with University of Nebraska at Omaha. *Accreditation:* NCATE. *Degree requirements:* For master's, thesis optional; for doctorate, comprehensive exam, thesis/dissertation. *Entrance requirements:* For master's, GRE or MAT; for doctorate, GRE General Test, administrative certification. Additional exam requirements/recommendations for international students: Required—TOEFL (minimum score 550 paper-based). Electronic applications accepted. *Faculty research:* Educational policy, school finance, school law, school restructuring, leadership behavior.

University of Nebraska–Lincoln, Graduate College, College of Education and Human Sciences, Interdepartmental Area of Administration, Curriculum and Instruction, Lincoln, NE 68588. Offers Ed D, PhD, JD/PhD. *Accreditation:* NCATE. Postbaccalaureate distance learning degree programs offered. *Degree requirements:* For doctorate, comprehensive exam, thesis/dissertation. *Entrance requirements:* For doctorate, GRE, curriculum vitae. Additional exam requirements/recommendations for international students: Required—TOEFL (minimum score 550 paper-based). Electronic applications accepted.

University of Nevada, Las Vegas, Graduate College, College of Education, Department of Educational Psychology and Higher Education, Las Vegas, NV 89154-3002. Offers educational leadership (Ed D, PhD); educational psychology (MS, PhD, Ed S), including learning and technology (PhD); higher education (M Ed, PhD, Certificate); PhD/JD. Part-time and evening/weekend programs available. *Faculty:* 19 full-time (12 women), 4 part-time/adjunct (2 women). *Students:* 56 full-time (44 women), 79 part-time (58 women); includes 40 minority (12 Black or African American, non-Hispanic/Latino; 1 American Indian or Alaska Native, non-Hispanic/Latino; 7 Asian, non-Hispanic/Latino; 10 Hispanic/Latino; 2 Native Hawaiian or other Pacific Islander, non-Hispanic/Latino; 8 Two or more races, non-Hispanic/Latino), 2 international. Average

age 35. 67 applicants, 64% accepted, 28 enrolled. In 2013, 22 master's, 36 doctorates, 10 other advanced degrees awarded. *Degree requirements:* For master's, comprehensive exam (for some programs), thesis (for some programs); for doctorate, comprehensive exam (for some programs), thesis/dissertation; for other advanced degree, comprehensive exam, thesis. *Entrance requirements:* For master's, GMAT or GRE General Test; for doctorate, GRE General Test, writing exam; for other advanced degree, GRE General Test. Additional exam requirements/recommendations for international students: Required—TOEFL (minimum score 550 paper-based; 80 iBT), IELTS (minimum score 7). *Application deadline:* For fall admission, 4/15 for domestic students, 5/1 for international students; for spring admission, 10/1 for international students. Application fee: $60 ($95 for international students). Electronic applications accepted. *Expenses:* Tuition, state resident: full-time $4752; part-time $264 per credit. Tuition, nonresident: full-time $18,662; part-time $554.50 per credit. *International tuition:* $18,952 full-time. *Required fees:* $532; $12 per credit. $266 per semester. One-time fee: $35. Tuition and fees vary according to course load and program. *Financial support:* In 2013–14, 48 students received support, including 39 research assistantships with partial tuition reimbursements available (averaging $11,046 per year), 9 teaching assistantships with partial tuition reimbursements available (averaging $10,922 per year); institutionally sponsored loans, scholarships/grants, health care benefits, and unspecified assistantships also available. Financial award application deadline: 3/1. *Faculty research:* Innovation and change in educational settings; educational policy, finance, and marketing; psycho-educational assessment; student retention, persistence, development, language, and culture; statistical modeling, program evaluation, qualitative and quantitative research methods. *Total annual research expenditures:* $158,645. *Unit head:* Dr. LeAnn Putney, Chair/Professor, 702-895-4879, Fax: 702-895-3492, E-mail: leann.putney@unlv.edu. *Application contact:* Graduate College Admissions Evaluator, 702-895-3320, Fax: 702-895-4180, E-mail: gradcollege@unlv.edu.
Website: http://education.unlv.edu/ephe/.

University of Nevada, Reno, Graduate School, College of Education, Department of Educational Leadership, Reno, NV 89557. Offers M Ed, MA, MS, Ed D, PhD, Ed S. *Accreditation:* NCATE. Terminal master's awarded for partial completion of doctoral program. *Degree requirements:* For master's, comprehensive exam, thesis optional; for doctorate, comprehensive exam, thesis/dissertation. *Entrance requirements:* For master's, minimum GPA of 2.75; for doctorate, GRE General Test, minimum GPA of 3.0. Additional exam requirements/recommendations for international students: Required—TOEFL (minimum score 500 paper-based; 61 iBT), IELTS (minimum score 6). Electronic applications accepted. *Faculty research:* Law, finance, supervision, organizational theory, principalship.

University of New England, College of Arts and Sciences, Doctoral Program in Educational Leadership, Biddeford, ME 04005-9526. Offers Ed D. Part-time programs available. Postbaccalaureate distance learning degree programs offered (no on-campus study). *Faculty:* 2 full-time, 1 part-time/adjunct. *Students:* 79 full-time (54 women), 2 part-time (both women); includes 11 minority (4 Black or African American, non-Hispanic/Latino; 5 Asian, non-Hispanic/Latino; 2 Two or more races, non-Hispanic/Latino). Average age 40. 114 applicants, 63% accepted, 54 enrolled. *Degree requirements:* For doctorate, thesis/dissertation. *Entrance requirements:* For doctorate, MS or MA from regionally-accredited institution, three letters of recommendation, current resume or curriculum vitae, essay, official transcripts from all colleges and universities attended, faculty interview. *Application deadline:* For fall admission, 6/1 for domestic and international students. Applications are processed on a rolling basis. Application fee: $40. Electronic applications accepted. *Financial support:* Application deadline: 5/1; applicants required to submit FAFSA. *Unit head:* Dr. Michelle Collay, Professor/Director, Online Doctoral Program in Educational Leadership, 207-602-2010, E-mail: mcollay@une.edu. *Application contact:* Dr. Cynthia Forrest, Vice President of Student Affairs, 207-221-4225, Fax: 207-523-1925, E-mail: gradadmissions@une.edu.
Website: http://www.une.edu/cas/education/doctoral/index.cfm.

University of New England, College of Arts and Sciences, Program in Education, Biddeford, ME 04005-9526. Offers advanced educational leadership (CAGS); career and technical education (MS Ed, CAGS); curriculum and instruction strategies (CAGS); curriculum and instruction strategy (MS Ed); educational leadership (MS Ed, CAGS); inclusion education (MS Ed); leadership, ethics and change (CAGS); literacy K-12 (MS Ed, CAGS); teaching methodologies (MS Ed). Part-time and evening/weekend programs available. Postbaccalaureate distance learning degree programs offered (no on-campus study). *Faculty:* 5 full-time (4 women), 17 part-time/adjunct (9 women). *Students:* 295 full-time (228 women), 233 part-time (175 women); includes 26 minority (19 Black or African American, non-Hispanic/Latino; 2 American Indian or Alaska Native, non-Hispanic/Latino; 2 Asian, non-Hispanic/Latino; 2 Hispanic/Latino; 1 Two or more races, non-Hispanic/Latino). Average age 37. 289 applicants, 84% accepted, 189 enrolled. In 2013, 257 master's, 106 CAGSs awarded. *Degree requirements:* For master's, collaborative action research project, integrative seminar portfolio. *Entrance requirements:* For master's, teaching certificate, 2 years of teaching experience. *Application deadline:* For fall admission, 9/15 for domestic students; for spring admission, 1/15 for domestic students. Applications are processed on a rolling basis. Application fee: $40. Electronic applications accepted. *Financial support:* Application deadline: 5/1; applicants required to submit FAFSA. *Faculty research:* Distance learning, effective teaching, transition planning, adult learning. *Unit head:* Paulette St. Ours, Associate Dean, College of Arts and Sciences, 207-602-2400, E-mail: pstours@une.edu. *Application contact:* Dr. Cynthia Forrest, Vice President for Student Affairs, 207-221-4225, Fax: 207-523-1925, E-mail: gradadmissions@une.edu.
Website: http://www.une.edu/cas/education/msonline.cfm.

University of New Hampshire, Graduate School, College of Liberal Arts, Department of Education, Program in Educational Administration, Durham, NH 03824. Offers Ed S, Postbaccalaureate Certificate. Part-time programs available. *Faculty:* 32 full-time. *Students:* 1 (woman) full-time, 17 part-time (8 women); includes 1 minority (Two or more races, non-Hispanic/Latino). Average age 42. 4 applicants, 100% accepted, 2 enrolled. In 2013, 10 Ed Ss awarded. *Entrance requirements:* For degree, GRE General Test. Additional exam requirements/recommendations for international students: Required—TOEFL (minimum score 550 paper-based; 80 iBT). *Application deadline:* For fall admission, 2/1 priority date for domestic students, 2/1 for international students; for spring admission, 12/1 for domestic students. Applications are processed on a rolling basis. Application fee: $65. *Expenses:* Tuition, state resident: full-time $13,500; part-time $750 per credit hour. Tuition, nonresident: full-time $26,200; part-time $1100 per credit hour. *Required fees:* $1741; $435.25 per term. Tuition and fees vary according to course level, course load, campus/location and program. *Financial support:* Fellowships, research assistantships, teaching assistantships, career-related internships or fieldwork, Federal Work-Study, scholarships/grants, and tuition waivers (full and partial) available. Support available to part-time students. Financial award application deadline: 2/15. *Faculty research:* School principalship, supervision, superintendency. *Unit head:* Dr. Mike Middleton, Chair, 603-862-7054, E-mail: education.department@unh.edu. *Application contact:* Lisa Wilder, Administrative Assistant, 603-862-2381, E-mail: education.department@unh.edu.
Website: http://www.unh.edu/education.

University of New Hampshire, Graduate School, College of Liberal Arts, Department of Education, Program in Teacher Leadership, Durham, NH 03824. Offers M Ed, Postbaccalaureate Certificate. Part-time programs available. *Faculty:* 32 full-time. *Students:* 10 part-time (7 women); includes 1 minority (Asian, non-Hispanic/Latino). Average age 34. 6 applicants, 67% accepted, 3 enrolled. In 2013, 3 master's awarded. *Degree requirements:* For master's, oral exam or thesis. *Entrance requirements:* For master's, GRE. Additional exam requirements/recommendations for international students: Required—TOEFL (minimum score 550 paper-based; 80 iBT). *Application deadline:* For fall admission, 3/1 for domestic and international students; for spring admission, 4/1 for domestic students. Applications are processed on a rolling basis. Application fee: $65. Electronic applications accepted. *Expenses:* Tuition, state resident: full-time $13,500; part-time $750 per credit hour. Tuition, nonresident: full-time $26,200; part-time $1100 per credit hour. *Required fees:* $1741; $435.25 per term. Tuition and fees vary according to course level, course load, campus/location and program. *Financial support:* Fellowships, research assistantships, teaching assistantships, Federal Work-Study, and scholarships/grants available. Support available to part-time students. Financial award application deadline: 2/15. *Unit head:* Dr. Mike Middleton, Chairperson, 603-862-7054, E-mail: education.department@unh.edu. *Application contact:* Lisa Wilder, Administrative Assistant, 603-862-2381, E-mail: education.department@unh.edu.
Website: http://www.unh.edu/education.

University of New Hampshire, Graduate School Manchester Campus, Manchester, NH 03101. Offers business administration (MBA); counseling (M Ed); education (M Ed, MAT); educational administration and supervision (M Ed, Ed S); information technology (MS); management of technology (MS); public administration (MPA); public health (MPH, Certificate); social work (MSW); software systems engineering (Certificate). Part-time and evening/weekend programs available. *Students:* 2 full-time (0 women), 5 part-time (0 women), 2 international. Average age 38. 6 applicants, 17% accepted, 1 enrolled. In 2013, 1 master's awarded. *Degree requirements:* For master's, thesis or alternative. *Entrance requirements:* Additional exam requirements/recommendations for international students: Required—TOEFL (minimum score 550 paper-based; 80 iBT). *Application deadline:* For fall admission, 6/1 for domestic students, 4/1 for international students; for spring admission, 12/1 for domestic students. Applications are processed on a rolling basis. Application fee: $65. Electronic applications accepted. *Expenses:* Tuition, state resident: full-time $13,500; part-time $750 per credit hour. Tuition, nonresident: full-time $26,200; part-time $1100 per credit hour. *Required fees:* $1741; $435.25 per term. Tuition and fees vary according to course level, course load, campus/location and program. *Financial support:* Fellowships, research assistantships, teaching assistantships, Federal Work-Study, scholarships/grants, health care benefits, and unspecified assistantships available. Support available to part-time students. Financial award application deadline: 3/1; financial award applicants required to submit FAFSA. *Unit head:* Candice Brown, Director, 603-641-4313, E-mail: unhm.gradcenter@unh.edu. *Application contact:* Graduate Admissions Office, 603-862-3000, Fax: 603-862-0275, E-mail: grad.school@unh.edu.
Website: http://www.gradschool.unh.edu/manchester/.

University of New Mexico, Graduate School, College of Education, Department of Teacher Education, Educational Leadership and Policy, Program in Educational Leadership, Albuquerque, NM 87131-2039. Offers MA, Ed D, Ed S. *Accreditation:* NCATE. Part-time and evening/weekend programs available. Postbaccalaureate distance learning degree programs offered. *Faculty:* 6 full-time (3 women), 1 part-time/adjunct (0 women). *Students:* 36 full-time (32 women), 78 part-time (54 women); includes 59 minority (4 Black or African American, non-Hispanic/Latino; 9 American Indian or Alaska Native, non-Hispanic/Latino; 2 Asian, non-Hispanic/Latino; 44 Hispanic/Latino), 1 international. Average age 40. 37 applicants, 46% accepted, 16 enrolled. In 2013, 14 master's, 5 doctorates, 17 other advanced degrees awarded. *Degree requirements:* For master's, comprehensive exam; for doctorate, comprehensive exam, thesis/dissertation. *Entrance requirements:* For master's, bachelor's degree; for doctorate, GRE, master's degree. *Application deadline:* For fall admission, 6/1 for domestic students; for spring admission, 10/1 for domestic students. Applications are processed on a rolling basis. Application fee: $50. Electronic applications accepted. *Financial support:* In 2013–14, 25 students received support, including 1 research assistantship (averaging $14,000 per year); career-related internships or fieldwork and scholarships/grants also available. Financial award application deadline: 3/1; financial award applicants required to submit FAFSA. *Faculty research:* K-20 educational and organizational leadership, individual and organizational learning, policy, legal and political contexts. *Unit head:* Dr. Patricia Boverie, Head, 505-277-2408, Fax: 505-277-5553, E-mail: pboverie@unm.edu. *Application contact:* Linda Wood, Information Contact, 505-277-0441, Fax: 505-277-5553, E-mail: woodl@unm.edu.
Website: http://coe.unm.edu/departments/elol/educational-leadership-program.html.

University of New Orleans, Graduate School, College of Education and Human Development, Department of Educational Leadership, Counseling, and Foundations, Program in Educational Leadership, New Orleans, LA 70148. Offers M Ed, PhD. *Accreditation:* NCATE. Evening/weekend programs available. Terminal master's awarded for partial completion of doctoral program. *Degree requirements:* For doctorate, variable foreign language requirement, thesis/dissertation. *Entrance requirements:* For master's and doctorate, GRE General Test. Additional exam requirements/recommendations for international students: Required—TOEFL (minimum score 550 paper-based; 79 iBT). Electronic applications accepted.

University of North Alabama, College of Education, Department of Elementary Education, Florence, AL 35632-0001. Offers collaborative teacher special education (MA Ed); elementary education (MA Ed, Ed S); instructional leadership (Ed S); teacher leader (Ed S). *Accreditation:* NCATE. Part-time and evening/weekend programs available. *Faculty:* 6 full-time (all women). *Students:* 7 full-time (6 women), 67 part-time (63 women); includes 6 minority (3 Black or African American, non-Hispanic/Latino; 3 American Indian or Alaska Native, non-Hispanic/Latino). Average age 32. 92 applicants, 87% accepted, 45 enrolled. In 2013, 25 master's awarded. *Degree requirements:* For master's, comprehensive exam. *Entrance requirements:* For master's, GRE, MAT, or NTE, minimum GPA of 2.5, Alabama Class B Certificate or equivalent, teaching experience. Additional exam requirements/recommendations for international students: Required—TOEFL (minimum score 550 paper-based; 79 iBT), IELTS (minimum score 6). *Application deadline:* For fall admission, 7/1 priority date for domestic students, 7/1 for international students; for spring admission, 12/1 for domestic and international students. Applications are processed on a rolling basis. Application fee: $25 ($50 for international students). Electronic applications accepted. *Expenses:* Tuition, state resident: full-time $4968; part-time $3312 per year. Tuition, nonresident: full-time $9936; part-time $6624 per year. *Required fees:* $970; $60.33 per credit. $362 per semester. *Financial support:* Federal Work-Study available. Support available to part-time students. Financial award application deadline: 4/1; financial award applicants required to submit FAFSA. *Unit head:* Dr. Victoria W. Hulsey, Chair, 256-765-5024, E-mail: vwhulsey@una.edu. *Application contact:* Russ Darracott, Graduate Admissions Counselor, 256-765-4447, E-mail: erdarracott@una.edu.
Website: http://www.una.edu/education/departments/elementary-education.html.

Educational Leadership and Administration

University of North Alabama, College of Education, Department of Secondary Education, Program in Education Leadership, Florence, AL 35632-0001. Offers Ed S. *Accreditation:* NCATE. Part-time and evening/weekend programs available. *Faculty:* 5 full-time (3 women). *Students:* 5 full-time (0 women), 63 part-time (42 women); includes 8 minority (6 Black or African American, non-Hispanic/Latino; 1 American Indian or Alaska Native, non-Hispanic/Latino; 1 Two or more races, non-Hispanic/Latino). Average age 39. 61 applicants, 84% accepted, 40 enrolled. In 2013, 4 Ed Ss awarded. *Entrance requirements:* Additional exam requirements/recommendations for international students: Required—TOEFL (minimum score 550 paper-based; 79 iBT), IELTS (minimum score 6). *Application deadline:* For fall admission, 7/1 priority date for domestic students, 7/1 for international students; for spring admission, 12/1 for domestic and international students. Applications are processed on a rolling basis. Application fee: $25 ($50 for international students). Electronic applications accepted. *Expenses:* Tuition, state resident: full-time $4968; part-time $3312 per year. Tuition, nonresident: full-time $9936; part-time $6624 per year. *Required fees:* $970; $60.33 per credit. $362 per semester. *Financial support:* Application deadline: 4/1; applicants required to submit FAFSA. *Unit head:* Dr. Beth H. Sewell, Chair, 256-765-4578, E-mail: bsewell@una.edu. *Application contact:* Russ Draccott, Graduate Admissions Counselor, 256-765-4447, E-mail: erdarracott@una.edu.
Website: http://www.una.edu/education.

The University of North Carolina at Chapel Hill, Graduate School, School of Education, Programs in Educational Leadership and School Administration, Chapel Hill, NC 27599. Offers educational leadership (Ed D); school administration (MSA). *Accreditation:* NCATE. Part-time programs available. *Degree requirements:* For master's, comprehensive exam; for doctorate, comprehensive exam, thesis/dissertation. *Entrance requirements:* For master's, GRE General Test or MAT, minimum GPA of 3.2 during last 2 years of undergraduate course work, 3 years of school-based professional experience; for doctorate, GRE General Test, minimum GPA of 3.2 during last 2 years of undergraduate course work, 3 years of school-based professional experience. Additional exam requirements/recommendations for international students: Required—TOEFL (minimum score 550 paper-based). *Faculty research:* Gender, race, and class issues; school leadership; school finance and reform.

The University of North Carolina at Charlotte, The Graduate School, College of Education, Department of Educational Leadership, Charlotte, NC 28223-0001. Offers curriculum and supervision (M Ed); educational leadership (Ed D); instructional systems technology (M Ed); school administration (MSA, Post-Master's Certificate). Part-time and evening/weekend programs available. *Faculty:* 24 full-time (13 women), 7 part-time/adjunct (5 women). *Students:* 28 full-time (20 women), 225 part-time (141 women); includes 65 minority (55 Black or African American, non-Hispanic/Latino; 3 Asian, non-Hispanic/Latino; 4 Hispanic/Latino; 3 Two or more races, non-Hispanic/Latino), 1 international. Average age 37. 71 applicants, 92% accepted, 59 enrolled. In 2013, 48 master's, 6 doctorates, 16 other advanced degrees awarded. *Degree requirements:* For master's, thesis. *Entrance requirements:* For master's and doctorate, GRE or MAT. Additional exam requirements/recommendations for international students: Required—TOEFL (minimum score 550 paper-based; 83 iBT). *Application deadline:* For fall admission, 5/1 priority date for domestic students, 5/1 for international students; for spring admission, 10/1 priority date for domestic students, 10/1 for international students. Applications are processed on a rolling basis. Application fee: $75. Electronic applications accepted. *Expenses:* Tuition, state resident: full-time $3522. Tuition, nonresident: full-time $16,051. *Required fees:* $2585. Tuition and fees vary according to course load and program. *Financial support:* In 2013–14, 7 students received support, including 6 research assistantships (averaging $8,163 per year); career-related internships or fieldwork, institutionally sponsored loans, scholarships/grants, unspecified assistantships, and administrative assistantships also available. Support available to part-time students. Financial award application deadline: 4/1; financial award applicants required to submit FAFSA. *Faculty research:* Educational leadership theory and practice, instructional systems technology, educational research methodology, curriculum and supervision in the schools, school law and finance. *Total annual research expenditures:* $1.2 million. *Unit head:* Dr. Jim Bird, Interim Chair, 704-687-1821, Fax: 704-687-3493, E-mail: jjbird@uncc.edu. *Application contact:* Kathy B. Giddings, Director of Graduate Admissions, 704-687-5503, Fax: 704-687-1668, E-mail: gradadm@uncc.edu.
Website: http://education.uncc.edu/eart.

The University of North Carolina at Charlotte, The Graduate School, College of Education, Interdisciplinary Education Programs, Charlotte, NC 28223-0001. Offers art education (MAT); dance education (MAT); elementary education (MAT); English as a second language (MAT); foreign language education (MAT); middle grades education (MAT); music education (MAT); secondary education (MAT); special education (MAT); teacher certification (Graduate Certificate); teaching (Graduate Certificate); theater education (MAT). Part-time programs available. *Students:* 206 full-time (165 women), 791 part-time (628 women); includes 342 minority (247 Black or African American, non-Hispanic/Latino; 16 Asian, non-Hispanic/Latino; 62 Hispanic/Latino; 17 Two or more races, non-Hispanic/Latino), 14 international. Average age 32. 564 applicants, 91% accepted, 414 enrolled. In 2013, 145 master's, 271 other advanced degrees awarded. Terminal master's awarded for partial completion of doctoral program. *Degree requirements:* For master's, thesis. *Entrance requirements:* For master's, GRE or MAT. Additional exam requirements/recommendations for international students: Required—TOEFL (minimum score 550 paper-based; 83 iBT). *Application deadline:* For fall admission, 5/1 priority date for domestic and international students; for spring admission, 10/1 priority date for domestic and international students. Applications are processed on a rolling basis. Application fee: $75. Electronic applications accepted. *Expenses:* Tuition, state resident: full-time $3522. Tuition, nonresident: full-time $16,051. *Required fees:* $2585. Tuition and fees vary according to course load and program. *Total annual research expenditures:* $43,031. *Unit head:* Dr. Warren DiBiase, Chair, 704-687-8881, Fax: 704-687-4705, E-mail: wjdibias@uncc.edu. *Application contact:* Kathy B. Giddings, Director of Graduate Admissions, 704-687-5503, Fax: 704-687-1668, E-mail: gradadm@uncc.edu.
Website: http://education.uncc.edu/academic-programs.

The University of North Carolina at Greensboro, Graduate School, School of Education, Department of Curriculum and Instruction, Greensboro, NC 27412-5001. Offers college teaching and adult learning (Certificate); curriculum and instruction (M Ed), including chemistry education, elementary education, English as a second language, French education, instructional technology, mathematics education, middle grades education, reading education, science education, social studies education, Spanish education; curriculum and teaching (PhD), including higher education, teacher education and development; English as a second language (Certificate); higher education (M Ed); supervision (M Ed). *Accreditation:* NCATE. Part-time programs available. *Degree requirements:* For doctorate, thesis/dissertation. *Entrance requirements:* For master's and doctorate, GRE General Test. Additional exam requirements/recommendations for international students: Required—TOEFL. Electronic applications accepted. *Faculty research:* Community college literacy program, middle school mathematics/computer mathematics.

The University of North Carolina at Greensboro, Graduate School, School of Education, Department of Educational Leadership and Cultural Foundations, Greensboro, NC 27412-5001. Offers curriculum and teaching (PhD), including cultural studies; educational leadership (Ed D, Ed S); school administration (MSA). *Accreditation:* NCATE. *Degree requirements:* For doctorate, thesis/dissertation. *Entrance requirements:* For master's, doctorate, and Ed S, GRE General Test. Additional exam requirements/recommendations for international students: Required—TOEFL. Electronic applications accepted.

The University of North Carolina at Pembroke, Graduate Studies, School of Education, Program in School Administration, Pembroke, NC 28372-1510. Offers MSA. Part-time and evening/weekend programs available. *Degree requirements:* For master's, internship. *Entrance requirements:* For master's, GRE General Test or MAT, minimum GPA of 3.0 in major, 2.5 overall; 3 years of teaching experience; two recommendations. Additional exam requirements/recommendations for international students: Required—TOEFL.

The University of North Carolina Wilmington, Watson College of Education, Department of Educational Leadership, Wilmington, NC 28403-3297. Offers educational leadership (MSA, Ed D), including educational leadership and administration (Ed D); school administration (MSA). Part-time and evening/weekend programs available. *Faculty:* 10 full-time (5 women). *Students:* 21 full-time (17 women), 108 part-time (74 women); includes 29 minority (22 Black or African American, non-Hispanic/Latino; 2 American Indian or Alaska Native, non-Hispanic/Latino; 3 Hispanic/Latino; 2 Two or more races, non-Hispanic/Latino), 2 international. Average age 38. 73 applicants, 93% accepted, 57 enrolled. In 2013, 8 master's, 4 doctorates awarded. *Degree requirements:* For master's, comprehensive exam, thesis or alternative; for doctorate, comprehensive exam, thesis/dissertation. *Entrance requirements:* For master's, GRE General Test, MAT, minimum B average in upper-division undergraduate course work. Additional exam requirements/recommendations for international students: Required—TOEFL (minimum score 550 paper-based; 79 iBT), IELTS (minimum score 6.5). *Application deadline:* For fall admission, 6/1 for domestic students. Applications are processed on a rolling basis. Application fee: $60. *Expenses:* Tuition, state resident: full-time $4163. Tuition, nonresident: full-time $16,098. *Financial support:* In 2013–14, teaching assistantships with full and partial tuition reimbursements (averaging $14,000 per year) were awarded; unspecified assistantships also available. Financial award application deadline: 3/15. *Unit head:* Dr. Susan Catapano, Chair, 910-962-2290, E-mail: catapano@uncw.edu. *Application contact:* Dr. Ron Vetter, Dean, Graduate School, 910-962-3224, E-mail: vetterr@uncw.edu.
Website: http://uncw.edu/ed/el/index.html.

University of North Dakota, Graduate School, College of Education and Human Development, Program in Educational Leadership, Grand Forks, ND 58202. Offers M Ed, MS, Ed D, PhD, Specialist. *Accreditation:* NCATE. Part-time and evening/weekend programs available. Postbaccalaureate distance learning degree programs offered (minimal on-campus study). *Degree requirements:* For master's and Specialist, comprehensive exam, thesis or alternative; for doctorate, comprehensive exam, thesis/dissertation, final exam. *Entrance requirements:* For master's, minimum GPA of 3.0; for doctorate, minimum GPA of 3.5. Additional exam requirements/recommendations for international students: Required—TOEFL (minimum score 550 paper-based; 79 iBT), IELTS (minimum score 6.5). Electronic applications accepted.

University of Northern Colorado, Graduate School, College of Education and Behavioral Sciences, Department of Leadership, Policy and Development: Higher Education and P-12 Education, Educational Leadership and Policy Studies Program, Greeley, CO 80639. Offers educational leadership (MA, Ed D, Ed S). *Accreditation:* NCATE. Part-time and evening/weekend programs available. Postbaccalaureate distance learning degree programs offered. *Degree requirements:* For master's, comprehensive exam, thesis or alternative; for doctorate, comprehensive exam, thesis/dissertation; for Ed S, comprehensive exam, thesis. *Entrance requirements:* For master's, resume, interview; for doctorate, GRE General Test, resume, interview; for Ed S, resume. Electronic applications accepted.

University of Northern Colorado, Graduate School, College of Education and Behavioral Sciences, School of Teacher Education, Program in Educational Studies, Greeley, CO 80639. Offers MAT, Ed D. Part-time and evening/weekend programs available. Electronic applications accepted.

University of Northern Iowa, Graduate College, College of Education, Department of Educational Leadership and Postsecondary Education, Programs in Principalship and Educational Leadership, Cedar Falls, IA 50614. Offers educational leadership (Ed D); principalship (MAE). Part-time and evening/weekend programs available. *Students:* 3 full-time (1 woman), 66 part-time (27 women); includes 5 minority (3 Black or African American, non-Hispanic/Latino; 2 Asian, non-Hispanic/Latino), 1 international. 34 applicants, 74% accepted, 21 enrolled. In 2013, 9 doctorates awarded. *Degree requirements:* For master's, comprehensive exam (for some programs), thesis or alternative, minimum of 1 year of successful teaching appropriate to the major; for doctorate, thesis/dissertation. *Entrance requirements:* For master's, minimum GPA of 3.0; for doctorate, GRE, master's degree, minimum GPA of 3.5. Additional exam requirements/recommendations for international students: Required—TOEFL (minimum score 500 paper-based; 61 iBT). *Application deadline:* For fall admission, 8/1 priority date for domestic students. Applications are processed on a rolling basis. Application fee: $50 ($70 for international students). Electronic applications accepted. *Financial support:* Career-related internships or fieldwork, Federal Work-Study, and tuition waivers (full and partial) available. Support available to part-time students. Financial award application deadline: 2/1. *Unit head:* Dr. Charles McNulty, Coordinator, 319-273-2605, Fax: 319-273-5175, E-mail: charles.mcnulty@uni.edu. *Application contact:* Laurie S. Russell, Record Analyst, 319-273-2623, Fax: 319-273-2885, E-mail: laurie.russell@uni.edu.
Website: http://www.uni.edu/coe/departments/educational-leadership-postsecondary-education/educational-leadership.

University of North Florida, College of Education and Human Services, Department of Leadership, School Counseling and Sport Management, Jacksonville, FL 32224. Offers counselor education (M Ed), including school counseling; educational leadership (M Ed, Ed D), including athletic administration (M Ed), educational leadership, educational technology (M Ed), instructional leadership (M Ed). Part-time and evening/weekend programs available. *Faculty:* 16 full-time (8 women), 1 (woman) part-time/adjunct. *Students:* 76 full-time (59 women), 212 part-time (153 women); includes 91 minority (65 Black or African American, non-Hispanic/Latino; 1 American Indian or Alaska Native, non-Hispanic/Latino; 3 Asian, non-Hispanic/Latino; 13 Hispanic/Latino; 1 Native Hawaiian or other Pacific Islander, non-Hispanic/Latino; 8 Two or more races, non-Hispanic/Latino), 6 international. Average age 35. 151 applicants, 60% accepted, 71 enrolled. In 2013, 59 master's, 12 doctorates awarded. *Degree requirements:* For doctorate, thesis/dissertation. *Entrance requirements:* For master's, GRE General Test, minimum GPA of 3.0 in last 60 hours, interview, 3 letters of recommendation; for doctorate, GRE General Test, master's degree, interview, 3 letters of recommendation, writing sample. Additional exam requirements/recommendations for international students: Required—TOEFL (minimum score 500 paper-based). *Application deadline:* For fall admission, 7/1 priority date for domestic students, 5/1 for international students;

for spring admission, 11/1 priority date for domestic students, 10/1 for international students. Application fee: $30. Electronic applications accepted. *Expenses:* Tuition, state resident: full-time $9794; part-time $408.10 per credit hour. Tuition, nonresident: full-time $22,383; part-time $932.61 per credit hour. *Required fees:* $2020; $84.20 per credit hour. Tuition and fees vary according to course load and program. *Financial support:* In 2013–14, 49 students received support, including 8 research assistantships (averaging $2,573 per year); teaching assistantships, career-related internships or fieldwork, Federal Work-Study, scholarships/grants, tuition waivers (partial), and unspecified assistantships also available. Support available to part-time students. Financial award application deadline: 4/1; financial award applicants required to submit FAFSA. *Faculty research:* Counseling: ethics; lesbian, bisexual and transgender issues; educational leadership: school culture and climate; educational assessment and accountability; school safety and student discipline. *Total annual research expenditures:* $128,099. *Unit head:* Dr. Jennifer Kane, Chair, 904-620-2465, E-mail: jkane@unf.edu. *Application contact:* Dr. Amanda Pascale, Director, The Graduate School, 904-620-1360, Fax: 904-620-1362, E-mail: graduateschool@unf.edu.
Website: http://www.unf.edu/coehs/lscsm/.

University of North Georgia, School of Education, Dahlonega, GA 30597. Offers art education (MAT); early childhood education (M Ed); English education (MAT); history education (MAT); math education (MAT); middle grades education (M Ed, MAT); physical education (MS); school leadership (Ed S); secondary education (M Ed), including English education, history education, mathematics education, physical education; teacher education (MAT). *Accreditation:* NCATE. Part-time and evening/weekend programs available. Postbaccalaureate distance learning degree programs offered (no on-campus study). *Degree requirements:* For master's, comprehensive exam, thesis optional. *Entrance requirements:* For master's, GRE or MAT, GACE, minimum GPA of 2.75; for Ed S, GRE General Test or MAT, 3 years of teaching experience, master's degree, minimum graduate GPA of 3.25, leadership position in the school. Additional exam requirements/recommendations for international students: Required—TOEFL (minimum score 550 paper-based; 79 iBT), IELTS (minimum score 6.5). Electronic applications accepted. *Faculty research:* Identification of professional development school structures supporting P-12 student achievement, impact of diverse field placement settings in teacher belief development among preservice teachers, use of inquiry methodology in social studies teaching with English language learners, use of instructional differentiation in the middle grades classroom, effects of international school placements on preservice teacher beliefs and attitudes.

University of North Texas, Robert B. Toulouse School of Graduate Studies, Denton, TN 76203-5017. Offers accounting (MS, PhD); applied anthropology (MA, MS); applied behavior analysis (Certificate); applied technology and performance improvement (M Ed, MS, PhD); art education (MA, PhD); art history (MA); art museum education (Certificate); arts leadership (Certificate); audiology (Au D); behavior analysis (MS); biochemistry and molecular biology (MS, PhD); biology (MA, MS, PhD); business (PhD); business computer information systems (PhD); chemistry (MS, PhD); clinical psychology (PhD); communication studies (MA, MS); computer engineering (MS); computer science (MS); computer science and engineering (PhD); counseling (M Ed, MS, PhD), including clinical mental health counseling (MS), college and university counseling (M Ed, MS), elementary school counseling (M Ed, MS), secondary school counseling (M Ed, MS); counseling psychology (PhD); creative writing (MA); criminal justice (MS); curriculum and instruction (M Ed, PhD), including curriculum studies (PhD), early childhood studies (PhD), language and literacy studies (PhD); decision sciences (MBA); design (MA, MFA), including fashion design (MFA), innovation studies, interior design (MFA); early childhood studies (MS); economics (MS); educational leadership (M Ed, Ed D, PhD); educational psychology (MS), including family studies, gifted and talented (MS, PhD), human development, learning and cognition, research, measurement and evaluation; educational research (PhD), including gifted and talented (MS, PhD), human development and family studies, psychological aspects of sports and exercise, research, measurement and statistics; electrical engineering (MS); emergency management (MPA); engineering systems (MS); English (MA, PhD); environmental science (MS, PhD); experimental psychology (PhD); finance (MBA, MS, PhD); financial management (MPA); French (MA); health psychology and behavioral medicine (PhD); health services management (MBA); higher education (M Ed, Ed D, PhD); history (MA, MS, PhD), including European history (PhD), military history (PhD), United States history (PhD); hospitality management (MS); human resources management (MPA); information science (MS, PhD); information technologies (MBA); information technology and decision sciences (MS); interdisciplinary studies (MA, MS); international sustainable tourism (MS); jazz studies (MM); journalism (MA, MJ, Graduate Certificate), including interactive and virtual digital communication (Graduate Certificate), narrative journalism (Graduate Certificate), public relations (Graduate Certificate); kinesiology (MS); learning technologies (MS, PhD); library science (MS); local government management (MPA); logistics and supply chain management (MBA, PhD); long-term care, senior housing, and aging services (MA, MS); management science (PhD); marketing (MBA, PhD); materials science and engineering (MS, PhD); mathematics (MA, PhD); merchandising (MS); music (MA, MM Ed, PhD), including ethnomusicology (MA), music education (MM Ed, PhD), music theory (MA, PhD), musicology (MA, PhD), performance (MA); nonprofit management (MPA); operations and supply chain management (MBA); performance (MM, DMA); philosophy (MA, PhD); physics (MS, PhD); political science (MA, MS, PhD); public administration and management (PhD), including emergency management, nonprofit management, public financial management, urban management; radio, television and film (MA, MFA); recreation, event and sport management (MS); rehabilitation counseling (MS, Certificate); sociology (MA, MS, PhD); Spanish (MA); special education (M Ed, PhD), including autism intervention (PhD), emotional/behavioral disorders (PhD), mild/moderate disabilities (PhD); speech-language pathology (MA, MS); strategic management (MBA); studio art (MFA); taxation (MS); teaching (M Ed); MBA/MS; MS/MPH; MSES/MBA. Part-time and evening/weekend programs available. Postbaccalaureate distance learning degree programs offered. *Faculty:* 661 full-time (213 women), 240 part-time/adjunct (144 women). *Students:* 3,106 full-time (1,620 women), 3,543 part-time (2,221 women); includes 1,740 minority (533 Black or African American, non-Hispanic/Latino; 15 American Indian or Alaska Native, non-Hispanic/Latino; 286 Asian, non-Hispanic/Latino; 746 Hispanic/Latino; 3 Native Hawaiian or other Pacific Islander, non-Hispanic/Latino; 157 Two or more races, non-Hispanic/Latino), 1,145 international. Average age 32. 6,289 applicants, 43% accepted, 1751 enrolled. In 2013, 1,778 master's, 239 doctorates, 10 other advanced degrees awarded. Terminal master's awarded for partial completion of doctoral program. *Degree requirements:* For master's, variable foreign language requirement, comprehensive exam (for some programs), thesis (for some programs); for doctorate, variable foreign language requirement, comprehensive exam (for some programs), thesis/dissertation; for other advanced degree, variable foreign language requirement, comprehensive exam (for some programs). *Entrance requirements:* For master's and doctorate, GRE, GMAT. Additional exam requirements/recommendations for international students: Required—TOEFL (minimum score 550 paper-based; 79 iBT). *Application deadline:* For fall admission, 7/15 for domestic students, 3/15 for international students; for spring admission, 11/15 for domestic students, 9/15 for international students; for summer admission, 5/1 for domestic students. Applications are processed on a rolling basis. Application fee: $60. Electronic applications accepted. *Financial support:* Fellowships with partial tuition reimbursements, research assistantships with partial tuition reimbursements, teaching assistantships, career-related internships or fieldwork, Federal Work-Study, institutionally sponsored loans, scholarships/grants, health care benefits, and library assistantships available. Support available to part-time students. Financial award applicants required to submit FAFSA. *Unit head:* Mark Wardell, Dean, 940-565-2383, E-mail: mark.wardell@unt.edu. *Application contact:* Toulouse School of Graduate Studies, 940-565-2383, Fax: 940-565-2141, E-mail: gradsch@unt.edu.
Website: http://tsgs.unt.edu/.

University of Oklahoma, Jeannine Rainbolt College of Education, Department of Educational Leadership and Policy Studies, Program in Educational Administration, Curriculum and Supervision, Norman, OK 73019. Offers M Ed, Ed D, PhD. *Accreditation:* NCATE. Part-time and evening/weekend programs available. *Students:* 28 full-time (19 women), 178 part-time (126 women); includes 36 minority (13 Black or African American, non-Hispanic/Latino; 11 American Indian or Alaska Native, non-Hispanic/Latino; 2 Asian, non-Hispanic/Latino; 6 Hispanic/Latino; 4 Two or more races, non-Hispanic/Latino), 1 international. Average age 36. 95 applicants, 85% accepted, 70 enrolled. In 2013, 28 master's, 8 doctorates awarded. Terminal master's awarded for partial completion of doctoral program. *Degree requirements:* For master's, thesis optional, comprehensive portfolio; for doctorate, variable foreign language requirement, thesis/dissertation, residency. *Entrance requirements:* For master's, bachelor's degree in education; minimum GPA of 3.0 in last 60 undergraduate hours; for doctorate, GRE, professional biography; career statement; 2 writing samples. Additional exam requirements/recommendations for international students: Required—TOEFL (minimum score 79 iBT). *Application deadline:* For fall admission, 4/15 for domestic and international students; for spring admission, 10/15 for domestic and international students. Applications are processed on a rolling basis. Application fee: $50 ($100 for international students). Electronic applications accepted. *Expenses:* Tuition, state resident: full-time $4205; part-time $175.20 per credit hour. Tuition, nonresident: full-time $16,205; part-time $675.20 per credit hour. *Required fees:* $2745; $103.85 per credit hour. $126.50 per semester. *Financial support:* In 2013–14, 89 students received support. Unspecified assistantships available. Financial award application deadline: 6/1; financial award applicants required to submit FAFSA. *Faculty research:* Moral-ethical leadership, Indian education, school-collective trust, school finance, diversity issues. *Unit head:* Dr. David Tan, Chair, 405-325-5986, Fax: 405-325-2403, E-mail: dtan@ou.edu. *Application contact:* Geri Evans, Graduate Programs Representative, 405-325-5978, Fax: 405-325-2403, E-mail: gevans@ou.edu.
Website: http://www.ou.edu/education/elps.

University of Oklahoma, Jeannine Rainbolt College of Education, Department of Instructional Leadership and Academic Curriculum, Norman, OK 73072. Offers communication, culture and pedagogy for Hispanic populations in educational settings (Graduate Certificate); instructional leadership and academic curriculum (M Ed, PhD), including bilingual education (PhD), early childhood education, elementary education, English education, instructional leadership, mathematics education, reading education, science education, science, technology, engineering and mathematics education (M Ed), secondary education, social studies education, teacher education (M Ed), world language education (M Ed). *Accreditation:* NCATE. Part-time and evening/weekend programs available. Postbaccalaureate distance learning degree programs offered (no on-campus study). *Faculty:* 22 full-time (15 women), 1 (woman) part-time/adjunct. *Students:* 64 full-time (49 women), 103 part-time (81 women); includes 33 minority (8 Black or African American, non-Hispanic/Latino; 9 American Indian or Alaska Native, non-Hispanic/Latino; 5 Asian, non-Hispanic/Latino; 4 Hispanic/Latino; 1 Native Hawaiian or other Pacific Islander, non-Hispanic/Latino; 6 Two or more races, non-Hispanic/Latino), 10 international. Average age 34. 50 applicants, 84% accepted, 36 enrolled. In 2013, 26 master's, 11 doctorates awarded. Terminal master's awarded for partial completion of doctoral program. *Degree requirements:* For master's, comprehensive exam (for some programs), thesis (for some programs); for doctorate, comprehensive exam, thesis/dissertation. *Entrance requirements:* For master's, essay; for doctorate, GRE, 3 recommendation letters; autobiography, statement of objectives; essay on chosen major; transcripts; writing sample. Additional exam requirements/recommendations for international students: Required—TOEFL (minimum score 79 iBT). *Application deadline:* For fall admission, 4/30 for domestic and international students; for spring admission, 10/31 for domestic and international students; for summer admission, 3/15 for domestic and international students. Applications are processed on a rolling basis. Application fee: $50 ($100 for international students). Electronic applications accepted. *Expenses:* Tuition, state resident: full-time $4205; part-time $175.20 per credit hour. Tuition, nonresident: full-time $16,205; part-time $675.20 per credit hour. *Required fees:* $2745; $103.85 per credit hour. $126.50 per semester. *Financial support:* In 2013–14, 98 students received support, including 10 research assistantships with partial tuition reimbursements available (averaging $10,671 per year), 7 teaching assistantships with partial tuition reimbursements available (averaging $10,753 per year); Federal Work-Study, institutionally sponsored loans, scholarships/grants, and unspecified assistantships also available. Support available to part-time students. Financial award application deadline: 6/1; financial award applicants required to submit FAFSA. *Total annual research expenditures:* $1 million. *Unit head:* Dr. Stacy Reeder, Chair/Graduate Liaison, 405-325-1498, Fax: 405-325-4061, E-mail: reeder@ou.edu. *Application contact:* Lynn Crussel, Graduate Programs Officer, 405-325-1498, Fax: 405-325-4061, E-mail: lcrussel@ou.edu.
Website: http://education.ou.edu/departments/ilac.

University of Pennsylvania, Graduate School of Education, Division of Teaching, Learning, and Leadership, Program in Educational Leadership, Philadelphia, PA 19104. Offers MS Ed, Ed D, PhD. Part-time programs available. *Students:* 19 full-time (10 women), 2 part-time (1 woman); includes 5 minority (2 Asian, non-Hispanic/Latino; 3 Two or more races, non-Hispanic/Latino). 21 applicants, 19% accepted, 3 enrolled. In 2013, 7 doctorates awarded. *Degree requirements:* For master's, comprehensive exam, thesis; for doctorate, comprehensive exam, thesis/dissertation, oral exams. *Entrance requirements:* For master's, GRE or MAT; for doctorate, GRE. *Application deadline:* For fall admission, 12/15 priority date for domestic students; for spring admission, 12/1 for domestic students. Applications are processed on a rolling basis. Application fee: $70. Electronic applications accepted. *Expenses:* Contact institution. *Financial support:* Institutionally sponsored loans, scholarships/grants, traineeships, health care benefits, and unspecified assistantships available. *Faculty research:* Public policy, curriculum and instruction, organization theory/leadership, school reform. *Unit head:* Dr. Andrew Porter, Dean, 215-898-7014. *Application contact:* 215-746-2566, E-mail: edwardsv@gse.upenn.edu.
Website: http://www.gse.upenn.edu.

University of Pennsylvania, Graduate School of Education, Division of Teaching, Learning, and Leadership, Program in School Leadership, Philadelphia, PA 19104. Offers MS Ed. *Students:* 33 full-time (15 women), 6 part-time (2 women); includes 11 minority (6 Black or African American, non-Hispanic/Latino; 5 Hispanic/Latino). 55 applicants, 84% accepted, 42 enrolled. In 2013, 30 master's awarded. *Degree requirements:* For master's, 360-hour internship, research project, paper. *Unit head:* Dr.

Educational Leadership and Administration

Andrew Porter, Dean, 215-898-7014. *Application contact:* Liz Ulivella, Coordinator, 215-746-2718, E-mail: ulivella@gse.upenn.edu. Website: http://www.gse.upenn.edu.

University of Pennsylvania, Graduate School of Education, Mid-Career Doctoral Program in Educational Leadership, Philadelphia, PA 19104. Offers Ed D. *Students:* 84 full-time (47 women); includes 46 minority (32 Black or African American, non-Hispanic/Latino; 2 American Indian or Alaska Native, non-Hispanic/Latino; 2 Asian, non-Hispanic/Latino; 7 Hispanic/Latino; 3 Two or more races, non-Hispanic/Latino). 76 applicants, 41% accepted, 26 enrolled. In 2013, 19 doctorates awarded. *Application deadline:* For fall admission, 2/1 for domestic students. *Unit head:* E-mail: midcareer@gse.upenn.edu. *Application contact:* Alyssa D'Alconzo, Associate Director, Admissions, 215-898-6415, Fax: 215-746-6884, E-mail: admissions@gse.upenn.edu. Website: http://www.gse.upenn.edu/degrees_programs/midcareer.

University of Pennsylvania, Graduate School of Education, Penn Chief Learning Officer (CLO) Executive Doctoral Program, Philadelphia, PA 19104. Offers Ed D. *Students:* 45 full-time (15 women), 1 part-time (0 women); includes 11 minority (4 Black or African American, non-Hispanic/Latino; 1 American Indian or Alaska Native, non-Hispanic/Latino; 2 Asian, non-Hispanic/Latino; 1 Hispanic/Latino; 3 Two or more races, non-Hispanic/Latino), 5 international. 54 applicants, 43% accepted, 22 enrolled. In 2013, 10 doctorates awarded. *Application deadline:* For fall admission, 7/15 for domestic students. *Unit head:* Dr. Andrew Porter, Dean, 215-898-7014. *Application contact:* Alyssa D'Alconzo, Associate Director, Admissions, 215-898-6415, Fax: 215-746-6884, E-mail: admissions@gse.upenn.edu. Website: http://pennclo.com/.

University of Phoenix–Bay Area Campus, College of Education, San Jose, CA 95134-1805. Offers administration and supervision (MA Ed); adult education and training (MA Ed); early childhood education (MA Ed); education (Ed S); educational leadership (Ed D); elementary teacher education (MA Ed); higher education administration (PhD); secondary teacher education (MA Ed); special education (MA Ed); teacher leadership (MA Ed). Evening/weekend programs available. Postbaccalaureate distance learning degree programs offered (no on-campus study). *Degree requirements:* For master's, thesis (for some programs). *Entrance requirements:* For master's, minimum undergraduate GPA of 2.5, 3 years of work experience. Additional exam requirements/recommendations for international students: Required—TOEFL (minimum score 550 paper-based; 79 iBT). Electronic applications accepted.

University of Phoenix–Chattanooga Campus, College of Education, Chattanooga, TN 37421-3707. Offers administration and supervision (MA Ed); curriculum and instruction (MA Ed); elementary teacher education (MA Ed); secondary teacher education (MA Ed).

University of Phoenix–Denver Campus, College of Education, Lone Tree, CO 80124-5453. Offers administration and supervision (MAEd); curriculum instruction (MAEd); elementary teacher education (MAEd); school counseling (MSC); secondary teacher education (MAEd). Evening/weekend programs available. *Degree requirements:* For master's, thesis (for some programs). *Entrance requirements:* For master's, minimum undergraduate GPA of 2.5, 3 years work experience. Additional exam requirements/recommendations for international students: Required—TOEFL (minimum score 550 paper-based; 79 iBT). Electronic applications accepted.

University of Phoenix–Hawaii Campus, College of Education, Honolulu, HI 96813-4317. Offers administration and supervision (MA Ed); curriculum and instruction (MA Ed); elementary education (MA Ed); secondary education (MA Ed); special education (MA Ed); teacher education for elementary licensure (MA Ed). Evening/weekend programs available. *Degree requirements:* For master's, thesis (for some programs). *Entrance requirements:* For master's, minimum undergraduate GPA of 2.5, 3 years of work experience. Additional exam requirements/recommendations for international students: Required—TOEFL (minimum score 550 paper-based; 79 iBT). Electronic applications accepted.

University of Phoenix–Idaho Campus, College of Education, Meridian, ID 83642-5114. Offers administration and supervision (MA Ed); curriculum and instruction (MA Ed); elementary teacher education (MA Ed); secondary teacher education (MA Ed). Evening/weekend programs available. *Degree requirements:* For master's, thesis (for some programs). *Entrance requirements:* For master's, minimum undergraduate GPA of 2.5, 3 years of work experience. Additional exam requirements/recommendations for international students: Required—TOEFL (minimum score 550 paper-based). Electronic applications accepted.

University of Phoenix–Kansas City Campus, College of Education, Kansas City, MO 64131. Offers administration and supervision (MA Ed). Postbaccalaureate distance learning degree programs offered.

University of Phoenix–Las Vegas Campus, College of Education, Las Vegas, NV 89135. Offers administration and supervision (MA Ed); curriculum and instruction (MA Ed); school counseling (MSC); teacher education-elementary licensure (MA Ed). Evening/weekend programs available. *Degree requirements:* For master's, thesis (for some programs). *Entrance requirements:* For master's, minimum undergraduate GPA of 2.5, 3 years of work experience. Additional exam requirements/recommendations for international students: Required—TOEFL (minimum score 550 paper-based; 79 iBT). Electronic applications accepted.

University of Phoenix–Madison Campus, College of Education, Madison, WI 53718-2416. Offers education (Ed S); educational leadership (Ed D); educational leadership: curriculum and instruction (Ed D); higher education administration (PhD).

University of Phoenix–Memphis Campus, College of Education, Cordova, TN 38018. Offers administration and supervision (MA Ed); curriculum and instruction (MA Ed); elementary teacher education (MA Ed); secondary teacher education (MA Ed).

University of Phoenix–Nashville Campus, College of Education, Nashville, TN 37214-5048. Offers administration and supervision (MA Ed); curriculum and instruction (MA Ed); elementary teacher education (MA Ed); secondary teacher education (MA Ed). Evening/weekend programs available. *Degree requirements:* For master's, thesis (for some programs). *Entrance requirements:* For master's, minimum undergraduate GPA of 2.5, 3 years work experience. Additional exam requirements/recommendations for international students: Required—TOEFL (minimum score 500 paper-based; 79 iBT). Electronic applications accepted.

University of Phoenix–New Mexico Campus, College of Education, Albuquerque, NM 87113-1570. Offers administration and supervision (MAEd); curriculum and instruction (MAEd); elementary teacher education (MAEd); school counseling (MSC); secondary teacher education (MAEd). Evening/weekend programs available. *Degree requirements:* For master's, thesis (for some programs). *Entrance requirements:* For master's, minimum undergraduate GPA of 2.5, 3 years of work experience. Additional exam requirements/recommendations for international students: Required—TOEFL (minimum score 550 paper-based; 79 iBT). Electronic applications accepted.

University of Phoenix–North Florida Campus, College of Education, Jacksonville, FL 32216-0959. Offers administration and supervision (MA Ed); curriculum and instruction (MA Ed), including computer education, mathematics education; early childhood

education (MA Ed); elementary teacher education (MA Ed); secondary teacher education (MA Ed). Evening/weekend programs available. *Degree requirements:* For master's, thesis (for some programs). *Entrance requirements:* For master's, 3 years of work experience, minimum undergraduate GPA of 2.5. Additional exam requirements/recommendations for international students: Required—TOEFL (minimum score 550 paper-based; 49 iBT). Electronic applications accepted.

University of Phoenix–Omaha Campus, College of Education, Omaha, NE 68154-5240. Offers administration and supervision (MA Ed); curriculum and instruction (MA Ed), including adult education, computer education, curriculum and instruction, English and language arts education, English as a second language, mathematics education; elementary teacher education (MA Ed); secondary teacher education (MA Ed); special education (MA Ed).

University of Phoenix–Online Campus, College of Education, Phoenix, AZ 85034-7209. Offers administration and supervision (MAEd, Certificate); adult education and training (MAEd); curriculum and instruction (MAEd), including computer education, curriculum and instruction, English as a second language, language arts, mathematics, reading; early childhood education (MAEd); educational studies (MAEd); elementary teacher education (MAEd), including early childhood, elementary teacher education, high school middle level, middle level; principal licensure (Certificate); secondary teacher education (MAEd); special education (MAEd, Certificate); teacher education (MAEd), including middle level generalist; teacher education middle level mathematics (MAEd), including middle level mathematics; teacher education middle level science (MAEd), including middle level science; teacher education secondary mathematics (MAEd); teacher education secondary science (MAEd); teacher leadership (MAEd); teachers of English learners (Certificate); transition to teaching (Certificate), including elementary education, secondary education. *Accreditation:* Teacher Education Accreditation Council. Evening/weekend programs available. Postbaccalaureate distance learning degree programs offered. *Entrance requirements:* Additional exam requirements/recommendations for international students: Required—TOEFL, TOEIC (Test of English as an International Communication), Berlitz Online English Proficiency Exam, PTE, or IELTS. Electronic applications accepted. *Expenses:* Contact institution.

University of Phoenix–Online Campus, School of Advanced Studies, Phoenix, AZ 85034-7209. Offers business administration (DBA); education (Ed S); educational leadership (Ed D), including curriculum and instruction, education technology, educational leadership; health administration (DHA); higher education administration (PhD); industrial/organizational psychology (PhD); nursing (PhD); organizational leadership (DM), including information systems and technology, organizational leadership. Evening/weekend programs available. Postbaccalaureate distance learning degree programs offered. *Degree requirements:* For doctorate, thesis/dissertation. *Entrance requirements:* Additional exam requirements/recommendations for international students: Required—TOEFL, TOEIC (Test of English as an International Communication), Berlitz Online English Proficiency Exam, PTE, or IELTS. Electronic applications accepted. *Expenses:* Contact institution.

University of Phoenix–Phoenix Campus, College of Education, Tempe, AZ 85282-2371. Offers administration and supervision (MA Ed); adult education and training (MA Ed); curriculum and instruction reading (MA Ed); early childhood education (MA Ed); education studies (MA Ed); elementary teacher education (MA Ed); secondary teacher education (MA Ed); special education (MA Ed); teacher leadership (MA Ed). Evening/weekend programs available. Postbaccalaureate distance learning degree programs offered. *Entrance requirements:* Additional exam requirements/recommendations for international students: Required—TOEFL, TOEIC (Test of English as an International Communication), Berlitz Online English Proficiency Exam, PTE, or IELTS. Electronic applications accepted. *Expenses:* Contact institution.

University of Phoenix–Puerto Rico Campus, College of Education, Guaynabo, PR 00968. Offers administration and supervision (MA Ed); early childhood education (MA Ed); school counselor (MSC). Evening/weekend programs available. *Degree requirements:* For master's, thesis (for some programs). *Entrance requirements:* For master's, minimum undergraduate GPA of 2.5, 3 years work experience. Additional exam requirements/recommendations for international students: Required—TOEFL (minimum score 550 paper-based; 79 iBT). Electronic applications accepted.

University of Phoenix–Richmond-Virginia Beach Campus, College of Education, Glen Allen, VA 23060. Offers administration and supervision (MA Ed); curriculum and instruction (MA Ed).

University of Phoenix–Southern Arizona Campus, College of Education, Tucson, AZ 85711. Offers administration and supervision (MA Ed); adult education and training (MA Ed); curriculum instruction (MA Ed); educational counseling (MA Ed); elementary teacher education (MA Ed); school counseling (MSC); secondary teacher education (MA Ed); special education (MA Ed, Certificate). Evening/weekend programs available. *Degree requirements:* For master's, thesis (for some programs). *Entrance requirements:* For master's, minimum undergraduate GPA of 2.5, 3 years of work experience. Additional exam requirements/recommendations for international students: Required—TOEFL (minimum score 550 paper-based; 79 iBT). Electronic applications accepted.

University of Phoenix–Southern California Campus, College of Education, Costa Mesa, CA 92626. Offers administration and supervision (MA Ed, Certificate); adult education and training (MA Ed); educational studies (MA Ed); elementary teacher education (MA Ed); secondary teacher education (MA Ed); teacher leadership (MA Ed); teachers of English learners (Certificate). Evening/weekend programs available. Postbaccalaureate distance learning degree programs offered. *Entrance requirements:* Additional exam requirements/recommendations for international students: Required—TOEFL, TOEIC (Test of English as an International Communication), Berlitz Online English Proficiency Exam, PTE, or IELTS. Electronic applications accepted. *Expenses:* Contact institution.

University of Phoenix–Southern Colorado Campus, College of Education, Colorado Springs, CO 80903. Offers administration and supervision (MA Ed); curriculum and instruction (MA Ed); elementary teacher education (MA Ed); principal licensure certification (Certificate); school counseling (MSC); secondary teacher education (MA Ed). Evening/weekend programs available. *Degree requirements:* For master's, thesis (for some programs). *Entrance requirements:* For master's, minimum undergraduate GPA of 2.5, 3 years of work experience. Additional exam requirements/recommendations for international students: Required—TOEFL (minimum score 550 paper-based; 79 iBT). Electronic applications accepted.

University of Phoenix–South Florida Campus, College of Education, Miramar, FL 33030. Offers administration and supervision (MA Ed); curriculum and instruction (MA Ed), including computer education, curriculum and instruction, mathematics education; early childhood education (MA Ed); elementary teacher education (MA Ed); secondary teacher education (MA Ed). Evening/weekend programs available. *Degree requirements:* For master's, thesis (for some programs). *Entrance requirements:* For master's, 3 years of work experience, minimum undergraduate GPA of 2.5. Additional exam requirements/recommendations for international students: Required—TOEFL (minimum score 550 paper-based; 79 iBT). Electronic applications accepted.

University of Phoenix–Springfield Campus, College of Education, Springfield, MO 65804-7211. Offers administration and supervision (MA Ed); curriculum and instruction (MA Ed), including computer education, curriculum and instruction, English and language arts education, English as a second language, mathematics education; English and language arts education (MA Ed).

University of Phoenix–Utah Campus, College of Education, Salt Lake City, UT 84123-4617. Offers administration and supervision (MA Ed); curriculum and instruction (MA Ed); elementary teacher education (MA Ed); school counseling (MSC); secondary teacher education (MA Ed); special education (MA Ed). Evening/weekend programs available. *Degree requirements:* For master's, thesis (for some programs). *Entrance requirements:* For master's, minimum undergraduate GPA of 2.5, 3 years work experience. Additional exam requirements/recommendations for international students: Required—TOEFL (minimum score 550 paper-based; 79 iBT). Electronic applications accepted.

University of Phoenix–Washington D.C. Campus, College of Education, Washington, DC 20001. Offers administration and supervision (MA Ed); adult education and training (MA Ed); computer education (MA Ed); curriculum and instruction (MA Ed, Ed D); early childhood education (MA Ed); education (Ed S); educational leadership (Ed D); educational technology (Ed D); elementary teacher education (MA Ed); English and language arts education (MA Ed); English as a second language (MA Ed); higher education administration (PhD); mathematics education (MA Ed); secondary teacher education (MA Ed); special education (MA Ed); teacher leadership (MA Ed).

University of Phoenix–West Florida Campus, College of Education, Temple Terrace, FL 33637. Offers administration and supervision (MA Ed); curriculum and instruction (MA Ed), including computer education, curriculum and instruction, mathematics education; curriculum and technology (MA Ed); early childhood education (MA Ed); elementary teacher education (MA Ed); secondary teacher education (MA Ed). Evening/weekend programs available. *Degree requirements:* For master's, thesis (for some programs). *Entrance requirements:* For master's, 3 years of work experience, minimum undergraduate GPA of 2.5. Additional exam requirements/recommendations for international students: Required—TOEFL (minimum score 550 paper-based; 79 iBT).

University of Pittsburgh, School of Education, Department of Administrative and Policy Studies, Program in School Leadership, Pittsburgh, PA 15260. Offers M Ed, Ed D, PhD. Part-time and evening/weekend programs available. *Faculty:* 18 full-time (8 women), 8 part-time/adjunct (3 women). *Students:* 15 full-time (10 women), 99 part-time (51 women); includes 10 minority (5 Black or African American, non-Hispanic/Latino; 1 Asian, non-Hispanic/Latino; 2 Hispanic/Latino; 2 Two or more races, non-Hispanic/Latino), 1 international. Average age 40. 21 applicants, 67% accepted, 13 enrolled. In 2013, 266 master's, 11 doctorates awarded. *Degree requirements:* For master's, thesis; for doctorate, thesis/dissertation. *Entrance requirements:* For doctorate, GRE General Test. Additional exam requirements/recommendations for international students: Required—TOEFL (minimum score 80 iBT). *Application deadline:* For fall admission, 2/15 priority date for domestic and international students; for spring admission, 11/1 priority date for domestic and international students. Applications are processed on a rolling basis. Application fee: $50. Electronic applications accepted. *Expenses:* Tuition, state resident: full-time $19,964; part-time $807 per credit. Tuition, nonresident: full-time $32,686; part-time $1337 per credit. *Required fees:* $740; $200. Tuition and fees vary according to program. *Financial support:* Fellowships, research assistantships, teaching assistantships, Federal Work-Study, institutionally sponsored loans, scholarships/grants, health care benefits, tuition waivers (partial), and unspecified assistantships available. Support available to part-time students. Financial award application deadline: 3/15; financial award applicants required to submit FAFSA. *Unit head:* Dr. Mary Margaret Kerr, Chair, 412-648-7205, Fax: 412-648-1784, E-mail: mmkerr@pitt.edu. *Application contact:* Norma Ann Yocco, Enrollment Manager, 412-648-2230, Fax: 412-648-1899, E-mail: soeinfo@pitt.edu. Website: http://www.education.pitt.edu/.

University of Portland, School of Education, Portland, OR 97203-5798. Offers education (MA, MAT); educational leadership (M Ed); English for speakers of other languages (M Ed); initial administrator licensure (M Ed); neuroeducation (Ed D); organizational leadership and development (Ed D); reading (M Ed); special education (M Ed). M Ed also available through the Graduate Outreach Program for teachers residing in the Oregon and Washington state areas. *Accreditation:* NCATE. Part-time and evening/weekend programs available. *Faculty:* 17 full-time (10 women), 12 part-time/adjunct (4 women). *Students:* 47 full-time (29 women), 214 part-time (155 women); includes 25 minority (1 Black or African American, non-Hispanic/Latino; 1 American Indian or Alaska Native, non-Hispanic/Latino; 8 Asian, non-Hispanic/Latino; 6 Hispanic/Latino; 6 Native Hawaiian or other Pacific Islander, non-Hispanic/Latino; 3 Two or more races, non-Hispanic/Latino), 63 international. Average age 32. In 2013, 96 master's awarded. *Entrance requirements:* For master's, minimum GPA of 3.0, teaching certificate, letters of recommendation, resume, statement of goals, official transcripts. Additional exam requirements/recommendations for international students: Required—TOEFL (minimum score 550 paper-based; 80 iBT), IELTS (minimum score 7). *Application deadline:* For fall admission, 7/15 priority date for domestic and international students; for spring admission, 12/15 priority date for domestic and international students. Applications are processed on a rolling basis. Application fee: $50. *Expenses:* Tuition: Part-time $1025 per credit hour. Tuition and fees vary according to program. *Financial support:* Federal Work-Study and scholarships/grants available. Support available to part-time students. Financial award application deadline: 3/1; financial award applicants required to submit FAFSA. *Faculty research:* Multicultural education, supervision/leadership. *Unit head:* Dr. Bruce Weitzel, Associate Dean, 503-943-7135, E-mail: soed@up.edu. *Application contact:* Dr. Matt Baasten, Assistant to the Provost and Dean of the Graduate School, 503-943-7107, Fax: 503-943-7315, E-mail: baasten@up.edu. Website: http://education.up.edu/default.aspx?cid-4318&pid-5590.

University of Prince Edward Island, Faculty of Education, Charlottetown, PE C1A 4P3, Canada. Offers leadership and learning (M Ed). Part-time programs available. *Degree requirements:* For master's, thesis. *Entrance requirements:* For master's, 2 years of professional experience, bachelor of education, professional certificate. Additional exam requirements/recommendations for international students: Required—TOEFL (minimum score 550 paper-based; 80 iBT), Canadian Academic English Language Assessment, Michigan English Language Assessment Battery, Canadian Test of English for Scholars and Trainees. *Faculty research:* Distance learning, aboriginal communities and education leadership development, international development, immersion language learning.

University of Puerto Rico, Río Piedras Campus, College of Education, Program in School Administration and Supervision, San Juan, PR 00931-3300. Offers M Ed, Ed D. Part-time programs available. *Degree requirements:* For master's, thesis; for doctorate, thesis/dissertation, internship. *Entrance requirements:* For master's, PAEG or GRE, minimum GPA of 3.0, letter of recommendation; for doctorate, GRE or PAEG, interview, master's degree, minimum GPA of 3.0, letter of recommendation.

University of Regina, Faculty of Graduate Studies and Research, Faculty of Education, Department of Educational Administration, Regina, SK S4S 0A2, Canada. Offers M Ed. Part-time programs available. *Faculty:* 42 full-time (23 women), 18 part-time/adjunct (10 women). *Students:* 11 full-time (all women), 57 part-time (30 women). 24 applicants, 58% accepted. In 2013, 16 master's awarded. *Degree requirements:* For master's, thesis (for some programs), practicum, project, or thesis. *Entrance requirements:* For master's, bachelor's degree in education, 2 years of teaching or other relevant professional experience. Additional exam requirements/recommendations for international students: Required—TOEFL (minimum score 580 paper-based; 80 iBT), IELTS (minimum score 6.5). *Application deadline:* For fall admission, 2/15 for domestic and international students; for winter admission, 10/15 for domestic and international students; for spring admission, 2/15 for domestic and international students. Application fee: $100. Electronic applications accepted. *Expenses: Tuition, area resident:* Full-time $4338 Canadian dollars. International tuition: $7338 Canadian dollars full-time. *Required fees:* $449.25 Canadian dollars. *Financial support:* In 2013–14, 1 fellowship (averaging $6,000 per year) was awarded; research assistantships and teaching assistantships also available. Financial award application deadline: 6/15. *Faculty research:* Legal aspects of school administration, economics of education, education planning, politics of education, administrative behavior in education. *Unit head:* Dr. Ken Montgomery, Associate Dean, Research and Graduate Programs in Education, 306-585-5031, Fax: 306-585-5387, E-mail: ken.montgomery@uregina.ca. *Application contact:* Tania Gates, Graduate Program Coordinator, 306-585-4506, Fax: 306-585-5387, E-mail: edgrad@uregina.ca.

University of Rochester, Margaret Warner Graduate School of Education and Human Development, Doctoral Programs in Education, Rochester, NY 14627. Offers counseling (Ed D); educational administration (Ed D); educational policy and theory (PhD); higher education (PhD); human development in educational context (PhD); teaching, curriculum, and change (PhD). *Expenses: Tuition:* Full-time $44,580; part-time $1394 per credit hour. *Required fees:* $492.

University of Rochester, Margaret Warner Graduate School of Education and Human Development, Master's Program in School Leadership, Rochester, NY 14627. Offers MS. *Expenses: Tuition:* Full-time $44,580; part-time $1394 per credit hour. *Required fees:* $492.

University of St. Francis, College of Education, Joliet, IL 60435-6169. Offers educational leadership (MS, Ed D); elementary education (M Ed); higher education (MS); reading (MS); secondary education (M Ed), including English education, math education, science education, social studies education, visual arts education; special education (M Ed); teaching and learning (MS). *Accreditation:* NCATE. Part-time and evening/weekend programs available. Postbaccalaureate distance learning degree programs offered (no on-campus study). *Faculty:* 10 full-time (8 women), 34 part-time/adjunct (25 women). *Students:* 14 full-time (13 women), 250 part-time (183 women); includes 34 minority (20 Black or African American, non-Hispanic/Latino; 1 American Indian or Alaska Native, non-Hispanic/Latino; 13 Hispanic/Latino), 1 international. Average age 36. 133 applicants, 62% accepted, 71 enrolled. In 2013, 147 master's awarded. *Degree requirements:* For doctorate, thesis/dissertation. *Entrance requirements:* For doctorate, master's degree, IL Type 75 or Principal's endorsement, interview, minimum undergraduate GPA of 3.0, professional portfolio, letter of recommendation. Additional exam requirements/recommendations for international students: Required—TOEFL (minimum score 550 paper-based; 79 iBT), IELTS (minimum score 6.5). *Application deadline:* Applications are processed on a rolling basis. Application fee: $30. Electronic applications accepted. Application fee is waived when completed online. *Expenses:* Contact institution. *Financial support:* In 2013–14, 10 students received support. Scholarships/grants, tuition waivers (partial), and unspecified assistantships available. Support available to part-time students. Financial award applicants required to submit FAFSA. *Unit head:* Dr. John Gambro, Dean, 815-740-3829, Fax: 815-740-2264, E-mail: jgambro@stfrancis.edu. *Application contact:* Sandra Sloka, Director of Admissions for Graduate and Degree Completion Programs, 800-735-7500, Fax: 815-740-3431, E-mail: ssloka@stfrancis.edu. Website: http://www.stfrancis.edu/academics/college-of-education/.

University of St. Thomas, Graduate Studies, School of Education, Department of Leadership, Policy and Administration, St. Paul, MN 55105-1096. Offers community education administration (MA); educational leadership (Ed S); educational leadership and administration (MA); international leadership (MA, Certificate); leadership (Ed D); leadership in student affairs (MA, Certificate); public policy and leadership (MA, Certificate); public safety and law enforcement leadership (MA). Part-time and evening/weekend programs available. Terminal master's awarded for partial completion of doctoral program. *Degree requirements:* For master's, thesis (for some programs); for doctorate, thesis/dissertation; for other advanced degree, thesis or alternative. *Entrance requirements:* For master's, minimum GPA of 3.0 or MAT; for doctorate, MAT, minimum graduate GPA of 3.5; for other advanced degree, minimum graduate GPA of 3.25 or MAT. Additional exam requirements/recommendations for international students: Required—TOEFL (minimum score 550 paper-based; 20 iBT). *Application deadline:* For fall admission, 6/1 priority date for domestic students; for spring admission, 11/1 priority date for domestic students. Applications are processed on a rolling basis. Application fee: $50. *Expenses:* Contact institution. *Financial support:* Fellowships, research assistantships, institutionally sponsored loans, and scholarships/grants available. Support available to part-time students. Financial award applicants required to submit FAFSA. *Unit head:* Dr. Kate M. Boyle, Chair, 651-962-4393, Fax: 651-962-4169, E-mail: kmboyle@stthomas.edu. *Application contact:* Jackie Grossklaus, Department Assistant, 651-962-4885, Fax: 651-962-4169, E-mail: jmgrossklaus@stthomas.edu.

University of St. Thomas, Graduate Studies, School of Education, Department of Special Education, St. Paul, MN 55105-1096. Offers autism spectrum disorders (MA, Certificate); developmental disabilities (MA); early childhood special education (MA); educational leadership (Ed S); emotional behavioral disorders (MA); gifted, creative, and talented education (MA); learning disabilities (MA); Orton-Gillingham reading (Certificate); special education (MA). *Accreditation:* NCATE. Part-time and evening/weekend programs available. *Degree requirements:* For master's, thesis; for other advanced degree, professional portfolio. *Entrance requirements:* For master's, minimum GPA of 3.0 or MAT; for other advanced degree, MAT or minimum GPA of 2.75. Additional exam requirements/recommendations for international students: Required—TOEFL (minimum score 550 paper-based; 80 iBT). *Application deadline:* For fall admission, 6/1 priority date for domestic students; for spring admission, 11/1 priority date for domestic students. Applications are processed on a rolling basis. Application fee: $50. *Financial support:* Fellowships, research assistantships, institutionally sponsored loans, and scholarships/grants available. Support available to part-time students. Financial award applicants required to submit FAFSA. *Faculty research:* Reading and math fluency, inclusion curriculum for developmental disorders, parent involvement in positive behavior supports, children's friendships, preschool inclusion. *Unit head:* Dr. Terri L. Vandercook, Chair, 651-962-4389, Fax: 651-962-4169, E-mail: tlvandercook@stthomas.edu. *Application contact:* Patricia L. Thomas, Department Assistant, 651-962-4980, Fax: 651-962-4169, E-mail: thom2319@stthomas.edu.

University of St. Thomas, School of Education, Houston, TX 77006-4696. Offers all level education (M Ed); bilingual/dual language (M Ed); Catholic school teaching (M Ed); Catholic/private school leadership (M Ed); counselor education (M Ed); curriculum and instruction (M Ed); educational leadership (M Ed); elementary teaching (M Ed); English

as a second language (M Ed); exceptionality/educational diagnostician (M Ed); exceptionality/special education (M Ed); generalist (M Ed); reading (M Ed); secondary teaching (M Ed). *Accreditation:* Teacher Education Accreditation Council. Part-time and evening/weekend programs available. Postbaccalaureate distance learning degree programs offered (no on-campus study). *Faculty:* 40 full-time (26 women), 43 part-time/adjunct (31 women). *Students:* 27 full-time (20 women), 1,091 part-time (981 women); includes 691 minority (247 Black or African American, non-Hispanic/Latino; 1 American Indian or Alaska Native, non-Hispanic/Latino; 44 Asian, non-Hispanic/Latino; 379 Hispanic/Latino; 2 Native Hawaiian or other Pacific Islander, non-Hispanic/Latino; 18 Two or more races, non-Hispanic/Latino), 28 international. Average age 36. 858 applicants, 83% accepted, 458 enrolled. In 2013, 454 master's awarded. *Degree requirements:* For master's, thesis, field experience. *Entrance requirements:* For master's, GRE or MAT if GPA is below 3.0, bachelor's degree; minimum GPA of 2.75 in bachelor's degree or last 60 credit hours; official transcripts from all institutions; goal statement of 250-300 words; 1 reference. Additional exam requirements/recommendations for international students: Required—TOEFL. *Application deadline:* Applications are processed on a rolling basis. Application fee: $35. Electronic applications accepted. *Expenses:* Contact institution. *Financial support:* In 2013–14, 41 students received support. Federal Work-Study, scholarships/grants, and state work-study, institutional employment available. Support available to part-time students. Financial award application deadline: 4/15; financial award applicants required to submit FAFSA. *Faculty research:* Leadership, diversity, personality traits, second language acquisition. *Unit head:* Dr. Robert LeBlanc, Dean, 713-525-3540, Fax: 713-525-3871, E-mail: education@stthom.edu. *Application contact:* Rita Paredes, Administrative Assistant, 713-525-3442, Fax: 713-525-3871, E-mail: rparede@stthom.edu. Website: http://www.stthom.edu/Academics/School_of_Education/Index.aqf.

University of San Diego, School of Leadership and Education Sciences, Department of Leadership Studies, San Diego, CA 92110-2492. Offers higher education leadership (MA); leadership studies (MA, PhD); nonprofit leadership and management (MA, Certificate). Part-time and evening/weekend programs available. *Faculty:* 10 full-time (6 women), 25 part-time/adjunct (17 women). *Students:* 25 full-time (17 women), 193 part-time (134 women); includes 115 minority (13 Black or African American, non-Hispanic/Latino; 2 American Indian or Alaska Native, non-Hispanic/Latino; 22 Asian, non-Hispanic/Latino; 23 Hispanic/Latino; 18 Native Hawaiian or other Pacific Islander, non-Hispanic/Latino; 37 Two or more races, non-Hispanic/Latino), 16 international. Average age 35. 254 applicants, 58% accepted, 85 enrolled. In 2013, 63 master's, 11 doctorates awarded. *Degree requirements:* For master's, thesis (for some programs), international experience; for doctorate, comprehensive exam, thesis/dissertation, international experience. *Entrance requirements:* For master's, minimum GPA of 3.0, interview; for doctorate, GRE, master's degree, minimum GPA of 3.5 (recommended), interview, resume. Additional exam requirements/recommendations for international students: Required—TOEFL (minimum score 580 paper-based; 83 iBT), TWE. *Application deadline:* For fall admission, 12/1 for domestic and international students. Application fee: $45. Electronic applications accepted. *Expenses: Tuition:* Full-time $23,580; part-time $1310 per credit. *Required fees:* $350. *Financial support:* In 2013–14, 160 students received support. Career-related internships or fieldwork, Federal Work-Study, institutionally sponsored loans, unspecified assistantships, and stipends available. Support available to part-time students. Financial award application deadline: 4/1; financial award applicants required to submit FAFSA. *Faculty research:* Higher education administration policy and relations, organizational leadership, nonprofits and philanthropy, student affairs leadership. *Unit head:* Dr. Afsaneh Nahavandi, Graduate Program Director, 619-260-4181, E-mail: anahavandi@sandiego.edu. *Application contact:* Monica Mahon, Associate Director of Graduate Admissions, 619-260-4524, Fax: 619-260-4158, E-mail: grads@sandiego.edu. Website: http://www.sandiego.edu/soles/departments/leadership-studies/.

University of San Francisco, School of Education, Catholic Educational Leadership Program, San Francisco, CA 94117-1080. Offers Catholic school leadership (MA, Ed D); Catholic school teaching (MA). *Faculty:* 2 full-time (1 woman), 3 part-time/adjunct (1 woman). *Students:* 12 full-time (5 women), 29 part-time (14 women); includes 6 minority (2 Black or African American, non-Hispanic/Latino; 1 Asian, non-Hispanic/Latino; 2 Hispanic/Latino; 1 Two or more races, non-Hispanic/Latino), 8 international. Average age 40. 20 applicants, 95% accepted, 11 enrolled. In 2013, 2 master's, 6 doctorates awarded. *Degree requirements:* For doctorate, thesis/dissertation. Application fee: $55 ($65 for international students). *Expenses: Tuition:* Full-time $21,150; part-time $1175 per unit. Tuition and fees vary according to course load, campus/location and program. *Financial support:* In 2013–14, 7 students received support. Fellowships, research assistantships, and teaching assistantships available. Financial award application deadline: 3/2; financial award applicants required to submit FAFSA. *Unit head:* Dr. Christopher Thomas, Chair, 415-422-2204. *Application contact:* Beth Teague, Associate Director of Graduate Outreach, 415-422-5467, E-mail: schoolofeducation@usfca.edu. Website: http://www.soe.usfca.edu/departments/leadership/cel_index.html.

University of San Francisco, School of Education, Organization and Leadership Program, San Francisco, CA 94117-1080. Offers MA, Ed D. Evening/weekend programs available. *Faculty:* 7 full-time (5 women), 10 part-time/adjunct (5 women). *Students:* 111 full-time (72 women), 50 part-time (33 women); includes 76 minority (19 Black or African American, non-Hispanic/Latino; 20 Asian, non-Hispanic/Latino; 27 Hispanic/Latino; 10 Two or more races, non-Hispanic/Latino), 10 international. Average age 35. 150 applicants, 69% accepted, 47 enrolled. In 2013, 32 master's, 15 doctorates awarded. *Degree requirements:* For doctorate, thesis/dissertation. *Application deadline:* For fall admission, 3/1 priority date for domestic and international students; for spring admission, 10/15 priority date for domestic and international students. Applications are processed on a rolling basis. Application fee: $55 ($65 for international students). Electronic applications accepted. *Expenses: Tuition:* Full-time $21,150; part-time $1175 per unit. Tuition and fees vary according to course load, campus/location and program. *Financial support:* In 2013–14, 43 students received support. Fellowships, research assistantships, and teaching assistantships available. Financial award application deadline: 3/2; financial award applicants required to submit FAFSA. *Unit head:* Dr. Christopher Thomas, Chair, 415-422-2204. *Application contact:* Amy Fogliani, Associate Director of Graduate Outreach, 415-422-5467, E-mail: schoolofeducation@usfca.edu. Website: http://www.soe.usfca.edu/departments/leadership/ol_index.html.

University of Saskatchewan, College of Graduate Studies and Research, College of Education, Department of Educational Administration, Saskatoon, SK S7N 5A2, Canada. Offers M Ed, PhD, Diploma. Part-time programs available. *Degree requirements:* For master's, thesis (for some programs); for doctorate, comprehensive exam (for some programs), thesis/dissertation. *Entrance requirements:* Additional exam requirements/recommendations for international students: Required—TOEFL (minimum score 80 iBT); Recommended—IELTS (minimum score 6.5). Electronic applications accepted. *Expenses: Tuition, area resident:* Full-time $3585 Canadian dollars; part-time $585 Canadian dollars per course. *Tuition, nonresident:* part-time $877 Canadian dollars per course. *International tuition:* $5377 Canadian dollars full-time. *Required fees:* $889.51 Canadian dollars.

The University of Scranton, College of Graduate and Continuing Education, Department of Education, Program in Educational Administration, Scranton, PA 18510. Offers MS. *Accreditation:* NCATE. Part-time and evening/weekend programs available. Postbaccalaureate distance learning degree programs offered (no on-campus study). *Students:* 90 full-time (55 women), 104 part-time (50 women); includes 32 minority (16 Black or African American, non-Hispanic/Latino; 1 American Indian or Alaska Native, non-Hispanic/Latino; 2 Asian, non-Hispanic/Latino; 12 Hispanic/Latino; 1 Two or more races, non-Hispanic/Latino). Average age 35. 42 applicants, 90% accepted. In 2013, 150 master's awarded. *Degree requirements:* For master's, comprehensive exam, capstone experience. *Entrance requirements:* For master's, minimum GPA of 3.0. Additional exam requirements/recommendations for international students: Required—TOEFL (minimum score 500 paper-based), IELTS (minimum score 6). *Application deadline:* Applications are processed on a rolling basis. Application fee: $0. *Financial support:* Teaching assistantships, career-related internships or fieldwork, Federal Work-Study, and unspecified assistantships available. Support available to part-time students. Financial award application deadline: 3/1. *Unit head:* Dr. Art Chambers, Director, 570-941-4668, Fax: 570-941-5515, E-mail: chambersa2@scranton.edu. *Application contact:* Joseph M. Roback, Director of Admissions, 570-941-4385, Fax: 570-941-5928, E-mail: robackj2@scranton.edu.

University of Sioux Falls, Fredrikson School of Education, Sioux Falls, SD 57105-1699. Offers educational administration (Ed S), including principal leadership, superintendent and district leadership; leadership in reading (M Ed); leadership in schools (M Ed); leadership in technology (M Ed); teaching (M Ed). Admission in summer only. *Accreditation:* NCATE. Part-time and evening/weekend programs available. *Degree requirements:* For master's, comprehensive exam (for some programs), research application project; for Ed S, comprehensive exam, portfolio. *Entrance requirements:* For master's, minimum GPA of 3.0, 1 year of teaching experience; for Ed S, minimum 3 years of teaching experience, minimum cumulative GPA of 3.5, 1 year of administrative experience. Additional exam requirements/recommendations for international students: Required—TOEFL. *Faculty research:* Reading, literacy, leadership.

University of South Africa, College of Human Sciences, Pretoria, South Africa. Offers adult education (M Ed); African languages (MA, PhD); African politics (MA, PhD); Afrikaans (MA, PhD); ancient history (MA, PhD); ancient Near Eastern studies (MA, PhD); anthropology (MA, PhD); applied linguistics (MA); Arabic (MA, PhD); archaeology (MA); art history (MA); Biblical archaeology (MA); Biblical studies (M Th, D Th, PhD); Christian spirituality (M Th, D Th); church history (M Th, D Th); classical studies (MA, PhD); clinical psychology (MA); communication (MA, PhD); comparative education (M Ed, Ed D); consulting psychology (D Admin, D Com, PhD); curriculum studies (M Ed, Ed D); development studies (M Admin, MA, D Admin, PhD); didactics (M Ed, Ed D); education (M Tech); education management (M Ed, Ed D); educational psychology (M Ed); English (MA); environmental education (M Ed); French (MA, PhD); German (MA, PhD); Greek (MA); guidance and counseling (M Ed); health studies (MA, PhD), including health sciences education (MA), health services management (MA), medical and surgical nursing science (critical care general) (MA), midwifery and neonatal nursing science (MA), trauma and emergency care (MA); history (MA, PhD); history of education (Ed D); inclusive education (M Ed, Ed D); information and communications technology policy and regulation (MA); information science (MA, MIS, PhD); international politics (MA, PhD); Islamic studies (MA, PhD); Italian (MA, PhD); Judaica (MA, PhD); linguistics (MA, PhD); mathematical education (M Ed); mathematics education (MA); missiology (M Th, D Th); modern Hebrew (MA, PhD); musicology (MA, MMus, D Mus, PhD); natural science education (M Ed); New Testament (M Th, D Th); Old Testament (D Th); pastoral therapy (M Th, D Th); philosophy (MA); philosophy of education (M Ed, Ed D); politics (MA, PhD); Portuguese (MA, PhD); practical theology (M Th, D Th); psychology (MA, MS, PhD); psychology of education (M Ed, Ed D); public health (MA); religious studies (MA, D Th, PhD); Romance languages (MA); Russian (MA, PhD); Semitic languages (MA, PhD); social behavior studies in HIV/AIDS (MA); social science (mental health) (MA); social science in development studies (MA); social science in psychology (MA); social science in social work (MA); social science in sociology (MA); social work (MSW, DSW, PhD); socio-education (M Ed, Ed D); sociolinguistics (MA); sociology (MA, PhD); Spanish (MA, PhD); systematic theology (M Th, D Th); TESOL (teaching English to speakers of other languages) (MA); theological ethics (M Th, D Th); theory of literature (MA, PhD); urban ministries (D Th); urban ministry (M Th).

University of South Alabama, Graduate School, College of Education, Department of Leadership and Teacher Education, Mobile, AL 36688-0002. Offers early childhood education (M Ed); educational administration (Ed S); educational leadership (M Ed); elementary education (M Ed); reading education (M Ed); science education (M Ed); secondary education (M Ed); special education (M Ed, Ed S). *Accreditation:* NCATE. Part-time programs available. *Faculty:* 17 full-time (11 women), 4 part-time/adjunct (all women). *Students:* 136 full-time (103 women), 78 part-time (67 women); includes 45 minority (40 Black or African American, non-Hispanic/Latino; 2 Asian, non-Hispanic/Latino; 1 Hispanic/Latino; 2 Two or more races, non-Hispanic/Latino). 90 applicants, 53% accepted, 45 enrolled. In 2013, 69 master's awarded. *Degree requirements:* For master's, comprehensive exam. *Entrance requirements:* For master's, GRE General Test or MAT, minimum GPA of 3.0. *Application deadline:* For fall admission, 7/15 priority date for domestic students, 6/15 priority date for international students; for spring admission, 12/1 priority date for domestic students, 11/1 priority date for international students. Applications are processed on a rolling basis. Application fee: $35. *Expenses:* Tuition, state resident: full-time $8976; part-time $374 per credit hour. Tuition, nonresident: full-time $17,952; part-time $748 per credit hour. *Financial support:* Research assistantships and career-related internships or fieldwork available. Support available to part-time students. Financial award application deadline: 4/1. *Unit head:* Dr. Harold Dodge, Jr., Chair, 251-380-2894. *Application contact:* Dr. Abigail Baxter, Director of Graduate Studies, 251-380-2738, Fax: 251-380-2748, E-mail: abaxter@southalabama.edu. Website: http://www.southalabama.edu/coe/lted.

University of South Carolina, The Graduate School, College of Education, Department of Educational Leadership and Policies, Program in Educational Administration, Columbia, SC 29208. Offers M Ed, PhD, Ed S. *Accreditation:* NCATE. Part-time and evening/weekend programs available. Postbaccalaureate distance learning degree programs offered (no on-campus study). *Degree requirements:* For master's, comprehensive exam, thesis (for some programs), foreign language (MA); for doctorate, comprehensive exam, thesis/dissertation. *Entrance requirements:* For master's, GRE General Test or MAT, letter of reference, resume; for doctorate and Ed S, GRE General Test or MAT, interview, letter of intent, letter of reference, transcripts, resum&e. Electronic applications accepted.

The University of South Dakota, Graduate School, School of Education, Division of Educational Administration, Vermillion, SD 57069-2390. Offers MA, Ed D, Ed S. *Accreditation:* NCATE. Part-time and evening/weekend programs available. Postbaccalaureate distance learning degree programs offered (no on-campus study). *Degree requirements:* For master's and Ed S, comprehensive exam, thesis or alternative; for doctorate, comprehensive exam, thesis/dissertation. *Entrance requirements:* For master's and doctorate, GRE General Test, MAT, minimum GPA of 2.7. Additional exam requirements/recommendations for international students:

Required—TOEFL (minimum score 550 paper-based; 79 iBT). Electronic applications accepted.

University of Southern California, Graduate School, Rossier School of Education, Doctor of Education Programs, Los Angeles, CA 90089. Offers educational psychology (Ed D); higher education administration (Ed D); K-12 leadership in urban school settings (Ed D); teacher education in multicultural societies (Ed D). Part-time and evening/weekend programs available. *Degree requirements:* For doctorate, thesis/dissertation. *Entrance requirements:* For doctorate, GRE. Additional exam requirements/recommendations for international students: Required—TOEFL (minimum score 100 iBT). Electronic applications accepted. *Faculty research:* Data-driven decision-making in K-12 schools and districts; examination of college and university leadership and management in U. S. and Asia; studies in facilitating student learning; organizational change and the role of leaders; leadership, diversity, learning and accountability.

University of Southern California, Graduate School, Rossier School of Education, Doctor of Philosophy in Education Programs, Los Angeles, CA 90089. Offers educational psychology (PhD); higher education administration and policy (PhD); K-12 policy and practice (PhD). *Degree requirements:* For doctorate, thesis/dissertation, 63 units; qualifying exam; dissertation proposal and defense. *Entrance requirements:* For doctorate, GRE. Additional exam requirements/recommendations for international students: Required—TOEFL (minimum score 100 iBT). Electronic applications accepted. *Faculty research:* Diversity in higher education, organizational change, educational psychology, policy and politics of educational reform, economics of education and education policy.

University of Southern Maine, College of Management and Human Service, School of Education and Human Development, Educational Leadership Program, Portland, ME 04104-9300. Offers assistant principal (Certificate); educational leadership (MS Ed, CAS). Part-time and evening/weekend programs available. Postbaccalaureate distance learning degree programs offered (minimal on-campus study). *Faculty:* 15 full-time (9 women), 11 part-time/adjunct (8 women). *Students:* 1 full-time (0 women), 77 part-time (58 women); includes 1 minority (American Indian or Alaska Native, non-Hispanic/Latino). Average age 40. 15 applicants, 100% accepted, 8 enrolled. In 2013, 18 master's, 35 CASs awarded. *Degree requirements:* For master's, thesis or alternative, practicum, internship; for other advanced degree, thesis or alternative. *Entrance requirements:* For master's, three years of documented teaching; for other advanced degree, master's degree. Additional exam requirements/recommendations for international students: Required—TOEFL (minimum score 550 paper-based; 79 iBT). *Application deadline:* For fall admission, 5/1 priority date for domestic students; for spring admission, 10/15 priority date for domestic students. Applications are processed on a rolling basis. Application fee: $65. Electronic applications accepted. *Expenses:* Tuition, state resident: part-time $380 per credit. Tuition, nonresident: part-time $1026 per credit. Part-time tuition and fees vary according to program. *Financial support:* Research assistantships, career-related internships or fieldwork, Federal Work-Study, institutionally sponsored loans, scholarships/grants, and unspecified assistantships available. Financial award application deadline: 3/1; financial award applicants required to submit FAFSA. *Faculty research:* Teaching strategies, technology-enhanced leadership, school-community partnerships, workforce development, higher education. *Unit head:* Dr. Jeffrey Beaudry, Chair, 270-780-5493, E-mail: jbeaudry@usm.maine.edu. *Application contact:* Mary Sloan, Assistant Dean of Graduate Studies and Director of Graduate Admissions, 207-780-4812, Fax: 207-780-4969, E-mail: gradstudies@usm.maine.edu.

University of Southern Mississippi, Graduate School, College of Education and Psychology, Department of Educational Leadership and School Counseling, Hattiesburg, MS 39401. Offers education (Ed D, PhD, Ed S), including educational leadership and school counseling (Ed D, PhD); educational administration (M Ed). Part-time programs available. *Faculty:* 9 full-time (5 women), 3 part-time/adjunct (1 woman). *Students:* 42 full-time (27 women), 158 part-time (110 women); includes 63 minority (53 Black or African American, non-Hispanic/Latino; 3 Asian, non-Hispanic/Latino; 2 Hispanic/Latino; 5 Two or more races, non-Hispanic/Latino). Average age 39. 35 applicants, 86% accepted, 19 enrolled. In 2013, 43 master's, 30 doctorates, 5 other advanced degrees awarded. *Degree requirements:* For master's, comprehensive exam, thesis optional, internship; for doctorate, comprehensive exam, thesis/dissertation; for Ed S, comprehensive exam, thesis optional. *Entrance requirements:* For master's, GRE General Test, minimum GPA of 2.75; for doctorate, GRE General Test, minimum GPA of 3.5; for Ed S, GRE General Test, minimum GPA of 3.25. Additional exam requirements/recommendations for international students: Required—TOEFL, IELTS. *Application deadline:* For fall admission, 3/1 priority date for domestic and international students; for spring admission, 1/10 for domestic and international students. Application fee: $50. *Financial support:* In 2013–14, research assistantships (averaging $9,000 per year), teaching assistantships (averaging $9,000 per year) were awarded; career-related internships or fieldwork, Federal Work-Study, institutionally sponsored loans, scholarships/grants, health care benefits, and unspecified assistantships also available. Financial award application deadline: 3/15; financial award applicants required to submit FAFSA. *Unit head:* Dr. Thelma Roberson, Interim Chair, 601-266-4556, Fax: 601-266-4233, E-mail: thelma.roberson@usm.edu. *Application contact:* Shonna Breland, Manager of Graduate Admissions, 601-266-6563, Fax: 601-266-5138.
Website: http://www.usm.edu/graduateschool/table.php.

University of Southern Mississippi, Graduate School, College of Education and Psychology, Department of Educational Studies and Research, Hattiesburg, MS 39406-0001. Offers adult education (Graduate Certificate); community college leadership (Graduate Certificate); counseling and personnel services (college) (M Ed); education (PhD, Ed S), including adult education, research, evaluation and statistics (PhD); education (Ed D), including educational administration, educational research; education: educational leadership and research (Ed S), including higher education administration; educational administration and supervision (M Ed); higher education administration (Ed D, PhD); institutional research (Graduate Certificate). *Faculty:* 7 full-time (1 woman), 5 part-time/adjunct (1 woman). *Students:* 32 full-time (21 women), 103 part-time (70 women); includes 44 minority (39 Black or African American, non-Hispanic/Latino; 2 Hispanic/Latino; 3 Two or more races, non-Hispanic/Latino), 4 international. Average age 36. 36 applicants, 72% accepted, 15 enrolled. In 2013, 18 master's, 9 doctorates, 7 other advanced degrees awarded. *Degree requirements:* For master's and other advanced degree, comprehensive exam, thesis (for some programs); for doctorate, comprehensive exam, thesis/dissertation. *Entrance requirements:* For master's, doctorate, and other advanced degree, GRE General Test, minimum GPA of 2.75. Additional exam requirements/recommendations for international students: Required—TOEFL. *Application deadline:* For fall admission, 2/1 for domestic students, 3/1 for international students. Applications are processed on a rolling basis. Application fee: $35. *Financial support:* Career-related internships or fieldwork, Federal Work-Study, and institutionally sponsored loans available. Financial award application deadline: 3/15; financial award applicants required to submit FAFSA. *Total annual research expenditures:* $88,500. *Unit head:* Dr. Thomas V. O'Brien, Chair, 601-266-6093, E-mail: thomas.obrien@usm.edu. *Application contact:* Shonna Breland, Manager of Graduate Admissions, 601-266-6563, Fax: 601-266-5138.
Website: http://www.usm.edu/cep/esr/.

University of South Florida, College of Education, Department of Educational Leadership and Policy Studies, Tampa, FL 33620-9951. Offers educational leadership (M Ed, Ed D, Ed S). Part-time programs available. *Degree requirements:* For master's, comprehensive exam, portfolio; for doctorate, comprehensive exam, thesis/dissertation, philosophies of inquiry; multiple research methods; for Ed S, comprehensive exam, thesis. *Entrance requirements:* For master's, minimum GPA of 3.0 in last 60 hours of coursework; Florida Professional Teaching Certificate; 2 years' post bachelor's teaching experience; for doctorate, GRE General Test, master's degree in educational leadership or educational leadership certification; for Ed S, GRE General Test, educational leadership certification. Additional exam requirements/recommendations for international students: Required—TOEFL (minimum score 550 paper-based; 79 iBT). Electronic applications accepted. *Faculty research:* Multicultural education and social justice, educational accountability policy, school reform, community development and school success, school governance, teacher and principal preparation.

University of South Florida, University College/Distance Education, Tampa, FL 33620-9951. *Unit head:* Kathy Barnes, Interdisciplinary Programs Coordinator, 813-974-8031, Fax: 813-974-7061, E-mail: barnesk@usf.edu. *Application contact:* Karen Tylinski, Metro Initiatives, 813-974-9943, Fax: 813-974-7061, E-mail: ktylinsk@usf.edu.
Website: http://uc.usf.edu/.

University of South Florida–St. Petersburg Campus, College of Education, St. Petersburg, FL 33701. Offers educational leadership development (M Ed); elementary education (MA), including math/science; English education (MA); middle grades STEM education (MS); reading education (MA). Part-time programs available. *Degree requirements:* For master's, comprehensive exam, practicum, internship, comprehensive portfolio. *Entrance requirements:* For master's, State of Florida General Knowledge Test (GKT), Florida Teaching Certificate (for non-initial certification programs), letters of recommendation. Additional exam requirements/recommendations for international students: Required—TOEFL (minimum score 550 paper-based; 79 iBT); Recommended—IELTS. Electronic applications accepted.

University of South Florida Sarasota-Manatee, College of Education, Sarasota, FL 34243. Offers education (MA); educational leadership (M Ed), including curriculum leadership, K-12, non-public/charter school leadership; English education (MA); teaching K-6 with ESOL endorsement (MAT). Part-time and evening/weekend programs available. *Faculty:* 7 full-time (all women), 5 part-time/adjunct (3 women). *Students:* 11 full-time (9 women), 43 part-time (33 women); includes 6 minority (2 Black or African American, non-Hispanic/Latino; 2 Hispanic/Latino; 1 Native Hawaiian or other Pacific Islander, non-Hispanic/Latino; 1 Two or more races, non-Hispanic/Latino). Average age 33. 46 applicants, 39% accepted, 15 enrolled. In 2013, 33 master's awarded. *Degree requirements:* For master's, comprehensive exam (for some programs). *Entrance requirements:* For master's, GRE (within last 5 years) or minimum GPA of 3.0, letters of recommendation. Additional exam requirements/recommendations for international students: Required—TOEFL (minimum score 550 paper-based; 79 iBT), IELTS (minimum score 6.5). *Application deadline:* For fall admission, 3/1 priority date for domestic students, 3/1 for international students; for spring admission, 10/1 priority date for domestic students, 10/1 for international students. Applications are processed on a rolling basis. Application fee: $30. Electronic applications accepted. *Expenses:* Tuition, state resident: full-time $10,029; part-time $418 per credit. Tuition, nonresident: full-time $20,727; part-time $863 per credit. *Required fees:* $10; $5. Tuition and fees vary according to program. *Financial support:* In 2013–14, 10 students received support. Career-related internships or fieldwork, institutionally sponsored loans, scholarships/grants, health care benefits, and unspecified assistantships available. Support available to part-time students. Financial award application deadline: 3/1; financial award applicants required to submit FAFSA. *Faculty research:* Child development, student achievement, inter-generational studies, equitable implementation of educational policy, linguistics and its applications. *Unit head:* Dr. Terry A. Osborn, Dean, 941-359-4531, Fax: 941-359-4778, E-mail: terryosborn@sar.usf.edu. *Application contact:* Andy Telatovich, Director, Admissions, 941-359-4330, Fax: 941-359-4585, E-mail: atelatovich@sar.usf.edu.
Website: http://usfsm.edu/college-of-education/.

The University of Tampa, Program in Teaching, Tampa, FL 33606-1490. Offers curricula and instructional leadership (M Ed); teaching (M Ed). Part-time and evening/weekend programs available. *Faculty:* 7 full-time (4 women), 6 part-time/adjunct (5 women). *Students:* 34 full-time (26 women), 47 part-time (32 women); includes 27 minority (11 Black or African American, non-Hispanic/Latino; 1 Asian, non-Hispanic/Latino; 11 Hispanic/Latino; 4 Two or more races, non-Hispanic/Latino), 3 international. Average age 32. 115 applicants, 54% accepted, 32 enrolled. In 2013, 9 master's awarded. *Entrance requirements:* For master's, Florida Teacher Certification Exam, PRAXIS, GRE, or GMAT, bachelor's degree in education or professional teaching certificate. Additional exam requirements/recommendations for international students: Required—TOEFL (minimum score 577 paper-based; 90 iBT), IELTS (minimum score 7). *Application deadline:* For fall admission, 5/1 for domestic students. Applications are processed on a rolling basis. Application fee: $40. Electronic applications accepted. *Expenses: Tuition:* Full-time $8928; part-time $558 per credit hour. *Required fees:* $80; $80 $40 per term. Tuition and fees vary according to program. *Financial support:* In 2013–14, 24 students received support. Scholarships/grants available. Financial award applicants required to submit FAFSA. *Faculty research:* Diversity in the classroom, technology integration, assessment methodologies, complex and ill-structured problem solving, and communities of practice. *Unit head:* Dr. Johnathan McKeown, Director, Education Master's Program, 813-257-6306, E-mail: jmckeown@ut.edu. *Application contact:* Brent Benner, Director of Admissions, 813-257-3642, E-mail: bbenner@ut.edu.
Website: http://www.ut.edu/graduate.

The University of Tennessee, Graduate School, College of Education, Health and Human Sciences, Program in Education, Knoxville, TN 37996. Offers art education (MS); counseling education (PhD); cultural studies in education (PhD); curriculum (MS, Ed S); curriculum, educational research and evaluation (Ed D, PhD); early childhood education (PhD); early childhood special education (MS); education of deaf and hard of hearing (MS); educational administration and policy studies (Ed D, PhD); educational administration and supervision (Ed S); educational psychology (Ed D, PhD); elementary education (MS, Ed S); elementary teaching (MS); English education (MS, Ed S); exercise science (PhD); foreign language/ESL education (MS, Ed S); instructional technology (MS, Ed D, PhD, Ed S); literacy, language and ESL education (PhD); literacy, language education, and ESL education (Ed D); mathematics education (MS, Ed S); modified and comprehensive special education (MS); reading education (MS, Ed S); school counseling (Ed S); school psychology (PhD, Ed S); science education (MS, Ed S); secondary teaching (MS); social foundations (MS); social science education (MS, Ed S); socio-cultural foundations of sports and education (PhD); special education (Ed S); teacher education (Ed D, PhD). *Accreditation:* NCATE. Part-time and evening/weekend programs available. *Degree requirements:* For master's and Ed S, thesis optional; for doctorate, variable foreign language requirement, thesis/dissertation. *Entrance requirements:* For master's, minimum GPA of 2.7; for doctorate and Ed S, GRE General Test, minimum GPA of 2.7. Additional exam requirements/recommendations for international students: Required—TOEFL. Electronic applications accepted. *Expenses:* Tuition, state resident: full-time $9540; part-time $531 per credit

hour. Tuition, nonresident: full-time $27,728; part-time $1542 per credit hour. *Required fees:* $1404; $67 per credit hour.

The University of Tennessee, Graduate School, College of Education, Health and Human Sciences, Program in Educational Administration and Policy Studies, Knoxville, TN 37996. Offers educational administration and policy studies (Ed D); educational administration and supervision (MS). *Accreditation:* NCATE. Part-time and evening/weekend programs available. Postbaccalaureate distance learning degree programs offered (no on-campus study). *Degree requirements:* For master's, thesis optional. *Entrance requirements:* For master's, minimum GPA of 2.7. Additional exam requirements/recommendations for international students: Required—TOEFL. Electronic applications accepted. *Expenses:* Tuition, state resident: full-time $9540; part-time $531 per credit hour. Tuition, nonresident: full-time $27,728; part-time $1542 per credit hour. *Required fees:* $1404; $67 per credit hour.

The University of Tennessee at Chattanooga, Graduate School, College of Health, Education and Professional Studies, School of Education, Chattanooga, TN 37403. Offers counseling (M Ed), including community counseling, school counseling; education (M Ed, Post-Master's Certificate), including elementary education (M Ed), school leadership, secondary education (M Ed), special education (M Ed); educational specialist (Ed S), including educational technology, school psychology; learning and leadership (Ed D), including educational leadership. *Accreditation:* ACA; NCATE. Part-time and evening/weekend programs available. Postbaccalaureate distance learning degree programs offered (no on-campus study). *Faculty:* 24 full-time (17 women), 6 part-time/adjunct (4 women). *Students:* 107 full-time (86 women), 263 part-time (192 women); includes 71 minority (46 Black or African American, non-Hispanic/Latino; 2 American Indian or Alaska Native, non-Hispanic/Latino; 5 Asian, non-Hispanic/Latino; 11 Hispanic/Latino; 7 Two or more races, non-Hispanic/Latino), 2 international. Average age 34. 121 applicants, 83% accepted, 67 enrolled. In 2013, 125 master's, 10 doctorates, 3 other advanced degrees awarded. *Degree requirements:* For master's, comprehensive exam, thesis optional, culminating experience; for doctorate, comprehensive exam, thesis/dissertation; for other advanced degree, internship. *Entrance requirements:* For master's, GRE General Test, PPST 1, teaching certificate; for doctorate, GRE General Test, master's degree, two years of practical work experience in organizational environment; for other advanced degree, GRE General Test, letters of reference. Additional exam requirements/recommendations for international students: Required—TOEFL (minimum score 550 paper-based; 79 iBT), IELTS (minimum score 6). *Application deadline:* For fall admission, 6/13 for domestic students, 6/1 for international students; for spring admission, 10/15 for domestic students, 10/1 for international students. Applications are processed on a rolling basis. Application fee: $30 ($35 for international students). Electronic applications accepted. *Financial support:* In 2013–14, 20 research assistantships with tuition reimbursements (averaging $6,340 per year), 4 teaching assistantships with tuition reimbursements (averaging $7,234 per year) were awarded; career-related internships or fieldwork, institutionally sponsored loans, scholarships/grants, and unspecified assistantships also available. Support available to part-time students. Financial award applicants required to submit FAFSA. *Faculty research:* School counseling, community counseling, elementary and secondary education, school leadership and administration. *Total annual research expenditures:* $967,880. *Unit head:* Dr. Linda Johnston, Director, 423-425-4122, Fax: 423-425-5380, E-mail: linda-johnston@utc.edu. *Application contact:* Dr. J. Randy Walker, Interim Dean of Graduate Studies, 423-425-4478, Fax: 423-425-5223, E-mail: randy-walker@utc.edu.
Website: http://www.utc.edu/school-education/abouttheschool/gradprograms.php.

The University of Tennessee at Martin, Graduate Programs, College of Education, Health and Behavioral Sciences, Program in Educational Leadership, Martin, TN 38238-1000. Offers MS Ed. Part-time programs available. *Students:* 1 full-time (0 women), 32 part-time (19 women); includes 7 minority (all Black or African American, non-Hispanic/Latino). 17 applicants, 35% accepted, 6 enrolled. In 2013, 10 master's awarded. *Degree requirements:* For master's, comprehensive exam. *Entrance requirements:* For master's, GRE General Test, minimum GPA of 2.5, letters of reference, teaching license, resume, teaching experience. Additional exam requirements/recommendations for international students: Required—TOEFL (minimum score 525 paper-based; 71 iBT). *Application deadline:* For fall admission, 7/29 priority date for domestic and international students; for spring admission, 12/12 priority date for domestic and international students. Applications are processed on a rolling basis. Application fee: $30 ($130 for international students). Electronic applications accepted. *Financial support:* Research assistantships with full tuition reimbursements, teaching assistantships with full tuition reimbursements, scholarships/grants, and unspecified assistantships available. Support available to part-time students. Financial award application deadline: 2/15; financial award applicants required to submit FAFSA. *Unit head:* Dr. Gail Stephens, Interim Dean, 731-881-7127, Fax: 731-881-7975, E-mail: gstephe6@utm.edu. *Application contact:* Jolene L. Cunningham, Student Services Specialist, 731-881-7012, Fax: 731-881-7499, E-mail: jcunningham@utm.edu.

The University of Texas at Arlington, Graduate School, College of Education and Health Professions, Department of Educational Leadership and Policy Studies, Arlington, TX 76019. Offers dual language (M Ed); education leadership and policy studies (PhD); higher education (M Ed); principal certification (M Ed). Part-time and evening/weekend programs available. Postbaccalaureate distance learning degree programs offered (no on-campus study). *Degree requirements:* For master's, 2 field-based practica; for doctorate, comprehensive exam, thesis/dissertation, 2 research-based practica. *Entrance requirements:* For master's, GRE, 3 references forms, minimum undergraduate GPA of 3.0 in the last 60 hours of course work; for doctorate, GRE, resume, statement of intent, 3 reference forms, applicable master's degree. *Faculty research:* Lived realities of students of color in K-16 contexts, K-16 faculty, K-16 policy and law, K-16 student access, K-16 student success.

The University of Texas at Austin, Graduate School, College of Education, Department of Educational Administration, Austin, TX 78712-1111. Offers M Ed, Ed D, PhD. *Degree requirements:* For doctorate, thesis/dissertation. *Entrance requirements:* For master's and doctorate, GRE General Test. Electronic applications accepted.

The University of Texas at Austin, Graduate School, College of Education, Department of Special Education, Austin, TX 78712-1111. Offers autism and developmental disabilities (Ed D, PhD); autism and developmental disability (M Ed, MA); early childhood special education (M Ed, MA, Ed D, PhD); learning disabilities (Ed D, PhD); learning disabilities/behavior disorders (M Ed, MA); multicultural special education (M Ed, MA, Ed D, PhD); rehabilitation counselor (M Ed); rehabilitation counselor education (Ed D, PhD); special education administration (Ed D, PhD). *Accreditation:* CORE. Part-time and evening/weekend programs available. Postbaccalaureate distance learning degree programs offered (no on-campus study). *Degree requirements:* For master's, thesis or alternative; for doctorate, thesis/dissertation. *Entrance requirements:* For master's and doctorate, GRE General Test. *Faculty research:* Anchored instruction, reading disabilities, multicultural/bilingual.

The University of Texas at Brownsville, Graduate Studies, College of Education, Brownsville, TX 78520-4991. Offers bilingual education (M Ed); counseling and guidance (M Ed); curriculum and instruction (M Ed); early childhood education (M Ed); educational leadership (M Ed); educational technology (M Ed); exercise science (MS); special education (M Ed). Part-time and evening/weekend programs available. Postbaccalaureate distance learning degree programs offered (no on-campus study). *Faculty:* 51 full-time (28 women). *Students:* 60 full-time (43 women), 496 part-time (363 women); includes 467 minority (4 Black or African American, non-Hispanic/Latino; 1 American Indian or Alaska Native, non-Hispanic/Latino; 10 Asian, non-Hispanic/Latino; 451 Hispanic/Latino; 1 Native Hawaiian or other Pacific Islander, non-Hispanic/Latino), 12 international. 161 applicants, 67% accepted, 81 enrolled. In 2013, 142 master's awarded. *Degree requirements:* For master's, comprehensive exam (for some programs), thesis optional, electronic portfolio. *Entrance requirements:* For master's, GRE General Test, curriculum vitae or resume, teaching certificate. Additional exam requirements/recommendations for international students: Required—TOEFL (minimum score 550 paper-based; 77 iBT). *Application deadline:* For fall admission, 7/1 priority date for domestic students, 7/1 for international students; for spring admission, 12/1 priority date for domestic students, 12/1 for international students. Applications are processed on a rolling basis. Application fee: $30. Electronic applications accepted. *Expenses:* Tuition, state resident: full-time $3444; part-time $1148 per semester. Tuition, nonresident: full-time $9816. *Required fees:* $1018; $221 per credit hour. $401 per semester. *Financial support:* In 2013–14, 136 students received support, including 6 research assistantships (averaging $10,000 per year); career-related internships or fieldwork, Federal Work-Study, scholarships/grants, tuition waivers (partial), and unspecified assistantships also available. Support available to part-time students. Financial award application deadline: 3/1; financial award applicants required to submit FAFSA. *Unit head:* Dr. Miguel Angel Escotet, Dean, 956-882-7220, Fax: 956-882-7431, E-mail: miguel.escotet@utb.edu. *Application contact:* Mari E. Stevens, Graduate Studies Specialist, 956-882-6587, Fax: 956-882-7279, E-mail: mari.stevens@utb.edu.
Website: http://www.utb.edu/vpaa/coe/Pages/default.aspx.

The University of Texas at El Paso, Graduate School, College of Education, Department of Educational Leadership and Foundations, El Paso, TX 79968-0001. Offers educational administration (M Ed); educational leadership and administration (Ed D). Part-time and evening/weekend programs available. *Degree requirements:* For master's, thesis optional; for doctorate, thesis/dissertation. *Entrance requirements:* For doctorate, GRE General Test, minimum graduate GPA of 3.0. Additional exam requirements/recommendations for international students: Required—TOEFL. Electronic applications accepted.

The University of Texas at San Antonio, College of Education and Human Development, Department of Educational Leadership and Policy Studies, San Antonio, TX 78249-0617. Offers educational leadership (Ed D); educational leadership and policy studies (M Ed), including educational leadership, higher education administration. Part-time programs available. *Faculty:* 22 full-time (10 women), 16 part-time/adjunct (11 women). *Students:* 62 full-time (43 women), 265 part-time (189 women); includes 216 minority (22 Black or African American, non-Hispanic/Latino; 1 American Indian or Alaska Native, non-Hispanic/Latino; 4 Asian, non-Hispanic/Latino; 183 Hispanic/Latino; 6 Two or more races, non-Hispanic/Latino), 3 international. Average age 36. 129 applicants, 86% accepted, 69 enrolled. In 2013, 129 master's, 9 doctorates awarded. *Degree requirements:* For master's, comprehensive exam, thesis or alternative; for doctorate, comprehensive exam, thesis/dissertation. *Entrance requirements:* For master's, transcripts, statement of purpose, resume or curriculum vitae; for doctorate, GRE General Test, minimum GPA of 3.5 in a master's program, resume, three letters of recommendation, statement of purpose. Additional exam requirements/recommendations for international students: Required—TOEFL (minimum score 550 paper-based; 79 iBT), IELTS (minimum score 6.5). *Application deadline:* For fall admission, 7/1 for domestic students, 4/1 for international students; for spring admission, 11/1 for domestic students, 9/1 for international students. Application fee: $45 ($80 for international students). *Expenses:* Tuition, state resident: full-time $4671. Tuition, nonresident: full-time $8708. *International tuition:* $17,415 full-time. *Required fees:* $1924.60. Tuition and fees vary according to course load and degree level. *Financial support:* In 2013–14, 6 students received support, including 6 fellowships with full and partial tuition reimbursements available (averaging $40,000 per year). Financial award application deadline: 2/1. *Faculty research:* Urban and international school leadership, student success, college access, higher education policy, multiculturalism, minority student achievement. *Unit head:* Dr. Bruce G. Barnett, Department Chair, 210-458-5413, Fax: 210-458-5848, E-mail: bruce.barnett@utsa.edu. *Application contact:* Elisha Reynolds, Student Development Specialist, 210-458-6620, Fax: 210-458-5848, E-mail: elisha.reynolds@utsa.edu.
Website: http://education.utsa.edu/educational_leadership_and_policy_studies/.

The University of Texas at Tyler, College of Education and Psychology, Department of Educational Leadership, Tyler, TX 75799-0001. Offers M Ed. Part-time and evening/weekend programs available. Postbaccalaureate distance learning degree programs offered (no on-campus study). *Degree requirements:* For master's, comprehensive exam, 2 years of teaching experience. *Entrance requirements:* For master's, GRE General Test. Additional exam requirements/recommendations for international students: Required—TOEFL. *Faculty research:* Effective schools, restructuring of schools, leadership.

The University of Texas of the Permian Basin, Office of Graduate Studies, School of Education, Program in Educational Leadership, Odessa, TX 79762-0001. Offers MA. *Degree requirements:* For master's, comprehensive exam (for some programs), thesis (for some programs). *Entrance requirements:* For master's, GRE General Test. Additional exam requirements/recommendations for international students: Required—TOEFL (minimum score 550 paper-based).

The University of Texas–Pan American, College of Education, Department of Educational Leadership, Edinburg, TX 78539. Offers M Ed, Ed D. Part-time and evening/weekend programs available. *Degree requirements:* For master's, comprehensive exam, thesis optional; for doctorate, comprehensive exam, thesis/dissertation. *Entrance requirements:* For master's, GRE; for doctorate, master's degree. Additional exam requirements/recommendations for international students: Required—TOEFL. Electronic applications accepted. *Expenses:* Tuition, state resident: full-time $5986; part-time $333 per credit hour. Tuition, nonresident: full-time $12,358; part-time $687 per credit hour. *Required fees:* $782. Tuition and fees vary according to program. *Faculty research:* Community perceptions of education, leadership and gender studies, continuous improvement processes, leadership.

University of the Cumberlands, Graduate Programs in Education, Williamsburg, KY 40769-1372. Offers all grades (P-12) (M Ed); business and marketing (MA Ed, MAT); counselor education and supervision (Ed D); director of pupil personnel (Certificate); director of special education (Certificate); educational administration and supervision (Ed S); educational leadership (Ed D); elementary education (MA Ed, MAT); instructional leadership - principalship (MA Ed); instructional leadership - school principal (Certificate); middle school education (MA Ed, MAT); reading and writing (MA Ed); school counseling (MA Ed); school superintendent (Certificate); secondary education (MA Ed, MAT); special education (MAT); supervisor of instruction (Certificate); teacher leader (MA Ed). Part-time and evening/weekend programs available. Postbaccalaureate distance learning degree programs offered. *Degree requirements:* For master's, comprehensive exam. Electronic applications accepted.

University of the Incarnate Word, School of Graduate Studies and Research, Dreeben School of Education, Programs in Education, San Antonio, TX 78209-6397. Offers adult education (M Ed, MA); cross-cultural education (M Ed, MA); early childhood literacy (M Ed, MA); general education (M Ed, MA); higher education (PhD); instructional technology (M Ed, MA); international education and entrepreneurship (PhD); kinesiology (M Ed, MA); literacy (M Ed, MA); organizational leadership (PhD); organizational learning and learning (M Ed, MA); reading (M Ed, MA); special education (M Ed, MA); teacher leadership (M Ed, MA). Part-time and evening/weekend programs available. *Faculty:* 17 full-time (9 women), 6 part-time/adjunct (all women). *Students:* 23 full-time (13 women), 187 part-time (122 women); includes 114 minority (24 Black or African American, non-Hispanic/Latino; 1 American Indian or Alaska Native, non-Hispanic/Latino; 3 Asian, non-Hispanic/Latino; 85 Hispanic/Latino; 1 Two or more races, non-Hispanic/Latino), 30 international. Average age 41. 52 applicants, 67% accepted, 25 enrolled. In 2013, 12 master's, 14 doctorates awarded. *Degree requirements:* For master's, capstone; for doctorate, thesis/dissertation, qualifying exam. *Entrance requirements:* For master's, baccalaureate degree; minimum foundation GPA of 2.5; interview; for doctorate, master's degree; interview; supervised writing sample. Additional exam requirements/recommendations for international students: Required—TOEFL (minimum score 560 paper-based; 83 iBT). *Application deadline:* Applications are processed on a rolling basis. Application fee: $20. Electronic applications accepted. *Expenses: Tuition:* Part-time $815 per credit hour. *Required fees:* $86 per credit hour. One-time fee: $40 part-time. Tuition and fees vary according to degree level and program. *Financial support:* In 2013–14, 5 research assistantships were awarded; Federal Work-Study and scholarships/grants also available. Financial award applicants required to submit FAFSA. *Unit head:* Dr. Denise Staudt, Dean, Dreeben School of Education, 210-829-2762, E-mail: staudt@uiwtx.edu. *Application contact:* Andrea Cyterski-Acosta, Dean of Enrollment, 210-829-6005, Fax: 210-829-3921, E-mail: admis@uiwtx.edu.
Website: http://www.uiw.edu/education/index.htm.

University of the Pacific, Gladys L. Benerd School of Education, Department of Educational Administration and Leadership, Stockton, CA 95211-0197. Offers educational administration (MA, Ed D). *Accreditation:* NCATE. *Faculty:* 4 full-time (2 women). *Students:* 45 full-time (25 women), 62 part-time (39 women); includes 43 minority (13 Black or African American, non-Hispanic/Latino; 8 Asian, non-Hispanic/Latino; 14 Hispanic/Latino; 8 Two or more races, non-Hispanic/Latino), 4 international. Average age 35. 67 applicants, 69% accepted, 27 enrolled. In 2013, 21 master's, 17 doctorates awarded. *Degree requirements:* For master's, thesis (for some programs); for doctorate, thesis/dissertation. *Entrance requirements:* For master's and doctorate, GRE General Test, GRE Subject Test. Additional exam requirements/recommendations for international students: Required—TOEFL (minimum score 475 paper-based). *Application deadline:* For fall admission, 3/1 priority date for domestic students; for spring admission, 10/1 priority date for domestic students. Applications are processed on a rolling basis. Application fee: $75. *Financial support:* In 2013–14, 1 teaching assistantship was awarded. Financial award application deadline: 3/1; financial award applicants required to submit FAFSA. *Unit head:* Dr. Linda Skrla, Chairperson, 209-946-2580, E-mail: lskrla@pacific.edu. *Application contact:* Office of Graduate Admissions, 209-946-2344.

University of the Southwest, Graduate Programs, Hobbs, NM 88240-9129. Offers business administration (MBA); curriculum and instruction (MSE); curriculum and instruction: bilingual (MSE); curriculum and instruction: TESOL (MSE); early childhood education (MSE); educational administration (MSE); mental health counseling (MSE); school counseling (MSE); special education (MSE); sports management (MBA). Part-time and evening/weekend programs available. Postbaccalaureate distance learning degree programs offered (no on-campus study). *Degree requirements:* For master's, comprehensive exam, thesis (for some programs). *Entrance requirements:* Additional exam requirements/recommendations for international students: Recommended—TOEFL. Electronic applications accepted.

The University of Toledo, College of Graduate Studies, Judith Herb College of Education, Department of Educational Foundations and Leadership, Toledo, OH 43606-3390. Offers educational administration and supervision (ME, DE, Ed S); educational psychology (ME, PhD); educational research and measurement (ME, PhD); educational sociology (PhD); educational theory and social foundations (ME); foundations of education (DE, PhD); history of education (PhD); philosophy of education (PhD). *Accreditation:* NCATE. Part-time and evening/weekend programs available. *Faculty:* 33. *Students:* 15 full-time (9 women), 84 part-time (57 women); includes 28 minority (21 Black or African American, non-Hispanic/Latino; 1 Asian, non-Hispanic/Latino; 5 Hispanic/Latino; 1 Two or more races, non-Hispanic/Latino), 2 international. Average age 42. 16 applicants, 63% accepted, 7 enrolled. In 2013, 16 master's, 4 doctorates awarded. *Degree requirements:* For master's, comprehensive exam, thesis or alternative; for doctorate, comprehensive exam, thesis/dissertation; for Ed S, thesis optional. *Entrance requirements:* For master's, doctorate, and Ed S, minimum cumulative GPA of 2.7 for all previous academic work, letters of recommendation. Additional exam requirements/recommendations for international students: Required—TOEFL (minimum score 550 paper-based; 80 iBT). *Application deadline:* For fall admission, 1/15 priority date for domestic and international students. Applications are processed on a rolling basis. Application fee: $45 ($75 for international students). Electronic applications accepted. *Financial support:* In 2013–14, 2 research assistantships with full and partial tuition reimbursements (averaging $7,500 per year), 2 teaching assistantships with full and partial tuition reimbursements (averaging $9,000 per year) were awarded; career-related internships or fieldwork, Federal Work-Study, institutionally sponsored loans, scholarships/grants, tuition waivers (full and partial), unspecified assistantships, and administrative assistantships also available. Support available to part-time students. Financial award applicants required to submit FAFSA. *Unit head:* Dr. Richard Welsch, Interim Chair, 419-530-2565, Fax: 419-530-8447, E-mail: richard.welsch@utoledo.edu. *Application contact:* Graduate School Office, 419-530-4723, Fax: 419-530-4724, E-mail: grdsch@utnet.utoledo.edu.
Website: http://www.utoledo.edu/eduhshs/.

University of Utah, Graduate School, College of Education, Department of Educational Leadership and Policy, Salt Lake City, UT 84112. Offers educational leadership and policy (Ed D, PhD); K-12 administrative licensure (M Ed); K-12 teacher instructional leadership (M Ed); student affairs (M Ed); MPA/PhD. Part-time and evening/weekend programs available. *Faculty:* 10 full-time (7 women), 4 part-time/adjunct (3 women). *Students:* 55 full-time (38 women), 65 part-time (40 women); includes 33 minority (5 Black or African American, non-Hispanic/Latino; 1 American Indian or Alaska Native, non-Hispanic/Latino; 3 Asian, non-Hispanic/Latino; 21 Hispanic/Latino; 3 Two or more races, non-Hispanic/Latino), 3 international. Average age 35. 123 applicants, 45% accepted, 51 enrolled. In 2013, 33 master's, 5 doctorates awarded. *Degree requirements:* For master's, comprehensive exam (for some programs), internship; for doctorate, thesis/dissertation, qualifying exam. *Entrance requirements:* For master's, minimum undergraduate GPA of 3.0, valid bachelor's degree, 3 years' teaching or leadership experience, Level 1 or 2 UT educator's license (for K-12 programs only); for doctorate, GRE General Test (taken with five years of applying), minimum undergraduate GPA of 3.0, valid master's degree. Additional exam requirements/recommendations for international students: Required—TOEFL (minimum score 500 paper-based). *Application deadline:* For fall and winter admission, 2/1 for domestic and international students; for summer admission, 1/15 for domestic and international students. Application fee: $55 ($65 for international students). Electronic applications accepted. *Expenses:* Tuition, state resident: full-time $5259. Tuition, nonresident: full-time $18,569. *Required fees:* $841. Tuition and fees vary according to course load. *Financial support:* In 2013–14, 86 students received support, including 7 fellowships (averaging $2,000 per year), research assistantships with full tuition reimbursements available (averaging $13,000 per year), 86 teaching assistantships with full tuition reimbursements available (averaging $13,000 per year); career-related internships or fieldwork, scholarships/grants, health care benefits, and unspecified assistantships also available. Financial award application deadline: 2/1. *Faculty research:* Education accountability, college student diversity, K-12 educational administration and school leadership, student affairs, higher education. *Total annual research expenditures:* $55,000. *Unit head:* Dr. Andrea Rorrer, Chair, 801-581-4207, Fax: 801-585-6756, E-mail: andrea.rorrer@utah.edu. *Application contact:* Marilynn S. Howard, Academic Coordinator, 801-581-6714, Fax: 801-585-6756, E-mail: marilynn.howard@utah.edu.
Website: http://elp.utah.edu/.

University of Vermont, Graduate College, College of Education and Social Services, Department of Leadership and Developmental Sciences, Program in Educational Leadership, Burlington, VT 05405. Offers M Ed. *Accreditation:* NCATE. *Students:* 19 (9 women); includes 2 minority (both Black or African American, non-Hispanic/Latino). 26 applicants, 77% accepted, 7 enrolled. In 2013, 9 master's awarded. *Degree requirements:* For master's, thesis or alternative. *Entrance requirements:* Additional exam requirements/recommendations for international students: Required—TOEFL (minimum score 550 paper-based; 80 iBT). *Application deadline:* For fall admission, 4/1 priority date for domestic students, 4/1 for international students; for spring admission, 11/15 priority date for domestic students, 11/15 for international students. Application fee: $65. Electronic applications accepted. *Financial support:* Research assistantships, teaching assistantships, and career-related internships or fieldwork available. Financial award application deadline: 3/1. *Unit head:* Dr. Deborah Hunter, Chairperson, 802-656-2030. *Application contact:* Dr. Kieran Killeen, Coordinator, 802-656-2936.

University of Vermont, Graduate College, College of Education and Social Services, Department of Leadership and Developmental Sciences, Program in Educational Leadership and Policy Studies, Burlington, VT 05405. Offers Ed D, PhD. *Accreditation:* NCATE. *Students:* 53 (30 women); includes 9 minority (2 Black or African American, non-Hispanic/Latino; 1 American Indian or Alaska Native, non-Hispanic/Latino; 6 Hispanic/Latino), 2 international. 34 applicants, 59% accepted, 16 enrolled. In 2013, 11 doctorates awarded. *Degree requirements:* For doctorate, thesis/dissertation. *Entrance requirements:* For doctorate, GRE, resume (for Ed D), writing sample. Additional exam requirements/recommendations for international students: Required—TOEFL (minimum score 550 paper-based; 80 iBT). *Application deadline:* For fall admission, 1/6 priority date for domestic students, 1/6 for international students. Application fee: $65. Electronic applications accepted. *Financial support:* Research assistantships and teaching assistantships available. *Unit head:* Prof. Cynthia Gerstl-Pepin, PhD Director and Coordinator, 802-656-2936. *Application contact:* Prof. Judith Aiken, Ed D Coordinator, 802-656-2936.

University of Vermont, Graduate College, College of Education and Social Services, Department of Leadership and Developmental Sciences, Program in Higher Education and Student Affairs Administration, Burlington, VT 05405. Offers M Ed. *Accreditation:* NCATE. *Students:* 32 (19 women); includes 11 minority (4 Black or African American, non-Hispanic/Latino; 2 Asian, non-Hispanic/Latino; 4 Hispanic/Latino; 1 Two or more races, non-Hispanic/Latino), 1 international. 189 applicants, 23% accepted, 17 enrolled. In 2013, 16 master's awarded. *Degree requirements:* For master's, thesis or alternative. *Entrance requirements:* For master's, resume. Additional exam requirements/recommendations for international students: Required—TOEFL (minimum score 550 paper-based; 80 iBT). *Application deadline:* For fall admission, 12/15 for domestic and international students. Applications are processed on a rolling basis. Application fee: $65. Electronic applications accepted. *Financial support:* Application deadline: 1/1. *Unit head:* Prof. Kathleen Manning, Director, 802-656-2030.

University of Victoria, Faculty of Graduate Studies, Faculty of Education, Department of Educational Psychology and Leadership Studies, Victoria, BC V8W 2Y2, Canada. Offers aboriginal communities counseling (M Ed); counseling (M Ed, MA); educational psychology (M Ed, MA, PhD), including counseling psychology (M Ed, MA), leadership studies (PhD), learning and development (MA, PhD), measurement and evaluation, special education (M Ed, MA); leadership studies (M Ed, MA). Part-time programs available. *Degree requirements:* For master's, thesis (for some programs), comprehensive exam (M Ed); for doctorate, comprehensive exam, thesis/dissertation, candidacy exam. *Entrance requirements:* For master's, 2 years of work experience in a relevant field; for doctorate, GRE, 2 years of work experience in a relevant field, minimum B average. Additional exam requirements/recommendations for international students: Required—TOEFL (minimum score 575 paper-based), IELTS (minimum score 7). *Faculty research:* Learning and development (child, adolescent and adult), special education and exceptional children.

University of Virginia, Curry School of Education, Department of Leadership, Foundations and Policy, Program in Administration and Supervision, Charlottesville, VA 22903. Offers M Ed, Ed D, Ed S. *Students:* 2 full-time (1 woman), 23 part-time (17 women); includes 1 minority (Asian, non-Hispanic/Latino). Average age 38. 20 applicants, 75% accepted, 13 enrolled. In 2013, 24 master's, 9 doctorates, 37 other advanced degrees awarded. *Entrance requirements:* For master's, doctorate, and Ed S, GRE General Test, letters of recommendation. *Application deadline:* Applications are processed on a rolling basis. Application fee: $60. Electronic applications accepted. *Expenses:* Tuition, state resident: part-time $334 per credit hour. Tuition, nonresident: part-time $1224 per credit hour. *Financial support:* Fellowships, research assistantships, and teaching assistantships available. Financial award applicants required to submit FAFSA. *Unit head:* Pam Tucker, Program Coordinator, 434-924-7846, E-mail: pdtucker@virginia.edu. *Application contact:* Lisa Miller, Assistant to the Chair, 434-982-2849, E-mail: lam3v@virginia.edu.
Website: http://curry.virginia.edu/academics/areas-of-study/administration-supervision.

University of Virginia, Curry School of Education, Program in Education, Charlottesville, VA 22903. Offers administration and supervision (PhD); applied developmental science (PhD); counselor education (PhD); curriculum and instruction (PhD); early childhood special education (MT); education evaluation (PhD); educational psychology (PhD); educational research (PhD); elementary education (MT); English education (MT, PhD); foreign language education (MT); higher education (PhD); instructional technology (PhD); kinesiology (MT, PhD); math education (PhD); reading education (PhD); research, statistics and evaluation (PhD); school psychology (PhD); science education (PhD); social studies education (MT, PhD); special education (PhD); world languages education (MT). *Students:* 474 full-time (379 women), 35 part-time (19 women); includes 89 minority (30 Black or African American, non-Hispanic/Latino; 1 American Indian or Alaska Native, non-Hispanic/Latino; 26 Asian, non-Hispanic/Latino; 19 Hispanic/Latino; 13 Two or more races, non-Hispanic/Latino), 21 international. Average age 26. 312 applicants, 49% accepted, 80 enrolled. In 2013, 137 master's, 38 doctorates awarded. *Degree requirements:* For master's, comprehensive exam (for

some programs), field project; for doctorate, comprehensive exam, thesis/dissertation. *Entrance requirements:* For doctorate, GRE General Test. Additional exam requirements/recommendations for international students: Required—TOEFL (minimum score 600 paper-based; 90 iBT), IELTS (minimum score 7). *Application deadline:* Applications are processed on a rolling basis. Application fee: $60. Electronic applications accepted. *Expenses:* Tuition, state resident: part-time $334 per credit hour. Tuition, nonresident: part-time $1224 per credit hour. *Financial support:* Fellowships, research assistantships, and teaching assistantships available. Financial award application deadline: 1/5; financial award applicants required to submit FAFSA. *Unit head:* Robert C. Pianta, Dean, 434-924-3334, E-mail: pianta@virginia.edu. *Application contact:* Office of Admissions and Student Services, 434-924-0742, E-mail: curry-admissions@virginia.edu.
Website: http://curry.virginia.edu/teacher-education.

University of Washington, Graduate School, College of Education, Seattle, WA 98195. Offers curriculum and instruction (M Ed, Ed D, PhD), including educational technology, general curriculum (Ed D, PhD), language, literacy, and culture, mathematics education, multicultural education, reading and language arts education (Ed D), science education, social studies education, teaching and curriculum (M Ed); educational leadership and policy studies (M Ed, Ed D, PhD), including administration (Ed D), educational policy, organization, and leadership (M Ed, PhD), higher education, leadership for learning (Ed D), social and cultural foundations of education (M Ed, PhD); educational psychology (M Ed, PhD), including educational psychology (PhD), human development and cognition (M Ed), learning sciences, measurement, statistics and research design (M Ed), school psychology (M Ed); instructional leadership (M Ed); intercollegiate athletic leadership (M Ed); special education (M Ed, Ed D, PhD), including early childhood special education (M Ed), emotional and behavioral disabilities (M Ed), learning disabilities (M Ed), low-incidence disabilities (M Ed), severe disabilities (M Ed), special education (Ed D, PhD); teacher education (MIT). *Accreditation:* APA. Part-time and evening/weekend programs available. *Degree requirements:* For master's, thesis optional; for doctorate, thesis/dissertation. *Entrance requirements:* For master's and doctorate, GRE General Test, minimum GPA of 3.0. Additional exam requirements/recommendations for international students: Required—TOEFL. Electronic applications accepted. *Faculty research:* School restructuring/effective schools, special education interventions, literacy and writing, technology, school partnerships, teacher preparation.

University of Washington, Bothell, Program in Education, Bothell, WA 98011-8246. Offers education (M Ed); leadership development for educators (M Ed); secondary/middle level endorsement (M Ed). Part-time and evening/weekend programs available. *Degree requirements:* For master's, thesis. *Entrance requirements:* Additional exam requirements/recommendations for international students: Required—TOEFL. Electronic applications accepted. *Faculty research:* Multicultural education in citizenship education, intercultural education, knowledge and practice in the principalship, educational public policy, national board certification for teachers, teacher learning in literacy, technology and its impact on teaching and learning of mathematics, reading assessments, professional development in literacy education and mobility, digital media, education and class.

University of Washington, Tacoma, Graduate Programs, Program in Education, Tacoma, WA 98402-3100. Offers education (M Ed); educational administration (principal or program administrator certification) (M Ed); elementary education teacher certification (M Ed); elementary education/special education teacher certification (M Ed); secondary science or math teacher certification (M Ed). Part-time and evening/weekend programs available. *Degree requirements:* For master's, culminating project. *Entrance requirements:* For master's, WEST-B, WEST-E (teacher certification programs only), official sealed transcript from every college/university attended, personal goal statement, letters of recommendation, copy of valid teaching certificate. Additional exam requirements/recommendations for international students: Required—TOEFL (minimum score 580 paper-based; 92 iBT). Electronic applications accepted. *Faculty research:* Global learning communities for English/Chinese languages, evaluation of mathematics and reading intervention programs, response to intervention, school-wide behavioral and emotional support, mathematics education and culturally responsive mathematics education.

The University of West Alabama, School of Graduate Studies, College of Education, Departments of Instructional Leadership and Support/Curriculum and Instruction, Program in Instructional Leadership, Livingston, AL 35470. Offers instructional leadership (M Ed, Ed S); teacher leader (Ed S). *Accreditation:* NCATE. Part-time and evening/weekend programs available. Postbaccalaureate distance learning degree programs offered (no on-campus study). *Faculty:* 2 full-time (both women), 14 part-time/adjunct (8 women). *Students:* 128 (84 women); includes 78 minority (77 Black or African American, non-Hispanic/Latino; 1 American Indian or Alaska Native, non-Hispanic/Latino). 43 applicants, 93% accepted, 33 enrolled. In 2013, 25 master's, 60 Ed Ss awarded. *Degree requirements:* For master's, comprehensive exam, thesis optional. *Entrance requirements:* For master's, GRE General Test, MAT, minimum GPA of 2.75. Additional exam requirements/recommendations for international students: Required—TOEFL (minimum score 500 paper-based; 61 iBT). *Application deadline:* For fall admission, 8/12 priority date for domestic students; for spring admission, 3/24 for domestic students. Applications are processed on a rolling basis. Application fee: $25 ($50 for international students). Electronic applications accepted. Tuition and fees vary according to course load. *Financial support:* Teaching assistantships, career-related internships or fieldwork, Federal Work-Study, scholarships/grants, and unspecified assistantships available. Support available to part-time students. Financial award application deadline: 3/1; financial award applicants required to submit FAFSA. *Unit head:* Dr. Reenay Rogers, Chair of Instructional Leadership and Support, 205-652-5423, Fax: 205-652-3706, E-mail: rrogers@uwa.edu. *Application contact:* Dr. Kathy Chandler, Dean of Graduate Studies, 205-652-3421, Fax: 205-652-3706, E-mail: kchandler@uwa.edu.
Website: http://www.uwa.edu/medinstructionalleadership.aspx.

University of West Florida, College of Professional Studies, Department of Applied Science, Technology and Administration, Program in Educational Leadership - ETMS, Pensacola, FL 32514-5750. Offers education and training management (M Ed). Part-time and evening/weekend programs available. Postbaccalaureate distance learning degree programs offered (no on-campus study). *Entrance requirements:* For master's, GRE, minimum undergraduate GPA of 3.0.

University of West Florida, College of Professional Studies, Department of Applied Science, Technology and Administration, Program in Instructional Technology, Pensacola, FL 32514-5750. Offers educational leadership (M Ed); instructional technology (M Ed). *Entrance requirements:* For master's, MAT, GRE or GMAT, letter of intent, names of references. Additional exam requirements/recommendations for international students: Required—TOEFL (minimum score 550 paper-based). Electronic applications accepted.

University of West Florida, College of Professional Studies, Department of Research and Advanced Studies, Pensacola, FL 32514-5750. Offers administration (MSA), including acquisition and contract administration, biomedical/pharmaceutical, criminal justice administration, database administration, education leadership, healthcare administration, human performance technology, leadership, nursing administration, public administration, software engineering and administration; college student personnel administration (M Ed), including college personnel administration, guidance and counseling; curriculum and instruction (M Ed, Ed S); educational leadership (M Ed); middle and secondary level education and ESOL (M Ed). Part-time and evening/weekend programs available. *Entrance requirements:* For master's, GRE or MAT, official transcripts; minimum undergraduate GPA of 3.0; letter of intent; three letters of recommendation; resume. Additional exam requirements/recommendations for international students: Required—TOEFL (minimum score 550 paper-based).

University of West Florida, College of Professional Studies, Ed D Programs, Specialization in Curriculum and Instruction: Administrative Studies, Pensacola, FL 32514-5750. Offers Ed D. *Degree requirements:* For doctorate, comprehensive exam, thesis/dissertation. *Entrance requirements:* For doctorate, GRE, MAT, or GMAT, letter of intent; writing sample; three letters of recommendation; two completed disposition assessment forms; written statement of goals; interview with admissions committee. Additional exam requirements/recommendations for international students: Required—TOEFL (minimum score 550 paper-based).

University of West Florida, College of Professional Studies, School of Education, Program in Educational Leadership, Pensacola, FL 32514-5750. Offers M Ed. *Accreditation:* NCATE. Part-time and evening/weekend programs available. Postbaccalaureate distance learning degree programs offered (no on-campus study). *Degree requirements:* For master's, thesis optional. *Entrance requirements:* For master's, GRE General Test or minimum GPA of 3.0. Additional exam requirements/recommendations for international students: Required—TOEFL (minimum score 550 paper-based).

University of West Florida, College of Professional Studies, School of Education, Program in Educational Leadership Specialist, Pensacola, FL 32514-5750. Offers Ed S. Part-time and evening/weekend programs available. Postbaccalaureate distance learning degree programs offered (no on-campus study). *Entrance requirements:* Additional exam requirements/recommendations for international students: Required—TOEFL (minimum score 550 paper-based).

University of West Georgia, College of Education, Department of Leadership and Instruction, Carrollton, GA 30118. Offers M Ed, MAT, Ed S. *Accreditation:* NCATE. Part-time and evening/weekend programs available. *Faculty:* 13 full-time (6 women), 1 part-time/adjunct (0 women). *Students:* 105 full-time (73 women), 136 part-time (85 women); includes 93 minority (84 Black or African American, non-Hispanic/Latino; 7 Hispanic/Latino; 1 Native Hawaiian or other Pacific Islander, non-Hispanic/Latino; 1 Two or more races, non-Hispanic/Latino), 2 international. Average age 35. 116 applicants, 84% accepted, 40 enrolled. In 2013, 41 master's, 21 other advanced degrees awarded. *Degree requirements:* For master's, comprehensive exam, internship; for Ed S, comprehensive exam, research project. *Entrance requirements:* For master's, minimum GPA of 2.7; for Ed S, master's degree, minimum graduate GPA of 3.0, district appointment. Additional exam requirements/recommendations for international students: Required—TOEFL (minimum score 523 paper-based; 69 iBT); Recommended—IELTS (minimum score 6). *Application deadline:* For fall admission, 7/21 for domestic students, 6/1 for international students; for spring admission, 10/15 for domestic and international students. Applications are processed on a rolling basis. Application fee: $40. Electronic applications accepted. *Expenses:* Tuition, state resident: full-time $4600; part-time $192 per semester hour. Tuition, nonresident: full-time $17,880; part-time $745 per semester hour. *Required fees:* $1858; $46.34 per semester hour. $512 per semester. Tuition and fees vary according to course load, degree level, campus/location and program. *Financial support:* In 2013–14, 9 students received support, including 1 research assistantship with full tuition reimbursement available (averaging $7,444 per year); career-related internships or fieldwork, scholarships/grants, and unspecified assistantships also available. Support available to part-time students. Financial award application deadline: 4/1; financial award applicants required to submit FAFSA. *Faculty research:* Assessment of online instruction, teaching methodology, career development in sport management. *Total annual research expenditures:* $811,000. *Unit head:* Dr. Frank Butts, Chair, 678-839-6530, Fax: 678-839-6195, E-mail: fbutts@westga.edu. *Application contact:* Deanna Richards, Coordinator, Graduate Studies, 678-839-5946, E-mail: drichard@westga.edu.
Website: http://www.westga.edu/coelai.

University of Wisconsin–Madison, Graduate School, School of Education, Department of Educational Leadership and Policy Analysis, Madison, WI 53706-1380. Offers administration (Certificate); educational policy (MS, PhD); global higher education (MS). *Degree requirements:* For doctorate, thesis/dissertation. *Entrance requirements:* For master's and doctorate, GRE General Test. *Application deadline:* For fall admission, 1/15 for domestic and international students. Application fee: $56. Electronic applications accepted. *Expenses:* Tuition, state resident: full-time $10,728; part-time $790 per credit. Tuition, nonresident: full-time $24,054; part-time $1623 per credit. *Required fees:* $1130; $119 per credit. *Financial support:* Fellowships with full tuition reimbursements, research assistantships with full tuition reimbursements, teaching assistantships with full tuition reimbursements, and project assistantships available. *Unit head:* Dr. Eric Camburn, Chair, 608-262-3106, E-mail: elpa@education.wisc.edu. *Application contact:* 608-262-2433, Fax: 608-262-5134, E-mail: gradadmiss@mail.bascom.wisc.edu.
Website: http://www.education.wisc.edu/elpa.

University of Wisconsin–Milwaukee, Graduate School, School of Education, Department of Administrative Leadership, Milwaukee, WI 53201-0413. Offers administrative leadership and supervision in education (MS); specialist in administrative leadership (Certificate); teaching and learning in higher education (Certificate). Part-time programs available. *Faculty:* 9 full-time (6 women), 1 part-time/adjunct (0 women). *Students:* 27 full-time (22 women), 147 part-time (100 women); includes 43 minority (24 Black or African American, non-Hispanic/Latino; 1 American Indian or Alaska Native, non-Hispanic/Latino; 4 Asian, non-Hispanic/Latino; 5 Hispanic/Latino; 9 Two or more races, non-Hispanic/Latino), 2 international. Average age 34. 112 applicants, 72% accepted, 52 enrolled. In 2013, 52 master's awarded. *Degree requirements:* For master's, comprehensive exam, thesis or alternative. *Entrance requirements:* For master's, GRE General Test. Additional exam requirements/recommendations for international students: Required—TOEFL (minimum score 550 paper-based; 79 iBT), IELTS (minimum score 6.5). *Application deadline:* For fall admission, 1/1 priority date for domestic students; for spring admission, 9/1 for domestic students. Applications are processed on a rolling basis. Application fee: $56 ($96 for international students). Electronic applications accepted. *Financial support:* In 2013–14, 2 fellowships were awarded; research assistantships, teaching assistantships, career-related internships or fieldwork, health care benefits, unspecified assistantships, and project assistantships also available. Support available to part-time students. Financial award application deadline: 4/15; financial award applicants required to submit FAFSA. *Unit head:* Larry Martin, Department Chair, 414-229-5754, Fax: 414-229-5300, E-mail: lmartin@uwm.edu. *Application contact:* General Information Contact, 414-229-4982, Fax: 414-229-6967, E-mail: gradschool@uwm.edu.
Website: http://www.uwm.edu/Dept/Ad_Ldsp/.

University of Wisconsin–Milwaukee, Graduate School, School of Education, Urban Education Doctoral Program, Milwaukee, WI 53201-0413. Offers adult, continuing and

higher education leadership (PhD); curriculum and instruction (PhD); educational administration (PhD); exceptional education (PhD); multicultural studies (PhD); social foundations of education (PhD). *Students:* 51 full-time (37 women), 40 part-time (25 women); includes 32 minority (16 Black or African American, non-Hispanic/Latino; 1 American Indian or Alaska Native, non-Hispanic/Latino; 3 Asian, non-Hispanic/Latino; 5 Hispanic/Latino; 7 Two or more races, non-Hispanic/Latino), 3 international. Average age 41. 25 applicants, 44% accepted, 4 enrolled. In 2013, 11 doctorates awarded. *Degree requirements:* For doctorate, comprehensive exam, thesis/dissertation. *Entrance requirements:* For doctorate, GRE General Test, minimum undergraduate GPA of 2.85, graduate 3.5. Additional exam requirements/recommendations for international students: Required—TOEFL (minimum score 550 paper-based; 79 iBT), IELTS (minimum score 6.5). *Application deadline:* For fall admission, 1/1 priority date for domestic students; for spring admission, 9/1 for domestic students. Applications are processed on a rolling basis. Application fee: $56 ($96 for international students). Electronic applications accepted. *Financial support:* In 2013–14, 11 fellowships, 1 teaching assistantship were awarded; research assistantships, career-related internships or fieldwork, health care benefits, unspecified assistantships, and project assistantships also available. Support available to part-time students. Financial award application deadline: 4/15; financial award applicants required to submit FAFSA. *Unit head:* Raji Swaminathan, Representative, 414-229-6740, Fax: 414-229-2920, E-mail: swaminar@uwm.edu. *Application contact:* General Information Contact, 414-229-4982, Fax: 414-229-6967, E-mail: gradschool@uwm.edu.
Website: http://www4.uwm.edu/soe/academics/urban_ed/.

University of Wisconsin–Oshkosh, Graduate Studies, College of Education and Human Services, Department of Educational Leadership and Human Services, Oshkosh, WI 54901. Offers educational leadership (MS). Part-time and evening/weekend programs available. *Degree requirements:* For master's, comprehensive exam, thesis optional. *Entrance requirements:* For master's, bachelor's degree in education or related field. Additional exam requirements/recommendations for international students: Required—TOEFL (minimum score 550 paper-based; 79 iBT). Electronic applications accepted. *Faculty research:* Supervision models, learning styles, total quality management, cooperative learning, school choice.

University of Wisconsin–Stevens Point, College of Professional Studies, School of Education, Program in Educational Administration, Stevens Point, WI 54481-3897. Offers MSE. Program offered jointly with University of Wisconsin–Superior. *Degree requirements:* For master's, comprehensive exam, thesis or alternative.

University of Wisconsin–Superior, Graduate Division, Department of Educational Administration, Superior, WI 54880-4500. Offers MSE, Ed S. Programs offered jointly with University of Wisconsin - Eau Claire, University of Wisconsin - Stevens Point. Part-time and evening/weekend programs available. Postbaccalaureate distance learning degree programs offered (minimal on-campus study). *Faculty:* 4 full-time (1 woman). *Students:* 15 full-time (9 women), 2 part-time (0 women). Average age 39. 5 applicants, 60% accepted, 3 enrolled. In 2013, 11 master's awarded. *Degree requirements:* For master's, thesis or alternative, research project or position paper, written exam; for Ed S, thesis, internship, oral and written exams. *Entrance requirements:* For master's, GRE General Test or MAT, minimum GPA of 2.75, teaching license, 3 years of teaching experience; for Ed S, MAT, GRE, master's degree, 3 years of teaching experience, teaching license. *Application deadline:* For fall admission, 4/1 priority date for domestic students; for spring admission, 10/15 priority date for domestic students. Applications are processed on a rolling basis. Application fee: $45. *Expenses:* Tuition, state resident: full-time $4526; part-time $649.24 per credit. Tuition, nonresident: full-time $9091; part-time $1156.51 per credit. *Financial support:* Career-related internships or fieldwork, Federal Work-Study, institutionally sponsored loans, scholarships/grants, tuition waivers (partial), and unspecified assistantships available. Support available to part-time students. Financial award application deadline: 4/15; financial award applicants required to submit FAFSA. *Faculty research:* Postsecondary disabilities, educational partnerships, K-12. *Unit head:* Terri Kronzer, Chairperson, 715-394-8506, E-mail: tkronzer@uwsuper.edu. *Application contact:* Suzie Finckler, Program Assistant/Status Examiner, 715-394-8295, Fax: 715-394-8146, E-mail: gradstudy@uwsuper.edu.

University of Wisconsin–Whitewater, School of Graduate Studies, College of Business and Economics, Program in School Business Management, Whitewater, WI 53190-1790. Offers MSE. Part-time and evening/weekend programs available. Postbaccalaureate distance learning degree programs offered (no on-campus study). *Entrance requirements:* For master's, minimum GPA of 2.75. Additional exam requirements/recommendations for international students: Required—TOEFL (minimum score 550 paper-based; 80 iBT), IELTS (minimum score 6). Electronic applications accepted.

University of Wisconsin–Whitewater, School of Graduate Studies, College of Education and Professional Studies, Department of Curriculum and Instruction, Whitewater, WI 53190-1790. Offers professional development (MS), including bilingual education, challenging advanced learners, curriculum and instruction, educational leadership, health, human performance and recreation, health, physical education and coaching, information technologies and libraries, reading. *Accreditation:* NCATE. Part-time and evening/weekend programs available. Postbaccalaureate distance learning degree programs offered. *Degree requirements:* For master's, thesis or integrated project. *Entrance requirements:* Additional exam requirements/recommendations for international students: Required—TOEFL (minimum score 550 paper-based; 80 iBT), IELTS (minimum score 6). Electronic applications accepted. *Faculty research:* Hybrid of exercise physiology and psychology; gender equity; education, pedagogy, and technology; comprehensive school health education.

University of Wyoming, College of Education, Programs in Educational Leadership, Laramie, WY 82071. Offers MA, Ed D, Certificate. Part-time programs available. Postbaccalaureate distance learning degree programs offered (minimal on-campus study). *Degree requirements:* For master's, thesis; for doctorate, comprehensive exam, thesis/dissertation; for Certificate, comprehensive exam, thesis, residency. *Entrance requirements:* For master's and Certificate, GRE; for doctorate, MA, 3 years' teaching experience. Additional exam requirements/recommendations for international students: Required—TOEFL (minimum score 520 paper-based). *Faculty research:* School leadership, leadership preparation, leadership skills.

Upper Iowa University, Online Master's Programs, Fayette, IA 52142-1857. Offers accounting (MBA); corporate financial management (MBA); global business (MBA); health and human services (MPA); higher education administration (MHEA); homeland security (MPA); human resources management (MBA); justice administration (MPA); organizational development (MBA); public personnel management (MPA); quality management (MBA). MBA also available at Madison, WI campus. Part-time programs available. Postbaccalaureate distance learning degree programs offered (no on-campus study). *Degree requirements:* For master's, research project. *Entrance requirements:* For master's, GMAT, GRE, or minimum GPA of 2.7 during last 60 hours. Additional exam requirements/recommendations for international students: Required—TOEFL (minimum score 570 paper-based). Electronic applications accepted. *Faculty research:* Total quality management, CQI, teams, organization culture and climate, management.

Ursuline College, School of Graduate Studies, Program in Educational Administration, Pepper Pike, OH 44124-4398. Offers MA. Part-time programs available. *Faculty:* 2 full-time (1 woman), 6 part-time/adjunct (3 women). *Students:* 6 full-time (4 women), 72 part-time (48 women); includes 18 minority (all Black or African American, non-Hispanic/Latino). Average age 37. 16 applicants, 94% accepted, 13 enrolled. In 2013, 18 master's awarded. *Degree requirements:* For master's, thesis or alternative. *Entrance requirements:* For master's, minimum undergraduate GPA of 3.0, teaching certificate, professional experience. Additional exam requirements/recommendations for international students: Required—TOEFL (minimum score 500 paper-based). *Application deadline:* For fall admission, 8/1 priority date for domestic students. Applications are processed on a rolling basis. Application fee: $25. *Expenses:* Contact institution. *Financial support:* In 2013–14, 13 students received support. Federal Work-Study available. Financial award application deadline: 3/1; financial award applicants required to submit FAFSA. *Unit head:* Martin Kane, Director, 440-646-8148, Fax: 440-646-8328, E-mail: mkane@ursuline.edu. *Application contact:* Stephanie Pratt, Graduate Admission Coordinator, 440-646-8119, Fax: 440-684-6138, E-mail: graduateadmissions@ursuline.edu.

Valdosta State University, Program in Educational Leadership, Valdosta, GA 31698. Offers higher education (M Ed); information technology (M Ed, Ed S); leadership (M Ed, Ed D, Ed S). *Accreditation:* NCATE. *Faculty:* 15 full-time (6 women). *Students:* 70 full-time (36 women), 94 part-time (64 women); includes 44 minority (37 Black or African American, non-Hispanic/Latino; 1 American Indian or Alaska Native, non-Hispanic/Latino; 2 Hispanic/Latino; 4 Two or more races, non-Hispanic/Latino), 4 international. Average age 28. 80 applicants, 94% accepted, 69 enrolled. In 2013, 36 master's, 17 doctorates awarded. *Degree requirements:* For master's, thesis (for some programs), comprehensive written and/or oral exams; for doctorate, thesis/dissertation, comprehensive written and/or oral exams; for Ed S, thesis. *Entrance requirements:* For master's and Ed S, GRE General Test or MAT; for doctorate, GRE General Test, minimum GPA of 3.5. Additional exam requirements/recommendations for international students: Required—TOEFL (minimum score 523 paper-based). *Application deadline:* For fall admission, 7/1 for domestic and international students; for spring admission, 11/15 for domestic and international students. Applications are processed on a rolling basis. Application fee: $35. Electronic applications accepted. *Expenses:* Tuition, state resident: full-time $4140; part-time $230 per credit hour. Tuition, nonresident: full-time $14,904; part-time $828 per credit hour. *Required fees:* $995 per semester. Tuition and fees vary according to course load. *Financial support:* In 2013–14, 3 students received support, including 4 research assistantships with full tuition reimbursements available (averaging $3,652 per year); institutionally sponsored loans, scholarships/grants, and unspecified assistantships also available. Support available to part-time students. Financial award application deadline: 7/1; financial award applicants required to submit FAFSA. *Faculty research:* Mentoring in higher education, contemporary issues in higher education. *Unit head:* Dr. Leon Pate, Interim Department Head, 229-333-5633, E-mail: jlpate@valdosta.edu. *Application contact:* Rebecca Petrella, Coordinator of Graduate Programs, 229-333-5694, Fax: 229-245-3853, E-mail: rlwaters@valdosta.edu.
Website: http://www.valdosta.edu/academics/graduate-school/our-programs/leadership.php.

Valparaiso University, Graduate School, Department of Education, Program in Instructional Leadership, Valparaiso, IN 46383. Offers M Ed. Part-time and evening/weekend programs available. Postbaccalaureate distance learning degree programs offered (minimal on-campus study). *Students:* 3 part-time (all women). Average age 27. *Degree requirements:* For master's, research project. *Entrance requirements:* For master's, valid teaching license, minimum undergraduate GPA of 3.0, two letters of recommendation. Additional exam requirements/recommendations for international students: Required—TOEFL (minimum score 550 paper-based; 80 iBT), IELTS (minimum score 6). *Application deadline:* Applications are processed on a rolling basis. Application fee: $30 ($50 for international students). Electronic applications accepted. *Expenses: Tuition:* Full-time $10,350; part-time $575 per credit hour. *Required fees:* $378; $101 per term. Tuition and fees vary according to course load and program. *Financial support:* Available to part-time students. Applicants required to submit FAFSA. *Unit head:* Dr. Jon Kilpinen, Acting Chair, Department of Education, 219-464-5314, Fax: 219-464-6720. *Application contact:* Jessica Choquette, Graduate Admissions Specialist, 219-464-5313, Fax: 219-464-5381, E-mail: jessica.choquette@valpo.edu.
Website: http://www.valpo.edu/grad/ed/instldrshp.php.

Vanderbilt University, Graduate School, Program in Leadership and Policy Studies, Nashville, TN 37240-1001. Offers MS, PhD. *Faculty:* 18 full-time (5 women), 3 part-time/adjunct (1 woman). *Students:* 36 full-time (18 women); includes 9 minority (3 Black or African American, non-Hispanic/Latino; 1 Asian, non-Hispanic/Latino; 4 Hispanic/Latino; 1 Two or more races, non-Hispanic/Latino), 5 international. Average age 31. 128 applicants, 7% accepted, 7 enrolled. In 2013, 1 master's, 6 doctorates awarded. *Degree requirements:* For doctorate, comprehensive exam, thesis/dissertation. *Entrance requirements:* For doctorate, GRE General Test. Additional exam requirements/recommendations for international students: Required—TOEFL (minimum score 570 paper-based; 88 iBT). *Application deadline:* For fall admission, 12/31 for domestic and international students. Electronic applications accepted. *Financial support:* Fellowships with full and partial tuition reimbursements, research assistantships with full tuition reimbursements, teaching assistantships with full tuition reimbursements, Federal Work-Study, institutionally sponsored loans, scholarships/grants, traineeships, and health care benefits available. Financial award application deadline: 1/15; financial award applicants required to submit CSS PROFILE or FAFSA. *Unit head:* Dr. Ron Zimmer, Director of Graduate Studies, 615-322-0722, Fax: 615-343-7094, E-mail: ronald.w.zimmer@vanderbilt.edu. *Application contact:* Rosie Moody, Administrative Assistant, 615-322-8019, Fax: 615-343-7094, E-mail: rosie.moody@vanderbilt.edu.
Website: http://peabody.vanderbilt.edu/departments/lpo/graduate_and_professional_programs/phd/index.php.

Vanderbilt University, Peabody College, Department of Leadership, Policy, and Organizations, Nashville, TN 37240-1001. Offers education policy (MPP); educational leadership and policy (Ed D); higher education (M Ed); higher education, leadership and policy (Ed D); international education policy and management (M Ed); leadership and organizational performance (M Ed). Part-time and evening/weekend programs available. *Faculty:* 30 full-time (13 women), 13 part-time/adjunct (6 women). *Students:* 183 full-time (128 women), 92 part-time (49 women); includes 59 minority (32 Black or African American, non-Hispanic/Latino; 8 Asian, non-Hispanic/Latino; 14 Hispanic/Latino; 5 Two or more races, non-Hispanic/Latino), 21 international. Average age 28. 464 applicants, 62% accepted, 123 enrolled. In 2013, 91 master's, 24 doctorates awarded. *Degree requirements:* For master's, comprehensive exam, thesis optional; for doctorate, thesis/dissertation, qualifying exams, residency. *Entrance requirements:* For master's and doctorate, GRE General Test. Additional exam requirements/recommendations for international students: Required—TOEFL (minimum score 550 paper-based; 80 iBT). *Application deadline:* For fall admission, 12/31 priority date for domestic and international students; for spring admission, 11/1 priority date for domestic and international students. Applications are processed on a rolling basis. Application fee: $0. Electronic applications accepted. *Financial support:* Fellowships with full and partial tuition reimbursements, research assistantships with full and partial tuition reimbursements, teaching assistantships with full and partial tuition reimbursements,

Federal Work-Study, institutionally sponsored loans, scholarships/grants, tuition waivers (partial), and unspecified assistantships available. Support available to part-time students. Financial award application deadline: 1/15; financial award applicants required to submit FAFSA. *Faculty research:* Higher education, educational leadership, education policy, economics of education, education accountability, school choice. *Unit head:* Dr. Ellen B. Goldring, Chair, 615-322-8000, Fax: 615-343-7094, E-mail: ellen.b.goldring@vanderbilt.edu. *Application contact:* Rosie Moody, Educational Coordinator, 615-322-8019, Fax: 615-343-7094, E-mail: rosie.moody@vanderbilt.edu.

Villanova University, Graduate School of Liberal Arts and Sciences, Department of Education and Counseling, Program in Teacher Leadership, Villanova, PA 19085-1699. Offers MA. Part-time and evening/weekend programs available. *Students:* 6 full-time (all women), 6 part-time (1 woman); includes 3 minority (1 Black or African American, non-Hispanic/Latino; 1 Asian, non-Hispanic/Latino; 1 Two or more races, non-Hispanic/Latino). Average age 30. In 2013, 2 master's awarded. *Degree requirements:* For master's, comprehensive exam. *Entrance requirements:* For master's, GRE or MAT, minimum GPA of 3.0. Additional exam requirements/recommendations for international students: Required—TOEFL. *Application deadline:* Applications are processed on a rolling basis. Application fee: $50. Electronic applications accepted. *Financial support:* Career-related internships or fieldwork and Federal Work-Study available. Financial award applicants required to submit FAFSA. *Unit head:* Dr. Edward Fierros, Chairperson, 610-519-4625. *Application contact:* Dean, Graduate School of Liberal Arts and Sciences.

Virginia Commonwealth University, Graduate School, School of Education, Doctoral Program in Education, Educational Leadership Track, Richmond, VA 23284-9005. Offers PhD. *Entrance requirements:* For doctorate, GRE. Additional exam requirements/recommendations for international students: Required—TOEFL (minimum score 600 paper-based; 100 iBT). Electronic applications accepted.

Virginia Commonwealth University, Graduate School, School of Education, Doctoral Program in Education, Instructional Leadership Track, Richmond, VA 23284-9005. Offers PhD. *Entrance requirements:* For doctorate, GRE. Additional exam requirements/recommendations for international students: Required—TOEFL (minimum score 600 paper-based; 100 iBT). Electronic applications accepted.

Virginia Polytechnic Institute and State University, Graduate School, College of Liberal Arts and Human Sciences, Blacksburg, VA 24061. Offers career and technical education (MS Ed, Ed D, PhD, Ed S); communication (MA); counselor education (MA Ed, Ed D, PhD, Ed S); creative writing (MFA); curriculum and instruction (MA Ed, Ed D, PhD, Ed S); educational leadership and policy studies (MA Ed, Ed D, PhD, Ed S); educational research and evaluation (PhD); English (MA); foreign languages, cultures, and literatures (MA); higher education and student affairs (MA Ed); history (MA); human development (MS, PhD); material culture and public humanities (MA); philosophy (MA); political science (MA); rhetoric and writing (PhD); science and technology studies (MS, PhD); social, political, ethical, and cultural thought (PhD); sociology (MS, PhD); theater arts (MFA). *Faculty:* 410 full-time (211 women), 6 part-time/adjunct (5 women). *Students:* 688 full-time (464 women), 576 part-time (372 women); includes 243 minority (144 Black or African American, non-Hispanic/Latino; 3 American Indian or Alaska Native, non-Hispanic/Latino; 29 Asian, non-Hispanic/Latino; 48 Hispanic/Latino; 1 Native Hawaiian or other Pacific Islander, non-Hispanic/Latino; 18 Two or more races, non-Hispanic/Latino), 84 international. Average age 34. 1,054 applicants, 48% accepted, 374 enrolled. In 2013, 314 master's, 74 doctorates, 14 other advanced degrees awarded. *Degree requirements:* For master's, comprehensive exam (for some programs), thesis (for some programs); for doctorate, comprehensive exam (for some programs), thesis/dissertation (for some programs). *Entrance requirements:* For master's and doctorate, GRE/GMAT (may vary by department). Additional exam requirements/recommendations for international students: Required—TOEFL (minimum score 550 paper-based). *Application deadline:* For fall admission, 8/1 for domestic students, 4/1 for international students; for spring admission, 1/1 for domestic students, 9/1 for international students. Applications are processed on a rolling basis. Application fee: $75. Electronic applications accepted. *Expenses:* Tuition, state resident: full-time $11,185; part-time $621.50 per credit hour. Tuition, nonresident: full-time $22,146; part-time $1230.25 per credit hour. *Required fees:* $2442; $449.25 per semester. Tuition and fees vary according to course load, campus/location and program. *Financial support:* In 2013–14, 19 research assistantships with full tuition reimbursements (averaging $17,115 per year), 205 teaching assistantships with full tuition reimbursements (averaging $14,433 per year) were awarded. Financial award application deadline: 3/1; financial award applicants required to submit FAFSA. *Total annual research expenditures:* $6.8 million. *Unit head:* Joan Hirt, Interim Dean, 540-231-6779, Fax: 540-231-7157, E-mail: jbhirt@vt.edu. *Application contact:* Melissa Elliott, Executive Assistant, 540-231-6779, Fax: 540-231-7157, E-mail: elliott1@vt.edu.
Website: http://www.clahs.vt.edu/.

Virginia State University, School of Graduate Studies, Research, and Outreach, School of Liberal Arts and Education, Department of Graduate Professional Education Programs, Program in Educational Administration and Supervision, Petersburg, VA 23806-0001. Offers M Ed, MS. *Accreditation:* NCATE. *Degree requirements:* For master's, thesis optional.

Wagner College, Division of Graduate Studies, Department of Education, Program in Educational Leadership, Staten Island, NY 10301-4495. Offers educational leadership (Certificate); school building leader (MS Ed). Part-time and evening/weekend programs available. *Entrance requirements:* For master's, minimum GPA of 3.0, valid initial NY State Certificate or equivalent, interview, recommendations. Electronic applications accepted. *Expenses: Tuition:* Full-time $17,496; part-time $972 per credit. Tuition and fees vary according to course load.

Walden University, Graduate Programs, Richard W. Riley College of Education and Leadership, Minneapolis, MN 55401. *Accreditation:* NCATE. Part-time and evening/weekend programs available. Postbaccalaureate distance learning degree programs offered (minimal on-campus study). *Faculty:* 23 full-time (15 women), 830 part-time/adjunct (569 women). *Students:* 8,671 full-time (7,197 women), 2,122 part-time (1,735 women); includes 4,734 minority (3,802 Black or African American, non-Hispanic/Latino; 50 American Indian or Alaska Native, non-Hispanic/Latino; 136 Asian, non-Hispanic/Latino; 539 Hispanic/Latino; 35 Native Hawaiian or other Pacific Islander, non-Hispanic/Latino; 172 Two or more races, non-Hispanic/Latino), 73 international. Average age 40. 2,646 applicants, 96% accepted, 2074 enrolled. In 2013, 2,214 master's, 354 doctorates, 479 other advanced degrees awarded. *Degree requirements:* For doctorate, thesis/dissertation (for some programs), residency; for other advanced degree, residency (for some programs). *Entrance requirements:* For master's, bachelor's degree or higher; minimum GPA of 2.5; official transcripts; goal statement (for some programs); access to computer and Internet; for doctorate, master's degree or higher; three years of related professional or academic experience (preferred); minimum GPA of 3.0; goal statement and current resume (select programs); official transcripts; access to computer and Internet; for other advanced degree, relevant work experience; access to computer and Internet. Additional exam requirements/recommendations for international students: Required—TOEFL (minimum score 550 paper-based; 79 iBT), IELTS (minimum score 6.5), Michigan English Language Assessment Battery (minimum score 82), or PTE. *Application deadline:* Applications are processed on a rolling basis. Application fee: $0. Electronic applications accepted. *Expenses: Tuition:* Full-time $11,813.55; part-time $500 per credit. *Required fees:* $618.76. *Financial support:* In 2013–14, 1 fellowship was awarded; Federal Work-Study, scholarships/grants, unspecified assistantships, and family tuition reduction, active duty/veteran tuition reduction, group tuition reduction, interest-free payment plans, employee tuition reduction also available. Support available to part-time students. Financial award applicants required to submit FAFSA. *Unit head:* Dr. Kate Steffens, Dean, 800-925-3368. *Application contact:* Jennifer Hall, Vice President of Enrollment Management, 866-4-WALDEN, E-mail: info@waldenu.edu.
Website: http://www.waldenu.edu/colleges-schools/riley-college-of-education/.

Walla Walla University, Graduate School, School of Education and Psychology, College Place, WA 99324-1198. Offers counseling psychology (MA); curriculum and instruction (M Ed, MA, MAT); educational leadership (M Ed, MA, MAT); literacy instruction (M Ed, MA, MAT); students at risk (M Ed, MA, MAT); teaching (MAT). Part-time programs available. *Entrance requirements:* For master's, GRE General Test, minimum GPA of 2.75. Additional exam requirements/recommendations for international students: Required—TOEFL (minimum score 550 paper-based; 79 iBT). Electronic applications accepted. *Faculty research:* Admissions/retention, instructional psychology, moral development, teaching of reading.

Walsh University, Graduate Studies, Program in Education, North Canton, OH 44720-3396. Offers 21st-century technologies (MA Ed); leadership (MA Ed); reading literacy (MA Ed); traditional program (MA Ed). *Accreditation:* NCATE. Part-time and evening/weekend programs available. *Faculty:* 6 full-time (3 women), 10 part-time/adjunct (all women). *Students:* 13 full-time (10 women), 18 part-time (14 women), 1 international. Average age 32. 16 applicants, 100% accepted, 6 enrolled. In 2013, 46 master's awarded. *Degree requirements:* For master's, comprehensive exam (for some programs), thesis optional, action research project or comprehensive exam. *Entrance requirements:* For master's, MAT (minimum score 396) or GRE (minimum scores: verbal 145, quantitative 146, combined 291, writing 3.0), interview, minimum GPA of 3.0, writing sample, 3 recommendation forms, notarized affidavit of good moral character. Additional exam requirements/recommendations for international students: Required—TOEFL (minimum score 500 paper-based; 61 iBT). *Application deadline:* For fall admission, 7/15 priority date for domestic students. Applications are processed on a rolling basis. Application fee: $25. Electronic applications accepted. *Expenses: Tuition:* Full-time $10,890; part-time $605 per credit hour. *Required fees:* $100; $100. *Financial support:* In 2013–14, 41 students received support, including 3 research assistantships with partial tuition reimbursements available (averaging $12,355 per year), 5 teaching assistantships (averaging $4,734 per year); scholarships/grants, tuition waivers (partial), and unspecified assistantships also available. Support available to part-time students. Financial award application deadline: 12/31; financial award applicants required to submit FAFSA. *Faculty research:* Technology in education, strategies for working with children with special needs, reading literacy, whole brain teaching, hybrid learning, online teaching, global learning. *Unit head:* Dr. Gary Jacobs, Director, 330-490-7336, Fax: 330-490-7326, E-mail: gjacobs@walsh.edu. *Application contact:* Audra Dice, Graduate and Transfer Admissions Counselor, 330-490-7181, Fax: 330-244-4680, E-mail: adice@walsh.edu.

Washburn University, College of Arts and Sciences, Department of Education, Topeka, KS 66621. Offers curriculum and instruction (M Ed); educational leadership (M Ed); reading (M Ed); special education (M Ed). *Accreditation:* NCATE. Part-time programs available. *Faculty:* 7 full-time (5 women). *Students:* 32 part-time (21 women). Average age 33. In 2013, 9 master's awarded. *Degree requirements:* For master's, comprehensive exam, thesis or alternative, portfolio, comprehensive paper, or action research project. *Entrance requirements:* For master's, department exam, GRE General Test, or MAT, minimum GPA of 3.0 in graduate coursework or last 60 hours of undergraduate coursework. Additional exam requirements/recommendations for international students: Required—TOEFL (minimum score 80 iBT). *Application deadline:* For fall admission, 8/1 for domestic and international students; for spring admission, 11/1 for domestic and international students. Applications are processed on a rolling basis. *Expenses:* Tuition, state resident: full-time $5850; part-time $325 per credit hour. Tuition, nonresident: full-time $11,916; part-time $662 per credit hour. *Required fees:* $86; $43 per semester. Tuition and fees vary according to program. *Financial support:* Federal Work-Study, institutionally sponsored loans, and scholarships/grants available. Support available to part-time students. Financial award applicants required to submit FAFSA. *Faculty research:* Reading/literature/literacy, foundations, special education, diversity, teaching and technology. *Unit head:* Dr. Donna Lalonde, Interim Chairperson, 785-670-1943, Fax: 785-670-1046, E-mail: donna.lalonde@washburn.edu. *Application contact:* Tara Porter, Licensure Officer, 785-670-1434, Fax: 785-670-1046, E-mail: tara.porter@washburn.edu.
Website: http://www.washburn.edu/academics/college-schools/arts-sciences/departments/education.

Washington State University, Graduate School, College of Education, Department of Educational Leadership and Counseling Psychology, Program in Educational Leadership, Pullman, WA 99164. Offers Ed M, MA, Ed D, PhD. *Degree requirements:* For master's, comprehensive exam (for some programs), thesis (for some programs), oral or written exam; for doctorate, comprehensive exam, thesis/dissertation, written and oral exam. *Entrance requirements:* For master's and doctorate, GRE General Test, minimum GPA of 3.0, 3 letters of recommendation, transcripts showing all college or university course work, statement of professional objectives, current curriculum vitae/resume. Additional exam requirements/recommendations for international students: Recommended—TOEFL (minimum score 550 paper-based; 80 iBT). Electronic applications accepted. *Faculty research:* Leadership and organizations, school as community, moral leadership and ethics, international education and cross-national partnerships, leadership practices and processes as suffused with and constituted by emotion work.

Washington State University, Graduate School, College of Education, Department of Teaching and Learning, Program in Teacher Leadership, Pullman, WA 99164. Offers Ed D. *Degree requirements:* For doctorate, comprehensive exam, thesis/dissertation, oral and written exam. *Entrance requirements:* For doctorate, transcripts showing all college or university course work, statement of professional objectives, current curriculum vitae/resume, writing sample. Additional exam requirements/recommendations for international students: Required—TOEFL (minimum score 550 paper-based; 80 iBT). Electronic applications accepted. *Faculty research:* K-20 curriculum change for teachers and higher education faculty in high stakes contexts, looking for solutions to the problems of inequalities in schools and society.

Washington State University Spokane, Graduate Programs, Education Department, Spokane, WA 99210. Offers curriculum and instruction (Ed M); educational leadership (Ed M, MA); principal (Certificate); program administrator (Certificate); superintendent (Certificate); teaching (MIT), including elementary, secondary. *Degree requirements:* For master's, comprehensive exam (for some programs), thesis (for some programs). *Entrance requirements:* For master's, GRE or GMAT, minimum GPA of 3.0, 3 letters of recommendation, resume. Additional exam requirements/recommendations for international students: Required—TOEFL (minimum score 550 paper-based).

Washington State University Tri-Cities, Graduate Programs, Program in Education, Richland, WA 99352-1671. Offers educational leadership (Ed M, Ed D); literacy (Ed M);

secondary certification (Ed M); teaching (MIT). Part-time programs available. *Degree requirements:* For master's, comprehensive exam, thesis or alternative; for doctorate, comprehensive exam, thesis/dissertation. *Entrance requirements:* For master's, GRE, minimum GPA of 3.0, Working with Youth form, Character and Fitness form, 3 letters of recommendation. Additional exam requirements/recommendations for international students: Required—TOEFL. Electronic applications accepted. *Faculty research:* Multicultural counseling, socio-cultural influences in schools, diverse learners, teacher education, K-12 educational leadership.

Wayland Baptist University, Graduate Programs, Program in Education, Plainview, TX 79072-6998. Offers education administration (M Ed); education diagnostics (M Ed); education literacy (M Ed); elementary certification (M Ed); English (M Ed); English as a second language (M Ed); higher education administration (M Ed); human resources (M Ed); instructional leadership (M Ed); instructional technology (M Ed); science education (M Ed); secondary certification (M Ed); social studies (M Ed); special education (M Ed). Part-time and evening/weekend programs available. Postbaccalaureate distance learning degree programs offered (no on-campus study). *Faculty:* 33 full-time (17 women), 28 part-time/adjunct (17 women). *Students:* 22 full-time (15 women), 316 part-time (189 women); includes 130 minority (48 Black or African American, non-Hispanic/Latino; 3 American Indian or Alaska Native, non-Hispanic/Latino; 71 Hispanic/Latino; 1 Native Hawaiian or other Pacific Islander, non-Hispanic/Latino; 7 Two or more races, non-Hispanic/Latino). Average age 39. 80 applicants, 96% accepted, 44 enrolled. In 2013, 170 master's awarded. *Degree requirements:* For master's, comprehensive exam, capstone course. *Entrance requirements:* For master's, GRE, GMAT or MAT. Additional exam requirements/recommendations for international students: Required—TOEFL (minimum score 500 paper-based; 61 iBT). *Application deadline:* Applications are processed on a rolling basis. Application fee: $50. Electronic applications accepted. *Expenses: Tuition:* Full-time $8190; part-time $455 per credit hour. *Required fees:* $970; $455 per credit hour. $485 per semester. *Financial support:* Federal Work-Study, institutionally sponsored loans, and scholarships/grants available. Support available to part-time students. Financial award application deadline: 5/1; financial award applicants required to submit FAFSA. *Unit head:* Dr. Jim Todd, Chairman, 806-291-1045, Fax: 806-291-1951. *Application contact:* Amanda Stanton, Coordinator of Graduate Studies, 806-291-3423, Fax: 806-291-1950, E-mail: stanton@wbu.edu.

Waynesburg University, Graduate and Professional Studies, Canonsburg, PA 15370. Offers business (MBA), including energy management, finance, health systems, human resources, leadership, market development; counseling (MA), including addictions counseling, clinical mental health; education (M Ed, MAT), including autism (M Ed), curriculum and instruction (M Ed), educational leadership (M Ed), online teaching (M Ed); nursing (MSN), including administration, education, informatics; nursing practice (DNP); special education (M Ed); technology (M Ed); MSN/MBA. *Accreditation:* AACN. Part-time and evening/weekend programs available. *Faculty:* 11 full-time (5 women), 136 part-time/adjunct (80 women). *Students:* 146 full-time (99 women), 419 part-time (268 women). In 2013, 290 master's, 7 doctorates awarded. *Degree requirements:* For doctorate, thesis/dissertation. *Entrance requirements:* Additional exam requirements/recommendations for international students: Required—TOEFL. *Application deadline:* For fall admission, 8/1 priority date for domestic students. Applications are processed on a rolling basis. Electronic applications accepted. *Financial support:* Available to part-time students. Application deadline: 5/1. *Unit head:* David Mariner, Dean, 724-743-4420, Fax: 724-743-4425, E-mail: dmariner@waynesburg.edu. *Application contact:* Dr. Michael Bednarski, Director of Enrollment, 724-743-4420, Fax: 724-743-4425, E-mail: mbednars@waynesburg.edu.
Website: http://www.waynesburg.edu/.

Wayne State College, School of Education and Counseling, Department of Educational Foundations and Leadership, Program in Educational Administration, Wayne, NE 68787. Offers educational administration (Ed S); elementary administration (MSE); elementary and secondary administration (MSE); secondary administration (MSE). *Accreditation:* NCATE. Part-time and evening/weekend programs available. *Degree requirements:* For master's, comprehensive exam, thesis optional, research paper. *Entrance requirements:* For master's, GRE General Test, minimum GPA of 2.5; for Ed S, GRE General Test, minimum GPA of 3.2. Additional exam requirements/recommendations for international students: Required—TOEFL (minimum score 550 paper-based). Electronic applications accepted.

Wayne State University, College of Education, Division of Administrative and Organizational Studies, Detroit, MI 48202. Offers college and university teaching (Certificate); educational administration and supervision (Ed S); educational leadership (M Ed); educational leadership and policy studies (Ed D, PhD); educational technology (Certificate); instructional technology (M Ed, Ed D, PhD, Ed S); online teaching (Certificate); secondary curriculum and instruction (Ed S); special education administration (Ed S). Part-time programs available. Postbaccalaureate distance learning degree programs offered. *Students:* 96 full-time (68 women), 207 part-time (137 women); includes 133 minority (115 Black or African American, non-Hispanic/Latino; 4 American Indian or Alaska Native, non-Hispanic/Latino; 2 Asian, non-Hispanic/Latino; 8 Hispanic/Latino; 4 Two or more races, non-Hispanic/Latino), 14 international. Average age 39. 127 applicants, 50% accepted, 42 enrolled. In 2013, 47 master's, 15 doctorates, 41 other advanced degrees awarded. *Degree requirements:* For doctorate, thesis/dissertation. *Entrance requirements:* For master's, baccalaureate degree from accredited U.S. institution or equivalent from college or university of government-recognized standing; minimum undergraduate GPA of 2.75 in upper-division coursework; for doctorate, GRE or MAT, interview; autobiography or curriculum vitae; references; master's degree; minimum undergraduate GPA of 3.0, graduate 3.75; 3 years of relevant experience; foundational course work; for other advanced degree, master's degree from accredited institution, minimum upper-division GPA of 2.6 or 3.4 master's, fulfillment of the special requirements of the area of concentration, 3 years of teaching experience (except for instructional technology). Additional exam requirements/recommendations for international students: Required—TOEFL (minimum score 550 paper-based; 79 iBT), Michigan English Language Assessment Battery (minimum score 85); Recommended—IELTS (minimum score 6.5), TWE (minimum score 5.5). *Application deadline:* For fall admission, 6/1 priority date for domestic students, 5/1 priority date for international students; for winter admission, 10/1 priority date for domestic students, 9/1 priority date for international students; for spring admission, 2/1 priority date for domestic students, 1/1 priority date for international students. Applications are processed on a rolling basis. Application fee: $0. Electronic applications accepted. *Expenses: Tuition,* state resident: part-time $554.15 per credit. Tuition, nonresident: part-time $1200.35 per credit. *Required fees:* $42.15 per credit. $268.30 per semester. Tuition and fees vary according to course load and program. *Financial support:* In 2013–14, 48 students received support, including 3 fellowships with tuition reimbursements available (averaging $15,541 per year), 4 research assistantships with tuition reimbursements available (averaging $16,508 per year); career-related internships or fieldwork, Federal Work-Study, scholarships/grants, health care benefits, and unspecified assistantships also available. Support available to part-time students. Financial award application deadline: 3/31; financial award applicants required to submit FAFSA. *Faculty research:* Total quality management, participatory management, administering educational technology, school improvement, principalship.

Total annual research expenditures: $6,888. *Unit head:* Dr. William Hill, Assistant Dean, 313-577-9316, E-mail: william_e_hill@wayne.edu. *Application contact:* Janice Green, Assistant Dean, 313-577-1605, E-mail: jwgreen@wayne.edu.
Website: http://coe.wayne.edu/aos/index.php.

Webster University, School of Education, Department of Multidisciplinary Studies, St. Louis, MO 63119-3194. Offers education leadership (Ed S); educational technology (MAT); educational technology leadership (Ed S); mathematics (MA); multidisciplinary studies (MAT); school psychology (Ed S); school systems, superintendency and leadership (Ed S); social science (MAT); special education (MA). Part-time programs available. *Entrance requirements:* For master's, minimum GPA of 2.5. Additional exam requirements/recommendations for international students: Required—TOEFL. *Expenses: Tuition:* Full-time $11,610; part-time $645 per credit hour. Tuition and fees vary according to campus/location and program.

Western Carolina University, Graduate School, College of Education and Allied Professions, School of Teaching and Learning, Cullowhee, NC 28723. Offers community college and higher education (MA Ed), including community college administration, community college teaching; comprehensive education (MA Ed, MAT); educational leadership (MA Ed, MSA, Ed D, Ed S), including educational leadership (MSA, Ed D, Ed S), educational supervision (MA Ed); teaching (MA Ed, MAT), including comprehensive education (MA Ed), physical education (MA Ed), teaching (MAT). *Accreditation:* NCATE. Part-time and evening/weekend programs available. Postbaccalaureate distance learning degree programs offered. *Degree requirements:* For master's, comprehensive exam; for doctorate, comprehensive exam, thesis/dissertation. *Entrance requirements:* For master's, GRE, appropriate undergraduate degree, 3 letters of recommendation; for doctorate, GRE General Test, minimum graduate GPA of 3.5, appropriate master's degree; for other advanced degree, GRE General Test, minimum graduate GPA of 3.5, work experience, appropriate master's degree. Additional exam requirements/recommendations for international students: Required—TOEFL (minimum score 550 paper-based; 79 iBT). *Faculty research:* Educational leadership, special education, rural education, organizational theory and practice, interinstitutional partnership, program evaluation.

Western Connecticut State University, Division of Graduate Studies, School of Professional Studies, Department of Education and Educational Psychology, Program in Instructional Leadership, Danbury, CT 06810-6885. Offers Ed D. Part-time programs available. *Degree requirements:* For doctorate, comprehensive exam, thesis/dissertation, completion of program in 6 years. *Entrance requirements:* For doctorate, GRE or MAT, resume, three recommendations (one in a supervisory capacity in an educational setting), satisfactory interview with WCSU representatives from the EdD Admissions Committee. Additional exam requirements/recommendations for international students: Recommended—TOEFL (minimum score 550 paper-based; 79 iBT), IELTS (minimum score 6). *Expenses:* Contact institution. *Faculty research:* Differentiated instruction, the transition of teacher learning, teacher retention, relationship building through the evaluation process, leadership development.

Western Governors University, Teachers College, Salt Lake City, UT 84107. Offers curriculum and instruction (MS); educational leadership (MS); educational studies (MA); educational studies (5-12) (MA), including mathematics; elementary education (K-8) (MAT, Postbaccalaureate Certificate); elementary education (PreK-8) (MAT); English language learning (K-12) (MA); instructional design (MAT); learning and technology (M Ed, MA); management and innovation (M Ed); mathematics (5-12) (MAT, Postbaccalaureate Certificate); mathematics (5-9) (MAT, Postbaccalaureate Certificate); mathematics education (5-12) (MA); mathematics education (5-9) (MA); mathematics education (K-6) (MA); measurement and evaluation (M Ed); science (5-12) (Postbaccalaureate Certificate); science (5-9) (MAT, Postbaccalaureate Certificate); science education (5-12) (MA), including biology, chemistry, geology, physics; science education (5-9) (MA); social science (5-12) (MAT, Postbaccalaureate Certificate); special education (MAT, MS). *Accreditation:* NCATE. Evening/weekend programs available. Postbaccalaureate distance learning degree programs offered (no on-campus study). *Degree requirements:* For master's, capstone project. *Entrance requirements:* For master's and Postbaccalaureate Certificate, Readiness Assessment, transcripts. Additional exam requirements/recommendations for international students: Required—TOEFL (minimum score 450 paper-based; 80 iBT). Electronic applications accepted. *Expenses:* Contact institution.

Western Illinois University, School of Graduate Studies, College of Education and Human Services, Department of Educational Leadership, Macomb, IL 61455-1390. Offers MS Ed, Ed D, Ed S. *Accreditation:* NCATE. Part-time and evening/weekend programs available. *Students:* 3 full-time (2 women), 181 part-time (80 women); includes 16 minority (7 Black or African American, non-Hispanic/Latino; 9 Hispanic/Latino). Average age 38. 30 applicants, 73% accepted. In 2013, 80 master's, 3 doctorates, 12 other advanced degrees awarded. *Degree requirements:* For master's, thesis or alternative; for doctorate, comprehensive exam, thesis/dissertation, electronic portfolio. *Entrance requirements:* For master's and Ed S, interview; for doctorate, GRE General Test. Additional exam requirements/recommendations for international students: Required—TOEFL (minimum score 575 paper-based; 88 iBT). *Application deadline:* Applications are processed on a rolling basis. Application fee: $30. Electronic applications accepted. *Financial support:* Applicants required to submit FAFSA. *Unit head:* Dr. Gloria Delany-Barmann, Interim Chairperson, 309-298-1070. *Application contact:* Dr. Nancy Parsons, Associate Provost and Director of Graduate Studies, 309-298-1806, Fax: 309-298-2345, E-mail: grad-office@wiu.edu.
Website: http://wiu.edu/edl.

Western Kentucky University, Graduate Studies, College of Education and Behavioral Sciences, Department of Educational Administration, Leadership, and Research, Bowling Green, KY 42101. Offers adult education (MAE); educational leadership (Ed D); school administration (Ed S); school principal (MAE). *Accreditation:* NCATE. Part-time and evening/weekend programs available. *Degree requirements:* For master's, comprehensive exam, thesis or applied project and oral defense; for Ed S, thesis. *Entrance requirements:* For master's, GRE General Test, minimum GPA of 2.75. Additional exam requirements/recommendations for international students: Required—TOEFL (minimum score 555 paper-based; 79 iBT). *Faculty research:* Principal internship, superintendent assessment, administrative leadership, group training for residential workers.

Western Michigan University, Graduate College, College of Education and Human Development, Department of Educational Leadership, Research and Technology, Kalamazoo, MI 49008. Offers educational leadership (MA, PhD, Ed S); educational technology (MA, Graduate Certificate); evaluation, measurement and research (MA, PhD).

Western New Mexico University, Graduate Division, School of Education, Silver City, NM 88062-0680. Offers bilingual education (MAT); counseling (MA); educational leadership (MA); elementary education (MAT); reading (MAT); school psychology (MA); secondary education (MAT); special education (MAT); TESOL (teaching English to speakers of other languages) (MAT). *Accreditation:* NCATE. *Degree requirements:* For master's, comprehensive exam. *Entrance requirements:* For master's, GRE General Test, GRE Subject Test, minimum GPA of 3.2 in last 64 hours of undergraduate study.

Educational Leadership and Administration

Additional exam requirements/recommendations for international students: Required—TOEFL (minimum score 550 paper-based). Electronic applications accepted.

Western State Colorado University, Graduate Programs in Education, Gunnison, CO 81231. Offers education administrator leadership (MA); reading leadership (MA); teacher leadership (MA). Postbaccalaureate distance learning degree programs offered (minimal on-campus study). *Degree requirements:* For master's, capstone.

Western Washington University, Graduate School, Woodring College of Education, Department of Educational Leadership, Educational Administration Program, Bellingham, WA 98225-5996. Offers M Ed. *Accreditation:* NCATE. Part-time programs available. *Degree requirements:* For master's, comprehensive exam, thesis optional. *Entrance requirements:* For master's, GRE General Test or MAT, minimum GPA of 3.0 in last 60 semester hours or last 90 quarter hours, certification. Additional exam requirements/recommendations for international students: Required—TOEFL (minimum score 567 paper-based). Electronic applications accepted. *Faculty research:* Principal efficacy, collaborative school leadership, school/university partnerships, case study methodology, ethical leadership.

Western Washington University, Graduate School, Woodring College of Education, Department of Educational Leadership, Program in Student Affairs Administration, Bellingham, WA 98225-5996. Offers M Ed. *Accreditation:* NCATE. Part-time programs available. *Degree requirements:* For master's, comprehensive exam, thesis optional, research project. *Entrance requirements:* For master's, GRE General Test or MAT, minimum GPA of 3.0 in last 60 semester hours or last 90 quarter hours. Additional exam requirements/recommendations for international students: Required—TOEFL (minimum score 567 paper-based). Electronic applications accepted. *Faculty research:* Outcomes assessment, adult learning, best practices/student affairs, college health promotion, cultural pluralism.

Westfield State University, Division of Graduate and Continuing Education, Department of Education, Program in School Administration, Westfield, MA 01086. Offers M Ed, CAGS. Part-time and evening/weekend programs available. *Degree requirements:* For master's, comprehensive exam, practicum; for CAGS, research-based field internship. *Entrance requirements:* For master's, GRE General Test or MAT, minimum undergraduate GPA of 2.7; for CAGS, master's degree. *Faculty research:* Collaborative teacher education, developmental early childhood education.

Westminster College, Programs in Education, Program in Administration, New Wilmington, PA 16172-0001. Offers M Ed, Certificate.

West Texas A&M University, College of Education and Social Sciences, Department of Education, Program in Educational Leadership, Canyon, TX 79016-0001. Offers M Ed. Part-time and evening/weekend programs available. Postbaccalaureate distance learning degree programs offered (minimal on-campus study). *Degree requirements:* For master's, comprehensive exam, thesis optional. *Entrance requirements:* For master's, GRE General Test. Additional exam requirements/recommendations for international students: Required—TOEFL (minimum score 550 paper-based). Electronic applications accepted. *Faculty research:* Teacher quality, leadership, recruitment, retention.

West Virginia University, College of Human Resources and Education, Department of Educational Leadership Studies, Morgantown, WV 26506. Offers educational leadership (Ed D); higher education administration (MA); public school administration (MA). *Accreditation:* NCATE. Part-time programs available. *Degree requirements:* For master's, content exams; for doctorate, comprehensive exam, thesis/dissertation. *Entrance requirements:* For master's, minimum GPA of 2.75 or MA Degree or MAT of 4107; for doctorate, GRE General Test or MAT, minimum GPA of 3.25. Additional exam requirements/recommendations for international students: Required—TOEFL. Electronic applications accepted. *Faculty research:* Evaluation, collective bargaining, educational law, international higher education, superintendency.

Wheeling Jesuit University, Department of Education, Wheeling, WV 26003-6295. Offers MEL. Part-time and evening/weekend programs available. Postbaccalaureate distance learning degree programs offered (no on-campus study). *Degree requirements:* For master's, thesis. *Entrance requirements:* For master's, GRE or MAT, minimum GPA of 2.5, professional teaching certificate. Additional exam requirements/recommendations for international students: Required—TOEFL (minimum score 600 paper-based; 100 iBT). Electronic applications accepted. Application fee is waived when completed online. *Faculty research:* Education leadership, school improvement, student achievement, leadership in special education.

Wheelock College, Graduate Programs, Division of Education, Boston, MA 02215-4176. Offers early childhood education (MS); education leadership (MS); elementary education (MS); language, literacy, and reading (MS); teaching students with moderate disabilities (MS). *Accreditation:* NCATE. Postbaccalaureate distance learning degree programs offered (minimal on-campus study). *Degree requirements:* For master's, comprehensive exam. *Entrance requirements:* Additional exam requirements/recommendations for international students: Required—TOEFL. Electronic applications accepted. *Faculty research:* Symbolic learning, emergent literacy, diversity inclusion, beginning reading language and culture, math education.

Whittier College, Graduate Programs, Department of Education and Child Development, Program in Educational Administration, Whittier, CA 90608-0634. Offers MA Ed. Part-time and evening/weekend programs available. *Degree requirements:* For master's, thesis. *Entrance requirements:* For master's, GRE General Test, MAT. *Faculty research:* Candidate leadership development.

Whitworth University, School of Education, Graduate Studies in Education, Program in Administration, Spokane, WA 99251-0001. Offers M Ed. *Accreditation:* NCATE. Part-time and evening/weekend programs available. *Degree requirements:* For master's, comprehensive exam, internship, practicum, research project, or thesis. *Entrance requirements:* For master's, GRE General Test, MAT. *Faculty research:* Rural staff development.

Wichita State University, Graduate School, College of Education, Department of Counseling, Educational Leadership, Educational and School Psychology, Wichita, KS 67260. Offers counseling (M Ed); educational leadership (M Ed, Ed D); educational psychology (M Ed); school psychology (Ed S). *Accreditation:* NCATE. Part-time and evening/weekend programs available. *Unit head:* Dr. Jean Patterson, Chairperson, 316-978-3325, Fax: 316-978-3102, E-mail: jean.patterson@wichita.edu. *Application contact:* Jordan Oleson, Admissions Coordinator, 316-978-3095, Fax: 316-978-3253, E-mail: jordan.oleson@wichita.edu.
Website: http://www.wichita.edu/.

Widener University, School of Human Service Professions, Center for Education, Chester, PA 19013-5792. Offers adult education (M Ed); counseling in higher education (M Ed); counselor education (M Ed); early childhood education (M Ed); educational foundations (M Ed); educational leadership (M Ed); educational psychology (M Ed); elementary education (M Ed); English and language arts (M Ed); health education (M Ed); higher education leadership (Ed D); home and school visitor (M Ed); human sexuality (M Ed, PhD); mathematics education (M Ed); middle school education (M Ed); principalship (M Ed); reading and language arts (Ed D); reading education (M Ed); school administration (Ed D); science education (M Ed); social studies education

(M Ed); special education (M Ed); technology education (M Ed). *Accreditation:* NCATE. Part-time and evening/weekend programs available. *Faculty:* 34 full-time (22 women), 37 part-time/adjunct (14 women). *Students:* 64 full-time (44 women), 209 part-time (146 women); includes 49 minority (39 Black or African American, non-Hispanic/Latino; 1 American Indian or Alaska Native, non-Hispanic/Latino; 4 Asian, non-Hispanic/Latino; 4 Hispanic/Latino; 1 Two or more races, non-Hispanic/Latino), 8 international. Average age 39. 139 applicants, 88% accepted. In 2013, 168 master's, 31 doctorates awarded. Terminal master's awarded for partial completion of doctoral program. *Degree requirements:* For doctorate, thesis/dissertation. *Entrance requirements:* For master's, minimum GPA of 2.5; for doctorate, GRE or MAT, minimum GPA of 2.0 (undergraduate), 3.5 (graduate). *Application deadline:* Applications are processed on a rolling basis. Application fee: $25 ($300 for international students). Electronic applications accepted. *Expenses:* Contact institution. *Financial support:* Career-related internships or fieldwork, tuition waivers (full and partial), and unspecified assistantships available. Support available to part-time students. Financial award application deadline: 5/1. *Faculty research:* Reading and cognition, adult education, technology education, educational leadership, special education. *Unit head:* Dr. Michael W. LeDoux, Associate Dean, 610-499-4294, Fax: 610-499-4623, E-mail: mwledoux@widener.edu. *Application contact:* Dr. Roberta Nolan, Director of Graduate Admissions, 610-499-4125, E-mail: rdnolan@widener.edu.

Wilkes University, College of Graduate and Professional Studies, School of Education, Wilkes-Barre, PA 18766-0002. Offers art and science of teaching (MS Ed); classroom technology (MS Ed); early childhood literacy (MS Ed); educational development and strategies (MS Ed); educational leadership (MS Ed); educational technology (Ed D); higher education administration (Ed D); instructional media (MS Ed); instructional technology (MS Ed); international school leadership (MS Ed); K-12 administration (Ed D); middle level education (MS Ed); online teaching (MS Ed); reading (MS Ed); school business leadership (MS Ed); secondary education (MS Ed), including biology, chemistry, English, history, mathematics; special education (MS Ed); teaching English as a second language (MS Ed); twenty-first century teaching and learning (MS Ed). Part-time and evening/weekend programs available. Postbaccalaureate distance learning degree programs offered (minimal on-campus study). *Students:* 46 full-time (37 women), 1,410 part-time (1,039 women); includes 67 minority (12 Black or African American, non-Hispanic/Latino; 2 American Indian or Alaska Native, non-Hispanic/Latino; 11 Asian, non-Hispanic/Latino; 28 Hispanic/Latino; 1 Native Hawaiian or other Pacific Islander, non-Hispanic/Latino; 13 Two or more races, non-Hispanic/Latino), 6 international. Average age 34. In 2013, 852 master's, 10 doctorates awarded. *Entrance requirements:* Additional exam requirements/recommendations for international students: Required—TOEFL (minimum score 550 paper-based; 79 iBT). *Application deadline:* Applications are processed on a rolling basis. Application fee: $45. Electronic applications accepted. *Expenses:* Contact institution. *Financial support:* Federal Work-Study and unspecified assistantships available. Financial award application deadline: 3/1; financial award applicants required to submit FAFSA. *Unit head:* Dr. Rhonda Waskiewicz, Interim Dean, Education, 570-408-4332, Fax: 570-408-7872, E-mail: rhonda.waskiewicz@wilkes.edu. *Application contact:* Joanne Thomas, Interim Director of Graduate Education, 570-408-4234, Fax: 570-408-7846, E-mail: joanne.thomas1@wilkes.edu.
Website: http://www.wilkes.edu/pages/383.asp.

William Paterson University of New Jersey, College of Education, Wayne, NJ 07470-8420. Offers curriculum and learning (M Ed); educational leadership (M Ed); reading (M Ed); special education and counseling services (M Ed), including counseling services, special education; teaching (MAT). *Accreditation:* NCATE. Part-time and evening/weekend programs available. Postbaccalaureate distance learning degree programs offered. *Faculty:* 33 full-time (8 women), 32 part-time/adjunct (9 women). *Students:* 118 full-time (92 women), 519 part-time (431 women); includes 134 minority (35 Black or African American, non-Hispanic/Latino; 1 American Indian or Alaska Native, non-Hispanic/Latino; 6 Asian, non-Hispanic/Latino; 86 Hispanic/Latino; 6 Two or more races, non-Hispanic/Latino). Average age 34. 439 applicants, 74% accepted, 240 enrolled. In 2013, 144 master's awarded. *Degree requirements:* For master's, comprehensive exam, thesis (for some programs), exit interview (for some programs), practicum/internship. *Entrance requirements:* For master's, GRE/MAT, minimum GPA of 2.75, teaching certificate. Additional exam requirements/recommendations for international students: Required—TOEFL (minimum score 550 paper-based; 79 iBT), IELTS (minimum score 6). *Application deadline:* For fall admission, 6/1 for domestic students, 5/1 for international students; for spring admission, 11/1 for domestic students, 10/1 for international students. Applications are processed on a rolling basis. Application fee: $50. Electronic applications accepted. *Financial support:* Research assistantships with full tuition reimbursements, career-related internships or fieldwork, Federal Work-Study, and unspecified assistantships available. Support available to part-time students. Financial award application deadline: 4/1; financial award applicants required to submit FAFSA. *Faculty research:* IPads in the classroom, characteristics of effective elementary teachers in language arts and mathematics, gender issues in science, after-school programs, middle class parents' roles and gentrifying school districts. *Unit head:* Dr. Candace Burns, Dean, 973-720-2137, Fax: 973-720-2955, E-mail: burnsc@wpunj.edu. *Application contact:* Liana Fornarotto, Assistant Director, Graduate Admissions, 973-720-3578, Fax: 973-720-2035, E-mail: fornarottol@wpunj.edu.
Website: http://www.wpunj.edu/coe.

William Woods University, Graduate and Adult Studies, Fulton, MO 65251-1098. Offers administration (M Ed, Ed S); athletic/activities administration (M Ed); curriculum and instruction (M Ed, Ed S); educational leadership (Ed D); equestrian education (M Ed); health management (MBA); human resources (MBA); leadership (MBA); marketing, advertising, and public relations (MBA); teaching and technology (M Ed). Part-time and evening/weekend programs available. *Faculty:* 231 part-time/adjunct (87 women). *Students:* 418 full-time (276 women), 716 part-time (433 women); includes 51 minority (34 Black or African American, non-Hispanic/Latino; 4 American Indian or Alaska Native, non-Hispanic/Latino; 5 Asian, non-Hispanic/Latino; 3 Hispanic/Latino; 5 Two or more races, non-Hispanic/Latino), 4 international. Average age 35. In 2013, 507 master's, 8 doctorates, 143 other advanced degrees awarded. *Degree requirements:* For master's, capstone course (MBA), action research (M Ed); for Ed S, field experience. *Entrance requirements:* Additional exam requirements/recommendations for international students: Required—TOEFL (minimum score 550 paper-based). *Application deadline:* Applications are processed on a rolling basis. Application fee: $0. Electronic applications accepted. *Expenses:* Contact institution. *Financial support:* Institutionally sponsored loans available. Financial award applicants required to submit FAFSA. *Unit head:* Dr. Michael Westerfield, Vice President and Dean of the Graduate College, 573-592-4383, Fax: 573-592-1164. *Application contact:* Jessica Brush, Director of Operations, 573-592-4227, Fax: 573-592-1164, E-mail: jessica.brush@williamwoods.ede.
Website: http://www.williamwoods.edu/evening_programs/index.asp.

Wilmington University, College of Education, New Castle, DE 19720-6491. Offers applied technology in education (M Ed); career and technical education (M Ed); educational leadership (Ed D); elementary and secondary school counseling (M Ed); elementary studies (M Ed); ESOL literacy (M Ed); higher education leadership (Ed D); instruction: gifted and talented (M Ed); instruction: teacher of reading (M Ed); instruction:

teaching and learning (M Ed); organizational leadership (Ed D); school leadership (M Ed); secondary education (MAT); special education (M Ed). *Accreditation:* NCATE. Part-time and evening/weekend programs available. *Entrance requirements:* For master's, 2 letters of recommendation, interview. Additional exam requirements/ recommendations for international students: Required—TOEFL (minimum score 500 paper-based). Electronic applications accepted.

Wingate University, Thayer School of Education, Wingate, NC 28174-0159. Offers community college leadership (Ed D); educational leadership (MA Ed, Ed D); elementary education (MA Ed, MAT); health and physical education (MA Ed); sport administration (MA Ed). *Accreditation:* NCATE. Part-time and evening/weekend programs available. *Degree requirements:* For master's, portfolio. *Entrance requirements:* For master's, GRE General Test or MAT, teaching certificate (MA Ed).

Winona State University, College of Education, Department of Education Leadership, Winona, MN 55987. Offers educational leadership (Ed S), including general superintendency, K-12 principalship; general school leadership (MS); K-12 principalship (MS); outdoor education/adventure-based leadership (MS); sports management (MS); teacher leadership (MS). *Accreditation:* NCATE. Part-time and evening/weekend programs available. *Degree requirements:* For master's, comprehensive exam, thesis optional; for Ed S, thesis optional.

Winthrop University, College of Education, Program in Educational Leadership, Rock Hill, SC 29733. Offers M Ed. *Entrance requirements:* For master's, GRE General Test or MAT, 3 years of experience, South Carolina Class III Teaching Certificate, recommendations from current principal and district-level administrator, pre-entrance assessment. Electronic applications accepted.

Worcester State University, Graduate Studies, Department of Education, Program in Leadership and Administration, Worcester, MA 01602-2597. Offers M Ed, CAGS, Postbaccalaureate Certificate. Part-time programs available. *Faculty:* 14 full-time (11 women), 22 part-time/adjunct (10 women). *Students:* 51 part-time (29 women); includes 2 minority (1 Black or African American, non-Hispanic/Latino; 1 Asian, non-Hispanic/ Latino). Average age 40. 80 applicants, 91% accepted, 3 enrolled. In 2013, 26 master's, 36 CAGSs awarded. *Degree requirements:* For master's, comprehensive exam (for some programs), thesis optional. *Entrance requirements:* For master's, GRE General Test or MAT, teaching certificate; for other advanced degree, Massachusetts Tests for Educator Licensure (communications and literacy skills), M Ed or master's degree in related field. Additional exam requirements/recommendations for international students: Required—TOEFL (minimum score 500 paper-based; 61 iBT). *Application deadline:* For fall admission, 6/15 for domestic and international students; for spring admission, 4/1 for domestic and international students. Applications are processed on a rolling basis. Application fee: $40. Electronic applications accepted. *Expenses: Tuition, area resident:* Part-time $150 per credit. Tuition, state resident: part-time $150 per credit. Tuition, nonresident: part-time $150 per credit. *Required fees:* $114.50 per credit. *Financial support:* Career-related internships or fieldwork, scholarships/grants, and unspecified assistantships available. Financial award application deadline: 3/1; financial award applicants required to submit FAFSA. *Unit head:* Dr. Audrey Wright, Coordinator, 508-929-8594, Fax: 508-929-8164, E-mail: awright1@worcester.edu. *Application contact:* Sara Grady, Assistant Dean of Graduate and Continuing Education, 508-929-8787, Fax: 508-929-8100, E-mail: sara.grady@worcester.edu.

Wright State University, School of Graduate Studies, College of Education and Human Services, Department of Educational Leadership, Program in Advanced Educational Leadership, Dayton, OH 45435. Offers advanced curriculum and instruction (Ed S); higher education-adult education (Ed S); superintendent (Ed S). *Accreditation:* NCATE. *Degree requirements:* For Ed S, thesis. *Entrance requirements:* For degree, GRE General Test, MAT. Additional exam requirements/recommendations for international students: Required—TOEFL.

Wright State University, School of Graduate Studies, College of Education and Human Services, Department of Educational Leadership, Programs in Educational Leadership, Dayton, OH 45435. Offers curriculum and instruction: teacher leader (MA); educational administrative specialist: teacher leader (M Ed); educational administrative specialist: vocational education administration (M Ed, MA); student affairs in higher education-administration (M Ed, MA). *Accreditation:* NCATE. *Degree requirements:* For master's, thesis (for some programs). *Entrance requirements:* For master's, GRE General Test, MAT. Additional exam requirements/recommendations for international students: Required—TOEFL.

Xavier University, College of Social Sciences, Health and Education, School of Education, Department of Educational Leadership and Human Resource Development, Program in Educational Administration, Cincinnati, OH 45207. Offers M Ed. Part-time and evening/weekend programs available. *Faculty:* 8 full-time (0 women), 16 part-time/ adjunct (2 women). *Students:* 3 full-time (2 women), 41 part-time (30 women); includes 2 minority (1 Black or African American, non-Hispanic/Latino; 1 Asian, non-Hispanic/ Latino), 2 international. Average age 32. 3 applicants, 100% accepted, 3 enrolled. In 2013, 30 master's awarded. *Degree requirements:* For master's, comprehensive exam, thesis. *Entrance requirements:* For master's, MAT or GRE. *Application deadline:* Applications are processed on a rolling basis. Application fee: $35. Electronic applications accepted. *Expenses: Tuition:* Part-time $594 per credit hour. *Required fees:* $3 per semester. *Financial support:* In 2013–14, 41 students received support. Tuition waivers (partial) and unspecified assistantships available. Financial award applicants required to submit FAFSA. *Faculty research:* Educational leadership, hidden curriculum, internship effectiveness, neuroleadership, school leadership. *Unit head:* Dr. Leo Bradley, Chair, 513-745-3701, Fax: 513-745-3504, E-mail: bradley@xavier.edu. *Application contact:* Roger Bosse, Graduate Services Director, 513-745-3357, Fax: 513-745-1048, E-mail: bosse@xavier.edu.
Website: http://www.xavier.edu/administration-grad/.

Xavier University of Louisiana, Graduate School, Programs in Education, New Orleans, LA 70125-1098. Offers curriculum and instruction (MA); education administration and supervision (MA); guidance and counseling (MA). *Accreditation:* NCATE. Part-time and evening/weekend programs available. *Degree requirements:* For master's, comprehensive exam, thesis or alternative. *Entrance requirements:* For master's, GRE General Test, MAT, minimum GPA of 2.5. Additional exam requirements/ recommendations for international students: Required—TOEFL.

Yeshiva University, Azrieli Graduate School of Jewish Education and Administration, New York, NY 10033-4391. Offers MS, Ed D, Specialist. Part-time and evening/ weekend programs available. Terminal master's awarded for partial completion of doctoral program. *Degree requirements:* For master's, one foreign language, student teaching experience, comprehensive exam or thesis; for doctorate, one foreign language, comprehensive exam, thesis/dissertation, certifying exams, internship; for Specialist, one foreign language, comprehensive exam, certifying exams, internship. *Entrance requirements:* For master's, GRE General Test, BA in Jewish studies or equivalent; for doctorate and Specialist, GRE General Test, master's degree in Jewish education, 2 years of teaching experience. *Expenses:* Contact institution. *Faculty research:* Social patterns of American and Israeli Jewish population, special education, adult education, technology in education, return to religious values.

York College of Pennsylvania, Department of Education, York, PA 17405-7199. Offers educational leadership (M Ed); reading specialist (M Ed). Part-time and evening/ weekend programs available. *Faculty:* 3 full-time (2 women), 8 part-time/adjunct (5 women). *Students:* 43 part-time (34 women); includes 1 minority (Hispanic/Latino). Average age 31. 15 applicants, 67% accepted, 7 enrolled. In 2013, 15 master's awarded. *Degree requirements:* For master's, comprehensive exam, thesis optional, portfolio. *Entrance requirements:* For master's, GRE, MAT or PRAXIS, letters of recommendation, portfolio. *Application deadline:* For fall admission, 7/15 priority date for domestic students; for spring admission, 11/15 priority date for domestic students; for summer admission, 4/15 priority date for domestic students. Applications are processed on a rolling basis. Application fee: $0. Electronic applications accepted. *Expenses: Tuition:* Full-time $12,870; part-time $715 per credit. *Required fees:* $1660; $360 per semester. Tuition and fees vary according to degree level. *Faculty research:* Mentoring, principal development, principal retention. *Unit head:* Dr. Philip Monteith, Director, 717-815-6406, E-mail: med@ycp.edu. *Application contact:* Irene Z. Altland, Administrative Assistant, 717-815-6406, Fax: 717-849-1629, E-mail: med@ycp.edu.
Website: http://www.ycp.edu/academics/academic-departments/education/.

Youngstown State University, Graduate School, Beeghly College of Education, Department of Educational Foundations, Research, Technology, and Leadership, Youngstown, OH 44555-0001. Offers educational administration (MS Ed); educational leadership (Ed D). *Accreditation:* NCATE. Part-time and evening/weekend programs available. *Degree requirements:* For master's, comprehensive exam; for doctorate, comprehensive exam, thesis/dissertation. *Entrance requirements:* For master's, GRE, MAT, or teaching certificate; minimum GPA of 2.7; for doctorate, GRE General Test, GRE Subject Test, interview, minimum GPA of 3.5. Additional exam requirements/ recommendations for international students: Required—TOEFL. *Faculty research:* Administrative theory, computer applications, education law, school and community relations, finance principalship.

Educational Measurement and Evaluation

American InterContinental University Online, Program in Education, Schaumburg, IL 60173. Offers curriculum and instruction (M Ed); educational assessment and evaluation (M Ed); instructional technology (M Ed); leadership of educational organizations (M Ed). Evening/weekend programs available. Postbaccalaureate distance learning degree programs offered (no on-campus study). *Entrance requirements:* Additional exam requirements/recommendations for international students: Required—TOEFL (minimum score 550 paper-based). Electronic applications accepted.

Baylor University, Graduate School, School of Education, Department of Educational Psychology, Waco, TX 76798-7301. Offers applied behavior analysis (MS Ed); educational psychology (MA, PhD); exceptionalities (PhD); learning and development (PhD); measurement (PhD); school psychology (Ed S). *Accreditation:* NCATE. *Faculty:* 12 full-time (7 women), 2 part-time/adjunct (1 woman). *Students:* 36 full-time (30 women), 6 part-time (all women); includes 8 minority (1 Black or African American, non-Hispanic/Latino; 3 Asian, non-Hispanic/Latino; 4 Hispanic/Latino), 2 international. Average age 29. 40 applicants, 38% accepted, 12 enrolled. In 2013, 4 master's, 8 doctorates, 8 other advanced degrees awarded. *Degree requirements:* For master's, thesis optional; for doctorate, comprehensive exam, thesis/dissertation; for Ed S, comprehensive exam, thesis or alternative. *Entrance requirements:* For master's, minimum GPA of 3.0; for doctorate, GRE General Test, master's degree; for Ed S, GRE General Test. Additional exam requirements/recommendations for international students: Required—TOEFL. *Application deadline:* For fall admission, 2/1 priority date for domestic and international students. Application fee: $50. Electronic applications accepted. *Expenses: Tuition:* Full-time $25,866; part-time $1437 per credit hour. *Required fees:* $2736; $152 per credit hour. Tuition and fees vary according to course load and program. *Financial support:* In 2013–14, 42 students received support, including 20 fellowships with full and partial tuition reimbursements available, 22 research assistantships with full and partial tuition reimbursements available; career-related internships or fieldwork, Federal Work-Study, institutionally sponsored loans, scholarships/grants, health care benefits, tuition waivers (full and partial), unspecified assistantships, and stipends also available. Financial award application deadline: 2/1; financial award applicants required to submit FAFSA. *Faculty research:* Individual differences, quantitative methods, gifted and talented, special education, school psychology, autism, applied behavior analysis, learning, human development. *Total annual research expenditures:* $248,000. *Unit head:* Dr. Marley W. Watkins, Professor and Chairman, 254-710-4234, Fax: 254-710-3987, E-mail: marley_watkins@baylor.edu. *Application contact:* Lisa Rowe, Office Manager, 254-710-3112, Fax: 254-710-3112, E-mail: lisa_rowe@baylor.edu.
Website: http://www.baylor.edu/soe/EDP/.

Boston College, Lynch Graduate School of Education, Program in Educational Research, Measurement, and Evaluation, Chestnut Hill, MA 02467-3800. Offers M Ed, PhD. Part-time and evening/weekend programs available. *Students:* 14 full-time (12 women), 1 (woman) part-time. 69 applicants, 42% accepted, 15 enrolled. In 2013, 9 master's, 2 doctorates awarded. Terminal master's awarded for partial completion of doctoral program. *Degree requirements:* For master's, comprehensive exam; for doctorate, comprehensive exam, thesis/dissertation. *Entrance requirements:* For master's, GRE General Test or MAT; for doctorate, GRE General Test. Additional exam requirements/recommendations for international students: Required—TOEFL (minimum score 100 iBT). *Application deadline:* For fall admission, 12/1 priority date for domestic and international students; for spring admission, 11/1 for domestic and international students. Application fee: $65. Electronic applications accepted. *Financial support:* Fellowships with full and partial tuition reimbursements, research assistantships with full and partial tuition reimbursements, teaching assistantships with full and partial tuition reimbursements, career-related internships or fieldwork, Federal Work-Study, institutionally sponsored loans, scholarships/grants, traineeships, health care benefits,

tuition waivers (full and partial), and unspecified assistantships available. Support available to part-time students. Financial award applicants required to submit FAFSA. *Faculty research:* Testing and educational public policy, statistical modeling, classroom use of technology, international comparisons of student achievement, psychometrics. *Unit head:* Dr. Larry Ludlow, Chairperson, 617-552-4214, Fax: 617-552-0398. *Application contact:* Domenic Lomanno, Director, Graduate Admission and Financial Aid, 617-552-4214, Fax: 617-552-0398, E-mail: lomanno@bc.edu.

Cambridge College, School of Education, Cambridge, MA 02138-5304. Offers autism specialist (M Ed); autism/behavior analyst (M Ed); behavior analyst (Post-Master's Certificate); behavioral management (M Ed); early childhood teacher (M Ed); education specialist in curriculum and instruction (CAGS); educational leadership (Ed D); elementary teacher (M Ed); English as a second language (M Ed, Certificate); general science (M Ed); health education (Post-Master's Certificate); health/family and consumer sciences (M Ed); history (M Ed); individualized (M Ed); information technology literacy (M Ed); instructional technology (M Ed); interdisciplinary studies (M Ed); library teacher (M Ed); literacy education (M Ed); mathematics (M Ed); mathematics specialist (Certificate); middle school mathematics and science (M Ed); school administration (M Ed, CAGS); school guidance counselor (M Ed); school nurse education (M Ed); school social worker/school adjustment counselor (M Ed); special education administrator (CAGS); special education/moderate disabilities (M Ed); teaching skills and methodologies (M Ed). Part-time and evening/weekend programs available. Postbaccalaureate distance learning degree programs offered (minimal on-campus study). *Degree requirements:* For master's, thesis, internship/practicum (licensure program only); for doctorate, thesis/dissertation; for other advanced degree, thesis. *Entrance requirements:* For master's, interview, resume, documentation of licensure, 2 professional references; for doctorate, official transcripts, interview, resume, documentation of licensure (if any), written personal statement/essay, portfolio of scholarly and professional work, qualifying assessment, 2 professional references, health insurance, immunizations form; for other advanced degree, official transcripts, interview, resume, documentation of licensure (if any), written personal statement/essay, 2 professional references, health insurance, immunizations form. Additional exam requirements/recommendations for international students: Required—TOEFL (minimum score 550 paper-based; 79 iBT), Michigan English Language Assessment Battery (minimum score 85); Recommended—IELTS (minimum score 6). Electronic applications accepted. *Expenses:* Contact institution. *Faculty research:* Adult education, accelerated learning, mathematics education, brain compatible learning, special education and law.

Claremont Graduate University, Graduate Programs, School of Educational Studies, Claremont, CA 91711-6160. Offers Africana education (Certificate); education and policy (MA, PhD); higher education/student affairs (MA, PhD); human development (MA, PhD); public school administration (MA, PhD); quantitative evaluation (MA, PhD); special education (MA, PhD); teacher education (MA); teaching and learning (MA, PhD); urban leadership (PhD); MBA/PhD. PhD program offered jointly with San Diego State University. Part-time programs available. *Faculty:* 16 full-time (9 women), 1 part-time/adjunct (0 women). *Students:* 224 full-time (158 women), 221 part-time (151 women); includes 229 minority (52 Black or African American, non-Hispanic/Latino; 3 American Indian or Alaska Native, non-Hispanic/Latino; 43 Asian, non-Hispanic/Latino; 113 Hispanic/Latino; 1 Native Hawaiian or other Pacific Islander, non-Hispanic/Latino; 17 Two or more races, non-Hispanic/Latino), 15 international. Average age 39. In 2013, 51 master's, 33 doctorates, 5 other advanced degrees awarded. Terminal master's awarded for partial completion of doctoral program. *Entrance requirements:* For master's and doctorate, GRE General Test. Additional exam requirements/recommendations for international students: Required—TOEFL (minimum score 550 paper-based; 80 iBT). *Application deadline:* For fall admission, 4/1 priority date for domestic and international students. Applications are processed on a rolling basis. Application fee: $80. Electronic applications accepted. *Expenses: Tuition:* Full-time $40,560; part-time $1690 per credit. *Required fees:* $275 per semester. Tuition and fees vary according to program. *Financial support:* Fellowships, research assistantships, Federal Work-Study, institutionally sponsored loans, and scholarships/grants available. Support available to part-time students. Financial award application deadline: 2/15; financial award applicants required to submit FAFSA. *Faculty research:* Education administration, K-12 and higher education, multicultural education, education policy, diversity in higher education, faculty issues. *Unit head:* Scott Thomas, Dean, 909-621-8075, Fax: 909-621-8734, E-mail: scott.thomas@cgu.edu. *Application contact:* Julia Wendt, Director of Central Recruitment, 909-607-3689, Fax: 909-607-7285, E-mail: admiss@cgu.edu.
Website: http://www.cgu.edu/pages/267.asp.

College of Saint Mary, Program in Education, Omaha, NE 68106. Offers assessment leadership (MSE); English as a second language (MSE). Part-time programs available. *Entrance requirements:* For master's, technology competency test or equivalent, minimum cumulative GPA of 3.0, teaching certificate, 2 letters of reference, resume.

Duquesne University, School of Education, Department of Foundations and Leadership, Program in Program Evaluation, Pittsburgh, PA 15282-0001. Offers MS Ed. Postbaccalaureate distance learning degree programs offered (minimal on-campus study). *Faculty:* 1 full-time (0 women). *Students:* 11 full-time (10 women); includes 2 minority (both Asian, non-Hispanic/Latino), 3 international. Average age 31. 11 applicants, 73% accepted, 7 enrolled. *Entrance requirements:* For master's, official transcripts, letter of recommendation, statement of purpose, interview. Additional exam requirements/recommendations for international students: Required—TOEFL (minimum score 550 paper-based; 80 iBT). *Application deadline:* Applications are processed on a rolling basis. Electronic applications accepted. *Expenses: Tuition:* Full-time $18,162; part-time $1009 per credit. *Required fees:* $1728; $96 per credit. Tuition and fees vary according to program. *Unit head:* Dr. Gibbs Kanyongo, Associate Professor and Director, 412-396-5190, Fax: 412-396-6017, E-mail: kanyongog@duq.edu. *Application contact:* Michael Dolinger, Director of Student and Academic Services, 412-396-6647, Fax: 412-396-5585, E-mail: dolingerm@duq.edu.
Website: http://www.duq.edu/academics/schools/education/graduate-programs-education/ms-education-program-evaluation.

Eastern Michigan University, Graduate School, College of Education, Department of Teacher Education, Programs in Educational Psychology and Assessment, Ypsilanti, MI 48197. Offers educational assessment (Graduate Certificate); educational psychology (MA), including development/personality, research and assessment, research and evaluation, the developing learner. *Accreditation:* NCATE. Part-time and evening/weekend programs available. Postbaccalaureate distance learning degree programs offered (minimal on-campus study). *Students:* 14 part-time (12 women); includes 2 minority (1 Black or African American, non-Hispanic/Latino; 1 Hispanic/Latino), 1 international. Average age 40. 6 applicants, 100% accepted, 4 enrolled. In 2013, 17 master's, 3 other advanced degrees awarded. *Degree requirements:* For master's, thesis or alternative. *Entrance requirements:* For master's, GRE. Additional exam requirements/recommendations for international students: Required—TOEFL. *Application deadline:* Applications are processed on a rolling basis. Application fee: $35. *Expenses:* Tuition, state resident: full-time $12,300; part-time $466 per credit hour. Tuition, nonresident: full-time $23,159; part-time $918 per credit hour. *Required fees:* $71 per credit hour. $46 per semester. One-time fee: $100. Tuition and fees vary according to course level and degree level. *Financial support:* Fellowships, research assistantships with full tuition reimbursements, teaching assistantships with full tuition reimbursements, career-related internships or fieldwork, Federal Work-Study, institutionally sponsored loans, scholarships/grants, tuition waivers (partial), and unspecified assistantships available. Support available to part-time students. Financial award applicants required to submit FAFSA. *Unit head:* Dr. Martha Kinney-Sedgwick, Interim Department Head, 734-487-3260, Fax: 734-487-2101, E-mail: mkinneys@emich.edu. *Application contact:* Dr. Patricia Pokay, Coordinator, 734-487-3260, Fax: 734-487-2101, E-mail: ppokay@emich.edu.

Florida State University, The Graduate School, College of Education, Department of Educational Leadership and Policy Studies, Program in Educational Leadership and Policy, Tallahassee, FL 32306. Offers education policy and evaluation (MS, PhD); educational leadership/administration (MS, PhD, Certificate, Ed S). Part-time and evening/weekend programs available. *Faculty:* 15 full-time (12 women). *Students:* 25 full-time (16 women), 97 part-time (63 women); includes 47 minority (23 Black or African American, non-Hispanic/Latino; 2 Asian, non-Hispanic/Latino; 21 Hispanic/Latino; 1 Two or more races, non-Hispanic/Latino), 6 international. Average age 36. 72 applicants, 56% accepted, 25 enrolled. In 2013, 24 master's, 4 doctorates, 16 other advanced degrees awarded. Terminal master's awarded for partial completion of doctoral program. *Degree requirements:* For master's and other advanced degree, comprehensive exam, thesis optional; for doctorate, comprehensive exam, thesis/dissertation. *Entrance requirements:* For master's, GRE General Test, minimum GPA of 3.0; for doctorate and other advanced degree, GRE General Test, minimum graduate GPA of 3.0. Additional exam requirements/recommendations for international students: Required—TOEFL (minimum score 550 paper-based; 80 iBT). *Application deadline:* For fall admission, 7/1 for domestic and international students; for winter admission, 11/1 for domestic and international students; for spring admission, 3/1 for domestic and international students. Application fee: $30. Electronic applications accepted. *Expenses:* Tuition, state resident: part-time $403.51 per credit hour. Tuition, nonresident: part-time $1004.85 per credit hour. *Required fees:* $75.81 per credit hour. One-time fee: $20 part-time. Tuition and fees vary according to course load, campus/location and student level. *Financial support:* Fellowships with full and partial tuition reimbursements, research assistantships with full and partial tuition reimbursements, teaching assistantships with full and partial tuition reimbursements, career-related internships or fieldwork, scholarships/grants, health care benefits, and unspecified assistantships available. Financial award application deadline: 1/15; financial award applicants required to submit FAFSA. *Faculty research:* Issues in higher education law; diversity, equity, and social justice; educational issues in Western and non-Western countries. *Unit head:* Dr. Stacey Rutledge, Program Coordinator, 850-644-8163, Fax: 850-644-1258, E-mail: sarutledge@fsu.edu. *Application contact:* Linda J. Lyons, Academic Support Assistant, 850-644-7077, Fax: 850-644-1258, E-mail: ljlyons@fsu.edu.
Website: http://www.coe.fsu.edu/Current-Students/Departments/Educational-Leadership-and-Policy-Studies-ELPS/Current-Students/Degree-Programs.

Florida State University, The Graduate School, College of Education, Department of Educational Psychology and Learning Systems, Program in Educational Psychology, Tallahassee, FL 32306. Offers learning and cognition (MS, PhD, Ed S); measurement and statistics (MS, PhD, Ed S); sport psychology (MS, PhD). *Faculty:* 10 full-time (6 women). *Students:* 97 full-time (52 women), 24 part-time (17 women); includes 26 minority (11 Black or African American, non-Hispanic/Latino; 1 American Indian or Alaska Native, non-Hispanic/Latino; 1 Asian, non-Hispanic/Latino; 12 Hispanic/Latino; 1 Two or more races, non-Hispanic/Latino), 47 international. Average age 31. 205 applicants, 35% accepted, 31 enrolled. In 2013, 12 master's, 7 doctorates awarded. *Degree requirements:* For master's, comprehensive exam, thesis optional; for doctorate, comprehensive exam, thesis/dissertation. *Entrance requirements:* For master's and doctorate, GRE General Test, minimum GPA of 3.0. Additional exam requirements/recommendations for international students: Required—TOEFL (minimum score 550 paper-based; 80 iBT). *Application deadline:* For fall admission, 7/1 for domestic and international students; for winter admission, 11/1 for domestic and international students; for spring admission, 3/1 for domestic and international students. Applications are processed on a rolling basis. Application fee: $30. Electronic applications accepted. *Expenses:* Tuition, state resident: part-time $403.51 per credit hour. Tuition, nonresident: part-time $1004.85 per credit hour. *Required fees:* $75.81 per credit hour. One-time fee: $20 part-time. Tuition and fees vary according to course load, campus/location and student level. *Financial support:* Fellowships with full and partial tuition reimbursements, research assistantships with full and partial tuition reimbursements, teaching assistantships with full and partial tuition reimbursements, career-related internships or fieldwork, scholarships/grants, health care benefits, and unspecified assistantships available. Financial award application deadline: 1/15; financial award applicants required to submit FAFSA. *Faculty research:* Meta analysis; item response theory (IRT)/mixture IRT; cognitive behavioral therapy (CBT); modeling, especially large data sets; learning and cognition, skill acquisition, self-perception, processes of motivation. *Unit head:* Dr. Betsy Becker, Chair, 850-644-2371, Fax: 850-644-8776, E-mail: bbecker@fsu.edu. *Application contact:* Peggy Lollie, Program Assistant, 850-644-8786, Fax: 850-644-8776, E-mail: plollie@fsu.edu.
Website: http://coe.fsu.edu/Academic-Programs/Departments/Educational-Psychology-and-Learning-Systems-EPLS/Degree-Programs/Educational-Psychology.

Georgia State University, College of Education, Department of Educational Policy Studies, Program in Educational Research, Atlanta, GA 30302-3083. Offers MS, PhD. MS offered jointly with Department of Counseling and Psychological Services. *Accreditation:* NCATE. Part-time programs available. *Students:* Average age 0. *Degree requirements:* For master's, 36 semester hours, thesis or project; for doctorate, comprehensive exam, thesis/dissertation, 69 semester hours. *Entrance requirements:* For master's and doctorate, GRE. Additional exam requirements/recommendations for international students: Required—TOEFL (minimum score 550 paper-based; 79 iBT) or IELTS (minimum score 6.5). *Application deadline:* For fall admission, 1/15 for domestic and international students; for winter admission, 2/1 for domestic students; for spring admission, 10/1 for domestic and international students. Applications are processed on a rolling basis. Application fee: $50. Electronic applications accepted. *Expenses: Tuition, area resident:* Full-time $4176; part-time $348 per credit hour. Tuition, state resident: full-time $14,544; part-time $1212 per credit hour. Tuition, nonresident: full-time $14,544; part-time $1212 per credit hour. Tuition and fees vary according to course load and program. *Financial support:* In 2013–14, research assistantships with full tuition reimbursements (averaging $10,886 per year) were awarded; fellowships, teaching assistantships with full tuition reimbursements, career-related internships or fieldwork, scholarships/grants, health care benefits, tuition waivers (full), and unspecified assistantships also available. Support available to part-time students. Financial award application deadline: 3/15. *Faculty research:* Program evaluation, item response theory, quantitative research methodology, qualitative research methodology, gender and identity studies. *Unit head:* Dr. Janice Fournillier, Associate Professor, 404-413-8030, Fax: 404-413-8003, E-mail: jfournillier@gsu.edu. *Application contact:* Aishah Cowan, Administrative Academic Specialist, 404-413-8273, Fax: 404-413-8003, E-mail: acowan@gsu.edu.
Website: http://education.gsu.edu/eps/4584.html.

Harvard University, Harvard Graduate School of Education, Doctoral Program in Education, Cambridge, MA 02138. Offers culture, communities and education (Ed D); education policy, leadership and instructional practice (Ed D); higher education (Ed D); human development and education (Ed D); quantitative policy analysis in education (Ed D). *Faculty:* 68 full-time (34 women), 77 part-time/adjunct (41 women). *Students:* 221 full-time (148 women), 8 part-time (4 women); includes 70 minority (28 Black or African American, non-Hispanic/Latino; 22 Asian, non-Hispanic/Latino; 14 Hispanic/Latino; 1 Native Hawaiian or other Pacific Islander, non-Hispanic/Latino; 5 Two or more races, non-Hispanic/Latino), 26 international. Average age 34. 472 applicants, 8% accepted, 25 enrolled. In 2013, 50 doctorates awarded. Terminal master's awarded for partial completion of doctoral program. *Degree requirements:* For doctorate, thesis/dissertation. *Entrance requirements:* For doctorate, GRE General Test, statement of purpose, 3 letters of recommendation, resume, official transcripts. Additional exam requirements/recommendations for international students: Required—TOEFL (minimum score 613 paper-based; 104 iBT), TWE (minimum score 5). *Application deadline:* For fall admission, 12/2 for domestic and international students. Application fee: $85. Electronic applications accepted. *Expenses:* Contact institution. *Financial support:* In 2013–14, 168 students received support, including 66 fellowships with full and partial tuition reimbursements available (averaging $15,034 per year), 48 research assistantships (averaging $11,714 per year), 190 teaching assistantships (averaging $6,097 per year); career-related internships or fieldwork, Federal Work-Study, institutionally sponsored loans, scholarships/grants, health care benefits, tuition waivers (full and partial), and unspecified assistantships also available. Support available to part-time students. Financial award application deadline: 2/1; financial award applicants required to submit FAFSA. *Faculty research:* Learning and development, educational leadership and organizations, education policy analysis. *Total annual research expenditures:* $34.3 million. *Unit head:* Dr. Barbara Selmo, Assistant Dean, 617-496-4406. *Application contact:* Information Contact, 617-495-3414, Fax: 617-496-3577, E-mail: gseadmissions@harvard.edu.
Website: http://gse.harvard.edu/.

Houston Baptist University, College of Education and Behavioral Sciences, Programs in Education, Houston, TX 77074-3298. Offers bilingual education (M Ed); counselor education (M Ed); curriculum and instruction (M Ed); educational administration (M Ed); educational diagnostician (M Ed); reading education (M Ed). Part-time programs available. Postbaccalaureate distance learning degree programs offered (no on-campus study). *Entrance requirements:* For master's, GRE General Test or MAT. Additional exam requirements/recommendations for international students: Required—TOEFL (minimum score 550 paper-based).

Indiana University Bloomington, School of Education, Department of Counseling and Educational Psychology, Bloomington, IN 47405-1006. Offers counseling (MS, PhD, Ed S); counselor education (MS, Ed S); educational psychology (MS, PhD); inquiry methodology (PhD); learning and developmental sciences (MS, PhD); school psychology (PhD, Ed S). *Accreditation:* ACA (one or more programs are accredited); APA (one or more programs are accredited); NCATE. Terminal master's awarded for partial completion of doctoral program. *Degree requirements:* For master's, thesis optional; for doctorate, thesis/dissertation; for Ed S, comprehensive exam or project. *Entrance requirements:* For master's, doctorate, and Ed S, GRE General Test. Additional exam requirements/recommendations for international students: Required—TOEFL. Electronic applications accepted. *Faculty research:* Counseling psychology, inquiry methodology, school psychology, learning sciences, human development, educational psychology.

Indiana University Bloomington, School of Education, Program in Inquiry Methodology, Bloomington, IN 47405-7000. Offers PhD.

Iowa State University of Science and Technology, Department of Educational Leadership and Policy Studies, Ames, IA 50011. Offers counselor education (M Ed, MS); educational administration (M Ed, MS); educational leadership (PhD); higher education (M Ed, MS); organizational learning and human resource development (M Ed, MS); research and evaluation (MS); student affairs (MS). *Degree requirements:* For master's, thesis or alternative; for doctorate, thesis/dissertation. *Entrance requirements:* For master's and doctorate, GRE General Test. Additional exam requirements/recommendations for international students: Required—TOEFL (minimum score 560 paper-based; 83 iBT), IELTS (minimum score 6.5). Electronic applications accepted.

James Madison University, The Graduate School, College of Health and Behavioral Studies, Department of Graduate Psychology, Program in Assessment and Measurement, Harrisonburg, VA 22807. Offers PhD. Part-time programs available. *Students:* 10 full-time (5 women), 3 part-time (2 women), 1 international. Average age 27. In 2013, 4 doctorates awarded. *Degree requirements:* For doctorate, thesis/dissertation. *Entrance requirements:* For doctorate, GRE General Test, 3 letters of recommendation, samples of professional writing, interview, professional curriculum vitae or resume, statement of interest in the program and professional goals. Additional exam requirements/recommendations for international students: Required—TOEFL. *Application deadline:* For fall admission, 2/1 priority date for domestic students. Applications are processed on a rolling basis. Application fee: $55. Electronic applications accepted. *Financial support:* In 2013–14, 7 students received support. 7 doctoral assistantships available. Financial award application deadline: 3/1; financial award applicants required to submit FAFSA. *Unit head:* Dr. Deborah L. Bandalos, Program Director, 540-568-7132, E-mail: bandaldl@jmu.edu. *Application contact:* Lynette M. Bible, Director of Graduate Admissions, 540-568-6395, Fax: 540-568-7860, E-mail: biblelm@jmu.edu.

Kent State University, Graduate School of Education, Health, and Human Services, School of Foundations, Leadership and Administration, Program in Evaluation and Measurement, Kent, OH 44242-0001. Offers M Ed, PhD. *Faculty:* 5 full-time (3 women), 5 part-time/adjunct (2 women). *Students:* 20 full-time (11 women), 10 part-time (3 women); includes 6 minority (2 Black or African American, non-Hispanic/Latino; 3 Asian, non-Hispanic/Latino; 1 Native Hawaiian or other Pacific Islander, non-Hispanic/Latino; 5 international. 33 applicants, 36% accepted. In 2013, 5 master's, 1 doctorate awarded. *Degree requirements:* For doctorate, comprehensive exam, thesis/dissertation. *Entrance requirements:* For master's, minimum GPA of 2.75, 2 letters of reference, goals statement; for doctorate, GRE, minimum GPA of 3.5 from master's degree, resume, 2 letters of reference, goal statement. Additional exam requirements/recommendations for international students: Required—TOEFL (minimum score 550 paper-based; 80 iBT). Application fee: $30 ($60 for international students). *Financial support:* In 2013–14, 4 research assistantships (averaging $12,000 per year), 1 teaching assistantship (averaging $12,000 per year) were awarded; fellowships, career-related internships or fieldwork, Federal Work-Study, institutionally sponsored loans, scholarships/grants, health care benefits, and unspecified assistantships also available. Support available to part-time students. *Unit head:* Dr. Tricia Niesz, Coordinator, 330-672-0591, E-mail: tniesz@kent.edu. *Application contact:* Nancy Miller, Academic Program Director, Office of Graduate Student Services, 330-672-2576, Fax: 330-672-9162, E-mail: ogs@kent.edu.
Website: http://www.kent.edu/ehhs/eval/.

Louisiana State University and Agricultural & Mechanical College, Graduate School, College of Human Sciences and Education, Department of Educational Theory, Policy and Practice, Baton Rouge, LA 70803. Offers counseling (M Ed, MA, Ed S); educational administration (M Ed, MA, PhD, Ed S); educational technology (MA); elementary education (M Ed, MAT); higher education (PhD); research methodology (PhD); secondary education (M Ed, MAT). PhD programs offered jointly with Louisiana State University in Shreveport. *Accreditation:* ACA (one or more programs are accredited); NCATE. Part-time and evening/weekend programs available. *Faculty:* 39 full-time (22 women). *Students:* 185 full-time (136 women), 177 part-time (140 women); includes 110 minority (90 Black or African American, non-Hispanic/Latino; 1 American Indian or Alaska Native, non-Hispanic/Latino; 5 Asian, non-Hispanic/Latino; 9 Hispanic/Latino; 5 Two or more races, non-Hispanic/Latino), 5 international. Average age 31. 167 applicants, 66% accepted, 76 enrolled. In 2013, 134 master's, 23 doctorates, 17 other advanced degrees awarded. Terminal master's awarded for partial completion of doctoral program. *Degree requirements:* For doctorate, thesis/dissertation; for Ed S, thesis optional. *Entrance requirements:* For master's and doctorate, GRE General Test, minimum GPA of 3.0. Additional exam requirements/recommendations for international students: Required—TOEFL (minimum score 550 paper-based; 79 iBT), IELTS (minimum score 6.5), or PTE (minimum score 59). *Application deadline:* For fall admission, 1/25 priority date for domestic students, 5/15 for international students; for spring admission, 10/15 for international students. Applications are processed on a rolling basis. Application fee: $50 ($70 for international students). Electronic applications accepted. *Financial support:* In 2013–14, 253 students received support, including 5 fellowships (averaging $32,204 per year), 27 research assistantships with full and partial tuition reimbursements available (averaging $10,199 per year), 68 teaching assistantships with full and partial tuition reimbursements available (averaging $12,316 per year); career-related internships or fieldwork, Federal Work-Study, institutionally sponsored loans, health care benefits, and unspecified assistantships also available. Support available to part-time students. Financial award applicants required to submit FAFSA. *Faculty research:* Literary, curriculum studies, science education, K-12 leadership, higher education. *Total annual research expenditures:* $735,835. *Unit head:* Dr. Earl Cheek, Jr., Chair, 225-578-1258, Fax: 225-578-2267, E-mail: echeek@lsu.edu. *Application contact:* Dr. Kristin Gansle, Graduate Coordinator, 225-578-6780, Fax: 225-578-2267, E-mail: kgansle@lsu.edu.

Loyola University Chicago, School of Education, Program in Research Methods, Chicago, IL 60660. Offers M Ed, MA, PhD. MA and PhD offered through the Graduate School. Part-time and evening/weekend programs available. *Faculty:* 3 full-time (all women), 3 part-time/adjunct (all women). *Students:* 19. Average age 25. 11 applicants, 55% accepted, 4 enrolled. In 2013, 2 master's, 3 doctorates awarded. *Degree requirements:* For master's, comprehensive exam (M Ed), thesis (MA); for doctorate, comprehensive exam, thesis/dissertation. *Entrance requirements:* For master's, GRE General Test, letters of recommendation, resume, minimum GPA of 3.0; for doctorate, GRE General Test, interview. Additional exam requirements/recommendations for international students: Required—TOEFL (minimum score 550 paper-based; 79 iBT). *Application deadline:* For fall admission, 12/1 for domestic and international students. Applications are processed on a rolling basis. Application fee: $50. Electronic applications accepted. Application fee is waived when completed online. *Expenses: Tuition:* Full-time $16,740; part-time $930 per credit. *Required fees:* $135 per semester. *Financial support:* In 2013–14, 2 research assistantships with full tuition reimbursements (averaging $12,000 per year) were awarded; institutionally sponsored loans, scholarships/grants, health care benefits, and unspecified assistantships also available. Support available to part-time students. Financial award application deadline: 2/1; financial award applicants required to submit FAFSA. *Faculty research:* Circular statistics, program evaluation, psychological measurement, infant attachment, adolescent development. *Unit head:* Dr. Meng-Jia Wu, Director, 312-915-7086, E-mail: mwu2@luc.edu. *Application contact:* Marie Rosin-Dittmar, Information Contact, 312-915-6800, E-mail: schleduc@luc.edu.

McNeese State University, Doré School of Graduate Studies, Burton College of Education, Office of Graduate Education Programs, Program in Special Education, Lake Charles, LA 70609. Offers advanced professional (M Ed); autism (M Ed); educational diagnostician (M Ed). *Entrance requirements:* For master's, GRE, teaching certificate.

McNeese State University, Doré School of Graduate Studies, Burton College of Education, Office of Student Teaching and Professional Education Services, Program in Educational Diagnostician, Lake Charles, LA 70609. Offers Graduate Certificate. *Entrance requirements:* For degree, bachelor's degree, teaching certificate.

Michigan State University, The Graduate School, College of Education, Department of Counseling, Educational Psychology and Special Education, East Lansing, MI 48824. Offers counseling (MA); educational psychology and educational technology (PhD); educational technology (MA); measurement and quantitative methods (PhD); rehabilitation counseling (MA); rehabilitation counselor education (PhD); school psychology (MA, PhD, Ed S); special education (MA, PhD). *Accreditation:* APA (one or more programs are accredited); CORE (one or more programs are accredited). Part-time programs available. *Entrance requirements:* Additional exam requirements/recommendations for international students: Required—TOEFL. Electronic applications accepted.

Mississippi State University, College of Education, Department of Counseling and Educational Psychology, Mississippi State, MS 39762. Offers college/postsecondary student counseling and personnel services (PhD); counselor education (MS), including clinical mental health, college counseling, rehabilitation, school counseling, student affairs in higher education; counselor education/student counseling and guidance services (PhD); education (Ed S), including counselor education, school psychology (PhD, Ed S); educational psychology (MS, PhD), including general education psychology (MS), general educational psychology (PhD), psychometry (MS), school psychology (PhD, Ed S). *Accreditation:* ACA (one or more programs are accredited); APA; CORE (one or more programs are accredited); NCATE. Part-time programs available. Postbaccalaureate distance learning degree programs offered (minimal on-campus study). *Faculty:* 17 full-time (13 women). *Students:* 137 full-time (104 women), 81 part-time (73 women); includes 57 minority (47 Black or African American, non-Hispanic/Latino; 4 American Indian or Alaska Native, non-Hispanic/Latino; 3 Asian, non-Hispanic/Latino; 1 Hispanic/Latino; 2 Two or more races, non-Hispanic/Latino), 5 international. Average age 32. 287 applicants, 36% accepted, 72 enrolled. In 2013, 70 master's, 3 doctorates, 4 other advanced degrees awarded. Terminal master's awarded for partial completion of doctoral program. *Degree requirements:* For master's, comprehensive exam, thesis optional; for doctorate, thesis/dissertation, comprehensive oral and written exam. *Entrance requirements:* For master's, GRE (taken within the last five years), BS with minimum GPA of 2.75 on last 60 hours; for doctorate, GRE, MS from CACREP- or CORE-accredited program in counseling; for Ed S, GRE, MS in counseling or related field, minimum GPA of 3.3 on all graduate work. Additional exam requirements/recommendations for international students: Required—TOEFL (minimum score 550 paper-based; 79 iBT); Recommended—IELTS (minimum score 6.5). *Application deadline:* For fall admission, 2/1 priority date for domestic and international students. Applications are processed on a rolling basis. Application fee: $60. Electronic applications accepted. *Financial support:* In 2013–14, 1 research assistantship (averaging $10,800 per year), 11 teaching assistantships with full tuition reimbursements (averaging $8,401 per year) were awarded; career-related internships

or fieldwork, Federal Work-Study, institutionally sponsored loans, and unspecified assistantships also available. Financial award application deadline: 2/1; financial award applicants required to submit FAFSA. *Faculty research:* HIV/AIDS in college population, substance abuse in youth and college students, ADHD and conduct disorders in youth, assessment and identification of early childhood disabilities, assessment and vocational transition of the disabled. *Unit head:* Dr. Daniel Wong, Professor/Head, 662-325-7928, Fax: 662-325-3263, E-mail: dwong@colled.msstate.edu. *Application contact:* Dr. Charles Palmer, Graduate Coordinator, Counselor Education, 662-325-7917, Fax: 662-325-3263, E-mail: cpalmer@colled.msstate.edu.
Website: http://www.cep.msstate.edu/.

Missouri Western State University, Program in Assessment, St. Joseph, MO 64507-2294. Offers autism spectrum disorders (MAS, Graduate Certificate); TESOL (MAS, Graduate Certificate); writing (MAS). Part-time programs available. *Students:* 6 full-time (4 women), 44 part-time (42 women); includes 4 minority (2 Black or African American, non-Hispanic/Latino; 1 Asian, non-Hispanic/Latino; 1 Hispanic/Latino), 1 international. Average age 36. 2 applicants, 50% accepted, 1 enrolled. In 2013, 9 master's, 7 other advanced degrees awarded. *Entrance requirements:* For master's, minimum GPA of 2.75. Additional exam requirements/recommendations for international students: Recommended—TOEFL (minimum score 500 paper-based; 61 iBT), IELTS (minimum score 5.5). *Application deadline:* For fall admission, 7/15 for domestic students, 6/15 for international students; for spring admission, 10/1 for domestic students, 10/15 for international students. Applications are processed on a rolling basis. Application fee: $45 ($50 for international students). Electronic applications accepted. *Expenses:* Tuition, state resident: full-time $6019; part-time $300.96 per credit hour. Tuition, nonresident: full-time $11,194; part-time $559.71 per credit hour. *Required fees:* $542; $99 per credit hour. $176 per semester. Tuition and fees vary according to course load and program. *Financial support:* Scholarships/grants and unspecified assistantships available. Support available to part-time students. *Unit head:* Dr. Susan Bashinski, Coordinator, 816-271-5629, E-mail: sbashinski@missouriwestern.edu. *Application contact:* Dr. Benjamin D. Caldwell, Dean of the Graduate School, 816-271-4394, Fax: 816-271-4525, E-mail: graduate@missouriwestern.edu.
Website: https://www.missouriwestern.edu/masa/.

New Mexico State University, Graduate School, College of Education, Department of Counseling and Educational Psychology, Las Cruces, NM 88003-8001. Offers counseling and guidance (MA), including counseling and guidance, educational diagnostics; counseling psychology (PhD); school psychology (Ed S). *Accreditation:* ACA; APA (one or more programs are accredited); NCATE. Part-time programs available. *Faculty:* 14 full-time (12 women). *Students:* 72 full-time (53 women), 23 part-time (17 women); includes 55 minority (3 Black or African American, non-Hispanic/Latino; 3 American Indian or Alaska Native, non-Hispanic/Latino; 4 Asian, non-Hispanic/Latino; 43 Hispanic/Latino; 2 Two or more races, non-Hispanic/Latino). Average age 31. 68 applicants, 35% accepted, 22 enrolled. In 2013, 16 master's, 5 doctorates, 9 other advanced degrees awarded. *Degree requirements:* For master's, comprehensive exam, thesis optional, internship; for doctorate, comprehensive exam, thesis/dissertation, internship; for Ed S, comprehensive exam, thesis or alternative, internship. *Entrance requirements:* For master's, doctorate, and Ed S, GRE General Test, minimum GPA of 3.0. Additional exam requirements/recommendations for international students: Required—IELTS (minimum score 6.5); Recommended—TOEFL (minimum score 550 paper-based; 79 iBT). *Application deadline:* For fall admission, 12/15 for domestic and international students; for winter admission, 1/15 for domestic and international students; for spring admission, 2/1 priority date for domestic students, 2/1 for international students. Application fee: $40 ($50 for international students). Electronic applications accepted. *Expenses:* Tuition, state resident: full-time $5398; part-time $224.90 per credit. Tuition, nonresident: full-time $18,821; part-time $784.20 per credit. *Required fees:* $1310; $54.60 per credit. *Financial support:* In 2013–14, 57 students received support, including 6 fellowships (averaging $4,050 per year), 6 research assistantships (averaging $10,227 per year), 16 teaching assistantships (averaging $9,456 per year); career-related internships or fieldwork, Federal Work-Study, institutionally sponsored loans, scholarships/grants, traineeships, health care benefits, and unspecified assistantships also available. Support available to part-time students. Financial award application deadline: 4/1; financial award applicants required to submit FAFSA. *Faculty research:* Multicultural counseling and training, integrative health psychology, social justice, academic success, mental health disparities. *Total annual research expenditures:* $99,768. *Unit head:* Dr. Elsa Corina Arroyos, Interim Head, 575-646-2121, Fax: 575-646-8035, E-mail: earroyos@nmsu.edu. *Application contact:* Jeanette Jones, Program Coordinator, 575-646-5485, Fax: 575-646-8035, E-mail: jjjones@nmsu.edu.
Website: http://cep.education.nmsu.edu.

North Carolina State University, Graduate School, College of Education, Department of Educational Leadership and Policy Studies, Program in Educational Research and Policy Analysis, Raleigh, NC 27695. Offers PhD. *Degree requirements:* For doctorate, thesis/dissertation. *Entrance requirements:* For doctorate, GRE General Test, minimum GPA of 3.0, interview, sample of work. Electronic applications accepted.

Ohio University, Graduate College, Gladys W. and David H. Patton College of Education and Human Services, Department of Educational Studies, Athens, OH 45701-2979. Offers computer education and technology (M Ed); cultural studies (M Ed); educational administration (M Ed, Ed D); educational research and evaluation (M Ed, PhD); instructional technology (PhD). Part-time and evening/weekend programs available. Postbaccalaureate distance learning degree programs offered (minimal on-campus study). *Degree requirements:* For master's, thesis or alternative; for doctorate, comprehensive exam, thesis/dissertation. *Entrance requirements:* For master's, GRE General Test (if GPA less than 2.9); for doctorate, GRE General Test, GRE Subject Test, minimum GPA of 2.9, work experience, 3 letters of reference, autobiography. Additional exam requirements/recommendations for international students: Required—TOEFL (minimum score 550 paper-based; 80 iBT) or IELTS (minimum score 6.5). Electronic applications accepted. *Faculty research:* Race, class and gender; computer programs; development and organization theory; evaluation/development of instruments, leadership.

Rutgers, The State University of New Jersey, New Brunswick, Graduate School of Education, Department of Educational Psychology, Program in Educational Statistics, Measurement and Evaluation, Piscataway, NJ 08854-8097. Offers Ed M. Part-time and evening/weekend programs available. *Entrance requirements:* For master's, GRE General Test, 3 letters of recommendation. Additional exam requirements/recommendations for international students: Required—TOEFL (minimum score 550 paper-based; 83 iBT). Electronic applications accepted. *Faculty research:* Program evaluation of student assessment, Type I error and power comparisons, test performance factors, theory building in participatory program evaluation, test validity in higher education admissions.

Seton Hall University, College of Education and Human Services, Department of Education Leadership, Management and Policy, South Orange, NJ 07079-2697. Offers college student personnel administration (MA); education research, assessment and program evaluation (PhD); higher education administration (Ed D, PhD); human resource training and development (MA); K–12 administration and supervision (Ed D, Exec Ed D, Ed S); K–12 leadership, management and policy (Ed D, Exec Ed D, Ed S). Part-time and evening/weekend programs available. Postbaccalaureate distance learning degree programs offered (no on-campus study). *Faculty:* 15 full-time (7 women), 21 part-time/adjunct (4 women). *Students:* 99 full-time (54 women), 454 part-time (208 women); includes 224 minority (144 Black or African American, non-Hispanic/Latino; 14 Asian, non-Hispanic/Latino; 65 Hispanic/Latino; 1 Native Hawaiian or other Pacific Islander, non-Hispanic/Latino), 17 international. Average age 38. 127 applicants, 89% accepted, 84 enrolled. In 2013, 85 master's, 15 doctorates, 14 other advanced degrees awarded. *Degree requirements:* For master's, comprehensive exam, thesis or alternative; for doctorate, thesis/dissertation, oral exam, written exam; for Ed S, internship, research project. *Entrance requirements:* For master's, GRE or MAT, minimum GPA of 3.0; for doctorate, GRE or MAT, interview, minimum GPA of 3.5; for Ed S, GRE or MAT, minimum GPA of 3.5. *Application deadline:* Applications are processed on a rolling basis. Application fee: $75. *Financial support:* In 2013–14, 2 research assistantships with full tuition reimbursements (averaging $4,500 per year) were awarded; unspecified assistantships also available. Financial award application deadline: 2/1; financial award applicants required to submit FAFSA. *Unit head:* Dr. Michael Osnato, Chair, 973-275-2446, E-mail: osnatomi@shu.edu. *Application contact:* Diana Minakakis, Director of Graduate Admissions, 973-275-2824, Fax: 973-275-2187, E-mail: diana.minakakis@shu.edu.

Southern Connecticut State University, School of Graduate Studies, School of Education, Department of Educational Leadership, New Haven, CT 06515-1355. Offers educational foundations (Diploma), including foundational studies; educational leadership (Ed D, Diploma); research, statistics, and measurement (MS). Part-time and evening/weekend programs available. *Entrance requirements:* For degree, master's degree, minimum GPA of 3.0, writing sample. Electronic applications accepted.

Southern Illinois University Carbondale, Graduate School, College of Education and Human Services, Department of Educational Psychology and Special Education, Program in Educational Psychology, Carbondale, IL 62901-4701. Offers counselor education (MS Ed, PhD); educational psychology (PhD); human learning and development (MS Ed); measurement and statistics (PhD). *Accreditation:* NCATE. *Faculty:* 19 full-time (9 women), 7 part-time/adjunct (2 women). *Students:* 40 full-time (30 women), 28 part-time (16 women); includes 13 minority (11 Black or African American, non-Hispanic/Latino; 1 Asian, non-Hispanic/Latino; 1 Hispanic/Latino), 11 international. Average age 36. 22 applicants, 50% accepted, 8 enrolled. In 2013, 6 master's, 1 doctorate awarded. *Degree requirements:* For master's, thesis; for doctorate, thesis/dissertation. *Entrance requirements:* For master's, GRE General Test, minimum GPA of 2.7; for doctorate, minimum GPA of 3.25. Additional exam requirements/recommendations for international students: Required—TOEFL. *Application deadline:* For fall admission, 6/15 priority date for domestic students. Applications are processed on a rolling basis. Application fee: $50. *Financial support:* In 2013–14, 36 students received support, including 2 fellowships with full tuition reimbursements available, 4 research assistantships with full tuition reimbursements available; teaching assistantships with full tuition reimbursements available, career-related internships or fieldwork, Federal Work-Study, institutionally sponsored loans, and tuition waivers (full) also available. Support available to part-time students. Financial award application deadline: 5/1. *Faculty research:* Career development, problem-solving, learning and instruction, cognitive development, family assessment. *Total annual research expenditures:* $10,000. *Unit head:* Dr. Lyle White, Chairperson, 618-536-7763, E-mail: lwhite@siu.edu. *Application contact:* Brenda Prell, Administrative Clerk, 618-453-6932, E-mail: bprell@siu.edu.

Southwestern Oklahoma State University, College of Professional and Graduate Studies, School of Behavioral Sciences and Education, Specialization in School Psychometry, Weatherford, OK 73096-3098. Offers M Ed. M Ed distance learning degree program offered to Oklahoma residents only. *Accreditation:* NCATE. Part-time and evening/weekend programs available. *Degree requirements:* For master's, exam. *Entrance requirements:* For master's, GRE General Test or minimum undergraduate GPA of 3.0, portfolio. Additional exam requirements/recommendations for international students: Required—TOEFL.

Sul Ross State University, Rio Grande College of Sul Ross State University, Alpine, TX 79832. Offers business administration (MBA); teacher education (M Ed), including bilingual education, counseling, educational diagnostics, elementary education, general education, reading, school administration, secondary education. Part-time and evening/weekend programs available. Postbaccalaureate distance learning degree programs offered (no on-campus study). *Degree requirements:* For master's, comprehensive exam, thesis optional, minimum GPA of 3.0. *Entrance requirements:* For master's, GMAT or GRE General Test, minimum GPA of 2.5 in last 60 hours of undergraduate work. Additional exam requirements/recommendations for international students: Required—TOEFL.

Sul Ross State University, School of Professional Studies, Department of Teacher Education, Program in Educational Diagnostics, Alpine, TX 79832. Offers M Ed, Certificate. Part-time and evening/weekend programs available. *Degree requirements:* For master's, thesis optional. *Entrance requirements:* For master's, GMAT or GRE General Test, minimum GPA of 2.5 in last 60 hours of undergraduate work.

Syracuse University, School of Education, Program in Instructional Design, Development, and Evaluation, Syracuse, NY 13244. Offers MS, PhD, CAS. Part-time programs available. *Students:* 35 full-time (23 women), 13 part-time (6 women); includes 6 minority (4 Black or African American, non-Hispanic/Latino; 1 American Indian or Alaska Native, non-Hispanic/Latino; 1 Asian, non-Hispanic/Latino), 18 international. Average age 34. 27 applicants, 59% accepted, 8 enrolled. In 2013, 10 master's, 7 doctorates awarded. *Degree requirements:* For master's, thesis or alternative; for doctorate, comprehensive exam, thesis/dissertation. *Entrance requirements:* For doctorate, GRE, interview, master's degree; for CAS, GRE (recommended), interview. Additional exam requirements/recommendations for international students: Required—TOEFL (minimum score 100 iBT). *Application deadline:* For fall admission, 1/15 priority date for domestic and international students; for spring admission, 10/15 priority date for domestic and international students. Applications are processed on a rolling basis. Application fee: $75. Electronic applications accepted. *Financial support:* Fellowships with full tuition reimbursements, research assistantships with full and partial tuition reimbursements, and teaching assistantships with full and partial tuition reimbursements available. Financial award application deadline: 1/1; financial award applicants required to submit FAFSA. *Faculty research:* Cultural pluralism and instructional design, corrections training, aging and learning, the University and social change, investigative evaluation. *Unit head:* Dr. Tiffany A. Koszalka, Chair, 315-443-3703, E-mail: takoszal@syr.edu. *Application contact:* Laurie Deyo, Graduate Recruiter, School of Education, 315-443-2505, E-mail: e-gradrcrt@syr.edu.
Website: http://soeweb.syr.edu/idde/instrucdesign.html.

Teachers College, Columbia University, Graduate Faculty of Education, Department of Human Development, Program in Measurement, Evaluation, and Statistics, New York, NY 10027. Offers MA, MS, Ed D, PhD. *Faculty:* 7 full-time, 1 part-time/adjunct. *Students:* 19 full-time (8 women), 20 part-time (8 women); includes 6 minority (2 Black or African American, non-Hispanic/Latino; 3 Asian, non-Hispanic/Latino; 1 Two or more races, non-Hispanic/Latino), 21 international. Average age 29. 41 applicants, 68%

accepted, 9 enrolled. In 2013, 6 master's, 9 doctorates awarded. *Degree requirements:* For master's, project; for doctorate, comprehensive exam, thesis/dissertation, empirical, research paper. *Entrance requirements:* For master's and doctorate, GRE. *Application deadline:* For fall admission, 12/15 for domestic students; for spring admission, 11/1 for domestic students. Applications are processed on a rolling basis. Application fee: $65. Electronic applications accepted. *Financial support:* Career-related internships or fieldwork, Federal Work-Study, institutionally sponsored loans, and tuition waivers (full and partial) available. Support available to part-time students. Financial award application deadline: 2/1; financial award applicants required to submit FAFSA. *Faculty research:* Probability and inference, potentially biased test items, research design, clustering and scaling methods for multivariate data. *Unit head:* Prof. Lawrence T. DeCarlo, Program Coordinator, 212-678-4037, E-mail: decarlo@tc.edu. *Application contact:* Melba Remice, Assistant Director of Admission, 212-678-4035, Fax: 212-678-4171, E-mail: ms2545@columbia.edu.
Website: http://www.tc.columbia.edu/hud/measurement/.

Tennessee Technological University, College of Graduate Studies, College of Education, Department of Curriculum and Instruction, Program in Exceptional Learning, Cookeville, TN 38505. Offers applied behavior analysis (PhD); literacy (PhD); program planning and evaluation (PhD); STEM education (PhD). Part-time and evening/weekend programs available. *Students:* 14 full-time (12 women), 22 part-time (16 women); includes 2 minority (1 Black or African American, non-Hispanic/Latino; 1 Two or more races, non-Hispanic/Latino), 1 international. 15 applicants, 47% accepted, 6 enrolled. In 2013, 1 doctorate awarded. *Degree requirements:* For doctorate, comprehensive exam, thesis/dissertation. *Entrance requirements:* For doctorate, GRE, minimum GPA of 3.0. Additional exam requirements/recommendations for international students: Required—TOEFL (minimum score 550 paper-based; 79 iBT), IELTS (minimum score 5.5), PTE (minimum score 53), or TOEIC (Test of English as an International Communication). *Application deadline:* For fall admission, 8/1 for domestic students, 5/1 for international students; for spring admission, 12/1 for domestic students, 10/1 for international students. Applications are processed on a rolling basis. Application fee: $35 ($40 for international students). Electronic applications accepted. *Expenses:* Tuition, state resident: full-time $9347; part-time $465 per credit hour. Tuition, nonresident: full-time $23,635; part-time $1152 per credit hour. *Financial support:* In 2013–14, 4 fellowships (averaging $8,000 per year), 10 research assistantships (averaging $12,000 per year), 1 teaching assistantship (averaging $12,000 per year) were awarded. Financial award application deadline: 4/1. *Unit head:* Dr. Lisa Zagumny, Director, 931-372-3078, Fax: 931-372-3517, E-mail: lzagumny@tntech.edu. *Application contact:* Shelia K. Kendrick, Coordinator of Graduate Studies, 931-372-3808, Fax: 931-372-3497, E-mail: skendrick@tntech.edu.
Website: https://www.tntech.edu/education/elphd/.

Texas A&M University–San Antonio, Department of Curriculum and Kinesiology, San Antonio, TX 78224. Offers bilingual education (MA); early childhood education (M Ed); kinesiology (MS); reading (MS); special education (M Ed), including educational diagnostician, instructional specialist. Part-time and evening/weekend programs available. *Degree requirements:* For master's, comprehensive exam, thesis or alternative. *Entrance requirements:* For master's, MAT. Additional exam requirements/recommendations for international students: Required—TOEFL (minimum score 550 paper-based; 80 iBT), IELTS (minimum score 6). Electronic applications accepted.

Université Laval, Faculty of Education, Department of Foundations and Interventions in Education, Québec, QC G1K 7P4, Canada. Offers educational administration and evaluation (MA, PhD); educational practice (Diploma), including educational pedagogy, pedagogy management and development, school adaptation; orientation sciences (MA, PhD). *Degree requirements:* For doctorate, comprehensive exam, thesis/dissertation. Electronic applications accepted.

University at Albany, State University of New York, School of Education, Department of Educational and Counseling Psychology, Albany, NY 12222-0001. Offers counseling psychology (MS, PhD, CAS); educational psychology (Ed D); educational psychology and statistics (MS); measurements and evaluation (Ed D); rehabilitation counseling (MS), including counseling psychology; school counselor (CAS); school psychology (Psy D, CAS); special education (MS); statistics and research design (Ed D). *Accreditation:* APA (one or more programs are accredited). Evening/weekend programs available. *Degree requirements:* For doctorate, thesis/dissertation. *Entrance requirements:* For doctorate, GRE General Test. Additional exam requirements/recommendations for international students: Required—TOEFL (minimum score 550 paper-based). Electronic applications accepted.

University of Arkansas, Graduate School, College of Education and Health Professions, Department of Curriculum and Instruction, Program in Educational Statistics and Research Methods, Fayetteville, AR 72701-1201. Offers MS, PhD. Electronic applications accepted.

The University of British Columbia, Faculty of Education, Department of Educational and Counseling Psychology, and Special Education, Vancouver, BC V6T 1Z1, Canada. Offers counseling psychology (M Ed, MA, PhD); development, learning and culture (PhD); guidance studies (Diploma); human development, learning and culture (M Ed, MA); measurement and evaluation and research methodology (M Ed); measurement, evaluation and research methodology (MA); measurement, evaluation, and research methodology (PhD); school psychology (M Ed, MA, PhD); special education (M Ed, MA, PhD, Diploma). Part-time programs available. *Degree requirements:* For master's, thesis (for some programs); for doctorate, comprehensive exam, thesis/dissertation. *Entrance requirements:* For master's, GRE General Test (counseling psychology MA); for doctorate, GRE General Test. Additional exam requirements/recommendations for international students: Required—TOEFL. Electronic applications accepted. *Expenses: Tuition, area resident:* Full-time $8000 Canadian dollars. *Faculty research:* Women, family, social problems, career transition, stress and coping problems.

University of Calgary, Faculty of Graduate Studies, Werklund School of Education, Graduate Division of Educational Research, Calgary, AB T2N 1N4, Canada. Offers adult learning (M Ed, MA, Ed D, PhD); curriculum and learning (M Ed, MA, Ed D, PhD); educational leadership (M Ed, MA, Ed D, PhD); languages and diversity (M Ed, MA, Ed D, PhD); learning sciences (M Ed, MA, Ed D, PhD). Ed D in educational leadership offered via distance delivery. Part-time and evening/weekend programs available. Postbaccalaureate distance learning degree programs offered (minimal on-campus study). *Degree requirements:* For master's, thesis (for some programs); for doctorate, thesis/dissertation, candidacy exam. *Entrance requirements:* For master's, minimum GPA of 3.0, 3 letters of reference; for doctorate, minimum GPA of 3.5, 3 letters of reference. Additional exam requirements/recommendations for international students: Required—TOEFL, IELTS. Electronic applications accepted. *Faculty research:* Curriculum, leadership, technology, contexts, gifted, second language teaching, work place and adult learning.

University of Colorado Boulder, Graduate School, School of Education, Division of Research and Evaluation Methodologies, Boulder, CO 80309. Offers PhD. *Accreditation:* NCATE. *Students:* 7 full-time (3 women), 2 part-time (1 woman); includes 1 minority (Native Hawaiian or other Pacific Islander, non-Hispanic/Latino), 1 international. Average age 32. 16 applicants, 19% accepted, 2 enrolled. *Degree requirements:* For doctorate, one foreign language, comprehensive exam, thesis/dissertation. *Entrance requirements:* For doctorate, GRE General Test, minimum undergraduate GPA of 2.75. *Application deadline:* For fall admission, 2/1 for domestic students, 12/1 for international students; for spring admission, 9/1 for domestic and international students. Application fee: $40 ($60 for international students). Electronic applications accepted. *Financial support:* In 2013–14, 24 students received support, including 1 fellowship (averaging $1,000 per year), 8 research assistantships with full and partial tuition reimbursements available (averaging $28,352 per year), 4 teaching assistantships with full and partial tuition reimbursements available (averaging $8,918 per year); institutionally sponsored loans, scholarships/grants, health care benefits, and unspecified assistantships also available. Financial award applicants required to submit FAFSA.
Website: http://www.colorado.edu/education/.

University of Colorado Denver, School of Education and Human Development, Program in Educational Leadership and Innovation, Denver, CO 80217-3364. Offers educational studies and research (PhD), including administrative leadership and policy, early childhood special education, math education, research, assessment and evaluation, science education, urban ecologies. Part-time and evening/weekend programs available. *Students:* 16 full-time (12 women), 12 part-time (9 women); includes 6 minority (2 Black or African American, non-Hispanic/Latino; 3 Asian, non-Hispanic/Latino; 1 Hispanic/Latino), 1 international. Average age 39. 16 applicants, 31% accepted, 4 enrolled. In 2013, 10 doctorates awarded. *Degree requirements:* For doctorate, comprehensive exam, thesis/dissertation, 75 credit hours (for PhD). *Entrance requirements:* For doctorate, GRE or equivalent, resume or curriculum vitae, letters of recommendation, master's degree or equivalent, completion of basic or advanced statistics course with minimum B grade. Additional exam requirements/recommendations for international students: Required—TOEFL (minimum score 537 paper-based; 75 iBT); Recommended—IELTS (minimum score 6.5). *Application deadline:* For fall admission, 5/1 priority date for domestic students, 4/15 priority date for international students. Applications are processed on a rolling basis. Application fee: $50 ($75 for international students). Electronic applications accepted. *Expenses:* Contact institution. *Financial support:* In 2013–14, 19 students received support. Fellowships, research assistantships, teaching assistantships, Federal Work-Study, institutionally sponsored loans, scholarships/grants, and traineeships available. Financial award application deadline: 4/1; financial award applicants required to submit FAFSA. *Faculty research:* Administrative leadership and policy studies, early childhood education, research in diversity, paraprofessionals in education, urban schools lab. *Unit head:* Dr. Deanna Sands, Associate Dean, Research and Professional Development, 303-315-4931, E-mail: deanna.sands@ucdenver.edu. *Application contact:* Student Services Center, 303-315-6300, Fax: 303-315-6311, E-mail: education@ucdenver.edu.
Website: http://www.ucdenver.edu/academics/colleges/SchoolOfEducation/Academics/Doctorate/Pages/PhD.aspx.

University of Colorado Denver, School of Education and Human Development, Programs in Educational and School Psychology, Denver, CO 80217. Offers educational psychology (MA), including educational assessment, educational psychology, human development, human learning, partner schools, research and evaluation; school psychology (Ed S). Part-time and evening/weekend programs available. *Students:* 145 full-time (118 women), 108 part-time (87 women); includes 34 minority (4 Black or African American, non-Hispanic/Latino; 3 Asian, non-Hispanic/Latino; 19 Hispanic/Latino; 8 Two or more races, non-Hispanic/Latino), 10 international. Average age 29. 189 applicants, 81% accepted, 120 enrolled. In 2013, 71 master's, 10 other advanced degrees awarded. *Degree requirements:* For master's, comprehensive exam, 9 hours of core courses, embedded within a minimum of 36 to 38 hours of relevant coursework, including an educational psychology practicum, independent study project or thesis (recommended); for Ed S, comprehensive exam, minimum of 75 semester hours (61 hours of coursework, 6 of 500-hour practicum in field, and 8 of 1200-hour internship); PRAXIS II. *Entrance requirements:* For master's, GRE if undergraduate GPA below 2.75, resume, three letters of recommendation, transcripts; for Ed S, GRE, resume, letters of recommendation, transcripts. Additional exam requirements/recommendations for international students: Required—TOEFL (minimum score 537 paper-based; 75 iBT); Recommended—IELTS (minimum score 6.5). *Application deadline:* For fall admission, 4/15 for domestic students, 4/1 for international students; for spring admission, 9/15 for domestic students, 9/1 for international students. Application fee: $50 ($75 for international students). Electronic applications accepted. *Expenses:* Contact institution. *Financial support:* In 2013–14, 5 students received support. Research assistantships, Federal Work-Study, institutionally sponsored loans, scholarships/grants, and traineeships available. Financial award application deadline: 4/1; financial award applicants required to submit FAFSA. *Faculty research:* Crisis response and intervention, school violence prevention, immigrant experience, educational environments for English language learners, culturally competent assessment and intervention, child and youth suicide. *Unit head:* Dr. Jung-In Kim, Assistant Professor of Educational Psychology, 303-315-4965, E-mail: jung-in.kim@ucdenver.edu. *Application contact:* Student Services Center, 303-315-6300, Fax: 303-315-6311, E-mail: education@ucdenver.edu.
Website: http://www.ucdenver.edu/academics/colleges/SchoolOfEducation/Academics/MASTERS/EPSY/Pages/default.aspx.

University of Connecticut, Graduate School, Neag School of Education, Department of Educational Psychology, Program in Measurement, Evaluation, and Assessment, Storrs, CT 06269. Offers MA, PhD, Post-Master's Certificate. Terminal master's awarded for partial completion of doctoral program. *Degree requirements:* For master's, comprehensive exam, thesis or alternative; for doctorate, thesis/dissertation. *Entrance requirements:* For doctorate, GRE General Test. Additional exam requirements/recommendations for international students: Required—TOEFL (minimum score 550 paper-based). Electronic applications accepted.

University of Florida, Graduate School, College of Education, School of Human Development and Organizational Studies in Education, Gainesville, FL 32611. Offers counseling and counselor education (Ed D, PhD), including counseling and counselor education, marriage and family counseling, mental health counseling, school counseling and guidance; educational leadership (M Ed, MAE, Ed D, PhD, Ed S), including educational leadership (Ed D, PhD), educational policy (Ed D, PhD); higher education administration (Ed D, PhD, Ed S), including education policy (Ed D), educational policy (Ed D, PhD), higher education administration (Ed D, PhD); marriage and family counseling (M Ed, MAE, Ed S); mental health counseling (M Ed, MAE, Ed S); research and evaluation methodology (M Ed, MAE, Ed D, PhD, Ed S); school counseling and guidance (M Ed, MAE, Ed S); student personnel in higher education (M Ed, MAE, Ed S). *Accreditation:* ACA (one or more programs are accredited); NCATE. Part-time programs available. Postbaccalaureate distance learning degree programs offered. *Faculty:* 20 full-time (11 women), 4 part-time/adjunct (1 woman). *Students:* 291 full-time (232 women), 212 part-time (157 women); includes 145 minority (71 Black or African American, non-Hispanic/Latino; 3 American Indian or Alaska Native, non-Hispanic/Latino; 11 Asian, non-Hispanic/Latino; 60 Hispanic/Latino), 38 international. Average age 31. 271 applicants, 42% accepted, 75 enrolled. In 2013, 71 master's, 31 doctorates, 62 other advanced degrees awarded. Terminal master's awarded for partial completion of doctoral program. *Degree requirements:* For master's, thesis optional; for doctorate,

comprehensive exam, thesis/dissertation. *Entrance requirements:* For master's and doctorate, GRE General Test, minimum GPA of 3.0 (undergraduate), 3.5 (graduate); for Ed S, GRE General Test. Additional exam requirements/recommendations for international students: Required—TOEFL (minimum score 550 paper-based; 80 iBT), IELTS (minimum score 6). *Application deadline:* Applications are processed on a rolling basis. Application fee: $30. Electronic applications accepted. *Expenses:* Tuition, state resident: full-time $12,640. Tuition, nonresident: full-time $30,000. *Financial support:* In 2013–14, 85 students received support, including 6 fellowships (averaging $12,190 per year), 48 research assistantships (averaging $15,155 per year), 50 teaching assistantships (averaging $9,080 per year); career-related internships or fieldwork and unspecified assistantships also available. Financial award applicants required to submit FAFSA. *Unit head:* Glenn E. Good, PhD, Dean and Professor, 352-273-4135, Fax: 352-846-2697, E-mail: ggood@ufl.edu. *Application contact:* Thomasenia L. Adams, PhD, Professor and Associate Dean, 352-273-4119, Fax: 352-846-2697, E-mail: tla@coe.ufl.edu.
Website: http://education.ufl.edu/hdose/.

University of Illinois at Chicago, Graduate College, College of Education, Department of Educational Psychology, Chicago, IL 60607-7128. Offers early childhood education (M Ed); educational psychology (PhD); measurement, evaluation, statistics, and assessment (M Ed); youth development (M Ed). Part-time programs available. Postbaccalaureate distance learning degree programs offered (no on-campus study). *Faculty:* 11 full-time (9 women), 4 part-time/adjunct (3 women). *Students:* 63 full-time (48 women), 108 part-time (80 women); includes 58 minority (27 Black or African American, non-Hispanic/Latino; 11 Asian, non-Hispanic/Latino; 17 Hispanic/Latino; 3 Two or more races, non-Hispanic/Latino), 11 international. Average age 33. 128 applicants, 69% accepted, 51 enrolled. In 2013, 41 master's, 2 doctorates awarded. *Expenses:* Tuition, state resident: full-time $11,066; part-time $3689 per term. Tuition, nonresident: full-time $23,064; part-time $7688 per term. *Required fees:* $3004; $1190 per term. Tuition and fees vary according to course level and program. *Total annual research expenditures:* $541,000. *Unit head:* Kimlerly Lawless, Chairperson, 312-996-2359, E-mail: klawless@uic.edu. *Application contact:* Receptionist, 312-413-2550, E-mail: gradcoll@uic.edu.
Website: http://education.uic.edu/academics-admissions/departments/department-educational-psychology#overview.

The University of Iowa, Graduate College, College of Education, Department of Psychological and Quantitative Foundations, Iowa City, IA 52242-1316. Offers counseling psychology (PhD); educational measurement and statistics (MA, PhD); educational psychology (MA, PhD); school psychology (PhD, Ed S). *Accreditation:* APA. *Degree requirements:* For master's, thesis optional, exam; for doctorate, comprehensive exam, thesis/dissertation; for Ed S, exam. *Entrance requirements:* For master's, doctorate, and Ed S, GRE General Test, minimum GPA of 3.0. Additional exam requirements/recommendations for international students: Required—TOEFL (minimum score 550 paper-based; 81 iBT). Electronic applications accepted.

The University of Kansas, Graduate Studies, School of Education, Department of Psychology and Research in Education, Program in Educational Psychology and Research, Lawrence, KS 66045. Offers MS Ed, PhD. *Faculty:* 21. *Students:* 35 full-time (26 women), 8 part-time (6 women); includes 3 minority (2 Black or African American, non-Hispanic/Latino; 1 Asian, non-Hispanic/Latino), 18 international. Average age 33. 16 applicants, 31% accepted, 2 enrolled. In 2013, 3 master's, 5 doctorates awarded. *Degree requirements:* For master's, thesis; for doctorate, comprehensive exam, thesis/dissertation. *Entrance requirements:* For master's, GRE General Test, minimum GPA of 3.0; for doctorate, GRE General Test. Additional exam requirements/recommendations for international students: Required—TOEFL. *Application deadline:* For fall admission, 12/15 for domestic and international students; for spring admission, 11/15 for domestic students. Application fee: $55 ($65 for international students). Electronic applications accepted. *Financial support:* Fellowships, research assistantships with full and partial tuition reimbursements, teaching assistantships with full and partial tuition reimbursements, career-related internships or fieldwork, institutionally sponsored loans, scholarships/grants, traineeships, health care benefits, tuition waivers (full and partial), and unspecified assistantships available. Support available to part-time students. Financial award application deadline: 2/1. *Faculty research:* Educational measurement, applied statistics, research design, program evaluation, learning and development. *Unit head:* William Skorupski, Director of Training, 785-864-3931, E-mail: bfrey@ku.edu. *Application contact:* Penny Fritts, Admissions Coordinator, 785-864-9645, Fax: 785-864-3820, E-mail: preadmit@ku.edu.
Website: http://www.soe.ku.edu/PRE/.

University of Kentucky, Graduate School, College of Education, Department of Educational Policy Studies and Evaluation, Lexington, KY 40506-0032. Offers educational policy studies and evaluation (Ed D); higher education (MS Ed, PhD); social and philosophical studies (MS Ed). *Accreditation:* NCATE. Terminal master's awarded for partial completion of doctoral program. *Degree requirements:* For master's, comprehensive exam, thesis optional; for doctorate, comprehensive exam, thesis/dissertation. *Entrance requirements:* For master's, GRE General Test, minimum undergraduate GPA of 2.75; for doctorate, GRE General Test, minimum graduate GPA of 3.0. Additional exam requirements/recommendations for international students: Required—TOEFL (minimum score 550 paper-based). Electronic applications accepted. *Faculty research:* Studies in higher education; comparative and international education; evaluation of educational programs, policies, and reform; student, teacher, and faculty cultures; gender and education.

University of Louisiana at Monroe, Graduate School, College of Arts, Education, and Sciences, School of Education, Program in Curriculum and Instruction, Monroe, LA 71209-0001. Offers art education (M Ed); biology education (M Ed); chemistry education (M Ed); curriculum and instruction (Ed D); early childhood education (M Ed); earth science education (M Ed); educational leadership (M Ed); elementary education (1-5) (M Ed); English as a second language (M Ed); English education (M Ed); family and consumer education (M Ed); French education (M Ed); history education (M Ed); math education (M Ed); middle school education (M Ed); music education (M Ed); reading education (K-12) (M Ed); Spanish education (M Ed); special education - academically gifted (M Ed); special education - early intervention (M Ed); special education - educational diagnostician (M Ed); special education - mild/moderate disabilities (M Ed); speech education (M Ed). *Accreditation:* NCATE. *Degree requirements:* For master's, comprehensive exam (for some programs), thesis; for doctorate, thesis/dissertation, internships. *Entrance requirements:* For master's, GRE General Test; for doctorate, GRE General Test, minimum undergraduate GPA of 2.75, graduate 3.25. Additional exam requirements/recommendations for international students: Required—TOEFL (minimum score 500 paper-based; 61 iBT). *Application deadline:* For fall admission, 8/24 priority date for domestic students, 7/1 for international students; for winter admission, 12/14 priority date for domestic students; for spring admission, 1/19 for domestic students, 11/1 for international students. Applications are processed on a rolling basis. Application fee: $20 ($30 for international students). Electronic applications accepted. *Expenses:* Tuition, state resident: full-time $6607. Tuition, nonresident: full-time $17,179. Full-time tuition and fees vary according to program. *Financial support:* Research assistantships, career-related internships or fieldwork, Federal Work-Study, and unspecified assistantships available. Financial award application deadline: 4/1; financial award applicants required to submit FAFSA. *Unit head:* Dr. Dorothy Schween, Director, 318-342-1268, Fax: 318-342-3131, E-mail: schween@ulm.edu. *Application contact:* Dr. Dorothy Schween, Director, 318-342-1268, Fax: 318-342-3131, E-mail: schween@ulm.edu.

University of Maryland, College Park, Academic Affairs, College of Education, Department of Human Development and Quantitative Methodology, College Park, MD 20742. Offers MA, Ed D, PhD. *Faculty:* 56 full-time (47 women), 12 part-time/adjunct (10 women). *Students:* 73 full-time (60 women), 46 part-time (36 women); includes 29 minority (8 Black or African American, non-Hispanic/Latino; 7 Asian, non-Hispanic/Latino; 10 Hispanic/Latino; 1 Native Hawaiian or other Pacific Islander, non-Hispanic/Latino; 3 Two or more races, non-Hispanic/Latino), 22 international. 162 applicants, 26% accepted, 26 enrolled. In 2013, 16 master's, 18 doctorates awarded. *Entrance requirements:* Additional exam requirements/recommendations for international students: Required—TOEFL. *Application deadline:* For fall admission, 3/15 for domestic students, 12/15 for international students; for spring admission, 10/1 for domestic students, 6/1 for international students. Application fee: $75. *Expenses:* Tuition, state resident: full-time $10,314; part-time $573 per credit hour. Tuition, nonresident: full-time $22,248; part-time $1236 per credit. *Required fees:* $1446; $403.15 per semester. Tuition and fees vary according to program. *Financial support:* In 2013–14, 9 fellowships with full tuition reimbursements (averaging $32,282 per year), 39 teaching assistantships (averaging $17,585 per year) were awarded. *Total annual research expenditures:* $3.4 million. *Unit head:* Nathan Fox, Chair, 301-405-2827, E-mail: fox@umd.edu. *Application contact:* Dr. Charles A. Caramello, Dean of Graduate School, 301-405-0358, Fax: 301-314-9305, E-mail: ccaramel@umd.edu.
Website: http://www.education.umd.edu/EDHI/.

University of Massachusetts Amherst, Graduate School, College of Education, Program in Education, Amherst, MA 01003. Offers bilingual/English as a second language/multicultural education (M Ed, Ed S); child study and early education (M Ed); children, families and schools (Ed D, Ed S); early childhood and elementary teacher education (M Ed); educational leadership (M Ed); educational policy and leadership (Ed D); higher education (M Ed); international education (M Ed); language, literacy and culture (Ed D); learning, media and technology (M Ed, Ed S); mathematics, science, and learning technologies (Ed D); psychometric methods, educational statistics and research methods (Ed D); reading and writing (M Ed); school counselor education (M Ed, Ed S); school psychology (Ed S); science education (Ed S); secondary teacher education (M Ed); social justice education (M Ed, Ed D, Ed S); special education (M Ed, Ed D, Ed S); teacher education and school improvement (Ed D, Ed S). *Accreditation:* NCATE. Part-time programs available. Postbaccalaureate distance learning degree programs offered (minimal on-campus study). *Faculty:* 95 full-time (55 women). *Students:* 357 full-time (240 women), 264 part-time (194 women); includes 114 minority (41 Black or African American, non-Hispanic/Latino; 4 American Indian or Alaska Native, non-Hispanic/Latino; 10 Asian, non-Hispanic/Latino; 47 Hispanic/Latino; 12 Two or more races, non-Hispanic/Latino), 100 international. Average age 34. 761 applicants, 51% accepted, 200 enrolled. In 2013, 186 master's, 31 doctorates, 22 other advanced degrees awarded. Terminal master's awarded for partial completion of doctoral program. *Degree requirements:* For doctorate, comprehensive exam, thesis/dissertation. *Entrance requirements:* Additional exam requirements/recommendations for international students: Required—TOEFL (minimum score 550 paper-based; 80 iBT), IELTS (minimum score 6.5). *Application deadline:* For fall admission, 1/15 for domestic and international students. Applications are processed on a rolling basis. Application fee: $75. Electronic applications accepted. *Financial support:* Fellowships with full and partial tuition reimbursements, research assistantships with full and partial tuition reimbursements, teaching assistantships with full and partial tuition reimbursements, career-related internships or fieldwork, Federal Work-Study, scholarships/grants, traineeships, health care benefits, tuition waivers (full and partial), and unspecified assistantships available. Support available to part-time students. Financial award application deadline: 1/15; financial award applicants required to submit FAFSA. *Unit head:* Dr. Linda L. Griffin, Graduate Program Director, 413-545-6984, Fax: 413-545-1523. *Application contact:* Lindsay DeSantis, Supervisor of Admissions, 413-545-0722, Fax: 413-577-0010, E-mail: gradadm@grad.umass.edu.
Website: http://www.umass.edu/education/.

University of Memphis, Graduate School, College of Education, Department of Counseling, Educational Psychology and Research, Memphis, TN 38152. Offers counseling (MS, Ed D), including community counseling (MS), rehabilitation counseling (MS), school counseling (MS); counseling psychology (PhD); educational psychology and research (MS, PhD), including educational psychology, educational research. *Accreditation:* ACA (one or more programs are accredited); APA (one or more programs are accredited); CORE (one or more programs are accredited); NCATE. *Faculty:* 27 full-time (13 women), 12 part-time/adjunct (9 women). *Students:* 137 full-time (105 women), 97 part-time (74 women); includes 60 minority (44 Black or African American, non-Hispanic/Latino; 1 American Indian or Alaska Native, non-Hispanic/Latino; 7 Hispanic/Latino; 8 Two or more races, non-Hispanic/Latino), 9 international. Average age 32. 129 applicants, 50% accepted, 30 enrolled. In 2013, 46 master's, 14 doctorates awarded. *Degree requirements:* For master's, comprehensive exam, thesis or alternative; for doctorate, comprehensive exam, thesis/dissertation. *Entrance requirements:* For master's, GRE General Test or MAT, minimum GPA of 2.5; for doctorate, GRE General Test. *Application deadline:* For fall admission, 10/1 for domestic students; for spring admission, 4/1 for domestic students. Application fee: $35 ($60 for international students). *Financial support:* In 2013–14, 130 students received support. Fellowships with full tuition reimbursements available, research assistantships with full tuition reimbursements available, teaching assistantships with full tuition reimbursements available, career-related internships or fieldwork, Federal Work-Study, scholarships/grants, and unspecified assistantships available. Financial award application deadline: 2/15; financial award applicants required to submit FAFSA. *Faculty research:* Anger management, aging and disability, supervision, multicultural counseling. *Unit head:* Dr. Douglas C. Strohmer, Chair, 901-678-2841, Fax: 901-678-5114. *Application contact:* Dr. Ernest A. Rakow, Associate Dean of Administration and Graduate Programs, 901-678-2399, Fax: 901-678-4778.
Website: http://coe.memphis.edu/cepr/.

University of Miami, Graduate School, School of Education and Human Development, Department of Educational and Psychological Studies, Program in Research, Measurement, and Evaluation, Coral Gables, FL 33124. Offers MS Ed, PhD. Part-time and evening/weekend programs available. *Faculty:* 3 full-time (2 women). *Students:* 2 full-time (both women), 3 part-time (all women); includes 2 minority (both Hispanic/Latino), 2 international. Average age 28. 9 applicants, 22% accepted, 2 enrolled. In 2013, 1 master's awarded. Terminal master's awarded for partial completion of doctoral program. *Degree requirements:* For master's, comprehensive exam, thesis optional; for doctorate, thesis/dissertation, qualifying exam. *Entrance requirements:* For master's and doctorate, GRE General Test. Additional exam requirements/recommendations for international students: Required—TOEFL (minimum score 550 paper-based; 80 iBT); Recommended—IELTS (minimum score 6.5). *Application deadline:* For fall admission, 10/1 for international students. Applications are processed on a rolling basis. Application fee: $65. Electronic applications accepted. *Financial support:* In 2013–14, 5 students

received support. Health care benefits and unspecified assistantships available. Support available to part-time students. Financial award application deadline: 3/1; financial award applicants required to submit FAFSA. *Faculty research:* Psychometric theory, computer-based testing, quantitative research methods. *Unit head:* Dr. Nicholas Myers, Associate Professor and Program Director, 305-284-9803, Fax: 305-284-3003, E-mail: nmyers@miami.edu. *Application contact:* Lois Heffernan, Graduate Admissions Coordinator, 305-284-2167, Fax: 305-284-9395, E-mail: lheffernan@miami.edu.
Website: http://www.education.miami.edu/program/Programs.asp?Program_ID=148&Src=Graduate.

University of Minnesota, Twin Cities Campus, Graduate School, College of Education and Human Development, Department of Organizational Leadership, Policy and Development, Program in Evaluation Studies, Minneapolis, MN 55455-0213. Offers MA, PhD. *Students:* 23 full-time (19 women), 18 part-time (15 women); includes 7 minority (3 Black or African American, non-Hispanic/Latino; 2 Asian, non-Hispanic/Latino; 2 Hispanic/Latino), 2 international. Average age 37. 13 applicants, 69% accepted. In 2013, 3 master's, 1 doctorate awarded. Application fee: $75 ($95 for international students). *Unit head:* Dr. Rebecca Ropers-Huilman, Chair, 612-624-1006, Fax: 612-624-3377, E-mail: ropers@umn.edu. *Application contact:* Dr. Jennifer Engler, Assistant Dean, 612-626-2887, Fax: 612-626-7496, E-mail: engle009@umn.edu.
Website: http://www.cehd.umn.edu/EdPA/Evaluation.

University of Missouri–St. Louis, College of Education, Division of Educational Leadership and Policy Studies, St. Louis, MO 63121. Offers adult and higher education (M Ed), including adult education, higher education; educational administration (M Ed, Ed S), including community education (M Ed), elementary education (M Ed), secondary education (M Ed); institutional research (Certificate). *Accreditation:* NCATE. Part-time and evening/weekend programs available. *Faculty:* 13 full-time (8 women), 5 part-time/adjunct (2 women). *Students:* 17 full-time (13 women), 154 part-time (114 women); includes 77 minority (75 Black or African American, non-Hispanic/Latino; 1 Asian, non-Hispanic/Latino; 1 Hispanic/Latino), 7 international. Average age 35. 120 applicants, 68% accepted, 40 enrolled. In 2013, 63 master's, 28 Certificates awarded. *Degree requirements:* For master's, comprehensive exam (for some programs); for other advanced degree, comprehensive exam (for some programs), thesis or alternative. *Entrance requirements:* Additional exam requirements/recommendations for international students: Recommended—TOEFL (minimum score 550 paper-based; 79 iBT), IELTS (minimum score 6.5). *Application deadline:* For fall admission, 7/1 priority date for domestic and international students; for spring admission, 12/1 priority date for domestic and international students. Applications are processed on a rolling basis. Application fee: $50 ($40 for international students). Electronic applications accepted. *Expenses:* Tuition, state resident: full-time $7364; part-time $409.10 per credit hour. Tuition, nonresident: full-time $19,162; part-time $1008.50 per credit hour. *Financial support:* In 2013–14, 1 research assistantship with full and partial tuition reimbursement (averaging $12,000 per year), teaching assistantships with full and partial tuition reimbursements (averaging $8,470 per year) were awarded. Financial award application deadline: 4/1; financial award applicants required to submit FAFSA. *Faculty research:* Educational policy research; philosophy of education; higher, adult, and vocational education; school initiatives, change, and reform. *Unit head:* Dr. E. Kathleen Sullivan Brown, Chair, 514-516-5944. *Application contact:* 314-516-5458, Fax: 314-516-6996, E-mail: gradadm@umsl.edu.
Website: http://coe.umsl.edu/web/divisions/elaps/index.html.

University of Missouri–St. Louis, College of Education, Division of Educational Psychology, Research, and Evaluation, St. Louis, MO 63121. Offers educational psychology (M Ed), including character and citizenship education, educational research and program evaluation; program evaluation and assessment (Certificate); school psychology (Ed S). *Faculty:* 12 full-time (5 women), 14 part-time/adjunct (5 women). *Students:* 19 full-time (17 women), 12 part-time (11 women); includes 3 minority (2 Black or African American, non-Hispanic/Latino; 1 Two or more races, non-Hispanic/Latino). Average age 29. 29 applicants, 66% accepted, 9 enrolled. In 2013, 8 Certificates awarded. *Degree requirements:* For other advanced degree, comprehensive exam, thesis or alternative, internship. *Entrance requirements:* For degree, GRE General Test, 2-4 letters of recommendation, personal interview. Additional exam requirements/recommendations for international students: Required—IELTS (minimum score 6.5); Recommended—TOEFL (minimum score 550 paper-based; 79 iBT). *Application deadline:* For fall admission, 2/15 for domestic and international students. Application fee: $50 ($40 for international students). Electronic applications accepted. *Expenses:* Tuition, state resident: full-time $7364; part-time $409.10 per credit hour. Tuition, nonresident: full-time $19,162; part-time $1008.50 per credit hour. *Financial support:* Application deadline: 4/1; applicants required to submit FAFSA. *Faculty research:* Child/adolescent psychology, quantitative and qualitative methodology, evaluation processes, measurement and assessment. *Unit head:* Dr. Donald Gouwens, Chairperson, 314-516-4773, Fax: 314-516-5784, E-mail: gouwensd@msx.umsl.edu. *Application contact:* 314-516-5458, Fax: 314-516-6996, E-mail: gradadm@umsl.edu.
Website: http://coe.umsl.edu/web/divisions/edpsych/index.html.

University of Nebraska–Lincoln, Graduate College, College of Education and Human Sciences, Department of Educational Psychology, Lincoln, NE 68588. Offers cognition, learning and development (MA); counseling psychology (MA); educational psychology (MA, Ed S); psychological studies in education (PhD), including cognition, learning and development, counseling psychology, quantitative, qualitative, and psychometric methods, school psychology; quantitative, qualitative, and psychometric methods (MA); school psychology (MA, Ed S). *Accreditation:* APA (one or more programs are accredited); NCATE. *Degree requirements:* For master's, thesis optional. *Entrance requirements:* For master's, GRE General Test. Additional exam requirements/recommendations for international students: Required—TOEFL (minimum score 500 paper-based). Electronic applications accepted. *Faculty research:* Measurement and assessment, metacognition, academic skills, child development, multicultural education and counseling.

University of New England, College of Arts and Sciences, Program in Education, Biddeford, ME 04005-9526. Offers advanced educational leadership (CAGS); career and technical education (MS Ed, CAGS); curriculum and instruction strategies (CAGS); curriculum and instruction strategy (MS Ed); educational leadership (MS Ed, CAGS); inclusion education (MS Ed); leadership, ethics and change (CAGS); literacy K-12 (MS Ed, CAGS); teaching methodologies (MS Ed). Part-time and evening/weekend programs available. Postbaccalaureate distance learning degree programs offered (no on-campus study). *Faculty:* 5 full-time (4 women), 17 part-time/adjunct (9 women). *Students:* 295 full-time (228 women), 233 part-time (175 women); includes 26 minority (19 Black or African American, non-Hispanic/Latino; 2 American Indian or Alaska Native, non-Hispanic/Latino; 2 Asian, non-Hispanic/Latino; 2 Hispanic/Latino; 1 Two or more races, non-Hispanic/Latino). Average age 37. 289 applicants, 84% accepted, 189 enrolled. In 2013, 257 master's, 106 CAGSs awarded. *Degree requirements:* For master's, collaborative action research project, integrative seminar portfolio. *Entrance requirements:* For master's, teaching certificate, 2 years of teaching experience. *Application deadline:* For fall admission, 9/15 for domestic students; for spring admission, 1/15 for domestic students. Applications are processed on a rolling basis. Application fee: $40. Electronic applications accepted. *Financial support:* Application deadline: 5/1; applicants required to submit FAFSA. *Faculty research:* Distance learning, effective teaching, transition planning, adult learning. *Unit head:* Paulette St. Ours, Associate Dean, College of Arts and Sciences, 207-602-2400, E-mail: pstours@une.edu. *Application contact:* Dr. Cynthia Forrest, Vice President for Student Affairs, 207-221-4225, Fax: 207-523-1925, E-mail: gradadmissions@une.edu.
Website: http://www.une.edu/cas/education/msonline.cfm.

The University of North Carolina at Chapel Hill, Graduate School, School of Education, Program in Education, Chapel Hill, NC 27599. Offers culture, curriculum and change (MA, PhD); early childhood, intervention and literacy (MA, PhD); educational psychology, measurement and evaluation (MA, PhD). *Accreditation:* NCATE. *Degree requirements:* For master's, thesis; for doctorate, comprehensive exam, thesis/dissertation. *Entrance requirements:* For master's, GRE General Test, minimum GPA of 3.0 during last 2 years of undergraduates course work; for doctorate, GRE General Test, minimum GPA of 3.0 during last 2 years of undergraduate course work. Additional exam requirements/recommendations for international students: Required—TOEFL (minimum score 550 paper-based). Electronic applications accepted.

The University of North Carolina at Greensboro, Graduate School, School of Education, Department of Educational Research Methodology, Greensboro, NC 27412-5001. Offers educational research, measurement and evaluation (PhD); MS/PhD. *Accreditation:* NCATE. *Degree requirements:* For doctorate, thesis/dissertation. *Entrance requirements:* For doctorate, GRE General Test. Additional exam requirements/recommendations for international students: Required—TOEFL. Electronic applications accepted.

University of North Dakota, Graduate School, College of Education and Human Development, Teaching and Learning Program, Grand Forks, ND 58202. Offers elementary education (Ed D, PhD); measurement and statistics (Ed D, PhD); secondary education (Ed D, PhD); special education (Ed D, PhD). *Accreditation:* NCATE. Postbaccalaureate distance learning degree programs offered (minimal on-campus study). *Degree requirements:* For doctorate, comprehensive exam, thesis/dissertation, final exam. *Entrance requirements:* For doctorate, minimum GPA of 3.5. Additional exam requirements/recommendations for international students: Required—TOEFL (minimum score 550 paper-based; 79 iBT), IELTS (minimum score 6.5). Electronic applications accepted.

University of Northern Colorado, Graduate School, College of Education and Behavioral Sciences, Department of Applied Statistics and Research Methods, Greeley, CO 80639. Offers MS, PhD. Part-time programs available. *Degree requirements:* For master's, comprehensive exam; for doctorate, comprehensive exam, thesis/dissertation. *Entrance requirements:* For master's, 3 letters of reference; for doctorate, GRE General Test, 3 letters of reference. Electronic applications accepted.

University of Northern Iowa, Graduate College, College of Education, Department of Educational Psychology and Foundations, Program in Educational Psychology: Context and Techniques of Assessment, Cedar Falls, IA 50614. Offers MAE. *Students:* 7 full-time (all women), 1 (woman) part-time. 24 applicants, 42% accepted, 8 enrolled. In 2013, 7 master's awarded. *Entrance requirements:* For master's, GRE, official transcripts, statement of purpose, three reference letters, writing sample. Application fee: $50 ($70 for international students). *Unit head:* Dr. Suzanne Freedman, Coordinator, 319-273-2483, Fax: 319-273-7732, E-mail: suzanne.freedman@uni.edu. *Application contact:* Laurie S. Russell, Record Analyst, 319-273-2623, Fax: 319-273-2885, E-mail: laurie.russell@uni.edu.

University of North Texas, Robert B. Toulouse School of Graduate Studies, Denton, TN 76203-5017. Offers accounting (MS, PhD); applied anthropology (MA, MS); applied behavior analysis (Certificate); applied technology and performance improvement (M Ed, MS, PhD); art education (MA, PhD); art history (MA); art museum education (Certificate); arts leadership (Certificate); audiology (Au D); behavior analysis (MS); biochemistry and molecular biology (MS, PhD); biology (MA, MS, PhD); business (PhD); business computer information systems (PhD); chemistry (MS, PhD); clinical psychology (PhD); communication studies (MA, MS); computer engineering (MS); computer science (MS); computer science and engineering (PhD); counseling (M Ed, MS, PhD), including clinical mental health counseling (MS), college and university counseling (M Ed, MS), elementary school counseling (M Ed, MS), secondary school counseling (M Ed, MS); counseling psychology (PhD); creative writing (MA); criminal justice (MS); curriculum and instruction (M Ed, PhD), including curriculum studies (PhD), early childhood studies (PhD), language and literacy studies (PhD); decision sciences (MBA); design (MA, MFA), including fashion design (MFA), innovation studies, interior design (MFA); early childhood studies (MS); economics (MS); educational leadership (M Ed, Ed D, PhD); educational psychology (MS), including family studies, gifted and talented (MS, PhD), human development, learning and cognition, research, measurement and evaluation; educational research (PhD), including gifted and talented (MS, PhD), human development and family studies, psychological aspects of sports and exercise, research, measurement and statistics; electrical engineering (MS); emergency management (MPA); engineering systems (MS); English (MA, PhD); environmental science (MS, PhD); experimental psychology (PhD); finance (MBA, MS, PhD); financial management (MPA); French (MA); health psychology and behavioral medicine (PhD); health services management (MBA); higher education (M Ed, Ed D, PhD); history (MA, MS, PhD), including European history (PhD), military history (PhD), United States history (PhD); hospitality management (MS); human resources management (MPA); information science (MS, PhD); information technologies (MBA); information technology and decision sciences (MS); interdisciplinary studies (MA, MS); international sustainable tourism (MS); jazz studies (MM); journalism (MA, MJ, Graduate Certificate), including interactive and virtual digital communication (Graduate Certificate), narrative journalism (Graduate Certificate), public relations (Graduate Certificate); kinesiology (MS); learning technologies (MS, PhD); library science (MS); local government management (MPA); logistics and supply chain management (MBA, PhD); long-term care, senior housing, and aging services (MA, MS); management science (PhD); marketing (MBA, PhD); materials science and engineering (MS, PhD); mathematics (MA, PhD); merchandising (MS); music (MA, MM Ed, PhD), including ethnomusicology (MA), music education (MM Ed, PhD), music theory (MA, PhD), musicology (MA, PhD), performance (MA); nonprofit management (MPA); operations and supply chain management (MBA); performance (MM, DMA); philosophy (MA, PhD); physics (MS, PhD); political science (MA, MS, PhD); public administration and management (PhD), including emergency management, nonprofit management, public financial management, urban management; radio, television and film (MA, MFA); recreation, event and sport management (MS); rehabilitation counseling (MS, Certificate); sociology (MA, MS, PhD); Spanish (MA); special education (M Ed, PhD), including autism intervention (PhD), emotional/behavioral disorders (PhD), mild/moderate disabilities (PhD); speech-language pathology (MA, MS); strategic management (MBA); studio art (MFA); taxation (MS); teaching (M Ed); MBA/MS; MS/MPH; MSES/MBA. Part-time and evening/weekend programs available. Postbaccalaureate distance learning degree programs offered. *Faculty:* 661 full-time (213 women), 240 part-time/adjunct (144 women). *Students:* 3,106 full-time (1,620 women), 3,543 part-time (2,221 women); includes 1,740 minority (533 Black or African American, non-Hispanic/Latino; 15 American Indian or Alaska Native, non-Hispanic/Latino; 286 Asian, non-Hispanic/Latino; 746 Hispanic/Latino; 3 Native Hawaiian or other Pacific Islander, non-Hispanic/Latino; 157 Two or

more races, non-Hispanic/Latino), 1,145 international. Average age 32. 6,289 applicants, 43% accepted, 1751 enrolled. In 2013, 1,778 master's, 239 doctorates, 10 other advanced degrees awarded. Terminal master's awarded for partial completion of doctoral program. *Degree requirements:* For master's, variable foreign language requirement, comprehensive exam (for some programs), thesis (for some programs); for doctorate, variable foreign language requirement, comprehensive exam (for some programs), thesis/dissertation; for other advanced degree, variable foreign language requirement, comprehensive exam (for some programs). *Entrance requirements:* For master's and doctorate, GRE, GMAT. Additional exam requirements/recommendations for international students: Required—TOEFL (minimum score 550 paper-based; 79 iBT). *Application deadline:* For fall admission, 7/15 for domestic students, 3/15 for international students; for spring admission, 11/15 for domestic students, 9/15 for international students; for summer admission, 5/1 for domestic students. Applications are processed on a rolling basis. Application fee: $60. Electronic applications accepted. *Financial support:* Fellowships with partial tuition reimbursements, research assistantships with partial tuition reimbursements, teaching assistantships, career-related internships or fieldwork, Federal Work-Study, institutionally sponsored loans, scholarships/grants, health care benefits, and library assistantships available. Support available to part-time students. Financial award applicants required to submit FAFSA. *Unit head:* Mark Wardell, Dean, 940-565-2383, E-mail: mark.wardell@unt.edu. *Application contact:* Toulouse School of Graduate Studies, 940-565-2383, Fax: 940-565-2141, E-mail: gradsch@unt.edu.
Website: http://tsgs.unt.edu/.

University of Oklahoma, Jeannine Rainbolt College of Education, Department of Educational Psychology, Norman, OK 73019. Offers community counseling (M Ed); counseling psychology (PhD); instructional psychology and technology (M Ed, PhD), including educational psychology and technology (M Ed), general (M Ed), instructional design (M Ed), instructional psychology and technology (PhD), integrating technology in teaching (M Ed), interactive learning technologies (M Ed), teaching and assessment (M Ed), teaching and learning (M Ed); school counseling (M Ed); special education (M Ed, PhD). *Accreditation:* NCATE. Part-time and evening/weekend programs available. *Faculty:* 24 full-time (18 women), 2 part-time/adjunct (1 woman). *Students:* 77 full-time (59 women), 90 part-time (69 women); includes 53 minority (15 Black or African American, non-Hispanic/Latino; 12 American Indian or Alaska Native, non-Hispanic/Latino; 2 Asian, non-Hispanic/Latino; 13 Hispanic/Latino; 11 Two or more races, non-Hispanic/Latino), 12 international. Average age 33. 130 applicants, 28% accepted, 34 enrolled. In 2013, 27 master's, 13 doctorates awarded. *Degree requirements:* For master's, comprehensive exam (for some programs), thesis (for some programs); for doctorate, comprehensive exam, thesis/dissertation. *Entrance requirements:* Additional exam requirements/recommendations for international students: Required—TOEFL (minimum score 79 iBT). *Application deadline:* For fall admission, 1/10 for domestic and international students. Application fee: $50 ($100 for international students). Electronic applications accepted. *Expenses:* Tuition, state resident: full-time $4205; part-time $175.20 per credit hour. Tuition, nonresident: full-time $16,205; part-time $675.20 per credit hour. *Required fees:* $2745; $103.85 per credit hour. $126.50 per semester. *Financial support:* In 2013–14, 108 students received support, including 3 fellowships with full tuition reimbursements available (averaging $5,000 per year), 13 research assistantships with partial tuition reimbursements available (averaging $12,565 per year), 7 teaching assistantships with partial tuition reimbursements available (averaging $10,569 per year); career-related internships or fieldwork, Federal Work-Study, scholarships/grants, health care benefits, and unspecified assistantships also available. Support available to part-time students. Financial award application deadline: 6/1; financial award applicants required to submit FAFSA. *Total annual research expenditures:* $898,873. *Unit head:* Dr. Xun Ge, Chair, 405-325-8418, Fax: 405-325-6655, E-mail: xge@ou.edu. *Application contact:* Shannon Vazquez, Graduate Programs Officer, 405-325-4525, Fax: 405-325-6655, E-mail: shannonv@ou.edu.
Website: http://www.ou.edu/content/education/edpy/.

University of Pennsylvania, Graduate School of Education, Division of Quantitative Methods, Program in Quantitative Methods, Philadelphia, PA 19104. Offers M Phil, MS, PhD. Part-time programs available. *Students:* 8 full-time (6 women); includes 2 minority (1 Asian, non-Hispanic/Latino; 1 Two or more races, non-Hispanic/Latino), 2 international. In 2013, 2 doctorates awarded. *Degree requirements:* For master's, exam; for doctorate, thesis/dissertation, exam. *Entrance requirements:* For master's, GRE General Test; for doctorate, GRE General Test, GRE Subject Test. *Application deadline:* For fall admission, 12/15 for domestic students. Applications are processed on a rolling basis. Application fee: $70. Electronic applications accepted. *Expenses:* Contact institution. *Financial support:* Fellowships and scholarships/grants available. Support available to part-time students. Financial award applicants required to submit FAFSA. *Faculty research:* Multivariate analysis of behavioral data, behavioral research design. *Unit head:* Dr. Andrew Porter, Dean, 215-898-7014. *Application contact:* 215-898-6415, Fax: 215-746-6884, E-mail: admissions@gse.upenn.edu.
Website: http://www.gse.upenn.edu/qm.

University of Pennsylvania, Graduate School of Education, Division of Quantitative Methods, Program in Statistics, Measurement, Assessment, and Research Technology (SMART), Philadelphia, PA 19104. Offers MS. *Students:* 15 full-time (12 women), 8 part-time (4 women); includes 2 minority (both Black or African American, non-Hispanic/Latino), 10 international. 126 applicants, 20% accepted, 14 enrolled. In 2013, 15 master's awarded. *Unit head:* Dr. Andrew Porter, Dean, 215-898-7014. *Application contact:* 215-898-6415, Fax: 215-746-6884, E-mail: admissions@gse.upenn.edu.
Website: http://www.gse.upenn.edu.

University of Pittsburgh, School of Education, Department of Psychology in Education, Program in Research Methodology, Pittsburgh, PA 15260. Offers M Ed, MA, PhD. Part-time and evening/weekend programs available. *Students:* 10 full-time (7 women), 22 part-time (14 women); includes 4 minority (1 Black or African American, non-Hispanic/Latino; 3 Asian, non-Hispanic/Latino), 12 international. Average age 34. 15 applicants, 87% accepted, 7 enrolled. In 2013, 2 master's, 3 doctorates awarded. Terminal master's awarded for partial completion of doctoral program. *Degree requirements:* For master's, thesis; for doctorate, thesis/dissertation. *Entrance requirements:* For doctorate, GRE General Test. Additional exam requirements/recommendations for international students: Required—TOEFL. *Application deadline:* For fall admission, 2/1 for domestic students. Application fee: $50. Electronic applications accepted. *Expenses:* Tuition, state resident: full-time $19,964; part-time $807 per credit. Tuition, nonresident: full-time $32,686; part-time $1337 per credit. *Required fees:* $740; $200. Tuition and fees vary according to program. *Financial support:* Fellowships, research assistantships with partial tuition reimbursements, Federal Work-Study, tuition waivers (partial), and unspecified assistantships available. Support available to part-time students. Financial award application deadline: 3/15; financial award applicants required to submit FAFSA. *Unit head:* Dr. Carl N. Johnson, Chairman, 412-624-6942, Fax: 412-624-7231, E-mail: johnson@pitt.edu. *Application contact:* Maggie Sikora, Graduate Enrollment Manager, 412-648-2230, Fax: 412-648-1899, E-mail: soeinfo@pitt.edu.
Website: http://www.education.pitt.edu/AcademicDepartments/PsychologyinEducation/Programs/ResearchMethodology.aspx.

University of Puerto Rico, Río Piedras Campus, College of Education, Program in Educational Research and Evaluation, San Juan, PR 00931-3300. Offers M Ed. Part-time programs available. *Degree requirements:* For master's, thesis. *Entrance requirements:* For master's, PAEG or GRE, interview, minimum GPA of 3.0, letter of recommendation.

University of St. Thomas, School of Education, Houston, TX 77006-4696. Offers all level education (M Ed); bilingual/dual language (M Ed); Catholic school teaching (M Ed); Catholic/private school leadership (M Ed); counselor education (M Ed); curriculum and instruction (M Ed); educational leadership (M Ed); elementary teaching (M Ed); English as a second language (M Ed); exceptionality/educational diagnostician (M Ed); exceptionality/special education (M Ed); generalist (M Ed); reading (M Ed); secondary teaching (M Ed). *Accreditation:* Teacher Education Accreditation Council. Part-time and evening/weekend programs available. Postbaccalaureate distance learning degree programs offered (no on-campus study). *Faculty:* 40 full-time (26 women), 43 part-time/adjunct (31 women). *Students:* 27 full-time (20 women), 1,091 part-time (981 women); includes 691 minority (247 Black or African American, non-Hispanic/Latino; 1 American Indian or Alaska Native, non-Hispanic/Latino; 44 Asian, non-Hispanic/Latino; 379 Hispanic/Latino; 2 Native Hawaiian or other Pacific Islander, non-Hispanic/Latino; 18 Two or more races, non-Hispanic/Latino), 28 international. Average age 36. 858 applicants, 83% accepted, 458 enrolled. In 2013, 454 master's awarded. *Degree requirements:* For master's, thesis, field experience. *Entrance requirements:* For master's, GRE or MAT if GPA is below 3.0, bachelor's degree; minimum GPA of 2.75 in bachelor's degree or last 60 credit hours; official transcripts from all institutions; goal statement of 250-300 words; 1 reference. Additional exam requirements/recommendations for international students: Required—TOEFL. *Application deadline:* Applications are processed on a rolling basis. Application fee: $35. Electronic applications accepted. *Expenses:* Contact institution. *Financial support:* In 2013–14, 41 students received support. Federal Work-Study, scholarships/grants, and state work-study, institutional employment available. Support available to part-time students. Financial award application deadline: 4/15; financial award applicants required to submit FAFSA. *Faculty research:* Leadership, diversity, personality traits, second language acquisition. *Unit head:* Dr. Robert LeBlanc, Dean, 713-525-3540, Fax: 713-525-3871, E-mail: education@stthom.edu. *Application contact:* Rita Paredes, Administrative Assistant, 713-525-3442, Fax: 713-525-3871, E-mail: rparede@stthom.edu.
Website: http://www.stthom.edu/Academics/School_of_Education/Index.aqf.

University of South Carolina, The Graduate School, College of Education, Department of Educational Studies, Program in Educational Psychology, Research, Columbia, SC 29208. Offers M Ed, PhD. *Accreditation:* NCATE. Part-time programs available. *Degree requirements:* For master's, comprehensive exam, thesis (for some programs); for doctorate, comprehensive exam, thesis/dissertation. *Entrance requirements:* For master's, GRE General Test; for doctorate, GRE General Test, interview. Electronic applications accepted. *Faculty research:* Problem solving, higher order thinking skills, psychometric research, methodology.

University of Southern Mississippi, Graduate School, College of Education and Psychology, Department of Educational Studies and Research, Hattiesburg, MS 39406-0001. Offers adult education (Graduate Certificate); community college leadership (Graduate Certificate); counseling and personnel services (college) (M Ed); education (PhD, Ed S), including adult education, research, evaluation and statistics (PhD); education (Ed D), including educational administration, educational research; education: educational leadership and research (Ed S), including higher education administration; educational administration and supervision (M Ed); higher education administration (Ed D, PhD); institutional research (Graduate Certificate). *Faculty:* 7 full-time (1 woman), 5 part-time/adjunct (1 woman). *Students:* 32 full-time (21 women), 103 part-time (70 women); includes 44 minority (39 Black or African American, non-Hispanic/Latino; 2 Hispanic/Latino; 3 Two or more races, non-Hispanic/Latino), 4 international. Average age 36. 36 applicants, 72% accepted, 15 enrolled. In 2013, 18 master's, 9 doctorates, 7 other advanced degrees awarded. *Degree requirements:* For master's and other advanced degree, comprehensive exam, thesis (for some programs); for doctorate, comprehensive exam, thesis/dissertation. *Entrance requirements:* For master's, doctorate, and other advanced degree, GRE General Test, minimum GPA of 2.75. Additional exam requirements/recommendations for international students: Required—TOEFL. *Application deadline:* For fall admission, 2/1 for domestic students, 3/1 for international students. Applications are processed on a rolling basis. Application fee: $35. *Financial support:* Career-related internships or fieldwork, Federal Work-Study, and institutionally sponsored loans available. Financial award application deadline: 3/15; financial award applicants required to submit FAFSA. *Total annual research expenditures:* $88,500. *Unit head:* Dr. Thomas V. O'Brien, Chair, 601-266-6093, E-mail: thomas.obrien@usm.edu. *Application contact:* Shonna Breland, Manager of Graduate Admissions, 601-266-6563, Fax: 601-266-5138.
Website: http://www.usm.edu/cep/esr/.

University of South Florida, College of Education, Department of Educational Measurement and Research, Tampa, FL 33620-9951. Offers measurement and evaluation (M Ed, PhD, Ed S). *Accreditation:* NCATE. Part-time programs available. *Degree requirements:* For master's, comprehensive exam; for doctorate, comprehensive exam, thesis/dissertation, philosophies of inquiry; multiple research methods. *Entrance requirements:* For master's, GRE General Test, minimum GPA of 3.0 in last 60 hours of course work; for doctorate, GRE General Test, minimum undergraduate GPA of 3.0 on upper-division coursework, master's degree or Ed S from regionally-accredited institution; for Ed S, GRE General Test, minimum undergraduate GPA of 3.0 on upper-division coursework, master's degree from regionally-accredited institution. Additional exam requirements/recommendations for international students: Required—TOEFL (minimum score 550 paper-based; 79 iBT). Electronic applications accepted. *Faculty research:* Multilevel modeling, methods for analyzing single case data, collaborative evaluation, validity of statistical inferences, secondary data analysis, effect sizes, meta-analyses.

University of South Florida, University College/Distance Education, Tampa, FL 33620-9951. *Unit head:* Kathy Barnes, Interdisciplinary Programs Coordinator, 813-974-8031, Fax: 813-974-7061, E-mail: barnesk@usf.edu. *Application contact:* Karen Tylinski, Metro Initiatives, 813-974-9943, Fax: 813-974-7061, E-mail: ktylinsk@usf.edu.
Website: http://uc.usf.edu/.

The University of Tennessee, Graduate School, College of Education, Health and Human Sciences, Program in Education, Knoxville, TN 37996. Offers art education (MS); counseling education (PhD); cultural studies in education (PhD); curriculum (MS, Ed S); curriculum, educational research and evaluation (Ed D, PhD); early childhood education (PhD); early childhood special education (MS); education of deaf and hard of hearing (MS); educational administration and policy studies (Ed D, PhD); educational administration and supervision (Ed S); educational psychology (Ed D, PhD); elementary education (MS, Ed S); elementary teaching (MS); English education (MS, Ed S); exercise science (PhD); foreign language/ESL education (MS, Ed S); instructional technology (MS, Ed D, PhD, Ed S); literacy, language and ESL education (PhD); literacy, language education, and ESL education (Ed D); mathematics education (MS, Ed S); modified and comprehensive special education (MS); reading education (MS, Ed S); school counseling (Ed S); school psychology (PhD, Ed S); science education

(MS, Ed S); secondary teaching (MS); social foundations (MS); social science education (MS, Ed S); socio-cultural foundations of sports and education (PhD); special education (Ed S); teacher education (Ed D, PhD). *Accreditation:* NCATE. Part-time and evening/weekend programs available. *Degree requirements:* For master's and Ed S, thesis optional; for doctorate, variable foreign language requirement, thesis/dissertation. *Entrance requirements:* For master's, minimum GPA of 2.7; for doctorate and Ed S, GRE General Test, minimum GPA of 2.7. Additional exam requirements/recommendations for international students: Required—TOEFL. Electronic applications accepted. *Expenses:* Tuition, state resident: full-time $9540; part-time $531 per credit hour. Tuition, nonresident: full-time $27,728; part-time $1542 per credit hour. *Required fees:* $1404; $67 per credit hour.

The University of Texas at El Paso, Graduate School, College of Education, Department of Educational Psychology and Special Services, El Paso, TX 79968-0001. Offers educational diagnostics (M Ed); guidance and counseling (M Ed); special education (M Ed). Part-time and evening/weekend programs available. *Degree requirements:* For master's, thesis optional. *Entrance requirements:* For master's, minimum GPA of 3.0. Additional exam requirements/recommendations for international students: Required—TOEFL. Electronic applications accepted.

The University of Texas–Pan American, College of Education, Department of Educational Psychology, Edinburg, TX 78539. Offers educational diagnostician (M Ed); gifted education (M Ed); guidance and counseling (M Ed); school psychology (MA); special education (M Ed). Part-time and evening/weekend programs available. *Degree requirements:* For master's, comprehensive exam (for some programs), thesis (for some programs). *Entrance requirements:* For master's, GRE General Test, interview. *Expenses:* Tuition, state resident: full-time $5986; part-time $333 per credit hour. Tuition, nonresident: full-time $12,358; part-time $687 per credit hour. *Required fees:* $782. Tuition and fees vary according to program. *Faculty research:* Reading instruction, assessment practice, behavior interventions consultation, mental retardation.

The University of Toledo, College of Graduate Studies, Judith Herb College of Education, Department of Educational Foundations and Leadership, Toledo, OH 43606-3390. Offers educational administration and supervision (ME, DE, Ed S); educational psychology (ME, PhD); educational research and measurement (ME, PhD); educational sociology (PhD); educational theory and social foundations (ME); foundations of education (DE, PhD); history of education (PhD); philosophy of education (PhD). *Accreditation:* NCATE. Part-time and evening/weekend programs available. *Faculty:* 33. *Students:* 15 full-time (9 women), 84 part-time (57 women); includes 28 minority (21 Black or African American, non-Hispanic/Latino; 1 Asian, non-Hispanic/Latino; 5 Hispanic/Latino; 1 Two or more races, non-Hispanic/Latino), 2 international. Average age 42. 16 applicants, 63% accepted, 7 enrolled. In 2013, 16 master's, 4 doctorates awarded. *Degree requirements:* For master's, comprehensive exam, thesis or alternative; for doctorate, comprehensive exam, thesis/dissertation; for Ed S, thesis optional. *Entrance requirements:* For master's, doctorate, and Ed S, minimum cumulative GPA of 2.7 for all previous academic work, letters of recommendation. Additional exam requirements/recommendations for international students: Required—TOEFL (minimum score 550 paper-based; 80 iBT). *Application deadline:* For fall admission, 1/15 priority date for domestic and international students. Applications are processed on a rolling basis. Application fee: $45 ($75 for international students). Electronic applications accepted. *Financial support:* In 2013–14, 2 research assistantships with full and partial tuition reimbursements (averaging $7,500 per year), 2 teaching assistantships with full and partial tuition reimbursements (averaging $9,000 per year) were awarded; career-related internships or fieldwork, Federal Work-Study, institutionally sponsored loans, scholarships/grants, tuition waivers (full and partial), unspecified assistantships, and administrative assistantships also available. Support available to part-time students. Financial award applicants required to submit FAFSA. *Unit head:* Dr. Richard Welsch, Interim Chair, 419-530-2565, Fax: 419-530-8447, E-mail: richard.welsch@utoledo.edu. *Application contact:* Graduate School Office, 419-530-4723, Fax: 419-530-4724, E-mail: grdsch@utnet.utoledo.edu. Website: http://www.utoledo.edu/eduhshs/.

University of Victoria, Faculty of Graduate Studies, Faculty of Education, Department of Educational Psychology and Leadership Studies, Victoria, BC V8W 2Y2, Canada. Offers aboriginal communities counseling (M Ed); counseling (M Ed, MA); educational psychology (M Ed, MA, PhD), including counseling psychology (M Ed, MA), leadership studies (PhD), learning and development (MA, PhD), measurement and evaluation, special education (M Ed, MA); leadership studies (M Ed, MA). Part-time programs available. *Degree requirements:* For master's, thesis (for some programs), comprehensive exam (M Ed); for doctorate, comprehensive exam, thesis/dissertation, candidacy exam. *Entrance requirements:* For master's, 2 years of work experience in a relevant field; for doctorate, GRE, 2 years of work experience in a relevant field, minimum B average. Additional exam requirements/recommendations for international students: Required—TOEFL (minimum score 575 paper-based), IELTS (minimum score 7). *Faculty research:* Learning and development (child, adolescent and adult), special education and exceptional children.

University of Virginia, Curry School of Education, Department of Leadership, Foundations and Policy, Educational Policy Studies Program, Charlottesville, VA 22903. Offers M Ed, Ed D. *Students:* 1 part-time (0 women). Average age 58. *Entrance requirements:* For master's and doctorate, GRE General Test, 2 letters of recommendation. Additional exam requirements/recommendations for international students: Required—TOEFL (minimum score 600 paper-based; 90 iBT), IELTS (minimum score 7). *Application deadline:* Applications are processed on a rolling basis. Application fee: $60. Electronic applications accepted. *Expenses:* Tuition, state resident: part-time $334 per credit hour. Tuition, nonresident: part-time $1224 per credit hour. *Financial support:* Fellowships, research assistantships, and teaching assistantships available. Financial award application deadline: 1/5; financial award applicants required to submit FAFSA. *Unit head:* James H. Wyckoff, Director, Educational Policy PhD Program, 434-924-0842, E-mail: jhw4n@virginia.edu. *Application contact:* Lisa Miller, Assistant to the Chair, 434-982-2849, E-mail: lam3v@virginia.edu. Website: http://curry.virginia.edu/academics/areas-of-study/education-policy.

University of Virginia, Curry School of Education, Department of Leadership, Foundations and Policy, Program in Educational Psychology, Charlottesville, VA 22903. Offers applied developmental science (M Ed); educational evaluation (M Ed); educational psychology (M Ed, Ed D, Ed S); educational research (Ed D); gifted education (M Ed); instructional technology (M Ed, Ed S); research statistics and evaluation (Ed D); school psychology (Ed D). *Students:* 21 full-time (14 women), 12 part-time (9 women); includes 9 minority (4 Black or African American, non-Hispanic/Latino; 2 Asian, non-Hispanic/Latino; 3 Hispanic/Latino), 2 international. Average age 32. 67 applicants, 78% accepted, 27 enrolled. In 2013, 42 master's, 1 doctorate awarded. *Degree requirements:* For master's, comprehensive exam. *Entrance requirements:* For master's and doctorate, GRE General Test, 2 letters of recommendation. Additional exam requirements/recommendations for international students: Required—TOEFL (minimum score 600 paper-based; 90 iBT), IELTS (minimum score 7). *Application deadline:* Applications are processed on a rolling basis. Application fee: $60. Electronic applications accepted. *Expenses:* Tuition, state resident: part-time $334 per credit hour.

Tuition, nonresident: part-time $1224 per credit hour. *Financial support:* Fellowships, research assistantships, and teaching assistantships available. Financial award application deadline: 1/5; financial award applicants required to submit FAFSA. *Unit head:* Leslie Booren, Managing Director, 434-243-2021, E-mail: booren@virginia.edu. Website: http://curry.virginia.edu/academics/areas-of-study/educational-psychology.

University of Virginia, Curry School of Education, Program in Education, Charlottesville, VA 22903. Offers administration and supervision (PhD); applied developmental science (PhD); counselor education (PhD); curriculum and instruction (PhD); early childhood special education (MT); education evaluation (PhD); educational psychology (PhD); educational research (PhD); elementary education (MT); English education (MT, PhD); foreign language education (MT); higher education (PhD); instructional technology (PhD); kinesiology (MT, PhD); math education (PhD); reading education (PhD); research, statistics and evaluation (PhD); school psychology (PhD); science education (PhD); social studies education (MT, PhD); special education (PhD); world languages education (MT). *Students:* 474 full-time (379 women), 35 part-time (19 women); includes 89 minority (30 Black or African American, non-Hispanic/Latino; 1 American Indian or Alaska Native, non-Hispanic/Latino; 26 Asian, non-Hispanic/Latino; 19 Hispanic/Latino; 13 Two or more races, non-Hispanic/Latino), 21 international. Average age 26. 312 applicants, 49% accepted, 80 enrolled. In 2013, 137 master's, 38 doctorates awarded. *Degree requirements:* For master's, comprehensive exam (for some programs), field project; for doctorate, comprehensive exam, thesis/dissertation. *Entrance requirements:* For doctorate, GRE General Test. Additional exam requirements/recommendations for international students: Required—TOEFL (minimum score 600 paper-based; 90 iBT), IELTS (minimum score 7). *Application deadline:* Applications are processed on a rolling basis. Application fee: $60. Electronic applications accepted. *Expenses:* Tuition, state resident: part-time $334 per credit hour. Tuition, nonresident: part-time $1224 per credit hour. *Financial support:* Fellowships, research assistantships, and teaching assistantships available. Financial award application deadline: 1/5; financial award applicants required to submit FAFSA. *Unit head:* Robert C. Pianta, Dean, 434-924-3334, E-mail: pianta@virginia.edu. *Application contact:* Office of Admissions and Student Services, 434-924-0742, E-mail: curry-admissions@virginia.edu. Website: http://curry.virginia.edu/teacher-education.

University of Washington, Graduate School, College of Education, Program in Educational Psychology, Seattle, WA 98195. Offers educational psychology (PhD); human development and cognition (M Ed); learning sciences (M Ed, PhD); measurement, statistics and research design (M Ed); school psychology (M Ed). *Accreditation:* APA. *Degree requirements:* For master's, thesis optional; for doctorate, thesis/dissertation. *Entrance requirements:* For master's and doctorate, GRE General Test, minimum GPA of 3.0. Additional exam requirements/recommendations for international students: Required—TOEFL.

University of West Georgia, College of Education, Program of School Improvement, Carrollton, GA 30118. Offers Ed D. Part-time and evening/weekend programs available. Postbaccalaureate distance learning degree programs offered (minimal on-campus study). *Faculty:* 1 (woman) full-time. *Students:* 1 full-time (0 women), 94 part-time (68 women); includes 27 minority (22 Black or African American, non-Hispanic/Latino; 2 Asian, non-Hispanic/Latino; 1 Hispanic/Latino; 2 Two or more races, non-Hispanic/Latino), 1 international. Average age 42. 5 applicants. In 2013, 5 doctorates awarded. *Degree requirements:* For doctorate, comprehensive exam, thesis/dissertation. *Entrance requirements:* For doctorate, GRE (minimum scores: 151 verbal, 145 quantitative; 300 combined), written essay, curriculum vitae, master's degree, minimum GPA of 3.0. Additional exam requirements/recommendations for international students: Required—TOEFL (minimum score 523 paper-based; 69 iBT); Recommended—IELTS (minimum score 6). *Application deadline:* For spring admission, 2/1 for domestic and international students. Application fee: $40. *Expenses:* Tuition, state resident: full-time $4600; part-time $192 per semester hour. Tuition, nonresident: full-time $17,880; part-time $745 per semester hour. *Required fees:* $1858; $46.34 per semester hour. $512 per semester. Tuition and fees vary according to course load, degree level, campus/location and program. *Financial support:* Scholarships/grants available. Support available to part-time students. Financial award application deadline: 4/1; financial award applicants required to submit FAFSA. *Faculty research:* Action research, leadership, teacher contract non-renewal, cyber-bullying, affective learning. *Unit head:* Dr. Lara Willox, Director, 678-839-6059, E-mail: lwillox@westga.edu. *Application contact:* Deanna Richards, Coordinator, Graduate Studies, 678-839-5946, E-mail: drichard@westga.edu. Website: http://www.westga.edu/eddsi.

University of Wisconsin–Milwaukee, Graduate School, School of Education, Department of Educational Psychology, Milwaukee, WI 53201-0413. Offers counseling psychology (PhD); educational statistics and measurement (MS, PhD); learning and development (MS, PhD); school and community counseling (MS); school psychology (PhD). *Accreditation:* APA. Part-time programs available. *Faculty:* 15 full-time (9 women), 1 (woman) part-time/adjunct. *Students:* 149 full-time (112 women), 41 part-time (27 women); includes 38 minority (12 Black or African American, non-Hispanic/Latino; 6 Asian, non-Hispanic/Latino; 5 Hispanic/Latino; 15 Two or more races, non-Hispanic/Latino), 9 international. Average age 31. 243 applicants, 52% accepted, 47 enrolled. In 2013, 61 master's, 5 doctorates awarded. *Degree requirements:* For master's, comprehensive exam, thesis; for doctorate, thesis/dissertation. *Entrance requirements:* For master's, minimum GPA of 3.0; for doctorate, GRE General Test, minimum GPA of 3.0. Additional exam requirements/recommendations for international students: Required—TOEFL (minimum score 550 paper-based; 79 iBT), IELTS (minimum score 6.5). *Application deadline:* For fall admission, 1/1 priority date for domestic students; for spring admission, 9/1 for domestic students. Applications are processed on a rolling basis. Application fee: $56 ($96 for international students). Electronic applications accepted. *Financial support:* In 2013–14, 14 fellowships, 1 research assistantship, 8 teaching assistantships were awarded; career-related internships or fieldwork, health care benefits, unspecified assistantships, and project assistantships also available. Support available to part-time students. Financial award application deadline: 4/15; financial award applicants required to submit FAFSA. *Unit head:* Nadya Fouad, Department Chair, 414-229-6830, Fax: 414-229-4939, E-mail: nadya@uwm.edu. *Application contact:* General Information Contact, 414-229-4982, Fax: 414-229-6967, E-mail: gradschool@uwm.edu. Website: http://www4.uwm.edu/soe/academics/ed_psych/.

Utah State University, School of Graduate Studies, Emma Eccles Jones College of Education and Human Services, Department of Psychology, Logan, UT 84322. Offers clinical/counseling/school psychology (PhD); research and evaluation methodology (PhD); school counseling (MS); school psychology (MS). *Accreditation:* APA (one or more programs are accredited). Part-time and evening/weekend programs available. Postbaccalaureate distance learning degree programs offered (no on-campus study). Terminal master's awarded for partial completion of doctoral program. *Degree requirements:* For master's, thesis (for some programs); for doctorate, thesis/dissertation. *Entrance requirements:* For master's, GRE General Test (school psychology), MAT (school counseling), minimum GPA of 3.5; for doctorate, GRE General Test, minimum GPA of 3.5. Additional exam requirements/recommendations for

international students: Required—TOEFL. *Faculty research:* Hearing loss detection in infancy, ADHD, eating disorders, domestic violence, neuropsychology, bilingual/Spanish speaking students/parents.

Utah State University, School of Graduate Studies, Emma Eccles Jones College of Education and Human Services, Doctoral Program in Education, Logan, UT 84322. Offers business information systems (Ed D, PhD); curriculum and instruction (Ed D, PhD); research and evaluation (PhD). *Degree requirements:* For doctorate, comprehensive exam, thesis/dissertation. *Entrance requirements:* For doctorate, GRE General Test, minimum GPA of 3.0, master's degree. Additional exam requirements/recommendations for international students: Required—TOEFL. Electronic applications accepted. *Faculty research:* Language and literacy development, math and science education, instructional technology, hearing problems/deafness, domestic violence and animal abuse.

Virginia Commonwealth University, Graduate School, School of Education, Doctoral Program in Education, Research and Evaluation Track, Richmond, VA 23284-9005. Offers PhD. *Entrance requirements:* For doctorate, GRE. Additional exam requirements/recommendations for international students: Required—TOEFL (minimum score 600 paper-based; 100 iBT). Electronic applications accepted.

Virginia Polytechnic Institute and State University, Graduate School, College of Liberal Arts and Human Sciences, Blacksburg, VA 24061. Offers career and technical education (MS Ed, Ed D, PhD, Ed S); communication (MA); counselor education (MA Ed, Ed D, PhD, Ed S); creative writing (MFA); curriculum and instruction (MA Ed, Ed D, PhD, Ed S); educational leadership and policy studies (MA Ed, Ed D, PhD, Ed S); educational research and evaluation (PhD); English (MA); foreign languages, cultures, and literatures (MA); higher education and student affairs (MA Ed); history (MA); human development (MS, PhD); material culture and public humanities (MA); philosophy (MA); political science (MA); rhetoric and writing (PhD); science and technology studies (MS, PhD); social, political, ethical, and cultural thought (PhD); sociology (MS, PhD); theater arts (MFA). *Faculty:* 410 full-time (211 women), 6 part-time/adjunct (5 women). *Students:* 688 full-time (464 women), 576 part-time (372 women); includes 243 minority (144 Black or African American, non-Hispanic/Latino; 3 American Indian or Alaska Native, non-Hispanic/Latino; 29 Asian, non-Hispanic/Latino; 48 Hispanic/Latino; 1 Native Hawaiian or other Pacific Islander, non-Hispanic/Latino; 18 Two or more races, non-Hispanic/Latino), 84 international. Average age 34. 1,054 applicants, 48% accepted, 374 enrolled. In 2013, 314 master's, 74 doctorates, 14 other advanced degrees awarded. *Degree requirements:* For master's, comprehensive exam (for some programs), thesis (for some programs); for doctorate, comprehensive exam (for some programs), thesis/dissertation (for some programs). *Entrance requirements:* For master's and doctorate, GRE/GMAT (may vary by department). Additional exam requirements/recommendations for international students: Required—TOEFL (minimum score 550 paper-based). *Application deadline:* For fall admission, 8/1 for domestic students, 4/1 for international students; for spring admission, 1/1 for domestic students, 9/1 for international students. Applications are processed on a rolling basis. Application fee: $75. Electronic applications accepted. *Expenses:* Tuition, state resident: full-time $11,185; part-time $621.50 per credit hour. Tuition, nonresident: full-time $22,146; part-time $1230.25 per credit hour. *Required fees:* $2442; $449.25 per semester. Tuition and fees vary according to course load, campus/location and program. *Financial support:* In 2013–14, 19 research assistantships with full tuition reimbursements (averaging $17,115 per year), 205 teaching assistantships with full tuition reimbursements (averaging $14,433 per year) were awarded. Financial award application deadline: 3/1; financial award applicants required to submit FAFSA. *Total annual research expenditures:* $6.8 million. *Unit head:* Joan Hirt, Interim Dean, 540-231-6779, Fax: 540-231-7157, E-mail: jbhirt@vt.edu. *Application contact:* Melissa Elliott, Executive Assistant, 540-231-6779, Fax: 540-231-7157, E-mail: elliott1@vt.edu. Website: http://www.clahs.vt.edu/.

Walden University, Graduate Programs, Richard W. Riley College of Education and Leadership, Minneapolis, MN 55401. *Accreditation:* NCATE. Part-time and evening/weekend programs available. Postbaccalaureate distance learning degree programs offered (minimal on-campus study). *Faculty:* 23 full-time (15 women), 830 part-time/adjunct (569 women). *Students:* 8,671 full-time (7,197 women), 2,122 part-time (1,735 women); includes 4,734 minority (3,802 Black or African American, non-Hispanic/Latino; 50 American Indian or Alaska Native, non-Hispanic/Latino; 136 Asian, non-Hispanic/Latino; 539 Hispanic/Latino; 35 Native Hawaiian or other Pacific Islander, non-Hispanic/Latino; 172 Two or more races, non-Hispanic/Latino), 73 international. Average age 40. 2,646 applicants, 96% accepted, 2074 enrolled. In 2013, 2,214 master's, 354 doctorates, 479 other advanced degrees awarded. *Degree requirements:* For doctorate, thesis/dissertation (for some programs), residency; for other advanced degree, residency (for some programs). *Entrance requirements:* For master's, bachelor's degree or higher; minimum GPA of 2.5; official transcripts; goal statement (for some programs); access to computer and Internet; for doctorate, master's degree or higher; three years of related professional or academic experience (preferred); minimum GPA of 3.0; goal statement and current resume (select programs); official transcripts; access to computer and Internet; for other advanced degree, relevant work experience; access to computer and Internet. Additional exam requirements/recommendations for international students: Required—TOEFL (minimum score 550 paper-based; 79 iBT), IELTS (minimum score 6.5), Michigan English Language Assessment Battery (minimum score 82), or PTE. *Application deadline:* Applications are processed on a rolling basis. Application fee: $0. Electronic applications accepted. *Expenses: Tuition:* Full-time $11,813.55; part-time $500 per credit. *Required fees:* $618.76. *Financial support:* In 2013–14, 1 fellowship was awarded; Federal Work-Study, scholarships/grants, unspecified assistantships, and family tuition reduction, active duty/veteran tuition reduction, group tuition reduction, interest-free payment plans, employee tuition reduction also available. Support available to part-time students. Financial award applicants required to submit FAFSA. *Unit head:* Dr. Kate Steffens, Dean, 800-925-3368. *Application contact:* Jennifer Hall, Vice President of Enrollment Management, 866-4-WALDEN, E-mail: info@waldenu.edu. Website: http://www.waldenu.edu/colleges-schools/riley-college-of-education/.

Washington University in St. Louis, Graduate School of Arts and Sciences, Department of Education, Program in Educational Research, St. Louis, MO 63130-4899. Offers PhD. *Entrance requirements:* For doctorate, GRE General Test. *Application deadline:* For fall admission, 1/15 priority date for domestic students. Applications are processed on a rolling basis. Application fee: $35. Electronic applications accepted. *Financial support:* Application deadline: 1/15. *Unit head:* Dr. William Tate, Chair, 314-935-6730.

Wayland Baptist University, Graduate Programs, Program in Education, Plainview, TX 79072-6998. Offers education administration (M Ed); education diagnostics (M Ed); education literacy (M Ed); elementary certification (M Ed); English (M Ed); English as a second language (M Ed); higher education administration (M Ed); human resources (M Ed); instructional leadership (M Ed); instructional technology (M Ed); science education (M Ed); secondary certification (M Ed); social studies (M Ed); special education (M Ed). Part-time and evening/weekend programs available. Postbaccalaureate distance learning degree programs offered (no on-campus study). *Faculty:* 33 full-time (17 women), 28 part-time/adjunct (17 women). *Students:* 22 full-time (15 women), 316 part-time (189 women); includes 130 minority (48 Black or African

American, non-Hispanic/Latino; 3 American Indian or Alaska Native, non-Hispanic/Latino; 71 Hispanic/Latino; 1 Native Hawaiian or other Pacific Islander, non-Hispanic/Latino; 7 Two or more races, non-Hispanic/Latino). Average age 39. 80 applicants, 96% accepted, 44 enrolled. In 2013, 170 master's awarded. *Degree requirements:* For master's, comprehensive exam, capstone course. *Entrance requirements:* For master's, GRE, GMAT or MAT. Additional exam requirements/recommendations for international students: Required—TOEFL (minimum score 500 paper-based; 61 iBT). *Application deadline:* Applications are processed on a rolling basis. Application fee: $50. Electronic applications accepted. *Expenses: Tuition:* Full-time $8190; part-time $455 per credit hour. *Required fees:* $970; $455 per credit hour. $485 per semester. *Financial support:* Federal Work-Study, institutionally sponsored loans, and scholarships/grants available. Support available to part-time students. Financial award application deadline: 5/1; financial award applicants required to submit FAFSA. *Unit head:* Dr. Jim Todd, Chairman, 806-291-1045, Fax: 806-291-1951. *Application contact:* Amanda Stanton, Coordinator of Graduate Studies, 806-291-3423, Fax: 806-291-1950, E-mail: stanton@wbu.edu.

Wayne State University, College of Education, Division of Theoretical and Behavioral Foundations, Detroit, MI 48202. Offers counseling (M Ed, MA, Ed D, PhD, Ed S); education evaluation and research (M Ed, Ed D, PhD); educational psychology (M Ed, PhD), including learning and instruction sciences (PhD), school psychology (PhD); educational sociology (M Ed); history and philosophy of education (M Ed); rehabilitation counseling and community inclusion (MA); school and community psychology (MA); school psychology (Certificate). *Accreditation:* ACA (one or more programs are accredited); CORE (one or more programs are accredited). Evening/weekend programs available. *Students:* 239 full-time (199 women), 214 part-time (190 women); includes 181 minority (141 Black or African American, non-Hispanic/Latino; 2 American Indian or Alaska Native, non-Hispanic/Latino; 14 Asian, non-Hispanic/Latino; 10 Hispanic/Latino; 1 Native Hawaiian or other Pacific Islander, non-Hispanic/Latino; 13 Two or more races, non-Hispanic/Latino), 21 international. Average age 33. 271 applicants, 35% accepted, 62 enrolled. In 2013, 55 master's, 19 doctorates, 8 other advanced degrees awarded. *Degree requirements:* For master's, thesis (for some programs); for doctorate, thesis/dissertation. *Entrance requirements:* For master's, GRE; for doctorate, GRE, interview, minimum GPA of 3.0, curriculum vitae, references. Additional exam requirements/recommendations for international students: Required—TOEFL (minimum score 550 paper-based; 79 iBT), Michigan English Language Assessment Battery (minimum score 85); Recommended—IELTS (minimum score 6.5), TWE (minimum score 5.5). *Application deadline:* For fall admission, 6/1 priority date for domestic students, 5/1 priority date for international students; for winter admission, 10/1 priority date for domestic students, 9/1 priority date for international students; for spring admission, 2/1 priority date for domestic students, 1/1 priority date for international students. Applications are processed on a rolling basis. Application fee: $0. Electronic applications accepted. *Expenses:* Tuition, state resident: part-time $554.15 per credit. Tuition, nonresident: part-time $1200.35 per credit. *Required fees:* $42.15 per credit. $268.30 per semester. Tuition and fees vary according to course load and program. *Financial support:* In 2013–14, 83 students received support, including 2 research assistantships with tuition reimbursements available (averaging $16,508 per year); fellowships with tuition reimbursements available, teaching assistantships with tuition reimbursements available, scholarships/grants, health care benefits, and unspecified assistantships also available. Financial award application deadline: 3/31; financial award applicants required to submit FAFSA. *Faculty research:* Adolescents at risk, supervision of counseling. *Unit head:* Dr. Joanne Holbert, Interim Assistant Dean, 313-577-1691, E-mail: jholbert@wayne.edu. *Application contact:* Janice Green, Assistant Dean, 313-577-1605, E-mail: jwgreen@wayne.edu.
Website: http://coe.wayne.edu/tbf/index.php.

Western Governors University, Teachers College, Salt Lake City, UT 84107. Offers curriculum and instruction (MS); educational leadership (MS); educational studies (MA); educational studies (5-12) (MA), including mathematics; elementary education (K-8) (MAT, Postbaccalaureate Certificate); elementary education (PreK-8) (MAT); English language learning (K-12) (MA); instructional design (MAT); learning and technology (M Ed, MA); management and innovation (M Ed); mathematics (5-12) (MAT, Postbaccalaureate Certificate); mathematics (5-9) (MAT, Postbaccalaureate Certificate); mathematics education (5-12) (MA); mathematics education (5-9) (MA); mathematics education (K-6) (MA); measurement and evaluation (M Ed); science (5-12) (Postbaccalaureate Certificate); science (5-9) (MAT, Postbaccalaureate Certificate); science education (5-12) (MA), including biology, chemistry, geology, physics; science education (5-9) (MA); social science (5-12) (MAT, Postbaccalaureate Certificate); special education (MAT, MS). *Accreditation:* NCATE. Evening/weekend programs available. Postbaccalaureate distance learning degree programs offered (no on-campus study). *Degree requirements:* For master's, capstone project. *Entrance requirements:* For master's and Postbaccalaureate Certificate, Readiness Assessment, transcripts. Additional exam requirements/recommendations for international students: Required—TOEFL (minimum score 450 paper-based; 80 iBT). Electronic applications accepted. *Expenses:* Contact institution.

Western Michigan University, Graduate College, College of Education and Human Development, Department of Educational Leadership, Research and Technology, Kalamazoo, MI 49008. Offers educational leadership (MA, PhD, Ed S); educational technology (MA, Graduate Certificate); evaluation, measurement and research (MA, PhD).

Western Michigan University, Graduate College, The Evaluation Center, Kalamazoo, MI 49008. Offers PhD.

West Texas A&M University, College of Education and Social Sciences, Department of Education, Program in Educational Diagnostician, Canyon, TX 79016-0001. Offers M Ed. Part-time programs available. Postbaccalaureate distance learning degree programs offered (minimal on-campus study). *Degree requirements:* For master's, comprehensive exam, thesis optional. *Entrance requirements:* For master's, GRE General Test, 3 years teaching experience, competency in diagnosis and prescription. Additional exam requirements/recommendations for international students: Required—TOEFL (minimum score 550 paper-based). Electronic applications accepted. *Faculty research:* Teacher preparation through web-based instruction, developmental disabilities.

Wilkes University, College of Graduate and Professional Studies, School of Education, Wilkes-Barre, PA 18766-0002. Offers art and science of teaching (MS Ed); classroom technology (MS Ed); early childhood literacy (MS Ed); educational development and strategies (MS Ed); educational leadership (MS Ed); educational technology (Ed D); higher education administration (Ed D); instructional media (MS Ed); instructional technology (MS Ed); international school leadership (MS Ed); K-12 administration (Ed D); middle level education (MS Ed); online teaching (MS Ed); reading (MS Ed); school business leadership (MS Ed); secondary education (MS Ed), including biology, chemistry, English, history, mathematics; special education (MS Ed); teaching English as a second language (MS Ed); twenty-first century teaching and learning (MS Ed). Part-time and evening/weekend programs available. Postbaccalaureate distance learning degree programs offered (minimal on-campus study). *Students:* 46 full-time (37 women), 1,410 part-time (1,039 women); includes 67 minority (12 Black or African

American, non-Hispanic/Latino; 2 American Indian or Alaska Native, non-Hispanic/Latino; 11 Asian, non-Hispanic/Latino; 28 Hispanic/Latino; 1 Native Hawaiian or other Pacific Islander, non-Hispanic/Latino; 13 Two or more races, non-Hispanic/Latino), 6 international. Average age 34. In 2013, 852 master's, 10 doctorates awarded. *Entrance requirements:* Additional exam requirements/recommendations for international students: Required—TOEFL (minimum score 550 paper-based; 79 iBT). *Application deadline:* Applications are processed on a rolling basis. Application fee: $45. Electronic applications accepted. *Expenses:* Contact institution. *Financial support:* Federal Work-

Study and unspecified assistantships available. Financial award application deadline: 3/1; financial award applicants required to submit FAFSA. *Unit head:* Dr. Rhonda Waskiewicz, Interim Dean, Education, 570-408-4332, Fax: 570-408-7872, E-mail: rhonda.waskiewicz@wilkes.edu. *Application contact:* Joanne Thomas, Interim Director of Graduate Education, 570-408-4234, Fax: 570-408-7846, E-mail: joanne.thomas1@wilkes.edu.
Website: http://www.wilkes.edu/pages/383.asp.

Educational Media/Instructional Technology

Abilene Christian University, Graduate School, College of Education and Human Services, Graduate Studies in Education, Leadership of Learning Program, Abilene, TX 79699-9100. Offers leadership of digital learning (M Ed, Certificate), including digital learning (M Ed), leadership of learning (Certificate); leadership of learning (M Ed), including conflict resolution, principalship. Part-time programs available. Postbaccalaureate distance learning degree programs offered (no on-campus study). *Students:* 28 full-time (24 women), 18 part-time (13 women); includes 14 minority (5 Black or African American, non-Hispanic/Latino; 1 American Indian or Alaska Native, non-Hispanic/Latino; 1 Asian, non-Hispanic/Latino; 7 Hispanic/Latino). 23 applicants, 83% accepted, 19 enrolled. In 2013, 34 master's awarded. *Degree requirements:* For master's, comprehensive exam, practicum. *Entrance requirements:* Additional exam requirements/recommendations for international students: Required—TOEFL (minimum score 550 paper-based; 90 iBT), IELTS (minimum score 6.5), PTE. *Application deadline:* For fall admission, 8/15 priority date for domestic students; for winter admission, 10/1 priority date for domestic students; for spring admission, 12/15 priority date for domestic students; for summer admission, 4/15 for domestic students. Applications are processed on a rolling basis. Application fee: $50. Electronic applications accepted. *Expenses:* Contact institution. *Financial support:* In 2013–14, 13 students received support. Application deadline: 4/1; applicants required to submit FAFSA. *Unit head:* Dr. Lloyd Goldsmith, Graduate Director, 325-674-2946, Fax: 325-674-2123, E-mail: lloyd.goldsmith@acu.edu. *Application contact:* Corey Patterson, Director of Graduate Admission and Recruiting, 325-674-6566, Fax: 325-674-6717, E-mail: gradinfo@acu.edu.

Acadia University, Faculty of Professional Studies, School of Education, Program in Curriculum Studies, Wolfville, NS B4P 2R6, Canada. Offers cultural and media studies (M Ed); learning and technology (M Ed); science, math and technology (M Ed). Part-time programs available. *Degree requirements:* For master's, thesis optional. *Entrance requirements:* For master's, B Ed or the equivalent, minimum B average in undergraduate course work, 2 years of teaching experience. Additional exam requirements/recommendations for international students: Required—TOEFL (minimum score 580 paper-based; 93 iBT), IELTS (minimum score 6.5). *Faculty research:* Literacy development, postmodern philosophy and curriculum theory, historiography, philosophy of education, learning and technology.

Adelphi University, Ruth S. Ammon School of Education, Program in Educational Leadership and Technology, Garden City, NY 11530-0701. Offers MA, Certificate. *Students:* 8 full-time (7 women), 8 part-time (7 women); includes 1 minority (Black or African American, non-Hispanic/Latino). Average age 39. In 2013, 4 other advanced degrees awarded. *Entrance requirements:* For master's, 2 letters of recommendation, resume, letter attesting to teaching experience (3 years full-time K-12). Additional exam requirements/recommendations for international students: Required—TOEFL (minimum score 550 paper-based; 80 iBT). *Application deadline:* For fall admission, 8/15 priority date for domestic students, 4/1 for international students; for spring admission, 1/15 priority date for domestic students, 11/1 for international students. Applications are processed on a rolling basis. Application fee: $50. Electronic applications accepted. *Expenses: Tuition:* Full-time $32,530; part-time $1010 per credit. *Required fees:* $1150. Tuition and fees vary according to degree level and program. *Financial support:* Research assistantships, career-related internships or fieldwork, Federal Work-Study, tuition waivers, and unspecified assistantships available. Financial award application deadline: 2/15; financial award applicants required to submit FAFSA. *Faculty research:* Technology methodology focusing on in-service and pre-service curriculum. *Unit head:* Dr. Devin Thornburg, Director, 516-877-4026, E-mail: thornburg@adelphi.edu. *Application contact:* Christine Murphy, Director of Admissions, 516-877-3050, Fax: 516-877-3039, E-mail: graduateadmissions@adelphi.edu.

Alabama State University, College of Education, Department of Instructional Support Programs, Montgomery, AL 36101-0271. Offers counselor education (M Ed, MS, Ed S), including general counseling (MS, Ed S), school counseling (M Ed, Ed S); educational administration (M Ed, Ed D, Ed S), including educational administration (Ed S), educational leadership, policy and law (Ed D), instructional leadership (M Ed); library education media (M Ed, Ed S). Part-time programs available. *Faculty:* 8 full-time (4 women), 14 part-time/adjunct (8 women). *Students:* 57 full-time (41 women), 175 part-time (126 women); includes 209 minority (203 Black or African American, non-Hispanic/Latino; 2 Asian, non-Hispanic/Latino; 4 Hispanic/Latino). Average age 39. 86 applicants, 48% accepted, 34 enrolled. In 2013, 28 master's, 14 doctorates, 7 other advanced degrees awarded. *Degree requirements:* For master's, comprehensive exam; for Ed S, comprehensive exam, thesis. *Entrance requirements:* For master's and Ed S, GRE General Test, MAT, writing competency test. Additional exam requirements/recommendations for international students: Required—TOEFL (minimum score 500 paper-based). *Application deadline:* For fall admission, 7/15 for domestic students; for spring admission, 12/15 for domestic students. Applications are processed on a rolling basis. Application fee: $10. *Expenses:* Tuition, state resident: full-time $7958; part-time $343 per credit hour. Tuition, nonresident: full-time $14,132; part-time $686 per credit hour. *Required fees:* $446 per term. One-time fee: $1784 full-time; $892 part-time. Tuition and fees vary according to course load. *Financial support:* In 2013–14, research assistantships (averaging $9,450 per year) were awarded. *Unit head:* Dr. Necoal Driver, Chair, 334-229-6882, Fax: 334-229-6904, E-mail: ndriver@alasu.edu. *Application contact:* Dr. Doris Screws, Dean of Graduate Studies, 334-229-4274, Fax: 334-229-4928, E-mail: dscrews@alasu.edu.
Website: http://www.alasu.edu/academics/colleges—departments/college-of-education/instructional-support-programs/index.aspx.

Alverno College, School of Education, Milwaukee, WI 53234-3922. Offers adaptive education (MA); administrative leadership (MA); adult education and organizational development (MA); adult educational and instructional design (MA); adult educational and instructional technology (MA); global connections in the humanities (MA); instructional leadership (MA); instructional technology for K-12 settings (MA); professional development (MA); reading education (MA); reading education with adaptive education (MA); science education (MA); teaching in alternative schools (MA). *Accreditation:* NCATE. Part-time and evening/weekend programs available. *Faculty:* 7 full-time (all women), 26 part-time/adjunct (23 women). *Students:* 48 full-time (41 women), 89 part-time (83 women); includes 41 minority (24 Black or African American, non-Hispanic/Latino; 3 Asian, non-Hispanic/Latino; 11 Hispanic/Latino; 3 Two or more races, non-Hispanic/Latino), 4 international. Average age 36. 89 applicants, 97% accepted, 59 enrolled. In 2013, 53 master's awarded. *Degree requirements:* For master's, presentation/defense of proposal, conference presentation of inquiry projects. *Entrance requirements:* For master's, bachelor's degree in related field, communication samples from work setting, 3 letters of recommendation. Additional exam requirements/recommendations for international students: Required—TOEFL. *Application deadline:* For fall admission, 7/15 priority date for domestic and international students; for spring admission, 12/15 priority date for domestic and international students. Applications are processed on a rolling basis. Application fee: $0. Electronic applications accepted. Application fee is waived when completed online. Tuition and fees vary according to program. *Financial support:* In 2013–14, 9 students received support. Federal Work-Study and scholarships/grants available. Support available to part-time students. Financial award application deadline: 4/15; financial award applicants required to submit FAFSA. *Faculty research:* Student self-assessment, self-reflection, integration of curriculum, identifying needs of students in strategic situations and designing appropriate classroom strategies. *Unit head:* Dr. Desiree Pointer-Mace, Associate Dean, Graduate Program, 414-382-6345, Fax: 414-382-6332, E-mail: desiree.pointer-mace@alverno.edu. *Application contact:* Mary Claire Jones, Senior Graduate Admissions Counselor, 414-382-6106, Fax: 414-382-6354, E-mail: maryclaire.jones@alverno.edu.

American College of Education, Graduate Programs, Chicago, IL 60606. Offers curriculum and instruction (M Ed), including bilingual, ESL; educational leadership (M Ed); educational technology (M Ed).

American InterContinental University Online, Program in Education, Schaumburg, IL 60173. Offers curriculum and instruction (M Ed); educational assessment and evaluation (M Ed); instructional technology (M Ed); leadership of educational organizations (M Ed). Evening/weekend programs available. Postbaccalaureate distance learning degree programs offered (no on-campus study). *Entrance requirements:* Additional exam requirements/recommendations for international students: Required—TOEFL (minimum score 550 paper-based). Electronic applications accepted.

American InterContinental University South Florida, Program in Instructional Technology, Weston, FL 33326. Offers M Ed. Part-time and evening/weekend programs available. *Entrance requirements:* Additional exam requirements/recommendations for international students: Required—TOEFL (minimum score 670 paper-based). Electronic applications accepted.

Antioch University New England, Graduate School, Department of Education, Experienced Educators Program, Keene, NH 03431-3552. Offers foundations of education (M Ed), including applied behavioral analysis, autism spectrum disorders, educating for sustainability, next-generation learning using technology, problem-based learning using critical skills, teacher leadership; principal certification (PMC). *Degree requirements:* For master's, thesis, practicum. *Entrance requirements:* For master's, previous course work and work experience in education. Additional exam requirements/recommendations for international students: Required—TOEFL (minimum score 550 paper-based). Electronic applications accepted. *Expenses:* Contact institution. *Faculty research:* Classroom action research, school restructuring, problem-based learning, brain-based learning.

Appalachian State University, Cratis D. Williams Graduate School, Department of Curriculum and Instruction, Boone, NC 28608. Offers curriculum specialist (MA); educational media (MA); elementary education (MA); middle grades education (MA), including language arts, mathematics, science, social studies. *Accreditation:* NCATE. Part-time and evening/weekend programs available. Postbaccalaureate distance learning degree programs offered (no on-campus study). *Degree requirements:* For master's, comprehensive exam, thesis or alternative. *Entrance requirements:* For master's, GRE General Test or MAT, 3 letters of recommendation. Additional exam requirements/recommendations for international students: Required—TOEFL (minimum score 570 paper-based; 79 iBT), IELTS (minimum score 6.5). Electronic applications accepted. *Faculty research:* Media literacy, elementary teaching, curriculum development, online learning environments.

Appalachian State University, Cratis D. Williams Graduate School, Department of Leadership and Educational Studies, Boone, NC 28608. Offers educational administration (Ed S); educational media (MA); higher education (MA, Ed S); library science (MLS); school administration (MSA). Part-time and evening/weekend programs available. Postbaccalaureate distance learning degree programs offered (no on-campus study). *Degree requirements:* For master's and Ed S, comprehensive exam, thesis optional. *Entrance requirements:* For master's and Ed S, GRE or MAT, 3 letters of recommendation. Additional exam requirements/recommendations for international students: Required—TOEFL (minimum score 570 paper-based; 79 iBT), IELTS (minimum score 6.5). Electronic applications accepted. *Faculty research:* Brain, learning and meditation; leadership of teaching and learning.

Arcadia University, Graduate Studies, School of Education, Glenside, PA 19038-3295. Offers art education (M Ed); computer education (CAS); curriculum (CAS); curriculum studies (M Ed); early childhood education (M Ed, CAS), including individualized (M Ed), master teacher (M Ed), research in child development (M Ed); educational leadership (M Ed, Ed D, CAS); elementary education (M Ed, CAS); English education (MA Ed); environmental education (MA Ed, CAS); history education (MA Ed); instructional technology (M Ed); language arts (M Ed, CAS); library science (M Ed); mathematics education (M Ed, MA Ed, CAS); music education (MA Ed); psychology (MA Ed); reading (M Ed, CAS); science education (M Ed, CAS); secondary education (M Ed, CAS); special education (M Ed, Ed D, CAS); theater arts (MA Ed); written communication (MA Ed). *Accreditation:* NASAD. Part-time and evening/weekend programs available.

Postbaccalaureate distance learning degree programs offered (minimal on-campus study). Electronic applications accepted. *Expenses:* Contact institution.

Argosy University, Atlanta, College of Education, Atlanta, GA 30328. Offers educational leadership (MAEd, Ed D, Ed S), including higher education administration (Ed D), K-12 education (Ed D); teaching and learning (MAEd, Ed D, Ed S), including education technology (Ed D), higher education (Ed D), K-12 education (Ed D).

Argosy University, Denver, College of Education, Denver, CO 80231. Offers community college executive leadership (Ed D); educational leadership (MA Ed, Ed D), including higher education (Ed D), K-12 education (Ed D); instructional leadership (MA Ed, Ed D), including higher education administration (Ed D), K-12 education (Ed D).

Argosy University, Nashville, College of Education, Program in Instructional Leadership, Nashville, TN 37214. Offers education technology (Ed D); higher education administration (Ed D); instructional leadership (MA Ed, Ed S); K-12 education (Ed D).

Argosy University, Orange County, College of Education, Orange, CA 92868. Offers community college executive leadership (Ed D); educational leadership (MA Ed, Ed D), including higher education administration (Ed D), K-12 education (Ed D); instructional leadership (MA Ed, Ed D), including education technology (Ed D), higher education (Ed D), K-12 education (Ed D), multiple subject teacher preparation (MA Ed), single subject teacher preparation (MA Ed).

Argosy University, Phoenix, College of Education, Phoenix, AZ 85021. Offers adult education and training (MA Ed); advanced educational administration (Ed D, Ed S); community college executive leadership (Ed D); educational administration (MA Ed); educational leadership (MA Ed, Ed D, Ed S), including education technology (Ed D), higher education administration (Ed D), K-12 education (Ed D); higher and postsecondary education (MA Ed); initial educational administration (Ed D, Ed S); school psychology (MA); teaching and learning (MA Ed, Ed D, Ed S), including education technology (Ed D), higher education (Ed D), K-12 education (Ed D).

Argosy University, San Francisco Bay Area, College of Education, Alameda, CA 94501. Offers community college executive leadership (Ed D); educational leadership (MA Ed, Ed D), including education technology (Ed D), higher education administration (Ed D), K-12 education (Ed D); instructional leadership (MA Ed, Ed D), including education technology (Ed D), higher education (Ed D), K-12 education (Ed D), multiple subject teacher preparation (MA Ed), single subject teacher preparation (MA Ed).

Argosy University, Sarasota, College of Education, Sarasota, FL 34235. Offers community college executive leadership (Ed D); educational leadership (MA Ed, Ed D, Ed S), including higher education administration (Ed D), K-12 education (Ed D); school counseling (MA, Ed S); school psychology (MA); teaching and learning (MA Ed, Ed D, Ed S), including education technology (Ed D), higher education (Ed D), K-12 education (Ed D).

Argosy University, Seattle, College of Education, Seattle, WA 98121. Offers adult education and training (MA Ed); community college executive leadership (Ed D); educational leadership (MA Ed, Ed D), including higher education administration (Ed D), K-12 education (Ed D); higher and postsecondary education (MA Ed); instructional leadership (MA Ed, Ed D), including education technology (Ed D), higher education (Ed D), K-12 education (Ed D).

Argosy University, Twin Cities, College of Education, Eagan, MN 55121. Offers advanced educational administration (Ed D, Ed S); educational leadership (MA Ed, Ed D, Ed S), including higher education administration (Ed D), K-12 education (Ed D); higher and postsecondary education (MA Ed); initial educational administration (Ed D, Ed S); instructional leadership (MA Ed, Ed D, Ed S), including education technology (Ed D), higher education (Ed D), K-12 education (Ed D).

Arizona State University at the Tempe campus, Mary Lou Fulton Teachers College, Program in Educational Technology, Phoenix, AZ 85069. Offers educational technology (M Ed, PhD); instructional design and performance improvement (Graduate Certificate); online teaching for grades K-12 (Graduate Certificate). Part-time and evening/weekend programs available. Postbaccalaureate distance learning degree programs offered (minimal on-campus study). Terminal master's awarded for partial completion of doctoral program. *Degree requirements:* For master's, thesis or alternative, applied project, interactive Program of Study (iPOS) submitted before completing 50 percent of required credit hours; for doctorate, comprehensive exam, thesis/dissertation, interactive Program of Study (iPOS) submitted before completing 50 percent of required credit hours. *Entrance requirements:* For master's, GRE (Verbal section) or MAT (for students with less than 3 years of professional experience as teacher, trainer or instructional designer), minimum GPA of 3.0 or equivalent in last 2 years of work leading to bachelor's degree, 3 letters of recommendation, personal statement, curriculum vitae or resume; for doctorate, GRE (minimum scores of 500 on each of the verbal and quantitative sections and 4 on the analytical writing section), minimum GPA of 3.2 or equivalent in last 2 years of work leading to bachelor's degree, 3 letters of recommendation, personal statement of professional goals, writing sample, curriculum vitae or resume. Additional exam requirements/recommendations for international students: Required—TOEFL (minimum score 600 paper-based; 100 iBT). Electronic applications accepted. *Faculty research:* Virtual environments; innovative technologies; theory, design, and implementation of computer-based learning environments; impact of technology into curricula on student achievement/attitude; electronic portfolios for learning and assessment.

Arkansas Tech University, College of Education, Russellville, AR 72801. Offers college student personnel (MS); elementary education (M Ed); instructional improvement (M Ed); instructional technology (M Ed); physical education (M Ed); teaching (MAT). *Accreditation:* NCATE. Part-time and evening/weekend programs available. Postbaccalaureate distance learning degree programs offered (no on-campus study). *Students:* 58 full-time (39 women), 304 part-time (240 women); includes 76 minority (58 Black or African American, non-Hispanic/Latino; 3 American Indian or Alaska Native, non-Hispanic/Latino; 4 Asian, non-Hispanic/Latino; 8 Hispanic/Latino; 3 Two or more races, non-Hispanic/Latino), 2 international. Average age 32. In 2013, 130 master's awarded. *Degree requirements:* For master's, comprehensive exam, thesis optional, action research project. *Entrance requirements:* Additional exam requirements/recommendations for international students: Required—TOEFL (minimum score 550 paper-based; 79 iBT), IELTS (minimum score 6.5). *Application deadline:* For fall admission, 3/1 priority date for domestic students, 5/1 priority date for international students; for spring admission, 10/1 priority date for domestic and international students. Applications are processed on a rolling basis. Application fee: $25 ($75 for international students). Electronic applications accepted. *Expenses:* Tuition, state resident: full-time $5976; part-time $249 per credit hour. Tuition, nonresident: full-time $11,952; part-time $498 per credit hour. *Required fees:* $411 per semester. Tuition and fees vary according to course load. *Financial support:* In 2013–14, research assistantships with full tuition reimbursements (averaging $4,800 per year), teaching assistantships with full tuition reimbursements (averaging $4,800 per year) were awarded; career-related internships or fieldwork, Federal Work-Study, scholarships/grants, health care benefits, and unspecified assistantships also available. Support available to part-time students. Financial award application deadline: 4/15; financial award applicants required to submit FAFSA. *Unit head:* Dr. Sherry Field, Dean, 479-968-0418, E-mail: sfield@atu.edu.

Application contact: Dr. Mary B. Gunter, Dean of Graduate College, 479-968-0398, Fax: 479-964-0542, E-mail: gradcollege@atu.edu. Website: http://www.atu.edu/education/.

Ashland University, Dwight Schar College of Education, Department of Curriculum and Instruction, Ashland, OH 44805-3702. Offers classroom instruction (M Ed); literacy (M Ed); technology facilitator (M Ed). *Accreditation:* NCATE. Part-time and evening/weekend programs available. *Degree requirements:* For master's, thesis or alternative, internship, practicum, inquiry seminar. *Entrance requirements:* For master's, teaching certificate or license, bachelor's degree, minimum cumulative GPA of 2.75. Additional exam requirements/recommendations for international students: Required—TOEFL. Electronic applications accepted. *Faculty research:* Gender equity, postmodern children's and young adult literature, outdoor/experimental education, re-examining literature study in middle grades, morality and giftedness.

Auburn University, Graduate School, College of Education, Department of Educational Foundations, Leadership, and Technology, Auburn University, AL 36849. Offers adult education (M Ed, MS, Ed D); curriculum and instruction (M Ed, MS, Ed D, Ed S); curriculum supervision (M Ed, MS, Ed D, Ed S); educational psychology (PhD); higher education administration (M Ed, MS, Ed D, Ed S); media instructional design (MS); media specialist (M Ed); school administration (M Ed, MS, Ed D, Ed S). *Accreditation:* NCATE. Part-time programs available. *Faculty:* 25 full-time (15 women), 6 part-time/adjunct (5 women). *Students:* 104 full-time (65 women), 250 part-time (140 women); includes 98 minority (90 Black or African American, non-Hispanic/Latino; 1 American Indian or Alaska Native, non-Hispanic/Latino; 4 Asian, non-Hispanic/Latino; 3 Hispanic/Latino), 14 international. Average age 36. 188 applicants, 66% accepted, 76 enrolled. In 2013, 51 master's, 22 doctorates, 10 other advanced degrees awarded. *Degree requirements:* For master's, thesis (for some programs); for doctorate, thesis/dissertation; for Ed S, field project. *Entrance requirements:* For master's, doctorate, and Ed S, GRE General Test. *Application deadline:* For fall admission, 7/7 for domestic students; for spring admission, 11/24 for domestic students. Applications are processed on a rolling basis. Application fee: $50 ($60 for international students). Electronic applications accepted. *Expenses:* Tuition, state resident: full-time $8262; part-time $459 per credit hour. Tuition, nonresident: full-time $24,786; part-time $1377 per credit hour. Tuition and fees vary according to degree level and program. *Financial support:* Teaching assistantships and Federal Work-Study available. Support available to part-time students. Financial award application deadline: 3/15; financial award applicants required to submit FAFSA. *Unit head:* Dr. Sherida Downer, Head, 334-844-4460. *Application contact:* Dr. George Flowers, Dean of the Graduate School, 334-844-4700. Website: http://www.education.auburn.edu/academic_departments/eflt/.

Auburn University at Montgomery, School of Education, Department of Foundations, Technology, and Secondary Education, Montgomery, AL 36124-4023. Offers instructional technology (M Ed); secondary education (M Ed, Ed S), including art education (M Ed), biology (M Ed), English language arts (M Ed), general science (M Ed), history (M Ed), mathematics (M Ed), social science (M Ed). *Accreditation:* NCATE. Part-time and evening/weekend programs available. *Faculty:* 6 full-time (2 women), 1 (woman) part-time/adjunct. *Students:* 47 full-time (22 women), 77 part-time (48 women); includes 30 minority (29 Black or African American, non-Hispanic/Latino; 1 Asian, non-Hispanic/Latino), 1 international. Average age 30. In 2013, 86 master's awarded. *Degree requirements:* For master's and Ed S, comprehensive exam, thesis optional. *Entrance requirements:* For master's, GRE General Test or MAT, certification, BS in teaching; for Ed S, GRE General Test or MAT, certification. *Application deadline:* Applications are processed on a rolling basis. Electronic applications accepted. *Expenses:* Tuition, state resident: full-time $5994; part-time $333 per credit hour. Tuition, nonresident: full-time $17,982; part-time $999 per credit hour. *Financial support:* Teaching assistantships, career-related internships or fieldwork, and scholarships/grants available. Support available to part-time students. Financial award application deadline: 3/1; financial award applicants required to submit FAFSA. *Unit head:* Dr. Sheila Austin, Dean, 334-244-3425, Fax: 334-244-3102, E-mail: saustin1@aum.edu. *Application contact:* Dr. Rhonda Morton, Associate Dean/Graduate Coordinator, 334-244-3287, Fax: 334-244-3978, E-mail: rmorton@aum.edu. Website: http://www.education.aum.edu/departments/foundations-technology-and-secondary-education.

Augustana College, MA in Education Program, Sioux Falls, SD 57197. Offers instructional strategies (MA); reading (MA); special populations (MA); technology (MA). *Accreditation:* NCATE. Part-time and evening/weekend programs available. Postbaccalaureate distance learning degree programs offered (no on-campus study). *Faculty:* 9 full-time (6 women). *Students:* 48 part-time (40 women). Average age 33. 55 applicants, 100% accepted, 49 enrolled. In 2013, 14 master's awarded. *Degree requirements:* For master's, thesis. *Entrance requirements:* For master's, appropriate bachelor's degree, minimum GPA of 3.0, teaching certificate. Additional exam requirements/recommendations for international students: Required—TOEFL (minimum score 550 paper-based). *Application deadline:* For spring admission, 4/1 priority date for domestic and international students. Applications are processed on a rolling basis. Application fee: $50. Electronic applications accepted. *Expenses:* Contact institution. *Financial support:* Application deadline: 3/1; applicants required to submit FAFSA. *Unit head:* Dr. Sheryl Feinstein, MA in Education Program Director, 605-274-5211, E-mail: sheryl.feinstein@augie.edu. *Application contact:* Nancy Wright, Graduate Coordinator, 605-274-4043, Fax: 605-274-4450, E-mail: graduate@augie.edu. Website: http://www.augie.edu/academics/graduate-education/master-arts-education.

Aurora University, College of Education, Aurora, IL 60506-4892. Offers curriculum and instruction (MA, Ed D); early childhood and special education (MA); education (MAT), including elementary certification; education and administration (Ed D); educational leadership (MEL); educational technology (MATL); reading instruction (MA); special education (MA). *Accreditation:* NCATE. Part-time and evening/weekend programs available. *Degree requirements:* For doctorate, comprehensive exam, thesis/dissertation. *Entrance requirements:* For master's, 2 years of teaching experience, valid teaching certificate. Additional exam requirements/recommendations for international students: Required—TOEFL (minimum score 550 paper-based). Electronic applications accepted. *Expenses:* Contact institution.

Avila University, School of Professional Studies, Kansas City, MO 64145-1698. Offers executive leadership development (MS); fundraising (MA); instructional design and technology (MA); leadership coaching (MS); organizational development (MS); project management (MA); strategic human resources (MS). Part-time and evening/weekend programs available. Postbaccalaureate distance learning degree programs offered (no on-campus study). *Faculty:* 2 full-time (1 woman), 10 part-time/adjunct (7 women). *Students:* 73 full-time (50 women), 68 part-time (54 women); includes 46 minority (33 Black or African American, non-Hispanic/Latino; 1 Asian, non-Hispanic/Latino; 11 Hispanic/Latino; 1 Two or more races, non-Hispanic/Latino), 11 international. Average age 38. 47 applicants, 64% accepted, 27 enrolled. In 2013, 42 master's awarded. *Degree requirements:* For master's, thesis optional. *Entrance requirements:* For master's, 2 letters of recommendation, minimum GPA of 3.0 during last 60 hours, resume, statement of intent. Additional exam requirements/recommendations for international students: Required—TOEFL. *Application deadline:* Applications are processed on a rolling basis. Application fee: $0. Electronic applications accepted.

Expenses: Tuition: Full-time $8430; part-time $468 per credit hour. *Required fees:* $648; $36 per credit hour. Tuition and fees vary according to program. *Financial support:* In 2013–14, 20 students received support. Unspecified assistantships available. Support available to part-time students. Financial award applicants required to submit FAFSA. *Unit head:* Dr. Steve Iliff, Dean, 816-501-3737, Fax: 816-941-4650, E-mail: advantage@ avila.edu. *Application contact:* Linda Dubar, School of Professional Studies, 816-501-3737, Fax: 816-941-4650, E-mail: advantage@avila.edu. Website: http://www.avila.edu/advantage.

Azusa Pacific University, School of Education, Department of Advanced Studies, Program in Digital Teaching and Learning, Azusa, CA 91702-7000. Offers MA Ed.

Azusa Pacific University, School of Education, Department of Advanced Studies, Program in Educational Technology, Azusa, CA 91702-7000. Offers M Ed. Part-time and evening/weekend programs available. *Degree requirements:* For master's, comprehensive exam, core exam, oral presentation. *Entrance requirements:* For master's, 12 units of course work in education, minimum GPA of 3.0.

Azusa Pacific University, School of Education, Department of Advanced Studies, Program in Educational Technology and Learning, Azusa, CA 91702-7000. Offers MA. Postbaccalaureate distance learning degree programs offered.

Azusa Pacific University, School of Education, Department of Special Education, Program in Special Education and Educational Technology, Azusa, CA 91702-7000. Offers M Ed.

Baldwin Wallace University, Graduate Programs, Division of Education, Specialization in Educational Technology, Berea, OH 44017-2088. Offers MA Ed. Part-time and evening/weekend programs available. *Faculty:* 1 full-time (0 women), 4 part-time/adjunct (1 woman). *Students:* 8 full-time (6 women), 11 part-time (4 women); includes 1 minority (Black or African American, non-Hispanic/Latino). Average age 32. 14 applicants, 71% accepted, 2 enrolled. In 2013, 18 master's awarded. *Degree requirements:* For master's, comprehensive exam, portfolio. *Entrance requirements:* For master's, bachelor's degree in field, MAT or minimum GPA of 2.75. Additional exam requirements/recommendations for international students: Required—TOEFL (minimum score 523 paper-based; 70 iBT). *Application deadline:* For fall admission, 8/15 priority date for domestic students; for spring admission, 12/15 priority date for domestic students. Applications are processed on a rolling basis. Application fee: $25. Electronic applications accepted. Application fee is waived when completed online. *Expenses:* Contact institution. *Financial support:* Career-related internships or fieldwork available. Support available to part-time students. Financial award application deadline: 5/1; financial award applicants required to submit FAFSA. *Faculty research:* No-cost software, online resources for building a classroom learning management system. *Unit head:* Dr. Karen Kaye, Chair, 440-826-2168, Fax: 440-826-3779, E-mail: kkaye@bw.edu. *Application contact:* Winifred W. Gerhardt, Director of Admission, Adult and Graduate Programs, 440-826-2222, Fax: 440-826-3830, E-mail: admission@bw.edu. Website: http://www.bw.edu/academics/mae/tech/.

Barry University, School of Education, Graduate Certificate Programs, Miami Shores, FL 33161-6695. Offers advanced teaching and learning with technology (Certificate); distance education (Certificate); higher education technology integration (Certificate); human resources: not for profit and religious organizations (Certificate); K-12 technology integration (Certificate).

Barry University, School of Education, Program in Educational Technology Applications, Miami Shores, FL 33161-6695. Offers educational computing and technology (MS, Ed S). Part-time and evening/weekend programs available. Postbaccalaureate distance learning degree programs offered (minimal on-campus study). *Degree requirements:* For master's and Ed S, comprehensive exam. *Entrance requirements:* For master's, GRE General Test or MAT, minimum GPA of 3.0; for Ed S, GRE General Test, minimum GPA of 3.0.

Barry University, School of Education, Program in Leadership and Education, Miami Shores, FL 33161-6695. Offers educational technology (PhD); exceptional student education (PhD); higher education administration (PhD); human resource development (PhD); leadership (PhD). Part-time and evening/weekend programs available. *Degree requirements:* For doctorate, thesis/dissertation. *Entrance requirements:* For doctorate, GRE General Test, minimum GPA of 3.25. Electronic applications accepted.

Barry University, School of Education, Program in Technology and TESOL, Miami Shores, FL 33161-6695. Offers MS, Ed S.

Bay Path College, Program in Higher Education Administration, Longmeadow, MA 01106-2292. Offers enrollment management (MS); general administration (MS); institutional advancement (MS); online teaching and program administration (MS). Part-time programs available. Postbaccalaureate distance learning degree programs offered (no on-campus study). *Students:* 3 full-time (2 women), 44 part-time (36 women); includes 8 minority (5 Black or African American, non-Hispanic/Latino; 1 Asian, non-Hispanic/Latino; 1 Hispanic/Latino; 1 Two or more races, non-Hispanic/Latino). Average age 37. 37 applicants, 81% accepted, 21 enrolled. In 2013, 16 master's awarded. *Degree requirements:* For master's, 8 core courses (24 credits) and 4 elective courses (12 credits) for a total of 36 credits. *Application deadline:* Applications are processed on a rolling basis. Application fee: $45. Electronic applications accepted. Application fee is waived when completed online. *Financial support:* In 2013–14, 9 students received support. Scholarships/grants available. Financial award applicants required to submit FAFSA. *Unit head:* Dr. Lauren Way, Program Director, 413-565-1193. *Application contact:* Lisa Adams, Director of Graduate Admissions, 413-565-1317, Fax: 413-565-1250, E-mail: ladams@baypath.edu. Website: http://graduate.baypath.edu/Graduate-Programs/Programs-Online/MS-Programs/Higher-Education-Administration.

Belhaven University, School of Education, Jackson, MS 39202-1789. Offers educational technology (M Ed); elementary education (M Ed, MAT); reading literacy (M Ed); secondary education (M Ed, MAT). Part-time and evening/weekend programs available. Postbaccalaureate distance learning degree programs offered (no on-campus study). *Faculty:* 7 full-time (6 women), 15 part-time/adjunct (10 women). *Students:* 1 full-time (0 women), 406 part-time (311 women); includes 254 minority (250 Black or African American, non-Hispanic/Latino; 2 Hispanic/Latino; 2 Two or more races, non-Hispanic/Latino). Average age 36. 273 applicants, 67% accepted, 162 enrolled. In 2013, 24 master's awarded. *Degree requirements:* For master's, comprehensive exam, portfolio. *Entrance requirements:* For master's, PRAXIS I and II, minimum GPA of 2.8. *Application deadline:* Applications are processed on a rolling basis. Application fee: $25. Electronic applications accepted. *Financial support:* Federal Work-Study, scholarships/grants, tuition waivers (full), and unspecified assistantships available. Support available to part-time students. Financial award applicants required to submit FAFSA. *Unit head:* Dr. David Hand, Dean, 601-965-7020, E-mail: dhand@belhaven.edu. *Application contact:* Amanda Slaughter, Assistant Vice President for Adult and Graduate Enrollment and Student Services, 601-968-8727, Fax: 601-968-5953, E-mail: gradadmission@ belhaven.edu. Website: http://graduateed.belhaven.edu.

Bellevue University, Graduate School, College of Professional Studies, Bellevue, NE 68005-3098. Offers instructional design and development (MS); justice administration and criminal management (MS); leadership (MA); organizational performance (MS); public administration (MPA); security management (MS).

Bloomsburg University of Pennsylvania, School of Graduate Studies, College of Science and Technology, Department of Instructional Technology, Bloomsburg, PA 17815-1301. Offers corporate instructional technology (MS); elearning developer (Certificate). Postbaccalaureate distance learning degree programs offered (no on-campus study). *Faculty:* 4 full-time (1 woman), 3 part-time/adjunct (1 woman). *Students:* 70 full-time (44 women), 20 part-time (9 women); includes 11 minority (5 Black or African American, non-Hispanic/Latino; 1 American Indian or Alaska Native, non-Hispanic/Latino; 3 Asian, non-Hispanic/Latino; 2 Hispanic/Latino), 7 international. Average age 32. 62 applicants, 85% accepted, 28 enrolled. In 2013, 52 master's awarded. *Degree requirements:* For master's, thesis optional. *Entrance requirements:* For master's, minimum QPA of 2.8, 3 letters of recommendation, personal statement. Additional exam requirements/recommendations for international students: Required—TOEFL (minimum score 550 paper-based). *Application deadline:* Applications are processed on a rolling basis. Application fee: $35 ($60 for international students). Electronic applications accepted. *Expenses:* Tuition, state resident: full-time $7956; part-time $442 per credit. Tuition, nonresident: full-time $11,934; part-time $663 per credit. *Required fees:* $95.50 per credit. $55 per semester. Tuition and fees vary according to course load. *Financial support:* Career-related internships or fieldwork and unspecified assistantships available. *Unit head:* Dr. Timothy Phillips, Coordinator, 570-389-4875, Fax: 570-389-4943, E-mail: tphillip@bloomu.edu. *Application contact:* Jennifer Richard, Administrative Assistant, 570-389-4015, Fax: 570-389-3054, E-mail: jrichard@bloomu.edu. Website: http://iit.bloomu.edu/.

Boise State University, College of Education, Department of Educational Technology, Boise, ID 83725-0399. Offers MET, MS, Ed D, Graduate Certificate. *Accreditation:* NCATE. Part-time programs available. Postbaccalaureate distance learning degree programs offered (no on-campus study). *Degree requirements:* For master's, thesis optional. *Entrance requirements:* For master's, minimum GPA of 3.0. Electronic applications accepted.

Boise State University, College of Engineering, Department of Instructional and Performance Technology, Boise, ID 83725-0399. Offers MS, Graduate Certificate. Part-time programs available. Postbaccalaureate distance learning degree programs offered (no on-campus study). *Degree requirements:* For master's, thesis optional. *Entrance requirements:* For master's, minimum GPA of 3.0. Electronic applications accepted.

Bowling Green State University, Graduate College, College of Education and Human Development, School of Education and Intervention Services, Intervention Services Division, Program in Special Education, Bowling Green, OH 43403. Offers assistive technology (M Ed); early childhood intervention (M Ed); gifted education (M Ed); hearing impaired intervention (M Ed); mild/moderate intervention (M Ed); moderate/intensive intervention (M Ed). *Accreditation:* NCATE. Part-time programs available. *Degree requirements:* For master's, thesis or alternative. *Entrance requirements:* For master's, GRE General Test. Additional exam requirements/recommendations for international students: Required—TOEFL. Electronic applications accepted. *Faculty research:* Reading and special populations, deafness, early childhood, gifted and talented, behavior disorders.

Bowling Green State University, Graduate College, College of Education and Human Development, School of Education and Intervention Services, Teaching and Learning Division, Program in Classroom Technology, Bowling Green, OH 43403. Offers M Ed. *Accreditation:* NCATE. Part-time and evening/weekend programs available. *Degree requirements:* For master's, thesis or alternative. *Entrance requirements:* For master's, GRE General Test. Additional exam requirements/recommendations for international students: Required—TOEFL. Electronic applications accepted.

Bridgewater State University, School of Graduate Studies, School of Education and Allied Studies, Department of Secondary Education and Professional Programs, Program in Instructional Technology, Bridgewater, MA 02325-0001. Offers M Ed. Part-time and evening/weekend programs available. *Entrance requirements:* For master's, GRE General Test or Massachusetts Test for Educator Licensure.

Brigham Young University, Graduate Studies, David O. McKay School of Education, Department of Instructional Psychology and Technology, Provo, UT 84602. Offers MS, PhD. *Faculty:* 9 full-time (0 women). *Students:* 57 full-time (22 women), 18 part-time (10 women); includes 4 minority (1 Asian, non-Hispanic/Latino; 1 Hispanic/Latino; 2 Native Hawaiian or other Pacific Islander, non-Hispanic/Latino), 2 international. Average age 36. 30 applicants, 67% accepted, 16 enrolled. In 2013, 7 master's, 5 doctorates awarded. *Degree requirements:* For master's, thesis; for doctorate, comprehensive exam, thesis/dissertation. *Entrance requirements:* For master's and doctorate, GRE General Test. Additional exam requirements/recommendations for international students: Required—TOEFL. *Application deadline:* For fall admission, 1/2 for domestic and international students; for winter admission, 2/1 for domestic and international students; for summer admission, 1/2 for domestic and international students. Application fee: $50. Electronic applications accepted. *Expenses: Tuition:* Full-time $6130; part-time $340 per credit hour. Tuition and fees vary according to program and student's religious affiliation. *Financial support:* In 2013–14, 21 students received support, including 14 research assistantships with full and partial tuition reimbursements available (averaging $10,000 per year), 16 teaching assistantships with full and partial tuition reimbursements available (averaging $6,500 per year); career-related internships or fieldwork, scholarships/grants, tuition waivers (full and partial), and unspecified assistantships also available. Support available to part-time students. *Faculty research:* Interactive learning, learning theory, instructional designed development, research and evaluation, measurement. *Unit head:* Dr. Andrew S. Gibbons, Chair, 801-422-5097, Fax: 801-422-0314, E-mail: andy_gibbons@byu.edu. *Application contact:* Michele Bray, Department Secretary, 801-422-2746, Fax: 801-422-0314, E-mail: michele_bray@byu.edu. Website: http://education.byu.edu/ipt/.

Brigham Young University, Graduate Studies, Ira A. Fulton College of Engineering and Technology, School of Technology, Provo, UT 84602-1001. Offers construction management (MS); information technology (MS); manufacturing systems (MS); technology and engineering education (MS). *Faculty:* 25 full-time (0 women). *Students:* 45 full-time (7 women); includes 2 minority (1 Black or African American, non-Hispanic/Latino; 1 Asian, non-Hispanic/Latino), 2 international. Average age 25. 18 applicants, 78% accepted, 13 enrolled. In 2013, 14 master's awarded. *Degree requirements:* For master's, thesis. *Entrance requirements:* For master's, GRE General Test; GMAT or GRE (for construction management emphasis), minimum GPA of 3.0 in last 60 hours of course work. Additional exam requirements/recommendations for international students: Required—TOEFL (minimum score 580 paper-based; 85 iBT). *Application deadline:* For fall admission, 2/15 for domestic and international students; for winter admission, 9/15 for domestic and international students; for spring admission, 2/15 for domestic and international students. Application fee: $50. Electronic applications accepted. *Expenses: Tuition:* Full-time $6130; part-time $340 per credit hour. Tuition and fees vary according to program and student's religious affiliation. *Financial support:* In 2013–14, 40 students received support, including 11 research assistantships (averaging $4,489 per year), 4 teaching assistantships (averaging $5,020 per year); scholarships/grants also available. *Faculty research:* Information assurance and security, HEI and databases;

manufacturing materials, processes and systems, innovation in construction management scheduling and delivery methods. *Total annual research expenditures:* $174,648. *Unit head:* Richard E. Fry, Director, 801-422-4445, Fax: 801-422-0490, E-mail: rfry@byu.edu. *Application contact:* Barry M. Lunt, Graduate Coordinator, 801-422-2264, Fax: 801-422-0490, E-mail: sotadminasst@byu.edu. Website: http://www.et.byu.edu/sot/.

Buffalo State College, State University of New York, The Graduate School, Faculty of Applied Science and Education, Department of Computer Information Systems, Program in Educational Computing, Buffalo, NY 14222-1095. Offers MS Ed. *Accreditation:* NCATE. Part-time and evening/weekend programs available. *Degree requirements:* For master's, thesis, project. *Entrance requirements:* Additional exam requirements/recommendations for international students: Required—TOEFL (minimum score 550 paper-based).

California Baptist University, Program in Education, Riverside, CA 92504-3206. Offers educational leadership for faith-based institutions (MS); educational leadership for public institutions (MS); educational technology (MS); instructional computer applications (MS); international education (MS); leadership and adult learning (MS); leadership and organizational studies (MS); reading (MS); school counseling (MS); school psychology (MS); science education (MS); special education in mild/moderate disabilities (MS); special education in moderate/severe disabilities (MS); teaching (MS); teaching and learning (MS); TESOL (teachers of English to speakers of other languages) (MS). Part-time and evening/weekend programs available. Postbaccalaureate distance learning degree programs offered (minimal on-campus study). *Faculty:* 18 full-time (9 women), 8 part-time/adjunct (5 women). *Students:* 158 full-time (127 women), 228 part-time (179 women); includes 159 minority (27 Black or African American, non-Hispanic/Latino; 4 American Indian or Alaska Native, non-Hispanic/Latino; 13 Asian, non-Hispanic/Latino; 107 Hispanic/Latino; 1 Native Hawaiian or other Pacific Islander, non-Hispanic/Latino; 7 Two or more races, non-Hispanic/Latino), 2 international. Average age 33. 298 applicants, 74% accepted, 113 enrolled. In 2013, 70 master's awarded. *Degree requirements:* For master's, comprehensive exam, project, or thesis. *Entrance requirements:* For master's, minimum undergraduate GPA of 3.0; 18 semester units of prerequisite course work in education; three recommendations; 500-word essay; interview. Additional exam requirements/recommendations for international students: Required—TOEFL (minimum score 80 iBT). *Application deadline:* For fall admission, 8/1 priority date for domestic students, 7/1 for international students; for spring admission, 12/1 priority date for domestic students, 11/1 for international students. Applications are processed on a rolling basis. Application fee: $45. Electronic applications accepted. *Expenses:* Contact institution. *Financial support:* Institutionally sponsored loans available. Financial award applicants required to submit CSS PROFILE or FAFSA. *Faculty research:* Leadership development, complexity theory, faith and learning, special education, social and philosophical contexts of education. *Unit head:* Dr. John Shoup, Dean, School of Education, 951-343-4205, Fax: 951-343-4516, E-mail: jshoup@calbaptist.edu. *Application contact:* Dr. Kathryn Norwood, Director, Master of Science Program in Education, 951-343-4760, E-mail: knorwood@calbaptist.edu. Website: http://www.calbaptist.edu/mastersined/.

California State Polytechnic University, Pomona, Academic Affairs, College of Education and Integrative Studies, Master's Programs in Education, Pomona, CA 91768-2557. Offers curriculum and instruction (MA); educational leadership (MA); educational multimedia (MA); special education (MA). *Students:* 39 full-time (26 women), 140 part-time (96 women); includes 91 minority (9 Black or African American, non-Hispanic/Latino; 1 American Indian or Alaska Native, non-Hispanic/Latino; 24 Asian, non-Hispanic/Latino; 53 Hispanic/Latino; 3 Native Hawaiian or other Pacific Islander, non-Hispanic/Latino; 1 Two or more races, non-Hispanic/Latino), 3 international. Average age 35. 64 applicants, 64% accepted, 25 enrolled. In 2013, 74 master's awarded. Application fee: $55. *Expenses:* Tuition, state resident: full-time $6738. Tuition, nonresident: full-time $12,690. *Required fees:* $878; $248 per credit hour. *Unit head:* Dr. Peggy Kelly, Dean, 909-869-2307, E-mail: pkelly@csupomona.edu. *Application contact:* Dr. Dorothy MacNevin, Co-Chair, Graduate Education Department, 909-869-2311, Fax: 909-869-4822, E-mail: dmacnevin@csupomona.edu.

California State University, Dominguez Hills, College of Education, Division of Graduate Education, Program in Technology-Based Education, Carson, CA 90747-0001. Offers MA, Certificate. Part-time and evening/weekend programs available. *Faculty:* 1 (woman) full-time. *Students:* 11 full-time (10 women), 17 part-time (10 women); includes 11 minority (5 Black or African American, non-Hispanic/Latino; 5 Hispanic/Latino; 1 Two or more races, non-Hispanic/Latino), 7 international. Average age 37. 17 applicants, 100% accepted, 13 enrolled. In 2013, 14 master's awarded. *Degree requirements:* For master's, comprehensive exam, thesis or alternative. *Entrance requirements:* For master's, minimum GPA of 2.75. *Application deadline:* For fall admission, 6/1 for domestic students. Application fee: $55. *Expenses:* Tuition, state resident: full-time $6738. Tuition, nonresident: full-time $13,434. *Required fees:* $622. *Faculty research:* Media literacy, assistive technology. *Unit head:* Dr. Peter Desberg, Unit Head, 310-243-3908, E-mail: pdesberg@csudh.edu. *Application contact:* Admissions Office, 310-243-3530. Website: http://www4.csudh.edu/coe/programs/grad-prgs/technology-based-edu/index.

California State University, East Bay, Office of Academic Programs and Graduate Studies, College of Education and Allied Studies, Department of Teacher Education, Hayward, CA 94542-3000. Offers education (MS), including curriculum, early childhood education, educational technology leadership, reading instruction. Postbaccalaureate distance learning degree programs offered. *Degree requirements:* For master's, project or thesis. *Entrance requirements:* For master's, minimum GPA of 3.0 in field, 2.5 overall; teaching experience; baccalaureate degree; 3 letters of recommendation. Additional exam requirements/recommendations for international students: Required—TOEFL (minimum score 550 paper-based), IELTS. Electronic applications accepted. *Faculty research:* Online, pedagogy, writing, learning, teaching.

California State University, Fullerton, Graduate Studies, College of Education, Department of Elementary and Bilingual Education, Fullerton, CA 92834-9480. Offers bilingual/bicultural education (MS); educational technology (MS); elementary curriculum and instruction (MS). *Accreditation:* NCATE. Part-time programs available. *Students:* 140 full-time (118 women), 97 part-time (89 women); includes 101 minority (3 Black or African American, non-Hispanic/Latino; 31 Asian, non-Hispanic/Latino; 61 Hispanic/Latino; 6 Two or more races, non-Hispanic/Latino). Average age 30. 184 applicants, 68% accepted, 99 enrolled. In 2013, 102 master's awarded. *Degree requirements:* For master's, comprehensive exam, project or thesis. *Entrance requirements:* For master's, minimum GPA of 2.5, teaching certificate. Application fee: $55. *Financial support:* Career-related internships or fieldwork, Federal Work-Study, institutionally sponsored loans, and scholarships/grants available. Support available to part-time students. Financial award application deadline: 3/1; financial award applicants required to submit FAFSA. *Faculty research:* Teacher training and tracking, model for improvement of teaching. *Unit head:* Lisa Kirtman, Chair, 657-278-4731. *Application contact:* Admissions/Applications, 657-278-2371.

California State University, Fullerton, Graduate Studies, College of Education, Program of Instructional Design and Technology, Fullerton, CA 92834-9480. Offers MS. Part-time programs available. Postbaccalaureate distance learning degree programs

offered. *Students:* 1 (woman) full-time, 44 part-time (29 women); includes 19 minority (5 Black or African American, non-Hispanic/Latino; 6 Asian, non-Hispanic/Latino; 6 Hispanic/Latino; 2 Two or more races, non-Hispanic/Latino). Average age 38. 48 applicants, 60% accepted, 26 enrolled. In 2013, 24 master's awarded. Application fee: $55. *Financial support:* Career-related internships or fieldwork, Federal Work-Study, institutionally sponsored loans, and scholarships/grants available. Support available to part-time students. Financial award application deadline: 3/1; financial award applicants required to submit FAFSA. *Unit head:* Dr. Jo Ann Carter-Wells, Chair, 657-278-3357. *Application contact:* Admissions/Applications, 657-278-2371.

California State University, Monterey Bay, College of Science, Media Arts and Technology, School of Information Technology and Communication Design, Seaside, CA 93955-8001. Offers interdisciplinary studies (MA), including instructional science and technology; management and information technology (MA). *Degree requirements:* For master's, capstone or thesis. *Entrance requirements:* For master's, GRE, 2 letters of recommendation, minimum GPA of 3.0, technology screening assessment. Additional exam requirements/recommendations for international students: Required—TOEFL (minimum score 550 paper-based; 71 iBT). Electronic applications accepted. *Faculty research:* Electronic commerce, e-learning, knowledge management, international business, business and public policy.

California State University, Northridge, Graduate Studies, College of Education, Department of Secondary Education, Northridge, CA 91330. Offers educational technology (MA); English education (MA); mathematics education (MA); secondary science education (MA); teaching and learning (MA). *Accreditation:* NCATE. Part-time programs available. *Degree requirements:* For master's, thesis optional. *Entrance requirements:* For master's, GRE General Test or minimum GPA of 3.0. Additional exam requirements/recommendations for international students: Required—TOEFL.

California State University, Sacramento, Office of Graduate Studies, College of Education, Department of Teacher Education, Sacramento, CA 95819. Offers behavioral sciences (MA), including gender equity studies; curriculum and instruction (MA); educational technology (MA); language and literacy (MA). Part-time programs available. *Entrance requirements:* Additional exam requirements/recommendations for international students: Required—TOEFL. *Application deadline:* For fall admission, 3/1 for domestic and international students; for spring admission, 9/15 for domestic students, 9/30 for international students. Applications are processed on a rolling basis. Application fee: $55. Electronic applications accepted. *Financial support:* Teaching assistantships, career-related internships or fieldwork, and Federal Work-Study available. Support available to part-time students. Financial award application deadline: 3/1; financial award applicants required to submit FAFSA. *Faculty research:* Technology integration and psychological implications for teaching and learning; inquiry-based research and learning in science and technology; uncovering the process of everyday creativity in teachers and other leaders; universal design as a foundation for inclusion; bullying, cyber-bullying and impact on school success; diversity, social justice in adult/vocational education. *Unit head:* Dr. Rita Johnson, Chair, 916-278-4356, E-mail: rjohnson@csus.edu. *Application contact:* Jose Martinez, Graduate Admissions Supervisor, 916-278-7871, E-mail: martinj@skymail.csus.edu. Website: http://www.edweb.csus.edu/edte.

California State University, San Bernardino, Graduate Studies, College of Education, Program in Instructional Technology, San Bernardino, CA 92407-2397. Offers MA. *Students:* 9 full-time (5 women), 30 part-time (21 women); includes 10 minority (1 Black or African American, non-Hispanic/Latino; 3 Asian, non-Hispanic/Latino; 6 Hispanic/Latino), 17 international. Average age 33. In 2013, 6 master's awarded. *Degree requirements:* For master's, comprehensive exam (for some programs), thesis optional, advancement to candidacy. *Entrance requirements:* For master's, minimum GPA of 2.5. *Application deadline:* For fall admission, 8/31 priority date for domestic students. Application fee: $55. *Unit head:* Dr. Herbert Brunkhorst, Chair, 909-537-5613, Fax: 909-537-7522, E-mail: hkbrunkh@csusb.edu. *Application contact:* Dr. Jeffrey Thompson, Dean of Graduate Studies, 909-537-5058, E-mail: jthompso@csusb.edu.

California State University, Stanislaus, College of Education, Program in Education (MA), Turlock, CA 95382. Offers curriculum and instruction (MA), including education technology, elementary education, multilingual education, physical education, reading, secondary education, special education; school administration (MA); school counseling (MA). Part-time and evening/weekend programs available. *Degree requirements:* For master's, comprehensive exam (for some programs), thesis (for some programs). *Entrance requirements:* For master's, MAT, GRE, or CBEST (varies by concentration), 3 letters of recommendation, personal statement. Additional exam requirements/recommendations for international students: Required—TOEFL (minimum score 550 paper-based). Electronic applications accepted. *Faculty research:* Children's perspectives on historical events, method elementary schools dual language education, K-12 reading programs.

Cambridge College, School of Education, Cambridge, MA 02138-5304. Offers autism specialist (M Ed); autism/behavior analyst (M Ed); behavior analyst (Post-Master's Certificate); behavioral management (M Ed); early childhood teacher (M Ed); education specialist in curriculum and instruction (CAGS); educational leadership (Ed D); elementary teacher (M Ed); English as a second language (M Ed, Certificate); general science (M Ed); health education (Post-Master's Certificate); health/family and consumer sciences (M Ed); history (M Ed); individualized (M Ed); information technology literacy (M Ed); instructional technology (M Ed); interdisciplinary studies (M Ed); library teacher (M Ed); literacy education (M Ed); mathematics (M Ed); mathematics specialist (Certificate); middle school mathematics and science (M Ed); school administration (M Ed, CAGS); school guidance counselor (M Ed); school nurse education (M Ed); school social worker/school adjustment counselor (M Ed); special education administrator (CAGS); special education/moderate disabilities (M Ed); teaching skills and methodologies (M Ed). Part-time and evening/weekend programs available. Postbaccalaureate distance learning degree programs offered (minimal on-campus study). *Degree requirements:* For master's, thesis, internship/practicum (licensure program only); for doctorate, thesis/dissertation; for other advanced degree, thesis. *Entrance requirements:* For master's, interview, resume, documentation of licensure, 2 professional references; for doctorate, official transcripts, interview, resume, documentation of licensure (if any), written personal statement/essay, portfolio of scholarly and professional work, qualifying assessment, 2 professional references, health insurance, immunizations form; for other advanced degree, official transcripts, interview, resume, documentation of licensure (if any), written personal statement/essay, 2 professional references, health insurance, immunizations form. Additional exam requirements/recommendations for international students: Required—TOEFL (minimum score 550 paper-based; 79 iBT), Michigan English Language Assessment Battery (minimum score 85); Recommended—IELTS (minimum score 6). Electronic applications accepted. *Expenses:* Contact institution. *Faculty research:* Adult education, accelerated learning, mathematics education, brain compatible learning, special education and law.

Canisius College, Graduate Division, School of Education and Human Services, Department of Graduate Education and Leadership, Buffalo, NY 14208-1098. Offers business and marketing education (MS Ed); college student personnel (MS Ed); deaf education (MS Ed); deaf/adolescent education, grades 7-12 (MS Ed); deaf/childhood

education, grades 1-6 (MS Ed); differentiated instruction (MS Ed); education administration (MS); educational administration (MS Ed); educational technologies (Certificate); gifted education extension (Certificate); literacy (MS Ed); reading (Certificate); school building leadership (MS Ed, Certificate); school district leadership (Certificate); teacher leader (Certificate); TESOL (MS Ed). *Accreditation:* NCATE. Part-time and evening/weekend programs available. Postbaccalaureate distance learning degree programs offered (minimal on-campus study). *Faculty:* 6 full-time (5 women), 33 part-time/adjunct (20 women). *Students:* 134 full-time (106 women), 267 part-time (213 women); includes 36 minority (22 Black or African American, non-Hispanic/Latino; 1 American Indian or Alaska Native, non-Hispanic/Latino; 3 Asian, non-Hispanic/Latino; 8 Hispanic/Latino; 2 Two or more races, non-Hispanic/Latino), 2 international. Average age 30. 282 applicants, 80% accepted, 120 enrolled. In 2013, 178 master's awarded. *Entrance requirements:* For master's, GRE if cumulative GPA less than 2.7, transcripts, two letters of recommendation. Additional exam requirements/recommendations for international students: Required—TOEFL (minimum score 550 paper-based, 80 iBT), IELTS (minimum score 6.5), or CAEL (minimum score 70). *Application deadline:* Applications are processed on a rolling basis. Application fee: $25. Electronic applications accepted. Application fee is waived when completed online. *Expenses: Tuition:* Part-time $750 per credit hour. *Financial support:* Career-related internships or fieldwork, Federal Work-Study, scholarships/grants, tuition waivers (partial), and unspecified assistantships available. Support available to part-time students. Financial award application deadline: 4/30; financial award applicants required to submit FAFSA. *Faculty research:* Asperger's disease, autism, private higher education, reading strategies. *Unit head:* Dr. Rosemary K. Murray, Chair/Associate Professor of Graduate Education and Leadership, 716-888-3723, E-mail: murray1@canisius.edu. *Application contact:* Julie A. Zulewski, Director of Graduate Admissions, 716-888-2548, Fax: 716-888-3195, E-mail: zulewskj@canisius.edu.
Website: http://www.canisius.edu/graduate/.

Capella University, School of Education, Doctoral Programs in Education, Minneapolis, MN 55402. Offers curriculum and instruction (PhD); educational leadership and management (Ed D); instructional design for online learning (PhD); K-12 studies in education (PhD); leadership for higher education (PhD); leadership in educational administration (PhD); postsecondary and adult education (PhD); professional studies in education (PhD); reading and literacy (Ed D); special education leadership (PhD); training and performance improvement (PhD).

Capella University, School of Education, Master's Programs in Education, Minneapolis, MN 55402. Offers adult education (MS); curriculum and instruction (MS); early childhood education (MS); enrollment management (MS); higher education leadership and management (MS); instructional design for online learning (MS); integrative studies (MS); K-12 studies in education (MS); leadership in educational administration (MS); reading and literacy (MS); special education teaching (MS).

Cardinal Stritch University, College of Education, Department of Educational Computing, Milwaukee, WI 53217-3985. Offers instructional technology (ME, MS). Part-time and evening/weekend programs available. *Degree requirements:* For master's, comprehensive exam, thesis, faculty recommendation. *Entrance requirements:* For master's, letters of recommendation (2), minimum GPA of 2.75.

Caribbean University, Graduate School, Bayamón, PR 00960-0493. Offers administration and supervision (MA Ed); criminal justice (MA); curriculum and instruction (MA Ed, PhD), including elementary education (MA Ed), English education (MA Ed), history education (MA Ed), mathematics education (MA Ed), primary education (MA Ed), science education (MA Ed), Spanish education (MA Ed); educational technology in instructional systems (MA Ed); gerontology (MSN); human resources (MBA); museology, archiving and art history (MA Ed); neonatal pediatrics (MSN); physical education (MA Ed); special education (MA Ed). *Entrance requirements:* For master's, interview, minimum GPA of 2.5.

Central Connecticut State University, School of Graduate Studies, School of Education and Professional Studies, Department of Educational Leadership, Program in Educational Technology and Media, New Britain, CT 06050-4010. Offers MS. Part-time and evening/weekend programs available. *Students:* 5 full-time (2 women), 27 part-time (18 women); includes 9 minority (3 Black or African American, non-Hispanic/Latino; 1 Asian, non-Hispanic/Latino; 5 Hispanic/Latino), 1 international. Average age 33. 15 applicants, 80% accepted, 11 enrolled. In 2013, 10 master's awarded. *Degree requirements:* For master's, thesis or alternative. *Entrance requirements:* For master's, minimum undergraduate GPA of 2.7. Additional exam requirements/recommendations for international students: Required—TOEFL (minimum score 550 paper-based; 79 iBT). *Application deadline:* For fall admission, 6/1 for domestic students, 5/1 for international students; for spring admission, 11/1 for domestic and international students. Applications are processed on a rolling basis. Application fee: $50. Electronic applications accepted. Part-time tuition and fees vary according to degree level. *Faculty research:* Design and development of multimedia packages, semiotics, perceptual theories, integrated media presentations, distance teaching. *Unit head:* Dr. Ellen Retelle, Chair, 860-832-2130, E-mail: retelleelm@ccsu.edu. *Application contact:* Patricia Gardner, Associate Director of Graduate Studies, 860-832-2350, Fax: 860-832-2362, E-mail: graduateadmissions@ccsu.edu.

Central Michigan University, Central Michigan University Global Campus, Program in Education, Mount Pleasant, MI 48859. Offers college teaching (Graduate Certificate); community college (MA); curriculum and instruction (MA); educational technology (MA); guidance and development (MA); reading and literacy K-12 (MA); school principalship (MA), including charter school leadership; training and development (MA). *Accreditation:* Teacher Education Accreditation Council. Part-time and evening/weekend programs available. *Entrance requirements:* For master's, minimum GPA of 2.7 in major. Additional exam requirements/recommendations for international students: Required—TOEFL. *Application deadline:* Applications are processed on a rolling basis. Application fee: $50. Electronic applications accepted. *Financial support:* Scholarships/grants available. Support available to part-time students. *Unit head:* Kaleb Patrick, Director, 989-774-3144, E-mail: patri1kg@cmich.edu. *Application contact:* 877-268-4636, E-mail: cmuglobal@cmich.edu.

Central Michigan University, College of Graduate Studies, College of Education and Human Services, Department of Educational Leadership, Mount Pleasant, MI 48859. Offers educational leadership (Ed D), including educational technology (Ed D, Ed S), higher education leadership, K-12 curriculum, K-12 leadership; general educational administration (Ed S), including administrative leadership K-12, educational technology (Ed D, Ed S), higher education administration, instructional leadership K-12; school principalship (MA), including charter school leadership, site-based leadership; student affairs administration (MA); teacher leadership (MA). Part-time and evening/weekend programs available. *Degree requirements:* For master's and Ed S, thesis or alternative; for doctorate, thesis/dissertation. *Entrance requirements:* For doctorate, GRE or MAT, master's degree, minimum GPA of 3.5, 3 years of professional education experience. Electronic applications accepted. *Faculty research:* Elementary administration, secondary administration, student achievement, in-service training, internships in administration.

Central Michigan University, College of Graduate Studies, College of Education and Human Services, Department of Teacher Education and Professional Development, Mount Pleasant, MI 48859. Offers educational technology (MA, Graduate Certificate); elementary education (MA), including classroom teaching, early childhood; reading and literacy K-12 (MA); secondary education (MA). Part-time and evening/weekend programs available. *Degree requirements:* For master's, thesis or alternative. Electronic applications accepted. *Faculty research:* Integrating literacy across the curriculum, science teaching and aesthetic learning in science, diversity education, educational technology, educational psychology and child development.

Chestnut Hill College, School of Graduate Studies, Department of Education, Program in Secondary Education, Philadelphia, PA 19118-2693. Offers instructional design and e-learning (M Ed); secondary education (CAS). Part-time and evening/weekend programs available. *Faculty:* 10 full-time (7 women), 48 part-time/adjunct (34 women). *Students:* 18 full-time (14 women), 51 part-time (31 women); includes 23 minority (15 Black or African American, non-Hispanic/Latino; 4 Asian, non-Hispanic/Latino; 4 Hispanic/Latino), 1 international. Average age 32. 36 applicants, 100% accepted. In 2013, 33 master's, 19 CASs awarded. *Degree requirements:* For master's, thesis optional. *Entrance requirements:* For master's, PRAXIS I or proof of teaching certification, letters of recommendation; writing sample; 6 graduate credits with minimum B grade if undergraduate GPA less than 3.0. Additional exam requirements/recommendations for international students: Required—TOEFL (minimum score 500 paper-based), IELTS (mnimum score 6.0), or TWE (minimum score 22). *Application deadline:* For fall admission, 7/1 for domestic and international students; for spring admission, 11/1 for domestic and international students; for summer admission, 4/1 for domestic and international students. Applications are processed on a rolling basis. *Expenses:* Contact institution. *Financial support:* Unspecified assistantships available. *Faculty research:* Science teaching. *Unit head:* Dr. Debra Chiaradonna, Chair, Department of Education, 215-248-7147, Fax: 215-248-7155, E-mail: chiaradonnad@chc.edu. *Application contact:* Jayne Mashett, Director of Admissions, School of Graduate Studies, 215-248-7020, Fax: 215-248-7161, E-mail: gradadmissions@chc.edu.
Website: http://www.chc.edu/Graduate/Programs/Masters/Education/.

Chestnut Hill College, School of Graduate Studies, Program in Instructional Technology, Philadelphia, PA 19118-2693. Offers instructional design and e-learning (MS); instructional technology specialist (MS, CAS). Part-time and evening/weekend programs available. *Faculty:* 1 full-time (0 women), 4 part-time/adjunct (0 women). *Students:* 4 full-time (3 women), 8 part-time (4 women), 5 international. Average age 33. 3 applicants, 100% accepted. In 2013, 7 master's, 1 other advanced degree awarded. *Degree requirements:* For master's, special project/internship. *Entrance requirements:* For master's, GRE General Test or MAT, letters of recommendation, writing sample. Additional exam requirements/recommendations for international students: Required—TOEFL (minimum score 500 paper-based), IELTS (mnimum score 6.0), or TWE (minimum score 22). *Application deadline:* For fall admission, 7/1 for domestic and international students; for spring admission, 11/1 for domestic and international students; for summer admission, 4/1 for domestic students. Applications are processed on a rolling basis. *Expenses:* Contact institution. *Financial support:* Unspecified assistantships available. *Faculty research:* Instructional design, learning management systems and related technologies, video as a teaching and learning tool, Web 2.0 technologies and virtual worlds as a learning tool, utilization of laptops and iPads in the classroom. *Unit head:* Dr. Yefim Kats, Coordinator, 215-248-7008, Fax: 215-248-7155, E-mail: katsy@chc.edu. *Application contact:* Jayne Mashett, Director of Admissions, School of Graduate Studies, 215-248-7020, Fax: 215-248-7161, E-mail: gradadmissions@chc.edu.
Website: http://www.chc.edu/Graduate/Programs/Masters/Instructional_Technology/.

Chicago State University, School of Graduate and Professional Studies, College of Education, Department of Reading, Elementary Education, Library Information and Media Studies, Program in Library Information and Media Studies, Chicago, IL 60628. Offers MS Ed. *Entrance requirements:* For master's, minimum GPA of 2.75.

Chicago State University, School of Graduate and Professional Studies, College of Education, Department of Technology and Education, Chicago, IL 60628. Offers secondary education (MAT); technology and education (MS Ed). Postbaccalaureate distance learning degree programs offered. *Degree requirements:* For master's, thesis optional. *Entrance requirements:* For master's, minimum GPA of 2.75.

Clarke University, Program in Education, Dubuque, IA 52001-3198. Offers early childhood/special education (MAE); educational administration: elementary and secondary (MAE); educational media: elementary and secondary (MAE); multi-categorical resource k-12 (MAE); multidisciplinary studies (MAE); reading: elementary (MAE); technology in education (MAE). Part-time and evening/weekend programs available. Postbaccalaureate distance learning degree programs offered (minimal on-campus study). *Faculty:* 10 full-time (9 women), 1 (woman) part-time/adjunct. *Students:* 5 full-time (3 women), 27 part-time (24 women); includes 2 minority (1 Black or African American, non-Hispanic/Latino; 1 American Indian or Alaska Native, non-Hispanic/Latino). In 2013, 11 master's awarded. *Degree requirements:* For master's, comprehensive exam, thesis optional. *Entrance requirements:* For master's, GRE General Test or MAT, minimum GPA of 2.75. *Application deadline:* Applications are processed on a rolling basis. Application fee: $25. Electronic applications accepted. *Expenses: Tuition:* Part-time $660 per credit. *Required fees:* $15 per credit. *Financial support:* Career-related internships or fieldwork available. Financial award applicants required to submit FAFSA. *Unit head:* Dr. Michele Slover, Chair, 319-588-6397, Fax: 319-584-8604. *Application contact:* Kara Shroeder, Information Contact, 563-588-6354, Fax: 563-588-6789, E-mail: graduate@clarke.edu.

Cleveland State University, College of Graduate Studies, College of Education and Human Services, Program in Urban Education, Specialization in Learning and Development, Cleveland, OH 44115. Offers PhD. Part-time programs available. *Faculty:* 17 full-time (9 women). *Students:* 8 full-time (5 women), 18 part-time (13 women); includes 10 minority (6 Black or African American, non-Hispanic/Latino; 3 Asian, non-Hispanic/Latino; 1 Hispanic/Latino), 5 international. Average age 43. 18 applicants, 28% accepted, 1 enrolled. In 2013, 9 doctorates awarded. *Degree requirements:* For doctorate, one foreign language, comprehensive exam, thesis/dissertation. *Entrance requirements:* For doctorate, General GRE Test (minimum score of 297 for combined Verbal and Quantitative exams, 4.0 preferred for Analytical Writing), minimum graduate GPA of 3.25 in educational psychology, school psychology and/or special education, curriculum vitae or resume, personal statement, 2 letters of recommendation. Additional exam requirements/recommendations for international students: Required—TOEFL (minimum score 525 paper-based), IELTS (minimum score 6). *Expenses:* Tuition, state resident: full-time $8335; part-time $521 per credit hour. Tuition, nonresident: full-time $15,670; part-time $979 per credit hour. *Required fees:* $50; $25 per semester. *Financial support:* In 2013–14, 5 students received support, including 1 research assistantship with full tuition reimbursement available, 2 teaching assistantships with full tuition reimbursements available (averaging $10,325 per year); tuition waivers also available. Support available to part-time students. Financial award application deadline: 4/1; financial award applicants required to submit FAFSA. *Faculty research:* The implications of human variability to instruction service delivery in educational and social

agencies. *Unit head:* Dr. Graham Stead, Director, Doctoral Studies, 216-875-9869, E-mail: g.b.stead@csuohio.edu. *Application contact:* Rita M. Grabowski, Administrative Coordinator, 216-687-4697, Fax: 216-875-9697, E-mail: r.grabowski@csuohio.edu. Website: http://www.csuohio.edu/cehs/departments/DOC/ld_doc.html.

College of Mount Saint Vincent, School of Professional and Continuing Studies, Department of Teacher Education, Riverdale, NY 10471-1093. Offers instructional technology and global perspectives (Certificate); middle level education (Certificate); multicultural studies (Certificate); urban and multicultural education (MS Ed). *Accreditation:* Teacher Education Accreditation Council. Part-time programs available. *Degree requirements:* For master's, comprehensive exam. *Entrance requirements:* For master's, interview, New York teaching certificate. Additional exam requirements/recommendations for international students: Required—TOEFL.

College of Saint Elizabeth, Department of Educational Leadership, Morristown, NJ 07960-6989. Offers accelerated certification for teaching (Certificate); assistive technology (Certificate); educational leadership (MA, Ed D); special education (MA). Part-time programs available. *Faculty:* 5 full-time (0 women), 21 part-time/adjunct (9 women). *Students:* 67 full-time (44 women), 146 part-time (117 women); includes 52 minority (36 Black or African American, non-Hispanic/Latino; 2 Asian, non-Hispanic/Latino; 12 Hispanic/Latino; 1 Native Hawaiian or other Pacific Islander, non-Hispanic/Latino; 1 Two or more races, non-Hispanic/Latino), 1 international. Average age 38. In 2013, 55 master's, 14 doctorates, 42 other advanced degrees awarded. *Degree requirements:* For master's, thesis or alternative; for doctorate, thesis/dissertation. *Entrance requirements:* For master's, personal written statement, interview, minimum undergraduate GPA of 3.0; for doctorate, master's degree. Additional exam requirements/recommendations for international students: Required—TOEFL. *Application deadline:* For fall admission, 6/30 priority date for domestic students; for spring admission, 11/30 for domestic students. Applications are processed on a rolling basis. Application fee: $35. Electronic applications accepted. *Expenses: Tuition:* Full-time $19,152; part-time $1064 per credit. *Financial support:* Career-related internships or fieldwork, tuition waivers (partial), and unspecified assistantships available. Support available to part-time students. Financial award application deadline: 3/15; financial award applicants required to submit FAFSA. *Faculty research:* Developmental stages for teaching and human services professionals, effectiveness of humanities core curriculum. *Unit head:* Dr. Joseph Ciccone, Associate Professor/Course of Study Coordinator, 973-290-4383, Fax: 973-290-4389, E-mail: jciccone@cse.edu. *Application contact:* Deborah S. Cobo, Associate Director for Graduate Admissions, 973-290-4194, Fax: 973-290-4710, E-mail: dscobo@cse.edu.
Website: http://www.cse.edu/academics/catalog/academic-programs/education.dot?tabID=tabMinor&divID=catalogMinor#maeducation.

The College of Saint Rose, Graduate Studies, School of Education, Department of Educational Psychology, Albany, NY 12203-1419. Offers applied technology education (MS Ed); educational psychology (MS Ed); instructional technology (Certificate); school psychology (MS Ed, Certificate). Part-time and evening/weekend programs available. *Entrance requirements:* For master's, minimum undergraduate GPA of 3.0. Additional exam requirements/recommendations for international students: Required—TOEFL (minimum score 550 paper-based). Electronic applications accepted.

The College of William and Mary, School of Education, Program in Education Policy, Planning, and Leadership, Williamsburg, VA 23187-8795. Offers curriculum and educational technology (Ed D, PhD); curriculum leadership (Ed D, PhD); educational leadership (M Ed), including higher education administration (M Ed, Ed D, PhD), K-12 administration and supervision; educational policy, planning, and leadership (Ed D, PhD), including general education administration, gifted education administration, higher education administration (M Ed, Ed D, PhD). *Accreditation:* NCATE. Part-time and evening/weekend programs available. *Faculty:* 10 full-time (5 women), 17 part-time/adjunct (13 women). *Students:* 64 full-time (52 women), 145 part-time (106 women); includes 46 minority (33 Black or African American, non-Hispanic/Latino; 3 Asian, non-Hispanic/Latino; 4 Hispanic/Latino; 6 Two or more races, non-Hispanic/Latino), 9 international. Average age 38. 133 applicants, 74% accepted, 72 enrolled. In 2013, 24 master's, 17 doctorates awarded. *Degree requirements:* For doctorate, comprehensive exam, thesis/dissertation. *Entrance requirements:* For master's, GRE or MAT, minimum GPA of 2.5; for doctorate, GRE or MAT, minimum GPA of 3.0. Additional exam requirements/recommendations for international students: Required—TOEFL, IELTS. *Application deadline:* For fall admission, 1/15 for domestic and international students. Application fee: $50. Electronic applications accepted. *Expenses:* Tuition, state resident: full-time $7120; part-time $405 per credit hour. Tuition, nonresident: full-time $21,639; part-time $1050 per credit hour. *Required fees:* $4764. *Financial support:* In 2013–14, 58 students received support, including 1 fellowship (averaging $20,000 per year), 51 research assistantships with full and partial tuition reimbursements available (averaging $16,551 per year); career-related internships or fieldwork, Federal Work-Study, institutionally sponsored loans, scholarships/grants, and unspecified assistantships also available. Support available to part-time students. Financial award application deadline: 1/15; financial award applicants required to submit FAFSA. *Faculty research:* Higher education policy, faculty incentives, history of adversity, resilience, leadership. *Unit head:* Dr. James Stronge, Area Coordinator, 757-221-2339, E-mail: jhstro@wm.edu. *Application contact:* Dorothy Smith Osborne, Assistant Dean for Academic Programs and Student Services, 757-221-2317, Fax: 757-221-2293, E-mail: dsosbo@wm.edu.
Website: http://education.wm.edu.

Colorado Christian University, Program in Curriculum and Instruction, Lakewood, CO 80226. Offers corporate education (MACI); early childhood educator (MACI); elementary educator (MACI); instructional technology (MACI); master educator (MACI); online course developer (MACI); online teaching and learning (MACI); special education generalist (MACI). Part-time and evening/weekend programs available. *Degree requirements:* For master's, thesis optional, practicum. *Entrance requirements:* For master's, interviews, letters of recommendation. Additional exam requirements/recommendations for international students: Required—TOEFL. Electronic applications accepted. *Expenses:* Contact institution.

Colorado State University–Pueblo, College of Education, Engineering and Professional Studies, Education Program, Pueblo, CO 81001-4901. Offers art education (M Ed); foreign language education (M Ed); health and physical education (M Ed); instructional technology (M Ed); linguistically diverse education (M Ed); music education (M Ed); special education (M Ed). *Accreditation:* Teacher Education Accreditation Council. Part-time programs available. *Degree requirements:* For master's, portfolio. *Entrance requirements:* For master's, 3 recommendations, teaching license. Additional exam requirements/recommendations for international students: Required—TOEFL (minimum score 500 paper-based). Electronic applications accepted. *Faculty research:* Portfolio assessment, math education, science education.

Columbia International University, Columbia Graduate School, Columbia, SC 29230-3122. Offers Bible teaching (MABT); Christian higher education leadership (Ed D); Christian school educational leadership (Ed D); counseling (MACN); curriculum and instruction (M Ed), including Christian school guidance, English as a second language, learning disabilities, school technology; early childhood and elementary education (MAT); educational administration (M Ed); teaching English as a foreign language

(Certificate); teaching English as a foreign language and intercultural studies (MATF). Part-time and evening/weekend programs available. *Degree requirements:* For master's, internships, professional project. *Entrance requirements:* For master's, Minnesota Multiphasic Personality Inventory, MAT, minimum GPA of 2.7. Additional exam requirements/recommendations for international students: Required—TOEFL. Electronic applications accepted.

Columbus State University, Graduate Studies, College of Education and Health Professions, Department of Teacher Education, Columbus, GA 31907-5645. Offers accomplished teaching (M Ed); early childhood education (M Ed, MAT, Ed S); middle grades education (M Ed, MAT, Ed S); school library media (M Ed, MAT); secondary education (M Ed, MAT, Ed S), including English/language arts (M Ed, Ed S), general science (M Ed), mathematics (M Ed, Ed S), science (Ed S), social science (M Ed, Ed S); special education (M Ed, MAT, Ed S), including general curriculum (M Ed, MAT); teacher leadership (M Ed). *Accreditation:* NCATE. Part-time and evening/weekend programs available. Postbaccalaureate distance learning degree programs offered (minimal on-campus study). *Faculty:* 17 full-time (12 women), 31 part-time/adjunct (28 women). *Students:* 59 full-time (48 women), 190 part-time (150 women); includes 85 minority (68 Black or African American, non-Hispanic/Latino; 1 American Indian or Alaska Native, non-Hispanic/Latino; 6 Asian, non-Hispanic/Latino; 4 Hispanic/Latino; 6 Two or more races, non-Hispanic/Latino), 2 international. Average age 34. 132 applicants, 58% accepted, 50 enrolled. In 2013, 86 master's, 26 other advanced degrees awarded. *Degree requirements:* For master's, thesis, exit exam; for Ed S, thesis or alternative. *Entrance requirements:* For master's, GRE General Test, minimum undergraduate GPA of 2.75; for Ed S, GRE General Test, minimum undergraduate GPA of 2.75, graduate 3.0. Additional exam requirements/recommendations for international students: Required—TOEFL (minimum score 550 paper-based; 79 iBT). *Application deadline:* For fall admission, 6/30 for domestic students, 5/1 for international students; for spring admission, 11/1 for domestic and international students; for summer admission, 3/1 for domestic and international students. Applications are processed on a rolling basis. Application fee: $40. Electronic applications accepted. *Expenses:* Tuition, state resident: full-time $4572; part-time $382 per credit hour. Tuition, nonresident: full-time $18,292; part-time $1526 per credit hour. *Required fees:* $1800; $196 per credit hour. Tuition and fees vary according to campus/location and program. *Financial support:* In 2013–14, 173 students received support, including 12 research assistantships with partial tuition reimbursements available (averaging $3,000 per year); career-related internships or fieldwork, Federal Work-Study, institutionally sponsored loans, scholarships/grants, tuition waivers (partial), and unspecified assistantships also available. Support available to part-time students. Financial award application deadline: 5/1; financial award applicants required to submit FAFSA. *Unit head:* Dr. Deirdre Greer, Department Chair, 706-507-8034, Fax: 706-568-3134, E-mail: greer_deirdre@columbusstate.edu. *Application contact:* Kristin Williams, Director of International and Graduate Recruitment, 706-507-8848, Fax: 706-568-5091, E-mail: williams_kristin@columbusstate.edu.
Website: http://te.columbusstate.edu/.

Concordia University, College of Education, Portland, OR 97211-6099. Offers career and technical education (M Ed); curriculum and instruction (M Ed), including adolescent literacy, career and technical education, e-learning/technology education, early childhood education, English for speakers of other languages, English language development, environmental education, mathematics, methods and curriculum, reading, science, teacher leadership, the inclusive classroom; early childhood (MAT); education leadership (Ed D); educational administration (M Ed); elementary education (MAT); secondary education (MAT); special education (M Ed); teacher leadership (Ed D). Part-time programs available. Postbaccalaureate distance learning degree programs offered (no on-campus study). *Degree requirements:* For master's, comprehensive exam, work samples/portfolio. *Entrance requirements:* For master's, California Basic Educational Skills Test or PRAXIS I, minimum undergraduate GPA of 2.8, graduate 3.0; 2 letters of recommendation. Additional exam requirements/recommendations for international students: Required—TOEFL (minimum score 525 paper-based). Electronic applications accepted. *Faculty research:* Learner-centered classroom, brain-based learning, future of online learning.

Concordia University, School of Education, Irvine, CA 92612-3299. Offers curriculum and instruction (MA); education and preliminary teaching credential (M Ed); educational administration and preliminary administrative services credential (MA); educational technology (MA); school counseling with pupil personnel services credential (MA). Part-time and evening/weekend programs available. Postbaccalaureate distance learning degree programs offered (no on-campus study). *Faculty:* 15 full-time (12 women), 96 part-time/adjunct (59 women). *Students:* 885 full-time (690 women), 96 part-time (74 women); includes 282 minority (39 Black or African American, non-Hispanic/Latino; 42 Asian, non-Hispanic/Latino; 182 Hispanic/Latino; 3 Native Hawaiian or other Pacific Islander, non-Hispanic/Latino; 16 Two or more races, non-Hispanic/Latino), 1 international. Average age 39. 402 applicants, 79% accepted, 311 enrolled. In 2013, 469 master's awarded. *Degree requirements:* For master's, action research project. *Entrance requirements:* For master's, California Basic Educational Skills Test, California Subject Examinations for Teachers (M Ed and MA in educational administration and preliminary administrative services credential), official college transcript(s), signed statement of intent, two references, copy of credential. Additional exam requirements/recommendations for international students: Required—TOEFL. *Application deadline:* For fall admission, 7/15 priority date for domestic students, 6/1 for international students; for spring admission, 11/30 priority date for domestic students, 10/1 for international students. Applications are processed on a rolling basis. Application fee: $50 ($125 for international students). Electronic applications accepted. *Expenses:* Contact institution. *Financial support:* In 2013–14, 23 students received support. Scholarships/grants and unspecified assistantships available. Financial award applicants required to submit FAFSA. *Unit head:* Dr. Janice Nelson, Dean, 949-214-3334, E-mail: janice.nelson@cui.edu. *Application contact:* Patty Hunt, Admissions Coordinator, 949-214-3362, Fax: 949-214-3362, E-mail: patricia.hunt@cui.edu.

Concordia University, School of Graduate Studies, Faculty of Arts and Science, Department of Education, Program in Educational Technology, Montréal, QC H3G 1M8, Canada. Offers MA, PhD. *Degree requirements:* For master's, one foreign language, thesis optional, internship; for doctorate, comprehensive exam, thesis/dissertation. *Entrance requirements:* For doctorate, MA in educational technology or equivalent. *Faculty research:* Instructional design and tele-education, educational cybernetics and systems analysis, media research and theory development, distance education.

Concordia University, School of Graduate Studies, Faculty of Arts and Science, Department of Education, Program in Instructional Technology, Montréal, QC H3G 1M8, Canada. Offers Diploma. *Entrance requirements:* For degree, BA in related field.

Concordia University Chicago, College of Graduate and Innovative Programs, Program in Educational Technology, River Forest, IL 60305-1499. Offers MA.

Concordia University, St. Paul, College of Education and Science, St. Paul, MN 55104-5494. Offers curriculum and instruction (MA Ed), including K-12 reading; differentiated instruction (MA Ed); early childhood education (MA Ed); educational leadership (MA Ed); educational technology (MA Ed); exercise science (MA); family life education (MA); K-12 principal licensure (Ed S); K-12 reading (Certificate); special

education (MA Ed, Certificate), including autism spectrum disorder (MA Ed), emotional and behavioral disorders (MA Ed), learning disabilities (MA Ed); sports management (MA); superintendent (Ed S). *Accreditation:* NCATE. Part-time and evening/weekend programs available. Postbaccalaureate distance learning degree programs offered (minimal on-campus study). *Faculty:* 12 full-time (7 women), 92 part-time/adjunct (49 women). *Students:* 915 full-time (659 women), 64 part-time (53 women); includes 99 minority (47 Black or African American, non-Hispanic/Latino; 5 American Indian or Alaska Native, non-Hispanic/Latino; 18 Asian, non-Hispanic/Latino; 15 Hispanic/Latino; 2 Native Hawaiian or other Pacific Islander, non-Hispanic/Latino; 12 Two or more races, non-Hispanic/Latino), 24 international. Average age 34. 664 applicants, 67% accepted, 411 enrolled. In 2013, 275 master's, 69 other advanced degrees awarded. *Degree requirements:* For master's, thesis (for some programs). *Entrance requirements:* For master's, official transcripts from regionally-accredited institution stating the conferral of a bachelor's degree with minimum cumulative GPA of 3.0; personal statement; professional resume; practitioner in field through work or volunteerism; resume. Additional exam requirements/recommendations for international students: Recommended—TOEFL (minimum score 547 paper-based; 78 iBT), IELTS (minimum score 6). *Application deadline:* For fall admission, 8/1 for domestic and international students; for spring admission, 12/1 for domestic and international students; for summer admission, 5/1 for domestic and international students. Applications are processed on a rolling basis. Application fee: $50. Electronic applications accepted. *Expenses: Tuition:* Full-time $6200; part-time $425 per credit. Tuition and fees vary according to degree level and program. *Financial support:* Applicants required to submit FAFSA. *Unit head:* Dr. Donald Helmstetter, Dean, 651-641-8227, Fax: 651-641-8807, E-mail: helmstetter@csp.edu. *Application contact:* Kimberly Craig, Director of Graduate and Cohort Admission, 651-603-6223, Fax: 651-603-6320, E-mail: craig@csp.edu.

Dakota State University, College of Education, Madison, SD 57042-1799. Offers instructional technology (MSET). *Accreditation:* NCATE. Part-time and evening/weekend programs available. Postbaccalaureate distance learning degree programs offered (minimal on-campus study). *Faculty:* 3 full-time (1 woman), 1 part-time/adjunct (0 women). *Students:* 2 full-time (0 women), 14 part-time (9 women); includes 3 minority (1 Asian, non-Hispanic/Latino; 2 Hispanic/Latino), 1 international. Average age 34. 3 applicants, 100% accepted, 3 enrolled. In 2013, 11 master's awarded. *Degree requirements:* For master's, thesis, portfolio. *Entrance requirements:* For master's, GRE General Test, demonstration of technology skills, minimum GPA of 2.7. Additional exam requirements/recommendations for international students: Required—TOEFL (minimum score 550 paper-based; 78 iBT). *Application deadline:* For fall admission, 6/15 for domestic and international students; for spring admission, 11/15 for domestic and international students. Applications are processed on a rolling basis. Application fee: $35 ($85 for international students). *Financial support:* In 2013–14, 9 students received support, including 3 fellowships with partial tuition reimbursements available (averaging $12,956 per year); research assistantships, teaching assistantships, Federal Work-Study, scholarships/grants, tuition waivers (partial), unspecified assistantships, and administrative assistantships also available. Support available to part-time students. Financial award applicants required to submit FAFSA. *Faculty research:* Educational technology evaluation, computer-supported collaborative learning, cognitive theory and visual representation of the effects of ambiquitous wireless computing on student learning and productivity. *Unit head:* Dr. Omar El-Gayar, Dean, 605-256-5799, Fax: 605-256-5093, E-mail: omar.el-gayar@dsu.edu. *Application contact:* Erin Blankespoor, Secretary, Office of Graduate Studies and Research, 605-256-5799, Fax: 605-256-5093, E-mail: erin.blankespoor@dsu.edu.
Website: http://www.dsu.edu/educate/index.aspx.

Delaware Valley College, Program in Educational Leadership, Doylestown, PA 18901-2697. Offers instruction, curriculum and technology (MS); school administration and leadership (MS). Part-time and evening/weekend programs available. *Entrance requirements:* For master's, minimum undergraduate GPA of 3.0.

DeSales University, Graduate Division, Division of Liberal Arts and Social Sciences, Program in Education, Center Valley, PA 18034-9568. Offers early childhood education Pre K-4 (M Ed); instructional technology for K-12 (M Ed); interdisciplinary (M Ed); secondary education (M Ed); special education (M Ed); teaching English to speakers of other languages (M Ed). Part-time and evening/weekend programs available. Postbaccalaureate distance learning degree programs offered (no on-campus study). *Degree requirements:* For master's, thesis project. *Entrance requirements:* Additional exam requirements/recommendations for international students: Required—TOEFL. *Application deadline:* Applications are processed on a rolling basis. Electronic applications accepted. *Expenses: Tuition:* Part-time $790 per credit. *Financial support:* Application deadline: 5/1. *Unit head:* Dr. Judith Rance-Roney, Chair, 610-282-1100 Ext. 1323, E-mail: judith.rance-roney@desales.edu. *Application contact:* Abigail Wernicki, Director of Graduate Admissions, 610-282-1100 Ext. 1768, E-mail: gradadmissions@desales.edu.

DeVry University, Graduate Programs, Downers Grove, IL 60515. Offers accounting and financial management (MAFM); business administration (MBA); education (MS); educational technology (MS); electrical engineering (MS); human resources management (MHRM); information systems management (MISM); network and communications management (MNCM); project management (MPM); public administration (MPA).

Dowling College, Graduate Programs in Education, Oakdale, NY 11769-1999. Offers adolescence education with middle childhood extension (MS); childhood and early childhood education (MS); childhood and gifted education (MS); childhood education (1-6) (MS); computers in education (AC); early childhood education (B-2) (MS); educational administration (Ed D); educational technology leadership (MS); educational technology specialist (AC); gifted education (AC); literacy education (MS, AC), including 5-12 (MS), B-12 (MS); literacy education (MS), including B-6; school building leader (AC); school district business leader (MBA, AC); school district leader (AC); special education (MS), including autism, severe disabilities; sport management (MS). *Accreditation:* NCATE. Part-time and evening/weekend programs available. Postbaccalaureate distance learning degree programs offered (minimal on-campus study). *Faculty:* 44 full-time (24 women), 17 part-time/adjunct (8 women). *Students:* 183 full-time (124 women), 314 part-time (231 women); includes 51 minority (19 Black or African American, non-Hispanic/Latino; 1 American Indian or Alaska Native, non-Hispanic/Latino; 3 Asian, non-Hispanic/Latino; 26 Hispanic/Latino; 2 Native Hawaiian or other Pacific Islander, non-Hispanic/Latino). Average age 32. 174 applicants, 80% accepted, 82 enrolled. In 2013, 198 master's, 33 doctorates, 48 other advanced degrees awarded. *Degree requirements:* For master's and AC, comprehensive exam; for doctorate, thesis/dissertation. *Entrance requirements:* For master's, minimum GPA of 3.0; for doctorate, GRE, master's degree; for AC, teaching certificate. Additional exam requirements/recommendations for international students: Required—TOEFL (minimum score 550 paper-based). *Application deadline:* For fall admission, 9/1 priority date for domestic students; for winter admission, 1/1 priority date for domestic students; for spring admission, 2/1 priority date for domestic students. Applications are processed on a rolling basis. Application fee: $50. Electronic applications accepted. *Expenses: Tuition:* Full-time $22,731; part-time $1029 per credit. *Required fees:* $956; $956. *Financial support:* Career-related internships or fieldwork and Federal Work-Study available. Support available to part-time students. Financial award application deadline: 6/30; financial award applicants required to submit FAFSA. *Faculty research:* Natural readers, Korean styles and learning strategies, mothers of children with disabilities, computers in instruction, cultural background and organizational roadblocks to problem solving. *Unit head:* Dr. Robert Manley, Dean, 631-244-3447, E-mail: manleyr@dowling.edu. *Application contact:* Mary Boullianne, Director of Admissions, 631-244-3274, Fax: 631-244-1059, E-mail: boulliam@dowling.edu.

Drexel University, College of Computing and Informatics, Master of Science in Library and Information Science Program, Philadelphia, PA 19104-2875. Offers archival studies (MS); competitive intelligence and knowledge management (MS); digital libraries (MS); library and information services (MS); school library media (MS); youth services (MS). Part-time and evening/weekend programs available. Postbaccalaureate distance learning degree programs offered (no on-campus study). *Faculty:* 31 full-time (20 women), 24 part-time/adjunct (15 women). *Students:* 136 full-time (99 women), 282 part-time (234 women); includes 55 minority (26 Black or African American, non-Hispanic/Latino; 4 American Indian or Alaska Native, non-Hispanic/Latino; 12 Asian, non-Hispanic/Latino; 13 Hispanic/Latino), 12 international. Average age 34. 277 applicants, 90% accepted, 116 enrolled. In 2013, 234 master's awarded. *Entrance requirements:* For master's, GRE General Test. Additional exam requirements/recommendations for international students: Required—TOEFL (minimum score 600 paper-based; 100 iBT). *Application deadline:* For fall admission, 8/1 for domestic and international students; for spring admission, 2/1 for domestic and international students. Applications are processed on a rolling basis. Electronic applications accepted. *Expenses:* Contact institution. *Financial support:* In 2013–14, 217 students received support, including 227 fellowships with partial tuition reimbursements available (averaging $22,500 per year); institutionally sponsored loans and scholarships/grants also available. Support available to part-time students. Financial award application deadline: 3/1; financial award applicants required to submit FAFSA. *Faculty research:* Library and information resources and services, knowledge organization and representation, information retrieval/information visualization/bibliometrics, information needs and behaviors, digital libraries. *Unit head:* Dr. David E. Fenske, Dean/Professor of Information Science, 215-895-2475, Fax: 215-895-6378, E-mail: fenske@drexel.edu. *Application contact:* Matthew Lechtenberg, Graduate Admissions Manager, 215-895-1951, Fax: 215-895-2303, E-mail: ml333@drexel.edu.
Website: http://cci.drexel.edu/academics/graduate-programs/ms-in-library-information-science.aspx.

Drexel University, Goodwin College of Professional Studies, School of Education, Philadelphia, PA 19104-2875. Offers educational administration (MS); educational improvement and transformation (MS); educational leadership and management (Ed D); educational leadership development and learning technologies (PhD); global and international education (MS); higher education (MS); human resources development (MS); learning technologies (MS); mathematics, learning and teaching (MS); special education (MS); teaching, learning and curriculum (MS). Part-time and evening/weekend programs available. Postbaccalaureate distance learning degree programs offered (no on-campus study). *Degree requirements:* For doctorate, thesis/dissertation. *Entrance requirements:* For doctorate, GRE or GMAT. Additional exam requirements/recommendations for international students: Required—TOEFL, IELTS. Electronic applications accepted. Application fee is waived when completed online. *Expenses:* Contact institution. *Faculty research:* Leadership development, mathematics education, literacy, autism, educational technology.

Drexel University, Goodwin College of Professional Studies, School of Technology and Professional Studies, Philadelphia, PA 19104-2875. Offers construction management (MS); creativity and innovation (MS); engineering technology (MS); food science (MS); hospitality management (MS); professional studies: creativity studies (MS); professional studies: e-learning leadership (MS); professional studies: homeland security management (MS); project management (MS); property management (MS); sport management (MS). Part-time and evening/weekend programs available. *Entrance requirements:* Additional exam requirements/recommendations for international students: Required—TOEFL, IELTS. Electronic applications accepted. Application fee is waived when completed online.

Drury University, Graduate Programs in Education, Springfield, MO 65802. Offers elementary education (M Ed); gifted education (M Ed); human services (M Ed); instructional mathematics K-8 (M Ed); instructional technology (M Ed); middle school teaching (M Ed); secondary education (M Ed); special education (M Ed); special reading (M Ed). *Accreditation:* NCATE. Part-time and evening/weekend programs available. *Degree requirements:* For master's, thesis. *Entrance requirements:* For master's, GRE or MAT, minimum GPA of 2.75. Additional exam requirements/recommendations for international students: Required—TOEFL. Electronic applications accepted. *Faculty research:* Cultural enrichment, research skills, parental involvement relating to reading skills, reading strategies for mainstreaming children.

Duquesne University, School of Education, Department of Instruction and Leadership, Program in Instructional Technology, Pittsburgh, PA 15282-0001. Offers MS Ed, Ed D, Post-Master's Certificate. Part-time and evening/weekend programs available. Postbaccalaureate distance learning degree programs offered (minimal on-campus study). *Faculty:* 3 full-time (1 woman). *Students:* 61 full-time (38 women), 7 part-time (5 women); includes 5 minority (3 Black or African American, non-Hispanic/Latino; 2 Hispanic/Latino), 6 international. Average age 34. 41 applicants, 41% accepted, 17 enrolled. In 2013, 31 master's, 2 doctorates awarded. *Degree requirements:* For master's, thesis optional; for doctorate, thesis/dissertation. *Entrance requirements:* For master's, bachelor's degree; for doctorate, GRE, master's degree; for Post-Master's Certificate, bachelor's/master's degree. Additional exam requirements/recommendations for international students: Required—TOEFL (minimum score 550 paper-based), IELTS (minimum score 7). *Application deadline:* For fall admission, 9/1 for domestic students; for spring admission, 1/1 for domestic students. Applications are processed on a rolling basis. Application fee: $0. Electronic applications accepted. Application fee is waived when completed online. *Expenses: Tuition:* Full-time $18,162; part-time $1009 per credit. *Required fees:* $1728; $96 per credit. Tuition and fees vary according to program. *Financial support:* Available to part-time students. *Unit head:* Dr. David Carbonara, Assistant Professor and Director, 412-396-4039, Fax: 412-396-1997, E-mail: carbonara@duq.edu. *Application contact:* Michael Dolinger, Director of Student and Academic Services, 412-396-6647, Fax: 412-396-5585, E-mail: dolingerm@duq.edu.
Website: http://www.duq.edu/academics/schools/education/graduate-programs/instructional-technology.

East Carolina University, Graduate School, College of Education, Department of Curriculum and Instruction, Greenville, NC 27858-4353. Offers assistive technology (Certificate); autism (Certificate); deaf/blindness (Certificate); elementary education (MA Ed); English education (MA Ed); history (MA Ed); middle grade education (MA Ed); reading education (MA Ed); special education (MA Ed); teaching (MAT). Part-time programs available. Postbaccalaureate distance learning degree programs offered. *Degree requirements:* For master's, comprehensive exam, thesis optional. *Entrance requirements:* For master's, GRE General Test or MAT, interview, bachelor's degree in related field, minimum GPA of 2.5, teaching license. Additional exam requirements/

recommendations for international students: Required—TOEFL. *Expenses:* Tuition, state resident: full-time $4223. Tuition, nonresident: full-time $16,540. *Required fees:* $2184.

East Carolina University, Graduate School, College of Education, Department of Mathematics, Science, and Instructional Technology Education, Greenville, NC 27858-4353. Offers computer-based instruction (Certificate); distance learning and administration (Certificate); instructional technology (MA Ed, MS); mathematics (MA Ed); performance improvement (Certificate); science education (MA, MA Ed); special endorsement in computer education (Certificate). Part-time and evening/weekend programs available. *Degree requirements:* For master's, comprehensive exam, thesis optional. *Entrance requirements:* For master's, GRE General Test or MAT, interview, minimum GPA of 2.5, bachelor's degree in related field, teaching license (MA Ed). Additional exam requirements/recommendations for international students: Required—TOEFL. *Expenses:* Tuition, state resident: full-time $4223. Tuition, nonresident: full-time $16,540. *Required fees:* $2184.

Eastern Connecticut State University, School of Education and Professional Studies/Graduate Division, Program in Educational Technology, Willimantic, CT 06226-2295. Offers MS. Part-time and evening/weekend programs available. *Degree requirements:* For master's, comprehensive exam or thesis. *Entrance requirements:* For master's, minimum GPA of 2.7. Additional exam requirements/recommendations for international students: Required—TOEFL (minimum score 550 paper-based). Electronic applications accepted.

Eastern Michigan University, Graduate School, College of Education, Department of Teacher Education, Program in Educational Media and Technology, Ypsilanti, MI 48197. Offers MA, Graduate Certificate. Part-time and evening/weekend programs available. Postbaccalaureate distance learning degree programs offered (minimal on-campus study). *Students:* 1 full-time (0 women), 54 part-time (34 women); includes 6 minority (3 Black or African American, non-Hispanic/Latino; 2 Asian, non-Hispanic/Latino; 1 Two or more races, non-Hispanic/Latino), 1 international. Average age 35. 19 applicants, 84% accepted, 9 enrolled. In 2013, 27 master's awarded. *Entrance requirements:* Additional exam requirements/recommendations for international students: Required—TOEFL. *Application deadline:* Applications are processed on a rolling basis. Application fee: $35. *Expenses:* Tuition, state resident: full-time $12,300; part-time $466 per credit hour. Tuition, nonresident: full-time $23,159; part-time $918 per credit hour. *Required fees:* $71 per credit hour. $46 per semester. One-time fee: $100. Tuition and fees vary according to course level and degree level. *Financial support:* Fellowships, research assistantships with full tuition reimbursements, teaching assistantships with full tuition reimbursements, career-related internships or fieldwork, Federal Work-Study, institutionally sponsored loans, scholarships/grants, tuition waivers (partial), and unspecified assistantships available. Support available to part-time students. Financial award applicants required to submit FAFSA. *Unit head:* Dr. Martha Kinney-Sedgwick, Interim Department Head, 734-487-3260, Fax: 734-487-2101, E-mail: mkinneys@emich.edu. *Application contact:* Dr. Toni Stokes Jones, Coordinator, 734-487-3260, Fax: 734-487-2101, E-mail: tjones1@emich.edu.

Eastern New Mexico University, Graduate School, College of Education and Technology, Department of Curriculum and Instruction, Portales, NM 88130. Offers bilingual education (M Ed); educational technology (M Ed); elementary education (M Ed); English as a second language (M Ed); pedagogy and learning (M Ed); professional technical education (M Ed); reading/literacy (M Ed). Part-time programs available. Postbaccalaureate distance learning degree programs offered (minimal on-campus study). *Degree requirements:* For master's, comprehensive exam, thesis optional. *Entrance requirements:* For master's, minimum GPA of 3.0, photocopy of teaching license, writing assessment, letter of recommendation. Additional exam requirements/recommendations for international students: Required—TOEFL (minimum score 550 paper-based; 79 iBT), IELTS (minimum score 6). Electronic applications accepted.

East Stroudsburg University of Pennsylvania, Graduate College, College of Education, Department of Media Communications and Technology, East Stroudsburg, PA 18301-2999. Offers instructional technology (M Ed). Part-time and evening/weekend programs available. Postbaccalaureate distance learning degree programs offered. *Faculty:* 4 full-time (3 women), 2 part-time/adjunct (1 woman). *Students:* 10 full-time (6 women), 13 part-time (9 women); includes 9 minority (5 Black or African American, non-Hispanic/Latino; 2 Hispanic/Latino; 1 Native Hawaiian or other Pacific Islander, non-Hispanic/Latino; 1 Two or more races, non-Hispanic/Latino), 4 international. Average age 29. 8 applicants, 75% accepted, 5 enrolled. In 2013, 11 master's awarded. *Degree requirements:* For master's, comprehensive exam, comprehensive portfolio, internship. *Entrance requirements:* For master's, two letters of recommendation, portfolio or interview, minimum overall undergraduate QPA of 2.5, internship. Additional exam requirements/recommendations for international students: Required—TOEFL (minimum score 560 paper-based; 83 iBT) or IELTS. *Application deadline:* For fall admission, 7/31 priority date for domestic students, 6/30 priority date for international students; for spring admission, 11/30 for domestic students, 10/31 for international students. Applications are processed on a rolling basis. Application fee: $50. Electronic applications accepted. *Expenses:* Tuition, state resident: full-time $7956; part-time $442 per credit. Tuition, nonresident: full-time $11,934; part-time $663 per credit. *Required fees:* $2129; $118 per credit. *Financial support:* Research assistantships with full and partial tuition reimbursements, career-related internships or fieldwork, Federal Work-Study, and institutionally sponsored loans available. Financial award application deadline: 3/1; financial award applicants required to submit FAFSA. *Unit head:* Dr. Beth Sockman, Graduate Coordinator, 570-422-3621, Fax: 570-422-3506, E-mail: bsockman@po-box.esu.edu. *Application contact:* Kevin Quintero, Graduate Admissions Coordinator, 570-422-3536, Fax: 570-422-2711, E-mail: kquintero@esu.edu.

East Tennessee State University, School of Graduate Studies, College of Education, Department of Curriculum and Instruction, Johnson City, TN 37614. Offers educational media and educational technology (M Ed), including educational communications and technology, school library media; elementary education (M Ed); reading (MA), including reading education, storytelling; school library professional (Post-Master's Certificate); secondary education (M Ed), including classroom technology, secondary education (M Ed, MAT); storytelling (Postbaccalaureate Certificate); teacher education with multiple levels (MAT), including elementary education, middle grades education, secondary education (M Ed, MAT). *Accreditation:* NCATE. Part-time and evening/weekend programs available. Postbaccalaureate distance learning degree programs offered (no on-campus study). *Faculty:* 25 full-time (18 women), 12 part-time/adjunct (8 women). *Students:* 66 full-time (50 women), 97 part-time (85 women); includes 5 minority (3 Black or African American, non-Hispanic/Latino; 2 Two or more races, non-Hispanic/Latino), 2 international. Average age 31. 144 applicants, 57% accepted, 70 enrolled. In 2013, 83 master's, 5 other advanced degrees awarded. *Degree requirements:* For master's, comprehensive exam, thesis optional, student teaching, practicum; for other advanced degree, field work (school library); culminating experience (storytelling). *Entrance requirements:* For master's, GRE, SAT, ACT, PRAXIS, minimum GPA of 3.0; for other advanced degree, master's degree, TN teaching license (for school library professional Post-Master's Certificate); three letters of recommendation (for storytelling Postbaccalaureate Certificate). Additional exam requirements/recommendations for international students: Required—TOEFL (minimum score 550 paper-based; 79 iBT). *Application deadline:* For fall admission, 6/1 for domestic students, 4/30 for international students; for spring admission, 11/1 for domestic students, 4/30 for international students. Application fee: $35 ($45 for international students). Electronic applications accepted. *Expenses:* Tuition, state resident: full-time $7900; part-time $395 per credit hour. Tuition, nonresident: full-time $21,960; part-time $1098 per credit hour. *Required fees:* $1345; $84 per credit hour. *Financial support:* In 2013–14, 43 students received support, including 6 research assistantships with full tuition reimbursements available (averaging $6,000 per year), 10 teaching assistantships with full tuition reimbursements available (averaging $6,000 per year); career-related internships or fieldwork, institutionally sponsored loans, scholarships/grants, and unspecified assistantships also available. Financial award application deadline: 7/1; financial award applicants required to submit FAFSA. *Faculty research:* Critical thinking; curriculum development in reading, math, and science education; cultural diversity; cognitive processes; effective teaching strategies. *Unit head:* Dr. Rhona Hurwitz, Chair, 423-439-7598, Fax: 423-439-8362, E-mail: hurwitz@etsu.edu. *Application contact:* Fiona Goodyear, Graduate Specialist, 423-439-6148, Fax: 423-439-5624, E-mail: goodyear@etsu.edu.
Website: http://www.etsu.edu/coe/cuai/.

Emporia State University, Department of Instructional Design and Technology, Emporia, KS 66801-5415. Offers MS. *Accreditation:* NCATE. Part-time programs available. Postbaccalaureate distance learning degree programs offered (minimal on-campus study). *Faculty:* 9 full-time (5 women). *Students:* 20 full-time (12 women), 84 part-time (62 women); includes 12 minority (6 Black or African American, non-Hispanic/Latino; 2 Asian, non-Hispanic/Latino; 3 Hispanic/Latino; 1 Two or more races, non-Hispanic/Latino), 22 international. 38 applicants, 95% accepted, 22 enrolled. In 2013, 45 master's awarded. *Degree requirements:* For master's, comprehensive exam (for some programs), thesis (for some programs), project. *Entrance requirements:* For master's, appropriate bachelor's degree, letters of recommendation. Additional exam requirements/recommendations for international students: Required—TOEFL (minimum score 520 paper-based; 68 iBT). *Application deadline:* For fall admission, 8/15 priority date for domestic students. Applications are processed on a rolling basis. Application fee: $30 ($75 for international students). Electronic applications accepted. *Expenses: Tuition, area resident:* Part-time $220 per credit hour. Tuition, state resident: part-time $220 per credit hour. Tuition, nonresident: part-time $685 per credit hour. *Required fees:* $73 per credit hour. *Financial support:* In 2013–14, 2 research assistantships (averaging $7,200 per year), 6 teaching assistantships with full tuition reimbursements (averaging $7,200 per year) were awarded; Federal Work-Study, institutionally sponsored loans, health care benefits, and unspecified assistantships also available. Financial award application deadline: 3/15; financial award applicants required to submit FAFSA. *Unit head:* Dr. Marcus Childress, Chair, 620-341-5627, E-mail: mchildre@emporia.edu. *Application contact:* Mary Sewell, Admissions Coordinator, 800-950-GRAD, Fax: 620-341-5909, E-mail: msewell@emporia.edu.
Website: http://www.emporia.edu/idt/.

Fairfield University, Graduate School of Education and Allied Professions, Fairfield, CT 06824-5195. Offers applied behavior analysis (ATC); applied psychology (MA); clinical mental health counseling (MA, CAS); early childhood studies (ATC); educational technology (MA); elementary education (MA, CAS); family studies (MA); integration of spirituality and religion in counseling (ATC); marriage and family therapy (MA); school counseling (MA, CAS); school psychology (MA, CAS); school-based marriage and family therapy (ATC); secondary education (MA); special education (MA, CAS); substance abuse counseling (ATC); teaching (Certificate); teaching and foundations (MA, CAS); TESOL, world languages, and bilingual education (MA, CAS). *Accreditation:* NCATE. Part-time and evening/weekend programs available. *Faculty:* 24 full-time (21 women), 39 part-time/adjunct (27 women). *Students:* 154 full-time (130 women), 307 part-time (248 women); includes 75 minority (14 Black or African American, non-Hispanic/Latino; 1 American Indian or Alaska Native, non-Hispanic/Latino; 10 Asian, non-Hispanic/Latino; 44 Hispanic/Latino; 6 Two or more races, non-Hispanic/Latino), 13 international. Average age 34. 263 applicants, 41% accepted, 91 enrolled. In 2013, 149 master's, 21 other advanced degrees awarded. *Degree requirements:* For master's, comprehensive exam. *Entrance requirements:* For master's, PRAXIS I (for certification programs), minimum GPA of 3.0, 2 recommendations, resume. Additional exam requirements/recommendations for international students: Required—TOEFL (minimum score 550 paper-based; 84 iBT) or IELTS (minimum score 7.5). *Application deadline:* For fall admission, 2/15 for international students; for spring admission, 10/1 for international students. Application fee: $60. Electronic applications accepted. *Expenses: Tuition:* Part-time $675 per credit hour. Tuition and fees vary according to program. *Financial support:* In 2013–14, 55 students received support. Career-related internships or fieldwork and unspecified assistantships available. Financial award applicants required to submit FAFSA. *Faculty research:* Literacy, adolescent psychology, special education, teaching development, mentoring for professional development, multicultural education. *Total annual research expenditures:* $325,000. *Unit head:* Dr. Robert D. Hannafin, Dean, 203-254-4250, Fax: 203-254-4241, E-mail: rhannafin@fairfield.edu. *Application contact:* Marianne Gumpper, Director of Graduate and Continuing Studies Admission, 203-254-4184, Fax: 203-254-4073, E-mail: gradadmis@fairfield.edu.
Website: http://www.fairfield.edu/academics/schoolscollegescenters/graduateschoolofeducationalliedprofessions/graduateprograms/.

Fairleigh Dickinson University, College at Florham, University College: Arts, Sciences, and Professional Studies, Peter Sammartino School of Education, Madison, NJ 07940-1099. Offers education for certified teachers (MA, Certificate); educational leadership (MA); instructional technology (Certificate); literacy/reading (Certificate); teaching (MAT).

Fairleigh Dickinson University, Metropolitan Campus, University College: Arts, Sciences, and Professional Studies, Peter Sammartino School of Education, Teaneck, NJ 07666-1914. Offers dyslexia specialist (Certificate); education for certified teachers (MA); educational leadership (MA); instructional technology (Certificate); learning disabilities (MA); literacy/reading (Certificate); multilingual education (MA); teacher of the handicapped (Certificate); teaching (MAT). *Accreditation:* Teacher Education Accreditation Council. Part-time programs available. *Degree requirements:* For master's, research project (MAT).

Fairmont State University, Programs in Education, Fairmont, WV 26554. Offers digital media, new literacies and learning (M Ed); education (MAT); exercise science, fitness and wellness (M Ed); online learning (M Ed); professional studies (M Ed); reading (M Ed); special education (M Ed). *Accreditation:* NCATE. Part-time and evening/weekend programs available. Postbaccalaureate distance learning degree programs offered. *Faculty:* 18 part-time/adjunct (11 women). *Students:* 75 full-time (55 women), 120 part-time (96 women); includes 11 minority (5 Black or African American, non-Hispanic/Latino; 2 American Indian or Alaska Native, non-Hispanic/Latino; 1 Asian, non-Hispanic/Latino; 1 Hispanic/Latino; 2 Two or more races, non-Hispanic/Latino), 1 international. Average age 32. 69 applicants, 86% accepted, 45 enrolled. In 2013, 82 master's awarded. *Entrance requirements:* For master's, GRE. Additional exam requirements/recommendations for international students: Required—TOEFL. *Application deadline:* For fall admission, 5/1 for domestic and international students.

Applications are processed on a rolling basis. Application fee: $40. *Expenses:* Tuition, state resident: full-time $6404; part-time $349 per credit hour. Tuition, nonresident: full-time $13,694; part-time $754 per credit hour. Part-time tuition and fees vary according to course load. *Financial support:* In 2013–14, 30 students received support. *Unit head:* Dr. Carolyn Crislip-Tacy, Interim Dean, School of Education, 304-367-4143, Fax: 304-367-4599, E-mail: carolyn.crislip-tacy@fairmontstate.edu. *Application contact:* Jack Kirby, Director of Graduate Studies, 304-367-4101, E-mail: jack.kirby@fairmontstate.edu.
Website: http://www.fairmontstate.edu/graduatestudies/default.asp.

Fitchburg State University, Division of Graduate and Continuing Education, Program in Applied Communications, Fitchburg, MA 01420-2697. Offers applied communications (MS, Certificate); health communication (MS); library media (MS); technical and professional writing (MS). Part-time and evening/weekend programs available. *Entrance requirements:* Additional exam requirements/recommendations for international students: Required—TOEFL (minimum score 550 paper-based; 79 iBT). Electronic applications accepted.

Florida Atlantic University, College of Education, Department of Teaching and Learning, Boca Raton, FL 33431-0991. Offers curriculum and instruction (M Ed), including art, biology, chemistry, English, French, German, mathematics, music, physics, Pre-K and primary education, reading, social sciences, Spanish; elementary education (M Ed); environmental education (M Ed); reading education (M Ed); social foundations of education (M Ed), including educational psychology, educational technology, multilingual education. *Accreditation:* NCATE. Part-time and evening/weekend programs available. *Faculty:* 16 full-time (12 women), 1 (woman) part-time/adjunct. *Students:* 56 full-time (46 women), 96 part-time (78 women); includes 39 minority (10 Black or African American, non-Hispanic/Latino; 6 Asian, non-Hispanic/Latino; 20 Hispanic/Latino; 3 Two or more races, non-Hispanic/Latino), 4 international. Average age 32. 101 applicants, 54% accepted, 42 enrolled. In 2013, 64 master's awarded. *Entrance requirements:* For master's, GRE General Test, minimum GPA of 3.0 in last 2 years of undergraduate course work. Additional exam requirements/recommendations for international students: Required—TOEFL (minimum score 500 paper-based; 61 iBT), IELTS (minimum score 6). *Application deadline:* For fall admission, 7/1 for domestic students, 2/15 for international students; for spring admission, 11/1 for domestic students, 7/15 for international students. Applications are processed on a rolling basis. Application fee: $30. *Expenses:* Tuition, state resident: full-time $6660; part-time $370 per credit hour. Tuition, nonresident: full-time $18,450; part-time $1025 per credit hour. Tuition and fees vary according to course load. *Financial support:* Fellowships with partial tuition reimbursements, research assistantships with partial tuition reimbursements, teaching assistantships with partial tuition reimbursements, career-related internships or fieldwork, scholarships/grants, and unspecified assistantships available. *Faculty research:* Technology, teaching English to speakers of other languages, math teaching, electronic portfolio assessment, global perspectives through social studies. *Unit head:* Dr. Barbara Ridener, Chairperson, 561-297-3588. *Application contact:* Dr. Eliah Watlington, Associate Dean, 561-296-8520, Fax: 261-297-2991, E-mail: ewatling@fau.edu.
Website: http://www.coe.fau.edu/academicdepartments/tl/.

Florida Gulf Coast University, College of Education, Program in Curriculum and Instruction, Fort Myers, FL 33965-6565. Offers curriculum and instruction (Ed D, Ed S); educational technology (M Ed, MA); English education (M Ed). Part-time and evening/weekend programs available. Postbaccalaureate distance learning degree programs offered (minimal on-campus study). *Degree requirements:* For master's, final project or portfolio. *Entrance requirements:* For master's, GRE General Test, MAT, minimum undergraduate GPA of 3.0 in last 2 years. Additional exam requirements/recommendations for international students: Required—TOEFL (minimum score 550 paper-based). Electronic applications accepted. *Faculty research:* Internet in schools, technology in pre-service and in-service teacher training.

Florida International University, College of Education, Department of Leadership and Professional Studies, Miami, FL 33199. Offers adult education and human resource development (MS, Ed D); counseling (MS), including rehabilitation counseling, school counseling; counselor education (MS), including clinical mental health counseling; educational administration and supervision (Ed D); educational leadership (MS, Certificate, Ed S); higher education (Ed D); higher education administration (MS); recreation and sport management (MS), including recreation and sport management, recreational therapy; school psychology (Ed S); urban education (MS), including instruction in urban settings, learning technologies, multicultural/bilingual, multicultural/TESOL, urban education. Part-time and evening/weekend programs available. *Degree requirements:* For doctorate, thesis/dissertation. *Entrance requirements:* For master's, minimum GPA of 3.0; for doctorate and other advanced degree, GRE General Test. Additional exam requirements/recommendations for international students: Required—TOEFL (minimum score 550 paper-based; 80 iBT), IELTS (minimum score 6.3). Electronic applications accepted.

Florida International University, College of Education, Department of Teaching and Learning, Miami, FL 33199. Offers art education (MA, MS); curriculum and instruction (MS, Ed D, PhD, Ed S), including curriculum development (MS), elementary education (MS), English education (MS), learning technologies (MS), mathematics education (MS), modern language education (MS), physical education (MS), science education (MS), social studies education (MS), special education (MS); early childhood education (MS); exceptional student education (Ed D); foreign language education (MS), including foreign language education, teaching English to speakers of other languages (TESOL); international/intercultural education (MS); language, literacy and culture (PhD); mathematics, science, and learning technologies (PhD); physical education (MS), including sport and fitness; reading education (MS). Part-time and evening/weekend programs available. *Degree requirements:* For doctorate, comprehensive exam, thesis/dissertation. *Entrance requirements:* For master's, GRE General Test, Florida General Knowledge Test or Florida College Level Academic Skills Test; for doctorate and Ed S, GRE General Test. Additional exam requirements/recommendations for international students: Required—TOEFL (minimum score 550 paper-based; 80 iBT), IELTS (minimum score 6.3). Electronic applications accepted.

Florida State University, The Graduate School, College of Education, Department of Educational Psychology and Learning Systems, Program in Instructional Systems, Tallahassee, FL 32306. Offers MS, PhD. *Faculty:* 6 full-time (4 women). *Students:* 65 full-time (39 women), 58 part-time (36 women); includes 24 minority (11 Black or African American, non-Hispanic/Latino; 5 Asian, non-Hispanic/Latino; 7 Hispanic/Latino; 1 Two or more races, non-Hispanic/Latino), 42 international. Average age 37. 60 applicants, 65% accepted, 25 enrolled. In 2013, 41 master's, 6 doctorates awarded. *Degree requirements:* For master's, comprehensive exam, thesis optional; for doctorate, comprehensive exam, thesis/dissertation. *Entrance requirements:* For master's and doctorate, GRE General Test, minimum GPA of 3.0. Additional exam requirements/recommendations for international students: Required—TOEFL (minimum score 550 paper-based; 80 iBT). *Application deadline:* For fall admission, 7/1 for domestic and international students; for winter admission, 11/1 for domestic and international students; for spring admission, 3/1 for domestic and international students. Applications are processed on a rolling basis. Application fee: $30. Electronic applications accepted.

Expenses: Tuition, state resident: part-time $403.51 per credit hour. Tuition, nonresident: part-time $1004.85 per credit hour. *Required fees:* $75.81 per credit hour. One-time fee: $20 part-time. Tuition and fees vary according to course load, campus/location and student level. *Financial support:* In 2013–14, 2 students received support. Fellowships with full and partial tuition reimbursements available, research assistantships with full and partial tuition reimbursements available, teaching assistantships with full and partial tuition reimbursements available, career-related internships or fieldwork, scholarships/grants, health care benefits, and unspecified assistantships available. Financial award applicants required to submit FAFSA. *Faculty research:* Human performance improvement, educational semiotics, development of software tools to measure online interaction among learners. *Unit head:* Dr. Vanessa Dennen, Program Leader, 850-644-8783, Fax: 850-644-8776, E-mail: vdennen@fsu.edu. *Application contact:* Mary Kate McKee, Program Coordinator, 850-644-8792, Fax: 850-644-8776, E-mail: mmckee@campus.fsu.edu.
Website: http://coe.fsu.edu/Academic-Programs/Departments/Educational-Psychology-and-Learning-Systems-EPLS/Degree-Programs/Instructional-Systems.

Fort Hays State University, Graduate School, College of Education and Technology, Department of Technology Studies, Hays, KS 67601-4099. Offers instructional technology (MS). *Degree requirements:* For master's, comprehensive exam, thesis or alternative. *Entrance requirements:* Additional exam requirements/recommendations for international students: Required—TOEFL (minimum score 550 paper-based). Electronic applications accepted.

Framingham State University, Continuing Education, Program in Curriculum and Instructional Technology, Framingham, MA 01701-9101. Offers M Ed. Postbaccalaureate distance learning degree programs offered.

Franklin University, Instructional Design and Performance Technology Program, Columbus, OH 43215-5399. Offers MS.

Fresno Pacific University, Graduate Programs, School of Education, Division of Foundations, Curriculum and Teaching, Program in School Library and Information Technology, Fresno, CA 93702-4709. Offers MA Ed. Part-time and evening/weekend programs available. *Students:* 1 (woman) full-time, 15 part-time (13 women); includes 1 minority (Black or African American, non-Hispanic/Latino). Average age 40. *Degree requirements:* For master's, thesis or alternative. *Entrance requirements:* Additional exam requirements/recommendations for international students: Required—TOEFL (minimum score 550 paper-based). *Application deadline:* For fall admission, 7/15 for domestic and international students; for spring admission, 11/15 for domestic and international students. Applications are processed on a rolling basis. Application fee: $90. Electronic applications accepted. *Expenses:* Tuition: Full-time $8910; part-time $495 per unit. *Required fees:* $270. Tuition and fees vary according to course load and program. *Financial support:* Scholarships/grants and tuition waivers (full and partial) available. Support available to part-time students. Financial award applicants required to submit FAFSA. *Unit head:* Jo Ellen Priest Misakian, Program Director, 559-453-2291, Fax: 559-453-7168, E-mail: jmisakian@fresno.edu. *Application contact:* Amanda Krum-Stovall, Director of Graduate Admissions, 559-453-2016, E-mail: amanda.krum-stovall@fresno.edu.
Website: http://grad.fresno.edu/programs/master-arts-education-school-library-and-information-technology-emphasis.

Fresno Pacific University, Graduate Programs, School of Education, Division of Mathematics/Science/Computer Education, Program in Educational Technology, Fresno, CA 93702-4709. Offers MA. Part-time and evening/weekend programs available. *Faculty:* 1 (woman) full-time. *Students:* 8 part-time (4 women); includes 2 minority (both Hispanic/Latino). Average age 44. In 2013, 4 master's awarded. *Degree requirements:* For master's, thesis or alternative. *Entrance requirements:* Additional exam requirements/recommendations for international students: Required—TOEFL (minimum score 550 paper-based). *Application deadline:* For fall admission, 7/15 for domestic and international students; for spring admission, 11/15 for domestic and international students. Applications are processed on a rolling basis. Application fee: $90. *Expenses:* Tuition: Full-time $8910; part-time $495 per unit. *Required fees:* $270. Tuition and fees vary according to course load and program. *Financial support:* Scholarships/grants and tuition waivers (full and partial) available. Support available to part-time students. Financial award applicants required to submit FAFSA. *Unit head:* Henrietta Siemens, Program Director, 559-453-7100, E-mail: hsiemens@fresno.edu. *Application contact:* Amanda Krum-Stovall, Director of Graduate Admissions, 559-453-2016, E-mail: amanda.krum-stovall@fresno.edu.
Website: http://grad.fresno.edu/programs/master-arts-educational-technology.

Frostburg State University, Graduate School, College of Education, Department of Educational Professions, Program in Curriculum and Instruction, Frostburg, MD 21532-1099. Offers educational technology (M Ed); elementary education (M Ed); secondary education (M Ed). Part-time and evening/weekend programs available. *Degree requirements:* For master's, thesis or alternative. *Entrance requirements:* For master's, teaching certificate. Additional exam requirements/recommendations for international students: Required—TOEFL. Electronic applications accepted. *Expenses: Tuition, area resident:* Part-time $340 per credit hour. Tuition, state resident: part-time $340 per credit hour. Tuition, nonresident: part-time $437 per credit hour.

Full Sail University, Education Media Design and Technology Master of Science Program - Online, Winter Park, FL 32792-7437. Offers MS. Postbaccalaureate distance learning degree programs offered (no on-campus study). *Entrance requirements:* Additional exam requirements/recommendations for international students: Required—TOEFL (minimum score 550 paper-based; 79 iBT).

George Fox University, College of Education, Educational Foundations and Leadership Program, Newberg, OR 97132-2697. Offers continuing administrator license (Certificate); curriculum and instruction (M Ed); educational leadership (M Ed, Ed D); ESOL (Certificate); higher education (M Ed); initial administrator license (Certificate); instructional leadership (Ed S); library media (M Ed, Certificate); literacy (M Ed); reading (M Ed); secondary education (M Ed). *Accreditation:* NCATE. Part-time and evening/weekend programs available. Postbaccalaureate distance learning degree programs offered (minimal on-campus study). *Faculty:* 7 full-time (3 women), 5 part-time/adjunct (4 women). *Students:* 194 part-time (128 women); includes 15 minority (1 Black or African American, non-Hispanic/Latino; 1 American Indian or Alaska Native, non-Hispanic/Latino; 3 Asian, non-Hispanic/Latino; 6 Hispanic/Latino; 1 Native Hawaiian or other Pacific Islander, non-Hispanic/Latino; 3 Two or more races, non-Hispanic/Latino), 2 international. Average age 42. 46 applicants, 85% accepted, 39 enrolled. In 2013, 15 master's, 16 doctorates, 106 Certificates awarded. *Degree requirements:* For master's, thesis (for some programs); for doctorate, comprehensive exam, thesis/dissertation, project. *Entrance requirements:* For master's, minimum undergraduate GPA of 3.0 during previous 2 years of course work, resume, 3 professional recommendations on university forms, official transcripts; for doctorate, GRE, master's degree with minimum GPA of 3.25, 3 years of relevant professional experience, interview, personal essay, scholarly work, 3 professional recommendations on university forms along with 3 written letters of recommendation, official transcripts. Additional exam requirements/recommendations for international students: Required—TOEFL (minimum score 577 paper-based; 90 iBT). *Application deadline:* For fall admission, 7/15 for domestic and

international students; for winter admission, 11/1 for domestic and international students; for spring admission, 4/1 for domestic and international students. Applications are processed on a rolling basis. Application fee: $40. Electronic applications accepted. *Expenses:* Contact institution. *Financial support:* Career-related internships or fieldwork available. Financial award applicants required to submit FAFSA. *Unit head:* Dr. Scot Headley, Professor/Chair, 503-554-2836, E-mail: sheadley@georgefox.edu. *Application contact:* Kipp Wilfong, Graduate Admissions Counselor, 800-631-0921, Fax: 503-554-3110, E-mail: kwilfong@georgefox.edu.
Website: http://www.georgefox.edu/education/index.html.

The George Washington University, Graduate School of Education and Human Development, Department of Educational Leadership, Program in Educational Technology Leadership, Washington, DC 20052. Offers MA Ed. *Accreditation:* NCATE. Part-time and evening/weekend programs available. *Students:* 1 (woman) full-time, 45 part-time (32 women); includes 14 minority (9 Black or African American, non-Hispanic/Latino; 1 Asian, non-Hispanic/Latino; 3 Hispanic/Latino; 1 Two or more races, non-Hispanic/Latino), 1 international. Average age 39. 26 applicants, 96% accepted, 17 enrolled. In 2013, 17 master's awarded. *Degree requirements:* For master's, comprehensive exam, thesis or alternative. *Entrance requirements:* For master's, GRE General Test or MAT, minimum GPA of 2.75. *Application deadline:* For fall admission, 1/15 priority date for domestic students; for spring admission, 10/1 for domestic students. Applications are processed on a rolling basis. Application fee: $75. *Expenses:* Contact institution. *Financial support:* Fellowships, research assistantships, teaching assistantships, and career-related internships or fieldwork available. Financial award application deadline: 1/15. *Faculty research:* Interactive multimedia, distance education, federal technology policy. *Unit head:* Dr. Michael Corry, Director, 202-994-9295, E-mail: mcorry@gwu.edu. *Application contact:* Sarah Lang, Director of Graduate Admissions, 202-994-1447, Fax: 202-994-7207, E-mail: slang@gwu.edu.

The George Washington University, Graduate School of Education and Human Development, Department of Educational Leadership, Program in Instructional Design, Washington, DC 20052. Offers Graduate Certificate. *Students:* 25 part-time (18 women); includes 5 minority (3 Black or African American, non-Hispanic/Latino; 2 Hispanic/Latino). Average age 45. 14 applicants, 100% accepted, 10 enrolled. In 2013, 7 Graduate Certificates awarded. *Unit head:* Virginia Roach, Chair, 202-994-3094, E-mail: vroach@gwu.edu. *Application contact:* Sarah Lang, Director of Graduate Admissions, 202-994-1447, Fax: 202-994-7207, E-mail: slang@gwu.edu.
Website: http://gsehd.gwu.edu/instructional-design-certificate.

The George Washington University, Graduate School of Education and Human Development, Department of Educational Leadership, Program in Integrating Technology into Education, Washington, DC 20052. Offers Graduate Certificate. *Students:* 1 (woman) part-time; minority (Hispanic/Latino). Average age 49. 2 applicants, 100% accepted. In 2013, 1 Graduate Certificate awarded. *Unit head:* Virginia Roach, Chair, 202-994-3094, E-mail: vroach@gwu.edu. *Application contact:* Sarah Lang, Director of Graduate Admissions, 202-994-1447, Fax: 202-994-7207, E-mail: slang@gwu.edu.
Website: http://gsehd.gwu.edu/integrating-technology-education-certificate.

The George Washington University, Graduate School of Education and Human Development, Department of Educational Leadership, Program in Leadership in Educational Technology, Washington, DC 20052. Offers Graduate Certificate. *Students:* 4 part-time (2 women); includes 1 minority (Black or African American, non-Hispanic/Latino). Average age 32. 2 applicants, 100% accepted, 2 enrolled. In 2013, 3 Graduate Certificates awarded. *Unit head:* Virginia Roach, Chair, 202-994-3094, E-mail: vroach@gwu.edu. *Application contact:* Sarah Lang, Director of Graduate Admissions, 202-994-1447, Fax: 202-994-7207, E-mail: slang@gwu.edu.
Website: http://gsehd.gwu.edu/programs/etl/certificate/let.

The George Washington University, Graduate School of Education and Human Development, Department of Educational Leadership, Program in Multimedia Development, Washington, DC 20052. Offers Graduate Certificate. *Students:* 2 part-time (1 woman); includes 1 minority (Black or African American, non-Hispanic/Latino). Average age 46. 2 applicants, 100% accepted, 1 enrolled. In 2013, 3 Graduate Certificates awarded. *Unit head:* Virginia Roach, Chair, 202-994-3094, E-mail: vroach@gwu.edu. *Application contact:* Sarah Lang, Director of Graduate Admissions, 202-994-1447, Fax: 202-994-7207, E-mail: slang@gwu.edu.
Website: http://gsehd.gwu.edu/multimedia-development-certificate.

The George Washington University, Graduate School of Education and Human Development, Department of Educational Leadership, Program in Training and Educational Technology, Washington, DC 20052. Offers Graduate Certificate. *Students:* 4 part-time (3 women); includes 1 minority (Black or African American, non-Hispanic/Latino). Average age 38. 8 applicants, 100% accepted, 2 enrolled. In 2013, 2 Graduate Certificates awarded. *Unit head:* Virginia Roach, Chair, 202-994-3094, E-mail: vroach@gwu.edu. *Application contact:* Sarah Lang, Director of Graduate Admissions, 202-994-1447, Fax: 202-994-7207, E-mail: slang@gwu.edu.
Website: http://gsehd.gwu.edu/training-and-educational-technology-certificate.

Georgia College & State University, Graduate School, The John H. Lounsbury College of Education, Program in Education/Instructional Technology, Milledgeville, GA 31061. Offers M Ed. Part-time and evening/weekend programs available. *Students:* 3 full-time (2 women), 21 part-time (11 women); includes 14 minority (13 Black or African American, non-Hispanic/Latino; 1 Hispanic/Latino). Average age 33. In 2013, 11 master's awarded. *Degree requirements:* For master's, comprehensive exam, minimum GPA of 3.0. *Entrance requirements:* For master's, on-site writing assessment, level 4 teaching certificate, 2 professional recommendations, transcripts, minimum GPA of 2.5, proof of immunization. Additional exam requirements/recommendations for international students: Required—TOEFL (minimum score 550 paper-based; 79 iBT). *Application deadline:* For fall admission, 7/1 priority date for domestic students, 4/1 priority date for international students; for spring admission, 11/15 priority date for domestic students, 9/1 priority date for international students. Applications are processed on a rolling basis. Application fee: $40. Electronic applications accepted. *Financial support:* Career-related internships or fieldwork and unspecified assistantships available. Support available to part-time students. *Application contact:* Shanda Brand, Graduate Admission Advisor, 478-445-1383, E-mail: shanda.brand@gcsu.edu.

Georgia College & State University, Graduate School, The John H. Lounsbury College of Education, Program in Library Media, Milledgeville, GA 31061. Offers M Ed. Part-time programs available. *Students:* 1 (woman) full-time, 10 part-time (all women); includes 4 minority (2 Black or African American, non-Hispanic/Latino; 1 American Indian or Alaska Native, non-Hispanic/Latino; 1 Hispanic/Latino). Average age 32. In 2013, 14 master's awarded. *Degree requirements:* For master's, comprehensive exam, minimum GPA of 3.0, complete program within 6 years of start date. *Entrance requirements:* For master's, GACE, writing assessment, 2 professional recommendations. Additional exam requirements/recommendations for international students: Recommended—TOEFL (minimum score 500 paper-based; 61 iBT), IELTS (minimum score 6). *Application deadline:* For fall admission, 7/1 for domestic students; for spring admission, 11/15 for domestic students; for summer admission, 4/1 for domestic students. Applications are processed on a rolling basis. Application fee: $35. *Unit head:* Dr. Diane Gregg, Program Coordinator, 478-445-1505, E-mail: diane.gregg@gcsu.edu. *Application contact:* Shanda Brand, Graduate Admissions Advisor, 478-445-1383, Fax: 478-445-6582, E-mail: shanda.brand@gcsu.edu.

Georgia Southern University, Jack N. Averitt College of Graduate Studies, College of Education, Department of Leadership, Technology, and Human Development, Program in Instructional Technology, Statesboro, GA 30460. Offers M Ed, Ed S. Part-time and evening/weekend programs available. Postbaccalaureate distance learning degree programs offered (no on-campus study). *Students:* 21 full-time (14 women), 189 part-time (156 women); includes 65 minority (56 Black or African American, non-Hispanic/Latino; 1 American Indian or Alaska Native, non-Hispanic/Latino; 1 Asian, non-Hispanic/Latino; 4 Hispanic/Latino; 3 Two or more races, non-Hispanic/Latino). Average age 35. 61 applicants, 92% accepted, 33 enrolled. In 2013, 74 master's, 9 Ed Ss awarded. *Degree requirements:* For master's, portfolio, transition point assessments. *Entrance requirements:* For master's, GRE General Test or MAT, minimum GPA of 2.5. Additional exam requirements/recommendations for international students: Required—TOEFL (minimum score 550 paper-based; 80 iBT), IELTS (minimum score 6). *Application deadline:* For fall admission, 3/1 priority date for domestic and international students; for spring admission, 10/1 priority date for domestic students, 10/1 for international students. Applications are processed on a rolling basis. Application fee: $50. Electronic applications accepted. *Expenses:* Tuition, state resident: full-time $7068; part-time $270 per semester hour. Tuition, nonresident: full-time $26,446; part-time $1077 per semester hour. *Required fees:* $2092. *Financial support:* Research assistantships, teaching assistantships, career-related internships or fieldwork, and scholarships/grants available. Support available to part-time students. Financial award application deadline: 4/15; financial award applicants required to submit FAFSA. *Faculty research:* Online learning in higher education and K-12, instructional technology leadership, school library media programs, twenty-first century skills, instructional technology in the content areas. *Unit head:* Dr. Chuck Hodges, Program Coordinator, 912-478-0497, Fax: 912-478-7104, E-mail: chodges@georgiasouthern.edu. *Application contact:* Amanda Gilliland, Coordinator for Graduate Student Recruitment, 912-478-5384, Fax: 912-478-0740, E-mail: gradadmissions@georgiasouthern.edu.
Website: http://coe.georgiasouthern.edu/itec/.

Georgia State University, College of Education, Department of Middle-Secondary Education and Instructional Technology, Atlanta, GA 30302-3083. Offers English education (M Ed, MAT); English speakers of other languages (MAT); instructional design and technology (MS); instructional technology (PhD), including alternative instructional delivery systems, consulting, instructional design, management, research; mathematics education (M Ed, MAT); middle level education (MAT); reading, language and literacy education (M Ed), including reading instruction; science education (MAT), including biology, broad field science, chemistry, earth science, physics; social studies education (M Ed, MAT), including economics (MAT), geography (MAT), history (MAT), political science (MAT); teaching and learning (PhD), including language and literacy, mathematics education, music education, science education, social studies, teaching and teacher education. *Accreditation:* NCATE. Part-time and evening/weekend programs available. Postbaccalaureate distance learning degree programs offered (minimal on-campus study). *Faculty:* 27 full-time (19 women). *Students:* 181 full-time (113 women), 203 part-time (145 women); includes 161 minority (127 Black or African American, non-Hispanic/Latino; 1 American Indian or Alaska Native, non-Hispanic/Latino; 10 Asian, non-Hispanic/Latino; 11 Hispanic/Latino; 1 Native Hawaiian or other Pacific Islander, non-Hispanic/Latino; 11 Two or more races, non-Hispanic/Latino), 9 international. Average age 36. 2 applicants, 50% accepted, 1 enrolled. In 2013, 213 master's, 17 doctorates awarded. *Degree requirements:* For master's, comprehensive exam (for some programs), thesis or alternative, exit portfolio; for doctorate, comprehensive exam, thesis/dissertation. *Entrance requirements:* For master's, GRE; GACE I (for initial teacher preparation degree programs), baccalaureate degree or equivalent, resume, goals statement, two letters of recommendation, minimum undergraduate GPA of 2.5; proof of initial teacher certification in the content area (for M Ed); for doctorate, GRE, resume, goals statement, writing sample, two letters of recommendation, minimum graduate GPA of 3.3, interview. Additional exam requirements/recommendations for international students: Required—TOEFL (minimum score 550 paper-based; 79 iBT) or IELTS (minimum score 6.5). *Application deadline:* For fall admission, 1/15 priority date for domestic and international students; for spring admission, 10/1 for domestic and international students. Application fee: $50. Electronic applications accepted. *Expenses: Tuition, area resident:* Full-time $4176; part-time $348 per credit hour. Tuition, state resident: full-time $14,544; part-time $1212 per credit hour. Tuition, nonresident: full-time $14,544; part-time $1212 per credit hour. Tuition and fees vary according to course load and program. *Financial support:* In 2013–14, fellowships with full tuition reimbursements (averaging $19,667 per year), research assistantships with full tuition reimbursements (averaging $5,436 per year), teaching assistantships with full tuition reimbursements (averaging $2,779 per year) were awarded; career-related internships or fieldwork, Federal Work-Study, scholarships/grants, health care benefits, tuition waivers (full and partial), and unspecified assistantships also available. Financial award application deadline: 3/15. *Faculty research:* Teacher education in language and literacy, mathematics, science, and social studies in urban middle and secondary school settings; learning technologies in school, community, and corporate settings; multicultural education and education for social justice; urban education; international education. *Unit head:* Dr. Dana L. Fox, Chair, 404-413-8060, Fax: 404-413-8063, E-mail: dfox@gsu.edu. *Application contact:* Bobbie Turner, Administrative Coordinator I, 404-413-8405, Fax: 404-413-8063, E-mail: bnturner@gsu.edu.
Website: http://msit.gsu.edu/msit_programs.htm.

Governors State University, College of Arts and Sciences, Program in Communication and Training, University Park, IL 60484. Offers communication studies (MA); instructional and training technology (MA); media communication (MA). Part-time and evening/weekend programs available. *Degree requirements:* For master's, thesis or alternative.

Graceland University, Gleazer School of Education, Independence, MO 64050. Offers differentiated instruction (M Ed); literacy and instruction (M Ed); management in the inclusive classroom (M Ed); mild/moderate special education (M Ed); technology integration (M Ed). *Accreditation:* NCATE. Part-time and evening/weekend programs available. Postbaccalaureate distance learning degree programs offered (no on-campus study). *Faculty:* 12 full-time (11 women), 18 part-time/adjunct (14 women). *Students:* 139 full-time (119 women), 18 part-time (14 women); includes 8 minority (3 Black or African American, non-Hispanic/Latino; 1 Asian, non-Hispanic/Latino; 4 Hispanic/Latino). Average age 36. 36 applicants, 81% accepted, 24 enrolled. In 2013, 196 master's awarded. *Degree requirements:* For master's, action research project. *Entrance requirements:* For master's, minimum GPA of 3.0, teaching certificate, current teaching contract. *Application deadline:* For fall admission, 7/15 for domestic students; for winter admission, 10/15 for domestic students; for spring admission, 1/15 priority date for domestic students. Application fee: $50. Electronic applications accepted. *Expenses: Tuition:* Part-time $450 per semester hour. Tuition and fees vary according to course load, degree level, campus/location and program. *Financial support:* Institutionally sponsored loans and scholarships/grants available. Financial award application deadline: 12/15; financial award applicants required to submit FAFSA. *Unit*

head: Dr. Scott Huddleston, Dean, 641-784-5000 Ext. 4744, E-mail: huddlest@graceland.edu. *Application contact:* Cathy Porter, Program Consultant, 816-423-4716, Fax: 816-833-2990, E-mail: cgporter@graceland.edu. Website: http://www.graceland.edu/education.

Grambling State University, School of Graduate Studies and Research, College of Education, Department of Educational Leadership, Grambling, LA 71245. Offers developmental education (MS, Ed D, PMC), including curriculum and instructional design (Ed D), English (MS), guidance and counseling (MS), higher education administration and management (Ed D), mathematics (MS), reading (MS), science (MS), student development and personnel services (Ed D); educational leadership (M Ed). Part-time and evening/weekend programs available. *Faculty:* 10 full-time (7 women). *Students:* 19 full-time (13 women), 89 part-time (70 women); includes 83 minority (82 Black or African American, non-Hispanic/Latino; 1 Hispanic/Latino), 6 international. Average age 40. In 2013, 13 master's, 6 doctorates, 1 other advanced degree awarded. *Degree requirements:* For master's, comprehensive exam, thesis (for some programs); for doctorate, comprehensive exam, thesis/dissertation. *Entrance requirements:* For master's, GRE, minimum GPA of 2.5 on last degree; for doctorate, GRE (minimum score 1000, 500 on Verbal), master's degree, minimum GPA of 3.0 on last degree. Additional exam requirements/recommendations for international students: Required—TOEFL (minimum score 500 paper-based; 62 iBT). *Application deadline:* For fall admission, 7/1 for domestic and international students; for spring admission, 12/1 for domestic and international students; for summer admission, 5/1 for domestic and international students. Applications are processed on a rolling basis. Application fee: $20 ($30 for international students). Electronic applications accepted. *Financial support:* Research assistantships, health care benefits, tuition waivers (full), and unspecified assistantships available. Financial award application deadline: 5/31; financial award applicants required to submit FAFSA. *Unit head:* Dr. Olatunde Ogunyemi, Department Head, 318-274-2549, Fax: 318-274-6249, E-mail: ogunyemio@gram.edu. *Application contact:* Brenda Cooper, Administrative Assistant III, 318-274-2238, Fax: 318-274-6249, E-mail: cooper@gram.edu. Website: http://www.gram.edu/academics/majors/education/departments/leadership/.

Grand Valley State University, College of Education, Programs in General Education, Allendale, MI 49401-9403. Offers adult and higher education (M Ed); early childhood education (M Ed); educational differentiation (M Ed); educational leadership (M Ed); educational technology integration (M Ed); elementary education (M Ed); middle level education (M Ed); school library media services (M Ed); secondary level education (M Ed); teaching English to speakers of other languages (M Ed). Part-time and evening/weekend programs available. Postbaccalaureate distance learning degree programs offered (minimal on-campus study). *Degree requirements:* For master's, thesis. *Entrance requirements:* For master's, GRE General Test or minimum GPA of 3.0. Additional exam requirements/recommendations for international students: Required—TOEFL. Electronic applications accepted. *Faculty research:* Effectiveness of technology in education, parental involvement, effective teaching, effective schools research.

Gratz College, Graduate Programs, Program in Educational Technology, Melrose Park, PA 19027. Offers Graduate Certificate. Postbaccalaureate distance learning degree programs offered. *Degree requirements:* For Graduate Certificate, final paper and project.

Harrisburg University of Science and Technology, Program in Learning Technologies, Harrisburg, PA 17101. Offers MS. Part-time and evening/weekend programs available. *Entrance requirements:* Additional exam requirements/recommendations for international students: Required—TOEFL (minimum score 520 paper-based; 80 iBT). Electronic applications accepted.

Harvard University, Extension School, Cambridge, MA 02138-3722. Offers applied sciences (CAS); biotechnology (ALM); educational technologies (ALM); educational technology (CET); English for graduate and professional studies (DGP); environmental management (ALM, CEM); information technology (ALM); journalism (ALM); liberal arts (ALM); management (ALM, CM); mathematics for teaching (ALM); museum studies (ALM); premedical studies (Diploma); publication and communication (CPC). Part-time and evening/weekend programs available. *Degree requirements:* For master's, thesis. *Entrance requirements:* For master's, 3 completed graduate courses with grade of B or higher. Additional exam requirements/recommendations for international students: Required—TOEFL (minimum score 600 paper-based), TWE (minimum score 5). *Expenses:* Contact institution.

Harvard University, Harvard Graduate School of Education, Master's Programs in Education, Cambridge, MA 02138. Offers arts in education (Ed M); education policy and management (Ed M); higher education (Ed M); human development and psychology (Ed M); international education policy (Ed M); language and literacy (Ed M); learning and teaching (Ed M); mind, brain, and education (Ed M); prevention science and practice (Ed M); school leadership (Ed M); special studies (Ed M); teacher education (Ed M); technology, innovation, and education (Ed M). Part-time programs available. *Faculty:* 68 full-time (34 women), 77 part-time/adjunct (41 women). *Students:* 557 full-time (410 women), 69 part-time (50 women); includes 179 minority (34 Black or African American, non-Hispanic/Latino; 1 American Indian or Alaska Native, non-Hispanic/Latino; 62 Asian, non-Hispanic/Latino; 52 Hispanic/Latino; 2 Native Hawaiian or other Pacific Islander, non-Hispanic/Latino; 28 Two or more races, non-Hispanic/Latino), 100 international. Average age 28. 1,756 applicants, 47% accepted, 589 enrolled. In 2013, 673 master's awarded. *Entrance requirements:* For master's, GRE General Test, statement of purpose, 3 letters of recommendation, resume, official transcripts. Additional exam requirements/recommendations for international students: Required—TOEFL (minimum score 613 paper-based; 104 iBT), TWE (minimum score 5). *Application deadline:* For fall admission, 1/3 for domestic and international students. Application fee: $85. Electronic applications accepted. *Expenses:* Contact institution. *Financial support:* In 2013–14, 375 students received support, including 12 fellowships with full and partial tuition reimbursements available (averaging $13,925 per year), 2 research assistantships (averaging $2,174 per year); career-related internships or fieldwork, Federal Work-Study, institutionally sponsored loans, scholarships/grants, health care benefits, tuition waivers (full and partial), and unspecified assistantships also available. Support available to part-time students. Financial award application deadline: 2/1; financial award applicants required to submit FAFSA. *Faculty research:* Learning and development, educational leadership and organizations, education policy analysis. *Total annual research expenditures:* $34.3 million. *Unit head:* Jennifer L. Petrallia, Assistant Dean, 617-495-8445. *Application contact:* Information Contact, 617-495-3414, Fax: 617-496-3577, E-mail: gseadmissions@harvard.edu. Website: http://www.gse.harvard.edu/.

Hofstra University, School of Education, Programs in Teaching - Elementary and Early Childhood Education, Hempstead, NY 11549. Offers early childhood and childhood education (MS Ed); early childhood education (MA, MS Ed); educational technology (MA); elementary education (MS Ed); literacy (MA); math specialist (Advanced Certificate); math, science, technology (MA); multiculturalism (MA).

Hofstra University, School of Education, Programs in Teaching - Secondary Education, Hempstead, NY 11549. Offers business education (MS Ed); education technology (Advanced Certificate); English education (MA, MS Ed); foreign language and TESOL

(MS Ed); foreign language education (MA, MS Ed), including French, German, Russian, Spanish; mathematics education (MA, MS Ed); science education (MA, MS Ed), including biology, chemistry, earth science, geology, physics; secondary education (Advanced Certificate); social studies education (MA, MS Ed); technology for learning (MA).

Idaho State University, Office of Graduate Studies, College of Education, Department of Educational Leadership and Instructional Design, Pocatello, ID 83209-8059. Offers educational administration (M Ed, 6th Year Certificate, Ed S); educational leadership (Ed D), including education training and development, educational administration, educational technology, higher education administration; educational leadership and instructional design (PhD); instructional technology (M Ed). Part-time programs available. *Degree requirements:* For master's, comprehensive exam, thesis optional, internship, oral exam or deferred thesis; for doctorate, comprehensive exam, thesis/dissertation, written exam; for other advanced degree, comprehensive exam, thesis (for some programs), written and oral exam. *Entrance requirements:* For master's, MAT, bachelor's degree, minimum GPA of 3.0, 1 year of training experience; for doctorate, GRE General Test or MAT, minimum GPA of 3.0 (undergraduate), 3.5 (graduate); departmental interview; for other advanced degree, GRE General Test, minimum GPA of 3.0, master's degree. Additional exam requirements/recommendations for international students: Required—TOEFL (minimum score 550 paper-based; 80 iBT). Electronic applications accepted. *Faculty research:* Educational leadership, gender issues in education and sport, staff development.

Idaho State University, Office of Graduate Studies, College of Education, Program in Instructional Methods and Technology, Pocatello, ID 83209. Offers instructional design (PhD); instructional technology (M Ed). Part-time programs available. *Degree requirements:* For master's, comprehensive exam, thesis optional, minimum 36 credits; for doctorate, comprehensive exam, thesis/dissertation (for some programs). *Entrance requirements:* For master's, GRE or MAT, bachelor's degree; for doctorate, GRE or MAT, master's degree. Additional exam requirements/recommendations for international students: Required—TOEFL (minimum score 550 paper-based; 80 iBT). Electronic applications accepted.

Indiana State University, College of Graduate and Professional Studies, College of Education, Department of Curriculum, Instruction, and Media Technology, Terre Haute, IN 47809. Offers curriculum and instruction (M Ed, PhD); educational technology (MS). *Accreditation:* NCATE. *Degree requirements:* For doctorate, thesis/dissertation. *Entrance requirements:* For doctorate, GRE General Test. Electronic applications accepted. *Faculty research:* Discipline FERPA reading, teacher strengths and needs.

Indiana University Bloomington, School of Education, Department of Instructional Systems Technology, Bloomington, IN 47405-1006. Offers MS, PhD. Postbaccalaureate distance learning degree programs offered (no on-campus study). Terminal master's awarded for partial completion of doctoral program. *Degree requirements:* For master's, thesis optional, portfolio; for doctorate, comprehensive exam, thesis/dissertation, dossier review. *Entrance requirements:* For master's and doctorate, GRE General Test, minimum GPA of 2.75. Additional exam requirements/recommendations for international students: Required—TOEFL. Electronic applications accepted. *Faculty research:* Instructional design and theory development, e-learning and distance education, systemic change, serious simulations and games, human performance improvement, technology integration in education.

Indiana University of Pennsylvania, School of Graduate Studies and Research, College of Education and Educational Technology, Department of Adult and Community Education, Program in Adult and Community Education/Communications Technology, Indiana, PA 15705-1087. Offers MA. Part-time and evening/weekend programs available. *Faculty:* 2 full-time (0 women). *Students:* 18 full-time (9 women), 6 part-time (5 women); includes 2 minority (1 Black or African American, non-Hispanic/Latino; 1 Hispanic/Latino), 7 international. Average age 30. 28 applicants, 75% accepted, 18 enrolled. In 2013, 19 master's awarded. *Degree requirements:* For master's, thesis optional. *Entrance requirements:* For master's, 2 letters of recommendation, resume. Additional exam requirements/recommendations for international students: Required—TOEFL (minimum score 540 paper-based; 76 iBT). *Application deadline:* Applications are processed on a rolling basis. Application fee: $50. Electronic applications accepted. *Expenses:* Tuition, state resident: full-time $3978; part-time $442 per credit. Tuition, nonresident: full-time $5967; part-time $663 per credit. *Required fees:* $2080; $115.55 per credit. $93 per semester. Tuition and fees vary according to degree level and program. *Financial support:* In 2013–14, 9 research assistantships with full and partial tuition reimbursements (averaging $5,138 per year) were awarded; fellowships, teaching assistantships, career-related internships or fieldwork, Federal Work-Study, scholarships/grants, and unspecified assistantships also available. Support available to part-time students. Financial award application deadline: 4/15; financial award applicants required to submit FAFSA. *Unit head:* Dr. Jeff Ritchey, Graduate Coordinator, 724-357-2470, E-mail: jeffrey.ritchey@iup.edu. Website: http://www.iup.edu/aect.

Indiana University of Pennsylvania, School of Graduate Studies and Research, College of Education and Educational Technology, Department of Communications Media, Indiana, PA 15705-1087. Offers adult education and communications technology (MA); communications media and instructional technology (PhD). Part-time and evening/weekend programs available. *Faculty:* 9 full-time (4 women). *Students:* 17 full-time (8 women), 43 part-time (19 women); includes 8 minority (3 Black or African American, non-Hispanic/Latino; 2 Asian, non-Hispanic/Latino; 3 Two or more races, non-Hispanic/Latino), 4 international. Average age 37. 47 applicants, 30% accepted, 11 enrolled. In 2013, 5 doctorates awarded. Terminal master's awarded for partial completion of doctoral program. *Degree requirements:* For doctorate, comprehensive exam, thesis/dissertation. *Entrance requirements:* For doctorate, GRE, goal statement, resume, writing sample, two letters of recommendation. Additional exam requirements/recommendations for international students: Required—TOEFL (minimum score 540 paper-based). *Application deadline:* Applications are processed on a rolling basis. Application fee: $50. Electronic applications accepted. *Expenses:* Tuition, state resident: full-time $3978; part-time $442 per credit. Tuition, nonresident: full-time $5967; part-time $663 per credit. *Required fees:* $2080; $115.55 per credit. $93 per semester. Tuition and fees vary according to degree level and program. *Financial support:* In 2013–14, 4 fellowships with full tuition reimbursements (averaging $2,282 per year), 12 research assistantships with full and partial tuition reimbursements (averaging $5,579 per year), 3 teaching assistantships with partial tuition reimbursements (averaging $22,848 per year) were awarded; career-related internships or fieldwork, Federal Work-Study, scholarships/grants, tuition waivers (full), and unspecified assistantships also available. Support available to part-time students. Financial award application deadline: 4/15; financial award applicants required to submit FAFSA. *Unit head:* Dr. Mark Piwinsky, Chairperson, 724-357-3954, Fax: 724-357-5503, E-mail: mark.piwinsky@iup.edu. *Application contact:* Dr. Gail Wilson, Graduate Coordinator, 724-357-3210, E-mail: b.g.wilson@iup.edu. Website: http://www.iup.edu/commmedia/.

Instituto Tecnológico y de Estudios Superiores de Monterrey, Campus Central de Veracruz, Graduate Programs, Córdoba, Mexico. Offers administration (MA); administration of information technologies (MTI); computer sciences (MCC); education

(MEE); educational institution administration (MAD); educational technology (MTE); electronic commerce (MCE); finance (MAF); humanistic studies (MEH); international business for Latin America (MNL); marketing (MMT); science (MCP). Part-time and evening/weekend programs available. Postbaccalaureate distance learning degree programs offered (minimal on-campus study). *Degree requirements:* For master's, thesis (for some programs). *Entrance requirements:* For master's, PAEP College Board. Electronic applications accepted.

Instituto Tecnológico y de Estudios Superiores de Monterrey, Campus Ciudad de México, Virtual University Division, Ciudad de Mexico, Mexico. Offers administration of information technologies (MA); computer sciences (MA); education (MA, PhD); educational technology (MA); environmental engineering (MA); environmental systems (MA); humanistic studies (MA); industrial engineering (MA); international business for Latin America (MA); quality systems (MA); quality systems and productivity (MA). Part-time and evening/weekend programs available. Postbaccalaureate distance learning degree programs offered (minimal on-campus study). *Entrance requirements:* For master's and doctorate, Instituto entrance exam. Additional exam requirements/recommendations for international students: Required—TOEFL.

Instituto Tecnológico y de Estudios Superiores de Monterrey, Campus Ciudad Juárez, Program in Educational Innovation, Ciudad Juárez, Mexico. Offers DE.

Instituto Tecnológico y de Estudios Superiores de Monterrey, Campus Ciudad Juárez, Program in Educational Technology, Ciudad Juárez, Mexico. Offers MTE.

Instituto Tecnológico y de Estudios Superiores de Monterrey, Campus Estado de México, Professional and Graduate Division, Estado de Mexico, Mexico. Offers administration of information technologies (MITA); architecture (M Arch); business administration (GMBA, MBA); computer sciences (MCS, PhD); education (M Ed); educational institution administration (MAD); educational technology and innovation (PhD); electronic commerce (MEC); environmental systems (MS); finance (MAF); humanistic studies (MHS); information sciences and knowledge management (MISKM); information systems (MS); manufacturing systems (MS); marketing (MEM); quality systems and productivity (MS); science and materials engineering (PhD); telecommunications management (MTM). Part-time programs available. Postbaccalaureate distance learning degree programs offered (minimal on-campus study). *Degree requirements:* For master's, one foreign language, thesis (for some programs); for doctorate, one foreign language, thesis/dissertation. *Entrance requirements:* For master's, E-PAEP 500, interview; for doctorate, E-PAEP 500, research proposal. Additional exam requirements/recommendations for international students: Required—TOEFL (minimum score 550 paper-based). *Faculty research:* Surface treatments by plasmas, mechanical properties, robotics, graphical computing, mechatronics security protocols.

Instituto Tecnológico y de Estudios Superiores de Monterrey, Campus Irapuato, Graduate Programs, Irapuato, Mexico. Offers administration (MBA); administration of information technology (MAIT); administration of telecommunications (MAT); architecture (M Arch); computer science (MCS); education (M Ed); educational administration (MEA); educational innovation and technology (DEIT); educational technology (MET); electronic commerce (MBA); environmental administration and planning (MEAP); environmental systems (MES); finances (MBA); humanistic studies (MHS); international management for Latin American executives (MIMLAE); library and information science (MLIS); manufacturing quality management (MMQM); marketing research (MBA).

Inter American University of Puerto Rico, Metropolitan Campus, Graduate Programs, Program in Educational Computing, San Juan, PR 00919-1293. Offers MA. *Degree requirements:* For master's, comprehensive exam, portfolio. *Entrance requirements:* For master's, GRE or EXADEP, minimum GPA of 2.5. Electronic applications accepted. *Faculty research:* Effectiveness of multimedia, World Wide Web for distance learning.

Iowa State University of Science and Technology, Department of Curriculum and Instruction, Ames, IA 50011. Offers curriculum and instructional technology (M Ed, MS, PhD); elementary education (M Ed, MS); historical, philosophical, and comparative studies in education (M Ed, MS); special education (M Ed, MS, PhD). *Degree requirements:* For master's, thesis or alternative; for doctorate, thesis/dissertation. *Entrance requirements:* For master's and doctorate, GRE General Test. Additional exam requirements/recommendations for international students: Required—TOEFL (minimum score 560 paper-based; 83 iBT), IELTS (minimum score 6.5). Electronic applications accepted.

Jackson State University, Graduate School, College of Education and Human Development, Department of Educational Leadership, Jackson, MS 39217. Offers education administration (Ed S); educational administration (MS Ed, PhD); secondary education (MS Ed, Ed S), including educational technology (MS Ed). *Accreditation:* NCATE. Part-time and evening/weekend programs available. *Degree requirements:* For master's, comprehensive exam, thesis or alternative; for doctorate, comprehensive exam, thesis/dissertation; for Ed S, comprehensive exam, thesis. *Entrance requirements:* For master's, GRE General Test; for doctorate, MAT, GRE, teaching experience. Additional exam requirements/recommendations for international students: Required—TOEFL (minimum score 520 paper-based; 67 iBT).

Jacksonville State University, College of Graduate Studies and Continuing Education, College of Education and Professional Studies, Program in Instructional Media, Jacksonville, AL 36265-1602. Offers MS Ed. Part-time and evening/weekend programs available. *Degree requirements:* For master's, comprehensive exam, thesis (for some programs). *Entrance requirements:* For master's, GRE General Test or MAT. Additional exam requirements/recommendations for international students: Required—TOEFL (minimum score 61 iBT). Electronic applications accepted.

John Hancock University, Program in Instructional Technology, Oakbrook Terrace, IL 60181. Offers MS. *Degree requirements:* For master's, research and field project.

Johns Hopkins University, School of Education, Certificate Programs in Education, Baltimore, MD 21218-2699. Offers advanced methods for differentiated instruction and inclusive education (Certificate); applied behavior analysis (Certificate); counseling (CAGS); data-based decision making and organizational improvement (Certificate); early intervention/preschool special education specialist (Certificate); education leadership for independent schools (Certificate); education of students with autism and other pervasive developmental disorders (Certificate); evidence-based teaching in the health professions (Certificate); gifted education (Certificate); K-8 mathematics lead-teacher (Certificate); K-8 STEM education lead-teacher (Certificate); leadership for school, family, and community collaboration (Certificate); leadership in technology integration (Certificate); mental health counseling (Certificate); mind, brain, and teaching (Certificate); school administration and supervision (Certificate); urban education (Certificate). Part-time and evening/weekend programs available. Postbaccalaureate distance learning degree programs offered (no on-campus study). *Students:* 7 full-time (4 women), 216 part-time (169 women); includes 66 minority (35 Black or African American, non-Hispanic/Latino; 17 Asian, non-Hispanic/Latino; 6 Hispanic/Latino; 8 Two or more races, non-Hispanic/Latino), 6 international. Average age 35. 257 applicants, 81% accepted, 62 enrolled. In 2013, 202 CAGSs awarded. *Entrance requirements:* For degree, bachelor's degree from regionally- or nationally-accredited institution (master's for some programs), minimum GPA of 3.0 in all previous programs of study, official transcripts from all post-secondary institutions attended, essay, curriculum vitae/resume, minimum of two letters of recommendation. Additional exam requirements/recommendations for international students: Required—TOEFL (minimum score 600 paper-based; 100 iBT) or IELTS (minimum score 7). *Application deadline:* For fall admission, 4/1 for domestic students; for spring admission, 10/1 for domestic students; for summer admission, 2/1 for domestic students. Application fee: $80. Electronic applications accepted. *Financial support:* Application deadline: 6/1; applicants required to submit FAFSA. *Unit head:* Dr. David A. Andrews, Dean, 410-516-7820, Fax: 410-516-6697, E-mail: davidandrews@jhu.edu. *Application contact:* Catherine Wilson, Associate Director of Admissions, 410-516-9797, Fax: 410-516-9799, E-mail: soe.info@jhu.edu.

Johns Hopkins University, School of Education, Master's Programs in Education, Baltimore, MD 21218-2699. Offers counseling (MS), including mental health counseling, school counseling; education (MS), including educational studies, gifted education, reading, school administration and supervision, technology for educators; elementary education (MAT); health professions (M Ed); intelligence analysis (MS); management (MS); secondary education (MAT); special education (MS), including early childhood special education, general special education studies, mild to moderate disabilities, severe disabilities. Part-time and evening/weekend programs available. Postbaccalaureate distance learning degree programs offered (no on-campus study). *Students:* 183 full-time (123 women), 1,001 part-time (757 women); includes 380 minority (160 Black or African American, non-Hispanic/Latino; 4 American Indian or Alaska Native, non-Hispanic/Latino; 91 Asian, non-Hispanic/Latino; 78 Hispanic/Latino; 4 Native Hawaiian or other Pacific Islander, non-Hispanic/Latino; 43 Two or more races, non-Hispanic/Latino), 28 international. Average age 28. 508 applicants, 90% accepted, 337 enrolled. In 2013, 565 degrees awarded. *Degree requirements:* For master's, comprehensive exam (for some programs), portfolio, capstone project and/or internship; PRAXIS II (for teacher preparation programs that lead to licensure). *Entrance requirements:* For master's, GRE (for full-time programs only); PRAXIS I or equivalent (for teacher preparation programs that lead to licensure), bachelor's degree from regionally- or nationally-accredited institution, minimum GPA of 3.0 in all previous programs of study, official transcripts from all post-secondary institutions attended, essay, curriculum vitae/resume, minimum of two letters of recommendation. Additional exam requirements/recommendations for international students: Required—TOEFL (minimum score 600 paper-based; 100 iBT) or IELTS (minimum score 7). *Application deadline:* For fall admission, 4/1 for domestic and international students; for spring admission, 10/1 for domestic and international students; for summer admission, 2/1 for domestic and international students. Application fee: $80. Electronic applications accepted. *Financial support:* Application deadline: 6/1; applicants required to submit FAFSA. *Unit head:* Dr. David A. Andrews, Dean, 410-516-7820, Fax: 410-516-6697, E-mail: davidandrews@jhu.edu. *Application contact:* Catherine Wilson, Associate Director of Admissions, 410-516-9797, Fax: 410-516-9799, E-mail: soe.info@jhu.edu.

Johnson University, Graduate and Professional Programs, Knoxville, TN 37998-1001. Offers educational technology (MA); intercultural studies (MA); leadership studies (PhD); marriage and family therapy/professional counseling (MA); New Testament (MA); school counseling (MA); teacher education (MA). *Degree requirements:* For master's, variable foreign language requirement, comprehensive exam, thesis (for some programs), internship (500 client contact hours). *Entrance requirements:* For master's, interview, minimum GPA of 3.0, 20 credits of course work in psychology, 15 credits of course work in Bible. Additional exam requirements/recommendations for international students: Required—TOEFL.

Jones International University, School of Education, Centennial, CO 80112. Offers adult education (M Ed); corporate training and knowledge management (M Ed); curriculum and instruction (M Ed), including elementary teacher licensure, secondary teacher licensure; e-learning technology and design (M Ed); educational leadership and administration (M Ed); educational leadership and administration: principal and administrator licensure (M Ed); elementary curriculum instruction and assessment (M Ed); higher education leadership and administration (M Ed); K-12 instructional technology (M Ed); K-12 instructional technology: teacher licensure (M Ed); secondary curriculum instruction and assessment (M Ed); technology and design (M Ed). Part-time and evening/weekend programs available. Postbaccalaureate distance learning degree programs offered (no on-campus study). *Entrance requirements:* For master's, minimum cumulative GPA of 2.5. Additional exam requirements/recommendations for international students: Recommended—TOEFL (minimum score 550 paper-based). Electronic applications accepted.

Kansas State University, Graduate School, College of Education, Department of Curriculum and Instruction, Manhattan, KS 66506. Offers career and technical education (Ed D, PhD); curriculum studies (Ed D, PhD); digital teaching and learning (MS); educational computing, design and online learning (MS); educational technology (Ed D, PhD); elementary/middle level curriculum and instruction (MS); English as a second language (MS); language/diversity education (Ed D, PhD); literacy education (Ed D, PhD); mathematics education (Ed D, PhD); middle level/secondary curriculum and instruction (MS); reading and language arts (MS); reading specialist endorsement (MS); science education (Ed D, PhD); social science education (Ed D, PhD); teacher education (Ed D, PhD); teacher leader/school improvement (MS, Ed D). *Accreditation:* NCATE. Part-time programs available. Postbaccalaureate distance learning degree programs offered (minimal on-campus study). *Faculty:* 18 full-time (13 women), 7 part-time/adjunct (4 women). *Students:* 39 full-time (23 women), 122 part-time (94 women); includes 19 minority (3 Black or African American, non-Hispanic/Latino; 2 Asian, non-Hispanic/Latino; 12 Hispanic/Latino; 2 Two or more races, non-Hispanic/Latino), 12 international. Average age 36. 80 applicants, 50% accepted, 34 enrolled. In 2013, 40 master's, 13 doctorates awarded. *Degree requirements:* For master's, comprehensive exam, portfolio, project, report or thesis; for doctorate, comprehensive exam, thesis/dissertation, preliminary exam. *Entrance requirements:* For master's, minimum GPA of 3.0, letters of recommendation; for doctorate, GRE, minimum GPA of 3.0, letters of recommendation, evidence of scholarly writing. Additional exam requirements/recommendations for international students: Required—TOEFL (minimum score 550 paper-based; 80 iBT). *Application deadline:* For fall admission, 3/1 priority date for domestic students, 2/1 priority date for international students; for spring admission, 10/1 priority date for domestic students, 8/1 priority date for international students. Applications are processed on a rolling basis. Application fee: $50 ($75 for international students). Electronic applications accepted. *Financial support:* In 2013–14, 1 research assistantship (averaging $16,900 per year), 8 teaching assistantships (averaging $12,466 per year) were awarded; career-related internships or fieldwork, institutionally sponsored loans, and scholarships/grants also available. Support available to part-time students. Financial award application deadline: 3/1; financial award applicants required to submit FAFSA. *Faculty research:* Literacy and technology, critical race theory and diversity, achievement gaps, school improvement, teacher education. *Total annual research expenditures:* $543,677. *Unit head:* Dr. Todd Goodson, Chair, 785-532-5904, Fax: 785-532-7304, E-mail: tgoodson@ksu.edu. *Application contact:* Dona Deam, Application Contact, 785-532-5595, Fax: 785-532-7304, E-mail: ddeam@ksu.edu. Website: http://www.coe.k-state.edu/departments/edci/.

Kaplan University, Davenport Campus, School of Teacher Education, Davenport, IA 52807-2095. Offers education (M Ed); secondary education (M Ed); teaching and learning (MA); teaching literacy and language: grades 6-12 (MA); teaching literacy and language: grades K-6 (MA); teaching mathematics: grades 6-8 (MA); teaching mathematics: grades 9-12 (MA); teaching mathematics: grades K-5 (MA); teaching science: grades 6-12 (MA); teaching science: grades K-6 (MA); teaching students with special needs (MA); teaching with technology (MA). Part-time and evening/weekend programs available. Postbaccalaureate distance learning degree programs offered (no on-campus study). *Entrance requirements:* Additional exam requirements/recommendations for international students: Required—TOEFL (minimum score 550 paper-based; 80 iBT).

Keiser University, EdS in Instructional Design and Technology Program, Ft. Lauderdale, FL 33309. Offers Ed S.

Keiser University, PhD in Instructional Design and Technology Program, Ft. Lauderdale, FL 33309. Offers PhD.

Kennesaw State University, Leland and Clarice C. Bagwell College of Education, Program in Graduate Education, Kennesaw, GA 30144-5591. Offers educational leadership (M Ed); educational leadership technology (M Ed); elementary and early childhood education (M Ed); instructional technology (M Ed); middle grades education (M Ed); reading (M Ed); secondary education (M Ed); special education (M Ed); teaching English to speakers of other languages (M Ed). *Accreditation:* NCATE. Part-time programs available. *Students:* 65 full-time (60 women), 229 part-time (158 women); includes 66 minority (46 Black or African American, non-Hispanic/Latino; 6 Asian, non-Hispanic/Latino; 9 Hispanic/Latino; 5 Two or more races, non-Hispanic/Latino), 1 international. Average age 34. 56 applicants, 86% accepted, 43 enrolled. In 2013, 109 master's awarded. *Degree requirements:* For master's, thesis or alternative. *Entrance requirements:* For master's, GRE General Test, T-4 state certification, minimum GPA of 2.75. Additional exam requirements/recommendations for international students: Required—TOEFL (minimum score 550 paper-based; 80 iBT), IELTS (minimum score 6.5). *Application deadline:* For fall admission, 7/1 for domestic and international students; for spring admission, 10/1 for domestic and international students; for summer admission, 4/15 for domestic and international students. Applications are processed on a rolling basis. Application fee: $60. Electronic applications accepted. *Expenses:* Tuition, state resident: full-time $4806; part-time $267 per semester hour. Tuition, nonresident: full-time $17,298; part-time $961 per semester hour. *Required fees:* $1834; $784.50 per semester. *Financial support:* In 2013–14, 10 research assistantships with tuition reimbursements (averaging $8,000 per year) were awarded; Federal Work-Study and unspecified assistantships also available. Support available to part-time students. Financial award application deadline: 4/1; financial award applicants required to submit FAFSA. *Unit head:* Melinda Ross, Administrative Coordinator for Graduate Programs in Education, 770-423-6043, E-mail: graded@kennesaw.edu. *Application contact:* Melinda Ross, Admissions Counselor, 770-423-6043, Fax: 770-423-6885, E-mail: ksugrad@kennesaw.edu.
Website: http://www.kennesaw.edu/education/grad/.

Kent State University, Graduate School of Education, Health, and Human Services, School of Lifespan Development and Educational Sciences, Program in Instructional Technology, Kent, OH 44242-0001. Offers computer technology (M Ed); general instructional technology (M Ed). *Accreditation:* NCATE. *Faculty:* 5 full-time (1 woman). *Students:* 6 full-time (3 women), 52 part-time (37 women); includes 4 minority (2 Black or African American, non-Hispanic/Latino; 2 Native Hawaiian or other Pacific Islander, non-Hispanic/Latino), 1 international. 28 applicants, 61% accepted. In 2013, 25 master's awarded. *Degree requirements:* For master's, thesis (for some programs). *Entrance requirements:* For master's, 2 letters of reference, goals statement, minimum GPA of 2.75. Additional exam requirements/recommendations for international students: Required—TOEFL (minimum score 550 paper-based; 80 iBT). *Application deadline:* Applications are processed on a rolling basis. Application fee: $30 ($60 for international students). *Financial support:* Research assistantships with full tuition reimbursements, teaching assistantships with full tuition reimbursements, Federal Work-Study, scholarships/grants, and unspecified assistantships available. Financial award application deadline: 4/1; financial award applicants required to submit FAFSA. *Faculty research:* Cooperative learning, aesthetics, computers in schools. *Unit head:* Dr. Drew Tiene, Coordinator, 330-672-0607, E-mail: dtiene@kent.edu. *Application contact:* Nancy Miller, Academic Program Director, Office of Graduate Student Services, 330-672-2576, Fax: 330-672-9162, E-mail: ogs@kent.edu.
Website: http://www.kent.edu/ehhs/itec/.

Kutztown University of Pennsylvania, College of Education, Program in Instructional Technology, Kutztown, PA 19530-0730. Offers M Ed. Part-time and evening/weekend programs available. *Students:* 1 (woman) full-time, 23 part-time (15 women). Average age 32. 9 applicants, 89% accepted, 7 enrolled. In 2013, 8 master's awarded. *Degree requirements:* For master's, comprehensive exam. *Entrance requirements:* Additional exam requirements/recommendations for international students: Required—TOEFL (minimum score 550 paper-based; 79 iBT). *Application deadline:* For fall admission, 8/1 priority date for domestic and international students; for spring admission, 12/1 priority date for domestic and international students. Applications are processed on a rolling basis. Application fee: $35. Electronic applications accepted. *Expenses: Tuition, area resident:* Part-time $442 per credit. Tuition, state resident: part-time $442 per credit. Tuition, nonresident: part-time $663 per credit. *Required fees:* $80 per credit. *Financial support:* Career-related internships or fieldwork, Federal Work-Study, scholarships/grants, and unspecified assistantships available. Financial award application deadline: 3/1; financial award applicants required to submit FAFSA. *Unit head:* Dr. Andrea Harmer, Chairperson, 610-683-4301, Fax: 610-683-1326, E-mail: harmer@kutztown.edu. *Application contact:* Kelly Hish, Admissions Clerk, 610-683-4200, Fax: 610-683-1393, E-mail: graduate@kutztown.edu.

Lamar University, College of Graduate Studies, College of Education and Human Development, Department of Educational Leadership, Beaumont, TX 77710. Offers counseling and development (M Ed, Certificate); education administration (M Ed); educational leadership (DE); principal (Certificate); school superintendent (Certificate); supervision (M Ed); technology application (Certificate). Part-time and evening/weekend programs available. Terminal master's awarded for partial completion of doctoral program. *Degree requirements:* For master's, comprehensive exam, thesis optional; for doctorate, thesis/dissertation. *Entrance requirements:* For master's, GRE General Test, minimum GPA of 2.5; for doctorate, GRE. Additional exam requirements/recommendations for international students: Required—TOEFL. *Faculty research:* School dropouts, suicide prevention in public school students, school climate and gifted performance, teacher evaluation.

La Salle University, College of Professional and Continuing Studies, Program in Instructional Technology Management, Philadelphia, PA 19141-1199. Offers MS, Certificate. Part-time and evening/weekend programs available. Postbaccalaureate distance learning degree programs offered (no on-campus study). *Faculty:* 5. *Students:* 37 part-time (26 women); includes 10 minority (8 Black or African American, non-Hispanic/Latino; 2 Asian, non-Hispanic/Latino). Average age 42. 6 applicants, 100% accepted, 4 enrolled. In 2013, 9 master's, 5 other advanced degrees awarded. *Degree requirements:* For master's, capstone project. *Entrance requirements:* For master's and

Certificate, baccalaureate degree; two letters of recommendation; 3 years of professional experience in corporate training, human resources, information technology or business. Additional exam requirements/recommendations for international students: Required—TOEFL. *Application deadline:* For fall admission, 8/15 priority date for domestic students, 7/15 for international students; for spring admission, 12/15 priority date for domestic students, 11/15 for international students; for summer admission, 4/15 priority date for domestic students, 3/15 for international students. Applications are processed on a rolling basis. Application fee: $35. Electronic applications accepted. Application fee is waived when completed online. *Expenses: Tuition:* Full-time $20,750; part-time $695 per credit hour. *Required fees:* $300; $200 per year. Tuition and fees vary according to program. *Financial support:* In 2013–14, 2 students received support. Federal Work-Study and scholarships/grants available. Support available to part-time students. Financial award application deadline: 8/31; financial award applicants required to submit FAFSA. *Unit head:* Dr. Bobbe G. Baggio, Director, 215-991-3682, Fax: 215-951-1276, E-mail: baggio@lasalle.edu. *Application contact:* Paul J. Reilly, Director of Marketing and Graduate Enrollment, 215-951-1946, Fax: 215-951-1462, E-mail: reilly@lasalle.edu.
Website: http://www.lasalle.edu/grad/index.php?section-itm&page-index.

Lawrence Technological University, College of Arts and Sciences, Southfield, MI 48075-1058. Offers computer science (MS); educational technology (MS); integrated science (MSE); science education (MSE); technical and professional communication (MS). Part-time and evening/weekend programs available. *Faculty:* 7 full-time (5 women), 14 part-time/adjunct (6 women). *Students:* 8 full-time (0 women), 74 part-time (38 women); includes 20 minority (12 Black or African American, non-Hispanic/Latino; 3 Asian, non-Hispanic/Latino; 1 Hispanic/Latino; 4 Two or more races, non-Hispanic/Latino), 12 international. Average age 35. 167 applicants, 47% accepted, 20 enrolled. In 2013, 26 master's awarded. *Degree requirements:* For master's, thesis (for some programs). *Entrance requirements:* Additional exam requirements/recommendations for international students: Required—TOEFL (minimum score 550 paper-based; 79 iBT). *Application deadline:* For fall admission, 8/1 priority date for domestic students, 5/29 for international students; for spring admission, 12/1 priority date for domestic students, 10/15 for international students. Applications are processed on a rolling basis. Application fee: $50. Electronic applications accepted. *Expenses: Tuition:* Full-time $14,112; part-time $1008 per credit hour. *Required fees:* $519. One-time fee: $519 part-time. *Financial support:* In 2013–14, 9 students received support, including 1 research assistantship (averaging $9,000 per year); Federal Work-Study also available. Financial award application deadline: 4/1; financial award applicants required to submit FAFSA. *Unit head:* Dr. Hsiao-Ping Moore, Dean, 248-204-3500, Fax: 248-204-3518, E-mail: scidean@ltu.edu. *Application contact:* Jane Rohrback, Director of Admissions, 248-204-3160, Fax: 248-204-2228, E-mail: admissions@ltu.edu.
Website: http://www.ltu.edu/arts_sciences/graduate.asp.

Lehigh University, College of Education, Program in Comparative and International Education, Bethlehem, PA 18015. Offers comparative and international education (MA, PhD); globalization and educational change (M Ed); international counseling (Certificate); international development in education (Certificate); special education (Certificate); technology use in schools (Certificate); TESOL (Certificate). Part-time and evening/weekend programs available. Postbaccalaureate distance learning degree programs offered (minimal on-campus study). *Faculty:* 4 full-time (2 women). *Students:* 20 full-time (18 women), 26 part-time (17 women); includes 3 minority (2 Asian, non-Hispanic/Latino; 1 Hispanic/Latino), 14 international. Average age 33. 59 applicants, 63% accepted, 10 enrolled. In 2013, 17 master's awarded. Terminal master's awarded for partial completion of doctoral program. *Degree requirements:* For master's, thesis (MA); for doctorate, comprehensive exam, thesis/dissertation. *Entrance requirements:* For master's, 2 letters of recommendation; for doctorate, GRE, transcripts, 2 letters of recommendation, essay, and TOEFL if International applicant. Additional exam requirements/recommendations for international students: Required—TOEFL (minimum score 600 paper-based; 93 iBT). *Application deadline:* For fall and spring admission, 2/1 for domestic and international students. Application fee: $65. Electronic applications accepted. *Financial support:* Application deadline: 3/15. *Faculty research:* Comparative education, rural education, gender equity in education, post-socialist education transformation, educational borrowing, comparing education systems, education policy and globalization, family-school relationships, China, international testing, social inequities. *Unit head:* Dr. Iveta Silova, Program Director and Associate Professor, 610-758-5750, Fax: 610-758-6223, E-mail: ism207@lehigh.edu. *Application contact:* Sharon Y. Warden, Coordinator, 610-758-3256, Fax: 610-758-6223, E-mail: sy00@lehigh.edu.
Website: http://www.lehigh.edu/education/cie.

Lehigh University, College of Education, Program in Teaching, Learning and Technology, Bethlehem, PA 18015. Offers instructional technology (MS); teaching, learning and technology (PhD); technology use in the schools (Graduate Certificate); M Ed/MA. Part-time and evening/weekend programs available. *Faculty:* 6 full-time (2 women), 4 part-time/adjunct (1 woman). *Students:* 34 full-time (26 women), 49 part-time (33 women); includes 9 minority (2 Black or African American, non-Hispanic/Latino; 3 Asian, non-Hispanic/Latino; 3 Hispanic/Latino; 1 Native Hawaiian or other Pacific Islander, non-Hispanic/Latino), 4 international. Average age 32. 77 applicants, 68% accepted, 12 enrolled. In 2013, 40 master's awarded. Terminal master's awarded for partial completion of doctoral program. *Degree requirements:* For doctorate, comprehensive exam, thesis/dissertation, qualifying exam. *Entrance requirements:* For master's, minimum GPA of 3.0, 2 letters of recommendation, essay, transcript; for doctorate, GRE General Test, minimum graduate GPA of 3.0, writing sample, 2 letters of recommendation, essay, transcript. Additional exam requirements/recommendations for international students: Required—TOEFL (minimum score 600 paper-based; 93 iBT). *Application deadline:* For fall admission, 2/1 for domestic and international students; for spring admission, 12/1 for domestic and international students. Applications are processed on a rolling basis. Application fee: $65. Electronic applications accepted. *Financial support:* Application deadline: 1/31. *Faculty research:* Teaching and learning, K-16 curriculum development, Web-based learning, teaching and technology, language and literacy. *Unit head:* Dr. Alec M. Bodzin, Director, 610-758-5095, Fax: 610-758-3243, E-mail: amb4@lehigh.edu. *Application contact:* Donna M. Johnson, Manager, Graduate Programs Admissions, 610-758-3231, Fax: 610-758-6223, E-mail: dmj4@lehigh.edu.
Website: http://coe.lehigh.edu/academics/disciplines/itech.

Lesley University, School of Education, Cambridge, MA 02138-2790. Offers arts, community, and education (M Ed); autism studies (Certificate); curriculum and instruction (M Ed, CAGS); early childhood education (M Ed); ecological teaching and learning (MS); educational studies (PhD), including adult learning, educational leadership, individually designed; elementary education (M Ed); emergent technologies for educators (Certificate); ESLArts: language learning through the arts (M Ed); high school education (M Ed); individually designed (M Ed); integrated teaching through the arts (M Ed); literacy for K-8 classroom teachers (M Ed); mathematics education (M Ed); middle school education (M Ed); moderate disabilities (M Ed); online learning (Certificate); reading (CAGS); science in education (M Ed); severe disabilities (M Ed); special needs (CAGS); specialist teacher of reading (M Ed); teacher of visual art (M Ed); technology in education (M Ed, CAGS). *Accreditation:* Teacher Education Accreditation Council. Part-time and evening/weekend programs available. Postbaccalaureate distance learning degree programs offered (no on-campus study). *Faculty:* 40 full-time

(30 women), 104 part-time/adjunct (77 women). *Students:* 453 full-time (381 women), 1,672 part-time (1,435 women); includes 284 minority (139 Black or African American, non-Hispanic/Latino; 11 American Indian or Alaska Native, non-Hispanic/Latino; 38 Asian, non-Hispanic/Latino; 58 Hispanic/Latino; 5 Native Hawaiian or other Pacific Islander, non-Hispanic/Latino; 33 Two or more races, non-Hispanic/Latino), 22 international. Average age 35. In 2013, 1,137 master's, 18 doctorates, 51 other advanced degrees awarded. *Degree requirements:* For master's, practicum; for doctorate, thesis/dissertation. *Entrance requirements:* For master's, Massachusetts Tests for Educator Licensure (MTEL), transcripts, statement of purpose, recommendations; interview (for special education); for doctorate, GRE General Test, transcripts, statement of purpose, recommendations, interview, master's degree, resume; for other advanced degree, interview, master's degree. Additional exam requirements/recommendations for international students: Required—TOEFL (minimum score 550 paper-based; 80 iBT). *Application deadline:* Applications are processed on a rolling basis. Application fee: $50. Electronic applications accepted. *Expenses: Tuition:* Part-time $900 per credit. *Financial support:* In 2013–14, 15 fellowships (averaging $3,600 per year) were awarded; career-related internships or fieldwork, Federal Work-Study, scholarships/grants, tuition waivers, and unspecified assistantships also available. Financial award application deadline: 4/15; financial award applicants required to submit FAFSA. *Faculty research:* Assessment in literacy, mathematics and science; autism spectrum disorders; instructional technology and online learning; multicultural education and English language learners. *Unit head:* Dr. Jack Gillette, Dean, 617-349-8401, Fax: 617-349-8607, E-mail: jgillett@lesley.edu. *Application contact:* Martha Sheehan, Director of Admissions, 888-LESLEYU, Fax: 617-349-8313, E-mail: info@lesley.edu.
Website: http://www.lesley.edu/soe.html.

Lewis University, College of Education, Program in Curriculum and Instruction: Instructional Technology, Romeoville, IL 60446. Offers M Ed. Part-time and evening/weekend programs available. *Students:* 13 part-time (10 women); includes 2 minority (both Black or African American, non-Hispanic/Latino). *Entrance requirements:* For master's, departmental qualifying exam, writing exam, minimum GPA of 2.75, 2 letters of recommendation, interview. Additional exam requirements/recommendations for international students: Required—TOEFL (minimum score 550 paper-based; 80 iBT). *Application deadline:* For fall admission, 5/1 priority date for international students; for spring admission, 11/15 priority date for international students. Applications are processed on a rolling basis. Application fee: $40. Electronic applications accepted. *Financial support:* Institutionally sponsored loans and unspecified assistantships available. Support available to part-time students. Financial award application deadline: 5/1; financial award applicants required to submit FAFSA. *Unit head:* Dr. Seung Kim, Program Director, 815-838-0500, E-mail: kimse@lewisu.edu. *Application contact:* Linda Campbell, Graduate Admission Counselor, 815-836-5610 Ext. 5704, Fax: 815-836-5578, E-mail: campbeli@lewisu.edu.

Liberty University, School of Education, Lynchburg, VA 24515. Offers administration and supervision (M Ed); curriculum and instruction (Ed D, Ed S); early childhood education (M Ed); educational leadership (Ed D, Ed S); educational technology and online instruction (M Ed); elementary education (M Ed, MAT); English (M Ed); gifted education (M Ed); history (M Ed); leadership (M Ed); math specialist (M Ed); middle grades (M Ed, MAT); outdoor adventure sport (MS); reading specialist (M Ed); school counseling (M Ed); secondary education (MAT); special education (M Ed, MAT); sport management (MS), including administration, outdoor recreation, sport management, tourism; sports administration (MS); student service (M Ed); teaching and learning (M Ed); tourism (MS). *Accreditation:* NCATE. Part-time programs available. Postbaccalaureate distance learning degree programs offered (minimal on-campus study). *Students:* 2,241 full-time (1,639 women), 4,413 part-time (3,240 women); includes 2,052 minority (1,588 Black or African American, non-Hispanic/Latino; 37 American Indian or Alaska Native, non-Hispanic/Latino; 67 Asian, non-Hispanic/Latino; 173 Hispanic/Latino; 37 Native Hawaiian or other Pacific Islander, non-Hispanic/Latino; 150 Two or more races, non-Hispanic/Latino), 15 international. Average age 37. 6,185 applicants, 43% accepted, 1603 enrolled. In 2013, 1,256 master's, 117 doctorates, 470 other advanced degrees awarded. *Degree requirements:* For doctorate, comprehensive exam, thesis/dissertation. *Entrance requirements:* For master's, GRE General Test or MAT (if taken in or before 1999), 2 letters of recommendation, minimum undergraduate GPA of 3.0, curriculum vitae; for doctorate and Ed S, GRE General Test or MAT (if taken before 1999), minimum master's GPA of 3.0, 3 years of teaching experience. Additional exam requirements/recommendations for international students: Required—TOEFL (minimum score 600 paper-based; 100 iBT). *Application deadline:* For fall admission, 6/1 for domestic students; for spring admission, 11/1 for domestic students. Applications are processed on a rolling basis. Application fee: $50. Electronic applications accepted. *Expenses:* Contact institution. *Financial support:* Federal Work-Study and tuition waivers (partial) available. *Faculty research:* Self-determination, character education, bibliotherapy, learning styles, distance education. *Unit head:* Dr. Karen L. Parker, Dean, 434-582-2195, Fax: 434-582-2468, E-mail: kparker@liberty.edu. *Application contact:* Jay Bridge, Director of Graduate Admissions, 800-424-9595, Fax: 800-628-7977, E-mail: gradadmissions@liberty.edu.
Website: http://www.liberty.edu/academics/education/graduate/.

Lindenwood University, Graduate Programs, School of Education, St. Charles, MO 63301-1695. Offers education (MA); educational administration (MA, Ed D, Ed S); human performance (MS); instructional leadership (Ed D, Ed S); library media (MA); professional counseling (MA); school administration (Ed S); school counseling (MA); teaching (MA); teaching English to speakers of other languages (MA). Part-time and evening/weekend programs available. Postbaccalaureate distance learning degree programs offered (no on-campus study). *Faculty:* 50 full-time (33 women), 228 part-time/adjunct (136 women). *Students:* 454 full-time (352 women), 1,772 part-time (1,351 women); includes 637 minority (545 Black or African American, non-Hispanic/Latino; 9 American Indian or Alaska Native, non-Hispanic/Latino; 9 Asian, non-Hispanic/Latino; 42 Hispanic/Latino; 32 Two or more races, non-Hispanic/Latino), 32 international. Average age 36. 644 applicants, 71% accepted, 401 enrolled. In 2013, 564 master's, 35 doctorates, 83 other advanced degrees awarded. *Degree requirements:* For master's, thesis (for some programs), minimum GPA of 3.0; for doctorate, thesis/dissertation, minimum GPA of 3.0; for Ed S, comprehensive exam, project, minimum GPA of 3.0. *Entrance requirements:* For master's, interview, minimum GPA of 3.0, writing sample, letter of recommendation; for doctorate, GRE, minimum graduate GPA of 3.4, resume, interview, writing sample, 4 letters of recommendation; for Ed S, master's degree in education, relevant work experience. Additional exam requirements/recommendations for international students: Required—TOEFL (minimum score 550 paper-based; 80 iBT). *Application deadline:* For fall admission, 8/26 priority date for domestic and international students; for spring admission, 1/27 priority date for domestic and international students. Applications are processed on a rolling basis. Application fee: $30 ($100 for international students). Electronic applications accepted. *Expenses: Tuition:* Full-time $14,800; part-time $428 per credit hour. *Required fees:* $350. Tuition and fees vary according to course level and course load. *Financial support:* In 2013–14, 385 students received support. Career-related internships or fieldwork, Federal Work-Study, institutionally sponsored loans, scholarships/grants, tuition waivers (partial), and unspecified assistantships available. Financial award application deadline: 6/30; financial award applicants required to submit FAFSA. *Unit head:* Dr. Cynthia Bice, Dean, 636-949-4618, Fax: 636-949-4197, E-mail: cbice@lindenwood.edu. *Application contact:* Brett Barger, Dean of Evening Admissions and Extension Campuses, 636-949-4934, Fax: 636-949-4109, E-mail: adultadmissions@lindenwood.edu.

Lipscomb University, Program in Education, Nashville, TN 37204-3951. Offers applied behavior analysis (Certificate); collaborative professional learning (M Ed, Ed S); educational leadership (M Ed, Ed S); English language learning (M Ed, Ed S); instructional coaching (Certificate); instructional practice (M Ed); learning organizations and strategic change (Ed D); math specialty (M Ed); reading specialty (M Ed, Ed S); special education (M Ed); teaching, learning, and leading (M Ed); technology integration (M Ed); technology integration specialist (Certificate). *Accreditation:* NCATE. Part-time and evening/weekend programs available. Postbaccalaureate distance learning degree programs offered (no on-campus study). *Faculty:* 19 full-time (13 women), 28 part-time/adjunct (22 women). *Students:* 171 full-time (123 women), 509 part-time (429 women); includes 118 minority (91 Black or African American, non-Hispanic/Latino; 1 American Indian or Alaska Native, non-Hispanic/Latino; 4 Asian, non-Hispanic/Latino; 15 Hispanic/Latino; 1 Native Hawaiian or other Pacific Islander, non-Hispanic/Latino; 6 Two or more races, non-Hispanic/Latino). Average age 32. 237 applicants, 65% accepted, 150 enrolled. In 2013, 212 master's awarded. *Degree requirements:* For master's, comprehensive exam, portfolio, research project and presentation; for doctorate, practical capstone project in experiential setting. *Entrance requirements:* For master's, MAT (minimum 31) or GRE General Test (minimum 294), 2 reference letters, goals statement, writing sample, interview; for doctorate, MAT or GRE General Test, 3 reference letters, artifact of demonstrated academic excellence, written personal statements, interview. Additional exam requirements/recommendations for international students: Required—TOEFL (minimum score 570 paper-based). *Application deadline:* For fall admission, 8/29 priority date for domestic students; for spring admission, 1/15 priority date for domestic students. Applications are processed on a rolling basis. Application fee: $50 ($75 for international students). *Expenses: Tuition:* Full-time $15,570; part-time $865 per credit hour. Tuition and fees vary according to degree level and program. *Financial support:* Scholarships/grants and unspecified assistantships available. Financial award applicants required to submit FAFSA. *Faculty research:* Facilitative learning styles, leadership, student assessment, interactive multimedia inclusion, learning organizations and strategic change. *Unit head:* Dr. Deborah Boyd, Director of Graduate Studies, 615-966-6263, E-mail: deborah.boyd@lipscomb.edu. *Application contact:* Kristin Baese, Director of Enrollment and Outreach, 615-966-7628 Ext. 6081, Fax: 615-966-5173, E-mail: kristin.baese@lipscomb.edu.
Website: http://www.lipscomb.edu/education/graduate-programs.

Long Island University–LIU Brooklyn, School of Education, Department of Teaching and Learning, Program in Computers in Education, Brooklyn, NY 11201-8423. Offers MS. *Degree requirements:* For master's, thesis optional. *Entrance requirements:* For master's, 2 letters of recommendation. Additional exam requirements/recommendations for international students: Required—TOEFL (minimum score 500 paper-based).

Long Island University–LIU Post, School of Education, Department of Educational Technology, Brookville, NY 11548-1300. Offers computers in education (MS). Part-time and evening/weekend programs available. *Degree requirements:* For master's, research project. *Entrance requirements:* For master's, interview; minimum GPA of 2.75 in major, 2.5 overall. Electronic applications accepted. *Faculty research:* Desktop publishing, higher-order thinking skills, interactive learning environments.

Longwood University, College of Graduate and Professional Studies, College of Education and Human Services, Farmville, VA 23909. Offers education (MS), including algebra and middle school math, counselor education, elementary and middle school math, elementary education, elementary education initial licensure, health and physical education, school librarianship, special education general curriculum, special education initial licensure; social work and communication sciences and disorders (MS). *Accreditation:* NCATE. Part-time and evening/weekend programs available. *Faculty:* 28 full-time (15 women), 9 part-time/adjunct (7 women). *Students:* 86 full-time (80 women), 187 part-time (173 women); includes 38 minority (26 Black or African American, non-Hispanic/Latino; 1 Asian, non-Hispanic/Latino; 5 Hispanic/Latino; 1 Native Hawaiian or other Pacific Islander, non-Hispanic/Latino; 5 Two or more races, non-Hispanic/Latino). 98 applicants, 89% accepted, 85 enrolled. In 2013, 132 master's awarded. *Degree requirements:* For master's, comprehensive exam (for some programs), thesis optional, professional portfolio, internship, clinical experience, or practicum. *Entrance requirements:* For master's, bachelor's degree from regionally-accredited institution, 2 recommendations, 500-word personal essay, official transcripts, minimum GPA of 2.75, valid teaching license (for some programs), passing Praxis I scores for initial teaching licensure programs. Additional exam requirements/recommendations for international students: Required—TOEFL (minimum score 570 paper-based), IELTS (minimum score 6.5). *Application deadline:* For fall admission, 5/1 priority date for domestic students; for spring admission, 10/1 priority date for domestic students; for summer admission, 2/1 priority date for domestic students. Applications are processed on a rolling basis. Application fee: $50. Electronic applications accepted. *Expenses:* Tuition, state resident: full-time $7506; part-time $327 per credit hour. Tuition, nonresident: full-time $17,100; part-time $837 per credit hour. Tuition and fees vary according to course load and campus/location. *Financial support:* Career-related internships or fieldwork and Federal Work-Study available. Financial award applicants required to submit FAFSA. *Unit head:* Dr. Peggy L. Tarpley, Chair of the Department of Education and Special Education, 434-395-2337, E-mail: tarpleypl@longwood.edu. *Application contact:* College of Graduate and Professional Studies, 434-395-2380, Fax: 434-395-2750, E-mail: graduate@longwood.edu.
Website: http://www.longwood.edu/cehs/.

Louisiana State University and Agricultural & Mechanical College, Graduate School, College of Human Sciences and Education, Department of Educational Theory, Policy and Practice, Baton Rouge, LA 70803. Offers counseling (M Ed, MA, Ed S); educational administration (M Ed, MA, PhD, Ed S); educational technology (MA); elementary education (M Ed, MAT); higher education (PhD); research methodology (PhD); secondary education (M Ed, MAT). PhD programs offered jointly with Louisiana State University in Shreveport. *Accreditation:* ACA (one or more programs are accredited); NCATE. Part-time and evening/weekend programs available. *Faculty:* 39 full-time (22 women). *Students:* 185 full-time (136 women), 177 part-time (140 women); includes 110 minority (90 Black or African American, non-Hispanic/Latino; 1 American Indian or Alaska Native, non-Hispanic/Latino; 5 Asian, non-Hispanic/Latino; 9 Hispanic/Latino; 5 Two or more races, non-Hispanic/Latino), 5 international. Average age 31. 167 applicants, 66% accepted, 76 enrolled. In 2013, 134 master's, 23 doctorates, 17 other advanced degrees awarded. Terminal master's awarded for partial completion of doctoral program. *Degree requirements:* For doctorate, thesis/dissertation; for Ed S, thesis optional. *Entrance requirements:* For master's and doctorate, GRE General Test, minimum GPA of 3.0. Additional exam requirements/recommendations for international students: Required—TOEFL (minimum score 550 paper-based; 79 IBT), IELTS (minimum score 6.5), or PTE (minimum score 59). *Application deadline:* For fall admission, 1/25 priority date for domestic students, 5/15 for international students; for spring admission, 10/15 for international students. Applications are processed on a rolling basis. Application fee: $50 ($70 for international students). Electronic applications

accepted. *Financial support:* In 2013–14, 253 students received support, including 5 fellowships (averaging $32,204 per year), 27 research assistantships with full and partial tuition reimbursements available (averaging $10,199 per year), 68 teaching assistantships with full and partial tuition reimbursements available (averaging $12,316 per year); career-related internships or fieldwork, Federal Work-Study, institutionally sponsored loans, health care benefits, and unspecified assistantships also available. Support available to part-time students. Financial award applicants required to submit FAFSA. *Faculty research:* Literary, curriculum studies, science education, K-12 leadership, higher education. *Total annual research expenditures:* $735,835. *Unit head:* Dr. Earl Cheek, Jr., Chair, 225-578-1258, Fax: 225-578-2267, E-mail: echeek@lsu.edu. *Application contact:* Dr. Kristin Gansle, Graduate Coordinator, 225-578-6780, Fax: 225-578-2267, E-mail: kgansle@lsu.edu.

Loyola University Chicago, School of Education, Program in Teaching and Learning, Chicago, IL 60660. Offers behavior intervention specialist (M Ed); elementary education (M Ed); English as a second language (Certificate); English language teaching and learning (M Ed); math education (M Ed); reading specialist (M Ed); reading teacher endorsement (Certificate); school technology (M Ed); science education (M Ed); secondary education (M Ed); special education (M Ed). *Accreditation:* NCATE. *Faculty:* 23 full-time (16 women), 49 part-time/adjunct (42 women). *Students:* 109. Average age 28. 104 applicants, 71% accepted, 44 enrolled. In 2013, 39 master's awarded. *Degree requirements:* For master's, comprehensive exam. *Entrance requirements:* For master's, Illinois Basic Skills Test, 3 letters of recommendation, minimum GPA of 3.0, resume. Additional exam requirements/recommendations for international students: Required—TOEFL (minimum score 550 paper-based; 79 iBT). *Application deadline:* For fall admission, 7/1 priority date for domestic and international students; for spring admission, 11/1 priority date for domestic and international students; for summer admission, 4/1 for domestic and international students. Applications are processed on a rolling basis. Application fee: $50. Electronic applications accepted. Application fee is waived when completed online. *Expenses: Tuition:* Full-time $16,740; part-time $930 per credit. *Required fees:* $135 per semester. *Financial support:* In 2013–14, 58 fellowships with partial tuition reimbursements were awarded; research assistantships, teaching assistantships, institutionally sponsored loans, scholarships/grants, and unspecified assistantships also available. Support available to part-time students. Financial award application deadline: 2/1; financial award applicants required to submit FAFSA. *Faculty research:* Positive behavior support, school reform, school improvement. *Unit head:* Dr. Ann Marie Ryan, Director, 312-915-7027, E-mail: aryan3@luc.edu. *Application contact:* Marie Rosin-Dittmar, Information Contact, 312-915-6800, E-mail: schleduc@luc.edu.

Loyola University Maryland, Graduate Programs, School of Education, Program in Educational Technology, Baltimore, MD 21210-2699. Offers M Ed, MA. Part-time programs available. *Degree requirements:* For master's, thesis. *Entrance requirements:* For master's, transcript, essay. Additional exam requirements/recommendations for international students: Required—TOEFL (minimum score 550 paper-based). Electronic applications accepted.

Marlboro College, Graduate and Professional Studies, Program in Teaching with Technology, Brattleboro, VT 05301. Offers MAT, Certificate. Part-time and evening/weekend programs available. Postbaccalaureate distance learning degree programs offered (minimal on-campus study). *Faculty:* 1 full-time (0 women), 10 part-time/adjunct (7 women). *Students:* 2 full-time (1 woman), 19 part-time (13 women). Average age 44. 6 applicants, 67% accepted, 2 enrolled. In 2013, 11 master's awarded. *Degree requirements:* For master's, 30 credits including capstone project. *Entrance requirements:* For master's, letter of intent, 2 letters of recommendation, transcripts. *Application deadline:* For fall admission, 7/1 priority date for domestic students; for winter admission, 11/1 priority date for domestic students; for spring admission, 3/1 priority date for domestic students. Applications are processed on a rolling basis. Application fee: $0. Electronic applications accepted. *Expenses: Tuition:* Part-time $685 per credit. Tuition and fees vary according to course load and program. *Financial support:* Applicants required to submit FAFSA. *Unit head:* Caleb Clark, Degree Chair, 802-258-9207, Fax: 802-258-9201, E-mail: cclark@marlboro.edu. *Application contact:* Matthew Livingston, Director of Graduate Admissions, 802-258-9209, Fax: 802-258-9201, E-mail: mlivingston@marlboro.edu.
Website: https://www.marlboro.edu/academics/graduate/mat.

Massachusetts College of Liberal Arts, Graduate Programs, North Adams, MA 01247-4100. Offers business (MBA); educational administration (M Ed); educational leadership (CAGS); instruction and curriculum (M Ed); instructional technology (M Ed); physical education and health (M Ed); reading (M Ed); special education (M Ed). Part-time and evening/weekend programs available. *Degree requirements:* For master's, thesis. *Entrance requirements:* For master's, writing sample.

McDaniel College, Graduate and Professional Studies, Program in School Librarianship, Westminster, MD 21157-4390. Offers MS. Part-time and evening/weekend programs available. *Degree requirements:* For master's, comprehensive exam, thesis optional. *Entrance requirements:* For master's, GRE General Test, MAT, or NTE/PRAXIS I, 3 letters of reference. Additional exam requirements/recommendations for international students: Required—TOEFL.

McNeese State University, Doré School of Graduate Studies, Burton College of Education, Office of Graduate Education Programs, Program in Educational Leadership, Lake Charles, LA 70609. Offers educational leadership (M Ed, Ed S); educational technology (Ed S). Evening/weekend programs available. *Degree requirements:* For Ed S, comprehensive exam. *Entrance requirements:* For master's, GRE, teaching certificate, 3 years of full-time teaching experience; for Ed S, teaching certificate, 3 years of teaching experience, 1 year of administration or supervision experience, master's degree with 12 semester hours in education.

McNeese State University, Doré School of Graduate Studies, Burton College of Education, Office of Graduate Education Programs, Program in Educational Technology Leadership, Lake Charles, LA 70609. Offers M Ed. Evening/weekend programs available. *Entrance requirements:* For master's, GRE, teaching certificate.

McNeese State University, Doré School of Graduate Studies, Burton College of Education, Office of Graduate Education Programs, Program in Instructional Technology, Lake Charles, LA 70609. Offers MS. Evening/weekend programs available. *Entrance requirements:* For master's, GRE.

Memorial University of Newfoundland, School of Graduate Studies, Faculty of Education, St. John's, NL A1C 5S7, Canada. Offers counseling psychology (M Ed); curriculum, teaching, and learning studies (M Ed); education (PhD); educational leadership studies (M Ed); information technology (M Ed); post-secondary studies (M Ed, Diploma), including health professional education (Diploma). Part-time programs available. *Degree requirements:* For master's, thesis optional, internship, paper folio, project; for doctorate, comprehensive exam, thesis/dissertation, thesis seminar, oral defense of thesis. *Entrance requirements:* For master's, undergraduate degree with at least 2nd class standing, 1-2 years work experience; for doctorate, minimum A average in graduate course work, MA in education, 2 years professional experience; for Diploma, 2nd class degree, 2 years of work experience with adult learners, appropriate academic qualifications and work experience in a health-related field. Electronic applications accepted. *Faculty research:* Critical thinking, literacy, cognitive studies and counseling, educational change, technology in instruction.

Miami University, College of Education, Health and Society, Department of Educational Psychology, Oxford, OH 45056. Offers educational psychology (M Ed); instructional design and technology (M Ed, MA); school psychology (MS, Ed S); special education (M Ed, MA). *Accreditation:* NCATE. *Students:* 45 full-time (35 women), 41 part-time (31 women); includes 8 minority (1 Black or African American, non-Hispanic/Latino; 1 American Indian or Alaska Native, non-Hispanic/Latino; 5 Asian, non-Hispanic/Latino; 1 Two or more races, non-Hispanic/Latino), 18 international. Average age 27. In 2013, 79 master's awarded. *Entrance requirements:* For degree, GRE General Test or MAT. Additional exam requirements/recommendations for international students: Recommended—TOEFL (minimum score 80 iBT), IELTS (minimum score 6.5), TSE (minimum score 54). Application fee: $50. Electronic applications accepted. *Expenses:* Tuition, state resident: full-time $12,634; part-time $526 per credit hour. Tuition, nonresident: full-time $27,892; part-time $1162 per credit hour. Part-time tuition and fees vary according to course load, campus/location and program. *Financial support:* Fellowships with full tuition reimbursements, research assistantships with full tuition reimbursements, teaching assistantships with full tuition reimbursements, career-related internships or fieldwork, Federal Work-Study, health care benefits, and unspecified assistantships available. Financial award application deadline: 2/15; financial award applicants required to submit FAFSA. *Unit head:* Dr. Susan Mosley-Howard, Chair, 513-529-6621, E-mail: edp@miamioh.edu. *Application contact:* 513-529-6621, E-mail: edp@miamioh.edu.
Website: http://www.MiamiOH.edu/EDP.

Michigan State University, The Graduate School, College of Education, Department of Counseling, Educational Psychology and Special Education, East Lansing, MI 48824. Offers counseling (MA); educational psychology and educational technology (PhD); educational technology (MA); measurement and quantitative methods (PhD); rehabilitation counseling (MA); rehabilitation counselor education (PhD); school psychology (MA, PhD, Ed S); special education (MA, PhD). *Accreditation:* APA (one or more programs are accredited); CORE (one or more programs are accredited). Part-time programs available. *Entrance requirements:* Additional exam requirements/recommendations for international students: Required—TOEFL. Electronic applications accepted.

MidAmerica Nazarene University, Graduate Studies in Education, Olathe, KS 66062-1899. Offers ESOL (M Ed); professional teaching (M Ed); special education (MA); technology enhanced teaching (M Ed). *Accreditation:* NCATE. Part-time and evening/weekend programs available. Postbaccalaureate distance learning degree programs offered (no on-campus study). *Degree requirements:* For master's, thesis or alternative, creative project, technology leadership practicum. *Entrance requirements:* For master's, minimum undergraduate GPA of 2.8, 2 years of teaching experience. *Expenses:* Contact institution.

Middle Tennessee State University, College of Graduate Studies, College of Education, Department of Educational Leadership, Program in Curriculum and Instruction, Murfreesboro, TN 37132. Offers curriculum and instruction (M Ed, Ed S); English as a second language (M Ed, Ed S); secondary education (M Ed); technology and curriculum design (Ed S). *Accreditation:* NCATE. Part-time and evening/weekend programs available. Postbaccalaureate distance learning degree programs offered. *Faculty:* 22 full-time (11 women), 22 part-time/adjunct (12 women). *Degree requirements:* For master's, comprehensive exam; for Ed S, comprehensive exam, thesis or alternative. *Entrance requirements:* For master's and Ed S, GRE, MAT or PRAXIS. Additional exam requirements/recommendations for international students: Required—TOEFL (minimum score 525 paper-based; 71 iBT) or IELTS (minimum score 6). *Application deadline:* For fall admission, 6/1 for domestic and international students. Applications are processed on a rolling basis. Application fee: $25 ($30 for international students). Electronic applications accepted. *Financial support:* Tuition waivers available. Support available to part-time students. Financial award application deadline: 5/1. *Unit head:* Dr. James Huffman, Chair, 615-898-2331, Fax: 615-898-2859, E-mail: jim.huffman@mtsu.edu. *Application contact:* Dr. Michael D. Allen, Vice Provost for Research and Dean, 615-898-2840, Fax: 615-904-8020, E-mail: michael.allen@mtsu.edu.

Midwestern State University, Graduate School, West College of Education, Programs in Educational Leadership and Technology, Wichita Falls, TX 76308. Offers bilingual education/English language learners (M Ed); educational leadership (M Ed); educational technology (M Ed). Part-time and evening/weekend programs available. *Degree requirements:* For master's, comprehensive exam. *Entrance requirements:* For master's, GRE General Test or MAT. Additional exam requirements/recommendations for international students: Required—TOEFL (minimum score 550 paper-based). *Application deadline:* For fall admission, 7/1 priority date for domestic students, 4/1 for international students; for spring admission, 11/1 priority date for domestic students, 8/1 for international students. Applications are processed on a rolling basis. Application fee: $35 ($50 for international students). Electronic applications accepted. *Expenses:* Tuition, state resident: full-time $3627; part-time $201.50 per credit hour. Tuition, nonresident: full-time $10,899; part-time $605.50 per credit hour. *Required fees:* $1357. *Financial support:* Career-related internships or fieldwork, Federal Work-Study, institutionally sponsored loans, scholarships/grants, tuition waivers (partial), and unspecified assistantships available. Support available to part-time students. Financial award application deadline: 3/1; financial award applicants required to submit FAFSA. *Faculty research:* Role of the principal in the twenty-first century, culturally proficient leadership, human diversity, immigration, teacher collaboration. *Unit head:* Dr. Pamela Whitehouse, Graduate Coordinator, 940-397-4139, Fax: 940-397-4694, E-mail: pamela.whitehouse@mwsu.edu. *Application contact:* Dr. Pamela Whitehouse, Graduate Coordinator, 940-397-4139, Fax: 940-397-4694, E-mail: pamela.whitehouse@mwsu.edu.
Website: http://www.mwsu.edu/academics/education/.

Minnesota State University Mankato, College of Graduate Studies, College of Education, Department of Educational Studies: K–12 and Secondary Programs, Program in Library Media Education, Mankato, MN 56001. Offers MS, Certificate. *Accreditation:* NCATE. Part-time programs available. *Students:* 3 full-time (2 women), 16 part-time (14 women). *Degree requirements:* For master's, comprehensive exam, thesis or alternative; for Certificate, comprehensive exam, thesis. *Entrance requirements:* For master's, GRE General Test (if GPA less than 3.0), minimum GPA of 3.0 during previous 2 years; for Certificate, minimum GPA of 3.0. Additional exam requirements/recommendations for international students: Required—TOEFL. *Application deadline:* For fall admission, 7/1 priority date for domestic students; for spring admission, 11/1 for domestic students. Applications are processed on a rolling basis. Application fee: $40. Electronic applications accepted. *Financial support:* Research assistantships with full tuition reimbursements, teaching assistantships with full tuition reimbursements, career-related internships or fieldwork, Federal Work-Study, and institutionally sponsored loans available. Support available to part-time students. Financial award application deadline: 3/15; financial award applicants required to submit

FAFSA. *Unit head:* Dr. Kitty Foord, Graduate Coordinator, 507-389-1965. *Application contact:* 507-389-2321, E-mail: grad@mnsu.edu. Website: http://ed.mnsu.edu/ksp/.

Misericordia University, College of Professional Studies and Social Sciences, Program in Education, Dallas, PA 18612-1098. Offers instructional technology (MS); reading specialist (MS); special education (MS). Part-time and evening/weekend programs available. *Faculty:* 1 full-time (0 women), 12 part-time/adjunct (8 women). *Students:* 44 part-time (35 women); includes 1 minority (Hispanic/Latino). Average age 32. In 2013, 24 master's awarded. *Entrance requirements:* For master's, minimum undergraduate GPA of 3.0. Additional exam requirements/recommendations for international students: Required—TOEFL. *Application deadline:* Applications are processed on a rolling basis. Application fee: $35. Electronic applications accepted. *Expenses: Tuition:* Full-time $14,450; part-time $680 per credit. Tuition and fees vary according to degree level. *Financial support:* In 2013–14, 11 students received support. Scholarships/grants available. Support available to part-time students. Financial award application deadline: 6/30; financial award applicants required to submit FAFSA. *Unit head:* Dr. Steven Broskoske, Associate Professor, Education Department, 570-674-6761, E-mail: sbroskos@misericordia.edu. *Application contact:* David Pasquini, Assistant Director of Admissions, 570-674-8183, Fax: 570-674-6232, E-mail: dpasquin@misericordia.edu. Website: http://www.misericordia.edu/ misericordia_pg.cfm?page_id=387&subcat_id=108.

Mississippi State University, College of Education, Department of Instructional Systems and Workforce Development, Mississippi State, MS 39762. Offers education (Ed S), including technology; instructional systems and workforce development (PhD); instructional technology (MSIT); technology (MS). *Faculty:* 8 full-time (5 women). *Students:* 20 full-time (9 women), 68 part-time (56 women); includes 59 minority (57 Black or African American, non-Hispanic/Latino; 2 Two or more races, non-Hispanic/Latino), 1 international. Average age 36. 54 applicants, 37% accepted, 19 enrolled. In 2013, 7 master's, 6 doctorates awarded. *Degree requirements:* For master's, thesis optional, comprehensive oral or written exam; for doctorate, thesis/dissertation, comprehensive oral and written exam; for Ed S, thesis, comprehensive written exam. *Entrance requirements:* For master's, GRE, minimum GPA of 2.75 on undergraduate work, 3.0 on graduate work; for doctorate, GRE, minimum GPA of 3.4 on graduate work; for Ed S, GRE, minimum GPA of 3.2, master's degree. Additional exam requirements/recommendations for international students: Required—TOEFL (minimum score 550 paper-based; 79 iBT); Recommended—IELTS (minimum score 6.5). *Application deadline:* For fall admission, 7/1 for domestic students, 5/1 for international students; for spring admission, 11/1 for domestic students, 9/1 for international students. Applications are processed on a rolling basis. Application fee: $60. Electronic applications accepted. *Financial support:* In 2013–14, 3 teaching assistantships with full tuition reimbursements (averaging $10,800 per year) were awarded; Federal Work-Study, institutionally sponsored loans, scholarships/grants, and unspecified assistantships also available. Financial award application deadline: 4/1; financial award applicants required to submit FAFSA. *Faculty research:* Computer technology, nontraditional students, interactive video, instructional technology, educational leadership. *Unit head:* Dr. Connie Forde, Professor and Department Head, 662-325-2281, Fax: 662-325-7599, E-mail: cforde@colled.msstate.edu. *Application contact:* Dr. James Adams, Associate Professor and Graduate Coordinator, 662-325-7563, Fax: 662-325-7258, E-mail: jadams@colled.msstate.edu. Website: http://www.iswd.msstate.edu.

Missouri Southern State University, Program in Instructional Technology, Joplin, MO 64801-1595. Offers MS Ed. Program offered jointly with Northwest Missouri State University. *Degree requirements:* For master's, comprehensive exam, research paper. *Entrance requirements:* For master's, GRE (minimum combined score of 700), writing assessment, minimum overall undergraduate GPA of 3.0.

Missouri State University, Graduate College, College of Education, Department of Reading, Foundations, and Technology, Program in Educational Technology, Springfield, MO 65897. Offers MS Ed. Part-time programs available. *Students:* 10 full-time (7 women), 33 part-time (23 women); includes 1 minority (Asian, non-Hispanic/Latino), 6 international. Average age 34. 11 applicants, 91% accepted, 7 enrolled. In 2013, 7 master's awarded. *Degree requirements:* For master's, comprehensive exam, thesis or alternative. *Entrance requirements:* Additional exam requirements/recommendations for international students: Required—TOEFL (minimum score 550 paper-based; 79 iBT). *Application deadline:* For fall admission, 7/20 for domestic students, 5/1 for international students; for spring admission, 12/20 for domestic students, 9/1 for international students. Applications are processed on a rolling basis. Application fee: $35 ($50 for international students). Electronic applications accepted. *Expenses:* Tuition, state resident: full-time $4500; part-time $250 per credit hour. Tuition, nonresident: full-time $9018; part-time $501 per credit hour. *Required fees:* $361 per semester. Tuition and fees vary according to course level, course load and program. *Financial support:* Federal Work-Study, institutionally sponsored loans, scholarships/grants, and unspecified assistantships available. Financial award application deadline: 3/31; financial award applicants required to submit FAFSA. *Unit head:* Dr. Ching-Wen Chang, Program Coordinator, 417-836-5353, E-mail: cchang@missouristate.edu. *Application contact:* Misty Stewart, Coordinator of Graduate Recruitment, 417-836-6079, Fax: 417-836-6200, E-mail: mistystewart@missouristate.edu. Website: http://education.missouristate.edu/rft/.

Montana State University Billings, College of Education, Department of Educational Theory and Practice, Option in Educational Technology, Billings, MT 59101-0298. Offers M Ed. *Accreditation:* NCATE. Part-time programs available. *Degree requirements:* For master's, professional paper or thesis. *Entrance requirements:* For master's, GRE General Test or MAT, minimum GPA of 3.0 (undergraduate), 3.25 (graduate). *Application deadline:* For fall admission, 7/15 for domestic students; for spring admission, 12/1 for domestic students. Applications are processed on a rolling basis. Application fee: $40. *Expenses:* Tuition, state resident: full-time $2653.75; part-time $1718 per semester. Tuition, nonresident: full-time $7015; part-time $4640 per semester. *Required fees:* $2445; $444 per credit. *Financial support:* Teaching assistantships, career-related internships or fieldwork, Federal Work-Study, institutionally sponsored loans, scholarships/grants, tuition waivers (partial), and unspecified assistantships available. Support available to part-time students. Financial award application deadline: 5/1; financial award applicants required to submit FAFSA. *Unit head:* Dr. Ken Miller, Chair, 406-657-2034, E-mail: kmiller@msubillings.edu. *Application contact:* David M. Sullivan, Graduate Studies Counselor, 406-657-2053, Fax: 406-657-2299, E-mail: dsullivan@msubillings.edu.

Montclair State University, The Graduate School, College of Education and Human Services, Department of Early Childhood, Elementary and Literacy Education, New Literacies, Digital Technologies and Learning Certificate Program, Montclair, NJ 07043-1624. Offers Certificate. Part-time and evening/weekend programs available. *Degree requirements:* For Certificate, comprehensive exam. *Entrance requirements:* Additional exam requirements/recommendations for international students: Required—TOEFL (minimum score 83 iBT), IELTS (minimum score 6.5). Electronic applications accepted.

Morehead State University, Graduate Programs, College of Education, Department of Foundational and Graduate Studies in Education, Morehead, KY 40351. Offers adult and higher education (MA, Ed S); certified professional counselor (Ed S); counseling P-12 (MA); curriculum and instruction (Ed S); educational technology (MA Ed); instructional leadership (Ed S); school administration (MA); school counseling (Ed S); teacher leader business and marketing content (MA Ed); teacher leader business and marketing technology (MA Ed); teacher leader educational technology (MA Ed); teacher leader English (MA Ed); teacher leader gifted education (MA Ed); teacher leader IECE certification (MA Ed); teacher leader interdisciplinary education P-5 (MA Ed); teacher leader middle grades (MA Ed); teacher leader non IECE certification (MA Ed); teacher leader reading/writing - non-certification (MA Ed); teacher leader reading/writing certification (MA Ed); teacher leader school communication - certification (MA Ed); teacher leader school communication - non-certification (MA Ed); teacher leader social studies (MA Ed); teacher leader special education (MA Ed). *Accreditation:* NCATE. Part-time and evening/weekend programs available. *Degree requirements:* For master's, thesis optional, oral and/or written comprehensive exams; for Ed S, thesis, oral exam. *Entrance requirements:* For master's, GRE General Test, minimum overall undergraduate GPA of 2.5; for Ed S, GRE General Test, interview, master's degree, minimum GPA of 3.5, work experience. Additional exam requirements/recommendations for international students: Required—TOEFL (minimum score 500 paper-based). Electronic applications accepted. *Faculty research:* Character education, school accountability, computer applications for school administrators.

National Louis University, National College of Education, Chicago, IL 60603. Offers administration and supervision (M Ed, Ed D, CAS, Ed S); curriculum and instruction (M Ed, MS Ed, CAS); early childhood administration (M Ed, CAS); early childhood education (M Ed, MAT, MS Ed, CAS); education (Ed D); educational psychology/human learning and development (M Ed, MS Ed, CAS, Ed S); elementary education (MAT); interdisciplinary curriculum and instruction (M Ed); mathematics education (M Ed, MS Ed, CAS); reading and language (M Ed, MS Ed, CAS); school psychology (M Ed, Ed S); science education (M Ed, MS Ed, CAS); secondary education (MAT); special education (M Ed, MAT, CAS); technology in education (M Ed, CAS). *Accreditation:* NCATE. Part-time and evening/weekend programs available. *Degree requirements:* For doctorate, comprehensive exam, thesis/dissertation. *Entrance requirements:* For master's, MAT or GRE, minimum GPA of 3.0; for doctorate, GRE General Test, minimum GPA of 3.25, interview, resume, writing sample, 4 recommendations. Additional exam requirements/recommendations for international students: Required—TOEFL (minimum score 550 paper-based; 79 iBT).

National University, Academic Affairs, School of Education, La Jolla, CA 92037-1011. Offers applied behavior analysis (Certificate); applied school leadership (MS); autism (Certificate); best practices (Certificate); e-teaching and learning (Certificate); early childhood education (Certificate); education (MA), including best practices (M Ed, MA), e-teaching and learning (M Ed, MA), education technology, teacher leadership (M Ed, MA), teaching and learning in a global society (M Ed, MA), teaching mathematics (M Ed, MA); education with preliminary multiple or single subject (M Ed), including best practices (M Ed, MA), e-teaching and learning (M Ed, MA), educational technology (M Ed, MA), teacher leadership (M Ed, MA), teaching and learning in a global society (M Ed, MA), teaching mathematics (M Ed, MA); educational administration (MS); educational and instructional technology (MS); educational counseling (MS); educational technology (Certificate); higher education administration (MS); innovative school leadership (MS); instructional leadership (MS); juvenile justice special education (MS); reading (Certificate); school psychology (MS); special education (MS), including deaf and hard-of-hearing, mild/moderate disabilities, moderate/severe disabilities; teacher leadership (Certificate); teaching (MA), including applied behavioral analysis, autism, best practices (M Ed, MA), e-teaching and learning (M Ed, MA), early childhood education, educational technology (M Ed, MA), reading, special education, teacher leadership (M Ed, MA), teaching and learning in a global society (M Ed, MA), teaching mathematics (M Ed, MA); teaching mathematics (Certificate). Part-time and evening/weekend programs available. Postbaccalaureate distance learning degree programs offered (no on-campus study). *Faculty:* 72 full-time (43 women), 287 part-time/adjunct (170 women). *Students:* 2,433 full-time (1,744 women), 2,017 part-time (1,371 women); includes 1,834 minority (358 Black or African American, non-Hispanic/Latino; 15 American Indian or Alaska Native, non-Hispanic/Latino; 250 Asian, non-Hispanic/Latino; 1,056 Hispanic/Latino; 29 Native Hawaiian or other Pacific Islander, non-Hispanic/Latino; 126 Two or more races, non-Hispanic/Latino), 1 international. Average age 34. 1,339 applicants, 100% accepted, 1035 enrolled. In 2013, 1,662 master's awarded. *Degree requirements:* For master's, thesis (for some programs). *Entrance requirements:* For master's, interview, minimum GPA of 2.5. Additional exam requirements/recommendations for international students: Required—TOEFL (minimum score 550 paper-based; 79 iBT), IELTS (minimum score 6). *Application deadline:* Applications are processed on a rolling basis. Application fee: $60 ($65 for international students). Electronic applications accepted. *Expenses: Tuition:* Full-time $13,824; part-time $1728 per course. One-time fee: $160. *Financial support:* Career-related internships or fieldwork, institutionally sponsored loans, scholarships/grants, and tuition waivers (partial) available. Support available to part-time students. Financial award application deadline: 6/30. *Faculty research:* Teacher education, special education, educational effectiveness, teaching abroad, school counseling. *Unit head:* School of Education, 800-628-8648, E-mail: soe@nu.edu. *Application contact:* Louis Cruz, Interim Vice President for Enrollment Services, 800-628-8648, E-mail: advisor@nu.edu. Website: http://www.nu.edu/OurPrograms/SchoolOfEducation.html.

Nazareth College of Rochester, Graduate Studies, Department of Education, Program in Educational Technology/Computer Education, Rochester, NY 14618-3790. Offers MS Ed. Part-time and evening/weekend programs available. *Entrance requirements:* For master's, minimum GPA of 3.0.

New Jersey City University, Graduate Studies and Continuing Education, Debra Cannon Partridge Wolfe College of Education, Concentration in Educational Technology, Jersey City, NJ 07305-1597. Offers educational technology (MA); educational technology leadership (Ed D). *Accreditation:* NCATE. Part-time and evening/weekend programs available. Postbaccalaureate distance learning degree programs offered (minimal on-campus study). *Faculty:* 4 full-time (2 women), 3 part-time/adjunct (1 woman). *Students:* 120 part-time (89 women); includes 31 minority (15 Black or African American, non-Hispanic/Latino; 3 Asian, non-Hispanic/Latino; 13 Hispanic/Latino). Average age 39. In 2013, 46 master's awarded. *Degree requirements:* For master's, internship. *Entrance requirements:* Additional exam requirements/recommendations for international students: Required—TOEFL (minimum score 61 iBT). *Application deadline:* For fall admission, 8/1 priority date for domestic students; for spring admission, 12/1 for domestic students. Applications are processed on a rolling basis. Application fee: $0. *Expenses: Tuition, area resident:* Part-time $527.90 per credit. Tuition, nonresident: part-time $947.75 per credit. *Financial support:* Unspecified assistantships available. *Unit head:* Dr. Cordelia Twomey, Chairperson, 201-200-3421, E-mail: ctwomey@njcu.edu. *Application contact:* Dr. William Bajor, Dean of Graduate Studies, 201-200-3409, Fax: 201-200-3411, E-mail: wbajor@njcu.edu.

New York Institute of Technology, School of Education, Department of Educational Leadership, Old Westbury, NY 11568-8000. Offers school leadership and technology

(Advanced Diploma). Part-time and evening/weekend programs available. *Faculty:* 11 part-time/adjunct (7 women). *Students:* 13 part-time (11 women); includes 3 minority (all Black or African American, non-Hispanic/Latino). Average age 37. 8 applicants, 100% accepted, 6 enrolled. In 2013, 14 Advanced Diplomas awarded. *Degree requirements:* For Advanced Diploma, internship. *Entrance requirements:* For degree, 3 years of full-time teaching experience, permanent teacher certification in New York state. Additional exam requirements/recommendations for international students: Required—TOEFL (minimum score 550 paper-based; 79 iBT), IELTS (minimum score 6). *Application deadline:* For fall admission, 7/1 for domestic students, 6/1 for international students; for spring admission, 12/1 for domestic and international students. Application fee: $50. *Expenses: Tuition:* Full-time $18,900; part-time $1050 per credit. *Financial support:* Career-related internships or fieldwork, scholarships/grants, health care benefits, tuition waivers, and unspecified assistantships available. Support available to part-time students. Financial award applicants required to submit FAFSA. *Unit head:* Dr. Sarah McPherson, Dean, 516-686-1053, Fax: 516-686-7655, E-mail: smcphers@nyit.edu. *Application contact:* Alice Dolitsky, Director, Graduate Admissions, 516-686-7520, Fax: 516-686-1116, E-mail: nyitgrad@nyit.edu.
Website: http://www.nyit.edu/education/leadership.

New York Institute of Technology, School of Education, Department of Instructional Technology, Old Westbury, NY 11568-8000. Offers computers in education (Advanced Certificate); distance learning (Advanced Certificate); emerging technologies for training (Advanced Certificate); instructional design for global e-learning (Advanced Certificate); instructional technology (MS); virtual education (Advanced Certificate). Part-time and evening/weekend programs available. Postbaccalaureate distance learning degree programs offered (minimal on-campus study). *Faculty:* 6 full-time (3 women), 38 part-time/adjunct (20 women). *Students:* 10 full-time (8 women), 111 part-time (74 women); includes 30 minority (12 Black or African American, non-Hispanic/Latino; 4 Asian, non-Hispanic/Latino; 13 Hispanic/Latino; 1 Two or more races, non-Hispanic/Latino), 3 international. Average age 32. 58 applicants, 76% accepted, 31 enrolled. In 2013, 67 master's, 1 other advanced degree awarded. *Degree requirements:* For master's, thesis. *Entrance requirements:* For master's, minimum QPA of 3.0; for Advanced Certificate, master's degree, minimum GPA of 3.0, 3 years of teaching experience, New York teaching certificate, 2 letters of recommendation. Additional exam requirements/recommendations for international students: Required—TOEFL (minimum score 550 paper-based; 79 iBT), IELTS (minimum score 6). *Application deadline:* For fall admission, 7/1 priority date for domestic students, 6/1 for international students; for spring admission, 12/1 priority date for domestic students, 12/1 for international students. Applications are processed on a rolling basis. Application fee: $50. Electronic applications accepted. *Expenses: Tuition:* Full-time $18,900; part-time $1050 per credit. *Financial support:* Research assistantships with partial tuition reimbursements, career-related internships or fieldwork, scholarships/grants, health care benefits, tuition waivers (full and partial), and unspecified assistantships available. Support available to part-time students. Financial award applicants required to submit FAFSA. *Faculty research:* Integration of information and communication technologies (ICTs) and social media into learning environments, urban K-12 teachers' effective use of technology to enhance student achievement, instructional design for online instruction, STEM education for K-12 teachers, collaborative and performance-based approaches to pedagogy and technology integration in the K-12 classroom, online learning in higher education. *Unit head:* Dr. Sarah McPherson, Department Chairperson, 516-686-1053, Fax: 516-686-7655, E-mail: smcphers@nyit.edu. *Application contact:* Alice Dolitsky, Director, Graduate Admissions, 516-686-7520, Fax: 516-686-1116, E-mail: nyitgrad@nyit.edu.
Website: http://www.nyit.edu/education/instructional_technology.

New York University, Steinhardt School of Culture, Education, and Human Development, Department of Administration, Leadership, and Technology, Program in Educational Communication and Technology, Brooklyn, NY 11201. Offers digital media design for learning (MA, Advanced Certificate); educational communication and technology (PhD); games for learning (MS). Part-time programs available. *Faculty:* 5 full-time (1 woman). *Students:* 40 full-time (27 women), 33 part-time (23 women); includes 21 minority (8 Black or African American, non-Hispanic/Latino; 1 American Indian or Alaska Native, non-Hispanic/Latino; 5 Asian, non-Hispanic/Latino; 5 Hispanic/Latino; 2 Two or more races, non-Hispanic/Latino), 20 international. Average age 41. 111 applicants, 57% accepted, 30 enrolled. In 2013, 12 master's awarded. *Degree requirements:* For master's, thesis (for some programs); for doctorate, thesis/dissertation. *Entrance requirements:* For doctorate, GRE General Test, interview; for Advanced Certificate, master's degree. Additional exam requirements/recommendations for international students: Required—TOEFL (minimum score 100 iBT). *Application deadline:* For fall admission, 12/1 priority date for domestic and international students; for spring admission, 10/1 for domestic and international students. Applications are processed on a rolling basis. Application fee: $75. Electronic applications accepted. *Expenses: Tuition:* Full-time $35,856; part-time $1494 per unit. *Required fees:* $1408; $64 per unit. $473 per term. Tuition and fees vary according to course load and program. *Financial support:* Fellowships with full and partial tuition reimbursements, research assistantships with full and partial tuition reimbursements, teaching assistantships with partial tuition reimbursements, career-related internships or fieldwork, Federal Work-Study, institutionally sponsored loans, scholarships/grants, tuition waivers (partial), and unspecified assistantships available. Support available to part-time students. Financial award application deadline: 2/1; financial award applicants required to submit FAFSA. *Faculty research:* Digital design for learning, critical evaluation of games, multimedia, cognitive science, individual differences in multimedia learning, serious games. *Unit head:* Prof. Jan L. Plass, Director, 212-998-5520, Fax: 212-995-4047, E-mail: jan.plass@nyu.edu. *Application contact:* 212-998-5030, Fax: 212-995-4328, E-mail: steinhardt.gradadmissions@nyu.edu.
Website: http://steinhardt.nyu.edu/alt/ect.

North Carolina Agricultural and Technical State University, School of Graduate Studies, School of Education, Department of Curriculum and Instruction, Greensboro, NC 27411. Offers elementary education (MA Ed); instructional technology (MS); reading education (MA Ed); teaching (MAT). *Accreditation:* NCATE. Part-time and evening/weekend programs available. *Degree requirements:* For master's, comprehensive exam, qualifying exam. *Entrance requirements:* For master's, GRE General Test, minimum GPA of 3.0.

North Carolina Central University, School of Education, Program in Educational Technology, Durham, NC 27707-3129. Offers MA. *Accreditation:* NCATE. Part-time and evening/weekend programs available. *Degree requirements:* For master's, comprehensive exam, thesis or alternative. *Entrance requirements:* For master's, GRE, minimum GPA of 3.0 in major, 2.5 overall. Additional exam requirements/recommendations for international students: Required—TOEFL. *Faculty research:* Role of media in school libraries, media and implications for educational gerontology.

North Carolina Central University, School of Education, Program in Instructional Technology, Durham, NC 27707-3129. Offers M Ed.

North Carolina State University, Graduate School, College of Education, Department of Curriculum and Instruction, Program in Instructional Technology, Raleigh, NC 27695. Offers M Ed, MS. *Entrance requirements:* For master's, MAT or GRE, minimum GPA of 3.0, 3 letters of reference.

North Carolina State University, Graduate School, College of Education, Department of Mathematics, Science, and Technology Education, Program in Technology Education, Raleigh, NC 27695. Offers M Ed, MS, Ed D. *Degree requirements:* For master's, thesis (for some programs); for doctorate, thesis/dissertation. *Entrance requirements:* For master's, GRE or MAT; for doctorate, GRE General Test or MAT, minimum GPA of 3.0, interview. Electronic applications accepted.

Northeastern State University, College of Education, Program in Library Media and Information Technology, Tahlequah, OK 74464-2399. Offers MS Ed. *Faculty:* 16 full-time (12 women), 7 part-time/adjunct (2 women). *Students:* 1 full-time (0 women), 32 part-time (28 women); includes 10 minority (4 American Indian or Alaska Native, non-Hispanic/Latino; 1 Hispanic/Latino; 5 Two or more races, non-Hispanic/Latino). Average age 34. In 2013, 32 master's awarded. *Entrance requirements:* Additional exam requirements/recommendations for international students: Required—TOEFL. *Application deadline:* For fall admission, 7/1 for domestic and international students; for spring admission, 11/1 for domestic and international students. Applications are processed on a rolling basis. Application fee: $25. Electronic applications accepted. *Expenses:* Tuition, state resident: full-time $3029; part-time $168.25 per credit hour. Tuition, nonresident: full-time $7709; part-time $428.25 per credit hour. *Required fees:* $35.90 per credit hour. *Unit head:* Dr. Barbara Ray, Head, 918-449-6451. *Application contact:* Margie Railey, Administrative Assistant, 918-456-5511 Ext. 2093, Fax: 918-458-2061, E-mail: railey@nsouk.edu.
Website: http://academics.nsuok.edu/education/DegreePrograms/GraduatePrograms/LibraryMediaInformationTechnology.aspx.

Northern Arizona University, Graduate College, College of Education, Department of Educational Specialties, Flagstaff, AZ 86011. Offers autism spectrum disorders (Certificate); bilingual/multicultural education (M Ed), including bilingual education, ESL education; career and technical education (M Ed, Certificate); early childhood special education (M Ed); educational technology (M Ed, Certificate); special education (M Ed). *Faculty:* 32 full-time (21 women), 4 part-time/adjunct (all women). *Students:* 68 full-time (48 women), 158 part-time (119 women); includes 93 minority (6 Black or African American, non-Hispanic/Latino; 29 American Indian or Alaska Native, non-Hispanic/Latino; 4 Asian, non-Hispanic/Latino; 53 Hispanic/Latino; 1 Native Hawaiian or other Pacific Islander, non-Hispanic/Latino), 6 international. Average age 37. 66 applicants, 95% accepted, 38 enrolled. In 2013, 121 master's, 3 Certificates awarded. *Degree requirements:* For master's, comprehensive exam (for some programs), thesis (for some programs). *Entrance requirements:* For master's, minimum GPA of 3.0. Additional exam requirements/recommendations for international students: Required—TOEFL (minimum score 550 paper-based; 80 iBT), IELTS (minimum score 7). *Application deadline:* For fall admission, 3/1 for international students; for spring admission, 9/15 for international students. Applications are processed on a rolling basis. Application fee: $65. Electronic applications accepted. *Financial support:* In 2013–14, 9 teaching assistantships with full tuition reimbursements (averaging $9,698 per year) were awarded. Financial award applicants required to submit FAFSA. *Unit head:* Dr. Laura Sujo-Montes, Chair, 928-523-0892, Fax: 928-523-1929, E-mail: laura.sujo-montes@nau.edu. *Application contact:* Laura Cook, Coordinator, 928-523-5342, Fax: 928-523-8950, E-mail: laura.cook@nau.edu.
Website: http://nau.edu/coe/ed-specialties/.

Northern Illinois University, Graduate School, College of Education, Department of Educational Technology, Research and Assessment, De Kalb, IL 60115-2854. Offers educational research and evaluation (MS); instructional technology (MS Ed, Ed D). Part-time and evening/weekend programs available. *Faculty:* 13 full-time (7 women). *Students:* 49 full-time (32 women), 137 part-time (92 women); includes 34 minority (18 Black or African American, non-Hispanic/Latino; 3 Asian, non-Hispanic/Latino; 9 Hispanic/Latino; 4 Two or more races, non-Hispanic/Latino), 24 international. Average age 40. 53 applicants, 85% accepted, 26 enrolled. In 2013, 40 master's, 4 doctorates awarded. Terminal master's awarded for partial completion of doctoral program. *Degree requirements:* For master's, comprehensive exam, thesis optional; for doctorate, thesis/dissertation, candidacy exam, dissertation defense. *Entrance requirements:* For master's, GRE General Test or MAT, minimum GPA of 2.75; for doctorate, GRE General Test or MAT, minimum undergraduate GPA of 2.75, 3.2 graduate. Additional exam requirements/recommendations for international students: Required—TOEFL (minimum score 550 paper-based). *Application deadline:* For fall admission, 6/1 for domestic students, 5/1 for international students; for spring admission, 11/1 for domestic students, 10/1 for international students. Applications are processed on a rolling basis. Application fee: $40. Electronic applications accepted. *Financial support:* In 2013–14, 5 research assistantships with full tuition reimbursements, 4 teaching assistantships with full tuition reimbursements were awarded; fellowships with full tuition reimbursements, career-related internships or fieldwork, Federal Work-Study, scholarships/grants, tuition waivers (full), and unspecified assistantships also available. Support available to part-time students. Financial award applicants required to submit FAFSA. *Faculty research:* Distance education, Web-based training, copyright assessment during student teaching, instructional software. *Unit head:* Dr. Wei-Chen Hung, Chair, 815-753-9339, E-mail: etra@niu.edu. *Application contact:* Graduate School Office, 815-753-0395, E-mail: gradsch@niu.edu.
Website: http://www.cedu.niu.edu/etra/index.html.

Northern State University, MS Ed Program in Instructional Design in E-learning, Aberdeen, SD 57401-7198. Offers MS Ed. Part-time programs available. Postbaccalaureate distance learning degree programs offered. *Faculty:* 2 full-time (0 women). *Students:* 1 (woman) full-time; minority (Asian, non-Hispanic/Latino). Average age 25. 11 applicants. In 2013, 1 master's awarded. *Degree requirements:* For master's, comprehensive exam, thesis optional. *Entrance requirements:* For master's, minimum GPA of 2.75. Additional exam requirements/recommendations for international students: Required—TOEFL (minimum score 550 paper-based; 78 iBT), IELTS (minimum score 6). *Application deadline:* For fall admission, 8/15 for domestic and international students; for spring admission, 12/15 for domestic and international students. Applications are processed on a rolling basis. Application fee: $35. Electronic applications accepted. *Expenses:* Tuition, state resident: full-time $3634. Tuition, nonresident: full-time $7690. One-time fee: $35 full-time. Part-time tuition and fees vary according to course load, degree level, campus/location and reciprocity agreements. *Financial support:* Career-related internships or fieldwork, Federal Work-Study, institutionally sponsored loans, scholarships/grants, and unspecified assistantships available. Support available to part-time students. Financial award application deadline: 3/1; financial award applicants required to submit FAFSA. *Unit head:* Dr. Constance Geier, Dean of Education, 605-626-2558, Fax: 605-626-7190, E-mail: connie.geier@northern.edu. *Application contact:* Tammy K. Griffith, Program Assistant, 605-626-2558, Fax: 605-626-7190, E-mail: tammy.griffith@northern.edu.

Northern State University, MS Program in Training and Development in E-learning, Aberdeen, SD 57401-7198. Offers MS. Part-time programs available. Postbaccalaureate distance learning degree programs offered (no on-campus study). *Faculty:* 2 full-time (0 women). *Students:* 1 full-time (0 women); minority (Asian, non-Hispanic/Latino). Average age 25. 2 applicants, 50% accepted, 1 enrolled. In 2013, 4 master's awarded. *Degree requirements:* For master's, comprehensive exam, thesis optional. *Entrance requirements:* For master's, minimum GPA of 2.75. Additional exam

requirements/recommendations for international students: Required—TOEFL (minimum score 550 paper-based; 78 iBT), IELTS (minimum score 6). *Application deadline:* Applications are processed on a rolling basis. Application fee: $35. Electronic applications accepted. *Expenses:* Tuition, state resident: full-time $3634. Tuition, nonresident: full-time $7690. One-time fee: $35 full-time. Part-time tuition and fees vary according to course load, degree level, campus/location and reciprocity agreements. *Financial support:* In 2013–14, 1 student received support. Career-related internships or fieldwork, Federal Work-Study, institutionally sponsored loans, and scholarships/grants available. Support available to part-time students. Financial award application deadline: 3/1; financial award applicants required to submit FAFSA. *Unit head:* Dr. Constance Geier, Dean of Education, 605-626-2558, Fax: 605-626-7190, E-mail: connie.geier@northern.edu. *Application contact:* Tammy K. Griffith, Program Assistant, 605-626-2558, Fax: 605-626-7190, E-mail: tammy.griffith@northern.edu.

Northwest Christian University, School of Education and Counseling, Eugene, OR 97401-3745. Offers clinical mental health counseling (MA); curriculum and instructional technology (M Ed); education (M Ed); school counseling (MA). Part-time and evening/weekend programs available. *Entrance requirements:* For master's, MAT, interview, minimum GPA of 3.0. Electronic applications accepted.

Northwestern State University of Louisiana, Graduate Studies and Research, College of Education and Human Development, Program in Educational Technology Leadership, Natchitoches, LA 71497. Offers M Ed. *Degree requirements:* For master's, comprehensive exam, thesis (for some programs). *Entrance requirements:* For master's, GRE General Test. Additional exam requirements/recommendations for international students: Required—TOEFL. Electronic applications accepted.

Northwestern State University of Louisiana, Graduate Studies and Research, College of Education and Human Development, Programs in Educational Leadership and Instruction, Natchitoches, LA 71497. Offers counseling (Ed S); educational leadership (M Ed, Ed S); educational technology (Ed S); elementary teaching (Ed S); reading (Ed S); secondary teaching (Ed S); special education (Ed S). *Accreditation:* NASAD. *Degree requirements:* For master's, comprehensive exam, thesis (for some programs). *Entrance requirements:* For master's and Ed S, GRE General Test. Additional exam requirements/recommendations for international students: Required—TOEFL. Electronic applications accepted.

Northwestern University, The Graduate School, School of Education and Social Policy, Program in Learning Sciences, Evanston, IL 60208. Offers MA, PhD. Admissions and degrees offered through The Graduate School. Terminal master's awarded for partial completion of doctoral program. *Degree requirements:* For master's, thesis or alternative, portfolio; for doctorate, thesis/dissertation, qualifying exam. *Entrance requirements:* For doctorate, GRE General Test. Additional exam requirements/recommendations for international students: Required—TOEFL (minimum score 600 paper-based; 100 iBT). Electronic applications accepted. *Expenses:* Contact institution. *Faculty research:* Technologically supported learning environments; inquiry-based learning in mathematics, science, and literacy; learning social contexts; cognitive models of learning and problem solving; changing roles for teachers involved in innovative design and practice.

Northwest Missouri State University, Graduate School, College of Arts and Sciences, Department of Mathematics, Computer Science and Information Systems, Program in Teaching Instructional Technology, Maryville, MO 64468-6001. Offers MS Ed. Part-time programs available. *Degree requirements:* For master's, comprehensive exam. *Entrance requirements:* For master's, GRE General Test, minimum GPA of 2.5, teaching certificate, writing sample. Additional exam requirements/recommendations for international students: Required—TOEFL (minimum score 550 paper-based).

Notre Dame de Namur University, Division of Academic Affairs, School of Education and Leadership, Program in Education, Belmont, CA 94002-1908. Offers curriculum and instruction (MA); disciplinary studies (MA); educational technology (MA); multiple subject teaching credential (Certificate); single subject teaching credential (Certificate). Part-time and evening/weekend programs available. *Degree requirements:* For master's, thesis (for some programs). *Entrance requirements:* For master's, CBEST, CSET, valid teaching credential or substantial teaching experience. Additional exam requirements/recommendations for international students: Required—TOEFL (minimum score 550 paper-based; 79 iBT). Electronic applications accepted.

Nova Southeastern University, Abraham S. Fischler School of Education, North Miami Beach, FL 33162. Offers education (MS, Ed D, Ed S); instructional design and diversity education (MS); instructional technology and distance education (MS); speech language pathology (MS, SLPD); teaching and learning (MA). Part-time and evening/weekend programs available. Postbaccalaureate distance learning degree programs offered. *Faculty:* 120 full-time (73 women), 279 part-time/adjunct (208 women). *Students:* 2,970 full-time (2,377 women), 3,619 part-time (2,946 women); includes 3,896 minority (2,352 Black or African American, non-Hispanic/Latino; 21 American Indian or Alaska Native, non-Hispanic/Latino; 90 Asian, non-Hispanic/Latino; 1,348 Hispanic/Latino; 6 Native Hawaiian or other Pacific Islander, non-Hispanic/Latino; 79 Two or more races, non-Hispanic/Latino), 39 international. Average age 40. 2,794 applicants, 53% accepted, 968 enrolled. In 2013, 1,103 master's, 426 doctorates, 349 other advanced degrees awarded. *Degree requirements:* For master's, practicum, internship; for doctorate, thesis/dissertation; for Ed S, thesis, practicum, internship. *Entrance requirements:* For master's, MAT or GRE (for some programs), CLAST, PRAXIS I, CBEST, General Knowledge Test, teaching certification, minimum GPA of 2.5, verification of teaching, BS; for doctorate, MAT or GRE, master's degree, minimum cumulative GPA of 3.0; for Ed S, MAT or GRE, master's degree, teaching certificate, minimum GPA of 3.0. Additional exam requirements/recommendations for international students: Recommended—TOEFL (minimum score 550 paper-based; 80 iBT), IELTS (minimum score 6). *Application deadline:* Applications are processed on a rolling basis. Application fee: $50. Electronic applications accepted. *Financial support:* In 2013–14, 68 students received support. Career-related internships or fieldwork and Federal Work-Study available. Support available to part-time students. Financial award application deadline: 4/15; financial award applicants required to submit FAFSA. *Faculty research:* Instructional technology and distance education, educational leadership, speech language pathology, quality of life. *Total annual research expenditures:* $1.8 million. *Unit head:* Dr. H. Wells Singleton, Provost/Dean, 954-262-8730, Fax: 954-262-3894, E-mail: singlew@nova.edu. *Application contact:* Dr. Timothy Shields, Dean of Student Affairs, 800-986-3223 Ext. 8500, E-mail: shieldsd@nova.edu. Website: http://www.fischlerschool.nova.edu/.

Oakland University, Graduate Study and Lifelong Learning, School of Education and Human Services, Department of Reading and Language Arts, Rochester, MI 48309-4401. Offers advanced microcomputer applications (Certificate); reading (Certificate); reading and language arts (MAT); reading education (PhD); reading, language arts and literature (Certificate). *Accreditation:* Teacher Education Accreditation Council. *Faculty:* 10 full-time (6 women), 7 part-time/adjunct (all women). *Students:* 25 full-time (24 women), 100 part-time (96 women); includes 11 minority (8 Black or African American, non-Hispanic/Latino; 1 Asian, non-Hispanic/Latino; 1 Hispanic/Latino; 1 Two or more races, non-Hispanic/Latino), 4 international. Average age 35. 45 applicants, 69% accepted, 31 enrolled. In 2013, 101 master's, 5 doctorates awarded. *Degree*

requirements: For doctorate, thesis/dissertation. *Entrance requirements:* For master's, minimum GPA of 3.0 for unconditional admission; for doctorate, MAT, minimum GPA of 3.0 for unconditional admission. *Application deadline:* For fall admission, 3/1 for domestic and international students. Application fee: $0. Electronic applications accepted. *Financial support:* Career-related internships or fieldwork, Federal Work-Study, institutionally sponsored loans, and tuition waivers (full) available. Financial award application deadline: 3/1; financial award applicants required to submit FAFSA. *Faculty research:* OSU-ARRA- Reading Recovery i3. *Total annual research expenditures:* $857,654. *Unit head:* Dr. Jane Cipielewski, Chair, 248-370-3065, Fax: 248-370-4367. *Application contact:* Dr. Toni Walters, Coordinator, 248-370-4205, Fax: 248-370-4367, E-mail: twalters@oakland.edu.

Ohio University, Graduate College, Gladys W. and David H. Patton College of Education and Human Services, Department of Educational Studies, Athens, OH 45701-2979. Offers computer education and technology (M Ed); cultural studies (M Ed); educational administration (M Ed, Ed D); educational research and evaluation (M Ed, PhD); instructional technology (PhD). Part-time and evening/weekend programs available. Postbaccalaureate distance learning degree programs offered (minimal on-campus study). *Degree requirements:* For master's, thesis or alternative; for doctorate, comprehensive exam, thesis/dissertation. *Entrance requirements:* For master's, GRE General Test (if GPA less than 2.9); for doctorate, GRE General Test, GRE Subject Test, minimum GPA of 2.9, work experience, 3 letters of reference, autobiography. Additional exam requirements/recommendations for international students: Required—TOEFL (minimum score 550 paper-based; 80 iBT) or IELTS (minimum score 6.5). Electronic applications accepted. *Faculty research:* Race, class and gender; computer programs; development and organization theory; evaluation/development of instruments, leadership.

Old Dominion University, Darden College of Education, Program in Elementary/Middle Education, Norfolk, VA 23529. Offers elementary education (MS Ed); instructional technology (MS Ed); library science (MS Ed); middle school education (MS Ed). *Accreditation:* NCATE. Part-time and evening/weekend programs available. Postbaccalaureate distance learning degree programs offered (no on-campus study). *Faculty:* 20 full-time (15 women), 31 part-time/adjunct (26 women). *Students:* 157 full-time (152 women), 91 part-time (77 women); includes 46 minority (17 Black or African American, non-Hispanic/Latino; 3 Asian, non-Hispanic/Latino; 17 Hispanic/Latino; 1 Native Hawaiian or other Pacific Islander, non-Hispanic/Latino; 8 Two or more races, non-Hispanic/Latino), 1 international. Average age 31. 291 applicants, 50% accepted, 123 enrolled. In 2013, 142 master's awarded. *Degree requirements:* For master's, comprehensive exam. *Entrance requirements:* For master's, GRE General Test or MAT; PRAXIS I, SAT or ACT, minimum GPA of 2.8. Additional exam requirements/recommendations for international students: Required—TOEFL (minimum score 600 paper-based). *Application deadline:* For fall admission, 6/1 priority date for domestic students; for winter admission, 11/1 priority date for domestic students; for spring admission, 3/1 priority date for domestic students. Applications are processed on a rolling basis. Application fee: $50. Electronic applications accepted. *Expenses:* Tuition, state resident: full-time $9888; part-time $412 per credit. Tuition, nonresident: full-time $25,152; part-time $1048 per credit. *Required fees:* $59 per semester. One-time fee: $50. *Financial support:* In 2013–14, 180 students received support. Application deadline: 2/15; applicants required to submit FAFSA. *Faculty research:* Education pre-K to 6, school librarianship. *Unit head:* Dr. Charlene Fleener, Graduate Program Director, 757-683-3284, Fax: 757-683-5862, E-mail: cfleener@odu.edu. *Application contact:* William Heffelfinger, Director of Graduate Admissions, 757-683-5554, Fax: 757-683-3255, E-mail: gradadmit@odu.edu. Website: http://education.odu.edu/eci/.

Old Dominion University, Darden College of Education, Program in Instructional Design and Technology, Norfolk, VA 23529. Offers PhD. Part-time and evening/weekend programs available. Postbaccalaureate distance learning degree programs offered (no on-campus study). *Faculty:* 4 full-time (3 women), 1 (woman) part-time/adjunct. *Students:* 8 full-time (4 women), 56 part-time (36 women); includes 9 minority (7 Black or African American, non-Hispanic/Latino; 1 Hispanic/Latino; 1 Two or more races, non-Hispanic/Latino), 3 international. Average age 42. 30 applicants, 43% accepted, 13 enrolled. In 2013, 3 doctorates awarded. *Degree requirements:* For doctorate, comprehensive exam, thesis/dissertation. *Entrance requirements:* For doctorate, GRE, references, interview, essay of 500 words. Additional exam requirements/recommendations for international students: Required—TOEFL (minimum score 550 paper-based). *Application deadline:* For fall admission, 6/1 priority date for domestic students, 2/1 priority date for international students; for winter admission, 11/1 priority date for domestic and international students. Applications are processed on a rolling basis. Application fee: $50. Electronic applications accepted. *Expenses:* Tuition, state resident: full-time $9888; part-time $412 per credit. Tuition, nonresident: full-time $25,152; part-time $1048 per credit. *Required fees:* $59 per semester. One-time fee: $50. *Financial support:* In 2013–14, 4 students received support, including 3 research assistantships with full tuition reimbursements available (averaging $15,000 per year); career-related internships or fieldwork and unspecified assistantships also available. Financial award application deadline: 2/15; financial award applicants required to submit FAFSA. *Faculty research:* Instructional design, cognitive load, distance education, pedagogical agents, human performance technology, gaming, simulation design, distance education. *Total annual research expenditures:* $2 million. *Unit head:* Dr. Gary R. Morrison, Graduate Program Director, 757-683-4305, Fax: 757-683-5227, E-mail: gmorriso@odu.edu. *Application contact:* Alice McAdory, Director of Admissions, 757-683-3685, Fax: 757-683-3255, E-mail: gradadmit@odu.edu. Website: http://education.odu.edu/eci/idt.

Old Dominion University, Darden College of Education, Programs in Secondary Education, Norfolk, VA 23529. Offers biology (MS Ed); chemistry (MS Ed); English (MS Ed); instructional technology (MS Ed); library science (MS Ed); secondary education (MS Ed). *Accreditation:* NCATE. Part-time and evening/weekend programs available. Postbaccalaureate distance learning degree programs offered (minimal on-campus study). *Faculty:* 13 full-time (7 women), 10 part-time/adjunct (7 women). *Students:* 74 full-time (56 women), 78 part-time (49 women); includes 25 minority (13 Black or African American, non-Hispanic/Latino; 6 Hispanic/Latino; 6 Two or more races, non-Hispanic/Latino). Average age 32. 75 applicants, 71% accepted, 53 enrolled. In 2013, 79 master's awarded. *Degree requirements:* For master's, comprehensive exam, thesis. *Entrance requirements:* For master's, GRE General Test or MAT, PRAXIS I (for licensure), minimum GPA of 2.8, teaching certificate. Additional exam requirements/recommendations for international students: Required—TOEFL. *Application deadline:* For fall admission, 6/1 for domestic and international students; for winter admission, 11/1 for domestic and international students; for spring admission, 3/1 for domestic and international students. Applications are processed on a rolling basis. Application fee: $50. Electronic applications accepted. *Expenses:* Tuition, state resident: full-time $9888; part-time $412 per credit. Tuition, nonresident: full-time $25,152; part-time $1048 per credit. *Required fees:* $59 per semester. One-time fee: $50. *Financial support:* In 2013–14, 56 students received support, including fellowships (averaging $15,000 per year), research assistantships with tuition reimbursements available (averaging $9,000 per year), teaching assistantships with tuition reimbursements available (averaging $15,000 per year). Financial award application deadline: 2/15;

financial award applicants required to submit FAFSA. *Faculty research:* Use of technology, writing project for teachers, geography teaching, reading. *Unit head:* Dr. Robert Lucking, Graduate Program Director, 757-683-5545, Fax: 757-683-5862, E-mail: rlucking@odu.edu. *Application contact:* William Heffelfinger, Director of Graduate Admissions, 757-683-5554, Fax: 757-683-3255, E-mail: gradadmit@odu.edu. Website: http://education.odu.edu/eci/secondary/.

Ottawa University, Graduate Studies-Arizona, Program in Education, Ottawa, KS 66067-3399. Offers community college counseling (MA); curriculum and instruction (MA); early childhood (MA); education intervention (MA); education leadership (MA); education technology (MA); Montessori early childhood education (MA); Montessori elementary education (MA); professional development (MA); school guidance counseling (MA); special education - cross categorical (MA). Programs offered in Mesa, Phoenix, Tempe and West Valley, AZ. *Accreditation:* NCATE. Part-time programs available. *Degree requirements:* For master's, thesis or alternative. *Entrance requirements:* For master's, minimum undergraduate GPA of 3.0, copy of current state certification or teaching license. Additional exam requirements/recommendations for international students: Required—TOEFL (minimum score 550 paper-based). Electronic applications accepted. *Expenses:* Contact institution.

Our Lady of the Lake University of San Antonio, School of Professional Studies, Program in Learning Resources Specialist, San Antonio, TX 78207-4689. Offers M Ed. Part-time and evening/weekend programs available. *Faculty:* 6 full-time (4 women), 3 part-time/adjunct (all women). *Students:* 1 applicant, 100% accepted. In 2013, 2 master's awarded. *Degree requirements:* For master's, comprehensive exam. *Entrance requirements:* For master's, GRE General Test or MAT. Additional exam requirements/recommendations for international students: Required—TOEFL. *Application deadline:* For fall admission, 4/1 priority date for domestic and international students; for spring admission, 11/1 priority date for domestic and international students; for summer admission, 4/1 priority date for domestic and international students. Applications are processed on a rolling basis. Application fee: $25 ($50 for international students). Electronic applications accepted. *Expenses: Tuition:* Full-time $9120; part-time $760 per credit. *Required fees:* $698; $334 per trimester. Tuition and fees vary according to course load, degree level, campus/location and program. *Financial support:* Research assistantships, teaching assistantships, career-related internships or fieldwork, Federal Work-Study, institutionally sponsored loans, scholarships/grants, and tuition waivers (partial) available. Support available to part-time students. Financial award application deadline: 4/15. *Faculty research:* Professional educator to understand and meet the comprehensive needs of a diverse student population, life-long learners, innovative practices. *Unit head:* Dr. Jerrie Jackson, Head, 210-434-6711 Ext. 2698, E-mail: jjackson@lake.ollusa.edu. *Application contact:* Graduate Admission, 210-431-3961, Fax: 210-431-4013, E-mail: gradadm@lake.ollusa.edu. Website: http://www.ollusa.edu/s/1190/ollu-3-column-noads.aspx?sid=1190&gid=1&pgid=3855.

Pace University, School of Education, New York, NY 10038. Offers adolescent education (MST); childhood education (MST); early childhood development, learning and intervention (MST); educational leadership (MS Ed); educational technology studies (MS); inclusive adolescent education (MST); literacy (MS Ed); school business management (Certificate); special education (MS Ed). *Accreditation:* NCATE. Part-time and evening/weekend programs available. *Students:* 186 full-time (154 women), 441 part-time (315 women); includes 209 minority (89 Black or African American, non-Hispanic/Latino; 2 American Indian or Alaska Native, non-Hispanic/Latino; 30 Asian, non-Hispanic/Latino; 74 Hispanic/Latino; 1 Native Hawaiian or other Pacific Islander, non-Hispanic/Latino; 13 Two or more races, non-Hispanic/Latino), 7 international. Average age 29. 207 applicants, 71% accepted, 105 enrolled. In 2013, 296 master's, 25 other advanced degrees awarded. *Degree requirements:* For master's, internship. *Entrance requirements:* For master's, interview, teaching certificate. Additional exam requirements/recommendations for international students: Required—TOEFL. *Application deadline:* For fall admission, 8/1 priority date for domestic students, 6/1 for international students; for spring admission, 12/1 priority date for domestic students, 10/1 for international students. Applications are processed on a rolling basis. Application fee: $70. Electronic applications accepted. *Expenses:* Contact institution. *Financial support:* Research assistantships, career-related internships or fieldwork, and Federal Work-Study available. Support available to part-time students. Financial award applicants required to submit FAFSA. *Faculty research:* Teacher education, technology in education, STEM, literacy education, special education. *Total annual research expenditures:* $1.3 million. *Unit head:* Dr. Andrea M. Spencer, Dean, School of Education, 914-773-3341, E-mail: aspencer@pace.edu. *Application contact:* Susan Ford-Goldschein, Director of Graduate Admissions, 212-346-1660, Fax: 212-346-1585, E-mail: gradnyc@pace.edu. Website: http://www.pace.edu/school-of-education.

Penn State University Park, Graduate School, College of Education, Department of Learning and Performance Systems, State College, PA 16802. Offers adult education (M Ed, D Ed, PhD, Certificate); instructional systems (Certificate); learning, design, and technology (M Ed, MS, D Ed, PhD, Certificate); organization development and change (MPS); workforce education and development (M Ed, MS, PhD). *Unit head:* Dr. David H. Monk, Dean, 814-865-2523, Fax: 814-865-0555, E-mail: dhm6@psu.edu. *Application contact:* Cynthia E. Nicosia, Director, Graduate Enrollment Services, 814-865-1834, Fax: 814-863-4627, E-mail: cey1@psu.edu. Website: http://www.ed.psu.edu/educ/lps/dept-lps.

Pepperdine University, Graduate School of Education and Psychology, Division of Education, Ed D Program in Learning Technologies, Malibu, CA 90263. Offers Ed D. Part-time and evening/weekend programs available. Postbaccalaureate distance learning degree programs offered (minimal on-campus study). *Faculty:* 50 full-time (29 women), 114 part-time/adjunct (68 women). *Students:* 36 full-time (25 women), 42 part-time (27 women); includes 26 minority (6 Black or African American, non-Hispanic/Latino; 1 American Indian or Alaska Native, non-Hispanic/Latino; 12 Asian, non-Hispanic/Latino; 4 Hispanic/Latino; 3 Native Hawaiian or other Pacific Islander, non-Hispanic/Latino). 42 applicants, 83% accepted, 20 enrolled. In 2013, 8 doctorates awarded. *Entrance requirements:* For doctorate, MAT or GRE verbal and quantitative sections (all taken within last five years), two recommendations; three-part statement describing vision for technology, experience/background in technology, and personal goals related to pursuit of degree (minimum of 2,000 words); personal interview. Additional exam requirements/recommendations for international students: Required—TOEFL. *Application deadline:* For fall admission, 3/1 priority date for domestic students. Tuition and fees vary according to program. *Financial support:* Applicants required to submit FAFSA. *Unit head:* Dr. Linda Polin, Director, 310-568-5641, E-mail: linda.polin@pepperdine.edu. *Application contact:* Jennifer Agatep, Admissions Manager, Education, 310-258-2850, E-mail: jennifer.agatep@pepperdine.edu. Website: http://gsep.pepperdine.edu/doctorate-learning-technologies/.

Pepperdine University, Graduate School of Education and Psychology, Division of Education, MA Program in Learning Technologies, Malibu, CA 90263. Offers MA. Part-time and evening/weekend programs available. Postbaccalaureate distance learning degree programs offered (minimal on-campus study). *Students:* 13 full-time (7 women); includes 3 minority (1 Black or African American, non-Hispanic/Latino; 1 Asian, non-

Hispanic/Latino; 1 Hispanic/Latino). *Entrance requirements:* For master's, personal interviews; two letters of recommendation; three-part statement describing vision for technology in educational settings, experience/background in technology, and personal goals related to pursuit of degree (minimum of 2000 words). Additional exam requirements/recommendations for international students: Required—TOEFL. *Application deadline:* For fall admission, 5/2 for domestic students. Applications are processed on a rolling basis. Application fee: $55. *Expenses:* Contact institution. *Financial support:* Research assistantships, institutionally sponsored loans, and scholarships/grants available. Support available to part-time students. Financial award application deadline: 7/1; financial award applicants required to submit FAFSA. *Unit head:* Dr. Paul Sparks, Director, 310-568-5600, E-mail: paul.sparks@pepperdine.edu. *Application contact:* Jennifer Agatep, Admissions Manager, Education, 310-258-2849, E-mail: jennifer.agatep@pepperdine.edu.

Piedmont College, School of Education, Demorest, GA 30535-0010. Offers art education (MAT); early childhood education (MA, MAT); instructional technology (MAT); middle grades education (MA, MAT); music education (MAT); secondary education (MA, MAT); special education (MA, MAT); teacher leadership (Ed S). Part-time and evening/weekend programs available. *Students:* 312 full-time (242 women), 694 part-time (563 women); includes 153 minority (103 Black or African American, non-Hispanic/Latino; 3 American Indian or Alaska Native, non-Hispanic/Latino; 17 Asian, non-Hispanic/Latino; 19 Hispanic/Latino; 11 Two or more races, non-Hispanic/Latino), 1 international. Average age 37. 165 applicants, 72% accepted, 118 enrolled. In 2013, 333 master's, 15 doctorates, 457 other advanced degrees awarded. *Degree requirements:* For master's, thesis, field experience in the classroom teaching; for doctorate, thesis/dissertation. *Entrance requirements:* For master's, GRE General Test, MAT, minimum undergraduate GPA of 2.5; for Ed S, minimum graduate GPA of 3.5, valid teaching certificate. Additional exam requirements/recommendations for international students: Required—TOEFL (minimum score 550 paper-based). *Application deadline:* For fall admission, 7/15 for domestic students; for spring admission, 12/1 for domestic students. Applications are processed on a rolling basis. Electronic applications accepted. *Expenses: Tuition:* Full-time $7992; part-time $444 per credit hour. *Financial support:* Career-related internships or fieldwork, Federal Work-Study, and unspecified assistantships available. Support available to part-time students. Financial award applicants required to submit FAFSA. *Unit head:* Dr. Don Gnecco, Dean, 706-778-3000 Ext. 1201, Fax: 706-776-9608, E-mail: dgnecco@piedmont.edu. *Application contact:* Kathleen Anderson, Director of Graduate Enrollment Management, 706-778-8500 Ext. 1181, Fax: 706-778-0150, E-mail: kanderson@piedmont.edu.

Pittsburg State University, Graduate School, College of Education, Department of Special Services and Leadership Studies, Program in Educational Technology, Pittsburg, KS 66762. Offers MS. *Accreditation:* NCATE. *Degree requirements:* For master's, thesis or alternative. *Entrance requirements:* For master's, GRE General Test or MAT.

Plymouth State University, College of Graduate Studies, Graduate Studies in Education, Program in Secondary Education, Plymouth, NH 03264-1595. Offers curriculum and instruction (M Ed); language education (M Ed); library media (M Ed); physical education (M Ed); social studies education (M Ed); special education (M Ed). Part-time and evening/weekend programs available. *Entrance requirements:* For master's, MAT.

Portland State University, Graduate Studies, School of Education, Department of Curriculum and Instruction, Portland, OR 97207-0751. Offers early childhood education (MA, MS); education (M Ed, MA, MS); educational leadership: curriculum and instruction (Ed D); educational media/school librarianship (MA, MS); elementary education (M Ed, MAT, MST); reading (MA, MS); secondary education (M Ed, MAT, MST). *Accreditation:* NCATE. Part-time programs available. *Faculty:* 22 full-time (15 women), 28 part-time/adjunct (20 women). *Students:* 29 full-time (23 women), 162 part-time (123 women); includes 26 minority (3 Black or African American, non-Hispanic/Latino; 6 Asian, non-Hispanic/Latino; 13 Hispanic/Latino; 4 Two or more races, non-Hispanic/Latino), 6 international. Average age 36. 145 applicants, 69% accepted, 93 enrolled. In 2013, 257 master's, 5 doctorates awarded. *Degree requirements:* For master's, comprehensive exam, thesis or alternative; for doctorate, thesis/dissertation. *Entrance requirements:* For master's, California Basic Educational Skills Test, minimum GPA of 3.0 in upper-division course work or 2.75 overall. Additional exam requirements/recommendations for international students: Required—TOEFL (minimum score 550 paper-based). *Application deadline:* For fall admission, 4/1 for domestic and international students; for winter admission, 9/1 for domestic and international students; for spring admission, 11/1 for domestic and international students. Applications are processed on a rolling basis. Application fee: $50. *Expenses:* Tuition, state resident: full-time $9207; part-time $341 per credit. Tuition, nonresident: full-time $14,391; part-time $533 per credit. *Required fees:* $1263; $22 per credit. $98 per quarter. One-time fee: $150. Tuition and fees vary according to program. *Financial support:* In 2013–14, 1 research assistantship with full tuition reimbursement (averaging $6,248 per year), 2 teaching assistantships with full tuition reimbursements (averaging $7,755 per year) were awarded; career-related internships or fieldwork, Federal Work-Study, and institutionally sponsored loans also available. Support available to part-time students. Financial award application deadline: 3/1; financial award applicants required to submit FAFSA. *Faculty research:* Early literacy, characteristics of successful teachers of at-risk students, participation of women/minorities in technology courses, selection of cooperating teachers. *Total annual research expenditures:* $1 million. *Unit head:* Christine Chaille, Head, 503-725-4753, Fax: 203-725-8475, E-mail: chaillec@pdx.edu. *Application contact:* Jake Fernandez, Department Assistant, 503-725-4756, Fax: 503-725-8475, E-mail: jifern@pdx.edu. Website: http://www.ed.pdx.edu/ci/.

Post University, Program in Education, Waterbury, CT 06723-2540. Offers education (M Ed); higher education administration (M Ed); instructional design and technology (M Ed); online teaching (M Ed); teaching and learning (M Ed); TESOL (teaching English to speakers of other languages) (M Ed). Postbaccalaureate distance learning degree programs offered.

Purdue University, Graduate School, College of Education, Department of Curriculum and Instruction, West Lafayette, IN 47907. Offers agricultural and extension education (PhD, Ed S); agriculture and extension education (MS, MS Ed); art education (PhD); curriculum studies (MS Ed, PhD, Ed S); educational technology (MS Ed, PhD, Ed S); elementary education (MS Ed); family and consumer sciences education (MS Ed, PhD, Ed S); foreign language education (MS Ed, PhD, Ed S); industrial technology (PhD, Ed S); language arts (MS Ed, PhD, Ed S); literacy (MS Ed, PhD, Ed S); mathematics/science education (MS, MS Ed, PhD, Ed S); social studies (MS Ed, PhD); social studies education (Ed S); vocational/industrial education (MS Ed, PhD, Ed S); vocational/technical education (MS Ed, PhD, Ed S). *Accreditation:* NCATE. Part-time and evening/weekend programs available. *Faculty:* 29 full-time (19 women), 33 part-time/adjunct (29 women). *Students:* 85 full-time (53 women), 271 part-time (195 women); includes 62 minority (19 Black or African American, non-Hispanic/Latino; 3 American Indian or Alaska Native, non-Hispanic/Latino; 13 Asian, non-Hispanic/Latino; 22 Hispanic/Latino; 1 Native Hawaiian or other Pacific Islander, non-Hispanic/Latino; 4 Two or more races, non-Hispanic/Latino), 41 international. Average age 36. 155 applicants, 71% accepted, 71 enrolled. In 2013, 60 master's, 20 doctorates awarded. *Degree requirements:* For

master's, thesis optional; for doctorate, thesis/dissertation, oral and written exams; for Ed S, oral presentation, project. *Entrance requirements:* For master's, GRE General Test (if undergraduate GPA is below 3.0), minimum undergraduate GPA of 3.0 or equivalent; for doctorate, GRE General Test (minimum combined verbal and quantitative score of 1000, 300 for new scoring), minimum undergraduate GPA of 3.0 or equivalent; master's degree with minimum GPA of 3.0 or equivalent; for Ed S, GRE General Test (minimum combined verbal and quantitative score of 1000, 300 for new scoring), minimum undergraduate GPA of 3.0 or equivalent; master's degree. Additional exam requirements/recommendations for international students: Required—TOEFL (minimum score 550 paper-based; 77 iBT). *Application deadline:* For fall admission, 12/15 for domestic students, 3/1 for international students; for spring admission, 9/15 for domestic students, 8/1 for international students. Application fee: $60 ($75 for international students). Electronic applications accepted. *Financial support:* Fellowships with full tuition reimbursements, research assistantships with full tuition reimbursements, teaching assistantships with full tuition reimbursements, career-related internships or fieldwork, and tuition waivers (full) available. Support available to part-time students. Financial award application deadline: 3/1; financial award applicants required to submit FAFSA. *Faculty research:* Literacy acquisition and development, teacher beliefs and knowledge, recruitment and retention of underrepresented students, economic education, literacy discourse. *Unit head:* Dr. Phillip J. VanFossen, Head, 765-494-7935, Fax: 765-496-1622, E-mail: vanfoss@purdue.edu. *Application contact:* Cindy Blankenship, Graduate Contact, 765-494-2345, Fax: 765-494-5832, E-mail: prater0@purdue.edu.
Website: http://www.edci.purdue.edu/.

Purdue University Calumet, Graduate Studies Office, School of Education, Program in Instructional Technology, Hammond, IN 46323-2094. Offers MS Ed. *Entrance requirements:* Additional exam requirements/recommendations for international students: Required—TOEFL.

Radford University, College of Graduate and Professional Studies, College of Education and Human Development, School of Teacher Education and Leadership, Program in Education, Radford, VA 24142. Offers curriculum and instruction (MS); early childhood education (MS); educational technology (MS); math education content area studies (MS). *Accreditation:* NCATE. Part-time and evening/weekend programs available. *Faculty:* 6 full-time (4 women), 2 part-time/adjunct (1 woman). *Students:* 68 full-time (53 women), 30 part-time (20 women); includes 6 minority (3 Black or African American, non-Hispanic/Latino; 1 Asian, non-Hispanic/Latino; 1 Hispanic/Latino; 1 Two or more races, non-Hispanic/Latino). Average age 28. 38 applicants, 100% accepted, 28 enrolled. In 2013, 42 master's awarded. *Degree requirements:* For master's, comprehensive exam. *Entrance requirements:* For master's, GRE, minimum GPA of 3.0, 2 letters of professional reference, personal statement, resume, official transcripts. Additional exam requirements/recommendations for international students: Required—TOEFL (minimum score 550 paper-based; 79 iBT). *Application deadline:* For fall admission, 2/15 priority date for domestic students, 12/1 for international students; for spring admission, 7/1 for international students. Applications are processed on a rolling basis. Application fee: $50. Electronic applications accepted. *Expenses:* Tuition, state resident: full-time $6800; part-time $283 per credit hour. Tuition, nonresident: full-time $15,610; part-time $627 per credit hour. *Required fees:* $2944; $123 per credit hour. Tuition and fees vary according to program. *Financial support:* In 2013–14, 24 students received support, including 19 research assistantships (averaging $7,105 per year); career-related internships or fieldwork, Federal Work-Study, institutionally sponsored loans, scholarships/grants, and unspecified assistantships also available. Financial award application deadline: 3/1; financial award applicants required to submit FAFSA. *Faculty research:* Pedagogy of mathematics education. *Unit head:* Dr. Kristan Morrison, Coordinator, 540-831-7120, Fax: 540-831-5059, E-mail: kmorrison12@radford.edu. *Application contact:* Rebecca Conner, Director, Graduate Enrollment, 540-831-6296, Fax: 540-831-6061, E-mail: gradcollege@radford.edu.
Website: http://www.radford.edu/content/cehd/home/departments/STEL/programs/education-master.html.

Ramapo College of New Jersey, Master of Science in Educational Technology Program, Mahwah, NJ 07430. Offers MS. Part-time and evening/weekend programs available. *Faculty:* 8 part-time/adjunct (5 women). *Students:* 84 part-time (61 women); includes 5 minority (1 Black or African American, non-Hispanic/Latino; 1 Asian, non-Hispanic/Latino; 3 Hispanic/Latino), 1 international. Average age 34. 68 applicants, 90% accepted, 49 enrolled. In 2013, 49 master's awarded. *Degree requirements:* For master's, capstone course. *Entrance requirements:* For master's, official transcript; personal statement; 2 letters of recommendation; resume (recommended with state-issued teaching certificate). Additional exam requirements/recommendations for international students: Required—TOEFL (minimum score 550 paper-based; 79 iBT); Recommended—IELTS (minimum score 6). *Application deadline:* For fall admission, 9/1 for domestic and international students; for spring admission, 1/29 for domestic students, 1/30 for international students. Applications are processed on a rolling basis. Application fee: $60. Electronic applications accepted. *Expenses: Tuition, area resident:* Part-time $582.45 per credit. Tuition, nonresident: part-time $748.70 per credit. *Required fees:* $127.05 per credit. *Financial support:* Institutionally sponsored loans and scholarships/grants available. Financial award application deadline: 3/1; financial award applicants required to submit FAFSA. *Faculty research:* Integrity technology in the curriculum of K-12 learning environment. *Unit head:* Dr. Richard Russo, Director of the Master in Educational Technology Program, 201-684-7899, Fax: 201-684-6699, E-mail: rrusso@ramapo.edu. *Application contact:* M. Joyce Wilson, Administrative Assistant, MSET Program, 201-684-7721, Fax: 201-684-6699, E-mail: mlafayet@ramapo.edu.
Website: http://www.ramapo.edu/mset/.

Regis University, College for Professional Studies, School of Education, Education Division, Denver, CO 80221-1099. Offers adult learning, training, and development (M Ed, Certificate); autism education (Certificate); curriculum, instruction, and assessment (M Ed); educational leadership (M Ed); gifted and talented education (M Ed); gifted/talented education (Certificate); initial licensure (M Ed); instructional technology (M Ed, Certificate); literacy (Certificate); reading (M Ed); school executive leadership (Certificate); space studies (M Ed). Program also offered in Henderson and Las Vegas (Summerlin), NV. *Accreditation:* Teacher Education Accreditation Council. Part-time and evening/weekend programs available. Postbaccalaureate distance learning degree programs offered (no on-campus study). *Degree requirements:* For master's, thesis. *Entrance requirements:* For master's, resume, minimum GPA of 2.75, criminal background check. Additional exam requirements/recommendations for international students: Required—TOEFL, TWE (minimum score 5). *Application deadline:* For fall admission, 7/23 priority date for domestic students; for winter admission, 9/17 priority date for domestic students; for spring admission, 12/3 priority date for domestic students. Applications are processed on a rolling basis. Application fee: $75. Electronic applications accepted. *Expenses:* Contact institution. *Financial support:* Federal Work-Study and scholarships/grants available. *Faculty research:* Issues of equity in the middle school classroom, professional learning communities, school reform, sociolinguistic and discursive obstacles to student integration, inclusive language arts curriculum. *Unit head:* Dr. Janna L. Oakes, Dean, 303-458-4302. *Application contact:* Information Contact, 303-458-4300, Fax: 303-964-5274, E-mail: masters@regis.edu.

The Richard Stockton College of New Jersey, School of Graduate and Continuing Studies, Program in Instructional Technology, Galloway, NJ 08205-9441. Offers MA. Part-time and evening/weekend programs available. *Faculty:* 3 full-time (2 women), 2 part-time/adjunct (0 women). *Students:* 1 (woman) full-time, 85 part-time (63 women); includes 8 minority (3 Black or African American, non-Hispanic/Latino; 1 Asian, non-Hispanic/Latino; 3 Hispanic/Latino; 1 Two or more races, non-Hispanic/Latino). Average age 39. 20 applicants, 85% accepted, 15 enrolled. In 2013, 6 master's awarded. *Degree requirements:* For master's, final project. *Entrance requirements:* For master's, GRE or MAT, minimum GPA of 3.0. Additional exam requirements/recommendations for international students: Required—TOEFL. *Application deadline:* For fall admission, 7/1 priority date for domestic students, 7/1 for international students; for spring admission, 12/1 for domestic students, 11/1 for international students. Applications are processed on a rolling basis. Application fee: $50. Electronic applications accepted. *Expenses: Tuition, area resident:* Part-time $559 per credit. Tuition, state resident: part-time $559 per credit. Tuition, nonresident: part-time $861 per credit. *Required fees:* $168.23 per credit. $75 per semester. Tuition and fees vary according to course load and degree level. *Financial support:* In 2013–14, 7 students received support, including 8 research assistantships with partial tuition reimbursements available; fellowships, career-related internships or fieldwork, Federal Work-Study, scholarships/grants, and unspecified assistantships also available. Support available to part-time students. Financial award application deadline: 3/1; financial award applicants required to submit FAFSA. *Faculty research:* Ethics, digital imaging, virtual reality in the classroom, 3D art in multimedia, technology projects for job-skills training, community computing networks. *Unit head:* Dr. Doug Harvey, Director, 609-626-3640, E-mail: mait@stockton.edu. *Application contact:* Tara Williams, Assistant Director of Graduate Enrollment, 609-626-3640, Fax: 609-626-6050, E-mail: gradschool@stockton.edu.
Website: http://www.stockton.edu/grad.

Robert Morris University Illinois, Morris Graduate School of Management, Chicago, IL 60605. Offers accounting (MBA); accounting/finance (MBA); business analytics (MIS); design and media (MM); educational technology (MM); health care administration (MM); higher education administration (MM); human resource management (MBA); information security (MIS); information systems (MIS); law enforcement administration (MM); management (MBA); management/finance (MBA); management/human resource management (MBA); mobile computing (MIS); sports administration (MM). Part-time and evening/weekend programs available. *Faculty:* 12 full-time (5 women), 18 part-time/adjunct (4 women). *Students:* 240 full-time (128 women), 195 part-time (127 women); includes 242 minority (147 Black or African American, non-Hispanic/Latino; 2 American Indian or Alaska Native, non-Hispanic/Latino; 24 Asian, non-Hispanic/Latino; 63 Hispanic/Latino; 1 Native Hawaiian or other Pacific Islander, non-Hispanic/Latino; 5 Two or more races, non-Hispanic/Latino), 26 international. Average age 33. 210 applicants, 63% accepted, 116 enrolled. In 2013, 278 master's awarded. *Entrance requirements:* For master's, official transcripts, two letters of recommendation. Additional exam requirements/recommendations for international students: Required—TOEFL (minimum score 550 paper-based). *Application deadline:* Applications are processed on a rolling basis. Application fee: $20 ($100 for international students). Electronic applications accepted. *Expenses: Tuition:* Full-time $14,400; part-time $2400 per course. *Financial support:* In 2013–14, 488 students received support. Federal Work-Study and scholarships/grants available. Support available to part-time students. Financial award applicants required to submit FAFSA. *Unit head:* Kayed Akkawi, Dean for Morris Graduate School of Management, 312-935-6050, Fax: 312-935-6020, E-mail: kakkawi@robertmorris.edu. *Application contact:* Fernando Villeda, Dean of Graduate Enrollment, 312-935-6050, Fax: 312-935-6020, E-mail: fvilleda@robertmorris.edu.

Rowan University, Graduate School, College of Education, Department of Teacher Education, Glassboro, NJ 08028-1701. Offers bilingual/bicultural education (CGS); collaborative teaching (MST); educational technology (CGS); elementary education (MST); elementary school teaching (MA); ESL education (CGS); foreign language education (MST); music education (MA); science teaching (MST); secondary education (MST); subject matter teaching (MA); teacher leadership (M Ed); teaching and learning (CGS); theatre education (MST). *Accreditation:* NCATE. Part-time and evening/weekend programs available. *Faculty:* 7 full-time (5 women), 1 (woman) part-time/adjunct. *Students:* 35 full-time (22 women), 78 part-time (66 women); includes 23 minority (4 Black or African American, non-Hispanic/Latino; 3 Asian, non-Hispanic/Latino; 16 Hispanic/Latino). Average age 28. 58 applicants, 100% accepted, 37 enrolled. In 2013, 12 master's awarded. *Degree requirements:* For master's, comprehensive exam, thesis. *Entrance requirements:* For master's, GRE General Test, PRAXIS I, PRAXIS II, interview, minimum GPA of 2.8. Additional exam requirements/recommendations for international students: Required—TOEFL. *Application deadline:* For spring admission, 2/15 priority date for domestic students. Applications are processed on a rolling basis. Application fee: $65. Electronic applications accepted. *Expenses: Tuition, area resident:* Part-time $638 per credit. Tuition, state resident: full-time $5742. *Required fees:* $142 per credit. Tuition and fees vary according to course level and program. *Financial support:* Career-related internships or fieldwork, scholarships/grants, health care benefits, and unspecified assistantships available. Support available to part-time students. *Unit head:* Dr. Horacio Sosa, Dean, College of Graduate and Continuing Education, 856-256-4747, Fax: 856-256-5638, E-mail: sosa@rowan.edu. *Application contact:* Karen Haynes, Graduate Coordinator, 856-256-4052, Fax: 856-256-4436, E-mail: haynes@rowan.edu.

Sacred Heart University, Graduate Programs, Isabelle Farrington College of Education, Department of Teacher Education, Fairfield, CT 06825-1000. Offers administration (CAS); advanced educational studies for teachers (CAS); educational technology (Certificate); teaching (MAT); TESOL (MAT); Web development (Certificate). *Faculty:* 14 full-time (7 women), 15 part-time/adjunct (8 women). *Students:* 210 full-time (155 women), 517 part-time (376 women); includes 78 minority (36 Black or African American, non-Hispanic/Latino; 1 American Indian or Alaska Native, non-Hispanic/Latino; 5 Asian, non-Hispanic/Latino; 31 Hispanic/Latino; 5 Two or more races, non-Hispanic/Latino). Average age 34. 90 applicants, 90% accepted, 75 enrolled. In 2013, 262 master's, 60 other advanced degrees awarded. *Entrance requirements:* For master's, bachelor's degree, copy of official teaching certificate, background check. Additional exam requirements/recommendations for international students: Required—PTE; Recommended—TOEFL (minimum score 570 paper-based; 80 iBT), IELTS (minimum score 6.5). *Application deadline:* Applications are processed on a rolling basis. Application fee: $60. Electronic applications accepted. *Expenses: Tuition:* Full-time $22,775; part-time $617 per credit. *Financial support:* Applicants required to submit FAFSA. *Unit head:* Dr. Jim Carl, Dean, 203-371-7800, Fax: 203-365-7513, E-mail: carlj@sacredheart.edu. *Application contact:* Kathy Dilks, Executive Director of Graduate Admissions, 203-365-7619, Fax: 203-365-4732, E-mail: gradstudies@sacredheart.edu.
Website: http://www.sacredheart.edu/academics/isabellefarringtoncollegeofeducation/.

Saginaw Valley State University, College of Education, Program in Instructional Technology, University Center, MI 48710. Offers MA. Part-time and evening/weekend programs available. *Students:* 9 full-time (5 women), 50 part-time (34 women); includes 6 minority (3 Black or African American, non-Hispanic/Latino; 1 American Indian or

Alaska Native, non-Hispanic/Latino; 2 Hispanic/Latino), 7 international. Average age 33. 14 applicants, 71% accepted, 7 enrolled. In 2013, 23 master's awarded. *Degree requirements:* For master's, capstone course or thesis. *Entrance requirements:* For master's, minimum GPA of 3.0. Additional exam requirements/recommendations for international students: Required—TOEFL (minimum score 550 paper-based; 79 iBT). *Application deadline:* For fall admission, 7/15 for international students; for winter admission, 11/15 for international students; for spring admission, 4/15 for international students. Applications are processed on a rolling basis. Application fee: $30 ($80 for international students). Electronic applications accepted. *Expenses:* Tuition, state resident: full-time $8933; part-time $496.30 per credit hour. Tuition, nonresident: full-time $16,806; part-time $933.65 per credit hour. *Required fees:* $263; $14.60 per credit hour. Tuition and fees vary according to degree level. *Financial support:* Federal Work-Study and scholarships/grants available. Support available to part-time students. Financial award applicants required to submit FAFSA. *Unit head:* Dr. Mary Harmon, Dean, 989-964-7107, Fax: 989-964-4563, E-mail: coeconnect@svsu.edu. *Application contact:* Jenna Briggs, Director, Graduate and International Admissions, 989-964-6096, Fax: 989-964-2788, E-mail: gradadm@svsu.edu.

St. Cloud State University, School of Graduate Studies, School of Education, Center for Information Media, St. Cloud, MN 56301-4498. Offers MS. Part-time and evening/weekend programs available. Postbaccalaureate distance learning degree programs offered (no on-campus study). *Degree requirements:* For master's, comprehensive exam, thesis or alternative. *Entrance requirements:* For master's, minimum overall GPA of 2.75 in previous undergraduate and graduate records or in last half of undergraduate work. Additional exam requirements/recommendations for international students: Required—Michigan English Language Assessment Battery; Recommended—TOEFL (minimum score 550 paper-based; 79 iBT), IELTS (minimum score 6.5). Electronic applications accepted.

Saint Joseph's University, College of Arts and Sciences, Department of Education, Philadelphia, PA 19131-1395. Offers curriculum supervisor (Certificate); educational leadership (MS, Ed D); elementary education (MS, Certificate); elementary/middle school education (Certificate); instructional technology (MS, Certificate); principal certification (Certificate); professional education (MS); reading specialist (MS, Certificate); reading supervisor (Certificate); secondary education (MS, Certificate); special education (MS, Certificate); superintendent's letter of eligibility (Certificate); supervisor of special education (Certificate). Part-time and evening/weekend programs available. Postbaccalaureate distance learning degree programs offered (no on-campus study). *Faculty:* 32 full-time (25 women), 75 part-time/adjunct (53 women). *Students:* 91 full-time (81 women), 858 part-time (656 women); includes 133 minority (96 Black or African American, non-Hispanic/Latino; 3 American Indian or Alaska Native, non-Hispanic/Latino; 9 Asian, non-Hispanic/Latino; 20 Hispanic/Latino; 5 Native Hawaiian or other Pacific Islander, non-Hispanic/Latino), 16 international. Average age 31. 359 applicants, 77% accepted, 203 enrolled. In 2013, 363 master's, 9 doctorates, 1 other advanced degree awarded. *Entrance requirements:* For master's, 2 letters of recommendation, minimum GPA of 3.0, official transcripts, personal statement; for doctorate, GRE, master's degree from accredited institution, minimum graduate GPA of 3.5, computer competence, commitment to participate in cohort, interview with program director. Additional exam requirements/recommendations for international students: Required—TOEFL (minimum score 550 paper-based; 79 iBT), IELTS (minimum score 6.5). *Application deadline:* For fall admission, 7/15 priority date for domestic students, 4/15 for international students; for winter admission, 11/15 for domestic students, 1/15 for international students; for spring admission, 11/15 priority date for domestic students, 10/15 for international students. Applications are processed on a rolling basis. Application fee: $35. Electronic applications accepted. *Expenses:* Contact institution. *Financial support:* Unspecified assistantships available. Financial award applicants required to submit FAFSA. *Faculty research:* Factors predicting early mathematics skills for low income children, early child care and development, preschool quality. *Total annual research expenditures:* $229,264. *Unit head:* Dr. John Vacca, Associate Dean, Education, 610-660-3131, E-mail: gradstudies@sju.edu. *Application contact:* Elisabeth Woodward, Director of Marketing and Admissions, Graduate Arts and Sciences, 610-660-3131, Fax: 610-660-3230, E-mail: gradstudies@sju.edu.
Website: http://sju.edu/int/academics/cas/grad/education/index.html.

Saint Leo University, Graduate Studies in Education, Saint Leo, FL 33574-6665. Offers educational leadership (M Ed); exceptional student education (M Ed); instructional design (MS); instructional leadership (M Ed); reading (M Ed). Part-time and evening/weekend programs available. Postbaccalaureate distance learning degree programs offered (minimal on-campus study). *Faculty:* 10 full-time (8 women), 31 part-time/adjunct (23 women). *Students:* 680 full-time (554 women), 4 part-time (all women); includes 83 minority (51 Black or African American, non-Hispanic/Latino; 2 Asian, non-Hispanic/Latino; 27 Hispanic/Latino; 3 Two or more races, non-Hispanic/Latino), 4 international. Average age 36. In 2013, 295 master's awarded. *Degree requirements:* For master's, comprehensive exam, appropriate State of Florida certification tests. *Entrance requirements:* For master's, GRE (minimum score of 1000) or MAT (minimum score of 410) if undergraduate GPA for last 60 hours of coursework was below 3.0 (for M Ed), bachelor's degree with minimum GPA of 3.0 for last 60 hours of coursework from regionally-accredited college or university, 2 recommendations, resume, statement of professional goals, copy of valid teaching certificate (for M Ed). Additional exam requirements/recommendations for international students: Required—TOEFL (minimum score 550 paper-based; 80 iBT). *Application deadline:* For fall admission, 7/1 priority date for domestic students, 7/1 for international students; for winter admission, 7/1 for international students; for spring admission, 11/1 priority date for domestic students. Applications are processed on a rolling basis. Application fee: $80. Electronic applications accepted. *Expenses:* Contact institution. *Financial support:* In 2013–14, 618 students received support. Career-related internships or fieldwork, Federal Work-Study, scholarships/grants, and health care benefits available. Financial award application deadline: 3/1; financial award applicants required to submit FAFSA. *Faculty research:* The role of the school leader in data analysis of student achievement, teacher recruitment, teacher effectiveness. *Unit head:* Dr. Sharyn Disabato, Director of Graduate Education, 352-588-8309, Fax: 352-588-8861, E-mail: med@saintleo.edu. *Application contact:* Joshua Stagner, Director of Graduate Admission, 800-707-8846, Fax: 352-588-7873, E-mail: grad.admissions@saintleo.edu.
Website: http://www.saintleo.edu/admissions/graduate.aspx.

Saint Mary's University of Minnesota, Schools of Graduate and Professional Programs, Graduate School of Education, Learning Design and Technology Program, Winona, MN 55987-1399. Offers M Ed. Postbaccalaureate distance learning degree programs offered (no on-campus study). *Unit head:* Nancy Van Erp, Associate Program Director, 320-260-5116, E-mail: nvanerp@smumn.edu. *Application contact:* Russell Kreager, Director of Admissions for Graduate and Professional Programs, 612-728-5207, Fax: 612-728-5121, E-mail: rkreager@smumn.edu.
Website: http://www.smumn.edu/graduate-home/areas-of-study/graduate-school-of-education/med-in-learning-design-technology.

Saint Michael's College, Graduate Programs, Program in Education, Colchester, VT 05439. Offers administration (M Ed, CAGS); arts in education (CAGS); curriculum and instruction (M Ed, CAGS); information technology (CAGS); reading (M Ed); special education (M Ed, CAGS); technology (M Ed). Part-time and evening/weekend programs available. *Degree requirements:* For master's, thesis. *Entrance requirements:* For master's, minimum GPA of 3.0. Electronic applications accepted. *Faculty research:* Integrative curriculum, moral and spiritual dimensions of education, learning styles, multiple intelligences, integrating technology into the curriculum.

St. Thomas University, School of Leadership Studies, Institute for Education, Miami Gardens, FL 33054-6459. Offers earth/space science (Certificate); educational administration (MS, Certificate); educational leadership (Ed D); elementary education (MS); ESOL (Certificate); gifted education (Certificate); instructional technology (MS, Certificate); professional/studies (Certificate); reading (MS, Certificate); special education (MS). Part-time and evening/weekend programs available. *Degree requirements:* For master's, comprehensive exam; for doctorate, comprehensive exam, thesis/dissertation. *Entrance requirements:* For master's, interview, minimum GPA of 3.0 or GRE; for doctorate, GRE or MAT. Additional exam requirements/recommendations for international students: Required—TOEFL (minimum score 550 paper-based; 79 iBT). Electronic applications accepted.

Saint Vincent College, Program in Education, Latrobe, PA 15650-2690. Offers curriculum and instruction (MS); educational media and technology (MS); environmental education (MS); school administration and supervision (MS); special education (MS). Part-time and evening/weekend programs available. *Degree requirements:* For master's, comprehensive exam. *Entrance requirements:* For master's, GRE (if undergraduate GPA less than 3.0). Additional exam requirements/recommendations for international students: Required—TOEFL (minimum score 550 paper-based). *Faculty research:* Assessment and instructional technology.

Saint Xavier University, Graduate Studies, School of Education, Chicago, IL 60655-3105. Offers counseling (MA); curriculum and instruction (MA); early childhood education (MA); educational administration (MA); elementary education (MA); individualized studies (MA), including educational technology, English as a second language (ESL), ISTEM (integrative science, technology, engineering, and math), science education; music education (MA); reading (MA); secondary education (MA); Spanish education (MA); special education (MA); teaching and leadership (MA). *Accreditation:* NCATE. Part-time and evening/weekend programs available. *Degree requirements:* For master's, thesis or project. *Entrance requirements:* For master's, minimum GPA of 3.0. *Expenses:* Contact institution.

Salem State University, School of Graduate Studies, Program in Library Media Studies, Salem, MA 01970-5353. Offers M Ed. *Accreditation:* NCATE. Part-time and evening/weekend programs available. *Students:* 1 (woman) full-time, 9 part-time (8 women). 6 applicants, 83% accepted, 5 enrolled. In 2013, 8 master's awarded. *Entrance requirements:* For master's, GRE or MAT. Additional exam requirements/recommendations for international students: Required—TOEFL (minimum score 550 paper-based; 80 iBT) or IELTS (minimum score 5.5). *Application deadline:* For fall admission, 5/1 for domestic students; for spring admission, 10/1 for domestic students. Applications are processed on a rolling basis. Application fee: $50. *Financial support:* Career-related internships or fieldwork, Federal Work-Study, scholarships/grants, and unspecified assistantships available. Support available to part-time students. Financial award application deadline: 5/1; financial award applicants required to submit FAFSA. *Application contact:* Dr. Lee A. Brossoit, Assistant Dean of Graduate Admissions, 978-542-6675, Fax: 978-542-7215, E-mail: lbrossoit@salemstate.edu.
Website: http://www.salemstate.edu/academics/schools/1563.php.

Sam Houston State University, College of Education and Applied Science, Department of Curriculum and Instruction, Huntsville, TX 77341. Offers curriculum and instruction (M Ed, MA); instructional technology (M Ed). *Accreditation:* NCATE. Part-time and evening/weekend programs available. *Faculty:* 19 full-time (13 women). *Students:* 53 full-time (39 women), 251 part-time (194 women); includes 124 minority (62 Black or African American, non-Hispanic/Latino; 1 American Indian or Alaska Native, non-Hispanic/Latino; 4 Asian, non-Hispanic/Latino; 47 Hispanic/Latino; 10 Two or more races, non-Hispanic/Latino), 4 international. Average age 32. 201 applicants, 94% accepted, 89 enrolled. In 2013, 114 master's awarded. *Degree requirements:* For master's, comprehensive exam, thesis optional. *Entrance requirements:* For master's, GRE General Test. Additional exam requirements/recommendations for international students: Required—TOEFL (minimum score 550 paper-based; 79 iBT), IELTS (minimum score 6.5). *Application deadline:* For fall admission, 8/1 for domestic students, 6/25 for international students; for spring admission, 12/1 for domestic students, 11/12 for international students. Applications are processed on a rolling basis. Application fee: $45 ($75 for international students). Electronic applications accepted. *Financial support:* In 2013–14, 3 research assistantships (averaging $9,542 per year) were awarded; career-related internships or fieldwork, Federal Work-Study, institutionally sponsored loans, scholarships/grants, tuition waivers (partial), and unspecified assistantships also available. Support available to part-time students. Financial award application deadline: 5/31; financial award applicants required to submit FAFSA. *Unit head:* Dr. Daphne Johnson, Chair, 936-294-3875, Fax: 936-294-1056, E-mail: edu_dxe@shsu.edu. *Application contact:* Molly Doughtie, Advisor, 936-294-1105, E-mail: edu_mej@shsu.edu.
Website: http://www.shsu.edu/~cai_www/.

San Diego State University, Graduate and Research Affairs, College of Education, Department of Educational Technology, San Diego, CA 92182. Offers educational technology (MA); educational technology and teaching and learning (Ed D). *Accreditation:* NCATE. Evening/weekend programs available. *Entrance requirements:* For master's, GRE General Test, letters of reference. Additional exam requirements/recommendations for international students: Required—TOEFL. Electronic applications accepted.

San Francisco State University, Division of Graduate Studies, College of Education, Department of Equity, Leadership Studies, and Instructional Technologies, Program in Instructional Technologies, San Francisco, CA 94132-1722. Offers MA. *Unit head:* Dr. David Hemphill, Interim Chair, 415-338-1653, E-mail: hemphill@sfsu.edu. *Application contact:* Dr. Pat Donohue, Program Coordinator, 415-338-1509, E-mail: pdonohue@sfsu.edu.
Website: http://www.sfsu.edu/~itec.

Seton Hall University, College of Education and Human Services, Department of Educational Studies, Program in Instructional Design, South Orange, NJ 07079-2697. Offers MA. Part-time and evening/weekend programs available. *Faculty:* 6 full-time (5 women), 7 part-time/adjunct (4 women). *Students:* 6 full-time (3 women), 41 part-time (31 women); includes 7 minority (4 Black or African American, non-Hispanic/Latino; 3 Hispanic/Latino), 2 international. Average age 38. 8 applicants, 100% accepted, 7 enrolled. In 2013, 13 degrees awarded. *Degree requirements:* For master's, comprehensive exam. *Entrance requirements:* For master's, GRE General Test or MAT, minimum GPA of 2.75. *Application deadline:* For fall admission, 5/1 for domestic students; for spring admission, 10/1 for domestic students. Applications are processed on a rolling basis. Application fee: $75. *Financial support:* Application deadline: 2/1. *Unit head:* Dr. Joseph Martinelli, Chair, 973-275-2733, E-mail: joseph.martinelli@shu.edu.

Application contact: Diana Minakakis, Associate Dean, 973-275-2824, Fax: 973-275-2187, E-mail: diana.minakakis@shu.edu.
Website: http://www.shu.edu/academics/education/ma-school-media-specialist/index.cfm.

Simmons College, Graduate School of Library and Information Science, Boston, MA 02115. Offers archives management (MS, Certificate); children's literature (MA); digital stewardship (Certificate); instructional technology (Certificate); library and information science (MS, PhD); managerial leadership in the informational professions (PhD); school library teacher (MS, Certificate); writing for children (MFA); MA/MA; MA/MAT; MA/MFA; MS/MA. *Accreditation:* ALA (one or more programs are accredited). Part-time and evening/weekend programs available. Postbaccalaureate distance learning degree programs offered (no on-campus study). *Students:* 55 full-time (45 women), 716 part-time (585 women); includes 81 minority (19 Black or African American, non-Hispanic/Latino; 1 American Indian or Alaska Native, non-Hispanic/Latino; 14 Asian, non-Hispanic/Latino; 32 Hispanic/Latino; 15 Two or more races, non-Hispanic/Latino), 9 international. 430 applicants, 82% accepted, 207 enrolled. In 2013, 281 master's, 4 doctorates awarded. *Degree requirements:* For master's, thesis optional, capstone project experience; for doctorate, comprehensive exam, 36 credit hours (includes 3-credit dissertation). *Entrance requirements:* For doctorate, GRE, transcripts, personal statement, resume, recommendations, master's degree. Additional exam requirements/recommendations for international students: Required—TOEFL (minimum score 550 paper-based; 79 iBT), IELTS (minimum score 7). *Application deadline:* For fall admission, 3/1 for domestic and international students; for spring admission, 9/1 for domestic and international students; for summer admission, 2/1 for domestic and international students. Applications are processed on a rolling basis. Application fee: $65. Electronic applications accepted. *Financial support:* In 2013–14, 67 students received support, including 5 fellowships with partial tuition reimbursements available (averaging $32,461 per year), 6 research assistantships (averaging $35,168 per year), 7 teaching assistantships with full and partial tuition reimbursements available (averaging $3,000 per year); scholarships/grants, tuition waivers, and unspecified assistantships also available. Financial award application deadline: 2/1; financial award applicants required to submit FAFSA. *Faculty research:* Archives and social justice, information-seeking behavior, information retrieval, organization of information, cultural heritage informatics. *Unit head:* Dr. Eileen G. Abels, Dean, 617-521-2869. *Application contact:* Sarah Petrakos, 617-521-2868, Fax: 617-521-3192, E-mail: gslisadm@simmons.edu.
Website: http://www.simmons.edu/gslis/.

Simon Fraser University, Office of Graduate Studies, Faculty of Education, Program in Educational Technology and Learning Design, Burnaby, BC V5A 1S6, Canada. Offers M Ed, MA, PhD. Part-time and evening/weekend programs available. *Degree requirements:* For master's, comprehensive exam (for some programs), thesis (for some programs); for doctorate, comprehensive exam, thesis/dissertation. *Entrance requirements:* For master's, minimum GPA of 3.0 (on scale of 4.33), or 3.33 based on last 60 credits of undergraduate courses; for doctorate, minimum GPA of 3.5 (on scale of 4.33). Additional exam requirements/recommendations for international students: Recommended—TOEFL (minimum score 580 paper-based; 93 iBT), IELTS (minimum score 7), TWE (minimum score 5). *Expenses: Tuition, area resident:* Full-time $5084 Canadian dollars. *Required fees:* $840 Canadian dollars. *Faculty research:* Integration of technological applications in post-secondary education, problems in learning and teaching science, gaming and simulation for learning, adaptive software for researching and promoting self-regulated learning, design and use of online environments for learning.

Southeastern Louisiana University, College of Education, Department of Educational Leadership and Technology, Hammond, LA 70402. Offers educational leadership (M Ed, Ed D); educational technology leadership (M Ed). Part-time and evening/weekend programs available. *Faculty:* 14 full-time (7 women), 1 part-time/adjunct (0 women). *Students:* 4 full-time (all women), 269 part-time (208 women); includes 78 minority (67 Black or African American, non-Hispanic/Latino; 7 Hispanic/Latino; 4 Two or more races, non-Hispanic/Latino), 1 international. Average age 37. 55 applicants, 87% accepted, 30 enrolled. In 2013, 94 master's, 4 doctorates awarded. *Degree requirements:* For master's, comprehensive exam; for doctorate, comprehensive exam, thesis/dissertation. *Entrance requirements:* For master's, GRE (verbal and quantitative); for doctorate, GRE, master's degree with minimum GPA of 3.25, 3.0 on the last 60 undergraduate hours. Additional exam requirements/recommendations for international students: Required—TOEFL (minimum score 500 paper-based; 61 iBT). *Application deadline:* For fall admission, 7/15 priority date for domestic students, 6/1 priority date for international students; for spring admission, 12/1 priority date for domestic students, 10/1 priority date for international students. Applications are processed on a rolling basis. Application fee: $20 ($30 for international students). Electronic applications accepted. *Expenses:* Tuition, state resident: full-time $5047. Tuition, nonresident: full-time $17,066. *Required fees:* $1213. Tuition and fees vary according to degree level. *Financial support:* Career-related internships or fieldwork, Federal Work-Study, institutionally sponsored loans, scholarships/grants, and unspecified assistantships available. Support available to part-time students. Financial award application deadline: 5/1; financial award applicants required to submit FAFSA. *Faculty research:* Technology leadership in schools, techno stress for educational leaders, dispositions of effective leaders. *Total annual research expenditures:* $3,692. *Unit head:* Dr. Jeffrey Oescher, Interim Department Head, 985-549-5713, Fax: 985-549-5712, E-mail: jeffrey.oescher@selu.edu. *Application contact:* Sandra Meyers, Graduate Admissions Analyst, 985-549-2066, Fax: 985-549-5632, E-mail: admissions@selu.edu.
Website: http://www.selu.edu/acad_research/depts/edlt.

Southeast Missouri State University, School of Graduate Studies, Department of Middle and Secondary Education, Cape Girardeau, MO 63701-4799. Offers secondary education (MA), including education studies, education technology. *Accreditation:* NCATE. Part-time programs available. *Faculty:* 5 full-time (3 women), 1 (woman) part-time/adjunct. *Students:* 6 full-time (4 women), 42 part-time (30 women); includes 4 minority (all Black or African American, non-Hispanic/Latino). Average age 30. 28 applicants, 100% accepted, 28 enrolled. In 2013, 8 master's awarded. *Degree requirements:* For master's, comprehensive exam, research paper. *Entrance requirements:* For master's, minimum undergraduate GPA of 2.75. Additional exam requirements/recommendations for international students: Required—TOEFL (minimum score 550 paper-based; 79 iBT), IELTS (minimum score 6), PTE (minimum score 53). *Application deadline:* For fall admission, 8/1 for domestic students, 6/1 for international students; for spring admission, 11/21 for domestic students, 10/1 for international students; for summer admission, 5/15 for domestic students. Applications are processed on a rolling basis. Application fee: $30 ($40 for international students). Electronic applications accepted. *Expenses:* Tuition, state resident: full-time $5139; part-time $285.50 per credit hour. Tuition, nonresident: full-time $9099; part-time $505.50 per credit hour. *Financial support:* In 2013–14, 7 students received support. Career-related internships or fieldwork, Federal Work-Study, scholarships/grants, traineeships, tuition waivers (full), and unspecified assistantships available. Financial award application deadline: 6/30; financial award applicants required to submit FAFSA. *Faculty research:* Pedagogy of teaching, multicultural education, reading and writing strategies, use of technology in the classroom. *Unit head:* Dr. Simin L. Cwick, Middle and Secondary Education Department Chair, 573-651-5965, E-mail: scwick@semo.edu. *Application contact:* Alisa Aleen McFerron, Assistant Director of Admissions for Operations, 573-651-5937, E-mail: amcferron@semo.edu.
Website: http://www5.semo.edu/middleandsec/.

Southern Illinois University Edwardsville, Graduate School, School of Education, Department of Educational Leadership, Program in Instructional Technology, Edwardsville, IL 62026. Offers MS Ed. *Accreditation:* NCATE. Part-time and evening/weekend programs available. *Students:* 3 full-time (1 woman), 53 part-time (34 women); includes 14 minority (10 Black or African American, non-Hispanic/Latino; 2 Hispanic/Latino; 2 Two or more races, non-Hispanic/Latino). 17 applicants, 94% accepted. In 2013, 11 master's awarded. *Degree requirements:* For master's, thesis or alternative, portfolio. *Entrance requirements:* Additional exam requirements/recommendations for international students: Required—TOEFL (minimum score 550 paper-based, 79 iBT), IELTS (minimum score 6.5), Michigan Test of English Language Proficiency or PTE. *Application deadline:* For fall admission, 7/18 for domestic students, 6/1 for international students; for spring admission, 12/12 for domestic students, 10/1 for international students; for summer admission, 4/24 for domestic students, 3/1 for international students. Applications are processed on a rolling basis. Application fee: $30. Electronic applications accepted. *Expenses:* Tuition, state resident: full-time $3551. Tuition, nonresident: full-time $8378. *Financial support:* In 2013–14, 2 research assistantships (averaging $9,585 per year), 3 teaching assistantships (averaging $9,585 per year) were awarded; fellowships, institutionally sponsored loans, scholarships/grants, and unspecified assistantships also available. Financial award application deadline: 3/1; financial award applicants required to submit FAFSA. *Unit head:* Dr. David Knowlton, Program Director, 618-650-3958, E-mail: dknowlt@siue.edu. *Application contact:* Melissa K. Mace, Assistant Director of Graduate and International Recruitment, 618-650-2756, Fax: 618-650-3618, E-mail: mmace@siue.edu.
Website: http://www.siue.edu/education/edld/.

Southern Illinois University Edwardsville, Graduate School, School of Education, Department of Educational Leadership, Program in Web-Based Learning, Edwardsville, IL 62026. Offers Postbaccalaureate Certificate. Part-time programs available. *Students:* 4 part-time (3 women). 1 applicant, 100% accepted. In 2013, 2 Postbaccalaureate Certificates awarded. *Entrance requirements:* Additional exam requirements/recommendations for international students: Required—TOEFL (minimum score 550 paper-based, 79 iBT), IELTS (minimum score 6.5), Michigan Test of English Language Proficiency or PTE. *Application deadline:* For fall admission, 7/18 for domestic students, 6/1 for international students; for spring admission, 12/12 for domestic students, 10/1 for international students; for summer admission, 4/24 for domestic students, 3/1 for international students. Applications are processed on a rolling basis. Application fee: $30. Electronic applications accepted. *Expenses:* Tuition, state resident: full-time $3551. Tuition, nonresident: full-time $8378. *Financial support:* Institutionally sponsored loans, scholarships/grants, and unspecified assistantships available. Financial award application deadline: 3/1; financial award applicants required to submit FAFSA. *Unit head:* Dr. David Knowlton, Program Director, 618-650-3958, E-mail: dknowlt@siue.edu. *Application contact:* Melissa K. Mace, Assistant Director of Graduate and International Recruitment, 618-650-2756, Fax: 618-650-3618, E-mail: mmace@siue.edu.
Website: http://www.siue.edu/education/edld/.

Southern New Hampshire University, School of Education, Manchester, NH 03106-1045. Offers business education (M Ed); child development (M Ed); curriculum and instruction (M Ed), including education leadership, reading, special education, technology integration; education (M Ed); educational leadership (M Ed, Ed D); educational studies (M Ed); elementary education (M Ed); English (MAT); English for speakers of other languages (M Ed); reading and writing specialist (M Ed); school business administration (Certificate); secondary education (M Ed); special education (M Ed); technology integration specialist (M Ed). Part-time and evening/weekend programs available. Postbaccalaureate distance learning degree programs offered (no on-campus study). *Degree requirements:* For master's, comprehensive exam (for some programs), thesis or alternative. *Entrance requirements:* For master's, PRAXIS I, minimum GPA of 2.75. Additional exam requirements/recommendations for international students: Required—TOEFL (minimum score 550 paper-based). Electronic applications accepted. *Expenses:* Contact institution.

Southern Polytechnic State University, School of Arts and Sciences, Department of English, Technical Communication, and Media Arts, Marietta, GA 30060-2896. Offers communications management (Postbaccalaureate Certificate); content development (Postbaccalaureate Certificate); information and instructional design (MSIID); information design and communication (MS); instructional design (Postbaccalaureate Certificate); technical communication (Graduate Certificate); visual communication and graphics (Postbaccalaureate Certificate). Part-time and evening/weekend programs available. Postbaccalaureate distance learning degree programs offered (no on-campus study). *Degree requirements:* For master's, thesis optional; for other advanced degree, thesis optional, 18 hours completed through thesis option (6 hours), internship option (6 hours) or advanced coursework option (6 hours). *Entrance requirements:* For master's, GRE, statement of purpose, writing sample, timed essay; for other advanced degree, writing sample, professional recommendations. Additional exam requirements/recommendations for international students: Required—TOEFL (minimum score 550 paper-based; 79 iBT), IELTS (minimum score 6.5). Electronic applications accepted. *Faculty research:* Usability, user-centered design, instructional design, information architecture, information design, content strategy.

Southern University and Agricultural and Mechanical College, Graduate School, College of Education, Department of Curriculum and Instruction, Baton Rouge, LA 70813. Offers elementary education (M Ed); media (M Ed); secondary education (M Ed). *Degree requirements:* For master's, comprehensive exam, thesis optional. *Entrance requirements:* For master's, GMAT or GRE General Test. Additional exam requirements/recommendations for international students: Required—TOEFL (minimum score 525 paper-based).

Stanford University, School of Education, Program in Learning, Design, and Technology, Stanford, CA 94305-9991. Offers MA. Electronic applications accepted. *Expenses: Tuition:* Full-time $42,690; part-time $949 per credit. *Required fees:* $185.

State University of New York College at Oneonta, Graduate Education, Division of Education, Oneonta, NY 13820-4015. Offers educational psychology and counseling (MS Ed, CAS), including school counselor K-12; educational technology specialist (MS Ed); elementary education and reading (MS Ed), including childhood education, literacy education; secondary education (MS Ed), including adolescence education; special education (MS Ed), including adolescence, childhood. *Accreditation:* NCATE. Part-time and evening/weekend programs available. *Entrance requirements:* For master's, GRE General Test.

State University of New York College at Potsdam, School of Education and Professional Studies, Program in Information and Communication Technology, Potsdam, NY 13676. Offers educational technology specialist (MS Ed); organizational performance, leadership and technology (MS Ed). Part-time and evening/weekend programs available. *Degree requirements:* For master's, culminating experience. *Entrance requirements:* For master's, minimum GPA of 3.0 in last 60 hours of course

work. Additional exam requirements/recommendations for international students: Required—TOEFL (minimum score 550 paper-based; 80 iBT), IELTS (minimum score 6). Electronic applications accepted.

State University of New York Empire State College, School for Graduate Studies, Programs in Education, Saratoga Springs, NY 12866-4391. Offers adult learning (MA); learning and emerging technologies (MA); teaching (MAT); teaching and learning (M Ed). Postbaccalaureate distance learning degree programs offered.

Stony Brook University, State University of New York, Graduate School, College of Engineering and Applied Sciences, Department of Technology and Society, Program in Educational Technology, Stony Brook, NY 11794. Offers MS. *Accreditation:* NCATE. *Application deadline:* For fall admission, 1/15 for domestic students; for spring admission, 10/1 for domestic students. Electronic applications accepted. *Expenses:* Tuition, state resident: full-time $9870; part-time $411 per credit. Tuition, nonresident: full-time $18,350; part-time $765 per credit. *Financial support:* Research assistantships and teaching assistantships available. *Unit head:* Dr. David Ferguson, Chair, 631-632-8770, E-mail: david.ferguson@stonybrook.edu. *Application contact:* Dr. Sheldon Reaven, Graduate Program Director, 631-632-8770, E-mail: sheldon.raven@sunysb.edu.
Website: http://www.stonybrook.edu/est/graduate/msedtech.shtml.

Stony Brook University, State University of New York, School of Professional Development, Stony Brook, NY 11794. Offers biology (MAT); chemistry (MAT); coaching (Graduate Certificate); earth science (MAT); educational computing (Graduate Certificate); educational leadership (Advanced Certificate); English (MAT); environmental management (Graduate Certificate); French (MAT); German (MAT); higher education administration (MA, Certificate); human resource management (MS, Graduate Certificate); industrial management (Graduate Certificate); information systems management (Graduate Certificate); Italian (MAT); liberal studies (MA); mathematics (MAT); operations research (Graduate Certificate); physics (MAT); school district business leadership (Advanced Certificate); social science and the professions (MPS), including environmental management, human resource management; social studies (MAT); Spanish (MAT). Part-time and evening/weekend programs available. Postbaccalaureate distance learning degree programs offered. *Faculty:* 2 full-time (1 woman), 70 part-time/adjunct (30 women). *Students:* 241 full-time (135 women), 954 part-time (673 women); includes 209 minority (65 Black or African American, non-Hispanic/Latino; 2 American Indian or Alaska Native, non-Hispanic/Latino; 32 Asian, non-Hispanic/Latino; 104 Hispanic/Latino; 6 Two or more races, non-Hispanic/Latino), 7 international. Average age 28. 353 applicants, 92% accepted, 248 enrolled. In 2013, 312 master's, 131 other advanced degrees awarded. *Degree requirements:* For master's, one foreign language, thesis or alternative. *Application deadline:* For fall admission, 1/15 for domestic students; for spring admission, 10/1 for domestic students. Applications are processed on a rolling basis. Application fee: $100. *Expenses:* Tuition, state resident: full-time $9870; part-time $411 per credit. Tuition, nonresident: full-time $18,350; part-time $765 per credit. *Financial support:* Fellowships, research assistantships, teaching assistantships, and career-related internships or fieldwork available. Support available to part-time students. *Unit head:* Dr. Thomas Sexton, Interim Dean, 631-632-7181, Fax: 631-632-9046, E-mail: thomas.sexton@stonybrook.edu. *Application contact:* 631-632-7050 Ext. 1, E-mail: spd@stonybrook.edu.
Website: http://www.stonybrook.edu/spd/.

Strayer University, Graduate Studies, Washington, DC 20005-2603. Offers accounting (MS); acquisition (MBA); business administration (MBA); communications technology (MS); educational management (M Ed); finance (MBA); health services administration (MHSA); hospitality and tourism management (MBA); human resource management (MBA); information systems (MS), including computer security management, decision support system management, enterprise resource management, network management, software engineering management, systems development management; management (MBA); management information systems (MS); marketing (MBA); professional accounting (MS), including accounting information systems, controllership, taxation; public administration (MPA); supply chain management (MBA); technology in education (M Ed). Programs also offered at campus locations in Birmingham, AL; Chamblee, GA; Cobb County, GA; Morrow, GA; White Marsh, MD; Charleston, SC; Columbia, SC; Greensboro, NC; Greenville, SC; Lexington, KY; Louisville, KY; Nashville, TN; North Raleigh, NC; Washington, DC. Part-time and evening/weekend programs available. Postbaccalaureate distance learning degree programs offered (minimal on-campus study). *Degree requirements:* For master's, thesis. *Entrance requirements:* For master's, GMAT, GRE General Test, bachelor's degree from an accredited college or university, minimum undergraduate GPA of 2.75. Electronic applications accepted.

Syracuse University, School of Education, Program in Educational Technology, Syracuse, NY 13244. Offers CAS. *Accreditation:* ACA. Part-time programs available. *Students:* 2 part-time (1 woman); includes 1 minority (American Indian or Alaska Native, non-Hispanic/Latino). Average age 39. In 2013, 1 CAS awarded. *Degree requirements:* For CAS, thesis or alternative. *Entrance requirements:* Additional exam requirements/recommendations for international students: Required—TOEFL (minimum score 100 iBT). *Application deadline:* For fall admission, 2/1 priority date for domestic and international students; for spring admission, 10/15 priority date for domestic and international students. Applications are processed on a rolling basis. Application fee: $75. Electronic applications accepted. *Financial support:* Application deadline: 1/1. *Faculty research:* Academics and athletics, drug free schools, group counseling, prejudice prevention, culture-centered counseling. *Unit head:* Dr. Tiffany A. Koszalka, Chair, 315-443-3703, E-mail: takoszal@syr.edu. *Application contact:* Laurie Deyo, Graduate Recruiter, School of Education, 315-443-2505, E-mail: e-gradrcrt@syr.edu.
Website: http://soeweb.syr.edu/chs/.

Syracuse University, School of Education, Program in Instructional Technology, Syracuse, NY 13244. Offers MS. Part-time programs available. *Students:* 2 full-time (1 woman), 3 part-time (1 woman); includes 1 minority (Hispanic/Latino). Average age 26. 4 applicants, 75% accepted, 1 enrolled. In 2013, 3 master's awarded. *Entrance requirements:* For master's, New York state teacher certification or eligibility for certification, resume. Additional exam requirements/recommendations for international students: Required—TOEFL (minimum score 100 iBT). *Application deadline:* For fall admission, 1/15 for domestic students, 1/15 priority date for international students. Application fee: $75. Electronic applications accepted. *Financial support:* Fellowships with full tuition reimbursements and research assistantships with full and partial tuition reimbursements available. Financial award application deadline: 1/1. *Unit head:* Dr. Tiffany A. Koszalka, Chair, 315-443-3703, E-mail: takoszal@syr.edu. *Application contact:* Laurie Deyo, Graduate Recruiter, School of Education, 315-443-2505, E-mail: e-gradrcrt@syr.edu.
Website: http://soeweb.syr.edu/academic/Instructional_Design_Development_and_Evaluation/graduate/masters/instructional_technology/default.aspx.

Syracuse University, School of Education, Program in Professional Practice in Educational Technology, Syracuse, NY 13244. Offers CAS. Part-time programs available. *Entrance requirements:* Additional exam requirements/recommendations for international students: Required—TOEFL (minimum score 100 iBT). *Application deadline:* For fall admission, 1/15 for domestic students, 1/14 priority date for international students. Applications are processed on a rolling basis. Application fee: $75. Electronic applications accepted. *Unit head:* Dr. Tiffany A. Koszalka, Chair, 315-443-3703, E-mail: takoszal@syr.edu. *Application contact:* Laurie Deyo, Graduate Recruiter, School of Education, 315-443-2505, E-mail: e-gradrcrt@syr.edu.
Website: http://soeweb.syr.edu/.

Syracuse University, School of Information Studies, Program in Library and Information Science: School Media, Syracuse, NY 13244. Offers MS. Part-time and evening/weekend programs available. Postbaccalaureate distance learning degree programs offered (minimal on-campus study). *Students:* 10 full-time (9 women), 12 part-time (11 women); includes 2 minority (1 Hispanic/Latino; 1 Two or more races, non-Hispanic/Latino). Average age 29. 16 applicants, 100% accepted, 10 enrolled. In 2013, 23 master's awarded. *Entrance requirements:* For master's, GRE. Additional exam requirements/recommendations for international students: Required—TOEFL (minimum score 100 iBT). *Application deadline:* For fall admission, 1/1 priority date for domestic and international students; for spring admission, 10/15 priority date for domestic and international students. Applications are processed on a rolling basis. Application fee: $75. Electronic applications accepted. *Financial support:* Fellowships with full tuition reimbursements, research assistantships with partial tuition reimbursements, and teaching assistantships with partial tuition reimbursements available. Financial award application deadline: 1/1. *Unit head:* Prof. Jill Hurst-Wahl, Program Director, 315-443-1070, E-mail: igrad@syr.edu. *Application contact:* Susan Corieri, Director of Enrollment Management, 315-443-2575, E-mail: ischool@syr.edu.
Website: http://ischool.syr.edu/academics/graduate/mls/mediaprogram/index.aspx.
See Display on page 1583 and Close-Up on page 1599.

Syracuse University, School of Information Studies, Program in School Media, Syracuse, NY 13244. Offers CAS. Part-time and evening/weekend programs available. Postbaccalaureate distance learning degree programs offered. *Students:* 2 part-time (both women). Average age 35. *Entrance requirements:* For degree, MS in library and information science. Additional exam requirements/recommendations for international students: Required—TOEFL (minimum score 100 iBT). *Application deadline:* For fall admission, 1/1 priority date for domestic and international students; for spring admission, 10/15 priority date for domestic and international students. Applications are processed on a rolling basis. Application fee: $75. Electronic applications accepted. *Financial support:* Application deadline: 1/1. *Unit head:* Prof. Jill Hurst-Wahl, Program Director, 315-443-1070, E-mail: igrad@syr.edu. *Application contact:* Susan Corieri, Director of Enrollment Management, 315-443-2575, E-mail: ist@syr.edu.
Website: http://ischool.syr.edu/.
See Display on page 1583 and Close-Up on page 1599.

Teachers College, Columbia University, Graduate Faculty of Education, Department of Math, Science and Technology, Program in Educational Media/Instructional Technology, New York, NY 10027. Offers Ed M, MA, Ed D. *Faculty:* 8 full-time, 6 part-time/adjunct. *Students:* 25 full-time (16 women), 74 part-time (41 women); includes 30 minority (8 Black or African American, non-Hispanic/Latino; 17 Asian, non-Hispanic/Latino; 3 Hispanic/Latino; 2 Two or more races, non-Hispanic/Latino), 38 international. Average age 33. 58 applicants, 76% accepted, 25 enrolled. In 2013, 20 master's, 8 doctorates awarded. *Degree requirements:* For master's, integrative project; for doctorate, comprehensive exam, thesis/dissertation. *Entrance requirements:* For doctorate, GRE General Test or MAT. *Application deadline:* For fall admission, 1/15 priority date for domestic students; for spring admission, 11/1 for domestic students; for summer admission, 1/15 priority date for domestic students. Applications are processed on a rolling basis. Application fee: $65. Electronic applications accepted. *Financial support:* Career-related internships or fieldwork, Federal Work-Study, institutionally sponsored loans, and tuition waivers (full and partial) available. Support available to part-time students. Financial award applicants required to submit FAFSA. *Faculty research:* Video and interactive learning. *Unit head:* Prof. Lalitha Vasudevan, Chair, 212-678-6660, E-mail: lmv2102@columbia.edu. *Application contact:* Deanna Ghozati, Assistant Director of Admission, 212-678-4018, Fax: 212-678-4171, E-mail: ghozati@tc.edu.
Website: http://www.tc.edu/mst/ccte/.

Tennessee Technological University, College of Graduate Studies, College of Education, Department of Curriculum and Instruction, Program in Educational Technology, Cookeville, TN 38505. Offers MA, Ed S. Part-time and evening/weekend programs available. *Students:* 3 full-time (1 woman), 15 part-time (12 women). 6 applicants, 67% accepted, 4 enrolled. *Degree requirements:* For master's, comprehensive exam, thesis or alternative. *Entrance requirements:* For master's, MAT or GRE. Additional exam requirements/recommendations for international students: Required—TOEFL (minimum score 527 paper-based; 71 iBT), IELTS (minimum score 5.5), PTE (minimum score 48), or TOEIC (Test of English as an International Communication). *Application deadline:* For fall admission, 8/1 for domestic students, 5/1 for international students; for spring admission, 12/1 for domestic students, 10/1 for international students. Application fee: $35 ($40 for international students). Electronic applications accepted. *Expenses:* Tuition, state resident: full-time $9347; part-time $465 per credit hour. Tuition, nonresident: full-time $23,635; part-time $1152 per credit hour. *Unit head:* Dr. Jeremy Wendt, Interim Chairperson, 931-372-3181, Fax: 931-372-6270, E-mail: jwendt@tntech.edu. *Application contact:* Shelia K. Kendrick, Coordinator of Graduate Studies, 931-372-3808, Fax: 931-372-3497, E-mail: skendrick@tntech.edu.

Texas A&M University, College of Education and Human Development, Department of Educational Psychology, College Station, TX 77843. Offers bilingual education (M Ed, MS); counseling psychology (PhD); educational psychology (M Ed, MS, PhD); educational technology (M Ed); school psychology (PhD); special education (M Ed, MS). *Accreditation:* APA (one or more programs are accredited). Part-time and evening/weekend programs available. Postbaccalaureate distance learning degree programs offered (no on-campus study). *Faculty:* 41. *Students:* 148 full-time (122 women), 143 part-time (124 women); includes 97 minority (15 Black or African American, non-Hispanic/Latino; 11 Asian, non-Hispanic/Latino; 66 Hispanic/Latino; 5 Two or more races, non-Hispanic/Latino), 49 international. Average age 31. 249 applicants, 52% accepted, 83 enrolled. In 2013, 43 master's, 22 doctorates awarded. *Degree requirements:* For master's, thesis optional; for doctorate, thesis/dissertation. *Entrance requirements:* For master's and doctorate, GRE General Test. Additional exam requirements/recommendations for international students: Required—TOEFL. Application fee: $50 ($75 for international students). Electronic applications accepted. *Expenses:* Tuition, state resident: full-time $4078; part-time $226.55 per credit hour. Tuition, nonresident: full-time $10,450; part-time $580.55 per credit hour. *Required fees:* $2328; $278.50 per credit hour. $642.45 per semester. *Financial support:* In 2013–14, fellowships (averaging $12,000 per year), research assistantships (averaging $9,000 per year), teaching assistantships (averaging $9,000 per year) were awarded; career-related internships or fieldwork, institutionally sponsored loans, scholarships/grants, and unspecified assistantships also available. Financial award applicants required to submit FAFSA. *Unit head:* Dr. Cathy Watson, Head, 979-845-1394, E-mail: cwatson@tamu.edu. *Application contact:* Christy Porter, Senior Academic Advisor, 979-845-1874, E-mail: csporter@tamu.edu.
Website: http://epsy.tamu.edu.

Educational Media/Instructional Technology

Texas A&M University–Commerce, Graduate School, College of Education and Human Services, Department of Educational Leadership, Commerce, TX 75429-3011. Offers educational administration (M Ed, Ed D); educational technology (M Ed, MS); higher education (MS, Ed D); training and development (MS). Part-time programs available. Terminal master's awarded for partial completion of doctoral program. *Degree requirements:* For master's, comprehensive exam, thesis (for some programs); for doctorate, thesis/dissertation, departmental qualifying exam. *Entrance requirements:* For master's, GRE General Test; for doctorate, GRE General Test, writing skills exam, interview. Electronic applications accepted. *Expenses:* Tuition, state resident: full-time $3630; part-time $2420 per year. Tuition, nonresident: full-time $9948; part-time $6632.16 per year. *Required fees:* $1006 per year. Tuition and fees vary according to course load. *Faculty research:* Property tax reform, politics of education, administrative stress.

Texas A&M University–Corpus Christi, Graduate Studies and Research, College of Education, Corpus Christi, TX 78412-5503. Offers counseling (MS, PhD), including counseling (MS), counselor education (PhD); curriculum and instruction (MS, Ed D); early childhood education (MS); educational administration (MS); educational leadership (Ed D); educational technology (MS); elementary education (MS); kinesiology (MS); reading (MS); secondary education (MS); special education (MS). Part-time and evening/weekend programs available. *Degree requirements:* For master's, comprehensive exam, thesis (for some programs); for doctorate, comprehensive exam, thesis/dissertation. *Entrance requirements:* For master's, GRE General Test. Additional exam requirements/recommendations for international students: Required—TOEFL. Electronic applications accepted.

Texas A&M University–Kingsville, College of Graduate Studies, College of Education, Department of Educational Leadership and Counseling, Program in Instructional Technology, Kingsville, TX 78363. Offers MS. *Faculty:* 9 full-time (5 women), 4 part-time/adjunct (2 women). *Students:* 8 full-time (5 women), 12 part-time (6 women); includes 16 minority (all Hispanic/Latino). Average age 37. 10 applicants, 100% accepted, 7 enrolled. In 2013, 5 master's awarded. *Degree requirements:* For master's, comprehensive exam, thesis or alternative, internship, project. *Entrance requirements:* For master's, GRE General Test, minimum GPA of 3.0. Additional exam requirements/recommendations for international students: Required—TOEFL. *Application deadline:* Applications are processed on a rolling basis. Application fee: $35 ($50 for international students). Electronic applications accepted. *Financial support:* Career-related internships or fieldwork and Federal Work-Study available. Support available to part-time students. Financial award applicants required to submit FAFSA. *Unit head:* Dr. Marybeth Green, Coordinator, 361-593-2895, E-mail: kumeg004@tamuk.edu. *Application contact:* Dr. Alberto M. Olivares, Dean, College of Graduate Studies, 361-593-2808, Fax: 361-593-3412, E-mail: a-olivares@tamuk.edu. Website: http://www.tamuk.edu/cehp/edlc/instructional-technology.html.

Texas A&M University–Texarkana, Graduate Studies and Research, College of Education and Liberal Arts, Texarkana, TX 75505-5518. Offers adult education (MS); curriculum and instruction (M Ed); education (MS); educational administration (M Ed); English (MA); instructional technology (MS); interdisciplinary studies (MA, MS); special education (MS). Part-time and evening/weekend programs available. *Degree requirements:* For master's, comprehensive exam (for some programs), thesis optional. *Entrance requirements:* For master's, minimum GPA of 2.5 on last 60 hours of bachelor's degree. Additional exam requirements/recommendations for international students: Required—TOEFL. Electronic applications accepted.

Texas State University, Graduate School, College of Education, Department of Curriculum and Instruction, Educational Technology Program, San Marcos, TX 78666. Offers M Ed. Part-time and evening/weekend programs available. *Faculty:* 3 full-time (1 woman). *Students:* 13 full-time (10 women), 22 part-time (16 women); includes 14 minority (1 Black or African American, non-Hispanic/Latino; 1 American Indian or Alaska Native, non-Hispanic/Latino; 2 Asian, non-Hispanic/Latino; 10 Hispanic/Latino). Average age 35. 14 applicants, 71% accepted, 9 enrolled. In 2013, 10 master's awarded. *Degree requirements:* For master's, comprehensive exam, thesis optional. *Entrance requirements:* For master's, minimum GPA of 2.75 in undergraduate work. Additional exam requirements/recommendations for international students: Required—TOEFL (minimum score 550 paper-based; 78 iBT). *Application deadline:* For fall admission, 6/15 priority date for domestic students, 6/1 for international students; for spring admission, 10/15 priority date for domestic students, 10/1 for international students. Applications are processed on a rolling basis. Application fee: $40 ($90 for international students). Electronic applications accepted. *Expenses:* Tuition, state resident: full-time $6663; part-time $278 per credit hour. Tuition, nonresident: full-time $15,159; part-time $632 per credit hour. *Required fees:* $1872; $54 per credit hour. $306 per term. Tuition and fees vary according to course load. *Financial support:* In 2013–14, 19 students received support, including 4 research assistantships (averaging $11,532 per year); teaching assistantships also available. Financial award application deadline: 4/1. *Unit head:* Dr. David Bynum, Graduate Advisor, 512-245-2038, Fax: 512-245-7911, E-mail: db15@txstate.edu. *Application contact:* Dr. Andrea Golato, Dean of Graduate School, 512-245-2581, Fax: 512-245-8365, E-mail: gradcollege@txstate.edu. Website: http://www.education.txstate.edu/ci/degrees-programs/graduate/edtech.html.

Texas Tech University, Graduate School, College of Education, Department of Educational Psychology and Leadership, Lubbock, TX 79409-1071. Offers counselor education (M Ed, PhD); educational leadership (M Ed, Ed D); educational psychology (M Ed, PhD); higher education (M Ed, Ed D); higher education research (PhD); instructional technology (M Ed, Ed D); special education (M Ed, Ed D, PhD). *Accreditation:* ACA; NCATE. Part-time and evening/weekend programs available. Postbaccalaureate distance learning degree programs offered (minimal on-campus study). *Faculty:* 42 full-time (20 women). *Students:* 220 full-time (171 women), 549 part-time (404 women); includes 219 minority (73 Black or African American, non-Hispanic/Latino; 5 American Indian or Alaska Native, non-Hispanic/Latino; 6 Asian, non-Hispanic/Latino; 122 Hispanic/Latino; 13 Two or more races, non-Hispanic/Latino), 48 international. Average age 36. 437 applicants, 72% accepted, 215 enrolled. In 2013, 137 master's, 38 doctorates awarded. Terminal master's awarded for partial completion of doctoral program. *Degree requirements:* For master's, comprehensive exam, thesis optional; for doctorate, comprehensive exam, thesis/dissertation. *Entrance requirements:* For master's, GRE (for some programs); for doctorate, GRE. Additional exam requirements/recommendations for international students: Required—TOEFL (minimum score 550 paper-based; 79 iBT). *Application deadline:* For fall admission, 6/1 priority date for domestic students, 1/15 priority date for international students; for spring admission, 9/1 priority date for domestic students, 6/15 priority date for international students. Applications are processed on a rolling basis. Application fee: $60. Electronic applications accepted. *Expenses:* Tuition, state resident: full-time $6062; part-time $252.57 per credit hour. Tuition, nonresident: full-time $14,558; part-time $606.57 per credit hour. *Required fees:* $2655; $35 per credit hour. $907.50 per semester. Tuition and fees vary according to course load. *Financial support:* In 2013–14, 188 students received support, including 179 fellowships (averaging $2,580 per year), 39 research assistantships (averaging $4,550 per year), 8 teaching assistantships (averaging $4,647 per year); scholarships/grants and unspecified assistantships also available. Support available to part-time students. Financial award application deadline: 1/3; financial

award applicants required to submit FAFSA. *Faculty research:* Cognitive, motivational, and developmental processes in learning; counseling education; instructional technology; generic special education and sensory impairment; community college administration; K-12 school administration. *Total annual research expenditures:* $708,063. *Unit head:* Dr. Fred Hartmeister, Chair, 806-834-0248, Fax: 806-742-2179, E-mail: fred.hartmeister@ttu.edu. *Application contact:* Pam Smith, Admissions Advisor, 806-834-2969, Fax: 806-742-2179, E-mail: pam.smith@ttu.edu. Website: http://www.educ.ttu.edu/.

Thomas Edison State College, Heavin School of Arts and Sciences, Program in Online Learning and Teaching, Trenton, NJ 08608-1176. Offers Graduate Certificate. Part-time programs available. Postbaccalaureate distance learning degree programs offered (no on-campus study). *Entrance requirements:* Additional exam requirements/recommendations for international students: Required—TOEFL (minimum score 550 paper-based; 79 iBT). Electronic applications accepted.

Touro College, Graduate School of Education, New York, NY 10010. Offers education and special education (MS); education biology (MS); instructional technology (MS); mathematics education (MS); school leadership (MS); teaching English to speakers of other languages (MS); teaching literacy (MS). Part-time and evening/weekend programs available. Postbaccalaureate distance learning degree programs offered (no on-campus study). *Faculty:* 75 full-time, 131 part-time/adjunct. *Students:* 327 full-time (272 women), 2,454 part-time (2,103 women); includes 840 minority (333 Black or African American, non-Hispanic/Latino; 4 American Indian or Alaska Native, non-Hispanic/Latino; 139 Asian, non-Hispanic/Latino; 334 Hispanic/Latino; 8 Native Hawaiian or other Pacific Islander, non-Hispanic/Latino; 22 Two or more races, non-Hispanic/Latino), 4 international. 1,422 applicants, 50% accepted, 675 enrolled. In 2013, 6 master's awarded. *Entrance requirements:* Additional exam requirements/recommendations for international students: Required—TOEFL (minimum score 83 iBT), IELTS (minimum score 6.5). *Application deadline:* For fall admission, 8/26 for domestic students, 7/15 for international students; for spring admission, 12/31 for domestic students, 12/15 for international students. Applications are processed on a rolling basis. Application fee: $50. *Financial support:* Federal Work-Study available. Financial award applicants required to submit FAFSA. *Faculty research:* Equity assistance, language development, scholar communications, Latin American studies and cultural sensitivity, behavior management techniques and strategies in special education. *Unit head:* Dr. LaMar Miller, Dean, 212-463-0400 Ext. 5561, Fax: 212-462-4889, E-mail: lpmiller@touro.edu. *Application contact:* Natalie Arroyo, Admissions, 212-463-0400.

Touro College, Graduate School of Technology, New York, NY 10010. Offers information systems (MS); instructional technology (MS); Web and multimedia design (MA). *Students:* 10 full-time (6 women), 226 part-time (111 women); includes 104 minority (39 Black or African American, non-Hispanic/Latino; 1 American Indian or Alaska Native, non-Hispanic/Latino; 39 Asian, non-Hispanic/Latino; 21 Hispanic/Latino; 4 Two or more races, non-Hispanic/Latino), 6 international. *Unit head:* Dr. Isaac Herskowitz, Dean of the Graduate School of Technology, 202-463-0400 Ext. 5231, E-mail: issac.herskowitz@touro.edu. Website: http://www.touro.edu/gst/.

Towson University, Program in Instructional Technology, Towson, MD 21252-0001. Offers instructional design and training (MS); instructional technology (Ed D). Part-time and evening/weekend programs available. *Students:* 12 full-time (10 women), 202 part-time (173 women); includes 26 minority (15 Black or African American, non-Hispanic/Latino; 6 Asian, non-Hispanic/Latino; 1 Hispanic/Latino; 1 Native Hawaiian or other Pacific Islander, non-Hispanic/Latino; 3 Two or more races, non-Hispanic/Latino), 4 international. *Degree requirements:* For master's, thesis optional; for doctorate, comprehensive exam, thesis/dissertation. *Entrance requirements:* For master's, minimum GPA of 3.0, technological literacy; for doctorate, GRE, master's degree in computer science, information systems, information technology, or closely-related areas; minimum GPA of 3.0; 2 letters of recommendation; letter of intent; writing sample; digital learning sample. Additional exam requirements/recommendations for international students: Required—TOEFL. *Application deadline:* For fall admission, 8/1 for domestic students, 7/15 for international students. Application fee: $45. Electronic applications accepted. *Financial support:* Application deadline: 4/1. *Unit head:* Dr. William Sadera, Graduate Program Director, 410-704-2731, E-mail: bsadera@towson.edu. *Application contact:* Alicia Arkell-Kleis, Information Contact, 410-704-6004, E-mail: grads@towson.edu.

Trident University International, College of Education, Program in Educational Leadership, Cypress, CA 90630. Offers e-learning leadership (MA Ed, PhD); educational leadership (MA Ed); higher education leadership (PhD); K-12 leadership (PhD). Part-time and evening/weekend programs available. Postbaccalaureate distance learning degree programs offered (no on-campus study). *Degree requirements:* For doctorate, comprehensive exam, thesis/dissertation, defense of dissertation. *Entrance requirements:* For master's, minimum GPA of 2.5 (students with GPA 3.0 or greater may transfer up to 30% of graduate level credits); for doctorate, minimum GPA of 3.4, course work in research methods or statistics. Additional exam requirements/recommendations for international students: Required—TOEFL. Electronic applications accepted.

Troy University, Graduate School, College of Education, Program in Postsecondary Education, Troy, AL 36082. Offers adult education (M Ed); biology (M Ed); criminal justice (M Ed); English (M Ed); foundations of education (M Ed); general science (M Ed); higher education administration (M Ed); history (M Ed); instructional technology (M Ed); mathematics (M Ed); music industry (M Ed); physical fitness (M Ed); political science (M Ed); public administration (M Ed); social science (M Ed); teaching English (M Ed). *Accreditation:* NCATE. Part-time and evening/weekend programs available. *Faculty:* 30 full-time (11 women), 8 part-time/adjunct (1 woman). *Students:* 17 full-time (13 women), 106 part-time (84 women); includes 55 minority (45 Black or African American, non-Hispanic/Latino; 3 Asian, non-Hispanic/Latino; 2 Hispanic/Latino; 5 Two or more races, non-Hispanic/Latino). Average age 34. 109 applicants, 83% accepted, 5 enrolled. In 2013, 130 master's awarded. *Degree requirements:* For master's, comprehensive exam (for some programs), thesis (for some programs), thesis or comprehensive exam. *Entrance requirements:* For master's, GRE (minimum score of 850 on old exam or 290 on new exam), GMAT (minimum score of 380), or MAT (minimum score of 385), bachelor's degree; minimum undergraduate GPA of 2.5 or 3.0 on last 30 semester hours, letter of recommendation. Additional exam requirements/recommendations for international students: Required—TOEFL (minimum score 523 paper-based; 70 iBT), IELTS (minimum score 6). *Application deadline:* Applications are processed on a rolling basis. Application fee: $50. Electronic applications accepted. *Expenses:* Tuition, state resident: full-time $6084; part-time $338 per credit hour. Tuition, nonresident: full-time $12,168; part-time $676 per credit hour. *Required fees:* $630; $35 per credit hour. $50 per semester. *Financial support:* Available to part-time students. Applicants required to submit FAFSA. *Unit head:* Dr. Jan Oliver, Associate Professor, 334-670-3444, Fax: 334-670-3474, E-mail: oliver@troy.edu. *Application contact:* Brenda K. Campbell, Director of Graduate Admissions, 334-670-3178, Fax: 334-670-3733, E-mail: bcamp@troy.edu.

Université Laval, Faculty of Education, Department of Teaching and Learning Studies, Programs in Teaching Technology, Québec, QC G1K 7P4, Canada. Offers MA, PhD. Terminal master's awarded for partial completion of doctoral program. *Degree requirements:* For master's, thesis (for some programs); for doctorate, comprehensive

exam, thesis/dissertation. *Entrance requirements:* For master's and doctorate, English exam (comprehension of written English), knowledge of French. Electronic applications accepted.

University at Albany, State University of New York, School of Education, Department of Educational Theory and Practice, Albany, NY 12222-0001. Offers curriculum and instruction (MS, Ed D, CAS); curriculum planning and development (MA); educational communications (MS, CAS). Evening/weekend programs available. *Degree requirements:* For doctorate, one foreign language, thesis/dissertation. *Entrance requirements:* For doctorate, GRE General Test. Additional exam requirements/ recommendations for international students: Required—TOEFL (minimum score 550 paper-based). Electronic applications accepted.

University at Buffalo, the State University of New York, Graduate School, Graduate School of Education, Department of Learning and Instruction, Buffalo, NY 14260. Offers biology education (Ed M, Certificate); chemistry education (Ed M, Certificate); childhood education (Ed M); childhood education with bilingual extension (Ed M); curriculum, instruction and the science of learning (PhD); early childhood education (Ed M); early childhood education with bilingual extension (birth-grade 2) (Ed M); earth science education (Ed M, Certificate); education studies (Ed M); educational technology and new literacies (Certificate); elementary education (Ed D); English education (Ed M, Certificate); English for speakers of other languages (Ed M); foreign and second language education (PhD); French education (Ed M, Certificate); German education (Ed M, Certificate); gifted education (Certificate); Latin education (Ed M, Certificate); literacy specialist (Ed M); literacy teaching and learning (Certificate); mathematics education (Ed M, Certificate); music education (Ed M, Certificate); physics education (Ed M, Certificate); science and the public (Ed M); social studies education (Ed M, Certificate); Spanish education (Ed M, Certificate); special education (PhD); teaching English to speakers of other languages (Ed M). Part-time and evening/weekend programs available. Postbaccalaureate distance learning degree programs offered (no on-campus study). *Faculty:* 31 full-time (23 women), 64 part-time/adjunct (53 women). *Students:* 275 full-time (215 women), 293 part-time (205 women); includes 35 minority (16 Black or African American, non-Hispanic/Latino; 5 American Indian or Alaska Native, non-Hispanic/Latino; 11 Asian, non-Hispanic/Latino; 3 Hispanic/Latino), 97 international. Average age 30. 544 applicants, 81% accepted, 246 enrolled. In 2013, 222 master's, 17 doctorates, 35 other advanced degrees awarded. *Degree requirements:* For master's, comprehensive exam; for doctorate, thesis/dissertation, research analysis exam, research experience component. *Entrance requirements:* For master's, content test in science and math, letters of reference; for doctorate, GRE General Test or MAT, interview, writing sample, letters of recommendation. Additional exam requirements/ recommendations for international students: Required—TOEFL (minimum score 600 paper-based; 96 iBT). *Application deadline:* For fall admission, 2/1 priority date for domestic and international students; for spring admission, 11/15 priority date for domestic students, 10/1 for international students. Applications are processed on a rolling basis. Application fee: $50. Electronic applications accepted. *Financial support:* In 2013–14, 50 fellowships (averaging $8,589 per year), 31 research assistantships with tuition reimbursements (averaging $11,406 per year) were awarded; teaching assistantships, career-related internships or fieldwork, Federal Work-Study, institutionally sponsored loans, scholarships/grants, tuition waivers, and unspecified assistantships also available. Financial award application deadline: 2/28; financial award applicants required to submit FAFSA. *Faculty research:* Science assessment, foreign language teaching and learning, early learning, new literacies, gender and education. *Total annual research expenditures:* $1.7 million. *Unit head:* Dr. Suzanne Miller, Chair, 716-645-2455, Fax: 716-645-3161, E-mail: smiller@buffalo.edu. *Application contact:* Cathy Dimino, Admissions Assistant, 716-645-2110, Fax: 716-645-7937, E-mail: cadimino@buffalo.edu.
Website: http://gse.buffalo.edu/lai.

University at Buffalo, the State University of New York, Graduate School, Graduate School of Education, Department of Library and Information Studies, Buffalo, NY 14260. Offers library and information studies (MLS, Certificate); library media specialist (MLS). *Accreditation:* ALA (one or more programs are accredited). Part-time programs available. Postbaccalaureate distance learning degree programs offered (no on-campus study). *Faculty:* 11 full-time (9 women), 20 part-time/adjunct (16 women). *Students:* 55 full-time (39 women), 149 part-time (123 women); includes 15 minority (9 Black or African American, non-Hispanic/Latino; 4 Asian, non-Hispanic/Latino; 2 Hispanic/ Latino). Average age 32. 155 applicants, 92% accepted, 87 enrolled. In 2013, 102 master's, 1 other advanced degree awarded. *Degree requirements:* For master's, thesis optional; for Certificate, thesis. *Entrance requirements:* For master's, letters of recommendation. Additional exam requirements/recommendations for international students: Required—TOEFL (minimum score 550 paper-based; 79 iBT). *Application deadline:* For fall admission, 4/1 priority date for domestic and international students; for spring admission, 10/15 priority date for domestic students, 10/15 for international students. Applications are processed on a rolling basis. Application fee: $50. Electronic applications accepted. *Financial support:* In 2013–14, 17 fellowships (averaging $2,776 per year), 4 research assistantships with tuition reimbursements (averaging $9,000 per year) were awarded; teaching assistantships, career-related internships or fieldwork, Federal Work-Study, institutionally sponsored loans, scholarships/grants, tuition waivers, and unspecified assistantships also available. Support available to part-time students. Financial award application deadline: 3/1; financial award applicants required to submit FAFSA. *Faculty research:* Information-seeking behavior, thesauri, impact of technology, questioning behaviors, educational informatics. *Total annual research expenditures:* $20,068. *Unit head:* Dr. Heidi Julien, Chair, 716-645-1474, Fax: 716-645-3775, E-mail: heidijul@buffalo.edu. *Application contact:* Pat Glinski, Admissions Assistant, 716-645-2110, Fax: 716-645-7937, E-mail: gse-info@buffalo.edu.
Website: http://www.gse.buffalo.edu/lis/.

University of Alaska Southeast, Graduate Programs, Program in Education, Juneau, AK 99801. Offers early childhood education (M Ed, MAT); educational technology (M Ed); elementary education (MAT); reading (M Ed); secondary education (MAT). *Accreditation:* NCATE. Part-time and evening/weekend programs available. Postbaccalaureate distance learning degree programs offered (minimal on-campus study). *Degree requirements:* For master's, comprehensive exam or project, portfolio. *Entrance requirements:* For master's, PRAXIS, minimum GPA of 3.0, writing sample, letters of recommendation. Electronic applications accepted. *Faculty research:* Applied classroom research, culturally responsive practices, action research, teaching effectiveness.

University of Alberta, Faculty of Graduate Studies and Research, Department of Educational Psychology, Edmonton, AB T6G 2E1, Canada. Offers counseling psychology (M Ed, PhD); educational psychology (M Ed, PhD); instructional technology (M Ed); school counseling (M Ed); school psychology (M Ed, PhD); special education (M Ed, PhD); special education-deafness studies (M Ed); teaching English as a second language (M Ed). Part-time programs available. *Degree requirements:* For master's, thesis optional; for doctorate, comprehensive exam, thesis/dissertation. *Entrance requirements:* For master's and doctorate, minimum GPA of 3.0. Additional exam requirements/recommendations for international students: Required—TOEFL. *Faculty research:* Human learning, development and assessment.

University of Arkansas, Graduate School, College of Education and Health Professions, Department of Curriculum and Instruction, Program in Educational Technology, Fayetteville, AR 72701-1201. Offers M Ed. *Accreditation:* NCATE. Part-time and evening/weekend programs available. *Entrance requirements:* For master's, GRE General Test, MAT or minimum GPA of 3.0. Electronic applications accepted.

University of Arkansas at Little Rock, Graduate School, College of Education, Department of Educational Leadership, Program in Learning Systems Technology, Little Rock, AR 72204-1099. Offers M Ed. *Degree requirements:* For master's, comprehensive exam or defense of portfolio. *Entrance requirements:* For master's, GRE General Test, interview, minimum GPA of 2.75. *Expenses:* Tuition, state resident: full-time $5690; part-time $284.50 per credit hour. Tuition, nonresident: full-time $13,030; part-time $651.50 per credit hour. *Required fees:* $1121; $672 per term. One-time fee: $40 full-time. *Faculty research:* Instructional program development, educational technology product development, educational technology management.

University of Central Arkansas, Graduate School, College of Education, Department of Leadership Studies, Program in Library Media and Information Technology, Conway, AR 72035-0001. Offers MS. Part-time and evening/weekend programs available. Postbaccalaureate distance learning degree programs offered (minimal on-campus study). *Degree requirements:* For master's, comprehensive exam. *Entrance requirements:* For master's, GRE General Test, minimum GPA of 2.7. Additional exam requirements/recommendations for international students: Required—TOEFL (minimum score 550 paper-based). Electronic applications accepted.

University of Central Florida, College of Education and Human Performance, Department of Educational and Human Sciences, Program in Instructional Design and Technology, Orlando, FL 32816. Offers instructional design and technology (MA); instructional design for simulations (Certificate). *Students:* 3 full-time (all women), 54 part-time (28 women); includes 15 minority (8 Black or African American, non-Hispanic/ Latino; 1 Asian, non-Hispanic/Latino; 5 Hispanic/Latino; 1 Two or more races, non-Hispanic/Latino), 2 international. Average age 38. 25 applicants, 72% accepted, 14 enrolled. In 2013, 22 master's, 3 other advanced degrees awarded. Application fee: $30. Electronic applications accepted. *Unit head:* Dr. Atsusi Hirumi, Program Coordinator, 407-823-1760, E-mail: atsusi.hirumi@ucf.edu. *Application contact:* Barbara Rodriguez Lamas, Director, Admissions and Student Services, 407-823-2766, Fax: 407-823-6442, E-mail: gradadmissions@ucf.edu.

University of Central Florida, College of Education and Human Performance, Education Doctoral Programs, Orlando, FL 32816. Offers communication sciences and disorders (PhD); counselor education (PhD); early childhood education (PhD); education (Ed D); elementary education (PhD); exceptional education (PhD); exercise physiology (PhD); higher education (PhD); hospitality education (PhD); instructional technology (PhD); mathematics education (PhD); reading education (PhD); science education (PhD); social science education (PhD); TESOL (PhD). *Students:* 137 full-time (94 women), 86 part-time (64 women); includes 45 minority (24 Black or African American, non-Hispanic/Latino; 5 Asian, non-Hispanic/Latino; 13 Hispanic/Latino; 3 Two or more races, non-Hispanic/Latino), 22 international. Average age 39. 132 applicants, 54% accepted, 54 enrolled. In 2013, 38 doctorates awarded. Application fee: $30. Electronic applications accepted. *Financial support:* In 2013–14, 84 students received support, including 38 fellowships with partial tuition reimbursements available (averaging $6,600 per year), 41 research assistantships with partial tuition reimbursements available (averaging $7,800 per year), 53 teaching assistantships with partial tuition reimbursements available (averaging $7,700 per year). *Unit head:* Dr. Edward Robinson, Director of Doctoral Programs, 407-823-6106, E-mail: edward.robinson@ucf.edu. *Application contact:* Barbara Rodriguez Lamas, Associate Director, Admissions and Student Services, 407-823-2766, Fax: 407-823-6442, E-mail: gradadmissions@ucf.edu.
Website: http://education.ucf.edu/departments.cfm.

University of Central Florida, College of Education and Human Performance, School of Teaching, Learning, and Leadership, Programs in Educational and Instructional Technology, Orlando, FL 32816. Offers e-learning (Certificate); educational technology (Certificate); instructional design and technology (MA), including e-learning, educational technology, instructional systems; instructional/educational technology (Certificate). *Students:* 8 full-time (7 women), 26 part-time (20 women); includes 8 minority (1 Black or African American, non-Hispanic/Latino; 2 Asian, non-Hispanic/Latino; 4 Hispanic/Latino; 1 Two or more races, non-Hispanic/Latino), 3 international. Average age 35. 14 applicants, 93% accepted, 9 enrolled. In 2013, 16 master's, 1 other advanced degree awarded. *Degree requirements:* For master's, thesis or alternative. *Application deadline:* For fall admission, 7/15 for domestic students; for spring admission, 12/1 for domestic students. Application fee: $30. Electronic applications accepted. *Financial support:* Career-related internships or fieldwork, Federal Work-Study, institutionally sponsored loans, tuition waivers (partial), and unspecified assistantships available. *Unit head:* Dr. Glenda A. Gunter, Program Coordinator, 407-823-3502, E-mail: glenda.gunter@ucf.edu. *Application contact:* Barbara Rodriguez Lamas, Director, Admissions and Student Support, 407-823-2766, Fax: 407-823-6442, E-mail: gradadmissions@ucf.edu.

University of Central Missouri, The Graduate School, Warrensburg, MO 6409. Offers accountancy (MA); accounting (MBA); applied mathematics (MS); aviation safety (MA); biology (MS); business administration (MBA); career and technical education leadership (MS); college student personnel administration (MS); communication (MA); computer science (MS); counseling (MS); criminal justice (MS); educational leadership (Ed D); educational technology (MS); elementary and early childhood education (MSE); English (MA); environmental studies (MA); finance (MBA); history (MA); human services/ educational technology (Ed S); human services/learning resources (Ed S); human services/professional counseling (Ed S); industrial hygiene (MS); industrial management (MS); information systems (MBA); information technology (MS); kinesiology (MS); library science and information services (MS); literacy education (MSE); marketing (MBA); mathematics (MS); music (MA); occupational safety management (MS); psychology (MS); rural family nursing (MS); school administration (MSE); social gerontology (MS); sociology (MA); special education (MSE); speech language pathology (MS); superintendency (Ed S); teaching (MAT); teaching English as a second language (MA); technology (MS); technology management (PhD); theatre (MA). Part-time programs available. *Faculty:* 233. *Students:* 890 full-time (396 women), 1,486 part-time (1,001 women); includes 192 minority (97 Black or African American, non-Hispanic/Latino; 9 American Indian or Alaska Native, non-Hispanic/Latino; 32 Asian, non-Hispanic/Latino; 40 Hispanic/Latino; 3 Native Hawaiian or other Pacific Islander, non-Hispanic/Latino; 11 Two or more races, non-Hispanic/Latino), 539 international. Average age 31. 1,953 applicants, 75% accepted. In 2013, 719 master's, 58 other advanced degrees awarded. *Degree requirements:* For master's and Ed S, comprehensive exam (for some programs), thesis (for some programs). *Entrance requirements:* Additional exam requirements/recommendations for international students: Required—TOEFL (minimum score 550 paper-based; 79 iBT). *Application deadline:* For fall admission, 6/1 for domestic students; for spring admission, 10/1 for domestic and international students. Applications are processed on a rolling basis. Application fee: $30 ($75 for international students). Electronic applications accepted. *Expenses:* Tuition, state resident: full-time $7326; part-time $276.25 per credit hour. Tuition, nonresident: full-time $13,956; part-time $552.50 per credit hour. *Required fees:* $29 per credit hour. *Financial support:* In

2013–14, 118 students received support, including 271 research assistantships with full and partial tuition reimbursements available (averaging $7,500 per year), 109 teaching assistantships with full and partial tuition reimbursements available (averaging $7,500 per year); career-related internships or fieldwork, Federal Work-Study, scholarships/grants, and administrative and laboratory assistantships also available. Support available to part-time students. Financial award application deadline: 3/1; financial award applicants required to submit FAFSA. *Unit head:* Dr. Joseph Vaughn, Assistant Provost for Research/Dean, 660-543-4092, Fax: 660-543-4778, E-mail: vaughn@ucmo.edu. *Application contact:* Brittany Lawrence, Graduate Student Services Coordinator, 660-543-4621, Fax: 660-543-4778, E-mail: gradinfo@ucmo.edu.
Website: http://www.ucmo.edu/graduate/.

University of Central Oklahoma, The Jackson College of Graduate Studies, College of Education and Professional Studies, Department of Advanced Professional and Special Services, Edmond, OK 73034-5209. Offers educational leadership (M Ed); library media education (M Ed); reading (M Ed); school counseling (M Ed); special education (M Ed), including mild/moderate disabilities, severe-profound/multiple disabilities, special education; speech-language pathology (MS). Part-time programs available. *Faculty:* 14 full-time (9 women), 16 part-time/adjunct (8 women). *Students:* 87 full-time (80 women), 298 part-time (251 women); includes 77 minority (32 Black or African American, non-Hispanic/Latino; 10 American Indian or Alaska Native, non-Hispanic/Latino; 2 Asian, non-Hispanic/Latino; 15 Hispanic/Latino; 18 Two or more races, non-Hispanic/Latino), 9 international. Average age 34. 147 applicants, 94% accepted, 89 enrolled. In 2013, 163 master's awarded. *Degree requirements:* For master's, comprehensive exam (for some programs), thesis (for some programs). *Entrance requirements:* For master's, GRE. Additional exam requirements/recommendations for international students: Required—TOEFL (minimum score 550 paper-based; 79 iBT), IELTS (minimum score 6.5). *Application deadline:* For fall admission, 7/1 for international students; for spring admission, 7/1 for international students. Applications are processed on a rolling basis. Application fee: $50. Electronic applications accepted. *Expenses:* Tuition, state resident: full-time $4137; part-time $206.85 per credit hour. Tuition, nonresident: full-time $10,359; part-time $517.95 per credit hour. *Required fees:* $481. Tuition and fees vary according to course load and program. *Financial support:* In 2013–14, 93 students received support, including 4 research assistantships with partial tuition reimbursements available (averaging $8,133 per year); teaching assistantships with partial tuition reimbursements available, career-related internships or fieldwork, scholarships/grants, tuition waivers (partial), and unspecified assistantships also available. Financial award application deadline: 3/31; financial award applicants required to submit FAFSA. *Faculty research:* Intellectual freedom, fair use copyright, technology integration, young adult literature, distance learning. *Unit head:* Dr. Patsy Couts, Chair, 405-974-3888, Fax: 405-974-3857, E-mail: pcouts@uco.edu. *Application contact:* Dr. Richard Bernard, Dean, Graduate College, 405-974-3493, Fax: 405-974-3852, E-mail: gradcoll@uco.edu.
Website: http://www.uco.edu/ceps/dept/apss/.

University of Colorado Denver, School of Education and Human Development, Information and Learning Technologies Program, Denver, CO 80217-3364. Offers e-learning design and implementation (MA); instructional design and adult learning (MA); K-12 teaching (MA). Part-time and evening/weekend programs available. Postbaccalaureate distance learning degree programs offered (no on-campus study). *Students:* 60 full-time (49 women), 59 part-time (43 women); includes 16 minority (2 Black or African American, non-Hispanic/Latino; 3 Asian, non-Hispanic/Latino; 10 Hispanic/Latino; 1 Two or more races, non-Hispanic/Latino), 1 international. Average age 38. 32 applicants, 88% accepted, 23 enrolled. In 2013, 47 master's awarded. *Degree requirements:* For master's, comprehensive exam (for some programs), comprehensive exam or online portfolio; 30 credit hours. *Entrance requirements:* For master's, GRE or MAT (if GPA is below 2.75), resume, statement of intent, three letters of recommendation. Additional exam requirements/recommendations for international students: Required—TOEFL (minimum score 537 paper-based; 75 iBT); Recommended—IELTS (minimum score 6.5). *Application deadline:* For fall admission, 5/15 for domestic students, 5/1 for international students; for spring admission, 11/15 for domestic students, 11/1 for international students. Application fee: $50 ($75 for international students). *Expenses:* Contact institution. *Financial support:* In 2013–14, 2 students received support. Fellowships, research assistantships, teaching assistantships, Federal Work-Study, institutionally sponsored loans, scholarships/grants, and traineeships available. Financial award application deadline: 4/1; financial award applicants required to submit FAFSA. *Faculty research:* Technology for educational management, instructional design foundations, e-Learning, educational design. *Unit head:* Brent Wilson, Professor, 303-315-4963, E-mail: brent.wilson@ucdenver.edu. *Application contact:* Hans Broers, Academic Advisor, 303-315-6351, Fax: 303-315-6311, E-mail: hans.broers@ucdenver.edu.
Website: http://www.ucdenver.edu/academics/colleges/SchoolOfEducation/Academics/MASTERS/ILT/Pages/default.aspx.

University of Connecticut, Graduate School, Neag School of Education, Department of Educational Psychology, Program in Learning Technology, Storrs, CT 06269. Offers MA, PhD, Post-Master's Certificate. *Accreditation:* NCATE. Terminal master's awarded for partial completion of doctoral program. *Degree requirements:* For master's, comprehensive exam, thesis or alternative; for doctorate, thesis/dissertation. *Entrance requirements:* For master's and doctorate, GRE General Test. Additional exam requirements/recommendations for international students: Required—TOEFL (minimum score 550 paper-based). Electronic applications accepted.

University of Dayton, Department of Teacher Education, Dayton, OH 45469-1300. Offers adolescence to young adult education (MS Ed); early childhood education (MS Ed); early childhood leadership and advocacy (MS Ed); interdisciplinary education studies (MS Ed); intervention specialist education, mild/moderate (MS Ed); literacy (MS Ed); middle childhood education (MS Ed); multi-age education (MS Ed); music education (MS Ed); teacher as leader (MS Ed); technology enhanced learning (MS Ed). Part-time and evening/weekend programs available. Postbaccalaureate distance learning degree programs offered (no on-campus study). *Faculty:* 19 full-time (13 women), 21 part-time/adjunct (18 women). *Students:* 69 full-time (57 women), 86 part-time (75 women); includes 16 minority (10 Black or African American, non-Hispanic/Latino; 2 Asian, non-Hispanic/Latino; 4 Hispanic/Latino), 10 international. Average age 31. 140 applicants, 54% accepted, 39 enrolled. In 2013, 93 master's awarded. *Degree requirements:* For master's, variable foreign language requirement, comprehensive exam (for some programs), thesis. *Entrance requirements:* For master's, GRE or MAT, minimum GPA of 2.75. Additional exam requirements/recommendations for international students: Required—TOEFL (minimum score 550 paper-based; 80 iBT), IELTS (minimum score 6.5). *Application deadline:* For fall admission, 3/1 for domestic students, 5/1 for international students; for winter admission, 7/1 for international students; for spring admission, 11/1 for international students. Applications are processed on a rolling basis. Application fee: $0 ($50 for international students). Electronic applications accepted. *Expenses:* Contact institution. *Financial support:* In 2013–14, 61 students received support, including 5 research assistantships with full tuition reimbursements available (averaging $8,720 per year), 3 teaching assistantships with full tuition reimbursements available (averaging $8,720 per year); career-related internships or fieldwork, institutionally sponsored loans, scholarships/grants, traineeships, health care benefits, and unspecified assistantships also available. Support available to part-time students. Financial award application deadline: 3/1; financial award applicants required to submit FAFSA. *Faculty research:* Diversity, literacy, art representation by young children, preservice teacher preparation. *Unit head:* Dr. Connie L. Bowman, Chair, 937-229-3305, E-mail: cbowman1@udayton.edu. *Application contact:* Gina Seiter, Graduate Program Advisor, 937-229-3103, E-mail: gseiter1@udayton.edu.

The University of Findlay, Office of Graduate Admissions, Findlay, OH 45840-3653. Offers athletic training (MAT); business (MBA), including health care management, hospitality management, organizational leadership, public management; education (MA Ed), including administration, children's literature, early childhood, human resource development, reading, science, special education, technology; environmental, safety and health management (MSEM); health informatics (MS); occupational therapy (MOT); pharmacy (Pharm D); physical therapy (DPT); physician assistant (MPA); rhetoric and writing (MA); teaching English to speakers of other languages (TESOL) and bilingual education (MA). Part-time and evening/weekend programs available. Postbaccalaureate distance learning degree programs offered (no on-campus study). *Faculty:* 209 full-time (98 women), 69 part-time/adjunct (38 women). *Students:* 551 full-time (332 women), 457 part-time (276 women); includes 77 minority (37 Black or African American, non-Hispanic/Latino; 1 American Indian or Alaska Native, non-Hispanic/Latino; 15 Asian, non-Hispanic/Latino; 23 Hispanic/Latino; 1 Native Hawaiian or other Pacific Islander, non-Hispanic/Latino), 135 international. Average age 28. 637 applicants, 66% accepted, 241 enrolled. In 2013, 267 master's, 91 doctorates awarded. *Degree requirements:* For master's, thesis, cumulative project, capstone project. *Entrance requirements:* For master's, GRE/GMAT, bachelor's degree from accredited institution, minimum undergraduate GPA of 2.5 in last 64 hours of course work; for doctorate, GRE, minimum cumulative GPA of 3.0. Additional exam requirements/recommendations for international students: Required—TOEFL (minimum score 80 iBT). *Application deadline:* Applications are processed on a rolling basis. Application fee: $25. Electronic applications accepted. *Expenses: Required fees:* $146 per semester. Tuition and fees vary according to degree level and program. *Financial support:* In 2013–14, 11 research assistantships with full and partial tuition reimbursements (averaging $4,000 per year), 10 teaching assistantships with full and partial tuition reimbursements (averaging $3,600 per year) were awarded; career-related internships or fieldwork, Federal Work-Study, health care benefits, and unspecified assistantships also available. Financial award application deadline: 4/1; financial award applicants required to submit FAFSA. *Unit head:* Christopher M. Harris, Director of Admissions, 419-434-4347, E-mail: harrisc1@findlay.edu. *Application contact:* Emily Ickes, Graduate Admissions Counselor, 419-434-6933, Fax: 419-434-4898, E-mail: ickese@findlay.edu.
Website: http://www.findlay.edu/admissions/graduate/Pages/default.aspx.

University of Georgia, College of Education, Department of Career and Information Studies, Athens, GA 30602. Offers learning, design, and technology (M Ed, PhD, Ed S), including instructional design and development (M Ed, Ed S), instructional technology (M Ed), learning, design, and technology (M Ed), school library media (M Ed, Ed S); workforce education (M Ed, MAT, Ed D, PhD, Ed S), including business education (MAT), family and consumer sciences education (MAT), health science and technology education (MAT), marketing education (MAT), technology education (MAT), trade and industry education (MAT). *Accreditation:* NCATE. *Entrance requirements:* For master's, GRE General Test, MAT; for doctorate, GRE General Test; for Ed S, GRE General Test or MAT. Electronic applications accepted.

University of Georgia, College of Education, Department of Educational Psychology and Instructional Technology, Athens, GA 30602. Offers education of the gifted (Ed D); educational psychology (M Ed, MA, Ed D, PhD, Ed S); instructional technology (M Ed, PhD, Ed S). *Accreditation:* NCATE. *Entrance requirements:* For master's and Ed S, GRE General Test or MAT; for doctorate, GRE General Test. Electronic applications accepted.

University of Hartford, College of Education, Nursing, and Health Professions, Program in Educational Technology, West Hartford, CT 06117-1599. Offers M Ed. *Accreditation:* NCATE. Part-time and evening/weekend programs available. *Degree requirements:* For master's, comprehensive exam. *Entrance requirements:* For master's, interview, 2 letters of recommendation. Additional exam requirements/recommendations for international students: Required—TOEFL (minimum score 550 paper-based). Electronic applications accepted.

University of Hawaii at Manoa, Graduate Division, College of Education, Department of Educational Technology, Honolulu, HI 96822. Offers M Ed. Part-time programs available. *Degree requirements:* For master's, thesis optional. *Entrance requirements:* Additional exam requirements/recommendations for international students: Required—TOEFL (minimum score 650 paper-based; 114 iBT), IELTS (minimum score 7). *Faculty research:* Distance education-interaction via electronic means.

University of Hawaii at Manoa, Graduate Division, College of Education, PhD in Education Program, Honolulu, HI 96822. Offers curriculum and instruction (PhD); educational administration (PhD); educational foundations (PhD); educational policy studies (PhD); educational technology (PhD); exceptionalities (PhD); kinesiology (PhD). Part-time and evening/weekend programs available. *Degree requirements:* For doctorate, thesis/dissertation. *Entrance requirements:* For doctorate, GRE General Test, sample of written work. Additional exam requirements/recommendations for international students: Required—TOEFL (minimum score 600 paper-based; 100 iBT), IELTS (minimum score 7).

University of Houston–Clear Lake, School of Education, Program in Curriculum and Instruction, Houston, TX 77058-1002. Offers curriculum and instruction (MS); early childhood education (MS); reading (MS); school library and information science (MS). Part-time and evening/weekend programs available. *Degree requirements:* For master's, thesis (for some programs). *Entrance requirements:* For master's, GRE or minimum GPA of 3.0 in last 60 hours. Additional exam requirements/recommendations for international students: Required—TOEFL (minimum score 550 paper-based). Electronic applications accepted.

University of Houston–Clear Lake, School of Education, Program in Foundations and Professional Studies, Houston, TX 77058-1002. Offers counseling (MS); instructional technology (MS); multicultural studies (MS). Part-time and evening/weekend programs available. *Degree requirements:* For master's, thesis optional. *Entrance requirements:* For master's, GRE or minimum GPA of 3.0 in last 60 hours. Additional exam requirements/recommendations for international students: Required—TOEFL (minimum score 550 paper-based). Electronic applications accepted.

The University of Kansas, Graduate Studies, School of Education, Department of Educational Leadership and Policy Studies, Program in Educational Technology, Lawrence, KS 66045. Offers MS Ed, PhD. *Faculty:* 15. *Students:* 11 full-time (8 women), 4 part-time (2 women); includes 1 minority (Hispanic/Latino), 9 international. Average age 33. 14 applicants, 57% accepted, 8 enrolled. In 2013, 8 master's awarded. *Degree requirements:* For doctorate, comprehensive exam. *Entrance requirements:* For master's, resume or electronic portfolio, statement of purpose, three letters of recommendation; for doctorate, GRE, resume or electronic portfolio, statement of purpose, three letters of recommendation, sample of academic writing. Additional exam requirements/recommendations for international students: Required—TOEFL, IELTS. *Unit head:* Ronald Aust, Coordinator, 785-864-4458, E-mail: aust@ku.edu. *Application*

contact: Denise Brubaker, Admissions Coordinator, 785-864-4458, Fax: 785-864-4697, E-mail: elps@ku.edu.
Website: http://edtech.ku.edu/.

University of Kentucky, Graduate School, College of Education, Department of Curriculum and Instruction, Lexington, KY 40506-0032. Offers curriculum and instruction (Ed D); elementary education (MA Ed); instructional system design (MS Ed); literacy (MA Ed); middle school education (MA Ed, MS Ed); secondary education (MA Ed, MS Ed). *Accreditation:* NCATE. *Degree requirements:* For master's, comprehensive exam, thesis optional; for doctorate, comprehensive exam, thesis/dissertation. *Entrance requirements:* For master's, GRE General Test, minimum undergraduate GPA of 2.75; for doctorate, GRE General Test, minimum graduate GPA of 3.0. Additional exam requirements/recommendations for international students: Required—TOEFL (minimum score 550 paper-based). Electronic applications accepted. *Faculty research:* Educational reform, multicultural education, classroom instructional practices, performance based assessment, primary school programs.

University of Maine, Graduate School, College of Education and Human Development, Department of Exercise Science and STEM Education, Orono, ME 04469. Offers classroom technology integrationist (CGS); education data specialist (CGS); educational technology coordinator (CGS); kinesiology and physical education (M Ed, MS); science education (M Ed, MS); STEM education (PhD). Part-time and evening/weekend programs available. *Students:* 25 full-time (13 women), 28 part-time (16 women); includes 5 minority (2 Black or African American, non-Hispanic/Latino; 2 American Indian or Alaska Native, non-Hispanic/Latino; 1 Asian, non-Hispanic/Latino), 2 international. Average age 34. 19 applicants, 84% accepted, 12 enrolled. In 2013, 6 master's awarded. *Degree requirements:* For master's, thesis (for some programs); for doctorate, comprehensive exam, thesis/dissertation. *Entrance requirements:* For master's, GRE General Test, MAT; for doctorate, GRE General Test. Additional exam requirements/recommendations for international students: Required—TOEFL. *Application deadline:* For fall admission, 1/15 for domestic students. Applications are processed on a rolling basis. Application fee: $65. Electronic applications accepted. *Expenses:* Tuition, state resident: full-time $7524. Tuition, nonresident: full-time $23,112. *Required fees:* $1970. *Financial support:* In 2013–14, 13 students received support, including 2 teaching assistantships (averaging $14,600 per year). Financial award application deadline: 3/1. *Faculty research:* Integration of technology in K-12 classrooms, instructional theory and practice in science, inquiry-based teaching, professional development, exercise science, adaptive physical education, neuromuscular function/dysfunction. *Unit head:* Dr. Janet Spector, Dean, 207-581-2441, Fax: 207-581-2423. *Application contact:* Scott G. Delcourt, Associate Dean of the Graduate School, 207-581-3291, Fax: 207-581-3232, E-mail: graduate@maine.edu.
Website: http://umaine.edu/edhd/.

University of Maryland, Baltimore County, Graduate School, College of Arts, Humanities and Social Sciences, Department of Education, Program in Instructional Systems Development, Halethorpe, MD 21227. Offers distance education (Graduate Certificate); instructional design for e-learning (Graduate Certificate); instructional systems development (MA, Graduate Certificate); instructional technology (Graduate Certificate). Part-time and evening/weekend programs available. Postbaccalaureate distance learning degree programs offered (no on-campus study). *Faculty:* 2 full-time (0 women), 13 part-time/adjunct (6 women). *Students:* 4 full-time (3 women), 155 part-time (118 women); includes 61 minority (48 Black or African American, non-Hispanic/Latino; 3 Asian, non-Hispanic/Latino; 4 Hispanic/Latino; 1 Native Hawaiian or other Pacific Islander, non-Hispanic/Latino; 5 Two or more races, non-Hispanic/Latino), 2 international. Average age 37. 88 applicants, 91% accepted, 60 enrolled. In 2013, 28 master's, 57 other advanced degrees awarded. *Degree requirements:* For master's, comprehensive exam (for some programs), portfolio (for some programs). *Entrance requirements:* Additional exam requirements/recommendations for international students: Required—TOEFL (minimum score 550 paper-based; 80 iBT). *Application deadline:* For fall admission, 6/1 priority date for domestic students, 1/1 priority date for international students; for spring admission, 11/1 priority date for domestic students, 6/1 for international students; for summer admission, 3/1 priority date for domestic students. Applications are processed on a rolling basis. Application fee: $50. Electronic applications accepted. One-time fee: $200 full-time. *Financial support:* Applicants required to submit FAFSA. *Faculty research:* E-learning, distance education, instructional design. *Unit head:* Dr. Greg Williams, Graduate Program Director, 443-543-5447, Fax: 443-543-5096, E-mail: gregw@umbc.edu. *Application contact:* Renee Eisenhuth, Graduate Program Coordinator, 443-543-5446, Fax: 443-543-5096, E-mail: reisen@umbc.edu.
Website: http://www.umbc.edu/isd.

University of Maryland, College Park, Academic Affairs, College of Education, Department of Education Policy and Leadership, College Park, MD 20742. Offers curriculum and educational communications (M Ed, MA, Ed D, PhD); social foundations of education (M Ed, MA, Ed D, PhD, CAGS). *Accreditation:* NCATE. Part-time and evening/weekend programs available. Postbaccalaureate distance learning degree programs offered (minimal on-campus study). *Students:* 1 (woman) full-time. In 2013, 1 doctorate awarded. *Degree requirements:* For master's, thesis or alternative, internship and/or field experience; for doctorate, comprehensive exam, thesis/dissertation, practicum or internship. *Entrance requirements:* For master's, GRE General Test or MAT, minimum GPA of 3.0, scholarly writing sample, 3 letters of recommendation; for doctorate, GRE General Test or MAT, scholarly writing sample; minimum undergraduate GPA of 3.0, graduate 3.5. *Application deadline:* For fall admission, 2/1 for domestic students, 9/1 for international students. *Expenses:* Tuition, state resident: full-time $10,314; part-time $573 per credit hour. Tuition, nonresident: full-time $22,248; part-time $1236 per credit. *Required fees:* $1446; $403.15 per semester. Tuition and fees vary according to program. *Financial support:* Career-related internships or fieldwork, Federal Work-Study, and scholarships/grants available. Support available to part-time students. Financial award applicants required to submit FAFSA. *Faculty research:* Educational technology, adult and higher education. *Unit head:* Francine Hultgren, Chair, 301-405-3117, E-mail: fh@umd.edu. *Application contact:* Dr. Charles A. Caramello, Dean of Graduate School, 301-405-0358, Fax: 301-314-9305, E-mail: ccaramel@umd.edu.

University of Massachusetts Amherst, Graduate School, College of Education, Program in Education, Amherst, MA 01003. Offers bilingual/English as a second language/multicultural education (M Ed, Ed S); child study and early education (M Ed); children, families and schools (Ed D, Ed S); early childhood and elementary teacher education (M Ed); educational leadership (M Ed); educational policy and leadership (Ed D); higher education (M Ed); international education (M Ed); language, literacy and culture (Ed D); learning, media and technology (M Ed, Ed S); mathematics, science, and learning technologies (Ed D); psychometric methods, educational statistics and research methods (Ed D); reading and writing (M Ed); school counselor education (M Ed, Ed S); school psychology (Ed S); science education (Ed S); secondary teacher education (M Ed); social justice education (M Ed, Ed D, Ed S); special education (M Ed, Ed D, Ed S); teacher education and school improvement (Ed D, Ed S). *Accreditation:* NCATE. Part-time programs available. Postbaccalaureate distance learning degree programs offered (minimal on-campus study). *Faculty:* 95 full-time (55 women). *Students:* 357 full-time (240 women), 264 part-time (194 women); includes 114 minority (41 Black or African American, non-Hispanic/Latino; 4 American Indian or Alaska Native, non-Hispanic/Latino; 10 Asian, non-Hispanic/Latino; 47 Hispanic/Latino; 12 Two or more races, non-Hispanic/Latino), 100 international. Average age 34. 761 applicants, 51% accepted, 200 enrolled. In 2013, 186 master's, 31 doctorates, 22 other advanced degrees awarded. Terminal master's awarded for partial completion of doctoral program. *Degree requirements:* For doctorate, comprehensive exam, thesis/dissertation. *Entrance requirements:* Additional exam requirements/recommendations for international students: Required—TOEFL (minimum score 550 paper-based; 80 iBT), IELTS (minimum score 6.5). *Application deadline:* For fall admission, 1/15 for domestic and international students. Applications are processed on a rolling basis. Application fee: $75. Electronic applications accepted. *Financial support:* Fellowships with full and partial tuition reimbursements, research assistantships with full and partial tuition reimbursements, teaching assistantships with full and partial tuition reimbursements, career-related internships or fieldwork, Federal Work-Study, scholarships/grants, traineeships, health care benefits, tuition waivers (full and partial), and unspecified assistantships available. Support available to part-time students. Financial award application deadline: 1/15; financial award applicants required to submit FAFSA. *Unit head:* Dr. Linda L. Griffin, Graduate Program Director, 413-545-6984, Fax: 413-545-1523. *Application contact:* Lindsay DeSantis, Supervisor of Admissions, 413-545-0722, Fax: 413-577-0010, E-mail: gradadm@grad.umass.edu.
Website: http://www.umass.edu/education/.

University of Memphis, Graduate School, College of Education, Department of Instruction and Curriculum Leadership, Memphis, TN 38152. Offers early childhood education (MAT, MS, Ed D); elementary education (MAT); instruction and curriculum (MS, Ed D); instruction design and technology (MS, Ed D); middle grades education (MAT); reading (MS, Ed D); secondary education (MAT); special education (MAT, MS, Ed D). *Accreditation:* NCATE (one or more programs are accredited). Part-time programs available. *Faculty:* 30 full-time (18 women), 16 part-time/adjunct (10 women). *Students:* 55 full-time (44 women), 370 part-time (300 women); includes 169 minority (153 Black or African American, non-Hispanic/Latino; 5 American Indian or Alaska Native, non-Hispanic/Latino; 1 Asian, non-Hispanic/Latino; 6 Hispanic/Latino; 4 Two or more races, non-Hispanic/Latino), 7 international. Average age 35. 181 applicants, 84% accepted, 21 enrolled. In 2013, 137 master's, 10 doctorates awarded. Terminal master's awarded for partial completion of doctoral program. *Degree requirements:* For master's, comprehensive exam, thesis or alternative; for doctorate, comprehensive exam, thesis/dissertation. *Entrance requirements:* For master's, GRE General Test, minimum GPA of 2.5; for doctorate, GRE General Test, GRE Subject Test, 2 years of teaching experience. *Application deadline:* For fall admission, 8/1 for domestic students; for spring admission, 12/1 for domestic students. Applications are processed on a rolling basis. Application fee: $35 ($60 for international students). Electronic applications accepted. *Financial support:* In 2013–14, 635 students received support. Research assistantships with full tuition reimbursements available, teaching assistantships with full tuition reimbursements available, career-related internships or fieldwork, Federal Work-Study, institutionally sponsored loans, scholarships/grants, traineeships, and unspecified assistantships available. Support available to part-time students. Financial award application deadline: 2/15; financial award applicants required to submit FAFSA. *Faculty research:* Effective urban teachers, preparation and retention of urban teachers, technology utilization in schools, field-based teacher preparation programs, effective use of online instruction. *Unit head:* Dr. Sandra Cooley-Nichols, Interim Chair, 901-678-2365. *Application contact:* Dr. Sally Blake, Director of Graduate Studies, 901-678-4861.
Website: http://www.memphis.edu/icl/.

University of Michigan, Horace H. Rackham School of Graduate Studies, School of Information, Ann Arbor, MI 48109-1285. Offers archives and records management (MSI); health informatics (MS); human computer interaction (MSI); information (PhD); information analysis and retrieval (MSI); information economics for management (MSI); library and information science (MSI); preservation of information (MSI); school library media (MSI); social computing (MSI). *Accreditation:* ALA (one or more programs are accredited). *Entrance requirements:* For master's and doctorate, GRE General Test. Additional exam requirements/recommendations for international students: Required—TOEFL (minimum score 600 paper-based; 100 iBT). Electronic applications accepted. Tuition and fees vary according to course level, course load, degree level, program and student level.

University of Michigan–Dearborn, College of Education, Health, and Human Services, Program in Educational Technology, Dearborn, MI 48128-1491. Offers MA. Part-time and evening/weekend programs available. Postbaccalaureate distance learning degree programs offered (no on-campus study). *Faculty:* 3 full-time (1 woman), 1 (woman) part-time/adjunct. *Students:* 2 full-time (0 women), 33 part-time (27 women); includes 5 minority (2 American Indian or Alaska Native, non-Hispanic/Latino; 1 Asian, non-Hispanic/Latino; 1 Hispanic/Latino; 1 Two or more races, non-Hispanic/Latino). 15 applicants, 73% accepted, 10 enrolled. In 2013, 2 master's awarded. *Entrance requirements:* Additional exam requirements/recommendations for international students: Required—TOEFL (minimum score 560 paper-based; 84 iBT), IELTS (minimum score 6.5). *Application deadline:* For fall admission, 8/1 priority date for domestic students, 5/1 priority date for international students; for winter admission, 12/1 priority date for domestic students, 9/1 priority date for international students; for spring admission, 4/1 priority date for domestic students, 1/1 priority date for international students. Applications are processed on a rolling basis. Application fee: $60. Electronic applications accepted. *Expenses:* Tuition, state resident: full-time $11,838; part-time $686 per credit hour. Tuition, nonresident: full-time $20,926; part-time $1206 per credit hour. *Required fees:* $760; $286 per semester. Tuition and fees vary according to course load and program. *Financial support:* Career-related internships or fieldwork and scholarships/grants available. Financial award applicants required to submit FAFSA. *Faculty research:* Educational technology, foundations, constructivist education. *Unit head:* Dr. Stein Brunvand, Coordinator, 313-583-6415, E-mail: sbrunvan@umich.edu. *Application contact:* Elizabeth Morden, Program Assistant, 313-593-6333, Fax: 313-593-4748, E-mail: emorden@umich.edu.
Website: http://cehhs.umd.umich.edu/cehhs_ma_ed_tech/.

University of Michigan–Flint, School of Education and Human Services, Department of Education, Flint, MI 48502-1950. Offers early childhood education (MA); educational technology (MA); elementary education with teaching certification (MA); literacy education (MA); special education (MA). Part-time programs available. *Faculty:* 14 full-time (12 women), 8 part-time/adjunct (4 women). *Students:* 27 full-time (24 women), 215 part-time (186 women); includes 22 minority (20 Black or African American, non-Hispanic/Latino; 2 American Indian or Alaska Native, non-Hispanic/Latino). Average age 35. 63 applicants, 86% accepted, 43 enrolled. In 2013, 91 master's awarded. *Entrance requirements:* For master's, BS with minimum GPA of 3.0. Additional exam requirements/recommendations for international students: Required—TOEFL (minimum score 560 paper-based; 84 iBT), IELTS (minimum score 6.5). *Application deadline:* For fall admission, 8/1 priority date for domestic students, 5/1 priority date for international students; for winter admission, 11/15 priority date for domestic students, 9/15 priority date for international students; for spring admission, 3/15 priority date for domestic students, 1/15 priority date for international students. Application fee: $55. *Expenses:* Contact institution. *Financial support:* Federal Work-Study, scholarships/grants, and

unspecified assistantships available. Support available to part-time students. Financial award application deadline: 6/1; financial award applicants required to submit FAFSA. *Unit head:* Dr. Beverly Schumer, Director, 810-424-5215, E-mail: bschumer@umflint.edu. *Application contact:* Beulah Alexander, Executive Secretary, 810-766-6879, Fax: 810-766-6891, E-mail: beulaha@umflint.edu.
Website: http://www.umflint.edu/education/graduate-programs.

University of Minnesota, Twin Cities Campus, Graduate School, College of Education and Human Development, Department of Curriculum and Instruction, Minneapolis, MN 55455-0213. Offers art education (M Ed, MA, PhD); children's literature (M Ed, MA, PhD); curriculum and instruction (MA, PhD); early childhood education (M Ed, PhD); elementary education (M Ed, MA, PhD); English education (MA, PhD); environmental education (M Ed); family education (M Ed, MA, Ed D, PhD); instructional systems and technology (M Ed, MA, PhD); language arts (MA, PhD); language immersion education (Certificate); literacy education (MA); mathematics education (MA, PhD); reading education (MA, PhD); science education (MA, PhD); second languages and cultures education (MA, PhD); social studies education (MA, PhD); teaching (M Ed), including Chinese, earth science, elementary special education, English, English as a second language, French, German, Hebrew, Japanese, life sciences, mathematics, middle school science, science, second languages and cultures, social studies, Spanish; technology enhanced learning (Certificate); writing education (M Ed, MA, PhD). *Faculty:* 29 full-time (16 women). *Students:* 425 full-time (301 women), 220 part-time (153 women); includes 85 minority (21 Black or African American, non-Hispanic/Latino; 6 American Indian or Alaska Native, non-Hispanic/Latino; 42 Asian, non-Hispanic/Latino; 16 Hispanic/Latino), 50 international. Average age 32. 551 applicants, 68% accepted, 340 enrolled. In 2013, 618 master's, 33 doctorates, 6 other advanced degrees awarded. Application fee: $75 ($95 for international students). *Financial support:* In 2013–14, 25 fellowships (averaging $28,500 per year), 23 research assistantships with full tuition reimbursements (averaging $8,082 per year), 81 teaching assistantships with full tuition reimbursements (averaging $9,974 per year) were awarded. *Faculty research:* Teaching and learning; quality of education; influence of cultural, linguistic, social, political, technological and economic factors on teaching, learning and educational research; relationship between educational practice and a democratic and just society. *Total annual research expenditures:* $272,048. *Unit head:* Dr. Nina Asher, Chair, 612-624-4772, Fax: 612-624-1357, E-mail: nasher@umn.edu. *Application contact:* Dr. Jennifer Engler, Assistant Dean, 612-626-2887, Fax: 612-626-7496, E-mail: engle009@umn.edu.
Website: http://www.cehd.umn.edu/ci.

University of Missouri, Graduate School, College of Education, School of Information Science and Learning Technologies, Columbia, MO 65211. Offers educational technology (M Ed, Ed S); information science and learning technology (PhD); library science (MA). *Accreditation:* ALA (one or more programs are accredited). Part-time and evening/weekend programs available. *Faculty:* 16 full-time (11 women), 1 (woman) part-time/adjunct. *Students:* 94 full-time (67 women), 258 part-time (178 women); includes 20 minority (8 Black or African American, non-Hispanic/Latino; 2 Asian, non-Hispanic/Latino; 7 Hispanic/Latino; 3 Two or more races, non-Hispanic/Latino), 15 international. Average age 35. 122 applicants, 81% accepted, 74 enrolled. In 2013, 140 master's, 7 doctorates, 22 other advanced degrees awarded. *Entrance requirements:* For master's, GRE General Test or MAT, minimum GPA of 3.0. Additional exam requirements/recommendations for international students: Required—TOEFL (minimum score 540 paper-based; 76 iBT). *Application deadline:* For fall admission, 2/15 priority date for domestic and international students; for winter admission, 9/15 priority date for domestic and international students; for spring admission, 3/1 priority date for domestic students. Applications are processed on a rolling basis. Application fee: $55 ($75 for international students). Electronic applications accepted. *Financial support:* Fellowships, teaching assistantships, scholarships/grants, health care benefits, and unspecified assistantships available. Support available to part-time students. *Faculty research:* Problem-based learning, technology usability in classrooms, computer-based performance support tools for children and youth with learning disabilities and/or emotional/behavioral disorders, engineering education collaboration environment, effectiveness of activities designed to recruit and retain women in engineering and science. *Unit head:* Dr. Joi L. Moore, Associate Division Director, 573-884-2877, E-mail: morrejoi@missouri.edu. *Application contact:* Amy Adam, Academic Advisor, 573-884-1391, E-mail: adamae@missouri.edu.
Website: http://education.missouri.edu/SISLT/.

University of Nebraska at Kearney, Graduate Programs, College of Education, Department of Teacher Education, Kearney, NE 68849-0001. Offers curriculum and instruction (MA Ed), including early childhood education, elementary education, English as a second language, instructional effectiveness, reading/special education, secondary education; instructional technology (MS Ed), including information technology, instructional technology, school librarian; reading PK-12 (MA Ed); special education (MA Ed), including advanced practitioner, gifted, mild/moderate. Part-time and evening/weekend programs available. *Degree requirements:* For master's, comprehensive exam, thesis optional. *Entrance requirements:* For master's, portfolio or GRE. Additional exam requirements/recommendations for international students: Required—TOEFL (minimum score 550 paper-based). Electronic applications accepted.

University of Nevada, Las Vegas, Graduate College, College of Education, Department of Educational Psychology and Higher Education, Las Vegas, NV 89154-3002. Offers educational leadership (Ed D, PhD); educational psychology (MS, PhD, Ed S), including learning and technology (PhD); higher education (M Ed, PhD, Certificate); PhD/JD. Part-time and evening/weekend programs available. *Faculty:* 19 full-time (12 women), 4 part-time/adjunct (2 women). *Students:* 56 full-time (44 women), 79 part-time (58 women); includes 40 minority (12 Black or African American, non-Hispanic/Latino; 1 American Indian or Alaska Native, non-Hispanic/Latino; 7 Asian, non-Hispanic/Latino; 10 Hispanic/Latino; 2 Native Hawaiian or other Pacific Islander, non-Hispanic/Latino; 8 Two or more races, non-Hispanic/Latino), 2 international. Average age 35. 67 applicants, 64% accepted, 28 enrolled. In 2013, 22 master's, 36 doctorates, 10 other advanced degrees awarded. *Degree requirements:* For master's, comprehensive exam (for some programs), thesis (for some programs); for doctorate, comprehensive exam (for some programs), thesis/dissertation; for other advanced degree, comprehensive exam, thesis. *Entrance requirements:* For master's, GMAT or GRE General Test; for doctorate, GRE General Test, writing exam; for other advanced degree, GRE General Test. Additional exam requirements/recommendations for international students: Required—TOEFL (minimum score 550 paper-based; 80 iBT), IELTS (minimum score 7). *Application deadline:* For fall admission, 4/15 for domestic students, 5/1 for international students; for spring admission, 10/1 for international students. Application fee: $60 ($95 for international students). Electronic applications accepted. *Expenses:* Tuition, state resident: full-time $4752; part-time $264 per credit. Tuition, nonresident: full-time $18,662; part-time $554.50 per credit. *International tuition:* $18,952 full-time. *Required fees:* $532; $12 per credit. $266 per semester. One-time fee: $35. Tuition and fees vary according to course load and program. *Financial support:* In 2013–14, 48 students received support, including 39 research assistantships with partial tuition reimbursements available (averaging $11,046 per year), 9 teaching assistantships with partial tuition reimbursements available (averaging $10,922 per year); institutionally sponsored loans, scholarships/grants, health care benefits, and unspecified assistantships also available. Financial award application deadline: 3/1. *Faculty research:* Innovation and change in educational settings; educational policy, finance, and marketing; psycho-educational assessment; student retention, persistence, development, language, and culture; statistical modeling, program evaluation, qualitative and quantitative research methods. *Total annual research expenditures:* $158,645. *Unit head:* Dr. LeAnn Putney, Chair/Professor, 702-895-4879, Fax: 702-895-3492, E-mail: leann.putney@unlv.edu. *Application contact:* Graduate College Admissions Evaluator, 702-895-3320, Fax: 702-895-4180, E-mail: gradcollege@unlv.edu.
Website: http://education.unlv.edu/ephe/.

University of New Mexico, Graduate School, Program in Organization, Information, and Learning Sciences, Albuquerque, NM 87131-2039. Offers MA, PhD, Ed S. *Accreditation:* NCATE. Part-time and evening/weekend programs available. Postbaccalaureate distance learning degree programs offered (no on-campus study). *Faculty:* 3 full-time (2 women). *Students:* 43 full-time (23 women), 73 part-time (54 women); includes 46 minority (5 Black or African American, non-Hispanic/Latino; 4 American Indian or Alaska Native, non-Hispanic/Latino; 3 Asian, non-Hispanic/Latino; 31 Hispanic/Latino; 3 Two or more races, non-Hispanic/Latino), 4 international. Average age 41. 34 applicants, 68% accepted, 20 enrolled. In 2013, 26 master's, 3 doctorates awarded. *Degree requirements:* For master's, comprehensive exam, thesis or alternative; for doctorate, comprehensive exam, thesis/dissertation. *Entrance requirements:* For master's, minimum GPA of 3.0 in last 60 hours of course work, bachelor's degree; for doctorate, GRE General Test, MAT, master's degree, minimum GPA of 3.5. Additional exam requirements/recommendations for international students: Required—TOEFL. *Application deadline:* For fall admission, 3/15 for domestic and international students; for spring admission, 10/15 for domestic and international students. Application fee: $50. Electronic applications accepted. *Financial support:* In 2013–14, 47 students received support, including 3 fellowships (averaging $2,290 per year), 3 research assistantships (averaging $8,333 per year), 2 teaching assistantships with tuition reimbursements available (averaging $8,396 per year); career-related internships or fieldwork also available. Financial award application deadline: 3/1; financial award applicants required to submit FAFSA. *Faculty research:* Adult learning, distance education, instructional multimedia, organizational learning and development, transformational learning, workplace and learning environment factors that enhance learning and productivity, program and organization evaluation and reform, effects of technology on learning and problem solving. *Total annual research expenditures:* $40,000. *Unit head:* Dr. Charlotte Gunawardens, Program Director, 505-277-5046, Fax: 505-277-1427, E-mail: lani@unm.edu. *Application contact:* Linda Wood, Program Coordinator, 505-277-4131, Fax: 505-277-1427, E-mail: woodl@unm.edu.
Website: http://oils.unm.edu/.

The University of North Carolina at Charlotte, The Graduate School, College of Education, Department of Educational Leadership, Charlotte, NC 28223-0001. Offers curriculum and supervision (M Ed); educational leadership (Ed D); instructional systems technology (M Ed); school administration (MSA, Post-Master's Certificate). Part-time and evening/weekend programs available. *Faculty:* 24 full-time (13 women), 7 part-time/adjunct (5 women). *Students:* 28 full-time (20 women), 225 part-time (141 women); includes 65 minority (55 Black or African American, non-Hispanic/Latino; 3 Asian, non-Hispanic/Latino; 4 Hispanic/Latino; 3 Two or more races, non-Hispanic/Latino), 1 international. Average age 37. 71 applicants, 92% accepted, 59 enrolled. In 2013, 48 master's, 6 doctorates, 16 other advanced degrees awarded. *Degree requirements:* For master's, thesis. *Entrance requirements:* For master's and doctorate, GRE or MAT. Additional exam requirements/recommendations for international students: Required—TOEFL (minimum score 550 paper-based; 83 iBT). *Application deadline:* For fall admission, 5/1 priority date for domestic students, 5/1 for international students; for spring admission, 10/1 priority date for domestic students, 10/1 for international students. Applications are processed on a rolling basis. Application fee: $75. Electronic applications accepted. *Expenses:* Tuition, state resident: full-time $3522. Tuition, nonresident: full-time $16,051. *Required fees:* $2585. Tuition and fees vary according to course load and program. *Financial support:* In 2013–14, 7 students received support, including 6 research assistantships (averaging $8,163 per year); career-related internships or fieldwork, institutionally sponsored loans, scholarships/grants, unspecified assistantships, and administrative assistantships also available. Support available to part-time students. Financial award application deadline: 4/1; financial award applicants required to submit FAFSA. *Faculty research:* Educational leadership theory and practice, instructional systems technology, educational research methodology, curriculum and supervision in the schools, school law and finance. *Total annual research expenditures:* $1.2 million. *Unit head:* Dr. Jim Bird, Interim Chair, 704-687-1821, Fax: 704-687-3493, E-mail: jjbird@uncc.edu. *Application contact:* Kathy B. Giddings, Director of Graduate Admissions, 704-687-5503, Fax: 704-687-1668, E-mail: gradadm@uncc.edu.
Website: http://education.uncc.edu/eart.

The University of North Carolina at Greensboro, Graduate School, School of Education, Department of Curriculum and Instruction, Greensboro, NC 27412-5001. Offers college teaching and adult learning (Certificate); curriculum and instruction (M Ed), including chemistry education, elementary education, English as a second language, French education, instructional technology, mathematics education, middle grades education, reading education, science education, social studies education, Spanish education; curriculum and teaching (PhD), including higher education, teacher education and development; English as a second language (Certificate); higher education (M Ed); supervision (M Ed). *Accreditation:* NCATE. Part-time programs available. *Degree requirements:* For doctorate, thesis/dissertation. *Entrance requirements:* For master's and doctorate, GRE General Test. Additional exam requirements/recommendations for international students: Required—TOEFL. Electronic applications accepted. *Faculty research:* Community college literacy program, middle school mathematics/computer mathematics.

The University of North Carolina Wilmington, Watson College of Education, Department of Instructional Technology, Foundations and Secondary Education, Wilmington, NC 28403-3297. Offers instructional technology (MS); secondary education (M Ed). *Faculty:* 17 full-time (10 women). *Students:* 55 full-time (44 women), 127 part-time (99 women); includes 29 minority (23 Black or African American, non-Hispanic/Latino; 1 American Indian or Alaska Native, non-Hispanic/Latino; 2 Hispanic/Latino; 3 Two or more races, non-Hispanic/Latino). Average age 31. 21 applicants, 95% accepted, 14 enrolled. In 2013, 12 master's awarded. *Degree requirements:* For master's, comprehensive exam, thesis or alternative. *Entrance requirements:* Additional exam requirements/recommendations for international students: Required—TOEFL (minimum score 550 paper-based; 79 iBT), IELTS (minimum score 6.5). *Application deadline:* For fall admission, 6/1 for domestic students. Applications are processed on a rolling basis. Application fee: $60. *Expenses:* Tuition, state resident: full-time $4163. Tuition, nonresident: full-time $16,098. *Financial support:* In 2013–14, teaching assistantships with full and partial tuition reimbursements (averaging $9,000 per year) were awarded. *Unit head:* Dr. Vance Durrington, Chair, 910-962-7539, E-mail: durringtonv@uncw.edu. *Application contact:* Dr. Mahnaz Moallem, Graduate Coordinator, 910-962-4183, E-mail: moallemm@uncw.edu.

University of North Dakota, Graduate School, College of Education and Human Development, Department of Instructional Design and Technology, Grand Forks, ND 58202. Offers M Ed, MS. *Degree requirements:* For master's, comprehensive exam, thesis or alternative. *Entrance requirements:* For master's, minimum GPA of 3.0. Additional exam requirements/recommendations for international students: Required— TOEFL (minimum score 550 paper-based; 79 iBT), IELTS (minimum score 6.5). Electronic applications accepted.

University of Northern Colorado, Graduate School, College of Education and Behavioral Sciences, Department of Educational Technology, Greeley, CO 80639. Offers educational technology (MA, PhD); school library education (MA). *Accreditation:* NCATE. Part-time programs available. Postbaccalaureate distance learning degree programs offered (minimal on-campus study). *Degree requirements:* For master's, comprehensive exam, thesis or alternative; for doctorate, comprehensive exam, thesis/ dissertation. *Entrance requirements:* For master's and doctorate, GRE General Test, 3 letters of reference. Electronic applications accepted.

University of Northern Iowa, Graduate College, College of Education, Department of Curriculum and Instruction, MA Program in Instructional Technology, Cedar Falls, IA 50614. Offers curriculum and instruction (MA); performance and training technology (MA); school library endorsement (MA). *Students:* 4 full-time (1 woman), 22 part-time (14 women); includes 3 minority (all Black or African American, non-Hispanic/Latino). 7 applicants, 57% accepted, 2 enrolled. In 2013, 12 master's awarded. *Degree requirements:* For master's, comprehensive exam, thesis or alternative. *Entrance requirements:* For master's, minimum GPA of 3.0. Additional exam requirements/ recommendations for international students: Required—TOEFL (minimum score 500 paper-based; 61 iBT). *Application deadline:* For fall admission, 8/1 priority date for domestic students. Applications are processed on a rolling basis. Application fee: $50 ($70 for international students). Electronic applications accepted. *Financial support:* Application deadline: 2/1. *Unit head:* Dr. Leigh Zeitz, Coordinator, 319-273-3249, Fax: 319-273-5886, E-mail: leigh.zeitz@uni.edu. *Application contact:* Laurie S. Russell, Record Analyst, 319-273-2623, Fax: 319-273-2885, E-mail: laurie.russell@uni.edu. Website: http://www.uni.edu/coe/departments/curriculum-instruction/instructional-technology.

University of Northern Iowa, Graduate College, College of Education, Department of Curriculum and Instruction, MA Program in School Library Studies, Cedar Falls, IA 50614. Offers MA. Part-time and evening/weekend programs available. *Students:* 2 full-time (both women), 44 part-time (42 women); includes 1 minority (Black or African American, non-Hispanic/Latino). 22 applicants, 73% accepted, 16 enrolled. In 2013, 19 master's awarded. *Degree requirements:* For master's, comprehensive exam (for some programs), thesis or alternative, comprehensive portfolio. *Entrance requirements:* For master's, minimum GPA of 3.0. Additional exam requirements/recommendations for international students: Required—TOEFL (minimum score 500 paper-based; 61 iBT). *Application deadline:* For fall admission, 8/1 priority date for domestic students. Applications are processed on a rolling basis. Application fee: $50 ($70 for international students). Electronic applications accepted. *Financial support:* Career-related internships or fieldwork, Federal Work-Study, scholarships/grants, and tuition waivers (full and partial) available. Support available to part-time students. Financial award application deadline: 2/1. *Unit head:* Dr. Karla Krueger, Coordinator, 319-273-7241, Fax: 319-273-5886, E-mail: karla.krueger@uni.edu. *Application contact:* Laurie S. Russell, Record Analyst, 319-273-2623, Fax: 319-273-2885, E-mail: laurie.russell@uni.edu. Website: http://www.uni.edu/coe/ci/slms/.

University of North Florida, College of Education and Human Services, Department of Leadership, School Counseling and Sport Management, Jacksonville, FL 32224. Offers counselor education (M Ed), including school counseling; educational leadership (M Ed, Ed D), including athletic administration (M Ed), educational leadership, educational technology (M Ed), instructional leadership (M Ed). Part-time and evening/weekend programs available. *Faculty:* 16 full-time (8 women), 1 (woman) part-time/adjunct. *Students:* 76 full-time (59 women), 212 part-time (153 women); includes 91 minority (65 Black or African American, non-Hispanic/Latino; 1 American Indian or Alaska Native, non-Hispanic/Latino; 3 Asian, non-Hispanic/Latino; 13 Hispanic/Latino; 1 Native Hawaiian or other Pacific Islander, non-Hispanic/Latino; 8 Two or more races, non-Hispanic/Latino), 6 international. Average age 35. 151 applicants, 60% accepted, 71 enrolled. In 2013, 59 master's, 12 doctorates awarded. *Degree requirements:* For doctorate, thesis/dissertation. *Entrance requirements:* For master's, GRE General Test, minimum GPA of 3.0 in last 60 hours, interview, 3 letters of recommendation; for doctorate, GRE General Test, master's degree, interview, 3 letters of recommendation, writing sample. Additional exam requirements/recommendations for international students: Required—TOEFL (minimum score 500 paper-based). *Application deadline:* For fall admission, 7/1 priority date for domestic students, 5/1 for international students; for spring admission, 11/1 priority date for domestic students, 10/1 for international students. Application fee: $30. Electronic applications accepted. *Expenses:* Tuition, state resident: full-time $9794; part-time $408.10 per credit hour. Tuition, nonresident: full-time $22,383; part-time $932.61 per credit hour. *Required fees:* $2020; $84.20 per credit hour. Tuition and fees vary according to course load and program. *Financial support:* In 2013–14, 49 students received support, including 8 research assistantships (averaging $2,573 per year); teaching assistantships, career-related internships or fieldwork, Federal Work-Study, scholarships/grants, tuition waivers (partial), and unspecified assistantships also available. Support available to part-time students. Financial award application deadline: 4/1; financial award applicants required to submit FAFSA. *Faculty research:* Counseling: ethics; lesbian, bisexual and transgender issues; educational leadership: school culture and climate; educational assessment and accountability; school safety and student discipline. *Total annual research expenditures:* $128,099. *Unit head:* Dr. Jennifer Kane, Chair, 904-620-2465, E-mail: jkane@unf.edu. *Application contact:* Dr. Amanda Pascale, Director, The Graduate School, 904-620-1360, Fax: 904-620-1362, E-mail: graduateschool@unf.edu. Website: http://www.unf.edu/coehs/lscsm/.

University of North Texas, Robert B. Toulouse School of Graduate Studies, Denton, TN 76203-5017. Offers accounting (MS, PhD); applied anthropology (MA, MS); applied behavior analysis (Certificate); applied technology and performance improvement (M Ed, MS, PhD); art education (MA, PhD); art history (MA); art museum education (Certificate); arts leadership (Certificate); audiology (Au D); behavior analysis (MS); biochemistry and molecular biology (MS, PhD); biology (MA, MS, PhD); business (PhD); business computer information systems (PhD); chemistry (MS, PhD); clinical psychology (PhD); communication studies (MA, MS); computer engineering (MS); computer science (MS); computer science and engineering (PhD); counseling (M Ed, MS, PhD), including clinical mental health counseling (MS), college and university counseling (M Ed, MS), elementary school counseling (M Ed, MS), secondary school counseling (M Ed, MS); counseling psychology (PhD); creative writing (MA); criminal justice (MS); curriculum and instruction (M Ed, PhD), including curriculum studies (PhD), early childhood studies (PhD), language and literacy studies (PhD); decision sciences (MBA); design (MA, MFA), including fashion design (MFA), innovation studies, interior design (MFA); early childhood studies (MS); economics (MS); educational leadership (M Ed, Ed D, PhD); educational psychology (MS), including family studies, gifted and talented (MS, PhD), human development, learning and cognition, research, measurement and evaluation;

educational research (PhD), including gifted and talented (MS, PhD), human development and family studies, psychological aspects of sports and exercise, research, measurement and statistics; electrical engineering (MS); emergency management (MPA); engineering systems (MS); English (MA, PhD); environmental science (MS, PhD); experimental psychology (PhD); finance (MBA, MS, PhD); financial management (MPA); French (MA); health psychology and behavioral medicine (PhD); health services management (MBA); higher education (M Ed, Ed D, PhD); history (MA, MS, PhD), including European history (PhD), military history (PhD), United States history (PhD); hospitality management (MS); human resources management (MPA); information science (MS, PhD); information technologies (MBA); information technology and decision sciences (MS); interdisciplinary studies (MA, MS); international sustainable tourism (MS); jazz studies (MM); journalism (MA, MJ, Graduate Certificate), including interactive and virtual digital communication (Graduate Certificate), narrative journalism (Graduate Certificate), public relations (Graduate Certificate); kinesiology (MS); learning technologies (MS, PhD); library science (MS); local government management (MPA); logistics and supply chain management (MBA, PhD); long-term care, senior housing, and aging services (MA, MS); management science (PhD); marketing (MBA, PhD); materials science and engineering (MS, PhD); mathematics (MA, PhD); merchandising (MS); music (MA, MM Ed, PhD), including ethnomusicology (MA), music education (MM Ed, PhD), music theory (MA, PhD), musicology (MA, PhD), performance (MA); nonprofit management (MPA); operations and supply chain management (MBA); performance (MM, DMA); philosophy (MA, PhD); physics (MS, PhD); political science (MA, MS, PhD); public administration and management (PhD), including emergency management, nonprofit management, public financial management, urban management; radio, television and film (MA, MFA); recreation, event and sport management (MS); rehabilitation counseling (MS, Certificate); sociology (MA, MS, PhD); Spanish (MA); special education (M Ed, PhD), including autism intervention (PhD), emotional/behavioral disorders (PhD), mild/moderate disabilities (PhD); speech-language pathology (MA, MS); strategic management (MBA); studio art (MFA); taxation (MS); teaching (M Ed); MBA/MS; MS/MPH; MSES/MBA. Part-time and evening/weekend programs available. Postbaccalaureate distance learning degree programs offered. *Faculty:* 661 full-time (213 women), 240 part-time/adjunct (144 women). *Students:* 3,106 full-time (1,620 women), 3,543 part-time (2,221 women); includes 1,740 minority (533 Black or African American, non-Hispanic/Latino; 15 American Indian or Alaska Native, non-Hispanic/Latino; 286 Asian, non-Hispanic/Latino; 746 Hispanic/Latino; 3 Native Hawaiian or other Pacific Islander, non-Hispanic/Latino; 157 Two or more races, non-Hispanic/Latino), 1,145 international. Average age 32. 6,289 applicants, 43% accepted, 1751 enrolled. In 2013, 1,778 master's, 239 doctorates, 10 other advanced degrees awarded. Terminal master's awarded for partial completion of doctoral program. *Degree requirements:* For master's, variable foreign language requirement, comprehensive exam (for some programs), thesis (for some programs); for doctorate, variable foreign language requirement, comprehensive exam (for some programs), thesis/dissertation; for other advanced degree, variable foreign language requirement, comprehensive exam (for some programs). *Entrance requirements:* For master's and doctorate, GRE, GMAT. Additional exam requirements/recommendations for international students: Required—TOEFL (minimum score 550 paper-based; 79 iBT). *Application deadline:* For fall admission, 7/15 for domestic students, 3/15 for international students; for spring admission, 11/15 for domestic students, 9/15 for international students; for summer admission, 5/1 for domestic students. Applications are processed on a rolling basis. Application fee: $60. Electronic applications accepted. *Financial support:* Fellowships with partial tuition reimbursements, research assistantships with partial tuition reimbursements, teaching assistantships, career-related internships or fieldwork, Federal Work-Study, institutionally sponsored loans, scholarships/grants, health care benefits, and library assistantships available. Support available to part-time students. Financial award applicants required to submit FAFSA. *Unit head:* Mark Wardell, Dean, 940-565-2383, E-mail: mark.wardell@unt.edu. *Application contact:* Toulouse School of Graduate Studies, 940-565-2383, Fax: 940-565-2141, E-mail: gradsch@unt.edu. Website: http://tsgs.unt.edu/.

University of Oklahoma, Jeannine Rainbolt College of Education, Department of Educational Psychology, Program in Instructional Psychology and Technology, Norman, OK 73019. Offers educational psychology and technology (M Ed); instructional psychology and technology (PhD). Part-time and evening/weekend programs available. *Students:* 19 full-time (12 women), 33 part-time (25 women); includes 16 minority (7 Black or African American, non-Hispanic/Latino; 2 American Indian or Alaska Native, non-Hispanic/Latino; 1 Asian, non-Hispanic/Latino; 3 Hispanic/Latino; 3 Two or more races, non-Hispanic/Latino), 8 international. Average age 34. 17 applicants, 76% accepted, 11 enrolled. In 2013, 7 master's, 1 doctorate awarded. *Degree requirements:* For master's, comprehensive exam, thesis optional; for doctorate, comprehensive exam, thesis/dissertation. *Entrance requirements:* For master's and doctorate, GRE. Additional exam requirements/recommendations for international students: Required—TOEFL (minimum score 79 iBT). *Application deadline:* For fall admission, 2/1 for domestic and international students; for spring admission, 10/15 for domestic students, 9/1 for international students. Application fee: $50 ($100 for international students). Electronic applications accepted. *Expenses:* Tuition, state resident: full-time $4205; part-time $175.20 per credit hour. Tuition, nonresident: full-time $16,205; part-time $675.20 per credit hour. *Required fees:* $2745; $103.85 per credit hour. $126.50 per semester. *Financial support:* In 2013–14, 32 students received support. Career-related internships or fieldwork, Federal Work-Study, scholarships/grants, health care benefits, and unspecified assistantships available. Support available to part-time students. Financial award application deadline: 6/1; financial award applicants required to submit FAFSA. *Faculty research:* Cognition and instruction, motivation and instruction, instructional design, technology integration in education, interactive learning technologies, measurement and assessment. *Unit head:* Dr. Barbara Greene, Program Coordinator, 405-325-1534, Fax: 405-325-6655, E-mail: barbara@ou.edu. *Application contact:* Shannon Vazquez, Graduate Programs Officer, 405-325-4525, Fax: 405-325-6655, E-mail: shannonv@ou.edu. Website: http://www.ou.edu/content/education/edpy/instructional-psychology-and-technology-degrees-and-programs/.

University of Pennsylvania, Graduate School of Education, Division of Teaching, Learning, and Leadership, Programs in Learning Science and Technologies, Philadelphia, PA 19104. Offers MS Ed. *Students:* 6 full-time (3 women), 5 part-time (3 women); includes 5 minority (2 Black or African American, non-Hispanic/Latino; 3 Asian, non-Hispanic/Latino), 1 international. 46 applicants, 72% accepted, 11 enrolled. In 2013, 2 master's awarded. *Degree requirements:* For master's, comprehensive exam or portfolio. *Entrance requirements:* For master's, GRE, MAT. *Application deadline:* For fall admission, 12/15 priority date for domestic students. Applications are processed on a rolling basis. Application fee: $70. Electronic applications accepted. *Expenses:* Contact institution. *Financial support:* Applicants required to submit FAFSA. *Unit head:* Dr. Andrew Porter, Dean, 215-898-7014. *Application contact:* 215-746-2566, E-mail: edwardsv@gse.upenn.edu. Website: http://www.gse.upenn.edu.

University of Phoenix–Online Campus, School of Advanced Studies, Phoenix, AZ 85034-7209. Offers business administration (DBA); education (Ed S); educational

leadership (Ed D), including curriculum and instruction, education technology, educational leadership; health administration (DHA); higher education administration (PhD); industrial/organizational psychology (PhD); nursing (PhD); organizational leadership (DM), including information systems and technology, organizational leadership. Evening/weekend programs available. Postbaccalaureate distance learning degree programs offered. *Degree requirements:* For doctorate, thesis/dissertation. *Entrance requirements:* Additional exam requirements/recommendations for international students: Required—TOEFL, TOEIC (Test of English as an International Communication), Berlitz Online English Proficiency Exam, PTE, or IELTS. Electronic applications accepted. *Expenses:* Contact institution.

University of Phoenix–Washington D.C. Campus, College of Education, Washington, DC 20001. Offers administration and supervision (MA Ed); adult education and training (MA Ed); computer education (MA Ed); curriculum and instruction (MA Ed, Ed D); early childhood education (MA Ed); education (Ed S); educational leadership (Ed D); educational technology (Ed D); elementary teacher education (MA Ed); English and language arts education (MA Ed); English as a second language (MA Ed); higher education administration (PhD); mathematics education (MA Ed); secondary teacher education (MA Ed); special education (MA Ed); teacher leadership (MA Ed).

University of Phoenix–West Florida Campus, College of Education, Temple Terrace, FL 33637. Offers administration and supervision (MA Ed); curriculum and instruction (MA Ed), including computer education, curriculum and instruction, mathematics education; curriculum and technology (MA Ed); early childhood education (MA Ed); elementary teacher education (MA Ed); secondary teacher education (MA Ed). Evening/weekend programs available. *Degree requirements:* For master's, thesis (for some programs). *Entrance requirements:* For master's, 3 years of work experience, minimum undergraduate GPA of 2.5. Additional exam requirements/recommendations for international students: Required—TOEFL (minimum score 550 paper-based; 79 iBT).

University of St. Thomas, Graduate Studies, School of Education, Department of Organization Learning and Development, St. Paul, MN 55105-1096. Offers human resources and change leadership (MA); learning, performance and technology (MA); organization development (Ed D). Part-time and evening/weekend programs available. Postbaccalaureate distance learning degree programs offered (minimal on-campus study). *Degree requirements:* For master's, practicum; for doctorate, comprehensive exam, thesis/dissertation. *Entrance requirements:* For master's, minimum GPA of 3.0, 2 letters of reference, personal statement, 2-5 years of organization experience; for doctorate, minimum GPA of 3.5, interview, 5-7 years of OD or leadership experience. Additional exam requirements/recommendations for international students: Required—TOEFL (minimum score 550 paper-based). *Application deadline:* For fall admission, 8/1 priority date for domestic and international students; for winter admission, 12/1 priority date for domestic students, 12/1 for international students; for spring admission, 12/1 priority date for domestic and international students. Applications are processed on a rolling basis. Application fee: $50. Electronic applications accepted. *Expenses:* Contact institution. *Financial support:* Fellowships, research assistantships, institutionally sponsored loans, and scholarships/grants available. Support available to part-time students. Financial award applicants required to submit FAFSA. *Faculty research:* Workplace conflict, physician leaders, virtual teams, technology use in schools/workplace, developing masterful practitioners. *Unit head:* Dr. David W. Jamieson, Chair, 651-962-4387, Fax: 651-962-4169, E-mail: djamieson@stthomas.edu. *Application contact:* Liz G. Knight, Program Manager, 651-962-4459, Fax: 651-962-4169, E-mail: egknight@stthomas.edu.

University of San Francisco, School of Education, Department of Learning and Instruction, San Francisco, CA 94117-1080. Offers digital technologies for teaching and learning (MA); learning and instruction (MA, Ed D); special education (MA, Ed D); teaching reading (MA). Part-time and evening/weekend programs available. *Faculty:* 7 full-time (4 women), 6 part-time/adjunct (4 women). *Students:* 76 full-time (59 women), 40 part-time (26 women); includes 35 minority (5 Black or African American, non-Hispanic/Latino; 2 American Indian or Alaska Native, non-Hispanic/Latino; 9 Asian, non-Hispanic/Latino; 16 Hispanic/Latino; 3 Two or more races, non-Hispanic/Latino), 5 international. Average age 39. 73 applicants, 86% accepted, 40 enrolled. In 2013, 14 master's, 7 doctorates awarded. *Degree requirements:* For doctorate, thesis/dissertation. *Application deadline:* For fall admission, 3/1 priority date for domestic and international students; for spring admission, 11/1 priority date for domestic and international students. Applications are processed on a rolling basis. Application fee: $55 ($65 for international students). Electronic applications accepted. *Expenses:* Tuition: Full-time $21,150; part-time $1175 per unit. Tuition and fees vary according to course load, campus/location and program. *Financial support:* In 2013–14, 14 students received support. Fellowships, research assistantships, and teaching assistantships available. Financial award application deadline: 3/2; financial award applicants required to submit FAFSA. *Unit head:* Dr. Patricia Busk, Chair, 415-422-6289. *Application contact:* Amy Fogliani, Associate Director of Graduate Outreach, 415-422-5467, E-mail: schoolofeducation@usfca.edu.

University of Sioux Falls, Fredrikson School of Education, Sioux Falls, SD 57105-1699. Offers educational administration (Ed S), including principal leadership, superintendent and district leadership; leadership in reading (M Ed); leadership in schools (M Ed); leadership in technology (M Ed); teaching (M Ed). Admission in summer only. *Accreditation:* NCATE. Part-time and evening/weekend programs available. *Degree requirements:* For master's, comprehensive exam (for some programs), research application project; for Ed S, comprehensive exam, portfolio. *Entrance requirements:* For master's, minimum GPA of 3.0, 1 year of teaching experience; for Ed S, minimum 3 years of teaching experience, minimum cumulative GPA of 3.5, 1 year of administrative experience. Additional exam requirements/recommendations for international students: Required—TOEFL. *Faculty research:* Reading, literacy, leadership.

University of South Africa, College of Human Sciences, Pretoria, South Africa. Offers adult education (M Ed); African languages (MA, PhD); African politics (MA, PhD); Afrikaans (MA, PhD); ancient history (MA, PhD); ancient Near Eastern studies (MA, PhD); anthropology (MA, PhD); applied linguistics (MA); Arabic (MA, PhD); archaeology (MA); art history (MA); Biblical archaeology (MA); Biblical studies (M Th, D Th, PhD); Christian spirituality (M Th, D Th); church history (M Th, D Th); classical studies (MA, PhD); clinical psychology (MA); communication (MA, PhD); comparative education (M Ed, Ed D); consulting psychology (D Admin, D Com, PhD); curriculum studies (M Ed, Ed D); development studies (M Admin, MA, D Admin, PhD); didactics (M Ed, Ed D); education (M Tech); education management (M Ed, Ed D); educational psychology (M Ed); English (MA); environmental education (M Ed); French (MA, PhD); German (MA, PhD); Greek (MA); guidance and counseling (M Ed); health studies (MA, PhD), including health sciences education (MA), health services management (MA), medical and surgical nursing science (critical care general) (MA), midwifery and neonatal nursing science (MA), trauma and emergency care (MA); history (MA, PhD); history of education (Ed D); inclusive education (M Ed, Ed D); information and communications technology policy and regulation (MA); information science (MA, MIS, PhD); international politics (MA, PhD); Islamic studies (MA, PhD); Italian (MA, PhD); Judaica (MA, PhD); linguistics (MA, PhD); mathematical education (M Ed); mathematics education (MA); missiology (M Th, D Th); modern Hebrew (MA, PhD); musicology (MA, MMus, D Mus, PhD); natural

science education (M Ed); New Testament (M Th, D Th); Old Testament (D Th); pastoral therapy (M Th, D Th); philosophy (MA); philosophy of education (M Ed, Ed D); politics (MA, PhD); Portuguese (MA, PhD); practical theology (M Th, D Th); psychology (MA, MS, PhD); psychology of education (M Ed, Ed D); public health (MA); religious studies (MA, D Th, PhD); Romance languages (MA); Russian (MA, PhD); Semitic languages (MA, PhD); social behavior studies in HIV/AIDS (MA); social science (mental health) (MA); social science in development studies (MA); social science in psychology (MA); social science in social work (MA); social science in sociology (MA); social work (MSW, DSW, PhD); socio-education (M Ed, Ed D); sociolinguistics (MA); sociology (MA, PhD); Spanish (MA, PhD); systematic theology (M Th, D Th); TESOL (teaching English to speakers of other languages) (MA); theological ethics (M Th, D Th); theory of literature (MA, PhD); urban ministries (D Th); urban ministry (M Th).

University of South Carolina, The Graduate School, College of Education, Department of Educational Studies, Program in Educational Technology, Columbia, SC 29208. Offers M Ed. *Accreditation:* NCATE. Part-time programs available. Postbaccalaureate distance learning degree programs offered. *Degree requirements:* For master's, comprehensive exam. *Entrance requirements:* For master's, GRE or MAT, interview, letters of intent and reference.

University of South Carolina Aiken, Program in Educational Technology, Aiken, SC 29801-6309. Offers M Ed. Part-time and evening/weekend programs available. Postbaccalaureate distance learning degree programs offered (no on-campus study). *Faculty:* 3 full-time (1 woman). *Students:* 1 (woman) full-time, 16 part-time (11 women); includes 3 minority (2 Black or African American, non-Hispanic/Latino; 1 Two or more races, non-Hispanic/Latino). Average age 38. 7 applicants, 100% accepted, 6 enrolled. In 2013, 4 master's awarded. *Degree requirements:* For master's, comprehensive exam, culminating electronic portfolio, professional conference presentations. *Entrance requirements:* For master's, GRE or MAT. Additional exam requirements/recommendations for international students: Required—TOEFL (minimum score 550 paper-based; 80 iBT). *Application deadline:* Applications are processed on a rolling basis. Application fee: $45. Electronic applications accepted. *Expenses:* Tuition, state resident: full-time $11,640; part-time $485 per credit hour. Tuition, nonresident: full-time $24,960; part-time $1040 per credit hour. *Required fees:* $9 per credit hour. $25 per semester. Full-time tuition and fees vary according to course load. *Financial support:* Career-related internships or fieldwork, Federal Work-Study, scholarships/grants, tuition waivers (partial), and unspecified assistantships available. Support available to part-time students. Financial award application deadline: 3/15; financial award applicants required to submit FAFSA. *Faculty research:* Integrating technology into the curriculum, multimedia in instructional design and delivery, online instruction, assistive technology, assessment technology. *Total annual research expenditures:* $387,567. *Unit head:* Dr. Tom Smyth, Education Technology Program Coordinator, 803-641-3527, E-mail: smyth@usca.edu. *Application contact:* Karen Morris, Graduate Studies Coordinator, 803-641-3489, E-mail: karenm@usca.edu. Website: http://edtech.usca.edu/.

The University of South Dakota, Graduate School, School of Education, Division of Curriculum and Instruction, Program in Technology for Education and Training, Vermillion, SD 57069-2390. Offers MS. Part-time and evening/weekend programs available. Postbaccalaureate distance learning degree programs offered (no on-campus study). *Degree requirements:* For master's, comprehensive exam, thesis or alternative. *Entrance requirements:* For master's, GRE, minimum GPA of 2.7. Additional exam requirements/recommendations for international students: Required—TOEFL (minimum score 550 paper-based; 79 iBT). Electronic applications accepted.

University of Southern Mississippi, Graduate School, College of Education and Psychology, Department of Curriculum, Instruction, and Special Education, Hattiesburg, MS 39406-0001. Offers elementary education (M Ed, PhD, Ed S); instructional technology (MS, PhD); secondary education (MAT); special education (M Ed, PhD, Ed S). Part-time programs available. *Faculty:* 23 full-time (17 women), 3 part-time/adjunct (2 women). *Students:* 20 full-time (19 women), 59 part-time (49 women); includes 18 minority (14 Black or African American, non-Hispanic/Latino; 3 Hispanic/Latino; 1 Two or more races, non-Hispanic/Latino). Average age 36. 21 applicants, 95% accepted, 17 enrolled. In 2013, 22 master's, 3 doctorates, 13 other advanced degrees awarded. *Degree requirements:* For master's and Ed S, comprehensive exam, thesis (for some programs); for doctorate, comprehensive exam, thesis/dissertation. *Entrance requirements:* For master's, GRE General Test, MAT, minimum GPA of 3.0; for doctorate, GRE General Test, minimum GPA of 3.5; for Ed S, GRE General Test, MAT, minimum GPA of 3.25. Additional exam requirements/recommendations for international students: Required—TOEFL, IELTS. *Application deadline:* For fall admission, 3/1 priority date for domestic students, 3/1 for international students; for spring admission, 1/10 priority date for domestic and international students. Applications are processed on a rolling basis. Application fee: $50. *Financial support:* In 2013–14, 9 research assistantships with tuition reimbursements (averaging $18,316 per year), 2 teaching assistantships with full tuition reimbursements (averaging $8,500 per year) were awarded; Federal Work-Study, institutionally sponsored loans, scholarships/grants, health care benefits, tuition waivers (partial), and unspecified assistantships also available. Financial award application deadline: 3/15; financial award applicants required to submit FAFSA. *Faculty research:* Mathematical problem solving, integrative curriculum, writing process, teacher education models. *Total annual research expenditures:* $100,000. *Unit head:* Dr. Ravic P. Ringlaben, Chair, 601-266-4547, Fax: 601-266-4175. *Application contact:* David Daves, Director of Graduate Studies, 601-266-6005, Fax: 601-266-4548. Website: http://www.usm.edu/graduateschool/table.php.

University of South Florida, College of Arts and Sciences, Department of World Languages, Tampa, FL 33620-9951. Offers applied linguistics: English as a second language (MA); French (MA); second language acquisition and instructional technology (PhD); Spanish (MA). Part-time and evening/weekend programs available. *Faculty:* 21 full-time (14 women). *Students:* 40 full-time (22 women), 18 part-time (12 women); includes 32 minority (5 Black or African American, non-Hispanic/Latino; 1 Asian, non-Hispanic/Latino; 26 Hispanic/Latino), 8 international. Average age 32. 41 applicants, 73% accepted, 19 enrolled. In 2013, 20 master's awarded. *Degree requirements:* For master's, one foreign language, comprehensive exam, thesis optional; for doctorate, one foreign language, comprehensive exam, thesis/dissertation. *Entrance requirements:* For master's, GRE General Test (minimum preferred scores of 430 verbal and 4 in analytic writing on old scoring, except for French program), minimum undergraduate GPA of 3.0; two-page statement of purpose (written in Spanish for Spanish program); oral interview (for Spanish and French programs); writing sample (for French program); 2-3 letters of recommendation; for doctorate, GRE General Test (minimum preferred scores of 500 verbal and 4 in analytical writing on old scoring), minimum GPA of 3.5 or international equivalent; master's degree or equivalent academic level; statement of purpose; current curriculum vitae; three letters of recommendation; personal interview with graduate faculty; evidence of research experience or scholarly promise. Additional exam requirements/recommendations for international students: Required—TOEFL (minimum score 600 paper-based; 80 iBT) or IELTS (minimum score 6.5) for MA; TOEFL (minimum score 550 paper-based; 80 iBT) or IELTS (minimum score 6.5) for PhD. *Application deadline:* For fall admission, 2/15 for domestic students, 1/2 for

international students; for spring admission, 10/15 for domestic students, 6/1 for international students. Application fee: $30. Electronic applications accepted. *Financial support:* In 2013–14, 43 students received support, including 43 teaching assistantships with full and partial tuition reimbursements available (averaging $10,152 per year); tuition waivers (partial) and unspecified assistantships also available. Financial award application deadline: 6/30. *Faculty research:* Second language acquisition, instructional technology, foreign language education, ESOL, distance learning. *Total annual research expenditures:* $87,194. *Unit head:* Dr. Stephan Schindler, Chair and Professor, 813-974-2548, Fax: 813-905-9937, E-mail: skschindler@.usf.edu. *Application contact:* Patricia Garcia, Academic Program Specialist, 813-974-2548, Fax: 813-905-9937, E-mail: pgarcia@usf.edu.
Website: http://languages.usf.edu/.

University of South Florida, College of Arts and Sciences, School of Information, Tampa, FL 33620-9951. Offers library and information science (MA), including youth services and school librarianship. *Accreditation:* ALA. Part-time and evening/weekend programs available. Postbaccalaureate distance learning degree programs offered (minimal on-campus study). *Faculty:* 14 full-time (8 women), 12 part-time/adjunct (8 women). *Students:* 68 full-time (59 women), 150 part-time (124 women); includes 45 minority (15 Black or African American, non-Hispanic/Latino; 1 American Indian or Alaska Native, non-Hispanic/Latino; 4 Asian, non-Hispanic/Latino; 22 Hispanic/Latino; 3 Two or more races, non-Hispanic/Latino), 2 international. Average age 35. 98 applicants, 73% accepted, 41 enrolled. In 2013, 117 master's awarded. *Degree requirements:* For master's, comprehensive exam, thesis optional. *Entrance requirements:* For master's, minimum GPA of 3.25 in upper-division course work, 3.5 in a completed master's degree program, or GRE; statement of purpose and goals, academic writing sample, three letters of recommendation. Additional exam requirements/recommendations for international students: Required—TOEFL (minimum score 550 paper-based; 79 iBT) or IELTS (minimum score 6.5). *Application deadline:* For fall admission, 6/1 for domestic students, 1/2 for international students; for spring admission, 10/15 for domestic students, 6/1 for international students. Applications are processed on a rolling basis. Application fee: $30. Electronic applications accepted. *Financial support:* Unspecified assistantships available. Financial award application deadline: 6/30. *Faculty research:* Youth services in libraries, community engagement and libraries, information architecture, biomedical informatics, health informatics. *Total annual research expenditures:* $49,361. *Unit head:* Dr. Jim Andrews, Director and Associate Professor, 813-974-2108, Fax: 813-974-6840, E-mail: jimandrews@usf.edu. *Application contact:* Dr. Diane Austin, Assistant Director, 813-974-6364, Fax: 813-974-6840, E-mail: dianeaustin@usf.edu.
Website: http://si.usf.edu/.

University of South Florida, College of Education, Department of Secondary Education, Tampa, FL 33620-9951. Offers English education (M Ed, MA, MAT, PhD); foreign language education/ESOL (M Ed, MA, MAT); instructional technology (M Ed, PhD, Ed S); mathematics education (M Ed, MA, MAT, PhD, Ed S); science education (M Ed, MA, MAT, PhD); second language acquisition/instructional technology (PhD); secondary education (M Ed, PhD); secondary education/TESOL (M Ed); social science education (M Ed, MA, MAT); teaching and learning in the content area (PhD). *Accreditation:* NCATE. Part-time and evening/weekend programs available. *Degree requirements:* For master's, variable foreign language requirement, comprehensive exam, project (for some programs); for doctorate, variable foreign language requirement, comprehensive exam, thesis/dissertation, philosophies of inquiry; multiple research methods. *Entrance requirements:* For master's, GRE General Test or General Knowledge Test, minimum GPA of 3.0; for doctorate, GRE General Test, minimum GPA of 3.5; for Ed S, GRE General Test. Additional exam requirements/recommendations for international students: Required—TOEFL (minimum score 550 paper-based; 79 iBT). Electronic applications accepted. *Faculty research:* English language learners/ multicultural, social science education, mathematics education, science education, instructional technology.

University of South Florida, University College/Distance Education, Tampa, FL 33620-9951. *Unit head:* Kathy Barnes, Interdisciplinary Programs Coordinator, 813-974-8031, Fax: 813-974-7061, E-mail: barnesk@usf.edu. *Application contact:* Karen Tylinski, Metro Initiatives, 813-974-9943, Fax: 813-974-7061, E-mail: ktylinsk@usf.edu.
Website: http://uc.usf.edu/.

The University of Tennessee, Graduate School, College of Education, Health and Human Sciences, Program in Education, Knoxville, TN 37996. Offers art education (MS); counseling education (PhD); cultural studies in education (PhD); curriculum (MS, Ed S); curriculum, educational research and evaluation (Ed D, PhD); early childhood education (PhD); early childhood special education (MS); education of deaf and hard of hearing (MS); educational administration and policy studies (Ed D, PhD); educational administration and supervision (Ed S); educational psychology (Ed D, PhD); elementary education (MS, Ed S); elementary teaching (MS); English education (MS, Ed S); exercise science (PhD); foreign language/ESL education (MS, Ed S); instructional technology (MS, Ed D, PhD, Ed S); literacy, language and ESL education (PhD); literacy, language education, and ESL education (Ed D); mathematics education (MS, Ed S); modified and comprehensive special education (MS); reading education (MS, Ed S); school counseling (Ed S); school psychology (PhD, Ed S); science education (MS, Ed S); secondary teaching (MS); social foundations (MS); social science education (MS, Ed S); socio-cultural foundations of sports and education (PhD); special education (Ed S); teacher education (Ed D, PhD). *Accreditation:* NCATE. Part-time and evening/ weekend programs available. *Degree requirements:* For master's and Ed S, thesis optional; for doctorate, variable foreign language requirement, thesis/dissertation. *Entrance requirements:* For master's, minimum GPA of 2.7; for doctorate and Ed S, GRE General Test, minimum GPA of 2.7. Additional exam requirements/ recommendations for international students: Required—TOEFL. Electronic applications accepted. *Expenses:* Tuition, state resident: full-time $9540; part-time $531 per credit hour. Tuition, nonresident: full-time $27,728; part-time $1542 per credit hour. *Required fees:* $1404; $67 per credit hour.

The University of Tennessee at Chattanooga, Graduate School, College of Health, Education and Professional Studies, School of Education, Chattanooga, TN 37403. Offers counseling (M Ed), including community counseling, school counseling; education (M Ed, Post-Master's Certificate), including elementary education (M Ed), school leadership, secondary education (M Ed), special education (M Ed); educational specialist (Ed S), including educational technology, school psychology; learning and leadership (Ed D), including educational leadership. *Accreditation:* ACA; NCATE. Part-time and evening/weekend programs available. Postbaccalaureate distance learning degree programs offered (no on-campus study). *Faculty:* 24 full-time (17 women), 6 part-time/adjunct (4 women). *Students:* 107 full-time (86 women), 263 part-time (192 women); includes 71 minority (46 Black or African American, non-Hispanic/Latino; 2 American Indian or Alaska Native, non-Hispanic/Latino; 5 Asian, non-Hispanic/Latino; 11 Hispanic/Latino; 7 Two or more races, non-Hispanic/Latino), 2 international. Average age 34. 121 applicants, 83% accepted, 67 enrolled. In 2013, 125 master's, 10 doctorates, 3 other advanced degrees awarded. *Degree requirements:* For master's, comprehensive exam, thesis optional, culminating experience; for doctorate, comprehensive exam, thesis/dissertation; for other advanced degree, internship. *Entrance requirements:* For master's, GRE General Test, PPST 1, teaching certificate; for doctorate, GRE General Test, master's degree, two years of practical work experience in organizational environment; for other advanced degree, GRE General Test, letters of reference. Additional exam requirements/recommendations for international students: Required—TOEFL (minimum score 550 paper-based; 79 iBT), IELTS (minimum score 6). *Application deadline:* For fall admission, 6/13 for domestic students, 6/1 for international students; for spring admission, 10/15 for domestic students, 10/1 for international students. Applications are processed on a rolling basis. Application fee: $30 ($35 for international students). Electronic applications accepted. *Financial support:* In 2013–14, 20 research assistantships with tuition reimbursements (averaging $6,340 per year), 4 teaching assistantships with tuition reimbursements (averaging $7,234 per year) were awarded; career-related internships or fieldwork, institutionally sponsored loans, scholarships/grants, and unspecified assistantships also available. Support available to part-time students. Financial award applicants required to submit FAFSA. *Faculty research:* School counseling, community counseling, elementary and secondary education, school leadership and administration. *Total annual research expenditures:* $967,880. *Unit head:* Dr. Linda Johnston, Director, 423-425-4122, Fax: 423-425-5380, E-mail: linda-johnston@utc.edu. *Application contact:* Dr. J. Randy Walker, Interim Dean of Graduate Studies, 423-425-4478, Fax: 423-425-5223, E-mail: randy-walker@utc.edu.
Website: http://www.utc.edu/school-education/abouttheschool/gradprograms.php.

The University of Texas at Austin, Graduate School, College of Education, Department of Curriculum and Instruction, Austin, TX 78712-1111. Offers bilingual/ bicultural education (M Ed, MA, PhD); cultural studies in education (M Ed, MA, PhD); early childhood education (M Ed, MA, PhD); language and literacy studies (M Ed, PhD); learning technologies (M Ed, MA, PhD); physical education (M Ed, MA, PhD). Terminal master's awarded for partial completion of doctoral program. *Degree requirements:* For doctorate, thesis/dissertation. *Entrance requirements:* For master's and doctorate, GRE General Test. Electronic applications accepted.

The University of Texas at Brownsville, Graduate Studies, College of Education, Brownsville, TX 78520-4991. Offers bilingual education (M Ed); counseling and guidance (M Ed); curriculum and instruction (M Ed); early childhood education (M Ed); educational leadership (M Ed); educational technology (M Ed); exercise science (MS); special education (M Ed). Part-time and evening/weekend programs available. Postbaccalaureate distance learning degree programs offered (no on-campus study). *Faculty:* 51 full-time (28 women). *Students:* 60 full-time (43 women), 496 part-time (363 women); includes 467 minority (4 Black or African American, non-Hispanic/Latino; 1 American Indian or Alaska Native, non-Hispanic/Latino; 10 Asian, non-Hispanic/Latino; 451 Hispanic/Latino; 1 Native Hawaiian or other Pacific Islander, non-Hispanic/Latino), 12 international. 161 applicants, 67% accepted, 81 enrolled. In 2013, 142 master's awarded. *Degree requirements:* For master's, comprehensive exam (for some programs), thesis optional, electronic portfolio. *Entrance requirements:* For master's, GRE General Test, curriculum vitae or resume, teaching certificate. Additional exam requirements/recommendations for international students: Required—TOEFL (minimum score 550 paper-based; 77 iBT). *Application deadline:* For fall admission, 7/1 priority date for domestic students, 7/1 for international students; for spring admission, 12/1 priority date for domestic students, 12/1 for international students. Applications are processed on a rolling basis. Application fee: $30. Electronic applications accepted. *Expenses:* Tuition, state resident: full-time $3444; part-time $1148 per semester. Tuition, nonresident: full-time $9816. *Required fees:* $1018; $221 per credit hour. $401 per semester. *Financial support:* In 2013–14, 136 students received support, including 6 research assistantships (averaging $10,000 per year); career-related internships or fieldwork, Federal Work-Study, scholarships/grants, tuition waivers (partial), and unspecified assistantships also available. Support available to part-time students. Financial award application deadline: 3/1; financial award applicants required to submit FAFSA. *Unit head:* Dr. Miguel Angel Escotet, Dean, 956-882-7220, Fax: 956-882-7431, E-mail: miguel.escotet@utb.edu. *Application contact:* Mari E. Stevens, Graduate Studies Specialist, 956-882-6587, Fax: 956-882-7279, E-mail: mari.stevens@utb.edu.
Website: http://www.utb.edu/vpaa/coe/Pages/default.aspx.

The University of Texas at San Antonio, College of Education and Human Development, Department of Interdisciplinary Learning and Teaching, San Antonio, TX 78249-0617. Offers education (MA), including curriculum and instruction, early childhood and elementary education, instructional technology, reading and literacy, special education; interdisciplinary learning and teaching (PhD). Part-time and evening/ weekend programs available. *Faculty:* 22 full-time (16 women), 1 (woman) part-time/ adjunct. *Students:* 109 full-time (80 women), 272 part-time (221 women); includes 209 minority (24 Black or African American, non-Hispanic/Latino; 3 American Indian or Alaska Native, non-Hispanic/Latino; 12 Asian, non-Hispanic/Latino; 166 Hispanic/Latino; 4 Two or more races, non-Hispanic/Latino), 40 international. Average age 33. 178 applicants, 87% accepted, 80 enrolled. In 2013, 136 master's, 7 doctorates awarded. *Degree requirements:* For master's, comprehensive exam, thesis optional, 36 hours of course work without thesis (33 with thesis); for doctorate, comprehensive exam, thesis/ dissertation, minimum of 60 semester credit hours. *Entrance requirements:* For master's, bachelor's degree with minimum GPA of 3.0 in last 60 hours of coursework; 18 hours of undergraduate coursework in education or related field; for doctorate, GRE, transcripts from all colleges and universities attended, professional vitae demonstrating experience in work environment where education was primary professional emphasis, 3 letters of recommendation, statement of purpose, minimum GPA of 3.5. Additional exam requirements/recommendations for international students: Required—TOEFL (minimum score 550 paper-based; 79 iBT), IELTS (minimum score 6.5). *Application deadline:* For fall admission, 7/1 for domestic students, 4/1 for international students; for spring admission, 11/1 for domestic students, 9/1 for international students. Applications are processed on a rolling basis. Application fee: $45 ($80 for international students). Electronic applications accepted. *Expenses:* Tuition, state resident: full-time $4671. Tuition, nonresident: full-time $8708. *International tuition:* $17,415 full-time. *Required fees:* $1924.60. Tuition and fees vary according to course load and degree level. *Financial support:* In 2013–14, 7 fellowships with partial tuition reimbursements (averaging $27,000 per year) were awarded; career-related internships or fieldwork, Federal Work-Study, and scholarships/grants also available. Support available to part-time students. *Faculty research:* Explorations of science, learning and teaching, family involvement in early childhood, culturally-responsive literacy instruction in diverse settings, STEM education, autism spectrum disorder. *Total annual research expenditures:* $5.9 million. *Unit head:* Dr. Maria R. Cortez, Department Chair, 210-458-5969, Fax: 210-458-7281, E-mail: mari.cortez@utsa.edu. *Application contact:* Erin Doran, Student Development Specialist, 210-458-7443, Fax: 210-458-7281, E-mail: erin.doran@utsa.edu.
Website: http://education.utsa.edu/interdisciplinary_learning_and_teaching/.

University of the Incarnate Word, School of Graduate Studies and Research, Dreeben School of Education, Programs in Education, San Antonio, TX 78209-6397. Offers adult education (M Ed, MA); cross-cultural education (M Ed, MA); early childhood literacy (M Ed, MA); general education (M Ed, MA); higher education (PhD); instructional technology (M Ed, MA); international education and entrepreneurship (PhD); kinesiology (M Ed, MA); literacy (M Ed, MA); organizational leadership (PhD); organizational learning and learning (M Ed, MA); reading (M Ed, MA); special education (M Ed, MA);

teacher leadership (M Ed, MA). Part-time and evening/weekend programs available. *Faculty:* 17 full-time (9 women), 6 part-time/adjunct (all women). *Students:* 23 full-time (13 women), 187 part-time (122 women); includes 114 minority (24 Black or African American, non-Hispanic/Latino; 1 American Indian or Alaska Native, non-Hispanic/Latino; 3 Asian, non-Hispanic/Latino; 85 Hispanic/Latino; 1 Two or more races, non-Hispanic/Latino), 30 international. Average age 41. 52 applicants, 67% accepted, 25 enrolled. In 2013, 12 master's, 14 doctorates awarded. *Degree requirements:* For master's, capstone; for doctorate, thesis/dissertation, qualifying exam. *Entrance requirements:* For master's, baccalaureate degree; minimum foundation GPA of 2.5; interview; for doctorate, master's degree; interview; supervised writing sample. Additional exam requirements/recommendations for international students: Required—TOEFL (minimum score 560 paper-based; 83 iBT). *Application deadline:* Applications are processed on a rolling basis. Application fee: $20. Electronic applications accepted. *Expenses: Tuition:* Part-time $815 per credit hour. *Required fees:* $86 per credit hour. One-time fee: $40 part-time. Tuition and fees vary according to degree level and program. *Financial support:* In 2013–14, 5 research assistantships were awarded; Federal Work-Study and scholarships/grants also available. Financial award applicants required to submit FAFSA. *Unit head:* Dr. Denise Staudt, Dean, Dreeben School of Education, 210-829-2762, E-mail: staudt@uiwtx.edu. *Application contact:* Andrea Cyterski-Acosta, Dean of Enrollment, 210-829-6005, Fax: 210-829-3921, E-mail: admis@uiwtx.edu.
Website: http://www.uiw.edu/education/index.htm.

University of the Incarnate Word, School of Graduate Studies and Research, H-E-B School of Business and Administration, Programs in Administration, San Antonio, TX 78209-6397. Offers adult education (MAA); communication arts (MAA); healthcare administration (MAA); instructional technology (MAA); nutrition (MAA); organizational development (MAA); sports management (MAA). Part-time and evening/weekend programs available. Postbaccalaureate distance learning degree programs offered (no on-campus study). *Faculty:* 20 full-time (10 women), 14 part-time/adjunct (6 women). *Students:* 31 full-time (22 women), 54 part-time (36 women); includes 61 minority (14 Black or African American, non-Hispanic/Latino; 1 Asian, non-Hispanic/Latino; 46 Hispanic/Latino), 6 international. Average age 31. 63 applicants, 68% accepted, 21 enrolled. In 2013, 35 master's awarded. *Degree requirements:* For master's, capstone. *Entrance requirements:* For master's, GRE, GMAT, undergraduate degree, minimum GPA of 2.5. Additional exam requirements/recommendations for international students: Required—TOEFL (minimum score 560 paper-based; 83 iBT). *Application deadline:* Applications are processed on a rolling basis. Application fee: $20. Electronic applications accepted. *Expenses: Tuition:* Part-time $815 per credit hour. *Required fees:* $86 per credit hour. One-time fee: $40 part-time. Tuition and fees vary according to degree level and program. *Financial support:* Federal Work-Study and scholarships/grants available. Financial award applicants required to submit FAFSA. *Unit head:* Dr. Mark Teachout, MAA Programs Director, 210-829-3177, Fax: 210-805-3564, E-mail: teachout@uiwtx.edu. *Application contact:* Andrea Cyterski-Acosta, Dean of Enrollment, 210-829-6005, Fax: 210-829-3921, E-mail: admis@uiwtx.edu.
Website: http://www.uiw.edu/maa/.

University of the Sacred Heart, Graduate Programs, Department of Education, Program in Instruction Systems and Education Technology, San Juan, PR 00914-0383. Offers M Ed. Part-time and evening/weekend programs available. *Degree requirements:* For master's, thesis. *Entrance requirements:* For master's, EXADEP, interview, minimum undergraduate GPA of 2.75.

The University of Toledo, College of Graduate Studies, Judith Herb College of Education, Department of Curriculum and Instruction, Toledo, OH 43606-3390. Offers art education (ME); career and technical education (ME); career-technical education (Ed S); curriculum and instruction (ME, PhD, Ed S); early childhood education (PhD, Ed S); education and biology (MES); education and chemistry (MES); education and economics (MAE); education and English (MAE); education and French (MAE); education and geography (MAE); education and geology (MES); education and German (MAE); education and history (MAE); education and mathematics (MAE, MES); education and physics (MES); education and political science (MAE); education and sociology (MAE); education and Spanish (MAE); educational media (PhD); educational technology (ME); educational technology: virtual educator (Certificate); elementary education (PhD); English as a second language (MAE); gifted and talented (PhD); middle childhood education licensure (ME); music education (MME); secondary education (PhD); secondary education licensure (ME); special education (PhD, Ed S). *Accreditation:* NCATE. Part-time and evening/weekend programs available. *Faculty:* 41. *Students:* 53 full-time (30 women), 154 part-time (111 women); includes 21 minority (16 Black or African American, non-Hispanic/Latino; 4 Hispanic/Latino; 1 Two or more races, non-Hispanic/Latino), 21 international. Average age 34. 82 applicants, 79% accepted, 47 enrolled. In 2013, 80 master's, 5 doctorates awarded. *Degree requirements:* For master's, comprehensive exam, thesis or alternative; for doctorate, comprehensive exam, thesis/dissertation; for other advanced degree, thesis optional. *Entrance requirements:* For master's, doctorate, and other advanced degree, minimum cumulative GPA of 2.7 for all previous academic work, letters of recommendation. Additional exam requirements/recommendations for international students: Required—TOEFL (minimum score 550 paper-based; 80 iBT). *Application deadline:* For fall admission, 1/15 priority date for domestic and international students. Applications are processed on a rolling basis. Application fee: $45 ($75 for international students). Electronic applications accepted. *Financial support:* In 2013–14, 5 research assistantships with full and partial tuition reimbursements (averaging $13,200 per year), 11 teaching assistantships with full and partial tuition reimbursements (averaging $8,809 per year) were awarded; career-related internships or fieldwork, Federal Work-Study, institutionally sponsored loans, scholarships/grants, tuition waivers (full and partial), unspecified assistantships, and administrative assistantships also available. Support available to part-time students. *Unit head:* Dr. Joan Kaderavek, Chair, 419-530-5373, E-mail: eigh.chiarelott@utoledo.edu. *Application contact:* Graduate School Office, 419-530-4723, Fax: 419-530-4724, E-mail: grdsch@utnet.utoledo.edu.
Website: http://www.utoledo.edu/eduhshs/.

University of Utah, Graduate School, College of Education, Department of Educational Psychology, Salt Lake City, UT 84112. Offers clinical mental health counseling (M Ed); counseling psychology (PhD); educational psychology (M Ed, MA, MS); elementary education (M Ed); instructional design and educational technology (M Ed); instructional design and technology (MS); learning and cognition (MS, PhD); reading and literacy (M Ed, MS, PhD); school counseling (M Ed); school psychology (M Ed, PhD); statistics (M Stat). *Accreditation:* APA (one or more programs are accredited). *Faculty:* 18 full-time (8 women), 20 part-time/adjunct (17 women). *Students:* 109 full-time (88 women), 108 part-time (68 women); includes 29 minority (2 Black or African American, non-Hispanic/Latino; 1 American Indian or Alaska Native, non-Hispanic/Latino; 7 Asian, non-Hispanic/Latino; 14 Hispanic/Latino; 1 Native Hawaiian or other Pacific Islander, non-Hispanic/Latino; 4 Two or more races, non-Hispanic/Latino), 7 international. Average age 32. 222 applicants, 35% accepted, 61 enrolled. In 2013, 51 master's, 10 doctorates awarded. *Degree requirements:* For master's, variable foreign language requirement, comprehensive exam (for some programs), thesis (for some programs), projects; for doctorate, variable foreign language requirement, comprehensive exam, thesis/dissertation, oral exam. *Entrance requirements:* For master's and doctorate, GRE General Test, minimum GPA of 3.0. Additional exam requirements/recommendations for international students: Required—TOEFL (minimum score 80 iBT). *Application deadline:* For fall admission, 4/1 for domestic and international students; for winter admission, 11/1 for domestic and international students; for spring admission, 3/15 for domestic and international students. Application fee: $55 ($65 for international students). Electronic applications accepted. *Expenses:* Contact institution. *Financial support:* In 2013–14, 81 students received support, including 29 fellowships with full and partial tuition reimbursements available (averaging $11,200 per year), 11 research assistantships with full and partial tuition reimbursements available (averaging $9,100 per year), 38 teaching assistantships with full and partial tuition reimbursements available (averaging $10,400 per year); career-related internships or fieldwork, Federal Work-Study, institutionally sponsored loans, scholarships/grants, health care benefits, and unspecified assistantships also available. Financial award application deadline: 4/1; financial award applicants required to submit FAFSA. *Faculty research:* Autism, computer technology and instruction, cognitive behavior, aging, group counseling. *Total annual research expenditures:* $441,375. *Unit head:* Dr. Anne E. Cook, Chair, 801-581-7148, Fax: 801-581-5566, E-mail: anne.cook@utah.edu. *Application contact:* JoLynn N. Yates, Academic Program Specialist, 801-581-7148, Fax: 801-581-5566, E-mail: jo.yates@utah.edu.
Website: http://www.ed.utah.edu/edps/.

University of Virginia, Curry School of Education, Department of Leadership, Foundations and Policy, Program in Educational Psychology, Charlottesville, VA 22903. Offers applied developmental science (M Ed); educational evaluation (M Ed); educational psychology (M Ed, Ed D, Ed S); educational research (Ed D); gifted education (M Ed); instructional technology (M Ed, Ed S); research statistics and evaluation (Ed D); school psychology (Ed D). *Students:* 21 full-time (14 women), 12 part-time (9 women); includes 9 minority (4 Black or African American, non-Hispanic/Latino; 2 Asian, non-Hispanic/Latino; 3 Hispanic/Latino), 2 international. Average age 32. 67 applicants, 78% accepted, 27 enrolled. In 2013, 42 master's, 1 doctorate awarded. *Degree requirements:* For master's, comprehensive exam. *Entrance requirements:* For master's and doctorate, GRE General Test, 2 letters of recommendation. Additional exam requirements/recommendations for international students: Required—TOEFL (minimum score 600 paper-based; 90 iBT), IELTS (minimum score 7). *Application deadline:* Applications are processed on a rolling basis. Application fee: $60. Electronic applications accepted. *Expenses:* Tuition, state resident: part-time $334 per credit hour. Tuition, nonresident: part-time $1224 per credit hour. *Financial support:* Fellowships, research assistantships, and teaching assistantships available. Financial award application deadline: 1/5; financial award applicants required to submit FAFSA. *Unit head:* Leslie Booren, Managing Director, 434-243-2021, E-mail: booren@virginia.edu.
Website: http://curry.virginia.edu/academics/areas-of-study/educational-psychology.

University of Virginia, Curry School of Education, Program in Education, Charlottesville, VA 22903. Offers administration and supervision (PhD); applied developmental science (PhD); counselor education (PhD); curriculum and instruction (PhD); early childhood special education (MT); education evaluation (PhD); educational psychology (PhD); educational research (PhD); elementary education (MT); English education (MT, PhD); foreign language education (MT); higher education (PhD); instructional technology (PhD); kinesiology (MT, PhD); math education (PhD); reading education (PhD); research, statistics and evaluation (PhD); school psychology (PhD); science education (PhD); social studies education (MT, PhD); special education (PhD); world languages education (MT). *Students:* 474 full-time (379 women), 35 part-time (19 women); includes 89 minority (30 Black or African American, non-Hispanic/Latino; 1 American Indian or Alaska Native, non-Hispanic/Latino; 26 Asian, non-Hispanic/Latino; 19 Hispanic/Latino; 13 Two or more races, non-Hispanic/Latino), 21 international. Average age 26. 312 applicants, 49% accepted, 80 enrolled. In 2013, 137 master's, 38 doctorates awarded. *Degree requirements:* For master's, comprehensive exam (for some programs), field project; for doctorate, comprehensive exam, thesis/dissertation. *Entrance requirements:* For doctorate, GRE General Test. Additional exam requirements/recommendations for international students: Required—TOEFL (minimum score 600 paper-based; 90 iBT), IELTS (minimum score 7). *Application deadline:* Applications are processed on a rolling basis. Application fee: $60. Electronic applications accepted. *Expenses:* Tuition, state resident: part-time $334 per credit hour. Tuition, nonresident: part-time $1224 per credit hour. *Financial support:* Fellowships, research assistantships, and teaching assistantships available. Financial award application deadline: 1/5; financial award applicants required to submit FAFSA. *Unit head:* Robert C. Pianta, Dean, 434-924-3334, E-mail: pianta@virginia.edu. *Application contact:* Office of Admissions and Student Services, 434-924-0742, E-mail: curry-admissions@virginia.edu.
Website: http://curry.virginia.edu/teacher-education.

University of Washington, Graduate School, College of Education, Seattle, WA 98195. Offers curriculum and instruction (M Ed, Ed D, PhD), including educational technology, general curriculum (Ed D, PhD), language, literacy, and culture, mathematics education, multicultural education, reading and language arts education (Ed D), science education, social studies education, teaching and curriculum (M Ed); educational leadership and policy studies (M Ed, Ed D, PhD), including administration (Ed D), educational policy, organization, and leadership (M Ed, PhD), higher education, leadership for learning (Ed D), social and cultural foundations of education (M Ed, PhD); educational psychology (M Ed, PhD), including educational psychology (PhD), human development and cognition (M Ed), learning sciences, measurement, statistics and research design (M Ed), school psychology (M Ed); instructional leadership (M Ed); intercollegiate athletic leadership (M Ed); special education (M Ed, Ed D, PhD), including early childhood special education (M Ed), emotional and behavioral disabilities (M Ed), learning disabilities (M Ed), low-incidence disabilities (M Ed), severe disabilities (M Ed), special education (Ed D, PhD); teacher education (MIT). *Accreditation:* APA. Part-time and evening/weekend programs available. *Degree requirements:* For master's, thesis optional; for doctorate, thesis/dissertation. *Entrance requirements:* For master's and doctorate, GRE General Test, minimum GPA of 3.0. Additional exam requirements/recommendations for international students: Required—TOEFL. Electronic applications accepted. *Faculty research:* School restructuring/effective schools, special education interventions, literacy and writing, technology, school partnerships, teacher preparation.

The University of West Alabama, School of Graduate Studies, College of Education, Departments of Instructional Leadership and Support/Curriculum and Instruction, Program in Library Media, Livingston, AL 35470. Offers M Ed, Ed S. Part-time and evening/weekend programs available. Postbaccalaureate distance learning degree programs offered (no on-campus study). *Faculty:* 2 full-time (both women), 14 part-time/adjunct (8 women). *Students:* 188 (184 women); includes 58 minority (53 Black or African American, non-Hispanic/Latino; 2 American Indian or Alaska Native, non-Hispanic/Latino; 3 Two or more races, non-Hispanic/Latino). 44 applicants, 98% accepted, 36 enrolled. In 2013, 65 master's, 17 Ed Ss awarded. *Degree requirements:* For master's, comprehensive exam, thesis optional. *Entrance requirements:* For master's, GRE General Test, MAT, minimum GPA of 2.75. Additional exam requirements/recommendations for international students: Required—TOEFL (minimum score 500 paper-based; 61 iBT). *Application deadline:* For fall admission, 8/12 priority date for domestic students; for spring admission, 3/24 for domestic students. Applications are processed on a rolling basis. Application fee: $25 ($50 for international

students). Electronic applications accepted. Tuition and fees vary according to course load. *Financial support:* Teaching assistantships, career-related internships or fieldwork, Federal Work-Study, scholarships/grants, and unspecified assistantships available. Support available to part-time students. Financial award application deadline: 3/1; financial award applicants required to submit FAFSA. *Unit head:* Dr. Reenay Rogers, Chair of Instructional Leadership and Support, 205-652-5423, Fax: 205-652-3706, E-mail: rrogers@uwa.edu. *Application contact:* Dr. Kathy Chandler, Dean of Graduate Studies, 205-652-3421, Fax: 205-652-3706, E-mail: kchandler@uwa.edu. Website: http://www.uwa.edu/medlibrarymedia.aspx.

University of West Florida, College of Professional Studies, Department of Applied Science, Technology and Administration, Program in Instructional Technology, Pensacola, FL 32514-5750. Offers educational leadership (M Ed); instructional technology (M Ed). *Entrance requirements:* For master's, MAT, GRE or GMAT, letter of intent, names of references. Additional exam requirements/recommendations for international students: Required—TOEFL (minimum score 550 paper-based). Electronic applications accepted.

University of West Florida, College of Professional Studies, Ed D Programs, Specialization in Curriculum and Instruction: Instructional Technology, Pensacola, FL 32514-5750. Offers Ed D. *Degree requirements:* For doctorate, comprehensive exam, thesis/dissertation. *Entrance requirements:* For doctorate, GRE, MAT, or GMAT, letter of intent; writing sample; three letters of recommendation; two completed disposition assessment forms; written statement of goals; interview with admissions committee. Additional exam requirements/recommendations for international students: Required—TOEFL (minimum score 550 paper-based).

University of West Georgia, College of Education, Department of Educational Technology and Foundations, Carrollton, GA 30118. Offers media (M Ed, Ed S). Part-time and evening/weekend programs available. Postbaccalaureate distance learning degree programs offered (no on-campus study). *Faculty:* 15 full-time (9 women), 1 (woman) part-time/adjunct. *Students:* 36 full-time (28 women), 308 part-time (260 women); includes 124 minority (111 Black or African American, non-Hispanic/Latino; 1 American Indian or Alaska Native, non-Hispanic/Latino; 2 Asian, non-Hispanic/Latino; 6 Hispanic/Latino; 1 Native Hawaiian or other Pacific Islander, non-Hispanic/Latino; 3 Two or more races, non-Hispanic/Latino). Average age 36. 126 applicants, 96% accepted, 58 enrolled. In 2013, 38 master's, 85 Ed Ss awarded. *Degree requirements:* For master's, comprehensive exam, electronic portfolio; for Ed S, comprehensive exam, research project. *Entrance requirements:* For master's, minimum GPA of 2.7, teaching certificate; for Ed S, master's degree, minimum graduate GPA of 3.0. Additional exam requirements/recommendations for international students: Required—TOEFL (minimum score 523 paper-based; 69 iBT); Recommended—IELTS (minimum score 6). *Application deadline:* For fall admission, 7/21 for domestic students, 6/1 for international students; for spring admission, 11/30 for domestic students, 10/15 for international students. Applications are processed on a rolling basis. Application fee: $40. Electronic applications accepted. *Expenses:* Tuition, state resident: full-time $4600; part-time $192 per semester hour. Tuition, nonresident: full-time $17,880; part-time $745 per semester hour. *Required fees:* $1858; $46.34 per semester hour. $512 per semester. Tuition and fees vary according to course load, degree level, campus/location and program. *Financial support:* In 2013–14, 6 students received support, including 2 research assistantships with full tuition reimbursements available (averaging $6,000 per year); career-related internships or fieldwork, scholarships/grants, and unspecified assistantships also available. Support available to part-time students. Financial award application deadline: 4/1; financial award applicants required to submit FAFSA. *Faculty research:* Distance education, technology integration, collaboration, e-books for children, instructional design. *Total annual research expenditures:* $94,000. *Unit head:* Dr. Stephen Bronack, Chair, 678-839-6188, Fax: 678-839-6153, E-mail: sbronack@westga.edu. *Application contact:* Deanna Richards, Coordinator, Graduate Studies, 678-839-5946, E-mail: drichard@westga.edu.
Website: http://www.westga.edu/coeei.

University of Wyoming, College of Education, Program in Instructional Technology, Laramie, WY 82071. Offers MS, Ed D, PhD. Part-time programs available. Postbaccalaureate distance learning degree programs offered (no on-campus study). *Degree requirements:* For master's, thesis or alternative; for doctorate, comprehensive exam, thesis/dissertation. *Entrance requirements:* For master's, GRE, minimum GPA of 3.0; for doctorate, MS or MA, minimum GPA of 3.0. Additional exam requirements/recommendations for international students: Required—TOEFL. Electronic applications accepted. *Faculty research:* Web based instruction, instructional decision, adult education history, literacy in adults, international distance education.

Utah State University, School of Graduate Studies, Emma Eccles Jones College of Education and Human Services, Department of Instructional Technology and Learning Sciences, Logan, UT 84322. Offers M Ed, MS, PhD, Ed S. Part-time and evening/weekend programs available. Postbaccalaureate distance learning degree programs offered (minimal on-campus study). Terminal master's awarded for partial completion of doctoral program. *Degree requirements:* For master's, thesis (for some programs); for doctorate, comprehensive exam, thesis/dissertation. *Entrance requirements:* For master's, GRE General Test or MAT, minimum GPA of 3.0, 3 recommendation letters; for doctorate, GRE General Test, minimum GPA of 3.0, 3 recommendation letters, transcripts, letter of intent; for Ed S, GRE General Test, GRE Subject Test, minimum GPA of 3.0. Additional exam requirements/recommendations for international students: Required—TOEFL (minimum score 550 paper-based). Electronic applications accepted. *Faculty research:* Interactive learning environments, computer-assisted instruction, learning, distance education, corporate training.

Utah Valley University, Program in Education, Orem, UT 84058-5999. Offers educational technology (M Ed); elementary mathematics (M Ed); English as a second language (M Ed); models of instruction (M Ed). *Accreditation:* Teacher Education Accreditation Council. Part-time programs available. *Faculty:* 4 full-time (2 women). *Students:* 107 part-time (76 women); includes 2 minority (1 Asian, non-Hispanic/Latino; 1 Hispanic/Latino). Average age 33. *Degree requirements:* For master's, project. *Entrance requirements:* For master's, GRE, 3 letters of recommendation, interview. Additional exam requirements/recommendations for international students: Required—TOEFL (minimum score 83 iBT). *Application deadline:* For fall admission, 3/31 for domestic and international students. Application fee: $45 ($100 for international students). Electronic applications accepted. *Expenses:* Tuition, state resident: full-time $8520; part-time $355 per credit. Tuition, nonresident: full-time $21,232; part-time $885 per credit. *Required fees:* $700; $350 per semester. Tuition and fees vary according to program. *Financial support:* Application deadline: 5/1; applicants required to submit FAFSA. *Unit head:* Parker Fewson, Dean, School of Education, 801-863-8006. *Application contact:* Mary Sowder, Coordinator of Graduate Studies, 801-863-6723.

Valley City State University, Online Master of Education Program, Valley City, ND 58072. Offers elementary education (M Ed); English education (M Ed); library and information technologies (M Ed); teaching and technology (M Ed); teaching English language learners (ELL) (M Ed); technology education (M Ed). *Accreditation:* NCATE. Part-time and evening/weekend programs available. Postbaccalaureate distance learning degree programs offered (no on-campus study). *Faculty:* 21 full-time (14 women), 7 part-time/adjunct (all women). *Students:* 2 full-time (both women), 151 part-time (102 women); includes 10 minority (1 Black or African American, non-Hispanic/Latino; 3 Asian, non-Hispanic/Latino; 2 Hispanic/Latino; 4 Two or more races, non-Hispanic/Latino), 1 international. Average age 34. 27 applicants, 93% accepted, 21 enrolled. In 2013, 45 master's awarded. *Degree requirements:* For master's, action research report, comprehensive portfolio. *Entrance requirements:* For master's, GRE, MAT, PRAXIS II or National Teaching Board for Professional Standards (if GPA is less than 3.0). Additional exam requirements/recommendations for international students: Required—TOEFL (minimum score 525 paper-based; 71 iBT); Recommended—IELTS (minimum score 5.5). *Application deadline:* For fall admission, 7/19 priority date for domestic and international students; for spring admission, 12/13 priority date for domestic and international students; for summer admission, 5/9 priority date for domestic and international students. Applications are processed on a rolling basis. Application fee: $35. Electronic applications accepted. *Expenses:* Contact institution. *Financial support:* In 2013–14, 24 students received support. Scholarships/grants and tuition waivers (full and partial) available. Financial award application deadline: 5/15; financial award applicants required to submit FAFSA. *Faculty research:* Academically at-risk students in higher education, communication pedagogy and technology, gender communication, computer-mediated communication, creativity in music, STEM education in K-12. *Total annual research expenditures:* $26,000. *Unit head:* Dr. Gary Thompson, Dean, 701-845-7197, E-mail: gary.thompson@vcsu.edu. *Application contact:* Misty Lindgren, Graduate Studies, 701-845-7303, Fax: 701-845-7190, E-mail: misty.lindgren@vcsu.edu.
Website: http://www.vcsu.edu/graduate.

Virginia Commonwealth University, Graduate School, School of Education, Program in Adult Learning, Richmond, VA 23284-9005. Offers adult literacy (M Ed); human resource development (M Ed); teaching and learning with technology (M Ed). *Accreditation:* NCATE. Part-time programs available. *Entrance requirements:* For master's, GRE General Test or MAT. Additional exam requirements/recommendations for international students: Required—TOEFL (minimum score 600 paper-based; 100 iBT). Electronic applications accepted. *Faculty research:* Adult development and learning, program planning and evaluation.

Virginia Polytechnic Institute and State University, VT Online, Blacksburg, VA 24061. Offers advanced transportation systems (Certificate); aerospace engineering (MS); agricultural and life sciences (MSLFS); business information systems (Graduate Certificate); career and technical education (MS); civil engineering (MS); computer engineering (M Eng, MS); decision support systems (Graduate Certificate); eLearning leadership (MA); electrical engineering (M Eng, MS); engineering administration (MEA); environmental engineering (Certificate); environmental politics and policy (Graduate Certificate); environmental sciences and engineering (MS); foundations of political analysis (Graduate Certificate); health product risk management (Graduate Certificate); industrial and systems engineering (MS); information policy and society (Graduate Certificate); information security (Graduate Certificate); information technology (MIT); instructional technology (MA); integrative STEM education (MA Ed); liberal arts (Graduate Certificate); life sciences: health product risk management (MS); natural resources (MNR, Graduate Certificate); networking (Graduate Certificate); nonprofit and nongovernmental organization management (Graduate Certificate); ocean engineering (MS); political science (MA); security studies (Graduate Certificate); software development (Graduate Certificate). *Expenses:* Tuition, state resident: full-time $11,185; part-time $621.50 per credit hour. Tuition, nonresident: full-time $22,146; part-time $1230.25 per credit hour. *Required fees:* $2442; $449.25 per semester. Tuition and fees vary according to course load, campus/location and program.

Walden University, Graduate Programs, Richard W. Riley College of Education and Leadership, Minneapolis, MN 55401. *Accreditation:* NCATE. Part-time and evening/weekend programs available. Postbaccalaureate distance learning degree programs offered (minimal on-campus study). *Faculty:* 23 full-time (15 women), 830 part-time/adjunct (569 women). *Students:* 8,671 full-time (7,197 women), 2,122 part-time (1,735 women); includes 4,734 minority (3,802 Black or African American, non-Hispanic/Latino; 50 American Indian or Alaska Native, non-Hispanic/Latino; 136 Asian, non-Hispanic/Latino; 539 Hispanic/Latino; 35 Native Hawaiian or other Pacific Islander, non-Hispanic/Latino; 172 Two or more races, non-Hispanic/Latino), 73 international. Average age 40. 2,646 applicants, 96% accepted, 2074 enrolled. In 2013, 2,214 master's, 354 doctorates, 479 other advanced degrees awarded. *Degree requirements:* For doctorate, thesis/dissertation (for some programs), residency; for other advanced degree, residency (for some programs). *Entrance requirements:* For master's, bachelor's degree or higher; minimum GPA of 2.5; official transcripts; goal statement (for some programs); access to computer and Internet; for doctorate, master's degree or higher; three years of related professional or academic experience (preferred); minimum GPA of 3.0; goal statement and current resume (select programs); official transcripts; access to computer and Internet; for other advanced degree, relevant work experience; access to computer and Internet. Additional exam requirements/recommendations for international students: Required—TOEFL (minimum score 550 paper-based; 79 iBT), IELTS (minimum score 6.5), Michigan English Language Assessment Battery (minimum score 82), or PTE. *Application deadline:* Applications are processed on a rolling basis. Application fee: $0. Electronic applications accepted. *Expenses: Tuition:* Full-time $11,813.55; part-time $500 per credit. *Required fees:* $618.76. *Financial support:* In 2013–14, 1 fellowship was awarded; Federal Work-Study, scholarships/grants, unspecified assistantships, and family tuition reduction, active duty/veteran tuition reduction, group tuition reduction, interest-free payment plans, employee tuition reduction also available. Support available to part-time students. Financial award applicants required to submit FAFSA. *Unit head:* Dr. Kate Steffens, Dean, 800-925-3368. *Application contact:* Jennifer Hall, Vice President of Enrollment Management, 866-4-WALDEN, E-mail: info@waldenu.edu.
Website: http://www.waldenu.edu/colleges-schools/riley-college-of-education/.

Walden University, Graduate Programs, School of Psychology, Minneapolis, MN 55401. Offers clinical psychology (MS), including counseling, general program; forensic psychology (MS), including forensic psychology in the community, general program, mental health applications, program planning and evaluation in forensic settings, psychology and legal systems; organizational psychology and development (Postbaccalaureate Certificate); psychology (MS, PhD), including applied psychology (MS), clinical psychology (PhD), counseling psychology (PhD), crisis management and response (MS), educational psychology, forensic psychology (PhD), general psychology, health psychology, leadership development and coaching (MS), media psychology (MS), organizational psychology, organizational psychology and nonprofit management (MS), psychology of culture (MS), psychology, public administration, and social change (MS), social psychology, terrorism and security (MS); psychology respecialization (Post-Doctoral Certificate); teaching online (Post-Master's Certificate). Part-time and evening/weekend programs available. Postbaccalaureate distance learning degree programs offered (minimal on-campus study). *Faculty:* 25 full-time (16 women), 272 part-time/adjunct (143 women). *Students:* 2,997 full-time (2,366 women), 1,450 part-time (1,149 women); includes 1,931 minority (1,326 Black or African American, non-Hispanic/Latino; 40 American Indian or Alaska Native, non-Hispanic/Latino; 88 Asian, non-Hispanic/Latino; 354 Hispanic/Latino; 11 Native Hawaiian or other Pacific Islander, non-Hispanic/Latino; 112 Two or more races, non-Hispanic/Latino), 30 international. Average age 41. 856 applicants, 94% accepted, 623 enrolled. In 2013, 483 master's, 146 doctorates, 5 other advanced degrees awarded. Terminal master's

awarded for partial completion of doctoral program. *Degree requirements:* For master's, thesis optional; for doctorate, thesis/dissertation, residency. *Entrance requirements:* For master's, bachelor's degree or higher; minimum GPA of 2.5; official transcripts; goal statement (for some programs); access to computer and Internet; for doctorate, master's degree or higher; three years of related professional or academic experience (preferred); minimum GPA of 3.0; goal statement and current resume (select programs); official transcripts; access to computer and Internet; for other advanced degree, relevant work experience; access to computer and Internet. Additional exam requirements/recommendations for international students: Required—TOEFL (minimum score 550 paper-based; 79 iBT), IELTS (minimum score 6.5), Michigan English Language Assessment Battery (minimum score 82), or PTE. *Application deadline:* Applications are processed on a rolling basis. Application fee: $0. Electronic applications accepted. *Expenses: Tuition:* Full-time $11,813.55; part-time $500 per credit. *Required fees:* $618.76. *Financial support:* Fellowships, Federal Work-Study, scholarships/grants, unspecified assistantships, and family tuition reduction, active duty/veteran tuition reduction, group tuition reduction, interest-free payment plans, employee tuition reduction available. Support available to part-time students. Financial award applicants required to submit FAFSA. *Unit head:* Dr. Marilyn Powell, Associate Dean, 800-925-3368. *Application contact:* Jennifer Hall, Vice President of Enrollment Management, 866-4-WALDEN, E-mail: info@waldenu.edu.
Website: http://www.waldenu.edu/programs/colleges-schools/psychology.

Walsh University, Graduate Studies, Program in Education, North Canton, OH 44720-3396. Offers 21st-century technologies (MA Ed); leadership (MA Ed); reading literacy (MA Ed); traditional program (MA Ed). *Accreditation:* NCATE. Part-time and evening/weekend programs available. *Faculty:* 6 full-time (3 women), 10 part-time/adjunct (all women). *Students:* 13 full-time (10 women), 18 part-time (14 women), 1 international. Average age 32. 16 applicants, 100% accepted, 6 enrolled. In 2013, 46 master's awarded. *Degree requirements:* For master's, comprehensive exam (for some programs), thesis optional, action research project or comprehensive exam. *Entrance requirements:* For master's, MAT (minimum score 396) or GRE (minimum scores: verbal 145, quantitative 146, combined 291, writing 3.0), interview, minimum GPA of 3.0, writing sample, 3 recommendation forms, notarized affidavit of good moral character. Additional exam requirements/recommendations for international students: Required—TOEFL (minimum score 500 paper-based; 61 iBT). *Application deadline:* For fall admission, 7/15 priority date for domestic students. Applications are processed on a rolling basis. Application fee: $25. Electronic applications accepted. *Expenses: Tuition:* Full-time $10,890; part-time $605 per credit hour. *Required fees:* $100; $100. *Financial support:* In 2013–14, 41 students received support, including 3 research assistantships with partial tuition reimbursements available (averaging $12,355 per year), 5 teaching assistantships (averaging $4,734 per year); scholarships/grants, tuition waivers (partial), and unspecified assistantships also available. Support available to part-time students. Financial award application deadline: 12/31; financial award applicants required to submit FAFSA. *Faculty research:* Technology in education, strategies for working with children with special needs, reading literacy, whole brain teaching, hybrid learning, online teaching, global learning. *Unit head:* Dr. Gary Jacobs, Director, 330-490-7336, Fax: 330-490-7326, E-mail: gjacobs@walsh.edu. *Application contact:* Audra Dice, Graduate and Transfer Admissions Counselor, 330-490-7181, Fax: 330-244-4680, E-mail: adice@walsh.edu.

Wayland Baptist University, Graduate Programs, Program in Education, Plainview, TX 79072-6998. Offers education administration (M Ed); education diagnostics (M Ed); education literacy (M Ed); elementary certification (M Ed); English (M Ed); English as a second language (M Ed); higher education administration (M Ed); human resources (M Ed); instructional leadership (M Ed); instructional technology (M Ed); science education (M Ed); secondary certification (M Ed); social studies (M Ed); special education (M Ed). Part-time and evening/weekend programs available. Postbaccalaureate distance learning degree programs offered (no on-campus study). *Faculty:* 33 full-time (17 women), 28 part-time/adjunct (17 women). *Students:* 22 full-time (15 women), 316 part-time (189 women); includes 130 minority (48 Black or African American, non-Hispanic/Latino; 3 American Indian or Alaska Native, non-Hispanic/Latino; 71 Hispanic/Latino; 1 Native Hawaiian or other Pacific Islander, non-Hispanic/Latino; 7 Two or more races, non-Hispanic/Latino). Average age 39. 80 applicants, 96% accepted, 44 enrolled. In 2013, 170 master's awarded. *Degree requirements:* For master's, comprehensive exam, capstone course. *Entrance requirements:* For master's, GRE, GMAT or MAT. Additional exam requirements/recommendations for international students: Required—TOEFL (minimum score 500 paper-based; 61 iBT). *Application deadline:* Applications are processed on a rolling basis. Application fee: $50. Electronic applications accepted. *Expenses: Tuition:* Full-time $8190; part-time $455 per credit hour. *Required fees:* $970; $455 per credit hour. $485 per semester. *Financial support:* Federal Work-Study, institutionally sponsored loans, and scholarships/grants available. Support available to part-time students. Financial award application deadline: 5/1; financial award applicants required to submit FAFSA. *Unit head:* Dr. Jim Todd, Chairman, 806-291-1045, Fax: 806-291-1951. *Application contact:* Amanda Stanton, Coordinator of Graduate Studies, 806-291-3423, Fax: 806-291-1950, E-mail: stanton@wbu.edu.

Waynesburg University, Graduate and Professional Studies, Canonsburg, PA 15370. Offers business (MBA), including energy management, finance, health systems, human resources, leadership, market development; counseling (MA), including addictions counseling, clinical mental health; education (M Ed, MAT), including autism (M Ed), curriculum and instruction (M Ed), educational leadership (M Ed), online teaching (M Ed); nursing (MSN), including administration, education, informatics; nursing practice (DNP); special education (M Ed); technology (M Ed); MSN/MBA. *Accreditation:* AACN. Part-time and evening/weekend programs available. *Faculty:* 11 full-time (5 women), 136 part-time/adjunct (80 women). *Students:* 146 full-time (99 women), 419 part-time (268 women). In 2013, 290 master's, 7 doctorates awarded. *Degree requirements:* For doctorate, thesis/dissertation. *Entrance requirements:* Additional exam requirements/recommendations for international students: Required—TOEFL. *Application deadline:* For fall admission, 8/1 priority date for domestic students. Applications are processed on a rolling basis. Electronic applications accepted. *Financial support:* Available to part-time students. Application deadline: 5/1. *Unit head:* David Mariner, Dean, 724-743-4420, Fax: 724-743-4425, E-mail: dmariner@waynesburg.edu. *Application contact:* Dr. Michael Bednarski, Director of Enrollment, 724-743-4420, Fax: 724-743-4425, E-mail: mbednars@waynesburg.edu.
Website: http://www.waynesburg.edu/.

Wayne State University, College of Education, Division of Administrative and Organizational Studies, Detroit, MI 48202. Offers college and university teaching (Certificate); educational administration and supervision (Ed S); educational leadership (M Ed); educational leadership and policy studies (Ed D, PhD); educational technology (Certificate); instructional technology (M Ed, Ed D, PhD, Ed S); online teaching (Certificate); secondary curriculum and instruction (Ed S); special education administration (Ed S). Part-time programs available. Postbaccalaureate distance learning degree programs offered. *Students:* 96 full-time (68 women), 207 part-time (137 women); includes 133 minority (115 Black or African American, non-Hispanic/Latino; 4 American Indian or Alaska Native, non-Hispanic/Latino; 2 Asian, non-Hispanic/Latino; 8 Hispanic/Latino; 4 Two or more races, non-Hispanic/Latino), 14 international. Average age 39. 127 applicants, 50% accepted, 42 enrolled. In 2013, 47 master's, 15 doctorates, 41 other advanced degrees awarded. *Degree requirements:* For doctorate, thesis/dissertation. *Entrance requirements:* For master's, baccalaureate degree from accredited U.S. institution or equivalent from college or university of government-recognized standing; minimum undergraduate GPA of 2.75 in upper-division coursework; for doctorate, GRE or MAT, interview; autobiography or curriculum vitae; references; master's degree; minimum undergraduate GPA of 3.0, graduate 3.75; 3 years of relevant experience; foundational course work; for other advanced degree, master's degree from accredited institution, minimum upper-division GPA of 2.6 or 3.4 master's, fulfillment of the special requirements of the area of concentration, 3 years of teaching experience (except for instructional technology). Additional exam requirements/recommendations for international students: Required—TOEFL (minimum score 550 paper-based; 79 iBT), Michigan English Language Assessment Battery (minimum score 85); Recommended—IELTS (minimum score 6.5), TWE (minimum score 5.5). *Application deadline:* For fall admission, 6/1 priority date for domestic students, 5/1 priority date for international students; for winter admission, 10/1 priority date for domestic students, 9/1 priority date for international students; for spring admission, 2/1 priority date for domestic students, 1/1 priority date for international students. Applications are processed on a rolling basis. Application fee: $0. Electronic applications accepted. *Expenses:* Tuition, state resident: part-time $554.15 per credit. Tuition, nonresident: part-time $1200.35 per credit. *Required fees:* $42.15 per credit. $268.30 per semester. Tuition and fees vary according to course load and program. *Financial support:* In 2013–14, 48 students received support, including 3 fellowships with tuition reimbursements available (averaging $15,541 per year), 4 research assistantships with tuition reimbursements available (averaging $16,508 per year); career-related internships or fieldwork, Federal Work-Study, scholarships/grants, health care benefits, and unspecified assistantships also available. Support available to part-time students. Financial award application deadline: 3/31; financial award applicants required to submit FAFSA. *Faculty research:* Total quality management, participatory management, administering educational technology, school improvement, principalship. *Total annual research expenditures:* $6,888. *Unit head:* Dr. William Hill, Assistant Dean, 313-577-9316, E-mail: william_e_hill@wayne.edu. *Application contact:* Janice Green, Assistant Dean, 313-577-1605, E-mail: jwgreen@wayne.edu.
Website: http://coe.wayne.edu/aos/index.php.

Wayne State University, School of Library and Information Science, Detroit, MI 48202. Offers academic libraries (MLIS); archival administration (MLIS, Certificate); general librarianship (MLIS); health sciences librarianship (MLIS); information management for librarians (Certificate); information science (MLIS); law librarianship (MLIS); library and information science (Spec); organization of information (MLIS); public libraries (MLIS); public library services to children and young adults (MLIS, Certificate); records management (MLIS); references services (MLIS); school library media specialist endorsement (MLIS); special libraries (MLIS); urban libraries (MLIS); MLIS/MA. *Accreditation:* ALA (one or more programs are accredited). Part-time and evening/weekend programs available. Postbaccalaureate distance learning degree programs offered (no on-campus study). *Faculty:* 13 full-time (9 women), 17 part-time/adjunct (13 women). *Students:* 112 full-time (80 women), 372 part-time (296 women); includes 65 minority (26 Black or African American, non-Hispanic/Latino; 11 Asian, non-Hispanic/Latino; 18 Hispanic/Latino; 10 Two or more races, non-Hispanic/Latino), 2 international. Average age 33. 275 applicants, 61% accepted, 109 enrolled. In 2013, 179 master's, 42 other advanced degrees awarded. *Entrance requirements:* For master's and other advanced degree, GRE or MAT (if undergraduate GPA is between 2.5 and 2.99), minimum undergraduate GPA of 3.0 or graduate degree, personal statement, resume or curriculum vitae. Additional exam requirements/recommendations for international students: Required—TOEFL (minimum score 550 paper-based; 79 iBT); Recommended—IELTS (minimum score 6.5), TWE (minimum score 5.5). *Application deadline:* For fall admission, 7/1 for domestic students, 5/1 priority date for international students; for winter admission, 10/1 for domestic students, 9/1 priority date for international students; for spring admission, 3/15 for domestic students, 1/1 priority date for international students. Applications are processed on a rolling basis. Application fee: $0. Electronic applications accepted. *Expenses:* Contact institution. *Financial support:* In 2013–14, 65 students received support. Fellowships with tuition reimbursements available, research assistantships with tuition reimbursements available, institutionally sponsored loans, scholarships/grants, and unspecified assistantships available. Support available to part-time students. Financial award application deadline: 3/31; financial award applicants required to submit FAFSA. *Faculty research:* Library services, information management issues, digital content management, library/community engagement, archives and preservation. *Unit head:* Dr. Stephen Bajjaly, Associate Dean and Professor, 313-577-0350, Fax: 313-577-7563, E-mail: bajjaly@wayne.edu. *Application contact:* Matthew Fredericks, Academic Services Officer I, 313-577-2446, Fax: 313-577-7563, E-mail: mfredericks@wayne.edu.
Website: http://slis.wayne.edu/.

Webster University, School of Education, Department of Multidisciplinary Studies, St. Louis, MO 63119-3194. Offers education leadership (Ed S); educational technology (MAT); educational technology leadership (Ed S); mathematics (MA); multidisciplinary studies (MAT); school psychology (Ed S); school systems, superintendency and leadership (Ed S); social science (MAT); special education (MA). Part-time programs available. *Entrance requirements:* For master's, minimum GPA of 2.5. Additional exam requirements/recommendations for international students: Required—TOEFL. *Expenses: Tuition:* Full-time $11,610; part-time $645 per credit hour. Tuition and fees vary according to campus/location and program.

West Chester University of Pennsylvania, College of Education, Department of Professional and Secondary Education, West Chester, PA 19383. Offers education for sustainability (Certificate); educational technology (Certificate); entrepreneurial education (Certificate); secondary education (M Ed). Part-time programs available. *Faculty:* 9 full-time (4 women). *Students:* 1 (woman) full-time, 20 part-time (14 women); includes 2 minority (1 Black or African American, non-Hispanic/Latino; 1 Two or more races, non-Hispanic/Latino). Average age 29. 19 applicants, 89% accepted, 12 enrolled. In 2013, 15 master's, 3 Certificates awarded. *Degree requirements:* For master's, comprehensive exam, thesis (for some programs), 36 credits. *Entrance requirements:* For master's, GRE or MAT, teaching certification (strongly recommended); for Certificate, minimum GPA of 3.0. Additional exam requirements/recommendations for international students: Required—TOEFL (minimum score 550 paper-based; 80 iBT). *Application deadline:* For fall admission, 4/15 priority date for domestic students, 3/15 for international students; for spring admission, 10/15 priority date for domestic students, 9/1 for international students. Applications are processed on a rolling basis. Application fee: $45. Electronic applications accepted. *Expenses:* Tuition, state resident: full-time $7956; part-time $442 per credit. Tuition, nonresident: full-time $11,934; part-time $663 per credit. *Required fees:* $2134.20; $106.24 per credit. Tuition and fees vary according to campus/location and program. *Financial support:* Unspecified assistantships available. Support available to part-time students. Financial award application deadline: 2/15; financial award applicants required to submit FAFSA. *Faculty research:* Technology integration: preparing our teachers for the twenty-first century, critical pedagogy. *Unit head:* Dr. John Elmore, Chair, 610-436-6934, Fax: 610-436-3102,

E-mail: jelmore@wcupa.edu. *Application contact:* Dr. Rob Haworth, Graduate Coordinator, 610-436-2246, Fax: 610-436-3102, E-mail: rhaworth@wcupa.edu. Website: http://www.wcupa.edu/_academics/sch_sed.prof&seced/.

West Chester University of Pennsylvania, College of Education, Department of Special Education, West Chester, PA 19383. Offers autism (Certificate); special education (M Ed); special education 7-12 (Certificate); special education PK-8 (Certificate); universal design for learning and assistive technology (Certificate). Programs available in traditional, distance, and blended formats. *Accreditation:* NCATE. Part-time programs available. Postbaccalaureate distance learning degree programs offered (no on-campus study). *Faculty:* 4 full-time (all women), 3 part-time/adjunct (2 women). *Students:* 7 full-time (6 women), 106 part-time (91 women); includes 7 minority (5 Black or African American, non-Hispanic/Latino; 1 Asian, non-Hispanic/Latino; 1 Hispanic/Latino), 1 international. Average age 29. 83 applicants, 89% accepted, 42 enrolled. In 2013, 30 master's, 2 Certificates awarded. *Degree requirements:* For master's, thesis optional, minimum GPA of 3.0, action research; for Certificate, minimum GPA of 3.0; modified student teaching. *Entrance requirements:* For master's, GRE if GPA below 3.0, two letters of recommendation; for Certificate, minimum GPA of 2.8 on last 48 credits or 3.0 overall undergraduate. Additional exam requirements/recommendations for international students: Required—TOEFL (minimum score 550 paper-based; 80 iBT). *Application deadline:* For fall admission, 4/15 priority date for domestic students, 3/15 for international students; for spring admission, 10/15 priority date for domestic students, 9/1 for international students. Applications are processed on a rolling basis. Application fee: $45. Electronic applications accepted. *Expenses:* Tuition, state resident: full-time $7956; part-time $442 per credit. Tuition, nonresident: full-time $11,934; part-time $663 per credit. *Required fees:* $2134.20; $106.24 per credit. Tuition and fees vary according to campus/location and program. *Financial support:* Unspecified assistantships available. Support available to part-time students. Financial award application deadline: 2/15; financial award applicants required to submit FAFSA. *Unit head:* Dr. Donna Wandry, Chair, 610-436-3431, Fax: 610-436-3102, E-mail: dwandry@wcupa.edu. *Application contact:* Dr. Vicki McGinley, Graduate Coordinator, 610-436-2867, E-mail: vmcginley@wcupa.edu. Website: http://www.wcupa.edu/_academics/sch_sed.earlyspecialed/.

Western Connecticut State University, Division of Graduate Studies, School of Professional Studies, Department of Education and Educational Psychology, Instructional Technology Option, Danbury, CT 06810-6885. Offers MS. Part-time programs available. *Degree requirements:* For master's, thesis or research project, completion of program in 6 years. *Entrance requirements:* For master's, minimum GPA of 2.8, teaching certificate. Additional exam requirements/recommendations for international students: Recommended—TOEFL (minimum score 550 paper-based; 79 iBT), IELTS (minimum score 6). *Faculty research:* Connectivism in education.

Western Governors University, Teachers College, Salt Lake City, UT 84107. Offers curriculum and instruction (MS); educational leadership (MS); educational studies (MA); educational studies (5-12) (MA), including mathematics; elementary education (K-8) (MAT, Postbaccalaureate Certificate); elementary education (PreK-8) (MAT); English language learning (K-12) (MA); instructional design (MAT); learning and technology (M Ed, MA); management and innovation (M Ed); mathematics (5-12) (MAT, Postbaccalaureate Certificate); mathematics (5-9) (MAT, Postbaccalaureate Certificate); mathematics education (5-12) (MA); mathematics education (5-9) (MA); mathematics education (K-6) (MA); measurement and evaluation (M Ed); science (5-12) (Postbaccalaureate Certificate); science (5-9) (MAT, Postbaccalaureate Certificate); science education (5-12) (MA), including biology, chemistry, geology, physics; science education (5-9) (MA); social science (5-12) (MAT, Postbaccalaureate Certificate); special education (MAT, MS). *Accreditation:* NCATE. Evening/weekend programs available. Postbaccalaureate distance learning degree programs offered (no on-campus study). *Degree requirements:* For master's, capstone project. *Entrance requirements:* For master's and Postbaccalaureate Certificate, Readiness Assessment, transcripts. Additional exam requirements/recommendations for international students: Required—TOEFL (minimum score 450 paper-based; 80 iBT). Electronic applications accepted. *Expenses:* Contact institution.

Western Illinois University, School of Graduate Studies, College of Education and Human Services, Department of Instructional Design and Technology, Macomb, IL 61455-1390. Offers distance learning (Certificate); educational technology specialist (Certificate); graphic applications (Certificate); instructional design and technology (MS); multimedia (Certificate); technology integration in education (Certificate); training development (Certificate). Part-time programs available. Postbaccalaureate distance learning degree programs offered (no on-campus study). *Students:* 28 full-time (11 women), 80 part-time (50 women); includes 17 minority (9 Black or African American, non-Hispanic/Latino; 1 American Indian or Alaska Native, non-Hispanic/Latino; 3 Asian, non-Hispanic/Latino; 3 Hispanic/Latino; 1 Two or more races, non-Hispanic/Latino), 8 international. Average age 35. In 2013, 23 master's, 7 other advanced degrees awarded. *Degree requirements:* For master's, thesis or alternative. *Entrance requirements:* Additional exam requirements/recommendations for international students: Required—TOEFL (minimum score 550 paper-based; 80 iBT). *Application deadline:* Applications are processed on a rolling basis. Application fee: $30. Electronic applications accepted. *Financial support:* In 2013–14, 12 students received support, including 5 research assistantships with full tuition reimbursements available (averaging $7,544 per year), 7 teaching assistantships with full tuition reimbursements available (averaging $8,688 per year). Financial award applicants required to submit FAFSA. *Unit head:* Dr. Hoyet Hemphill, Chairperson, 309-298-1952. *Application contact:* Dr. Nancy Parsons, Associate Provost and Director of Graduate Studies, 309-298-1806, Fax: 309-298-2345, E-mail: grad-office@wiu.edu. Website: http://wiu.edu/idt.

Western Kentucky University, Graduate Studies, College of Education and Behavioral Sciences, School of Teacher Education, Bowling Green, KY 42101. Offers elementary education (MAE, Ed S); exceptional education: learning and behavioral disorders (MAE); exceptional education: moderate and severe disabilities (MAE); instructional design (MS); interdisciplinary early childhood education (MAE); library media education (MS); literacy education (MAE); middle grades education (MAE); secondary education (MAE, Ed S). Part-time and evening/weekend programs available. Postbaccalaureate distance learning degree programs offered (minimal on-campus study). *Degree requirements:* For master's, comprehensive exam. *Entrance requirements:* For master's, GRE General Test. Additional exam requirements/recommendations for international students: Required—TOEFL (minimum score 555 paper-based; 79 iBT). *Faculty research:* Teacher preparation in moderate/severe disabilities.

Western Michigan University, Graduate College, College of Education and Human Development, Department of Educational Leadership, Research and Technology, Kalamazoo, MI 49008. Offers educational leadership (MA, PhD, Ed S); educational technology (MA, Graduate Certificate); evaluation, measurement and research (MA, PhD).

Western Oregon University, Graduate Programs, College of Education, Division of Teacher Education, Program in Information Technology, Monmouth, OR 97361-1394. Offers MS Ed. *Accreditation:* NCATE. Part-time and evening/weekend programs available. Postbaccalaureate distance learning degree programs offered (minimal on-

campus study). *Degree requirements:* For master's, written exams. *Entrance requirements:* For master's, interview, minimum GPA of 3.0, teaching license. Additional exam requirements/recommendations for international students: Required—TOEFL (minimum score 550 paper-based; 79 iBT), IELTS (minimum score 6.5). *Faculty research:* Impact of technology on teaching and learning.

Westfield State University, Division of Graduate and Continuing Education, Department of Education, Program in Technology for Educators, Westfield, MA 01086. Offers M Ed. Part-time and evening/weekend programs available. *Degree requirements:* For master's, comprehensive exam or project. *Entrance requirements:* For master's, GRE General Test or MAT, minimum undergraduate GPA of 2.7.

West Texas A&M University, College of Education and Social Sciences, Department of Education, Program in Instructional Design and Technology, Canyon, TX 79016-0001. Offers M Ed. Part-time and evening/weekend programs available. Postbaccalaureate distance learning degree programs offered (minimal on-campus study). *Degree requirements:* For master's, comprehensive exam, thesis optional. *Entrance requirements:* For master's, GRE General Test, approval from the instructional technology admissions committee. Additional exam requirements/recommendations for international students: Required—TOEFL (minimum score 550 paper-based). Electronic applications accepted. *Faculty research:* Mathematics and science instruction, technology, developing online courses for freshmen, integrity of online courses.

West Virginia University, College of Human Resources and Education, Department of Technology, Learning and Culture, Program in Instructional Design and Technology, Morgantown, WV 26506. Offers MA, Ed D. *Accreditation:* NCATE. *Degree requirements:* For master's, thesis; for doctorate, thesis/dissertation. *Entrance requirements:* For master's, GRE General Test, minimum GPA of 2.75; for doctorate, GRE, minimum GPA of 2.75. Additional exam requirements/recommendations for international students: Required—TOEFL. *Faculty research:* Appropriate technology, alternative energy, computer applications for education and training, telecommunication, professional development.

Widener University, School of Human Service Professions, Center for Education, Chester, PA 19013-5792. Offers adult education (M Ed); counseling in higher education (M Ed); counselor education (M Ed); early childhood education (M Ed); educational foundations (M Ed); educational leadership (M Ed); educational psychology (M Ed); elementary education (M Ed); English and language arts (M Ed); health education (M Ed); higher education leadership (Ed D); home and school visitor (M Ed); human sexuality (M Ed, PhD); mathematics education (M Ed); middle school education (M Ed); principalship (M Ed); reading and language arts (Ed D); reading education (M Ed); school administration (Ed D); science education (M Ed); social studies education (M Ed); special education (M Ed); technology education (M Ed). *Accreditation:* NCATE. Part-time and evening/weekend programs available. *Faculty:* 34 full-time (22 women), 37 part-time/adjunct (14 women). *Students:* 64 full-time (44 women), 209 part-time (146 women); includes 49 minority (39 Black or African American, non-Hispanic/Latino; 1 American Indian or Alaska Native, non-Hispanic/Latino; 4 Asian, non-Hispanic/Latino; 4 Hispanic/Latino; 1 Two or more races, non-Hispanic/Latino), 8 international. Average age 39. 139 applicants, 88% accepted. In 2013, 168 master's, 31 doctorates awarded. Terminal master's awarded for partial completion of doctoral program. *Degree requirements:* For doctorate, thesis/dissertation. *Entrance requirements:* For master's, minimum GPA of 2.5; for doctorate, GRE or MAT, minimum GPA of 2.0 (undergraduate), 3.5 (graduate). *Application deadline:* Applications are processed on a rolling basis. Application fee: $25 ($300 for international students). Electronic applications accepted. *Expenses:* Contact institution. *Financial support:* Career-related internships or fieldwork, tuition waivers (full and partial), and unspecified assistantships available. Support available to part-time students. Financial award application deadline: 5/1. *Faculty research:* Reading and cognition, adult education, technology education, educational leadership, special education. *Unit head:* Dr. Michael W. LeDoux, Associate Dean, 610-499-4294, Fax: 610-499-4623, E-mail: mwledoux@widener.edu. *Application contact:* Dr. Roberta Nolan, Director of Graduate Admissions, 610-499-4125, E-mail: rdnolan@widener.edu.

Wilkes University, College of Graduate and Professional Studies, School of Education, Wilkes-Barre, PA 18766-0002. Offers art and science of teaching (MS Ed); classroom technology (MS Ed); early childhood literacy (MS Ed); educational development and strategies (MS Ed); educational leadership (MS Ed); educational technology (Ed D); higher education administration (Ed D); instructional media (MS Ed); instructional technology (MS Ed); international school leadership (MS Ed); K-12 administration (Ed D); middle level education (MS Ed); online teaching (MS Ed); reading (MS Ed); school business leadership (MS Ed); secondary education (MS Ed), including biology, chemistry, English, history, mathematics; special education (MS Ed); teaching English as a second language (MS Ed); twenty-first century teaching and learning (MS Ed). Part-time and evening/weekend programs available. Postbaccalaureate distance learning degree programs offered (minimal on-campus study). *Students:* 46 full-time (37 women), 1,410 part-time (1,039 women); includes 67 minority (12 Black or African American, non-Hispanic/Latino; 2 American Indian or Alaska Native, non-Hispanic/Latino; 11 Asian, non-Hispanic/Latino; 28 Hispanic/Latino; 1 Native Hawaiian or other Pacific Islander, non-Hispanic/Latino; 13 Two or more races, non-Hispanic/Latino), 6 international. Average age 34. In 2013, 852 master's, 10 doctorates awarded. *Entrance requirements:* Additional exam requirements/recommendations for international students: Required—TOEFL (minimum score 550 paper-based; 79 iBT). *Application deadline:* Applications are processed on a rolling basis. Application fee: $45. Electronic applications accepted. *Expenses:* Contact institution. *Financial support:* Federal Work-Study and unspecified assistantships available. Financial award application deadline: 3/1; financial award applicants required to submit FAFSA. *Unit head:* Dr. Rhonda Waskiewicz, Interim Dean, Education, 570-408-4332, Fax: 570-408-7872, E-mail: rhonda.waskiewicz@wilkes.edu. *Application contact:* Joanne Thomas, Interim Director of Graduate Education, 570-408-4234, Fax: 570-408-7846, E-mail: joanne.thomas1@wilkes.edu. Website: http://www.wilkes.edu/pages/383.asp.

William Woods University, Graduate and Adult Studies, Fulton, MO 65251-1098. Offers administration (M Ed, Ed S); athletic/activities administration (M Ed); curriculum and instruction (M Ed, Ed S); educational leadership (Ed D); equestrian education (M Ed); health management (MBA); human resources (MBA); leadership (MBA); marketing, advertising, and public relations (MBA); teaching and technology (M Ed). Part-time and evening/weekend programs available. *Faculty:* 231 part-time/adjunct (87 women). *Students:* 418 full-time (276 women), 716 part-time (433 women); includes 51 minority (34 Black or African American, non-Hispanic/Latino; 4 American Indian or Alaska Native, non-Hispanic/Latino; 5 Asian, non-Hispanic/Latino; 3 Hispanic/Latino; 5 Two or more races, non-Hispanic/Latino), 4 international. Average age 35. In 2013, 507 master's, 8 doctorates, 143 other advanced degrees awarded. *Degree requirements:* For master's, capstone course (MBA), action research (M Ed); for Ed S, field experience. *Entrance requirements:* Additional exam requirements/recommendations for international students: Required—TOEFL (minimum score 550 paper-based). *Application deadline:* Applications are processed on a rolling basis. Application fee: $0. Electronic applications accepted. *Expenses:* Contact institution. *Financial support:* Institutionally sponsored loans available. Financial award applicants required to submit

FAFSA. *Unit head:* Dr. Michael Westerfield, Vice President and Dean of the Graduate College, 573-592-4383, Fax: 573-592-1164. *Application contact:* Jessica Brush, Director of Operations, 573-592-4227, Fax: 573-592-1164, E-mail: jessica.brush@williamwoods.ede.
Website: http://www.williamwoods.edu/evening_programs/index.asp.

Wilmington University, College of Education, New Castle, DE 19720-6491. Offers applied technology in education (M Ed); career and technical education (M Ed); educational leadership (Ed D); elementary and secondary school counseling (M Ed); elementary studies (M Ed); ESOL literacy (M Ed); higher education leadership (Ed D); instruction: gifted and talented (M Ed); instruction: teacher of reading (M Ed); instruction: teaching and learning (M Ed); organizational leadership (Ed D); school leadership (M Ed); secondary education (MAT); special education (M Ed). *Accreditation:* NCATE. Part-time and evening/weekend programs available. *Entrance requirements:* For master's, 2 letters of recommendation, interview. Additional exam requirements/recommendations for international students: Required—TOEFL (minimum score 500 paper-based). Electronic applications accepted.

Worcester Polytechnic Institute, Graduate Studies and Research, Program in Learning Sciences and Technologies, Worcester, MA 01609-2280. Offers MS, PhD. Program offered jointly between Department of Social Science and Policy Studies and Department of Computer Science. Part-time and evening/weekend programs available. *Students:* 5 full-time (1 woman), 4 part-time (all women); includes 1 minority (Hispanic/Latino), 2 international. 12 applicants, 100% accepted, 7 enrolled. In 2013, 2 master's, 1 doctorate awarded. *Entrance requirements:* For master's and doctorate, GRE (strongly recommended), statement of purpose, brief sample of scholarly writing. Additional exam requirements/recommendations for international students: Required—TOEFL (minimum score 563 paper-based; 84 iBT), IELTS (minimum score 7). *Application deadline:* For fall admission, 1/1 for domestic and international students; for spring admission, 10/1 for domestic and international students. Applications are processed on a rolling basis. Application fee: $70. Electronic applications accepted. *Financial support:* Research assistantships and teaching assistantships available. *Unit head:* Janice Gobert, Co-Director, 508-831-5296, E-mail: jgobert@wpi.edu. *Application contact:* Lynne Dougherty, Administrative Assistant, 508-831-5301, Fax: 508-831-5717, E-mail: grad@wpi.edu.
Website: http://www.wpi.edu/academics/Majors/LST/progra586.html.

Youngstown State University, Graduate School, Beeghly College of Education, Department of Teacher Education, Youngstown, OH 44555-0001. Offers adolescent/young adult education (MS Ed); content area concentration (MS Ed); early childhood education (MS Ed); educational technology (MS Ed); literacy (MS Ed); middle childhood education (MS Ed); special education (MS Ed), including gifted and talented education, special education. *Accreditation:* NCATE. Part-time and evening/weekend programs available. *Degree requirements:* For master's, comprehensive exam. *Entrance requirements:* For master's, GRE, MAT, or teaching certificate; minimum GPA of 2.7. Additional exam requirements/recommendations for international students: Required—TOEFL. *Faculty research:* Multicultural literacy, hands-on mathematics teaching, integrated instruction, reading comprehension, emergent curriculum.

Educational Policy

Alabama State University, College of Education, Department of Instructional Support Programs, Montgomery, AL 36101-0271. Offers counselor education (M Ed, MS, Ed S), including general counseling (MS, Ed S); school counseling (M Ed, Ed S); educational administration (M Ed, Ed D, Ed S), including educational administration (Ed S), educational leadership, policy and law (Ed D), instructional leadership (M Ed); library education media (M Ed, Ed S). Part-time programs available. *Faculty:* 8 full-time (4 women), 14 part-time/adjunct (8 women). *Students:* 57 full-time (41 women), 175 part-time (126 women); includes 209 minority (203 Black or African American, non-Hispanic/Latino; 2 Asian, non-Hispanic/Latino; 4 Hispanic/Latino). Average age 39. 86 applicants, 48% accepted, 34 enrolled. In 2013, 28 master's, 14 doctorates, 7 other advanced degrees awarded. *Degree requirements:* For master's, comprehensive exam; for Ed S, comprehensive exam, thesis. *Entrance requirements:* For master's and Ed S, GRE General Test, MAT, writing competency test. Additional exam requirements/recommendations for international students: Required—TOEFL (minimum score 500 paper-based). *Application deadline:* For fall admission, 7/15 for domestic students; for spring admission, 12/15 for domestic students. Applications are processed on a rolling basis. Application fee: $10. *Expenses:* Tuition, state resident: full-time $7958; part-time $343 per credit hour. Tuition, nonresident: full-time $14,132; part-time $686 per credit hour. *Required fees:* $446 per term. One-time fee: $1784 full-time; $892 part-time. Tuition and fees vary according to course load. *Financial support:* In 2013–14, research assistantships (averaging $9,450 per year) were awarded. *Unit head:* Dr. Necoal Driver, Chair, 334-229-6882, Fax: 334-229-6904, E-mail: ndriver@alasu.edu. *Application contact:* Dr. Doris Screws, Dean of Graduate Studies, 334-229-4274, Fax: 334-229-4928, E-mail: dscrews@alasu.edu.
Website: http://www.alasu.edu/academics/colleges—departments/college-of-education/instructional-support-programs/index.aspx.

Arizona State University at the Tempe campus, Mary Lou Fulton Teachers College, Program in Educational Leadership and Policy Studies, Phoenix, AZ 85069. Offers PhD. Fall admission only. *Degree requirements:* For doctorate, comprehensive exam, thesis/dissertation, interactive Program of Study (iPOS) submitted before completing 50 percent of required credit hours. *Entrance requirements:* For doctorate, GRE, minimum GPA of 3.0 or equivalent in last 2 years of work leading to bachelor's degree, 3 letters of recommendation, personal statement, writing sample, curriculum vitae or resume. Additional exam requirements/recommendations for international students: Required—TOEFL (minimum score 80 iBT), TOEFL, IELTS, or PTE. Electronic applications accepted. *Expenses:* Contact institution. *Faculty research:* Education policy analysis, school finance and quantitative methods, school improvement in ethnically, linguistically and economically diverse communities, parent/teacher engagement, school choice, accountability polices, school finance litigation, school segregation.

The Catholic University of America, School of Arts and Sciences, Department of Education, Washington, DC 20064. Offers Catholic educational leadership and policy studies (PhD); Catholic school leadership (MA); education (Certificate); educational psychology (PhD); secondary education (MA); special education (MA). *Accreditation:* NCATE. Part-time programs available. *Faculty:* 9 full-time (8 women), 4 part-time/adjunct (all women). *Students:* 9 full-time (6 women), 44 part-time (37 women); includes 8 minority (3 Black or African American, non-Hispanic/Latino; 3 Hispanic/Latino; 2 Two or more races, non-Hispanic/Latino), 2 international. Average age 34. 53 applicants, 53% accepted, 17 enrolled. In 2013, 18 master's, 2 doctorates awarded. *Degree requirements:* For master's, comprehensive exam, thesis or alternative; for doctorate, comprehensive exam, thesis/dissertation; for Certificate, action research project. *Entrance requirements:* For master's and doctorate, GRE General Test or MAT, statement of purpose, official copies of academic transcripts, three letters of recommendation, interview; for Certificate, PRAXIS I, statement of purpose, official copies of academic transcripts, three letters of recommendation, interview. Additional exam requirements/recommendations for international students: Required—TOEFL (minimum score 580 paper-based). *Application deadline:* For fall admission, 8/1 priority date for domestic students, 7/15 for international students; for spring admission, 12/1 priority date for domestic students, 10/15 for international students. Applications are processed on a rolling basis. Application fee: $55. Electronic applications accepted. *Expenses:* Tuition: Full-time $38,500; part-time $1490 per credit hour. *Required fees:* $400; $1525 per credit hour. One-time fee: $425. Tuition and fees vary according to program. *Financial support:* Fellowships, research assistantships, teaching assistantships, Federal Work-Study, scholarships/grants, tuition waivers (full and partial), and unspecified assistantships available. Financial award application deadline: 2/1; financial award applicants required to submit FAFSA. *Faculty research:* Special education, early childhood education, educational psychology, Catholic school administration, leadership and policy studies, counseling, curriculum and instruction. *Total annual research expenditures:* $65,883. *Unit head:* Dr. Merylann J. Schuttloffel, Chair, 202-319-5805, Fax: 202-319-5815, E-mail: schuttloffel@cua.edu. *Application contact:* Andrew Woodall, Director of Graduate Admissions, 202-319-5057, Fax: 202-319-6533, E-mail: cua-admissions@cua.edu.
Website: http://education.cua.edu/.

Cleveland State University, College of Graduate Studies, College of Education and Human Services, Program in Urban Education, Specialization in Policy Studies, Cleveland, OH 44115. Offers PhD. Part-time programs available. *Faculty:* 6 full-time (1 woman). *Students:* 8 full-time (5 women), 11 part-time (7 women); includes 7 minority (5 Black or African American, non-Hispanic/Latino; 1 Hispanic/Latino; 1 Two or more races, non-Hispanic/Latino). Average age 39. 6 applicants, 33% accepted. In 2013, 2 doctorates awarded. *Degree requirements:* For doctorate, one foreign language, comprehensive exam, thesis/dissertation. *Entrance requirements:* For doctorate, General GRE Test (minimum score of 297 for combined Verbal and Quantitative exams, 4.0 preferred for Analytical Writing), minimum graduate GPA of 3.25, curriculum vitae or resume, personal statement, 2 letters of recommendation. Additional exam requirements/recommendations for international students: Required—TOEFL (minimum score 525 paper-based), IELTS (minimum score 6). *Expenses:* Tuition, state resident: full-time $8335; part-time $521 per credit hour. Tuition, nonresident: full-time $15,670; part-time $979 per credit hour. *Required fees:* $50; $25 per semester. *Financial support:* In 2013–14, 5 students received support, including 2 research assistantships with full tuition reimbursements available, 1 teaching assistantship with full tuition reimbursement available (averaging $8,850 per year); tuition waivers (full and partial) also available. Support available to part-time students. Financial award application deadline: 4/1; financial award applicants required to submit FAFSA. *Faculty research:* Historical, theoretical and practical aspects of educational policy formation; relationship of educational policy within the larger context of urban affairs, public policy, and school reform. *Unit head:* Dr. Graham Stead, Director, 216-875-9869, Fax: 216-875-9697, E-mail: g.b.stead@csuohio.edu. *Application contact:* Rita M. Grabowski, Administrative Coordinator, 216-687-4697, Fax: 216-875-9697, E-mail: r.grabowski@csuohio.edu.
Website: http://www.csuohio.edu/cehs/departments/DOC/ep_doc.html.

The College of William and Mary, School of Education, Program in Education Policy, Planning, and Leadership, Williamsburg, VA 23187-8795. Offers curriculum and educational technology (Ed D, PhD); curriculum leadership (Ed D, PhD); educational leadership (M Ed), including higher education administration (M Ed, Ed D, PhD), K-12 administration and supervision; educational policy, planning, and leadership (Ed D, PhD), including general education administration, gifted education administration, higher education administration (M Ed, Ed D, PhD). *Accreditation:* NCATE. Part-time and evening/weekend programs available. *Faculty:* 10 full-time (5 women), 17 part-time/adjunct (13 women). *Students:* 64 full-time (52 women), 145 part-time (106 women); includes 46 minority (33 Black or African American, non-Hispanic/Latino; 3 Asian, non-Hispanic/Latino; 4 Hispanic/Latino; 6 Two or more races, non-Hispanic/Latino), 9 international. Average age 38. 133 applicants, 74% accepted, 72 enrolled. In 2013, 24 master's, 17 doctorates awarded. *Degree requirements:* For doctorate, comprehensive exam, thesis/dissertation. *Entrance requirements:* For master's, GRE or MAT, minimum GPA of 2.5; for doctorate, GRE or MAT, minimum GPA of 3.0. Additional exam requirements/recommendations for international students: Required—TOEFL, IELTS. *Application deadline:* For fall admission, 1/15 for domestic and international students. Application fee: $50. Electronic applications accepted. *Expenses:* Tuition, state resident: full-time $7120; part-time $405 per credit hour. Tuition, nonresident: full-time $21,639; part-time $1050 per credit hour. *Required fees:* $4764. *Financial support:* In 2013–14, 58 students received support, including 1 fellowship (averaging $20,000 per year), 51 research assistantships with full and partial tuition reimbursements available (averaging $16,551 per year); career-related internships or fieldwork, Federal Work-Study, institutionally sponsored loans, scholarships/grants, and unspecified assistantships also available. Support available to part-time students. Financial award application deadline: 1/15; financial award applicants required to submit FAFSA. *Faculty research:* Higher education policy, faculty incentives, history of adversity, resilience, leadership. *Unit head:* Dr. James Stronge, Area Coordinator, 757-221-2339, E-mail: jhstro@wm.edu. *Application contact:* Dorothy Smith Osborne, Assistant Dean for Academic Programs and Student Services, 757-221-2317, Fax: 757-221-2293, E-mail: dsosbo@wm.edu.
Website: http://education.wm.edu.

Cornell University, Graduate School, Graduate Fields of Agriculture and Life Sciences, Field of Education, Ithaca, NY 14853-0001. Offers adult and extension education (MPS, MS, PhD); learning, teaching, and social policy (MPS, MS, PhD); mathematics 7-12 (MS). *Faculty:* 21 full-time (8 women). *Students:* 14 full-time (9 women); includes 2 minority (1 Asian, non-Hispanic/Latino; 1 Hispanic/Latino), 1 international. Average age 32. 20 applicants, 20% accepted, 2 enrolled. In 2013, 17 master's, 4 doctorates awarded. Terminal master's awarded for partial completion of doctoral program. *Degree requirements:* For master's, thesis (MS); for doctorate, comprehensive exam, thesis/dissertation. *Entrance requirements:* For master's and doctorate, GRE General Test,

sample of written work (recommended), 2 letters of recommendation. Additional exam requirements/recommendations for international students: Required—TOEFL (minimum score 550 paper-based; 77 iBT). *Application deadline:* For fall admission, 2/15 for domestic students. Application fee: $95. Electronic applications accepted. *Financial support:* In 2013–14, 4 students received support, including 3 fellowships with full tuition reimbursements available, 1 research assistantship with full tuition reimbursement available; teaching assistantships with full tuition reimbursements available, institutionally sponsored loans, scholarships/grants, health care benefits, tuition waivers (full and partial), and unspecified assistantships also available. Financial award applicants required to submit FAFSA. *Faculty research:* Moral development and professional ethics, public issues education and community development, socio/political issues in public education, teacher education and curriculum in agricultural science and mathematics, extension research. *Unit head:* Director of Graduate Studies, 607-255-4278, Fax: 607-255-7905. *Application contact:* Graduate Field Assistant, 607-255-4278, Fax: 607-255-7905, E-mail: rh22@cornell.edu.
Website: http://www.gradschool.cornell.edu/fields.php?id-80&a-2.

Florida State University, The Graduate School, College of Education, Department of Educational Leadership and Policy Studies, Program in Educational Leadership and Policy, Tallahassee, FL 32306. Offers education policy and evaluation (MS, PhD); educational leadership/administration (MS, PhD, Certificate, Ed S). Part-time and evening/weekend programs available. *Faculty:* 15 full-time (12 women). *Students:* 25 full-time (16 women), 97 part-time (63 women); includes 47 minority (23 Black or African American, non-Hispanic/Latino; 2 Asian, non-Hispanic/Latino; 21 Hispanic/Latino; 1 Two or more races, non-Hispanic/Latino), 6 international. Average age 36. 72 applicants, 56% accepted, 25 enrolled. In 2013, 24 master's, 4 doctorates, 16 other advanced degrees awarded. Terminal master's awarded for partial completion of doctoral program. *Degree requirements:* For master's and other advanced degree, comprehensive exam, thesis optional; for doctorate, comprehensive exam, thesis/dissertation. *Entrance requirements:* For master's, GRE General Test, minimum GPA of 3.0; for doctorate and other advanced degree, GRE General Test, minimum graduate GPA of 3.0. Additional exam requirements/recommendations for international students: Required—TOEFL (minimum score 550 paper-based; 80 iBT). *Application deadline:* For fall admission, 7/1 for domestic and international students; for winter admission, 11/1 for domestic and international students; for spring admission, 3/1 for domestic and international students. Application fee: $30. Electronic applications accepted. *Expenses:* Tuition, state resident: part-time $403.51 per credit hour. Tuition, nonresident: part-time $1004.85 per credit hour. *Required fees:* $75.81 per credit hour. One-time fee: $20 part-time. Tuition and fees vary according to course load, campus/location and student level. *Financial support:* Fellowships with full and partial tuition reimbursements, research assistantships with full and partial tuition reimbursements, teaching assistantships with full and partial tuition reimbursements, career-related internships or fieldwork, scholarships/grants, health care benefits, and unspecified assistantships available. Financial award application deadline: 1/15; financial award applicants required to submit FAFSA. *Faculty research:* Issues in higher education law; diversity, equity, and social justice; educational issues in Western and non-Western countries. *Unit head:* Dr. Stacey Rutledge, Program Coordinator, 850-644-8163, Fax: 850-644-1258, E-mail: sarutledge@fsu.edu. *Application contact:* Linda J. Lyons, Academic Support Assistant, 850-644-7077, Fax: 850-644-1258, E-mail: ljlyons@fsu.edu.
Website: http://www.coe.fsu.edu/Current-Students/Departments/Educational-Leadership-and-Policy-Studies-ELPS/Current-Students/Degree-Programs.

The George Washington University, Graduate School of Education and Human Development, Department of Educational Leadership, Program in Educational Administration and Policy Studies, Washington, DC 20052. Offers education policy (Ed D); educational administration (Ed D). Educational administration program offered at Newport News and Alexandria, VA. *Accreditation:* NCATE. *Students:* 6 full-time (4 women), 146 part-time (106 women); includes 48 minority (35 Black or African American, non-Hispanic/Latino; 7 Asian, non-Hispanic/Latino; 5 Hispanic/Latino; 1 Native Hawaiian or other Pacific Islander, non-Hispanic/Latino), 3 international. Average age 40. 31 applicants, 48% accepted, 4 enrolled. In 2013, 14 doctorates awarded. *Degree requirements:* For doctorate, comprehensive exam, thesis/dissertation. *Entrance requirements:* For doctorate, GRE General Test or MAT, interview, minimum GPA of 3.3. *Application deadline:* For fall admission, 1/15 priority date for domestic students; for spring admission, 10/1 for domestic students. Applications are processed on a rolling basis. Application fee: $75. *Financial support:* In 2013–14, 9 students received support. Fellowships, research assistantships, teaching assistantships, career-related internships or fieldwork, Federal Work-Study, and tuition waivers (partial) available. Financial award application deadline: 1/15; financial award applicants required to submit FAFSA. *Unit head:* Prof. Yas Nakib, Program Coordinator, 202-994-8816, E-mail: nakib@gwu.edu. *Application contact:* Sarah Lang, Director, Admissions and Marketing, 202-994-1447, Fax: 202-994-7207, E-mail: slang@gwu.edu.

The George Washington University, Graduate School of Education and Human Development, Department of Educational Leadership, Program in Education Policy Studies, Washington, DC 20052. Offers MA Ed. *Accreditation:* NCATE. *Students:* 6 full-time (3 women), 8 part-time (7 women); includes 4 minority (2 Black or African American, non-Hispanic/Latino; 2 Hispanic/Latino). Average age 29. 47 applicants, 83% accepted, 10 enrolled. In 2013, 10 master's awarded. *Degree requirements:* For master's, comprehensive exam. *Entrance requirements:* For master's, GRE General Test or MAT, interview, minimum GPA of 2.75. *Application deadline:* For fall admission, 1/15 priority date for domestic students; for spring admission, 10/1 for domestic students. Applications are processed on a rolling basis. Application fee: $75. *Financial support:* In 2013–14, 10 students received support. Fellowships, career-related internships or fieldwork, Federal Work-Study, and tuition waivers (partial) available. Financial award application deadline: 1/15. *Unit head:* Prof. Yas Nakib, Coordinator, 202-994-8816, E-mail: nakib@gwu.edu. *Application contact:* Sarah Lang, Director of Graduate Admissions, 202-994-1447, Fax: 202-994-7207, E-mail: slang@gwu.edu.

Georgia State University, College of Education, Department of Educational Policy Studies, Atlanta, GA 30302-3083. Offers educational leadership (M Ed, Ed D, Ed S), including educational leadership, urban teacher leadership (M Ed); educational research (MS, PhD); social foundations of education (MS, PhD). Part-time programs available. *Faculty:* 12 full-time (6 women). *Students:* 60 full-time (43 women), 105 part-time (73 women); includes 83 minority (66 Black or African American, non-Hispanic/Latino; 1 American Indian or Alaska Native, non-Hispanic/Latino; 3 Asian, non-Hispanic/Latino; 7 Hispanic/Latino; 1 Native Hawaiian or other Pacific Islander, non-Hispanic/Latino; 5 Two or more races, non-Hispanic/Latino), 3 international. Average age 38. 76 applicants, 38% accepted, 21 enrolled. In 2013, 24 master's, 6 doctorates, 19 other advanced degrees awarded. *Degree requirements:* For master's, thesis optional, 36 semester hours; for doctorate, comprehensive exam, thesis/dissertation, 54 semester hours (for EdD); 69 semester hours (for PhD); for Ed S, thesis, 30 semester hours of coursework. *Entrance requirements:* For master's, GRE; for doctorate and Ed S, GRE, MAT. Additional exam requirements/recommendations for international students: Required—TOEFL (minimum score 550 paper-based; 79 iBT) or IELTS (minimum score 6.5). *Application deadline:* For fall admission, 1/15 for domestic and international students; for winter admission, 2/1 for domestic and international students; for spring admission, 10/1 for domestic and international students. Applications are processed on a rolling basis.

Application fee: $50. Electronic applications accepted. *Expenses: Tuition, area resident:* Full-time $4176; part-time $348 per credit hour. Tuition, state resident: full-time $14,544; part-time $1212 per credit hour. Tuition, nonresident: full-time $14,544; part-time $1212 per credit hour. Tuition and fees vary according to course load and program. *Financial support:* In 2013–14, fellowships with full tuition reimbursements (averaging $23,000 per year), research assistantships with full tuition reimbursements (averaging $27,671 per year), teaching assistantships with full tuition reimbursements (averaging $2,300 per year) were awarded; career-related internships or fieldwork, institutionally sponsored loans, scholarships/grants, health care benefits, tuition waivers (full), and unspecified assistantships also available. Support available to part-time students. Financial award application deadline: 3/15. *Faculty research:* Social and cultural influences on schools, equity and social justice, research methodology, program evaluation, leadership and instruction in schools. *Unit head:* Dr. Bill Curlette, Chair, 404-413-8030, Fax: 404-413-8003, E-mail: wcurlette@gsu.edu. *Application contact:* Aishah Cowan, Administrative Academic Specialist, 404-413-8273, Fax: 404-413-8033, E-mail: acowan@gsu.edu.
Website: http://education.gsu.edu/eps/index.htm.

Harvard University, Harvard Graduate School of Education, Master's Programs in Education, Cambridge, MA 02138. Offers arts in education (Ed M); education policy and management (Ed M); higher education (Ed M); human development and psychology (Ed M); international education policy (Ed M); language and literacy (Ed M); learning and teaching (Ed M); mind, brain, and education (Ed M); prevention science and practice (Ed M); school leadership (Ed M); special studies (Ed M); teacher education (Ed M); technology, innovation, and education (Ed M). Part-time programs available. *Faculty:* 68 full-time (34 women), 77 part-time/adjunct (41 women). *Students:* 557 full-time (410 women), 69 part-time (50 women); includes 179 minority (34 Black or African American, non-Hispanic/Latino; 1 American Indian or Alaska Native, non-Hispanic/Latino; 62 Asian, non-Hispanic/Latino; 52 Hispanic/Latino; 2 Native Hawaiian or other Pacific Islander, non-Hispanic/Latino; 28 Two or more races, non-Hispanic/Latino), 100 international. Average age 28. 1,756 applicants, 47% accepted, 589 enrolled. In 2013, 673 master's awarded. *Entrance requirements:* For master's, GRE General Test, statement of purpose, 3 letters of recommendation, resume, official transcripts. Additional exam requirements/recommendations for international students: Required—TOEFL (minimum score 613 paper-based; 104 iBT), TWE (minimum score 5). *Application deadline:* For fall admission, 1/3 for domestic and international students. Application fee: $85. Electronic applications accepted. *Expenses:* Contact institution. *Financial support:* In 2013–14, 375 students received support, including 12 fellowships with full and partial tuition reimbursements available (averaging $13,925 per year), 2 research assistantships (averaging $2,174 per year); career-related internships or fieldwork, Federal Work-Study, institutionally sponsored loans, scholarships/grants, health care benefits, tuition waivers (full and partial), and unspecified assistantships also available. Support available to part-time students. Financial award application deadline: 2/1; financial award applicants required to submit FAFSA. *Faculty research:* Learning and development, educational leadership and organizations, education policy analysis. *Total annual research expenditures:* $34.3 million. *Unit head:* Jennifer L. Petrallia, Assistant Dean, 617-495-8445. *Application contact:* Information Contact, 617-495-3414, Fax: 617-496-3577, E-mail: gseadmissions@harvard.edu.
Website: http://www.gse.harvard.edu/.

Hofstra University, School of Education, Programs in Educational Policy and Leadership, Hempstead, NY 11549. Offers educational and policy leadership (MS Ed, Ed D), including K-12 (MS Ed), K-12/higher education (Ed D); educational policy and leadership (Advanced Certificate), including school district business leader; foundations of education (MA, Advanced Certificate); higher education leadership and policy studies (MS Ed).

Howard University, School of Education, Department of Educational Leadership and Policy Studies, Washington, DC 20059. Offers educational administration (Ed D); educational administration and supervision (M Ed, CAGS). Part-time programs available. *Faculty:* 5 full-time (2 women), 7 part-time/adjunct (2 women). *Students:* 33 full-time (26 women), 53 part-time (33 women); includes 72 minority (71 Black or African American, non-Hispanic/Latino; 1 American Indian or Alaska Native, non-Hispanic/Latino), 10 international. Average age 40. 54 applicants, 70% accepted, 10 enrolled. In 2013, 4 master's, 4 doctorates awarded. *Degree requirements:* For master's, comprehensive exam, School Leaders Licensure Assessment, practicum; for doctorate, comprehensive exam, thesis/dissertation, internship; for CAGS, thesis. *Entrance requirements:* For master's, minimum GPA of 2.7; for doctorate, minimum GPA of 3.0. Additional exam requirements/recommendations for international students: Required—TOEFL (minimum score 550 paper-based; 79 iBT). *Application deadline:* For fall admission, 4/15 priority date for domestic students, 4/1 for international students; for spring admission, 11/15 for domestic students. Applications are processed on a rolling basis. Application fee: $45. Electronic applications accepted. *Financial support:* In 2013–14, 4 students received support, including 4 fellowships with full and partial tuition reimbursements available (averaging $15,000 per year); career-related internships or fieldwork, Federal Work-Study, institutionally sponsored loans, scholarships/grants, tuition waivers (full and partial), and unspecified assistantships also available. Financial award application deadline: 3/15; financial award applicants required to submit FAFSA. *Unit head:* Dr. Dawn G. Williams, Chair, Department of Educational Administration and Policy, 202-806-7342, Fax: 202-806-5310, E-mail: dgwilliams@howard.edu. *Application contact:* Naomi Black, Administrative Assistant, Department of Educational Administration and Policy, 202-806-7342, Fax: 202-806-5310, E-mail: nblack@howard.edu.
Website: http://www.howard.edu/schooleducation/departments/elps/ELPS_Overview.html.

Illinois State University, Graduate School, College of Education, Department of Curriculum and Instruction, Normal, IL 61790-2200. Offers curriculum and instruction (MS, MS Ed, Ed D); educational policies (Ed D); postsecondary education (Ed D); reading (MS Ed); supervision (Ed D). *Accreditation:* NCATE. *Degree requirements:* For master's, variable foreign language requirement, thesis or alternative; for doctorate, variable foreign language requirement, thesis/dissertation, 2 terms of residency, internship. *Entrance requirements:* For master's, GRE General Test, minimum GPA of 3.0 in last 60 hours of course work; for doctorate, GRE General Test. *Faculty research:* In-service and pre-service teacher education for teachers of English language learners; teachers for all children: developing a model for alternative, bilingual elementary certification for paraprofessionals in Illinois; Illinois Geographic Alliance, Connections Project.

Indiana University Bloomington, School of Education, Department of Educational Leadership and Policy Studies, Bloomington, IN 47405-7000. Offers education policy studies (PhD); educational leadership (MS, Ed D, Ed S); higher education (MS, Ed D, PhD); history and philosophy of education (MS); history of education (PhD); international and comparative education (MS, PhD); philosophy of education (PhD); student affairs administration (MS). *Accreditation:* NCATE. Part-time and evening/weekend programs available. *Degree requirements:* For master's, thesis optional; for doctorate, comprehensive exam, thesis/dissertation; for Ed S, comprehensive exam or project. *Entrance requirements:* For master's, doctorate, and Ed S, GRE General Test.

Additional exam requirements/recommendations for international students: Required—TOEFL (minimum score 79 iBT). Electronic applications accepted. *Faculty research:* Student engagement at higher education institutions in the nation, Reading First professional development initiative, state finance policy on financial access to higher education, school reform, special needs studies.

Johns Hopkins University, School of Education, Doctoral Programs in Education, Baltimore, MD 21218-2699. Offers Ed D, PhD. Part-time and evening/weekend programs available. Postbaccalaureate distance learning degree programs offered (no on-campus study). *Students:* 19 full-time (16 women), 80 part-time (53 women); includes 33 minority (18 Black or African American, non-Hispanic/Latino; 4 Asian, non-Hispanic/Latino; 8 Hispanic/Latino; 3 Two or more races, non-Hispanic/Latino), 3 international. Average age 38. 202 applicants, 38% accepted, 58 enrolled. In 2013, 4 doctorates awarded. *Degree requirements:* For doctorate, comprehensive exam (for some programs), thesis/dissertation. *Entrance requirements:* For doctorate, GRE (for PhD students only), master's degree from regionally- or nationally-accredited institution, minimum GPA of 3.0 (for EdD only), official transcripts from all post-secondary institutions attended, three letters of recommendation, curriculum vitae/resume, personal statement. Additional exam requirements/recommendations for international students: Required—TOEFL (minimum score 600 paper-based; 100 iBT) or IELTS (minimum score 7). Application fee: $80. Electronic applications accepted. *Financial support:* In 2013–14, 13 fellowships, 4 research assistantships, 1 teaching assistantship were awarded. Financial award application deadline: 6/1; financial award applicants required to submit FAFSA. *Unit head:* Dr. David A. Andrews, Dean, 410-516-7820, Fax: 410-516-6697, E-mail: davidandrews@jhu.edu. *Application contact:* Catherine Wilson, Associate Director of Admissions, 410-516-9797, Fax: 410-516-9799, E-mail: soe.info@jhu.edu.

Loyola University Chicago, School of Education, Program in Cultural and Educational Policy Studies, Chicago, IL 60660. Offers M Ed, MA, PhD. Part-time programs available. *Faculty:* 5 full-time (2 women), 9 part-time/adjunct (6 women). *Students:* 63. Average age 30. 61 applicants, 57% accepted, 20 enrolled. In 2013, 12 master's, 5 doctorates awarded. *Degree requirements:* For master's, comprehensive exam (M Ed), thesis (MA); for doctorate, comprehensive exam, thesis/dissertation, oral candidacy exam. *Entrance requirements:* For master's, letters of recommendation, minimum GPA of 3.0; for doctorate, GRE General Test, interview, letter of recommendation, resume, minimum GPA of 3.0. Additional exam requirements/recommendations for international students: Required—TOEFL (minimum score 550 paper-based; 79 iBT). *Application deadline:* For fall admission, 12/1 for domestic and international students; for spring admission, 11/1 for domestic and international students. Applications are processed on a rolling basis. Application fee: $50. Application fee is waived when completed online. *Expenses: Tuition:* Full-time $16,740; part-time $930 per credit. *Required fees:* $135 per semester. *Financial support:* In 2013–14, 15 fellowships with partial tuition reimbursements, 6 research assistantships with full tuition reimbursements (averaging $12,000 per year) were awarded; career-related internships or fieldwork, institutionally sponsored loans, scholarships/grants, health care benefits, tuition waivers (partial), and unspecified assistantships also available. Support available to part-time students. Financial award application deadline: 2/1; financial award applicants required to submit FAFSA. *Faculty research:* Politics of education, cultural foundations, policy studies, qualitative research methods, multicultural diversity. *Unit head:* Dr. Noah Sobe, Director, 312-915-6954, E-mail: nsobe@luc.edu. *Application contact:* Marie Rosin-Dittmar, Information Contact, 312-915-6800, E-mail: schleduc@luc.edu.

Marquette University, Graduate School, College of Education, Department of Educational Policy and Leadership, Milwaukee, WI 53201-1881. Offers college student personnel administration (M Ed); curriculum and instruction (MA); education (MA); educational administration (M Ed); educational policy and foundations (MA); elementary education (Certificate); literacy (MA); principal (Certificate); reading specialist (Certificate); reading teacher (Certificate); secondary education (Certificate); superintendent (Certificate). Part-time and evening/weekend programs available. *Faculty:* 15 full-time (10 women), 3 part-time/adjunct (2 women). *Students:* 39 full-time (31 women), 107 part-time (70 women); includes 19 minority (7 Black or African American, non-Hispanic/Latino; 2 American Indian or Alaska Native, non-Hispanic/Latino; 3 Asian, non-Hispanic/Latino; 6 Hispanic/Latino; 1 Two or more races, non-Hispanic/Latino), 2 international. Average age 30. 144 applicants, 74% accepted, 67 enrolled. In 2013, 48 master's, 4 doctorates, 12 other advanced degrees awarded. Terminal master's awarded for partial completion of doctoral program. *Degree requirements:* For master's, comprehensive exam, thesis (for some programs); for doctorate, thesis/dissertation, qualifying exam, supporting minor. *Entrance requirements:* For master's, GRE General Test or MAT, official transcripts from all current and previous colleges/universities except Marquette, three letters of recommendation, statement of purpose; for doctorate, GRE General Test, MAT, sample of written work, official transcripts from all current and previous colleges/universities except Marquette, three letters of recommendation, statement of purpose, resume/curriculum vitae; for Certificate, GRE General Test or MAT, master's degree. Additional exam requirements/recommendations for international students: Required—TOEFL (minimum score 530 paper-based). *Application deadline:* For fall admission, 1/15 for domestic and international students. Application fee: $50. *Expenses:* Contact institution. *Financial support:* In 2013–14, 130 students received support, including 1 fellowship with full tuition reimbursement available (averaging $18,780 per year), 5 research assistantships with full tuition reimbursements available (averaging $13,404 per year); health care benefits, tuition waivers (partial), and unspecified assistantships also available. Support available to part-time students. Financial award application deadline: 2/15. *Faculty research:* Leadership; social justice in education; development of lifelong learners; race, class, and schooling in historical perspective; urban teacher education. *Unit head:* Dr. Ellen Eckman, Chair, 414-288-1561, E-mail: ellen.eckman@marquette.edu. *Application contact:* Dr. Sharon Chubbuck, Associate Professor, 414-288-5895.

Michigan State University, The Graduate School, College of Education, Program in Educational Policy, East Lansing, MI 48824. Offers PhD. *Entrance requirements:* Additional exam requirements/recommendations for international students: Required—TOEFL. Electronic applications accepted.

New York University, Steinhardt School of Culture, Education, and Human Development, Department of Humanities and Social Sciences in the Professions, Program in Sociology of Education, New York, NY 10003. Offers education policy (MA); social and cultural studies of education (MA); sociology of education (PhD). Part-time programs available. *Faculty:* 14 full-time (7 women). *Students:* 32 full-time (29 women), 30 part-time (24 women); includes 21 minority (7 Black or African American, non-Hispanic/Latino; 6 Asian, non-Hispanic/Latino; 5 Hispanic/Latino; 3 Two or more races, non-Hispanic/Latino), 18 international. Average age 28. 102 applicants, 43% accepted, 9 enrolled. In 2013, 6 master's, 1 doctorate awarded. *Degree requirements:* For master's, thesis (for some programs); for doctorate, thesis/dissertation. *Entrance requirements:* For master's, letters of recommendation; for doctorate, GRE General Test, interview. Additional exam requirements/recommendations for international students: Required—TOEFL (minimum score 100 iBT). *Application deadline:* For fall admission, 12/1 priority date for domestic and international students; for spring admission, 11/1 for domestic and international students. Applications are processed on a rolling basis. Application fee: $75. Electronic applications accepted. *Expenses: Tuition:* Full-time $35,856; part-time $1494 per unit. *Required fees:* $1408; $64 per unit. $473 per term. Tuition and fees vary according to course load and program. *Financial support:* Fellowships with full and partial tuition reimbursements, Federal Work-Study, institutionally sponsored loans, scholarships/grants, and tuition waivers (partial) available. Support available to part-time students. Financial award application deadline: 2/1; financial award applicants required to submit FAFSA. *Faculty research:* Legal and institutional environments of schools; social inequality; high school reform and achievement; urban schooling, economics and education, educational policy. *Unit head:* Prof. Lisa Stulberg, Program Director, 212-992-9373, Fax: 212-995-4832, E-mail: lisa.stulberg@nyu.edu. *Application contact:* 212-998-5030, Fax: 212-995-4328, E-mail: steinhardt.gradadmissions@nyu.edu.
Website: http://steinhardt.nyu.edu/humsocsci/sociology.

Niagara University, Graduate Division of Education, Concentration in Educational Leadership, Niagara Falls, NY 14109. Offers leadership and policy (PhD); school administration/supervision (MS Ed); school building leader (MS Ed, Certificate); school business administration (MS Ed); school district business leader (Certificate); school district leader (MS Ed, Certificate). Part-time and evening/weekend programs available. Postbaccalaureate distance learning degree programs offered (no on-campus study). *Students:* 38 full-time (23 women), 82 part-time (51 women); includes 12 minority (9 Black or African American, non-Hispanic/Latino; 1 Asian, non-Hispanic/Latino; 2 Hispanic/Latino), 44 international. Average age 39. In 2013, 48 master's, 8 other advanced degrees awarded. *Entrance requirements:* For master's, GRE General Test or MAT; for Certificate, GRE General Test and GRE Subject Test or MAT. Additional exam requirements/recommendations for international students: Required—TOEFL (minimum score 550 paper-based, 79 iBT) or IELTS (minimum score 6). *Application deadline:* For fall admission, 8/1 for domestic students. Applications are processed on a rolling basis. Application fee: $30. *Expenses:* Contact institution. *Financial support:* In 2013–14, 1 research assistantship with full and partial tuition reimbursement was awarded; teaching assistantships with full and partial tuition reimbursements, career-related internships or fieldwork, Federal Work-Study, scholarships/grants, and unspecified assistantships also available. Support available to part-time students. Financial award application deadline: 4/15. *Unit head:* Dr. Kristine Augustyniak, Chair, 716-286-8548, E-mail: kma@niagara.edu. *Application contact:* Dr. Debra A. Colley, Dean of Education, 716-286-8560, Fax: 716-286-8561, E-mail: dcolley@niagara.edu.
Website: http://www.niagara.edu/educational-leadership-online.

The Ohio State University, Graduate School, College of Education and Human Ecology, Department of Educational Studies, Columbus, OH 43210. Offers M Ed, MA, PhD, Ed S. *Accreditation:* NCATE. Part-time programs available. *Faculty:* 32. *Students:* 325 full-time (223 women), 135 part-time (84 women); includes 92 minority (47 Black or African American, non-Hispanic/Latino; 1 American Indian or Alaska Native, non-Hispanic/Latino; 7 Asian, non-Hispanic/Latino; 27 Hispanic/Latino; 10 Two or more races, non-Hispanic/Latino), 37 international. Average age 31. In 2013, 128 master's, 31 doctorates, 5 other advanced degrees awarded. *Degree requirements:* For master's, thesis optional; for doctorate, thesis/dissertation. *Entrance requirements:* For master's and doctorate, GRE General Test. Additional exam requirements/recommendations for international students: Required—TOEFL (minimum score 550 paper-based; 79 iBT), Michigan English Language Assessment Battery (minimum score 82); Recommended—IELTS (minimum score 7). *Application deadline:* For fall admission, 12/1 priority date for domestic and international students; for winter admission, 12/1 for domestic students; 11/1 for international students; for spring admission, 11/1 priority date for domestic and international students. Applications are processed on a rolling basis. Application fee: $60 ($70 for international students). Electronic applications accepted. *Financial support:* Fellowships with tuition reimbursements, research assistantships with tuition reimbursements, teaching assistantships with tuition reimbursements, Federal Work-Study, institutionally sponsored loans, and unspecified assistantships available. Support available to part-time students. *Unit head:* Eric Anderman, Chair, 614-688-3484, E-mail: anderman.1@osu.edu. *Application contact:* Deb Zabloudil, Director of Graduate Student Services, 614-688-4007, E-mail: zabloudil.1@osu.edu.
Website: http://ehe.osu.edu/educational-studies/.

Penn State University Park, Graduate School, College of Education, Department of Education Policy Studies, State College, PA 16802. Offers college student affairs (M Ed); educational leadership (M Ed, D Ed, PhD, Certificate); educational theory and policy (MA, PhD); higher education (M Ed, D Ed, PhD). *Accreditation:* NCATE. *Unit head:* Dr. David H. Monk, Dean, 814-865-2523, Fax: 814-865-0555, E-mail: dhm6@psu.edu. *Application contact:* Cynthia E. Nicosia, Director, Graduate Enrollment Services, 814-865-1834, Fax: 814-863-4627, E-mail: cey1@psu.edu.
Website: http://www.ed.psu.edu/educ/eps/.

Rutgers, The State University of New Jersey, Camden, Graduate School of Arts and Sciences, Department of Public Policy and Administration, Camden, NJ 08102. Offers education policy and leadership (MPA); international public service and development (MPA); public management (MPA); JD/MPA; MPA/MA. *Accreditation:* NASPAA. Part-time and evening/weekend programs available. *Degree requirements:* For master's, directed study, research workshop, 42 credits. *Entrance requirements:* For master's, GRE General Test, GMAT or LSAT, 3 letters of recommendation; resume. Additional exam requirements/recommendations for international students: Required—TOEFL (minimum score 550 paper-based), IELTS. Electronic applications accepted. *Faculty research:* Nonprofit management, county and municipal administration, health and human services, government communication, administrative law, educational finance.

Rutgers, The State University of New Jersey, New Brunswick, Graduate School of Education, Doctoral Program in Education, New Brunswick, NJ 08901. Offers educational policy (PhD); educational psychology (PhD); literacy education (PhD); mathematics education (PhD). Part-time programs available. *Degree requirements:* For doctorate, thesis/dissertation, qualifying exam. *Entrance requirements:* For doctorate, GRE General Test, GRE Subject Test (mathematics education). Additional exam requirements/recommendations for international students: Required—TOEFL (minimum score 575 paper-based; 83 iBT). Electronic applications accepted. *Faculty research:* Literacy education, math education, educational psychology, educational policy, learning sciences.

Syracuse University, School of Education, Program in Instructional Design Foundation, Syracuse, NY 13244. Offers CAS. Part-time programs available. *Entrance requirements:* For degree, GRE (recommended). *Application deadline:* For fall admission, 1/15 priority date for domestic and international students; for spring admission, 10/15 priority date for domestic and international students. Application fee: $75. *Unit head:* Dr. Tiffany A. Koszalka, Chair, 315-443-3703, E-mail: takoszal@syr.edu. *Application contact:* Laurie Deyo, Graduate Recruiter, School of Education, 315-443-2505, E-mail: e-gradrcrt@syr.edu.
Website: http://soe.syr.edu/.

University of Alberta, Faculty of Graduate Studies and Research, Department of Educational Policy Studies, Edmonton, AB T6G 2E1, Canada. Offers adult education (M Ed, Ed D, PhD); educational administration and leadership (M Ed, Ed D, PhD, Postgraduate Diploma); First Nations education (M Ed, Ed D, PhD); theoretical, cultural

and international studies in education (M Ed, Ed D, PhD). *Degree requirements:* For master's, thesis (for some programs); for doctorate, thesis/dissertation. *Entrance requirements:* For master's, minimum GPA of 6.5 on a 9.0 scale; for doctorate, minimum GPA of 7.5 on a 9.0 scale. Additional exam requirements/recommendations for international students: Required—TOEFL (minimum score 580 paper-based). Electronic applications accepted.

University of Arkansas, Graduate School, College of Education and Health Professions, Department of Education Reform, Fayetteville, AR 72701-1201. Offers education policy (PhD). Electronic applications accepted.

The University of British Columbia, Faculty of Education, Department of Educational Studies, Vancouver, BC V6T 1Z1, Canada. Offers adult education (M Ed, MA); adult learning and global change (M Ed); educational administration (M Ed, MA); educational leadership and policy (Ed D); educational studies (PhD); higher education (M Ed, MA); society, culture and politics in education (M Ed, MA). Part-time and evening/weekend programs available. Terminal master's awarded for partial completion of doctoral program. *Degree requirements:* For master's, thesis; for doctorate, comprehensive exam, thesis/dissertation, master's thesis. *Entrance requirements:* For master's, minimum B+ average, 4-year undergraduate degree, field-related experience; for doctorate, minimum B+ average, 4-year undergraduate degree, master's degree, field-related experience. Additional exam requirements/recommendations for international students: Required—TOEFL (minimum score 600 paper-based; 100 iBT) or IELTS (minimum score 6.5). Electronic applications accepted. *Expenses: Tuition, area resident:* Full-time $8000 Canadian dollars. *Faculty research:* Educational leadership educational administration adult education politics in education, global change and adult learning.

University of Colorado Boulder, Graduate School, School of Education, Division of Educational Foundations, Policy, and Practice, Boulder, CO 80309. Offers MA, PhD. *Students:* 31 full-time (18 women), 10 part-time (7 women); includes 15 minority (5 Black or African American, non-Hispanic/Latino; 3 Asian, non-Hispanic/Latino; 6 Hispanic/Latino; 1 Two or more races, non-Hispanic/Latino). Average age 33. 51 applicants, 39% accepted, 6 enrolled. In 2013, 10 master's, 4 doctorates awarded. *Entrance requirements:* For master's, minimum undergraduate GPA of 2.75. *Application deadline:* For fall admission, 2/1 for domestic students, 12/1 for international students; for spring admission, 9/1 for domestic and international students. Electronic applications accepted. *Financial support:* In 2013–14, 77 students received support, including 4 fellowships (averaging $6,891 per year), 18 research assistantships with full and partial tuition reimbursements available (averaging $20,481 per year), 14 teaching assistantships with full and partial tuition reimbursements available (averaging $19,454 per year); institutionally sponsored loans, scholarships/grants, health care benefits, and unspecified assistantships also available. Financial award applicants required to submit FAFSA.
Website: http://www.colorado.edu/education/.

University of Colorado Denver, School of Education and Human Development, Program in Educational Leadership and Innovation, Denver, CO 80217-3364. Offers educational studies and research (PhD), including administrative leadership and policy, early childhood special education, math education, research, assessment and evaluation, science education, urban ecologies. Part-time and evening/weekend programs available. *Students:* 16 full-time (12 women), 12 part-time (9 women); includes 6 minority (2 Black or African American, non-Hispanic/Latino; 3 Asian, non-Hispanic/Latino; 1 Hispanic/Latino), 1 international. Average age 39. 16 applicants, 31% accepted, 4 enrolled. In 2013, 10 doctorates awarded. *Degree requirements:* For doctorate, comprehensive exam, thesis/dissertation, 75 credit hours (for PhD). *Entrance requirements:* For doctorate, GRE or equivalent, resume or curriculum vitae, letters of recommendation, master's degree or equivalent, completion of basic or advanced statistics course with minimum B grade. Additional exam requirements/recommendations for international students: Required—TOEFL (minimum score 537 paper-based; 75 iBT); Recommended—IELTS (minimum score 6.5). *Application deadline:* For fall admission, 5/1 priority date for domestic students, 4/15 priority date for international students. Applications are processed on a rolling basis. Application fee: $50 ($75 for international students). Electronic applications accepted. *Expenses:* Contact institution. *Financial support:* In 2013–14, 19 students received support. Fellowships, research assistantships, teaching assistantships, Federal Work-Study, institutionally sponsored loans, scholarships/grants, and traineeships available. Financial award application deadline: 4/1; financial award applicants required to submit FAFSA. *Faculty research:* Administrative leadership and policy studies, early childhood education, research in diversity, paraprofessionals in education, urban schools lab. *Unit head:* Dr. Deanna Sands, Associate Dean, Research and Professional Development, 303-315-4931, E-mail: deanna.sands@ucdenver.edu. *Application contact:* Student Services Center, 303-315-6300, Fax: 303-315-6311, E-mail: education@ucdenver.edu.
Website: http://www.ucdenver.edu/academics/colleges/SchoolOfEducation/Academics/Doctorate/Pages/PhD.aspx.

University of Denver, Morgridge College of Education, Denver, CO 80208. Offers child, family and school psychology (MA, PhD, Ed S); counseling psychology (MA, PhD); curriculum and instruction (MA, Ed D, PhD); curriculum instruction and teaching (Certificate); early childhood special education (MA); educational leadership and policy studies (MA, Ed D, PhD, Certificate); higher education (MA, Ed D, PhD); law librarianship (Certificate); library and information science (MLIS); research methods and statistics (MA, PhD). *Accreditation:* ALA; APA (one or more programs are accredited). Part-time and evening/weekend programs available. Postbaccalaureate distance learning degree programs offered (no on-campus study). *Faculty:* 35 full-time (21 women), 63 part-time/adjunct (43 women). *Students:* 435 full-time (332 women), 414 part-time (297 women); includes 194 minority (45 Black or African American, non-Hispanic/Latino; 9 American Indian or Alaska Native, non-Hispanic/Latino; 16 Asian, non-Hispanic/Latino; 96 Hispanic/Latino; 2 Native Hawaiian or other Pacific Islander, non-Hispanic/Latino; 26 Two or more races, non-Hispanic/Latino), 14 international. Average age 32. 672 applicants, 61% accepted, 193 enrolled. In 2013, 248 master's, 30 doctorates, 130 other advanced degrees awarded. Terminal master's awarded for partial completion of doctoral program. *Degree requirements:* For master's, comprehensive exam; for doctorate, 2 foreign languages, comprehensive exam, thesis/dissertation. *Entrance requirements:* For master's and doctorate, GRE General Test or GMAT. Additional exam requirements/recommendations for international students: Required—TOEFL (minimum score 550 paper-based; 80 iBT). *Application deadline:* Applications are processed on a rolling basis. Application fee: $65. Electronic applications accepted. *Financial support:* In 2013–14, 706 students received support, including 54 research assistantships with full and partial tuition reimbursements available (averaging $15,599 per year), 77 teaching assistantships with full and partial tuition reimbursements available (averaging $12,804 per year); career-related internships or fieldwork, Federal Work-Study, institutionally sponsored loans, scholarships/grants, and unspecified assistantships also available. Support available to part-time students. Financial award application deadline: 2/15; financial award applicants required to submit FAFSA. *Faculty research:* Principal and teacher preparation, development and assessments, gifted education, service-learning, early childhood, mathematics education, access to higher education. *Total annual research expenditures:* $6.3 million. *Unit head:* Dr. Karen Riley, Interim Dean, 303-871-3665, E-mail: karen.riley@du.edu. *Application contact:* Jodi Dye, Assistant Director of Admissions, 303-871-2510, E-mail: jodi.dye@du.edu.
Website: http://morgridge.du.edu/.

University of Florida, Graduate School, College of Education, School of Human Development and Organizational Studies in Education, Gainesville, FL 32611. Offers counseling and counselor education (Ed D, PhD), including counseling and counselor education, marriage and family counseling, mental health counseling, school counseling and guidance; educational leadership (M Ed, MAE, Ed D, PhD, Ed S), including educational leadership (Ed D, PhD), educational policy (Ed D, PhD); higher education administration (Ed D, PhD, Ed S), including education policy (Ed D), educational policy (Ed D, PhD), higher education administration (Ed D, PhD); marriage and family counseling (M Ed, MAE, Ed S); mental health counseling (M Ed, MAE, Ed S); research and evaluation methodology (M Ed, MAE, Ed D, PhD, Ed S); school counseling and guidance (M Ed, MAE, Ed S); student personnel in higher education (M Ed, MAE, Ed S). *Accreditation:* ACA (one or more programs are accredited); NCATE. Part-time programs available. Postbaccalaureate distance learning degree programs offered. *Faculty:* 20 full-time (11 women), 4 part-time/adjunct (1 woman). *Students:* 291 full-time (232 women), 212 part-time (157 women); includes 145 minority (71 Black or African American, non-Hispanic/Latino; 3 American Indian or Alaska Native, non-Hispanic/Latino; 11 Asian, non-Hispanic/Latino; 60 Hispanic/Latino), 38 international. Average age 31. 271 applicants, 42% accepted, 75 enrolled. In 2013, 71 master's, 31 doctorates, 62 other advanced degrees awarded. Terminal master's awarded for partial completion of doctoral program. *Degree requirements:* For master's, thesis optional; for doctorate, comprehensive exam, thesis/dissertation. *Entrance requirements:* For master's and doctorate, GRE General Test, minimum GPA of 3.0 (undergraduate), 3.5 (graduate); for Ed S, GRE General Test. Additional exam requirements/recommendations for international students: Required—TOEFL (minimum score 550 paper-based; 80 iBT), IELTS (minimum score 6). *Application deadline:* Applications are processed on a rolling basis. Application fee: $30. Electronic applications accepted. *Expenses:* Tuition, state resident: full-time $12,640. Tuition, nonresident: full-time $30,000. *Financial support:* In 2013–14, 85 students received support, including 6 fellowships (averaging $12,190 per year), 48 research assistantships (averaging $15,155 per year), 50 teaching assistantships (averaging $9,080 per year); career-related internships or fieldwork and unspecified assistantships also available. Financial award applicants required to submit FAFSA. *Unit head:* Glenn E. Good, PhD, Dean and Professor, 352-273-4135, Fax: 352-846-2697, E-mail: ggood@ufl.edu. *Application contact:* Thomasenia L. Adams, PhD, Professor and Associate Dean, 352-273-4119, Fax: 352-846-2697, E-mail: tla@coe.ufl.edu.
Website: http://education.ufl.edu/hdose/.

University of Florida, Graduate School, College of Liberal Arts and Sciences, Department of Political Science, Gainesville, FL 32611. Offers educational policy (PhD); international development policy and administration (MA, Certificate); international relations (MA, MAT); political campaigning (MA, Certificate); political science (MA, PhD); public affairs (MA, Certificate); tropical conservation and development (PhD); JD/MA. *Faculty:* 25 full-time (9 women), 4 part-time/adjunct (1 woman). *Students:* 110 full-time (46 women), 20 part-time (8 women); includes 28 minority (13 Black or African American, non-Hispanic/Latino; 6 Asian, non-Hispanic/Latino; 9 Hispanic/Latino), 33 international. Average age 30. 151 applicants, 48% accepted, 23 enrolled. In 2013, 32 master's, 6 doctorates awarded. Terminal master's awarded for partial completion of doctoral program. *Degree requirements:* For master's, variable foreign language requirement, comprehensive exam (for some programs), thesis or alternative, internship (for some programs); for doctorate, variable foreign language requirement, comprehensive exam, thesis/dissertation. *Entrance requirements:* For master's and doctorate, GRE General Test, minimum GPA of 3.0. Additional exam requirements/recommendations for international students: Required—TOEFL (minimum score 550 paper-based; 80 iBT), IELTS (minimum score 6). *Application deadline:* For fall admission, 1/1 priority date for domestic students, 1/1 for international students. Applications are processed on a rolling basis. Application fee: $30. Electronic applications accepted. *Expenses:* Tuition, state resident: full-time $12,640. Tuition, nonresident: full-time $30,000. *Financial support:* In 2013–14, 73 students received support, including 27 fellowships (averaging $17,625 per year), 15 research assistantships (averaging $11,460 per year), 64 teaching assistantships (averaging $9,920 per year); career-related internships or fieldwork, Federal Work-Study, institutionally sponsored loans, and unspecified assistantships also available. Financial award application deadline: 1/15; financial award applicants required to submit FAFSA. *Faculty research:* American political institutions, comparative democratization, political theory and judgment, religion and politics, theories of international relations. *Unit head:* Ido Oren, PhD, Professor and Chair, 352-273-2393, Fax: 352-392-8127, E-mail: oren@ufl.edu. *Application contact:* Leslie Anderson, PhD, Graduate Coordinator, 352-273-3725, Fax: 352-392-8127, E-mail: landerso@ufl.edu.
Website: http://polisci.ufl.edu/.

University of Georgia, College of Education, Department of Lifelong Education, Administration and Policy, Athens, GA 30602. Offers adult education (M Ed, Ed D, PhD, Ed S); educational administration and policy (M Ed, PhD, Ed S); educational leadership (Ed D); human resource and organizational design (M Ed). *Accreditation:* NCATE. *Entrance requirements:* For master's and Ed S, GRE General Test or MAT; for doctorate, GRE General Test. Electronic applications accepted.

University of Hawaii at Manoa, Graduate Division, College of Education, PhD in Education Program, Honolulu, HI 96822. Offers curriculum and instruction (PhD); educational administration (PhD); educational foundations (PhD); educational policy studies (PhD); educational technology (PhD); exceptionalities (PhD); kinesiology (PhD). Part-time and evening/weekend programs available. *Degree requirements:* For doctorate, thesis/dissertation. *Entrance requirements:* For doctorate, GRE General Test, sample of written work. Additional exam requirements/recommendations for international students: Required—TOEFL (minimum score 600 paper-based; 100 iBT), IELTS (minimum score 7).

University of Illinois at Chicago, Graduate College, College of Education, Department of Educational Policy Studies, Chicago, IL 60607-7128. Offers policy studies (M Ed); policy studies in urban education (PhD); urban education leadership (Ed D). *Faculty:* 12 full-time (6 women). *Students:* 45 full-time (33 women), 103 part-time (69 women); includes 78 minority (38 Black or African American, non-Hispanic/Latino; 4 Asian, non-Hispanic/Latino; 31 Hispanic/Latino; 5 Two or more races, non-Hispanic/Latino), 2 international. Average age 36. 71 applicants, 44% accepted, 22 enrolled. In 2013, 14 master's, 16 doctorates awarded. *Expenses:* Tuition, state resident: full-time $11,066; part-time $3689 per term. Tuition, nonresident: full-time $23,064; part-time $7688 per term. *Required fees:* $3004; $1190 per term. Tuition and fees vary according to course level and program. *Total annual research expenditures:* $290,000. *Unit head:* Prof. David Mayrowetz, Chair, 312-996-3326, E-mail: dmayro@uic.edu. *Application contact:* Receptionist, 312-413-2550, E-mail: gradcoll@uic.edu.
Website: http://education.uic.edu.

University of Illinois at Urbana–Champaign, Graduate College, College of Education, Department of Education Policy, Organization, and Leadership, Champaign, IL 61820.

Educational Policy

Offers educational organization and leadership (Ed M, MS, Ed D, PhD, CAS); educational policy studies (Ed M, MA, PhD); human resource education (Ed M, MS, Ed D, PhD, CAS). Part-time programs available. Postbaccalaureate distance learning degree programs offered (no on-campus study). *Students:* 518 (342 women). Application fee: $75 ($90 for international students). *Unit head:* James Anderson, Head, 217-333-2446, Fax: 217-244-5632, E-mail: janders@illinois.edu. *Application contact:* Rebecca Grady, Office Support Specialist, 217-265-5404, Fax: 217-244-5632, E-mail: rgrady@illinois.edu.
Website: http://education.illinois.edu/epol.

The University of Iowa, Graduate College, College of Education, Department of Educational Policy and Leadership Studies, Iowa City, IA 52242-1316. Offers educational leadership (MA, PhD, Ed S); higher education and student affairs (MA, PhD); schools, culture, and society (MA, PhD). *Degree requirements:* For master's and Ed S, exam; for doctorate, comprehensive exam, thesis/dissertation. *Entrance requirements:* For master's, doctorate, and Ed S, GRE General Test, minimum GPA of 3.0. Additional exam requirements/recommendations for international students: Required—TOEFL (minimum score 550 paper-based; 81 iBT). Electronic applications accepted.

The University of Kansas, Graduate Studies, School of Education, Department of Educational Leadership and Policy Studies, Education Leadership and Policy Program, Lawrence, KS 66045-3101. Offers educational administration (Ed D, PhD); foundations (PhD); higher education (Ed D, PhD); policy studies (PhD). Part-time and evening/weekend programs available. *Faculty:* 15. *Students:* 106 full-time (63 women), 46 part-time (19 women); includes 32 minority (10 Black or African American, non-Hispanic/Latino; 4 American Indian or Alaska Native, non-Hispanic/Latino; 6 Asian, non-Hispanic/Latino; 7 Hispanic/Latino; 5 Two or more races, non-Hispanic/Latino), 27 international. Average age 37. 63 applicants, 71% accepted, 32 enrolled. In 2013, 31 doctorates awarded. *Degree requirements:* For doctorate, comprehensive exam, thesis/dissertation. *Entrance requirements:* For doctorate, GRE General Test, minimum graduate GPA of 3.5. Additional exam requirements/recommendations for international students: Required—TOEFL (minimum score 570 paper-based; 80 iBT). *Application deadline:* For fall admission, 7/1 for domestic and international students; for spring admission, 11/1 for domestic and international students. Applications are processed on a rolling basis. Application fee: $55 ($65 for international students). Electronic applications accepted. *Financial support:* Fellowships, research assistantships with full and partial tuition reimbursements, teaching assistantships with full and partial tuition reimbursements, scholarships/grants, and unspecified assistantships available. Financial award application deadline: 3/15. *Faculty research:* Historical and philosophical issues in education, education policy and leadership, higher education faculty, research on college students, education technology. *Unit head:* Dr. Susan Twombly, Chair, 785-864-9721, Fax: 785-864-4697, E-mail: stwombly@ku.edu. *Application contact:* Denise Brubaker, Admissions Coordinator, 785-864-7973, Fax: 785-864-4697, E-mail: brubaker@ku.edu.
Website: http://elps.soe.ku.edu/.

University of Kentucky, Graduate School, College of Education, Department of Educational Policy Studies and Evaluation, Lexington, KY 40506-0032. Offers educational policy studies and evaluation (Ed D); higher education (MS Ed, PhD); social and philosophical studies (MS Ed). *Accreditation:* NCATE. Terminal master's awarded for partial completion of doctoral program. *Degree requirements:* For master's, comprehensive exam, thesis optional; for doctorate, comprehensive exam, thesis/dissertation. *Entrance requirements:* For master's, GRE General Test, minimum undergraduate GPA of 2.75; for doctorate, GRE General Test, minimum graduate GPA of 3.0. Additional exam requirements/recommendations for international students: Required—TOEFL (minimum score 550 paper-based). Electronic applications accepted. *Faculty research:* Studies in higher education; comparative and international education; evaluation of educational programs, policies, and reform; student, teacher, and faculty cultures; gender and education.

University of Maryland, Baltimore County, Graduate School, College of Arts, Humanities and Social Sciences, Department of Public Policy, Program in Public Policy, Baltimore, MD 21250. Offers economics (PhD); educational policy (MPP, PhD); evaluation and analytical methods (MPP, PhD); health policy (MPP, PhD); policy history (PhD); public management (MPP, PhD); urban policy (MPP, PhD). Part-time and evening/weekend programs available. *Faculty:* 10 full-time (2 women). *Students:* 60 full-time (35 women), 76 part-time (41 women); includes 29 minority (15 Black or African American, non-Hispanic/Latino; 8 Asian, non-Hispanic/Latino; 3 Hispanic/Latino; 1 Native Hawaiian or other Pacific Islander, non-Hispanic/Latino; 2 Two or more races, non-Hispanic/Latino), 13 international. Average age 36. 91 applicants, 55% accepted, 22 enrolled. In 2013, 11 master's, 8 doctorates awarded. Terminal master's awarded for partial completion of doctoral program. *Degree requirements:* For master's, thesis optional, public analysis paper, internship for pre-service students; for doctorate, comprehensive exam, thesis/dissertation, comprehensive and field qualifying exams. *Entrance requirements:* For master's and doctorate, GRE General Test, 3 academic letters of reference, transcripts, resume, research paper. Additional exam requirements/recommendations for international students: Required—TOEFL (minimum score 550 paper-based; 80 iBT). *Application deadline:* For fall admission, 1/15 priority date for domestic students, 1/1 priority date for international students; for spring admission, 11/1 priority date for domestic students, 5/1 priority date for international students. Applications are processed on a rolling basis. Application fee: $50. Electronic applications accepted. One-time fee: $200 full-time. *Financial support:* In 2013–14, 26 students received support, including 4 fellowships with full tuition reimbursements available (averaging $12,000 per year), 23 research assistantships with full tuition reimbursements available (averaging $20,000 per year), 1 teaching assistantship with full tuition reimbursement available (averaging $20,000 per year); career-related internships or fieldwork, Federal Work-Study, scholarships/grants, health care benefits, and unspecified assistantships also available. Support available to part-time students. Financial award application deadline: 1/15; financial award applicants required to submit FAFSA. *Faculty research:* Health policy, education policy, urban policy, public management, evaluation and analytical methods. *Unit head:* Dr. Donald F. Norris, Chair, 410-455-1455, E-mail: norris@umbc.edu. *Application contact:* Sally F. Helms, Administrator of Academic Affairs, 410-455-3202, Fax: 410-455-1172, E-mail: gradposi@umbc.edu.
Website: http://www.umbc.edu/pubpol.

University of Massachusetts Amherst, Graduate School, College of Education, Program in Education, Amherst, MA 01003. Offers bilingual/English as a second language/multicultural education (M Ed, Ed S); child study and early education (M Ed); children, families and schools (Ed D, Ed S); early childhood and elementary teacher education (M Ed); educational leadership (M Ed); educational policy and leadership (Ed D); higher education (M Ed); international education (M Ed); language, literacy and culture (Ed D); learning, media and technology (M Ed, Ed S); mathematics, science, and learning technologies (Ed D); psychometric methods, educational statistics and research methods (Ed D); reading and writing (M Ed); school counselor education (M Ed, Ed S); school psychology (Ed S); science education (Ed S); secondary teacher education (M Ed); social justice education (M Ed, Ed D, Ed S); special education (M Ed, Ed D, Ed S); teacher education and school improvement (Ed D, Ed S). *Accreditation:* NCATE. Part-time programs available. Postbaccalaureate distance learning degree programs offered (minimal on-campus study). *Faculty:* 95 full-time (55 women). *Students:* 357 full-time (240 women), 264 part-time (194 women); includes 114 minority (41 Black or African American, non-Hispanic/Latino; 4 American Indian or Alaska Native, non-Hispanic/Latino; 10 Asian, non-Hispanic/Latino; 47 Hispanic/Latino; 12 Two or more races, non-Hispanic/Latino), 100 international. Average age 34. 761 applicants, 51% accepted, 200 enrolled. In 2013, 186 master's, 31 doctorates, 22 other advanced degrees awarded. Terminal master's awarded for partial completion of doctoral program. *Degree requirements:* For doctorate, comprehensive exam, thesis/dissertation. *Entrance requirements:* Additional exam requirements/recommendations for international students: Required—TOEFL (minimum score 550 paper-based; 80 iBT), IELTS (minimum score 6.5). *Application deadline:* For fall admission, 1/15 for domestic and international students. Applications are processed on a rolling basis. Application fee: $75. Electronic applications accepted. *Financial support:* Fellowships with full and partial tuition reimbursements, research assistantships with full and partial tuition reimbursements, teaching assistantships with full and partial tuition reimbursements, career-related internships or fieldwork, Federal Work-Study, scholarships/grants, traineeships, health care benefits, tuition waivers (full and partial), and unspecified assistantships available. Support available to part-time students. Financial award application deadline: 1/15; financial award applicants required to submit FAFSA. *Unit head:* Dr. Linda L. Griffin, Graduate Program Director, 413-545-6984, Fax: 413-545-1523. *Application contact:* Lindsay DeSantis, Supervisor of Admissions, 413-545-0722, Fax: 413-577-0010, E-mail: gradadm@grad.umass.edu.
Website: http://www.umass.edu/education/.

University of Minnesota, Twin Cities Campus, Graduate School, College of Education and Human Development, Department of Organizational Leadership, Policy and Development, Minneapolis, MN 55455-0213. Offers adult education (M Ed, MA, Ed D, PhD, Certificate); agricultural, food and environmental education (M Ed, MA, Ed D, PhD); business and industry education (M Ed, MA, Ed D, PhD); business education (M Ed); comparative and international development education (MA, PhD); disability policy and services (Certificate); educational administration (MA, Ed D, PhD); evaluation studies (MA, PhD); higher education (MA, PhD); human resource development (M Ed, MA, Ed D, PhD, Certificate); marketing education (M Ed); postsecondary administration (Ed D); program evaluation (Certificate); school-to-work (Certificate); staff development (Certificate); teacher leadership (M Ed); technical education (Certificate); technology education (M Ed, MA); work and human resource education (M Ed, MA, Ed D, PhD); youth development leadership (M Ed). *Faculty:* 29 full-time (12 women). *Students:* 229 full-time (149 women), 352 part-time (227 women); includes 108 minority (46 Black or African American, non-Hispanic/Latino; 7 American Indian or Alaska Native, non-Hispanic/Latino; 36 Asian, non-Hispanic/Latino; 19 Hispanic/Latino), 62 international. Average age 38. 416 applicants, 63% accepted, 132 enrolled. In 2013, 84 master's, 56 doctorates, 120 other advanced degrees awarded. Application fee: $75 ($95 for international students). *Financial support:* In 2013–14, 2 fellowships (averaging $26,250 per year), 41 research assistantships with full tuition reimbursements (averaging $9,917 per year), 17 teaching assistantships with full tuition reimbursements (averaging $9,447 per year) were awarded. *Faculty research:* Organizational change in schools, universities, and other organizations; international education and development; program evaluation to facilitate organizational reform; international human resource development and change; interactions of gender and race/ethnicity on learning and leadership; development of initiatives to develop intercultural sensitivity and global awareness; leadership theory and development in educational, work-based, and other organizations. *Total annual research expenditures:* $836,434. *Unit head:* Dr. Rebecca Ropers-Huilman, Chair, 612-624-1006, Fax: 612-624-3377, E-mail: ropers@umn.edu. *Application contact:* Dr. Jennifer Engler, Assistant Dean, 612-626-2887, Fax: 612-626-7496, E-mail: engle009@umn.edu.
Website: http://www.cehd.umn.edu/olpd/.

University of Pennsylvania, Graduate School of Education, Division of Education Policy, Philadelphia, PA 19104. Offers MS Ed, PhD. *Students:* 27 full-time (18 women), 3 part-time (2 women); includes 7 minority (3 Black or African American, non-Hispanic/Latino; 2 Asian, non-Hispanic/Latino; 1 Hispanic/Latino; 1 Native Hawaiian or other Pacific Islander, non-Hispanic/Latino), 6 international. 187 applicants, 39% accepted, 20 enrolled. In 2013, 20 master's, 1 doctorate awarded. *Unit head:* Dr. Andrew Porter, Dean, 215-898-7014. *Application contact:* 215-898-6415, Fax: 215-746-6884, E-mail: admissions@gse.upenn.edu.
Website: http://www.gse.upenn.edu.

University of Pittsburgh, School of Education, Learning Sciences and Policy Program, Pittsburgh, PA 15260. Offers PhD. Part-time and evening/weekend programs available. *Faculty:* 5 full-time (3 women). *Students:* 9 full-time (7 women), 3 part-time (2 women); includes 3 minority (1 Black or African American, non-Hispanic/Latino; 1 Asian, non-Hispanic/Latino; 1 Two or more races, non-Hispanic/Latino), 1 international. Average age 36. 17 applicants, 6% accepted. In 2013, 3 doctorates awarded. *Degree requirements:* For doctorate, comprehensive exam, thesis/dissertation. *Entrance requirements:* Additional exam requirements/recommendations for international students: Required—TOEFL (minimum score 550 paper-based; 80 iBT). *Application deadline:* For fall admission, 2/1 priority date for domestic and international students; for spring admission, 11/15 for domestic students, 7/1 priority date for international students. Application fee: $50. *Expenses:* Tuition, state resident: full-time $19,964; part-time $807 per credit. Tuition, nonresident: full-time $32,686; part-time $1337 per credit. *Required fees:* $740; $200. Tuition and fees vary according to program. *Financial support:* Fellowships with full and partial tuition reimbursements, research assistantships with full and partial tuition reimbursements, and teaching assistantships with full and partial tuition reimbursements available. Financial award applicants required to submit FAFSA. *Unit head:* Dr. Mary Kay Stein, Head, 412-648-7116, E-mail: mkstein@pitt.edu. *Application contact:* Maggie Sikora, Graduate Enrollment Manager, 412-648-2230, Fax: 412-648-1899, E-mail: soeinfo@pitt.edu.
Website: http://www.education.pitt.edu/lsap/.

University of Rochester, Margaret Warner Graduate School of Education and Human Development, Doctoral Programs in Education, Rochester, NY 14627. Offers counseling (Ed D); educational administration (Ed D); educational policy and theory (PhD); higher education (PhD); human development in educational context (PhD); teaching, curriculum, and change (PhD). *Expenses: Tuition:* Full-time $44,580; part-time $1394 per credit hour. *Required fees:* $492.

University of Rochester, Margaret Warner Graduate School of Education and Human Development, Master's Program in Educational Policy, Rochester, NY 14627. Offers MS. *Expenses: Tuition:* Full-time $44,580; part-time $1394 per credit hour. *Required fees:* $492.

University of St. Thomas, Graduate Studies, School of Education, Department of Leadership, Policy and Administration, St. Paul, MN 55105-1096. Offers community education administration (MA); educational leadership (Ed S); educational leadership and administration (MA); international leadership (MA, Certificate); leadership (Ed D); leadership in student affairs (MA, Certificate); public policy and leadership (MA, Certificate); public safety and law enforcement leadership (MA). Part-time and evening/

weekend programs available. Terminal master's awarded for partial completion of doctoral program. *Degree requirements:* For master's, thesis (for some programs); for doctorate, thesis/dissertation; for other advanced degree, thesis or alternative. *Entrance requirements:* For master's, minimum GPA of 3.0 or MAT; for doctorate, MAT, minimum graduate GPA of 3.5; for other advanced degree, minimum graduate GPA of 3.25 or MAT. Additional exam requirements/recommendations for international students: Required—TOEFL (minimum score 550 paper-based; 20 iBT). *Application deadline:* For fall admission, 6/1 priority date for domestic students; for spring admission, 11/1 priority date for domestic students. Applications are processed on a rolling basis. Application fee: $50. *Expenses:* Contact institution. *Financial support:* Fellowships, research assistantships, institutionally sponsored loans, and scholarships/grants available. Support available to part-time students. Financial award applicants required to submit FAFSA. *Unit head:* Dr. Kate M. Boyle, Chair, 651-962-4393, Fax: 651-962-4169, E-mail: kmboyle@stthomas.edu. *Application contact:* Jackie Grossklaus, Department Assistant, 651-962-4885, Fax: 651-962-4169, E-mail: jmgrossklaus@stthomas.edu.

University of Southern California, Graduate School, Rossier School of Education, Doctor of Philosophy in Education Programs, Los Angeles, CA 90089. Offers educational psychology (PhD); higher education administration and policy (PhD); K-12 policy and practice (PhD). *Degree requirements:* For doctorate, thesis/dissertation, 63 units; qualifying exam; dissertation proposal and defense. *Entrance requirements:* For doctorate, GRE. Additional exam requirements/recommendations for international students: Required—TOEFL (minimum score 100 iBT). Electronic applications accepted. *Faculty research:* Diversity in higher education, organizational change, educational psychology, policy and politics of educational reform, economics of education and education policy.

The University of Texas at Arlington, Graduate School, College of Education and Health Professions, Department of Educational Leadership and Policy Studies, Arlington, TX 76019. Offers dual language (M Ed); education leadership and policy studies (PhD); higher education (M Ed); principal certification (M Ed). Part-time and evening/weekend programs available. Postbaccalaureate distance learning degree programs offered (no on-campus study). *Degree requirements:* For master's, 2 field-based practica; for doctorate, comprehensive exam, thesis/dissertation, 2 research-based practica. *Entrance requirements:* For master's, GRE, 3 references forms, minimum undergraduate GPA of 3.0 in the last 60 hours of course work; for doctorate, GRE, resume, statement of intent, 3 reference forms, applicable master's degree. *Faculty research:* Lived realities of students of color in K-16 contexts, K-16 faculty, K-16 policy and law, K-16 student access, K-16 student success.

University of Washington, Graduate School, College of Education, Seattle, WA 98195. Offers curriculum and instruction (M Ed, Ed D, PhD), including educational technology, general curriculum (Ed D, PhD), language, literacy, and culture, mathematics education, multicultural education, reading and language arts education (Ed D), science education, social studies education, teaching and curriculum (M Ed); educational leadership and policy studies (M Ed, Ed D, PhD), including administration (Ed D), educational policy, organization, and leadership (M Ed, PhD), higher education, leadership for learning (Ed D), social and cultural foundations of education (M Ed, PhD); educational psychology (M Ed, PhD), including educational psychology (PhD), human development and cognition (M Ed), learning sciences, measurement, statistics and research design (M Ed), school psychology (M Ed); instructional leadership (M Ed); intercollegiate athletic leadership (M Ed); special education (M Ed, Ed D, PhD), including early childhood special education (M Ed), emotional and behavioral disabilities (M Ed), learning disabilities (M Ed), low-incidence disabilities (M Ed), severe disabilities (M Ed), special education (Ed D, PhD); teacher education (MIT). *Accreditation:* APA. Part-time and evening/weekend programs available. *Degree requirements:* For master's, thesis optional; for doctorate, thesis/dissertation. *Entrance requirements:* For master's and doctorate, GRE General Test, minimum GPA of 3.0. Additional exam requirements/recommendations for international students: Required—TOEFL. Electronic applications accepted. *Faculty research:* School restructuring/effective schools, special education interventions, literacy and writing, technology, school partnerships, teacher preparation.

The University of Western Ontario, Faculty of Graduate Studies, Social Sciences Division, Faculty of Education, Program in Educational Studies, London, ON N6A 5B8, Canada. Offers curriculum studies (M Ed); educational policy studies (M Ed); educational psychology/special education (M Ed). Part-time programs available. *Faculty research:* Reflective practice, gender and schooling, feminist pedagogy, narrative inquiry, second language, multiculturalism in Canada, education and law.

University of Wisconsin–Madison, Graduate School, School of Education, Department of Educational Leadership and Policy Analysis, Madison, WI 53706-1380. Offers administration (Certificate); educational policy (MS, PhD); global higher education (MS). *Degree requirements:* For doctorate, thesis/dissertation. *Entrance requirements:* For master's and doctorate, GRE General Test. *Application deadline:* For fall admission, 1/15 for domestic and international students. Application fee: $56. Electronic applications accepted. *Expenses:* Tuition, state resident: full-time $10,728; part-time $790 per credit. Tuition, nonresident: full-time $24,054; part-time $1623 per credit. *Required fees:* $1130; $119 per credit. *Financial support:* Fellowships with full tuition reimbursements, research assistantships with full tuition reimbursements, teaching assistantships with full tuition reimbursements, and project assistantships available. *Unit head:* Dr. Eric Camburn, Chair, 608-262-3106, E-mail: elpa@education.wisc.edu. *Application contact:* 608-262-2433, Fax: 608-262-5134, E-mail: gradadmiss@mail.bascom.wisc.edu.
Website: http://www.education.wisc.edu/elpa.

University of Wisconsin–Madison, Graduate School, School of Education, Department of Educational Policy Studies, Madison, WI 53706-1380. Offers MA, PhD. *Degree requirements:* For doctorate, thesis/dissertation. *Entrance requirements:* For master's and doctorate, GRE General Test. *Application deadline:* For fall admission, 1/1 for domestic and international students; for spring admission, 10/15 for domestic and international students. Application fee: $56. Electronic applications accepted. *Expenses:* Tuition, state resident: full-time $10,728; part-time $790 per credit. Tuition, nonresident: full-time $24,054; part-time $1623 per credit. *Required fees:* $1130; $119 per credit. *Financial support:* Project assistantships available. *Unit head:* Dr. Stacey Lee, Chair, 608-262-1760, E-mail: slee@education.wisc.edu. *Application contact:* 608-262-2433, Fax: 608-262-5134, E-mail: gradadmiss@mail.bascom.wisc.edu.
Website: http://www.education.wisc.edu/eps.

Vanderbilt University, Peabody College, Department of Leadership, Policy, and Organizations, Nashville, TN 37240-1001. Offers education policy (MPP); educational leadership and policy (Ed D); higher education (M Ed); higher education, leadership and policy (Ed D); international education policy and management (M Ed); leadership and organizational performance (M Ed). Part-time and evening/weekend programs available. *Faculty:* 30 full-time (13 women), 13 part-time/adjunct (6 women). *Students:* 183 full-time (128 women), 92 part-time (49 women); includes 59 minority (32 Black or African American, non-Hispanic/Latino; 8 Asian, non-Hispanic/Latino; 14 Hispanic/Latino; 5 Two or more races, non-Hispanic/Latino), 21 international. Average age 28. 464 applicants, 62% accepted, 123 enrolled. In 2013, 91 master's, 24 doctorates awarded. *Degree requirements:* For master's, comprehensive exam, thesis optional; for doctorate, thesis/dissertation, qualifying exams, residency. *Entrance requirements:* For master's and doctorate, GRE General Test. Additional exam requirements/recommendations for international students: Required—TOEFL (minimum score 550 paper-based; 80 iBT). *Application deadline:* For fall admission, 12/31 priority date for domestic and international students; for spring admission, 11/1 priority date for domestic and international students. Applications are processed on a rolling basis. Application fee: $0. Electronic applications accepted. *Financial support:* Fellowships with full and partial tuition reimbursements, research assistantships with full and partial tuition reimbursements, teaching assistantships with full and partial tuition reimbursements, Federal Work-Study, institutionally sponsored loans, scholarships/grants, tuition waivers (partial), and unspecified assistantships available. Support available to part-time students. Financial award application deadline: 1/15; financial award applicants required to submit FAFSA. *Faculty research:* Higher education, educational leadership, education policy, economics of education, education accountability, school choice. *Unit head:* Dr. Ellen B. Goldring, Chair, 615-322-8000, Fax: 615-343-7094, E-mail: ellen.b.goldring@vanderbilt.edu. *Application contact:* Rosie Moody, Educational Coordinator, 615-322-8019, Fax: 615-343-7094, E-mail: rosie.moody@vanderbilt.edu.

Virginia Commonwealth University, Graduate School, School of Education, Doctoral Program in Education, Richmond, VA 23284-9005. Offers educational leadership (PhD); educational psychology (PhD); instructional leadership (PhD); leadership (Ed D); research and evaluation (PhD); special education and disability leadership (PhD); urban services leadership (PhD). *Accreditation:* NCATE. Part-time programs available. *Degree requirements:* For doctorate, thesis/dissertation. *Entrance requirements:* For doctorate, GRE (for PhD), MAT (for Ed D), interview, master's degree, writing sample. Additional exam requirements/recommendations for international students: Required—TOEFL (minimum score 600 paper-based; 100 iBT). Electronic applications accepted.

Virginia Polytechnic Institute and State University, Graduate School, College of Liberal Arts and Human Sciences, Blacksburg, VA 24061. Offers career and technical education (MS Ed, Ed D, PhD, Ed S); communication (MA); counselor education (MA Ed, Ed D, PhD, Ed S); creative writing (MFA); curriculum and instruction (MA Ed, Ed D, PhD, Ed S); educational leadership and policy studies (MA Ed, Ed D, PhD, Ed S); educational research and evaluation (PhD); English (MA); foreign languages, cultures, and literatures (MA); higher education and student affairs (MA Ed); history (MA); human development (MS, PhD); material culture and public humanities (MA); philosophy (MA); political science (MA); rhetoric and writing (PhD); science and technology studies (MS, PhD); social, political, ethical, and cultural thought (PhD); sociology (MS, PhD); theater arts (MFA). *Faculty:* 410 full-time (211 women), 6 part-time/adjunct (5 women). *Students:* 688 full-time (464 women), 576 part-time (372 women); includes 243 minority (144 Black or African American, non-Hispanic/Latino; 3 American Indian or Alaska Native, non-Hispanic/Latino; 29 Asian, non-Hispanic/Latino; 48 Hispanic/Latino; 1 Native Hawaiian or other Pacific Islander, non-Hispanic/Latino; 18 Two or more races, non-Hispanic/Latino), 84 international. Average age 34. 1,054 applicants, 48% accepted, 374 enrolled. In 2013, 314 master's, 74 doctorates, 14 other advanced degrees awarded. *Degree requirements:* For master's, comprehensive exam (for some programs), thesis (for some programs); for doctorate, comprehensive exam (for some programs), thesis/dissertation (for some programs). *Entrance requirements:* For master's and doctorate, GRE/GMAT (may vary by department). Additional exam requirements/recommendations for international students: Required—TOEFL (minimum score 550 paper-based). *Application deadline:* For fall admission, 8/1 for domestic students, 4/1 for international students; for spring admission, 1/1 for domestic students, 9/1 for international students. Applications are processed on a rolling basis. Application fee: $75. Electronic applications accepted. *Expenses:* Tuition, state resident: full-time $11,185; part-time $621.50 per credit hour. Tuition, nonresident: full-time $22,146; part-time $1230.25 per credit hour. *Required fees:* $2442; $449.25 per semester. Tuition and fees vary according to course load, campus/location and program. *Financial support:* In 2013–14, 19 research assistantships with full tuition reimbursements (averaging $17,115 per year), 205 teaching assistantships with full tuition reimbursements (averaging $14,433 per year) were awarded. Financial award application deadline: 3/1; financial award applicants required to submit FAFSA. *Total annual research expenditures:* $6.8 million. *Unit head:* Joan Hirt, Interim Dean, 540-231-6779, Fax: 540-231-7157, E-mail: jbhirt@vt.edu. *Application contact:* Melissa Elliott, Executive Assistant, 540-231-6779, Fax: 540-231-7157, E-mail: elliott1@vt.edu.
Website: http://www.clahs.vt.edu/.

Walden University, Graduate Programs, Richard W. Riley College of Education and Leadership, Minneapolis, MN 55401. *Accreditation:* NCATE. Part-time and evening/weekend programs available. Postbaccalaureate distance learning degree programs offered (minimal on-campus study). *Faculty:* 23 full-time (15 women), 830 part-time/adjunct (569 women). *Students:* 8,671 full-time (7,197 women), 2,122 part-time (1,735 women); includes 4,734 minority (3,802 Black or African American, non-Hispanic/Latino; 50 American Indian or Alaska Native, non-Hispanic/Latino; 136 Asian, non-Hispanic/Latino; 539 Hispanic/Latino; 35 Native Hawaiian or other Pacific Islander, non-Hispanic/Latino; 172 Two or more races, non-Hispanic/Latino), 73 international. Average age 40. 2,646 applicants, 96% accepted, 2074 enrolled. In 2013, 2,214 master's, 354 doctorates, 479 other advanced degrees awarded. *Degree requirements:* For doctorate, thesis/dissertation (for some programs), residency; for other advanced degree, residency (for some programs). *Entrance requirements:* For master's, bachelor's degree or higher; minimum GPA of 2.5; official transcripts; goal statement (for some programs); access to computer and Internet; for doctorate, master's degree or higher; three years of related professional or academic experience (preferred); minimum GPA of 3.0; goal statement and current resume (select programs); official transcripts; access to computer and Internet; for other advanced degree, relevant work experience; access to computer and Internet. Additional exam requirements/recommendations for international students: Required—TOEFL (minimum score 550 paper-based; 79 iBT), IELTS (minimum score 6.5), Michigan English Language Assessment Battery (minimum score 82), or PTE. *Application deadline:* Applications are processed on a rolling basis. Application fee: $0. Electronic applications accepted. *Expenses: Tuition:* Full-time $11,813.55; part-time $500 per credit. *Required fees:* $618.76. *Financial support:* In 2013–14, 1 fellowship was awarded; Federal Work-Study, scholarships/grants, unspecified assistantships, and family tuition reduction, active duty/veteran tuition reduction, group tuition reduction, interest-free payment plans, employee tuition reduction also available. Support available to part-time students. Financial award applicants required to submit FAFSA. *Unit head:* Dr. Kate Steffens, Dean, 800-925-3368. *Application contact:* Jennifer Hall, Vice President of Enrollment Management, 866-4-WALDEN, E-mail: info@waldenu.edu.
Website: http://www.waldenu.edu/colleges-schools/riley-college-of-education/.

Wayne State University, College of Education, Division of Administrative and Organizational Studies, Detroit, MI 48202. Offers college and university teaching (Certificate); educational administration and supervision (Ed S); educational leadership (M Ed); educational leadership and policy studies (Ed D, PhD); educational technology (Certificate); instructional technology (M Ed, Ed D, PhD, Ed S); online teaching (Certificate); secondary curriculum and instruction (Ed S); special education administration (Ed S). Part-time programs available. Postbaccalaureate distance learning degree programs offered. *Students:* 96 full-time (68 women), 207 part-time (137 women); includes 133 minority (115 Black or African American, non-Hispanic/Latino; 4 American Indian or Alaska Native, non-Hispanic/Latino; 2 Asian, non-Hispanic/Latino; 8 Hispanic/Latino; 4 Two or more races, non-Hispanic/Latino), 14 international. Average

age 39. 127 applicants, 50% accepted, 42 enrolled. In 2013, 47 master's, 15 doctorates, 41 other advanced degrees awarded. *Degree requirements:* For doctorate, thesis/dissertation. *Entrance requirements:* For master's, baccalaureate degree from accredited U.S. institution or equivalent from college or university of government-recognized standing; minimum undergraduate GPA of 2.75 in upper-division coursework; for doctorate, GRE or MAT, interview; autobiography or curriculum vitae; references; master's degree; minimum undergraduate GPA of 3.0, graduate 3.75; 3 years of relevant experience; foundational course work; for other advanced degree, master's degree from accredited institution, minimum upper-division GPA of 2.6 or 3.4 master's, fulfillment of the special requirements of the area of concentration, 3 years of teaching experience (except for instructional technology). Additional exam requirements/recommendations for international students: Required—TOEFL (minimum score 550 paper-based; 79 iBT), Michigan English Language Assessment Battery (minimum score 85); Recommended—IELTS (minimum score 6.5), TWE (minimum score 5.5). *Application deadline:* For fall admission, 6/1 priority date for domestic students, 5/1 priority date for international students; for winter admission, 10/1 priority date for domestic students, 9/1 priority date for international students; for spring admission, 2/1 priority date for domestic students, 1/1 priority date for international students. Applications are processed on a rolling basis. Application fee: $0. Electronic applications accepted. *Expenses:* Tuition, state resident: part-time $554.15 per credit. Tuition, nonresident: part-time $1200.35 per credit. *Required fees:* $42.15 per credit. $268.30 per semester. Tuition and fees vary according to course load and program. *Financial support:* In 2013–14, 48 students received support, including 3 fellowships with tuition reimbursements available (averaging $15,541 per year), 4 research assistantships with tuition reimbursements available (averaging $16,508 per year); career-related internships or fieldwork, Federal Work-Study, scholarships/grants, health care benefits, and unspecified assistantships also available. Support available to part-time students. Financial award application deadline: 3/31; financial award applicants required to submit FAFSA. *Faculty research:* Total quality management, participatory management, administering educational technology, school improvement, principalship. *Total annual research expenditures:* $6,888. *Unit head:* Dr. William Hill, Assistant Dean, 313-577-9316, E-mail: william_e_hill@wayne.edu. *Application contact:* Janice Green, Assistant Dean, 313-577-1605, E-mail: jwgreen@wayne.edu.
Website: http://coe.wayne.edu/aos/index.php.

Educational Psychology

Alliant International University–Irvine, Shirley M. Hufstedler School of Education, Educational Psychology Programs, Irvine, CA 92606. Offers educational psychology (Psy D); pupil personnel services (Credential); school psychology (MA). Part-time programs available. *Students:* 13 full-time (10 women), 13 part-time (10 women); includes 17 minority (3 Black or African American, non-Hispanic/Latino; 5 Asian, non-Hispanic/Latino; 7 Hispanic/Latino; 2 Two or more races, non-Hispanic/Latino). Average age 32. 16 applicants, 88% accepted, 12 enrolled. In 2013, 4 master's, 6 doctorates, 12 other advanced degrees awarded. *Degree requirements:* For doctorate, thesis/dissertation. *Entrance requirements:* For master's, minimum GPA of 2.5, letters of recommendation; for doctorate, interview, minimum GPA of 3.0, letters of recommendation. Additional exam requirements/recommendations for international students: Required—TOEFL (minimum score 550 paper-based; 80 iBT), TWE (minimum score 5). *Application deadline:* For fall admission, 7/1 priority date for domestic and international students; for spring admission, 12/1 priority date for domestic and international students. Application fee: $65. *Financial support:* Career-related internships or fieldwork, Federal Work-Study, institutionally sponsored loans, and scholarships/grants available. Financial award application deadline: 2/15; financial award applicants required to submit FAFSA. *Faculty research:* School-based mental health. *Unit head:* Dr. Don Wofford, Program Director, 949-833-2651, Fax: 949-833-3507, E-mail: admissions@alliant.edu. *Application contact:* Alliant International University Central Contact Center, 866-U-ALLIANT, Fax: 858-635-4555, E-mail: admissions@alliant.edu.

Alliant International University–Los Angeles, Shirley M. Hufstedler School of Education, Educational Psychology Programs, Alhambra, CA 91803-1360. Offers educational psychology (Psy D); pupil personnel services (Credential); school psychology (MA). Part-time programs available. *Students:* 4 full-time (3 women), 19 part-time (16 women); includes 15 minority (2 Black or African American, non-Hispanic/Latino; 2 Asian, non-Hispanic/Latino; 8 Hispanic/Latino; 3 Two or more races, non-Hispanic/Latino). Average age 35. 16 applicants, 81% accepted, 6 enrolled. In 2013, 6 master's, 7 doctorates awarded. *Degree requirements:* For doctorate, comprehensive exam, thesis/dissertation. *Entrance requirements:* For master's, minimum GPA of 2.5, letters of recommendation; for doctorate, interview, minimum GPA of 3.0, letters of recommendation. Additional exam requirements/recommendations for international students: Required—TOEFL (minimum score 550 paper-based), TWE (minimum score 5). *Application deadline:* For fall admission, 4/15 priority date for domestic and international students; for spring admission, 12/1 priority date for domestic and international students. Applications are processed on a rolling basis. Application fee: $65. Electronic applications accepted. *Financial support:* Career-related internships or fieldwork, Federal Work-Study, institutionally sponsored loans, and scholarships/grants available. Financial award application deadline: 2/15; financial award applicants required to submit FAFSA. *Faculty research:* Early identification and intervention with high-risk preschoolers, pediatric neuropsychology, interpersonal violence, ADHD, learning theories. *Unit head:* Dr. Steven Fisher, Program Director, 858-635-4825, Fax: 626-284-0550, E-mail: admissions@alliant.edu. *Application contact:* Alliant International University Central Contact Center, 866-U-ALLIANT, Fax: 858-635-4555, E-mail: admissions@alliant.edu.
Website: http://www.alliant.edu/hsoe/.

Alliant International University–San Diego, Shirley M. Hufstedler School of Education, Educational Psychology Programs, San Diego, CA 92131-1799. Offers educational psychology (Psy D); pupil personnel services (Credential); school neuropsychology (Certificate); school psychology (MA); school-based mental health (Certificate). Part-time programs available. *Faculty:* 1 full-time (0 women), 14 part-time/adjunct (9 women). *Students:* 20 full-time (19 women), 13 part-time (all women); includes 16 minority (2 Black or African American, non-Hispanic/Latino; 13 Hispanic/Latino; 1 Two or more races, non-Hispanic/Latino), 1 international. Average age 30. 23 applicants, 87% accepted, 15 enrolled. In 2013, 8 master's, 6 doctorates awarded. *Degree requirements:* For doctorate, comprehensive exam, thesis/dissertation, internship. *Entrance requirements:* For master's, minimum GPA of 2.5, letters of recommendation; for doctorate, minimum GPA of 3.0, letters of recommendation. Additional exam requirements/recommendations for international students: Required—TOEFL (minimum score 550 paper-based; 80 iBT), TWE (minimum score 5). *Application deadline:* For fall admission, 4/15 priority date for domestic and international students; for spring admission, 11/3 priority date for domestic and international students. Applications are processed on a rolling basis. Application fee: $65. Electronic applications accepted. *Financial support:* Career-related internships or fieldwork, Federal Work-Study, institutionally sponsored loans, and scholarships/grants available. Financial award application deadline: 2/15; financial award applicants required to submit FAFSA. *Faculty research:* School-based mental health, pupil personnel services, childhood mood, school-based assessment. *Unit head:* Dr. Steve Fisher, Program Director, 828-635-4825, Fax: 858-635-4739, E-mail: admissions@alliant.edu. *Application contact:* Alliant International University Central Contact Center, 866-U-ALLIANT, Fax: 858-635-4555, E-mail: admissions@alliant.edu.
Website: http://www.alliant.edu/hsoe.

Alliant International University–San Francisco, Shirley M. Hufstedler School of Education, Educational Psychology Programs, San Francisco, CA 94133-1221. Offers educational psychology (Psy D); pupil personnel services (Credential); school psychology (MA). Part-time programs available. *Faculty:* 1 full-time (0 women), 9 part-time/adjunct (7 women). *Students:* 16 full-time (11 women), 15 part-time (12 women); includes 19 minority (2 Black or African American, non-Hispanic/Latino; 7 Asian, non-Hispanic/Latino; 6 Hispanic/Latino; 4 Two or more races, non-Hispanic/Latino), 2 international. Average age 32. 34 applicants, 88% accepted, 18 enrolled. In 2013, 6 master's, 5 doctorates, 5 other advanced degrees awarded. Terminal master's awarded for partial completion of doctoral program. *Degree requirements:* For doctorate, thesis/dissertation. *Entrance requirements:* For master's, minimum GPA of 3.0, letters of recommendation; for doctorate, interview, minimum GPA of 3.0, letters of recommendation. Additional exam requirements/recommendations for international students: Required—TOEFL (minimum score 550 paper-based), TWE (minimum score 5). *Application deadline:* For fall admission, 7/1 priority date for domestic and international students; for spring admission, 12/1 priority date for domestic and international students. Applications are processed on a rolling basis. Application fee: $55. Electronic applications accepted. *Financial support:* Career-related internships or fieldwork, Federal Work-Study, institutionally sponsored loans, and scholarships/grants available. Financial award application deadline: 2/15; financial award applicants required to submit FAFSA. *Faculty research:* Social skills, ADHD, cognitive functioning and learning, innovative teaching methods. *Unit head:* Dr. Steven Fisher, Systemwide Program Director, 415-955-2087, Fax: 415-955-2179, E-mail: admissions@alliant.edu. *Application contact:* Alliant International University Central Contact Center, 866-U-ALLIANT, Fax: 858-635-4555, E-mail: admissions@alliant.edu.

American International College, School of Graduate and Adult Education, Graduate Psychology Department, Educational Psychology Program, Springfield, MA 01109-3189. Offers MA, Ed D. Part-time and evening/weekend programs available. *Faculty:* 2 full-time (1 woman), 4 part-time/adjunct (2 women). *Students:* 55 full-time (44 women), 21 part-time (18 women); includes 10 minority (4 Black or African American, non-Hispanic/Latino; 2 Asian, non-Hispanic/Latino; 2 Hispanic/Latino; 1 Native Hawaiian or other Pacific Islander, non-Hispanic/Latino; 1 Two or more races, non-Hispanic/Latino). Average age 38. 48 applicants, 88% accepted, 29 enrolled. In 2013, 24 master's, 6 doctorates awarded. *Degree requirements:* For doctorate, comprehensive exam, thesis/dissertation. *Entrance requirements:* For master's, graduate of accredited four-year college with minimum GPA of 2.67; for doctorate, minimum GPA of 3.25; master's degree (preferred). Additional exam requirements/recommendations for international students: Required—TOEFL or IELTS. *Application deadline:* For fall admission, 7/1 priority date for domestic students, 4/1 priority date for international students; for spring admission, 10/1 priority date for domestic and international students. Applications are processed on a rolling basis. Application fee: $50. Electronic applications accepted. *Expenses: Tuition:* Full-time $14,040; part-time $780 per credit. Tuition and fees vary according to course load, degree level and program. *Financial support:* In 2013–14, 6 students received support, including 6 fellowships with full tuition reimbursements available (averaging $1,500 per year); career-related internships or fieldwork and unspecified assistantships also available. Support available to part-time students. Financial award application deadline: 4/1; financial award applicants required to submit FAFSA. *Unit head:* Dr. John DeFrancesco, Director, 413-205-3343, Fax: 413-205-3943, E-mail: john.defrancesco@aic.edu. *Application contact:* Kerry Barnes, Director of Graduate Admissions, 413-205-3703, Fax: 413-205-3051, E-mail: kerry.barnes@aic.edu.
Website: http://www.aic.edu/academics.

Andrews University, School of Graduate Studies, School of Education, Department of Graduate Psychology and Counseling, Program in Educational and Developmental Psychology, Berrien Springs, MI 49104. Offers educational and developmental psychology (MA); educational psychology (Ed D, PhD). *Students:* 9 full-time (4 women), 19 part-time (17 women); includes 9 minority (5 Black or African American, non-Hispanic/Latino; 3 Asian, non-Hispanic/Latino; 1 Hispanic/Latino), 6 international. Average age 35. 26 applicants, 62% accepted, 7 enrolled. In 2013, 10 master's awarded. *Degree requirements:* For master's, thesis optional. *Entrance requirements:* For master's, GRE. Additional exam requirements/recommendations for international students: Required—TOEFL (minimum score 550 paper-based). *Application deadline:* Applications are processed on a rolling basis. Application fee: $40. *Unit head:* Dr. Jimmy Kijai, Coordinator, 269-471-6240. *Application contact:* Monica Wringer, Supervisor of Graduate Admission, 800-253-2874, Fax: 269-471-6321, E-mail: graduate@andrews.edu.

Auburn University, Graduate School, College of Education, Department of Educational Foundations, Leadership, and Technology, Auburn University, AL 36849. Offers adult education (M Ed, MS, Ed D); curriculum and instruction (M Ed, MS, Ed D, Ed S); curriculum supervision (M Ed, MS, Ed D, Ed S); educational psychology (PhD); higher education administration (M Ed, MS, Ed D, Ed S); media instructional design (MS); media specialist (M Ed); school administration (M Ed, MS, Ed D, Ed S). *Accreditation:* NCATE. Part-time programs available. *Faculty:* 25 full-time (15 women), 6 part-time/adjunct (5 women). *Students:* 104 full-time (65 women), 250 part-time (140 women); includes 98 minority (90 Black or African American, non-Hispanic/Latino; 1 American Indian or Alaska Native, non-Hispanic/Latino; 4 Asian, non-Hispanic/Latino; 3 Hispanic/Latino), 14 international. Average age 36. 188 applicants, 66% accepted, 76 enrolled. In 2013, 51 master's, 22 doctorates, 10 other advanced degrees awarded. *Degree requirements:* For master's, thesis (for some programs); for doctorate, thesis/dissertation; for Ed S, field project. *Entrance requirements:* For master's, doctorate, and Ed S, GRE General Test. *Application deadline:* For fall admission, 7/7 for domestic

students; for spring admission, 11/24 for domestic students. Applications are processed on a rolling basis. Application fee: $50 ($60 for international students). Electronic applications accepted. *Expenses:* Tuition, state resident: full-time $8262; part-time $459 per credit hour. Tuition, nonresident: full-time $24,786; part-time $1377 per credit hour. Tuition and fees vary according to degree level and program. *Financial support:* Teaching assistantships and Federal Work-Study available. Support available to part-time students. Financial award application deadline: 3/15; financial award applicants required to submit FAFSA. *Unit head:* Dr. Sherida Downer, Head, 334-844-4460. *Application contact:* Dr. George Flowers, Dean of the Graduate School, 334-844-4700. Website: http://www.education.auburn.edu/academic_departments/eflt/.

Ball State University, Graduate School, Teachers College, Department of Educational Psychology, Program in Educational Psychology, Muncie, IN 47306-1099. Offers MA, PhD, Ed S. *Accreditation:* NCATE. *Students:* 20 full-time (14 women), 28 part-time (20 women); includes 7 minority (4 Black or African American, non-Hispanic/Latino; 2 American Indian or Alaska Native, non-Hispanic/Latino; 1 Hispanic/Latino), 1 international. Average age 27. 38 applicants, 29% accepted, 3 enrolled. In 2013, 20 master's, 5 doctorates, 8 other advanced degrees awarded. *Degree requirements:* For doctorate, thesis/dissertation; for Ed S, thesis. *Entrance requirements:* For master's and Ed S, GRE General Test; for doctorate, GRE General Test, minimum graduate GPA of 3.2. Application fee: $50. *Financial support:* In 2013-14, 33 students received support, including 35 teaching assistantships with full tuition reimbursements available (averaging $10,722 per year); research assistantships with tuition reimbursements available also available. Financial award application deadline: 3/1. *Unit head:* Dr. Felicia Dixon, Head, 785-285-8500, Fax: 785-285-3653. *Application contact:* Dr. Robert Morris, Associate Provost for Research and Dean of the Graduate School, 765-285-1300, E-mail: rmorris@bsu.edu.
Website: http://www.bsu.edu/teachers/departments/edpsy/.

Baylor University, Graduate School, School of Education, Department of Educational Psychology, Waco, TX 76798-7301. Offers applied behavior analysis (MS Ed); educational psychology (MA, PhD); exceptionalities (PhD); learning and development (PhD); measurement (PhD); school psychology (Ed S). *Accreditation:* NCATE. *Faculty:* 12 full-time (7 women), 2 part-time/adjunct (1 woman). *Students:* 36 full-time (30 women), 6 part-time (all women); includes 8 minority (1 Black or African American, non-Hispanic/Latino; 3 Asian, non-Hispanic/Latino; 4 Hispanic/Latino), 2 international. Average age 29. 40 applicants, 38% accepted, 12 enrolled. In 2013, 4 master's, 8 doctorates, 8 other advanced degrees awarded. *Degree requirements:* For master's, thesis optional; for doctorate, comprehensive exam, thesis/dissertation; for Ed S, comprehensive exam, thesis or alternative. *Entrance requirements:* For master's, minimum GPA of 3.0; for doctorate, GRE General Test, master's degree; for Ed S, GRE General Test. Additional exam requirements/recommendations for international students: Required—TOEFL. *Application deadline:* For fall admission, 2/1 priority date for domestic and international students. Application fee: $50. Electronic applications accepted. *Expenses: Tuition:* Full-time $25,866; part-time $1437 per credit hour. *Required fees:* $2736; $152 per credit hour. Tuition and fees vary according to course load and program. *Financial support:* In 2013-14, 42 students received support, including 20 fellowships with full and partial tuition reimbursements available, 22 research assistantships with full and partial tuition reimbursements available; career-related internships or fieldwork, Federal Work-Study, institutionally sponsored loans, scholarships/grants, health care benefits, tuition waivers (full and partial), unspecified assistantships and stipends also available. Financial award application deadline: 2/1; financial award applicants required to submit FAFSA. *Faculty research:* Individual differences, quantitative methods, gifted and talented, special education, school psychology, autism, applied behavior analysis, learning, human development. *Total annual research expenditures:* $248,000. *Unit head:* Dr. Marley W. Watkins, Professor and Chairman, 254-710-4234, Fax: 254-710-3987, E-mail: marley_watkins@baylor.edu. *Application contact:* Lisa Rowe, Office Manager, 254-710-3112, Fax: 254-710-3112, E-mail: lisa_rowe@baylor.edu.
Website: http://www.baylor.edu/soe/EDP/.

Boston College, Lynch Graduate School of Education, Program in Applied Developmental and Educational Psychology, Chestnut Hill, MA 02467-3800. Offers MA, PhD. Part-time and evening/weekend programs available. *Students:* 14 full-time (13 women), 3 part-time (all women). 137 applicants, 34% accepted, 17 enrolled. In 2013, 15 master's, 2 doctorates awarded. Terminal master's awarded for partial completion of doctoral program. *Degree requirements:* For master's, comprehensive exam; for doctorate, comprehensive exam, thesis/dissertation. *Entrance requirements:* For master's and doctorate, GRE General Test. Additional exam requirements/recommendations for international students: Required—TOEFL (minimum score 100 iBT). *Application deadline:* For fall admission, 12/1 priority date for domestic and international students; for spring admission, 11/1 for domestic and international students. Application fee: $65. Electronic applications accepted. *Financial support:* Fellowships with full and partial tuition reimbursements, research assistantships with full and partial tuition reimbursements, teaching assistantships with full and partial tuition reimbursements, career-related internships or fieldwork, Federal Work-Study, scholarships/grants, traineeships, health care benefits, tuition waivers (full and partial), and unspecified assistantships available. Support available to part-time students. Financial award applicants required to submit FAFSA. *Faculty research:* Cognitive learning and culture, effects of social policy reform on children and families, psychosocial trauma, human rights and international justice, positive youth development, children and adolescents living in poverty. *Unit head:* Dr. M. Brinton Lykes, Chairperson, 617-552-4214, Fax: 617-552-0812. *Application contact:* Domenic Lomanno, Director, Graduate Admission and Financial Aid, 617-552-4214, Fax: 617-552-0398, E-mail: lomanno@bc.edu.

Brigham Young University, Graduate Studies, David O. McKay School of Education, Department of Instructional Psychology and Technology, Provo, UT 84602. Offers MS, PhD. *Faculty:* 9 full-time (0 women). *Students:* 57 full-time (22 women), 18 part-time (10 women); includes 4 minority (1 Asian, non-Hispanic/Latino; 1 Hispanic/Latino; 2 Native Hawaiian or other Pacific Islander, non-Hispanic/Latino), 2 international. Average age 36. 30 applicants, 67% accepted, 16 enrolled. In 2013, 7 master's, 5 doctorates awarded. *Degree requirements:* For master's, thesis; for doctorate, comprehensive exam, thesis/dissertation. *Entrance requirements:* For master's and doctorate, GRE General Test. Additional exam requirements/recommendations for international students: Required—TOEFL. *Application deadline:* For fall admission, 1/2 for domestic and international students; for winter admission, 2/1 for domestic and international students; for summer admission, 1/2 for domestic and international students. Application fee: $50. Electronic applications accepted. *Expenses: Tuition:* Full-time $6130; part-time $340 per credit hour. Tuition and fees vary according to program and student's religious affiliation. *Financial support:* In 2013-14, 21 students received support, including 14 research assistantships with full and partial tuition reimbursements available (averaging $10,000 per year), 16 teaching assistantships with full and partial tuition reimbursements available (averaging $6,500 per year); career-related internships or fieldwork, scholarships/grants, tuition waivers (full and partial), and unspecified assistantships also available. Support available to part-time students. *Faculty research:* Interactive learning, learning theory, instructional designed development, research and evaluation, measurement. *Unit head:* Dr. Andrew S. Gibbons, Chair, 801-422-5097, Fax: 801-422-

0314, E-mail: andy_gibbons@byu.edu. *Application contact:* Michele Bray, Department Secretary, 801-422-2746, Fax: 801-422-0314, E-mail: michele_bray@byu.edu. Website: http://education.byu.edu/ipt/.

California Coast University, School of Education, Santa Ana, CA 92701. Offers administration (M Ed); curriculum and instruction (M Ed); educational administration (Ed D); educational psychology (Ed D); organizational leadership (Ed D). Postbaccalaureate distance learning degree programs offered (no on-campus study).

California State University, Long Beach, Graduate Studies, College of Education, Department of Advanced Studies in Education and Counseling, Program in Educational Psychology, Long Beach, CA 90840. Offers MA. *Degree requirements:* For master's, thesis. *Entrance requirements:* For master's, GRE General Test, minimum GPA of 2.75. Electronic applications accepted.

California State University, Northridge, Graduate Studies, College of Education, Department of Educational Psychology and Counseling, Northridge, CA 91330. Offers counseling (MS), including career counseling, college counseling and student services, marriage and family therapy, school counseling, school psychology; educational psychology (MA Ed), including development, learning, and instruction, early childhood education. *Accreditation:* ACA (one or more programs are accredited); NCATE. Part-time and evening/weekend programs available. *Entrance requirements:* For master's, GRE General Test or minimum GPA of 3.0. Additional exam requirements/recommendations for international students: Required—TOEFL.

Capella University, Harold Abel School of Social and Behavioral Science, Doctoral Programs in Psychology, Minneapolis, MN 55402. Offers addiction psychology (PhD); clinical psychology (Psy D); educational psychology (PhD); general advanced studies in human behavior (PhD); general psychology (PhD); industrial/organizational psychology (PhD); school psychology (Psy D).

Capella University, Harold Abel School of Social and Behavioral Science, Master's Programs in Psychology, Minneapolis, MN 55402. Offers applied behavior analysis (MS); clinical psychology (MS); counseling psychology (MS); educational psychology (MS); evaluation, research, and measurement (MS); general advanced studies in human behavior (MS); general psychology (MS); industrial/organizational psychology (MS); leadership coaching psychology (MS); school psychology (MS); sport psychology (MS).

The Catholic University of America, School of Arts and Sciences, Department of Education, Washington, DC 20064. Offers Catholic educational leadership and policy studies (PhD); Catholic school leadership (MA); education (Certificate); educational psychology (PhD); secondary education (MA); special education (MA). *Accreditation:* NCATE. Part-time programs available. *Faculty:* 9 full-time (8 women), 4 part-time/adjunct (all women). *Students:* 9 full-time (6 women), 44 part-time (37 women); includes 8 minority (3 Black or African American, non-Hispanic/Latino; 3 Hispanic/Latino; 2 Two or more races, non-Hispanic/Latino), 2 international. Average age 34. 53 applicants, 53% accepted, 17 enrolled. In 2013, 18 master's, 2 doctorates awarded. *Degree requirements:* For master's, comprehensive exam, thesis or alternative; for doctorate, comprehensive exam, thesis/dissertation; for Certificate, action research project. *Entrance requirements:* For master's and doctorate, GRE General Test or MAT, statement of purpose, official copies of academic transcripts, three letters of recommendation, interview; for Certificate, PRAXIS I, statement of purpose, official copies of academic transcripts, three letters of recommendation, interview. Additional exam requirements/recommendations for international students: Required—TOEFL (minimum score 580 paper-based). *Application deadline:* For fall admission, 8/1 priority date for domestic students, 7/15 for international students; for spring admission, 12/1 priority date for domestic students, 10/15 for international students. Applications are processed on a rolling basis. Application fee: $55. Electronic applications accepted. *Expenses: Tuition:* Full-time $38,500; part-time $1490 per credit hour. *Required fees:* $400; $1525 per credit hour. One-time fee: $425. Tuition and fees vary according to program. *Financial support:* Fellowships, research assistantships, teaching assistantships, Federal Work-Study, scholarships/grants, tuition waivers (full and partial), and unspecified assistantships available. Financial award application deadline: 2/1; financial award applicants required to submit FAFSA. *Faculty research:* Special education, early childhood education, educational psychology, Catholic school administration, leadership and policy studies, counseling, curriculum and instruction. *Total annual research expenditures:* $65,883. *Unit head:* Dr. Merylann J. Schuttloffel, Chair, 202-319-5805, Fax: 202-319-5815, E-mail: schuttloffel@cua.edu. *Application contact:* Andrew Woodall, Director of Graduate Admissions, 202-319-5057, Fax: 202-319-6533, E-mail: cua-admissions@cua.edu.
Website: http://education.cua.edu/.

Chapman University, College of Educational Studies, Orange, CA 92866. Offers communication sciences and disorders (MS); counseling (MA), including school counseling (MA, Credential); education (PhD), including cultural and curricular studies, disability studies, leadership studies, school psychology (PhD, Credential); educational psychology (MA); leadership development (MA); pupil personnel services (Credential), including school counseling (MA, Credential), school psychology (PhD, Credential); school psychology (Ed S); single subject (Credential); special education (MA, Credential), including mild/moderate (Credential), moderate/severe (Credential); speech language pathology (Credential); teaching (MA), including elementary education, secondary education. *Accreditation:* Teacher Education Accreditation Council. Part-time and evening/weekend programs available. *Faculty:* 29 full-time (18 women), 56 part-time/adjunct (38 women). *Students:* 251 full-time (208 women), 194 part-time (150 women); includes 185 minority (13 Black or African American, non-Hispanic/Latino; 61 Asian, non-Hispanic/Latino; 97 Hispanic/Latino; 1 Native Hawaiian or other Pacific Islander, non-Hispanic/Latino; 13 Two or more races, non-Hispanic/Latino), 7 international. Average age 29. 580 applicants, 42% accepted, 166 enrolled. In 2013, 140 master's, 10 doctorates awarded. *Entrance requirements:* Additional exam requirements/recommendations for international students: Required—TOEFL (minimum score 550 paper-based; 80 iBT). *Application deadline:* Applications are processed on a rolling basis. Application fee: $60. Electronic applications accepted. Tuition and fees vary according to program. *Financial support:* Fellowships and scholarships/grants available. Financial award application deadline: 6/30; financial award applicants required to submit FAFSA. *Unit head:* Dr. Don Cardinal, Dean, 714-997-6781, E-mail: cardinal@chapman.edu. *Application contact:* Admissions Coordinator, 714-997-6714. Website: http://www.chapman.edu/CES/.

Clark Atlanta University, School of Education, Department of Counseling and Psychological Studies, Atlanta, GA 30314. Offers MA. *Accreditation:* ACA. Part-time programs available. *Faculty:* 4 full-time (1 woman), 4 part-time/adjunct (2 women). *Students:* 33 full-time (28 women), 5 part-time (all women); includes 36 minority (all Black or African American, non-Hispanic/Latino). Average age 26. 23 applicants, 96% accepted, 17 enrolled. In 2013, 10 master's awarded. *Degree requirements:* For master's, comprehensive exam. *Entrance requirements:* For master's, GRE General Test, minimum undergraduate GPA of 2.6. Additional exam requirements/recommendations for international students: Required—TOEFL (minimum score 500 paper-based; 61 iBT). *Application deadline:* For fall admission, 4/1 for domestic and international students; for spring admission, 11/1 for domestic and international

students. Applications are processed on a rolling basis. Application fee: $40 ($55 for international students). Electronic applications accepted. *Expenses: Tuition:* Full-time $14,616; part-time $812 per credit hour. *Required fees:* $706; $353 per semester. *Financial support:* Career-related internships or fieldwork, Federal Work-Study, scholarships/grants, and unspecified assistantships available. Support available to part-time students. Financial award application deadline: 4/30; financial award applicants required to submit FAFSA. *Unit head:* Dr. Noran Moffett, Interim Chairperson, 404-880-6330, E-mail: nmoffett@cau.edu. *Application contact:* Michelle Clark-Davis, Graduate Program Admissions, 404-880-6605, E-mail: cauadmissions@cau.edu.

The College of Saint Rose, Graduate Studies, School of Education, Department of Educational Psychology, Albany, NY 12203-1419. Offers applied technology education (MS Ed); educational psychology (MS Ed); instructional technology (Certificate); school psychology (MS Ed, Certificate). Part-time and evening/weekend programs available. *Entrance requirements:* For master's, minimum undergraduate GPA of 3.0. Additional exam requirements/recommendations for international students: Required—TOEFL (minimum score 550 paper-based). Electronic applications accepted.

Dowling College, Graduate Programs in Education, Oakdale, NY 11769-1999. Offers adolescence education with middle childhood extension (MS); childhood and early childhood education (MS); childhood and gifted education (MS); childhood education (1-6) (MS); computers in education (AC); early childhood education (B-2) (MS); educational administration (Ed D); educational technology leadership (MS); educational technology specialist (AC); gifted education (AC); literacy education (MS, AC), including 5-12 (MS), B-12 (MS); literacy education (MS), including B-6; school building leader (AC); school district business leader (MBA, AC); school district leader (AC); special education (MS), including autism, severe disabilities; sport management (MS). *Accreditation:* NCATE. Part-time and evening/weekend programs available. Postbaccalaureate distance learning degree programs offered (minimal on-campus study). *Faculty:* 44 full-time (24 women), 17 part-time/adjunct (8 women). *Students:* 183 full-time (124 women), 314 part-time (231 women); includes 51 minority (19 Black or African American, non-Hispanic/Latino; 1 American Indian or Alaska Native, non-Hispanic/Latino; 3 Asian, non-Hispanic/Latino; 26 Hispanic/Latino; 2 Native Hawaiian or other Pacific Islander, non-Hispanic/Latino). Average age 32. 174 applicants, 80% accepted, 82 enrolled. In 2013, 198 master's, 33 doctorates, 48 other advanced degrees awarded. *Degree requirements:* For master's and AC, comprehensive exam; for doctorate, thesis/dissertation. *Entrance requirements:* For master's, minimum GPA of 3.0; for doctorate, GRE, master's degree; for AC, teaching certificate. Additional exam requirements/recommendations for international students: Required—TOEFL (minimum score 550 paper-based). *Application deadline:* For fall admission, 9/1 priority date for domestic students; for winter admission, 1/1 priority date for domestic students; for spring admission, 2/1 priority date for domestic students. Applications are processed on a rolling basis. Application fee: $50. Electronic applications accepted. *Expenses: Tuition:* Full-time $22,731; part-time $1029 per credit. *Required fees:* $956; $956. *Financial support:* Career-related internships or fieldwork and Federal Work-Study available. Support available to part-time students. Financial award application deadline: 6/30; financial award applicants required to submit FAFSA. *Faculty research:* Natural readers, Korean styles and learning strategies, mothers of children with disabilities, computers in instruction, cultural background and organizational roadblocks to problem solving. *Unit head:* Dr. Robert Manley, Dean, 631-244-3447, E-mail: manleyr@dowling.edu. *Application contact:* Mary Boullianne, Director of Admissions, 631-244-3274, Fax: 631-244-1059, E-mail: boulliam@dowling.edu.

Eastern Michigan University, Graduate School, College of Education, Department of Teacher Education, Programs in Educational Psychology and Assessment, Ypsilanti, MI 48197. Offers educational assessment (Graduate Certificate); educational psychology (MA), including development/personality, research and assessment, research and evaluation, the developing learner. *Accreditation:* NCATE. Part-time and evening/weekend programs available. Postbaccalaureate distance learning degree programs offered (minimal on-campus study). *Students:* 14 part-time (12 women); includes 2 minority (1 Black or African American, non-Hispanic/Latino; 1 Hispanic/Latino), 1 international. Average age 40. 6 applicants, 100% accepted, 4 enrolled. In 2013, 17 master's, 3 other advanced degrees awarded. *Degree requirements:* For master's, thesis or alternative. *Entrance requirements:* For master's, GRE. Additional exam requirements/recommendations for international students: Required—TOEFL. *Application deadline:* Applications are processed on a rolling basis. Application fee: $35. *Expenses:* Tuition, state resident: full-time $12,300; part-time $466 per credit hour. Tuition, nonresident: full-time $23,159; part-time $918 per credit hour. *Required fees:* $71 per credit hour. $46 per semester. One-time fee: $100. Tuition and fees vary according to course level and degree level. *Financial support:* Fellowships, research assistantships with full tuition reimbursements, teaching assistantships with full tuition reimbursements, career-related internships or fieldwork, Federal Work-Study, institutionally sponsored loans, scholarships/grants, tuition waivers (partial), and unspecified assistantships available. Support available to part-time students. Financial award applicants required to submit FAFSA. *Unit head:* Dr. Martha Kinney-Sedgwick, Interim Department Head, 734-487-3260, Fax: 734-487-2101, E-mail: mkinneys@emich.edu. *Application contact:* Dr. Patricia Pokay, Coordinator, 734-487-3260, Fax: 734-487-2101, E-mail: ppokay@emich.edu.

Edinboro University of Pennsylvania, School of Education, Department of Professional Studies, Edinboro, PA 16444. Offers counseling (MA); educational leadership (M Ed); educational psychology (M Ed); reading (M Ed); school psychology (MS, Ed S). Part-time and evening/weekend programs available. *Degree requirements:* For master's, thesis or alternative, competency exam; for Ed S, thesis or alternative. *Entrance requirements:* For master's and Ed S, GRE or MAT, minimum QPA of 2.5. Electronic applications accepted.

Florida Atlantic University, College of Education, Department of Teaching and Learning, Boca Raton, FL 33431-0991. Offers curriculum and instruction (M Ed), including art, biology, chemistry, English, French, German, mathematics, music, physics, Pre-K and primary education, reading, social sciences, Spanish; elementary education (M Ed); environmental education (M Ed); reading education (M Ed); social foundations of education (M Ed), including educational psychology, educational technology, multilingual education. *Accreditation:* NCATE. Part-time and evening/weekend programs available. *Faculty:* 16 full-time (12 women), 1 (woman) part-time/adjunct. *Students:* 56 full-time (46 women), 96 part-time (78 women); includes 39 minority (10 Black or African American, non-Hispanic/Latino; 6 Asian, non-Hispanic/Latino; 20 Hispanic/Latino; 3 Two or more races, non-Hispanic/Latino), 4 international. Average age 32. 101 applicants, 54% accepted, 42 enrolled. In 2013, 64 master's awarded. *Entrance requirements:* For master's, GRE General Test, minimum GPA of 3.0 in last 2 years of undergraduate course work. Additional exam requirements/recommendations for international students: Required—TOEFL (minimum score 500 paper-based; 61 iBT), IELTS (minimum score 6). *Application deadline:* For fall admission, 7/1 for domestic students, 2/15 for international students; for spring admission, 11/1 for domestic students, 7/15 for international students. Applications are processed on a rolling basis. Application fee: $30. *Expenses:* Tuition, state resident: full-time $6660; part-time $370 per credit hour. Tuition, nonresident: full-time $18,450; part-time $1025 per credit hour. Tuition and fees vary according to course load. *Financial support:* Fellowships with partial tuition reimbursements, research assistantships with partial tuition reimbursements, teaching assistantships with partial tuition reimbursements, career-related internships or fieldwork, scholarships/grants, and unspecified assistantships available. *Faculty research:* Technology, teaching English to speakers of other languages, math teaching, electronic portfolio assessment, global perspectives through social studies. *Unit head:* Dr. Barbara Ridener, Chairperson, 561-297-3588. *Application contact:* Dr. Eliah Watlington, Associate Dean, 561-296-8520, Fax: 261-297-2991, E-mail: ewatling@fau.edu.
Website: http://www.coe.fau.edu/academicdepartments/tl/.

Florida State University, The Graduate School, College of Education, Department of Educational Psychology and Learning Systems, Program in Educational Psychology, Tallahassee, FL 32306. Offers learning and cognition (MS, PhD, Ed S); measurement and statistics (MS, PhD, Ed S); sport psychology (MS, PhD). *Faculty:* 10 full-time (6 women). *Students:* 97 full-time (52 women), 24 part-time (17 women); includes 26 minority (11 Black or African American, non-Hispanic/Latino; 1 American Indian or Alaska Native, non-Hispanic/Latino; 1 Asian, non-Hispanic/Latino; 12 Hispanic/Latino; 1 Two or more races, non-Hispanic/Latino), 47 international. Average age 31. 205 applicants, 35% accepted, 31 enrolled. In 2013, 12 master's, 7 doctorates awarded. *Degree requirements:* For master's, comprehensive exam, thesis optional; for doctorate, comprehensive exam, thesis/dissertation. *Entrance requirements:* For master's and doctorate, GRE General Test, minimum GPA of 3.0. Additional exam requirements/recommendations for international students: Required—TOEFL (minimum score 550 paper-based; 80 iBT). *Application deadline:* For fall admission, 7/1 for domestic and international students; for winter admission, 11/1 for domestic and international students; for spring admission, 3/1 for domestic and international students. Applications are processed on a rolling basis. Application fee: $30. Electronic applications accepted. *Expenses:* Tuition, state resident: part-time $403.51 per credit hour. Tuition, nonresident: part-time $1004.85 per credit hour. *Required fees:* $75.81 per credit hour. One-time fee: $20 part-time. Tuition and fees vary according to course load, campus/location and student level. *Financial support:* Fellowships with full and partial tuition reimbursements, research assistantships with full and partial tuition reimbursements, teaching assistantships with full and partial tuition reimbursements, career-related internships or fieldwork, scholarships/grants, health care benefits, and unspecified assistantships available. Financial award application deadline: 1/15; financial award applicants required to submit FAFSA. *Faculty research:* Meta analysis; item response theory (IRT)/mixture IRT; cognitive behavioral therapy (CBT); modeling, especially large data sets; learning and cognition, skill acquisition, self-perception, processes of motivation. *Unit head:* Dr. Betsy Becker, Chair, 850-644-2371, Fax: 850-644-8776, E-mail: bbecker@fsu.edu. *Application contact:* Peggy Lollie, Program Assistant, 850-644-8786, Fax: 850-644-8776, E-mail: plollie@fsu.edu.
Website: http://coe.fsu.edu/Academic-Programs/Departments/Educational-Psychology-and-Learning-Systems-EPLS/Degree-Programs/Educational-Psychology.

Fordham University, Graduate School of Education, Division of Psychological and Educational Services, New York, NY 10023. Offers counseling and personnel services (MSE, Adv C); counseling psychology (PhD); educational psychology (MSE, PhD); school psychology (PhD); urban and urban bilingual school psychology (Adv C). *Accreditation:* APA (one or more programs are accredited); NCATE. *Degree requirements:* For doctorate, thesis/dissertation. *Entrance requirements:* For doctorate, GRE General Test.

George Mason University, College of Education and Human Development, Program in Educational Psychology, Fairfax, VA 22030. Offers MS. *Faculty:* 7 full-time (6 women), 2 part-time/adjunct (both women). *Students:* 6 full-time (4 women), 31 part-time (29 women); includes 12 minority (5 Black or African American, non-Hispanic/Latino; 4 Asian, non-Hispanic/Latino; 3 Hispanic/Latino). Average age 33. 32 applicants, 72% accepted, 13 enrolled. In 2013, 9 master's awarded. *Entrance requirements:* For master's, GRE, official transcripts; 3 letters of recommendation; expanded goals statement. Additional exam requirements/recommendations for international students: Required—TOEFL (minimum score 575 paper-based; 88 iBT), IELTS (minimum score 6.5), PTE. *Application deadline:* For fall admission, 4/1 for domestic students; for spring admission, 11/1 for domestic students. Application fee: $65 ($80 for international students). *Expenses:* Tuition, state resident: full-time $9350; part-time $390 per credit. Tuition, nonresident: full-time $25,754; part-time $1073 per credit. *Required fees:* $2688; $112 per credit. *Financial support:* In 2013–14, 1 student received support, including 1 research assistantship with full and partial tuition reimbursement available (averaging $4,573 per year); career-related internships or fieldwork, Federal Work-Study, scholarships/grants, unspecified assistantships, and health care benefits (for full-time research or teaching assistantship recipients) also available. Support available to part-time students. Financial award application deadline: 3/1; financial award applicants required to submit FAFSA. *Faculty research:* Learning, cognition, motivation measurement, evaluation assessment, educational policy. *Unit head:* Anastasia Kitsantas, Division Director, 703-993-2688, Fax: 703-993-3678, E-mail: akitsant@gmu.edu. *Application contact:* Kim Howe, Office Manager, 703-993-3679, Fax: 703-993-3678, E-mail: khowe1@gmu.edu.
Website: http://gse.gmu.edu/programs/edpsych/.

Georgia State University, College of Education, Department of Educational Psychology and Special Education, Program in Educational Psychology, Atlanta, GA 30302-3083. Offers MS, PhD. *Accreditation:* NCATE. Part-time and evening/weekend programs available. Postbaccalaureate distance learning degree programs offered. *Students:* Average age 0. *Degree requirements:* For master's, comprehensive exam (for some programs), thesis (for some programs); for doctorate, comprehensive exam, thesis/dissertation. *Entrance requirements:* For master's and doctorate, GRE. Additional exam requirements/recommendations for international students: Required—TOEFL (minimum score 550 paper-based; 79 iBT) or IELTS (minimum score 6.5). *Application deadline:* For fall admission, 1/15 for domestic and international students; for winter admission, 9/1 for domestic and international students. Applications are processed on a rolling basis. Application fee: $50. Electronic applications accepted. *Expenses: Tuition, area resident:* Full-time $4176; part-time $348 per credit hour. Tuition, state resident: full-time $14,544; part-time $1212 per credit hour. Tuition, nonresident: full-time $14,544; part-time $1212 per credit hour. Tuition and fees vary according to course load and program. *Financial support:* In 2013–14, fellowships with full tuition reimbursements (averaging $28,000 per year) were awarded; research assistantships with full tuition reimbursements, teaching assistantships with full tuition reimbursements, institutionally sponsored loans, scholarships/grants, tuition waivers, and unspecified assistantships also available. Financial award applicants required to submit FAFSA. *Faculty research:* Language and literacy, social emotional development, cognitive development, applied behavior analysis, motivation and metacognition. *Unit head:* Dr. Miles Anthony Irving, Program Coordinator, 404-413-3808, E-mail: iam@gsu.edu. *Application contact:* Sandy Vaughn, Senior Administrative Coordinator, 404-413-8318, E-mail: svaughn@gsu.edu.
Website: http://education.gsu.edu/EPSE/epse_programs.htm.

The Graduate Center, City University of New York, Graduate Studies, Program in Educational Psychology, New York, NY 10016-4039. Offers PhD. *Accreditation:* APA. *Degree requirements:* For doctorate, 2 foreign languages, thesis/dissertation. *Entrance requirements:* For doctorate, GRE General Test, interview, minimum GPA of 3.0.

Additional exam requirements/recommendations for international students: Required—TOEFL. Electronic applications accepted.

Harvard University, Harvard Graduate School of Education, Master's Programs in Education, Cambridge, MA 02138. Offers arts in education (Ed M); education policy and management (Ed M); higher education (Ed M); human development and psychology (Ed M); international education policy (Ed M); language and literacy (Ed M); learning and teaching (Ed M); mind, brain, and education (Ed M); prevention science and practice (Ed M); school leadership (Ed M); special studies (Ed M); teacher education (Ed M); technology, innovation, and education (Ed M). Part-time programs available. *Faculty:* 68 full-time (34 women), 77 part-time/adjunct (41 women). *Students:* 557 full-time (410 women), 69 part-time (50 women); includes 179 minority (34 Black or African American, non-Hispanic/Latino; 1 American Indian or Alaska Native, non-Hispanic/Latino; 62 Asian, non-Hispanic/Latino; 52 Hispanic/Latino; 2 Native Hawaiian or other Pacific Islander, non-Hispanic/Latino; 28 Two or more races, non-Hispanic/Latino), 100 international. Average age 28. 1,756 applicants, 47% accepted, 589 enrolled. In 2013, 673 master's awarded. *Entrance requirements:* For master's, GRE General Test, statement of purpose, 3 letters of recommendation, resume, official transcripts. Additional exam requirements/recommendations for international students: Required—TOEFL (minimum score 613 paper-based; 104 iBT), TWE (minimum score 5). *Application deadline:* For fall admission, 1/3 for domestic and international students. Application fee: $85. Electronic applications accepted. *Expenses:* Contact institution. *Financial support:* In 2013–14, 375 students received support, including 12 fellowships with full and partial tuition reimbursements available (averaging $13,925 per year), 2 research assistantships (averaging $2,174 per year); career-related internships or fieldwork, Federal Work-Study, institutionally sponsored loans, scholarships/grants, health care benefits, tuition waivers (full and partial), and unspecified assistantships also available. Support available to part-time students. Financial award application deadline: 2/1; financial award applicants required to submit FAFSA. *Faculty research:* Learning and development, educational leadership and organizations, education policy analysis. *Total annual research expenditures:* $34.3 million. *Unit head:* Jennifer L. Petrallia, Assistant Dean, 617-495-8445. *Application contact:* Information Contact, 617-495-3414, Fax: 617-496-3577, E-mail: gseadmissions@harvard.edu. Website: http://www.gse.harvard.edu/.

Holy Names University, Graduate Division, Department of Education, Oakland, CA 94619-1699. Offers educational therapy (Certificate); mild/moderate disabilities (Ed S); multiple subject teaching (Credential); single subject teaching (Credential); teaching English as a second language (TESL) (M Ed); urban education: educational therapy (M Ed); urban education: K-12 education (M Ed); urban education: special education (M Ed). Part-time programs available. *Faculty:* 4 full-time, 14 part-time/adjunct. *Students:* 25 full-time (19 women), 127 part-time (93 women); includes 74 minority (37 Black or African American, non-Hispanic/Latino; 7 Asian, non-Hispanic/Latino; 28 Hispanic/Latino; 1 Native Hawaiian or other Pacific Islander, non-Hispanic/Latino; 1 Two or more races, non-Hispanic/Latino), 2 international. Average age 35. 72 applicants, 75% accepted, 37 enrolled. In 2013, 15 master's, 22 Certificates awarded. *Degree requirements:* For master's, comprehensive exam, research paper, thesis or project. *Entrance requirements:* For master's, minimum undergraduate GPA of 2.6 overall, 3.0 in major, personal statement, two recommendations, interview. Additional exam requirements/recommendations for international students: Required—TOEFL (minimum score 550 paper-based; 79 iBT). *Application deadline:* For fall admission, 8/1 priority date for domestic students, 7/15 for international students; for spring admission, 12/1 priority date for domestic students, 12/1 for international students; for summer admission, 5/1 priority date for domestic students, 5/1 for international students. Applications are processed on a rolling basis. Application fee: $65. Electronic applications accepted. Application fee is waived when completed online. *Expenses:* Tuition: Part-time $866 per unit. *Financial support:* Career-related internships or fieldwork, Federal Work-Study, scholarships/grants, and unspecified assistantships available. Support available to part-time students. Financial award application deadline: 3/2; financial award applicants required to submit FAFSA. *Faculty research:* Cognitive development, language development, learning handicaps. *Unit head:* Dr. Kimberly Mayfiel, 510-436-1396, Fax: 510-436-1325, E-mail: mayfield@hnu.edu. *Application contact:* Graduate Admission, 800-430-1321, Fax: 510-436-1325, E-mail: graduateadmissions@hnu.edu. Website: http://www.hnu.edu/academics/graduatePrograms/education.html.

Howard University, School of Education, Department of Human Development and Psychoeducational Studies, Program in Educational Psychology, Washington, DC 20059-0002. Offers PhD. Part-time programs available. *Faculty:* 3 full-time (all women), 2 part-time/adjunct (both women). *Students:* 8 full-time (6 women), 8 part-time (5 women); includes 12 minority (all Black or African American, non-Hispanic/Latino), 3 international. Average age 31. 7 applicants, 71% accepted, 1 enrolled. In 2013, 1 doctorate awarded. *Degree requirements:* For doctorate, one foreign language, comprehensive exam, thesis/dissertation, expository writing exam, internship. *Entrance requirements:* For doctorate, GRE General Test, minimum GPA of 3.4. Additional exam requirements/recommendations for international students: Required—TOEFL (minimum score 550 paper-based; 79 iBT). *Application deadline:* For fall admission, 2/15 priority date for domestic students; for spring admission, 11/1 for domestic students. Applications are processed on a rolling basis. Application fee: $45. Electronic applications accepted. *Financial support:* Fellowships with full and partial tuition reimbursements, career-related internships or fieldwork, Federal Work-Study, institutionally sponsored loans, scholarships/grants, and tuition waivers (full and partial) available. Financial award application deadline: 3/15; financial award applicants required to submit FAFSA. *Unit head:* Dr. Kyndra Middleton, Assistant Professor/Coordinator, 202-806-6515, Fax: 202-806-5205, E-mail: kyndra.middleton@howard.edu. *Application contact:* Georgina Jarrett, Administration Assistant, Department of Human Development and Psychoeducational Studies, 202-806-7351, Fax: 202-806-5205, E-mail: gjarrett@howard.edu.

Illinois State University, Graduate School, College of Arts and Sciences, Department of Psychology, Normal, IL 61790-2200. Offers psychology (MA, MS), including clinical psychology, counseling psychology, developmental psychology, educational psychology, experimental psychology, measurement-evaluation, organizational-industrial psychology; school psychology (PhD, SSP). *Accreditation:* APA. *Degree requirements:* For master's, thesis or alternative; for doctorate, variable foreign language requirement, thesis/dissertation, 2 terms of residency, internship, practicum. *Entrance requirements:* For master's, GRE General Test, GRE Subject Test, minimum GPA of 3.0 in last 60 hours of course work; for doctorate, GRE General Test. *Faculty research:* Comprehensive evaluation system for the central region professional development grant, Illinois school psychology internship consortium, for children's sake.

Indiana University Bloomington, School of Education, Department of Counseling and Educational Psychology, Bloomington, IN 47405-1006. Offers counseling (MS, PhD, Ed S); counselor education (MS, Ed S); educational psychology (MS, PhD); inquiry methodology (PhD); learning and developmental sciences (MS, PhD); school psychology (PhD, Ed S). *Accreditation:* ACA (one or more programs are accredited); APA (one or more programs are accredited); NCATE. Terminal master's awarded for partial completion of doctoral program. *Degree requirements:* For master's, thesis optional; for doctorate, thesis/dissertation; for Ed S, comprehensive exam or project. *Entrance requirements:* For master's, doctorate, and Ed S, GRE General Test. Additional exam requirements/recommendations for international students: Required—TOEFL. Electronic applications accepted. *Faculty research:* Counseling psychology, inquiry methodology, school psychology, learning sciences, human development, educational psychology.

Indiana University of Pennsylvania, School of Graduate Studies and Research, College of Education and Educational Technology, Department of Educational and School Psychology, Program in Educational Psychology, Indiana, PA 15705-1087. Offers M Ed, Certificate. *Accreditation:* NCATE. Part-time programs available. *Faculty:* 8 full-time (2 women). *Students:* 14 full-time (11 women). Average age 24. 25 applicants, 56% accepted, 13 enrolled. In 2013, 18 master's awarded. *Degree requirements:* For master's, thesis optional. *Entrance requirements:* For master's, GRE General Test, 2 letters of recommendation. Additional exam requirements/recommendations for international students: Required—TOEFL (minimum score 540 paper-based; 76 iBT). *Application deadline:* For fall admission, 2/1 priority date for domestic students. Application fee: $50. Electronic applications accepted. *Expenses:* Tuition, state resident: full-time $3978; part-time $442 per credit. Tuition, nonresident: full-time $5967; part-time $663 per credit. *Required fees:* $2080; $115.55 per credit. $93 per semester. Tuition and fees vary according to degree level and program. *Financial support:* In 2013–14, 12 research assistantships with full and partial tuition reimbursements (averaging $4,760 per year) were awarded; fellowships with full tuition reimbursements, teaching assistantships with partial tuition reimbursements, career-related internships or fieldwork, Federal Work-Study, scholarships/grants, and unspecified assistantships also available. Support available to part-time students. Financial award application deadline: 4/15; financial award applicants required to submit FAFSA. *Unit head:* Dr. Mark R. McGowan, Graduate Coordinator, 724-357-2174, E-mail: mmcgowan@iup.edu. Website: http://www.iup.edu/upper.aspx?id-49407.

Instituto Tecnologico de Santo Domingo, Graduate School, Area of Humanities and Social Sciences, Santo Domingo, Dominican Republic. Offers accounting (Certificate); adult education (Certificate); applied linguistics (MA); economics (MA); education (M Ed); educational psychology (MA, Certificate); gender and development (MA, Certificate); humanistic studies (MA); international marketing management (Certificate); international relations in the Caribbean basin (Certificate); intervention systems in family therapy (MA); linguistic and literary communication (Certificate); pedagogical support (MA); social science education (M Ed); sustainable human development (MA); terminal illness and death psychology (Certificate); youth and adult education (M Ed).

John Carroll University, Graduate School, Department of Education and Allied Studies, Program in Educational and School Psychology, University Heights, OH 44118-4581. Offers M Ed, MA. *Accreditation:* NCATE. Part-time and evening/weekend programs available. *Degree requirements:* For master's, comprehensive exam, research essay or thesis (MA only). *Entrance requirements:* For master's, GRE General Test or MAT, minimum GPA of 2.75, Educ. or Psych. degree, questionnaire, interview. Electronic applications accepted.

Kent State University, Graduate School of Education, Health, and Human Services, School of Lifespan Development and Educational Sciences, Program in Educational Psychology, Kent, OH 44242-0001. Offers M Ed, MA, PhD. *Faculty:* 3 full-time (1 woman), 1 (woman) part-time/adjunct. *Students:* 34 full-time (18 women), 15 part-time (8 women); includes 4 minority (2 American Indian or Alaska Native, non-Hispanic/Latino; 1 Asian, non-Hispanic/Latino; 1 Hispanic/Latino), 6 international. 23 applicants, 35% accepted. In 2013, 5 master's, 5 doctorates awarded. *Degree requirements:* For master's, thesis optional; for doctorate, comprehensive exam, thesis/dissertation. *Entrance requirements:* For master's, 2 letters of reference, minimum GPA of 3.5, goals statement; for doctorate, GRE, 2 letters of reference, minimum undergraduate GPA of 3.0, goals statement, resume, interview. Additional exam requirements/recommendations for international students: Required—TOEFL (minimum score 550 paper-based; 80 iBT). *Application deadline:* Applications are processed on a rolling basis. Application fee: $30 ($60 for international students). Electronic applications accepted. *Financial support:* In 2013–14, 2 research assistantships (averaging $12,000 per year), 3 teaching assistantships (averaging $12,000 per year) were awarded; Federal Work-Study, scholarships/grants, health care benefits, and unspecified assistantships also available. *Unit head:* Dr. Drew Tiene, Coordinator, 330-672-0607, E-mail: dtiene@kent.edu. *Application contact:* Nancy Miller, Academic Program Director, Office of Graduate Student Services, 330-672-2576, Fax: 330-672-9162, E-mail: ogs@kent.edu. Website: http://www.kent.edu/ehhs/edpf/.

La Sierra University, School of Education, Department of School Psychology and Counseling, Riverside, CA 92515. Offers counseling (MA); educational psychology (Ed S); school psychology (Ed S). Part-time and evening/weekend programs available. *Degree requirements:* For master's, thesis optional; for Ed S, practicum (educational psychology). *Entrance requirements:* For master's, California Basic Educational Skills Test, NTE, minimum GPA of 3.0; for Ed S, minimum GPA of 3.3. *Faculty research:* Equivalent score scales, self perception.

Long Island University–Hudson at Westchester, Programs in Education-School Counselor and School Psychology, Purchase, NY 10577. Offers school counselor (MS Ed); school psychologist (MS Ed). Part-time and evening/weekend programs available.

Loyola University Chicago, School of Education, Program in Educational Psychology, Chicago, IL 60660. Offers M Ed. Part-time and evening/weekend programs available. *Faculty:* 8 full-time (5 women), 5 part-time/adjunct (1 woman). *Students:* 25. Average age 28. 83 applicants, 70% accepted, 24 enrolled. In 2013, 22 master's awarded. Terminal master's awarded for partial completion of doctoral program. *Degree requirements:* For master's, comprehensive exam, thesis (for some programs). *Entrance requirements:* For master's, GRE General Test, letters of recommendation, minimum GPA of 3.0. Additional exam requirements/recommendations for international students: Required—TOEFL (minimum score 550 paper-based; 79 iBT). *Application deadline:* For fall admission, 12/1 for domestic and international students. Application fee: $50. Electronic applications accepted. Application fee is waived when completed online. *Expenses:* Tuition: Full-time $16,740; part-time $930 per credit. *Required fees:* $135 per semester. *Financial support:* Institutionally sponsored loans and scholarships/grants available. Support available to part-time students. Financial award application deadline: 2/1; financial award applicants required to submit FAFSA. *Faculty research:* Learning theory and teaching; cognitive, social, and cultural constructivism; school reform; workplace training and adult education. *Unit head:* Dr. Lynne Golomb, Director, 312-915-6218, E-mail: lgolomb@luc.edu. *Application contact:* Marie Rosin-Dittmar, Information Contact, 312-915-6800, E-mail: schleduc@luc.edu.

McGill University, Faculty of Graduate and Postdoctoral Studies, Faculty of Education, Department of Educational and Counseling Psychology, Montréal, QC H3A 2T5, Canada. Offers counseling psychology (MA, PhD); educational psychology (M Ed, MA, PhD); school/applied child psychology and applied developmental psychology (M Ed, MA, PhD, Diploma), including school psychology. *Accreditation:* APA.

Educational Psychology

Memorial University of Newfoundland, School of Graduate Studies, Faculty of Education, St. John's, NL A1C 5S7, Canada. Offers counseling psychology (M Ed); curriculum, teaching, and learning studies (M Ed); education (PhD); educational leadership studies (M Ed); information technology (M Ed); post-secondary studies (M Ed, Diploma), including health professional education (Diploma). Part-time programs available. *Degree requirements:* For master's, thesis optional, internship, paper folio, project; for doctorate, comprehensive exam, thesis/dissertation, thesis seminar, oral defense of thesis. *Entrance requirements:* For master's, undergraduate degree with at least 2nd class standing, 1-2 years work experience; for doctorate, minimum A average in graduate course work, MA in education, 2 years professional experience; for Diploma, 2nd class degree, 2 years of work experience with adult learners, appropriate academic qualifications and work experience in a health-related field. Electronic applications accepted. *Faculty research:* Critical thinking, literacy, cognitive studies and counseling, educational change, technology in instruction.

Miami University, College of Education, Health and Society, Department of Educational Psychology, Oxford, OH 45056. Offers educational psychology (M Ed); instructional design and technology (M Ed, MA); school psychology (MS, Ed S); special education (M Ed, MA). *Accreditation:* NCATE. *Students:* 45 full-time (35 women), 41 part-time (31 women); includes 8 minority (1 Black or African American, non-Hispanic/Latino; 1 American Indian or Alaska Native, non-Hispanic/Latino; 5 Asian, non-Hispanic/Latino; 1 Two or more races, non-Hispanic/Latino), 18 international. Average age 27. In 2013, 79 master's awarded. *Entrance requirements:* For degree, GRE General Test or MAT. Additional exam requirements/recommendations for international students: Recommended—TOEFL (minimum score 80 iBT), IELTS (minimum score 6.5), TSE (minimum score 54). Application fee: $50. Electronic applications accepted. *Expenses:* Tuition, state resident: full-time $12,634; part-time $526 per credit hour. Tuition, nonresident: full-time $27,892; part-time $1162 per credit hour. Part-time tuition and fees vary according to course load, campus/location and program. *Financial support:* Fellowships with full tuition reimbursements, research assistantships with full tuition reimbursements, teaching assistantships with full tuition reimbursements, career-related internships or fieldwork, Federal Work-Study, health care benefits, and unspecified assistantships available. Financial award application deadline: 2/15; financial award applicants required to submit FAFSA. *Unit head:* Dr. Susan Mosley-Howard, Chair, 513-529-6621, E-mail: edp@miamioh.edu. *Application contact:* 513-529-6621, E-mail: edp@miamioh.edu.
Website: http://www.MiamiOH.edu/EDP.

Michigan School of Professional Psychology, MA and Psy D Programs in Clinical Psychology, Farmington Hills, MI 48334. Offers MA, Psy D. Part-time programs available. *Faculty:* 9 full-time (4 women), 17 part-time/adjunct (12 women). *Students:* 86 full-time, 75 part-time; includes 34 minority (23 Black or African American, non-Hispanic/Latino; 5 Asian, non-Hispanic/Latino; 3 Hispanic/Latino; 3 Two or more races, non-Hispanic/Latino). 160 applicants, 56% accepted, 85 enrolled. In 2013, 35 master's, 16 doctorates awarded. *Degree requirements:* For master's, practicum; for doctorate, comprehensive exam, thesis/dissertation, internship, practicum. *Entrance requirements:* For master's, undergraduate degree from accredited institution with minimum GPA of 2.5; major in psychology, social work, or counseling (if major is not in one of these areas, 3 prerequisite courses are required: Introduction to Psychology, Abnormal Psychology, Developmental Psychology); for doctorate, GRE General Test, undergraduate degree from accredited institution with minimum GPA of 2.5; graduate degree in psychology, social work, or counseling from accredited institution with minimum GPA of 3.25; graduate-level practicum. Additional exam requirements/recommendations for international students: Required—TOEFL (minimum score 550 paper-based; 79 iBT). *Application deadline:* Applications are processed on a rolling basis. Application fee: $75. Electronic applications accepted. *Expenses: Tuition:* Full-time $28,500. Tuition and fees vary according to course load, degree level and program. *Financial support:* In 2013–14, 6 students received support, including 3 research assistantships (averaging $1,200 per year), 4 teaching assistantships (averaging $1,200 per year); career-related internships or fieldwork, institutionally sponsored loans, scholarships/grants, and unspecified assistantships also available. Support available to part-time students. Financial award application deadline: 6/30; financial award applicants required to submit FAFSA. *Faculty research:* Qualitative research, existential, phenomenological psychology, multicultural, humanistic. *Unit head:* Dr. Lee Bach, Program Director, 248-476-1122, Fax: 248-476-1125. *Application contact:* Amanda Ming, Admissions and Recruitment Coordinator, 248-476-1122 Ext. 117, Fax: 248-476-1125, E-mail: aming@mispp.edu.
Website: http://www.mispp.edu.

Michigan State University, The Graduate School, College of Education, Department of Counseling, Educational Psychology and Special Education, East Lansing, MI 48824. Offers counseling (MA); educational psychology and educational technology (PhD); educational technology (MA); measurement and quantitative methods (PhD); rehabilitation counseling (MA); rehabilitation counselor education (PhD); school psychology (MA, PhD, Ed S); special education (MA, PhD). *Accreditation:* APA (one or more programs are accredited); CORE (one or more programs are accredited). Part-time programs available. *Entrance requirements:* Additional exam requirements/recommendations for international students: Required—TOEFL. Electronic applications accepted.

Middle Tennessee State University, College of Graduate Studies, College of Behavioral and Health Sciences, Department of Psychology, Program in Psychology, Murfreesboro, TN 37132. Offers curriculum and instruction/school psychology (Ed S); psychology (MA). Part-time and evening/weekend programs available. Postbaccalaureate distance learning degree programs offered. *Faculty:* 33 full-time (12 women), 1 (woman) part-time/adjunct. *Students:* 62 full-time (48 women), 54 part-time (44 women); includes 17 minority (9 Black or African American, non-Hispanic/Latino; 1 American Indian or Alaska Native, non-Hispanic/Latino; 4 Asian, non-Hispanic/Latino; 1 Hispanic/Latino; 2 Two or more races, non-Hispanic/Latino). 240 applicants, 79% accepted. In 2013, 33 master's awarded. *Degree requirements:* For master's, comprehensive exam, thesis. *Entrance requirements:* For master's, GRE. Additional exam requirements/recommendations for international students: Required—TOEFL (minimum score 525 paper-based; 71 iBT) or IELTS (minimum score 6). *Application deadline:* For fall admission, 6/1 for domestic and international students. Applications are processed on a rolling basis. Application fee: $25 ($30 for international students). Electronic applications accepted. *Financial support:* In 2013–14, 16 students received support. Tuition waivers available. Support available to part-time students. Financial award application deadline: 5/1. *Faculty research:* Health psychology, industrial/organizational psychology, experimental psychology. *Unit head:* Dr. Greg Schmidt, Chair, 615-898-2706, Fax: 615-898-5027, E-mail: greg.schmidt@mtsu.edu. *Application contact:* Dr. Michael D. Allen, Vice Provost for Research and Dean, 615-898-2840, Fax: 615-904-8020, E-mail: michael.allen@mtsu.edu.

Mississippi State University, College of Education, Department of Counseling and Educational Psychology, Mississippi State, MS 39762. Offers college/postsecondary student counseling and personnel services (PhD); counselor education (MS), including clinical mental health, college counseling, rehabilitation, school counseling, student affairs in higher education; counselor education/student counseling and guidance services (PhD); education (Ed S), including counselor education, school psychology (PhD, Ed S); educational psychology (MS, PhD), including general education psychology (MS), general educational psychology (PhD), psychometry (MS), school psychology (PhD, Ed S). *Accreditation:* ACA (one or more programs are accredited); APA; CORE (one or more programs are accredited); NCATE. Part-time programs available. Postbaccalaureate distance learning degree programs offered (minimal on-campus study). *Faculty:* 17 full-time (13 women). *Students:* 137 full-time (104 women), 81 part-time (73 women); includes 57 minority (47 Black or African American, non-Hispanic/Latino; 4 American Indian or Alaska Native, non-Hispanic/Latino; 3 Asian, non-Hispanic/Latino; 1 Hispanic/Latino; 2 Two or more races, non-Hispanic/Latino), 5 international. Average age 32. 287 applicants, 36% accepted, 72 enrolled. In 2013, 70 master's, 3 doctorates, 4 other advanced degrees awarded. Terminal master's awarded for partial completion of doctoral program. *Degree requirements:* For master's, comprehensive exam, thesis optional; for doctorate, thesis/dissertation, comprehensive oral and written exam. *Entrance requirements:* For master's, GRE (taken within the last five years), BS with minimum GPA of 2.75 on last 60 hours; for doctorate, GRE, MS from CACREP- or CORE-accredited program in counseling; for Ed S, GRE, MS in counseling or related field, minimum GPA of 3.3 on all graduate work. Additional exam requirements/recommendations for international students: Required—TOEFL (minimum score 550 paper-based; 79 iBT); Recommended—IELTS (minimum score 6.5). *Application deadline:* For fall admission, 2/1 priority date for domestic and international students. Applications are processed on a rolling basis. Application fee: $60. Electronic applications accepted. *Financial support:* In 2013–14, 1 research assistantship (averaging $10,800 per year), 11 teaching assistantships with full tuition reimbursements (averaging $8,401 per year) were awarded; career-related internships or fieldwork, Federal Work-Study, institutionally sponsored loans, and unspecified assistantships also available. Financial award application deadline: 2/1; financial award applicants required to submit FAFSA. *Faculty research:* HIV/AIDS in college population, substance abuse in youth and college students, ADHD and conduct disorders in youth, assessment and identification of early childhood disabilities, assessment and vocational transition of the disabled. *Unit head:* Dr. Daniel Wong, Professor/Head, 662-325-7928, Fax: 662-325-3263, E-mail: dwong@colled.msstate.edu. *Application contact:* Dr. Charles Palmer, Graduate Coordinator, Counselor Education, 662-325-7917, Fax: 662-325-3263, E-mail: cpalmer@colled.msstate.edu.
Website: http://www.cep.msstate.edu/.

Mount Saint Vincent University, Graduate Programs, Faculty of Education, Program in Educational Psychology, Halifax, NS B3M 2J6, Canada. Offers education of the blind or visually impaired (M Ed, MA Ed); education of the deaf or hard of hearing (M Ed, MA Ed); educational psychology (MA-R); human relations (M Ed, MA Ed). Part-time and evening/weekend programs available. Postbaccalaureate distance learning degree programs offered (minimal on-campus study). *Degree requirements:* For master's, thesis (for some programs). *Entrance requirements:* For master's, bachelor's degree in related field, 1 year of teaching experience. Electronic applications accepted. *Faculty research:* Personality measurement, values reasoning, aggression and sexuality, power and control, quantitative and qualitative research methodologies.

National Louis University, National College of Education, Chicago, IL 60603. Offers administration and supervision (M Ed, Ed D, CAS, Ed S); curriculum and instruction (M Ed, MS Ed, CAS); early childhood administration (M Ed, CAS); early childhood education (M Ed, MAT, MS Ed, CAS); education (Ed D); educational psychology/human learning and development (M Ed, MS Ed, CAS, Ed S); elementary education (MAT); interdisciplinary curriculum and instruction (M Ed); mathematics education (M Ed, MS Ed, CAS); reading and language (M Ed, MS Ed, CAS); school psychology (M Ed, Ed S); science education (M Ed, MS Ed, CAS); secondary education (MAT); special education (M Ed, MAT, CAS); technology in education (M Ed, CAS). *Accreditation:* NCATE. Part-time and evening/weekend programs available. *Degree requirements:* For doctorate, comprehensive exam, thesis/dissertation. *Entrance requirements:* For master's, MAT or GRE, minimum GPA of 3.0; for doctorate, GRE General Test, minimum GPA of 3.25, interview, resume, writing sample, 4 recommendations. Additional exam requirements/recommendations for international students: Required—TOEFL (minimum score 550 paper-based; 79 iBT).

New Jersey City University, Graduate Studies and Continuing Education, William J. Maxwell College of Arts and Sciences, Program in Educational Psychology, Jersey City, NJ 07305-1597. Offers educational psychology (MA); school psychology (PD). Part-time and evening/weekend programs available. *Faculty:* 1 full-time (0 women), 3 part-time/adjunct (0 women). *Students:* 7 full-time (3 women), 8 part-time (all women); includes 6 minority (1 Asian, non-Hispanic/Latino; 5 Hispanic/Latino). Average age 28. In 2013, 12 master's, 5 other advanced degrees awarded. *Degree requirements:* For PD, summer internship or externship. *Entrance requirements:* For degree, GRE General Test. Additional exam requirements/recommendations for international students: Required—TOEFL (minimum score 61 iBT). *Application deadline:* For fall admission, 8/1 priority date for domestic students; for spring admission, 12/1 for domestic students. Applications are processed on a rolling basis. Application fee: $0. *Expenses: Tuition, area resident:* Part-time $527.90 per credit. Tuition, nonresident: part-time $947.75 per credit. *Financial support:* Unspecified assistantships available. *Unit head:* Dr. James Lennon, Director, 201-200-3309, E-mail: jlennon@njcu.edu. *Application contact:* Dr. William Bajor, Dean of Graduate Studies, 201-200-3409, Fax: 201-200-3411, E-mail: wbajor@njcu.edu.

New York University, Steinhardt School of Culture, Education, and Human Development, Department of Applied Psychology, Programs in Educational and Developmental Psychology, New York, NY 10003. Offers human development and social intervention (MA); psychological development (PhD); psychology and social intervention (PhD). *Accreditation:* APA (one or more programs are accredited). Part-time programs available. *Faculty:* 24 full-time (16 women). *Students:* 60 full-time (52 women), 8 part-time (7 women); includes 26 minority (6 Black or African American, non-Hispanic/Latino; 6 Asian, non-Hispanic/Latino; 13 Hispanic/Latino; 1 Two or more races, non-Hispanic/Latino), 17 international. Average age 27. 174 applicants, 48% accepted, 26 enrolled. In 2013, 27 master's, 4 doctorates awarded. *Degree requirements:* For master's, thesis (for some programs); for doctorate, thesis/dissertation. *Entrance requirements:* For doctorate, GRE General Test, interview. Additional exam requirements/recommendations for international students: Required—TOEFL. *Application deadline:* For fall admission, 12/1 priority date for domestic and international students. Applications are processed on a rolling basis. Application fee: $75. Electronic applications accepted. *Expenses: Tuition:* Full-time $35,856; part-time $1494 per unit. *Required fees:* $1408; $64 per unit. $473 per term. Tuition and fees vary according to course load and program. *Financial support:* Teaching assistantships with partial tuition reimbursements, career-related internships or fieldwork, Federal Work-Study, institutionally sponsored loans, and tuition waivers (partial) available. Support available to part-time students. Financial award application deadline: 2/1; financial award applicants required to submit FAFSA. *Faculty research:* Schools and communities, self-regulation and academic achievement, intervention and social change, trauma and resilience, cognition. *Unit head:* Prof. Niobe Way, Director, 212-998-5563, Fax: 212-995-4358, E-mail: niobe.way@nyu.edu. *Application contact:* 212-998-5030, Fax: 212-995-4328, E-mail: steinhardt.gradadmissions@nyu.edu.
Website: http://steinhardt.nyu.edu/appsych.

Northern Arizona University, Graduate College, College of Education, Department of Educational Psychology, Flagstaff, AZ 86011. Offers counseling (MA); educational psychology (PhD), including counseling psychology, school psychology; human relations (M Ed); school counseling (M Ed); school psychology (Ed S); student affairs (M Ed). Part-time programs available. Postbaccalaureate distance learning degree programs offered. *Faculty:* 22 full-time (9 women), 3 part-time/adjunct (1 woman). *Students:* 232 full-time (175 women), 237 part-time (187 women); includes 155 minority (21 Black or African American, non-Hispanic/Latino; 27 American Indian or Alaska Native, non-Hispanic/Latino; 3 Asian, non-Hispanic/Latino; 91 Hispanic/Latino; 1 Native Hawaiian or other Pacific Islander, non-Hispanic/Latino; 12 Two or more races, non-Hispanic/Latino), 4 international. Average age 34. 234 applicants, 71% accepted, 101 enrolled. In 2013, 232 master's, 6 doctorates awarded. Terminal master's awarded for partial completion of doctoral program. *Degree requirements:* For master's, internship (for some programs); for doctorate, comprehensive exam, thesis/dissertation, internship. *Entrance requirements:* Additional exam requirements/recommendations for international students: Required—TOEFL (minimum score 550 paper-based; 80 iBT), IELTS (minimum score 7). *Application deadline:* For fall admission, 9/15 for domestic students; for spring admission, 1/15 for domestic students. Applications are processed on a rolling basis. Application fee: $65. Electronic applications accepted. *Financial support:* In 2013–14, 20 students received support, including 11 teaching assistantships with full tuition reimbursements available (averaging $9,660 per year); research assistantships, career-related internships or fieldwork, Federal Work-Study, scholarships/grants, health care benefits, tuition waivers (full and partial), and unspecified assistantships also available. Financial award applicants required to submit FAFSA. *Unit head:* Dr. Robert Horn, Chair, 928-523-0362, Fax: 928-523-9284, E-mail: robert.horn@nau.edu. *Application contact:* Hope DeMello, Administrative Assistant, 928-523-7103, Fax: 928-523-9284, E-mail: eps@nau.edu.
Website: http://nau.edu/coe/ed-psych/.

Northern Illinois University, Graduate School, College of Education, Department of Leadership, Educational Psychology and Foundations, De Kalb, IL 60115-2854. Offers educational administration (MS Ed, Ed D, Ed S); educational psychology (MS Ed, Ed D); foundations of education (MS Ed); school business management (MS Ed). Part-time and evening/weekend programs available. Postbaccalaureate distance learning degree programs offered (minimal on-campus study). *Faculty:* 23 full-time (12 women). *Students:* 7 full-time (4 women), 221 part-time (125 women); includes 36 minority (17 Black or African American, non-Hispanic/Latino; 18 Hispanic/Latino; 1 Two or more races, non-Hispanic/Latino), 2 international. Average age 40. 52 applicants, 71% accepted, 15 enrolled. In 2013, 76 master's, 14 doctorates, 18 other advanced degrees awarded. *Degree requirements:* For master's, comprehensive exam, thesis optional; for doctorate, thesis/dissertation, candidacy exam, dissertation defense. *Entrance requirements:* For master's, minimum undergraduate GPA of 2.75; for doctorate, GRE General Test, minimum undergraduate GPA of 2.75, 3.2 graduate; for Ed S, GRE General Test, minimum GPA of 2.75 (undergraduate), 3.2 (graduate). Additional exam requirements/recommendations for international students: Required—TOEFL (minimum score 550 paper-based). *Application deadline:* For fall admission, 6/1 for domestic students, 5/1 for international students; for spring admission, 11/1 for domestic students, 10/1 for international students. Applications are processed on a rolling basis. Application fee: $40. Electronic applications accepted. *Financial support:* In 2013–14, 2 research assistantships with full tuition reimbursements were awarded; fellowships with full tuition reimbursements, teaching assistantships with full tuition reimbursements, career-related internships or fieldwork, Federal Work-Study, scholarships/grants, tuition waivers (full), and staff assistantships also available. Support available to part-time students. Financial award applicants required to submit FAFSA. *Faculty research:* Interpersonal forgiveness, learner-centered education, psychedelic studies, senior theory, professional growth. *Unit head:* Dr. Patrick A. Roberts, Acting Chair, 815-753-4404, E-mail: lepf@niu.edu. *Application contact:* Graduate School Office, 815-753-0395, E-mail: gradsch@niu.edu.
Website: http://cedu.niu.edu/LEPF/.

Oklahoma State University, College of Education, School of Applied Health and Educational Psychology, Stillwater, OK 74078. Offers applied behavioral studies (Ed D); applied health and educational psychology (MS, PhD, Ed S). *Accreditation:* APA (one or more programs are accredited). Part-time programs available. *Faculty:* 40 full-time (21 women), 17 part-time/adjunct (10 women). *Students:* 172 full-time (121 women), 187 part-time (123 women); includes 88 minority (19 Black or African American, non-Hispanic/Latino; 13 American Indian or Alaska Native, non-Hispanic/Latino; 6 Asian, non-Hispanic/Latino; 25 Hispanic/Latino; 25 Two or more races, non-Hispanic/Latino), 10 international. Average age 32. 303 applicants, 31% accepted, 75 enrolled. In 2013, 56 master's, 31 doctorates awarded. *Degree requirements:* For master's, thesis (for some programs); for doctorate, comprehensive exam, thesis/dissertation. *Entrance requirements:* For master's and doctorate, GRE or GMAT. Additional exam requirements/recommendations for international students: Required—TOEFL (minimum score 550 paper-based; 79 iBT). *Application deadline:* For fall admission, 3/1 priority date for international students; for spring admission, 8/1 priority date for international students. Applications are processed on a rolling basis. Application fee: $40 ($75 for international students). Electronic applications accepted. *Expenses:* Tuition, state resident: full-time $4272; part-time $178 per credit hour. Tuition, nonresident: full-time $17,472; part-time $709 per credit hour. *Required fees:* $2413.20; $100.55 per credit hour. One-time fee: $50 full-time. Part-time tuition and fees vary according to course load and campus/location. *Financial support:* In 2013–14, 26 research assistantships (averaging $9,164 per year), 58 teaching assistantships (averaging $8,917 per year) were awarded; career-related internships or fieldwork, Federal Work-Study, scholarships/grants, health care benefits, tuition waivers (partial), and unspecified assistantships also available. Support available to part-time students. Financial award application deadline: 3/1; financial award applicants required to submit FAFSA. *Unit head:* Dr. John Romans, Interim Head, 405-744-6040, Fax: 405-744-6779, E-mail: steve.harrist@okstate.edu.
Website: http://education.okstate.edu/sahep.

Penn State University Park, Graduate School, College of Education, Department of Educational Psychology, Counseling and Special Education, State College, PA 16802. Offers counselor education (M Ed, D Ed, PhD, Certificate); educational psychology (MS, PhD, Certificate); school psychology (M Ed, MS, PhD, Certificate); special education (M Ed, MS, PhD, Certificate). *Unit head:* Dr. David H. Monk, Dean, 814-865-2523, Fax: 814-865-0555, E-mail: dhm6@psu.edu. *Application contact:* Cynthia E. Nicosia, Director, Graduate Enrollment Services, 814-865-1834, Fax: 814-863-4627, E-mail: cey1@psu.edu.
Website: http://www.ed.psu.edu/educ/epcse.

Pontifical Catholic University of Puerto Rico, College of Education, Program in Educational Psychology, Ponce, PR 00717-0777. Offers M Ed. *Degree requirements:* For master's, comprehensive exam, thesis (for some programs). *Entrance requirements:* For master's, GRE, 2 letters of recommendation, interview, minimum GPA of 2.75.

Purdue University, Graduate School, College of Education, Department of Educational Studies, West Lafayette, IN 47907. Offers administration (MS Ed, PhD, Ed S); counseling and development (MS Ed, PhD); education of the gifted (MS Ed); educational psychology (MS Ed, PhD); foundations of education (MS Ed, PhD); higher education administration (MS Ed, PhD); special education (MS Ed, PhD). *Accreditation:* ACA (one or more programs are accredited); NCATE (one or more programs are accredited). Part-time and evening/weekend programs available. *Faculty:* 21 full-time (17 women), 7 part-time/adjunct (4 women). *Students:* 102 full-time (73 women), 45 part-time (27 women); includes 23 minority (10 Black or African American, non-Hispanic/Latino; 5 Asian, non-Hispanic/Latino; 5 Hispanic/Latino; 3 Two or more races, non-Hispanic/Latino), 32 international. Average age 35. 165 applicants, 40% accepted, 33 enrolled. In 2013, 26 master's, 21 doctorates awarded. *Degree requirements:* For master's, thesis optional; for doctorate, thesis/dissertation, oral and written exams; for Ed S, oral presentation, project. *Entrance requirements:* For master's, GRE General Test (except for special education if undergraduate GPA is higher than a 3.0), minimum undergraduate GPA of 3.0; for doctorate and Ed S, GRE General Test (minimum combined score of 1000, 300 for new scoring), minimum undergraduate GPA of 3.0. Additional exam requirements/recommendations for international students: Required—TOEFL (minimum score 550 paper-based; 77 iBT), TWE (minimum score 5). *Application deadline:* Applications are processed on a rolling basis. Application fee: $60 ($75 for international students). Electronic applications accepted. *Financial support:* Fellowships with full tuition reimbursements, research assistantships with full tuition reimbursements, teaching assistantships with full tuition reimbursements, career-related internships or fieldwork, and tuition waivers (full) available. Support available to part-time students. Financial award application deadline: 3/1; financial award applicants required to submit FAFSA. *Faculty research:* Motivation, learning disabilities, school learning, group processes, cognitive development. *Unit head:* Dr. Ala Samarapungavan, Head, 765-494-9170, Fax: 765-496-1228, E-mail: ala@purdue.edu. *Application contact:* Cindy Blankenship, Graduate Contact, 765-494-2345, Fax: 765-494-5832, E-mail: prater0@purdue.edu.
Website: http://www.edst.purdue.edu/.

Regent University, Graduate School, School of Education, Virginia Beach, VA 23464-9800. Offers adult education (Ed D, PhD); advanced educational leadership (Ed D, PhD); career switcher with licensure (M Ed), including alternative licensure; character education (Ed D, PhD); Christian education leadership (Ed D); Christian school administration (M Ed); curriculum and instruction (M Ed); distance education (Ed D, PhD); educational leadership (M Ed); educational leadership - special education (Ed S); educational psychology (Ed D); elementary education (M Ed); higher education (Ed D, PhD); higher education leadership and management (Ed D); K-12 school leadership (Ed D, PhD); leadership in mathematics education (M Ed); reading specialist (M Ed); special education (M Ed, Ed D, PhD); student affairs (M Ed); TESOL (M Ed), including adult education, PreK-12. *Accreditation:* Teacher Education Accreditation Council. Part-time and evening/weekend programs available. Postbaccalaureate distance learning degree programs offered (minimal on-campus study). *Faculty:* 25 full-time (12 women), 50 part-time/adjunct (31 women). *Students:* 100 full-time (78 women), 754 part-time (614 women); includes 225 minority (191 Black or African American, non-Hispanic/Latino; 1 American Indian or Alaska Native, non-Hispanic/Latino; 7 Asian, non-Hispanic/Latino; 26 Hispanic/Latino), 16 international. Average age 39. 487 applicants, 63% accepted, 233 enrolled. In 2013, 202 master's, 19 doctorates awarded. *Degree requirements:* For master's, thesis or alternative; for doctorate, comprehensive exam, thesis/dissertation. *Entrance requirements:* For master's, MAT, minimum undergraduate GPA of 2.75, writing sample, resume, recommendations, interview; for doctorate, GRE, writing sample, 3 years of relevant professional experience, master's-level paper, copies of published work, resume, transcripts, interview, recommendations. Additional exam requirements/recommendations for international students: Required—TOEFL (minimum score 577 paper-based). *Application deadline:* For fall admission, 4/1 priority date for domestic students; for spring admission, 10/15 priority date for domestic students. Applications are processed on a rolling basis. Application fee: $50. Electronic applications accepted. Tuition and fees vary according to course load and degree level. *Financial support:* Fellowships, career-related internships or fieldwork, scholarships/grants, tuition waivers (full and partial), and unspecified assistantships available. Support available to part-time students. Financial award application deadline: 4/1; financial award applicants required to submit FAFSA. *Faculty research:* Character development and discipline for children, education leadership development, diversity in schools, classroom management, technology in education settings. *Unit head:* Dr. Alan Arroyo, Dean, 757-352-4261, Fax: 757-352-4318, E-mail: alanarr@regent.edu. *Application contact:* Matthew Chadwick, Director of Enrollment Support Services, 800-373-5504, Fax: 757-352-4381, E-mail: admissions@regent.edu.
Website: http://www.regent.edu/education/.

Rutgers, The State University of New Jersey, New Brunswick, Graduate School of Education, Department of Educational Psychology, Program in Learning, Cognition and Development, Piscataway, NJ 08854-8097. Offers Ed M. Part-time and evening/weekend programs available. *Entrance requirements:* For master's, GRE General Test, 3 letters of recommendation. Additional exam requirements/recommendations for international students: Required—TOEFL (minimum score 550 paper-based; 83 iBT). Electronic applications accepted. *Faculty research:* Cognitive development, gender roles, cognition and instruction, peer learning, infancy and early childhood.

Rutgers, The State University of New Jersey, New Brunswick, Graduate School of Education, Doctoral Program in Education, New Brunswick, NJ 08901. Offers educational policy (PhD); educational psychology (PhD); literacy education (PhD); mathematics education (PhD). Part-time programs available. *Degree requirements:* For doctorate, thesis/dissertation, qualifying exam. *Entrance requirements:* For doctorate, GRE General Test, GRE Subject Test (mathematics education). Additional exam requirements/recommendations for international students: Required—TOEFL (minimum score 575 paper-based; 83 iBT). Electronic applications accepted. *Faculty research:* Literacy education, math education, educational psychology, educational policy, learning sciences.

Simon Fraser University, Office of Graduate Studies, Faculty of Education, Program in Educational Psychology, Burnaby, BC V5A 1S6, Canada. Offers M Ed, MA, PhD. Part-time and evening/weekend programs available. *Degree requirements:* For master's, comprehensive exam (for some programs), thesis (for some programs), project or thesis; for doctorate, comprehensive exam, thesis/dissertation. *Entrance requirements:* For master's, minimum GPA of 3.0 (on scale of 4.33), or 3.33 based on last 60 credits of undergraduate courses; for doctorate, GRE, minimum GPA of 3.5 (on scale of 4.33). Additional exam requirements/recommendations for international students: Recommended—TOEFL (minimum score 580 paper-based; 93 iBT), IELTS (minimum score 7), TWE (minimum score 5). Electronic applications accepted. *Expenses: Tuition, area resident:* Full-time $5084 Canadian dollars. *Required fees:* $840 Canadian dollars. *Faculty research:* Autism and social interaction; cultural and personal dimensions in psychological development; early childhood education; social and emotional development; historical emergence, practice, and ongoing development of the constructs of learning disabilities.

Southern Illinois University Carbondale, Graduate School, College of Education and Human Services, Department of Educational Psychology and Special Education, Program in Educational Psychology, Carbondale, IL 62901-4701. Offers counselor education (MS Ed, PhD); educational psychology (PhD); human learning and

development (MS Ed); measurement and statistics (PhD). *Accreditation:* NCATE. *Faculty:* 19 full-time (9 women), 7 part-time/adjunct (2 women). *Students:* 40 full-time (30 women), 28 part-time (16 women); includes 13 minority (11 Black or African American, non-Hispanic/Latino; 1 Asian, non-Hispanic/Latino; 1 Hispanic/Latino), 11 international. Average age 36. 22 applicants, 50% accepted, 8 enrolled. In 2013, 6 master's, 1 doctorate awarded. *Degree requirements:* For master's, thesis; for doctorate, thesis/dissertation. *Entrance requirements:* For master's, GRE General Test, minimum GPA of 2.7; for doctorate, minimum GPA of 3.25. Additional exam requirements/recommendations for international students: Required—TOEFL. *Application deadline:* For fall admission, 6/15 priority date for domestic students. Applications are processed on a rolling basis. Application fee: $50. *Financial support:* In 2013–14, 36 students received support, including 2 fellowships with full tuition reimbursements available, 4 research assistantships with full tuition reimbursements available; teaching assistantships with full tuition reimbursements available, career-related internships or fieldwork, Federal Work-Study, institutionally sponsored loans, and tuition waivers (full) also available. Support available to part-time students. Financial award application deadline: 5/1. *Faculty research:* Career development, problem-solving, learning and instruction, cognitive development, family assessment. *Total annual research expenditures:* $10,000. *Unit head:* Dr. Lyle White, Chairperson, 618-536-7763, E-mail: lwhite@siu.edu. *Application contact:* Brenda Prell, Administrative Clerk, 618-453-6932, E-mail: bprell@siu.edu.

State University of New York College at Oneonta, Graduate Education, Division of Education, Department of Educational Psychology and Counseling, Oneonta, NY 13820-4015. Offers school counselor K-12 (MS Ed, CAS). *Accreditation:* NCATE. Part-time and evening/weekend programs available. *Degree requirements:* For master's, comprehensive exam. *Entrance requirements:* For master's, GRE General Test.

Teachers College, Columbia University, Graduate Faculty of Education, Department of Health and Behavioral Studies, Program in Applied Educational Psychology-School Psychology, New York, NY 10027. Offers Ed M, MA, Ed D, PhD. *Accreditation:* APA (one or more programs are accredited). *Faculty:* 5 full-time. *Students:* 35 full-time (32 women), 48 part-time (43 women); includes 12 minority (1 Black or African American, non-Hispanic/Latino; 5 Asian, non-Hispanic/Latino; 6 Hispanic/Latino), 5 international. Average age 26. 111 applicants, 38% accepted, 21 enrolled. In 2013, 39 master's, 4 doctorates awarded. *Degree requirements:* For master's, project; for doctorate, comprehensive exam, thesis/dissertation. *Entrance requirements:* For master's, GRE General Test (for Ed M); for doctorate, GRE General Test. *Application deadline:* For fall admission, 12/15 for domestic students. Application fee: $65. *Financial support:* Fellowships, research assistantships, career-related internships or fieldwork, Federal Work-Study, institutionally sponsored loans, and tuition waivers (full and partial) available. Support available to part-time students. Financial award application deadline: 2/1; financial award applicants required to submit FAFSA. *Faculty research:* Psychoeducational assessment, observation and concept acquisition in young children, reading, mathematical thinking, memory. *Unit head:* Prof. Marla Brassard, Chair, 212-678-3368, E-mail: brassard@tc.edu. *Application contact:* Peter Shon, Assistant Director of Admission, 212-678-3305, Fax: 212-678-4171, E-mail: shon@exchange.tc.columbia.edu.
Website: http://www.tc.edu/hbs/SchoolPsych/.

Teachers College, Columbia University, Graduate Faculty of Education, Department of Human Development, Program in Educational Psychology-Human Cognition and Learning, New York, NY 10027-6696. Offers Ed M, MA, Ed D, PhD. *Accreditation:* APA (one or more programs are accredited). Part-time programs available. *Faculty:* 5 full-time, 4 part-time/adjunct. *Students:* 29 full-time (19 women), 73 part-time (55 women); includes 36 minority (10 Black or African American, non-Hispanic/Latino; 13 Asian, non-Hispanic/Latino; 9 Hispanic/Latino; 2 Native Hawaiian or other Pacific Islander, non-Hispanic/Latino; 2 Two or more races, non-Hispanic/Latino), 28 international. Average age 31. 51 applicants, 90% accepted, 23 enrolled. In 2013, 10 master's, 10 doctorates awarded. Terminal master's awarded for partial completion of doctoral program. *Degree requirements:* For master's, integrative paper; for doctorate, thesis/dissertation, integrative project. *Entrance requirements:* For doctorate, GRE General Test. *Application deadline:* For fall admission, 1/15 for domestic students; for spring admission, 12/1 for domestic students. Application fee: $65. *Financial support:* Fellowships, research assistantships, career-related internships or fieldwork, Federal Work-Study, institutionally sponsored loans, and tuition waivers (full and partial) available. Support available to part-time students. Financial award application deadline: 2/1. *Faculty research:* Early reading, text comprehension, learning disabilities, mathematical thinking, reasoning. *Unit head:* Prof. Deanna Kuhn, Program Coordinator, 212-678-3885, E-mail: dk100@columbia.edu. *Application contact:* David Estrella, Associate Director of Admission, 212-678-3710, Fax: 212-678-4171, E-mail: tcinfo@tc.edu.
Website: http://www.tc.columbia.edu/hud/CogStudies/.

Temple University, College of Education, Department of Psychological Studies in Education, Program in Educational Psychology, Philadelphia, PA 19122-6096. Offers Ed M. Part-time and evening/weekend programs available. *Faculty:* 10 full-time (6 women). *Students:* 29 full-time (22 women), 33 part-time (23 women); includes 15 minority (10 Black or African American, non-Hispanic/Latino; 1 Asian, non-Hispanic/Latino; 3 Hispanic/Latino; 1 Two or more races, non-Hispanic/Latino), 2 international. 24 applicants, 38% accepted, 6 enrolled. In 2013, 4 master's awarded. *Degree requirements:* For master's, thesis or alternative. *Entrance requirements:* For master's, GRE General Test or MAT, 2 letters of recommendation, goal statement, resume. Additional exam requirements/recommendations for international students: Required—TOEFL (minimum score 550 paper-based; 79 iBT). *Application deadline:* For fall admission, 12/1 for domestic students, 9/1 for international students; for spring admission, 11/1 for domestic students, 8/1 for international students. Applications are processed on a rolling basis. Application fee: $60. Electronic applications accepted. *Financial support:* In 2013–14, 10 students received support, including 6 research assistantships with full tuition reimbursements available (averaging $20,333 per year), 4 teaching assistantships with full tuition reimbursements available (averaging $17,046 per year); fellowships, career-related internships or fieldwork, Federal Work-Study, scholarships/grants, and unspecified assistantships also available. Financial award application deadline: 1/15; financial award applicants required to submit FAFSA. *Faculty research:* Cognitive development, human development, research methodologies, quantitative research, applied data analysis. *Unit head:* Dr. Avi Kaplan, Program Coordinator, E-mail: avi.kaplan@temple.edu. *Application contact:* Felicia Neuber, Enrollment Management, 215-204-8011, E-mail: educate@temple.edu.
Website: http://education.temple.edu/edpsych/masters-program.

Tennessee Technological University, College of Graduate Studies, College of Education, Department of Counseling and Psychology, Cookeville, TN 38505. Offers agency counseling (Ed S); case management and supervision (MA); educational psychology (MA, Ed S); mental health counseling (MA); school counseling (MA, Ed S); school psychology (MA, Ed S). *Accreditation:* NCATE (one or more programs are accredited). Part-time and evening/weekend programs available. *Faculty:* 24 full-time (6 women). *Students:* 50 full-time (31 women), 36 part-time (31 women); includes 14 minority (7 Black or African American, non-Hispanic/Latino; 1 Asian, non-Hispanic/Latino; 2 Hispanic/Latino; 4 Two or more races, non-Hispanic/Latino). Average age 27. 50 applicants, 62% accepted, 17 enrolled. In 2013, 23 master's, 12 other advanced degrees awarded. *Degree requirements:* For master's and Ed S, comprehensive exam, thesis or alternative. *Entrance requirements:* For master's, GRE; for Ed S, MAT or GRE. Additional exam requirements/recommendations for international students: Required—TOEFL (minimum score 527 paper-based; 71 iBT), IELTS (minimum score 5.5), PTE (minimum score 48), or TOEIC (Test of English as an International Communication). *Application deadline:* For fall admission, 8/1 for domestic students, 5/1 for international students; for spring admission, 12/1 for domestic students, 10/1 for international students. Applications are processed on a rolling basis. Application fee: $35 ($40 for international students). Electronic applications accepted. *Expenses:* Tuition, state resident: full-time $9347; part-time $465 per credit hour. Tuition, nonresident: full-time $23,635; part-time $1152 per credit hour. *Financial support:* In 2013–14, 1 fellowship (averaging $8,000 per year), 8 research assistantships (averaging $4,000 per year), 3 teaching assistantships (averaging $4,000 per year) were awarded; career-related internships or fieldwork also available. Financial award application deadline: 4/1. *Unit head:* Dr. Barry Stein, Interim Chairperson, 931-372-3457, Fax: 931-372-6319, E-mail: bstein@tntech.edu. *Application contact:* Shelia K. Kendrick, Coordinator of Graduate Studies, 931-372-3808, Fax: 931-372-3497, E-mail: skendrick@tntech.edu.

Texas A&M University, College of Education and Human Development, Department of Educational Psychology, College Station, TX 77843. Offers bilingual education (M Ed, MS); counseling psychology (PhD); educational psychology (M Ed, MS, PhD); educational technology (M Ed); school psychology (PhD); special education (M Ed, MS). *Accreditation:* APA (one or more programs are accredited). Part-time and evening/weekend programs available. Postbaccalaureate distance learning degree programs offered (no on-campus study). *Faculty:* 41. *Students:* 148 full-time (122 women), 143 part-time (124 women); includes 97 minority (15 Black or African American, non-Hispanic/Latino; 11 Asian, non-Hispanic/Latino; 66 Hispanic/Latino; 5 Two or more races, non-Hispanic/Latino), 49 international. Average age 31. 249 applicants, 52% accepted, 83 enrolled. In 2013, 43 master's, 22 doctorates awarded. *Degree requirements:* For master's, thesis optional; for doctorate, thesis/dissertation. *Entrance requirements:* For master's and doctorate, GRE General Test. Additional exam requirements/recommendations for international students: Required—TOEFL. Application fee: $50 ($75 for international students). Electronic applications accepted. *Expenses:* Tuition, state resident: full-time $4078; part-time $226.55 per credit hour. Tuition, nonresident: full-time $10,450; part-time $580.55 per credit hour. *Required fees:* $2328; $278.50 per credit hour. $642.45 per semester. *Financial support:* In 2013–14, fellowships (averaging $12,000 per year), research assistantships (averaging $9,000 per year), teaching assistantships (averaging $9,000 per year) were awarded; career-related internships or fieldwork, institutionally sponsored loans, scholarships/grants, and unspecified assistantships also available. Financial award applicants required to submit FAFSA. *Unit head:* Dr. Cathy Watson, Head, 979-845-1394, E-mail: cwatson@tamu.edu. *Application contact:* Christy Porter, Senior Academic Advisor, 979-845-1874, E-mail: csporter@tamu.edu.
Website: http://epsy.tamu.edu.

Texas Christian University, College of Education, Program in Counseling, Fort Worth, TX 76129-0002. Offers counseling (M Ed); counseling and counselor education (PhD); school counseling (Certificate). Part-time and evening/weekend programs available. *Students:* 18 full-time (15 women), 35 part-time (32 women); includes 14 minority (4 Black or African American, non-Hispanic/Latino; 2 Asian, non-Hispanic/Latino; 7 Hispanic/Latino; 1 Two or more races, non-Hispanic/Latino). Average age 30. 30 applicants, 47% accepted, 8 enrolled. In 2013, 14 master's awarded. *Degree requirements:* For master's, oral exam; for doctorate, comprehensive exam, thesis/dissertation. *Entrance requirements:* For master's and doctorate, GRE, interview. Additional exam requirements/recommendations for international students: Required—TOEFL (minimum score 550 paper-based; 80 iBT). *Application deadline:* For fall admission, 11/16 for domestic and international students; for winter admission, 2/1 for domestic and international students; for spring admission, 3/1 for domestic and international students. Application fee: $60. Electronic applications accepted. *Expenses: Tuition:* Part-time $1270 per credit hour. Tuition and fees vary according to course load and program. *Financial support:* Teaching assistantships with full tuition reimbursements, career-related internships or fieldwork, scholarships/grants, and unspecified assistantships available. Financial award application deadline: 2/1; financial award applicants required to submit FAFSA. *Unit head:* Dr. Jan Lacina, Associate Dean, 817-257-6786, E-mail: j.lacina@tcu.edu. *Application contact:* Lori Kimball, Administrative Program Specialist, 817-257-7661, E-mail: l.kimball@tcu.edu.
Website: http://www.coe.tcu.edu/graduate-students-graduate-programs.asp.

Texas Christian University, College of Science and Engineering, Department of Psychology, Fort Worth, TX 76129-0002. Offers developmental trauma (MS); experimental psychology (PhD), including behavioral neuroscience, cognition, learning, social; psychology (MA, MS). *Faculty:* 11 full-time (4 women), 1 part-time/adjunct (0 women). *Students:* 7 full-time (5 women), 21 part-time (9 women); includes 1 minority (Hispanic/Latino), 4 international. Average age 27. 35 applicants, 29% accepted, 9 enrolled. In 2013, 9 master's, 3 doctorates awarded. Terminal master's awarded for partial completion of doctoral program. *Degree requirements:* For master's, thesis; for doctorate, thesis/dissertation. *Entrance requirements:* For master's and doctorate, GRE General Test. Additional exam requirements/recommendations for international students: Recommended—TOEFL. *Application deadline:* For fall admission, 12/30 for domestic and international students; for spring admission, 12/1 for domestic students. Application fee: $60. Electronic applications accepted. *Expenses:* Contact institution. *Financial support:* In 2013–14, 28 students received support. Teaching assistantships with full tuition reimbursements available and unspecified assistantships available. Financial award application deadline: 12/30. *Faculty research:* Neural and behavioral mechanisms mediating after damage to the brain, neural immune interactions, physiological psychology, learning, bird song, qualitative methods, parenting and attachment. *Unit head:* Dr. Charles Lord, Director of Graduate Studies, 817-257-6425, Fax: 817-257-7681, E-mail: c.lord@tcu.edu. *Application contact:* Cindy Hayes, Administrative Assistant, 817-257-7410, Fax: 817-257-7681, E-mail: c.hayes@tcu.edu.
Website: http://www.psy.tcu.edu/gradpro.html.

Texas Tech University, Graduate School, College of Education, Department of Educational Psychology and Leadership, Lubbock, TX 79409-1071. Offers counselor education (M Ed, PhD); educational leadership (M Ed, Ed D); educational psychology (M Ed, PhD); higher education (M Ed, Ed D); higher education research (PhD); instructional technology (M Ed, Ed D); special education (M Ed, Ed D, PhD). *Accreditation:* ACA; NCATE. Part-time and evening/weekend programs available. Postbaccalaureate distance learning degree programs offered (minimal on-campus study). *Faculty:* 42 full-time (20 women). *Students:* 220 full-time (171 women), 549 part-time (404 women); includes 219 minority (73 Black or African American, non-Hispanic/Latino; 5 American Indian or Alaska Native, non-Hispanic/Latino; 6 Asian, non-Hispanic/Latino; 122 Hispanic/Latino; 13 Two or more races, non-Hispanic/Latino), 48 international. Average age 36. 437 applicants, 72% accepted, 215 enrolled. In 2013, 137 master's, 38 doctorates awarded. Terminal master's awarded for partial completion of doctoral program. *Degree requirements:* For master's, comprehensive exam, thesis optional; for doctorate, comprehensive exam, thesis/dissertation. *Entrance*

requirements: For master's, GRE (for some programs); for doctorate, GRE. Additional exam requirements/recommendations for international students: Required—TOEFL (minimum score 550 paper-based; 79 iBT). *Application deadline:* For fall admission, 6/1 priority date for domestic students, 1/15 priority date for international students; for spring admission, 9/1 priority date for domestic students, 6/15 priority date for international students. Applications are processed on a rolling basis. Application fee: $60. Electronic applications accepted. *Expenses:* Tuition, state resident: full-time $6062; part-time $252.57 per credit hour. Tuition, nonresident: full-time $14,558; part-time $606.57 per credit hour. *Required fees:* $2655; $35 per credit hour. $907.50 per semester. Tuition and fees vary according to course load. *Financial support:* In 2013–14, 188 students received support, including 179 fellowships (averaging $2,580 per year), 39 research assistantships (averaging $4,550 per year), 8 teaching assistantships (averaging $4,647 per year); scholarships/grants and unspecified assistantships also available. Support available to part-time students. Financial award application deadline: 1/3; financial award applicants required to submit FAFSA. *Faculty research:* Cognitive, motivational, and developmental processes in learning; counseling education; instructional technology; generic special education and sensory impairment; community college administration; K-12 school administration. *Total annual research expenditures:* $708,063. *Unit head:* Dr. Fred Hartmeister, Chair, 806-834-0248, Fax: 806-742-2179, E-mail: fred.hartmeister@ttu.edu. *Application contact:* Pam Smith, Admissions Advisor, 806-834-2969, Fax: 806-742-2179, E-mail: pam.smith@ttu.edu.
Website: http://www.educ.ttu.edu/.

Universidad de Iberoamerica, Graduate School, San Jose, Costa Rica. Offers clinical neuropsychology (PhD); clinical psychology (M Psych); educational psychology (M Psych); forensic psychology (M Psych); hospital management (MHA); intensive care nursing (MN); medicine (MD).

Université de Moncton, Faculty of Education, Graduate Studies in Education, Moncton, NB E1A 3E9, Canada. Offers educational psychology (M Ed, MA Ed); guidance (M Ed, MA Ed); school administration (M Ed, MA Ed); teaching (M Ed, MA Ed). Part-time programs available. *Degree requirements:* For master's, proficiency in English and French. *Entrance requirements:* For master's, minimum GPA of 3.0. *Faculty research:* Guidance, ethnolinguistic vitality, children's rights, ecological education, entrepreneurship.

Université de Montréal, Faculty of Education, Department of Psychopedagogy and Andragogy, Montréal, QC H3C 3J7, Canada. Offers M Ed, MA, PhD, DESS. Part-time and evening/weekend programs available. Terminal master's awarded for partial completion of doctoral program. *Degree requirements:* For master's, thesis (for some programs); for doctorate, thesis/dissertation, general exam. *Entrance requirements:* For doctorate, MA or M Ed. Electronic applications accepted.

Université du Québec à Trois-Rivières, Graduate Programs, Program in Psychoeducation, Trois-Rivières, QC G9A 5H7, Canada. Offers M Ed, PhD. M Ed offered jointly with Université du Québec en Outaouais. *Entrance requirements:* For master's, appropriate bachelor's degree, proficiency in French. *Faculty research:* Troubled youth intervention.

Université du Québec en Outaouais, Graduate Programs, Program in Psychoéducation, Gatineau, QC J8X 3X7, Canada. Offers M Ed, MA. Part-time programs available. *Degree requirements:* For master's, thesis (for some programs). *Entrance requirements:* For master's, appropriate bachelor's degree, proficiency in French.

Université Laval, Faculty of Education, Department of Teaching and Learning Studies, Programs in Educational Psychology, Québec, QC G1K 7P4, Canada. Offers MA, PhD. Terminal master's awarded for partial completion of doctoral program. *Degree requirements:* For master's, thesis (for some programs); for doctorate, comprehensive exam, thesis/dissertation. *Entrance requirements:* For master's and doctorate, English exam (comprehension of written English), knowledge of French. Electronic applications accepted. *Faculty research:* Emotional, social, and cognitive development; learning and motivation in school; language development; reading acquisition; computer and learning strategies.

University at Albany, State University of New York, School of Education, Department of Educational and Counseling Psychology, Albany, NY 12222-0001. Offers counseling psychology (MS, PhD, CAS); educational psychology (Ed D); educational psychology and statistics (MS); measurements and evaluation (Ed D); rehabilitation counseling (MS), including counseling psychology; school counselor (CAS); school psychology (Psy D, CAS); special education (MS); statistics and research design (Ed D). *Accreditation:* APA (one or more programs are accredited). Evening/weekend programs available. *Degree requirements:* For doctorate, thesis/dissertation. *Entrance requirements:* For doctorate, GRE General Test. Additional exam requirements/recommendations for international students: Required—TOEFL (minimum score 550 paper-based). Electronic applications accepted.

University at Buffalo, the State University of New York, Graduate School, Graduate School of Education, Department of Counseling, School, and Educational Psychology, Buffalo, NY 14260. Offers counseling/school psychology (PhD); counselor education (PhD); education studies (Ed M); educational psychology (MA, PhD); mental health counseling (MS, Certificate); rehabilitation counseling (MS, Advanced Certificate); school counseling (Ed M, Certificate). *Accreditation:* CORE (one or more programs are accredited). Part-time programs available. Postbaccalaureate distance learning degree programs offered (no on-campus study). *Faculty:* 20 full-time (12 women), 36 part-time/adjunct (29 women). *Students:* 167 full-time (134 women), 131 part-time (109 women); includes 44 minority (24 Black or African American, non-Hispanic/Latino; 5 American Indian or Alaska Native, non-Hispanic/Latino; 6 Asian, non-Hispanic/Latino; 9 Hispanic/Latino), 18 international. Average age 31. 333 applicants, 54% accepted, 120 enrolled. In 2013, 64 master's, 15 doctorates, 19 other advanced degrees awarded. *Degree requirements:* For master's, comprehensive exam (for some programs), thesis (for some programs); for doctorate, comprehensive exam, thesis/dissertation. *Entrance requirements:* For master's, GRE General Test, interview, letters of reference; for doctorate, GRE General Test, interview, letters of reference, writing sample. Additional exam requirements/recommendations for international students: Required—TOEFL (minimum score 79 iBT). *Application deadline:* For fall admission, 2/1 priority date for domestic and international students. Application fee: $50. Electronic applications accepted. *Financial support:* In 2013–14, 21 fellowships (averaging $13,105 per year), 23 research assistantships with tuition reimbursements (averaging $9,652 per year) were awarded; teaching assistantships, career-related internships or fieldwork, Federal Work-Study, institutionally sponsored loans, scholarships/grants, tuition waivers, and unspecified assistantships also available. Financial award application deadline: 2/1; financial award applicants required to submit FAFSA. *Faculty research:* Multicultural counseling, class size effects, good work in counseling, eating disorders, outcome assessment, change agents and therapeutic factors in group counseling. *Total annual research expenditures:* $1.9 million. *Unit head:* Dr. Timothy Janikowski, Chair, 716-645-2484, Fax: 716-645-6616, E-mail: tjanikow@buffalo.edu. *Application contact:* Joanne Laska, Admissions Assistant, 716-645-2110, Fax: 716-645-7937, E-mail: jlaska@buffalo.edu.
Website: http://gse.buffalo.edu/csep.

University of Alberta, Faculty of Graduate Studies and Research, Department of Educational Psychology, Edmonton, AB T6G 2E1, Canada. Offers counseling psychology (M Ed, PhD); educational psychology (M Ed, PhD); instructional technology (M Ed); school counseling (M Ed); school psychology (M Ed, PhD); special education (M Ed, PhD); special education-deafness studies (M Ed); teaching English as a second language (M Ed). Part-time programs available. *Degree requirements:* For master's, thesis optional; for doctorate, comprehensive exam, thesis/dissertation. *Entrance requirements:* For master's and doctorate, minimum GPA of 3.0. Additional exam requirements/recommendations for international students: Required—TOEFL. *Faculty research:* Human learning, development and assessment.

The University of Arizona, College of Education, Department of Educational Psychology, Tucson, AZ 85721. Offers educational psychology (MA, PhD, Ed S); school counseling and guidance (M Ed). *Accreditation:* APA (one or more programs are accredited). Part-time programs available. *Faculty:* 2 full-time (1 woman). *Students:* 33 full-time (22 women), 9 part-time (6 women); includes 13 minority (2 Black or African American, non-Hispanic/Latino; 1 American Indian or Alaska Native, non-Hispanic/Latino; 5 Hispanic/Latino; 1 Native Hawaiian or other Pacific Islander, non-Hispanic/Latino; 4 Two or more races, non-Hispanic/Latino), 5 international. Average age 31. 30 applicants, 43% accepted, 5 enrolled. In 2013, 9 master's, 4 doctorates awarded. Terminal master's awarded for partial completion of doctoral program. *Degree requirements:* For master's, comprehensive exam (for some programs), thesis optional; for doctorate, comprehensive exam, thesis/dissertation. *Entrance requirements:* For master's, minimum GPA of 3.0, 3 letters of recommendation, 500-word professional writing sample; for doctorate, GRE General Test, minimum GPA of 3.0, 3 letters of recommendation, statement of purpose, 500-word professional writing sample. Additional exam requirements/recommendations for international students: Required—TOEFL (minimum score 600 paper-based). *Application deadline:* For fall admission, 3/1 for domestic students; for spring admission, 10/1 for domestic students. Applications are processed on a rolling basis. Application fee: $75. Electronic applications accepted. *Expenses:* Tuition, state resident: full-time $11,526. Tuition, nonresident: full-time $27,398. *Financial support:* In 2013–14, 6 research assistantships with full tuition reimbursements (averaging $19,036 per year), 9 teaching assistantships with full tuition reimbursements (averaging $17,672 per year) were awarded; career-related internships or fieldwork, scholarships/grants, health care benefits, tuition waivers (partial), and unspecified assistantships also available. *Faculty research:* School reform, motivational learning in classroom settings, measurement and evaluation of learning outcomes, student resilience, preadolescent and adolescent development. *Unit head:* Dr. Mary McCaslin, Department Head, 520-621-1906, Fax: 520-621-2909, E-mail: mccaslin@email.arizona.edu. *Application contact:* Toni Sollars, Administrative Associate, 520-621-7828, Fax: 520-621-2909, E-mail: tsollars@u.arizona.edu.
Website: http://www.coe.arizona.edu/ep.

University of California, Davis, Graduate Studies, Graduate Group in Education, Davis, CA 95616. Offers education (MA, Ed D); instructional studies (PhD); psychological studies (PhD); sociocultural studies (PhD). Ed D offered jointly with California State University, Fresno. Terminal master's awarded for partial completion of doctoral program. *Degree requirements:* For master's, comprehensive exam (for some programs), thesis (for some programs); for doctorate, thesis/dissertation. *Entrance requirements:* For master's and doctorate, GRE. Additional exam requirements/recommendations for international students: Required—TOEFL (minimum score 550 paper-based). Electronic applications accepted. *Faculty research:* Language and literacy, mathematics education, science education, teacher development, school psychology.

University of California, Riverside, Graduate Division, Graduate School of Education, Riverside, CA 92521-0102. Offers autism (M Ed); diversity and equity (M Ed); education specialist (Credential); education, society and culture (MA, PhD); educational psychology (MA, PhD); general education (M Ed); higher education administration and policy (M Ed, PhD); multiple subject (Credential); reading (M Ed); school psychology (PhD); single subject (Credential); special education (M Ed, MA, PhD); TESOL (M Ed). *Faculty:* 22 full-time (11 women), 14 part-time/adjunct (10 women). *Students:* 218 full-time (148 women); includes 95 minority (10 Black or African American, non-Hispanic/Latino; 30 Asian, non-Hispanic/Latino; 49 Hispanic/Latino; 6 Two or more races, non-Hispanic/Latino), 12 international. Average age 31. 236 applicants, 66% accepted, 78 enrolled. In 2013, 66 master's, 13 doctorates, 86 other advanced degrees awarded. Terminal master's awarded for partial completion of doctoral program. *Degree requirements:* For master's, thesis optional, comprehensive exams or thesis (MA), case study or analytical report (M Ed); for doctorate, thesis/dissertation, written and oral qualifying exams, college teaching practicum. *Entrance requirements:* For master's, GRE General Test (for MA); CBEST and CSET (for M Ed in general education only), UCR Extension TESOL certificate (for M Ed with TESOL emphasis only); for doctorate, GRE General Test, writing sample; for Credential, CBEST, CSET. Additional exam requirements/recommendations for international students: Required—TOEFL (minimum score 550 paper-based; 80 iBT), IELTS (minimum score 7). *Application deadline:* For fall admission, 9/1 for domestic students, 5/1 for international students; for winter admission, 11/15 for domestic students, 7/1 for international students; for spring admission, 3/1 for domestic students, 10/1 for international students. Applications are processed on a rolling basis. Application fee: $80 ($100 for international students). Electronic applications accepted. *Financial support:* In 2013–14, 58 students received support, including 31 fellowships with full tuition reimbursements available, 11 research assistantships with full tuition reimbursements available (averaging $14,691 per year), 5 teaching assistantships with full tuition reimbursements available (averaging $17,655 per year); career-related internships or fieldwork, Federal Work-Study, institutionally sponsored loans, scholarships/grants, and unspecified assistantships also available. Financial award application deadline: 1/5. *Faculty research:* Responsiveness to intervention, faculty core, response to intervention of English language learners, advanced modeling techniques, study on social capital, trust, and motivation. *Total annual research expenditures:* $1.9 million. *Unit head:* Prof. Douglas Mitchell, Interim Dean and Professor, 951-827-5802, Fax: 951-827-3942, E-mail: douglas.mitchell@ucr.edu. *Application contact:* Prof. Michael Orosco, Assistant Professor and Graduate Advisor of Admissions, 951-827-6362, Fax: 951-827-3291, E-mail: edgrad@ucr.edu.
Website: http://www.education.ucr.edu/.

University of Colorado Boulder, Graduate School, School of Education, Division of Educational and Psychological Studies, Boulder, CO 80309. Offers MA, PhD. *Accreditation:* NCATE. *Students:* 15 full-time (11 women), 2 part-time (1 woman); includes 8 minority (1 Black or African American, non-Hispanic/Latino; 5 Hispanic/Latino; 2 Two or more races, non-Hispanic/Latino). Average age 32. 29 applicants, 24% accepted, 6 enrolled. In 2013, 2 master's, 1 doctorate awarded. Terminal master's awarded for partial completion of doctoral program. *Degree requirements:* For master's, comprehensive exam, thesis or alternative; for doctorate, one foreign language, comprehensive exam, thesis/dissertation. *Entrance requirements:* For master's, GRE General Test or MAT, minimum undergraduate GPA of 2.75; for doctorate, GRE General Test. *Application deadline:* For fall admission, 2/1 for domestic students, 12/1 for international students; for spring admission, 9/1 for domestic and international students. Application fee: $50 ($60 for international students). Electronic applications accepted. *Financial support:* In 2013–14, 49 students received support, including 6

fellowships (averaging $2,877 per year), 11 research assistantships with full and partial tuition reimbursements available (averaging $33,687 per year), 6 teaching assistantships with full and partial tuition reimbursements available (averaging $11,447 per year); institutionally sponsored loans, scholarships/grants, health care benefits, and unspecified assistantships also available. Financial award applicants required to submit FAFSA.
Website: http://www.colorado.edu/education/.

University of Colorado Denver, School of Education and Human Development, Programs in Educational and School Psychology, Denver, CO 80217. Offers educational psychology (MA), including educational assessment, educational psychology, human development, human learning, partner schools, research and evaluation; school psychology (Ed S). Part-time and evening/weekend programs available. *Students:* 145 full-time (118 women), 108 part-time (87 women); includes 34 minority (4 Black or African American, non-Hispanic/Latino; 3 Asian, non-Hispanic/Latino; 19 Hispanic/Latino; 8 Two or more races, non-Hispanic/Latino), 10 international. Average age 29. 189 applicants, 81% accepted, 120 enrolled. In 2013, 71 master's, 10 other advanced degrees awarded. *Degree requirements:* For master's, comprehensive exam, 9 hours of core courses, embedded within a minimum of 36 to 38 hours of relevant coursework, including an educational psychology practicum, independent study project or thesis (recommended); for Ed S, comprehensive exam, minimum of 75 semester hours (61 hours of coursework, 6 of 500-hour practicum in field, and 8 of 1200-hour internship); PRAXIS II. *Entrance requirements:* For master's, GRE if undergraduate GPA below 2.75, resume, three letters of recommendation, transcripts; for Ed S, GRE, resume, letters of recommendation, transcripts. Additional exam requirements/recommendations for international students: Required—TOEFL (minimum score 537 paper-based; 75 iBT); Recommended—IELTS (minimum score 6.5). *Application deadline:* For fall admission, 4/15 for domestic students, 4/1 for international students; for spring admission, 9/15 for domestic students, 9/1 for international students. Application fee: $50 ($75 for international students). Electronic applications accepted. *Expenses:* Contact institution. *Financial support:* In 2013–14, 5 students received support. Research assistantships, Federal Work-Study, institutionally sponsored loans, scholarships/grants, and traineeships available. Financial award application deadline: 4/1; financial award applicants required to submit FAFSA. *Faculty research:* Crisis response and intervention, school violence prevention, immigrant experience, educational environments for English language learners, culturally competent assessment and intervention, child and youth suicide. *Unit head:* Dr. Jung-In Kim, Assistant Professor of Educational Psychology, 303-315-4965, E-mail: jung-in.kim@ucdenver.edu. *Application contact:* Student Services Center, 303-315-6300, Fax: 303-315-6311, E-mail: education@ucdenver.edu.
Website: http://www.ucdenver.edu/academics/colleges/SchoolOfEducation/Academics/MASTERS/EPSY/Pages/default.aspx.

University of Connecticut, Graduate School, Neag School of Education, Department of Educational Psychology, Storrs, CT 06269. Offers cognition and instruction (MA, PhD, Post-Master's Certificate); counseling psychology (MA, PhD, Post-Master's Certificate), including counseling psychology (PhD), school counseling (MA, Post-Master's Certificate); gifted and talented education (MA, PhD, Post-Master's Certificate); learning technology (MA, PhD, Post-Master's Certificate); measurement, evaluation, and assessment (MA, PhD, Post-Master's Certificate); school psychology (MA, PhD, Post-Master's Certificate); special education (MA, PhD, Post-Master's Certificate). *Degree requirements:* For master's, comprehensive exam; for doctorate, thesis/dissertation. *Entrance requirements:* For doctorate, GRE General Test. Additional exam requirements/recommendations for international students: Required—TOEFL (minimum score 550 paper-based). Electronic applications accepted.

University of Georgia, College of Education, Department of Educational Psychology and Instructional Technology, Athens, GA 30602. Offers education of the gifted (Ed D); educational psychology (M Ed, MA, Ed D, PhD, Ed S); instructional technology (M Ed, PhD, Ed S). *Accreditation:* NCATE. *Entrance requirements:* For master's and Ed S, GRE General Test or MAT; for doctorate, GRE General Test. Electronic applications accepted.

University of Hawaii at Manoa, Graduate Division, College of Education, Department of Educational Psychology, Honolulu, HI 96822. Offers M Ed, PhD. Part-time programs available. *Degree requirements:* For master's, thesis optional; for doctorate, comprehensive exam, thesis/dissertation. *Entrance requirements:* Additional exam requirements/recommendations for international students: Required—TOEFL (minimum score 600 paper-based; 100 iBT), IELTS (minimum score 7). *Faculty research:* Human learning and development, measurement, research methods, statistics.

University of Houston, College of Education, Department of Educational Psychology, Houston, TX 77204. Offers administration and supervision - higher education (M Ed); counseling (M Ed); counseling psychology (PhD); educational psychology (M Ed); school psychology (PhD); school psychology and individual differences (PhD); special education (M Ed). *Accreditation:* NCATE. Part-time and evening/weekend programs available. Postbaccalaureate distance learning degree programs offered (no on-campus study). *Degree requirements:* For master's, comprehensive exam or thesis; for doctorate, comprehensive exam, thesis/dissertation. *Entrance requirements:* For master's, GRE, transcripts, 3 letters of recommendation, curriculum vita, goal statement; for doctorate, GRE, transcripts, 3 letters of recommendation, curriculum vita, goal statement, writing sample, interview. Additional exam requirements/recommendations for international students: Required—TOEFL (minimum score 550 paper-based; 79 iBT), IELTS (minimum score 6.5). Electronic applications accepted. *Faculty research:* Evidence-based assessment and intervention, multicultural issues in psychology, social and cultural context of learning, systemic barriers to college, motivational aspects of self-regulated learning.

University of Illinois at Chicago, Graduate College, College of Education, Department of Educational Psychology, Chicago, IL 60607-7128. Offers early childhood education (M Ed); educational psychology (PhD); measurement, evaluation, statistics, and assessment (M Ed); youth development (M Ed). Part-time programs available. Postbaccalaureate distance learning degree programs offered (no on-campus study). *Faculty:* 11 full-time (9 women), 4 part-time/adjunct (3 women). *Students:* 63 full-time (48 women), 108 part-time (80 women); includes 58 minority (27 Black or African American, non-Hispanic/Latino; 11 Asian, non-Hispanic/Latino; 17 Hispanic/Latino; 3 Two or more races, non-Hispanic/Latino), 11 international. Average age 33. 128 applicants, 69% accepted, 51 enrolled. In 2013, 41 master's, 2 doctorates awarded. *Expenses:* Tuition, state resident: full-time $11,066; part-time $3689 per term. Tuition, nonresident: full-time $23,064; part-time $7688 per term. *Required fees:* $3004; $1190 per term. Tuition and fees vary according to course level and program. *Total annual research expenditures:* $541,000. *Unit head:* Kimlerly Lawless, Chairperson, 312-996-2359, E-mail: klawless@uic.edu. *Application contact:* Receptionist, 312-413-2550, E-mail: gradcoll@uic.edu.
Website: http://education.uic.edu/academics-admissions/departments/department-educational-psychology#overview.

University of Illinois at Urbana–Champaign, Graduate College, College of Education, Department of Educational Psychology, Champaign, IL 61820. Offers Ed M, MA, MS, PhD, CAS. *Accreditation:* APA (one or more programs are accredited). Part-time programs available. Postbaccalaureate distance learning degree programs offered (no on-campus study). *Students:* 84 (60 women). Application fee: $75 ($90 for international students). *Unit head:* Jose Mestre, Chair, 217-333-0098, Fax: 217-244-7620, E-mail: mestre@illinois.edu. *Application contact:* Myranda Lyons, Office Support Specialist, 217-244-3391, Fax: 217-244-7620, E-mail: mjlyons@illinois.edu.
Website: http://education.illinois.edu/EDPSY/.

The University of Iowa, Graduate College, College of Education, Department of Psychological and Quantitative Foundations, Iowa City, IA 52242-1316. Offers counseling psychology (PhD); educational measurement and statistics (MA, PhD); educational psychology (MA, PhD); school psychology (PhD, Ed S). *Accreditation:* APA. *Degree requirements:* For master's, thesis optional, exam; for doctorate, comprehensive exam, thesis/dissertation; for Ed S, exam. *Entrance requirements:* For master's, doctorate, and Ed S, GRE General Test, minimum GPA of 3.0. Additional exam requirements/recommendations for international students: Required—TOEFL (minimum score 550 paper-based; 81 iBT). Electronic applications accepted.

The University of Kansas, Graduate Studies, School of Education, Department of Psychology and Research in Education, Program in Educational Psychology and Research, Lawrence, KS 66045. Offers MS Ed, PhD. *Faculty:* 21. *Students:* 35 full-time (26 women), 8 part-time (6 women); includes 3 minority (2 Black or African American, non-Hispanic/Latino; 1 Asian, non-Hispanic/Latino), 18 international. Average age 33. 16 applicants, 31% accepted, 2 enrolled. In 2013, 3 master's, 5 doctorates awarded. *Degree requirements:* For master's, thesis; for doctorate, comprehensive exam, thesis/dissertation. *Entrance requirements:* For master's, GRE General Test, minimum GPA of 3.0; for doctorate, GRE General Test. Additional exam requirements/recommendations for international students: Required—TOEFL. *Application deadline:* For fall admission, 12/15 for domestic and international students; for spring admission, 11/15 for domestic students. Application fee: $55 ($65 for international students). Electronic applications accepted. *Financial support:* Fellowships, research assistantships with full and partial tuition reimbursements, teaching assistantships with full and partial tuition reimbursements, career-related internships or fieldwork, institutionally sponsored loans, scholarships/grants, traineeships, health care benefits, tuition waivers (full and partial), and unspecified assistantships available. Support available to part-time students. Financial award application deadline: 2/1. *Faculty research:* Educational measurement, applied statistics, research design, program evaluation, learning and development. *Unit head:* William Skorupski, Director of Training, 785-864-3931, E-mail: bfrey@ku.edu. *Application contact:* Penny Fritts, Admissions Coordinator, 785-864-9645, Fax: 785-864-3820, E-mail: preadmit@ku.edu.
Website: http://www.soe.ku.edu/PRE/.

University of Kentucky, Graduate School, College of Education, Department of Educational, School, and Counseling Psychology, Lexington, KY 40506-0032. Offers counseling psychology (PhD, Ed S); educational psychology (Ed D); school psychology (PhD, Ed S). *Accreditation:* APA (one or more programs are accredited); NCATE. *Degree requirements:* For doctorate, comprehensive exam, thesis/dissertation; for Ed S, comprehensive exam. *Entrance requirements:* For doctorate, GRE General Test, minimum graduate GPA of 3.0; for Ed S, GRE General Test. Additional exam requirements/recommendations for international students: Required—TOEFL (minimum score 550 paper-based). Electronic applications accepted.

University of Louisville, Graduate School, College of Education and Human Development, Department of Educational and Counseling Psychology, Louisville, KY 40292-0001. Offers counseling and personnel services (M Ed, PhD). *Accreditation:* APA; NCATE. Part-time and evening/weekend programs available. *Faculty:* 15 full-time (8 women), 4 part-time/adjunct (2 women). *Students:* 192 full-time (158 women), 72 part-time (55 women); includes 59 minority (38 Black or African American, non-Hispanic/Latino; 1 American Indian or Alaska Native, non-Hispanic/Latino; 5 Asian, non-Hispanic/Latino; 9 Hispanic/Latino; 6 Two or more races, non-Hispanic/Latino), 7 international. Average age 29. 222 applicants, 50% accepted, 77 enrolled. In 2013, 46 master's, 2 doctorates awarded. *Degree requirements:* For doctorate, comprehensive exam, thesis/dissertation. *Entrance requirements:* For master's and doctorate, GRE General Test. Additional exam requirements/recommendations for international students: Required—TOEFL (minimum score 560 paper-based; 83 iBT). *Application deadline:* For fall admission, 5/1 priority date for international students; for winter admission, 11/1 for international students; for summer admission, 4/1 priority date for international students. Application fee: $60. Electronic applications accepted. *Expenses:* Tuition, state resident: full-time $10,788; part-time $599 per credit hour. Tuition, nonresident: full-time $22,446; part-time $1247 per credit hour. *Required fees:* $196. Tuition and fees vary according to program and reciprocity agreements. *Financial support:* Fellowships, research assistantships, teaching assistantships, career-related internships or fieldwork, Federal Work-Study, scholarships/grants, health care benefits, and unspecified assistantships available. Financial award application deadline: 6/1; financial award applicants required to submit FAFSA. *Faculty research:* Classroom processes, school outcomes, adolescent and adult development issues/prevention and treatment, multicultural counseling, spirituality, therapeutic outcomes, college student success, college student affairs administration, career development. *Unit head:* Dr. Michael Cuyjet, Acting Chair, 502-852-0628, Fax: 502-852-0629, E-mail: cuyjet@louisville.edu. *Application contact:* Libby Leggett, Director, Graduate Admissions, 502-852-3101, Fax: 502-852-6536, E-mail: gradadm@louisville.edu.
Website: http://www.louisville.edu/education/departments/ecpy.

The University of Manchester, School of Education, Manchester, United Kingdom. Offers counseling (D Couns); counseling psychology (D Couns); education (M Phil, Ed D, PhD); educational and child psychology (Ed D); educational psychology (Ed D).

University of Manitoba, Faculty of Graduate Studies, Faculty of Education, Department of Educational Administration, Foundations and Psychology, Winnipeg, MB R3T 2N2, Canada. Offers adult and post-secondary education (M Ed); educational administration (M Ed); guidance and counseling (M Ed); inclusive special education (M Ed); social foundations of education (M Ed). *Degree requirements:* For master's, thesis or alternative.

University of Memphis, Graduate School, College of Education, Department of Counseling, Educational Psychology and Research, Memphis, TN 38152. Offers counseling (MS, Ed D), including community counseling (MS), rehabilitation counseling (MS), school counseling (MS); counseling psychology (PhD); educational psychology and research (MS, PhD), including educational psychology, educational research. *Accreditation:* ACA (one or more programs are accredited); APA (one or more programs are accredited); CORE (one or more programs are accredited); NCATE. *Faculty:* 27 full-time (13 women), 12 part-time/adjunct (9 women). *Students:* 137 full-time (105 women), 97 part-time (74 women); includes 60 minority (44 Black or African American, non-Hispanic/Latino; 1 American Indian or Alaska Native, non-Hispanic/Latino; 7 Hispanic/Latino; 8 Two or more races, non-Hispanic/Latino), 9 international. Average age 32. 129 applicants, 50% accepted, 30 enrolled. In 2013, 46 master's, 14 doctorates awarded. *Degree requirements:* For master's, comprehensive exam, thesis or alternative; for doctorate, comprehensive exam, thesis/dissertation. *Entrance requirements:* For master's, GRE General Test or MAT, minimum GPA of 2.5; for doctorate, GRE General Test. *Application deadline:* For fall admission, 10/1 for domestic students; for spring admission, 4/1 for domestic students. Application fee: $35 ($60 for international

students). *Financial support:* In 2013–14, 130 students received support. Fellowships with full tuition reimbursements available, research assistantships with full tuition reimbursements available, teaching assistantships with full tuition reimbursements available, career-related internships or fieldwork, Federal Work-Study, scholarships/grants, and unspecified assistantships available. Financial award application deadline: 2/15; financial award applicants required to submit FAFSA. *Faculty research:* Anger management, aging and disability, supervision, multicultural counseling. *Unit head:* Dr. Douglas C. Strohmer, Chair, 901-678-2841, Fax: 901-678-5114. *Application contact:* Dr. Ernest A. Rakow, Associate Dean of Administration and Graduate Programs, 901-678-2399, Fax: 901-678-4778.
Website: http://coe.memphis.edu/cepr/.

University of Minnesota, Twin Cities Campus, Graduate School, College of Education and Human Development, Department of Educational Psychology, Minneapolis, MN 55455-0213. Offers counseling and student personnel psychology (MA, PhD, Ed S); early childhood education (M Ed, MA, PhD); educational psychology (PhD); psychological foundations of education (MA, PhD, Ed S); school psychology (MA, PhD, Ed S); special education (M Ed, MA, PhD, Ed S); talent development and gifted education (Certificate). *Accreditation:* APA (one or more programs are accredited). *Faculty:* 31 full-time (15 women). *Students:* 276 full-time (215 women), 1,982 part-time (65 women); includes 47 minority (12 Black or African American, non-Hispanic/Latino; 4 American Indian or Alaska Native, non-Hispanic/Latino; 16 Asian, non-Hispanic/Latino; 15 Hispanic/Latino), 45 international. Average age 29. 342 applicants, 47% accepted, 97 enrolled. In 2013, 109 master's, 26 doctorates, 30 other advanced degrees awarded. Application fee: $75 ($95 for international students). *Financial support:* In 2013–14, 5 fellowships (averaging $21,623 per year), 62 research assistantships (averaging $10,081 per year), 31 teaching assistantships (averaging $7,120 per year) were awarded. *Faculty research:* Learning, cognitive and social processes; multicultural education and counseling; measurement and statistical processes; performance assessment; instructional design/strategies for students with special needs. *Total annual research expenditures:* $3.5 million. *Unit head:* Geoff Maruyama, Chair, 612-625-5861, Fax: 612-624-8241, E-mail: geoff@umn.edu. *Application contact:* Dr. Jennifer Engler, Assistant Dean, 612-626-2887, Fax: 612-626-7496, E-mail: engle009@umn.edu.
Website: http://www.cehd.umn.edu/EdPsych.

University of Missouri, Graduate School, College of Education, Department of Educational, School, and Counseling Psychology, Columbia, MO 65211. Offers counseling psychology (M Ed, MA, PhD, Ed S); educational psychology (M Ed, MA, PhD, Ed S); learning and instruction (M Ed); school psychology (M Ed, MA, PhD, Ed S). *Accreditation:* APA (one or more programs are accredited). Part-time programs available. *Faculty:* 25 full-time (13 women), 4 part-time/adjunct (2 women). *Students:* 191 full-time (125 women), 143 part-time (80 women); includes 72 minority (38 Black or African American, non-Hispanic/Latino; 5 Asian, non-Hispanic/Latino; 21 Hispanic/Latino; 8 Two or more races, non-Hispanic/Latino), 35 international. Average age 29. 354 applicants, 38% accepted, 116 enrolled. In 2013, 59 master's, 16 doctorates, 13 other advanced degrees awarded. *Degree requirements:* For doctorate, thesis/dissertation. *Entrance requirements:* For master's, doctorate, and Ed S, GRE General Test, minimum GPA of 3.0. Additional exam requirements/recommendations for international students: Required—TOEFL (minimum score 580 paper-based; 92 iBT). *Application deadline:* For fall admission, 12/1 priority date for domestic and international students. Applications are processed on a rolling basis. Application fee: $55 ($75 for international students). Electronic applications accepted. *Financial support:* Fellowships, research assistantships, teaching assistantships, institutionally sponsored loans, traineeships, health care benefits, and unspecified assistantships available. Support available to part-time students. *Faculty research:* Out-of-school learning, social cognitive career theory, black psychology and the intersectionality of social identities, test session behavior. *Unit head:* Dr. Matthew Martens, Division Executive Director, 573-882-9434, E-mail: martensmp@missouri.edu. *Application contact:* Latoya Luther, Senior Secretary, 573-882-7732, E-mail: lutherl@missouri.edu.
Website: http://education.missouri.edu/ESCP/.

University of Missouri–St. Louis, College of Education, Interdisciplinary Doctoral Programs, St. Louis, MO 63121. Offers adult and higher education (Ed D); counseling (PhD); counselor education (Ed D); educational administration (Ed D); educational leadership and policy studies (PhD); educational psychology (PhD); teaching-learning processes (Ed D, PhD). *Faculty:* 72 full-time (33 women). *Students:* 58 full-time (46 women), 240 part-time (154 women); includes 106 minority (86 Black or African American, non-Hispanic/Latino; 4 American Indian or Alaska Native, non-Hispanic/Latino; 6 Asian, non-Hispanic/Latino; 8 Hispanic/Latino; 2 Two or more races, non-Hispanic/Latino), 9 international. Average age 42. 67 applicants, 58% accepted, 24 enrolled. In 2013, 24 doctorates awarded. *Degree requirements:* For doctorate, thesis/dissertation. *Entrance requirements:* For doctorate, GRE General Test, 3 letters of recommendation; personal interview. Additional exam requirements/recommendations for international students: Recommended—TOEFL (minimum score 550 paper-based; 79 iBT), IELTS (minimum score 6.5). *Application deadline:* For fall admission, 3/1 for domestic and international students; for spring admission, 10/1 for domestic and international students. Application fee: $50 ($40 for international students). Electronic applications accepted. *Expenses:* Tuition, state resident: full-time $7364; part-time $409.10 per credit hour. Tuition, nonresident: full-time $19,162; part-time $1008.50 per credit hour. *Financial support:* In 2013–14, 13 research assistantships (averaging $12,240 per year), 9 teaching assistantships (averaging $12,240 per year) were awarded. Financial award application deadline: 4/1; financial award applicants required to submit FAFSA. *Faculty research:* Higher education law and policy, gender and higher education, student retention, lifelong learning orientation, school counselor's role in violence prevention. *Unit head:* Dr. Kathleen Haywood, Director of Graduate Studies, 314-516-5483, Fax: 314-516-5227, E-mail: kathleen_haywood@umsl.edu. *Application contact:* 314-516-5458, Fax: 314-516-6996, E-mail: gradadm@umsl.edu.

University of Nebraska–Lincoln, Graduate College, College of Education and Human Sciences, Department of Educational Psychology, Lincoln, NE 68588. Offers cognition, learning and development (MA); counseling psychology (MA); educational psychology (MA, Ed S); psychological studies in education (PhD), including cognition, learning and development, counseling psychology, quantitative, qualitative, and psychometric methods, school psychology; quantitative, qualitative, and psychometric methods (MA); school psychology (MA, Ed S). *Accreditation:* APA (one or more programs are accredited); NCATE. *Degree requirements:* For master's, thesis optional. *Entrance requirements:* For master's, GRE General Test. Additional exam requirements/recommendations for international students: Required—TOEFL (minimum score 500 paper-based). Electronic applications accepted. *Faculty research:* Measurement and assessment, metacognition, academic skills, child development, multicultural education and counseling.

University of Nevada, Las Vegas, Graduate College, College of Education, Department of Educational Psychology and Higher Education, Las Vegas, NV 89154-3002. Offers educational leadership (Ed D, PhD); educational psychology (MS, PhD, Ed S), including learning and technology (PhD); higher education (M Ed, PhD, Certificate); PhD/JD. Part-time and evening/weekend programs available. *Faculty:* 19

full-time (12 women), 4 part-time/adjunct (2 women). *Students:* 56 full-time (44 women), 79 part-time (58 women); includes 40 minority (12 Black or African American, non-Hispanic/Latino; 1 American Indian or Alaska Native, non-Hispanic/Latino; 7 Asian, non-Hispanic/Latino; 10 Hispanic/Latino; 2 Native Hawaiian or other Pacific Islander, non-Hispanic/Latino; 8 Two or more races, non-Hispanic/Latino), 2 international. Average age 35. 67 applicants, 64% accepted, 28 enrolled. In 2013, 22 master's, 36 doctorates, 10 other advanced degrees awarded. *Degree requirements:* For master's, comprehensive exam (for some programs), thesis (for some programs); for doctorate, comprehensive exam (for some programs), thesis/dissertation; for other advanced degree, comprehensive exam, thesis. *Entrance requirements:* For master's, GMAT or GRE General Test; for doctorate, GRE General Test, writing exam; for other advanced degree, GRE General Test. Additional exam requirements/recommendations for international students: Required—TOEFL (minimum score 550 paper-based; 80 iBT), IELTS (minimum score 7). *Application deadline:* For fall admission, 4/15 for domestic students, 5/1 for international students; for spring admission, 10/1 for international students. Application fee: $60 ($95 for international students). Electronic applications accepted. *Expenses:* Tuition, state resident: full-time $4752; part-time $264 per credit. Tuition, nonresident: full-time $18,662; part-time $554.50 per credit. *International tuition:* $18,952 full-time. *Required fees:* $532; $12 per credit. $266 per semester. One-time fee: $35. Tuition and fees vary according to course load and program. *Financial support:* In 2013–14, 48 students received support, including 39 research assistantships with partial tuition reimbursements available (averaging $11,046 per year), 9 teaching assistantships with partial tuition reimbursements available (averaging $10,922 per year); institutionally sponsored loans, scholarships/grants, health care benefits, and unspecified assistantships also available. Financial award application deadline: 3/1. *Faculty research:* Innovation and change in educational settings; educational policy, finance, and marketing; psycho-educational assessment; student retention, persistence, development, language, and culture; statistical modeling, program evaluation, qualitative and quantitative research methods. *Total annual research expenditures:* $158,645. *Unit head:* Dr. LeAnn Putney, Chair/Professor, 702-895-4879, Fax: 702-895-3492, E-mail: leann.putney@unlv.edu. *Application contact:* Graduate College Admissions Evaluator, 702-895-3320, Fax: 702-895-4180, E-mail: gradcollege@unlv.edu.
Website: http://education.unlv.edu/ephe/.

University of Nevada, Reno, Graduate School, College of Education, Department of Counseling and Educational Psychology, Reno, NV 89557. Offers M Ed, MA, MS, Ed D, PhD, Ed S. *Accreditation:* ACA (one or more programs are accredited); NCATE. Terminal master's awarded for partial completion of doctoral program. *Degree requirements:* For master's, comprehensive exam, thesis optional; for doctorate, comprehensive exam, thesis/dissertation, qualifying exam. *Entrance requirements:* For master's, GRE, minimum GPA of 2.75; for doctorate, GRE, minimum GPA of 3.0. Additional exam requirements/recommendations for international students: Required—TOEFL (minimum score 500 paper-based; 61 iBT), IELTS (minimum score 6). Electronic applications accepted. *Faculty research:* Marriage and family counseling, substance abuse attitudes of teachers, current supply of counseling educators, HIV-positive services for patients, family counseling for youth at risk.

University of New Mexico, Graduate School, College of Education, Department of Individual, Family and Community Education, Program in Educational Psychology, Albuquerque, NM 87131. Offers MA, PhD. *Accreditation:* NCATE. Part-time and evening/weekend programs available. *Faculty:* 5 full-time (2 women), 2 part-time/adjunct (0 women). *Students:* 17 full-time (11 women), 14 part-time (11 women); includes 11 minority (4 American Indian or Alaska Native, non-Hispanic/Latino; 7 Hispanic/Latino). Average age 38. 8 applicants, 63% accepted, 5 enrolled. In 2013, 2 master's, 2 doctorates awarded. Terminal master's awarded for partial completion of doctoral program. *Degree requirements:* For master's, comprehensive exam (for some programs), thesis (for some programs); for doctorate, comprehensive exam, thesis/dissertation. *Entrance requirements:* For master's, GRE General Test or MAT, minimum GPA of 3.0 in last 2 years of undergraduate study, 3 letters of reference, interview with 3 faculty; for doctorate, GRE General Test or MAT, minimum GPA of 3.0 in last 2 years of undergraduate study, 3 letters of reference, interview with 3 faculty, writing sample. Additional exam requirements/recommendations for international students: Required—TOEFL. *Application deadline:* For fall admission, 3/1 for domestic and international students; for spring admission, 10/1 for domestic and international students. Application fee: $50. Electronic applications accepted. *Financial support:* In 2013–14, 14 students received support, including 8 teaching assistantships with full and partial tuition reimbursements available (averaging $9,070 per year); unspecified assistantships also available. Financial award application deadline: 3/1; financial award applicants required to submit FAFSA. *Faculty research:* Measurement and assessment, cognitive strategies, accountability, motivation, instructional technology, educational research, human lifespan development, beliefs. *Unit head:* Dr. Jay Parkes, Department Chair, 505-277-3320, Fax: 505-277-8361, E-mail: edpsy@unm.edu. *Application contact:* Cynthia Salas, Department Administrator, 505-277-4535, Fax: 505-277-8361, E-mail: divbse@unm.edu.
Website: http://coe.unm.edu/departments/ifce/educational-psychology.html.

The University of North Carolina at Chapel Hill, Graduate School, School of Education, Program in Education, Chapel Hill, NC 27599. Offers culture, curriculum and change (MA, PhD); early childhood, intervention and literacy (MA, PhD); educational psychology, measurement and evaluation (MA, PhD). *Accreditation:* NCATE. *Degree requirements:* For master's, thesis; for doctorate, comprehensive exam, thesis/dissertation. *Entrance requirements:* For master's, GRE General Test, minimum GPA of 3.0 during last 2 years of undergraduates course work; for doctorate, GRE General Test, minimum GPA of 3.0 during last 2 years of undergraduate course work. Additional exam requirements/recommendations for international students: Required—TOEFL (minimum score 550 paper-based). Electronic applications accepted.

University of Northern Colorado, Graduate School, College of Education and Behavioral Sciences, School of Psychological Sciences, Program in Educational Psychology, Greeley, CO 80639. Offers early childhood education (MA); educational psychology (MA, PhD). *Accreditation:* NCATE. Part-time programs available. *Degree requirements:* For master's, comprehensive exam, thesis or alternative; for doctorate, comprehensive exam, thesis/dissertation. *Entrance requirements:* For master's, GRE General Test, letters of recommendation; for doctorate, GRE General Test, letters of recommendation, resume. Electronic applications accepted.

University of Northern Iowa, Graduate College, College of Education, Department of Educational Psychology and Foundations, Program in Educational Psychology: Professional Development for Teachers, Cedar Falls, IA 50614. Offers MAE. Postbaccalaureate distance learning degree programs offered (no on-campus study). *Students:* 2 full-time (1 woman), 36 part-time (31 women); includes 4 minority (3 Black or African American, non-Hispanic/Latino; 1 Two or more races, non-Hispanic/Latino), 4 international. 10 applicants, 60% accepted, 4 enrolled. In 2013, 9 master's awarded. Application fee: $50 ($70 for international students). *Unit head:* Dr. Radhi Al-Mabuk, Coordinator, 319-273-2609, Fax: 319-273-7732, E-mail: radhi.al-mabuk@uni.edu. *Application contact:* Laurie S. Russell, Record Analyst, 319-273-2623, Fax: 319-273-2885, E-mail: laurie.russell@uni.edu.

Educational Psychology

University of North Texas, Robert B. Toulouse School of Graduate Studies, Denton, TN 76203-5017. Offers accounting (MS, PhD); applied anthropology (MA, MS); applied behavior analysis (Certificate); applied technology and performance improvement (M Ed, MS, PhD); art education (MA, PhD); art history (MA); art museum education (Certificate); arts leadership (Certificate); audiology (Au D); behavior analysis (MS); biochemistry and molecular biology (MS, PhD); biology (MA, MS, PhD); business (PhD); business computer information systems (PhD); chemistry (MS, PhD); clinical psychology (PhD); communication studies (MA, MS); computer engineering (MS); computer science (MS); computer science and engineering (PhD); counseling (M Ed, MS, PhD), including clinical mental health counseling (MS), college and university counseling (M Ed, MS), elementary school counseling (M Ed, MS), secondary school counseling (M Ed, MS); counseling psychology (PhD); creative writing (MA); criminal justice (MS); curriculum and instruction (M Ed, PhD), including curriculum studies (PhD), early childhood studies (PhD), language and literacy studies (PhD); decision sciences (MBA); design (MA, MFA), including fashion design (MFA), innovation studies, interior design (MFA); early childhood studies (MS); economics (MS); educational leadership (M Ed, Ed D, PhD); educational psychology (MS), including family studies, gifted and talented (MS, PhD), human development, learning and cognition, research, measurement and evaluation; educational research (PhD), including gifted and talented (MS, PhD), human development and family studies, psychological aspects of sports and exercise, research, measurement and statistics; electrical engineering (MS); emergency management (MPA); engineering systems (MS); English (MA, PhD); environmental science (MS, PhD); experimental psychology (PhD); finance (MBA, MS, PhD); financial management (MPA); French (MA); health psychology and behavioral medicine (PhD); health services management (MBA); higher education (M Ed, Ed D, PhD); history (MA, MS, PhD), including European history (PhD), military history (PhD), United States history (PhD); hospitality management (MS); human resources management (MPA); information science (MS, PhD); information technologies (MBA); information technology and decision sciences (MS); interdisciplinary studies (MA, MS); international sustainable tourism (MS); jazz studies (MM); journalism (MA, MJ, Graduate Certificate), including interactive and virtual digital communication (Graduate Certificate), narrative journalism (Graduate Certificate), public relations (Graduate Certificate); kinesiology (MS); learning technologies (MS, PhD); library science (MS); local government management (MPA); logistics and supply chain management (MBA, PhD); long-term care, senior housing, and aging services (MA, MS); management science (PhD); marketing (MBA, PhD); materials science and engineering (MS, PhD); mathematics (MA, PhD); merchandising (MS); music (MA, MM Ed, PhD), including ethnomusicology (MA), music education (MM Ed, PhD), music theory (MA, PhD), musicology (MA, PhD), performance (MA); nonprofit management (MPA); operations and supply chain management (MBA); performance (MM, DMA); philosophy (MA, PhD); physics (MS, PhD); political science (MA, MS, PhD); public administration and management (PhD), including emergency management, nonprofit management, public financial management, urban management; radio, television and film (MA, MFA); recreation, event and sport management (MS); rehabilitation counseling (MS, Certificate); sociology (MA, MS, PhD); Spanish (MA); special education (M Ed, PhD), including autism intervention (PhD), emotional/behavioral disorders (PhD), mild/moderate disabilities (PhD); speech-language pathology (MA, MS); strategic management (MBA); studio art (MFA); taxation (MS); teaching (M Ed); MBA/MS; MS/MPH; MSES/MBA. Part-time and evening/weekend programs available. Postbaccalaureate distance learning degree programs offered. *Faculty:* 661 full-time (213 women), 240 part-time/adjunct (144 women). *Students:* 3,106 full-time (1,620 women), 3,543 part-time (2,221 women); includes 1,740 minority (533 Black or African American, non-Hispanic/Latino; 15 American Indian or Alaska Native, non-Hispanic/Latino; 286 Asian, non-Hispanic/Latino; 746 Hispanic/Latino; 3 Native Hawaiian or other Pacific Islander, non-Hispanic/Latino; 157 Two or more races, non-Hispanic/Latino), 1,145 international. Average age 32. 6,289 applicants, 43% accepted, 1751 enrolled. In 2013, 1,778 master's, 239 doctorates, 10 other advanced degrees awarded. Terminal master's awarded for partial completion of doctoral program. *Degree requirements:* For master's, variable foreign language requirement, comprehensive exam (for some programs), thesis (for some programs); for doctorate, variable foreign language requirement, comprehensive exam (for some programs), thesis/dissertation; for other advanced degree, variable foreign language requirement, comprehensive exam (for some programs). *Entrance requirements:* For master's and doctorate, GRE, GMAT. Additional exam requirements/recommendations for international students: Required—TOEFL (minimum score 550 paper-based; 79 iBT). *Application deadline:* For fall admission, 7/15 for domestic students, 3/15 for international students; for spring admission, 11/15 for domestic students, 9/15 for international students; for summer admission, 5/1 for domestic students. Applications are processed on a rolling basis. Application fee: $60. Electronic applications accepted. *Financial support:* Fellowships with partial tuition reimbursements, research assistantships with partial tuition reimbursements, teaching assistantships, career-related internships or fieldwork, Federal Work-Study, institutionally sponsored loans, scholarships/grants, health care benefits, and library assistantships available. Support available to part-time students. Financial award applicants required to submit FAFSA. *Unit head:* Mark Wardell, Dean, 940-565-2383, E-mail: mark.wardell@unt.edu. *Application contact:* Toulouse School of Graduate Studies, 940-565-2383, Fax: 940-565-2141, E-mail: gradsch@unt.edu.
Website: http://tsgs.unt.edu/.

University of Oklahoma, Jeannine Rainbolt College of Education, Department of Educational Psychology, Program in Instructional Psychology and Technology, Norman, OK 73019. Offers educational psychology and technology (M Ed); instructional psychology and technology (PhD). Part-time and evening/weekend programs available. *Students:* 19 full-time (12 women), 33 part-time (25 women); includes 16 minority (7 Black or African American, non-Hispanic/Latino; 2 American Indian or Alaska Native, non-Hispanic/Latino; 1 Asian, non-Hispanic/Latino; 3 Hispanic/Latino; 3 Two or more races, non-Hispanic/Latino), 8 international. Average age 34. 17 applicants, 76% accepted, 11 enrolled. In 2013, 7 master's, 1 doctorate awarded. *Degree requirements:* For master's, comprehensive exam, thesis optional; for doctorate, comprehensive exam, thesis/dissertation. *Entrance requirements:* For master's and doctorate, GRE. Additional exam requirements/recommendations for international students: Required—TOEFL (minimum score 79 iBT). *Application deadline:* For fall admission, 2/1 for domestic and international students; for spring admission, 10/15 for domestic students, 9/1 for international students. Application fee: $50 ($100 for international students). Electronic applications accepted. *Expenses:* Tuition, state resident: full-time $4205; part-time $175.20 per credit hour. Tuition, nonresident: full-time $16,205; part-time $675.20 per credit hour. *Required fees:* $2745; $103.85 per credit hour. $126.50 per semester. *Financial support:* In 2013–14, 32 students received support. Career-related internships or fieldwork, Federal Work-Study, scholarships/grants, health care benefits, and unspecified assistantships available. Support available to part-time students. Financial award application deadline: 6/1; financial award applicants required to submit FAFSA. *Faculty research:* Cognition and instruction, motivation and instruction, instructional design, technology integration in education, interactive learning technologies, measurement and assessment. *Unit head:* Dr. Barbara Greene, Program Coordinator, 405-325-1534, Fax: 405-325-6655, E-mail: barbara@ou.edu. *Application contact:* Shannon Vazquez, Graduate Programs Officer, 405-325-4525, Fax: 405-325-6655, E-mail: shannonv@ou.edu.
Website: http://www.ou.edu/content/education/edpy/instructional-psychology-and-technology-degrees-and-programs/.

University of Phoenix–Southern Arizona Campus, College of Education, Tucson, AZ 85711. Offers administration and supervision (MA Ed); adult education and training (MA Ed); curriculum instruction (MA Ed); educational counseling (MA Ed); elementary teacher education (MA Ed); school counseling (MSC); secondary teacher education (MA Ed); special education (MA Ed, Certificate). Evening/weekend programs available. *Degree requirements:* For master's, thesis (for some programs). *Entrance requirements:* For master's, minimum undergraduate GPA of 2.5, 3 years of work experience. Additional exam requirements/recommendations for international students: Required—TOEFL (minimum score 550 paper-based; 79 iBT). Electronic applications accepted.

University of Regina, Faculty of Graduate Studies and Research, Faculty of Education, Department of Educational Psychology, Regina, SK S4S 0A2, Canada. Offers M Ed. Part-time programs available. *Faculty:* 42 full-time (23 women), 18 part-time/adjunct (10 women). *Students:* 13 full-time (9 women), 29 part-time (27 women). 23 applicants, 39% accepted. In 2013, 24 master's awarded. *Degree requirements:* For master's, thesis (for some programs), practicum, project, or thesis. *Entrance requirements:* For master's, bachelor's degree in education. Additional exam requirements/recommendations for international students: Required—TOEFL (minimum score 580 paper-based; 80 iBT), IELTS (minimum score 6.5). *Application deadline:* For fall admission, 2/15 for domestic and international students; for winter admission, 10/15 for domestic and international students; for spring admission, 2/15 for domestic and international students. Application fee: $100. Electronic applications accepted. *Expenses: Tuition, area resident:* Full-time $4338 Canadian dollars. *International tuition:* $7338 Canadian dollars full-time. *Required fees:* $449.25 Canadian dollars. *Financial support:* In 2013–14, 3 fellowships (averaging $6,000 per year) were awarded; research assistantships, teaching assistantships, career-related internships or fieldwork, and scholarships/grants also available. Financial award application deadline: 6/15. *Faculty research:* Theories of counseling, psychology of learning, aptitude and achievement analysis, education and vocational guidance, resilience: re-conceptualizing PRAXIS. *Unit head:* Dr. Ken Montgomery, Associate Dean, Research and Graduate Programs, 306-585-5031, Fax: 306-585-5387, E-mail: ken.montgomery@uregina.ca. *Application contact:* Tania Gates, Graduate Program Coordinator, 306-585-4506, Fax: 306-585-5387, E-mail: edgrad@uregina.ca.

University of Saskatchewan, College of Graduate Studies and Research, College of Education, Department of Educational Psychology and Special Education, Saskatoon, SK S7N 5A2, Canada. Offers M Ed, PhD, Diploma. *Degree requirements:* For master's, thesis (for some programs); for doctorate, comprehensive exam (for some programs), thesis/dissertation. *Entrance requirements:* Additional exam requirements/recommendations for international students: Required—TOEFL (minimum score 80 iBT); Recommended—IELTS (minimum score 6.5). Electronic applications accepted. *Expenses: Tuition, area resident:* Full-time $3585 Canadian dollars; part-time $585 Canadian dollars per course. Tuition, nonresident: part-time $877 Canadian dollars per course. *International tuition:* $5377 Canadian dollars full-time. *Required fees:* $889.51 Canadian dollars.

University of South Africa, College of Human Sciences, Pretoria, South Africa. Offers adult education (M Ed); African languages (MA, PhD); African politics (MA, PhD); Afrikaans (MA, PhD); ancient history (MA, PhD); ancient Near Eastern studies (MA, PhD); anthropology (MA, PhD); applied linguistics (MA); Arabic (MA, PhD); archaeology (MA); art history (MA); Biblical archaeology (MA); Biblical studies (M Th, D Th, PhD); Christian spirituality (M Th, D Th); church history (M Th, D Th); classical studies (MA, PhD); clinical psychology (MA); communication (MA, PhD); comparative education (M Ed, Ed D); consulting psychology (D Admin, D Com, PhD); curriculum studies (M Ed, Ed D); development studies (M Admin, MA, D Admin, PhD); didactics (M Ed, Ed D); education (M Tech); education management (M Ed, Ed D); educational psychology (M Ed); English (MA); environmental education (M Ed); French (MA, PhD); German (MA, PhD); Greek (MA); guidance and counseling (M Ed); health studies (MA, PhD), including health sciences education (MA), health services management (MA), medical and surgical nursing science (critical care general) (MA), midwifery and neonatal nursing science (MA), trauma and emergency care (MA); history (MA, PhD); history of education (Ed D); inclusive education (M Ed, Ed D); information and communications technology policy and regulation (MA); information science (MA, MIS, PhD); international politics (MA, PhD); Islamic studies (MA, PhD); Italian (MA, PhD); Judaica (MA, PhD); linguistics (MA, PhD); mathematical education (M Ed); mathematics education (MA); missiology (M Th, D Th); modern Hebrew (MA, PhD); musicology (MA, MMus, D Mus, PhD); natural science education (M Ed); New Testament (M Th, D Th); Old Testament (D Th); pastoral therapy (M Th, D Th); philosophy (MA); philosophy of education (M Ed, Ed D); politics (MA, PhD); Portuguese (MA, PhD); practical theology (M Th, D Th); psychology (MA, MS, PhD); psychology of education (M Ed, Ed D); public health (MA); religious studies (MA, D Th, PhD); Romance languages (MA); Russian (MA, PhD); Semitic languages (MA, PhD); social behavior studies in HIV/AIDS (MA); social science (mental health) (MA); social science in development studies (MA); social science in psychology (MA); social science in social work (MA); social science in sociology (MA); social work (MSW, DSW, PhD); socio-education (M Ed, Ed D); sociolinguistics (MA); sociology (MA, PhD); Spanish (MA, PhD); systematic theology (M Th, D Th); TESOL (teaching English to speakers of other languages) (MA); theological ethics (M Th, D Th); theory of literature (MA, PhD); urban ministries (D Th); urban ministry (M Th).

University of South Carolina, The Graduate School, College of Education, Department of Educational Studies, Program in Educational Psychology, Research, Columbia, SC 29208. Offers M Ed, PhD. *Accreditation:* NCATE. Part-time programs available. *Degree requirements:* For master's, comprehensive exam, thesis (for some programs); for doctorate, comprehensive exam, thesis/dissertation. *Entrance requirements:* For master's, GRE General Test; for doctorate, GRE General Test, interview. Electronic applications accepted. *Faculty research:* Problem solving, higher order thinking skills, psychometric research, methodology.

The University of South Dakota, Graduate School, School of Education, Division of Counseling and Psychology in Education, Vermillion, SD 57069-2390. Offers counseling (MA, PhD, Ed S); human development and educational psychology (MA, PhD, Ed S); school psychology (PhD, Ed S). *Accreditation:* ACA (one or more programs are accredited); NCATE. Part-time programs available. *Degree requirements:* For master's and Ed S, comprehensive exam, thesis or alternative; for doctorate, comprehensive exam, thesis/dissertation. *Entrance requirements:* For master's and doctorate, GRE General Test, minimum GPA of 3.0. Additional exam requirements/recommendations for international students: Required—TOEFL (minimum score 550 paper-based; 79 iBT). Electronic applications accepted.

University of Southern California, Graduate School, Rossier School of Education, Doctor of Education Programs, Los Angeles, CA 90089. Offers educational psychology (Ed D); higher education administration (Ed D); K-12 leadership in urban school settings (Ed D); teacher education in multicultural societies (Ed D). Part-time and evening/weekend programs available. *Degree requirements:* For doctorate, thesis/dissertation. *Entrance requirements:* For doctorate, GRE. Additional exam requirements/recommendations for international students: Required—TOEFL (minimum score 100

iBT). Electronic applications accepted. *Faculty research:* Data-driven decision-making in K-12 schools and districts; examination of college and university leadership and management in U. S. and Asia; studies in facilitating student learning; organizational change and the role of leaders; leadership, diversity, learning and accountability.

University of Southern California, Graduate School, Rossier School of Education, Doctor of Philosophy in Education Programs, Los Angeles, CA 90089. Offers educational psychology (PhD); higher education administration and policy (PhD); K-12 policy and practice (PhD). *Degree requirements:* For doctorate, thesis/dissertation, 63 units; qualifying exam; dissertation proposal and defense. *Entrance requirements:* For doctorate, GRE. Additional exam requirements/recommendations for international students: Required—TOEFL (minimum score 100 iBT). Electronic applications accepted. *Faculty research:* Diversity in higher education, organizational change, educational psychology, policy and politics of educational reform, economics of education and education policy.

University of Southern Maine, College of Management and Human Service, School of Education and Human Development, Program in Educational Psychology, Portland, ME 04104-9300. Offers applied behavior analysis (MS, Certificate); response to intervention: academic (CGS); response to intervention: behavior (CGS). Part-time and evening/weekend programs available. *Faculty:* 4 full-time (2 women), 1 (woman) part-time/adjunct. *Students:* 3 full-time (2 women), 24 part-time (14 women); includes 4 minority (1 American Indian or Alaska Native, non-Hispanic/Latino; 1 Asian, non-Hispanic/Latino; 1 Native Hawaiian or other Pacific Islander, non-Hispanic/Latino; 1 Two or more races, non-Hispanic/Latino). Average age 31. 16 applicants, 81% accepted, 12 enrolled. In 2013, 10 master's, 11 other advanced degrees awarded. *Entrance requirements:* For master's, GRE or MAT. Additional exam requirements/recommendations for international students: Required—TOEFL (minimum score 550 paper-based; 79 iBT). *Application deadline:* For fall admission, 5/1 priority date for domestic students; for spring admission, 10/15 priority date for domestic students. Applications are processed on a rolling basis. Application fee: $65. Electronic applications accepted. *Expenses:* Tuition, state resident: part-time $380 per credit. Tuition, nonresident: part-time $1026 per credit. Part-time tuition and fees vary according to program. *Financial support:* Federal Work-Study, institutionally sponsored loans, scholarships/grants, and unspecified assistantships available. Support available to part-time students. Financial award application deadline: 3/1. *Faculty research:* Applied behavior analysis, functional behavioral analysis, positive behavioral interventions and supports. *Unit head:* Dr. Rachel Brown, Program Director, 207-228-8322, E-mail: rbrown@usm.maine.edu. *Application contact:* Mary Sloan, Assistant Dean of Graduate Studies and Director of Graduate Admissions, 207-780-4812, E-mail: gradstudies@usm.maine.edu.
Website: http://usm.maine.edu/educational-psychology.

The University of Tennessee, Graduate School, College of Education, Health and Human Sciences, Department of Educational Psychology and Counseling, Knoxville, TN 37996. Offers adult education (MS); applied educational psychology (MS); collaborative learning (Ed D); college student personnel (MS); mental health counseling (MS); rehabilitation counseling (MS); school counseling (MS). *Accreditation:* ACA (one or more programs are accredited); CORE (one or more programs are accredited); NCATE. Part-time and evening/weekend programs available. *Degree requirements:* For master's, thesis optional. *Entrance requirements:* For master's, GRE General Test, minimum GPA of 2.7. Additional exam requirements/recommendations for international students: Required—TOEFL. Electronic applications accepted. *Expenses:* Tuition, state resident: full-time $9540; part-time $531 per credit hour. Tuition, nonresident: full-time $27,728; part-time $1542 per credit hour. *Required fees:* $1404; $67 per credit hour.

The University of Tennessee, Graduate School, College of Education, Health and Human Sciences, Program in Education, Knoxville, TN 37996. Offers art education (MS); counseling education (PhD); cultural studies in education (PhD); curriculum (MS, Ed S); curriculum, educational research and evaluation (Ed D, PhD); early childhood education (PhD); early childhood special education (MS); education of deaf and hard of hearing (MS); educational administration and policy studies (Ed D, PhD); educational administration and supervision (Ed S); educational psychology (Ed D, PhD); elementary education (MS, Ed S); elementary teaching (MS); English education (MS, Ed S); exercise science (PhD); foreign language/ESL education (MS, Ed S); instructional technology (MS, Ed D, PhD, Ed S); literacy, language and ESL education (PhD); literacy, language education, and ESL education (Ed D); mathematics education (MS, Ed S); modified and comprehensive special education (MS); reading education (MS, Ed S); school counseling (Ed S); school psychology (PhD, Ed S); science education (MS, Ed S); secondary teaching (MS); social foundations (MS); social science education (MS, Ed S); socio-cultural foundations of sports and education (PhD); special education (Ed S); teacher education (Ed D, PhD). *Accreditation:* NCATE. Part-time and evening/weekend programs available. *Degree requirements:* For master's and Ed S, thesis optional; for doctorate, variable foreign language requirement, thesis/dissertation. *Entrance requirements:* For master's, minimum GPA of 2.7; for doctorate and Ed S, GRE General Test, minimum GPA of 2.7. Additional exam requirements/recommendations for international students: Required—TOEFL. Electronic applications accepted. *Expenses:* Tuition, state resident: full-time $9540; part-time $531 per credit hour. Tuition, nonresident: full-time $27,728; part-time $1542 per credit hour. *Required fees:* $1404; $67 per credit hour.

The University of Texas at Austin, Graduate School, College of Education, Department of Educational Psychology, Austin, TX 78712-1111. Offers academic educational psychology (M Ed, MA); counseling psychology (PhD); counselor education (M Ed); human development, culture and learning sciences (PhD); program evaluation (MA); quantitative methods (M Ed, MA, PhD); school psychology (MA, PhD). *Accreditation:* APA (one or more programs are accredited). *Degree requirements:* For master's, thesis optional; for doctorate, thesis/dissertation. *Entrance requirements:* For master's and doctorate, GRE General Test, 3 letters of recommendation. Additional exam requirements/recommendations for international students: Required—TOEFL.

The University of Texas at El Paso, Graduate School, College of Education, Department of Educational Psychology and Special Services, El Paso, TX 79968-0001. Offers educational diagnostics (M Ed); guidance and counseling (M Ed); special education (M Ed). Part-time and evening/weekend programs available. *Degree requirements:* For master's, thesis optional. *Entrance requirements:* For master's, minimum GPA of 3.0. Additional exam requirements/recommendations for international students: Required—TOEFL. Electronic applications accepted.

The University of Texas–Pan American, College of Education, Department of Educational Psychology, Edinburg, TX 78539. Offers educational diagnostician (M Ed); gifted education (M Ed); guidance and counseling (M Ed); school psychology (MA); special education (M Ed). Part-time and evening/weekend programs available. *Degree requirements:* For master's, comprehensive exam (for some programs), thesis (for some programs). *Entrance requirements:* For master's, GRE General Test, interview. *Expenses:* Tuition, state resident: full-time $5986; part-time $333 per credit hour. Tuition, nonresident: full-time $12,358; part-time $687 per credit hour. *Required fees:* $782. Tuition and fees vary according to program. *Faculty research:* Reading instruction, assessment practice, behavior interventions consultation, mental retardation.

University of the Incarnate Word, Extended Academic Programs, Programs in Psychology, San Antonio, TX 78209-6397. Offers educational psychology (MS); industrial and organizational psychology (MS); sport psychology (MS). *Students:* 9 part-time (8 women); includes 5 minority (1 Black or African American, non-Hispanic/Latino; 1 Asian, non-Hispanic/Latino; 3 Hispanic/Latino). Average age 32. 9 applicants, 100% accepted, 5 enrolled. *Expenses: Tuition:* Part-time $815 per credit hour. *Required fees:* $86 per credit hour. One-time fee: $40 part-time. Tuition and fees vary according to degree level and program. *Unit head:* Dr. Cyndi Porter, Vice President, 877-603-1130, E-mail: porter@uiwtx.edu. *Application contact:* Julie Weber, Director of Marketing and Recruitment, 210-318-1876, Fax: 210-829-2756, E-mail: eapadmission@uiwtx.edu.

University of the Pacific, Gladys L. Benerd School of Education, Department of Educational and School Psychology, Stockton, CA 95211-0197. Offers educational psychology (MA, Ed D); school psychology (Ed S). *Accreditation:* NCATE. *Faculty:* 3 full-time (all women). *Students:* 8 full-time (7 women), 13 part-time (12 women); includes 9 minority (1 American Indian or Alaska Native, non-Hispanic/Latino; 3 Asian, non-Hispanic/Latino; 4 Hispanic/Latino; 1 Two or more races, non-Hispanic/Latino). Average age 28. 11 applicants, 64% accepted, 6 enrolled. In 2013, 9 master's, 1 doctorate awarded. *Degree requirements:* For master's, thesis; for doctorate, thesis/dissertation. *Entrance requirements:* For master's and doctorate, GRE General Test, GRE Subject Test. Additional exam requirements/recommendations for international students: Required—TOEFL (minimum score 475 paper-based). *Application deadline:* For fall admission, 3/1 priority date for domestic students; for spring admission, 10/1 priority date for domestic students. Applications are processed on a rolling basis. Application fee: $75. *Financial support:* In 2013–14, 4 teaching assistantships were awarded. Financial award application deadline: 3/1; financial award applicants required to submit FAFSA. *Unit head:* Dr. Linda Webster, Chairperson, 209-946-2559, E-mail: lwebster@pacific.edu. *Application contact:* Office of Graduate Admissions, 209-946-2344.

The University of Toledo, College of Graduate Studies, Judith Herb College of Education, Department of Educational Foundations and Leadership, Toledo, OH 43606-3390. Offers educational administration and supervision (ME, DE, Ed S); educational psychology (ME, PhD); educational research and measurement (ME, PhD); educational sociology (PhD); educational theory and social foundations (ME); foundations of education (DE, PhD); history of education (PhD); philosophy of education (PhD). *Accreditation:* NCATE. Part-time and evening/weekend programs available. *Faculty:* 33. *Students:* 15 full-time (9 women), 84 part-time (57 women); includes 28 minority (21 Black or African American, non-Hispanic/Latino; 1 Asian, non-Hispanic/Latino; 5 Hispanic/Latino; 1 Two or more races, non-Hispanic/Latino), 2 international. Average age 42. 16 applicants, 63% accepted, 7 enrolled. In 2013, 16 master's, 4 doctorates awarded. *Degree requirements:* For master's, comprehensive exam, thesis or alternative; for doctorate, comprehensive exam, thesis/dissertation; for Ed S, thesis optional. *Entrance requirements:* For master's, doctorate, and Ed S, minimum cumulative GPA of 2.7 for all previous academic work, letters of recommendation. Additional exam requirements/recommendations for international students: Required—TOEFL (minimum score 550 paper-based; 80 iBT). *Application deadline:* For fall admission, 1/15 priority date for domestic and international students. Applications are processed on a rolling basis. Application fee: $45 ($75 for international students). Electronic applications accepted. *Financial support:* In 2013–14, 2 research assistantships with full and partial tuition reimbursements (averaging $7,500 per year), 2 teaching assistantships with full and partial tuition reimbursements (averaging $9,000 per year) were awarded; career-related internships or fieldwork, Federal Work-Study, institutionally sponsored loans, scholarships/grants, tuition waivers (full and partial), unspecified assistantships, and administrative assistantships also available. Support available to part-time students. Financial award applicants required to submit FAFSA. *Unit head:* Dr. Richard Welsch, Interim Chair, 419-530-2565, Fax: 419-530-8447, E-mail: richard.welsch@utoledo.edu. *Application contact:* Graduate School Office, 419-530-4723, Fax: 419-530-4724, E-mail: grdsch@utnet.utoledo.edu.
Website: http://www.utoledo.edu/eduhshs/.

University of Utah, Graduate School, College of Education, Department of Educational Psychology, Salt Lake City, UT 84112. Offers clinical mental health counseling (M Ed); counseling psychology (PhD); educational psychology (M Ed, MA, MS); elementary education (M Ed); instructional design and educational technology (M Ed); instructional design and technology (MS); learning and cognition (MS, PhD); reading and literacy (M Ed, MS, PhD); school counseling (M Ed); school psychology (M Ed, PhD); statistics (M Stat). *Accreditation:* APA (one or more programs are accredited). *Faculty:* 18 full-time (8 women), 20 part-time/adjunct (17 women). *Students:* 109 full-time (88 women), 108 part-time (68 women); includes 29 minority (2 Black or African American, non-Hispanic/Latino; 1 American Indian or Alaska Native, non-Hispanic/Latino; 7 Asian, non-Hispanic/Latino; 14 Hispanic/Latino; 1 Native Hawaiian or other Pacific Islander, non-Hispanic/Latino; 4 Two or more races, non-Hispanic/Latino), 7 international. Average age 32. 222 applicants, 35% accepted, 61 enrolled. In 2013, 51 master's, 10 doctorates awarded. *Degree requirements:* For master's, variable foreign language requirement, comprehensive exam (for some programs), thesis (for some programs), projects; for doctorate, variable foreign language requirement, comprehensive exam, thesis/dissertation, oral exam. *Entrance requirements:* For master's and doctorate, GRE General Test, minimum GPA of 3.0. Additional exam requirements/recommendations for international students: Required—TOEFL (minimum score 80 iBT). *Application deadline:* For fall admission, 4/1 for domestic and international students; for winter admission, 11/1 for domestic and international students; for spring admission, 3/15 for domestic and international students. Application fee: $55 ($65 for international students). Electronic applications accepted. *Expenses:* Contact institution. *Financial support:* In 2013–14, 81 students received support, including 29 fellowships with full and partial tuition reimbursements available (averaging $11,200 per year), 11 research assistantships with full and partial tuition reimbursements available (averaging $9,100 per year), 38 teaching assistantships with full and partial tuition reimbursements available (averaging $10,400 per year); career-related internships or fieldwork, Federal Work-Study, institutionally sponsored loans, scholarships/grants, health care benefits, and unspecified assistantships also available. Financial award application deadline: 4/1; financial award applicants required to submit FAFSA. *Faculty research:* Autism, computer technology and instruction, cognitive behavior, aging, group counseling. *Total annual research expenditures:* $441,375. *Unit head:* Dr. Anne E. Cook, Chair, 801-581-7148, Fax: 801-581-5566, E-mail: anne.cook@utah.edu. *Application contact:* JoLynn N. Yates, Academic Program Specialist, 801-581-7148, Fax: 801-581-5566, E-mail: jo.yates@utah.edu.
Website: http://www.ed.utah.edu/edps/.

University of Utah, Graduate School, Interdepartmental Program in Statistics, Salt Lake City, UT 84112-1107. Offers biostatistics (M Stat); econometrics (M Stat); educational psychology (M Stat); mathematics (M Stat); sociology (M Stat). Part-time programs available. *Students:* 28 full-time (11 women), 60 part-time (31 women); includes 18 minority (4 Black or African American, non-Hispanic/Latino; 9 Asian, non-Hispanic/Latino; 3 Hispanic/Latino; 2 Two or more races, non-Hispanic/Latino), 29 international. Average age 32. 50 applicants, 70% accepted, 33 enrolled. In 2013, 25 master's awarded. *Degree requirements:* For master's, comprehensive exam (for some programs), projects. *Entrance requirements:* For master's, GRE General Test (for all but biostatistics); GRE Subject Test (for mathematics), minimum GPA of 3.0; course work in

calculus, matrix theory, statistics. Additional exam requirements/recommendations for international students: Required—TOEFL (minimum score 500 paper-based; 61 iBT). *Application deadline:* For fall admission, 7/1 for domestic students, 4/1 for international students. Applications are processed on a rolling basis. Application fee: $55 ($65 for international students). Electronic applications accepted. *Expenses:* Tuition, state resident: full-time $5259. Tuition, nonresident: full-time $18,569. *Required fees:* $841. Tuition and fees vary according to course load. *Financial support:* In 2013–14, 10 students received support, including 10 research assistantships with full and partial tuition reimbursements available (averaging $1,000 per year); career-related internships or fieldwork, scholarships/grants, and unspecified assistantships also available. *Faculty research:* Biostatistics, sociology, economics, educational psychology, mathematics. *Unit head:* Xiaoming Sheng, PhD, Chair, University Statistics Committee, 801-213-3729, E-mail: xiaoming.sheng@utah.edu. *Application contact:* Laura Egbert, Coordinator, 801-585-6853, E-mail: laura.egbert@utah.edu.
Website: http://www.mstat.utah.edu.

University of Victoria, Faculty of Graduate Studies, Faculty of Education, Department of Educational Psychology and Leadership Studies, Victoria, BC V8W 2Y2, Canada. Offers aboriginal communities counseling (M Ed); counseling (M Ed, MA); educational psychology (M Ed, MA, PhD), including counseling psychology (M Ed, MA), leadership studies (PhD), learning and development (MA, PhD), measurement and evaluation, special education (M Ed, MA); leadership studies (M Ed, MA). Part-time programs available. *Degree requirements:* For master's, thesis (for some programs), comprehensive exam (M Ed); for doctorate, comprehensive exam, thesis/dissertation, candidacy exam. *Entrance requirements:* For master's, 2 years of work experience in a relevant field; for doctorate, GRE, 2 years of work experience in a relevant field, minimum B average. Additional exam requirements/recommendations for international students: Required—TOEFL (minimum score 575 paper-based), IELTS (minimum score 7). *Faculty research:* Learning and development (child, adolescent and adult), special education and exceptional children.

University of Virginia, Curry School of Education, Department of Leadership, Foundations and Policy, Program in Educational Psychology, Charlottesville, VA 22903. Offers applied developmental science (M Ed); educational evaluation (M Ed); educational psychology (M Ed, Ed D, Ed S); educational research (Ed D); gifted education (M Ed); instructional technology (M Ed, Ed S); research statistics and evaluation (Ed D); school psychology (Ed D). *Students:* 21 full-time (14 women), 12 part-time (9 women); includes 9 minority (4 Black or African American, non-Hispanic/Latino; 2 Asian, non-Hispanic/Latino; 3 Hispanic/Latino), 2 international. Average age 32. 67 applicants, 78% accepted, 27 enrolled. In 2013, 42 master's, 1 doctorate awarded. *Degree requirements:* For master's, comprehensive exam. *Entrance requirements:* For master's and doctorate, GRE General Test, 2 letters of recommendation. Additional exam requirements/recommendations for international students: Required—TOEFL (minimum score 600 paper-based; 90 iBT), IELTS (minimum score 7). *Application deadline:* Applications are processed on a rolling basis. Application fee: $60. Electronic applications accepted. *Expenses:* Tuition, state resident: part-time $334 per credit hour. Tuition, nonresident: part-time $1224 per credit hour. *Financial support:* Fellowships, research assistantships, and teaching assistantships available. Financial award application deadline: 1/5; financial award applicants required to submit FAFSA. *Unit head:* Leslie Booren, Managing Director, 434-243-2021, E-mail: booren@virginia.edu.
Website: http://curry.virginia.edu/academics/areas-of-study/educational-psychology.

University of Virginia, Curry School of Education, Program in Education, Charlottesville, VA 22903. Offers administration and supervision (PhD); applied developmental science (PhD); counselor education (PhD); curriculum and instruction (PhD); early childhood special education (MT); education evaluation (PhD); educational psychology (PhD); educational research (PhD); elementary education (MT); English education (MT, PhD); foreign language education (MT); higher education (PhD); instructional technology (PhD); kinesiology (MT, PhD); math education (PhD); reading education (PhD); research, statistics and evaluation (PhD); school psychology (PhD); science education (PhD); social studies education (MT, PhD); special education (PhD); world languages education (MT). *Students:* 474 full-time (379 women), 35 part-time (19 women); includes 89 minority (30 Black or African American, non-Hispanic/Latino; 1 American Indian or Alaska Native, non-Hispanic/Latino; 26 Asian, non-Hispanic/Latino; 19 Hispanic/Latino; 13 Two or more races, non-Hispanic/Latino), 21 international. Average age 26. 312 applicants, 49% accepted, 80 enrolled. In 2013, 137 master's, 38 doctorates awarded. *Degree requirements:* For master's, comprehensive exam (for some programs), field project; for doctorate, comprehensive exam, thesis/dissertation. *Entrance requirements:* For doctorate, GRE General Test. Additional exam requirements/recommendations for international students: Required—TOEFL (minimum score 600 paper-based; 90 iBT), IELTS (minimum score 7). *Application deadline:* Applications are processed on a rolling basis. Application fee: $60. Electronic applications accepted. *Expenses:* Tuition, state resident: part-time $334 per credit hour. Tuition, nonresident: part-time $1224 per credit hour. *Financial support:* Fellowships, research assistantships, and teaching assistantships available. Financial award application deadline: 1/5; financial award applicants required to submit FAFSA. *Unit head:* Robert C. Pianta, Dean, 434-924-3334, E-mail: pianta@virginia.edu. *Application contact:* Office of Admissions and Student Services, 434-924-0742, E-mail: curry-admissions@virginia.edu.
Website: http://curry.virginia.edu/teacher-education.

University of Washington, Graduate School, College of Education, Program in Educational Psychology, Seattle, WA 98195. Offers educational psychology (PhD); human development and cognition (M Ed); learning sciences (M Ed, PhD); measurement, statistics and research design (M Ed); school psychology (M Ed). *Accreditation:* APA. *Degree requirements:* For master's, thesis optional; for doctorate, thesis/dissertation. *Entrance requirements:* For master's and doctorate, GRE General Test, minimum GPA of 3.0. Additional exam requirements/recommendations for international students: Required—TOEFL.

The University of Western Ontario, Faculty of Graduate Studies, Social Sciences Division, Faculty of Education, Program in Educational Studies, London, ON N6A 5B8, Canada. Offers curriculum studies (M Ed); educational policy studies (M Ed); educational psychology/special education (M Ed). Part-time programs available. *Faculty research:* Reflective practice, gender and schooling, feminist pedagogy, narrative inquiry, second language, multiculturalism in Canada, education and law.

University of Wisconsin–Madison, Graduate School, School of Education, Department of Educational Psychology, Madison, WI 53706-1380. Offers MS, PhD. *Accreditation:* APA (one or more programs are accredited). *Degree requirements:* For doctorate, thesis/dissertation. *Entrance requirements:* For master's and doctorate, GRE General Test. *Application deadline:* For fall admission, 12/1 for domestic and international students; for spring admission, 10/1 for domestic and international students. Application fee: $56. Electronic applications accepted. *Expenses:* Tuition, state resident: full-time $10,728; part-time $790 per credit. Tuition, nonresident: full-time $24,054; part-time $1623 per credit. *Required fees:* $1130; $119 per credit. *Financial support:* Fellowships with full tuition reimbursements, research assistantships with full tuition reimbursements, teaching assistantships with full tuition reimbursements, and project assistantships available. *Unit head:* Dr. David Kaplan, Chair, 608-262-3432,

E-mail: edpsych@education.wisc.edu. *Application contact:* 608-262-2433, Fax: 608-262-5134, E-mail: gradadmiss@mail.bascom.wisc.edu.
Website: http://www.education.wisc.edu/edpsych/.

University of Wisconsin–Milwaukee, Graduate School, School of Education, Department of Educational Psychology, Milwaukee, WI 53201-0413. Offers counseling psychology (PhD); educational statistics and measurement (MS, PhD); learning and development (MS, PhD); school and community counseling (MS); school psychology (PhD). *Accreditation:* APA. Part-time programs available. *Faculty:* 15 full-time (9 women), 1 (woman) part-time/adjunct. *Students:* 149 full-time (112 women), 41 part-time (27 women); includes 38 minority (12 Black or African American, non-Hispanic/Latino; 6 Asian, non-Hispanic/Latino; 5 Hispanic/Latino; 15 Two or more races, non-Hispanic/Latino), 9 international. Average age 31. 243 applicants, 52% accepted, 47 enrolled. In 2013, 61 master's, 5 doctorates awarded. *Degree requirements:* For master's, comprehensive exam, thesis; for doctorate, thesis/dissertation. *Entrance requirements:* For master's, minimum GPA of 3.0; for doctorate, GRE General Test, minimum GPA of 3.0. Additional exam requirements/recommendations for international students: Required—TOEFL (minimum score 550 paper-based; 79 iBT), IELTS (minimum score 6.5). *Application deadline:* For fall admission, 1/1 priority date for domestic students; for spring admission, 9/1 for domestic students. Applications are processed on a rolling basis. Application fee: $56 ($96 for international students). Electronic applications accepted. *Financial support:* In 2013–14, 14 fellowships, 1 research assistantship, 8 teaching assistantships were awarded; career-related internships or fieldwork, health care benefits, unspecified assistantships, and project assistantships also available. Support available to part-time students. Financial award application deadline: 4/15; financial award applicants required to submit FAFSA. *Unit head:* Nadya Fouad, Department Chair, 414-229-6830, Fax: 414-229-4939, E-mail: nadya@uwm.edu. *Application contact:* General Information Contact, 414-229-4982, Fax: 414-229-6967, E-mail: gradschool@uwm.edu.
Website: http://www4.uwm.edu/soe/academics/ed_psych/.

Virginia Commonwealth University, Graduate School, School of Education, Doctoral Program in Education, Educational Psychology Track, Richmond, VA 23284-9005. Offers PhD. *Entrance requirements:* For doctorate, GRE. Additional exam requirements/recommendations for international students: Required—TOEFL (minimum score 600 paper-based; 100 iBT). Electronic applications accepted.

Walden University, Graduate Programs, School of Psychology, Minneapolis, MN 55401. Offers clinical psychology (MS), including counseling, general program; forensic psychology (MS), including forensic psychology in the community, general program, mental health applications, program planning and evaluation in forensic settings, psychology and legal systems; organizational psychology and development (Postbaccalaureate Certificate); psychology (MS, PhD), including applied psychology (MS), clinical psychology (PhD), counseling psychology (PhD), crisis management and response (MS), educational psychology, forensic psychology (PhD), general psychology, health psychology, leadership development and coaching (MS), media psychology (MS), organizational psychology, organizational psychology and nonprofit management (MS), psychology of culture (MS), psychology, public administration, and social change (MS), social psychology, terrorism and security (MS); psychology respecialization (Post-Doctoral Certificate); teaching online (Post-Master's Certificate). Part-time and evening/weekend programs available. Postbaccalaureate distance learning degree programs offered (minimal on-campus study). *Faculty:* 25 full-time (16 women), 272 part-time/adjunct (143 women). *Students:* 2,997 full-time (2,366 women), 1,450 part-time (1,149 women); includes 1,931 minority (1,326 Black or African American, non-Hispanic/Latino; 40 American Indian or Alaska Native, non-Hispanic/Latino; 88 Asian, non-Hispanic/Latino; 354 Hispanic/Latino; 11 Native Hawaiian or other Pacific Islander, non-Hispanic/Latino; 112 Two or more races, non-Hispanic/Latino), 30 international. Average age 41. 856 applicants, 94% accepted, 623 enrolled. In 2013, 483 master's, 146 doctorates, 5 other advanced degrees awarded. Terminal master's awarded for partial completion of doctoral program. *Degree requirements:* For master's, thesis optional; for doctorate, thesis/dissertation, residency. *Entrance requirements:* For master's, bachelor's degree or higher; minimum GPA of 2.5; official transcripts; goal statement (for some programs); access to computer and Internet; for doctorate, master's degree or higher; three years of related professional or academic experience (preferred); minimum GPA of 3.0; goal statement and current resume (select programs); official transcripts; access to computer and Internet; for other advanced degree, relevant work experience; access to computer and Internet. Additional exam requirements/recommendations for international students: Required—TOEFL (minimum score 550 paper-based; 79 iBT), IELTS (minimum score 6.5), Michigan English Language Assessment Battery (minimum score 82), or PTE. *Application deadline:* Applications are processed on a rolling basis. Application fee: $0. Electronic applications accepted. *Expenses:* Tuition: Full-time $11,813.55; part-time $500 per credit. *Required fees:* $618.76. *Financial support:* Fellowships, Federal Work-Study, scholarships/grants, unspecified assistantships, and family tuition reduction, active duty/veteran tuition reduction, group tuition reduction, interest-free payment plans, employee tuition reduction available. Support available to part-time students. Financial award applicants required to submit FAFSA. *Unit head:* Dr. Marilyn Powell, Associate Dean, 800-925-3368. *Application contact:* Jennifer Hall, Vice President of Enrollment Management, 866-4-WALDEN, E-mail: info@waldenu.edu.
Website: http://www.waldenu.edu/programs/colleges-schools/psychology.

Washington State University, Graduate School, College of Education, Department of Educational Leadership and Counseling Psychology, Program in Educational Psychology, Pullman, WA 99164. Offers Ed M, MA, PhD. *Degree requirements:* For master's, comprehensive exam (for some programs), thesis (for some programs), written or oral exam; for doctorate, comprehensive exam, thesis/dissertation, written and oral exam. *Entrance requirements:* For master's and doctorate, GRE General Test, minimum GPA of 3.0, 3 letters of recommendation, transcripts showing all college or university course work, statement of professional objectives, current curriculum vitae/resume. Additional exam requirements/recommendations for international students: Required—TOEFL (minimum score 550 paper-based; 80 iBT). Electronic applications accepted. *Faculty research:* Intersection of educational psychology, learning sciences, instructional design and technology, educational and psychological measurement issues.

Wayne State University, College of Education, Division of Theoretical and Behavioral Foundations, Detroit, MI 48202. Offers counseling (M Ed, MA, Ed D, PhD, Ed S); education evaluation and research (M Ed, Ed D, PhD); educational psychology (M Ed, PhD), including learning and instruction sciences (PhD), school psychology (PhD); educational sociology (M Ed); history and philosophy of education (M Ed); rehabilitation counseling and community inclusion (MA); school and community psychology (MA); school psychology (Certificate). *Accreditation:* ACA (one or more programs are accredited); CORE (one or more programs are accredited). Evening/weekend programs available. *Students:* 239 full-time (199 women), 214 part-time (190 women); includes 181 minority (141 Black or African American, non-Hispanic/Latino; 2 American Indian or Alaska Native, non-Hispanic/Latino; 14 Asian, non-Hispanic/Latino; 10 Hispanic/Latino; 1 Native Hawaiian or other Pacific Islander, non-Hispanic/Latino; 13 Two or more races, non-Hispanic/Latino), 21 international. Average age 33. 271 applicants, 35% accepted,

62 enrolled. In 2013, 55 master's, 19 doctorates, 8 other advanced degrees awarded. *Degree requirements:* For master's, thesis (for some programs); for doctorate, thesis/dissertation. *Entrance requirements:* For master's, GRE; for doctorate, GRE, interview, minimum GPA of 3.0, curriculum vitae, references. Additional exam requirements/recommendations for international students: Required—TOEFL (minimum score 550 paper-based; 79 iBT), Michigan English Language Assessment Battery (minimum score 85); Recommended—IELTS (minimum score 6.5), TWE (minimum score 5.5). *Application deadline:* For fall admission, 6/1 priority date for domestic students, 5/1 priority date for international students; for winter admission, 10/1 priority date for domestic students, 9/1 priority date for international students; for spring admission, 2/1 priority date for domestic students, 1/1 priority date for international students. Applications are processed on a rolling basis. Application fee: $0. Electronic applications accepted. *Expenses:* Tuition, state resident: part-time $554.15 per credit. Tuition, nonresident: part-time $1200.35 per credit. *Required fees:* $42.15 per credit. $268.30 per semester. Tuition and fees vary according to course load and program. *Financial support:* In 2013–14, 83 students received support, including 2 research assistantships with tuition reimbursements available (averaging $16,508 per year); fellowships with tuition reimbursements available, teaching assistantships with tuition reimbursements available, scholarships/grants, health care benefits, and unspecified assistantships also available. Financial award application deadline: 3/31; financial award applicants required to submit FAFSA. *Faculty research:* Adolescents at risk, supervision of counseling. *Unit head:* Dr. Joanne Holbert, Interim Assistant Dean, 313-577-1691, E-mail: jholbert@wayne.edu. *Application contact:* Janice Green, Assistant Dean, 313-577-1605, E-mail: jwgreen@wayne.edu.
Website: http://coe.wayne.edu/tbf/index.php.

Webster University, School of Education, Department of Multidisciplinary Studies, St. Louis, MO 63119-3194. Offers education leadership (Ed S); educational technology (MAT); educational technology leadership (Ed S); mathematics (MA); multidisciplinary studies (MAT); school psychology (Ed S); school systems, superintendency and leadership (Ed S); social science (MAT); special education (MA). Part-time programs available. *Entrance requirements:* For master's, minimum GPA of 2.5. Additional exam requirements/recommendations for international students: Required—TOEFL. *Expenses: Tuition:* Full-time $11,610; part-time $645 per credit hour. Tuition and fees vary according to campus/location and program.

West Virginia University, College of Human Resources and Education, Department of Technology, Learning and Culture, Program in Educational Psychology, Morgantown, WV 26506. Offers MA. *Accreditation:* NCATE. Evening/weekend programs available. *Degree requirements:* For master's, thesis, content exams. *Entrance requirements:* For master's, GRE General Test (minimum score 1100 verbal and quantitative) or MAT (minimum score 55), minimum GPA of 3.0, interview. Additional exam requirements/recommendations for international students: Required—TOEFL (minimum score 550

paper-based). *Faculty research:* Learning, development, instructional design, stimulus control, rehabilitation.

Wichita State University, Graduate School, College of Education, Department of Counseling, Educational Leadership, Educational and School Psychology, Wichita, KS 67260. Offers counseling (M Ed); educational leadership (M Ed, Ed D); educational psychology (M Ed); school psychology (Ed S). *Accreditation:* NCATE. Part-time and evening/weekend programs available. *Unit head:* Dr. Jean Patterson, Chairperson, 316-978-3325, Fax: 316-978-3102, E-mail: jean.patterson@wichita.edu. *Application contact:* Jordan Oleson, Admissions Coordinator, 316-978-3095, Fax: 316-978-3253, E-mail: jordan.oleson@wichita.edu.
Website: http://www.wichita.edu/.

Widener University, School of Human Service Professions, Center for Education, Chester, PA 19013-5792. Offers adult education (M Ed); counseling in higher education (M Ed); counselor education (M Ed); early childhood education (M Ed); educational foundations (M Ed); educational leadership (M Ed); educational psychology (M Ed); elementary education (M Ed); English and language arts (M Ed); health education (M Ed); higher education leadership (Ed D); home and school visitor (M Ed); human sexuality (M Ed, PhD); mathematics education (M Ed); middle school education (M Ed); principalship (M Ed); reading and language arts (Ed D); reading education (M Ed); school administration (Ed D); science education (M Ed); social studies education (M Ed); special education (M Ed); technology education (M Ed). *Accreditation:* NCATE. Part-time and evening/weekend programs available. *Faculty:* 34 full-time (22 women), 37 part-time/adjunct (14 women). *Students:* 64 full-time (44 women), 209 part-time (146 women); includes 49 minority (39 Black or African American, non-Hispanic/Latino; 1 American Indian or Alaska Native, non-Hispanic/Latino; 4 Asian, non-Hispanic/Latino; 4 Hispanic/Latino; 1 Two or more races, non-Hispanic/Latino), 8 international. Average age 39. 139 applicants, 88% accepted. In 2013, 168 master's, 31 doctorates awarded. Terminal master's awarded for partial completion of doctoral program. *Degree requirements:* For doctorate, thesis/dissertation. *Entrance requirements:* For master's, minimum GPA of 2.5; for doctorate, GRE or MAT, minimum GPA of 2.0 (undergraduate), 3.5 (graduate). *Application deadline:* Applications are processed on a rolling basis. Application fee: $25 ($300 for international students). Electronic applications accepted. *Expenses:* Contact institution. *Financial support:* Career-related internships or fieldwork, tuition waivers (full and partial), and unspecified assistantships available. Support available to part-time students. Financial award application deadline: 5/1. *Faculty research:* Reading and cognition, adult education, technology education, educational leadership, special education. *Unit head:* Dr. Michael W. LeDoux, Associate Dean, 610-499-4294, Fax: 610-499-4623, E-mail: mwledoux@widener.edu. *Application contact:* Dr. Roberta Nolan, Director of Graduate Admissions, 610-499-4125, E-mail: rdnolan@widener.edu.

Foundations and Philosophy of Education

Antioch University New England, Graduate School, Department of Education, Experienced Educators Program, Keene, NH 03431-3552. Offers foundations of education (M Ed), including applied behavioral analysis, autism spectrum disorders, educating for sustainability, next-generation learning using technology, problem-based learning using critical skills, teacher leadership; principal certification (PMC). *Degree requirements:* For master's, thesis, practicum. *Entrance requirements:* For master's, previous course work and work experience in education. Additional exam requirements/recommendations for international students: Required—TOEFL (minimum score 550 paper-based). Electronic applications accepted. *Expenses:* Contact institution. *Faculty research:* Classroom action research, school restructuring, problem-based learning, brain-based learning.

Arizona State University at the Tempe campus, Mary Lou Fulton Teachers College, Program in Social and Philosophical Foundations of Education, Phoenix, AZ 85069. Offers MA. Part-time and evening/weekend programs available. *Degree requirements:* For master's, thesis optional, interactive Program of Study (iPOS) submitted before completing 50 percent of required credit hours. *Entrance requirements:* For master's, minimum GPA of 3.0 or equivalent in last 2 years of work leading to bachelor's degree, 3 letters of recommendation, professional statement, curriculum vitae or resume. Additional exam requirements/recommendations for international students: Required—TOEFL (minimum score 80 iBT), TOEFL, IELTS, or PTE. Electronic applications accepted.

Arkansas State University, Graduate School, College of Education and Behavioral Science, School of Teacher Education and Leadership, Jonesboro, AR 72467. Offers community college administration (SCCT); curriculum and instruction (MSE); early childhood education (MAT, MSE); early childhood services (MS); educational leadership (MSE, Ed D, PhD, Ed S); educational theory and practice (MSE); middle level education (MAT, MSE); reading (MSE, Ed S); special education - gifted, talented, and creative (MSE); special education - instructional specialist grades 4-12 (MSE); special education - instructional specialist grades P-4 (MSE). *Accreditation:* NCATE. Part-time programs available. Postbaccalaureate distance learning degree programs offered. *Faculty:* 28 full-time (16 women). *Students:* 77 full-time (68 women), 1,934 part-time (1,449 women); includes 361 minority (290 Black or African American, non-Hispanic/Latino; 11 American Indian or Alaska Native, non-Hispanic/Latino; 3 Asian, non-Hispanic/Latino; 26 Hispanic/Latino; 1 Native Hawaiian or other Pacific Islander, non-Hispanic/Latino; 30 Two or more races, non-Hispanic/Latino), 5 international. Average age 36. 1,627 applicants, 71% accepted, 770 enrolled. In 2013, 1,182 master's, 12 doctorates, 76 other advanced degrees awarded. *Degree requirements:* For master's, comprehensive exam, thesis or alternative; for doctorate, comprehensive exam, thesis/dissertation; for other advanced degree, comprehensive exam. *Entrance requirements:* For master's, GRE General Test or MAT, appropriate bachelor's degree, official transcripts, immunization records, letters of reference, interview; for doctorate, GRE General Test or MAT, interview, master's degree, letters of reference, official transcript, personal statement, writing sample, immunization records; for other advanced degree, GRE General Test or MAT, interview, master's degree, official transcript, immunization records, letters of reference, 3 years of teaching experience, teaching license. Additional exam requirements/recommendations for international students: Required—TOEFL (minimum score 550 paper-based; 79 iBT), IELTS (minimum score 6), PTE (minimum score 56). *Application deadline:* For fall admission, 7/1 for domestic and international students; for spring admission, 11/15 for domestic students, 11/14 for international students. Applications are processed on a rolling basis. Electronic applications accepted. *Expenses:* Tuition, state resident: full-time $4284; part-time $238 per credit hour. Tuition, nonresident: full-time $8568; part-time $476 per credit hour. *International tuition:* $9268 full-time. *Required fees:* $1098;

$61 per credit hour. $25 per term. Tuition and fees vary according to course load and program. *Financial support:* In 2013–14, 20 students received support. Fellowships, teaching assistantships, career-related internships or fieldwork, scholarships/grants, and unspecified assistantships available. Financial award application deadline: 7/1; financial award applicants required to submit FAFSA. *Unit head:* Dr. Annette Hux, Interim Chair, 870-972-3059, Fax: 870-972-3344, E-mail: ahux@astate.edu. *Application contact:* Vickey Ring, Graduate Admissions Coordinator, 870-972-3029, Fax: 870-972-3857, E-mail: vickeyring@astate.edu.
Website: http://www.astate.edu/college/education/departments/school-of-teacher-education-and-leadership/index.dot.

Ashland University, Dwight Schar College of Education, Department of Educational Foundations, Ashland, OH 44805-3702. Offers teacher leader (M Ed). Part-time and evening/weekend programs available. *Degree requirements:* For master's, inquiry seminar, internship, or thesis. *Entrance requirements:* For master's, teaching certificate or license, bachelor's degree, minimum cumulative GPA of 2.75. Additional exam requirements/recommendations for international students: Required—TOEFL. Electronic applications accepted. *Faculty research:* Character education, teacher reflection, religion and education, professional education, environmental education.

Azusa Pacific University, School of Education, Department of Foundations and Transdisciplinary Studies, Azusa, CA 91702-7000. Offers curriculum and instruction in multicultural contexts (MA Ed); teaching (MA Ed).

Ball State University, Graduate School, Teachers College, Department of Educational Studies, Program in Educational Studies, Muncie, IN 47306-1099. Offers PhD. *Students:* 6 full-time (4 women), 15 part-time (7 women); includes 1 minority (Hispanic/Latino), 1 international. 14 applicants, 50% accepted, 4 enrolled. In 2013, 1 doctorate awarded. *Financial support:* In 2013–14, 6 students received support, including 13 teaching assistantships with full tuition reimbursements available (averaging $9,411 per year). *Unit head:* Dr. Jayne Beilke, Chairman, 765-285-5460, Fax: 765-285-5489, E-mail: jbeilke@bsu.edu. *Application contact:* Dr. Robert Morris, Associate Provost for Research and Dean of the Graduate School, 765-285-1300, E-mail: rmorris@bsu.edu.

Bank Street College of Education, Graduate School, Studies in Education Program, New York, NY 10025. Offers Ed M, MS Ed. *Degree requirements:* For master's, thesis. *Entrance requirements:* For master's, interview, essays. Additional exam requirements/recommendations for international students: Required—TOEFL (minimum score 600 paper-based; 100 iBT), IELTS (minimum score 7). Electronic applications accepted.

Binghamton University, State University of New York, Graduate School, School of Education, Program in Educational Theory and Practice, Vestal, NY 13850. Offers educational leadership (Certificate); educational studies (MS); educational theory and practice (Ed D). MS program also offered for working teachers in Greater New Orleans. *Students:* 6 full-time (5 women), 83 part-time (67 women); includes 12 minority (7 Black or African American, non-Hispanic/Latino; 1 American Indian or Alaska Native, non-Hispanic/Latino; 2 Asian, non-Hispanic/Latino; 2 Hispanic/Latino), 6 international. Average age 42. 36 applicants, 50% accepted, 12 enrolled. In 2013, 16 master's, 3 doctorates, 6 other advanced degrees awarded. *Degree requirements:* For doctorate, thesis/dissertation. *Entrance requirements:* For doctorate, GRE General Test, writing sample. Additional exam requirements/recommendations for international students: Required—TOEFL (minimum score 550 paper-based; 80 iBT). *Application deadline:* For fall admission, 2/1 priority date for domestic and international students. Applications are processed on a rolling basis. Application fee: $75. Electronic applications accepted. *Financial support:* In 2013–14, 11 students received support, including 1 fellowship with full tuition reimbursement available (averaging $15,500 per year), 1 teaching

assistantship with full tuition reimbursement available (averaging $15,500 per year); career-related internships or fieldwork, Federal Work-Study, institutionally sponsored loans, scholarships/grants, health care benefits, tuition waivers (full), and unspecified assistantships also available. Financial award application deadline: 2/15; financial award applicants required to submit FAFSA. *Unit head:* Dr. S. G. Grant, Dean of The Graduate School of Education, 607-777-6041, E-mail: jcarpent@binghamton.edu. *Application contact:* Kishan Zuber, Recruiting and Admissions Coordinator, 607-777-2151, Fax: 607-777-2501, E-mail: kzuber@binghamton.edu.
Website: http://www2.binghamton.edu/gse/doctoral-program/index.html.

Brigham Young University, Graduate Studies, David O. McKay School of Education, Department of Educational Leadership and Foundations, Provo, UT 84602. Offers M Ed, Ed D. Part-time and evening/weekend programs available. *Faculty:* 10 full-time (2 women), 2 part-time/adjunct (0 women). *Students:* 7 full-time (5 women), 67 part-time (25 women); includes 5 minority (1 Asian, non-Hispanic/Latino; 2 Hispanic/Latino; 2 Native Hawaiian or other Pacific Islander, non-Hispanic/Latino), 5 international. Average age 37. 55 applicants, 51% accepted, 26 enrolled. In 2013, 25 master's, 5 doctorates awarded. *Degree requirements:* For master's, comprehensive exam, thesis or alternative; for doctorate, comprehensive exam, thesis/dissertation. *Entrance requirements:* For master's, GRE, MAT, LSAT, GMAT; for doctorate, GRE, LSAT, GMAT. Additional exam requirements/recommendations for international students: Required—TOEFL (minimum score 580 paper-based; 85 iBT). *Application deadline:* For fall and spring admission, 2/15 for domestic and international students; for summer admission, 3/1 for domestic and international students. Application fee: $50. Electronic applications accepted. *Expenses: Tuition:* Full-time $6130; part-time $340 per credit hour. Tuition and fees vary according to program and student's religious affiliation. *Financial support:* In 2013–14, research assistantships (averaging $950 per year) were awarded. Financial award application deadline: 9/1. *Faculty research:* Mentoring, pre-service training of administrators, policy development, cross-cultural studies of educational leadership. *Unit head:* Dr. Sterling Clint Hilton, Chair, 801-422-4291, Fax: 801-422-0196, E-mail: edlfsec@byu.edu. *Application contact:* Bonnie Bennett, Department Secretary, 801-422-3813, Fax: 801-422-0196, E-mail: bonnie_bennett@byu.edu.
Website: http://education.byu.edu/edlf/.

Central Connecticut State University, School of Graduate Studies, School of Education and Professional Studies, Department of Teacher Education, Program in Educational Foundations Policy/Secondary Education, New Britain, CT 06050-4010. Offers MS. Part-time and evening/weekend programs available. *Students:* 2 part-time (both women). Average age 43. *Degree requirements:* For master's, comprehensive exam, thesis or alternative. *Entrance requirements:* For master's, minimum undergraduate GPA of 2.7. Additional exam requirements/recommendations for international students: Required—TOEFL (minimum score 550 paper-based; 79 iBT). *Application deadline:* For fall admission, 6/1 for domestic students, 5/1 for international students; for spring admission, 11/1 for domestic and international students. Applications are processed on a rolling basis. Application fee: $50. Electronic applications accepted. Part-time tuition and fees vary according to degree level. *Unit head:* Dr. Aram Ayalon, Chair, 860-832-2415, E-mail: casellar@ccsu.edu. *Application contact:* Patricia Gardner, Associate Director of Graduate Studies, 860-832-2350, Fax: 860-832-2362, E-mail: graduateadmissions@ccsu.edu.

Central Washington University, Graduate Studies and Research, College of Education and Professional Studies, Department of Educational Foundations and Curriculum, Ellensburg, WA 98926. Offers master teacher (M Ed). Part-time programs available. *Degree requirements:* For master's, comprehensive exam (for some programs), thesis or alternative. *Entrance requirements:* For master's, 1 year contracted teaching experience. Additional exam requirements/recommendations for international students: Required—TOEFL (minimum score 550 paper-based; 79 iBT), IELTS (minimum score 6.5). Electronic applications accepted.

Chicago State University, School of Graduate and Professional Studies, College of Education, Department of Educational Leadership, Curriculum and Foundations, Program in Curriculum and Instruction, Chicago, IL 60628. Offers instructional foundations (MS Ed). *Degree requirements:* For master's, comprehensive exam, thesis optional. *Entrance requirements:* For master's, minimum GPA of 2.75.

Columbia University, Graduate School of Arts and Sciences, New York, NY 10027. Offers African-American studies (MA); American studies (MA); anthropology (MA, PhD); art history and archaeology (MA, PhD); astronomy (PhD); biological sciences (PhD); biotechnology (MA); chemical physics (PhD); chemistry (PhD); classical studies (MA, PhD); classics (MA, PhD); climate and society (MA); earth and environmental sciences (PhD); East Asia: regional studies (MA); East Asian languages and cultures (MA, PhD); ecology, evolution and environmental biology (MA), including conservation biology; ecology, evolution, and environmental biology (PhD), including ecology and evolutionary biology, evolutionary primatology; economics (PhD); English and comparative literature (MA, PhD); French and Romance philology (MA, PhD); Germanic languages (MA, PhD); global French studies (MA); Hispanic cultural studies (MA); history (PhD); history and literature (MA); human rights studies (MA); Islamic studies (MA); Italian (MA, PhD); Japanese pedagogy (MA); Jewish studies (MA); Latin America and the Caribbean: regional studies (MA); Latin American and Iberian cultures (PhD); mathematics (MA, PhD), including finance (MA); medieval and Renaissance studies (MA); Middle Eastern, South Asian, and African studies (MA, PhD); modern art: critical and curatorial studies (MA); modern European studies (MA); museum anthropology (MA); music (DMA, PhD); oral history (MA); philosophical foundations of physics (MA); philosophy (MA, PhD); physics (PhD); political science (MA, PhD); psychology (PhD); quantitative methods in the social sciences (MA); religion (MA, PhD); Russia, Eurasia and East Europe: regional studies (MA); Russian translation (MA); Slavic cultures (MA); Slavic languages (MA, PhD); sociology (MA, PhD); South Asian studies (MA); statistics (MA, PhD); theatre (PhD); JD/PhD; MA/MS; MD/PhD; MPA/MA. Dual-degree programs require admission to both Graduate School of Arts and Sciences and another Columbia school. Part-time and evening/weekend programs available. *Faculty:* 808 full-time (310 women). *Students:* 2,755 full-time, 354 part-time; includes 493 minority (80 Black or African American, non-Hispanic/Latino; 6 American Indian or Alaska Native, non-Hispanic/Latino; 215 Asian, non-Hispanic/Latino; 135 Hispanic/Latino; 3 Native Hawaiian or other Pacific Islander, non-Hispanic/Latino; 54 Two or more races, non-Hispanic/Latino), 1,433 international. 12,949 applicants, 19% accepted, 998 enrolled. In 2013, 969 master's, 461 doctorates awarded. Terminal master's awarded for partial completion of doctoral program. *Degree requirements:* For master's, thesis (for some programs); for doctorate, comprehensive exam, thesis/dissertation. *Entrance requirements:* For master's and doctorate, GRE General Test, GRE Subject Test (for some programs). Application fee: $105. Electronic applications accepted. *Financial support:* Application deadline: 12/15. *Faculty research:* Humanities, natural sciences, social sciences. *Unit head:* Carlos J. Alonso, Dean of the Graduate School of Arts and Sciences, 212-854-5177. *Application contact:* GSAS Office of Admissions, 212-854-8903, E-mail: gsas-admissions@columbia.edu.
Website: http://gsas.columbia.edu/.

Curry College, Graduate Studies, Program in Education, Milton, MA 02186-9984. Offers elementary education (M Ed); foundations (non-license) (M Ed); reading (M Ed, Certificate); special education (M Ed). Part-time and evening/weekend programs available. *Degree requirements:* For master's, project or thesis. *Entrance requirements:* For master's, interview, recommendations, resume, written statement. Additional exam requirements/recommendations for international students: Required—TOEFL (minimum score 550 paper-based; 80 iBT). *Expenses:* Contact institution. *Faculty research:* Classroom trauma, therapeutic writing, inclusionary practices.

DePaul University, College of Education, Chicago, IL 60614. Offers bilingual bicultural education (M Ed, MA); counseling (M Ed, MA), including clinical mental health counseling, college student development, school counseling; curriculum studies (M Ed, MA, Ed D); early childhood education (M Ed, MA, Ed D); educating adults (MA); educational leadership (M Ed, MA, Ed D), including administration and supervision (M Ed, MA), principal preparation (M Ed, MA); elementary education (MA); mathematics education (MA); mathematics for teaching (MS); middle school mathematics education (MS); reading specialist (M Ed, MA); secondary education (M Ed); social and cultural foundations in education (MA); special education (M Ed, MA); world languages education (M Ed, MA). Part-time and evening/weekend programs available. Postbaccalaureate distance learning degree programs offered (no on-campus study). *Faculty:* 61 full-time (35 women), 59 part-time/adjunct (43 women). *Students:* 628 full-time (486 women), 324 part-time (243 women); includes 304 minority (144 Black or African American, non-Hispanic/Latino; 1 American Indian or Alaska Native, non-Hispanic/Latino; 38 Asian, non-Hispanic/Latino; 98 Hispanic/Latino; 23 Two or more races, non-Hispanic/Latino), 24 international. Average age 30. In 2013, 465 master's, 4 doctorates awarded. *Degree requirements:* For doctorate, thesis/dissertation. *Application deadline:* For fall admission, 8/15 for domestic students; for winter admission, 12/1 for domestic students; for spring admission, 3/1 for domestic students. Applications are processed on a rolling basis. Application fee: $40. Electronic applications accepted. Tuition and fees vary according to course level, course load and degree level. *Financial support:* Application deadline: 12/31; applicants required to submit FAFSA. *Unit head:* Dr. Paul Zionts, Dean, 773-325-7581, Fax: 773-325-7713, E-mail: pzionts@depaul.edu. *Application contact:* Farrah Dalal, Assistant Director, 773-325-2465, Fax: 773-325-2270, E-mail: fdalal@depaul.edu.
Website: http://education.depaul.edu.

Duquesne University, School of Education, Department of Foundations and Leadership, Program in Educational Studies, Pittsburgh, PA 15282-0001. Offers MS Ed. Part-time and evening/weekend programs available. Postbaccalaureate distance learning degree programs offered (no on-campus study). *Faculty:* 1 (woman) full-time. *Students:* 15 full-time (9 women), 18 part-time (14 women); includes 8 minority (5 Black or African American, non-Hispanic/Latino; 1 Hispanic/Latino; 2 Two or more races, non-Hispanic/Latino), 12 international. Average age 39. 19 applicants, 21% accepted, 4 enrolled. In 2013, 9 master's awarded. *Degree requirements:* For master's, thesis optional. *Entrance requirements:* For master's, bachelor's degree. Additional exam requirements/recommendations for international students: Required—TOEFL (minimum score 550 paper-based), IELTS (minimum score 7). *Application deadline:* For fall admission, 9/1 for domestic students; for spring admission, 1/1 for domestic students. Applications are processed on a rolling basis. Application fee: $0. Electronic applications accepted. *Expenses: Tuition:* Full-time $18,162; part-time $1009 per credit. *Required fees:* $1728; $96 per credit. Tuition and fees vary according to program. *Financial support:* Research assistantships available. Support available to part-time students. *Unit head:* Dr. Connie Marie Moss, Associate Professor and Director, 412-396-4778, Fax: 412-396-5454, E-mail: moss@duq.edu. *Application contact:* Michael Dolinger, Director of Student and Academic Services, 412-396-6647, Fax: 412-396-5585, E-mail: dolingerm@duq.edu.
Website: http://www.duq.edu/academics/schools/education/graduate-programs-education/ms-educational-studies.

Eastern Michigan University, Graduate School, College of Education, Department of Teacher Education, Program in Social Foundations, Ypsilanti, MI 48197. Offers MA. *Accreditation:* NCATE. Part-time and evening/weekend programs available. Postbaccalaureate distance learning degree programs offered (minimal on-campus study). *Students:* 3 full-time (2 women), 16 part-time (13 women); includes 7 minority (4 Black or African American, non-Hispanic/Latino; 1 American Indian or Alaska Native, non-Hispanic/Latino; 1 Asian, non-Hispanic/Latino; 1 Two or more races, non-Hispanic/Latino). Average age 33. 5 applicants, 80% accepted, 2 enrolled. In 2013, 8 master's awarded. *Entrance requirements:* For master's, GRE. Additional exam requirements/recommendations for international students: Required—TOEFL. *Application deadline:* Applications are processed on a rolling basis. Application fee: $35. *Expenses:* Tuition, state resident: full-time $12,300; part-time $466 per credit hour. Tuition, nonresident: full-time $23,159; part-time $918 per credit hour. *Required fees:* $71 per credit hour. $46 per semester. One-time fee: $100. Tuition and fees vary according to course level and degree level. *Financial support:* Fellowships, research assistantships with full tuition reimbursements, teaching assistantships with full tuition reimbursements, career-related internships or fieldwork, Federal Work-Study, institutionally sponsored loans, scholarships/grants, tuition waivers (partial), and unspecified assistantships available. Support available to part-time students. Financial award applicants required to submit FAFSA. *Unit head:* Dr. Martha Kinney-Sedgwick, Interim Department Head, 734-487-3260, Fax: 734-487-2101, E-mail: mkinneys@emich.edu. *Application contact:* Dr. Joe Ramsey, Coordinator, 734-487-3260, Fax: 734-487-2101, E-mail: pramsey1@emich.edu.

Fairfield University, Graduate School of Education and Allied Professions, Fairfield, CT 06824-5195. Offers applied behavior analysis (ATC); applied psychology (MA); clinical mental health counseling (MA, CAS); early childhood studies (ATC); educational technology (MA); elementary education (MA, CAS); family studies (MA); integration of spirituality and religion in counseling (ATC); marriage and family therapy (MA); school counseling (MA, CAS); school psychology (MA, CAS); school-based marriage and family therapy (ATC); secondary education (MA); special education (MA, CAS); substance abuse counseling (ATC); teaching (Certificate); teaching and foundations (MA, CAS); TESOL, world languages, and bilingual education (MA, CAS). *Accreditation:* NCATE. Part-time and evening/weekend programs available. *Faculty:* 24 full-time (21 women), 39 part-time/adjunct (27 women). *Students:* 154 full-time (130 women), 307 part-time (248 women); includes 75 minority (14 Black or African American, non-Hispanic/Latino; 1 American Indian or Alaska Native, non-Hispanic/Latino; 10 Asian, non-Hispanic/Latino; 44 Hispanic/Latino; 6 Two or more races, non-Hispanic/Latino), 13 international. Average age 34. 263 applicants, 41% accepted, 91 enrolled. In 2013, 149 master's, 21 other advanced degrees awarded. *Degree requirements:* For master's, comprehensive exam. *Entrance requirements:* For master's, PRAXIS I (for certification programs), minimum GPA of 3.0, 2 recommendations, resume. Additional exam requirements/recommendations for international students: Required—TOEFL (minimum score 550 paper-based; 84 iBT) or IELTS (minimum score 7.5). *Application deadline:* For fall admission, 2/15 for international students; for spring admission, 10/1 for international students. Application fee: $60. Electronic applications accepted. *Expenses: Tuition:* Part-time $675 per credit hour. Tuition and fees vary according to program. *Financial support:* In 2013–14, 55 students received support. Career-related internships or fieldwork and unspecified assistantships available. Financial award applicants required to submit FAFSA. *Faculty research:* Literacy, adolescent psychology, special education, teaching development, mentoring for professional development, multicultural

education. *Total annual research expenditures:* $325,000. *Unit head:* Dr. Robert D. Hannafin, Dean, 203-254-4250, Fax: 203-254-4241, E-mail: rhannafin@fairfield.edu. *Application contact:* Marianne Gumpper, Director of Graduate and Continuing Studies Admission, 203-254-4184, Fax: 203-254-4073, E-mail: gradadmis@fairfield.edu.
Website: http://www.fairfield.edu/academics/schoolscollegescenters/graduateschoolofeducationalliedprofessions/graduateprograms/.

Fairleigh Dickinson University, Metropolitan Campus, University College: Arts, Sciences, and Professional Studies, School of Computer Sciences and Engineering, Program in Mathematical Foundation, Teaneck, NJ 07666-1914. Offers MS.

Florida Atlantic University, College of Education, Department of Teaching and Learning, Boca Raton, FL 33431-0991. Offers curriculum and instruction (M Ed), including art, biology, chemistry, English, French, German, mathematics, music, physics, Pre-K and primary education, reading, social sciences, Spanish; elementary education (M Ed); environmental education (M Ed); reading education (M Ed); social foundations of education (M Ed), including educational psychology, educational technology, multilingual education. *Accreditation:* NCATE. Part-time and evening/weekend programs available. *Faculty:* 16 full-time (12 women), 1 (woman) part-time/adjunct. *Students:* 56 full-time (46 women), 96 part-time (78 women); includes 39 minority (10 Black or African American, non-Hispanic/Latino; 6 Asian, non-Hispanic/Latino; 20 Hispanic/Latino; 3 Two or more races, non-Hispanic/Latino), 4 international. Average age 32. 101 applicants, 54% accepted, 42 enrolled. In 2013, 64 master's awarded. *Entrance requirements:* For master's, GRE General Test, minimum GPA of 3.0 in last 2 years of undergraduate course work. Additional exam requirements/recommendations for international students: Required—TOEFL (minimum score 500 paper-based; 61 iBT), IELTS (minimum score 6). *Application deadline:* For fall admission, 7/1 for domestic students, 2/15 for international students; for spring admission, 11/1 for domestic students, 7/15 for international students. Applications are processed on a rolling basis. Application fee: $30. *Expenses:* Tuition, state resident: full-time $6660; part-time $370 per credit hour. Tuition, nonresident: full-time $18,450; part-time $1025 per credit hour. Tuition and fees vary according to course load. *Financial support:* Fellowships with partial tuition reimbursements, research assistantships with partial tuition reimbursements, teaching assistantships with partial tuition reimbursements, career-related internships or fieldwork, scholarships/grants, and unspecified assistantships available. *Faculty research:* Technology, teaching English to speakers of other languages, math teaching, electronic portfolio assessment, global perspectives through social studies. *Unit head:* Dr. Barbara Ridener, Chairperson, 561-297-3588. *Application contact:* Dr. Eliah Watlington, Associate Dean, 561-296-8520, Fax: 261-297-2991, E-mail: ewatling@fau.edu.
Website: http://www.coe.fau.edu/academicdepartments/tl/.

Florida State University, The Graduate School, College of Education, Department of Educational Leadership and Policy Studies, Program in Social, History and Philosophy of Education, Tallahassee, FL 32306. Offers history and philosophy of education (MS, PhD); international and intercultural education (PhD). *Faculty:* 5 full-time (3 women). *Students:* 29 full-time (20 women), 10 part-time (5 women); includes 6 minority (4 Black or African American, non-Hispanic/Latino; 2 Hispanic/Latino), 16 international. Average age 34. 35 applicants, 69% accepted, 13 enrolled. In 2013, 5 master's, 2 doctorates awarded. *Degree requirements:* For master's, comprehensive exam, thesis optional; for doctorate, comprehensive exam, thesis/dissertation. *Entrance requirements:* For master's and doctorate, GRE General Test, minimum GPA of 3.0. Additional exam requirements/recommendations for international students: Required—TOEFL (minimum score 550 paper-based; 80 iBT). *Application deadline:* For fall admission, 7/1 for domestic and international students; for winter admission, 11/1 for domestic and international students; for spring admission, 3/1 for domestic and international students. Application fee: $30. Electronic applications accepted. *Expenses:* Tuition, state resident: part-time $403.51 per credit hour. Tuition, nonresident: part-time $1004.85 per credit hour. *Required fees:* $75.81 per credit hour. One-time fee: $20 part-time. Tuition and fees vary according to course load, campus/location and student level. *Financial support:* Fellowships with full and partial tuition reimbursements, research assistantships with full and partial tuition reimbursements, teaching assistantships with full and partial tuition reimbursements, career-related internships or fieldwork, scholarships/grants, health care benefits, and unspecified assistantships available. Financial award applicants required to submit FAFSA. *Faculty research:* Social, historical, philosophical content of educational policies; religion, gender, diversity, and social justice in educational policy. *Unit head:* Dr. Jeffrey A. Milligan, Assistant Professor/Coordinator, 850-644-8171, Fax: 850-644-1258, E-mail: jmilligan@fsu.edu. *Application contact:* Linda J. Lyons, Academic Support Assistant, 850-644-7077, Fax: 850-644-1258, E-mail: ljlyons@fsu.edu.
Website: http://www.coe.fsu.edu/SHPFE.

The George Washington University, Graduate School of Education and Human Development, Department of Curriculum and Pedagogy, Program in Professional Teaching Standards, Washington, DC 20052. Offers Graduate Certificate. In 2013, 8 Graduate Certificates awarded. *Unit head:* Dr. Colin Green, Chair, 202-994-0997, E-mail: colgreen@gwu.edu. *Application contact:* Sarah Lang, Director of Graduate Admissions, 202-994-1447, Fax: 202-994-7207, E-mail: slang@gwu.edu.
Website: http://gsehd.gwu.edu/academics/programs/certificates/professional-teaching-standards/overview.

Georgia State University, College of Education, Department of Educational Policy Studies, Program in Social Foundations of Education, Atlanta, GA 30302-3083. Offers MS, PhD. *Accreditation:* NCATE. Part-time programs available. *Students:* Average age 0. *Degree requirements:* For master's, 36 semester hours, thesis or project; for doctorate, comprehensive exam, thesis/dissertation, 69 semester hours. *Entrance requirements:* For master's and doctorate, GRE. Additional exam requirements/recommendations for international students: Required—TOEFL (minimum score 550 paper-based; 79 iBT) or IELTS (minimum score 6.5). *Application deadline:* For fall admission, 1/15 for domestic and international students; for winter admission, 2/1 for domestic students; for spring admission, 10/1 for domestic and international students. Applications are processed on a rolling basis. Application fee: $50. Electronic applications accepted. *Expenses: Tuition, area resident:* Full-time $4176; part-time $348 per credit hour. Tuition, state resident: full-time $14,544; part-time $1212 per credit hour. Tuition, nonresident: full-time $14,544; part-time $1212 per credit hour. Tuition and fees vary according to course load and program. *Financial support:* In 2013–14, research assistantships with full tuition reimbursements (averaging $10,886 per year) were awarded; fellowships, teaching assistantships with full tuition reimbursements, career-related internships or fieldwork, institutionally sponsored loans, scholarships/grants, health care benefits, tuition waivers, and unspecified assistantships also available. Financial award application deadline: 3/15. *Faculty research:* Social and cultural Influences on schools, globalization and the workforce, history of women teachers in the U.S., school-corporate nexes, curriculum transformation for equity and inclusion. *Unit head:* Dr. Richard Lakes, Professor, 404-413-8030, Fax: 404-413-8003, E-mail: rlakes@gsu.edu. *Application contact:* Aishah Cowan, Administrative Academic Specialist, 404-413-8273, Fax: 404-413-8033, E-mail: acowan@gau.edu.
Website: http://education.gsu.edu/eps/6092.html.

Harvard University, Extension School, Cambridge, MA 02138-3722. Offers applied sciences (CAS); biotechnology (ALM); educational technologies (ALM); educational technology (CET); English for graduate and professional studies (DGP); environmental management (ALM, CEM); information technology (ALM); journalism (ALM); liberal arts (ALM); management (ALM, CM); mathematics for teaching (ALM); museum studies (ALM); premedical studies (Diploma); publication and communication (CPC). Part-time and evening/weekend programs available. *Degree requirements:* For master's, thesis. *Entrance requirements:* For master's, 3 completed graduate courses with grade of B or higher. Additional exam requirements/recommendations for international students: Required—TOEFL (minimum score 600 paper-based), TWE (minimum score 5). *Expenses:* Contact institution.

Hofstra University, School of Education, Programs in Educational Policy and Leadership, Hempstead, NY 11549. Offers educational and policy leadership (MS Ed, Ed D), including K-12 (MS Ed), K-12/higher education (Ed D); educational policy and leadership (Advanced Certificate), including school district business leader; foundations of education (MA, Advanced Certificate); higher education leadership and policy studies (MS Ed).

Indiana University Bloomington, School of Education, Department of Educational Leadership and Policy Studies, Bloomington, IN 47405-7000. Offers education policy studies (PhD); educational leadership (MS, Ed D, Ed S); higher education (MS, Ed D, PhD); history and philosophy of education (MS); history of education (PhD); international and comparative education (MS, PhD); philosophy of education (PhD); student affairs administration (MS). *Accreditation:* NCATE. Part-time and evening/weekend programs available. *Degree requirements:* For master's, thesis optional; for doctorate, comprehensive exam, thesis/dissertation; for Ed S, comprehensive exam or project. *Entrance requirements:* For master's, doctorate, and Ed S, GRE General Test. Additional exam requirements/recommendations for international students: Required—TOEFL (minimum score 79 iBT). Electronic applications accepted. *Faculty research:* Student engagement at higher education institutions in the nation, Reading First professional development initiative, state finance policy on financial access to higher education, school reform, special needs studies.

Indiana University Bloomington, University Graduate School, College of Arts and Sciences, Department of East Asian Languages and Cultures, Bloomington, IN 47408. Offers Chinese (MA, PhD); Chinese language pedagogy (MA); East Asian studies (MA); Japanese (MA, PhD); Japanese language pedagogy (MA). Part-time programs available. *Faculty:* 17 full-time (7 women), 17 part-time/adjunct (8 women). *Students:* 16 full-time (7 women), 18 part-time (13 women); includes 2 minority (1 Black or African American, non-Hispanic/Latino; 1 Hispanic/Latino), 16 international. 93 applicants, 40% accepted, 18 enrolled. In 2013, 9 master's, 2 doctorates awarded. *Degree requirements:* For master's, one foreign language, thesis; for doctorate, 2 foreign languages, comprehensive exam, thesis/dissertation. *Entrance requirements:* Additional exam requirements/recommendations for international students: Required—TOEFL (minimum score 93 iBT). *Application deadline:* For fall admission, 1/15 for domestic students, 12/1 for international students. Application fee: $55 ($65 for international students). Electronic applications accepted. *Financial support:* In 2013–14, fellowships with full tuition reimbursements (averaging $15,000 per year), teaching assistantships with full tuition reimbursements (averaging $15,750 per year) were awarded. Financial award application deadline: 2/15. *Faculty research:* Modern East Asian history; politics and society; traditional Chinese thought and society; medieval and premodern Japanese history, literature and society; modern Chinese and Japanese film and literature; Chinese, Japanese, Korean language and linguistics. *Unit head:* Prof. Natsuko Tsujimura, Chair, 812-855-0856, Fax: 812-855-6402, E-mail: tsujimur@indiana.edu. *Application contact:* Rachel Gray, Graduate Secretary, 812-856-4959, E-mail: rtgray@indiana.edu.
Website: http://www.indiana.edu/~ealc/index.shtml.

Iowa State University of Science and Technology, Department of Curriculum and Instruction, Ames, IA 50011. Offers curriculum and instructional technology (M Ed, MS, PhD); elementary education (M Ed, MS); historical, philosophical, and comparative studies in education (M Ed, MS); special education (M Ed, MS, PhD). *Degree requirements:* For master's, thesis or alternative; for doctorate, thesis/dissertation. *Entrance requirements:* For master's and doctorate, GRE General Test. Additional exam requirements/recommendations for international students: Required—TOEFL (minimum score 560 paper-based; 83 iBT), IELTS (minimum score 6.5). Electronic applications accepted.

Kent State University, Graduate School of Education, Health, and Human Services, School of Foundations, Leadership and Administration, Program in Cultural Foundations, Kent, OH 44242-0001. Offers M Ed, MA, PhD. *Accreditation:* NCATE. *Faculty:* 4 full-time (all women), 1 (woman) part-time/adjunct. *Students:* 24 full-time (16 women), 22 part-time (15 women); includes 20 minority (12 Black or African American, non-Hispanic/Latino; 5 Asian, non-Hispanic/Latino; 2 Hispanic/Latino; 1 Two or more races, non-Hispanic/Latino), 7 international. 26 applicants, 27% accepted. In 2013, 4 master's, 1 doctorate awarded. *Degree requirements:* For master's, thesis optional; for doctorate, comprehensive exam, thesis/dissertation. *Entrance requirements:* For master's, minimum GPA of 2.75, 2 letters of reference, goal statement; for doctorate, GRE General Test, minimum GPA of 3.5, master's degree, resume, interview, goal statement, 2 letters of reference. Additional exam requirements/recommendations for international students: Required—TOEFL (minimum score 550 paper-based; 80 iBT). *Application deadline:* Applications are processed on a rolling basis. Application fee: $30 ($60 for international students). Electronic applications accepted. *Financial support:* In 2013–14, 1 research assistantship with full tuition reimbursement (averaging $12,000 per year), 1 teaching assistantship with full tuition reimbursement (averaging $12,000 per year) were awarded; career-related internships or fieldwork, Federal Work-Study, institutionally sponsored loans, scholarships/grants, health care benefits, and unspecified assistantships also available. Support available to part-time students. Financial award application deadline: 4/1; financial award applicants required to submit FAFSA. *Faculty research:* Public politics, intercultural communication and training, research paradigms, comparative and international education. *Unit head:* Dr. Averil McClelland, Coordinator, 330-672-0594, E-mail: amcclell@kent.edu. *Application contact:* Nancy Miller, Academic Program Director, Office of Graduate Student Services, 330-672-2576, Fax: 330-672-9162, E-mail: ogs@kent.edu.
Website: http://www.kent.edu/ehhs/cult/.

Marquette University, Graduate School, College of Education, Department of Educational Policy and Leadership, Milwaukee, WI 53201-1881. Offers college student personnel administration (M Ed); curriculum and instruction (MA); education (MA); educational administration (M Ed); educational policy and foundations (MA); elementary education (Certificate); literacy (MA); principal (Certificate); reading specialist (Certificate); reading teacher (Certificate); secondary education (Certificate); superintendent (Certificate). Part-time and evening/weekend programs available. *Faculty:* 15 full-time (10 women), 3 part-time/adjunct (2 women). *Students:* 39 full-time (31 women), 107 part-time (70 women); includes 19 minority (7 Black or African American, non-Hispanic/Latino; 2 American Indian or Alaska Native, non-Hispanic/Latino; 3 Asian, non-Hispanic/Latino; 6 Hispanic/Latino; 1 Two or more races, non-Hispanic/Latino), 2 international. Average age 30. 144 applicants, 74% accepted, 67

enrolled. In 2013, 48 master's, 4 doctorates, 12 other advanced degrees awarded. Terminal master's awarded for partial completion of doctoral program. *Degree requirements:* For master's, comprehensive exam, thesis (for some programs); for doctorate, thesis/dissertation, qualifying exam, supporting minor. *Entrance requirements:* For master's, GRE General Test or MAT, official transcripts from all current and previous colleges/universities except Marquette, three letters of recommendation, statement of purpose; for doctorate, GRE General Test, MAT, sample of written work, official transcripts from all current and previous colleges/universities except Marquette, three letters of recommendation, statement of purpose, resume/curriculum vitae; for Certificate, GRE General Test or MAT, master's degree. Additional exam requirements/recommendations for international students: Required—TOEFL (minimum score 530 paper-based). *Application deadline:* For fall admission, 1/15 for domestic and international students. Application fee: $50. *Expenses:* Contact institution. *Financial support:* In 2013–14, 130 students received support, including 1 fellowship with full tuition reimbursement available (averaging $18,780 per year), 5 research assistantships with full tuition reimbursements available (averaging $13,404 per year); health care benefits, tuition waivers (partial), and unspecified assistantships also available. Support available to part-time students. Financial award application deadline: 2/15. *Faculty research:* Leadership; social justice in education; development of lifelong learners; race, class, and schooling in historical perspective; urban teacher education. *Unit head:* Dr. Ellen Eckman, Chair, 414-288-1561, E-mail: ellen.eckman@marquette.edu. *Application contact:* Dr. Sharon Chubbuck, Associate Professor, 414-288-5895.

McGill University, Faculty of Graduate and Postdoctoral Studies, Faculty of Education, Department of Integrated Studies in Education, Montréal, QC H3A 2T5, Canada. Offers culture and values in education (MA, PhD); curriculum studies (MA); educational leadership (MA, Certificate); educational studies (PhD); integrated studies in education (M Ed); second language education (MA, PhD).

Millersville University of Pennsylvania, College of Graduate and Professional Studies, School of Education, Department of Educational Foundations, Millersville, PA 17551-0302. Offers leadership for teaching and learning (M Ed); special education (M Ed). Part-time and evening/weekend programs available. *Faculty:* 13 full-time (7 women), 18 part-time/adjunct (11 women). *Students:* 1 (woman) full-time, 43 part-time (27 women); includes 4 minority (2 Black or African American, non-Hispanic/Latino; 1 American Indian or Alaska Native, non-Hispanic/Latino; 1 Hispanic/Latino). Average age 31. 6 applicants, 100% accepted, 6 enrolled. In 2013, 18 master's awarded. *Degree requirements:* For master's, graded portfolio. *Entrance requirements:* For master's, GRE or MAT, 3 letters of recommendation, official transcripts, goal statement, PA teacher certificate. Additional exam requirements/recommendations for international students: Required—TOEFL (minimum score 550 paper-based, 79 iBT) or IELTS (minimum score 6). *Application deadline:* For fall admission, 1/15 priority date for domestic and international students; for winter admission, 10/1 priority date for domestic and international students; for spring admission, 10/1 priority date for domestic and international students. Applications are processed on a rolling basis. Application fee: $40. Electronic applications accepted. *Expenses:* Tuition, state resident: full-time $7956; part-time $442 per credit. Tuition, nonresident: full-time $11,934; part-time $663 per credit. *Required fees:* $2196; $122 per credit. Tuition and fees vary according to course load. *Financial support:* In 2013–14, 2 students received support, including 2 research assistantships with full tuition reimbursements available (averaging $3,750 per year); institutionally sponsored loans and unspecified assistantships also available. Support available to part-time students. Financial award application deadline: 3/15; financial award applicants required to submit FAFSA. *Faculty research:* Teacher development, math learning disabilities, motivation for learning, gender studies, inclusive education. *Unit head:* Dr. John R. Ward, Chair, 717-871-3835, Fax: 717-871-2376, E-mail: john.ward@millersville.edu. *Application contact:* Dr. Victor S. DeSantis, Dean of College of Graduate and Professional Studies/Associate Provost for Civic and Community Engagement, 717-872-3099, Fax: 717-872-3453, E-mail: victor.desantis@millersville.edu.
Website: http://www.millersville.edu/edfoundations/.

Montclair State University, The Graduate School, College of Education and Human Services, Department of Educational Foundations, Montclair, NJ 07043-1624. Offers educational foundations (Certificate); pedagogy and philosophy (Ed D). Part-time and evening/weekend programs available. *Entrance requirements:* For doctorate, GRE General Test, 3 years of classroom teaching experience, interview, writing sample. Additional exam requirements/recommendations for international students: Required—TOEFL (minimum score 83 iBT) or IELTS. Electronic applications accepted. *Faculty research:* Pragmatism and education: theoretical and practical, history of education, children and philosophy, academic development, developing theory and practice - transforming K-12 school pedagogy.

Mount Saint Vincent University, Graduate Programs, Faculty of Education, Program in Educational Foundations, Halifax, NS B3M 2J6, Canada. Offers M Ed, MA Ed, MA-R. Part-time and evening/weekend programs available. *Degree requirements:* For master's, thesis (for some programs). *Entrance requirements:* For master's, bachelor's degree in related field, minimum B average. Electronic applications accepted. *Faculty research:* Research paradigms, moral aspects of education and teaching, private/independent schools, theory of critical thinking, teachers as workers and as agents of social change.

New York University, Steinhardt School of Culture, Education, and Human Development, Department of Humanities and Social Sciences in the Professions, Program in History of Education, New York, NY 10003. Offers MA, PhD. Part-time programs available. *Faculty:* 2 full-time (0 women). *Students:* 2 full-time (1 woman). Average age 26. 11 applicants, 18% accepted, 1 enrolled. In 2013, 1 master's awarded. *Degree requirements:* For master's, thesis (for some programs); for doctorate, thesis/dissertation. *Entrance requirements:* For doctorate, GRE General Test, interview. Additional exam requirements/recommendations for international students: Required—TOEFL (minimum score 100 iBT). *Application deadline:* For fall admission, 12/1 priority date for domestic and international students; for spring admission, 10/1 for domestic and international students. Applications are processed on a rolling basis. Application fee: $75. Electronic applications accepted. *Expenses: Tuition:* Full-time $35,856; part-time $1494 per unit. *Required fees:* $1408; $64 per unit. $473 per term. Tuition and fees vary according to course load and program. *Financial support:* Fellowships with full and partial tuition reimbursements, Federal Work-Study, institutionally sponsored loans, scholarships/grants, and tuition waivers (partial) available. Support available to part-time students. Financial award application deadline: 2/1; financial award applicants required to submit FAFSA. *Faculty research:* American educational thought, democratic community and education, twentieth-century history of education, Jewish history. *Unit head:* Dr. Jonathan L. Zimmerman, Director, 212-998-5049, Fax: 212-995-4832, E-mail: jlzimm@aol.com. *Application contact:* 212-998-5030, Fax: 212-995-4328, E-mail: steinhardt.gradadmissions@nyu.edu.
Website: http://steinhardt.nyu.edu/humsocsci/history.

Niagara University, Graduate Division of Education, Concentration in Foundations of Teaching, Niagara Falls, NY 14109. Offers MS Ed. *Accreditation:* NCATE. Part-time programs available. *Students:* 1 (woman) full-time, 5 part-time (2 women). Average age 30. In 2013, 5 master's awarded. *Degree requirements:* For master's, thesis. *Entrance requirements:* For master's, GRE General Test or MAT. Additional exam requirements/recommendations for international students: Required—TOEFL (minimum score 550 paper-based, 79 iBT) or IELTS (minimum score 6). *Application deadline:* For fall admission, 8/1 for domestic students. Applications are processed on a rolling basis. Application fee: $30. *Expenses:* Contact institution. *Financial support:* Research assistantships with full and partial tuition reimbursements, teaching assistantships with full and partial tuition reimbursements, career-related internships or fieldwork, Federal Work-Study, scholarships/grants, and unspecified assistantships available. Financial award application deadline: 4/15; financial award applicants required to submit FAFSA. *Unit head:* Dr. Leticia Hahn, 716-286-8760, E-mail: lhahn@niagara.edu. *Application contact:* Dr. Debra A. Colley, Dean of Education, 716-286-8560, Fax: 716-286-8560, E-mail: dcolley@niagara.edu.
Website: http://www.niagara.edu/foundations-of-teaching-math-science-and-technology-education.

Northeastern State University, College of Education, Department of Educational Foundations and Leadership, Tahlequah, OK 74464-2399. Offers higher education leadership (MS); school administration (M Ed); teaching (M Ed). Part-time and evening/weekend programs available. *Faculty:* 14 full-time (10 women), 6 part-time/adjunct (2 women). *Students:* 35 full-time (13 women), 154 part-time (69 women); includes 72 minority (9 Black or African American, non-Hispanic/Latino; 50 American Indian or Alaska Native, non-Hispanic/Latino; 2 Asian, non-Hispanic/Latino; 3 Hispanic/Latino; 8 Two or more races, non-Hispanic/Latino). Average age 37. In 2013, 31 master's awarded. *Degree requirements:* For master's, thesis. *Entrance requirements:* For master's, MAT or GRE. Additional exam requirements/recommendations for international students: Required—TOEFL. *Application deadline:* For fall admission, 6/1 priority date for domestic students. Applications are processed on a rolling basis. Application fee: $25. Electronic applications accepted. *Expenses:* Tuition, state resident: full-time $3029; part-time $168.25 per credit hour. Tuition, nonresident: full-time $7709; part-time $428.25 per credit hour. *Required fees:* $35.90 per credit hour. *Financial support:* Teaching assistantships and Federal Work-Study available. Financial award application deadline: 3/1. *Unit head:* Dr. Renee Cambiano, Head, 918-444-3741, E-mail: cambiare@nsuok.edu. *Application contact:* Margie Railey, Administrative Assistant, 918-456-5511 Ext. 2093, Fax: 918-458-2061, E-mail: railey@nsouk.edu.
Website: http://academics.nsuok.edu/education/COEDepartments/EducationalFoundationsLeadership.aspx.

Northern Arizona University, Graduate College, College of Education, Department of Educational Leadership, Flagstaff, AZ 86011. Offers community college/higher education (M Ed); educational foundations (M Ed); educational leadership (M Ed, Ed D); principal (Certificate); principal K-12 (M Ed); school leadership K-12 (M Ed); superintendent (Certificate). Part-time programs available. *Faculty:* 22 full-time (9 women). *Students:* 159 full-time (103 women), 528 part-time (331 women); includes 199 minority (36 Black or African American, non-Hispanic/Latino; 20 American Indian or Alaska Native, non-Hispanic/Latino; 11 Asian, non-Hispanic/Latino; 115 Hispanic/Latino; 1 Native Hawaiian or other Pacific Islander, non-Hispanic/Latino; 16 Two or more races, non-Hispanic/Latino). Average age 38. 211 applicants, 97% accepted, 148 enrolled. In 2013, 269 master's, 20 doctorates, 47 Certificates awarded. *Degree requirements:* For master's, comprehensive exam, thesis (for some programs); for doctorate, comprehensive exam, thesis/dissertation. *Entrance requirements:* For master's, minimum GPA of 3.0; for doctorate, GRE or MAT, minimum GPA of 3.5. Additional exam requirements/recommendations for international students: Required—TOEFL (minimum score 550 paper-based; 80 iBT), IELTS (minimum score 7). *Application deadline:* For fall admission, 3/1 priority date for international students; for spring admission, 9/15 priority date for international students. Applications are processed on a rolling basis. Application fee: $65. Electronic applications accepted. *Financial support:* In 2013–14, 1 research assistantship with full tuition reimbursement (averaging $12,000 per year) was awarded. Financial award applicants required to submit FAFSA. *Unit head:* Dr. Michael Schwanenberger, Chair, 928-523-4212, Fax: 928-523-1929, E-mail: michael.schwanenberger@nau.edu. *Application contact:* Jennifer Offutt, Administrative Assistant, 928-523-5098, Fax: 928-523-1929, E-mail: jennifer.offutt@nau.edu.
Website: http://nau.edu/coe/ed-leadership/.

Northern Illinois University, Graduate School, College of Education, Department of Leadership, Educational Psychology and Foundations, De Kalb, IL 60115-2854. Offers educational administration (MS Ed, Ed D, Ed S); educational psychology (MS Ed, Ed D); foundations of education (MS Ed); school business management (MS Ed). Part-time and evening/weekend programs available. Postbaccalaureate distance learning degree programs offered (minimal on-campus study). *Faculty:* 23 full-time (12 women). *Students:* 7 full-time (4 women), 221 part-time (125 women); includes 36 minority (17 Black or African American, non-Hispanic/Latino; 18 Hispanic/Latino; 1 Two or more races, non-Hispanic/Latino), 2 international. Average age 40. 52 applicants, 71% accepted, 15 enrolled. In 2013, 76 master's, 14 doctorates, 18 other advanced degrees awarded. *Degree requirements:* For master's, comprehensive exam, thesis optional; for doctorate, thesis/dissertation, candidacy exam, dissertation defense. *Entrance requirements:* For master's, minimum undergraduate GPA of 2.75; for doctorate, GRE General Test, minimum undergraduate GPA of 2.75, 3.2 graduate; for Ed S, GRE General Test, minimum GPA of 2.75 (undergraduate), 3.2 (graduate). Additional exam requirements/recommendations for international students: Required—TOEFL (minimum score 550 paper-based). *Application deadline:* For fall admission, 6/1 for domestic students, 5/1 for international students; for spring admission, 11/1 for domestic students, 10/1 for international students. Applications are processed on a rolling basis. Application fee: $40. Electronic applications accepted. *Financial support:* In 2013–14, 2 research assistantships with full tuition reimbursements were awarded; fellowships with full tuition reimbursements, teaching assistantships with full tuition reimbursements, career-related internships or fieldwork, Federal Work-Study, scholarships/grants, tuition waivers (full), and staff assistantships also available. Support available to part-time students. Financial award applicants required to submit FAFSA. *Faculty research:* Interpersonal forgiveness, learner-centered education, psychedelic studies, senior theory, professional growth. *Unit head:* Dr. Patrick A. Roberts, Acting Chair, 815-753-4404, E-mail: lepf@niu.edu. *Application contact:* Graduate School Office, 815-753-0395, E-mail: gradsch@niu.edu.
Website: http://cedu.niu.edu/LEPF/.

Oakland University, Graduate Study and Lifelong Learning, School of Education and Human Services, Department of Teacher Development and Educational Studies, Rochester, MI 48309-4401. Offers education studies (M Ed); secondary education (MAT). *Faculty:* 6 full-time (3 women), 17 part-time/adjunct (11 women). *Students:* 85 full-time (71 women), 151 part-time (99 women); includes 42 minority (24 Black or African American, non-Hispanic/Latino; 2 American Indian or Alaska Native, non-Hispanic/Latino; 9 Asian, non-Hispanic/Latino; 7 Hispanic/Latino), 3 international. Average age 30. 175 applicants, 47% accepted, 76 enrolled. In 2013, 69 master's awarded. *Entrance requirements:* For master's, minimum GPA of 3.0 for unconditional admission. *Application deadline:* For fall admission, 3/1 for domestic students. Application fee: $35. Electronic applications accepted. *Financial support:* Federal Work-Study, institutionally sponsored loans, and tuition waivers (full) available. Financial award application deadline: 3/1; financial award applicants required to submit FAFSA.

Total annual research expenditures: $182,162. *Unit head:* Dr. Dyanne M. Tracy, Chair, 248-370-3064, Fax: 248-370-4605, E-mail: dtracy@oakland.edu. *Application contact:* Christina J. Grabowski, Associate Director of Graduate Study and Lifelong Learning, 248-370-3167, Fax: 248-370-4114, E-mail: grabowsk@oakland.edu.

Purdue University, Graduate School, College of Education, Department of Educational Studies, West Lafayette, IN 47907. Offers administration (MS Ed, PhD, Ed S); counseling and development (MS Ed, PhD); education of the gifted (MS Ed); educational psychology (MS Ed, PhD); foundations of education (MS Ed, PhD); higher education administration (MS Ed, PhD); special education (MS Ed, PhD). *Accreditation:* ACA (one or more programs are accredited); NCATE (one or more programs are accredited). Part-time and evening/weekend programs available. *Faculty:* 21 full-time (17 women), 7 part-time/adjunct (4 women). *Students:* 102 full-time (73 women), 45 part-time (27 women); includes 23 minority (10 Black or African American, non-Hispanic/Latino; 5 Asian, non-Hispanic/Latino; 5 Hispanic/Latino; 3 Two or more races, non-Hispanic/Latino), 32 international. Average age 35. 165 applicants, 40% accepted, 33 enrolled. In 2013, 26 master's, 21 doctorates awarded. *Degree requirements:* For master's, thesis optional; for doctorate, thesis/dissertation, oral and written exams; for Ed S, oral presentation, project. *Entrance requirements:* For master's, GRE General Test (except for special education if undergraduate GPA is higher than a 3.0), minimum undergraduate GPA of 3.0; for doctorate and Ed S, GRE General Test (minimum combined score of 1000, 300 for new scoring), minimum undergraduate GPA of 3.0. Additional exam requirements/recommendations for international students: Required—TOEFL (minimum score 550 paper-based; 77 iBT), TWE (minimum score 5). *Application deadline:* Applications are processed on a rolling basis. Application fee: $60 ($75 for international students). Electronic applications accepted. *Financial support:* Fellowships with full tuition reimbursements, research assistantships with full tuition reimbursements, teaching assistantships with full tuition reimbursements, career-related internships or fieldwork, and tuition waivers (full) available. Support available to part-time students. Financial award application deadline: 3/1; financial award applicants required to submit FAFSA. *Faculty research:* Motivation, learning disabilities, school learning, group processes, cognitive development. *Unit head:* Dr. Ala Samrapungavan, Head, 765-494-9170, Fax: 765-496-1228, E-mail: ala@purdue.edu. *Application contact:* Cindy Blankenship, Graduate Contact, 765-494-2345, Fax: 765-494-5832, E-mail: prater0@purdue.edu.
Website: http://www.edst.purdue.edu/.

Rutgers, The State University of New Jersey, New Brunswick, Graduate School of Education, Department of Educational Theory, Policy and Administration, Program in Social and Philosophical Foundations of Education, Piscataway, NJ 08854-8097. Offers Ed M, Ed D. Part-time and evening/weekend programs available. *Degree requirements:* For doctorate, thesis/dissertation, qualifying exam. *Entrance requirements:* For master's, GRE General Test; for doctorate, GRE General Test, writing sample. Additional exam requirements/recommendations for international students: Required—TOEFL. Electronic applications accepted. *Faculty research:* Anthropology, history, sociology, philosophy, comparative education.

Saint Louis University, Graduate Education, College of Education and Public Service, Department of Educational Studies, St. Louis, MO 63103-2097. Offers curriculum and instruction (MA, Ed D, PhD); educational foundations (MA, Ed D, PhD); special education (MA); teaching (MAT). *Accreditation:* NCATE. Part-time programs available. *Degree requirements:* For master's, comprehensive exam; for doctorate, comprehensive exam, thesis/dissertation, preliminary oral and written exams. *Entrance requirements:* For master's, GRE General Test or MAT, letters of recommendation, resume; for doctorate, GRE General Test, letters of recommendation, resumé, goal statement, transcripts. Additional exam requirements/recommendations for international students: Required—TOEFL (minimum score 525 paper-based). Electronic applications accepted. *Faculty research:* Teacher preparation, multicultural issues, children with special needs, qualitative research in education, inclusion.

Simon Fraser University, Office of Graduate Studies, Faculty of Education, Programs in Curriculum and Instruction, Burnaby, BC V5A 1S6, Canada. Offers curriculum and instruction (M Ed); curriculum and instruction foundations (M Ed, MA); curriculum theory and implementation (PhD); educational practice (M Ed); philosophy of education (PhD). *Degree requirements:* For master's, comprehensive exam (for some programs), thesis (for some programs); for doctorate, comprehensive exam, thesis/dissertation. *Entrance requirements:* For master's, minimum GPA of 3.0 (on scale of 4.33) or 3.33 based on the last 60 credits of undergraduate courses; for doctorate, minimum GPA of 3.5 (on scale of 4.33). Additional exam requirements/recommendations for international students: Recommended—TOEFL (minimum score 580 paper-based; 93 iBT), IELTS (minimum score 7), TWE (minimum score 5). Electronic applications accepted. *Expenses: Tuition, area resident:* Full-time $5084 Canadian dollars. *Required fees:* $840 Canadian dollars. *Faculty research:* Philosophy of education, applied and comparative epistemology, ethics and moral education, critical multicultural practices.

Southeast Missouri State University, School of Graduate Studies, Department of Middle and Secondary Education, Cape Girardeau, MO 63701-4799. Offers secondary education (MA), including education studies, education technology. *Accreditation:* NCATE. Part-time programs available. *Faculty:* 5 full-time (3 women), 1 (woman) part-time/adjunct. *Students:* 6 full-time (4 women), 42 part-time (30 women); includes 4 minority (all Black or African American, non-Hispanic/Latino). Average age 30. 28 applicants, 100% accepted, 28 enrolled. In 2013, 8 master's awarded. *Degree requirements:* For master's, comprehensive exam, research paper. *Entrance requirements:* For master's, minimum undergraduate GPA of 2.75. Additional exam requirements/recommendations for international students: Required—TOEFL (minimum score 550 paper-based; 79 iBT), IELTS (minimum score 6), PTE (minimum score 53). *Application deadline:* For fall admission, 8/1 for domestic students, 6/1 for international students; for spring admission, 11/21 for domestic students, 10/1 for international students; for summer admission, 5/15 for domestic students. Applications are processed on a rolling basis. Application fee: $30 ($40 for international students). Electronic applications accepted. *Expenses:* Tuition, state resident: full-time $5139; part-time $285.50 per credit hour. Tuition, nonresident: full-time $9099; part-time $505.50 per credit hour. *Financial support:* In 2013–14, 7 students received support. Career-related internships or fieldwork, Federal Work-Study, scholarships/grants, traineeships, tuition waivers (full), and unspecified assistantships available. Financial award application deadline: 6/30; financial award applicants required to submit FAFSA. *Faculty research:* Pedagogy of teaching, multicultural education, reading and writing strategies, use of technology in the classroom. *Unit head:* Dr. Simin L. Cwick, Middle and Secondary Education Department Chair, 573-651-5965, E-mail: scwick@semo.edu. *Application contact:* Alisa Aleen McFerron, Assistant Director of Admissions for Operations, 573-651-5937, E-mail: amcferron@semo.edu.
Website: http://www5.semo.edu/middleandsec/.

Southern Connecticut State University, School of Graduate Studies, School of Education, Department of Educational Leadership, New Haven, CT 06515-1355. Offers educational foundations (Diploma), including foundational studies; educational leadership (Ed D, Diploma); research, statistics, and measurement (MS). Part-time and evening/weekend programs available. *Entrance requirements:* For degree, master's degree, minimum GPA of 3.0, writing sample. Electronic applications accepted.

Southern Illinois University Edwardsville, Graduate School, School of Education, Department of Educational Leadership, Program in Learning, Culture, and Society, Edwardsville, IL 62026. Offers MS Ed. Part-time programs available. *Students:* 1 (woman) full-time, 12 part-time (9 women); includes 5 minority (2 Black or African American, non-Hispanic/Latino; 1 Asian, non-Hispanic/Latino; 2 Hispanic/Latino). 6 applicants, 67% accepted. In 2013, 5 master's awarded. *Degree requirements:* For master's, thesis or alternative, project, oral defense. *Entrance requirements:* Additional exam requirements/recommendations for international students: Required—TOEFL (minimum score 550 paper-based, 79 iBT), IELTS (minimum score 6.5), Michigan Test of English Language Proficiency or PTE. *Application deadline:* For fall admission, 7/18 for domestic students, 6/1 for international students; for spring admission, 12/12 for domestic students, 10/1 for international students; for summer admission, 4/24 for domestic students, 3/1 for international students. Applications are processed on a rolling basis. Application fee: $30. Electronic applications accepted. *Expenses:* Tuition, state resident: full-time $3551. Tuition, nonresident: full-time $8378. *Financial support:* In 2013–14, 1 research assistantship with full tuition reimbursement (averaging $9,585 per year), 4 teaching assistantships with tuition reimbursements (averaging $9,585 per year) were awarded; fellowships, institutionally sponsored loans, scholarships/grants, and unspecified assistantships also available. Financial award application deadline: 3/1; financial award applicants required to submit FAFSA. *Unit head:* Dr. Laurel Puchner, Director, 618-650-3286, E-mail: lpuchne@siue.edu. *Application contact:* Melissa K. Mace, Assistant Director of Graduate and International Recruitment, 618-650-2756, Fax: 618-650-3618, E-mail: mmace@siue.edu.
Website: http://www.siue.edu/education/edld/.

Spring Hill College, Graduate Programs, Program in Education, Mobile, AL 36608-1791. Offers early childhood education (MAT, MS Ed); educational theory (MS Ed); elementary education (MAT, MS Ed); secondary education (MAT, MS Ed). Part-time programs available. *Faculty:* 3 full-time (all women). *Students:* 2 full-time (both women), 17 part-time (14 women); includes 2 minority (both Black or African American, non-Hispanic/Latino). Average age 32. In 2013, 7 master's awarded. *Degree requirements:* For master's, comprehensive exam, completion of program within 6 calendar years of entrance into graduate studies at Spring Hill; documentation of course field assignments (MS) or completion of internship (MAT). *Entrance requirements:* For master's, GRE, MAT, or PRAXIS (varies by program), bachelor's degree with minimum undergraduate GPA of 3.0; class B certificate (MS) or minimum number of hours in specific fields (MAT). Additional exam requirements/recommendations for international students: Required—TOEFL (minimum score 550 paper-based; 80 iBT), IELTS (minimum score 6.5), CPE or CAE (minimum score C), Michigan English Language Assessment Battery (minimum score 90). *Application deadline:* For fall admission, 8/1 priority date for domestic and international students; for spring admission, 12/1 priority date for domestic and international students. Applications are processed on a rolling basis. Application fee: $25 ($35 for international students). Electronic applications accepted. *Expenses:* Contact institution. *Financial support:* Applicants required to submit FAFSA. *Unit head:* Dr. Lori P. Aultman, Chair of Teacher Education, 251-380-3473, Fax: 251-460-2184, E-mail: laultman@shc.edu. *Application contact:* Donna B. Tarasavage, Associate Director, Academic Affairs, 251-380-3067, Fax: 251-460-2182, E-mail: dtarasavage@shc.edu.
Website: http://www.shc.edu/page/teacher-education.

Syracuse University, School of Education, Program in Cultural Foundations of Education, Syracuse, NY 13244. Offers MS, PhD, CAS. Part-time programs available. *Students:* 39 full-time (26 women), 17 part-time (8 women); includes 18 minority (9 Black or African American, non-Hispanic/Latino; 2 Asian, non-Hispanic/Latino; 4 Hispanic/Latino; 1 Native Hawaiian or other Pacific Islander, non-Hispanic/Latino; 2 Two or more races, non-Hispanic/Latino), 7 international. Average age 33. 42 applicants, 69% accepted, 7 enrolled. In 2013, 17 master's, 4 doctorates awarded. *Degree requirements:* For master's, thesis or alternative; for doctorate, comprehensive exam, thesis/dissertation. *Entrance requirements:* For doctorate, GRE, master's degree, writing sample; interview (recommended). Additional exam requirements/recommendations for international students: Required—TOEFL (minimum score 100 iBT). *Application deadline:* For fall admission, 12/1 priority date for domestic and international students; for spring admission, 10/15 priority date for domestic and international students. Applications are processed on a rolling basis. Application fee: $75. Electronic applications accepted. *Financial support:* Fellowships with full tuition reimbursements, research assistantships with full and partial tuition reimbursements, and teaching assistantships with full and partial tuition reimbursements available. Financial award application deadline: 1/1; financial award applicants required to submit FAFSA. *Faculty research:* Gender and education, history of women's education, the role of science in liberal education, student attrition. *Unit head:* Dr. Barbara Applebaum, Chair, 315-443-3343, E-mail: bappleba@syr.edu. *Application contact:* Laurie Deyo, Graduate Recruiter, School of Education, 315-443-2505, E-mail: e-gradrcrt@syr.edu.
Website: http://soeweb.syr.edu/cfe/culturalfound.html.

Teachers College, Columbia University, Graduate Faculty of Education, Department of Arts and Humanities, Program in Philosophy and Education, New York, NY 10027. Offers Ed M, MA, Ed D, PhD. *Faculty:* 2 full-time. *Students:* 11 full-time (6 women), 39 part-time (19 women); includes 14 minority (1 Black or African American, non-Hispanic/Latino; 1 Asian, non-Hispanic/Latino; 9 Hispanic/Latino; 1 Native Hawaiian or other Pacific Islander, non-Hispanic/Latino; 2 Two or more races, non-Hispanic/Latino), 12 international. Average age 30. 36 applicants, 67% accepted, 12 enrolled. In 2013, 12 master's, 1 doctorate awarded. *Degree requirements:* For master's, project; for doctorate, one foreign language, thesis/dissertation. *Entrance requirements:* For master's, previous course work in philosophy; for doctorate, GRE, previous course work in philosophy (Ed D), undergraduate degree in philosophy (PhD). *Application deadline:* For fall admission, 1/15 priority date for domestic students; for spring admission, 11/1 for domestic students. Applications are processed on a rolling basis. Application fee: $65. *Financial support:* Career-related internships or fieldwork, Federal Work-Study, institutionally sponsored loans, and tuition waivers (full and partial) available. Support available to part-time students. Financial award application deadline: 2/1. *Faculty research:* Philosophy and its relationship to educational thought, ethics and education, social theory and ideology. *Unit head:* Prof. David T. Hansen, Program Coordinator, 212-678-8239, E-mail: hansen@tc.edu. *Application contact:* Thomas P. Rock, Director of Admissions, 212-678-3083, Fax: 212-678-4171, E-mail: rock@tc.edu.
Website: http://www.tc.edu/philosophy/.

Troy University, Graduate School, College of Education, Program in Postsecondary Education, Troy, AL 36082. Offers adult education (M Ed); biology (M Ed); criminal justice (M Ed); English (M Ed); foundations of education (M Ed); general science (M Ed); higher education administration (M Ed); history (M Ed); instructional technology (M Ed); mathematics (M Ed); music industry (M Ed); physical fitness (M Ed); political science (M Ed); public administration (M Ed); social science (M Ed); teaching English (M Ed). *Accreditation:* NCATE. Part-time and evening/weekend programs available. *Faculty:* 30 full-time (11 women), 8 part-time/adjunct (1 woman). *Students:* 17 full-time (13 women), 106 part-time (84 women); includes 55 minority (45 Black or African American, non-Hispanic/Latino; 3 Asian, non-Hispanic/Latino; 2 Hispanic/Latino; 5 Two or more races, non-Hispanic/Latino). Average age 34. 109 applicants, 83% accepted, 5 enrolled. In 2013, 130 master's awarded. *Degree requirements:* For master's, comprehensive exam

(for some programs), thesis (for some programs), thesis or comprehensive exam. *Entrance requirements:* For master's, GRE (minimum score of 850 on old exam or 290 on new exam), GMAT (minimum score of 380), or MAT (minimum score of 385), bachelor's degree; minimum undergraduate GPA of 2.5 or 3.0 on last 30 semester hours, letter of recommendation. Additional exam requirements/recommendations for international students: Required—TOEFL (minimum score 523 paper-based; 70 iBT), IELTS (minimum score 6). *Application deadline:* Applications are processed on a rolling basis. Application fee: $50. Electronic applications accepted. *Expenses:* Tuition, state resident: full-time $6084; part-time $338 per credit hour. Tuition, nonresident: full-time $12,168; part-time $676 per credit hour. *Required fees:* $630; $35 per credit hour. $50 per semester. *Financial support:* Available to part-time students. Applicants required to submit FAFSA. *Unit head:* Dr. Jan Oliver, Associate Professor, 334-670-3444, Fax: 334-670-3474, E-mail: oliver@troy.edu. *Application contact:* Brenda K. Campbell, Director of Graduate Admissions, 334-670-3178, Fax: 334-670-3733, E-mail: bcamp@troy.edu.

University at Buffalo, the State University of New York, Graduate School, Graduate School of Education, Department of Educational Leadership and Policy, Buffalo, NY 14260. Offers education studies (Ed M); educational administration (Ed M, Ed D, PhD); educational culture, policy and society (PhD); higher education administration (Ed M, PhD); school building leadership (Certificate); school business and human resource administration (Certificate); school district business leadership (Certificate); school district leadership (Certificate). Part-time and evening/weekend programs available. *Faculty:* 13 full-time (7 women), 8 part-time/adjunct (all women). *Students:* 65 full-time (40 women), 139 part-time (83 women); includes 40 minority (24 Black or African American, non-Hispanic/Latino; 6 Asian, non-Hispanic/Latino; 10 Hispanic/Latino), 15 international. Average age 35. 159 applicants, 71% accepted, 65 enrolled. In 2013, 44 master's, 14 doctorates, 19 other advanced degrees awarded. *Degree requirements:* For master's, comprehensive exam (for some programs), thesis optional; for doctorate, comprehensive exam, thesis/dissertation. *Entrance requirements:* For master's, interview, letters of reference; for doctorate, GRE General Test or MAT, writing sample, letters of reference. Additional exam requirements/recommendations for international students: Required—TOEFL (minimum score 550 paper-based; 79 iBT). *Application deadline:* For fall admission, 2/1 priority date for domestic students, 2/1 for international students; for spring admission, 11/15 priority date for domestic students, 10/1 for international students. Applications are processed on a rolling basis. Application fee: $50. Electronic applications accepted. *Financial support:* In 2013–14, 20 fellowships (averaging $6,639 per year), 6 research assistantships with tuition reimbursements (averaging $10,500 per year) were awarded; career-related internships or fieldwork, Federal Work-Study, institutionally sponsored loans, scholarships/grants, health care benefits, tuition waivers, and unspecified assistantships also available. Financial award application deadline: 3/15; financial award applicants required to submit FAFSA. *Faculty research:* College access and choice, school leadership preparation and practice, public policy, curriculum and pedagogy, comparative and international education. *Total annual research expenditures:* $455,347. *Unit head:* Dr. Janina C. Brutt-Griffler, Chair, 716-645-2471, Fax: 716-645-2481, E-mail: bruttg@buffalo.edu. *Application contact:* Ryan Taugrin, Admission and Student Services Coordinator, 716-645-2110, Fax: 716-645-7937, E-mail: ryantaug@buffalo.edu.
Website: http://gse.buffalo.edu/elp.

The University of British Columbia, Faculty of Education, Department of Educational Studies, Vancouver, BC V6T 1Z1, Canada. Offers adult education (M Ed, MA); adult learning and global change (M Ed); educational administration (M Ed, MA); educational leadership and policy (Ed D); educational studies (PhD); higher education (M Ed, MA); society, culture and politics in education (M Ed, MA). Part-time and evening/weekend programs available. Terminal master's awarded for partial completion of doctoral program. *Degree requirements:* For master's, thesis; for doctorate, comprehensive exam, thesis/dissertation, master's thesis. *Entrance requirements:* For master's, minimum B+ average, 4-year undergraduate degree, field-related experience; for doctorate, minimum B+ average, 4-year undergraduate degree, master's degree, field-related experience. Additional exam requirements/recommendations for international students: Required—TOEFL (minimum score 600 paper-based; 100 iBT) or IELTS (minimum score 6.5). Electronic applications accepted. *Expenses: Tuition, area resident:* Full-time $8000 Canadian dollars. *Faculty research:* Educational leadership educational administration adult education politics in education, global change and adult learning.

University of California, Riverside, Graduate Division, Graduate School of Education, Riverside, CA 92521-0102. Offers autism (M Ed); diversity and equity (M Ed); education specialist (Credential); education, society and culture (MA, PhD); educational psychology (MA, PhD); general education (M Ed); higher education administration and policy (M Ed, PhD); multiple subject (Credential); reading (M Ed); school psychology (PhD); single subject (Credential); special education (M Ed, MA, PhD); TESOL (M Ed). *Faculty:* 22 full-time (11 women), 14 part-time/adjunct (10 women). *Students:* 218 full-time (148 women); includes 95 minority (10 Black or African American, non-Hispanic/Latino; 30 Asian, non-Hispanic/Latino; 49 Hispanic/Latino; 6 Two or more races, non-Hispanic/Latino), 12 international. Average age 31. 236 applicants, 66% accepted, 78 enrolled. In 2013, 66 master's, 13 doctorates, 86 other advanced degrees awarded. Terminal master's awarded for partial completion of doctoral program. *Degree requirements:* For master's, thesis optional, comprehensive exams or thesis (MA), case study or analytical report (M Ed); for doctorate, thesis/dissertation, written and oral qualifying exams, college teaching practicum. *Entrance requirements:* For master's, GRE General Test (for MA); CBEST and CSET (for M Ed in general education only), UCR Extension TESOL certificate (for M Ed with TESOL emphasis only); for doctorate, GRE General Test, writing sample; for Credential, CBEST, CSET. Additional exam requirements/recommendations for international students: Required—TOEFL (minimum score 550 paper-based; 80 iBT), IELTS (minimum score 7). *Application deadline:* For fall admission, 9/1 for domestic students, 5/1 for international students; for winter admission, 11/15 for domestic students, 7/1 for international students; for spring admission, 3/1 for domestic students, 10/1 for international students. Applications are processed on a rolling basis. Application fee: $80 ($100 for international students). Electronic applications accepted. *Financial support:* In 2013–14, 58 students received support, including 31 fellowships with full tuition reimbursements available, 11 research assistantships with full tuition reimbursements available (averaging $14,691 per year), 5 teaching assistantships with full tuition reimbursements available (averaging $17,655 per year); career-related internships or fieldwork, Federal Work-Study, institutionally sponsored loans, scholarships/grants, and unspecified assistantships also available. Financial award application deadline: 1/5. *Faculty research:* Responsiveness to intervention, faculty core, response to intervention of English language learners, advanced modeling techniques, study on social capital, trust, and motivation. *Total annual research expenditures:* $1.9 million. *Unit head:* Prof. Douglas Mitchell, Interim Dean and Professor, 951-827-5802, Fax: 951-827-3942, E-mail: douglas.mitchell@ucr.edu. *Application contact:* Prof. Michael Orosco, Assistant Professor and Graduate Advisor of Admissions, 951-827-6362, Fax: 951-827-3291, E-mail: edgrad@ucr.edu.
Website: http://www.education.ucr.edu/.

University of Cincinnati, Graduate School, College of Education, Criminal Justice, and Human Services, Division of Educational Studies, Program in Educational Studies, Cincinnati, OH 45221. Offers M Ed, PhD. *Accreditation:* NCATE. Part-time programs available. *Degree requirements:* For master's, thesis optional; for doctorate, comprehensive exam, thesis/dissertation. *Entrance requirements:* For master's, GRE General Test; for doctorate, GRE General Test, GRE Subject Test. Additional exam requirements/recommendations for international students: Required—TOEFL (minimum score 520 paper-based), OEPT 3. Electronic applications accepted.

University of Connecticut, Graduate School, Neag School of Education, Department of Educational Leadership, Center for Education Policy Analysis, Storrs, CT 06269. Offers PhD. *Accreditation:* NCATE. *Degree requirements:* For doctorate, thesis/dissertation. *Entrance requirements:* For doctorate, GRE General Test. Additional exam requirements/recommendations for international students: Required—TOEFL (minimum score 550 paper-based). Electronic applications accepted.

University of Hawaii at Manoa, Graduate Division, College of Education, Department of Educational Foundations, Honolulu, HI 96822. Offers M Ed. Part-time and evening/weekend programs available. *Degree requirements:* For master's, thesis optional. *Entrance requirements:* Additional exam requirements/recommendations for international students: Required—TOEFL (minimum score 580 paper-based; 92 iBT), IELTS (minimum score 5). *Faculty research:* Multicultural-ethnic education, comparative education, educational policy, interdisciplinary inquiry, moral/political education.

University of Hawaii at Manoa, Graduate Division, College of Education, PhD in Education Program, Honolulu, HI 96822. Offers curriculum and instruction (PhD); educational administration (PhD); educational foundations (PhD); educational policy studies (PhD); educational technology (PhD); exceptionalities (PhD); kinesiology (PhD). Part-time and evening/weekend programs available. *Degree requirements:* For doctorate, thesis/dissertation. *Entrance requirements:* For doctorate, GRE General Test, sample of written work. Additional exam requirements/recommendations for international students: Required—TOEFL (minimum score 600 paper-based; 100 iBT), IELTS (minimum score 7).

University of Houston, College of Education, Department of Educational Leadership and Cultural Studies, Houston, TX 77204. Offers administration and supervision (M Ed, Ed D); higher education (M Ed); historical, social, and cultural foundations of education (M Ed). *Accreditation:* NCATE. Part-time and evening/weekend programs available. *Degree requirements:* For master's, comprehensive exam or thesis; for doctorate, comprehensive exam, thesis/dissertation. *Entrance requirements:* For master's, GRE General Test, minimum cumulative GPA of 2.6, 3 letters of recommendation, resume/vitae, goal statement; for doctorate, GRE General Test, minimum cumulative GPA of 2.6, 3 letters of recommendation, resume/vitae, goal statement, writing sample, interview. Additional exam requirements/recommendations for international students: Required—TOEFL (minimum score 550 paper-based; 79 iBT). Electronic applications accepted. *Faculty research:* Change, supervision, multiculturalism, evaluation, policy.

University of Houston–Clear Lake, School of Education, Program in Foundations and Professional Studies, Houston, TX 77058-1002. Offers counseling (MS); instructional technology (MS); multicultural studies (MS). Part-time and evening/weekend programs available. *Degree requirements:* For master's, thesis optional. *Entrance requirements:* For master's, GRE or minimum GPA of 3.0 in last 60 hours. Additional exam requirements/recommendations for international students: Required—TOEFL (minimum score 550 paper-based). Electronic applications accepted.

The University of Iowa, Graduate College, College of Education, Department of Educational Policy and Leadership Studies, Program in Schools, Culture, and Society, Iowa City, IA 52242-1316. Offers MA, PhD. *Degree requirements:* For master's, thesis optional, exam; for doctorate, comprehensive exam, thesis/dissertation. *Entrance requirements:* For master's and doctorate, GRE General Test, minimum GPA of 3.0. Additional exam requirements/recommendations for international students: Required—TOEFL (minimum score 550 paper-based; 81 iBT). Electronic applications accepted.

The University of Iowa, Graduate College, College of Education, Department of Psychological and Quantitative Foundations, Iowa City, IA 52242-1316. Offers counseling psychology (PhD); educational measurement and statistics (MA, PhD); educational psychology (MA, PhD); school psychology (PhD, Ed S). *Accreditation:* APA. *Degree requirements:* For master's, thesis optional, exam; for doctorate, comprehensive exam, thesis/dissertation; for Ed S, exam. *Entrance requirements:* For master's, doctorate, and Ed S, GRE General Test, minimum GPA of 3.0. Additional exam requirements/recommendations for international students: Required—TOEFL (minimum score 550 paper-based; 81 iBT). Electronic applications accepted.

The University of Kansas, Graduate Studies, School of Education, Department of Educational Leadership and Policy Studies, Education Leadership and Policy Program, Lawrence, KS 66045-3101. Offers educational administration (Ed D, PhD); foundations (PhD); higher education (Ed D, PhD); policy studies (PhD). Part-time and evening/weekend programs available. *Faculty:* 15. *Students:* 106 full-time (63 women), 46 part-time (19 women); includes 32 minority (10 Black or African American, non-Hispanic/Latino; 4 American Indian or Alaska Native, non-Hispanic/Latino; 6 Asian, non-Hispanic/Latino; 7 Hispanic/Latino; 5 Two or more races, non-Hispanic/Latino), 27 international. Average age 37. 63 applicants, 71% accepted, 32 enrolled. In 2013, 31 doctorates awarded. *Degree requirements:* For doctorate, comprehensive exam, thesis/dissertation. *Entrance requirements:* For doctorate, GRE General Test, minimum graduate GPA of 3.5. Additional exam requirements/recommendations for international students: Required—TOEFL (minimum score 570 paper-based; 80 iBT). *Application deadline:* For fall admission, 7/1 for domestic and international students; for spring admission, 11/1 for domestic and international students. Applications are processed on a rolling basis. Application fee: $55 ($65 for international students). Electronic applications accepted. *Financial support:* Fellowships, research assistantships with full and partial tuition reimbursements, teaching assistantships with full and partial tuition reimbursements, scholarships/grants, and unspecified assistantships available. Financial award application deadline: 3/15. *Faculty research:* Historical and philosophical issues in education, education policy and leadership, higher education faculty, research on college students, education technology. *Unit head:* Dr. Susan Twombly, Chair, 785-864-9721, Fax: 785-864-4697, E-mail: stwombly@ku.edu. *Application contact:* Denise Brubaker, Admissions Coordinator, 785-864-7973, Fax: 785-864-4697, E-mail: brubaker@ku.edu.
Website: http://elps.soe.ku.edu/.

The University of Kansas, Graduate Studies, School of Education, Department of Educational Leadership and Policy Studies, Program in Foundations of Education, Lawrence, KS 66045. Offers historical, philosophical, and social foundations of education (MS Ed, PhD). Part-time and evening/weekend programs available. *Faculty:* 15. *Students:* 2 full-time (1 woman), 4 part-time (3 women), 2 international. Average age 36. 7 applicants, 71% accepted, 1 enrolled. In 2013, 1 master's awarded. *Degree requirements:* For master's, thesis optional; for doctorate, comprehensive exam, thesis/dissertation. *Entrance requirements:* For master's, minimum GPA of 3.0; for doctorate, GRE General Test, minimum graduate GPA of 3.5. Additional exam requirements/recommendations for international students: Required—TOEFL (minimum score 570 paper-based; 80 iBT). *Application deadline:* For fall admission, 7/1 for domestic and international students; for spring admission, 11/1 for domestic and international students. Applications are processed on a rolling basis. Application fee: $55 ($65 for international students). Electronic applications accepted. *Financial support:*

Fellowships, research assistantships with full and partial tuition reimbursements, and teaching assistantships with full and partial tuition reimbursements available. Financial award application deadline: 3/15. *Faculty research:* Historical, social, and philosophical issues in education. *Unit head:* Dr. Susan Twombly, Chair, 785-864-9721, Fax: 785-864-4697, E-mail: stwombly@ku.edu. *Application contact:* Denise Brubaker, Admissions Coordinator, 785-864-7973, Fax: 785-864-4697, E-mail: brubaker@ku.edu.
Website: http://elps.soe.ku.edu/academics/social-cultural-studies/mse.

University of Manitoba, Faculty of Graduate Studies, Faculty of Education, Department of Educational Administration, Foundations and Psychology, Winnipeg, MB R3T 2N2, Canada. Offers adult and post-secondary education (M Ed); educational administration (M Ed); guidance and counseling (M Ed); inclusive special education (M Ed); social foundations of education (M Ed). *Degree requirements:* For master's, thesis or alternative.

University of Maryland, College Park, Academic Affairs, College of Education, Department of Education Policy and Leadership, College Park, MD 20742. Offers curriculum and educational communications (M Ed, MA, Ed D, PhD); social foundations of education (M Ed, MA, Ed D, PhD, CAGS). *Accreditation:* NCATE. Part-time and evening/weekend programs available. Postbaccalaureate distance learning degree programs offered (minimal on-campus study). *Students:* 1 (woman) full-time. In 2013, 1 doctorate awarded. *Degree requirements:* For master's, thesis or alternative, internship and/or field experience; for doctorate, comprehensive exam, thesis/dissertation, practicum or internship. *Entrance requirements:* For master's, GRE General Test or MAT, minimum GPA of 3.0, scholarly writing sample, 3 letters of recommendation; for doctorate, GRE General Test or MAT, scholarly writing sample; minimum undergraduate GPA of 3.0, graduate 3.5. *Application deadline:* For fall admission, 2/1 for domestic students, 9/1 for international students. *Expenses:* Tuition, state resident: full-time $10,314; part-time $573 per credit hour. Tuition, nonresident: full-time $22,248; part-time $1236 per credit. *Required fees:* $1446; $403.15 per semester. Tuition and fees vary according to program. *Financial support:* Career-related internships or fieldwork, Federal Work-Study, and scholarships/grants available. Support available to part-time students. Financial award applicants required to submit FAFSA. *Faculty research:* Educational technology, adult and higher education. *Unit head:* Francine Hultgren, Chair, 301-405-3117, E-mail: fh@umd.edu. *Application contact:* Dr. Charles A. Caramello, Dean of Graduate School, 301-405-0358, Fax: 301-314-9305, E-mail: ccaramel@umd.edu.

University of Minnesota, Twin Cities Campus, Graduate School, College of Education and Human Development, Department of Educational Psychology, Program in Psychological Foundations of Education, Minneapolis, MN 55455-0213. Offers MA, PhD, Ed S. *Students:* 54 full-time (36 women), 14 part-time (9 women); includes 10 minority (3 Black or African American, non-Hispanic/Latino; 1 American Indian or Alaska Native, non-Hispanic/Latino; 3 Asian, non-Hispanic/Latino; 3 Hispanic/Latino), 23 international. Average age 33. 66 applicants, 38% accepted, 8 enrolled. In 2013, 10 doctorates awarded. Application fee: $75 ($95 for international students). *Unit head:* Geoff Maruyama, Chair, 612-625-5861, Fax: 612-624-8241, E-mail: geoff@umn.edu. *Application contact:* Dr. Jennifer Engler, Assistant Dean, 612-626-2887, Fax: 612-626-7496, E-mail: engle009@umn.edu.
Website: http://www.cehd.umn.edu/EdPsych/Foundations.

University of New Mexico, Graduate School, College of Education, Department of Language, Literacy and Sociocultural Studies, Program in Language, Literacy and Sociocultural Studies, Albuquerque, NM 87131. Offers American Indian education (MA); bilingual education (MA, PhD); educational linguistics (PhD); educational thought and sociocultural studies (MA, PhD); literacy/language arts (MA, PhD); social studies (MA); TESOL (MA, PhD). *Faculty:* 10 full-time (6 women), 3 part-time/adjunct (1 woman). *Students:* 63 full-time (48 women), 117 part-time (105 women); includes 96 minority (8 Black or African American, non-Hispanic/Latino; 16 American Indian or Alaska Native, non-Hispanic/Latino; 6 Asian, non-Hispanic/Latino; 62 Hispanic/Latino; 4 Two or more races, non-Hispanic/Latino), 20 international. Average age 39. 67 applicants, 63% accepted, 30 enrolled. In 2013, 30 master's, 8 doctorates awarded. *Degree requirements:* For master's, comprehensive exam, thesis optional; for doctorate, comprehensive exam, thesis/dissertation, research skills. *Entrance requirements:* For master's, letter of intent, 3 letters of recommendation, resume, BA/BS, department demographic form, transcripts; for doctorate, writing sample, letter of intent, 3 letters of recommendation, resume, BA/BS, MA, department demographic form, transcripts. Additional exam requirements/recommendations for international students: Required—TOEFL. *Application deadline:* For fall admission, 12/1 for domestic and international students; for spring admission, 9/15 for domestic and international students. Application fee: $50. Electronic applications accepted. *Financial support:* In 2013–14, 7 students received support, including 7 fellowships (averaging $3,170 per year), 1,318 teaching assistantships with tuition reimbursements available (averaging $3,789 per year); research assistantships, career-related internships or fieldwork, institutionally sponsored loans, scholarships/grants, and unspecified assistantships also available. Support available to part-time students. Financial award application deadline: 3/1; financial award applicants required to submit FAFSA. *Faculty research:* School reform, professional development, history of education, Native American education, politics of education, feminism and issues of sexual identity, critical race theory, bilingualism, literacy reading, adolescent literature, second language acquisition, critical theory and schooling, indigenous languages. *Unit head:* Dr. Lois M. Meyer, Chair, 505-277-7244, Fax: 505-277-8362, E-mail: lsmeyer@unm.edu. *Application contact:* Debra Schaffer, Administrative Assistant, 505-277-0437, Fax: 505-277-8362, E-mail: schaffer@unm.edu.
Website: http://coe.unm.edu/departments/department-of-language-literacy-and-sociocultural-studies/llss-program.html.

University of Pennsylvania, Graduate School of Education, Division of Education, Culture and Society, Program in Education, Culture and Society, Philadelphia, PA 19104. Offers MS Ed, PhD. *Students:* 37 full-time (27 women), 4 part-time (all women); includes 18 minority (11 Black or African American, non-Hispanic/Latino; 4 Asian, non-Hispanic/Latino; 3 Hispanic/Latino), 7 international. 197 applicants, 26% accepted, 18 enrolled. In 2013, 14 master's, 2 doctorates awarded. *Unit head:* Dr. Andrew Porter, Dean, 215-898-7014. *Application contact:* 215-898-6415, Fax: 215-746-6884, E-mail: admissions@gse.upenn.edu.
Website: http://www.gse.upenn.edu.

University of Pittsburgh, School of Education, Department of Administrative and Policy Studies, Program in Social and Comparative Analysis in Education, Pittsburgh, PA 15260. Offers M Ed, MA, Ed D, PhD. Evening/weekend programs available. *Students:* 65 full-time (47 women), 27 part-time (20 women); includes 15 minority (5 Black or African American, non-Hispanic/Latino; 5 Asian, non-Hispanic/Latino; 5 Hispanic/Latino), 23 international. Average age 36. 45 applicants, 76% accepted, 16 enrolled. In 2013, 11 master's, 8 doctorates awarded. *Degree requirements:* For master's, thesis; for doctorate, thesis/dissertation. *Entrance requirements:* For doctorate, GRE General Test. Additional exam requirements/recommendations for international students: Required—TOEFL (minimum score 80 iBT). *Application deadline:* For fall admission, 2/1 priority date for domestic and international students; for spring admission, 11/15 priority date for domestic students, 7/1 priority date for international students. Applications are processed on a rolling basis. Application fee: $50. Electronic applications accepted. *Expenses:* Tuition, state resident: full-time $19,964; part-time $807 per credit. Tuition, nonresident: full-time $32,686; part-time $1337 per credit. *Required fees:* $740; $200. Tuition and fees vary according to program. *Financial support:* Research assistantships, teaching assistantships, Federal Work-Study, institutionally sponsored loans, scholarships/grants, health care benefits, tuition waivers (partial), and unspecified assistantships available. Support available to part-time students. Financial award application deadline: 3/15; financial award applicants required to submit FAFSA. *Unit head:* Dr. Mary Margaret Kerr, Chair, 412-648-7205, Fax: 412-648-1784, E-mail: mmkerr@pitt.edu. *Application contact:* Norma Ann McMichael, Graduate Enrollment Manager, 412-648-2230, Fax: 412-648-1899, E-mail: soeinfo@pitt.edu.
Website: http://www.education.pitt.edu/AcademicDepartments/AdministrativePolicyStudies/Programs/SocialComparativeAnalysisinEducation.aspx.

University of Rochester, Margaret Warner Graduate School of Education and Human Development, Doctoral Programs in Education, Rochester, NY 14627. Offers counseling (Ed D); educational administration (Ed D); educational policy and theory (PhD); higher education (PhD); human development in educational context (PhD); teaching, curriculum, and change (PhD). *Expenses: Tuition:* Full-time $44,580; part-time $1394 per credit hour. *Required fees:* $492.

University of Saskatchewan, College of Graduate Studies and Research, College of Education, Department of Educational Foundations, Saskatoon, SK S7N 5A2, Canada. Offers M Ed, MC Ed, PhD, Diploma. Part-time programs available. *Degree requirements:* For master's, thesis (for some programs); for doctorate, comprehensive exam (for some programs), thesis/dissertation. *Entrance requirements:* Additional exam requirements/recommendations for international students: Required—TOEFL (minimum score 80 iBT); Recommended—IELTS (minimum score 6.5). Electronic applications accepted. *Expenses: Tuition, area resident:* Full-time $3585 Canadian dollars; part-time $585 Canadian dollars per course. Tuition, nonresident: part-time $877 Canadian dollars per course. *International tuition:* $5377 Canadian dollars full-time. *Required fees:* $889.51 Canadian dollars. *Faculty research:* Indian and northern education, adult and continuing education, international education.

University of South Africa, College of Human Sciences, Pretoria, South Africa. Offers adult education (M Ed); African languages (MA, PhD); African politics (MA, PhD); Afrikaans (MA, PhD); ancient history (MA, PhD); ancient Near Eastern studies (MA, PhD); anthropology (MA, PhD); applied linguistics (MA); Arabic (MA, PhD); archaeology (MA); art history (MA); Biblical archaeology (MA); Biblical studies (M Th, D Th, PhD); Christian spirituality (M Th, D Th); church history (M Th, D Th); classical studies (MA, PhD); clinical psychology (MA); communication (MA, PhD); comparative education (M Ed, Ed D); consulting psychology (D Admin, D Com, PhD); curriculum studies (M Ed, Ed D); development studies (M Admin, MA, D Admin, PhD); didactics (M Ed, Ed D); education (M Tech); education management (M Ed, Ed D); educational psychology (M Ed); English (MA); environmental education (M Ed); French (MA, PhD); German (MA, PhD); Greek (MA); guidance and counseling (M Ed); health studies (MA, PhD), including health sciences education (MA), health services management (MA), medical and surgical nursing science (critical care general) (MA), midwifery and neonatal nursing science (MA), trauma and emergency care (MA); history (MA, PhD); history of education (Ed D); inclusive education (M Ed, Ed D); information and communications technology policy and regulation (MA); information science (MA, MIS, PhD); international politics (MA, PhD); Islamic studies (MA, PhD); Italian (MA, PhD); Judaica (MA, PhD); linguistics (MA, PhD); mathematical education (M Ed); mathematics education (MA); missiology (M Th, D Th); modern Hebrew (MA, PhD); musicology (MA, MMus, D Mus, PhD); natural science education (M Ed); New Testament (M Th, D Th); Old Testament (D Th); pastoral therapy (M Th, D Th); philosophy (MA); philosophy of education (M Ed, Ed D); politics (MA, PhD); Portuguese (MA, PhD); practical theology (M Th, D Th); psychology (MA, MS, PhD); psychology of education (M Ed, Ed D); public health (MA); religious studies (MA, D Th, PhD); Romance languages (MA); Russian (MA, PhD); Semitic languages (MA, PhD); social behavior studies in HIV/AIDS (MA); social science (mental health) (MA); social science in development studies (MA); social science in psychology (MA); social science in social work (MA); social science in sociology (MA); social work (MSW, DSW, PhD); socio-education (M Ed, Ed D); sociolinguistics (MA); sociology (MA, PhD); Spanish (MA, PhD); systematic theology (M Th, D Th); TESOL (teaching English to speakers of other languages) (MA); theological ethics (M Th, D Th); theory of literature (MA, PhD); urban ministries (D Th); urban ministry (M Th).

University of South Carolina, The Graduate School, College of Education, Department of Educational Studies, Program in Foundations in Education, Columbia, SC 29208. Offers PhD. *Accreditation:* NCATE. Part-time programs available. *Degree requirements:* For doctorate, comprehensive exam, thesis/dissertation. *Entrance requirements:* For doctorate, GRE General Test or MAT, interview. Electronic applications accepted. *Faculty research:* Oral history, educational biography, home schooling, international education.

The University of Tennessee, Graduate School, College of Education, Health and Human Sciences, Program in Education, Knoxville, TN 37996. Offers art education (MS); counseling education (PhD); cultural studies in education (PhD); curriculum (MS, Ed S); curriculum, educational research and evaluation (Ed D, PhD); early childhood education (PhD); early childhood special education (MS); education of deaf and hard of hearing (MS); educational administration and policy studies (Ed D, PhD); educational administration and supervision (Ed S); educational psychology (Ed D, PhD); elementary education (MS, Ed S); elementary teaching (MS); English education (MS, Ed S); exercise science (PhD); foreign language/ESL education (MS, Ed S); instructional technology (MS, Ed D, PhD, Ed S); literacy, language and ESL education (PhD); literacy, language education, and ESL education (Ed D); mathematics education (MS, Ed S); modified and comprehensive special education (MS); reading education (MS, Ed S); school counseling (Ed S); school psychology (PhD, Ed S); science education (MS, Ed S); secondary teaching (MS); social foundations (MS); social science education (MS, Ed S); socio-cultural foundations of sports and education (PhD); special education (Ed S); teacher education (Ed D, PhD). *Accreditation:* NCATE. Part-time and evening/weekend programs available. *Degree requirements:* For master's and Ed S, thesis optional; for doctorate, variable foreign language requirement, thesis/dissertation. *Entrance requirements:* For master's, minimum GPA of 2.7; for doctorate and Ed S, GRE General Test, minimum GPA of 2.7. Additional exam requirements/recommendations for international students: Required—TOEFL. Electronic applications accepted. *Expenses:* Tuition, state resident: full-time $9540; part-time $531 per credit hour. Tuition, nonresident: full-time $27,728; part-time $1542 per credit hour. *Required fees:* $1404; $67 per credit hour.

The University of Texas of the Permian Basin, Office of Graduate Studies, School of Education, Program in Professional Education, Odessa, TX 79762-0001. Offers MA. *Degree requirements:* For master's, comprehensive exam (for some programs), thesis (for some programs). *Entrance requirements:* For master's, GRE General Test. Additional exam requirements/recommendations for international students: Required—TOEFL (minimum score 550 paper-based).

The University of Toledo, College of Graduate Studies, Judith Herb College of Education, Department of Educational Foundations and Leadership, Toledo, OH 43606-

3390. Offers educational administration and supervision (ME, DE, Ed S); educational psychology (ME, PhD); educational research and measurement (ME, PhD); educational sociology (PhD); educational theory and social foundations (ME); foundations of education (DE, PhD); history of education (PhD); philosophy of education (PhD). *Accreditation:* NCATE. Part-time and evening/weekend programs available. *Faculty:* 33. *Students:* 15 full-time (9 women), 84 part-time (57 women); includes 28 minority (21 Black or African American, non-Hispanic/Latino; 1 Asian, non-Hispanic/Latino; 5 Hispanic/Latino; 1 Two or more races, non-Hispanic/Latino), 2 international. Average age 42. 16 applicants, 63% accepted, 7 enrolled. In 2013, 16 master's, 4 doctorates awarded. *Degree requirements:* For master's, comprehensive exam, thesis or alternative; for doctorate, comprehensive exam, thesis/dissertation; for Ed S, thesis optional. *Entrance requirements:* For master's, doctorate, and Ed S, minimum cumulative GPA of 2.7 for all previous academic work, letters of recommendation. Additional exam requirements/recommendations for international students: Required—TOEFL (minimum score 550 paper-based; 80 iBT). *Application deadline:* For fall admission, 1/15 priority date for domestic and international students. Applications are processed on a rolling basis. Application fee: $45 ($75 for international students). Electronic applications accepted. *Financial support:* In 2013–14, 2 research assistantships with full and partial tuition reimbursements (averaging $7,500 per year), 2 teaching assistantships with full and partial tuition reimbursements (averaging $9,000 per year) were awarded; career-related internships or fieldwork, Federal Work-Study, institutionally sponsored loans, scholarships/grants, tuition waivers (full and partial), unspecified assistantships, and administrative assistantships also available. Support available to part-time students. Financial award applicants required to submit FAFSA. *Unit head:* Dr. Richard Welsch, Interim Chair, 419-530-2565, Fax: 419-530-8447, E-mail: richard.welsch@utoledo.edu. *Application contact:* Graduate School Office, 419-530-4723, Fax: 419-530-4724, E-mail: grdsch@utnet.utoledo.edu.
Website: http://www.utoledo.edu/eduhshs/.

University of Utah, Graduate School, College of Education, Department of Education, Culture, and Society, Salt Lake City, UT 84112. Offers M Ed, MA, MS, PhD. Evening/weekend programs available. *Faculty:* 12 full-time (8 women), 1 part-time/adjunct (0 women). *Students:* 61 full-time (40 women), 42 part-time (25 women); includes 42 minority (5 Black or African American, non-Hispanic/Latino; 1 American Indian or Alaska Native, non-Hispanic/Latino; 5 Asian, non-Hispanic/Latino; 25 Hispanic/Latino; 2 Native Hawaiian or other Pacific Islander, non-Hispanic/Latino; 4 Two or more races, non-Hispanic/Latino), 5 international. Average age 35. 62 applicants, 76% accepted, 30 enrolled. In 2013, 18 master's, 3 doctorates awarded. *Degree requirements:* For master's, comprehensive exam, thesis (for some programs); for doctorate, thesis/dissertation. *Entrance requirements:* For master's and doctorate, minimum GPA of 3.0. Additional exam requirements/recommendations for international students: Required—TOEFL (minimum score 650 paper-based; 114 iBT). *Application deadline:* For fall admission, 2/1 priority date for domestic and international students. Application fee: $55 ($65 for international students). Electronic applications accepted. *Expenses:* Tuition, state resident: full-time $5259. Tuition, nonresident: full-time $18,569. *Required fees:* $841. Tuition and fees vary according to course load. *Financial support:* In 2013–14, 8 students received support, including 8 teaching assistantships with full tuition reimbursements available (averaging $15,000 per year); tuition waivers (full) and unspecified assistantships also available. Financial award application deadline: 4/1; financial award applicants required to submit FAFSA. *Faculty research:* History, philosophy and sociology of education, language, culture and curriculum. *Total annual research expenditures:* $6,404. *Unit head:* Dr. Ed Buendia, Department Chair, 801-581-7803, Fax: 801-587-7801, E-mail: ed.buendia@utah.edu. *Application contact:* Amy Suzanne Wright, Academic Support Specialist, 801-587-7814, E-mail: amy.wright@utah.edu.
Website: http://www.ed.utah.edu/ecs/.

University of Victoria, Faculty of Graduate Studies, Faculty of Education, Department of Curriculum and Instruction, Victoria, BC V8W 2Y2, Canada. Offers art education (M Ed, PhD); curriculum studies (M Ed, MA, PhD); early childhood education (M Ed, PhD); educational studies (PhD); language and literacy (M Ed, MA, PhD); mathematics (M Ed, MA, PhD); music education (M Ed, MA, PhD); science (M Ed, MA, PhD); social studies (M Ed, MA); social, cultural and foundational studies (MA, PhD); technology and environmental education (PhD). Part-time programs available. *Degree requirements:* For master's, thesis, project (M Ed); for doctorate, comprehensive exam, thesis/dissertation. *Entrance requirements:* For master's, minimum B average. Additional exam requirements/recommendations for international students: Required—TOEFL (minimum score 575 paper-based), IELTS (minimum score 7). Electronic applications accepted. *Faculty research:* Elementary and secondary English, language arts, curriculum theory and practice, educational media and technology, educational administration and leadership, history and philosophy of education.

University of Washington, Graduate School, College of Education, Seattle, WA 98195. Offers curriculum and instruction (M Ed, Ed D, PhD), including educational technology, general curriculum (Ed D, PhD), language, literacy, and culture, mathematics education, multicultural education, reading and language arts education (Ed D), science education, social studies education, teaching and curriculum (M Ed); educational leadership and policy studies (M Ed, Ed D, PhD), including administration (Ed D), educational policy, organization, and leadership (M Ed, PhD), higher education, leadership for learning (Ed D), social and cultural foundations of education (M Ed, PhD); educational psychology (M Ed, PhD), including educational psychology (PhD), human development and cognition (M Ed), learning sciences, measurement, statistics and research design (M Ed), school psychology (M Ed); instructional leadership (M Ed); intercollegiate athletic leadership (M Ed); special education (M Ed, Ed D, PhD), including early childhood special education (M Ed), emotional and behavioral disabilities (M Ed), learning disabilities (M Ed), low-incidence disabilities (M Ed), severe disabilities (M Ed), special education (Ed D, PhD); teacher education (MIT). *Accreditation:* APA. Part-time and evening/weekend programs available. *Degree requirements:* For master's, thesis optional; for doctorate, thesis/dissertation. *Entrance requirements:* For master's and doctorate, GRE General Test, minimum GPA of 3.0. Additional exam requirements/recommendations for international students: Required—TOEFL. Electronic applications accepted. *Faculty research:* School restructuring/effective schools, special education interventions, literacy and writing, technology, school partnerships, teacher preparation.

University of West Georgia, College of Education, Department of Educational Technology and Foundations, Carrollton, GA 30118. Offers media (M Ed, Ed S). Part-time and evening/weekend programs available. Postbaccalaureate distance learning degree programs offered (no on-campus study). *Faculty:* 15 full-time (9 women), 1 (woman) part-time/adjunct. *Students:* 36 full-time (28 women), 308 part-time (260 women); includes 124 minority (111 Black or African American, non-Hispanic/Latino; 1 American Indian or Alaska Native, non-Hispanic/Latino; 2 Asian, non-Hispanic/Latino; 6 Hispanic/Latino; 1 Native Hawaiian or other Pacific Islander, non-Hispanic/Latino; 3 Two or more races, non-Hispanic/Latino). Average age 36. 126 applicants, 96% accepted, 58 enrolled. In 2013, 38 master's, 85 Ed Ss awarded. *Degree requirements:* For master's, comprehensive exam, electronic portfolio; for Ed S, comprehensive exam, research project. *Entrance requirements:* For master's, minimum GPA of 2.7, teaching certificate; for Ed S, master's degree, minimum graduate GPA of 3.0. Additional exam requirements/recommendations for international students: Required—TOEFL (minimum score 523 paper-based; 69 iBT); Recommended—IELTS (minimum score 6). *Application deadline:* For fall admission, 7/21 for domestic students, 6/1 for international students; for spring admission, 11/30 for domestic students, 10/15 for international students. Applications are processed on a rolling basis. Application fee: $40. Electronic applications accepted. *Expenses:* Tuition, state resident: full-time $4600; part-time $192 per semester hour. Tuition, nonresident: full-time $17,880; part-time $745 per semester hour. *Required fees:* $1858; $46.34 per semester hour. $512 per semester. Tuition and fees vary according to course load, degree level, campus/location and program. *Financial support:* In 2013–14, 6 students received support, including 2 research assistantships with full tuition reimbursements available (averaging $6,000 per year); career-related internships or fieldwork, scholarships/grants, and unspecified assistantships also available. Support available to part-time students. Financial award application deadline: 4/1; financial award applicants required to submit FAFSA. *Faculty research:* Distance education, technology integration, collaboration, e-books for children, instructional design. *Total annual research expenditures:* $94,000. *Unit head:* Dr. Stephen Bronack, Chair, 678-839-6188, Fax: 678-839-6153, E-mail: sbronack@westga.edu. *Application contact:* Deanna Richards, Coordinator, Graduate Studies, 678-839-5946, E-mail: drichard@westga.edu.
Website: http://www.westga.edu/coeei.

University of Wisconsin–Milwaukee, Graduate School, School of Education, MS Program in Cultural Foundations of Education, Milwaukee, WI 53201-0413. Offers MS. Part-time programs available. *Students:* 17 full-time (13 women), 30 part-time (23 women); includes 20 minority (13 Black or African American, non-Hispanic/Latino; 4 Hispanic/Latino; 3 Two or more races, non-Hispanic/Latino), 2 international. Average age 34. 32 applicants, 50% accepted, 8 enrolled. In 2013, 14 master's awarded. *Degree requirements:* For master's, thesis or alternative. *Entrance requirements:* Additional exam requirements/recommendations for international students: Required—TOEFL (minimum score 550 paper-based; 79 iBT), IELTS (minimum score 6.5). *Application deadline:* For fall admission, 1/1 priority date for domestic students; for spring admission, 9/1 for domestic students. Applications are processed on a rolling basis. Application fee: $56 ($96 for international students). Electronic applications accepted. *Financial support:* In 2013–14, 3 fellowships with full tuition reimbursements were awarded; research assistantships, teaching assistantships, career-related internships or fieldwork, health care benefits, and unspecified assistantships also available. Support available to part-time students. Financial award application deadline: 4/15; financial award applicants required to submit FAFSA. *Faculty research:* Human relations in education, international and multicultural education. *Unit head:* Aaron Schutz, Representative, 414-229-4150, E-mail: schutz@uwm.edu. *Application contact:* General Information Contact, 414-229-4982, Fax: 414-229-6967, E-mail: gradschool@uwm.edu.
Website: http://www4.uwm.edu/soe/academics/ed_policy/cfe.cfm.

University of Wisconsin–Milwaukee, Graduate School, School of Education, Urban Education Doctoral Program, Milwaukee, WI 53201-0413. Offers adult, continuing and higher education leadership (PhD); curriculum and instruction (PhD); educational administration (PhD); exceptional education (PhD); multicultural studies (PhD); social foundations of education (PhD). *Students:* 51 full-time (37 women), 40 part-time (25 women); includes 32 minority (16 Black or African American, non-Hispanic/Latino; 1 American Indian or Alaska Native, non-Hispanic/Latino; 3 Asian, non-Hispanic/Latino; 5 Hispanic/Latino; 7 Two or more races, non-Hispanic/Latino), 3 international. Average age 41. 25 applicants, 44% accepted, 4 enrolled. In 2013, 11 doctorates awarded. *Degree requirements:* For doctorate, comprehensive exam, thesis/dissertation. *Entrance requirements:* For doctorate, GRE General Test, minimum undergraduate GPA of 2.85, graduate 3.5. Additional exam requirements/recommendations for international students: Required—TOEFL (minimum score 550 paper-based; 79 iBT), IELTS (minimum score 6.5). *Application deadline:* For fall admission, 1/1 priority date for domestic students; for spring admission, 9/1 for domestic students. Applications are processed on a rolling basis. Application fee: $56 ($96 for international students). Electronic applications accepted. *Financial support:* In 2013–14, 11 fellowships, 1 teaching assistantship were awarded; research assistantships, career-related internships or fieldwork, health care benefits, unspecified assistantships, and project assistantships also available. Support available to part-time students. Financial award application deadline: 4/15; financial award applicants required to submit FAFSA. *Unit head:* Raji Swaminathan, Representative, 414-229-6740, Fax: 414-229-2920, E-mail: swaminar@uwm.edu. *Application contact:* General Information Contact, 414-229-4982, Fax: 414-229-6967, E-mail: gradschool@uwm.edu.
Website: http://www4.uwm.edu/soe/academics/urban_ed/.

Wayne State University, College of Education, Division of Theoretical and Behavioral Foundations, Detroit, MI 48202. Offers counseling (M Ed, MA, Ed D, PhD, Ed S); education evaluation and research (M Ed, Ed D, PhD); educational psychology (M Ed, PhD), including learning and instruction sciences (PhD), school psychology (PhD); educational sociology (M Ed); history and philosophy of education (M Ed); rehabilitation counseling and community inclusion (MA); school and community psychology (MA); school psychology (Certificate). *Accreditation:* ACA (one or more programs are accredited); CORE (one or more programs are accredited). Evening/weekend programs available. *Students:* 239 full-time (199 women), 214 part-time (190 women); includes 181 minority (141 Black or African American, non-Hispanic/Latino; 2 American Indian or Alaska Native, non-Hispanic/Latino; 14 Asian, non-Hispanic/Latino; 10 Hispanic/Latino; 1 Native Hawaiian or other Pacific Islander, non-Hispanic/Latino; 13 Two or more races, non-Hispanic/Latino), 21 international. Average age 33. 271 applicants, 35% accepted, 62 enrolled. In 2013, 55 master's, 19 doctorates, 8 other advanced degrees awarded. *Degree requirements:* For master's, thesis (for some programs); for doctorate, thesis/dissertation. *Entrance requirements:* For master's, GRE; for doctorate, GRE, interview, minimum GPA of 3.0, curriculum vitae, references. Additional exam requirements/recommendations for international students: Required—TOEFL (minimum score 550 paper-based; 79 iBT), Michigan English Language Assessment Battery (minimum score 85); Recommended—IELTS (minimum score 6.5), TWE (minimum score 5.5). *Application deadline:* For fall admission, 6/1 priority date for domestic students, 5/1 priority date for international students; for winter admission, 10/1 priority date for domestic students, 9/1 priority date for international students; for spring admission, 2/1 priority date for domestic students, 1/1 priority date for international students. Applications are processed on a rolling basis. Application fee: $0. Electronic applications accepted. *Expenses:* Tuition, state resident: part-time $554.15 per credit. Tuition, nonresident: part-time $1200.35 per credit. *Required fees:* $42.15 per credit. $268.30 per semester. Tuition and fees vary according to course load and program. *Financial support:* In 2013–14, 83 students received support, including 2 research assistantships with tuition reimbursements available (averaging $16,508 per year); fellowships with tuition reimbursements available, teaching assistantships with tuition reimbursements available, scholarships/grants, health care benefits, and unspecified assistantships also available. Financial award application deadline: 3/31; financial award applicants required to submit FAFSA. *Faculty research:* Adolescents at risk, supervision of counseling. *Unit head:* Dr. Joanne Holbert, Interim Assistant Dean, 313-577-1691, E-mail: jholbert@wayne.edu. *Application contact:* Janice Green, Assistant Dean, 313-577-1605, E-mail: jwgreen@wayne.edu.
Website: http://coe.wayne.edu/tbf/index.php.

Western Illinois University, School of Graduate Studies, College of Education and Human Services, Department of Educational and Interdisciplinary Studies, Program in Educational and Interdisciplinary Studies, Macomb, IL 61455-1390. Offers educational and interdisciplinary studies (MS Ed); teaching English to speakers of other languages (Certificate). *Accreditation:* NCATE. Part-time programs available. *Students:* 13 full-time (11 women), 36 part-time (28 women); includes 11 minority (3 Black or African American, non-Hispanic/Latino; 1 Asian, non-Hispanic/Latino; 6 Hispanic/Latino; 1 Two or more races, non-Hispanic/Latino), 2 international. Average age 34. In 2013, 16 master's, 5 Certificates awarded. *Degree requirements:* For master's, thesis or alternative. *Entrance requirements:* For master's, minimum GPA of 2.75, interview. Additional exam requirements/recommendations for international students: Required—TOEFL (minimum score 550 paper-based; 80 iBT). *Application deadline:* Applications are processed on a rolling basis. Application fee: $30. Electronic applications accepted. *Financial support:* In 2013–14, 9 students received support, including 5 research assistantships with full tuition reimbursements available (averaging $7,544 per year), 4 teaching assistantships with full tuition reimbursements available (averaging $8,688 per year). Financial award applicants required to submit FAFSA. *Unit head:* Dr. Gloria Delany-Barmann, Chairperson, 309-298-1183. *Application contact:* Dr. Nancy Parsons, Associate Provost and Director of Graduate Studies, 309-298-1806, Fax: 309-298-2345, E-mail: grad-office@wiu.edu.
Website: http://wiu.edu/eis.

Widener University, School of Human Service Professions, Center for Education, Chester, PA 19013-5792. Offers adult education (M Ed); counseling in higher education (M Ed); counselor education (M Ed); early childhood education (M Ed); educational foundations (M Ed); educational leadership (M Ed); educational psychology (M Ed); elementary education (M Ed); English and language arts (M Ed); health education (M Ed); higher education leadership (Ed D); home and school visitor (M Ed); human sexuality (M Ed, PhD); mathematics education (M Ed); middle school education (M Ed); principalship (M Ed); reading and language arts (Ed D); reading education (M Ed); school administration (Ed D); science education (M Ed); social studies education (M Ed); special education (M Ed); technology education (M Ed). *Accreditation:* NCATE. Part-time and evening/weekend programs available. *Faculty:* 34 full-time (22 women), 37 part-time/adjunct (14 women). *Students:* 64 full-time (44 women), 209 part-time (146 women); includes 49 minority (39 Black or African American, non-Hispanic/Latino; 1 American Indian or Alaska Native, non-Hispanic/Latino; 4 Asian, non-Hispanic/Latino; 4 Hispanic/Latino; 1 Two or more races, non-Hispanic/Latino), 8 international. Average age 39. 139 applicants, 88% accepted. In 2013, 168 master's, 31 doctorates awarded. Terminal master's awarded for partial completion of doctoral program. *Degree requirements:* For doctorate, thesis/dissertation. *Entrance requirements:* For master's, minimum GPA of 2.5; for doctorate, GRE or MAT, minimum GPA of 2.0 (undergraduate), 3.5 (graduate). *Application deadline:* Applications are processed on a rolling basis. Application fee: $25 ($300 for international students). Electronic applications accepted. *Expenses:*. Contact institution. *Financial support:* Career-related internships or fieldwork, tuition waivers (full and partial), and unspecified assistantships available. Support available to part-time students. Financial award application deadline: 5/1. *Faculty research:* Reading and cognition, adult education, technology education, educational leadership, special education. *Unit head:* Dr. Michael W. LeDoux, Associate Dean, 610-499-4294, Fax: 610-499-4623, E-mail: mwledoux@widener.edu. *Application contact:* Dr. Roberta Nolan, Director of Graduate Admissions, 610-499-4125, E-mail: rdnolan@widener.edu.

International and Comparative Education

American University, College of Arts and Sciences, Washington, DC 20016-8012. Offers addiction and addictive behavior (Certificate); anthropology (PhD); applied microeconomics (Certificate); applied statistics (Certificate); art history (MA); arts management (MA, Certificate); Asian studies (Certificate); audio production (Certificate); audio technology (MA); behavior, cognition, and neuroscience (PhD); bilingual education (MA, Certificate); biology (MA, MS); chemistry (MS); clinical psychology (PhD); computer science (MS, Certificate); creative writing (MFA); curriculum and instruction (M Ed, Certificate); economics (MA, PhD); environmental assessment (Certificate); environmental science (MS); ethics, peace, and global affairs (MA); gender analysis in economics (Certificate); health promotion management (MS); history (MA, PhD); international arts management (Certificate); international economic relations (Certificate); international economics (MA); international training and education (MA); literature (MA); mathematics (MA); North American studies (Certificate); nutrition education (MS, Certificate); philosophy (MA); professional science: biotechnology (MS); professional science: environmental assessment (MS); professional science: quantitative analysis (MS); psychobiology of healing (Certificate); psychology (MA); psychology: general (PhD); public anthropology (MA, Certificate); public sociology (Certificate); social research (Certificate); sociology (MA); Spanish: Latin American studies (MA); special education: learning disabilities (MA); statistics (MS); studio art (MFA); teaching (MAT); teaching English as a foreign language (MA); teaching: early childhood (Certificate); teaching: elementary (Certificate); teaching: ESOL (Certificate); teaching: secondary (Certificate); technology in arts management (Certificate); TESOL (MA); translation: French (Certificate); translation: Russian (Certificate); translation: Spanish (Certificate); women's, gender, and sexuality studies (Certificate). Part-time and evening/weekend programs available. Postbaccalaureate distance learning degree programs offered (no on-campus study). *Faculty:* 358 full-time (187 women), 254 part-time/adjunct (127 women). *Students:* 627 full-time (411 women), 416 part-time (300 women); includes 206 minority (91 Black or African American, non-Hispanic/Latino; 5 American Indian or Alaska Native, non-Hispanic/Latino; 32 Asian, non-Hispanic/Latino; 64 Hispanic/Latino; 1 Native Hawaiian or other Pacific Islander, non-Hispanic/Latino; 13 Two or more races, non-Hispanic/Latino), 124 international. Average age 29. 1,672 applicants, 52% accepted, 361 enrolled. In 2013, 382 master's, 38 doctorates, 33 other advanced degrees awarded. Terminal master's awarded for partial completion of doctoral program. *Degree requirements:* For master's, comprehensive exam (for some programs), thesis (for some programs); for doctorate, comprehensive exam (for some programs), thesis/dissertation. *Entrance requirements:* For master's, GRE, minimum GPA of 3.0 in last 60 credit hours, letter of recommendation, statement of purpose, resume, unofficial transcript; for doctorate, GRE, minimum GPA of 3.0 for all graduate work, letter of recommendation, statement of purpose, resume, unofficial transcript. Additional exam requirements/recommendations for international students: Required—TOEFL (minimum score 600 paper-based; 100 iBT), IELTS (minimum score 7). *Application deadline:* For fall admission, 2/1 for domestic students; for spring admission, 10/1 for domestic students. Applications are processed on a rolling basis. Application fee: $55. Electronic applications accepted. *Expenses: Tuition:* Full-time $25,920; part-time $1482 per credit hour. *Required fees:* $430. Tuition and fees vary according to course load and program. *Financial support:* Fellowships, research assistantships with full and partial tuition reimbursements, teaching assistantships with full and partial tuition reimbursements, career-related internships or fieldwork, Federal Work-Study, institutionally sponsored loans, scholarships/grants, traineeships, tuition waivers (full and partial), and unspecified assistantships available. Support available to part-time students. Financial award applicants required to submit FAFSA. *Unit head:* Dr. Peter Starr, Dean, 202-885-2446, Fax: 202-885-2429, E-mail: pstarr@american.edu. *Application contact:* Kathleen Clowery, Associate Director, Graduate Enrollment Management, 202-885-3621, Fax: 202-885-1505, E-mail: clowery@american.edu. Website: http://www.american.edu/cas/.

The American University in Cairo, Graduate School of Education, New Cairo, Egypt. Offers international and comparative education (MA). Part-time programs available. *Faculty:* 8 full-time (6 women). *Students:* 14 full-time (9 women), 58 part-time (46 women), 12 international. 52 applicants, 87% accepted, 19 enrolled. In 2013, 12 master's awarded. *Degree requirements:* For master's, thesis. *Entrance requirements:* Additional exam requirements/recommendations for international students: Required—TOEFL (minimum score 450 paper-based; 45 iBT), IELTS (minimum score 5). *Application deadline:* For fall admission, 1/30 priority date for domestic and international students; for spring admission, 11/1 priority date for domestic and international students. Applications are processed on a rolling basis. Application fee: $50. Electronic applications accepted. Tuition and fees vary according to course level, course load and program. *Financial support:* Fellowships with partial tuition reimbursements, scholarships/grants, and tuition waivers available. Financial award application deadline: 7/1. *Unit head:* Dr. Samiha Peterson, Interim Dean, 20-2-2615-1490, E-mail: peterss@ aucegypt.edu. *Application contact:* Anna Arejman, Admissions Counselor, 212-730-8800 Ext. 4528, E-mail: arejman@aucegypt.edu.
Website: http://www.aucegypt.edu/GSE/Pages/default.aspx.

Bowling Green State University, Graduate College, College of Education and Human Development, School of Leadership and Policy Studies, Program in Cross-Cultural and International Education, Bowling Green, OH 43403. Offers MA. Part-time programs available. *Degree requirements:* For master's, thesis or alternative. *Entrance requirements:* For master's, GRE General Test. Additional exam requirements/recommendations for international students: Required—TOEFL.

California Baptist University, Program in Education, Riverside, CA 92504-3206. Offers educational leadership for faith-based institutions (MS); educational leadership for public institutions (MS); educational technology (MS); instructional computer applications (MS); international education (MS); leadership and adult learning (MS); leadership and organizational studies (MS); reading (MS); school counseling (MS); school psychology (MS); science education (MS); special education in mild/moderate disabilities (MS); special education in moderate/severe disabilities (MS); teaching (MS); teaching and learning (MS); TESOL (teachers of English to speakers of other languages) (MS). Part-time and evening/weekend programs available. Postbaccalaureate distance learning degree programs offered (minimal on-campus study). *Faculty:* 18 full-time (9 women), 8 part-time/adjunct (5 women). *Students:* 158 full-time (127 women), 228 part-time (179 women); includes 159 minority (27 Black or African American, non-Hispanic/Latino; 4 American Indian or Alaska Native, non-Hispanic/Latino; 13 Asian, non-Hispanic/Latino; 107 Hispanic/Latino; 1 Native Hawaiian or other Pacific Islander, non-Hispanic/Latino; 7 Two or more races, non-Hispanic/Latino), 2 international. Average age 33. 298 applicants, 74% accepted, 113 enrolled. In 2013, 70 master's awarded. *Degree requirements:* For master's, comprehensive exam, project, or thesis. *Entrance requirements:* For master's, minimum undergraduate GPA of 3.0; 18 semester units of prerequisite course work in education; three recommendations; 500-word essay; interview. Additional exam requirements/recommendations for international students: Required—TOEFL (minimum score 80 iBT). *Application deadline:* For fall admission, 8/1 priority date for domestic students, 7/1 for international students; for spring admission, 12/1 priority date for domestic students, 11/1 for international students. Applications are processed on a rolling basis. Application fee: $45. Electronic applications accepted. *Expenses:* Contact institution. *Financial support:* Institutionally sponsored loans available. Financial award applicants required to submit CSS PROFILE or FAFSA. *Faculty research:* Leadership development, complexity theory, faith and learning, special education, social and philosophical contexts of education. *Unit head:* Dr. John Shoup, Dean, School of Education, 951-343-4205, Fax: 951-343-4516, E-mail: jshoup@calbaptist.edu. *Application contact:* Dr. Kathryn Norwood, Director, Master of Science Program in Education, 951-343-4760, E-mail: knorwood@calbaptist.edu. Website: http://www.calbaptist.edu/mastersined/.

California State University, Dominguez Hills, College of Extended and International Education, Carson, CA 90747-0001. Offers MA, MS. Part-time and evening/weekend programs available. Postbaccalaureate distance learning degree programs offered. *Faculty:* 3 full-time (0 women), 46 part-time/adjunct (17 women). *Students:* 9 full-time (4 women), 518 part-time (276 women); includes 167 minority (39 Black or African American, non-Hispanic/Latino; 4 American Indian or Alaska Native, non-Hispanic/Latino; 61 Asian, non-Hispanic/Latino; 48 Hispanic/Latino; 1 Native Hawaiian or other Pacific Islander, non-Hispanic/Latino; 14 Two or more races, non-Hispanic/Latino), 40 international. Average age 41. 125 applicants, 96% accepted, 69 enrolled. In 2013, 82 master's awarded. *Degree requirements:* For master's, thesis. *Entrance requirements:* Additional exam requirements/recommendations for international students: Required—TOEFL. Application fee: $55. Electronic applications accepted. *Expenses:* Contact institution. *Unit head:* Dr. Joanne Zitelli, Acting Dean, 310-243-3739, Fax: 310-516-4423, E-mail: jzitelli@csudh.edu. *Application contact:* Dr. Timothy Mozia, Director of Operations, 310-243-3741, E-mail: tmozia@csudh.edu.
Website: http://www.csudh.edu/ee/.

The College of New Jersey, Graduate Studies, Office of Global Programs, Program in Overseas Education, Ewing, NJ 08628. Offers M Ed, Certificate. Part-time programs available. *Degree requirements:* For master's, comprehensive exam. *Entrance requirements:* For master's, GRE, minimum GPA of 3.0 in field or 2.75 overall; for Certificate, previous master's degree or higher. Additional exam requirements/recommendations for international students: Required—TOEFL. Electronic applications accepted.

Drexel University, Goodwin College of Professional Studies, School of Education, Philadelphia, PA 19104-2875. Offers educational administration (MS); educational improvement and transformation (MS); educational leadership and management (Ed D); educational leadership development and learning technologies (PhD); global and

international education (MS); higher education (MS); human resources development (MS); learning technologies (MS); mathematics, learning and teaching (MS); special education (MS); teaching, learning and curriculum (MS). Part-time and evening/weekend programs available. Postbaccalaureate distance learning degree programs offered (no on-campus study). *Degree requirements:* For doctorate, thesis/dissertation. *Entrance requirements:* For doctorate, GRE or GMAT. Additional exam requirements/recommendations for international students: Required—TOEFL, IELTS. Electronic applications accepted. Application fee is waived when completed online. *Expenses:* Contact institution. *Faculty research:* Leadership development, mathematics education, literacy, autism, educational technology.

Florida International University, College of Education, Department of Teaching and Learning, Miami, FL 33199. Offers art education (MA, MS); curriculum and instruction (MS, Ed D, PhD, Ed S), including curriculum development (MS), elementary education (MS), English education (MS), learning technologies (MS), mathematics education (MS), modern language education (MS), physical education (MS), science education (MS), social studies education (MS), special education (MS); early childhood education (MS); exceptional student education (Ed D); foreign language education (MS), including foreign language education, teaching English to speakers of other languages (TESOL); international/intercultural education (MS); language, literacy and culture (PhD); mathematics, science, and learning technologies (PhD); physical education (MS), including sport and fitness; reading education (MS). Part-time and evening/weekend programs available. *Degree requirements:* For doctorate, comprehensive exam, thesis/dissertation. *Entrance requirements:* For master's, GRE General Test, Florida General Knowledge Test or Florida College Level Academic Skills Test; for doctorate and Ed S, GRE General Test. Additional exam requirements/recommendations for international students: Required—TOEFL (minimum score 550 paper-based; 80 iBT), IELTS (minimum score 6.3). Electronic applications accepted.

Florida State University, The Graduate School, College of Education, Department of Educational Leadership and Policy Studies, Program in Social, History and Philosophy of Education, Tallahassee, FL 32306. Offers history and philosophy of education (MS, PhD); international and intercultural education (PhD). *Faculty:* 5 full-time (3 women). *Students:* 29 full-time (20 women), 10 part-time (5 women); includes 6 minority (4 Black or African American, non-Hispanic/Latino; 2 Hispanic/Latino), 16 international. Average age 34. 35 applicants, 69% accepted, 13 enrolled. In 2013, 5 master's, 2 doctorates awarded. *Degree requirements:* For master's, comprehensive exam, thesis optional; for doctorate, comprehensive exam, thesis/dissertation. *Entrance requirements:* For master's and doctorate, GRE General Test, minimum GPA of 3.0. Additional exam requirements/recommendations for international students: Required—TOEFL (minimum score 550 paper-based; 80 iBT). *Application deadline:* For fall admission, 7/1 for domestic and international students; for winter admission, 11/1 for domestic and international students; for spring admission, 3/1 for domestic and international students. Application fee: $30. Electronic applications accepted. *Expenses:* Tuition, state resident: part-time $403.51 per credit hour. Tuition, nonresident: part-time $1004.85 per credit hour. *Required fees:* $75.81 per credit hour. One-time fee: $20 part-time. Tuition and fees vary according to course load, campus/location and student level. *Financial support:* Fellowships with full and partial tuition reimbursements, research assistantships with full and partial tuition reimbursements, teaching assistantships with full and partial tuition reimbursements, career-related internships or fieldwork, scholarships/grants, health care benefits, and unspecified assistantships available. Financial award applicants required to submit FAFSA. *Faculty research:* Social, historical, philosophical content of educational policies; religion, gender, diversity, and social justice in educational policy. *Unit head:* Dr. Jeffrey A. Milligan, Assistant Professor/Coordinator, 850-644-8171, Fax: 850-644-1258, E-mail: jmilligan@fsu.edu. *Application contact:* Linda J. Lyons, Academic Support Assistant, 850-644-7077, Fax: 850-644-1258, E-mail: ljlyons@fsu.edu.
Website: http://www.coe.fsu.edu/SHPFE.

Gallaudet University, The Graduate School, Washington, DC 20002-3625. Offers ASL/English bilingual early childhood education: birth to 5 (Certificate); audiology (Au D); clinical psychology (PhD); critical studies in the education of deaf learners (PhD); deaf and hard of hearing infants, toddlers, and their families (Certificate); deaf education (Ed S); deaf education: advanced studies (MA); deaf education: special programs (MA); deaf history (Certificate); deaf studies (MA, Certificate); educating deaf students with disabilities (Certificate); education: teacher preparation (MA), including deaf education, early childhood education and deaf education, elementary education and deaf education, secondary education and deaf education; educational neuroscience (PhD); hearing, speech and language sciences (MS, PhD); international development (MA); interpretation (MA, PhD), including combined interpreting practice and research (MA), interpreting research (MA); linguistics (MA, PhD); mental health counseling (MA); peer mentoring (Certificate); public administration (MPA); school counseling (MA); school psychology (Psy S); sign language teaching (MA); social work (MSW); speech-language pathology (MS). Part-time programs available. *Faculty:* 55 full-time (37 women). *Students:* 361 full-time (279 women), 108 part-time (73 women); includes 98 minority (39 Black or African American, non-Hispanic/Latino; 1 American Indian or Alaska Native, non-Hispanic/Latino; 12 Asian, non-Hispanic/Latino; 36 Hispanic/Latino; 1 Native Hawaiian or other Pacific Islander, non-Hispanic/Latino; 9 Two or more races, non-Hispanic/Latino), 31 international. Average age 30. 602 applicants, 49% accepted, 177 enrolled. In 2013, 140 master's, 32 doctorates, 11 other advanced degrees awarded. Terminal master's awarded for partial completion of doctoral program. *Degree requirements:* For master's, comprehensive exam (for some programs), thesis optional; for doctorate, comprehensive exam, thesis/dissertation. *Entrance requirements:* For master's and doctorate, GRE General Test or MAT, letters of recommendation, interviews, goals statement, ASL proficiency interview, written English competency. Additional exam requirements/recommendations for international students: Required—TOEFL. *Application deadline:* For fall admission, 2/15 for domestic students. Applications are processed on a rolling basis. Application fee: $75. Electronic applications accepted. *Expenses: Tuition:* Full-time $14,774; part-time $821 per credit. *Required fees:* $198 per semester. *Financial support:* In 2013–14, 325 students received support. Fellowships, research assistantships, teaching assistantships, career-related internships or fieldwork, Federal Work-Study, scholarships/grants, tuition waivers (partial), and unspecified assistantships available. Support available to part-time students. Financial award applicants required to submit FAFSA. *Faculty research:* Bimodal bilingualism development, cochlear implants, telecommunications access, cancer genetics, linguistics, visual language and visual learning, advancement of avatar and robotics translation, algal productivity and physiology in the Anacostia River. *Unit head:* Dr. Carol J. Erting, Dean, Research, Graduate School, Continuing Studies, and International Programs, 202-651-5520, Fax: 202-651-5027, E-mail: carol.erting@gallaudet.edu. *Application contact:* Wednesday Luria, Coordinator of Prospective Graduate Student Services, 202-651-5400, Fax: 202-651-5295, E-mail: graduate.school@gallaudet.edu.
Website: http://www.gallaudet.edu/x26696.xml.

George Mason University, College of Humanities and Social Sciences, Program in Global Affairs, Fairfax, VA 22030. Offers MA. *Faculty:* 16 full-time (6 women), 1 part-time/adjunct (0 women). *Students:* 22 full-time (18 women), 35 part-time (25 women); includes 12 minority (3 Black or African American, non-Hispanic/Latino; 2 Asian, non-Hispanic/Latino; 6 Hispanic/Latino; 1 Two or more races, non-Hispanic/Latino), 2 international. Average age 27. 86 applicants, 55% accepted, 16 enrolled. In 2013, 19 master's awarded. *Degree requirements:* For master's, capstone seminar. *Entrance requirements:* For master's, GRE, expanded goals statement, 2 letters of recommendation, evidence of professional competency in a second language tested through Language Testing International or other means approved by the department. Additional exam requirements/recommendations for international students: Required—TOEFL (minimum score 575 paper-based; 88 iBT), IELTS (minimum score 6.5), PTE. *Application deadline:* For fall admission, 3/15 for domestic students, 2/15 for international students; for spring admission, 10/15 for domestic students, 9/15 for international students. Application fee: $65 ($80 for international students). *Expenses:* Tuition, state resident: full-time $9350; part-time $390 per credit. Tuition, nonresident: full-time $25,754; part-time $1073 per credit. *Required fees:* $2688; $112 per credit. *Financial support:* Career-related internships or fieldwork, Federal Work-Study, and health care benefits (for full-time research or teaching assistantship recipients) available. Financial award application deadline: 3/1; financial award applicants required to submit FAFSA. *Unit head:* Lisa C. Breglia, Director, 703-993-9184, Fax: 703-993-1244, E-mail: lbreglia@gmu.edu. *Application contact:* Erin McSherry, Graduate Coordinator/Academic Advisor/Program Assistant, 703-993-5056, Fax: 703-993-1244, E-mail: emcsherr@gmu.edu.

The George Washington University, Graduate School of Education and Human Development, Department of Educational Leadership, Program in International Education, Washington, DC 20052. Offers MA Ed. *Accreditation:* NCATE. *Students:* 27 full-time (24 women), 43 part-time (all women); includes 10 minority (1 Black or African American, non-Hispanic/Latino; 3 Asian, non-Hispanic/Latino; 4 Hispanic/Latino; 2 Two or more races, non-Hispanic/Latino), 12 international. Average age 29. 115 applicants, 91% accepted, 26 enrolled. In 2013, 32 master's awarded. *Degree requirements:* For master's, comprehensive exam. *Entrance requirements:* For master's, GRE General Test or MAT, minimum GPA of 2.75. *Application deadline:* For fall admission, 1/15 priority date for domestic students; for spring admission, 10/1 for domestic students. Applications are processed on a rolling basis. Application fee: $75. *Financial support:* In 2013–14, 13 students received support. Fellowships, research assistantships, career-related internships or fieldwork, Federal Work-Study, and tuition waivers available. Financial award application deadline: 1/15; financial award applicants required to submit FAFSA. *Faculty research:* Education and development. *Unit head:* Dr. William K. Cummings, Coordinator, 202-994-4698, E-mail: wkcum@gwu.edu. *Application contact:* Sarah Lang, Director of Graduate Admissions, 202-994-1447, Fax: 202-994-7207, E-mail: slang@gwu.edu.

Harvard University, Harvard Graduate School of Education, Master's Programs in Education, Cambridge, MA 02138. Offers arts in education (Ed M); education policy and management (Ed M); higher education (Ed M); human development and psychology (Ed M); international education policy (Ed M); language and literacy (Ed M); learning and teaching (Ed M); mind, brain, and education (Ed M); prevention science and practice (Ed M); school leadership (Ed M); special studies (Ed M); teacher education (Ed M); technology, innovation, and education (Ed M). Part-time programs available. *Faculty:* 68 full-time (34 women), 77 part-time/adjunct (41 women). *Students:* 557 full-time (410 women), 69 part-time (50 women); includes 179 minority (34 Black or African American, non-Hispanic/Latino; 1 American Indian or Alaska Native, non-Hispanic/Latino; 62 Asian, non-Hispanic/Latino; 52 Hispanic/Latino; 2 Native Hawaiian or other Pacific Islander, non-Hispanic/Latino; 28 Two or more races, non-Hispanic/Latino), 100 international. Average age 28. 1,756 applicants, 47% accepted, 589 enrolled. In 2013, 673 master's awarded. *Entrance requirements:* For master's, GRE General Test, statement of purpose, 3 letters of recommendation, resume, official transcripts. Additional exam requirements/recommendations for international students: Required—TOEFL (minimum score 613 paper-based; 104 iBT), TWE (minimum score 5). *Application deadline:* For fall admission, 1/3 for domestic and international students. Application fee: $85. Electronic applications accepted. *Expenses:* Contact institution. *Financial support:* In 2013–14, 375 students received support, including 12 fellowships with full and partial tuition reimbursements available (averaging $13,925 per year), 2 research assistantships (averaging $2,174 per year); career-related internships or fieldwork, Federal Work-Study, institutionally sponsored loans, scholarships/grants, health care benefits, tuition waivers (full and partial), and unspecified assistantships also available. Support available to part-time students. Financial award application deadline: 2/1; financial award applicants required to submit FAFSA. *Faculty research:* Learning and development, educational leadership and organizations, education policy analysis. *Total annual research expenditures:* $34.3 million. *Unit head:* Jennifer L. Petrallia, Assistant Dean, 617-495-8445. *Application contact:* Information Contact, 617-495-3414, Fax: 617-496-3577, E-mail: gseadmissions@harvard.edu.
Website: http://www.gse.harvard.edu/.

Indiana University Bloomington, School of Education, Department of Educational Leadership and Policy Studies, Bloomington, IN 47405-7000. Offers education policy studies (PhD); educational leadership (MS, Ed D, Ed S); higher education (MS, Ed D, PhD); history and philosophy of education (MS); history of education (PhD); international and comparative education (MS, PhD); philosophy of education (PhD); student affairs administration (MS). *Accreditation:* NCATE. Part-time and evening/weekend programs available. *Degree requirements:* For master's, thesis optional; for doctorate, comprehensive exam, thesis/dissertation; for Ed S, comprehensive exam or project. *Entrance requirements:* For master's, doctorate, and Ed S, GRE General Test. Additional exam requirements/recommendations for international students: Required—TOEFL (minimum score 79 iBT). Electronic applications accepted. *Faculty research:* Student engagement at higher education institutions in the nation, Reading First professional development initiative, state finance policy on financial access to higher education, school reform, special needs studies.

Lehigh University, College of Education, Program in Comparative and International Education, Bethlehem, PA 18015. Offers comparative and international education (MA, PhD); globalization and educational change (M Ed); international counseling (Certificate); international development in education (Certificate); special education (Certificate); technology use in schools (Certificate); TESOL (Certificate). Part-time and evening/weekend programs available. Postbaccalaureate distance learning degree programs offered (minimal on-campus study). *Faculty:* 4 full-time (2 women). *Students:* 20 full-time (18 women), 26 part-time (17 women); includes 3 minority (2 Asian, non-Hispanic/Latino; 1 Hispanic/Latino), 14 international. Average age 33. 59 applicants, 63% accepted, 10 enrolled. In 2013, 17 master's awarded. Terminal master's awarded for partial completion of doctoral program. *Degree requirements:* For master's, thesis (MA); for doctorate, comprehensive exam, thesis/dissertation. *Entrance requirements:* For master's, 2 letters of recommendation; for doctorate, GRE, transcripts, 2 letters of recommendation, essay, and TOEFL if International applicant. Additional exam requirements/recommendations for international students: Required—TOEFL (minimum score 600 paper-based; 93 iBT). *Application deadline:* For fall and spring admission, 2/1 for domestic and international students. Application fee: $65. Electronic applications accepted. *Financial support:* Application deadline: 3/15. *Faculty research:* Comparative education, rural education, gender equity in education, post-socialist education transformation, educational borrowing, comparing education systems, education policy and globalization, family-school relationships, China, international testing, social

inequities. *Unit head:* Dr. Iveta Silova, Program Director and Associate Professor, 610-758-5750, Fax: 610-758-6223, E-mail: ism207@lehigh.edu. *Application contact:* Sharon Y. Warden, Coordinator, 610-758-3256, Fax: 610-758-6223, E-mail: sy00@lehigh.edu. Website: http://www.lehigh.edu/education/cie.

Louisiana State University and Agricultural & Mechanical College, Graduate School, College of Human Sciences and Education, School of Human Resource Education and Workforce Development, Baton Rouge, LA 70803. Offers agriculture and extension education and youth development (MS, PhD); career and technical education (MS, PhD); comprehensive vocational education (MS, PhD); extension and international education (MS, PhD); human resource and leadership development (MS, PhD); industrial education (MS); vocational agriculture education (MS, PhD); vocational business education (MS); vocational home economics education (MS). *Accreditation:* NCATE. Part-time programs available. *Faculty:* 10 full-time (5 women). *Students:* 46 full-time (28 women), 138 part-time (96 women); includes 65 minority (52 Black or African American, non-Hispanic/Latino; 2 American Indian or Alaska Native, non-Hispanic/Latino; 2 Asian, non-Hispanic/Latino; 6 Hispanic/Latino; 3 Two or more races, non-Hispanic/Latino), 6 international. Average age 35. 120 applicants, 62% accepted, 49 enrolled. In 2013, 23 master's, 14 doctorates awarded. Terminal master's awarded for partial completion of doctoral program. *Degree requirements:* For master's, thesis (for some programs); for doctorate, thesis/dissertation. *Entrance requirements:* For master's and doctorate, GRE General Test, minimum GPA of 3.0. Additional exam requirements/recommendations for international students: Required—TOEFL (minimum score 550 paper-based; 79 iBT), IELTS (minimum score 6.5), or PTE (minimum score 59). *Application deadline:* For fall admission, 1/25 priority date for domestic students, 5/15 for international students; for spring admission, 10/15 for international students. Applications are processed on a rolling basis. Application fee: $50 ($70 for international students). Electronic applications accepted. *Financial support:* In 2013–14, 85 students received support, including 4 fellowships with full and partial tuition reimbursements available (averaging $31,175 per year), 9 research assistantships with full and partial tuition reimbursements available (averaging $15,422 per year), 14 teaching assistantships with partial tuition reimbursements available (averaging $14,289 per year); career-related internships or fieldwork, Federal Work-Study, institutionally sponsored loans, health care benefits, tuition waivers (full and partial), and unspecified assistantships also available. Financial award application deadline: 3/1; financial award applicants required to submit FAFSA. *Faculty research:* Adult education, history and philosophy of vocational education, curriculum and instruction, career decision-making. *Total annual research expenditures:* $4,454. *Unit head:* Dr. Ed Holton, Director, 225-578-5748, Fax: 225-578-5755, E-mail: eholton@lsu.edu. Website: http://www.lsu.edu/hrleader/.

Monterey Institute of International Studies, Graduate School of International Policy and Management, Program in International Education Management, Monterey, CA 93940-2691. Offers MA. *Degree requirements:* For master's, one foreign language. *Entrance requirements:* For master's, minimum GPA of 3.0, proficiency in a foreign language. Additional exam requirements/recommendations for international students: Required—TOEFL (minimum score 550 paper-based; 80 iBT). Electronic applications accepted. Application fee is waived when completed online. *Expenses: Tuition:* Full-time $34,970; part-time $1665 per credit. *Required fees:* $28 per semester.

Morehead State University, Graduate Programs, College of Education, Department of Curriculum and Instruction, Morehead, KY 40351. Offers curriculum and instruction (Ed S); elementary education (MA Ed), including elementary education, international education, middle school education, reading; secondary education (MA Ed); special education (MA Ed); teaching (MAT). Part-time and evening/weekend programs available. *Degree requirements:* For master's, comprehensive exam, thesis optional; for Ed S, thesis, oral exam. *Entrance requirements:* For master's, GRE General Test, minimum GPA of 2.75, teaching certificate; for Ed S, GRE General Test, interview, master's degree, minimum GPA of 3.5, work experience. Additional exam requirements/recommendations for international students: Required—TOEFL (minimum score 500 paper-based). Electronic applications accepted. *Faculty research:* Communicative competence of learning-disabled students, teaching social studies in elementary schools, ungraded primary school organization, study skills.

National University, Academic Affairs, School of Education, La Jolla, CA 92037-1011. Offers applied behavior analysis (Certificate); applied school leadership (MS); autism (Certificate); best practices (Certificate); e-teaching and learning (Certificate); early childhood education (Certificate); education (MA), including best practices (M Ed, MA), e-teaching and learning (M Ed, MA), education technology, teacher leadership (M Ed, MA), teaching and learning in a global society (M Ed, MA), teaching mathematics (M Ed, MA); education with preliminary multiple or single subject (M Ed), including best practices (M Ed, MA), e-teaching and learning (M Ed, MA), educational technology (M Ed, MA), teacher leadership (M Ed, MA), teaching and learning in a global society (M Ed, MA), teaching mathematics (M Ed, MA); educational administration (MS); educational and instructional technology (MS); educational counseling (MS); educational technology (Certificate); higher education administration (MS); innovative school leadership (MS); instructional leadership (MS); juvenile justice special education (MS); reading (Certificate); school psychology (MS); special education (MS), including deaf and hard-of-hearing, mild/moderate disabilities, moderate/severe disabilities; teacher leadership (Certificate); teaching (MA), including applied behavioral analysis, autism, best practices (M Ed, MA), e-teaching and learning (M Ed, MA), early childhood education, educational technology (M Ed, MA), reading, special education, teacher leadership (M Ed, MA), teaching and learning in a global society (M Ed, MA), teaching mathematics (M Ed, MA); teaching mathematics (Certificate). Part-time and evening/weekend programs available. Postbaccalaureate distance learning degree programs offered (no on-campus study). *Faculty:* 72 full-time (43 women), 287 part-time/adjunct (170 women). *Students:* 2,433 full-time (1,744 women), 2,017 part-time (1,371 women); includes 1,834 minority (358 Black or African American, non-Hispanic/Latino; 15 American Indian or Alaska Native, non-Hispanic/Latino; 250 Asian, non-Hispanic/Latino; 1,056 Hispanic/Latino; 29 Native Hawaiian or other Pacific Islander, non-Hispanic/Latino; 126 Two or more races, non-Hispanic/Latino), 1 international. Average age 34. 1,339 applicants, 100% accepted, 1035 enrolled. In 2013, 1,662 master's awarded. *Degree requirements:* For master's, thesis (for some programs). *Entrance requirements:* For master's, interview, minimum GPA of 2.5. Additional exam requirements/recommendations for international students: Required—TOEFL (minimum score 550 paper-based; 79 iBT), IELTS (minimum score 6). *Application deadline:* Applications are processed on a rolling basis. Application fee: $60 ($65 for international students). Electronic applications accepted. *Expenses: Tuition:* Full-time $13,824; part-time $1728 per course. One-time fee: $160. *Financial support:* Career-related internships or fieldwork, institutionally sponsored loans, scholarships/grants, and tuition waivers (partial) available. Support available to part-time students. Financial award application deadline: 6/30. *Faculty research:* Teacher education, special education, educational effectiveness, teaching abroad, school counseling. *Unit head:* School of Education, 800-628-8648, E-mail: soe@nu.edu. *Application contact:* Louis Cruz, Interim Vice President for Enrollment Services, 800-628-8648, E-mail: advisor@nu.edu. Website: http://www.nu.edu/OurPrograms/SchoolOfEducation.html.

New York University, Steinhardt School of Culture, Education, and Human Development, Department of Humanities and Social Sciences in the Professions, Program in International Education, New York, NY 10003. Offers cross cultural exchange and training (PhD); international education (MA, PhD, Advanced Certificate). Part-time programs available. *Faculty:* 3 full-time (2 women). *Students:* 68 full-time (57 women), 58 part-time (51 women); includes 36 minority (8 Black or African American, non-Hispanic/Latino; 11 Asian, non-Hispanic/Latino; 15 Hispanic/Latino; 2 Two or more races, non-Hispanic/Latino), 22 international. Average age 34. 223 applicants, 65% accepted, 47 enrolled. In 2013, 58 master's, 2 doctorates awarded. *Degree requirements:* For master's, thesis (for some programs); for doctorate, thesis/dissertation. *Entrance requirements:* For doctorate, GRE General Test, interview; for Advanced Certificate, master's degree. Additional exam requirements/recommendations for international students: Required—TOEFL (minimum score 100 iBT). *Application deadline:* For fall admission, 12/1 priority date for domestic and international students; for spring admission, 10/1 for domestic and international students. Applications are processed on a rolling basis. Application fee: $75. Electronic applications accepted. *Expenses: Tuition:* Full-time $35,856; part-time $1494 per unit. *Required fees:* $1408; $64 per unit. $473 per term. Tuition and fees vary according to course load and program. *Financial support:* Fellowships with full and partial tuition reimbursements, career-related internships or fieldwork, Federal Work-Study, institutionally sponsored loans, and scholarships/grants available. Support available to part-time students. Financial award application deadline: 2/1; financial award applicants required to submit FAFSA. *Faculty research:* Civic education, ethnic identity among students and teachers, comparative education, education during emergencies, cross-cultural exchange. *Unit head:* Dr. Philip M. Hosay, Director, 212-998-5496, Fax: 212-995-4832, E-mail: pmh2@nyu.edu. *Application contact:* 212-998-5030, Fax: 212-995-4328, E-mail: steinhardt.gradadmissions@nyu.edu. Website: http://steinhardt.nyu.edu/humsocsci/international.

New York University, Steinhardt School of Culture, Education, and Human Development, Department of Teaching and Learning, Program in English Education, New York, NY 10012-1019. Offers clinically-based English education, grades 7-12 (MA, Postbaccalaureate Certificate); English education (Advanced Certificate); English education, grades 7-12 (MA); literature, reading, and media education (PhD), including applied linguistics, comparative education. *Accreditation:* Teacher Education Accreditation Council. Part-time programs available. *Faculty:* 6 full-time (4 women). *Students:* 21 full-time (15 women), 34 part-time (24 women); includes 24 minority (9 Black or African American, non-Hispanic/Latino; 5 Asian, non-Hispanic/Latino; 9 Hispanic/Latino; 1 Two or more races, non-Hispanic/Latino), 1 international. Average age 31. 104 applicants, 75% accepted, 28 enrolled. In 2013, 26 master's, 2 doctorates awarded. *Degree requirements:* For master's, thesis (for some programs); for doctorate, thesis/dissertation. *Entrance requirements:* For doctorate, GRE General Test, interview; for other advanced degree, master's degree. Additional exam requirements/recommendations for international students: Required—TOEFL (minimum score 100 iBT). *Application deadline:* For fall admission, 12/1 priority date for domestic and international students; for spring admission, 10/1 for domestic and international students. Applications are processed on a rolling basis. Application fee: $75. Electronic applications accepted. *Expenses: Tuition:* Full-time $35,856; part-time $1494 per unit. *Required fees:* $1408; $64 per unit. $473 per term. Tuition and fees vary according to course load and program. *Financial support:* Fellowships with full and partial tuition reimbursements, teaching assistantships with full and partial tuition reimbursements, career-related internships or fieldwork, Federal Work-Study, institutionally sponsored loans, scholarships/grants, tuition waivers (partial), and unspecified assistantships available. Support available to part-time students. Financial award application deadline: 2/1; financial award applicants required to submit FAFSA. *Faculty research:* Making meaning of literature, teaching of literature, urban adolescent literacy and equity, literacy development and globalization, digital media and literacy. *Unit head:* Prof. Sarah W. Beck, Chairperson, 212-998-5473, Fax: 212-995-4049, E-mail: sarah.beck@nyu.edu. *Application contact:* 212-998-5030, Fax: 212-995-4328, E-mail: steinhardt.gradadmissions@nyu.edu. Website: http://steinhardt.nyu.edu/teachlearn/english.

New York University, Steinhardt School of Culture, Education, and Human Development, Department of Teaching and Learning, Program in Social Studies Education, New York, NY 10003. Offers history, social studies, and global education (PhD); teaching art and social studies 7-12 (MA); teaching social studies 7-12 (MA). *Accreditation:* Teacher Education Accreditation Council. Part-time and evening/weekend programs available. *Faculty:* 3 full-time (2 women). *Students:* 5 full-time (3 women), 5 part-time (2 women); includes 4 minority (all Hispanic/Latino). Average age 27. 48 applicants, 88% accepted, 6 enrolled. In 2013, 23 master's awarded. *Degree requirements:* For master's, thesis (for some programs). *Entrance requirements:* Additional exam requirements/recommendations for international students: Required—TOEFL (minimum score 100 iBT). *Application deadline:* For fall admission, 2/1 priority date for domestic and international students; for spring admission, 10/1 for domestic and international students. Applications are processed on a rolling basis. Application fee: $75. Electronic applications accepted. *Expenses: Tuition:* Full-time $35,856; part-time $1494 per unit. *Required fees:* $1408; $64 per unit. $473 per term. Tuition and fees vary according to course load and program. *Financial support:* Career-related internships or fieldwork, Federal Work-Study, institutionally sponsored loans, scholarships/grants, and tuition waivers (partial) available. Support available to part-time students. Financial award application deadline: 2/1; financial award applicants required to submit FAFSA. *Faculty research:* Social studies education reform, ethnography and oral history, civic education, labor history and social studies curriculum, material culture. *Unit head:* 212-998-5460, Fax: 212-995-4049. *Application contact:* 212-998-5030, Fax: 212-995-4328, E-mail: steinhardt.gradadmissions@nyu.edu. Website: http://steinhardt.nyu.edu/teachlearn/social_studies.

SIT Graduate Institute, Graduate Programs, Master's Programs in Intercultural Service, Leadership, and Management, Brattleboro, VT 05302-0676. Offers conflict transformation (MA); intercultural service, leadership, and management (MA); international education (MA); sustainable development (MA). Postbaccalaureate distance learning degree programs offered (minimal on-campus study). *Degree requirements:* For master's, one foreign language, thesis. *Entrance requirements:* For master's, 4 letters of reference. Additional exam requirements/recommendations for international students: Required—TOEFL, IELTS. *Faculty research:* Intercultural communication, conflict resolution, international education, world issues, international affairs.

Stanford University, School of Education, Program in International Comparative Education, Stanford, CA 94305-9991. Offers MA, PhD. *Expenses: Tuition:* Full-time $42,690; part-time $949 per credit. *Required fees:* $185.

Teachers College, Columbia University, Graduate Faculty of Education, Department of International and Transcultural Studies, Program in Comparative and International Education, New York, NY 10027. Offers Ed M, MA, Ed D, PhD. *Faculty:* 11 full-time, 3 part-time/adjunct. *Students:* 14 full-time (all women), 20 part-time (14 women); includes 8 minority (1 Black or African American, non-Hispanic/Latino; 2 Asian, non-Hispanic/Latino; 3 Hispanic/Latino; 2 Native Hawaiian or other Pacific Islander, non-Hispanic/

Latino), 11 international. Average age 29. 71 applicants, 44% accepted, 13 enrolled. In 2013, 4 master's, 5 doctorates awarded. *Degree requirements:* For master's, integrative project; for doctorate, variable foreign language requirement, comprehensive exam, thesis/dissertation. *Entrance requirements:* For doctorate, academic writing sample. *Application deadline:* For fall admission, 12/15 for domestic students. Application fee: $65. Electronic applications accepted. *Financial support:* Career-related internships or fieldwork, Federal Work-Study, institutionally sponsored loans, and tuition waivers (full and partial) available. Support available to part-time students. Financial award application deadline: 2/1; financial award applicants required to submit FAFSA. *Faculty research:* Comparative analysis of national educational systems, identity and community in local and transcultural settings. *Unit head:* Prof. Regina Cortina, Program Coordinator, 212-678-7401, E-mail: cortina@tc.columbia.edu. *Application contact:* Deanna Ghozati, Assistant Director of Admission, 212-678-4018, Fax: 212-678-4171, E-mail: ghozati@tc.edu.
Website: http://www.tc.columbia.edu/its/cie%26ied/.

Teachers College, Columbia University, Graduate Faculty of Education, Department of International and Transcultural Studies, Program in International Educational Development, New York, NY 10027. Offers Ed M, MA, Ed D, PhD. *Faculty:* 11 full-time, 3 part-time/adjunct. *Students:* 77 full-time (59 women), 128 part-time (109 women); includes 63 minority (13 Black or African American, non-Hispanic/Latino; 27 Asian, non-Hispanic/Latino; 17 Hispanic/Latino; 6 Two or more races, non-Hispanic/Latino), 67 international. Average age 28. 258 applicants, 71% accepted, 78 enrolled. In 2013, 61 master's, 7 doctorates awarded. *Degree requirements:* For master's, integrative project; for doctorate, comprehensive exam, thesis/dissertation. *Entrance requirements:* For master's, master's degree (for Ed M applicants); for doctorate, master's degree. Additional exam requirements/recommendations for international students: Required—TOEFL (minimum score 600 paper-based). *Application deadline:* For fall admission, 1/15 priority date for domestic students; for spring admission, 12/1 for domestic students. Application fee: $65. Electronic applications accepted. *Financial support:* Career-related internships or fieldwork, Federal Work-Study, institutionally sponsored loans, and tuition waivers (full and partial) available. Support available to part-time students. Financial award application deadline: 2/1; financial award applicants required to submit FAFSA. *Faculty research:* Application of formal and nonformal education to programs of social and economic development in Third World countries. *Unit head:* Prof. Regina Cortina, Program Coordinator, 212-678-7401, E-mail: cortina@tc.edu. *Application contact:* Deanna Ghozati, Assistant Director of Admission, 212-678-4018, Fax: 212-678-4171, E-mail: ghozati@tc.edu.
Website: http://www.tc.columbia.edu/its/cie&ied/.

University of Bridgeport, School of Education, Department of Education, Bridgeport, CT 06604. Offers education (MS); educational management (Ed D, Diploma), including intermediate administrator or supervisor (Diploma), leadership (Ed D); elementary education (MS, Diploma), including early childhood education, elementary education; middle school education (MS); music education (MS); remedial reading and language arts (Diploma); secondary education (MS, Diploma), including computer specialist (Diploma), international education (Diploma), reading specialist, secondary education. Part-time and evening/weekend programs available. *Faculty:* 12 full-time (5 women), 108 part-time/adjunct (60 women). *Students:* 155 full-time (108 women), 139 part-time (98 women); includes 48 minority (22 Black or African American, non-Hispanic/Latino; 9 Asian, non-Hispanic/Latino; 15 Hispanic/Latino; 2 Two or more races, non-Hispanic/Latino), 2 international. Average age 30. 306 applicants, 55% accepted, 107 enrolled. In 2013, 153 master's, 16 other advanced degrees awarded. *Degree requirements:* For master's, final exam, final project, or thesis; for doctorate, comprehensive exam, thesis/dissertation; for Diploma, thesis or alternative, final project. *Entrance requirements:* For master's, minimum undergraduate QPA of 2.67; for doctorate, GRE, MAT; for Diploma, GRE General Test or MAT, minimum graduate QPA of 3.0. Additional exam requirements/recommendations for international students: Recommended—TOEFL (minimum score 550 paper-based; 80 iBT), IELTS (minimum score 6.5). *Application deadline:* For fall admission, 8/1 priority date for domestic and international students; for spring admission, 12/1 priority date for domestic and international students. Applications are processed on a rolling basis. Application fee: $50. Electronic applications accepted. *Expenses:* Contact institution. *Financial support:* In 2013–14, 120 students received support. Fellowships, research assistantships, teaching assistantships, career-related internships or fieldwork, Federal Work-Study, and institutionally sponsored loans available. Support available to part-time students. Financial award application deadline: 6/1; financial award applicants required to submit FAFSA. *Faculty research:* Self-concept, internship assessment, stress and situational development, follow-up of graduation, trend analysis. *Unit head:* Dr. Allen P. Cook, Dean, 203-576-4192, Fax: 203-576-4200, E-mail: acook@bridgeport.edu. *Application contact:* Leanne Proctor, Director of Graduate Admissions, 203-576-4552, Fax: 203-576-4941, E-mail: admit@bridgeport.edu.

University of Central Florida, College of Education and Human Performance, School of Teaching, Learning, and Leadership, Applied Learning and Instruction Program, Orlando, FL 32816. Offers applied learning and instruction (MA); community college education (Certificate); gifted education (Certificate); global and comparative education (Certificate); initial teacher professional preparation (Certificate); urban education (Certificate). *Accreditation:* NCATE. Part-time and evening/weekend programs available. *Students:* 11 full-time (9 women), 80 part-time (62 women); includes 27 minority (10 Black or African American, non-Hispanic/Latino; 2 Asian, non-Hispanic/Latino; 13 Hispanic/Latino; 2 Two or more races, non-Hispanic/Latino). Average age 33. 61 applicants, 70% accepted, 29 enrolled. In 2013, 19 master's, 26 other advanced degrees awarded. *Degree requirements:* For Certificate, thesis or alternative, final exam. *Entrance requirements:* For degree, GRE General Test, minimum GPA of 3.0, resume. Additional exam requirements/recommendations for international students: Required—TOEFL. *Application deadline:* For fall admission, 2/20 for domestic students; for spring admission, 9/20 for domestic students. Application fee: $30. Electronic applications accepted. *Financial support:* In 2013–14, 3 students received support, including 1 research assistantship with partial tuition reimbursement available (averaging $8,100 per year), 2 teaching assistantships with partial tuition reimbursements available (averaging $6,900 per year); fellowships, career-related internships or fieldwork, Federal Work-Study, institutionally sponsored loans, and unspecified assistantships also available. Financial award application deadline: 3/1; financial award applicants required to submit FAFSA. *Unit head:* Dr. Bobby Hoffman, Program Coordinator, 407-823-1770, E-mail: bobby.hoffman@ucf.edu. *Application contact:* Barbara Rodriguez Lamas, Director, Admissions and Student Services, 407-823-2766, Fax: 407-823-6442, E-mail: gradadmissions@ucf.edu.
Website: http://education.ucf.edu/departments.cfm.

University of Massachusetts Amherst, Graduate School, College of Education, Program in Education, Amherst, MA 01003. Offers bilingual/English as a second language/multicultural education (M Ed, Ed S); child study and early education (M Ed); children, families and schools (Ed D, Ed S); early childhood and elementary teacher education (M Ed); educational leadership (M Ed); educational policy and leadership (Ed D); higher education (M Ed); international education (M Ed); language, literacy and culture (Ed D); learning, media and technology (M Ed, Ed S); mathematics, science, and learning technologies (Ed D); psychometric methods, educational statistics and research methods (Ed D); reading and writing (M Ed); school counselor education (M Ed, Ed S); school psychology (Ed S); science education (Ed S); secondary teacher education (M Ed); social justice education (M Ed, Ed D, Ed S); special education (M Ed, Ed D, Ed S); teacher education and school improvement (Ed D, Ed S). *Accreditation:* NCATE. Part-time programs available. Postbaccalaureate distance learning degree programs offered (minimal on-campus study). *Faculty:* 95 full-time (55 women). *Students:* 357 full-time (240 women), 264 part-time (194 women); includes 114 minority (41 Black or African American, non-Hispanic/Latino; 4 American Indian or Alaska Native, non-Hispanic/Latino; 10 Asian, non-Hispanic/Latino; 47 Hispanic/Latino; 12 Two or more races, non-Hispanic/Latino), 100 international. Average age 34. 761 applicants, 51% accepted, 200 enrolled. In 2013, 186 master's, 31 doctorates, 22 other advanced degrees awarded. Terminal master's awarded for partial completion of doctoral program. *Degree requirements:* For doctorate, comprehensive exam, thesis/dissertation. *Entrance requirements:* Additional exam requirements/recommendations for international students: Required—TOEFL (minimum score 550 paper-based; 80 iBT), IELTS (minimum score 6.5). *Application deadline:* For fall admission, 1/15 for domestic and international students. Applications are processed on a rolling basis. Application fee: $75. Electronic applications accepted. *Financial support:* Fellowships with full and partial tuition reimbursements, research assistantships with full and partial tuition reimbursements, teaching assistantships with full and partial tuition reimbursements, career-related internships or fieldwork, Federal Work-Study, scholarships/grants, traineeships, health care benefits, tuition waivers (full and partial), and unspecified assistantships available. Support available to part-time students. Financial award application deadline: 1/15; financial award applicants required to submit FAFSA. *Unit head:* Dr. Linda L. Griffin, Graduate Program Director, 413-545-6984, Fax: 413-545-1523. *Application contact:* Lindsay DeSantis, Supervisor of Admissions, 413-545-0722, Fax: 413-577-0010, E-mail: gradadm@grad.umass.edu.
Website: http://www.umass.edu/education/.

University of Minnesota, Twin Cities Campus, Graduate School, College of Education and Human Development, Department of Organizational Leadership, Policy and Development, Program in Comparative and International Development Education, Minneapolis, MN 55455-0213. Offers MA, PhD. *Students:* 51 full-time (36 women), 43 part-time (29 women); includes 13 minority (4 Black or African American, non-Hispanic/Latino; 1 American Indian or Alaska Native, non-Hispanic/Latino; 6 Asian, non-Hispanic/Latino; 2 Hispanic/Latino), 18 international. Average age 34. 62 applicants, 69% accepted, 4 enrolled. In 2013, 14 master's, 7 doctorates awarded. Application fee: $75 ($95 for international students). *Unit head:* Dr. Rebecca Ropers-Huilman, Chair, 612-624-1006, Fax: 612-624-3377, E-mail: ropers@umn.edu. *Application contact:* Dr. Jennifer Engler, Assistant Dean, 612-626-2887, Fax: 612-626-7496, E-mail: engle009@umn.edu.
Website: http://www.cehd.umn.edu/EdPA/CIDE.

University of Pennsylvania, Graduate School of Education, Division of Education, Culture and Society, Program in International Educational Development, Philadelphia, PA 19104. Offers MS Ed. *Students:* 33 full-time (26 women), 5 part-time (all women); includes 9 minority (3 Black or African American, non-Hispanic/Latino; 1 Asian, non-Hispanic/Latino; 2 Hispanic/Latino; 3 Two or more races, non-Hispanic/Latino), 13 international. 131 applicants, 67% accepted, 37 enrolled. In 2013, 24 master's awarded. *Unit head:* Dr. Andrew Porter, Dean, 215-898-7014. *Application contact:* 215-898-6415, Fax: 215-746-6884, E-mail: admissions@gse.upenn.edu.
Website: http://www.gse.upenn.edu/iedp.

University of Pittsburgh, School of Education, Department of Administrative and Policy Studies, Program in Social and Comparative Analysis in Education, Pittsburgh, PA 15260. Offers M Ed, MA, Ed D, PhD. Evening/weekend programs available. *Students:* 65 full-time (47 women), 27 part-time (20 women); includes 15 minority (5 Black or African American, non-Hispanic/Latino; 5 Asian, non-Hispanic/Latino; 5 Hispanic/Latino), 23 international. Average age 36. 45 applicants, 76% accepted, 16 enrolled. In 2013, 11 master's, 8 doctorates awarded. *Degree requirements:* For master's, thesis; for doctorate, thesis/dissertation. *Entrance requirements:* For doctorate, GRE General Test. Additional exam requirements/recommendations for international students: Required—TOEFL (minimum score 80 iBT). *Application deadline:* For fall admission, 2/1 priority date for domestic and international students; for spring admission, 11/15 priority date for domestic students, 7/1 priority date for international students. Applications are processed on a rolling basis. Application fee: $50. Electronic applications accepted. *Expenses:* Tuition, state resident: full-time $19,964; part-time $807 per credit. Tuition, nonresident: full-time $32,686; part-time $1337 per credit. *Required fees:* $740; $200. Tuition and fees vary according to program. *Financial support:* Research assistantships, teaching assistantships, Federal Work-Study, institutionally sponsored loans, scholarships/grants, health care benefits, tuition waivers (partial), and unspecified assistantships available. Support available to part-time students. Financial award application deadline: 3/15; financial award applicants required to submit FAFSA. *Unit head:* Dr. Mary Margaret Kerr, Chair, 412-648-7205, Fax: 412-648-1784, E-mail: mmkerr@pitt.edu. *Application contact:* Norma Ann McMichael, Graduate Enrollment Manager, 412-648-2230, Fax: 412-648-1899, E-mail: soeinfo@pitt.edu.
Website: http://www.education.pitt.edu/AcademicDepartments/AdministrativePolicyStudies/Programs/SocialComparativeAnalysisinEducation.aspx.

University of San Francisco, School of Education, Department of International and Multicultural Education, San Francisco, CA 94117-1080. Offers human rights education (MA); international and multicultural education (MA, Ed D); multicultural literature for children and young adults (MA); teaching English to speakers of other languages (MA). Evening/weekend programs available. *Faculty:* 2 full-time (both women), 9 part-time/adjunct (5 women). *Students:* 132 full-time (99 women), 62 part-time (53 women); includes 90 minority (12 Black or African American, non-Hispanic/Latino; 26 Asian, non-Hispanic/Latino; 39 Hispanic/Latino; 1 Native Hawaiian or other Pacific Islander, non-Hispanic/Latino; 12 Two or more races, non-Hispanic/Latino), 30 international. Average age 35. 202 applicants, 80% accepted, 60 enrolled. In 2013, 41 master's, 10 doctorates awarded. *Degree requirements:* For doctorate, thesis/dissertation. *Application deadline:* For fall admission, 3/1 priority date for domestic students, 3/1 for international students; for spring admission, 10/15 priority date for domestic and international students. Applications are processed on a rolling basis. Application fee: $55 ($65 for international students). Electronic applications accepted. *Expenses: Tuition:* Full-time $21,150; part-time $1175 per unit. Tuition and fees vary according to course load, campus/location and program. *Financial support:* In 2013–14, 18 students received support. Fellowships, research assistantships, and teaching assistantships available. Financial award application deadline: 3/2; financial award applicants required to submit FAFSA. *Unit head:* Dr. Katz Susan, Chair, 415-422-6878. *Application contact:* Amy Fogliani, Associate Director of Graduate Outreach, 415-422-5467, E-mail: schoolofeducation@usfca.edu.

University of South Africa, College of Human Sciences, Pretoria, South Africa. Offers adult education (M Ed); African languages (MA, PhD); African politics (MA, PhD); Afrikaans (MA, PhD); ancient history (MA, PhD); ancient Near Eastern studies (MA, PhD); anthropology (MA, PhD); applied linguistics (MA); Arabic (MA, PhD); archaeology (MA); art history (MA); Biblical archaeology (MA); Biblical studies (M Th, D Th, PhD);

Christian spirituality (M Th, D Th); church history (M Th, D Th); classical studies (MA, PhD); clinical psychology (MA); communication (MA, PhD); comparative education (M Ed, Ed D); consulting psychology (D Admin, D Com, PhD); curriculum studies (M Ed, Ed D); development studies (M Admin, MA, D Admin, PhD); didactics (M Ed, Ed D); education (M Tech); education management (M Ed, Ed D); educational psychology (M Ed); English (MA); environmental education (M Ed); French (MA, PhD); German (MA, PhD); Greek (MA); guidance and counseling (M Ed); health studies (MA, PhD), including health sciences education (MA), health services management (MA), medical and surgical nursing science (critical care general) (MA), midwifery and neonatal nursing science (MA), trauma and emergency care (MA); history (MA, PhD); history of education (Ed D); inclusive education (M Ed, Ed D); information and communications technology policy and regulation (MA); information science (MA, MIS, PhD); international politics (MA, PhD); Islamic studies (MA, PhD); Italian (MA, PhD); Judaica (MA, PhD); linguistics (MA, PhD); mathematical education (M Ed); mathematics education (MA); missiology (M Th, D Th); modern Hebrew (MA, PhD); musicology (MA, MMus, D Mus, PhD); natural science education (M Ed); New Testament (M Th, D Th); Old Testament (D Th); pastoral therapy (M Th, D Th); philosophy (MA); philosophy of education (M Ed, Ed D); politics (MA, PhD); Portuguese (MA, PhD); practical theology (M Th, D Th); psychology (MA, MS, PhD); psychology of education (M Ed, Ed D); public health (MA); religious studies (MA, D Th, PhD); Romance languages (MA); Russian (MA, PhD); Semitic languages (MA, PhD); social behavior studies in HIV/AIDS (MA); social science (mental health) (MA); social science in development studies (MA); social science in psychology (MA); social science in social work (MA); social science in sociology (MA); social work (MSW, DSW, PhD); socio-education (M Ed, Ed D); sociolinguistics (MA); sociology (MA, PhD); Spanish (MA, PhD); systematic theology (M Th, D Th); TESOL (teaching English to speakers of other languages) (MA); theological ethics (M Th, D Th); theory of literature (MA, PhD); urban ministries (D Th); urban ministry (M Th).

University of Wisconsin–Madison, Graduate School, School of Education, Department of Educational Leadership and Policy Analysis, Madison, WI 53706-1380. Offers administration (Certificate); educational policy (MS, PhD); global higher education (MS). *Degree requirements:* For doctorate, thesis/dissertation. *Entrance requirements:* For master's and doctorate, GRE General Test. *Application deadline:* For fall admission, 1/15 for domestic and international students. *Application fee:* $56. Electronic applications accepted. *Expenses:* Tuition, state resident: full-time $10,728; part-time $790 per credit. Tuition, nonresident: full-time $24,054; part-time $1623 per credit. *Required fees:* $1130; $119 per credit. *Financial support:* Fellowships with full tuition reimbursements, research assistantships with full tuition reimbursements, teaching assistantships with full tuition reimbursements, and project assistantships available. *Unit head:* Dr. Eric Camburn, Chair, 608-262-3106, E-mail: elpa@education.wisc.edu. *Application contact:* 608-262-2433, Fax: 608-262-5134, E-mail: gradadmiss@mail.bascom.wisc.edu.
Website: http://www.education.wisc.edu/elpa.

Valparaiso University, Graduate School, Program in Comparative Global Inquiry, Valparaiso, IN 46383. Offers MA. Part-time and evening/weekend programs available. *Students:* 1 (woman) part-time. Average age 25. *Degree requirements:* For master's, thesis. *Entrance requirements:* For master's, undergraduate degree from accredited college or university; minimum GPA of 3.3 (preferred); essay indicating expected personal and professional outcomes from the program; recommendations from faculty advisors or instructors. Additional exam requirements/recommendations for international students: Required—TOEFL (minimum score 550 paper-based; 80 iBT), IELTS (minimum score 6). *Application deadline:* Applications are processed on a rolling basis. *Application fee:* $30 ($50 for international students). Electronic applications accepted. *Expenses: Tuition:* Full-time $10,350; part-time $575 per credit hour. *Required fees:* $378; $101 per term. Tuition and fees vary according to course load and program. *Financial support:* Available to part-time students. Applicants required to submit FAFSA. *Unit head:* Dr. Jennifer A. Ziegler, Dean, Graduate School and Continuing Education, 219-464-5313, Fax: 219-464-5381, E-mail: jennifer.ziegler@valpo.edu. *Application contact:* Jessica Choquette, Graduate Admissions Specialist, 219-464-5313, Fax: 219-464-5381, E-mail: jessica.choquette@valpo.edu.
Website: http://www.valpo.edu/grad/globinquiry/globalinquiry.php.

Vanderbilt University, Peabody College, Department of Leadership, Policy, and Organizations, Nashville, TN 37240-1001. Offers education policy (MPP); educational leadership and policy (Ed D); higher education (M Ed); higher education, leadership and policy (Ed D); international education policy and management (M Ed); leadership and organizational performance (M Ed). Part-time and evening/weekend programs available. *Faculty:* 30 full-time (13 women), 13 part-time/adjunct (6 women). *Students:* 183 full-time (128 women), 92 part-time (49 women); includes 59 minority (32 Black or African American, non-Hispanic/Latino; 8 Asian, non-Hispanic/Latino; 14 Hispanic/Latino; 5 Two or more races, non-Hispanic/Latino), 21 international. Average age 28. 464 applicants, 62% accepted, 123 enrolled. In 2013, 91 master's, 24 doctorates awarded. *Degree requirements:* For master's, comprehensive exam, thesis optional; for doctorate, thesis/dissertation, qualifying exams, residency. *Entrance requirements:* For master's and doctorate, GRE General Test. Additional exam requirements/recommendations for international students: Required—TOEFL (minimum score 550 paper-based; 80 iBT). *Application deadline:* For fall admission, 12/31 priority date for domestic and international students; for spring admission, 11/1 priority date for domestic and international students. Applications are processed on a rolling basis. *Application fee:* $0.

Electronic applications accepted. *Financial support:* Fellowships with full and partial tuition reimbursements, research assistantships with full and partial tuition reimbursements, teaching assistantships with full and partial tuition reimbursements, Federal Work-Study, institutionally sponsored loans, scholarships/grants, tuition waivers (partial), and unspecified assistantships available. Support available to part-time students. Financial award application deadline: 1/15; financial award applicants required to submit FAFSA. *Faculty research:* Higher education, educational leadership, education policy, economics of education, education accountability, school choice. *Unit head:* Dr. Ellen B. Goldring, Chair, 615-322-8000, Fax: 615-343-7094, E-mail: ellen.b.goldring@vanderbilt.edu. *Application contact:* Rosie Moody, Educational Coordinator, 615-322-8019, Fax: 615-343-7094, E-mail: rosie.moody@vanderbilt.edu.

Walden University, Graduate Programs, Richard W. Riley College of Education and Leadership, Minneapolis, MN 55401. *Accreditation:* NCATE. Part-time and evening/weekend programs available. Postbaccalaureate distance learning degree programs offered (minimal on-campus study). *Faculty:* 23 full-time (15 women), 830 part-time/adjunct (569 women). *Students:* 8,671 full-time (7,197 women), 2,122 part-time (1,735 women); includes 4,734 minority (3,802 Black or African American, non-Hispanic/Latino; 50 American Indian or Alaska Native, non-Hispanic/Latino; 136 Asian, non-Hispanic/Latino; 539 Hispanic/Latino; 35 Native Hawaiian or other Pacific Islander, non-Hispanic/Latino; 172 Two or more races, non-Hispanic/Latino), 73 international. Average age 40. 2,646 applicants, 96% accepted, 2074 enrolled. In 2013, 2,214 master's, 354 doctorates, 479 other advanced degrees awarded. *Degree requirements:* For doctorate, thesis/dissertation (for some programs), residency; for other advanced degree, residency (for some programs). *Entrance requirements:* For master's, bachelor's degree or higher; minimum GPA of 2.5; official transcripts; goal statement (for some programs); access to computer and Internet; for doctorate, master's degree or higher; three years of related professional or academic experience (preferred); minimum GPA of 3.0; goal statement and current resume (select programs); official transcripts; access to computer and Internet; for other advanced degree, relevant work experience; access to computer and Internet. Additional exam requirements/recommendations for international students: Required—TOEFL (minimum score 550 paper-based; 79 iBT), IELTS (minimum score 6.5), Michigan English Language Assessment Battery (minimum score 82), or PTE. *Application deadline:* Applications are processed on a rolling basis. *Application fee:* $0. Electronic applications accepted. *Expenses: Tuition:* Full-time $11,813.55; part-time $500 per credit. *Required fees:* $618.76. *Financial support:* In 2013–14, 1 fellowship was awarded; Federal Work-Study, scholarships/grants, unspecified assistantships, and family tuition reduction, active duty/veteran tuition reduction, group tuition reduction, interest-free payment plans, employee tuition reduction also available. Support available to part-time students. Financial award applicants required to submit FAFSA. *Unit head:* Dr. Kate Steffens, Dean, 800-925-3368. *Application contact:* Jennifer Hall, Vice President of Enrollment Management, 866-4-WALDEN, E-mail: info@waldenu.edu.
Website: http://www.waldenu.edu/colleges-schools/riley-college-of-education/.

Wilkes University, College of Graduate and Professional Studies, School of Education, Wilkes-Barre, PA 18766-0002. Offers art and science of teaching (MS Ed); classroom technology (MS Ed); early childhood literacy (MS Ed); educational development and strategies (MS Ed); educational leadership (MS Ed); educational technology (Ed D); higher education administration (Ed D); instructional media (MS Ed); instructional technology (MS Ed); international school leadership (MS Ed); K-12 administration (Ed D); middle level education (MS Ed); online teaching (MS Ed); reading (MS Ed); school business leadership (MS Ed); secondary education (MS Ed), including biology, chemistry, English, history, mathematics; special education (MS Ed); teaching English as a second language (MS Ed); twenty-first century teaching and learning (MS Ed). Part-time and evening/weekend programs available. Postbaccalaureate distance learning degree programs offered (minimal on-campus study). *Students:* 46 full-time (37 women), 1,410 part-time (1,039 women); includes 67 minority (12 Black or African American, non-Hispanic/Latino; 2 American Indian or Alaska Native, non-Hispanic/Latino; 11 Asian, non-Hispanic/Latino; 28 Hispanic/Latino; 1 Native Hawaiian or other Pacific Islander, non-Hispanic/Latino; 13 Two or more races, non-Hispanic/Latino), 6 international. Average age 34. In 2013, 852 master's, 10 doctorates awarded. *Entrance requirements:* Additional exam requirements/recommendations for international students: Required—TOEFL (minimum score 550 paper-based; 79 iBT). *Application deadline:* Applications are processed on a rolling basis. *Application fee:* $45. Electronic applications accepted. *Expenses:* Contact institution. *Financial support:* Federal Work-Study and unspecified assistantships available. Financial award application deadline: 3/1; financial award applicants required to submit FAFSA. *Unit head:* Dr. Rhonda Waskiewicz, Interim Dean, Education, 570-408-4332, Fax: 570-408-7872, E-mail: rhonda.waskiewicz@wilkes.edu. *Application contact:* Joanne Thomas, Interim Director of Graduate Education, 570-408-4234, Fax: 570-408-7846, E-mail: joanne.thomas1@wilkes.edu.
Website: http://www.wilkes.edu/pages/383.asp.

Wright State University, School of Graduate Studies, College of Liberal Arts, Program in Applied Behavioral Science, Dayton, OH 45435. Offers criminal justice and social problems (MA); international and comparative politics (MA). *Degree requirements:* For master's, thesis optional. *Entrance requirements:* Additional exam requirements/recommendations for international students: Required—TOEFL. *Faculty research:* Training and development, criminal justice and social problems, community systems, human factors, industrial/organizational psychology.

Student Affairs

Alliant International University–Los Angeles, Shirley M. Hufstedler School of Education, Educational Psychology Programs, Alhambra, CA 91803-1360. Offers educational psychology (Psy D); pupil personnel services (Credential); school psychology (MA). Part-time programs available. *Students:* 4 full-time (3 women), 19 part-time (16 women); includes 15 minority (2 Black or African American, non-Hispanic/Latino; 2 Asian, non-Hispanic/Latino; 8 Hispanic/Latino; 3 Two or more races, non-Hispanic/Latino). Average age 35. 16 applicants, 81% accepted, 6 enrolled. In 2013, 6 master's, 7 doctorates awarded. *Degree requirements:* For doctorate, comprehensive exam, thesis/dissertation. *Entrance requirements:* For master's, minimum GPA of 2.5, letters of recommendation; for doctorate, interview, minimum GPA of 3.0, letters of recommendation. Additional exam requirements/recommendations for international students: Required—TOEFL (minimum score 550 paper-based), TWE (minimum score 5). *Application deadline:* For fall admission, 4/15 priority date for domestic and international students; for spring admission, 12/1 priority date for domestic and international students. Applications are processed on a rolling basis. *Application fee:* $65. Electronic applications accepted. *Financial support:* Career-related internships or fieldwork, Federal Work-Study, institutionally sponsored loans, and scholarships/grants

available. Financial award application deadline: 2/15; financial award applicants required to submit FAFSA. *Faculty research:* Early identification and intervention with high-risk preschoolers, pediatric neuropsychology, interpersonal violence, ADHD, learning theories. *Unit head:* Dr. Steven Fisher, Program Director, 858-635-4825, Fax: 626-284-0550, E-mail: admissions@alliant.edu. *Application contact:* Alliant International University Central Contact Center, 866-U-ALLIANT, Fax: 858-635-4555, E-mail: admissions@alliant.edu.
Website: http://www.alliant.edu/hsoe/.

Alliant International University–San Diego, Shirley M. Hufstedler School of Education, Educational Psychology Programs, San Diego, CA 92131-1799. Offers educational psychology (Psy D); pupil personnel services (Credential); school neuropsychology (Certificate); school psychology (MA); school-based mental health (Certificate). Part-time programs available. *Faculty:* 1 full-time (0 women), 14 part-time/adjunct (9 women). *Students:* 20 full-time (19 women), 13 part-time (all women); includes 16 minority (2 Black or African American, non-Hispanic/Latino; 13 Hispanic/Latino; 1 Two or more races, non-Hispanic/Latino), 1 international. Average age 30. 23

applicants, 87% accepted, 15 enrolled. In 2013, 8 master's, 6 doctorates awarded. *Degree requirements:* For doctorate, comprehensive exam, thesis/dissertation, internship. *Entrance requirements:* For master's, minimum GPA of 2.5, letters of recommendation; for doctorate, minimum GPA of 3.0, letters of recommendation. Additional exam requirements/recommendations for international students: Required—TOEFL (minimum score 550 paper-based; 80 iBT), TWE (minimum score 5). *Application deadline:* For fall admission, 4/15 priority date for domestic and international students; for spring admission, 11/3 priority date for domestic and international students. Applications are processed on a rolling basis. Application fee: $65. Electronic applications accepted. *Financial support:* Career-related internships or fieldwork, Federal Work-Study, institutionally sponsored loans, and scholarships/grants available. Financial award application deadline: 2/15; financial award applicants required to submit FAFSA. *Faculty research:* School-based mental health, pupil personnel services, childhood mood, school-based assessment. *Unit head:* Dr. Steve Fisher, Program Director, 828-635-4825, Fax: 858-635-4739, E-mail: admissions@alliant.edu. *Application contact:* Alliant International University Central Contact Center, 866-U-ALLIANT, Fax: 858-635-4555, E-mail: admissions@alliant.edu.
Website: http://www.alliant.edu/hsoe.

Appalachian State University, Cratis D. Williams Graduate School, Department of Human Development and Psychological Counseling, Boone, NC 28608. Offers clinical mental health counseling (MA); college student development (MA); marriage and family therapy (MA); school counseling (MA). *Accreditation:* AAMFT/COAMFTE; ACA; NCATE. Part-time programs available. *Degree requirements:* For master's, comprehensive exam (for some programs), thesis optional, internships. *Entrance requirements:* For master's, GRE General Test, 3 letters of recommendation. Additional exam requirements/recommendations for international students: Required—TOEFL (minimum score 570 paper-based; 79 iBT), IELTS (minimum score 6.5). Electronic applications accepted. *Faculty research:* Multicultural counseling, addictions counseling, play therapy, expressive arts, child and adolescent therapy, sexual abuse counseling.

Arkansas State University, Graduate School, College of Education and Behavioral Science, Department of Psychology and Counseling, Jonesboro, AR 72467. Offers college student personnel services (MS); mental health counseling (Certificate); psychology and counseling (Ed S); rehabilitation counseling (MRC); school counseling (MSE); student affairs (Certificate). *Accreditation:* ACA (one or more programs are accredited); CORE (one or more programs are accredited); NCATE. Part-time programs available. *Faculty:* 15 full-time (9 women). *Students:* 50 full-time (33 women), 73 part-time (56 women); includes 33 minority (31 Black or African American, non-Hispanic/Latino; 1 American Indian or Alaska Native, non-Hispanic/Latino; 1 Two or more races, non-Hispanic/Latino), 1 international. Average age 32. 87 applicants, 53% accepted, 42 enrolled. In 2013, 17 master's, 11 other advanced degrees awarded. *Degree requirements:* For master's and other advanced degree, comprehensive exam, thesis or alternative. *Entrance requirements:* For master's, GRE General Test or MAT (for MSE), appropriate bachelor's degree, interview, letters of reference, official transcripts, immunization records, written statement, 2-3 page autobiography; for other advanced degree, GRE General Test, interview, master's degree, letters of reference, official transcript, personal statement, immunization records. Additional exam requirements/recommendations for international students: Required—TOEFL (minimum score 550 paper-based; 79 iBT), IELTS (minimum score 6), PTE (minimum score 56). *Application deadline:* Applications are processed on a rolling basis. Application fee: $30 ($40 for international students). Electronic applications accepted. *Expenses:* Tuition, state resident: full-time $4284; part-time $238 per credit hour. Tuition, nonresident: full-time $8568; part-time $476 per credit hour. *International tuition:* $9268 full-time. *Required fees:* $1098; $61 per credit hour. $25 per term. Tuition and fees vary according to course load and program. *Financial support:* In 2013–14, 17 students received support. Teaching assistantships, career-related internships or fieldwork, scholarships/grants, and unspecified assistantships available. Financial award application deadline: 7/1; financial award applicants required to submit FAFSA. *Unit head:* Dr. Loretta McGregor, Chair, 870-972-3064, Fax: 870-972-3962, E-mail: lmcgregor@astate.edu. *Application contact:* Vickey Ring, Graduate Admissions Coordinator, 870-972-3029, Fax: 870-972-3857, E-mail: vickeyring@astate.edu.
Website: http://www.astate.edu/college/education/departments/psychology-and-counseling/index.dot.

Arkansas Tech University, College of Education, Russellville, AR 72801. Offers college student personnel (MS); elementary education (M Ed); instructional improvement (M Ed); instructional technology (M Ed); physical education (M Ed); teaching (MAT). *Accreditation:* NCATE. Part-time and evening/weekend programs available. Postbaccalaureate distance learning degree programs offered (no on-campus study). *Students:* 58 full-time (39 women), 304 part-time (240 women); includes 76 minority (58 Black or African American, non-Hispanic/Latino; 3 American Indian or Alaska Native, non-Hispanic/Latino; 4 Asian, non-Hispanic/Latino; 8 Hispanic/Latino; 3 Two or more races, non-Hispanic/Latino), 2 international. Average age 32. In 2013, 130 master's awarded. *Degree requirements:* For master's, comprehensive exam, thesis optional, action research project. *Entrance requirements:* Additional exam requirements/recommendations for international students: Required—TOEFL (minimum score 550 paper-based; 79 iBT), IELTS (minimum score 6.5). *Application deadline:* For fall admission, 3/1 priority date for domestic students, 5/1 priority date for international students; for spring admission, 10/1 priority date for domestic and international students. Applications are processed on a rolling basis. Application fee: $25 ($75 for international students). Electronic applications accepted. *Expenses:* Tuition, state resident: full-time $5976; part-time $249 per credit hour. Tuition, nonresident: full-time $11,952; part-time $498 per credit hour. *Required fees:* $411 per semester. Tuition and fees vary according to course load. *Financial support:* In 2013–14, research assistantships with full tuition reimbursements (averaging $4,800 per year), teaching assistantships with full tuition reimbursements (averaging $4,800 per year) were awarded; career-related internships or fieldwork, Federal Work-Study, scholarships/grants, health care benefits, and unspecified assistantships also available. Support available to part-time students. Financial award application deadline: 4/15; financial award applicants required to submit FAFSA. *Unit head:* Dr. Sherry Field, Dean, 479-968-0418, E-mail: sfield@atu.edu. *Application contact:* Dr. Mary B. Gunter, Dean of Graduate College, 479-968-0398, Fax: 479-964-0542, E-mail: gradcollege@atu.edu.
Website: http://www.atu.edu/education/.

Ashland University, Dwight Schar College of Education, Department of Educational Administration, Ashland, OH 44805-3702. Offers curriculum specialist (M Ed); principalship (M Ed); pupil services (M Ed). Part-time programs available. *Degree requirements:* For master's, thesis or alternative, internship. *Entrance requirements:* For master's, teaching certificate or license, bachelor's degree, minimum cumulative GPA of 2.75. Additional exam requirements/recommendations for international students: Required—TOEFL. Electronic applications accepted. *Faculty research:* Gender and religious considerations in employment, Interstate School Leaders Licensure Consortium (ISLLC) standards, adjunct faculty training, politics of school finance, ethnicity and employment.

Azusa Pacific University, School of Behavioral and Applied Sciences, Department of Higher Education and Organizational Leadership, Program in College Student Affairs, Azusa, CA 91702-7000. Offers M Ed. Part-time and evening/weekend programs available. *Degree requirements:* For master's, exam. *Entrance requirements:* For master's, 12 units of course work in social science, minimum GPA of 3.0.

Binghamton University, State University of New York, Graduate School, College of Community and Public Affairs, Department of Student Affairs Administration, Vestal, NY 13850. Offers MS. *Faculty:* 3 full-time (2 women), 1 part-time/adjunct (0 women). *Students:* 37 full-time (26 women), 11 part-time (6 women); includes 7 minority (1 Black or African American, non-Hispanic/Latino; 1 Asian, non-Hispanic/Latino; 5 Hispanic/Latino). Average age 27. 32 applicants, 94% accepted, 19 enrolled. In 2013, 17 master's awarded. Application fee: $75. *Financial support:* In 2013–14, 32 students received support. Career-related internships or fieldwork, Federal Work-Study, institutionally sponsored loans, scholarships/grants, health care benefits, and unspecified assistantships available. Financial award application deadline: 2/15; financial award applicants required to submit FAFSA. *Unit head:* Dr. Mary Ann Swain, Chair, 607-777-9219, E-mail: mswain@binghamton.edu. *Application contact:* Kishan Zuber, Recruiting and Admissions Coordinator, 607-777-2151, Fax: 607-777-2501, E-mail: kzuber@binghamton.edu.
Website: http://www2.binghamton.edu/ccpa/student-affairs-administration/.

Bloomsburg University of Pennsylvania, School of Graduate Studies, College of Education, Department of Educational Studies and Secondary Education, Program in School Counseling and Student Affairs, Bloomsburg, PA 17815-1301. Offers college student affairs (M Ed); elementary school (M Ed); secondary school (M Ed). *Faculty:* 5 full-time (3 women), 5 part-time/adjunct (2 women). *Students:* 8 full-time (6 women), 59 part-time (40 women); includes 16 minority (10 Black or African American, non-Hispanic/Latino; 4 Hispanic/Latino; 2 Two or more races, non-Hispanic/Latino), 1 international. Average age 25. 48 applicants, 79% accepted, 30 enrolled. *Degree requirements:* For master's, practicum. *Entrance requirements:* For master's, 3 letters of recommendation, resume, minimum QPA of 3.0, personal statement, interview. Additional exam requirements/recommendations for international students: Required—TOEFL. Application fee: $35 ($60 for international students). Electronic applications accepted. *Expenses:* Tuition, state resident: full-time $7956; part-time $442 per credit. Tuition, nonresident: full-time $11,934; part-time $663 per credit. *Required fees:* $95.50 per credit. $55 per semester. Tuition and fees vary according to course load. *Unit head:* Dr. Tegan Kotarski, College of Education Graduate Coordinator, 570-389-3883, Fax: 570-389-5049, E-mail: tkotarsk@bloomu.edu. *Application contact:* Jennifer Richard, Administrative Assistant, 570-389-4015, Fax: 570-389-3054, E-mail: jrichard@bloomu.edu.
Website: http://www.bloomu.edu/gradschool/counseling-student-affairs.

Bob Jones University, Graduate Programs, Greenville, SC 29614. Offers accountancy (MS); Bible (MA); Bible translation (MA); Biblical studies (Certificate); broadcast management (MS); business administration (MBA); church history (MA, PhD); church ministries (MA); church music (MM); cinema and video production (MA); counseling (MS); curriculum and instruction (Ed D); divinity (M Div); dramatic production (MA); educational leadership (MS, Ed D, Ed S); elementary education (M Ed, MAT); English (M Ed, MA, MAT); fine arts (MA); graphic design (MA); history (M Ed, MA); illustration (MA); interpretative speech (MA); mathematics (M Ed, MAT); medical missions (Certificate); ministry (MM, D Min); multi-categorical special education (M Ed, MAT); music (M Ed); New Testament interpretation (PhD); Old Testament interpretation (PhD); orchestral instrument performance (MM); organ performance (MM); pastoral studies (MA); personnel services (MS, Ed S); piano pedagogy (MM); piano performance (MM); platform arts (MA); radio and television broadcasting (MS); rhetoric and public address (MA); secondary education (M Ed); studio art (MA); teaching Bible (MA); theology (MA, PhD); voice performance (MM); youth ministries (MA); M Div/MM.

Bowling Green State University, Graduate College, College of Education and Human Development, School of Leadership and Policy Studies, Program in College Student Personnel, Bowling Green, OH 43403. Offers MA. Part-time programs available. *Degree requirements:* For master's, thesis or alternative. *Entrance requirements:* For master's, GRE General Test, interview. Additional exam requirements/recommendations for international students: Required—TOEFL. Electronic applications accepted. *Faculty research:* Adult learning, legal issues, moral and ethical development.

Bucknell University, Graduate Studies, College of Arts and Sciences, Department of Education, Lewisburg, PA 17837. Offers college student personnel (MS Ed). Part-time programs available. *Degree requirements:* For master's, comprehensive exam (for some programs), thesis or alternative. *Entrance requirements:* For master's, GRE General Test, minimum GPA of 3.0. Additional exam requirements/recommendations for international students: Required—TOEFL (minimum score 600 paper-based).

Buffalo State College, State University of New York, The Graduate School, Faculty of Applied Science and Education, Department of Educational Foundations, Program in Student Personnel Administration, Buffalo, NY 14222-1095. Offers MS. *Degree requirements:* For master's, comprehensive exam. *Entrance requirements:* For master's, minimum GPA of 2.75 in last 60 hours of undergraduate course work. Additional exam requirements/recommendations for international students: Required—TOEFL (minimum score 550 paper-based).

California State University, Bakersfield, Division of Graduate Studies, School of Social Sciences and Education, Program in Counseling, Bakersfield, CA 93311. Offers school counseling (MS); student affairs (MS). *Accreditation:* NCATE. *Degree requirements:* For master's, thesis or alternative, culminating projects. *Entrance requirements:* For master's, CBEST (school counseling). *Application deadline:* Applications are processed on a rolling basis. Application fee: $55. *Unit head:* Julia Bavier, Evaluator, Advanced Educational Studies, 661-654-3193, Fax: 661-665-6916, E-mail: jbavier@csub.edu. *Application contact:* Debbie Blowers, Assistant Director of Admissions, 661-664-3381, E-mail: dblowers@csub.edu.
Website: http://www.csub.edu/sse/departments/advancededucationalstudies/educational_counseling/index.html.

California State University, Long Beach, Graduate Studies, College of Education, Department of Advanced Studies in Education and Counseling, Master of Science in Counseling Program, Long Beach, CA 90840. Offers marriage and family therapy (MS); school counseling (MS); student development in higher education (MS). *Accreditation:* NCATE. *Degree requirements:* For master's, comprehensive exam or thesis. Electronic applications accepted.

California State University, Sacramento, Office of Graduate Studies, College of Education, Department of Educational Leadership and Policy Studies, Sacramento, CA 95819. Offers educational leadership (MA), including PreK-12; higher education leadership (MA), including community college leadership, student services. Part-time programs available. *Degree requirements:* For master's, thesis or project; writing proficiency exam. *Entrance requirements:* For master's, minimum GPA of 2.5. Additional exam requirements/recommendations for international students: Required—TOEFL. *Application deadline:* For fall admission, 3/1 for domestic and international students; for spring admission, 9/30 for international students. Applications are processed on a rolling basis. Application fee: $55. Electronic applications accepted. *Financial support:* Career-related internships or fieldwork and Federal Work-Study available. Support available to part-time students. Financial award application deadline: 3/1; financial award applicants

required to submit FAFSA. *Unit head:* Dr. Francisco Reveles, Chair, 916-278-5388, Fax: 916-278-4608, E-mail: revelesf@csus.edu. *Application contact:* Jose Martinez, Graduate Admissions Supervisor, 916-278-7871, E-mail: martinj@skymail.csus.edu. Website: http://www.edweb.csus.edu/edlp.

Canisius College, Graduate Division, School of Education and Human Services, Department of Graduate Education and Leadership, Buffalo, NY 14208-1098. Offers business and marketing education (MS Ed); college student personnel (MS Ed); deaf education (MS Ed); deaf/adolescent education, grades 7-12 (MS Ed); deaf/childhood education, grades 1-6 (MS Ed); differentiated instruction (MS Ed); education administration (MS); educational administration (MS Ed); educational technologies (Certificate); gifted education extension (Certificate); literacy (MS Ed); reading (Certificate); school building leadership (MS Ed, Certificate); school district leadership (Certificate); teacher leader (Certificate); TESOL (MS Ed). *Accreditation:* NCATE. Part-time and evening/weekend programs available. Postbaccalaureate distance learning degree programs offered (minimal on-campus study). *Faculty:* 6 full-time (5 women), 33 part-time/adjunct (20 women). *Students:* 134 full-time (106 women), 267 part-time (213 women); includes 36 minority (22 Black or African American, non-Hispanic/Latino; 1 American Indian or Alaska Native, non-Hispanic/Latino; 3 Asian, non-Hispanic/Latino; 8 Hispanic/Latino; 2 Two or more races, non-Hispanic/Latino), 2 international. Average age 30. 282 applicants, 80% accepted, 120 enrolled. In 2013, 178 master's awarded. *Entrance requirements:* For master's, GRE if cumulative GPA less than 2.7, transcripts, two letters of recommendation. Additional exam requirements/recommendations for international students: Required—TOEFL (minimum score 550 paper-based, 80 iBT), IELTS (minimum score 6.5), or CAEL (minimum score 70). *Application deadline:* Applications are processed on a rolling basis. Application fee: $25. Electronic applications accepted. Application fee is waived when completed online. *Expenses: Tuition:* Part-time $750 per credit hour. *Financial support:* Career-related internships or fieldwork, Federal Work-Study, scholarships/grants, tuition waivers (partial), and unspecified assistantships available. Support available to part-time students. Financial award application deadline: 4/30; financial award applicants required to submit FAFSA. *Faculty research:* Asperger's disease, autism, private higher education, reading strategies. *Unit head:* Dr. Rosemary K. Murray, Chair/Associate Professor of Graduate Education and Leadership, 716-888-3723, E-mail: murray1@canisius.edu. *Application contact:* Julie A. Zulewski, Director of Graduate Admissions, 716-888-2548, Fax: 716-888-3195, E-mail: zulewskj@canisius.edu.
Website: http://www.canisius.edu/graduate/.

Central Michigan University, College of Graduate Studies, College of Education and Human Services, Department of Educational Leadership, Mount Pleasant, MI 48859. Offers educational leadership (Ed D), including educational technology (Ed D, Ed S); higher education leadership, K-12 curriculum, K-12 leadership; general educational administration (Ed S), including administrative leadership K-12, educational technology (Ed D, Ed S); higher education administration, instructional leadership K-12; school principalship (MA), including charter school leadership, site-based leadership; student affairs administration (MA); teacher leadership (MA). Part-time and evening/weekend programs available. *Degree requirements:* For master's and Ed S, thesis or alternative; for doctorate, thesis/dissertation. *Entrance requirements:* For doctorate, GRE or MAT, master's degree, minimum GPA of 3.5, 3 years of professional education experience. Electronic applications accepted. *Faculty research:* Elementary administration, secondary administration, student achievement, in-service training, internships in administration.

The Citadel, The Military College of South Carolina, Citadel Graduate College, School of Education, Program in Guidance and Counseling, Charleston, SC 29409. Offers elementary/secondary school counseling (M Ed); student affairs and college counseling (M Ed). *Accreditation:* ACA; NCATE. Part-time and evening/weekend programs available. *Faculty:* 10 full-time (6 women), 8 part-time/adjunct (3 women). *Students:* 15 full-time (14 women), 40 part-time (35 women); includes 13 minority (12 Black or African American, non-Hispanic/Latino; 1 Two or more races, non-Hispanic/Latino). Average age 30. In 2013, 27 master's awarded. *Degree requirements:* For master's, comprehensive exam, practicum or internship. *Entrance requirements:* For master's, GRE (minimum score 290; 900 on old scoring system) or MAT (minimum score 396), minimum undergraduate GPA of 3.0, 3 letters of reference, group interview. Additional exam requirements/recommendations for international students: Required—TOEFL (minimum score 550 paper-based; 79 iBT). *Application deadline:* For fall admission, 6/1 for domestic students; for spring admission, 10/1 for domestic students. Application fee: $30. Electronic applications accepted. *Expenses: Tuition, area resident:* Part-time $525 per credit hour. Tuition, state resident: part-time $525 per credit hour. Tuition, nonresident: part-time $865 per credit hour. *Financial support:* Career-related internships or fieldwork, health care benefits, and unspecified assistantships available. Support available to part-time students. Financial award application deadline: 7/1; financial award applicants required to submit FAFSA. *Unit head:* Dr. George T. Williams, Director, 843-953-2205, Fax: 843-953-7258, E-mail: williamsg@citadel.edu. *Application contact:* Dr. Robert H. McNamara, Associate Provost, The Citadel Graduate College, 843-953-5089, Fax: 843-953-7630, E-mail: cgc@citadel.edu.
Website: http://www.citadel.edu/education/counselor.html.

Claremont Graduate University, Graduate Programs, School of Educational Studies, Claremont, CA 91711-6160. Offers Africana education (Certificate); education and policy (MA, PhD); higher education/student affairs (MA, PhD); human development (MA, PhD); public school administration (MA, PhD); quantitative evaluation (MA, PhD); special education (MA, PhD); teacher education (MA); teaching and learning (MA, PhD); urban leadership (PhD); MBA/PhD. PhD program offered jointly with San Diego State University. Part-time programs available. *Faculty:* 16 full-time (9 women), 1 part-time/adjunct (0 women). *Students:* 224 full-time (158 women), 221 part-time (151 women); includes 229 minority (52 Black or African American, non-Hispanic/Latino; 3 American Indian or Alaska Native, non-Hispanic/Latino; 43 Asian, non-Hispanic/Latino; 113 Hispanic/Latino; 1 Native Hawaiian or other Pacific Islander, non-Hispanic/Latino; 17 Two or more races, non-Hispanic/Latino), 15 international. Average age 39. In 2013, 51 master's, 33 doctorates, 5 other advanced degrees awarded. Terminal master's awarded for partial completion of doctoral program. *Entrance requirements:* For master's and doctorate, GRE General Test. Additional exam requirements/recommendations for international students: Required—TOEFL (minimum score 550 paper-based; 80 iBT). *Application deadline:* For fall admission, 4/1 priority date for domestic and international students. Applications are processed on a rolling basis. Application fee: $80. Electronic applications accepted. *Expenses: Tuition:* Full-time $40,560; part-time $1690 per credit. Required fees: $275 per semester. Tuition and fees vary according to program. *Financial support:* Fellowships, research assistantships, Federal Work-Study, institutionally sponsored loans, and scholarships/grants available. Support available to part-time students. Financial award application deadline: 2/15; financial award applicants required to submit FAFSA. *Faculty research:* Education administration, K-12 and higher education, multicultural education, education policy, diversity in higher education, faculty issues. *Unit head:* Scott Thomas, Dean, 909-621-8075, Fax: 909-621-8734, E-mail: scott.thomas@cgu.edu. *Application contact:* Julia Wendt, Director of Central Recruitment, 909-607-3689, Fax: 909-607-7285, E-mail: admiss@cgu.edu.
Website: http://www.cgu.edu/pages/267.asp.

Clemson University, Graduate School, College of Health, Education, and Human Development, Eugene T. Moore School of Education, Program in Counselor Education, Clemson, SC 29634. Offers clinical mental health counseling (M Ed); community mental health (M Ed); school counseling (K-12) (M Ed); student affairs (higher education) (M Ed). *Accreditation:* ACA; NCATE. Part-time and evening/weekend programs available. *Students:* 135 full-time (109 women), 14 part-time (10 women); includes 29 minority (17 Black or African American, non-Hispanic/Latino; 3 Asian, non-Hispanic/Latino; 6 Hispanic/Latino; 1 Native Hawaiian or other Pacific Islander, non-Hispanic/Latino; 2 Two or more races, non-Hispanic/Latino), 1 international. Average age 24. 271 applicants, 43% accepted, 63 enrolled. In 2013, 47 master's awarded. *Degree requirements:* For master's, comprehensive exam. *Entrance requirements:* For master's, GRE General Test. Additional exam requirements/recommendations for international students: Required—TOEFL; Recommended—IELTS. *Application deadline:* For fall admission, 2/1 priority date for domestic students; for spring admission, 10/1 for domestic students. Applications are processed on a rolling basis. Application fee: $70 ($80 for international students). Electronic applications accepted. *Expenses:* Contact institution. *Financial support:* In 2013–14, 84 students received support, including 9 research assistantships with partial tuition reimbursements available (averaging $7,586 per year), 3 teaching assistantships with partial tuition reimbursements available (averaging $22,987 per year); institutionally sponsored loans, health care benefits, and unspecified assistantships also available. Financial award application deadline: 6/1; financial award applicants required to submit FAFSA. *Faculty research:* At-risk youth, ethnic identity development across the life span, postsecondary transitions and college readiness, distance and distributed learning environments, the student veteran experience in college, student development theory. *Unit head:* Dr. Michael J. Padilla, Director/Associate Dean, 864-656-4444, Fax: 864-656-0311, E-mail: padilla@clemson.edu. *Application contact:* Dr. David Fleming, Graduate Coordinator, 864-656-1881, Fax: 864-656-0311, E-mail: dflemin@clemson.edu.

College of Saint Elizabeth, Department of Psychology, Morristown, NJ 07960-6989. Offers counseling psychology (MA); forensic psychology (MA); mental health counseling (Certificate); student affairs in higher education (Certificate). Part-time programs available. *Faculty:* 2 full-time (1 woman), 4 part-time/adjunct (3 women). *Students:* 55 full-time (50 women), 33 part-time (31 women); includes 25 minority (11 Black or African American, non-Hispanic/Latino; 1 Asian, non-Hispanic/Latino; 13 Hispanic/Latino), 1 international. Average age 30. In 2013, 31 master's, 5 other advanced degrees awarded. *Degree requirements:* For master's, thesis or alternative. *Entrance requirements:* For master's, minimum GPA of 3.0, BA in psychology (preferred), 12 credits of course work in psychology. Additional exam requirements/recommendations for international students: Required—TOEFL. *Application deadline:* For fall admission, 4/1 priority date for domestic students; for spring admission, 11/15 for domestic students. Applications are processed on a rolling basis. Application fee: $35. Electronic applications accepted. *Expenses: Tuition:* Full-time $19,152; part-time $1064 per credit. *Financial support:* Career-related internships or fieldwork, tuition waivers (partial), and unspecified assistantships available. Support available to part-time students. Financial award application deadline: 3/15; financial award applicants required to submit FAFSA. *Unit head:* Dr. Thomas C. Barrett, Coordinator, Graduate and Doctoral Programs in Psychology, 973-290-4106, Fax: 973-290-4676, E-mail: tbarrett@cse.edu. *Application contact:* Deborah S. Cobo, Associate Director of Graduate Admissions, 973-290-4194, Fax: 973-290-4710, E-mail: dscobo@cse.edu.
Website: http://www.cse.edu/academics/academic-programs/human-social-dev/psychology/.

The College of Saint Rose, Graduate Studies, School of Education, Program in College Student Services Administration, Albany, NY 12203-1419. Offers MS Ed. *Accreditation:* NCATE. Part-time and evening/weekend programs available. *Degree requirements:* For master's, comprehensive exam or thesis. *Entrance requirements:* For master's, interview, minimum undergraduate GPA of 3.0, 9 hours of psychology coursework. Additional exam requirements/recommendations for international students: Required—TOEFL (minimum score 550 paper-based). Electronic applications accepted.

Colorado State University, Graduate School, College of Health and Human Sciences, School of Education, Fort Collins, CO 80523-1588. Offers adult education and training (M Ed); community college leadership (PhD); counseling and career development (M Ed); education and human resource studies (M Ed, PhD); educational leadership (M Ed, PhD); interdisciplinary studies (PhD); organizational performance and change (M Ed, PhD); student affairs in higher education (MS). *Accreditation:* ACA; Teacher Education Accreditation Council. Part-time and evening/weekend programs available. *Faculty:* 19 full-time (10 women). *Students:* 84 full-time (60 women), 545 part-time (356 women); includes 115 minority (26 Black or African American, non-Hispanic/Latino; 5 American Indian or Alaska Native, non-Hispanic/Latino; 13 Asian, non-Hispanic/Latino; 56 Hispanic/Latino; 15 Two or more races, non-Hispanic/Latino), 22 international. Average age 37. 475 applicants, 38% accepted, 147 enrolled. In 2013, 1,157 master's, 43 doctorates awarded. *Degree requirements:* For master's, comprehensive exam, thesis optional; for doctorate, comprehensive exam, thesis/dissertation, minimum of 60 credits. *Entrance requirements:* For master's and doctorate, GRE, minimum GPA of 3.0. Additional exam requirements/recommendations for international students: Required—TOEFL (minimum score 550 paper-based; 80 iBT), IELTS. *Application deadline:* For fall admission, 3/1 priority date for domestic and international students; for spring admission, 9/1 for domestic and international students. Applications are processed on a rolling basis. Application fee: $50. Electronic applications accepted. *Expenses:* Tuition, state resident: full-time $9075.40; part-time $504 per credit. Tuition, nonresident: full-time $22,248; part-time $1236 per credit. Required fees: $1819; $60 per credit. *Financial support:* In 2013–14, 7 students received support, including 1 research assistantship with partial tuition reimbursement available (averaging $16,135 per year), 6 teaching assistantships with partial tuition reimbursements available (averaging $10,106 per year); career-related internships or fieldwork, scholarships/grants, and unspecified assistantships also available. Financial award application deadline: 3/1; financial award applicants required to submit FAFSA. *Faculty research:* Issues in STEM education, diversity and multiculturalism, teacher education leadership, distance learning and teaching. Total annual research expenditures: $498,539. *Unit head:* Dr. Daniel H. Robinson, Director, 970-491-6316, Fax: 970-491-1317, E-mail: dan.robinson@colostate.edu. *Application contact:* Kelli M. Clark, Academic Coordinator, 970-491-2093, Fax: 970-491-1317, E-mail: kelli.clark@colostate.edu.
Website: http://www.soe.chhs.colostate.edu/.

Concordia University Wisconsin, Graduate Programs, School of Business and Legal Studies, Program in Student Personnel Administration, Mequon, WI 53097-2402. Offers MSSPA. *Degree requirements:* For master's, comprehensive exam, thesis or alternative. *Entrance requirements:* Additional exam requirements/recommendations for international students: Required—TOEFL.

Creighton University, Graduate School, College of Arts and Sciences, Department of Education, Program in Counselor Education, Omaha, NE 68178-0001. Offers college student affairs (MS); community counseling (MS); elementary school guidance (MS); secondary school guidance (MS). Part-time and evening/weekend programs available. Postbaccalaureate distance learning degree programs offered (minimal on-campus study). *Faculty:* 4 full-time (2 women). *Students:* 24 part-time (20 women), 1

international. Average age 36. 8 applicants, 63% accepted, 4 enrolled. In 2013, 8 master's awarded. *Degree requirements:* For master's, comprehensive exam. *Entrance requirements:* For master's, GRE General Test, resume, 3 letters of recommendation, personal statement, background check. Additional exam requirements/recommendations for international students: Required—TOEFL (minimum score 550 paper-based; 80 iBT). *Application deadline:* For fall admission, 7/1 for domestic students, 3/1 for international students; for winter admission, 10/1 for domestic students, 7/1 for international students; for spring admission, 3/1 for domestic students, 9/1 for international students; for summer admission, 3/1 for domestic and international students. Applications are processed on a rolling basis. Application fee: $50. Electronic applications accepted. *Expenses: Tuition:* Full-time $13,608; part-time $756 per credit hour. *Required fees:* $149 per semester. Tuition and fees vary according to course load, campus/location, program, reciprocity agreements and student's religious affiliation. *Financial support:* Scholarships/grants available. Support available to part-time students. Financial award applicants required to submit FAFSA. *Unit head:* Dr. Jeffrey Smith, Associate Professor of Education, 402-280-2413, E-mail: jefsmith@creighton.edu. *Application contact:* Valerie Mattix, Senior Program Coordinator, 402-280-2425, Fax: 402-280-2423, E-mail: valeriemattix@creighton.edu.

DePaul University, College of Education, Chicago, IL 60614. Offers bilingual bicultural education (M Ed, MA); counseling (M Ed, MA), including clinical mental health counseling, college student development, school counseling; curriculum studies (M Ed, MA, Ed D); early childhood education (M Ed, MA, Ed D); educating adults (MA); educational leadership (M Ed, MA, Ed D), including administration and supervision (M Ed, MA), principal preparation (M Ed, MA); elementary education (MA); mathematics education (MA); mathematics for teaching (MS); middle school mathematics education (MS); reading specialist (M Ed, MA); secondary education (M Ed); social and cultural foundations in education (MA); special education (M Ed, MA); world languages education (M Ed, MA). Part-time and evening/weekend programs available. Postbaccalaureate distance learning degree programs offered (no on-campus study). *Faculty:* 61 full-time (35 women), 59 part-time/adjunct (43 women). *Students:* 628 full-time (486 women), 324 part-time (243 women); includes 304 minority (144 Black or African American, non-Hispanic/Latino; 1 American Indian or Alaska Native, non-Hispanic/Latino; 38 Asian, non-Hispanic/Latino; 98 Hispanic/Latino; 23 Two or more races, non-Hispanic/Latino), 24 international. Average age 30. In 2013, 465 master's, 4 doctorates awarded. *Degree requirements:* For doctorate, thesis/dissertation. *Application deadline:* For fall admission, 8/15 for domestic students; for winter admission, 12/1 for domestic students; for spring admission, 3/1 for domestic students. Applications are processed on a rolling basis. Application fee: $40. Electronic applications accepted. Tuition and fees vary according to course level, course load and degree level. *Financial support:* Application deadline: 12/31; applicants required to submit FAFSA. *Unit head:* Dr. Paul Zionts, Dean, 773-325-7581, Fax: 773-325-7713, E-mail: pzionts@depaul.edu. *Application contact:* Farrah Dalal, Assistant Director, 773-325-2465, Fax: 773-325-2270, E-mail: fdalal@depaul.edu.
Website: http://education.depaul.edu.

Eastern Illinois University, Graduate School, College of Education and Professional Studies, Department of Counseling and Student Development, Charleston, IL 61920-3099. Offers clinical counseling (MS); college student affairs (MS); school counseling (MS). *Accreditation:* ACA; NCATE. Part-time and evening/weekend programs available. *Degree requirements:* For master's, comprehensive exam. *Entrance requirements:* For master's, GRE General Test or MAT. *Expenses: Tuition, area resident:* Part-time $283 per credit hour. Tuition, state resident: part-time $283 per credit hour. Tuition, nonresident: part-time $679 per credit hour.

Fresno Pacific University, Graduate Programs, School of Education, Division of Pupil Personnel Services, Fresno, CA 93702-4709. Offers board certified associate behavior analyst (Certificate); school counseling (MA); school psychology (MA). Part-time programs available. *Degree requirements:* For master's, thesis or alternative. *Entrance requirements:* Additional exam requirements/recommendations for international students: Required—TOEFL (minimum score 550 paper-based). *Application deadline:* For fall admission, 7/15 for domestic and international students; for spring admission, 11/15 for domestic and international students. Applications are processed on a rolling basis. Application fee: $90. *Expenses: Tuition:* Full-time $8910; part-time $495 per unit. *Required fees:* $270. Tuition and fees vary according to course load and program. *Financial support:* Applicants required to submit FAFSA. *Unit head:* Diane Talbot, Program Director, 559-453-2014, E-mail: diane.talbot@fresno.edu. *Application contact:* Amanda Krum-Stovall, Director of Graduate Admissions, 559-453-2016, E-mail: amanda.krum-stovall@fresno.edu.

Grambling State University, School of Graduate Studies and Research, College of Education, Department of Educational Leadership, Grambling, LA 71245. Offers developmental education (MS, Ed D, PMC), including curriculum and instructional design (Ed D), English (MS), guidance and counseling (MS), higher education administration and management (Ed D), mathematics (MS), reading (MS), science (MS), student development and personnel services (Ed D); educational leadership (M Ed). Part-time and evening/weekend programs available. *Faculty:* 10 full-time (7 women). *Students:* 19 full-time (13 women), 89 part-time (70 women); includes 83 minority (82 Black or African American, non-Hispanic/Latino; 1 Hispanic/Latino), 6 international. Average age 40. In 2013, 13 master's, 6 doctorates, 1 other advanced degree awarded. *Degree requirements:* For master's, comprehensive exam, thesis (for some programs); for doctorate, comprehensive exam, thesis/dissertation. *Entrance requirements:* For master's, GRE, minimum GPA of 2.5 on last degree; for doctorate, GRE (minimum score 1000, 500 on Verbal), master's degree, minimum GPA of 3.0 on last degree. Additional exam requirements/recommendations for international students: Required—TOEFL (minimum score 500 paper-based; 62 iBT). *Application deadline:* For fall admission, 7/1 for domestic and international students; for spring admission, 12/1 for domestic and international students; for summer admission, 5/1 for domestic and international students. Applications are processed on a rolling basis. Application fee: $20 ($30 for international students). Electronic applications accepted. *Financial support:* Research assistantships, health care benefits, tuition waivers (full), and unspecified assistantships available. Financial award application deadline: 5/31; financial award applicants required to submit FAFSA. *Unit head:* Dr. Olatunde Ogunyemi, Department Head, 318-274-2549, Fax: 318-274-6249, E-mail: ogunyemio@gram.edu. *Application contact:* Brenda Cooper, Administrative Assistant III, 318-274-2238, Fax: 318-274-6249, E-mail: cooper@gram.edu.
Website: http://www.gram.edu/academics/majors/education/departments/leadership/.

Hampton University, Graduate College, College of Education and Continuing Studies, Program in Counseling, Hampton, VA 23668. Offers college student development (MA); community agency counseling (MA); pastoral counseling (MA); school counseling (MA). *Accreditation:* NCATE. Part-time and evening/weekend programs available. *Entrance requirements:* For master's, GRE General Test.

Illinois State University, Graduate School, College of Education, Department of Educational Administration and Foundations, Program in College Student Personnel Administration, Normal, IL 61790-2200. Offers MS.

Indiana State University, College of Graduate and Professional Studies, College of Education, Department of Educational Leadership, Administration, and Foundations, Terre Haute, IN 47809. Offers educational administration (PhD); leadership in higher education (PhD); school administration (Ed S); school administration and supervision (M Ed); student affairs in higher education (MS). *Accreditation:* NCATE. Part-time and evening/weekend programs available. Terminal master's awarded for partial completion of doctoral program. *Degree requirements:* For master's, thesis; for doctorate, thesis/dissertation. *Entrance requirements:* For master's, GRE General Test, minimum undergraduate GPA of 2.5; for doctorate, GRE General Test, minimum undergraduate GPA of 3.5; for Ed S, GRE General Test, minimum graduate GPA of 3.25. Electronic applications accepted.

Indiana University of Pennsylvania, School of Graduate Studies and Research, College of Education and Educational Technology, Department of Student Affairs in Higher Education, Indiana, PA 15705-1087. Offers MA. *Accreditation:* NCATE. Part-time programs available. *Faculty:* 4 full-time (2 women). *Students:* 57 full-time (45 women), 7 part-time (2 women); includes 8 minority (5 Black or African American, non-Hispanic/Latino; 1 Asian, non-Hispanic/Latino; 2 Hispanic/Latino). Average age 24. 137 applicants, 54% accepted, 26 enrolled. In 2013, 30 master's awarded. *Degree requirements:* For master's, comprehensive exam, thesis optional. *Entrance requirements:* For master's, resume, interview, 2 letters of recommendation, writing sample, minimum GPA of 2.8. Additional exam requirements/recommendations for international students: Required—TOEFL (minimum score 540 paper-based). *Application deadline:* For fall admission, 1/15 priority date for domestic students. Application fee: $50. Electronic applications accepted. *Expenses:* Tuition, state resident: full-time $3978; part-time $442 per credit. Tuition, nonresident: full-time $5967; part-time $663 per credit. *Required fees:* $2080; $115.55 per credit. $93 per semester. Tuition and fees vary according to degree level and program. *Financial support:* In 2013–14, 23 research assistantships with full and partial tuition reimbursements (averaging $5,216 per year) were awarded; fellowships, career-related internships or fieldwork, Federal Work-Study, scholarships/grants, and unspecified assistantships also available. Support available to part-time students. Financial award application deadline: 4/15; financial award applicants required to submit FAFSA. *Unit head:* Dr. John Wesley Lowery, Chairperson, 724-357-4535, E-mail: jlowery@iup.edu. *Application contact:* Paula Stossel, Assistant Dean for Administration, 724-357-4511, Fax: 724-357-4862, E-mail: graduate-admissions@iup.edu.
Website: http://www.iup.edu/sahe.

Indiana University–Purdue University Indianapolis, School of Education, Indianapolis, IN 46202-2896. Offers computer education (Certificate); curriculum and instruction (MS); early childhood (MS); educational leadership (MS, Certificate); English as a second language (Certificate); higher education and student affairs (MS); kindergarten (Certificate); language education (MS); reading (Certificate); school counseling (MS); special education (MS, Certificate). Part-time and evening/weekend programs available. *Faculty:* 41 full-time, 80 part-time/adjunct. *Students:* 113 full-time (78 women), 263 part-time (200 women); includes 88 minority (51 Black or African American, non-Hispanic/Latino; 1 American Indian or Alaska Native, non-Hispanic/Latino; 10 Asian, non-Hispanic/Latino; 19 Hispanic/Latino; 7 Two or more races, non-Hispanic/Latino), 5 international. Average age 33. 93 applicants, 54% accepted, 40 enrolled. In 2013, 179 master's awarded. *Degree requirements:* For master's, thesis optional. *Entrance requirements:* For master's, GRE General Test, minimum GPA of 3.0. Additional exam requirements/recommendations for international students: Required—TOEFL. *Application deadline:* For fall admission, 5/1 priority date for domestic students; for spring admission, 11/1 for domestic students. Application fee: $55 ($65 for international students). *Financial support:* Fellowships, research assistantships with partial tuition reimbursements, teaching assistantships, Federal Work-Study, institutionally sponsored loans, scholarships/grants, and tuition waivers (partial) available. Support available to part-time students. *Faculty research:* Teachers in the process of change, learning cycles, children's concepts of science. *Total annual research expenditures:* $614,458. *Unit head:* Dr. Pat Rogan, Executive Associate Dean, 317-274-6862, E-mail: progan@iupui.edu. *Application contact:* Donnella Dillon, Graduate Admissions Coordinator, 317-274-0645, E-mail: dmdillon@iupui.edu.
Website: http://education.iupui.edu/.

Iowa State University of Science and Technology, Department of Educational Leadership and Policy Studies, Ames, IA 50011. Offers counselor education (M Ed, MS); educational administration (M Ed, MS); educational leadership (PhD); higher education (M Ed, MS); organizational learning and human resource development (M Ed, MS); research and evaluation (MS); student affairs (MS). *Degree requirements:* For master's, thesis or alternative; for doctorate, thesis/dissertation. *Entrance requirements:* For master's and doctorate, GRE General Test. Additional exam requirements/recommendations for international students: Required—TOEFL (minimum score 560 paper-based; 83 iBT), IELTS (minimum score 6.5). Electronic applications accepted.

Kansas State University, Graduate School, College of Education, Department of Special Education, Counseling and Student Affairs, Manhattan, KS 66506. Offers academic advising (MS); counseling and student development (MS, Ed D, PhD), including college student development (MS), counselor education and supervision (PhD), school counseling (MS), student affairs in higher education (PhD); special education (MS, Ed D). *Accreditation:* ACA; NCATE. Part-time programs available. *Faculty:* 18 full-time (8 women), 15 part-time/adjunct (5 women). *Students:* 117 full-time (80 women), 327 part-time (257 women); includes 83 minority (42 Black or African American, non-Hispanic/Latino; 2 American Indian or Alaska Native, non-Hispanic/Latino; 9 Asian, non-Hispanic/Latino; 23 Hispanic/Latino; 1 Native Hawaiian or other Pacific Islander, non-Hispanic/Latino; 6 Two or more races, non-Hispanic/Latino), 9 international. Average age 33. 247 applicants, 69% accepted, 117 enrolled. In 2013, 117 master's, 7 doctorates awarded. *Degree requirements:* For master's, comprehensive exam; for doctorate, comprehensive exam, thesis/dissertation. *Entrance requirements:* For master's, minimum undergraduate GPA of 3.0; for doctorate, GRE General Test, minimum GPA of 3.0 in last 60 hours. Additional exam requirements/recommendations for international students: Required—TOEFL. *Application deadline:* For fall admission, 2/1 priority date for domestic and international students; for spring admission, 8/1 priority date for domestic and international students. Applications are processed on a rolling basis. Application fee: $50 ($75 for international students). Electronic applications accepted. *Financial support:* In 2013–14, 3 teaching assistantships (averaging $18,090 per year) were awarded; career-related internships or fieldwork, institutionally sponsored loans, and scholarships/grants also available. Financial award application deadline: 3/1; financial award applicants required to submit FAFSA. *Faculty research:* Counseling supervision, academic advising, career development, student development, universal design for learning, autism, learning disabilities. *Unit head:* Kenneth Hughey, Head, 785-532-6445, Fax: 785-532-7304, E-mail: khughey@ksu.edu. *Application contact:* Dona Deam, Application Contact, 785-532-5595, Fax: 785-532-7304, E-mail: ddeam@ksu.edu.
Website: http://www.coe.k-state.edu/departments/secsa/.

Kaplan University, Davenport Campus, School of Higher Education Studies, Davenport, IA 52807-2095. Offers college administration and leadership (MS); college teaching and learning (MS); student services (MS). Part-time and evening/weekend programs available. Postbaccalaureate distance learning degree programs offered (no on-campus study). *Entrance requirements:* Additional exam requirements/

recommendations for international students: Required—TOEFL (minimum score 550 paper-based; 80 iBT).

Kent State University, Graduate School of Education, Health, and Human Services, School of Foundations, Leadership and Administration, Program in Higher Education and Student Personnel, Kent, OH 44242-0001. Offers M Ed. *Accreditation:* NCATE. Part-time and evening/weekend programs available. *Faculty:* 5 full-time (3 women), 3 part-time/adjunct (2 women). *Students:* 82 full-time (60 women), 23 part-time (20 women); includes 19 minority (10 Black or African American, non-Hispanic/Latino; 1 American Indian or Alaska Native, non-Hispanic/Latino; 1 Asian, non-Hispanic/Latino; 2 Hispanic/Latino; 5 Native Hawaiian or other Pacific Islander, non-Hispanic/Latino), 2 international. 182 applicants, 15% accepted. In 2013, 35 master's awarded. *Entrance requirements:* For master's, GRE if undergraduate GPA is below 3.0, resume, interview, 2 letters of recommendation, goals statement. Additional exam requirements/ recommendations for international students: Required—TOEFL (minimum score 550 paper-based; 80 iBT). *Application deadline:* Applications are processed on a rolling basis. Application fee: $30 ($60 for international students). Electronic applications accepted. *Financial support:* In 2013–14, 2 research assistantships with full tuition reimbursements (averaging $8,500 per year) were awarded; teaching assistantships with full tuition reimbursements, Federal Work-Study, scholarships/grants, and unspecified assistantships also available. Financial award application deadline: 4/1; financial award applicants required to submit FAFSA. *Faculty research:* History/ sociology of higher education, organization and administration in higher education. *Unit head:* Dr. Mark Kretovics, Coordinator, 330-672-0642, E-mail: mkretov1@kent.edu. *Application contact:* Nancy Miller, Academic Program Director, Office of Graduate Student Services, 330-672-2576, Fax: 330-672-9162, E-mail: ogs@kent.edu.

Lamar University, College of Graduate Studies, College of Education and Human Development, Department of Counseling and Special Populations, Beaumont, TX 77710. Offers counseling and development (M Ed); school counseling (M Ed); special education (M Ed); student affairs (Certificate).

Lee University, Graduate Studies in Counseling, Cleveland, TN 37320-3450. Offers college student development (MS); holistic child development (MS); marriage and family therapy (MS); mental health counseling (MS); school counseling (MS). Part-time programs available. *Faculty:* 9 full-time (3 women), 4 part-time/adjunct (0 women). *Students:* 65 full-time (52 women), 37 part-time (32 women); includes 16 minority (7 Black or African American, non-Hispanic/Latino; 1 Asian, non-Hispanic/Latino; 7 Hispanic/Latino; 1 Native Hawaiian or other Pacific Islander, non-Hispanic/Latino). Average age 27. 52 applicants, 75% accepted, 28 enrolled. In 2013, 42 master's awarded. *Degree requirements:* For master's, variable foreign language requirement, comprehensive exam, thesis, internship. *Entrance requirements:* For master's, GRE General Test or MAT, minimum undergraduate GPA of 3.0, 3 letters of recommendation, interview, official transcripts, essay. Additional exam requirements/recommendations for international students: Required—TOEFL (minimum score 450 paper-based). *Application deadline:* For fall admission, 4/1 priority date for domestic and international students; for spring admission, 10/1 priority date for domestic and international students. Applications are processed on a rolling basis. Application fee: $25. *Expenses: Tuition:* Full-time $9900; part-time $550 per credit hour. *Required fees:* $35 per term. One-time fee: $25. *Financial support:* In 2013–14, 52 students received support, including 1 teaching assistantship (averaging $250 per year); career-related internships or fieldwork, Federal Work-Study, institutionally sponsored loans, scholarships/grants, and unspecified assistantships also available. Financial award application deadline: 3/1; financial award applicants required to submit FAFSA. *Unit head:* Dr. Trevor Milliron, Director, 423-614-8126, Fax: 423-614-8129, E-mail: tmilliron@leeuniversity.edu. *Application contact:* Vicki Glasscock, Graduate Admissions Director, 423-614-8059, E-mail: vglasscock@leeuniversity.edu.
Website: http://www.leeuniversity.edu/academics/graduate/counseling/.

Lee University, Program in Education, Cleveland, TN 37320-3450. Offers college student development (MS); curriculum and instruction (M Ed, Ed S); educational leadership (M Ed, Ed S); elementary education (MAT); higher education administration (MS); middle grades (MAT); secondary education (MAT); special education (M Ed); special education (secondary) (MAT). Part-time programs available. *Faculty:* 14 full-time (7 women), 6 part-time/adjunct (3 women). *Students:* 30 full-time (23 women), 62 part-time (37 women); includes 8 minority (3 Black or African American, non-Hispanic/Latino; 1 American Indian or Alaska Native, non-Hispanic/Latino; 2 Asian, non-Hispanic/Latino; 2 Hispanic/Latino). Average age 30. 40 applicants, 100% accepted, 30 enrolled. In 2013, 117 master's, 2 other advanced degrees awarded. *Degree requirements:* For master's, variable foreign language requirement, comprehensive exam, thesis, internship. *Entrance requirements:* For master's, MAT or GRE General Test, minimum GPA of 2.75, 3 letters of recommendation, interview, writing sample, official transcripts. Additional exam requirements/recommendations for international students: Required—TOEFL (minimum score 450 paper-based). *Application deadline:* For fall admission, 4/1 priority date for domestic and international students; for spring admission, 10/1 priority date for domestic and international students. Applications are processed on a rolling basis. Application fee: $25. *Expenses: Tuition:* Full-time $9900; part-time $550 per credit hour. *Required fees:* $35 per term. One-time fee: $25. *Financial support:* In 2013–14, 47 students received support, including 1 teaching assistantship (averaging $1,500 per year); career-related internships or fieldwork, Federal Work-Study, institutionally sponsored loans, scholarships/grants, and unspecified assistantships also available. Financial award application deadline: 3/1; financial award applicants required to submit FAFSA. *Unit head:* Dr. Gary Riggins, Director, 423-614-8193. *Application contact:* Vicki Glasscock, Graduate Admissions Director, 423-614-8059, E-mail: vglasscock@leeuniversity.edu.
Website: http://www.leeuniversity.edu/academics/graduate/education.

Lewis University, College of Arts and Sciences, Program in Organizational Leadership, Romeoville, IL 60446. Offers coaching (MA); higher education/student services (MA); non-for-profit management (MA); organizational management (MA); public administration (MA); training and development (MA). Part-time and evening/weekend programs available. Postbaccalaureate distance learning degree programs offered (no on-campus study). *Students:* 24 full-time (21 women), 200 part-time (152 women); includes 87 minority (60 Black or African American, non-Hispanic/Latino; 2 American Indian or Alaska Native, non-Hispanic/Latino; 4 Asian, non-Hispanic/Latino; 20 Hispanic/ Latino; 1 Two or more races, non-Hispanic/Latino), 1 international. Average age 36. *Entrance requirements:* For master's, bachelor's degree, at least 24 years of age, minimum of 3 years of work experience, minimum GPA of 3.0, letter of recommendation. Additional exam requirements/recommendations for international students: Required—TOEFL (minimum score 550 paper-based; 80 iBT). *Application deadline:* For fall admission, 5/1 priority date for international students; for spring admission, 11/15 priority date for international students. Applications are processed on a rolling basis. Application fee: $40. Electronic applications accepted. *Financial support:* Tuition waivers and unspecified assistantships available. Financial award application deadline: 5/1; financial award applicants required to submit FAFSA. *Unit head:* Dr. Keith Lavine, Chair of Organizational Leadership, 815-838-0500, E-mail: lavineke@lewisu.edu. *Application contact:* Julie Branchaw, Assistant Director, Graduate and Adult Admission, 815-836-5574, Fax: 815-836-5578, E-mail: branchju@lewisu.edu.

Liberty University, School of Education, Lynchburg, VA 24515. Offers administration and supervision (M Ed); curriculum and instruction (Ed D, Ed S); early childhood education (M Ed); educational leadership (Ed D, Ed S); educational technology and online instruction (M Ed); elementary education (M Ed, MAT); English (M Ed); gifted education (M Ed); history (M Ed); leadership (M Ed); math specialist (M Ed); middle grades (M Ed, MAT); outdoor adventure sport (MS); reading specialist (M Ed); school counseling (M Ed); secondary education (MAT); special education (M Ed, MAT); sport management (MS), including administration, outdoor recreation, sport management, tourism; sports administration (MS); student service (M Ed); teaching and learning (M Ed); tourism (MS). *Accreditation:* NCATE. Part-time programs available. Postbaccalaureate distance learning degree programs offered (minimal on-campus study). *Students:* 2,241 full-time (1,639 women), 4,413 part-time (3,240 women); includes 2,052 minority (1,588 Black or African American, non-Hispanic/Latino; 37 American Indian or Alaska Native, non-Hispanic/Latino; 67 Asian, non-Hispanic/Latino; 173 Hispanic/Latino; 37 Native Hawaiian or other Pacific Islander, non-Hispanic/Latino; 150 Two or more races, non-Hispanic/Latino), 15 international. Average age 37. 6,185 applicants, 43% accepted, 1603 enrolled. In 2013, 1,256 master's, 117 doctorates, 470 other advanced degrees awarded. *Degree requirements:* For doctorate, comprehensive exam, thesis/dissertation. *Entrance requirements:* For master's, GRE General Test or MAT (if taken in or before 1999), 2 letters of recommendation, minimum undergraduate GPA of 3.0, curriculum vitae; for doctorate and Ed S, GRE General Test or MAT (if taken before 1999), minimum master's GPA of 3.0, 3 years of teaching experience. Additional exam requirements/recommendations for international students: Required—TOEFL (minimum score 600 paper-based; 100 iBT). *Application deadline:* For fall admission, 6/ 1 for domestic students; for spring admission, 11/1 for domestic students. Applications are processed on a rolling basis. Application fee: $50. Electronic applications accepted. *Expenses:* Contact institution. *Financial support:* Federal Work-Study and tuition waivers (partial) available. *Faculty research:* Self-determination, character education, bibliotherapy, learning styles, distance education. *Unit head:* Dr. Karen L. Parker, Dean, 434-582-2195, Fax: 434-582-2468, E-mail: kparker@liberty.edu. *Application contact:* Jay Bridge, Director of Graduate Admissions, 800-424-9595, Fax: 800-628-7977, E-mail: gradadmissions@liberty.edu.
Website: http://www.liberty.edu/academics/education/graduate/.

Manhattan College, Graduate Programs, School of Education and Health, Program in Counseling, Riverdale, NY 10471. Offers bilingual pupil personnel services (Professional Diploma); mental health counseling (MS, Professional Diploma); school counseling (MA, Professional Diploma). Part-time and evening/weekend programs available. *Faculty:* 2 full-time (1 woman), 16 part-time/adjunct (9 women). *Students:* 64 full-time (51 women), 55 part-time (45 women); includes 64 minority (25 Black or African American, non-Hispanic/Latino; 11 Asian, non-Hispanic/Latino; 28 Hispanic/Latino). 123 applicants, 89% accepted, 58 enrolled. In 2013, 42 master's, 4 other advanced degrees awarded. *Degree requirements:* For master's, thesis, internship. *Entrance requirements:* For master's, minimum GPA of 3.0. Additional exam requirements/recommendations for international students: Recommended—TOEFL. *Application deadline:* For fall admission, 7/1 priority date for domestic students; for spring admission, 12/20 priority date for domestic students. Applications are processed on a rolling basis. Application fee: $60. *Expenses: Tuition:* Part-time $890 per credit. Part-time tuition and fees vary according to program. *Financial support:* In 2013–14, 1 research assistantship with partial tuition reimbursement (averaging $18,000 per year) was awarded; Federal Work-Study, scholarships/grants, health care benefits, and unspecified assistantships also available. Financial award application deadline: 2/1; financial award applicants required to submit FAFSA. *Faculty research:* College advising, cognition, family counseling, group dynamics, cultural attitudes, bullying. *Unit head:* Dr. Corine Fitzpatrick, Director, 718-862-7497, Fax: 718-862-7472, E-mail: corine.fitzpatrick@manhattan.edu. *Application contact:* William Bisset, Vice President for Enrollment, 718-862-7199, Fax: 718-862-8019, E-mail: william.bisset@manhattan.edu.

Marquette University, Graduate School, College of Education, Department of Educational Policy and Leadership, Milwaukee, WI 53201-1881. Offers college student personnel administration (M Ed); curriculum and instruction (MA); education (MA); educational administration (M Ed); educational policy and foundations (MA); elementary education (Certificate); literacy (MA); principal (Certificate); reading specialist (Certificate); reading teacher (Certificate); secondary education (Certificate); superintendent (Certificate). Part-time and evening/weekend programs available. *Faculty:* 15 full-time (10 women), 3 part-time/adjunct (2 women). *Students:* 39 full-time (31 women), 107 part-time (70 women); includes 19 minority (7 Black or African American, non-Hispanic/Latino; 2 American Indian or Alaska Native, non-Hispanic/ Latino; 3 Asian, non-Hispanic/Latino; 6 Hispanic/Latino; 1 Two or more races, non-Hispanic/Latino), 2 international. Average age 30. 144 applicants, 74% accepted, 67 enrolled. In 2013, 48 master's, 4 doctorates, 12 other advanced degrees awarded. Terminal master's awarded for partial completion of doctoral program. *Degree requirements:* For master's, comprehensive exam, thesis (for some programs); for doctorate, thesis/dissertation, qualifying exam, supporting minor. *Entrance requirements:* For master's, GRE General Test or MAT, official transcripts from all current and previous colleges/universities except Marquette, three letters of recommendation, statement of purpose; for doctorate, GRE General Test, MAT, sample of written work, official transcripts from all current and previous colleges/universities except Marquette, three letters of recommendation, statement of purpose, resume/ curriculum vitae; for Certificate, GRE General Test or MAT, master's degree. Additional exam requirements/recommendations for international students: Required—TOEFL (minimum score 530 paper-based). *Application deadline:* For fall admission, 1/15 for domestic and international students. Application fee: $50. *Expenses:* Contact institution. *Financial support:* In 2013–14, 130 students received support, including 1 fellowship with full tuition reimbursement available (averaging $18,780 per year), 5 research assistantships with full tuition reimbursements available (averaging $13,404 per year); health care benefits, tuition waivers (partial), and unspecified assistantships also available. Support available to part-time students. Financial award application deadline: 2/15. *Faculty research:* Leadership; social justice in education; development of lifelong learners; race, class, and schooling in historical perspective; urban teacher education. *Unit head:* Dr. Ellen Eckman, Chair, 414-288-1561, E-mail: ellen.eckman@marquette.edu. *Application contact:* Dr. Sharon Chubbuck, Associate Professor, 414-288-5895.

Massachusetts School of Professional Psychology, Graduate Programs, Boston, MA 02132. Offers applied psychology in higher education student personnel administration (MA); clinical psychology (Psy D); counseling psychology (MA); counseling psychology and community mental health (MA); counseling psychology and global mental health (MA); executive coaching (Graduate Certificate); forensic and counseling psychology (MA); leadership psychology (Psy D); organizational psychology (MA); primary care psychology (MA); respecialization in clinical psychology (Certificate); school psychology (Psy D); MA/CAGS. *Accreditation:* APA. *Degree requirements:* For master's, comprehensive exam (for some programs); for doctorate, thesis/dissertation (for some programs). Electronic applications accepted.

Merrimack College, School of Education, North Andover, MA 01845-5800. Offers community engagement (M Ed), including community organizations, higher education, K-12 education; early childhood education (M Ed); elementary education (M Ed);

English as a second language (PreK-6) (M Ed); English language learners (M Ed); general studies (M Ed); higher education (M Ed), including leadership and organizational development, student affairs; middle (M Ed); moderate disabilities (PreK-8) (M Ed); secondary (M Ed); teacher leadership (CAGS), including instructional leadership, reading specialist. Part-time and evening/weekend programs available. *Faculty:* 4 full-time (all women), 23 part-time/adjunct (15 women). *Students:* 127 full-time (104 women), 61 part-time (52 women); includes 3 minority (1 Asian, non-Hispanic/Latino; 2 Hispanic/Latino), 2 international. Average age 25. 403 applicants, 47% accepted, 138 enrolled. In 2013, 140 master's awarded. *Degree requirements:* For master's, practicum, portfolio, and state test (for licensure track); capstone (for higher education and community engagement tracks). *Entrance requirements:* For master's, MTEL (Massachusetts Tests for Educator Licensure), official transcripts from other colleges, resume, personal statement, 2 letters of recommendation, additional essay requirements for fellowships. Additional exam requirements/recommendations for international students: Required—TOEFL (minimum score 84 iBT), IELTS (minimum score 6.5). *Application deadline:* For fall admission, 8/15 for domestic and international students; for winter admission, 12/1 for domestic students, 11/15 for international students; for spring admission, 1/10 for domestic and international students; for summer admission, 5/10 for domestic and international students. Applications are processed on a rolling basis. Application fee: $0. Electronic applications accepted. Tuition and fees vary according to course load and program. *Financial support:* In 2013–14, 91 fellowships with full tuition reimbursements were awarded; career-related internships or fieldwork, scholarships/grants, and health care benefits also available. Support available to part-time students. Financial award applicants required to submit FAFSA. *Faculty research:* Expressive language, civic engagement, family life education, reading genres, the psychological process of aging. *Application contact:* Kristen English, Interim Director of Graduate Admission, 978-837-5073, E-mail: englishkr@merrimack.edu.
Website: http://www.merrimack.edu/academics/graduate/education/.

Messiah College, Program in Higher Education, Mechanicsburg, PA 17055. Offers college athletics management (MA); self-designed concentration (MA); student affairs (MA). Part-time programs available. Electronic applications accepted. *Expenses: Tuition:* Part-time $595 per credit hour. *Required fees:* $30 per course. *Faculty research:* College athletics management, assessment and student learning outcomes, the life and legacy of Ernest L. Boyer, common learning, student affairs practice.

Miami University, College of Education, Health and Society, Department of Educational Leadership, Oxford, OH 45056. Offers educational administration (Ed D, PhD); school leadership (M Ed); student affairs in higher education (MS, PhD). *Accreditation:* NCATE. Part-time and evening/weekend programs available. *Students:* 99 full-time (65 women), 90 part-time (61 women); includes 44 minority (29 Black or African American, non-Hispanic/Latino; 2 Asian, non-Hispanic/Latino; 9 Hispanic/Latino; 4 Two or more races, non-Hispanic/Latino), 8 international. Average age 34. In 2013, 82 master's, 10 doctorates awarded. *Entrance requirements:* Additional exam requirements/recommendations for international students: Required—TOEFL (minimum score 550 paper-based). Application fee: $50. Electronic applications accepted. *Expenses:* Tuition, state resident: full-time $12,634; part-time $526 per credit hour. Tuition, nonresident: full-time $27,892; part-time $1162 per credit hour. Part-time tuition and fees vary according to course load, campus/location and program. *Financial support:* Research assistantships with full and partial tuition reimbursements, teaching assistantships with partial tuition reimbursements, career-related internships or fieldwork, Federal Work-Study, scholarships/grants, health care benefits, tuition waivers (partial), and unspecified assistantships available. Financial award application deadline: 2/15; financial award applicants required to submit FAFSA. *Unit head:* Dr. Kathleen Knight Abowitz, Chair, 513-529-6825, E-mail: knightk2@miamioh.edu. *Application contact:* Dr. Thomas Poetter, Professor and Director of Graduate Studies, 513-529-6853, E-mail: poettets@miamioh.edu.
Website: http://www.MiamiOH.edu/EDL.

Minnesota State University Mankato, College of Graduate Studies, College of Education, Department of Counseling and Student Personnel, Mankato, MN 56001. Offers college student affairs (MS); counselor education and supervision (Ed D); marriage and family counseling (Certificate); mental health counseling (MS); professional school counseling (MS). *Accreditation:* ACA (one or more programs are accredited); NCATE. *Students:* 69 full-time (59 women), 45 part-time (33 women). *Degree requirements:* For master's, comprehensive exam, thesis or alternative. *Entrance requirements:* For master's, GRE General Test or MAT (if GPA less than 3.0 for last 2 years), minimum GPA of 3.0 during previous 2 years, 3 letters of reference. Additional exam requirements/recommendations for international students: Required—TOEFL. *Application deadline:* For fall admission, 1/15 priority date for domestic students. Applications are processed on a rolling basis. Application fee: $40. Electronic applications accepted. *Financial support:* Research assistantships with full tuition reimbursements, teaching assistantships with full tuition reimbursements, career-related internships or fieldwork, Federal Work-Study, institutionally sponsored loans, and unspecified assistantships available. Support available to part-time students. Financial award application deadline: 3/15; financial award applicants required to submit FAFSA. *Unit head:* Dr. Richard Auger, Chairperson, 507-389-5658. *Application contact:* 507-389-2321, E-mail: grad@mnsu.edu.

Mississippi State University, College of Education, Department of Counseling and Educational Psychology, Mississippi State, MS 39762. Offers college/postsecondary student counseling and personnel services (PhD); counselor education (MS), including clinical mental health, college counseling, rehabilitation, school counseling, student affairs in higher education; counselor education/student counseling and guidance services (PhD); education (Ed S), including counselor education, school psychology (PhD, Ed S); educational psychology (MS, PhD), including general education psychology (MS), general educational psychology (PhD), psychometry (MS), school psychology (PhD, Ed S). *Accreditation:* ACA (one or more programs are accredited); APA; CORE (one or more programs are accredited); NCATE. Part-time programs available. Postbaccalaureate distance learning degree programs offered (minimal on-campus study). *Faculty:* 17 full-time (13 women). *Students:* 137 full-time (104 women), 81 part-time (73 women); includes 57 minority (47 Black or African American, non-Hispanic/Latino; 4 American Indian or Alaska Native, non-Hispanic/Latino; 3 Asian, non-Hispanic/Latino; 1 Hispanic/Latino; 2 Two or more races, non-Hispanic/Latino), 5 international. Average age 32. 287 applicants, 36% accepted, 72 enrolled. In 2013, 70 master's, 3 doctorates, 4 other advanced degrees awarded. Terminal master's awarded for partial completion of doctoral program. *Degree requirements:* For master's, comprehensive exam, thesis optional; for doctorate, thesis/dissertation, comprehensive oral and written exam. *Entrance requirements:* For master's, GRE (taken within the last five years), BS with minimum GPA of 2.75 on last 60 hours; for doctorate, GRE, MS from CACREP- or CORE-accredited program in counseling; for Ed S, GRE, MS in counseling or related field, minimum GPA of 3.3 on all graduate work. Additional exam requirements/recommendations for international students: Required—TOEFL (minimum score 550 paper-based; 79 iBT); Recommended—IELTS (minimum score 6.5). *Application deadline:* For fall admission, 2/1 priority date for domestic and international students. Applications are processed on a rolling basis. Application fee: $60. Electronic applications accepted. *Financial support:* In 2013–14, 1 research assistantship (averaging $10,800 per year), 11 teaching assistantships with full tuition reimbursements (averaging $8,401 per year) were awarded; career-related internships or fieldwork, Federal Work-Study, institutionally sponsored loans, and unspecified assistantships also available. Financial award application deadline: 2/1; financial award applicants required to submit FAFSA. *Faculty research:* HIV/AIDS in college population, substance abuse in youth and college students, ADHD and conduct disorders in youth, assessment and identification of early childhood disabilities, assessment and vocational transition of the disabled. *Unit head:* Dr. Daniel Wong, Professor/Head, 662-325-7928, Fax: 662-325-3263, E-mail: dwong@colled.msstate.edu. *Application contact:* Dr. Charles Palmer, Graduate Coordinator, Counselor Education, 662-325-7917, Fax: 662-325-3263, E-mail: cpalmer@colled.msstate.edu.
Website: http://www.cep.msstate.edu/.

Missouri State University, Graduate College, College of Education, Department of Counseling, Leadership, and Special Education, Program in Student Affairs in Higher Education, Springfield, MO 65897. Offers MS. Part-time programs available. *Students:* 38 full-time (26 women), 6 part-time (all women); includes 8 minority (4 Black or African American, non-Hispanic/Latino; 2 Hispanic/Latino; 2 Two or more races, non-Hispanic/Latino). Average age 27. 26 applicants, 100% accepted, 14 enrolled. In 2013, 22 master's awarded. *Degree requirements:* For master's, comprehensive exam, thesis or alternative. *Entrance requirements:* For master's, statement of purpose; three references. Additional exam requirements/recommendations for international students: Required—TOEFL (minimum score 550 paper-based; 79 iBT). *Application deadline:* For fall admission, 7/20 priority date for domestic students, 5/1 for international students; for spring admission, 12/20 priority date for domestic students, 9/1 for international students. Applications are processed on a rolling basis. Application fee: $35 ($50 for international students). Electronic applications accepted. *Expenses:* Tuition, state resident: full-time $4500; part-time $250 per credit hour. Tuition, nonresident: full-time $9018; part-time $501 per credit hour. *Required fees:* $361 per semester. Tuition and fees vary according to course level, course load and program. *Financial support:* Federal Work-Study, institutionally sponsored loans, scholarships/grants, and unspecified assistantships available. Financial award application deadline: 3/31; financial award applicants required to submit FAFSA. *Unit head:* Dr. Gilbert Brown, Program Director, 417-836-4428, E-mail: gilbertbrown@missouristate.edu. *Application contact:* Misty Stewart, Coordinator of Graduate Recruitment, 417-836-6079, Fax: 417-836-6200, E-mail: mistystewart@missouristate.edu.
Website: http://education.missouristate.edu/edadmin/MSEDSA.htm.

Monmouth University, The Graduate School, School of Education, West Long Branch, NJ 07764-1898. Offers applied behavioral analysis (Certificate); autism (Certificate); initial certification (MAT), including elementary level, K-12, secondary level; principal (MS Ed); principal/school administrator (MS Ed); reading specialist (MS Ed); school counseling (MS Ed); special education (MS Ed), including autism, learning disabilities teacher consultant, teacher of students with disabilities, teaching in inclusive settings; speech-language pathology (MS Ed); student affairs and college counseling (MS Ed); teaching English to speakers of other languages (TESOL) (Certificate). *Accreditation:* NCATE. Part-time and evening/weekend programs available. *Faculty:* 15 full-time (11 women), 19 part-time/adjunct (17 women). *Students:* 125 full-time (97 women), 168 part-time (146 women); includes 38 minority (12 Black or African American, non-Hispanic/Latino; 5 Asian, non-Hispanic/Latino; 16 Hispanic/Latino; 5 Two or more races, non-Hispanic/Latino). Average age 28. 176 applicants, 90% accepted, 112 enrolled. In 2013, 147 master's awarded. *Entrance requirements:* For master's, GRE within last 5 years (for MS Ed in speech-language pathology), minimum GPA of 3.0 in major; 2 letters of recommendation (for some programs), resume, personal statement or essay (depending on degree program). Additional exam requirements/recommendations for international students: Required—TOEFL (minimum score 550 paper-based; 79 iBT), IELTS (minimum score 6), Michigan English Language Assessment Battery (minimum score 77). *Application deadline:* For fall admission, 7/15 priority date for domestic students, 7/1 for international students; for spring admission, 11/15 priority date for domestic students, 11/1 for international students. Applications are processed on a rolling basis. Application fee: $50. Electronic applications accepted. *Expenses: Tuition:* Part-time $1004 per credit hour. *Required fees:* $157 per semester. *Financial support:* In 2013–14, 191 students received support, including 159 fellowships (averaging $2,786 per year), 30 research assistantships (averaging $8,755 per year); career-related internships or fieldwork, scholarships/grants, and unspecified assistantships also available. Support available to part-time students. Financial award applicants required to submit FAFSA. *Faculty research:* Multicultural literacy, science and mathematics teaching strategies, teacher as reflective practitioner, children with disabilities. *Unit head:* Dr. Jason Barr, Program Director, 732-263-5238, Fax: 732-263-5277, E-mail: jbarr@monmouth.edu. *Application contact:* Lauren Vento-Cifelli, Associate Vice President of Undergraduate and Graduate Admission, 732-571-3452, Fax: 732-263-5123, E-mail: gradadm@monmouth.edu.
Website: http://www.monmouth.edu/academics/schools/education/default.asp.

New York University, Steinhardt School of Culture, Education, and Human Development, Department of Administration, Leadership, and Technology, Program in Higher Education, New York, NY 10003. Offers higher education (Ed D, PhD); higher education and student affairs (MA). *Accreditation:* Teacher Education Accreditation Council. Part-time programs available. *Faculty:* 8 full-time (5 women). *Students:* 17 full-time (13 women), 136 part-time (41 women); includes 64 minority (20 Black or African American, non-Hispanic/Latino; 1 American Indian or Alaska Native, non-Hispanic/Latino; 18 Asian, non-Hispanic/Latino; 22 Hispanic/Latino; 3 Two or more races, non-Hispanic/Latino), 7 international. Average age 35. 268 applicants, 22% accepted, 51 enrolled. In 2013, 27 master's, 10 doctorates awarded. *Degree requirements:* For master's, thesis (for some programs); for doctorate, thesis/dissertation. *Entrance requirements:* For master's, interview, 2 letters of recommendation; for doctorate, GRE General Test, interview. Additional exam requirements/recommendations for international students: Required—TOEFL (minimum score 100 iBT). *Application deadline:* For fall admission, 12/1 priority date for domestic and international students; for spring admission, 10/1 for domestic and international students. Applications are processed on a rolling basis. Application fee: $75. Electronic applications accepted. *Expenses: Tuition:* Full-time $35,856; part-time $1494 per unit. *Required fees:* $1408; $64 per unit. $473 per term. Tuition and fees vary according to course load and program. *Financial support:* Fellowships with full and partial tuition reimbursements, career-related internships or fieldwork, Federal Work-Study, institutionally sponsored loans, scholarships/grants, tuition waivers (partial), and unspecified assistantships available. Support available to part-time students. Financial award application deadline: 2/1; financial award applicants required to submit FAFSA. *Faculty research:* Organizational theory and culture, systemic change, leadership development, access, equity and diversity. *Unit head:* Prof. Ann Marcus, Director, 212-998-5005, Fax: 212-995-4041, E-mail: alm1@nyu.edu. *Application contact:* 212-998-5030, Fax: 212-995-4328, E-mail: steinhardt.gradadmissions@nyu.edu.
Website: http://steinhardt.nyu.edu/alt/highered.

Northern Arizona University, Graduate College, College of Education, Department of Educational Psychology, Flagstaff, AZ 86011. Offers counseling (MA); educational psychology (PhD), including counseling psychology, school psychology; human relations (M Ed); school counseling (M Ed); school psychology (Ed S); student affairs (M Ed). Part-time programs available. Postbaccalaureate distance learning degree programs offered. *Faculty:* 22 full-time (9 women), 3 part-time/adjunct (1 woman).

Students: 232 full-time (175 women), 237 part-time (187 women); includes 155 minority (21 Black or African American, non-Hispanic/Latino; 27 American Indian or Alaska Native, non-Hispanic/Latino; 3 Asian, non-Hispanic/Latino; 91 Hispanic/Latino; 1 Native Hawaiian or other Pacific Islander, non-Hispanic/Latino; 12 Two or more races, non-Hispanic/Latino), 4 international. Average age 34. 234 applicants, 71% accepted, 101 enrolled. In 2013, 232 master's, 6 doctorates awarded. Terminal master's awarded for partial completion of doctoral program. *Degree requirements:* For master's, internship (for some programs); for doctorate, comprehensive exam, thesis/dissertation, internship. *Entrance requirements:* Additional exam requirements/recommendations for international students: Required—TOEFL (minimum score 550 paper-based; 80 iBT), IELTS (minimum score 7). *Application deadline:* For fall admission, 9/15 for domestic students; for spring admission, 1/15 for domestic students. Applications are processed on a rolling basis. Application fee: $65. Electronic applications accepted. *Financial support:* In 2013–14, 20 students received support, including 11 teaching assistantships with full tuition reimbursements available (averaging $9,660 per year); research assistantships, career-related internships or fieldwork, Federal Work-Study, scholarships/grants, health care benefits, tuition waivers (full and partial), and unspecified assistantships also available. Financial award applicants required to submit FAFSA. *Unit head:* Dr. Robert Horn, Chair, 928-523-0362, Fax: 928-523-9284, E-mail: robert.horn@nau.edu. *Application contact:* Hope DeMello, Administrative Assistant, 928-523-7103, Fax: 928-523-9284, E-mail: eps@nau.edu.
Website: http://nau.edu/coe/ed-psych/.

Northwestern State University of Louisiana, Graduate Studies and Research, College of Education and Human Development, Program in Student Affairs in Higher Education, Natchitoches, LA 71497. Offers MA. *Accreditation:* NCATE. *Degree requirements:* For master's, comprehensive exam, thesis or alternative. *Entrance requirements:* For master's, GRE General Test, GRE Subject Test, minimum undergraduate GPA of 2.5. Additional exam requirements/recommendations for international students: Required—TOEFL. Electronic applications accepted.

Nova Southeastern University, Graduate School of Humanities and Social Sciences, Fort Lauderdale, FL 33314-7796. Offers advanced conflict resolution practice (Graduate Certificate); advanced family systems (Graduate Certificate); college student affairs (MS); college student personnel administration (Graduate Certificate); conflict analysis and resolution (MS, PhD); cross-disciplinary studies (MA); family studies (Graduate Certificate); family systems healthcare (Graduate Certificate); family therapy (MS, PhD); marriage and family therapy (DMFT); national security affairs (MS); peace studies (Graduate Certificate); qualitative research (Graduate Certificate); solution focused coaching (Graduate Certificate). *Accreditation:* AAMFT/COAMFTE (one or more programs are accredited). Part-time and evening/weekend programs available. Postbaccalaureate distance learning degree programs offered (minimal on-campus study). *Faculty:* 26 full-time (14 women), 34 part-time/adjunct (18 women). *Students:* 443 full-time (327 women), 383 part-time (260 women); includes 444 minority (259 Black or African American, non-Hispanic/Latino; 2 American Indian or Alaska Native, non-Hispanic/Latino; 18 Asian, non-Hispanic/Latino; 144 Hispanic/Latino; 21 Two or more races, non-Hispanic/Latino), 51 international. Average age 37. 406 applicants, 89% accepted, 280 enrolled. In 2013, 127 master's, 28 doctorates, 14 other advanced degrees awarded. *Degree requirements:* For master's, thesis optional, comprehensive exams, portfolios (for some programs), table-top exams (for some programs); for doctorate, comprehensive exam, thesis/dissertation, qualifying exams, portfolios (for some programs). *Entrance requirements:* For master's, interview, minimum GPA of 3.0, writing sample; for doctorate, interview, minimum GPA of 3.5, master's degree in related field, writing sample; for Graduate Certificate, minimum GPA of 3.0. Additional exam requirements/recommendations for international students: Required—TOEFL. *Application deadline:* For fall admission, 5/17 priority date for domestic and international students; for winter admission, 12/1 priority date for domestic and international students; for spring admission, 4/1 priority date for domestic and international students. Applications are processed on a rolling basis. Application fee: $50. Electronic applications accepted. *Financial support:* In 2013–14, 21 students received support, including 35 research assistantships (averaging $13,800 per year); career-related internships or fieldwork, Federal Work-Study, scholarships/grants, and unspecified assistantships also available. Financial award application deadline: 4/1; financial award applicants required to submit CSS PROFILE. *Faculty research:* Conflict resolution, family therapy, peace research, international conflict, multi-disciplinary studies, college student affairs, national security affairs, health care conflict resolution, family systems health care, advanced family systems, qualitative research, solution-focused coaching. *Unit head:* Dr. Honggang Yang, Dean, 954-262-3016, Fax: 954-262-3968, E-mail: yangh@nova.edu. *Application contact:* Marcia Arango, Student Recruitment Coordinator, 954-262-3006, Fax: 954-262-3968, E-mail: marango@nsu.nova.edu.
Website: http://shss.nova.edu/.

Ohio University, Graduate College, Gladys W. and David H. Patton College of Education and Human Services, Department of Counseling and Higher Education, Athens, OH 45701-2979. Offers college student personnel (M Ed); community/agency counseling (M Ed); counselor education (PhD); higher education (PhD); rehabilitation counseling (M Ed); school counseling (M Ed). *Accreditation:* ACA; CORE. Part-time and evening/weekend programs available. *Degree requirements:* For master's, comprehensive exam (for some programs), thesis or alternative; for doctorate, comprehensive exam, thesis/dissertation. *Entrance requirements:* For master's, GRE General Test or MAT (if GPA less than 2.9), 3 letters of reference; for doctorate, GRE General Test, work experience, minimum GPA of 3.4. Additional exam requirements/recommendations for international students: Required—TOEFL (minimum score 550 paper-based; 80 iBT) or IELTS (minimum score 6.5). Electronic applications accepted. *Faculty research:* Youth violence, gender studies, student affairs, chemical dependency, disabilities issues.

Oregon State University, College of Education, Program in College Student Services Administration, Corvallis, OR 97331. Offers Ed M, MS. *Faculty:* 4 full-time (all women), 1 (woman) part-time/adjunct. *Students:* 36 full-time (25 women), 1 (woman) part-time; includes 17 minority (1 Black or African American, non-Hispanic/Latino; 1 Asian, non-Hispanic/Latino; 11 Hispanic/Latino; 4 Two or more races, non-Hispanic/Latino). Average age 27. 77 applicants, 36% accepted, 16 enrolled. In 2013, 20 master's awarded. *Degree requirements:* For master's, thesis or alternative. *Entrance requirements:* For master's, minimum GPA of 3.0 in last 90 hours of course work. Additional exam requirements/recommendations for international students: Required—TOEFL (minimum score 80 iBT), IELTS (minimum score 6.5). *Application deadline:* For fall admission, 12/16 for domestic students. Applications are processed on a rolling basis. Application fee: $60. *Expenses:* Tuition, state resident: full-time $11,664; part-time $432 per credit hour. Tuition, nonresident: full-time $19,197; part-time $711 per credit hour. *Required fees:* $1446; $443 per quarter. One-time fee: $300. Tuition and fees vary according to course load and program. *Financial support:* Teaching assistantships, career-related internships or fieldwork, Federal Work-Study, and institutionally sponsored loans available. Support available to part-time students. Financial award application deadline: 2/1. *Faculty research:* Improvement of student activities, administering recreational sports programs. *Unit head:* Dr. Larry Flick, Dean, 541-737-3664, E-mail: larry.flick@oregonstate.edu. *Application contact:* Kim McAloney, 541-737-9035, E-mail: kim.mcaloney@oregonstate.edu.
Website: http://education.oregonstate.edu/college-student-services-administration.

Penn State University Park, Graduate School, College of Education, Department of Education Policy Studies, State College, PA 16802. Offers college student affairs (M Ed); educational leadership (M Ed, D Ed, PhD, Certificate); educational theory and policy (MA, PhD); higher education (M Ed, D Ed, PhD). *Accreditation:* NCATE. *Unit head:* Dr. David H. Monk, Dean, 814-865-2523, Fax: 814-865-0555, E-mail: dhm6@psu.edu. *Application contact:* Cynthia E. Nicosia, Director, Graduate Enrollment Services, 814-865-1834, Fax: 814-863-4627, E-mail: cey1@psu.edu.
Website: http://www.ed.psu.edu/educ/eps/.

Providence University College & Theological Seminary, Theological Seminary, Otterburne, MB R0A 1G0, Canada. Offers children's ministry (Certificate); Christian studies (MA, Certificate); counseling (MA); cross-cultural discipleship (Certificate); divinity (M Div); educational studies (MA), including counseling psychology, educational ministries, student development, teaching English to speakers of other languages, training teachers of English to speakers of other languages; global studies (MA); lay counseling (Diploma); ministry (D Min); teaching English to speakers of other languages (Certificate); theological studies (MA); training teacher of English to speakers of other languages (Certificate); youth ministry (Certificate). *Accreditation:* ATS. Part-time programs available. *Degree requirements:* For master's, variable foreign language requirement, thesis (for some programs); for doctorate, thesis/dissertation. *Entrance requirements:* Additional exam requirements/recommendations for international students: Recommended—TOEFL (minimum score 550 paper-based). *Faculty research:* Studies in Isaiah, theology of sin.

Regent University, Graduate School, School of Education, Virginia Beach, VA 23464-9800. Offers adult education (Ed D, PhD); advanced educational leadership (Ed D, PhD); career switcher with licensure (M Ed), including alternative licensure; character education (Ed D, PhD); Christian education leadership (Ed D); Christian school administration (M Ed); curriculum and instruction (M Ed); distance education (Ed D, PhD); educational leadership (M Ed); educational leadership - special education (Ed S); educational psychology (Ed D); elementary education (M Ed); higher education (Ed D, PhD); higher education leadership and management (Ed D); K-12 school leadership (Ed D, PhD); leadership in mathematics education (M Ed); reading specialist (M Ed); special education (M Ed, Ed D, PhD); student affairs (M Ed); TESOL (M Ed), including adult education, PreK-12. *Accreditation:* Teacher Education Accreditation Council. Part-time and evening/weekend programs available. Postbaccalaureate distance learning degree programs offered (minimal on-campus study). *Faculty:* 25 full-time (12 women), 50 part-time/adjunct (31 women). *Students:* 100 full-time (78 women), 754 part-time (614 women); includes 225 minority (191 Black or African American, non-Hispanic/Latino; 1 American Indian or Alaska Native, non-Hispanic/Latino; 7 Asian, non-Hispanic/Latino; 26 Hispanic/Latino), 16 international. Average age 39. 487 applicants, 63% accepted, 233 enrolled. In 2013, 202 master's, 19 doctorates awarded. *Degree requirements:* For master's, thesis or alternative; for doctorate, comprehensive exam, thesis/dissertation. *Entrance requirements:* For master's, MAT, minimum undergraduate GPA of 2.75, writing sample, resume, recommendations, interview; for doctorate, GRE, writing sample, 3 years of relevant professional experience, master's-level paper, copies of published work, resume, transcripts, interview, recommendations. Additional exam requirements/recommendations for international students: Required—TOEFL (minimum score 577 paper-based). *Application deadline:* For fall admission, 4/1 priority date for domestic students; for spring admission, 10/15 priority date for domestic students. Applications are processed on a rolling basis. Application fee: $50. Electronic applications accepted. Tuition and fees vary according to course load and degree level. *Financial support:* Fellowships, career-related internships or fieldwork, scholarships/grants, tuition waivers (full and partial), and unspecified assistantships available. Support available to part-time students. Financial award application deadline: 4/1; financial award applicants required to submit FAFSA. *Faculty research:* Character development and discipline for children, education leadership development, diversity in schools, classroom management, technology in education settings. *Unit head:* Dr. Alan Arroyo, Dean, 757-352-4261, Fax: 757-352-4318, E-mail: alanarr@regent.edu. *Application contact:* Matthew Chadwick, Director of Enrollment Support Services, 800-373-5504, Fax: 757-352-4381, E-mail: admissions@regent.edu.
Website: http://www.regent.edu/education/.

Rutgers, The State University of New Jersey, New Brunswick, Graduate School of Education, Department of Educational Psychology, Program in College Student Affairs, Piscataway, NJ 08854-8097. Offers Ed M. *Accreditation:* ACA. *Degree requirements:* For master's, comprehensive exam. *Entrance requirements:* For master's, GRE General Test, 3 letters of recommendation, resume. Additional exam requirements/recommendations for international students: Required—TOEFL (minimum score 550 paper-based; 83 iBT). Electronic applications accepted. *Faculty research:* Higher education equality, Latino college student experience.

St. Cloud State University, School of Graduate Studies, School of Education, Department of Educational Leadership and Higher Education, Program in College Counseling and Student Development, St. Cloud, MN 56301-4498. Offers MS. *Degree requirements:* For master's, comprehensive exam, thesis or alternative. *Entrance requirements:* For master's, GRE General Test, minimum GPA of 2.75. Additional exam requirements/recommendations for international students: Required—Michigan English Language Assessment Battery; Recommended—TOEFL (minimum score 550 paper-based), IELTS (minimum score 6.5). Electronic applications accepted.

St. Edward's University, New College, Program in College Student Development, Austin, TX 78704. Offers MA. Part-time and evening/weekend programs available. *Students:* 19 part-time (15 women); includes 6 minority (1 Black or African American, non-Hispanic/Latino; 5 Hispanic/Latino). Average age 36. 16 applicants, 75% accepted, 6 enrolled. In 2013, 10 master's awarded. *Entrance requirements:* For master's, GRE, minimum GPA of 3.0 in last 60 hours or 2.75 overall. Additional exam requirements/recommendations for international students: Required—TOEFL (minimum score 79 iBT) or IELTS (minimum score 6). *Application deadline:* For fall admission, 6/1 priority date for domestic and international students; for spring admission, 10/1 priority date for domestic and international students; for summer admission, 3/1 priority date for domestic and international students. Applications are processed on a rolling basis. Application fee: $50. Electronic applications accepted. *Expenses: Tuition:* Full-time $20,664; part-time $1148 per credit hour. *Required fees:* $50 per trimester. Full-time tuition and fees vary according to course load and program. *Unit head:* Dr. Richard A. Parsells, Director, 512-637-1978, Fax: 512-448-8492, E-mail: richp@stedwards.edu. *Application contact:* Office of Admission, 512-448-8500, Fax: 512-464-8877, E-mail: seu.admit@stedwards.edu.
Website: http://www.stedwards.edu.

Saint Louis University, Graduate Education, College of Education and Public Service and Graduate Education, Department of Educational Leadership and Higher Education, St. Louis, MO 63103-2097. Offers Catholic school leadership (MA); educational administration (MA, Ed D, PhD, Ed S); higher education (MA, Ed D, PhD); student personnel administration (MA). *Accreditation:* NCATE. Part-time programs available. *Degree requirements:* For master's, comprehensive written and oral exam; for

doctorate, comprehensive exam, thesis/dissertation, preliminary oral and written exams. *Entrance requirements:* For master's, GRE General Test, MAT, LSAT, GMAT or MCAT, letters of recommendation, resume; for doctorate and Ed S, GRE General Test, LSAT, GMAT or MCAT, letters of recommendation, resumé, goal statement, transcripts. Additional exam requirements/recommendations for international students: Required—TOEFL (minimum score 525 paper-based). Electronic applications accepted. *Faculty research:* Superintendent of schools, school finance, school facilities, student personal administration, building leadership.

San Jose State University, Graduate Studies and Research, Connie L. Lurie College of Education, Department of Counselor Education, San Jose, CA 95192-0001. Offers MA. *Accreditation:* NCATE. Evening/weekend programs available. *Degree requirements:* For master's, thesis or alternative. Electronic applications accepted.

Seton Hall University, College of Education and Human Services, Department of Education Leadership, Management and Policy, Program in College Student Personnel Administration, South Orange, NJ 07079-2697. Offers MA. Part-time and evening/weekend programs available. *Faculty:* 12 full-time (4 women), 1 part-time/adjunct (0 women). *Students:* 3 full-time (1 woman), 7 part-time (4 women); includes 4 minority (2 Black or African American, non-Hispanic/Latino; 1 Asian, non-Hispanic/Latino; 1 Hispanic/Latino). Average age 33. 12 applicants, 100% accepted, 4 enrolled. In 2013, 3 master's awarded. *Entrance requirements:* For master's, GRE or MAT (within past 5 years), minimum GPA of 3.0. Additional exam requirements/recommendations for international students: Required—TOEFL. *Application deadline:* Applications are processed on a rolling basis. Application fee: $75. *Unit head:* Dr. Rong Chen, Program Director, 973-275-2823, Fax: 973-275-2187, E-mail: rong.chen@shu.edu. *Application contact:* Diana Minakakis, Director of Graduate Admissions, 973-761-9668, Fax: 973-275-2187, E-mail: diana.minakakis@shu.edu.
Website: http://www.shu.edu/academics/education/ma-college-administration/index.cfm.

Shippensburg University of Pennsylvania, School of Graduate Studies, College of Education and Human Services, Department of Counseling, Shippensburg, PA 17257-2299. Offers clinical mental health counseling (MS); college counseling (MS); college student personnel (MS); couple and family counseling (Certificate); school counseling (M Ed). *Accreditation:* ACA (one or more programs are accredited); NCATE. Part-time and evening/weekend programs available. *Faculty:* 8 full-time (3 women), 3 part-time/adjunct (2 women). *Students:* 87 full-time (70 women), 53 part-time (42 women); includes 23 minority (15 Black or African American, non-Hispanic/Latino; 1 American Indian or Alaska Native, non-Hispanic/Latino; 2 Asian, non-Hispanic/Latino; 1 Hispanic/Latino; 4 Two or more races, non-Hispanic/Latino). Average age 28. 101 applicants, 54% accepted, 38 enrolled. In 2013, 47 master's awarded. *Degree requirements:* For master's, fieldwork, research project, internship, candidacy. *Entrance requirements:* For master's, GRE or MAT (for clinical mental health, student personnel, and college counseling applicants if GPA is less than 2.75), minimum GPA of 2.75 (3.0 for M Ed), resume, 3 letters of recommendation, one year of relevant work experience, on-campus interview, autobiographical statement. Additional exam requirements/recommendations for international students: Required—TOEFL (minimum score 580 paper-based); Recommended—IELTS (minimum score 6). *Application deadline:* For fall admission, 4/30 for international students; for spring admission, 9/30 for international students. Applications are processed on a rolling basis. Application fee: $45. Electronic applications accepted. *Expenses: Tuition, area resident:* Part-time $442 per credit. Tuition, state resident: part-time $442 per credit. Tuition, nonresident: part-time $663 per credit. *Required fees:* $127 per credit. *Financial support:* In 2013–14, 60 research assistantships with full tuition reimbursements (averaging $5,000 per year) were awarded; career-related internships or fieldwork, scholarships/grants, unspecified assistantships, and resident hall director and student payroll positions also available. Support available to part-time students. Financial award application deadline: 3/1; financial award applicants required to submit FAFSA. *Unit head:* Dr. Kurt L. Kraus, Chairperson, 717-477-1603, Fax: 717-477-4016, E-mail: klkrau@ship.edu. *Application contact:* Jeremy R. Goshorn, Assistant Dean of Graduate Admissions, 717-477-1231, Fax: 717-477-4016, E-mail: jrgoshorn@ship.edu.
Website: http://www.ship.edu/counsel/.

Slippery Rock University of Pennsylvania, Graduate Studies (Recruitment), College of Education, Department of Counseling and Development, Slippery Rock, PA 16057-1383. Offers community counseling (MA), including addiction, adult, child/adolescent, older adult, youth; school counseling (M Ed); student affairs (MA), including higher education; student affairs in higher education (MA), including college counseling. *Accreditation:* ACA (one or more programs are accredited); NCATE. Part-time and evening/weekend programs available. *Faculty:* 9 full-time (5 women). *Students:* 85 full-time (69 women), 26 part-time (21 women); includes 9 minority (7 Black or African American, non-Hispanic/Latino; 1 American Indian or Alaska Native, non-Hispanic/Latino; 1 Hispanic/Latino). Average age 28. 137 applicants, 49% accepted, 51 enrolled. In 2013, 45 master's awarded. *Degree requirements:* For master's, comprehensive exam, thesis (for some programs). *Entrance requirements:* For master's, GRE General Test, MAT, minimum GPA of 2.75 or 3.0 (depending on program), personal statement, three letters of recommendation, interview. Additional exam requirements/recommendations for international students: Required—TOEFL (minimum score 550 paper-based; 80 iBT). *Application deadline:* For fall admission, 1/15 priority date for domestic and international students. Application fee: $25 ($30 for international students). Electronic applications accepted. *Expenses:* Tuition, state resident: full-time $7956; part-time $442 per credit. Tuition, nonresident: full-time $11,934; part-time $663 per credit. *Required fees:* $2896; $148 per credit. Tuition and fees vary according to degree level and program. *Financial support:* Career-related internships or fieldwork, Federal Work-Study, institutionally sponsored loans, scholarships/grants, tuition waivers (partial), and unspecified assistantships available. Support available to part-time students. Financial award application deadline: 5/1; financial award applicants required to submit FAFSA. *Unit head:* Dr. Donald Strano, Graduate Coordinator, 724-738-2035, Fax: 724-738-4859, E-mail: donald.strano@sru.edu. *Application contact:* Brandi Weber-Mortimer, Director of Graduate Admissions, 724-738-2051, Fax: 724-738-2146, E-mail: graduate.admissions@sru.edu.

Springfield College, Graduate Programs, Programs in Psychology and Counseling, Springfield, MA 01109-3797. Offers athletic counseling (M Ed, MS, Psy D, CAGS); clinical mental health counseling (Psy D); couples and family therapy (Psy D); industrial/organizational psychology (M Ed, MS, CAGS); marriage and family therapy (M Ed, MS, CAGS); mental health counseling (M Ed, MS, CAGS); school guidance and counseling (M Ed, MS, CAGS); student personnel in higher education (M Ed, MS, CAGS). Part-time programs available. *Faculty:* 13 full-time (6 women), 12 part-time/adjunct (3 women). *Students:* 151 full-time, 52 part-time. Average age 30. 198 applicants, 73% accepted, 74 enrolled. In 2013, 84 master's, 4 other advanced degrees awarded. *Degree requirements:* For master's, research project, portfolio; for doctorate, dissertation project, 1500 hours of counseling psychology practicum, full-year internship. *Entrance requirements:* Additional exam requirements/recommendations for international students: Required—TOEFL (minimum score 550 paper-based). *Application deadline:* For fall admission, 1/15 priority date for domestic students, 1/15 for international students; for winter admission, 11/1 for domestic and international students; for spring

admission, 11/1 for domestic and international students. Applications are processed on a rolling basis. Application fee: $50. Electronic applications accepted. *Expenses: Tuition:* Full-time $13,620; part-time $908 per credit. *Financial support:* Fellowships with partial tuition reimbursements, teaching assistantships with partial tuition reimbursements, career-related internships or fieldwork, Federal Work-Study, institutionally sponsored loans, and unspecified assistantships available. Financial award application deadline: 3/1; financial award applicants required to submit FAFSA. *Unit head:* Dr. Allison Cumming-McCann, Graduate Program Director, 413-748-3075, Fax: 413-748-3854, E-mail: acumming@springfieldcollege.edu. *Application contact:* Evelyn Cohen, Director of Graduate Admissions, 413-748-3225, E-mail: ecohen@springfieldcollege.edu.
Website: http://www.springfieldcollege.edu/academic-programs/psychology-department/graduate-programs-in-psychology/index#.U1F-dKJWiSo.

State University of New York at Plattsburgh, Division of Education, Health, and Human Services, Department of Counselor Education, Plattsburgh, NY 12901-2681. Offers clinical mental health counseling (MS, Advanced Certificate); school counselor (MS Ed, CAS); student affairs counseling (MS). *Accreditation:* ACA (one or more programs are accredited); Teacher Education Accreditation Council. Part-time programs available. *Students:* 50 full-time (36 women), 14 part-time (10 women); includes 9 minority (4 Black or African American, non-Hispanic/Latino; 5 Hispanic/Latino), 3 international. Average age 27. *Entrance requirements:* For master's, GRE General Test or MAT, minimum GPA of 2.8. Additional exam requirements/recommendations for international students: Required—TOEFL. *Application deadline:* For fall admission, 2/15 priority date for domestic students; for spring admission, 10/15 priority date for domestic students. Applications are processed on a rolling basis. Application fee: $75. *Financial support:* Research assistantships, teaching assistantships, career-related internships or fieldwork, Federal Work-Study, and administrative assistantships, editorial assistantships available. Support available to part-time students. Financial award application deadline: 4/15; financial award applicants required to submit FAFSA. *Faculty research:* Campus violence, program accreditation, substance abuse, vocational assessment, group counseling, divorce. *Unit head:* Dr. Julia Davis, Coordinator, 518-564-4179, E-mail: jdavi004@plattsburgh.edu. *Application contact:* Betsy Kane, Director, Graduate Admissions, 518-564-4723, Fax: 518-564-4722, E-mail: bkane002@plattsburgh.edu.

Syracuse University, School of Education, Program in Student Affairs Counseling, Syracuse, NY 13244. Offers MS. Part-time programs available. *Students:* 3 full-time (all women), 5 part-time (all women); includes 3 minority (1 Black or African American, non-Hispanic/Latino; 1 Asian, non-Hispanic/Latino; 1 Hispanic/Latino). Average age 28. 11 applicants, 36% accepted, 1 enrolled. In 2013, 2 master's awarded. *Entrance requirements:* For master's, GRE General Test or MAT, interview. Additional exam requirements/recommendations for international students: Required—TOEFL (minimum score 100 iBT). *Application deadline:* For fall admission, 1/15 priority date for domestic and international students; for spring admission, 10/15 priority date for domestic and international students. Applications are processed on a rolling basis. Application fee: $75. Electronic applications accepted. *Financial support:* Fellowships with full tuition reimbursements and teaching assistantships with full and partial tuition reimbursements available. Financial award application deadline: 1/1. *Unit head:* Dr. Derek Seward, 315-443-2266, E-mail: bernard@syr.edu. *Application contact:* Laurie Deyo, Graduate Recruiter, School of Education, 315-443-2505, E-mail: dxseward@syr.ed.
Website: http://soeweb.syr.edu/.

Texas State University, Graduate School, College of Education, Department of Counseling, Leadership, Adult Education, and School Psychology, Program of Student Affairs in Higher Education, San Marcos, TX 78666. Offers M Ed. *Accreditation:* ACA. Part-time and evening/weekend programs available. *Faculty:* 4 full-time (2 women), 2 part-time/adjunct (1 woman). *Students:* 34 full-time (24 women), 3 part-time (all women); includes 19 minority (6 Black or African American, non-Hispanic/Latino; 13 Hispanic/Latino), 1 international. Average age 24. 50 applicants, 48% accepted, 18 enrolled. In 2013, 22 master's awarded. *Degree requirements:* For master's, comprehensive exam, thesis (for some programs). *Entrance requirements:* For master's, GRE General Test, minimum GPA of 3.0 in last 60 hours of course work. Additional exam requirements/recommendations for international students: Required—TOEFL (minimum score 550 paper-based; 78 iBT). *Application deadline:* For fall admission, 4/15 for domestic students, 3/15 for international students; for spring admission, 10/1 for domestic and international students. Applications are processed on a rolling basis. Application fee: $40 ($90 for international students). Electronic applications accepted. *Expenses:* Tuition, state resident: full-time $6663; part-time $278 per credit hour. Tuition, nonresident: full-time $15,159; part-time $632 per credit hour. *Required fees:* $1872; $54 per credit hour. $306 per term. Tuition and fees vary according to course load. *Financial support:* In 2013–14, 25 students received support, including 33 research assistantships (averaging $11,663 per year); teaching assistantships, career-related internships or fieldwork, Federal Work-Study, and institutionally sponsored loans also available. Support available to part-time students. Financial award application deadline: 4/1; financial award applicants required to submit FAFSA. *Unit head:* Dr. Paige Haber-Curran, Graduate Advisor, 512-245-7628, Fax: 512-245-8872, E-mail: ph31@txstate.edu. *Application contact:* Dr. Andrea Golato, Dean of Graduate School, 512-245-2581, Fax: 512-245-8365, E-mail: gradcollege@txstate.edu.
Website: http://www.txstate.edu/clas/Student-Affairs/student-affairs-in-higher-ed2.html.

University of Bridgeport, School of Arts and Sciences, Department of Counseling, Bridgeport, CT 06604. Offers clinical mental health counseling (MS); college student personnel (MS); community counseling (MS); human resource development (MS); human service (MS). Part-time and evening/weekend programs available. *Faculty:* 7 full-time (4 women), 13 part-time/adjunct (7 women). *Students:* 28 full-time (22 women), 79 part-time (61 women); includes 60 minority (45 Black or African American, non-Hispanic/Latino; 11 Hispanic/Latino; 4 Two or more races, non-Hispanic/Latino), 3 international. Average age 34. 124 applicants, 46% accepted, 29 enrolled. In 2013, 26 master's awarded. *Degree requirements:* For master's, thesis, project. *Entrance requirements:* Additional exam requirements/recommendations for international students: Recommended—TOEFL (minimum score 550 paper-based; 80 iBT), IELTS (minimum score 6.5). *Application deadline:* For fall admission, 8/1 priority date for domestic and international students; for spring admission, 12/1 priority date for domestic and international students. Applications are processed on a rolling basis. Application fee: $50. Electronic applications accepted. *Expenses:* Contact institution. *Financial support:* In 2013–14, 27 students received support. Fellowships, research assistantships, teaching assistantships, career-related internships or fieldwork, Federal Work-Study, and institutionally sponsored loans available. Support available to part-time students. Financial award application deadline: 6/1; financial award applicants required to submit FAFSA. *Faculty research:* Corporate elder care programs. *Unit head:* Dr. Sara L. Connolly, Director, Division of Counseling and Human Resources, 203-576-4183, Fax: 203-576-4219, E-mail: sconnoll@bridgeport.edu. *Application contact:* Leanne Proctor, Director of Graduate Admissions, 203-576-4552, Fax: 203-576-4941, E-mail: admit@bridgeport.edu.

University of Central Arkansas, Graduate School, College of Education, Department of Leadership Studies, Program in College Student Personnel, Conway, AR 72035-0001. Offers MS. *Degree requirements:* For master's, comprehensive exam, thesis.

Entrance requirements: For master's, GRE General Test, minimum GPA of 2.7. Additional exam requirements/recommendations for international students: Required—TOEFL (minimum score 550 paper-based). Electronic applications accepted. *Expenses:* Contact institution.

University of Central Florida, College of Education and Human Performance, Department of Educational and Human Sciences, Program in Educational Leadership, Orlando, FL 32816. Offers educational leadership (MA, Ed D), including community college education (MA), higher education (Ed D), student personnel (MA). Part-time and evening/weekend programs available. *Students:* 108 full-time (79 women), 259 part-time (180 women); includes 105 minority (43 Black or African American, non-Hispanic/Latino; 1 American Indian or Alaska Native, non-Hispanic/Latino; 8 Asian, non-Hispanic/Latino; 49 Hispanic/Latino; 4 Two or more races, non-Hispanic/Latino), 1 international. Average age 33. 218 applicants, 82% accepted, 117 enrolled. In 2013, 42 master's, 22 doctorates awarded. *Degree requirements:* For master's, thesis or alternative; for doctorate, thesis/dissertation, candidacy exam. *Entrance requirements:* For master's, GRE General Test; for doctorate, GRE General Test, GRE Subject Test, minimum GPA of 3.0, resume. Additional exam requirements/recommendations for international students: Required—TOEFL. *Application deadline:* For fall admission, 2/20 priority date for domestic students; for spring admission, 9/20 priority date for domestic students. Application fee: $30. Electronic applications accepted. *Financial support:* In 2013–14, 14 students received support, including 2 fellowships with partial tuition reimbursements available (averaging $2,800 per year), 12 research assistantships with partial tuition reimbursements available (averaging $6,700 per year), 1 teaching assistantship with partial tuition reimbursement available (averaging $6,600 per year); career-related internships or fieldwork, Federal Work-Study, institutionally sponsored loans, tuition waivers (partial), and unspecified assistantships also available. Financial award application deadline: 3/1; financial award applicants required to submit FAFSA. *Unit head:* Dr. Kenneth Murray, Program Coordinator, 407-832-1468, E-mail: kenneth.murray@ucf.edu. *Application contact:* Barbara Rodriguez Lamas, Director, Admissions and Student Services, 407-823-2766, Fax: 407-823-6442, E-mail: gradadmissions@ucf.edu.
Website: http://education.ucf.edu/departments.cfm.

University of Central Missouri, The Graduate School, Warrensburg, MO 6409. Offers accountancy (MA); accounting (MBA); applied mathematics (MS); aviation safety (MA); biology (MS); business administration (MBA); career and technical education leadership (MS); college student personnel administration (MS); communication (MA); computer science (MS); counseling (MS); criminal justice (MS); educational leadership (Ed D); educational technology (MS); elementary and early childhood education (MSE); English (MA); environmental studies (MA); finance (MBA); history (MA); human services/educational technology (Ed S); human services/learning resources (Ed S); human services/professional counseling (Ed S); industrial hygiene (MS); industrial management (MS); information systems (MBA); information technology (MS); kinesiology (MS); library science and information services (MS); literacy education (MSE); marketing (MBA); mathematics (MS); music (MA); occupational safety management (MS); psychology (MS); rural family nursing (MS); school administration (MSE); social gerontology (MS); sociology (MA); special education (MSE); speech language pathology (MS); superintendency (Ed S); teaching (MAT); teaching English as a second language (MA); technology (MS); technology management (PhD); theatre (MA). Part-time programs available. *Faculty:* 233. *Students:* 890 full-time (396 women), 1,486 part-time (1,001 women); includes 192 minority (97 Black or African American, non-Hispanic/Latino; 9 American Indian or Alaska Native, non-Hispanic/Latino; 32 Asian, non-Hispanic/Latino; 40 Hispanic/Latino; 3 Native Hawaiian or other Pacific Islander, non-Hispanic/Latino; 11 Two or more races, non-Hispanic/Latino), 539 international. Average age 31. 1,953 applicants, 75% accepted. In 2013, 719 master's, 58 other advanced degrees awarded. *Degree requirements:* For master's and Ed S, comprehensive exam (for some programs), thesis (for some programs). *Entrance requirements:* Additional exam requirements/recommendations for international students: Required—TOEFL (minimum score 550 paper-based; 79 iBT). *Application deadline:* For fall admission, 6/1 for domestic students; for spring admission, 10/1 for domestic and international students. Applications are processed on a rolling basis. Application fee: $30 ($75 for international students). Electronic applications accepted. *Expenses:* Tuition, state resident: full-time $7326; part-time $276.25 per credit hour. Tuition, nonresident: full-time $13,956; part-time $552.50 per credit hour. *Required fees:* $29 per credit hour. *Financial support:* In 2013–14, 118 students received support, including 271 research assistantships with full and partial tuition reimbursements available (averaging $7,500 per year), 109 teaching assistantships with full and partial tuition reimbursements available (averaging $7,500 per year); career-related internships or fieldwork, Federal Work-Study, scholarships/grants, and administrative and laboratory assistantships also available. Support available to part-time students. Financial award application deadline: 3/1; financial award applicants required to submit FAFSA. *Unit head:* Dr. Joseph Vaughn, Assistant Provost for Research/Dean, 660-543-4092, Fax: 660-543-4778, E-mail: vaughn@ucmo.edu. *Application contact:* Brittany Lawrence, Graduate Student Services Coordinator, 660-543-4621, Fax: 660-543-4778, E-mail: gradinfo@ucmo.edu.
Website: http://www.ucmo.edu/graduate/.

University of Central Oklahoma, The Jackson College of Graduate Studies, College of Education and Professional Studies, Department of Adult Education and Safety Science, Edmond, OK 73034-5209. Offers adult and higher education (M Ed), including adult and higher education, interdisciplinary studies, student personnel, training. Part-time programs available. *Faculty:* 7 full-time (4 women), 12 part-time/adjunct (5 women). *Students:* 37 full-time (23 women), 91 part-time (57 women); includes 50 minority (24 Black or African American, non-Hispanic/Latino; 3 American Indian or Alaska Native, non-Hispanic/Latino; 5 Asian, non-Hispanic/Latino; 12 Hispanic/Latino; 6 Two or more races, non-Hispanic/Latino), 5 international. Average age 36. 59 applicants, 78% accepted, 28 enrolled. In 2013, 17 master's awarded. *Degree requirements:* For master's, comprehensive exam (for some programs), thesis (for some programs). *Entrance requirements:* For master's, GRE General Test. Additional exam requirements/recommendations for international students: Required—TOEFL (minimum score 550 paper-based; 79 iBT), IELTS (minimum score 6.5). *Application deadline:* For fall admission, 7/1 for international students; for spring admission, 11/1 for international students. Applications are processed on a rolling basis. Application fee: $50. Electronic applications accepted. *Expenses:* Tuition, state resident: full-time $4137; part-time $206.85 per credit hour. Tuition, nonresident: full-time $10,359; part-time $517.95 per credit hour. *Required fees:* $481. Tuition and fees vary according to course load and program. *Financial support:* In 2013–14, 31 students received support, including 2 research assistantships with partial tuition reimbursements available (averaging $2,958 per year), 1 teaching assistantship with partial tuition reimbursement available (averaging $15,382 per year); career-related internships or fieldwork, scholarships/grants, tuition waivers (partial), and unspecified assistantships also available. Financial award application deadline: 3/31; financial award applicants required to submit FAFSA. *Faculty research:* Violence in the workplace/schools, aging issues, trade and industrial education. *Unit head:* Dr. Candy Sebert, Chair, 405-974-5780, Fax: 405-974-3822. *Application contact:* Dr. Richard Bernard, Dean, Graduate College, 405-974-3493, Fax: 405-974-3852, E-mail: gradcoll@uco.edu.

University of Dayton, Department of Counselor Education and Human Services, Dayton, OH 45469-1300. Offers clinical mental health counseling (MS Ed); college student personnel (MS Ed); higher education administration (MS Ed); human services (MS Ed); school counseling (MS Ed); school psychology (MS Ed, Ed S). *Accreditation:* ACA; NCATE. Part-time and evening/weekend programs available. *Faculty:* 11 full-time (7 women), 46 part-time/adjunct (31 women). *Students:* 212 full-time (170 women), 151 part-time (118 women); includes 73 minority (61 Black or African American, non-Hispanic/Latino; 1 Asian, non-Hispanic/Latino; 8 Hispanic/Latino; 3 Two or more races, non-Hispanic/Latino), 4 international. Average age 32. 295 applicants, 47% accepted, 103 enrolled. In 2013, 147 master's, 5 Ed Ss awarded. *Degree requirements:* For master's, comprehensive exam (for some programs), thesis (for some programs), exit exam. *Entrance requirements:* For master's, MAT or GRE (if GPA less than 2.75), interview, writing sample. Additional exam requirements/recommendations for international students: Required—TOEFL (minimum score 550 paper-based; 80 iBT). *Application deadline:* For fall admission, 4/10 for domestic students, 4/10 priority date for international students; for winter admission, 9/10 for domestic students, 7/1 for international students; for spring admission, 9/10 for domestic students, 9/10 priority date for international students. Application fee: $0 ($50 for international students). Electronic applications accepted. *Expenses: Tuition:* Full-time $10,296; part-time $858 per credit hour. *Required fees:* $50; $25. *Financial support:* In 2013–14, 10 research assistantships with full tuition reimbursements (averaging $8,720 per year) were awarded; career-related internships or fieldwork, institutionally sponsored loans, health care benefits, and unspecified assistantships also available. Financial award application deadline: 3/1; financial award applicants required to submit FAFSA. *Faculty research:* Mindfulness, forgiveness in relationships, positive psychology in couples counseling, traumatic brain injury responses, college student development. *Unit head:* Dr. Molly Schaller, Chairperson, 937-229-3644, Fax: 937-229-1055, E-mail: mschaller1@udayton.edu. *Application contact:* Kathleen Brown, Administrative Assistant, 937-229-3644, Fax: 937-229-1055, E-mail: kbrown1@udayton.edu.
Website: http://www.udayton.edu/education/edc/index.php.

University of Florida, Graduate School, College of Education, School of Human Development and Organizational Studies in Education, Gainesville, FL 32611. Offers counseling and counselor education (Ed D, PhD), including counseling and counselor education, marriage and family counseling, mental health counseling, school counseling and guidance; educational leadership (M Ed, MAE, Ed D, PhD, Ed S), including educational leadership (Ed D, PhD), educational policy (Ed D, PhD); higher education administration (Ed D, PhD, Ed S), including education policy (Ed D), educational policy (Ed D, PhD), higher education administration (Ed D, PhD); marriage and family counseling (M Ed, MAE, Ed S); mental health counseling (M Ed, MAE, Ed S); research and evaluation methodology (M Ed, MAE, Ed D, PhD, Ed S); school counseling and guidance (M Ed, MAE, Ed S); student personnel in higher education (M Ed, MAE, Ed S). *Accreditation:* ACA (one or more programs are accredited); NCATE. Part-time programs available. Postbaccalaureate distance learning degree programs offered. *Faculty:* 20 full-time (11 women), 4 part-time/adjunct (1 woman). *Students:* 291 full-time (232 women), 212 part-time (157 women); includes 145 minority (71 Black or African American, non-Hispanic/Latino; 3 American Indian or Alaska Native, non-Hispanic/Latino; 11 Asian, non-Hispanic/Latino; 60 Hispanic/Latino), 38 international. Average age 31. 271 applicants, 42% accepted, 75 enrolled. In 2013, 71 master's, 31 doctorates, 62 other advanced degrees awarded. Terminal master's awarded for partial completion of doctoral program. *Degree requirements:* For master's, thesis optional; for doctorate, comprehensive exam, thesis/dissertation. *Entrance requirements:* For master's and doctorate, GRE General Test, minimum GPA of 3.0 (undergraduate), 3.5 (graduate); for Ed S, GRE General Test. Additional exam requirements/recommendations for international students: Required—TOEFL (minimum score 550 paper-based; 80 iBT), IELTS (minimum score 6). *Application deadline:* Applications are processed on a rolling basis. Application fee: $30. Electronic applications accepted. *Expenses:* Tuition, state resident: full-time $12,640. Tuition, nonresident: full-time $30,000. *Financial support:* In 2013–14, 85 students received support, including 6 fellowships (averaging $12,190 per year), 48 research assistantships (averaging $15,155 per year), 50 teaching assistantships (averaging $9,080 per year); career-related internships or fieldwork and unspecified assistantships also available. Financial award applicants required to submit FAFSA. *Unit head:* Glenn E. Good, PhD, Dean and Professor, 352-273-4135, Fax: 352-846-2697, E-mail: ggood@ufl.edu. *Application contact:* Thomasenia L. Adams, PhD, Professor and Associate Dean, 352-273-4119, Fax: 352-846-2697, E-mail: tla@coe.ufl.edu.
Website: http://education.ufl.edu/hdose/.

University of Georgia, College of Education, Department of Counseling and Human Development Services, Athens, GA 30602. Offers college student affairs administration (M Ed, PhD); counseling and student personnel (PhD); counseling psychology (PhD); professional counseling (M Ed); professional school counseling (Ed S); recreation and leisure studies (M Ed, MA, PhD). *Accreditation:* ACA (one or more programs are accredited); APA (one or more programs are accredited); NCATE. *Degree requirements:* For master's, thesis (MA); for doctorate, variable foreign language requirement, thesis/dissertation. *Entrance requirements:* For master's, GRE General Test or MAT; for doctorate, GRE General Test. Electronic applications accepted.

The University of Iowa, Graduate College, College of Education, Department of Educational Policy and Leadership Studies, Program in Higher Education and Student Affairs, Iowa City, IA 52242-1316. Offers MA, PhD. *Degree requirements:* For master's, exam; for doctorate, comprehensive exam, thesis/dissertation. *Entrance requirements:* For master's and doctorate, GRE General Test, minimum GPA of 3.0. Additional exam requirements/recommendations for international students: Required—TOEFL (minimum score 550 paper-based; 81 iBT). Electronic applications accepted.

University of Louisville, Graduate School, College of Education and Human Development, Department of Educational and Counseling Psychology, Louisville, KY 40292-0001. Offers counseling and personnel services (M Ed, PhD). *Accreditation:* APA; NCATE. Part-time and evening/weekend programs available. *Faculty:* 15 full-time (8 women), 4 part-time/adjunct (2 women). *Students:* 192 full-time (158 women), 72 part-time (55 women); includes 59 minority (38 Black or African American, non-Hispanic/Latino; 1 American Indian or Alaska Native, non-Hispanic/Latino; 5 Asian, non-Hispanic/Latino; 9 Hispanic/Latino; 6 Two or more races, non-Hispanic/Latino), 7 international. Average age 29. 222 applicants, 50% accepted, 77 enrolled. In 2013, 46 master's, 2 doctorates awarded. *Degree requirements:* For doctorate, comprehensive exam, thesis/dissertation. *Entrance requirements:* For master's and doctorate, GRE General Test. Additional exam requirements/recommendations for international students: Required—TOEFL (minimum score 560 paper-based; 83 iBT). *Application deadline:* For fall admission, 5/1 priority date for international students; for winter admission, 11/1 for international students; for summer admission, 4/1 priority date for international students. Application fee: $60. Electronic applications accepted. *Expenses:* Tuition, state resident: full-time $10,788; part-time $599 per credit hour. Tuition, nonresident: full-time $22,446; part-time $1247 per credit hour. *Required fees:* $196. Tuition and fees vary according to program and reciprocity agreements. *Financial support:* Fellowships, research assistantships, teaching assistantships, career-related internships or fieldwork, Federal Work-Study, scholarships/grants, health care benefits, and unspecified assistantships available. Financial award application deadline: 6/1; financial award

Student Affairs

applicants required to submit FAFSA. *Faculty research:* Classroom processes, school outcomes, adolescent and adult development issues/prevention and treatment, multicultural counseling, spirituality, therapeutic outcomes, college student success, college student affairs administration, career development. *Unit head:* Dr. Michael Cuyjet, Acting Chair, 502-852-0628, Fax: 502-852-0629, E-mail: cuyjet@louisville.edu. *Application contact:* Libby Leggett, Director, Graduate Admissions, 502-852-3101, Fax: 502-852-6536, E-mail: gradadm@louisville.edu.
Website: http://www.louisville.edu/education/departments/ecpy.

University of Mary, School of Education and Behavioral Sciences, Department of Behavioral Sciences, Bismarck, ND 58504-9652. Offers addiction counseling (MSC); community counseling (MSC); school counseling (MSC); student affairs counseling (MSC). Part-time programs available. Postbaccalaureate distance learning degree programs offered (minimal on-campus study). *Degree requirements:* For master's, thesis, internship. *Entrance requirements:* For master's, coursework/experience in psychology, statistics, minimum GPA of 3.0. Additional exam requirements/recommendations for international students: Required—TOEFL (minimum score 500 paper-based; 71 iBT).

University of Maryland, College Park, Academic Affairs, College of Education, Department of Counseling, Higher Education and Special Education, College Park, MD 20742. Offers college student personnel (M Ed, MA); college student personnel administration (PhD); community counseling (CAGS); community/career counseling (M Ed, MA); counseling and personnel services (M Ed, MA, PhD), including art therapy (M Ed), college student personnel (M Ed), counseling and personnel services (PhD), counseling psychology (M Ed), mental health counseling (M Ed), school counseling (M Ed); counseling psychology (PhD); counselor education (PhD); rehabilitation counseling (M Ed, MA, AGSC); school counseling (M Ed, MA); school psychology (M Ed, MA, PhD). *Accreditation:* ACA (one or more programs are accredited); APA (one or more programs are accredited); NCATE. Part-time and evening/weekend programs available. Postbaccalaureate distance learning degree programs offered (no on-campus study). *Faculty:* 63 full-time (43 women), 9 part-time/adjunct (8 women). *Students:* 244 full-time (189 women), 76 part-time (54 women); includes 96 minority (40 Black or African American, non-Hispanic/Latino; 1 American Indian or Alaska Native, non-Hispanic/Latino; 23 Asian, non-Hispanic/Latino; 26 Hispanic/Latino; 6 Two or more races, non-Hispanic/Latino), 34 international. 623 applicants, 21% accepted, 83 enrolled. In 2013, 64 master's, 41 doctorates awarded. *Degree requirements:* For master's, thesis (for some programs); for doctorate, thesis/dissertation. *Entrance requirements:* For master's, GRE General Test or MAT, minimum GPA of 3.0, 3 letters of recommendation; for doctorate, GRE General Test or MAT, minimum GPA of 3.5, 3 letters of recommendation. Additional exam requirements/recommendations for international students: Required—TOEFL. *Application deadline:* For fall admission, 12/1 for domestic students, 12/15 for international students; for spring admission, 12/1 for domestic students, 6/1 for international students. Applications are processed on a rolling basis. Application fee: $75. Electronic applications accepted. *Expenses:* Tuition, state resident: full-time $10,314; part-time $573 per credit hour. Tuition, nonresident: full-time $22,248; part-time $1236 per credit. *Required fees:* $1446; $403.15 per semester. Tuition and fees vary according to program. *Financial support:* In 2013–14, 31 fellowships with full and partial tuition reimbursements (averaging $21,772 per year), 7 research assistantships with tuition reimbursements (averaging $17,202 per year), 100 teaching assistantships with tuition reimbursements (averaging $16,637 per year) were awarded; career-related internships or fieldwork, Federal Work-Study, and scholarships/grants also available. Support available to part-time students. Financial award applicants required to submit FAFSA. *Faculty research:* Educational psychology, counseling, health. *Total annual research expenditures:* $3.2 million. *Unit head:* Dennis Kivlighan, Chair, 301-405-2858, E-mail: dennisk@umd.edu. *Application contact:* Dr. Charles A. Caramello, Dean of Graduate School, 301-405-0358, Fax: 301-314-9305, E-mail: ccaramel@umd.edu.

University of Minnesota, Twin Cities Campus, Graduate School, College of Education and Human Development, Department of Educational Psychology, Program in Counseling and Student Personnel Psychology, Minneapolis, MN 55455-0213. Offers MA, PhD, Ed S. *Students:* 90 full-time (72 women), 13 part-time (9 women); includes 20 minority (5 Black or African American, non-Hispanic/Latino; 2 American Indian or Alaska Native, non-Hispanic/Latino; 6 Asian, non-Hispanic/Latino; 7 Hispanic/Latino), 15 international. Average age 28. 134 applicants, 56% accepted, 37 enrolled. In 2013, 31 master's, 6 doctorates awarded. Application fee: $75 ($95 for international students). *Unit head:* Geoff Maruyama, Chair, 612-624-1003, Fax: 612-625-5861, E-mail: geoff@umn.edu. *Application contact:* Dr. Jennifer Engler, Assistant Dean, 612-626-2887, Fax: 612-626-7496, E-mail: engle009@umn.edu.
Website: http://www.cehd.umn.edu/EdPsych/CSPP.

University of Mississippi, Graduate School, School of Education, Department of Leadership and Counselor Education, Oxford, MS 38677. Offers counselor education (M Ed, PhD); educational leadership (M Ed, PhD, Ed S); higher education/student personnel (MA, PhD); play therapy (Ed S). *Accreditation:* ACA; NCATE. *Faculty:* 13 full-time (6 women), 9 part-time/adjunct (6 women). *Students:* 155 full-time (123 women), 181 part-time (127 women); includes 136 minority (116 Black or African American, non-Hispanic/Latino; 3 American Indian or Alaska Native, non-Hispanic/Latino; 8 Hispanic/Latino; 9 Two or more races, non-Hispanic/Latino), 6 international. In 2013, 104 master's, 9 doctorates awarded. *Degree requirements:* For doctorate, thesis/dissertation. *Entrance requirements:* For master's, GRE General Test, minimum GPA of 3.0; for doctorate, GRE General Test. Additional exam requirements/recommendations for international students: Required—TOEFL. *Application deadline:* For fall admission, 4/1 for domestic students; for spring admission, 10/1 for domestic students. Applications are processed on a rolling basis. Application fee: $40. Electronic applications accepted. *Financial support:* Scholarships/grants available. Financial award application deadline: 3/1; financial award applicants required to submit FAFSA. *Unit head:* Dr. Timothy Letzring, Chair, 662-915-7069, Fax: 662-915-7230. *Application contact:* Dr. Christy M. Wyandt, Associate Dean, 662-915-7474, Fax: 662-915-7577, E-mail: cwyandt@olemiss.edu.
Website: http://education.olemiss.edu/dco/leadership_counselor_education.html.

University of Nebraska at Kearney, Graduate Programs, College of Education, Department of Counseling and School Psychology, Kearney, NE 68849-0001. Offers clinical mental health counseling (MS Ed); school counseling (MS Ed), including elementary, secondary, student affairs; school psychology (Ed S). *Accreditation:* ACA; NCATE. Part-time and evening/weekend programs available. *Degree requirements:* For master's, thesis optional; for Ed S, thesis. *Entrance requirements:* For master's and Ed S, personal statement, recommendations, resume, interview. Additional exam requirements/recommendations for international students: Required—TOEFL (minimum score: 550 paper-based, 79 iBT) or IELTS (6.5). Electronic applications accepted. *Faculty research:* Multicultural counseling and diversity issues, team decision-making, adult development, women's issues, brief therapy.

University of Northern Colorado, Graduate School, College of Education and Behavioral Sciences, Department of Leadership, Policy and Development: Higher Education and P-12 Education, Program in Higher Education and Student Affairs Leadership, Greeley, CO 80639. Offers PhD. Part-time programs available. *Entrance*

requirements: For doctorate, GRE General Test, transcripts, 3 letters of recommendation. Electronic applications accepted.

University of Northern Iowa, Graduate College, College of Education, Department of Educational Leadership and Postsecondary Education, MAE Program in Postsecondary Education: Student Affairs, Cedar Falls, IA 50614. Offers MAE. *Students:* 20 full-time (14 women), 7 part-time (6 women); includes 4 minority (1 Black or African American, non-Hispanic/Latino; 1 Asian, non-Hispanic/Latino; 2 Hispanic/Latino). 66 applicants, 42% accepted, 13 enrolled. In 2013, 17 master's awarded. *Degree requirements:* For master's, comprehensive exam, thesis or alternative. *Entrance requirements:* For master's, minimum GPA of 3.0. Additional exam requirements/recommendations for international students: Required—TOEFL (minimum score 500 paper-based; 61 iBT). *Application deadline:* For fall admission, 8/1 priority date for domestic students. Applications are processed on a rolling basis. Application fee: $50 ($70 for international students). Electronic applications accepted. *Financial support:* Career-related internships or fieldwork, Federal Work-Study, scholarships/grants, and tuition waivers (full) available. Financial award application deadline: 2/1. *Unit head:* Dr. Michael Waggoner, Coordinator, 319-273-2605, Fax: 319-273-5175, E-mail: mike.waggoner@uni.edu. *Application contact:* Laurie S. Russell, Record Analyst, 319-273-2623, Fax: 319-273-2885, E-mail: laurie.russell@uni.edu.
Website: http://www.uni.edu/coe/departments/educational-leadership-postsecondary-education/postsecondary-education.

University of Rhode Island, Graduate School, College of Human Science and Services, Department of Human Development and Family Studies, Kingston, RI 02881. Offers college student personnel (MS); human development and family studies (MS); marriage and family therapy (MS). *Accreditation:* AAMFT/COAMFTE. Part-time programs available. *Faculty:* 14 full-time (11 women), 1 part-time/adjunct (0 women). *Students:* 41 full-time (36 women), 6 part-time (3 women); includes 8 minority (5 Black or African American, non-Hispanic/Latino; 1 Asian, non-Hispanic/Latino; 1 Hispanic/Latino; 1 Two or more races, non-Hispanic/Latino), 1 international. In 2013, 29 master's awarded. *Degree requirements:* For master's, comprehensive exam (for some programs), thesis optional. *Entrance requirements:* For master's, GRE or MAT, 2 letters of recommendation; resume (for college student personnel specialization). Additional exam requirements/recommendations for international students: Required—TOEFL (minimum score 550 paper-based). *Application deadline:* For fall admission, 1/15 for domestic and international students. Application fee: $65. Electronic applications accepted. *Expenses:* Tuition, state resident: full-time $11,532; part-time $641 per credit. Tuition, nonresident: full-time $23,606; part-time $1311 per credit. *Required fees:* $1388; $36 per credit. $35 per semester. One-time fee: $130. *Financial support:* Application deadline: 1/15; applicants required to submit FAFSA. *Total annual research expenditures:* $256,058. *Unit head:* Dr. Karen McCurdy, Chair, 401-874-5960, Fax: 401-874-4020, E-mail: kmccurdy@uri.edu. *Application contact:* Graduate Admissions, 401-874-2872, E-mail: gradadm@etal.uri.edu.
Website: http://www.uri.edu/hss/hdf/.

University of Rochester, Margaret Warner Graduate School of Education and Human Development, Master's Program in Higher Education, Rochester, NY 14627. Offers higher education (MS); higher education student affairs (MS). *Expenses:* Tuition: Full-time $44,580; part-time $1394 per credit hour. *Required fees:* $492.

University of St. Thomas, Graduate Studies, School of Education, Department of Leadership, Policy and Administration, St. Paul, MN 55105-1096. Offers community education administration (MA); educational leadership (Ed S); educational leadership and administration (MA); international leadership (MA, Certificate); leadership (Ed D); leadership in student affairs (MA, Certificate); public policy and leadership (MA, Certificate); public safety and law enforcement leadership (MA). Part-time and evening/weekend programs available. Terminal master's awarded for partial completion of doctoral program. *Degree requirements:* For master's, thesis (for some programs); for doctorate, thesis/dissertation; for other advanced degree, thesis or alternative. *Entrance requirements:* For master's, minimum GPA of 3.0 or MAT; for doctorate, MAT, minimum graduate GPA of 3.5; for other advanced degree, minimum graduate GPA of 3.25 or MAT. Additional exam requirements/recommendations for international students: Required—TOEFL (minimum score 550 paper-based; 20 iBT). *Application deadline:* For fall admission, 6/1 priority date for domestic students; for spring admission, 11/1 priority date for domestic students. Applications are processed on a rolling basis. Application fee: $50. *Expenses:* Contact institution. *Financial support:* Fellowships, research assistantships, institutionally sponsored loans, and scholarships/grants available. Support available to part-time students. Financial award applicants required to submit FAFSA. *Unit head:* Dr. Kate M. Boyle, Chair, 651-962-4393, Fax: 651-962-4169, E-mail: kmboyle@stthomas.edu. *Application contact:* Jackie Grossklaus, Department Assistant, 651-962-4885, Fax: 651-962-4169, E-mail: jmgrossklaus@stthomas.edu.

University of South Carolina, The Graduate School, College of Education, Department of Educational Leadership and Policies, Program in Higher Education and Student Affairs, Columbia, SC 29208. Offers M Ed. *Accreditation:* NCATE. Part-time programs available. *Degree requirements:* For master's, comprehensive exam, thesis (for some programs). *Entrance requirements:* For master's, GRE General Test or MAT, letters of reference. Electronic applications accepted. *Faculty research:* Minorities in higher education, community college transfer problem, federal role in educational research.

University of Southern California, Graduate School, Rossier School of Education, Master's Programs in Education, Los Angeles, CA 90089-4038. Offers educational counseling (ME); marriage, family and child counseling (MMFT); postsecondary administration and student affairs [PASA] (ME); school counseling (ME); teaching (online) (MAT); teaching and teaching credential (MAT); teaching English to speakers of other languages (MAT). Part-time and evening/weekend programs available. Postbaccalaureate distance learning degree programs offered (no on-campus study). *Degree requirements:* For master's, thesis optional. *Entrance requirements:* For master's, GRE (for all programs except MAT). Additional exam requirements/recommendations for international students: Required—TOEFL (minimum score 100 iBT). Electronic applications accepted. *Faculty research:* College access and equity, preparing teachers for culturally diverse populations, sociocultural basis of learning as mediated by instruction with focus on reading and literacy in English learners, social and political aspects of teaching and learning English, school counselor development and training.

University of Southern Mississippi, Graduate School, College of Education and Psychology, Department of Educational Studies and Research, Hattiesburg, MS 39406-0001. Offers adult education (Graduate Certificate); community college leadership (Graduate Certificate); counseling and personnel services (college) (M Ed); education (PhD, Ed S), including adult education, research, evaluation and statistics (PhD); education (Ed D), including educational administration, educational research; education: educational leadership and research (Ed S), including higher education administration; educational administration and supervision (M Ed); higher education administration (Ed D, PhD); institutional research (Graduate Certificate). *Faculty:* 7 full-time (1 woman), 5 part-time/adjunct (1 woman). *Students:* 32 full-time (21 women), 103 part-time (70 women); includes 44 minority (39 Black or African American, non-Hispanic/Latino; 2 Hispanic/Latino; 3 Two or more races, non-Hispanic/Latino), 4 international. Average age 36. 36 applicants, 72% accepted, 15 enrolled. In 2013, 18 master's, 9 doctorates, 7

other advanced degrees awarded. *Degree requirements:* For master's and other advanced degree, comprehensive exam, thesis (for some programs); for doctorate, comprehensive exam, thesis/dissertation. *Entrance requirements:* For master's, doctorate, and other advanced degree, GRE General Test, minimum GPA of 2.75. Additional exam requirements/recommendations for international students: Required—TOEFL. *Application deadline:* For fall admission, 2/1 for domestic students, 3/1 for international students. Applications are processed on a rolling basis. Application fee: $35. *Financial support:* Career-related internships or fieldwork, Federal Work-Study, and institutionally sponsored loans available. Financial award application deadline: 3/15; financial award applicants required to submit FAFSA. *Total annual research expenditures:* $88,500. *Unit head:* Dr. Thomas V. O'Brien, Chair, 601-266-6093, E-mail: thomas.obrien@usm.edu. *Application contact:* Shonna Breland, Manager of Graduate Admissions, 601-266-6563, Fax: 601-266-5138. Website: http://www.usm.edu/cep/esr/.

University of South Florida, College of Education, Department of Psychological and Social Foundations, Tampa, FL 33620-9951. Offers college student affairs (M Ed); counselor education (MA, PhD, Ed S); interdisciplinary (PhD, Ed S); school psychology (PhD, Ed S). Part-time and evening/weekend programs available. *Degree requirements:* For master's, comprehensive exam, thesis (for some programs); for doctorate, comprehensive exam, thesis/dissertation, multiple research methods; philosophies of inquiry (for some programs). *Entrance requirements:* For master's, GRE General Test, minimum GPA of 3.5 in last 60 hours of course work; for doctorate, GRE General Test, MAT, minimum GPA of 3.5 in last 60 hours of course work; for Ed S, GRE General Test. Additional exam requirements/recommendations for international students: Required—TOEFL (minimum score 550 paper-based; 79 iBT). Electronic applications accepted. *Faculty research:* College student affairs, counselor education, educational psychology, school psychology, social foundations.

University of South Florida, University College/Distance Education, Tampa, FL 33620-9951. *Unit head:* Kathy Barnes, Interdisciplinary Programs Coordinator, 813-974-8031, Fax: 813-974-7061, E-mail: barnesk@usf.edu. *Application contact:* Karen Tylinski, Metro Initiatives, 813-974-9943, Fax: 813-974-7061, E-mail: ktylinsk@usf.edu. Website: http://uc.usf.edu/.

The University of Tennessee, Graduate School, College of Education, Health and Human Sciences, Department of Educational Psychology and Counseling, Program in College Student Personnel, Knoxville, TN 37996. Offers MS. *Accreditation:* NCATE. Part-time programs available. *Degree requirements:* For master's, thesis optional. *Entrance requirements:* For master's, GRE General Test, minimum GPA of 2.7. Additional exam requirements/recommendations for international students: Required—TOEFL. Electronic applications accepted. *Expenses:* Tuition, state resident: full-time $9540; part-time $531 per credit hour. Tuition, nonresident: full-time $27,728; part-time $1542 per credit hour. *Required fees:* $1404; $67 per credit hour.

University of the Cumberlands, Graduate Programs in Education, Williamsburg, KY 40769-1372. Offers all grades (P-12) (M Ed); business and marketing (MA Ed, MAT); counselor education and supervision (Ed D); director of pupil personnel (Certificate); director of special education (Certificate); educational administration and supervision (Ed S); educational leadership (Ed D); elementary education (MA Ed, MAT); instructional leadership - principalship (MA Ed); instructional leadership - school principal (Certificate); middle school education (MA Ed, MAT); reading and writing (MA Ed); school counseling (MA Ed); school superintendent (Certificate); secondary education (MA Ed, MAT); special education (MAT); supervisor of instruction (Certificate); teacher leader (MA Ed). Part-time and evening/weekend programs available. Postbaccalaureate distance learning degree programs offered. *Degree requirements:* For master's, comprehensive exam. Electronic applications accepted.

University of Utah, Graduate School, College of Education, Department of Educational Leadership and Policy, Salt Lake City, UT 84112. Offers educational leadership and policy (Ed D, PhD); K-12 administrative licensure (M Ed); K-12 teacher instructional leadership (M Ed); student affairs (M Ed); MPA/PhD. Part-time and evening/weekend programs available. *Faculty:* 10 full-time (7 women), 4 part-time/adjunct (3 women). *Students:* 55 full-time (38 women), 65 part-time (40 women); includes 33 minority (5 Black or African American, non-Hispanic/Latino; 1 American Indian or Alaska Native, non-Hispanic/Latino; 3 Asian, non-Hispanic/Latino; 21 Hispanic/Latino; 3 Two or more races, non-Hispanic/Latino), 3 international. Average age 35. 123 applicants, 45% accepted, 51 enrolled. In 2013, 33 master's, 5 doctorates awarded. *Degree requirements:* For master's, comprehensive exam (for some programs), internship; for doctorate, thesis/dissertation, qualifying exam. *Entrance requirements:* For master's, minimum undergraduate GPA of 3.0, valid bachelor's degree, 3 years' teaching or leadership experience, Level 1 or 2 UT educator's license (for K-12 programs only); for doctorate, GRE General Test (taken with five years of applying), minimum undergraduate GPA of 3.0, valid master's degree. Additional exam requirements/recommendations for international students: Required—TOEFL (minimum score 500 paper-based). *Application deadline:* For fall and winter admission, 2/1 for domestic and international students; for summer admission, 1/15 for domestic and international students. Application fee: $55 ($65 for international students). Electronic applications accepted. *Expenses:* Tuition, state resident: full-time $5259. Tuition, nonresident: full-time $18,569. *Required fees:* $841. Tuition and fees vary according to course load. *Financial support:* In 2013–14, 86 students received support, including 7 fellowships (averaging $2,000 per year), research assistantships with full tuition reimbursements available (averaging $13,000 per year), 86 teaching assistantships with full tuition reimbursements available (averaging $13,000 per year); career-related internships or fieldwork, scholarships/grants, health care benefits, and unspecified assistantships also available. Financial award application deadline: 2/1. *Faculty research:* Education accountability, college student diversity, K-12 educational administration and school leadership, student affairs, higher education. *Total annual research expenditures:* $55,000. *Unit head:* Dr. Andrea Rorrer, Chair, 801-581-4207, Fax: 801-585-6756, E-mail: andrea.rorrer@utah.edu. *Application contact:* Marilynn S. Howard, Academic Coordinator, 801-581-6714, Fax: 801-585-6756, E-mail: marilynn.howard@utah.edu. Website: http://elp.utah.edu/.

University of Virginia, Curry School of Education, Department of Leadership, Foundations and Policy, Program in Higher Education, Charlottesville, VA 22903. Offers higher education (Ed S); student affairs practice (M Ed). *Students:* 30 full-time (22 women), 17 part-time (6 women); includes 7 minority (3 Black or African American, non-Hispanic/Latino; 2 Asian, non-Hispanic/Latino; 2 Hispanic/Latino), 1 international. Average age 30. 14 applicants, 57% accepted, 6 enrolled. In 2013, 28 master's awarded. *Entrance requirements:* For master's, doctorate, and Ed S, GRE General Test, 2 letters of recommendation. Additional exam requirements/recommendations for international students: Required—TOEFL (minimum score 600 paper-based; 90 iBT), IELTS (minimum score 7). *Application deadline:* Applications are processed on a rolling basis. Application fee: $60. Electronic applications accepted. *Expenses:* Tuition, state resident: part-time $334 per credit hour. Tuition, nonresident: part-time $1224 per credit hour. *Financial support:* Fellowships, research assistantships, and teaching assistantships available. Financial award applicants required to submit FAFSA. *Unit*

head: Karen Kurotsuchi Inkelas, Associate Professor and Director, 434-243-1943, E-mail: highered@virginia.edu. *Application contact:* Assistant to the Chair. Website: http://curry.virginia.edu/academics/areas-of-study/higher-education.

The University of West Alabama, School of Graduate Studies, College of Education, Departments of Instructional Leadership and Support/Curriculum and Instruction, Program in Continuing Education, Livingston, AL 35470. Offers college student development (MSCE); continuing education (MSCE); counseling and psychology (MSCE); family counseling (MSCE); guidance and counseling (MSCE). *Accreditation:* NCATE. Part-time and evening/weekend programs available. Postbaccalaureate distance learning degree programs offered (no on-campus study). *Faculty:* 16 full-time (10 women), 38 part-time/adjunct (28 women). *Students:* 757 (662 women); includes 581 minority (572 Black or African American, non-Hispanic/Latino; 3 American Indian or Alaska Native, non-Hispanic/Latino; 1 Asian, non-Hispanic/Latino; 3 Hispanic/Latino; 2 Two or more races, non-Hispanic/Latino). 212 applicants, 100% accepted, 173 enrolled. In 2013, 152 master's awarded. *Degree requirements:* For master's, comprehensive exam, thesis optional. *Entrance requirements:* For master's, GRE General Test, MAT, minimum GPA of 2.75. Additional exam requirements/recommendations for international students: Required—TOEFL (minimum score 500 paper-based; 61 iBT). *Application deadline:* For fall admission, 8/12 priority date for domestic students; for spring admission, 3/24 for domestic students. Applications are processed on a rolling basis. Application fee: $25 ($50 for international students). Electronic applications accepted. Tuition and fees vary according to course load. *Financial support:* Teaching assistantships, career-related internships or fieldwork, Federal Work-Study, scholarships/grants, and unspecified assistantships available. Support available to part-time students. Financial award applicants required to submit FAFSA. *Unit head:* Dr. Reenay Rogers, Chair of Instructional Leadership and Support, 205-652-5423, Fax: 205-652-3706, E-mail: rrogers@uwa.edu. *Application contact:* Dr. Kathy Chandler, Dean of Graduate Studies, 205-652-3421, Fax: 205-652-3670, E-mail: kchandler@uwa.edu.

University of West Florida, College of Professional Studies, Department of Research and Advanced Studies, Program in College Student Personnel Administration, Pensacola, FL 32514-5750. Offers college personnel administration (M Ed); guidance and counseling (M Ed). Part-time and evening/weekend programs available. *Degree requirements:* For master's, internship. *Entrance requirements:* For master's, GRE General Test, minimum GPA of 3.0. Additional exam requirements/recommendations for international students: Required—TOEFL (minimum score 550 paper-based).

University of Wisconsin–La Crosse, Graduate Studies, College of Liberal Studies, Department of Student Affairs Administration in Higher Education, La Crosse, WI 54601-3742. Offers MS Ed. Part-time programs available. Postbaccalaureate distance learning degree programs offered (no on-campus study). *Faculty:* 2 full-time (1 woman). *Students:* 49 full-time (35 women), 46 part-time (36 women); includes 18 minority (5 Black or African American, non-Hispanic/Latino; 1 American Indian or Alaska Native, non-Hispanic/Latino; 4 Asian, non-Hispanic/Latino; 4 Hispanic/Latino; 4 Two or more races, non-Hispanic/Latino), 1 international. Average age 27. 136 applicants, 40% accepted, 48 enrolled. In 2013, 48 master's awarded. *Degree requirements:* For master's, comprehensive exam (for some programs), thesis optional, electronic portfolio, applied research project. *Entrance requirements:* For master's, interview, writing sample, references, experience in the field. Additional exam requirements/recommendations for international students: Required—TOEFL (minimum score 550 paper-based; 79 iBT). *Application deadline:* For fall admission, 2/1 priority date for domestic and international students. Electronic applications accepted. *Financial support:* Research assistantships with partial tuition reimbursements, Federal Work-Study, scholarships/grants, and health care benefits available. Support available to part-time students. Financial award application deadline: 3/15; financial award applicants required to submit FAFSA. *Unit head:* Dr. Jodie Rindt, Director, 608-785-6450, E-mail: rindt.jodi@uwlax.edu. *Application contact:* Corey Sjoquist, Director of Admissions, 608-785-8939, E-mail: admissions@uwlax.edu. Website: http://www.uwlax.edu/saa/.

University of Wyoming, College of Education, Programs in Counselor Education, Laramie, WY 82071. Offers community mental health (MS); counselor education and supervision (PhD); school counseling (MS); student affairs (MS). *Accreditation:* ACA (one or more programs are accredited). *Degree requirements:* For master's, comprehensive exam (for some programs), thesis optional; for doctorate, thesis/dissertation, video demonstration. *Entrance requirements:* For master's, interview, background check; for doctorate, video tape session, interview, writing sample, master's degree, background check. Additional exam requirements/recommendations for international students: Required—TOEFL. *Faculty research:* Wyoming SAGE photovoice project; accountable school counseling programs; GLBT issues; addictions; play therapy-early childhood mental health.

Virginia Commonwealth University, Graduate School, School of Education, Program in Counselor Education, Richmond, VA 23284-9005. Offers college student development and counseling (M Ed); school counseling (M Ed). *Accreditation:* ACA; NCATE. *Entrance requirements:* For master's, GRE General Test or MAT. Additional exam requirements/recommendations for international students: Required—TOEFL (minimum score 600 paper-based; 100 iBT). Electronic applications accepted.

Virginia Polytechnic Institute and State University, Graduate School, College of Liberal Arts and Human Sciences, Blacksburg, VA 24061. Offers career and technical education (MS Ed, Ed D, PhD, Ed S); communication (MA); counselor education (MA Ed, Ed D, PhD, Ed S); creative writing (MFA); curriculum and instruction (MA Ed, Ed D, PhD, Ed S); educational leadership and policy studies (MA Ed, Ed D, PhD, Ed S); educational research and evaluation (PhD); English (MA); foreign languages, cultures, and literatures (MA); higher education and student affairs (MA Ed); history (MA); human development (MS, PhD); material culture and public humanities (MA); philosophy (MA); political science (MA); rhetoric and writing (PhD); science and technology studies (MS, PhD); social, political, ethical, and cultural thought (PhD); sociology (MS, PhD); theater arts (MFA). *Faculty:* 410 full-time (211 women), 6 part-time/adjunct (5 women). *Students:* 688 full-time (464 women), 576 part-time (372 women); includes 243 minority (144 Black or African American, non-Hispanic/Latino; 3 American Indian or Alaska Native, non-Hispanic/Latino; 29 Asian, non-Hispanic/Latino; 48 Hispanic/Latino; 1 Native Hawaiian or other Pacific Islander, non-Hispanic/Latino; 18 Two or more races, non-Hispanic/Latino), 84 international. Average age 34. 1,054 applicants, 48% accepted, 374 enrolled. In 2013, 314 master's, 74 doctorates, 14 other advanced degrees awarded. *Degree requirements:* For master's, comprehensive exam (for some programs), thesis (for some programs); for doctorate, comprehensive exam (for some programs), thesis/dissertation (for some programs). *Entrance requirements:* For master's and doctorate, GRE/GMAT (may vary by department). Additional exam requirements/recommendations for international students: Required—TOEFL (minimum score 550 paper-based). *Application deadline:* For fall admission, 8/1 for domestic students, 4/1 for international students; for spring admission, 1/1 for domestic students, 9/1 for international students. Applications are processed on a rolling basis. Application fee: $75. Electronic applications accepted. *Expenses:* Tuition, state resident: full-time $11,185; part-time $621.50 per credit hour. Tuition, nonresident: full-time $22,146; part-time $1230.25 per credit hour. *Required fees:* $2442; $449.25 per semester. Tuition and

fees vary according to course load, campus/location and program. *Financial support:* In 2013–14, 19 research assistantships with full tuition reimbursements (averaging $17,115 per year), 205 teaching assistantships with full tuition reimbursements (averaging $14,433 per year) were awarded. Financial award application deadline: 3/1; financial award applicants required to submit FAFSA. *Total annual research expenditures:* $6.8 million. *Unit head:* Joan Hirt, Interim Dean, 540-231-6779, Fax: 540-231-7157, E-mail: jbhirt@vt.edu. *Application contact:* Melissa Elliott, Executive Assistant, 540-231-6779, Fax: 540-231-7157, E-mail: elliott1@vt.edu.
Website: http://www.clahs.vt.edu/.

Walsh University, Graduate Studies, Program in Counseling and Human Development, North Canton, OH 44720-3396. Offers clinical mental health counseling (MA); school counseling (MA); student affairs in higher education (MA). *Accreditation:* ACA. Part-time and evening/weekend programs available. *Faculty:* 5 full-time (all women), 6 part-time/adjunct (2 women). *Students:* 38 full-time (27 women), 47 part-time (41 women); includes 3 minority (2 Black or African American, non-Hispanic/Latino; 1 Hispanic/Latino), 2 international. Average age 28. 94 applicants, 37% accepted, 26 enrolled. In 2013, 21 master's awarded. *Degree requirements:* For master's, comprehensive exam, internship, practicum. *Entrance requirements:* For master's, GRE (minimum score of 145 verbal and 146 quantitative) or MAT (minimum score of 397), interview, minimum GPA of 3.0, writing sample, reference forms, notarized affidavit of good moral conduct. Additional exam requirements/recommendations for international students: Required—TOEFL (minimum score 500 paper-based; 61 iBT). *Application deadline:* For fall admission, 7/15 priority date for domestic students. Applications are processed on a rolling basis. Application fee: $25. Electronic applications accepted. *Expenses: Tuition:* Full-time $10,890; part-time $605 per credit hour. *Required fees:* $100; $100. *Financial support:* In 2013–14, 73 students received support, including 3 research assistantships with partial tuition reimbursements available (averaging $8,065 per year), 11 teaching assistantships with partial tuition reimbursements available (averaging $5,610 per year); scholarships/grants, tuition waivers (full and partial), and unspecified assistantships also available. Support available to part-time students. Financial award application deadline: 12/31. *Faculty research:* Clinical training and supervision of clinical mental health counselors, supervision of school counselors, cross-cultural training in counselor education, outcomes in adventure-based therapies with children, counseling for intimate partner violence and relational issues, refugee mental health and trauma, career counseling for refugees using ecological and social learning models, integration of neuroscience and culture in clinical mental health counseling. *Unit head:* Dr. Linda Barclay, Program Director, 330-490-7264, Fax: 330-490-7323, E-mail: lbarclay@walsh.edu. *Application contact:* Audra Dice, Graduate and Transfer Admissions Counselor, 330-490-7181, Fax: 330-244-4925, E-mail: adice@walsh.edu.
Website: http://www.walsh.edu/counseling-graduate-program.

West Chester University of Pennsylvania, College of Education, Department of Counselor Education, West Chester, PA 19383. Offers counseling (Teaching Certificate); elementary school counseling (M Ed); higher education counseling (MS); higher education counseling/student affairs (Certificate); secondary school counseling (M Ed). *Accreditation:* ACA; NCATE. Part-time and evening/weekend programs available. *Faculty:* 10 full-time (6 women), 7 part-time/adjunct (5 women). *Students:* 116 full-time (100 women), 110 part-time (93 women); includes 36 minority (19 Black or African American, non-Hispanic/Latino; 2 American Indian or Alaska Native, non-Hispanic/Latino; 2 Asian, non-Hispanic/Latino; 7 Hispanic/Latino; 6 Two or more races, non-Hispanic/Latino). Average age 28. 145 applicants, 76% accepted, 59 enrolled. In 2013, 83 master's awarded. *Degree requirements:* For master's, comprehensive exam. *Entrance requirements:* For master's, minimum GPA of 3.0, three letters of reference. Additional exam requirements/recommendations for international students: Required—TOEFL (minimum score 550 paper-based; 80 iBT). *Application deadline:* For fall admission, 4/15 priority date for domestic students, 3/15 for international students; for spring admission, 10/15 priority date for domestic students, 9/1 for international students. Applications are processed on a rolling basis. Application fee: $45. Electronic applications accepted. *Expenses:* Tuition, state resident: full-time $7956; part-time $442 per credit. Tuition, nonresident: full-time $11,934; part-time $663 per credit. *Required fees:* $2134.20; $106.24 per credit. Tuition and fees vary according to campus/location and program. *Financial support:* Unspecified assistantships available. Support available to part-time students. Financial award application deadline: 2/15; financial award applicants required to submit FAFSA. *Faculty research:* Teacher and student cognition, adolescent cognitive development, college counseling, motivational interviewing. *Unit head:* Dr. Kathryn (Tina) Alessandria, Chair, 610-436-2559, Fax: 610-425-7432, E-mail: kalessandria@wcupa.edu. *Application contact:* Dr. Eric W. Owens, Graduate Coordinator, 610-436-2559, Fax: 610-425-7432, E-mail: eowens@wcupa.edu.
Website: http://www.wcupa.edu/_academics/sch_sed.counseling&edpsych/.

Western Illinois University, School of Graduate Studies, College of Education and Human Services, Department of Educational and Interdisciplinary Studies, Program in College Student Personnel, Macomb, IL 61455-1390. Offers MS. *Accreditation:* NCATE. Part-time programs available. *Students:* 45 full-time (32 women); includes 11 minority (6 Black or African American, non-Hispanic/Latino; 2 Asian, non-Hispanic/Latino; 2 Hispanic/Latino; 1 Two or more races, non-Hispanic/Latino). Average age 22. In 2013, 24 master's awarded. *Degree requirements:* For master's, thesis or alternative. *Entrance requirements:* For master's, interview. Additional exam requirements/recommendations for international students: Required—TOEFL (minimum score 550 paper-based; 80 iBT). *Application deadline:* For fall admission, 1/15 priority date for domestic students. Applications are processed on a rolling basis. Application fee: $30. Electronic applications accepted. *Financial support:* In 2013–14, 45 students received support, including 45 research assistantships with full tuition reimbursements available (averaging $7,544 per year). Financial award applicants required to submit FAFSA. *Unit head:* Dr. Tracy Davis, Coordinator, 309-298-1183. *Application contact:* Dr. Nancy Parsons, Associate Provost and Director of Graduate Studies, 309-298-1806, Fax: 309-298-2345, E-mail: grad-office@wiu.edu.
Website: http://wiu.edu/csp/.

Western Kentucky University, Graduate Studies, College of Education and Behavioral Sciences, Department of Counseling and Student Affairs, Bowling Green, KY 42101. Offers counseling (MA Ed), including marriage and family therapy, mental health counseling; school counseling (P-12) (MA Ed); student affairs in higher education (MA Ed). *Accreditation:* ACA; NCATE. Part-time and evening/weekend programs available. *Degree requirements:* For master's, comprehensive exam, thesis optional. *Entrance requirements:* For master's, GRE General Test. Additional exam requirements/recommendations for international students: Required—TOEFL (minimum score 555 paper-based; 79 iBT). *Faculty research:* Counselor education, research for residential workers.

Section 24
Instructional Levels

This section contains a directory of institutions offering graduate work in instructional levels. Additional information about programs listed in the directory may be obtained by writing directly to the dean of a graduate school or chair of a department at the address given in the directory.

For programs offering related work, see also in this book *Administration, Instruction, and Theory; Education; Leisure Studies and Recreation; Physical Education and Kinesiology; Special Focus;* and *Subject Areas.* In other guides in this series:

Graduate Programs in the Humanities, Arts & Social Sciences
See *Psychology and Counseling (School Psychology)*

Graduate Programs in the Biological/Biomedical Sciences and Health-Related Medical Professions
See *Health-Related Professions*

CONTENTS

Program Directories

Adult Education	950
Community College Education	960
Early Childhood Education	963
Elementary Education	997
Higher Education	1042
Middle School Education	1066
Secondary Education	1082

Adult Education

Alverno College, School of Education, Milwaukee, WI 53234-3922. Offers adaptive education (MA); administrative leadership (MA); adult education and organizational development (MA); adult educational and instructional design (MA); adult educational and instructional technology (MA); global connections in the humanities (MA); instructional leadership (MA); instructional technology for K-12 settings (MA); professional development (MA); reading education (MA); reading education with adaptive education (MA); science education (MA); teaching in alternative schools (MA). *Accreditation:* NCATE. Part-time and evening/weekend programs available. *Faculty:* 7 full-time (all women), 26 part-time/adjunct (23 women). *Students:* 48 full-time (41 women), 89 part-time (83 women); includes 41 minority (24 Black or African American, non-Hispanic/Latino; 3 Asian, non-Hispanic/Latino; 11 Hispanic/Latino; 3 Two or more races, non-Hispanic/Latino), 4 international. Average age 36. 89 applicants, 97% accepted, 59 enrolled. In 2013, 53 master's awarded. *Degree requirements:* For master's, presentation/defense of proposal, conference presentation of inquiry projects. *Entrance requirements:* For master's, bachelor's degree in related field, communication samples from work setting, 3 letters of recommendation. Additional exam requirements/recommendations for international students: Required—TOEFL. *Application deadline:* For fall admission, 7/15 priority date for domestic and international students; for spring admission, 12/15 priority date for domestic and international students. Applications are processed on a rolling basis. *Application fee:* $0. Electronic applications accepted. Application fee is waived when completed online. Tuition and fees vary according to program. *Financial support:* In 2013–14, 9 students received support. Federal Work-Study and scholarships/grants available. Support available to part-time students. Financial award application deadline: 4/15; financial award applicants required to submit FAFSA. *Faculty research:* Student self-assessment, self-reflection, integration of curriculum, identifying needs of students in strategic situations and designing appropriate classroom strategies. *Unit head:* Dr. Desiree Pointer-Mace, Associate Dean, Graduate Program, 414-382-6345, Fax: 414-382-6332, E-mail: desiree.pointer-mace@alverno.edu. *Application contact:* Mary Claire Jones, Senior Graduate Admissions Counselor, 414-382-6106, Fax: 414-382-6354, E-mail: maryclaire.jones@alverno.edu.

Argosy University, Chicago, College of Education, Chicago, IL 60601. Offers adult education and training (MA Ed); community college executive leadership (Ed D); educational leadership (MA Ed, Ed D, Ed S), including district leadership (Ed D), higher education administration (Ed D), K-12 education (Ed D); instructional leadership (Ed D, Ed S), including higher education (Ed D), K-12 education (Ed D). Postbaccalaureate distance learning degree programs offered (minimal on-campus study).

Argosy University, Hawai`i, College of Education, Honolulu, HI 96813. Offers adult education and training (MAEd); educational leadership (Ed D), including higher education administration, K-12 education; instructional leadership (Ed D), including higher education, K-12 education; school psychology (MA).

Argosy University, Phoenix, College of Education, Phoenix, AZ 85021. Offers adult education and training (MA Ed); advanced educational administration (Ed D, Ed S); community college executive leadership (Ed D); educational administration (MA Ed); educational leadership (MA Ed, Ed D, Ed S), including education technology (Ed D), higher education administration (Ed D), K-12 education (Ed D); higher and postsecondary education (MA Ed); initial educational administration (Ed D, Ed S); school psychology (MA); teaching and learning (MA Ed, Ed D, Ed S), including education technology (Ed D), higher education (Ed D), K-12 education (Ed D).

Argosy University, Seattle, College of Education, Seattle, WA 98121. Offers adult education and training (MA Ed); community college executive leadership (Ed D); educational leadership (MA Ed, Ed D), including higher education administration (Ed D), K-12 education (Ed D); higher and postsecondary education (MA Ed); instructional leadership (MA Ed, Ed D), including education technology (Ed D), higher education (Ed D), K-12 education (Ed D).

Armstrong State University, School of Graduate Studies, Department of Adolescent and Adult Education, Savannah, GA 31419-1997. Offers adolescent and adult education (Certificate); adult education and community leadership (M Ed); curriculum and instruction (M Ed); secondary education (MAT). Part-time and evening/weekend programs available. Postbaccalaureate distance learning degree programs offered (minimal on-campus study). *Faculty:* 10 full-time (8 women), 2 part-time/adjunct (1 woman). *Students:* 35 full-time (29 women), 80 part-time (57 women); includes 34 minority (31 Black or African American, non-Hispanic/Latino; 1 Asian, non-Hispanic/Latino; 2 Hispanic/Latino). Average age 34. 61 applicants, 79% accepted, 43 enrolled. In 2013, 59 master's awarded. *Degree requirements:* For master's, comprehensive exam (for some programs), thesis (for some programs). *Entrance requirements:* For master's, GRE, MAT, minimum GPA of 2.5 and disposition statement (for MAT), 3.0 and clear certification (for M Ed). Additional exam requirements/recommendations for international students: Required—TOEFL (minimum score 523 paper-based). *Application deadline:* For fall admission, 6/30 priority date for domestic students, 5/1 priority date for international students; for spring admission, 11/15 priority date for domestic students, 9/15 priority date for international students; for summer admission, 4/15 priority date for domestic students, 9/15 for international students. Applications are processed on a rolling basis. *Application fee:* $30. Electronic applications accepted. *Expenses:* Tuition, state resident: part-time $201 per credit hour. Tuition, nonresident: part-time $745 per credit hour. *Required fees:* $310 per semester. Tuition and fees vary according to course load, campus/location and program. *Financial support:* In 2013–14, research assistantships with full tuition reimbursements (averaging $5,000 per year) were awarded; career-related internships or fieldwork, Federal Work-Study, scholarships/grants, and unspecified assistantships also available. Support available to part-time students. Financial award application deadline: 3/15; financial award applicants required to submit FAFSA. *Faculty research:* Women's issues, education pedagogy, reading, heat of body metabolism, geographic education. *Unit head:* Dr. Patrick Thomas, Interim Department Head, 912-344-2562, Fax: 912-344-3496, E-mail: patrick.thomas@armstrong.edu. *Application contact:* Jill Bell, Director, Graduate Enrollment Services, 912-344-2798, Fax: 912-344-3488, E-mail: graduate@armstrong.edu. Website: http://www.armstrong.edu/Education/adolescent_adult_education2/aaed_welcome.

Athabasca University, Centre for Integrated Studies, Athabasca, AB T9S 3A3, Canada. Offers adult education (MA); community studies (MA); cultural studies (MA); educational studies (MA); global change (MA); work, organization, and leadership (MA). Part-time and evening/weekend programs available. Postbaccalaureate distance learning degree programs offered (no on-campus study). *Degree requirements:* For master's, project. *Entrance requirements:* Additional exam requirements/recommendations for international students: Required—TOEFL (minimum score 560 paper-based). Electronic applications accepted. *Faculty research:* Women's history, literature and culture studies, sustainable development, labor and education.

Auburn University, Graduate School, College of Education, Department of Educational Foundations, Leadership, and Technology, Auburn University, AL 36849. Offers adult education (M Ed, MS, Ed D); curriculum and instruction (M Ed, MS, Ed D, Ed S); curriculum supervision (M Ed, MS, Ed D, Ed S); educational psychology (PhD); higher education administration (M Ed, MS, Ed D, Ed S); media instructional design (MS); media specialist (M Ed); school administration (M Ed, MS, Ed D, Ed S). *Accreditation:* NCATE. Part-time programs available. *Faculty:* 25 full-time (15 women), 6 part-time/adjunct (5 women). *Students:* 104 full-time (65 women), 250 part-time (140 women); includes 98 minority (90 Black or African American, non-Hispanic/Latino; 1 American Indian or Alaska Native, non-Hispanic/Latino; 4 Asian, non-Hispanic/Latino; 3 Hispanic/Latino), 14 international. Average age 36. 188 applicants, 66% accepted, 76 enrolled. In 2013, 51 master's, 22 doctorates, 10 other advanced degrees awarded. *Degree requirements:* For master's, thesis (for some programs); for doctorate, thesis/dissertation; for Ed S, field project. *Entrance requirements:* For master's, doctorate, and Ed S, GRE General Test. *Application deadline:* For fall admission, 7/7 for domestic students; for spring admission, 11/24 for domestic students. Applications are processed on a rolling basis. *Application fee:* $50 ($60 for international students). Electronic applications accepted. *Expenses:* Tuition, state resident: full-time $8262; part-time $459 per credit hour. Tuition, nonresident: full-time $24,786; part-time $1377 per credit hour. Tuition and fees vary according to degree level and program. *Financial support:* Teaching assistantships and Federal Work-Study available. Support available to part-time students. Financial award application deadline: 3/15; financial award applicants required to submit FAFSA. *Unit head:* Dr. Sherida Downer, Head, 334-844-4460. *Application contact:* Dr. George Flowers, Dean of the Graduate School, 334-844-4700. Website: http://www.education.auburn.edu/academic_departments/eflt/.

Ball State University, Graduate School, Teachers College, Department of Educational Studies, Program in Adult Education, Muncie, IN 47306-1099. Offers adult and community education (MA); adult, community, and higher education (Ed D). *Accreditation:* NCATE. *Students:* 24 full-time (17 women), 58 part-time (46 women); includes 16 minority (11 Black or African American, non-Hispanic/Latino; 1 American Indian or Alaska Native, non-Hispanic/Latino; 3 Hispanic/Latino; 1 Two or more races, non-Hispanic/Latino), 1 international. Average age 34. 22 applicants, 64% accepted, 7 enrolled. In 2013, 22 master's, 8 doctorates awarded. *Degree requirements:* For doctorate, thesis/dissertation. *Entrance requirements:* For doctorate, GRE General Test, minimum graduate GPA of 3.2. *Application fee:* $50. *Financial support:* In 2013–14, 17 students received support. Career-related internships or fieldwork available. Financial award application deadline: 3/1. *Faculty research:* Community education, executive development for public services, applied gerontology. *Unit head:* Dr. Jayne Beilke, Director of Doctoral Program, 765-285-5460, Fax: 765-285-5489, E-mail: jbeilke@bsu.edu. *Application contact:* Dr. Robert Morris, Associate Provost for Research and Dean of the Graduate School, 765-285-1300, E-mail: rmorris@bsu.edu.

Buffalo State College, State University of New York, The Graduate School, Faculty of Applied Science and Education, Department of Educational Foundations, Program in Adult Education, Buffalo, NY 14222-1095. Offers adult education (MS, Certificate); human resources development (Certificate). Part-time and evening/weekend programs available. Postbaccalaureate distance learning degree programs offered (no on-campus study). *Degree requirements:* For master's, comprehensive exam. *Entrance requirements:* Additional exam requirements/recommendations for international students: Required—TOEFL (minimum score 550 paper-based).

California Baptist University, Program in Education, Riverside, CA 92504-3206. Offers educational leadership for faith-based institutions (MS); educational leadership for public institutions (MS); educational technology (MS); instructional computer applications (MS); international education (MS); leadership and adult learning (MS); leadership and organizational studies (MS); reading (MS); school counseling (MS); school psychology (MS); science education (MS); special education in mild/moderate disabilities (MS); special education in moderate/severe disabilities (MS); teaching (MS); teaching and learning (MS); TESOL (teachers of English to speakers of other languages) (MS). Part-time and evening/weekend programs available. Postbaccalaureate distance learning degree programs offered (minimal on-campus study). *Faculty:* 18 full-time (9 women), 8 part-time/adjunct (5 women). *Students:* 158 full-time (127 women), 228 part-time (179 women); includes 159 minority (27 Black or African American, non-Hispanic/Latino; 4 American Indian or Alaska Native, non-Hispanic/Latino; 13 Asian, non-Hispanic/Latino; 107 Hispanic/Latino; 1 Native Hawaiian or other Pacific Islander, non-Hispanic/Latino; 7 Two or more races, non-Hispanic/Latino), 2 international. Average age 33. 298 applicants, 74% accepted, 113 enrolled. In 2013, 70 master's awarded. *Degree requirements:* For master's, comprehensive exam, project, or thesis. *Entrance requirements:* For master's, minimum undergraduate GPA of 3.0; 18 semester units of prerequisite course work in education; three recommendations; 500-word essay; interview. Additional exam requirements/recommendations for international students: Required—TOEFL (minimum score 80 iBT). *Application deadline:* For fall admission, 8/1 priority date for domestic students, 7/1 for international students; for spring admission, 12/1 priority date for domestic students, 11/1 for international students. Applications are processed on a rolling basis. *Application fee:* $45. Electronic applications accepted. *Expenses:* Contact institution. *Financial support:* Institutionally sponsored loans available. Financial award applicants required to submit CSS PROFILE or FAFSA. *Faculty research:* Leadership development, complexity theory, faith and learning, special education, social and philosophical contexts of education. *Unit head:* Dr. John Shoup, Dean, School of Education, 951-343-4205, Fax: 951-343-4516, E-mail: jshoup@calbaptist.edu. *Application contact:* Dr. Kathryn Norwood, Director, Master of Science Program in Education, 951-343-4760, E-mail: knorwood@calbaptist.edu. Website: http://www.calbaptist.edu/mastersined/.

California Baptist University, Program in Leadership and Adult Learning, Riverside, CA 92504-3206. Offers MA. Part-time and evening/weekend programs available. *Degree requirements:* For master's, professional training or leadership tactics. *Entrance requirements:* For master's, minimum undergraduate GPA of 2.75, bachelor's degree transcripts, three recommendations, essay, resume. Additional exam requirements/recommendations for international students: Required—TOEFL (minimum score 80 iBT). *Application deadline:* For fall admission, 8/1 priority date for domestic students, 7/1 for international students; for spring admission, 12/1 priority date for domestic students, 11/1 for international students. Applications are processed on a rolling basis. Application fee: $45. Electronic applications accepted. *Expenses:* Contact institution. *Financial support:* Applicants required to submit CSS PROFILE or FAFSA. *Unit head:* Dr. John Shoup, Dean, School of Education, 951-343-4205, E-mail: jshoup@calbaptist.edu. *Application contact:* Fax: 877-228-8877. Website: http://www.calbaptist.edu/explore-cbu/schools-colleges/school-education/programs/graduate/master-arts-leadership-and-adult-learning/.

Capella University, School of Education, Doctoral Programs in Education, Minneapolis, MN 55402. Offers curriculum and instruction (PhD); educational leadership and management (Ed D); instructional design for online learning (PhD); K-12 studies in education (PhD); leadership for higher education (PhD); leadership in educational administration (PhD); postsecondary and adult education (PhD); professional studies in education (PhD); reading and literacy (Ed D); special education leadership (PhD); training and performance improvement (PhD).

Capella University, School of Education, Master's Programs in Education, Minneapolis, MN 55402. Offers adult education (MS); curriculum and instruction (MS); early childhood education (MS); enrollment management (MS); higher education leadership and management (MS); instructional design for online learning (MS); integrative studies (MS); K-12 studies in education (MS); leadership in educational administration (MS); reading and literacy (MS); special education teaching (MS).

Cleveland State University, College of Graduate Studies, College of Education and Human Services, Department of Counseling, Administration, Supervision and Adult Learning (CASAL), Cleveland, OH 44115. Offers adult learning and development (M Ed); chemical dependency counseling (Certificate); clinical mental health counseling (M Ed); early childhood mental health counseling (Certificate); educational administration and supervision (M Ed); organizational leadership (M Ed); school administration (Ed S); school counseling (M Ed). *Accreditation:* ACA (one or more programs are accredited). Part-time and evening/weekend programs available. *Faculty:* 15 full-time (8 women), 19 part-time/adjunct (10 women). *Students:* 79 full-time (61 women), 237 part-time (188 women); includes 101 minority (86 Black or African American, non-Hispanic/Latino; 3 Asian, non-Hispanic/Latino; 11 Hispanic/Latino; 1 Two or more races, non-Hispanic/Latino), 8 international. Average age 36. 131 applicants, 69% accepted, 49 enrolled. In 2013, 99 master's, 7 Certificates awarded. *Degree requirements:* For master's, comprehensive exam (for some programs), thesis optional, internship. *Entrance requirements:* For master's, GRE General Test or MAT, letter of recommendation and minimum GPA of 2.75 (for counseling); 2 letters of recommendation and interviews (for organizational leadership). Additional exam requirements/recommendations for international students: Required—TOEFL (minimum score 525 paper-based), IELTS (minimum score 6). *Application deadline:* For fall admission, 6/21 for domestic students, 5/15 for international students; for spring admission, 8/31 for domestic students, 11/1 for international students. Application fee: $30. Electronic applications accepted. *Expenses:* Tuition, state resident: full-time $8335; part-time $521 per credit hour. Tuition, nonresident: full-time $15,670; part-time $979 per credit hour. *Required fees:* $50; $25 per semester. *Financial support:* In 2013–14, 19 students received support, including 10 research assistantships with full and partial tuition reimbursements available (averaging $11,882 per year), 5 teaching assistantships with full and partial tuition reimbursements available (averaging $11,882 per year); scholarships/grants and unspecified assistantships also available. Support available to part-time students. *Faculty research:* Education law, career development, bullying, psychopharmacology, counseling and spirituality. *Total annual research expenditures:* $225,821. *Unit head:* Dr. Ann L. Bauer, Chairperson, 216-687-4582, Fax: 216-687-5378, E-mail: a.l.bauer@csuohio.edu. *Application contact:* Deborah L. Brown, Interim Assistant Director, Graduate Admissions, 216-523-7572, Fax: 216-687-5400, E-mail: d.l.brown@csuohio.edu.
Website: http://www.csuohio.edu/cehs/departments/CASAL/casal_dept.html.

Cleveland State University, College of Graduate Studies, College of Education and Human Services, Program in Urban Education, Specialization in Adult, Continuing, and Higher Education, Cleveland, OH 44115. Offers PhD. Part-time programs available. *Faculty:* 4 full-time (3 women). *Students:* 2 full-time (both women), 10 part-time (6 women); includes 4 minority (all Black or African American, non-Hispanic/Latino). Average age 46. *Degree requirements:* For doctorate, one foreign language, comprehensive exam, thesis/dissertation. *Entrance requirements:* For doctorate, General GRE Test (minimum score of 297 for combined Verbal and Quantitative exams, 4.0 preferred for Analytical Writing), minimum graduate GPA of 3.25, curriculum vitae or resume, personal statement, 2 letters of recommendation. Additional exam requirements/recommendations for international students: Required—TOEFL (minimum score 525 paper-based), IELTS (minimum score 6). *Expenses:* Tuition, state resident: full-time $8335; part-time $521 per credit hour. Tuition, nonresident: full-time $15,670; part-time $979 per credit hour. *Required fees:* $50; $25 per semester. *Financial support:* In 2013–14, 2 students received support, including 1 research assistantship with full tuition reimbursement available, 1 teaching assistantship with full tuition reimbursement available (averaging $11,800 per year); tuition waivers (full) also available. Support available to part-time students. Financial award application deadline: 4/1; financial award applicants required to submit FAFSA. *Faculty research:* Adult education research, practice in diverse contexts. *Unit head:* Dr. Graham Stead, Director, Doctoral Studies, 216-875-9869, E-mail: g.b.stead@csuohio.edu. *Application contact:* Rita M. Grabowski, Administrative Coordinator, 216-687-4697, Fax: 216-875-9697, E-mail: r.grabowski@csuohio.edu.
Website: http://www.csuohio.edu/cehs/departments/DOC/lll_doc.html.

Colorado State University, Graduate School, College of Health and Human Sciences, School of Education, Fort Collins, CO 80523-1588. Offers adult education and training (M Ed); community college leadership (PhD); counseling and career development (M Ed); education and human resource studies (M Ed, PhD); educational leadership (M Ed, PhD); interdisciplinary studies (PhD); organizational performance and change (M Ed, PhD); student affairs in higher education (MS). *Accreditation:* ACA; Teacher Education Accreditation Council. Part-time and evening/weekend programs available. *Faculty:* 19 full-time (10 women). *Students:* 84 full-time (60 women), 545 part-time (356 women); includes 115 minority (26 Black or African American, non-Hispanic/Latino; 5 American Indian or Alaska Native, non-Hispanic/Latino; 13 Asian, non-Hispanic/Latino; 56 Hispanic/Latino; 15 Two or more races, non-Hispanic/Latino), 22 international. Average age 37. 475 applicants, 38% accepted, 147 enrolled. In 2013, 1,157 master's, 43 doctorates awarded. *Degree requirements:* For master's, comprehensive exam, thesis optional; for doctorate, comprehensive exam, thesis/dissertation, minimum of 60 credits. *Entrance requirements:* For master's and doctorate, GRE, minimum GPA of 3.0. Additional exam requirements/recommendations for international students: Required—TOEFL (minimum score 550 paper-based; 80 iBT), IELTS. *Application deadline:* For fall admission, 3/1 priority date for domestic and international students; for spring admission, 9/1 for domestic and international students. Applications are processed on a rolling basis. Application fee: $50. Electronic applications accepted. *Expenses:* Tuition, state resident: full-time $9075.40; part-time $504 per credit. Tuition, nonresident: full-time $22,248; part-time $1236 per credit. *Required fees:* $1819; $60 per credit. *Financial support:* In 2013–14, 7 students received support, including 1 research assistantship with partial tuition reimbursement available (averaging $16,135 per year), 6 teaching assistantships with partial tuition reimbursements available (averaging $10,106 per year); career-related internships or fieldwork, scholarships/grants, and unspecified assistantships also available. Financial award application deadline: 3/1; financial award applicants required to submit FAFSA. *Faculty research:* Issues in STEM education, diversity and multiculturalism, teacher education leadership, distance learning and teaching. *Total annual research expenditures:* $498,539. *Unit head:* Dr. Daniel H. Robinson, Director, 970-491-6316, Fax: 970-491-1317, E-mail: dan.robinson@colostate.edu. *Application contact:* Kelli M. Clark, Academic Coordinator, 970-491-2093, Fax: 970-491-1317, E-mail: kelli.clark@colostate.edu.
Website: http://www.soe.chhs.colostate.edu/.

Concordia University, School of Graduate Studies, Faculty of Arts and Science, Department of Education, Program in Adult Education, Montréal, QC H3G 1M8, Canada. Offers Diploma. *Degree requirements:* For Diploma, internship. *Entrance requirements:* For degree, interview. *Faculty research:* Staff development, human relations training, adult learning, professional development, learning in the workplace.

Concordia University, School of Graduate Studies, Faculty of Arts and Science, Department of Education, Program in Educational Studies, Montréal, QC H3G 1M8, Canada. Offers MA. *Degree requirements:* For master's, one foreign language, thesis optional. *Faculty research:* Social aspects of microtechnology, gender and education, minorities and immigrants in Canadian education, professional development, political education.

Coppin State University, Division of Graduate Studies, Division of Education, Department of Adult and General Education, Baltimore, MD 21216-3698. Offers MS. Part-time and evening/weekend programs available. *Degree requirements:* For master's, thesis optional, research paper, internship. *Entrance requirements:* For master's, GRE or PRAXIS, minimum GPA of 2.5, interview, resume, references.

Cornell University, Graduate School, Graduate Fields of Agriculture and Life Sciences, Field of Education, Ithaca, NY 14853-0001. Offers adult and extension education (MPS, MS, PhD); learning, teaching, and social policy (MPS, MS, PhD); mathematics 7-12 (MS). *Faculty:* 21 full-time (8 women). *Students:* 14 full-time (9 women); includes 2 minority (1 Asian, non-Hispanic/Latino; 1 Hispanic/Latino), 1 international. Average age 32. 20 applicants, 20% accepted, 2 enrolled. In 2013, 17 master's, 4 doctorates awarded. Terminal master's awarded for partial completion of doctoral program. *Degree requirements:* For master's, thesis (MS); for doctorate, comprehensive exam, thesis/dissertation. *Entrance requirements:* For master's and doctorate, GRE General Test, sample of written work (recommended), 2 letters of recommendation. Additional exam requirements/recommendations for international students: Required—TOEFL (minimum score 550 paper-based; 77 iBT). *Application deadline:* For fall admission, 2/15 for domestic students. Application fee: $95. Electronic applications accepted. *Financial support:* In 2013–14, 4 students received support, including 3 fellowships with full tuition reimbursements available, 1 research assistantship with full tuition reimbursement available; teaching assistantships with full tuition reimbursements available, institutionally sponsored loans, scholarships/grants, health care benefits, tuition waivers (full and partial), and unspecified assistantships also available. Financial award applicants required to submit FAFSA. *Faculty research:* Moral development and professional ethics, public issues education and community development, socio/political issues in public education, teacher education and curriculum in agricultural science and mathematics, extension research. *Unit head:* Director of Graduate Studies, 607-255-4278, Fax: 607-255-7905. *Application contact:* Graduate Field Assistant, 607-255-4278, Fax: 607-255-7905, E-mail: rh22@cornell.edu.
Website: http://www.gradschool.cornell.edu/fields.php?id-80&a-2.

Dallas Theological Seminary, Graduate Programs, Dallas, TX 75204-6499. Offers adult education (Th M); apologetics (Th M); Bible backgrounds (Th M); Bible translation (Th M); Biblical and theological studies (Certificate); biblical counseling (MA); biblical exegesis and linguistics (MA); biblical exposition (PhD); biblical studies (MA); Biblical theology (Th M); children's education (Th M); Christian education (MA, D Min); Christian leadership (MA); cross-cultural ministries (MA); educational administration (Th M); educational leadership (Th M); evangelism and discipleship (Th M); exposition of Biblical books (Th M); family life education (Th M); general studies (Th M); Hebrew and cognate studies (Th M); hermeneutics (Th M); historical theology (Th M); homiletics (Th M); intercultural ministries (Th M); Jesus studies (Th M); leadership studies (Th M); media and communication (MA); media arts (Th M); ministry (D Min); ministry with women (Th M); New Testament studies (Th M, PhD); Old Testament studies (Th M, PhD); parachurch ministries (Th M); pastoral care and counseling (Th M); pastoral theology and practice (Th M); philosophy (Th M); sacred theology (STM); spiritual formation (Th M); systematic theology (Th M); teaching in Christian institutions (Th M); theological studies (PhD); urban ministries (Th M); worship studies (Th M); youth education (Th M). *Accreditation:* ATS (one or more programs are accredited). Part-time programs available. Postbaccalaureate distance learning degree programs offered (no on-campus study). *Faculty:* 66 full-time (4 women), 35 part-time/adjunct (8 women). *Students:* 901 full-time (252 women), 1,210 part-time (432 women); includes 552 minority (232 Black or African American, non-Hispanic/Latino; 5 American Indian or Alaska Native, non-Hispanic/Latino; 172 Asian, non-Hispanic/Latino; 104 Hispanic/Latino; 4 Native Hawaiian or other Pacific Islander, non-Hispanic/Latino; 35 Two or more races, non-Hispanic/Latino), 258 international. Average age 36. 978 applicants, 89% accepted, 607 enrolled. In 2013, 358 master's, 27 doctorates, 34 other advanced degrees awarded. *Degree requirements:* For master's, variable foreign language requirement, thesis (for some programs); for doctorate, 2 foreign languages, thesis/dissertation. *Entrance requirements:* For master's, GRE or MAT (if minimum undergraduate cumulative GPA is below 2.5 or undergraduate degree is unaccredited). Additional exam requirements/recommendations for international students: Required—TOEFL (minimum score 575 paper-based; 85 iBT), TWE. *Application deadline:* For fall admission, 7/1 for domestic students, 1/1 for international students; for winter admission, 11/1 for domestic students; for spring admission, 11/1 for domestic students. Applications are processed on a rolling basis. Application fee: $50. Electronic applications accepted. *Financial support:* In 2013–14, 1,042 students received support. Career-related internships or fieldwork, scholarships/grants, and tuition waivers (full and partial) available. Financial award application deadline: 2/28. *Unit head:* Dr. Mark L. Bailey, President, 214-887-5004, Fax: 214-887-5532. *Application contact:* Greg Hatteberg, Director of Admissions and Student Advising, 214-887-5040, Fax: 214-841-3664, E-mail: admissions@dts.edu.

Defiance College, Program in Education, Defiance, OH 43512-1610. Offers adolescent and young adult licensure (MA); mild and moderate intervention specialist (MA). Part-time programs available. *Degree requirements:* For master's, thesis (for some programs). *Entrance requirements:* For master's, teaching certificate.

Delaware State University, Graduate Programs, College of Education, Health and Public Policy, Program in Adult Literacy and Basic Education, Dover, DE 19901-2277. Offers MA. *Entrance requirements:* Additional exam requirements/recommendations for international students: Required—TOEFL (minimum score 550 paper-based). Electronic applications accepted.

DePaul University, College of Education, Chicago, IL 60614. Offers bilingual bicultural education (M Ed, MA); counseling (M Ed, MA), including clinical mental health counseling, college student development, school counseling; curriculum studies (M Ed, MA, Ed D); early childhood education (M Ed, MA, Ed D); educating adults (MA); educational leadership (M Ed, MA, Ed D), including administration and supervision (M Ed, MA), principal preparation (M Ed, MA); elementary education (MA); mathematics education (MA); mathematics for teaching (MS); middle school mathematics education (MS); reading specialist (M Ed, MA); secondary education (M Ed); social and cultural foundations in education (MA); special education (M Ed, MA); world languages education (M Ed, MA). Part-time and evening/weekend programs available.

Adult Education

Postbaccalaureate distance learning degree programs offered (no on-campus study). *Faculty:* 61 full-time (35 women), 59 part-time/adjunct (43 women). *Students:* 628 full-time (486 women), 324 part-time (243 women); includes 304 minority (144 Black or African American, non-Hispanic/Latino; 1 American Indian or Alaska Native, non-Hispanic/Latino; 38 Asian, non-Hispanic/Latino; 98 Hispanic/Latino; 23 Two or more races, non-Hispanic/Latino), 24 international. Average age 30. In 2013, 465 master's, 4 doctorates awarded. *Degree requirements:* For doctorate, thesis/dissertation. *Application deadline:* For fall admission, 8/15 for domestic students; for winter admission, 12/1 for domestic students; for spring admission, 3/1 for domestic students. Applications are processed on a rolling basis. Application fee: $40. Electronic applications accepted. Tuition and fees vary according to course level, course load and degree level. *Financial support:* Application deadline: 12/31; applicants required to submit FAFSA. *Unit head:* Dr. Paul Zionts, Dean, 773-325-7581, Fax: 773-325-7713, E-mail: pzionts@depaul.edu. *Application contact:* Farrah Dalal, Assistant Director, 773-325-2465, Fax: 773-325-2270, E-mail: fdalal@depaul.edu.
Website: http://education.depaul.edu.

DePaul University, School for New Learning, Chicago, IL 60604. Offers applied professional studies (MA); applied technology (MS); educating adults (MA). Part-time and evening/weekend programs available. *Faculty:* 16 full-time (12 women), 6 part-time/adjunct (5 women). *Students:* 24 full-time (18 women), 122 part-time (95 women); includes 93 minority (70 Black or African American, non-Hispanic/Latino; 5 Asian, non-Hispanic/Latino; 13 Hispanic/Latino; 5 Two or more races, non-Hispanic/Latino). Average age 45. In 2013, 38 master's awarded. *Degree requirements:* For master's, thesis or alternative. *Application deadline:* For fall admission, 9/1 for domestic students; for spring admission, 3/1 for domestic students. Applications are processed on a rolling basis. Electronic applications accepted. Tuition and fees vary according to course level, course load and degree level. *Financial support:* Applicants required to submit FAFSA. *Unit head:* Dr. Russ Rogers, Program Director, 312-362-8512, Fax: 312-362-8809, E-mail: rrogers@depaul.edu. *Application contact:* Sarah Hellstrom, Assistant Director, 312-362-5744, Fax: 312-362-8809, E-mail: shellstr@depaul.edu.
Website: http://snl.depaul.edu/.

East Carolina University, Graduate School, College of Education, Department of Higher, Adult, and Counselor Education, Greenville, NC 27858-4353. Offers adult education (MA Ed); counselor education (MS); higher education administration (Ed D). *Accreditation:* NCATE. Part-time and evening/weekend programs available. *Degree requirements:* For master's, comprehensive exam, thesis optional. *Entrance requirements:* For master's, GRE General Test or MAT, interview, minimum GPA of 2.5, bachelor's degree in related field, teaching license (MA Ed). Additional exam requirements/recommendations for international students: Required—TOEFL. *Expenses:* Tuition, state resident: full-time $4223. Tuition, nonresident: full-time $16,540. *Required fees:* $2184.

Eastern Washington University, Graduate Studies, College of Arts, Letters and Education, Department of Education, Program in Adult Education, Cheney, WA 99004-2431. Offers M Ed. *Students:* 10 full-time (5 women), 14 part-time (7 women); includes 5 minority (1 Black or African American, non-Hispanic/Latino; 2 Asian, non-Hispanic/Latino; 2 Hispanic/Latino). Average age 41. 6 applicants, 50% accepted, 3 enrolled. In 2013, 3 master's awarded. *Degree requirements:* For master's, comprehensive exam, thesis or alternative. *Entrance requirements:* For master's, minimum GPA of 3.0. *Application deadline:* For fall admission, 4/1 priority date for domestic students; for spring admission, 1/15 for domestic students. Applications are processed on a rolling basis. Application fee: $35. *Financial support:* In 2013–14, teaching assistantships with partial tuition reimbursements (averaging $7,000 per year) were awarded; career-related internships or fieldwork, Federal Work-Study, institutionally sponsored loans, scholarships/grants, health care benefits, tuition waivers (partial), and unspecified assistantships also available. Support available to part-time students. Financial award application deadline: 2/1; financial award applicants required to submit FAFSA. *Unit head:* Robin Showalter, Program Coordinator, 509-359-6492, E-mail: rshowalter@mail.ewu.edu. *Application contact:* Dr. Kevin Pyatt, Graduate Program Coordinator, 509-359-6091, Fax: 509-359-4822.

Edgewood College, Program in Education, Madison, WI 53711-1997. Offers adult learning (MA Ed); bilingual teaching and learning (MA Ed); director of instruction (Certificate); director of special education and pupil services (Certificate); education (MA Ed); educational administration (MA Ed); educational leadership (Ed D); professional studies (MA Ed); program coordinator (Certificate); reading administration (MA Ed); school business administration (Certificate); school principalship K-12 (Certificate); special education (MA Ed); sustainability leadership (MA Ed); teaching and learning (MA Ed); teaching English to speakers of other languages (TESOL) (MA Ed). *Accreditation:* NCATE (one or more programs are accredited). Part-time and evening/weekend programs available. *Students:* 159 full-time (95 women), 164 part-time (121 women); includes 61 minority (19 Black or African American, non-Hispanic/Latino; 9 Asian, non-Hispanic/Latino; 25 Hispanic/Latino; 8 Two or more races, non-Hispanic/Latino), 27 international. Average age 36. In 2013, 51 master's, 22 doctorates awarded. *Degree requirements:* For master's, practicum, research project; for doctorate, comprehensive exam, thesis/dissertation. *Entrance requirements:* For master's, minimum GPA of 2.75, 2 letters of recommendation, personal statement; for doctorate, resume, letter of intent, 2 letters of recommendation, interview, writing sample. Additional exam requirements/recommendations for international students: Required—TOEFL (minimum score 525 paper-based; 72 iBT). *Application deadline:* For fall admission, 8/15 for domestic students, 5/1 for international students; for spring admission, 1/8 for domestic students, 11/1 for international students. Applications are processed on a rolling basis. Application fee: $30. Electronic applications accepted. *Unit head:* Dr. Timothy Slekar, Dean, E-mail: tslekar@edgewood.edu. *Application contact:* Joann Eastman, Admissions Counselor, 608-663-3250, Fax: 608-663-2214, E-mail: gps@edgewood.edu.
Website: http://www.edgewood.edu/Academics/School-of-Education.

Florida Agricultural and Mechanical University, Division of Graduate Studies, Research, and Continuing Education, College of Education, Department of Educational Leadership and Human Services, Tallahassee, FL 32307-3200. Offers administration and supervision (M Ed, MS Ed, PhD); adult education (M Ed, MS Ed); educational leadership (PhD); guidance and counseling (M Ed, MS Ed). *Accreditation:* NCATE. *Degree requirements:* For master's, thesis (for some programs); for doctorate, thesis/dissertation. *Entrance requirements:* For master's, GRE General Test, minimum GPA of 3.0. Additional exam requirements/recommendations for international students: Required—TOEFL.

Florida Atlantic University, College of Education, Department of Educational Leadership and Research Methodology, Boca Raton, FL 33431-0991. Offers adult and community education (M Ed, PhD, Ed S); educational leadership (M Ed, PhD, Ed S); higher education (M Ed, PhD); K-12 school leadership (M Ed, PhD, Ed S). *Accreditation:* NCATE. Part-time and evening/weekend programs available. Postbaccalaureate distance learning degree programs offered (minimal on-campus study). *Faculty:* 19 full-time (9 women), 16 part-time/adjunct (7 women). *Students:* 97 full-time (72 women), 227 part-time (150 women); includes 140 minority (83 Black or African American, non-Hispanic/Latino; 8 Asian, non-Hispanic/Latino; 41 Hispanic/Latino; 8 Two or more races,

non-Hispanic/Latino), 2 international. Average age 37. 180 applicants, 50% accepted, 74 enrolled. In 2013, 80 master's, 11 doctorates, 19 other advanced degrees awarded. *Degree requirements:* For doctorate, comprehensive exam, thesis/dissertation, departmental qualifying exam; for Ed S, departmental qualifying exam. *Entrance requirements:* For master's, GRE General Test, minimum GPA of 3.0 during previous 2 years; for doctorate, GRE General Test, minimum GPA of 3.5; for Ed S, GRE General Test. Additional exam requirements/recommendations for international students: Required—TOEFL (minimum score 500 paper-based; 61 iBT), IELTS (minimum score 6). *Application deadline:* For fall admission, 7/1 for domestic students, 2/15 for international students; for spring admission, 9/15 for domestic students, 7/15 for international students. Applications are processed on a rolling basis. Application fee: $30. Electronic applications accepted. *Expenses:* Tuition, state resident: full-time $6660; part-time $370 per credit hour. Tuition, nonresident: full-time $18,450; part-time $1025 per credit hour. Tuition and fees vary according to course load. *Financial support:* Fellowships, research assistantships, teaching assistantships, career-related internships or fieldwork, and tuition waivers (partial) available. *Faculty research:* Self-directed learning, school reform issues, legal issues, mentoring, school leadership. *Unit head:* Dr. Robert E. Shockley, Chair, 561-297-3550, Fax: 561-297-3618, E-mail: shockley@fau.edu. *Application contact:* Kathy DuBois, Senior Secretary, 561-297-3550, Fax: 561-297-3618, E-mail: edleadership@fau.edu.
Website: http://www.coe.fau.edu/academicdepartments/el/.

Florida International University, College of Education, Department of Leadership and Professional Studies, Miami, FL 33199. Offers adult education and human resource development (MS, Ed D); counseling (MS), including rehabilitation counseling, school counseling; counselor education (MS), including clinical mental health counseling; educational administration and supervision (Ed D); educational leadership (MS, Certificate, Ed S); higher education (Ed D); higher education administration (MS); recreation and sport management (MS), including recreation and sport management, recreational therapy; school psychology (Ed S); urban education (MS), including instruction in urban settings, learning technologies, multicultural/bilingual, multicultural/TESOL, urban education. Part-time and evening/weekend programs available. *Degree requirements:* For doctorate, thesis/dissertation. *Entrance requirements:* For master's, minimum GPA of 3.0; for doctorate and other advanced degree, GRE General Test. Additional exam requirements/recommendations for international students: Required—TOEFL (minimum score 550 paper-based; 80 iBT), IELTS (minimum score 6.3). Electronic applications accepted.

Fordham University, Graduate School of Education, Division of Curriculum and Teaching, New York, NY 10023. Offers adult education (MS, MSE); bilingual teacher education (MSE); curriculum and teaching (MSE); early childhood education (MSE); elementary education (MST); language, literacy, and learning (PhD); reading education (MSE, Adv C); secondary education (MAT, MSE); special education (MSE, Adv C); teaching English as a second language (MSE). *Accreditation:* NCATE. *Degree requirements:* For doctorate, thesis/dissertation; for Adv C, thesis. *Entrance requirements:* For doctorate, MAT, GRE General Test.

The George Washington University, Graduate School of Education and Human Development, Department of Human and Organizational Learning, Program in Design and Assessment of Adult Learning, Washington, DC 20052. Offers Graduate Certificate. *Students:* 1 part-time (0 women). Average age 36. 1 applicant, 100% accepted, 1 enrolled. *Entrance requirements:* For degree, two letters of recommendation, resume, statement of purpose. Electronic applications accepted. *Unit head:* Dr. Mary Hatwood Futrell, Dean, 202-994-6161, Fax: 202-994-7207, E-mail: mfutrell@gwu.edu. *Application contact:* Sarah Lang, Director of Graduate Admissions, 202-994-1447, Fax: 202-994-7207, E-mail: slang@gwu.edu.
Website: http://gsehd.gwu.edu/design-and-assessment-adult-learning-certificate.

Grand Valley State University, College of Education, Programs in General Education, Allendale, MI 49401-9403. Offers adult and higher education (M Ed); early childhood education (M Ed); educational differentiation (M Ed); educational leadership (M Ed); educational technology integration (M Ed); elementary education (M Ed); middle level education (M Ed); school library media services (M Ed); secondary level education (M Ed); teaching English to speakers of other languages (M Ed). Part-time and evening/weekend programs available. Postbaccalaureate distance learning degree programs offered (minimal on-campus study). *Degree requirements:* For master's, thesis. *Entrance requirements:* For master's, GRE General Test or minimum GPA of 3.0. Additional exam requirements/recommendations for international students: Required—TOEFL. Electronic applications accepted. *Faculty research:* Effectiveness of technology in education, parental involvement, effective teaching, effective schools research.

Indiana University of Pennsylvania, School of Graduate Studies and Research, College of Education and Educational Technology, Department of Adult and Community Education, Program in Adult and Community Education, Indiana, PA 15705-1087. Offers MA. Part-time programs available. Postbaccalaureate distance learning degree programs offered (no on-campus study). *Faculty:* 2 full-time (0 women). *Students:* 6 full-time (4 women), 21 part-time (18 women); includes 4 minority (all Black or African American, non-Hispanic/Latino), 1 international. Average age 38. 22 applicants, 64% accepted, 10 enrolled. In 2013, 6 master's awarded. *Degree requirements:* For master's, thesis optional. *Entrance requirements:* For master's, goal statement, letters of recommendation, official transcripts. Additional exam requirements/recommendations for international students: Required—TOEFL (minimum score 540 paper-based; 76 iBT). *Application deadline:* Applications are processed on a rolling basis. Application fee: $50. Electronic applications accepted. *Expenses:* Tuition, state resident: full-time $3978; part-time $442 per credit. Tuition, nonresident: full-time $5967; part-time $663 per credit. *Required fees:* $2080; $115.55 per credit. $93 per semester. Tuition and fees vary according to degree level and program. *Financial support:* In 2013–14, 3 research assistantships with full and partial tuition reimbursements (averaging $2,480 per year) were awarded; career-related internships or fieldwork, Federal Work-Study, scholarships/grants, and unspecified assistantships also available. Support available to part-time students. Financial award application deadline: 4/15; financial award applicants required to submit FAFSA. *Unit head:* Dr. Gary Dean, Chairperson, 724-357-2470, E-mail: gjdean@iup.edu.
Website: http://www.iup.edu/grad/ace/default.aspx.

Indiana University of Pennsylvania, School of Graduate Studies and Research, College of Education and Educational Technology, Department of Adult and Community Education, Program in Adult and Community Education/Communications Technology, Indiana, PA 15705-1087. Offers MA. Part-time and evening/weekend programs available. *Faculty:* 2 full-time (0 women). *Students:* 18 full-time (9 women), 6 part-time (5 women); includes 2 minority (1 Black or African American, non-Hispanic/Latino; 1 Hispanic/Latino), 7 international. Average age 30. 28 applicants, 75% accepted, 18 enrolled. In 2013, 19 master's awarded. *Degree requirements:* For master's, thesis optional. *Entrance requirements:* For master's, 2 letters of recommendation, resume. Additional exam requirements/recommendations for international students: Required—TOEFL (minimum score 540 paper-based; 76 iBT). *Application deadline:* Applications are processed on a rolling basis. Application fee: $50. Electronic applications accepted. *Expenses:* Tuition, state resident: full-time $3978; part-time $442 per credit. Tuition, nonresident: full-time $5967; part-time $663 per credit. *Required fees:* $2080; $115.55

per credit. $93 per semester. Tuition and fees vary according to degree level and program. *Financial support:* In 2013–14, 9 research assistantships with full and partial tuition reimbursements (averaging $5,138 per year) were awarded; fellowships, teaching assistantships, career-related internships or fieldwork, Federal Work-Study, scholarships/grants, and unspecified assistantships also available. Support available to part-time students. Financial award application deadline: 4/15; financial award applicants required to submit FAFSA. *Unit head:* Dr. Jeff Ritchey, Graduate Coordinator, 724-357-2470, E-mail: jeffrey.ritchey@iup.edu.
Website: http://www.iup.edu/aect.

Indiana University of Pennsylvania, School of Graduate Studies and Research, College of Education and Educational Technology, Department of Communications Media, Indiana, PA 15705-1087. Offers adult education and communications technology (MA); communications media and instructional technology (PhD). Part-time and evening/weekend programs available. *Faculty:* 9 full-time (4 women). *Students:* 17 full-time (8 women), 43 part-time (19 women); includes 8 minority (3 Black or African American, non-Hispanic/Latino; 2 Asian, non-Hispanic/Latino; 3 Two or more races, non-Hispanic/Latino), 4 international. Average age 37. 47 applicants, 30% accepted, 11 enrolled. In 2013, 5 doctorates awarded. Terminal master's awarded for partial completion of doctoral program. *Degree requirements:* For doctorate, comprehensive exam, thesis/dissertation. *Entrance requirements:* For doctorate, GRE, goal statement, resume, writing sample, two letters of recommendation. Additional exam requirements/recommendations for international students: Required—TOEFL (minimum score 540 paper-based). *Application deadline:* Applications are processed on a rolling basis. Application fee: $50. Electronic applications accepted. *Expenses:* Tuition, state resident: full-time $3978; part-time $442 per credit. Tuition, nonresident: full-time $5967; part-time $663 per credit. *Required fees:* $2080; $115.55 per credit. $93 per semester. Tuition and fees vary according to degree level and program. *Financial support:* In 2013–14, 4 fellowships with full tuition reimbursements (averaging $2,282 per year), 12 research assistantships with full and partial tuition reimbursements (averaging $5,579 per year), 3 teaching assistantships with partial tuition reimbursements (averaging $22,848 per year) were awarded; career-related internships or fieldwork, Federal Work-Study, scholarships/grants, tuition waivers (full), and unspecified assistantships also available. Support available to part-time students. Financial award application deadline: 4/15; financial award applicants required to submit FAFSA. *Unit head:* Dr. Mark Piwinsky, Chairperson, 724-357-3954, Fax: 724-357-5503, E-mail: mark.piwinsky@iup.edu. *Application contact:* Dr. Gail Wilson, Graduate Coordinator, 724-357-3210, E-mail: b.g.wilson@iup.edu.
Website: http://www.iup.edu/commmedia/.

Instituto Tecnologico de Santo Domingo, Graduate School, Area of Humanities and Social Sciences, Santo Domingo, Dominican Republic. Offers accounting (Certificate); adult education (Certificate); applied linguistics (MA); economics (MA); education (M Ed); educational psychology (MA, Certificate); gender and development (MA, Certificate); humanistic studies (MA); international marketing management (Certificate); international relations in the Caribbean basin (Certificate); intervention systems in family therapy (MA); linguistic and literary communication (Certificate); pedagogical support (MA); social science education (M Ed); sustainable human development (MA); terminal illness and death psychology (Certificate); youth and adult education (M Ed).

Jones International University, School of Education, Centennial, CO 80112. Offers adult education (M Ed); corporate training and knowledge management (M Ed); curriculum and instruction (M Ed), including elementary teacher licensure, secondary teacher licensure; e-learning technology and design (M Ed); educational leadership and administration (M Ed); educational leadership and administration: principal and administrator licensure (M Ed); elementary curriculum instruction and assessment (M Ed); higher education leadership and administration (M Ed); K-12 instructional technology (M Ed); K-12 instructional technology: teacher licensure (M Ed); secondary curriculum instruction and assessment (M Ed); technology and design (M Ed). Part-time and evening/weekend programs available. Postbaccalaureate distance learning degree programs offered (no on-campus study). *Entrance requirements:* For master's, minimum cumulative GPA of 2.5. Additional exam requirements/recommendations for international students: Recommended—TOEFL (minimum score 550 paper-based). Electronic applications accepted.

Kansas State University, Graduate School, College of Education, Department of Educational Leadership, Manhattan, KS 66506. Offers adult, occupational and continuing education (MS, Ed D, PhD); educational leadership (MS, Ed D). *Accreditation:* NCATE. *Faculty:* 11 full-time (6 women), 3 part-time/adjunct (2 women). *Students:* 46 full-time (13 women), 206 part-time (106 women); includes 33 minority (14 Black or African American, non-Hispanic/Latino; 2 Asian, non-Hispanic/Latino; 12 Hispanic/Latino; 5 Two or more races, non-Hispanic/Latino), 4 international. Average age 39. 76 applicants, 72% accepted, 48 enrolled. In 2013, 94 master's, 7 doctorates awarded. *Degree requirements:* For master's, comprehensive exam; for doctorate, comprehensive exam, thesis/dissertation. *Entrance requirements:* For master's, minimum undergraduate GPA of 3.0; for doctorate, GRE General Test, minimum GPA of 3.0 in last 60 hours. Additional exam requirements/recommendations for international students: Required—TOEFL. *Application deadline:* For fall admission, 2/1 priority date for domestic and international students; for spring admission, 8/1 priority date for domestic and international students. Applications are processed on a rolling basis. Application fee: $50 ($75 for international students). Electronic applications accepted. *Financial support:* Career-related internships or fieldwork, institutionally sponsored loans, and scholarships/grants available. Support available to part-time students. Financial award application deadline: 3/1; financial award applicants required to submit FAFSA. *Faculty research:* Educational law, school finance, school facilities, organizational leadership, adult learning, distance learning/education. *Total annual research expenditures:* $7,569. *Unit head:* David C. Thompson, Head, 785-532-5535, Fax: 785-532-7304, E-mail: thomsond@ksu.edu. *Application contact:* Dona Deam, Applications Contact, 785-532-5595, Fax: 785-532-7304, E-mail: ddeam@ksu.edu.
Website: http://www.coe.k-state.edu/departments/edlea/index.html.

Lesley University, School of Education, Cambridge, MA 02138-2790. Offers arts, community, and education (M Ed); autism studies (Certificate); curriculum and instruction (M Ed, CAGS); early childhood education (M Ed); ecological teaching and learning (MS); educational studies (PhD), including adult learning, educational leadership, individually designed; elementary education (M Ed); emergent technologies for educators (Certificate); ESLArts: language learning through the arts (M Ed); high school education (M Ed); individually designed (M Ed); integrated teaching through the arts (M Ed); literacy for K-8 classroom teachers (M Ed); mathematics education (M Ed); middle school education (M Ed); moderate disabilities (M Ed); online learning (Certificate); reading (CAGS); science in education (M Ed); severe disabilities (M Ed); special needs (CAGS); specialist teacher of reading (M Ed); teacher of visual art (M Ed); technology in education (M Ed, CAGS). *Accreditation:* Teacher Education Accreditation Council. Part-time and evening/weekend programs available. Postbaccalaureate distance learning degree programs offered (no on-campus study). *Faculty:* 40 full-time (30 women), 104 part-time/adjunct (77 women). *Students:* 453 full-time (381 women), 1,672 part-time (1,435 women); includes 284 minority (139 Black or African American, non-Hispanic/Latino; 11 American Indian or Alaska Native, non-Hispanic/Latino; 38 Asian, non-Hispanic/Latino; 58 Hispanic/Latino; 5 Native Hawaiian or other Pacific Islander, non-Hispanic/Latino; 33 Two or more races, non-Hispanic/Latino), 22 international. Average age 35. In 2013, 1,137 master's, 18 doctorates, 51 other advanced degrees awarded. *Degree requirements:* For master's, practicum; for doctorate, thesis/dissertation. *Entrance requirements:* For master's, Massachusetts Tests for Educator Licensure (MTEL), transcripts, statement of purpose, recommendations; interview (for special education); for doctorate, GRE General Test, transcripts, statement of purpose, recommendations, interview, master's degree, resume; for other advanced degree, interview, master's degree. Additional exam requirements/recommendations for international students: Required—TOEFL (minimum score 550 paper-based; 80 iBT). *Application deadline:* Applications are processed on a rolling basis. Application fee: $50. Electronic applications accepted. *Expenses: Tuition:* Part-time $900 per credit. *Financial support:* In 2013–14, 15 fellowships (averaging $3,600 per year) were awarded; career-related internships or fieldwork, Federal Work-Study, scholarships/grants, tuition waivers, and unspecified assistantships also available. Financial award application deadline: 4/15; financial award applicants required to submit FAFSA. *Faculty research:* Assessment in literacy, mathematics and science; autism spectrum disorders; instructional technology and online learning; multicultural education and English language learners. *Unit head:* Dr. Jack Gillette, Dean, 617-349-8401, Fax: 617-349-8607, E-mail: jgillett@lesley.edu. *Application contact:* Martha Sheehan, Director of Admissions, 888-LESLEYU, Fax: 617-349-8313, E-mail: info@lesley.edu.
Website: http://www.lesley.edu/soe.html.

Louisiana Tech University, Graduate School, College of Education, Department of Curriculum, Instruction and Leadership, Ruston, LA 71272. Offers curriculum and instruction (M Ed, Ed D), including adult education (M Ed), early childhood (M Ed), English education (M Ed), mathematics education (M Ed), science education (M Ed), social studies education (M Ed), special education (M Ed); educational leadership (M Ed, Ed D). *Accreditation:* NCATE. Part-time programs available. *Degree requirements:* For doctorate, thesis/dissertation. *Entrance requirements:* For master's and doctorate, GRE General Test. *Application deadline:* For fall admission, 7/29 for domestic students; for spring admission, 2/3 for domestic students. Application fee: $20 ($30 for international students). *Financial support:* Fellowships, research assistantships, and teaching assistantships available. Financial award application deadline: 2/1. *Unit head:* Dr. Pauline Leonard, Head, 318-257-4609, Fax: 318-257-2379. *Application contact:* Dr. John Harrison, Associate Dean of Graduate Studies, 318-257-3229, Fax: 318-257-2379, E-mail: johnharrison@latech.edu.
Website: http://www.latech.edu/education/cil/.

Marshall University, Academic Affairs Division, College of Education and Professional Development, Programs in Adult and Technical Education, Huntington, WV 25755. Offers MS. *Accreditation:* NCATE. Evening/weekend programs available. *Students:* 34 full-time (21 women), 51 part-time (33 women); includes 8 minority (7 Black or African American, non-Hispanic/Latino; 1 Hispanic/Latino), 12 international. Average age 37. In 2013, 22 master's awarded. *Degree requirements:* For master's, thesis optional, comprehensive assessment. Application fee: $40. *Unit head:* Dr. Michael Cunningham, Program Coordinator, 304-746-1902, E-mail: mcunningham@marshall.edu. *Application contact:* Graduate Admission.

Memorial University of Newfoundland, School of Graduate Studies, Faculty of Education, St. John's, NL A1C 5S7, Canada. Offers counseling psychology (M Ed); curriculum, teaching, and learning studies (M Ed); education (PhD); educational leadership studies (M Ed); information technology (M Ed); post-secondary studies (M Ed, Diploma), including health professional education (Diploma). Part-time programs available. *Degree requirements:* For master's, thesis optional, internship, paper folio, project; for doctorate, comprehensive exam, thesis/dissertation, thesis seminar, oral defense of thesis. *Entrance requirements:* For master's, undergraduate degree with at least 2nd class standing, 1-2 years work experience; for doctorate, minimum A average in graduate course work, MA in education, 2 years professional experience; for Diploma, 2nd class degree, 2 years of work experience with adult learners, appropriate academic qualifications and work experience in a health-related field. Electronic applications accepted. *Faculty research:* Critical thinking, literacy, cognitive studies and counseling, educational change, technology in instruction.

Merrimack College, School of Education, North Andover, MA 01845-5800. Offers community engagement (M Ed), including community organizations, higher education, K-12 education; early childhood education (M Ed); elementary education (M Ed); English as a second language (PreK-6) (M Ed); English language learners (M Ed); general studies (M Ed); higher education (M Ed), including leadership and organizational development, student affairs; middle (M Ed); moderate disabilities (PreK-8) (M Ed); secondary (M Ed); teacher leadership (CAGS), including instructional leadership, reading specialist. Part-time and evening/weekend programs available. *Faculty:* 4 full-time (all women), 23 part-time/adjunct (15 women). *Students:* 127 full-time (104 women), 61 part-time (52 women); includes 3 minority (1 Asian, non-Hispanic/Latino; 2 Hispanic/Latino), 2 international. Average age 25. 403 applicants, 47% accepted, 138 enrolled. In 2013, 140 master's awarded. *Degree requirements:* For master's, practicum, portfolio, and state test (for licensure track); capstone (for higher education and community engagement tracks). *Entrance requirements:* For master's, MTEL (Massachusetts Tests for Educator Licensure), official transcripts from other colleges, resume, personal statement, 2 letters of recommendation, additional essay requirements for fellowships. Additional exam requirements/recommendations for international students: Required—TOEFL (minimum score 84 iBT), IELTS (minimum score 6.5). *Application deadline:* For fall admission, 8/15 for domestic and international students; for winter admission, 12/1 for domestic students, 11/15 for international students; for spring admission, 1/10 for domestic and international students; for summer admission, 5/10 for domestic and international students. Applications are processed on a rolling basis. Application fee: $0. Electronic applications accepted. Tuition and fees vary according to course load and program. *Financial support:* In 2013–14, 91 fellowships with full tuition reimbursements were awarded; career-related internships or fieldwork, scholarships/grants, and health care benefits also available. Support available to part-time students. Financial award applicants required to submit FAFSA. *Faculty research:* Expressive language, civic engagement, family life education, reading genres, the psychological process of aging. *Application contact:* Kristen English, Interim Director of Graduate Admission, 978-837-5073, E-mail: englishkr@merrimack.edu.
Website: http://www.merrimack.edu/academics/graduate/education/.

Michigan State University, The Graduate School, College of Education, Department of Educational Administration, East Lansing, MI 48824. Offers higher, adult and lifelong education (MA, PhD); K–12 educational administration (MA, PhD, Ed S); student affairs administration (MA). Part-time programs available. *Entrance requirements:* Additional exam requirements/recommendations for international students: Required—TOEFL. Electronic applications accepted.

Montana State University, College of Graduate Studies, College of Education, Health, and Human Development, Department of Education, Bozeman, MT 59717. Offers adult and higher education (Ed D); curriculum and instruction (M Ed, Ed D), including professional educator (M Ed), technology education (M Ed); education (M Ed), including adult and higher education, educational leadership, school counseling; educational

leadership (Ed D, Ed S). *Accreditation:* Teacher Education Accreditation Council. Part-time programs available. Postbaccalaureate distance learning degree programs offered (minimal on-campus study). *Degree requirements:* For master's, comprehensive exam; for doctorate, comprehensive exam, thesis/dissertation. *Entrance requirements:* For master's, GRE, 3 letters of reference, essays, BA transcripts; for doctorate, GRE, MAT, 3 letters of reference, essay, BA and M Ed transcripts; for Ed S, PRAXIS. Additional exam requirements/recommendations for international students: Required—TOEFL (minimum score 550 paper-based). Electronic applications accepted. *Faculty research:* Critical literacy; standards-based education; school Improvement, organizational change, leadership in rural education, leadership in Indian education; student Learning; multicultural/culturally responsive education for social justice Native American indigenous education, community-centered education teacher preparation.

Morehead State University, Graduate Programs, College of Education, Department of Foundational and Graduate Studies in Education, Morehead, KY 40351. Offers adult and higher education (MA, Ed S); certified professional counselor (Ed S); counseling P-12 (MA); curriculum and instruction (Ed S); educational technology (MA Ed); instructional leadership (Ed S); school administration (MA); school counseling (Ed S); teacher leader business and marketing content (MA Ed); teacher leader business and marketing technology (MA Ed); teacher leader educational technology (MA Ed); teacher leader English (MA Ed); teacher leader gifted education (MA Ed); teacher leader IECE certification (MA Ed); teacher leader interdisciplinary education P-5 (MA Ed); teacher leader middle grades (MA Ed); teacher leader non IECE certification (MA Ed); teacher leader reading/writing - non-certification (MA Ed); teacher leader reading/writing certification (MA Ed); teacher leader school communication - certification (MA Ed); teacher leader school communication - non-certification (MA Ed); teacher leader social studies (MA Ed); teacher leader special education (MA Ed). *Accreditation:* NCATE. Part-time and evening/weekend programs available. *Degree requirements:* For master's, thesis optional, oral and/or written comprehensive exams; for Ed S, thesis, oral exam. *Entrance requirements:* For master's, GRE General Test, minimum overall undergraduate GPA of 2.5; for Ed S, GRE General Test, interview, master's degree, minimum GPA of 3.5, work experience. Additional exam requirements/recommendations for international students: Required—TOEFL (minimum score 500 paper-based). Electronic applications accepted. *Faculty research:* Character education, school accountability, computer applications for school administrators.

Mount Saint Vincent University, Graduate Programs, Faculty of Education, Program in Adult Education, Halifax, NS B3M 2J6, Canada. Offers M Ed, MA Ed, MA-R. Part-time and evening/weekend programs available. Postbaccalaureate distance learning degree programs offered (minimal on-campus study). *Degree requirements:* For master's, thesis (for some programs), practicum. *Entrance requirements:* For master's, bachelor's degree in related field, minimum B average. Electronic applications accepted.

National Louis University, College of Arts and Sciences, Chicago, IL 60603. Offers adult education (Ed D); counseling and human services (MS); language and academic development (M Ed, Certificate); psychology (MA, PhD, Certificate); public policy (MA); written communication (MS, Certificate). Part-time and evening/weekend programs available. Postbaccalaureate distance learning degree programs offered (minimal on-campus study). *Degree requirements:* For master's and Certificate, comprehensive exam (for some programs), thesis (for some programs); for doctorate, thesis/dissertation. *Entrance requirements:* For master's, MAT or GRE, 3 professional or academic references, interview, minimum GPA of 3.0; for doctorate, GRE General Test, MAT, or Watson-Glaser Critical Thinking Appraisal, three professional or academic references, statement of academic and professional goals, 3 years of experience in field, interview, master's degree, resume, writing sample; for Certificate, GRE, MAT, or Watson-Glaser Critical Thinking Appraisal, three professional or academic references, statement of academic and professional goals, interview, minimum GPA of 3.0. Additional exam requirements/recommendations for international students: Required—Department of Language Studies Assessment or TOEFL (minimum score 550 paper-based; 79 iBT). Electronic applications accepted.

North Carolina Agricultural and Technical State University, School of Graduate Studies, School of Education, Department of Human Development and Services, Greensboro, NC 27411. Offers adult education (MS); counseling (MS); school administration (MS). *Accreditation:* ACA. Part-time and evening/weekend programs available. *Degree requirements:* For master's, comprehensive exam, thesis, qualifying exam. *Entrance requirements:* For master's, GRE General Test, minimum GPA of 3.0.

North Carolina State University, Graduate School, College of Education, Department of Adult and Higher Education, Program in Adult and Community College Education, Raleigh, NC 27695. Offers M Ed, MS, Ed D. *Degree requirements:* For master's, thesis (for some programs); for doctorate, thesis/dissertation. *Entrance requirements:* For master's and doctorate, GRE or MAT. Electronic applications accepted.

North Dakota State University, College of Graduate and Interdisciplinary Studies, College of Human Development and Education, School of Education, Fargo, ND 58108. Offers agricultural education (M Ed, MS), including agricultural education, agricultural extension education (MS); counseling (M Ed, MS, PhD); curriculum and instruction (M Ed, MS); education (PhD); educational leadership (M Ed, MS, Ed S); family and consumer sciences education (M Ed, MS); history education (M Ed, MS); institutional analysis (Ed D); mathematics education (M Ed, MS); music education (M Ed, MS); occupational and adult education (Ed D); science education (M Ed, MS). *Accreditation:* NCATE. Part-time and evening/weekend programs available. Postbaccalaureate distance learning degree programs offered (minimal on-campus study). *Faculty:* 25 full-time (11 women), 1 (woman) part-time/adjunct. *Students:* 110 full-time (82 women), 123 part-time (85 women); includes 14 minority (4 Black or African American, non-Hispanic/Latino; 4 American Indian or Alaska Native, non-Hispanic/Latino; 1 Native Hawaiian or other Pacific Islander, non-Hispanic/Latino; 5 Two or more races, non-Hispanic/Latino), 10 international. Average age 28. 57 applicants, 81% accepted, 42 enrolled. In 2013, 38 master's, 9 doctorates awarded. *Degree requirements:* For master's, comprehensive exam; for doctorate, thesis/dissertation; for Ed S, thesis. *Entrance requirements:* For degree, GRE General Test, master's degree, minimum GPA of 3.25. Additional exam requirements/recommendations for international students: Required—TOEFL. *Application deadline:* Applications are processed on a rolling basis. Application fee: $45 ($60 for international students). *Financial support:* Research assistantships, teaching assistantships, career-related internships or fieldwork, Federal Work-Study, institutionally sponsored loans, and tuition waivers (full) available. Financial award application deadline: 4/15. *Unit head:* Dr. William Martin, Chair, 701-231-7202, Fax: 701-231-7416, E-mail: william.martin@ndsu.edu. *Application contact:* Sonya Goergen, Marketing, Recruitment, and Public Relations Coordinator, 701-231-7033, Fax: 701-231-6524.
Website: http://www.ndsu.nodak.edu/school_of_education/.

Northern Illinois University, Graduate School, College of Education, Department of Counseling, Adult and Higher Education, De Kalb, IL 60115-2854. Offers adult and higher education (MS Ed, Ed D); counseling (MS Ed, Ed D). *Accreditation:* ACA. Part-time and evening/weekend programs available. *Faculty:* 19 full-time (11 women), 2 part-time/adjunct (1 woman). *Students:* 121 full-time (94 women), 252 part-time (182 women); includes 149 minority (102 Black or African American, non-Hispanic/Latino; 1 American Indian or Alaska Native, non-Hispanic/Latino; 11 Asian, non-Hispanic/Latino; 28 Hispanic/Latino; 7 Two or more races, non-Hispanic/Latino), 9 international. Average age 36. 115 applicants, 48% accepted, 37 enrolled. In 2013, 73 master's, 19 doctorates awarded. Terminal master's awarded for partial completion of doctoral program. *Degree requirements:* For master's, comprehensive exam, thesis optional; for doctorate, thesis/dissertation, candidacy exam, dissertation defense. *Entrance requirements:* For master's, GRE General Test or MAT, minimum undergraduate GPA of 2.75, interview (for counseling); for doctorate, GRE General Test, minimum undergraduate GPA of 2.75, 3.2 graduate, interview (for counseling). Additional exam requirements/recommendations for international students: Required—TOEFL (minimum score 550 paper-based). *Application deadline:* For fall admission, 6/1 for domestic students, 5/1 for international students; for spring admission, 11/1 for domestic students, 10/1 for international students. Applications are processed on a rolling basis. Application fee: $40. Electronic applications accepted. *Financial support:* In 2013–14, 13 research assistantships with full tuition reimbursements, 2 teaching assistantships with full tuition reimbursements were awarded; fellowships with full tuition reimbursements, career-related internships or fieldwork, Federal Work-Study, scholarships/grants, tuition waivers (full), and staff assistantships also available. Support available to part-time students. Financial award applicants required to submit FAFSA. *Unit head:* Dr. Suzanne Degges-White, Interim Chair, 815-753-1448, E-mail: cahe@niu.edu. *Application contact:* Graduate School Office, 815-753-0395, E-mail: gradsch@niu.edu.
Website: http://www.cedu.niu.edu/cahe/index.html.

Northwestern Oklahoma State University, School of Professional Studies, Program in Adult Education Management and Administration, Alva, OK 73717-2799. Offers M Ed. Part-time programs available. *Degree requirements:* For master's, thesis optional, portfolio. *Entrance requirements:* For master's, GRE or MAT, minimum GPA of 2.75.

Northwestern State University of Louisiana, Graduate Studies and Research, College of Education and Human Development, Program in Adult and Continuing Education, Natchitoches, LA 71497. Offers MA. *Degree requirements:* For master's, comprehensive exam, thesis or alternative. *Entrance requirements:* For master's, GRE General Test, minimum undergraduate GPA of 2.5. Additional exam requirements/recommendations for international students: Required—TOEFL. Electronic applications accepted.

Oregon State University, College of Education, Program in Adult Education, Corvallis, OR 97331. Offers Ed M, MAIS. *Accreditation:* NCATE. Part-time programs available. *Faculty:* 4 full-time (all women), 1 (woman) part-time/adjunct. *Students:* 1 full-time (0 women), 23 part-time (16 women); includes 6 minority (1 Black or African American, non-Hispanic/Latino; 1 Asian, non-Hispanic/Latino; 2 Hispanic/Latino; 2 Two or more races, non-Hispanic/Latino). Average age 41. 29 applicants, 48% accepted, 13 enrolled. In 2013, 12 master's awarded. *Degree requirements:* For master's, thesis or alternative. *Entrance requirements:* For master's, minimum GPA of 3.0 in last 90 hours. Additional exam requirements/recommendations for international students: Required—TOEFL (minimum score 575 paper-based). *Application deadline:* For fall admission, 3/31 for domestic students. Applications are processed on a rolling basis. Application fee: $60. *Expenses:* Tuition, state resident: full-time $11,664; part-time $432 per credit hour. Tuition, nonresident: full-time $19,197; part-time $711 per credit hour. *Required fees:* $1446; $443 per quarter. One-time fee: $300. Tuition and fees vary according to course load and program. *Financial support:* Research assistantships, teaching assistantships, career-related internships or fieldwork, Federal Work-Study, and institutionally sponsored loans available. Support available to part-time students. Financial award application deadline: 2/1. *Faculty research:* Adult training and developmental psychology, cross-cultural communication, leadership development and human relations, adult literacy. *Unit head:* Dr. Larry Flick, Dean, 541-737-3664, E-mail: larry.flick@oregonstate.edu. *Application contact:* Shelley Dubkin-Lee, Adult Education Advisor, 541-737-5963, E-mail: shelley.dubkin-lee@oregonstate.edu.
Website: http://education.oregonstate.edu/adult-education-masters-degree-program.

Penn State University Park, Graduate School, College of Education, Department of Learning and Performance Systems, State College, PA 16802. Offers adult education (M Ed, D Ed, PhD, Certificate); instructional systems (Certificate); learning, design, and technology (M Ed, MS, D Ed, PhD, Certificate); organization development and change (MPS); workforce education and development (M Ed, MS, PhD). *Unit head:* Dr. David H. Monk, Dean, 814-865-2523, Fax: 814-865-0555, E-mail: dhm6@psu.edu. *Application contact:* Cynthia E. Nicosia, Director, Graduate Enrollment Services, 814-865-1834, Fax: 814-863-4627, E-mail: cey1@psu.edu.
Website: http://www.ed.psu.edu/educ/lps/dept-lps.

Plymouth State University, College of Graduate Studies, Graduate Studies in Education, Program in Learning, Leadership and Community, Plymouth, NH 03264-1595. Offers Ed D. *Degree requirements:* For doctorate, thesis/dissertation.

Portland State University, Graduate Studies, School of Education, Department of Educational Policy, Foundations, and Administrative Studies, Portland, OR 97207-0751. Offers educational leadership (MA, MS, Ed D); postsecondary, adult and continuing education (Ed D). *Accreditation:* NCATE. Part-time and evening/weekend programs available. *Faculty:* 14 full-time (9 women), 9 part-time/adjunct (5 women). *Students:* 231 full-time (154 women), 382 part-time (256 women); includes 139 minority (22 Black or African American, non-Hispanic/Latino; 8 American Indian or Alaska Native, non-Hispanic/Latino; 24 Asian, non-Hispanic/Latino; 59 Hispanic/Latino; 3 Native Hawaiian or other Pacific Islander, non-Hispanic/Latino; 23 Two or more races, non-Hispanic/Latino), 11 international. Average age 38. 210 applicants, 60% accepted, 125 enrolled. In 2013, 79 master's, 13 doctorates awarded. *Degree requirements:* For master's, thesis or alternative, written exam or research project; for doctorate, comprehensive exam, thesis/dissertation. *Entrance requirements:* For master's, California Basic Educational Skills Test, minimum GPA of 3.0 in upper-division course work or 2.75 overall; for doctorate, GRE General Test or MAT. Additional exam requirements/recommendations for international students: Required—TOEFL (minimum score 550 paper-based). *Application deadline:* For fall admission, 4/1 for domestic and international students; for winter admission, 9/1 for domestic and international students; for spring admission, 11/1 for domestic and international students. Applications are processed on a rolling basis. Application fee: $50. *Expenses:* Tuition, state resident: full-time $9207; part-time $341 per credit. Tuition, nonresident: full-time $14,391; part-time $533 per credit. *Required fees:* $1263; $22 per credit. $98 per quarter. One-time fee: $150. Tuition and fees vary according to program. *Financial support:* Career-related internships or fieldwork, Federal Work-Study, and institutionally sponsored loans available. Support available to part-time students. Financial award application deadline: 3/1; financial award applicants required to submit FAFSA. *Faculty research:* Leadership development and research, principals and urban schools, accelerated schools, cooperative learning, family involvement in schools. *Total annual research expenditures:* $43,200. *Unit head:* Candyce Reynolds, Chair, 503-725-4657, Fax: 503-725-8475, E-mail: reynoldsc@pdx.edu. *Application contact:* Mindy Friend, Department Assistant, 503-725-4716, Fax: 503-725-8475, E-mail: mfriend@pdx.edu.
Website: http://www.ed.pdx.edu/epfa/.

Regent University, Graduate School, School of Education, Virginia Beach, VA 23464-9800. Offers adult education (Ed D, PhD); advanced educational leadership (Ed D, PhD); career switcher with licensure (M Ed), including alternative licensure; character education (Ed D, PhD); Christian education leadership (Ed D); Christian school

administration (M Ed); curriculum and instruction (M Ed); distance education (Ed D, PhD); educational leadership (M Ed); educational leadership - special education (Ed S); educational psychology (Ed D); elementary education (M Ed); higher education (Ed D, PhD); higher education leadership and management (Ed D); K-12 school leadership (Ed D, PhD); leadership in mathematics education (M Ed); reading specialist (M Ed); special education (M Ed, Ed D, PhD); student affairs (M Ed); TESOL (M Ed), including adult education, PreK-12. *Accreditation:* Teacher Education Accreditation Council. Part-time and evening/weekend programs available. Postbaccalaureate distance learning degree programs offered (minimal on-campus study). *Faculty:* 25 full-time (12 women), 50 part-time/adjunct (31 women). *Students:* 100 full-time (78 women), 754 part-time (614 women); includes 225 minority (191 Black or African American, non-Hispanic/Latino; 1 American Indian or Alaska Native, non-Hispanic/Latino; 7 Asian, non-Hispanic/Latino; 26 Hispanic/Latino), 16 international. Average age 39. 487 applicants, 63% accepted, 233 enrolled. In 2013, 202 master's, 19 doctorates awarded. *Degree requirements:* For master's, thesis or alternative; for doctorate, comprehensive exam, thesis/dissertation. *Entrance requirements:* For master's, MAT, minimum undergraduate GPA of 2.75, writing sample, resume, recommendations, interview; for doctorate, GRE, writing sample, 3 years of relevant professional experience, master's-level paper, copies of published work, resume, transcripts, interview, recommendations. Additional exam requirements/recommendations for international students: Required—TOEFL (minimum score 577 paper-based). *Application deadline:* For fall admission, 4/1 priority date for domestic students; for spring admission, 10/15 priority date for domestic students. Applications are processed on a rolling basis. Application fee: $50. Electronic applications accepted. Tuition and fees vary according to course load and degree level. *Financial support:* Fellowships, career-related internships or fieldwork, scholarships/grants, tuition waivers (full and partial), and unspecified assistantships available. Support available to part-time students. Financial award application deadline: 4/1; financial award applicants required to submit FAFSA. *Faculty research:* Character development and discipline for children, education leadership development, diversity in schools, classroom management, technology in education settings. *Unit head:* Dr. Alan Arroyo, Dean, 757-352-4261, Fax: 757-352-4318, E-mail: alanarr@regent.edu. *Application contact:* Matthew Chadwick, Director of Enrollment Support Services, 800-373-5504, Fax: 757-352-4381, E-mail: admissions@regent.edu.
Website: http://www.regent.edu/education/.

Regis University, College for Professional Studies, School of Education, Education Division, Denver, CO 80221-1099. Offers adult learning, training, and development (M Ed, Certificate); autism education (Certificate); curriculum, instruction, and assessment (M Ed); educational leadership (M Ed); gifted and talented education (M Ed); gifted/talented education (Certificate); initial licensure (M Ed); instructional technology (M Ed, Certificate); literacy (Certificate); reading (M Ed); school executive leadership (Certificate); space studies (M Ed). Program also offered in Henderson and Las Vegas (Summerlin), NV. *Accreditation:* Teacher Education Accreditation Council. Part-time and evening/weekend programs available. Postbaccalaureate distance learning degree programs offered (no on-campus study). *Degree requirements:* For master's, thesis. *Entrance requirements:* For master's, resume, minimum GPA of 2.75, criminal background check. Additional exam requirements/recommendations for international students: Required—TOEFL, TWE (minimum score 5). *Application deadline:* For fall admission, 7/23 priority date for domestic students; for winter admission, 9/17 priority date for domestic students; for spring admission, 12/3 priority date for domestic students. Applications are processed on a rolling basis. Application fee: $75. Electronic applications accepted. *Expenses:* Contact institution. *Financial support:* Federal Work-Study and scholarships/grants available. *Faculty research:* Issues of equity in the middle school classroom, professional learning communities, school reform, sociolinguistic and discursive obstacles to student integration, inclusive language arts curriculum. *Unit head:* Dr. Janna L. Oakes, Dean, 303-458-4302. *Application contact:* Information Contact, 303-458-4300, Fax: 303-964-5274, E-mail: masters@regis.edu.

St. Francis Xavier University, Graduate Studies, Department of Adult Education, Antigonish, NS B2G 2W5, Canada. Offers M Ad Ed. Part-time programs available. Postbaccalaureate distance learning degree programs offered (minimal on-campus study). *Degree requirements:* For master's, thesis. *Entrance requirements:* For master's, minimum undergraduate B average, 2 years of work experience in field. Additional exam requirements/recommendations for international students: Required—TOEFL (minimum score 580 paper-based). *Faculty research:* Adult learning and development, religious education, women's issues, literacy, action research.

Saint Joseph's College of Maine, Master of Science in Education Program, Standish, ME 04084. Offers adult education and training (MS Ed); Catholic school leadership (MS Ed); health care educator (MS Ed); school educator (MS Ed). Program available by correspondence. Part-time programs available. Postbaccalaureate distance learning degree programs offered (minimal on-campus study). Electronic applications accepted.

Saint Joseph's University, College of Arts and Sciences, Organization Development and Leadership Programs, Philadelphia, PA 19131-1395. Offers adult learning and training (MS, Certificate); organization dynamics and leadership (MS, Certificate); organizational psychology and development (MS, Certificate). Part-time and evening/weekend programs available. Postbaccalaureate distance learning degree programs offered (no on-campus study). *Faculty:* 2 full-time (both women), 16 part-time/adjunct (9 women). *Students:* 7 full-time (3 women), 233 part-time (154 women); includes 94 minority (59 Black or African American, non-Hispanic/Latino; 17 American Indian or Alaska Native, non-Hispanic/Latino; 9 Asian, non-Hispanic/Latino; 7 Hispanic/Latino; 1 Native Hawaiian or other Pacific Islander, non-Hispanic/Latino; 1 Two or more races, non-Hispanic/Latino), 3 international. Average age 38. 100 applicants, 78% accepted, 50 enrolled. In 2013, 65 master's awarded. *Entrance requirements:* For master's, GRE (if GPA less than 2.7), minimum GPA of 2.7, 2 letters of recommendation, resume, personal statement. Additional exam requirements/recommendations for international students: Required—TOEFL (minimum score 550 paper-based; 80 iBT). *Application deadline:* For fall admission, 7/15 priority date for domestic students, 4/15 for international students; for winter admission, 1/15 for international students; for spring admission, 11/15 priority date for domestic students, 10/15 for international students. Applications are processed on a rolling basis. Application fee: $35. Electronic applications accepted. *Expenses:* Tuition: Part-time $786 per credit hour. Tuition and fees vary according to degree level and program. *Financial support:* Applicants required to submit FAFSA. *Unit head:* Dr. Felice Tilin, Director, 610-660-1575, E-mail: ftilin@sju.edu. *Application contact:* Elisabeth Woodward, Director of Marketing and Admissions, Graduate Arts and Sciences, 610-660-3131, Fax: 610-660-3230, E-mail: gradstudies@sju.edu.
Website: http://www.sju.edu/majors-programs/graduate-arts-sciences/masters/organization-development-and-leadership-ms.

San Francisco State University, Division of Graduate Studies, College of Education, Department of Equity, Leadership Studies, and Instructional Technologies, Program in Adult Education, San Francisco, CA 94132-1722. Offers adult education (MA); designated subjects (Credential). *Accreditation:* NCATE. *Unit head:* Dr. David Hemphill,

Interim Chair, 415-338-1653, E-mail: hemphill@sfsu.edu. *Application contact:* Dr. Ming Yeh Lee, Graduate Coordinator, 415-338-1081, E-mail: mylee@sfsu.edu.
Website: http://coe.sfsu.edu/elsit.

Seattle University, College of Education, Program in Adult Education and Training, Seattle, WA 98122-1090. Offers M Ed, MA, Certificate. *Accreditation:* NCATE. Part-time and evening/weekend programs available. *Faculty:* 1 full-time (0 women), 2 part-time/adjunct (1 woman). *Students:* 14 full-time (9 women); includes 4 minority (1 Black or African American, non-Hispanic/Latino; 1 Asian, non-Hispanic/Latino; 2 Hispanic/Latino). Average age 34. 3 applicants, 67% accepted, 2 enrolled. In 2013, 5 master's awarded. *Degree requirements:* For master's, comprehensive exam. *Entrance requirements:* For master's, GRE, MAT, or minimum GPA of 3.0; 1 year of related experience. Additional exam requirements/recommendations for international students: Required—TOEFL. *Application deadline:* For fall admission, 8/20 priority date for domestic students; for winter admission, 11/20 for domestic students; for spring admission, 2/20 for domestic students. Applications are processed on a rolling basis. Application fee: $55. *Financial support:* In 2013–14, 1 student received support. Career-related internships or fieldwork and Federal Work-Study available. Support available to part-time students. Financial award applicants required to submit FAFSA. *Unit head:* Dr. Carol Weaver, Director, 206-296-5908, E-mail: cweaver@seattleu.edu. *Application contact:* Janet Shandley, Associate Dean of Graduate Admissions, 206-296-5900, Fax: 206-298-5656, E-mail: grad_admissions@seattleu.edu.
Website: http://www.seattleu.edu/coe/adedm/Default.aspx?id=11190.

State University of New York Empire State College, School for Graduate Studies, Programs in Education, Saratoga Springs, NY 12866-4391. Offers adult learning (MA); learning and emerging technologies (MA); teaching (MAT); teaching and learning (M Ed). Postbaccalaureate distance learning degree programs offered.

Teachers College, Columbia University, Graduate Faculty of Education, Department of Organization and Leadership, Adult Education Guided Intensive Study (AEGIS) Program, New York, NY 10027. Offers Ed D. *Accreditation:* NCATE. *Faculty:* 5 full-time, 3 part-time/adjunct. *Students:* 36 full-time (22 women), 18 part-time (7 women); includes 25 minority (15 Black or African American, non-Hispanic/Latino; 7 Asian, non-Hispanic/Latino; 3 Hispanic/Latino), 2 international. Average age 45. 1 applicant. In 2013, 1 doctorate awarded. *Degree requirements:* For doctorate, comprehensive exam, thesis/dissertation, qualifying paper. *Entrance requirements:* For doctorate, 3-5 years of professional experience. *Application deadline:* For fall admission, 10/1 for domestic students. Application fee: $65. Electronic applications accepted. *Financial support:* Career-related internships or fieldwork, Federal Work-Study, institutionally sponsored loans, and tuition waivers (full and partial) available. Support available to part-time students. Financial award applicants required to submit FAFSA. *Faculty research:* Adult learning, perspective transformation, training and evaluation, workplace learning, theory to practice. *Unit head:* Lyle Yorks, Program Coordinator, 212-678-3820, E-mail: ly84@columbia.edu. *Application contact:* Debbie Lesperance, Assistant Director of Admission, 212-678-3710, Fax: 212-678-4171.
Website: http://www.tc.columbia.edu/o&l/adulted/index.asp?Id-Program+Informationnfo-AEGIS.

Texas A&M University–Kingsville, College of Graduate Studies, College of Education, Department of Education, Program in Adult Education, Kingsville, TX 78363. Offers M Ed. Program offered jointly with Texas A&M University. Part-time and evening/weekend programs available. *Faculty:* 10 full-time (8 women), 9 part-time/adjunct (5 women). *Students:* 3 full-time (all women), 19 part-time (15 women); includes 16 minority (1 Black or African American, non-Hispanic/Latino; 15 Hispanic/Latino). Average age 41. 5 applicants, 100% accepted, 4 enrolled. In 2013, 9 master's awarded. *Degree requirements:* For master's, comprehensive exam, mini-thesis. *Entrance requirements:* For master's, GRE General Test, MAT, minimum GPA of 3.0. *Application deadline:* For fall admission, 6/1 for domestic students; for spring admission, 11/15 for domestic students. Applications are processed on a rolling basis. Application fee: $35 ($50 for international students). *Financial support:* Federal Work-Study and institutionally sponsored loans available. Support available to part-time students. Financial award application deadline: 5/15. *Faculty research:* Continuing education efforts in south Texas, adult education methodologies. *Unit head:* Dr. Travis Polk, Chair, 361-593-3204. *Application contact:* Dr. Alberto M. Olivares, Dean, College of Graduate Studies, 361-593-2808, Fax: 361-593-3412, E-mail: a-olivares@tamuk.edu.

Texas A&M University–Texarkana, Graduate Studies and Research, College of Education and Liberal Arts, Texarkana, TX 75505-5518. Offers adult education (MS); curriculum and instruction (M Ed); education (MS); educational administration (M Ed); English (MA); instructional technology (MS); interdisciplinary studies (MA, MS); special education (MS). Part-time and evening/weekend programs available. *Degree requirements:* For master's, comprehensive exam (for some programs), thesis optional. *Entrance requirements:* For master's, minimum GPA of 2.5 on last 60 hours of bachelor's degree. Additional exam requirements/recommendations for international students: Required—TOEFL. Electronic applications accepted.

Texas State University, Graduate School, College of Education, Department of Counseling, Leadership, Adult Education, and School Psychology, Program in Adult, Professional and Community Education, San Marcos, TX 78666. Offers PhD. Part-time programs available. *Faculty:* 2 full-time (1 woman), 2 part-time/adjunct (0 women). *Students:* 40 full-time (34 women), 44 part-time (24 women); includes 43 minority (18 Black or African American, non-Hispanic/Latino; 3 Asian, non-Hispanic/Latino; 22 Hispanic/Latino), 3 international. Average age 42. 68 applicants, 47% accepted, 26 enrolled. In 2013, 16 doctorates awarded. *Entrance requirements:* For doctorate, master's degree with minimum GPA of 3.5 in all related course work. Additional exam requirements/recommendations for international students: Required—TOEFL (minimum score 550 paper-based; 78 iBT). *Application deadline:* For fall admission, 6/15 for domestic students, 6/1 for international students; for spring admission, 10/1 for domestic and international students. Applications are processed on a rolling basis. Application fee: $40 ($90 for international students). Electronic applications accepted. *Expenses:* Tuition, state resident: full-time $6663; part-time $278 per credit hour. Tuition, nonresident: full-time $15,159; part-time $632 per credit hour. *Required fees:* $1872; $54 per credit hour. $306 per term. Tuition and fees vary according to course load. *Financial support:* In 2013–14, 26 students received support, including 5 research assistantships (averaging $23,967 per year), 18 teaching assistantships (averaging $26,968 per year); career-related internships or fieldwork, Federal Work-Study, and institutionally sponsored loans also available. Support available to part-time students. Financial award application deadline: 4/1; financial award applicants required to submit FAFSA. *Faculty research:* Systems of learning, community building, community youth development, culturally responsive learning. *Unit head:* Dr. Ann K. Brooks, PhD Program Director, 512-245-1936, Fax: 512-245-8872, E-mail: ab41@txstate.edu. *Application contact:* Dr. Andrea Golato, Dean of Graduate School, 512-245-2531, Fax: 512-245-8365, E-mail: gradcollege@txstate.edu.
Website: http://www.txstate.edu/edphd/Majors/apce.html.

Trident University International, College of Education, Program in Education, Cypress, CA 90630. Offers adult education (MA Ed); aviation education (MA Ed); children's literacy development (MA Ed); e-learning (MA Ed); early childhood education (MA Ed); enrollment management (MA Ed); higher education (MA Ed); teaching and

instruction (MA Ed); training and development (MA Ed). Part-time and evening/weekend programs available. Postbaccalaureate distance learning degree programs offered (no on-campus study). *Degree requirements:* For master's, capstone project with integrative paper. *Entrance requirements:* For master's, minimum GPA of 2.5 (students with GPA 3.0 or greater may transfer up to 30% of graduate level credits). Additional exam requirements/recommendations for international students: Required—TOEFL (minimum score 525 paper-based). Electronic applications accepted.

Troy University, Graduate School, College of Education, Program in Adult Education, Troy, AL 36082. Offers MS. Part-time and evening/weekend programs available. *Faculty:* 7 full-time (3 women), 6 part-time/adjunct (1 woman). *Students:* 20 full-time (15 women), 91 part-time (69 women); includes 81 minority (77 Black or African American, non-Hispanic/Latino; 4 Hispanic/Latino). Average age 41. 22 applicants, 100% accepted, 22 enrolled. In 2013, 11 master's awarded. *Degree requirements:* For master's, comprehensive exam, capstone course or thesis. *Entrance requirements:* For master's, GRE (minimum score of 850 on old exam or 294 on new exam), GMAT (minimum score of 380), or MAT (minimum score of 385), bachelor's degree; minimum undergraduate GPA of 2.5 or 3.0 on last 30 semester hours, letter of recommendation. Additional exam requirements/recommendations for international students: Required—TOEFL (minimum score 523 paper-based; 70 iBT), IELTS (minimum score 6). *Application deadline:* Applications are processed on a rolling basis. Application fee: $50. Electronic applications accepted. *Expenses:* Tuition, state resident: full-time $6084; part-time $338 per credit hour. Tuition, nonresident: full-time $12,168; part-time $676 per credit hour. *Required fees:* $630; $35 per credit hour. $50 per semester. *Unit head:* Dr. Dianne Rosse-Mims, Coordinator, 678-625-5762, Fax: 678-625-5268, E-mail: droseer-mims@troy.edu. *Application contact:* Brenda K Campbell, Graduate Actions Coordinator, 334-670-3178, Fax: 334-670-3733, E-mail: bcamp@troy.edu.

Troy University, Graduate School, College of Education, Program in Postsecondary Education, Troy, AL 36082. Offers adult education (M Ed); biology (M Ed); criminal justice (M Ed); English (M Ed); foundations of education (M Ed); general science (M Ed); higher education administration (M Ed); history (M Ed); instructional technology (M Ed); mathematics (M Ed); music industry (M Ed); physical fitness (M Ed); political science (M Ed); public administration (M Ed); social science (M Ed); teaching English (M Ed). *Accreditation:* NCATE. Part-time and evening/weekend programs available. *Faculty:* 30 full-time (11 women), 8 part-time/adjunct (1 woman). *Students:* 17 full-time (13 women), 106 part-time (84 women); includes 55 minority (45 Black or African American, non-Hispanic/Latino; 3 Asian, non-Hispanic/Latino; 2 Hispanic/Latino; 5 Two or more races, non-Hispanic/Latino). Average age 34. 109 applicants, 83% accepted, 5 enrolled. In 2013, 130 master's awarded. *Degree requirements:* For master's, comprehensive exam (for some programs), thesis (for some programs), thesis or comprehensive exam. *Entrance requirements:* For master's, GRE (minimum score of 850 on old exam or 290 on new exam), GMAT (minimum score of 380), or MAT (minimum score of 385), bachelor's degree; minimum undergraduate GPA of 2.5 or 3.0 on last 30 semester hours, letter of recommendation. Additional exam requirements/recommendations for international students: Required—TOEFL (minimum score 523 paper-based; 70 iBT), IELTS (minimum score 6). *Application deadline:* Applications are processed on a rolling basis. Application fee: $50. Electronic applications accepted. *Expenses:* Tuition, state resident: full-time $6084; part-time $338 per credit hour. Tuition, nonresident: full-time $12,168; part-time $676 per credit hour. *Required fees:* $630; $35 per credit hour. $50 per semester. *Financial support:* Available to part-time students. Applicants required to submit FAFSA. *Unit head:* Dr. Jan Oliver, Associate Professor, 334-670-3444, Fax: 334-670-3474, E-mail: oliver@troy.edu. *Application contact:* Brenda K. Campbell, Director of Graduate Admissions, 334-670-3178, Fax: 334-670-3733, E-mail: bcamp@troy.edu.

Tusculum College, Graduate School, Program in Education, Greeneville, TN 37743-9997. Offers adult education (MA Ed); K–12 (MA Ed). Evening/weekend programs available. *Degree requirements:* For master's, thesis or alternative. *Entrance requirements:* For master's, 3 years of work experience, minimum GPA of 2.75.

Universidad del Este, Graduate School, Carolina, PR 00984. Offers accounting (MBA); adult education (M Ed); agribusiness (MBA); criminal justice and criminology (MA); curriculum and instruction - early education (M Ed); curriculum and instruction - elementary (M Ed); curriculum and instruction - English (M Ed); curriculum and instruction - Spanish (M Ed); human resources (MBA); information security management (MBA); information technology and Web business development (MBA); management (MBA); public policy (MPA); social work (MA), including clinical social work; special education (M Ed); strategic leadership (MBA). *Students:* 464 full-time (322 women), 669 part-time (499 women); all minorities (all Hispanic/Latino). Average age 35. 693 applicants, 61% accepted, 332 enrolled. In 2013, 228 master's awarded. *Unit head:* Jose R. Clintron, Dean, 787-257-7373 Ext. 3007, E-mail: ue_jcintron@suagm.edu. *Application contact:* Clotilde Santiago, Director of Admissions, 787-257-7373 Ext. 3400, E-mail: ue_csantiago@suagm.edu.

Universidad Metropolitana, School of Education, Program in Teaching of Physical Education, San Juan, PR 00928-1150. Offers teaching of adult physical education (M Ed); teaching of elementary physical education (M Ed); teaching of secondary physical education (M Ed). *Degree requirements:* For master's, thesis or alternative. *Entrance requirements:* For master's, EXADEP, interview. Electronic applications accepted.

University of Alberta, Faculty of Graduate Studies and Research, Department of Educational Policy Studies, Edmonton, AB T6G 2E1, Canada. Offers adult education (M Ed, Ed D, PhD); educational administration and leadership (M Ed, Ed D, PhD, Postgraduate Diploma); First Nations education (M Ed, Ed D, PhD); theoretical, cultural and international studies in education (M Ed, Ed D, PhD). *Degree requirements:* For master's, thesis (for some programs); for doctorate, thesis/dissertation. *Entrance requirements:* For master's, minimum GPA of 6.5 on a 9.0 scale; for doctorate, minimum GPA of 7.5 on a 9.0 scale. Additional exam requirements/recommendations for international students: Required—TOEFL (minimum score 580 paper-based). Electronic applications accepted.

University of Arkansas at Little Rock, Graduate School, College of Education, Department of Counseling, Adult and Rehabilitation Education, Program in Adult Education, Little Rock, AR 72204-1099. Offers M Ed. *Accreditation:* NCATE. Part-time programs available. *Degree requirements:* For master's, comprehensive exam. *Entrance requirements:* For master's, interview, minimum GPA of 2.75, GRE General Test or teaching certificate. *Expenses:* Tuition, state resident: full-time $5690; part-time $284.50 per credit hour. Tuition, nonresident: full-time $13,030; part-time $651.50 per credit hour. *Required fees:* $1121; $672 per term. One-time fee: $40 full-time. *Faculty research:* Adult literacy, volunteer training, in-services education.

The University of British Columbia, Faculty of Education, Department of Educational Studies, Vancouver, BC V6T 1Z1, Canada. Offers adult education (M Ed, MA); adult learning and global change (M Ed); educational administration (M Ed, MA); educational leadership and policy (Ed D); educational studies (PhD); higher education (M Ed, MA); society, culture and politics in education (M Ed, MA). Part-time and evening/weekend programs available. Terminal master's awarded for partial completion of doctoral program. *Degree requirements:* For master's, thesis; for doctorate, comprehensive

exam, thesis/dissertation, master's thesis. *Entrance requirements:* For master's, minimum B+ average, 4-year undergraduate degree, field-related experience; for doctorate, minimum B+ average, 4-year undergraduate degree, master's degree, field-related experience. Additional exam requirements/recommendations for international students: Required—TOEFL (minimum score 600 paper-based; 100 iBT) or IELTS (minimum score 6.5). Electronic applications accepted. *Expenses: Tuition, area resident:* Full-time $8000 Canadian dollars. *Faculty research:* Educational leadership educational administration adult education politics in education, global change and adult learning.

University of Calgary, Faculty of Graduate Studies, Werklund School of Education, Graduate Division of Educational Research, Calgary, AB T2N 1N4, Canada. Offers adult learning (M Ed, MA, Ed D, PhD); curriculum and learning (M Ed, MA, Ed D, PhD); educational leadership (M Ed, MA, Ed D, PhD); languages and diversity (M Ed, MA, Ed D, PhD); learning sciences (M Ed, MA, Ed D, PhD). Ed D in educational leadership offered via distance delivery. Part-time and evening/weekend programs available. Postbaccalaureate distance learning degree programs offered (minimal on-campus study). *Degree requirements:* For master's, thesis (for some programs); for doctorate, thesis/dissertation, candidacy exam. *Entrance requirements:* For master's, minimum GPA of 3.0, 3 letters of reference; for doctorate, minimum GPA of 3.5, 3 letters of reference. Additional exam requirements/recommendations for international students: Required—TOEFL, IELTS. Electronic applications accepted. *Faculty research:* Curriculum, leadership, technology, contexts, gifted, second language teaching, work place and adult learning.

University of Central Arkansas, Graduate School, College of Education, Department of Leadership Studies, Conway, AR 72035-0001. Offers college student personnel (MS); district-level administration (PMC); educational leadership - district level (Ed S); instructional technology (MS); library media and information technology (MS); school counseling (MS); school leadership (MS); school-based leadership adult education program administration (PMC); school-based leadership building administration (PMC); school-based leadership curriculum administration (PMC); school-based leadership gifted and talented program administration (PMC); school-based leadership special education program administration (PMC). *Accreditation:* NCATE. Part-time and evening/weekend programs available. Postbaccalaureate distance learning degree programs offered (minimal on-campus study). *Degree requirements:* For master's and other advanced degree, comprehensive exam. *Entrance requirements:* For master's, GRE. Additional exam requirements/recommendations for international students: Required—TOEFL (minimum score 80 iBT). Electronic applications accepted. *Expenses:* Contact institution.

University of Central Oklahoma, The Jackson College of Graduate Studies, College of Education and Professional Studies, Department of Adult Education and Safety Science, Edmond, OK 73034-5209. Offers adult and higher education (M Ed), including adult and higher education, interdisciplinary studies, student personnel, training. Part-time programs available. *Faculty:* 7 full-time (4 women), 12 part-time/adjunct (5 women). *Students:* 37 full-time (23 women), 91 part-time (57 women); includes 50 minority (24 Black or African American, non-Hispanic/Latino; 3 American Indian or Alaska Native, non-Hispanic/Latino; 5 Asian, non-Hispanic/Latino; 12 Hispanic/Latino; 6 Two or more races, non-Hispanic/Latino), 5 international. Average age 36. 59 applicants, 78% accepted, 28 enrolled. In 2013, 17 master's awarded. *Degree requirements:* For master's, comprehensive exam (for some programs), thesis (for some programs). *Entrance requirements:* For master's, GRE General Test. Additional exam requirements/recommendations for international students: Required—TOEFL (minimum score 550 paper-based; 79 iBT), IELTS (minimum score 6.5). *Application deadline:* For fall admission, 7/1 for international students; for spring admission, 11/1 for international students. Applications are processed on a rolling basis. Application fee: $50. Electronic applications accepted. *Expenses:* Tuition, state resident: full-time $4137; part-time $206.85 per credit hour. Tuition, nonresident: full-time $10,359; part-time $517.95 per credit hour. *Required fees:* $481. Tuition and fees vary according to course load and program. *Financial support:* In 2013–14, 31 students received support, including 2 research assistantships with partial tuition reimbursements available (averaging $2,958 per year), 1 teaching assistantship with partial tuition reimbursement available (averaging $15,382 per year); career-related internships or fieldwork, scholarships/grants, tuition waivers (partial), and unspecified assistantships also available. Financial award application deadline: 3/31; financial award applicants required to submit FAFSA. *Faculty research:* Violence in the workplace/schools, aging issues, trade and industrial education. *Unit head:* Dr. Candy Sebert, Chair, 405-974-5780, Fax: 405-974-3822. *Application contact:* Dr. Richard Bernard, Dean, Graduate College, 405-974-3493, Fax: 405-974-3852, E-mail: gradcoll@uco.edu.

University of Cincinnati, Graduate School, College of Education, Criminal Justice, and Human Services, Division of Teacher Education, Cincinnati, OH 45221. Offers curriculum and instruction (M Ed, Ed D); deaf studies (Certificate); early childhood education (M Ed); middle childhood education (M Ed); postsecondary literacy instruction (Certificate); reading/literacy (M Ed, Ed D); secondary education (M Ed); special education (M Ed, Ed D); teaching English as a second language (M Ed, Ed D, Certificate); teaching science (MS). Part-time programs available. *Degree requirements:* For doctorate, thesis/dissertation. *Entrance requirements:* For master's, GRE General Test. Additional exam requirements/recommendations for international students: Required—TOEFL (minimum score 550 paper-based). Electronic applications accepted.

University of Colorado Denver, School of Education and Human Development, Information and Learning Technologies Program, Denver, CO 80217-3364. Offers e-learning design and implementation (MA); instructional design and adult learning (MA); K-12 teaching (MA). Part-time and evening/weekend programs available. Postbaccalaureate distance learning degree programs offered (no on-campus study). *Students:* 60 full-time (49 women), 59 part-time (43 women); includes 16 minority (2 Black or African American, non-Hispanic/Latino; 3 Asian, non-Hispanic/Latino; 10 Hispanic/Latino; 1 Two or more races, non-Hispanic/Latino), 1 international. Average age 38. 32 applicants, 88% accepted, 23 enrolled. In 2013, 47 master's awarded. *Degree requirements:* For master's, comprehensive exam (for some programs), comprehensive exam or online portfolio; 30 credit hours. *Entrance requirements:* For master's, GRE or MAT (if GPA is below 2.75), resume, statement of intent, three letters of recommendation. Additional exam requirements/recommendations for international students: Required—TOEFL (minimum score 537 paper-based; 75 iBT); Recommended—IELTS (minimum score 6.5). *Application deadline:* For fall admission, 5/15 for domestic students, 5/1 for international students; for spring admission, 11/15 for domestic students, 11/1 for international students. Application fee: $50 ($75 for international students). *Expenses:* Contact institution. *Financial support:* In 2013–14, 2 students received support. Fellowships, research assistantships, teaching assistantships, Federal Work-Study, institutionally sponsored loans, scholarships/grants, and traineeships available. Financial award application deadline: 4/1; financial award applicants required to submit FAFSA. *Faculty research:* Technology for educational management, instructional design foundations, e-Learning, educational design. *Unit head:* Brent Wilson, Professor, 303-315-4963, E-mail: brent.wilson@

ucdenver.edu. *Application contact:* Hans Broers, Academic Advisor, 303-315-6351, Fax: 303-315-6311, E-mail: hans.broers@ucdenver.edu. Website: http://www.ucdenver.edu/academics/colleges/SchoolOfEducation/Academics/MASTERS/ILT/Pages/default.aspx.

University of Connecticut, Graduate School, Neag School of Education, Department of Educational Leadership, Field of Adult Learning, Storrs, CT 06269. Offers MA, PhD. *Accreditation:* NCATE. Terminal master's awarded for partial completion of doctoral program. *Degree requirements:* For master's, comprehensive exam, thesis or alternative; for doctorate, thesis/dissertation. *Entrance requirements:* For master's and doctorate, GRE General Test. Additional exam requirements/recommendations for international students: Required—TOEFL (minimum score 550 paper-based). Electronic applications accepted.

University of Georgia, College of Education, Department of Lifelong Education, Administration and Policy, Athens, GA 30602. Offers adult education (M Ed, Ed D, PhD, Ed S); educational administration and policy (M Ed, PhD, Ed S); educational leadership (Ed D); human resource and organizational design (M Ed). *Accreditation:* NCATE. *Entrance requirements:* For master's and Ed S, GRE General Test or MAT; for doctorate, GRE General Test. Electronic applications accepted.

University of Houston–Victoria, School of Education and Human Development, Victoria, TX 77901-4450. Offers administration and supervision (M Ed); adult and higher education (M Ed); counseling (M Ed); curriculum and instruction (M Ed); special education (M Ed). Part-time and evening/weekend programs available. Postbaccalaureate distance learning degree programs offered (minimal on-campus study). *Faculty:* 22 full-time (19 women). *Students:* 56 full-time (52 women), 325 part-time (274 women); includes 211 minority (113 Black or African American, non-Hispanic/Latino; 2 American Indian or Alaska Native, non-Hispanic/Latino; 16 Asian, non-Hispanic/Latino; 68 Hispanic/Latino; 12 Two or more races, non-Hispanic/Latino), 3 international. *Degree requirements:* For master's, comprehensive exam, project or thesis. *Entrance requirements:* For master's, GRE General Test. Additional exam requirements/recommendations for international students: Required—TOEFL. *Application deadline:* For fall admission, 6/1 for international students; for spring admission, 10/1 for international students. Applications are processed on a rolling basis. Application fee: $0. Electronic applications accepted. *Expenses:* Tuition, state resident: full-time $4534; part-time $251 per credit hour. Tuition, nonresident: full-time $10,906; part-time $606 per contact hour. *Required fees:* $68 per semester hour. Tuition and fees vary according to course load. *Financial support:* In 2013–14, research assistantships with partial tuition reimbursements (averaging $2,000 per year), teaching assistantships with partial tuition reimbursements (averaging $2,000 per year) were awarded; Federal Work-Study, scholarships/grants, and unspecified assistantships also available. Support available to part-time students. Financial award application deadline: 4/15; financial award applicants required to submit FAFSA. *Faculty research:* Reading and language arts education, evaluation and diagnosis of special children's abilities. *Unit head:* Freddie W. Litton, Dean, 361-570-4260, Fax: 361-580-5580. *Application contact:* Sandy Hybner, Senior Recruitment Coordinator, 361-570-4252, Fax: 361-580-5580, E-mail: hybners@uhv.edu. Website: http://www.uhv.edu/edu/.

University of Manitoba, Faculty of Graduate Studies, Faculty of Education, Department of Educational Administration, Foundations and Psychology, Winnipeg, MB R3T 2N2, Canada. Offers adult and post-secondary education (M Ed); educational administration (M Ed); guidance and counseling (M Ed); inclusive special education (M Ed); social foundations of education (M Ed). *Degree requirements:* For master's, thesis or alternative.

University of Memphis, Graduate School, College of Education, Department of Leadership, Memphis, TN 38152. Offers adult education (Ed D); educational leadership (Ed D); higher education (Ed D); leadership (MS); policy studies (Ed D); school administration and supervision (MS). *Accreditation:* NCATE. Part-time and evening/weekend programs available. Postbaccalaureate distance learning degree programs offered (minimal on-campus study). *Faculty:* 12 full-time (4 women), 2 part-time/adjunct (0 women). *Students:* 12 full-time (8 women), 138 part-time (87 women); includes 86 minority (79 Black or African American, non-Hispanic/Latino; 1 Asian, non-Hispanic/Latino; 1 Hispanic/Latino; 5 Two or more races, non-Hispanic/Latino), 1 international. Average age 40. 65 applicants, 66% accepted, 10 enrolled. In 2013, 12 master's, 13 doctorates awarded. *Degree requirements:* For master's, comprehensive exam, thesis optional; for doctorate, comprehensive exam, thesis/dissertation. *Entrance requirements:* For master's and doctorate, GRE. *Application deadline:* For fall admission, 4/1 for domestic students; for spring admission, 10/1 for domestic students. Application fee: $35 ($60 for international students). Electronic applications accepted. *Financial support:* In 2013–14, 70 students received support. Research assistantships with full tuition reimbursements available, teaching assistantships, Federal Work-Study, scholarships/grants, and unspecified assistantships available. Financial award application deadline: 2/15; financial award applicants required to submit FAFSA. *Faculty research:* School improvement, social justice, online learning, adult learning, diversity. *Unit head:* Katrina Mayer, Interim Chair, 901-678-2466, E-mail: kmeyer@memphis.edu. *Application contact:* Larry McNeal, Professor, School Administration and Supervision Programs, 901-678-2369, E-mail: lmcneal1@memphis.edu. Website: http://www.memphis.edu/lead.

University of Minnesota, Twin Cities Campus, Graduate School, College of Education and Human Development, Department of Organizational Leadership, Policy and Development, Program in Adult Education, Minneapolis, MN 55455-0213. Offers M Ed, MA, Ed D, PhD, Certificate. *Students:* 2 full-time (1 woman), 8 part-time (5 women); includes 2 minority (1 Black or African American, non-Hispanic/Latino; 1 Asian, non-Hispanic/Latino). Average age 42. 15 applicants, 87% accepted, 9 enrolled. In 2013, 12 master's, 10 other advanced degrees awarded. Application fee: $75 ($95 for international students). *Unit head:* Dr. Rebecca Ropers-Huilman, Chair, 612-626-9809, Fax: 612-624-2231, E-mail: ropers@umn.edu. *Application contact:* Dr. Jennifer Engler, Assistant Dean, 612-626-2887, Fax: 612-626-7496, E-mail: engle009@umn.edu. Website: http://www.education.umn.edu/edpa/.

University of Missouri, Graduate School, College of Education, Department of Educational Leadership and Policy Analysis, Columbia, MO 65211. Offers education administration (M Ed, MA, Ed D, PhD, Ed S); higher and adult education (M Ed, MA, Ed D, PhD, Ed S). Part-time programs available. *Faculty:* 15 full-time (8 women), 5 part-time/adjunct (4 women). *Students:* 118 full-time (67 women), 273 part-time (158 women); includes 52 minority (30 Black or African American, non-Hispanic/Latino; 1 American Indian or Alaska Native, non-Hispanic/Latino; 4 Asian, non-Hispanic/Latino; 10 Hispanic/Latino; 7 Two or more races, non-Hispanic/Latino), 18 international. Average age 37. 233 applicants, 62% accepted, 120 enrolled. In 2013, 35 master's, 70 doctorates, 31 other advanced degrees awarded. *Degree requirements:* For doctorate, variable foreign language requirement, comprehensive exam (for some programs), thesis/dissertation. *Entrance requirements:* For master's, doctorate, and Ed S, minimum GPA of 3.0. Additional exam requirements/recommendations for international students: Required—TOEFL (minimum score 500 paper-based; 61 iBT), IELTS (minimum score 5.5). *Application deadline:* For fall admission, 1/15 priority date for domestic and international students; for winter admission, 9/15 priority date for domestic and

international students; for spring admission, 10/15 for domestic students. Applications are processed on a rolling basis. Application fee: $55 ($75 for international students). Electronic applications accepted. *Financial support:* Fellowships with full tuition reimbursements, research assistantships with full tuition reimbursements, teaching assistantships with full tuition reimbursements, institutionally sponsored loans, scholarships/grants, health care benefits, and unspecified assistantships available. *Faculty research:* Administrative communication and behavior, middle schools leadership, administration of special education. *Unit head:* Dr. Jeni Hart, Associate Division Director, 573-882-4225, E-mail: hartjl@missouri.edu. *Application contact:* Betty Kissane, Office Support Assistant IV, 573-882-8221, E-mail: kissaneb@missouri.edu. Website: http://elpa.missouri.edu/.

University of Missouri–St. Louis, College of Education, Division of Educational Leadership and Policy Studies, St. Louis, MO 63121. Offers adult and higher education (M Ed), including adult education, higher education; educational administration (M Ed, Ed S), including community education (M Ed), elementary education (M Ed), secondary education (M Ed); institutional research (Certificate). *Accreditation:* NCATE. Part-time and evening/weekend programs available. *Faculty:* 13 full-time (8 women), 5 part-time/adjunct (2 women). *Students:* 17 full-time (13 women), 154 part-time (114 women); includes 77 minority (75 Black or African American, non-Hispanic/Latino; 1 Asian, non-Hispanic/Latino; 1 Hispanic/Latino), 7 international. Average age 35. 120 applicants, 68% accepted, 40 enrolled. In 2013, 63 master's, 28 Certificates awarded. *Degree requirements:* For master's, comprehensive exam (for some programs); for other advanced degree, comprehensive exam (for some programs), thesis or alternative. *Entrance requirements:* Additional exam requirements/recommendations for international students: Recommended—TOEFL (minimum score 550 paper-based; 79 iBT), IELTS (minimum score 6.5). *Application deadline:* For fall admission, 7/1 priority date for domestic and international students; for spring admission, 12/1 priority date for domestic and international students. Applications are processed on a rolling basis. Application fee: $50 ($40 for international students). Electronic applications accepted. *Expenses:* Tuition, state resident: full-time $7364; part-time $409.10 per credit hour. Tuition, nonresident: full-time $19,162; part-time $1008.50 per credit hour. *Financial support:* In 2013–14, 1 research assistantship with full and partial tuition reimbursement (averaging $12,000 per year), teaching assistantships with full and partial tuition reimbursements (averaging $8,470 per year) were awarded. Financial award application deadline: 4/1; financial award applicants required to submit FAFSA. *Faculty research:* Educational policy research; philosophy of education; higher, adult, and vocational education; school initiatives, change, and reform. *Unit head:* Dr. E. Kathleen Sullivan Brown, Chair, 514-516-5944. *Application contact:* 314-516-5458, Fax: 314-516-6996, E-mail: gradadm@umsl.edu. Website: http://coe.umsl.edu/web/divisions/elaps/index.html.

University of Missouri–St. Louis, College of Education, Interdisciplinary Doctoral Programs, St. Louis, MO 63121. Offers adult and higher education (Ed D); counseling (PhD); counselor education (Ed D); educational administration (Ed D); educational leadership and policy studies (PhD); educational psychology (PhD); teaching-learning processes (Ed D, PhD). *Faculty:* 72 full-time (33 women). *Students:* 58 full-time (46 women), 240 part-time (154 women); includes 106 minority (86 Black or African American, non-Hispanic/Latino; 4 American Indian or Alaska Native, non-Hispanic/Latino; 6 Asian, non-Hispanic/Latino; 8 Hispanic/Latino; 2 Two or more races, non-Hispanic/Latino), 9 international. Average age 42. 67 applicants, 58% accepted, 24 enrolled. In 2013, 24 doctorates awarded. *Degree requirements:* For doctorate, thesis/dissertation. *Entrance requirements:* For doctorate, GRE General Test, 3 letters of recommendation; personal interview. Additional exam requirements/recommendations for international students: Recommended—TOEFL (minimum score 550 paper-based; 79 iBT), IELTS (minimum score 6.5). *Application deadline:* For fall admission, 3/1 for domestic and international students; for spring admission, 10/1 for domestic and international students. Application fee: $50 ($40 for international students). Electronic applications accepted. *Expenses:* Tuition, state resident: full-time $7364; part-time $409.10 per credit hour. Tuition, nonresident: full-time $19,162; part-time $1008.50 per credit hour. *Financial support:* In 2013–14, 13 research assistantships (averaging $12,240 per year), 9 teaching assistantships (averaging $12,240 per year) were awarded. Financial award application deadline: 4/1; financial award applicants required to submit FAFSA. *Faculty research:* Higher education law and policy, gender and higher education, student retention, lifelong learning orientation, school counselor's role in violence prevention. *Unit head:* Dr. Kathleen Haywood, Director of Graduate Studies, 314-516-5483, Fax: 314-516-5227, E-mail: kathleen_haywood@umsl.edu. *Application contact:* 314-516-5458, Fax: 314-516-6996, E-mail: gradadm@umsl.edu.

University of Nebraska–Lincoln, Graduate College, College of Education and Human Sciences, Department of Teaching, Learning and Teacher Education, Lincoln, NE 68588. Offers adult and continuing education (MA); educational studies (Ed D, PhD), including special education (Ed D); teaching, learning and teacher education (M Ed, MA, MST, Ed D, PhD); vocational and adult education (M Ed, MA). *Accreditation:* NCATE. *Degree requirements:* For master's, thesis optional. *Entrance requirements:* Additional exam requirements/recommendations for international students: Required—TOEFL (minimum score 550 paper-based). Electronic applications accepted. *Faculty research:* Teacher education, instructional leadership, literacy education, technology, improvement of school curriculum.

The University of North Carolina at Greensboro, Graduate School, School of Education, Department of Curriculum and Instruction, Greensboro, NC 27412-5001. Offers college teaching and adult learning (Certificate); curriculum and instruction (M Ed), including chemistry education, elementary education, English as a second language, French education, instructional technology, mathematics education, middle grades education, reading education, science education, social studies education, Spanish education; curriculum and teaching (PhD), including higher education, teacher education and development; English as a second language (Certificate); higher education (M Ed); supervision (M Ed). *Accreditation:* NCATE. Part-time programs available. *Degree requirements:* For doctorate, thesis/dissertation. *Entrance requirements:* For master's and doctorate, GRE General Test. Additional exam requirements/recommendations for international students: Required—TOEFL. Electronic applications accepted. *Faculty research:* Community college literacy program, middle school mathematics/computer mathematics.

University of North Florida, College of Education and Human Services, Department of Foundations and Secondary Education, Jacksonville, FL 32224. Offers adult learning (M Ed); professional education (M Ed). *Accreditation:* NCATE. Part-time and evening/weekend programs available. *Faculty:* 12 full-time (5 women). *Students:* 1 (woman) full-time, 13 part-time (10 women); includes 4 minority (2 Black or African American, non-Hispanic/Latino; 1 Asian, non-Hispanic/Latino; 1 Hispanic/Latino). Average age 33. 13 applicants, 69% accepted, 7 enrolled. In 2013, 2 master's awarded. *Entrance requirements:* For master's, GRE General Test, minimum GPA of 3.0 in last 60 hours, interview, 3 letters of recommendation. Additional exam requirements/recommendations for international students: Required—TOEFL (minimum score 500 paper-based; 61 iBT). *Application deadline:* For fall admission, 7/1 priority date for domestic students, 5/1 for international students; for spring admission, 11/1 priority date for domestic students, 10/1 for international students. Application fee: $30. Electronic applications accepted.

Adult Education

Expenses: Tuition, state resident: full-time $9794; part-time $408.10 per credit hour. Tuition, nonresident: full-time $22,383; part-time $932.61 per credit hour. *Required fees:* $2020; $84.20 per credit hour. Tuition and fees vary according to course load and program. *Financial support:* In 2013–14, 11 students received support, including 1 research assistantship (averaging $4,264 per year); teaching assistantships, career-related internships or fieldwork, Federal Work-Study, and tuition waivers (partial) also available. Support available to part-time students. Financial award application deadline: 4/1; financial award applicants required to submit FAFSA. *Faculty research:* Using children's literature to enhance metalinguistic awareness, education, oral language diagnosis of middle-schoolers, science inquiry teaching and learning. *Total annual research expenditures:* $821. *Unit head:* Dr. Jeffery Cornett, Chair, 904-620-2610, Fax: 904-620-1821, E-mail: jcornett@unf.edu. *Application contact:* Dr. Amanda Pascale, Director, The Graduate School, 904-620-1360, Fax: 904-620-1362, E-mail: graduateschool@unf.edu.
Website: http://www.unf.edu/coehs/fse/.

University of Oklahoma, Jeannine Rainbolt College of Education, Department of Educational Leadership and Policy Studies, Program in Adult and Higher Education, Norman, OK 73019. Offers M Ed, PhD. *Accreditation:* NCATE. Part-time and evening/weekend programs available. *Students:* 140 full-time (72 women), 74 part-time (49 women); includes 65 minority (31 Black or African American, non-Hispanic/Latino; 13 American Indian or Alaska Native, non-Hispanic/Latino; 2 Asian, non-Hispanic/Latino; 10 Hispanic/Latino; 9 Two or more races, non-Hispanic/Latino), 5 international. Average age 29. 122 applicants, 71% accepted, 62 enrolled. In 2013, 69 master's, 3 doctorates awarded. *Degree requirements:* For master's, comprehensive exam; for doctorate, variable foreign language requirement, thesis/dissertation. *Entrance requirements:* For master's, minimum GPA of 3.0 in last 60 hours of undergraduate course work; for doctorate, GRE General Test, resume, 3 letters of reference, scholarly writing sample. Additional exam requirements/recommendations for international students: Required—TOEFL (minimum score 79 iBT). *Application deadline:* For fall admission, 2/1 for domestic and international students; for spring admission, 10/1 for domestic and international students; for summer admission, 4/1 for domestic and international students. Application fee: $50 ($100 for international students). Electronic applications accepted. *Expenses:* Tuition, state resident: full-time $4205; part-time $175.20 per credit hour. Tuition, nonresident: full-time $16,205; part-time $675.20 per credit hour. *Required fees:* $2745; $103.85 per credit hour. $126.50 per semester. *Financial support:* In 2013–14, 179 students received support. Unspecified assistantships available. Financial award application deadline: 6/1; financial award applicants required to submit FAFSA. *Faculty research:* Student-athlete development, equity in higher education, e-learning, student identity, diversity issues. *Unit head:* Dr. David Tan, Chair, 405-325-5986, Fax: 405-325-2403, E-mail: dtan@ou.edu. *Application contact:* Geri Evans, Graduate Programs Representative, 405-325-5978, Fax: 405-325-2403, E-mail: gevans@ou.edu.
Website: http://www.ou.edu/education/elps.

University of Phoenix–Bay Area Campus, College of Education, San Jose, CA 95134-1805. Offers administration and supervision (MA Ed); adult education and training (MA Ed); early childhood education (MA Ed); education (Ed S); educational leadership (Ed D); elementary teacher education (MA Ed); higher education administration (PhD); secondary teacher education (MA Ed); special education (MA Ed); teacher leadership (MA Ed). Evening/weekend programs available. Postbaccalaureate distance learning degree programs offered (no on-campus study). *Degree requirements:* For master's, thesis (for some programs). *Entrance requirements:* For master's, minimum undergraduate GPA of 2.5, 3 years of work experience. Additional exam requirements/recommendations for international students: Required—TOEFL (minimum score 550 paper-based; 79 iBT). Electronic applications accepted.

University of Phoenix–Omaha Campus, College of Education, Omaha, NE 68154-5240. Offers administration and supervision (MA Ed); curriculum and instruction (MA Ed), including adult education, computer education, curriculum and instruction, English and language arts education, English as a second language, mathematics education; elementary teacher education (MA Ed); secondary teacher education (MA Ed); special education (MA Ed).

University of Phoenix–Online Campus, College of Education, Phoenix, AZ 85034-7209. Offers administration and supervision (MAEd, Certificate); adult education and training (MAEd); curriculum and instruction (MAEd), including computer education, curriculum and instruction, English as a second language, language arts, mathematics, reading; early childhood education (MAEd); educational studies (MAEd); elementary teacher education (MAEd), including early childhood, elementary teacher education, high school middle level, middle level; principal licensure (Certificate); secondary teacher education (MAEd); special education (MAEd, Certificate); teacher education (MAEd), including middle level generalist; teacher education middle level mathematics (MAEd), including middle level mathematics; teacher education middle level science (MAEd), including middle level science; teacher education secondary mathematics (MAEd); teacher education secondary science (MAEd); teacher leadership (MAEd); teachers of English learners (Certificate); transition to teaching (Certificate), including elementary education, secondary education. *Accreditation:* Teacher Education Accreditation Council. Evening/weekend programs available. Postbaccalaureate distance learning degree programs offered. *Entrance requirements:* Additional exam requirements/recommendations for international students: Required—TOEFL, TOEIC (Test of English as an International Communication), Berlitz Online English Proficiency Exam, PTE, or IELTS. Electronic applications accepted. *Expenses:* Contact institution.

University of Phoenix–Phoenix Campus, College of Education, Tempe, AZ 85282-2371. Offers administration and supervision (MA Ed); adult education and training (MA Ed); curriculum and instruction reading (MA Ed); early childhood education (MA Ed); education studies (MA Ed); elementary teacher education (MA Ed); secondary teacher education (MA Ed); special education (MA Ed); teacher leadership (MA Ed). Evening/weekend programs available. Postbaccalaureate distance learning degree programs offered. *Entrance requirements:* Additional exam requirements/recommendations for international students: Required—TOEFL, TOEIC (Test of English as an International Communication), Berlitz Online English Proficiency Exam, PTE, or IELTS. Electronic applications accepted. *Expenses:* Contact institution.

University of Phoenix–Sacramento Valley Campus, College of Education, Sacramento, CA 95833-3632. Offers adult education (MA Ed); curriculum instruction (MA Ed); elementary teacher education (MA Ed); secondary teacher education (MA Ed); teacher education (Certificate). Evening/weekend programs available. *Degree requirements:* For master's, thesis (for some programs). *Entrance requirements:* For master's, 3 years of work experience, minimum undergraduate GPA of 2.5. Additional exam requirements/recommendations for international students: Required—TOEFL (minimum score 550 paper-based; 79 iBT). Electronic applications accepted.

University of Phoenix–Southern Arizona Campus, College of Education, Tucson, AZ 85711. Offers administration and supervision (MA Ed); adult education and training (MA Ed); curriculum instruction (MA Ed); educational counseling (MA Ed); elementary teacher education (MA Ed); school counseling (MSC); secondary teacher education (MA Ed); special education (MA Ed, Certificate). Evening/weekend programs available. *Degree requirements:* For master's, thesis (for some programs). *Entrance requirements:* For master's, minimum undergraduate GPA of 2.5, 3 years of work experience. Additional exam requirements/recommendations for international students: Required—TOEFL (minimum score 550 paper-based; 79 iBT). Electronic applications accepted.

University of Phoenix–Southern California Campus, College of Education, Costa Mesa, CA 92626. Offers administration and supervision (MA Ed, Certificate); adult education and training (MA Ed); educational studies (MA Ed); elementary teacher education (MA Ed); secondary teacher education (MA Ed); teacher leadership (MA Ed); teachers of English learners (Certificate). Evening/weekend programs available. Postbaccalaureate distance learning degree programs offered. *Entrance requirements:* Additional exam requirements/recommendations for international students: Required—TOEFL, TOEIC (Test of English as an International Communication), Berlitz Online English Proficiency Exam, PTE, or IELTS. Electronic applications accepted. *Expenses:* Contact institution.

University of Phoenix–Washington D.C. Campus, College of Education, Washington, DC 20001. Offers administration and supervision (MA Ed); adult education and training (MA Ed); computer education (MA Ed); curriculum and instruction (MA Ed, Ed D); early childhood education (MA Ed); education (Ed S); educational leadership (Ed D); educational technology (Ed D); elementary teacher education (MA Ed); English and language arts education (MA Ed); English as a second language (MA Ed); higher education administration (PhD); mathematics education (MA Ed); secondary teacher education (MA Ed); special education (MA Ed); teacher leadership (MA Ed).

University of Regina, Faculty of Graduate Studies and Research, Faculty of Education, Department of Adult Education, Regina, SK S4S 0A2, Canada. Offers MA Ed. Part-time programs available. *Faculty:* 42 full-time (23 women), 18 part-time/adjunct (10 women). *Students:* 5 full-time (all women), 11 part-time (9 women). 2 applicants, 50% accepted. In 2013, 10 master's awarded. *Degree requirements:* For master's, thesis (for some programs), practicum, project, or thesis. *Entrance requirements:* For master's, bachelor's degree in education, 2 years of teaching or other relevant professional experience. Additional exam requirements/recommendations for international students: Required—TOEFL (minimum score 580 paper-based; 80 iBT), IELTS (minimum score 6.5). *Application deadline:* For fall admission, 2/15 for domestic and international students; for winter admission, 10/15 for domestic and international students; for spring admission, 2/15 for domestic students. Application fee: $100. Electronic applications accepted. *Expenses: Tuition, area resident:* Full-time $4338 Canadian dollars. *International tuition:* $7338 Canadian dollars full-time. *Required fees:* $449.25 Canadian dollars. *Financial support:* In 2013–14, 3 fellowships (averaging $6,000 per year), 2 teaching assistantships (averaging $2,356 per year) were awarded; research assistantships and scholarships/grants also available. Financial award application deadline: 6/15. *Faculty research:* Program and instruction. *Unit head:* Dr. Ken Montgomery, Associate Dean, Research and Graduate Programs in Education, 306-585-5031, Fax: 306-585-5387, E-mail: ken.montgomery@uregina.ca. *Application contact:* Tania Gates, Graduate Program Coordinator, 306-585-4506, Fax: 306-585-5387, E-mail: edgrad@uregina.ca.

University of Rhode Island, Graduate School, College of Human Science and Services, School of Education, Kingston, RI 02881. Offers adult education (MA); education (PhD); elementary education (MA); music education (MM); reading education (MA); secondary education (MA); special education (MA); MS/PhD. *Accreditation:* NCATE. Part-time and evening/weekend programs available. *Faculty:* 16 full-time (9 women). *Students:* 64 full-time (48 women), 91 part-time (68 women); includes 17 minority (8 Black or African American, non-Hispanic/Latino; 2 American Indian or Alaska Native, non-Hispanic/Latino; 2 Asian, non-Hispanic/Latino; 3 Hispanic/Latino; 2 Two or more races, non-Hispanic/Latino), 6 international. In 2013, 47 master's, 11 doctorates awarded. *Degree requirements:* For master's, comprehensive exam (for some programs), thesis optional; for doctorate, comprehensive exam, thesis/dissertation. *Entrance requirements:* For master's, 2 letters of recommendation; interview (for special education applicants); for doctorate, GRE, 3 letters of recommendation, resume. Additional exam requirements/recommendations for international students: Required—TOEFL (minimum score 600 paper-based; 100 iBT). *Application deadline:* For fall admission, 1/31 for domestic and international students. Application fee: $65. Electronic applications accepted. *Expenses:* Tuition, state resident: full-time $11,532; part-time $641 per credit. Tuition, nonresident: full-time $23,606; part-time $1311 per credit. *Required fees:* $1388; $36 per credit. $35 per semester. One-time fee: $130. *Financial support:* In 2013–14, 2 research assistantships with full and partial tuition reimbursements (averaging $11,883 per year), 4 teaching assistantships with full and partial tuition reimbursements (averaging $8,488 per year) were awarded; career-related internships or fieldwork also available. Financial award application deadline: 1/31; financial award applicants required to submit FAFSA. *Total annual research expenditures:* $1.1 million. *Unit head:* Dr. David Byrd, Director, 401-874-5484, Fax: 401-874-5471, E-mail: dbyrd@uri.edu. *Application contact:* Graduate Admissions, 401-874-2872, E-mail: gradadm@etal.uri.edu.
Website: http://www.uri.edu/hss/education/.

University of South Africa, College of Human Sciences, Pretoria, South Africa. Offers adult education (M Ed); African languages (MA, PhD); African politics (MA, PhD); Afrikaans (MA, PhD); ancient history (MA, PhD); ancient Near Eastern studies (MA, PhD); anthropology (MA, PhD); applied linguistics (MA); Arabic (MA, PhD); archaeology (MA); art history (MA); Biblical archaeology (MA); Biblical studies (M Th, D Th, PhD); Christian spirituality (M Th, D Th); church history (M Th, D Th); classical studies (MA, PhD); clinical psychology (MA); communication (MA, PhD); comparative education (M Ed, Ed D); consulting psychology (D Admin, D Com, PhD); curriculum studies (M Ed, Ed D); development studies (M Admin, MA, D Admin, PhD); didactics (M Ed, Ed D); education (M Tech); education management (M Ed, Ed D); educational psychology (M Ed); English (MA); environmental education (M Ed); French (MA, PhD); German (MA, PhD); Greek (MA); guidance and counseling (M Ed); health studies (MA, PhD), including health sciences education (MA), health services management (MA), medical and surgical nursing science (critical care general) (MA), midwifery and neonatal nursing science (MA), trauma and emergency care (MA); history (MA, PhD); history of education (Ed D); inclusive education (M Ed, Ed D); information and communications technology policy and regulation (MA); information science (MA, MIS, PhD); international politics (MA, PhD); Islamic studies (MA, PhD); Italian (MA, PhD); Judaica (MA, PhD); linguistics (MA, PhD); mathematical education (M Ed); mathematics education (MA); missiology (M Th, D Th); modern Hebrew (MA, PhD); musicology (MA, MMus, D Mus, PhD); natural science education (M Ed); New Testament (M Th, D Th); Old Testament (D Th); pastoral therapy (M Th, D Th); philosophy (MA); philosophy of education (M Ed, Ed D); politics (MA, PhD); Portuguese (MA, PhD); practical theology (M Th, D Th); psychology (MA, MS, PhD); psychology of education (M Ed, Ed D); public health (MA); religious studies (MA, D Th, PhD); Romance languages (MA); Russian (MA, PhD); Semitic languages (MA, PhD); social behavior studies in HIV/AIDS (MA); social science (mental health) (MA); social science in development studies (MA); social science in psychology (MA); social science in social work (MA); social science in sociology (MA); social work (MSW, DSW, PhD); socio-education (M Ed, Ed D); sociolinguistics (MA); sociology (MA, PhD); Spanish (MA, PhD); systematic theology (M Th, D Th); TESOL (teaching English to speakers of other languages) (MA); theological ethics (M Th, D Th); theory of literature (MA, PhD); urban ministries (D Th); urban ministry (M Th).

University of Southern Maine, College of Management and Human Service, School of Education and Human Development, Program in Adult Education, Portland, ME 04104-9300. Offers adult and higher education (MS); adult learning (CAS). *Accreditation:* Teacher Education Accreditation Council. Part-time and evening/weekend programs available. Postbaccalaureate distance learning degree programs offered (minimal on-campus study). *Faculty:* 3 full-time (1 woman), 2 part-time/adjunct (1 woman). *Students:* 4 full-time (3 women), 37 part-time (33 women); includes 1 minority (Hispanic/Latino). Average age 42. 16 applicants, 69% accepted, 9 enrolled. In 2013, 16 master's, 2 other advanced degrees awarded. *Degree requirements:* For master's and CAS, thesis or alternative. *Entrance requirements:* For master's, interview; for CAS, master's degree. Additional exam requirements/recommendations for international students: Required—TOEFL (minimum score 550 paper-based; 79 iBT). *Application deadline:* For fall admission, 5/1 priority date for domestic students; for spring admission, 10/15 priority date for domestic students. Applications are processed on a rolling basis. Application fee: $65. Electronic applications accepted. *Expenses:* Tuition, state resident: part-time $380 per credit. Tuition, nonresident: part-time $1026 per credit. Part-time tuition and fees vary according to program. *Financial support:* Research assistantships, career-related internships or fieldwork, Federal Work-Study, institutionally sponsored loans, scholarships/grants, and unspecified assistantships available. Support available to part-time students. Financial award application deadline: 3/1; financial award applicants required to submit FAFSA. *Faculty research:* Older learners, lifelong learning institutes, teaching and learning in later age. *Unit head:* Dr. E. Michael Brady, Program Coordinator, 207-780-5312, E-mail: mbrady@usm.maine.edu. *Application contact:* Mary Sloan, Assistant Dean of Graduate Studies and Director of Graduate Admissions, 207-780-4812, Fax: 207-780-4969, E-mail: gradstudies@usm.maine.edu.
Website: http://usm.maine.edu/adult-education.

University of Southern Mississippi, Graduate School, College of Education and Psychology, Department of Educational Studies and Research, Hattiesburg, MS 39406-0001. Offers adult education (Graduate Certificate); community college leadership (Graduate Certificate); counseling and personnel services (college) (M Ed); education (PhD, Ed S), including adult education, research, evaluation and statistics (PhD); education (Ed D), including educational administration, educational research; education: educational leadership and research (Ed S), including higher education administration; educational administration and supervision (M Ed); higher education administration (Ed D, PhD); institutional research (Graduate Certificate). *Faculty:* 7 full-time (1 woman), 5 part-time/adjunct (1 woman). *Students:* 32 full-time (21 women), 103 part-time (70 women); includes 44 minority (39 Black or African American, non-Hispanic/Latino; 2 Hispanic/Latino; 3 Two or more races, non-Hispanic/Latino), 4 international. Average age 36. 36 applicants, 72% accepted, 15 enrolled. In 2013, 18 master's, 9 doctorates, 7 other advanced degrees awarded. *Degree requirements:* For master's and other advanced degree, comprehensive exam, thesis (for some programs); for doctorate, comprehensive exam, thesis/dissertation. *Entrance requirements:* For master's, doctorate, and other advanced degree, GRE General Test, minimum GPA of 2.75. Additional exam requirements/recommendations for international students: Required—TOEFL. *Application deadline:* For fall admission, 2/1 for domestic students, 3/1 for international students. Applications are processed on a rolling basis. Application fee: $35. *Financial support:* Career-related internships or fieldwork, Federal Work-Study, and institutionally sponsored loans available. Financial award application deadline: 3/15; financial award applicants required to submit FAFSA. *Total annual research expenditures:* $88,500. *Unit head:* Dr. Thomas V. O'Brien, Chair, 601-266-6093, E-mail: thomas.obrien@usm.edu. *Application contact:* Shonna Breland, Manager of Graduate Admissions, 601-266-6563, Fax: 601-266-5138.
Website: http://www.usm.edu/cep/esr/.

University of South Florida, College of Education, Department of Adult, Career and Higher Education, Tampa, FL 33620-9951. Offers adult education (MA, Ed D, PhD, Ed S); career and technical education (MA); career and workforce education (PhD); higher education/community college teaching (MA, Ed D, PhD); vocational education (Ed S). Part-time programs available. Postbaccalaureate distance learning degree programs offered (minimal on-campus study). *Degree requirements:* For master's, comprehensive exam; for doctorate, comprehensive exam, thesis/dissertation, philosophies of inquiry; multiple research methods; for Ed S, comprehensive exam, thesis. *Entrance requirements:* For master's, minimum GPA of 3.0 in last 60 hours of course work; for doctorate and Ed S, GRE General Test, GRE Writing Test. Additional exam requirements/recommendations for international students: Required—TOEFL (minimum score 500 paper-based; 91 iBT). Electronic applications accepted. *Faculty research:* Community college leadership; integration of academic, career and technical education; competency-based education; continuing education administration; adult learning and development.

University of South Florida, University College/Distance Education, Tampa, FL 33620-9951. *Unit head:* Kathy Barnes, Interdisciplinary Programs Coordinator, 813-974-8031, Fax: 813-974-7061, E-mail: barnesk@usf.edu. *Application contact:* Karen Tylinski, Metro Initiatives, 813-974-9943, Fax: 813-974-7061, E-mail: ktylinsk@usf.edu.
Website: http://uc.usf.edu/.

The University of Tennessee, Graduate School, College of Education, Health and Human Sciences, Department of Educational Psychology and Counseling, Knoxville, TN 37996. Offers adult education (MS); applied educational psychology (MS); collaborative learning (Ed D); college student personnel (MS); mental health counseling (MS); rehabilitation counseling (MS); school counseling (MS). *Accreditation:* ACA (one or more programs are accredited); CORE (one or more programs are accredited); NCATE. Part-time and evening/weekend programs available. *Degree requirements:* For master's, thesis optional. *Entrance requirements:* For master's, GRE General Test, minimum GPA of 2.7. Additional exam requirements/recommendations for international students: Required—TOEFL. Electronic applications accepted. *Expenses:* Tuition, state resident: full-time $9540; part-time $531 per credit hour. Tuition, nonresident: full-time $27,728; part-time $1542 per credit hour. *Required fees:* $1404; $67 per credit hour.

University of the Incarnate Word, School of Graduate Studies and Research, Dreeben School of Education, Programs in Education, San Antonio, TX 78209-6397. Offers adult education (M Ed, MA); cross-cultural education (M Ed, MA); early childhood literacy (M Ed, MA); general education (M Ed, MA); higher education (PhD); instructional technology (M Ed, MA); international education and entrepreneurship (PhD); kinesiology (M Ed, MA); literacy (M Ed, MA); organizational leadership (PhD); organizational learning and learning (M Ed, MA); reading (M Ed, MA); special education (M Ed, MA); teacher leadership (M Ed, MA). Part-time and evening/weekend programs available. *Faculty:* 17 full-time (9 women), 6 part-time/adjunct (all women). *Students:* 23 full-time (13 women), 187 part-time (122 women); includes 114 minority (24 Black or African American, non-Hispanic/Latino; 1 American Indian or Alaska Native, non-Hispanic/Latino; 3 Asian, non-Hispanic/Latino; 85 Hispanic/Latino; 1 Two or more races, non-Hispanic/Latino), 30 international. Average age 41. 52 applicants, 67% accepted, 25 enrolled. In 2013, 12 master's, 14 doctorates awarded. *Degree requirements:* For master's, capstone; for doctorate, thesis/dissertation, qualifying exam. *Entrance requirements:* For master's, baccalaureate degree; minimum foundation GPA of 2.5; interview; for doctorate, master's degree; interview; supervised writing sample. Additional exam requirements/recommendations for international students: Required—

TOEFL (minimum score 560 paper-based; 83 iBT). *Application deadline:* Applications are processed on a rolling basis. Application fee: $20. Electronic applications accepted. *Expenses: Tuition:* Part-time $815 per credit hour. *Required fees:* $86 per credit hour. One-time fee: $40 part-time. Tuition and fees vary according to degree level and program. *Financial support:* In 2013–14, 5 research assistantships were awarded; Federal Work-Study and scholarships/grants also available. Financial award applicants required to submit FAFSA. *Unit head:* Dr. Denise Staudt, Dean, Dreeben School of Education, 210-829-2762, E-mail: staudt@uiwtx.edu. *Application contact:* Andrea Cyterski-Acosta, Dean of Enrollment, 210-829-6005, Fax: 210-829-3921, E-mail: admis@uiwtx.edu.
Website: http://www.uiw.edu/education/index.htm.

University of the Incarnate Word, School of Graduate Studies and Research, H-E-B School of Business and Administration, Programs in Administration, San Antonio, TX 78209-6397. Offers adult education (MAA); communication arts (MAA); healthcare administration (MAA); instructional technology (MAA); nutrition (MAA); organizational development (MAA); sports management (MAA). Part-time and evening/weekend programs available. Postbaccalaureate distance learning degree programs offered (no on-campus study). *Faculty:* 20 full-time (10 women), 14 part-time/adjunct (6 women). *Students:* 31 full-time (22 women), 54 part-time (36 women); includes 61 minority (14 Black or African American, non-Hispanic/Latino; 1 Asian, non-Hispanic/Latino; 46 Hispanic/Latino), 6 international. Average age 31. 63 applicants, 68% accepted, 21 enrolled. In 2013, 35 master's awarded. *Degree requirements:* For master's, capstone. *Entrance requirements:* For master's, GRE, GMAT, undergraduate degree, minimum GPA of 2.5. Additional exam requirements/recommendations for international students: Required—TOEFL (minimum score 560 paper-based; 83 iBT). *Application deadline:* Applications are processed on a rolling basis. Application fee: $20. Electronic applications accepted. *Expenses: Tuition:* Part-time $815 per credit hour. *Required fees:* $86 per credit hour. One-time fee: $40 part-time. Tuition and fees vary according to degree level and program. *Financial support:* Federal Work-Study and scholarships/grants available. Financial award applicants required to submit FAFSA. *Unit head:* Dr. Mark Teachout, MAA Programs Director, 210-829-3177, Fax: 210-805-3564, E-mail: teachout@uiwtx.edu. *Application contact:* Andrea Cyterski-Acosta, Dean of Enrollment, 210-829-6005, Fax: 210-829-3921, E-mail: admis@uiwtx.edu.
Website: http://www.uiw.edu/maa/.

The University of West Alabama, School of Graduate Studies, College of Education, Departments of Instructional Leadership and Support/Curriculum and Instruction, Program in Continuing Education, Livingston, AL 35470. Offers college student development (MSCE); continuing education (MSCE); counseling and psychology (MSCE); family counseling (MSCE); guidance and counseling (MSCE). *Accreditation:* NCATE. Part-time and evening/weekend programs available. Postbaccalaureate distance learning degree programs offered (no on-campus study). *Faculty:* 16 full-time (10 women), 38 part-time/adjunct (28 women). *Students:* 757 (662 women); includes 581 minority (572 Black or African American, non-Hispanic/Latino; 3 American Indian or Alaska Native, non-Hispanic/Latino; 1 Asian, non-Hispanic/Latino; 3 Hispanic/Latino; 2 Two or more races, non-Hispanic/Latino). 212 applicants, 100% accepted, 173 enrolled. In 2013, 152 master's awarded. *Degree requirements:* For master's, comprehensive exam, thesis optional. *Entrance requirements:* For master's, GRE General Test, MAT, minimum GPA of 2.75. Additional exam requirements/recommendations for international students: Required—TOEFL (minimum score 500 paper-based; 61 iBT). *Application deadline:* For fall admission, 8/12 priority date for domestic students; for spring admission, 3/24 for domestic students. Applications are processed on a rolling basis. Application fee: $25 ($50 for international students). Electronic applications accepted. Tuition and fees vary according to course load. *Financial support:* Teaching assistantships, career-related internships or fieldwork, Federal Work-Study, scholarships/grants, and unspecified assistantships available. Support available to part-time students. Financial award applicants required to submit FAFSA. *Unit head:* Dr. Reenay Rogers, Chair of Instructional Leadership and Support, 205-652-5423, Fax: 205-652-3706, E-mail: rrogers@uwa.edu. *Application contact:* Dr. Kathy Chandler, Dean of Graduate Studies, 205-652-3421, Fax: 205-652-3670, E-mail: kchandler@uwa.edu.

University of Wisconsin–Milwaukee, Graduate School, School of Education, Urban Education Doctoral Program, Milwaukee, WI 53201-0413. Offers adult, continuing and higher education leadership (PhD); curriculum and instruction (PhD); educational administration (PhD); exceptional education (PhD); multicultural studies (PhD); social foundations of education (PhD). *Students:* 51 full-time (37 women), 40 part-time (25 women); includes 32 minority (16 Black or African American, non-Hispanic/Latino; 1 American Indian or Alaska Native, non-Hispanic/Latino; 3 Asian, non-Hispanic/Latino; 5 Hispanic/Latino; 7 Two or more races, non-Hispanic/Latino), 3 international. Average age 41. 25 applicants, 44% accepted, 4 enrolled. In 2013, 11 doctorates awarded. *Degree requirements:* For doctorate, comprehensive exam, thesis/dissertation. *Entrance requirements:* For doctorate, GRE General Test, minimum undergraduate GPA of 2.85, graduate 3.5. Additional exam requirements/recommendations for international students: Required—TOEFL (minimum score 550 paper-based; 79 iBT), IELTS (minimum score 6.5). *Application deadline:* For fall admission, 1/1 priority date for domestic students; for spring admission, 9/1 for domestic students. Applications are processed on a rolling basis. Application fee: $56 ($96 for international students). Electronic applications accepted. *Financial support:* In 2013–14, 11 fellowships, 1 teaching assistantship were awarded; research assistantships, career-related internships or fieldwork, health care benefits, unspecified assistantships, and project assistantships also available. Support available to part-time students. Financial award application deadline: 4/15; financial award applicants required to submit FAFSA. *Unit head:* Raji Swaminathan, Representative, 414-229-6740, Fax: 414-229-2920, E-mail: swaminar@uwm.edu. *Application contact:* General Information Contact, 414-229-4982, Fax: 414-229-6967, E-mail: gradschool@uwm.edu.
Website: http://www4.uwm.edu/soe/academics/urban_ed/.

University of Wisconsin–Platteville, School of Graduate Studies, College of Liberal Arts and Education, School of Education, Platteville, WI 53818-3099. Offers adult education (MSE); elementary education (MSE); English education (MSE); middle school education (MSE); secondary education (MSE). *Accreditation:* NCATE. Part-time programs available. *Faculty:* 5 full-time (3 women), 13 part-time/adjunct (7 women). *Students:* 90 full-time (70 women), 30 part-time (16 women); includes 25 minority (21 Black or African American, non-Hispanic/Latino; 1 American Indian or Alaska Native, non-Hispanic/Latino; 2 Asian, non-Hispanic/Latino; 1 Hispanic/Latino), 3 international. 45 applicants, 96% accepted, 38 enrolled. In 2013, 82 master's awarded. *Degree requirements:* For master's, comprehensive exam, thesis or alternative. *Entrance requirements:* Additional exam requirements/recommendations for international students: Required—TOEFL (minimum score 500 paper-based; 61 iBT), IELTS (minimum score 6). *Application deadline:* For fall admission, 7/1 priority date for domestic students; for spring admission, 11/1 for domestic students. Applications are processed on a rolling basis. Application fee: $56. Electronic applications accepted. *Financial support:* Research assistantships with partial tuition reimbursements, career-related internships or fieldwork, Federal Work-Study, institutionally sponsored loans, scholarships/grants, and unspecified assistantships available. Support available to part-time students. Financial award applicants required to submit FAFSA. *Unit head:* Dr.

Karen Stinson, Director, 608-342-1131, Fax: 608-342-1133, E-mail: stinsonk@uwplatt.edu. *Application contact:* Dee Dunbar, School of Graduate Studies, 608-342-1322, Fax: 608-342-1389, E-mail: dunbard@uwplatt.edu.
Website: http://www.uwplatt.edu/.

Virginia Commonwealth University, Graduate School, School of Education, Program in Adult Learning, Richmond, VA 23284-9005. Offers adult literacy (M Ed); human resource development (M Ed); teaching and learning with technology (M Ed). *Accreditation:* NCATE. Part-time programs available. *Entrance requirements:* For master's, GRE General Test or MAT. Additional exam requirements/recommendations for international students: Required—TOEFL (minimum score 600 paper-based; 100 iBT). Electronic applications accepted. *Faculty research:* Adult development and learning, program planning and evaluation.

Walden University, Graduate Programs, Richard W. Riley College of Education and Leadership, Minneapolis, MN 55401. *Accreditation:* NCATE. Part-time and evening/weekend programs available. Postbaccalaureate distance learning degree programs offered (minimal on-campus study). *Faculty:* 23 full-time (15 women), 830 part-time/adjunct (569 women). *Students:* 8,671 full-time (7,197 women), 2,122 part-time (1,735 women); includes 4,734 minority (3,802 Black or African American, non-Hispanic/Latino; 50 American Indian or Alaska Native, non-Hispanic/Latino; 136 Asian, non-Hispanic/Latino; 539 Hispanic/Latino; 35 Native Hawaiian or other Pacific Islander, non-Hispanic/Latino; 172 Two or more races, non-Hispanic/Latino), 73 international. Average age 40. 2,646 applicants, 96% accepted, 2074 enrolled. In 2013, 2,214 master's, 354 doctorates, 479 other advanced degrees awarded. *Degree requirements:* For doctorate, thesis/dissertation (for some programs), residency; for other advanced degree, residency (for some programs). *Entrance requirements:* For master's, bachelor's degree or higher; minimum GPA of 2.5; official transcripts; goal statement (for some programs); access to computer and Internet; for doctorate, master's degree or higher; three years of related professional or academic experience (preferred); minimum GPA of 3.0; goal statement and current resume (select programs); official transcripts; access to computer and Internet; for other advanced degree, relevant work experience; access to computer and Internet. Additional exam requirements/recommendations for international students: Required—TOEFL (minimum score 550 paper-based; 79 iBT), IELTS (minimum score 6.5), Michigan English Language Assessment Battery (minimum score 82), or PTE. *Application deadline:* Applications are processed on a rolling basis. Application fee: $0. Electronic applications accepted. *Expenses: Tuition:* Full-time $11,813.55; part-time $500 per credit. *Required fees:* $618.76. *Financial support:* In 2013–14, 1 fellowship was awarded; Federal Work-Study, scholarships/grants, unspecified assistantships, and family tuition reduction, active duty/veteran tuition reduction, group tuition reduction, interest-free payment plans, employee tuition reduction also available. Support available to part-time students. Financial award applicants required to submit FAFSA. *Unit head:* Dr. Kate Steffens, Dean, 800-925-3368. *Application contact:* Jennifer Hall, Vice President of Enrollment Management, 866-4-WALDEN, E-mail: info@waldenu.edu.
Website: http://www.waldenu.edu/colleges-schools/riley-college-of-education/.

Western Kentucky University, Graduate Studies, College of Education and Behavioral Sciences, Department of Educational Administration, Leadership, and Research, Bowling Green, KY 42101. Offers adult education (MAE); educational leadership (Ed D); school administration (Ed S); school principal (MAE). *Accreditation:* NCATE. Part-time and evening/weekend programs available. *Degree requirements:* For master's, comprehensive exam, thesis or applied project and oral defense; for Ed S, thesis. *Entrance requirements:* For master's, GRE General Test, minimum GPA of 2.75. Additional exam requirements/recommendations for international students: Required—TOEFL (minimum score 555 paper-based; 79 iBT). *Faculty research:* Principal internship, superintendent assessment, administrative leadership, group training for residential workers.

Western Washington University, Graduate School, Woodring College of Education, Department of Educational Leadership, Program in Continuing and College Education, Bellingham, WA 98225-5996. Offers M Ed. Part-time and evening/weekend programs available. Postbaccalaureate distance learning degree programs offered (minimal on-campus study). *Degree requirements:* For master's, comprehensive exam, thesis optional. *Entrance requirements:* For master's, GRE General Test or MAT, minimum GPA of 3.0 in last 60 semester hours or last 90 quarter hours. Additional exam requirements/recommendations for international students: Required—TOEFL (minimum score 567 paper-based). Electronic applications accepted. *Faculty research:* Transfer of learning, postsecondary faculty development, action research as professional development, literacy education in community colleges, adult education in the Middle East, distance learning tools for graduate students.

Widener University, School of Human Service Professions, Center for Education, Chester, PA 19013-5792. Offers adult education (M Ed); counseling in higher education (M Ed); counselor education (M Ed); early childhood education (M Ed); educational foundations (M Ed); educational leadership (M Ed); educational psychology (M Ed); elementary education (M Ed); English and language arts (M Ed); health education (M Ed); higher education leadership (Ed D); home and school visitor (M Ed); human sexuality (M Ed, PhD); mathematics education (M Ed); middle school education (M Ed); principalship (M Ed); reading and language arts (Ed D); reading education (M Ed); school administration (Ed D); science education (M Ed); social studies education (M Ed); special education (M Ed); technology education (M Ed). *Accreditation:* NCATE. Part-time and evening/weekend programs available. *Faculty:* 34 full-time (22 women), 37 part-time/adjunct (14 women). *Students:* 64 full-time (44 women), 209 part-time (146 women); includes 49 minority (39 Black or African American, non-Hispanic/Latino; 1 American Indian or Alaska Native, non-Hispanic/Latino; 4 Asian, non-Hispanic/Latino; 4 Hispanic/Latino; 1 Two or more races, non-Hispanic/Latino), 8 international. Average age 39. 139 applicants, 88% accepted. In 2013, 168 master's, 31 doctorates awarded. Terminal master's awarded for partial completion of doctoral program. *Degree requirements:* For doctorate, thesis/dissertation. *Entrance requirements:* For master's, minimum GPA of 2.5; for doctorate, GRE or MAT, minimum GPA of 2.0 (undergraduate), 3.5 (graduate). *Application deadline:* Applications are processed on a rolling basis. Application fee: $25 ($300 for international students). Electronic applications accepted. *Expenses:* Contact institution. *Financial support:* Career-related internships or fieldwork, tuition waivers (full and partial), and unspecified assistantships available. Support available to part-time students. Financial award application deadline: 5/1. *Faculty research:* Reading and cognition, adult education, technology education, educational leadership, special education. *Unit head:* Dr. Michael W. LeDoux, Associate Dean, 610-499-4294, Fax: 610-499-4623, E-mail: mwledoux@widener.edu. *Application contact:* Dr. Roberta Nolan, Director of Graduate Admissions, 610-499-4125, E-mail: rdnolan@widener.edu.

Wright State University, School of Graduate Studies, College of Education and Human Services, Department of Educational Leadership, Program in Advanced Educational Leadership, Dayton, OH 45435. Offers advanced curriculum and instruction (Ed S); higher education-adult education (Ed S); superintendent (Ed S). *Accreditation:* NCATE. *Degree requirements:* For Ed S, thesis. *Entrance requirements:* For degree, GRE General Test, MAT. Additional exam requirements/recommendations for international students: Required—TOEFL.

Community College Education

Argosy University, Chicago, College of Education, Chicago, IL 60601. Offers adult education and training (MA Ed); community college executive leadership (Ed D); educational leadership (MA Ed, Ed D, Ed S), including district leadership (Ed D), higher education administration (Ed D), K-12 education (Ed D); instructional leadership (Ed D, Ed S), including higher education (Ed D), K-12 education (Ed D). Postbaccalaureate distance learning degree programs offered (minimal on-campus study).

Argosy University, Denver, College of Education, Denver, CO 80231. Offers community college executive leadership (Ed D); educational leadership (MA Ed, Ed D), including higher education (Ed D), K-12 education (Ed D); instructional leadership (MA Ed, Ed D), including higher education administration (Ed D), K-12 education (Ed D).

Argosy University, Inland Empire, College of Education, Ontario, CA 91761. Offers community college executive leadership (Ed D); educational leadership (MA Ed, Ed D), including higher education administration (Ed D), K-12 education (Ed D); instructional leadership (MA Ed, Ed D), including higher education (Ed D), K-12 education (Ed D), multiple subject teacher preparation (MA Ed), single subject teacher preparation (MA Ed).

Argosy University, Los Angeles, College of Education, Santa Monica, CA 90045. Offers community college executive leadership (Ed D); educational leadership (MA Ed, Ed D), including higher education administration (Ed D), K-12 education (Ed D); instructional leadership (MA Ed, Ed D), including higher education (Ed D), K-12 education (Ed D), multiple subject teacher preparation (MA Ed), single subject teacher preparation (MA Ed).

Argosy University, Orange County, College of Education, Orange, CA 92868. Offers community college executive leadership (Ed D); educational leadership (MA Ed, Ed D), including higher education administration (Ed D), K-12 education (Ed D); instructional leadership (MA Ed, Ed D), including education technology (Ed D), higher education (Ed D), K-12 education (Ed D), multiple subject teacher preparation (MA Ed), single subject teacher preparation (MA Ed).

Argosy University, Phoenix, College of Education, Phoenix, AZ 85021. Offers adult education and training (MA Ed); advanced educational administration (Ed D, Ed S); community college executive leadership (Ed D); educational administration (MA Ed); educational leadership (MA Ed, Ed D, Ed S), including education technology (Ed D), higher education administration (Ed D), K-12 education (Ed D); higher and postsecondary education (MA Ed); initial educational administration (Ed D, Ed S); school psychology (MA); teaching and learning (MA Ed, Ed D, Ed S), including education technology (Ed D), higher education (Ed D), K-12 education (Ed D).

Argosy University, San Diego, College of Education, San Diego, CA 92108. Offers community college executive leadership (Ed D); educational leadership (MA Ed, Ed D), including higher education administration (Ed D), K-12 education (Ed D); instructional leadership (MA Ed, Ed D), including higher education (Ed D), K-12 education (Ed D).

Argosy University, San Francisco Bay Area, College of Education, Alameda, CA 94501. Offers community college executive leadership (Ed D); educational leadership (MA Ed, Ed D), including education technology (Ed D), higher education administration (Ed D), K-12 education (Ed D); instructional leadership (MA Ed, Ed D), including education technology (Ed D), higher education (Ed D), K-12 education (Ed D), multiple subject teacher preparation (MA Ed), single subject teacher preparation (MA Ed).

Argosy University, Schaumburg, College of Education, Schaumburg, IL 60173-5403. Offers community college executive leadership (Ed D); educational leadership (MA Ed, Ed D, Ed S), including district leadership (Ed D), higher education administration (Ed D), K-12 education (Ed D); instructional leadership (Ed D, Ed S), including higher education (Ed D), K-12 education (Ed D).

Argosy University, Seattle, College of Education, Seattle, WA 98121. Offers adult education and training (MA Ed); community college executive leadership (Ed D); educational leadership (MA Ed, Ed D), including higher education administration (Ed D), K-12 education (Ed D); higher and postsecondary education (MA Ed); instructional leadership (MA Ed, Ed D), including education technology (Ed D), higher education (Ed D), K-12 education (Ed D).

Argosy University, Tampa, College of Education, Tampa, FL 33607. Offers community college executive leadership (Ed D); educational leadership (MA Ed, Ed D, Ed S), including higher education administration (Ed D), K-12 education (Ed D); school counseling (MA); teaching and learning (MA Ed, Ed D, Ed S), including higher education (Ed D), K-12 education (Ed D).

Argosy University, Washington DC, College of Education, Arlington, VA 22209. Offers community college executive leadership (Ed D); educational leadership (MA Ed, Ed D, Ed S), including higher education administration (Ed D), K-12 education (Ed D); instructional leadership (MA Ed, Ed D, Ed S), including higher education (Ed D), K-12 education (Ed D).

Arkansas State University, Graduate School, College of Education and Behavioral Science, School of Teacher Education and Leadership, Jonesboro, AR 72467. Offers community college administration (SCCT); curriculum and instruction (MSE); early childhood education (MAT, MSE); early childhood services (MS); educational leadership (MSE, Ed D, PhD, Ed S); educational theory and practice (MSE); middle level education (MAT, MSE); reading (MSE, Ed S); special education - gifted, talented, and creative (MSE); special education - instructional specialist grades 4-12 (MSE); special education - instructional specialist grades P-4 (MSE). *Accreditation:* NCATE. Part-time programs available. Postbaccalaureate distance learning degree programs offered. *Faculty:* 28 full-time (16 women). *Students:* 77 full-time (68 women), 1,934 part-time (1,449 women); includes 361 minority (290 Black or African American, non-Hispanic/Latino; 11 American Indian or Alaska Native, non-Hispanic/Latino; 3 Asian, non-Hispanic/Latino; 26 Hispanic/Latino; 1 Native Hawaiian or other Pacific Islander, non-Hispanic/Latino; 30 Two or more races, non-Hispanic/Latino), 5 international. Average age 36. 1,627 applicants, 71%

accepted, 770 enrolled. In 2013, 1,182 master's, 12 doctorates, 76 other advanced degrees awarded. *Degree requirements:* For master's, comprehensive exam, thesis or alternative; for doctorate, comprehensive exam, thesis/dissertation; for other advanced degree, comprehensive exam. *Entrance requirements:* For master's, GRE General Test or MAT, appropriate bachelor's degree, official transcripts, immunization records, letters of reference, interview; for doctorate, GRE General Test or MAT, interview, master's degree, letters of reference, official transcript, personal statement, writing sample, immunization records; for other advanced degree, GRE General Test or MAT, interview, master's degree, official transcript, immunization records, letters of reference, 3 years of teaching experience, teaching license. Additional exam requirements/recommendations for international students: Required—TOEFL (minimum score 550 paper-based; 79 iBT), IELTS (minimum score 6), PTE (minimum score 56). *Application deadline:* For fall admission, 7/1 for domestic and international students; for spring admission, 11/15 for domestic students, 11/14 for international students. Applications are processed on a rolling basis. Electronic applications accepted. *Expenses:* Tuition, state resident: full-time $4284; part-time $238 per credit hour. Tuition, nonresident: full-time $8568; part-time $476 per credit hour. *International tuition:* $9268 full-time. *Required fees:* $1098; $61 per credit hour. $25 per term. Tuition and fees vary according to course load and program. *Financial support:* In 2013–14, 20 students received support. Fellowships, teaching assistantships, career-related internships or fieldwork, scholarships/grants, and unspecified assistantships available. Financial award application deadline: 7/1; financial award applicants required to submit FAFSA. *Unit head:* Dr. Annette Hux, Interim Chair, 870-972-3059, Fax: 870-972-3344, E-mail: ahux@astate.edu. *Application contact:* Vickey Ring, Graduate Admissions Coordinator, 870-972-3029, Fax: 870-972-3857, E-mail: vickeyring@astate.edu.
Website: http://www.astate.edu/college/education/departments/school-of-teacher-education-and-leadership/index.dot.

California State University, Fullerton, Graduate Studies, College of Education, Department of Educational Leadership, Fullerton, CA 92834-9480. Offers community college educational leadership (Ed D); educational administration (MS); higher education (MS); pre K-12 educational leadership (Ed D). *Accreditation:* NCATE. Part-time programs available. *Students:* 2 full-time (0 women), 230 part-time (147 women); includes 133 minority (26 Black or African American, non-Hispanic/Latino; 33 Asian, non-Hispanic/Latino; 67 Hispanic/Latino; 7 Two or more races, non-Hispanic/Latino), 12 international. Average age 36. 192 applicants, 48% accepted, 84 enrolled. In 2013, 52 master's, 26 doctorates awarded. *Degree requirements:* For master's, thesis or alternative, project. *Entrance requirements:* For master's, minimum GPA of 2.5. Application fee: $55. *Financial support:* Career-related internships or fieldwork, Federal Work-Study, institutionally sponsored loans, and scholarships/grants available. Support available to part-time students. Financial award application deadline: 3/1; financial award applicants required to submit FAFSA. *Faculty research:* Creation of a substance abuse prevention training and demonstration program. *Unit head:* Jennifer Goldstein, Head, 657-278-3963. *Application contact:* Admissions/Applications, 657-278-2371.

California State University, Sacramento, Office of Graduate Studies, College of Education, Department of Educational Leadership and Policy Studies, Sacramento, CA 95819. Offers educational leadership (MA), including PreK-12; higher education leadership (MA), including community college leadership, student services. Part-time programs available. *Degree requirements:* For master's, thesis or project; writing proficiency exam. *Entrance requirements:* For master's, minimum GPA of 2.5. Additional exam requirements/recommendations for international students: Required—TOEFL. *Application deadline:* For fall admission, 3/1 for domestic and international students; for spring admission, 9/30 for international students. Applications are processed on a rolling basis. Application fee: $55. Electronic applications accepted. *Financial support:* Career-related internships or fieldwork and Federal Work-Study available. Support available to part-time students. Financial award application deadline: 3/1; financial award applicants required to submit FAFSA. *Unit head:* Dr. Francisco Reveles, Chair, 916-278-5388, Fax: 916-278-4608, E-mail: revelesf@csus.edu. *Application contact:* Jose Martinez, Graduate Admissions Supervisor, 916-278-7871, E-mail: martinj@skymail.csus.edu.
Website: http://www.edweb.csus.edu/edlp.

California State University, Stanislaus, College of Education, Programs in Educational Leadership (Ed D), Turlock, CA 95382. Offers community college leadership (Ed D); P-12 leadership (Ed D). Part-time and evening/weekend programs available. *Degree requirements:* For doctorate, thesis/dissertation. *Entrance requirements:* For doctorate, GRE, minimum GPA of 3.0, 3 letters of reference, interview, personal statement. Additional exam requirements/recommendations for international students: Required—TOEFL (minimum score 550 paper-based). Electronic applications accepted.

Central Michigan University, Central Michigan University Global Campus, Program in Education, Mount Pleasant, MI 48859. Offers college teaching (Graduate Certificate); community college (MA); curriculum and instruction (MA); educational technology (MA); guidance and development (MA); reading and literacy K-12 (MA); school principalship (MA), including charter school leadership; training and development (MA). *Accreditation:* Teacher Education Accreditation Council. Part-time and evening/weekend programs available. *Entrance requirements:* For master's, minimum GPA of 2.7 in major. Additional exam requirements/recommendations for international students: Required—TOEFL. *Application deadline:* Applications are processed on a rolling basis. Application fee: $50. Electronic applications accepted. *Financial support:* Scholarships/grants available. Support available to part-time students. *Unit head:* Kaleb Patrick, Director, 989-774-3144, E-mail: patri1kg@cmich.edu. *Application contact:* 877-268-4636, E-mail: cmuglobal@cmich.edu.

Colorado State University, Graduate School, College of Health and Human Sciences, School of Education, Fort Collins, CO 80523-1588. Offers adult education and training (M Ed); community college leadership (PhD); counseling and career development (M Ed); education and human resource studies (M Ed, PhD); educational leadership (M Ed, PhD); interdisciplinary studies (PhD); organizational performance and change (M Ed, PhD); student affairs in higher education (MS). *Accreditation:* ACA; Teacher Education Accreditation Council. Part-time and evening/weekend programs available. *Faculty:* 19 full-time (10 women). *Students:* 84 full-time (60 women), 545 part-time (356 women); includes 115 minority (26 Black or African American, non-Hispanic/Latino; 5 American Indian or Alaska Native, non-Hispanic/Latino; 13 Asian, non-Hispanic/Latino; 56 Hispanic/Latino; 15 Two or more races, non-Hispanic/Latino), 22 international. Average age 37. 475 applicants, 38% accepted, 147 enrolled. In 2013, 1,157 master's, 43 doctorates awarded. *Degree requirements:* For master's, comprehensive exam, thesis optional; for doctorate, comprehensive exam, thesis/dissertation, minimum of 60 credits. *Entrance requirements:* For master's and doctorate, GRE, minimum GPA of 3.0. Additional exam requirements/recommendations for international students: Required—TOEFL (minimum score 550 paper-based; 80 iBT), IELTS. *Application deadline:* For fall admission, 3/1 priority date for domestic and international students; for spring admission, 9/1 for domestic and international students. Applications are processed on a rolling basis. Application fee: $50. Electronic applications accepted. *Expenses:* Tuition, state resident: full-time $9075.40; part-time $504 per credit. Tuition, nonresident: full-time $22,248; part-time $1236 per credit. *Required fees:* $1819; $60 per credit. *Financial support:* In 2013–14, 7 students received support, including 1 research assistantship with partial tuition reimbursement available (averaging $16,135 per year), 6 teaching assistantships with partial tuition reimbursements available (averaging $10,106 per year); career-related internships or fieldwork, scholarships/grants, and unspecified assistantships also available. Financial award application deadline: 3/1; financial award applicants required to submit FAFSA. *Faculty research:* Issues in STEM education, diversity and multiculturalism, teacher education leadership, distance learning and teaching. *Total annual research expenditures:* $498,539. *Unit head:* Dr. Daniel H. Robinson, Director, 970-491-6316, Fax: 970-491-1317, E-mail: dan.robinson@colostate.edu. *Application contact:* Kelli M. Clark, Academic Coordinator, 970-491-2093, Fax: 970-491-1317, E-mail: kelli.clark@colostate.edu.
Website: http://www.soe.chhs.colostate.edu/.

East Carolina University, Graduate School, Thomas Harriot College of Arts and Sciences, Department of Mathematics, Greenville, NC 27858-4353. Offers mathematics (MA); mathematics in the community college (MA); statistics (MA, Certificate). Part-time and evening/weekend programs available. *Degree requirements:* For master's, comprehensive exam. *Entrance requirements:* For master's, GRE General Test, MAT. Additional exam requirements/recommendations for international students: Required—TOEFL. *Expenses:* Tuition, state resident: full-time $4223. Tuition, nonresident: full-time $16,540. *Required fees:* $2184.

Eastern Illinois University, Graduate School, College of Arts and Humanities, Department of Communication Studies, Charleston, IL 61920-3099. Offers community college pedagogy (MA). Part-time programs available. *Faculty:* 11 full-time (2 women). *Degree requirements:* For master's, comprehensive exam (for some programs), thesis optional, major paper. *Application deadline:* For fall admission, 3/31 priority date for domestic students. Applications are processed on a rolling basis. Application fee: $30. *Expenses: Tuition, area resident:* Part-time $283 per credit hour. Tuition, state resident: part-time $283 per credit hour. Tuition, nonresident: part-time $679 per credit hour. *Financial support:* In 2013–14, 1 research assistantship with full tuition reimbursement (averaging $8,100 per year), 6 teaching assistantships with full tuition reimbursements (averaging $8,100 per year) were awarded. *Unit head:* Dr. Stephen King, Chairperson, 217-581-2016, E-mail: saking@eiu.edu. *Application contact:* Dr. Matt Gill, Coordinator, 217-581-6306, E-mail: mjgill@eiu.edu.

Elizabeth City State University, School of Mathematics, Science and Technology, Master of Science in Mathematics Program, Elizabeth City, NC 27909-7806. Offers applied mathematics (MS); community college teaching (MS); mathematics education (MS); remote sensing (MS). Part-time and evening/weekend programs available. *Faculty:* 7 full-time (2 women). *Students:* 25 part-time (13 women); includes 19 minority (all Black or African American, non-Hispanic/Latino). Average age 25. 5 applicants, 80% accepted, 4 enrolled. In 2013, 18 degrees awarded. *Degree requirements:* For master's, thesis. *Entrance requirements:* For master's, MAT and/or GRE, minimum GPA of 3.0, 3 letters of recommendation, two official transcripts from all undergraduate/graduate schools attended, typewritten one-page request for entry into program that includes description of student's educational preparation. Additional exam requirements/recommendations for international students: Required—TOEFL (minimum score 550 paper-based, 80 iBT) or IELTS (minimum score 6.5). *Application deadline:* For fall admission, 7/15 priority date for domestic and international students; for spring admission, 11/15 priority date for domestic and international students; for summer admission, 3/15 priority date for domestic and international students. Applications are processed on a rolling basis. Application fee: $30. Electronic applications accepted. *Expenses:* Tuition, state resident: full-time $2916; part-time $364.48 per credit. Tuition, nonresident: full-time $14,199; part-time $1774.83 per credit. *Required fees:* $2972.23; $206.58 per credit. $571.06 per semester. *Financial support:* In 2013–14, 22 students received support, including 3 research assistantships (averaging $19,000 per year), 2 teaching assistantships (averaging $18,000 per year); scholarships/grants and tuition waivers also available. Financial award application deadline: 6/30; financial award applicants required to submit FAFSA. *Faculty research:* Oceanic temperature effects, mathematics strategies in elementary schools, multimedia, Antarctic temperature mapping, computer networks, water quality, remote sensing, polar ice, satellite imagery. *Total annual research expenditures:* $25,000. *Unit head:* Dr. Farrah Jackson, Chair, 252-335-8549, Fax: 252-335-3487, E-mail: fmjackson@mail.ecsu.edu. *Application contact:* Dr. Paula S. Viltz, Interim Dean, School of Education and Psychology and Graduate Education, 252-335-3297, Fax: 252-335-3146, E-mail: psviltz@mail.ecsu.edu.
Website: http://www.ecsu.edu/academics/mathsciencetechnology/.

Ferris State University, Extended and International Operations, Big Rapids, MI 49307. Offers community college leadership (Ed D). Evening/weekend programs available. Postbaccalaureate distance learning degree programs offered (minimal on-campus study). *Faculty:* 26 part-time/adjunct (16 women). *Students:* 59 full-time (31 women); includes 14 minority (10 Black or African American, non-Hispanic/Latino; 2 Asian, non-Hispanic/Latino; 1 Hispanic/Latino; 1 Two or more races, non-Hispanic/Latino). Average age 44. 40 applicants, 85% accepted, 29 enrolled. In 2013, 5 doctorates awarded. *Degree requirements:* For doctorate, thesis/dissertation, e-portfolio demonstrating completion of program outcomes. *Entrance requirements:* For doctorate, master's degree with minimum GPA of 3.25, fierce commitment to the mission of community colleges, essay, writing samples. *Application deadline:* For fall admission, 12/15 for domestic and international students; for winter admission, 1/27 for domestic and international students; for spring admission, 4/18 for domestic and international students. Applications are processed on a rolling basis. Application fee: $30. Electronic applications accepted. Application fee is waived when completed online. *Expenses:* Contact institution. *Financial support:* In 2013–14, 10 students received support. Applicants required to submit FAFSA. *Unit head:* Dr. Roberta Teahen, Director, 231-591-3805, E-mail: robertateahen@ferris.edu. *Application contact:* Andrea Wigrau, Assistant Director, 231-591-2710, Fax: 231-591-3539, E-mail: andreawigrau@ferris.edu.

Fielding Graduate University, Graduate Programs, School of Educational Leadership for Change, Santa Barbara, CA 93105-3814. Offers collaborative educational leadership (MA), including charter school leadership, dual language; educational administration (Graduate Certificate); educational leadership and change (Ed D), including community college leadership and change. Postbaccalaureate distance learning degree programs offered (minimal on-campus study). *Faculty:* 9 full-time (6 women), 10 part-time/adjunct (6 women). *Students:* 172 full-time (121 women), 8 part-time (5 women); includes 109 minority (39 Black or African American, non-Hispanic/Latino; 19 American Indian or Alaska Native, non-Hispanic/Latino; 8 Asian, non-Hispanic/Latino; 34 Hispanic/Latino; 2 Native Hawaiian or other Pacific Islander, non-Hispanic/Latino; 7 Two or more races, non-Hispanic/Latino). Average age 48. 40 applicants, 98% accepted, 28 enrolled. In 2013, 45 doctorates awarded. *Degree requirements:* For master's, capstone research project; for doctorate, comprehensive exam, thesis/dissertation. *Entrance requirements:* For master's, BA from regionally accredited institution or equivalent with minimum GPA of 2.5; for doctorate, BA or MA from regionally accredited institution or equivalent, resume, 2 letters of recommendation, statement of purpose, reflective essay; for Graduate Certificate, BA from regionally-accredited institution or equivalent. *Application deadline:* For fall admission, 6/10 for domestic and international students; for spring admission, 11/19 for domestic and international students. Application fee: $75. Electronic applications accepted. *Expenses:* Contact institution. *Financial support:* In

2013–14, 90 students received support. Scholarships/grants, health care benefits, and tuition waivers (partial) available. Support available to part-time students. Financial award applicants required to submit FAFSA. *Unit head:* Dr. Mario R. Borunda, Dean, 805-898-2940, E-mail: mborunda@fielding.edu. *Application contact:* Admission Counselor, 800-340-1099 Ext. 4098, Fax: 805-687-9793, E-mail: elcadmissions@fielding.edu.
Website: http://www.fielding.edu/programs/elc/default.aspx.

Florida State University, The Graduate School, College of Arts and Sciences, Department of Biological Science, Masters in Science Teaching Program, Tallahassee, FL 32306. Offers community college science teaching (MST); secondary science teaching (MST). *Faculty:* 2 full-time (both women). *Students:* 4 full-time (2 women). Average age 27. 3 applicants, 67% accepted, 2 enrolled. In 2013, 4 master's awarded. *Degree requirements:* For master's, thesis or alternative, teacher work sample (action research). *Entrance requirements:* For master's, GRE. *Application deadline:* For fall admission, 7/1 for domestic students; for spring admission, 11/1 for domestic students; for summer admission, 3/1 for domestic students. Application fee: $30. Electronic applications accepted. *Expenses:* Tuition, state resident: part-time $403.51 per credit hour. Tuition, nonresident: part-time $1004.85 per credit hour. *Required fees:* $75.81 per credit hour. One-time fee: $20 part-time. Tuition and fees vary according to course load, campus/location and student level. *Faculty research:* Science and mathematics education, science and mathematics teacher preparation. *Total annual research expenditures:* $500,000. *Unit head:* Dr. Don R. Levitan, Chairman and Professor, Department of Biological Science, 850-644-4424, Fax: 850-645-8447, E-mail: levitan@bio.fsu.edu. *Application contact:* Erica M. Staehling, Director, Master's in Science Teaching Program, 850-644-1142, Fax: 850-644-0643, E-mail: staehling@bio.fsu.edu.
Website: http://bio.fsu.edu/osta/tpp.php.

George Mason University, College of Humanities and Social Sciences, Higher Education Program, Fairfax, VA 22030. Offers college teaching (Certificate); community college education (DA Ed); higher education administration (Certificate). *Faculty:* 4 full-time (all women), 1 (woman) part-time/adjunct. *Students:* 1 (woman) full-time, 44 part-time (28 women); includes 11 minority (7 Black or African American, non-Hispanic/Latino; 2 Asian, non-Hispanic/Latino; 2 Hispanic/Latino), 1 international. Average age 44. 12 applicants, 50% accepted, 5 enrolled. In 2013, 6 doctorates, 5 Certificates awarded. *Degree requirements:* For doctorate, thesis/dissertation, internship. *Entrance requirements:* For doctorate, GRE, 3 letters of recommendation; writing sample; resume; master's degree; expanded goals statement; official transcripts; for Certificate, official transcripts; expanded goals statement; 3 letters of recommendation; resume. Additional exam requirements/recommendations for international students: Required—TOEFL (minimum score 570 paper-based; 88 iBT), IELTS (minimum score 6.5), PTE. *Application deadline:* For fall admission, 4/15 priority date for domestic students; for spring admission, 11/1 priority date for domestic students. Application fee: $65 ($80 for international students). Electronic applications accepted. *Expenses:* Tuition, state resident: full-time $9350; part-time $390 per credit. Tuition, nonresident: full-time $25,754; part-time $1073 per credit. *Required fees:* $2688; $112 per credit. *Financial support:* In 2013–14, 1 student received support, including 1 teaching assistantship (averaging $20,000 per year); career-related internships or fieldwork, Federal Work-Study, scholarships/grants, unspecified assistantships, and health care benefits (for full-time research or teaching assistantship recipients) also available. Support available to part-time students. Financial award application deadline: 3/1; financial award applicants required to submit FAFSA. *Faculty research:* Leadership, the scholarship of teaching, learning, and assessment; ethical leadership; assessment; information technology; diversity. *Total annual research expenditures:* $984. *Unit head:* Jan Arminio, Director, 703-993-2064, Fax: 703-993-2307, E-mail: jarminio@gmu.edu. *Application contact:* Helen C. Zhao, Administrative Coordinator, 703-993-2310, Fax: 703-993-2307, E-mail: hzhao2@gmu.edu.
Website: http://highered.gmu.edu/.

George Mason University, College of Humanities and Social Sciences, Interdisciplinary Studies Program, Fairfax, VA 22030. Offers community college teaching (MAIS); computational social science (MAIS); energy and sustainability (MAIS); film and video studies (MAIS); folklore studies (MAIS); higher education administration (MAIS); neuroethics (MAIS); religion, culture and values (MAIS); social entrepreneurship (MAIS); war and military in society (MAIS); women and gender studies (MAIS). *Faculty:* 10 full-time (3 women), 7 part-time/adjunct (3 women). *Students:* 31 full-time (17 women), 79 part-time (50 women); includes 30 minority (17 Black or African American, non-Hispanic/Latino; 4 Asian, non-Hispanic/Latino; 6 Hispanic/Latino; 3 Two or more races, non-Hispanic/Latino), 3 international. Average age 33. 78 applicants, 59% accepted, 25 enrolled. In 2013, 32 master's awarded. *Degree requirements:* For master's, project or thesis. *Entrance requirements:* For master's, 3 letters of recommendation; writing sample; official transcript; resume. Additional exam requirements/recommendations for international students: Required—TOEFL (minimum score 570 paper-based; 88 iBT), IELTS (minimum score 6.5), PTE. *Application deadline:* For fall admission, 3/1 priority date for domestic students; for spring admission, 10/15 for domestic students. Application fee: $65 ($80 for international students). Electronic applications accepted. *Expenses:* Tuition, state resident: full-time $9350; part-time $390 per credit. Tuition, nonresident: full-time $25,754; part-time $1073 per credit. *Required fees:* $2688; $112 per credit. *Financial support:* In 2013–14, 8 students received support, including 3 research assistantships with full and partial tuition reimbursements available (averaging $10,238 per year), 5 teaching assistantships with full and partial tuition reimbursements available (averaging $7,655 per year); career-related internships or fieldwork, Federal Work-Study, scholarships/grants, unspecified assistantships, and health care benefits (for full-time research or teaching assistantship recipients) also available. Support available to part-time students. Financial award application deadline: 3/1; financial award applicants required to submit FAFSA. *Faculty research:* Combined English and folklore, religious and cultural studies (Christianity and Muslim society). *Unit head:* Jan Arminio, Interim Director, 703-993-2064, Fax: 703-993-2307, E-mail: jarminio@gmu.edu. *Application contact:* Becky Durham, Administrative Coordinator, 703-993-8762, Fax: 703-993-5585, E-mail: rdurham4@gmu.edu.
Website: http://mais.gmu.edu.

Mississippi State University, College of Education, Department of Leadership and Foundations, Mississippi State, MS 39762. Offers community college education (MAT); community college leadership (PhD); education (Ed S), including school administration; elementary, middle and secondary education administration (PhD); school administration (MS); workforce education leadership (MS). MS in workforce educational leadership held jointly with Alcorn State University. *Faculty:* 9 full-time (3 women). *Students:* 50 full-time (26 women), 156 part-time (100 women); includes 104 minority (99 Black or African American, non-Hispanic/Latino; 1 American Indian or Alaska Native, non-Hispanic/Latino; 1 Asian, non-Hispanic/Latino; 1 Hispanic/Latino; 1 Native Hawaiian or other Pacific Islander, non-Hispanic/Latino; 1 Two or more races, non-Hispanic/Latino). Average age 39. 121 applicants, 32% accepted, 33 enrolled. In 2013, 47 master's, 15 doctorates, 7 other advanced degrees awarded. *Degree requirements:* For master's and Ed S, comprehensive exam, thesis; for doctorate, comprehensive exam, thesis/dissertation. *Entrance requirements:* For master's, GRE, minimum GPA of 2.75 in junior and senior courses; for doctorate, GRE, minimum GPA of 3.4 on previous graduate work; for Ed S, GRE, minimum GPA of 3.2, master's degree. Additional exam requirements/recommendations for international students: Required—TOEFL (minimum score 550 paper-based; 79 iBT); Recommended—IELTS (minimum score 6.5). *Application deadline:* For fall admission, 7/1 for domestic students, 5/1 for international students; for spring admission, 11/1 for domestic students, 9/1 for international students. Application fee: $60. *Financial support:* In 2013–14, 3 research assistantships with full tuition reimbursements (averaging $12,400 per year), 1 teaching assistantship with full tuition reimbursement (averaging $10,194 per year) were awarded; Federal Work-Study, institutionally sponsored loans, and unspecified assistantships also available. Financial award application deadline: 4/1; financial award applicants required to submit FAFSA. *Unit head:* Dr. David Morse, Interim Department Head and Professor, 662-325-0969, Fax: 662-325-0975, E-mail: dmorse@colled.msstate.edu.
Website: http://www.leadershipandfoundations.msstate.edu/.

Morgan State University, School of Graduate Studies, School of Education and Urban Studies, Department of Advanced Studies, Leadership and Policy, Program in Community College Leadership, Baltimore, MD 21251. Offers Ed D. *Accreditation:* NCATE. Part-time and evening/weekend programs available. *Degree requirements:* For doctorate, comprehensive exam, thesis/dissertation. *Entrance requirements:* For doctorate, GRE General Test or MAT. Additional exam requirements/recommendations for international students: Required—TOEFL (minimum score 550 paper-based). *Faculty research:* Multicultural education, cooperative learning, psychology of cognition.

North Carolina State University, Graduate School, College of Education, Department of Adult and Higher Education, Program in Adult and Community College Education, Raleigh, NC 27695. Offers M Ed, MS, Ed D. *Degree requirements:* For master's, thesis (for some programs); for doctorate, thesis/dissertation. *Entrance requirements:* For master's and doctorate, GRE or MAT. Electronic applications accepted.

Northern Arizona University, Graduate College, College of Education, Department of Educational Leadership, Flagstaff , AZ 86011. Offers community college/higher education (M Ed); educational foundations (M Ed); educational leadership (M Ed, Ed D); principal (Certificate); principal K-12 (M Ed); school leadership K-12 (M Ed); superintendent (Certificate). Part-time programs available. *Faculty:* 22 full-time (9 women). *Students:* 159 full-time (103 women), 528 part-time (331 women); includes 199 minority (36 Black or African American, non-Hispanic/Latino; 20 American Indian or Alaska Native, non-Hispanic/Latino; 11 Asian, non-Hispanic/Latino; 115 Hispanic/Latino; 1 Native Hawaiian or other Pacific Islander, non-Hispanic/Latino; 16 Two or more races, non-Hispanic/Latino). Average age 38. 211 applicants, 97% accepted, 148 enrolled. In 2013, 269 master's, 20 doctorates, 47 Certificates awarded. *Degree requirements:* For master's, comprehensive exam, thesis (for some programs); for doctorate, comprehensive exam, thesis/dissertation. *Entrance requirements:* For master's, minimum GPA of 3.0; for doctorate, GRE or MAT, minimum GPA of 3.5. Additional exam requirements/recommendations for international students: Required—TOEFL (minimum score 550 paper-based; 80 iBT), IELTS (minimum score 7). *Application deadline:* For fall admission, 3/1 priority date for international students; for spring admission, 9/15 priority date for international students. Applications are processed on a rolling basis. Application fee: $65. Electronic applications accepted. *Financial support:* In 2013–14, 1 research assistantship with full tuition reimbursement (averaging $12,000 per year) was awarded. Financial award applicants required to submit FAFSA. *Unit head:* Dr. Michael Schwanenberger, Chair, 928-523-4212, Fax: 928-523-1929, E-mail: michael.schwanenberger@nau.edu. *Application contact:* Jennifer Offutt, Administrative Assistant, 928-523-5098, Fax: 928-523-1929, E-mail: jennifer.offutt@nau.edu.
Website: http://nau.edu/coe/ed-leadership/.

Old Dominion University, Darden College of Education, Doctoral Program in Community College Leadership, Norfolk, VA 23529. Offers PhD. Part-time programs available. Postbaccalaureate distance learning degree programs offered (minimal on-campus study). *Faculty:* 2 full-time (0 women), 1 (woman) part-time/adjunct. *Students:* 9 full-time (3 women), 38 part-time (22 women); includes 11 minority (8 Black or African American, non-Hispanic/Latino; 2 Asian, non-Hispanic/Latino; 1 Hispanic/Latino). Average age 45. 11 applicants, 82% accepted, 9 enrolled. In 2013, 7 doctorates awarded. *Degree requirements:* For doctorate, comprehensive exam, thesis/dissertation, internship. *Entrance requirements:* For doctorate, GRE, master's degree, minimum GPA of 3.5, 3 letters of reference, essay, interview with faculty. Additional exam requirements/recommendations for international students: Required—TOEFL (minimum score 600 paper-based). *Application deadline:* For spring admission, 2/1 for domestic students, 2/1 priority date for international students. Application fee: $50. Electronic applications accepted. *Expenses:* Tuition, state resident: full-time $9888; part-time $412 per credit. Tuition, nonresident: full-time $25,152; part-time $1048 per credit. *Required fees:* $59 per semester. One-time fee: $50. *Financial support:* In 2013–14, 12 fellowships with partial tuition reimbursements (averaging $1,500 per year), 1 research assistantship with full tuition reimbursement (averaging $15,000 per year) were awarded; career-related internships or fieldwork and unspecified assistantships also available. Financial award application deadline: 4/15. *Faculty research:* Rural community colleges, inter-institutional collaboration in higher education. *Unit head:* Dr. Chris Glass, Interim Graduate Program Director, 757-683-4118, Fax: 757-683-5756, E-mail: cglass@odu.edu. *Application contact:* Vanessa Malo-Kurzinski, Office Manager, 757-683-4344, Fax: 757-683-5756, E-mail: vmaloku@odu.edu.
Website: http://education.odu.edu/efl/academics/commcollege/.

Old Dominion University, Darden College of Education, Programs in Occupational and Technical Studies, Norfolk, VA 23529. Offers business and industry training (MS); career and technical education (MS, PhD); community college teaching (MS); human resources training (PhD); STEM education (MS); technology education (PhD). *Accreditation:* NCATE (one or more programs are accredited). Part-time and evening/weekend programs available. Postbaccalaureate distance learning degree programs offered (minimal on-campus study). *Faculty:* 6 full-time (2 women), 2 part-time/adjunct (both women). *Students:* 8 full-time (3 women), 41 part-time (21 women); includes 19 minority (13 Black or African American, non-Hispanic/Latino; 1 American Indian or Alaska Native, non-Hispanic/Latino; 1 Asian, non-Hispanic/Latino; 3 Hispanic/Latino; 1 Two or more races, non-Hispanic/Latino), 2 international. Average age 43. 12 applicants, 83% accepted, 10 enrolled. In 2013, 16 master's, 8 doctorates awarded. *Degree requirements:* For master's, comprehensive exam, thesis optional, writing exam, candidacy exam; for doctorate, comprehensive exam, thesis/dissertation, writing exam, candidacy exam. *Entrance requirements:* For master's, GRE General Test or MAT, minimum GPA of 2.8, 2 letters of reference; for doctorate, GRE, minimum GPA of 3.0, 3 letters of reference. Additional exam requirements/recommendations for international students: Required—TOEFL. *Application deadline:* For fall admission, 6/1 priority date for domestic students, 6/1 for international students; for winter admission, 11/1 priority date for domestic students, 11/1 for international students; for spring admission, 3/1 priority date for domestic students, 3/1 for international students. Applications are processed on a rolling basis. Application fee: $50. Electronic applications accepted. *Expenses:* Tuition, state resident: full-time $9888; part-time $412 per credit. Tuition, nonresident: full-time $25,152; part-time $1048 per credit. *Required fees:* $59 per semester. One-time fee: $50. *Financial support:* In 2013–14, 19 students received support, including fellowships with full tuition reimbursements available (averaging $15,000 per year), research assistantships with partial tuition reimbursements available (averaging $9,000 per year), 2 teaching assistantships with partial tuition

reimbursements available (averaging $15,000 per year); career-related internships or fieldwork, scholarships/grants, tuition waivers (partial), and unspecified assistantships also available. Support available to part-time students. Financial award application deadline: 2/15; financial award applicants required to submit FAFSA. *Faculty research:* Training and development, marketing, technology, special populations, STEM education. *Total annual research expenditures:* $799,773. *Unit head:* Dr. Cynthia L. Tomovic, Graduate Program Director, 757-683-5228, Fax: 757-683-5228, E-mail: ctomovic@odu.edu. *Application contact:* William Heffelfinger, Director of Graduate Admissions, 757-683-5554, Fax: 757-683-3255, E-mail: gradadmit@odu.edu.
Website: http://education.odu.edu/ots/.

Pittsburg State University, Graduate School, College of Education, Department of Special Services and Leadership Studies, Program in Community College and Higher Education, Pittsburg, KS 66762. Offers Ed S. *Accreditation:* NCATE.

University of Central Florida, College of Education and Human Performance, Department of Educational and Human Sciences, Program in Educational Leadership, Orlando, FL 32816. Offers educational leadership (MA, Ed D), including community college education (MA), higher education (Ed D), student personnel (MA). Part-time and evening/weekend programs available. *Students:* 108 full-time (79 women), 259 part-time (180 women); includes 105 minority (43 Black or African American, non-Hispanic/Latino; 1 American Indian or Alaska Native, non-Hispanic/Latino; 8 Asian, non-Hispanic/Latino; 49 Hispanic/Latino; 4 Two or more races, non-Hispanic/Latino), 1 international. Average age 33. 218 applicants, 82% accepted, 117 enrolled. In 2013, 42 master's, 22 doctorates awarded. *Degree requirements:* For master's, thesis or alternative; for doctorate, thesis/dissertation, candidacy exam. *Entrance requirements:* For master's, GRE General Test; for doctorate, GRE General Test, GRE Subject Test, minimum GPA of 3.0, resume. Additional exam requirements/recommendations for international students: Required—TOEFL. *Application deadline:* For fall admission, 2/20 priority date for domestic students; for spring admission, 9/20 priority date for domestic students. Application fee: $30. Electronic applications accepted. *Financial support:* In 2013–14, 14 students received support, including 2 fellowships with partial tuition reimbursements available (averaging $2,800 per year), 12 research assistantships with partial tuition reimbursements available (averaging $6,700 per year), 1 teaching assistantship with partial tuition reimbursement available (averaging $6,600 per year); career-related internships or fieldwork, Federal Work-Study, institutionally sponsored loans, tuition waivers (partial), and unspecified assistantships also available. Financial award application deadline: 3/1; financial award applicants required to submit FAFSA. *Unit head:* Dr. Kenneth Murray, Program Coordinator, 407-832-1468, E-mail: kenneth.murray@ucf.edu. *Application contact:* Barbara Rodriguez Lamas, Director, Admissions and Student Services, 407-823-2766, Fax: 407-823-6442, E-mail: gradadmissions@ucf.edu.
Website: http://education.ucf.edu/departments.cfm.

University of Central Florida, College of Education and Human Performance, School of Teaching, Learning, and Leadership, Applied Learning and Instruction Program, Orlando, FL 32816. Offers applied learning and instruction (MA); community college education (Certificate); gifted education (Certificate); global and comparative education (Certificate); initial teacher professional preparation (Certificate); urban education (Certificate). *Accreditation:* NCATE. Part-time and evening/weekend programs available. *Students:* 11 full-time (9 women), 80 part-time (62 women); includes 27 minority (10 Black or African American, non-Hispanic/Latino; 2 Asian, non-Hispanic/Latino; 13 Hispanic/Latino; 2 Two or more races, non-Hispanic/Latino). Average age 33. 61 applicants, 70% accepted, 29 enrolled. In 2013, 19 master's, 26 other advanced degrees awarded. *Degree requirements:* For Certificate, thesis or alternative, final exam. *Entrance requirements:* For degree, GRE General Test, minimum GPA of 3.0, resume. Additional exam requirements/recommendations for international students: Required—TOEFL. *Application deadline:* For fall admission, 2/20 for domestic students; for spring admission, 9/20 for domestic students. Application fee: $30. Electronic applications accepted. *Financial support:* In 2013–14, 3 students received support, including 1 research assistantship with partial tuition reimbursement available (averaging $8,100 per year), 2 teaching assistantships with partial tuition reimbursements available (averaging $6,900 per year); fellowships, career-related internships or fieldwork, Federal Work-Study, institutionally sponsored loans, and unspecified assistantships also available. Financial award application deadline: 3/1; financial award applicants required to submit FAFSA. *Unit head:* Dr. Bobby Hoffman, Program Coordinator, 407-823-1770, E-mail: bobby.hoffman@ucf.edu. *Application contact:* Barbara Rodriguez Lamas, Director, Admissions and Student Services, 407-823-2766, Fax: 407-823-6442, E-mail: gradadmissions@ucf.edu.
Website: http://education.ucf.edu/departments.cfm.

University of Northern Iowa, Graduate College, College of Humanities, Arts and Sciences, Department of Mathematics, Program in Mathematics, Cedar Falls, IA 50614. Offers community college teaching (MA); mathematics (MA); secondary teaching (MA). *Students:* 5 full-time (1 woman), 23 part-time (13 women); includes 1 minority (Black or African American, non-Hispanic/Latino). 8 applicants, 50% accepted, 2 enrolled. In 2013, 4 master's awarded. Application fee: $50 ($70 for international students). *Unit head:* Dr. Michael Prophet, Coordinator, 319-273-2104, Fax: 319-273-2546, E-mail: mike.prophet@uni.edu. *Application contact:* Laurie S. Russell, Record Analyst, 319-273-2623, Fax: 319-273-2885, E-mail: laurie.russell@uni.edu.

University of Southern Mississippi, Graduate School, College of Education and Psychology, Department of Educational Studies and Research, Hattiesburg, MS 39406-0001. Offers adult education (Graduate Certificate); community college leadership (Graduate Certificate); counseling and personnel services (college) (M Ed); education (PhD, Ed S), including adult education, research, evaluation and statistics (PhD); education (Ed D), including educational administration, educational research; education: educational leadership and research (Ed S), including higher education administration; educational administration and supervision (M Ed); higher education administration (Ed D, PhD); institutional research (Graduate Certificate). *Faculty:* 7 full-time (1 woman), 5 part-time/adjunct (1 woman). *Students:* 32 full-time (21 women), 103 part-time (70 women); includes 44 minority (39 Black or African American, non-Hispanic/Latino; 2 Hispanic/Latino; 3 Two or more races, non-Hispanic/Latino), 4 international. Average age 36. 36 applicants, 72% accepted, 15 enrolled. In 2013, 18 master's, 9 doctorates, 7 other advanced degrees awarded. *Degree requirements:* For master's and other advanced degree, comprehensive exam, thesis (for some programs); for doctorate, comprehensive exam, thesis/dissertation. *Entrance requirements:* For master's, doctorate, and other advanced degree, GRE General Test, minimum GPA of 2.75. Additional exam requirements/recommendations for international students: Required—TOEFL. *Application deadline:* For fall admission, 2/1 for domestic students, 3/1 for international students. Applications are processed on a rolling basis. Application fee: $35. *Financial support:* Career-related internships or fieldwork, Federal Work-Study, and institutionally sponsored loans available. Financial award application deadline: 3/15; financial award applicants required to submit FAFSA. *Total annual research expenditures:* $88,500. *Unit head:* Dr. Thomas V. O'Brien, Chair, 601-266-6093, E-mail: thomas.obrien@usm.edu. *Application contact:* Shonna Breland, Manager of Graduate Admissions, 601-266-6563, Fax: 601-266-5138.
Website: http://www.usm.edu/cep/esr/.

University of South Florida, College of Education, Department of Adult, Career and Higher Education, Tampa, FL 33620-9951. Offers adult education (MA, Ed D, PhD, Ed S); career and technical education (MA); career and workforce education (PhD); higher education/community college teaching (MA, Ed D, PhD); vocational education (Ed S). Part-time programs available. Postbaccalaureate distance learning degree programs offered (minimal on-campus study). *Degree requirements:* For master's, comprehensive exam; for doctorate, comprehensive exam, thesis/dissertation, philosophies of inquiry; multiple research methods; for Ed S, comprehensive exam, thesis. *Entrance requirements:* For master's, minimum GPA of 3.0 in last 60 hours of course work; for doctorate and Ed S, GRE General Test, GRE Writing Test. Additional exam requirements/recommendations for international students: Required—TOEFL (minimum score 500 paper-based; 91 iBT). Electronic applications accepted. *Faculty research:* Community college leadership; integration of academic, career and technical education; competency-based education; continuing education administration; adult learning and development.

Walden University, Graduate Programs, Richard W. Riley College of Education and Leadership, Minneapolis, MN 55401. *Accreditation:* NCATE. Part-time and evening/weekend programs available. Postbaccalaureate distance learning degree programs offered (minimal on-campus study). *Faculty:* 23 full-time (15 women), 830 part-time/adjunct (569 women). *Students:* 8,671 full-time (7,197 women), 2,122 part-time (1,735 women); includes 4,734 minority (3,802 Black or African American, non-Hispanic/Latino; 50 American Indian or Alaska Native, non-Hispanic/Latino; 136 Asian, non-Hispanic/Latino; 539 Hispanic/Latino; 35 Native Hawaiian or other Pacific Islander, non-Hispanic/Latino; 172 Two or more races, non-Hispanic/Latino), 73 international. Average age 40. 2,646 applicants, 96% accepted, 2074 enrolled. In 2013, 2,214 master's, 354 doctorates, 479 other advanced degrees awarded. *Degree requirements:* For doctorate, thesis/dissertation (for some programs), residency; for other advanced degree, residency (for some programs). *Entrance requirements:* For master's, bachelor's degree or higher; minimum GPA of 2.5; official transcripts; goal statement (for some programs); access to computer and Internet; for doctorate, master's degree or higher; three years of related professional or academic experience (preferred); minimum GPA of 3.0; goal statement and current resume (select programs); official transcripts; access to computer and Internet; for other advanced degree, relevant work experience; access to computer and Internet. Additional exam requirements/recommendations for international students: Required—TOEFL (minimum score 550 paper-based; 79 iBT), IELTS (minimum score 6.5), Michigan English Language Assessment Battery (minimum score 82), or PTE. *Application deadline:* Applications are processed on a rolling basis. Application fee: $0. Electronic applications accepted. *Expenses: Tuition:* Full-time $11,813.55; part-time $500 per credit. *Required fees:* $618.76. *Financial support:* In 2013–14, 1 fellowship was awarded; Federal Work-Study, scholarships/grants, unspecified assistantships, and family tuition reduction, active duty/veteran tuition reduction, group tuition reduction, interest-free payment plans, employee tuition reduction also available. Support available to part-time students. Financial award applicants required to submit FAFSA. *Unit head:* Dr. Kate Steffens, Dean, 800-925-3368. *Application contact:* Jennifer Hall, Vice President of Enrollment Management, 866-4-WALDEN, E-mail: info@waldenu.edu.
Website: http://www.waldenu.edu/colleges-schools/riley-college-of-education/.

Western Carolina University, Graduate School, College of Education and Allied Professions, School of Teaching and Learning, Cullowhee, NC 28723. Offers community college and higher education (MA Ed), including community college administration, community college teaching; comprehensive education (MA Ed, MAT); educational leadership (MA Ed, MSA, Ed D, Ed S), including educational leadership (MSA, Ed D, Ed S), educational supervision (MA Ed); teaching (MA Ed, MAT), including comprehensive education (MA Ed), physical education (MA Ed), teaching (MAT). *Accreditation:* NCATE. Part-time and evening/weekend programs available. Postbaccalaureate distance learning degree programs offered. *Degree requirements:* For master's, comprehensive exam; for doctorate, comprehensive exam, thesis/dissertation. *Entrance requirements:* For master's, GRE, appropriate undergraduate degree, 3 letters of recommendation; for doctorate, GRE General Test, minimum graduate GPA of 3.5, appropriate master's degree; for other advanced degree, GRE General Test, minimum graduate GPA of 3.5, work experience, appropriate master's degree. Additional exam requirements/recommendations for international students: Required—TOEFL (minimum score 550 paper-based; 79 iBT). *Faculty research:* Educational leadership, special education, rural education, organizational theory and practice, interinstitutional partnership, program evaluation.

Wingate University, Thayer School of Education, Wingate, NC 28174-0159. Offers community college leadership (Ed D); educational leadership (MA Ed, Ed D); elementary education (MA Ed, MAT); health and physical education (MA Ed); sport administration (MA Ed). *Accreditation:* NCATE. Part-time and evening/weekend programs available. *Degree requirements:* For master's, portfolio. *Entrance requirements:* For master's, GRE General Test or MAT, teaching certificate (MA Ed).

Early Childhood Education

Alabama Agricultural and Mechanical University, School of Graduate Studies, School of Education, Area in Elementary and Early Childhood Education, Huntsville, AL 35811. Offers early childhood education (MS Ed, Ed S); elementary education (MS Ed, Ed S). *Accreditation:* NCATE. Evening/weekend programs available. *Degree requirements:* For master's, comprehensive exam; for Ed S, thesis. *Entrance requirements:* For master's, GRE General Test. Additional exam requirements/recommendations for international students: Required—TOEFL (minimum score 500 paper-based; 61 iBT). Electronic applications accepted. *Faculty research:* Multicultural education, learning styles, diagnostic-prescriptive instruction.

Alabama State University, College of Education, Department of Curriculum and Instruction, Montgomery, AL 36101-0271. Offers early childhood education (M Ed, Ed S); elementary education (M Ed, Ed S); secondary education (M Ed, Ed S), including

biology education, English language arts education (M Ed), history education, math education, music education (M Ed), reading education (M Ed), social science education; special education (M Ed). Part-time programs available. *Faculty:* 11 full-time (8 women), 13 part-time/adjunct (10 women). *Students:* 32 full-time (19 women), 162 part-time (136 women); includes 189 minority (187 Black or African American, non-Hispanic/Latino; 1 Hispanic/Latino; 1 Two or more races, non-Hispanic/Latino). Average age 33. 99 applicants, 45% accepted, 34 enrolled. In 2013, 74 master's, 20 Ed Ss awarded. *Degree requirements:* For master's, comprehensive exam, thesis optional; for Ed S, comprehensive exam, thesis. *Entrance requirements:* For master's, GRE General Test, MAT, writing competency test; for Ed S, writing competency test, GRE, MAT. Additional exam requirements/recommendations for international students: Required—TOEFL (minimum score 500 paper-based). *Application deadline:* For fall admission, 7/15 for domestic students; for spring admission, 12/15 for domestic students. Applications are processed on a rolling basis. Application fee: $25. *Expenses:* Tuition, state resident: full-time $7958; part-time $343 per credit hour. Tuition, nonresident: full-time $14,132; part-time $686 per credit hour. *Required fees:* $446 per term. One-time fee: $1784 full-time; $892 part-time. Tuition and fees vary according to course load. *Financial support:* In 2013–14, research assistantships (averaging $9,450 per year) were awarded. *Unit head:* Dr. Joyce Johnson, Acting Chairperson, 334-229-4485, Fax: 334-229-5603, E-mail: jjohnson@alasu.edu. *Application contact:* Dr. William Person, Dean of Graduate Studies, 334-229-4274, Fax: 334-229-4928, E-mail: wperson@alasu.edu.
Website: http://www.alasu.edu/academics/colleges—departments/college-of-education/curriculum—instruction/index.aspx.

Albany State University, College of Education, Albany, GA 31705-2717. Offers early childhood education (M Ed); education specialist (Ed S); educational leadership and administration (M Ed); health, physical education and recreation (M Ed); middle grades education (M Ed); school counseling (M Ed); special education (M Ed). *Accreditation:* NCATE. Part-time and evening/weekend programs available. Postbaccalaureate distance learning degree programs offered (minimal on-campus study). *Degree requirements:* For master's, comprehensive exam, internship, GACE Content Exam. *Entrance requirements:* For master's, GRE or MAT. Electronic applications accepted. *Faculty research:* GACE preparation, STEM (science, technology, engineering, and mathematics), technology education, special education, professional teacher development, health implications liberation philosophy, NET-Q, learning community, disabled or at-risk students.

Albright College, Graduate Division, Reading, PA 19612-5234. Offers early childhood education (MS); elementary education (MS); English as a second language (MA); general education (MA); special education (MS). Part-time and evening/weekend programs available. *Degree requirements:* For master's, thesis. *Entrance requirements:* For master's, GRE General Test or MAT, minimum undergraduate GPA of 3.0, 2 letters of recommendation, interview. Additional exam requirements/recommendations for international students: Recommended—TOEFL (minimum score 525 paper-based). Electronic applications accepted.

American International College, School of Graduate and Adult Education, Department of Education, Springfield, MA 01109-3189. Offers early childhood education (M Ed, CAGS); educational leadership and supervision (Ed D); elementary education (M Ed, CAGS); middle/secondary education (M Ed, CAGS); moderate disabilities (M Ed, CAGS); reading (M Ed, CAGS); school adjustment counseling (MA, CAGS); school guidance counseling (MA, CAGS); school leadership preparation (M Ed, CAGS); teaching and learning (Ed D). Evening/weekend programs available. *Faculty:* 11 full-time (9 women), 235 part-time/adjunct. *Students:* 1,530 full-time (1,219 women), 184 part-time (143 women); includes 100 minority (58 Black or African American, non-Hispanic/Latino; 3 American Indian or Alaska Native, non-Hispanic/Latino; 14 Asian, non-Hispanic/Latino; 6 Hispanic/Latino; 19 Two or more races, non-Hispanic/Latino). Average age 36. 695 applicants, 82% accepted, 508 enrolled. In 2013, 449 master's, 17 doctorates, 135 other advanced degrees awarded. Terminal master's awarded for partial completion of doctoral program. *Degree requirements:* For master's, comprehensive exam (for some programs), thesis (for some programs), practicum/culminating experience; for doctorate, comprehensive exam (for some programs), thesis/dissertation; for CAGS, practicum/culminating experience. *Entrance requirements:* For master's, graduate of accredited four-year college with minimum B-average in undergraduate course work; for doctorate, master's degree, minimum GPA of 3.0; for CAGS, M Ed or master's degree in field related to licensure from accredited institution. Additional exam requirements/recommendations for international students: Required—TOEFL or IELTS. *Application deadline:* For fall admission, 7/1 for domestic and international students; for spring admission, 12/1 for domestic and international students. Applications are processed on a rolling basis. Application fee: $50. Electronic applications accepted. *Expenses: Tuition:* Full-time $14,040; part-time $780 per credit. Tuition and fees vary according to course load, degree level and program. *Financial support:* Career-related internships or fieldwork available. Financial award applicants required to submit FAFSA. *Unit head:* Esta Sobey, Associate Dean, 413-205-3453, Fax: 413-205-3943, E-mail: esta.sobey@aic.edu. *Application contact:* Kaitlyn Rickard, Director of XCP Admissions, 413-205-3090, Fax: 413-205-3911, E-mail: kaitlyn.rickard@aic.edu.
Website: http://www.aic.edu/academics.

American University, College of Arts and Sciences, Washington, DC 20016-8012. Offers addiction and addictive behavior (Certificate); anthropology (PhD); applied microeconomics (Certificate); applied statistics (Certificate); art history (MA); arts management (MA, Certificate); Asian studies (Certificate); audio production (Certificate); audio technology (MA); behavior, cognition, and neuroscience (PhD); bilingual education (MA, Certificate); biology (MA, MS); chemistry (MS); clinical psychology (PhD); computer science (MS, Certificate); creative writing (MFA); curriculum and instruction (M Ed, Certificate); economics (MA, PhD); environmental assessment (Certificate); environmental science (MS); ethics, peace, and global affairs (MA); gender analysis in economics (Certificate); health promotion management (MS); history (MA, PhD); international arts management (Certificate); international economic relations (Certificate); international economics (MA); international training and education (MA); literature (MA); mathematics (MA); North American studies (Certificate); nutrition education (MS, Certificate); philosophy (MA); professional science: biotechnology (MS); professional science: environmental assessment (MS); professional science: quantitative analysis (MS); psychobiology of healing (Certificate); psychology (MA); psychology: general (PhD); public anthropology (MA, Certificate); public sociology (Certificate); social research (Certificate); sociology (MA); Spanish: Latin American studies (MA); special education: learning disabilities (MA); statistics (MS); studio art (MFA); teaching (MAT); teaching English as a foreign language (MA); teaching: early childhood (Certificate); teaching: elementary (Certificate); teaching: ESOL (Certificate); teaching: secondary (Certificate); technology in arts management (Certificate); TESOL (MA); translation: French (Certificate); translation: Russian (Certificate); translation: Spanish (Certificate); women's, gender, and sexuality studies (Certificate). Part-time and evening/weekend programs available. Postbaccalaureate distance learning degree programs offered (no on-campus study). *Faculty:* 358 full-time (187 women), 254 part-time/adjunct (127 women). *Students:* 627 full-time (411 women), 416 part-time (300 women); includes 206 minority (91 Black or African American, non-Hispanic/Latino; 5 American Indian or Alaska Native, non-Hispanic/Latino; 32 Asian, non-Hispanic/Latino; 64 Hispanic/Latino; 1 Native Hawaiian or other Pacific Islander, non-Hispanic/Latino; 13 Two or more races, non-Hispanic/Latino), 124 international. Average age 29. 1,672 applicants, 52% accepted, 361 enrolled. In 2013, 382 master's, 38 doctorates, 33 other advanced degrees awarded. Terminal master's awarded for partial completion of doctoral program. *Degree requirements:* For master's, comprehensive exam (for some programs), thesis (for some programs); for doctorate, comprehensive exam (for some programs), thesis/dissertation. *Entrance requirements:* For master's, GRE, minimum GPA of 3.0 in last 60 credit hours, letter of recommendation, statement of purpose, resume, unofficial transcript; for doctorate, GRE, minimum GPA of 3.0 for all graduate work, letter of recommendation, statement of purpose, resume, unofficial transcript. Additional exam requirements/recommendations for international students: Required—TOEFL (minimum score 600 paper-based; 100 iBT), IELTS (minimum score 7). *Application deadline:* For fall admission, 2/1 for domestic students; for spring admission, 10/1 for domestic students. Applications are processed on a rolling basis. Application fee: $55. Electronic applications accepted. *Expenses: Tuition:* Full-time $25,920; part-time $1482 per credit hour. *Required fees:* $430. Tuition and fees vary according to course load and program. *Financial support:* Fellowships, research assistantships with full and partial tuition reimbursements, teaching assistantships with full and partial tuition reimbursements, career-related internships or fieldwork, Federal Work-Study, institutionally sponsored loans, scholarships/grants, traineeships, tuition waivers (full and partial), and unspecified assistantships available. Support available to part-time students. Financial award applicants required to submit FAFSA. *Unit head:* Dr. Peter Starr, Dean, 202-885-2446, Fax: 202-885-2429, E-mail: pstarr@american.edu. *Application contact:* Kathleen Clowery, Associate Director, Graduate Enrollment Management, 202-885-3621, Fax: 202-885-1505, E-mail: clowery@american.edu.
Website: http://www.american.edu/cas/.

Anna Maria College, Graduate Division, Program in Education, Paxton, MA 01612. Offers early childhood education (M Ed); education (CAGS); elementary education (M Ed); English language arts (M Ed); visual arts (M Ed). Part-time and evening/weekend programs available. *Entrance requirements:* For master's, bachelor's degree in liberal arts or sciences, minimum GPA of 3.0. Additional exam requirements/recommendations for international students: Required—TOEFL (minimum score 500 paper-based). Electronic applications accepted.

Antioch University New England, Graduate School, Department of Education, Integrated Learning Program, Keene, NH 03431-3552. Offers early childhood education (M Ed); elementary education (M Ed), including arts and humanities, science and environmental education; special education (M Ed). *Degree requirements:* For master's, internship. *Entrance requirements:* For master's, previous course work or work experience in education. Additional exam requirements/recommendations for international students: Required—TOEFL (minimum score 550 paper-based). Electronic applications accepted. *Expenses:* Contact institution. *Faculty research:* Problem-based learning, place-based education, mathematics education, democratic classrooms, art education.

Arcadia University, Graduate Studies, School of Education, Glenside, PA 19038-3295. Offers art education (M Ed); computer education (CAS); curriculum (CAS); curriculum studies (M Ed); early childhood education (M Ed, CAS), including individualized (M Ed), master teacher (M Ed), research in child development (M Ed); educational leadership (M Ed, Ed D, CAS); elementary education (M Ed, CAS); English education (MA Ed); environmental education (MA Ed, CAS); history education (MA Ed); instructional technology (M Ed); language arts (M Ed, CAS); library science (M Ed); mathematics education (M Ed, MA Ed, CAS); music education (MA Ed); psychology (MA Ed); reading (M Ed, CAS); science education (M Ed, CAS); secondary education (M Ed, CAS); special education (M Ed, Ed D, CAS); theater arts (MA Ed); written communication (MA Ed). *Accreditation:* NASAD. Part-time and evening/weekend programs available. Postbaccalaureate distance learning degree programs offered (minimal on-campus study). Electronic applications accepted. *Expenses:* Contact institution.

Arkansas State University, Graduate School, College of Education and Behavioral Science, School of Teacher Education and Leadership, Jonesboro, AR 72467. Offers community college administration (SCCT); curriculum and instruction (MSE); early childhood education (MAT, MSE); early childhood services (MS); educational leadership (MSE, Ed D, PhD, Ed S); educational theory and practice (MSE); middle level education (MAT, MSE); reading (MSE, Ed S); special education - gifted, talented, and creative (MSE); special education - instructional specialist grades 4-12 (MSE); special education - instructional specialist grades P-4 (MSE). *Accreditation:* NCATE. Part-time programs available. Postbaccalaureate distance learning degree programs offered. *Faculty:* 28 full-time (16 women). *Students:* 77 full-time (68 women), 1,934 part-time (1,449 women); includes 361 minority (290 Black or African American, non-Hispanic/Latino; 11 American Indian or Alaska Native, non-Hispanic/Latino; 3 Asian, non-Hispanic/Latino; 26 Hispanic/Latino; 1 Native Hawaiian or other Pacific Islander, non-Hispanic/Latino; 30 Two or more races, non-Hispanic/Latino), 5 international. Average age 36. 1,627 applicants, 71% accepted, 770 enrolled. In 2013, 1,182 master's, 12 doctorates, 76 other advanced degrees awarded. *Degree requirements:* For master's, comprehensive exam, thesis or alternative; for doctorate, comprehensive exam, thesis/dissertation; for other advanced degree, comprehensive exam. *Entrance requirements:* For master's, GRE General Test or MAT, appropriate bachelor's degree, official transcripts, immunization records, letters of reference, interview; for doctorate, GRE General Test or MAT, interview, master's degree, letters of reference, official transcript, personal statement, writing sample, immunization records; for other advanced degree, GRE General Test or MAT, interview, master's degree, official transcript, immunization records, letters of reference, 3 years of teaching experience, teaching license. Additional exam requirements/recommendations for international students: Required—TOEFL (minimum score 550 paper-based; 79 iBT), IELTS (minimum score 6), PTE (minimum score 56). *Application deadline:* For fall admission, 7/1 for domestic and international students; for spring admission, 11/15 for domestic students, 11/14 for international students. Applications are processed on a rolling basis. Electronic applications accepted. *Expenses:* Tuition, state resident: full-time $4284; part-time $238 per credit hour. Tuition, nonresident: full-time $8568; part-time $476 per credit hour. *International tuition:* $9268 full-time. *Required fees:* $1098; $61 per credit hour. $25 per term. Tuition and fees vary according to course load and program. *Financial support:* In 2013–14, 20 students received support. Fellowships, teaching assistantships, career-related internships or fieldwork, scholarships/grants, and unspecified assistantships available. Financial award application deadline: 7/1; financial award applicants required to submit FAFSA. *Unit head:* Dr. Annette Hux, Interim Chair, 870-972-3059, Fax: 870-972-3344, E-mail: ahux@astate.edu. *Application contact:* Vickey Ring, Graduate Admissions Coordinator, 870-972-3029, Fax: 870-972-3857, E-mail: vickeyring@astate.edu.
Website: http://www.astate.edu/college/education/departments/school-of-teacher-education-and-leadership/index.dot.

Armstrong State University, School of Graduate Studies, Department of Childhood and Exceptional Student Education, Savannah, GA 31419-1997. Offers early childhood education (M Ed, MAT); reading endorsement (Certificate); special education (M Ed, MAT). *Accreditation:* NCATE. Part-time and evening/weekend programs available. Postbaccalaureate distance learning degree programs offered (minimal on-campus study). *Faculty:* 12 full-time (9 women), 4 part-time/adjunct (0 women). *Students:* 26 full-

time (22 women), 208 part-time (186 women); includes 74 minority (66 Black or African American, non-Hispanic/Latino; 1 Asian, non-Hispanic/Latino; 5 Hispanic/Latino; 2 Two or more races, non-Hispanic/Latino), 1 international. Average age 33. 107 applicants, 70% accepted, 69 enrolled. In 2013, 122 master's, 64 other advanced degrees awarded. *Degree requirements:* For master's, comprehensive exam. *Entrance requirements:* For master's, GRE General Test or MAT. Additional exam requirements/recommendations for international students: Required—TOEFL (minimum score 523 paper-based). *Application deadline:* For fall admission, 6/30 priority date for domestic students, 5/1 priority date for international students; for spring admission, 11/15 priority date for domestic students, 9/15 priority date for international students; for summer admission, 4/15 priority date for domestic students, 9/15 for international students. Applications are processed on a rolling basis. Application fee: $30. Electronic applications accepted. *Expenses:* Tuition, state resident: part-time $201 per credit hour. Tuition, nonresident: part-time $745 per credit hour. *Required fees:* $310 per semester. Tuition and fees vary according to course load, campus/location and program. *Financial support:* In 2013–14, research assistantships with full tuition reimbursements (averaging $5,000 per year) were awarded; career-related internships or fieldwork, Federal Work-Study, scholarships/grants, and unspecified assistantships also available. Support available to part-time students. Financial award application deadline: 3/15; financial award applicants required to submit FAFSA. *Faculty research:* Literacy, instructional design, poetry, working with local schools. *Unit head:* Dr. John Hobe, Department Head, 912-344-2564, Fax: 912-344-3443, E-mail: john.hobe@armstrong.edu. *Application contact:* Jill Bell, Director, Graduate Enrollment Services, 912-344-2798, Fax: 912-344-3488, E-mail: graduate@armstrong.edu.
Website: http://www.armstrong.edu/Education/childhood_exceptional_education2/ceed_welcome.

Auburn University, Graduate School, College of Education, Department of Curriculum and Teaching, Auburn University, AL 36849. Offers business education (M Ed, MS, PhD); early childhood education (M Ed, MS, PhD, Ed S); elementary education (M Ed, MS, PhD, Ed S); foreign languages (M Ed, MS); music education (M Ed, MS, PhD, Ed S); postsecondary education (PhD); reading education (PhD, Ed S); secondary education (M Ed, MS, PhD, Ed S), including English language arts, mathematics, science, social studies. *Accreditation:* NASM (one or more programs are accredited); NCATE. Part-time programs available. *Faculty:* 29 full-time (21 women), 4 part-time/adjunct (all women). *Students:* 61 full-time (40 women), 153 part-time (108 women); includes 37 minority (32 Black or African American, non-Hispanic/Latino; 2 Asian, non-Hispanic/Latino; 3 Hispanic/Latino), 1 international. Average age 34. 150 applicants, 59% accepted, 74 enrolled. In 2013, 70 master's, 6 doctorates, 26 other advanced degrees awarded. *Degree requirements:* For master's, thesis (for some programs); for doctorate, thesis/dissertation; for Ed S, field project. *Entrance requirements:* For master's, doctorate, and Ed S, GRE General Test. *Application deadline:* For fall admission, 7/7 for domestic students; for spring admission, 11/24 for domestic students. Applications are processed on a rolling basis. Application fee: $50 ($60 for international students). Electronic applications accepted. *Expenses:* Tuition, state resident: full-time $8262; part-time $459 per credit hour. Tuition, nonresident: full-time $24,786; part-time $1377 per credit hour. Tuition and fees vary according to degree level and program. *Financial support:* Fellowships, teaching assistantships, career-related internships or fieldwork, and Federal Work-Study available. Support available to part-time students. Financial award application deadline: 3/15; financial award applicants required to submit FAFSA. *Faculty research:* Emerging literacy, reading attitudes, music for at-risk youth, portfolio assessment. *Unit head:* Dr. Kimberly Walls, Head, 334-844-4434. *Application contact:* Dr. George Flowers, Dean of the Graduate School, 334-844-2125.
Website: http://education.auburn.edu/academic_departments/curr/.

Auburn University, Graduate School, College of Education, Department of Special Education, Rehabilitation, Counseling and School Psychology, Auburn University, AL 36849. Offers collaborative teacher special education (M Ed, MS); early childhood special education (M Ed, MS); rehabilitation counseling (M Ed, MS, PhD). *Accreditation:* CORE; NCATE. Part-time programs available. *Faculty:* 18 full-time (14 women), 8 part-time/adjunct (7 women). *Students:* 142 full-time (118 women), 80 part-time (64 women); includes 57 minority (53 Black or African American, non-Hispanic/Latino; 1 American Indian or Alaska Native, non-Hispanic/Latino; 2 Asian, non-Hispanic/Latino; 1 Hispanic/Latino). Average age 30. 239 applicants, 42% accepted, 83 enrolled. In 2013, 59 master's, 10 doctorates awarded. *Degree requirements:* For master's, thesis (for some programs); for doctorate, thesis/dissertation. *Entrance requirements:* For master's, GRE General Test; for doctorate, GRE General Test, interview. *Application deadline:* For fall admission, 7/7 for domestic students; for spring admission, 11/24 for domestic students. Applications are processed on a rolling basis. Application fee: $50 ($60 for international students). Electronic applications accepted. *Expenses:* Tuition, state resident: full-time $8262; part-time $459 per credit hour. Tuition, nonresident: full-time $24,786; part-time $1377 per credit hour. Tuition and fees vary according to degree level and program. *Financial support:* Research assistantships, teaching assistantships, and Federal Work-Study available. Support available to part-time students. Financial award application deadline: 3/15; financial award applicants required to submit FAFSA. *Faculty research:* Emotional conflict/behavior disorders, gifted and talented, learning disabilities, mental retardation, multi-handicapped. *Unit head:* Dr. E. Davis Martin, Jr., Head, 334-844-7676. *Application contact:* Dr. George Flowers, Dean of the Graduate School, 334-844-2125.

Auburn University at Montgomery, School of Education, Department of Counselor, Leadership, and Special Education, Montgomery, AL 36124-4023. Offers counseling education (M Ed, Ed S), including counseling and development (Ed S); school counseling (Ed S); early childhood special education (M Ed); instructional leadership (Ed S); special education (Ed S); special education/collaborative teacher (M Ed). *Accreditation:* ACA; NCATE. Part-time and evening/weekend programs available. *Faculty:* 6 full-time (5 women), 2 part-time/adjunct (1 woman). *Students:* 15 full-time (11 women), 55 part-time (42 women); includes 32 minority (31 Black or African American, non-Hispanic/Latino; 1 Hispanic/Latino). Average age 33. In 2013, 22 master's awarded. *Degree requirements:* For master's and Ed S, comprehensive exam. *Entrance requirements:* For master's, GRE General Test or MAT, certification, BS in teaching; for Ed S, GRE General Test or MAT, certification. *Application deadline:* Applications are processed on a rolling basis. Electronic applications accepted. *Expenses:* Tuition, state resident: full-time $5994; part-time $333 per credit hour. Tuition, nonresident: full-time $17,982; part-time $999 per credit hour. *Financial support:* Career-related internships or fieldwork and scholarships/grants available. Support available to part-time students. Financial award application deadline: 3/1; financial award applicants required to submit FAFSA. *Unit head:* Dr. Sheila Austin, Dean, 334-244-3425, Fax: 334-244-3102, E-mail: saustin1@aum.edu. *Application contact:* Dr. Rhonda Morton, Associate Dean/Graduate Coordinator, 334-244-3287, Fax: 334-244-3978, E-mail: rmorton@aum.edu.
Website: http://www.aum.edu/Education.

Auburn University at Montgomery, School of Education, Department of Early Childhood, Elementary, and Reading Education, Montgomery, AL 36124-4023. Offers collaborative teacher (Ed S); early childhood education (Ed S); elementary education (M Ed, Ed S). *Accreditation:* NCATE. Part-time and evening/weekend programs available. *Faculty:* 4 full-time (all women). *Students:* 27 full-time (26 women), 67 part-time (64 women); includes 32 minority (29 Black or African American, non-Hispanic/Latino; 2 Asian, non-Hispanic/Latino; 1 Hispanic/Latino). Average age 34. In 2013, 44

master's, 11 Ed Ss awarded. *Degree requirements:* For master's and Ed S, comprehensive exam. *Entrance requirements:* For master's, GRE General Test or MAT, certification, BS in teaching; for Ed S, GRE General Test or MAT, certification. *Application deadline:* Applications are processed on a rolling basis. Electronic applications accepted. *Expenses:* Tuition, state resident: full-time $5994; part-time $333 per credit hour. Tuition, nonresident: full-time $17,982; part-time $999 per credit hour. *Financial support:* Teaching assistantships, career-related internships or fieldwork, and scholarships/grants available. Support available to part-time students. Financial award application deadline: 3/1; financial award applicants required to submit FAFSA. *Unit head:* Dr. Lynne Mills, Head, 334-244-3283, Fax: 334-244-3835, E-mail: lmills@mail.aum.edu. *Application contact:* Dr. Rhonda Morton, Associate Dean/Graduate Coordinator, 334-244-3287, Fax: 334-244-3978, E-mail: rmorton@aum.edu.
Website: http://www.aum.edu/Education.

Aurora University, College of Education, Aurora, IL 60506-4892. Offers curriculum and instruction (MA, Ed D); early childhood and special education (MA); education (MAT), including elementary certification; education and administration (Ed D); educational leadership (MEL); educational technology (MATL); reading instruction (MA); special education (MA). *Accreditation:* NCATE. Part-time and evening/weekend programs available. *Degree requirements:* For doctorate, comprehensive exam, thesis/dissertation. *Entrance requirements:* For master's, 2 years of teaching experience, valid teaching certificate. Additional exam requirements/recommendations for international students: Required—TOEFL (minimum score 550 paper-based). Electronic applications accepted. *Expenses:* Contact institution.

Averett University, Master in Education Program, Danville, VA 24541-3692. Offers administration and supervision (M Ed); art (M Ed); biology (M Ed); chemistry (M Ed); curriculum and instruction (M Ed); early childhood (M Ed); English (M Ed); mathematics (M Ed); middle grades (M Ed); physical science (M Ed); reading specialist (M Ed); science (M Ed); special education (M Ed); special education learning disability (M Ed). Program offered on Danville Campus only. Part-time and evening/weekend programs available. *Faculty:* 4 full-time (3 women), 13 part-time/adjunct (8 women). *Students:* 43 full-time (35 women), 44 part-time (35 women); includes 7 minority (all Black or African American, non-Hispanic/Latino). *Degree requirements:* For master's, 30-credit core curriculum, minimum GPA of 3.0 throughout program, completion of degree requirements within six years from start of program. *Entrance requirements:* For master's, PRAXIS I, GRE, or MAT; writing proficiency test, minimum cumulative GPA of 3.0 over the last 60 hours of undergraduate study toward a baccalaureate degree, three letters of recommendation, Virginia teaching license (or eligibility). Additional exam requirements/recommendations for international students: Required—TOEFL (minimum score 600 paper-based; 100 iBT). *Application deadline:* Applications are processed on a rolling basis. Application fee: $100. *Expenses:* Contact institution. *Financial support:* Career-related internships or fieldwork, Federal Work-Study, and scholarships/grants available. Financial award application deadline: 4/1; financial award applicants required to submit FAFSA. *Unit head:* Wilfred Lawrence, Department Chair of Education, 434-791-5752, E-mail: priedel@averett.edu. *Application contact:* Christy Pack, Executive Director of Enrollment, 804-887-8612, E-mail: dpack@averett.edu.
Website: http://www.averett.edu/adultprograms/degrees/MEDtrad.php.

Bank Street College of Education, Graduate School, Program in Early Childhood Education, New York, NY 10025. Offers MS Ed. *Degree requirements:* For master's, thesis. *Entrance requirements:* For master's, interview, essays. Additional exam requirements/recommendations for international students: Required—TOEFL (minimum score 600 paper-based; 100 iBT), IELTS (minimum score 7). Electronic applications accepted. *Faculty research:* Play in early childhood settings, early childhood learning environments, family-teacher interaction, child-centered education, developmental interaction.

Bank Street College of Education, Graduate School, Program in Infant and Family Development and Early Intervention, New York, NY 10025. Offers infant and family development (MS Ed); infant and family early childhood special and general education (MS Ed); infant and family/early childhood special education (Ed M). *Degree requirements:* For master's, thesis. *Entrance requirements:* For master's, interview, essays. Additional exam requirements/recommendations for international students: Required—TOEFL (minimum score 600 paper-based; 100 iBT), IELTS (minimum score 7). Electronic applications accepted. *Faculty research:* Early intervention, early attachment practice in infant and toddler childcare, parenting skills in adolescents.

Bank Street College of Education, Graduate School, Program in Reading and Literacy, New York, NY 10025. Offers advanced literacy specialization (Ed M); reading and literacy (MS Ed); teaching literacy (MS Ed); teaching literacy and childhood general education (MS Ed). *Degree requirements:* For master's, thesis. *Entrance requirements:* For master's, interview, essays. Additional exam requirements/recommendations for international students: Required—TOEFL (minimum score 600 paper-based; 100 iBT), IELTS (minimum score 7). Electronic applications accepted. *Faculty research:* Language development, children's literature, whole language, the reading and writing processes, reading difficulties in multicultural classrooms.

Bank Street College of Education, Graduate School, Programs in Educational Leadership, New York, NY 10025. Offers early childhood leadership (MS Ed); educational leadership (MS Ed); leadership for educational change (Ed M, MS Ed); leadership in community-based learning (MS Ed); leadership in mathematics education (MS Ed); leadership in museum education (MS Ed); leadership in the arts: creative writing (MS Ed); leadership in the arts: visual arts (MS Ed). *Degree requirements:* For master's, thesis. *Entrance requirements:* For master's, interview, essays, minimum of 2 years experience as a classroom teacher. Additional exam requirements/recommendations for international students: Required—TOEFL (minimum score 600 paper-based; 100 iBT), IELTS (minimum score 7). Electronic applications accepted. *Faculty research:* Leadership in urban schools, leadership in small schools, mathematics in elementary schools, professional development in early childhood, leadership in arts education, leadership in special education, museum leadership, community-based leadership.

Barry University, School of Education, Program in Curriculum and Instruction, Miami Shores, FL 33161-6695. Offers accomplished teacher (Ed S); culture, language and literacy (TESOL) (PhD); curriculum evaluation and research (PhD); early childhood (Ed S); early childhood education (PhD); elementary (Ed S); elementary education (PhD); ESOL (Ed S); gifted (Ed S); Montessori (Ed S); PKP/elementary (Ed S); reading (Ed S); reading, language and cognition (PhD). *Entrance requirements:* For doctorate, GRE, minimum GPA of 3.25.

Barry University, School of Education, Program in Montessori Education, Miami Shores, FL 33161-6695. Offers MS, Ed S. Part-time and evening/weekend programs available. *Degree requirements:* For master's, comprehensive exam, practicum; for Ed S, practicum. *Entrance requirements:* For master's, GRE General Test or MAT, minimum GPA of 3.0; for Ed S, GRE General Test, minimum GPA of 3.0. Electronic applications accepted.

Barry University, School of Education, Program in Pre-Kindergarten and Primary Education, Miami Shores, FL 33161-6695. Offers pre-k/primary (MS); pre-k/primary/ESOL (MS). Part-time and evening/weekend programs available. *Degree requirements:*

Early Childhood Education

For master's, comprehensive exam, practicum. *Entrance requirements:* For master's, GRE General Test or MAT, minimum GPA of 3.0. Electronic applications accepted.

Bayamón Central University, Graduate Programs, Program in Education, Bayamón, PR 00960-1725. Offers administration and supervision (MA Ed); commercial education (MA Ed); elementary education (K–3) (MA Ed); family counseling (Graduate Certificate); guidance and counseling (MA Ed); pre-elementary teacher (MA Ed); rehabilitation counseling (MA Ed); special education (MA Ed), including attention deficit disorder, education of the autistic, learning disabilities. Part-time and evening/weekend programs available. *Degree requirements:* For master's, comprehensive exam. *Entrance requirements:* For master's, EXADEP, bachelor's degree in education or related field.

Berry College, Graduate Programs, Graduate Programs in Education, Program in Early Childhood Education, Mount Berry, GA 30149-0159. Offers M Ed, MAT. *Accreditation:* NCATE. Part-time programs available. *Faculty:* 10 part-time/adjunct (5 women). *Students:* 7 full-time (6 women), 9 part-time (7 women); includes 1 minority (Hispanic/Latino). Average age 33. In 2013, 7 master's awarded. *Degree requirements:* For master's, thesis, portfolio, oral exams. *Entrance requirements:* For master's, GRE General Test or MAT, minimum GPA of 2.5. Additional exam requirements/recommendations for international students: Required—TOEFL (minimum score 550 paper-based). *Application deadline:* For fall admission, 7/25 for domestic students, 5/1 for international students; for spring admission, 12/1 for domestic students, 10/1 for international students. Applications are processed on a rolling basis. Application fee: $25 ($30 for international students). *Expenses:* Contact institution. *Financial support:* In 2013–14, 7 students received support, including 4 research assistantships with full tuition reimbursements available (averaging $4,608 per year); scholarships/grants and unspecified assistantships also available. Support available to part-time students. Financial award application deadline: 3/1; financial award applicants required to submit FAFSA. *Unit head:* Dr. Jacqueline McDowell, Dean, 706-236-1717, Fax: 706-238-5827, E-mail: jmcdowell@berry.edu. *Application contact:* Brett Kennedy, Assistant Vice President of Enrollment Management, 706-236-2215, Fax: 706-290-2178, E-mail: admissions@berry.edu.
Website: http://www.berry.edu/academics/education/graduate/.

Binghamton University, State University of New York, Graduate School, School of Education, Program in Childhood Education, Vestal, NY 13850. Offers MS Ed. *Accreditation:* Teacher Education Accreditation Council. Part-time and evening/weekend programs available. *Entrance requirements:* For master's, GRE General Test. Additional exam requirements/recommendations for international students: Required—TOEFL (minimum score 550 paper-based; 80 iBT). *Application deadline:* For fall admission, 2/1 priority date for domestic and international students; for spring admission, 10/15 priority date for domestic and international students. Applications are processed on a rolling basis. Application fee: $75. Electronic applications accepted. *Financial support:* Career-related internships or fieldwork, Federal Work-Study, institutionally sponsored loans, scholarships/grants, health care benefits, tuition waivers (full), and unspecified assistantships available. Financial award application deadline: 2/15; financial award applicants required to submit FAFSA. *Unit head:* Dr. S. G. Grant, Coordinator, 607-777-7329, E-mail: sggrant@binghamton.edu. *Application contact:* Kishan Zuber, Recruiting and Admissions Coordinator, 607-777-2151, Fax: 607-777-2501, E-mail: kzuber@binghamton.edu.

Biola University, School of Education, La Mirada, CA 90639-0001. Offers apologetics (MA Ed); curriculum and instruction (MA Ed, MAT, Certificate); early childhood (MA Ed, MAT); history and philosophy of science (MA Ed, MAT); linguistics and inter-cultural studies (MAT); linguistics and international studies (MA Ed); multiple subject (MAT); single subject (MAT); special education (MA Ed, MAT, Certificate); TESOL (MA Ed, MAT). Part-time and evening/weekend programs available. Postbaccalaureate distance learning degree programs offered (no on-campus study). *Faculty:* 14. *Students:* 51 full-time (38 women), 101 part-time (83 women); includes 47 minority (8 Black or African American, non-Hispanic/Latino; 1 American Indian or Alaska Native, non-Hispanic/Latino; 32 Asian, non-Hispanic/Latino; 6 Two or more races, non-Hispanic/Latino), 4 international. In 2013, 33 master's awarded. *Entrance requirements:* For master's, CBEST, CSET. Additional exam requirements/recommendations for international students: Required—TOEFL (minimum score 100 iBT). *Application deadline:* For fall admission, 7/1 for domestic students, 6/1 for international students; for spring admission, 12/1 for domestic students; for summer admission, 5/1 for domestic students. Applications are processed on a rolling basis. Application fee: $55. Electronic applications accepted. *Financial support:* Scholarships/grants available. Support available to part-time students. Financial award applicants required to submit FAFSA. *Faculty research:* Early childhood education, elementary education, special education, curriculum development, teacher preparation. *Unit head:* Dr. June Hetzel, Dean, 562-903-4715. *Application contact:* Graduate Admissions Office, 562-903-4752, E-mail: graduate.admissions@biola.edu.
Website: http://education.biola.edu/.

Bloomsburg University of Pennsylvania, School of Graduate Studies, College of Education, Department of Early Childhood and Adolescent Education, Program in Early Childhood Education, Bloomsburg, PA 17815-1301. Offers M Ed. *Accreditation:* NCATE. *Faculty:* 13 full-time (5 women), 3 part-time/adjunct (2 women). *Students:* 3 full-time (all women), 5 part-time (all women). Average age 30. 9 applicants, 78% accepted, 2 enrolled. In 2013, 19 master's awarded. *Degree requirements:* For master's, thesis. *Entrance requirements:* For master's, MAT, GRE, minimum QPA of 3.0, U.S. citizenship. Additional exam requirements/recommendations for international students: Required—TOEFL. *Application deadline:* Applications are processed on a rolling basis. Application fee: $35 ($60 for international students). Electronic applications accepted. *Expenses:* Tuition, state resident: full-time $7956; part-time $442 per credit. Tuition, nonresident: full-time $11,934; part-time $663 per credit. *Required fees:* $95.50 per credit. $55 per semester. Tuition and fees vary according to course load. *Financial support:* Unspecified assistantships available. *Unit head:* Dr. Tegan Kotarski, College of Education Graduate Coordinator, 570-389-3883, Fax: 570-389-5049, E-mail: tkotarsk@bloomu.edu. *Application contact:* Jennifer Richard, Administrative Assistant, 570-389-4015, Fax: 570-389-3054, E-mail: jrichard@bloomu.edu.
Website: http://www.bloomu.edu/gradschool/early-childhood-education.

Boise State University, College of Education, Department of Early Childhood Education, Boise, ID 83725-0399. Offers M Ed, MA. *Accreditation:* NCATE. Part-time programs available. *Degree requirements:* For master's, thesis optional. *Entrance requirements:* For master's, minimum GPA of 3.0. Electronic applications accepted.

Bowling Green State University, Graduate College, College of Education and Human Development, School of Education and Intervention Services, Intervention Services Division, Program in Special Education, Bowling Green, OH 43403. Offers assistive technology (M Ed); early childhood intervention (M Ed); gifted education (M Ed); hearing impaired intervention (M Ed); mild/moderate intervention (M Ed); moderate/intensive intervention (M Ed). *Accreditation:* NCATE. Part-time programs available. *Degree requirements:* For master's, thesis or alternative. *Entrance requirements:* For master's, GRE General Test. Additional exam requirements/recommendations for international students: Required—TOEFL. Electronic applications accepted. *Faculty research:* Reading and special populations, deafness, early childhood, gifted and talented, behavior disorders.

Brenau University, Sydney O. Smith Graduate School, School of Education, Gainesville, GA 30501. Offers early childhood (Ed S); early childhood education (M Ed, MAT); middle grades (Ed S); middle grades education (M Ed, MAT); secondary education (MAT); special education (M Ed, MAT). *Accreditation:* NCATE. Part-time and evening/weekend programs available. Postbaccalaureate distance learning degree programs offered (no on-campus study). *Degree requirements:* For master's, thesis optional, comprehensive exam or applied research project, effective portfolio; for Ed S, thesis, applied research project. *Entrance requirements:* For master's, GRE, MAT, interview, minimum GPA of 3.0, 3 references, writing samples; for Ed S, GRE, MAT, master's degree, minimum GPA of 3.0, writing sample, letters of reference. Additional exam requirements/recommendations for international students: Required—TOEFL (minimum score 500 paper-based; 61 iBT); Recommended—IELTS (minimum score 5). Electronic applications accepted. *Expenses:* Contact institution.

Bridgewater State University, School of Graduate Studies, School of Education and Allied Studies, Department of Elementary and Early Childhood Education, Program in Early Childhood Education, Bridgewater, MA 02325-0001. Offers M Ed. *Accreditation:* NCATE. Part-time and evening/weekend programs available. *Entrance requirements:* For master's, GRE General Test or Massachusetts Test for Educator Licensure.

Brooklyn College of the City University of New York, Division of Graduate Studies, School of Education, Program in Early Childhood Education, Brooklyn, NY 11210-2889. Offers birth-grade 2 (MS Ed). Part-time and evening/weekend programs available. *Entrance requirements:* For master's, LAST, bachelor's degree in early childhood education, resume, 2 letters of recommendation, essay. Additional exam requirements/recommendations for international students: Required—TOEFL (minimum score 500 paper-based; 61 iBT). Electronic applications accepted. *Faculty research:* Children's narrations, language acquisition, culture and education.

Buffalo State College, State University of New York, The Graduate School, Faculty of Applied Science and Education, Department of Elementary Education and Reading, Program in Elementary Education, Buffalo, NY 14222-1095. Offers childhood education (grades 1-6) (MS Ed); early childhood and childhood curriculum and instruction (MS Ed); early childhood education (birth-grade 2) (MS Ed). *Accreditation:* NCATE. Part-time programs available. *Degree requirements:* For master's, thesis or project. *Entrance requirements:* For master's, minimum GPA of 2.5 in last 60 hours, New York teaching certificate. Additional exam requirements/recommendations for international students: Required—TOEFL (minimum score 550 paper-based).

California State University, East Bay, Office of Academic Programs and Graduate Studies, College of Education and Allied Studies, Department of Teacher Education, Hayward, CA 94542-3000. Offers education (MS), including curriculum, early childhood education, educational technology leadership, reading instruction. Postbaccalaureate distance learning degree programs offered. *Degree requirements:* For master's, project or thesis. *Entrance requirements:* For master's, minimum GPA of 3.0 in field, 2.5 overall; teaching experience; baccalaureate degree; 3 letters of recommendation. Additional exam requirements/recommendations for international students: Required—TOEFL (minimum score 550 paper-based), IELTS. Electronic applications accepted. *Faculty research:* Online, pedagogy, writing, learning, teaching.

California State University, Fresno, Division of Graduate Studies, School of Education and Human Development, Department of Literacy and Early Education, Fresno, CA 93740-8027. Offers education (MA), including early childhood education, reading/language arts. *Accreditation:* NCATE. Part-time and evening/weekend programs available. *Degree requirements:* For master's, thesis or alternative. *Entrance requirements:* For master's, GRE General Test, MAT, minimum GPA of 2.75. Additional exam requirements/recommendations for international students: Required—TOEFL. Electronic applications accepted. *Faculty research:* Reading recovery, monitoring/tutoring programs, character and academics, professional ethics, low-performing partnership schools.

California State University, Northridge, Graduate Studies, College of Education, Department of Educational Psychology and Counseling, Northridge, CA 91330. Offers counseling (MS), including career counseling, college counseling and student services, marriage and family therapy, school counseling, school psychology; educational psychology (MA Ed), including development, learning, and instruction, early childhood education. *Accreditation:* ACA (one or more programs are accredited); NCATE. Part-time and evening/weekend programs available. *Entrance requirements:* For master's, GRE General Test or minimum GPA of 3.0. Additional exam requirements/recommendations for international students: Required—TOEFL.

Cambridge College, School of Education, Cambridge, MA 02138-5304. Offers autism specialist (M Ed); autism/behavior analyst (M Ed); behavior analyst (Post-Master's Certificate); behavioral management (M Ed); early childhood teacher (M Ed); education specialist in curriculum and instruction (CAGS); educational leadership (Ed D); elementary teacher (M Ed); English as a second language (M Ed, Certificate); general science (M Ed); health education (Post-Master's Certificate); health/family and consumer sciences (M Ed); history (M Ed); individualized (M Ed); information technology literacy (M Ed); instructional technology (M Ed); interdisciplinary studies (M Ed); library teacher (M Ed); literacy education (M Ed); mathematics (M Ed); mathematics specialist (Certificate); middle school mathematics and science (M Ed); school administration (M Ed, CAGS); school guidance counselor (M Ed); school nurse education (M Ed); school social worker/school adjustment counselor (M Ed); special education administrator (CAGS); special education/moderate disabilities (M Ed); teaching skills and methodologies (M Ed). Part-time and evening/weekend programs available. Postbaccalaureate distance learning degree programs offered (minimal on-campus study). *Degree requirements:* For master's, thesis, internship/practicum (licensure program only); for doctorate, thesis/dissertation; for other advanced degree, thesis. *Entrance requirements:* For master's, interview, resume, documentation of licensure, 2 professional references; for doctorate, official transcripts, interview, resume, documentation of licensure (if any), written personal statement/essay, portfolio of scholarly and professional work, qualifying assessment, 2 professional references, health insurance, immunizations form; for other advanced degree, official transcripts, interview, resume, documentation of licensure (if any), written personal statement/essay, 2 professional references, health insurance, immunizations form. Additional exam requirements/recommendations for international students: Required—TOEFL (minimum score 550 paper-based; 79 iBT), Michigan English Language Assessment Battery (minimum score 85); Recommended—IELTS (minimum score 6). Electronic applications accepted. *Expenses:* Contact institution. *Faculty research:* Adult education, accelerated learning, mathematics education, brain compatible learning, special education and law.

Canisius College, Graduate Division, School of Education and Human Services, Department of Teacher Education, Buffalo, NY 14208-1098. Offers adolescence education (MS Ed); childhood education (MS Ed); general education (MS Ed); special education (MS), including adolescence special education, advanced special education, childhood education grade 1-6, childhood special education. Part-time and evening/weekend programs available. Postbaccalaureate distance learning degree programs offered (minimal on-campus study). *Faculty:* 23 full-time (18 women), 10 part-time/adjunct (4 women). *Students:* 87 full-time (58 women), 32 part-time (27 women);

includes 8 minority (4 Black or African American, non-Hispanic/Latino; 3 Asian, non-Hispanic/Latino; 1 Two or more races, non-Hispanic/Latino), 14 international. Average age 29. 73 applicants, 68% accepted, 23 enrolled. In 2013, 135 master's awarded. *Degree requirements:* For master's, research project or thesis, project internship. *Entrance requirements:* For master's, GRE if cumulative GPA is less than 2.7, transcripts, letters of recommendation. Additional exam requirements/recommendations for international students: Required—TOEFL (minimum score 550 paper-based, 80 iBT), IELTS (minimum score 6.5), or CAEL (minimum score 70). *Application deadline:* Applications are processed on a rolling basis. Application fee: $25. Electronic applications accepted. Application fee is waived when completed online. *Expenses: Tuition:* Part-time $750 per credit hour. *Financial support:* Career-related internships or fieldwork, Federal Work-Study, scholarships/grants, tuition waivers (partial), and unspecified assistantships available. Support available to part-time students. Financial award application deadline: 4/30; financial award applicants required to submit FAFSA. *Unit head:* Dr. Julie Henry, Chair/Professor, 716-888-3729, E-mail: henry1@canisius.edu. *Application contact:* Julie A. Zulewski, Director of Graduate Admissions, 716-555-2548, Fax: 716-888-3195, E-mail: zulewskj@canisius.edu.
Website: http://www.canisius.edu/academics/graduate/.

Capella University, School of Education, Master's Programs in Education, Minneapolis, MN 55402. Offers adult education (MS); curriculum and instruction (MS); early childhood education (MS); enrollment management (MS); higher education leadership and management (MS); instructional design for online learning (MS); integrative studies (MS); K-12 studies in education (MS); leadership in educational administration (MS); reading and literacy (MS); special education teaching (MS).

Caribbean University, Graduate School, Bayamón, PR 00960-0493. Offers administration and supervision (MA Ed); criminal justice (MA); curriculum and instruction (MA Ed, PhD), including elementary education (MA Ed), English education (MA Ed), history education (MA Ed), mathematics education (MA Ed), primary education (MA Ed), science education (MA Ed), Spanish education (MA Ed); educational technology in instructional systems (MA Ed); gerontology (MSN); human resources (MBA); museology, archiving and art history (MA Ed); neonatal pediatrics (MSN); physical education (MA Ed); special education (MA Ed). *Entrance requirements:* For master's, interview, minimum GPA of 2.5.

Carlow University, School of Education, Program in Early Childhood Education, Pittsburgh, PA 15213-3165. Offers M Ed. Part-time and evening/weekend programs available. Postbaccalaureate distance learning degree programs offered (no on-campus study). *Students:* 14 full-time (12 women), 19 part-time (18 women); includes 4 minority (all Black or African American, non-Hispanic/Latino). Average age 34. 6 applicants, 100% accepted, 5 enrolled. In 2013, 8 master's awarded. *Degree requirements:* For master's, thesis or alternative. *Entrance requirements:* Additional exam requirements/recommendations for international students: Required—TOEFL. *Application deadline:* For fall admission, 6/15 priority date for domestic and international students; for spring admission, 11/15 priority date for domestic and international students. Applications are processed on a rolling basis. Application fee: $20. Electronic applications accepted. Application fee is waived when completed online. *Expenses: Tuition:* Full-time $9523; part-time $744 per credit. Tuition and fees vary according to course load, degree level and program. *Financial support:* Application deadline: 4/1; applicants required to submit FAFSA. *Faculty research:* Understanding children's play, infant and toddler development, effects of violence on children, supervision and staff development. *Unit head:* Dr. Marilyn Llewellyn, Dean, 412-578-6011, Fax: 412-578-0816, E-mail: llewellynmj@carlow.edu. *Application contact:* Jo Danhires, Administrative Assistant, Admissions, 412-578-6092, Fax: 412-578-6321, E-mail: gradstudies@carlow.edu.
Website: http://www.carlow.edu/.

Carlow University, School of Education, Program in Early Childhood Supervision, Pittsburgh, PA 15213-3165. Offers M Ed. Part-time and evening/weekend programs available. *Students:* 1 (woman) full-time, 3 part-time (2 women); includes 2 minority (both Black or African American, non-Hispanic/Latino). Average age 46. 2 applicants, 100% accepted, 1 enrolled. In 2013, 2 master's awarded. *Degree requirements:* For master's, thesis or alternative. *Entrance requirements:* Additional exam requirements/recommendations for international students: Required—TOEFL. *Application deadline:* For fall admission, 6/15 priority date for domestic and international students; for spring admission, 11/15 priority date for domestic and international students. Applications are processed on a rolling basis. Application fee: $20. Electronic applications accepted. Application fee is waived when completed online. *Expenses: Tuition:* Full-time $9523; part-time $744 per credit. Tuition and fees vary according to course load, degree level and program. *Financial support:* Federal Work-Study and scholarships/grants available. Support available to part-time students. Financial award application deadline: 4/1; financial award applicants required to submit FAFSA. *Faculty research:* Leadership styles, learning styles, feminist pedagogy. *Unit head:* Dr. Marilyn Llewellyn, Dean, 412-578-6011, Fax: 412-578-0816, E-mail: llewellynmj@carlow.edu. *Application contact:* Jo Danhires, Administrative Assistant, Admissions, 412-578-6059, Fax: 412-578-6321, E-mail: gradstudies@carlow.edu.

Carlow University, School of Education, Program in Education, Pittsburgh, PA 15213-3165. Offers art education (M Ed); early childhood education (M Ed); secondary education (M Ed); special education (M Ed). Part-time and evening/weekend programs available. *Students:* 42 full-time (37 women), 36 part-time (34 women); includes 9 minority (6 Black or African American, non-Hispanic/Latino; 1 Asian, non-Hispanic/Latino; 2 Two or more races, non-Hispanic/Latino). Average age 31. 27 applicants, 100% accepted, 19 enrolled. In 2013, 17 master's awarded. *Entrance requirements:* For master's, resume, 3 letters of recommendation, minimum GPA of 3.0, interview. Additional exam requirements/recommendations for international students: Required—TOEFL. *Application deadline:* For fall admission, 6/15 priority date for domestic and international students; for spring admission, 11/15 priority date for domestic and international students. Applications are processed on a rolling basis. Application fee: $20. Electronic applications accepted. Application fee is waived when completed online. *Expenses: Tuition:* Full-time $9523; part-time $744 per credit. Tuition and fees vary according to course load, degree level and program. *Financial support:* Applicants required to submit FAFSA. *Unit head:* Dr. Marilyn Llewellyn, Dean, 412-578-6011, Fax: 412-578-0816, E-mail: llewellynmj@carlow.edu. *Application contact:* Jo Danhires, Administrative Assistant, Admissions, 412-578-6089, Fax: 412-578-6321, E-mail: gradstudies@carlow.edu.
Website: http://www.carlow.edu.

Central Connecticut State University, School of Graduate Studies, School of Education and Professional Studies, Department of Teacher Education, Program in Early Childhood Education, New Britain, CT 06050-4010. Offers MS. Part-time and evening/weekend programs available. *Students:* 1 (woman) full-time, 16 part-time (all women); includes 2 minority (1 Black or African American, non-Hispanic/Latino; 1 Two or more races, non-Hispanic/Latino). Average age 36. 6 applicants, 67% accepted, 3 enrolled. In 2013, 3 master's awarded. *Degree requirements:* For master's, comprehensive exam, thesis or alternative. *Entrance requirements:* For master's, minimum undergraduate GPA of 2.7. Additional exam requirements/recommendations for international students: Required—TOEFL (minimum score 550 paper-based; 79 iBT). *Application deadline:* For fall admission, 6/1 for domestic students, 5/1 for international students; for spring admission, 11/1 for domestic and international students. Applications are processed on a rolling basis. Application fee: $50. Electronic applications accepted. Part-time tuition and fees vary according to degree level. *Faculty research:* Pre-kindergarten and early learning research, early learning environments. *Unit head:* Dr. Aram Ayalon, Chair, 860-832-2415, E-mail: ayalona@ccsu.edu. *Application contact:* Patricia Gardner, Associate Director of Graduate Studies, 860-832-2350, Fax: 860-832-2362, E-mail: graduateadmissions@ccsu.edu.

Central Michigan University, College of Graduate Studies, College of Education and Human Services, Department of Teacher Education and Professional Development, Mount Pleasant, MI 48859. Offers educational technology (MA, Graduate Certificate); elementary education (MA), including classroom teaching, early childhood; reading and literacy K-12 (MA); secondary education (MA). Part-time and evening/weekend programs available. *Degree requirements:* For master's, thesis or alternative. Electronic applications accepted. *Faculty research:* Integrating literacy across the curriculum, science teaching and aesthetic learning in science, diversity education, educational technology, educational psychology and child development.

Chaminade University of Honolulu, Graduate Services, Program in Education, Honolulu, HI 96816-1578. Offers child development (M Ed); early childhood education (M Ed); educational leadership (M Ed); elementary education (MAT); instructional leadership (M Ed); Montessori education (M Ed); secondary education (MAT), including English, math, science, social studies; special education (MAT). Part-time and evening/weekend programs available. Postbaccalaureate distance learning degree programs offered (minimal on-campus study). *Degree requirements:* For master's, thesis or alternative. *Entrance requirements:* For master's, PRAXIS (for MAT only), minimum GPA of 2.75, 3 letters of recommendation. Additional exam requirements/recommendations for international students: Required—TOEFL (minimum score 550 paper-based). Electronic applications accepted. *Faculty research:* Peace and curriculum education.

Champlain College, Graduate Studies, Burlington, VT 05402-0670. Offers business (MBA); digital forensic management (MS); digital forensic science (MS); early childhood education (M Ed); emergent media (MFA, MS); health care administration (MS); law (MS); managing innovation and information technology (MS); mediation and applied conflict studies (MS). MS in emergent media program held in Shanghai. Part-time programs available. Postbaccalaureate distance learning degree programs offered (no on-campus study). *Faculty:* 13 full-time (2 women), 34 part-time/adjunct (14 women). *Students:* 303 full-time (191 women), 104 part-time (58 women); includes 38 minority (21 Black or African American, non-Hispanic/Latino; 8 Asian, non-Hispanic/Latino; 7 Hispanic/Latino; 2 Two or more races, non-Hispanic/Latino), 4 international. Average age 37. In 2013, 169 master's awarded. *Degree requirements:* For master's, capstone project. *Entrance requirements:* Additional exam requirements/recommendations for international students: Required—TOEFL (minimum score 550 paper-based; 80 iBT). *Application deadline:* For fall admission, 8/1 priority date for domestic and international students; for spring admission, 1/1 priority date for domestic and international students. Applications are processed on a rolling basis. Electronic applications accepted. *Expenses: Tuition:* Full-time $18,456; part-time $769 per credit. Tuition and fees vary according to program. *Financial support:* Applicants required to submit FAFSA. *Unit head:* Dr. Donald Haggerty, Associate Provost of Graduate Studies, 802-865-6496, Fax: 802-865-6447, E-mail: haggerty@champlain.edu. *Application contact:* Matt Manz, Assistant Director, Graduate Admission, 800-383-6603, E-mail: mmanz@champlain.edu.
Website: http://www.champlain.edu/academics/graduate-studies.

Chatham University, Program in Education, Pittsburgh, PA 15232-2826. Offers early childhood education (MAT); elementary education (MAT); environmental education (K-12) (MAT); secondary art (MAT); secondary biology education (MAT); secondary chemistry education (MAT); secondary English education (MAT); secondary math education (MAT); secondary physics education (MAT); secondary social studies education (MAT); special education (MAT). *Faculty:* 1 (woman) full-time, 5 part-time/adjunct (4 women). *Students:* 19 full-time (15 women), 4 part-time (all women); includes 2 minority (1 Black or African American, non-Hispanic/Latino; 1 Asian, non-Hispanic/Latino), 2 international. Average age 28. 22 applicants, 73% accepted, 6 enrolled. In 2013, 20 master's awarded. *Degree requirements:* For master's, thesis, teaching experience. *Entrance requirements:* For master's, minimum GPA of 3.0, sample of written work, recommendation letters. Additional exam requirements/recommendations for international students: Required—TOEFL (minimum score 600 paper-based; 100 iBT), IELTS (minimum score 7), TWE. *Application deadline:* For fall admission, 4/1 priority date for domestic and international students; for spring admission, 11/1 priority date for domestic students, 10/1 priority date for international students. Applications are processed on a rolling basis. Application fee: $45. Electronic applications accepted. Application fee is waived when completed online. *Expenses: Tuition:* Full-time $14,886; part-time $827 per credit hour. One-time fee: $396 full-time. *Financial support:* Career-related internships or fieldwork available. Financial award applicants required to submit FAFSA. *Faculty research:* Gifted education, environmental education, technology in education, writing as learning, class size and achievement. *Unit head:* Dr. Edward Donovan, Director of Education Programs, 412-365-2773, E-mail: edonovan@chatham.edu. *Application contact:* Katie Noel, Assistant Director of Graduate Admission, 412-365-2758, Fax: 412-365-1609, E-mail: gradadmissions@chatham.edu.
Website: http://www.chatham.edu/mat.

Chestnut Hill College, School of Graduate Studies, Department of Education, Program in Early Education, Philadelphia, PA 19118-2693. Offers early education (M Ed, CAS); Montessori education (CAS). Part-time and evening/weekend programs available. *Faculty:* 10 full-time (7 women), 48 part-time/adjunct (34 women). *Students:* 5 full-time (all women), 66 part-time (60 women); includes 27 minority (19 Black or African American, non-Hispanic/Latino; 2 Asian, non-Hispanic/Latino; 5 Hispanic/Latino; 1 Two or more races, non-Hispanic/Latino). Average age 33. 29 applicants, 97% accepted. In 2013, 15 master's, 14 CASs awarded. *Degree requirements:* For master's, thesis optional. *Entrance requirements:* For master's, PRAXIS I or proof of teaching certification, writing sample, letters of recommendation, 6 graduate credits with minimum B grade if undergraduate GPA is below 3.0. Additional exam requirements/recommendations for international students: Required—TOEFL (minimum score 500 paper-based), IELTS (mnimum score 6.0), or TWE (minimum score 22). *Application deadline:* For fall admission, 7/1 for domestic and international students; for spring admission, 11/1 for domestic and international students; for summer admission, 4/1 for domestic and international students. Applications are processed on a rolling basis. *Expenses:* Contact institution. *Financial support:* Unspecified assistantships available. *Faculty research:* Gender issues, early childhood education standardized testing. *Unit head:* Dr. Debra Chiaradonna, Chair, Education Department, 215-248-7127, Fax: 215-148-7155, E-mail: chiaradonnad@chc.edu. *Application contact:* Jayne Mashett, Director of Admissions, School of Graduate Studies, 215-248-7020, Fax: 215-248-7161, E-mail: gradadmissions@chc.edu.
Website: http://www.chc.edu/Graduate/Programs/Masters/Education/.

Chicago State University, School of Graduate and Professional Studies, College of Education, Department of Special Education, Early Childhood Education and Bilingual Education, Program in Early Childhood Education, Chicago, IL 60628. Offers MAT,

Early Childhood Education

MS Ed. *Accreditation:* NCATE. *Degree requirements:* For master's, thesis optional. *Entrance requirements:* For master's, minimum GPA of 2.75.

City College of the City University of New York, Graduate School, School of Education, Department of Childhood Education, New York, NY 10031-9198. Offers MS. *Accreditation:* NCATE. *Degree requirements:* For master's, thesis. *Entrance requirements:* For master's, Liberal Arts and Sciences Test (LAST), Content Specialty Test (CST). Additional exam requirements/recommendations for international students: Required—TOEFL.

Clarion University of Pennsylvania, Office of Transfer, Adult and Graduate Admissions, Master of Education Program, Clarion, PA 16214. Offers curriculum and instruction (M Ed); early childhood (M Ed); math education (M Ed); reading (M Ed); science education (M Ed); special education (M Ed); technology (M Ed). *Accreditation:* NCATE. Part-time programs available. Postbaccalaureate distance learning degree programs offered (no on-campus study). *Faculty:* 17 full-time (10 women). *Students:* 231 full-time (191 women), 535 part-time (448 women); includes 39 minority (12 Black or African American, non-Hispanic/Latino; 8 Asian, non-Hispanic/Latino; 11 Hispanic/Latino; 1 Native Hawaiian or other Pacific Islander, non-Hispanic/Latino; 7 Two or more races, non-Hispanic/Latino). Average age 31. 28 applicants, 75% accepted, 18 enrolled. In 2013, 99 master's awarded. *Degree requirements:* For master's, comprehensive exam, thesis, or portfolio. *Entrance requirements:* For master's, minimum QPA of 3.0. Additional exam requirements/recommendations for international students: Required—TOEFL (minimum score 550 paper-based; 80 iBT), IELTS (minimum score 7). *Application deadline:* For fall admission, 8/1 for domestic students, 4/15 for international students; for spring admission, 8/1 for domestic students, 9/15 for international students. Applications are processed on a rolling basis. Application fee: $40. Electronic applications accepted. *Expenses:* Tuition, state resident: part-time $442 per credit. Tuition, nonresident: part-time $451 per credit. *Required fees:* $142.40 per semester. One-time fee: $150 part-time. *Financial support:* In 2013–14, 8 research assistantships with full and partial tuition reimbursements (averaging $9,420 per year) were awarded; career-related internships or fieldwork also available. Support available to part-time students. Financial award application deadline: 3/1. *Unit head:* Ray Puller, Interim Dean, 814-393-2146, Fax: 514-393-2446, E-mail: rpuller@clarion.edu. *Application contact:* Susan Staub, Assistant Director, Graduate Programs, 814-393-2337, Fax: 814-393-2722, E-mail: gradstudies@clarion.edu.
Website: http://www.clarion.edu/25887/.

Clarke University, Program in Education, Dubuque, IA 52001-3198. Offers early childhood/special education (MAE); educational administration: elementary and secondary (MAE); educational media: elementary and secondary (MAE); multi-categorical resource k-12 (MAE); multidisciplinary studies (MAE); reading: elementary (MAE); technology in education (MAE). Part-time and evening/weekend programs available. Postbaccalaureate distance learning degree programs offered (minimal on-campus study). *Faculty:* 10 full-time (9 women), 1 (woman) part-time/adjunct. *Students:* 5 full-time (3 women), 27 part-time (24 women); includes 2 minority (1 Black or African American, non-Hispanic/Latino; 1 American Indian or Alaska Native, non-Hispanic/Latino). In 2013, 11 master's awarded. *Degree requirements:* For master's, comprehensive exam, thesis optional. *Entrance requirements:* For master's, GRE General Test or MAT, minimum GPA of 2.75. *Application deadline:* Applications are processed on a rolling basis. Application fee: $25. Electronic applications accepted. *Expenses: Tuition:* Part-time $660 per credit. *Required fees:* $15 per credit. *Financial support:* Career-related internships or fieldwork available. Financial award applicants required to submit FAFSA. *Unit head:* Dr. Michele Slover, Chair, 319-588-6397, Fax: 319-584-8604. *Application contact:* Kara Shroeder, Information Contact, 563-588-6354, Fax: 563-588-6789, E-mail: graduate@clarke.edu.

Cleveland State University, College of Graduate Studies, College of Education and Human Services, Department of Teacher Education, Cleveland, OH 44115. Offers art education (M Ed); early childhood education (M Ed); foreign language education (M Ed); mathematics and science education (M Ed); middle childhood education (M Ed); special education (M Ed), including mild/moderate disabilities, moderate/intensive disabilities; teaching English to speakers of other languages (M Ed). Part-time and evening/weekend programs available. *Faculty:* 20 full-time (12 women), 26 part-time/adjunct (20 women). *Students:* 108 full-time (78 women), 311 part-time (252 women); includes 103 minority (80 Black or African American, non-Hispanic/Latino; 2 Asian, non-Hispanic/Latino; 10 Hispanic/Latino; 1 Native Hawaiian or other Pacific Islander, non-Hispanic/Latino; 10 Two or more races, non-Hispanic/Latino), 52 international. Average age 32. 177 applicants, 55% accepted, 68 enrolled. In 2013, 192 master's awarded. *Degree requirements:* For master's, comprehensive exam (for some programs), thesis or alternative. *Entrance requirements:* For master's, GRE General Test or MAT, minimum GPA of 2.75. Additional exam requirements/recommendations for international students: Required—TOEFL (minimum score 525 paper-based), IELTS (minimum score 6). *Application deadline:* For fall admission, 7/15 priority date for domestic students. Applications are processed on a rolling basis. Application fee: $30. *Expenses:* Tuition, state resident: full-time $8335; part-time $521 per credit hour. Tuition, nonresident: full-time $15,670; part-time $979 per credit hour. *Required fees:* $50; $25 per semester. *Financial support:* In 2013–14, 12 research assistantships with full tuition reimbursements (averaging $3,480 per year) were awarded; tuition waivers (partial) and unspecified assistantships also available. *Faculty research:* Early literacy, professional development in reading, reading recovery, dual language, induction programs. *Total annual research expenditures:* $6.2 million. *Unit head:* Dr. Clifford T. Bennett, Chairperson, 216-523-7105, Fax: 216-687-5379, E-mail: c.t.bennett@csuohio.edu. *Application contact:* Deborah L. Brown, Interim Assistant Director, Graduate Admissions, 216-523-7572, E-mail: d.l.brown@csuohio.edu.
Website: http://www.csuohio.edu/cehs/departments/TE/te_dept.html.

The College at Brockport, State University of New York, School of Education and Human Services, Department of Education and Human Development, Program in Childhood Curriculum Specialist, Brockport, NY 14420-2997. Offers MS Ed. *Accreditation:* NCATE. Part-time programs available. *Students:* 1 (woman) full-time, 18 part-time (13 women); includes 3 minority (1 Asian, non-Hispanic/Latino; 1 Hispanic/Latino; 1 Two or more races, non-Hispanic/Latino). 1 applicant, 100% accepted. In 2013, 11 master's awarded. *Degree requirements:* For master's, thesis or alternative. *Entrance requirements:* For master's, minimum GPA of 3.0, letters of recommendation; statement of objectives; current resume. Additional exam requirements/recommendations for international students: Required—TOEFL (minimum score 550 paper-based; 79 iBT), IELTS (minimum score 6.5). *Application deadline:* For fall admission, 3/15 priority date for domestic and international students; for spring admission, 10/15 priority date for domestic and international students. Application fee: $80. Electronic applications accepted. *Expenses:* Tuition, state resident: full-time $9870. Tuition, nonresident: full-time $18,350. *Required fees:* $1848. *Financial support:* Federal Work-Study, scholarships/grants, and unspecified assistantships available. Support available to part-time students. Financial award application deadline: 3/15; financial award applicants required to submit FAFSA. *Unit head:* Dr. Don Halquist, Chairperson, 585-395-5550, Fax: 585-395-2172, E-mail: snovinge@brockport.edu. *Application contact:* Michael Harrison, Coordinator of Certification and Graduate Advisement, 585-395-2326, Fax: 585-395-2172, E-mail: mharriso@brockport.edu.
Website: http://www.brockport.edu/ehd.

College of Charleston, Graduate School, School of Education, Health, and Human Performance, Department of Elementary and Early Childhood Education, Program in Early Childhood Education, Charleston, SC 29424-0001. Offers MAT. *Accreditation:* NCATE. Part-time and evening/weekend programs available. *Degree requirements:* For master's, thesis or alternative, written qualifying exam, student teaching experience (MAT). *Entrance requirements:* For master's, GRE, minimum GPA of 2.5, 2 letters of recommendation. Additional exam requirements/recommendations for international students: Required—TOEFL (minimum score 81 iBT). Electronic applications accepted. *Faculty research:* Teacher education and creative arts, integrated curriculum, multicultural awareness, teaching models, cooperative learning.

The College of New Jersey, Graduate Studies, School of Education, Department of Elementary and Early Childhood Education, Program in School Personnel Licensure: Preschool-Grade 3, Ewing, NJ 08628. Offers M Ed, MAT. Part-time programs available. *Entrance requirements:* For master's, GRE, minimum GPA of 3.0 in field or 2.75 overall. Additional exam requirements/recommendations for international students: Required—TOEFL. Electronic applications accepted.

The College of New Rochelle, Graduate School, Division of Education, Program in Elementary Education/Early Childhood Education, New Rochelle, NY 10805-2308. Offers MS Ed. Part-time programs available. *Degree requirements:* For master's, comprehensive exam (for some programs), thesis (for some programs), practicum. *Entrance requirements:* For master's, interview, minimum GPA of 3.0 in field, 2.7 overall. *Expenses: Tuition:* Part-time $894 per credit. *Required fees:* $300 per semester. One-time fee: $200. Tuition and fees vary according to course load.

The College of Saint Rose, Graduate Studies, School of Education, Department of Special Education and Inclusive Education, Albany, NY 12203-1419. Offers birth-grade 2 special education (MS Ed); grades 1-6 special education (MS Ed); grades 1-6 special education and childhood education (MS Ed); grades 7-12 adolescence education and special education (MS Ed); grades 7-12 special education (MS Ed); professional special education (MS Ed). *Accreditation:* NCATE. Part-time and evening/weekend programs available. *Degree requirements:* For master's, comprehensive exam (for some programs), thesis or alternative, research project. *Entrance requirements:* For master's, minimum undergraduate GPA of 3.0. Additional exam requirements/recommendations for international students: Required—TOEFL (minimum score 550 paper-based). Electronic applications accepted.

The College of Saint Rose, Graduate Studies, School of Education, Department of Teacher Education, Albany, NY 12203-1419. Offers adolescence education (MS Ed); childhood education (MS Ed); curriculum and instruction (MS Ed); early childhood education (MS Ed). Part-time and evening/weekend programs available. *Entrance requirements:* For master's, minimum undergraduate GPA of 3.0. Additional exam requirements/recommendations for international students: Required—TOEFL (minimum score 550 paper-based). Electronic applications accepted.

Colorado Christian University, Program in Curriculum and Instruction, Lakewood, CO 80226. Offers corporate education (MACI); early childhood educator (MACI); elementary educator (MACI); instructional technology (MACI); master educator (MACI); online course developer (MACI); online teaching and learning (MACI); special education generalist (MACI). Part-time and evening/weekend programs available. *Degree requirements:* For master's, thesis optional, practicum. *Entrance requirements:* For master's, interviews, letters of recommendation. Additional exam requirements/recommendations for international students: Required—TOEFL. Electronic applications accepted. *Expenses:* Contact institution.

Columbia International University, Columbia Graduate School, Columbia, SC 29230-3122. Offers Bible teaching (MABT); Christian higher education leadership (Ed D); Christian school educational leadership (Ed D); counseling (MACN); curriculum and instruction (M Ed), including Christian school guidance, English as a second language, learning disabilities, school technology; early childhood and elementary education (MAT); educational administration (M Ed); teaching English as a foreign language (Certificate); teaching English as a foreign language and intercultural studies (MATF). Part-time and evening/weekend programs available. *Degree requirements:* For master's, internships, professional project. *Entrance requirements:* For master's, Minnesota Multiphasic Personality Inventory, MAT, minimum GPA of 2.7. Additional exam requirements/recommendations for international students: Required—TOEFL. Electronic applications accepted.

Columbus State University, Graduate Studies, College of Education and Health Professions, Department of Teacher Education, Columbus, GA 31907-5645. Offers accomplished teaching (M Ed); early childhood education (M Ed, MAT, Ed S); middle grades education (M Ed, MAT, Ed S); school library media (M Ed, MAT); secondary education (M Ed, MAT, Ed S), including English/language arts (M Ed, Ed S), general science (M Ed), mathematics (M Ed, Ed S), science (Ed S), social science (M Ed, Ed S); special education (M Ed, MAT, Ed S), including general curriculum (M Ed, MAT); teacher leadership (M Ed). *Accreditation:* NCATE. Part-time and evening/weekend programs available. Postbaccalaureate distance learning degree programs offered (minimal on-campus study). *Faculty:* 17 full-time (12 women), 31 part-time/adjunct (28 women). *Students:* 59 full-time (48 women), 190 part-time (150 women); includes 85 minority (68 Black or African American, non-Hispanic/Latino; 1 American Indian or Alaska Native, non-Hispanic/Latino; 6 Asian, non-Hispanic/Latino; 4 Hispanic/Latino; 6 Two or more races, non-Hispanic/Latino), 2 international. Average age 34. 132 applicants, 58% accepted, 50 enrolled. In 2013, 86 master's, 26 other advanced degrees awarded. *Degree requirements:* For master's, thesis, exit exam; for Ed S, thesis or alternative. *Entrance requirements:* For master's, GRE General Test, minimum undergraduate GPA of 2.75; for Ed S, GRE General Test, minimum undergraduate GPA of 2.75, graduate 3.0. Additional exam requirements/recommendations for international students: Required—TOEFL (minimum score 550 paper-based; 79 iBT). *Application deadline:* For fall admission, 6/30 for domestic students, 5/1 for international students; for spring admission, 11/1 for domestic and international students; for summer admission, 3/1 for domestic and international students. Applications are processed on a rolling basis. Application fee: $40. Electronic applications accepted. *Expenses:* Tuition, state resident: full-time $4572; part-time $382 per credit hour. Tuition, nonresident: full-time $18,292; part-time $1526 per credit hour. *Required fees:* $1800; $196 per credit hour. Tuition and fees vary according to campus/location and program. *Financial support:* In 2013–14, 173 students received support, including 12 research assistantships with partial tuition reimbursements available (averaging $3,000 per year); career-related internships or fieldwork, Federal Work-Study, institutionally sponsored loans, scholarships/grants, tuition waivers (partial), and unspecified assistantships also available. Support available to part-time students. Financial award application deadline: 5/1; financial award applicants required to submit FAFSA. *Unit head:* Dr. Deirdre Greer, Department Chair, 706-507-8034, Fax: 706-568-3134, E-mail: greer_deirdre@columbusstate.edu. *Application contact:* Kristin Williams, Director of International and

Graduate Recruitment, 706-507-8848, Fax: 706-568-5091, E-mail: williams_kristin@columbusstate.edu. Website: http://te.columbusstate.edu/.

Concordia University, College of Education, Portland, OR 97211-6099. Offers career and technical education (M Ed); curriculum and instruction (M Ed), including adolescent literacy, career and technical education, e-learning/technology education, early childhood education, English for speakers of other languages, English language development, environmental education, mathematics, methods and curriculum, reading, science, teacher leadership, the inclusive classroom; early childhood (MAT); education leadership (Ed D); educational administration (M Ed); elementary education (MAT); secondary education (MAT); special education (M Ed); teacher leadership (Ed D). Part-time programs available. Postbaccalaureate distance learning degree programs offered (no on-campus study). *Degree requirements:* For master's, comprehensive exam, work samples/portfolio. *Entrance requirements:* For master's, California Basic Educational Skills Test or PRAXIS I, minimum undergraduate GPA of 2.8, graduate 3.0; 2 letters of recommendation. Additional exam requirements/recommendations for international students: Required—TOEFL (minimum score 525 paper-based). Electronic applications accepted. *Faculty research:* Learner-centered classroom, brain-based learning, future of online learning.

Concordia University Chicago, College of Education, Program in Early Childhood Education, River Forest, IL 60305-1499. Offers MA, Ed D. Part-time and evening/weekend programs available. *Degree requirements:* For master's, comprehensive exam, thesis. *Entrance requirements:* For master's, minimum GPA of 2.9; for doctorate, MAT or GRE, minimum graduate GPA of 3.5. Additional exam requirements/recommendations for international students: Required—TOEFL (minimum score 550 paper-based). Electronic applications accepted. *Faculty research:* Child care training project, "Children in Worship" project, ethical development of children.

Concordia University Chicago, College of Education, Program in Teaching, River Forest, IL 60305-1499. Offers early childhood education (MAT); elementary education (MAT); secondary education (MAT). *Degree requirements:* For master's, thesis or alternative. *Entrance requirements:* For master's, minimum GPA of 2.9. Additional exam requirements/recommendations for international students: Required—TOEFL (minimum score 550 paper-based). Electronic applications accepted.

Concordia University, Nebraska, Graduate Programs in Education, Program in Early Childhood Education, Seward, NE 68434-1556. Offers M Ed. *Accreditation:* NCATE. Part-time programs available. *Degree requirements:* For master's, comprehensive exam, thesis or alternative. *Entrance requirements:* For master's, GRE, MAT, or NTE, minimum GPA of 3.0, BS in education or equivalent. Additional exam requirements/recommendations for international students: Required—TOEFL.

Concordia University, St. Paul, College of Education and Science, St. Paul, MN 55104-5494. Offers curriculum and instruction (MA Ed), including K-12 reading; differentiated instruction (MA Ed); early childhood education (MA Ed); educational leadership (MA Ed); educational technology (MA Ed); exercise science (MA); family life education (MA); K-12 principal licensure (Ed S); K-12 reading (Certificate); special education (MA Ed, Certificate), including autism spectrum disorder (MA Ed), emotional and behavioral disorders (MA Ed), learning disabilities (MA Ed); sports management (MA); superintendent (Ed S). *Accreditation:* NCATE. Part-time and evening/weekend programs available. Postbaccalaureate distance learning degree programs offered (minimal on-campus study). *Faculty:* 12 full-time (7 women), 92 part-time/adjunct (49 women). *Students:* 915 full-time (659 women), 64 part-time (53 women); includes 99 minority (47 Black or African American, non-Hispanic/Latino; 5 American Indian or Alaska Native, non-Hispanic/Latino; 18 Asian, non-Hispanic/Latino; 15 Hispanic/Latino; 2 Native Hawaiian or other Pacific Islander, non-Hispanic/Latino; 12 Two or more races, non-Hispanic/Latino), 24 international. Average age 34. 664 applicants, 67% accepted, 411 enrolled. In 2013, 275 master's, 69 other advanced degrees awarded. *Degree requirements:* For master's, thesis (for some programs). *Entrance requirements:* For master's, official transcripts from regionally-accredited institution stating the conferral of a bachelor's degree with minimum cumulative GPA of 3.0; personal statement; professional resume; practitioner in field through work or volunteerism; resume. Additional exam requirements/recommendations for international students: Recommended—TOEFL (minimum score 547 paper-based; 78 iBT), IELTS (minimum score 6). *Application deadline:* For fall admission, 8/1 for domestic and international students; for spring admission, 12/1 for domestic and international students; for summer admission, 5/1 for domestic and international students. Applications are processed on a rolling basis. Application fee: $50. Electronic applications accepted. *Expenses: Tuition:* Full-time $6200; part-time $425 per credit. Tuition and fees vary according to degree level and program. *Financial support:* Applicants required to submit FAFSA. *Unit head:* Dr. Donald Helmstetter, Dean, 651-641-8227, Fax: 651-641-8807, E-mail: helmstetter@csp.edu. *Application contact:* Kimberly Craig, Director of Graduate and Cohort Admission, 651-603-6223, Fax: 651-603-6320, E-mail: craig@csp.edu.

Concordia University Wisconsin, Graduate Programs, Department of Education, Program in Early Childhood, Mequon, WI 53097-2402. Offers MS Ed. *Degree requirements:* For master's, comprehensive exam, thesis or alternative. *Entrance requirements:* For master's, minimum GPA of 3.0, teaching license. Additional exam requirements/recommendations for international students: Required—TOEFL.

Daemen College, Education Department, Amherst, NY 14226-3592. Offers adolescence education (MS); childhood education (MS); childhood special education (MS); childhood special-alternative certification (MS); early childhood special-alternative certification (MS). Part-time programs available. *Degree requirements:* For master's, thesis optional, research thesis in lieu of comprehensive exam; completion of degree within 5 years. *Entrance requirements:* For master's, 2 letters of recommendation (professional and character), proof of initial certificate of license for professional programs, resume. Additional exam requirements/recommendations for international students: Required—TOEFL (minimum score 500 paper-based; 63 iBT), IELTS (minimum score 5.5). Electronic applications accepted. *Faculty research:* Transition for students with disabilities, early childhood special education, traumatic brain injury (TBI), reading assessment.

Dallas Baptist University, Dorothy M. Bush College of Education, Teaching Program, Dallas, TX 75211-9299. Offers distance learning (MAT); early childhood (MAT); elementary (MAT); English as a second language (MAT); Montessori (MAT); multisensory (MAT); secondary (MAT). Part-time and evening/weekend programs available. *Entrance requirements:* For master's, GRE General Test, minimum GPA of 3.0. Additional exam requirements/recommendations for international students: Required—TOEFL, IELTS. *Application deadline:* Applications are processed on a rolling basis. Application fee: $25. Electronic applications accepted. *Expenses: Tuition:* Full-time $13,410; part-time $745 per credit hour. *Required fees:* $300; $150 per semester. Tuition and fees vary according to degree level. *Financial support:* Federal Work-Study, institutionally sponsored loans, scholarships/grants, and tuition waivers (full and partial) available. Support available to part-time students. Financial award applicants required to submit FAFSA. *Unit head:* Dr. Carolyn Spain, Director, 214-333-5217, E-mail:

graduate@dbu.edu. *Application contact:* Kit P. Montgomery, Director of Graduate Programs, 214-333-5242, Fax: 214-333-5579, E-mail: graduate@dbu.edu. Website: http://www3.dbu.edu/graduate/mat.asp.

DePaul University, College of Education, Chicago, IL 60614. Offers bilingual bicultural education (M Ed, MA); counseling (M Ed, MA), including clinical mental health counseling, college student development, school counseling; curriculum studies (M Ed, MA, Ed D); early childhood education (M Ed, MA, Ed D); educating adults (MA); educational leadership (M Ed, MA, Ed D), including administration and supervision (M Ed, MA), principal preparation (M Ed, MA); elementary education (MA); mathematics education (MA); mathematics for teaching (MS); middle school mathematics education (MS); reading specialist (M Ed, MA); secondary education (M Ed); social and cultural foundations in education (MA); special education (M Ed, MA); world languages education (M Ed, MA). Part-time and evening/weekend programs available. Postbaccalaureate distance learning degree programs offered (no on-campus study). *Faculty:* 61 full-time (35 women), 59 part-time/adjunct (43 women). *Students:* 628 full-time (486 women), 324 part-time (243 women); includes 304 minority (144 Black or African American, non-Hispanic/Latino; 1 American Indian or Alaska Native, non-Hispanic/Latino; 38 Asian, non-Hispanic/Latino; 98 Hispanic/Latino; 23 Two or more races, non-Hispanic/Latino), 24 international. Average age 30. In 2013, 465 master's, 4 doctorates awarded. *Degree requirements:* For doctorate, thesis/dissertation. *Application deadline:* For fall admission, 8/15 for domestic students; for winter admission, 12/1 for domestic students; for spring admission, 3/1 for domestic students. Applications are processed on a rolling basis. Application fee: $40. Electronic applications accepted. Tuition and fees vary according to course level, course load and degree level. *Financial support:* Application deadline: 12/31; applicants required to submit FAFSA. *Unit head:* Dr. Paul Zionts, Dean, 773-325-7581, Fax: 773-325-7713, E-mail: pzionts@depaul.edu. *Application contact:* Farrah Dalal, Assistant Director, 773-325-2465, Fax: 773-325-2270, E-mail: fdalal@depaul.edu. Website: http://education.depaul.edu.

DeSales University, Graduate Division, Division of Liberal Arts and Social Sciences, Program in Education, Center Valley, PA 18034-9568. Offers early childhood education Pre K-4 (M Ed); instructional technology for K-12 (M Ed); interdisciplinary (M Ed); secondary education (M Ed); special education (M Ed); teaching English to speakers of other languages (M Ed). Part-time and evening/weekend programs available. Postbaccalaureate distance learning degree programs offered (no on-campus study). *Degree requirements:* For master's, thesis project. *Entrance requirements:* Additional exam requirements/recommendations for international students: Required—TOEFL. *Application deadline:* Applications are processed on a rolling basis. Electronic applications accepted. *Expenses: Tuition:* Part-time $790 per credit. *Financial support:* Application deadline: 5/1. *Unit head:* Dr. Judith Rance-Roney, Chair, 610-282-1100 Ext. 1323, E-mail: judith.rance-roney@desales.edu. *Application contact:* Abigail Wernicki, Director of Graduate Admissions, 610-282-1100 Ext. 1768, E-mail: gradadmissions@desales.edu.

Dominican University, School of Education, River Forest, IL 60305-1099. Offers curriculum and instruction (MA Ed); early childhood education (MS); education (MAT); educational administration (MA); elementary education (MA Ed); English as a second language (MA Ed); reading (MA Ed); special education (MS). Part-time and evening/weekend programs available. Postbaccalaureate distance learning degree programs offered (no on-campus study). *Faculty:* 19 full-time (14 women), 51 part-time/adjunct (42 women). *Students:* 18 full-time (13 women), 334 part-time (274 women); includes 76 minority (26 Black or African American, non-Hispanic/Latino; 9 Asian, non-Hispanic/Latino; 41 Hispanic/Latino). Average age 32. 119 applicants, 77% accepted, 70 enrolled. In 2013, 246 master's awarded. *Entrance requirements:* For master's, Illinois Test of Basic Skills. Additional exam requirements/recommendations for international students: Required—TOEFL (minimum score 550 paper-based; 79 iBT). *Application deadline:* Applications are processed on a rolling basis. Application fee: $25. *Expenses:* Contact institution. *Financial support:* In 2013–14, 97 students received support. Career-related internships or fieldwork, scholarships/grants, and tuition waivers (partial) available. Support available to part-time students. Financial award application deadline: 8/15; financial award applicants required to submit FAFSA. *Faculty research:* Governance of private education institutions, reading and language arts, inclusion, organizational planning, leadership and vision. *Unit head:* Dr. Colleen Reardon, Dean, 718-524-6643, Fax: 708-524-6665, E-mail: creardon@dom.edu. *Application contact:* Keven Hansen, Coordinator of Recruitment and Admissions, 708-524-6921, Fax: 708-524-6665, E-mail: educate@dom.edu. Website: http://educate.dom.edu/.

Dowling College, Graduate Programs in Education, Oakdale, NY 11769-1999. Offers adolescence education with middle childhood extension (MS); childhood and early childhood education (MS); childhood and gifted education (MS); childhood education (1-6) (MS); computers in education (AC); early childhood education (B-2) (MS); educational administration (Ed D); educational technology leadership (MS); educational technology specialist (AC); gifted education (AC); literacy education (MS, AC), including 5-12 (MS), B-12 (MS); literacy education (MS), including B-6; school building leader (AC); school district business leader (MBA, AC); school district leader (AC); special education (MS), including autism, severe disabilities; sport management (MS). *Accreditation:* NCATE. Part-time and evening/weekend programs available. Postbaccalaureate distance learning degree programs offered (minimal on-campus study). *Faculty:* 44 full-time (24 women), 17 part-time/adjunct (8 women). *Students:* 183 full-time (124 women), 314 part-time (231 women); includes 51 minority (19 Black or African American, non-Hispanic/Latino; 1 American Indian or Alaska Native, non-Hispanic/Latino; 3 Asian, non-Hispanic/Latino; 26 Hispanic/Latino; 2 Native Hawaiian or other Pacific Islander, non-Hispanic/Latino). Average age 32. 174 applicants, 80% accepted, 82 enrolled. In 2013, 198 master's, 33 doctorates, 48 other advanced degrees awarded. *Degree requirements:* For master's and AC, comprehensive exam; for doctorate, thesis/dissertation. *Entrance requirements:* For master's, minimum GPA of 3.0; for doctorate, GRE, master's degree; for AC, teaching certificate. Additional exam requirements/recommendations for international students: Required—TOEFL (minimum score 550 paper-based). *Application deadline:* For fall admission, 9/1 priority date for domestic students; for winter admission, 1/1 priority date for domestic students; for spring admission, 2/1 priority date for domestic students. Applications are processed on a rolling basis. Application fee: $50. Electronic applications accepted. *Expenses: Tuition:* Full-time $22,731; part-time $1029 per credit. *Required fees:* $956; $956. *Financial support:* Career-related internships or fieldwork and Federal Work-Study available. Support available to part-time students. Financial award application deadline: 6/30; financial award applicants required to submit FAFSA. *Faculty research:* Natural readers, Korean styles and learning strategies, mothers of children with disabilities, computers in instruction, cultural background and organizational roadblocks to problem solving. *Unit head:* Dr. Robert Manley, Dean, 631-244-3447, E-mail: manleyr@dowling.edu. *Application contact:* Mary Boullianne, Director of Admissions, 631-244-3274, Fax: 631-244-1059, E-mail: boulliam@dowling.edu.

Duquesne University, School of Education, Department of Instruction and Leadership, Program in Early Level (PreK-4) Education, Pittsburgh, PA 15282-0001. Offers MS Ed. Part-time and evening/weekend programs available. *Faculty:* 2 full-time (both women).

Early Childhood Education

Students: 31 full-time (29 women), 2 part-time (both women); includes 7 minority (2 Black or African American, non-Hispanic/Latino; 1 Asian, non-Hispanic/Latino; 4 Hispanic/Latino), 1 international. Average age 27. 22 applicants, 77% accepted, 9 enrolled. In 2013, 20 master's awarded. *Degree requirements:* For master's, thesis optional. *Entrance requirements:* For master's, bachelor's degree. Additional exam requirements/recommendations for international students: Required—TOEFL (minimum score 550 paper-based), IELTS (minimum score 7). *Application deadline:* For fall admission, 9/1 for domestic students; for spring admission, 1/1 for domestic students. Applications are processed on a rolling basis. Electronic applications accepted. Application fee is waived when completed online. *Expenses: Tuition:* Full-time $18,162; part-time $1009 per credit. *Required fees:* $1728; $96 per credit. Tuition and fees vary according to program. *Unit head:* Dr. Julia Williams, Assistant Professor, 412-396-6098, Fax: 412-396-5388, E-mail: williamsj@duq.edu. *Application contact:* Michael Dolinger, Director of Student and Academic Services, 412-396-6647, Fax: 412-396-5585, E-mail: dolingerm@duq.edu.
Website: http://www.duq.edu/academics/schools/education/graduate-programs/ms-early-level-prek-4.

East Carolina University, Graduate School, College of Human Ecology, Department of Child Development and Family Relations, Greenville, NC 27858-4353. Offers birth through kindergarten education (MA Ed); child development and family relations (MS); family and consumer sciences (MA Ed); marriage and family therapy (MS). *Accreditation:* AAMFT/COAMFTE. Part-time programs available. *Degree requirements:* For master's, comprehensive exam, thesis optional. *Expenses:* Tuition, state resident: full-time $4223. Tuition, nonresident: full-time $16,540. *Required fees:* $2184. *Faculty research:* Child care quality, mental health delivery systems for children, family violence.

Eastern Connecticut State University, School of Education and Professional Studies/Graduate Division, Program in Early Childhood Education, Willimantic, CT 06226-2295. Offers MS. *Accreditation:* NCATE. Part-time and evening/weekend programs available. *Degree requirements:* For master's, comprehensive exam or thesis. *Entrance requirements:* For master's, PRAXIS I, minimum GPA of 2.7. Additional exam requirements/recommendations for international students: Required—TOEFL (minimum score 550 paper-based).

Eastern Illinois University, Graduate School, College of Education and Professional Studies, Department of Early Childhood, Elementary and Middle Level Education, Charleston, IL 61920-3099. Offers elementary education (MS Ed). *Accreditation:* NCATE. Part-time programs available. *Degree requirements:* For master's, comprehensive exam. *Expenses: Tuition, area resident:* Part-time $283 per credit hour. Tuition, state resident: part-time $283 per credit hour. Tuition, nonresident: part-time $679 per credit hour.

Eastern Michigan University, Graduate School, College of Education, Department of Teacher Education, Program in Early Childhood Education, Ypsilanti, MI 48197. Offers MA. *Accreditation:* NCATE. Part-time and evening/weekend programs available. *Students:* 50 part-time (all women); includes 4 minority (1 Black or African American, non-Hispanic/Latino; 1 American Indian or Alaska Native, non-Hispanic/Latino; 1 Asian, non-Hispanic/Latino; 1 Hispanic/Latino). Average age 34. 11 applicants, 100% accepted, 3 enrolled. In 2013, 17 master's awarded. *Degree requirements:* For master's, thesis optional. *Entrance requirements:* For master's, GRE. Additional exam requirements/recommendations for international students: Required—TOEFL. *Application deadline:* Applications are processed on a rolling basis. Application fee: $35. *Expenses:* Tuition, state resident: full-time $12,300; part-time $466 per credit hour. Tuition, nonresident: full-time $23,159; part-time $918 per credit hour. *Required fees:* $71 per credit hour. $46 per semester. One-time fee: $100. Tuition and fees vary according to course level and degree level. *Financial support:* Fellowships and teaching assistantships available. Support available to part-time students. Financial award applicants required to submit FAFSA. *Unit head:* Dr. Martha Kinney-Sedgwick, Interim Department Head, 734-487-3260, Fax: 734-487-2101, E-mail: mkinneys@emich.edu. *Application contact:* Dr. Brigid Beaubien, Coordinator, 734-487-3260, Fax: 734-487-2101, E-mail: brigid.beaubien@emich.edu.

Eastern Nazarene College, Adult and Graduate Studies, Division of Teacher Education, Quincy, MA 02170. Offers administration (M Ed); early childhood education (M Ed, Certificate); elementary education (M Ed, Certificate); English as a second language (Certificate); instructional enrichment and development (Certificate); middle school education (M Ed, Certificate); moderate special needs education (Certificate); principal (Certificate); program development and supervision (Certificate); secondary education (M Ed, Certificate); special education administrator (Certificate); special needs (M Ed); supervisor (Certificate); teacher of reading (M Ed, Certificate). M Ed also available through weekend program for administration, special needs, and teacher of reading only. Part-time and evening/weekend programs available. *Entrance requirements:* Additional exam requirements/recommendations for international students: Required—TOEFL (minimum score 550 paper-based).

Eastern New Mexico University, Graduate School, College of Education and Technology, Department of Educational Studies, Program in Special Education, Portales, NM 88130. Offers early childhood special education (M Sp Ed); general (M Sp Ed). Part-time programs available. *Degree requirements:* For master's, comprehensive exam, thesis optional. *Entrance requirements:* For master's, minimum GPA of 3.0, letter of recommendation, photocopy of teaching license or confirmation of entrance into alternative licensure program, writing assessment, 2 letters of application, special education license or minimum 30 hours of undergraduate course work. Additional exam requirements/recommendations for international students: Required—TOEFL (minimum score 550 paper-based; 79 iBT), IELTS (minimum score 6). Electronic applications accepted.

Eastern University, Graduate Education Programs, St. Davids, PA 19087-3696. Offers ESL program specialist (K-12) (Certificate); general supervisor (PreK-12) (Certificate); health and physical education (K-12) (Certificate); middle level (4-8) (Certificate); multicultural education (M Ed); pre K-4 (Certificate); pre K-4 with special education (Certificate); reading (M Ed); reading specialist (K-12) (Certificate); reading supervisor (K-12) (Certificate); school health services (M Ed); school health supervisor (Certificate); school nurse (Certificate); school principalship (K-12) (Certificate); secondary biology education (7-12) (Certificate); secondary chemistry education (7-12) (Certificate); secondary communication education (7-12) (Certificate); secondary education (7-12) (Certificate); secondary English education (7-12) (Certificate); secondary math education (7-12) (Certificate); secondary social studies education (7-12) (Certificate); special education (M Ed); special education (7-12) (Certificate); special education (Pre K-8) (Certificate); special education supervisor (N-12) (Certificate); TESOL (M Ed); world language (Certificate), including French, Mandarin Chinese, Spanish. Part-time and evening/weekend programs available. Postbaccalaureate distance learning degree programs offered (no on-campus study). *Faculty:* 22 full-time (11 women), 26 part-time/adjunct (18 women). *Students:* 77 full-time (58 women), 223 part-time (149 women); includes 112 minority (81 Black or African American, non-Hispanic/Latino; 1 American Indian or Alaska Native, non-Hispanic/Latino; 9 Asian, non-Hispanic/Latino; 18 Hispanic/Latino; 1 Native Hawaiian or other Pacific Islander, non-Hispanic/Latino; 2 Two or more races, non-Hispanic/Latino), 7 international. Average age 34. 94 applicants, 100% accepted, 81 enrolled. In 2013, 120 master's awarded. *Entrance requirements:* For

master's, minimum GPA of 2.5 (for M Ed); for Certificate, minimum GPA of 3.0 for certifications. Additional exam requirements/recommendations for international students: Required—TOEFL. *Application deadline:* For fall admission, 8/14 for domestic students; for spring admission, 12/20 for domestic students. Applications are processed on a rolling basis. Application fee: $35. Application fee is waived when completed online. *Expenses: Tuition:* Full-time $15,600; part-time $650 per credit. *Required fees:* $27.50 per semester. One-time fee: $50. Tuition and fees vary according to course load, degree level and program. *Financial support:* In 2013–14, 84 students received support, including 6 research assistantships with partial tuition reimbursements available (averaging $7,710 per year); scholarships/grants and unspecified assistantships also available. Financial award application deadline: 3/15; financial award applicants required to submit FAFSA. *Unit head:* Harry Gutelius, Associate Dean, 610-341-1729. *Application contact:* Michael Perpiglia, Associate Director of Enrollment, 610-341-5947, Fax: 484-581-1276, E-mail: mperpigl@eastern.edu.
Website: http://www.eastern.edu/academics/programs/loeb-school-education-0/graduateprograms.

Eastern Washington University, Graduate Studies, College of Arts, Letters and Education, Department of Education, Program in Early Childhood Education, Cheney, WA 99004-2431. Offers M Ed. *Students:* 5 applicants, 20% accepted. *Entrance requirements:* For master's, minimum GPA of 3.0. *Unit head:* Robin Showalter, Program Coordinator, 509-359-6492, E-mail: rshowalter@mail.ewu.edu. *Application contact:* Dr. Kevin Pyatt, Graduate Program Coordinator, 509-359-6091, E-mail: kpyatt@ewu.edu.

East Tennessee State University, School of Graduate Studies, College of Education, Department of Teaching and Learning, Johnson City, TN 37614. Offers early childhood education (MA, PhD), including initial licensure PreK-3 (MA), master teacher (MA), researcher (MA); early childhood education emergent inquiry (Post-Master's Certificate); special education (M Ed), including advanced practitioner, early childhood special education, special education. Part-time programs available. *Faculty:* 8 full-time (7 women), 4 part-time/adjunct (3 women). *Students:* 45 full-time (43 women), 43 part-time (40 women); includes 5 minority (2 Black or African American, non-Hispanic/Latino; 1 Asian, non-Hispanic/Latino; 2 Hispanic/Latino), 4 international. Average age 36. 75 applicants, 64% accepted, 41 enrolled. *Entrance requirements:* For master's, PRAXIS I or Tennessee teaching license (for special education only), minimum GPA of 3.0 (or complete probationary period with no grade lower than B for first 9 graduate hours for early childhood education); for doctorate, GRE General Test, professional resume; master's degree in early childhood or related field; interview; for Post-Master's Certificate, bachelor's or master's degree in early childhood or related field; two years of experience working with young children (preferred). Additional exam requirements/recommendations for international students: Required—TOEFL (minimum score 550 paper-based; 79 iBT). *Application deadline:* For fall admission, 3/15 for domestic and international students. Application fee: $35 ($45 for international students). *Expenses:* Tuition, state resident: full-time $7900; part-time $395 per credit hour. Tuition, nonresident: full-time $21,960; part-time $1098 per credit hour. *Required fees:* $1345; $84 per credit hour. *Financial support:* In 2013–14, 31 students received support, including 5 fellowships with full tuition reimbursements available (averaging $18,000 per year), 7 research assistantships with full tuition reimbursements available (averaging $6,000 per year), 4 teaching assistantships with full tuition reimbursements available (averaging $6,000 per year); career-related internships or fieldwork, institutionally sponsored loans, scholarships/grants, and unspecified assistantships also available. Financial award application deadline: 7/1; financial award applicants required to submit FAFSA. *Faculty research:* Teaching students with significant disabilities, problem solving in toddlers, children and their development and learning, connecting classroom environment to student engagement in PreK-3, bilingual education in Ecuador, positive discipline/behavior support programs, early childhood relationships, international and comparative special education. *Unit head:* Dr. Pamela Evanshen, Chair, 423-439-7694, E-mail: evanshep@etsu.edu. *Application contact:* Fiona Goodyear, School of Graduate Studies, 423-439-6148, Fax: 423-439-5624, E-mail: goodyear@etsu.edu.
Website: http://www.etsu.edu/coe/teachlearn/default.aspx.

Edinboro University of Pennsylvania, School of Education, Department of Early Childhood and Special Education, Edinboro, PA 16444. Offers early childhood education (M Ed); special education (M Ed). Part-time and evening/weekend programs available. *Degree requirements:* For master's, thesis or alternative, competency exam. *Entrance requirements:* For master's, GRE or MAT, minimum QPA of 2.5. Electronic applications accepted.

Elms College, Division of Education, Chicopee, MA 01013-2839. Offers early childhood education (MAT); education (M Ed, CAGS); elementary education (MAT); English as a second language (MAT); reading (MAT); secondary education (MAT), including biology education, English education, Spanish education; special education (MAT). Part-time and evening/weekend programs available. *Degree requirements:* For master's, thesis (for some programs). *Entrance requirements:* For master's, Massachusetts Educators Certification Test, minimum GPA of 3.0; for CAGS, master's degree in education. Additional exam requirements/recommendations for international students: Required—TOEFL.

Emporia State University, Program in Early Childhood Education, Emporia, KS 66801-5415. Offers early childhood curriculum (MS); early childhood special education (MS). *Accreditation:* NCATE. Part-time programs available. Postbaccalaureate distance learning degree programs offered. *Faculty:* 31 full-time (24 women), 4 part-time/adjunct (2 women). *Students:* 3 full-time (all women), 69 part-time (68 women); includes 7 minority (2 Black or African American, non-Hispanic/Latino; 5 Hispanic/Latino), 1 international. 29 applicants, 93% accepted, 17 enrolled. In 2013, 7 master's awarded. *Degree requirements:* For master's, comprehensive exam or thesis, practicum. *Entrance requirements:* For master's, GRE General Test or MAT, essay exam, appropriate bachelor's degree, letters of recommendation. Additional exam requirements/recommendations for international students: Required—TOEFL (minimum score 520 paper-based; 68 iBT). *Application deadline:* For fall admission, 8/15 priority date for domestic students. Applications are processed on a rolling basis. Application fee: $30 ($75 for international students). Electronic applications accepted. *Expenses: Tuition, area resident:* Part-time $220 per credit hour. Tuition, state resident: part-time $220 per credit hour. Tuition, nonresident: part-time $685 per credit hour. *Required fees:* $73 per credit hour. *Financial support:* In 2013–14, 1 research assistantship with full tuition reimbursement (averaging $7,200 per year), 4 teaching assistantships with full tuition reimbursements (averaging $7,200 per year) were awarded; Federal Work-Study, institutionally sponsored loans, health care benefits, and unspecified assistantships also available. Financial award application deadline: 3/15; financial award applicants required to submit FAFSA. *Unit head:* Dr. Jean Morrow, Chair, 620-341-5766, E-mail: jmorrow@emporia.edu. *Application contact:* Mary Sewell, Admissions Coordinator, 800-950-GRAD, Fax: 620-341-5909, E-mail: msewell@emporia.edu.

Endicott College, Van Loan School of Graduate and Professional Studies, Program in Montessori Integrative Learning, Beverly, MA 01915-2096. Offers M Ed. *Faculty:* 1 full-time (0 women), 2 part-time/adjunct (both women). *Students:* 43 full-time (34 women), 8 part-time (all women); includes 1 minority (Asian, non-Hispanic/Latino). Average age 37. 36 applicants, 92% accepted, 30 enrolled. In 2013, 5 master's awarded. *Entrance requirements:* Additional exam requirements/recommendations for international

students: Required—TOEFL. *Application deadline:* Applications are processed on a rolling basis. *Financial support:* Applicants required to submit FAFSA. *Unit head:* Dr. Enid E. Larsen, Assistant Dean, Graduate and Professional Studies, 978-232-2198. *Application contact:* Dr. Mary Huegel, Vice President and Dean of the School of Graduate and Professional Studies, 978-232-2084, Fax: 978-232-3000, E-mail: mhuegel@endicott.edu.

Erikson Institute, Erikson Institute, Chicago, IL 60654. Offers child development (MS); early childhood education (M Ed, MS, PhD). PhD offered through the Graduate School. *Accreditation:* NCA. *Degree requirements:* For master's, comprehensive exam, internship; for doctorate, one foreign language, comprehensive exam, thesis/dissertation. *Entrance requirements:* For master's, experience working with young children, interview; for doctorate, GRE General Test, interview. *Faculty research:* Early childhood development, cognitive development, sociocultural contexts, early childhood education, family and culture, early literacy.

Erikson Institute, Academic Programs, Program in Early Childhood Education, Chicago, IL 60654. Offers MS. *Degree requirements:* For master's, comprehensive exam. *Entrance requirements:* For master's, 3 letters of recommendation, minimum GPA of 2.75. Additional exam requirements/recommendations for international students: Required—TOEFL.

Fairfield University, Graduate School of Education and Allied Professions, Fairfield, CT 06824-5195. Offers applied behavior analysis (ATC); applied psychology (MA); clinical mental health counseling (MA, CAS); early childhood studies (ATC); educational technology (MA); elementary education (MA, CAS); family studies (MA); integration of spirituality and religion in counseling (ATC); marriage and family therapy (MA); school counseling (MA, CAS); school psychology (MA, CAS); school-based marriage and family therapy (ATC); secondary education (MA); special education (MA, CAS); substance abuse counseling (ATC); teaching (Certificate); teaching and foundations (MA, CAS); TESOL, world languages, and bilingual education (MA, CAS). *Accreditation:* NCATE. Part-time and evening/weekend programs available. *Faculty:* 24 full-time (21 women), 39 part-time/adjunct (27 women). *Students:* 154 full-time (130 women), 307 part-time (248 women); includes 75 minority (14 Black or African American, non-Hispanic/Latino; 1 American Indian or Alaska Native, non-Hispanic/Latino; 10 Asian, non-Hispanic/Latino; 44 Hispanic/Latino; 6 Two or more races, non-Hispanic/Latino), 13 international. Average age 34. 263 applicants, 41% accepted, 91 enrolled. In 2013, 149 master's, 21 other advanced degrees awarded. *Degree requirements:* For master's, comprehensive exam. *Entrance requirements:* For master's, PRAXIS I (for certification programs), minimum GPA of 3.0, 2 recommendations, resume. Additional exam requirements/recommendations for international students: Required—TOEFL (minimum score 550 paper-based; 84 iBT) or IELTS (minimum score 7.5). *Application deadline:* For fall admission, 2/15 for international students; for spring admission, 10/1 for international students. Application fee: $60. Electronic applications accepted. *Expenses: Tuition:* Part-time $675 per credit hour. Tuition and fees vary according to program. *Financial support:* In 2013–14, 55 students received support. Career-related internships or fieldwork and unspecified assistantships available. Financial award applicants required to submit FAFSA. *Faculty research:* Literacy, adolescent psychology, special education, teaching development, mentoring for professional development, multicultural education. *Total annual research expenditures:* $325,000. *Unit head:* Dr. Robert D. Hannafin, Dean, 203-254-4250, Fax: 203-254-4241, E-mail: rhannafin@fairfield.edu. *Application contact:* Marianne Gumpper, Director of Graduate and Continuing Studies Admission, 203-254-4184, Fax: 203-254-4073, E-mail: gradadmis@fairfield.edu. Website: http://www.fairfield.edu/academics/schoolscollegescenters/graduateschoolofeducationalliedprofessions/graduateprograms/.

Fitchburg State University, Division of Graduate and Continuing Education, Program in Early Childhood Education, Fitchburg, MA 01420-2697. Offers M Ed. *Accreditation:* NCATE. Part-time and evening/weekend programs available. *Entrance requirements:* Additional exam requirements/recommendations for international students: Recommended—TOEFL (minimum score 550 paper-based; 79 iBT). Electronic applications accepted.

Five Towns College, Department of Music, Dix Hills, NY 11746-6055. Offers childhood education (MS Ed); composition and arranging (DMA); jazz/commercial music (MM); music education (MM, DMA); music history and literature (DMA); music performance (DMA). Part-time programs available. *Faculty:* 6 full-time (2 women), 10 part-time/adjunct (0 women). *Students:* 14 full-time (3 women), 28 part-time (12 women); includes 6 minority (3 Black or African American, non-Hispanic/Latino; 1 Asian, non-Hispanic/Latino; 2 Hispanic/Latino), 7 international. Average age 27. 19 applicants, 58% accepted, 9 enrolled. In 2013, 17 master's, 3 doctorates awarded. *Degree requirements:* For master's, thesis, exams, major composition or capstone project, recital; for doctorate, comprehensive exam, thesis/dissertation, final oral exam. *Entrance requirements:* For master's, audition, bachelor's degree in music or music education, minimum GPA of 2.75, 36 hours of course work in performance; for doctorate, master's degree in music or music education, minimum GPA of 3.0, 3 letters of recommendation, audition. Additional exam requirements/recommendations for international students: Required—TOEFL (minimum score 520 paper-based; 85 iBT); Recommended—IELTS (minimum score 7). *Application deadline:* For fall admission, 9/1 for domestic and international students; for spring admission, 1/25 for domestic and international students. Applications are processed on a rolling basis. Application fee: $50. Electronic applications accepted. *Expenses: Tuition:* Full-time $14,400; part-time $600 per credit. *Required fees:* $60 per semester. One-time fee: $85. Tuition and fees vary according to degree level. *Financial support:* Fellowships with tuition reimbursements, teaching assistantships with tuition reimbursements, and tuition waivers (partial) available. Financial award applicants required to submit FAFSA. *Faculty research:* Teaching methods, teaching strategies and techniques, analysis of modern music, jazz. *Unit head:* Dr. Jill Miller-Thorn, Dean of Graduate Music Studies, 631-656-2142, Fax: 631-656-2172, E-mail: jill.millerthorn@ftc.edu. *Application contact:* Jerry Cohen, Dean of Enrollment, 631-656-2110, Fax: 631-656-2172, E-mail: jerry.cohen@ftc.edu.

Florida Agricultural and Mechanical University, Division of Graduate Studies, Research, and Continuing Education, College of Education, Department of Elementary Education, Tallahassee, FL 32307-3200. Offers early childhood and elementary education (M Ed, MS Ed). *Accreditation:* NCATE. *Degree requirements:* For master's, thesis (for some programs). *Entrance requirements:* For master's, GRE General Test, minimum GPA of 3.0. Additional exam requirements/recommendations for international students: Required—TOEFL.

Florida Atlantic University, College of Education, Department of Curriculum, Culture, and Educational Inquiry, Boca Raton, FL 33431-0991. Offers curriculum and instruction (M Ed, PhD, Ed S); early childhood education (M Ed); multicultural education (M Ed); TESOL and bilingual education (MA). Part-time and evening/weekend programs available. *Faculty:* 9 full-time (8 women), 3 part-time/adjunct (all women). *Students:* 17 full-time (14 women), 119 part-time (93 women); includes 41 minority (18 Black or African American, non-Hispanic/Latino; 4 Asian, non-Hispanic/Latino; 18 Hispanic/Latino; 1 Two or more races, non-Hispanic/Latino), 5 international. Average age 36. 49 applicants, 39% accepted, 13 enrolled. In 2013, 31 master's, 2 other advanced degrees awarded. *Entrance requirements:* Additional exam requirements/recommendations for international students: Required—TOEFL (minimum score 500 paper-based; 61 iBT),

IELTS (minimum score 6). *Application deadline:* For fall admission, 7/1 for domestic students, 2/15 for international students; for spring admission, 11/1 for domestic students, 7/15 for international students. Application fee: $30. *Expenses:* Tuition, state resident: full-time $6660; part-time $370 per credit hour. Tuition, nonresident: full-time $18,450; part-time $1025 per credit hour. Tuition and fees vary according to course load. *Faculty research:* Multicultural education, early intervention strategies, family literacy, religious diversity in schools, early childhood curriculum. *Unit head:* Dr. Emery Hyslop-Margison, Interim Chair, 561-297-3965, E-mail: ehyslopmargison@fau.edu. *Application contact:* Dr. Eliah Watlington, Associate Dean, 561-296-8520, Fax: 261-297-2991, E-mail: ewatling@fau.edu. Website: http://www.coe.fau.edu/academicdepartments/ccei/.

Florida Atlantic University, College of Education, Department of Teaching and Learning, Boca Raton, FL 33431-0991. Offers curriculum and instruction (M Ed), including art, biology, chemistry, English, French, German, mathematics, music, physics, Pre-K and primary education, reading, social sciences, Spanish; elementary education (M Ed); environmental education (M Ed); reading education (M Ed); social foundations of education (M Ed), including educational psychology, educational technology, multilingual education. *Accreditation:* NCATE. Part-time and evening/weekend programs available. *Faculty:* 16 full-time (12 women), 1 (woman) part-time/adjunct. *Students:* 56 full-time (46 women), 96 part-time (78 women); includes 39 minority (10 Black or African American, non-Hispanic/Latino; 6 Asian, non-Hispanic/Latino; 20 Hispanic/Latino; 3 Two or more races, non-Hispanic/Latino), 4 international. Average age 32. 101 applicants, 54% accepted, 42 enrolled. In 2013, 64 master's awarded. *Entrance requirements:* For master's, GRE General Test, minimum GPA of 3.0 in last 2 years of undergraduate course work. Additional exam requirements/recommendations for international students: Required—TOEFL (minimum score 500 paper-based; 61 iBT), IELTS (minimum score 6). *Application deadline:* For fall admission, 7/1 for domestic students, 2/15 for international students; for spring admission, 11/1 for domestic students, 7/15 for international students. Applications are processed on a rolling basis. Application fee: $30. *Expenses:* Tuition, state resident: full-time $6660; part-time $370 per credit hour. Tuition, nonresident: full-time $18,450; part-time $1025 per credit hour. Tuition and fees vary according to course load. *Financial support:* Fellowships with partial tuition reimbursements, research assistantships with partial tuition reimbursements, teaching assistantships with partial tuition reimbursements, career-related internships or fieldwork, scholarships/grants, and unspecified assistantships available. *Faculty research:* Technology, teaching English to speakers of other languages, math teaching, electronic portfolio assessment, global perspectives through social studies. *Unit head:* Dr. Barbara Ridener, Chairperson, 561-297-3588. *Application contact:* Dr. Eliah Watlington, Associate Dean, 561-296-8520, Fax: 261-297-2991, E-mail: ewatling@fau.edu. Website: http://www.coe.fau.edu/academicdepartments/tl/.

Florida International University, College of Education, Department of Teaching and Learning, Miami, FL 33199. Offers art education (MA, MS); curriculum and instruction (MS, Ed D, PhD, Ed S), including curriculum development (MS), elementary education (MS), English education (MS), learning technologies (MS), mathematics education (MS), modern language education (MS), physical education (MS), science education (MS), social studies education (MS), special education (MS), early childhood education (MS); exceptional student education (Ed D); foreign language education (MS), including foreign language education, teaching English to speakers of other languages (TESOL); international/intercultural education (MS); language, literacy and culture (PhD); mathematics, science, and learning technologies (PhD); physical education (MS), including sport and fitness; reading education (MS). Part-time and evening/weekend programs available. *Degree requirements:* For doctorate, comprehensive exam, thesis/dissertation. *Entrance requirements:* For master's, GRE General Test, Florida General Knowledge Test or Florida College Level Academic Skills Test; for doctorate and Ed S, GRE General Test. Additional exam requirements/recommendations for international students: Required—TOEFL (minimum score 550 paper-based; 80 iBT), IELTS (minimum score 6.3). Electronic applications accepted.

Florida State University, The Graduate School, College of Education, School of Teacher Education, Tallahassee, FL 32306. Offers curriculum and instruction (MS, MST, PhD, Ed S), including early childhood education (MS, PhD, Ed S), elementary education (MS, PhD, Ed S), English education (MS, PhD, Ed S), English teaching (MST), exceptional student education (MST), foreign and second language education (MS, PhD, Ed S), foreign and second language teaching (MST), math education (MS, PhD, Ed S), math teaching (MST), reading education and language arts (MS, PhD, Ed S), science education (MS, PhD, Ed S), social science education (MS, PhD, Ed S), social science teaching (MST), special education (MS, PhD, Ed S), special education studies (MST), visual disabilities (MS, Ed S). Part-time programs available. *Faculty:* 30 full-time (20 women), 22 part-time/adjunct (18 women). *Students:* 183 full-time (151 women), 92 part-time (80 women); includes 47 minority (20 Black or African American, non-Hispanic/Latino; 3 American Indian or Alaska Native, non-Hispanic/Latino; 1 Asian, non-Hispanic/Latino; 20 Hispanic/Latino; 3 Two or more races, non-Hispanic/Latino), 61 international. Average age 30. 199 applicants, 79% accepted, 86 enrolled. In 2013, 119 master's, 9 doctorates, 4 other advanced degrees awarded. *Degree requirements:* For master's and Ed S, comprehensive exam, thesis optional; for doctorate, comprehensive exam, thesis/dissertation, preliminary exam, prospectus defense. *Entrance requirements:* For master's, doctorate, and Ed S, GRE General Test, minimum GPA of 3.0. Additional exam requirements/recommendations for international students: Required—TOEFL (minimum score 550 paper-based; 80 iBT). *Application deadline:* For fall admission, 7/1 for domestic and international students; for winter admission, 10/1 for domestic students, 11/1 for international students; for spring admission, 3/1 for domestic and international students. Applications are processed on a rolling basis. Application fee: $30. Electronic applications accepted. *Expenses:* Tuition, state resident: part-time $403.51 per credit hour. Tuition, nonresident: part-time $1004.85 per credit hour. *Required fees:* $75.81 per credit hour. One-time fee: $20 part-time. Tuition and fees vary according to course load, campus/location and student level. *Financial support:* In 2013–14, 113 students received support, including 55 research assistantships with full and partial tuition reimbursements available, 18 teaching assistantships with full and partial tuition reimbursements available; fellowships with full and partial tuition reimbursements available, career-related internships or fieldwork, scholarships/grants, health care benefits, and unspecified assistantships also available. Financial award application deadline: 1/15; financial award applicants required to submit FAFSA. *Faculty research:* Effective intervention and assessment strategies to improve reading skills; literacy teaching and learning through technology; understanding of student sense-making through instructions, especially STEM learning for all students; international education and consequences of globalization; support professional teacher development and adoption of effective/transformative practices. *Total annual research expenditures:* $1.3 million. *Unit head:* Dr. Sherry Southerland, Chair, 850-644-4880, Fax: 850-644-7736, E-mail: ssoutherland@admin.fsu.edu. *Application contact:* Dawn Matthews, Academic Support Assistant, 850-644-2122, Fax: 850-644-7736, E-mail: dmatthews@fsu.edu. Website: http://www.coe.fsu.edu/STE.

Fordham University, Graduate School of Education, Division of Curriculum and Teaching, New York, NY 10023. Offers adult education (MS, MSE); bilingual teacher

education (MSE); curriculum and teaching (MSE); early childhood education (MSE); elementary education (MST); language, literacy, and learning (PhD); reading education (MSE, Adv C); secondary education (MAT, MSE); special education (MSE, Adv C); teaching English as a second language (MSE). *Accreditation:* NCATE. *Degree requirements:* For doctorate, thesis/dissertation; for Adv C, thesis. *Entrance requirements:* For doctorate, MAT, GRE General Test.

Framingham State University, Continuing Education, Program in Early Childhood Education, Framingham, MA 01701-9101. Offers M Ed.

Francis Marion University, Graduate Programs, School of Education, Florence, SC 29502-0547. Offers early childhood education (M Ed); elementary education (M Ed); learning disabilities (M Ed, MAT); remedial education (M Ed); secondary education (M Ed). *Accreditation:* NCATE. Part-time programs available. *Faculty:* 17 full-time (12 women). *Students:* 5 full-time (3 women), 79 part-time (63 women); includes 33 minority (all Black or African American, non-Hispanic/Latino). Average age 34. 327 applicants, 42% accepted, 135 enrolled. In 2013, 45 master's awarded. *Degree requirements:* For master's, comprehensive exam. *Entrance requirements:* For master's, GRE General Test, MAT, NTE, or PRAXIS II. *Application deadline:* For fall admission, 3/15 priority date for domestic students; for spring admission, 10/15 priority date for domestic students. Application fee: $33. *Expenses:* Tuition, state resident: full-time $9184; part-time $459.20 per credit hour. Tuition, nonresident: full-time $18,368; part-time $918.40 per credit hour. *Required fees:* $13.50 per credit hour. $92 per semester. Tuition and fees vary according to program. *Financial support:* In 2013–14, 2 research assistantships (averaging $6,000 per year) were awarded; scholarships/grants and unspecified assistantships also available. Support available to part-time students. Financial award application deadline: 3/1; financial award applicants required to submit FAFSA. *Faculty research:* Identification and alternate assessment of at-risk students. *Unit head:* Dr. Shirley Carr Bausmith, Dean, 843-661-1460, Fax: 843-661-4647. *Application contact:* Rannie Gamble, Administrative Manager, 843-661-1286, Fax: 843-661-4688, E-mail: rgamble@fmarion.edu.

Furman University, Graduate Division, Department of Education, Greenville, SC 29613. Offers curriculum and instruction (MA); early childhood education (MA); educational leadership (Ed S); English as a second language (MA); literacy (MA); school leadership (MA); special education (MA). *Accreditation:* NCATE. Part-time programs available. Postbaccalaureate distance learning degree programs offered (minimal on-campus study). *Degree requirements:* For master's, comprehensive exam (for some programs), thesis or alternative. *Entrance requirements:* For master's, PRAXIS II. *Faculty research:* Literacy, pedagogy and practice, social justice, advanced leadership, achievement in high poverty schools.

Gallaudet University, The Graduate School, Washington, DC 20002-3625. Offers ASL/English bilingual early childhood education: birth to 5 (Certificate); audiology (Au D); clinical psychology (PhD); critical studies in the education of deaf learners (PhD); deaf and hard of hearing infants, toddlers, and their families (Certificate); deaf education (Ed S); deaf education: advanced studies (MA); deaf education: special programs (MA); deaf history (Certificate); deaf studies (MA, Certificate); educating deaf students with disabilities (Certificate); education: teacher preparation (MA), including deaf education, early childhood education and deaf education, elementary education and deaf education, secondary education and deaf education; educational neuroscience (PhD); hearing, speech and language sciences (MS, PhD); international development (MA); interpretation (MA, PhD), including combined interpreting practice and research (MA), interpreting research (MA); linguistics (MA, PhD); mental health counseling (MA); peer mentoring (Certificate); public administration (MPA); school counseling (MA); school psychology (Psy S); sign language teaching (MA); social work (MSW); speech-language pathology (MS). Part-time programs available. *Faculty:* 55 full-time (37 women). *Students:* 361 full-time (279 women), 108 part-time (73 women); includes 98 minority (39 Black or African American, non-Hispanic/Latino; 1 American Indian or Alaska Native, non-Hispanic/Latino; 12 Asian, non-Hispanic/Latino; 36 Hispanic/Latino; 1 Native Hawaiian or other Pacific Islander, non-Hispanic/Latino; 9 Two or more races, non-Hispanic/Latino), 31 international. Average age 30. 602 applicants, 49% accepted, 177 enrolled. In 2013, 140 master's, 32 doctorates, 11 other advanced degrees awarded. Terminal master's awarded for partial completion of doctoral program. *Degree requirements:* For master's, comprehensive exam (for some programs), thesis optional; for doctorate, comprehensive exam, thesis/dissertation. *Entrance requirements:* For master's and doctorate, GRE General Test or MAT, letters of recommendation, interviews, goals statement, ASL proficiency interview, written English competency. Additional exam requirements/recommendations for international students: Required—TOEFL. *Application deadline:* For fall admission, 2/15 for domestic students. Applications are processed on a rolling basis. Application fee: $75. Electronic applications accepted. *Expenses: Tuition:* Full-time $14,774; part-time $821 per credit. *Required fees:* $198 per semester. *Financial support:* In 2013–14, 325 students received support. Fellowships, research assistantships, teaching assistantships, career-related internships or fieldwork, Federal Work-Study, scholarships/grants, tuition waivers (partial), and unspecified assistantships available. Support available to part-time students. Financial award applicants required to submit FAFSA. *Faculty research:* Bimodal bilingualism development, cochlear implants, telecommunications access, cancer genetics, linguistics, visual language and visual learning, advancement of avatar and robotics translation, algal productivity and physiology in the Anacostia River. *Unit head:* Dr. Carol J. Erting, Dean, Research, Graduate School, Continuing Studies, and International Programs, 202-651-5520, Fax: 202-651-5027, E-mail: carol.erting@gallaudet.edu. *Application contact:* Wednesday Luria, Coordinator of Prospective Graduate Student Services, 202-651-5400, Fax: 202-651-5295, E-mail: graduate.school@gallaudet.edu.
Website: http://www.gallaudet.edu/x26696.xml.

The George Washington University, Graduate School of Education and Human Development, Department of Special Education and Disability Studies, Program in Early Childhood Special Education, Washington, DC 20052. Offers MA Ed. *Accreditation:* NCATE. *Students:* 20 full-time (19 women), 14 part-time (12 women); includes 9 minority (6 Black or African American, non-Hispanic/Latino; 2 Asian, non-Hispanic/Latino; 1 Two or more races, non-Hispanic/Latino), 3 international. Average age 31. 43 applicants, 98% accepted, 11 enrolled. In 2013, 20 master's awarded. *Degree requirements:* For master's, comprehensive exam. *Entrance requirements:* For master's, GRE General Test or MAT, minimum GPA of 2.75. *Application deadline:* For fall admission, 1/15 priority date for domestic students; for spring admission, 10/1 for domestic students. Applications are processed on a rolling basis. Application fee: $75. *Financial support:* In 2013–14, 19 students received support. Fellowships, career-related internships or fieldwork, Federal Work-Study, and tuition waivers (full) available. Financial award application deadline: 1/15; financial award applicants required to submit FAFSA. *Faculty research:* Computer-assisted instruction and learning, disabled learner assessment of preschool, handicapped children. *Unit head:* Dr. Marian H. Jarrett, Faculty Coordinator, 202-994-1509, E-mail: mjarrett@gwu.edu. *Application contact:* Sarah Lang, Director of Graduate Admissions, 202-994-1447, Fax: 202-994-7207, E-mail: slang@gwu.edu.

Georgia College & State University, Graduate School, The John H. Lounsbury College of Education, Program in Early Childhood Education, Milledgeville, GA 31061.

Offers M Ed, Ed S. *Accreditation:* NCATE. Part-time and evening/weekend programs available. *Students:* 1 (woman) full-time, 8 part-time (7 women); includes 4 minority (3 Black or African American, non-Hispanic/Latino; 1 Hispanic/Latino). Average age 28. In 2013, 16 master's awarded. *Degree requirements:* For master's, comprehensive exam, exit portfolio; for Ed S, comprehensive exam, electronic portfolio presentation. *Entrance requirements:* For master's, on-site writing assessment, level 4 teaching certificate, 2 recommendations, minimum GPA of 2.75; for Ed S, on-site writing assessment, master's degree, 2 years of teaching experience, 2 professional recommendations, level 5 teacher certification, minimum GPA of 3.25. Additional exam requirements/recommendations for international students: Recommended—TOEFL (minimum score 550 paper-based; 79 iBT). *Application deadline:* For fall admission, 7/1 priority date for domestic students; for spring admission, 11/15 priority date for domestic students. Applications are processed on a rolling basis. Application fee: $40. Electronic applications accepted. *Financial support:* In 2013–14, 1 research assistantship was awarded; career-related internships or fieldwork, Federal Work-Study, and unspecified assistantships also available. Support available to part-time students. Financial award applicants required to submit FAFSA. *Application contact:* Shanda Brand, Graduate Coordinator, 478-445-1383, E-mail: shanda.brand@gcsu.edu.

Georgia Southern University, Jack N. Averitt College of Graduate Studies, College of Education, Department of Teaching and Learning, Program in Early Childhood Education, Statesboro, GA 30460. Offers M Ed, Ed S. *Accreditation:* NCATE. Part-time and evening/weekend programs available. *Students:* 32 full-time (29 women), 38 part-time (37 women); includes 15 minority (all Black or African American, non-Hispanic/Latino). Average age 32. 29 applicants, 62% accepted, 13 enrolled. *Degree requirements:* For master's, portfolio, transition point assessments, exit assessment. *Entrance requirements:* For master's, GRE General Test or MAT, minimum cumulative GPA of 2.5. Additional exam requirements/recommendations for international students: Required—TOEFL (minimum score 550 paper-based; 80 iBT). *Application deadline:* For fall admission, 3/1 priority date for domestic and international students; for spring admission, 10/1 priority date for domestic students, 10/1 for international students. Applications are processed on a rolling basis. Application fee: $50. Electronic applications accepted. *Expenses:* Tuition, state resident: full-time $7068; part-time $270 per semester hour. Tuition, nonresident: full-time $26,446; part-time $1077 per semester hour. *Required fees:* $2092. *Financial support:* Career-related internships or fieldwork, Federal Work-Study, scholarships/grants, tuition waivers (partial), and unspecified assistantships available. Support available to part-time students. Financial award application deadline: 4/15; financial award applicants required to submit FAFSA. *Faculty research:* Technology, effective instructional strategies, multiculturalism, children's literature, school violence. *Unit head:* Dr. Hsiu-Lien Lu, Program Coordinator, 912-478-0210, Fax: 912-478-0026, E-mail: hlu@georgiasouthern.edu. *Application contact:* Amanda Gilliland, Coordinator for Graduate Student Recruitment, 912-478-2302, Fax: 912-478-0740, E-mail: gradadmissions@georgiasouthern.edu. Website: http://coe.georgiasouthern.edu/eced/.

Georgia Southwestern State University, Graduate Studies, School of Education, Americus, GA 31709-4693. Offers early childhood education (M Ed, Ed S); health and physical education (M Ed); middle grades education (M Ed, Ed S); reading (M Ed); secondary education (M Ed); special education (M Ed). *Accreditation:* NCATE. *Degree requirements:* For master's, comprehensive exam. *Entrance requirements:* For master's, GRE General Test or MAT, minimum GPA of 2.5; for Ed S, GRE General Test or MAT, minimum graduate GPA of 3.25, M Ed from accredited college or university, 3 years teaching experience. Electronic applications accepted.

Georgia State University, College of Education, Department of Early Childhood Education, Atlanta, GA 30302-3083. Offers early childhood and elementary education (PhD); early childhood education (M Ed, Ed S); mathematics education (M Ed); urban education (M Ed). *Accreditation:* NCATE. Part-time and evening/weekend programs available. *Faculty:* 20 full-time (16 women). *Students:* 104 full-time (93 women), 37 part-time (36 women); includes 70 minority (54 Black or African American, non-Hispanic/Latino; 7 Asian, non-Hispanic/Latino; 6 Hispanic/Latino; 3 Two or more races, non-Hispanic/Latino), 2 international. Average age 29. 51 applicants, 55% accepted, 27 enrolled. In 2013, 73 master's, 1 doctorate, 17 other advanced degrees awarded. *Degree requirements:* For master's, comprehensive exam (for some programs), thesis (for some programs); for doctorate, comprehensive exam, thesis/dissertation (for some programs); for Ed S, comprehensive exam (for some programs). *Entrance requirements:* For master's, GRE, undergraduate diploma; for doctorate and Ed S, GRE, master's degree. Additional exam requirements/recommendations for international students: Required—TOEFL (minimum score 550 paper-based; 79 iBT) or IELTS (minimum score 6.5). *Application deadline:* Applications are processed on a rolling basis. Application fee: $50. Electronic applications accepted. *Expenses: Tuition, area resident:* Full-time $4176; part-time $348 per credit hour. Tuition, state resident: full-time $14,544; part-time $1212 per credit hour. Tuition, nonresident: full-time $14,544; part-time $1212 per credit hour. Tuition and fees vary according to course load and program. *Financial support:* In 2013–14, fellowships with full tuition reimbursements (averaging $24,000 per year), research assistantships with full and partial tuition reimbursements (averaging $4,000 per year), teaching assistantships with full tuition reimbursements (averaging $2,000 per year) were awarded; career-related internships or fieldwork, Federal Work-Study, institutionally sponsored loans, scholarships/grants, traineeships, health care benefits, tuition waivers (partial), and unspecified assistantships also available. Support available to part-time students. Financial award applicants required to submit FAFSA. *Faculty research:* Teacher development; language arts/literacy education; mathematics education; intersection of science, urban, and multicultural education; diversity in education. *Unit head:* Dr. Barbara Meyers, Department Chair, 404-413-8021, Fax: 404-413-8023, E-mail: barbara@gsu.edu. *Application contact:* Elaine King Jones, Administrative Curriculum Specialist, 404-413-8234, Fax: 404-413-8023, E-mail: ekjones@gsu.edu.
Website: http://education.gsu.edu/ece/index.htm.

Georgia State University, College of Education, Department of Educational Psychology and Special Education, Program in Education of Students with Exceptionalities, Atlanta, GA 30302-3083. Offers autism spectrum disorders (PhD); behavior disorders (PhD); communication disorders (PhD); early childhood special education (PhD); learning disabilities (PhD); mental retardation (PhD); orthopedic impairments (PhD); sensory impairments (PhD). *Accreditation:* NCATE. Part-time and evening/weekend programs available. *Students:* Average age 0. *Degree requirements:* For doctorate, comprehensive exam, thesis/dissertation. *Entrance requirements:* Additional exam requirements/recommendations for international students: Required—TOEFL (minimum score 550 paper-based; 79 iBT) or IELTS (minimum score 6.5). *Application deadline:* For fall admission, 6/1 for domestic and international students; for winter admission, 11/1 for domestic and international students; for spring admission, 5/1 for domestic and international students. Application fee: $50. Electronic applications accepted. *Expenses: Tuition, area resident:* Full-time $4176; part-time $348 per credit hour. Tuition, state resident: full-time $14,544; part-time $1212 per credit hour. Tuition, nonresident: full-time $14,544; part-time $1212 per credit hour. Tuition and fees vary according to course load and program. *Financial support:* In 2013–14, fellowships with full tuition reimbursements (averaging $28,000 per year), research assistantships with full tuition reimbursements (averaging $2,000 per year) were awarded; scholarships/

grants, health care benefits, and unspecified assistantships also available. *Faculty research:* Academic and behavioral supports for students with emotional/behavior disorders; academic interventions for learning disabilities; cultural, socioeconomic, and linguistic diversity; language and literacy development, disorders, and instruction. *Unit head:* Dr. Kristine Jolivette, Associate Professor, 404-413-8040, Fax: 404-413-8043, E-mail: kjolivette@gsu.edu. *Application contact:* Sandy Vaughn, Senior Administrative Coordinator, 404-413-8318, Fax: 404-413-8043, E-mail: svaughn@gsu.edu.
Website: http://education.gsu.edu/EPSE/4922.html.

Georgia State University, College of Education, Department of Educational Psychology and Special Education, Program in Multiple and Severe Disabilities, Atlanta, GA 30302-3083. Offers early childhood special education general curriculum (M Ed); special education adapted curriculum (intellectual disability) (M Ed); special education deaf education (M Ed); special education general/adapted (autism spectrum disorders) (M Ed); special education physical and health disabilities (orthopedic impairments) (M Ed). *Accreditation:* NCATE. Part-time programs available. *Students:* Average age 0. *Degree requirements:* For master's, variable foreign language requirement, comprehensive exam, thesis (for some programs). *Entrance requirements:* For master's, GRE. Additional exam requirements/recommendations for international students: Required—TOEFL (minimum score 550 paper-based; 79 iBT) or IELTS (minimum score 6.5). *Application deadline:* For fall admission, 6/1 for domestic and international students; for winter admission, 11/1 for domestic and international students; for spring admission, 5/1 for domestic and international students. Application fee: $50. Electronic applications accepted. *Expenses: Tuition, area resident:* Full-time $4176; part-time $348 per credit hour. Tuition, state resident: full-time $14,544; part-time $1212 per credit hour. Tuition, nonresident: full-time $14,544; part-time $1212 per credit hour. Tuition and fees vary according to course load and program. *Financial support:* In 2013–14, fellowships with full tuition reimbursements (averaging $25,000 per year), research assistantships with full tuition reimbursements (averaging $2,000 per year) were awarded; teaching assistantships with full tuition reimbursements, scholarships/grants, health care benefits, and unspecified assistantships also available. *Faculty research:* Literacy, language, behavioral supports. *Unit head:* Dr. Kathryn Wolff Heller, Professor, 404-413-8040, E-mail: kheller@gsu.edu. *Application contact:* Sandy Vaughn, Senior Administrative Coordinator, 404-413-8318, Fax: 404-413-8043, E-mail: svaughn@gsu.edu.
Website: http://education.gsu.edu/EPSE/4637.html.

Golden Gate Baptist Theological Seminary, Graduate and Professional Programs, Mill Valley, CA 94941-3197. Offers divinity (M Div); early childhood education (Certificate); education leadership (MAEL, Diploma); ministry (D Min); theological studies (MTS); theology (Th M); youth ministry (Certificate). *Accreditation:* ACIPE; ATS (one or more programs are accredited). Part-time and evening/weekend programs available. *Degree requirements:* For master's, thesis (for some programs); for doctorate, 2 foreign languages, thesis/dissertation. *Entrance requirements:* For doctorate, MAT. Additional exam requirements/recommendations for international students: Required—TOEFL (minimum score 550 paper-based). Electronic applications accepted.

Governors State University, College of Education, Program in Early Childhood Education, University Park, IL 60484. Offers MA. *Accreditation:* NCATE. *Degree requirements:* For master's, comprehensive exam, practicum. *Entrance requirements:* For master's, minimum GPA of 2.75 in last 60 hours of undergraduate course work, 3.0 graduate.

Grand Valley State University, College of Education, Program in Special Education, Allendale, MI 49401-9403. Offers cognitive impairment (M Ed); early childhood developmental delay (M Ed); emotional impairment (M Ed); learning disabilities (M Ed); special education (M Ed). *Accreditation:* NCATE. Part-time and evening/weekend programs available. *Degree requirements:* For master's, thesis. *Entrance requirements:* For master's, GRE General Test or minimum GPA of 3.0. Additional exam requirements/recommendations for international students: Required—TOEFL. Electronic applications accepted. *Faculty research:* Evaluation of special education program effects, adaptive behavior assessment, language development, writing disorders, comparative effects of presentation methods.

Grand Valley State University, College of Education, Programs in General Education, Allendale, MI 49401-9403. Offers adult and higher education (M Ed); early childhood education (M Ed); educational differentiation (M Ed); educational leadership (M Ed); educational technology integration (M Ed); elementary education (M Ed); middle level education (M Ed); school library media services (M Ed); secondary level education (M Ed); teaching English to speakers of other languages (M Ed). Part-time and evening/weekend programs available. Postbaccalaureate distance learning degree programs offered (minimal on-campus study). *Degree requirements:* For master's, thesis. *Entrance requirements:* For master's, GRE General Test or minimum GPA of 3.0. Additional exam requirements/recommendations for international students: Required—TOEFL. Electronic applications accepted. *Faculty research:* Effectiveness of technology in education, parental involvement, effective teaching, effective schools research.

Hampton University, Graduate College, College of Education and Continuing Studies, Program in Teaching, Hampton, VA 23668. Offers early childhood education (MT); middle school education (MT); music education (MT); secondary education (MT); special education (MT). *Entrance requirements:* For master's, GRE General Test.

Harding University, Cannon-Clary College of Education, Searcy, AR 72149-0001. Offers advanced studies in teaching and learning (M Ed); art (MSE); behavioral science (MSE); counseling (MS, Ed S); early childhood special education (M Ed, MSE); education (MSE); educational leadership (M Ed, Ed S); elementary education (M Ed); English (MSE); French (MSE); history/social science (MSE); kinesiology (MSE); math (MSE); reading (M Ed); secondary education (M Ed); Spanish (MSE); teaching (MAT); teaching English as a second language (MSE). *Accreditation:* NCATE. Part-time and evening/weekend programs available. *Faculty:* 13 full-time (5 women), 42 part-time/adjunct (24 women). *Students:* 154 full-time (119 women), 393 part-time (270 women); includes 108 minority (81 Black or African American, non-Hispanic/Latino; 5 American Indian or Alaska Native, non-Hispanic/Latino; 5 Asian, non-Hispanic/Latino; 9 Hispanic/Latino; 8 Two or more races, non-Hispanic/Latino), 15 international. Average age 36. 187 applicants, 79% accepted, 135 enrolled. In 2013, 138 master's, 17 other advanced degrees awarded. *Degree requirements:* For master's, comprehensive exam (for some programs), thesis optional, portfolio(s); for Ed S, comprehensive exam, portfolio, project. *Entrance requirements:* For master's, GRE, MAT, PRAXIS; for Ed S, MAT or GRE. Additional exam requirements/recommendations for international students: Required—TOEFL (minimum score 550 paper-based; 79 iBT). *Application deadline:* For fall admission, 8/1 for domestic and international students; for spring admission, 1/1 for domestic and international students. Applications are processed on a rolling basis. Application fee: $35. *Expenses: Tuition:* Full-time $11,574; part-time $643 per credit hour. *Required fees:* $432; $24 per credit hour. Tuition and fees vary according to course load, degree level and program. *Financial support:* In 2013–14, 36 students received support. Unspecified assistantships available. *Faculty research:* Reading, comprehension, school violence, educational technology, behavior, college choice, differentiated instruction, brain-based teaching. *Unit head:* Dr. Clara Carroll, Chair, 501-279-4501, Fax: 501-279-4083, E-mail: ccarroll@harding.edu. *Application contact:* Information Contact, 501-279-4315, E-mail: gradstudiesedu@harding.edu.
Website: http://www.harding.edu/education.

Hebrew College, Shoolman Graduate School of Jewish Education, Newton Centre, MA 02459. Offers early childhood Jewish education (Certificate); Jewish day school education (Certificate); Jewish education (MJ Ed); Jewish family education (Certificate); Jewish special education (Certificate); Jewish youth education, informal education and camping (Certificate). Part-time and evening/weekend programs available. Postbaccalaureate distance learning degree programs offered. *Degree requirements:* For master's, one foreign language. *Entrance requirements:* For master's, GRE, interview. Additional exam requirements/recommendations for international students: Required—TOEFL.

Henderson State University, Graduate Studies, Teachers College, Department of Advanced Instructional Studies, Arkadelphia, AR 71999-0001. Offers early childhood (P-4) (MSE); education (MAT); English as a second language (Graduate Certificate); instructional facilitator (Graduate Certificate); middle school (MSE); reading (MSE); special education (MSE). *Accreditation:* NCATE. Part-time programs available. *Faculty:* 7 full-time (3 women), 2 part-time/adjunct (both women). *Students:* 1 (woman) full-time, 99 part-time (88 women); includes 20 minority (13 Black or African American, non-Hispanic/Latino; 1 American Indian or Alaska Native, non-Hispanic/Latino; 5 Hispanic/Latino; 1 Two or more races, non-Hispanic/Latino), 1 international. Average age 36. 7 applicants, 100% accepted, 7 enrolled. In 2013, 45 master's awarded. *Entrance requirements:* For master's, GRE General Test or MAT, minimum GPA of 2.7, teacher certification. Additional exam requirements/recommendations for international students: Required—TOEFL (minimum score 600 paper-based); Recommended—IELTS (minimum score 6.5). *Application deadline:* For fall admission, 8/1 priority date for domestic students, 6/30 priority date for international students; for spring admission, 1/1 priority date for domestic students, 11/30 priority date for international students. Applications are processed on a rolling basis. Application fee: $25 ($75 for international students). *Expenses:* Tuition, state resident: full-time $4284; part-time $238 per credit hour. Tuition, nonresident: full-time $8802; part-time $489 per credit hour. Tuition and fees vary according to course load and campus/location. *Financial support:* In 2013–14, 1 teaching assistantship with partial tuition reimbursement (averaging $4,000 per year) was awarded; scholarships/grants and unspecified assistantships also available. *Unit head:* Dr. Gary Smithey, Chairperson, 870-230-5361, Fax: 870-230-5455, E-mail: smitheg@hsu.edu. *Application contact:* Dr. Ken Taylor, Graduate Dean, 870-230-5126, Fax: 870-230-5479, E-mail: taylorke@hsu.edu.

Hofstra University, School of Education, Programs in Special Education, Hempstead, NY 11549. Offers applied behavior analysis (Advanced Certificate); early childhood special education (MS Ed, Advanced Certificate); gifted education (Advanced Certificate); inclusive early childhood special education (MS Ed); inclusive elementary special education (MS Ed); inclusive secondary special education (MS Ed); secondary education generalist (MS Ed), including students with disabilities 7-12; special education (MA, MS Ed, Advanced Certificate, PD); special education assessment and diagnosis (Advanced Certificate); special education generalist (MS Ed), including extension in secondary education; teaching students with severe or multiple disabilities (Advanced Certificate).

Hofstra University, School of Education, Programs in Teaching - Elementary and Early Childhood Education, Hempstead, NY 11549. Offers early childhood and childhood education (MS Ed); early childhood education (MA, MS Ed); educational technology (MA); elementary education (MS Ed); literacy (MA); math specialist (Advanced Certificate); math, science, technology (MA); multiculturalism (MA).

Holy Family University, Graduate School, School of Education, Master of Education Programs, Philadelphia, PA 19114. Offers early elementary education (PreK-Grade 4) (M Ed); education leadership (M Ed); general education (M Ed); middle level education (Grades 4-8) (M Ed); reading specialist (M Ed); secondary education (Grades 7-12) (M Ed); special education (M Ed); TESOL and literacy (M Ed). *Expenses: Tuition:* Full-time $12,060. *Required fees:* $250. Tuition and fees vary according to degree level. *Unit head:* Dr. Leonard Soroka, Dean, 267-341-3565, Fax: 215-824-2438, E-mail: lsoroka@holyfamily.edu. *Application contact:* Gidget Marie Montelibano, Associate Director of Graduate Admissions, 267-341-3358, Fax: 215-637-1478, E-mail: gmontelibano@holyfamily.edu.

Hood College, Graduate School, Department of Education, Frederick, MD 21701-8575. Offers curriculum and instruction (MS), including early childhood education, elementary education, elementary school science and mathematics, secondary education, special education; educational leadership (MS, Certificate); reading specialization (MS); STEM (Certificate). *Accreditation:* NCATE. Part-time and evening/weekend programs available. *Faculty:* 4 full-time (3 women), 33 part-time/adjunct (25 women). *Students:* 1 (woman) full-time, 340 part-time (282 women); includes 59 minority (31 Black or African American, non-Hispanic/Latino; 1 American Indian or Alaska Native, non-Hispanic/Latino; 10 Asian, non-Hispanic/Latino; 13 Hispanic/Latino; 4 Two or more races, non-Hispanic/Latino). Average age 33. 97 applicants, 99% accepted, 86 enrolled. In 2013, 64 master's, 40 other advanced degrees awarded. *Degree requirements:* For master's, action research project, portfolio (reading). *Entrance requirements:* For master's, minimum GPA of 2.75, teaching certification. Additional exam requirements/recommendations for international students: Required—TOEFL (minimum score 575 paper-based; 89 iBT), IELTS (minimum score 6.5). *Application deadline:* For fall admission, 7/15 priority date for domestic students, 7/15 for international students; for spring admission, 12/1 priority date for domestic students, 12/1 for international students. Applications are processed on a rolling basis. Application fee: $35. Electronic applications accepted. Application fee is waived when completed online. *Expenses: Tuition:* Part-time $405 per credit. *Required fees:* $100 per semester. *Financial support:* In 2013–14, 1 student received support. Tuition waivers (partial) and unspecified assistantships available. Financial award applicants required to submit FAFSA. *Faculty research:* Leadership, action research, brain research, learning styles. *Unit head:* Dr. Ellen Koitz, Chairperson, 301-696-3466, Fax: 301-696-3597, E-mail: koitz@hood.edu. *Application contact:* Dr. Maria Green Cowles, Dean of Graduate School, 301-696-3811, Fax: 301-696-3597, E-mail: gofurther@hood.edu.
Website: http://www.hood.edu/academics/education/index.html.

Hunter College of the City University of New York, Graduate School, School of Education, Department of Curriculum and Teaching, New York, NY 10065-5085. Offers bilingual education (MS); corrective reading (K-12) (MS Ed); early childhood education (MS); educational supervision and administration (AC); elementary education (MS); literacy education (MS); teaching English as a second language (MA). *Faculty:* 18 full-time (10 women), 38 part-time/adjunct (26 women). *Students:* 61 full-time (54 women), 665 part-time (542 women); includes 256 minority (53 Black or African American, non-Hispanic/Latino; 1 American Indian or Alaska Native, non-Hispanic/Latino; 76 Asian, non-Hispanic/Latino; 126 Hispanic/Latino), 19 international. Average age 30. 443 applicants, 61% accepted, 176 enrolled. In 2013, 279 master's, 28 other advanced degrees awarded. *Degree requirements:* For master's, thesis; for AC, portfolio review. *Entrance requirements:* For degree, minimum B average in graduate course work, teaching certificate, minimum 3 years of full-time teaching experience, interview, 2 letters of support. Additional exam requirements/recommendations for international

students: Required—TOEFL, TWE. *Application deadline:* For fall admission, 4/1 for domestic students; for spring admission, 11/1 for domestic students. Applications are processed on a rolling basis. Application fee: $125. *Financial support:* Federal Work-Study, scholarships/grants, and tuition waivers (partial) available. Support available to part-time students. *Faculty research:* Teacher opportunity corps (mentor program for first-year teachers), adult literacy, student literacy corporation. *Unit head:* Dr. Jennifer Tuten, Head, 212-777-4686, E-mail: jtuten@hunter.cuny.edu. *Application contact:* Milena Solo, Director for Graduate Admissions, 212-772-4482, E-mail: milena.solo@hunter.cuny.edu.
Website: http://www.hunter.cuny.edu/school-of-education/departments/curriculum-teaching.

Indiana State University, College of Graduate and Professional Studies, College of Education, Department of Elementary, Early and Special Education, Terre Haute, IN 47809. Offers early childhood education (M Ed); elementary education (M Ed); MA/MS. *Accreditation:* NCATE. Electronic applications accepted.

Indiana University–Purdue University Indianapolis, School of Education, Indianapolis, IN 46202-2896. Offers computer education (Certificate); curriculum and instruction (MS); early childhood (MS); educational leadership (MS, Certificate); English as a second language (Certificate); higher education and student affairs (MS); kindergarten (Certificate); language education (MS); reading (Certificate); school counseling (MS); special education (MS, Certificate). Part-time and evening/weekend programs available. *Faculty:* 41 full-time, 80 part-time/adjunct. *Students:* 113 full-time (78 women), 263 part-time (200 women); includes 88 minority (51 Black or African American, non-Hispanic/Latino; 1 American Indian or Alaska Native, non-Hispanic/Latino; 10 Asian, non-Hispanic/Latino; 19 Hispanic/Latino; 7 Two or more races, non-Hispanic/Latino), 5 international. Average age 33. 93 applicants, 54% accepted, 40 enrolled. In 2013, 179 master's awarded. *Degree requirements:* For master's, thesis optional. *Entrance requirements:* For master's, GRE General Test, minimum GPA of 3.0. Additional exam requirements/recommendations for international students: Required—TOEFL. *Application deadline:* For fall admission, 5/1 priority date for domestic students; for spring admission, 11/1 for domestic students. Application fee: $55 ($65 for international students). *Financial support:* Fellowships, research assistantships with partial tuition reimbursements, teaching assistantships, Federal Work-Study, institutionally sponsored loans, scholarships/grants, and tuition waivers (partial) available. Support available to part-time students. *Faculty research:* Teachers in the process of change, learning cycles, children's concepts of science. *Total annual research expenditures:* $614,458. *Unit head:* Dr. Pat Rogan, Executive Associate Dean, 317-274-6862, E-mail: progan@iupui.edu. *Application contact:* Donnella Dillon, Graduate Admissions Coordinator, 317-274-0645, E-mail: dmdillon@iupui.edu.
Website: http://education.iupui.edu/.

Inter American University of Puerto Rico, Guayama Campus, Department of Education and Social Sciences, Guayama, PR 00785. Offers early childhood education (0-4 years) (M Ed); elementary education (M Ed). Part-time programs available. *Entrance requirements:* For master's, GRE, MAT, EXADEP, letters of recommendation, minimum GPA of 2.5. Electronic applications accepted.

Iona College, School of Arts and Science, Department of Education, New Rochelle, NY 10801-1890. Offers adolescence education: biology (MS Ed, MST); adolescence education: English (MS Ed, MST); adolescence education: Italian (MS Ed, MST); adolescence education: mathematics (MS Ed, MST); adolescence education: social studies (MS Ed, MST); adolescence education: Spanish (MS Ed, MST); adolescence special education 5-12 (MST); adolescence special education and literacy (MS Ed); childhood and special education (MST); childhood education (MST); early childhood and childhood (MST); educational leadership (MS Ed); literacy education: birth-grade 6 (MS Ed). *Accreditation:* NCATE. Part-time and evening/weekend programs available. *Faculty:* 11 full-time (9 women), 7 part-time/adjunct (6 women). *Students:* 34 full-time (25 women), 61 part-time (47 women); includes 5 minority (2 Asian, non-Hispanic/Latino; 3 Hispanic/Latino), 1 international. Average age 25. 27 applicants, 93% accepted, 16 enrolled. In 2013, 54 master's awarded. *Degree requirements:* For master's, thesis or alternative. *Entrance requirements:* For master's, minimum GPA of 3.0, NY State teaching certificate (for all MS Ed programs). Additional exam requirements/recommendations for international students: Required—TOEFL (minimum score 550 paper-based; 80 iBT), IELTS (minimum score 6.5). *Application deadline:* For fall admission, 8/1 priority date for domestic students, 5/1 priority date for international students; for spring admission, 1/1 priority date for domestic students, 9/1 priority date for international students. Applications are processed on a rolling basis. Application fee: $50. Electronic applications accepted. *Expenses: Tuition:* Part-time $948 per credit. *Required fees:* $235 per term. *Financial support:* In 2013–14, 84 students received support. Unspecified assistantships available. Support available to part-time students. Financial award application deadline: 4/15; financial award applicants required to submit FAFSA. *Faculty research:* Reading/writing, educational technology, administration, early literacy assessment, literacy development. *Unit head:* Margaret Smith, PhD, Chair, 914-633-2210, Fax: 914-633-2608, E-mail: msmith@iona.edu. *Application contact:* Veronica Jarek-Prinz, Director, Graduate Admissions, 914-633-2420, Fax: 914-633-2277, E-mail: vjarekprinz@iona.edu.
Website: http://www.iona.edu/Academics/School-of-Arts-Science/Departments/Education/Graduate-Programs.aspx.

Jackson State University, Graduate School, College of Education and Human Development, Department of Elementary and Early Childhood Education, Jackson, MS 39217. Offers early childhood education (MS Ed, Ed D); elementary education (MS Ed, Ed S). *Accreditation:* NCATE. Evening/weekend programs available. Terminal master's awarded for partial completion of doctoral program. *Degree requirements:* For master's, comprehensive exam, thesis or alternative; for doctorate, comprehensive exam, thesis/dissertation. *Entrance requirements:* For master's, GRE General Test; for doctorate, MAT, teaching experience. Additional exam requirements/recommendations for international students: Required—TOEFL (minimum score 520 paper-based; 67 iBT).

Jacksonville State University, College of Graduate Studies and Continuing Education, College of Education and Professional Studies, Program in Early Childhood Education, Jacksonville, AL 36265-1602. Offers MS Ed. *Accreditation:* NCATE. Part-time and evening/weekend programs available. *Degree requirements:* For master's, comprehensive exam, thesis (for some programs). *Entrance requirements:* For master's, GRE General Test or MAT. Additional exam requirements/recommendations for international students: Required—TOEFL (minimum score 61 iBT). Electronic applications accepted.

James Madison University, The Graduate School, College of Education, Early, Elementary, and Reading Education Department, Harrisonburg, VA 22807. Offers early childhood education (MAT); elementary education (MAT); reading education (M Ed). *Students:* Average age 27. *Entrance requirements:* Additional exam requirements/recommendations for international students: Required—TOEFL. *Application deadline:* For fall admission, 5/1 for domestic students; for spring admission, 9/1 for domestic students. Applications are processed on a rolling basis. Application fee: $55. Electronic applications accepted. *Financial support:* Application deadline: 3/1; applicants required to submit FAFSA. *Unit head:* Dr. Martha Ross, Academic Unit Head, 540-568-6255. *Application contact:* Lynette M. Bible, Director of Graduate Admissions, 540-568-6395, Fax: 540-568-7860, E-mail: biblelm@jmu.edu.

John Carroll University, Graduate School, Department of Education and Allied Studies, Program in School Based Early Childhood Education, University Heights, OH 44118-4581. Offers M Ed. *Accreditation:* NCATE. *Degree requirements:* For master's, comprehensive exam. *Entrance requirements:* For master's, GRE General Test or MAT, minimum GPA of 2.75, interview. Additional exam requirements/recommendations for international students: Required—TOEFL. Electronic applications accepted.

John Hancock University, Program in Education, Oakbrook Terrace, IL 60181. Offers early childhood education (MA Ed); education (MA Ed); teacher as a leader (MA Ed). *Degree requirements:* For master's, thesis or capstone.

Johns Hopkins University, School of Education, Certificate Programs in Education, Baltimore, MD 21218-2699. Offers advanced methods for differentiated instruction and inclusive education (Certificate); applied behavior analysis (Certificate); counseling (CAGS); data-based decision making and organizational improvement (Certificate); early intervention/preschool special education specialist (Certificate); education leadership for independent schools (Certificate); education of students with autism and other pervasive developmental disorders (Certificate); evidence-based teaching in the health professions (Certificate); gifted education (Certificate); K-8 mathematics lead-teacher (Certificate); K-8 STEM education lead-teacher (Certificate); leadership for school, family, and community collaboration (Certificate); leadership in technology integration (Certificate); mental health counseling (Certificate); mind, brain, and teaching (Certificate); school administration and supervision (Certificate); urban education (Certificate). Part-time and evening/weekend programs available. Postbaccalaureate distance learning degree programs offered (no on-campus study). *Students:* 7 full-time (4 women), 216 part-time (169 women); includes 66 minority (35 Black or African American, non-Hispanic/Latino; 17 Asian, non-Hispanic/Latino; 6 Hispanic/Latino; 8 Two or more races, non-Hispanic/Latino), 6 international. Average age 35. 257 applicants, 81% accepted, 62 enrolled. In 2013, 202 CAGSs awarded. *Entrance requirements:* For degree, bachelor's degree from regionally- or nationally-accredited institution (master's for some programs), minimum GPA of 3.0 in all previous programs of study, official transcripts from all post-secondary institutions attended, essay, curriculum vitae/resume, minimum of two letters of recommendation. Additional exam requirements/recommendations for international students: Required—TOEFL (minimum score 600 paper-based; 100 iBT) or IELTS (minimum score 7). *Application deadline:* For fall admission, 4/1 for domestic students; for spring admission, 10/1 for domestic students; for summer admission, 2/1 for domestic students. Application fee: $80. Electronic applications accepted. *Financial support:* Application deadline: 6/1; applicants required to submit FAFSA. *Unit head:* Dr. David A. Andrews, Dean, 410-516-7820, Fax: 410-516-6697, E-mail: davidandrews@jhu.edu. *Application contact:* Catherine Wilson, Associate Director of Admissions, 410-516-9797, Fax: 410-516-9799, E-mail: soe.info@jhu.edu.

Johns Hopkins University, School of Education, Master's Programs in Education, Baltimore, MD 21218-2699. Offers counseling (MS), including mental health counseling, school counseling; education (MS), including educational studies, gifted education, reading, school administration and supervision, technology for educators; elementary education (MAT); health professions (M Ed); intelligence analysis (MS); management (MS); secondary education (MAT); special education (MS), including early childhood special education, general special education studies, mild to moderate disabilities, severe disabilities. Part-time and evening/weekend programs available. Postbaccalaureate distance learning degree programs offered (no on-campus study). *Students:* 183 full-time (123 women), 1,001 part-time (757 women); includes 380 minority (160 Black or African American, non-Hispanic/Latino; 4 American Indian or Alaska Native, non-Hispanic/Latino; 91 Asian, non-Hispanic/Latino; 78 Hispanic/Latino; 4 Native Hawaiian or other Pacific Islander, non-Hispanic/Latino; 43 Two or more races, non-Hispanic/Latino), 28 international. Average age 28. 508 applicants, 90% accepted, 337 enrolled. In 2013, 565 degrees awarded. *Degree requirements:* For master's, comprehensive exam (for some programs), portfolio, capstone project and/or internship; PRAXIS II (for teacher preparation programs that lead to licensure). *Entrance requirements:* For master's, GRE (for full-time programs only); PRAXIS I or equivalent (for teacher preparation programs that lead to licensure), bachelor's degree from regionally- or nationally-accredited institution, minimum GPA of 3.0 in all previous programs of study, official transcripts from all post-secondary institutions attended, essay, curriculum vitae/resume, minimum of two letters of recommendation. Additional exam requirements/recommendations for international students: Required—TOEFL (minimum score 600 paper-based; 100 iBT) or IELTS (minimum score 7). *Application deadline:* For fall admission, 4/1 for domestic and international students; for spring admission, 10/1 for domestic and international students; for summer admission, 2/1 for domestic and international students. Application fee: $80. Electronic applications accepted. *Financial support:* Application deadline: 6/1; applicants required to submit FAFSA. *Unit head:* Dr. David A. Andrews, Dean, 410-516-7820, Fax: 410-516-6697, E-mail: davidandrews@jhu.edu. *Application contact:* Catherine Wilson, Associate Director of Admissions, 410-516-9797, Fax: 410-516-9799, E-mail: soe.info@jhu.edu.

Jose Maria Vargas University, Program in Preschool Education, Pembroke Pines, FL 33026. Offers MS.

Kansas State University, Graduate School, College of Human Ecology, School of Family Studies and Human Services, Manhattan, KS 66506. Offers communication sciences and disorders (MS); conflict resolution (Graduate Certificate); early childhood education (MS); family and community services (MS); family studies (MS, PhD); life span human development (MS, PhD); marriage and family therapy (MS, PhD); personal financial planning (MS, PhD, Graduate Certificate); youth development (MS, Graduate Certificate). *Accreditation:* AAMFT/COAMFTE; ASHA. Part-time programs available. Postbaccalaureate distance learning degree programs offered (no on-campus study). *Faculty:* 34 full-time (22 women), 11 part-time/adjunct (8 women). *Students:* 68 full-time (56 women), 131 part-time (86 women); includes 42 minority (19 Black or African American, non-Hispanic/Latino; 2 American Indian or Alaska Native, non-Hispanic/Latino; 4 Asian, non-Hispanic/Latino; 14 Hispanic/Latino; 1 Native Hawaiian or other Pacific Islander, non-Hispanic/Latino; 2 Two or more races, non-Hispanic/Latino), 3 international. Average age 31. 248 applicants, 29% accepted, 48 enrolled. In 2013, 35 master's, 7 doctorates awarded. *Degree requirements:* For master's, thesis or alternative. *Entrance requirements:* For master's, GRE, minimum GPA of 3.0 in last 2 years of undergraduate study; for doctorate, GRE. Additional exam requirements/recommendations for international students: Required—TOEFL (minimum score 600 paper-based). *Application deadline:* For fall admission, 2/1 priority date for domestic students, 1/1 priority date for international students; for spring admission, 10/1 priority date for domestic students, 8/1 priority date for international students; for summer admission, 2/1 priority date for domestic students, 12/1 priority date for international students. Applications are processed on a rolling basis. Application fee: $50 ($75 for international students). Electronic applications accepted. *Financial support:* In 2013–14, 63 students received support, including 45 research assistantships (averaging $13,500 per year), 18 teaching assistantships with full tuition reimbursements available (averaging $11,000 per year). Financial award application deadline: 3/1. *Faculty research:* Health and security of military families, personal and family risk assessment and evaluation, disorders of communication and swallowing, families and health. *Total*

annual research expenditures: $14.9 million. *Unit head:* Dr. Maurice MacDonald, Director, 785-532-5510, Fax: 785-532-5505, E-mail: morey@ksu.edu. *Application contact:* Connie Fechter, Administrative Specialist, 785-532-5510, Fax: 785-532-5505, E-mail: fechter@ksu.edu.
Website: http://www.he.k-state.edu/fshs/.

Kean University, College of Education, Program in Early Childhood Education, Union, NJ 07083. Offers administration in early childhood and family studies (MA); advanced curriculum and teaching (MA); classroom instruction (MA), including preschool-third grade; education for family living (MA). *Accreditation:* NCATE. Part-time programs available. *Faculty:* 22 full-time (12 women). *Students:* 3 full-time (2 women), 30 part-time (all women); includes 14 minority (4 Black or African American, non-Hispanic/Latino; 4 Asian, non-Hispanic/Latino; 6 Hispanic/Latino), 1 international. Average age 31. 29 applicants, 79% accepted, 15 enrolled. In 2013, 15 master's awarded. *Degree requirements:* For master's, portfolio. *Entrance requirements:* For master's, GRE General Test, PRAXIS Early Childhood Content Knowledge (for some programs), minimum GPA of 3.0, 2 letters of recommendation, teacher certification (for some programs), personal statement, official transcripts, resume. Additional exam requirements/recommendations for international students: Required—TOEFL (minimum score 550 paper-based; 79 iBT). *Application deadline:* For fall admission, 6/1 for domestic and international students; for spring admission, 12/1 for domestic and international students. Applications are processed on a rolling basis. Application fee: $75 ($150 for international students). Electronic applications accepted. *Expenses:* Tuition, state resident: full-time $12,099; part-time $589 per credit. Tuition, nonresident: full-time $16,399; part-time $722 per credit. *Required fees:* $3050; $139 per credit. Part-time tuition and fees vary according to course level, course load, degree level and program. *Financial support:* In 2013–14, research assistantships with full tuition reimbursements (averaging $3,713 per year) were awarded; unspecified assistantships also available. Financial award applicants required to submit FAFSA. *Unit head:* Dr. Polly Ashelman, Program Coordinator, 908-737-3785, E-mail: pashelma@kean.edu. *Application contact:* Ann-Marie Kay, Assistant Director of Graduate Admissions, 908-737-5922, Fax: 908-737-5925, E-mail: akay@kean.edu.
Website: http://grad.kean.edu/masters-programs/administration-early-childhood-family-studies.

Kennesaw State University, Leland and Clarice C. Bagwell College of Education, Program in Graduate Education, Kennesaw, GA 30144-5591. Offers educational leadership (M Ed); educational leadership technology (M Ed); elementary and early childhood education (M Ed); instructional technology (M Ed); middle grades education (M Ed); reading (M Ed); secondary education (M Ed); special education (M Ed); teaching English to speakers of other languages (M Ed). *Accreditation:* NCATE. Part-time programs available. *Students:* 65 full-time (60 women), 229 part-time (158 women); includes 66 minority (46 Black or African American, non-Hispanic/Latino; 6 Asian, non-Hispanic/Latino; 9 Hispanic/Latino; 5 Two or more races, non-Hispanic/Latino), 1 international. Average age 34. 56 applicants, 86% accepted, 43 enrolled. In 2013, 109 master's awarded. *Degree requirements:* For master's, thesis or alternative. *Entrance requirements:* For master's, GRE General Test, T-4 state certification, minimum GPA of 2.75. Additional exam requirements/recommendations for international students: Required—TOEFL (minimum score 550 paper-based; 80 iBT), IELTS (minimum score 6.5). *Application deadline:* For fall admission, 7/1 for domestic and international students; for spring admission, 10/1 for domestic and international students; for summer admission, 4/15 for domestic and international students. Applications are processed on a rolling basis. Application fee: $60. Electronic applications accepted. *Expenses:* Tuition, state resident: full-time $4806; part-time $267 per semester hour. Tuition, nonresident: full-time $17,298; part-time $961 per semester hour. *Required fees:* $1834; $784.50 per semester. *Financial support:* In 2013–14, 10 research assistantships with tuition reimbursements (averaging $8,000 per year) were awarded; Federal Work-Study and unspecified assistantships also available. Support available to part-time students. Financial award application deadline: 4/1; financial award applicants required to submit FAFSA. *Unit head:* Melinda Ross, Administrative Coordinator for Graduate Programs in Education, 770-423-6043, E-mail: graded@kennesaw.edu. *Application contact:* Melinda Ross, Admissions Counselor, 770-423-6043, Fax: 770-423-6885, E-mail: ksugrad@kennesaw.edu.
Website: http://www.kennesaw.edu/education/grad/.

Kent State University, Graduate School of Education, Health, and Human Services, School of Lifespan Development and Educational Sciences, Program in Special Education, Kent, OH 44242-0001. Offers deaf education (M Ed); early childhood education (M Ed); educational interpreter K-12 (M Ed); general special education (M Ed); gifted education (M Ed); mild/moderate intervention (M Ed); special education (PhD, Ed S); transition to work (M Ed). *Accreditation:* NCATE. *Faculty:* 11 full-time (6 women), 12 part-time/adjunct (all women). *Students:* 75 full-time (61 women), 59 part-time (50 women); includes 15 minority (12 Black or African American, non-Hispanic/Latino; 1 Asian, non-Hispanic/Latino; 2 Native Hawaiian or other Pacific Islander, non-Hispanic/Latino), 8 international. 80 applicants, 35% accepted. In 2013, 44 master's, 4 doctorates awarded. *Degree requirements:* For doctorate, comprehensive exam, thesis/dissertation. *Entrance requirements:* For master's, minimum undergraduate GPA of 2.75, moral character form, 2 letters of reference, goals statement; for doctorate and Ed S, GRE General Test, goals statement, 2 letters of reference, interview, resume. Additional exam requirements/recommendations for international students: Required—TOEFL (minimum score 550 paper-based; 80 iBT). *Application deadline:* Applications are processed on a rolling basis. Application fee: $30 ($60 for international students). Electronic applications accepted. *Financial support:* In 2013–14, 6 research assistantships with full tuition reimbursements (averaging $9,667 per year), 1 teaching assistantship with full tuition reimbursement (averaging $12,000 per year) were awarded; career-related internships or fieldwork, Federal Work-Study, institutionally sponsored loans, scholarships/grants, health care benefits, and unspecified assistantships also available. Support available to part-time students. Financial award application deadline: 4/1; financial award applicants required to submit FAFSA. *Faculty research:* Social/emotional needs of gifted, inclusion transition services, early intervention/ecobehavioral assessments, applied behavioral analysis. *Unit head:* Sonya Wisdom, Coordinator, 330-672-0578, E-mail: swisdom@kent.edu. *Application contact:* Nancy Miller, Academic Program Director, Office of Graduate Student Services, 330-672-2576, Fax: 330-672-9162, E-mail: ogs@kent.edu.
Website: http://www.kent.edu/ehhs/sped/.

Kent State University, Graduate School of Education, Health, and Human Services, School of Teaching, Learning and Curriculum Studies, Program in Early Childhood Education, Kent, OH 44242-0001. Offers M Ed, MA, MAT. *Accreditation:* NCATE. *Faculty:* 4 full-time (all women), 2 part-time/adjunct (both women). *Students:* 15 full-time (14 women), 2 part-time (1 woman); includes 1 minority (Asian, non-Hispanic/Latino), 1 international. 46 applicants, 30% accepted. In 2013, 3 master's awarded. *Degree requirements:* For master's, thesis (for some programs). *Entrance requirements:* For master's, GRE General Test (for licensure), 2 letters of reference, goals statement. Additional exam requirements/recommendations for international students: Required—TOEFL (minimum score 550 paper-based; 80 iBT). *Application deadline:* For spring admission, 3/1 for domestic students. Applications are processed on a rolling basis. Application fee: $30 ($60 for international students). Electronic applications accepted.

Financial support: Research assistantships with full tuition reimbursements, teaching assistantships, Federal Work-Study, scholarships/grants, and unspecified assistantships available. Financial award application deadline: 4/1; financial award applicants required to submit FAFSA. *Faculty research:* Parent-child relationships, professional preparation, curriculum and assessment. *Unit head:* Martha Lash, Coordinator, 330-672-0628, E-mail: mlash@kent.edu. *Application contact:* Nancy Miller, Academic Program Director, Office of Graduate Student Services, 330-672-2576, Fax: 330-672-9162, E-mail: ogs@kent.edu.

Keuka College, Program in Childhood Education/Literacy, Keuka Park, NY 14478-0098. Offers MS. Part-time and evening/weekend programs available. *Faculty:* 5 part-time/adjunct (3 women). *Students:* 4 full-time (all women), 14 part-time (all women). 9 applicants, 100% accepted, 9 enrolled. In 2013, 11 master's awarded. *Degree requirements:* For master's, thesis, research project, portfolio. *Entrance requirements:* For master's, minimum undergraduate GPA of 3.0, 2 letters of recommendation, provisional New York state certification. Additional exam requirements/recommendations for international students: Required—TOEFL (minimum score 550 paper-based). *Application deadline:* For fall admission, 8/15 priority date for domestic students; for winter admission, 12/15 priority date for domestic students; for spring admission, 4/15 priority date for domestic students. Applications are processed on a rolling basis. Application fee: $30. *Expenses:* Contact institution. *Faculty research:* Reading and writing across the curriculum, science education, elementary mathematics education, special education, critical thinking. *Unit head:* Dr. Patricia Pulver, Director of Graduate Program in Education, 315-279-5688 Ext. 5662, E-mail: ppulver@keuka.edu. *Application contact:* Jack Farrel, Dean of Enrollment, 315-279-5296.

La Salle University, School of Arts and Sciences, Program in Education, Philadelphia, PA 19141-1199. Offers American studies (MA); autism spectrum disorders (MA, Certificate); bilingual/bicultural studies (MA); classroom management (MA, Certificate); dual early childhood and special education (MA); dual middle-level science and math and special education secondary education (MA); education (MA); English (MA); English as a second language (Certificate); instructional coach (Certificate); instructional leadership (MA); reading specialist (MA, Certificate); secondary education (MA); special education (MA, Certificate). Part-time and evening/weekend programs available. *Faculty:* 5 full-time (4 women), 16 part-time/adjunct (10 women). *Students:* 18 full-time (13 women), 137 part-time (112 women); includes 33 minority (24 Black or African American, non-Hispanic/Latino; 9 Hispanic/Latino), 4 international. Average age 32. 47 applicants, 96% accepted, 28 enrolled. In 2013, 58 master's, 20 other advanced degrees awarded. *Degree requirements:* For master's, comprehensive exam. *Entrance requirements:* For master's and Certificate, MAT or GRE, 2 letters of recommendation. Additional exam requirements/recommendations for international students: Required—TOEFL. *Application deadline:* For fall admission, 8/15 priority date for domestic students, 7/15 for international students; for spring admission, 12/15 priority date for domestic students, 11/15 for international students; for summer admission, 4/15 priority date for domestic students, 3/15 for international students. Applications are processed on a rolling basis. Application fee: $35. Electronic applications accepted. Application fee is waived when completed online. *Expenses:* Contact institution. *Financial support:* In 2013–14, 28 students received support. Career-related internships or fieldwork, Federal Work-Study, and scholarships/grants available. Support available to part-time students. Financial award application deadline: 8/31; financial award applicants required to submit FAFSA. *Unit head:* Dr. Greer Richardson, Interim Director, 215-951-1806, Fax: 215-951-1843, E-mail: graded@lasalle.edu. *Application contact:* Paul J. Reilly, Assistant Vice President, Enrollment Services, 215-951-1946, Fax: 215-951-1462, E-mail: reilly@lasalle.edu.
Website: http://www.lasalle.edu/grad/index.php?section-education&page-index.

Lehman College of the City University of New York, Division of Education, Department of Early Childhood and Elementary Education, Program in Early Childhood Education, Bronx, NY 10468-1589. Offers MS Ed. *Accreditation:* NCATE. Part-time and evening/weekend programs available. *Entrance requirements:* For master's, minimum GPA of 2.7. *Faculty research:* TV programming, literacy, children's trauma conceptualization.

Le Moyne College, Department of Education, Syracuse, NY 13214. Offers adolescent education (MS Ed, MST); adolescent education/special education (MS Ed, MST); adolescent English (MST), including grades 7-12 (MS Ed, MST); adolescent English/special education (MST), including grades 7-12 (MS Ed, MST); adolescent foreign language (MST), including grades 7-12 (MS Ed, MST); adolescent history (MST), including grades 7-12 (MS Ed, MST); childhood education (MS Ed); childhood education/special education (MS Ed); elementary education (MS Ed); general education (MS Ed); inclusive childhood education (MST); literacy education (MS Ed), including birth to grade 6, grades 5-12; school building leader (MS Ed); school building leadership (CAS); school district business leader (MS Ed, CAS); school district leader (MS Ed); school district leadership (CAS); secondary education (MS Ed); special education (MS Ed); students with disabilities-generalist (MS Ed), including grades 7-12 (MS Ed, MST); teaching English to speakers of other languages (MS Ed); urban studies (MS Ed). *Accreditation:* Teacher Education Accreditation Council. Part-time and evening/weekend programs available. *Faculty:* 8 full-time (5 women), 61 part-time/adjunct (38 women). *Students:* 24 full-time (20 women), 178 part-time (133 women); includes 22 minority (12 Black or African American, non-Hispanic/Latino; 1 American Indian or Alaska Native, non-Hispanic/Latino; 3 Asian, non-Hispanic/Latino; 6 Hispanic/Latino), 1 international. Average age 31. 248 applicants, 90% accepted, 86 enrolled. In 2013, 158 master's, 37 CASs awarded. *Degree requirements:* For master's, thesis. *Entrance requirements:* For master's, GRE General Test, bachelor's degree, 2 letters of recommendation, written statement, transcripts. Additional exam requirements/recommendations for international students: Required—TOEFL (minimum score 550 paper-based; 79 iBT). *Application deadline:* For fall admission, 4/1 priority date for domestic and international students; for spring admission, 10/1 priority date for domestic and international students; for summer admission, 3/1 priority date for domestic and international students. Applications are processed on a rolling basis. Application fee: $50. *Expenses:* Contact institution. *Financial support:* In 2013–14, 26 students received support. Career-related internships or fieldwork and health care benefits available. Support available to part-time students. Financial award applicants required to submit FAFSA. *Faculty research:* Minority teachers, special education, multiculturalism, literacy, technology, media literacy learning, autism, school district organization, service-learning, higher level problem solving, teacher leadership. *Unit head:* Dr. Suzanne L. Gilmour, Chair, Department of Education/Director of Graduate Education Programs, 315-445-4376, Fax: 315-445-4744, E-mail: gilmous@lemoyne.edu. *Application contact:* Kristen P. Trapasso, Senior Director of Enrollment Management, 315-445-4265, Fax: 315-445-6092, E-mail: trapaskp@lemoyne.edu.
Website: http://www.lemoyne.edu/education.

Lenoir-Rhyne University, Graduate Programs, School of Education, Program in Birth through Kindergarten Education, Hickory, NC 28601. Offers MA. Part-time and evening/weekend programs available. *Degree requirements:* For master's, comprehensive exam, thesis optional. *Entrance requirements:* For master's, GRE General Test or MAT, minimum undergraduate GPA of 2.7, graduate 3.0. Additional exam requirements/

recommendations for international students: Required—TOEFL (minimum score 600 paper-based). Electronic applications accepted.

Lesley University, School of Education, Cambridge, MA 02138-2790. Offers arts, community, and education (M Ed); autism studies (Certificate); curriculum and instruction (M Ed, CAGS); early childhood education (M Ed); ecological teaching and learning (MS); educational studies (PhD), including adult learning, educational leadership, individually designed; elementary education (M Ed); emergent technologies for educators (Certificate); ESLArts: language learning through the arts (M Ed); high school education (M Ed); individually designed (M Ed); integrated teaching through the arts (M Ed); literacy for K-8 classroom teachers (M Ed); mathematics education (M Ed); middle school education (M Ed); moderate disabilities (M Ed); online learning (Certificate); reading (CAGS); science in education (M Ed); severe disabilities (M Ed); special needs (CAGS); specialist teacher of reading (M Ed); teacher of visual art (M Ed); technology in education (M Ed, CAGS). *Accreditation:* Teacher Education Accreditation Council. Part-time and evening/weekend programs available. Postbaccalaureate distance learning degree programs offered (no on-campus study). *Faculty:* 40 full-time (30 women), 104 part-time/adjunct (77 women). *Students:* 453 full-time (381 women), 1,672 part-time (1,435 women); includes 284 minority (139 Black or African American, non-Hispanic/Latino; 11 American Indian or Alaska Native, non-Hispanic/Latino; 38 Asian, non-Hispanic/Latino; 58 Hispanic/Latino; 5 Native Hawaiian or other Pacific Islander, non-Hispanic/Latino; 33 Two or more races, non-Hispanic/Latino), 22 international. Average age 35. In 2013, 1,137 master's, 18 doctorates, 51 other advanced degrees awarded. *Degree requirements:* For master's, practicum; for doctorate, thesis/dissertation. *Entrance requirements:* For master's, Massachusetts Tests for Educator Licensure (MTEL), transcripts, statement of purpose, recommendations; interview (for special education); for doctorate, GRE General Test, transcripts, statement of purpose, recommendations, interview, master's degree, resume; for other advanced degree, interview, master's degree. Additional exam requirements/recommendations for international students: Required—TOEFL (minimum score 550 paper-based; 80 iBT). *Application deadline:* Applications are processed on a rolling basis. Application fee: $50. Electronic applications accepted. *Expenses: Tuition:* Part-time $900 per credit. *Financial support:* In 2013–14, 15 fellowships (averaging $3,600 per year) were awarded; career-related internships or fieldwork, Federal Work-Study, scholarships/grants, tuition waivers, and unspecified assistantships also available. Financial award application deadline: 4/15; financial award applicants required to submit FAFSA. *Faculty research:* Assessment in literacy, mathematics and science; autism spectrum disorders; instructional technology and online learning; multicultural education and English language learners. *Unit head:* Dr. Jack Gillette, Dean, 617-349-8401, Fax: 617-349-8607, E-mail: jgillett@lesley.edu. *Application contact:* Martha Sheehan, Director of Admissions, 888-LESLEYU, Fax: 617-349-8313, E-mail: info@lesley.edu.
Website: http://www.lesley.edu/soe.html.

Lewis & Clark College, Graduate School of Education and Counseling, Department of Teacher Education, Program in Early Childhood/Elementary Education, Portland, OR 97219-7899. Offers MAT. *Accreditation:* NCATE. *Entrance requirements:* For master's, minimum undergraduate GPA of 2.75; history of work, either volunteer or paid, with children in grades K-6. Additional exam requirements/recommendations for international students: Required—TOEFL (minimum score 575 paper-based). Electronic applications accepted. *Faculty research:* Classroom ethnography, assessing student learning, reading, moral development, language arts.

Lewis University, College of Education, Romeoville, IL 60446. Offers advanced study in education (CAS), including general administrative, superintendent endorsement; curriculum and instruction: instructional technology (M Ed); early childhood education (MA); educational leadership (M Ed, MA); educational leadership for teaching and learning (Ed D); elementary education (MA); English as a second language (M Ed); instructional technology (M Ed); reading and literacy (M Ed, MA); secondary education (MA), including biology, chemistry, English, history, math, physics, psychology and social science; special education (MA). *Accreditation:* NCATE. Part-time and evening/weekend programs available. *Students:* 75 full-time (58 women), 362 part-time (281 women); includes 90 minority (48 Black or African American, non-Hispanic/Latino; 6 Asian, non-Hispanic/Latino; 33 Hispanic/Latino; 3 Two or more races, non-Hispanic/Latino), 6 international. *Degree requirements:* For master's, thesis optional; for doctorate, thesis/dissertation. *Entrance requirements:* For master's, departmental qualifying exam, writing exam, minimum GPA of 2.75, 3 letters of recommendation, interview. Additional exam requirements/recommendations for international students: Required—TOEFL (minimum score 550 paper-based; 80 iBT). *Application deadline:* For fall admission, 5/1 priority date for international students; for spring admission, 11/15 priority date for international students. Applications are processed on a rolling basis. Application fee: $40. Electronic applications accepted. *Financial support:* Federal Work-Study, scholarships/grants, tuition waivers (partial), and unspecified assistantships available. Financial award application deadline: 5/1; financial award applicants required to submit FAFSA. *Unit head:* Dr. Pamela Jessee, Dean, 815-836-5316, E-mail: jesseepa@lewisu.edu. *Application contact:* Linda Campbell, Graduate Admission Counselor, 815-836-5704, Fax: 815-836-5578, E-mail: campbeli@lewisu.edu.

Liberty University, School of Education, Lynchburg, VA 24515. Offers administration and supervision (M Ed); curriculum and instruction (Ed D, Ed S); early childhood education (M Ed); educational leadership (Ed D, Ed S); educational technology and online instruction (M Ed); elementary education (M Ed, MAT); English (M Ed); gifted education (M Ed); history (M Ed); leadership (M Ed); math specialist (M Ed); middle grades (M Ed, MAT); outdoor adventure sport (MS); reading specialist (M Ed); school counseling (M Ed); secondary education (MAT); special education (M Ed, MAT); sport management (MS), including administration, outdoor recreation, sport management, tourism; sports administration (MS); student service (M Ed); teaching and learning (M Ed); tourism (MS). *Accreditation:* NCATE. Part-time programs available. Postbaccalaureate distance learning degree programs offered (minimal on-campus study). *Students:* 2,241 full-time (1,639 women), 4,413 part-time (3,240 women); includes 2,052 minority (1,588 Black or African American, non-Hispanic/Latino; 37 American Indian or Alaska Native, non-Hispanic/Latino; 67 Asian, non-Hispanic/Latino; 173 Hispanic/Latino; 37 Native Hawaiian or other Pacific Islander, non-Hispanic/Latino; 150 Two or more races, non-Hispanic/Latino), 15 international. Average age 37. 6,185 applicants, 43% accepted, 1603 enrolled. In 2013, 1,256 master's, 117 doctorates, 470 other advanced degrees awarded. *Degree requirements:* For doctorate, comprehensive exam, thesis/dissertation. *Entrance requirements:* For master's, GRE General Test or MAT (if taken in or before 1999), 2 letters of recommendation, minimum undergraduate GPA of 3.0, curriculum vitae; for doctorate and Ed S, GRE General Test or MAT (if taken before 1999), minimum master's GPA of 3.0, 3 years of teaching experience. Additional exam requirements/recommendations for international students: Required—TOEFL (minimum score 600 paper-based; 100 iBT). *Application deadline:* For fall admission, 6/1 for domestic students; for spring admission, 11/1 for domestic students. Applications are processed on a rolling basis. Application fee: $50. Electronic applications accepted. *Expenses:* Contact institution. *Financial support:* Federal Work-Study and tuition waivers (partial) available. *Faculty research:* Self-determination, character education, bibliotherapy, learning styles, distance education. *Unit head:* Dr. Karen L. Parker, Dean, 434-582-2195, Fax: 434-582-2468, E-mail: kparker@liberty.edu. *Application contact:* Jay Bridge, Director of Graduate Admissions, 800-424-9595, Fax: 800-628-7977, E-mail: gradadmissions@liberty.edu.
Website: http://www.liberty.edu/academics/education/graduate/.

Lincoln University, Graduate Programs, Philadelphia , PA 19104. Offers early childhood education (M Ed); educational leadership (M Ed); human resources (MSA), including finance, human resources management; human services (MHS); reading (MSR). Evening/weekend programs available. *Faculty:* 10 full-time (4 women), 34 part-time/adjunct (19 women). *Students:* 224 full-time (145 women), 115 part-time (74 women); includes 328 minority (311 Black or African American, non-Hispanic/Latino; 17 Hispanic/Latino). Average age 40. 237 applicants, 65% accepted, 64 enrolled. In 2013, 155 master's awarded. *Degree requirements:* For master's, thesis. *Entrance requirements:* For master's, working as full-time, paid staff member in the human services field, at least one year of paid experience in this field, and undergraduate degree in human services or a related field from an accredited institution (for MHS). *Application deadline:* For fall admission, 6/1 priority date for domestic and international students. Applications are processed on a rolling basis. Application fee: $50. *Expenses:* Tuition, state resident: full-time $10,106; part-time $567 per hour. Tuition, nonresident: full-time $17,636; part-time $949 per hour. *Financial support:* Application deadline: 8/1. *Unit head:* Dr. Cheryl Gooch, Dean, School of Humanities and Graduate Studies, 484-365-7664, E-mail: cgooch@lincoln.edu. *Application contact:* Jernice Lea, Director of Graduate Admissions, 215-590-8233, Fax: 215-387-3859, E-mail: jlea@lincoln.edu.
Website: http://www.lincoln.edu/academicaffairs/uc.html.

Long Island University–Brentwood Campus, School of Education, Brentwood, NY 11717. Offers childhood education (MS); early childhood education (MS); literacy (MS); mental health counseling (MS); school counseling (MS); special education (MS). Part-time and evening/weekend programs available.

Long Island University–Hudson at Rockland, Graduate School, Program in Curriculum and Instruction, Orangeburg, NY 10962. Offers adolescence education (MS Ed); childhood education (MS Ed). Part-time and evening/weekend programs available. *Degree requirements:* For master's, LAST and CST exams. *Entrance requirements:* For master's, college transcripts, letters of recommendation, personal statement.

Long Island University–Hudson at Westchester, Programs in Education-Teaching, Program in Early Childhood Education, Purchase, NY 10577. Offers MS Ed, Advanced Certificate.

Long Island University–LIU Post, School of Education, Department of Curriculum and Instruction, Brookville, NY 11548-1300. Offers adolescence education (MS); adolescence education: biology (MS); adolescence education: earth science (MS); adolescence education: English (MS); adolescence education: mathematics (MS); adolescence education: social studies (MS); adolescence education: Spanish (MS); art education (MS); bilingual education (MS); childhood education (MS); early childhood education (MS); middle childhood education (MS); music education (MS); teaching English to speakers of other languages (MS). Part-time and evening/weekend programs available. *Degree requirements:* For master's, comprehensive exam or thesis, student teaching. *Entrance requirements:* For master's, minimum GPA of 2.75 in major, 2.5 overall. Electronic applications accepted. *Faculty research:* Ethics and education, teaching strategies.

Long Island University–Riverhead, Education Division, Program in Childhood Education, Riverhead, NY 11901. Offers childhood education (MS Ed); elementary education (MS Ed). *Accreditation:* Teacher Education Accreditation Council. *Degree requirements:* For master's, thesis. *Entrance requirements:* For master's, minimum undergraduate GPA of 2.75, on-campus writing sample. Additional exam requirements/recommendations for international students: Required—TOEFL (minimum score 550 paper-based). Electronic applications accepted.

Louisiana Tech University, Graduate School, College of Education, Department of Curriculum, Instruction and Leadership, Ruston, LA 71272. Offers curriculum and instruction (M Ed, Ed D), including adult education (M Ed), early childhood (M Ed), English education (M Ed), mathematics education (M Ed), science education (M Ed), social studies education (M Ed), special education (M Ed); educational leadership (M Ed, Ed D). *Accreditation:* NCATE. Part-time programs available. *Degree requirements:* For doctorate, thesis/dissertation. *Entrance requirements:* For master's and doctorate, GRE General Test. *Application deadline:* For fall admission, 7/29 for domestic students; for spring admission, 2/3 for domestic students. Application fee: $20 ($30 for international students). *Financial support:* Fellowships, research assistantships, and teaching assistantships available. Financial award application deadline: 2/1. *Unit head:* Dr. Pauline Leonard, Head, 318-257-4609, Fax: 318-257-2379. *Application contact:* Dr. John Harrison, Associate Dean of Graduate Studies, 318-257-3229, Fax: 318-257-2379, E-mail: johnharrison@latech.edu.
Website: http://www.latech.edu/education/cil/.

Loyola Marymount University, School of Education, Department of Elementary and Secondary Education, Program in Early Childhood Education, Los Angeles, CA 90045. Offers MA. Part-time and evening/weekend programs available. *Faculty:* 5 full-time (4 women), 19 part-time/adjunct (11 women). *Students:* 27 full-time (22 women), 2 part-time (both women); includes 17 minority (3 Black or African American, non-Hispanic/Latino; 3 Asian, non-Hispanic/Latino; 11 Hispanic/Latino). Average age 27. 25 applicants, 80% accepted, 17 enrolled. In 2013, 17 master's awarded. *Degree requirements:* For master's, comprehensive exam. *Entrance requirements:* For master's, 3 letters of recommendation. Additional exam requirements/recommendations for international students: Required—TOEFL (minimum score 600 paper-based; 100 iBT). *Application deadline:* For fall admission, 6/15 for domestic students. Application fee: $50. Electronic applications accepted. *Financial support:* In 2013–14, 15 students received support, including 1 research assistantship (averaging $1,440 per year); scholarships/grants and unspecified assistantships also available. Support available to part-time students. Financial award application deadline: 6/30; financial award applicants required to submit FAFSA. *Total annual research expenditures:* $132,233. *Unit head:* Dr. Leslie Ponciano, Program Director, 310-338-6595, E-mail: lponcian@lmu.edu. *Application contact:* Chake H. Kouyoumjian, Director, Graduate Admissions, 310-338-2721, E-mail: ckouyoum@lmu.edu.
Website: http://soe.lmu.edu/admissions/programs/earlychildhoodeducation/.

Loyola University Maryland, Graduate Programs, School of Education, Program in Montessori Education, Baltimore, MD 21210-2699. Offers elementary education (M Ed); Montessori education (CAS); primary education (M Ed). *Accreditation:* NCATE. *Entrance requirements:* For master's, essay, 3 letters of recommendation, transcripts, resume. Additional exam requirements/recommendations for international students: Required—TOEFL (minimum score 550 paper-based).

Loyola University Maryland, Graduate Programs, School of Education, Program in Special Education, Baltimore, MD 21210-2699. Offers early childhood education (M Ed, CAS); elementary/middle education (M Ed, CAS); secondary education (M Ed, CAS). *Accreditation:* NCATE. Part-time programs available. *Entrance requirements:* For master's, transcript, essay, letter of recommendation. Additional exam requirements/recommendations for international students: Required—TOEFL (minimum score 550 paper-based). Electronic applications accepted.

Manhattan College, Graduate Programs, School of Education and Health, Program in Special Education, Riverdale, NY 10471. Offers adolescent special education generalist in English, math or social studies (MS Ed); autism spectrum disorder (Certificate); bilingual special education (Professional Diploma); dual childhood/special education (MS Ed); special education (MS Ed). Part-time and evening/weekend programs available. *Faculty:* 8 full-time (5 women), 16 part-time/adjunct (12 women). *Students:* 30 full-time (28 women), 68 part-time (61 women). Average age 24. 86 applicants, 94% accepted, 76 enrolled. In 2013, 37 master's awarded. *Degree requirements:* For master's, thesis, internship (if not certified). *Entrance requirements:* For master's, minimum GPA of 3.0. Additional exam requirements/recommendations for international students: Required—TOEFL (minimum score 550 paper-based). *Application deadline:* For fall admission, 8/10 priority date for domestic students; for spring admission, 1/7 priority date for domestic students. Applications are processed on a rolling basis. Application fee: $60. *Expenses:* Contact institution. *Financial support:* Federal Work-Study, scholarships/grants, and unspecified assistantships available. Financial award application deadline: 2/1. *Unit head:* Dr. Elizabeth Mary Kosky, Director of Childhood/Adolescent Special Education Programs, 718-862-7969, Fax: 718-862-7816, E-mail: elizabeth.kosky@manhattan.edu. *Application contact:* William Bisset, Information Contact, 718-862-8000, E-mail: william.bisset@manhattan.edu. Website: http://www.manhattan.edu/academics/education/special-education-dept.

Manhattanville College, School of Education, Program in Childhood Education, Purchase, NY 10577-2132. Offers childhood and special education (MPS); childhood education (MAT); special education childhood (MPS). Part-time and evening/weekend programs available. *Degree requirements:* For master's, comprehensive exam or research project, field experience. *Entrance requirements:* For master's, minimum undergraduate GPA of 3.0, 2 letters of recommendation. Additional exam requirements/recommendations for international students: Required—TOEFL.

Manhattanville College, School of Education, Program in Early Childhood Education, Purchase, NY 10577-2132. Offers early childhood education (MAT); early childhood and special education (birth-grade 2) (MPS); early childhood education (birth-grade 2) (MAT); special education (birth-grade 2) (MPS); special education (birth-grade 6) (MPS). Part-time and evening/weekend programs available. *Degree requirements:* For master's, comprehensive exam or research project, field experience. *Entrance requirements:* For master's, minimum undergraduate GPA of 3.0, 2 letters of recommendation. Additional exam requirements/recommendations for international students: Required—TOEFL. Electronic applications accepted.

Marshall University, Academic Affairs Division, College of Education and Professional Development, Program in Early Childhood Education, Huntington, WV 25755. Offers MA. *Accreditation:* NCATE. Evening/weekend programs available. *Students:* 7 part-time (all women). Average age 32. In 2013, 2 master's awarded. *Degree requirements:* For master's, thesis optional, comprehensive or oral assessment. *Entrance requirements:* For master's, GRE General Test or MAT. Application fee: $40. *Unit head:* Dr. Lisa Heaton, Director, 304-746-2026, E-mail: heaton@marshall.edu. *Application contact:* Information Contact, Graduate Admissions, 304-746-1900, Fax: 304-746-1902, E-mail: services@marshall.edu.

Maryville University of Saint Louis, School of Education, St. Louis, MO 63141-7299. Offers art education (MA Ed); early childhood education (MA Ed); educational leadership (Ed D); educational leadership: principal certification (MA Ed); elementary education (MA Ed); gifted education (MA Ed); higher education leadership (Ed D); literacy specialist (MA Ed); middle grades education (MA Ed); secondary teaching and inquiry (MA Ed); teacher as leader (MA Ed); teacher leadership (Ed D). *Accreditation:* NCATE. Part-time and evening/weekend programs available. *Faculty:* 10 full-time (6 women), 17 part-time/adjunct (13 women). *Students:* 21 full-time (17 women), 238 part-time (167 women); includes 64 minority (54 Black or African American, non-Hispanic/Latino; 2 Asian, non-Hispanic/Latino; 4 Hispanic/Latino; 4 Two or more races, non-Hispanic/Latino), 2 international. Average age 39. In 2013, 61 master's, 40 doctorates awarded. *Degree requirements:* For master's, thesis, project. *Entrance requirements:* For master's, minimum cumulative GPA of 3.0, 3 professional recommendations, essays, interview with program faculty; for doctorate, minimum GPA of 3.0, 3 professional recommendations, essay, interview, on-site writing sample. Additional exam requirements/recommendations for international students: Required—TOEFL (minimum score 550 paper-based). *Application deadline:* Applications are processed on a rolling basis. Application fee: $40 ($60 for international students). Electronic applications accepted. Application fee is waived when completed online. *Expenses:* Tuition: Full-time $23,812; part-time $728 per credit hour. *Required fees:* $395 per year. Tuition and fees vary according to course load, degree level and program. *Financial support:* Career-related internships or fieldwork, Federal Work-Study, tuition waivers (partial), and professional educator discounts available. Financial award application deadline: 3/1; financial award applicants required to submit FAFSA. *Faculty research:* Collaboration with public schools, pre-service program development, mathematics, diversity, literacy. *Unit head:* Dr. Cathy Bear, Dean, 314-529-9692, Fax: 314-529-9921, E-mail: cbear@maryville.edu. *Application contact:* Holly Stanwich, Graduate Admissions Coordinator, 314-529-9542, Fax: 314-529-9921, E-mail: teachered@maryville.edu. Website: http://www.maryville.edu/ed/graduate-programs/.

Marywood University, Academic Affairs, Reap College of Education and Human Development, Department of Education, Program in Early Childhood Intervention, Scranton, PA 18509-1598. Offers birth to age 9 (MS). *Accreditation:* NCATE. *Entrance requirements:* Additional exam requirements/recommendations for international students: Required—TOEFL (minimum score 550 paper-based; 79 iBT). *Application deadline:* For fall admission, 4/1 priority date for domestic students, 3/31 priority date for international students; for spring admission, 11/1 priority date for domestic students, 8/31 priority date for international students. Applications are processed on a rolling basis. Application fee: $35. Electronic applications accepted. *Expenses: Tuition:* Part-time $775 per credit. Tuition and fees vary according to degree level. *Financial support:* Career-related internships or fieldwork, scholarships/grants, and unspecified assistantships available. Support available to part-time students. Financial award application deadline: 6/30; financial award applicants required to submit FAFSA. *Faculty research:* Montessori education, developmentally-appropriate practice, child care environment. *Unit head:* Dr. Patricia S. Arter, Chairperson, 570-348-6211 Ext. 2511, E-mail: psarter@marywood.edu. *Application contact:* Tammy Manka, Assistant Director of Graduate Admissions, 570-348-6211 Ext. 2322, E-mail: tmanka@marywood.edu. Website: http://www.marywood.edu/education/graduate-programs/ms-early-childhood-intervention.html.

McNeese State University, Doré School of Graduate Studies, Burton College of Education, Office of Graduate Education Programs, Program in Curriculum and Instruction, Lake Charles, LA 70609. Offers early childhood education (M Ed); elementary education (M Ed); reading (M Ed); secondary education (M Ed). Evening/weekend programs available. *Entrance requirements:* For master's, GRE, teaching certificate.

McNeese State University, Doré School of Graduate Studies, Burton College of Education, Office of Student Teaching and Professional Education Services, Program in Early Childhood Education Grades PK-3, Lake Charles, LA 70609. Offers

Postbaccalaureate Certificate. *Entrance requirements:* For degree, PRAXIS, 2 letters of recommendation, autobiography.

Mercer University, Graduate Studies, Cecil B. Day Campus, Tift College of Education (Atlanta), Macon, GA 31207-0003. Offers curriculum and instruction (PhD); early childhood education (M Ed, MAT, Ed S); educational leadership (PhD, Ed S); higher education leadership (M Ed); independent and charter school leadership (M Ed); middle grades education (M Ed, MAT); reading education (M Ed); school counseling (Ed S); secondary education (M Ed, MAT); teacher leadership (Ed S). *Accreditation:* NCATE. Part-time and evening/weekend programs available. *Faculty:* 40 full-time (20 women), 9 part-time/adjunct (4 women). *Students:* 240 full-time (197 women), 382 part-time (320 women); includes 343 minority (315 Black or African American, non-Hispanic/Latino; 4 American Indian or Alaska Native, non-Hispanic/Latino; 9 Asian, non-Hispanic/Latino; 9 Hispanic/Latino; 1 Native Hawaiian or other Pacific Islander, non-Hispanic/Latino; 5 Two or more races, non-Hispanic/Latino), 4 international. Average age 36. In 2013, 233 master's, 24 doctorates, 47 other advanced degrees awarded. *Degree requirements:* For master's and Ed S, research project; for doctorate, comprehensive exam, thesis/dissertation. *Entrance requirements:* For master's, GRE or MAT, minimum undergraduate GPA of 2.75; for doctorate, GRE; for Ed S, GRE or MAT, minimum GPA of 3.25; for EDS degrees in educational leadership and teacher leadership: 3 years of certified teaching experience. Additional exam requirements/recommendations for international students: Required—TOEFL. *Application deadline:* For fall admission, 8/1 for domestic and international students; for spring admission, 12/1 for domestic and international students; for summer admission, 5/1 for domestic and international students. Applications are processed on a rolling basis. Application fee: $25. *Expenses:* Contact institution. *Financial support:* Federal Work-Study available. Support available to part-time students. Financial award application deadline: 5/1. *Faculty research:* Educational technology, multicultural and minority issues in education, educational leadership (P-12 and higher education), school discipline and school bullying, standards-based mathematics education. *Unit head:* Dr. Paige L. Tompkins, Interim Dean, 478-301-5397, Fax: 478-301-2280, E-mail: tompkins_pl@mercer.edu. *Application contact:* Dr. Allison Gilmore, Associate Dean for Graduate Teacher Education, 678-547-6333, Fax: 678-547-6055, E-mail: gilmore_a@mercer.edu. Website: http://www.mercer.edu/education/.

Mercy College, School of Education, Program in Early Childhood Education, Dobbs Ferry, NY 10522-1189. Offers MS. Part-time and evening/weekend programs available. Postbaccalaureate distance learning degree programs offered (no on-campus study). *Students:* 314 full-time (309 women), 258 part-time (245 women); includes 205 minority (99 Black or African American, non-Hispanic/Latino; 5 Asian, non-Hispanic/Latino; 96 Hispanic/Latino; 5 Two or more races, non-Hispanic/Latino), 2 international. Average age 32. 294 applicants, 76% accepted, 169 enrolled. In 2013, 440 master's awarded. *Degree requirements:* For master's, comprehensive exam (for some programs). *Entrance requirements:* For master's, resume, undergraduate transcript. Additional exam requirements/recommendations for international students: Required—TOEFL (minimum score 600 paper-based; 100 iBT), IELTS (minimum score 8). *Application deadline:* For fall admission, 8/1 for international students. Applications are processed on a rolling basis. Application fee: $40. Electronic applications accepted. *Expenses: Tuition:* Full-time $19,344; part-time $806 per credit. *Required fees:* $580; $806 per credit. $145 per term. Tuition and fees vary according to course load, degree level and program. *Financial support:* Career-related internships or fieldwork, Federal Work-Study, scholarships/grants, and unspecified assistantships available. Support available to part-time students. Financial award applicants required to submit FAFSA. *Unit head:* Dr. Alfred S. Posamentier, Dean for the School of Education, 914-674-7350, E-mail: aposamentier@mercy.edu. *Application contact:* Allison Gurdineer, Senior Director of Admissions, 877-637-2946, Fax: 914-674-7382, E-mail: admissions@mercy.edu. Website: https://www.mercy.edu/academics/school-of-education/department-of-early-childhood-childhood-education/ms-in-childhood-education-birth-grade-2/.

Merrimack College, School of Education, North Andover, MA 01845-5800. Offers community engagement (M Ed), including community organizations, higher education, K-12 education; early childhood education (M Ed); elementary education (M Ed); English as a second language (PreK-6) (M Ed); English language learners (M Ed); general studies (M Ed); higher education (M Ed), including leadership and organizational development, student affairs; middle (M Ed); moderate disabilities (PreK-8) (M Ed); secondary (M Ed); teacher leadership (CAGS), including instructional leadership, reading specialist. Part-time and evening/weekend programs available. *Faculty:* 4 full-time (all women), 23 part-time/adjunct (15 women). *Students:* 127 full-time (104 women), 61 part-time (52 women); includes 3 minority (1 Asian, non-Hispanic/Latino; 2 Hispanic/Latino), 2 international. Average age 25. 403 applicants, 47% accepted, 138 enrolled. In 2013, 140 master's awarded. *Degree requirements:* For master's, practicum, portfolio, and state test (for licensure track); capstone (for higher education and community engagement tracks). *Entrance requirements:* For master's, MTEL (Massachusetts Tests for Educator Licensure), official transcripts from other colleges, resume, personal statement, 2 letters of recommendation, additional essay requirements for fellowships. Additional exam requirements/recommendations for international students: Required—TOEFL (minimum score 84 iBT), IELTS (minimum score 6.5). *Application deadline:* For fall admission, 8/15 for domestic and international students; for winter admission, 12/1 for domestic students, 11/15 for international students; for spring admission, 1/10 for domestic and international students; for summer admission, 5/10 for domestic and international students. Applications are processed on a rolling basis. Application fee: $0. Electronic applications accepted. Tuition and fees vary according to course load and program. *Financial support:* In 2013–14, 91 fellowships with full tuition reimbursements were awarded; career-related internships or fieldwork, scholarships/grants, and health care benefits also available. Support available to part-time students. Financial award applicants required to submit FAFSA. *Faculty research:* Expressive language, civic engagement, family life education, reading genres, the psychological process of aging. *Application contact:* Kristen English, Interim Director of Graduate Admission, 978-837-5073, E-mail: englishkr@merrimack.edu. Website: http://www.merrimack.edu/academics/graduate/education/.

Middle Tennessee State University, College of Graduate Studies, College of Education, Department of Elementary and Special Education, Major in Curriculum and Instruction, Murfreesboro, TN 37132. Offers early childhood education (M Ed); elementary education (M Ed, Ed S); middle school education (M Ed). *Accreditation:* NCATE. Part-time and evening/weekend programs available. Postbaccalaureate distance learning degree programs offered. *Faculty:* 14 full-time (9 women), 7 part-time/adjunct (all women). *Degree requirements:* For master's, comprehensive exam; for Ed S, comprehensive exam, thesis or alternative. *Entrance requirements:* For master's and Ed S, GRE, MAT or PRAXIS. Additional exam requirements/recommendations for international students: Required—TOEFL (minimum score 525 paper-based; 71 iBT) or IELTS (minimum score 6). *Application deadline:* For fall admission, 8/1 priority date for domestic students. Applications are processed on a rolling basis. Application fee: $25. Electronic applications accepted. *Financial support:* Tuition waivers available. Support available to part-time students. Financial award application deadline: 5/1. *Unit head:* Dr. Kathleen Burriss, Interim Chair, 615-898-2680, Fax: 615-898-5309, E-mail: kathleen.burriss@mtsu.edu. *Application contact:* Dr. Michael D. Allen, Vice Provost for

Research and Dean, 615-898-2840, Fax: 615-904-8020, E-mail: michael.allen@mtsu.edu.

Millersville University of Pennsylvania, College of Graduate and Professional Studies, School of Education, Department of Elementary and Early Childhood Education, Program in Early Childhood Education, Millersville, PA 17551-0302. Offers M Ed. Part-time and evening/weekend programs available. *Faculty:* 17 full-time (11 women), 18 part-time/adjunct (15 women). *Students:* 4 full-time (all women), 17 part-time (all women); includes 1 minority (Black or African American, non-Hispanic/Latino). Average age 30. 6 applicants, 100% accepted, 5 enrolled. In 2013, 5 master's awarded. *Degree requirements:* For master's, thesis optional. *Entrance requirements:* For master's, GRE or MAT, 3 letters of recommendation; copy of teaching certificate, goal statement, official transcripts. Additional exam requirements/recommendations for international students: Required—TOEFL (minimum score 550 paper-based, 79 iBT) or IELTS (minimum score 6). *Application deadline:* For fall admission, 1/15 priority date for domestic and international students; for winter admission, 10/1 priority date for domestic and international students; for spring admission, 10/1 priority date for domestic and international students. Applications are processed on a rolling basis. Application fee: $40. Electronic applications accepted. *Expenses:* Tuition, state resident: full-time $7956; part-time $442 per credit. Tuition, nonresident: full-time $11,934; part-time $663 per credit. *Required fees:* $2196; $122 per credit. Tuition and fees vary according to course load. *Financial support:* In 2013–14, 1 student received support, including 1 research assistantship with full tuition reimbursement available (averaging $5,000 per year); institutionally sponsored loans and unspecified assistantships also available. Support available to part-time students. Financial award application deadline: 3/15; financial award applicants required to submit FAFSA. *Faculty research:* Play, creativity, professional development, professional development schools. *Unit head:* Dr. Marcia L. Nell, Coordinator, 717-872-2170, Fax: 717-871-5462, E-mail: marcia.nell@millersville.edu. *Application contact:* Dr. Victor S. DeSantis, Dean of College of Graduate and Professional Studies/Associate Provost for Civic and Community Engagement, 717-872-3099, Fax: 717-872-3453, E-mail: victor.desantis@millersville.edu.
Website: http://www.millersville.edu/academics/educ/eled/graduate.php.

Mills College, Graduate Studies, Program in Infant Mental Health, Oakland, CA 94613-1000. Offers MA. Part-time programs available. *Faculty:* 2 full-time (both women). *Students:* 12 full-time (all women); includes 3 minority (1 Black or African American, non-Hispanic/Latino; 1 Hispanic/Latino; 1 Two or more races, non-Hispanic/Latino). Average age 27. 10 applicants, 70% accepted, 6 enrolled. In 2013, 11 master's awarded. *Entrance requirements:* For master's, bachelor's degree, preferably in psychology, and the following prerequisite courses: fundamentals of psychology, developmental psychology, psychopathology, analytical methods/statistics, research methods; three letters of recommendation; statement of purpose essay. Additional exam requirements/recommendations for international students: Required—TOEFL (minimum score 550 paper-based; 80 iBT) or IELTS (minimum score 6). *Application deadline:* For fall admission, 12/31 priority date for domestic students, 12/15 for international students. Applications are processed on a rolling basis. *Expenses: Tuition:* Full-time $29,860. *Required fees:* $1134. Part-time tuition and fees vary according to course load, degree level and program. *Financial support:* In 2013–14, 12 fellowships with full and partial tuition reimbursements (averaging $9,225 per year) were awarded; scholarships/grants also available. Financial award application deadline: 2/1; financial award applicants required to submit FAFSA. *Faculty research:* Development and sequelae of attachment in children and adults in normative and clinical/risk populations, identifying the mental health needs of young children who have experienced extraordinary traumatic situations during critical points in their early development, examining the effects of early childhood trauma, work on helping professionals' psychological well-being. *Unit head:* Linda Perez, Professor of Education, 510-430-2328, Fax: 510-430-2159, E-mail: lmperez@mills.edu. *Application contact:* Shrim Bathey, Director of Graduate Admission, 510-430-3309, Fax: 510-430-2159, E-mail: grad-admission@mills.edu.
Website: http://www.mills.edu/imh/.

Mills College, Graduate Studies, School of Education, Oakland, CA 94613-1000. Offers child life in hospitals (MA); early childhood education (MA); education (MA), including art education, curriculum and instruction, elementary education, English education, foreign language education, mathematics education, science education, secondary education, social studies education, teaching; educational leadership (MA, Ed D). Part-time and evening/weekend programs available. *Faculty:* 10 full-time (7 women), 13 part-time/adjunct (10 women). *Students:* 154 full-time (136 women), 54 part-time (47 women); includes 96 minority (32 Black or African American, non-Hispanic/Latino; 1 American Indian or Alaska Native, non-Hispanic/Latino; 23 Asian, non-Hispanic/Latino; 27 Hispanic/Latino; 1 Native Hawaiian or other Pacific Islander, non-Hispanic/Latino; 12 Two or more races, non-Hispanic/Latino), 2 international. Average age 25. 222 applicants, 89% accepted, 110 enrolled. In 2013, 96 master's, 38 doctorates awarded. Terminal master's awarded for partial completion of doctoral program. *Degree requirements:* For master's, comprehensive exam, thesis (for some programs); for doctorate, thesis/dissertation. *Entrance requirements:* For master's, statement of purpose, official transcript, 3 recommendations. Additional exam requirements/recommendations for international students: Required—TOEFL (minimum score 550 paper-based; 80 iBT) or IELTS (minimum score 6). *Application deadline:* For fall admission, 12/31 priority date for domestic students, 12/15 for international students; for spring admission, 11/1 priority date for domestic students, 10/1 for international students. Applications are processed on a rolling basis. Application fee: $50. Electronic applications accepted. *Expenses: Tuition:* Full-time $29,860. *Required fees:* $1134. Part-time tuition and fees vary according to course load, degree level and program. *Financial support:* In 2013–14, 130 students received support, including 130 fellowships with full and partial tuition reimbursements available (averaging $7,565 per year); career-related internships or fieldwork and scholarships/grants also available. Support available to part-time students. Financial award application deadline: 2/1; financial award applicants required to submit FAFSA. *Faculty research:* Early childhood education, teacher preparation, educational leadership. *Total annual research expenditures:* $3.5 million. *Unit head:* Dr. Katherine Schultz, Department Head, 510-430-3384, Fax: 510-430-2159, E-mail: kschultz@mills.edu. *Application contact:* Shrim Bathey, Director of Graduate Admission, 510-430-3309, Fax: 510-430-2159, E-mail: grad-admission@mills.edu.
Website: http://www.mills.edu/education.

Minnesota State University Mankato, College of Graduate Studies, College of Education, Department of Elementary and Early Childhood Education, Mankato, MN 56001. Offers MS, Certificate. *Accreditation:* NCATE. Part-time programs available. *Students:* 6 full-time (all women), 89 part-time (84 women). *Degree requirements:* For master's, comprehensive exam, thesis or alternative. *Entrance requirements:* For master's, GRE General Test or MAT, minimum GPA of 3.0 during previous 2 years. Additional exam requirements/recommendations for international students: Required—TOEFL. *Application deadline:* For fall admission, 7/1 priority date for domestic students; for spring admission, 11/1 for domestic students. Applications are processed on a rolling basis. Application fee: $40. Electronic applications accepted. *Financial support:* Application deadline: 3/15; applicants required to submit FAFSA. *Unit head:* Dr. Peggy Ballard, Graduate Coordinator, 507-389-1516. *Application contact:* 507-389-2321, E-mail: grad@mnsu.edu.
Website: http://ed.mnsu.edu/eec/.

Minot State University, Graduate School, Program in Special Education, Minot, ND 58707-0002. Offers education of the deaf (MS); learning disabilities (MS); special education strategist (MS), including early childhood special education, severe multiple handicaps. *Accreditation:* NCATE. *Degree requirements:* For master's, comprehensive exam (for some programs), thesis (for some programs). *Entrance requirements:* For master's, GRE General Test or minimum GPA of 3.0. Additional exam requirements/recommendations for international students: Required—TOEFL. *Faculty research:* Special education team diagnostic unit; individual diagnostic assessments of mentally retarded, learning-disabled, hearing-impaired, and speech-impaired youth; educational programming for the hearing impaired.

Mississippi State University, College of Education, Department of Curriculum, Instruction and Special Education, Mississippi State, MS 39762. Offers curriculum and instruction (PhD), including early childhood education (MS, PhD), elementary education (PhD, Ed S), general curriculum and instruction, reading education, secondary education (PhD, Ed S), special education (PhD, Ed S); education (Ed S), including elementary education (PhD, Ed S), secondary education (PhD, Ed S), special education (PhD, Ed S); elementary education (MS), including early childhood education (MS, PhD), general elementary education, middle level education; middle level alternate route (MAT); secondary education (MS); secondary teacher alternate route (MAT); special education (MS). *Accreditation:* NCATE. Part-time and evening/weekend programs available. *Faculty:* 11 full-time (9 women). *Students:* 58 full-time (40 women), 143 part-time (100 women); includes 62 minority (56 Black or African American, non-Hispanic/Latino; 2 American Indian or Alaska Native, non-Hispanic/Latino; 3 Hispanic/Latino; 1 Two or more races, non-Hispanic/Latino). Average age 33. 181 applicants, 32% accepted, 52 enrolled. In 2013, 44 master's, 1 doctorate, 7 other advanced degrees awarded. *Degree requirements:* For master's, comprehensive exam; for doctorate, thesis/dissertation; for Ed S, comprehensive exam, thesis or alternative. *Entrance requirements:* For master's, GRE, minimum GPA of 2.75 in junior and senior year, eligibility for initial teacher certification; for doctorate, GRE, minimum GPA of 3.4 on previous graduate work; for Ed S, GRE, minimum GPA of 3.2 on master's degree. Additional exam requirements/recommendations for international students: Required—TOEFL (minimum score 550 paper-based; 79 iBT); Recommended—IELTS (minimum score 6.5). *Application deadline:* For fall admission, 3/1 priority date for domestic students, 5/1 for international students; for spring admission, 9/1 priority date for domestic students, 9/1 for international students. Applications are processed on a rolling basis. Application fee: $60. Electronic applications accepted. *Financial support:* In 2013–14, 7 research assistantships with full and partial tuition reimbursements (averaging $9,623 per year), 2 teaching assistantships (averaging $11,382 per year) were awarded; Federal Work-Study, institutionally sponsored loans, scholarships/grants, and unspecified assistantships also available. Financial award application deadline: 4/1; financial award applicants required to submit FAFSA. *Faculty research:* Early childhood education, reading, rural schools, multicultural education, use of technology in instruction. *Unit head:* Dr. Devon Brenner, Professor and Interim Head, 662-325-7119, Fax: 662-325-7857, E-mail: devon@ra.msstate.edu. *Application contact:* Dr. Dana Franz, Graduate Coordinator, 662-325-3703, Fax: 662-325-7857, E-mail: tstevonson@colled.msstate.edu.
Website: http://www.cise.msstate.edu/.

Missouri Southern State University, Program in Early Childhood Education, Joplin, MO 64801-1595. Offers MS Ed. Program offered jointly with Northwest Missouri State University. *Accreditation:* NCATE. *Entrance requirements:* For master's, GRE, minimum cumulative undergraduate GPA of 2.5.

Missouri State University, Graduate College, College of Education, Department of Childhood Education and Family Studies, Springfield, MO 65897. Offers early childhood and family development (MS); elementary education (MS Ed). Part-time programs available. *Faculty:* 12 full-time (9 women), 2 part-time/adjunct (both women). *Students:* 15 full-time (all women), 87 part-time (85 women); includes 9 minority (3 Black or African American, non-Hispanic/Latino; 1 American Indian or Alaska Native, non-Hispanic/Latino; 5 Hispanic/Latino), 3 international. Average age 30. 47 applicants, 100% accepted, 31 enrolled. In 2013, 23 master's awarded. *Degree requirements:* For master's, comprehensive exam. *Entrance requirements:* For master's, GRE, minimum GPA of 3.0. Additional exam requirements/recommendations for international students: Required—TOEFL (minimum score 550 paper-based; 79 iBT). *Application deadline:* For fall admission, 7/20 priority date for domestic students, 5/1 for international students; for spring admission, 12/20 priority date for domestic students, 9/1 for international students. Applications are processed on a rolling basis. Application fee: $35 ($50 for international students). Electronic applications accepted. *Expenses:* Tuition, state resident: full-time $4500; part-time $250 per credit hour. Tuition, nonresident: full-time $9018; part-time $501 per credit hour. *Required fees:* $361 per semester. Tuition and fees vary according to course level, course load and program. *Financial support:* Federal Work-Study, institutionally sponsored loans, scholarships/grants, and unspecified assistantships available. Financial award applicants required to submit FAFSA. *Unit head:* Dr. Donna Breault, Department Head, 417-836-3262, Fax: 417-836-8900, E-mail: cefs@missouristate.edu. *Application contact:* Misty Stewart, Coordinator of Graduate Recruitment, 417-836-6079, Fax: 417-836-6200, E-mail: mistystewart@missouristate.edu.
Website: http://education.missouristate.edu/cefs/.

Montclair State University, The Graduate School, College of Education and Human Services, Department of Early Childhood, Elementary and Literacy Education, Program in Early Childhood and Elementary Education, Montclair, NJ 07043-1624. Offers M Ed. Part-time and evening/weekend programs available. *Degree requirements:* For master's, comprehensive exam, thesis or alternative. *Entrance requirements:* For master's, GRE General Test, interview, 2 letters of recommendation. Additional exam requirements/recommendations for international students: Required—TOEFL (minimum score 83 iBT), IELTS (minimum score 6.5). Electronic applications accepted.

Montclair State University, The Graduate School, College of Education and Human Services, Department of Early Childhood, Elementary and Literacy Education, Program in Teaching Early Childhood, Montclair, NJ 07043-1624. Offers MAT. *Degree requirements:* For master's, comprehensive exam, thesis or alternative. *Entrance requirements:* For master's, GRE General Test, interview, essay, 2 letters of recommendation. Additional exam requirements/recommendations for international students: Required—TOEFL (minimum score 83 iBT), IELTS (minimum score 6.5). Electronic applications accepted.

Mount St. Joseph University, Graduate Education Program, Cincinnati, OH 45233-1670. Offers adolescent to young adult education (MA); dyslexia (Certificate); inclusive early childhood education (MA); instructional leadership (MA); middle childhood education (MA); multicultural special education (MA); Pre-K special needs (Certificate); principal licensure (MA); reading (Certificate); reading science (MA). *Accreditation:* Teacher Education Accreditation Council. Part-time and evening/weekend programs available. *Faculty:* 10 full-time (7 women), 7 part-time/adjunct (6 women). *Students:* 28 full-time (25 women), 95 part-time (76 women); includes 27 minority (19 Black or African

American, non-Hispanic/Latino; 6 Hispanic/Latino; 2 Two or more races, non-Hispanic/Latino). Average age 36. 73 applicants, 44% accepted, 30 enrolled. In 2013, 69 master's awarded. *Degree requirements:* For master's, research project, student teaching, clinical and field-based experiences. *Entrance requirements:* For master's, GRE, PRAXIS II in teaching content area (math or science), 2 letters of recommendation, interview, resume. Additional exam requirements/recommendations for international students: Required—TOEFL (minimum score 560 paper-based; 83 iBT). *Application deadline:* Applications are processed on a rolling basis. Application fee: $50. Electronic applications accepted. *Expenses: Tuition:* Full-time $18,400; part-time $575 per credit hour. *Required fees:* $450; $450 per year. Part-time tuition and fees vary according to course load, degree level and program. *Financial support:* Scholarships/grants available. Financial award applicants required to submit FAFSA. *Faculty research:* Foreign and second language learning problems/reading disabilities/hyperlexia, multicultural/bilingual special education, alternative educator licensure, science education, pedagogical content knowledge. *Unit head:* Dr. Mary West, Chair, 513-244-3263, Fax: 513-244-4867, E-mail: mary_west@mail.msj.edu. *Application contact:* Mary Brigham, Assistant Director of Graduate Recruitment, 513-244-4233, Fax: 513-244-4629, E-mail: mary_brigham@mail.msj.edu.
Website: http://www.msj.edu/academics/graduate-programs/master-of-arts-initial-teacher-licensure-programs/.

Mount Saint Mary College, Division of Education, Newburgh, NY 12550-3494. Offers adolescence and special education (MS Ed); adolescence education (MS Ed); childhood and special education (MS Ed); childhood education (MS Ed); literacy (5-12) (Advanced Certificate); literacy (birth-6) (Advanced Certificate); literacy and special education (MS Ed); literacy/childhood (MS Ed); middle school (5-6) (MS Ed); middle school (7-9) (MS Ed); special education (1-6) (MS Ed); special education (7-12) (MS Ed). *Accreditation:* NCATE. Part-time and evening/weekend programs available. *Faculty:* 11 full-time (9 women), 9 part-time/adjunct (4 women). *Students:* 29 full-time (19 women), 142 part-time (117 women); includes 22 minority (5 Black or African American, non-Hispanic/Latino; 16 Hispanic/Latino; 1 Two or more races, non-Hispanic/Latino). Average age 29. 51 applicants, 65% accepted, 27 enrolled. In 2013, 72 master's awarded. *Application deadline:* Applications are processed on a rolling basis. Application fee: $45. Application fee is waived when completed online. *Expenses: Tuition:* Full-time $13,356; part-time $742 per credit. *Required fees:* $70 per semester. *Financial support:* In 2013–14, 69 students received support. Unspecified assistantships available. Financial award application deadline: 4/15; financial award applicants required to submit FAFSA. *Faculty research:* Learning and teaching styles, computers in special education, language development. *Unit head:* Dr. William Swart, Graduate Coordinator, 845-569-3149, Fax: 845-569-3535, E-mail: william.swart@msmc.edu. *Application contact:* Lisa Gallina, Director of Admissions for Graduate Programs and Adult Degree Completion, 845-569-3166, Fax: 845-569-3450, E-mail: lisa.gallina@msmc.edu.
Website: http://www.msmc.edu/Academics/Graduate_Programs/Master_of_Science_in_Education.

Murray State University, College of Education, Department of Early Childhood and Elementary Education, Program in Interdisciplinary Early Childhood Education, Murray, KY 42071. Offers MA Ed. Part-time programs available. *Degree requirements:* For master's, portfolio. *Entrance requirements:* For master's, minimum GPA of 2.5 for conditional admittance, 3.0 for unconditional.

National Louis University, National College of Education, Chicago, IL 60603. Offers administration and supervision (M Ed, Ed D, CAS, Ed S); curriculum and instruction (M Ed, MS Ed, CAS); early childhood administration (M Ed, CAS); early childhood education (M Ed, MAT, MS Ed, CAS); education (Ed D); educational psychology/human learning and development (M Ed, MS Ed, CAS, Ed S); elementary education (MAT); interdisciplinary curriculum and instruction (M Ed); mathematics education (M Ed, MS Ed, CAS); reading and language (M Ed, MS Ed, CAS); school psychology (M Ed, Ed S); science education (M Ed, MS Ed, CAS); secondary education (MAT); special education (M Ed, MAT, CAS); technology in education (M Ed, CAS). *Accreditation:* NCATE. Part-time and evening/weekend programs available. *Degree requirements:* For doctorate, comprehensive exam, thesis/dissertation. *Entrance requirements:* For master's, MAT or GRE, minimum GPA of 3.0; for doctorate, GRE General Test, minimum GPA of 3.25, interview, resume, writing sample, 4 recommendations. Additional exam requirements/recommendations for international students: Required—TOEFL (minimum score 550 paper-based; 79 iBT).

National University, Academic Affairs, School of Education, La Jolla, CA 92037-1011. Offers applied behavior analysis (Certificate); applied school leadership (MS); autism (Certificate); best practices (Certificate); e-teaching and learning (Certificate); early childhood education (Certificate); education (MA), including best practices (M Ed, MA), e-teaching and learning (M Ed, MA), education technology, teacher leadership (M Ed, MA), teaching and learning in a global society (M Ed, MA), teaching mathematics (M Ed, MA); education with preliminary multiple or single subject (M Ed), including best practices (M Ed, MA), e-teaching and learning (M Ed, MA), educational technology (M Ed, MA), teacher leadership (M Ed, MA), teaching and learning in a global society (M Ed, MA), teaching mathematics (M Ed, MA); educational administration (MS); educational and instructional technology (MS); educational counseling (MS); educational technology (Certificate); higher education administration (MS); innovative school leadership (MS); instructional leadership (MS); juvenile justice special education (MS); reading (Certificate); school psychology (MS); special education (MS), including deaf and hard-of-hearing, mild/moderate disabilities, moderate/severe disabilities; teacher leadership (Certificate); teaching (MA), including applied behavioral analysis, autism, best practices (M Ed, MA), e-teaching and learning (M Ed, MA), early childhood education, educational technology (M Ed, MA), reading, special education, teacher leadership (M Ed, MA), teaching and learning in a global society (M Ed, MA), teaching mathematics (M Ed, MA); teaching mathematics (Certificate). Part-time and evening/weekend programs available. Postbaccalaureate distance learning degree programs offered (no on-campus study). *Faculty:* 72 full-time (43 women), 287 part-time/adjunct (170 women). *Students:* 2,433 full-time (1,744 women), 2,017 part-time (1,371 women); includes 1,834 minority (358 Black or African American, non-Hispanic/Latino; 15 American Indian or Alaska Native, non-Hispanic/Latino; 250 Asian, non-Hispanic/Latino; 1,056 Hispanic/Latino; 29 Native Hawaiian or other Pacific Islander, non-Hispanic/Latino; 126 Two or more races, non-Hispanic/Latino; 1 international. Average age 34. 1,339 applicants, 100% accepted, 1035 enrolled. In 2013, 1,662 master's awarded. *Degree requirements:* For master's, thesis (for some programs). *Entrance requirements:* For master's, interview, minimum GPA of 2.5. Additional exam requirements/recommendations for international students: Required—TOEFL (minimum score 550 paper-based; 79 iBT), IELTS (minimum score 6). *Application deadline:* Applications are processed on a rolling basis. Application fee: $60 ($65 for international students). Electronic applications accepted. *Expenses: Tuition:* Full-time $13,824; part-time $1728 per course. One-time fee: $160. *Financial support:* Career-related internships or fieldwork, institutionally sponsored loans, scholarships/grants, and tuition waivers (partial) available. Support available to part-time students. Financial award application deadline: 6/30. *Faculty research:* Teacher education, special education, educational effectiveness, teaching abroad, school counseling. *Unit head:* School of Education, 800-

628-8648, E-mail: soe@nu.edu. *Application contact:* Louis Cruz, Interim Vice President for Enrollment Services, 800-628-8648, E-mail: advisor@nu.edu.
Website: http://www.nu.edu/OurPrograms/SchoolOfEducation.html.

Nazareth College of Rochester, Graduate Studies, Department of Education, Program in Inclusive Education-Early Childhood Level, Rochester, NY 14618-3790. Offers MS Ed. *Accreditation:* Teacher Education Accreditation Council. Part-time and evening/weekend programs available. *Entrance requirements:* For master's, minimum GPA of 3.0.

New Jersey City University, Graduate Studies and Continuing Education, Debra Cannon Partridge Wolfe College of Education, Department of Early Childhood Education, Jersey City, NJ 07305-1597. Offers MA. Part-time and evening/weekend programs available. *Faculty:* 11 full-time (9 women), 11 part-time/adjunct (all women). *Students:* 15 full-time (14 women), 48 part-time (47 women); includes 35 minority (11 Black or African American, non-Hispanic/Latino; 4 Asian, non-Hispanic/Latino; 20 Hispanic/Latino), 1 international. Average age 34. In 2013, 29 master's awarded. *Entrance requirements:* Additional exam requirements/recommendations for international students: Required—TOEFL (minimum score 61 iBT). *Application deadline:* For fall admission, 8/1 priority date for domestic students; for spring admission, 12/1 for domestic students. Applications are processed on a rolling basis. Application fee: $0. *Expenses: Tuition, area resident:* Part-time $527.90 per credit. Tuition, nonresident: part-time $947.75 per credit. *Financial support:* Career-related internships or fieldwork and unspecified assistantships available. *Unit head:* Dr. Regina Adesanya, Coordinator, 201-200-2114, E-mail: radesanya@njcu.edu. *Application contact:* Dr. William Bajor, Dean of Graduate Studies, 201-200-3409, Fax: 201-200-3411, E-mail: wbajor@njcu.edu.

New York Institute of Technology, School of Education, Department of Education, Old Westbury, NY 11568-8000. Offers adolescence education: mathematics (MS); adolescence education: science (MS); childhood education (MS); science, technology, engineering, and math education (Advanced Certificate); teaching 21st century skills (Advanced Certificate). Part-time and evening/weekend programs available. Postbaccalaureate distance learning degree programs offered (minimal on-campus study). *Faculty:* 1 (woman) full-time, 6 part-time/adjunct (3 women). *Students:* 13 full-time (11 women), 21 part-time (19 women); includes 7 minority (2 Black or African American, non-Hispanic/Latino; 3 Asian, non-Hispanic/Latino; 1 Hispanic/Latino; 1 Two or more races, non-Hispanic/Latino), 1 international. Average age 31. 32 applicants, 75% accepted, 13 enrolled. In 2013, 6 master's, 58 other advanced degrees awarded. *Entrance requirements:* Additional exam requirements/recommendations for international students: Required—TOEFL (minimum score 550 paper-based; 79 iBT), IELTS (minimum score 6). *Application deadline:* For fall admission, 7/1 priority date for domestic students, 6/1 for international students; for spring admission, 12/1 priority date for domestic students, 12/1 for international students. Applications are processed on a rolling basis. Application fee: $50. Electronic applications accepted. *Expenses: Tuition:* Full-time $18,900; part-time $1050 per credit. *Financial support:* Research assistantships with partial tuition reimbursements, career-related internships or fieldwork, scholarships/grants, health care benefits, tuition waivers (full and partial), and unspecified assistantships available. Support available to part-time students. Financial award applicants required to submit FAFSA. *Faculty research:* Evolving definition of new literacies and its impact on teaching and learning (twenty-first century skills), new literacies practices in teacher education, teachers' professional development, English language and literacy learning through mobile learning, teaching reading to culturally and linguistically diverse children. *Unit head:* Dr. Hui-Yin Hsu, Associate Professor, 516-686-1322, Fax: 516-686-7655, E-mail: hhsu02@nyit.edu. *Application contact:* Alice Dolitsky, Director, Graduate Admissions, 516-686-7520, Fax: 516-686-1116, E-mail: nyitgrad@nyit.edu.
Website: http://www.nyit.edu/education/departments.

New York University, Steinhardt School of Culture, Education, and Human Development, Department of Teaching and Learning, Program in Early Childhood and Childhood Education, New York, NY 10003. Offers childhood education (MA), including childhood education, special education; early childhood and childhood education (PhD); early childhood education (MA); early childhood education/early childhood special education (MA). *Accreditation:* Teacher Education Accreditation Council. Part-time programs available. *Faculty:* 10 full-time (all women). *Students:* 75 full-time (67 women), 27 part-time (26 women); includes 40 minority (6 Black or African American, non-Hispanic/Latino; 1 American Indian or Alaska Native, non-Hispanic/Latino; 18 Asian, non-Hispanic/Latino; 12 Hispanic/Latino; 3 Two or more races, non-Hispanic/Latino), 11 international. Average age 28. 122 applicants, 59% accepted, 14 enrolled. In 2013, 64 master's, 2 doctorates awarded. *Degree requirements:* For master's, thesis (for some programs); for doctorate, thesis/dissertation. *Entrance requirements:* For doctorate, GRE General Test, interview. Additional exam requirements/recommendations for international students: Required—TOEFL (minimum score 100 iBT). *Application deadline:* For fall admission, 12/1 priority date for domestic and international students; for spring admission, 11/1 for domestic and international students. Applications are processed on a rolling basis. Application fee: $75. Electronic applications accepted. *Expenses: Tuition:* Full-time $35,856; part-time $1494 per unit. *Required fees:* $1408; $64 per unit. $473 per term. Tuition and fees vary according to course load and program. *Financial support:* Fellowships with full and partial tuition reimbursements, career-related internships or fieldwork, Federal Work-Study, institutionally sponsored loans, scholarships/grants, tuition waivers (partial), and unspecified assistantships available. Support available to part-time students. Financial award application deadline: 2/1; financial award applicants required to submit FAFSA. *Faculty research:* Teacher evaluation and beliefs about teaching, early literacy development, language arts, child development and education, cultural differences. *Unit head:* 212-998-5460, Fax: 212-995-4049. *Application contact:* 212-998-5030, Fax: 212-995-4328, E-mail: steinhardt.gradadmissions@nyu.edu.
Website: http://steinhardt.nyu.edu/teachlearn/childhood.

New York University, Steinhardt School of Culture, Education, and Human Development, Department of Teaching and Learning, Program in Special Education, New York, NY 10012-1019. Offers childhood (MA); early childhood (MA). *Accreditation:* Teacher Education Accreditation Council. Part-time programs available. *Faculty:* 11 full-time (8 women). *Students:* 10 full-time (all women), 3 part-time (all women); includes 7 minority (2 Asian, non-Hispanic/Latino; 4 Hispanic/Latino; 1 Two or more races, non-Hispanic/Latino), 1 international. Average age 25. 132 applicants, 74% accepted, 34 enrolled. In 2013, 9 master's awarded. *Degree requirements:* For master's, thesis (for some programs). *Entrance requirements:* Additional exam requirements/recommendations for international students: Required—TOEFL (minimum score 100 iBT). *Application deadline:* For fall admission, 2/1 priority date for domestic and international students. Applications are processed on a rolling basis. Application fee: $75. Electronic applications accepted. *Expenses: Tuition:* Full-time $35,856; part-time $1494 per unit. *Required fees:* $1408; $64 per unit. $473 per term. Tuition and fees vary according to course load and program. *Financial support:* Career-related internships or fieldwork, Federal Work-Study, institutionally sponsored loans, scholarships/grants, and tuition waivers (partial) available. Support available to part-time students. Financial award application deadline: 2/1; financial award applicants required to submit FAFSA.

Early Childhood Education

Faculty research: Special education referrals, attention deficit disorders in children, mainstreaming, curriculum-based assessment and program implementation, special education policy. *Unit head:* Prof. Joan Rosenberg, 212-998-5554, Fax: 212-995-4049, E-mail: joanrosenberg@nyu.edu. *Application contact:* 212-998-5030, Fax: 212-995-4328, E-mail: steinhardt.gradadmissions@nyu.edu.
Website: http://steinhardt.nyu.edu/teachlearn/special/ma.

Niagara University, Graduate Division of Education, Concentration in Teacher Education, Niagara Falls, NY 14109. Offers early childhood and childhood education (MS Ed, Certificate); middle and adolescence education (MS Ed, Certificate); special education (grades 1-12) (MS Ed, Certificate); teaching English to speakers of other languages (MS Ed). *Accreditation:* NCATE. *Students:* 168 full-time (130 women), 40 part-time (28 women); includes 11 minority (4 Black or African American, non-Hispanic/Latino; 1 Asian, non-Hispanic/Latino; 5 Hispanic/Latino; 1 Native Hawaiian or other Pacific Islander, non-Hispanic/Latino), 101 international. Average age 27. In 2013, 131 master's, 1 Certificate awarded. *Entrance requirements:* For master's, GRE General Test or MAT. Additional exam requirements/recommendations for international students: Required—TOEFL (minimum score 550 paper-based, 79 iBT) or IELTS (minimum score 6). *Application deadline:* For fall admission, 8/1 for domestic students. Applications are processed on a rolling basis. Application fee: $30. *Expenses:* Contact institution. *Financial support:* Research assistantships with full and partial tuition reimbursements, teaching assistantships with full and partial tuition reimbursements, career-related internships or fieldwork, Federal Work-Study, scholarships/grants, and unspecified assistantships available. Financial award application deadline: 4/15; financial award applicants required to submit FAFSA. *Unit head:* Dr. Chandra Foote, Chair, 716-286-8549. *Application contact:* Dr. Debra A. Colley, Dean of Education, 716-286-8560, Fax: 716-286-8561, E-mail: dcolley@niagara.edu.
Website: http://www.niagara.edu/teacher-education.

Norfolk State University, School of Graduate Studies, School of Education, Department of Early Childhood and Elementary Education, Norfolk, VA 23504. Offers early childhood education (MAT); pre-elementary education (MA). *Accreditation:* NCATE. Part-time programs available. *Students:* 5 full-time (all women), 10 part-time (all women); includes 12 minority (all Black or African American, non-Hispanic/Latino). In 2013, 7 master's awarded. *Degree requirements:* For master's, comprehensive exam, thesis or alternative. *Entrance requirements:* For master's, PRAXIS I and II, minimum GPA of 2.5, letters of recommendation, interview. *Application deadline:* For fall admission, 3/1 for domestic students; for spring admission, 10/1 for domestic students. Applications are processed on a rolling basis. Application fee: $30. *Financial support:* Fellowships and career-related internships or fieldwork available. Financial award application deadline: 4/15; financial award applicants required to submit FAFSA. *Faculty research:* Parent involvement in education. *Unit head:* Dr. Arletha McSwain, Head, 757-823-8702, Fax: 757-823-8133, E-mail: amcswain@nsu.edu. *Application contact:* Dr. Mona Thornton, Coordinator, 757-823-9021, Fax: 757-823-8133, E-mail: mthornton@nsu.edu.

North Carolina Agricultural and Technical State University, School of Graduate Studies, School of Agriculture and Environmental Sciences, Department of Family and Consumer Sciences, Greensboro, NC 27411. Offers child development early education and family studies (MAT); family and consumer sciences (MAT); food and nutrition (MS). Part-time and evening/weekend programs available. *Degree requirements:* For master's, comprehensive exam, thesis or alternative, qualifying exam. *Entrance requirements:* For master's, GRE General Test, minimum GPA of 2.6.

Northeastern Illinois University, College of Graduate Studies and Research, College of Education, Program in Early Childhood Education, Chicago, IL 60625-4699. Offers MAT. *Degree requirements:* For master's, practicum, internship, research project. *Entrance requirements:* For master's, bachelor's degree from accredited college or university; minimum undergraduate GPA of 3.0; three professional references. Electronic applications accepted.

Northeastern State University, College of Education, Department of Curriculum and Instruction, Program in Early Childhood Education, Tahlequah, OK 74464-2399. Offers M Ed. Part-time and evening/weekend programs available. *Faculty:* 17 full-time (13 women), 7 part-time/adjunct (2 women). *Students:* 3 full-time (all women), 17 part-time (16 women); includes 6 minority (2 Black or African American, non-Hispanic/Latino; 1 American Indian or Alaska Native, non-Hispanic/Latino; 2 Hispanic/Latino; 1 Two or more races, non-Hispanic/Latino). Average age 35. In 2013, 2 master's awarded. *Degree requirements:* For master's, thesis. *Entrance requirements:* For master's, GRE or MAT, minimum GPA of 2.5. Additional exam requirements/recommendations for international students: Required—TOEFL. *Application deadline:* For fall admission, 6/1 priority date for domestic students. Applications are processed on a rolling basis. Application fee: $25. Electronic applications accepted. *Expenses:* Tuition, state resident: full-time $3029; part-time $168.25 per credit hour. Tuition, nonresident: full-time $7709; part-time $428.25 per credit hour. *Required fees:* $35.90 per credit hour. *Financial support:* Teaching assistantships and Federal Work-Study available. Financial award application deadline: 3/1. *Unit head:* Dr. Anita Ede, Chair, 918-449-6523, E-mail: edear@nsuok.edu. *Application contact:* Margie Railey, Administrative Assistant, 918-456-5511 Ext. 2093, Fax: 918-458-2061, E-mail: railey@nsouk.edu.
Website: http://academics.nsuok.edu/education/GraduatePrograms/EarlyChildhood.aspx.

Northern Arizona University, Graduate College, College of Education, Department of Teaching and Learning, Flagstaff , AZ 86011. Offers early childhood education (M Ed); elementary education (M Ed); secondary education (M Ed). Part-time programs available. *Faculty:* 33 full-time (26 women), 3 part-time/adjunct (all women). *Students:* 146 full-time (119 women), 188 part-time (169 women); includes 91 minority (5 Black or African American, non-Hispanic/Latino; 16 American Indian or Alaska Native, non-Hispanic/Latino; 1 Asian, non-Hispanic/Latino; 65 Hispanic/Latino; 4 Two or more races, non-Hispanic/Latino), 2 international. Average age 35. 114 applicants, 94% accepted, 67 enrolled. In 2013, 205 master's awarded. *Degree requirements:* For master's, comprehensive exam (for some programs), thesis (for some programs). *Entrance requirements:* For master's, minimum GPA of 3.0. Additional exam requirements/recommendations for international students: Required—TOEFL (minimum score 550 paper-based; 80 iBT), IELTS (minimum score 7). *Application deadline:* For fall admission, 3/1 priority date for international students; for spring admission, 9/15 priority date for international students. Applications are processed on a rolling basis. Application fee: $65. Electronic applications accepted. *Financial support:* In 2013–14, 6 teaching assistantships with full tuition reimbursements (averaging $9,698 per year) were awarded; Federal Work-Study, scholarships/grants, health care benefits, tuition waivers (full and partial), and unspecified assistantships also available. Financial award applicants required to submit FAFSA. *Unit head:* Dr. Pamela Powell, Chair, 928-523-5644, Fax: 928-523-1929, E-mail: pamela.powell@nau.edu. *Application contact:* Kay Quillen, Administrative Assistant, 928-523-9316, Fax: 928-523-1929, E-mail: kay.quillen@nau.edu.
Website: http://nau.edu/coe/teaching-and-learning/.

Northern Illinois University, Graduate School, College of Education, Department of Special and Early Education, De Kalb, IL 60115-2854. Offers curriculum and instruction (MS Ed, Ed D), including curriculum leadership (Ed D), elementary education (Ed D), secondary education (Ed D); early childhood education (MS Ed); elementary education (MS Ed); special education (MS Ed). Part-time and evening/weekend programs available. *Faculty:* 22 full-time (14 women), 2 part-time/adjunct (both women). *Students:* 52 full-time (41 women), 168 part-time (137 women); includes 29 minority (11 Black or African American, non-Hispanic/Latino; 7 Asian, non-Hispanic/Latino; 6 Hispanic/Latino; 5 Two or more races, non-Hispanic/Latino), 3 international. Average age 36. 38 applicants, 63% accepted, 18 enrolled. In 2013, 59 master's, 15 doctorates awarded. *Degree requirements:* For master's, comprehensive exam, thesis optional; for doctorate, thesis/dissertation, candidacy exam, dissertation defense. *Entrance requirements:* For master's, GRE General Test or MAT, minimum undergraduate GPA of 2.75; for doctorate, GRE General Test or MAT, minimum undergraduate GPA of 2.75, graduate 3.2. Additional exam requirements/recommendations for international students: Required—TOEFL (minimum score 550 paper-based). *Application deadline:* For fall admission, 6/1 for domestic students, 5/1 for international students; for spring admission, 11/1 for domestic students, 10/1 for international students. Applications are processed on a rolling basis. Application fee: $40. Electronic applications accepted. *Financial support:* In 2013–14, 24 research assistantships with full tuition reimbursements were awarded; fellowships with full tuition reimbursements, teaching assistantships with full tuition reimbursements, career-related internships or fieldwork, Federal Work-Study, scholarships/grants, tuition waivers (full), and unspecified assistantships also available. Support available to part-time students. Financial award applicants required to submit FAFSA. *Faculty research:* Teacher certification, stress reduction during student teaching, teaching history, portfolios in student teaching. *Unit head:* Dr. Barbara Schwartz-Bechet, Interim Chair, 815-753-1619, E-mail: seed@niu.edu. *Application contact:* Gail Myers, Clerk, Graduate Advising, 815-753-0381, E-mail: gmyers@niu.edu.
Website: http://www.cedu.niu.edu/seed/.

Northwestern State University of Louisiana, Graduate Studies and Research, College of Education and Human Development, Program in Early Childhood Education, Natchitoches, LA 71497. Offers early childhood education and teaching (M Ed, MAT). *Degree requirements:* For master's, comprehensive exam, thesis or alternative. *Entrance requirements:* For master's, GRE General Test. Additional exam requirements/recommendations for international students: Required—TOEFL. Electronic applications accepted.

Northwest Missouri State University, Graduate School, College of Education and Human Services, Department of Professional Education, Program in Teaching: Early Childhood, Maryville, MO 64468-6001. Offers MS Ed. *Accreditation:* NCATE. Part-time programs available. *Degree requirements:* For master's, comprehensive exam. *Entrance requirements:* For master's, GRE General Test, teaching certificate, minimum undergraduate GPA of 2.75, writing sample. Additional exam requirements/recommendations for international students: Required—TOEFL (minimum score 550 paper-based).

Oakland University, Graduate Study and Lifelong Learning, School of Education and Human Services, Department of Human Development and Child Studies, Program in Early Childhood Education, Rochester, MI 48309-4401. Offers early childhood education (M Ed, PhD, Certificate); early mathematics education (Certificate). *Accreditation:* Teacher Education Accreditation Council. *Students:* 15 full-time (all women), 73 part-time (70 women); includes 12 minority (10 Black or African American, non-Hispanic/Latino; 2 Asian, non-Hispanic/Latino), 1 international. Average age 36. 66 applicants, 94% accepted, 59 enrolled. In 2013, 49 master's, 2 doctorates awarded. *Degree requirements:* For doctorate, thesis/dissertation. *Entrance requirements:* For master's, minimum GPA of 3.0 for unconditional admission; for doctorate, GRE General Test, minimum GPA of 3.0 for unconditional admission. Additional exam requirements/recommendations for international students: Required—TOEFL (minimum score 550 paper-based). *Application deadline:* For fall admission, 5/1 for domestic students, 5/1 priority date for international students; for winter admission, 2/1 for domestic students, 9/1 priority date for international students. Application fee: $0. *Financial support:* Career-related internships or fieldwork, Federal Work-Study, institutionally sponsored loans, and tuition waivers (full) available. Financial award application deadline: 3/1; financial award applicants required to submit FAFSA. *Unit head:* Dr. Sherri Oden, Coordinator, 248-370-3027, E-mail: oden@oakland.edu. *Application contact:* Christina J. Grabowski, Associate Director of Graduate Study and Lifelong Learning, 248-370-3167, Fax: 248-370-4114, E-mail: grabowsk@oakland.edu.

The Ohio State University at Lima, Graduate Programs, Lima, OH 45804. Offers early childhood education (M Ed); education (MA); middle childhood education (M Ed); social work (MSW). Part-time programs available. *Faculty:* 37. *Students:* 8 full-time (6 women), 8 part-time (7 women). Average age 31. Terminal master's awarded for partial completion of doctoral program. *Degree requirements:* For master's, comprehensive exam (for some programs), thesis (for some programs). *Entrance requirements:* For master's, GRE, minimum GPA of 3.0. Additional exam requirements/recommendations for international students: Required—TOEFL (minimum score 550 paper-based, 79 iBT), IELTS (minimum score 7), or Michigan English Language Assessment Battery (minimum score 82). *Application deadline:* For fall admission, 6/1 for domestic and international students; for spring admission, 10/15 for domestic and international students. Applications are processed on a rolling basis. Application fee: $60 ($70 for international students). Electronic applications accepted. *Financial support:* Application deadline: 2/15. *Unit head:* Dr. Gregory Rose, Interim Dean and Director, 419-995-8481, E-mail: rose.9@osu.edu. *Application contact:* Graduate Admissions, 614-292-9444, Fax: 614-292-3895, E-mail: gradadmissions@osu.edu.

The Ohio State University at Marion, Graduate Programs, Marion, OH 43302-5695. Offers early childhood education (pre-K to grade 3) (M Ed); education - teaching and learning (MA); middle childhood education (grades 4-9) (M Ed). Part-time programs available. *Faculty:* 38. *Students:* 17 full-time (13 women); includes 1 minority (Asian, non-Hispanic/Latino). Average age 27. *Degree requirements:* For master's, comprehensive exam (for some programs), thesis (for some programs). *Entrance requirements:* For master's, GRE, minimum undergraduate GPA of 3.0. Additional exam requirements/recommendations for international students: Required—TOEFL (minimum score 550 paper-based, 79 iBT), IELTS (minimum score 7) or Michigan English Language Assessment Battery (minimum score 82). *Application deadline:* For fall admission, 6/1 for domestic students, 6/1 priority date for international students; for spring admission, 10/15 for domestic students, 10/15 priority date for international students. Applications are processed on a rolling basis. Application fee: $60 ($70 for international students). Electronic applications accepted. *Financial support:* Application deadline: 2/15; applicants required to submit FAFSA. *Unit head:* Dr. Gregory S. Rose, Dean/Director, 740-725-6218, E-mail: rose.9@osu.edu. *Application contact:* Graduate Admissions, 614-292-9444, Fax: 614-292-3895, E-mail: gradadmissions@osu.edu.

The Ohio State University–Mansfield Campus, Graduate Programs, Mansfield, OH 44906-1599. Offers early childhood education (M Ed); education (MA); middle childhood education (M Ed); social work (MSW). Part-time programs available. *Faculty:* 40. *Students:* 18 full-time (17 women), 30 part-time (29 women). Average age 31. *Degree requirements:* For master's, comprehensive exam (for some programs), thesis (for some programs). *Entrance requirements:* For master's, GRE, minimum GPA of 3.0. Additional exam requirements/recommendations for international students: Required—TOEFL

(minimum 550 paper-based, 79 iBT), IELTS (minimum score 7) or Michigan English Language Assessment Battery (minimum score 82). *Application deadline:* For fall admission, 6/1 for domestic and international students; for spring admission, 10/15 for domestic and international students. Applications are processed on a rolling basis. Application fee: $60 ($70 for international students). Electronic applications accepted. *Financial support:* Teaching assistantships with full tuition reimbursements, Federal Work-Study, and scholarships/grants available. Support available to part-time students. Financial award application deadline: 2/15. *Unit head:* Dr. Stephen M. Gavazzi, Dean and Director, 419-755-4221, Fax: 419-755-4241, E-mail: gavazzi.1@osu.edu. *Application contact:* Graduate Admissions, 614-292-9444, Fax: 614-292-3895, E-mail: gradadmissions@osu.edu.

The Ohio State University–Newark Campus, Graduate Programs, Newark, OH 43055-1797. Offers early/middle childhood education (M Ed); education - teaching and learning (MA); social work (MSW). Part-time programs available. *Faculty:* 53. *Students:* 10 full-time (9 women), 27 part-time (24 women); includes 3 minority (1 Black or African American, non-Hispanic/Latino; 2 Hispanic/Latino). Average age 35. Terminal master's awarded for partial completion of doctoral program. *Degree requirements:* For master's, comprehensive exam (for some programs), thesis (for some programs). *Entrance requirements:* For master's, GRE, minimum GPA of 3.0. Additional exam requirements/recommendations for international students: Required—TOEFL (minimum score 550 paper-based; 79 iBT), IELTS (minimum score 7), or Michigan English Language Assessment Battery (minimum score 82). *Application deadline:* For fall admission, 6/1 for domestic and international students; for spring admission, 10/15 for domestic students, 2/1 for international students. Applications are processed on a rolling basis. Application fee: $60 ($70 for international students). Electronic applications accepted. *Financial support:* Application deadline: 2/15. *Unit head:* Dr. William L. MacDonald, Dean/Director, 740-366-9333 Ext. 330, E-mail: macdonald.24@osu.edu. *Application contact:* Graduate Admissions, 614-292-9444, Fax: 614-292-3985, E-mail: gradadmissions@osu.edu.

Oklahoma City University, Petree College of Arts and Sciences, Programs in Education, Oklahoma City, OK 73106-1402. Offers applied behavioral studies (M Ed); early childhood education (M Ed), including Montessori education; elementary education (M Ed), including Montessori education. Part-time and evening/weekend programs available. *Students:* 35 full-time (20 women), 9 part-time (7 women); includes 17 minority (12 Black or African American, non-Hispanic/Latino; 1 American Indian or Alaska Native, non-Hispanic/Latino; 1 Asian, non-Hispanic/Latino; 3 Two or more races, non-Hispanic/Latino), 6 international. Average age 32. 49 applicants, 61% accepted, 20 enrolled. In 2013, 24 master's awarded. *Entrance requirements:* For master's, bachelor's degree from accredited institution, minimum GPA of 3.0, essay, recommendation letters. Additional exam requirements/recommendations for international students: Required—TOEFL (minimum score 550 paper-based; 80 iBT). *Application deadline:* Applications are processed on a rolling basis. Application fee: $50. Electronic applications accepted. *Expenses: Tuition:* Full-time $16,848; part-time $936 per credit hour. Tuition and fees vary according to course load, degree level and program. *Financial support:* Career-related internships or fieldwork, Federal Work-Study, institutionally sponsored loans, scholarships/grants, and tuition waivers available. Support available to part-time students. Financial award application deadline: 6/1; financial award applicants required to submit FAFSA. *Faculty research:* Adult literacy, cognition, reading strategies. *Unit head:* Dr. Lois Lawler-Brown, Chair, 405-208-5374, Fax: 405-208-6012, E-mail: llbrown@okcu.edu. *Application contact:* Heidi Puckett, Director of Graduate Admissions, 800-633-7242, Fax: 405-208-5916, E-mail: gadmissions@okcu.edu.
Website: http://www.okcu.edu/petree/education/graduate.aspx.

Old Dominion University, Darden College of Education, Program in Early Childhood Education, Norfolk, VA 23529. Offers MS Ed, PhD. *Accreditation:* NCATE. Part-time and evening/weekend programs available. *Faculty:* 5 full-time (4 women), 7 part-time/adjunct (6 women). *Students:* 16 full-time (all women), 15 part-time (14 women); includes 8 minority (6 Black or African American, non-Hispanic/Latino; 1 Asian, non-Hispanic/Latino; 1 Hispanic/Latino), 2 international. Average age 33. 43 applicants, 42% accepted, 18 enrolled. In 2013, 19 master's awarded. *Degree requirements:* For master's, comprehensive exam, written exams; for doctorate, comprehensive exam, thesis/dissertation. *Entrance requirements:* For master's, GRE General Test, PRAXIS I, minimum undergraduate GPA of 2.8; for doctorate, GRE General Test. Additional exam requirements/recommendations for international students: Required—TOEFL. *Application deadline:* For fall admission, 6/1 for domestic students; for winter admission, 11/1 for domestic students; for spring admission, 3/1 for domestic students. Applications are processed on a rolling basis. Application fee: $50. *Expenses:* Tuition, state resident: full-time $9888; part-time $412 per credit. Tuition, nonresident: full-time $25,152; part-time $1048 per credit. *Required fees:* $59 per semester. One-time fee: $50. *Financial support:* In 2013–14, fellowships with full tuition reimbursements (averaging $15,000 per year), 2 research assistantships (averaging $9,000 per year), 2 teaching assistantships with full tuition reimbursements (averaging $15,000 per year) were awarded. Financial award application deadline: 2/15; financial award applicants required to submit FAFSA. *Faculty research:* Child abuse, day care, parenting, discipline (positive), bullying. *Unit head:* Dr. Charlene Fleener, Graduate Program Director, 757-683-3284, Fax: 757-683-5862, E-mail: cfleener@odu.edu. *Application contact:* William Heffelfinger, Director of Graduate Admissions, 757-683-5554, Fax: 757-683-3255, E-mail: gradadmit@odu.edu.
Website: http://education.odu.edu/esse/academics/degrees/ecedeg.shtml.

Ottawa University, Graduate Studies-Arizona, Program in Education, Ottawa, KS 66067-3399. Offers community college counseling (MA); curriculum and instruction (MA); early childhood (MA); education intervention (MA); education leadership (MA); education technology (MA); Montessori early childhood education (MA); Montessori elementary education (MA); professional development (MA); school guidance counseling (MA); special education - cross categorical (MA). Programs offered in Mesa, Phoenix, Tempe and West Valley, AZ. *Accreditation:* NCATE. Part-time programs available. *Degree requirements:* For master's, thesis or alternative. *Entrance requirements:* For master's, minimum undergraduate GPA of 3.0, copy of current state certification or teaching license. Additional exam requirements/recommendations for international students: Required—TOEFL (minimum score 550 paper-based). Electronic applications accepted. *Expenses:* Contact institution.

Our Lady of the Lake University of San Antonio, School of Professional Studies, Program in Curriculum and Instruction, San Antonio, TX 78207-4689. Offers bilingual education (M Ed); early childhood education (M Ed); English as a second language (M Ed); integrated math teaching (M Ed); integrated science teaching (M Ed); reading specialist (M Ed). Part-time and evening/weekend programs available. *Faculty:* 6 full-time (4 women), 3 part-time/adjunct (all women). *Students:* 4 full-time (all women), 84 part-time (72 women); includes 52 minority (2 Black or African American, non-Hispanic/Latino; 2 Asian, non-Hispanic/Latino; 48 Hispanic/Latino). Average age 40. 9 applicants, 56% accepted, 1 enrolled. In 2013, 8 master's awarded. *Degree requirements:* For master's, comprehensive exam. *Entrance requirements:* For master's, GRE General Test or MAT. Additional exam requirements/recommendations for international students: Required—TOEFL. *Application deadline:* For fall admission, 4/1 priority date for domestic and international students; for spring admission, 11/1 priority date for domestic and international students; for summer admission, 2/1 priority date for domestic students, 4/1 priority date for international students. Applications are processed on a rolling basis. Application fee: $25 ($50 for international students). Electronic applications accepted. *Expenses: Tuition:* Full-time $9120; part-time $760 per credit. *Required fees:* $698; $334 per trimester. Tuition and fees vary according to course load, degree level, campus/location and program. *Financial support:* Research assistantships, teaching assistantships, career-related internships or fieldwork, Federal Work-Study, institutionally sponsored loans, scholarships/grants, and tuition waivers (partial) available. Support available to part-time students. Financial award application deadline: 4/1. *Faculty research:* Professional educator to understand and meet the comprehensive needs of a diverse student population, life-long learners, innovative practices. *Unit head:* Dr. Jerrie Jackson, 210-434-6711 Ext. 2698, E-mail: jjackson@lake.ollusa.edu. *Application contact:* Graduate Admission, 210-431-3961, Fax: 210-431-4013, E-mail: gradadm@lake.ollusa.edu.
Website: http://www.ollusa.edu/s/1190/ollu-3-column-noads.aspx?sid=1190&gid=1&pgid=4173.

Pace University, School of Education, New York, NY 10038. Offers adolescent education (MST); childhood education (MST); early childhood development, learning and intervention (MST); educational leadership (MS Ed); educational technology studies (MS); inclusive adolescent education (MST); literacy (MS Ed); school business management (Certificate); special education (MS Ed). *Accreditation:* NCATE. Part-time and evening/weekend programs available. *Students:* 186 full-time (154 women), 441 part-time (315 women); includes 209 minority (89 Black or African American, non-Hispanic/Latino; 2 American Indian or Alaska Native, non-Hispanic/Latino; 30 Asian, non-Hispanic/Latino; 74 Hispanic/Latino; 1 Native Hawaiian or other Pacific Islander, non-Hispanic/Latino; 13 Two or more races, non-Hispanic/Latino), 7 international. Average age 29. 207 applicants, 71% accepted, 105 enrolled. In 2013, 296 master's, 25 other advanced degrees awarded. *Degree requirements:* For master's, internship. *Entrance requirements:* For master's, interview, teaching certificate. Additional exam requirements/recommendations for international students: Required—TOEFL. *Application deadline:* For fall admission, 8/1 priority date for domestic students, 6/1 for international students; for spring admission, 12/1 priority date for domestic students, 10/1 for international students. Applications are processed on a rolling basis. Application fee: $70. Electronic applications accepted. *Expenses:* Contact institution. *Financial support:* Research assistantships, career-related internships or fieldwork, and Federal Work-Study available. Support available to part-time students. Financial award applicants required to submit FAFSA. *Faculty research:* Teacher education, technology in education, STEM, literacy education, special education. *Total annual research expenditures:* $1.3 million. *Unit head:* Dr. Andrea M. Spencer, Dean, School of Education, 914-773-3341, E-mail: aspencer@pace.edu. *Application contact:* Susan Ford-Goldschein, Director of Graduate Admissions, 212-346-1660, Fax: 212-346-1585, E-mail: gradnyc@pace.edu.
Website: http://www.pace.edu/school-of-education.

Pacific University, College of Education, Forest Grove, OR 97116-1797. Offers early childhood education (MAT); education (MAE); elementary education (MAT); high school education (MAT); middle school education (MAT); special education (MAT); visual function in learning (M Ed). *Accreditation:* NCATE. Part-time and evening/weekend programs available. *Degree requirements:* For master's, research project. *Entrance requirements:* For master's, California Basic Educational Skills Test, PRAXIS II, minimum undergraduate GPA of 2.75, 3.0 graduate. Additional exam requirements/recommendations for international students: Required—TOEFL. Electronic applications accepted. *Expenses:* Contact institution. *Faculty research:* Defining a culturally competent classroom, technology in the k-12 classroom, Socratic seminars, social studies education.

Piedmont College, School of Education, Demorest, GA 30535-0010. Offers art education (MAT); early childhood education (MA, MAT); instructional technology (MAT); middle grades education (MA, MAT); music education (MAT); secondary education (MA, MAT); special education (MA, MAT); teacher leadership (Ed S). Part-time and evening/weekend programs available. *Students:* 312 full-time (242 women), 694 part-time (563 women); includes 153 minority (103 Black or African American, non-Hispanic/Latino; 3 American Indian or Alaska Native, non-Hispanic/Latino; 17 Asian, non-Hispanic/Latino; 19 Hispanic/Latino; 11 Two or more races, non-Hispanic/Latino), 1 international. Average age 37. 165 applicants, 72% accepted, 118 enrolled. In 2013, 333 master's, 15 doctorates, 457 other advanced degrees awarded. *Degree requirements:* For master's, thesis, field experience in the classroom teaching; for doctorate, thesis/dissertation. *Entrance requirements:* For master's, GRE General Test, MAT, minimum undergraduate GPA of 2.5; for Ed S, minimum graduate GPA of 3.5, valid teaching certificate. Additional exam requirements/recommendations for international students: Required—TOEFL (minimum score 550 paper-based). *Application deadline:* For fall admission, 7/15 for domestic students; for spring admission, 12/1 for domestic students. Applications are processed on a rolling basis. Electronic applications accepted. *Expenses: Tuition:* Full-time $7992; part-time $444 per credit hour. *Financial support:* Career-related internships or fieldwork, Federal Work-Study, and unspecified assistantships available. Support available to part-time students. Financial award applicants required to submit FAFSA. *Unit head:* Dr. Don Gnecco, Dean, 706-778-3000 Ext. 1201, Fax: 706-776-9608, E-mail: dgnecco@piedmont.edu. *Application contact:* Kathleen Anderson, Director of Graduate Enrollment Management, 706-778-8500 Ext. 1181, Fax: 706-778-0150, E-mail: kanderson@piedmont.edu.

Pittsburg State University, Graduate School, College of Education, Department of Curriculum and Instruction, Pittsburg, KS 66762. Offers classroom reading teacher (MS); early childhood education (MS); elementary education (MS); reading (MS); reading specialist (MS); secondary education (MS); teaching (MAT). *Accreditation:* NCATE. *Degree requirements:* For master's, thesis or alternative. *Entrance requirements:* For master's, GRE or MAT.

Pontificia Universidad Catolica Madre y Maestra, Graduate School, Faculty of Sciences and Humanities, Santiago, Dominican Republic. Offers architecture (M Arch), including architecture of interiors, architecture of tourist lodgings, landscaping; early childhood education (M Ed).

Portland State University, Graduate Studies, School of Education, Department of Curriculum and Instruction, Portland, OR 97207-0751. Offers early childhood education (MA, MS); education (M Ed, MA, MS); educational leadership: curriculum and instruction (Ed D); educational media/school librarianship (MA, MS); elementary education (M Ed, MAT, MST); reading (MA, MS); secondary education (M Ed, MAT, MST). *Accreditation:* NCATE. Part-time programs available. *Faculty:* 22 full-time (15 women), 28 part-time/adjunct (20 women). *Students:* 29 full-time (23 women), 162 part-time (123 women); includes 26 minority (3 Black or African American, non-Hispanic/Latino; 6 Asian, non-Hispanic/Latino; 13 Hispanic/Latino; 4 Two or more races, non-Hispanic/Latino), 6 international. Average age 36. 145 applicants, 69% accepted, 93 enrolled. In 2013, 257 master's, 5 doctorates awarded. *Degree requirements:* For master's, comprehensive exam, thesis or alternative; for doctorate, thesis/dissertation. *Entrance requirements:* For master's, California Basic Educational Skills Test, minimum GPA of 3.0 in upper-division course work or 2.75 overall. Additional exam requirements/recommendations for

international students: Required—TOEFL (minimum score 550 paper-based). *Application deadline:* For fall admission, 4/1 for domestic and international students; for winter admission, 9/1 for domestic and international students; for spring admission, 11/1 for domestic and international students. Applications are processed on a rolling basis. Application fee: $50. *Expenses:* Tuition, state resident: full-time $9207; part-time $341 per credit. Tuition, nonresident: full-time $14,391; part-time $533 per credit. *Required fees:* $1263; $22 per credit. $98 per quarter. One-time fee: $150. Tuition and fees vary according to program. *Financial support:* In 2013–14, 1 research assistantship with full tuition reimbursement (averaging $6,248 per year), 2 teaching assistantships with full tuition reimbursements (averaging $7,755 per year) were awarded; career-related internships or fieldwork, Federal Work-Study, and institutionally sponsored loans also available. Support available to part-time students. Financial award application deadline: 3/1; financial award applicants required to submit FAFSA. *Faculty research:* Early literacy, characteristics of successful teachers of at-risk students, participation of women/minorities in technology courses, selection of cooperating teachers. *Total annual research expenditures:* $1 million. *Unit head:* Christine Chaille, Head, 503-725-4753, Fax: 203-725-8475, E-mail: chaillec@pdx.edu. *Application contact:* Jake Fernandez, Department Assistant, 503-725-4756, Fax: 503-725-8475, E-mail: jifern@pdx.edu.
Website: http://www.ed.pdx.edu/ci/.

Prescott College, Graduate Programs, Program in Education, Prescott, AZ 86301. Offers early childhood education (MA); early childhood special education (MA); education (MA); elementary education (MA); environmental education leadership and administration (MA); equine-assisted learning (MA); school guidance counseling (MA); secondary education (MA); special education: learning disabilities (MA); special education: mental retardation (MA); special education: serious emotional disabilities (MA); student-directed independent study (MA); sustainability education (PhD). Part-time programs available. Postbaccalaureate distance learning degree programs offered (minimal on-campus study). *Degree requirements:* For master's, thesis, fieldwork or internship, practicum; for doctorate, thesis/dissertation. *Entrance requirements:* For master's, 2 letters of recommendation, resume; for doctorate, 3 letters of recommendation, resume, official transcripts, personal statement, program proposal. Additional exam requirements/recommendations for international students: Required—TOEFL (minimum score 500 paper-based). Electronic applications accepted.

Queens College of the City University of New York, Division of Graduate Studies, Division of Education, Department of Elementary and Early Childhood Education, Flushing, NY 11367-1597. Offers bilingual education (MS Ed); childhood education (MA); early childhood education (MA); elementary education (MS Ed, AC); literacy (MS Ed). Part-time and evening/weekend programs available. *Degree requirements:* For master's, research project; for AC, thesis optional. *Entrance requirements:* For master's, minimum GPA of 3.0. Additional exam requirements/recommendations for international students: Required—TOEFL.

Radford University, College of Graduate and Professional Studies, College of Education and Human Development, School of Teacher Education and Leadership, Program in Education, Radford, VA 24142. Offers curriculum and instruction (MS); early childhood education (MS); educational technology (MS); math education content area studies (MS). *Accreditation:* NCATE. Part-time and evening/weekend programs available. *Faculty:* 6 full-time (4 women), 2 part-time/adjunct (1 woman). *Students:* 68 full-time (53 women), 30 part-time (20 women); includes 6 minority (3 Black or African American, non-Hispanic/Latino; 1 Asian, non-Hispanic/Latino; 1 Hispanic/Latino; 1 Two or more races, non-Hispanic/Latino). Average age 28. 38 applicants, 100% accepted, 28 enrolled. In 2013, 42 master's awarded. *Degree requirements:* For master's, comprehensive exam. *Entrance requirements:* For master's, GRE, minimum GPA of 3.0, 2 letters of professional reference, personal statement, resume, official transcripts. Additional exam requirements/recommendations for international students: Required—TOEFL (minimum score 550 paper-based; 79 iBT). *Application deadline:* For fall admission, 2/15 priority date for domestic students, 12/1 for international students; for spring admission, 7/1 for international students. Applications are processed on a rolling basis. Application fee: $50. Electronic applications accepted. *Expenses:* Tuition, state resident: full-time $6800; part-time $283 per credit hour. Tuition, nonresident: full-time $15,610; part-time $627 per credit hour. *Required fees:* $2944; $123 per credit hour. Tuition and fees vary according to program. *Financial support:* In 2013–14, 24 students received support, including 19 research assistantships (averaging $7,105 per year); career-related internships or fieldwork, Federal Work-Study, institutionally sponsored loans, scholarships/grants, and unspecified assistantships also available. Financial award application deadline: 3/1; financial award applicants required to submit FAFSA. *Faculty research:* Pedagogy of mathematics education. *Unit head:* Dr. Kristan Morrison, Coordinator, 540-831-7120, Fax: 540-831-5059, E-mail: kmorrison12@radford.edu. *Application contact:* Rebecca Conner, Director, Graduate Enrollment, 540-831-6296, Fax: 540-831-6061, E-mail: gradcollege@radford.edu.
Website: http://www.radford.edu/content/cehd/home/departments/STEL/programs/education-master.html.

Radford University, College of Graduate and Professional Studies, College of Education and Human Development, School of Teacher Education and Leadership, Program in Special Education, Radford, VA 24142. Offers adapted curriculum (MS); autism studies (Certificate); early childhood special education (MS); general curriculum (MS); hearing impairments (MS); visual impairment (MS). *Accreditation:* NCATE. Part-time and evening/weekend programs available. *Faculty:* 8 full-time (7 women), 5 part-time/adjunct (all women). *Students:* 27 full-time (22 women), 27 part-time (22 women). Average age 28. 21 applicants, 100% accepted, 18 enrolled. In 2013, 46 master's, 2 other advanced degrees awarded. *Degree requirements:* For master's, comprehensive exam. *Entrance requirements:* For master's, GRE, minimum GPA of 2.75, 3 letters of reference, resume, personal essay, official transcripts. Additional exam requirements/recommendations for international students: Required—TOEFL (minimum score 550 paper-based; 79 iBT). *Application deadline:* For fall admission, 2/15 for domestic students, 12/1 for international students; for spring admission, 7/1 for international students. Applications are processed on a rolling basis. Application fee: $50. Electronic applications accepted. *Expenses:* Tuition, state resident: full-time $6800; part-time $283 per credit hour. Tuition, nonresident: full-time $15,610; part-time $627 per credit hour. *Required fees:* $2944; $123 per credit hour. Tuition and fees vary according to program. *Financial support:* In 2013–14, 6 students received support, including 5 research assistantships (averaging $6,300 per year); career-related internships or fieldwork, Federal Work-Study, institutionally sponsored loans, scholarships/grants, and unspecified assistantships also available. Financial award application deadline: 3/1; financial award applicants required to submit FAFSA. *Faculty research:* Collaborative new visions for alignment in elementary, reading and special education teacher preparation; Project MERGE: Merging Expertise for Results in the General Education Curriculum. *Unit head:* Dr. Brenda Tyler, Coordinator, 540-831-5868, Fax: 540-831-5059, E-mail: ruspecialed@radford.edu. *Application contact:* Rebecca Conner, Director, Graduate Enrollment, 540-831-6296, Fax: 540-831-6061, E-mail: gradcollege@radford.edu.
Website: http://www.radford.edu/content/cehd/home/departments/STEL/programs/special-educationms.html.

Reinhardt University, Program in Early Childhood Education, Waleska, GA 30183-2981. Offers M Ed, MAT. Part-time and evening/weekend programs available. Postbaccalaureate distance learning degree programs offered. *Degree requirements:* For master's, comprehensive exam. *Entrance requirements:* For master's, GACE, background check. Additional exam requirements/recommendations for international students: Required—TOEFL. Electronic applications accepted.

Rhode Island College, School of Graduate Studies, Feinstein School of Education and Human Development, Department of Elementary Education, Providence, RI 02908-1991. Offers early childhood education (M Ed); elementary education (M Ed, MAT); reading (M Ed). *Accreditation:* NCATE. Part-time and evening/weekend programs available. *Faculty:* 11 full-time (9 women), 2 part-time/adjunct (both women). *Students:* 16 full-time (12 women), 51 part-time (49 women); includes 5 minority (1 Black or African American, non-Hispanic/Latino; 3 Hispanic/Latino; 1 Two or more races, non-Hispanic/Latino). Average age 37. In 2013, 29 master's awarded. *Degree requirements:* For master's, comprehensive exam (for some programs), comprehensive assessment. *Entrance requirements:* For master's, GRE General Test or MAT, PRAXIS II (elementary content knowledge), undergraduate transcripts; minimum undergraduate GPA of 3.0; 3 letters of recommendation. Additional exam requirements/recommendations for international students: Recommended—TOEFL (minimum score 550 paper-based; 79 iBT). *Application deadline:* For fall admission, 3/1 for domestic students; for spring admission, 11/1 for domestic students. Applications are processed on a rolling basis. Application fee: $50. *Expenses:* Tuition, state resident: full-time $8928; part-time $372 per credit hour. Tuition, nonresident: full-time $17,376; part-time $724 per credit hour. *Required fees:* $602; $22 per credit. $72 per term. *Financial support:* Teaching assistantships with full tuition reimbursements, Federal Work-Study, scholarships/grants, and health care benefits available. Support available to part-time students. Financial award application deadline: 5/15; financial award applicants required to submit FAFSA. *Unit head:* Dr. Patricia Cordeiro, Chair, 401-456-8016. *Application contact:* Graduate Studies, 401-456-8700.
Website: http://www.ric.edu/elementaryEducation/.

Rivier University, School of Graduate Studies, Department of Education, Nashua, NH 03060. Offers curriculum and instruction (M Ed); early childhood education (M Ed); educational administration (M Ed); educational studies (M Ed); elementary education (M Ed); elementary education and general special education (M Ed); emotional and behavioral disorders (M Ed); general social education (M Ed); leadership and learning (Ed D, CAGS); learning disabilities (M Ed); learning disabilities and reading (M Ed); mental health counseling (MA); reading (M Ed); school counseling (M Ed). Part-time and evening/weekend programs available. *Degree requirements:* For master's, comprehensive exam (for some programs), internships. *Entrance requirements:* For master's, GRE General Test or MAT.

Roberts Wesleyan College, Department of Teacher Education, Rochester, NY 14624-1997. Offers adolescence education (M Ed); childhood and special education (M Ed); literacy education (M Ed); special education online (M Ed). Part-time and evening/weekend programs available. *Faculty:* 10 full-time (7 women), 12 part-time/adjunct (6 women). *Students:* 37 full-time (29 women), 10 part-time (6 women); includes 16 minority (15 Black or African American, non-Hispanic/Latino; 1 Hispanic/Latino). Average age 33. 72 applicants, 63% accepted, 34 enrolled. In 2013, 20 master's awarded. *Degree requirements:* For master's, thesis. *Application deadline:* For fall admission, 6/1 for domestic and international students; for spring admission, 11/1 for domestic and international students; for summer admission, 3/1 for domestic and international students. Applications are processed on a rolling basis. Electronic applications accepted. Application fee is waived when completed online. *Expenses: Tuition:* Full-time $12,816; part-time $712 per credit hour. One-time fee: $300. Tuition and fees vary according to course load and program. *Financial support:* In 2013–14, 7 students received support. Career-related internships or fieldwork available. Financial award application deadline: 9/1; financial award applicants required to submit FAFSA. *Unit head:* Dr. Sharon Harris-Ewing, Chair, 585-594-6935, E-mail: harrisewing_sharon@roberts.edu. *Application contact:* Paul Ziegler, Director of Marketing and Recruitment for Teacher Education, 585-594-6146, Fax: 585-594-6108, E-mail: ziegler_paul@roberts.edu.
Website: https://www.roberts.edu/department-of-teacher-education.aspx.

Rockford University, Graduate Studies, Department of Education, Program in Early Childhood Education, Rockford, IL 61108-2393. Offers MAT. Part-time and evening/weekend programs available. *Degree requirements:* For master's, thesis optional. *Entrance requirements:* For master's, GRE General Test, basic skills test (for students seeking certification), 3 letters of recommendation. Additional exam requirements/recommendations for international students: Required—TOEFL. Electronic applications accepted.

Roosevelt University, Graduate Division, College of Education, Department of Teaching and Learning, Chicago, IL 60605. Offers early childhood education (MA); elementary education (MA); special education (MA).

Rutgers, The State University of New Jersey, New Brunswick, Graduate School of Education, Department of Learning and Teaching, Program in Early Childhood/Elementary Education, Piscataway, NJ 08854-8097. Offers Ed M, Ed D. Part-time programs available. Terminal master's awarded for partial completion of doctoral program. *Degree requirements:* For master's, comprehensive exam (for some programs); for doctorate, thesis/dissertation, qualifying exam. *Entrance requirements:* For master's, GRE General Test, minimum GPA of 3.0; for doctorate, GRE General Test, minimum GPA of 3.5. Additional exam requirements/recommendations for international students: Required—TOEFL. Electronic applications accepted.

Saginaw Valley State University, College of Education, Program in Early Childhood Education, University Center, MI 48710. Offers MAT. *Accreditation:* NCATE. Part-time and evening/weekend programs available. *Students:* 5 full-time (all women), 95 part-time (93 women); includes 2 minority (both Black or African American, non-Hispanic/Latino), 3 international. Average age 34. 23 applicants, 100% accepted, 11 enrolled. In 2013, 23 master's awarded. *Degree requirements:* For master's, capstone course. *Entrance requirements:* For master's, minimum GPA of 3.0, teaching certificate. Additional exam requirements/recommendations for international students: Required—TOEFL (minimum score 550 paper-based; 79 iBT). *Application deadline:* For fall admission, 7/15 for international students; for winter admission, 11/15 for international students; for spring admission, 4/15 for international students. Applications are processed on a rolling basis. Application fee: $30 ($80 for international students). Electronic applications accepted. *Expenses:* Tuition, state resident: full-time $8933; part-time $496.30 per credit hour. Tuition, nonresident: full-time $16,806; part-time $933.65 per credit hour. *Required fees:* $263; $14.60 per credit hour. Tuition and fees vary according to degree level. *Financial support:* Federal Work-Study and scholarships/grants available. Support available to part-time students. Financial award applicants required to submit FAFSA. *Unit head:* Dr. Mary Harmon, Dean, 989-964-7107, Fax: 989-964-4563, E-mail: coeconnect@svsu.edu. *Application contact:* Jenna Briggs, Director, Graduate and International Admissions, 989-964-6096, Fax: 989-964-2788, E-mail: gradadm@svsu.edu.

St. Bonaventure University, School of Graduate Studies, School of Education, Literacy Programs, St. Bonaventure, NY 14778-2284. Offers adolescent literacy 5-12 (MS Ed); childhood literacy B-6 (MS Ed). Program offered in Olean and Buffalo Center (Hamburg, NY). *Accreditation:* NCATE. Part-time and evening/weekend programs available. *Faculty:* 2 full-time (both women), 1 (woman) part-time/adjunct. *Students:* 14 full-time (13 women), 14 part-time (13 women). Average age 29. 19 applicants, 100% accepted, 13 enrolled. In 2013, 27 master's awarded. *Degree requirements:* For master's, comprehensive exam, thesis optional, literacy coaching internship, portfolio. *Entrance requirements:* For master's, interview, writing sample, minimum undergraduate GPA of 3.0, two letters of recommendation, teaching certificate in matching area, transcripts. Additional exam requirements/recommendations for international students: Required—TOEFL (minimum score 550 paper-based; 80 iBT). *Application deadline:* For fall admission, 6/15 priority date for domestic students, 2/1 for international students; for spring admission, 11/15 priority date for domestic students, 7/1 for international students. Applications are processed on a rolling basis. Application fee: $0. Electronic applications accepted. *Financial support:* In 2013–14, 4 research assistantships with full and partial tuition reimbursements were awarded; Federal Work-Study, scholarships/grants, health care benefits, and unspecified assistantships also available. Support available to part-time students. Financial award application deadline: 4/15; financial award applicants required to submit FAFSA. *Unit head:* Dr. Karen M. Wieland, Program Director, 716-375-2369, Fax: 716-375-2360, E-mail: kwieland@sbu.edu. *Application contact:* Bruce Campbell, Director of Graduate Admissions, 716-375-2429, Fax: 716-375-4015, E-mail: gradsch@sbu.edu.
Website: http://www.sbu.edu/academics/schools/education/graduate-degrees-certificates/msed-in-childhood-literacy.

St. Catherine University, Graduate Programs, Program in Education - Montessori Education, St. Paul, MN 55105. Offers MA.

St. John's University, The School of Education, Department of Curriculum and Instruction, Program in Early Childhood Education, Queens, NY 11439. Offers MS Ed. Part-time and evening/weekend programs available. *Students:* 18 full-time (all women), 25 part-time (all women); includes 22 minority (7 Black or African American, non-Hispanic/Latino; 5 Asian, non-Hispanic/Latino; 10 Hispanic/Latino), 2 international. Average age 29. 44 applicants, 91% accepted, 14 enrolled. In 2013, 16 master's awarded. *Degree requirements:* For master's, comprehensive exam. *Entrance requirements:* For master's, minimum GPA of 3.0, 2 letters of recommendation, qualification for the New York State provisional (initial) teaching certificate, transcript, personal statement. Additional exam requirements/recommendations for international students: Required—TOEFL (minimum score 600 paper-based; 100 iBT), IELTS (minimum score 5.5). *Application deadline:* For fall admission, 8/17 for domestic students, 5/1 priority date for international students; for spring admission, 1/5 for domestic students, 11/1 priority date for international students. Applications are processed on a rolling basis. Application fee: $70. Electronic applications accepted. *Expenses: Tuition:* Full-time $19,800; part-time $1100 per credit. *Required fees:* $170 per semester. *Financial support:* Research assistantships available. *Faculty research:* Improving children's learning in math, science and technology; health and nutrition education to prevent obesity; oral language and literacy development in diverse populations; home-school collaborations in literacy among young ELLS; multicultural and international education; bilingual education; at-risk children; arts education; parent, home and community partnership; special needs and inclusive education. *Unit head:* Dr. Judith McVarish, Chair, 718-990-2334, E-mail: mcvarisj@stjohns.edu. *Application contact:* Dr. Kelly K. Ronayne, Associate Dean of Graduate Admissions, 718-990-2304, Fax: 718-990-2343, E-mail: graded@stjohns.edu.

St. Joseph's College, Long Island Campus, Program in Infant/Toddler Early Childhood Special Education, Patchogue, NY 11772-2399. Offers MA. Part-time and evening/weekend programs available. *Degree requirements:* For master's, thesis, full-time practicum experience. *Entrance requirements:* For master's, 1 course in child development, 2 courses in special education, minimum undergraduate GPA of 3.0, New York state teaching certificate, interview. Additional exam requirements/recommendations for international students: Required—TOEFL (minimum score 550 paper-based).

St. Joseph's College, New York, Graduate Programs, Program in Education, Field of Infant/Toddler Early Childhood Special Education, Brooklyn, NY 11205-3688. Offers MA.

Saint Mary's College of California, Kalmanovitz School of Education, Program in Early Childhood Education, Moraga, CA 94575. Offers curriculum and instruction (MA); supervision and leadership (MA). Part-time and evening/weekend programs available. *Degree requirements:* For master's, thesis or alternative. *Entrance requirements:* For master's, interview, minimum GPA of 3.0.

Saint Mary's College of California, Kalmanovitz School of Education, Program in Montessori Education, Moraga, CA 94575. Offers reading and language arts (M Ed, MA).

Saint Xavier University, Graduate Studies, School of Education, Chicago, IL 60655-3105. Offers counseling (MA); curriculum and instruction (MA); early childhood education (MA); educational administration (MA); elementary education (MA); individualized studies (MA), including educational technology, English as a second language (ESL), ISTEM (integrative science, technology, engineering, and math), science education; music education (MA); reading (MA); secondary education (MA); Spanish education (MA); special education (MA); teaching and leadership (MA). *Accreditation:* NCATE. Part-time and evening/weekend programs available. *Degree requirements:* For master's, thesis or project. *Entrance requirements:* For master's, minimum GPA of 3.0. *Expenses:* Contact institution.

Salem State University, School of Graduate Studies, Program in Early Childhood Education, Salem, MA 01970-5353. Offers M Ed. *Accreditation:* NCATE. Part-time and evening/weekend programs available. *Students:* 3 full-time (all women), 26 part-time (all women). 9 applicants, 67% accepted, 5 enrolled. In 2013, 12 master's awarded. *Entrance requirements:* For master's, GRE or MAT. Additional exam requirements/recommendations for international students: Required—TOEFL (minimum score 550 paper-based; 80 iBT) or IELTS (minimum score 5.5). *Application deadline:* For fall admission, 4/1 for domestic students; for spring admission, 10/1 for domestic students. Applications are processed on a rolling basis. Application fee: $50. *Financial support:* Career-related internships or fieldwork, Federal Work-Study, scholarships/grants, and unspecified assistantships available. Support available to part-time students. Financial award application deadline: 4/1; financial award applicants required to submit FAFSA. *Application contact:* Dr. Lee A. Brossoit, Assistant Dean of Graduate Admissions, 978-542-6673, Fax: 978-542-7215, E-mail: lbrossoit@salemstate.edu.
Website: http://www.salemstate.edu/academics/schools/12545.php.

Samford University, Orlean Bullard Beeson School of Education, Birmingham, AL 35229. Offers early childhood/elementary education (MS Ed); educational leadership (MS Ed, Ed D); gifted education (MS Ed); instructional leadership (MS Ed, Ed S); secondary collaboration (MS Ed); M Div/MS Ed. *Accreditation:* NCATE. Part-time and evening/weekend programs available. *Faculty:* 10 full-time (5 women), 16 part-time/adjunct (15 women). *Students:* 40 full-time (25 women), 210 part-time (156 women); includes 39 minority (33 Black or African American, non-Hispanic/Latino; 3 American Indian or Alaska Native, non-Hispanic/Latino; 2 Asian, non-Hispanic/Latino; 1 Hispanic/Latino), 4 international. Average age 38. 81 applicants, 89% accepted, 70 enrolled. In 2013, 94 master's, 21 doctorates, 16 other advanced degrees awarded. *Degree requirements:* For master's and Ed S, comprehensive exam; for doctorate, comprehensive exam, thesis/dissertation. *Entrance requirements:* For master's, GRE (minimum score of 295) or MAT (minimum score of 396); waived if previously completed a graduate degree, writing sample, statement of purpose, 3 letters of recommendation, 2 original copies of all transcripts, minimum GPA of 2.75, teaching certificate; for doctorate, minimum GPA of 3.7, professional resume, writing sample, 3 letters of recommendation, 1 original copy of all transcripts; for Ed S, master's degree, teaching certificate, minimum GPA of 3.25, 3 letters of recommendation, 2 original copies of all transcripts, writing sample, statement of purpose. Additional exam requirements/recommendations for international students: Required—TOEFL (minimum score 90 iBT), IELTS (minimum score 7). *Application deadline:* For fall admission, 7/30 for domestic and international students; for winter admission, 4/5 for domestic students; for spring admission, 12/5 for domestic and international students; for summer admission, 4/18 for domestic and international students. Applications are processed on a rolling basis. Application fee: $35. Electronic applications accepted. *Expenses: Tuition:* Full-time $11,552; part-time $722 per credit. *Required fees:* $500; $250 per term. *Financial support:* In 2013–14, 162 students received support. Research assistantships, career-related internships or fieldwork, Federal Work-Study, scholarships/grants, and tuition waivers (partial) available. Support available to part-time students. Financial award applicants required to submit FAFSA. *Faculty research:* Research on gifted/high ability students (K-12), school law, the characteristics of beginning teachers, the nature of school reform, school culture, quality improvement in education, K-12 student achievement, reading research, classroom management, reading intervention, schema theory. *Unit head:* Dr. Maurice Persall, Chair, Department of Educational Leadership, 205-726-2019, E-mail: jmpersal@samford.edu. *Application contact:* Brooke Gilreath Karr, Graduate Admissions Coordinator, 205-729-2783, Fax: 205-726-4233, E-mail: kbgilrea@samford.edu.
Website: http://www.samford.edu/education/.

San Francisco State University, Division of Graduate Studies, College of Education, Department of Elementary Education, Program in Early Childhood Education, San Francisco, CA 94132-1722. Offers MA. *Accreditation:* NCATE. *Unit head:* Dr. Debra Luna, Chair, 415-338-1562, E-mail: dluna@sfsu.edu. *Application contact:* Dr. Barbara Henderson, MA Program Coordinator, 415-338-1319, E-mail: barbarah@sfsu.edu.
Website: http://coe.sfsu.edu/eed/early-childhood-education.

San Francisco State University, Division of Graduate Studies, College of Education, Department of Special Education, San Francisco, CA 94132-1722. Offers autism spectrum (AC); communicative disorders (MS); early childhood special education (AC); guide dog mobility (AC); orientation and mobility (MA, Credential); special education (MA, PhD). PhD offered jointly with University of California, Berkeley. *Accreditation:* NCATE. *Unit head:* Dr. Nancy Robinson, Interim Chair, 415-338-1161, E-mail: spedcd@sfsu.edu. *Application contact:* Louise Guy, Office Coordinator, 415-338-1161, E-mail: lguy@sfsu.edu.
Website: http://coe.sfsu.edu/sped.

Shippensburg University of Pennsylvania, School of Graduate Studies, College of Education and Human Services, Department of Teacher Education, Shippensburg, PA 17257-2299. Offers curriculum and instruction (M Ed), including biology, early childhood education, elementary education, geography/earth science, history, mathematics, middle level education, modern languages; reading (M Ed). *Accreditation:* NCATE. Part-time and evening/weekend programs available. *Faculty:* 13 full-time (9 women), 2 part-time/adjunct (both women). *Students:* 6 full-time (all women), 72 part-time (61 women); includes 5 minority (1 Black or African American, non-Hispanic/Latino; 1 Asian, non-Hispanic/Latino; 2 Hispanic/Latino; 1 Two or more races, non-Hispanic/Latino), 1 international. Average age 30. 55 applicants, 60% accepted, 24 enrolled. In 2013, 63 master's awarded. *Degree requirements:* For master's, comprehensive exam (for some programs), thesis optional, practicum or internship; capstone seminar (for some programs). *Entrance requirements:* For master's, MAT or GRE (if GPA less than 2.75), interview, 3 letters of reference, questionnaire of teaching background and future goals. Additional exam requirements/recommendations for international students: Required—TOEFL (minimum score 580 paper-based); Recommended—IELTS (minimum score 6). *Application deadline:* For fall admission, 4/1 priority date for domestic students, 4/30 for international students; for spring admission, 9/1 priority date for domestic students, 9/30 for international students. Applications are processed on a rolling basis. Application fee: $45. Electronic applications accepted. *Expenses: Tuition, area resident:* Part-time $442 per credit. Tuition, state resident: part-time $442 per credit. Tuition, nonresident: part-time $663 per credit. *Required fees:* $127 per credit. *Financial support:* In 2013–14, 4 research assistantships with full tuition reimbursements (averaging $5,000 per year) were awarded; career-related internships or fieldwork, scholarships/grants, unspecified assistantships, and resident hall director and student payroll positions also available. Support available to part-time students. Financial award application deadline: 3/1; financial award applicants required to submit FAFSA. *Unit head:* Dr. Christine A. Royce, Chairperson, 717-477-1688, Fax: 717-477-4046, E-mail: caroyc@ship.edu. *Application contact:* Jeremy R. Goshorn, Assistant Dean of Graduate Admissions, 717-477-1231, Fax: 717-477-4016, E-mail: jrgoshorn@ship.edu.
Website: http://www.ship.edu/teacher/.

Siena Heights University, Graduate College, Adrian, MI 49221-1796. Offers clinical mental health counseling (MA); education leadership (Specialist); leadership (MA), including health care, higher education leadership, organizational; teacher education (MA), including early childhood, early childhood: Montessori-based, education leadership: principal, elementary education, K-12 reading, leadership: higher education, secondary education, K-12 reading, special education, K-12 cognitive impairment, special education, K-12 learning disabled. Part-time and evening/weekend programs available. *Faculty:* 37. *Students:* 9 full-time (7 women), 251 part-time (179 women). In 2013, 32 master's awarded. *Degree requirements:* For master's, thesis, presentation. *Entrance requirements:* For master's, minimum GPA of 3.0, current resume, essay, all post-secondary transcripts, 3 letters of reference, conviction disclosure form; copy of teaching certificate (for some education programs); for Specialist, master's degree, minimum GPA of 3.0, current resume, essay, all post-secondary transcripts, 3 letters of reference, conviction disclosure form; copy of teaching certificate (for some education programs). *Application deadline:* Applications are processed on a rolling basis. Application fee: $50. *Expenses: Tuition:* Part-time $535 per semester hour. *Required fees:* $130 per semester. *Financial support:* Career-related internships or fieldwork, Federal Work-Study, and resident assistantships available. Financial award application deadline: 9/1; financial award applicants required to submit FAFSA. *Unit head:* Dr. Linda S. Pettit, Dean, Graduate College, 517-264-7661, Fax: 517-264-7714, E-mail: lpettit@sienahts.edu.
Website: http://www.sienaheights.edu.

Sonoma State University, School of Education, Rohnert Park, CA 94928. Offers curriculum, teaching, and learning (MA); early childhood education (MA); education (Ed D); educational administration (MA); multiple subject (Credential); reading and

literacy (MA); single subject (Credential); special education (MA, Credential). *Accreditation:* NCATE. Part-time and evening/weekend programs available. *Faculty:* 11 full-time (9 women), 1 (woman) part-time/adjunct. *Students:* 162 full-time (119 women), 165 part-time (125 women); includes 61 minority (4 Black or African American, non-Hispanic/Latino; 1 American Indian or Alaska Native, non-Hispanic/Latino; 12 Asian, non-Hispanic/Latino; 29 Hispanic/Latino; 1 Native Hawaiian or other Pacific Islander, non-Hispanic/Latino; 14 Two or more races, non-Hispanic/Latino), 1 international. Average age 33. 314 applicants, 82% accepted, 75 enrolled. In 2013, 41 master's, 287 other advanced degrees awarded. *Degree requirements:* For master's, thesis or alternative. *Entrance requirements:* For master's, minimum GPA of 2.5. Additional exam requirements/recommendations for international students: Required—TOEFL (minimum score 500 paper-based). Application fee: $55. *Expenses:* Tuition, state resident: full-time $8500. Tuition, nonresident: full-time $12,964. *Required fees:* $1762. *Financial support:* In 2013–14, 1 research assistantship (averaging $1,876 per year) was awarded; fellowships, career-related internships or fieldwork, and Federal Work-Study also available. Support available to part-time students. Financial award application deadline: 3/2; financial award applicants required to submit FAFSA. *Unit head:* Dr. Carlos Ayala, Dean, 707-664-4412, E-mail: carlos.ayala@sonoma.edu. *Application contact:* Dr. Jennifer Mahdavi, Coordinator of Graduate Studies, 707-664-3311, E-mail: jennifer.mahdavi@sonoma.edu.
Website: http://www.sonoma.edu/education/.

South Carolina State University, School of Graduate and Professional Studies, Department of Education, Orangeburg, SC 29117-0001. Offers early childhood and special education (M Ed); early childhood education (MAT); elementary education (M Ed, MAT); general science (MAT); mathematics (MAT); secondary education (M Ed), including biology education, business education, counselor education, English education, home economics education, industrial education, mathematics education, science education, social studies education; special education (M Ed), including emotionally handicapped, learning disabilities, mentally handicapped. *Accreditation:* NCATE. Part-time and evening/weekend programs available. *Faculty:* 9 full-time (3 women), 4 part-time/adjunct (3 women). *Students:* 32 full-time (26 women), 33 part-time (26 women); includes 63 minority (61 Black or African American, non-Hispanic/Latino; 2 Asian, non-Hispanic/Latino). Average age 31. 21 applicants, 100% accepted, 21 enrolled. In 2013, 15 master's awarded. *Degree requirements:* For master's, thesis optional, departmental qualifying exam. *Entrance requirements:* For master's, GRE General Test, NTE, interview, teaching certificate. *Application deadline:* For fall admission, 6/15 priority date for domestic students, 6/15 for international students; for spring admission, 11/1 for domestic and international students. Applications are processed on a rolling basis. Application fee: $25. Electronic applications accepted. *Expenses:* Tuition, state resident: full-time $8906; part-time $543 per credit hour. Tuition, nonresident: full-time $18,040; part-time $1051 per credit hour. *Financial support:* Fellowships, career-related internships or fieldwork, Federal Work-Study, and institutionally sponsored loans available. Financial award application deadline: 6/1. *Faculty research:* Critical thinking, child abuse, stress, test-taking skills, conflict resolution, mainstreaming. *Unit head:* Dr. Margaret Evelyn Fields, Interim Chair, 803-536-7098, Fax: 803-516-4568, E-mail: efields@scsu.edu. *Application contact:* Curtis Foskey, Coordinator of Graduate Studies, 803-536-8419, Fax: 803-536-8812, E-mail: cfoskey@scsu.edu.

Southern Oregon University, Graduate Studies, School of Education, Ashland, OR 97520. Offers elementary education (MA Ed, MS Ed), including classroom teacher, early childhood, handicapped learner, reading, supervision; secondary education (MA Ed, MS Ed), including classroom teacher, handicapped learner, reading, supervision; teaching (MAT). Postbaccalaureate distance learning degree programs offered (minimal on-campus study). *Faculty:* 23 full-time (16 women), 21 part-time/adjunct (20 women). *Students:* 92 full-time (68 women), 118 part-time (88 women); includes 19 minority (1 Black or African American, non-Hispanic/Latino; 1 American Indian or Alaska Native, non-Hispanic/Latino; 2 Asian, non-Hispanic/Latino; 10 Hispanic/Latino; 5 Two or more races, non-Hispanic/Latino), 5 international. Average age 36. 22 applicants, 59% accepted, 12 enrolled. In 2013, 127 master's awarded. *Degree requirements:* For master's, thesis optional. *Entrance requirements:* For master's, GRE General Test, minimum cumulative GPA of 3.0 in the last 90 quarter credits (60 semester credits) of undergraduate coursework. Additional exam requirements/recommendations for international students: Required—TOEFL (minimum score 540 paper-based; 76 iBT), IELTS (minimum score 6), ELPT (minimum score 964) or ELS (minimum score 112). *Application deadline:* For fall admission, 7/31 priority date for domestic and international students; for winter admission, 11/15 priority date for domestic and international students; for spring admission, 1/7 priority date for domestic and international students. Applications are processed on a rolling basis. Application fee: $50. Electronic applications accepted. *Expenses:* Tuition, state resident: full-time $13,635; part-time $378.72 per credit hour. Tuition, nonresident: full-time $17,042; part-time $473.40 per credit hour. *Required fees:* $408 per quarter. *Financial support:* Research assistantships with partial tuition reimbursements, career-related internships or fieldwork, institutionally sponsored loans, scholarships/grants, and unspecified assistantships available. *Unit head:* Dr. Gerry McCain, Graduate Program Coordinator, 541-552-6934, E-mail: mccaing@sou.edu. *Application contact:* Kelly Moutsatson, Director of Admissions, 541-552-6411, Fax: 541-552-8403, E-mail: admissions@sou.edu.
Website: http://www.sou.edu/education/.

Southwestern Oklahoma State University, College of Professional and Graduate Studies, School of Behavioral Sciences and Education, Specialization in Early Childhood Education, Weatherford, OK 73096-3098. Offers M Ed. M Ed distance learning degree program offered to Oklahoma residents only. *Accreditation:* NCATE. Part-time and evening/weekend programs available. *Degree requirements:* For master's, exam. *Entrance requirements:* For master's, GRE General Test or minimum undergraduate GPA of 3.0. Additional exam requirements/recommendations for international students: Required—TOEFL.

Southwest Minnesota State University, Department of Education, Marshall, MN 56258. Offers ESL (MS); math (MS); reading (MS); special education (MS), including developmental disabilities, early childhood education, emotional behavioral disorders, learning disabilities; teaching, learning and leadership (MS). Part-time and evening/weekend programs available. Postbaccalaureate distance learning degree programs offered (no on-campus study). *Entrance requirements:* Additional exam requirements/recommendations for international students: Required—TOEFL or IELTS; Recommended—TOEFL (minimum score 550 paper-based; 80 iBT), IELTS.

Springfield College, Graduate Programs, Program in Education, Springfield, MA 01109-3797. Offers counseling and secondary education (M Ed, MS); early childhood education (M Ed, MS); education (M Ed, MS); educational administration (M Ed, MS); educational studies (M Ed, MS); elementary education (M Ed, MS); secondary education (M Ed, MS); special education (M Ed, MS). Part-time and evening/weekend programs available. *Faculty:* 6 full-time. *Students:* 47 full-time. 45 applicants, 87% accepted, 35 enrolled. In 2013, 15 master's awarded. *Entrance requirements:* Additional exam requirements/recommendations for international students: Required—TOEFL (minimum score 550 paper-based); Recommended—IELTS (minimum score 6). *Application deadline:* For fall admission, 1/15 for domestic and international students; for winter admission, 11/1 for domestic and international students; for spring admission, 11/1 for domestic and international students. Applications are processed on a rolling basis. Application fee: $50. Electronic applications accepted. *Expenses: Tuition:* Full-time $13,620; part-time $908 per credit. *Financial support:* Fellowships with partial tuition reimbursements, teaching assistantships with partial tuition reimbursements, career-related internships or fieldwork, Federal Work-Study, institutionally sponsored loans, and unspecified assistantships available. Financial award application deadline: 3/1; financial award applicants required to submit FAFSA. *Unit head:* Jennifer Johnston, Program Coordinator, 413-748-3348, E-mail: jjohnston@springfieldcollege.edu. *Application contact:* Evelyn Cohen, Associate Director of Graduate Admissions, 413-748-3479, Fax: 413-748-3694, E-mail: ecohen@springfieldcollege.edu.

Spring Hill College, Graduate Programs, Program in Education, Mobile, AL 36608-1791. Offers early childhood education (MAT, MS Ed); educational theory (MS Ed); elementary education (MAT, MS Ed); secondary education (MAT, MS Ed). Part-time programs available. *Faculty:* 3 full-time (all women). *Students:* 2 full-time (both women), 17 part-time (14 women); includes 2 minority (both Black or African American, non-Hispanic/Latino). Average age 32. In 2013, 7 master's awarded. *Degree requirements:* For master's, comprehensive exam, completion of program within 6 calendar years of entrance into graduate studies at Spring Hill; documentation of course field assignments (MS) or completion of internship (MAT). *Entrance requirements:* For master's, GRE, MAT, or PRAXIS (varies by program), bachelor's degree with minimum undergraduate GPA of 3.0; class B certificate (MS) or minimum number of hours in specific fields (MAT). Additional exam requirements/recommendations for international students: Required—TOEFL (minimum score 550 paper-based; 80 iBT), IELTS (minimum score 6.5), CPE or CAE (minimum score C), Michigan English Language Assessment Battery (minimum score 90). *Application deadline:* For fall admission, 8/1 priority date for domestic and international students; for spring admission, 12/1 priority date for domestic and international students. Applications are processed on a rolling basis. Application fee: $25 ($35 for international students). Electronic applications accepted. *Expenses:* Contact institution. *Financial support:* Applicants required to submit FAFSA. *Unit head:* Dr. Lori P. Aultman, Chair of Teacher Education, 251-380-3473, Fax: 251-460-2184, E-mail: laultman@shc.edu. *Application contact:* Donna B. Tarasavage, Associate Director, Academic Affairs, 251-380-3067, Fax: 251-460-2182, E-mail: dtarasavage@shc.edu.
Website: http://www.shc.edu/page/teacher-education.

State University of New York at New Paltz, Graduate School, School of Education, Department of Educational Studies, Program in Special Education, New Paltz, NY 12561. Offers adolescence special education (7-12) (MS Ed); adolescence special education and literacy education (MS Ed); childhood special education (1-6) (MS Ed); childhood special education and literacy education (MS Ed); early childhood special education (B-2) (MS Ed). *Accreditation:* NCATE. Part-time and evening/weekend programs available. *Faculty:* 6 full-time (4 women), 9 part-time/adjunct (all women). *Students:* 42 full-time (35 women), 35 part-time (24 women); includes 11 minority (1 Asian, non-Hispanic/Latino; 8 Hispanic/Latino; 2 Two or more races, non-Hispanic/Latino). Average age 27. 63 applicants, 73% accepted, 24 enrolled. In 2013, 43 master's awarded. *Degree requirements:* For master's, portfolio. *Entrance requirements:* For master's, minimum GPA of 3.0 (3.2 for special education and literacy programs), New York state teaching certificate. Additional exam requirements/recommendations for international students: Required—TOEFL (minimum score 550 paper-based; 80 iBT), IELTS (minimum score 6.5). *Application deadline:* For fall admission, 3/15 priority date for domestic students, 3/15 for international students; for spring admission, 11/1 for domestic and international students. Application fee: $50. Electronic applications accepted. *Expenses:* Tuition, state resident: full-time $9870; part-time $411 per credit. Tuition, nonresident: full-time $18,350; part-time $765 per credit. *Required fees:* $1213. Tuition and fees vary according to program. *Financial support:* Application deadline: 8/1. *Unit head:* Dr. Jane Sileo, Coordinator, 845-257-2835, E-mail: sileoj@newpaltz.edu. *Application contact:* Caroline Murphy, Graduate Admissions Advisor, 845-257-3285, E-mail: gradschool@newpaltz.edu.
Website: http://www.newpaltz.edu/edstudies/special_ed.html.

State University of New York at New Paltz, Graduate School, School of Education, Department of Elementary Education, New Paltz, NY 12561. Offers childhood education 1-6 (MS Ed, MST), including childhood education 1-6 (MST), early childhood B-2 (MS Ed), mathematics, science and technology (MS Ed), reading/literacy (MS Ed); literacy education 5-12 (MS Ed); literacy education and childhood special education (MS Ed); literacy education B-6 (MS Ed). *Accreditation:* NCATE. Part-time and evening/weekend programs available. *Faculty:* 11 full-time (10 women), 9 part-time/adjunct (8 women). *Students:* 51 full-time (47 women), 128 part-time (117 women); includes 13 minority (2 Black or African American, non-Hispanic/Latino; 11 Hispanic/Latino). Average age 27. 103 applicants, 89% accepted, 57 enrolled. In 2013, 96 master's awarded. *Degree requirements:* For master's, comprehensive exam (for some programs), portfolio. *Entrance requirements:* For master's, GRE or MAT (for MST), minimum GPA of 3.0 (3.2 for literacy and special education), New York state teaching certificate (for MS Ed). Additional exam requirements/recommendations for international students: Required—TOEFL (minimum score 550 paper-based; 80 iBT), IELTS (minimum score 6.5). *Application deadline:* For fall admission, 4/1 for domestic and international students; for spring admission, 11/15 for domestic and international students. Application fee: $50. Electronic applications accepted. *Expenses:* Tuition, state resident: full-time $9870; part-time $411 per credit. Tuition, nonresident: full-time $18,350; part-time $765 per credit. *Required fees:* $1213. Tuition and fees vary according to program. *Financial support:* Application deadline: 8/1. *Faculty research:* Multi-sensory teaching methods, volunteer tutoring programs for struggling readers, school readiness and transition, math/science/technology, university-school partnerships. *Unit head:* Dr. Andrea Noel, Chair, 845-257-2860, E-mail: noela@newpaltz.edu. *Application contact:* Caroline Murphy, Graduate Admissions Advisor, 845-257-3285, Fax: 845-257-3284, E-mail: gradschool@newpaltz.edu.
Website: http://www.newpaltz.edu/elementaryed/.

State University of New York at Oswego, Graduate Studies, School of Education, Department of Curriculum and Instruction, Oswego, NY 13126. Offers adolescence education (MST); art education (MAT); childhood education (MST); elementary education (MS Ed); literacy education (MS Ed); secondary education (MS Ed); special education (MS Ed). Part-time and evening/weekend programs available. *Degree requirements:* For master's, comprehensive exam (for some programs), thesis optional. *Entrance requirements:* For master's, GRE General Test, minimum GPA of 2.7, provisional teaching certificate. Additional exam requirements/recommendations for international students: Required—TOEFL (minimum score 560 paper-based). *Faculty research:* Classroom applications for microcomputers; classroom questioning, wait-time, and achievement; values clarification and academic achievement.

State University of New York at Plattsburgh, Division of Education, Health, and Human Services, Program in Early Childhood Education, Plattsburgh, NY 12901-2681. Offers early childhood birth-grade 6 (Advanced Certificate). *Students:* 1 (woman) full-time. *Unit head:* Dr. Heidi Schnackenberg, Coordinator, 518-564-5143, E-mail:

schnachl@plattsburgh.edu. *Application contact:* Betsy Kane, Director, Graduate Admissions, 518-564-4723, Fax: 518-564-4722, E-mail: bkane002@plattsburgh.edu.

State University of New York College at Cortland, Graduate Studies, School of Education, Program in Childhood/Early Child Education, Cortland, NY 13045. Offers MS Ed, MST. *Accreditation:* NCATE. *Expenses:* Tuition, state resident: full-time $9870; part-time $411 per credit hour. Tuition, nonresident: full-time $18,350; part-time $765 per credit hour. *Required fees:* $1458; $65 per credit hour.

State University of New York College at Geneseo, Graduate Studies, School of Education, Program in Early Childhood Education, Geneseo, NY 14454-1401. Offers MS Ed. Part-time and evening/weekend programs available. *Degree requirements:* For master's, thesis optional. *Application deadline:* For fall admission, 3/1 priority date for domestic students; for spring admission, 10/1 for domestic students. Application fee: $50. *Expenses:* Tuition, state resident: full-time $8790; part-time $411 per credit hour. Tuition, nonresident: full-time $18,350; part-time $765 per credit hour. *Required fees:* $795; $32.90 per credit hour. *Financial support:* Scholarships/grants, health care benefits, and unspecified assistantships available. Support available to part-time students. Financial award application deadline: 4/1; financial award applicants required to submit FAFSA. *Unit head:* Dr. Anjoo Sikka, Dean of School of Education, 585-245-5151, Fax: 585-245-5220, E-mail: sikka@geneseo.edu. *Application contact:* Tracy Peterson, Director of Student Success, 585-245-5443, Fax: 585-245-5220, E-mail: peterson@geneseo.edu.

State University of New York College at Potsdam, School of Education and Professional Studies, Program in Special Education, Potsdam, NY 13676. Offers adolescence (grades 7-12) (MS Ed); childhood (grades 1-6) (MS Ed); early childhood (birth-grade 2) (MS Ed). *Accreditation:* NCATE. Part-time programs available. *Degree requirements:* For master's, culminating experience. *Entrance requirements:* For master's, minimum GPA of 3.0 in last 60 hours of course work. Additional exam requirements/recommendations for international students: Required—TOEFL (minimum score 550 paper-based; 80 iBT), IELTS (minimum score 6). Electronic applications accepted.

Stephen F. Austin State University, Graduate School, College of Education, Department of Elementary Education, Program in Early Childhood Education, Nacogdoches, TX 75962. Offers M Ed. *Accreditation:* NCATE. *Degree requirements:* For master's, comprehensive exam. *Entrance requirements:* For master's, GRE General Test. Additional exam requirements/recommendations for international students: Required—TOEFL (minimum score 550 paper-based).

Syracuse University, School of Education, Program in Early Childhood Special Education, Syracuse, NY 13244. Offers MS. Part-time programs available. *Students:* 19 full-time (18 women), 6 part-time (all women); includes 6 minority (2 Black or African American, non-Hispanic/Latino; 1 American Indian or Alaska Native, non-Hispanic/Latino; 1 Asian, non-Hispanic/Latino; 1 Hispanic/Latino; 1 Two or more races, non-Hispanic/Latino). Average age 29. 17 applicants, 65% accepted, 4 enrolled. In 2013, 13 master's awarded. *Entrance requirements:* For master's, interview. Additional exam requirements/recommendations for international students: Required—TOEFL (minimum score 100 iBT). *Application deadline:* For fall admission, 1/15 for domestic students, 1/15 priority date for international students; for spring admission, 10/15 priority date for domestic and international students. Applications are processed on a rolling basis. Application fee: $75. Electronic applications accepted. *Financial support:* Fellowships with full tuition reimbursements and teaching assistantships with full and partial tuition reimbursements available. Financial award application deadline: 1/1; financial award applicants required to submit FAFSA. *Unit head:* Dr. Gail Ensher, Director, 315-443-9650. *Application contact:* Laurie Deyo, Graduate Recruiter, School of Education, 315-443-2505, E-mail: e-gradrcrt@syr.edu. Website: http://soeweb.syr.edu/.

Teachers College, Columbia University, Graduate Faculty of Education, Department of Curriculum and Teaching, Program in Early Childhood Education, New York, NY 10027. Offers Ed M, MA, Ed D. *Accreditation:* NCATE. *Faculty:* 6 full-time, 3 part-time/adjunct. *Students:* 12 full-time (all women), 27 part-time (25 women); includes 14 minority (2 Black or African American, non-Hispanic/Latino; 6 Asian, non-Hispanic/Latino; 2 Hispanic/Latino; 4 Two or more races, non-Hispanic/Latino), 9 international. Average age 28. 51 applicants, 51% accepted, 18 enrolled. In 2013, 15 master's, 1 doctorate awarded. *Degree requirements:* For master's, culminating project; for doctorate, thesis/dissertation. *Entrance requirements:* For doctorate, GRE General Test or MAT. *Application deadline:* For fall admission, 1/2 priority date for domestic students; for spring admission, 4/15 for domestic students. Application fee: $65. Electronic applications accepted. *Financial support:* Career-related internships or fieldwork, Federal Work-Study, institutionally sponsored loans, and tuition waivers (full and partial) available. Support available to part-time students. Financial award applicants required to submit FAFSA. *Faculty research:* Infancy, child development, children and family, policy and program, childhood bilingualism. *Unit head:* Prof. Mariana Souto-Manning, Program Coordinator, 212-678-3970, E-mail: ms3983@columbia.edu. *Application contact:* Peter Shon, Assistant Director of Admission, 212-678-3305, Fax: 212-678-4171, E-mail: shon@exchange.tc.columbia.edu.
Website: http://www.tc.columbia.edu/c&t/childEd/.

Teachers College, Columbia University, Graduate Faculty of Education, Department of Curriculum and Teaching, Program in Early Childhood Special Education, New York, NY 10027-6696. Offers Ed M, MA. *Accreditation:* NCATE. *Faculty:* 6 full-time, 3 part-time/adjunct. *Students:* 22 full-time (21 women), 51 part-time (49 women); includes 30 minority (3 Black or African American, non-Hispanic/Latino; 9 Asian, non-Hispanic/Latino; 10 Hispanic/Latino; 8 Two or more races, non-Hispanic/Latino), 6 international. Average age 26. 112 applicants, 66% accepted, 30 enrolled. In 2013, 34 master's awarded. *Degree requirements:* For master's, culminating project. *Application deadline:* For fall admission, 1/15 priority date for domestic students. Application fee: $65. Electronic applications accepted. *Financial support:* Research assistantships, teaching assistantships, career-related internships or fieldwork, Federal Work-Study, institutionally sponsored loans, and tuition waivers (full and partial) available. Support available to part-time students. Financial award application deadline: 2/1; financial award applicants required to submit FAFSA. *Faculty research:* Curriculum development, infants, urban education, visually-impaired infants. *Unit head:* Prof. Mariana Souto-Manning, Program Coordinator, 212-678-3970, E-mail: ms3983@columbia.edu. *Application contact:* Peter Shon, Assistant Director of Admission, 212-678-3305, Fax: 212-678-4171, E-mail: shon@exchange.tc.columbia.edu.

Tennessee Technological University, College of Graduate Studies, College of Education, Department of Curriculum and Instruction, Program in Early Childhood Education, Cookeville, TN 38505. Offers MA, Ed S. *Accreditation:* NCATE. Part-time and evening/weekend programs available. *Faculty:* 2 full-time (both women). *Students:* 9 full-time (all women), 8 part-time (7 women); includes 2 minority (both Black or African American, non-Hispanic/Latino). Average age 27. 9 applicants, 100% accepted, 5 enrolled. In 2013, 3 master's, 1 other advanced degree awarded. *Degree requirements:* For master's and Ed S, comprehensive exam, thesis or alternative. *Entrance requirements:* For master's, and Ed S, MAT or GRE. Additional exam requirements/recommendations for international students: Required—TOEFL (minimum score 527

paper-based; 71 iBT), IELTS (minimum score 5.5), PTE (minimum score 48), or TOEIC (Test of English as an International Communication). *Application deadline:* For fall admission, 8/1 priority date for domestic students, 5/1 for international students; for spring admission, 12/1 for domestic students, 10/1 for international students. Application fee: $35 ($40 for international students). Electronic applications accepted. *Expenses:* Tuition, state resident: full-time $9347; part-time $465 per credit hour. Tuition, nonresident: full-time $23,635; part-time $1152 per credit hour. *Financial support:* In 2013–14, research assistantships (averaging $4,000 per year), teaching assistantships (averaging $4,000 per year) were awarded; fellowships and career-related internships or fieldwork also available. Financial award application deadline: 4/1. *Unit head:* Dr. Jeremy Wendt, Interim Chairperson, 931-372-3181, Fax: 931-372-6270, E-mail: jwendt@tntech.edu. *Application contact:* Shelia K. Kendrick, Coordinator of Graduate Studies, 931-372-3808, Fax: 931-372-3497, E-mail: skendrick@tntech.edu.

Texas A&M University–Commerce, Graduate School, College of Education and Human Services, Department of Curriculum and Instruction, Commerce, TX 75429-3011. Offers bilingual/ESL education (M Ed, MS); early childhood education (M Ed, MS); elementary education (M Ed, MS); reading (M Ed, MS); secondary education (M Ed, MS); supervision, curriculum and instruction: elementary education (Ed D). MS and M Ed programs in early childhood education offered jointly with Texas Woman's University and University of North Texas. Part-time programs available. Terminal master's awarded for partial completion of doctoral program. *Degree requirements:* For master's, comprehensive exam, thesis (for some programs); for doctorate, 2 foreign languages, thesis/dissertation, departmental qualifying exam. *Entrance requirements:* For master's and doctorate, GRE General Test. Electronic applications accepted. *Expenses:* Tuition, state resident: full-time $3630; part-time $2420 per year. Tuition, nonresident: full-time $9948; part-time $6632.16 per year. *Required fees:* $1006 per year. Tuition and fees vary according to course load. *Faculty research:* Literacy and learning, early childhood, preservice teacher education, technology.

Texas A&M University–Corpus Christi, Graduate Studies and Research, College of Education, Corpus Christi, TX 78412-5503. Offers counseling (MS, PhD), including counseling (MS), counselor education (PhD); curriculum and instruction (MS, Ed D); early childhood education (MS); educational administration (MS); educational leadership (Ed D); educational technology (MS); elementary education (MS); kinesiology (MS); reading (MS); secondary education (MS); special education (MS). Part-time and evening/weekend programs available. *Degree requirements:* For master's, comprehensive exam, thesis (for some programs); for doctorate, comprehensive exam, thesis/dissertation. *Entrance requirements:* For master's, GRE General Test. Additional exam requirements/recommendations for international students: Required—TOEFL. Electronic applications accepted.

Texas A&M University–Kingsville, College of Graduate Studies, College of Education, Department of Education, Program in Early Childhood Education, Kingsville, TX 78363. Offers M Ed. Part-time and evening/weekend programs available. *Faculty:* 9 full-time (5 women), 4 part-time/adjunct (2 women). *Students:* 1 (woman) full-time, 20 part-time (all women); includes 18 minority (2 Black or African American, non-Hispanic/Latino; 16 Hispanic/Latino). Average age 32. 6 applicants, 100% accepted, 6 enrolled. In 2013, 3 master's awarded. *Degree requirements:* For master's, comprehensive exam, mini-thesis. *Entrance requirements:* For master's, GRE General Test, MAT, minimum GPA of 3.0. *Application deadline:* For fall admission, 6/1 for domestic students; for spring admission, 11/15 for domestic students. Applications are processed on a rolling basis. Application fee: $35 ($50 for international students). *Financial support:* Application deadline: 5/15. *Unit head:* Director, 361-593-3203. *Application contact:* Dr. Alberto M. Olivares, Dean, College of Graduate Studies, 361-593-2808, Fax: 361-593-3412, E-mail: a-olivares@tamuk.edu.

Texas A&M University–San Antonio, Department of Curriculum and Kinesiology, San Antonio, TX 78224. Offers bilingual education (MA); early childhood education (M Ed); kinesiology (MS); reading (MS); special education (M Ed), including educational diagnostician, instructional specialist. Part-time and evening/weekend programs available. *Degree requirements:* For master's, comprehensive exam, thesis or alternative. *Entrance requirements:* For master's, MAT. Additional exam requirements/recommendations for international students: Required—TOEFL (minimum score 550 paper-based; 80 iBT), IELTS (minimum score 6). Electronic applications accepted.

Texas Woman's University, Graduate School, College of Professional Education, Department of Family Sciences, Denton, TX 76201. Offers child development (MS); counseling and development (MS); early childhood development and education (PhD); early childhood education (M Ed, MA, MS); family studies (MS, PhD); family therapy (MS, PhD). *Accreditation:* ACA (one or more programs are accredited). Part-time and evening/weekend programs available. *Faculty:* 23 full-time (18 women), 11 part-time/adjunct (9 women). *Students:* 138 full-time (130 women), 296 part-time (272 women); includes 198 minority (117 Black or African American, non-Hispanic/Latino; 5 American Indian or Alaska Native, non-Hispanic/Latino; 15 Asian, non-Hispanic/Latino; 61 Hispanic/Latino), 18 international. Average age 35. 187 applicants, 41% accepted, 56 enrolled. In 2013, 88 master's, 12 doctorates awarded. Terminal master's awarded for partial completion of doctoral program. *Degree requirements:* For master's, comprehensive exam (for some programs), thesis (for some programs); for doctorate, comprehensive exam, thesis/dissertation. *Entrance requirements:* Additional exam requirements/recommendations for international students: Required—TOEFL (minimum score 550 paper-based; 79 iBT). *Application deadline:* For fall admission, 7/1 priority date for domestic students, 2/15 for international students; for spring admission, 9/15 priority date for domestic students, 7/1 for international students. Applications are processed on a rolling basis. Application fee: $50 ($75 for international students). Electronic applications accepted. *Expenses:* Tuition, state resident: full-time $4182; part-time $233.32 per credit hour. Tuition, nonresident: full-time $10,716; part-time $595.32 per credit hour. *Financial support:* In 2013–14, 137 students received support, including 15 research assistantships (averaging $5,637 per year), 8 teaching assistantships (averaging $5,637 per year); career-related internships or fieldwork, Federal Work-Study, institutionally sponsored loans, scholarships/grants, traineeships, health care benefits, and unspecified assistantships also available. Support available to part-time students. Financial award application deadline: 3/1; financial award applicants required to submit FAFSA. *Faculty research:* Parenting/parent education, military families, play therapy, family sexuality, diversity, healthy relationships/healthy marriages, childhood obesity, male communication. *Unit head:* Dr. Karen Petty, Chair, 940-898-2685, Fax: 940-898-2676, E-mail: famsci@twu.edu. *Application contact:* Dr. Samuel Wheeler, Assistant Director of Admissions, 940-898-3188, Fax: 940-898-3081, E-mail: wheelersr@twu.edu.
Website: http://www.twu.edu/family-sciences/.

Towson University, Program in Early Childhood Education, Towson, MD 21252-0001. Offers M Ed, CAS. *Accreditation:* NCATE. Part-time and evening/weekend programs available. *Students:* 16 full-time (all women), 153 part-time (149 women); includes 30 minority (16 Black or African American, non-Hispanic/Latino; 9 Asian, non-Hispanic/Latino; 4 Hispanic/Latino; 1 Two or more races, non-Hispanic/Latino), 4 international. *Degree requirements:* For master's, thesis optional. *Entrance requirements:* For master's, bachelor's degree with minimum GPA of 3.0, resume, teacher certification, work experience or course work in early childhood education; for CAS, master's degree

in early childhood education or related field from nationally-accredited institution; minimum overall GPA of 3.75 for graduate work; resume; 3 letters of recommendation. *Application deadline:* Applications are processed on a rolling basis. Application fee: $45. Electronic applications accepted. *Financial support:* Application deadline: 4/1. *Unit head:* Dr. Janese Daniels, Graduate Program Director, 410-704-4832, E-mail: jdaniels@towson.edu. *Application contact:* Alicia Arkell-Kleis, Information Contact, 410-704-6004, Fax: 410-704-4675, E-mail: grads@towson.edu. Website: http://grad.towson.edu/program/master/eced-med/.

Trident University International, College of Education, Program in Education, Cypress, CA 90630. Offers adult education (MA Ed); aviation education (MA Ed); children's literacy development (MA Ed); e-learning (MA Ed); early childhood education (MA Ed); enrollment management (MA Ed); higher education (MA Ed); teaching and instruction (MA Ed); training and development (MA Ed). Part-time and evening/weekend programs available. Postbaccalaureate distance learning degree programs offered (no on-campus study). *Degree requirements:* For master's, capstone project with integrative paper. *Entrance requirements:* For master's, minimum GPA of 2.5 (students with GPA 3.0 or greater may transfer up to 30% of graduate level credits). Additional exam requirements/recommendations for international students: Required—TOEFL (minimum score 525 paper-based). Electronic applications accepted.

Trinity Washington University, School of Education, Washington, DC 20017-1094. Offers clinical mental health counseling (MA); early childhood education (MAT); educating for change (M Ed); educational administration (MSA); elementary education (MAT); reading (M Ed); school counseling (MA); secondary education (MAT), including English, social studies; special education (MAT). *Accreditation:* NCATE. Part-time and evening/weekend programs available. *Degree requirements:* For master's, thesis (for some programs), capstone project(s). *Entrance requirements:* For master's, PRAXIS I, minimum GPA of 2.8. Additional exam requirements/recommendations for international students: Required—TOEFL (minimum score 550 paper-based). *Application deadline:* For fall admission, 4/1 priority date for domestic students; for winter admission, 11/1 priority date for domestic students; for spring admission, 11/1 priority date for domestic students. Applications are processed on a rolling basis. Application fee: $40. *Expenses: Tuition:* Part-time $715 per credit. *Financial support:* Career-related internships or fieldwork, health care benefits, and unspecified assistantships available. Support available to part-time students. Financial award application deadline: 4/1; financial award applicants required to submit FAFSA. *Faculty research:* Technology, literacy, special education, organizations, inclusion models. *Unit head:* Dr. Janet Stocks, Dean, 202-884-9380, Fax: 202-884-9506, E-mail: stocksj@trinitydc.edu. *Application contact:* Erika Davis, Director of Admissions for School of Education, 202-884-9400, Fax: 202-884-9229, E-mail: daviser@trinitydc.edu. Website: http://www.trinitydc.edu/education/.

Troy University, Graduate School, College of Education, Program in Early Childhood Education, Troy, AL 36082. Offers MS, Ed S. Part-time and evening/weekend programs available. Postbaccalaureate distance learning degree programs offered. *Faculty:* 2 full-time (both women), 2 part-time/adjunct (both women). *Students:* 2 full-time (both women), 6 part-time (all women); includes 1 minority (Black or African American, non-Hispanic/Latino). Average age 27. 12 applicants, 50% accepted, 3 enrolled. In 2013, 1 master's awarded. *Entrance requirements:* For master's, GRE (minimum score of 850 on old exam or 290 on new exam), GMAT (minimum score of 380), or MAT (minimum score of 385), bachelor's degree; minimum undergraduate GPA of 2.5 or 3.0 on last 30 semester hours, letter of recommendation. Additional exam requirements/recommendations for international students: Required—TOEFL (minimum score 523 paper-based; 70 iBT), IELTS (minimum score 6). Application fee: $50. *Expenses: Tuition,* state resident: full-time $6084; part-time $338 per credit hour. Tuition, nonresident: full-time $12,168; part-time $676 per credit hour. *Required fees:* $630; $35 per credit hour. $50 per semester. *Unit head:* Dr. Jan Oliver, Associate Professor, 334-670-3444, Fax: 334-670-3474, E-mail: oliverj@troy.edu. *Application contact:* Brenda K. Campbell, Director of Graduate Admissions, 334-670-3178, Fax: 334-670-3733, E-mail: bcamp@troy.edu.

Tufts University, Graduate School of Arts and Sciences, Eliot-Pearson Department of Child Study and Human Development, Medford, MA 02155. Offers child study and human development (MA, PhD); early childhood education (MAT). Part-time programs available. *Faculty:* 16 full-time, 12 part-time/adjunct. *Students:* 111 full-time (94 women); includes 20 minority (6 Black or African American, non-Hispanic/Latino; 3 Asian, non-Hispanic/Latino; 8 Hispanic/Latino; 3 Two or more races, non-Hispanic/Latino), 16 international. Average age 27. 126 applicants, 68% accepted, 42 enrolled. In 2013, 27 master's, 10 doctorates awarded. *Degree requirements:* For master's, thesis (for some programs); for doctorate, thesis/dissertation. *Entrance requirements:* For master's and doctorate, GRE General Test. Additional exam requirements/recommendations for international students: Required—TOEFL (minimum score 550 paper-based; 80 iBT), IELTS (minimum score 6.5). *Application deadline:* For fall admission, 12/1 priority date for domestic and international students. Applications are processed on a rolling basis. Application fee: $75. Electronic applications accepted. *Financial support:* Fellowships, research assistantships with full and partial tuition reimbursements, teaching assistantships with full and partial tuition reimbursements, Federal Work-Study, scholarships/grants, tuition waivers (partial), and unspecified assistantships available. Support available to part-time students. Financial award application deadline: 5/15; financial award applicants required to submit FAFSA. *Unit head:* David Henry Feldman, Chair, 617-627-3355. *Application contact:* Ellen Pinderhughes, Graduate Advisor, 617-627-3355. Website: http://ase.tufts.edu/epcd.

United States University, School of Education, Cypress, CA 90630. Offers administration (MA Ed); early childhood education (MA Ed); general (MA Ed); higher education administration (MA Ed); Spanish language education (MA Ed); special education (MA Ed). *Degree requirements:* For master's, portfolio. *Entrance requirements:* For master's, minimum undergraduate GPA of 2.5. Additional exam requirements/recommendations for international students: Required—TOEFL (minimum score 500 paper-based; 61 iBT).

Universidad del Turabo, Graduate Programs, Programs in Education, Program in Teaching at Primary Level, Gurabo, PR 00778-3030. Offers M Ed.

University at Buffalo, the State University of New York, Graduate School, Graduate School of Education, Department of Learning and Instruction, Buffalo, NY 14260. Offers biology education (Ed M, Certificate); chemistry education (Ed M, Certificate); childhood education (Ed M); childhood education with bilingual extension (Ed M); curriculum, instruction and the science of learning (PhD); early childhood education (Ed M); early childhood education with bilingual extension (birth-grade 2) (Ed M); earth science education (Ed M, Certificate); education studies (Ed M); educational technology and new literacies (Certificate); elementary education (Ed D); English education (Ed M, Certificate); English for speakers of other languages (Ed M); foreign and second language education (PhD); French education (Ed M, Certificate); German education (Ed M, Certificate); gifted education (Certificate); Latin education (Ed M, Certificate); literacy specialist (Ed M); literacy teaching and learning (Certificate); mathematics education (Ed M, Certificate); music education (Ed M, Certificate); physics education (Ed M, Certificate); science and the public (Ed M); social studies education (Ed M,

Certificate); Spanish education (Ed M, Certificate); special education (PhD); teaching English to speakers of other languages (Ed M). Part-time and evening/weekend programs available. Postbaccalaureate distance learning degree programs offered (no on-campus study). *Faculty:* 31 full-time (23 women), 64 part-time/adjunct (53 women). *Students:* 275 full-time (215 women), 293 part-time (205 women); includes 35 minority (16 Black or African American, non-Hispanic/Latino; 5 American Indian or Alaska Native, non-Hispanic/Latino; 11 Asian, non-Hispanic/Latino; 3 Hispanic/Latino), 97 international. Average age 30. 544 applicants, 81% accepted, 246 enrolled. In 2013, 222 master's, 17 doctorates, 35 other advanced degrees awarded. *Degree requirements:* For master's, comprehensive exam; for doctorate, thesis/dissertation, research analysis exam, research experience component. *Entrance requirements:* For master's, content test in science and math, letters of reference; for doctorate, GRE General Test or MAT, interview, writing sample, letters of recommendation. Additional exam requirements/recommendations for international students: Required—TOEFL (minimum score 600 paper-based; 96 iBT). *Application deadline:* For fall admission, 2/1 priority date for domestic and international students; for spring admission, 11/15 priority date for domestic students, 10/1 for international students. Applications are processed on a rolling basis. Application fee: $50. Electronic applications accepted. *Financial support:* In 2013–14, 50 fellowships (averaging $8,589 per year), 31 research assistantships with tuition reimbursements (averaging $11,406 per year) were awarded; teaching assistantships, career-related internships or fieldwork, Federal Work-Study, institutionally sponsored loans, scholarships/grants, tuition waivers, and unspecified assistantships also available. Financial award application deadline: 2/28; financial award applicants required to submit FAFSA. *Faculty research:* Science assessment, foreign language teaching and learning, early learning, new literacies, gender and education. *Total annual research expenditures:* $1.7 million. *Unit head:* Dr. Suzanne Miller, Chair, 716-645-2455, Fax: 716-645-3161, E-mail: smiller@buffalo.edu. *Application contact:* Cathy Dimino, Admissions Assistant, 716-645-2110, Fax: 716-645-7937, E-mail: cadimino@buffalo.edu. Website: http://gse.buffalo.edu/lai.

The University of Alabama at Birmingham, School of Education, Program in Early Childhood Education, Birmingham, AL 35294. Offers MA Ed, PhD. *Accreditation:* NCATE. *Degree requirements:* For master's, comprehensive exam, thesis optional; for doctorate, thesis/dissertation. *Entrance requirements:* For master's, GRE General Test, MAT, or NTE, minimum GPA of 3.0; for doctorate, GRE General Test, MAT, minimum GPA of 3.25. Electronic applications accepted.

University of Alaska Anchorage, College of Education, Program in Special Education, Anchorage, AK 99508. Offers early childhood special education (M Ed); special education (M Ed, Certificate). Part-time programs available. *Degree requirements:* For master's, comprehensive exam (for some programs), thesis or alternative. *Entrance requirements:* For master's, GRE or MAT, interview, minimum GPA of 2.75. Additional exam requirements/recommendations for international students: Required—TOEFL (minimum score 550 paper-based). *Faculty research:* Mild disabilities, substance abuse issues for educators, partnerships to improve at-risk youth, analysis of planning models for teachers in special education.

University of Alaska Southeast, Graduate Programs, Program in Education, Juneau, AK 99801. Offers early childhood education (M Ed, MAT); educational technology (M Ed); elementary education (MAT); reading (M Ed); secondary education (MAT). *Accreditation:* NCATE. Part-time and evening/weekend programs available. Postbaccalaureate distance learning degree programs offered (minimal on-campus study). *Degree requirements:* For master's, comprehensive exam or project, portfolio. *Entrance requirements:* For master's, PRAXIS, minimum GPA of 3.0, writing sample, letters of recommendation. Electronic applications accepted. *Faculty research:* Applied classroom research, culturally responsive practices, action research, teaching effectiveness.

University of Arkansas, Graduate School, College of Education and Health Professions, Department of Curriculum and Instruction, Program in Childhood Education, Fayetteville, AR 72701-1201. Offers MAT. *Accreditation:* NCATE. Electronic applications accepted.

University of Arkansas at Little Rock, Graduate School, College of Education, Department of Teacher Education, Program in Early Childhood Education, Little Rock, AR 72204-1099. Offers M Ed. *Expenses:* Tuition, state resident: full-time $5690; part-time $284.50 per credit hour. Tuition, nonresident: full-time $13,030; part-time $651.50 per credit hour. *Required fees:* $1121; $672 per term. One-time fee: $40 full-time.

University of Arkansas at Pine Bluff, School of Education, Pine Bluff, AR 71601-2799. Offers early childhood education (M Ed); secondary education (M Ed), including English education, mathematics education, physical education, science education, social studies education; teaching (MAT). *Accreditation:* NCATE. Part-time and evening/weekend programs available. *Degree requirements:* For master's, comprehensive exam. *Entrance requirements:* For master's, GRE, minimum GPA of 2.75, NTE or Standard Arkansas Teaching Certificate. *Faculty research:* Teacher certification, accreditation, assessment, standards, portfolio development, rehabilitation, technology.

University of Bridgeport, School of Education, Department of Education, Bridgeport, CT 06604. Offers education (MS); educational management (Ed D, Diploma), including intermediate administrator or supervisor (Diploma), leadership (Ed D); elementary education (MS, Diploma), including early childhood education, elementary education; middle school education (MS); music education (MS); remedial reading and language arts (Diploma); secondary education (MS, Diploma), including computer specialist (Diploma), international education (Diploma), reading specialist, secondary education. Part-time and evening/weekend programs available. *Faculty:* 12 full-time (5 women), 108 part-time/adjunct (60 women). *Students:* 155 full-time (108 women), 139 part-time (98 women); includes 48 minority (22 Black or African American, non-Hispanic/Latino; 9 Asian, non-Hispanic/Latino; 15 Hispanic/Latino; 2 Two or more races, non-Hispanic/Latino), 2 international. Average age 30. 306 applicants, 55% accepted, 107 enrolled. In 2013, 153 master's, 16 other advanced degrees awarded. *Degree requirements:* For master's, final exam, final project, or thesis; for doctorate, comprehensive exam, thesis/dissertation; for Diploma, thesis or alternative, final project. *Entrance requirements:* For master's, minimum undergraduate QPA of 2.67; for doctorate, GRE, MAT; for Diploma, GRE General Test or MAT, minimum graduate QPA of 3.0. Additional exam requirements/recommendations for international students: Recommended—TOEFL (minimum score 550 paper-based; 80 iBT), IELTS (minimum score 6.5). *Application deadline:* For fall admission, 8/1 priority date for domestic and international students; for spring admission, 12/1 priority date for domestic and international students. Applications are processed on a rolling basis. Application fee: $50. Electronic applications accepted. *Expenses:* Contact institution. *Financial support:* In 2013–14, 120 students received support. Fellowships, research assistantships, teaching assistantships, career-related internships or fieldwork, Federal Work-Study, and institutionally sponsored loans available. Support available to part-time students. Financial award application deadline: 6/1; financial award applicants required to submit FAFSA. *Faculty research:* Self-concept, internship assessment, stress and situational development, follow-up of graduation, trend analysis. *Unit head:* Dr. Allen P. Cook, Dean, 203-576-4192, Fax: 203-576-4200, E-mail: acook@bridgeport.edu. *Application contact:* Leanne Proctor, Director

of Graduate Admissions, 203-576-4552, Fax: 203-576-4941, E-mail: admit@bridgeport.edu.

The University of British Columbia, Faculty of Education, Centre for Cross-Faculty Inquiry in Education, Vancouver, BC V6T 1Z1, Canada. Offers curriculum and instruction (M Ed, MA, PhD); early childhood education (M Ed, MA). Part-time and evening/weekend programs available. *Students:* 81 full-time, 43 part-time. 58 applicants, 72% accepted, 27 enrolled. Terminal master's awarded for partial completion of doctoral program. *Degree requirements:* For master's, thesis (MA); for doctorate, thesis/dissertation. *Entrance requirements:* Additional exam requirements/recommendations for international students: Required—TOEFL (minimum score 567 paper-based). *Application deadline:* For fall admission, 1/1 for domestic and international students. Application fee: $90 Canadian dollars ($150 Canadian dollars for international students). Electronic applications accepted. *Expenses: Tuition, area resident:* Full-time $8000 Canadian dollars. *Financial support:* In 2013–14, 20 students received support. Fellowships with tuition reimbursements available, research assistantships with tuition reimbursements available, teaching assistantships with tuition reimbursements available, institutionally sponsored loans, scholarships/grants, and tuition waivers (full and partial) available.

University of Central Florida, College of Education and Human Performance, Education Doctoral Programs, Orlando, FL 32816. Offers communication sciences and disorders (PhD); counselor education (PhD); early childhood education (PhD); education (Ed D); elementary education (PhD); exceptional education (PhD); exercise physiology (PhD); higher education (PhD); hospitality education (PhD); instructional technology (PhD); mathematics education (PhD); reading education (PhD); science education (PhD); social science education (PhD); TESOL (PhD). *Students:* 137 full-time (94 women), 86 part-time (64 women); includes 45 minority (24 Black or African American, non-Hispanic/Latino; 5 Asian, non-Hispanic/Latino; 13 Hispanic/Latino; 3 Two or more races, non-Hispanic/Latino), 22 international. Average age 39. 132 applicants, 54% accepted, 54 enrolled. In 2013, 38 doctorates awarded. Application fee: $30. Electronic applications accepted. *Financial support:* In 2013–14, 84 students received support, including 38 fellowships with partial tuition reimbursements available (averaging $6,600 per year), 41 research assistantships with partial tuition reimbursements available (averaging $7,800 per year), 53 teaching assistantships with partial tuition reimbursements available (averaging $7,700 per year). *Unit head:* Dr. Edward Robinson, Director of Doctoral Programs, 407-823-6106, E-mail: edward.robinson@ucf.edu. *Application contact:* Barbara Rodriguez Lamas, Associate Director, Admissions and Student Services, 407-823-2766, Fax: 407-823-6442, E-mail: gradadmissions@ucf.edu.
Website: http://education.ucf.edu/departments.cfm.

University of Central Missouri, The Graduate School, Warrensburg, MO 6409. Offers accountancy (MA); accounting (MBA); applied mathematics (MS); aviation safety (MA); biology (MS); business administration (MBA); career and technical education leadership (MS); college student personnel administration (MS); communication (MA); computer science (MS); counseling (MS); criminal justice (MS); educational leadership (Ed D); educational technology (MS); elementary and early childhood education (MSE); English (MA); environmental studies (MA); finance (MBA); history (MA); human services/educational technology (Ed S); human services/learning resources (Ed S); human services/professional counseling (Ed S); industrial hygiene (MS); industrial management (MS); information systems (MBA); information technology (MS); kinesiology (MS); library science and information services (MS); literacy education (MSE); marketing (MBA); mathematics (MS); music (MA); occupational safety management (MS); psychology (MS); rural family nursing (MS); school administration (MSE); social gerontology (MS); sociology (MA); special education (MSE); speech language pathology (MS); superintendency (Ed S); teaching (MAT); teaching English as a second language (MA); technology (MS); technology management (PhD); theatre (MA). Part-time programs available. *Faculty:* 233. *Students:* 890 full-time (396 women), 1,486 part-time (1,001 women); includes 192 minority (97 Black or African American, non-Hispanic/Latino; 9 American Indian or Alaska Native, non-Hispanic/Latino; 32 Asian, non-Hispanic/Latino; 40 Hispanic/Latino; 3 Native Hawaiian or other Pacific Islander, non-Hispanic/Latino; 11 Two or more races, non-Hispanic/Latino), 539 international. Average age 31. 1,953 applicants, 75% accepted. In 2013, 719 master's, 58 other advanced degrees awarded. *Degree requirements:* For master's and Ed S, comprehensive exam (for some programs), thesis (for some programs). *Entrance requirements:* Additional exam requirements/recommendations for international students: Required—TOEFL (minimum score 550 paper-based; 79 iBT). *Application deadline:* For fall admission, 6/1 for domestic students; for spring admission, 10/1 for domestic and international students. Applications are processed on a rolling basis. Application fee: $30 ($75 for international students). Electronic applications accepted. *Expenses: Tuition, state resident:* full-time $7326; part-time $276.25 per credit hour. Tuition, nonresident: full-time $13,956; part-time $552.50 per credit hour. *Required fees:* $29 per credit hour. *Financial support:* In 2013–14, 118 students received support, including 271 research assistantships with full and partial tuition reimbursements available (averaging $7,500 per year), 109 teaching assistantships with full and partial tuition reimbursements available (averaging $7,500 per year); career-related internships or fieldwork, Federal Work-Study, scholarships/grants, and administrative and laboratory assistantships also available. Support available to part-time students. Financial award application deadline: 3/1; financial award applicants required to submit FAFSA. *Unit head:* Dr. Joseph Vaughn, Assistant Provost for Research/Dean, 660-543-4092, Fax: 660-543-4778, E-mail: vaughn@ucmo.edu. *Application contact:* Brittany Lawrence, Graduate Student Services Coordinator, 660-543-4621, Fax: 660-543-4778, E-mail: gradinfo@ucmo.edu.
Website: http://www.ucmo.edu/graduate/.

University of Central Oklahoma, The Jackson College of Graduate Studies, College of Education and Professional Studies, Department of Curriculum and Instruction, Edmond, OK 73034-5209. Offers bilingual education/teaching English as a second language (M Ed); early childhood education (M Ed); elementary education (M Ed). Part-time programs available. *Faculty:* 8 full-time (6 women), 10 part-time/adjunct (8 women). *Students:* 50 full-time (46 women), 68 part-time (61 women); includes 21 minority (7 Black or African American, non-Hispanic/Latino; 1 American Indian or Alaska Native, non-Hispanic/Latino; 3 Asian, non-Hispanic/Latino; 8 Hispanic/Latino; 2 Two or more races, non-Hispanic/Latino), 51 international. Average age 34. 55 applicants, 91% accepted, 25 enrolled. In 2013, 65 master's awarded. *Degree requirements:* For master's, comprehensive exam (for some programs), thesis optional. *Entrance requirements:* For master's, GRE General Test. Additional exam requirements/recommendations for international students: Required—TOEFL (minimum score 550 paper-based; 79 iBT), IELTS (minimum score 6.5). *Application deadline:* For fall admission, 7/1 for international students; for spring admission, 11/1 for international students. Applications are processed on a rolling basis. Application fee: $50. Electronic applications accepted. *Expenses: Tuition, state resident:* full-time $4137; part-time $206.85 per credit hour. Tuition, nonresident: full-time $10,359; part-time $517.95 per credit hour. *Required fees:* $481. Tuition and fees vary according to course load and program. *Financial support:* In 2013–14, 26 students received support, including research assistantships with partial tuition reimbursements available (averaging $5,454 per year), teaching assistantships with partial tuition reimbursements available (averaging $9,478 per year); Federal Work-Study, scholarships/grants, tuition waivers

(partial), and unspecified assistantships also available. Financial award application deadline: 3/31; financial award applicants required to submit FAFSA. *Faculty research:* Tourette's syndrome, bilingual education, science education, language development/disorders. *Unit head:* Dr. Paulette Shreck, Chair, 405-974-5721, Fax: 405-974-3858, E-mail: pshreck@uco.edu. *Application contact:* Dr. Richard Bernard, Dean, Graduate College, 405-974-3493, Fax: 405-974-3852, E-mail: gradcoll@uco.edu.

University of Cincinnati, Graduate School, College of Education, Criminal Justice, and Human Services, Division of Teacher Education, Program in Early Childhood Education, Cincinnati, OH 45221. Offers M Ed. *Accreditation:* NCATE. Part-time programs available. *Degree requirements:* For master's, thesis or alternative. *Entrance requirements:* For master's, GRE General Test. Additional exam requirements/recommendations for international students: Required—TOEFL (minimum score 610 paper-based), TWE (minimum score 5), OEPT. Electronic applications accepted.

University of Colorado Denver, School of Education and Human Development, Early Childhood Education Program, Denver, CO 80217. Offers early childhood education (MA); special education (MA). *Accreditation:* NCATE. Part-time and evening/weekend programs available. Postbaccalaureate distance learning degree programs offered (no on-campus study). *Students:* 121 full-time (113 women), 42 part-time (41 women); includes 18 minority (1 Black or African American, non-Hispanic/Latino; 2 American Indian or Alaska Native, non-Hispanic/Latino; 3 Asian, non-Hispanic/Latino; 8 Hispanic/Latino; 4 Two or more races, non-Hispanic/Latino), 11 international. Average age 32. 71 applicants, 66% accepted, 28 enrolled. In 2013, 73 master's awarded. *Degree requirements:* For master's, comprehensive exam, fieldwork, practica, 40 credit hours. *Entrance requirements:* For master's, GRE or MAT (if GPA is below 2.75), minimum GPA of 2.75, resume, three letters of recommendation. Additional exam requirements/recommendations for international students: Required—TOEFL (minimum score 537 paper-based; 75 iBT); Recommended—IELTS (minimum score 6.5). *Application deadline:* For fall admission, 4/15 for domestic students, 4/1 for international students; for spring admission, 9/15 for domestic students, 9/1 for international students. Application fee: $50 ($75 for international students). Electronic applications accepted. *Expenses:* Contact institution. *Financial support:* In 2013–14, 3 students received support. Research assistantships, teaching assistantships, Federal Work-Study, institutionally sponsored loans, scholarships/grants, and traineeships available. Financial award application deadline: 4/1; financial award applicants required to submit FAFSA. *Faculty research:* Early childhood growth and development, faculty development, adult learning, gender and equity issues, research methodology. *Unit head:* Lori Ryan, Professor, 303-315-2578, E-mail: lori.ryan@ucdenver.edu. *Application contact:* Jason Clark, Director of Recruitment and Retention, 300-315-0183, E-mail: jason.clark@ucdenver.edu.
Website: http://www.ucdenver.edu/academics/colleges/SchoolOfEducation/Academics/MASTERS/ECE/Pages/EarlyChildhoodEducation.aspx.

University of Colorado Denver, School of Education and Human Development, Program in Educational Leadership and Innovation, Denver, CO 80217-3364. Offers educational studies and research (PhD), including administrative leadership and policy, early childhood special education, math education, research, assessment and evaluation, science education, urban ecologies. Part-time and evening/weekend programs available. *Students:* 16 full-time (12 women), 12 part-time (9 women); includes 6 minority (2 Black or African American, non-Hispanic/Latino; 3 Asian, non-Hispanic/Latino; 1 Hispanic/Latino), 1 international. Average age 39. 16 applicants, 31% accepted, 4 enrolled. In 2013, 10 doctorates awarded. *Degree requirements:* For doctorate, comprehensive exam, thesis/dissertation, 75 credit hours (for PhD). *Entrance requirements:* For doctorate, GRE or equivalent, resume or curriculum vitae, letters of recommendation, master's degree or equivalent, completion of basic or advanced statistics course with minimum B grade. Additional exam requirements/recommendations for international students: Required—TOEFL (minimum score 537 paper-based; 75 iBT); Recommended—IELTS (minimum score 6.5). *Application deadline:* For fall admission, 5/1 priority date for domestic students, 4/15 priority date for international students. Applications are processed on a rolling basis. Application fee: $50 ($75 for international students). Electronic applications accepted. *Expenses:* Contact institution. *Financial support:* In 2013–14, 19 students received support. Fellowships, research assistantships, teaching assistantships, Federal Work-Study, institutionally sponsored loans, scholarships/grants, and traineeships available. Financial award application deadline: 4/1; financial award applicants required to submit FAFSA. *Faculty research:* Administrative leadership and policy studies, early childhood education, research in diversity, paraprofessionals in education, urban schools lab. *Unit head:* Dr. Deanna Sands, Associate Dean, Research and Professional Development, 303-315-4931, E-mail: deanna.sands@ucdenver.edu. *Application contact:* Student Services Center, 303-315-6300, Fax: 303-315-6311, E-mail: education@ucdenver.edu.
Website: http://www.ucdenver.edu/academics/colleges/SchoolOfEducation/Academics/Doctorate/Pages/PhD.aspx.

University of Dayton, Department of Teacher Education, Dayton, OH 45469-1300. Offers adolescence to young adult education (MS Ed); early childhood education (MS Ed); early childhood leadership and advocacy (MS Ed); interdisciplinary education studies (MS Ed); intervention specialist education, mild/moderate (MS Ed); literacy (MS Ed); middle childhood education (MS Ed); multi-age education (MS Ed); music education (MS Ed); teacher as leader (MS Ed); technology enhanced learning (MS Ed). Part-time and evening/weekend programs available. Postbaccalaureate distance learning degree programs offered (no on-campus study). *Faculty:* 19 full-time (13 women), 21 part-time/adjunct (18 women). *Students:* 69 full-time (57 women), 86 part-time (75 women); includes 16 minority (10 Black or African American, non-Hispanic/Latino; 2 Asian, non-Hispanic/Latino; 4 Hispanic/Latino), 10 international. Average age 31. 140 applicants, 54% accepted, 39 enrolled. In 2013, 93 master's awarded. *Degree requirements:* For master's, variable foreign language requirement, comprehensive exam (for some programs), thesis. *Entrance requirements:* For master's, GRE or MAT, minimum GPA of 2.75. Additional exam requirements/recommendations for international students: Required—TOEFL (minimum score 550 paper-based; 80 iBT), IELTS (minimum score 6.5). *Application deadline:* For fall admission, 3/1 for domestic students, 5/1 for international students; for winter admission, 7/1 for international students; for spring admission, 11/1 for international students. Applications are processed on a rolling basis. Application fee: $0 ($50 for international students). Electronic applications accepted. *Expenses:* Contact institution. *Financial support:* In 2013–14, 61 students received support, including 5 research assistantships with full tuition reimbursements available (averaging $8,720 per year), 3 teaching assistantships with full tuition reimbursements available (averaging $8,720 per year); career-related internships or fieldwork, institutionally sponsored loans, scholarships/grants, traineeships, health care benefits, and unspecified assistantships also available. Support available to part-time students. Financial award application deadline: 3/1; financial award applicants required to submit FAFSA. *Faculty research:* Diversity, literacy, art representation by young children, preservice teacher preparation. *Unit head:* Dr. Connie L. Bowman, Chair, 937-229-3305, E-mail: cbowman1@udayton.edu. *Application contact:* Gina Seiter, Graduate Program Advisor, 937-229-3103, E-mail: gseiter1@udayton.edu.

University of Denver, Morgridge College of Education, Denver, CO 80208. Offers child, family and school psychology (MA, PhD, Ed S); counseling psychology (MA, PhD);

curriculum and instruction (MA, Ed D, PhD); curriculum instruction and teaching (Certificate); early childhood special education (MA); educational leadership and policy studies (MA, Ed D, PhD, Certificate); higher education (MA, Ed D, PhD); law librarianship (Certificate); library and information science (MLIS); research methods and statistics (MA, PhD). *Accreditation:* ALA; APA (one or more programs are accredited). Part-time and evening/weekend programs available. Postbaccalaureate distance learning degree programs offered (no on-campus study). *Faculty:* 35 full-time (21 women), 63 part-time/adjunct (43 women). *Students:* 435 full-time (332 women), 414 part-time (297 women); includes 194 minority (45 Black or African American, non-Hispanic/Latino; 9 American Indian or Alaska Native, non-Hispanic/Latino; 16 Asian, non-Hispanic/Latino; 96 Hispanic/Latino; 2 Native Hawaiian or other Pacific Islander, non-Hispanic/Latino; 26 Two or more races, non-Hispanic/Latino), 14 international. Average age 32. 672 applicants, 61% accepted, 193 enrolled. In 2013, 248 master's, 30 doctorates, 130 other advanced degrees awarded. Terminal master's awarded for partial completion of doctoral program. *Degree requirements:* For master's, comprehensive exam; for doctorate, 2 foreign languages, comprehensive exam, thesis/dissertation. *Entrance requirements:* For master's and doctorate, GRE General Test or GMAT. Additional exam requirements/recommendations for international students: Required—TOEFL (minimum score 550 paper-based; 80 iBT). *Application deadline:* Applications are processed on a rolling basis. Application fee: $65. Electronic applications accepted. *Financial support:* In 2013–14, 706 students received support, including 54 research assistantships with full and partial tuition reimbursements available (averaging $15,599 per year), 77 teaching assistantships with full and partial tuition reimbursements available (averaging $12,804 per year); career-related internships or fieldwork, Federal Work-Study, institutionally sponsored loans, scholarships/grants, and unspecified assistantships also available. Support available to part-time students. Financial award application deadline: 2/15; financial award applicants required to submit FAFSA. *Faculty research:* Principal and teacher preparation, development and assessments, gifted education, service-learning, early childhood, mathematics education, access to higher education. *Total annual research expenditures:* $6.3 million. *Unit head:* Dr. Karen Riley, Interim Dean, 303-871-3665, E-mail: karen.riley@du.edu. *Application contact:* Jodi Dye, Assistant Director of Admissions, 303-871-2510, E-mail: jodi.dye@du.edu.
Website: http://morgridge.du.edu/.

The University of Findlay, Office of Graduate Admissions, Findlay, OH 45840-3653. Offers athletic training (MAT); business (MBA), including health care management, hospitality management, organizational leadership, public management; education (MA Ed), including administration, children's literature, early childhood, human resource development, reading, science, special education, technology; environmental, safety and health management (MSEM); health informatics (MS); occupational therapy (MOT); pharmacy (Pharm D); physical therapy (DPT); physician assistant (MPA); rhetoric and writing (MA); teaching English to speakers of other languages (TESOL) and bilingual education (MA). Part-time and evening/weekend programs available. Postbaccalaureate distance learning degree programs offered (no on-campus study). *Faculty:* 209 full-time (98 women), 69 part-time/adjunct (38 women). *Students:* 551 full-time (332 women), 457 part-time (276 women); includes 77 minority (37 Black or African American, non-Hispanic/Latino; 1 American Indian or Alaska Native, non-Hispanic/Latino; 15 Asian, non-Hispanic/Latino; 23 Hispanic/Latino; 1 Native Hawaiian or other Pacific Islander, non-Hispanic/Latino), 135 international. Average age 28. 637 applicants, 66% accepted, 241 enrolled. In 2013, 267 master's, 91 doctorates awarded. *Degree requirements:* For master's, thesis, cumulative project, capstone project. *Entrance requirements:* For master's, GRE/GMAT, bachelor's degree from accredited institution, minimum undergraduate GPA of 2.5 in last 64 hours of course work; for doctorate, GRE, minimum cumulative GPA of 3.0. Additional exam requirements/recommendations for international students: Required—TOEFL (minimum score 80 iBT). *Application deadline:* Applications are processed on a rolling basis. Application fee: $25. Electronic applications accepted. *Expenses: Required fees:* $146 per semester. Tuition and fees vary according to degree level and program. *Financial support:* In 2013–14, 11 research assistantships with full and partial tuition reimbursements (averaging $4,000 per year), 10 teaching assistantships with full and partial tuition reimbursements (averaging $3,600 per year) were awarded; career-related internships or fieldwork, Federal Work-Study, health care benefits, and unspecified assistantships also available. Financial award application deadline: 4/1; financial award applicants required to submit FAFSA. *Unit head:* Christopher M. Harris, Director of Admissions, 419-434-4347, E-mail: harrisc1@findlay.edu. *Application contact:* Emily Ickes, Graduate Admissions Counselor, 419-434-6933, Fax: 419-434-4898, E-mail: ickese@findlay.edu.
Website: http://www.findlay.edu/admissions/graduate/Pages/default.aspx.

University of Florida, Graduate School, College of Education, Department of Special Education, School Psychology and Early Childhood Studies, Gainesville, FL 32611. Offers early childhood education (M Ed, MAE); school psychology (M Ed, MAE, Ed D, PhD, Ed S); special education (M Ed, MAE, Ed D, PhD, Ed S). *Accreditation:* NCATE. Part-time and evening/weekend programs available. Postbaccalaureate distance learning degree programs offered (no on-campus study). *Faculty:* 22 full-time (17 women), 1 (woman) part-time/adjunct. *Students:* 130 full-time (120 women), 41 part-time (34 women); includes 50 minority (19 Black or African American, non-Hispanic/Latino; 8 Asian, non-Hispanic/Latino; 23 Hispanic/Latino), 9 international. Average age 29. 114 applicants, 37% accepted, 18 enrolled. In 2013, 64 master's, 17 doctorates, 12 other advanced degrees awarded. *Degree requirements:* For master's, comprehensive exam (for some programs), thesis (MAE); for doctorate, comprehensive exam, thesis/dissertation. *Entrance requirements:* For master's and doctorate, GRE General Test, minimum GPA of 3.0; for Ed S, GRE General Test. Additional exam requirements/recommendations for international students: Required—TOEFL (minimum score 550 paper-based; 80 iBT), IELTS (minimum score 6). *Application deadline:* For fall admission, 11/1 priority date for domestic students. Applications are processed on a rolling basis. Application fee: $30. Electronic applications accepted. *Expenses:* Tuition, state resident: full-time $12,640. Tuition, nonresident: full-time $30,000. *Financial support:* In 2013–14, 55 students received support, including 45 research assistantships (averaging $15,225 per year), 27 teaching assistantships (averaging $9,655 per year); career-related internships or fieldwork and unspecified assistantships also available. Financial award application deadline: 11/15; financial award applicants required to submit FAFSA. *Faculty research:* Teacher quality/teacher education, early childhood, autism, instructional interventions in reading and mathematics, behavioral interventions. *Unit head:* Jean Crockett, PhD, Chair and Associate Professor, 352-273-4292, Fax: 352-392-2655, E-mail: crocketj@coe.ufl.edu. *Application contact:* Nancy L. Waldron, PhD, Professor and Graduate Coordinator, 352-273-4284, Fax: 352-392-2655, E-mail: waldron@coe.ufl.edu.
Website: http://education.ufl.edu/sespecs/.

University of Georgia, College of Education, Department of Elementary and Social Studies Education, Athens, GA 30602. Offers early childhood education (M Ed, MAT, PhD, Ed S), including child and family development (MAT); elementary education (PhD); middle school education (M Ed, PhD, Ed S); social studies education (M Ed, Ed D, PhD, Ed S). *Entrance requirements:* For master's and Ed S, GRE General Test or MAT; for doctorate, GRE General Test. Electronic applications accepted.

University of Hartford, College of Education, Nursing, and Health Professions, Program in Early Childhood Education, West Hartford, CT 06117-1599. Offers M Ed. *Accreditation:* NCATE. Part-time and evening/weekend programs available. *Degree requirements:* For master's, comprehensive exam. *Entrance requirements:* For master's, PRAXIS I or waiver, interview, 2 letters of recommendation. Additional exam requirements/recommendations for international students: Required—TOEFL (minimum score 550 paper-based). Electronic applications accepted.

University of Hawaii at Manoa, Graduate Division, College of Education, Department of Curriculum Studies, Program in Early Childhood Education, Honolulu, HI 96822. Offers M Ed. *Accreditation:* NCATE. Part-time programs available. *Degree requirements:* For master's, thesis optional. *Entrance requirements:* Additional exam requirements/recommendations for international students: Required—TOEFL (minimum score 580 paper-based; 92 iBT), IELTS (minimum score 5).

University of Houston–Clear Lake, School of Education, Program in Curriculum and Instruction, Houston, TX 77058-1002. Offers curriculum and instruction (MS); early childhood education (MS); reading (MS); school library and information science (MS). Part-time and evening/weekend programs available. *Degree requirements:* For master's, thesis (for some programs). *Entrance requirements:* For master's, GRE or minimum GPA of 3.0 in last 60 hours. Additional exam requirements/recommendations for international students: Required—TOEFL (minimum score 550 paper-based). Electronic applications accepted.

University of Illinois at Chicago, Graduate College, College of Education, Department of Educational Psychology, Chicago, IL 60607-7128. Offers early childhood education (M Ed); educational psychology (PhD); measurement, evaluation, statistics, and assessment (M Ed); youth development (M Ed). Part-time programs available. Postbaccalaureate distance learning degree programs offered (no on-campus study). *Faculty:* 11 full-time (9 women), 4 part-time/adjunct (3 women). *Students:* 63 full-time (48 women), 108 part-time (80 women); includes 58 minority (27 Black or African American, non-Hispanic/Latino; 11 Asian, non-Hispanic/Latino; 17 Hispanic/Latino; 3 Two or more races, non-Hispanic/Latino), 11 international. Average age 33. 128 applicants, 69% accepted, 51 enrolled. In 2013, 41 master's, 2 doctorates awarded. *Expenses:* Tuition, state resident: full-time $11,066; part-time $3689 per term. Tuition, nonresident: full-time $23,064; part-time $7688 per term. *Required fees:* $3004; $1190 per term. Tuition and fees vary according to course level and program. *Total annual research expenditures:* $541,000. *Unit head:* Kimlerly Lawless, Chairperson, 312-996-2359, E-mail: klawless@uic.edu. *Application contact:* Receptionist, 312-413-2550, E-mail: gradcoll@uic.edu.
Website: http://education.uic.edu/academics-admissions/departments/department-educational-psychology#overview.

University of Kentucky, Graduate School, College of Education, Department of Early Childhood, Special Education, and Rehabilitation Counseling, Lexington, KY 40506-0032. Offers early childhood (MS Ed); rehabilitation counseling (MRC); special education (MS Ed, Ed D). *Accreditation:* CORE; NCATE. Terminal master's awarded for partial completion of doctoral program. *Degree requirements:* For master's, comprehensive exam, thesis optional; for doctorate, comprehensive exam, thesis/dissertation. *Entrance requirements:* For master's, GRE General Test, minimum undergraduate GPA of 2.75; for doctorate, GRE General Test, minimum graduate GPA of 3.0. Additional exam requirements/recommendations for international students: Required—TOEFL (minimum score 550 paper-based). Electronic applications accepted. *Faculty research:* Applied behavior analysis applications in special education, single subject research design in classroom settings, transition research across life span, rural special education personnel.

University of Louisiana at Monroe, Graduate School, College of Arts, Education, and Sciences, School of Education, Program in Curriculum and Instruction, Monroe, LA 71209-0001. Offers art education (M Ed); biology education (M Ed); chemistry education (M Ed); curriculum and instruction (Ed D); early childhood education (M Ed); earth science education (M Ed); educational leadership (M Ed); elementary education (1-5) (M Ed); English as a second language (M Ed); English education (M Ed); family and consumer education (M Ed); French education (M Ed); history education (M Ed); math education (M Ed); middle school education (M Ed); music education (M Ed); reading education (K-12) (M Ed); Spanish education (M Ed); special education - academically gifted (M Ed); special education - early intervention (M Ed); special education - educational diagnostician (M Ed); special education - mild/moderate disabilities (M Ed); speech education (M Ed). *Accreditation:* NCATE. *Degree requirements:* For master's, comprehensive exam (for some programs), thesis; for doctorate, thesis/dissertation, internships. *Entrance requirements:* For master's, GRE General Test; for doctorate, GRE General Test, minimum undergraduate GPA of 2.75, graduate 3.25. Additional exam requirements/recommendations for international students: Required—TOEFL (minimum score 500 paper-based; 61 iBT). *Application deadline:* For fall admission, 8/24 priority date for domestic students, 7/1 for international students; for winter admission, 12/14 priority date for domestic students; for spring admission, 1/19 for domestic students, 11/1 for international students. Applications are processed on a rolling basis. Application fee: $20 ($30 for international students). Electronic applications accepted. *Expenses:* Tuition, state resident: full-time $6607. Tuition, nonresident: full-time $17,179. Full-time tuition and fees vary according to program. *Financial support:* Research assistantships, career-related internships or fieldwork, Federal Work-Study, and unspecified assistantships available. Financial award application deadline: 4/1; financial award applicants required to submit FAFSA. *Unit head:* Dr. Dorothy Schween, Director, 318-342-1268, Fax: 318-342-3131, E-mail: schween@ulm.edu. *Application contact:* Dr. Dorothy Schween, Director, 318-342-1268, Fax: 318-342-3131, E-mail: schween@ulm.edu.

University of Louisville, Graduate School, College of Education and Human Development, Department of Teaching and Learning, Louisville, KY 40292-0001. Offers art education (MAT); curriculum and instruction (PhD); early elementary education (MAT); instructional technology (M Ed); interdisciplinary early childhood education (MAT); middle school education (MAT); music education (MAT); secondary education (MAT); special education (MAT); teacher leadership (M Ed). Part-time and evening/weekend programs available. *Students:* 137 full-time (93 women), 208 part-time (131 women); includes 44 minority (25 Black or African American, non-Hispanic/Latino; 1 American Indian or Alaska Native, non-Hispanic/Latino; 3 Asian, non-Hispanic/Latino; 12 Hispanic/Latino; 3 Two or more races, non-Hispanic/Latino), 2 international. Average age 32. 150 applicants, 51% accepted, 54 enrolled. In 2013, 127 master's, 5 doctorates awarded. *Degree requirements:* For doctorate, comprehensive exam, thesis/dissertation. *Entrance requirements:* For master's, GRE General Test, PRAXIS II (for some programs); for doctorate, GRE General Test. Additional exam requirements/recommendations for international students: Required—TOEFL (minimum score 560 paper-based; 83 iBT). *Application deadline:* For fall admission, 5/1 priority date for international students; for spring admission, 11/1 priority date for international students; for summer admission, 4/1 priority date for international students. Application fee: $60. Electronic applications accepted. *Expenses:* Tuition, state resident: full-time $10,788; part-time $599 per credit hour. Tuition, nonresident: full-time $22,446; part-time $1247 per credit hour. *Required fees:* $196. Tuition and fees vary according to program and reciprocity agreements. *Financial support:* Fellowships, research assistantships,

teaching assistantships, career-related internships or fieldwork, Federal Work-Study, scholarships/grants, and unspecified assistantships available. Financial award application deadline: 6/1; financial award applicants required to submit FAFSA. *Faculty research:* Mathematics teacher education and ongoing professional development in pedagogy and content knowledge; development of literacy, including early literacy in science and mathematics and literacy development for English language learners; immersive visualizations for promoting STEM education from nanoscience to cosmic scales; evidence-based practices for students with disabilities; urban education, including teacher response to intervention systems in schools and cross-cultural competence. *Unit head:* Dr. Ann E. Larson, Acting Chair, 502-852-6431, Fax: 502-852-1497, E-mail: ann@louisville.edu. *Application contact:* Libby Leggett, Director, Graduate Admissions, 502-852-3101, Fax: 502-852-6536, E-mail: gradadm@louisville.edu.
Website: http://louisville.edu/delphi.

University of Maine, Graduate School, College of Education and Human Development, Department of Teacher and Counselor Education, Orono, ME 04469. Offers counselor education (M Ed, MA, MS, CAS); early childhood teacher (CGS); education (PhD), including counselor education, literacy education, prevention and intervention studies; elementary education (M Ed, CAS); individualized education (M Ed); literacy education (M Ed, MS, CAS); response to intervention for behavior (CGS); secondary education (M Ed, MAT, CAS); social studies education (M Ed); special education (M Ed, CAS); teacher consultant in writing (CGS). Part-time programs available. *Students:* 147 full-time (118 women), 15 part-time (2 women); includes 8 minority (4 Black or African American, non-Hispanic/Latino; 2 American Indian or Alaska Native, non-Hispanic/Latino; 1 Hispanic/Latino; 1 Two or more races, non-Hispanic/Latino), 3 international. Average age 37. 100 applicants, 58% accepted, 50 enrolled. In 2013, 83 master's, 5 doctorates, 17 other advanced degrees awarded. *Degree requirements:* For master's, thesis (for some programs); for doctorate, comprehensive exam, thesis/dissertation. *Entrance requirements:* For master's, GRE General Test, MAT. Additional exam requirements/recommendations for international students: Required—TOEFL. *Application deadline:* For fall admission, 2/1 priority date for domestic students. Applications are processed on a rolling basis. Application fee: $65. Electronic applications accepted. *Expenses:* Tuition, state resident: full-time $7524. Tuition, nonresident: full-time $23,112. *Required fees:* $1970. *Financial support:* In 2013–14, 46 students received support, including 1 research assistantship (averaging $14,600 per year), 11 teaching assistantships (averaging $14,600 per year). Financial award application deadline: 3/1. *Unit head:* Dr. Janet Spector, Coordinator, 207-581-2459. *Application contact:* Scott G. Delcourt, Associate Dean of the Graduate School, 207-581-3291, Fax: 207-581-3232, E-mail: graduate@maine.edu.
Website: http://umaine.edu/edhd/.

University of Maine at Farmington, Program in Education, Farmington, ME 04938-1990. Offers early childhood education (MS Ed); educational leadership (MS Ed). *Accreditation:* NCATE. Part-time and evening/weekend programs available. Postbaccalaureate distance learning degree programs offered (minimal on-campus study). *Faculty:* 10 full-time (9 women), 4 part-time/adjunct (2 women). *Students:* 43 full-time (38 women); includes 2 minority (1 American Indian or Alaska Native, non-Hispanic/Latino; 1 Hispanic/Latino). *Degree requirements:* For master's, capstone project (for educational leadership). *Entrance requirements:* For master's, baccalaureate degree from accredited institution, valid teaching certificate or professional experience in education, professional employment by school district or other educational institution, minimum of two years' experience in professional education. *Application deadline:* Applications are processed on a rolling basis. Application fee: $60. *Expenses:* Tuition, state resident: full-time $4930; part-time $379 per credit. Tuition, nonresident: full-time $7150; part-time $550 per credit. *Required fees:* $84 per semester. One-time fee: $100. *Faculty research:* School improvement strategies, technology integration. *Application contact:* Graduate Studies, 207-778-7502, Fax: 207-778-8134, E-mail: umfmasters@maine.edu.
Website: http://www2.umf.maine.edu/gradstudies/.

University of Mary, School of Education and Behavioral Sciences, Department of Education, Bismarck, ND 58504-9652. Offers college teaching (M Ed); curriculum, instruction and assessment (M Ed); early childhood education (M Ed); early childhood special education (M Ed); elementary administration (M Ed); emotional disorders (M Ed); learning disabilities (M Ed); reading (M Ed); secondary administration (M Ed); special education strategist (M Ed). Part-time programs available. *Degree requirements:* For master's, portfolio or thesis. *Entrance requirements:* For master's, interview, letters of reference, minimum GPA of 2.5. Additional exam requirements/recommendations for international students: Required—TOEFL (minimum score 500 paper-based; 71 iBT). Electronic applications accepted. *Faculty research:* Innovative pedagogy in higher education, technology in education, content standards, children of poverty, children with diverse learning needs.

University of Maryland, Baltimore County, Graduate School, College of Arts, Humanities and Social Sciences, Department of Education, Program in Teaching, Baltimore, MD 21250. Offers early childhood education (MAT); elementary education (MAT); secondary education (MAT), including art, biology, chemistry, dance, earth/space science, English, foreign language, mathematics, music, physics, social studies, theatre. Part-time and evening/weekend programs available. *Faculty:* 24 full-time (18 women), 25 part-time/adjunct (19 women). *Students:* 49 full-time (34 women), 35 part-time (23 women); includes 19 minority (9 Black or African American, non-Hispanic/Latino; 3 Asian, non-Hispanic/Latino; 6 Hispanic/Latino; 1 Two or more races, non-Hispanic/Latino). Average age 30. 40 applicants, 95% accepted, 35 enrolled. In 2013, 106 master's awarded. *Degree requirements:* For master's, comprehensive exam (for some programs), thesis (for some programs). *Entrance requirements:* For master's, PRAXIS I or SAT (minimum score of 1000), minimum GPA of 3.0. Additional exam requirements/recommendations for international students: Required—TOEFL. *Application deadline:* For fall admission, 6/1 for domestic students; for spring admission, 11/1 for domestic students. Applications are processed on a rolling basis. Application fee: $50. Electronic applications accepted. One-time fee: $200 full-time. *Financial support:* In 2013–14, 6 students received support, including teaching assistantships with full and partial tuition reimbursements available (averaging $12,000 per year); career-related internships or fieldwork, Federal Work-Study, scholarships/grants, tuition waivers, and unspecified assistantships also available. Financial award application deadline: 3/1. *Faculty research:* STEM teacher education, culturally sensitive pedagogy, ESOL/bilingual education, early childhood education, language, literacy and culture. *Unit head:* Dr. Susan M. Blunck, Graduate Program Director, 410-455-2869, Fax: 410-455-3986, E-mail: blunck@umbc.edu. *Application contact:* Dr. Susan M. Blunck, Graduate Program Director, 410-455-2869, Fax: 410-455-3986, E-mail: blunck@umbc.edu.
Website: http://www.umbc.edu/education/.

University of Massachusetts Amherst, Graduate School, College of Education, Program in Education, Amherst, MA 01003. Offers bilingual/English as a second language/multicultural education (M Ed, Ed S); child study and early education (M Ed); children, families and schools (Ed D, Ed S); early childhood and elementary teacher education (M Ed); educational leadership (M Ed); educational policy and leadership (Ed D); higher education (M Ed); international education (M Ed); language, literacy and culture (Ed D); learning, media and technology (M Ed, Ed S); mathematics, science, and learning technologies (Ed D); psychometric methods, educational statistics and research methods (Ed D); reading and writing (M Ed); school counselor education (M Ed, Ed S); school psychology (Ed S); science education (Ed S); secondary teacher education (M Ed); social justice education (M Ed, Ed D, Ed S); special education (M Ed, Ed D, Ed S); teacher education and school improvement (Ed D, Ed S). *Accreditation:* NCATE. Part-time programs available. Postbaccalaureate distance learning degree programs offered (minimal on-campus study). *Faculty:* 95 full-time (55 women). *Students:* 357 full-time (240 women), 264 part-time (194 women); includes 114 minority (41 Black or African American, non-Hispanic/Latino; 4 American Indian or Alaska Native, non-Hispanic/Latino; 10 Asian, non-Hispanic/Latino; 47 Hispanic/Latino; 12 Two or more races, non-Hispanic/Latino), 100 international. Average age 34. 761 applicants, 51% accepted, 200 enrolled. In 2013, 186 master's, 31 doctorates, 22 other advanced degrees awarded. Terminal master's awarded for partial completion of doctoral program. *Degree requirements:* For doctorate, comprehensive exam, thesis/dissertation. *Entrance requirements:* Additional exam requirements/recommendations for international students: Required—TOEFL (minimum score 550 paper-based; 80 iBT), IELTS (minimum score 6.5). *Application deadline:* For fall admission, 1/15 for domestic and international students. Applications are processed on a rolling basis. Application fee: $75. Electronic applications accepted. *Financial support:* Fellowships with full and partial tuition reimbursements, research assistantships with full and partial tuition reimbursements, teaching assistantships with full and partial tuition reimbursements, career-related internships or fieldwork, Federal Work-Study, scholarships/grants, traineeships, health care benefits, tuition waivers (full and partial), and unspecified assistantships available. Support available to part-time students. Financial award application deadline: 1/15; financial award applicants required to submit FAFSA. *Unit head:* Dr. Linda L. Griffin, Graduate Program Director, 413-545-6984, Fax: 413-545-1523. *Application contact:* Lindsay DeSantis, Supervisor of Admissions, 413-545-0722, Fax: 413-577-0010, E-mail: gradadm@grad.umass.edu.
Website: http://www.umass.edu/education/.

University of Memphis, Graduate School, College of Education, Department of Instruction and Curriculum Leadership, Memphis, TN 38152. Offers early childhood education (MAT, MS, Ed D); elementary education (MAT); instruction and curriculum (MS, Ed D); instruction design and technology (MS, Ed D); middle grades education (MAT); reading (MS, Ed D); secondary education (MAT); special education (MAT, MS, Ed D). *Accreditation:* NCATE (one or more programs are accredited). Part-time programs available. *Faculty:* 30 full-time (18 women), 16 part-time/adjunct (10 women). *Students:* 55 full-time (44 women), 370 part-time (300 women); includes 169 minority (153 Black or African American, non-Hispanic/Latino; 5 American Indian or Alaska Native, non-Hispanic/Latino; 1 Asian, non-Hispanic/Latino; 6 Hispanic/Latino; 4 Two or more races, non-Hispanic/Latino), 7 international. Average age 35. 181 applicants, 84% accepted, 21 enrolled. In 2013, 137 master's, 10 doctorates awarded. Terminal master's awarded for partial completion of doctoral program. *Degree requirements:* For master's, comprehensive exam, thesis or alternative; for doctorate, comprehensive exam, thesis/dissertation. *Entrance requirements:* For master's, GRE General Test, minimum GPA of 2.5; for doctorate, GRE General Test, GRE Subject Test, 2 years of teaching experience. *Application deadline:* For fall admission, 8/1 for domestic students; for spring admission, 12/1 for domestic students. Applications are processed on a rolling basis. Application fee: $35 ($60 for international students). Electronic applications accepted. *Financial support:* In 2013–14, 635 students received support. Research assistantships with full tuition reimbursements available, teaching assistantships with full tuition reimbursements available, career-related internships or fieldwork, Federal Work-Study, institutionally sponsored loans, scholarships/grants, traineeships, and unspecified assistantships available. Support available to part-time students. Financial award application deadline: 2/15; financial award applicants required to submit FAFSA. *Faculty research:* Effective urban teachers, preparation and retention of urban teachers, technology utilization in schools, field-based teacher preparation programs, effective use of online instruction. *Unit head:* Dr. Sandra Cooley-Nichols, Interim Chair, 901-678-2365. *Application contact:* Dr. Sally Blake, Director of Graduate Studies, 901-678-4861.
Website: http://www.memphis.edu/icl/.

University of Miami, Graduate School, School of Education and Human Development, Department of Teaching and Learning, Program in Early Childhood Special Education, Coral Gables, FL 33124. Offers MS Ed, Ed S. Part-time and evening/weekend programs available. *Faculty:* 4 full-time (3 women), 6 part-time/adjunct (all women). *Students:* 31 part-time (29 women); includes 22 minority (5 Black or African American, non-Hispanic/Latino; 1 Asian, non-Hispanic/Latino; 14 Hispanic/Latino; 2 Two or more races, non-Hispanic/Latino). Average age 35. 30 applicants, 70% accepted, 21 enrolled. In 2013, 1 master's awarded. *Degree requirements:* For master's, electronic portfolio. *Entrance requirements:* For master's, GRE General Test. Additional exam requirements/recommendations for international students: Required—TOEFL (minimum score 550 paper-based; 80 iBT); Recommended—IELTS (minimum score 6.5). *Application deadline:* For fall admission, 6/30 for domestic students. Application fee: $65. Electronic applications accepted. *Financial support:* In 2013–14, 30 students received support. Application deadline: 3/1; applicants required to submit FAFSA. *Unit head:* Dr. Elizabeth Harry, Department Chairperson and Program Director, 305-284-4961, Fax: 305-284-6998, E-mail: bharry@miami.edu. *Application contact:* Maria Papazian, Graduate Admissions Coordinator, 305-284-2963, Fax: 305-284-6998, E-mail: m.papazian@miami.edu.
Website: http://www.education.miami.edu/program/Programs.asp?Program_ID=43&Src=Graduate.

University of Michigan–Dearborn, College of Education, Health, and Human Services, Program in Early Childhood Education, Dearborn, MI 48128-1491. Offers MA. Part-time and evening/weekend programs available. Postbaccalaureate distance learning degree programs offered (minimal on-campus study). *Faculty:* 2 full-time (both women), 1 (woman) part-time/adjunct. *Students:* 3 full-time (all women), 18 part-time (all women); includes 3 minority (2 Hispanic/Latino; 1 Two or more races, non-Hispanic/Latino), 2 international. Average age 34. 9 applicants, 67% accepted, 5 enrolled. *Entrance requirements:* Additional exam requirements/recommendations for international students: Required—TOEFL (minimum score 560 paper-based; 84 iBT), IELTS (minimum score 6.5). *Application deadline:* For fall admission, 8/1 priority date for domestic students, 5/1 for international students; for winter admission, 12/1 priority date for domestic students, 9/1 for international students; for spring admission, 4/1 priority date for domestic students, 1/1 for international students. Applications are processed on a rolling basis. Application fee: $60. Electronic applications accepted. *Expenses:* Tuition, state resident: full-time $11,838; part-time $686 per credit hour. Tuition, nonresident: full-time $20,926; part-time $1206 per credit hour. *Required fees:* $760; $286 per semester. Tuition and fees vary according to course load and program. *Financial support:* Career-related internships or fieldwork and scholarships/grants available. Financial award applicants required to submit FAFSA. *Faculty research:* Early childhood education, constructivist education, assessment. *Unit head:* Dr. Seong Hong, Coordinator, 313-593-3613, E-mail: seong@umich.edu. *Application contact:* Elizabeth Morden, Program Assistant, 313-593-6333, Fax: 313-593-4748, E-mail: emorden@umich.edu.
Website: http://cehhs.umd.umich.edu/cehhs_maeced/.

Early Childhood Education

University of Michigan–Flint, School of Education and Human Services, Department of Education, Flint, MI 48502-1950. Offers early childhood education (MA); educational technology (MA); elementary education with teaching certification (MA); literacy education (MA); special education (MA). Part-time programs available. *Faculty:* 14 full-time (12 women), 8 part-time/adjunct (4 women). *Students:* 27 full-time (24 women), 215 part-time (186 women); includes 22 minority (20 Black or African American, non-Hispanic/Latino; 2 American Indian or Alaska Native, non-Hispanic/Latino). Average age 35. 63 applicants, 86% accepted, 43 enrolled. In 2013, 91 master's awarded. *Entrance requirements:* For master's, BS with minimum GPA of 3.0. Additional exam requirements/recommendations for international students: Required—TOEFL (minimum score 560 paper-based; 84 iBT), IELTS (minimum score 6.5). *Application deadline:* For fall admission, 8/1 priority date for domestic students, 5/1 priority date for international students; for winter admission, 11/15 priority date for domestic students, 9/15 priority date for international students; for spring admission, 3/15 priority date for domestic students, 1/15 priority date for international students. Application fee: $55. *Expenses:* Contact institution. *Financial support:* Federal Work-Study, scholarships/grants, and unspecified assistantships available. Support available to part-time students. Financial award application deadline: 6/1; financial award applicants required to submit FAFSA. *Unit head:* Dr. Beverly Schumer, Director, 810-424-5215, E-mail: bschumer@umflint.edu. *Application contact:* Beulah Alexander, Executive Secretary, 810-766-6879, Fax: 810-766-6891, E-mail: beulaha@umflint.edu.
Website: http://www.umflint.edu/education/graduate-programs.

University of Minnesota, Twin Cities Campus, Graduate School, College of Education and Human Development, Department of Curriculum and Instruction, Minneapolis, MN 55455-0213. Offers art education (M Ed, MA, PhD); children's literature (M Ed, MA, PhD); curriculum and instruction (MA, PhD); early childhood education (M Ed, PhD); elementary education (M Ed, MA, PhD); English education (MA, PhD); environmental education (M Ed); family education (M Ed, MA, Ed D, PhD); instructional systems and technology (M Ed, MA, PhD); language arts (MA, PhD); language immersion education (Certificate); literacy education (MA); mathematics education (MA, PhD); reading education (MA, PhD); science education (MA, PhD); second languages and cultures education (MA, PhD); social studies education (MA, PhD); teaching (M Ed), including Chinese, earth science, elementary special education, English, English as a second language, French, German, Hebrew, Japanese, life sciences, mathematics, middle school science, science, second languages and cultures, social studies, Spanish; technology enhanced learning (Certificate); writing education (M Ed, MA, PhD). *Faculty:* 29 full-time (16 women). *Students:* 425 full-time (301 women), 220 part-time (153 women); includes 85 minority (21 Black or African American, non-Hispanic/Latino; 6 American Indian or Alaska Native, non-Hispanic/Latino; 42 Asian, non-Hispanic/Latino; 16 Hispanic/Latino), 50 international. Average age 32. 551 applicants, 68% accepted, 340 enrolled. In 2013, 618 master's, 33 doctorates, 6 other advanced degrees awarded. Application fee: $75 ($95 for international students). *Financial support:* In 2013–14, 25 fellowships (averaging $28,500 per year), 23 research assistantships with full tuition reimbursements (averaging $8,082 per year), 81 teaching assistantships with full tuition reimbursements (averaging $9,974 per year) were awarded. *Faculty research:* Teaching and learning; quality of education; influence of cultural, linguistic, social, political, technological and economic factors on teaching, learning and educational research; relationship between educational practice and a democratic and just society. *Total annual research expenditures:* $272,048. *Unit head:* Dr. Nina Asher, Chair, 612-624-4772, Fax: 612-624-1357, E-mail: nasher@umn.edu. *Application contact:* Dr. Jennifer Engler, Assistant Dean, 612-626-2887, Fax: 612-626-7496, E-mail: engle009@umn.edu.
Website: http://www.cehd.umn.edu/ci.

University of Minnesota, Twin Cities Campus, Graduate School, College of Education and Human Development, Department of Educational Psychology, Minneapolis, MN 55455-0213. Offers counseling and student personnel psychology (MA, PhD, Ed S); early childhood education (M Ed, MA, PhD); educational psychology (PhD); psychological foundations of education (MA, PhD, Ed S); school psychology (MA, PhD, Ed S); special education (M Ed, MA, PhD, Ed S); talent development and gifted education (Certificate). *Accreditation:* APA (one or more programs are accredited). *Faculty:* 31 full-time (15 women). *Students:* 276 full-time (215 women), 1,982 part-time (65 women); includes 47 minority (12 Black or African American, non-Hispanic/Latino; 4 American Indian or Alaska Native, non-Hispanic/Latino; 16 Asian, non-Hispanic/Latino; 15 Hispanic/Latino), 45 international. Average age 29. 342 applicants, 47% accepted, 97 enrolled. In 2013, 109 master's, 26 doctorates, 30 other advanced degrees awarded. Application fee: $75 ($95 for international students). *Financial support:* In 2013–14, 5 fellowships (averaging $21,623 per year), 62 research assistantships (averaging $10,081 per year), 31 teaching assistantships (averaging $7,120 per year) were awarded. *Faculty research:* Learning, cognitive and social processes; multicultural education and counseling; measurement and statistical processes; performance assessment; instructional design/strategies for students with special needs. *Total annual research expenditures:* $3.5 million. *Unit head:* Geoff Maruyama, Chair, 612-625-5861, Fax: 612-624-8241, E-mail: geoff@umn.edu. *Application contact:* Dr. Jennifer Engler, Assistant Dean, 612-626-2887, Fax: 612-626-7496, E-mail: engle009@umn.edu.
Website: http://www.cehd.umn.edu/EdPsych.

University of Minnesota, Twin Cities Campus, Graduate School, College of Education and Human Development, Institute of Child Development, Minneapolis, MN 55455-0213. Offers child psychology (MA, PhD); early childhood education (M Ed, MA, PhD); school psychology (MA, PhD). *Faculty:* 17 full-time (8 women). *Students:* 61 full-time (54 women), 17 part-time (all women); includes 10 minority (3 Black or African American, non-Hispanic/Latino; 2 Asian, non-Hispanic/Latino; 5 Hispanic/Latino), 6 international. Average age 28. 125 applicants, 25% accepted, 24 enrolled. In 2013, 55 master's, 6 doctorates awarded. Application fee: $75 ($95 for international students). *Financial support:* In 2013–14, 21 fellowships (averaging $20,606 per year), 12 research assistantships with full tuition reimbursements (averaging $9,058 per year), 23 teaching assistantships with full tuition reimbursements (averaging $9,182 per year) were awarded. *Faculty research:* Developmental affective and cognitive neuroscience; developmental psychopathology; intervention and prevention science; social and emotional development; cognitive, language, and perceptual development. *Total annual research expenditures:* $8.4 million. *Unit head:* Dr. Megan Gunnar, Director, 612-624-2846, Fax: 612-624-6373, E-mail: gunnar@umn.edu. *Application contact:* Dr. Jennifer Engler, Assistant Dean, 612-626-2887, Fax: 612-626-7496, E-mail: engle009@umn.edu.
Website: http://www.cehd.umn.edu/ICD.

University of Missouri, Graduate School, College of Education, Department of Learning, Teaching and Curriculum, Columbia, MO 65211. Offers agricultural education (M Ed, PhD, Ed S); art education (M Ed, PhD, Ed S); business and office education (M Ed, PhD, Ed S); early childhood education (M Ed, PhD, Ed S); elementary education (M Ed, PhD, Ed S); English education (M Ed, PhD, Ed S); foreign language education (M Ed, PhD, Ed S); health education and promotion (M Ed, PhD); learning and instruction (M Ed); marketing education (M Ed, PhD, Ed S); mathematics education (M Ed, PhD, Ed S); music education (M Ed, PhD, Ed S); reading education (M Ed, PhD, Ed S); science education (M Ed, PhD, Ed S); social studies education (M Ed, PhD,

Ed S); vocational education (M Ed, PhD, Ed S). Part-time programs available. *Faculty:* 26 full-time (16 women), 3 part-time/adjunct (2 women). *Students:* 186 full-time (143 women), 197 part-time (172 women); includes 19 minority (4 Black or African American, non-Hispanic/Latino; 4 Asian, non-Hispanic/Latino; 6 Hispanic/Latino; 5 Two or more races, non-Hispanic/Latino), 25 international. Average age 31. 288 applicants, 65% accepted, 160 enrolled. In 2013, 202 master's, 18 doctorates, 7 other advanced degrees awarded. Terminal master's awarded for partial completion of doctoral program. *Degree requirements:* For doctorate, thesis/dissertation. *Entrance requirements:* For master's and Ed S, GRE General Test or MAT, minimum GPA of 3.0; for doctorate, GRE General Test, minimum GPA of 3.0. Additional exam requirements/recommendations for international students: Required—TOEFL (minimum score 600 paper-based; 100 iBT). *Application deadline:* For fall admission, 12/1 priority date for domestic and international students. Applications are processed on a rolling basis. Application fee: $55 ($75 for international students). Electronic applications accepted. *Financial support:* Fellowships, research assistantships, teaching assistantships, institutionally sponsored loans, traineeships, health care benefits, and unspecified assistantships available. Support available to part-time students. *Faculty research:* Curriculum development and research, teacher education, art education, business and marketing, early childhood education, English education, literacy/reading education, mathematics education, music education, science education, social studies education. *Unit head:* Dr. James Tarr, Associate Division Director, 573-882-4034, E-mail: tarrj@missouri.edu. *Application contact:* Fran Colley, Academic Advisor, 573-882-6462, E-mail: colleyf@missouri.edu.
Website: http://education.missouri.edu/LTC/.

University of Missouri–St. Louis, College of Education, Division of Teaching and Learning, St. Louis, MO 63121. Offers autism studies (Certificate); elementary education (M Ed), including early childhood, general, reading; secondary education (M Ed), including curriculum and instruction, general, middle level education, reading, teaching English to speakers of other languages (TESOL); secondary school teaching (Certificate); special education (M Ed), including autism and developmental disabilities, cross-categorical disabilities, early childhood; teaching English to speakers of other languages (Certificate). Part-time and evening/weekend programs available. *Faculty:* 20 full-time (11 women), 1 (woman) part-time/adjunct. *Students:* 42 full-time (33 women), 578 part-time (442 women); includes 152 minority (101 Black or African American, non-Hispanic/Latino; 1 American Indian or Alaska Native, non-Hispanic/Latino; 20 Asian, non-Hispanic/Latino; 23 Hispanic/Latino; 7 Two or more races, non-Hispanic/Latino), 19 international. Average age 29. 245 applicants, 97% accepted, 166 enrolled. In 2013, 219 master's, 14 Certificates awarded. *Degree requirements:* For master's, comprehensive exam. *Entrance requirements:* Additional exam requirements/recommendations for international students: Recommended—TOEFL (minimum score 550 paper-based; 79 iBT), IELTS (minimum score 6.5). *Application deadline:* For fall admission, 7/1 priority date for domestic and international students; for spring admission, 12/1 priority date for domestic and international students. Application fee: $50 ($40 for international students). Electronic applications accepted. *Expenses:* Tuition, state resident: full-time $7364; part-time $409.10 per credit hour. Tuition, nonresident: full-time $19,162; part-time $1008.50 per credit hour. *Financial support:* Application deadline: 4/1; applicants required to submit FAFSA. *Unit head:* Dr. Patricia Kopetz, Chair, 314-516-5791. *Application contact:* 314-516-5458, Fax: 314-516-6996, E-mail: gadadm@umsl.edu.
Website: http://coe.umsl.edu/web/divisions/teach-learn/index.html.

University of Nebraska at Kearney, Graduate Programs, College of Education, Department of Teacher Education, Kearney, NE 68849-0001. Offers curriculum and instruction (MA Ed), including early childhood education, elementary education, English as a second language, instructional effectiveness, reading/special education, secondary education; instructional technology (MS Ed), including information technology, instructional technology, school librarian; reading PK-12 (MA Ed); special education (MA Ed), including advanced practitioner, gifted, mild/moderate. Part-time and evening/weekend programs available. *Degree requirements:* For master's, comprehensive exam, thesis optional. *Entrance requirements:* For master's, portfolio or GRE. Additional exam requirements/recommendations for international students: Required—TOEFL (minimum score 550 paper-based). Electronic applications accepted.

University of Nebraska–Lincoln, Graduate College, College of Education and Human Sciences, Department of Child, Youth and Family Studies, Lincoln, NE 68588. Offers child development/early childhood education (MS, PhD); child, youth and family studies (MS); family and consumer sciences education (MS, PhD); family financial planning (MS); family science (MS, PhD); gerontology (PhD); human sciences (PhD), including child, youth and family studies, gerontology, medical family therapy; marriage and family therapy (MS); medical family therapy (PhD); youth development (MS). *Accreditation:* AAMFT/COAMFTE (one or more programs are accredited). Postbaccalaureate distance learning degree programs offered. *Degree requirements:* For master's, thesis optional. *Entrance requirements:* For master's, GRE. Additional exam requirements/recommendations for international students: Required—TOEFL (minimum score 550 paper-based). Electronic applications accepted. *Faculty research:* Marriage and family therapy, child development/early childhood education, family financial management.

University of Nevada, Las Vegas, Graduate College, College of Education, Department of Educational and Clinical Studies, Las Vegas, NV 89154-3066. Offers addiction studies (Advanced Certificate); counselor education (Ed D, Ed S), including clinical mental health (Ed D), school counseling (Ed S); mental health counseling (Advanced Certificate); rehabilitation counseling (Advanced Certificate); special education (MS, Ed D, PhD, Ed S), including early childhood education (Ed D), special education (Ed D). Part-time and evening/weekend programs available. *Faculty:* 16 full-time (7 women), 17 part-time/adjunct (16 women). *Students:* 161 full-time (136 women), 184 part-time (148 women); includes 153 minority (31 Black or African American, non-Hispanic/Latino; 13 Asian, non-Hispanic/Latino; 53 Hispanic/Latino; 3 Native Hawaiian or other Pacific Islander, non-Hispanic/Latino; 53 Two or more races, non-Hispanic/Latino), 14 international. Average age 33. 140 applicants, 84% accepted, 100 enrolled. In 2013, 133 master's, 11 doctorates, 2 other advanced degrees awarded. *Degree requirements:* For master's, comprehensive exam (for some programs), thesis (for some programs); for other advanced degree, thesis (for some programs). *Entrance requirements:* Additional exam requirements/recommendations for international students: Required—TOEFL (minimum score 550 paper-based; 80 iBT), IELTS (minimum score 7). *Application deadline:* For fall admission, 2/1 for domestic students, 5/1 for international students; for spring admission, 10/1 for domestic and international students. Application fee: $60 ($95 for international students). Electronic applications accepted. *Expenses:* Tuition, state resident: full-time $4752; part-time $264 per credit. Tuition, nonresident: full-time $18,662; part-time $554.50 per credit. *International tuition:* $18,952 full-time. *Required fees:* $532; $12 per credit. $266 per semester. One-time fee: $35. Tuition and fees vary according to course load and program. *Financial support:* In 2013–14, 35 students received support, including 27 research assistantships with partial tuition reimbursements available (averaging $9,213 per year), 8 teaching assistantships with partial tuition reimbursements available (averaging $11,438 per year); institutionally sponsored loans, scholarships/grants, health care benefits, and unspecified assistantships also available. Financial award application deadline: 3/1. *Faculty research:* Multicultural issues in counseling, academic interventions for students with disabilities, rough and tumble play in early childhood, inclusive strategies for students with disabilities, addictions. *Total annual research expenditures:* $343,782. *Unit head:*

Dr. Thomas Pierce, Interim Chair/Associate Professor, 702-895-1104, Fax: 702-895-5550, E-mail: tom.pierce@unlv.edu. *Application contact:* Graduate College Admissions Evaluator, 702-895-3320, Fax: 702-895-4180, E-mail: gradcollege@unlv.edu.
Website: http://education.unlv.edu/ecs/.

University of New Hampshire, Graduate School, College of Liberal Arts, Department of Education, Program in Early Childhood Education, Durham, NH 03824. Offers early childhood education (M Ed, Postbaccalaureate Certificate); special needs (M Ed). Part-time programs available. *Faculty:* 32 full-time. *Students:* 9 full-time (all women), 7 part-time (6 women); includes 2 minority (1 Black or African American, non-Hispanic/Latino; 1 Hispanic/Latino), 1 international. Average age 29. 13 applicants, 69% accepted, 8 enrolled. In 2013, 7 master's, 2 other advanced degrees awarded. *Degree requirements:* For master's, thesis or alternative. *Entrance requirements:* For master's, GRE General Test. Additional exam requirements/recommendations for international students: Required—TOEFL (minimum score 550 paper-based; 80 iBT). *Application deadline:* For fall admission, 2/1 priority date for domestic students, 2/1 for international students; for spring admission, 12/1 for domestic students. Applications are processed on a rolling basis. Application fee: $65. Electronic applications accepted. *Expenses:* Tuition, state resident: full-time $13,500; part-time $750 per credit hour. Tuition, nonresident: full-time $26,200; part-time $1100 per credit hour. *Required fees:* $1741; $435.25 per term. Tuition and fees vary according to course level, course load, campus/location and program. *Financial support:* In 2013–14, 8 students received support, including 1 teaching assistantship; fellowships, research assistantships, career-related internships or fieldwork, Federal Work-Study, scholarships/grants, and tuition waivers (full and partial) also available. Support available to part-time students. Financial award application deadline: 2/15. *Faculty research:* Young children with special needs. *Unit head:* Dr. Mike Middleton, Chairperson, 603-862-7054, E-mail: education.department@unh.edu. *Application contact:* Lisa Wilder, Administrative Assistant, 603-862-2381, E-mail: education.department@unh.edu.
Website: http://www.unh.edu/education.

University of New Mexico, Graduate School, College of Education, Department of Teacher Education, Educational Leadership and Policy, Program in Multicultural Teacher and Childhood Education, Albuquerque, NM 87131-2039. Offers Ed D, PhD. *Accreditation:* NCATE. Part-time programs available. *Faculty:* 16 full-time (14 women). *Students:* 4 full-time (3 women), 11 part-time (8 women); includes 8 minority (all Hispanic/Latino). Average age 49. 1 applicant, 100% accepted. In 2013, 2 doctorates awarded. *Degree requirements:* For doctorate, comprehensive exam, thesis/dissertation. *Entrance requirements:* For doctorate, GRE, master's degree, minimum GPA of 3.0, 3 years of teaching experience, 3-5 letters of reference, 1 letter of intent, professional writing sample. Additional exam requirements/recommendations for international students: Required—TOEFL (minimum score 550 paper-based). *Application deadline:* For fall admission, 1/15 priority date for domestic students, 1/15 for international students; for spring admission, 10/30 for domestic and international students. Application fee: $50. Electronic applications accepted. *Financial support:* In 2013–14, 10 students received support, including 2 research assistantships (averaging $22,000 per year), 3 teaching assistantships with partial tuition reimbursements available (averaging $8,628 per year); fellowships, scholarships/grants, and unspecified assistantships also available. Financial award application deadline: 3/1; financial award applicants required to submit FAFSA. *Faculty research:* Teacher education, clinical preparation, reflective practice, science education, mathematics education, social justice, technology education, media literacy. *Unit head:* Dr. Cheryl Torrez, Department Chair, 505-277-9611, Fax: 505-277-0455, E-mail: ted@unm.edu. *Application contact:* Robert Romero, Program Coordinator, 505-277-0513, Fax: 505-277-0455, E-mail: ted@unm.edu.
Website: http://coe.unm.edu/departments/teacher-ed/grad-degrees-certs/mctc-edd-phd.html.

The University of North Carolina at Chapel Hill, Graduate School, School of Education, Master of Education Program for Experienced Teachers: Early Childhood Intervention and Family Support, Chapel Hill, NC 27599. Offers M Ed. *Accreditation:* NCATE. Part-time programs available. *Degree requirements:* For master's, comprehensive exam. *Entrance requirements:* For master's, minimum GPA of 3.0 during last 2 years of undergraduate course work. Electronic applications accepted.

The University of North Carolina at Chapel Hill, Graduate School, School of Education, Program in Education, Chapel Hill, NC 27599. Offers culture, curriculum and change (MA, PhD); early childhood, intervention and literacy (MA, PhD); educational psychology, measurement and evaluation (MA, PhD). *Accreditation:* NCATE. *Degree requirements:* For master's, thesis; for doctorate, comprehensive exam, thesis/dissertation. *Entrance requirements:* For master's, GRE General Test, minimum GPA of 3.0 during last 2 years of undergraduate course work; for doctorate, GRE General Test, minimum GPA of 3.0 during last 2 years of undergraduate course work. Additional exam requirements/recommendations for international students: Required—TOEFL (minimum score 550 paper-based). Electronic applications accepted.

The University of North Carolina at Greensboro, Graduate School, School of Education, Department of Specialized Education Services, Greensboro, NC 27412-5001. Offers cross-categorical special education (M Ed); interdisciplinary studies in special education (M Ed); leadership early care and education (Certificate); special education (M Ed, PhD). *Degree requirements:* For master's, thesis or alternative. *Entrance requirements:* For master's, GRE General Test. Additional exam requirements/recommendations for international students: Required—TOEFL. Electronic applications accepted.

The University of North Carolina Wilmington, Watson College of Education, Department of Early Childhood, Elementary, Middle, Literacy and Special Education, Wilmington, NC 28403-3297. Offers MAT. *Accreditation:* NCATE. Part-time and evening/weekend programs available. *Faculty:* 21 full-time (17 women). *Students:* 47 full-time (36 women), 13 part-time (11 women); includes 9 minority (5 Black or African American, non-Hispanic/Latino; 2 Hispanic/Latino; 2 Two or more races, non-Hispanic/Latino), 3 international. Average age 31. 36 applicants, 97% accepted, 33 enrolled. In 2013, 24 master's awarded. *Degree requirements:* For master's, comprehensive exam. *Entrance requirements:* For master's, GRE General Test, MAT, minimum B average in upper-division undergraduate course work. *Application deadline:* For fall admission, 6/1 for domestic students. Applications are processed on a rolling basis. Application fee: $60. *Expenses:* Tuition, state resident: full-time $4163. Tuition, nonresident: full-time $16,098. *Financial support:* Career-related internships or fieldwork, Federal Work-Study, and unspecified assistantships available. Support available to part-time students. Financial award application deadline: 3/15. *Unit head:* Dr. Tracy Hargrove, Chair, 910-962-3240, Fax: 910-962-3988, E-mail: hargrovet@uncw.edu. *Application contact:* Dr. Ron Vetter, Dean, Graduate School, 910-962-3224, Fax: 910-962-3787, E-mail: vetterr@uncw.edu.

University of North Dakota, Graduate School, College of Education and Human Development, Program in Early Childhood Education, Grand Forks, ND 58202. Offers MS. *Accreditation:* NCATE. Part-time programs available. *Degree requirements:* For master's, comprehensive exam, thesis or alternative. *Entrance requirements:* For master's, minimum GPA of 3.0. Additional exam requirements/recommendations for international students: Required—TOEFL (minimum score 550 paper-based; 79 iBT), IELTS (minimum score 6.5). Electronic applications accepted.

University of Northern Colorado, Graduate School, College of Education and Behavioral Sciences, School of Psychological Sciences, Program in Educational Psychology, Greeley, CO 80639. Offers early childhood education (MA); educational psychology (MA, PhD). *Accreditation:* NCATE. Part-time programs available. *Degree requirements:* For master's, comprehensive exam, thesis or alternative; for doctorate, comprehensive exam, thesis/dissertation. *Entrance requirements:* For master's, GRE General Test, letters of recommendation; for doctorate, GRE General Test, letters of recommendation, resume. Electronic applications accepted.

University of Northern Iowa, Graduate College, College of Education, Department of Curriculum and Instruction, MAE Program in Early Childhood Education, Cedar Falls, IA 50614. Offers curriculum and instruction (MAE). *Students:* 23 part-time (all women); includes 1 minority (Black or African American, non-Hispanic/Latino). In 2013, 12 master's awarded. *Degree requirements:* For master's, comprehensive exam, thesis or alternative. *Entrance requirements:* For master's, minimum GPA of 3.0. Additional exam requirements/recommendations for international students: Required—TOEFL (minimum score 500 paper-based; 61 iBT). *Application deadline:* For fall admission, 8/1 priority date for domestic students. Applications are processed on a rolling basis. Application fee: $50 ($70 for international students). Electronic applications accepted. *Financial support:* Application deadline: 2/1. *Unit head:* Dr. Gloria Kirkland-Holmes, Coordinator, 319-273-2007, Fax: 319-273-5886, E-mail: gloria.holmes@uni.edu. *Application contact:* Laurie S. Russell, Record Analyst, 319-273-2623, Fax: 319-273-2885, E-mail: laurie.russell@uni.edu.
Website: http://www.uni.edu/coe/departments/curriculum-instruction/early-childhood-education.

University of North Georgia, School of Education, Dahlonega, GA 30597. Offers art education (MAT); early childhood education (M Ed); English education (MAT); history education (MAT); math education (MAT); middle grades education (M Ed, MAT); physical education (MS); school leadership (Ed S); secondary education (M Ed), including English education, history education, mathematics education, physical education; teacher education (MAT). *Accreditation:* NCATE. Part-time and evening/weekend programs available. Postbaccalaureate distance learning degree programs offered (no on-campus study). *Degree requirements:* For master's, comprehensive exam, thesis optional. *Entrance requirements:* For master's, GRE or MAT, GACE, minimum GPA of 2.75; for Ed S, GRE General Test or MAT, 3 years of teaching experience, master's degree, minimum graduate GPA of 3.25, leadership position in the school. Additional exam requirements/recommendations for international students: Required—TOEFL (minimum score 550 paper-based; 79 iBT), IELTS (minimum score 6.5). Electronic applications accepted. *Faculty research:* Identification of professional development school structures supporting P-12 student achievement, impact of diverse field placement settings in teacher belief development among preservice teachers, use of inquiry methodology in social studies teaching with English language learners, use of instructional differentiation in the middle grades classroom, effects of international school placements on preservice teacher beliefs and attitudes.

University of North Texas, Robert B. Toulouse School of Graduate Studies, Denton, TN 76203-5017. Offers accounting (MS, PhD); applied anthropology (MA, MS); applied behavior analysis (Certificate); applied technology and performance improvement (M Ed, MS, PhD); art education (MA, PhD); art history (MA); art museum education (Certificate); arts leadership (Certificate); audiology (Au D); behavior analysis (MS); biochemistry and molecular biology (MS, PhD); biology (MA, MS, PhD); business (PhD); business computer information systems (PhD); chemistry (MS, PhD); clinical psychology (PhD); communication studies (MA, MS); computer engineering (MS); computer science (MS); computer science and engineering (PhD); counseling (M Ed, MS, PhD), including clinical mental health counseling (MS), college and university counseling (M Ed, MS), elementary school counseling (M Ed, MS), secondary school counseling (M Ed, MS); counseling psychology (PhD); creative writing (MA); criminal justice (MS); curriculum and instruction (M Ed, PhD), including curriculum studies (PhD), early childhood studies (PhD), language and literacy studies (PhD); decision sciences (MBA); design (MA, MFA), including fashion design (MFA), innovation studies, interior design (MFA); early childhood studies (MS); economics (MS); educational leadership (M Ed, Ed D, PhD); educational psychology (MS), including family studies, gifted and talented (MS, PhD), human development, learning and cognition, research, measurement and evaluation; educational research (PhD), including gifted and talented (MS, PhD), human development and family studies, psychological aspects of sports and exercise, research, measurement and statistics; electrical engineering (MS); emergency management (MPA); engineering systems (MS); English (MA, PhD); environmental science (MS, PhD); experimental psychology (PhD); finance (MBA, MS, PhD); financial management (MPA); French (MA); health psychology and behavioral medicine (PhD); health services management (MBA); higher education (M Ed, Ed D, PhD); history (MA, MS, PhD), including European history (PhD), military history (PhD), United States history (PhD); hospitality management (MS); human resources management (MPA); information science (MS, PhD); information technologies (MBA); information technology and decision sciences (MS); interdisciplinary studies (MA, MS); international sustainable tourism (MS); jazz studies (MM); journalism (MA, MJ, Graduate Certificate), including interactive and virtual digital communication (Graduate Certificate), narrative journalism (Graduate Certificate), public relations (Graduate Certificate); kinesiology (MS); learning technologies (MS, PhD); library science (MS); local government management (MPA); logistics and supply chain management (MBA, PhD); long-term care, senior housing, and aging services (MA, MS); management science (PhD); marketing (MBA, PhD); materials science and engineering (MS, PhD); mathematics (MA, PhD); merchandising (MS); music (MA, MM Ed, PhD), including ethnomusicology (MA), music education (MM Ed, PhD), music theory (MA, PhD), musicology (MA, PhD), performance (MA); nonprofit management (MPA); operations and supply chain management (MBA); performance (MM, DMA); philosophy (MA, PhD); physics (MS, PhD); political science (MA, MS, PhD); public administration and management (PhD), including emergency management, nonprofit management, public financial management, urban management; radio, television and film (MA, MFA); recreation, event and sport management (MS); rehabilitation counseling (MS, Certificate); sociology (MA, MS, PhD); Spanish (MA); special education (M Ed, PhD), including autism intervention (PhD), emotional/behavioral disorders (PhD), mild/moderate disabilities (PhD); speech-language pathology (MA, MS); strategic management (MBA); studio art (MFA); taxation (MS); teaching (M Ed); MBA/MS; MS/MPH; MSES/MBA. Part-time and evening/weekend programs available. Postbaccalaureate distance learning degree programs offered. *Faculty:* 661 full-time (213 women), 240 part-time/adjunct (144 women). *Students:* 3,106 full-time (1,620 women), 3,543 part-time (2,221 women); includes 1,740 minority (533 Black or African American, non-Hispanic/Latino; 15 American Indian or Alaska Native, non-Hispanic/Latino; 286 Asian, non-Hispanic/Latino; 746 Hispanic/Latino; 3 Native Hawaiian or other Pacific Islander, non-Hispanic/Latino; 157 Two or more races, non-Hispanic/Latino), 1,145 international. Average age 32. 6,289 applicants, 43% accepted, 1751 enrolled. In 2013, 1,778 master's, 239 doctorates, 10 other advanced degrees awarded. Terminal master's awarded for partial completion of doctoral program. *Degree requirements:* For master's, variable foreign language requirement, comprehensive exam (for some programs), thesis (for some programs); for

doctorate, variable foreign language requirement, comprehensive exam (for some programs), thesis/dissertation; for other advanced degree, variable foreign language requirement, comprehensive exam (for some programs). *Entrance requirements:* For master's and doctorate, GRE, GMAT. Additional exam requirements/recommendations for international students: Required—TOEFL (minimum score 550 paper-based; 79 iBT). *Application deadline:* For fall admission, 7/15 for domestic students, 3/15 for international students; for spring admission, 11/15 for domestic students, 9/15 for international students; for summer admission, 5/1 for domestic students. Applications are processed on a rolling basis. Application fee: $60. Electronic applications accepted. *Financial support:* Fellowships with partial tuition reimbursements, research assistantships with partial tuition reimbursements, teaching assistantships, career-related internships or fieldwork, Federal Work-Study, institutionally sponsored loans, scholarships/grants, health care benefits, and library assistantships available. Support available to part-time students. Financial award applicants required to submit FAFSA. *Unit head:* Mark Wardell, Dean, 940-565-2383, E-mail: mark.wardell@unt.edu. *Application contact:* Toulouse School of Graduate Studies, 940-565-2383, Fax: 940-565-2141, E-mail: gradsch@unt.edu.
Website: http://tsgs.unt.edu/.

University of Oklahoma, Jeannine Rainbolt College of Education, Department of Instructional Leadership and Academic Curriculum, Norman, OK 73072. Offers communication, culture and pedagogy for Hispanic populations in educational settings (Graduate Certificate); instructional leadership and academic curriculum (M Ed, PhD), including bilingual education (PhD), early childhood education, elementary education, English education, instructional leadership, mathematics education, reading education, science education, science, technology, engineering and mathematics education (M Ed), secondary education, social studies education, teacher education (M Ed), world language education (M Ed). *Accreditation:* NCATE. Part-time and evening/weekend programs available. Postbaccalaureate distance learning degree programs offered (no on-campus study). *Faculty:* 22 full-time (15 women), 1 (woman) part-time/adjunct. *Students:* 64 full-time (49 women), 103 part-time (81 women); includes 33 minority (8 Black or African American, non-Hispanic/Latino; 9 American Indian or Alaska Native, non-Hispanic/Latino; 5 Asian, non-Hispanic/Latino; 4 Hispanic/Latino; 1 Native Hawaiian or other Pacific Islander, non-Hispanic/Latino; 6 Two or more races, non-Hispanic/Latino), 10 international. Average age 34. 50 applicants, 84% accepted, 36 enrolled. In 2013, 26 master's, 11 doctorates awarded. Terminal master's awarded for partial completion of doctoral program. *Degree requirements:* For master's, comprehensive exam (for some programs), thesis (for some programs); for doctorate, comprehensive exam, thesis/dissertation. *Entrance requirements:* For master's, essay; for doctorate, GRE, 3 recommendation letters; autobiography, statement of objectives; essay on chosen major; transcripts; writing sample. Additional exam requirements/recommendations for international students: Required—TOEFL (minimum score 79 iBT). *Application deadline:* For fall admission, 4/30 for domestic and international students; for spring admission, 10/31 for domestic and international students; for summer admission, 3/15 for domestic and international students. Applications are processed on a rolling basis. Application fee: $50 ($100 for international students). Electronic applications accepted. *Expenses:* Tuition, state resident: full-time $4205; part-time $175.20 per credit hour. Tuition, nonresident: full-time $16,205; part-time $675.20 per credit hour. *Required fees:* $2745; $103.85 per credit hour. $126.50 per semester. *Financial support:* In 2013–14, 98 students received support, including 10 research assistantships with partial tuition reimbursements available (averaging $10,671 per year), 7 teaching assistantships with partial tuition reimbursements available (averaging $10,753 per year); Federal Work-Study, institutionally sponsored loans, scholarships/grants, and unspecified assistantships also available. Support available to part-time students. Financial award application deadline: 6/1; financial award applicants required to submit FAFSA. *Total annual research expenditures:* $1 million. *Unit head:* Dr. Stacy Reeder, Chair/Graduate Liaison, 405-325-1498, Fax: 405-325-4061, E-mail: reeder@ou.edu. *Application contact:* Lynn Crussel, Graduate Programs Officer, 405-325-1498, Fax: 405-325-4061, E-mail: lcrussel@ou.edu.
Website: http://education.ou.edu/departments/ilac.

University of Phoenix–Bay Area Campus, College of Education, San Jose, CA 95134-1805. Offers administration and supervision (MA Ed); adult education and training (MA Ed); early childhood education (MA Ed); education (Ed S); educational leadership (Ed D); elementary teacher education (MA Ed); higher education administration (PhD); secondary teacher education (MA Ed); special education (MA Ed); teacher leadership (MA Ed). Evening/weekend programs available. Postbaccalaureate distance learning degree programs offered (no on-campus study). *Degree requirements:* For master's, thesis (for some programs). *Entrance requirements:* For master's, minimum undergraduate GPA of 2.5, 3 years of work experience. Additional exam requirements/recommendations for international students: Required—TOEFL (minimum score 550 paper-based; 79 iBT). Electronic applications accepted.

University of Phoenix–Louisiana Campus, College of Education, Metairie, LA 70001-2082. Offers curriculum and instruction (MA Ed); early childhood education (MA Ed). Postbaccalaureate distance learning degree programs offered. *Degree requirements:* For master's, thesis. *Entrance requirements:* For master's, minimum undergraduate GPA of 2.5, 3 years work experience. Additional exam requirements/recommendations for international students: Required—TOEFL (minimum score 550 paper-based; 79 iBT).

University of Phoenix–North Florida Campus, College of Education, Jacksonville, FL 32216-0959. Offers administration and supervision (MA Ed); curriculum and instruction (MA Ed), including computer education, mathematics education; early childhood education (MA Ed); elementary teacher education (MA Ed); secondary teacher education (MA Ed). Evening/weekend programs available. *Degree requirements:* For master's, thesis (for some programs). *Entrance requirements:* For master's, 3 years of work experience, minimum undergraduate GPA of 2.5. Additional exam requirements/recommendations for international students: Required—TOEFL (minimum score 550 paper-based; 49 iBT). Electronic applications accepted.

University of Phoenix–Online Campus, College of Education, Phoenix, AZ 85034-7209. Offers administration and supervision (MAEd, Certificate); adult education and training (MAEd); curriculum and instruction (MAEd), including computer education, curriculum and instruction, English as a second language, language arts, mathematics, reading; early childhood education (MAEd); educational studies (MAEd); elementary teacher education (MAEd), including early childhood, elementary teacher education, high school middle level, middle level; principal licensure (Certificate); secondary teacher education (MAEd); special education (MAEd, Certificate); teacher education (MAEd), including middle level generalist; teacher education middle level mathematics (MAEd), including middle level mathematics; teacher education middle level science (MAEd), including middle level science; teacher education secondary mathematics (MAEd); teacher education secondary science (MAEd); teacher leadership (MAEd); teachers of English learners (Certificate); transition to teaching (Certificate), including elementary education, secondary education. *Accreditation:* Teacher Education Accreditation Council. Evening/weekend programs available. Postbaccalaureate distance learning degree programs offered. *Entrance requirements:* Additional exam requirements/recommendations for international students: Required—TOEFL, TOEIC (Test of English as an International Communication), Berlitz Online English Proficiency Exam, PTE, or IELTS. Electronic applications accepted. *Expenses:* Contact institution.

University of Phoenix–Oregon Campus, College of Education, Tigard, OR 97223. Offers curriculum and instruction (MA Ed); early childhood education (MA Ed); elementary education (MA Ed), including early childhood specialization, middle level specialization; secondary education (MA Ed). Evening/weekend programs available. *Degree requirements:* For master's, thesis (for some programs). *Entrance requirements:* For master's, minimum undergraduate GPA of 2.5, 3 years work experience. Additional exam requirements/recommendations for international students: Required—TOEFL (minimum score 550 paper-based; 79 iBT). Electronic applications accepted.

University of Phoenix–Phoenix Campus, College of Education, Tempe, AZ 85282-2371. Offers administration and supervision (MA Ed); adult education and training (MA Ed); curriculum and instruction reading (MA Ed); early childhood education (MA Ed); education studies (MA Ed); elementary teacher education (MA Ed); secondary teacher education (MA Ed); special education (MA Ed); teacher leadership (MA Ed). Evening/weekend programs available. Postbaccalaureate distance learning degree programs offered. *Entrance requirements:* Additional exam requirements/recommendations for international students: Required—TOEFL, TOEIC (Test of English as an International Communication), Berlitz Online English Proficiency Exam, PTE, or IELTS. Electronic applications accepted. *Expenses:* Contact institution.

University of Phoenix–Puerto Rico Campus, College of Education, Guaynabo, PR 00968. Offers administration and supervision (MA Ed); early childhood education (MA Ed); school counselor (MSC). Evening/weekend programs available. *Degree requirements:* For master's, thesis (for some programs). *Entrance requirements:* For master's, minimum undergraduate GPA of 2.5, 3 years work experience. Additional exam requirements/recommendations for international students: Required—TOEFL (minimum score 550 paper-based; 79 iBT). Electronic applications accepted.

University of Phoenix–South Florida Campus, College of Education, Miramar, FL 33030. Offers administration and supervision (MA Ed); curriculum and instruction (MA Ed), including computer education, curriculum and instruction, mathematics education; early childhood education (MA Ed); elementary teacher education (MA Ed); secondary teacher education (MA Ed). Evening/weekend programs available. *Degree requirements:* For master's, thesis (for some programs). *Entrance requirements:* For master's, 3 years of work experience, minimum undergraduate GPA of 2.5. Additional exam requirements/recommendations for international students: Required—TOEFL (minimum score 550 paper-based; 79 iBT). Electronic applications accepted.

University of Phoenix–Washington D.C. Campus, College of Education, Washington, DC 20001. Offers administration and supervision (MA Ed); adult education and training (MA Ed); computer education (MA Ed); curriculum and instruction (MA Ed, Ed D); early childhood education (MA Ed); education (Ed S); educational leadership (Ed D); educational technology (Ed D); elementary teacher education (MA Ed); English and language arts education (MA Ed); English as a second language (MA Ed); higher education administration (PhD); mathematics education (MA Ed); secondary teacher education (MA Ed); special education (MA Ed); teacher leadership (MA Ed).

University of Phoenix–West Florida Campus, College of Education, Temple Terrace, FL 33637. Offers administration and supervision (MA Ed); curriculum and instruction (MA Ed), including computer education, curriculum and instruction, mathematics education; curriculum and technology (MA Ed); early childhood education (MA Ed); elementary teacher education (MA Ed); secondary teacher education (MA Ed). Evening/weekend programs available. *Degree requirements:* For master's, thesis (for some programs). *Entrance requirements:* For master's, 3 years of work experience, minimum undergraduate GPA of 2.5. Additional exam requirements/recommendations for international students: Required—TOEFL (minimum score 550 paper-based; 79 iBT).

University of Pittsburgh, School of Education, Department of Instruction and Learning, Program in Early Childhood Education, Pittsburgh, PA 15260. Offers M Ed. Part-time and evening/weekend programs available. *Students:* 16 full-time (all women), 2 part-time (both women); includes 2 minority (1 Black or African American, non-Hispanic/Latino; 1 Two or more races, non-Hispanic/Latino), 5 international. Average age 27. 10 applicants, 70% accepted, 5 enrolled. In 2013, 3 master's awarded. *Degree requirements:* For master's, thesis. *Entrance requirements:* For master's, PRAXIS I. Additional exam requirements/recommendations for international students: Required—TOEFL. *Application deadline:* For fall admission, 2/1 for domestic students. Application fee: $50. Electronic applications accepted. *Expenses:* Tuition, state resident: full-time $19,964; part-time $807 per credit. Tuition, nonresident: full-time $32,686; part-time $1337 per credit. *Required fees:* $740; $200. Tuition and fees vary according to program. *Financial support:* Career-related internships or fieldwork, Federal Work-Study, institutionally sponsored loans, and tuition waivers (partial) available. Support available to part-time students. Financial award application deadline: 3/15; financial award applicants required to submit FAFSA. *Unit head:* Dr. Richard Donato, Chairman, 412-624-7248, Fax: 412-648-7081, E-mail: donato@pitt.edu. *Application contact:* Dr. Marjie Schermer, Graduate Enrollment Manager, 412-648-2230, Fax: 412-648-1899, E-mail: soeinfo@pitt.edu.
Website: http://www.education.pitt.edu/.

University of Pittsburgh, School of Education, Department of Instruction and Learning, Program in Special Education, Pittsburgh, PA 15260. Offers applied behavior analysis (M Ed); combined studies in early childhood and special education (M Ed); early education of disabled students (M Ed); education of students with mental and physical disabilities (M Ed); general special education (M Ed); special education (Ed D, PhD); special education teacher preparation K-8 (M Ed); special education with academic instruction certification (M Ed); vision studies (M Ed). Part-time and evening/weekend programs available. *Students:* 72 full-time (66 women), 91 part-time (83 women); includes 8 minority (3 Black or African American, non-Hispanic/Latino; 1 Asian, non-Hispanic/Latino; 1 Hispanic/Latino; 3 Two or more races, non-Hispanic/Latino), 3 international. Average age 30. 91 applicants, 85% accepted, 56 enrolled. In 2013, 68 master's, 4 doctorates awarded. *Degree requirements:* For master's, thesis; for doctorate, thesis/dissertation. *Entrance requirements:* For master's, PRAXIS I; for doctorate, GRE General Test. Additional exam requirements/recommendations for international students: Required—TOEFL. *Application deadline:* For fall admission, 2/1 priority date for domestic students; for spring admission, 11/1 priority date for domestic students. Applications are processed on a rolling basis. Application fee: $50. *Expenses:* Tuition, state resident: full-time $19,964; part-time $807 per credit. Tuition, nonresident: full-time $32,686; part-time $1337 per credit. *Required fees:* $740; $200. Tuition and fees vary according to program. *Financial support:* Research assistantships, teaching assistantships, career-related internships or fieldwork, Federal Work-Study, and tuition waivers (partial) available. Support available to part-time students. Financial award application deadline: 3/15; financial award applicants required to submit FAFSA. *Unit head:* Dr. Richard Donato, Chairman, 412-624-7248, Fax: 412-648-7081, E-mail: donato@pitt.edu. *Application contact:* Norma Ann McMichael, Graduate Enrollment Manager, 412-648-2230, Fax: 412-648-1899, E-mail: soeinfo@pitt.edu.
Website: http://www.education.pitt.edu/AcademicDepartments/InstructionLearning/Programs/GeneralSpecialEducation.aspx.

University of Puerto Rico, Río Piedras Campus, College of Education, Program in Early Child Education, San Juan, PR 00931-3300. Offers M Ed. Part-time programs available. *Degree requirements:* For master's, thesis. *Entrance requirements:* For master's, EXADEP, GRE General Test or PAEG, interview, minimum GPA of 3.0, letter of recommendation.

University of St. Thomas, Graduate Studies, School of Education, Department of Special Education, St. Paul, MN 55105-1096. Offers autism spectrum disorders (MA, Certificate); developmental disabilities (MA); early childhood special education (MA); educational leadership (Ed S); emotional behavioral disorders (MA); gifted, creative, and talented education (MA); learning disabilities (MA); Orton-Gillingham reading (Certificate); special education (MA). *Accreditation:* NCATE. Part-time and evening/weekend programs available. *Degree requirements:* For master's, thesis; for other advanced degree, professional portfolio. *Entrance requirements:* For master's, minimum GPA of 3.0 or MAT; for other advanced degree, MAT or minimum GPA of 2.75. Additional exam requirements/recommendations for international students: Required—TOEFL (minimum score 550 paper-based; 80 iBT). *Application deadline:* For fall admission, 6/1 priority date for domestic students; for spring admission, 11/1 priority date for domestic students. Applications are processed on a rolling basis. Application fee: $50. *Financial support:* Fellowships, research assistantships, institutionally sponsored loans, and scholarships/grants available. Support available to part-time students. Financial award applicants required to submit FAFSA. *Faculty research:* Reading and math fluency, inclusion curriculum for developmental disorders, parent involvement in positive behavior supports, children's friendships, preschool inclusion. *Unit head:* Dr. Terri L. Vandercook, Chair, 651-962-4389, Fax: 651-962-4169, E-mail: tlvandercook@stthomas.edu. *Application contact:* Patricia L. Thomas, Department Assistant, 651-962-4980, Fax: 651-962-4169, E-mail: thom2319@stthomas.edu.

The University of Scranton, College of Graduate and Continuing Education, Department of Education, Scranton, PA 18510. Offers curriculum and instruction (MA, MS); early childhood education (MS); educational administration (MS); reading education (MS); secondary education (MS). *Accreditation:* NCATE. Part-time and evening/weekend programs available. Postbaccalaureate distance learning degree programs offered (no on-campus study). *Faculty:* 17 full-time (11 women), 47 part-time/adjunct (18 women). *Students:* 169 full-time (106 women), 175 part-time (116 women); includes 45 minority (21 Black or African American, non-Hispanic/Latino; 1 American Indian or Alaska Native, non-Hispanic/Latino; 4 Asian, non-Hispanic/Latino; 18 Hispanic/Latino; 1 Two or more races, non-Hispanic/Latino), 2 international. Average age 28. 91 applicants, 92% accepted. In 2013, 291 master's awarded. *Degree requirements:* For master's, comprehensive exam, thesis (for some programs), capstone experience. *Entrance requirements:* For master's, minimum GPA of 3.0. Additional exam requirements/recommendations for international students: Required—TOEFL (minimum score 500 paper-based), IELTS (minimum score 6). *Application deadline:* Applications are processed on a rolling basis. Application fee: $0. *Financial support:* In 2013–14, 14 students received support, including 14 teaching assistantships with full and partial tuition reimbursements available (averaging $4,400 per year); fellowships, career-related internships or fieldwork, Federal Work-Study, and unspecified assistantships also available. Support available to part-time students. Financial award application deadline: 3/1. *Faculty research:* Meta-analysis as a research tool, family involvement in school activities, effect of curriculum integration on student learning and attitude, the effects of inclusion on students, development of emotional intelligence of young children. *Unit head:* Dr. Art Chambers, Chair, 570-941-4668, Fax: 570-941-5515, E-mail: lchambersa2@scranton.edu. *Application contact:* Joseph M. Roback, Director of Admissions, 570-941-4385, Fax: 570-941-5928, E-mail: robackj2@scranton.edu.
Website: http://matrix.scranton.edu/academics/pcps/education/.

University of South Alabama, Graduate School, College of Education, Department of Leadership and Teacher Education, Mobile, AL 36688-0002. Offers early childhood education (M Ed); educational administration (Ed S); educational leadership (M Ed); elementary education (M Ed); reading education (M Ed); science education (M Ed); secondary education (M Ed); special education (M Ed, Ed S). *Accreditation:* NCATE. Part-time programs available. *Faculty:* 17 full-time (11 women), 4 part-time/adjunct (all women). *Students:* 136 full-time (103 women), 78 part-time (67 women); includes 45 minority (40 Black or African American, non-Hispanic/Latino; 2 Asian, non-Hispanic/Latino; 1 Hispanic/Latino; 2 Two or more races, non-Hispanic/Latino). 90 applicants, 53% accepted, 45 enrolled. In 2013, 69 master's awarded. *Degree requirements:* For master's, comprehensive exam. *Entrance requirements:* For master's, GRE General Test or MAT, minimum GPA of 3.0. *Application deadline:* For fall admission, 7/15 priority date for domestic students, 6/15 priority date for international students; for spring admission, 12/1 priority date for domestic students, 11/1 priority date for international students. Applications are processed on a rolling basis. Application fee: $35. *Expenses:* Tuition, state resident: full-time $8976; part-time $374 per credit hour. Tuition, nonresident: full-time $17,952; part-time $748 per credit hour. *Financial support:* Research assistantships and career-related internships or fieldwork available. Support available to part-time students. Financial award application deadline: 4/1. *Unit head:* Dr. Harold Dodge, Jr., Chair, 251-380-2894. *Application contact:* Dr. Abigail Baxter, Director of Graduate Studies, 251-380-2738, Fax: 251-380-2748, E-mail: abaxter@southalabama.edu.
Website: http://www.southalabama.edu/coe/lted.

University of South Carolina, The Graduate School, College of Education, Department of Instruction and Teacher Education, Program in Early Childhood Education, Columbia, SC 29208. Offers M Ed, Ed D, PhD. *Accreditation:* NCATE. *Degree requirements:* For master's, comprehensive exam; for doctorate, one foreign language, comprehensive exam, thesis/dissertation. *Entrance requirements:* For master's, GRE General Test, MAT, interview; for doctorate, GRE General Test, MAT, interview, teaching experience. *Faculty research:* Parent involvement, play, multicultural education, global education.

University of South Carolina Upstate, Graduate Programs, Spartanburg, SC 29303-4999. Offers early childhood education (M Ed); elementary education (M Ed); informatics (MS); special education: visual impairment (M Ed). *Accreditation:* NCATE. Part-time and evening/weekend programs available. *Faculty:* 8 full-time (6 women), 5 part-time/adjunct (4 women). *Students:* 10 full-time (4 women), 13 part-time (11 women); includes 8 minority (6 Black or African American, non-Hispanic/Latino; 2 Two or more races, non-Hispanic/Latino). Average age 33. In 2013, 11 master's awarded. *Degree requirements:* For master's, professional portfolio. *Entrance requirements:* For master's, GRE General Test or MAT, interview, minimum undergraduate GPA of 2.5, teaching certificate, 2 letters of recommendation. *Application deadline:* Applications are processed on a rolling basis. Application fee: $40. *Expenses:* Tuition, state resident: full-time $11,272; part-time $470 per semester hour. Tuition, nonresident: full-time $24,196; part-time $1008 per semester hour. Tuition and fees vary according to course load and program. *Financial support:* Institutionally sponsored loans and institutional work-study available. Financial award application deadline: 7/15; financial award applicants required to submit FAFSA. *Faculty research:* Promoting university diversity awareness, rough and tumble play, social justice education, American Indian literatures and cultures, diversity and multicultural education, science teaching strategy. *Unit head:* Dr. Tina Herzberg, Director of Graduate Programs, 864-503-5572, Fax: 864-503-5573, E-mail: rstevens@uscupstate.edu. *Application contact:* Donette Stewart, Associate Vice Chancellor for Enrollment Services, 864-503-5280, E-mail: dstewart@uscupstate.edu.
Website: http://www.uscupstate.edu/graduate/.

University of Southern Maine, College of Management and Human Service, School of Education and Human Development, Teaching and Learning Extended Teacher Education Program, Portland, ME 04104-9300. Offers Montessori early childhood teacher education (MS Ed); teaching and learning (MS Ed). Part-time programs available. Postbaccalaureate distance learning degree programs offered (minimal on-campus study). *Faculty:* 15 full-time (9 women), 11 part-time/adjunct (8 women). *Students:* 76 full-time (56 women), 53 part-time (38 women); includes 7 minority (1 Black or African American, non-Hispanic/Latino; 3 American Indian or Alaska Native, non-Hispanic/Latino; 1 Asian, non-Hispanic/Latino; 1 Hispanic/Latino; 1 Two or more races, non-Hispanic/Latino). Average age 30. 101 applicants, 69% accepted, 57 enrolled. In 2013, 75 master's awarded. *Degree requirements:* For master's, thesis or alternative, portfolio, internship. *Entrance requirements:* For master's, PRAXIS, interview. Additional exam requirements/recommendations for international students: Required—TOEFL (minimum score 550 paper-based; 79 iBT). *Application deadline:* For fall admission, 1/2 priority date for domestic students. Application fee: $65. Electronic applications accepted. *Expenses:* Tuition, state resident: part-time $380 per credit. Tuition, nonresident: part-time $1026 per credit. Part-time tuition and fees vary according to program. *Financial support:* Career-related internships or fieldwork, Federal Work-Study, institutionally sponsored loans, scholarships/grants, and unspecified assistantships available. Support available to part-time students. Financial award application deadline: 3/1; financial award applicants required to submit FAFSA. *Faculty research:* Democracy in education, multicultural education, social justice in teacher education, teacher identity. *Unit head:* Dr. Flynn Ross, Chair, 207-780-5768, E-mail: fross@usm.maine.edu. *Application contact:* Mary Sloan, Assistant Dean of Graduate Studies and Director of Graduate Admissions, 207-780-4812, E-mail: gradstudies@usm.maine.edu.

University of South Florida, College of Education, Department of Childhood Education, Tampa, FL 33620-9951. Offers early childhood education (M Ed, MA, PhD); elementary education (MA, MAT, PhD); reading/language arts (MA, PhD, Ed S). *Accreditation:* NCATE. Part-time and evening/weekend programs available. *Degree requirements:* For master's, comprehensive exam; for doctorate, comprehensive exam, thesis/dissertation, philosophies of inquiry; multiple research methods. *Entrance requirements:* For master's, GRE (if GPA less than 3.0), minimum GPA of 3.0 in last 60 hours of course work; for doctorate, GRE General Test, minimum GPA of 3.0 undergraduate, 3.5 graduate; interview; for Ed S, GRE General Test, interview. Additional exam requirements/recommendations for international students: Required—TOEFL (minimum score 550 paper-based). Electronic applications accepted. *Faculty research:* Evaluating interventions for struggling readers, prevention and intervention services for young children at risk for behavioral and mental health challenges, preservice teacher education and young adolescent middle school experience, art and inquiry-based approaches to teaching and learning, study of children's writing development.

The University of Tennessee, Graduate School, College of Education, Health and Human Sciences, Department of Child and Family Studies, Knoxville, TN 37996. Offers child and family studies (MS); early childhood education (MS). Part-time programs available. *Degree requirements:* For master's, thesis or alternative. *Entrance requirements:* For master's, GRE General Test, minimum GPA of 2.7. Additional exam requirements/recommendations for international students: Required—TOEFL. Electronic applications accepted. *Expenses:* Tuition, state resident: full-time $9540; part-time $531 per credit hour. Tuition, nonresident: full-time $27,728; part-time $1542 per credit hour. *Required fees:* $1404; $67 per credit hour.

The University of Tennessee, Graduate School, College of Education, Health and Human Sciences, Program in Education, Knoxville, TN 37996. Offers art education (MS); counseling education (PhD); cultural studies in education (PhD); curriculum (MS, Ed S); curriculum, educational research and evaluation (Ed D, PhD); early childhood education (PhD); early childhood special education (MS); education of deaf and hard of hearing (MS); educational administration and policy studies (Ed D, PhD); educational administration and supervision (Ed S); educational psychology (Ed D, PhD); elementary education (MS, Ed S); elementary teaching (MS); English education (MS, Ed S); exercise science (PhD); foreign language/ESL education (MS, Ed S); instructional technology (MS, Ed D, PhD, Ed S); literacy, language and ESL education (PhD); literacy, language education, and ESL education (Ed D); mathematics education (MS, Ed S); modified and comprehensive special education (MS); reading education (MS, Ed S); school counseling (Ed S); school psychology (PhD, Ed S); science education (MS, Ed S); secondary teaching (MS); social foundations (MS); social science education (MS, Ed S); socio-cultural foundations of sports and education (PhD); special education (Ed S); teacher education (Ed D, PhD). *Accreditation:* NCATE. Part-time and evening/weekend programs available. *Degree requirements:* For master's and Ed S, thesis optional; for doctorate, variable foreign language requirement, thesis/dissertation. *Entrance requirements:* For master's, minimum GPA of 2.7; for doctorate and Ed S, GRE General Test, minimum GPA of 2.7. Additional exam requirements/recommendations for international students: Required—TOEFL. Electronic applications accepted. *Expenses:* Tuition, state resident: full-time $9540; part-time $531 per credit hour. Tuition, nonresident: full-time $27,728; part-time $1542 per credit hour. *Required fees:* $1404; $67 per credit hour.

The University of Texas at Austin, Graduate School, College of Education, Department of Curriculum and Instruction, Austin, TX 78712-1111. Offers bilingual/bicultural education (M Ed, MA, PhD); cultural studies in education (M Ed, MA, PhD); early childhood education (M Ed, MA, PhD); language and literacy studies (M Ed, PhD); learning technologies (M Ed, MA, PhD); physical education (M Ed, MA, PhD). Terminal master's awarded for partial completion of doctoral program. *Degree requirements:* For doctorate, thesis/dissertation. *Entrance requirements:* For master's and doctorate, GRE General Test. Electronic applications accepted.

The University of Texas at Austin, Graduate School, College of Education, Department of Special Education, Austin, TX 78712-1111. Offers autism and developmental disabilities (Ed D, PhD); autism and developmental disability (M Ed, MA); early childhood special education (M Ed, MA, Ed D, PhD); learning disabilities (Ed D, PhD); learning disabilities/behavior disorders (M Ed, MA); multicultural special education (M Ed, MA, Ed D, PhD); rehabilitation counselor (M Ed); rehabilitation counselor education (Ed D, PhD); special education administration (Ed D, PhD). *Accreditation:* CORE. Part-time and evening/weekend programs available. Postbaccalaureate distance learning degree programs offered (no on-campus study). *Degree requirements:* For master's, thesis or alternative; for doctorate, thesis/dissertation. *Entrance requirements:* For master's and doctorate, GRE General Test. *Faculty research:* Anchored instruction, reading disabilities, multicultural/bilingual.

The University of Texas at Brownsville, Graduate Studies, College of Education, Brownsville, TX 78520-4991. Offers bilingual education (M Ed); counseling and guidance (M Ed); curriculum and instruction (M Ed); early childhood education (M Ed); educational leadership (M Ed); educational technology (M Ed); exercise science (MS); special education (M Ed). Part-time and evening/weekend programs available.

Postbaccalaureate distance learning degree programs offered (no on-campus study). *Faculty:* 51 full-time (28 women). *Students:* 60 full-time (43 women), 496 part-time (363 women); includes 467 minority (4 Black or African American, non-Hispanic/Latino; 1 American Indian or Alaska Native, non-Hispanic/Latino; 10 Asian, non-Hispanic/Latino; 451 Hispanic/Latino; 1 Native Hawaiian or other Pacific Islander, non-Hispanic/Latino), 12 international. 161 applicants, 67% accepted, 81 enrolled. In 2013, 142 master's awarded. *Degree requirements:* For master's, comprehensive exam (for some programs), thesis optional, electronic portfolio. *Entrance requirements:* For master's, GRE General Test, curriculum vitae or resume, teaching certificate. Additional exam requirements/recommendations for international students: Required—TOEFL (minimum score 550 paper-based; 77 iBT). *Application deadline:* For fall admission, 7/1 priority date for domestic students, 7/1 for international students; for spring admission, 12/1 priority date for domestic students, 12/1 for international students. Applications are processed on a rolling basis. Application fee: $30. Electronic applications accepted. *Expenses:* Tuition, state resident: full-time $3444; part-time $1148 per semester. Tuition, nonresident: full-time $9816. *Required fees:* $1018; $221 per credit hour. $401 per semester. *Financial support:* In 2013–14, 136 students received support, including 6 research assistantships (averaging $10,000 per year); career-related internships or fieldwork, Federal Work-Study, scholarships/grants, tuition waivers (partial), and unspecified assistantships also available. Support available to part-time students. Financial award application deadline: 3/1; financial award applicants required to submit FAFSA. *Unit head:* Dr. Miguel Angel Escotet, Dean, 956-882-7220, Fax: 956-882-7431, E-mail: miguel.escotet@utb.edu. *Application contact:* Mari E. Stevens, Graduate Studies Specialist, 956-882-6587, Fax: 956-882-7279, E-mail: mari.stevens@utb.edu.
Website: http://www.utb.edu/vpaa/coe/Pages/default.aspx.

The University of Texas at San Antonio, College of Education and Human Development, Department of Interdisciplinary Learning and Teaching, San Antonio, TX 78249-0617. Offers education (MA), including curriculum and instruction, early childhood and elementary education, instructional technology, reading and literacy, special education; interdisciplinary learning and teaching (PhD). Part-time and evening/weekend programs available. *Faculty:* 22 full-time (16 women), 1 (woman) part-time/adjunct. *Students:* 109 full-time (80 women), 272 part-time (221 women); includes 209 minority (24 Black or African American, non-Hispanic/Latino; 3 American Indian or Alaska Native, non-Hispanic/Latino; 12 Asian, non-Hispanic/Latino; 166 Hispanic/Latino; 4 Two or more races, non-Hispanic/Latino), 40 international. Average age 33. 178 applicants, 87% accepted, 80 enrolled. In 2013, 136 master's, 7 doctorates awarded. *Degree requirements:* For master's, comprehensive exam, thesis optional, 36 hours of course work without thesis (33 with thesis); for doctorate, comprehensive exam, thesis/dissertation, minimum of 60 semester credit hours. *Entrance requirements:* For master's, bachelor's degree with minimum GPA of 3.0 in last 60 hours of coursework; 18 hours of undergraduate coursework in education or related field; for doctorate, GRE, transcripts from all colleges and universities attended, professional vitae demonstrating experience in work environment where education was primary professional emphasis, 3 letters of recommendation, statement of purpose, minimum GPA of 3.5. Additional exam requirements/recommendations for international students: Required—TOEFL (minimum score 550 paper-based; 79 iBT), IELTS (minimum score 6.5). *Application deadline:* For fall admission, 7/1 for domestic students, 4/1 for international students; for spring admission, 11/1 for domestic students, 9/1 for international students. Applications are processed on a rolling basis. Application fee: $45 ($80 for international students). Electronic applications accepted. *Expenses:* Tuition, state resident: full-time $4671. Tuition, nonresident: full-time $8708. *International tuition:* $17,415 full-time. *Required fees:* $1924.60. Tuition and fees vary according to course load and degree level. *Financial support:* In 2013–14, 7 fellowships with partial tuition reimbursements (averaging $27,000 per year) were awarded; career-related internships or fieldwork, Federal Work-Study, and scholarships/grants also available. Support available to part-time students. *Faculty research:* Explorations of science, learning and teaching, family involvement in early childhood, culturally-responsive literacy instruction in diverse settings, STEM education, autism spectrum disorder. *Total annual research expenditures:* $5.9 million. *Unit head:* Dr. Maria R. Cortez, Department Chair, 210-458-5969, Fax: 210-458-7281, E-mail: mari.cortez@utsa.edu. *Application contact:* Erin Doran, Student Development Specialist, 210-458-7443, Fax: 210-458-7281, E-mail: erin.doran@utsa.edu.
Website: http://education.utsa.edu/interdisciplinary_learning_and_teaching/.

The University of Texas at Tyler, College of Education and Psychology, School of Education, Tyler, TX 75799-0001. Offers early childhood education (M Ed, MA); reading (M Ed, MA); special education (M Ed, MA). Part-time and evening/weekend programs available. *Degree requirements:* For master's, comprehensive exam, thesis (for some programs), research project. *Entrance requirements:* For master's, GRE General Test. Additional exam requirements/recommendations for international students: Required—TOEFL. Electronic applications accepted. *Faculty research:* Improving quality in childcare settings, play and creativity, teacher interactions, effects of modeling on early childhood teachers, biofeedback, literacy instruction.

The University of Texas of the Permian Basin, Office of Graduate Studies, School of Education, Program in Early Childhood Education, Odessa, TX 79762-0001. Offers MA. *Degree requirements:* For master's, comprehensive exam (for some programs), thesis (for some programs). *Entrance requirements:* For master's, GRE General Test. Additional exam requirements/recommendations for international students: Required—TOEFL (minimum score 550 paper-based).

The University of Texas–Pan American, College of Education, Department of Curriculum and Instruction: Elementary and Secondary, Edinburg, TX 78539. Offers bilingual education (M Ed); early childhood education (M Ed); elementary education (M Ed); reading (M Ed); secondary education (M Ed). Part-time programs available. *Degree requirements:* For master's, comprehensive exam, thesis optional. *Entrance requirements:* For master's, GRE. Additional exam requirements/recommendations for international students: Required—TOEFL, IELTS. *Expenses:* Tuition, state resident: full-time $5986; part-time $333 per credit hour. Tuition, nonresident: full-time $12,358; part-time $687 per credit hour. *Required fees:* $782. Tuition and fees vary according to program. *Faculty research:* Dual language instruction, literacy and technology, teacher education in diverse populations, mathematics and science education.

University of the District of Columbia, College of Arts and Sciences, Department of Education, Program in Early Childhood Education, Washington, DC 20008-1175. Offers MA. *Accreditation:* NCATE. Part-time programs available. *Degree requirements:* For master's, comprehensive exam, research paper. *Entrance requirements:* For master's, GRE General Test, writing proficiency exam, minimum GPA of 3.0. *Expenses: Tuition, area resident:* Full-time $7883.28; part-time $437.96 per credit hour. Tuition, state resident: full-time $8923.14. Tuition, nonresident: full-time $15,163; part-time $842.40 per credit hour. *Required fees:* $620; $30 per credit hour.

University of the Incarnate Word, School of Graduate Studies and Research, Dreeben School of Education, Programs in Education, San Antonio, TX 78209-6397. Offers adult education (M Ed, MA); cross-cultural education (M Ed, MA); early childhood literacy (M Ed, MA); general education (M Ed, MA); higher education (PhD); instructional technology (M Ed, MA); international education and entrepreneurship (PhD); kinesiology (M Ed, MA); literacy (M Ed, MA); organizational leadership (PhD); organizational learning and learning (M Ed, MA); reading (M Ed, MA); special education (M Ed, MA); teacher leadership (M Ed, MA). Part-time and evening/weekend programs available. *Faculty:* 17 full-time (9 women), 6 part-time/adjunct (all women). *Students:* 23 full-time (13 women), 187 part-time (122 women); includes 114 minority (24 Black or African American, non-Hispanic/Latino; 1 American Indian or Alaska Native, non-Hispanic/Latino; 3 Asian, non-Hispanic/Latino; 85 Hispanic/Latino; 1 Two or more races, non-Hispanic/Latino), 30 international. Average age 41. 52 applicants, 67% accepted, 25 enrolled. In 2013, 12 master's, 14 doctorates awarded. *Degree requirements:* For master's, capstone; for doctorate, thesis/dissertation, qualifying exam. *Entrance requirements:* For master's, baccalaureate degree; minimum foundation GPA of 2.5; interview; for doctorate, master's degree; interview; supervised writing sample. Additional exam requirements/recommendations for international students: Required—TOEFL (minimum score 560 paper-based; 83 iBT). *Application deadline:* Applications are processed on a rolling basis. Application fee: $20. Electronic applications accepted. *Expenses: Tuition:* Part-time $815 per credit hour. *Required fees:* $86 per credit hour. One-time fee: $40 part-time. Tuition and fees vary according to degree level and program. *Financial support:* In 2013–14, 5 research assistantships were awarded; Federal Work-Study and scholarships/grants also available. Financial award applicants required to submit FAFSA. *Unit head:* Dr. Denise Staudt, Dean, Dreeben School of Education, 210-829-2762, E-mail: staudt@uiwtx.edu. *Application contact:* Andrea Cyterski-Acosta, Dean of Enrollment, 210-829-6005, Fax: 210-829-3921, E-mail: admis@uiwtx.edu.
Website: http://www.uiw.edu/education/index.htm.

University of the Sacred Heart, Graduate Programs, Department of Education, San Juan, PR 00914-0383. Offers early childhood education (M Ed); information technology and multimedia (Certificate); instruction systems and education technology (M Ed), including English, information technology and multimedia, instructional design, mathematics, Spanish. Part-time and evening/weekend programs available. *Degree requirements:* For master's, thesis. *Entrance requirements:* For master's, EXADEP, minimum undergraduate GPA of 2.75, interview.

University of the Southwest, Graduate Programs, Hobbs, NM 88240-9129. Offers business administration (MBA); curriculum and instruction (MSE); curriculum and instruction: bilingual (MSE); curriculum and instruction: TESOL (MSE); early childhood education (MSE); educational administration (MSE); mental health counseling (MSE); school counseling (MSE); special education (MSE); sports management (MBA). Part-time and evening/weekend programs available. Postbaccalaureate distance learning degree programs offered (no on-campus study). *Degree requirements:* For master's, comprehensive exam, thesis (for some programs). *Entrance requirements:* Additional exam requirements/recommendations for international students: Recommended—TOEFL. Electronic applications accepted.

The University of Toledo, College of Graduate Studies, Judith Herb College of Education, Department of Curriculum and Instruction, Toledo, OH 43606-3390. Offers art education (ME); career and technical education (ME); career-technical education (Ed S); curriculum and instruction (ME, PhD, Ed S); early childhood education (PhD, Ed S); education and biology (MES); education and chemistry (MES); education and economics (MAE); education and English (MAE); education and French (MAE); education and geography (MAE); education and geology (MES); education and German (MAE); education and history (MAE); education and mathematics (MAE, MES); education and physics (MES); education and political science (MAE); education and sociology (MAE); education and Spanish (MAE); educational media (PhD); educational technology (ME); educational technology: virtual educator (Certificate); elementary education (PhD); English as a second language (MAE); gifted and talented (PhD); middle childhood education licensure (ME); music education (MME); secondary education (PhD); secondary education licensure (ME); special education (PhD, Ed S). *Accreditation:* NCATE. Part-time and evening/weekend programs available. *Faculty:* 41. *Students:* 53 full-time (30 women), 154 part-time (111 women); includes 21 minority (16 Black or African American, non-Hispanic/Latino; 4 Hispanic/Latino; 1 Two or more races, non-Hispanic/Latino), 21 international. Average age 34. 82 applicants, 79% accepted, 47 enrolled. In 2013, 80 master's, 5 doctorates awarded. *Degree requirements:* For master's, comprehensive exam, thesis or alternative; for doctorate, comprehensive exam, thesis/dissertation; for other advanced degree, thesis optional. *Entrance requirements:* For master's, doctorate, and other advanced degree, minimum cumulative GPA of 2.7 for all previous academic work, letters of recommendation. Additional exam requirements/recommendations for international students: Required—TOEFL (minimum score 550 paper-based; 80 iBT). *Application deadline:* For fall admission, 1/15 priority date for domestic and international students. Applications are processed on a rolling basis. Application fee: $45 ($75 for international students). Electronic applications accepted. *Financial support:* In 2013–14, 5 research assistantships with full and partial tuition reimbursements (averaging $13,200 per year), 11 teaching assistantships with full and partial tuition reimbursements (averaging $8,809 per year) were awarded; career-related internships or fieldwork, Federal Work-Study, institutionally sponsored loans, scholarships/grants, tuition waivers (full and partial), unspecified assistantships, and administrative assistantships also available. Support available to part-time students. *Unit head:* Dr. Joan Kaderavek, Chair, 419-530-5373, E-mail: eigh.chiarelott@utoledo.edu. *Application contact:* Graduate School Office, 419-530-4723, Fax: 419-530-4724, E-mail: grdsch@utnet.utoledo.edu.
Website: http://www.utoledo.edu/eduhshs/.

The University of Toledo, College of Graduate Studies, Judith Herb College of Education, Department of Early Childhood, Physical and Special Education, Toledo, OH 43606-3390. Offers early childhood education (ME); physical education (ME); special education (ME). Part-time programs available. *Faculty:* 25. *Students:* 9 full-time (all women), 89 part-time (80 women); includes 16 minority (13 Black or African American, non-Hispanic/Latino; 3 Hispanic/Latino), 1 international. Average age 32. 28 applicants, 75% accepted, 16 enrolled. In 2013, 47 master's awarded. *Degree requirements:* For master's, thesis. *Entrance requirements:* For master's, minimum cumulative GPA of 2.7 for all previous academic work, letters of recommendation. Additional exam requirements/recommendations for international students: Required—TOEFL (minimum score 550 paper-based; 80 iBT). *Application deadline:* For fall admission, 1/15 priority date for domestic and international students. Applications are processed on a rolling basis. Application fee: $45 ($75 for international students). Electronic applications accepted. *Financial support:* In 2013–14, 3 teaching assistantships with full and partial tuition reimbursements (averaging $4,500 per year) were awarded; career-related internships or fieldwork, Federal Work-Study, institutionally sponsored loans, scholarships/grants, tuition waivers (full and partial), unspecified assistantships, and administrative assistantships also available. Support available to part-time students. *Unit head:* Dr. Richard Welsch, Chair, 419-530-7736, E-mail: richard.welsch@utoledo.edu. *Application contact:* Graduate School Office, 419-530-4723, Fax: 419-530-4724, E-mail: grdsch@utnet.utoledo.edu.
Website: http://www.utoledo.edu/eduhshs/.

University of Utah, Graduate School, College of Education, Department of Special Education, Salt Lake City, UT 84112. Offers deaf and hard of hearing (M Ed); deaf/blind (M Ed); early childhood hearing impairments (M Ed, MS); early childhood special education (M Ed, MS, PhD); early childhood vision impairments (M Ed, MS); hearing

impairments (MS); mild/moderate (MS); mild/moderate disabilities (M Ed, MS, PhD); professional practice (M Ed); research in special education (MS); research without licensure (MS); severe (MS); severe disabilities (M Ed, MS, PhD); vision impairments (M Ed, MS). Part-time and evening/weekend programs available. Postbaccalaureate distance learning degree programs offered (no on-campus study). *Faculty:* 9 full-time (6 women), 8 part-time/adjunct (7 women). *Students:* 28 full-time (23 women), 12 part-time (10 women); includes 7 minority (2 Black or African American, non-Hispanic/Latino; 3 Hispanic/Latino; 1 Native Hawaiian or other Pacific Islander, non-Hispanic/Latino; 1 Two or more races, non-Hispanic/Latino), 1 international. Average age 33. 15 applicants, 93% accepted, 13 enrolled. In 2013, 36 master's, 4 doctorates awarded. Terminal master's awarded for partial completion of doctoral program. *Degree requirements:* For master's, comprehensive exam, thesis (for some programs), qualifying exam; for doctorate, thesis/dissertation, qualifying exam. *Entrance requirements:* For master's, GRE or Analytical Writing portion of GRE plus PRAXIS I, minimum GPA of 3.0; for doctorate, GRE General Test (minimum scores: Verbal 600; Quantitative 600; Analytical/Writing 4), minimum GPA of 3.0 (3.5 recommended). Additional exam requirements/recommendations for international students: Required—TOEFL (minimum score 600 paper-based; 100 iBT); Recommended—IELTS (minimum score 7). *Application deadline:* For fall admission, 3/1 for domestic and international students; for spring admission, 11/1 for domestic and international students. Application fee: $55 ($65 for international students). Electronic applications accepted. *Expenses:* Contact institution. *Financial support:* In 2013–14, 27 students received support, including 27 fellowships with full and partial tuition reimbursements available (averaging $5,015 per year), 4 teaching assistantships with full tuition reimbursements available (averaging $17,175 per year); research assistantships and career-related internships or fieldwork also available. Support available to part-time students. Financial award application deadline: 3/1; financial award applicants required to submit FAFSA. *Faculty research:* Inclusive education, positive behavior support, reading, instruction and intervention strategies. *Total annual research expenditures:* $5,926. *Unit head:* Dr. Robert E. O'Neill, Chair, 801-581-8121, Fax: 801-585-6476, E-mail: rob.oneill@utah.edu. *Application contact:* Patty Davis, Academic Advisor, 801-581-4764, Fax: 801-585-6476, E-mail: patty.davis@utah.edu.
Website: http://www.ed.utah.edu/sped/.

University of Victoria, Faculty of Graduate Studies, Faculty of Education, Department of Curriculum and Instruction, Victoria, BC V8W 2Y2, Canada. Offers art education (M Ed, PhD); curriculum studies (M Ed, MA, PhD); early childhood education (M Ed, PhD); educational studies (PhD); language and literacy (M Ed, MA, PhD); mathematics (M Ed, MA, PhD); music education (M Ed, MA, PhD); science (M Ed, MA, PhD); social studies (M Ed, MA); social, cultural and foundational studies (MA, PhD); technology and environmental education (PhD). Part-time programs available. *Degree requirements:* For master's, thesis, project (M Ed); for doctorate, comprehensive exam, thesis/dissertation. *Entrance requirements:* For master's, minimum B average. Additional exam requirements/recommendations for international students: Required—TOEFL (minimum score 575 paper-based), IELTS (minimum score 7). Electronic applications accepted. *Faculty research:* Elementary and secondary English, language arts, curriculum theory and practice, educational media and technology, educational administration and leadership, history and philosophy of education.

University of Virginia, Curry School of Education, Program in Education, Charlottesville, VA 22903. Offers administration and supervision (PhD); applied developmental science (PhD); counselor education (PhD); curriculum and instruction (PhD); early childhood special education (MT); education evaluation (PhD); educational psychology (PhD); educational research (PhD); elementary education (MT); English education (MT, PhD); foreign language education (MT); higher education (PhD); instructional technology (PhD); kinesiology (MT, PhD); math education (PhD); reading education (PhD); research, statistics and evaluation (PhD); school psychology (PhD); science education (PhD); social studies education (MT, PhD); special education (PhD); world languages education (MT). *Students:* 474 full-time (379 women), 35 part-time (19 women); includes 89 minority (30 Black or African American, non-Hispanic/Latino; 1 American Indian or Alaska Native, non-Hispanic/Latino; 26 Asian, non-Hispanic/Latino; 19 Hispanic/Latino; 13 Two or more races, non-Hispanic/Latino), 21 international. Average age 26. 312 applicants, 49% accepted, 80 enrolled. In 2013, 137 master's, 38 doctorates awarded. *Degree requirements:* For master's, comprehensive exam (for some programs), field project; for doctorate, comprehensive exam, thesis/dissertation. *Entrance requirements:* For doctorate, GRE General Test. Additional exam requirements/recommendations for international students: Required—TOEFL (minimum score 600 paper-based; 90 iBT), IELTS (minimum score 7). *Application deadline:* Applications are processed on a rolling basis. Application fee: $60. Electronic applications accepted. *Expenses:* Tuition, state resident: part-time $334 per credit hour. Tuition, nonresident: part-time $1224 per credit hour. *Financial support:* Fellowships, research assistantships, and teaching assistantships available. Financial award application deadline: 1/5; financial award applicants required to submit FAFSA. *Unit head:* Robert C. Pianta, Dean, 434-924-3334, E-mail: pianta@virginia.edu. *Application contact:* Office of Admissions and Student Services, 434-924-0742, E-mail: curry-admissions@virginia.edu.
Website: http://curry.virginia.edu/teacher-education.

The University of West Alabama, School of Graduate Studies, College of Education, Departments of Instructional Leadership and Support/Curriculum and Instruction, Program in Early Childhood Education, Livingston, AL 35470. Offers early childhood development (Ed S); early childhood education (M Ed). *Accreditation:* NCATE. Part-time and evening/weekend programs available. Postbaccalaureate distance learning degree programs offered (no on-campus study). *Faculty:* 10 full-time (8 women), 29 part-time/adjunct (21 women). *Students:* 58 (all women); includes 23 minority (all Black or African American, non-Hispanic/Latino). 19 applicants, 95% accepted, 14 enrolled. In 2013, 11 master's, 6 Ed Ss awarded. *Degree requirements:* For master's, comprehensive exam, thesis optional. *Entrance requirements:* For master's, GRE General Test, MAT, minimum GPA of 2.75. Additional exam requirements/recommendations for international students: Required—TOEFL (minimum score 500 paper-based; 61 iBT). *Application deadline:* For fall admission, 8/12 priority date for domestic students; for spring admission, 3/24 for domestic students. Applications are processed on a rolling basis. Application fee: $25 ($50 for international students). Electronic applications accepted. Tuition and fees vary according to course load. *Financial support:* Teaching assistantships, career-related internships or fieldwork, Federal Work-Study, scholarships/grants, and unspecified assistantships available. Support available to part-time students. Financial award applicants required to submit FAFSA. *Unit head:* Dr. Esther Howard, Chair of Curriculum and Instruction, 205-652-3428, Fax: 205-652-3706, E-mail: ehoward@uwa.edu. *Application contact:* Dr. Kathy Chandler, Dean of Graduate Studies, 205-652-3421, Fax: 205-652-3706, E-mail: kchandler@uwa.edu.
Website: http://www.uwa.edu/earlychildhoodeducationp3.aspx.

University of West Florida, College of Professional Studies, School of Education, Program in Curriculum and Instruction, Pensacola, FL 32514-5750. Offers curriculum and instruction: special education (M Ed); elementary education (M Ed); primary education (M Ed). Part-time and evening/weekend programs available. *Entrance requirements:* For master's, GRE (minimum score 450 verbal) or MAT (minimum score 396) if bachelor's GPA less than 3.0, state teaching certification; letter of intent; two professional references. Additional exam requirements/recommendations for international students: Required—TOEFL (minimum score 550 paper-based).

University of West Georgia, College of Education, Department of Learning and Teaching, Carrollton, GA 30118. Offers early childhood education (M Ed, Ed S); reading education (M Ed); special education (M Ed, Ed S). *Accreditation:* ACA; NCATE. Part-time and evening/weekend programs available. *Faculty:* 10 full-time (9 women), 3 part-time/adjunct (all women). *Students:* 50 full-time (44 women), 228 part-time (204 women); includes 112 minority (102 Black or African American, non-Hispanic/Latino; 6 Hispanic/Latino; 4 Two or more races, non-Hispanic/Latino), 2 international. Average age 34. 198 applicants, 57% accepted, 46 enrolled. In 2013, 73 master's, 31 Ed Ss awarded. *Degree requirements:* For master's and Ed S, comprehensive exam. *Entrance requirements:* For master's, undergraduate degree in early childhood, elementary (P-5), middle grades (4-8), special education; one year of teaching experience; minimum overall GPA of 2.7; clear and renewable level 4 teaching certificate; for Ed S, master's degree in early childhood or elementary education; minimum overall GPA of 3.0 in graduate work; level 5 teaching certificate. Additional exam requirements/recommendations for international students: Required—TOEFL (minimum score 523 paper-based; 69 iBT); Recommended—IELTS (minimum score 6). *Application deadline:* For fall admission, 7/21 for domestic students, 6/1 for international students; for spring admission, 1/30 for domestic students, 10/15 for international students. Applications are processed on a rolling basis. Application fee: $40. Electronic applications accepted. *Expenses:* Tuition, state resident: full-time $4600; part-time $192 per semester hour. Tuition, nonresident: full-time $17,880; part-time $745 per semester hour. *Required fees:* $1858; $46.34 per semester hour. $512 per semester. Tuition and fees vary according to course load, degree level, campus/location and program. *Financial support:* In 2013–14, 10 students received support, including 1 research assistantship with full tuition reimbursement available (averaging $2,963 per year); scholarships/grants and unspecified assistantships also available. Support available to part-time students. Financial award application deadline: 4/1; financial award applicants required to submit FAFSA. *Faculty research:* Early childhood education, social justice, action research. *Total annual research expenditures:* $274,000. *Unit head:* Dr. Donna Harkins, Chair, 678-839-6066, Fax: 678-839-6063, E-mail: dharkins@westga.edu. *Application contact:* Dr. Jill Drake, Coordinator, Early Childhood Education, 678-839-6080, Fax: 678-839-6063, E-mail: jdrake@westga.edu.
Website: http://www.westga.edu/coeelce.

University of Wisconsin–Milwaukee, Graduate School, School of Education, Department of Curriculum and Instruction, Milwaukee, WI 53201-0413. Offers curriculum planning and instruction improvement (MS); early childhood education (MS); elementary education (MS); junior high/middle school education (MS); reading education (MS); secondary education (MS); teaching in an urban setting (MS). Part-time programs available. *Faculty:* 18 full-time (13 women). *Students:* 17 full-time (10 women), 46 part-time (42 women); includes 15 minority (7 Black or African American, non-Hispanic/Latino; 1 Asian, non-Hispanic/Latino; 7 Two or more races, non-Hispanic/Latino), 1 international. Average age 32. 35 applicants, 69% accepted, 11 enrolled. In 2013, 31 master's awarded. *Degree requirements:* For master's, thesis or alternative. *Entrance requirements:* Additional exam requirements/recommendations for international students: Required—TOEFL (minimum score 550 paper-based; 79 iBT), IELTS (minimum score 6.5). *Application deadline:* For fall admission, 1/1 priority date for domestic students; for spring admission, 9/1 for domestic students. Applications are processed on a rolling basis. Application fee: $56 ($96 for international students). Electronic applications accepted. *Financial support:* In 2013–14, 1 fellowship was awarded; research assistantships, teaching assistantships, career-related internships or fieldwork, health care benefits, unspecified assistantships, and project assistantships also available. Support available to part-time students. Financial award application deadline: 4/15; financial award applicants required to submit FAFSA. *Unit head:* Raquel Oxford, Department Chair, 414-229-4884, Fax: 414-229-5571, E-mail: roxford@uwm.edu. *Application contact:* General Information Contact, 414-229-4982, Fax: 414-229-6967, E-mail: gradschool@uwm.edu.
Website: http://www.uwm.edu/SOE/.

University of Wisconsin–Oshkosh, Graduate Studies, College of Education and Human Services, Department of Special Education, Oshkosh, WI 54901. Offers cross-categorical (MSE); early childhood: exceptional education needs (MSE); non-licensure (MSE). Part-time and evening/weekend programs available. *Degree requirements:* For master's, comprehensive exam (for some programs), thesis or alternative, field report. *Entrance requirements:* For master's, interview, minimum GPA of 3.0, teaching license, letters of recommendation. Additional exam requirements/recommendations for international students: Required—TOEFL (minimum score 550 paper-based; 79 iBT). Electronic applications accepted. *Faculty research:* Private agency contributions to the disabled, graduation requirements for exceptional education needs students, direct instruction in spelling for learning disabled, effects of behavioral parent training, secondary education programming issues.

Ursuline College, School of Graduate Studies, Program in Education, Pepper Pike, OH 44124-4398. Offers art education (MA); early childhood education (MA); language arts education (MA); life science education (MA); math education (MA); middle school education (MA); social studies education (MA); special education (MA). *Accreditation:* NCATE. *Faculty:* 4 full-time (all women), 7 part-time/adjunct (5 women). *Students:* 18 full-time (16 women), 7 part-time (all women); includes 8 minority (4 Black or African American, non-Hispanic/Latino; 2 Asian, non-Hispanic/Latino; 2 Hispanic/Latino). Average age 34. 1 applicant, 100% accepted, 1 enrolled. In 2013, 25 master's awarded. *Degree requirements:* For master's, comprehensive exam. *Entrance requirements:* For master's, minimum undergraduate GPA of 3.0. Additional exam requirements/recommendations for international students: Required—TOEFL (minimum score 500 paper-based). *Application deadline:* For fall admission, 8/1 priority date for domestic students. Applications are processed on a rolling basis. Application fee: $25. *Expenses:* Contact institution. *Financial support:* In 2013–14, 1 student received support. Federal Work-Study available. Financial award application deadline: 3/1. *Unit head:* Dr. Edna West, Director, Master's Apprentice Program, 440-646-6134, Fax: 440-646-8328, E-mail: ewest@ursuline.edu. *Application contact:* Stephanie Pratt, Graduate Admission Coordinator, 440-646-8119, Fax: 440-684-6138, E-mail: graduateadmissions@ursuline.edu.

Valdosta State University, Department of Early Childhood and Special Education, Valdosta, GA 31698. Offers early childhood (M Ed); special education (M Ed, MAT, Ed S). *Accreditation:* ASHA (one or more programs are accredited); NCATE. Part-time and evening/weekend programs available. Postbaccalaureate distance learning degree programs offered (no on-campus study). *Faculty:* 9 full-time (8 women), 4 part-time/adjunct (all women). *Students:* 31 full-time (27 women), 13 part-time (10 women); includes 11 minority (8 Black or African American, non-Hispanic/Latino; 1 Asian, non-Hispanic/Latino; 1 Hispanic/Latino; 1 Two or more races, non-Hispanic/Latino). Average age 23. 13 applicants, 92% accepted, 12 enrolled. In 2013, 23 master's awarded. *Degree requirements:* For master's, thesis (for some programs), comprehensive written and/or oral exams; for Ed S, thesis. *Entrance requirements:* For master's, GRE General Test or MAT, minimum GPA of 2.5; for Ed S, GRE General Test or MAT, minimum GPA of 3.0. Additional exam requirements/recommendations for international students:

Required—TOEFL (minimum score 523 paper-based). *Application deadline:* For fall and spring admission, 7/1 for domestic and international students. Applications are processed on a rolling basis. Application fee: $35. Electronic applications accepted. *Expenses:* Tuition, state resident: full-time $4140; part-time $230 per credit hour. Tuition, nonresident: full-time $14,904; part-time $828 per credit hour. *Required fees:* $995 per semester. Tuition and fees vary according to course load. *Financial support:* In 2013–14, 4 students received support, including 5 research assistantships with full tuition reimbursements available (averaging $3,252 per year); institutionally sponsored loans, scholarships/grants, and unspecified assistantships also available. Support available to part-time students. Financial award application deadline: 7/1; financial award applicants required to submit FAFSA. *Unit head:* Dr. Festus Obiakor, Head, 229-333-5929, E-mail: feobiakor@valdosta.edu. *Application contact:* Rebecca Petrella, Graduate Admissions Coordinator, 229-333-5694, Fax: 229-245-3853, E-mail: rlwaters@valdosta.edu.
Website: http://www.valdosta.edu/colleges/education/early-childhood-and-special-education/welcome.php.

Virginia Commonwealth University, Graduate School, School of Education, Program in Special Education, Richmond, VA 23284-9005. Offers autism spectrum disorders (Certificate); disability leadership (Certificate); early childhood (M Ed); general education (M Ed); severe disabilities (M Ed). *Accreditation:* NCATE. *Degree requirements:* For master's, comprehensive exam. *Entrance requirements:* For master's, GRE General Test or MAT. Additional exam requirements/recommendations for international students: Required—TOEFL (minimum score 600 paper-based; 100 iBT). Electronic applications accepted.

Virginia Commonwealth University, Graduate School, School of Education, Program in Teaching and Learning, Richmond, VA 23284-9005. Offers early and elementary education (MT); health and physical education (MT); secondary 6-12 education (MT); secondary education (Certificate). *Accreditation:* NCATE. Part-time programs available. *Entrance requirements:* For master's, GRE General Test or MAT. Additional exam requirements/recommendations for international students: Required—TOEFL (minimum score 600 paper-based; 100 iBT). Electronic applications accepted.

Wagner College, Division of Graduate Studies, Department of Education, Program in Early Childhood Education/Special Education (Birth-Grade 2), Staten Island, NY 10301-4495. Offers MS Ed. Part-time and evening/weekend programs available. *Degree requirements:* For master's, thesis. *Entrance requirements:* For master's, minimum GPA of 3.0, valid initial NY State Certificate or equivalent, interview, recommendations. Electronic applications accepted. *Expenses: Tuition:* Full-time $17,496; part-time $972 per credit. Tuition and fees vary according to course load.

Walden University, Graduate Programs, Richard W. Riley College of Education and Leadership, Minneapolis, MN 55401. *Accreditation:* NCATE. Part-time and evening/weekend programs available. Postbaccalaureate distance learning degree programs offered (minimal on-campus study). *Faculty:* 23 full-time (15 women), 830 part-time/adjunct (569 women). *Students:* 8,671 full-time (7,197 women), 2,122 part-time (1,735 women); includes 4,734 minority (3,802 Black or African American, non-Hispanic/Latino; 50 American Indian or Alaska Native, non-Hispanic/Latino; 136 Asian, non-Hispanic/Latino; 539 Hispanic/Latino; 35 Native Hawaiian or other Pacific Islander, non-Hispanic/Latino; 172 Two or more races, non-Hispanic/Latino), 73 international. Average age 40. 2,646 applicants, 96% accepted, 2074 enrolled. In 2013, 2,214 master's, 354 doctorates, 479 other advanced degrees awarded. *Degree requirements:* For doctorate, thesis/dissertation (for some programs), residency; for other advanced degree, residency (for some programs). *Entrance requirements:* For master's, bachelor's degree or higher; minimum GPA of 2.5; official transcripts; goal statement (for some programs); access to computer and Internet; for doctorate, master's degree or higher; three years of related professional or academic experience (preferred); minimum GPA of 3.0; goal statement and current resume (select programs); official transcripts; access to computer and Internet; for other advanced degree, relevant work experience; access to computer and Internet. Additional exam requirements/recommendations for international students: Required—TOEFL (minimum score 550 paper-based; 79 iBT), IELTS (minimum score 6.5), Michigan English Language Assessment Battery (minimum score 82), or PTE. *Application deadline:* Applications are processed on a rolling basis. Application fee: $0. Electronic applications accepted. *Expenses: Tuition:* Full-time $11,813.55; part-time $500 per credit. *Required fees:* $618.76. *Financial support:* In 2013–14, 1 fellowship was awarded; Federal Work-Study, scholarships/grants, unspecified assistantships, and family tuition reduction, active duty/veteran tuition reduction, group tuition reduction, interest-free payment plans, employee tuition reduction also available. Support available to part-time students. Financial award applicants required to submit FAFSA. *Unit head:* Dr. Kate Steffens, Dean, 800-925-3368. *Application contact:* Jennifer Hall, Vice President of Enrollment Management, 866-4-WALDEN, E-mail: info@waldenu.edu.
Website: http://www.waldenu.edu/colleges-schools/riley-college-of-education/.

Wayne State College, School of Education and Counseling, Department of Educational Foundations and Leadership, Program in Curriculum and Instruction, Wayne, NE 68787. Offers alternative education (MSE); business and information technology education (MSE); communication arts education (MSE); early childhood education (MSE); elementary education (MSE); English as a second language (MSE); English education (MSE); family and consumer sciences education (MSE); industrial technology and vocational education (MSE); learning communities (MSE); mathematics education (MSE); music education (MSE); science education (MSE); social science education (MSE). *Accreditation:* NCATE. Part-time and evening/weekend programs available. *Degree requirements:* For master's, comprehensive exam, thesis optional. *Entrance requirements:* For master's, GRE General Test. Additional exam requirements/recommendations for international students: Required—TOEFL (minimum score 550 paper-based).

Wayne State University, College of Education, Division of Teacher Education, Detroit, MI 48202. Offers art education (M Ed), including art therapy; autism spectrum disorders (Certificate); bilingual/bicultural education (M Ed, Certificate); career and technical education (M Ed, Certificate); cognitive impairment (Certificate); curriculum and instruction (Ed D, PhD, Ed S), including art education (PhD), bilingual education (Ed D, Ed S), bilingual-bicultural education (PhD), career and technical education (MAT, Ed D, PhD, Ed S), early childhood education (MAT, Ed D, PhD, Ed S), elementary education, English as a second language (MAT, Ed D, Ed S), English education (MAT, Ed D, PhD, Ed S), foreign language education (MAT, PhD), K-12 curriculum, mathematics education (MAT, Ed D, PhD, Ed S), science education (MAT, Ed D, PhD, Ed S), secondary education, social studies education (MAT, Ed S), social studies education: secondary (Ed D, PhD); early childhood education (M Ed, Certificate); elementary education (M Ed, MAT), including children's literature (MAT), early childhood education (MAT, Ed D, PhD, Ed S), general elementary education (MAT); elementary or secondary education (MAT), including bilingual/bicultural education, English as a second language (MAT, Ed D, Ed S), mathematics education (MAT, Ed D, PhD, Ed S), science education (MAT, Ed D, PhD, Ed S), social studies education (MAT, Ed S); emotionally impaired (Certificate); English as a second language (Certificate); English education (M Ed), including secondary; foreign language education (M Ed); K-12 reading specialist (Certificate); learning disabilities (Certificate); mathematics education (M Ed), including secondary; reading (M Ed, Ed S); reading, language and literature (Ed D); science education (M Ed), including secondary; secondary education (MAT), including art education (K-12), career and technical education (MAT, Ed D, PhD, Ed S), English education (MAT, Ed D, PhD, Ed S), foreign language education (MAT, PhD), kinesiology; social studies education (M Ed), including secondary; special education (M Ed, MAT, Ed D, PhD, Ed S); visual arts education (Certificate). Part-time programs available. *Faculty:* 36 full-time (25 women), 55 part-time/adjunct (43 women). *Students:* 218 full-time (163 women), 448 part-time (344 women); includes 218 minority (177 Black or African American, non-Hispanic/Latino; 2 American Indian or Alaska Native, non-Hispanic/Latino; 11 Asian, non-Hispanic/Latino; 19 Hispanic/Latino; 1 Native Hawaiian or other Pacific Islander, non-Hispanic/Latino; 8 Two or more races, non-Hispanic/Latino), 10 international. Average age 37. 258 applicants, 30% accepted, 52 enrolled. In 2013, 183 master's, 10 doctorates, 35 other advanced degrees awarded. *Degree requirements:* For master's, thesis, essay or project (for some M Ed programs), professional field experience (for MAT programs); for doctorate, thesis/dissertation. *Entrance requirements:* For master's, Michigan Basic Skills Test (MA in teaching), admission to the graduate school, verification of participation in group work with children and Michigan State Police Criminal Background check; for doctorate, minimum undergraduate GPA of 3.0, graduate 3.5; interview, curriculum vitae; references. Additional exam requirements/recommendations for international students: Required—TOEFL (minimum score 550 paper-based; 79 iBT), TWE (minimum score 5.5), Michigan English Language Assessment Battery (minimum score 85); Recommended—IELTS (minimum score 6.5). *Application deadline:* For fall admission, 6/1 priority date for domestic students, 5/1 priority date for international students; for winter admission, 10/1 priority date for domestic students, 9/1 priority date for international students; for spring admission, 2/1 priority date for domestic students, 1/1 priority date for international students. Applications are processed on a rolling basis. Application fee: $0. Electronic applications accepted. *Expenses:* Tuition, state resident: part-time $554.15 per credit. Tuition, nonresident: part-time $1200.35 per credit. *Required fees:* $42.15 per credit. $268.30 per semester. Tuition and fees vary according to course load and program. *Financial support:* In 2013–14, 83 students received support, including 1 fellowship (averaging $16,842 per year), 1 research assistantship with tuition reimbursement available (averaging $21,229 per year); career-related internships or fieldwork, Federal Work-Study, scholarships/grants, health care benefits, and unspecified assistantships also available. Support available to part-time students. Financial award application deadline: 3/31; financial award applicants required to submit FAFSA. *Faculty research:* Improving students' skill achievement in mathematics; improving elementary children's understanding of informational text; teachers' use of their pedagogical and mathematical knowledge in the interactive work of teaching; the intersection of identity construction in teaching and learning; identifying effective methods of literacy instruction and assessments for bilingual students in elementary language arts classrooms. *Total annual research expenditures:* $368,105. *Unit head:* Dr. Kathleen Crawford-McKinney, Assistant Dean, 313-577-0122. *Application contact:* Janice Green, Assistant Dean, 313-577-1605, E-mail: jwgreen@wayne.edu.
Website: http://coe.wayne.edu/ted/index.php.

Webster University, School of Education, Department of Communication Arts, Reading and Early Childhood, St. Louis, MO 63119-3194. Offers early childhood education (MAT); elementary education (MAT); middle school education (MAT). *Entrance requirements:* For master's, minimum GPA of 2.5. Additional exam requirements/recommendations for international students: Required—TOEFL. *Expenses: Tuition:* Full-time $11,610; part-time $645 per credit hour. Tuition and fees vary according to campus/location and program.

Wesleyan College, Department of Education, Program in Early Childhood Education, Macon, GA 31210-4462. Offers MA. Part-time programs available. *Degree requirements:* For master's, thesis or alternative, practicum, professional portfolio. *Entrance requirements:* For master's, GRE or MAT, interview, teaching certificate, 3 letters of recommendation. Additional exam requirements/recommendations for international students: Required—TOEFL.

West Chester University of Pennsylvania, College of Education, Department of Early and Middle Grades, West Chester, PA 19383. Offers applied studies in teaching and learning (M Ed); early childhood education (M Ed, Teaching Certificate); early grades preparation (Teaching Certificate); elementary education (Teaching Certificate); middle grades preparation (Teaching Certificate). *Accreditation:* NCATE. Part-time and evening/weekend programs available. *Faculty:* 5 full-time (all women), 1 part-time/adjunct (0 women). *Students:* 26 full-time (17 women), 68 part-time (58 women); includes 11 minority (7 Black or African American, non-Hispanic/Latino; 1 American Indian or Alaska Native, non-Hispanic/Latino; 1 Asian, non-Hispanic/Latino; 2 Hispanic/Latino), 3 international. Average age 31. 41 applicants, 83% accepted, 8 enrolled. In 2013, 17 master's, 3 other advanced degrees awarded. *Degree requirements:* For master's, teacher research project, portfolio. *Entrance requirements:* For master's, minimum GPA of 3.0, teacher certification (for applied studies in teaching and learning track), one year of full-time teaching experience; for Teaching Certificate, math, social studies, or science concentration exams (for middle grades preparation), minimum GPA of 3.0. Additional exam requirements/recommendations for international students: Required—TOEFL (minimum score 550 paper-based; 80 iBT). *Application deadline:* For fall admission, 4/15 priority date for domestic students, 3/15 for international students; for spring admission, 10/15 priority date for domestic students. Applications are processed on a rolling basis. Application fee: $45. Electronic applications accepted. *Expenses:* Tuition, state resident: full-time $7956; part-time $442 per credit. Tuition, nonresident: full-time $11,934; part-time $663 per credit. *Required fees:* $2134.20; $106.24 per credit. Tuition and fees vary according to campus/location and program. *Financial support:* Unspecified assistantships available. Support available to part-time students. Financial award application deadline: 2/15; financial award applicants required to submit FAFSA. *Faculty research:* Cooperative learning, creative expression and critical thinking, teacher research, learning styles, middle school education. *Unit head:* Dr. Heather Leaman, Chair, 610-436-2944, Fax: 610-436-3102, E-mail: hleaman@wcupa.edu. *Application contact:* Dr. Connie DiLucchio, Graduate Coordinator, 610-436-3323, Fax: 610-436-3102, E-mail: cdilucchio@wcupa.edu.

Western Kentucky University, Graduate Studies, College of Education and Behavioral Sciences, School of Teacher Education, Bowling Green, KY 42101. Offers elementary education (MAE, Ed S); exceptional education: learning and behavioral disorders (MAE); exceptional education: moderate and severe disabilities (MAE); instructional design (MS); interdisciplinary early childhood education (MAE); library media education (MS); literacy education (MAE); middle grades education (MAE); secondary education (MAE, Ed S). Part-time and evening/weekend programs available. Postbaccalaureate distance learning degree programs offered (minimal on-campus study). *Degree requirements:* For master's, comprehensive exam. *Entrance requirements:* For master's, GRE General Test. Additional exam requirements/recommendations for international students: Required—TOEFL (minimum score 555 paper-based; 79 iBT). *Faculty research:* Teacher preparation in moderate/severe disabilities.

Western Oregon University, Graduate Programs, College of Education, Division of Special Education, Program in Early Childhood Special Education, Monmouth, OR 97361-1394. Offers MS Ed. *Accreditation:* NCATE. Part-time and evening/weekend programs available. *Degree requirements:* For master's, thesis optional, written exam,

portfolio. *Entrance requirements:* For master's, CBEST, PRAXIS or GRE General Test, minimum GPA of 3.0, teaching license. Additional exam requirements/recommendations for international students: Required—TOEFL (minimum score 550 paper-based; 79 iBT), IELTS (minimum score 6.5). *Faculty research:* High school through university articulation, career development for early childhood educators professional collaboration/cooperation.

Westfield State University, Division of Graduate and Continuing Education, Department of Education, Program in Early Childhood Education, Westfield, MA 01086. Offers M Ed. *Accreditation:* NCATE. Part-time and evening/weekend programs available. *Degree requirements:* For master's, comprehensive exam, practicum. *Entrance requirements:* For master's, GRE General Test or MAT, minimum undergraduate GPA of 2.7.

West Virginia University, College of Human Resources and Education, Department of Special Education, Morgantown, WV 26506. Offers autism spectrum disorder (5-adult) (MA); autism spectrum disorder (K-6) (MA); early intervention/early childhood special education (MA); gifted education (1-12) (MA); low vision (PreK-adult) (MA); multicategorical special education (5-adult) (MA); multicategorical special education (K-6) (MA); severe/multiple disabilities (K-adult) (MA); special education (MA, Ed D); vision impairments (PreK-adult) (MA). *Accreditation:* NCATE. Part-time and evening/weekend programs available. Postbaccalaureate distance learning degree programs offered (no on-campus study). *Degree requirements:* For master's, thesis optional; for doctorate, comprehensive exam, thesis/dissertation. *Entrance requirements:* For master's, minimum GPA of 2.75 passing scores on PRAXIS PPST; for doctorate, GRE General Test or MAT. Additional exam requirements/recommendations for international students: Required—TOEFL.

Wheelock College, Graduate Programs, Division of Education, Boston, MA 02215-4176. Offers early childhood education (MS); education leadership (MS); elementary education (MS); language, literacy, and reading (MS); teaching students with moderate disabilities (MS). *Accreditation:* NCATE. Postbaccalaureate distance learning degree programs offered (minimal on-campus study). *Degree requirements:* For master's, comprehensive exam. *Entrance requirements:* Additional exam requirements/recommendations for international students: Required—TOEFL. Electronic applications accepted. *Faculty research:* Symbolic learning, emergent literacy, diversity inclusion, beginning reading language and culture, math education.

Wichita State University, Graduate School, College of Education, Department of Curriculum and Instruction, Wichita, KS 67260. Offers curriculum and instruction (M Ed); special education (M Ed), including adaptive, early childhood unified (M Ed, MAT), functional, gifted; teaching (MAT), including curriculum and instruction, early childhood unified (M Ed, MAT). *Accreditation:* NCATE. Part-time and evening/weekend programs available. *Entrance requirements:* For master's, MAT, minimum GPA of 2.75. *Unit head:* Dr. Janice Ewing, Chairperson, 316-978-3322, E-mail: janice.ewing@wichita.edu. *Application contact:* Jordan Oleson, Admission Coordinator, 316-978-3095, Fax: 316-978-3253, E-mail: jordan.oleson@wichita.edu.

Widener University, School of Human Service Professions, Center for Education, Chester, PA 19013-5792. Offers adult education (M Ed); counseling in higher education (M Ed); counselor education (M Ed); early childhood education (M Ed); educational foundations (M Ed); educational leadership (M Ed); educational psychology (M Ed); elementary education (M Ed); English and language arts (M Ed); health education (M Ed); higher education leadership (Ed D); home and school visitor (M Ed); human sexuality (M Ed, PhD); mathematics education (M Ed); middle school education (M Ed); principalship (M Ed); reading and language arts (Ed D); reading education (M Ed); school administration (Ed D); science education (M Ed); social studies education (M Ed); special education (M Ed); technology education (M Ed). *Accreditation:* NCATE. Part-time and evening/weekend programs available. *Faculty:* 34 full-time (22 women), 37 part-time/adjunct (14 women). *Students:* 64 full-time (44 women), 209 part-time (146 women); includes 49 minority (39 Black or African American, non-Hispanic/Latino; 1 American Indian or Alaska Native, non-Hispanic/Latino; 4 Asian, non-Hispanic/Latino; 4 Hispanic/Latino; 1 Two or more races, non-Hispanic/Latino), 8 international. Average age 39. 139 applicants, 88% accepted. In 2013, 168 master's, 31 doctorates awarded. Terminal master's awarded for partial completion of doctoral program. *Degree requirements:* For doctorate, thesis/dissertation. *Entrance requirements:* For master's, minimum GPA of 2.5; for doctorate, GRE or MAT, minimum GPA of 2.0 (undergraduate), 3.5 (graduate). *Application deadline:* Applications are processed on a rolling basis. Application fee: $25 ($300 for international students). Electronic applications accepted. *Expenses:* Contact institution. *Financial support:* Career-related internships or fieldwork, tuition waivers (full and partial), and unspecified assistantships available. Support available to part-time students. Financial award application deadline: 5/1. *Faculty research:* Reading and cognition, adult education, technology education, educational leadership, special education. *Unit head:* Dr. Michael W. LeDoux, Associate Dean, 610-499-4294, Fax: 610-499-4623, E-mail: mwledoux@widener.edu. *Application contact:* Dr. Roberta Nolan, Director of Graduate Admissions, 610-499-4125, E-mail: rdnolan@widener.edu.

Wilkes University, College of Graduate and Professional Studies, School of Education, Wilkes-Barre, PA 18766-0002. Offers art and science of teaching (MS Ed); classroom technology (MS Ed); early childhood literacy (MS Ed); educational development and strategies (MS Ed); educational leadership (MS Ed); educational technology (Ed D); higher education administration (Ed D); instructional media (MS Ed); instructional technology (MS Ed); international school leadership (MS Ed); K-12 administration

(Ed D); middle level education (MS Ed); online teaching (MS Ed); reading (MS Ed); school business leadership (MS Ed); secondary education (MS Ed), including biology, chemistry, English, history, mathematics; special education (MS Ed); teaching English as a second language (MS Ed); twenty-first century teaching and learning (MS Ed). Part-time and evening/weekend programs available. Postbaccalaureate distance learning degree programs offered (minimal on-campus study). *Students:* 46 full-time (37 women), 1,410 part-time (1,039 women); includes 67 minority (12 Black or African American, non-Hispanic/Latino; 2 American Indian or Alaska Native, non-Hispanic/Latino; 11 Asian, non-Hispanic/Latino; 28 Hispanic/Latino; 1 Native Hawaiian or other Pacific Islander, non-Hispanic/Latino; 13 Two or more races, non-Hispanic/Latino), 6 international. Average age 34. In 2013, 852 master's, 10 doctorates awarded. *Entrance requirements:* Additional exam requirements/recommendations for international students: Required—TOEFL (minimum score 550 paper-based; 79 iBT). *Application deadline:* Applications are processed on a rolling basis. Application fee: $45. Electronic applications accepted. *Expenses:* Contact institution. *Financial support:* Federal Work-Study and unspecified assistantships available. Financial award application deadline: 3/1; financial award applicants required to submit FAFSA. *Unit head:* Dr. Rhonda Waskiewicz, Interim Dean, Education, 570-408-4332, Fax: 570-408-7872, E-mail: rhonda.waskiewicz@wilkes.edu. *Application contact:* Joanne Thomas, Interim Director of Graduate Education, 570-408-4234, Fax: 570-408-7846, E-mail: joanne.thomas1@wilkes.edu.
Website: http://www.wilkes.edu/pages/383.asp.

Worcester State University, Graduate Studies, Department of Education, Program in Early Childhood Education, Worcester, MA 01602-2597. Offers M Ed. Part-time and evening/weekend programs available. *Faculty:* 14 full-time (11 women), 22 part-time/adjunct (10 women). *Students:* 1 (woman) full-time, 16 part-time (all women); includes 1 minority (Asian, non-Hispanic/Latino). Average age 35. 13 applicants, 46% accepted, 2 enrolled. In 2013, 7 master's awarded. *Degree requirements:* For master's, comprehensive exam (for some programs), thesis optional. *Entrance requirements:* For master's, GRE General Test or MAT, teaching certificate. Additional exam requirements/recommendations for international students: Required—TOEFL (minimum score 500 paper-based; 61 iBT). *Application deadline:* For fall admission, 6/15 for domestic and international students; for spring admission, 4/1 for domestic and international students. Applications are processed on a rolling basis. Application fee: $40. Electronic applications accepted. *Expenses: Tuition, area resident:* Part-time $150 per credit. Tuition, state resident: part-time $150 per credit. Tuition, nonresident: part-time $150 per credit. *Required fees:* $114.50 per credit. *Financial support:* Career-related internships or fieldwork, scholarships/grants, and unspecified assistantships available. Financial award application deadline: 3/1; financial award applicants required to submit FAFSA. *Unit head:* Dr. Carol Donnelly, Coordinator, 508-929-8667, Fax: 508-929-8164, E-mail: cdonnelly@worcester.edu. *Application contact:* Sara Grady, Assistant Dean of Graduate and Continuing Education, 508-929-8787, Fax: 508-929-8100, E-mail: sara.grady@worcester.edu.

Wright State University, School of Graduate Studies, College of Education and Human Services, Department of Teacher Education, Program in Early Childhood Education, Dayton, OH 45435. Offers M Ed, MA. *Accreditation:* NCATE. *Degree requirements:* For master's, thesis (for some programs). *Entrance requirements:* For master's, GRE General Test, MAT. Additional exam requirements/recommendations for international students: Required—TOEFL.

Xavier University, College of Social Sciences, Health and Education, School of Education, Department of Childhood Education and Literacy, Montessori Program, Cincinnati, OH 45207. Offers M Ed. Part-time programs available. *Faculty:* 4 full-time (all women), 9 part-time/adjunct (7 women). *Students:* 23 full-time (20 women), 9 part-time (6 women); includes 6 minority (2 Black or African American, non-Hispanic/Latino; 2 Asian, non-Hispanic/Latino; 1 Hispanic/Latino; 1 Two or more races, non-Hispanic/Latino), 3 international. Average age 30. 8 applicants, 100% accepted, 5 enrolled. In 2013, 14 master's awarded. *Degree requirements:* For master's, comprehensive exam, research project or thesis. *Entrance requirements:* For master's, MAT or GRE. Additional exam requirements/recommendations for international students: Required—TOEFL (minimum score 550 paper-based; 79 iBT). *Application deadline:* Applications are processed on a rolling basis. Application fee: $35. Electronic applications accepted. *Expenses: Tuition:* Part-time $594 per credit hour. *Required fees:* $3 per semester. *Financial support:* In 2013–14, 23 students received support. Unspecified assistantships available. Financial award applicants required to submit FAFSA. *Faculty research:* First-year teacher retention, teaching efficacy of science educators, adolescents' literacy practices, family resiliency, preparing culturally responsive teachers. *Unit head:* Gina Taliaferro Lofquist, Director, 513-745-1072, Fax: 513-745-4378, E-mail: lofquistgm@xavier.edu. *Application contact:* Roger Bosse, Graduate Services Director, 513-745-3357, Fax: 513-745-1048, E-mail: bosse@xavier.edu.
Website: http://www.xavier.edu/montessori-grad/.

Youngstown State University, Graduate School, Beeghly College of Education, Department of Teacher Education, Program in Early Childhood Education, Youngstown, OH 44555-0001. Offers MS Ed. *Accreditation:* NCATE. Part-time and evening/weekend programs available. *Degree requirements:* For master's, comprehensive exam. *Entrance requirements:* For master's, GRE, MAT, or teaching certificate; minimum GPA of 2.7. Additional exam requirements/recommendations for international students: Required—TOEFL.

Elementary Education

Acacia University, American Graduate School of Education, Tempe, AZ 85284. Offers educational administration (M Ed); elementary education (MA); English as a second language (M Ed); secondary education (MA); special education (M Ed).

Adelphi University, Ruth S. Ammon School of Education, Program in Childhood Education, Garden City, NY 11530-0701. Offers MA. Part-time and evening/weekend programs available. *Students:* 60 full-time (59 women), 12 part-time (all women); includes 13 minority (2 Black or African American, non-Hispanic/Latino; 4 Asian, non-Hispanic/Latino; 6 Hispanic/Latino; 1 Two or more races, non-Hispanic/Latino). Average age 25. In 2013, 12 master's awarded. *Entrance requirements:* For master's, 2 letters of recommendation, resume. Additional exam requirements/recommendations for international students: Required—TOEFL (minimum score 550 paper-based; 80 iBT). *Application deadline:* For fall admission, 4/1 for international students; for spring admission, 11/1 for international students. Application fee: $50. Electronic applications accepted. *Expenses: Tuition:* Full-time $32,530; part-time $1010 per credit. *Required*

fees: $1150. Tuition and fees vary according to degree level and program. *Financial support:* Teaching assistantships, career-related internships or fieldwork, Federal Work-Study, institutionally sponsored loans, tuition waivers, and unspecified assistantships available. Support available to part-time students. Financial award application deadline: 2/15; financial award applicants required to submit FAFSA. *Faculty research:* Diversity; parental involvement; teacher education; psychoanalytic understanding of racial formation; relationships between ideology, language, culture and individual subject formation. *Unit head:* Dr. Carl Mirra, Director, 516-877-4137, E-mail: mirra@adelphi.edu. *Application contact:* Christine Murphy, Director of Admissions, 516-877-3050, Fax: 516-877-3039, E-mail: graduateadmissions@adelphi.edu.

Alabama Agricultural and Mechanical University, School of Graduate Studies, School of Education, Area in Elementary and Early Childhood Education, Huntsville, AL 35811. Offers early childhood education (MS Ed, Ed S); elementary education (MS Ed, Ed S). *Accreditation:* NCATE. Evening/weekend programs available. *Degree*

requirements: For master's, comprehensive exam; for Ed S, thesis. *Entrance requirements:* For master's, GRE General Test. Additional exam requirements/recommendations for international students: Required—TOEFL (minimum score 500 paper-based; 61 iBT). Electronic applications accepted. *Faculty research:* Multicultural education, learning styles, diagnostic-prescriptive instruction.

Alabama State University, College of Education, Department of Curriculum and Instruction, Montgomery, AL 36101-0271. Offers early childhood education (M Ed, Ed S); elementary education (M Ed, Ed S); secondary education (M Ed, Ed S), including biology education, English language arts education (M Ed), history education, math education, music education (M Ed), reading education (M Ed), social science education; special education (M Ed). Part-time programs available. *Faculty:* 11 full-time (8 women), 13 part-time/adjunct (10 women). *Students:* 32 full-time (19 women), 162 part-time (136 women); includes 189 minority (187 Black or African American, non-Hispanic/Latino; 1 Hispanic/Latino; 1 Two or more races, non-Hispanic/Latino). Average age 33. 99 applicants, 45% accepted, 34 enrolled. In 2013, 74 master's, 20 Ed Ss awarded. *Degree requirements:* For master's, comprehensive exam, thesis optional; for Ed S, comprehensive exam, thesis. *Entrance requirements:* For master's, GRE General Test, MAT, writing competency test; for Ed S, writing competency test, GRE, MAT. Additional exam requirements/recommendations for international students: Required—TOEFL (minimum score 500 paper-based). *Application deadline:* For fall admission, 7/15 for domestic students; for spring admission, 12/15 for domestic students. Applications are processed on a rolling basis. Application fee: $25. *Expenses:* Tuition, state resident: full-time $7958; part-time $343 per credit hour. Tuition, nonresident: full-time $14,132; part-time $686 per credit hour. *Required fees:* $446 per term. One-time fee: $1784 full-time; $892 part-time. Tuition and fees vary according to course load. *Financial support:* In 2013–14, research assistantships (averaging $9,450 per year) were awarded. *Unit head:* Dr. Joyce Johnson, Acting Chairperson, 334-229-4485, Fax: 334-229-5603, E-mail: jjohnson@alasu.edu. *Application contact:* Dr. William Person, Dean of Graduate Studies, 334-229-4274, Fax: 334-229-4928, E-mail: wperson@alasu.edu.
Website: http://www.alasu.edu/academics/colleges—departments/college-of-education/curriculum—instruction/index.aspx.

Alaska Pacific University, Graduate Programs, Education Department, Program in Teaching, Anchorage, AK 99508-4672. Offers teaching (K-8) (MAT). *Degree requirements:* For master's, research project. *Entrance requirements:* For master's, GRE or MAT, PRAXIS, minimum GPA of 3.0.

Albright College, Graduate Division, Reading, PA 19612-5234. Offers early childhood education (MS); elementary education (MS); English as a second language (MA); general education (MA); special education (MS). Part-time and evening/weekend programs available. *Degree requirements:* For master's, thesis. *Entrance requirements:* For master's, GRE General Test or MAT, minimum undergraduate GPA of 3.0, 2 letters of recommendation, interview. Additional exam requirements/recommendations for international students: Recommended—TOEFL (minimum score 525 paper-based). Electronic applications accepted.

Alcorn State University, School of Graduate Studies, School of Psychology and Education, Alcorn State, MS 39096-7500. Offers agricultural education (MS Ed); elementary education (MS Ed, Ed S); guidance and counseling (MS Ed); industrial education (MS Ed); secondary education (MS Ed), including health and physical education; special education (MS Ed). *Accreditation:* NCATE. *Degree requirements:* For master's, thesis optional.

American International College, School of Graduate and Adult Education, Department of Education, Springfield, MA 01109-3189. Offers early childhood education (M Ed, CAGS); educational leadership and supervision (Ed D); elementary education (M Ed, CAGS); middle/secondary education (M Ed, CAGS); moderate disabilities (M Ed, CAGS); reading (M Ed, CAGS); school adjustment counseling (MA, CAGS); school guidance counseling (MA, CAGS); school leadership preparation (M Ed, CAGS); teaching and learning (Ed D). Evening/weekend programs available. *Faculty:* 11 full-time (9 women), 235 part-time/adjunct. *Students:* 1,530 full-time (1,219 women), 184 part-time (143 women); includes 100 minority (58 Black or African American, non-Hispanic/Latino; 3 American Indian or Alaska Native, non-Hispanic/Latino; 14 Asian, non-Hispanic/Latino; 6 Hispanic/Latino; 19 Two or more races, non-Hispanic/Latino). Average age 36. 695 applicants, 82% accepted, 508 enrolled. In 2013, 449 master's, 17 doctorates, 135 other advanced degrees awarded. Terminal master's awarded for partial completion of doctoral program. *Degree requirements:* For master's, comprehensive exam (for some programs), thesis (for some programs), practicum/culminating experience; for doctorate, comprehensive exam (for some programs), thesis/dissertation; for CAGS, practicum/culminating experience. *Entrance requirements:* For master's, graduate of accredited four-year college with minimum B-average in undergraduate course work; for doctorate, master's degree, minimum GPA of 3.0; for CAGS, M Ed or master's degree in field related to licensure from accredited institution. Additional exam requirements/recommendations for international students: Required—TOEFL or IELTS. *Application deadline:* For fall admission, 7/1 for domestic and international students; for spring admission, 12/1 for domestic and international students. Applications are processed on a rolling basis. Application fee: $50. Electronic applications accepted. *Expenses: Tuition:* Full-time $14,040; part-time $780 per credit. Tuition and fees vary according to course load, degree level and program. *Financial support:* Career-related internships or fieldwork available. Financial award applicants required to submit FAFSA. *Unit head:* Esta Sobey, Associate Dean, 413-205-3453, Fax: 413-205-3943, E-mail: esta.sobey@aic.edu. *Application contact:* Kaitlyn Rickard, Director of XCP Admissions, 413-205-3090, Fax: 413-205-3911, E-mail: kaitlyn.rickard@aic.edu.
Website: http://www.aic.edu/academics.

American Public University System, AMU/APU Graduate Programs, Charles Town, WV 25414. Offers accounting (MBA, MS); criminal justice (MA), including business administration, emergency and disaster management, general (MA, MS); educational leadership (M Ed); emergency and disaster management (MA); entrepreneurship (MBA); environmental policy and management (MS), including environmental planning, environmental sustainability, fish and wildlife management, general (MA, MS), global environmental management; finance (MBA); general (MBA); global business management (MBA); history (MA), including American history, ancient and classical history, European history, global history, public history; homeland security (MA), including business administration, counter-terrorism studies, criminal justice, cyber, emergency management and public health, intelligence studies, transportation security; homeland security resource allocation (MBA); humanities (MA); information technology (MS), including digital forensics, enterprise software development, information assurance and security, IT project management; information technology management (MBA); intelligence studies (MA), including criminal intelligence, cyber, general (MA, MS), homeland security, intelligence analysis, intelligence collection, intelligence management, intelligence operations, terrorism studies; international relations and conflict resolution (MA), including comparative and security issues, conflict resolution, international and transnational security issues, peacekeeping; legal studies (MA); management (MA), including defense management, general (MA, MS), human resource management, organizational leadership, public administration; marketing (MBA); military history (MA), including American military history, American Revolution, civil war, war since 1945, World War II; military studies (MA), including joint warfare, strategic leadership; national security studies (MA), including general (MA, MS), homeland security, regional security studies, security and intelligence analysis, terrorism studies; nonprofit management (MBA); political science (MA), including American politics and government, comparative government and development, general (MA, MS), international relations, public policy; psychology (MA), including general (MA, MS), maritime engineering management, reverse logistics management; public administration (MPA), including disaster management, environmental policy, health policy, human resources, national security, organizational management, security management; public health (MPH); reverse logistics management (MA); school counseling (M Ed); security management (MA); space studies (MS), including aerospace science, general (MA, MS), planetary science; sports and health sciences (MS); teaching (M Ed), including curriculum and instruction for elementary teachers, elementary reading, English language learners, instructional leadership, online learning, special education; transportation and logistics management (MA), including general (MA, MS), maritime engineering management, reverse logistics management. Programs offered via distance learning only. Part-time and evening/weekend programs available. Postbaccalaureate distance learning degree programs offered (no on-campus study). *Faculty:* 432 full-time (242 women), 1,722 part-time/adjunct (829 women). *Students:* 511 full-time (241 women), 10,947 part-time (4,294 women); includes 3,760 minority (2,058 Black or African American, non-Hispanic/Latino; 88 American Indian or Alaska Native, non-Hispanic/Latino; 293 Asian, non-Hispanic/Latino; 876 Hispanic/Latino; 91 Native Hawaiian or other Pacific Islander, non-Hispanic/Latino; 354 Two or more races, non-Hispanic/Latino), 134 international. Average age 36. In 2013, 3,323 master's awarded. *Degree requirements:* For master's, comprehensive exam or practicum. *Entrance requirements:* For master's, official transcript showing earned bachelor's degree from institution accredited by recognized accrediting body. Additional exam requirements/recommendations for international students: Required—TOEFL (minimum score 550 paper-based), IELTS (minimum score 6.5). *Application deadline:* Applications are processed on a rolling basis. Application fee: $0. Electronic applications accepted. *Expenses: Tuition:* Part-time $325 per semester hour. *Financial support:* Applicants required to submit FAFSA. *Faculty research:* Military history, criminal justice, management performance, national security. *Unit head:* Dr. Karan Powell, Executive Vice President and Provost, 877-468-6268, Fax: 304-724-3780. *Application contact:* Terry Grant, Vice President of Enrollment Management, 877-468-6268, Fax: 304-724-3780, E-mail: info@apus.edu.
Website: http://www.apus.edu.

American University, College of Arts and Sciences, Washington, DC 20016-8012. Offers addiction and addictive behavior (Certificate); anthropology (PhD); applied microeconomics (Certificate); applied statistics (Certificate); art history (MA); arts management (MA, Certificate); Asian studies (Certificate); audio production (Certificate); audio technology (MA); behavior, cognition, and neuroscience (PhD); bilingual education (MA, Certificate); biology (MA, MS); chemistry (MS); clinical psychology (PhD); computer science (MS, Certificate); creative writing (MFA); curriculum and instruction (M Ed, Certificate); economics (MA, PhD); environmental assessment (Certificate); environmental science (MS); ethics, peace, and global affairs (MA); gender analysis in economics (Certificate); health promotion management (MS); history (MA, PhD); international arts management (Certificate); international economic relations (Certificate); international economics (MA); international training and education (MA); literature (MA); mathematics (MA); North American studies (Certificate); nutrition education (MS, Certificate); philosophy (MA); professional science: biotechnology (MS); professional science: environmental assessment (MS); professional science: quantitative analysis (MS); psychobiology of healing (Certificate); psychology (MA); psychology: general (PhD); public anthropology (MA, Certificate); public sociology (Certificate); social research (Certificate); sociology (MA); Spanish: Latin American studies (MA); special education: learning disabilities (MA); statistics (MS); studio art (MFA); teaching (MAT); teaching English as a foreign language (MA); teaching: early childhood (Certificate); teaching: elementary (Certificate); teaching: ESOL (Certificate); teaching: secondary (Certificate); technology in arts management (Certificate); TESOL (MA); translation: French (Certificate); translation: Russian (Certificate); translation: Spanish (Certificate); women's, gender, and sexuality studies (Certificate). Part-time and evening/weekend programs available. Postbaccalaureate distance learning degree programs offered (no on-campus study). *Faculty:* 358 full-time (187 women), 254 part-time/adjunct (127 women). *Students:* 627 full-time (411 women), 416 part-time (300 women); includes 206 minority (91 Black or African American, non-Hispanic/Latino; 5 American Indian or Alaska Native, non-Hispanic/Latino; 32 Asian, non-Hispanic/Latino; 64 Hispanic/Latino; 1 Native Hawaiian or other Pacific Islander, non-Hispanic/Latino; 13 Two or more races, non-Hispanic/Latino), 124 international. Average age 29. 1,672 applicants, 52% accepted, 361 enrolled. In 2013, 382 master's, 38 doctorates, 33 other advanced degrees awarded. Terminal master's awarded for partial completion of doctoral program. *Degree requirements:* For master's, comprehensive exam (for some programs), thesis (for some programs); for doctorate, comprehensive exam (for some programs), thesis/dissertation. *Entrance requirements:* For master's, GRE, minimum GPA of 3.0 in last 60 credit hours, letter of recommendation, statement of purpose, resume, unofficial transcript; for doctorate, GRE, minimum GPA of 3.0 for all graduate work, letter of recommendation, statement of purpose, resume, unofficial transcript. Additional exam requirements/recommendations for international students: Required—TOEFL (minimum score 600 paper-based; 100 iBT), IELTS (minimum score 7). *Application deadline:* For fall admission, 2/1 for domestic students; for spring admission, 10/1 for domestic students. Applications are processed on a rolling basis. Application fee: $55. Electronic applications accepted. *Expenses: Tuition:* Full-time $25,920; part-time $1482 per credit hour. *Required fees:* $430. Tuition and fees vary according to course load and program. *Financial support:* Fellowships, research assistantships with full and partial tuition reimbursements, teaching assistantships with full and partial tuition reimbursements, career-related internships or fieldwork, Federal Work-Study, institutionally sponsored loans, scholarships/grants, traineeships, tuition waivers (full and partial), and unspecified assistantships available. Support available to part-time students. Financial award applicants required to submit FAFSA. *Unit head:* Dr. Peter Starr, Dean, 202-885-2446, Fax: 202-885-2429, E-mail: pstarr@american.edu. *Application contact:* Kathleen Clowery, Associate Director, Graduate Enrollment Management, 202-885-3621, Fax: 202-885-1505, E-mail: clowery@american.edu.
Website: http://www.american.edu/cas/.

American University of Puerto Rico, Program in Education, Bayamón, PR 00960-2037. Offers art education (M Ed); elementary education 4-6 (M Ed); elementary education K-3 (M Ed); general science education (M Ed); physical education (M Ed); special education (M Ed). *Faculty:* 17 part-time/adjunct (7 women). *Students:* 55 full-time (42 women), 105 part-time (96 women); all minorities (all Hispanic/Latino). Average age 33. 120 applicants, 99% accepted, 81 enrolled. In 2013, 52 master's awarded. *Entrance requirements:* For master's, EXADEP, GRE, or MAT, 2 letters of recommendation, minimum GPA of 2.5. *Application deadline:* For fall admission, 8/1 for domestic students; for winter admission, 10/18 for domestic students; for spring admission, 3/15 for domestic students. Applications are processed on a rolling basis. Application fee: $25. *Expenses: Tuition:* Part-time $240 per credit. Tuition and fees vary according to course load. *Unit head:* Dr. Jose A. Ramirez-Figueroa, Education and

Technology Department Director/Chancellor, 787-620-2040 Ext. 2010, Fax: 787-620-2958, E-mail: jramirez@aupr.edu. *Application contact:* Keren I. Llanos-Figueroa, Information Contact, 787-620-2040 Ext. 2021, Fax: 787-785-7377, E-mail: oficnaadmisiones@aupr.edu.

Andrews University, School of Graduate Studies, School of Education, Department of Teaching, Learning, and Curriculum, Berrien Springs, MI 49104. Offers curriculum and instruction (MA, Ed D, PhD, Ed S); elementary education (MAT); secondary education (MAT), including biology, education, English, English as a second language, French, history, physics; teacher education (MAT). *Faculty:* 7 full-time (4 women). *Students:* 16 full-time (11 women), 26 part-time (22 women); includes 14 minority (11 Black or African American, non-Hispanic/Latino; 1 Asian, non-Hispanic/Latino; 1 Hispanic/Latino; 1 Two or more races, non-Hispanic/Latino), 13 international. Average age 40. 33 applicants, 42% accepted, 3 enrolled. In 2013, 7 master's, 1 doctorate, 1 other advanced degree awarded. *Entrance requirements:* For master's, GRE Subject Test. Additional exam requirements/recommendations for international students: Required—TOEFL (minimum score 550 paper-based). *Application deadline:* For fall admission, 8/15 for domestic students. Applications are processed on a rolling basis. Application fee: $40. *Unit head:* Dr. Lee C. Davidson, Chair, 269-471-6364. *Application contact:* Monica Wringer, Supervisor of Graduate Admission, 800-253-2874, Fax: 269-471-6321, E-mail: graduate@andrews.edu.

Anna Maria College, Graduate Division, Program in Education, Paxton, MA 01612. Offers early childhood education (M Ed); education (CAGS); elementary education (M Ed); English language arts (M Ed); visual arts (M Ed). Part-time and evening/weekend programs available. *Entrance requirements:* For master's, bachelor's degree in liberal arts or sciences, minimum GPA of 3.0. Additional exam requirements/recommendations for international students: Required—TOEFL (minimum score 500 paper-based). Electronic applications accepted.

Antioch University New England, Graduate School, Department of Education, Integrated Learning Program, Keene, NH 03431-3552. Offers early childhood education (M Ed); elementary education (M Ed), including arts and humanities, science and environmental education; special education (M Ed). *Degree requirements:* For master's, internship. *Entrance requirements:* For master's, previous course work or work experience in education. Additional exam requirements/recommendations for international students: Required—TOEFL (minimum score 550 paper-based). Electronic applications accepted. *Expenses:* Contact institution. *Faculty research:* Problem-based learning, place-based education, mathematics education, democratic classrooms, art education.

Antioch University New England, Graduate School, Department of Education, Waldorf Teacher Training Program, Keene, NH 03431-3552. Offers elementary education (M Ed, Certificate). *Degree requirements:* For master's, thesis (for some programs), internship. *Entrance requirements:* For master's, foundation studies in anthroposophy or equivalent. Additional exam requirements/recommendations for international students: Required—TOEFL (minimum score 550 paper-based). Electronic applications accepted. *Expenses:* Contact institution. *Faculty research:* Teacher renewal, early childhood education, collaborative leadership.

Appalachian State University, Cratis D. Williams Graduate School, Department of Curriculum and Instruction, Boone, NC 28608. Offers curriculum specialist (MA); educational media (MA); elementary education (MA); middle grades education (MA), including language arts, mathematics, science, social studies. *Accreditation:* NCATE. Part-time and evening/weekend programs available. Postbaccalaureate distance learning degree programs offered (no on-campus study). *Degree requirements:* For master's, comprehensive exam, thesis or alternative. *Entrance requirements:* For master's, GRE General Test or MAT, 3 letters of recommendation. Additional exam requirements/recommendations for international students: Required—TOEFL (minimum score 570 paper-based; 79 iBT), IELTS (minimum score 6.5). Electronic applications accepted. *Faculty research:* Media literacy, elementary teaching, curriculum development, online learning environments.

Arcadia University, Graduate Studies, School of Education, Glenside, PA 19038-3295. Offers art education (M Ed); computer education (CAS); curriculum (CAS); curriculum studies (M Ed); early childhood education (M Ed, CAS), including individualized (M Ed), master teacher (M Ed), research in child development (M Ed); educational leadership (M Ed, Ed D, CAS); elementary education (M Ed, CAS); English education (MA Ed); environmental education (MA Ed, CAS); history education (MA Ed); instructional technology (M Ed); language arts (M Ed, CAS); library science (M Ed); mathematics education (M Ed, MA Ed, CAS); music education (MA Ed); psychology (MA Ed); reading (M Ed, CAS); science education (M Ed, CAS); secondary education (M Ed, CAS); special education (M Ed, Ed D, CAS); theater arts (MA Ed); written communication (MA Ed). *Accreditation:* NASAD. Part-time and evening/weekend programs available. Postbaccalaureate distance learning degree programs offered (minimal on-campus study). Electronic applications accepted. *Expenses:* Contact institution.

Argosy University, Atlanta, College of Education, Atlanta, GA 30328. Offers educational leadership (MAEd, Ed D, Ed S), including higher education administration (Ed D), K-12 education (Ed D); teaching and learning (MAEd, Ed D, Ed S), including education technology (Ed D), higher education (Ed D), K-12 education (Ed D).

Argosy University, Chicago, College of Education, Chicago, IL 60601. Offers adult education and training (MA Ed); community college executive leadership (Ed D); educational leadership (MA Ed, Ed D, Ed S), including district leadership (Ed D), higher education administration (Ed D), K-12 education (Ed D); instructional leadership (Ed D, Ed S), including higher education (Ed D), K-12 education (Ed D). Postbaccalaureate distance learning degree programs offered (minimal on-campus study).

Argosy University, Denver, College of Education, Denver, CO 80231. Offers community college executive leadership (Ed D); educational leadership (MA Ed, Ed D), including higher education (Ed D), K-12 education (Ed D); instructional leadership (MA Ed, Ed D), including higher education administration (Ed D), K-12 education (Ed D).

Argosy University, Hawai`i, College of Education, Honolulu, HI 96813. Offers adult education and training (MAEd); educational leadership (Ed D), including higher education administration, K-12 education; instructional leadership (Ed D), including higher education, K-12 education; school psychology (MA).

Argosy University, Inland Empire, College of Education, Ontario, CA 91761. Offers community college executive leadership (Ed D); educational leadership (MA Ed, Ed D), including higher education administration (Ed D), K-12 education (Ed D); instructional leadership (MA Ed, Ed D), including higher education (Ed D), K-12 education (Ed D), multiple subject teacher preparation (MA Ed), single subject teacher preparation (MA Ed).

Argosy University, Los Angeles, College of Education, Santa Monica, CA 90045. Offers community college executive leadership (Ed D); educational leadership (MA Ed, Ed D), including higher education administration (Ed D), K-12 education (Ed D); instructional leadership (MA Ed, Ed D), including higher education (Ed D), K-12 education (Ed D), multiple subject teacher preparation (MA Ed), single subject teacher preparation (MA Ed).

Argosy University, Nashville, College of Education, Program in Educational Leadership, Nashville, TN 37214. Offers educational leadership (MA Ed, Ed S); higher education administration (Ed D); K-12 education (Ed D).

Argosy University, Nashville, College of Education, Program in Instructional Leadership, Nashville, TN 37214. Offers education technology (Ed D); higher education administration (Ed D); instructional leadership (MA Ed, Ed S); K-12 education (Ed D).

Argosy University, Orange County, College of Education, Orange, CA 92868. Offers community college executive leadership (Ed D); educational leadership (MA Ed, Ed D), including higher education administration (Ed D), K-12 education (Ed D); instructional leadership (MA Ed, Ed D), including education technology (Ed D), higher education (Ed D), K-12 education (Ed D), multiple subject teacher preparation (MA Ed), single subject teacher preparation (MA Ed).

Argosy University, Phoenix, College of Education, Phoenix, AZ 85021. Offers adult education and training (MA Ed); advanced educational administration (Ed D, Ed S); community college executive leadership (Ed D); educational administration (MA Ed); educational leadership (MA Ed, Ed D, Ed S), including education technology (Ed D), higher education administration (Ed D), K-12 education (Ed D); higher and postsecondary education (MA Ed); initial educational administration (Ed D, Ed S); school psychology (MA); teaching and learning (MA Ed, Ed D, Ed S), including education technology (Ed D), higher education (Ed D), K-12 education (Ed D).

Argosy University, San Diego, College of Education, San Diego, CA 92108. Offers community college executive leadership (Ed D); educational leadership (MA Ed, Ed D), including higher education administration (Ed D), K-12 education (Ed D); instructional leadership (MA Ed, Ed D), including higher education (Ed D), K-12 education (Ed D).

Argosy University, San Francisco Bay Area, College of Education, Alameda, CA 94501. Offers community college executive leadership (Ed D); educational leadership (MA Ed, Ed D), including education technology (Ed D), higher education administration (Ed D), K-12 education (Ed D); instructional leadership (MA Ed, Ed D), including education technology (Ed D), higher education (Ed D), K-12 education (Ed D), multiple subject teacher preparation (MA Ed), single subject teacher preparation (MA Ed).

Argosy University, Sarasota, College of Education, Sarasota, FL 34235. Offers community college executive leadership (Ed D); educational leadership (MA Ed, Ed D, Ed S), including higher education administration (Ed D), K-12 education (Ed D); school counseling (MA, Ed S); school psychology (MA); teaching and learning (MA Ed, Ed D, Ed S), including education technology (Ed D), higher education (Ed D), K-12 education (Ed D).

Argosy University, Schaumburg, College of Education, Schaumburg, IL 60173-5403. Offers community college executive leadership (Ed D); educational leadership (MA Ed, Ed D, Ed S), including district leadership (Ed D), higher education administration (Ed D), K-12 education (Ed D); instructional leadership (Ed D, Ed S), including higher education (Ed D), K-12 education (Ed D).

Argosy University, Seattle, College of Education, Seattle, WA 98121. Offers adult education and training (MA Ed); community college executive leadership (Ed D); educational leadership (MA Ed, Ed D), including higher education administration (Ed D), K-12 education (Ed D); higher and postsecondary education (MA Ed); instructional leadership (MA Ed, Ed D), including education technology (Ed D), higher education (Ed D), K-12 education (Ed D).

Argosy University, Tampa, College of Education, Tampa, FL 33607. Offers community college executive leadership (Ed D); educational leadership (MA Ed, Ed D, Ed S), including higher education administration (Ed D), K-12 education (Ed D); school counseling (MA); teaching and learning (MA Ed, Ed D, Ed S), including higher education (Ed D), K-12 education (Ed D).

Argosy University, Twin Cities, College of Education, Eagan, MN 55121. Offers advanced educational administration (Ed D, Ed S); educational leadership (MA Ed, Ed D, Ed S), including higher education administration (Ed D), K-12 education (Ed D); higher and postsecondary education (MA Ed); initial educational administration (Ed D, Ed S); instructional leadership (MA Ed, Ed D, Ed S), including education technology (Ed D), higher education (Ed D), K-12 education (Ed D).

Argosy University, Washington DC, College of Education, Arlington, VA 22209. Offers community college executive leadership (Ed D); educational leadership (MA Ed, Ed D, Ed S), including higher education administration (Ed D), K-12 education (Ed D); instructional leadership (MA Ed, Ed D, Ed S), including higher education (Ed D), K-12 education (Ed D).

Arizona State University at the Tempe campus, Mary Lou Fulton Teachers College, Program in Curriculum and Instruction, Phoenix, AZ 85069. Offers curriculum and instruction (M Ed, MA, PhD); elementary education (M Ed); physical education (MPE); secondary education (M Ed). Part-time and evening/weekend programs available. Postbaccalaureate distance learning degree programs offered (minimal on-campus study). Terminal master's awarded for partial completion of doctoral program. *Degree requirements:* For master's, thesis or alternative, applied project, interactive Program of Study (iPOS) submitted before completing 50 percent of required credit hours; for doctorate, comprehensive exam, thesis/dissertation, interactive Program of Study (iPOS) submitted before completing 50 percent of required credit hours. *Entrance requirements:* For master's, GRE or GMAT (for some programs), minimum GPA of 3.0 or equivalent in last 2 years of work leading to bachelor's degree, 3 letters of recommendation, personal statement describing research and career goals, curriculum vitae or resume, IVP fingerprint clearance card (for those seeking Arizona certification); for doctorate, GRE or GMAT (depending on program), minimum GPA of 3.0 or equivalent in last 2 years of work leading to bachelor's degree, 3 letters of recommendation, personal statement describing research and career goals, curriculum vitae or resume. Additional exam requirements/recommendations for international students: Required—TOEFL, IELTS, or PTE. Electronic applications accepted. *Expenses:* Contact institution. *Faculty research:* Early childhood, media and computers, elementary education, secondary education, English education, bilingual education, language and literacy, science education, engineering education, exercise and wellness education.

Arkansas State University, Graduate School, College of Education and Behavioral Science, School of Teacher Education and Leadership, Jonesboro, AR 72467. Offers community college administration (SCCT); curriculum and instruction (MSE); early childhood education (MAT, MSE); early childhood services (MS); educational leadership (MSE, Ed D, PhD, Ed S); educational theory and practice (MSE); middle level education (MAT, MSE); reading (MSE, Ed S); special education - gifted, talented, and creative (MSE); special education - instructional specialist grades 4-12 (MSE); special education - instructional specialist grades P-4 (MSE). *Accreditation:* NCATE. Part-time programs available. Postbaccalaureate distance learning degree programs offered. *Faculty:* 28 full-time (16 women). *Students:* 77 full-time (68 women), 1,934 part-time (1,449 women); includes 361 minority (290 Black or African American, non-Hispanic/Latino; 11 American Indian or Alaska Native, non-Hispanic/Latino; 3 Asian, non-Hispanic/Latino; 26 Hispanic/Latino; 1 Native Hawaiian or other Pacific Islander, non-Hispanic/Latino; 30 Two or more races, non-Hispanic/Latino), 5 international. Average age 36. 1,627 applicants, 71% accepted, 770 enrolled. In 2013, 1,182 master's, 12 doctorates, 76 other advanced

degrees awarded. *Degree requirements:* For master's, comprehensive exam, thesis or alternative; for doctorate, comprehensive exam, thesis/dissertation; for other advanced degree, comprehensive exam. *Entrance requirements:* For master's, GRE General Test or MAT, appropriate bachelor's degree, official transcripts, immunization records, letters of reference, interview; for doctorate, GRE General Test or MAT, interview, master's degree, letters of reference, official transcript, personal statement, writing sample, immunization records; for other advanced degree, GRE General Test or MAT, interview, master's degree, official transcript, immunization records, letters of reference, 3 years of teaching experience, teaching license. Additional exam requirements/recommendations for international students: Required—TOEFL (minimum score 550 paper-based; 79 iBT), IELTS (minimum score 6), PTE (minimum score 56). *Application deadline:* For fall admission, 7/1 for domestic and international students; for spring admission, 11/15 for domestic students, 11/14 for international students. Applications are processed on a rolling basis. Electronic applications accepted. *Expenses:* Tuition, state resident: full-time $4284; part-time $238 per credit hour. Tuition, nonresident: full-time $8568; part-time $476 per credit hour. *International tuition:* $9268 full-time. *Required fees:* $1098; $61 per credit hour. $25 per term. Tuition and fees vary according to course load and program. *Financial support:* In 2013–14, 20 students received support. Fellowships, teaching assistantships, career-related internships or fieldwork, scholarships/grants, and unspecified assistantships available. Financial award application deadline: 7/1; financial award applicants required to submit FAFSA. *Unit head:* Dr. Annette Hux, Interim Chair, 870-972-3059, Fax: 870-972-3344, E-mail: ahux@astate.edu. *Application contact:* Vickey Ring, Graduate Admissions Coordinator, 870-972-3029, Fax: 870-972-3857, E-mail: vickeyring@astate.edu.
Website: http://www.astate.edu/college/education/departments/school-of-teacher-education-and-leadership/index.dot.

Arkansas Tech University, College of Education, Russellville, AR 72801. Offers college student personnel (MS); elementary education (M Ed); instructional improvement (M Ed); instructional technology (M Ed); physical education (M Ed); teaching (MAT). *Accreditation:* NCATE. Part-time and evening/weekend programs available. Postbaccalaureate distance learning degree programs offered (no on-campus study). *Students:* 58 full-time (39 women), 304 part-time (240 women); includes 76 minority (58 Black or African American, non-Hispanic/Latino; 3 American Indian or Alaska Native, non-Hispanic/Latino; 4 Asian, non-Hispanic/Latino; 8 Hispanic/Latino; 3 Two or more races, non-Hispanic/Latino), 2 international. Average age 32. In 2013, 130 master's awarded. *Degree requirements:* For master's, comprehensive exam, thesis optional, action research project. *Entrance requirements:* Additional exam requirements/recommendations for international students: Required—TOEFL (minimum score 550 paper-based; 79 iBT), IELTS (minimum score 6.5). *Application deadline:* For fall admission, 3/1 priority date for domestic students, 5/1 priority date for international students; for spring admission, 10/1 priority date for domestic and international students. Applications are processed on a rolling basis. Application fee: $25 ($75 for international students). Electronic applications accepted. *Expenses:* Tuition, state resident: full-time $5976; part-time $249 per credit hour. Tuition, nonresident: full-time $11,952; part-time $498 per credit hour. *Required fees:* $411 per semester. Tuition and fees vary according to course load. *Financial support:* In 2013–14, research assistantships with full tuition reimbursements (averaging $4,800 per year), teaching assistantships with full tuition reimbursements (averaging $4,800 per year) were awarded; career-related internships or fieldwork, Federal Work-Study, scholarships/grants, health care benefits, and unspecified assistantships also available. Support available to part-time students. Financial award application deadline: 4/15; financial award applicants required to submit FAFSA. *Unit head:* Dr. Sherry Field, Dean, 479-968-0418, E-mail: sfield@atu.edu. *Application contact:* Dr. Mary B. Gunter, Dean of Graduate College, 479-968-0398, Fax: 479-964-0542, E-mail: gradcollege@atu.edu.
Website: http://www.atu.edu/education/.

Auburn University, Graduate School, College of Education, Department of Curriculum and Teaching, Auburn University, AL 36849. Offers business education (M Ed, MS, PhD); early childhood education (M Ed, MS, PhD, Ed S); elementary education (M Ed, MS, PhD, Ed S); foreign languages (M Ed, MS); music education (M Ed, MS, PhD, Ed S); postsecondary education (PhD); reading education (PhD, Ed S); secondary education (M Ed, MS, PhD, Ed S), including English language arts, mathematics, science, social studies. *Accreditation:* NASM (one or more programs are accredited); NCATE. Part-time programs available. *Faculty:* 29 full-time (21 women), 4 part-time/adjunct (all women). *Students:* 61 full-time (40 women), 153 part-time (108 women); includes 37 minority (32 Black or African American, non-Hispanic/Latino; 2 Asian, non-Hispanic/Latino; 3 Hispanic/Latino), 1 international. Average age 34. 150 applicants, 59% accepted, 74 enrolled. In 2013, 70 master's, 6 doctorates, 26 other advanced degrees awarded. *Degree requirements:* For master's, thesis (for some programs); for doctorate, thesis/dissertation; for Ed S, field project. *Entrance requirements:* For master's, doctorate, and Ed S, GRE General Test. *Application deadline:* For fall admission, 7/7 for domestic students; for spring admission, 11/24 for domestic students. Applications are processed on a rolling basis. Application fee: $50 ($60 for international students). Electronic applications accepted. *Expenses:* Tuition, state resident: full-time $8262; part-time $459 per credit hour. Tuition, nonresident: full-time $24,786; part-time $1377 per credit hour. Tuition and fees vary according to degree level and program. *Financial support:* Fellowships, teaching assistantships, career-related internships or fieldwork, and Federal Work-Study available. Support available to part-time students. Financial award application deadline: 3/15; financial award applicants required to submit FAFSA. *Faculty research:* Emerging literacy, reading attitudes, music for at-risk youth, portfolio assessment. *Unit head:* Dr. Kimberly Walls, Head, 334-844-4434. *Application contact:* Dr. George Flowers, Dean of the Graduate School, 334-844-2125.
Website: http://education.auburn.edu/academic_departments/curr/.

Auburn University at Montgomery, School of Education, Department of Early Childhood, Elementary, and Reading Education, Montgomery, AL 36124-4023. Offers collaborative teacher (Ed S); early childhood education (Ed S); elementary education (M Ed, Ed S). *Accreditation:* NCATE. Part-time and evening/weekend programs available. *Faculty:* 4 full-time (all women). *Students:* 27 full-time (26 women), 67 part-time (64 women); includes 32 minority (29 Black or African American, non-Hispanic/Latino; 2 Asian, non-Hispanic/Latino; 1 Hispanic/Latino). Average age 34. In 2013, 44 master's, 11 Ed Ss awarded. *Degree requirements:* For master's and Ed S, comprehensive exam. *Entrance requirements:* For master's, GRE General Test or MAT, certification, BS in teaching; for Ed S, GRE General Test or MAT, certification. *Application deadline:* Applications are processed on a rolling basis. Electronic applications accepted. *Expenses:* Tuition, state resident: full-time $5994; part-time $333 per credit hour. Tuition, nonresident: full-time $17,982; part-time $999 per credit hour. *Financial support:* Teaching assistantships, career-related internships or fieldwork, and scholarships/grants available. Support available to part-time students. Financial award application deadline: 3/1; financial award applicants required to submit FAFSA. *Unit head:* Dr. Lynne Mills, Head, 334-244-3283, Fax: 334-244-3835, E-mail: lmills@mail.aum.edu. *Application contact:* Dr. Rhonda Morton, Associate Dean/Graduate Coordinator, 334-244-3287, Fax: 334-244-3978, E-mail: rmorton@aum.edu.
Website: http://www.aum.edu/Education.

Aurora University, College of Education, Aurora, IL 60506-4892. Offers curriculum and instruction (MA, Ed D); early childhood and special education (MA); education (MAT), including elementary certification; education and administration (Ed D); educational leadership (MEL); educational technology (MATL); reading instruction (MA); special education (MA). *Accreditation:* NCATE. Part-time and evening/weekend programs available. *Degree requirements:* For doctorate, comprehensive exam, thesis/dissertation. *Entrance requirements:* For master's, 2 years of teaching experience, valid teaching certificate. Additional exam requirements/recommendations for international students: Required—TOEFL (minimum score 550 paper-based). Electronic applications accepted. *Expenses:* Contact institution.

Austin Peay State University, College of Graduate Studies, College of Education, Department of Educational Specialties, Clarksville, TN 37044. Offers administration and supervision (Ed S); curriculum and instruction (MA Ed); education leadership (MA Ed); elementary education (Ed S); secondary education (Ed S); special education (MA Ed). Part-time and evening/weekend programs available. Postbaccalaureate distance learning degree programs offered. *Faculty:* 8 full-time (5 women), 4 part-time/adjunct (3 women). *Students:* 6 full-time (5 women), 87 part-time (73 women); includes 10 minority (5 Black or African American, non-Hispanic/Latino; 1 American Indian or Alaska Native, non-Hispanic/Latino; 1 Asian, non-Hispanic/Latino; 1 Hispanic/Latino; 2 Two or more races, non-Hispanic/Latino). Average age 35. 11 applicants, 82% accepted, 6 enrolled. In 2013, 37 master's, 6 Ed Ss awarded. *Degree requirements:* For master's, comprehensive exam, thesis optional. *Entrance requirements:* For master's, GRE General Test, 3 letters of recommendation, minimum undergraduate GPA of 2.75. Additional exam requirements/recommendations for international students: Required—TOEFL (minimum score 500 paper-based). *Application deadline:* For fall admission, 8/5 priority date for domestic students. Applications are processed on a rolling basis. Application fee: $25. Electronic applications accepted. *Expenses:* Tuition, state resident: full-time $7500; part-time $375 per credit hour. Tuition, nonresident: full-time $20,800; part-time $1040 per credit hour. *Required fees:* $1284; $64.20 per credit hour. *Financial support:* Career-related internships or fieldwork, Federal Work-Study, institutionally sponsored loans, scholarships/grants, and unspecified assistantships available. Support available to part-time students. Financial award application deadline: 3/1; financial award applicants required to submit FAFSA. *Unit head:* Dr. Moniqueka Gold, Chair, 931-221-7696, Fax: 931-221-1292, E-mail: goldm@apsu.edu. *Application contact:* June D. Lee, Graduate Coordinator, 800-859-4723, Fax: 931-221-7641, E-mail: gradadmissions@apsu.edu.

Austin Peay State University, College of Graduate Studies, College of Education, Department of Teaching and Learning, Clarksville, TN 37044. Offers elementary education K-6 (MAT); reading (MA Ed); secondary education 7-12 (MAT); special education K-12 (MAT). Part-time and evening/weekend programs available. Postbaccalaureate distance learning degree programs offered. *Faculty:* 7 full-time (4 women), 5 part-time/adjunct (all women). *Students:* 70 full-time (59 women), 77 part-time (55 women); includes 23 minority (10 Black or African American, non-Hispanic/Latino; 2 Asian, non-Hispanic/Latino; 5 Hispanic/Latino; 6 Two or more races, non-Hispanic/Latino). Average age 33. 50 applicants, 90% accepted, 37 enrolled. In 2013, 60 master's awarded. *Degree requirements:* For master's, comprehensive exam, thesis optional. *Entrance requirements:* For master's, GRE General Test, 3 letters of recommendation, minimum undergraduate GPA of 2.75. Additional exam requirements/recommendations for international students: Required—TOEFL (minimum score 500 paper-based). *Application deadline:* For fall admission, 8/5 priority date for domestic students. Applications are processed on a rolling basis. Application fee: $25. Electronic applications accepted. *Expenses:* Tuition, state resident: full-time $7500; part-time $375 per credit hour. Tuition, nonresident: full-time $20,800; part-time $1040 per credit hour. *Required fees:* $1284; $64.20 per credit hour. *Financial support:* Career-related internships or fieldwork, Federal Work-Study, institutionally sponsored loans, scholarships/grants, and unspecified assistantships available. Support available to part-time students. Financial award application deadline: 3/1; financial award applicants required to submit FAFSA. *Unit head:* Dr. Rebecca McMahan, Chair, 931-221-7513, Fax: 931-221-1292, E-mail: mcmahanb@apsu.edu. *Application contact:* June D. Lee, Graduate Coordinator, 800-859-4723, Fax: 931-221-7641, E-mail: gradadmissions@apsu.edu.

Ball State University, Graduate School, Teachers College, Department of Elementary Education, Muncie, IN 47306-1099. Offers MAE, Ed D, PhD. *Accreditation:* NCATE. *Faculty:* 10 full-time (7 women), 1 (woman) part-time/adjunct. *Students:* 13 full-time (all women), 143 part-time (135 women); includes 5 minority (1 Black or African American, non-Hispanic/Latino; 1 American Indian or Alaska Native, non-Hispanic/Latino; 3 Hispanic/Latino). Average age 25. 43 applicants, 65% accepted, 21 enrolled. In 2013, 234 master's, 4 doctorates awarded. *Degree requirements:* For doctorate, thesis/dissertation. *Entrance requirements:* For doctorate, GRE General Test, interview, minimum graduate GPA of 3.2. Application fee: $50. *Financial support:* In 2013–14, 6 students received support, including 12 teaching assistantships with full tuition reimbursements available (averaging $10,468 per year); research assistantships with full tuition reimbursements available also available. Financial award application deadline: 3/1. *Unit head:* Dr. John Jacobson, Dean of Elementary Education, 765-285-5251, E-mail: jejacobson@bsu.edu. *Application contact:* Harold Roberts, Assistant to Department Chair, 765-285-9046, E-mail: hlroberts@bsu.edu.
Website: http://www.bsu.edu/elementaryeducation/.

Bank Street College of Education, Graduate School, Program in Elementary/Childhood Education, New York, NY 10025. Offers early childhood and elementary/childhood education (MS Ed); elementary/childhood education (MS Ed). *Degree requirements:* For master's, thesis. *Entrance requirements:* For master's, interview, essays. Additional exam requirements/recommendations for international students: Required—TOEFL (minimum score 600 paper-based; 100 iBT), IELTS (minimum score 7). Electronic applications accepted. *Faculty research:* Social studies in the elementary grades, urban education, experiential learning, child-centered classrooms.

Barry University, School of Education, Program in Curriculum and Instruction, Miami Shores, FL 33161-6695. Offers accomplished teacher (Ed S); culture, language and literacy (TESOL) (PhD); curriculum evaluation and research (PhD); early childhood (Ed S); early childhood education (PhD); elementary (Ed S); elementary education (PhD); ESOL (Ed S); gifted (Ed S); Montessori (Ed S); PKP/elementary (Ed S); reading (Ed S); reading, language and cognition (PhD). *Entrance requirements:* For doctorate, GRE, minimum GPA of 3.25.

Barry University, School of Education, Program in Elementary Education, Miami Shores, FL 33161-6695. Offers elementary education (MS); elementary education/ESOL (MS). Part-time and evening/weekend programs available. *Degree requirements:* For master's, comprehensive exam, practicum. *Entrance requirements:* For master's, GRE General Test or MAT, minimum GPA of 3.0. Electronic applications accepted.

Barton College, Program in Elementary Education, Wilson, NC 27893-7000. Offers M Ed. *Entrance requirements:* For master's, MAT or GRE taken within last five years, bachelor's degree from accredited college or university, minimum GPA of 3.0 for undergraduate work (recommended), official transcript, one year of teaching experience, copy of recognized teaching license in elementary education, personal statement, recommendation form from current employer or administrator, interview. Additional exam requirements/recommendations for international students: Required—TOEFL (minimum score 550 paper-based). Electronic applications accepted.

Bayamón Central University, Graduate Programs, Program in Education, Bayamón, PR 00960-1725. Offers administration and supervision (MA Ed); commercial education (MA Ed); elementary education (K–3) (MA Ed); family counseling (Graduate Certificate); guidance and counseling (MA Ed); pre-elementary teacher (MA Ed); rehabilitation counseling (MA Ed); special education (MA Ed), including attention deficit disorder, education of the autistic, learning disabilities. Part-time and evening/weekend programs available. *Degree requirements:* For master's, comprehensive exam. *Entrance requirements:* For master's, EXADEP, bachelor's degree in education or related field.

Belhaven University, School of Education, Jackson, MS 39202-1789. Offers educational technology (M Ed); elementary education (M Ed, MAT); reading literacy (M Ed); secondary education (M Ed, MAT). Part-time and evening/weekend programs available. Postbaccalaureate distance learning degree programs offered (no on-campus study). *Faculty:* 7 full-time (6 women), 15 part-time/adjunct (10 women). *Students:* 1 full-time (0 women), 406 part-time (311 women); includes 254 minority (250 Black or African American, non-Hispanic/Latino; 2 Hispanic/Latino; 2 Two or more races, non-Hispanic/Latino). Average age 36. 273 applicants, 67% accepted, 162 enrolled. In 2013, 24 master's awarded. *Degree requirements:* For master's, comprehensive exam, portfolio. *Entrance requirements:* For master's, PRAXIS I and II, minimum GPA of 2.8. *Application deadline:* Applications are processed on a rolling basis. Application fee: $25. Electronic applications accepted. *Financial support:* Federal Work-Study, scholarships/grants, tuition waivers (full), and unspecified assistantships available. Support available to part-time students. Financial award applicants required to submit FAFSA. *Unit head:* Dr. David Hand, Dean, 601-965-7020, E-mail: dhand@belhaven.edu. *Application contact:* Amanda Slaughter, Assistant Vice President for Adult and Graduate Enrollment and Student Services, 601-968-8727, Fax: 601-968-5953, E-mail: gradadmission@belhaven.edu.
Website: http://graduateed.belhaven.edu.

Bellarmine University, Annsley Frazier Thornton School of Education, Louisville, KY 40205-0671. Offers education and social change (PhD); elementary education (MA Ed, MAT); learning and behavior disorders (MA Ed, MAT); middle grades education (MA Ed, MAT); principalship (Ed S); reading and writing (MA Ed); secondary education (MAT); teacher leadership (MA Ed). *Accreditation:* NCATE. Part-time and evening/weekend programs available. *Faculty:* 13 full-time (7 women), 14 part-time/adjunct (9 women). *Students:* 60 full-time (47 women), 191 part-time (140 women); includes 35 minority (22 Black or African American, non-Hispanic/Latino; 1 American Indian or Alaska Native, non-Hispanic/Latino; 3 Asian, non-Hispanic/Latino; 5 Hispanic/Latino; 4 Two or more races, non-Hispanic/Latino). Average age 33. In 2013, 108 master's awarded. *Degree requirements:* For master's, comprehensive exam, thesis (for some programs); for doctorate, comprehensive exam, thesis/dissertation. *Entrance requirements:* For master's, GRE, baccalaureate degree from accredited institution; minimum overall GPA of 2.75, 3.0 in major; letters of recommendation; valid Kentucky provisional or professional certificate; for doctorate, GRE, minimum GPA of 3.5 in all graduate coursework; baccalaureate and master's degrees in education (MA, MS) or fields directly relevant to education; three letters of recommendation; two essays (no more than 1000 words each); interview. Additional exam requirements/recommendations for international students: Required—TOEFL (minimum score 550 paper-based; 80 iBT). *Application deadline:* Applications are processed on a rolling basis. Application fee: $25. *Expenses:* Contact institution. *Financial support:* Scholarships/grants available. Financial award applicants required to submit FAFSA. *Faculty research:* Literacy, service-learning, dispositions, educational technology, special education. *Unit head:* Dr. Robert Cooter, Dean, 502-272-8191, Fax: 502-272-8189, E-mail: rcooter@bellarmine.edu. *Application contact:* Theresa Klapheke, Administrative Director of Graduate Programs, 502-272-8271, Fax: 502-272-8002, E-mail: tklapheke@bellarmine.edu.
Website: http://www.bellarmine.edu/education/graduate.

Benedictine University, Graduate Programs, Program in Education, Lisle, IL 60532-0900. Offers curriculum and instruction and collaborative teaching (M Ed); elementary education (MA Ed); leadership and administration (M Ed); reading and literacy (M Ed); secondary education (MA Ed); special education (MA Ed). Part-time and evening/weekend programs available. *Students:* 6 full-time (all women), 124 part-time (106 women); includes 14 minority (8 Black or African American, non-Hispanic/Latino; 1 American Indian or Alaska Native, non-Hispanic/Latino; 2 Asian, non-Hispanic/Latino; 3 Hispanic/Latino). 21 applicants, 62% accepted, 8 enrolled. In 2013, 120 master's awarded. *Degree requirements:* For master's, comprehensive exam, thesis (for some programs). *Entrance requirements:* For master's, GRE or MAT. Additional exam requirements/recommendations for international students: Required—TOEFL (minimum score 550 paper-based). *Application deadline:* For fall admission, 9/1 for domestic students; for winter admission, 12/1 for domestic students; for spring admission, 2/15 for domestic students. Applications are processed on a rolling basis. Application fee: $40. Electronic applications accepted. *Expenses:* Contact institution. *Financial support:* Career-related internships or fieldwork and health care benefits available. Support available to part-time students. *Unit head:* MeShelda Jackson, Director, 630-829-6282, E-mail: mjackson@ben.edu. *Application contact:* Kari Gibbons, Associate Vice President, Enrollment Center, 630-829-6200, Fax: 630-829-6584, E-mail: kgibbons@ben.edu.

Benedictine University at Springfield, Program in Elementary Education, Springfield, IL 62702. Offers MA Ed. *Degree requirements:* For master's, student teaching. *Entrance requirements:* For master's, official transcript, minimum cumulative GPA of 3.0, 3 letters of recommendation, statement of goals.

Bethel University, Graduate School, St. Paul, MN 55112-6999. Offers autism spectrum disorders (Certificate); business administration (MBA); communication (MA); counseling psychology (MA); educational leadership (Ed D); gerontology (MA); international baccalaureate education (Certificate); K-12 education (MA); literacy education (MA, Certificate); nurse educator (Certificate); nurse leader (Certificate); nurse-midwifery (MS); nursing (MS); physician assistant (MS); postsecondary teaching (Certificate); special education (MA); strategic leadership (MA); teaching (MA). Part-time and evening/weekend programs available. Postbaccalaureate distance learning degree programs offered (no on-campus study). *Faculty:* 13 full-time (7 women), 89 part-time/adjunct (43 women). *Students:* 692 full-time (457 women), 573 part-time (371 women); includes 170 minority (86 Black or African American, non-Hispanic/Latino; 1 American Indian or Alaska Native, non-Hispanic/Latino; 49 Asian, non-Hispanic/Latino; 20 Hispanic/Latino; 1 Native Hawaiian or other Pacific Islander, non-Hispanic/Latino; 13 Two or more races, non-Hispanic/Latino), 21 international. Average age 37. In 2013, 166 master's, 9 doctorates, 11 other advanced degrees awarded. *Degree requirements:* For master's, comprehensive exam (for some programs), thesis (for some programs); for doctorate, comprehensive exam, thesis/dissertation. *Entrance requirements:* Additional exam requirements/recommendations for international students: Required—TOEFL (minimum score 550 paper-based; 80 iBT). *Application deadline:* Applications are processed on a rolling basis. Electronic applications accepted. Tuition and fees vary according to course load, degree level and program. *Financial support:* Teaching assistantships, career-related internships or fieldwork, and scholarships/grants available. Support available to part-time students. Financial award applicants required to submit FAFSA. *Unit head:* Dick Crombie, Vice-President/Dean, 651-635-8000, Fax:

651-635-8004, E-mail: gs@bethel.edu. *Application contact:* Director of Admissions, 651-635-8000, Fax: 651-635-8004, E-mail: gs@bethel.edu.
Website: http://gs.bethel.edu/.

Bloomsburg University of Pennsylvania, School of Graduate Studies, College of Education, Department of Educational Studies and Secondary Education, Program in School Counseling and Student Affairs, Bloomsburg, PA 17815-1301. Offers college student affairs (M Ed); elementary school (M Ed); secondary school (M Ed). *Faculty:* 5 full-time (3 women), 5 part-time/adjunct (2 women). *Students:* 8 full-time (6 women), 59 part-time (40 women); includes 16 minority (10 Black or African American, non-Hispanic/Latino; 4 Hispanic/Latino; 2 Two or more races, non-Hispanic/Latino), 1 international. Average age 25. 48 applicants, 79% accepted, 30 enrolled. *Degree requirements:* For master's, practicum. *Entrance requirements:* For master's, 3 letters of recommendation, resume, minimum QPA of 3.0, personal statement, interview. Additional exam requirements/recommendations for international students: Required—TOEFL. Application fee: $35 ($60 for international students). Electronic applications accepted. *Expenses:* Tuition, state resident: full-time $7956; part-time $442 per credit. Tuition, nonresident: full-time $11,934; part-time $663 per credit. *Required fees:* $95.50 per credit. $55 per semester. Tuition and fees vary according to course load. *Unit head:* Dr. Tegan Kotarski, College of Education Graduate Coordinator, 570-389-3883, Fax: 570-389-5049, E-mail: tkotarsk@bloomu.edu. *Application contact:* Jennifer Richard, Administrative Assistant, 570-389-4015, Fax: 570-389-3054, E-mail: jrichard@bloomu.edu.
Website: http://www.bloomu.edu/gradschool/counseling-student-affairs.

Blue Mountain College, Program in Elementary Education, Blue Mountain, MS 38610. Offers M Ed. Part-time and evening/weekend programs available. *Faculty:* 3 full-time (all women). *Students:* 6 full-time (all women), 2 part-time (both women); includes 1 minority (Black or African American, non-Hispanic/Latino). 4 applicants, 100% accepted, 4 enrolled. In 2013, 3 master's awarded. *Degree requirements:* For master's, comprehensive exam. *Entrance requirements:* For master's, PRAXIS, GRE or MAT, official transcripts; bachelor's degree in a field of education from accredited university or college; teaching certificate; three recommendations. Additional exam requirements/recommendations for international students: Required—TOEFL (minimum score 550 paper-based). *Application deadline:* For fall admission, 7/1 priority date for domestic students; for spring admission, 1/1 priority date for domestic students; for summer admission, 5/1 priority date for domestic students. Applications are processed on a rolling basis. Application fee: $25. Electronic applications accepted. *Expenses: Tuition:* Full-time $8550; part-time $285 per hour. *Required fees:* $1160; $335 per term. *Financial support:* Scholarships/grants available. Financial award application deadline: 6/30; financial award applicants required to submit FAFSA. *Unit head:* Dr. Jenetta R. Waddell, Dean of Graduate Studies, 662-685-4771 Ext. 118, Fax: 662-815-2919, E-mail: jwaddell@bmc.edu. *Application contact:* Jean Harrington, Administrative Assistant, 662-685-4771 Ext. 238, Fax: 662-815-2919, E-mail: jharrington@bmc.edu.
Website: http://www.bmc.edu/master_of_education.asp.

Bob Jones University, Graduate Programs, Greenville, SC 29614. Offers accountancy (MS); Bible (MA); Bible translation (MA); Biblical studies (Certificate); broadcast management (MS); business administration (MBA); church history (MA, PhD); church ministries (MA); church music (MM); cinema and video production (MA); counseling (MS); curriculum and instruction (Ed D); divinity (M Div); dramatic production (MA); educational leadership (MS, Ed D, Ed S); elementary education (M Ed, MAT); English (M Ed, MA, MAT); fine arts (MA); graphic design (MA); history (M Ed, MA); illustration (MA); interpretative speech (MA); mathematics (M Ed, MAT); medical missions (Certificate); ministry (MM, D Min); multi-categorical special education (M Ed, MAT); music (M Ed); New Testament interpretation (PhD); Old Testament interpretation (PhD); orchestral instrument performance (MM); organ performance (MM); pastoral studies (MA); personnel services (MS, Ed S); piano pedagogy (MM); piano performance (MM); platform arts (MA); radio and television broadcasting (MS); rhetoric and public address (MA); secondary education (M Ed); studio art (MA); teaching Bible (MA); theology (MA, PhD); voice performance (MM); youth ministries (MA); M Div/MM.

Boston College, Lynch Graduate School of Education, Program in Elementary Education, Chestnut Hill, MA 02467-3800. Offers M Ed, MAT. *Accreditation:* Teacher Education Accreditation Council. Part-time and evening/weekend programs available. *Students:* 13 full-time (9 women), 4 part-time (all women). 81 applicants, 70% accepted, 17 enrolled. In 2013, 29 master's awarded. *Degree requirements:* For master's, comprehensive exam. *Entrance requirements:* For master's, GRE General Test or MAT. Additional exam requirements/recommendations for international students: Required—TOEFL (minimum score 100 iBT). *Application deadline:* For fall admission, 12/1 priority date for domestic and international students; for spring admission, 11/1 for domestic and international students. Application fee: $65. Electronic applications accepted. *Financial support:* Fellowships with full and partial tuition reimbursements, research assistantships with full and partial tuition reimbursements, teaching assistantships with full and partial tuition reimbursements, career-related internships or fieldwork, Federal Work-Study, scholarships/grants, traineeships, health care benefits, tuition waivers (full and partial), and unspecified assistantships available. Support available to part-time students. Financial award applicants required to submit FAFSA. *Faculty research:* Cross-cultural studies in teaching, learning or supervision, curriculum design, teacher research. *Unit head:* Dr. Alec Peck, Chairperson, 617-552-4214, Fax: 617-552-0398. *Application contact:* Domenic Lomanno, Director, Graduate Admission and Financial Aid, 617-552-4214, Fax: 617-552-0398, E-mail: lomanno@bc.edu.

Bowie State University, Graduate Programs, Program in Elementary Education, Bowie, MD 20715-9465. Offers M Ed. *Accreditation:* NCATE. Part-time and evening/weekend programs available. *Degree requirements:* For master's, comprehensive exam, thesis optional, research paper. *Entrance requirements:* For master's, minimum GPA of 2.5, teaching certificate, teaching experience. Electronic applications accepted. *Expenses:* Tuition, state resident: full-time $8665. Tuition, nonresident: full-time $16,007. *Required fees:* $1927.

Brandeis University, Graduate School of Arts and Sciences, Teaching Program, Waltham, MA 02454-9110. Offers Jewish day school (MAT); public elementary education (MAT); secondary education (MAT), including Bible, biology, chemistry, Chinese, English, history, math, physics. *Degree requirements:* For master's, internship, research project. *Entrance requirements:* For master's, GRE General Test or MAT, official transcript(s), 3 letters of recommendation, resume, statement of purpose. Additional exam requirements/recommendations for international students: Required—TOEFL (minimum score 600 paper-based; 100 iBT), PTE (minimum score 68); Recommended—IELTS (minimum score 7). Electronic applications accepted. *Expenses:* Contact institution. *Faculty research:* Teacher education, education, teaching, elementary education, secondary education, Jewish education, English, history, biology, chemistry, physics, math, Chinese, Bible/Tanakh.

Bridgewater State University, School of Graduate Studies, School of Education and Allied Studies, Department of Elementary and Early Childhood Education, Program in Elementary Education, Bridgewater, MA 02325-0001. Offers M Ed. *Accreditation:* NCATE. Part-time and evening/weekend programs available. *Entrance requirements:* For master's, GRE General Test or Massachusetts Test for Educator Licensure.

Elementary Education

Brooklyn College of the City University of New York, Division of Graduate Studies, School of Education, Program in Childhood Education, Brooklyn, NY 11210-2889. Offers bilingual education (MS Ed); liberal arts (MS Ed); mathematics (MS Ed); science/ environmental education (MS Ed). Part-time and evening/weekend programs available. *Entrance requirements:* For master's, LAST, interview, previous course work in education, writing sample, resume, 2 letters of recommendation. Additional exam requirements/recommendations for international students: Required—TOEFL (minimum score 500 paper-based; 61 iBT). Electronic applications accepted. *Faculty research:* Emotional intelligence, multiculturalism, arts immersion, the Holocaust.

Brown University, Graduate School, Department of Education, Providence, RI 02912. Offers teaching (MAT), including elementary education, English, history/social studies, science, secondary education; urban education policy (AM). *Degree requirements:* For master's, student teaching, portfolio. *Entrance requirements:* For master's, GRE General Test, letters of recommendation, interview. Additional exam requirements/ recommendations for international students: Recommended—TOEFL.

Buffalo State College, State University of New York, The Graduate School, Faculty of Applied Science and Education, Department of Elementary Education and Reading, Program in Elementary Education, Buffalo, NY 14222-1095. Offers childhood education (grades 1-6) (MS Ed); early childhood and childhood curriculum and instruction (MS Ed); early childhood education (birth-grade 2) (MS Ed). *Accreditation:* NCATE. Part-time programs available. *Degree requirements:* For master's, thesis or project. *Entrance requirements:* For master's, minimum GPA of 2.5 in last 60 hours, New York teaching certificate. Additional exam requirements/recommendations for international students: Required—TOEFL (minimum score 550 paper-based).

California Lutheran University, Graduate Studies, Graduate School of Education, Thousand Oaks, CA 91360-2787. Offers counseling and guidance (MS), including college student personnel, counseling and guidance; educational leadership (MA, Ed D), including educational leadership (K-12) (Ed D), higher education leadership (Ed D); special education (MS); teacher leadership (M Ed); teaching (M Ed). *Accreditation:* NCATE. Part-time and evening/weekend programs available. *Faculty:* 18 full-time (14 women), 28 part-time/adjunct (20 women). *Students:* 327 full-time (260 women), 96 part-time (77 women); includes 150 minority (7 Black or African American, non-Hispanic/ Latino; 20 Asian, non-Hispanic/Latino; 112 Hispanic/Latino; 11 Two or more races, non-Hispanic/Latino), 1 international. Average age 33. 123 applicants, 85% accepted, 80 enrolled. In 2013, 117 master's, 9 doctorates awarded. *Entrance requirements:* For master's, GRE General Test, interview, minimum GPA of 3.0. *Application deadline:* For fall admission, 7/1 priority date for domestic students; for spring admission, 11/1 priority date for domestic students; for summer admission, 4/1 priority date for domestic students. Applications are processed on a rolling basis. Application fee: $50. *Unit head:* Dr. Robert Fraisse, Dean, 805-493-3421. *Application contact:* 805-493-3325, Fax: 805-493-3861, E-mail: clugrad@callutheran.edu.

California State University, Fullerton, Graduate Studies, College of Education, Department of Elementary and Bilingual Education, Fullerton, CA 92834-9480. Offers bilingual/bicultural education (MS); educational technology (MS); elementary curriculum and instruction (MS). *Accreditation:* NCATE. Part-time programs available. *Students:* 140 full-time (118 women), 97 part-time (89 women); includes 101 minority (3 Black or African American, non-Hispanic/Latino; 31 Asian, non-Hispanic/Latino; 61 Hispanic/ Latino; 6 Two or more races, non-Hispanic/Latino). Average age 30. 184 applicants, 68% accepted, 99 enrolled. In 2013, 102 master's awarded. *Degree requirements:* For master's, comprehensive exam, project or thesis. *Entrance requirements:* For master's, minimum GPA of 2.5, teaching certificate. Application fee: $55. *Financial support:* Career-related internships or fieldwork, Federal Work-Study, institutionally sponsored loans, and scholarships/grants available. Support available to part-time students. Financial award application deadline: 3/1; financial award applicants required to submit FAFSA. *Faculty research:* Teacher training and tracking, model for improvement of teaching. *Unit head:* Lisa Kirtman, Chair, 657-278-4731. *Application contact:* Admissions/Applications, 657-278-2371.

California State University, Long Beach, Graduate Studies, College of Education, Department of Teacher Education, Long Beach, CA 90840. Offers elementary education (MA); secondary education (MA). Part-time and evening/weekend programs available. *Degree requirements:* For master's, comprehensive exam or thesis. *Entrance requirements:* For master's, GRE General Test, minimum GPA of 2.75. Electronic applications accepted. *Faculty research:* Teacher stress and burnout, new teacher induction.

California State University, Los Angeles, Graduate Studies, Charter College of Education, Division of Curriculum and Instruction, Los Angeles, CA 90032-8530. Offers elementary teaching (MA); reading (MA); secondary teaching (MA). Part-time and evening/weekend programs available. *Faculty:* 4 full-time (2 women), 12 part-time/ adjunct (8 women). *Students:* 144 full-time (104 women), 119 part-time (91 women); includes 188 minority (13 Black or African American, non-Hispanic/Latino; 39 Asian, non-Hispanic/Latino; 130 Hispanic/Latino; 6 Two or more races, non-Hispanic/Latino), 12 international. Average age 33. 78 applicants, 73% accepted, 41 enrolled. In 2013, 87 master's awarded. *Entrance requirements:* For master's, minimum GPA of 2.75 in last 90 units of course work, teaching certificate. Additional exam requirements/ recommendations for international students: Required—TOEFL (minimum score 500 paper-based). *Application deadline:* For fall admission, 5/1 for domestic and international students. Applications are processed on a rolling basis. Application fee: $55. Electronic applications accepted. *Financial support:* Federal Work-Study available. Support available to part-time students. Financial award application deadline: 3/1. *Faculty research:* Media, language arts, mathematics, computers, drug-free schools. *Unit head:* Dr. Gay Yuen, Acting Chair, 323-343-4350, Fax: 323-343-5458, E-mail: gyuen@calstatela.edu. *Application contact:* Dr. Larry Fritz, Dean of Graduate Studies, 323-343-3827, Fax: 323-343-5653, E-mail: lfritz@calstatela.edu. Website: http://www.calstatela.edu/academic/ccoe/index_edci.htm.

California State University, Northridge, Graduate Studies, College of Education, Department of Elementary Education, Northridge, CA 91330. Offers curriculum and instruction (MA); language and literacy (MA); multilingual/multicultural education (MA); teaching and learning (MA). *Accreditation:* NCATE. Part-time and evening/weekend programs available. *Degree requirements:* For master's, comprehensive exam. *Entrance requirements:* For master's, GRE General Test or minimum GPA of 3.0. Additional exam requirements/recommendations for international students: Required—TOEFL.

California State University, Stanislaus, College of Education, Program in Education (MA), Turlock, CA 95382. Offers curriculum and instruction (MA), including education technology, elementary education, multilingual education, physical education, reading, secondary education, special education; school administration (MA); school counseling (MA). Part-time and evening/weekend programs available. *Degree requirements:* For master's, comprehensive exam (for some programs), thesis (for some programs). *Entrance requirements:* For master's, MAT, GRE, or CBEST (varies by concentration), 3 letters of recommendation, personal statement. Additional exam requirements/ recommendations for international students: Required—TOEFL (minimum score 550 paper-based). Electronic applications accepted. *Faculty research:* Children's

perspectives on historical events, method elementary schools dual language education, K-12 reading programs.

California University of Pennsylvania, School of Graduate Studies and Research, College of Education and Human Services, Department of Elementary Education, California, PA 15419-1394. Offers reading specialist (M Ed). *Accreditation:* NCATE. Part-time and evening/weekend programs available. *Degree requirements:* For master's, comprehensive exam, thesis optional. *Entrance requirements:* For master's, MAT, PRAXIS, minimum GPA of 3.0, state police clearances. Additional exam requirements/recommendations for international students: Required—TOEFL (minimum score 550 paper-based; 80 iBT). Electronic applications accepted. *Faculty research:* English as a second language, adult literacy, emerging literacy, diagnosis and remediation, phonemic awareness.

Cambridge College, School of Education, Cambridge, MA 02138-5304. Offers autism specialist (M Ed); autism/behavior analyst (M Ed); behavior analyst (Post-Master's Certificate); behavioral management (M Ed); early childhood teacher (M Ed); education specialist in curriculum and instruction (CAGS); educational leadership (Ed D); elementary teacher (M Ed); English as a second language (M Ed, Certificate); general science (M Ed); health education (Post-Master's Certificate); health/family and consumer sciences (M Ed); history (M Ed); individualized (M Ed); information technology literacy (M Ed); instructional technology (M Ed); interdisciplinary studies (M Ed); library teacher (M Ed); literacy education (M Ed); mathematics (M Ed); mathematics specialist (Certificate); middle school mathematics and science (M Ed); school administration (M Ed, CAGS); school guidance counselor (M Ed); school nurse education (M Ed); school social worker/school adjustment counselor (M Ed); special education administrator (CAGS); special education/moderate disabilities (M Ed); teaching skills and methodologies (M Ed). Part-time and evening/weekend programs available. Postbaccalaureate distance learning degree programs offered (minimal on-campus study). *Degree requirements:* For master's, thesis, internship/practicum (licensure program only); for doctorate, thesis/dissertation; for other advanced degree, thesis. *Entrance requirements:* For master's, interview, resume, documentation of licensure, 2 professional references; for doctorate, official transcripts, interview, resume, documentation of licensure (if any), written personal statement/essay, portfolio of scholarly and professional work, qualifying assessment, 2 professional references, health insurance, immunizations form; for other advanced degree, official transcripts, interview, resume, documentation of licensure (if any), written personal statement/ essay, 2 professional references, health insurance, immunizations form. Additional exam requirements/recommendations for international students: Required—TOEFL (minimum score 550 paper-based; 79 iBT), Michigan English Language Assessment Battery (minimum score 85); Recommended—IELTS (minimum score 6). Electronic applications accepted. *Expenses:* Contact institution. *Faculty research:* Adult education, accelerated learning, mathematics education, brain compatible learning, special education and law.

Campbell University, Graduate and Professional Programs, School of Education, Buies Creek, NC 27506. Offers administration (MSA); community counseling (MA); elementary education (M Ed); English education (M Ed); interdisciplinary studies (M Ed); mathematics education (M Ed); middle grades education (M Ed); physical education (M Ed); school counseling (M Ed); secondary education (M Ed); social science education (M Ed). *Accreditation:* NCATE. Part-time and evening/weekend programs available. *Degree requirements:* For master's, comprehensive exam. *Entrance requirements:* For master's, GRE General Test, minimum GPA of 2.7. *Faculty research:* Spiritual values and wellness issues in counseling, stress and professional burnout among counselors, thinking strategies, leadership, adaptive technology.

Canisius College, Graduate Division, School of Education and Human Services, Department of Graduate Education and Leadership, Buffalo, NY 14208-1098. Offers business and marketing education (MS Ed); college student personnel (MS Ed); deaf education (MS Ed); deaf/adolescent education, grades 7-12 (MS Ed); deaf/childhood education, grades 1-6 (MS Ed); differentiated instruction (MS Ed); education administration (MS); educational administration (MS Ed); educational technologies (Certificate); gifted education extension (Certificate); literacy (MS Ed); reading (Certificate); school building leadership (MS Ed, Certificate); school district leadership (Certificate); teacher leader (Certificate); TESOL (MS Ed). *Accreditation:* NCATE. Part-time and evening/weekend programs available. Postbaccalaureate distance learning degree programs offered (minimal on-campus study). *Faculty:* 6 full-time (5 women), 33 part-time/adjunct (20 women). *Students:* 134 full-time (106 women), 267 part-time (213 women); includes 36 minority (22 Black or African American, non-Hispanic/Latino; 1 American Indian or Alaska Native, non-Hispanic/Latino; 3 Asian, non-Hispanic/Latino; 8 Hispanic/Latino; 2 Two or more races, non-Hispanic/Latino), 2 international. Average age 30. 282 applicants, 80% accepted, 120 enrolled. In 2013, 178 master's awarded. *Entrance requirements:* For master's, GRE if cumulative GPA less than 2.7, transcripts, two letters of recommendation. Additional exam requirements/recommendations for international students: Required—TOEFL (minimum score 550 paper-based, 80 iBT), IELTS (minimum score 6.5), or CAEL (minimum score 70). *Application deadline:* Applications are processed on a rolling basis. Application fee: $25. Electronic applications accepted. Application fee is waived when completed online. *Expenses:* Tuition: Part-time $750 per credit hour. *Financial support:* Career-related internships or fieldwork, Federal Work-Study, scholarships/grants, tuition waivers (partial), and unspecified assistantships available. Support available to part-time students. Financial award application deadline: 4/30; financial award applicants required to submit FAFSA. *Faculty research:* Asperger's disease, autism, private higher education, reading strategies. *Unit head:* Dr. Rosemary K. Murray, Chair/Associate Professor of Graduate Education and Leadership, 716-888-3723, E-mail: murray1@canisius.edu. *Application contact:* Julie A. Zulewski, Director of Graduate Admissions, 716-888-2548, Fax: 716-888-3195, E-mail: zulewskj@canisius.edu. Website: http://www.canisius.edu/graduate/.

Capella University, School of Education, Doctoral Programs in Education, Minneapolis, MN 55402. Offers curriculum and instruction (PhD); educational leadership and management (Ed D); instructional design for online learning (PhD); K-12 studies in education (PhD); leadership for higher education (PhD); leadership in educational administration (PhD); postsecondary and adult education (PhD); professional studies in education (PhD); reading and literacy (Ed D); special education leadership (PhD); training and performance improvement (PhD).

Capella University, School of Education, Master's Programs in Education, Minneapolis, MN 55402. Offers adult education (MS); curriculum and instruction (MS); early childhood education (MS); enrollment management (MS); higher education leadership and management (MS); instructional design for online learning (MS); integrative studies (MS); K-12 studies in education (MS); leadership in educational administration (MS); reading and literacy (MS); special education teaching (MS).

Caribbean University, Graduate School, Bayamón, PR 00960-0493. Offers administration and supervision (MA Ed); criminal justice (MA); curriculum and instruction (MA Ed, PhD), including elementary education (MA Ed), English education (MA Ed), history education (MA Ed), mathematics education (MA Ed), primary education (MA Ed), science education (MA Ed), Spanish education (MA Ed); educational technology in instructional systems (MA Ed); gerontology (MSN); human resources (MBA);

museology, archiving and art history (MA Ed); neonatal pediatrics (MSN); physical education (MA Ed); special education (MA Ed). *Entrance requirements:* For master's, interview, minimum GPA of 2.5.

Carson-Newman University, Graduate Program in Education, Jefferson City, TN 37760. Offers curriculum and instruction (M Ed); educational leadership (M Ed); elementary education (MAT); school counseling (MS); secondary education (MAT); teaching English as a second language (MATESL). *Accreditation:* NCATE. Part-time and evening/weekend programs available. *Faculty:* 5 full-time (2 women), 10 part-time/adjunct (3 women). *Students:* 25 full-time (12 women), 100 part-time (70 women); includes 8 minority (4 Black or African American, non-Hispanic/Latino; 1 Asian, non-Hispanic/Latino; 1 Hispanic/Latino; 2 Two or more races, non-Hispanic/Latino), 1 international. Average age 32. In 2013, 34 master's awarded. *Degree requirements:* For master's, thesis or alternative. *Entrance requirements:* For master's, NTE, minimum GPA of 3.0 in major, 2.5 overall. *Application deadline:* For fall admission, 7/15 priority date for domestic students. Applications are processed on a rolling basis. Application fee: $25 ($50 for international students). *Expenses: Tuition:* Part-time $390 per credit hour. *Financial support:* Federal Work-Study and unspecified assistantships available. Financial award application deadline: 4/1; financial award applicants required to submit FAFSA. *Unit head:* Dr. Sharon Teets, Chair, 865-471-3461. *Application contact:* Graduate Admissions and Services Adviser, 865-471-3460, Fax: 865-471-3875.

Catawba College, Master's Program in Elementary Education, Salisbury, NC 28144-2488. Offers elementary education (M Ed). *Accreditation:* NCATE. Part-time and evening/weekend programs available. *Faculty:* 4 full-time (3 women). *Students:* 12 part-time (all women); includes 2 minority (1 Black or African American, non-Hispanic/Latino; 1 Hispanic/Latino). Average age 33. 1 applicant, 100% accepted, 1 enrolled. In 2013, 8 master's awarded. *Degree requirements:* For master's, portfolio. *Entrance requirements:* For master's, NTE, PRAXIS II, minimum undergraduate GPA of 3.0, valid teaching license, official transcripts, 3 references, essay, interview, practicing teacher. *Application deadline:* For fall admission, 7/1 for domestic students; for spring admission, 12/1 for domestic students. Applications are processed on a rolling basis. Application fee: $25. *Expenses: Tuition:* Part-time $170 per credit hour. *Financial support:* Scholarships/grants available. Financial award applicants required to submit FAFSA. *Unit head:* Dr. Rhonda L. Truitt, Chair, Department of Teacher Education, 704-637-4468, Fax: 704-637-4732, E-mail: rltruitt@catawba.edu. *Application contact:* Dr. Lou W. Kasias, Director, Graduate Program, 704-637-4462, Fax: 704-637-4732, E-mail: lakasias@catawba.edu.
Website: http://www.catawba.edu/academic/teachereducation/grad/.

Centenary College of Louisiana, Graduate Programs, Department of Education, Shreveport, LA 71104. Offers administration (M Ed); elementary education (MAT); secondary education (MAT); supervision of instruction (M Ed). Part-time and evening/weekend programs available. *Degree requirements:* For master's, comprehensive exam. *Entrance requirements:* For master's, GRE General Test (M Ed), PRAXIS I and PRAXIS II (MAT), teacher certification (M Ed), minimum GPA of 2.5. *Expenses:* Contact institution. *Faculty research:* Teachers as advocates for teachers, portfolio assessment, disabled readers.

Central Connecticut State University, School of Graduate Studies, School of Education and Professional Studies, Department of Teacher Education, Program in Elementary Education, New Britain, CT 06050-4010. Offers MS, Certificate. Part-time and evening/weekend programs available. *Students:* 10 full-time (8 women), 16 part-time (14 women); includes 4 minority (all Black or African American, non-Hispanic/Latino). Average age 29. 20 applicants, 60% accepted, 5 enrolled. In 2013, 10 master's awarded. *Degree requirements:* For master's, comprehensive exam, thesis or alternative; for Certificate, qualifying exam. *Entrance requirements:* For master's, minimum undergraduate GPA of 2.7, teacher certification. Additional exam requirements/recommendations for international students: Required—TOEFL (minimum score 550 paper-based; 79 iBT). *Application deadline:* For fall admission, 6/1 for domestic students, 5/1 for international students; for spring admission, 11/1 for domestic and international students. Applications are processed on a rolling basis. Application fee: $50. Electronic applications accepted. Part-time tuition and fees vary according to degree level. *Faculty research:* Elementary school curriculum, changing school populations, multicultural education, professional development. *Unit head:* Dr. Aram Ayalon, Chair, 860-832-2415, E-mail: casellar@ccsu.edu. *Application contact:* Patricia Gardner, Associate Director of Graduate Studies, 860-832-2350, Fax: 860-832-2362, E-mail: graduateadmissions@ccsu.edu.

Central Michigan University, College of Graduate Studies, College of Education and Human Services, Department of Teacher Education and Professional Development, Mount Pleasant, MI 48859. Offers educational technology (MA, Graduate Certificate); elementary education (MA), including classroom teaching, early childhood; reading and literacy K-12 (MA); secondary education (MA). Part-time and evening/weekend programs available. *Degree requirements:* For master's, thesis or alternative. Electronic applications accepted. *Faculty research:* Integrating literacy across the curriculum, science teaching and aesthetic learning in science, diversity education, educational technology, educational psychology and child development.

Chadron State College, School of Professional and Graduate Studies, Department of Education, Chadron, NE 69337. Offers business (MA Ed); community counseling (MA Ed); educational administration (MS Ed, Sp Ed); elementary education (MS Ed); history (MA Ed); language and literature (MA Ed); secondary administration (MS Ed); secondary education (MS Ed). *Accreditation:* NCATE. Part-time and evening/weekend programs available. Postbaccalaureate distance learning degree programs offered. *Degree requirements:* For master's, thesis optional. *Entrance requirements:* For master's, GRE General Test, GRE Writing Test, minimum GPA of 2.75 or 12 graduate hours at CSC with minimum GPA of 3.25. Additional exam requirements/recommendations for international students: Required—TOEFL. Electronic applications accepted. *Faculty research:* Rural education, technology, mental health.

Chaminade University of Honolulu, Graduate Services, Program in Education, Honolulu, HI 96816-1578. Offers child development (M Ed); early childhood education (M Ed); educational leadership (M Ed); elementary education (MAT); instructional leadership (M Ed); Montessori education (M Ed); secondary education (MAT), including English, math, science, social studies; special education (MAT). Part-time and evening/weekend programs available. Postbaccalaureate distance learning degree programs offered (minimal on-campus study). *Degree requirements:* For master's, thesis or alternative. *Entrance requirements:* For master's, PRAXIS (for MAT only), minimum GPA of 2.75, 3 letters of recommendation. Additional exam requirements/recommendations for international students: Required—TOEFL (minimum score 550 paper-based). Electronic applications accepted. *Faculty research:* Peace and curriculum education.

Chapman University, College of Educational Studies, Orange, CA 92866. Offers communication sciences and disorders (MS); counseling (MA), including school counseling (MA, Credential); education (PhD), including cultural and curricular studies, disability studies, leadership studies, school psychology (PhD, Credential); educational psychology (MA); leadership development (MA); pupil personnel services (Credential), including school counseling (MA, Credential), school psychology (PhD, Credential);

school psychology (Ed S); single subject (Credential); special education (MA, Credential), including mild/moderate (Credential), moderate/severe (Credential); speech language pathology (Credential); teaching (MA), including elementary education, secondary education. *Accreditation:* Teacher Education Accreditation Council. Part-time and evening/weekend programs available. *Faculty:* 29 full-time (18 women), 56 part-time/adjunct (38 women). *Students:* 251 full-time (208 women), 194 part-time (150 women); includes 185 minority (13 Black or African American, non-Hispanic/Latino; 61 Asian, non-Hispanic/Latino; 97 Hispanic/Latino; 1 Native Hawaiian or other Pacific Islander, non-Hispanic/Latino; 13 Two or more races, non-Hispanic/Latino), 7 international. Average age 29. 580 applicants, 42% accepted, 166 enrolled. In 2013, 140 master's, 10 doctorates awarded. *Entrance requirements:* Additional exam requirements/recommendations for international students: Required—TOEFL (minimum score 550 paper-based; 80 iBT). *Application deadline:* Applications are processed on a rolling basis. Application fee: $60. Electronic applications accepted. Tuition and fees vary according to program. *Financial support:* Fellowships and scholarships/grants available. Financial award application deadline: 6/30; financial award applicants required to submit FAFSA. *Unit head:* Dr. Don Cardinal, Dean, 714-997-6781, E-mail: cardinal@chapman.edu. *Application contact:* Admissions Coordinator, 714-997-6714.
Website: http://www.chapman.edu/CES/.

Charleston Southern University, School of Education, Charleston, SC 29423-8087. Offers elementary administration and supervision (M Ed); elementary education (M Ed). *Accreditation:* NCATE. Part-time and evening/weekend programs available. *Degree requirements:* For master's, thesis optional. *Entrance requirements:* For master's, GRE or MAT. Additional exam requirements/recommendations for international students: Required—TOEFL (minimum score 550 paper-based; 79 iBT). *Expenses:* Contact institution.

Chatham University, Program in Education, Pittsburgh, PA 15232-2826. Offers early childhood education (MAT); elementary education (MAT); environmental education (K-12) (MAT); secondary art (MAT); secondary biology education (MAT); secondary chemistry education (MAT); secondary English education (MAT); secondary math education (MAT); secondary physics education (MAT); secondary social studies education (MAT); special education (MAT). *Faculty:* 1 (woman) full-time, 5 part-time/adjunct (4 women). *Students:* 19 full-time (15 women), 4 part-time (all women); includes 2 minority (1 Black or African American, non-Hispanic/Latino; 1 Asian, non-Hispanic/Latino), 2 international. Average age 28. 22 applicants, 73% accepted, 6 enrolled. In 2013, 20 master's awarded. *Degree requirements:* For master's, thesis, teaching experience. *Entrance requirements:* For master's, minimum GPA of 3.0, sample of written work, recommendation letters. Additional exam requirements/recommendations for international students: Required—TOEFL (minimum score 600 paper-based; 100 iBT), IELTS (minimum score 7), TWE. *Application deadline:* For fall admission, 4/1 priority date for domestic and international students; for spring admission, 11/1 priority date for domestic students, 10/1 priority date for international students. Applications are processed on a rolling basis. Application fee: $45. Electronic applications accepted. Application fee is waived when completed online. *Expenses: Tuition:* Full-time $14,886; part-time $827 per credit hour. One-time fee: $396 full-time. *Financial support:* Career-related internships or fieldwork available. Financial award applicants required to submit FAFSA. *Faculty research:* Gifted education, environmental education, technology in education, writing as learning, class size and achievement. *Unit head:* Dr. Edward Donovan, Director of Education Programs, 412-365-2773, E-mail: edonovan@chatham.edu. *Application contact:* Katie Noel, Assistant Director of Graduate Admission, 412-365-2758, Fax: 412-365-1609, E-mail: gradadmissions@chatham.edu.
Website: http://www.chatham.edu/mat.

Chestnut Hill College, School of Graduate Studies, Department of Education, Program in Middle Education, Philadelphia, PA 19118-2693. Offers elementary/middle education (M Ed, CAS). Part-time and evening/weekend programs available. *Faculty:* 10 full-time (7 women), 48 part-time/adjunct (34 women). *Students:* 13 full-time (11 women), 96 part-time (78 women); includes 30 minority (22 Black or African American, non-Hispanic/Latino; 1 American Indian or Alaska Native, non-Hispanic/Latino; 1 Asian, non-Hispanic/Latino; 4 Hispanic/Latino; 2 Two or more races, non-Hispanic/Latino). Average age 31. 28 applicants, 100% accepted. In 2013, 51 master's, 11 CASs awarded. *Degree requirements:* For master's, thesis optional. *Entrance requirements:* For master's, PRAXIS I or proof of teaching certification, letters of recommendation, writing sample, 6 graduate credits with minimum B grade if undergraduate GPA less than 3.0. Additional exam requirements/recommendations for international students: Required—TOEFL (minimum score 500 paper-based), IELTS (mnimum score 6.0), or TWE (minimum score 22). *Application deadline:* For fall admission, 7/1 for domestic and international students; for spring admission, 11/1 for domestic and international students; for summer admission, 4/1 for domestic and international students. Applications are processed on a rolling basis. *Expenses:* Contact institution. *Financial support:* Unspecified assistantships available. *Faculty research:* Inclusive education, cultural issues in education. *Unit head:* Dr. Debra Chiaradonna, Chair, Department of Education, 215-248-7147, Fax: 215-248-7155, E-mail: chiaradonnad@chc.edu. *Application contact:* Jayne Mashett, Director of Admissions, School of Graduate Studies, 215-248-7020, Fax: 215-248-7161, E-mail: gradadmissions@chc.edu.
Website: http://www.chc.edu/Graduate/Programs/Masters/Education/.

Cheyney University of Pennsylvania, Graduate Programs, Program in Elementary Education, Cheyney, PA 19319. Offers M Ed. Part-time and evening/weekend programs available. *Degree requirements:* For master's, thesis. *Entrance requirements:* For master's, GRE General Test, MAT, minimum GPA of 2.75. Electronic applications accepted.

Chicago State University, School of Graduate and Professional Studies, College of Education, Department of Reading, Elementary Education, Library Information and Media Studies, Program in Elementary Education, Chicago, IL 60628. Offers MAT. *Accreditation:* NCATE. *Degree requirements:* For master's, comprehensive exam, thesis optional. *Entrance requirements:* For master's, minimum GPA of 3.0 in last 60 hours.

Christopher Newport University, Graduate Studies, Department of Teacher Preparation, Newport News, VA 23606-3072. Offers art (PK-12) (MAT); biology (6-12) (MAT); chemistry (6-12) (MAT); computer science (6-12) (MAT); elementary (PK-6) (MAT); English (6-12) (MAT); English as second language (PK-12) (MAT); French (PK-12) (MAT); history and social science (6-12) (MAT); mathematics (6-12) (MAT); music (PK-12) (MAT), including choral, instrumental; physics (6-12) (MAT); Spanish (PK-12) (MAT). Part-time programs available. *Faculty:* 15 full-time (7 women), 14 part-time/adjunct (13 women). *Students:* 74 full-time (64 women), 2 part-time (both women); includes 6 minority (4 Hispanic/Latino; 2 Two or more races, non-Hispanic/Latino). Average age 23. 90 applicants, 100% accepted, 67 enrolled. In 2013, 96 master's awarded. *Degree requirements:* For master's, comprehensive exam, thesis or alternative. *Entrance requirements:* For master's, PRAXIS I, minimum GPA of 3.0. Additional exam requirements/recommendations for international students: Required—TOEFL (minimum score 580 paper-based; 92 iBT). *Application deadline:* For fall admission, 4/1 for international students; for spring admission, 10/15 for domestic students, 10/1 for international students; for summer admission, 1/15 for domestic students, 3/1 for international students. Applications are processed on a rolling basis. Application fee: $50. Electronic applications accepted. *Expenses: Tuition, area resident:*

Part-time $498 per credit hour. Tuition, state resident: part-time $498 per credit hour. Tuition, nonresident: part-time $899 per credit hour. *Financial support:* In 2013–14, 3 students received support, including 3 research assistantships with full tuition reimbursements available (averaging $2,000 per year); career-related internships or fieldwork, Federal Work-Study, and unspecified assistantships also available. Financial award application deadline: 3/1; financial award applicants required to submit FAFSA. *Faculty research:* Early literacy development, instructional innovations, professional teaching standards, multicultural issues, aesthetic education. *Total annual research expenditures:* $24,000. *Unit head:* Dr. Marsha Sprague, Director, 757-594-7388, Fax: 757-594-7803, E-mail: msprague@cnu.edu. *Application contact:* Lyn Sawyer, Associate Director, Graduate Admissions, 757-594-7544, Fax: 757-594-7649, E-mail: gradstdy@cnu.edu.

The Citadel, The Military College of South Carolina, Citadel Graduate College, School of Education, Program in Guidance and Counseling, Charleston, SC 29409. Offers elementary/secondary school counseling (M Ed); student affairs and college counseling (M Ed). *Accreditation:* ACA; NCATE. Part-time and evening/weekend programs available. *Faculty:* 10 full-time (6 women), 8 part-time/adjunct (3 women). *Students:* 15 full-time (14 women), 40 part-time (35 women); includes 13 minority (12 Black or African American, non-Hispanic/Latino; 1 Two or more races, non-Hispanic/Latino). Average age 30. In 2013, 27 master's awarded. *Degree requirements:* For master's, comprehensive exam, practicum or internship. *Entrance requirements:* For master's, GRE (minimum score 290; 900 on old scoring system) or MAT (minimum score 396), minimum undergraduate GPA of 3.0, 3 letters of reference, group interview. Additional exam requirements/recommendations for international students: Required—TOEFL (minimum score 550 paper-based; 79 iBT). *Application deadline:* For fall admission, 6/1 for domestic students; for spring admission, 10/1 for domestic students. Application fee: $30. Electronic applications accepted. *Expenses: Tuition, area resident:* Part-time $525 per credit hour. Tuition, state resident: part-time $525 per credit hour. Tuition, nonresident: part-time $865 per credit hour. *Financial support:* Career-related internships or fieldwork, health care benefits, and unspecified assistantships available. Support available to part-time students. Financial award application deadline: 7/1; financial award applicants required to submit FAFSA. *Unit head:* Dr. George T. Williams, Director, 843-953-2205, Fax: 843-953-7258, E-mail: williamsg@citadel.edu. *Application contact:* Dr. Robert H. McNamara, Associate Provost, The Citadel Graduate College, 843-953-5089, Fax: 843-953-7630, E-mail: cgc@citadel.edu.
Website: http://www.citadel.edu/education/counselor.html.

City University of Seattle, Graduate Division, Albright School of Education, Bellevue, WA 98005. Offers administrator certification (Certificate); curriculum and instruction (M Ed); educational leadership (Ed D); elementary education (MIT); guidance and counseling (M Ed); higher education leadership (Ed D); leadership (M Ed); leadership and school counseling (M Ed); organizational leadership (Ed D); reading and literacy (M Ed); special education (MIT); superintendent certification (Certificate). Part-time and evening/weekend programs available. Postbaccalaureate distance learning degree programs offered (no on-campus study). *Degree requirements:* For master's, comprehensive exam (for some programs), thesis (for some programs); for doctorate, comprehensive exam, thesis/dissertation. *Entrance requirements:* Additional exam requirements/recommendations for international students: Required—TOEFL (minimum score 567 paper-based; 87 iBT); Recommended—IELTS. Electronic applications accepted. *Expenses:* Contact institution.

Clemson University, Graduate School, College of Health, Education, and Human Development, Eugene T. Moore School of Education, Program in Teaching and Learning, Clemson, SC 29634. Offers elementary education (M Ed); English education (M Ed); mathematics education (M Ed); science education (M Ed); social studies education (M Ed). *Students:* 6 full-time (5 women), 8 part-time (7 women), 3 international. Average age 28. 6 applicants, 100% accepted, 4 enrolled. In 2013, 9 master's awarded. *Entrance requirements:* For master's, GRE, baccalaureate degree from regionally-accredited institution, official transcripts, copy of valid teaching certificate, two letters of recommendation. *Financial support:* In 2013–14, 1 teaching assistantship (averaging $6,812 per year) was awarded. *Unit head:* Dr. Michael J. Padilla, Director/Associate Dean, 864-656-4444, Fax: 864-656-0311, E-mail: padilla@clemson.edu. *Application contact:* Dr. David Fleming, Graduate Programs Coordinator, 864-656-1881, Fax: 864-656-0311, E-mail: dflemin@clemson.edu.
Website: http://www.grad.clemson.edu/programs/Teaching-Learning/.

College of Charleston, Graduate School, School of Education, Health, and Human Performance, Department of Elementary and Early Childhood Education, Program in Elementary Education, Charleston, SC 29424-0001. Offers MAT. *Accreditation:* NCATE. Part-time and evening/weekend programs available. *Degree requirements:* For master's, thesis or alternative, written qualifying exam, student teaching experience. *Entrance requirements:* For master's, GRE, 2 letters of recommendation. Additional exam requirements/recommendations for international students: Required—TOEFL (minimum score 81 iBT). Electronic applications accepted.

The College of New Jersey, Graduate Studies, School of Education, Department of Elementary and Early Childhood Education, Program in Elementary Education, Ewing, NJ 08628. Offers M Ed, MAT. *Accreditation:* NCATE. Part-time programs available. *Degree requirements:* For master's, comprehensive exam. *Entrance requirements:* For master's, GRE General Test, minimum GPA of 3.0 in field or 2.75 overall. Additional exam requirements/recommendations for international students: Required—TOEFL. Electronic applications accepted.

The College of New Rochelle, Graduate School, Division of Education, Program in Elementary Education/Early Childhood Education, New Rochelle, NY 10805-2308. Offers MS Ed. Part-time programs available. *Degree requirements:* For master's, comprehensive exam (for some programs), thesis (for some programs), practicum. *Entrance requirements:* For master's, interview, minimum GPA of 3.0 in field, 2.7 overall. *Expenses: Tuition:* Part-time $894 per credit. *Required fees:* $300 per semester. One-time fee: $200. Tuition and fees vary according to course load.

College of St. Joseph, Graduate Programs, Division of Education, Program in Elementary Education, Rutland, VT 05701-3899. Offers M Ed. Part-time and evening/weekend programs available. *Degree requirements:* For master's, comprehensive exam. *Entrance requirements:* For master's, PRAXIS I (for initial licensure), official college transcripts; 2 letters of reference; minimum GPA of 3.0 (initial licensure) or 2.7 (nonlicensure); interview. Additional exam requirements/recommendations for international students: Required—TOEFL (minimum score 550 paper-based). Electronic applications accepted.

College of Staten Island of the City University of New York, Graduate Programs, School of Education, Program in Childhood Education, Staten Island, NY 10314-6600. Offers MS Ed. Part-time and evening/weekend programs available. *Faculty:* 5 full-time (4 women), 4 part-time/adjunct (2 women). *Students:* 9 full-time, 89 part-time. Average age 30. 49 applicants, 57% accepted, 14 enrolled. In 2013, 48 master's awarded. *Degree requirements:* For master's, 2 foreign languages, thesis, educational research project. *Entrance requirements:* For master's, relevant bachelor's degree, letters of recommendation, one- or two-page personal statement. Additional exam requirements/recommendations for international students: Required—TOEFL (minimum score 550 paper-based; 79 iBT), IELTS (minimum score 6.5). *Application deadline:* For fall admission, 4/25 for domestic and international students; for spring admission, 11/15 for domestic and international students. Applications are processed on a rolling basis. Application fee: $125. Electronic applications accepted. *Expenses:* Tuition, state resident: full-time $9240; part-time $385 per credit hour. Tuition, nonresident: full-time $17,040; part-time $710 per credit hour. *Required fees:* $428; $128 per term. *Financial support:* In 2013–14, 1 student received support. Career-related internships or fieldwork, Federal Work-Study, and scholarships/grants available. Support available to part-time students. Financial award applicants required to submit FAFSA. *Unit head:* Dr. Vivian Shulman, Graduate Program Coordinator, 718-982-4086, Fax: 718-982-3743, E-mail: vivian.shulman@csi.cuny.edu. *Application contact:* Sasha Spence, Assistant Director for Graduate Admissions, 718-982-2019, Fax: 718-982-2500, E-mail: sasha.spence@csi.cuny.edu.
Website: http://csivc.csi.cuny.edu/education/files.

The College of William and Mary, School of Education, Program in Curriculum and Instruction, Williamsburg, VA 23187-8795. Offers elementary education (MA Ed); gifted education (MA Ed); literacy leadership (MA Ed); math specialist (MA Ed); secondary education (MA Ed), including English education, mathematics education, modern foreign languages education, science education, social studies education; special education (MA Ed), including collaborating master educator, general curriculum. *Accreditation:* NCATE. Part-time programs available. *Faculty:* 15 full-time (10 women), 44 part-time/adjunct (38 women). *Students:* 66 full-time (55 women), 27 part-time (26 women); includes 17 minority (4 Black or African American, non-Hispanic/Latino; 1 American Indian or Alaska Native, non-Hispanic/Latino; 3 Asian, non-Hispanic/Latino; 5 Hispanic/Latino; 4 Two or more races, non-Hispanic/Latino). Average age 28. 179 applicants, 72% accepted, 92 enrolled. In 2013, 76 master's awarded. *Degree requirements:* For master's, project. *Entrance requirements:* For master's, GRE or MAT, minimum GPA of 2.5. Additional exam requirements/recommendations for international students: Required—TOEFL, IELTS. *Application deadline:* For fall admission, 1/15 for domestic and international students; for spring admission, 10/1 for domestic and international students. Application fee: $50. Electronic applications accepted. *Expenses:* Tuition, state resident: full-time $7120; part-time $405 per credit hour. Tuition, nonresident: full-time $21,639; part-time $1050 per credit hour. *Required fees:* $4764. *Financial support:* In 2013–14, 49 students received support, including 6 research assistantships with full and partial tuition reimbursements available (averaging $8,269 per year); career-related internships or fieldwork, Federal Work-Study, institutionally sponsored loans, scholarships/grants, and unspecified assistantships also available. Financial award application deadline: 1/15; financial award applicants required to submit FAFSA. *Faculty research:* National Council of Teachers of Mathematics standards, counseling, self-concept and self-esteem, special education, curriculum development. *Unit head:* Dr. Mark Hofer, Area Coordinator, 757-221-1713, E-mail: mjhofe@wm.edu. *Application contact:* Dorothy Smith Osborne, Assistant Dean for Academic Programs and Student Services, 757-221-2317, Fax: 757-221-2293, E-mail: dsosbo@wm.edu.
Website: http://education.wm.edu.

Colorado Christian University, Program in Curriculum and Instruction, Lakewood, CO 80226. Offers corporate education (MACI); early childhood educator (MACI); elementary educator (MACI); instructional technology (MACI); master educator (MACI); online course developer (MACI); online teaching and learning (MACI); special education generalist (MACI). Part-time and evening/weekend programs available. *Degree requirements:* For master's, thesis optional, practicum. *Entrance requirements:* For master's, interviews, letters of recommendation. Additional exam requirements/recommendations for international students: Required—TOEFL. Electronic applications accepted. *Expenses:* Contact institution.

The Colorado College, Education Department, Program in Elementary Education, Colorado Springs, CO 80903-3294. Offers elementary school teaching (MAT). *Degree requirements:* For master's, thesis, internship. Electronic applications accepted.

Columbia College, Graduate Programs, Department of Education, Columbia, SC 29203-5998. Offers divergent learning (M Ed); higher education administration (M Ed). *Accreditation:* NCATE. Part-time and evening/weekend programs available. Postbaccalaureate distance learning degree programs offered. *Faculty:* 3 full-time (1 woman), 18 part-time/adjunct (10 women). *Students:* 113 full-time (96 women), 2 part-time (1 woman); includes 50 minority (46 Black or African American, non-Hispanic/Latino; 2 American Indian or Alaska Native, non-Hispanic/Latino; 2 Asian, non-Hispanic/Latino). Average age 27. 108 applicants, 81% accepted, 77 enrolled. In 2013, 106 master's awarded. *Degree requirements:* For master's, thesis. *Entrance requirements:* For master's, GRE General Test, MAT, 2 recommendations, current South Carolina teaching certificate, minimum GPA of 3.2. *Application deadline:* For fall admission, 8/22 for domestic students. Application fee: $50. *Expenses:* Contact institution. *Financial support:* Available to part-time students. Application deadline: 7/1; applicants required to submit FAFSA. *Unit head:* Dr. Chris Burkett, Chair, 803-786-3782, Fax: 803-786-3034, E-mail: chrisburkett@colacoll.edu. *Application contact:* Carolyn Emeneker, Director of Graduate School and Evening College Admissions, 803-786-3766, Fax: 803-786-3674, E-mail: emeneker@colacoll.edu.

Columbia International University, Columbia Graduate School, Columbia, SC 29230-3122. Offers Bible teaching (MABT); Christian higher education leadership (Ed D); Christian school educational leadership (Ed D); counseling (MACN); curriculum and instruction (M Ed), including Christian school guidance, English as a second language, learning disabilities, school technology; early childhood and elementary education (MAT); educational administration (M Ed); teaching English as a foreign language (Certificate); teaching English as a foreign language and intercultural studies (MATF). Part-time and evening/weekend programs available. *Degree requirements:* For master's, internships, professional project. *Entrance requirements:* For master's, Minnesota Multiphasic Personality Inventory, MAT, minimum GPA of 2.7. Additional exam requirements/recommendations for international students: Required—TOEFL. Electronic applications accepted.

Concordia University, College of Education, Portland, OR 97211-6099. Offers career and technical education (M Ed); curriculum and instruction (M Ed), including adolescent literacy, career and technical education, e-learning/technology education, early childhood education, English for speakers of other languages, English language development, environmental education, mathematics, methods and curriculum, reading, science, teacher leadership, the inclusive classroom; early childhood (MAT); education leadership (Ed D); educational administration (M Ed); elementary education (MAT); secondary education (MAT); special education (M Ed); teacher leadership (Ed D). Part-time programs available. Postbaccalaureate distance learning degree programs offered (no on-campus study). *Degree requirements:* For master's, comprehensive exam, work samples/portfolio. *Entrance requirements:* For master's, California Basic Educational Skills Test or PRAXIS I, minimum undergraduate GPA of 2.8, graduate 3.0; 2 letters of recommendation. Additional exam requirements/recommendations for international students: Required—TOEFL (minimum score 525 paper-based). Electronic applications accepted. *Faculty research:* Learner-centered classroom, brain-based learning, future of online learning.

Concordia University Chicago, College of Education, Program in Teaching, River Forest, IL 60305-1499. Offers early childhood education (MAT); elementary education

(MAT); secondary education (MAT). *Degree requirements:* For master's, thesis or alternative. *Entrance requirements:* For master's, minimum GPA of 2.9. Additional exam requirements/recommendations for international students: Required—TOEFL (minimum score 550 paper-based). Electronic applications accepted.

Concordia University, Nebraska, Graduate Programs in Education, Program in Educational Administration, Seward, NE 68434-1556. Offers elementary and secondary education (M Ed); elementary education (M Ed); secondary education (M Ed). *Accreditation:* NCATE. Part-time programs available. *Degree requirements:* For master's, thesis or alternative. *Entrance requirements:* For master's, GRE, MAT, or NTE, BS in education or equivalent, minimum GPA of 3.0.

Converse College, School of Education and Graduate Studies, Program in Elementary Education, Spartanburg, SC 29302-0006. Offers M Ed, MAT. Part-time programs available. *Degree requirements:* For master's, capstone paper. *Entrance requirements:* For master's, NTE or PRAXIS II (M Ed), minimum GPA of 2.75, 2 recommendations. Electronic applications accepted.

Creighton University, Graduate School, College of Arts and Sciences, Department of Education, Program in Teaching, Omaha, NE 68178-0001. Offers elementary teaching (M Ed); secondary teaching (M Ed). Part-time and evening/weekend programs available. *Faculty:* 12 full-time (6 women). *Students:* 16 full-time (14 women), 18 part-time (11 women); includes 2 minority (both Black or African American, non-Hispanic/Latino). Average age 25. In 2013, 13 master's awarded. *Entrance requirements:* For master's, 3 letters of recommendation, 2 writing samples. Additional exam requirements/recommendations for international students: Required—TOEFL (minimum score 550 paper-based; 80 iBT). *Application deadline:* For fall admission, 7/1 priority date for domestic students, 3/1 priority date for international students; for winter admission, 12/1 priority date for domestic students, 6/1 priority date for international students; for spring admission, 3/1 priority date for domestic and international students; for summer admission, 3/1 for domestic and international students. Application fee: $50. Electronic applications accepted. *Expenses: Tuition:* Full-time $13,608; part-time $756 per credit hour. *Required fees:* $149 per semester. Tuition and fees vary according to course load, campus/location, program, reciprocity agreements and student's religious affiliation. *Financial support:* Scholarships/grants and tuition waivers (partial) available. Support available to part-time students. Financial award applicants required to submit FAFSA. *Unit head:* Dr. Lynn Olson, Director, 402-280-2554, E-mail: lolson@creighton.edu. *Application contact:* Valerie Mattix, Senior Program Coordinator, 402-280-2425, Fax: 402-280-2423, E-mail: valeriemattix@creighton.edu.

Curry College, Graduate Studies, Program in Education, Milton, MA 02186-9984. Offers elementary education (M Ed); foundations (non-license) (M Ed); reading (M Ed, Certificate); special education (M Ed). Part-time and evening/weekend programs available. *Degree requirements:* For master's, project or thesis. *Entrance requirements:* For master's, interview, recommendations, resume, written statement. Additional exam requirements/recommendations for international students: Required—TOEFL (minimum score 550 paper-based; 80 iBT). *Expenses:* Contact institution. *Faculty research:* Classroom trauma, therapeutic writing, inclusionary practices.

Dallas Baptist University, Dorothy M. Bush College of Education, Teaching Program, Dallas, TX 75211-9299. Offers distance learning (MAT); early childhood (MAT); elementary (MAT); English as a second language (MAT); Montessori (MAT); multisensory (MAT); secondary (MAT). Part-time and evening/weekend programs available. *Entrance requirements:* For master's, GRE General Test, minimum GPA of 3.0. Additional exam requirements/recommendations for international students: Required—TOEFL, IELTS. *Application deadline:* Applications are processed on a rolling basis. Application fee: $25. Electronic applications accepted. *Expenses: Tuition:* Full-time $13,410; part-time $745 per credit hour. *Required fees:* $300; $150 per semester. Tuition and fees vary according to degree level. *Financial support:* Federal Work-Study, institutionally sponsored loans, scholarships/grants, and tuition waivers (full and partial) available. Support available to part-time students. Financial award applicants required to submit FAFSA. *Unit head:* Dr. Carolyn Spain, Director, 214-333-5217, E-mail: graduate@dbu.edu. *Application contact:* Kit P. Montgomery, Director of Graduate Programs, 214-333-5242, Fax: 214-333-5579, E-mail: graduate@dbu.edu.
Website: http://www3.dbu.edu/graduate/mat.asp.

Delta State University, Graduate Programs, College of Education, Division of Teacher Education, Programs in Elementary Education, Cleveland, MS 38733-0001. Offers M Ed, MAT, Ed S. *Accreditation:* NCATE. Part-time and evening/weekend programs available. *Faculty:* 5 full-time (3 women). *Students:* 8 full-time (7 women), 120 part-time (112 women); includes 33 minority (30 Black or African American, non-Hispanic/Latino; 2 Hispanic/Latino; 1 Two or more races, non-Hispanic/Latino), 1 international. Average age 33. 35 applicants, 100% accepted, 27 enrolled. *Degree requirements:* For master's, thesis optional. *Entrance requirements:* For master's, GRE General Test; for Ed S, master's degree, teaching certificate. *Application deadline:* For fall admission, 8/1 priority date for domestic students; for spring admission, 12/1 priority date for domestic students. Applications are processed on a rolling basis. Application fee: $0. *Expenses:* Tuition, state resident: full-time $3006; part-time $334 per credit hour. Tuition, nonresident: full-time $3006; part-time $334 per credit hour. *Financial support:* Research assistantships, career-related internships or fieldwork, Federal Work-Study, and institutionally sponsored loans available. Support available to part-time students. Financial award application deadline: 6/1. *Unit head:* Dr. Corlis Snow, Head, 662-846-3000. *Application contact:* Dr. Albert Nylander, Dean of Graduate Studies, 662-846-4875, Fax: 662-846-4313, E-mail: grad-info@deltastate.edu.

Delta State University, Graduate Programs, College of Education, Thad Cochran Center for Rural School Leadership and Research, Program in Professional Studies, Cleveland, MS 38733-0001. Offers counselor education (Ed D); educational leadership (Ed D); elementary education (Ed D); higher education (Ed D). Part-time and evening/weekend programs available. *Students:* 3 full-time (all women), 90 part-time (58 women); includes 31 minority (all Black or African American, non-Hispanic/Latino), 1 international. Average age 38. 44 applicants, 95% accepted, 28 enrolled. In 2013, 2 doctorates awarded. *Degree requirements:* For doctorate, thesis/dissertation. *Entrance requirements:* For doctorate, GRE General Test. *Application deadline:* For fall admission, 8/1 priority date for domestic students; for spring admission, 12/1 priority date for domestic students. Applications are processed on a rolling basis. Application fee: $0. *Expenses:* Tuition, state resident: full-time $3006; part-time $334 per credit hour. Tuition, nonresident: full-time $3006; part-time $334 per credit hour. *Financial support:* Research assistantships, career-related internships or fieldwork, Federal Work-Study, and institutionally sponsored loans available. Support available to part-time students. Financial award application deadline: 6/1. *Unit head:* Dr. Dan McFall, Interim Chair, 662-846-4395, Fax: 662-846-4402. *Application contact:* Dr. Albert Nylander, Dean of Graduate Studies, 662-846-4875, Fax: 662-846-4313, E-mail: grad-info@deltastate.edu.

DePaul University, College of Education, Chicago, IL 60614. Offers bilingual bicultural education (M Ed, MA); counseling (M Ed, MA), including clinical mental health counseling, college student development, school counseling; curriculum studies (M Ed, MA, Ed D); early childhood education (M Ed, MA, Ed D); educating adults (MA); educational leadership (M Ed, MA, Ed D), including administration and supervision (M Ed, MA), principal preparation (M Ed, MA); elementary education (MA); mathematics education (MA); mathematics for teaching (MS); middle school mathematics education (MS); reading specialist (M Ed, MA); secondary education (M Ed, MA); social and cultural foundations in education (MA); special education (M Ed, MA); world languages education (M Ed, MA). Part-time and evening/weekend programs available. Postbaccalaureate distance learning degree programs offered (no on-campus study). *Faculty:* 61 full-time (35 women), 59 part-time/adjunct (43 women). *Students:* 628 full-time (486 women), 324 part-time (243 women); includes 304 minority (144 Black or African American, non-Hispanic/Latino; 1 American Indian or Alaska Native, non-Hispanic/Latino; 38 Asian, non-Hispanic/Latino; 98 Hispanic/Latino; 23 Two or more races, non-Hispanic/Latino), 24 international. Average age 30. In 2013, 465 master's, 4 doctorates awarded. *Degree requirements:* For doctorate, thesis/dissertation. *Application deadline:* For fall admission, 8/15 for domestic students; for winter admission, 12/1 for domestic students; for spring admission, 3/1 for domestic students. Applications are processed on a rolling basis. Application fee: $40. Electronic applications accepted. Tuition and fees vary according to course level, course load and degree level. *Financial support:* Application deadline: 12/31; applicants required to submit FAFSA. *Unit head:* Dr. Paul Zionts, Dean, 773-325-7581, Fax: 773-325-7713, E-mail: pzionts@depaul.edu. *Application contact:* Farrah Dalal, Assistant Director, 773-325-2465, Fax: 773-325-2270, E-mail: fdalal@depaul.edu.
Website: http://education.depaul.edu.

Dominican College, Division of Teacher Education, Orangeburg, NY 10962-1210. Offers MS Ed. Part-time and evening/weekend programs available. Postbaccalaureate distance learning degree programs offered (minimal on-campus study). *Faculty:* 4 full-time (2 women), 4 part-time/adjunct (2 women). *Students:* 65 part-time (53 women). In 2013, 22 master's awarded. *Degree requirements:* For master's, comprehensive exam (for some programs). *Entrance requirements:* Additional exam requirements/recommendations for international students: Required—TOEFL. *Application deadline:* Applications are processed on a rolling basis. *Expenses: Tuition:* Part-time $815 per credit. *Required fees:* $180 per semester. *Financial support:* Application deadline: 2/15; applicants required to submit FAFSA. *Unit head:* Dr. Mike Kelly, Director, 845-848-4090, Fax: 845-359-7802, E-mail: mike.kelly@dc.edu. *Application contact:* Joyce Elbe, Director of Admissions, 845-848-7896 Ext. 15, Fax: 845-365-3150, E-mail: admissions@dc.edu.

Dominican University, School of Education, River Forest, IL 60305-1099. Offers curriculum and instruction (MA Ed); early childhood education (MS); education (MAT); educational administration (MA); elementary education (MA Ed); English as a second language (MA Ed); reading (MA Ed); special education (MS). Part-time and evening/weekend programs available. Postbaccalaureate distance learning degree programs offered (no on-campus study). *Faculty:* 19 full-time (14 women), 51 part-time/adjunct (42 women). *Students:* 18 full-time (13 women), 334 part-time (274 women); includes 76 minority (26 Black or African American, non-Hispanic/Latino; 9 Asian, non-Hispanic/Latino; 41 Hispanic/Latino). Average age 32. 119 applicants, 77% accepted, 70 enrolled. In 2013, 246 master's awarded. *Entrance requirements:* For master's, Illinois Test of Basic Skills. Additional exam requirements/recommendations for international students: Required—TOEFL (minimum score 550 paper-based; 79 iBT). *Application deadline:* Applications are processed on a rolling basis. Application fee: $25. *Expenses:* Contact institution. *Financial support:* In 2013–14, 97 students received support. Career-related internships or fieldwork, scholarships/grants, and tuition waivers (partial) available. Support available to part-time students. Financial award application deadline: 8/15; financial award applicants required to submit FAFSA. *Faculty research:* Governance of private education institutions, reading and language arts, inclusion, organizational planning, leadership and vision. *Unit head:* Dr. Colleen Reardon, Dean, 718-524-6643, Fax: 708-524-6665, E-mail: creardon@dom.edu. *Application contact:* Keven Hansen, Coordinator of Recruitment and Admissions, 708-524-6921, Fax: 708-524-6665, E-mail: educate@dom.edu.
Website: http://educate.dom.edu/.

Dowling College, Graduate Programs in Education, Oakdale, NY 11769-1999. Offers adolescence education with middle childhood extension (MS); childhood and early childhood education (MS); childhood and gifted education (MS); childhood education (1-6) (MS); computers in education (AC); early childhood education (B-2) (MS); educational administration (Ed D); educational technology leadership (MS); educational technology specialist (AC); gifted education (AC); literacy education (MS, AC), including 5-12 (MS), B-12 (MS); literacy education (MS), including B-6; school building leader (AC); school district business leader (MBA, AC); school district leader (AC); special education (MS), including autism, severe disabilities; sport management (MS). *Accreditation:* NCATE. Part-time and evening/weekend programs available. Postbaccalaureate distance learning degree programs offered (minimal on-campus study). *Faculty:* 44 full-time (24 women), 17 part-time/adjunct (8 women). *Students:* 183 full-time (124 women), 314 part-time (231 women); includes 51 minority (19 Black or African American, non-Hispanic/Latino; 1 American Indian or Alaska Native, non-Hispanic/Latino; 3 Asian, non-Hispanic/Latino; 26 Hispanic/Latino; 2 Native Hawaiian or other Pacific Islander, non-Hispanic/Latino). Average age 32. 174 applicants, 80% accepted, 82 enrolled. In 2013, 198 master's, 33 doctorates, 48 other advanced degrees awarded. *Degree requirements:* For master's and AC, comprehensive exam; for doctorate, thesis/dissertation. *Entrance requirements:* For master's, minimum GPA of 3.0; for doctorate, GRE, master's degree; for AC, teaching certificate. Additional exam requirements/recommendations for international students: Required—TOEFL (minimum score 550 paper-based). *Application deadline:* For fall admission, 9/1 priority date for domestic students; for winter admission, 1/1 priority date for domestic students; for spring admission, 2/1 priority date for domestic students. Applications are processed on a rolling basis. Application fee: $50. Electronic applications accepted. *Expenses: Tuition:* Full-time $22,731; part-time $1029 per credit. *Required fees:* $956; $956. *Financial support:* Career-related internships or fieldwork and Federal Work-Study available. Support available to part-time students. Financial award application deadline: 6/30; financial award applicants required to submit FAFSA. *Faculty research:* Natural readers, Korean styles and learning strategies, mothers of children with disabilities, computers in instruction, cultural background and organizational roadblocks to problem solving. *Unit head:* Dr. Robert Manley, Dean, 631-244-3447, E-mail: manleyr@dowling.edu. *Application contact:* Mary Boullianne, Director of Admissions, 631-244-3274, Fax: 631-244-1059, E-mail: boulliam@dowling.edu.

Drury University, Graduate Programs in Education, Springfield, MO 65802. Offers elementary education (M Ed); gifted education (M Ed); human services (M Ed); instructional mathematics K-8 (M Ed); instructional technology (M Ed); middle school teaching (M Ed); secondary education (M Ed); special education (M Ed); special reading (M Ed). *Accreditation:* NCATE. Part-time and evening/weekend programs available. *Degree requirements:* For master's, thesis. *Entrance requirements:* For master's, GRE or MAT, minimum GPA of 2.75. Additional exam requirements/recommendations for international students: Required—TOEFL. Electronic applications accepted. *Faculty research:* Cultural enrichment, research skills, parental involvement relating to reading skills, reading strategies for mainstreaming children.

Duquesne University, School of Education, Department of Instruction and Leadership, Program in Secondary Education, Pittsburgh, PA 15282-0001. Offers biology (MS Ed);

chemistry (MS Ed); English (MS Ed); K-12 education (MS Ed), including Latin; mathematics (MS Ed); physics (MS Ed); social studies (MS Ed). Part-time and evening/weekend programs available. *Faculty:* 4 full-time (2 women). *Students:* 44 full-time (23 women), 3 part-time (2 women); includes 7 minority (6 Black or African American, non-Hispanic/Latino; 1 Two or more races, non-Hispanic/Latino), 1 international. Average age 27. 43 applicants, 35% accepted, 15 enrolled. In 2013, 28 master's awarded. *Degree requirements:* For master's, thesis optional. *Entrance requirements:* For master's, letters of recommendation, letter of intent, interview, bachelor's degree. Additional exam requirements/recommendations for international students: Required—TOEFL (minimum score 550 paper-based), IELTS (minimum score 7). *Application deadline:* For fall admission, 9/1 for domestic students; for spring admission, 1/1 for domestic students. Applications are processed on a rolling basis. Application fee: $0. Electronic applications accepted. Application fee is waived when completed online. *Expenses: Tuition:* Full-time $18,162; part-time $1009 per credit. *Required fees:* $1728; $96 per credit. Tuition and fees vary according to program. *Financial support:* Research assistantships and Federal Work-Study available. Support available to part-time students. *Unit head:* Dr. Melissa Boston, Associate Professor and Director, 412-396-6109, E-mail: bostonm@duq.edu. *Application contact:* Michael Dolinger, Director of Student and Academic Services, 412-396-6647, Fax: 412-396-5585, E-mail: dolingerm@duq.edu.
Website: http://www.duq.edu/academics/schools/education/graduate-programs-education/ms-ed-secondary-education.

D'Youville College, Department of Education, Buffalo, NY 14201-1084. Offers educational leadership (Ed D); elementary education (MS Ed, Teaching Certificate); secondary education (MS Ed, Teaching Certificate); special education (MS Ed). Part-time and evening/weekend programs available. *Students:* 96 full-time (68 women), 91 part-time (60 women); includes 14 minority (9 Black or African American, non-Hispanic/Latino; 1 American Indian or Alaska Native, non-Hispanic/Latino; 4 Hispanic/Latino), 90 international. Average age 32. 383 applicants, 48% accepted, 104 enrolled. In 2013, 128 master's awarded. *Degree requirements:* For master's, one foreign language, comprehensive exam, project or thesis. *Entrance requirements:* For master's, GRE (if GPA less than 2.75), minimum GPA of 3.0. Additional exam requirements/recommendations for international students: Required—TOEFL (minimum score 500 paper-based). *Application deadline:* For fall admission, 5/1 priority date for international students; for spring admission, 9/1 priority date for international students. Applications are processed on a rolling basis. Application fee: $25. Electronic applications accepted. *Financial support:* Career-related internships or fieldwork, Federal Work-Study, institutionally sponsored loans, scholarships/grants, tuition waivers (full and partial), and unspecified assistantships available. Support available to part-time students. Financial award application deadline: 3/1; financial award applicants required to submit FAFSA. *Faculty research:* Developmental disabilities, multiculturalism, early childhood education. *Unit head:* Dr. Hilary Lochte, Chair, 716-829-8110, Fax: 716-829-7660. *Application contact:* Mark Pavone, Graduate Admissions Director, 716-829-8400, Fax: 716-829-7900, E-mail: graduateadmissions@dyc.edu.

East Carolina University, Graduate School, College of Education, Department of Business and Information Technologies Education, Greenville, NC 27858-4353. Offers business education (MA Ed); elementary education (MAT); English education (MAT); family and consumer science (MAT); health education (MAT); Hispanic studies (MAT); history education (MAT); marketing education (MA Ed); middle grades education (MAT); music education (MAT); physical education (MAT); science education (MAT); special education (MAT), including general curriculum; vocation education (MS). *Accreditation:* NCATE. Part-time and evening/weekend programs available. Postbaccalaureate distance learning degree programs offered (no on-campus study). *Degree requirements:* For master's, comprehensive exam, thesis optional. *Entrance requirements:* For master's, GRE or MAT, minimum GPA of 2.5, bachelor's degree in related field, teaching license (MA Ed). Additional exam requirements/recommendations for international students: Required—TOEFL. *Expenses:* Tuition, state resident: full-time $4223. Tuition, nonresident: full-time $16,540. *Required fees:* $2184.

East Carolina University, Graduate School, College of Education, Department of Curriculum and Instruction, Greenville, NC 27858-4353. Offers assistive technology (Certificate); autism (Certificate); deaf/blindness (Certificate); elementary education (MA Ed); English education (MA Ed); history (MA Ed); middle grade education (MA Ed); reading education (MA Ed); special education (MA Ed); teaching (MAT). Part-time programs available. Postbaccalaureate distance learning degree programs offered. *Degree requirements:* For master's, comprehensive exam, thesis optional. *Entrance requirements:* For master's, GRE General Test or MAT, interview, bachelor's degree in related field, minimum GPA of 2.5, teaching license. Additional exam requirements/recommendations for international students: Required—TOEFL. *Expenses:* Tuition, state resident: full-time $4223. Tuition, nonresident: full-time $16,540. *Required fees:* $2184.

Eastern Connecticut State University, School of Education and Professional Studies/Graduate Division, Program in Elementary Education, Willimantic, CT 06226-2295. Offers MS. *Accreditation:* NCATE. Part-time and evening/weekend programs available. *Degree requirements:* For master's, comprehensive exam or thesis. *Entrance requirements:* For master's, PRAXIS I, minimum GPA of 2.7, teaching certificate. Additional exam requirements/recommendations for international students: Required—TOEFL (minimum score 550 paper-based).

Eastern Illinois University, Graduate School, College of Education and Professional Studies, Department of Early Childhood, Elementary and Middle Level Education, Charleston, IL 61920-3099. Offers elementary education (MS Ed). *Accreditation:* NCATE. Part-time programs available. *Degree requirements:* For master's, comprehensive exam. *Expenses: Tuition, area resident:* Part-time $283 per credit hour. Tuition, state resident: part-time $283 per credit hour. Tuition, nonresident: part-time $679 per credit hour.

Eastern Kentucky University, The Graduate School, College of Education, Department of Curriculum and Instruction, Richmond, KY 40475-3102. Offers elementary education (MA Ed), including early elementary education, reading; library science (MA Ed); music education (MA Ed); secondary and higher education (MA Ed), including secondary education; teaching (MAT). *Accreditation:* NCATE. Part-time programs available. *Degree requirements:* For master's, portfolio is part of exam. *Entrance requirements:* For master's, GRE General Test, PRAXIS II (KY), minimum GPA of 2.5. *Faculty research:* Technology in education, reading instruction, e-portfolios, induction to teacher education, dispositions of teachers.

Eastern Michigan University, Graduate School, College of Education, Department of Teacher Education, Programs in K–12 Education, Ypsilanti, MI 48197. Offers curriculum and instruction (MA); elementary education (MA); K-12 education (MA); middle school education (MA); secondary school education (MA). *Accreditation:* NCATE. Part-time and evening/weekend programs available. Postbaccalaureate distance learning degree programs offered (minimal on-campus study). *Students:* 11 full-time (4 women), 46 part-time (31 women); includes 8 minority (4 Black or African American, non-Hispanic/Latino; 1 American Indian or Alaska Native, non-Hispanic/Latino; 3 Hispanic/Latino). Average age 36. 41 applicants, 78% accepted, 20 enrolled. In 2013, 5 master's awarded. *Entrance requirements:* For master's, GRE. Additional exam requirements/recommendations for international students: Required—TOEFL. *Application deadline:* Applications are processed on a rolling basis. Application fee: $35. *Expenses:* Tuition, state resident: full-time $12,300; part-time $466 per credit hour. Tuition, nonresident: full-time $23,159; part-time $918 per credit hour. *Required fees:* $71 per credit hour. $46 per semester. One-time fee: $100. Tuition and fees vary according to course level and degree level. *Financial support:* Fellowships, research assistantships with full tuition reimbursements, teaching assistantships with full tuition reimbursements, career-related internships or fieldwork, Federal Work-Study, institutionally sponsored loans, scholarships/grants, tuition waivers (partial), and unspecified assistantships available. Support available to part-time students. Financial award applicants required to submit FAFSA. *Unit head:* Dr. Martha Kinney-Sedgwick, Interim Department Head, 734-487-3260, Fax: 734-487-2101, E-mail: mkinneys@emich.edu. *Application contact:* Dr. Ethan Lowenstein, Coordinator, 734-487-3260, Fax: 734-487-2101, E-mail: elowste@emich.edu.

Eastern Nazarene College, Adult and Graduate Studies, Division of Teacher Education, Quincy, MA 02170. Offers administration (M Ed); early childhood education (M Ed, Certificate); elementary education (M Ed, Certificate); English as a second language (Certificate); instructional enrichment and development (Certificate); middle school education (M Ed, Certificate); moderate special needs education (Certificate); principal (Certificate); program development and supervision (Certificate); secondary education (M Ed, Certificate); special education administrator (Certificate); special needs (M Ed); supervisor (Certificate); teacher of reading (M Ed, Certificate). M Ed also available through weekend program for administration, special needs, and teacher of reading only. Part-time and evening/weekend programs available. *Entrance requirements:* Additional exam requirements/recommendations for international students: Required—TOEFL (minimum score 550 paper-based).

Eastern New Mexico University, Graduate School, College of Education and Technology, Department of Curriculum and Instruction, Portales, NM 88130. Offers bilingual education (M Ed); educational technology (M Ed); elementary education (M Ed); English as a second language (M Ed); pedagogy and learning (M Ed); professional technical education (M Ed); reading/literacy (M Ed). Part-time programs available. Postbaccalaureate distance learning degree programs offered (minimal on-campus study). *Degree requirements:* For master's, comprehensive exam, thesis optional. *Entrance requirements:* For master's, minimum GPA of 3.0, photocopy of teaching license, writing assessment, letter of recommendation. Additional exam requirements/recommendations for international students: Required—TOEFL (minimum score 550 paper-based; 79 iBT), IELTS (minimum score 6). Electronic applications accepted.

Eastern Oregon University, Program in Elementary Education, La Grande, OR 97850-2899. Offers MAT. Part-time programs available. Postbaccalaureate distance learning degree programs offered (minimal on-campus study). *Degree requirements:* For master's, thesis. *Entrance requirements:* For master's, NTE.

Eastern University, Graduate Education Programs, St. Davids, PA 19087-3696. Offers ESL program specialist (K-12) (Certificate); general supervisor (PreK-12) (Certificate); health and physical education (K-12) (Certificate); middle level (4-8) (Certificate); multicultural education (M Ed); pre K-4 (Certificate); pre K-4 with special education (Certificate); reading (M Ed); reading specialist (K-12) (Certificate); reading supervisor (K-12) (Certificate); school health services (M Ed); school health supervisor (Certificate); school nurse (Certificate); school principalship (K-12) (Certificate); secondary biology education (7-12) (Certificate); secondary chemistry education (7-12) (Certificate); secondary communication education (7-12) (Certificate); secondary education (7-12) (Certificate); secondary English education (7-12) (Certificate); secondary math education (7-12) (Certificate); secondary social studies education (7-12) (Certificate); special education (M Ed); special education (7-12) (Certificate); special education (Pre K-8) (Certificate); special education supervisor (N-12) (Certificate); TESOL (M Ed); world language (Certificate), including French, Mandarin Chinese, Spanish. Part-time and evening/weekend programs available. Postbaccalaureate distance learning degree programs offered (no on-campus study). *Faculty:* 22 full-time (11 women), 26 part-time/adjunct (18 women). *Students:* 77 full-time (58 women), 223 part-time (149 women); includes 112 minority (81 Black or African American, non-Hispanic/Latino; 1 American Indian or Alaska Native, non-Hispanic/Latino; 9 Asian, non-Hispanic/Latino; 18 Hispanic/Latino; 1 Native Hawaiian or other Pacific Islander, non-Hispanic/Latino; 2 Two or more races, non-Hispanic/Latino), 7 international. Average age 34. 94 applicants, 100% accepted, 81 enrolled. In 2013, 120 master's awarded. *Entrance requirements:* For master's, minimum GPA of 2.5 (for M Ed); for Certificate, minimum GPA of 3.0 for certifications. Additional exam requirements/recommendations for international students: Required—TOEFL. *Application deadline:* For fall admission, 8/14 for domestic students; for spring admission, 12/20 for domestic students. Applications are processed on a rolling basis. Application fee: $35. Application fee is waived when completed online. *Expenses: Tuition:* Full-time $15,600; part-time $650 per credit. *Required fees:* $27.50 per semester. One-time fee: $50. Tuition and fees vary according to course load, degree level and program. *Financial support:* In 2013–14, 84 students received support, including 6 research assistantships with partial tuition reimbursements available (averaging $7,710 per year); scholarships/grants and unspecified assistantships also available. Financial award application deadline: 3/15; financial award applicants required to submit FAFSA. *Unit head:* Harry Gutelius, Associate Dean, 610-341-1729. *Application contact:* Michael Perpiglia, Associate Director of Enrollment, 610-341-5947, Fax: 484-581-1276, E-mail: mperpigl@eastern.edu.
Website: http://www.eastern.edu/academics/programs/loeb-school-education-0/graduateprograms.

Eastern Washington University, Graduate Studies, College of Arts, Letters and Education, Department of Education, Program in Elementary Teaching, Cheney, WA 99004-2431. Offers M Ed. *Students:* 11 full-time (5 women), 1 (woman) part-time; includes 1 minority (Black or African American, non-Hispanic/Latino). 5 applicants, 20% accepted. In 2013, 12 master's awarded. *Degree requirements:* For master's, comprehensive exam. *Entrance requirements:* For master's, minimum GPA of 3.0. *Application deadline:* For fall admission, 4/1 priority date for domestic students; for spring admission, 1/15 for domestic students. Applications are processed on a rolling basis. Application fee: $50. *Financial support:* In 2013–14, teaching assistantships with partial tuition reimbursements (averaging $7,000 per year) were awarded; career-related internships or fieldwork, Federal Work-Study, institutionally sponsored loans, scholarships/grants, health care benefits, tuition waivers (partial), and unspecified assistantships also available. Support available to part-time students. Financial award application deadline: 2/1; financial award applicants required to submit FAFSA. *Unit head:* Robin Showalter, Program Coordinator, 509-359-6492, E-mail: rshowalter@mail.ewu.edu. *Application contact:* Dr. Judy Leach, Adviser, 509-359-2500, Fax: 509-359-4822.

East Stroudsburg University of Pennsylvania, Graduate College, College of Education, Program in Elementary Education, East Stroudsburg, PA 18301-2999. Offers M Ed. Part-time and evening/weekend programs available. Postbaccalaureate distance learning degree programs offered. *Faculty:* 3 full-time (2 women). *Students:* 1 (woman) full-time, 12 part-time (all women); includes 3 minority (1 Black or African American, non-Hispanic/Latino; 2 Hispanic/Latino). Average age 32. 13 applicants, 54% accepted, 6

enrolled. In 2013, 10 master's awarded. *Degree requirements:* For master's, comprehensive exam, professional portfolio, curriculum project or action research. *Entrance requirements:* For master's, PRAXIS/teacher certification, letter of recommendation, Pennsylvania Department of Education requirements. Additional exam requirements/recommendations for international students: Required—TOEFL (minimum score 560 paper-based; 83 iBT) or IELTS. *Application deadline:* For fall admission, 7/31 priority date for domestic students, 6/30 priority date for international students; for spring admission, 11/30 for domestic students, 10/31 for international students. Applications are processed on a rolling basis. Application fee: $50. Electronic applications accepted. *Expenses:* Tuition, state resident: full-time $7956; part-time $442 per credit. Tuition, nonresident: full-time $11,934; part-time $663 per credit. *Required fees:* $2129; $118 per credit. *Financial support:* Research assistantships with full and partial tuition reimbursements, Federal Work-Study, and institutionally sponsored loans available. Financial award application deadline: 3/1; financial award applicants required to submit FAFSA. *Unit head:* Dr. Paula Kelberman, Graduate Coordinator, 570-422-3365, Fax: 570-422-3942, E-mail: pkelberman@po-box.esu.edu. *Application contact:* Kevin Quintero, Graduate Admissions Coordinator, 570-422-3536, Fax: 570-422-2711, E-mail: kquintero@esu.edu.

East Tennessee State University, School of Graduate Studies, College of Education, Department of Curriculum and Instruction, Johnson City, TN 37614. Offers educational media and educational technology (M Ed), including educational communications and technology, school library media; elementary education (M Ed); reading (MA), including reading education, storytelling; school library professional (Post-Master's Certificate); secondary education (M Ed), including classroom technology, secondary education (M Ed, MAT); storytelling (Postbaccalaureate Certificate); teacher education with multiple levels (MAT), including elementary education, middle grades education, secondary education (M Ed, MAT). *Accreditation:* NCATE. Part-time and evening/weekend programs available. Postbaccalaureate distance learning degree programs offered (no on-campus study). *Faculty:* 25 full-time (18 women), 12 part-time/adjunct (8 women). *Students:* 66 full-time (50 women), 97 part-time (85 women); includes 5 minority (3 Black or African American, non-Hispanic/Latino; 2 Two or more races, non-Hispanic/Latino), 2 international. Average age 31. 144 applicants, 57% accepted, 70 enrolled. In 2013, 83 master's, 5 other advanced degrees awarded. *Degree requirements:* For master's, comprehensive exam, thesis optional, student teaching, practicum; for other advanced degree, field work (school library); culminating experience (storytelling). *Entrance requirements:* For master's, GRE, SAT, ACT, PRAXIS, minimum GPA of 3.0; for other advanced degree, master's degree, TN teaching license (for school library professional Post-Master's Certificate); three letters of recommendation (for storytelling Postbaccalaureate Certificate). Additional exam requirements/recommendations for international students: Required—TOEFL (minimum score 550 paper-based; 79 iBT). *Application deadline:* For fall admission, 6/1 for domestic students, 4/30 for international students; for spring admission, 11/1 for domestic students, 4/30 for international students. Application fee: $35 ($45 for international students). Electronic applications accepted. *Expenses:* Tuition, state resident: full-time $7900; part-time $395 per credit hour. Tuition, nonresident: full-time $21,960; part-time $1098 per credit hour. *Required fees:* $1345; $84 per credit hour. *Financial support:* In 2013–14, 43 students received support, including 6 research assistantships with full tuition reimbursements available (averaging $6,000 per year), 10 teaching assistantships with full tuition reimbursements available (averaging $6,000 per year); career-related internships or fieldwork, institutionally sponsored loans, scholarships/grants, and unspecified assistantships also available. Financial award application deadline: 7/1; financial award applicants required to submit FAFSA. *Faculty research:* Critical thinking; curriculum development in reading, math, and science education; cultural diversity; cognitive processes; effective teaching strategies. *Unit head:* Dr. Rhona Hurwitz, Chair, 423-439-7598, Fax: 423-439-8362, E-mail: hurwitz@etsu.edu. *Application contact:* Fiona Goodyear, Graduate Specialist, 423-439-6148, Fax: 423-439-5624, E-mail: goodyear@etsu.edu.
Website: http://www.etsu.edu/coe/cuai/.

Edinboro University of Pennsylvania, School of Education, Department of Elementary, Middle and Secondary Education, Edinboro, PA 16444. Offers elementary education (M Ed); middle/secondary instruction (M Ed). Part-time and evening/weekend programs available. *Degree requirements:* For master's, comprehensive exam, thesis or alternative, project. *Entrance requirements:* For master's, GRE or MAT, minimum QPA of 2.5. Electronic applications accepted.

Elizabeth City State University, School of Education and Psychology, Master of Education in Elementary Education Program, Elizabeth City, NC 27909-7806. Offers M Ed. *Accreditation:* NCATE. Part-time and evening/weekend programs available. *Faculty:* 4 full-time (3 women), 1 (woman) part-time/adjunct. *Students:* 2 full-time (both women), 12 part-time (10 women); includes 6 minority (5 Black or African American, non-Hispanic/Latino; 1 Two or more races, non-Hispanic/Latino). Average age 35. 1 applicant, 100% accepted. In 2013, 7 master's awarded. *Degree requirements:* For master's, comprehensive exam, thesis or alternative, electronic transformational teaching project. *Entrance requirements:* For master's, GRE and/or MAT, minimum GPA of 3.0, 3 letters of recommendation, 2 official transcripts from all undergraduate/graduate schools attended, teacher license, typewritten 2-page essay specifying educational philosophy. Additional exam requirements/recommendations for international students: Required—TOEFL (minimum score 550 paper-based, 80 iBT) or IELTS (minimum score 6.5). *Application deadline:* For fall admission, 7/15 priority date for domestic and international students; for spring admission, 11/15 priority date for domestic and international students; for summer admission, 3/15 priority date for domestic and international students. Applications are processed on a rolling basis. Application fee: $30. Electronic applications accepted. *Expenses:* Tuition, state resident: full-time $2916; part-time $364.48 per credit. Tuition, nonresident: full-time $14,199; part-time $1774.83 per credit. *Required fees:* $2972.23; $206.58 per credit. $571.06 per semester. *Financial support:* Scholarships/grants available. Financial award application deadline: 6/30; financial award applicants required to submit FAFSA. *Faculty research:* Diverse learners, disproportionality, inclusionary classrooms, international curriculum development. *Unit head:* Dr. John Dixon, Jr., Chair, 252-335-3342, Fax: 252-335-3037, E-mail: jadixon@mail.ecsu.edu. *Application contact:* Dr. Paula S. Viltz, Interim Dean, School of Education and Psychology, 252-335-3455, Fax: 252-335-3146, E-mail: psviltz@mail.ecsu.edu.

Elms College, Division of Education, Chicopee, MA 01013-2839. Offers early childhood education (MAT); education (M Ed, CAGS); elementary education (MAT); English as a second language (MAT); reading (MAT); secondary education (MAT), including biology education, English education, Spanish education; special education (MAT). Part-time and evening/weekend programs available. *Degree requirements:* For master's, thesis (for some programs). *Entrance requirements:* For master's, Massachusetts Educators Certification Test, minimum GPA of 3.0; for CAGS, master's degree in education. Additional exam requirements/recommendations for international students: Required—TOEFL.

Elon University, Program in Education, Elon, NC 27244-2010. Offers elementary education (M Ed); gifted education (M Ed); special education (M Ed). *Accreditation:* NCATE. Part-time programs available. *Faculty:* 16 full-time (13 women), 3 part-time/

adjunct (2 women). *Students:* 62 part-time (53 women); includes 11 minority (5 Black or African American, non-Hispanic/Latino; 1 Asian, non-Hispanic/Latino; 5 Hispanic/Latino). Average age 33. 35 applicants, 94% accepted, 29 enrolled. *Entrance requirements:* For master's, GRE, MAT. Additional exam requirements/recommendations for international students: Required—TOEFL (minimum score 550 paper-based; 79 iBT). *Application deadline:* For winter admission, 6/1 priority date for domestic students. Applications are processed on a rolling basis. Application fee: $50. Electronic applications accepted. *Expenses:* Contact institution. *Financial support:* In 2013–14, 5 students received support. Federal Work-Study and scholarships/grants available. Support available to part-time students. Financial award application deadline: 6/1; financial award applicants required to submit FAFSA. *Faculty research:* Teaching reading to low-achieving second and third graders, pre- and post-student teaching attitudes, children's writing, whole language methodology, critical creative thinking. *Unit head:* Dr. Angela Owusu-Ansah, Director and Associate Dean of Education, 336-278-5885, Fax: 336-278-5919, E-mail: aansah@elon.edu. *Application contact:* Art Fadde, Director of Graduate Admissions, 800-334-8448 Ext. 3, Fax: 336-278-7699, E-mail: afadde@elon.edu.
Website: http://www.elon.edu/med/.

Emmanuel College, Graduate Studies, Graduate Programs in Education, Boston, MA 02115. Offers educational leadership (CAGS); elementary education (MAT); school administration (M Ed); secondary education (MAT). Part-time and evening/weekend programs available. *Faculty:* 3 full-time (all women), 10 part-time/adjunct (7 women). *Students:* 11 full-time (7 women), 22 part-time (13 women); includes 4 minority (3 Black or African American, non-Hispanic/Latino; 1 Native Hawaiian or other Pacific Islander, non-Hispanic/Latino). Average age 30. In 2013, 15 master's, 1 other advanced degree awarded. *Degree requirements:* For master's, 36 credits, including 6-credit practicum. *Entrance requirements:* For master's and CAGS, transcripts from all regionally-accredited institutions attended (showing proof of bachelor's degree completion), 2 letters of recommendation, essay, resume, interview. Additional exam requirements/recommendations for international students: Required—TOEFL (minimum score 600 paper-based; 106 iBT) or IELTS (minimum score 6.5). *Application deadline:* For fall admission, 7/31 priority date for domestic students; for spring admission, 11/30 priority date for domestic students. Applications are processed on a rolling basis. Application fee: $0. Electronic applications accepted. *Financial support:* Applicants required to submit FAFSA. *Unit head:* Sandy Robbins, Dean of Enrollment, 617-735-9700, Fax: 617-507-0434, E-mail: graduatestudies@emmanuel.edu. *Application contact:* Enrollment Counselor, 617-735-9700, Fax: 617-507-0434, E-mail: graduatestudies@emmanuel.edu.
Website: http://www.emmanuel.edu/graduate-studies-nursing/academics/education.html.

Emporia State University, Program in Master Teacher, Emporia, KS 66801-5415. Offers elementary subject matter (MS); reading (MS). *Accreditation:* NCATE. Part-time programs available. *Students:* 3 full-time (all women), 60 part-time (59 women); includes 3 minority (1 Black or African American, non-Hispanic/Latino; 1 Hispanic/Latino; 1 Two or more races, non-Hispanic/Latino). 19 applicants, 79% accepted, 13 enrolled. In 2013, 22 master's awarded. *Degree requirements:* For master's, comprehensive exam or thesis, practicum. *Entrance requirements:* For master's, GRE General Test or MAT, essay exam, appropriate bachelor's degree, letters of recommendation. Additional exam requirements/recommendations for international students: Required—TOEFL (minimum score 520 paper-based; 68 iBT). *Application deadline:* For fall admission, 8/15 priority date for domestic students. Applications are processed on a rolling basis. Application fee: $30 ($75 for international students). Electronic applications accepted. *Expenses:* Tuition, area resident: Part-time $220 per credit hour. Tuition, state resident: part-time $220 per credit hour. Tuition, nonresident: part-time $685 per credit hour. *Required fees:* $73 per credit hour. *Financial support:* Federal Work-Study, institutionally sponsored loans, health care benefits, and unspecified assistantships available. Financial award application deadline: 3/15; financial award applicants required to submit FAFSA. *Unit head:* Dr. Jean Morrow, Chair, 620-341-5766, E-mail: jmorrow@emporia.edu. *Application contact:* Mary Sewell, Admissions Coordinator, 800-950-GRAD, Fax: 620-341-5909, E-mail: msewell@emporia.edu.

Endicott College, Van Loan School of Graduate and Professional Studies, Program in Elementary Education, Beverly, MA 01915-2096. Offers M Ed. Part-time and evening/weekend programs available. *Faculty:* 6 part-time/adjunct (3 women). *Students:* 5 full-time (all women), 4 part-time (all women); includes 3 minority (2 Black or African American, non-Hispanic/Latino; 1 Hispanic/Latino). Average age 33. 12 applicants, 58% accepted, 6 enrolled. In 2013, 3 master's awarded. *Degree requirements:* For master's, comprehensive exam. *Entrance requirements:* For master's, MAT or GRE, Massachusetts teaching certificate, 2 professional letters of recommendation. Additional exam requirements/recommendations for international students: Required—TOEFL. *Application deadline:* Applications are processed on a rolling basis. Application fee: $50. Electronic applications accepted. *Financial support:* Career-related internships or fieldwork, Federal Work-Study, and institutionally sponsored loans available. Financial award applicants required to submit FAFSA. *Unit head:* Dr. John D. MacLean, Jr., Director of Licensure Programs, 978-232-2408, E-mail: jmaclean@endicott.edu. *Application contact:* Vice President and Dean of the School of Graduate and Professional Studies.
Website: http://www.endicott.edu/GradProf.aspx.

Fairfield University, Graduate School of Education and Allied Professions, Fairfield, CT 06824-5195. Offers applied behavior analysis (ATC); applied psychology (MA); clinical mental health counseling (MA, CAS); early childhood studies (ATC); educational technology (MA); elementary education (MA, CAS); family studies (MA); integration of spirituality and religion in counseling (ATC); marriage and family therapy (MA); school counseling (MA, CAS); school psychology (MA, CAS); school-based marriage and family therapy (ATC); secondary education (MA); special education (MA, CAS); substance abuse counseling (ATC); teaching (Certificate); teaching and foundations (MA, CAS); TESOL, world languages, and bilingual education (MA, CAS). *Accreditation:* NCATE. Part-time and evening/weekend programs available. *Faculty:* 24 full-time (21 women), 39 part-time/adjunct (27 women). *Students:* 154 full-time (130 women), 307 part-time (248 women); includes 75 minority (14 Black or African American, non-Hispanic/Latino; 1 American Indian or Alaska Native, non-Hispanic/Latino; 10 Asian, non-Hispanic/Latino; 44 Hispanic/Latino; 6 Two or more races, non-Hispanic/Latino), 13 international. Average age 34. 263 applicants, 41% accepted, 91 enrolled. In 2013, 149 master's, 21 other advanced degrees awarded. *Degree requirements:* For master's, comprehensive exam. *Entrance requirements:* For master's, PRAXIS I (for certification programs), minimum GPA of 3.0, 2 recommendations, resume. Additional exam requirements/recommendations for international students: Required—TOEFL (minimum score 550 paper-based; 84 iBT) or IELTS (minimum score 7.5). *Application deadline:* For fall admission, 2/15 for international students; for spring admission, 10/1 for international students. Application fee: $60. Electronic applications accepted. *Expenses:* Tuition: Part-time $675 per credit hour. Tuition and fees vary according to program. *Financial support:* In 2013–14, 55 students received support. Career-related internships or fieldwork and unspecified assistantships available. Financial award applicants required to submit FAFSA. *Faculty research:* Literacy, adolescent psychology, special education, teaching development, mentoring for professional development, multicultural

education. *Total annual research expenditures:* $325,000. *Unit head:* Dr. Robert D. Hannafin, Dean, 203-254-4250, Fax: 203-254-4241, E-mail: rhannafin@fairfield.edu. *Application contact:* Marianne Gumpper, Director of Graduate and Continuing Studies Admission, 203-254-4184, Fax: 203-254-4073, E-mail: gradadmis@fairfield.edu. Website: http://www.fairfield.edu/academics/schoolscollegescenters/graduateschoolofeducationalliedprofessions/graduateprograms/.

Fayetteville State University, Graduate School, Programs in Middle Grades, Secondary and Special Education and Elementary Education, Fayetteville, NC 28301-4298. Offers biology (MA Ed); elementary education (MA Ed); history (MA Ed); mathematics (MA Ed); middle grades (MA Ed); political science (MA Ed); reading (MA Ed); sociology (MA Ed); special education (MA Ed), including behavioral-emotional handicaps, mentally handicapped, specific training disability. *Accreditation:* NCATE. Part-time and evening/weekend programs available. *Faculty:* 12 full-time (8 women), 4 part-time/adjunct (3 women). *Students:* 25 full-time (22 women), 49 part-time (45 women); includes 51 minority (48 Black or African American, non-Hispanic/Latino; 1 American Indian or Alaska Native, non-Hispanic/Latino; 2 Hispanic/Latino). Average age 35. 5 applicants, 100% accepted, 5 enrolled. In 2013, 29 master's awarded. *Degree requirements:* For master's, comprehensive exam, internship. *Application deadline:* For fall admission, 4/15 for domestic students; for spring admission, 10/15 for domestic students. Applications are processed on a rolling basis. Application fee: $40. Electronic applications accepted. *Faculty research:* Students with disabilities and selected leadership behaviors, new vision for professional development, gifted and talented students, emotional and behavioral disabilities, professional development for high school biology teachers. *Unit head:* Dr. Kimberly Smith-Burton, Interim Chair, 910-672-1182, E-mail: cbarringerbrown@uncfsu.edu. *Application contact:* Katrina Hoffman, Graduate Admission Officer, 910-672-1374, Fax: 910-672-1470, E-mail: khoffma1@uncfsu.edu.

Fitchburg State University, Division of Graduate and Continuing Education, Program in Elementary Education, Fitchburg, MA 01420-2697. Offers M Ed. *Accreditation:* NCATE. Part-time and evening/weekend programs available. *Entrance requirements:* Additional exam requirements/recommendations for international students: Required—TOEFL (minimum score 550 paper-based; 79 iBT). Electronic applications accepted.

Florida Agricultural and Mechanical University, Division of Graduate Studies, Research, and Continuing Education, College of Education, Department of Elementary Education, Tallahassee, FL 32307-3200. Offers early childhood and elementary education (M Ed, MS Ed). *Accreditation:* NCATE. *Degree requirements:* For master's, thesis (for some programs). *Entrance requirements:* For master's, GRE General Test, minimum GPA of 3.0. Additional exam requirements/recommendations for international students: Required—TOEFL.

Florida Atlantic University, College of Education, Department of Teaching and Learning, Boca Raton, FL 33431-0991. Offers curriculum and instruction (M Ed), including art, biology, chemistry, English, French, German, mathematics, music, physics, Pre-K and primary education, reading, social sciences, Spanish; elementary education (M Ed); environmental education (M Ed); reading education (M Ed); social foundations of education (M Ed), including educational psychology, educational technology, multilingual education. *Accreditation:* NCATE. Part-time and evening/weekend programs available. *Faculty:* 16 full-time (12 women), 1 (woman) part-time/adjunct. *Students:* 56 full-time (46 women), 96 part-time (78 women); includes 39 minority (10 Black or African American, non-Hispanic/Latino; 6 Asian, non-Hispanic/Latino; 20 Hispanic/Latino; 3 Two or more races, non-Hispanic/Latino), 4 international. Average age 32. 101 applicants, 54% accepted, 42 enrolled. In 2013, 64 master's awarded. *Entrance requirements:* For master's, GRE General Test, minimum GPA of 3.0 in last 2 years of undergraduate course work. Additional exam requirements/recommendations for international students: Required—TOEFL (minimum score 500 paper-based; 61 iBT), IELTS (minimum score 6). *Application deadline:* For fall admission, 7/1 for domestic students, 2/15 for international students; for spring admission, 11/1 for domestic students, 7/15 for international students. Applications are processed on a rolling basis. Application fee: $30. *Expenses:* Tuition, state resident: full-time $6660; part-time $370 per credit hour. Tuition, nonresident: full-time $18,450; part-time $1025 per credit hour. Tuition and fees vary according to course load. *Financial support:* Fellowships with partial tuition reimbursements, research assistantships with partial tuition reimbursements, teaching assistantships with partial tuition reimbursements, career-related internships or fieldwork, scholarships/grants, and unspecified assistantships available. *Faculty research:* Technology, teaching English to speakers of other languages, math teaching, electronic portfolio assessment, global perspectives through social studies. *Unit head:* Dr. Barbara Ridener, Chairperson, 561-297-3588. *Application contact:* Dr. Eliah Watlington, Associate Dean, 561-296-8520, Fax: 261-297-2991, E-mail: ewatling@fau.edu. Website: http://www.coe.fau.edu/academicdepartments/tl/.

Florida Institute of Technology, Graduate Programs, College of Science, Department of Education and Interdisciplinary Studies, Melbourne, FL 32901-6975. Offers computer education (MS); elementary science education (M Ed); environmental education (MS); interdisciplinary science (MS); mathematics education (MS, PhD, Ed S); science education (MS, PhD, Ed S), including informal science education (MS); teaching (MAT). Part-time and evening/weekend programs available. *Faculty:* 4 full-time (1 woman), 5 part-time/adjunct (2 women). *Students:* 47 full-time (29 women), 40 part-time (25 women); includes 10 minority (4 Black or African American, non-Hispanic/Latino; 4 Asian, non-Hispanic/Latino; 2 Hispanic/Latino), 48 international. Average age 32. 90 applicants, 63% accepted, 23 enrolled. In 2013, 16 master's awarded. Terminal master's awarded for partial completion of doctoral program. *Degree requirements:* For master's, comprehensive exam (for some programs), thesis optional; for doctorate, comprehensive exam, thesis/dissertation; for Ed S, comprehensive exam. *Entrance requirements:* For master's, minimum GPA of 3.0, resume, 3 letters of recommendation (elementary science education), statement of objectives; for doctorate, minimum GPA of 3.2, resume, 3 letters of recommendation, statement of objectives, 3 years of teaching experience (recommended); for Ed S, minimum GPA of 3.0, resume, 3 letters of recommendation, statement of objectives. Additional exam requirements/recommendations for international students: Required—TOEFL (minimum score 550 paper-based; 79 iBT). *Application deadline:* For fall admission, 4/1 for international students; for spring admission, 9/30 for international students. Applications are processed on a rolling basis. Electronic applications accepted. *Expenses: Tuition:* Full-time $20,214; part-time $1123 per credit. Tuition and fees vary according to campus/location. *Financial support:* In 2013–14, 2 teaching assistantships with full and partial tuition reimbursements (averaging $12,623 per year) were awarded; research assistantships with full and partial tuition reimbursements, career-related internships or fieldwork, institutionally sponsored loans, tuition waivers (partial), unspecified assistantships, and tuition remissions also available. Support available to part-time students. Financial award application deadline: 3/1; financial award applicants required to submit FAFSA. *Faculty research:* Measurement and evaluation, computers in education, educational technology. *Total annual research expenditures:* $644,517. *Unit head:* Dr. Kastro Hamed, Department Head, 321-674-8126, Fax: 321-674-7598, E-mail: khamed@fit.edu. *Application contact:* Cheryl A. Brown, Associate Director of Graduate Admissions, 321-674-7581, Fax: 321-723-9468, E-mail: cbrown@fit.edu. Website: http://cos.fit.edu/education/.

Florida International University, College of Education, Department of Teaching and Learning, Miami, FL 33199. Offers art education (MA, MS); curriculum and instruction (MS, Ed D, PhD, Ed S), including curriculum development (MS), elementary education (MS), English education (MS), learning technologies (MS), mathematics education (MS), modern language education (MS), physical education (MS), science education (MS), social studies education (MS), special education (MS); early childhood education (MS); exceptional student education (Ed D); foreign language education (MS), including foreign language education, teaching English to speakers of other languages (TESOL); international/intercultural education (MS); language, literacy and culture (PhD); mathematics, science, and learning technologies (PhD); physical education (MS), including sport and fitness; reading education (MS). Part-time and evening/weekend programs available. *Degree requirements:* For doctorate, comprehensive exam, thesis/dissertation. *Entrance requirements:* For master's, GRE General Test, Florida General Knowledge Test or Florida College Level Academic Skills Test; for doctorate and Ed S, GRE General Test. Additional exam requirements/recommendations for international students: Required—TOEFL (minimum score 550 paper-based; 80 iBT), IELTS (minimum score 6.3). Electronic applications accepted.

Florida Memorial University, School of Education, Miami-Dade, FL 33054. Offers elementary education (MS); exceptional student education (MS); reading (MS). *Degree requirements:* For master's, comprehensive exam or thesis, field and clinical experiences, exit exam. *Entrance requirements:* For master's, GRE, CLAST, PRAXIS I, baccalaureate or graduate degree with minimum GPA of 3.0 in last 60 hours, 3 recommendations. Additional exam requirements/recommendations for international students: Recommended—TOEFL.

Florida State University, The Graduate School, College of Education, School of Teacher Education, Tallahassee, FL 32306. Offers curriculum and instruction (MS, MST, PhD, Ed S), including early childhood education (MS, PhD, Ed S), elementary education (MS, PhD, Ed S), English education (MS, PhD, Ed S), English teaching (MST), exceptional student education (MST), foreign and second language education (MS, PhD, Ed S), foreign and second language teaching (MST), math education (MS, PhD, Ed S), math teaching (MST), reading education and language arts (MS, PhD, Ed S), science education (MS, PhD, Ed S), social science education (MS, PhD, Ed S), social science teaching (MST), special education (MS, PhD, Ed S), special education studies (MST), visual disabilities (MS, Ed S). Part-time programs available. *Faculty:* 30 full-time (20 women), 22 part-time/adjunct (18 women). *Students:* 183 full-time (151 women), 92 part-time (80 women); includes 47 minority (20 Black or African American, non-Hispanic/Latino; 3 American Indian or Alaska Native, non-Hispanic/Latino; 1 Asian, non-Hispanic/Latino; 20 Hispanic/Latino; 3 Two or more races, non-Hispanic/Latino), 61 international. Average age 30. 199 applicants, 79% accepted, 86 enrolled. In 2013, 119 master's, 9 doctorates, 4 other advanced degrees awarded. *Degree requirements:* For master's and Ed S, comprehensive exam, thesis optional; for doctorate, comprehensive exam, thesis/dissertation, preliminary exam, prospectus defense. *Entrance requirements:* For master's, doctorate, and Ed S, GRE General Test, minimum GPA of 3.0. Additional exam requirements/recommendations for international students: Required—TOEFL (minimum score 550 paper-based; 80 iBT). *Application deadline:* For fall admission, 7/1 for domestic and international students; for winter admission, 10/1 for domestic students, 11/1 for international students; for spring admission, 3/1 for domestic and international students. Applications are processed on a rolling basis. Application fee: $30. Electronic applications accepted. *Expenses:* Tuition, state resident: part-time $403.51 per credit hour. Tuition, nonresident: part-time $1004.85 per credit hour. *Required fees:* $75.81 per credit hour. One-time fee: $20 part-time. Tuition and fees vary according to course load, campus/location and student level. *Financial support:* In 2013–14, 113 students received support, including 55 research assistantships with full and partial tuition reimbursements available, 18 teaching assistantships with full and partial tuition reimbursements available; fellowships with full and partial tuition reimbursements available, career-related internships or fieldwork, scholarships/grants, health care benefits, and unspecified assistantships also available. Financial award application deadline: 1/15; financial award applicants required to submit FAFSA. *Faculty research:* Effective intervention and assessment strategies to improve reading skills; literacy teaching and learning through technology; understanding of student sense-making through instructions, especially STEM learning for all students; international education and consequences of globalization; support professional teacher development and adoption of effective/transformative practices. *Total annual research expenditures:* $1.3 million. *Unit head:* Dr. Sherry Southerland, Chair, 850-644-4880, Fax: 850-644-7736, E-mail: ssoutherland@admin.fsu.edu. *Application contact:* Dawn Matthews, Academic Support Assistant, 850-644-2122, Fax: 850-644-7736, E-mail: dmatthews@fsu.edu. Website: http://www.coe.fsu.edu/STE.

Fordham University, Graduate School of Education, Division of Curriculum and Teaching, New York, NY 10023. Offers adult education (MS, MSE); bilingual teacher education (MSE); curriculum and teaching (MSE); early childhood education (MSE); elementary education (MST); language, literacy, and learning (PhD); reading education (MSE, Adv C); secondary education (MAT, MSE); special education (MSE, Adv C); teaching English as a second language (MSE). *Accreditation:* NCATE. *Degree requirements:* For doctorate, thesis/dissertation; for Adv C, thesis. *Entrance requirements:* For doctorate, MAT, GRE General Test.

Framingham State University, Continuing Education, Program in Elementary Education, Framingham, MA 01701-9101. Offers M Ed.

Francis Marion University, Graduate Programs, School of Education, Florence, SC 29502-0547. Offers early childhood education (M Ed); elementary education (M Ed); learning disabilities (M Ed, MAT); remedial education (M Ed); secondary education (M Ed). *Accreditation:* NCATE. Part-time programs available. *Faculty:* 17 full-time (12 women). *Students:* 5 full-time (3 women), 79 part-time (63 women); includes 33 minority (all Black or African American, non-Hispanic/Latino). Average age 34. 327 applicants, 42% accepted, 135 enrolled. In 2013, 45 master's awarded. *Degree requirements:* For master's, comprehensive exam. *Entrance requirements:* For master's, GRE General Test, MAT, NTE, or PRAXIS II. *Application deadline:* For fall admission, 3/15 priority date for domestic students; for spring admission, 10/15 priority date for domestic students. Application fee: $33. *Expenses:* Tuition, state resident: full-time $9184; part-time $459.20 per credit hour. Tuition, nonresident: full-time $18,368; part-time $918.40 per credit hour. *Required fees:* $13.50 per credit hour. $92 per semester. Tuition and fees vary according to program. *Financial support:* In 2013–14, 2 research assistantships (averaging $6,000 per year) were awarded; scholarships/grants and unspecified assistantships also available. Support available to part-time students. Financial award application deadline: 3/1; financial award applicants required to submit FAFSA. *Faculty research:* Identification and alternate assessment of at-risk students. *Unit head:* Dr. Shirley Carr Bausmith, Dean, 843-661-1460, Fax: 843-661-4647. *Application contact:* Rannie Gamble, Administrative Manager, 843-661-1286, Fax: 843-661-4688, E-mail: rgamble@fmarion.edu.

Frostburg State University, Graduate School, College of Education, Department of Educational Professions, Program in Curriculum and Instruction, Frostburg, MD 21532-1099. Offers educational technology (M Ed); elementary education (M Ed); secondary education (M Ed). Part-time and evening/weekend programs available. *Degree requirements:* For master's, thesis or alternative. *Entrance requirements:* For master's, teaching certificate. Additional exam requirements/recommendations for international students: Required—TOEFL. Electronic applications accepted. *Expenses: Tuition, area resident:* Part-time $340 per credit hour. Tuition, state resident: part-time $340 per credit hour. Tuition, nonresident: part-time $437 per credit hour.

Frostburg State University, Graduate School, College of Education, Department of Educational Professions, Program in Elementary Teaching, Frostburg, MD 21532-1099. Offers MAT. *Accreditation:* NCATE. *Degree requirements:* For master's, thesis or alternative, PRAXIS II. *Entrance requirements:* For master's, PRAXIS I, entry portfolio. Additional exam requirements/recommendations for international students: Required—TOEFL. Electronic applications accepted. *Expenses: Tuition, area resident:* Part-time $340 per credit hour. Tuition, state resident: part-time $340 per credit hour. Tuition, nonresident: part-time $437 per credit hour.

Gallaudet University, The Graduate School, Washington, DC 20002-3625. Offers ASL/English bilingual early childhood education: birth to 5 (Certificate); audiology (Au D); clinical psychology (PhD); critical studies in the education of deaf learners (PhD); deaf and hard of hearing infants, toddlers, and their families (Certificate); deaf education (Ed S); deaf education: advanced studies (MA); deaf education: special programs (MA); deaf history (Certificate); deaf studies (MA, Certificate); educating deaf students with disabilities (Certificate); education: teacher preparation (MA), including deaf education, early childhood education and deaf education, elementary education and deaf education, secondary education and deaf education; educational neuroscience (PhD); hearing, speech and language sciences (MS, PhD); international development (MA); interpretation (MA, PhD), including combined interpreting practice and research (MA), interpreting research (MA); linguistics (MA, PhD); mental health counseling (MA); peer mentoring (Certificate); public administration (MPA); school counseling (MA); school psychology (Psy S); sign language teaching (MA); social work (MSW); speech-language pathology (MS). Part-time programs available. *Faculty:* 55 full-time (37 women). *Students:* 361 full-time (279 women), 108 part-time (73 women); includes 98 minority (39 Black or African American, non-Hispanic/Latino; 1 American Indian or Alaska Native, non-Hispanic/Latino; 12 Asian, non-Hispanic/Latino; 36 Hispanic/Latino; 1 Native Hawaiian or other Pacific Islander, non-Hispanic/Latino; 9 Two or more races, non-Hispanic/Latino), 31 international. Average age 30. 602 applicants, 49% accepted, 177 enrolled. In 2013, 140 master's, 32 doctorates, 11 other advanced degrees awarded. Terminal master's awarded for partial completion of doctoral program. *Degree requirements:* For master's, comprehensive exam (for some programs), thesis optional; for doctorate, comprehensive exam, thesis/dissertation. *Entrance requirements:* For master's and doctorate, GRE General Test or MAT, letters of recommendation, interviews, goals statement, ASL proficiency interview, written English competency. Additional exam requirements/recommendations for international students: Required—TOEFL. *Application deadline:* For fall admission, 2/15 for domestic students. Applications are processed on a rolling basis. Application fee: $75. Electronic applications accepted. *Expenses: Tuition:* Full-time $14,774; part-time $821 per credit. *Required fees:* $198 per semester. *Financial support:* In 2013–14, 325 students received support. Fellowships, research assistantships, teaching assistantships, career-related internships or fieldwork, Federal Work-Study, scholarships/grants, tuition waivers (partial), and unspecified assistantships available. Support available to part-time students. Financial award applicants required to submit FAFSA. *Faculty research:* Bimodal bilingualism development, cochlear implants, telecommunications access, cancer genetics, linguistics, visual language and visual learning, advancement of avatar and robotics translation, algal productivity and physiology in the Anacostia River. *Unit head:* Dr. Carol J. Erting, Dean, Research, Graduate School, Continuing Studies, and International Programs, 202-651-5520, Fax: 202-651-5027, E-mail: carol.erting@gallaudet.edu. *Application contact:* Wednesday Luria, Coordinator of Prospective Graduate Student Services, 202-651-5400, Fax: 202-651-5295, E-mail: graduate.school@gallaudet.edu.
Website: http://www.gallaudet.edu/x26696.xml.

Gardner-Webb University, Graduate School, School of Education, Program in Elementary Education, Boiling Springs, NC 28017. Offers MA. *Accreditation:* NCATE. Part-time and evening/weekend programs available. *Students:* 139 full-time (136 women), 25 part-time (22 women); includes 33 minority (27 Black or African American, non-Hispanic/Latino; 1 American Indian or Alaska Native, non-Hispanic/Latino; 1 Asian, non-Hispanic/Latino; 4 Hispanic/Latino). Average age 33. 68 applicants, 47% accepted, 14 enrolled. In 2013, 12 master's awarded. *Degree requirements:* For master's, comprehensive exam. *Entrance requirements:* For master's, GRE General Test or NTE, PRAXIS, minimum GPA of 2.5. *Application deadline:* For fall admission, 8/1 priority date for domestic students. Applications are processed on a rolling basis. Application fee: $40. Electronic applications accepted. *Expenses: Tuition:* Full-time $7200; part-time $400 per credit hour. Tuition and fees vary according to course load and program. *Financial support:* Unspecified assistantships available. *Unit head:* Dr. Alan D. Eury, Chair, 704-406-4402, Fax: 704-406-3921, E-mail: dsimmons@gardner-webb.edu. *Application contact:* Office of Graduate Admissions, 877-498-4723, Fax: 704-406-3895, E-mail: gradinfo@gardner-webb.edu.

The George Washington University, Graduate School of Education and Human Development, Department of Curriculum and Pedagogy, Program in Elementary Education, Washington, DC 20052. Offers M Ed. *Accreditation:* NCATE. Part-time programs available. *Students:* 15 full-time (all women), 2 part-time (both women); includes 2 minority (1 Black or African American, non-Hispanic/Latino; 1 Two or more races, non-Hispanic/Latino), 1 international. Average age 26. 30 applicants, 100% accepted, 13 enrolled. In 2013, 19 master's awarded. *Degree requirements:* For master's, comprehensive exam. *Entrance requirements:* For master's, GRE General Test or MAT, minimum GPA of 2.75. *Application deadline:* For fall admission, 1/15 priority date for domestic students; for spring admission, 10/1 for domestic students. Applications are processed on a rolling basis. Application fee: $75. *Financial support:* In 2013–14, 25 students received support. Fellowships, career-related internships or fieldwork, Federal Work-Study, and tuition waivers (partial) available. Financial award application deadline: 1/15; financial award applicants required to submit FAFSA. *Faculty research:* Issues in teacher training. *Unit head:* Dr. Sylven S. Beck, Director, 202-994-3365, E-mail: sbeck@gwu.edu. *Application contact:* Sarah Lang, Director of Graduate Admissions, 202-994-1447, Fax: 202-994-7207, E-mail: slang@gwu.edu.

Georgia Southern University, Jack N. Averitt College of Graduate Studies, College of Education, Department of Teaching and Learning, Program in P-12 Education, Statesboro, GA 30460. Offers MAT. *Students:* 4 full-time (all women); includes 3 minority (all Hispanic/Latino). Average age 28. 5 applicants, 100% accepted. In 2013, 2 master's awarded. *Expenses: Tuition,* state resident: full-time $7068; part-time $270 per semester hour. Tuition, nonresident: full-time $26,446; part-time $1077 per semester hour. *Required fees:* $2092. *Financial support:* In 2013–14, 4 students received support. *Unit head:* Dr. Greg Chamblee, Program Coordinator, 912-478-5783, Fax: 912-478-0026, E-mail: gchamblee@georgiasouthern.edu. *Application contact:* Amanda

Gilliland, Coordinator for Graduate Student Recruitment, 912-478-5384, Fax: 912-478-0740, E-mail: gradschool@georgiasouthern.edu.

Georgia State University, College of Education, Department of Early Childhood Education, Atlanta, GA 30302-3083. Offers early childhood and elementary education (PhD); early childhood education (M Ed, Ed S); mathematics education (M Ed); urban education (M Ed). *Accreditation:* NCATE. Part-time and evening/weekend programs available. *Faculty:* 20 full-time (16 women). *Students:* 104 full-time (93 women), 37 part-time (36 women); includes 70 minority (54 Black or African American, non-Hispanic/Latino; 7 Asian, non-Hispanic/Latino; 6 Hispanic/Latino; 3 Two or more races, non-Hispanic/Latino), 2 international. Average age 29. 51 applicants, 55% accepted, 27 enrolled. In 2013, 73 master's, 1 doctorate, 17 other advanced degrees awarded. *Degree requirements:* For master's, comprehensive exam (for some programs), thesis (for some programs); for doctorate, comprehensive exam, thesis/dissertation (for some programs); for Ed S, comprehensive exam (for some programs). *Entrance requirements:* For master's, GRE, undergraduate diploma; for doctorate and Ed S, GRE, master's degree. Additional exam requirements/recommendations for international students: Required—TOEFL (minimum score 550 paper-based; 79 iBT) or IELTS (minimum score 6.5). *Application deadline:* Applications are processed on a rolling basis. Application fee: $50. Electronic applications accepted. *Expenses: Tuition, area resident:* Full-time $4176; part-time $348 per credit hour. Tuition, state resident: full-time $14,544; part-time $1212 per credit hour. Tuition, nonresident: full-time $14,544; part-time $1212 per credit hour. Tuition and fees vary according to course load and program. *Financial support:* In 2013–14, fellowships with full tuition reimbursements (averaging $24,000 per year), research assistantships with full and partial tuition reimbursements (averaging $4,000 per year), teaching assistantships with full tuition reimbursements (averaging $2,000 per year) were awarded; career-related internships or fieldwork, Federal Work-Study, institutionally sponsored loans, scholarships/grants, traineeships, health care benefits, tuition waivers (partial), and unspecified assistantships also available. Support available to part-time students. Financial award applicants required to submit FAFSA. *Faculty research:* Teacher development; language arts/literacy education; mathematics education; intersection of science, urban, and multicultural education; diversity in education. *Unit head:* Dr. Barbara Meyers, Department Chair, 404-413-8021, Fax: 404-413-8023, E-mail: barbara@gsu.edu. *Application contact:* Elaine King Jones, Administrative Curriculum Specialist, 404-413-8234, Fax: 404-413-8023, E-mail: ekjones@gsu.edu.
Website: http://education.gsu.edu/ece/index.htm.

Grand Canyon University, College of Education, Phoenix, AZ 85017-1097. Offers curriculum and instruction (M Ed); education administration (M Ed); elementary education (M Ed); secondary education (M Ed); special education (M Ed); teaching (MA). Part-time and evening/weekend programs available. Postbaccalaureate distance learning degree programs offered (no on-campus study). *Degree requirements:* For master's, publishable research paper (M Ed), e-portfolio. *Entrance requirements:* For master's, undergraduate degree from accredited, GCU-approved college, university, or program with minimum GPA 2.8. Additional exam requirements/recommendations for international students: Required—TOEFL (minimum score 550 paper-based; 79 iBT), IELTS (minimum score 6). Electronic applications accepted.

Grand Valley State University, College of Education, Programs in General Education, Allendale, MI 49401-9403. Offers adult and higher education (M Ed); early childhood education (M Ed); educational differentiation (M Ed); educational leadership (M Ed); educational technology integration (M Ed); elementary education (M Ed); middle level education (M Ed); school library media services (M Ed); secondary level education (M Ed); teaching English to speakers of other languages (M Ed). Part-time and evening/weekend programs available. Postbaccalaureate distance learning degree programs offered (minimal on-campus study). *Degree requirements:* For master's, thesis. *Entrance requirements:* For master's, GRE General Test or minimum GPA of 3.0. Additional exam requirements/recommendations for international students: Required—TOEFL. Electronic applications accepted. *Faculty research:* Effectiveness of technology in education, parental involvement, effective teaching, effective schools research.

Greensboro College, Program in Education, Greensboro, NC 27401-1875. Offers elementary education (M Ed); special education (M Ed). Part-time and evening/weekend programs available. *Degree requirements:* For master's, thesis. *Entrance requirements:* For master's, GRE, teacher license, 2 years of teaching experience, 2 letters of recommendation. Additional exam requirements/recommendations for international students: Required—TOEFL (minimum score 550 paper-based). Electronic applications accepted.

Greenville College, Program in Education, Greenville, IL 62246-0159. Offers education (MAT); elementary education (MAE); secondary education (MAE). *Degree requirements:* For master's, thesis (for some programs). *Entrance requirements:* For master's, GRE, Illinois Basic Skills Test, teacher certification. Electronic applications accepted.

Hampton University, Graduate College, College of Education and Continuing Studies, Program in Elementary Education, Hampton, VA 23668. Offers MA. *Accreditation:* NCATE. Part-time and evening/weekend programs available. *Entrance requirements:* For master's, GRE General Test.

Harding University, Cannon-Clary College of Education, Searcy, AR 72149-0001. Offers advanced studies in teaching and learning (M Ed); art (MSE); behavioral science (MSE); counseling (MS, Ed S); early childhood special education (M Ed, MSE); education (MSE); educational leadership (M Ed, Ed S); elementary education (M Ed); English (MSE); French (MSE); history/social science (MSE); kinesiology (MSE); math (MSE); reading (M Ed); secondary education (M Ed); Spanish (MSE); teaching (MAT); teaching English as a second language (MSE). *Accreditation:* NCATE. Part-time and evening/weekend programs available. *Faculty:* 13 full-time (5 women), 42 part-time/adjunct (24 women). *Students:* 154 full-time (119 women), 393 part-time (270 women); includes 108 minority (81 Black or African American, non-Hispanic/Latino; 5 American Indian or Alaska Native, non-Hispanic/Latino; 5 Asian, non-Hispanic/Latino; 9 Hispanic/Latino; 8 Two or more races, non-Hispanic/Latino), 15 international. Average age 36. 187 applicants, 79% accepted, 135 enrolled. In 2013, 138 master's, 17 other advanced degrees awarded. *Degree requirements:* For master's, comprehensive exam (for some programs), thesis optional, portfolio(s); for Ed S, comprehensive exam, portfolio, project. *Entrance requirements:* For master's, GRE, MAT, PRAXIS; for Ed S, MAT or GRE. Additional exam requirements/recommendations for international students: Required—TOEFL (minimum score 550 paper-based; 79 iBT). *Application deadline:* For fall admission, 8/1 for domestic and international students; for spring admission, 1/1 for domestic and international students. Applications are processed on a rolling basis. Application fee: $35. *Expenses: Tuition:* Full-time $11,574; part-time $643 per credit hour. *Required fees:* $432; $24 per credit hour. Tuition and fees vary according to course load, degree level and program. *Financial support:* In 2013–14, 36 students received support. Unspecified assistantships available. *Faculty research:* Reading, comprehension, school violence, educational technology, behavior, college choice, differentiated instruction, brain-based teaching. *Unit head:* Dr. Clara Carroll, Chair, 501-279-4501, Fax: 501-279-4083, E-mail: ccarroll@harding.edu. *Application contact:* Information Contact, 501-279-4315, E-mail: gradstudiesedu@harding.edu.
Website: http://www.harding.edu/education.

Elementary Education

Hawai'i Pacific University, College of Humanities and Social Sciences, Program in Elementary Education, Honolulu, HI 96813. Offers M Ed. Part-time and evening/weekend programs available. *Faculty:* 4 full-time (2 women), 4 part-time/adjunct (3 women). *Students:* 21 full-time (16 women), 1 (woman) part-time; includes 11 minority (3 Asian, non-Hispanic/Latino; 1 Hispanic/Latino; 7 Two or more races, non-Hispanic/Latino). Average age 30. 19 applicants, 68% accepted, 13 enrolled. In 2013, 1 master's awarded. *Financial support:* In 2013–14, 8 students received support. Career-related internships or fieldwork, Federal Work-Study, scholarships/grants, and tuition waivers available. *Unit head:* Dr. Valentina Abordonado, Program Chair, 808-544-1143, Fax: 808-544-0841, E-mail: vabordonado@hpu.edu. *Application contact:* Rumi Yoshida, Associate Director of Graduate Admissions, 808-543-8034, Fax: 808-544-0280, E-mail: grad@hpu.edu.
Website: http://www.hpu.edu/CHSS/Education/MEDEE/index.html.

High Point University, Norcross Graduate School, High Point, NC 27262-3598. Offers business administration (MBA); educational leadership (M Ed); elementary education (M Ed); history (MA); nonprofit management (MA); secondary math (M Ed); special education (M Ed); strategic communication (MA); teaching elementary education k-6 (MAT); teaching secondary mathematics 9-12 (MAT). *Accreditation:* NCATE. Part-time and evening/weekend programs available. *Degree requirements:* For master's, comprehensive exam (for some programs), thesis (for some programs). *Entrance requirements:* For master's, GMAT (MBA), GRE, MAT, minimum GPA of 3.0. Additional exam requirements/recommendations for international students: Required—TOEFL (minimum score 550 paper-based). Electronic applications accepted.

Hofstra University, School of Education, Programs in Educational Policy and Leadership, Hempstead, NY 11549. Offers educational and policy leadership (MS Ed, Ed D), including K-12 (MS Ed), K-12/higher education (Ed D); educational policy and leadership (Advanced Certificate), including school district business leader; foundations of education (MA, Advanced Certificate); higher education leadership and policy studies (MS Ed).

Hofstra University, School of Education, Programs in Literacy, Hempstead, NY 11549. Offers advanced literacy studies (PD), including birth-grade 6 (MA, MS Ed, PD); advanced literary studies (PD), including grades 5-12 (MA, PD); birth-grade 6 (MS Ed, Advanced Certificate); grades 5-12 (Advanced Certificate); literacy studies (Ed D, PhD); special education (MS Ed), including birth-grade 2, birth-grade 6 (MA, MS Ed, PD); teaching of writing (MA), including birth-grade 6 (MA, MS Ed, PD), grades 5-12 (MA, PD).

Hofstra University, School of Education, Programs in Special Education, Hempstead, NY 11549. Offers applied behavior analysis (Advanced Certificate); early childhood special education (MS Ed, Advanced Certificate); gifted education (Advanced Certificate); inclusive early childhood special education (MS Ed); inclusive elementary special education (MS Ed); inclusive secondary special education (MS Ed); secondary education generalist (MS Ed), including students with disabilities 7-12; special education (MA, MS Ed, Advanced Certificate, PD); special education assessment and diagnosis (Advanced Certificate); special education generalist (MS Ed), including extension in secondary education; teaching students with severe or multiple disabilities (Advanced Certificate).

Hofstra University, School of Education, Programs in Teaching - Elementary and Early Childhood Education, Hempstead, NY 11549. Offers early childhood and childhood education (MS Ed); early childhood education (MA, MS Ed); educational technology (MA); elementary education (MS Ed); literacy (MA); math specialist (Advanced Certificate); math, science, technology (MA); multiculturalism (MA).

Holy Family University, Graduate School, School of Education, Master of Education Programs, Philadelphia, PA 19114. Offers early elementary education (PreK-Grade 4) (M Ed); education leadership (M Ed); general education (M Ed); middle level education (Grades 4-8) (M Ed); reading specialist (M Ed); secondary education (Grades 7-12) (M Ed); special education (M Ed); TESOL and literacy (M Ed). *Expenses: Tuition:* Full-time $12,060. *Required fees:* $250. Tuition and fees vary according to degree level. *Unit head:* Dr. Leonard Soroka, Dean, 267-341-3565, Fax: 215-824-2438, E-mail: lsoroka@holyfamily.edu. *Application contact:* Gidget Marie Montelibano, Associate Director of Graduate Admissions, 267-341-3358, Fax: 215-637-1478, E-mail: gmontelibano@holyfamily.edu.

Hood College, Graduate School, Department of Education, Frederick, MD 21701-8575. Offers curriculum and instruction (MS), including early childhood education, elementary education, elementary school science and mathematics, secondary education, special education; educational leadership (MS, Certificate); reading specialization (MS); STEM (Certificate). *Accreditation:* NCATE. Part-time and evening/weekend programs available. *Faculty:* 4 full-time (3 women), 33 part-time/adjunct (25 women). *Students:* 1 (woman) full-time, 340 part-time (282 women); includes 59 minority (31 Black or African American, non-Hispanic/Latino; 1 American Indian or Alaska Native, non-Hispanic/Latino; 10 Asian, non-Hispanic/Latino; 13 Hispanic/Latino; 4 Two or more races, non-Hispanic/Latino). Average age 33. 97 applicants, 99% accepted, 86 enrolled. In 2013, 64 master's, 40 other advanced degrees awarded. *Degree requirements:* For master's, action research project, portfolio (reading). *Entrance requirements:* For master's, minimum GPA of 2.75, teaching certification. Additional exam requirements/recommendations for international students: Required—TOEFL (minimum score 575 paper-based; 89 iBT), IELTS (minimum score 6.5). *Application deadline:* For fall admission, 7/15 priority date for domestic students, 7/15 for international students; for spring admission, 12/1 priority date for domestic students, 12/1 for international students. Applications are processed on a rolling basis. Application fee: $35. Electronic applications accepted. Application fee is waived when completed online. *Expenses: Tuition:* Part-time $405 per credit. *Required fees:* $100 per semester. *Financial support:* In 2013–14, 1 student received support. Tuition waivers (partial) and unspecified assistantships available. Financial award applicants required to submit FAFSA. *Faculty research:* Leadership, action research, brain research, learning styles. *Unit head:* Dr. Ellen Koitz, Chairperson, 301-696-3466, Fax: 301-696-3597, E-mail: koitz@hood.edu. *Application contact:* Dr. Maria Green Cowles, Dean of Graduate School, 301-696-3811, Fax: 301-696-3597, E-mail: gofurther@hood.edu.
Website: http://www.hood.edu/academics/education/index.html.

Hope International University, School of Graduate and Professional Studies, Program in Education, Fullerton, CA 92831-3138. Offers education administration (MA); elementary education (ME); secondary education (ME). Part-time and evening/weekend programs available. *Degree requirements:* For master's, comprehensive exam (for some programs), thesis. *Entrance requirements:* For master's, minimum GPA of 3.0, 2 references. Additional exam requirements/recommendations for international students: Required—TOEFL (minimum score 550 paper-based; 86 iBT); Recommended—IELTS (minimum score 6.5). Electronic applications accepted. *Expenses:* Contact institution. *Faculty research:* Distance education.

Howard University, School of Education, Department of Curriculum and Instruction, Program in Elementary Education, Washington, DC 20059-0002. Offers M Ed. *Accreditation:* NCATE. *Faculty:* 4 full-time (all women). *Students:* 4 full-time (3 women), 8 part-time (6 women); all minorities (all Black or African American, non-Hispanic/Latino). Average age 30. In 2013, 8 master's awarded. *Degree requirements:* For master's, comprehensive exam, expository writing exam, internships, seminar paper. *Entrance requirements:* For master's, PRAXIS I, GRE, minimum GPA of 2.7. Additional exam requirements/recommendations for international students: Required—TOEFL (minimum score 550 paper-based; 79 iBT). *Application deadline:* For fall admission, 2/15 priority date for domestic students; for spring admission, 11/1 for domestic students. Applications are processed on a rolling basis. Application fee: $45. Electronic applications accepted. *Financial support:* In 2013–14, 1 student received support, including 1 fellowship with full and partial tuition reimbursement available (averaging $15,000 per year); career-related internships or fieldwork, Federal Work-Study, scholarships/grants, tuition waivers (full and partial), and unspecified assistantships also available. Financial award application deadline: 3/15; financial award applicants required to submit FAFSA. *Unit head:* Dr. Kenneth Anderson, Chair, Department of Curriculum and Instruction, 202-806-5300, Fax: 202-806-5297, E-mail: kenneth.anderson@howard.edu. *Application contact:* June L. Harris, Administrative Assistant, Department of Curriculum and Instruction, 202-806-7343, Fax: 202-806-5297, E-mail: jlharris@howard.edu.

Hunter College of the City University of New York, Graduate School, School of Education, Department of Curriculum and Teaching and Department of Educational Foundations and Counseling Programs, Program in Elementary Education, New York, NY 10065-5085. Offers MS. *Accreditation:* NCATE. *Faculty:* 3 full-time (all women), 10 part-time/adjunct (9 women). *Students:* 51 full-time (44 women), 307 part-time (274 women); includes 119 minority (27 Black or African American, non-Hispanic/Latino; 31 Asian, non-Hispanic/Latino; 61 Hispanic/Latino), 9 international. Average age 23. 198 applicants, 63% accepted, 70 enrolled. In 2013, 209 master's awarded. *Degree requirements:* For master's, thesis, integrative seminar, New York State Teacher Certification Exams, student teaching. *Entrance requirements:* For master's, minimum undergraduate GPA of 2.8, writing sample. Additional exam requirements/recommendations for international students: Required—TOEFL, TWE. *Application deadline:* For fall admission, 4/1 for domestic students, 2/1 for international students; for spring admission, 11/1 for domestic students, 9/1 for international students. Application fee: $125. *Financial support:* Federal Work-Study, scholarships/grants, and tuition waivers (partial) available. Support available to part-time students. *Faculty research:* Urban education, multicultural education, gifted education, educational technology, cultural cognition. *Unit head:* Dr. Christina Taharally, Program Coordinator, 212-772-4679, E-mail: christina.taharally@hunter.cuny.edu. *Application contact:* Milena Solo, Director for Graduate Admissions, 212-772-4480, E-mail: admissions@hunter.cuny.edu. Website: http://www.hunter.cuny.edu/school-of-education/programs/graduate/childhood-math-science.

Idaho State University, Office of Graduate Studies, College of Education, Department of Educational Foundations, Pocatello, ID 83209-8059. Offers child and family studies (M Ed); curriculum leadership (M Ed); education (M Ed); educational administration (M Ed); educational foundations (5th Year Certificate); elementary education (M Ed), including K-12 education, literacy, secondary education. Part-time programs available. *Degree requirements:* For master's, comprehensive exam, thesis optional, oral exam, written exam; for 5th Year Certificate, comprehensive exam, thesis (for some programs), oral exam, written exam. *Entrance requirements:* For master's, GRE General Test or MAT, minimum undergraduate GPA of 3.0; for 5th Year Certificate, GRE General Test, minimum undergraduate GPA of 3.0, master's degree. Additional exam requirements/recommendations for international students: Required—TOEFL (minimum score 550 paper-based; 80 iBT). Electronic applications accepted. *Faculty research:* Child and families studies; business education; special education; math, science, and technology education.

Immaculata University, College of Graduate Studies, Program in Educational Leadership and Administration, Immaculata, PA 19345. Offers educational leadership and administration (MA, Ed D); elementary education (Certificate); school principal (Certificate); school superintendent (Certificate); secondary education (Certificate); special education (Certificate). Part-time and evening/weekend programs available. *Degree requirements:* For master's, comprehensive exam, thesis optional; for doctorate, comprehensive exam, thesis/dissertation. *Entrance requirements:* For master's, GRE or MAT, minimum GPA of 3.0; for doctorate, GRE General Test or MAT, minimum GPA of 3.5. Additional exam requirements/recommendations for international students: Required—TOEFL. Electronic applications accepted. *Faculty research:* Cooperative learning, school-based management, whole language, performance assessment.

Indiana State University, College of Graduate and Professional Studies, College of Education, Department of Elementary, Early and Special Education, Terre Haute, IN 47809. Offers early childhood education (M Ed); elementary education (M Ed); MA/MS. *Accreditation:* NCATE. Electronic applications accepted.

Indiana University Bloomington, School of Education, Department of Curriculum and Instruction, Bloomington, IN 47405-7000. Offers art education (MS, Ed D, PhD); curriculum studies (Ed D, PhD); elementary education (MS, Ed D, PhD, Ed S); mathematics education (MS, Ed D, PhD); science education (MS, Ed D, PhD); secondary education (MS, Ed D, PhD); social studies education (MS, PhD); special education (PhD, Ed S). *Accreditation:* NCATE. Part-time and evening/weekend programs available. Terminal master's awarded for partial completion of doctoral program. *Degree requirements:* For doctorate, thesis/dissertation; for Ed S, comprehensive exam or project. *Entrance requirements:* For master's, doctorate, and Ed S, GRE General Test. Electronic applications accepted.

Indiana University Kokomo, Division of Education, Kokomo, IN 46904-9003. Offers elementary education (MS Ed). *Accreditation:* NCATE. Part-time and evening/weekend programs available. *Faculty:* 1 full-time (0 women). *Students:* 3 full-time (1 woman), 14 part-time (7 women); includes 1 minority (Asian, non-Hispanic/Latino). Average age 36. 1 applicant. *Degree requirements:* For master's, thesis optional, research project. *Entrance requirements:* For master's, GRE General Test, minimum GPA of 2.5. *Application deadline:* For fall admission, 8/1 for domestic students; for spring admission, 12/1 for domestic students. Applications are processed on a rolling basis. *Financial support:* Fellowships and minority teacher scholarships available. *Faculty research:* Reading, teaching effectiveness, portfolio, curriculum development. *Unit head:* Dr. Shirley Aamidor, Dean, 765-455-9441, E-mail: mseduc@iuk.edu. *Application contact:* Admissions Office, 765-455-9357.

Indiana University Northwest, School of Education, Gary, IN 46408-1197. Offers educational leadership (MS Ed); elementary education (MS Ed); secondary education (MS Ed). *Accreditation:* NCATE. Part-time and evening/weekend programs available. *Faculty:* 5 full-time (2 women). *Students:* 19 full-time (17 women), 119 part-time (98 women); includes 79 minority (63 Black or African American, non-Hispanic/Latino; 3 Asian, non-Hispanic/Latino; 12 Hispanic/Latino; 1 Two or more races, non-Hispanic/Latino), 1 international. Average age 37. 25 applicants, 92% accepted, 16 enrolled. In 2013, 69 master's awarded. *Entrance requirements:* For master's, GRE General Test or MAT, minimum GPA of 3.0. *Application deadline:* For fall admission, 7/15 priority date for domestic students; for spring admission, 11/15 for domestic students. *Unit head:* Dr. Stanley E. Wigle, Dean, 219-980-6989, E-mail: swigle@iun.edu. *Application contact:* Admissions Counselor, 219-980-6760, Fax: 219-980-7103.
Website: http://www.iun.edu/education/degrees/masters.htm.

Indiana University–Purdue University Fort Wayne, College of Education and Public Policy, Department of Educational Studies, Fort Wayne, IN 46805-1499. Offers elementary education (MS Ed); secondary education (MS Ed). *Accreditation:* NCATE. Part-time programs available. *Faculty:* 13 full-time (6 women). *Students:* 5 part-time (2 women); includes 1 minority (Hispanic/Latino). Average age 40. 2 applicants, 100% accepted, 2 enrolled. In 2013, 20 master's awarded. *Entrance requirements:* For master's, minimum GPA of 2.5, three professional letters of recommendation. Additional exam requirements/recommendations for international students: Required—TOEFL (minimum score 550 paper-based; 79 iBT). *Application deadline:* For fall admission, 4/1 priority date for domestic and international students. Applications are processed on a rolling basis. Application fee: $55. *Financial support:* In 2013–14, 1 teaching assistantship with partial tuition reimbursement (averaging $13,322 per year) was awarded; scholarships/grants also available. Support available to part-time students. Financial award application deadline: 3/1; financial award applicants required to submit FAFSA. *Faculty research:* Student course evaluation (SET) in higher education, North Korea's food shortage. *Unit head:* Dr. Terri Swim, Chair, 260-481-6442, Fax: 260-481-5408, E-mail: swimt@ipfw.edu. *Application contact:* Vicky L. Schmidt, Graduate Recorder, 260-481-6450, Fax: 260-481-5408, E-mail: schmidt@ipfw.edu. Website: http://www.ipfw.edu/education.

Indiana University South Bend, School of Education, South Bend, IN 46634-7111. Offers counseling and human services (MS Ed); elementary and secondary education leadership (MS Ed); elementary education (MS Ed); secondary education (MS Ed); special education (MAT, MS Ed). *Accreditation:* NCATE. Part-time and evening/weekend programs available. *Faculty:* 21 full-time (11 women), 9 part-time/adjunct (3 women). *Students:* 12 full-time (8 women), 103 part-time (85 women); includes 18 minority (8 Black or African American, non-Hispanic/Latino; 1 Asian, non-Hispanic/Latino; 5 Hispanic/Latino; 4 Two or more races, non-Hispanic/Latino), 3 international. Average age 36. 24 applicants, 63% accepted, 9 enrolled. In 2013, 41 master's awarded. *Degree requirements:* For master's, thesis or alternative, exit project. *Entrance requirements:* For master's, letters of recommendation, GRE or minimum GPA of 3.0. Additional exam requirements/recommendations for international students: Required—TOEFL. *Application deadline:* For fall admission, 7/1 for domestic students; for spring admission, 11/1 for domestic students. Applications are processed on a rolling basis. Electronic applications accepted. *Financial support:* Career-related internships or fieldwork available. Support available to part-time students. Financial award application deadline: 3/1; financial award applicants required to submit FAFSA. *Faculty research:* Professional dispositions, early childhood literacy, online learning, program assessments, problem-based learning. *Unit head:* Dr. Marvin Lynn, Dean, 574-520-4339. *Application contact:* Yvonne Walker, Student Services Representative, 574-520-4185, E-mail: ydwalker@iusb.edu. Website: http://www.iusb.edu/~edud/.

Indiana University Southeast, School of Education, New Albany, IN 47150-6405. Offers counselor education (MS Ed); elementary education (MS Ed); secondary education (MS Ed). *Accreditation:* NCATE. Part-time and evening/weekend programs available. *Students:* 23 full-time (21 women), 324 part-time (248 women); includes 44 minority (34 Black or African American, non-Hispanic/Latino; 1 American Indian or Alaska Native, non-Hispanic/Latino; 1 Asian, non-Hispanic/Latino; 5 Hispanic/Latino; 3 Two or more races, non-Hispanic/Latino). Average age 33. 36 applicants, 81% accepted, 25 enrolled. In 2013, 147 master's awarded. *Entrance requirements:* For master's, minimum undergraduate GPA of 2.5, graduate 3.0. *Application deadline:* Applications are processed on a rolling basis. *Financial support:* Career-related internships or fieldwork, Federal Work-Study, and institutionally sponsored loans available. Support available to part-time students. Financial award applicants required to submit FAFSA. *Faculty research:* Learning styles, technology, constructivism, group process, innovative math strategies. *Unit head:* Dr. Gloria Murray, Dean, 812-941-2169, Fax: 812-941-2667, E-mail: soeinfo@ius.edu. *Application contact:* Admissions Counselor, 812-941-2212, Fax: 812-941-2595, E-mail: admissions@ius.edu. Website: http://www.ius.edu/education/.

Inter American University of Puerto Rico, Aguadilla Campus, Graduate School, Aguadilla, PR 00605. Offers accounting (MBA); counseling psychology specializing in family (MS); criminal justice (MA); educative management and leadership (MA); elementary education (M Ed); finance (MBA); human resources (MBA); industrial management (MBA); management information systems (MBA); marketing (MBA). Part-time and evening/weekend programs available. *Degree requirements:* For master's, comprehensive exam. *Entrance requirements:* For master's, EXADEP, 2 letters of recommendation, minimum GPA of 2.5. Electronic applications accepted.

Inter American University of Puerto Rico, Arecibo Campus, Programs in Education, Arecibo, PR 00614-4050. Offers administration and educational supervision (MA Ed); counseling and guidance (MA Ed); curriculum and teaching (MA Ed), including biology education, English as a second language, history education, math education, Spanish; elementary education (MA Ed). *Degree requirements:* For master's, comprehensive exam, thesis optional. *Entrance requirements:* For master's, GRE, EXADEP, bachelor's degree in education or teaching license (administration and supervision) or courses in education and psychology (counseling and guidance), minimum GPA of 2.5 in last 60 credits.

Inter American University of Puerto Rico, Barranquitas Campus, Program in Education, Barranquitas, PR 00794. Offers curriculum and teaching (M Ed), including biology education, English as a second language, history education, mathematics education, Spanish; educational leadership and management (MA); elementary education (M Ed); information and library service technology (M Ed); special education (MA). *Degree requirements:* For master's, comprehensive exam, thesis optional. *Entrance requirements:* For master's, EXADEP, letter of recommendation. Electronic applications accepted.

Inter American University of Puerto Rico, Guayama Campus, Department of Education and Social Sciences, Guayama, PR 00785. Offers early childhood education (0-4 years) (M Ed); elementary education (M Ed). Part-time programs available. *Entrance requirements:* For master's, GRE, MAT, EXADEP, letters of recommendation, minimum GPA of 2.5. Electronic applications accepted.

Inter American University of Puerto Rico, Metropolitan Campus, Graduate Programs, Program in Elementary Education, San Juan, PR 00919-1293. Offers MA. *Degree requirements:* For master's, comprehensive exam. *Entrance requirements:* For master's, GRE or EXADEP, interview. Electronic applications accepted.

Inter American University of Puerto Rico, Ponce Campus, Graduate School, Mercedita, PR 00715-1602. Offers accounting (MBA); biology (M Ed); chemistry (M Ed); criminal justice (MA); elementary education (M Ed); English as a Second Language (M Ed); finance (MBA); history (M Ed); human resources (MBA); marketing (MBA); mathematics (M Ed); Spanish (M Ed). *Entrance requirements:* For master's, minimum GPA of 2.5.

Inter American University of Puerto Rico, San Germán Campus, Graduate Studies Center, Program in Elementary Education, San Germán, PR 00683-5008. Offers MA. Part-time and evening/weekend programs available. *Faculty:* 9 full-time (6 women), 13 part-time/adjunct (7 women). *Students:* 17 full-time (16 women), 2 part-time (both

women); all minorities (all Hispanic/Latino). 6 applicants, 100% accepted, 6 enrolled. In 2013, 1 master's awarded. *Degree requirements:* For master's, comprehensive exam. *Entrance requirements:* For master's, GRE General Test or EXADEP, minimum GPA of 3.0. Application fee: $31. *Expenses: Tuition:* Full-time $2424; part-time $202 per credit hour. *Required fees:* $260 per semester. Tuition and fees vary according to course level, course load, degree level and program. *Financial support:* Teaching assistantships, Federal Work-Study, and unspecified assistantships available. *Unit head:* Dr. Elba T. Irizarry, Director of Graduate Studies Center, 787-264-1912 Ext. 7357, Fax: 787-892-6350, E-mail: elbat@sg.inter.edu. *Application contact:* Dr. Evelyn Acevedo, Coordinator, 787-264-1912, E-mail: eacevedo@intersg.edu.

Iona College, School of Arts and Science, Department of Education, New Rochelle, NY 10801-1890. Offers adolescence education: biology (MS Ed, MST); adolescence education: English (MS Ed, MST); adolescence education: Italian (MS Ed, MST); adolescence education: mathematics (MS Ed, MST); adolescence education: social studies (MS Ed, MST); adolescence education: Spanish (MS Ed, MST); adolescence special education 5-12 (MST); adolescence special education and literacy (MS Ed); childhood and special education (MST); childhood education (MST); early childhood and childhood (MST); educational leadership (MS Ed); literacy education: birth-grade 6 (MS Ed). *Accreditation:* NCATE. Part-time and evening/weekend programs available. *Faculty:* 11 full-time (9 women), 7 part-time/adjunct (6 women). *Students:* 34 full-time (25 women), 61 part-time (47 women); includes 5 minority (2 Asian, non-Hispanic/Latino; 3 Hispanic/Latino; 1 international. Average age 25. 27 applicants, 93% accepted, 16 enrolled. In 2013, 54 master's awarded. *Degree requirements:* For master's, thesis or alternative. *Entrance requirements:* For master's, minimum GPA of 3.0, NY State teaching certificate (for all MS Ed programs). Additional exam requirements/recommendations for international students: Required—TOEFL (minimum score 550 paper-based; 80 iBT), IELTS (minimum score 6.5). *Application deadline:* For fall admission, 8/1 priority date for domestic students, 5/1 priority date for international students; for spring admission, 1/1 priority date for domestic students, 9/1 priority date for international students. Applications are processed on a rolling basis. Application fee: $50. Electronic applications accepted. *Expenses: Tuition:* Part-time $948 per credit. *Required fees:* $235 per term. *Financial support:* In 2013–14, 84 students received support. Unspecified assistantships available. Support available to part-time students. Financial award application deadline: 4/15; financial award applicants required to submit FAFSA. *Faculty research:* Reading/writing, educational technology, administration, early literacy assessment, literacy development. *Unit head:* Margaret Smith, PhD, Chair, 914-633-2210, Fax: 914-633-2608, E-mail: msmith@iona.edu. *Application contact:* Veronica Jarek-Prinz, Director, Graduate Admissions, 914-633-2420, Fax: 914-633-2277, E-mail: vjarekprinz@iona.edu. Website: http://www.iona.edu/Academics/School-of-Arts-Science/Departments/Education/Graduate-Programs.aspx.

Iowa State University of Science and Technology, Department of Curriculum and Instruction, Ames, IA 50011. Offers curriculum and instructional technology (M Ed, MS, PhD); elementary education (M Ed, MS); historical, philosophical, and comparative studies in education (M Ed, MS); special education (M Ed, MS, PhD). *Degree requirements:* For master's, thesis or alternative; for doctorate, thesis/dissertation. *Entrance requirements:* For master's and doctorate, GRE General Test. Additional exam requirements/recommendations for international students: Required—TOEFL (minimum score 560 paper-based; 83 iBT), IELTS (minimum score 6.5). Electronic applications accepted.

Ithaca College, School of Humanities and Sciences, Program in Childhood Education, Grades 1-6, Ithaca, NY 14850. Offers MS. Part-time programs available. *Faculty:* 31 full-time (11 women). *Students:* 9 full-time (6 women). Average age 30. 21 applicants, 67% accepted, 9 enrolled. In 2013, 7 master's awarded. *Degree requirements:* For master's, thesis or alternative, student teaching. *Entrance requirements:* For master's, minimum GPA of 3.0. Additional exam requirements/recommendations for international students: Required—TOEFL (minimum score 550 paper-based; 80 iBT). *Application deadline:* For fall admission, 2/15 for domestic and international students; for spring admission, 12/1 for domestic and international students. Applications are processed on a rolling basis. Application fee: $40. Electronic applications accepted. *Expenses:* Contact institution. *Financial support:* In 2013–14, 6 students received support, including 6 teaching assistantships (averaging $8,792 per year); career-related internships or fieldwork, Federal Work-Study, scholarships/grants, and unspecified assistantships also available. Support available to part-time students. Financial award application deadline: 2/15; financial award applicants required to submit CSS PROFILE or FAFSA. *Faculty research:* Teacher preparation (elementary and secondary education), equity and social justice in education, language and literacy, multicultural education/sociocultural studies, reflective practice and teacher research. *Unit head:* Dr. Linda Hanrahan, Chairperson, 607-274-3143, Fax: 607-274-1263, E-mail: gps@ithaca.edu. *Application contact:* Gerard Turbide, Director, Office of Admission, 607-274-3143, Fax: 607-274-1263, E-mail: gps@ithaca.edu. Website: http://www.ithaca.edu/gradprograms/education/programs/childhooded.

Jackson State University, Graduate School, College of Education and Human Development, Department of Elementary and Early Childhood Education, Jackson, MS 39217. Offers early childhood education (MS Ed, Ed D); elementary education (MS Ed, Ed S). *Accreditation:* NCATE. Evening/weekend programs available. Terminal master's awarded for partial completion of doctoral program. *Degree requirements:* For master's, comprehensive exam, thesis or alternative; for doctorate, comprehensive exam, thesis/dissertation. *Entrance requirements:* For master's, GRE General Test; for doctorate, MAT, teaching experience. Additional exam requirements/recommendations for international students: Required—TOEFL (minimum score 520 paper-based; 67 iBT).

Jacksonville State University, College of Graduate Studies and Continuing Education, College of Education and Professional Studies, Program in Elementary Education, Jacksonville, AL 36265-1602. Offers MS Ed. *Accreditation:* NCATE. Part-time and evening/weekend programs available. *Degree requirements:* For master's, comprehensive exam, thesis (for some programs). *Entrance requirements:* For master's, GRE General Test or MAT. Additional exam requirements/recommendations for international students: Required—TOEFL (minimum score 61 iBT). Electronic applications accepted.

James Madison University, The Graduate School, College of Education, Early, Elementary, and Reading Education Department, Harrisonburg, VA 22807. Offers early childhood education (MAT); elementary education (MAT); reading education (M Ed). *Students:* Average age 27. *Entrance requirements:* Additional exam requirements/recommendations for international students: Required—TOEFL. *Application deadline:* For fall admission, 5/1 for domestic students; for spring admission, 9/1 for domestic students. Applications are processed on a rolling basis. Application fee: $55. Electronic applications accepted. *Financial support:* Application deadline: 3/1; applicants required to submit FAFSA. *Unit head:* Dr. Martha Ross, Academic Unit Head, 540-568-6255. *Application contact:* Lynette M. Bible, Director of Graduate Admissions, 540-568-6395, Fax: 540-568-7860, E-mail: biblelm@jmu.edu.

Johns Hopkins University, School of Education, Master's Programs in Education, Baltimore, MD 21218-2699. Offers counseling (MS), including mental health counseling, school counseling; education (MS), including educational studies, gifted education,

reading, school administration and supervision, technology for educators; elementary education (MAT); health professions (M Ed); intelligence analysis (MS); management (MS); secondary education (MAT); special education (MS), including early childhood special education, general special education studies, mild to moderate disabilities, severe disabilities. Part-time and evening/weekend programs available. Postbaccalaureate distance learning degree programs offered (no on-campus study). *Students:* 183 full-time (123 women), 1,001 part-time (757 women); includes 380 minority (160 Black or African American, non-Hispanic/Latino; 4 American Indian or Alaska Native, non-Hispanic/Latino; 91 Asian, non-Hispanic/Latino; 78 Hispanic/Latino; 4 Native Hawaiian or other Pacific Islander, non-Hispanic/Latino; 43 Two or more races, non-Hispanic/Latino), 28 international. Average age 28. 508 applicants, 90% accepted, 337 enrolled. In 2013, 565 degrees awarded. *Degree requirements:* For master's, comprehensive exam (for some programs), portfolio, capstone project and/or internship; PRAXIS II (for teacher preparation programs that lead to licensure). *Entrance requirements:* For master's, GRE (for full-time programs only); PRAXIS I or equivalent (for teacher preparation programs that lead to licensure), bachelor's degree from regionally- or nationally-accredited institution, minimum GPA of 3.0 in all previous programs of study, official transcripts from all post-secondary institutions attended, essay, curriculum vitae/resume, minimum of two letters of recommendation. Additional exam requirements/recommendations for international students: Required—TOEFL (minimum score 600 paper-based; 100 iBT) or IELTS (minimum score 7). *Application deadline:* For fall admission, 4/1 for domestic and international students; for spring admission, 10/1 for domestic and international students; for summer admission, 2/1 for domestic and international students. Application fee: $80. Electronic applications accepted. *Financial support:* Application deadline: 6/1; applicants required to submit FAFSA. *Unit head:* Dr. David A. Andrews, Dean, 410-516-7820, Fax: 410-516-6697, E-mail: davidandrews@jhu.edu. *Application contact:* Catherine Wilson, Associate Director of Admissions, 410-516-9797, Fax: 410-516-9799, E-mail: soe.info@jhu.edu.

Johnson & Wales University, MAT Program in Teacher Education, Providence, RI 02903-3703. Offers business education and secondary special education (MAT); elementary education and elementary special education (MAT); elementary education and elementary/secondary special education (MAT); elementary education and secondary special education (MAT); food service education (MAT). Part-time and evening/weekend programs available. *Entrance requirements:* For master's, MAT, minimum GPA of 2.75. Additional exam requirements/recommendations for international students: Required—TOEFL (minimum score 550 paper-based) or IELTS (recommended). *Faculty research:* Secondary education, student teaching, educational reform, evaluation procedures.

Jones International University, School of Education, Centennial, CO 80112. Offers adult education (M Ed); corporate training and knowledge management (M Ed); curriculum and instruction (M Ed), including elementary teacher licensure, secondary teacher licensure; e-learning technology and design (M Ed); educational leadership and administration (M Ed); educational leadership and administration: principal and administrator licensure (M Ed); elementary curriculum instruction and assessment (M Ed); higher education leadership and administration (M Ed); K-12 instructional technology (M Ed); K-12 instructional technology: teacher licensure (M Ed); secondary curriculum instruction and assessment (M Ed); technology and design (M Ed). Part-time and evening/weekend programs available. Postbaccalaureate distance learning degree programs offered (no on-campus study). *Entrance requirements:* For master's, minimum cumulative GPA of 2.5. Additional exam requirements/recommendations for international students: Recommended—TOEFL (minimum score 550 paper-based). Electronic applications accepted.

Kansas State University, Graduate School, College of Education, Department of Curriculum and Instruction, Manhattan, KS 66506. Offers career and technical education (Ed D, PhD); curriculum studies (Ed D, PhD); digital teaching and learning (MS); educational computing, design and online learning (MS); educational technology (Ed D, PhD); elementary/middle level curriculum and instruction (MS); English as a second language (MS); language/diversity education (Ed D, PhD); literacy education (Ed D, PhD); mathematics education (Ed D, PhD); middle level/secondary curriculum and instruction (MS); reading and language arts (MS); reading specialist endorsement (MS); science education (Ed D, PhD); social science education (Ed D, PhD); teacher education (Ed D, PhD); teacher leader/school improvement (MS, Ed D). *Accreditation:* NCATE. Part-time programs available. Postbaccalaureate distance learning degree programs offered (minimal on-campus study). *Faculty:* 18 full-time (13 women), 7 part-time/adjunct (4 women). *Students:* 39 full-time (23 women), 122 part-time (94 women); includes 19 minority (3 Black or African American, non-Hispanic/Latino; 2 Asian, non-Hispanic/Latino; 12 Hispanic/Latino; 2 Two or more races, non-Hispanic/Latino), 12 international. Average age 36. 80 applicants, 50% accepted, 34 enrolled. In 2013, 40 master's, 13 doctorates awarded. *Degree requirements:* For master's, comprehensive exam, portfolio, project, report or thesis; for doctorate, comprehensive exam, thesis/dissertation, preliminary exam. *Entrance requirements:* For master's, minimum GPA of 3.0, letters of recommendation; for doctorate, GRE, minimum GPA of 3.0, letters of recommendation, evidence of scholarly writing. Additional exam requirements/recommendations for international students: Required—TOEFL (minimum score 550 paper-based; 80 iBT). *Application deadline:* For fall admission, 3/1 priority date for domestic students, 2/1 priority date for international students; for spring admission, 10/1 priority date for domestic students, 8/1 priority date for international students. Applications are processed on a rolling basis. Application fee: $50 ($75 for international students). Electronic applications accepted. *Financial support:* In 2013-14, 1 research assistantship (averaging $16,900 per year), 8 teaching assistantships (averaging $12,466 per year) were awarded; career-related internships or fieldwork, institutionally sponsored loans, and scholarships/grants also available. Support available to part-time students. Financial award application deadline: 3/1; financial award applicants required to submit FAFSA. *Faculty research:* Literacy and technology, critical race theory and diversity, achievement gaps, school improvement, teacher education. *Total annual research expenditures:* $543,677. *Unit head:* Dr. Todd Goodson, Chair, 785-532-5904, Fax: 785-532-7304, E-mail: tgoodson@ksu.edu. *Application contact:* Dona Deam, Application Contact, 785-532-5595, Fax: 785-532-7304, E-mail: ddeam@ksu.edu. Website: http://www.coe.k-state.edu/departments/edci/.

Kennesaw State University, Leland and Clarice C. Bagwell College of Education, Program in Graduate Education, Kennesaw, GA 30144-5591. Offers educational leadership (M Ed); educational leadership technology (M Ed); elementary and early childhood education (M Ed); instructional technology (M Ed); middle grades education (M Ed); reading (M Ed); secondary education (M Ed); special education (M Ed); teaching English to speakers of other languages (M Ed). *Accreditation:* NCATE. Part-time programs available. *Students:* 65 full-time (60 women), 229 part-time (158 women); includes 66 minority (46 Black or African American, non-Hispanic/Latino; 6 Asian, non-Hispanic/Latino; 9 Hispanic/Latino; 5 Two or more races, non-Hispanic/Latino), 1 international. Average age 34. 56 applicants, 86% accepted, 43 enrolled. In 2013, 109 master's awarded. *Degree requirements:* For master's, thesis or alternative. *Entrance requirements:* For master's, GRE General Test, T-4 state certification, minimum GPA of 2.75. Additional exam requirements/recommendations for international students: Required—TOEFL (minimum score 550 paper-based; 80 iBT), IELTS (minimum score 6.5). *Application deadline:* For fall admission, 7/1 for domestic and international

students; for spring admission, 10/1 for domestic and international students; for summer admission, 4/15 for domestic and international students. Applications are processed on a rolling basis. Application fee: $60. Electronic applications accepted. *Expenses:* Tuition, state resident: full-time $4806; part-time $267 per semester hour. Tuition, nonresident: full-time $17,298; part-time $961 per semester hour. *Required fees:* $1834; $784.50 per semester. *Financial support:* In 2013-14, 10 research assistantships with tuition reimbursements (averaging $8,000 per year) were awarded; Federal Work-Study and unspecified assistantships also available. Support available to part-time students. Financial award application deadline: 4/1; financial award applicants required to submit FAFSA. *Unit head:* Melinda Ross, Administrative Coordinator for Graduate Programs in Education, 770-423-6043, E-mail: graded@kennesaw.edu. *Application contact:* Melinda Ross, Admissions Counselor, 770-423-6043, Fax: 770-423-6885, E-mail: ksugrad@kennesaw.edu. Website: http://www.kennesaw.edu/education/grad/.

Kutztown University of Pennsylvania, College of Education, Program in Elementary Education, Kutztown, PA 19530-0730. Offers M Ed. *Accreditation:* NCATE. Part-time and evening/weekend programs available. *Faculty:* 6 full-time (all women), 1 (woman) part-time/adjunct. *Students:* 5 full-time (all women), 12 part-time (11 women). Average age 28. 11 applicants, 36% accepted, 2 enrolled. In 2013, 5 master's awarded. *Degree requirements:* For master's, comprehensive exam, thesis optional, comprehensive project. *Entrance requirements:* For master's, GRE General Test. Additional exam requirements/recommendations for international students: Required—TOEFL (minimum score 550 paper-based; 79 iBT). *Application deadline:* For fall admission, 8/1 priority date for domestic and international students; for spring admission, 12/1 priority date for domestic and international students. Applications are processed on a rolling basis. Application fee: $35. Electronic applications accepted. *Expenses: Tuition, area resident:* Part-time $442 per credit. Tuition, state resident: part-time $442 per credit. Tuition, nonresident: part-time $663 per credit. *Required fees:* $80 per credit. *Financial support:* Career-related internships or fieldwork, Federal Work-Study, scholarships/grants, and unspecified assistantships available. Financial award application deadline: 3/1; financial award applicants required to submit FAFSA. *Faculty research:* Whole language, middle schools, cooperative learning discussion techniques, oral reading techniques, hemisphericity. *Unit head:* Dr. Jeanie Burnett, Chairperson, 610-683-4286, Fax: 610-683-1327, E-mail: burnett@kutztown.edu. *Application contact:* Kelly Hish, Admissions Clerk, 610-683-4200, Fax: 610-683-1393, E-mail: graduate@kutztown.edu.

Lake Forest College, Master of Arts in Teaching Program, Lake Forest, IL 60045. Offers elementary education (MAT); K-12 French (MAT); K-12 music (MAT); K-12 Spanish (MAT); K-12 visual art (MAT); secondary biology (MAT); secondary chemistry (MAT); secondary English (MAT); secondary history (MAT); secondary mathematics (MAT). *Degree requirements:* For master's, comprehensive exam, portfolio. *Entrance requirements:* For master's, GRE.

Lancaster Bible College, Graduate School, Lancaster, PA 17601-5036. Offers adult ministries (MA); Bible (MA); children and family ministry (MA); church planting (MA); consulting resource teacher (M Ed); elementary school counseling (M Ed); leadership (PhD); leadership studies (MA); marriage and family counseling (MA); mental health counseling (MA); pastoral studies (MA); secondary school counseling (M Ed); sports ministry (MA); student ministry (MA); town and country ministry (MA). Part-time and evening/weekend programs available. *Degree requirements:* For master's, comprehensive exam (for some programs), thesis (for some programs). *Entrance requirements:* For master's, bachelor's degree with a minimum of 30 credits of course work in Bible, minimum undergraduate GPA of 3.0, interview. Additional exam requirements/recommendations for international students: Required—TOEFL.

Lander University, School of Education, Greenwood, SC 29649-2099. Offers elementary education (M Ed); teaching (MAT). *Accreditation:* NCATE. Part-time programs available. *Degree requirements:* For master's, comprehensive exam, thesis or alternative. *Entrance requirements:* For master's, GRE General Test. Additional exam requirements/recommendations for international students: Required—TOEFL (minimum score 550 paper-based). Electronic applications accepted.

Langston University, School of Education and Behavioral Sciences, Langston, OK 73050. Offers bilingual/multicultural (M Ed); elementary education (M Ed); English as a second language (M Ed); rehabilitation counseling (M Sc); urban education (M Ed). *Accreditation:* CORE; NCATE (one or more programs are accredited). Part-time programs available. *Degree requirements:* For master's, comprehensive exam, thesis optional. *Entrance requirements:* For master's, GRE, writing skills test, minimum GPA of 2.5, 3 letters of recommendation. Additional exam requirements/recommendations for international students: Required—TOEFL, TWE. *Faculty research:* Bilingual/multicultural education, financing post-secondary education.

Lasell College, Graduate and Professional Studies in Education, Newton, MA 02466-2709. Offers elementary education (M Ed); special education (M Ed), including moderate disabilities. Part-time and evening/weekend programs available. Postbaccalaureate distance learning degree programs offered. *Faculty:* 2 full-time (both women), 5 part-time/adjunct (4 women). *Students:* 8 full-time (7 women), 23 part-time (22 women); includes 5 minority (4 Black or African American, non-Hispanic/Latino; 1 Hispanic/Latino). Average age 28. 25 applicants, 64% accepted, 15 enrolled. In 2013, 2 master's awarded. *Entrance requirements:* For master's, bachelor's degree from an accredited institution. Additional exam requirements/recommendations for international students: Required—TOEFL (minimum score 550 paper-based; 79 iBT), IELTS. *Application deadline:* For fall admission, 8/31 priority date for domestic students, 6/30 priority date for international students; for spring admission, 12/31 priority date for domestic students, 10/31 priority date for international students. Applications are processed on a rolling basis. Electronic applications accepted. *Expenses: Tuition:* Part-time $575 per credit. *Required fees:* $80 per semester. *Financial support:* Available to part-time students. Application deadline: 8/31; applicants required to submit FAFSA. *Unit head:* Dr. Joan Dolamore, Dean of Graduate and Professional Studies, 617-243-2485, Fax: 617-243-2450, E-mail: gradinfo@lasell.edu. *Application contact:* Adrienne Franciosi, Director of Graduate Admission, 617-243-2214, Fax: 617-243-2450, E-mail: gradinfo@lasell.edu. Website: http://www.lasell.edu/Academics/Graduate-and-Professional-Studies/Master-of-Education.html.

Lee University, Program in Education, Cleveland, TN 37320-3450. Offers college student development (MS); curriculum and instruction (M Ed, Ed S); educational leadership (M Ed, Ed S); elementary education (MAT); higher education administration (MS); middle grades (MAT); secondary education (MAT); special education (M Ed); special education (secondary) (MAT). Part-time programs available. *Faculty:* 14 full-time (7 women), 6 part-time/adjunct (3 women). *Students:* 30 full-time (23 women), 62 part-time (37 women); includes 8 minority (3 Black or African American, non-Hispanic/Latino; 1 American Indian or Alaska Native, non-Hispanic/Latino; 2 Asian, non-Hispanic/Latino; 2 Hispanic/Latino). Average age 30. 40 applicants, 100% accepted, 30 enrolled. In 2013, 117 master's, 2 other advanced degrees awarded. *Degree requirements:* For master's, variable foreign language requirement, comprehensive exam, thesis, internship. *Entrance requirements:* For master's, MAT or GRE General Test, minimum GPA of 2.75, 3 letters of recommendation, interview, writing sample, official transcripts. Additional exam requirements/recommendations for international students: Required—

TOEFL (minimum score 450 paper-based). *Application deadline:* For fall admission, 4/1 priority date for domestic and international students; for spring admission, 10/1 priority date for domestic and international students. Applications are processed on a rolling basis. Application fee: $25. *Expenses: Tuition:* Full-time $9900; part-time $550 per credit hour. *Required fees:* $35 per term. One-time fee: $25. *Financial support:* In 2013–14, 47 students received support, including 1 teaching assistantship (averaging $1,500 per year); career-related internships or fieldwork, Federal Work-Study, institutionally sponsored loans, scholarships/grants, and unspecified assistantships also available. Financial award application deadline: 3/1; financial award applicants required to submit FAFSA. *Unit head:* Dr. Gary Riggins, Director, 423-614-8193. *Application contact:* Vicki Glasscock, Graduate Admissions Director, 423-614-8059, E-mail: vglasscock@leeuniversity.edu.
Website: http://www.leeuniversity.edu/academics/graduate/education.

Lehman College of the City University of New York, Division of Education, Department of Early Childhood and Elementary Education, Program in Elementary Education, Bronx, NY 10468-1589. Offers MS Ed. *Accreditation:* NCATE. Part-time and evening/weekend programs available. *Degree requirements:* For master's, thesis. *Entrance requirements:* For master's, minimum GPA of 3.0. *Faculty research:* POS network, emotional and intellectual learning, realistic picture books.

Le Moyne College, Department of Education, Syracuse, NY 13214. Offers adolescent education (MS Ed, MST); adolescent education/special education (MS Ed, MST); adolescent English (MST), including grades 7-12 (MS Ed, MST); adolescent English/special education (MST), including grades 7-12 (MS Ed, MST); adolescent foreign language (MST), including grades 7-12 (MS Ed, MST); adolescent history (MST), including grades 7-12 (MS Ed, MST); childhood education (MS Ed); childhood education/special education (MS Ed); elementary education (MS Ed); general education (MS Ed); inclusive childhood education (MST); literacy education (MS Ed), including birth to grade 6, grades 5-12; school building leader (MS Ed); school building leadership (CAS); school district business leader (MS Ed, CAS); school district leader (MS Ed); school district leadership (CAS); secondary education (MS Ed); special education (MS Ed); students with disabilities-generalist (MS Ed), including grades 7-12 (MS Ed, MST); teaching English to speakers of other languages (MS Ed); urban studies (MS Ed). *Accreditation:* Teacher Education Accreditation Council. Part-time and evening/weekend programs available. *Faculty:* 8 full-time (5 women), 61 part-time/adjunct (38 women). *Students:* 24 full-time (20 women), 178 part-time (133 women); includes 22 minority (12 Black or African American, non-Hispanic/Latino; 1 American Indian or Alaska Native, non-Hispanic/Latino; 3 Asian, non-Hispanic/Latino; 6 Hispanic/Latino), 1 international. Average age 31. 248 applicants, 90% accepted, 86 enrolled. In 2013, 158 master's, 37 CASs awarded. *Degree requirements:* For master's, thesis. *Entrance requirements:* For master's, GRE General Test, bachelor's degree, 2 letters of recommendation, written statement, transcripts. Additional exam requirements/recommendations for international students: Required—TOEFL (minimum score 550 paper-based; 79 iBT). *Application deadline:* For fall admission, 4/1 priority date for domestic and international students; for spring admission, 10/1 priority date for domestic and international students; for summer admission, 3/1 priority date for domestic and international students. Applications are processed on a rolling basis. Application fee: $50. *Expenses:* Contact institution. *Financial support:* In 2013–14, 26 students received support. Career-related internships or fieldwork and health care benefits available. Support available to part-time students. Financial award applicants required to submit FAFSA. *Faculty research:* Minority teachers, special education, multiculturalism, literacy, technology, media literacy learning, autism, school district organization, service-learning, higher level problem solving, teacher leadership. *Unit head:* Dr. Suzanne L. Gilmour, Chair, Department of Education/Director of Graduate Education Programs, 315-445-4376, Fax: 315-445-4744, E-mail: gilmous@lemoyne.edu. *Application contact:* Kristen P. Trapasso, Senior Director of Enrollment Management, 315-445-4265, Fax: 315-445-6092, E-mail: trapaskp@lemoyne.edu.
Website: http://www.lemoyne.edu/education.

Lesley University, School of Education, Cambridge, MA 02138-2790. Offers arts, community, and education (M Ed); autism studies (Certificate); curriculum and instruction (M Ed, CAGS); early childhood education (M Ed); ecological teaching and learning (MS); educational studies (PhD), including adult learning, educational leadership, individually designed; elementary education (M Ed); emergent technologies for educators (Certificate); ESLArts: language learning through the arts (M Ed); high school education (M Ed); individually designed (M Ed); integrated teaching through the arts (M Ed); literacy for K-8 classroom teachers (M Ed); mathematics education (M Ed); middle school education (M Ed); moderate disabilities (M Ed); online learning (Certificate); reading (CAGS); science in education (M Ed); severe disabilities (M Ed); special needs (CAGS); specialist teacher of reading (M Ed); teacher of visual art (M Ed); technology in education (M Ed, CAGS). *Accreditation:* Teacher Education Accreditation Council. Part-time and evening/weekend programs available. Postbaccalaureate distance learning degree programs offered (no on-campus study). *Faculty:* 40 full-time (30 women), 104 part-time/adjunct (77 women). *Students:* 453 full-time (381 women), 1,672 part-time (1,435 women); includes 284 minority (139 Black or African American, non-Hispanic/Latino; 11 American Indian or Alaska Native, non-Hispanic/Latino; 38 Asian, non-Hispanic/Latino; 58 Hispanic/Latino; 5 Native Hawaiian or other Pacific Islander, non-Hispanic/Latino; 33 Two or more races, non-Hispanic/Latino), 22 international. Average age 35. In 2013, 1,137 master's, 18 doctorates, 51 other advanced degrees awarded. *Degree requirements:* For master's, practicum; for doctorate, thesis/dissertation. *Entrance requirements:* For master's, Massachusetts Tests for Educator Licensure (MTEL), transcripts, statement of purpose, recommendations; interview (for special education); for doctorate, GRE General Test, transcripts, statement of purpose, recommendations, interview, master's degree, resume; for other advanced degree, interview, master's degree. Additional exam requirements/recommendations for international students: Required—TOEFL (minimum score 550 paper-based; 80 iBT). *Application deadline:* Applications are processed on a rolling basis. Application fee: $50. Electronic applications accepted. *Expenses: Tuition:* Part-time $900 per credit. *Financial support:* In 2013–14, 15 fellowships (averaging $3,600 per year) were awarded; career-related internships or fieldwork, Federal Work-Study, scholarships/grants, tuition waivers, and unspecified assistantships also available. Financial award application deadline: 4/15; financial award applicants required to submit FAFSA. *Faculty research:* Assessment in literacy, mathematics and science; autism spectrum disorders; instructional technology and online learning; multicultural education and English language learners. *Unit head:* Dr. Jack Gillette, Dean, 617-349-8401, Fax: 617-349-8607, E-mail: jgillett@lesley.edu. *Application contact:* Martha Sheehan, Director of Admissions, 888-LESLEYU, Fax: 617-349-8313, E-mail: info@lesley.edu.
Website: http://www.lesley.edu/soe.html.

Lewis & Clark College, Graduate School of Education and Counseling, Department of Teacher Education, Program in Early Childhood/Elementary Education, Portland, OR 97219-7899. Offers MAT. *Accreditation:* NCATE. *Entrance requirements:* For master's, minimum undergraduate GPA of 2.75; history of work, either volunteer or paid, with children in grades K-6. Additional exam requirements/recommendations for international students: Required—TOEFL (minimum score 575 paper-based). Electronic applications accepted. *Faculty research:* Classroom ethnography, assessing student learning, reading, moral development, language arts.

Lewis University, College of Education, Program in Elementary Education, Romeoville, IL 60446. Offers MA. *Students:* 4 full-time (all women), 34 part-time (27 women); includes 11 minority (2 Black or African American, non-Hispanic/Latino; 1 Asian, non-Hispanic/Latino; 7 Hispanic/Latino; 1 Two or more races, non-Hispanic/Latino), 1 international. Average age 32. *Entrance requirements:* For master's, departmental qualifying exam, writing exam, minimum GPA of 2.75, 2 letters of recommendation, interview. Additional exam requirements/recommendations for international students: Required—TOEFL (minimum score 550 paper-based; 80 iBT). *Application deadline:* For fall admission, 5/1 priority date for international students; for spring admission, 11/15 priority date for international students. Application fee: $40. Electronic applications accepted. *Financial support:* Federal Work-Study, scholarships/grants, and unspecified assistantships available. Financial award application deadline: 5/1; financial award applicants required to submit FAFSA. *Unit head:* Dr. Suzanne O'Brien, Program Director, 815-836-5632, E-mail: obriensu@lewisu.edu. *Application contact:* Linda Campbell, Graduate Admission Counselor, 815-838-5610 Ext. 5704, E-mail: campbeli@lewisu.edu.

Liberty University, School of Education, Lynchburg, VA 24515. Offers administration and supervision (M Ed); curriculum and instruction (Ed D, Ed S); early childhood education (M Ed); educational leadership (Ed D, Ed S); educational technology and online instruction (M Ed); elementary education (M Ed, MAT); English (M Ed); gifted education (M Ed); history (M Ed); leadership (M Ed); math specialist (M Ed); middle grades (M Ed, MAT); outdoor adventure sport (MS); reading specialist (M Ed); school counseling (M Ed); secondary education (MAT); special education (M Ed, MAT); sport management (MS), including administration, outdoor recreation, sport management, tourism; sports administration (MS); student service (M Ed); teaching and learning (M Ed); tourism (MS). *Accreditation:* NCATE. Part-time programs available. Postbaccalaureate distance learning degree programs offered (minimal on-campus study). *Students:* 2,241 full-time (1,639 women), 4,413 part-time (3,240 women); includes 2,052 minority (1,588 Black or African American, non-Hispanic/Latino; 37 American Indian or Alaska Native, non-Hispanic/Latino; 67 Asian, non-Hispanic/Latino; 173 Hispanic/Latino; 37 Native Hawaiian or other Pacific Islander, non-Hispanic/Latino; 150 Two or more races, non-Hispanic/Latino), 15 international. Average age 37. 6,185 applicants, 43% accepted, 1603 enrolled. In 2013, 1,256 master's, 117 doctorates, 470 other advanced degrees awarded. *Degree requirements:* For doctorate, comprehensive exam, thesis/dissertation. *Entrance requirements:* For master's, GRE General Test or MAT (if taken in or before 1999), 2 letters of recommendation, minimum undergraduate GPA of 3.0, curriculum vitae; for doctorate and Ed S, GRE General Test or MAT (if taken before 1999), minimum master's GPA of 3.0, 3 years of teaching experience. Additional exam requirements/recommendations for international students: Required—TOEFL (minimum score 600 paper-based; 100 iBT). *Application deadline:* For fall admission, 6/1 for domestic students; for spring admission, 11/1 for domestic students. Applications are processed on a rolling basis. Application fee: $50. Electronic applications accepted. *Expenses:* Contact institution. *Financial support:* Federal Work-Study and tuition waivers (partial) available. *Faculty research:* Self-determination, character education, bibliotherapy, learning styles, distance education. *Unit head:* Dr. Karen L. Parker, Dean, 434-582-2195, Fax: 434-582-2468, E-mail: kparker@liberty.edu. *Application contact:* Jay Bridge, Director of Graduate Admissions, 800-424-9595, Fax: 800-628-7977, E-mail: gradadmissions@liberty.edu.
Website: http://www.liberty.edu/academics/education/graduate/.

Lincoln University, Graduate Studies, Jefferson City, MO 65101. Offers business administration (MBA), including accounting, entrepreneurship, management, public administration and policy; educational leadership (Ed S), including elementary leadership, secondary leadership, superintendency; guidance and counseling (M Ed), including community/agency counseling, elementary school, secondary school; history (MA); school administration and supervision (M Ed), including elementary school administration, secondary school administration, special education administration; school teaching (M Ed), including elementary school teaching, secondary school teaching; sociology (MA); sociology/criminal justice (MA). Part-time and evening/weekend programs available. Postbaccalaureate distance learning degree programs offered (minimal on-campus study). *Students:* 42 full-time (29 women), 109 part-time (66 women); includes 51 minority (37 Black or African American, non-Hispanic/Latino; 10 American Indian or Alaska Native, non-Hispanic/Latino; 1 Asian, non-Hispanic/Latino; 2 Hispanic/Latino; 1 Two or more races, non-Hispanic/Latino), 10 international. Average age 33. 84 applicants, 76% accepted, 51 enrolled. In 2013, 73 master's, 6 other advanced degrees awarded. *Degree requirements:* For master's and Ed S, comprehensive exam, thesis optional. *Entrance requirements:* For master's and Ed S, GRE, MAT or GMAT, minimum GPA of 2.75 in major, 2.5 overall; 3 letters of recommendation; minimum C average in English composition; personal statement of purpose. Additional exam requirements/recommendations for international students: Required—TOEFL (minimum score 500 paper-based; 61 iBT). *Application deadline:* For fall admission, 8/1 priority date for domestic and international students; for spring admission, 12/1 priority date for domestic and international students; for summer admission, 5/1 priority date for domestic and international students. Applications are processed on a rolling basis. Application fee: $30. *Expenses:* Tuition, state resident: full-time $6840; part-time $285 per credit hour. Tuition, nonresident: full-time $12,720; part-time $530 per credit hour. *Required fees:* $587; $587 per year. Tuition and fees vary according to course load. *Financial support:* Federal Work-Study and scholarships/grants available. Support available to part-time students. Financial award application deadline: 3/1; financial award applicants required to submit FAFSA. *Unit head:* Dr. Linda S. Bickel, Dean, 573-681-5247, Fax: 573-681-5106, E-mail: gradschool@lincolnu.edu. *Application contact:* Irasema Steck, Administrative Assistant, 573-681-5247, Fax: 573-681-5106, E-mail: gradschool@lincolnu.edu.
Website: http://www.lincolnu.edu/web/graduate-studies/graduate-studies.

Lock Haven University of Pennsylvania, College of Liberal Arts and Education, Lock Haven, PA 17745-2390. Offers alternative education (M Ed); educational leadership (M Ed); teaching and learning (M Ed). *Accreditation:* NCATE. Part-time and evening/weekend programs available. Postbaccalaureate distance learning degree programs offered (no on-campus study). *Degree requirements:* For master's, thesis. *Entrance requirements:* For master's, minimum undergraduate GPA of 3.0. Additional exam requirements/recommendations for international students: Required—TOEFL. *Application deadline:* Applications are processed on a rolling basis. Application fee: $25. Electronic applications accepted. *Expenses: Tuition, area resident:* Part-time $442 per credit hour. Tuition, state resident: part-time $442 per credit hour. Tuition, nonresident: part-time $663 per credit hour. *Required fees:* $208.45 per credit hour. Tuition and fees vary according to program. *Financial support:* Unspecified assistantships available. Financial award application deadline: 8/1. *Unit head:* Dr. Susan Rimby, Dean, 570-484-2137, E-mail: ser1116@lhup.edu. *Application contact:* Kelly Hibbler, Assistant to the Dean, 570-484-2147, Fax: 570-484-2734, E-mail: khibbler@lhup.edu.
Website: http://www.lhup.edu/colleges/liberal_arts_education/.

Long Island University–Hudson at Rockland, Graduate School, Program in Curriculum and Instruction, Orangeburg, NY 10962. Offers adolescence education

(MS Ed); childhood education (MS Ed). Part-time and evening/weekend programs available. *Degree requirements:* For master's, LAST and CST exams. *Entrance requirements:* For master's, college transcripts, letters of recommendation, personal statement.

Long Island University–Hudson at Westchester, Programs in Education-Teaching, Purchase, NY 10577. Offers early childhood education (MS Ed, Advanced Certificate); elementary education (MS Ed, Advanced Certificate); literacy education (MS Ed, Advanced Certificate); second language, TESOL, bilingual education (MS Ed, Advanced Certificate); special education and secondary education (MS Ed, Advanced Certificate). *Accreditation:* Teacher Education Accreditation Council. Part-time and evening/weekend programs available. *Degree requirements:* For master's, comprehensive exam.

Long Island University–LIU Brooklyn, School of Education, Department of Teaching and Learning, Program in Elementary Education, Brooklyn, NY 11201-8423. Offers MS Ed. Part-time and evening/weekend programs available. *Degree requirements:* For master's, thesis optional. *Entrance requirements:* For master's, 2 letters of recommendation. Additional exam requirements/recommendations for international students: Required—TOEFL (minimum score 500 paper-based). Electronic applications accepted.

Long Island University–LIU Post, School of Education, Department of Curriculum and Instruction, Brookville, NY 11548-1300. Offers adolescence education (MS); adolescence education: biology (MS); adolescence education: earth science (MS); adolescence education: English (MS); adolescence education: mathematics (MS); adolescence education: social studies (MS); adolescence education: Spanish (MS); art education (MS); bilingual education (MS); childhood education (MS); early childhood education (MS); middle childhood education (MS); music education (MS); teaching English to speakers of other languages (MS). Part-time and evening/weekend programs available. *Degree requirements:* For master's, comprehensive exam or thesis, student teaching. *Entrance requirements:* For master's, minimum GPA of 2.75 in major, 2.5 overall. Electronic applications accepted. *Faculty research:* Ethics and education, teaching strategies.

Long Island University–Riverhead, Education Division, Program in Childhood Education, Riverhead, NY 11901. Offers childhood education (MS Ed); elementary education (MS Ed). *Accreditation:* Teacher Education Accreditation Council. *Degree requirements:* For master's, thesis. *Entrance requirements:* For master's, minimum undergraduate GPA of 2.75, on-campus writing sample. Additional exam requirements/recommendations for international students: Required—TOEFL (minimum score 550 paper-based). Electronic applications accepted.

Longwood University, College of Graduate and Professional Studies, College of Education and Human Services, Farmville, VA 23909. Offers education (MS), including algebra and middle school math, counselor education, elementary and middle school math, elementary education, elementary education initial licensure, health and physical education, school librarianship, special education general curriculum, special education initial licensure; social work and communication sciences and disorders (MS). *Accreditation:* NCATE. Part-time and evening/weekend programs available. *Faculty:* 28 full-time (15 women), 9 part-time/adjunct (7 women). *Students:* 86 full-time (80 women), 187 part-time (173 women); includes 38 minority (26 Black or African American, non-Hispanic/Latino; 1 Asian, non-Hispanic/Latino; 5 Hispanic/Latino; 1 Native Hawaiian or other Pacific Islander, non-Hispanic/Latino; 5 Two or more races, non-Hispanic/Latino). 98 applicants, 89% accepted, 85 enrolled. In 2013, 132 master's awarded. *Degree requirements:* For master's, comprehensive exam (for some programs), thesis optional, professional portfolio, internship, clinical experience, or practicum. *Entrance requirements:* For master's, bachelor's degree from regionally-accredited institution, 2 recommendations, 500-word personal essay, official transcripts, minimum GPA of 2.75, valid teaching license (for some programs), passing Praxis I scores for initial teaching licensure programs. Additional exam requirements/recommendations for international students: Required—TOEFL (minimum score 570 paper-based), IELTS (minimum score 6.5). *Application deadline:* For fall admission, 5/1 priority date for domestic students; for spring admission, 10/1 priority date for domestic students; for summer admission, 2/1 priority date for domestic students. Applications are processed on a rolling basis. Application fee: $50. Electronic applications accepted. *Expenses:* Tuition, state resident: full-time $7506; part-time $327 per credit hour. Tuition, nonresident: full-time $17,100; part-time $837 per credit hour. Tuition and fees vary according to course load and campus/location. *Financial support:* Career-related internships or fieldwork and Federal Work-Study available. Financial award applicants required to submit FAFSA. *Unit head:* Dr. Peggy L. Tarpley, Chair of the Department of Education and Special Education, 434-395-2337, E-mail: tarpleypl@longwood.edu. *Application contact:* College of Graduate and Professional Studies, 434-395-2380, Fax: 434-395-2750, E-mail: graduate@longwood.edu.
Website: http://www.longwood.edu/cehs/.

Louisiana State University and Agricultural & Mechanical College, Graduate School, College of Human Sciences and Education, Department of Educational Theory, Policy and Practice, Baton Rouge, LA 70803. Offers counseling (M Ed, MA, Ed S); educational administration (M Ed, MA, PhD, Ed S); educational technology (MA); elementary education (M Ed, MAT); higher education (PhD); research methodology (PhD); secondary education (M Ed, MAT). PhD programs offered jointly with Louisiana State University in Shreveport. *Accreditation:* ACA (one or more programs are accredited); NCATE. Part-time and evening/weekend programs available. *Faculty:* 39 full-time (22 women). *Students:* 185 full-time (136 women), 177 part-time (140 women); includes 110 minority (90 Black or African American, non-Hispanic/Latino; 1 American Indian or Alaska Native, non-Hispanic/Latino; 5 Asian, non-Hispanic/Latino; 9 Hispanic/Latino; 5 Two or more races, non-Hispanic/Latino), 5 international. Average age 31. 167 applicants, 66% accepted, 76 enrolled. In 2013, 134 master's, 23 doctorates, 17 other advanced degrees awarded. Terminal master's awarded for partial completion of doctoral program. *Degree requirements:* For doctorate, thesis/dissertation; for Ed S, thesis optional. *Entrance requirements:* For master's and doctorate, GRE General Test, minimum GPA of 3.0. Additional exam requirements/recommendations for international students: Required—TOEFL (minimum score 550 paper-based; 79 IBT), IELTS (minimum score 6.5), or PTE (minimum score 59). *Application deadline:* For fall admission, 1/25 priority date for domestic students, 5/15 for international students; for spring admission, 10/15 for international students. Applications are processed on a rolling basis. Application fee: $50 ($70 for international students). Electronic applications accepted. *Financial support:* In 2013–14, 253 students received support, including 5 fellowships (averaging $32,204 per year), 27 research assistantships with full and partial tuition reimbursements available (averaging $10,199 per year), 68 teaching assistantships with full and partial tuition reimbursements available (averaging $12,316 per year); career-related internships or fieldwork, Federal Work-Study, institutionally sponsored loans, health care benefits, and unspecified assistantships also available. Support available to part-time students. Financial award applicants required to submit FAFSA. *Faculty research:* Literary, curriculum studies, science education, K-12 leadership, higher education. *Total annual research expenditures:* $735,835. *Unit head:* Dr. Earl Cheek, Jr., Chair, 225-578-1258, Fax: 225-578-2267, E-mail: echeek@lsu.edu. *Application contact:* Dr. Kristin Gansle, Graduate Coordinator, 225-578-6780, Fax: 225-578-2267, E-mail: kgansle@lsu.edu.

Loyola Marymount University, School of Education, Department of Elementary and Secondary Education, Program in Elementary Education, Los Angeles, CA 90045. Offers MA. Part-time and evening/weekend programs available. *Faculty:* 5 full-time (4 women), 19 part-time/adjunct (11 women). *Students:* 90 full-time (77 women), 19 part-time (18 women); includes 60 minority (6 Black or African American, non-Hispanic/Latino; 1 American Indian or Alaska Native, non-Hispanic/Latino; 11 Asian, non-Hispanic/Latino; 39 Hispanic/Latino; 3 Two or more races, non-Hispanic/Latino). Average age 29. 76 applicants, 71% accepted, 45 enrolled. In 2013, 51 master's awarded. *Degree requirements:* For master's, comprehensive exam. *Entrance requirements:* For master's, CBEST, CSET, 3 letters of recommendation. Additional exam requirements/recommendations for international students: Required—TOEFL (minimum score 600 paper-based; 100 iBT). *Application deadline:* For fall admission, 6/15 for domestic students; for spring admission, 11/15 for domestic students. Application fee: $50. Electronic applications accepted. *Financial support:* In 2013–14, 68 students received support, including 1 research assistantship (averaging $432 per year); scholarships/grants and unspecified assistantships also available. Support available to part-time students. Financial award application deadline: 6/30; financial award applicants required to submit FAFSA. *Unit head:* Dr. Irene Oliver, Chair, 310-338-7302, E-mail: ioliver@lmu.edu. *Application contact:* Chake H. Kouyoumjian, Director, Graduate Admissions, 310-338-2721, E-mail: ckouyoum@lmu.edu.
Website: http://soe.lmu.edu/admissions/programs/tcp/elementaryeducation/.

Loyola University Chicago, School of Education, Program in Teaching and Learning, Chicago, IL 60660. Offers behavior intervention specialist (M Ed); elementary education (M Ed); English as a second language (Certificate); English language teaching and learning (M Ed); math education (M Ed); reading specialist (M Ed); reading teacher endorsement (Certificate); school technology (M Ed); science education (M Ed); secondary education (M Ed); special education (M Ed). *Accreditation:* NCATE. *Faculty:* 23 full-time (16 women), 49 part-time/adjunct (42 women). *Students:* 109. Average age 28. 104 applicants, 71% accepted, 44 enrolled. In 2013, 39 master's awarded. *Degree requirements:* For master's, comprehensive exam. *Entrance requirements:* For master's, Illinois Basic Skills Test, 3 letters of recommendation, minimum GPA of 3.0, resume. Additional exam requirements/recommendations for international students: Required—TOEFL (minimum score 550 paper-based; 79 iBT). *Application deadline:* For fall admission, 7/1 priority date for domestic and international students; for spring admission, 11/1 priority date for domestic and international students; for summer admission, 4/1 for domestic and international students. Applications are processed on a rolling basis. Application fee: $50. Electronic applications accepted. Application fee is waived when completed online. *Expenses: Tuition:* Full-time $16,740; part-time $930 per credit. *Required fees:* $135 per semester. *Financial support:* In 2013–14, 58 fellowships with partial tuition reimbursements were awarded; research assistantships, teaching assistantships, institutionally sponsored loans, scholarships/grants, and unspecified assistantships also available. Support available to part-time students. Financial award application deadline: 2/1; financial award applicants required to submit FAFSA. *Faculty research:* Positive behavior support, school reform, school improvement. *Unit head:* Dr. Ann Marie Ryan, Director, 312-915-7027, E-mail: aryan3@luc.edu. *Application contact:* Marie Rosin-Dittmar, Information Contact, 312-915-6800, E-mail: schleduc@luc.edu.

Loyola University Maryland, Graduate Programs, School of Education, Master of Arts in Teaching Program, Baltimore, MD 21210-2699. Offers elementary/middle education (MAT); secondary education (MAT); secondary education: biology (MAT); secondary education: chemistries (MAT); secondary education: earth science (MAT); secondary education: English (MAT); secondary education: mathematics (MAT); secondary education: physics (MAT). Part-time programs available. *Entrance requirements:* For master's, essay, 2 letters of recommendation, resume, transcipt. Additional exam requirements/recommendations for international students: Required—TOEFL (minimum score 550 paper-based).

Loyola University Maryland, Graduate Programs, School of Education, Program in Montessori Education, Baltimore, MD 21210-2699. Offers elementary education (M Ed); Montessori education (CAS); primary education (M Ed). *Accreditation:* NCATE. *Entrance requirements:* For master's, essay, 3 letters of recommendation, transcripts, resume. Additional exam requirements/recommendations for international students: Required—TOEFL (minimum score 550 paper-based).

Loyola University Maryland, Graduate Programs, School of Education, Program in Special Education, Baltimore, MD 21210-2699. Offers early childhood education (M Ed, CAS); elementary/middle education (M Ed, CAS); secondary education (M Ed, CAS). *Accreditation:* NCATE. Part-time programs available. *Entrance requirements:* For master's, transcript, essay, letter of recommendation. Additional exam requirements/recommendations for international students: Required—TOEFL (minimum score 550 paper-based). Electronic applications accepted.

Maharishi University of Management, Graduate Studies, Department of Education, Fairfield, IA 52557. Offers teaching elementary education (MA); teaching secondary education (MA). *Degree requirements:* For master's, thesis or alternative. *Entrance requirements:* For master's, GRE, minimum GPA of 3.0. Additional exam requirements/recommendations for international students: Required—TOEFL. *Faculty research:* Unified field-based approach to education, moral climate, scientific study of teaching.

Manhattanville College, School of Education, Program in Childhood Education, Purchase, NY 10577-2132. Offers childhood and special education (MPS); childhood education (MAT); special education childhood (MPS). Part-time and evening/weekend programs available. *Degree requirements:* For master's, comprehensive exam or research project, field experience. *Entrance requirements:* For master's, minimum undergraduate GPA of 3.0, 2 letters of recommendation. Additional exam requirements/recommendations for international students: Required—TOEFL.

Mansfield University of Pennsylvania, Graduate Studies, Department of Education and Special Education, Mansfield, PA 16933. Offers elementary education (M Ed); secondary education (MS); special education (M Ed). *Accreditation:* NCATE (one or more programs are accredited). Part-time and evening/weekend programs available. Postbaccalaureate distance learning degree programs offered (no on-campus study). *Degree requirements:* For master's, comprehensive exam, thesis optional. *Entrance requirements:* For master's, minimum GPA of 3.0. Additional exam requirements/recommendations for international students: Required—TOEFL (minimum score 550 paper-based). Electronic applications accepted.

Marquette University, Graduate School, College of Education, Department of Educational Policy and Leadership, Milwaukee, WI 53201-1881. Offers college student personnel administration (M Ed); curriculum and instruction (MA); education (MA); educational administration (M Ed); educational policy and foundations (MA); elementary education (Certificate); literacy (MA); principal (Certificate); reading specialist (Certificate); reading teacher (Certificate); secondary education (Certificate); superintendent (Certificate). Part-time and evening/weekend programs available. *Faculty:* 15 full-time (10 women), 3 part-time/adjunct (2 women). *Students:* 39 full-time (31 women), 107 part-time (70 women); includes 19 minority (7 Black or African American, non-Hispanic/Latino; 2 American Indian or Alaska Native, non-Hispanic/Latino; 3 Asian, non-Hispanic/Latino; 6 Hispanic/Latino; 1 Two or more races, non-

Hispanic/Latino), 2 international. Average age 30. 144 applicants, 74% accepted, 67 enrolled. In 2013, 48 master's, 4 doctorates, 12 other advanced degrees awarded. Terminal master's awarded for partial completion of doctoral program. *Degree requirements:* For master's, comprehensive exam, thesis (for some programs); for doctorate, thesis/dissertation, qualifying exam, supporting minor. *Entrance requirements:* For master's, GRE General Test or MAT, official transcripts from all current and previous colleges/universities except Marquette, three letters of recommendation, statement of purpose; for doctorate, GRE General Test, MAT, sample of written work, official transcripts from all current and previous colleges/universities except Marquette, three letters of recommendation, statement of purpose, resume/curriculum vitae; for Certificate, GRE General Test or MAT, master's degree. Additional exam requirements/recommendations for international students: Required—TOEFL (minimum score 530 paper-based). *Application deadline:* For fall admission, 1/15 for domestic and international students. Application fee: $50. *Expenses:* Contact institution. *Financial support:* In 2013–14, 130 students received support, including 1 fellowship with full tuition reimbursement available (averaging $18,780 per year), 5 research assistantships with full tuition reimbursements available (averaging $13,404 per year); health care benefits, tuition waivers (partial), and unspecified assistantships also available. Support available to part-time students. Financial award application deadline: 2/15. *Faculty research:* Leadership; social justice in education; development of lifelong learners; race, class, and schooling in historical perspective; urban teacher education. *Unit head:* Dr. Ellen Eckman, Chair, 414-288-1561, E-mail: ellen.eckman@marquette.edu. *Application contact:* Dr. Sharon Chubbuck, Associate Professor, 414-288-5895.

Marshall University, Academic Affairs Division, College of Education and Professional Development, Program in Elementary Education, Huntington, WV 25755. Offers MA. *Accreditation:* NCATE. Part-time and evening/weekend programs available. *Students:* 11 full-time (10 women), 58 part-time (54 women); includes 3 minority (2 Black or African American, non-Hispanic/Latino; 1 Two or more races, non-Hispanic/Latino). Average age 34. In 2013, 27 master's awarded. *Degree requirements:* For master's, thesis optional, comprehensive or oral assessment, research project. *Entrance requirements:* For master's, GRE General Test or MAT. Application fee: $40. *Financial support:* Federal Work-Study, tuition waivers (full and partial), and unspecified assistantships available. Support available to part-time students. Financial award applicants required to submit FAFSA. *Unit head:* Dr. Lisa Heaton, Director, 304-746-2026, E-mail: heaton@marshall.edu. *Application contact:* Information Contact, Graduate Admissions, 304-746-1900, Fax: 304-746-1902, E-mail: services@marshall.edu.

Mars Hill University, Adult and Graduate Studies, Mars Hill, NC 28754. Offers elementary education (K-6) (M Ed). *Degree requirements:* For master's, project.

Mary Baldwin College, Graduate Studies, Program in Teaching, Staunton, VA 24401-3610. Offers elementary education (MAT); middle grades education (MAT). *Accreditation:* Teacher Education Accreditation Council.

Marygrove College, Graduate Division, Sage Program, Detroit, MI 48221-2599. Offers M Ed. *Entrance requirements:* For master's, Michigan Teacher Test for Certification.

Marymount University, School of Education and Human Services, Program in Education, Arlington, VA 22207-4299. Offers counselor education and supervision (Ed D); elementary education (M Ed); English as a second language (M Ed); professional studies (M Ed); secondary education (M Ed); special education: general curriculum (M Ed). *Accreditation:* NCATE. Part-time and evening/weekend programs available. *Faculty:* 8 full-time (6 women), 13 part-time/adjunct (9 women). *Students:* 76 full-time (67 women), 83 part-time (70 women); includes 30 minority (12 Black or African American, non-Hispanic/Latino; 2 American Indian or Alaska Native, non-Hispanic/Latino; 9 Asian, non-Hispanic/Latino; 6 Hispanic/Latino; 1 Two or more races, non-Hispanic/Latino), 12 international. Average age 31. 63 applicants, 95% accepted, 44 enrolled. In 2013, 88 master's awarded. *Degree requirements:* For master's, thesis or alternative; for doctorate, thesis/dissertation. *Entrance requirements:* For master's, GRE or MAT and PRAXIS I or SAT/ACT and VCLA, 2 letters of recommendation, resume, interview. Additional exam requirements/recommendations for international students: Required—TOEFL (minimum score 600 paper-based; 96 iBT), IELTS (minimum score 6.5). *Application deadline:* For fall admission, 7/1 for international students. Applications are processed on a rolling basis. Application fee: $40. Electronic applications accepted. *Expenses: Tuition:* Part-time $850 per credit. *Required fees:* $10 per credit. One-time fee: $200 part-time. Tuition and fees vary according to program. *Financial support:* In 2013–14, 41 students received support, including 4 research assistantships with full and partial tuition reimbursements available, 1 teaching assistantship with full and partial tuition reimbursement available; career-related internships or fieldwork, Federal Work-Study, scholarships/grants, and unspecified assistantships also available. Support available to part-time students. Financial award applicants required to submit FAFSA. *Unit head:* Dr. Lisa Turissini, Chair, 703-526-1668, Fax: 703-284-1631, E-mail: lisa.turissini@marymount.edu. *Application contact:* Francesca Reed, Director, Graduate Admissions, 703-284-5901, Fax: 703-527-3815, E-mail: grad.admissions@marymount.edu.
Website: http://www.marymount.edu/academics/schools/sehs/grad.aspx.

Maryville University of Saint Louis, School of Education, St. Louis, MO 63141-7299. Offers art education (MA Ed); early childhood education (MA Ed); educational leadership (Ed D); educational leadership: principal certification (MA Ed); elementary education (MA Ed); gifted education (MA Ed); higher education leadership (Ed D); literacy specialist (MA Ed); middle grades education (MA Ed); secondary teaching and inquiry (MA Ed); teacher as leader (MA Ed); teacher leadership (Ed D). *Accreditation:* NCATE. Part-time and evening/weekend programs available. *Faculty:* 10 full-time (6 women), 17 part-time/adjunct (13 women). *Students:* 21 full-time (17 women), 238 part-time (167 women); includes 64 minority (54 Black or African American, non-Hispanic/Latino; 2 Asian, non-Hispanic/Latino; 4 Hispanic/Latino; 4 Two or more races, non-Hispanic/Latino), 2 international. Average age 39. In 2013, 61 master's, 40 doctorates awarded. *Degree requirements:* For master's, thesis, project. *Entrance requirements:* For master's, minimum cumulative GPA of 3.0, 3 professional recommendations, essays, interview with program faculty; for doctorate, minimum GPA of 3.0, 3 professional recommendations, essay, interview, on-site writing sample. Additional exam requirements/recommendations for international students: Required—TOEFL (minimum score 550 paper-based). *Application deadline:* Applications are processed on a rolling basis. Application fee: $40 ($60 for international students). Electronic applications accepted. Application fee is waived when completed online. *Expenses: Tuition:* Full-time $23,812; part-time $728 per credit hour. *Required fees:* $395 per year. Tuition and fees vary according to course load, degree level and program. *Financial support:* Career-related internships or fieldwork, Federal Work-Study, tuition waivers (partial), and professional educator discounts available. Financial award application deadline: 3/1; financial award applicants required to submit FAFSA. *Faculty research:* Collaboration with public schools, pre-service program development, mathematics, diversity, literacy. *Unit head:* Dr. Cathy Bear, Dean, 314-529-9692, Fax: 314-529-9921, E-mail: cbear@maryville.edu. *Application contact:* Holly Stanwich, Graduate Admissions Coordinator, 314-529-9542, Fax: 314-529-9921, E-mail: teachered@maryville.edu.
Website: http://www.maryville.edu/ed/graduate-programs/.

Marywood University, Academic Affairs, Reap College of Education and Human Development, Department of Education, Program in PK-4 Certification, Scranton, PA 18509-1598. Offers MAT. *Accreditation:* NCATE. *Entrance requirements:* Additional exam requirements/recommendations for international students: Required—TOEFL (minimum score 550 paper-based; 79 iBT). *Application deadline:* For fall admission, 4/1 priority date for domestic students, 3/31 priority date for international students; for spring admission, 11/1 priority date for domestic students, 8/31 priority date for international students. Applications are processed on a rolling basis. Application fee: $35. Electronic applications accepted. *Expenses: Tuition:* Part-time $775 per credit. Tuition and fees vary according to degree level. *Financial support:* Research assistantships, career-related internships or fieldwork, scholarships/grants, and unspecified assistantships available. Support available to part-time students. Financial award application deadline: 6/30; financial award applicants required to submit FAFSA. *Unit head:* Dr. Patricia S. Arter, Chairperson, 570-348-6211 Ext. 2511, E-mail: psarter@marywood.edu. *Application contact:* Tammy Manka, Assistant Director of Graduate Admissions, 570-348-6211 Ext. 2322, E-mail: tmanka@marywood.edu.
Website: http://www.marywood.edu/education/graduate-programs/mat-elementary.html.

McDaniel College, Graduate and Professional Studies, Program in Elementary and Secondary Education, Westminster, MD 21157-4390. Offers elementary education (MS); secondary education (MS). *Accreditation:* NCATE. Part-time and evening/weekend programs available. *Degree requirements:* For master's, comprehensive exam (for some programs), thesis optional. *Entrance requirements:* For master's, GRE General Test, MAT, or NTE/PRAXIS I, 3 letters of reference. Additional exam requirements/recommendations for international students: Required—TOEFL.

McNeese State University, Doré School of Graduate Studies, Burton College of Education, Office of Graduate Education Programs, Program in Curriculum and Instruction, Lake Charles, LA 70609. Offers early childhood education (M Ed); elementary education (M Ed); reading (M Ed); secondary education (M Ed). Evening/weekend programs available. *Entrance requirements:* For master's, GRE, teaching certificate.

McNeese State University, Doré School of Graduate Studies, Burton College of Education, Office of Graduate Education Programs, Program in Elementary Education, Lake Charles, LA 70609. Offers MAT. Evening/weekend programs available. *Degree requirements:* For master's, comprehensive exam, field experiences. *Entrance requirements:* For master's, GRE General Test, PRAXIS I and II, autobiography, two letters of recommendation.

McNeese State University, Doré School of Graduate Studies, Burton College of Education, Office of Student Teaching and Professional Education Services, Program in Elementary Education Grades 1-5, Lake Charles, LA 70609. Offers Postbaccalaureate Certificate. *Entrance requirements:* For degree, PRAXIS, 2 letters of recommendation, autobiography.

Medaille College, Program in Education, Buffalo, NY 14214-2695. Offers adolescent education (MS Ed); curriculum and instruction (MS Ed); education preparation (MS Ed); literacy (MS Ed); special education (MS). *Accreditation:* Teacher Education Accreditation Council. Part-time and evening/weekend programs available. *Faculty:* 12 full-time (9 women), 28 part-time/adjunct (19 women). *Students:* 159 full-time (123 women), 25 part-time (22 women); includes 8 minority (5 Black or African American, non-Hispanic/Latino; 3 Hispanic/Latino), 88 international. Average age 29. 209 applicants, 96% accepted, 61 enrolled. In 2013, 253 master's awarded. *Degree requirements:* For master's, comprehensive exam (for some programs), thesis or alternative. *Entrance requirements:* For master's, minimum undergraduate GPA of 2.7. Additional exam requirements/recommendations for international students: Required—TOEFL (minimum score 550 paper-based). *Application deadline:* For fall admission, 8/15 priority date for domestic students; for spring admission, 1/15 priority date for domestic students. Applications are processed on a rolling basis. Application fee: $35. Electronic applications accepted. *Financial support:* Federal Work-Study available. Financial award applicants required to submit FAFSA. *Faculty research:* Curriculum planning, truancy, tracking minority students, curriculum design, mentoring students. *Unit head:* Dr. Illana Lane, Dean, School of Education, 716-880-2553, E-mail: ilane@medaille.edu. *Application contact:* E-mail: sageadmissions@medaille.edu.
Website: http://www.medaille.edu.

Mercy College, School of Education, Program in Childhood Education, Dobbs Ferry, NY 10522-1189. Offers MS. Part-time and evening/weekend programs available. Postbaccalaureate distance learning degree programs offered (no on-campus study). *Students:* 94 full-time (80 women), 142 part-time (120 women); includes 136 minority (72 Black or African American, non-Hispanic/Latino; 1 American Indian or Alaska Native, non-Hispanic/Latino; 3 Asian, non-Hispanic/Latino; 58 Hispanic/Latino; 2 Two or more races, non-Hispanic/Latino). Average age 32. 141 applicants, 58% accepted, 57 enrolled. In 2013, 16 master's awarded. *Degree requirements:* For master's, comprehensive exam (for some programs), thesis (for some programs). *Entrance requirements:* For master's, resume, undergraduate transcript. Additional exam requirements/recommendations for international students: Required—TOEFL (minimum score 600 paper-based; 100 iBT), IELTS (minimum score 8). *Application deadline:* For fall admission, 8/1 for international students. Applications are processed on a rolling basis. Application fee: $40. Electronic applications accepted. *Expenses: Tuition:* Full-time $19,344; part-time $806 per credit. *Required fees:* $580; $806 per credit. $145 per term. Tuition and fees vary according to course load, degree level and program. *Financial support:* Career-related internships or fieldwork, Federal Work-Study, scholarships/grants, and unspecified assistantships available. Financial award applicants required to submit FAFSA. *Unit head:* Dr. Alfred S. Posamentier, Dean for the School of Education, 914-674-7350, E-mail: aposamentier@mercy.edu. *Application contact:* Alison Gurdineer, Senior Director of Admissions, 877-637-2946, Fax: 914-674-7382, E-mail: admissions@mercy.edu.
Website: https://www.mercy.edu/academics/school-of-education/department-of-early-childhood-childhood-education/ms-in-childhood-education-grades-1-6/.

Merrimack College, School of Education, North Andover, MA 01845-5800. Offers community engagement (M Ed), including community organizations, higher education, K-12 education; early childhood education (M Ed); elementary education (M Ed); English as a second language (PreK-6) (M Ed); English language learners (M Ed); general studies (M Ed); higher education (M Ed), including leadership and organizational development, student affairs; middle (M Ed); moderate disabilities (PreK-8) (M Ed); secondary (M Ed); teacher leadership (CAGS), including instructional leadership, reading specialist. Part-time and evening/weekend programs available. *Faculty:* 4 full-time (all women), 23 part-time/adjunct (15 women). *Students:* 127 full-time (104 women), 61 part-time (52 women); includes 3 minority (1 Asian, non-Hispanic/Latino; 2 Hispanic/Latino), 2 international. Average age 25. 403 applicants, 47% accepted, 138 enrolled. In 2013, 140 master's awarded. *Degree requirements:* For master's, practicum, portfolio, and state test (for licensure track); capstone (for higher education and community engagement tracks). *Entrance requirements:* For master's, MTEL (Massachusetts Tests for Educator Licensure), official transcripts from other colleges, resume, personal statement, 2 letters of recommendation, additional essay requirements for fellowships. Additional exam requirements/recommendations for international students: Required—TOEFL (minimum score 84 iBT), IELTS (minimum

score 6.5). *Application deadline:* For fall admission, 8/15 for domestic and international students; for winter admission, 12/1 for domestic students, 11/15 for international students; for spring admission, 1/10 for domestic and international students; for summer admission, 5/10 for domestic and international students. Applications are processed on a rolling basis. Application fee: $0. Electronic applications accepted. Tuition and fees vary according to course load and program. *Financial support:* In 2013–14, 91 fellowships with full tuition reimbursements were awarded; career-related internships or fieldwork, scholarships/grants, and health care benefits also available. Support available to part-time students. Financial award applicants required to submit FAFSA. *Faculty research:* Expressive language, civic engagement, family life education, reading genres, the psychological process of aging. *Application contact:* Kristen English, Interim Director of Graduate Admission, 978-837-5073, E-mail: englishkr@merrimack.edu.
Website: http://www.merrimack.edu/academics/graduate/education/.

Metropolitan College of New York, Program in Childhood Education, New York, NY 10013. Offers MS. *Degree requirements:* For master's, one foreign language. *Entrance requirements:* For master's, Liberal Arts and Sciences Test (LAST) recommended, minimum GPA of 3.0, 2 letters of reference, writing sample, interview. Additional exam requirements/recommendations for international students: Required—TOEFL (minimum score 600 paper-based). *Expenses:* Contact institution. *Faculty research:* Classroom management, learner autonomy, teacher research, math and gender, intelligence.

Metropolitan State University of Denver, School of Professional Studies, Denver, CO 80217-3362. Offers elementary education (MAT); special education (MAT).

Miami University, College of Education, Health and Society, Department of Teacher Education, Oxford, OH 45056. Offers adolescent education (M Ed); elementary education (M Ed, MAT); reading education (M Ed); secondary education (MAT). Part-time and evening/weekend programs available. *Students:* 31 full-time (21 women), 26 part-time (23 women); includes 8 minority (3 Black or African American, non-Hispanic/Latino; 1 Asian, non-Hispanic/Latino; 2 Hispanic/Latino; 2 Two or more races, non-Hispanic/Latino), 2 international. Average age 31. In 2013, 31 master's awarded. *Entrance requirements:* Additional exam requirements/recommendations for international students: Recommended—TOEFL (minimum score 80 iBT), IELTS (minimum score 6.5), TSE (minimum score 54). *Application deadline:* Applications are processed on a rolling basis. Application fee: $50. Electronic applications accepted. *Expenses:* Tuition, state resident: full-time $12,634; part-time $526 per credit hour. Tuition, nonresident: full-time $27,892; part-time $1162 per credit hour. Part-time tuition and fees vary according to course load, campus/location and program. *Financial support:* Research assistantships with full tuition reimbursements, teaching assistantships with full tuition reimbursements, career-related internships or fieldwork, Federal Work-Study, scholarships/grants, health care benefits, tuition waivers, and unspecified assistantships available. Financial award application deadline: 2/15. *Unit head:* Dr. Paula Saine, Interim Co-Chair, 513-529-6443, Fax: 513-529-4931, E-mail: sainep@miamioh.edu. *Application contact:* Linda Dennett, Program Associate, 513-529-5708, E-mail: dennetlg@miamioh.edu.
Website: http://www.MiamiOH.edu/edt.

Middle Tennessee State University, College of Graduate Studies, College of Education, Department of Elementary and Special Education, Major in Curriculum and Instruction, Murfreesboro, TN 37132. Offers early childhood education (M Ed); elementary education (M Ed, Ed S); middle school education (M Ed). *Accreditation:* NCATE. Part-time and evening/weekend programs available. Postbaccalaureate distance learning degree programs offered. *Faculty:* 14 full-time (9 women), 7 part-time/adjunct (all women). *Degree requirements:* For master's, comprehensive exam; for Ed S, comprehensive exam, thesis or alternative. *Entrance requirements:* For master's and Ed S, GRE, MAT or PRAXIS. Additional exam requirements/recommendations for international students: Required—TOEFL (minimum score 525 paper-based; 71 iBT) or IELTS (minimum score 6). *Application deadline:* For fall admission, 8/1 priority date for domestic students. Applications are processed on a rolling basis. Application fee: $25. Electronic applications accepted. *Financial support:* Tuition waivers available. Support available to part-time students. Financial award application deadline: 5/1. *Unit head:* Dr. Kathleen Burriss, Interim Chair, 615-898-2680, Fax: 615-898-5309, E-mail: kathleen.burriss@mtsu.edu. *Application contact:* Dr. Michael D. Allen, Vice Provost for Research and Dean, 615-898-2840, Fax: 615-904-8020, E-mail: michael.allen@mtsu.edu.

Millersville University of Pennsylvania, College of Graduate and Professional Studies, School of Education, Department of Elementary and Early Childhood Education, Program in Elementary Education, Millersville, PA 17551-0302. Offers M Ed. *Accreditation:* NCATE. Part-time and evening/weekend programs available. *Faculty:* 17 full-time (11 women), 18 part-time/adjunct (15 women). *Students:* 2 full-time (1 woman), 5 part-time (all women). Average age 32. In 2013, 12 master's awarded. *Degree requirements:* For master's, comprehensive exam, thesis optional. *Entrance requirements:* For master's, GRE or MAT, 3 letters of recommendation, copy of teaching certificate, goal statement, official transcripts. Additional exam requirements/recommendations for international students: Required—TOEFL (minimum score 550 paper-based, 79 iBT) or IELTS (minimum score 6). *Application deadline:* For fall admission, 1/15 priority date for domestic and international students; for winter admission, 10/1 priority date for domestic and international students; for spring admission, 10/1 priority date for domestic and international students. Applications are processed on a rolling basis. Application fee: $40. Electronic applications accepted. *Expenses:* Tuition, state resident: full-time $7956; part-time $442 per credit. Tuition, nonresident: full-time $11,934; part-time $663 per credit. *Required fees:* $2196; $122 per credit. Tuition and fees vary according to course load. *Financial support:* Research assistantships with full tuition reimbursements, institutionally sponsored loans, and unspecified assistantships available. Support available to part-time students. Financial award application deadline: 3/15; financial award applicants required to submit FAFSA. *Faculty research:* Multicultural education, diversity education, teacher candidates' reflections on white privilege, challenges facing children of new immigrants. *Unit head:* Dr. Kazi I. Hossain, Coordinator, 717-871-2265, Fax: 717-871-5462, E-mail: kazi.hossain@millersville.edu. *Application contact:* Dr. Victor S. DeSantis, Dean of College of Graduate and Professional Studies/Associate Provost for Civic and Community Engagement, 717-872-3099, Fax: 717-872-3453, E-mail: victor.desantis@millersville.edu.
Website: http://www.millersville.edu/academics/educ/eled/graduate.php.

Mills College, Graduate Studies, School of Education, Oakland, CA 94613-1000. Offers child life in hospitals (MA); early childhood education (MA); education (MA), including art education, curriculum and instruction, elementary education, English education, foreign language education, mathematics education, science education, secondary education, social studies education, teaching; educational leadership (MA, Ed D). Part-time and evening/weekend programs available. *Faculty:* 10 full-time (7 women), 13 part-time/adjunct (10 women). *Students:* 154 full-time (136 women), 54 part-time (47 women); includes 96 minority (32 Black or African American, non-Hispanic/Latino; 1 American Indian or Alaska Native, non-Hispanic/Latino; 23 Asian, non-Hispanic/Latino; 27 Hispanic/Latino; 1 Native Hawaiian or other Pacific Islander, non-Hispanic/Latino; 12 Two or more races, non-Hispanic/Latino), 2 international. Average age 25. 222 applicants, 89% accepted, 110 enrolled. In 2013, 96 master's, 38 doctorates awarded. Terminal master's awarded for partial completion of doctoral program. *Degree requirements:* For master's, comprehensive exam, thesis (for some programs); for doctorate, thesis/dissertation. *Entrance requirements:* For master's, statement of purpose, official transcript, 3 recommendations. Additional exam requirements/recommendations for international students: Required—TOEFL (minimum score 550 paper-based; 80 iBT) or IELTS (minimum score 6). *Application deadline:* For fall admission, 12/31 priority date for domestic students, 12/15 for international students; for spring admission, 11/1 priority date for domestic students, 10/1 for international students. Applications are processed on a rolling basis. Application fee: $50. Electronic applications accepted. *Expenses: Tuition:* Full-time $29,860. *Required fees:* $1134. Part-time tuition and fees vary according to course load, degree level and program. *Financial support:* In 2013–14, 130 students received support, including 130 fellowships with full and partial tuition reimbursements available (averaging $7,565 per year); career-related internships or fieldwork and scholarships/grants also available. Support available to part-time students. Financial award application deadline: 2/1; financial award applicants required to submit FAFSA. *Faculty research:* Early childhood education, teacher preparation, educational leadership. *Total annual research expenditures:* $3.5 million. *Unit head:* Dr. Katherine Schultz, Department Head, 510-430-3384, Fax: 510-430-2159, E-mail: kschultz@mills.edu. *Application contact:* Shrim Bathey, Director of Graduate Admission, 510-430-3309, Fax: 510-430-2159, E-mail: grad-admission@mills.edu.
Website: http://www.mills.edu/education.

Minnesota State University Mankato, College of Graduate Studies, College of Education, Department of Elementary and Early Childhood Education, Mankato, MN 56001. Offers MS, Certificate. *Accreditation:* NCATE. Part-time programs available. *Students:* 6 full-time (all women), 89 part-time (84 women). *Degree requirements:* For master's, comprehensive exam, thesis or alternative. *Entrance requirements:* For master's, GRE General Test or MAT, minimum GPA of 3.0 during previous 2 years. Additional exam requirements/recommendations for international students: Required—TOEFL. *Application deadline:* For fall admission, 7/1 priority date for domestic students; for spring admission, 11/1 for domestic students. Applications are processed on a rolling basis. Application fee: $40. Electronic applications accepted. *Financial support:* Application deadline: 3/15; applicants required to submit FAFSA. *Unit head:* Dr. Peggy Ballard, Graduate Coordinator, 507-389-1516. *Application contact:* 507-389-2321, E-mail: grad@mnsu.edu.
Website: http://ed.mnsu.edu/eec/.

Minot State University, Graduate School, Teacher Education and Human Performance Department, Minot, ND 58707-0002. Offers elementary education (M Ed). *Accreditation:* NCATE. *Degree requirements:* For master's, thesis. *Entrance requirements:* For master's, 2 years of teaching experience, bachelor's degree in education, minimum GPA of 2.75. Additional exam requirements/recommendations for international students: Required—TOEFL. *Faculty research:* Technology, personnel-teaching efficacy, reflective teaching.

Mississippi College, Graduate School, School of Education, Department of Teacher Education and Leadership, Clinton, MS 39058. Offers art (M Ed); biological science (M Ed); business education (M Ed); computer science (M Ed); dyslexia therapy (M Ed); educational leadership (M Ed, Ed D, Ed S); elementary education (M Ed, Ed S); English (M Ed); higher education administration (MS); mathematics (M Ed); secondary education (M Ed); social studies (history) (M Ed); teaching arts (M Ed). Part-time programs available. Postbaccalaureate distance learning degree programs offered (no on-campus study). *Degree requirements:* For master's, comprehensive exam, thesis optional. *Entrance requirements:* For master's, NTE. Additional exam requirements/recommendations for international students: Recommended—TOEFL, IELTS. Electronic applications accepted.

Mississippi State University, College of Education, Department of Curriculum, Instruction and Special Education, Mississippi State, MS 39762. Offers curriculum and instruction (PhD), including early childhood education (MS, PhD), elementary education (PhD, Ed S), general curriculum and instruction, reading education, secondary education (PhD, Ed S), special education (PhD, Ed S); education (Ed S), including elementary education (PhD, Ed S), secondary education (PhD, Ed S), special education (PhD, Ed S); elementary education (MS), including early childhood education (MS, PhD), general elementary education, middle level education; middle level alternate route (MAT); secondary education (MS); secondary teacher alternate route (MAT); special education (MS). *Accreditation:* NCATE. Part-time and evening/weekend programs available. *Faculty:* 11 full-time (9 women). *Students:* 58 full-time (40 women), 143 part-time (100 women); includes 62 minority (56 Black or African American, non-Hispanic/Latino; 2 American Indian or Alaska Native, non-Hispanic/Latino; 3 Hispanic/Latino; 1 Two or more races, non-Hispanic/Latino). Average age 33. 181 applicants, 32% accepted, 52 enrolled. In 2013, 44 master's, 1 doctorate, 7 other advanced degrees awarded. *Degree requirements:* For master's, comprehensive exam; for doctorate, thesis/dissertation; for Ed S, comprehensive exam, thesis or alternative. *Entrance requirements:* For master's, GRE, minimum GPA of 2.75 in junior and senior year, eligibility for initial teacher certification; for doctorate, GRE, minimum GPA of 3.4 on previous graduate work; for Ed S, GRE, minimum GPA of 3.2 on master's degree. Additional exam requirements/recommendations for international students: Required—TOEFL (minimum score 550 paper-based; 79 iBT); Recommended—IELTS (minimum score 6.5). *Application deadline:* For fall admission, 3/1 priority date for domestic students, 5/1 for international students; for spring admission, 9/1 priority date for domestic students, 9/1 for international students. Applications are processed on a rolling basis. Application fee: $60. Electronic applications accepted. *Financial support:* In 2013–14, 7 research assistantships with full and partial tuition reimbursements (averaging $9,623 per year), 2 teaching assistantships (averaging $11,382 per year) were awarded; Federal Work-Study, institutionally sponsored loans, scholarships/grants, and unspecified assistantships also available. Financial award application deadline: 4/1; financial award applicants required to submit FAFSA. *Faculty research:* Early childhood education, reading, rural schools, multicultural education, use of technology in instruction. *Unit head:* Dr. Devon Brenner, Professor and Interim Head, 662-325-7119, Fax: 662-325-7857, E-mail: devon@ra.msstate.edu. *Application contact:* Dr. Dana Franz, Graduate Coordinator, 662-325-3703, Fax: 662-325-7857, E-mail: tstevonson@colled.msstate.edu.
Website: http://www.cise.msstate.edu/.

Mississippi State University, College of Education, Department of Leadership and Foundations, Mississippi State, MS 39762. Offers community college education (MAT); community college leadership (PhD); education (Ed S), including school administration; elementary, middle and secondary education administration (PhD); school administration (MS); workforce education leadership (MS). MS in workforce educational leadership held jointly with Alcorn State University. *Faculty:* 9 full-time (3 women). *Students:* 50 full-time (26 women), 156 part-time (100 women); includes 104 minority (99 Black or African American, non-Hispanic/Latino; 1 American Indian or Alaska Native, non-Hispanic/Latino; 1 Asian, non-Hispanic/Latino; 1 Hispanic/Latino; 1 Native Hawaiian or other Pacific Islander, non-Hispanic/Latino; 1 Two or more races, non-Hispanic/Latino). Average age 39. 121 applicants, 32% accepted, 33 enrolled. In 2013, 47 master's, 15 doctorates, 7 other advanced degrees awarded. *Degree requirements:* For

master's and Ed S, comprehensive exam, thesis; for doctorate, comprehensive exam, thesis/dissertation. *Entrance requirements:* For master's, GRE, minimum GPA of 2.75 in junior and senior courses; for doctorate, GRE, minimum GPA of 3.4 on previous graduate work; for Ed S, GRE, minimum GPA of 3.2, master's degree. Additional exam requirements/recommendations for international students: Required—TOEFL (minimum score 550 paper-based; 79 iBT); Recommended—IELTS (minimum score 6.5). *Application deadline:* For fall admission, 7/1 for domestic students, 5/1 for international students; for spring admission, 11/1 for domestic students, 9/1 for international students. *Application fee:* $60. *Financial support:* In 2013–14, 3 research assistantships with full tuition reimbursements (averaging $12,400 per year), 1 teaching assistantship with full tuition reimbursement (averaging $10,194 per year) were awarded; Federal Work-Study, institutionally sponsored loans, and unspecified assistantships also available. Financial award application deadline: 4/1; financial award applicants required to submit FAFSA. *Unit head:* Dr. David Morse, Interim Department Head and Professor, 662-325-0969, Fax: 662-325-0975, E-mail: dmorse@colled.msstate.edu. Website: http://www.leadershipandfoundations.msstate.edu/.

Mississippi Valley State University, Department of Education, Itta Bena, MS 38941-1400. Offers education (MAT); elementary education (MA). *Accreditation:* NCATE.

Missouri State University, Graduate College, College of Education, Department of Childhood Education and Family Studies, Program in Elementary Education, Springfield, MO 65897. Offers MS Ed. Part-time and evening/weekend programs available. Postbaccalaureate distance learning degree programs offered (minimal on-campus study). *Students:* 9 full-time (all women), 57 part-time (56 women); includes 3 minority (1 American Indian or Alaska Native, non-Hispanic/Latino; 2 Hispanic/Latino). Average age 34. 24 applicants, 100% accepted, 19 enrolled. In 2013, 19 master's awarded. *Degree requirements:* For master's, comprehensive exam, thesis or alternative. *Entrance requirements:* For master's, GRE (if GPA less than 3.0), minimum GPA of 2.75, teaching certificate. Additional exam requirements/recommendations for international students: Required—TOEFL (minimum score 550 paper-based; 79 iBT). *Application deadline:* For fall admission, 7/20 priority date for domestic students, 5/1 for international students; for spring admission, 12/20 priority date for domestic students, 9/1 for international students. Applications are processed on a rolling basis. Application fee: $35 ($50 for international students). Electronic applications accepted. *Expenses:* Tuition, state resident: full-time $4500; part-time $250 per credit hour. Tuition, nonresident: full-time $9018; part-time $501 per credit hour. *Required fees:* $361 per semester. Tuition and fees vary according to course level, course load and program. *Financial support:* Federal Work-Study, institutionally sponsored loans, and scholarships/grants available. Financial award application deadline: 3/31; financial award applicants required to submit FAFSA. *Unit head:* Dr. Cynthia Wilson-Hail, Program Coordinator, 417-836-6065, E-mail: cindywilson@missouristate.edu. *Application contact:* Misty Stewart, Coordinator of Graduate Recruitment, 417-836-6079, Fax: 417-836-6200, E-mail: mistystewart@missouristate.edu. Website: http://education.missouristate.edu/ele/.

Missouri State University, Graduate College, College of Education, Department of Counseling, Leadership, and Special Education, Program in Counseling, Springfield, MO 65897. Offers counseling and assessment (Ed S); elementary school counseling (MS); mental health counseling (MS); secondary school counseling (MS). Part-time and evening/weekend programs available. *Students:* 51 full-time (44 women), 66 part-time (54 women); includes 11 minority (2 Black or African American, non-Hispanic/Latino; 1 American Indian or Alaska Native, non-Hispanic/Latino; 1 Asian, non-Hispanic/Latino; 4 Hispanic/Latino; 3 Two or more races, non-Hispanic/Latino), 4 international. Average age 33. 59 applicants, 51% accepted, 16 enrolled. In 2013, 39 master's awarded. *Degree requirements:* For master's, comprehensive exam, thesis or alternative. *Entrance requirements:* For master's, GRE or MAT, minimum GPA of 2.75. Additional exam requirements/recommendations for international students: Required—TOEFL (minimum score 550 paper-based; 79 iBT). *Application deadline:* For fall admission, 2/1 priority date for domestic students, 1/1 priority date for international students; for spring admission, 10/1 priority date for domestic students, 9/1 priority date for international students. Application fee: $35 ($50 for international students). Electronic applications accepted. *Expenses:* Tuition, state resident: full-time $4500; part-time $250 per credit hour. Tuition, nonresident: full-time $9018; part-time $501 per credit hour. *Required fees:* $361 per semester. Tuition and fees vary according to course level, course load and program. *Financial support:* Federal Work-Study, institutionally sponsored loans, scholarships/grants, and unspecified assistantships available. Financial award application deadline: 3/31; financial award applicants required to submit FAFSA. *Unit head:* Dr. Jeffrey Cornelius-White, Program Coordinator, 417-836-6517, Fax: 417-836-4918, E-mail: jcornelius-white@missouristate.edu. *Application contact:* Misty Stewart, Coordinator of Admissions and Recruitment, 417-836-6079, Fax: 417-836-6200, E-mail: mistystewart@missouristate.edu. Website: http://education.missouristate.edu/clse/.

Missouri State University, Graduate College, College of Education, Department of Counseling, Leadership, and Special Education, Program in Educational Administration, Springfield, MO 65897. Offers educational administration (MS Ed, Ed S); elementary education (MS Ed); elementary principal (Ed S); secondary education (MS Ed); secondary principal (Ed S); superintendent (Ed S). Part-time and evening/weekend programs available. *Students:* 30 full-time (22 women), 88 part-time (56 women); includes 7 minority (1 Black or African American, non-Hispanic/Latino; 1 American Indian or Alaska Native, non-Hispanic/Latino; 3 Hispanic/Latino; 2 Two or more races, non-Hispanic/Latino), 2 international. Average age 35. 49 applicants, 100% accepted, 44 enrolled. In 2013, 57 master's, 16 Ed Ss awarded. *Degree requirements:* For master's and Ed S, comprehensive exam, thesis or alternative. *Entrance requirements:* For master's, minimum GPA of 2.75; for Ed S, GRE General Test, MAT, minimum GPA of 2.75. Additional exam requirements/recommendations for international students: Required—TOEFL (minimum score 550 paper-based; 79 iBT). *Application deadline:* For fall admission, 7/20 priority date for domestic students, 5/1 for international students; for spring admission, 12/20 priority date for domestic students, 9/1 for international students. Applications are processed on a rolling basis. Application fee: $35 ($50 for international students). Electronic applications accepted. *Expenses:* Tuition, state resident: full-time $4500; part-time $250 per credit hour. Tuition, nonresident: full-time $9018; part-time $501 per credit hour. *Required fees:* $361 per semester. Tuition and fees vary according to course level, course load and program. *Financial support:* Career-related internships or fieldwork, Federal Work-Study, institutionally sponsored loans, scholarships/grants, and unspecified assistantships available. Financial award application deadline: 3/31; financial award applicants required to submit FAFSA. *Unit head:* Dr. Kim Finch, Program Coordinator, 417-836-5192, Fax: 417-836-4918, E-mail: kimfinch@missouristate.edu. *Application contact:* Misty Stewart, Coordinator of Admissions and Recruitment, 417-836-6079, Fax: 417-836-6200, E-mail: mistystewart@missouristate.edu. Website: http://education.missouristate.edu/edadmin/.

Monmouth University, The Graduate School, School of Education, West Long Branch, NJ 07764-1898. Offers applied behavioral analysis (Certificate); autism (Certificate); initial certification (MAT), including elementary level, K-12, secondary level; principal (MS Ed); principal/school administrator (MS Ed); reading specialist (MS Ed); school counseling (MS Ed); special education (MS Ed), including autism, learning disabilities teacher consultant, teacher of students with disabilities, teaching in inclusive settings; speech-language pathology (MS Ed); student affairs and college counseling (MS Ed); teaching English to speakers of other languages (TESOL) (Certificate). *Accreditation:* NCATE. Part-time and evening/weekend programs available. *Faculty:* 15 full-time (11 women), 19 part-time/adjunct (17 women). *Students:* 125 full-time (97 women), 168 part-time (146 women); includes 38 minority (12 Black or African American, non-Hispanic/Latino; 5 Asian, non-Hispanic/Latino; 16 Hispanic/Latino; 5 Two or more races, non-Hispanic/Latino). Average age 28. 176 applicants, 90% accepted, 112 enrolled. In 2013, 147 master's awarded. *Entrance requirements:* For master's, GRE within last 5 years (for MS Ed in speech-language pathology), minimum GPA of 3.0 in major; 2 letters of recommendation (for some programs), resume, personal statement or essay (depending on degree program). Additional exam requirements/recommendations for international students: Required—TOEFL (minimum score 550 paper-based; 79 iBT), IELTS (minimum score 6), Michigan English Language Assessment Battery (minimum score 77). *Application deadline:* For fall admission, 7/15 priority date for domestic students, 7/1 for international students; for spring admission, 11/15 priority date for domestic students, 11/1 for international students. Applications are processed on a rolling basis. Application fee: $50. Electronic applications accepted. *Expenses:* Tuition: Part-time $1004 per credit hour. *Required fees:* $157 per semester. *Financial support:* In 2013–14, 191 students received support, including 159 fellowships (averaging $2,786 per year), 30 research assistantships (averaging $8,755 per year); career-related internships or fieldwork, scholarships/grants, and unspecified assistantships also available. Support available to part-time students. Financial award applicants required to submit FAFSA. *Faculty research:* Multicultural literacy, science and mathematics teaching strategies, teacher as reflective practitioner, children with disabilities. *Unit head:* Dr. Jason Barr, Program Director, 732-263-5238, Fax: 732-263-5277, E-mail: jbarr@monmouth.edu. *Application contact:* Lauren Vento-Cifelli, Associate Vice President of Undergraduate and Graduate Admission, 732-571-3452, Fax: 732-263-5123, E-mail: gradadm@monmouth.edu. Website: http://www.monmouth.edu/academics/schools/education/default.asp.

Montclair State University, The Graduate School, College of Education and Human Services, Department of Early Childhood, Elementary and Literacy Education, Program in Early Childhood and Elementary Education, Montclair, NJ 07043-1624. Offers M Ed. Part-time and evening/weekend programs available. *Degree requirements:* For master's, comprehensive exam, thesis or alternative. *Entrance requirements:* For master's, GRE General Test, interview, 2 letters of recommendation. Additional exam requirements/recommendations for international students: Required—TOEFL (minimum score 83 iBT), IELTS (minimum score 6.5). Electronic applications accepted.

Montclair State University, The Graduate School, College of Education and Human Services, Department of Early Childhood, Elementary and Literacy Education, Program in Teaching Elementary Education, Montclair, NJ 07043-1624. Offers MAT. *Degree requirements:* For master's, comprehensive exam, thesis or alternative. *Entrance requirements:* For master's, GRE General Test, interview, essay, 2 letters of recommendation. Additional exam requirements/recommendations for international students: Required—TOEFL (minimum score 83 iBT), IELTS (minimum score 6.5). Electronic applications accepted.

Morehead State University, Graduate Programs, College of Education, Department of Curriculum and Instruction, Morehead, KY 40351. Offers curriculum and instruction (Ed S); elementary education (MA Ed), including elementary education, international education, middle school education, reading; secondary education (MA Ed); special education (MA Ed); teaching (MAT). Part-time and evening/weekend programs available. *Degree requirements:* For master's, comprehensive exam, thesis optional; for Ed S, thesis, oral exam. *Entrance requirements:* For master's, GRE General Test, minimum GPA of 2.75, teaching certificate; for Ed S, GRE General Test, interview, master's degree, minimum GPA of 3.5, work experience. Additional exam requirements/recommendations for international students: Required—TOEFL (minimum score 500 paper-based). Electronic applications accepted. *Faculty research:* Communicative competence of learning-disabled students, teaching social studies in elementary schools, ungraded primary school organization, study skills.

Morehead State University, Graduate Programs, College of Education, Department of Foundational and Graduate Studies in Education, Morehead, KY 40351. Offers adult and higher education (MA, Ed S); certified professional counselor (Ed S); counseling P-12 (MA); curriculum and instruction (Ed S); educational technology (MA Ed); instructional leadership (Ed S); school administration (MA); school counseling (Ed S); teacher leader business and marketing content (MA Ed); teacher leader business and marketing technology (MA Ed); teacher leader educational technology (MA Ed); teacher leader English (MA Ed); teacher leader gifted education (MA Ed); teacher leader IECE certification (MA Ed); teacher leader interdisciplinary education P-5 (MA Ed); teacher leader middle grades (MA Ed); teacher leader non IECE certification (MA Ed); teacher leader reading/writing - non-certification (MA Ed); teacher leader reading/writing certification (MA Ed); teacher leader school communication - certification (MA Ed); teacher leader school communication - non-certification (MA Ed); teacher leader social studies (MA Ed); teacher leader special education (MA Ed). *Accreditation:* NCATE. Part-time and evening/weekend programs available. *Degree requirements:* For master's, thesis optional, oral and/or written comprehensive exams; for Ed S, thesis, oral exam. *Entrance requirements:* For master's, GRE General Test, minimum overall undergraduate GPA of 2.5; for Ed S, GRE General Test, interview, master's degree, minimum GPA of 3.5, work experience. Additional exam requirements/recommendations for international students: Required—TOEFL (minimum score 500 paper-based). Electronic applications accepted. *Faculty research:* Character education, school accountability, computer applications for school administrators.

Morgan State University, School of Graduate Studies, School of Education and Urban Studies, MAT Program, Baltimore, MD 21251. Offers elementary education (MAT); high school education (MAT); middle school education (MAT). Part-time programs available. *Degree requirements:* For master's, comprehensive exam. *Entrance requirements:* For master's, GRE General Test or MAT. *Faculty research:* Multicultural education, cooperative learning, psychology of cognition.

Mount Saint Mary College, Division of Education, Newburgh, NY 12550-3494. Offers adolescence and special education (MS Ed); adolescence education (MS Ed); childhood and special education (MS Ed); childhood education (MS Ed); literacy (5-12) (Advanced Certificate); literacy (birth-6) (Advanced Certificate); literacy and special education (MS Ed); literacy/childhood (MS Ed); middle school (5-6) (MS Ed); middle school (7-9) (MS Ed); special education (1-6) (MS Ed); special education (7-12) (MS Ed). *Accreditation:* NCATE. Part-time and evening/weekend programs available. *Faculty:* 11 full-time (9 women), 9 part-time/adjunct (4 women). *Students:* 29 full-time (19 women), 142 part-time (117 women); includes 22 minority (5 Black or African American, non-Hispanic/Latino; 16 Hispanic/Latino; 1 Two or more races, non-Hispanic/Latino). Average age 29. 51 applicants, 65% accepted, 27 enrolled. In 2013, 72 master's awarded. *Application deadline:* Applications are processed on a rolling basis. Application fee: $45. Application fee is waived when completed online. *Expenses:* Tuition: Full-time $13,356; part-time $742 per credit. *Required fees:* $70 per semester. *Financial support:* In 2013–14, 69 students received support. Unspecified assistantships available. Financial award application deadline: 4/15; financial award

applicants required to submit FAFSA. *Faculty research:* Learning and teaching styles, computers in special education, language development. *Unit head:* Dr. William Swart, Graduate Coordinator, 845-569-3149, Fax: 845-569-3535, E-mail: william.swart@msmc.edu. *Application contact:* Lisa Gallina, Director of Admissions for Graduate Programs and Adult Degree Completion, 845-569-3166, Fax: 845-569-3450, E-mail: lisa.gallina@msmc.edu.
Website: http://www.msmc.edu/Academics/Graduate_Programs/Master_of_Science_in_Education.

Mount Saint Vincent University, Graduate Programs, Faculty of Education, Program in Elementary Education, Halifax, NS B3M 2J6, Canada. Offers M Ed, MA Ed, MA-R. Part-time and evening/weekend programs available. Postbaccalaureate distance learning degree programs offered (minimal on-campus study). *Degree requirements:* For master's, thesis (for some programs). *Entrance requirements:* For master's, bachelor's degree in education, 1 year of teaching experience. Electronic applications accepted. *Faculty research:* Curriculum theory, mathematics education, philosophy in teacher education, science education, literacy education.

Murray State University, College of Education, Department of Early Childhood and Elementary Education, Programs in Elementary Education/Reading and Writing, Murray, KY 42071. Offers elementary education (MA Ed, Ed S); reading and writing (MA Ed). *Accreditation:* NCATE. Part-time programs available. *Degree requirements:* For master's, comprehensive exam, thesis optional; for Ed S, comprehensive exam. *Entrance requirements:* For master's, minimum GPA of 2.5 for conditional admittance, 3.0 for unconditional; for Ed S, GRE General Test or MAT. Additional exam requirements/recommendations for international students: Required—TOEFL.

National Louis University, National College of Education, Chicago, IL 60603. Offers administration and supervision (M Ed, Ed D, CAS, Ed S); curriculum and instruction (M Ed, MS Ed, CAS); early childhood administration (M Ed, CAS); early childhood education (M Ed, MAT, MS Ed, CAS); education (Ed D); educational psychology/human learning and development (M Ed, MS Ed, CAS, Ed S); elementary education (MAT); interdisciplinary curriculum and instruction (M Ed); mathematics education (M Ed, MS Ed, CAS); reading and language (M Ed, MS Ed, CAS); school psychology (M Ed, Ed S); science education (M Ed, MS Ed, CAS); secondary education (MAT); special education (M Ed, MAT, CAS); technology in education (M Ed, CAS). *Accreditation:* NCATE. Part-time and evening/weekend programs available. *Degree requirements:* For doctorate, comprehensive exam, thesis/dissertation. *Entrance requirements:* For master's, MAT or GRE, minimum GPA of 3.0; for doctorate, GRE General Test, minimum GPA of 3.25, interview, resume, writing sample, 4 recommendations. Additional exam requirements/recommendations for international students: Required—TOEFL (minimum score 550 paper-based; 79 iBT).

Nazareth College of Rochester, Graduate Studies, Department of Education, Program in Inclusive Education-Childhood Level, Rochester, NY 14618-3790. Offers MS Ed. *Accreditation:* Teacher Education Accreditation Council. *Entrance requirements:* For master's, minimum GPA of 3.0.

New Jersey City University, Graduate Studies and Continuing Education, Debra Cannon Partridge Wolfe College of Education, Department of Elementary and Secondary Education, Jersey City, NJ 07305-1597. Offers elementary education (MAT); secondary education (MAT). Part-time and evening/weekend programs available. *Faculty:* 16 full-time (14 women), 8 part-time/adjunct (4 women). *Students:* 14 full-time (12 women), 23 part-time (11 women); includes 15 minority (6 Black or African American, non-Hispanic/Latino; 2 Asian, non-Hispanic/Latino; 7 Hispanic/Latino). Average age 33. In 2013, 21 master's awarded. *Entrance requirements:* Additional exam requirements/recommendations for international students: Required—TOEFL (minimum score 61 iBT). *Application deadline:* For fall admission, 8/1 priority date for domestic students; for spring admission, 12/1 for domestic students. Applications are processed on a rolling basis. Application fee: $0. *Expenses: Tuition, area resident:* Part-time $527.90 per credit. Tuition, nonresident: part-time $947.75 per credit. *Financial support:* Teaching assistantships, career-related internships or fieldwork, and unspecified assistantships available. *Unit head:* Dr. Althea Hall, Coordinator, 201-200-2101, E-mail: ahall@njcu.edu. *Application contact:* Dr. William Bajor, Dean of Graduate Studies, 201-200-3409, Fax: 201-200-3411, E-mail: wbajor@njcu.edu.

New York University, Steinhardt School of Culture, Education, and Human Development, Department of Teaching and Learning, Program in Early Childhood and Childhood Education, New York, NY 10003. Offers childhood education (MA), including childhood education, special education; early childhood and childhood education (PhD); early childhood education (MA); early childhood education/early childhood special education (MA). *Accreditation:* Teacher Education Accreditation Council. Part-time programs available. *Faculty:* 10 full-time (all women). *Students:* 75 full-time (67 women), 27 part-time (26 women); includes 40 minority (6 Black or African American, non-Hispanic/Latino; 1 American Indian or Alaska Native, non-Hispanic/Latino; 18 Asian, non-Hispanic/Latino; 12 Hispanic/Latino; 3 Two or more races, non-Hispanic/Latino), 11 international. Average age 28. 122 applicants, 59% accepted, 14 enrolled. In 2013, 64 master's, 2 doctorates awarded. *Degree requirements:* For master's, thesis (for some programs); for doctorate, thesis/dissertation. *Entrance requirements:* For doctorate, GRE General Test, interview. Additional exam requirements/recommendations for international students: Required—TOEFL (minimum score 100 iBT). *Application deadline:* For fall admission, 12/1 priority date for domestic and international students; for spring admission, 11/1 for domestic and international students. Applications are processed on a rolling basis. Application fee: $75. Electronic applications accepted. *Expenses: Tuition:* Full-time $35,856; part-time $1494 per unit. *Required fees:* $1408; $64 per unit. $473 per term. Tuition and fees vary according to course load and program. *Financial support:* Fellowships with full and partial tuition reimbursements, career-related internships or fieldwork, Federal Work-Study, institutionally sponsored loans, scholarships/grants, tuition waivers (partial), and unspecified assistantships available. Support available to part-time students. Financial award application deadline: 2/1; financial award applicants required to submit FAFSA. *Faculty research:* Teacher evaluation and beliefs about teaching, early literacy development, language arts, child development and education, cultural differences. *Unit head:* 212-998-5460, Fax: 212-995-4049. *Application contact:* 212-998-5030, Fax: 212-995-4328, E-mail: steinhardt.gradadmissions@nyu.edu.
Website: http://steinhardt.nyu.edu/teachlearn/childhood.

Niagara University, Graduate Division of Education, Concentration in Teacher Education, Niagara Falls, NY 14109. Offers early childhood and childhood education (MS Ed, Certificate); middle and adolescence education (MS Ed, Certificate); special education (grades 1-12) (MS Ed, Certificate); teaching English to speakers of other languages (MS Ed). *Accreditation:* NCATE. *Students:* 168 full-time (130 women), 40 part-time (28 women); includes 11 minority (4 Black or African American, non-Hispanic/Latino; 1 Asian, non-Hispanic/Latino; 5 Hispanic/Latino; 1 Native Hawaiian or other Pacific Islander, non-Hispanic/Latino), 101 international. Average age 27. In 2013, 131 master's, 1 Certificate awarded. *Entrance requirements:* For master's, GRE General Test or MAT. Additional exam requirements/recommendations for international students: Required—TOEFL (minimum score 550 paper-based, 79 iBT) or IELTS (minimum score 6). *Application deadline:* For fall admission, 8/1 for domestic students. Applications are processed on a rolling basis. Application fee: $30. *Expenses:* Contact institution. *Financial support:* Research assistantships with full and partial tuition reimbursements, teaching assistantships with full and partial tuition reimbursements, career-related internships or fieldwork, Federal Work-Study, scholarships/grants, and unspecified assistantships available. Financial award application deadline: 4/15; financial award applicants required to submit FAFSA. *Unit head:* Dr. Chandra Foote, Chair, 716-286-8549. *Application contact:* Dr. Debra A. Colley, Dean of Education, 716-286-8560, Fax: 716-286-8561, E-mail: dcolley@niagara.edu.
Website: http://www.niagara.edu/teacher-education.

North Carolina Agricultural and Technical State University, School of Graduate Studies, School of Education, Department of Curriculum and Instruction, Program in Elementary Education, Greensboro, NC 27411. Offers MA Ed. *Accreditation:* NCATE. Part-time and evening/weekend programs available. *Degree requirements:* For master's, comprehensive exam, research project or comprehensive portfolio. *Entrance requirements:* For master's, GRE General Test, minimum GPA of 3.0.

North Carolina Central University, School of Education, Department of Curriculum, Instruction and Professional Studies, Durham, NC 27707-3129. Offers curriculum and instruction (MA), including elementary education, middle grades education. *Accreditation:* NCATE. Part-time and evening/weekend programs available. *Degree requirements:* For master's, comprehensive exam, thesis or alternative. *Entrance requirements:* For master's, minimum GPA of 3.0 in major, 2.5 overall. Additional exam requirements/recommendations for international students: Required—TOEFL. *Faculty research:* Simulation of decision-making behavior of school boards.

North Carolina State University, Graduate School, College of Education, Department of Elementary Education, Raleigh, NC 27695. Offers M Ed. *Entrance requirements:* For master's, MAT or GRE, 3 letters of reference.

Northeastern Illinois University, College of Graduate Studies and Research, College of Education, MAT Program in Language Arts - Elementary Education, Chicago, IL 60625-4699. Offers MAT.

Northeastern Illinois University, College of Graduate Studies and Research, College of Education, MSI Program in Language Arts - Elementary Education, Chicago, IL 60625-4699. Offers MSI. *Entrance requirements:* For master's, minimum undergraduate GPA of 2.75; current valid state teaching certificate; 18 credit hours of undergraduate coursework in English literature and composition, linguistics, and/or speech; 15 credit hours of undergraduate coursework in education; two letters of recommendation; official transcripts.

Northeastern University, School of Education, Boston, MA 02115-5096. Offers curriculum, teaching, learning, and leadership (Ed D); elementary licensure (MAT); higher education administration (MAT, Ed D); Jewish education leadership (Ed D); learning and instruction (M Ed); organizational leadership studies (Ed D); secondary licensure (MAT); special education (M Ed). Part-time and evening/weekend programs available.

Northern Arizona University, Graduate College, College of Education, Department of Teaching and Learning, Flagstaff , AZ 86011. Offers early childhood education (M Ed); elementary education (M Ed); secondary education (M Ed). Part-time programs available. *Faculty:* 33 full-time (26 women), 3 part-time/adjunct (all women). *Students:* 146 full-time (119 women), 188 part-time (169 women); includes 91 minority (5 Black or African American, non-Hispanic/Latino; 16 American Indian or Alaska Native, non-Hispanic/Latino; 1 Asian, non-Hispanic/Latino; 65 Hispanic/Latino; 4 Two or more races, non-Hispanic/Latino), 2 international. Average age 35. 114 applicants, 94% accepted, 67 enrolled. In 2013, 205 master's awarded. *Degree requirements:* For master's, comprehensive exam (for some programs), thesis (for some programs). *Entrance requirements:* For master's, minimum GPA of 3.0. Additional exam requirements/recommendations for international students: Required—TOEFL (minimum score 550 paper-based; 80 iBT), IELTS (minimum score 7). *Application deadline:* For fall admission, 3/1 priority date for international students; for spring admission, 9/15 priority date for international students. Applications are processed on a rolling basis. Application fee: $65. Electronic applications accepted. *Financial support:* In 2013–14, 6 teaching assistantships with full tuition reimbursements (averaging $9,698 per year) were awarded; Federal Work-Study, scholarships/grants, health care benefits, tuition waivers (full and partial), and unspecified assistantships also available. Financial award applicants required to submit FAFSA. *Unit head:* Dr. Pamela Powell, Chair, 928-523-5644, Fax: 928-523-1929, E-mail: pamela.powell@nau.edu. *Application contact:* Kay Quillen, Administrative Assistant, 928-523-9316, Fax: 928-523-1929, E-mail: kay.quillen@nau.edu.
Website: http://nau.edu/coe/teaching-and-learning/.

Northern Illinois University, Graduate School, College of Education, Department of Special and Early Education, De Kalb, IL 60115-2854. Offers curriculum and instruction (MS Ed, Ed D), including curriculum leadership (Ed D), elementary education (Ed D), secondary education (Ed D); early childhood education (MS Ed); elementary education (MS Ed); special education (MS Ed). Part-time and evening/weekend programs available. *Faculty:* 22 full-time (14 women), 2 part-time/adjunct (both women). *Students:* 52 full-time (41 women), 168 part-time (137 women); includes 29 minority (11 Black or African American, non-Hispanic/Latino; 7 Asian, non-Hispanic/Latino; 6 Hispanic/Latino; 5 Two or more races, non-Hispanic/Latino), 3 international. Average age 36. 38 applicants, 63% accepted, 18 enrolled. In 2013, 59 master's, 15 doctorates awarded. *Degree requirements:* For master's, comprehensive exam, thesis optional; for doctorate, thesis/dissertation, candidacy exam, dissertation defense. *Entrance requirements:* For master's, GRE General Test or MAT, minimum undergraduate GPA of 2.75; for doctorate, GRE General Test or MAT, minimum undergraduate GPA of 2.75, graduate 3.2. Additional exam requirements/recommendations for international students: Required—TOEFL (minimum score 550 paper-based). *Application deadline:* For fall admission, 6/1 for domestic students, 5/1 for international students; for spring admission, 11/1 for domestic students, 10/1 for international students. Applications are processed on a rolling basis. Application fee: $40. Electronic applications accepted. *Financial support:* In 2013–14, 24 research assistantships with full tuition reimbursements were awarded; fellowships with full tuition reimbursements, teaching assistantships with full tuition reimbursements, career-related internships or fieldwork, Federal Work-Study, scholarships/grants, tuition waivers (full), and unspecified assistantships also available. Support available to part-time students. Financial award applicants required to submit FAFSA. *Faculty research:* Teacher certification, stress reduction during student teaching, teaching history, portfolios in student teaching. *Unit head:* Dr. Barbara Schwartz-Bechet, Interim Chair, 815-753-1619, E-mail: seed@niu.edu. *Application contact:* Gail Myers, Clerk, Graduate Advising, 815-753-0381, E-mail: gmyers@niu.edu.
Website: http://www.cedu.niu.edu/seed/.

Northern Michigan University, College of Graduate Studies, College of Health Sciences and Professional Studies, School of Education, Leadership and Public Service, Program in Elementary Education, Marquette, MI 49855-5301. Offers MAE. Part-time programs available. *Students:* 7 full-time (5 women), 30 part-time (29 women). In 2013, 16 master's awarded. *Degree requirements:* For master's, thesis or alternative. *Entrance requirements:* For master's, minimum GPA of 3.0. *Application deadline:* For fall admission, 7/1 priority date for domestic students; for spring admission, 11/1 for

domestic students. Applications are processed on a rolling basis. Application fee: $25. *Expenses:* Tuition, state resident: part-time $427 per credit. Tuition, nonresident: part-time $614.50 per credit. *Required fees:* $325 per semester. Tuition and fees vary according to course load and program. *Financial support:* Teaching assistantships, Federal Work-Study, and institutionally sponsored loans available. Support available to part-time students. Financial award application deadline: 3/1. *Faculty research:* Whole language research, literature-based reading, essential elements of instruction, supervision and improvement of instruction. *Unit head:* Rodney Clarken, Associate Dean, 906-227-1880, E-mail: rclarken@nmu.edu. *Application contact:* Nancy E. Carter, Coordinator, 906-227-1625.

Northwestern Oklahoma State University, School of Professional Studies, Program in Elementary Education, Alva, OK 73717-2799. Offers M Ed. *Accreditation:* NCATE. Part-time programs available. *Degree requirements:* For master's, thesis optional, portfolio. *Entrance requirements:* For master's, GRE General Test or MAT, minimum GPA of 2.75.

Northwestern State University of Louisiana, Graduate Studies and Research, College of Education and Human Development, Program in Elementary Education, Natchitoches, LA 71497. Offers MAT. *Degree requirements:* For master's, comprehensive exam, thesis or alternative. *Entrance requirements:* For master's, GRE General Test, minimum undergraduate GPA of 2.5. Additional exam requirements/recommendations for international students: Required—TOEFL. Electronic applications accepted.

Northwestern State University of Louisiana, Graduate Studies and Research, College of Education and Human Development, Programs in Educational Leadership and Instruction, Natchitoches, LA 71497. Offers counseling (Ed S); educational leadership (M Ed, Ed S); educational technology (Ed S); elementary teaching (Ed S); reading (Ed S); secondary teaching (Ed S); special education (Ed S). *Accreditation:* NASAD. *Degree requirements:* For master's, comprehensive exam, thesis (for some programs). *Entrance requirements:* For master's and Ed S, GRE General Test. Additional exam requirements/recommendations for international students: Required—TOEFL. Electronic applications accepted.

Northwestern University, The Graduate School, School of Education and Social Policy, Education and Social Policy Program, Evanston, IL 60035. Offers elementary teaching (MS); secondary teaching (MS); teacher leadership (MS). Part-time and evening/weekend programs available. *Degree requirements:* For master's, research project. *Entrance requirements:* For master's, GRE General Test, Illinois State Board of Education Basic Skills Exam (secondary and elementary), bachelor's degree. Additional exam requirements/recommendations for international students: Recommended—TOEFL. Electronic applications accepted. *Faculty research:* Cultural context and literacy, philosophy of education and interpretive discussion, productivity, enhancing research and teaching, motivation, new and junior faculty issues, professional development for K-12 teachers to improve math and science teaching, female/underrepresented students/faculty in STEM disciplines.

Northwest Missouri State University, Graduate School, College of Education and Human Services, Department of Professional Education, Program in Educational Leadership, Maryville, MO 64468-6001. Offers educational leadership: elementary (MS Ed); educational leadership: K-12 (MS Ed); educational leadership: secondary (MS Ed); elementary principalship (Ed S); secondary principalship (Ed S); superintendency (Ed S). *Accreditation:* NCATE. Part-time programs available. *Degree requirements:* For master's, comprehensive exam; for Ed S, comprehensive exam, thesis. *Entrance requirements:* For master's, GRE General Test, minimum undergraduate GPA of 2.75, teaching certificate, writing sample; for Ed S, minimum graduate GPA of 3.25. Additional exam requirements/recommendations for international students: Required—TOEFL (minimum score 550 paper-based).

Northwest Missouri State University, Graduate School, College of Education and Human Services, Department of Professional Education, Program in Teaching: Elementary Self Contained, Maryville, MO 64468-6001. Offers MS Ed. *Accreditation:* NCATE. Part-time programs available. *Degree requirements:* For master's, comprehensive exam. *Entrance requirements:* For master's, GRE General Test, minimum undergraduate GPA of 2.75, teaching certificate, writing sample. Additional exam requirements/recommendations for international students: Required—TOEFL (minimum score 550 paper-based). Electronic applications accepted.

Nyack College, School of Education, Nyack, NY 10960-3698. Offers childhood education (MS); childhood special education (MS); TESOL (MAT, MS). Part-time programs available. Postbaccalaureate distance learning degree programs offered (no on-campus study). *Students:* 37 full-time (31 women), 14 part-time (10 women); includes 34 minority (22 Black or African American, non-Hispanic/Latino; 3 Asian, non-Hispanic/Latino; 9 Hispanic/Latino), 2 international. Average age 34. In 2013, 11 master's awarded. *Degree requirements:* For master's, comprehensive exam, clinical experience. *Entrance requirements:* For master's, LAST (Liberal Arts and Sciences Test), transcripts, autobiography and statement on reasons for pursuing graduate study in education, recommendations, 6 credits of language, evidence of computer literacy, introductory course in psychology. Additional exam requirements/recommendations for international students: Required—TOEFL (minimum score 550 paper-based). *Application deadline:* Applications are processed on a rolling basis. Application fee: $30. Electronic applications accepted. *Expenses:* Contact institution. *Financial support:* Scholarships/grants available. Financial award applicants required to submit FAFSA. *Unit head:* Dr. JoAnn Looney, Dean, 845-675-4538, Fax: 845-358-0874. *Application contact:* Traci Piescki, Director of Admissions, 800-541-6891, Fax: 845-348-3912, E-mail: admissions.grad@nyack.edu.
Website: http://www.nyack.edu/edu.

Occidental College, Graduate Studies, Department of Education, Los Angeles, CA 90041-3314. Offers elementary education (MAT), including liberal studies; secondary education (MAT), including English and comparative literary studies, history, life science, mathematics, physical science, social science, Spanish. Part-time programs available. *Degree requirements:* For master's, comprehensive exam, synthesis paper. *Entrance requirements:* For master's, GRE General Test, minimum GPA of 3.0. Additional exam requirements/recommendations for international students: Required—TOEFL (minimum score 625 paper-based). *Expenses:* Contact institution. *Faculty research:* Preparing teacher-leaders, curriculum development.

Oklahoma City University, Petree College of Arts and Sciences, Programs in Education, Oklahoma City, OK 73106-1402. Offers applied behavioral studies (M Ed); early childhood education (M Ed), including Montessori education; elementary education (M Ed), including Montessori education. Part-time and evening/weekend programs available. *Students:* 35 full-time (20 women), 9 part-time (7 women); includes 17 minority (12 Black or African American, non-Hispanic/Latino; 1 American Indian or Alaska Native, non-Hispanic/Latino; 1 Asian, non-Hispanic/Latino; 3 Two or more races, non-Hispanic/Latino), 6 international. Average age 32. 49 applicants, 61% accepted, 20 enrolled. In 2013, 24 master's awarded. *Entrance requirements:* For master's, bachelor's degree from accredited institution, minimum GPA of 3.0, essay, recommendation letters. Additional exam requirements/recommendations for international students: Required—TOEFL (minimum score 550 paper-based; 80 iBT). *Application deadline:* Applications are processed on a rolling basis. Application fee: $50. Electronic applications accepted. *Expenses: Tuition:* Full-time $16,848; part-time $936 per credit hour. Tuition and fees vary according to course load, degree level and program. *Financial support:* Career-related internships or fieldwork, Federal Work-Study, institutionally sponsored loans, scholarships/grants, and tuition waivers available. Support available to part-time students. Financial award application deadline: 6/1; financial award applicants required to submit FAFSA. *Faculty research:* Adult literacy, cognition, reading strategies. *Unit head:* Dr. Lois Lawler-Brown, Chair, 405-208-5374, Fax: 405-208-6012, E-mail: llbrown@okcu.edu. *Application contact:* Heidi Puckett, Director of Graduate Admissions, 800-633-7242, Fax: 405-208-5916, E-mail: gadmissions@okcu.edu.
Website: http://www.okcu.edu/petree/education/graduate.aspx.

Old Dominion University, Darden College of Education, Program in Elementary/Middle Education, Norfolk, VA 23529. Offers elementary education (MS Ed); instructional technology (MS Ed); library science (MS Ed); middle school education (MS Ed). *Accreditation:* NCATE. Part-time and evening/weekend programs available. Postbaccalaureate distance learning degree programs offered (no on-campus study). *Faculty:* 20 full-time (15 women), 31 part-time/adjunct (26 women). *Students:* 157 full-time (152 women), 91 part-time (77 women); includes 46 minority (17 Black or African American, non-Hispanic/Latino; 3 Asian, non-Hispanic/Latino; 17 Hispanic/Latino; 1 Native Hawaiian or other Pacific Islander, non-Hispanic/Latino; 8 Two or more races, non-Hispanic/Latino), 1 international. Average age 31. 291 applicants, 50% accepted, 123 enrolled. In 2013, 142 master's awarded. *Degree requirements:* For master's, comprehensive exam. *Entrance requirements:* For master's, GRE General Test or MAT; PRAXIS I, SAT or ACT, minimum GPA of 2.8. Additional exam requirements/recommendations for international students: Required—TOEFL (minimum score 600 paper-based). *Application deadline:* For fall admission, 6/1 priority date for domestic students; for winter admission, 11/1 priority date for domestic students; for spring admission, 3/1 priority date for domestic students. Applications are processed on a rolling basis. Application fee: $50. Electronic applications accepted. *Expenses:* Tuition, state resident: full-time $9888; part-time $412 per credit. Tuition, nonresident: full-time $25,152; part-time $1048 per credit. *Required fees:* $59 per semester. One-time fee: $50. *Financial support:* In 2013–14, 180 students received support. Application deadline: 2/15; applicants required to submit FAFSA. *Faculty research:* Education pre-K to 6, school librarianship. *Unit head:* Dr. Charlene Fleener, Graduate Program Director, 757-683-3284, Fax: 757-683-5862, E-mail: cfleener@odu.edu. *Application contact:* William Heffelfinger, Director of Graduate Admissions, 757-683-5554, Fax: 757-683-3255, E-mail: gradadmit@odu.edu.
Website: http://education.odu.edu/eci/.

Olivet Nazarene University, Graduate School, Division of Education, Program in Elementary Education, Bourbonnais, IL 60914. Offers MAT. *Accreditation:* NCATE. Evening/weekend programs available. *Degree requirements:* For master's, thesis or alternative.

Ottawa University, Graduate Studies-Arizona, Program in Education, Ottawa, KS 66067-3399. Offers community college counseling (MA); curriculum and instruction (MA); early childhood (MA); education intervention (MA); education leadership (MA); education technology (MA); Montessori early childhood education (MA); Montessori elementary education (MA); professional development (MA); school guidance counseling (MA); special education - cross categorical (MA). Programs offered in Mesa, Phoenix, Tempe and West Valley, AZ. *Accreditation:* NCATE. Part-time programs available. *Degree requirements:* For master's, thesis or alternative. *Entrance requirements:* For master's, minimum undergraduate GPA of 3.0, copy of current state certification or teaching license. Additional exam requirements/recommendations for international students: Required—TOEFL (minimum score 550 paper-based). Electronic applications accepted. *Expenses:* Contact institution.

Our Lady of the Lake University of San Antonio, School of Professional Studies, Program in Early Elementary Education, San Antonio, TX 78207-4689. Offers M Ed. Part-time and evening/weekend programs available. *Faculty:* 6 full-time (4 women), 3 part-time/adjunct (all women). *Students:* 1 (woman) full-time, 1 (woman) part-time; both minorities (both Hispanic/Latino). Average age 44. In 2013, 1 master's awarded. *Degree requirements:* For master's, comprehensive exam, thesis optional. *Entrance requirements:* For master's, GRE General Test or MAT. Additional exam requirements/recommendations for international students: Required—TOEFL. *Application deadline:* For fall admission, 4/1 priority date for domestic and international students; for spring admission, 11/1 priority date for domestic and international students; for summer admission, 2/1 priority date for domestic and international students. Applications are processed on a rolling basis. Application fee: $25 ($50 for international students). Electronic applications accepted. *Expenses: Tuition:* Full-time $9120; part-time $760 per credit. *Required fees:* $698; $334 per trimester. Tuition and fees vary according to course load, degree level, campus/location and program. *Financial support:* Research assistantships, teaching assistantships, career-related internships or fieldwork, Federal Work-Study, institutionally sponsored loans, scholarships/grants, and tuition waivers (partial) available. Support available to part-time students. Financial award application deadline: 4/1. *Faculty research:* Professional educator to understand and meet the comprehensive needs of a diverse student population, life-long learners, innovative practices. *Unit head:* Dr. Jerrie Jackson, 210-434-6711 Ext. 2698, E-mail: jjackson@lake.ollusa.edu. *Application contact:* Graduate Admission, 210-431-3961, Fax: 210-431-4013, E-mail: gradadm@lake.ollusa.edu.
Website: http://www.ollusa.edu/s/1190/ollu-3-column-noads.aspx?sid=1190&gid=1&pgid=3855.

Our Lady of the Lake University of San Antonio, School of Professional Studies, Program in Generic Special Education, San Antonio, TX 78207-4689. Offers elementary education (M Ed). Part-time and evening/weekend programs available. *Faculty:* 6 full-time (4 women), 3 part-time/adjunct (all women). *Students:* 9 full-time (7 women), 4 part-time (all women); includes 9 minority (1 Black or African American, non-Hispanic/Latino; 8 Hispanic/Latino). Average age 37. 10 applicants, 90% accepted, 5 enrolled. In 2013, 6 master's awarded. *Degree requirements:* For master's, comprehensive exam, thesis optional, examination for the Certification of Education in Texas. *Entrance requirements:* For master's, GRE General Test or MAT. Additional exam requirements/recommendations for international students: Required—TOEFL. *Application deadline:* For fall admission, 4/1 priority date for domestic and international students; for spring admission, 11/1 priority date for domestic and international students; for summer admission, 2/1 priority date for domestic and international students. Applications are processed on a rolling basis. Application fee: $25 ($50 for international students). Electronic applications accepted. *Expenses: Tuition:* Full-time $9120; part-time $760 per credit. *Required fees:* $698; $334 per trimester. Tuition and fees vary according to course load, degree level, campus/location and program. *Financial support:* Research assistantships, teaching assistantships, career-related internships or fieldwork, Federal Work-Study, institutionally sponsored loans, scholarships/grants, and tuition waivers (partial) available. Support available to part-time students. Financial award application deadline: 4/15. *Faculty research:* Professional educator to understand and meet the comprehensive needs of a diverse student population, life-long learners, innovative practices. *Unit head:* Dr. Jerrie Jackson, Coordinator, 210-434-6711 Ext. 2698, E-mail:

jjackson@lake.ollusa.edu. *Application contact:* Graduate Admission, 210-434-6711 Ext. 3961, Fax: 210-431-4013, E-mail: gradadm@lake.ollusa.edu. Website: http://www.ollusa.edu/s/1190/ollu-3-column-noads.aspx?sid=1190&gid=1&pgid=3855.

Pace University, School of Education, New York, NY 10038. Offers adolescent education (MST); childhood education (MST); early childhood development, learning and intervention (MST); educational leadership (MS Ed); educational technology studies (MS); inclusive adolescent education (MST); literacy (MS Ed); school business management (Certificate); special education (MS Ed). *Accreditation:* NCATE. Part-time and evening/weekend programs available. *Students:* 186 full-time (154 women), 441 part-time (315 women); includes 209 minority (89 Black or African American, non-Hispanic/Latino; 2 American Indian or Alaska Native, non-Hispanic/Latino; 30 Asian, non-Hispanic/Latino; 74 Hispanic/Latino; 1 Native Hawaiian or other Pacific Islander, non-Hispanic/Latino; 13 Two or more races, non-Hispanic/Latino), 7 international. Average age 29. 207 applicants, 71% accepted, 105 enrolled. In 2013, 296 master's, 25 other advanced degrees awarded. *Degree requirements:* For master's, internship. *Entrance requirements:* For master's, interview, teaching certificate. Additional exam requirements/recommendations for international students: Required—TOEFL. *Application deadline:* For fall admission, 8/1 priority date for domestic students, 6/1 for international students; for spring admission, 12/1 priority date for domestic students, 10/1 for international students. Applications are processed on a rolling basis. Application fee: $70. Electronic applications accepted. *Expenses:* Contact institution. *Financial support:* Research assistantships, career-related internships or fieldwork, and Federal Work-Study available. Support available to part-time students. Financial award applicants required to submit FAFSA. *Faculty research:* Teacher education, technology in education, STEM, literacy education, special education. *Total annual research expenditures:* $1.3 million. *Unit head:* Dr. Andrea M. Spencer, Dean, School of Education, 914-773-3341, E-mail: aspencer@pace.edu. *Application contact:* Susan Ford-Goldschein, Director of Graduate Admissions, 212-346-1660, Fax: 212-346-1585, E-mail: gradnyc@pace.edu.
Website: http://www.pace.edu/school-of-education.

Pacific Union College, Education Department, Angwin, CA 94508-9707. Offers education (M Ed); elementary teaching (MAT); secondary teaching (MAT). Part-time programs available. *Faculty:* 3 full-time (1 woman), 3 part-time/adjunct (all women). *Students:* 3 full-time (2 women), 11 part-time (7 women); includes 4 minority (1 Black or African American, non-Hispanic/Latino; 2 Asian, non-Hispanic/Latino; 1 Hispanic/Latino). Average age 35. In 2013, 2 master's awarded. *Degree requirements:* For master's, thesis, action research project, field experiences. *Entrance requirements:* For master's, GRE (for M Ed), two interviews, teaching credential, letters of recommendation, essay. *Application deadline:* Applications are processed on a rolling basis. Application fee: $0. *Expenses: Tuition:* Full-time $26,550; part-time $770 per quarter hour. *Required fees:* $930. Full-time tuition and fees vary according to course load and student's religious affiliation. Part-time tuition and fees vary according to class time and student's religious affiliation. *Financial support:* In 2013–14, 2 students received support. Scholarships/grants available. Support available to part-time students. *Faculty research:* Choice theory. *Unit head:* Prof. Thomas Lee, Chair, 707-965-6646, Fax: 707-965-6645, E-mail: tdlee@puc.edu. *Application contact:* Marsha Crow, Assistant Chair/Accreditation and Certification Specialist/Credential Analyst, 707-965-6643, Fax: 707-965-6645, E-mail: mcrow@puc.edu.
Website: http://www.puc.edu/academics/departments/education/.

Pacific University, College of Education, Forest Grove, OR 97116-1797. Offers early childhood education (MAT); education (MAE); elementary education (MAT); high school education (MAT); middle school education (MAT); special education (MAT); visual function in learning (M Ed). *Accreditation:* NCATE. Part-time and evening/weekend programs available. *Degree requirements:* For master's, research project. *Entrance requirements:* For master's, California Basic Educational Skills Test, PRAXIS II, minimum undergraduate GPA of 2.75, 3.0 graduate. Additional exam requirements/recommendations for international students: Required—TOEFL. Electronic applications accepted. *Expenses:* Contact institution. *Faculty research:* Defining a culturally competent classroom, technology in the k-12 classroom, Socratic seminars, social studies education.

Pfeiffer University, Program in Elementary Education, Misenheimer, NC 28109-0960. Offers MAT, MS. *Accreditation:* NCATE. *Entrance requirements:* For master's, GRE, MAT, minimum GPA of 2.75.

Pittsburg State University, Graduate School, College of Education, Department of Curriculum and Instruction, Pittsburg, KS 66762. Offers classroom reading teacher (MS); early childhood education (MS); elementary education (MS); reading (MS); reading specialist (MS); secondary education (MS); teaching (MAT). *Accreditation:* NCATE. *Degree requirements:* For master's, thesis or alternative. *Entrance requirements:* For master's, GRE or MAT.

Plymouth State University, College of Graduate Studies, Graduate Studies in Education, Program in Elementary Education, Plymouth, NH 03264-1595. Offers M Ed. *Accreditation:* NCATE. Part-time and evening/weekend programs available. *Degree requirements:* For master's, capstone project. *Entrance requirements:* For master's, MAT, minimum GPA of 3.0.

Portland State University, Graduate Studies, School of Education, Department of Curriculum and Instruction, Portland, OR 97207-0751. Offers early childhood education (MA, MS); education (M Ed, MA, MS); educational leadership: curriculum and instruction (Ed D); educational media/school librarianship (MA, MS); elementary education (M Ed, MAT, MST); reading (MA, MS); secondary education (M Ed, MAT, MST). *Accreditation:* NCATE. Part-time programs available. *Faculty:* 22 full-time (15 women), 28 part-time/adjunct (20 women). *Students:* 29 full-time (23 women), 162 part-time (123 women); includes 26 minority (3 Black or African American, non-Hispanic/Latino; 6 Asian, non-Hispanic/Latino; 13 Hispanic/Latino; 4 Two or more races, non-Hispanic/Latino), 6 international. Average age 36. 145 applicants, 69% accepted, 93 enrolled. In 2013, 257 master's, 5 doctorates awarded. *Degree requirements:* For master's, comprehensive exam, thesis or alternative; for doctorate, thesis/dissertation. *Entrance requirements:* For master's, California Basic Educational Skills Test, minimum GPA of 3.0 in upper-division course work or 2.75 overall. Additional exam requirements/recommendations for international students: Required—TOEFL (minimum score 550 paper-based). *Application deadline:* For fall admission, 4/1 for domestic and international students; for winter admission, 9/1 for domestic and international students; for spring admission, 11/1 for domestic and international students. Applications are processed on a rolling basis. Application fee: $50. *Expenses:* Tuition, state resident: full-time $9207; part-time $341 per credit. Tuition, nonresident: full-time $14,391; part-time $533 per credit. *Required fees:* $1263; $22 per credit. $98 per quarter. One-time fee: $150. Tuition and fees vary according to program. *Financial support:* In 2013–14, 1 research assistantship with full tuition reimbursement (averaging $6,248 per year), 2 teaching assistantships with full tuition reimbursements (averaging $7,755 per year) were awarded; career-related internships or fieldwork, Federal Work-Study, and institutionally sponsored loans also available. Support available to part-time students. Financial award application deadline: 3/1; financial award applicants required to submit FAFSA. *Faculty research:* Early literacy, characteristics of successful teachers of at-risk students, participation of women/minorities in technology courses, selection of cooperating teachers. *Total annual research expenditures:* $1 million. *Unit head:* Christine Chaille, Head, 503-725-4753, Fax: 203-725-8475, E-mail: chaillec@pdx.edu. *Application contact:* Jake Fernandez, Department Assistant, 503-725-4756, Fax: 503-725-8475, E-mail: jifern@pdx.edu.
Website: http://www.ed.pdx.edu/ci/.

Prescott College, Graduate Programs, Program in Education, Prescott, AZ 86301. Offers early childhood education (MA); early childhood special education (MA); education (MA); elementary education (MA); environmental education leadership and administration (MA); equine-assisted learning (MA); school guidance counseling (MA); secondary education (MA); special education: learning disabilities (MA); special education: mental retardation (MA); special education: serious emotional disabilities (MA); student-directed independent study (MA); sustainability education (PhD). Part-time programs available. Postbaccalaureate distance learning degree programs offered (minimal on-campus study). *Degree requirements:* For master's, thesis, fieldwork or internship, practicum; for doctorate, thesis/dissertation. *Entrance requirements:* For master's, 2 letters of recommendation, resume; for doctorate, 3 letters of recommendation, resume, official transcripts, personal statement, program proposal. Additional exam requirements/recommendations for international students: Required—TOEFL (minimum score 500 paper-based). Electronic applications accepted.

Providence College, Program in Special Education, Providence, RI 02918. Offers special education (M Ed), including elementary teaching, secondary teaching. Part-time and evening/weekend programs available. *Faculty:* 9 part-time/adjunct (5 women). *Students:* 7 full-time (5 women), 18 part-time (15 women). Average age 29. 3 applicants, 33% accepted. In 2013, 15 master's awarded. *Degree requirements:* For master's, comprehensive exam. *Entrance requirements:* For master's, GRE General Test. Additional exam requirements/recommendations for international students: Required—TOEFL (minimum score 550 paper-based; 80 iBT). *Application deadline:* For fall admission, 8/1 priority date for domestic and international students; for spring admission, 12/1 priority date for domestic and international students. Applications are processed on a rolling basis. Application fee: $55. *Expenses: Tuition:* Part-time $432 per credit. *Required fees:* $432 per credit. *Financial support:* Career-related internships or fieldwork and unspecified assistantships available. Support available to part-time students. Financial award application deadline: 8/1; financial award applicants required to submit FAFSA. *Unit head:* Barbara Vigeant, Director, 401-865-2912, Fax: 401-865-1147, E-mail: bvigeant@providence.edu. *Application contact:* Rev. Mark D. Nowel, Dean of Undergraduate and Graduate Studies, 401-865-2649, Fax: 401-865-1496, E-mail: mnowel@providence.edu.
Website: http://www.providence.edu/professional-studies/graduate-degrees/Pages/master-education-specialed.aspx.

Providence College, Programs in Administration, Providence, RI 02918. Offers elementary administration (M Ed); secondary administration (M Ed). Part-time and evening/weekend programs available. *Faculty:* 14 part-time/adjunct (6 women). *Students:* 5 full-time (1 woman), 50 part-time (31 women). Average age 37. 9 applicants, 100% accepted, 8 enrolled. In 2013, 33 master's awarded. *Degree requirements:* For master's, comprehensive exam, portfolio. *Entrance requirements:* For master's, GRE General Test. Additional exam requirements/recommendations for international students: Required—TOEFL (minimum score 550 paper-based; 80 iBT). *Application deadline:* For fall admission, 8/1 priority date for domestic and international students; for spring admission, 12/1 priority date for domestic and international students. Applications are processed on a rolling basis. Application fee: $55. *Expenses: Tuition:* Part-time $432 per credit. *Required fees:* $432 per credit. *Financial support:* Career-related internships or fieldwork, institutionally sponsored loans, and unspecified assistantships available. Support available to part-time students. Financial award application deadline: 8/1; financial award applicants required to submit FAFSA. *Unit head:* Francis J. Leary, Director, 401-865-2881, E-mail: fleary@providence.edu. *Application contact:* Rev. Mark D. Nowel, Dean of Undergraduate and Graduate Studies, 401-865-2649, Fax: 401-865-1496, E-mail: mnowel@providence.edu.
Website: http://www.providence.edu/professional-studies/graduate-degrees/Pages/master-education-administration.aspx.

Purdue University, Graduate School, College of Education, Department of Curriculum and Instruction, West Lafayette, IN 47907. Offers agricultural and extension education (PhD, Ed S); agriculture and extension education (MS, MS Ed); art education (PhD); curriculum studies (MS Ed, PhD, Ed S); educational technology (MS Ed, PhD, Ed S); elementary education (MS Ed); family and consumer sciences education (MS Ed, PhD, Ed S); foreign language education (MS Ed, PhD, Ed S); industrial technology (PhD, Ed S); language arts (MS Ed, PhD, Ed S); literacy (MS Ed, PhD, Ed S); mathematics/science education (MS, MS Ed, PhD, Ed S); social studies (MS Ed, PhD); social studies education (Ed S); vocational/industrial education (MS Ed, PhD, Ed S); vocational/technical education (MS Ed, PhD, Ed S). *Accreditation:* NCATE. Part-time and evening/weekend programs available. *Faculty:* 29 full-time (19 women), 33 part-time/adjunct (29 women). *Students:* 85 full-time (53 women), 271 part-time (195 women); includes 62 minority (19 Black or African American, non-Hispanic/Latino; 3 American Indian or Alaska Native, non-Hispanic/Latino; 13 Asian, non-Hispanic/Latino; 22 Hispanic/Latino; 1 Native Hawaiian or other Pacific Islander, non-Hispanic/Latino; 4 Two or more races, non-Hispanic/Latino), 41 international. Average age 36. 155 applicants, 71% accepted, 71 enrolled. In 2013, 60 master's, 20 doctorates awarded. *Degree requirements:* For master's, thesis optional; for doctorate, thesis/dissertation, oral and written exams; for Ed S, oral presentation, project. *Entrance requirements:* For master's, GRE General Test (if undergraduate GPA is below 3.0), minimum undergraduate GPA of 3.0 or equivalent; for doctorate, GRE General Test (minimum combined verbal and quantitative score of 1000, 300 for new scoring), minimum undergraduate GPA of 3.0 or equivalent; master's degree with minimum GPA of 3.0 or equivalent; for Ed S, GRE General Test (minimum combined verbal and quantitative score of 1000, 300 for new scoring), minimum undergraduate GPA of 3.0 or equivalent; master's degree. Additional exam requirements/recommendations for international students: Required—TOEFL (minimum score 550 paper-based; 77 iBT). *Application deadline:* For fall admission, 12/15 for domestic students, 3/1 for international students; for spring admission, 9/15 for domestic students, 8/1 for international students. Application fee: $60 ($75 for international students). Electronic applications accepted. *Financial support:* Fellowships with full tuition reimbursements, research assistantships with full tuition reimbursements, teaching assistantships with full tuition reimbursements, career-related internships or fieldwork, and tuition waivers (full) available. Support available to part-time students. Financial award application deadline: 3/1; financial award applicants required to submit FAFSA. *Faculty research:* Literacy acquisition and development, teacher beliefs and knowledge, recruitment and retention of underrepresented students, economic education, literacy discourse. *Unit head:* Dr. Phillip J. VanFossen, Head, 765-494-7935, Fax: 765-496-1622, E-mail: vanfoss@purdue.edu. *Application contact:* Cindy Blankenship, Graduate Contact, 765-494-2345, Fax: 765-494-5832, E-mail: prater0@purdue.edu.
Website: http://www.edci.purdue.edu/.

Purdue University North Central, Program in Education, Westville, IN 46391-9542. Offers elementary education (MS Ed). *Accreditation:* NCATE. Part-time and evening/weekend programs available. *Degree requirements:* For master's, one foreign language.

Entrance requirements: For master's, GRE, minimum GPA of 3.0. Electronic applications accepted. *Faculty research:* Diversity, integration.

Queens College of the City University of New York, Division of Graduate Studies, Division of Education, Department of Elementary and Early Childhood Education, Flushing, NY 11367-1597. Offers bilingual education (MS Ed); childhood education (MA); early childhood education (MA); elementary education (MS Ed, AC); literacy (MS Ed). Part-time and evening/weekend programs available. *Degree requirements:* For master's, research project; for AC, thesis optional. *Entrance requirements:* For master's, minimum GPA of 3.0. Additional exam requirements/recommendations for international students: Required—TOEFL.

Queens University of Charlotte, Wayland H. Cato, Jr. School of Education, Charlotte, NC 28274-0002. Offers education in literacy (M Ed); elementary education (MAT); school administration (MSA). *Accreditation:* NCATE. Part-time and evening/weekend programs available. *Degree requirements:* For master's, comprehensive exam. *Entrance requirements:* For master's, GRE General Test. *Expenses:* Contact institution.

Quinnipiac University, School of Education, Program in Elementary Education, Hamden, CT 06518-1940. Offers MAT. *Accreditation:* NCATE. *Faculty:* 14 full-time (7 women), 46 part-time/adjunct (27 women). *Students:* 55 full-time (53 women), 3 part-time (2 women); includes 4 minority (1 Black or African American, non-Hispanic/Latino; 1 American Indian or Alaska Native, non-Hispanic/Latino; 2 Hispanic/Latino). 55 applicants, 93% accepted, 48 enrolled. In 2013, 53 master's awarded. *Entrance requirements:* For master's, PRAXIS I, minimum GPA of 2.67, interview. *Application deadline:* For fall admission, 4/1 priority date for domestic students. Applications are processed on a rolling basis. Application fee: $45. Electronic applications accepted. *Expenses: Tuition:* Part-time $920 per credit. *Required fees:* $37 per credit. *Financial support:* Career-related internships or fieldwork, tuition waivers (full and partial), and unspecified assistantships available. Support available to part-time students. Financial award application deadline: 6/1; financial award applicants required to submit FAFSA. *Faculty research:* Multicultural and urban education/leadership, challenges of teaching diverse learners, scholarship of teaching and learning, technology and teaching, humor and education. *Unit head:* Mordechai Gordon, Program Director, E-mail: mordechai.gordon@quinnipiac.edu. *Application contact:* Office of Graduate Admissions, 203-582-8672, Fax: 203-582-3443, E-mail: graduate@quinnipiac.edu.
Website: http://www.quinnipiac.edu/gradeducation.

Regent University, Graduate School, School of Education, Virginia Beach, VA 23464-9800. Offers adult education (Ed D, PhD); advanced educational leadership (Ed D, PhD); career switcher with licensure (M Ed), including alternative licensure; character education (Ed D, PhD); Christian education leadership (Ed D); Christian school administration (M Ed); curriculum and instruction (M Ed); distance education (Ed D, PhD); educational leadership (M Ed); educational leadership - special education (Ed S); educational psychology (Ed D); elementary education (M Ed); higher education (Ed D, PhD); higher education leadership and management (Ed D); K-12 school leadership (Ed D, PhD); leadership in mathematics education (M Ed); reading specialist (M Ed); special education (M Ed, Ed D, PhD); student affairs (M Ed); TESOL (M Ed), including adult education, PreK-12. *Accreditation:* Teacher Education Accreditation Council. Part-time and evening/weekend programs available. Postbaccalaureate distance learning degree programs offered (minimal on-campus study). *Faculty:* 25 full-time (12 women), 50 part-time/adjunct (31 women). *Students:* 100 full-time (78 women), 754 part-time (614 women); includes 225 minority (191 Black or African American, non-Hispanic/Latino; 1 American Indian or Alaska Native, non-Hispanic/Latino; 7 Asian, non-Hispanic/Latino; 26 Hispanic/Latino), 16 international. Average age 39. 487 applicants, 63% accepted, 233 enrolled. In 2013, 202 master's, 19 doctorates awarded. *Degree requirements:* For master's, thesis or alternative; for doctorate, comprehensive exam, thesis/dissertation. *Entrance requirements:* For master's, MAT, minimum undergraduate GPA of 2.75, writing sample, resume, recommendations, interview; for doctorate, GRE, writing sample, 3 years of relevant professional experience, master's-level paper, copies of published work, resume, transcripts, interview, recommendations. Additional exam requirements/recommendations for international students: Required—TOEFL (minimum score 577 paper-based). *Application deadline:* For fall admission, 4/1 priority date for domestic students; for spring admission, 10/15 priority date for domestic students. Applications are processed on a rolling basis. Application fee: $50. Electronic applications accepted. Tuition and fees vary according to course load and degree level. *Financial support:* Fellowships, career-related internships or fieldwork, scholarships/grants, tuition waivers (full and partial), and unspecified assistantships available. Support available to part-time students. Financial award application deadline: 4/1; financial award applicants required to submit FAFSA. *Faculty research:* Character development and discipline for children, education leadership development, diversity in schools, classroom management, technology in education settings. *Unit head:* Dr. Alan Arroyo, Dean, 757-352-4261, Fax: 757-352-4318, E-mail: alanarr@regent.edu. *Application contact:* Matthew Chadwick, Director of Enrollment Support Services, 800-373-5504, Fax: 757-352-4381, E-mail: admissions@regent.edu.
Website: http://www.regent.edu/education/.

Regis College, Department of Education, Weston, MA 02493. Offers elementary teacher (MAT); higher education leadership (Ed D); reading (MAT); special education (MAT). Part-time and evening/weekend programs available. *Degree requirements:* For master's, thesis. *Entrance requirements:* For master's, GRE or MAT. Additional exam requirements/recommendations for international students: Required—TOEFL. Electronic applications accepted. *Faculty research:* Reflective teaching, gender-based education, integrated teaching.

Rhode Island College, School of Graduate Studies, Feinstein School of Education and Human Development, Department of Elementary Education, Providence, RI 02908-1991. Offers early childhood education (M Ed); elementary education (M Ed, MAT); reading (M Ed). *Accreditation:* NCATE. Part-time and evening/weekend programs available. *Faculty:* 11 full-time (9 women), 2 part-time/adjunct (both women). *Students:* 16 full-time (12 women), 51 part-time (49 women); includes 5 minority (1 Black or African American, non-Hispanic/Latino; 3 Hispanic/Latino; 1 Two or more races, non-Hispanic/Latino). Average age 37. In 2013, 29 master's awarded. *Degree requirements:* For master's, comprehensive exam (for some programs), comprehensive assessment. *Entrance requirements:* For master's, GRE General Test or MAT, PRAXIS II (elementary content knowledge), undergraduate transcripts; minimum undergraduate GPA of 3.0; 3 letters of recommendation. Additional exam requirements/recommendations for international students: Recommended—TOEFL (minimum score 550 paper-based; 79 iBT). *Application deadline:* For fall admission, 3/1 for domestic students; for spring admission, 11/1 for domestic students. Applications are processed on a rolling basis. Application fee: $50. *Expenses:* Tuition, state resident: full-time $8928; part-time $372 per credit hour. Tuition, nonresident: full-time $17,376; part-time $724 per credit hour. *Required fees:* $602; $22 per credit. $72 per term. *Financial support:* Teaching assistantships with full tuition reimbursements, Federal Work-Study, scholarships/grants, and health care benefits available. Support available to part-time students. Financial award application deadline: 5/15; financial award applicants required to submit FAFSA. *Unit head:* Dr. Patricia Cordeiro, Chair, 401-456-8016. *Application contact:* Graduate Studies, 401-456-8700.
Website: http://www.ric.edu/elementaryEducation/.

Rider University, Department of Graduate Education, Leadership and Counseling, Teacher Certification Program, Lawrenceville, NJ 08648-3001. Offers business education (Certificate); elementary education (Certificate); English as a second language (Certificate); English education (Certificate); mathematics education (Certificate); preschool to grade 3 (Certificate); science education (Certificate); social studies education (Certificate); world languages (Certificate), including French, German, Spanish. Part-time programs available. *Degree requirements:* For Certificate, internship, professional portfolio. *Entrance requirements:* For degree, PRAXIS, resume. Additional exam requirements/recommendations for international students: Required—TOEFL (minimum score 550 paper-based). Electronic applications accepted. *Faculty research:* Conceptual foundations for optimal development of creativity; creative theory, cognitive processes in mathematics learning, teacher collaboration.

Rivier University, School of Graduate Studies, Department of Education, Nashua, NH 03060. Offers curriculum and instruction (M Ed); early childhood education (M Ed); educational administration (M Ed); educational studies (M Ed); elementary education (M Ed); elementary education and general special education (M Ed); emotional and behavioral disorders (M Ed); general social education (M Ed); leadership and learning (Ed D, CAGS); learning disabilities (M Ed); learning disabilities and reading (M Ed); mental health counseling (MA); reading (M Ed); school counseling (M Ed). Part-time and evening/weekend programs available. *Degree requirements:* For master's, comprehensive exam (for some programs), internships. *Entrance requirements:* For master's, GRE General Test or MAT.

Rockford University, Graduate Studies, Department of Education, Program in Elementary Education, Rockford, IL 61108-2393. Offers MAT. Part-time and evening/weekend programs available. *Degree requirements:* For master's, thesis optional. *Entrance requirements:* For master's, GRE General Test, basic skills test (for students seeking certification), 3 letters of recommendation. Additional exam requirements/recommendations for international students: Required—TOEFL (minimum score 550 paper-based; 79 iBT). Electronic applications accepted.

Roger Williams University, School of Education, Program in Elementary Education, Bristol, RI 02809. Offers MAT. Part-time and evening/weekend programs available. *Faculty:* 5 full-time (4 women), 8 part-time/adjunct (7 women). *Students:* 21 full-time (17 women), 20 part-time (17 women); includes 4 minority (2 Asian, non-Hispanic/Latino; 1 Native Hawaiian or other Pacific Islander, non-Hispanic/Latino; 1 Two or more races, non-Hispanic/Latino). Average age 30. 14 applicants, 64% accepted, 7 enrolled. In 2013, 7 master's awarded. *Degree requirements:* For master's, state-mandated exams. *Entrance requirements:* For master's, resume, 3 letters of recommendation. Additional exam requirements/recommendations for international students: Recommended—TOEFL (minimum score 85 iBT), IELTS. *Application deadline:* Applications are processed on a rolling basis. Application fee: $50. Electronic applications accepted. *Expenses:* Contact institution. *Financial support:* In 2013–14, 19 students received support. Application deadline: 6/15; applicants required to submit FAFSA. *Faculty research:* Assistive technology; standards-based curricular development; professional development strategies, instruction, and assessment. *Unit head:* Dr. Rachel McCormack, Program Director, 401-254-3019, Fax: 401-254-3710, E-mail: rmccormack@rwu.edu. *Application contact:* Jamie Grenon, Director of Graduate Admissions, 401-254-6000, Fax: 401-254-3557, E-mail: gradadmit@rwu.edu.
Website: http://www.rwu.edu/academics/departments/education.htm#elementarygraduate.

Rollins College, Hamilton Holt School, Graduate Studies in Education, Winter Park, FL 32789. Offers elementary education (M Ed, MAT). Part-time and evening/weekend programs available. *Faculty:* 6 full-time (3 women), 5 part-time/adjunct (2 women). *Students:* 12 full-time (6 women), 20 part-time (15 women); includes 7 minority (3 Black or African American, non-Hispanic/Latino; 1 Asian, non-Hispanic/Latino; 3 Hispanic/Latino), 2 international. Average age 32. 4 applicants, 100% accepted, 4 enrolled. In 2013, 8 master's awarded. *Degree requirements:* For master's, comprehensive exam, Professional Education Test (PED) and Subject Area Examination (SAE) of the Florida Teacher Certification Examinations (FTCE), successful review of the Expanded Teacher Education Portfolio (ETEP), successful completion of all required coursework. *Entrance requirements:* For master's, General Knowledge Test of the Florida Teacher Certification Examination (FTCE), official transcripts, letter(s) of recommendation, essay. Additional exam requirements/recommendations for international students: Required—TOEFL (minimum score 550 paper-based; 80 iBT). *Application deadline:* For fall admission, 8/11 for domestic students; for spring admission, 12/10 for domestic students. Applications are processed on a rolling basis. Application fee: $50. *Expenses:* Contact institution. *Financial support:* In 2013–14, 13 students received support. Federal Work-Study, scholarships/grants, and unspecified assistantships available. Support available to part-time students. Financial award applicants required to submit FAFSA. *Unit head:* Dr. J. Scott Hewit, Faculty Director, 407-646-2300, E-mail: shewit@rollins.edu. *Application contact:* 407-646-1568, Fax: 407-975-6430.
Website: http://www.rollins.edu/holt/graduate/gse.html.

Roosevelt University, Graduate Division, College of Education, Department of Teaching and Learning, Program in Elementary Education, Chicago, IL 60605. Offers MA.

Rosemont College, Schools of Graduate and Professional Studies, Graduate Education PreK-4 Program, Rosemont, PA 19010-1699. Offers elementary certification (MA); PreK-4 (MA). Part-time and evening/weekend programs available. *Degree requirements:* For master's, thesis optional. *Entrance requirements:* For master's, minimum college GPA of 3.0, 3 letters of recommendation. Additional exam requirements/recommendations for international students: Required—TOEFL. Electronic applications accepted. Application fee is waived when completed online.

Rowan University, Graduate School, College of Education, Department of Teacher Education, Program in Elementary Education, Glassboro, NJ 08028-1701. Offers MST. *Faculty:* 2 full-time (1 woman). *Students:* 7 full-time (6 women); includes 1 minority (Asian, non-Hispanic/Latino). Average age 24. In 2013, 10 master's awarded. *Expenses: Tuition, area resident:* Part-time $638 per credit. Tuition, state resident: full-time $5742. *Required fees:* $142 per credit. Tuition and fees vary according to course level and program. *Unit head:* Dr. Horacio Sosa, Dean, College of Graduate and Continuing Education, 856-256-4747, Fax: 856-256-5638, E-mail: sosa@rowan.edu. *Application contact:* Admissions and Enrollment Services, 856-256-5435, Fax: 856-256-5637.

Rutgers, The State University of New Jersey, New Brunswick, Graduate School of Education, Department of Learning and Teaching, Program in Early Childhood/Elementary Education, Piscataway, NJ 08854-8097. Offers Ed M, Ed D. Part-time programs available. Terminal master's awarded for partial completion of doctoral program. *Degree requirements:* For master's, comprehensive exam (for some programs); for doctorate, thesis/dissertation, qualifying exam. *Entrance requirements:* For master's, GRE General Test, minimum GPA of 3.0; for doctorate, GRE General Test, minimum GPA of 3.5. Additional exam requirements/recommendations for international students: Required—TOEFL. Electronic applications accepted.

Sacred Heart University, Graduate Programs, Isabelle Farrington College of Education, Fairfield, CT 06825-1000. Offers administration (CAS); educational

technology (MAT); elementary education (MAT); leadership/literacy (CAS), including literacy; reading (CAS); secondary education (MAT); teaching (CAS). Part-time and evening/weekend programs available. *Faculty:* 23 full-time (13 women), 32 part-time/adjunct (14 women). *Students:* 210 full-time (155 women), 603 part-time (451 women); includes 86 minority (38 Black or African American, non-Hispanic/Latino; 1 American Indian or Alaska Native, non-Hispanic/Latino; 6 Asian, non-Hispanic/Latino; 35 Hispanic/Latino; 6 Two or more races, non-Hispanic/Latino). Average age 35. 278 applicants, 95% accepted, 227 enrolled. In 2013, 262 master's, 72 other advanced degrees awarded. *Degree requirements:* For master's, comprehensive exam (for some programs), thesis (for some programs). *Entrance requirements:* For master's, PRAXIS (teacher certification/MAT), minimum GPA of 2.75; for CAS, PRAXIS I, minimum GPA of 2.75. Additional exam requirements/recommendations for international students: Required—PTE; Recommended—TOEFL (minimum score 570 paper-based; 80 iBT), IELTS (minimum score 6.5). *Application deadline:* Applications are processed on a rolling basis. Application fee: $60. Electronic applications accepted. *Expenses:* Contact institution. *Financial support:* Teaching assistantships with partial tuition reimbursements, career-related internships or fieldwork, institutionally sponsored loans, traineeships, tuition waivers (partial), and unspecified assistantships available. Support available to part-time students. Financial award applicants required to submit FAFSA. *Faculty research:* Reading education, learning theory, teacher preparation, education of underachievers. *Unit head:* Dr. Jim Carl, Dean, 203-396-8454, Fax: 203-365-7513, E-mail: carlj@sacredheart.edu. *Application contact:* Kathy Dilks, Executive Director of Graduate Admissions, 203-365-7619, Fax: 203-365-4732, E-mail: gradstudies@sacredheart.edu.
Website: http://www.sacredheart.edu/academics/isabellefarringtoncollegeofeducation/.

Sage Graduate School, Esteves School of Education, Program in Childhood Education, Troy, NY 12180-4115. Offers MS Ed. *Accreditation:* NCATE. Part-time and evening/weekend programs available. *Faculty:* 11 full-time (6 women), 33 part-time/adjunct (25 women). *Students:* 2 full-time (both women), 5 part-time (all women). Average age 31. 10 applicants, 40% accepted, 1 enrolled. In 2013, 5 master's awarded. *Degree requirements:* For master's, thesis. *Entrance requirements:* For master's, minimum GPA of 2.75, resume, 2 letters of recommendation, interview, assessment of writing skills. Additional exam requirements/recommendations for international students: Required—TOEFL (minimum score 550 paper-based). *Application deadline:* Applications are processed on a rolling basis. Application fee: $40. *Expenses: Tuition:* Full-time $11,880; part-time $660 per credit hour. *Financial support:* Federal Work-Study, scholarships/grants, and unspecified assistantships available. Support available to part-time students. Financial award application deadline: 3/1; financial award applicants required to submit FAFSA. *Faculty research:* The effects of teachers' personal characteristics on the instructional process. *Unit head:* Dr. Lori Quigley, Dean, Esteves School of Education, 518-244-2326, Fax: 518-244-4571, E-mail: l.quigley@sage.edu. *Application contact:* Dr. Soyong Lee, Chair/Associate Professor, 518-244-2370, Fax: 518-244-2334, E-mail: lees2@sage.edu.

Sage Graduate School, Esteves School of Education, Program in Childhood Education/Literacy, Troy, NY 12180-4115. Offers MS. Part-time and evening/weekend programs available. *Faculty:* 10 full-time (5 women), 33 part-time/adjunct (25 women). *Students:* 1 (woman) full-time, 9 part-time (7 women); includes 1 minority (Hispanic/Latino). Average age 25. 7 applicants, 29% accepted, 2 enrolled. In 2013, 7 master's awarded. *Degree requirements:* For master's, thesis optional. *Entrance requirements:* For master's, minimum GPA of 2.75, resume, 2 letters of recommendation, interview, assessment of writing skills. Additional exam requirements/recommendations for international students: Required—TOEFL (minimum score 550 paper-based). *Application deadline:* Applications are processed on a rolling basis. Application fee: $40. *Expenses: Tuition:* Full-time $11,880; part-time $660 per credit hour. *Financial support:* Fellowships, research assistantships, Federal Work-Study, scholarships/grants, and unspecified assistantships available. Support available to part-time students. Financial award application deadline: 3/1. *Unit head:* Dr. Lori Quigley, Dean, Esteves School of Education, 518-244-2326, Fax: 518-244-4571, E-mail: l.quigley@sage.edu. *Application contact:* Mary Grace Luibrand, Director, 518-244-4578, Fax: 518-244-4571, E-mail: luibrm@sage.edu.

Sage Graduate School, Esteves School of Education, Program in Childhood Special Education, Troy, NY 12180-4115. Offers MS Ed. *Accreditation:* NCATE. Part-time and evening/weekend programs available. *Faculty:* 10 full-time (5 women), 33 part-time/adjunct (25 women). *Students:* 2 full-time (both women), 10 part-time (9 women); includes 2 minority (1 Black or African American, non-Hispanic/Latino; 1 Hispanic/Latino). Average age 24. 15 applicants, 53% accepted, 2 enrolled. In 2013, 4 master's awarded. *Degree requirements:* For master's, thesis optional. *Entrance requirements:* For master's, minimum GPA of 2.75, resume, 2 letters of recommendation, interview, assessment of writing skills. Additional exam requirements/recommendations for international students: Required—TOEFL (minimum score 550 paper-based). *Application deadline:* Applications are processed on a rolling basis. Application fee: $40. *Expenses: Tuition:* Full-time $11,880; part-time $660 per credit hour. *Financial support:* Fellowships, research assistantships, Federal Work-Study, scholarships/grants, and unspecified assistantships available. Support available to part-time students. Financial award application deadline: 3/1; financial award applicants required to submit FAFSA. *Faculty research:* Effective behavioral strategies for classroom instruction. *Unit head:* Dr. Lori Quigley, Dean, Esteves School of Education, 518-244-2326, Fax: 518-244-4571, E-mail: l.quigley@sage.edu. *Application contact:* Mary Grace Luibrand, Director, 518-244-4578, Fax: 518-244-4571, E-mail: luibrm@sage.edu.

Saginaw Valley State University, College of Education, Program in Elementary Classroom Teaching, University Center, MI 48710. Offers MAT. *Accreditation:* NCATE. Part-time and evening/weekend programs available. *Students:* 14 part-time (all women); includes 2 minority (1 Black or African American, non-Hispanic/Latino; 1 Hispanic/Latino). Average age 34. In 2013, 2 master's awarded. *Degree requirements:* For master's, capstone course. *Entrance requirements:* For master's, minimum GPA of 3.0, teaching certificate. Additional exam requirements/recommendations for international students: Required—TOEFL (minimum score 550 paper-based; 79 iBT). *Application deadline:* For fall admission, 7/15 for international students; for winter admission, 11/15 for international students; for spring admission, 4/15 for international students. Applications are processed on a rolling basis. Application fee: $30 ($80 for international students). Electronic applications accepted. *Expenses:* Tuition, state resident: full-time $8933; part-time $496.30 per credit hour. Tuition, nonresident: full-time $16,806; part-time $933.65 per credit hour. *Required fees:* $263; $14.60 per credit hour. Tuition and fees vary according to degree level. *Financial support:* Federal Work-Study and scholarships/grants available. Support available to part-time students. Financial award applicants required to submit FAFSA. *Unit head:* Dr. Mary Harmon, Dean, 989-964-7107, Fax: 989-964-4563, E-mail: coeconnect@svsu.edu. *Application contact:* Jenna Briggs, Director, Graduate and International Admissions, 989-964-6096, Fax: 989-964-2788, E-mail: gradadm@svsu.edu.

Saginaw Valley State University, College of Education, Program in Natural Science Teaching, University Center, MI 48710. Offers elementary school (MAT); middle school (MAT); secondary school (MAT). *Accreditation:* NCATE. Part-time and evening/weekend programs available. *Students:* 1 (woman) part-time. Average age 43. In 2013, 8 master's awarded. *Degree requirements:* For master's, capstone course. *Entrance requirements:* For master's, minimum GPA of 3.0, teaching certificate. Additional exam requirements/recommendations for international students: Required—TOEFL (minimum score 550 paper-based; 79 iBT). *Application deadline:* For fall admission, 7/15 for international students; for winter admission, 11/15 for international students; for spring admission, 4/15 for international students. Applications are processed on a rolling basis. Application fee: $30 ($80 for international students). Electronic applications accepted. *Expenses:* Tuition, state resident: full-time $8933; part-time $496.30 per credit hour. Tuition, nonresident: full-time $16,806; part-time $933.65 per credit hour. *Required fees:* $263; $14.60 per credit hour. Tuition and fees vary according to degree level. *Financial support:* Federal Work-Study and scholarships/grants available. Support available to part-time students. Financial award applicants required to submit FAFSA. *Unit head:* Dr. Mary Harmon, Dean, 989-964-7107, Fax: 989-964-4563, E-mail: coeconnect@svsu.edu. *Application contact:* Jenna Briggs, Director, Graduate and International Admissions, 989-964-6096, Fax: 989-964-2788, E-mail: gradadm@svsu.edu.

St. John Fisher College, Ralph C. Wilson Jr. School of Education, Program in Childhood Education/Special Education, Rochester, NY 14618-3597. Offers childhood education (MS); childhood education/special education (Certificate). Part-time and evening/weekend programs available. *Faculty:* 3 full-time (1 woman), 4 part-time/adjunct (all women). *Students:* 38 full-time (32 women), 6 part-time (5 women); includes 7 minority (2 Black or African American, non-Hispanic/Latino; 2 Asian, non-Hispanic/Latino; 3 Hispanic/Latino). Average age 29. 40 applicants, 90% accepted, 27 enrolled. In 2013, 12 master's awarded. *Degree requirements:* For master's, field experience, student teaching, LAST. *Entrance requirements:* For master's, 2 letters of recommendation, personal statement, current resume. Additional exam requirements/recommendations for international students: Required—TOEFL (minimum score 575 paper-based; 80 iBT). *Application deadline:* Applications are processed on a rolling basis. Application fee: $30. Electronic applications accepted. *Expenses: Tuition:* Part-time $795 per credit hour. *Required fees:* $10 per credit hour. Tuition and fees vary according to course load, degree level and program. *Financial support:* In 2013–14, 9 students received support. Scholarships/grants available. Financial award applicants required to submit FAFSA. *Faculty research:* Professional development, science assessment, multi-cultural, educational technology. *Unit head:* Dr. Susan Schultz, Program Director, 585-385-7296, E-mail: sschultz@sjfc.edu. *Application contact:* Jose Perales, Director of Graduate Admissions, 585-385-8067, E-mail: jperales@sjfc.edu.
Website: http://www.sjfc.edu/admissions/graduate/programs/childhood.dot.

St. John's University, The School of Education, Department of Curriculum and Instruction, Program in Childhood Education, Queens, NY 11439. Offers MS Ed. Part-time and evening/weekend programs available. *Students:* 9 full-time (6 women), 32 part-time (29 women); includes 17 minority (7 Black or African American, non-Hispanic/Latino; 3 Asian, non-Hispanic/Latino; 6 Hispanic/Latino; 1 Native Hawaiian or other Pacific Islander, non-Hispanic/Latino), 1 international. Average age 31. 28 applicants, 75% accepted, 6 enrolled. In 2013, 29 master's awarded. *Degree requirements:* For master's, comprehensive exam. *Entrance requirements:* For master's, minimum GPA of 3.0, qualification for New York State provisional (initial) teaching certificate, 2 letters of recommendation, transcript, personal statement. Additional exam requirements/recommendations for international students: Required—TOEFL (minimum score 600 paper-based; 100 iBT), IELTS (minimum score 5.5). *Application deadline:* For fall admission, 8/17 for domestic students, 5/1 priority date for international students; for spring admission, 1/5 for domestic students, 11/1 priority date for international students. Applications are processed on a rolling basis. Application fee: $70. Electronic applications accepted. *Expenses: Tuition:* Full-time $19,800; part-time $1100 per credit. *Required fees:* $170 per semester. *Financial support:* Research assistantships available. *Faculty research:* Self determination in the special education setting; parent, teacher, and student views on testing in elementary school. *Unit head:* Dr. Judith McVarish, Chair, 718-990-2334, E-mail: mcvarisj@stjohns.edu. *Application contact:* Dr. Kelly K. Ronayne, Associate Dean of Graduate Admissions, 718-990-2304, Fax: 718-990-2343, E-mail: graded@stjohns.edu.

Saint Joseph's University, College of Arts and Sciences, Department of Education, Philadelphia, PA 19131-1395. Offers curriculum supervisor (Certificate); educational leadership (MS, Ed D); elementary education (MS, Certificate); elementary/middle school education (Certificate); instructional technology (MS, Certificate); principal certification (Certificate); professional education (MS); reading specialist (MS, Certificate); reading supervisor (Certificate); secondary education (MS, Certificate); special education (MS, Certificate); superintendent's letter of eligibility (Certificate); supervisor of special education (Certificate). Part-time and evening/weekend programs available. Postbaccalaureate distance learning degree programs offered (no on-campus study). *Faculty:* 32 full-time (25 women), 75 part-time/adjunct (53 women). *Students:* 91 full-time (81 women), 858 part-time (656 women); includes 133 minority (96 Black or African American, non-Hispanic/Latino; 3 American Indian or Alaska Native, non-Hispanic/Latino; 9 Asian, non-Hispanic/Latino; 20 Hispanic/Latino; 5 Native Hawaiian or other Pacific Islander, non-Hispanic/Latino), 16 international. Average age 31. 359 applicants, 77% accepted, 203 enrolled. In 2013, 363 master's, 9 doctorates, 1 other advanced degree awarded. *Entrance requirements:* For master's, 2 letters of recommendation, minimum GPA of 3.0, official transcripts, personal statement; for doctorate, GRE, master's degree from accredited institution, minimum graduate GPA of 3.5, computer competence, commitment to participate in cohort, interview with program director. Additional exam requirements/recommendations for international students: Required—TOEFL (minimum score 550 paper-based; 79 iBT), IELTS (minimum score 6.5). *Application deadline:* For fall admission, 7/15 priority date for domestic students, 4/15 for international students; for winter admission, 11/15 for domestic students, 1/15 for international students; for spring admission, 11/15 priority date for domestic students, 10/15 for international students. Applications are processed on a rolling basis. Application fee: $35. Electronic applications accepted. *Expenses:* Contact institution. *Financial support:* Unspecified assistantships available. Financial award applicants required to submit FAFSA. *Faculty research:* Factors predicting early mathematics skills for low income children, early child care and development, preschool quality. *Total annual research expenditures:* $229,264. *Unit head:* Dr. John Vacca, Associate Dean, Education, 610-660-3131, E-mail: gradstudies@sju.edu. *Application contact:* Elisabeth Woodward, Director of Marketing and Admissions, Graduate Arts and Sciences, 610-660-3131, Fax: 610-660-3230, E-mail: gradstudies@sju.edu.
Website: http://sju.edu/int/academics/cas/grad/education/index.html.

Saint Mary's University of Minnesota, Schools of Graduate and Professional Programs, Graduate School of Education, Instruction Program, Winona, MN 55987-1399. Offers MA, Certificate. *Unit head:* Kellie Schmitz, Director, 507-457-6619, E-mail: kschmitz@smumn.edu. *Application contact:* Russell Kreager, Director of Admissions for Graduate and Professional Programs, 612-728-5207, Fax: 612-728-5121, E-mail: rkreager@smumn.edu.
Website: http://www.smumn.edu/graduate-home/areas-of-study/graduate-school-of-education/ma-in-instruction.

Saint Peter's University, Graduate Programs in Education, Program in Teaching, Jersey City, NJ 07306-5997. Offers 6-8 middle school education (MA Ed, Certificate); K-12 secondary education (MA Ed, Certificate); K-5 elementary education (MA Ed,

Certificate). Part-time and evening/weekend programs available. *Degree requirements:* For master's, comprehensive exam. *Entrance requirements:* For master's, GRE or MAT. Additional exam requirements/recommendations for international students: Required—TOEFL. Electronic applications accepted.

St. Thomas Aquinas College, Division of Teacher Education, Sparkill, NY 10976. Offers adolescence education (MST); childhood and special education (MST); childhood education (MST); educational leadership (MS Ed); reading (MS Ed, PMC); special education (MS Ed, PMC); teaching (MS Ed), including elementary education, middle school education, secondary education. *Accreditation:* NCATE. Part-time and evening/weekend programs available. *Degree requirements:* For master's, comprehensive exam, comprehensive professional portfolio; for PMC, action research project. *Entrance requirements:* For master's, New York State Qualifying Exam, GRE General Test or minimum GPA of 3.0, teaching certificate; for PMC, GRE General Test or minimum GPA of 3.0. Electronic applications accepted. *Faculty research:* Computer applications in education, adolescent special education students, literacy development, inclusive practices for special education students.

St. Thomas University, School of Leadership Studies, Institute for Education, Miami Gardens, FL 33054-6459. Offers earth/space science (Certificate); educational administration (MS, Certificate); educational leadership (Ed D); elementary education (MS); ESOL (Certificate); gifted education (Certificate); instructional technology (MS, Certificate); professional/studies (Certificate); reading (MS, Certificate); special education (MS). Part-time and evening/weekend programs available. *Degree requirements:* For master's, comprehensive exam; for doctorate, comprehensive exam, thesis/dissertation. *Entrance requirements:* For master's, interview, minimum GPA of 3.0 or GRE; for doctorate, GRE or MAT. Additional exam requirements/recommendations for international students: Required—TOEFL (minimum score 550 paper-based; 79 iBT). Electronic applications accepted.

Saint Xavier University, Graduate Studies, School of Education, Chicago, IL 60655-3105. Offers counseling (MA); curriculum and instruction (MA); early childhood education (MA); educational administration (MA); elementary education (MA); individualized studies (MA), including educational technology, English as a second language (ESL), ISTEM (integrative science, technology, engineering, and math), science education; music education (MA); reading (MA); secondary education (MA); Spanish education (MA); special education (MA); teaching and leadership (MA). *Accreditation:* NCATE. Part-time and evening/weekend programs available. *Degree requirements:* For master's, thesis or project. *Entrance requirements:* For master's, minimum GPA of 3.0. *Expenses:* Contact institution.

Salem College, Department of Education, Winston-Salem, NC 27101. Offers art education (MAT); elementary education (M Ed, MAT); language and literacy (M Ed); middle school education (MAT); school counseling (M Ed); second language studies (MAT); secondary education (MAT); special education (M Ed, MAT). *Accreditation:* NCATE. Part-time and evening/weekend programs available. Postbaccalaureate distance learning degree programs offered (minimal on-campus study). *Degree requirements:* For master's, practicum (MAT), project (M Ed), oral and written comprehensive exams. *Entrance requirements:* For master's, minimum GPA of 2.5. *Faculty research:* Content area reading strategies, literacy development, brain compatible instruction.

Salem State University, School of Graduate Studies, Program in Elementary Education, Salem, MA 01970-5353. Offers M Ed. *Accreditation:* NCATE. Part-time and evening/weekend programs available. *Students:* 13 full-time (10 women), 46 part-time (43 women); includes 2 minority (both Asian, non-Hispanic/Latino). 20 applicants, 100% accepted, 16 enrolled. In 2013, 33 master's awarded. *Entrance requirements:* For master's, GRE or MAT. Additional exam requirements/recommendations for international students: Required—TOEFL (minimum score 550 paper-based; 80 iBT) or IELTS (minimum score 5.5). *Application deadline:* For fall admission, 5/1 for domestic students; for spring admission, 10/1 for domestic students. Applications are processed on a rolling basis. Application fee: $50. *Financial support:* Career-related internships or fieldwork, Federal Work-Study, scholarships/grants, and unspecified assistantships available. Support available to part-time students. Financial award application deadline: 5/1; financial award applicants required to submit FAFSA. *Application contact:* Dr. Lee A. Brossoit, Assistant Dean of Graduate Admissions, 978-542-6673, Fax: 978-542-7215, E-mail: lbrossoit@salemstate.edu.
Website: http://www.salemstate.edu/academics/schools/12559.php.

Salem State University, School of Graduate Studies, Program in Spanish, Salem, MA 01970-5353. Offers MAT. Part-time and evening/weekend programs available. *Students:* 2 full-time (1 woman), 17 part-time (15 women); includes 6 minority (all Hispanic/Latino). 2 applicants, 50% accepted, 1 enrolled. In 2013, 6 master's awarded. *Entrance requirements:* For master's, GRE or MAT. Additional exam requirements/recommendations for international students: Required—TOEFL (minimum score 550 paper-based; 80 iBT) or IELTS (minimum score 5.5). *Application deadline:* For fall admission, 5/1 for domestic students; for spring admission, 10/1 for domestic students. Applications are processed on a rolling basis. Application fee: $50. *Financial support:* Career-related internships or fieldwork, Federal Work-Study, scholarships/grants, and unspecified assistantships available. Support available to part-time students. Financial award application deadline: 5/1; financial award applicants required to submit FAFSA. *Application contact:* Dr. Lee A. Brossoit, Assistant Dean of Graduate Admissions, 978-542-6675, Fax: 978-542-7215, E-mail: lbrossoit@salemstate.edu.
Website: http://www.salemstate.edu/academics/schools/6646.php.

Samford University, Orlean Bullard Beeson School of Education, Birmingham, AL 35229. Offers early childhood/elementary education (MS Ed); educational leadership (MS Ed, Ed D); gifted education (MS Ed); instructional leadership (MS Ed, Ed S); secondary collaboration (MS Ed); M Div/MS Ed. *Accreditation:* NCATE. Part-time and evening/weekend programs available. *Faculty:* 10 full-time (5 women), 16 part-time/adjunct (15 women). *Students:* 40 full-time (25 women), 210 part-time (156 women); includes 39 minority (33 Black or African American, non-Hispanic/Latino; 3 American Indian or Alaska Native, non-Hispanic/Latino; 2 Asian, non-Hispanic/Latino; 1 Hispanic/Latino), 4 international. Average age 38. 81 applicants, 89% accepted, 70 enrolled. In 2013, 94 master's, 21 doctorates, 16 other advanced degrees awarded. *Degree requirements:* For master's and Ed S, comprehensive exam; for doctorate, comprehensive exam, thesis/dissertation. *Entrance requirements:* For master's, GRE (minimum score of 295) or MAT (minimum score of 396); waived if previously completed a graduate degree, writing sample, statement of purpose, 3 letters of recommendation, 2 original copies of all transcripts, minimum GPA of 2.75, teaching certificate; for doctorate, minimum GPA of 3.7, professional resume, writing sample, 3 letters of recommendation, 1 original copy of all transcripts; for Ed S, master's degree, teaching certificate, minimum GPA of 3.25, 3 letters of recommendation, 2 original copies of all transcripts, writing sample, statement of purpose. Additional exam requirements/recommendations for international students: Required—TOEFL (minimum score 90 iBT), IELTS (minimum score 7). *Application deadline:* For fall admission, 7/30 for domestic and international students; for winter admission, 4/5 for domestic students; for spring admission, 12/5 for domestic and international students; for summer admission, 4/18 for domestic and international students. Applications are processed on a rolling basis. Application fee: $35. Electronic applications accepted. *Expenses: Tuition:* Full-

time $11,552; part-time $722 per credit. *Required fees:* $500; $250 per term. *Financial support:* In 2013–14, 162 students received support. Research assistantships, career-related internships or fieldwork, Federal Work-Study, scholarships/grants, and tuition waivers (partial) available. Support available to part-time students. Financial award applicants required to submit FAFSA. *Faculty research:* Research on gifted/high ability students (K-12), school law, the characteristics of beginning teachers, the nature of school reform, school culture, quality improvement in education, K-12 student achievement, reading research, classroom management, reading intervention, schema theory. *Unit head:* Dr. Maurice Persall, Chair, Department of Educational Leadership, 205-726-2019, E-mail: jmpersal@samford.edu. *Application contact:* Brooke Gilreath Karr, Graduate Admissions Coordinator, 205-729-2783, Fax: 205-726-4233, E-mail: kbgilrea@samford.edu.
Website: http://www.samford.edu/education/.

San Diego State University, Graduate and Research Affairs, College of Education, School of Teacher Education, Program in Elementary Curriculum and Instruction, San Diego, CA 92182. Offers MA. *Accreditation:* NCATE. Evening/weekend programs available. *Entrance requirements:* For master's, GRE General Test, letters of reference. Additional exam requirements/recommendations for international students: Required—TOEFL. Electronic applications accepted.

San Francisco State University, Division of Graduate Studies, College of Education, Department of Elementary Education, Program in Elementary Education, San Francisco, CA 94132-1722. Offers MA. *Accreditation:* NCATE. *Unit head:* Dr. Debra Luna, Chair, 415-338-1562, E-mail: dluna@sfsu.edu. *Application contact:* Dr. Stephanie Sisk-Hilton, MA Program Coordinator, 415-338-3442, E-mail: halcyon@sfsu.edu.
Website: http://coe.sfsu.edu/eed.

San Jose State University, Graduate Studies and Research, Connie L. Lurie College of Education, Department of Elementary Education, San Jose, CA 95192-0001. Offers curriculum and instruction (MA); reading (Certificate). *Accreditation:* NCATE. *Degree requirements:* For master's, thesis or alternative. Electronic applications accepted.

Seton Hill University, Program in Elementary Education/Middle Level Education, Greensburg, PA 15601. Offers MA, Certificate. Part-time and evening/weekend programs available. Postbaccalaureate distance learning degree programs offered (minimal on-campus study). *Faculty:* 7 full-time (6 women), 6 part-time/adjunct (3 women). *Students:* 4 full-time (3 women), 3 part-time (2 women). Average age 29. 5 applicants, 80% accepted, 4 enrolled. In 2013, 1 master's awarded. *Entrance requirements:* For master's, teacher's certification, 3 letters of recommendation, personal statement, transcripts, resume. Additional exam requirements/recommendations for international students: Required—TOEFL (minimum score 600 paper-based; 100 iBT), IELTS (minimum score 6.5). *Application deadline:* Applications are processed on a rolling basis. Application fee: $0. Electronic applications accepted. *Expenses: Tuition:* Full-time $14,220; part-time $790 per credit. *Required fees:* $700; $34 per credit. $50 per semester. *Financial support:* Scholarships/grants and tuition discounts available. Financial award application deadline: 8/15. *Faculty research:* Autism spectrum disorder, assessment rubrics, brain-based teaching and learning, administration in public education, early intervention, STEM. *Unit head:* Dr. Audrey Quinlan, Director, 724-830-4734, E-mail: quinlan@setonhill.edu. *Application contact:* Laurel Komarny, Program Counselor, 724-838-4209, E-mail: lkomarny@setonhill.edu.
Website: http://www.setonhill.edu/academics/graduate_programs/elementary_middle_level_education.

Shippensburg University of Pennsylvania, School of Graduate Studies, College of Education and Human Services, Department of Teacher Education, Shippensburg, PA 17257-2299. Offers curriculum and instruction (M Ed), including biology, early childhood education, elementary education, geography/earth science, history, mathematics, middle level education, modern languages; reading (M Ed). *Accreditation:* NCATE. Part-time and evening/weekend programs available. *Faculty:* 13 full-time (9 women), 2 part-time/adjunct (both women). *Students:* 6 full-time (all women), 72 part-time (61 women); includes 5 minority (1 Black or African American, non-Hispanic/Latino; 1 Asian, non-Hispanic/Latino; 2 Hispanic/Latino; 1 Two or more races, non-Hispanic/Latino), 1 international. Average age 30. 55 applicants, 60% accepted, 24 enrolled. In 2013, 63 master's awarded. *Degree requirements:* For master's, comprehensive exam (for some programs), thesis optional, practicum or internship; capstone seminar (for some programs). *Entrance requirements:* For master's, MAT or GRE (if GPA less than 2.75), interview, 3 letters of reference, questionnaire of teaching background and future goals. Additional exam requirements/recommendations for international students: Required—TOEFL (minimum score 580 paper-based); Recommended—IELTS (minimum score 6). *Application deadline:* For fall admission, 4/1 priority date for domestic students, 4/30 for international students; for spring admission, 9/1 priority date for domestic students, 9/30 for international students. Applications are processed on a rolling basis. Application fee: $45. Electronic applications accepted. *Expenses: Tuition, area resident:* Part-time $442 per credit. Tuition, state resident: part-time $442 per credit. Tuition, nonresident: part-time $663 per credit. *Required fees:* $127 per credit. *Financial support:* In 2013–14, 4 research assistantships with full tuition reimbursements (averaging $5,000 per year) were awarded; career-related internships or fieldwork, scholarships/grants, unspecified assistantships, and resident hall director and student payroll positions also available. Support available to part-time students. Financial award application deadline: 3/1; financial award applicants required to submit FAFSA. *Unit head:* Dr. Christine A. Royce, Chairperson, 717-477-1688, Fax: 717-477-4046, E-mail: caroyc@ship.edu. *Application contact:* Jeremy R. Goshorn, Assistant Dean of Graduate Admissions, 717-477-1231, Fax: 717-477-4016, E-mail: jrgoshorn@ship.edu.
Website: http://www.ship.edu/teacher/.

Siena Heights University, Graduate College, Adrian, MI 49221-1796. Offers clinical mental health counseling (MA); education leadership (Specialist); leadership (MA), including health care, higher education leadership, organizational; teacher education (MA), including early childhood, early childhood: Montessori-based, education leadership: principal, elementary education, K-12 reading, leadership: higher education, secondary education, K-12 reading, special education, K-12 cognitive impairment, special education, K-12 learning disabled. Part-time and evening/weekend programs available. *Faculty:* 37. *Students:* 9 full-time (7 women), 251 part-time (179 women). In 2013, 32 master's awarded. *Degree requirements:* For master's, thesis, presentation. *Entrance requirements:* For master's, minimum GPA of 3.0, current resume, essay, all post-secondary transcripts, 3 letters of reference, conviction disclosure form; copy of teaching certificate (for some education programs); for Specialist, master's degree, minimum GPA of 3.0, current resume, essay, all post-secondary transcripts, 3 letters of reference, conviction disclosure form; copy of teaching certificate (for some education programs). *Application deadline:* Applications are processed on a rolling basis. Application fee: $50. *Expenses: Tuition:* Part-time $535 per semester hour. *Required fees:* $130 per semester. *Financial support:* Career-related internships or fieldwork, Federal Work-Study, and resident assistantships available. Financial award application deadline: 9/1; financial award applicants required to submit FAFSA. *Unit head:* Dr. Linda S. Pettit, Dean, Graduate College, 517-264-7661, Fax: 517-264-7714, E-mail: lpettit@sienahts.edu.
Website: http://www.sienaheights.edu.

Elementary Education

Sierra Nevada College, Teacher Education Program, Incline Village, NV 89451. Offers advanced teaching and leadership (M Ed); elementary education (MAT); secondary education (MAT). Part-time and evening/weekend programs available. Postbaccalaureate distance learning degree programs offered (minimal on-campus study). *Degree requirements:* For master's, comprehensive exam, thesis, PRAXIS I and II. *Entrance requirements:* For master's, 2 letters of recommendation, minimum GPA of 3.0. Electronic applications accepted.

Simmons College, School of Social Work, Boston, MA 02115. Offers assistive technology (MS Ed, Ed S); behavior analysis (MS, PhD, Ed S); education (MA, CAGS); language and literacy (MS Ed, Ed S); social work (MSW, PhD); special education (MS Ed), including moderate disabilities, severe disabilities; teaching (MAT), including elementary education, general education, high school education; teaching English as a second language (MA, CAGS); urban leadership (MSW); MSW/MBA. *Accreditation:* CSWE (one or more programs are accredited). Part-time programs available. Postbaccalaureate distance learning degree programs offered (no on-campus study). *Students:* 519 full-time (454 women), 703 part-time (604 women); includes 192 minority (61 Black or African American, non-Hispanic/Latino; 1 American Indian or Alaska Native, non-Hispanic/Latino; 35 Asian, non-Hispanic/Latino; 71 Hispanic/Latino; 2 Native Hawaiian or other Pacific Islander, non-Hispanic/Latino; 22 Two or more races, non-Hispanic/Latino), 16 international. 952 applicants, 66% accepted, 353 enrolled. In 2013, 159 master's, 2 doctorates awarded. Terminal master's awarded for partial completion of doctoral program. *Degree requirements:* For master's, thesis (for some programs); for doctorate, comprehensive exam (for some programs), thesis/dissertation (for some programs). *Entrance requirements:* For master's, GRE, MAT, MTEL (for different programs); for doctorate, GRE, BCBA Analyst Exam. Additional exam requirements/recommendations for international students: Required—TOEFL (minimum score 600 paper-based; 100 iBT). *Application deadline:* Applications are processed on a rolling basis. Application fee: $45. Electronic applications accepted. *Financial support:* Teaching assistantships and scholarships/grants available. *Unit head:* Dr. Stefan Krug, Dean, 617-521-3924. *Application contact:* Carlos D. Frontado, Director of Admissions, 617-521-3920, Fax: 617-521-3980, E-mail: ssw@simmons.edu. Website: http://www.simmons.edu/ssw/.

Sinte Gleska University, Graduate Education Program, Mission, SD 57555. Offers elementary education (M Ed). Part-time and evening/weekend programs available. *Degree requirements:* For master's, thesis. *Entrance requirements:* For master's, 2 years of experience in elementary education, minimum GPA of 2.5, South Dakota elementary education certification. *Faculty research:* American Indian graduate education, teaching of Native American students.

Slippery Rock University of Pennsylvania, Graduate Studies (Recruitment), College of Education, Department of Elementary Education and Early Childhood, Slippery Rock, PA 16057-1383. Offers elementary education (M Ed), including K-12 reading specialist, math/science K-8, reading, reading specialist-instructional coach: literacy. *Accreditation:* NCATE. Part-time and evening/weekend programs available. Postbaccalaureate distance learning degree programs offered (no on-campus study). *Faculty:* 2 full-time (both women). *Students:* 4 full-time (all women), 23 part-time (all women); includes 1 minority (Black or African American, non-Hispanic/Latino). Average age 28. 47 applicants, 79% accepted, 11 enrolled. In 2013, 36 master's awarded. *Entrance requirements:* For master's, GRE General Test, MAT, minimum GPA of 3.0, resume, teaching certification, letters of recommendation, transcripts (depending on program). Additional exam requirements/recommendations for international students: Required—TOEFL (minimum score 550 paper-based; 80 iBT). *Application deadline:* For fall admission, 3/1 priority date for domestic students, 5/1 priority date for international students; for spring admission, 10/1 priority date for domestic students, 9/1 priority date for international students. Applications are processed on a rolling basis. Application fee: $25 ($30 for international students). Electronic applications accepted. *Expenses:* Tuition, state resident: full-time $7956; part-time $442 per credit. Tuition, nonresident: full-time $11,934; part-time $663 per credit. *Required fees:* $2896; $148 per credit. Tuition and fees vary according to degree level and program. *Financial support:* Career-related internships or fieldwork, Federal Work-Study, institutionally sponsored loans, scholarships/grants, tuition waivers (partial), and unspecified assistantships available. Support available to part-time students. Financial award application deadline: 5/1; financial award applicants required to submit FAFSA. *Unit head:* Dr. Suzanne Rose, Graduate Coordinator, 724-738-2042, Fax: 724-738-2779, E-mail: suzanne.rose@sru.edu. *Application contact:* Brandi Weber-Mortimer, Director of Graduate Admissions, 724-738-2051, Fax: 724-738-2146, E-mail: graduate.admissions@sru.edu.

Smith College, Graduate and Special Programs, Department of Education and Child Study, Program in Elementary Education, Northampton, MA 01063. Offers MAT. Part-time programs available. *Faculty:* 6 full-time (4 women), 3 part-time/adjunct (2 women). *Students:* 8 full-time (6 women), 2 part-time (both women); includes 1 minority (Asian, non-Hispanic/Latino). Average age 28. 18 applicants, 89% accepted, 10 enrolled. In 2013, 15 master's awarded. *Entrance requirements:* Additional exam requirements/recommendations for international students: Required—TOEFL (minimum score 595 paper-based; 97 iBT). *Application deadline:* For fall admission, 4/1 for domestic students, 1/15 priority date for international students; for spring admission, 12/1 for domestic students. Application fee: $60. *Expenses: Tuition:* Full-time $32,160; part-time $1340 per credit. *Financial support:* In 2013–14, 7 students received support, including 3 fellowships with full tuition reimbursements available; career-related internships or fieldwork, institutionally sponsored loans, and scholarships/grants also available. Support available to part-time students. Financial award application deadline: 1/15. *Unit head:* Alan Rudnitsky, Graduate Student Adviser, 413-585-3261, E-mail: arudnits@smith.edu. *Application contact:* Ruth Morgan, Administrative Assistant, 413-585-3050, Fax: 413-585-3054, E-mail: gradstdy@smith.edu. Website: http://www.smith.edu/educ/.

South Carolina State University, School of Graduate and Professional Studies, Department of Education, Orangeburg, SC 29117-0001. Offers early childhood and special education (M Ed); early childhood education (MAT); elementary education (M Ed, MAT); general science (MAT); mathematics (MAT); secondary education (M Ed), including biology education, business education, counselor education, English education, home economics education, industrial education, mathematics education, science education, social studies education; special education (M Ed), including emotionally handicapped, learning disabilities, mentally handicapped. *Accreditation:* NCATE. Part-time and evening/weekend programs available. *Faculty:* 9 full-time (3 women), 4 part-time/adjunct (3 women). *Students:* 32 full-time (26 women), 33 part-time (26 women); includes 63 minority (61 Black or African American, non-Hispanic/Latino; 2 Asian, non-Hispanic/Latino). Average age 31. 21 applicants, 100% accepted, 21 enrolled. In 2013, 15 master's awarded. *Degree requirements:* For master's, thesis optional, departmental qualifying exam. *Entrance requirements:* For master's, GRE General Test, NTE, interview, teaching certificate. *Application deadline:* For fall admission, 6/15 priority date for domestic students, 6/15 for international students; for spring admission, 11/1 for domestic and international students. Applications are processed on a rolling basis. Application fee: $25. Electronic applications accepted. *Expenses:* Tuition, state resident: full-time $8906; part-time $543 per credit hour. Tuition, nonresident: full-time $18,040; part-time $1051 per credit hour. *Financial*

support: Fellowships, career-related internships or fieldwork, Federal Work-Study, and institutionally sponsored loans available. Financial award application deadline: 6/1. *Faculty research:* Critical thinking, child abuse, stress, test-taking skills, conflict resolution, mainstreaming. *Unit head:* Dr. Margaret Evelyn Fields, Interim Chair, 803-536-7098, Fax: 803-516-4568, E-mail: efields@scsu.edu. *Application contact:* Curtis Foskey, Coordinator of Graduate Studies, 803-536-8419, Fax: 803-536-8812, E-mail: cfoskey@scsu.edu.

Southeastern Louisiana University, College of Education, Department of Teaching and Learning, Hammond, LA 70402. Offers curriculum and instruction (M Ed); elementary education (MAT); special education (M Ed); special education: early interventionist (MAT). *Accreditation:* NCATE. Part-time and evening/weekend programs available. *Faculty:* 11 full-time (9 women). *Students:* 40 full-time (38 women), 191 part-time (165 women); includes 55 minority (35 Black or African American, non-Hispanic/Latino; 1 American Indian or Alaska Native, non-Hispanic/Latino; 4 Asian, non-Hispanic/Latino; 13 Hispanic/Latino; 2 Two or more races, non-Hispanic/Latino), 2 international. Average age 34. 35 applicants, 66% accepted, 20 enrolled. In 2013, 50 master's awarded. *Degree requirements:* For master's, comprehensive exam (for some programs), thesis (for some programs), action research project, oral defense of research project, portfolio, teaching certificate, minimum cumulative GPA of 3.0. *Entrance requirements:* For master's, GRE (verbal and quantitative), PRAXIS (MAT). Additional exam requirements/recommendations for international students: Required—TOEFL (minimum score 500 paper-based; 61 iBT). *Application deadline:* For fall admission, 7/15 priority date for domestic students, 6/1 priority date for international students; for spring admission, 12/1 priority date for domestic students, 10/1 priority date for international students. Applications are processed on a rolling basis. Application fee: $20 ($30 for international students). Electronic applications accepted. *Expenses:* Tuition, state resident: full-time $5047. Tuition, nonresident: full-time $17,066. *Required fees:* $1213. Tuition and fees vary according to degree level. *Financial support:* Career-related internships or fieldwork, Federal Work-Study, institutionally sponsored loans, scholarships/grants, and unspecified assistantships available. Support available to part-time students. Financial award application deadline: 5/1; financial award applicants required to submit FAFSA. *Faculty research:* ESL, dyslexia, pre-service teachers, inclusion, early childhood education. *Total annual research expenditures:* $45,104. *Unit head:* Dr. Cynthia Elliott, Interim Department Head, 985-549-2221, Fax: 985-549-5009, E-mail: celliott@selu.edu. *Application contact:* Sandra Meyers, Graduate Admissions Analyst, 985-549-5620, Fax: 985-549-5632, E-mail: admissions@selu.edu. Website: http://www.selu.edu/acad_research/depts/teach_lrn/index.html.

Southeastern University, College of Education, Lakeland, FL 33801-6099. Offers educational leadership (M Ed); elementary education (M Ed); teaching and learning (M Ed).

Southeast Missouri State University, School of Graduate Studies, Department of Educational Leadership and Counseling, Program in Educational Administration, Cape Girardeau, MO 63701-4799. Offers educational administration (Ed S); educational leadership development (Ed S); elementary administration and supervision (MA); higher education administration (MA); school administration (MA); secondary administration and supervision (MA); teacher leadership (MA). *Accreditation:* NCATE. Part-time and evening/weekend programs available. *Faculty:* 6 full-time (3 women), 4 part-time/adjunct (1 woman). *Students:* 48 full-time (27 women), 181 part-time (118 women); includes 18 minority (11 Black or African American, non-Hispanic/Latino; 1 American Indian or Alaska Native, non-Hispanic/Latino; 2 Asian, non-Hispanic/Latino; 3 Hispanic/Latino; 1 Two or more races, non-Hispanic/Latino), 2 international. Average age 34. 83 applicants, 100% accepted, 83 enrolled. In 2013, 88 master's, 28 other advanced degrees awarded. *Degree requirements:* For master's and Ed S, comprehensive exam, thesis or alternative, paper. *Entrance requirements:* For master's, minimum undergraduate GPA of 2.75, valid teacher certification; for Ed S, minimum graduate GPA of 3.5; master's degree; valid teaching certificate. Additional exam requirements/recommendations for international students: Required—TOEFL (minimum score 550 paper-based; 79 iBT), IELTS (minimum score 6), PTE (minimum score 53). *Application deadline:* For fall admission, 8/1 for domestic students, 6/1 for international students; for spring admission, 11/21 for domestic students, 10/1 for international students; for summer admission, 5/15 for domestic students. Applications are processed on a rolling basis. Application fee: $30 ($40 for international students). Electronic applications accepted. *Expenses:* Tuition, state resident: full-time $5139; part-time $285.50 per credit hour. Tuition, nonresident: full-time $9099; part-time $505.50 per credit hour. *Financial support:* In 2013–14, 25 students received support. Career-related internships or fieldwork, Federal Work-Study, scholarships/grants, traineeships, tuition waivers (full), and unspecified assistantships available. Financial award application deadline: 6/30; financial award applicants required to submit FAFSA. *Faculty research:* Learning and the technology push, administration and student success, ethics of leaders. *Unit head:* Dr. Ruth Ann Williams, Professor/Interim Chair, Department of Educational Leadership and Counseling, 573-651-2417, E-mail: raroberts@semo.edu. *Application contact:* Alisa Aleen McFerron, Assistant Director of Admissions for Operations, 573-651-5937, E-mail: amcferron@semo.edu. Website: http://www4.semo.edu/edadmin/admin.

Southeast Missouri State University, School of Graduate Studies, Department of Elementary, Early and Special Education, Program in Elementary Education, Cape Girardeau, MO 63701-4799. Offers MA. *Accreditation:* NCATE. Part-time and evening/weekend programs available. Postbaccalaureate distance learning degree programs offered (no on-campus study). *Faculty:* 12 full-time (10 women). *Students:* 2 full-time (both women), 32 part-time (31 women); includes 2 minority (both Black or African American, non-Hispanic/Latino). Average age 33. 13 applicants, 100% accepted, 13 enrolled. In 2013, 9 master's awarded. *Degree requirements:* For master's, comprehensive exam, action research project. *Entrance requirements:* For master's, GRE General Test, MAT, or PRAXIS, minimum undergraduate GPA of 2.75; valid elementary or secondary teaching certificate. Additional exam requirements/recommendations for international students: Required—TOEFL (minimum score 550 paper-based; 79 iBT), IELTS (minimum score 6), PTE (minimum score 53). *Application deadline:* For fall admission, 8/1 for domestic students, 6/1 for international students; for spring admission, 11/21 for domestic students, 10/1 for international students; for summer admission, 5/15 for domestic students. Applications are processed on a rolling basis. Application fee: $30 ($40 for international students). Electronic applications accepted. *Expenses:* Tuition, state resident: full-time $5139; part-time $285.50 per credit hour. Tuition, nonresident: full-time $9099; part-time $505.50 per credit hour. *Financial support:* In 2013–14, 3 students received support. Career-related internships or fieldwork, Federal Work-Study, scholarships/grants, traineeships, tuition waivers (full), and unspecified assistantships available. Financial award application deadline: 6/30; financial award applicants required to submit FAFSA. *Unit head:* Dr. Julie Ray, Department of Elementary, Early, and Special Education Chair and Professor, 573-651-2444, E-mail: jaray@semo.edu. *Application contact:* Dr. Cindy Gordinier-Harkey, Assistant Professor, 573-651-2122, E-mail: cgordinier@semo.edu. Website: http://www.semo.edu/eese/.

Southern Arkansas University–Magnolia, Graduate Programs, Magnolia, AR 71753. Offers agriculture (MS); business administration (MBA); computer and information

sciences (MS); education (M Ed), including counseling and development, curriculum and instruction, educational administration and supervision, elementary education, reading, secondary education, TESOL; kinesiology (M Ed); library media and information specialist (M Ed); mental health and clinical counseling (MS); public administration (MPA); school counseling (M Ed); teaching (MAT). *Accreditation:* NCATE. Part-time and evening/weekend programs available. Postbaccalaureate distance learning degree programs offered. *Faculty:* 34 full-time (15 women), 8 part-time/adjunct (5 women). *Students:* 48 full-time (22 women), 269 part-time (167 women); includes 85 minority (78 Black or African American, non-Hispanic/Latino; 2 Asian, non-Hispanic/Latino; 2 Hispanic/Latino; 1 Native Hawaiian or other Pacific Islander, non-Hispanic/Latino; 2 Two or more races, non-Hispanic/Latino), 5 international. Average age 33. 149 applicants, 73% accepted, 109 enrolled. In 2013, 149 master's awarded. *Degree requirements:* For master's, comprehensive exam (for some programs), thesis optional. *Entrance requirements:* For master's, GRE, MAT or GMAT, minimum GPA of 2.5. Additional exam requirements/recommendations for international students: Required—TOEFL, IELTS. *Application deadline:* For fall admission, 7/10 for domestic and international students; for winter admission, 12/1 for domestic and international students; for spring admission, 12/1 for domestic and international students; for summer admission, 4/1 for domestic students. Applications are processed on a rolling basis. Application fee: $25 ($50 for international students). Electronic applications accepted. *Expenses:* Tuition, state resident: part-time $254 per credit hour. Tuition, nonresident: part-time $370 per credit hour. *Required fees:* $136 per credit hour. $259 per semester. Tuition and fees vary according to course load and program. *Financial support:* Career-related internships or fieldwork, Federal Work-Study, scholarships/grants, tuition waivers (full), and unspecified assistantships available. Financial award applicants required to submit FAFSA. *Faculty research:* Alternative certification for teachers, supervision of instruction, instructional leadership, counseling. *Unit head:* Dr. Kim Bloss, Dean, School of Graduate Studies, 870-235-4150, Fax: 870-235-5227, E-mail: kkbloss@saumag.edu. *Application contact:* Shrijana Malaka, Admissions Specialist, 870-235-4150, Fax: 870-235-5227, E-mail: smalakar@saumag.edu.
Website: http://www.saumag.edu/graduate.

Southern Connecticut State University, School of Graduate Studies, School of Education, Department of Elementary Education, New Haven, CT 06515-1355. Offers classroom teacher specialist (Diploma); educational coach (Diploma); elementary education (MS). *Accreditation:* NCATE. Part-time and evening/weekend programs available. *Degree requirements:* For master's, thesis or alternative. *Entrance requirements:* For master's, interview, minimum QPA of 2.5; for Diploma, master's degree. Electronic applications accepted.

Southern New Hampshire University, School of Education, Manchester, NH 03106-1045. Offers business education (M Ed); child development (M Ed); curriculum and instruction (M Ed), including education leadership, reading, special education, technology integration; education (M Ed); educational leadership (M Ed, Ed D); educational studies (M Ed); elementary education (M Ed); English (MAT); English for speakers of other languages (M Ed); reading and writing specialist (M Ed); school business administration (Certificate); secondary education (M Ed); special education (M Ed); technology integration specialist (M Ed). Part-time and evening/weekend programs available. Postbaccalaureate distance learning degree programs offered (no on-campus study). *Degree requirements:* For master's, comprehensive exam (for some programs), thesis or alternative. *Entrance requirements:* For master's, PRAXIS I, minimum GPA of 2.75. Additional exam requirements/recommendations for international students: Required—TOEFL (minimum score 550 paper-based). Electronic applications accepted. *Expenses:* Contact institution.

Southern Oregon University, Graduate Studies, School of Education, Ashland, OR 97520. Offers elementary education (MA Ed, MS Ed), including classroom teacher, early childhood, handicapped learner, reading, supervision; secondary education (MA Ed, MS Ed), including classroom teacher, handicapped learner, reading, supervision; teaching (MAT). Postbaccalaureate distance learning degree programs offered (minimal on-campus study). *Faculty:* 23 full-time (16 women), 21 part-time/adjunct (20 women). *Students:* 92 full-time (68 women), 118 part-time (88 women); includes 19 minority (1 Black or African American, non-Hispanic/Latino; 1 American Indian or Alaska Native, non-Hispanic/Latino; 2 Asian, non-Hispanic/Latino; 10 Hispanic/Latino; 5 Two or more races, non-Hispanic/Latino), 5 international. Average age 36. 22 applicants, 59% accepted, 12 enrolled. In 2013, 127 master's awarded. *Degree requirements:* For master's, thesis optional. *Entrance requirements:* For master's, GRE General Test, minimum cumulative GPA of 3.0 in the last 90 quarter credits (60 semester credits) of undergraduate coursework. Additional exam requirements/recommendations for international students: Required—TOEFL (minimum score 540 paper-based; 76 iBT), IELTS (minimum score 6), ELPT (minimum score 964) or ELS (minimum score 112). *Application deadline:* For fall admission, 7/31 priority date for domestic and international students; for winter admission, 11/15 priority date for domestic and international students; for spring admission, 1/7 priority date for domestic and international students. Applications are processed on a rolling basis. Application fee: $50. Electronic applications accepted. *Expenses:* Tuition, state resident: full-time $13,635; part-time $378.72 per credit hour. Tuition, nonresident: full-time $17,042; part-time $473.40 per credit hour. *Required fees:* $408 per quarter. *Financial support:* Research assistantships with partial tuition reimbursements, career-related internships or fieldwork, institutionally sponsored loans, scholarships/grants, and unspecified assistantships available. *Unit head:* Dr. Gerry McCain, Graduate Program Coordinator, 541-552-6934, E-mail: mccaing@sou.edu. *Application contact:* Kelly Moutsatson, Director of Admissions, 541-552-6411, Fax: 541-552-8403, E-mail: admissions@sou.edu.
Website: http://www.sou.edu/education/.

Southern University and Agricultural and Mechanical College, Graduate School, College of Education, Department of Curriculum and Instruction, Baton Rouge, LA 70813. Offers elementary education (M Ed); media (M Ed); secondary education (M Ed). *Degree requirements:* For master's, comprehensive exam, thesis optional. *Entrance requirements:* For master's, GMAT or GRE General Test. Additional exam requirements/recommendations for international students: Required—TOEFL (minimum score 525 paper-based).

Southwestern Oklahoma State University, College of Professional and Graduate Studies, School of Behavioral Sciences and Education, Specialization in Elementary Education, Weatherford, OK 73096-3098. Offers M Ed. M Ed distance learning degree program offered to Oklahoma residents only. *Accreditation:* NCATE. Part-time and evening/weekend programs available. *Degree requirements:* For master's, exam. *Entrance requirements:* For master's, GRE General Test or minimum undergraduate GPA of 3.0. Additional exam requirements/recommendations for international students: Required—TOEFL.

Spalding University, Graduate Studies, College of Education, Programs in Education, Louisville, KY 40203-2188. Offers art teacher education (MAT); business teacher education (MAT); elementary school education (MAT); foreign language (MAT); general education (MA Ed); high school education (MAT); middle school education (MAT); school administration (MA Ed); secondary education (MAT); special education (learning and behavioral disorders) (MAT); student guidance counselor (MA); teacher education and professional development (MAT). *Accreditation:* NCATE. Part-time and evening/weekend programs available. *Faculty:* 12 full-time (11 women), 6 part-time/adjunct (4 women). *Students:* 92 full-time (63 women), 36 part-time (29 women); includes 43 minority (41 Black or African American, non-Hispanic/Latino; 2 Two or more races, non-Hispanic/Latino). Average age 35. 77 applicants, 48% accepted, 30 enrolled. In 2013, 81 master's awarded. *Degree requirements:* For master's, portfolio, final project, clinical experience. *Entrance requirements:* For master's, GRE General Test or MAT, interview, letters of recommendation, resume. Additional exam requirements/recommendations for international students: Required—TOEFL (minimum score 535 paper-based). *Application deadline:* Applications are processed on a rolling basis. Application fee: $30. Electronic applications accepted. *Expenses: Tuition:* Full-time $21,450. *Required fees:* $810. Tuition and fees vary according to course load, degree level, program and student level. *Financial support:* Scholarships/grants, traineeships, and unspecified assistantships available. Financial award application deadline: 3/30; financial award applicants required to submit FAFSA. *Faculty research:* Instructional technology, achievement gap, classroom management, assessment. *Unit head:* Dr. Beverly Keepers, Dean, 502-588-7121, Fax: 502-585-7123, E-mail: bkeepers@spalding.edu. *Application contact:* Bonnie Caughron, Administrative Assistant, College of Education, 502-873-4262, E-mail: bcaughron@spalding.edu.

Springfield College, Graduate Programs, Program in Education, Springfield, MA 01109-3797. Offers counseling and secondary education (M Ed, MS); early childhood education (M Ed, MS); education (M Ed, MS); educational administration (M Ed, MS); educational studies (M Ed, MS); elementary education (M Ed, MS); secondary education (M Ed, MS); special education (M Ed, MS). Part-time and evening/weekend programs available. *Faculty:* 6 full-time. *Students:* 47 full-time. 45 applicants, 87% accepted, 35 enrolled. In 2013, 15 master's awarded. *Entrance requirements:* Additional exam requirements/recommendations for international students: Required—TOEFL (minimum score 550 paper-based); Recommended—IELTS (minimum score 6). *Application deadline:* For fall admission, 1/15 for domestic and international students; for winter admission, 11/1 for domestic and international students; for spring admission, 11/1 for domestic and international students. Applications are processed on a rolling basis. Application fee: $50. Electronic applications accepted. *Expenses: Tuition:* Full-time $13,620; part-time $908 per credit. *Financial support:* Fellowships with partial tuition reimbursements, teaching assistantships with partial tuition reimbursements, career-related internships or fieldwork, Federal Work-Study, institutionally sponsored loans, and unspecified assistantships available. Financial award application deadline: 3/1; financial award applicants required to submit FAFSA. *Unit head:* Jennifer Johnston, Program Coordinator, 413-748-3348, E-mail: jjohnston@springfieldcollege.edu. *Application contact:* Evelyn Cohen, Associate Director of Graduate Admissions, 413-748-3479, Fax: 413-748-3694, E-mail: ecohen@springfieldcollege.edu.

Spring Hill College, Graduate Programs, Program in Education, Mobile, AL 36608-1791. Offers early childhood education (MAT, MS Ed); educational theory (MS Ed); elementary education (MAT, MS Ed); secondary education (MAT, MS Ed). Part-time programs available. *Faculty:* 3 full-time (all women). *Students:* 2 full-time (both women), 17 part-time (14 women); includes 2 minority (both Black or African American, non-Hispanic/Latino). Average age 32. In 2013, 7 master's awarded. *Degree requirements:* For master's, comprehensive exam, completion of program within 6 calendar years of entrance into graduate studies at Spring Hill; documentation of course field assignments (MS) or completion of internship (MAT). *Entrance requirements:* For master's, GRE, MAT, or PRAXIS (varies by program), bachelor's degree with minimum undergraduate GPA of 3.0; class B certificate (MS) or minimum number of hours in specific fields (MAT). Additional exam requirements/recommendations for international students: Required—TOEFL (minimum score 550 paper-based; 80 iBT), IELTS (minimum score 6.5), CPE or CAE (minimum score C), Michigan English Language Assessment Battery (minimum score 90). *Application deadline:* For fall admission, 8/1 priority date for domestic and international students; for spring admission, 12/1 priority date for domestic and international students. Applications are processed on a rolling basis. Application fee: $25 ($35 for international students). Electronic applications accepted. *Expenses:* Contact institution. *Financial support:* Applicants required to submit FAFSA. *Unit head:* Dr. Lori P. Aultman, Chair of Teacher Education, 251-380-3473, Fax: 251-460-2184, E-mail: laultman@shc.edu. *Application contact:* Donna B. Tarasavage, Associate Director, Academic Affairs, 251-380-3067, Fax: 251-460-2182, E-mail: dtarasavage@shc.edu.
Website: http://www.shc.edu/page/teacher-education.

Stanford University, School of Education, Teacher Education Program, Stanford, CA 94305-9991. Offers elementary (MAE); secondary (MAE). *Degree requirements:* For master's, thesis. *Entrance requirements:* For master's, GRE General Test. Electronic applications accepted. *Expenses: Tuition:* Full-time $42,690; part-time $949 per credit. *Required fees:* $185.

State University of New York at Fredonia, Graduate Studies, College of Education, Program in Elementary Education, Fredonia, NY 14063-1136. Offers MS Ed. *Accreditation:* NCATE. Part-time and evening/weekend programs available. *Degree requirements:* For master's, thesis optional. *Expenses:* Tuition, state resident: full-time $7398; part-time $411 per credit hour. Tuition, nonresident: full-time $13,770; part-time $765 per credit hour. *Required fees:* $1143.90; $63.55 per credit hour. Tuition and fees vary according to course load.

State University of New York at New Paltz, Graduate School, School of Education, Department of Elementary Education, New Paltz, NY 12561. Offers childhood education 1-6 (MS Ed, MST), including childhood education 1-6 (MST), early childhood B-2 (MS Ed), mathematics, science and technology (MS Ed), reading/literacy (MS Ed); literacy education 5-12 (MS Ed); literacy education and childhood special education (MS Ed); literacy education B-6 (MS Ed). *Accreditation:* NCATE. Part-time and evening/weekend programs available. *Faculty:* 11 full-time (10 women), 9 part-time/adjunct (8 women). *Students:* 51 full-time (47 women), 128 part-time (117 women); includes 13 minority (2 Black or African American, non-Hispanic/Latino; 11 Hispanic/Latino). Average age 27. 103 applicants, 89% accepted, 57 enrolled. In 2013, 96 master's awarded. *Degree requirements:* For master's, comprehensive exam (for some programs), portfolio. *Entrance requirements:* For master's, GRE or MAT (for MST), minimum GPA of 3.0 (3.2 for literacy and special education), New York state teaching certificate (for MS Ed). Additional exam requirements/recommendations for international students: Required—TOEFL (minimum score 550 paper-based; 80 iBT), IELTS (minimum score 6.5). *Application deadline:* For fall admission, 4/1 for domestic and international students; for spring admission, 11/15 for domestic and international students. Application fee: $50. Electronic applications accepted. *Expenses:* Tuition, state resident: full-time $9870; part-time $411 per credit. Tuition, nonresident: full-time $18,350; part-time $765 per credit. *Required fees:* $1213. Tuition and fees vary according to program. *Financial support:* Application deadline: 8/1. *Faculty research:* Multi-sensory teaching methods, volunteer tutoring programs for struggling readers, school readiness and transition, math/science/technology, university-school partnerships. *Unit head:* Dr. Andrea Noel, Chair, 845-257-2860, E-mail: noela@newpaltz.edu. *Application contact:* Caroline Murphy, Graduate Admissions Advisor, 845-257-3285, Fax: 845-257-3284, E-mail: gradschool@newpaltz.edu.
Website: http://www.newpaltz.edu/elementaryed/.

Elementary Education

State University of New York at Oswego, Graduate Studies, School of Education, Department of Curriculum and Instruction, Oswego, NY 13126. Offers adolescence education (MST); art education (MAT); childhood education (MST); elementary education (MS Ed); literacy education (MS Ed); secondary education (MS Ed); special education (MS Ed). Part-time and evening/weekend programs available. *Degree requirements:* For master's, comprehensive exam (for some programs), thesis optional. *Entrance requirements:* For master's, GRE General Test, minimum GPA of 2.7, provisional teaching certificate. Additional exam requirements/recommendations for international students: Required—TOEFL (minimum score 560 paper-based). *Faculty research:* Classroom applications for microcomputers; classroom questioning, wait-time, and achievement; values clarification and academic achievement.

State University of New York at Plattsburgh, Division of Education, Health, and Human Services, Program in Early Childhood Education, Plattsburgh, NY 12901-2681. Offers early childhood birth-grade 6 (Advanced Certificate). *Students:* 1 (woman) full-time. *Unit head:* Dr. Heidi Schnackenberg, Coordinator, 518-564-5143, E-mail: schnachl@plattsburgh.edu. *Application contact:* Betsy Kane, Director, Graduate Admissions, 518-564-4723, Fax: 518-564-4722, E-mail: bkane002@plattsburgh.edu.

State University of New York at Plattsburgh, Division of Education, Health, and Human Services, Program in Teacher Education: Adolescence, Plattsburgh, NY 12901-2681. Offers adolescence education (MST); biology 7-12 (MST); chemistry 7-12 (MST); earth science 7-12 (MST); English 7-12 (MST); French 7-12 (MST); mathematics 7-12 (MST); physics 7-12 (MST); social studies 7-12 (MST); Spanish 7-12 (MST). *Accreditation:* Teacher Education Accreditation Council. Part-time and evening/weekend programs available. *Students:* 75 full-time (47 women), 5 part-time (3 women); includes 10 minority (1 Black or African American, non-Hispanic/Latino; 4 Asian, non-Hispanic/Latino; 5 Hispanic/Latino), 1 international. Average age 25. *Entrance requirements:* For master's, minimum GPA of 2.75. Additional exam requirements/recommendations for international students: Required—TOEFL. *Application deadline:* For fall admission, 2/15 priority date for domestic students. Applications are processed on a rolling basis. Application fee: $75. *Financial support:* Application deadline: 4/15; applicants required to submit FAFSA. *Unit head:* Dr. Robert Ackland, Coordinator, 518-564-5131, E-mail: acklanrt@plattsburgh.edu. *Application contact:* Betsy Kane, Director, Graduate Admissions, 518-564-4723, Fax: 518-564-4722, E-mail: bkane002@plattsburgh.edu.

State University of New York at Plattsburgh, Division of Education, Health, and Human Services, Program in Teacher Education: Childhood, Plattsburgh, NY 12901-2681. Offers childhood education (grades 1-6) (MST). *Accreditation:* Teacher Education Accreditation Council. Part-time and evening/weekend programs available. *Students:* 9 full-time (6 women). Average age 33. *Entrance requirements:* For master's, minimum GPA of 2.75. Additional exam requirements/recommendations for international students: Required—TOEFL. *Application deadline:* For fall admission, 2/15 priority date for domestic students. Applications are processed on a rolling basis. Application fee: $75. *Financial support:* Federal Work-Study available. Support available to part-time students. Financial award application deadline: 4/15; financial award applicants required to submit FAFSA. *Unit head:* Dr. Robert Ackland, Coordinator, 518-564-5131, E-mail: acklanrt@plattsburgh.edu. *Application contact:* Betsy Kane, Director, Graduate Admissions, 518-564-4723, Fax: 518-564-4722, E-mail: bkane002@plattsburgh.edu.

State University of New York College at Oneonta, Graduate Education, Division of Education, Department of Elementary Education and Reading, Oneonta, NY 13820-4015. Offers childhood education (MS Ed); literacy education (MS Ed). *Accreditation:* NCATE. Part-time and evening/weekend programs available. *Entrance requirements:* For master's, GRE General Test.

State University of New York College at Potsdam, School of Education and Professional Studies, Program in Curriculum and Instruction, Potsdam, NY 13676. Offers childhood education (MST); curriculum and instruction (MS Ed). *Accreditation:* NCATE. Postbaccalaureate distance learning degree programs offered (minimal on-campus study). *Degree requirements:* For master's, thesis (for some programs). *Entrance requirements:* For master's, minimum GPA of 2.75 in last 60 credit hours of undergraduate study. Additional exam requirements/recommendations for international students: Required—TOEFL (minimum score 550 paper-based; 80 iBT), IELTS (minimum score 6). Electronic applications accepted.

State University of New York College at Potsdam, School of Education and Professional Studies, Program in Special Education, Potsdam, NY 13676. Offers adolescence (grades 7-12) (MS Ed); childhood (grades 1-6) (MS Ed); early childhood (birth-grade 2) (MS Ed). *Accreditation:* NCATE. Part-time programs available. *Degree requirements:* For master's, culminating experience. *Entrance requirements:* For master's, minimum GPA of 3.0 in last 60 hours of course work. Additional exam requirements/recommendations for international students: Required—TOEFL (minimum score 550 paper-based; 80 iBT), IELTS (minimum score 6). Electronic applications accepted.

Stephen F. Austin State University, Graduate School, College of Education, Department of Elementary Education, Program in Elementary Education, Nacogdoches, TX 75962. Offers M Ed. *Accreditation:* NCATE. *Degree requirements:* For master's, comprehensive exam. *Entrance requirements:* For master's, GRE General Test. Additional exam requirements/recommendations for international students: Required—TOEFL.

Sul Ross State University, Rio Grande College of Sul Ross State University, Alpine, TX 79832. Offers business administration (MBA); teacher education (M Ed), including bilingual education, counseling, educational diagnostics, elementary education, general education, reading, school administration, secondary education. Part-time and evening/weekend programs available. Postbaccalaureate distance learning degree programs offered (no on-campus study). *Degree requirements:* For master's, comprehensive exam, thesis optional, minimum GPA of 3.0. *Entrance requirements:* For master's, GMAT or GRE General Test, minimum GPA of 2.5 in last 60 hours of undergraduate work. Additional exam requirements/recommendations for international students: Required—TOEFL.

Temple University, College of Education, Department of Psychological Studies in Education, Department of Educational Leadership and Policy Studies, Philadelphia, PA 19122-6096. Offers educational leadership (Ed D), including higher education, K-12. Part-time and evening/weekend programs available. *Faculty:* 7 full-time (3 women). *Students:* 10 full-time (7 women), 66 part-time (42 women); includes 20 minority (15 Black or African American, non-Hispanic/Latino; 1 American Indian or Alaska Native, non-Hispanic/Latino; 1 Asian, non-Hispanic/Latino; 3 Hispanic/Latino), 24 international. 58 applicants, 69% accepted, 24 enrolled. In 2013, 6 master's awarded. Terminal master's awarded for partial completion of doctoral program. *Degree requirements:* For master's, comprehensive exam, thesis or alternative, internship; for doctorate, thesis/dissertation, preliminary exam. *Entrance requirements:* For master's, GRE General Test or MAT, minimum undergraduate GPA of 3.0, 2 letters of recommendation, goal statement, resume; for doctorate, GRE General Test or MAT, minimum undergraduate GPA of 3.0, 3 letters of recommendation, goal statement, resume. Additional exam requirements/recommendations for international students: Required—TOEFL (minimum score 550 paper-based; 79 iBT). *Application deadline:* For fall admission, 1/5 for domestic students, 10/7 for international students; for spring admission, 11/1 for domestic students, 11/3 for international students. Application fee: $60. Electronic applications accepted. *Financial support:* In 2013–14, 2 students received support, including 1 research assistantship with full tuition reimbursement available (averaging $20,333 per year), 1 teaching assistantship with full tuition reimbursement available (averaging $17,046 per year); career-related internships or fieldwork, Federal Work-Study, scholarships/grants, health care benefits, and unspecified assistantships also available. Financial award application deadline: 1/15; financial award applicants required to submit FAFSA. *Faculty research:* School leadership, educational policy, educational accountability, democratic leadership, equity and access. *Unit head:* Dr. Joan Shapiro, Professor, 215-204-6645, E-mail: joan.shapiro@temple.edu. *Application contact:* Felicia Neuber, Enrollment Management, 215-204-8011, E-mail: educate@temple.edu. Website: http://education.temple.edu/leadership.

Tennessee State University, The School of Graduate Studies and Research, College of Education, Department of Teaching and Learning, Nashville, TN 37209-1561. Offers curriculum and instruction (M Ed, Ed D); elementary education (M Ed); special education (M Ed). *Accreditation:* NCATE. *Degree requirements:* For doctorate, thesis/dissertation. *Entrance requirements:* For master's, GRE General Test, GRE Subject Test, or MAT, minimum GPA of 2.5; for doctorate, GRE General Test, GRE Subject Test, or MAT, minimum GPA of 3.25. Electronic applications accepted. *Faculty research:* Multicultural education, teacher education reform, whole language, interactive video teaching, English as a second language.

Tennessee Technological University, College of Graduate Studies, College of Education, Department of Curriculum and Instruction, Program in Elementary Education, Cookeville, TN 38505. Offers MA, Ed S. *Accreditation:* NCATE. Part-time and evening/weekend programs available. *Faculty:* 8 full-time (2 women). *Students:* 11 full-time (10 women), 22 part-time (18 women); includes 1 minority (Black or African American, non-Hispanic/Latino). Average age 27. 12 applicants, 92% accepted, 8 enrolled. In 2013, 13 master's awarded. *Degree requirements:* For master's and Ed S, comprehensive exam, thesis or alternative. *Entrance requirements:* For master's and Ed S, MAT or GRE. Additional exam requirements/recommendations for international students: Required—TOEFL (minimum score 527 paper-based; 71 iBT), IELTS (minimum score 5.5), PTE (minimum score 48), or TOEIC (Test of English as an International Communication). *Application deadline:* For fall admission, 8/1 for domestic students, 5/1 for international students; for spring admission, 12/1 for domestic students, 10/1 for international students. Applications are processed on a rolling basis. Application fee: $35 ($40 for international students). Electronic applications accepted. *Expenses:* Tuition, state resident: full-time $9347; part-time $465 per credit hour. Tuition, nonresident: full-time $23,635; part-time $1152 per credit hour. *Financial support:* In 2013–14, 1 fellowship (averaging $8,000 per year), research assistantships (averaging $4,000 per year), 1 teaching assistantship (averaging $4,000 per year) were awarded; career-related internships or fieldwork also available. Financial award application deadline: 4/1. *Faculty research:* Educational television art program. *Unit head:* Dr. Jeremy Wendt, Interim Chairperson, 931-372-3181, Fax: 931-372-6270, E-mail: jwendt@tntech.edu. *Application contact:* Shelia K. Kendrick, Coordinator of Graduate Studies, 931-372-3808, Fax: 931-372-3497, E-mail: skendrick@tntech.edu.

Tennessee Technological University, College of Graduate Studies, College of Education, Department of Exercise Science, Physical Education and Wellness, Cookeville, TN 38505. Offers adapted physical education (MA); elementary/middle school physical education (MA); lifetime wellness (MA); sport management (MA). *Accreditation:* NCATE. Part-time programs available. Postbaccalaureate distance learning degree programs offered (no on-campus study). *Faculty:* 7 full-time (0 women). *Students:* 10 full-time (0 women), 38 part-time (11 women); includes 5 minority (all Black or African American, non-Hispanic/Latino). Average age 27. 38 applicants, 58% accepted, 20 enrolled. In 2013, 23 master's awarded. *Degree requirements:* For master's, comprehensive exam, thesis or alternative. *Entrance requirements:* For master's, MAT or GRE. Additional exam requirements/recommendations for international students: Required—TOEFL (minimum score 527 paper-based; 71 iBT), IELTS (minimum score 5.5), PTE (minimum score 48), or TOEIC (Test of English as an International Communication). *Application deadline:* For fall admission, 8/1 for domestic students, 5/1 for international students; for spring admission, 12/1 for domestic students, 10/1 for international students. Applications are processed on a rolling basis. Application fee: $35 ($40 for international students). Electronic applications accepted. *Expenses:* Tuition, state resident: full-time $9347; part-time $465 per credit hour. Tuition, nonresident: full-time $23,635; part-time $1152 per credit hour. *Financial support:* In 2013–14, fellowships (averaging $8,000 per year), 3 research assistantships (averaging $4,000 per year), 4 teaching assistantships (averaging $4,000 per year) were awarded; career-related internships or fieldwork also available. Financial award application deadline: 4/1. *Unit head:* Dr. John Steven Smith, Interim Chairperson, 931-372-3467, Fax: 931-372-6319, E-mail: jssmith@tntech.edu. *Application contact:* Shelia K. Kendrick, Coordinator of Graduate Studies, 931-372-3808, Fax: 931-372-3497, E-mail: skendrick@tntech.edu.

Texas A&M University–Commerce, Graduate School, College of Education and Human Services, Department of Curriculum and Instruction, Commerce, TX 75429-3011. Offers bilingual/ESL education (M Ed, MS); early childhood education (M Ed, MS); elementary education (M Ed, MS); reading (M Ed, MS); secondary education (M Ed, MS); supervision, curriculum and instruction: elementary education (Ed D). MS and M Ed programs in early childhood education offered jointly with Texas Woman's University and University of North Texas. Part-time programs available. Terminal master's awarded for partial completion of doctoral program. *Degree requirements:* For master's, comprehensive exam, thesis (for some programs); for doctorate, 2 foreign languages, thesis/dissertation, departmental qualifying exam. *Entrance requirements:* For master's and doctorate, GRE General Test. Electronic applications accepted. *Expenses:* Tuition, state resident: full-time $3630; part-time $2420 per year. Tuition, nonresident: full-time $9948; part-time $6632.16 per year. *Required fees:* $1006 per year. Tuition and fees vary according to course load. *Faculty research:* Literacy and learning, early childhood, preservice teacher education, technology.

Texas A&M University–Corpus Christi, Graduate Studies and Research, College of Education, Program in Elementary Education, Corpus Christi, TX 78412-5503. Offers MS. Part-time and evening/weekend programs available. *Degree requirements:* For master's, comprehensive exam, thesis (for some programs). *Entrance requirements:* For master's, GRE General Test. Additional exam requirements/recommendations for international students: Required—TOEFL. Electronic applications accepted.

Texas Christian University, College of Education, Program in Elementary Education, Fort Worth, TX 76129-0002. Offers M Ed. Part-time and evening/weekend programs available. *Students:* 4 full-time (all women). 2 applicants, 100% accepted, 1 enrolled. In 2013, 4 master's awarded. *Degree requirements:* For master's, comprehensive exam, thesis. *Entrance requirements:* Additional exam requirements/recommendations for international students: Required—TOEFL (minimum score 550 paper-based; 80 iBT). *Application deadline:* For fall admission, 11/16 for domestic and international students; for spring admission, 3/1 for domestic and international students. Application fee: $60. Electronic applications accepted. *Expenses: Tuition:* Part-time $1270 per credit hour. Tuition and fees vary according to course load and program. *Financial support:* Teaching assistantships with full tuition reimbursements, career-related internships or

fieldwork, scholarships/grants, and unspecified assistantships available. Financial award application deadline: 3/1. *Unit head:* Dr. Jan Lacina, Associate Dean, 817-257-6786, E-mail: j.lacina@tcu.edu. *Application contact:* Lori Kimball, Academic Program Specialist, 817-257-7661, E-mail: l.kimball@tcu.edu.
Website: http://www.coe.tcu.edu/graduate-students-graduate-programs.asp.

Texas Christian University, College of Education, Program in Elementary (Four-One Option), Fort Worth, TX 76129-0002. Offers M Ed. Part-time and evening/weekend programs available. *Students:* 3 full-time (all women). 6 applicants, 67% accepted, 3 enrolled. In 2013, 7 master's awarded. *Degree requirements:* For master's, comprehensive exam, thesis. *Entrance requirements:* Additional exam requirements/recommendations for international students: Required—TOEFL (minimum score 550 paper-based; 80 iBT). *Application deadline:* For fall admission, 11/16 for domestic and international students; for spring admission, 3/1 for domestic and international students. Application fee: $60. Electronic applications accepted. *Expenses: Tuition:* Part-time $1270 per credit hour. Tuition and fees vary according to course load and program. *Financial support:* Teaching assistantships with full tuition reimbursements, career-related internships or fieldwork, scholarships/grants, and unspecified assistantships available. Financial award application deadline: 3/1; financial award applicants required to submit FAFSA. *Unit head:* Dr. Jan Lacina, Associate Dean, 817-257-6786, E-mail: j.lacina@tcu.edu. *Application contact:* Lori Kimball, Academic Program Specialist, 817-257-7661, E-mail: l.kimball@tcu.edu.
Website: http://www.coe.tcu.edu/graduate-students-graduate-programs.asp.

Texas State University, Graduate School, College of Education, Department of Curriculum and Instruction, Program in Elementary Education, San Marcos, TX 78666. Offers M Ed, MA. Part-time and evening/weekend programs available. *Faculty:* 20 full-time (15 women), 4 part-time/adjunct (all women). *Students:* 100 full-time (96 women), 107 part-time (97 women); includes 61 minority (12 Black or African American, non-Hispanic/Latino; 3 American Indian or Alaska Native, non-Hispanic/Latino; 6 Asian, non-Hispanic/Latino; 37 Hispanic/Latino; 3 Two or more races, non-Hispanic/Latino), 3 international. Average age 32. 95 applicants, 89% accepted, 55 enrolled. In 2013, 107 master's awarded. *Degree requirements:* For master's, comprehensive exam, thesis (for some programs). *Entrance requirements:* For master's, minimum GPA of 2.75 in last 60 hours of course work, teaching experience. Additional exam requirements/recommendations for international students: Required—TOEFL (minimum score 550 paper-based; 78 iBT). *Application deadline:* For fall admission, 6/15 priority date for domestic students, 6/1 for international students; for spring admission, 10/15 priority date for domestic students, 10/1 for international students. Applications are processed on a rolling basis. Application fee: $40 ($90 for international students). Electronic applications accepted. *Expenses:* Tuition, state resident: full-time $6663; part-time $278 per credit hour. Tuition, nonresident: full-time $15,159; part-time $632 per credit hour. *Required fees:* $1872; $54 per credit hour. $306 per term. Tuition and fees vary according to course load. *Financial support:* In 2013–14, 110 students received support, including 16 research assistantships (averaging $13,966 per year), 3 teaching assistantships (averaging $11,377 per year); career-related internships or fieldwork, Federal Work-Study, and institutionally sponsored loans also available. Support available to part-time students. Financial award application deadline: 4/1; financial award applicants required to submit FAFSA. *Faculty research:* Novice teacher induction, developmental education research, college and career initiative, teacher preparation academy, creative science. *Total annual research expenditures:* $1.5 million. *Unit head:* Dr. Priscilla Crawford, Graduate Advisor, 512-245-2041, Fax: 512-245-7911, E-mail: ph12@txstate.edu. *Application contact:* Dr. Andrea Golato, Dean of Graduate School, 512-245-2581, Fax: 512-245-8365, E-mail: gradcollege@txstate.edu.
Website: http://www.education.txstate.edu/ci/degrees-programs/graduate/elementary-education.html.

Texas State University, Graduate School, College of Education, Department of Curriculum and Instruction, Program in Elementary Education-Bilingual/Bicultural, San Marcos, TX 78666. Offers M Ed, MA. Part-time programs available. *Faculty:* 5 full-time (all women). *Students:* 6 full-time (all women), 13 part-time (11 women); includes 16 minority (all Hispanic/Latino), 1 international. Average age 34. 14 applicants, 79% accepted, 7 enrolled. In 2013, 5 master's awarded. *Degree requirements:* For master's, comprehensive exam, thesis optional. *Entrance requirements:* For master's, minimum GPA of 2.75 in last 60 hours of course work, teaching experience. Additional exam requirements/recommendations for international students: Required—TOEFL (minimum score 550 paper-based; 78 iBT). *Application deadline:* For fall admission, 6/15 priority date for domestic students, 6/1 for international students; for spring admission, 10/15 priority date for domestic students, 10/1 for international students. Applications are processed on a rolling basis. Application fee: $40 ($90 for international students). Electronic applications accepted. *Expenses:* Tuition, state resident: full-time $6663; part-time $278 per credit hour. Tuition, nonresident: full-time $15,159; part-time $632 per credit hour. *Required fees:* $1872; $54 per credit hour. $306 per term. Tuition and fees vary according to course load. *Financial support:* In 2013–14, 15 students received support, including 2 teaching assistantships (averaging $11,280 per year); research assistantships, career-related internships or fieldwork, Federal Work-Study, institutionally sponsored loans, and unspecified assistantships also available. Support available to part-time students. Financial award application deadline: 4/1; financial award applicants required to submit FAFSA. *Unit head:* Dr. Roxanne Cuellar Allsup, Graduate Advisor, 512-245-7486, Fax: 512-245-7911, E-mail: ra17@txstate.edu. *Application contact:* Dr. Andrea Golato, Dean of Graduate School, 512-245-2581, Fax: 512-245-8365, E-mail: gradcollege@txstate.edu.
Website: http://www.education.txstate.edu/ci/degrees-programs/graduate/elementary-education.html.

Texas State University, Graduate School, College of Science and Engineering, Interdisciplinary Studies Program in Elementary Mathematics, Science, and Technology, San Marcos, TX 78666. Offers MSIS. *Students:* 3 full-time (2 women); includes 1 minority (Hispanic/Latino), 1 international. Average age 24. 1 applicant, 100% accepted. In 2013, 2 master's awarded. *Degree requirements:* For master's, comprehensive exam, thesis optional. *Entrance requirements:* For master's, minimum GPA of 2.75 in the last 60 hours of undergraduate work. Additional exam requirements/recommendations for international students: Required—TOEFL (minimum score 550 paper-based; 78 iBT). *Application deadline:* For fall admission, 6/15 priority date for domestic students, 6/1 priority date for international students; for spring admission, 10/15 priority date for domestic students, 10/1 priority date for international students. Applications are processed on a rolling basis. Application fee: $40 ($90 for international students). Electronic applications accepted. *Expenses:* Tuition, state resident: full-time $6663; part-time $278 per credit hour. Tuition, nonresident: full-time $15,159; part-time $632 per credit hour. *Required fees:* $1872; $54 per credit hour. $306 per term. Tuition and fees vary according to course load. *Financial support:* In 2013–14, 1 student received support, including 1 teaching assistantship (averaging $11,568 per year); research assistantships, Federal Work-Study, institutionally sponsored loans, scholarships/grants, health care benefits, and unspecified assistantships also available. Support available to part-time students. Financial award application deadline: 4/1; financial award applicants required to submit FAFSA. *Unit head:* Dr. Sandra West Moody, Acting Dean, 512-245-3360, Fax: 512-245-8095, E-mail: sw04@txstate.edu. *Application contact:* Dr. Andrea Golato, Dean of Graduate School, 512-245-2581, Fax: 512-245-8365, E-mail: gradcollege@txstate.edu.

Texas Tech University, Graduate School, College of Education, Department of Curriculum and Instruction, Lubbock, TX 79409-1071. Offers bilingual education (M Ed); curriculum and instruction (M Ed, PhD); elementary education (M Ed); language/literacy education (M Ed); multidisciplinary science (MS); secondary education (M Ed). *Accreditation:* NCATE. Part-time programs available. Postbaccalaureate distance learning degree programs offered (minimal on-campus study). *Faculty:* 27 full-time (21 women). *Students:* 49 full-time (40 women), 194 part-time (149 women); includes 74 minority (13 Black or African American, non-Hispanic/Latino; 6 Asian, non-Hispanic/Latino; 50 Hispanic/Latino; 5 Two or more races, non-Hispanic/Latino), 20 international. Average age 38. 105 applicants, 66% accepted, 46 enrolled. In 2013, 48 master's, 14 doctorates awarded. *Degree requirements:* For master's, comprehensive exam (for some programs), thesis optional; for doctorate, comprehensive exam, thesis/dissertation. *Entrance requirements:* For master's, bachelor's degree; resume; letter of intent; academic writing sample; 2 letters of recommendation; for doctorate, GRE, master's degree; resume; letter of intent; academic writing sample; 3 letters of recommendation. Additional exam requirements/recommendations for international students: Required—TOEFL (minimum score 550 paper-based; 79 iBT). *Application deadline:* For fall admission, 6/1 priority date for domestic students, 1/15 priority date for international students; for spring admission, 9/1 priority date for domestic students, 6/15 priority date for international students. Applications are processed on a rolling basis. Application fee: $60. Electronic applications accepted. *Expenses:* Tuition, state resident: full-time $6062; part-time $252.57 per credit hour. Tuition, nonresident: full-time $14,558; part-time $606.57 per credit hour. *Required fees:* $2655; $35 per credit hour. $907.50 per semester. Tuition and fees vary according to course load. *Financial support:* In 2013–14, 94 students received support, including 89 fellowships (averaging $2,276 per year), 14 research assistantships (averaging $5,226 per year), 6 teaching assistantships (averaging $4,517 per year); career-related internships or fieldwork, Federal Work-Study, institutionally sponsored loans, scholarships/grants, traineeships, health care benefits, and unspecified assistantships also available. Support available to part-time students. Financial award application deadline: 2/1; financial award applicants required to submit FAFSA. *Faculty research:* Teacher education, curriculum studies, bilingual education, science and math education, language and literacy education. *Total annual research expenditures:* $413,968. *Unit head:* Dr. Margaret Ann Price, Department Chair, Curriculum and Instruction, 806-834-4347, E-mail: peggie.price@ttu.edu. *Application contact:* Stephenie A. Jones, Administrative Assistant, 806-834-2751, Fax: 806-742-2179, E-mail: stephenie.a.jones@ttu.edu.
Website: http://www.educ.ttu.edu.

Towson University, Program in Elementary Education, Towson, MD 21252-0001. Offers M Ed. *Accreditation:* NCATE. Part-time and evening/weekend programs available. *Students:* 25 part-time (all women); includes 5 minority (2 Black or African American, non-Hispanic/Latino; 1 Asian, non-Hispanic/Latino; 2 Hispanic/Latino). *Entrance requirements:* For master's, minimum GPA of 3.0, bachelor's degree in education, certified in teaching or eligibility for certification. Application fee: $45. Electronic applications accepted. *Financial support:* Application deadline: 4/1. *Unit head:* Dr. Todd Kenreich, Graduate Program Director, 410-704-5897, E-mail: tkenreich@towson.edu. *Application contact:* Alicia Arkell-Kleis, Information Contact, 410-704-6004, Fax: 410-704-4675, E-mail: grads@towson.edu.
Website: http://grad.towson.edu/program/master/eled-med/.

Trevecca Nazarene University, Graduate Education Program, Nashville, TN 37210-2877. Offers curriculum, assessment, and instruction K-12 (M Ed); educational leadership (M Ed); English language learners (PreK-12) (M Ed); leadership and professional practice (Ed D); library and information science (MLI Sc); teacher leader (M Ed); teaching (MAE, MAT), including teaching 7-12 (MAT), teaching K-6 (MAT); visual impairments special education (M Ed). *Accreditation:* NCATE. Part-time and evening/weekend programs available. Postbaccalaureate distance learning degree programs offered. *Faculty:* 19 full-time (17 women), 14 part-time/adjunct (5 women). *Students:* 186 full-time (137 women), 134 part-time (94 women); includes 93 minority (87 Black or African American, non-Hispanic/Latino; 1 American Indian or Alaska Native, non-Hispanic/Latino; 2 Asian, non-Hispanic/Latino; 1 Hispanic/Latino; 1 Native Hawaiian or other Pacific Islander, non-Hispanic/Latino; 1 Two or more races, non-Hispanic/Latino), 2 international. In 2013, 201 master's, 40 doctorates awarded. *Degree requirements:* For master's, comprehensive exam, exit assessment/e-portfolio; for doctorate, thesis/dissertation, proposal study, symposium presentation. *Entrance requirements:* For master's, GRE with minimum score of 378 or MAT with minimum score of 290, ACT with minimum score of 22 or SAT with minimum score of 1020 (for MAT programs only); PRAXIS (for MAT and MAE programs), minimum GPA of 2.7, official transcript from regionally accredited institution, 3+ years successful teaching experience (Teacher Leader and Education Leadership majors), technology pre-assessment written requirements (some majors); for doctorate, GRE or MAT, minimum GPA of 3.4, official transcript from regionally-accredited institution, resume, writing sample, interview, reference forms. Additional exam requirements/recommendations for international students: Required—TOEFL (minimum score 550 paper-based). *Application deadline:* Applications are processed on a rolling basis. *Expenses:* Contact institution. *Financial support:* Applicants required to submit FAFSA. *Unit head:* Dr. Suzie Harris, Dean, School of Education/Director of Graduate Education Programs, 615-248-1201, Fax: 615-248-1597, E-mail: admissions_ged@trevecca.edu. *Application contact:* 615-248-1529, E-mail: cll@trevecca.edu.
Website: http://www.trevecca.edu/academics/schools-colleges/education/.

Trinity Washington University, School of Education, Washington, DC 20017-1094. Offers clinical mental health counseling (MA); early childhood education (MAT); educating for change (M Ed); educational administration (MSA); elementary education (MAT); reading (M Ed); school counseling (MA); secondary education (MAT), including English, social studies; special education (MAT). *Accreditation:* NCATE. Part-time and evening/weekend programs available. *Degree requirements:* For master's, thesis (for some programs), capstone project(s). *Entrance requirements:* For master's, PRAXIS I, minimum GPA of 2.8. Additional exam requirements/recommendations for international students: Required—TOEFL (minimum score 550 paper-based). *Application deadline:* For fall admission, 4/1 priority date for domestic students; for winter admission, 11/1 priority date for domestic students; for spring admission, 11/1 priority date for domestic students. Applications are processed on a rolling basis. Application fee: $40. *Expenses: Tuition:* Part-time $715 per credit. *Financial support:* Career-related internships or fieldwork, health care benefits, and unspecified assistantships available. Support available to part-time students. Financial award application deadline: 4/1; financial award applicants required to submit FAFSA. *Faculty research:* Technology, literacy, special education, organizations, inclusion models. *Unit head:* Dr. Janet Stocks, Dean, 202-884-9380, Fax: 202-884-9506, E-mail: stocksj@trinitydc.edu. *Application contact:* Erika Davis, Director of Admissions for School of Education, 202-884-9400, Fax: 202-884-9229, E-mail: daviser@trinitydc.edu.
Website: http://www.trinitydc.edu/education/.

Troy University, Graduate School, College of Education, Program in K–6 Elementary and Collaborative Education, Troy, AL 36082. Offers alternative K-6 elementary (MS);

elementary education (Ed S); traditional K-6 elementary (MS). *Accreditation:* NCATE. Part-time and evening/weekend programs available. *Faculty:* 26 full-time (20 women), 16 part-time/adjunct (9 women). *Students:* 72 full-time (68 women), 131 part-time (123 women); includes 81 minority (72 Black or African American, non-Hispanic/Latino; 3 American Indian or Alaska Native, non-Hispanic/Latino; 3 Hispanic/Latino; 3 Two or more races, non-Hispanic/Latino). Average age 31. 63 applicants, 83% accepted, 41 enrolled. In 2013, 79 master's, 40 other advanced degrees awarded. *Degree requirements:* For master's, comprehensive exam, thesis. *Entrance requirements:* For master's, GRE (minimum score of 850 on old exam or 286 on new exam) or GMAT (minimum score of 380), bachelor's degree; minimum undergraduate GPA of 2.5 or 3.0 on last 30 semester hours, letter of recommendation; for Ed S, GRE (minimum score of 850 on old exam or 286 on new exam) or GMAT (minimum score of 380), Alabama Class A certificate or equivalent, master's degree, minimum graduate GPA of 3.0. Additional exam requirements/recommendations for international students: Required—TOEFL (minimum score 523 paper-based; 70 iBT), IELTS (minimum score 5.5). *Application deadline:* Applications are processed on a rolling basis. Application fee: $50. Electronic applications accepted. *Expenses:* Tuition, state resident: full-time $6084; part-time $338 per credit hour. Tuition, nonresident: full-time $12,168; part-time $676 per credit hour. *Required fees:* $630; $35 per credit hour. $50 per semester. *Financial support:* Available to part-time students. Applicants required to submit FAFSA. *Unit head:* Dr. Jan Oliver, Associate Professor, 334-670-3444, Fax: 334-670-3474, E-mail: oliverj@troy.edu. *Application contact:* Brenda K. Campbell, Director of Graduate Admissions, 334-670-3178, Fax: 334-670-3733, E-mail: bcamp@troy.edu.

Tufts University, Graduate School of Arts and Sciences, Department of Education, Program in Education, Medford, MA 02155. Offers educational studies (MA); elementary education (MAT); middle and secondary education (MA, MAT); museum education (MA); secondary education (MA); STEM education (MS, PhD). *Faculty:* 13 full-time, 9 part-time/adjunct. *Students:* 85 full-time (72 women); includes 19 minority (4 Black or African American, non-Hispanic/Latino; 1 American Indian or Alaska Native, non-Hispanic/Latino; 3 Asian, non-Hispanic/Latino; 7 Hispanic/Latino; 4 Two or more races, non-Hispanic/Latino), 5 international. Average age 27. 154 applicants, 69% accepted, 50 enrolled. In 2013, 84 master's awarded. *Degree requirements:* For master's, thesis optional; for doctorate, thesis/dissertation. *Entrance requirements:* For master's and doctorate, GRE General Test. Additional exam requirements/recommendations for international students: Required—TOEFL (minimum score 550 paper-based; 80 iBT), IELTS (minimum score 6.5). *Application deadline:* For fall admission, 1/2 for domestic and international students; for spring admission, 10/15 for domestic students, 9/15 for international students. Applications are processed on a rolling basis. Application fee: $75. Electronic applications accepted. *Financial support:* Teaching assistantships with full and partial tuition reimbursements, Federal Work-Study, scholarships/grants, and tuition waivers (full and partial) available. Support available to part-time students. Financial award application deadline: 1/2. *Unit head:* Hammer David, Chair, 617-627-3244, Fax: 617-627-3901. *Application contact:* Patricia Romeo, Information Contact, 617-627-3244.

Union College, Graduate Programs, Department of Education, Program in Elementary Education, Barbourville, KY 40906-1499. Offers MA. *Degree requirements:* For master's, thesis optional. *Entrance requirements:* For master's, GRE General Test, NTE.

Universidad del Este, Graduate School, Carolina, PR 00984. Offers accounting (MBA); adult education (M Ed); agribusiness (MBA); criminal justice and criminology (MA); curriculum and instruction - early education (M Ed); curriculum and instruction - elementary (M Ed); curriculum and instruction - English (M Ed); curriculum and instruction - Spanish (M Ed); human resources (MBA); information security management (MBA); information technology and Web business development (MBA); management (MBA); public policy (MPA); social work (MA), including clinical social work; special education (M Ed); strategic leadership (MBA). *Students:* 464 full-time (322 women), 669 part-time (499 women); all minorities (all Hispanic/Latino). Average age 35. 693 applicants, 61% accepted, 332 enrolled. In 2013, 228 master's awarded. *Unit head:* Jose R. Clintron, Dean, 787-257-7373 Ext. 3007, E-mail: ue_jcintron@suagm.edu. *Application contact:* Clotilde Santiago, Director of Admissions, 787-257-7373 Ext. 3400, E-mail: ue_csantiago@suagm.edu.

Universidad Metropolitana, School of Education, Program in Teaching of Physical Education, San Juan, PR 00928-1150. Offers teaching of adult physical education (M Ed); teaching of elementary physical education (M Ed); teaching of secondary physical education (M Ed). *Degree requirements:* For master's, thesis or alternative. *Entrance requirements:* For master's, EXADEP, interview. Electronic applications accepted.

Université de Sherbrooke, Faculty of Education, Program in Elementary Education, Sherbrooke, QC J1K 2R1, Canada. Offers M Ed, Diploma. Part-time and evening/weekend programs available. *Degree requirements:* For master's, thesis.

University at Buffalo, the State University of New York, Graduate School, Graduate School of Education, Department of Learning and Instruction, Buffalo, NY 14260. Offers biology education (Ed M, Certificate); chemistry education (Ed M, Certificate); childhood education (Ed M); childhood education with bilingual extension (Ed M); curriculum, instruction and the science of learning (PhD); early childhood education (Ed M); early childhood education with bilingual extension (birth-grade 2) (Ed M); earth science education (Ed M, Certificate); education studies (Ed M); educational technology and new literacies (Certificate); elementary education (Ed D); English education (Ed M, Certificate); English for speakers of other languages (Ed M); foreign and second language education (PhD); French education (Ed M, Certificate); German education (Ed M, Certificate); gifted education (Certificate); Latin education (Ed M, Certificate); literacy specialist (Ed M); literacy teaching and learning (Certificate); mathematics education (Ed M, Certificate); music education (Ed M, Certificate); physics education (Ed M, Certificate); science and the public (Ed M); social studies education (Ed M, Certificate); Spanish education (Ed M, Certificate); special education (PhD); teaching English to speakers of other languages (Ed M). Part-time and evening/weekend programs available. Postbaccalaureate distance learning degree programs offered (no on-campus study). *Faculty:* 31 full-time (23 women), 64 part-time/adjunct (53 women). *Students:* 275 full-time (215 women), 293 part-time (205 women); includes 35 minority (16 Black or African American, non-Hispanic/Latino; 5 American Indian or Alaska Native, non-Hispanic/Latino; 11 Asian, non-Hispanic/Latino; 3 Hispanic/Latino), 97 international. Average age 30. 544 applicants, 81% accepted, 246 enrolled. In 2013, 222 master's, 17 doctorates, 35 other advanced degrees awarded. *Degree requirements:* For master's, comprehensive exam; for doctorate, thesis/dissertation, research analysis exam, research experience component. *Entrance requirements:* For master's, content test in science and math, letters of reference; for doctorate, GRE General Test or MAT, interview, writing sample, letters of recommendation. Additional exam requirements/recommendations for international students: Required—TOEFL (minimum score 600 paper-based; 96 iBT). *Application deadline:* For fall admission, 2/1 priority date for domestic and international students; for spring admission, 11/15 priority date for domestic students, 10/1 for international students. Applications are processed on a rolling basis. Application fee: $50. Electronic applications accepted. *Financial support:* In 2013–14, 50 fellowships (averaging $8,589 per year), 31 research assistantships with tuition reimbursements (averaging $11,406 per year) were awarded; teaching assistantships, career-related internships or fieldwork, Federal Work-Study, institutionally sponsored loans, scholarships/grants, tuition waivers, and unspecified assistantships also available. Financial award application deadline: 2/28; financial award applicants required to submit FAFSA. *Faculty research:* Science assessment, foreign language teaching and learning, early learning, new literacies, gender and education. *Total annual research expenditures:* $1.7 million. *Unit head:* Dr. Suzanne Miller, Chair, 716-645-2455, Fax: 716-645-3161, E-mail: smiller@buffalo.edu. *Application contact:* Cathy Dimino, Admissions Assistant, 716-645-2110, Fax: 716-645-7937, E-mail: cadimino@buffalo.edu.
Website: http://gse.buffalo.edu/lai.

The University of Akron, Graduate School, College of Education, Department of Curricular and Instructional Studies, Program in Elementary Education, Akron, OH 44325. Offers elementary education (PhD); elementary education - literacy (MA); elementary education with licensure (MS). *Accreditation:* NCATE. *Students:* 5 full-time (all women), 29 part-time (28 women); includes 5 minority (2 Black or African American, non-Hispanic/Latino; 1 Asian, non-Hispanic/Latino; 1 Hispanic/Latino; 1 Two or more races, non-Hispanic/Latino), 2 international. Average age 39. 8 applicants, 50% accepted, 3 enrolled. In 2013, 3 master's, 2 doctorates awarded. *Degree requirements:* For master's, comprehensive exam, thesis optional; for doctorate, variable foreign language requirement, comprehensive exam, thesis/dissertation, written and oral exams. *Entrance requirements:* For master's, minimum GPA of 2.75, valid teaching license; for doctorate, MAT or GRE, minimum GPA of 3.5, three letters of recommendation, statement of purpose indicating career goals and research interest, controlled department writing sample, completion of Agreement to Advise Form, current curriculum vitae, at least three years of teaching experience. Additional exam requirements/recommendations for international students: Required—TOEFL (minimum score 550 paper-based; 79 iBT). *Application deadline:* For fall admission, 3/1 for domestic and international students; for spring admission, 10/1 for domestic and international students. Applications are processed on a rolling basis. Application fee: $30 ($40 for international students). Electronic applications accepted. *Expenses:* Tuition, state resident: full-time $7430; part-time $412.80 per credit hour. Tuition, nonresident: full-time $12,722; part-time $706.80 per credit hour. *Required fees:* $53 per credit hour. $12 per semester. Tuition and fees vary according to course load and program. *Unit head:* Dr. Sandra Coyner, Interim Chair, 330-972-5822, E-mail: scoyner@uakron.edu.

The University of Alabama, Graduate School, College of Education, Department of Curriculum and Instruction, Tuscaloosa, AL 35487. Offers elementary education (MA, Ed D, PhD, Ed S); secondary education (MA, Ed D, PhD, Ed S). Part-time and evening/weekend programs available. Postbaccalaureate distance learning degree programs offered (no on-campus study). *Faculty:* 20 full-time (15 women), 2 part-time/adjunct (both women). *Students:* 78 full-time (59 women), 102 part-time (81 women); includes 22 minority (18 Black or African American, non-Hispanic/Latino; 1 Hispanic/Latino; 3 Two or more races, non-Hispanic/Latino), 6 international. Average age 33. 71 applicants, 62% accepted, 33 enrolled. In 2013, 107 master's, 13 doctorates, 9 other advanced degrees awarded. *Degree requirements:* For master's, comprehensive exam, thesis (for some programs); for doctorate, comprehensive exam, thesis/dissertation; for Ed S, comprehensive exam, thesis optional. *Entrance requirements:* For master's, doctorate, and Ed S, MAT and/or GRE. Additional exam requirements/recommendations for international students: Recommended—TOEFL (minimum score 550 paper-based), IELTS (minimum score 6.5). *Application deadline:* For fall admission, 7/1 priority date for domestic students, 1/15 priority date for international students; for spring admission, 11/1 priority date for domestic students, 6/1 priority date for international students; for summer admission, 3/1 priority date for domestic and international students. Applications are processed on a rolling basis. Application fee: $50 ($60 for international students). Electronic applications accepted. *Expenses:* Tuition, state resident: full-time $9450. Tuition, nonresident: full-time $23,950. *Financial support:* In 2013–14, 14 students received support, including 10 research assistantships with tuition reimbursements available (averaging $9,844 per year), 4 teaching assistantships with tuition reimbursements available (averaging $9,844 per year); institutionally sponsored loans, traineeships, and unspecified assistantships also available. Financial award applicants required to submit FAFSA. *Faculty research:* Teacher education, diversity, integration of curriculum, technology, pedagogical content knowledge. *Total annual research expenditures:* $141,733. *Unit head:* Dr. Cynthia Sunal, Chair, 205-348-8264, Fax: 205-348-9863, E-mail: cvsunal@bamaed.ua.edu. *Application contact:* Dr. Kathy S. Wetzel, Assistant Dean for Student Services, 205-348-1154, Fax: 205-348-0080, E-mail: kwetzel@bamaed.ua.edu.
Website: http://courseleaf.ua.edu/education/curriculumandinstruction/.

The University of Alabama at Birmingham, School of Education, Program in Elementary Education, Birmingham, AL 35294. Offers MA Ed. *Accreditation:* NCATE. Part-time programs available. *Degree requirements:* For master's, thesis optional. *Entrance requirements:* For master's, GRE General Test, MAT, or NTE, minimum GPA of 3.0. Electronic applications accepted.

University of Alaska Fairbanks, School of Education, Program in Education, Fairbanks, AK 99775. Offers curriculum and instruction (M Ed); education (M Ed, Graduate Certificate); elementary education (M Ed); language and literacy (M Ed); reading (M Ed); secondary education (M Ed); special education (M Ed). *Faculty:* 23 full-time (14 women), 1 part-time/adjunct (0 women). *Students:* 37 full-time (26 women), 78 part-time (54 women); includes 15 minority (6 American Indian or Alaska Native, non-Hispanic/Latino; 6 Hispanic/Latino; 3 Two or more races, non-Hispanic/Latino), 2 international. Average age 34. 37 applicants, 68% accepted, 19 enrolled. In 2013, 39 master's, 28 other advanced degrees awarded. *Degree requirements:* For master's, comprehensive exam, thesis, oral defense. *Entrance requirements:* Additional exam requirements/recommendations for international students: Required—TOEFL (minimum score 550 paper-based; 80 iBT). *Application deadline:* For fall admission, 5/1 for domestic students, 3/1 for international students; for spring admission, 10/15 for domestic students, 8/1 for international students. Applications are processed on a rolling basis. Application fee: $60. Electronic applications accepted. *Expenses:* Tuition, state resident: full-time $7254; part-time $403 per credit. Tuition, nonresident: full-time $14,814; part-time $823 per credit. Tuition and fees vary according to course level, course load and reciprocity agreements. *Financial support:* In 2013–14, 1 teaching assistantship with tuition reimbursement (averaging $11,011 per year) was awarded; fellowships with tuition reimbursements, research assistantships with tuition reimbursements, career-related internships or fieldwork, Federal Work-Study, scholarships/grants, health care benefits, and unspecified assistantships also available. Support available to part-time students. Financial award application deadline: 6/1; financial award applicants required to submit FAFSA. *Unit head:* Allan Morotti, Interim Dean, 907-474-7341, Fax: 907-474-5451, E-mail: uaf-soe-school@alaska.edu. *Application contact:* Libby Eddy, Director of Admissions, 907-474-7500, Fax: 907-474-7097, E-mail: admissions@uaf.edu.
Website: https://sites.google.com/a/alaska.edu/soe-graduate/.

University of Alaska Southeast, Graduate Programs, Program in Education, Juneau, AK 99801. Offers early childhood education (M Ed, MAT); educational technology

(M Ed); elementary education (MAT); reading (M Ed); secondary education (MAT). *Accreditation:* NCATE. Part-time and evening/weekend programs available. Postbaccalaureate distance learning degree programs offered (minimal on-campus study). *Degree requirements:* For master's, comprehensive exam or project, portfolio. *Entrance requirements:* For master's, PRAXIS, minimum GPA of 3.0, writing sample, letters of recommendation. Electronic applications accepted. *Faculty research:* Applied classroom research, culturally responsive practices, action research, teaching effectiveness.

University of Alberta, Faculty of Graduate Studies and Research, Department of Elementary Education, Edmonton, AB T6G 2E1, Canada. Offers M Ed, Ed D, PhD. Part-time and evening/weekend programs available. Postbaccalaureate distance learning degree programs offered (minimal on-campus study). *Degree requirements:* For master's, thesis (for some programs); for doctorate, thesis/dissertation. *Entrance requirements:* For master's and doctorate, 1 year of teaching experience, minimum GPA of 6.5 on a 9.0 scale. *Faculty research:* Literacy education, early childhood education, teacher education, curriculum studies, instructional studies.

The University of Arizona, College of Education, Department of Teaching, Learning and Sociocultural Studies, Program in Teaching and Teacher Education, Tucson, AZ 85721. Offers M Ed, MA, PhD. Part-time and evening/weekend programs available. *Faculty:* 24 full-time (19 women), 1 (woman) part-time/adjunct. *Students:* 90 full-time (61 women), 37 part-time (24 women); includes 31 minority (3 Black or African American, non-Hispanic/Latino; 2 Asian, non-Hispanic/Latino; 18 Hispanic/Latino; 8 Two or more races, non-Hispanic/Latino), 7 international. Average age 36. 111 applicants, 71% accepted, 57 enrolled. In 2013, 70 master's, 3 doctorates awarded. *Degree requirements:* For master's, thesis optional; for doctorate, comprehensive exam, thesis/dissertation. *Entrance requirements:* For master's, writing sample, 1 year of teaching experience, 3 letters of recommendation; for doctorate, GRE General Test (minimum score 1000), minimum GPA of 3.5, 2 years of teaching experience, 3 letters of recommendation, writing sample. Additional exam requirements/recommendations for international students: Required—TOEFL (minimum score 550 paper-based; 79 iBT). *Application deadline:* For fall admission, 2/1 for domestic students, 12/1 for international students; for spring admission, 10/1 for domestic students, 6/1 for international students. Applications are processed on a rolling basis. Application fee: $75. Electronic applications accepted. *Expenses:* Tuition, state resident: full-time $11,526. Tuition, nonresident: full-time $27,398. *Financial support:* In 2013–14, 19 research assistantships with full tuition reimbursements (averaging $19,534 per year), 25 teaching assistantships with full tuition reimbursements (averaging $16,157 per year) were awarded; career-related internships or fieldwork, scholarships/grants, health care benefits, tuition waivers (full and partial), and unspecified assistantships also available. Financial award application deadline: 4/15. *Faculty research:* Staff development, science education, environmental education, math education. *Total annual research expenditures:* $1.7 million. *Unit head:* Dr. Bruce Johnson, Department Head, 520-621-7820, E-mail: brucej@email.arizona.edu. *Application contact:* Information Contact, 520-621-6993, E-mail: ttegrad@email.arizona.edu.
Website: https://www.coe.arizona.edu/tls/degrees_programs.

University of Bridgeport, School of Education, Department of Education, Bridgeport, CT 06604. Offers education (MS); educational management (Ed D, Diploma), including intermediate administrator or supervisor (Diploma), leadership (Ed D); elementary education (MS, Diploma), including early childhood education, elementary education; middle school education (MS); music education (MS); remedial reading and language arts (Diploma); secondary education (MS, Diploma), including computer specialist (Diploma), international education (Diploma), reading specialist, secondary education. Part-time and evening/weekend programs available. *Faculty:* 12 full-time (5 women), 108 part-time/adjunct (60 women). *Students:* 155 full-time (108 women), 139 part-time (98 women); includes 48 minority (22 Black or African American, non-Hispanic/Latino; 9 Asian, non-Hispanic/Latino; 15 Hispanic/Latino; 2 Two or more races, non-Hispanic/Latino), 2 international. Average age 30. 306 applicants, 55% accepted, 107 enrolled. In 2013, 153 master's, 16 other advanced degrees awarded. *Degree requirements:* For master's, final exam, final project, or thesis; for doctorate, comprehensive exam, thesis/dissertation; for Diploma, thesis or alternative, final project. *Entrance requirements:* For master's, minimum undergraduate QPA of 2.67; for doctorate, GRE, MAT; for Diploma, GRE General Test or MAT, minimum graduate QPA of 3.0. Additional exam requirements/recommendations for international students: Recommended—TOEFL (minimum score 550 paper-based; 80 iBT), IELTS (minimum score 6.5). *Application deadline:* For fall admission, 8/1 priority date for domestic and international students; for spring admission, 12/1 priority date for domestic and international students. Applications are processed on a rolling basis. Application fee: $50. Electronic applications accepted. *Expenses:* Contact institution. *Financial support:* In 2013–14, 120 students received support. Fellowships, research assistantships, teaching assistantships, career-related internships or fieldwork, Federal Work-Study, and institutionally sponsored loans available. Support available to part-time students. Financial award application deadline: 6/1; financial award applicants required to submit FAFSA. *Faculty research:* Self-concept, internship assessment, stress and situational development, follow-up of graduation, trend analysis. *Unit head:* Dr. Allen P. Cook, Dean, 203-576-4192, Fax: 203-576-4200, E-mail: acook@bridgeport.edu. *Application contact:* Leanne Proctor, Director of Graduate Admissions, 203-576-4552, Fax: 203-576-4941, E-mail: admit@bridgeport.edu.

University of California, Irvine, Department of Education, Irvine, CA 92697. Offers educational administration (Ed D); educational administration and leadership (Ed D); elementary and secondary education (MAT). Part-time and evening/weekend programs available. *Students:* 254 full-time (194 women), 4 part-time (3 women); includes 125 minority (1 Black or African American, non-Hispanic/Latino; 69 Asian, non-Hispanic/Latino; 41 Hispanic/Latino; 2 Native Hawaiian or other Pacific Islander, non-Hispanic/Latino; 12 Two or more races, non-Hispanic/Latino), 11 international. Average age 28. 506 applicants, 70% accepted, 200 enrolled. In 2013, 133 master's, 17 doctorates awarded. *Degree requirements:* For doctorate, thesis/dissertation. *Entrance requirements:* For master's, GRE, minimum GPA of 3.0; for doctorate, GRE General Test, minimum GPA of 3.0. Additional exam requirements/recommendations for international students: Required—TOEFL (minimum score 550 paper-based). *Application deadline:* For fall admission, 1/2 priority date for domestic students, 1/2 for international students. Application fee: $80 ($100 for international students). Electronic applications accepted. *Financial support:* Fellowships, research assistantships with full tuition reimbursements, institutionally sponsored loans, traineeships, health care benefits, and unspecified assistantships available. Financial award application deadline: 3/1; financial award applicants required to submit FAFSA. *Faculty research:* Education technology, learning theory, social theory, cultural diversity, postmodernism. *Unit head:* Deborah L. Vandell, Dean, 949-824-8026, Fax: 949-824-3968, E-mail: dvandell@uci.edu. *Application contact:* Judi Conroy, Director of Student Services, 949-824-7465, Fax: 949-824-9103, E-mail: jconroy@uci.edu.
Website: http://www.gse.uci.edu/.

University of Central Florida, College of Education and Human Performance, Education Doctoral Programs, Orlando, FL 32816. Offers communication sciences and disorders (PhD); counselor education (PhD); early childhood education (PhD); education (Ed D); elementary education (PhD); exceptional education (PhD); exercise physiology (PhD); higher education (PhD); hospitality education (PhD); instructional technology (PhD); mathematics education (PhD); reading education (PhD); science education (PhD); social science education (PhD); TESOL (PhD). *Students:* 137 full-time (94 women), 86 part-time (64 women); includes 45 minority (24 Black or African American, non-Hispanic/Latino; 5 Asian, non-Hispanic/Latino; 13 Hispanic/Latino; 3 Two or more races, non-Hispanic/Latino), 22 international. Average age 39. 132 applicants, 54% accepted, 54 enrolled. In 2013, 38 doctorates awarded. Application fee: $30. Electronic applications accepted. *Financial support:* In 2013–14, 84 students received support, including 38 fellowships with partial tuition reimbursements available (averaging $6,600 per year), 41 research assistantships with partial tuition reimbursements available (averaging $7,800 per year), 53 teaching assistantships with partial tuition reimbursements available (averaging $7,700 per year). *Unit head:* Dr. Edward Robinson, Director of Doctoral Programs, 407-823-6106, E-mail: edward.robinson@ucf.edu. *Application contact:* Barbara Rodriguez Lamas, Associate Director, Admissions and Student Services, 407-823-2766, Fax: 407-823-6442, E-mail: gradadmissions@ucf.edu.
Website: http://education.ucf.edu/departments.cfm.

University of Central Florida, College of Education and Human Performance, School of Teaching, Learning, and Leadership, Program in Elementary Education, Orlando, FL 32816. Offers M Ed, MA. *Accreditation:* NCATE. *Students:* 30 full-time (28 women), 55 part-time (49 women); includes 23 minority (7 Black or African American, non-Hispanic/Latino; 2 Asian, non-Hispanic/Latino; 13 Hispanic/Latino; 1 Two or more races, non-Hispanic/Latino), 4 international. Average age 31. 56 applicants, 79% accepted, 25 enrolled. In 2013, 40 master's awarded. *Degree requirements:* For master's, thesis or alternative. *Application deadline:* For fall admission, 7/15 for domestic students; for spring admission, 12/15 for domestic students. Application fee: $30. Electronic applications accepted. *Financial support:* In 2013–14, 2 students received support, including 2 research assistantships (averaging $6,900 per year); career-related internships or fieldwork, Federal Work-Study, institutionally sponsored loans, tuition waivers (partial), and unspecified assistantships also available. *Unit head:* Dr. Karri J. Williams, Program Coordinator, 407-433-7922, E-mail: karri.williams@ucf.edu. *Application contact:* Barbara Rodriguez Lamas, Director, Admissions and Student Services, 321-823-2766, Fax: 407-823-6442, E-mail: gradadmissions@ucf.edu.

University of Central Missouri, The Graduate School, Warrensburg, MO 6409. Offers accountancy (MA); accounting (MBA); applied mathematics (MS); aviation safety (MA); biology (MS); business administration (MBA); career and technical education leadership (MS); college student personnel administration (MS); communication (MA); computer science (MS); counseling (MS); criminal justice (MS); educational leadership (Ed D); educational technology (MS); elementary and early childhood education (MSE); English (MA); environmental studies (MA); finance (MBA); history (MA); human services/educational technology (Ed S); human services/learning resources (Ed S); human services/professional counseling (Ed S); industrial hygiene (MS); industrial management (MS); information systems (MBA); information technology (MS); kinesiology (MS); library science and information services (MS); literacy education (MSE); marketing (MBA); mathematics (MS); music (MA); occupational safety management (MS); psychology (MS); rural family nursing (MS); school administration (MSE); social gerontology (MS); sociology (MA); special education (MSE); speech language pathology (MS); superintendency (Ed S); teaching (MAT); teaching English as a second language (MA); technology (MS); technology management (PhD); theatre (MA). Part-time programs available. *Faculty:* 233. *Students:* 890 full-time (396 women), 1,486 part-time (1,001 women); includes 192 minority (97 Black or African American, non-Hispanic/Latino; 9 American Indian or Alaska Native, non-Hispanic/Latino; 32 Asian, non-Hispanic/Latino; 40 Hispanic/Latino; 3 Native Hawaiian or other Pacific Islander, non-Hispanic/Latino; 11 Two or more races, non-Hispanic/Latino), 539 international. Average age 31. 1,953 applicants, 75% accepted. In 2013, 719 master's, 58 other advanced degrees awarded. *Degree requirements:* For master's and Ed S, comprehensive exam (for some programs), thesis (for some programs). *Entrance requirements:* Additional exam requirements/recommendations for international students: Required—TOEFL (minimum score 550 paper-based; 79 iBT). *Application deadline:* For fall admission, 6/1 for domestic students; for spring admission, 10/1 for domestic and international students. Applications are processed on a rolling basis. Application fee: $30 ($75 for international students). Electronic applications accepted. *Expenses:* Tuition, state resident: full-time $7326; part-time $276.25 per credit hour. Tuition, nonresident: full-time $13,956; part-time $552.50 per credit hour. *Required fees:* $29 per credit hour. *Financial support:* In 2013–14, 118 students received support, including 271 research assistantships with full and partial tuition reimbursements available (averaging $7,500 per year), 109 teaching assistantships with full and partial tuition reimbursements available (averaging $7,500 per year); career-related internships or fieldwork, Federal Work-Study, scholarships/grants, and administrative and laboratory assistantships also available. Support available to part-time students. Financial award application deadline: 3/1; financial award applicants required to submit FAFSA. *Unit head:* Dr. Joseph Vaughn, Assistant Provost for Research/Dean, 660-543-4092, Fax: 660-543-4778, E-mail: vaughn@ucmo.edu. *Application contact:* Brittany Lawrence, Graduate Student Services Coordinator, 660-543-4621, Fax: 660-543-4778, E-mail: gradinfo@ucmo.edu.
Website: http://www.ucmo.edu/graduate/.

University of Central Oklahoma, The Jackson College of Graduate Studies, College of Education and Professional Studies, Department of Curriculum and Instruction, Edmond, OK 73034-5209. Offers bilingual education/teaching English as a second language (M Ed); early childhood education (M Ed); elementary education (M Ed). Part-time programs available. *Faculty:* 8 full-time (6 women), 10 part-time/adjunct (8 women). *Students:* 50 full-time (46 women), 68 part-time (61 women); includes 21 minority (7 Black or African American, non-Hispanic/Latino; 1 American Indian or Alaska Native, non-Hispanic/Latino; 3 Asian, non-Hispanic/Latino; 8 Hispanic/Latino; 2 Two or more races, non-Hispanic/Latino), 51 international. Average age 34. 55 applicants, 91% accepted, 25 enrolled. In 2013, 65 master's awarded. *Degree requirements:* For master's, comprehensive exam (for some programs), thesis optional. *Entrance requirements:* For master's, GRE General Test. Additional exam requirements/recommendations for international students: Required—TOEFL (minimum score 550 paper-based; 79 iBT), IELTS (minimum score 6.5). *Application deadline:* For fall admission, 7/1 for international students; for spring admission, 11/1 for international students. Applications are processed on a rolling basis. Application fee: $50. Electronic applications accepted. *Expenses:* Tuition, state resident: full-time $4137; part-time $206.85 per credit hour. Tuition, nonresident: full-time $10,359; part-time $517.95 per credit hour. *Required fees:* $481. Tuition and fees vary according to course load and program. *Financial support:* In 2013–14, 26 students received support, including research assistantships with partial tuition reimbursements available (averaging $5,454 per year), teaching assistantships with partial tuition reimbursements available (averaging $9,478 per year); Federal Work-Study, scholarships/grants, tuition waivers (partial), and unspecified assistantships also available. Financial award application deadline: 3/31; financial award applicants required to submit FAFSA. *Faculty research:* Tourette's syndrome, bilingual education, science education, language development/disorders. *Unit head:* Dr. Paulette Shreck, Chair, 405-974-5721, Fax: 405-974-3858,

Elementary Education

E-mail: pshreck@uco.edu. *Application contact:* Dr. Richard Bernard, Dean, Graduate College, 405-974-3493, Fax: 405-974-3852, E-mail: gradcoll@uco.edu.

University of Cincinnati, Graduate School, College of Education, Criminal Justice, and Human Services, Division of Teacher Education, Program in Middle Childhood Education, Cincinnati, OH 45221. Offers M Ed. *Accreditation:* NCATE. Part-time programs available. *Degree requirements:* For master's, thesis or alternative. *Entrance requirements:* For master's, GRE General Test. Additional exam requirements/recommendations for international students: Required—TOEFL (minimum score 550 paper-based), TWE (minimum score 4.5), OEPT. Electronic applications accepted.

University of Colorado Denver, School of Education and Human Development, Information and Learning Technologies Program, Denver, CO 80217-3364. Offers e-learning design and implementation (MA); instructional design and adult learning (MA); K-12 teaching (MA). Part-time and evening/weekend programs available. Postbaccalaureate distance learning degree programs offered (no on-campus study). *Students:* 60 full-time (49 women), 59 part-time (43 women); includes 16 minority (2 Black or African American, non-Hispanic/Latino; 3 Asian, non-Hispanic/Latino; 10 Hispanic/Latino; 1 Two or more races, non-Hispanic/Latino), 1 international. Average age 38. 32 applicants, 88% accepted, 23 enrolled. In 2013, 47 master's awarded. *Degree requirements:* For master's, comprehensive exam (for some programs), comprehensive exam or online portfolio; 30 credit hours. *Entrance requirements:* For master's, GRE or MAT (if GPA is below 2.75), resume, statement of intent, three letters of recommendation. Additional exam requirements/recommendations for international students: Required—TOEFL (minimum score 537 paper-based; 75 iBT); Recommended—IELTS (minimum score 6.5). *Application deadline:* For fall admission, 5/15 for domestic students, 5/1 for international students; for spring admission, 11/15 for domestic students, 11/1 for international students. Application fee: $50 ($75 for international students). *Expenses:* Contact institution. *Financial support:* In 2013–14, 2 students received support. Fellowships, research assistantships, teaching assistantships, Federal Work-Study, institutionally sponsored loans, scholarships/grants, and traineeships available. Financial award application deadline: 4/1; financial award applicants required to submit FAFSA. *Faculty research:* Technology for educational management, instructional design foundations, e-Learning, educational design. *Unit head:* Brent Wilson, Professor, 303-315-4963, E-mail: brent.wilson@ucdenver.edu. *Application contact:* Hans Broers, Academic Advisor, 303-315-6351, Fax: 303-315-6311, E-mail: hans.broers@ucdenver.edu.
Website: http://www.ucdenver.edu/academics/colleges/SchoolOfEducation/Academics/MASTERS/ILT/Pages/default.aspx.

University of Colorado Denver, School of Education and Human Development, Teacher Education Programs, Denver, CO 80217. Offers elementary linguistically diverse education (MA); elementary math and science education (MA); elementary math education (MA); elementary reading and writing (MA); elementary science education (MA); secondary English education (MA); secondary linguistically diverse education (MA); secondary math education (MA); secondary reading and writing (MA); secondary science education (MA); special education (MA). *Accreditation:* NCATE. Part-time and evening/weekend programs available. *Students:* 269 full-time (208 women), 141 part-time (111 women); includes 55 minority (4 Black or African American, non-Hispanic/Latino; 1 American Indian or Alaska Native, non-Hispanic/Latino; 10 Asian, non-Hispanic/Latino; 39 Hispanic/Latino; 1 Two or more races, non-Hispanic/Latino), 7 international. Average age 31. 97 applicants, 81% accepted, 62 enrolled. In 2013, 180 master's awarded. *Degree requirements:* For master's, comprehensive exam. *Entrance requirements:* For master's, GRE or MAT (for those with GPA below 2.75), transcripts, resume, letters of recommendation. Additional exam requirements/recommendations for international students: Required—TOEFL (minimum score 537 paper-based; 75 iBT); Recommended—IELTS (minimum score 6.5). *Application deadline:* For fall admission, 4/15 priority date for domestic students, 4/1 for international students; for spring admission, 9/15 priority date for domestic students, 9/1 for international students. Applications are processed on a rolling basis. Application fee: $50 ($75 for international students). Electronic applications accepted. *Expenses:* Contact institution. *Financial support:* In 2013–14, 42 students received support. Fellowships, research assistantships, teaching assistantships, Federal Work-Study, institutionally sponsored loans, scholarships/grants, and traineeships available. Financial award application deadline: 4/1; financial award applicants required to submit FAFSA. *Faculty research:* Linguistically diverse education/ESL, elementary reading and writing, elementary teacher education, secondary teacher education, special education. *Unit head:* Cindy Gutierrez, Director, 303-315-4982, E-mail: cindy.gutierrez@ucdenver.edu. *Application contact:* Lori Sisneros, Student Services Center, 303-315-4979, E-mail: education@ucdenver.edu.
Website: http://www.ucdenver.edu/academics/colleges/SchoolOfEducation/Academics/MASTERS/Pages/default.aspx.

University of Connecticut, Graduate School, Neag School of Education, Department of Curriculum and Instruction, Program in Elementary Education, Storrs, CT 06269. Offers MA, PhD, Post-Master's Certificate. *Accreditation:* NCATE. Terminal master's awarded for partial completion of doctoral program. *Degree requirements:* For master's, comprehensive exam, thesis or alternative; for doctorate, thesis/dissertation. *Entrance requirements:* For doctorate, GRE General Test. Additional exam requirements/recommendations for international students: Required—TOEFL (minimum score 550 paper-based). Electronic applications accepted.

University of Florida, Graduate School, College of Education, School of Teaching and Learning, Gainesville, FL 32611. Offers curriculum and instruction (M Ed, MAE, Ed D, PhD, Ed S), including bilingual/ESOL specialization; elementary education (M Ed, MAE); English education (M Ed, MAE); mathematics education (M Ed, MAE); reading education (M Ed, MAE); science education (M Ed, MAE); social studies education (M Ed, MAE). *Accreditation:* NCATE. Part-time and evening/weekend programs available. Postbaccalaureate distance learning degree programs offered (no on-campus study). *Faculty:* 24 full-time (17 women), 12 part-time/adjunct (7 women). *Students:* 201 full-time (162 women), 325 part-time (255 women); includes 124 minority (36 Black or African American, non-Hispanic/Latino; 4 American Indian or Alaska Native, non-Hispanic/Latino; 10 Asian, non-Hispanic/Latino; 74 Hispanic/Latino), 47 international. Average age 34. 220 applicants, 55% accepted, 64 enrolled. In 2013, 215 master's, 15 doctorates, 14 other advanced degrees awarded. Terminal master's awarded for partial completion of doctoral program. *Degree requirements:* For master's, comprehensive exam (for some programs), thesis (for some programs); for doctorate, comprehensive exam (for some programs), thesis/dissertation (for some programs). *Entrance requirements:* For master's and doctorate, GRE General Test, minimum GPA of 3.0; for Ed S, GRE General Test. Additional exam requirements/recommendations for international students: Required—TOEFL (minimum score 550 paper-based; 80 iBT), IELTS (minimum score 6). *Application deadline:* For fall admission, 2/15 for domestic students, 12/1 for international students; for spring admission, 9/15 for domestic students, 3/1 for international students. Applications are processed on a rolling basis. Application fee: $30. Electronic applications accepted. *Expenses:* Tuition, state resident: full-time $12,640. Tuition, nonresident: full-time $30,000. *Financial support:* In 2013–14, 52 students received support, including 3 fellowships (averaging $2,365 per year), 20 research assistantships (averaging $11,715 per year), 58 teaching assistantships (averaging $8,410 per year); career-related internships or fieldwork and unspecified assistantships also available. Financial award applicants required to submit FAFSA. *Faculty research:* Early childhood, child and adolescents, diverse learners, race/ethnicity issues, teacher education, professional development, language and literacy development, policy development. *Unit head:* Elizabeth Bondy, PhD, Interim Director and Professor, 352-273-4242, Fax: 352-392-9193, E-mail: bondy@coe.ufl.edu. *Application contact:* Sevan Terzian, Graduate Coordinator, 352-273-4216, Fax: 352-392-9193, E-mail: sterzian@coe.ufl.edu.
Website: http://education.ufl.edu/school-teaching-learning/.

University of Georgia, College of Education, Department of Elementary and Social Studies Education, Athens, GA 30602. Offers early childhood education (M Ed, MAT, PhD, Ed S), including child and family development (MAT); elementary education (PhD); middle school education (M Ed, PhD, Ed S); social studies education (M Ed, Ed D, PhD, Ed S). *Entrance requirements:* For master's and Ed S, GRE General Test or MAT; for doctorate, GRE General Test. Electronic applications accepted.

University of Hartford, College of Education, Nursing, and Health Professions, Program in Elementary and Special Education, West Hartford, CT 06117-1599. Offers elementary education (M Ed). *Accreditation:* NCATE. Part-time and evening/weekend programs available. *Degree requirements:* For master's, comprehensive exam. *Entrance requirements:* For master's, PRAXIS I or waiver, interview, 2 letters of recommendation. Additional exam requirements/recommendations for international students: Required—TOEFL (minimum score 550 paper-based). Electronic applications accepted.

University of Houston–Downtown, College of Public Service, Department of Urban Education, Houston, TX 77002. Offers curriculum and instruction (MAT); elementary (EC-6) generalist certification (MAT); elementary/middle school (4-8) generalist certification (MAT); secondary education certification (MAT). Part-time and evening/weekend programs available. Postbaccalaureate distance learning degree programs offered. *Faculty:* 7 full-time (3 women). *Students:* 4 full-time (3 women), 28 part-time (19 women); includes 22 minority (14 Black or African American, non-Hispanic/Latino; 1 Asian, non-Hispanic/Latino; 6 Hispanic/Latino; 1 Two or more races, non-Hispanic/Latino). Average age 36. 31 applicants, 87% accepted, 27 enrolled. In 2013, 10 master's awarded. *Degree requirements:* For master's, capstone course with completed project, position paper, grant proposal, empirical study, curriculum development/revision, or advanced technology project presented at annual Graduate Project Exhibition. *Entrance requirements:* For master's, GRE, personal statement, 3 recommendation forms. Additional exam requirements/recommendations for international students: Required—TOEFL (minimum score 550 paper-based; 80 iBT). *Application deadline:* For fall admission, 7/15 for domestic and international students; for spring admission, 11/15 for domestic and international students. Application fee: $35 ($60 for international students). Electronic applications accepted. *Expenses:* Tuition, state resident: full-time $4212; part-time $234 per credit hour. Tuition, nonresident: full-time $9684; part-time $538 per credit hour. *Required fees:* $1074. Tuition and fees vary according to program. *Financial support:* Scholarships/grants available. Financial award applicants required to submit FAFSA. *Unit head:* Dr. Viola Garcia, Department Chair, 713-221-8165, Fax: 713-226-5294, E-mail: garciav@uhd.edu. *Application contact:* Ceshia Love, Assistant Director of Graduate Admissions, 713-221-8093, Fax: 713-223-7408, E-mail: gradadmissions@uhd.edu.
Website: http://www.uhd.edu/academic/colleges/publicservice/urbaned/.

University of Illinois at Chicago, Graduate College, College of Education, Department of Curriculum and Instruction, Chicago, IL 60607-7128. Offers curriculum studies (PhD); educational studies (M Ed); elementary education (M Ed); instructional leadership (M Ed); literacy, language and culture (M Ed, PhD); science education (M Ed); secondary education (M Ed). Part-time and evening/weekend programs available. *Faculty:* 20 full-time (10 women), 10 part-time/adjunct (8 women). *Students:* 124 full-time (89 women), 155 part-time (117 women); includes 117 minority (51 Black or African American, non-Hispanic/Latino; 19 Asian, non-Hispanic/Latino; 43 Hispanic/Latino; 4 Two or more races, non-Hispanic/Latino), 11 international. Average age 32. 154 applicants, 70% accepted, 74 enrolled. In 2013, 108 master's, 16 doctorates awarded. *Degree requirements:* For doctorate, thesis/dissertation. *Entrance requirements:* For master's, minimum GPA of 2.75; for doctorate, GRE General Test, minimum GPA of 2.75. Additional exam requirements/recommendations for international students: Required—TOEFL. *Application deadline:* For fall admission, 1/9 for domestic and international students; for spring admission, 10/1 for domestic and international students. Applications are processed on a rolling basis. Application fee: $40 ($50 for international students). Electronic applications accepted. *Expenses:* Tuition, state resident: full-time $11,066; part-time $3689 per term. Tuition, nonresident: full-time $23,064; part-time $7688 per term. *Required fees:* $3004; $1190 per term. Tuition and fees vary according to course level and program. *Financial support:* In 2013–14, 101 students received support, including 4 fellowships with full tuition reimbursements available; research assistantships with full tuition reimbursements available, teaching assistantships with full tuition reimbursements available, career-related internships or fieldwork, Federal Work-Study, institutionally sponsored loans, traineeships, tuition waivers (full), and unspecified assistantships also available. Support available to part-time students. Financial award application deadline: 3/1; financial award applicants required to submit FAFSA. *Faculty research:* Curriculum theory, curriculum development, research on teaching, curriculum and context, reading/literacy. *Total annual research expenditures:* $70,000. *Unit head:* Prof. Alfred Tatum, Associate Professor/Director/Chair, 312-413-3883, Fax: 312-996-8134, E-mail: atatum1@uic.edu.
Website: http://education.uic.edu.

University of Indianapolis, Graduate Programs, School of Education, Indianapolis, IN 46227-3697. Offers art education (MAT); biology (MAT); chemistry (MAT); curriculum and instruction (MA); earth sciences (MAT); education (MA, MAT); educational leadership (MA); elementary education (MA); English (MAT); French (MAT); math (MAT); physical education (MAT); physics (MAT); secondary education (MA), including art education, education, English education, social studies education; social studies (MAT); Spanish (MAT). *Accreditation:* NCATE. Part-time and evening/weekend programs available. *Faculty:* 5 full-time (4 women), 2 part-time/adjunct (1 woman). *Students:* 19 full-time (9 women), 54 part-time (27 women); includes 13 minority (5 Black or African American, non-Hispanic/Latino; 1 Asian, non-Hispanic/Latino; 5 Hispanic/Latino; 2 Two or more races, non-Hispanic/Latino), 1 international. Average age 32. In 2013, 52 master's awarded. *Entrance requirements:* For master's, GRE Subject Test, PRAXIS I, minimum GPA of 2.5, 3 letters of recommendation, interview. Additional exam requirements/recommendations for international students: Required—TOEFL (minimum score 550 paper-based). *Application deadline:* Applications are processed on a rolling basis. Application fee: $50. *Expenses: Tuition:* Full-time $5436; part-time $810 per credit hour. *Financial support:* Federal Work-Study available. Financial award application deadline: 5/1; financial award applicants required to submit FAFSA. *Faculty research:* Assessment of teacher education, perceptions of prospective teachers by parents. *Unit head:* Dr. Kathy Moran, Dean, 317-788-3285, Fax: 317-788-3300, E-mail: kmoran@uindy.edu. *Application contact:* Jeni Kirby, Administrative Assistant, Teacher Education, 317-788-2113, E-mail: kirbyj@uindy.edu.
Website: http://education.uindy.edu/.

The University of Iowa, Graduate College, College of Education, Department of Teaching and Learning, Program in Education, Iowa City, IA 52242-1316. Offers art education (MA); developmental reading (MA); elementary education (MA); English education (MA, MAT); foreign and second language education (MAT); foreign language education (MA); foreign language/ESL education (PhD); language, literacy and culture (PhD); mathematics education (MA, MAT, PhD); music education (MM, PhD); science education (MA); secondary education (MA); social studies (MA, PhD). *Degree requirements:* For master's, thesis optional, exam; for doctorate, comprehensive exam, thesis/dissertation. *Entrance requirements:* For master's and doctorate, GRE General Test, minimum GPA of 3.0. Additional exam requirements/recommendations for international students: Required—TOEFL (minimum score 550 paper-based; 81 iBT). Electronic applications accepted.

University of Kentucky, Graduate School, College of Education, Department of Curriculum and Instruction, Lexington, KY 40506-0032. Offers curriculum and instruction (Ed D); elementary education (MA Ed); instructional system design (MS Ed); literacy (MA Ed); middle school education (MA Ed, MS Ed); secondary education (MA Ed, MS Ed). *Accreditation:* NCATE. *Degree requirements:* For master's, comprehensive exam, thesis optional; for doctorate, comprehensive exam, thesis/dissertation. *Entrance requirements:* For master's, GRE General Test, minimum undergraduate GPA of 2.75; for doctorate, GRE General Test, minimum graduate GPA of 3.0. Additional exam requirements/recommendations for international students: Required—TOEFL (minimum score 550 paper-based). Electronic applications accepted. *Faculty research:* Educational reform, multicultural education, classroom instructional practices, performance based assessment, primary school programs.

University of La Verne, Regional and Online Campuses, Graduate Programs, Central Coast/Vandenberg Air Force Base Campuses, La Verne, CA 91750-4443. Offers business administration for experienced professionals (MBA), including health services management, information technology; education (special emphasis) (M Ed); educational counseling (MS); educational leadership (M Ed); multiple subject (elementary) (Credential); preliminary administrative services (Credential); pupil personnel services (Credential); single subject (secondary) (Credential). Part-time programs available. *Faculty:* 11 part-time/adjunct (2 women). *Students:* 17 full-time (7 women), 34 part-time (22 women); includes 15 minority (1 Black or African American, non-Hispanic/Latino; 1 American Indian or Alaska Native, non-Hispanic/Latino; 1 Asian, non-Hispanic/Latino; 10 Hispanic/Latino; 2 Two or more races, non-Hispanic/Latino). Average age 38. In 2013, 25 master's awarded. *Application deadline:* Applications are processed on a rolling basis. Application fee: $50. *Expenses:* Contact institution. *Financial support:* Institutionally sponsored loans available. Financial award application deadline: 3/2; financial award applicants required to submit FAFSA. *Unit head:* Kitt Vincent, Director, Central Coast Campus, 805-788-6202, Fax: 805-788-6201, E-mail: kvincent@laverne.edu. *Application contact:* Gene Teal, Admissions, 805-788-6205, Fax: 805-788-6201, E-mail: eteal@laverne.edu.
Website: http://www.laverne.edu/locations.

University of La Verne, Regional and Online Campuses, Graduate Programs, High Desert Campus, Victorville, CA 92392. Offers business administration for experienced professionals (MBA); educational counseling (MS); educational leadership (M Ed); multiple subject (elementary) (Credential); preliminary administrative services (Credential); pupil personnel services (Credential); single subject (secondary) (Credential). *Faculty:* 3 part-time/adjunct (0 women). *Students:* 10 full-time (6 women), 17 part-time (12 women); includes 14 minority (3 Black or African American, non-Hispanic/Latino; 3 Asian, non-Hispanic/Latino; 6 Hispanic/Latino; 1 Native Hawaiian or other Pacific Islander, non-Hispanic/Latino; 1 Two or more races, non-Hispanic/Latino). Average age 38. In 2013, 6 master's awarded. *Application deadline:* Applications are processed on a rolling basis. Application fee: $50. *Expenses:* Contact institution. *Financial support:* Application deadline: 3/2; applicants required to submit FAFSA. *Unit head:* Juli Roberts, Regional Campus Director, 760-955-6448, Fax: 760-843-9505, E-mail: jroberts@laverne.edu. *Application contact:* Donald Parker, Associate Director of Admissions, 760-955-6477, E-mail: dparker@laverne.edu.
Website: http://www.laverne.edu/locations/victorville/.

University of La Verne, Regional and Online Campuses, Graduate Programs, Kern County Campus, Bakersfield, CA 93301. Offers business administration for experienced professionals (MBA-EP); education (special emphasis) (M Ed); educational counseling (MS); educational leadership (M Ed); health administration (MHA); leadership and management (MS); mild/moderate education specialist preliminary (Credential); multiple subject (elementary) (Credential); organizational leadership (Ed D); preliminary administrative services (Credential); single subject (secondary) (Credential); special education studies (MS). Part-time and evening/weekend programs available. *Faculty:* 2 part-time/adjunct (1 woman). *Students:* 1 (woman) full-time, 5 part-time (3 women); includes 4 minority (3 Hispanic/Latino; 1 Two or more races, non-Hispanic/Latino). Average age 36. In 2013, 4 master's awarded. *Application deadline:* Applications are processed on a rolling basis. Application fee: $50. *Expenses:* Contact institution. *Financial support:* Institutionally sponsored loans available. Financial award application deadline: 3/2; financial award applicants required to submit FAFSA. *Unit head:* Nora Dominguez, Regional Campus Director, 661-861-6802, E-mail: ndominguez@laverne.edu. *Application contact:* Regina Benavides, Associate Director of Admissions, 661-861-6807, E-mail: rbenavides@laverne.edu.
Website: http://laverne.edu/locations/bakersfield/.

University of La Verne, Regional and Online Campuses, Graduate Programs, Ventura County/Point Mugu Naval Air Station Campuses, Oxnard, CA 93036. Offers business administration for experienced professionals (MS); educational counseling (MS); educational leadership (M Ed); leadership and management (MS); multiple subject (elementary) (Credential); pupil personnel services (Credential); single subject (secondary) (Credential). Part-time and evening/weekend programs available. *Faculty:* 12 part-time/adjunct (2 women). *Students:* 34 full-time (13 women), 37 part-time (20 women); includes 39 minority (3 Black or African American, non-Hispanic/Latino; 2 American Indian or Alaska Native, non-Hispanic/Latino; 3 Asian, non-Hispanic/Latino; 29 Hispanic/Latino; 2 Two or more races, non-Hispanic/Latino). Average age 38. In 2013, 31 master's awarded. Application fee: $50. *Expenses:* Contact institution. *Financial support:* Institutionally sponsored loans available. Financial award application deadline: 3/2; financial award applicants required to submit FAFSA. *Unit head:* Jamie Dempsey, Director, Point Mugu, 661-986-6902, E-mail: jdempsey@laverne.edu. *Application contact:* Kevin Laack, Regional Campus Director, Ventura, 805-981-6022, E-mail: klaack@laverne.edu.
Website: http://laverne.edu/locations/oxnard/.

University of Louisiana at Monroe, Graduate School, College of Arts, Education, and Sciences, School of Education, Program in Curriculum and Instruction, Monroe, LA 71209-0001. Offers art education (M Ed); biology education (M Ed); chemistry education (M Ed); curriculum and instruction (Ed D); early childhood education (M Ed); earth science education (M Ed); educational leadership (M Ed); elementary education (1-5) (M Ed); English as a second language (M Ed); English education (M Ed); family and consumer education (M Ed); French education (M Ed); history education (M Ed); math education (M Ed); middle school education (M Ed); music education (M Ed); reading education (K-12) (M Ed); Spanish education (M Ed); special education - academically

gifted (M Ed); special education - early intervention (M Ed); special education - educational diagnostician (M Ed); special education - mild/moderate disabilities (M Ed); speech education (M Ed). *Accreditation:* NCATE. *Degree requirements:* For master's, comprehensive exam (for some programs), thesis; for doctorate, thesis/dissertation, internships. *Entrance requirements:* For master's, GRE General Test; for doctorate, GRE General Test, minimum undergraduate GPA of 2.75, graduate 3.25. Additional exam requirements/recommendations for international students: Required—TOEFL (minimum score 500 paper-based; 61 iBT). *Application deadline:* For fall admission, 8/24 priority date for domestic students, 7/1 for international students; for winter admission, 12/14 priority date for domestic students; for spring admission, 1/19 for domestic students, 11/1 for international students. Applications are processed on a rolling basis. Application fee: $20 ($30 for international students). Electronic applications accepted. *Expenses:* Tuition, state resident: full-time $6607. Tuition, nonresident: full-time $17,179. Full-time tuition and fees vary according to program. *Financial support:* Research assistantships, career-related internships or fieldwork, Federal Work-Study, and unspecified assistantships available. Financial award application deadline: 4/1; financial award applicants required to submit FAFSA. *Unit head:* Dr. Dorothy Schween, Director, 318-342-1268, Fax: 318-342-3131, E-mail: schween@ulm.edu. *Application contact:* Dr. Dorothy Schween, Director, 318-342-1268, Fax: 318-342-3131, E-mail: schween@ulm.edu.

University of Louisiana at Monroe, Graduate School, College of Arts, Education, and Sciences, School of Education, Program in Elementary Education, Monroe, LA 71209-0001. Offers MAT. *Accreditation:* NCATE. Part-time and evening/weekend programs available. *Degree requirements:* For master's, thesis optional. *Entrance requirements:* For master's, GRE General Test, minimum GPA of 2.5. Additional exam requirements/recommendations for international students: Required—TOEFL (minimum score 500 paper-based; 61 iBT). *Application deadline:* For fall admission, 8/24 for domestic students, 7/1 for international students; for winter admission, 12/14 priority date for domestic students; for spring admission, 1/19 for domestic students, 11/1 for international students. Applications are processed on a rolling basis. Application fee: $20 ($30 for international students). Electronic applications accepted. *Expenses:* Tuition, state resident: full-time $6607. Tuition, nonresident: full-time $17,179. Full-time tuition and fees vary according to program. *Financial support:* Career-related internships or fieldwork, Federal Work-Study, and unspecified assistantships available. Financial award application deadline: 4/1; financial award applicants required to submit FAFSA. *Faculty research:* Student attitudes. *Unit head:* Dr. Dorothy Schween, Director, 318-342-1268, E-mail: schween@ulm.edu. *Application contact:* Dr. Dorothy Schween, Director, 318-342-1268, E-mail: schween@ulm.edu.

University of Louisville, Graduate School, College of Education and Human Development, Department of Teaching and Learning, Louisville, KY 40292-0001. Offers art education (MAT); curriculum and instruction (PhD); early elementary education (MAT); instructional technology (M Ed); interdisciplinary early childhood education (MAT); middle school education (MAT); music education (MAT); secondary education (MAT); special education (MAT); teacher leadership (M Ed). Part-time and evening/weekend programs available. *Students:* 137 full-time (93 women), 208 part-time (131 women); includes 44 minority (25 Black or African American, non-Hispanic/Latino; 1 American Indian or Alaska Native, non-Hispanic/Latino; 3 Asian, non-Hispanic/Latino; 12 Hispanic/Latino; 3 Two or more races, non-Hispanic/Latino), 2 international. Average age 32. 150 applicants, 51% accepted, 54 enrolled. In 2013, 127 master's, 5 doctorates awarded. *Degree requirements:* For doctorate, comprehensive exam, thesis/dissertation. *Entrance requirements:* For master's, GRE General Test, PRAXIS II (for some programs); for doctorate, GRE General Test. Additional exam requirements/recommendations for international students: Required—TOEFL (minimum score 560 paper-based; 83 iBT). *Application deadline:* For fall admission, 5/1 priority date for international students; for spring admission, 11/1 priority date for international students; for summer admission, 4/1 priority date for international students. Application fee: $60. Electronic applications accepted. *Expenses:* Tuition, state resident: full-time $10,788; part-time $599 per credit hour. Tuition, nonresident: full-time $22,446; part-time $1247 per credit hour. *Required fees:* $196. Tuition and fees vary according to program and reciprocity agreements. *Financial support:* Fellowships, research assistantships, teaching assistantships, career-related internships or fieldwork, Federal Work-Study, scholarships/grants, and unspecified assistantships available. Financial award application deadline: 6/1; financial award applicants required to submit FAFSA. *Faculty research:* Mathematics teacher education and ongoing professional development in pedagogy and content knowledge; development of literacy, including early literacy in science and mathematics and literacy development for English language learners; immersive visualizations for promoting STEM education from nanoscience to cosmic scales; evidence-based practices for students with disabilities; urban education, including teacher response to intervention systems in schools and cross-cultural competence. *Unit head:* Dr. Ann E. Larson, Acting Chair, 502-852-6431, Fax: 502-852-1497, E-mail: ann@louisville.edu. *Application contact:* Libby Leggett, Director, Graduate Admissions, 502-852-3101, Fax: 502-852-6536, E-mail: gradadm@louisville.edu.
Website: http://louisville.edu/delphi.

University of Maine, Graduate School, College of Education and Human Development, Department of Teacher and Counselor Education, Orono, ME 04469. Offers counselor education (M Ed, MA, MS, CAS); early childhood teacher (CGS); education (PhD), including counselor education, literacy education, prevention and intervention studies; elementary education (M Ed, CAS); individualized education (M Ed); literacy education (M Ed, MS, CAS); response to intervention for behavior (CGS); secondary education (M Ed, MAT, CAS); social studies education (M Ed); special education (M Ed, CAS); teacher consultant in writing (CGS). Part-time programs available. *Students:* 147 full-time (118 women), 15 part-time (2 women); includes 8 minority (4 Black or African American, non-Hispanic/Latino; 2 American Indian or Alaska Native, non-Hispanic/Latino; 1 Hispanic/Latino; 1 Two or more races, non-Hispanic/Latino), 3 international. Average age 37. 100 applicants, 58% accepted, 50 enrolled. In 2013, 83 master's, 5 doctorates, 17 other advanced degrees awarded. *Degree requirements:* For master's, thesis (for some programs); for doctorate, comprehensive exam, thesis/dissertation. *Entrance requirements:* For master's, GRE General Test, MAT. Additional exam requirements/recommendations for international students: Required—TOEFL. *Application deadline:* For fall admission, 2/1 priority date for domestic students. Applications are processed on a rolling basis. Application fee: $65. Electronic applications accepted. *Expenses:* Tuition, state resident: full-time $7524. Tuition, nonresident: full-time $23,112. *Required fees:* $1970. *Financial support:* In 2013–14, 46 students received support, including 1 research assistantship (averaging $14,600 per year), 11 teaching assistantships (averaging $14,600 per year). Financial award application deadline: 3/1. *Unit head:* Dr. Janet Spector, Coordinator, 207-581-2459. *Application contact:* Scott G. Delcourt, Associate Dean of the Graduate School, 207-581-3291, Fax: 207-581-3232, E-mail: graduate@maine.edu.
Website: http://umaine.edu/edhd/.

University of Mary Hardin-Baylor, Graduate Studies in Education, Belton, TX 76513. Offers administration of intervention programs (M Ed); curriculum and instruction (M Ed); educational administration (M Ed, Ed D), including higher education (Ed D), leadership in nursing education (Ed D), P-12 (Ed D). Part-time and evening/weekend programs available. *Faculty:* 13 full-time (10 women), 6 part-time/adjunct (2 women). *Students:* 46

full-time (33 women), 61 part-time (40 women); includes 35 minority (15 Black or African American, non-Hispanic/Latino; 1 American Indian or Alaska Native, non-Hispanic/Latino; 19 Hispanic/Latino), 1 international. Average age 38. 72 applicants, 88% accepted, 47 enrolled. In 2013, 13 master's, 30 doctorates awarded. *Degree requirements:* For master's, comprehensive exam; for doctorate, thesis/dissertation. *Entrance requirements:* For master's, minimum GPA of 3.0, interview; for doctorate, minimum GPA of 3.5, interview, essay, resume, employment verification, employer letter of support, 3 letters of recommendation. Additional exam requirements/recommendations for international students: Required—TOEFL (minimum score 550 paper-based; 80 iBT), IELTS (minimum score 6). *Application deadline:* For fall admission, 6/1 for domestic students, 6/15 priority date for international students; for spring admission, 11/1 for domestic students, 10/15 priority date for international students. Applications are processed on a rolling basis. Application fee: $35 ($135 for international students). Electronic applications accepted. *Expenses: Tuition:* Full-time $14,130; part-time $785 per credit hour. *Required fees:* $1350; $75 per credit hour. $50 per term. *Financial support:* Federal Work-Study and scholarships (for some active duty military personnel only) available. Support available to part-time students. Financial award application deadline: 6/1; financial award applicants required to submit FAFSA. *Unit head:* Dr. Marlene Zipperlen, Dean, College of Education/Director, Doctor of Education Program, 254-295-4572, Fax: 254-295-4480, E-mail: mzipperlen@umhb.edu. *Application contact:* Melissa Ford, Director of Graduate Admissions, 254-295-4020, Fax: 254-295-5038, E-mail: mford@umhb.edu.
Website: http://graduate.umhb.edu/education/.

University of Maryland, Baltimore County, Graduate School, College of Arts, Humanities and Social Sciences, Department of Education, Program in Teaching, Baltimore, MD 21250. Offers early childhood education (MAT); elementary education (MAT); secondary education (MAT), including art, biology, chemistry, dance, earth/space science, English, foreign language, mathematics, music, physics, social studies, theatre. Part-time and evening/weekend programs available. *Faculty:* 24 full-time (18 women), 25 part-time/adjunct (19 women). *Students:* 49 full-time (34 women), 35 part-time (23 women); includes 19 minority (9 Black or African American, non-Hispanic/Latino; 3 Asian, non-Hispanic/Latino; 6 Hispanic/Latino; 1 Two or more races, non-Hispanic/Latino). Average age 30. 40 applicants, 95% accepted, 35 enrolled. In 2013, 106 master's awarded. *Degree requirements:* For master's, comprehensive exam (for some programs), thesis (for some programs). *Entrance requirements:* For master's, PRAXIS I or SAT (minimum score of 1000), minimum GPA of 3.0. Additional exam requirements/recommendations for international students: Required—TOEFL. *Application deadline:* For fall admission, 6/1 for domestic students; for spring admission, 11/1 for domestic students. Applications are processed on a rolling basis. Application fee: $50. Electronic applications accepted. One-time fee: $200 full-time. *Financial support:* In 2013–14, 6 students received support, including teaching assistantships with full and partial tuition reimbursements available (averaging $12,000 per year); career-related internships or fieldwork, Federal Work-Study, scholarships/grants, tuition waivers, and unspecified assistantships also available. Financial award application deadline: 3/1. *Faculty research:* STEM teacher education, culturally sensitive pedagogy, ESOL/bilingual education, early childhood education, language, literacy and culture. *Unit head:* Dr. Susan M. Blunck, Graduate Program Director, 410-455-2869, Fax: 410-455-3986, E-mail: blunck@umbc.edu. *Application contact:* Dr. Susan M. Blunck, Graduate Program Director, 410-455-2869, Fax: 410-455-3986, E-mail: blunck@umbc.edu.
Website: http://www.umbc.edu/education/.

University of Mary Washington, College of Education, Fredericksburg, VA 22401. Offers education (M Ed); elementary education (MS). Part-time and evening/weekend programs available. *Faculty:* 18 full-time (16 women), 30 part-time/adjunct (23 women). *Students:* 42 full-time (37 women), 212 part-time (180 women); includes 22 minority (3 Black or African American, non-Hispanic/Latino; 4 Asian, non-Hispanic/Latino; 6 Hispanic/Latino; 9 Two or more races, non-Hispanic/Latino). Average age 31. 238 applicants, 61% accepted, 86 enrolled. In 2013, 132 master's awarded. *Degree requirements:* For master's, one foreign language, comprehensive exam (for some programs). *Entrance requirements:* For master's, PRAXIS I or Virginia Department of Education accepted equivalent. Additional exam requirements/recommendations for international students: Required—TOEFL (minimum score 570 paper-based; 88 iBT), IELTS (minimum score 6.5). *Application deadline:* For fall admission, 4/15 for domestic and international students; for spring admission, 9/15 for domestic and international students. Applications are processed on a rolling basis. Application fee: $50. Electronic applications accepted. Application fee is waived when completed online. *Expenses: Tuition, area resident:* Part-time $444 per credit hour. Tuition, state resident: part-time $444 per credit hour. Tuition, nonresident: part-time $883 per credit hour. *Required fees:* $30 per semester. *Financial support:* In 2013–14, 20 students received support, including 3 fellowships with partial tuition reimbursements available (averaging $9,000 per year); research assistantships, teaching assistantships, and scholarships/grants also available. Financial award application deadline: 4/25; financial award applicants required to submit FAFSA. *Unit head:* Dr. Mary L. Gendernalik-Cooper, Dean, 540-654-1290. *Application contact:* Dre N. Anthes, Director of Graduate Admissions, 540-286-8030, Fax: 540-286-8085, E-mail: aanthes@umw.edu.
Website: http://www.umw.edu/education/.

University of Massachusetts Amherst, Graduate School, College of Education, Program in Education, Amherst, MA 01003. Offers bilingual/English as a second language/multicultural education (M Ed, Ed S); child study and early education (M Ed); children, families and schools (Ed D, Ed S); early childhood and elementary teacher education (M Ed); educational leadership (M Ed); educational policy and leadership (Ed D); higher education (M Ed); international education (M Ed); language, literacy and culture (Ed D); learning, media and technology (M Ed, Ed S); mathematics, science, and learning technologies (Ed D); psychometric methods, educational statistics and research methods (Ed D); reading and writing (M Ed); school counselor education (M Ed, Ed S); school psychology (Ed S); science education (Ed S); secondary teacher education (M Ed); social justice education (M Ed, Ed D, Ed S); special education (M Ed, Ed D, Ed S); teacher education and school improvement (Ed D, Ed S). *Accreditation:* NCATE. Part-time programs available. Postbaccalaureate distance learning degree programs offered (minimal on-campus study). *Faculty:* 95 full-time (55 women). *Students:* 357 full-time (240 women), 264 part-time (194 women); includes 114 minority (41 Black or African American, non-Hispanic/Latino; 4 American Indian or Alaska Native, non-Hispanic/Latino; 10 Asian, non-Hispanic/Latino; 47 Hispanic/Latino; 12 Two or more races, non-Hispanic/Latino), 100 international. Average age 34. 761 applicants, 51% accepted, 200 enrolled. In 2013, 186 master's, 31 doctorates, 22 other advanced degrees awarded. Terminal master's awarded for partial completion of doctoral program. *Degree requirements:* For doctorate, comprehensive exam, thesis/dissertation. *Entrance requirements:* Additional exam requirements/recommendations for international students: Required—TOEFL (minimum score 550 paper-based; 80 iBT), IELTS (minimum score 6.5). *Application deadline:* For fall admission, 1/15 for domestic and international students. Applications are processed on a rolling basis. Application fee: $75. Electronic applications accepted. *Financial support:* Fellowships with full and partial tuition reimbursements, research assistantships with full and partial tuition reimbursements, teaching assistantships with full and partial tuition reimbursements, career-related internships or fieldwork, Federal Work-Study, scholarships/grants, traineeships, health care benefits, tuition waivers (full and partial), and unspecified assistantships available. Support available to part-time students. Financial award application deadline: 1/15; financial award applicants required to submit FAFSA. *Unit head:* Dr. Linda L. Griffin, Graduate Program Director, 413-545-6984, Fax: 413-545-1523. *Application contact:* Lindsay DeSantis, Supervisor of Admissions, 413-545-0722, Fax: 413-577-0010, E-mail: gradadm@grad.umass.edu.
Website: http://www.umass.edu/education/.

University of Massachusetts Boston, Office of Graduate Studies, Graduate College of Education, School Organization, Curriculum and Instruction Department, Boston, MA 02125-3393. Offers education (M Ed, Ed D), including elementary and secondary education/certification (M Ed), higher education administration (Ed D), teacher certification (M Ed), urban school leadership (Ed D); educational administration (M Ed, CAGS); special education (M Ed). *Degree requirements:* For master's and CAGS, comprehensive exam; for doctorate, comprehensive exam, thesis/dissertation. *Entrance requirements:* For master's, GRE General Test or MAT; for doctorate, GRE General Test or MAT, minimum GPA of 2.75; for CAGS, minimum GPA of 2.75.

University of Massachusetts Boston, Office of Graduate Studies, Graduate College of Education, School Organization, Curriculum and Instruction Department, Program in Education, Track in Elementary and Secondary Education/Certification, Boston, MA 02125-3393. Offers M Ed. Part-time and evening/weekend programs available. *Degree requirements:* For master's, comprehensive exam, thesis optional, practicum. *Entrance requirements:* For master's, GRE General Test or MAT, minimum GPA of 3.0, 2 years of teaching experience. *Faculty research:* Anti-bias education, inclusionary curriculum and instruction, creativity and learning, science, technology and society, teaching of reading.

University of Memphis, Graduate School, College of Education, Department of Instruction and Curriculum Leadership, Memphis, TN 38152. Offers early childhood education (MAT, MS, Ed D); elementary education (MAT); instruction and curriculum (MS, Ed D); instruction design and technology (MS, Ed D); middle grades education (MAT); reading (MS, Ed D); secondary education (MAT); special education (MAT, MS, Ed D). *Accreditation:* NCATE (one or more programs are accredited). Part-time programs available. *Faculty:* 30 full-time (18 women), 16 part-time/adjunct (10 women). *Students:* 55 full-time (44 women), 370 part-time (300 women); includes 169 minority (153 Black or African American, non-Hispanic/Latino; 5 American Indian or Alaska Native, non-Hispanic/Latino; 1 Asian, non-Hispanic/Latino; 6 Hispanic/Latino; 4 Two or more races, non-Hispanic/Latino), 7 international. Average age 35. 181 applicants, 84% accepted, 21 enrolled. In 2013, 137 master's, 10 doctorates awarded. Terminal master's awarded for partial completion of doctoral program. *Degree requirements:* For master's, comprehensive exam, thesis or alternative; for doctorate, comprehensive exam, thesis/dissertation. *Entrance requirements:* For master's, GRE General Test, minimum GPA of 2.5; for doctorate, GRE General Test, GRE Subject Test, 2 years of teaching experience. *Application deadline:* For fall admission, 8/1 for domestic students; for spring admission, 12/1 for domestic students. Applications are processed on a rolling basis. Application fee: $35 ($60 for international students). Electronic applications accepted. *Financial support:* In 2013–14, 635 students received support. Research assistantships with full tuition reimbursements available, teaching assistantships with full tuition reimbursements available, career-related internships or fieldwork, Federal Work-Study, institutionally sponsored loans, scholarships/grants, traineeships, and unspecified assistantships available. Support available to part-time students. Financial award application deadline: 2/15; financial award applicants required to submit FAFSA. *Faculty research:* Effective urban teachers, preparation and retention of urban teachers, technology utilization in schools, field-based teacher preparation programs, effective use of online instruction. *Unit head:* Dr. Sandra Cooley-Nichols, Interim Chair, 901-678-2365. *Application contact:* Dr. Sally Blake, Director of Graduate Studies, 901-678-4861.
Website: http://www.memphis.edu/icl/.

University of Michigan–Flint, School of Education and Human Services, Department of Education, Flint, MI 48502-1950. Offers early childhood education (MA); educational technology (MA); elementary education with teaching certification (MA); literacy education (MA); special education (MA). Part-time programs available. *Faculty:* 14 full-time (12 women), 8 part-time/adjunct (4 women). *Students:* 27 full-time (24 women), 215 part-time (186 women); includes 22 minority (20 Black or African American, non-Hispanic/Latino; 2 American Indian or Alaska Native, non-Hispanic/Latino). Average age 35. 63 applicants, 86% accepted, 43 enrolled. In 2013, 91 master's awarded. *Entrance requirements:* For master's, BS with minimum GPA of 3.0. Additional exam requirements/recommendations for international students: Required—TOEFL (minimum score 560 paper-based; 84 iBT), IELTS (minimum score 6.5). *Application deadline:* For fall admission, 8/1 priority date for domestic students, 5/1 priority date for international students; for winter admission, 11/15 priority date for domestic students, 9/15 priority date for international students; for spring admission, 3/15 priority date for domestic students, 1/15 priority date for international students. Application fee: $55. *Expenses:* Contact institution. *Financial support:* Federal Work-Study, scholarships/grants, and unspecified assistantships available. Support available to part-time students. Financial award application deadline: 6/1; financial award applicants required to submit FAFSA. *Unit head:* Dr. Beverly Schumer, Director, 810-424-5215, E-mail: bschumer@umflint.edu. *Application contact:* Beulah Alexander, Executive Secretary, 810-766-6879, Fax: 810-766-6891, E-mail: beulaha@umflint.edu.
Website: http://www.umflint.edu/education/graduate-programs.

University of Minnesota, Twin Cities Campus, Graduate School, College of Education and Human Development, Department of Curriculum and Instruction, Minneapolis, MN 55455-0213. Offers art education (M Ed, MA, PhD); children's literature (M Ed, MA, PhD); curriculum and instruction (MA, PhD); early childhood education (M Ed, PhD); elementary education (M Ed, MA, PhD); English education (MA, PhD); environmental education (M Ed); family education (M Ed, MA, Ed D, PhD); instructional systems and technology (M Ed, MA, PhD); language arts (MA, PhD); language immersion education (Certificate); literacy education (MA); mathematics education (MA, PhD); reading education (MA, PhD); science education (MA, PhD); second languages and cultures education (MA, PhD); social studies education (MA, PhD); teaching (M Ed), including Chinese, earth science, elementary special education, English, English as a second language, French, German, Hebrew, Japanese, life sciences, mathematics, middle school science, science, second languages and cultures, social studies, Spanish; technology enhanced learning (Certificate); writing education (M Ed, MA, PhD). *Faculty:* 29 full-time (16 women). *Students:* 425 full-time (301 women), 220 part-time (153 women); includes 85 minority (21 Black or African American, non-Hispanic/Latino; 6 American Indian or Alaska Native, non-Hispanic/Latino; 42 Asian, non-Hispanic/Latino; 16 Hispanic/Latino), 50 international. Average age 32. 551 applicants, 68% accepted, 340 enrolled. In 2013, 618 master's, 33 doctorates, 6 other advanced degrees awarded. Application fee: $75 ($95 for international students). *Financial support:* In 2013–14, 25 fellowships (averaging $28,500 per year), 23 research assistantships with full tuition reimbursements (averaging $8,082 per year), 81 teaching assistantships with full tuition reimbursements (averaging $9,974 per year) were awarded. *Faculty research:* Teaching and learning; quality of education; influence of cultural, linguistic, social, political, technological and economic factors on teaching, learning and educational research; relationship between educational practice and a democratic and just society. *Total annual research*

expenditures: $272,048. *Unit head:* Dr. Nina Asher, Chair, 612-624-4772, Fax: 612-624-1357, E-mail: nasher@umn.edu. *Application contact:* Dr. Jennifer Engler, Assistant Dean, 612-626-2887, Fax: 612-626-7496, E-mail: engle009@umn.edu.
Website: http://www.cehd.umn.edu/ci.

University of Mississippi, Graduate School, School of Education, Department of Teacher Education, Oxford, MS 38677. Offers curriculum and instruction (MA); elementary education (M Ed, Ed D, Ed S); literacy education (M Ed); secondary education (M Ed, PhD, Ed S); special education (M Ed, PhD, Ed S). *Accreditation:* NCATE. *Faculty:* 42 full-time (29 women), 25 part-time/adjunct (22 women). *Students:* 70 full-time (59 women), 194 part-time (156 women); includes 67 minority (60 Black or African American, non-Hispanic/Latino; 1 Asian, non-Hispanic/Latino; 4 Hispanic/Latino; 2 Two or more races, non-Hispanic/Latino), 1 international. In 2013, 122 master's, 1 doctorate awarded. *Degree requirements:* For master's, thesis (for some programs); for doctorate, one foreign language, thesis/dissertation. *Entrance requirements:* For master's, GRE General Test, minimum GPA of 3.0; for doctorate, GRE General Test. Additional exam requirements/recommendations for international students: Required—TOEFL. *Application deadline:* For fall admission, 7/1 for domestic students; for spring admission, 10/1 for domestic students. Applications are processed on a rolling basis. Application fee: $40. *Financial support:* Scholarships/grants available. Financial award application deadline: 3/1; financial award applicants required to submit FAFSA. *Unit head:* Dr. Susan McClelland, Interim Chair, 662-915-7350. *Application contact:* Dr. Christy M. Wyandt, Associate Dean, 662-915-7474, Fax: 662-915-7577, E-mail: cwyandt@olemiss.edu.
Website: http://education.olemiss.edu/dco/teacher_education.html.

University of Missouri, Graduate School, College of Education, Department of Learning, Teaching and Curriculum, Columbia, MO 65211. Offers agricultural education (M Ed, PhD, Ed S); art education (M Ed, PhD, Ed S); business and office education (M Ed, PhD, Ed S); early childhood education (M Ed, PhD, Ed S); elementary education (M Ed, PhD, Ed S); English education (M Ed, PhD, Ed S); foreign language education (M Ed, PhD, Ed S); health education and promotion (M Ed, PhD); learning and instruction (M Ed); marketing education (M Ed, PhD, Ed S); mathematics education (M Ed, PhD, Ed S); music education (M Ed, PhD, Ed S); reading education (M Ed, PhD, Ed S); science education (M Ed, PhD, Ed S); social studies education (M Ed, PhD, Ed S); vocational education (M Ed, PhD, Ed S). Part-time programs available. *Faculty:* 26 full-time (16 women), 3 part-time/adjunct (2 women). *Students:* 186 full-time (143 women), 197 part-time (172 women); includes 19 minority (4 Black or African American, non-Hispanic/Latino; 4 Asian, non-Hispanic/Latino; 6 Hispanic/Latino; 5 Two or more races, non-Hispanic/Latino), 25 international. Average age 31. 288 applicants, 65% accepted, 160 enrolled. In 2013, 202 master's, 18 doctorates, 7 other advanced degrees awarded. Terminal master's awarded for partial completion of doctoral program. *Degree requirements:* For doctorate, thesis/dissertation. *Entrance requirements:* For master's and Ed S, GRE General Test or MAT, minimum GPA of 3.0; for doctorate, GRE General Test, minimum GPA of 3.0. Additional exam requirements/recommendations for international students: Required—TOEFL (minimum score 600 paper-based; 100 iBT). *Application deadline:* For fall admission, 12/1 priority date for domestic and international students. Applications are processed on a rolling basis. Application fee: $55 ($75 for international students). Electronic applications accepted. *Financial support:* Fellowships, research assistantships, teaching assistantships, institutionally sponsored loans, traineeships, health care benefits, and unspecified assistantships available. Support available to part-time students. *Faculty research:* Curriculum development and research, teacher education, art education, business and marketing, early childhood education, English education, literacy/reading education, mathematics education, music education, science education, social studies education. *Unit head:* Dr. James Tarr, Associate Division Director, 573-882-4034, E-mail: tarrj@missouri.edu. *Application contact:* Fran Colley, Academic Advisor, 573-882-6462, E-mail: colleyf@missouri.edu.
Website: http://education.missouri.edu/LTC/.

University of Missouri–St. Louis, College of Education, Division of Counseling, St. Louis, MO 63121. Offers clinical mental health counseling (M Ed); elementary school counseling (M Ed); secondary school counseling (M Ed). *Accreditation:* ACA; NCATE. Part-time and evening/weekend programs available. *Faculty:* 6 full-time (3 women), 19 part-time/adjunct (13 women). *Students:* 65 full-time (53 women), 131 part-time (108 women); includes 46 minority (32 Black or African American, non-Hispanic/Latino; 1 American Indian or Alaska Native, non-Hispanic/Latino; 3 Asian, non-Hispanic/Latino; 6 Hispanic/Latino; 4 Two or more races, non-Hispanic/Latino), 2 international. Average age 32. 73 applicants, 73% accepted, 37 enrolled. In 2013, 54 master's awarded. *Degree requirements:* For master's, comprehensive exam. *Entrance requirements:* For master's, 3 letters of recommendation. Additional exam requirements/recommendations for international students: Recommended—TOEFL (minimum score 550 paper-based; 79 iBT), IELTS (minimum score 6.5). *Application deadline:* For fall admission, 6/1 for domestic and international students; for spring admission, 10/1 for domestic and international students. Application fee: $50 ($40 for international students). Electronic applications accepted. *Expenses:* Tuition, state resident: full-time $7364; part-time $409.10 per credit hour. Tuition, nonresident: full-time $19,162; part-time $1008.50 per credit hour. *Financial support:* In 2013–14, 1 research assistantship with full and partial tuition reimbursement (averaging $12,500 per year), 2 teaching assistantships with full and partial tuition reimbursements (averaging $8,470 per year) were awarded. Financial award application deadline: 4/1; financial award applicants required to submit FAFSA. *Faculty research:* Vocational interests, self-concept, decision-making factors, developmental differences. *Unit head:* Dr. Mark Pope, Chair, 314-516-5782. *Application contact:* 314-516-5458, Fax: 314-516-6996, E-mail: gradadm@umsl.edu.

University of Missouri–St. Louis, College of Education, Division of Teaching and Learning, St. Louis, MO 63121. Offers autism studies (Certificate); elementary education (M Ed), including early childhood, general, reading; secondary education (M Ed), including curriculum and instruction, general, middle level education, reading, teaching English to speakers of other languages (TESOL); secondary school teaching (Certificate); special education (M Ed), including autism and developmental disabilities, cross-categorical disabilities, early childhood; teaching English to speakers of other languages (Certificate). Part-time and evening/weekend programs available. *Faculty:* 20 full-time (11 women), 1 (woman) part-time/adjunct. *Students:* 42 full-time (33 women), 578 part-time (442 women); includes 152 minority (101 Black or African American, non-Hispanic/Latino; 1 American Indian or Alaska Native, non-Hispanic/Latino; 20 Asian, non-Hispanic/Latino; 23 Hispanic/Latino; 7 Two or more races, non-Hispanic/Latino), 19 international. Average age 29. 245 applicants, 97% accepted, 166 enrolled. In 2013, 219 master's, 14 Certificates awarded. *Degree requirements:* For master's, comprehensive exam. *Entrance requirements:* Additional exam requirements/recommendations for international students: Recommended—TOEFL (minimum score 550 paper-based; 79 iBT), IELTS (minimum score 6.5). *Application deadline:* For fall admission, 7/1 priority date for domestic and international students; for spring admission, 12/1 priority date for domestic and international students. Application fee: $50 ($40 for international students). Electronic applications accepted. *Expenses:* Tuition, state resident: full-time $7364; part-time $409.10 per credit hour. Tuition, nonresident: full-time $19,162; part-time $1008.50 per credit hour. *Financial support:* Application deadline: 4/1; applicants

required to submit FAFSA. *Unit head:* Dr. Patricia Kopetz, Chair, 314-516-5791. *Application contact:* 314-516-5458, Fax: 314-516-6996, E-mail: gadadm@umsl.edu. Website: http://coe.umsl.edu/web/divisions/teach-learn/index.html.

University of Montevallo, College of Education, Program in Elementary Education, Montevallo, AL 35115. Offers M Ed. *Accreditation:* NCATE. Part-time programs available. *Students:* 26 full-time (21 women), 29 part-time (27 women); includes 14 minority (13 Black or African American, non-Hispanic/Latino; 1 Two or more races, non-Hispanic/Latino). In 2013, 26 master's awarded. *Degree requirements:* For master's, comprehensive exam. *Entrance requirements:* For master's, GRE General Test, MAT, minimum undergraduate GPA of 2.5. Additional exam requirements/recommendations for international students: Required—TOEFL (minimum score 550 paper-based). *Application deadline:* For fall admission, 7/15 for domestic students; for spring admission, 11/15 for domestic students. Application fee: $25. *Financial support:* Federal Work-Study, scholarships/grants, and unspecified assistantships available. *Unit head:* Dr. Anna E. McEwan, Dean, 205-665-6360, E-mail: mcewanae@montevallo.edu. *Application contact:* Kevin Thornthwaite, Director, Graduate Admissions and Records, 205-665-6350, E-mail: graduate@montevallo.edu.
Website: http://www.montevallo.edu/education/college-of-education/traditional-masters-degrees/elementary-secondary-p-12-education/.

University of Nebraska at Kearney, Graduate Programs, College of Education, Department of Teacher Education, Kearney, NE 68849-0001. Offers curriculum and instruction (MA Ed), including early childhood education, elementary education, English as a second language, instructional effectiveness, reading/special education, secondary education; instructional technology (MS Ed), including information technology, instructional technology, school librarian; reading PK-12 (MA Ed); special education (MA Ed), including advanced practitioner, gifted, mild/moderate. Part-time and evening/weekend programs available. *Degree requirements:* For master's, comprehensive exam, thesis optional. *Entrance requirements:* For master's, portfolio or GRE. Additional exam requirements/recommendations for international students: Required—TOEFL (minimum score 550 paper-based). Electronic applications accepted.

University of Nebraska at Omaha, Graduate Studies, College of Education, Department of Teacher Education, Program in Elementary Education, Omaha, NE 68182. Offers MS. *Accreditation:* NCATE. Part-time and evening/weekend programs available. *Faculty:* 11 full-time (8 women). *Students:* 5 full-time (4 women), 135 part-time (127 women); includes 15 minority (3 Black or African American, non-Hispanic/Latino; 2 Asian, non-Hispanic/Latino; 8 Hispanic/Latino; 2 Two or more races, non-Hispanic/Latino). Average age 33. 18 applicants, 83% accepted, 12 enrolled. In 2013, 33 master's awarded. *Degree requirements:* For master's, comprehensive exam (for some programs), thesis (for some programs). *Entrance requirements:* For master's, minimum GPA of 3.0, transcripts. Additional exam requirements/recommendations for international students: Required—TOEFL, IELTS, PTE. *Application deadline:* For fall admission, 8/1 priority date for domestic students; for spring admission, 12/1 priority date for domestic students; for summer admission, 6/1 for domestic students. Applications are processed on a rolling basis. Application fee: $45. Electronic applications accepted. *Financial support:* In 2013–14, 3 students received support, including 2 research assistantships with tuition reimbursements available, 1 teaching assistantship with tuition reimbursement available; fellowships, Federal Work-Study, institutionally sponsored loans, scholarships/grants, tuition waivers (full), and unspecified assistantships also available. Support available to part-time students. Financial award application deadline: 3/1. *Unit head:* Dr. Sarah Edwards, Chairperson, 402-554-3512. *Application contact:* Dr. Wilma Kuhlman, Graduate Program Chair, 402-554-3926, E-mail: graduate@unomaha.edu.

University of Nevada, Reno, Graduate School, College of Education, Department of Curriculum, Teaching and Learning, Program in Elementary Education, Reno, NV 89557. Offers M Ed, MA, MS. *Degree requirements:* For master's, thesis optional. *Entrance requirements:* For master's, GRE General Test, minimum GPA of 2.75. Additional exam requirements/recommendations for international students: Required—TOEFL (minimum score 500 paper-based; 61 iBT), IELTS (minimum score 6). Electronic applications accepted. *Faculty research:* Child development, educational trends.

University of New Hampshire, Graduate School, College of Liberal Arts, Department of Education, Program in Elementary Education, Durham, NH 03824. Offers M Ed. Part-time programs available. *Faculty:* 32 full-time. *Students:* 38 full-time (all women), 32 part-time (all women); includes 6 minority (3 Black or African American, non-Hispanic/Latino; 2 Hispanic/Latino; 1 Two or more races, non-Hispanic/Latino). Average age 24. 41 applicants, 85% accepted, 30 enrolled. In 2013, 53 master's awarded. *Degree requirements:* For master's, thesis or alternative. *Entrance requirements:* For master's, GRE General Test. Additional exam requirements/recommendations for international students: Required—TOEFL (minimum score 550 paper-based; 80 iBT). *Application deadline:* For fall admission, 4/1 priority date for domestic students, 4/1 for international students; for spring admission, 11/1 for domestic students. Applications are processed on a rolling basis. Application fee: $65. Electronic applications accepted. *Expenses:* Tuition, state resident: full-time $13,500; part-time $750 per credit hour. Tuition, nonresident: full-time $26,200; part-time $1100 per credit hour. *Required fees:* $1741; $435.25 per term. Tuition and fees vary according to course level, course load, campus/location and program. *Financial support:* In 2013–14, 5 students received support, including 2 teaching assistantships; fellowships, research assistantships, career-related internships or fieldwork, Federal Work-Study, scholarships/grants, and tuition waivers (full and partial) also available. Support available to part-time students. Financial award application deadline: 2/15. *Faculty research:* Pre-service teacher education. *Unit head:* Dr. Mike Middleton, Chairperson, 603-862-7054, E-mail: education.department@unh.edu. *Application contact:* Lisa Wilder, Administrative Assistant, 603-862-2381, E-mail: education.department@unh.edu.
Website: http://www.unh.edu/education.

University of New Mexico, Graduate School, College of Education, Department of Teacher Education, Educational Leadership and Policy, Program in Elementary Education, Albuquerque, NM 87131-2039. Offers math, science, environmental and technology education (MA). Part-time programs available. *Faculty:* 10 full-time (7 women). *Students:* 27 full-time (20 women), 85 part-time (71 women); includes 54 minority (4 Black or African American, non-Hispanic/Latino; 10 American Indian or Alaska Native, non-Hispanic/Latino; 3 Asian, non-Hispanic/Latino; 33 Hispanic/Latino; 2 Native Hawaiian or other Pacific Islander, non-Hispanic/Latino; 2 Two or more races, non-Hispanic/Latino). Average age 34. 50 applicants, 58% accepted, 21 enrolled. In 2013, 102 master's awarded. *Degree requirements:* For master's, comprehensive exam, thesis optional. *Entrance requirements:* For master's, minimum overall GPA of 3.0, some experience working with students, NMTA or teacher's license, 3 letters of reference, letter of intent. Additional exam requirements/recommendations for international students: Required—TOEFL (minimum score 550 paper-based). *Application deadline:* For fall admission, 2/15 for domestic students; for spring admission, 10/1 for domestic students. Application fee: $50. Electronic applications accepted. *Financial support:* In 2013–14, 127 students received support, including 1 fellowship (averaging $2,000 per year); career-related internships or fieldwork, scholarships/grants, and unspecified assistantships also available. Financial award application deadline: 4/15; financial award applicants required to submit FAFSA. *Faculty*

Elementary Education

research: Elementary education, science education, technology education, reflective practice, teacher education. *Unit head:* Dr. Cheryl Torrez, Chair, 505-277-0911, Fax: 505-277-0455, E-mail: ted@unm.edu. *Application contact:* Lea Briggs, Administrative Assistant, 505-277-9439, Fax: 505-277-0455, E-mail: ted@unm.edu.
Website: http://ted.unm.edu.

University of North Alabama, College of Education, Department of Elementary Education, Program in Elementary Education, Florence, AL 35632-0001. Offers MA Ed, Ed S. *Accreditation:* NCATE. Part-time and evening/weekend programs available. *Faculty:* 6 full-time (all women). *Students:* 5 full-time (4 women), 51 part-time (49 women); includes 5 minority (3 Black or African American, non-Hispanic/Latino; 2 American Indian or Alaska Native, non-Hispanic/Latino). Average age 33. 80 applicants, 86% accepted, 45 enrolled. In 2013, 18 master's awarded. *Degree requirements:* For master's, comprehensive exam. *Entrance requirements:* For master's, GRE, MAT, or NTE, minimum GPA of 2.5, Alabama Class B Certificate or equivalent, teaching experience. Additional exam requirements/recommendations for international students: Required—TOEFL (minimum score 550 paper-based; 79 iBT), IELTS (minimum score 6). *Application deadline:* For fall admission, 7/1 priority date for domestic students, 7/1 for international students; for spring admission, 12/1 for domestic and international students. Applications are processed on a rolling basis. Application fee: $25 ($50 for international students). Electronic applications accepted. *Expenses:* Tuition, state resident: full-time $4968; part-time $3312 per year. Tuition, nonresident: full-time $9936; part-time $6624 per year. *Required fees:* $970; $60.33 per credit. $362 per semester. *Financial support:* Federal Work-Study available. Support available to part-time students. Financial award application deadline: 4/1; financial award applicants required to submit FAFSA. *Unit head:* Dr. Victoria W. Hulsey, Chair, 256-765-5024, E-mail: vwhulsey@una.edu. *Application contact:* Russ Darracott, Graduate Admissions Counselor, 256-765-4447, E-mail: erdarracott@una.edu.

The University of North Carolina at Charlotte, The Graduate School, College of Education, Department of Reading and Elementary Education, Charlotte, NC 28223-0001. Offers elementary education (M Ed); reading, language and literacy (M Ed). Part-time and evening/weekend programs available. Postbaccalaureate distance learning degree programs offered (no on-campus study). *Faculty:* 27 full-time (15 women), 3 part-time/adjunct (2 women). *Students:* 16 full-time (15 women), 78 part-time (76 women); includes 12 minority (7 Black or African American, non-Hispanic/Latino; 1 American Indian or Alaska Native, non-Hispanic/Latino; 3 Hispanic/Latino; 1 Two or more races, non-Hispanic/Latino). Average age 31. 45 applicants, 91% accepted, 31 enrolled. In 2013, 10 master's awarded. *Degree requirements:* For master's, thesis or alternative. *Entrance requirements:* For master's, GRE or MAT. Additional exam requirements/recommendations for international students: Required—TOEFL (minimum score 557 paper-based; 83 iBT). *Application deadline:* For fall admission, 5/1 priority date for domestic students, 5/1 for international students; for spring admission, 10/1 priority date for domestic students, 10/1 for international students. Applications are processed on a rolling basis. Application fee: $75. Electronic applications accepted. *Expenses:* Tuition, state resident: full-time $3522. Tuition, nonresident: full-time $16,051. *Required fees:* $2585. Tuition and fees vary according to course load and program. *Financial support:* In 2013–14, 1 student received support, including 1 teaching assistantship (averaging $7,500 per year); career-related internships or fieldwork, institutionally sponsored loans, scholarships/grants, and unspecified assistantships also available. Support available to part-time students. Financial award application deadline: 4/1; financial award applicants required to submit FAFSA. *Total annual research expenditures:* $81,584. *Unit head:* Dr. Janice Hinson, Chair, 704-687-8019, Fax: 704-687-1631, E-mail: jhinso42@uncc.edu. *Application contact:* Kathy B. Giddings, Director of Graduate Admissions, 704-687-5503, Fax: 704-687-1668, E-mail: gradadm@uncc.edu.
Website: http://education.uncc.edu/reel.

The University of North Carolina at Greensboro, Graduate School, School of Education, Department of Curriculum and Instruction, Program in Curriculum and Teaching, Greensboro, NC 27412-5001. Offers higher education (PhD); teacher education and development (PhD). *Accreditation:* NCATE. *Degree requirements:* For doctorate, comprehensive exam, thesis/dissertation. *Entrance requirements:* For doctorate, GRE General Test. Additional exam requirements/recommendations for international students: Required—TOEFL. Electronic applications accepted.

The University of North Carolina at Pembroke, Graduate Studies, School of Education, Program in Elementary Education, Pembroke, NC 28372-1510. Offers MA Ed. *Accreditation:* NCATE. Part-time and evening/weekend programs available. Postbaccalaureate distance learning degree programs offered. *Degree requirements:* For master's, comprehensive exam, thesis optional. *Entrance requirements:* For master's, GRE General Test or MAT, minimum GPA of 3.0 in major, 2.5 overall; teaching license; two years of full-time teaching experience (recommended). Additional exam requirements/recommendations for international students: Required—TOEFL.

The University of North Carolina Wilmington, Watson College of Education, Department of Early Childhood, Elementary, Middle, Literacy and Special Education, Wilmington, NC 28403-3297. Offers MAT. *Accreditation:* NCATE. Part-time and evening/weekend programs available. *Faculty:* 21 full-time (17 women). *Students:* 47 full-time (36 women), 13 part-time (11 women); includes 9 minority (5 Black or African American, non-Hispanic/Latino; 2 Hispanic/Latino; 2 Two or more races, non-Hispanic/Latino), 3 international. Average age 31. 36 applicants, 97% accepted, 33 enrolled. In 2013, 24 master's awarded. *Degree requirements:* For master's, comprehensive exam. *Entrance requirements:* For master's, GRE General Test, MAT, minimum B average in upper-division undergraduate course work. *Application deadline:* For fall admission, 6/1 for domestic students. Applications are processed on a rolling basis. Application fee: $60. *Expenses:* Tuition, state resident: full-time $4163. Tuition, nonresident: full-time $16,098. *Financial support:* Career-related internships or fieldwork, Federal Work-Study, and unspecified assistantships available. Support available to part-time students. Financial award application deadline: 3/15. *Unit head:* Dr. Tracy Hargrove, Chair, 910-962-3240, Fax: 910-962-3988, E-mail: hargrovet@uncw.edu. *Application contact:* Dr. Ron Vetter, Dean, Graduate School, 910-962-3224, Fax: 910-962-3787, E-mail: vetterr@uncw.edu.

University of North Dakota, Graduate School, College of Education and Human Development, Program in Elementary Education, Grand Forks, ND 58202. Offers M Ed, MS. *Accreditation:* NCATE. Part-time programs available. Postbaccalaureate distance learning degree programs offered (minimal on-campus study). *Degree requirements:* For master's, comprehensive exam, thesis or alternative. *Entrance requirements:* For master's, minimum GPA of 3.0. Additional exam requirements/recommendations for international students: Required—TOEFL (minimum score 550 paper-based; 79 iBT), IELTS (minimum score 6.5). Electronic applications accepted. *Faculty research:* Whole language, multicultural education, child-focused learning, experiential science, cooperative learning.

University of North Dakota, Graduate School, College of Education and Human Development, Teaching and Learning Program, Grand Forks, ND 58202. Offers elementary education (Ed D, PhD); measurement and statistics (Ed D, PhD); secondary education (Ed D, PhD); special education (Ed D, PhD). *Accreditation:* NCATE. Postbaccalaureate distance learning degree programs offered (minimal on-campus study). *Degree requirements:* For doctorate, comprehensive exam, thesis/dissertation, final exam. *Entrance requirements:* For doctorate, minimum GPA of 3.5. Additional exam requirements/recommendations for international students: Required—TOEFL (minimum score 550 paper-based; 79 iBT), IELTS (minimum score 6.5). Electronic applications accepted.

University of Northern Iowa, Graduate College, College of Education, Department of Curriculum and Instruction, MAE Program in Elementary Education, Cedar Falls, IA 50614. Offers curriculum and instruction (MAE). Part-time and evening/weekend programs available. *Students:* 23 part-time (20 women). 1 applicant. In 2013, 12 master's awarded. *Degree requirements:* For master's, comprehensive exam, thesis or alternative. *Entrance requirements:* For master's, minimum GPA of 3.0. Additional exam requirements/recommendations for international students: Required—TOEFL (minimum score 500 paper-based; 61 iBT). *Application deadline:* For fall admission, 8/1 priority date for domestic students. Applications are processed on a rolling basis. Application fee: $50 ($70 for international students). *Financial support:* Career-related internships or fieldwork, Federal Work-Study, and tuition waivers (full and partial) available. Support available to part-time students. Financial award application deadline: 2/1. *Unit head:* Dr. Sarah Montgomery, Coordinator, 319-273-6757, Fax: 319-273-5886, E-mail: sarah.montgomery@uni.edu. *Application contact:* Laurie S. Russell, Record Analyst, 319-273-2623, Fax: 319-273-2885, E-mail: laurie.russell@uni.edu.
Website: http://www.uni.edu/continuinged/distance/programs/degrees/elementary-education-mae.

University of North Florida, College of Education and Human Services, Department of Childhood Education, Jacksonville, FL 32224. Offers literacy K-12 (M Ed); professional education - elementary education (M Ed); TESOL K-12 (M Ed). *Accreditation:* NCATE. Part-time and evening/weekend programs available. *Faculty:* 10 full-time (8 women). *Students:* 11 full-time (10 women), 24 part-time (18 women); includes 6 minority (1 Black or African American, non-Hispanic/Latino; 1 Asian, non-Hispanic/Latino; 4 Hispanic/Latino), 1 international. Average age 33. 24 applicants, 79% accepted, 10 enrolled. In 2013, 21 master's awarded. *Entrance requirements:* For master's, GRE General Test, minimum GPA of 3.0 in last 60 hours, 3 letters of recommendation, interview. Additional exam requirements/recommendations for international students: Required—TOEFL (minimum score 500 paper-based). *Application deadline:* For fall admission, 7/1 priority date for domestic students, 5/1 for international students; for spring admission, 11/1 priority date for domestic students, 10/1 for international students. Application fee: $30. Electronic applications accepted. *Expenses:* Tuition, state resident: full-time $9794; part-time $408.10 per credit hour. Tuition, nonresident: full-time $22,383; part-time $932.61 per credit hour. *Required fees:* $2020; $84.20 per credit hour. Tuition and fees vary according to course load and program. *Financial support:* In 2013–14, 8 students received support, including 2 research assistantships (averaging $5,183 per year); Federal Work-Study, tuition waivers (partial), and unspecified assistantships also available. Support available to part-time students. Financial award application deadline: 4/1; financial award applicants required to submit FAFSA. *Faculty research:* The social context of and processes in learning, inter-disciplinary instruction, cross-cultural conflict resolution, the Vygotskian perspective on literacy diagnosis and instruction, performance poetry and teaching the language arts through drama. *Total annual research expenditures:* $2,158. *Unit head:* Dr. John Venn, Chair, 904-620-5352, Fax: 904-620-1025, E-mail: j.venn@unf.edu. *Application contact:* Dr. Amanda Pascale, Director, The Graduate School, 904-620-1360, Fax: 904-620-1362, E-mail: graduateschool@unf.edu.
Website: http://www.unf.edu/coehs/celt/.

University of Oklahoma, Jeannine Rainbolt College of Education, Department of Instructional Leadership and Academic Curriculum, Norman, OK 73072. Offers communication, culture and pedagogy for Hispanic populations in educational settings (Graduate Certificate); instructional leadership and academic curriculum (M Ed, PhD), including bilingual education (PhD), early childhood education, elementary education, English education, instructional leadership, mathematics education, reading education, science education, science, technology, engineering and mathematics education (M Ed), secondary education, social studies education, teacher education (M Ed), world language education (M Ed). *Accreditation:* NCATE. Part-time and evening/weekend programs available. Postbaccalaureate distance learning degree programs offered (no on-campus study). *Faculty:* 22 full-time (15 women), 1 (woman) part-time/adjunct. *Students:* 64 full-time (49 women), 103 part-time (81 women); includes 33 minority (8 Black or African American, non-Hispanic/Latino; 9 American Indian or Alaska Native, non-Hispanic/Latino; 5 Asian, non-Hispanic/Latino; 4 Hispanic/Latino; 1 Native Hawaiian or other Pacific Islander, non-Hispanic/Latino; 6 Two or more races, non-Hispanic/Latino), 10 international. Average age 34. 50 applicants, 84% accepted, 36 enrolled. In 2013, 26 master's, 11 doctorates awarded. Terminal master's awarded for partial completion of doctoral program. *Degree requirements:* For master's, comprehensive exam (for some programs), thesis (for some programs); for doctorate, comprehensive exam, thesis/dissertation. *Entrance requirements:* For master's, essay; for doctorate, GRE, 3 recommendation letters; autobiography, statement of objectives; essay on chosen major; transcripts; writing sample. Additional exam requirements/recommendations for international students: Required—TOEFL (minimum score 79 iBT). *Application deadline:* For fall admission, 4/30 for domestic and international students; for spring admission, 10/31 for domestic and international students; for summer admission, 3/15 for domestic and international students. Applications are processed on a rolling basis. Application fee: $50 ($100 for international students). Electronic applications accepted. *Expenses:* Tuition, state resident: full-time $4205; part-time $175.20 per credit hour. Tuition, nonresident: full-time $16,205; part-time $675.20 per credit hour. *Required fees:* $2745; $103.85 per credit hour. $126.50 per semester. *Financial support:* In 2013–14, 98 students received support, including 10 research assistantships with partial tuition reimbursements available (averaging $10,671 per year), 7 teaching assistantships with partial tuition reimbursements available (averaging $10,753 per year); Federal Work-Study, institutionally sponsored loans, scholarships/grants, and unspecified assistantships also available. Support available to part-time students. Financial award application deadline: 6/1; financial award applicants required to submit FAFSA. *Total annual research expenditures:* $1 million. *Unit head:* Dr. Stacy Reeder, Chair/Graduate Liaison, 405-325-1498, Fax: 405-325-4061, E-mail: reeder@ou.edu. *Application contact:* Lynn Crussel, Graduate Programs Officer, 405-325-1498, Fax: 405-325-4061, E-mail: lcrussel@ou.edu.
Website: http://education.ou.edu/departments/ilac.

University of Pennsylvania, Graduate School of Education, Division of Teaching, Learning, and Leadership, Teacher Education Program, Philadelphia, PA 19104. Offers elementary education (MS Ed); secondary education (MS Ed). *Students:* 59 full-time (42 women); includes 15 minority (2 Black or African American, non-Hispanic/Latino; 10 Asian, non-Hispanic/Latino; 2 Hispanic/Latino; 1 Two or more races, non-Hispanic/Latino), 1 international. 157 applicants, 70% accepted, 66 enrolled. In 2013, 80 master's awarded. *Degree requirements:* For master's, comprehensive exam or portfolio. *Entrance requirements:* For master's, GRE General Test, MAT. *Application deadline:* For fall admission, 12/15 priority date for domestic students. Applications are processed on a rolling basis. Application fee: $70. Electronic applications accepted. *Expenses:* Contact institution. *Financial support:* Fellowships available. Financial award applicants required to submit FAFSA. *Unit head:* Dr. Andrew Porter, Dean, 215-898-7014.

Application contact: Maureen Cotterill, Program Manager, 215-898-7364, E-mail: maureenc@gse.upenn.edu.
Website: http://www.gse.upenn.edu/tll.

University of Phoenix–Bay Area Campus, College of Education, San Jose, CA 95134-1805. Offers administration and supervision (MA Ed); adult education and training (MA Ed); early childhood education (MA Ed); education (Ed S); educational leadership (Ed D); elementary teacher education (MA Ed); higher education administration (PhD); secondary teacher education (MA Ed); special education (MA Ed); teacher leadership (MA Ed). Evening/weekend programs available. Postbaccalaureate distance learning degree programs offered (no on-campus study). *Degree requirements:* For master's, thesis (for some programs). *Entrance requirements:* For master's, minimum undergraduate GPA of 2.5, 3 years of work experience. Additional exam requirements/recommendations for international students: Required—TOEFL (minimum score 550 paper-based; 79 iBT). Electronic applications accepted.

University of Phoenix–Central Valley Campus, College of Education, Fresno, CA 93720-1562. Offers curriculum and instruction (MA Ed); curriculum and instruction-computer education (MA Ed); elementary teacher education (MA Ed); secondary teacher education (MA Ed).

University of Phoenix–Chattanooga Campus, College of Education, Chattanooga, TN 37421-3707. Offers administration and supervision (MA Ed); curriculum and instruction (MA Ed); elementary teacher education (MA Ed); secondary teacher education (MA Ed).

University of Phoenix–Denver Campus, College of Education, Lone Tree, CO 80124-5453. Offers administration and supervision (MAEd); curriculum instruction (MAEd); elementary teacher education (MAEd); school counseling (MSC); secondary teacher education (MAEd). Evening/weekend programs available. *Degree requirements:* For master's, thesis (for some programs). *Entrance requirements:* For master's, minimum undergraduate GPA of 2.5, 3 years work experience. Additional exam requirements/recommendations for international students: Required—TOEFL (minimum score 550 paper-based; 79 iBT). Electronic applications accepted.

University of Phoenix–Hawaii Campus, College of Education, Honolulu, HI 96813-4317. Offers administration and supervision (MA Ed); curriculum and instruction (MA Ed); elementary education (MA Ed); secondary education (MA Ed); special education (MA Ed); teacher education for elementary licensure (MA Ed). Evening/weekend programs available. *Degree requirements:* For master's, thesis (for some programs). *Entrance requirements:* For master's, minimum undergraduate GPA of 2.5, 3 years of work experience. Additional exam requirements/recommendations for international students: Required—TOEFL (minimum score 550 paper-based; 79 iBT). Electronic applications accepted.

University of Phoenix–Idaho Campus, College of Education, Meridian, ID 83642-5114. Offers administration and supervision (MA Ed); curriculum and instruction (MA Ed); elementary teacher education (MA Ed); secondary teacher education (MA Ed). Evening/weekend programs available. *Degree requirements:* For master's, thesis (for some programs). *Entrance requirements:* For master's, minimum undergraduate GPA of 2.5, 3 years of work experience. Additional exam requirements/recommendations for international students: Required—TOEFL (minimum score 550 paper-based). Electronic applications accepted.

University of Phoenix–Indianapolis Campus, College of Education, Indianapolis, IN 46250-932. Offers elementary teacher education (MA Ed); secondary teacher education (MA Ed).

University of Phoenix–Las Vegas Campus, College of Education, Las Vegas, NV 89135. Offers administration and supervision (MA Ed); curriculum and instruction (MA Ed); school counseling (MSC); teacher education-elementary licensure (MA Ed). Evening/weekend programs available. *Degree requirements:* For master's, thesis (for some programs). *Entrance requirements:* For master's, minimum undergraduate GPA of 2.5, 3 years of work experience. Additional exam requirements/recommendations for international students: Required—TOEFL (minimum score 550 paper-based; 79 iBT). Electronic applications accepted.

University of Phoenix–Memphis Campus, College of Education, Cordova, TN 38018. Offers administration and supervision (MA Ed); curriculum and instruction (MA Ed); elementary teacher education (MA Ed); secondary teacher education (MA Ed).

University of Phoenix–Nashville Campus, College of Education, Nashville, TN 37214-5048. Offers administration and supervision (MA Ed); curriculum and instruction (MA Ed); elementary teacher education (MA Ed); secondary teacher education (MA Ed). Evening/weekend programs available. *Degree requirements:* For master's, thesis (for some programs). *Entrance requirements:* For master's, minimum undergraduate GPA of 2.5, 3 years work experience. Additional exam requirements/recommendations for international students: Required—TOEFL (minimum score 500 paper-based; 79 iBT). Electronic applications accepted.

University of Phoenix–New Mexico Campus, College of Education, Albuquerque, NM 87113-1570. Offers administration and supervision (MAEd); curriculum and instruction (MAEd); elementary teacher education (MAEd); school counseling (MSC); secondary teacher education (MAEd). Evening/weekend programs available. *Degree requirements:* For master's, thesis (for some programs). *Entrance requirements:* For master's, minimum undergraduate GPA of 2.5, 3 years of work experience. Additional exam requirements/recommendations for international students: Required—TOEFL (minimum score 550 paper-based; 79 iBT). Electronic applications accepted.

University of Phoenix–North Florida Campus, College of Education, Jacksonville, FL 32216-0959. Offers administration and supervision (MA Ed); curriculum and instruction (MA Ed), including computer education, mathematics education; early childhood education (MA Ed); elementary teacher education (MA Ed); secondary teacher education (MA Ed). Evening/weekend programs available. *Degree requirements:* For master's, thesis (for some programs). *Entrance requirements:* For master's, 3 years of work experience, minimum undergraduate GPA of 2.5. Additional exam requirements/recommendations for international students: Required—TOEFL (minimum score 550 paper-based; 49 iBT). Electronic applications accepted.

University of Phoenix–Omaha Campus, College of Education, Omaha, NE 68154-5240. Offers administration and supervision (MA Ed); curriculum and instruction (MA Ed), including adult education, computer education, curriculum and instruction, English and language arts education, English as a second language, mathematics education; elementary teacher education (MA Ed); secondary teacher education (MA Ed); special education (MA Ed).

University of Phoenix–Online Campus, College of Education, Phoenix, AZ 85034-7209. Offers administration and supervision (MAEd, Certificate); adult education and training (MAEd); curriculum and instruction (MAEd), including computer education, curriculum and instruction, English as a second language, language arts, mathematics, reading; early childhood education (MAEd); educational studies (MAEd); elementary teacher education (MAEd), including early childhood, elementary teacher education, high school middle level, middle level; principal licensure (Certificate); secondary teacher education (MAEd); special education (MAEd, Certificate); teacher education (MAEd), including middle level generalist; teacher education middle level mathematics (MAEd), including middle level mathematics; teacher education middle level science (MAEd), including middle level science; teacher education secondary mathematics (MAEd); teacher education secondary science (MAEd); teacher leadership (MAEd); teachers of English learners (Certificate); transition to teaching (Certificate), including elementary education, secondary education. *Accreditation:* Teacher Education Accreditation Council. Evening/weekend programs available. Postbaccalaureate distance learning degree programs offered. *Entrance requirements:* Additional exam requirements/recommendations for international students: Required—TOEFL, TOEIC (Test of English as an International Communication), Berlitz Online English Proficiency Exam, PTE, or IELTS. Electronic applications accepted. *Expenses:* Contact institution.

University of Phoenix–Oregon Campus, College of Education, Tigard, OR 97223. Offers curriculum and instruction (MA Ed); early childhood education (MA Ed); elementary education (MA Ed), including early childhood specialization, middle level specialization; secondary education (MA Ed). Evening/weekend programs available. *Degree requirements:* For master's, thesis (for some programs). *Entrance requirements:* For master's, minimum undergraduate GPA of 2.5, 3 years work experience. Additional exam requirements/recommendations for international students: Required—TOEFL (minimum score 550 paper-based; 79 iBT). Electronic applications accepted.

University of Phoenix–Phoenix Campus, College of Education, Tempe, AZ 85282-2371. Offers administration and supervision (MA Ed); adult education and training (MA Ed); curriculum and instruction reading (MA Ed); early childhood education (MA Ed); education studies (MA Ed); elementary teacher education (MA Ed); secondary teacher education (MA Ed); special education (MA Ed); teacher leadership (MA Ed). Evening/weekend programs available. Postbaccalaureate distance learning degree programs offered. *Entrance requirements:* Additional exam requirements/recommendations for international students: Required—TOEFL, TOEIC (Test of English as an International Communication), Berlitz Online English Proficiency Exam, PTE, or IELTS. Electronic applications accepted. *Expenses:* Contact institution.

University of Phoenix–Sacramento Valley Campus, College of Education, Sacramento, CA 95833-3632. Offers adult education (MA Ed); curriculum instruction (MA Ed); elementary teacher education (MA Ed); secondary teacher education (MA Ed); teacher education (Certificate). Evening/weekend programs available. *Degree requirements:* For master's, thesis (for some programs). *Entrance requirements:* For master's, 3 years of work experience, minimum undergraduate GPA of 2.5. Additional exam requirements/recommendations for international students: Required—TOEFL (minimum score 550 paper-based; 79 iBT). Electronic applications accepted.

University of Phoenix–San Diego Campus, College of Education, San Diego, CA 92123. Offers curriculum and instruction (MA Ed), including computer education, curriculum and instruction, English as a second language; elementary teacher education (MA Ed); secondary teacher education (MA Ed). Evening/weekend programs available. *Degree requirements:* For master's, thesis (for some programs). *Entrance requirements:* For master's, 3 years of work experience, minimum undergraduate GPA of 3.0. Additional exam requirements/recommendations for international students: Required—TOEFL (minimum score 550 paper-based; 79 iBT). Electronic applications accepted.

University of Phoenix–Southern Arizona Campus, College of Education, Tucson, AZ 85711. Offers administration and supervision (MA Ed); adult education and training (MA Ed); curriculum instruction (MA Ed); educational counseling (MA Ed); elementary teacher education (MA Ed); school counseling (MSC); secondary teacher education (MA Ed); special education (MA Ed, Certificate). Evening/weekend programs available. *Degree requirements:* For master's, thesis (for some programs). *Entrance requirements:* For master's, minimum undergraduate GPA of 2.5, 3 years of work experience. Additional exam requirements/recommendations for international students: Required—TOEFL (minimum score 550 paper-based; 79 iBT). Electronic applications accepted.

University of Phoenix–Southern California Campus, College of Education, Costa Mesa, CA 92626. Offers administration and supervision (MA Ed, Certificate); adult education and training (MA Ed); educational studies (MA Ed); elementary teacher education (MA Ed); secondary teacher education (MA Ed); teacher leadership (MA Ed); teachers of English learners (Certificate). Evening/weekend programs available. Postbaccalaureate distance learning degree programs offered. *Entrance requirements:* Additional exam requirements/recommendations for international students: Required—TOEFL, TOEIC (Test of English as an International Communication), Berlitz Online English Proficiency Exam, PTE, or IELTS. Electronic applications accepted. *Expenses:* Contact institution.

University of Phoenix–Southern Colorado Campus, College of Education, Colorado Springs, CO 80903. Offers administration and supervision (MA Ed); curriculum and instruction (MA Ed); elementary teacher education (MA Ed); principal licensure certification (Certificate); school counseling (MSC); secondary teacher education (MA Ed). Evening/weekend programs available. *Degree requirements:* For master's, thesis (for some programs). *Entrance requirements:* For master's, minimum undergraduate GPA of 2.5, 3 years of work experience. Additional exam requirements/recommendations for international students: Required—TOEFL (minimum score 550 paper-based; 79 iBT). Electronic applications accepted.

University of Phoenix–South Florida Campus, College of Education, Miramar, FL 33030. Offers administration and supervision (MA Ed); curriculum and instruction (MA Ed), including computer education, curriculum and instruction, mathematics education; early childhood education (MA Ed); elementary teacher education (MA Ed); secondary teacher education (MA Ed). Evening/weekend programs available. *Degree requirements:* For master's, thesis (for some programs). *Entrance requirements:* For master's, 3 years of work experience, minimum undergraduate GPA of 2.5. Additional exam requirements/recommendations for international students: Required—TOEFL (minimum score 550 paper-based; 79 iBT). Electronic applications accepted.

University of Phoenix–Utah Campus, College of Education, Salt Lake City, UT 84123-4617. Offers administration and supervision (MA Ed); curriculum and instruction (MA Ed); elementary teacher education (MA Ed); school counseling (MSC); secondary teacher education (MA Ed); special education (MA Ed). Evening/weekend programs available. *Degree requirements:* For master's, thesis (for some programs). *Entrance requirements:* For master's, minimum undergraduate GPA of 2.5, 3 years work experience. Additional exam requirements/recommendations for international students: Required—TOEFL (minimum score 550 paper-based; 79 iBT). Electronic applications accepted.

University of Phoenix–Washington D.C. Campus, College of Education, Washington, DC 20001. Offers administration and supervision (MA Ed); adult education and training (MA Ed); computer education (MA Ed); curriculum and instruction (MA Ed, Ed D); early childhood education (MA Ed); education (Ed S); educational leadership (Ed D); educational technology (Ed D); elementary teacher education (MA Ed); English and language arts education (MA Ed); English as a second language (MA Ed); higher education administration (PhD); mathematics education (MA Ed); secondary teacher education (MA Ed); special education (MA Ed); teacher leadership (MA Ed).

University of Phoenix–West Florida Campus, College of Education, Temple Terrace, FL 33637. Offers administration and supervision (MA Ed); curriculum and instruction

(MA Ed), including computer education, curriculum and instruction, mathematics education; curriculum and technology (MA Ed); early childhood education (MA Ed); elementary teacher education (MA Ed); secondary teacher education (MA Ed). Evening/weekend programs available. *Degree requirements:* For master's, thesis (for some programs). *Entrance requirements:* For master's, 3 years of work experience, minimum undergraduate GPA of 2.5. Additional exam requirements/recommendations for international students: Required—TOEFL (minimum score 550 paper-based; 79 iBT).

University of Pittsburgh, School of Education, Department of Instruction and Learning, Program in Elementary Education, Pittsburgh, PA 15260. Offers M Ed, MAT. *Students:* 4 full-time (all women), 20 part-time (19 women); includes 6 minority (4 Black or African American, non-Hispanic/Latino; 1 Asian, non-Hispanic/Latino; 1 Two or more races, non-Hispanic/Latino). Average age 31. 13 applicants, 92% accepted, 8 enrolled. In 2013, 54 master's awarded. *Degree requirements:* For master's, thesis. *Entrance requirements:* For master's, PRAXIS I. Additional exam requirements/recommendations for international students: Required—TOEFL. *Application deadline:* For fall admission, 2/1 for domestic students. Application fee: $50. Electronic applications accepted. *Expenses:* Tuition, state resident: full-time $19,964; part-time $807 per credit. Tuition, nonresident: full-time $32,686; part-time $1337 per credit. *Required fees:* $740; $200. Tuition and fees vary according to program. *Financial support:* In 2013–14, fellowships (averaging $1,000 per year) were awarded; career-related internships or fieldwork, Federal Work-Study, traineeships, and tuition waivers (partial) also available. Support available to part-time students. Financial award application deadline: 3/15; financial award applicants required to submit FAFSA. *Unit head:* Dr. Richard Donato, Chairman, 412-624-7248, Fax: 412-648-7081, E-mail: donato@pitt.edu. *Application contact:* Dr. Marjie Schermer, Graduate Enrollment Manager, 412-648-2230, Fax: 412-648-1899, E-mail: soeinfo@pitt.edu.

University of Pittsburgh, School of Education, Department of Instruction and Learning, Program in Special Education, Pittsburgh, PA 15260. Offers applied behavior analysis (M Ed); combined studies in early childhood and special education (M Ed); early education of disabled students (M Ed); education of students with mental and physical disabilities (M Ed); general special education (M Ed); special education (Ed D, PhD); special education teacher preparation K-8 (M Ed); special education with academic instruction certification (M Ed); vision studies (M Ed). Part-time and evening/weekend programs available. *Students:* 72 full-time (66 women), 91 part-time (83 women); includes 8 minority (3 Black or African American, non-Hispanic/Latino; 1 Asian, non-Hispanic/Latino; 1 Hispanic/Latino; 3 Two or more races, non-Hispanic/Latino). 3 international. Average age 30. 91 applicants, 85% accepted, 56 enrolled. In 2013, 68 master's, 4 doctorates awarded. *Degree requirements:* For master's, thesis; for doctorate, thesis/dissertation. *Entrance requirements:* For master's, PRAXIS I; for doctorate, GRE General Test. Additional exam requirements/recommendations for international students: Required—TOEFL. *Application deadline:* For fall admission, 2/1 priority date for domestic students; for spring admission, 11/1 priority date for domestic students. Applications are processed on a rolling basis. Application fee: $50. *Expenses:* Tuition, state resident: full-time $19,964; part-time $807 per credit. Tuition, nonresident: full-time $32,686; part-time $1337 per credit. *Required fees:* $740; $200. Tuition and fees vary according to program. *Financial support:* Research assistantships, teaching assistantships, career-related internships or fieldwork, Federal Work-Study, and tuition waivers (partial) available. Support available to part-time students. Financial award application deadline: 3/15; financial award applicants required to submit FAFSA. *Unit head:* Dr. Richard Donato, Chairman, 412-624-7248, Fax: 412-648-7081, E-mail: donato@pitt.edu. *Application contact:* Norma Ann McMichael, Graduate Enrollment Manager, 412-648-2230, Fax: 412-648-1899, E-mail: soeinfo@pitt.edu. Website: http://www.education.pitt.edu/AcademicDepartments/InstructionLearning/Programs/GeneralSpecialEducation.aspx.

University of Puget Sound, Graduate Studies, School of Education, Program in Teaching, Tacoma, WA 98416. Offers elementary education (MAT); secondary education (MAT). *Accreditation:* NASM. *Degree requirements:* For master's, capstone course. *Entrance requirements:* For master's, GRE General Test, WEST-B, WEST-E in content area, minimum baccalaureate GPA of 3.0. Additional exam requirements/recommendations for international students: Required—TOEFL (minimum score 550 paper-based; 90 iBT). Electronic applications accepted. *Expenses:* Contact institution. *Faculty research:* Mathematics education, professional development, social studies education, gender studies.

University of Rhode Island, Graduate School, College of Human Science and Services, School of Education, Kingston, RI 02881. Offers adult education (MA); education (PhD); elementary education (MA); music education (MM); reading education (MA); secondary education (MA); special education (MA); MS/PhD. *Accreditation:* NCATE. Part-time and evening/weekend programs available. *Faculty:* 16 full-time (9 women). *Students:* 64 full-time (48 women), 91 part-time (68 women); includes 17 minority (8 Black or African American, non-Hispanic/Latino; 2 American Indian or Alaska Native, non-Hispanic/Latino; 2 Asian, non-Hispanic/Latino; 3 Hispanic/Latino; 2 Two or more races, non-Hispanic/Latino), 6 international. In 2013, 47 master's, 11 doctorates awarded. *Degree requirements:* For master's, comprehensive exam (for some programs), thesis optional; for doctorate, comprehensive exam, thesis/dissertation. *Entrance requirements:* For master's, 2 letters of recommendation; interview (for special education applicants); for doctorate, GRE, 3 letters of recommendation, resume. Additional exam requirements/recommendations for international students: Required—TOEFL (minimum score 600 paper-based; 100 iBT). *Application deadline:* For fall admission, 1/31 for domestic and international students. Application fee: $65. Electronic applications accepted. *Expenses:* Tuition, state resident: full-time $11,532; part-time $641 per credit. Tuition, nonresident: full-time $23,606; part-time $1311 per credit. *Required fees:* $1388; $36 per credit. $35 per semester. One-time fee: $130. *Financial support:* In 2013–14, 2 research assistantships with full and partial tuition reimbursements (averaging $11,883 per year), 4 teaching assistantships with full and partial tuition reimbursements (averaging $8,488 per year) were awarded; career-related internships or fieldwork also available. Financial award application deadline: 1/31; financial award applicants required to submit FAFSA. *Total annual research expenditures:* $1.1 million. *Unit head:* Dr. David Byrd, Director, 401-874-5484, Fax: 401-874-5471, E-mail: dbyrd@uri.edu. *Application contact:* Graduate Admissions, 401-874-2872, E-mail: gradadm@etal.uri.edu. Website: http://www.uri.edu/hss/education/.

University of St. Francis, College of Education, Joliet, IL 60435-6169. Offers educational leadership (MS, Ed D); elementary education (M Ed); higher education (MS); reading (MS); secondary education (M Ed), including English education, math education, science education, social studies education, visual arts education; special education (M Ed); teaching and learning (MS). *Accreditation:* NCATE. Part-time and evening/weekend programs available. Postbaccalaureate distance learning degree programs offered (no on-campus study). *Faculty:* 10 full-time (8 women), 34 part-time/adjunct (25 women). *Students:* 14 full-time (13 women), 250 part-time (183 women); includes 34 minority (20 Black or African American, non-Hispanic/Latino; 1 American Indian or Alaska Native, non-Hispanic/Latino; 13 Hispanic/Latino), 1 international. Average age 36. 133 applicants, 62% accepted, 71 enrolled. In 2013, 147 master's awarded. *Degree requirements:* For doctorate, thesis/dissertation. *Entrance*

requirements: For doctorate, master's degree, IL Type 75 or Principal's endorsement, interview, minimum undergraduate GPA of 3.0, professional portfolio, letter of recommendation. Additional exam requirements/recommendations for international students: Required—TOEFL (minimum score 550 paper-based; 79 iBT), IELTS (minimum score 6.5). *Application deadline:* Applications are processed on a rolling basis. Application fee: $30. Electronic applications accepted. Application fee is waived when completed online. *Expenses:* Contact institution. *Financial support:* In 2013–14, 10 students received support. Scholarships/grants, tuition waivers (partial), and unspecified assistantships available. Support available to part-time students. Financial award applicants required to submit FAFSA. *Unit head:* Dr. John Gambro, Dean, 815-740-3829, Fax: 815-740-2264, E-mail: jgambro@stfrancis.edu. *Application contact:* Sandra Sloka, Director of Admissions for Graduate and Degree Completion Programs, 800-735-7500, Fax: 815-740-3431, E-mail: ssloka@stfrancis.edu. Website: http://www.stfrancis.edu/academics/college-of-education/.

University of Saint Mary, Graduate Programs, Program in Elementary Education, Leavenworth, KS 66048-5082. Offers MA. *Students:* 27 full-time (18 women); includes 4 minority (2 Black or African American, non-Hispanic/Latino; 2 Hispanic/Latino). *Entrance requirements:* For master's, PPST, minimum GPA of 2.75, interview, essay, two letters of reference. *Expenses: Tuition:* Part-time $550 per credit hour. *Application contact:* Dr. Ron Logan, Graduate Dean, 913-345-8288, Fax: 913-345-2802, E-mail: loganr@stmary.edu.

University of St. Thomas, Graduate Studies, School of Education, Department of Teacher Education, St. Paul, MN 55105-1096. Offers curriculum and instruction (MA), including elementary, individualized, K-12, secondary; elementary education (MA); English as a second language (MA); math education (Certificate); multicultural education (Certificate); reading (MA, Certificate), including elementary (MA), K-12 (MA). *Accreditation:* NCATE. Part-time and evening/weekend programs available. *Entrance requirements:* For master's, minimum GPA of 3.0 or MAT. Additional exam requirements/recommendations for international students: Required—TOEFL (minimum score 550 paper-based; 80 iBT). *Application deadline:* For fall admission, 6/1 for domestic students; for spring admission, 11/1 for domestic students. Applications are processed on a rolling basis. Application fee: $50. *Financial support:* Fellowships, research assistantships, institutionally sponsored loans, and scholarships/grants available. Support available to part-time students. Financial award applicants required to submit FAFSA. *Unit head:* Dr. Jan L. H. Frank, Chair, 651-962-4446, Fax: 651-962-4169, E-mail: jlhfrank@stthomas.edu. *Application contact:* Rosemary R. Barreto, Department Assistant, 651-962-4420, Fax: 651-962-4169, E-mail: barr7879@stthomas.edu.

University of St. Thomas, School of Education, Houston, TX 77006-4696. Offers all level education (M Ed); bilingual/dual language (M Ed); Catholic school teaching (M Ed); Catholic/private school leadership (M Ed); counselor education (M Ed); curriculum and instruction (M Ed); educational leadership (M Ed); elementary teaching (M Ed); English as a second language (M Ed); exceptionality/educational diagnostician (M Ed); exceptionality/special education (M Ed); generalist (M Ed); reading (M Ed); secondary teaching (M Ed). *Accreditation:* Teacher Education Accreditation Council. Part-time and evening/weekend programs available. Postbaccalaureate distance learning degree programs offered (no on-campus study). *Faculty:* 40 full-time (26 women), 43 part-time/adjunct (31 women). *Students:* 27 full-time (20 women), 1,091 part-time (981 women); includes 691 minority (247 Black or African American, non-Hispanic/Latino; 1 American Indian or Alaska Native, non-Hispanic/Latino; 44 Asian, non-Hispanic/Latino; 379 Hispanic/Latino; 2 Native Hawaiian or other Pacific Islander, non-Hispanic/Latino; 18 Two or more races, non-Hispanic/Latino), 28 international. Average age 36. 858 applicants, 83% accepted, 458 enrolled. In 2013, 454 master's awarded. *Degree requirements:* For master's, thesis, field experience. *Entrance requirements:* For master's, GRE or MAT if GPA is below 3.0, bachelor's degree; minimum GPA of 2.75 in bachelor's degree or last 60 credit hours; official transcripts from all institutions; goal statement of 250-300 words; 1 reference. Additional exam requirements/recommendations for international students: Required—TOEFL. *Application deadline:* Applications are processed on a rolling basis. Application fee: $35. Electronic applications accepted. *Expenses:* Contact institution. *Financial support:* In 2013–14, 41 students received support. Federal Work-Study, scholarships/grants, and state work-study, institutional employment available. Support available to part-time students. Financial award application deadline: 4/15; financial award applicants required to submit FAFSA. *Faculty research:* Leadership, diversity, personality traits, second language acquisition. *Unit head:* Dr. Robert LeBlanc, Dean, 713-525-3540, Fax: 713-525-3871, E-mail: education@stthom.edu. *Application contact:* Rita Paredes, Administrative Assistant, 713-525-3442, Fax: 713-525-3871, E-mail: rparede@stthom.edu. Website: http://www.stthom.edu/Academics/School_of_Education/Index.aqf.

University of South Alabama, Graduate School, College of Education, Department of Leadership and Teacher Education, Mobile, AL 36688-0002. Offers early childhood education (M Ed); educational administration (Ed S); educational leadership (M Ed); elementary education (M Ed); reading education (M Ed); science education (M Ed); secondary education (M Ed); special education (M Ed, Ed S). *Accreditation:* NCATE. Part-time programs available. *Faculty:* 17 full-time (11 women), 4 part-time/adjunct (all women). *Students:* 136 full-time (103 women), 78 part-time (67 women); includes 45 minority (40 Black or African American, non-Hispanic/Latino; 2 Asian, non-Hispanic/Latino; 1 Hispanic/Latino; 2 Two or more races, non-Hispanic/Latino). 90 applicants, 53% accepted, 45 enrolled. In 2013, 69 master's awarded. *Degree requirements:* For master's, comprehensive exam. *Entrance requirements:* For master's, GRE General Test or MAT, minimum GPA of 3.0. *Application deadline:* For fall admission, 7/15 priority date for domestic students, 6/15 priority date for international students; for spring admission, 12/1 priority date for domestic students, 11/1 priority date for international students. Applications are processed on a rolling basis. Application fee: $35. *Expenses:* Tuition, state resident: full-time $8976; part-time $374 per credit hour. Tuition, nonresident: full-time $17,952; part-time $748 per credit hour. *Financial support:* Research assistantships and career-related internships or fieldwork available. Support available to part-time students. Financial award application deadline: 4/1. *Unit head:* Dr. Harold Dodge, Jr., Chair, 251-380-2894. *Application contact:* Dr. Abigail Baxter, Director of Graduate Studies, 251-380-2738, Fax: 251-380-2748, E-mail: abaxter@southalabama.edu. Website: http://www.southalabama.edu/coe/lted.

University of South Carolina, The Graduate School, College of Education, Department of Instruction and Teacher Education, Program in Elementary Education, Columbia, SC 29208. Offers MAT, Ed D, PhD. *Accreditation:* NCATE. *Degree requirements:* For master's, comprehensive exam; for doctorate, one foreign language, comprehensive exam, thesis/dissertation. *Entrance requirements:* For master's, GRE General Test, MAT, interview, letters of reference, resume; for doctorate, GRE General Test, MAT, interview, letters of reference, letters of intent, resum&e, transcript. *Faculty research:* Children's conception of science, whole language, middle school curriculum.

University of South Carolina Upstate, Graduate Programs, Spartanburg, SC 29303-4999. Offers early childhood education (M Ed); elementary education (M Ed); informatics (MS); special education: visual impairment (M Ed). *Accreditation:* NCATE. Part-time and evening/weekend programs available. *Faculty:* 8 full-time (6 women), 5

part-time/adjunct (4 women). *Students:* 10 full-time (4 women), 13 part-time (11 women); includes 8 minority (6 Black or African American, non-Hispanic/Latino; 2 Two or more races, non-Hispanic/Latino). Average age 33. In 2013, 11 master's awarded. *Degree requirements:* For master's, professional portfolio. *Entrance requirements:* For master's, GRE General Test or MAT, interview, minimum undergraduate GPA of 2.5, teaching certificate, 2 letters of recommendation. *Application deadline:* Applications are processed on a rolling basis. Application fee: $40. *Expenses:* Tuition, state resident: full-time $11,272; part-time $470 per semester hour. Tuition, nonresident: full-time $24,196; part-time $1008 per semester hour. Tuition and fees vary according to course load and program. *Financial support:* Institutionally sponsored loans and institutional work-study available. Financial award application deadline: 7/15; financial award applicants required to submit FAFSA. *Faculty research:* Promoting university diversity awareness, rough and tumble play, social justice education, American Indian literatures and cultures, diversity and multicultural education, science teaching strategy. *Unit head:* Dr. Tina Herzberg, Director of Graduate Programs, 864-503-5572, Fax: 864-503-5573, E-mail: rstevens@uscupstate.edu. *Application contact:* Donette Stewart, Associate Vice Chancellor for Enrollment Services, 864-503-5280, E-mail: dstewart@uscupstate.edu. Website: http://www.uscupstate.edu/graduate/.

The University of South Dakota, Graduate School, School of Education, Division of Curriculum and Instruction, Program in Elementary Education, Vermillion, SD 57069-2390. Offers MA. *Accreditation:* NCATE. Part-time programs available. Postbaccalaureate distance learning degree programs offered. *Degree requirements:* For master's, comprehensive exam, thesis or alternative. *Entrance requirements:* For master's, GRE General Test, MAT, minimum GPA of 2.7. Additional exam requirements/recommendations for international students: Required—TOEFL (minimum score 550 paper-based; 79 iBT). Electronic applications accepted.

University of Southern Indiana, Graduate Studies, College of Science, Engineering, and Education, Department of Teacher Education, Program in Elementary Education, Evansville, IN 47712-3590. Offers MS. *Accreditation:* NCATE. Part-time and evening/weekend programs available. *Faculty:* 8 full-time (7 women), 3 part-time/adjunct (1 woman). *Students:* 34 part-time (all women); includes 2 minority (1 Black or African American, non-Hispanic/Latino; 1 Two or more races, non-Hispanic/Latino), 1 international. Average age 32. 11 applicants, 73% accepted, 6 enrolled. In 2013, 11 master's awarded. *Entrance requirements:* For master's, GRE General Test, NTE or PRAXIS I, minimum GPA of 3.0, teaching license. Additional exam requirements/recommendations for international students: Required—TOEFL (minimum score 550 paper-based; 79 iBT), IELTS (minimum score 6). *Application deadline:* For fall admission, 7/1 priority date for domestic students. Applications are processed on a rolling basis. Application fee: $40. Electronic applications accepted. *Expenses:* Tuition, state resident: full-time $5567; part-time $309 per credit hour. Tuition, nonresident: full-time $10,977; part-time $610 per credit. *Required fees:* $23 per semester. *Financial support:* In 2013–14, 2 students received support. Federal Work-Study, scholarships/grants, tuition waivers (full and partial), and unspecified assistantships available. Financial award application deadline: 3/1; financial award applicants required to submit FAFSA. *Unit head:* Dr. Vella Goebel, Coordinator, 812-461-5306, E-mail: vgoebel@usi.edu. *Application contact:* Dr. Mayola Rowser, Interim Director, Graduate Studies, 812-465-7016, Fax: 812-464-1956, E-mail: mrowser@usi.edu. Website: http://www.usi.edu/science/teacher-education/programs/mse.

University of Southern Mississippi, Graduate School, College of Education and Psychology, Department of Curriculum, Instruction, and Special Education, Hattiesburg, MS 39406-0001. Offers elementary education (M Ed, PhD, Ed S); instructional technology (MS, PhD); secondary education (MAT); special education (M Ed, PhD, Ed S). Part-time programs available. *Faculty:* 23 full-time (17 women), 3 part-time/adjunct (2 women). *Students:* 20 full-time (19 women), 59 part-time (49 women); includes 18 minority (14 Black or African American, non-Hispanic/Latino; 3 Hispanic/Latino; 1 Two or more races, non-Hispanic/Latino). Average age 36. 21 applicants, 95% accepted, 17 enrolled. In 2013, 22 master's, 3 doctorates, 13 other advanced degrees awarded. *Degree requirements:* For master's and Ed S, comprehensive exam, thesis (for some programs); for doctorate, comprehensive exam, thesis/dissertation. *Entrance requirements:* For master's, GRE General Test, MAT, minimum GPA of 3.0; for doctorate, GRE General Test, minimum GPA of 3.5; for Ed S, GRE General Test, MAT, minimum GPA of 3.25. Additional exam requirements/recommendations for international students: Required—TOEFL, IELTS. *Application deadline:* For fall admission, 3/1 priority date for domestic students, 3/1 for international students; for spring admission, 1/10 priority date for domestic and international students. Applications are processed on a rolling basis. Application fee: $50. *Financial support:* In 2013–14, 9 research assistantships with tuition reimbursements (averaging $18,316 per year), 2 teaching assistantships with full tuition reimbursements (averaging $8,500 per year) were awarded; Federal Work-Study, institutionally sponsored loans, scholarships/grants, health care benefits, tuition waivers (partial), and unspecified assistantships also available. Financial award application deadline: 3/15; financial award applicants required to submit FAFSA. *Faculty research:* Mathematical problem solving, integrative curriculum; writing process, teacher education models. *Total annual research expenditures:* $100,000. *Unit head:* Dr. Ravic P. Ringlaben, Chair, 601-266-4547, Fax: 601-266-4175. *Application contact:* David Daves, Director of Graduate Studies, 601-266-6005, Fax: 601-266-4548. Website: http://www.usm.edu/graduateschool/table.php.

University of South Florida, College of Education, Department of Childhood Education, Tampa, FL 33620-9951. Offers early childhood education (M Ed, MA, PhD); elementary education (MA, MAT, PhD); reading/language arts (MA, PhD, Ed S). *Accreditation:* NCATE. Part-time and evening/weekend programs available. *Degree requirements:* For master's, comprehensive exam; for doctorate, comprehensive exam, thesis/dissertation, philosophies of inquiry; multiple research methods. *Entrance requirements:* For master's, GRE (if GPA less than 3.0), minimum GPA of 3.0 in last 60 hours of course work; for doctorate, GRE General Test, minimum GPA of 3.0 undergraduate, 3.5 graduate; interview; for Ed S, GRE General Test, interview. Additional exam requirements/recommendations for international students: Required—TOEFL (minimum score 550 paper-based). Electronic applications accepted. *Faculty research:* Evaluating interventions for struggling readers, prevention and intervention services for young children at risk for behavioral and mental health challenges, preservice teacher education and young adolescent middle school experience, art and inquiry-based approaches to teaching and learning, study of children's writing development.

University of South Florida–St. Petersburg Campus, College of Education, St. Petersburg, FL 33701. Offers educational leadership development (M Ed); elementary education (MA), including math/science; English education (MA); middle grades STEM education (MS); reading education (MA). Part-time programs available. *Degree requirements:* For master's, comprehensive exam, practicum, internship, comprehensive portfolio. *Entrance requirements:* For master's, State of Florida General Knowledge Test (GKT), Florida Teaching Certificate (for non-initial certification programs), letters of recommendation. Additional exam requirements/recommendations for international students: Required—TOEFL (minimum score 550 paper-based; 79 iBT); Recommended—IELTS. Electronic applications accepted.

The University of Tennessee, Graduate School, College of Education, Health and Human Sciences, Program in Education, Knoxville, TN 37996. Offers art education (MS); counseling education (PhD); cultural studies in education (PhD); curriculum (MS, Ed S); curriculum, educational research and evaluation (Ed D, PhD); early childhood education (PhD); early childhood special education (MS); education of deaf and hard of hearing (MS); educational administration and policy studies (Ed D, PhD); educational administration and supervision (Ed S); educational psychology (Ed D, PhD); elementary education (MS, Ed S); elementary teaching (MS); English education (MS, Ed S); exercise science (PhD); foreign language/ESL education (MS, Ed S); instructional technology (MS, Ed D, PhD, Ed S); literacy, language and ESL education (PhD); literacy, language education, and ESL education (Ed D); mathematics education (MS, Ed S); modified and comprehensive special education (MS); reading education (MS, Ed S); school counseling (Ed S); school psychology (PhD, Ed S); science education (MS, Ed S); secondary teaching (MS); social foundations (MS); social science education (MS, Ed S); socio-cultural foundations of sports and education (PhD); special education (Ed S); teacher education (Ed D, PhD). *Accreditation:* NCATE. Part-time and evening/weekend programs available. *Degree requirements:* For master's and Ed S, thesis optional; for doctorate, variable foreign language requirement, thesis/dissertation. *Entrance requirements:* For master's, minimum GPA of 2.7; for doctorate and Ed S, GRE General Test, minimum GPA of 2.7. Additional exam requirements/recommendations for international students: Required—TOEFL. Electronic applications accepted. *Expenses:* Tuition, state resident: full-time $9540; part-time $531 per credit hour. Tuition, nonresident: full-time $27,728; part-time $1542 per credit hour. *Required fees:* $1404; $67 per credit hour.

The University of Tennessee at Chattanooga, Graduate School, College of Health, Education and Professional Studies, School of Education, Chattanooga, TN 37403. Offers counseling (M Ed), including community counseling, school counseling; education (M Ed, Post-Master's Certificate), including elementary education (M Ed), school leadership, secondary education (M Ed), special education (M Ed); educational specialist (Ed S), including educational technology, school psychology; learning and leadership (Ed D), including educational leadership. *Accreditation:* ACA; NCATE. Part-time and evening/weekend programs available. Postbaccalaureate distance learning degree programs offered (no on-campus study). *Faculty:* 24 full-time (17 women), 6 part-time/adjunct (4 women). *Students:* 107 full-time (86 women), 263 part-time (192 women); includes 71 minority (46 Black or African American, non-Hispanic/Latino; 2 American Indian or Alaska Native, non-Hispanic/Latino; 5 Asian, non-Hispanic/Latino; 11 Hispanic/Latino; 7 Two or more races, non-Hispanic/Latino), 2 international. Average age 34. 121 applicants, 83% accepted, 67 enrolled. In 2013, 125 master's, 10 doctorates, 3 other advanced degrees awarded. *Degree requirements:* For master's, comprehensive exam, thesis optional, culminating experience; for doctorate, comprehensive exam, thesis/dissertation; for other advanced degree, internship. *Entrance requirements:* For master's, GRE General Test, PPST 1, teaching certificate; for doctorate, GRE General Test, master's degree, two years of practical work experience in organizational environment; for other advanced degree, GRE General Test, letters of reference. Additional exam requirements/recommendations for international students: Required—TOEFL (minimum score 550 paper-based; 79 iBT), IELTS (minimum score 6). *Application deadline:* For fall admission, 6/13 for domestic students, 6/1 for international students; for spring admission, 10/15 for domestic students, 10/1 for international students. Applications are processed on a rolling basis. Application fee: $30 ($35 for international students). Electronic applications accepted. *Financial support:* In 2013–14, 20 research assistantships with tuition reimbursements (averaging $6,340 per year), 4 teaching assistantships with tuition reimbursements (averaging $7,234 per year) were awarded; career-related internships or fieldwork, institutionally sponsored loans, scholarships/grants, and unspecified assistantships also available. Support available to part-time students. Financial award applicants required to submit FAFSA. *Faculty research:* School counseling, community counseling, elementary and secondary education, school leadership and administration. *Total annual research expenditures:* $967,880. *Unit head:* Dr. Linda Johnston, Director, 423-425-4122, Fax: 423-425-5380, E-mail: linda-johnston@utc.edu. *Application contact:* Dr. J. Randy Walker, Interim Dean of Graduate Studies, 423-425-4478, Fax: 423-425-5223, E-mail: randy-walker@utc.edu. Website: http://www.utc.edu/school-education/abouttheschool/gradprograms.php.

The University of Tennessee at Martin, Graduate Programs, College of Education, Health and Behavioral Sciences, Program in Teaching, Martin, TN 38238-1000. Offers curriculum and instruction (MS Ed), including 7-12, K-6; initial licensure (MS Ed), including elementary, secondary; initial licensure K-12 (MS Ed), including physical education, special education; interdisciplinary (MS Ed). Part-time programs available. *Students:* 20 full-time (14 women), 88 part-time (65 women); includes 9 minority (8 Black or African American, non-Hispanic/Latino; 1 Two or more races, non-Hispanic/Latino). 78 applicants, 64% accepted, 33 enrolled. In 2013, 32 master's awarded. *Degree requirements:* For master's, comprehensive exam. *Entrance requirements:* For master's, GRE General Test, minimum GPA of 2.5. Additional exam requirements/recommendations for international students: Required—TOEFL (minimum score 525 paper-based; 71 iBT). *Application deadline:* For fall admission, 7/29 priority date for domestic students, 7/29 for international students; for spring admission, 12/12 priority date for domestic students, 12/12 for international students. Applications are processed on a rolling basis. Application fee: $30 ($130 for international students). Electronic applications accepted. *Financial support:* Research assistantships with full tuition reimbursements, teaching assistantships with full tuition reimbursements, career-related internships or fieldwork, scholarships/grants, and unspecified assistantships available. Financial award application deadline: 3/1. *Faculty research:* Special education, science/math/technology, school reform, reading. *Unit head:* Dr. Gail Stephens, Interim Dean, 731-881-7127, Fax: 731-881-7975, E-mail: gstephe6@utm.edu. *Application contact:* Jolene L. Cunningham, Student Services Specialist, 731-881-7012, Fax: 731-881-7499, E-mail: jcunningham@utm.edu.

The University of Texas–Pan American, College of Education, Department of Curriculum and Instruction: Elementary and Secondary, Edinburg, TX 78539. Offers bilingual education (M Ed); early childhood education (M Ed); elementary education (M Ed); reading (M Ed); secondary education (M Ed). Part-time programs available. *Degree requirements:* For master's, comprehensive exam, thesis optional. *Entrance requirements:* For master's, GRE. Additional exam requirements/recommendations for international students: Required—TOEFL, IELTS. *Expenses:* Tuition, state resident: full-time $5986; part-time $333 per credit hour. Tuition, nonresident: full-time $12,358; part-time $687 per credit hour. *Required fees:* $782. Tuition and fees vary according to program. *Faculty research:* Dual language instruction, literacy and technology, teacher education in diverse populations, mathematics and science education.

University of the Cumberlands, Graduate Programs in Education, Williamsburg, KY 40769-1372. Offers all grades (P-12) (M Ed); business and marketing (MA Ed, MAT); counselor education and supervision (Ed D); director of pupil personnel (Certificate); director of special education (Certificate); educational administration and supervision (Ed S); educational leadership (Ed D); elementary education (MA Ed, MAT); instructional leadership - principalship (MA Ed); instructional leadership - school principal (Certificate); middle school education (MA Ed, MAT); reading and writing (MA Ed); school counseling (MA Ed); school superintendent (Certificate); secondary

education (MA Ed, MAT); special education (MAT); supervisor of instruction (Certificate); teacher leader (MA Ed). Part-time and evening/weekend programs available. Postbaccalaureate distance learning degree programs offered. *Degree requirements:* For master's, comprehensive exam. Electronic applications accepted.

University of the Incarnate Word, School of Graduate Studies and Research, Dreeben School of Education, Program in Teaching, San Antonio, TX 78209-6397. Offers all-level teaching (MAT); elementary teaching (MAT); secondary teaching (MAT). Part-time and evening/weekend programs available. *Faculty:* 17 full-time (9 women), 6 part-time/adjunct (all women). *Students:* 1 full-time (0 women), 45 part-time (40 women); includes 28 minority (1 Black or African American, non-Hispanic/Latino; 26 Hispanic/Latino; 1 Two or more races, non-Hispanic/Latino). Average age 26. 17 applicants, 88% accepted, 8 enrolled. In 2013, 6 master's awarded. *Degree requirements:* For master's, internship. *Entrance requirements:* For master's, GRE, Texas Higher Education Assessment test (THEA), interview. Additional exam requirements/recommendations for international students: Required—TOEFL (minimum score 560 paper-based; 83 iBT). *Application deadline:* Applications are processed on a rolling basis. Application fee: $20. Electronic applications accepted. *Expenses: Tuition:* Part-time $815 per credit hour. *Required fees:* $86 per credit hour. One-time fee: $40 part-time. Tuition and fees vary according to degree level and program. *Financial support:* Federal Work-Study and scholarships/grants available. Financial award applicants required to submit FAFSA. *Unit head:* Dr. Elda Martinez, Director of Teacher Education, 210-832-3297, Fax: 210-829-3134, E-mail: eemartin@uiwtx.edu. *Application contact:* Andrea Cyterski-Acosta, Dean of Enrollment, 210-829-6005, Fax: 210-829-3921, E-mail: admis@uiwtx.edu.
Website: http://www.uiw.edu/education/graduate.html.

The University of Toledo, College of Graduate Studies, Judith Herb College of Education, Department of Curriculum and Instruction, Toledo, OH 43606-3390. Offers art education (ME); career and technical education (ME); career-technical education (Ed S); curriculum and instruction (ME, PhD, Ed S); early childhood education (PhD, Ed S); education and biology (MES); education and chemistry (MES); education and economics (MAE); education and English (MAE); education and French (MAE); education and geography (MAE); education and geology (MES); education and German (MAE); education and history (MAE); education and mathematics (MAE, MES); education and physics (MES); education and political science (MAE); education and sociology (MAE); education and Spanish (MAE); educational media (PhD); educational technology (ME); educational technology: virtual educator (Certificate); elementary education (PhD); English as a second language (MAE); gifted and talented (PhD); middle childhood education licensure (ME); music education (MME); secondary education (PhD); secondary education licensure (ME); special education (PhD, Ed S). *Accreditation:* NCATE. Part-time and evening/weekend programs available. *Faculty:* 41. *Students:* 53 full-time (30 women), 154 part-time (111 women); includes 21 minority (16 Black or African American, non-Hispanic/Latino; 4 Hispanic/Latino; 1 Two or more races, non-Hispanic/Latino), 21 international. Average age 34. 82 applicants, 79% accepted, 47 enrolled. In 2013, 80 master's, 5 doctorates awarded. *Degree requirements:* For master's, comprehensive exam, thesis or alternative; for doctorate, comprehensive exam, thesis/dissertation; for other advanced degree, thesis optional. *Entrance requirements:* For master's, doctorate, and other advanced degree, minimum cumulative GPA of 2.7 for all previous academic work, letters of recommendation. Additional exam requirements/recommendations for international students: Required—TOEFL (minimum score 550 paper-based; 80 iBT). *Application deadline:* For fall admission, 1/15 priority date for domestic and international students. Applications are processed on a rolling basis. Application fee: $45 ($75 for international students). Electronic applications accepted. *Financial support:* In 2013–14, 5 research assistantships with full and partial tuition reimbursements (averaging $13,200 per year), 11 teaching assistantships with full and partial tuition reimbursements (averaging $8,809 per year) were awarded; career-related internships or fieldwork, Federal Work-Study, institutionally sponsored loans, scholarships/grants, tuition waivers (full and partial), unspecified assistantships, and administrative assistantships also available. Support available to part-time students. *Unit head:* Dr. Joan Kaderavek, Chair, 419-530-5373, E-mail: eigh.chiarelott@utoledo.edu. *Application contact:* Graduate School Office, 419-530-4723, Fax: 419-530-4724, E-mail: grdsch@utnet.utoledo.edu.
Website: http://www.utoledo.edu/eduhshs/.

The University of Tulsa, Graduate School, College of Arts and Sciences, School of Urban Education, Program in Education, Tulsa, OK 74104-3189. Offers education (MA); elementary certification (M Ed); secondary certification (M Ed). Part-time programs available. *Faculty:* 7 full-time (3 women). *Students:* 4 full-time (1 woman), 1 part-time (0 women), 1 international. Average age 30. 5 applicants, 80% accepted, 3 enrolled. In 2013, 10 master's awarded. *Degree requirements:* For master's, thesis optional. *Entrance requirements:* For master's, GRE General Test. Additional exam requirements/recommendations for international students: Required—TOEFL (minimum score 577 paper-based; 91 iBT), IELTS (minimum score 6.5). *Application deadline:* Applications are processed on a rolling basis. Application fee: $40. Electronic applications accepted. *Expenses: Tuition:* Full-time $19,566; part-time $1087 per credit hour. *Required fees:* $1690; $5 per credit hour. $160 per semester. Tuition and fees vary according to course load. *Financial support:* In 2013–14, 5 students received support, including 5 teaching assistantships with full and partial tuition reimbursements available (averaging $12,310 per year); fellowships with full and partial tuition reimbursements available, research assistantships with full and partial tuition reimbursements available, Federal Work-Study, scholarships/grants, health care benefits, tuition waivers (full and partial), and unspecified assistantships also available. Support available to part-time students. Financial award application deadline: 2/1; financial award applicants required to submit FAFSA. *Faculty research:* Elementary and secondary education; educational foundations; language, discourse and development. *Unit head:* Dr. Kara Gae Neal, Chair, 918-631-2541, Fax: 918-631-2238, E-mail: karagae-neal@utulsa.edu. *Application contact:* Dr. David Brown, Advisor, 918-631-2719, Fax: 918-631-2133, E-mail: david-brown@utulsa.edu.

University of Utah, Graduate School, College of Education, Department of Educational Leadership and Policy, Salt Lake City, UT 84112. Offers educational leadership and policy (Ed D, PhD); K-12 administrative licensure (M Ed); K-12 teacher instructional leadership (M Ed); student affairs (M Ed); MPA/PhD. Part-time and evening/weekend programs available. *Faculty:* 10 full-time (7 women), 4 part-time/adjunct (3 women). *Students:* 55 full-time (38 women), 65 part-time (40 women); includes 33 minority (5 Black or African American, non-Hispanic/Latino; 1 American Indian or Alaska Native, non-Hispanic/Latino; 3 Asian, non-Hispanic/Latino; 21 Hispanic/Latino; 3 Two or more races, non-Hispanic/Latino), 3 international. Average age 35. 123 applicants, 45% accepted, 51 enrolled. In 2013, 33 master's, 5 doctorates awarded. *Degree requirements:* For master's, comprehensive exam (for some programs), internship; for doctorate, thesis/dissertation, qualifying exam. *Entrance requirements:* For master's, minimum undergraduate GPA of 3.0, valid bachelor's degree, 3 years' teaching or leadership experience, Level 1 or 2 UT educator's license (for K-12 programs only); for doctorate, GRE General Test (taken with five years of applying), minimum undergraduate GPA of 3.0, valid master's degree. Additional exam requirements/recommendations for international students: Required—TOEFL (minimum score 500 paper-based). *Application deadline:* For fall and winter admission, 2/1 for domestic and international students; for summer admission, 1/15 for domestic and international students. Application fee: $55 ($65 for international students). Electronic applications accepted. *Expenses:* Tuition, state resident: full-time $5259. Tuition, nonresident: full-time $18,569. *Required fees:* $841. Tuition and fees vary according to course load. *Financial support:* In 2013–14, 86 students received support, including 7 fellowships (averaging $2,000 per year), research assistantships with full tuition reimbursements available (averaging $13,000 per year), 86 teaching assistantships with full tuition reimbursements available (averaging $13,000 per year); career-related internships or fieldwork, scholarships/grants, health care benefits, and unspecified assistantships also available. Financial award application deadline: 2/1. *Faculty research:* Education accountability, college student diversity, K-12 educational administration and school leadership, student affairs, higher education. *Total annual research expenditures:* $55,000. *Unit head:* Dr. Andrea Rorrer, Chair, 801-581-4207, Fax: 801-585-6756, E-mail: andrea.rorrer@utah.edu. *Application contact:* Marilynn S. Howard, Academic Coordinator, 801-581-6714, Fax: 801-585-6756, E-mail: marilynn.howard@utah.edu.
Website: http://elp.utah.edu/.

University of Utah, Graduate School, College of Education, Department of Educational Psychology, Salt Lake City, UT 84112. Offers clinical mental health counseling (M Ed); counseling psychology (PhD); educational psychology (M Ed, MA, MS); elementary education (M Ed); instructional design and educational technology (M Ed); instructional design and technology (MS); learning and cognition (MS, PhD); reading and literacy (M Ed, MS, PhD); school counseling (M Ed); school psychology (M Ed, PhD); statistics (M Stat). *Accreditation:* APA (one or more programs are accredited). *Faculty:* 18 full-time (8 women), 20 part-time/adjunct (17 women). *Students:* 109 full-time (88 women), 108 part-time (68 women); includes 29 minority (2 Black or African American, non-Hispanic/Latino; 1 American Indian or Alaska Native, non-Hispanic/Latino; 7 Asian, non-Hispanic/Latino; 14 Hispanic/Latino; 1 Native Hawaiian or other Pacific Islander, non-Hispanic/Latino; 4 Two or more races, non-Hispanic/Latino), 7 international. Average age 32. 222 applicants, 35% accepted, 61 enrolled. In 2013, 51 master's, 10 doctorates awarded. *Degree requirements:* For master's, variable foreign language requirement, comprehensive exam (for some programs), thesis (for some programs), projects; for doctorate, variable foreign language requirement, comprehensive exam, thesis/dissertation, oral exam. *Entrance requirements:* For master's and doctorate, GRE General Test, minimum GPA of 3.0. Additional exam requirements/recommendations for international students: Required—TOEFL (minimum score 80 iBT). *Application deadline:* For fall admission, 4/1 for domestic and international students; for winter admission, 11/1 for domestic and international students; for spring admission, 3/15 for domestic and international students. Application fee: $55 ($65 for international students). Electronic applications accepted. *Expenses:* Contact institution. *Financial support:* In 2013–14, 81 students received support, including 29 fellowships with full and partial tuition reimbursements available (averaging $11,200 per year), 11 research assistantships with full and partial tuition reimbursements available (averaging $9,100 per year), 38 teaching assistantships with full and partial tuition reimbursements available (averaging $10,400 per year); career-related internships or fieldwork, Federal Work-Study, institutionally sponsored loans, scholarships/grants, health care benefits, and unspecified assistantships also available. Financial award application deadline: 4/1; financial award applicants required to submit FAFSA. *Faculty research:* Autism, computer technology and instruction, cognitive behavior, aging, group counseling. *Total annual research expenditures:* $441,375. *Unit head:* Dr. Anne E. Cook, Chair, 801-581-7148, Fax: 801-581-5566, E-mail: anne.cook@utah.edu. *Application contact:* JoLynn N. Yates, Academic Program Specialist, 801-581-7148, Fax: 801-581-5566, E-mail: jo.yates@utah.edu.
Website: http://www.ed.utah.edu/edps/.

University of Virginia, Curry School of Education, Department of Curriculum, Instruction, and Special Education, Program in Curriculum and Instruction, Charlottesville, VA 22903. Offers curriculum and instruction (M Ed, Ed S); elementary education (M Ed, Ed D); English (M Ed, Ed D); foreign language (M Ed); mathematics (M Ed, Ed D); reading (M Ed, Ed D, Ed S); science (Ed D); social studies (M Ed). *Students:* 42 full-time (30 women), 37 part-time (32 women); includes 4 minority (1 Black or African American, non-Hispanic/Latino; 2 Hispanic/Latino; 1 Two or more races, non-Hispanic/Latino), 1 international. Average age 31. 76 applicants, 74% accepted, 39 enrolled. In 2013, 84 master's, 3 doctorates, 23 other advanced degrees awarded. *Degree requirements:* For master's, comprehensive exam (for some programs); for doctorate, comprehensive exam, thesis/dissertation; for Ed S, comprehensive exam. *Entrance requirements:* For master's, doctorate, and Ed S, GRE General Test, 2 letters of recommendation. Additional exam requirements/recommendations for international students: Required—TOEFL (minimum score 600 paper-based; 90 iBT), IELTS (minimum score 7). *Application deadline:* Applications are processed on a rolling basis. Application fee: $60. Electronic applications accepted. *Expenses:* Tuition, state resident: part-time $334 per credit hour. Tuition, nonresident: part-time $1224 per credit hour. *Financial support:* Fellowships with tuition reimbursements, research assistantships with tuition reimbursements, and teaching assistantships with tuition reimbursements available. Financial award application deadline: 1/5; financial award applicants required to submit FAFSA. *Unit head:* Stephanie van Hover, Chair, 434-924-0841, E-mail: sdv2w@virginia.edu. *Application contact:* Karen Dwier, Information Contact, 434-924-0831, E-mail: kgd9g@virginia.edu.
Website: http://curry.virginia.edu/academics/areas-of-study/curriculum-teaching-learning.

University of Virginia, Curry School of Education, Program in Education, Charlottesville, VA 22903. Offers administration and supervision (PhD); applied developmental science (PhD); counselor education (PhD); curriculum and instruction (PhD); early childhood special education (MT); education evaluation (PhD); educational psychology (PhD); educational research (PhD); elementary education (MT); English education (MT, PhD); foreign language education (MT); higher education (PhD); instructional technology (PhD); kinesiology (MT, PhD); math education (PhD); reading education (PhD); research, statistics and evaluation (PhD); school psychology (PhD); science education (PhD); social studies education (MT, PhD); special education (PhD); world languages education (MT). *Students:* 474 full-time (379 women), 35 part-time (19 women); includes 89 minority (30 Black or African American, non-Hispanic/Latino; 1 American Indian or Alaska Native, non-Hispanic/Latino; 26 Asian, non-Hispanic/Latino; 19 Hispanic/Latino; 13 Two or more races, non-Hispanic/Latino), 21 international. Average age 26. 312 applicants, 49% accepted, 80 enrolled. In 2013, 137 master's, 38 doctorates awarded. *Degree requirements:* For master's, comprehensive exam (for some programs), field project; for doctorate, comprehensive exam, thesis/dissertation. *Entrance requirements:* For doctorate, GRE General Test. Additional exam requirements/recommendations for international students: Required—TOEFL (minimum score 600 paper-based; 90 iBT), IELTS (minimum score 7). *Application deadline:* Applications are processed on a rolling basis. Application fee: $60. Electronic applications accepted. *Expenses:* Tuition, state resident: part-time $334 per credit hour. Tuition, nonresident: part-time $1224 per credit hour. *Financial support:* Fellowships, research assistantships, and teaching assistantships available. Financial award application deadline: 1/5; financial award applicants required to submit FAFSA. *Unit head:* Robert C. Pianta, Dean, 434-924-3334, E-mail: pianta@virginia.edu. *Application*

contact: Office of Admissions and Student Services, 434-924-0742, E-mail: curry-admissions@virginia.edu.
Website: http://curry.virginia.edu/teacher-education.

University of Washington, Tacoma, Graduate Programs, Program in Education, Tacoma, WA 98402-3100. Offers education (M Ed); educational administration (principal or program administrator certification) (M Ed); elementary education teacher certification (M Ed); elementary education/special education teacher certification (M Ed); secondary science or math teacher certification (M Ed). Part-time and evening/weekend programs available. *Degree requirements:* For master's, culminating project. *Entrance requirements:* For master's, WEST-B, WEST-E (teacher certification programs only), official sealed transcript from every college/university attended, personal goal statement, letters of recommendation, copy of valid teaching certificate. Additional exam requirements/recommendations for international students: Required—TOEFL (minimum score 580 paper-based; 92 iBT). Electronic applications accepted. *Faculty research:* Global learning communities for English/Chinese languages, evaluation of mathematics and reading intervention programs, response to intervention, school-wide behavioral and emotional support, mathematics education and culturally responsive mathematics education.

The University of West Alabama, School of Graduate Studies, College of Education, Departments of Instructional Leadership and Support/Curriculum and Instruction, Program in Elementary Education, Livingston, AL 35470. Offers M Ed, Ed S. *Accreditation:* NCATE. Part-time and evening/weekend programs available. Postbaccalaureate distance learning degree programs offered (no on-campus study). *Faculty:* 13 full-time (11 women), 39 part-time/adjunct (29 women). *Students:* 292 (283 women); includes 174 minority (168 Black or African American, non-Hispanic/Latino; 3 American Indian or Alaska Native, non-Hispanic/Latino; 1 Asian, non-Hispanic/Latino; 2 Hispanic/Latino). 112 applicants, 97% accepted, 79 enrolled. In 2013, 104 master's, 52 Ed Ss awarded. *Degree requirements:* For master's, comprehensive exam, thesis optional. *Entrance requirements:* For master's, GRE General Test, MAT, minimum GPA of 2.75. Additional exam requirements/recommendations for international students: Required—TOEFL (minimum score 500 paper-based; 61 iBT). *Application deadline:* For fall admission, 8/12 priority date for domestic students; for spring admission, 3/24 for domestic students. Applications are processed on a rolling basis. Application fee: $25 ($50 for international students). Electronic applications accepted. Tuition and fees vary according to course load. *Financial support:* Teaching assistantships, career-related internships or fieldwork, Federal Work-Study, scholarships/grants, and unspecified assistantships available. Support available to part-time students. Financial award application deadline: 3/1; financial award applicants required to submit FAFSA. *Unit head:* Dr. Esther Howard, Chair of Curriculum and Instruction, 205-652-3428, Fax: 205-652-3706, E-mail: ehoward@uwa.edu. *Application contact:* Dr. Kathy Chandler, Dean of Graduate Studies, 205-652-3421, Fax: 205-652-3706, E-mail: kchandler@uwa.edu. Website: http://www.uwa.edu/elementaryeducationk6.aspx.

University of West Florida, College of Professional Studies, School of Education, Program in Curriculum and Instruction, Pensacola, FL 32514-5750. Offers curriculum and instruction: special education (M Ed); elementary education (M Ed); primary education (M Ed). Part-time and evening/weekend programs available. *Entrance requirements:* For master's, GRE (minimum score 450 verbal) or MAT (minimum score 396) if bachelor's GPA less than 3.0, state teaching certification; letter of intent; two professional references. Additional exam requirements/recommendations for international students: Required—TOEFL (minimum score 550 paper-based).

University of Wisconsin–La Crosse, Graduate Studies, College of Liberal Studies, Department of Educational Studies, La Crosse, WI 54601-3742. Offers professional development (ME-PD), including elementary education, K-12, professional development, secondary education; professional development learning community (ME-PD). Part-time programs available. *Faculty:* 6 full-time (4 women), 4 part-time/adjunct (all women). *Students:* 2 full-time (1 woman), 27 part-time (24 women); includes 2 minority (both Asian, non-Hispanic/Latino). Average age 30. 21 applicants, 100% accepted, 21 enrolled. In 2013, 61 master's awarded. *Entrance requirements:* Additional exam requirements/recommendations for international students: Required—TOEFL (minimum score 550 paper-based; 79 iBT). *Application deadline:* Applications are processed on a rolling basis. Electronic applications accepted. *Financial support:* Research assistantships, Federal Work-Study, scholarships/grants, health care benefits, and tuition waivers (partial) available. Support available to part-time students. Financial award application deadline: 3/15; financial award applicants required to submit FAFSA. *Unit head:* Dr. Carol Angell, E-mail: cangell@uwlax.edu. *Application contact:* Corey Sjoquist, Director of Admissions, 608-785-8939, E-mail: admissions@uwlax.edu. Website: http://www.uwlax.edu/educational-studies/.

University of Wisconsin–Milwaukee, Graduate School, School of Education, Department of Curriculum and Instruction, Milwaukee, WI 53201-0413. Offers curriculum planning and instruction improvement (MS); early childhood education (MS); elementary education (MS); junior high/middle school education (MS); reading education (MS); secondary education (MS); teaching in an urban setting (MS). Part-time programs available. *Faculty:* 18 full-time (13 women). *Students:* 17 full-time (10 women), 46 part-time (42 women); includes 15 minority (7 Black or African American, non-Hispanic/Latino; 1 Asian, non-Hispanic/Latino; 7 Two or more races, non-Hispanic/Latino), 1 international. Average age 32. 35 applicants, 69% accepted, 11 enrolled. In 2013, 31 master's awarded. *Degree requirements:* For master's, thesis or alternative. *Entrance requirements:* Additional exam requirements/recommendations for international students: Required—TOEFL (minimum score 550 paper-based; 79 iBT), IELTS (minimum score 6.5). *Application deadline:* For fall admission, 1/1 priority date for domestic students; for spring admission, 9/1 for domestic students. Applications are processed on a rolling basis. Application fee: $56 ($96 for international students). Electronic applications accepted. *Financial support:* In 2013–14, 1 fellowship was awarded; research assistantships, teaching assistantships, career-related internships or fieldwork, health care benefits, unspecified assistantships, and project assistantships also available. Support available to part-time students. Financial award application deadline: 4/15; financial award applicants required to submit FAFSA. *Unit head:* Raquel Oxford, Department Chair, 414-229-4884, Fax: 414-229-5571, E-mail: roxford@uwm.edu. *Application contact:* General Information Contact, 414-229-4982, Fax: 414-229-6967, E-mail: gradschool@uwm.edu.
Website: http://www.uwm.edu/SOE/.

University of Wisconsin–Platteville, School of Graduate Studies, College of Liberal Arts and Education, School of Education, Platteville, WI 53818-3099. Offers adult education (MSE); elementary education (MSE); English education (MSE); middle school education (MSE); secondary education (MSE). *Accreditation:* NCATE. Part-time programs available. *Faculty:* 5 full-time (3 women), 13 part-time/adjunct (7 women). *Students:* 90 full-time (70 women), 30 part-time (16 women); includes 25 minority (21 Black or African American, non-Hispanic/Latino; 1 American Indian or Alaska Native, non-Hispanic/Latino; 2 Asian, non-Hispanic/Latino; 1 Hispanic/Latino), 3 international. 45 applicants, 96% accepted, 38 enrolled. In 2013, 82 master's awarded. *Degree requirements:* For master's, comprehensive exam, thesis or alternative. *Entrance requirements:* Additional exam requirements/recommendations for international students: Required—TOEFL (minimum score 500 paper-based; 61 iBT), IELTS

(minimum score 6). *Application deadline:* For fall admission, 7/1 priority date for domestic students; for spring admission, 11/1 for domestic students. Applications are processed on a rolling basis. Application fee: $56. Electronic applications accepted. *Financial support:* Research assistantships with partial tuition reimbursements, career-related internships or fieldwork, Federal Work-Study, institutionally sponsored loans, scholarships/grants, and unspecified assistantships available. Support available to part-time students. Financial award applicants required to submit FAFSA. *Unit head:* Dr. Karen Stinson, Director, 608-342-1131, Fax: 608-342-1133, E-mail: stinsonk@uwplatt.edu. *Application contact:* Dee Dunbar, School of Graduate Studies, 608-342-1322, Fax: 608-342-1389, E-mail: dunbard@uwplatt.edu.
Website: http://www.uwplatt.edu/.

University of Wisconsin–River Falls, Outreach and Graduate Studies, College of Education and Professional Studies, Department of Teacher Education, River Falls, WI 54022. Offers elementary education (MSE); professional development shared inquiry communities (MSE); reading (MSE). Part-time programs available. *Degree requirements:* For master's, comprehensive exam, thesis or alternative. *Entrance requirements:* For master's, minimum GPA of 2.75. Additional exam requirements/recommendations for international students: Required—TOEFL (minimum score 500 paper-based; 65 iBT), IELTS (minimum score 5.5). Electronic applications accepted.

University of Wisconsin–Stevens Point, College of Fine Arts and Communication, Department of Music, Stevens Point, WI 54481-3897. Offers elementary/secondary (MM Ed); studio pedagogy (MM Ed); Suzuki talent education (MM Ed). *Accreditation:* NASM. Part-time programs available. *Degree requirements:* For master's, thesis or alternative. *Entrance requirements:* For master's, teaching certificate. *Faculty research:* Music education, music composition, music performance.

University of Wisconsin–Stevens Point, College of Professional Studies, School of Education, Program in Elementary Education, Stevens Point, WI 54481-3897. Offers MSE. Part-time programs available. *Degree requirements:* For master's, comprehensive exam, thesis or alternative. *Entrance requirements:* For master's, teacher certification, minimum undergraduate GPA of 3.0. Additional exam requirements/recommendations for international students: Required—TOEFL (minimum score 523 paper-based). *Faculty research:* Gifted education, early childhood special education, curriculum and instruction, standards-based education.

Utah State University, School of Graduate Studies, Emma Eccles Jones College of Education and Human Services, Program in Elementary Education, Logan, UT 84322. Offers M Ed, MA, MS. Part-time programs available. Postbaccalaureate distance learning degree programs offered (no on-campus study). *Degree requirements:* For master's, comprehensive exam (for some programs), thesis (for some programs). *Entrance requirements:* For master's, GRE General Test or MAT, minimum GPA of 3.0, teaching certificate, 3 recommendations, 1 year teaching department record. Additional exam requirements/recommendations for international students: Required—TOEFL. *Faculty research:* Teacher education, supervision, gifted and talented education, language arts/writing, early childhood education.

Utah Valley University, Program in Education, Orem, UT 84058-5999. Offers educational technology (M Ed); elementary mathematics (M Ed); English as a second language (M Ed); models of instruction (M Ed). *Accreditation:* Teacher Education Accreditation Council. Part-time programs available. *Faculty:* 4 full-time (2 women). *Students:* 107 part-time (76 women); includes 2 minority (1 Asian, non-Hispanic/Latino; 1 Hispanic/Latino). Average age 33. *Degree requirements:* For master's, project. *Entrance requirements:* For master's, GRE, 3 letters of recommendation, interview. Additional exam requirements/recommendations for international students: Required—TOEFL (minimum score 83 iBT). *Application deadline:* For fall admission, 3/31 for domestic and international students. Application fee: $45 ($100 for international students). Electronic applications accepted. *Expenses:* Tuition, state resident: full-time $8520; part-time $355 per credit. Tuition, nonresident: full-time $21,232; part-time $885 per credit. *Required fees:* $700; $350 per semester. Tuition and fees vary according to program. *Financial support:* Application deadline: 5/1; applicants required to submit FAFSA. *Unit head:* Parker Fewson, Dean, School of Education, 801-863-8006. *Application contact:* Mary Sowder, Coordinator of Graduate Studies, 801-863-6723.

Valley City State University, Online Master of Education Program, Valley City, ND 58072. Offers elementary education (M Ed); English education (M Ed); library and information technologies (M Ed); teaching and technology (M Ed); teaching English language learners (ELL) (M Ed); technology education (M Ed). *Accreditation:* NCATE. Part-time and evening/weekend programs available. Postbaccalaureate distance learning degree programs offered (no on-campus study). *Faculty:* 21 full-time (14 women), 7 part-time/adjunct (all women). *Students:* 2 full-time (both women), 151 part-time (102 women); includes 10 minority (1 Black or African American, non-Hispanic/Latino; 3 Asian, non-Hispanic/Latino; 2 Hispanic/Latino; 4 Two or more races, non-Hispanic/Latino), 1 international. Average age 34. 27 applicants, 93% accepted, 21 enrolled. In 2013, 45 master's awarded. *Degree requirements:* For master's, action research report, comprehensive portfolio. *Entrance requirements:* For master's, GRE, MAT, PRAXIS II or National Teaching Board for Professional Standards (if GPA is less than 3.0). Additional exam requirements/recommendations for international students: Required—TOEFL (minimum score 525 paper-based; 71 iBT); Recommended—IELTS (minimum score 5.5). *Application deadline:* For fall admission, 7/19 priority date for domestic and international students; for spring admission, 12/13 priority date for domestic and international students; for summer admission, 5/9 priority date for domestic and international students. Applications are processed on a rolling basis. Application fee: $35. Electronic applications accepted. *Expenses:* Contact institution. *Financial support:* In 2013–14, 24 students received support. Scholarships/grants and tuition waivers (full and partial) available. Financial award application deadline: 5/15; financial award applicants required to submit FAFSA. *Faculty research:* Academically at-risk students in higher education, communication pedagogy and technology, gender communication, computer-mediated communication, creativity in music, STEM education in K-12. *Total annual research expenditures:* $26,000. *Unit head:* Dr. Gary Thompson, Dean, 701-845-7197, E-mail: gary.thompson@vcsu.edu. *Application contact:* Misty Lindgren, Graduate Studies, 701-845-7303, Fax: 701-845-7190, E-mail: misty.lindgren@vcsu.edu.
Website: http://www.vcsu.edu/graduate.

Vanderbilt University, Peabody College, Department of Teaching and Learning, Nashville, TN 37240-1001. Offers elementary education (M Ed); English language learners (M Ed); learning and instruction (M Ed); learning, diversity, and urban studies (M Ed); reading education (M Ed); secondary education (M Ed). *Accreditation:* NCATE. *Faculty:* 35 full-time (25 women), 20 part-time/adjunct (14 women). *Students:* 103 full-time (74 women), 44 part-time (39 women); includes 22 minority (8 Black or African American, non-Hispanic/Latino; 5 Asian, non-Hispanic/Latino; 5 Hispanic/Latino; 1 Native Hawaiian or other Pacific Islander, non-Hispanic/Latino; 3 Two or more races, non-Hispanic/Latino), 21 international. Average age 25. 264 applicants, 73% accepted, 57 enrolled. In 2013, 95 master's awarded. *Degree requirements:* For master's, comprehensive exam, thesis optional. *Entrance requirements:* For master's, GRE General Test, MAT. Additional exam requirements/recommendations for international students: Required—TOEFL (minimum score 550 paper-based; 80 iBT). *Application deadline:* For fall admission, 12/31 priority date for domestic and international students;

for spring admission, 11/1 priority date for domestic and international students. Applications are processed on a rolling basis. Application fee: $0. Electronic applications accepted. *Financial support:* Fellowships with full and partial tuition reimbursements, research assistantships with full and partial tuition reimbursements, teaching assistantships with full and partial tuition reimbursements, Federal Work-Study, institutionally sponsored loans, scholarships/grants, tuition waivers (partial), and unspecified assistantships available. Support available to part-time students. Financial award application deadline: 1/15; financial award applicants required to submit FAFSA. *Faculty research:* Learning environments for mathematics of space and motion, visual programming tools for children's learning of basic science concepts, pathways for elementary and middle school children's learning about measurement and statistics, early reading intervention, professional development for ambitious mathematics teaching. *Unit head:* Dr. Rogers Hall, Chair, 615-322-8100, Fax: 615-322-8999, E-mail: rogers.hall@vanderbilt.edu. *Application contact:* Angela Saylor, Educational Coordinator, 615-322-8092, Fax: 615-322-8999, E-mail: angela.saylor@vanderbilt.edu.

Virginia Commonwealth University, Graduate School, School of Education, Program in Teaching and Learning, Richmond, VA 23284-9005. Offers early and elementary education (MT); health and physical education (MT); secondary 6-12 education (MT); secondary education (Certificate). *Accreditation:* NCATE. Part-time programs available. *Entrance requirements:* For master's, GRE General Test or MAT. Additional exam requirements/recommendations for international students: Required—TOEFL (minimum score 600 paper-based; 100 iBT). Electronic applications accepted.

Wagner College, Division of Graduate Studies, Department of Education, Program in Childhood Education/Special Education, Staten Island, NY 10301-4495. Offers MS Ed. Part-time and evening/weekend programs available. *Degree requirements:* For master's, thesis (for some programs). *Entrance requirements:* For master's, minimum GPA of 3.0, interview, recommendations. Additional exam requirements/recommendations for international students: Required—TOEFL. Electronic applications accepted. *Expenses: Tuition:* Full-time $17,496; part-time $972 per credit. Tuition and fees vary according to course load.

Walden University, Graduate Programs, Richard W. Riley College of Education and Leadership, Minneapolis, MN 55401. *Accreditation:* NCATE. Part-time and evening/weekend programs available. Postbaccalaureate distance learning degree programs offered (minimal on-campus study). *Faculty:* 23 full-time (15 women), 830 part-time/adjunct (569 women). *Students:* 8,671 full-time (7,197 women), 2,122 part-time (1,735 women); includes 4,734 minority (3,802 Black or African American, non-Hispanic/Latino; 50 American Indian or Alaska Native, non-Hispanic/Latino; 136 Asian, non-Hispanic/Latino; 539 Hispanic/Latino; 35 Native Hawaiian or other Pacific Islander, non-Hispanic/Latino; 172 Two or more races, non-Hispanic/Latino), 73 international. Average age 40. 2,646 applicants, 96% accepted, 2074 enrolled. In 2013, 2,214 master's, 354 doctorates, 479 other advanced degrees awarded. *Degree requirements:* For doctorate, thesis/dissertation (for some programs), residency; for other advanced degree, residency (for some programs). *Entrance requirements:* For master's, bachelor's degree or higher; minimum GPA of 2.5; official transcripts; goal statement (for some programs); access to computer and Internet; for doctorate, master's degree or higher; three years of related professional or academic experience (preferred); minimum GPA of 3.0; goal statement and current resume (select programs); official transcripts; access to computer and Internet; for other advanced degree, relevant work experience; access to computer and Internet. Additional exam requirements/recommendations for international students: Required—TOEFL (minimum score 550 paper-based; 79 iBT), IELTS (minimum score 6.5), Michigan English Language Assessment Battery (minimum score 82), or PTE. *Application deadline:* Applications are processed on a rolling basis. Application fee: $0. Electronic applications accepted. *Expenses: Tuition:* Full-time $11,813.55; part-time $500 per credit. *Required fees:* $618.76. *Financial support:* In 2013–14, 1 fellowship was awarded; Federal Work-Study, scholarships/grants, unspecified assistantships, and family tuition reduction, active duty/veteran tuition reduction, group tuition reduction, interest-free payment plans, employee tuition reduction also available. Support available to part-time students. Financial award applicants required to submit FAFSA. *Unit head:* Dr. Kate Steffens, Dean, 800-925-3368. *Application contact:* Jennifer Hall, Vice President of Enrollment Management, 866-4-WALDEN, E-mail: info@waldenu.edu. Website: http://www.waldenu.edu/colleges-schools/riley-college-of-education/.

Washington State University, Graduate School, College of Education, Department of Teaching and Learning, Program in Teaching, Pullman, WA 99164. Offers elementary education (MIT), including K-8; secondary education (MIT). *Degree requirements:* For master's, comprehensive exam, written and oral exam. *Entrance requirements:* For master's, WEST-B; WEST-E, minimum GPA of 3.0, letters of recommendation, letter of intent, current resume, writing sample, transcripts. Additional exam requirements/recommendations for international students: Required—TOEFL (minimum score 550 paper-based; 80 iBT). Electronic applications accepted.

Washington State University Spokane, Graduate Programs, Education Department, Spokane, WA 99210. Offers curriculum and instruction (Ed M); educational leadership (Ed M, MA); principal (Certificate); program administrator (Certificate); superintendent (Certificate); teaching (MIT), including elementary, secondary. *Degree requirements:* For master's, comprehensive exam (for some programs), thesis (for some programs). *Entrance requirements:* For master's, GRE or GMAT, minimum GPA of 3.0, 3 letters of recommendation, resume. Additional exam requirements/recommendations for international students: Required—TOEFL (minimum score 550 paper-based).

Washington University in St. Louis, Graduate School of Arts and Sciences, Department of Education, Program in Elementary Education, St. Louis, MO 63130-4899. Offers MA Ed. *Degree requirements:* For master's, thesis or alternative. *Entrance requirements:* For master's, GRE General Test or MAT. *Application deadline:* For fall admission, 1/15 priority date for domestic students. Applications are processed on a rolling basis. Application fee: $35. Electronic applications accepted. *Financial support:* Career-related internships or fieldwork available. Financial award application deadline: 1/15. *Unit head:* Dr. William Tate, Chair, 314-935-6730.

Wayland Baptist University, Graduate Programs, Program in Education, Plainview, TX 79072-6998. Offers education administration (M Ed); education diagnostics (M Ed); education literacy (M Ed); elementary certification (M Ed); English (M Ed); English as a second language (M Ed); higher education administration (M Ed); human resources (M Ed); instructional leadership (M Ed); instructional technology (M Ed); science education (M Ed); secondary certification (M Ed); social studies (M Ed); special education (M Ed). Part-time and evening/weekend programs available. Postbaccalaureate distance learning degree programs offered (no on-campus study). *Faculty:* 33 full-time (17 women), 28 part-time/adjunct (17 women). *Students:* 22 full-time (15 women), 316 part-time (189 women); includes 130 minority (48 Black or African American, non-Hispanic/Latino; 3 American Indian or Alaska Native, non-Hispanic/Latino; 71 Hispanic/Latino; 1 Native Hawaiian or other Pacific Islander, non-Hispanic/Latino; 7 Two or more races, non-Hispanic/Latino). Average age 39. 80 applicants, 96% accepted, 44 enrolled. In 2013, 170 master's awarded. *Degree requirements:* For master's, comprehensive exam, capstone course. *Entrance requirements:* For master's, GRE, GMAT or MAT. Additional exam requirements/recommendations for international students: Required—TOEFL (minimum score 500 paper-based; 61 iBT). *Application deadline:* Applications are processed on a rolling basis. Application fee: $50. Electronic applications accepted. *Expenses: Tuition:* Full-time $8190; part-time $455 per credit hour. *Required fees:* $970; $455 per credit hour. $485 per semester. *Financial support:* Federal Work-Study, institutionally sponsored loans, and scholarships/grants available. Support available to part-time students. Financial award application deadline: 5/1; financial award applicants required to submit FAFSA. *Unit head:* Dr. Jim Todd, Chairman, 806-291-1045, Fax: 806-291-1951. *Application contact:* Amanda Stanton, Coordinator of Graduate Studies, 806-291-3423, Fax: 806-291-1950, E-mail: stanton@wbu.edu.

Wayne State College, School of Education and Counseling, Department of Educational Foundations and Leadership, Program in Curriculum and Instruction, Wayne, NE 68787. Offers alternative education (MSE); business and information technology education (MSE); communication arts education (MSE); early childhood education (MSE); elementary education (MSE); English as a second language (MSE); English education (MSE); family and consumer sciences education (MSE); industrial technology and vocational education (MSE); learning communities (MSE); mathematics education (MSE); music education (MSE); science education (MSE); social science education (MSE). *Accreditation:* NCATE. Part-time and evening/weekend programs available. *Degree requirements:* For master's, comprehensive exam, thesis optional. *Entrance requirements:* For master's, GRE General Test. Additional exam requirements/recommendations for international students: Required—TOEFL (minimum score 550 paper-based).

Wayne State University, College of Education, Division of Kinesiology, Health and Sports Studies, Detroit, MI 48202. Offers adapted physical education (Certificate); coaching (Certificate); elementary physical education (Certificate); exercise and sport science (M Ed); health education (M Ed, Certificate); kinesiology (M Ed, PhD), including exercise and sport science (PhD), physical education pedagogy (PhD); physical education (M Ed); secondary physical education (Certificate); sports administration (MA); wellness clinician/research (M Ed). Part-time programs available. *Students:* 42 full-time (27 women), 78 part-time (38 women); includes 43 minority (35 Black or African American, non-Hispanic/Latino; 1 Asian, non-Hispanic/Latino; 5 Hispanic/Latino; 2 Two or more races, non-Hispanic/Latino), 5 international. Average age 30. 120 applicants, 48% accepted, 30 enrolled. In 2013, 32 master's awarded. *Degree requirements:* For master's, thesis (for some programs); for doctorate, thesis/dissertation. *Entrance requirements:* For master's and doctorate, minimum undergraduate GPA of 3.0, undergraduate degree directly relating to the field of specialization being applied for, or undergraduate degree accompanied by extensive educational background in a closely-related field. Additional exam requirements/recommendations for international students: Required—TOEFL (minimum score 79 iBT), TWE (minimum score 5.5), Michigan English Language Assessment Battery (minimum score 85); Recommended—IELTS (minimum score 6.5). *Application deadline:* For fall admission, 6/1 priority date for domestic students, 5/1 priority date for international students; for winter admission, 10/1 priority date for domestic students, 9/1 priority date for international students; for spring admission, 2/1 priority date for domestic students, 1/1 priority date for international students. Applications are processed on a rolling basis. Application fee: $0. Electronic applications accepted. *Expenses:* Tuition, state resident: part-time $554.15 per credit. Tuition, nonresident: part-time $1200.35 per credit. *Required fees:* $42.15 per credit. $268.30 per semester. Tuition and fees vary according to course load and program. *Financial support:* In 2013–14, 22 students received support, including 4 fellowships with tuition reimbursements available (averaging $13,050 per year), 5 research assistantships with tuition reimbursements available (averaging $16,508 per year); career-related internships or fieldwork, Federal Work-Study, scholarships/grants, health care benefits, and unspecified assistantships also available. Support available to part-time students. Financial award application deadline: 3/31; financial award applicants required to submit FAFSA. *Faculty research:* Exercise and sport science, nutrition and physical activity interventions, school and community health, obesity prevention. *Total annual research expenditures:* $1.3 million. *Unit head:* Dr. Nate McCaughtry, Assistant Dean, Division of Kinesiology, Health and Sport Studies/Director, Center for School Health, 313-577-0014, Fax: 313-577-5002, E-mail: aj4391@wayne.edu. *Application contact:* Janice Green, Assistant Dean, 313-577-1605, E-mail: jwgreen@wayne.edu. Website: http://coe.wayne.edu/kinesiology/index.php.

Wayne State University, College of Education, Division of Teacher Education, Detroit, MI 48202. Offers art education (M Ed), including art therapy; autism spectrum disorders (Certificate); bilingual/bicultural education (M Ed, Certificate); career and technical education (M Ed, Certificate); cognitive impairment (Certificate); curriculum and instruction (Ed D, PhD, Ed S), including art education (PhD), bilingual education (Ed D, Ed S), bilingual-bicultural education (PhD), career and technical education (MAT, Ed D, PhD, Ed S), early childhood education (MAT, Ed D, PhD, Ed S), elementary education, English as a second language (MAT, Ed D, Ed S), English education (MAT, Ed D, PhD, Ed S), foreign language education (MAT, PhD), K-12 curriculum, mathematics education (MAT, Ed D, PhD, Ed S), science education (MAT, Ed D, PhD, Ed S), secondary education, social studies education (MAT, Ed S), social studies education: secondary (Ed D, PhD); early childhood education (M Ed, Certificate); elementary education (M Ed, MAT), including children's literature (MAT), early childhood education (MAT, Ed D, PhD, Ed S), general elementary education (MAT); elementary or secondary education (MAT), including bilingual/bicultural education, English as a second language (MAT, Ed D, Ed S), mathematics education (MAT, Ed D, PhD, Ed S), science education (MAT, Ed D, PhD, Ed S), social studies education (MAT, Ed S); emotionally impaired (Certificate); English as a second language (Certificate); English education (M Ed), including secondary; foreign language education (M Ed); K-12 reading specialist (Certificate); learning disabilities (Certificate); mathematics education (M Ed), including secondary; reading (M Ed, Ed S); reading, language and literature (Ed D); science education (M Ed), including secondary; secondary education (MAT), including art education (K-12), career and technical education (MAT, Ed D, PhD, Ed S), English education (MAT, Ed D, PhD, Ed S), foreign language education (MAT, PhD), kinesiology; social studies education (M Ed), including secondary; special education (M Ed, MAT, Ed D, PhD, Ed S); visual arts education (Certificate). Part-time programs available. *Faculty:* 36 full-time (25 women), 55 part-time/adjunct (43 women). *Students:* 218 full-time (163 women), 448 part-time (344 women); includes 218 minority (177 Black or African American, non-Hispanic/Latino; 2 American Indian or Alaska Native, non-Hispanic/Latino; 11 Asian, non-Hispanic/Latino; 19 Hispanic/Latino; 1 Native Hawaiian or other Pacific Islander, non-Hispanic/Latino; 8 Two or more races, non-Hispanic/Latino), 10 international. Average age 37. 258 applicants, 30% accepted, 52 enrolled. In 2013, 183 master's, 10 doctorates, 35 other advanced degrees awarded. *Degree requirements:* For master's, thesis, essay or project (for some M Ed programs), professional field experience (for MAT programs); for doctorate, thesis/dissertation. *Entrance requirements:* For master's, Michigan Basic Skills Test (MA in teaching), admission to the graduate school, verification of participation in group work with children and Michigan State Police Criminal Background check; for doctorate, minimum undergraduate GPA of 3.0, graduate 3.5; interview, curriculum vitae; references. Additional exam requirements/recommendations for international students: Required—TOEFL (minimum score 550 paper-based; 79 iBT), TWE (minimum score 5.5), Michigan English Language Assessment Battery (minimum score 85); Recommended—IELTS (minimum score 6.5). *Application deadline:* For fall admission, 6/1 priority date for domestic students, 5/1 priority date for international students; for winter admission, 10/1

priority date for domestic students, 9/1 priority date for international students; for spring admission, 2/1 priority date for domestic students, 1/1 priority date for international students. Applications are processed on a rolling basis. Application fee: $0. Electronic applications accepted. *Expenses:* Tuition, state resident: part-time $554.15 per credit. Tuition, nonresident: part-time $1200.35 per credit. *Required fees:* $42.15 per credit. $268.30 per semester. Tuition and fees vary according to course load and program. *Financial support:* In 2013–14, 83 students received support, including 1 fellowship (averaging $16,842 per year), 1 research assistantship with tuition reimbursement available (averaging $21,229 per year); career-related internships or fieldwork, Federal Work-Study, scholarships/grants, health care benefits, and unspecified assistantships also available. Support available to part-time students. Financial award application deadline: 3/31; financial award applicants required to submit FAFSA. *Faculty research:* Improving students' skill achievement in mathematics; improving elementary children's understanding of informational text; teachers' use of their pedagogical and mathematical knowledge in the interactive work of teaching; the intersection of identity construction in teaching and learning; identifying effective methods of literacy instruction and assessments for bilingual students in elementary language arts classrooms. *Total annual research expenditures:* $368,105. *Unit head:* Dr. Kathleen Crawford-McKinney, Assistant Dean, 313-577-0122. *Application contact:* Janice Green, Assistant Dean, 313-577-1605, E-mail: jwgreen@wayne.edu.
Website: http://coe.wayne.edu/ted/index.php.

Webster University, School of Education, Department of Communication Arts, Reading and Early Childhood, St. Louis, MO 63119-3194. Offers early childhood education (MAT); elementary education (MAT); middle school education (MAT). *Entrance requirements:* For master's, minimum GPA of 2.5. Additional exam requirements/recommendations for international students: Required—TOEFL. *Expenses: Tuition:* Full-time $11,610; part-time $645 per credit hour. Tuition and fees vary according to campus/location and program.

West Chester University of Pennsylvania, College of Education, Department of Early and Middle Grades, West Chester, PA 19383. Offers applied studies in teaching and learning (M Ed); early childhood education (M Ed, Teaching Certificate); early grades preparation (Teaching Certificate); elementary education (Teaching Certificate); middle grades preparation (Teaching Certificate). *Accreditation:* NCATE. Part-time and evening/weekend programs available. *Faculty:* 5 full-time (all women), 1 part-time/adjunct (0 women). *Students:* 26 full-time (17 women), 68 part-time (58 women); includes 11 minority (7 Black or African American, non-Hispanic/Latino; 1 American Indian or Alaska Native, non-Hispanic/Latino; 1 Asian, non-Hispanic/Latino; 2 Hispanic/Latino), 3 international. Average age 31. 41 applicants, 83% accepted, 8 enrolled. In 2013, 17 master's, 3 other advanced degrees awarded. *Degree requirements:* For master's, teacher research project, portfolio. *Entrance requirements:* For master's, minimum GPA of 3.0, teacher certification (for applied studies in teaching and learning track), one year of full-time teaching experience; for Teaching Certificate, math, social studies, or science concentration exams (for middle grades preparation), minimum GPA of 3.0. Additional exam requirements/recommendations for international students: Required—TOEFL (minimum score 550 paper-based; 80 iBT). *Application deadline:* For fall admission, 4/15 priority date for domestic students, 3/15 for international students; for spring admission, 10/15 priority date for domestic students. Applications are processed on a rolling basis. Application fee: $45. Electronic applications accepted. *Expenses:* Tuition, state resident: full-time $7956; part-time $442 per credit. Tuition, nonresident: full-time $11,934; part-time $663 per credit. *Required fees:* $2134.20; $106.24 per credit. Tuition and fees vary according to campus/location and program. *Financial support:* Unspecified assistantships available. Support available to part-time students. Financial award application deadline: 2/15; financial award applicants required to submit FAFSA. *Faculty research:* Cooperative learning, creative expression and critical thinking, teacher research, learning styles, middle school education. *Unit head:* Dr. Heather Leaman, Chair, 610-436-2944, Fax: 610-436-3102, E-mail: hleaman@wcupa.edu. *Application contact:* Dr. Connie DiLucchio, Graduate Coordinator, 610-436-3323, Fax: 610-436-3102, E-mail: cdilucchio@wcupa.edu.

West Chester University of Pennsylvania, College of Education, Department of Special Education, West Chester, PA 19383. Offers autism (Certificate); special education (M Ed); special education 7-12 (Certificate); special education PK-8 (Certificate); universal design for learning and assistive technology (Certificate). Programs available in traditional, distance, and blended formats. *Accreditation:* NCATE. Part-time programs available. Postbaccalaureate distance learning degree programs offered (no on-campus study). *Faculty:* 4 full-time (all women), 3 part-time/adjunct (2 women). *Students:* 7 full-time (6 women), 106 part-time (91 women); includes 7 minority (5 Black or African American, non-Hispanic/Latino; 1 Asian, non-Hispanic/Latino; 1 Hispanic/Latino), 1 international. Average age 29. 83 applicants, 89% accepted, 42 enrolled. In 2013, 30 master's, 2 Certificates awarded. *Degree requirements:* For master's, thesis optional, minimum GPA of 3.0, action research; for Certificate, minimum GPA of 3.0; modified student teaching. *Entrance requirements:* For master's, GRE if GPA below 3.0, two letters of recommendation; for Certificate, minimum GPA of 2.8 on last 48 credits or 3.0 overall undergraduate. Additional exam requirements/recommendations for international students: Required—TOEFL (minimum score 550 paper-based; 80 iBT). *Application deadline:* For fall admission, 4/15 priority date for domestic students, 3/15 for international students; for spring admission, 10/15 priority date for domestic students, 9/1 for international students. Applications are processed on a rolling basis. Application fee: $45. Electronic applications accepted. *Expenses:* Tuition, state resident: full-time $7956; part-time $442 per credit. Tuition, nonresident: full-time $11,934; part-time $663 per credit. *Required fees:* $2134.20; $106.24 per credit. Tuition and fees vary according to campus/location and program. *Financial support:* Unspecified assistantships available. Support available to part-time students. Financial award application deadline: 2/15; financial award applicants required to submit FAFSA. *Unit head:* Dr. Donna Wandry, Chair, 610-436-3431, Fax: 610-436-3102, E-mail: dwandry@wcupa.edu. *Application contact:* Dr. Vicki McGinley, Graduate Coordinator, 610-436-2867, E-mail: vmcginley@wcupa.edu.
Website: http://www.wcupa.edu/_academics/sch_sed.earlyspecialed/.

Western Governors University, Teachers College, Salt Lake City, UT 84107. Offers curriculum and instruction (MS); educational leadership (MS); educational studies (MA); educational studies (5-12) (MA), including mathematics; elementary education (K-8) (MAT, Postbaccalaureate Certificate); elementary education (PreK-8) (MAT); English language learning (K-12) (MA); instructional design (MAT); learning and technology (M Ed, MA); management and innovation (M Ed); mathematics (5-12) (MAT, Postbaccalaureate Certificate); mathematics (5-9) (MAT, Postbaccalaureate Certificate); mathematics education (5-12) (MA); mathematics education (5-9) (MA); mathematics education (K-6) (MA); measurement and evaluation (M Ed); science (5-12) (Postbaccalaureate Certificate); science (5-9) (MAT, Postbaccalaureate Certificate); science education (5-12) (MA), including biology, chemistry, geology, physics; science education (5-9) (MA); social science (5-12) (MAT, Postbaccalaureate Certificate); special education (MAT, MS). *Accreditation:* NCATE. Evening/weekend programs available. Postbaccalaureate distance learning degree programs offered (no on-campus study). *Degree requirements:* For master's, capstone project. *Entrance requirements:* For master's and Postbaccalaureate Certificate, Readiness Assessment, transcripts. Additional exam requirements/recommendations for international students: Required—

TOEFL (minimum score 450 paper-based; 80 iBT). Electronic applications accepted. *Expenses:* Contact institution.

Western Illinois University, School of Graduate Studies, College of Education and Human Services, Department of Curriculum and Instruction, Program in Elementary Education, Macomb, IL 61455-1390. Offers MS Ed. *Accreditation:* NCATE. Part-time programs available. *Students:* 1 (woman) full-time, 72 part-time (64 women); includes 4 minority (1 Black or African American, non-Hispanic/Latino; 2 Hispanic/Latino; 1 Two or more races, non-Hispanic/Latino). Average age 32. In 2013, 26 master's awarded. *Degree requirements:* For master's, thesis or alternative. *Entrance requirements:* Additional exam requirements/recommendations for international students: Required—TOEFL (minimum score 550 paper-based; 80 iBT). *Application deadline:* Applications are processed on a rolling basis. Application fee: $30. Electronic applications accepted. *Financial support:* In 2013–14, 1 student received support, including 1 research assistantship with full tuition reimbursement available (averaging $7,544 per year). Financial award applicants required to submit FAFSA. *Unit head:* Dr. Anne Gregory, Chairperson, 309-298-1961. *Application contact:* Dr. Nancy Parsons, Assistant Director of Graduate Studies, 309-298-1806, Fax: 309-298-2345, E-mail: grad-office@wiu.edu.
Website: http://wiu.edu/curriculum.

Western Kentucky University, Graduate Studies, College of Education and Behavioral Sciences, School of Teacher Education, Bowling Green, KY 42101. Offers elementary education (MAE, Ed S); exceptional education: learning and behavioral disorders (MAE); exceptional education: moderate and severe disabilities (MAE); instructional design (MS); interdisciplinary early childhood education (MAE); library media education (MS); literacy education (MAE); middle grades education (MAE); secondary education (MAE, Ed S). Part-time and evening/weekend programs available. Postbaccalaureate distance learning degree programs offered (minimal on-campus study). *Degree requirements:* For master's, comprehensive exam. *Entrance requirements:* For master's, GRE General Test. Additional exam requirements/recommendations for international students: Required—TOEFL (minimum score 555 paper-based; 79 iBT). *Faculty research:* Teacher preparation in moderate/severe disabilities.

Western New England University, College of Arts and Sciences, Program in Elementary Education, Springfield, MA 01119. Offers M Ed. Part-time and evening/weekend programs available. *Faculty:* 3 full-time (2 women). *Students:* 11 part-time (all women); includes 1 minority (Black or African American, non-Hispanic/Latino). Average age 28. 19 applicants. In 2013, 11 master's awarded. *Entrance requirements:* For master's, two letters of recommendation, official transcript, personal statement, resume, copy of initial teacher's license. Additional exam requirements/recommendations for international students: Required—TOEFL. *Application deadline:* Applications are processed on a rolling basis. Application fee: $30. Electronic applications accepted. Tuition and fees vary according to program. *Financial support:* Application deadline: 4/15; applicants required to submit FAFSA. *Unit head:* Dr. Saeed Ghahramani, Dean, 413-782-1218, Fax: 413-796-2118, E-mail: sghahram@wne.edu. *Application contact:* Matthew Fox, Director of Admissions for Graduate Students and Adult Learners, 413-782-1517, Fax: 413-782-1777, E-mail: study@wne.edu.
Website: http://www1.wne.edu/artsandsciences/index.cfm?selection=doc.1672.

Western New Mexico University, Graduate Division, School of Education, Silver City, NM 88062-0680. Offers bilingual education (MAT); counseling (MA); educational leadership (MA); elementary education (MAT); reading (MAT); school psychology (MA); secondary education (MAT); special education (MAT); TESOL (teaching English to speakers of other languages) (MAT). *Accreditation:* NCATE. *Degree requirements:* For master's, comprehensive exam. *Entrance requirements:* For master's, GRE General Test, GRE Subject Test, minimum GPA of 3.2 in last 64 hours of undergraduate study. Additional exam requirements/recommendations for international students: Required—TOEFL (minimum score 550 paper-based). Electronic applications accepted.

Western Washington University, Graduate School, Woodring College of Education, Department of Elementary Education, Bellingham, WA 98225-5996. Offers M Ed. *Accreditation:* NCATE. Part-time programs available. *Degree requirements:* For master's, comprehensive exam, thesis optional. *Entrance requirements:* For master's, GRE General Test or MAT, minimum GPA of 3.0 in last 60 semester hours or last 90 quarter hours, elementary teaching certificate. Additional exam requirements/recommendations for international students: Required—TOEFL (minimum score 567 paper-based). Electronic applications accepted. *Faculty research:* Teacher learning through National Board certification.

Westfield State University, Division of Graduate and Continuing Education, Department of Education, Program in Elementary Education, Westfield, MA 01086. Offers M Ed. *Accreditation:* NCATE. Part-time and evening/weekend programs available. *Degree requirements:* For master's, comprehensive exam, practicum. *Entrance requirements:* For master's, GRE General Test or MAT, minimum undergraduate GPA of 2.7.

West Virginia University, College of Human Resources and Education, Department of Curriculum and Instruction/Literacy Studies, Program in Elementary Education, Morgantown, WV 26506. Offers MA. Students enter program as undergraduates. *Accreditation:* NCATE. Part-time programs available. *Degree requirements:* For master's, thesis optional, content exams. *Entrance requirements:* For master's, minimum GPA of 2.75. Additional exam requirements/recommendations for international students: Required—TOEFL. Electronic applications accepted. *Faculty research:* Teacher education, school reform, teacher and student attitudes, curriculum development, education technology.

Wheaton College, Graduate School, Department of Education, Wheaton, IL 60187-5593. Offers elementary education (MAT); secondary education (MAT). *Accreditation:* NCATE. *Degree requirements:* For master's, thesis or alternative. *Entrance requirements:* For master's, GRE General Test or MAT. Additional exam requirements/recommendations for international students: Required—TOEFL (minimum score 550 paper-based; 80 iBT), IELTS (minimum score 6.5). Electronic applications accepted.

Wheelock College, Graduate Programs, Division of Education, Boston, MA 02215-4176. Offers early childhood education (MS); education leadership (MS); elementary education (MS); language, literacy, and reading (MS); teaching students with moderate disabilities (MS). *Accreditation:* NCATE. Postbaccalaureate distance learning degree programs offered (minimal on-campus study). *Degree requirements:* For master's, comprehensive exam. *Entrance requirements:* Additional exam requirements/recommendations for international students: Required—TOEFL. Electronic applications accepted. *Faculty research:* Symbolic learning, emergent literacy, diversity inclusion, beginning reading language and culture, math education.

Whittier College, Graduate Programs, Department of Education and Child Development, Program in Elementary Education, Whittier, CA 90608-0634. Offers MA Ed. Part-time and evening/weekend programs available. *Degree requirements:* For master's, thesis. *Entrance requirements:* For master's, GRE General Test, MAT.

Whitworth University, School of Education, Graduate Studies in Education, Spokane, WA 99251-0001. Offers administration (M Ed); counseling (M Ed), including school counselors, social agency/church setting; elementary education (M Ed); gifted and talented (MAT); secondary education (M Ed); special education (MAT); teaching (MIT).

Accreditation: NCATE. Part-time and evening/weekend programs available. *Degree requirements:* For master's, comprehensive exam, thesis (for some programs). *Entrance requirements:* For master's, GRE General Test, MAT. Additional exam requirements/recommendations for international students: Required—TOEFL. *Faculty research:* Rural program development, mainstreaming, special needs learners.

Widener University, School of Human Service Professions, Center for Education, Chester, PA 19013-5792. Offers adult education (M Ed); counseling in higher education (M Ed); counselor education (M Ed); early childhood education (M Ed); educational foundations (M Ed); educational leadership (M Ed); educational psychology (M Ed); elementary education (M Ed); English and language arts (M Ed); health education (M Ed); higher education leadership (Ed D); home and school visitor (M Ed); human sexuality (M Ed, PhD); mathematics education (M Ed); middle school education (M Ed); principalship (M Ed); reading and language arts (Ed D); reading education (M Ed); school administration (Ed D); science education (M Ed); social studies education (M Ed); special education (M Ed); technology education (M Ed). *Accreditation:* NCATE. Part-time and evening/weekend programs available. *Faculty:* 34 full-time (22 women), 37 part-time/adjunct (14 women). *Students:* 64 full-time (44 women), 209 part-time (146 women); includes 49 minority (39 Black or African American, non-Hispanic/Latino; 1 American Indian or Alaska Native, non-Hispanic/Latino; 4 Asian, non-Hispanic/Latino; 4 Hispanic/Latino; 1 Two or more races, non-Hispanic/Latino), 8 international. Average age 39. 139 applicants, 88% accepted. In 2013, 168 master's, 31 doctorates awarded. Terminal master's awarded for partial completion of doctoral program. *Degree requirements:* For doctorate, thesis/dissertation. *Entrance requirements:* For master's, minimum GPA of 2.5; for doctorate, GRE or MAT, minimum GPA of 2.0 (undergraduate), 3.5 (graduate). *Application deadline:* Applications are processed on a rolling basis. Application fee: $25 ($300 for international students). Electronic applications accepted. *Expenses:* Contact institution. *Financial support:* Career-related internships or fieldwork, tuition waivers (full and partial), and unspecified assistantships available. Support available to part-time students. Financial award application deadline: 5/1. *Faculty research:* Reading and cognition, adult education, technology education, educational leadership, special education. *Unit head:* Dr. Michael W. LeDoux, Associate Dean, 610-499-4294, Fax: 610-499-4623, E-mail: mwledoux@widener.edu. *Application contact:* Dr. Roberta Nolan, Director of Graduate Admissions, 610-499-4125, E-mail: rdnolan@widener.edu.

William Carey University, School of Education, Hattiesburg, MS 39401-5499. Offers art education (M Ed); art of teaching (M Ed); elementary education (M Ed, Ed S); English education (M Ed); gifted education (M Ed); history and social science (M Ed); mild/moderate disabilities (M Ed); secondary education (M Ed). *Accreditation:* NCATE. Part-time programs available. *Degree requirements:* For master's, comprehensive exam. *Entrance requirements:* For master's, GRE, MAT, minimum GPA of 2.5, Class A teacher's license. Additional exam requirements/recommendations for international students: Required—TOEFL (minimum score 550 paper-based).

Wilmington University, College of Education, New Castle, DE 19720-6491. Offers applied technology in education (M Ed); career and technical education (M Ed); educational leadership (Ed D); elementary and secondary school counseling (M Ed); elementary studies (M Ed); ESOL literacy (M Ed); higher education leadership (Ed D); instruction: gifted and talented (M Ed); instruction: teacher of reading (M Ed); instruction: teaching and learning (M Ed); organizational leadership (Ed D); school leadership (M Ed); secondary education (MAT); special education (M Ed). *Accreditation:* NCATE. Part-time and evening/weekend programs available. *Entrance requirements:* For master's, 2 letters of recommendation, interview. Additional exam requirements/recommendations for international students: Required—TOEFL (minimum score 500 paper-based). Electronic applications accepted.

Wilson College, Program in Education, Chambersburg, PA 17201-1285. Offers M Ed. Evening/weekend programs available. *Degree requirements:* For master's, project. *Entrance requirements:* For master's, PRAXIS, minimum undergraduate cumulative GPA of 3.0, 2 letters of recommendation, current certification for eligibility to teach in grades K-12, resume, personal interview. Electronic applications accepted.

Wingate University, Thayer School of Education, Wingate, NC 28174-0159. Offers community college leadership (Ed D); educational leadership (MA Ed, Ed D); elementary education (MA Ed, MAT); health and physical education (MA Ed); sport administration (MA Ed). *Accreditation:* NCATE. Part-time and evening/weekend programs available. *Degree requirements:* For master's, portfolio. *Entrance requirements:* For master's, GRE General Test or MAT, teaching certificate (MA Ed).

Winston-Salem State University, Program in Elementary Education, Winston-Salem, NC 27110-0003. Offers M Ed. *Accreditation:* NCATE. Part-time and evening/weekend programs available. Postbaccalaureate distance learning degree programs offered (minimal on-campus study). *Entrance requirements:* For master's, GRE, MAT, NC teacher licensure. Electronic applications accepted. *Faculty research:* Action research on issues in elementary classroom.

Worcester State University, Graduate Studies, Department of Education, Program in Elementary Education, Worcester, MA 01602-2597. Offers M Ed. Part-time and evening/weekend programs available. *Faculty:* 14 full-time (11 women), 22 part-time/adjunct (10 women). *Students:* 4 full-time (all women), 21 part-time (all women); includes 3 minority (1 Black or African American, non-Hispanic/Latino; 1 American Indian or Alaska Native, non-Hispanic/Latino; 1 Two or more races, non-Hispanic/Latino). Average age 32. 8 applicants, 75% accepted, 4 enrolled. In 2013, 7 master's awarded. *Degree requirements:* For master's, comprehensive exam (for some programs), thesis optional. *Entrance requirements:* For master's, GRE General Test or MAT, elementary teaching certificate. Additional exam requirements/recommendations for international students: Required—TOEFL (minimum score 500 paper-based; 61 iBT). *Application deadline:* For fall admission, 6/15 for domestic and international students; for spring admission, 4/1 for domestic and international students. Applications are processed on a rolling basis. Application fee: $40. Electronic applications accepted. *Expenses: Tuition, area resident:* Part-time $150 per credit. Tuition, state resident: part-time $150 per credit. Tuition, nonresident: part-time $150 per credit. *Required fees:* $114.50 per credit. *Financial support:* Career-related internships or fieldwork, scholarships/grants, and unspecified assistantships available. Financial award application deadline: 3/1; financial award applicants required to submit FAFSA. *Faculty research:* Contemporary elementary education, social studies in the elementary school. *Unit head:* Dr. Christine Bebas, Coordinator, 508-929-8753, Fax: 508-929-8164, E-mail: cbebas@worcester.edu. *Application contact:* Sara Grady, Assistant Dean of Graduate and Continuing Education, 508-929-8787, Fax: 508-929-8100, E-mail: sara.grady@worcester.edu.

Wright State University, School of Graduate Studies, College of Education and Human Services, Department of Teacher Education, Programs in Classroom Teacher Education, Dayton, OH 45435. Offers M Ed, MA. *Accreditation:* NCATE. *Degree requirements:* For master's, thesis (for some programs). *Entrance requirements:* For master's, GRE General Test, MAT, PRAXIS II. Additional exam requirements/recommendations for international students: Required—TOEFL.

Xavier University, College of Social Sciences, Health and Education, School of Education, Department of Childhood Education and Literacy, Program in Elementary Education, Cincinnati, OH 45207. Offers M Ed. Part-time programs available. *Faculty:* 4 full-time (2 women), 1 part-time/adjunct (0 women). *Students:* 38 full-time (32 women), 39 part-time (34 women); includes 3 minority (2 Hispanic/Latino; 1 Two or more races, non-Hispanic/Latino). Average age 32. 19 applicants, 95% accepted, 13 enrolled. In 2013, 32 master's awarded. *Degree requirements:* For master's, comprehensive exam, research project or thesis. *Entrance requirements:* For master's, GRE or MAT. Additional exam requirements/recommendations for international students: Required—TOEFL (minimum score 550 paper-based; 79 iBT). *Application deadline:* Applications are processed on a rolling basis. Application fee: $35. Electronic applications accepted. *Expenses: Tuition:* Part-time $594 per credit hour. *Required fees:* $3 per semester. *Financial support:* In 2013–14, 53 students received support. Unspecified assistantships available. Financial award applicants required to submit FAFSA. *Faculty research:* First-year teacher retention, teaching efficacy of science educators, adolescents' literacy practices, family resiliency, preparing culturally responsive teachers. *Unit head:* Dr. Cynthia Geer, Department Chairperson/Professor, 513-745-3262, Fax: 513-745-3504, E-mail: geer@xavier.edu. *Application contact:* Roger Bosse, Graduate Services Director, 513-745-3357, Fax: 513-745-1048, E-mail: bosse@xavier.edu.
Website: http://www.xavier.edu/elementary-grad/.

Higher Education

Abilene Christian University, Graduate School, College of Education and Human Services, Program in Higher Education, Abilene, TX 79699-9100. Offers M Ed. Part-time programs available. Postbaccalaureate distance learning degree programs offered (minimal on-campus study). *Faculty:* 1 full-time (0 women). *Students:* 53 full-time (37 women), 16 part-time (11 women); includes 25 minority (14 Black or African American, non-Hispanic/Latino; 1 Asian, non-Hispanic/Latino; 7 Hispanic/Latino; 3 Two or more races, non-Hispanic/Latino), 1 international. 39 applicants, 97% accepted, 30 enrolled. In 2013, 21 master's awarded. *Degree requirements:* For master's, internship capstone. *Entrance requirements:* Additional exam requirements/recommendations for international students: Required—TOEFL (minimum score 550 paper-based; 90 iBT), IELTS (minimum score 6.5), PTE. *Application deadline:* For fall admission, 8/15 priority date for domestic students; for winter admission, 10/1 priority date for domestic students; for spring admission, 12/15 priority date for domestic students; for summer admission, 4/15 for domestic students. Applications are processed on a rolling basis. Application fee: $100. Electronic applications accepted. *Expenses:* Contact institution. *Financial support:* In 2013–14, 4 students received support. Application deadline: 4/1; applicants required to submit FAFSA. *Unit head:* Dr. Jason Morris, Graduate Advisor, 325-674-2838, Fax: 325-674-2123, E-mail: morrisj@acu.edu. *Application contact:* Corey Patterson, Director of Graduate Admission and Recruiting, 325-674-6566, Fax: 325-674-6717, E-mail: gradinfo@acu.edu.
Website: http://www.acu.edu/hied.

Alliant International University–San Diego, Shirley M. Hufstedler School of Education, Educational Leadership Programs, San Diego, CA 92131-1799. Offers educational administration (MA); educational leadership and management (K-12) (Ed D); higher education (Ed D, Certificate); preliminary administrative services (Credential). Part-time programs available. *Faculty:* 4 full-time (2 women), 3 part-time/adjunct (2 women). *Students:* 8 full-time (3 women), 25 part-time (14 women); includes 15 minority (6 Black or African American, non-Hispanic/Latino; 4 Asian, non-Hispanic/Latino; 5 Hispanic/Latino), 4 international. Average age 43. 21 applicants, 71% accepted, 11 enrolled. In 2013, 1 master's, 3 doctorates awarded. *Degree requirements:* For doctorate, comprehensive exam, thesis/dissertation. *Entrance requirements:* For master's, minimum GPA of 2.5, letters of recommendation; for doctorate, minimum GPA of 3.0, letters of recommendation. Additional exam requirements/recommendations for international students: Required—TOEFL (minimum score 550 paper-based; 80 iBT), TWE (minimum score 5). *Application deadline:* For fall admission, 4/15 priority date for domestic and international students; for spring admission, 11/3 priority date for domestic and international students; for summer admission, 2/15 for domestic and international students. Applications are processed on a rolling basis. Application fee: $65. Electronic applications accepted. *Financial support:* Federal Work-Study, institutionally sponsored loans, and scholarships/grants available. Financial award application deadline: 2/15; financial award applicants required to submit FAFSA. *Faculty research:* Global education, women and international educational opportunities. *Unit head:* Dr. Trudy Day, Program Director, Educational Policy and Practice Programs, 415-955-2102, Fax: 415-955-2179, E-mail: admissions@alliant.edu. *Application contact:* Alliant International University Central Contact Center, 866-U-ALLIANT, Fax: 858-635-4555, E-mail: admissions@alliant.edu.

Alliant International University–San Francisco, Shirley M. Hufstedler School of Education, Educational Leadership Programs, San Francisco, CA 94133-1221. Offers community college administration (Ed D); educational administration (MA); educational leadership and management (K-12) (Ed D); higher education (Ed D); preliminary administrative services (Credential). Part-time programs available. *Faculty:* 5 full-time (2 women), 2 part-time/adjunct (both women). *Students:* 1 (woman) full-time, 5 part-time (1 woman); includes 4 minority (1 Asian, non-Hispanic/Latino; 2 Hispanic/Latino; 1 Two or more races, non-Hispanic/Latino), 1 international. Average age 45. In 2013, 1 doctorate awarded. *Degree requirements:* For doctorate, comprehensive exam, thesis/dissertation. *Entrance requirements:* For master's and doctorate, minimum GPA of 3.0, letters of recommendation. Additional exam requirements/recommendations for international students: Required—TOEFL (minimum score 550 paper-based; 80 iBT), TWE (minimum score 5). *Application deadline:* For fall admission, 7/1 priority date for domestic and international students; for spring admission, 12/1 priority date for domestic and international students. Applications are processed on a rolling basis. Application fee: $65. Electronic applications accepted. *Financial support:* Federal Work-Study, institutionally sponsored loans, and scholarships/grants available. Financial award application deadline: 2/15; financial award applicants required to submit FAFSA. *Faculty research:* Leadership in higher education, community colleges. *Unit head:* Dr. Ed Shenk, Educational Policy and Practice Director, 415-955-2193, Fax: 415-955-2179, E-mail:

admissions@alliant.edu. *Application contact:* Alliant International University Central Contact Center, 866-U-ALLIANT, Fax: 858-635-4555, E-mail: admissions@alliant.edu. Website: http://www.alliant.edu/gsoe/.

Andrews University, School of Graduate Studies, School of Education, Department of Leadership and Educational Administration, Berrien Springs, MI 49104. Offers educational administration and leadership (MA, Ed D, PhD, Ed S); higher education administration (MA, Ed D, PhD, Ed S); leadership (MA, Ed D, PhD, Ed S). *Faculty:* 6 full-time (3 women). *Students:* 2 full-time (1 woman), 123 part-time (57 women); includes 41 minority (26 Black or African American, non-Hispanic/Latino; 3 Asian, non-Hispanic/Latino; 10 Hispanic/Latino; 2 Two or more races, non-Hispanic/Latino), 25 international. Average age 50. 57 applicants, 46% accepted, 13 enrolled. In 2013, 11 master's, 13 doctorates awarded. *Degree requirements:* For doctorate, thesis/dissertation. *Entrance requirements:* For master's, GRE. Additional exam requirements/recommendations for international students: Required—TOEFL (minimum score 550 paper-based). *Application deadline:* Applications are processed on a rolling basis. Application fee: $40. *Unit head:* Dr. Robson Marinho, Chair, 269-471-3487. *Application contact:* Monica Wringer, Supervisor of Graduate Admission, 800-253-2874, Fax: 269-471-6321, E-mail: graduate@andrews.edu.

Angelo State University, College of Graduate Studies, College of Education, Department of Curriculum and Instruction, Program in Student Development and Leadership in Higher Education, San Angelo, TX 76909. Offers M Ed. Part-time and evening/weekend programs available. *Degree requirements:* For master's, comprehensive exam. *Entrance requirements:* Additional exam requirements/recommendations for international students: Required—TOEFL or IELTS. Electronic applications accepted.

Appalachian State University, Cratis D. Williams Graduate School, Department of Leadership and Educational Studies, Boone, NC 28608. Offers educational administration (Ed S); educational media (MA); higher education (MA, Ed S); library science (MLS); school administration (MSA). Part-time and evening/weekend programs available. Postbaccalaureate distance learning degree programs offered (no on-campus study). *Degree requirements:* For master's and Ed S, comprehensive exam, thesis optional. *Entrance requirements:* For master's and Ed S, GRE or MAT, 3 letters of recommendation. Additional exam requirements/recommendations for international students: Required—TOEFL (minimum score 570 paper-based; 79 iBT), IELTS (minimum score 6.5). Electronic applications accepted. *Faculty research:* Brain, learning and meditation; leadership of teaching and learning.

Argosy University, Atlanta, College of Education, Atlanta, GA 30328. Offers educational leadership (MAEd, Ed D, Ed S), including higher education administration (Ed D), K-12 education (Ed D); teaching and learning (MAEd, Ed D, Ed S), including education technology (Ed D), higher education (Ed D), K-12 education (Ed D).

Argosy University, Chicago, College of Education, Chicago, IL 60601. Offers adult education and training (MA Ed); community college executive leadership (Ed D); educational leadership (MA Ed, Ed D, Ed S), including district leadership (Ed D), higher education administration (Ed D), K-12 education (Ed D); instructional leadership (Ed D, Ed S), including higher education (Ed D), K-12 education (Ed D). Postbaccalaureate distance learning degree programs offered (minimal on-campus study).

Argosy University, Dallas, College of Education, Farmers Branch, TX 75244. Offers educational administration (MA Ed); educational leadership (Ed D); higher and postsecondary education (MA Ed); instructional leadership (MA Ed); school psychology (MA).

Argosy University, Denver, College of Education, Denver, CO 80231. Offers community college executive leadership (Ed D); educational leadership (MA Ed, Ed D), including higher education (Ed D), K-12 education (Ed D); instructional leadership (MA Ed, Ed D), including higher education administration (Ed D), K-12 education (Ed D).

Argosy University, Hawai`i, College of Education, Honolulu, HI 96813. Offers adult education and training (MAEd); educational leadership (Ed D), including higher education administration, K-12 education; instructional leadership (Ed D), including higher education, K-12 education; school psychology (MA).

Argosy University, Inland Empire, College of Education, Ontario, CA 91761. Offers community college executive leadership (Ed D); educational leadership (MA Ed, Ed D), including higher education administration (Ed D), K-12 education (Ed D); instructional leadership (MA Ed, Ed D), including higher education (Ed D), K-12 education (Ed D), multiple subject teacher preparation (MA Ed), single subject teacher preparation (MA Ed).

Argosy University, Los Angeles, College of Education, Santa Monica, CA 90045. Offers community college executive leadership (Ed D); educational leadership (MA Ed, Ed D), including higher education administration (Ed D), K-12 education (Ed D); instructional leadership (MA Ed, Ed D), including higher education (Ed D), K-12 education (Ed D), multiple subject teacher preparation (MA Ed), single subject teacher preparation (MA Ed).

Argosy University, Nashville, College of Education, Program in Educational Leadership, Nashville, TN 37214. Offers educational leadership (MA Ed, Ed S); higher education administration (Ed D); K-12 education (Ed D).

Argosy University, Nashville, College of Education, Program in Instructional Leadership, Nashville, TN 37214. Offers education technology (Ed D); higher education administration (Ed D); instructional leadership (MA Ed, Ed S); K-12 education (Ed D).

Argosy University, Orange County, College of Education, Orange, CA 92868. Offers community college executive leadership (Ed D); educational leadership (MA Ed, Ed D), including higher education administration (Ed D), K-12 education (Ed D); instructional leadership (MA Ed, Ed D), including education technology (Ed D), higher education (Ed D), K-12 education (Ed D), multiple subject teacher preparation (MA Ed), single subject teacher preparation (MA Ed).

Argosy University, Phoenix, College of Education, Phoenix, AZ 85021. Offers adult education and training (MA Ed); advanced educational administration (Ed D, Ed S); community college executive leadership (Ed D); educational administration (MA Ed); educational leadership (MA Ed, Ed D, Ed S), including education technology (Ed D), higher education administration (Ed D), K-12 education (Ed D); higher and postsecondary education (MA Ed); initial educational administration (Ed D, Ed S); school psychology (MA); teaching and learning (MA Ed, Ed D, Ed S), including education technology (Ed D), higher education (Ed D), K-12 education (Ed D).

Argosy University, San Diego, College of Education, San Diego, CA 92108. Offers community college executive leadership (Ed D); educational leadership (MA Ed, Ed D), including higher education administration (Ed D), K-12 education (Ed D); instructional leadership (MA Ed, Ed D), including higher education (Ed D), K-12 education (Ed D).

Argosy University, San Francisco Bay Area, College of Education, Alameda, CA 94501. Offers community college executive leadership (Ed D); educational leadership (MA Ed, Ed D), including education technology (Ed D), higher education administration (Ed D), K-12 education (Ed D); instructional leadership (MA Ed, Ed D), including education technology (Ed D), higher education (Ed D), K-12 education (Ed D), multiple subject teacher preparation (MA Ed), single subject teacher preparation (MA Ed).

Argosy University, Sarasota, College of Education, Sarasota, FL 34235. Offers community college executive leadership (Ed D); educational leadership (MA Ed, Ed D, Ed S), including higher education administration (Ed D), K-12 education (Ed D); school counseling (MA, Ed S); school psychology (MA); teaching and learning (MA Ed, Ed D, Ed S), including education technology (Ed D), higher education (Ed D), K-12 education (Ed D).

Argosy University, Schaumburg, College of Education, Schaumburg, IL 60173-5403. Offers community college executive leadership (Ed D); educational leadership (MA Ed, Ed D, Ed S), including district leadership (Ed D), higher education administration (Ed D), K-12 education (Ed D); instructional leadership (Ed D, Ed S), including higher education (Ed D), K-12 education (Ed D).

Argosy University, Seattle, College of Education, Seattle, WA 98121. Offers adult education and training (MA Ed); community college executive leadership (Ed D); educational leadership (MA Ed, Ed D), including higher education administration (Ed D), K-12 education (Ed D); higher and postsecondary education (MA Ed); instructional leadership (MA Ed, Ed D), including education technology (Ed D), higher education (Ed D), K-12 education (Ed D).

Argosy University, Tampa, College of Education, Tampa, FL 33607. Offers community college executive leadership (Ed D); educational leadership (MA Ed, Ed D, Ed S), including higher education administration (Ed D), K-12 education (Ed D); school counseling (MA); teaching and learning (MA Ed, Ed D, Ed S), including higher education (Ed D), K-12 education (Ed D).

Argosy University, Twin Cities, College of Education, Eagan, MN 55121. Offers advanced educational administration (Ed D, Ed S); educational leadership (MA Ed, Ed D, Ed S), including higher education administration (Ed D), K-12 education (Ed D); higher and postsecondary education (MA Ed); initial educational administration (Ed D, Ed S); instructional leadership (MA Ed, Ed D, Ed S), including education technology (Ed D), higher education (Ed D), K-12 education (Ed D).

Argosy University, Washington DC, College of Education, Arlington, VA 22209. Offers community college executive leadership (Ed D); educational leadership (MA Ed, Ed D, Ed S), including higher education administration (Ed D), K-12 education (Ed D); instructional leadership (MA Ed, Ed D, Ed S), including higher education (Ed D), K-12 education (Ed D).

Arizona State University at the Tempe campus, Mary Lou Fulton Teachers College, Program in Higher and Post-Secondary Education, Phoenix, AZ 85069. Offers M Ed. Part-time and evening/weekend programs available. *Degree requirements:* For master's, thesis or alternative, applied project, interactive Program of Study (iPOS) submitted before completing 50 percent of required credit hours. *Entrance requirements:* For master's, minimum GPA of 3.0 or equivalent in last 2 years of work leading to bachelor's degree, 3 letters of recommendation, personal statement describing research and career goals, curriculum vitae or resume. Additional exam requirements/recommendations for international students: Required—TOEFL (minimum score 80 iBT), TOEFL, IELTS, or PTE. Electronic applications accepted.

Auburn University, Graduate School, College of Education, Department of Curriculum and Teaching, Auburn University, AL 36849. Offers business education (M Ed, MS, PhD); early childhood education (M Ed, MS, PhD, Ed S); elementary education (M Ed, MS, PhD, Ed S); foreign languages (M Ed, MS); music education (M Ed, MS, PhD, Ed S); postsecondary education (PhD); reading education (PhD, Ed S); secondary education (M Ed, MS, PhD, Ed S), including English language arts, mathematics, science, social studies. *Accreditation:* NASM (one or more programs are accredited); NCATE. Part-time programs available. *Faculty:* 29 full-time (21 women), 4 part-time/adjunct (all women). *Students:* 61 full-time (40 women), 153 part-time (108 women); includes 37 minority (32 Black or African American, non-Hispanic/Latino; 2 Asian, non-Hispanic/Latino; 3 Hispanic/Latino), 1 international. Average age 34. 150 applicants, 59% accepted, 74 enrolled. In 2013, 70 master's, 6 doctorates, 26 other advanced degrees awarded. *Degree requirements:* For master's, thesis (for some programs); for doctorate, thesis/dissertation; for Ed S, field project. *Entrance requirements:* For master's, doctorate, and Ed S, GRE General Test. *Application deadline:* For fall admission, 7/7 for domestic students; for spring admission, 11/24 for domestic students. Applications are processed on a rolling basis. Application fee: $50 ($60 for international students). Electronic applications accepted. *Expenses:* Tuition, state resident: full-time $8262; part-time $459 per credit hour. Tuition, nonresident: full-time $24,786; part-time $1377 per credit hour. Tuition and fees vary according to degree level and program. *Financial support:* Fellowships, teaching assistantships, career-related internships or fieldwork, and Federal Work-Study available. Support available to part-time students. Financial award application deadline: 3/15; financial award applicants required to submit FAFSA. *Faculty research:* Emerging literacy, reading attitudes, music for at-risk youth, portfolio assessment. *Unit head:* Dr. Kimberly Walls, Head, 334-844-4434. *Application contact:* Dr. George Flowers, Dean of the Graduate School, 334-844-2125. Website: http://education.auburn.edu/academic_departments/curr/.

Auburn University, Graduate School, College of Education, Department of Educational Foundations, Leadership, and Technology, Auburn University, AL 36849. Offers adult education (M Ed, MS, Ed D); curriculum and instruction (M Ed, MS, Ed D, Ed S); curriculum supervision (M Ed, MS, Ed D, Ed S); educational psychology (PhD); higher education administration (M Ed, MS, Ed D, Ed S); media instructional design (MS); media specialist (M Ed); school administration (M Ed, MS, Ed D, Ed S). *Accreditation:* NCATE. Part-time programs available. *Faculty:* 25 full-time (15 women), 6 part-time/adjunct (5 women). *Students:* 104 full-time (65 women), 250 part-time (140 women); includes 98 minority (90 Black or African American, non-Hispanic/Latino; 1 American Indian or Alaska Native, non-Hispanic/Latino; 4 Asian, non-Hispanic/Latino; 3 Hispanic/Latino), 14 international. Average age 36. 188 applicants, 66% accepted, 76 enrolled. In 2013, 51 master's, 22 doctorates, 10 other advanced degrees awarded. *Degree requirements:* For master's, thesis (for some programs); for doctorate, thesis/dissertation; for Ed S, field project. *Entrance requirements:* For master's, doctorate, and Ed S, GRE General Test. *Application deadline:* For fall admission, 7/7 for domestic students; for spring admission, 11/24 for domestic students. Applications are processed on a rolling basis. Application fee: $50 ($60 for international students). Electronic applications accepted. *Expenses:* Tuition, state resident: full-time $8262; part-time $459 per credit hour. Tuition, nonresident: full-time $24,786; part-time $1377 per credit hour. Tuition and fees vary according to degree level and program. *Financial support:* Teaching assistantships and Federal Work-Study available. Support available to part-time students. Financial award application deadline: 3/15; financial award applicants required to submit FAFSA. *Unit head:* Dr. Sherida Downer, Head, 334-844-4460. *Application contact:* Dr. George Flowers, Dean of the Graduate School, 334-844-4700. Website: http://www.education.auburn.edu/academic_departments/eflt/.

Azusa Pacific University, School of Behavioral and Applied Sciences, Department of Doctoral Higher Education, Azusa, CA 91702-7000. Offers educational leadership (Ed D); higher education leadership (Ed D).

Azusa Pacific University, School of Behavioral and Applied Sciences, Department of Higher Education and Organizational Leadership, Program in College Student Affairs, Azusa, CA 91702-7000. Offers M Ed. Part-time and evening/weekend programs

available. *Degree requirements:* For master's, exam. *Entrance requirements:* For master's, 12 units of course work in social science, minimum GPA of 3.0.

Ball State University, Graduate School, Teachers College, Department of Educational Studies, Program in Adult Education, Muncie, IN 47306-1099. Offers adult and community education (MA); adult, community, and higher education (Ed D). *Accreditation:* NCATE. *Students:* 24 full-time (17 women), 58 part-time (46 women); includes 16 minority (11 Black or African American, non-Hispanic/Latino; 1 American Indian or Alaska Native, non-Hispanic/Latino; 3 Hispanic/Latino; 1 Two or more races, non-Hispanic/Latino), 1 international. Average age 34. 22 applicants, 64% accepted, 7 enrolled. In 2013, 22 master's, 8 doctorates awarded. *Degree requirements:* For doctorate, thesis/dissertation. *Entrance requirements:* For doctorate, GRE General Test, minimum graduate GPA of 3.2. Application fee: $50. *Financial support:* In 2013–14, 17 students received support. Career-related internships or fieldwork available. Financial award application deadline: 3/1. *Faculty research:* Community education, executive development for public services, applied gerontology. *Unit head:* Dr. Jayne Beilke, Director of Doctoral Program, 765-285-5460, Fax: 765-285-5489, E-mail: jbeilke@bsu.edu. *Application contact:* Dr. Robert Morris, Associate Provost for Research and Dean of the Graduate School, 765-285-1300, E-mail: rmorris@bsu.edu.

Ball State University, Graduate School, Teachers College, Department of Educational Studies, Program in Student Affairs Administration in Higher Education, Muncie, IN 47306-1099. Offers MA. *Accreditation:* NCATE. *Students:* 40 full-time (25 women); includes 7 minority (4 Black or African American, non-Hispanic/Latino; 1 Asian, non-Hispanic/Latino; 1 Hispanic/Latino; 1 Native Hawaiian or other Pacific Islander, non-Hispanic/Latino). Average age 22. 216 applicants, 15% accepted, 29 enrolled. In 2013, 32 master's awarded. *Entrance requirements:* For master's, GRE General Test, interview. Application fee: $50. *Financial support:* In 2013–14, 41 students received support, including 40 research assistantships with full tuition reimbursements available (averaging $15,978 per year), 10 teaching assistantships with full tuition reimbursements available (averaging $10,771 per year). Financial award application deadline: 3/1. *Unit head:* Dr. Jayne Beilke, Director, 765-285-5460, Fax: 765-285-2464, E-mail: jbeilke@bsu.edu. *Application contact:* Dr. Roger Wessel, Professor of Higher Education, 765-285-5486, E-mail: rwessel@bsu.edu.
Website: http://www.bsu.edu/teachers/departments/edstudies/.

Barry University, School of Education, Program in Higher Education Administration, Miami Shores, FL 33161-6695. Offers MS. Part-time and evening/weekend programs available. *Degree requirements:* For master's, comprehensive exam. *Entrance requirements:* For master's, GRE General Test or MAT, minimum GPA of 3.0. Electronic applications accepted.

Barry University, School of Education, Program in Leadership and Education, Miami Shores, FL 33161-6695. Offers educational technology (PhD); exceptional student education (PhD); higher education administration (PhD); human resource development (PhD); leadership (PhD). Part-time and evening/weekend programs available. *Degree requirements:* For doctorate, thesis/dissertation. *Entrance requirements:* For doctorate, GRE General Test, minimum GPA of 3.25. Electronic applications accepted.

Baruch College of the City University of New York, School of Public Affairs, Program in Higher Education Administration, New York, NY 10010-5585. Offers MS Ed. Part-time and evening/weekend programs available. *Entrance requirements:* For master's, GRE General Test. Additional exam requirements/recommendations for international students: Required—TOEFL. Electronic applications accepted. *Expenses:* Contact institution.

Bay Path College, Program in Higher Education Administration, Longmeadow, MA 01106-2292. Offers enrollment management (MS); general administration (MS); institutional advancement (MS); online teaching and program administration (MS). Part-time programs available. Postbaccalaureate distance learning degree programs offered (no on-campus study). *Students:* 3 full-time (2 women), 44 part-time (36 women); includes 8 minority (5 Black or African American, non-Hispanic/Latino; 1 Asian, non-Hispanic/Latino; 1 Hispanic/Latino; 1 Two or more races, non-Hispanic/Latino). Average age 37. 37 applicants, 81% accepted, 21 enrolled. In 2013, 16 master's awarded. *Degree requirements:* For master's, 8 core courses (24 credits) and 4 elective courses (12 credits) for a total of 36 credits. *Application deadline:* Applications are processed on a rolling basis. Application fee: $45. Electronic applications accepted. Application fee is waived when completed online. *Financial support:* In 2013–14, 9 students received support. Scholarships/grants available. Financial award applicants required to submit FAFSA. *Unit head:* Dr. Lauren Way, Program Director, 413-565-1193. *Application contact:* Lisa Adams, Director of Graduate Admissions, 413-565-1317, Fax: 413-565-1250, E-mail: ladams@baypath.edu.
Website: http://graduate.baypath.edu/Graduate-Programs/Programs-Online/MS-Programs/Higher-Education-Administration.

Bay Path College, Program in Strategic Fundraising and Philanthropy, Longmeadow, MA 01106-2292. Offers higher education (MS); non-profit fundraising administration (MS). Part-time and evening/weekend programs available. Postbaccalaureate distance learning degree programs offered (no on-campus study). *Students:* 9 part-time (8 women). Average age 33. 7 applicants, 71% accepted, 2 enrolled. In 2013, 13 master's awarded. *Degree requirements:* For master's, 36 hours of coursework inluding portfolio. *Application deadline:* Applications are processed on a rolling basis. Application fee: $45. Electronic applications accepted. Application fee is waived when completed online. *Expenses:* Contact institution. *Financial support:* In 2013–14, 6 students received support. Scholarships/grants available. Financial award applicants required to submit FAFSA. *Unit head:* Jeffrey Greim, Program Director, 413-565-1045. *Application contact:* Lisa Adams, Director of Graduate Admissions, 413-565-1317, Fax: 413-565-1250, E-mail: ladams@baypath.edu.
Website: http://graduate.baypath.edu/Graduate-Programs/Programs-On-Campus/MS-Programs/Strategic-Fundraising-and-Philanthropy.

Benedictine University, Graduate Programs, Program in Higher Education and Organizational Change, Lisle, IL 60532-0900. Offers Ed D. *Students:* 43 full-time (30 women), 47 part-time (30 women); includes 26 minority (18 Black or African American, non-Hispanic/Latino; 2 Asian, non-Hispanic/Latino; 6 Hispanic/Latino). 32 applicants, 94% accepted, 26 enrolled. In 2013, 9 doctorates awarded. Application fee: $40. *Expenses: Tuition:* Part-time $590 per credit hour. *Unit head:* Dr. Sunil Chand, Director, 630-829-1930, E-mail: schand@ben.edu. *Application contact:* Kari Gibbons, Associate Vice President, Enrollment Center, 630-829-6200, Fax: 630-829-6584, E-mail: kgibbons@ben.edu.

Bethel University, Graduate School, St. Paul, MN 55112-6999. Offers autism spectrum disorders (Certificate); business administration (MBA); communication (MA); counseling psychology (MA); educational leadership (Ed D); gerontology (MA); international baccalaureate education (Certificate); K-12 education (MA); literacy education (MA, Certificate); nurse educator (Certificate); nurse leader (Certificate); nurse-midwifery (MS); nursing (MS); physician assistant (MS); postsecondary teaching (Certificate); special education (MA); strategic leadership (MA); teaching (MA). Part-time and evening/weekend programs available. Postbaccalaureate distance learning degree programs offered (no on-campus study). *Faculty:* 13 full-time (7 women), 89 part-time/adjunct (43 women). *Students:* 692 full-time (457 women), 573 part-time (371 women); includes 170 minority (86 Black or African American, non-Hispanic/Latino; 1 American Indian or Alaska Native, non-Hispanic/Latino; 49 Asian, non-Hispanic/Latino; 20 Hispanic/Latino; 1 Native Hawaiian or other Pacific Islander, non-Hispanic/Latino; 13 Two or more races, non-Hispanic/Latino), 21 international. Average age 37. In 2013, 166 master's, 9 doctorates, 11 other advanced degrees awarded. *Degree requirements:* For master's, comprehensive exam (for some programs), thesis (for some programs); for doctorate, comprehensive exam, thesis/dissertation. *Entrance requirements:* Additional exam requirements/recommendations for international students: Required—TOEFL (minimum score 550 paper-based; 80 iBT). *Application deadline:* Applications are processed on a rolling basis. Electronic applications accepted. Tuition and fees vary according to course load, degree level and program. *Financial support:* Teaching assistantships, career-related internships or fieldwork, and scholarships/grants available. Support available to part-time students. Financial award applicants required to submit FAFSA. *Unit head:* Dick Crombie, Vice-President/Dean, 651-635-8000, Fax: 651-635-8004, E-mail: gs@bethel.edu. *Application contact:* Director of Admissions, 651-635-8000, Fax: 651-635-8004, E-mail: gs@bethel.edu.
Website: http://gs.bethel.edu/.

Boston College, Lynch Graduate School of Education, Program in Higher Education, Chestnut Hill, MA 02467-3800. Offers MA, PhD, JD/MA, MBA/MA. *Accreditation:* Teacher Education Accreditation Council. Part-time and evening/weekend programs available. *Students:* 18 full-time (12 women), 28 part-time (21 women). 300 applicants, 48% accepted, 46 enrolled. In 2013, 42 master's, 4 doctorates awarded. Terminal master's awarded for partial completion of doctoral program. *Degree requirements:* For master's, comprehensive exam; for doctorate, comprehensive exam, thesis/dissertation. *Entrance requirements:* For master's, GRE General Test or MAT; for doctorate, GRE General Test. Additional exam requirements/recommendations for international students: Required—TOEFL (minimum score 100 iBT). *Application deadline:* For fall admission, 12/1 priority date for domestic and international students; for spring admission, 11/1 for domestic and international students. Application fee: $65. Electronic applications accepted. *Financial support:* Fellowships with full and partial tuition reimbursements, research assistantships with full and partial tuition reimbursements, teaching assistantships with full and partial tuition reimbursements, career-related internships or fieldwork, Federal Work-Study, scholarships/grants, traineeships, health care benefits, tuition waivers (full and partial), and unspecified assistantships available. Support available to part-time students. Financial award applicants required to submit FAFSA. *Faculty research:* Student affairs; race, culture and gender in higher education; international education; college student development; Catholic higher education; organizational analysis. *Unit head:* Dr. Ana M. Martinez-Aleman, Chairperson, 617-552-4214, Fax: 617-552-0398. *Application contact:* Domenic Lomanno, Director, Graduate Admission and Financial Aid, 617-552-4214, Fax: 617-552-0398, E-mail: lomanno@bc.edu.

Bowling Green State University, Graduate College, College of Education and Human Development, School of Leadership and Policy Studies, Program in Higher Education Administration, Bowling Green, OH 43403. Offers PhD. *Accreditation:* NCATE. Part-time programs available. *Degree requirements:* For doctorate, comprehensive exam, thesis/dissertation. *Entrance requirements:* For doctorate, GRE General Test. Additional exam requirements/recommendations for international students: Required—TOEFL. Electronic applications accepted. *Faculty research:* Adult learners, legal issues, intellectual development.

California Lutheran University, Graduate Studies, Graduate School of Education, Thousand Oaks, CA 91360-2787. Offers counseling and guidance (MS), including college student personnel, counseling and guidance; educational leadership (MA, Ed D), including educational leadership (K-12) (Ed D), higher education leadership (Ed D); special education (MS); teacher leadership (M Ed); teaching (M Ed). *Accreditation:* NCATE. Part-time and evening/weekend programs available. *Faculty:* 18 full-time (14 women), 28 part-time/adjunct (20 women). *Students:* 327 full-time (260 women), 96 part-time (77 women); includes 150 minority (7 Black or African American, non-Hispanic/Latino; 20 Asian, non-Hispanic/Latino; 112 Hispanic/Latino; 11 Two or more races, non-Hispanic/Latino), 1 international. Average age 33. 123 applicants, 85% accepted, 80 enrolled. In 2013, 117 master's, 9 doctorates awarded. *Entrance requirements:* For master's, GRE General Test, interview, minimum GPA of 3.0. *Application deadline:* For fall admission, 7/1 priority date for domestic students; for spring admission, 11/1 priority date for domestic students; for summer admission, 4/1 priority date for domestic students. Applications are processed on a rolling basis. Application fee: $50. *Unit head:* Dr. Robert Fraisse, Dean, 805-493-3421. *Application contact:* 805-493-3325, Fax: 805-493-3861, E-mail: clugrad@callutheran.edu.

California State University, Fullerton, Graduate Studies, College of Education, Department of Educational Leadership, Fullerton, CA 92834-9480. Offers community college educational leadership (Ed D); educational administration (MS); higher education (MS); pre K-12 educational leadership (Ed D). *Accreditation:* NCATE. Part-time programs available. *Students:* 2 full-time (0 women), 230 part-time (147 women); includes 133 minority (26 Black or African American, non-Hispanic/Latino; 33 Asian, non-Hispanic/Latino; 67 Hispanic/Latino; 7 Two or more races, non-Hispanic/Latino), 12 international. Average age 36. 192 applicants, 48% accepted, 84 enrolled. In 2013, 52 master's, 26 doctorates awarded. *Degree requirements:* For master's, thesis or alternative, project. *Entrance requirements:* For master's, minimum GPA of 2.5. Application fee: $55. *Financial support:* Career-related internships or fieldwork, Federal Work-Study, institutionally sponsored loans, and scholarships/grants available. Support available to part-time students. Financial award application deadline: 3/1; financial award applicants required to submit FAFSA. *Faculty research:* Creation of a substance abuse prevention training and demonstration program. *Unit head:* Jennifer Goldstein, Head, 657-278-3963. *Application contact:* Admissions/Applications, 657-278-2371.

California State University, Long Beach, Graduate Studies, College of Education, Department of Advanced Studies in Education and Counseling, Master of Science in Counseling Program, Long Beach, CA 90840. Offers marriage and family therapy (MS); school counseling (MS); student development in higher education (MS). *Accreditation:* NCATE. *Degree requirements:* For master's, comprehensive exam or thesis. Electronic applications accepted.

California State University, Sacramento, Office of Graduate Studies, College of Education, Department of Educational Leadership and Policy Studies, Sacramento, CA 95819. Offers educational leadership (MA), including PreK-12; higher education leadership (MA), including community college leadership, student services. Part-time programs available. *Degree requirements:* For master's, thesis or project; writing proficiency exam. *Entrance requirements:* For master's, minimum GPA of 2.5. Additional exam requirements/recommendations for international students: Required—TOEFL. *Application deadline:* For fall admission, 3/1 for domestic and international students; for spring admission, 9/30 for international students. Applications are processed on a rolling basis. Application fee: $55. Electronic applications accepted. *Financial support:* Career-related internships or fieldwork and Federal Work-Study available. Support available to part-time students. Financial award application deadline: 3/1; financial award applicants required to submit FAFSA. *Unit head:* Dr. Francisco Reveles, Chair, 916-278-5388, Fax:

916-278-4608, E-mail: revelesf@csus.edu. *Application contact:* Jose Martinez, Graduate Admissions Supervisor, 916-278-7871, E-mail: martinj@skymail.csus.edu. Website: http://www.edweb.csus.edu/edlp.

Capella University, School of Education, Doctoral Programs in Education, Minneapolis, MN 55402. Offers curriculum and instruction (PhD); educational leadership and management (Ed D); instructional design for online learning (PhD); K-12 studies in education (PhD); leadership for higher education (PhD); leadership in educational administration (PhD); postsecondary and adult education (PhD); professional studies in education (PhD); reading and literacy (Ed D); special education leadership (PhD); training and performance improvement (PhD).

Capella University, School of Education, Master's Programs in Education, Minneapolis, MN 55402. Offers adult education (MS); curriculum and instruction (MS); early childhood education (MS); enrollment management (MS); higher education leadership and management (MS); instructional design for online learning (MS); integrative studies (MS); K-12 studies in education (MS); leadership in educational administration (MS); reading and literacy (MS); special education teaching (MS).

Central Michigan University, Central Michigan University Global Campus, Program in Education, Mount Pleasant, MI 48859. Offers college teaching (Graduate Certificate); community college (MA); curriculum and instruction (MA); educational technology (MA); guidance and development (MA); reading and literacy K-12 (MA); school principalship (MA), including charter school leadership; training and development (MA). *Accreditation:* Teacher Education Accreditation Council. Part-time and evening/weekend programs available. *Entrance requirements:* For master's, minimum GPA of 2.7 in major. Additional exam requirements/recommendations for international students: Required—TOEFL. *Application deadline:* Applications are processed on a rolling basis. Application fee: $50. Electronic applications accepted. *Financial support:* Scholarships/grants available. Support available to part-time students. *Unit head:* Kaleb Patrick, Director, 989-774-3144, E-mail: patri1kg@cmich.edu. *Application contact:* 877-268-4636, E-mail: cmuglobal@cmich.edu.

Central Michigan University, College of Graduate Studies, College of Education and Human Services, Department of Educational Leadership, Mount Pleasant, MI 48859. Offers educational leadership (Ed D), including educational technology (Ed D, Ed S), higher education leadership, K-12 curriculum, K-12 leadership; general educational administration (Ed S), including administrative leadership K-12, educational technology (Ed D, Ed S), higher education administration, instructional leadership K-12; school principalship (MA), including charter school leadership, site-based leadership; student affairs administration (MA); teacher leadership (MA). Part-time and evening/weekend programs available. *Degree requirements:* For master's and Ed S, thesis or alternative; for doctorate, thesis/dissertation. *Entrance requirements:* For doctorate, GRE or MAT, master's degree, minimum GPA of 3.5, 3 years of professional education experience. Electronic applications accepted. *Faculty research:* Elementary administration, secondary administration, student achievement, in-service training, internships in administration.

Chicago State University, School of Graduate and Professional Studies, College of Education, Department of Educational Leadership, Curriculum and Foundations, Program in Educational Leadership, Chicago, IL 60628. Offers educational leadership (Ed D); general administration (MA); higher education administration (MA). *Accreditation:* NCATE. *Degree requirements:* For master's, comprehensive exam, thesis optional. *Entrance requirements:* For master's, minimum GPA of 2.75.

City University of Seattle, Graduate Division, Albright School of Education, Bellevue, WA 98005. Offers administrator certification (Certificate); curriculum and instruction (M Ed); educational leadership (Ed D); elementary education (MIT); guidance and counseling (M Ed); higher education leadership (Ed D); leadership (M Ed); leadership and school counseling (M Ed); organizational leadership (Ed D); reading and literacy (M Ed); special education (MIT); superintendent certification (Certificate). Part-time and evening/weekend programs available. Postbaccalaureate distance learning degree programs offered (no on-campus study). *Degree requirements:* For master's, comprehensive exam (for some programs), thesis (for some programs); for doctorate, comprehensive exam, thesis/dissertation. *Entrance requirements:* Additional exam requirements/recommendations for international students: Required—TOEFL (minimum score 567 paper-based; 87 iBT); Recommended—IELTS. Electronic applications accepted. *Expenses:* Contact institution.

Claremont Graduate University, Graduate Programs, School of Educational Studies, Claremont, CA 91711-6160. Offers Africana education (Certificate); education and policy (MA, PhD); higher education/student affairs (MA, PhD); human development (MA, PhD); public school administration (MA, PhD); quantitative evaluation (MA, PhD); special education (MA, PhD); teacher education (MA); teaching and learning (MA, PhD); urban leadership (PhD); MBA/PhD. PhD program offered jointly with San Diego State University. Part-time programs available. *Faculty:* 16 full-time (9 women), 1 part-time/adjunct (0 women). *Students:* 224 full-time (158 women), 221 part-time (151 women); includes 229 minority (52 Black or African American, non-Hispanic/Latino; 3 American Indian or Alaska Native, non-Hispanic/Latino; 43 Asian, non-Hispanic/Latino; 113 Hispanic/Latino; 1 Native Hawaiian or other Pacific Islander, non-Hispanic/Latino; 17 Two or more races, non-Hispanic/Latino), 15 international. Average age 39. In 2013, 51 master's, 33 doctorates, 5 other advanced degrees awarded. Terminal master's awarded for partial completion of doctoral program. *Entrance requirements:* For master's and doctorate, GRE General Test. Additional exam requirements/recommendations for international students: Required—TOEFL (minimum score 550 paper-based; 80 iBT). *Application deadline:* For fall admission, 4/1 priority date for domestic and international students. Applications are processed on a rolling basis. Application fee: $80. Electronic applications accepted. *Expenses: Tuition:* Full-time $40,560; part-time $1690 per credit. *Required fees:* $275 per semester. Tuition and fees vary according to program. *Financial support:* Fellowships, research assistantships, Federal Work-Study, institutionally sponsored loans, and scholarships/grants available. Support available to part-time students. Financial award application deadline: 2/15; financial award applicants required to submit FAFSA. *Faculty research:* Education administration, K-12 and higher education, multicultural education, education policy, diversity in higher education, faculty issues. *Unit head:* Scott Thomas, Dean, 909-621-8075, Fax: 909-621-8734, E-mail: scott.thomas@cgu.edu. *Application contact:* Julia Wendt, Director of Central Recruitment, 909-607-3689, Fax: 909-607-7285, E-mail: admiss@cgu.edu.
Website: http://www.cgu.edu/pages/267.asp.

Clemson University, Graduate School, College of Health, Education, and Human Development, Eugene T. Moore School of Education, Program in Educational Leadership, Clemson, SC 29634. Offers higher education (PhD); K-12 (PhD). *Accreditation:* NCATE. Part-time and evening/weekend programs available. *Students:* 26 full-time (13 women), 76 part-time (46 women); includes 28 minority (25 Black or African American, non-Hispanic/Latino; 2 Hispanic/Latino; 1 Two or more races, non-Hispanic/Latino), 2 international. Average age 37. 26 applicants, 54% accepted, 13 enrolled. In 2013, 13 doctorates awarded. *Degree requirements:* For doctorate, comprehensive exam, thesis/dissertation, preliminary exam. *Entrance requirements:* For doctorate, GRE General Test, master's degree in related field. Additional exam requirements/recommendations for international students: Required—TOEFL; Recommended—IELTS. *Application deadline:* For fall admission, 3/1 for domestic and international students; for spring admission, 10/1 for domestic and international students. Application fee: $70 ($80 for international students). Electronic applications accepted. *Financial support:* In 2013–14, 19 students received support, including 2 fellowships with full and partial tuition reimbursements available (averaging $5,000 per year), 12 research assistantships with partial tuition reimbursements available (averaging $14,221 per year); teaching assistantships with partial tuition reimbursements available, institutionally sponsored loans, health care benefits, and unspecified assistantships also available. Financial award application deadline: 6/1; financial award applicants required to submit FAFSA. *Faculty research:* Higher education leadership, P-12 educational leadership. *Unit head:* Dr. Michael J. Padilla, Director/Associate Dean, 864-656-4444, Fax: 864-656-0311, E-mail: padilla@clemson.edu. *Application contact:* Dr. David Fleming, Graduate Coordinator, 864-656-1881, Fax: 864-656-0311, E-mail: dflemin@clemson.edu.

Cleveland State University, College of Graduate Studies, College of Education and Human Services, Program in Urban Education, Specialization in Adult, Continuing, and Higher Education, Cleveland, OH 44115. Offers PhD. Part-time programs available. *Faculty:* 4 full-time (3 women). *Students:* 2 full-time (both women), 10 part-time (6 women); includes 4 minority (all Black or African American, non-Hispanic/Latino). Average age 46. *Degree requirements:* For doctorate, one foreign language, comprehensive exam, thesis/dissertation. *Entrance requirements:* For doctorate, General GRE Test (minimum score of 297 for combined Verbal and Quantitative exams, 4.0 preferred for Analytical Writing), minimum graduate GPA of 3.25, curriculum vitae or resume, personal statement, 2 letters of recommendation. Additional exam requirements/recommendations for international students: Required—TOEFL (minimum score 525 paper-based), IELTS (minimum score 6). *Expenses:* Tuition, state resident: full-time $8335; part-time $521 per credit hour. Tuition, nonresident: full-time $15,670; part-time $979 per credit hour. *Required fees:* $50; $25 per semester. *Financial support:* In 2013–14, 2 students received support, including 1 research assistantship with full tuition reimbursement available, 1 teaching assistantship with full tuition reimbursement available (averaging $11,800 per year); tuition waivers (full) also available. Support available to part-time students. Financial award application deadline: 4/1; financial award applicants required to submit FAFSA. *Faculty research:* Adult education research, practice in diverse contexts. *Unit head:* Dr. Graham Stead, Director, Doctoral Studies, 216-875-9869, E-mail: g.b.stead@csuohio.edu. *Application contact:* Rita M. Grabowski, Administrative Coordinator, 216-687-4697, Fax: 216-875-9697, E-mail: r.grabowski@csuohio.edu.
Website: http://www.csuohio.edu/cehs/departments/DOC/lll_doc.html.

College of Saint Elizabeth, Department of Psychology, Morristown, NJ 07960-6989. Offers counseling psychology (MA); forensic psychology (MA); mental health counseling (Certificate); student affairs in higher education (Certificate). Part-time programs available. *Faculty:* 2 full-time (1 woman), 4 part-time/adjunct (3 women). *Students:* 55 full-time (50 women), 33 part-time (31 women); includes 25 minority (11 Black or African American, non-Hispanic/Latino; 1 Asian, non-Hispanic/Latino; 13 Hispanic/Latino), 1 international. Average age 30. In 2013, 31 master's, 5 other advanced degrees awarded. *Degree requirements:* For master's, thesis or alternative. *Entrance requirements:* For master's, minimum GPA of 3.0, BA in psychology (preferred), 12 credits of course work in psychology. Additional exam requirements/recommendations for international students: Required—TOEFL. *Application deadline:* For fall admission, 4/1 priority date for domestic students; for spring admission, 11/15 for domestic students. Applications are processed on a rolling basis. Application fee: $35. Electronic applications accepted. *Expenses: Tuition:* Full-time $19,152; part-time $1064 per credit. *Financial support:* Career-related internships or fieldwork, tuition waivers (partial), and unspecified assistantships available. Support available to part-time students. Financial award application deadline: 3/15; financial award applicants required to submit FAFSA. *Unit head:* Dr. Thomas C. Barrett, Coordinator, Graduate and Doctoral Programs in Psychology, 973-290-4106, Fax: 973-290-4676, E-mail: tbarrett@cse.edu. *Application contact:* Deborah S. Cobo, Associate Director of Graduate Admissions, 973-290-4194, Fax: 973-290-4710, E-mail: dscobo@cse.edu.
Website: http://www.cse.edu/academics/academic-programs/human-social-dev/psychology/.

The College of Saint Rose, Graduate Studies, School of Education, Program in Higher Education Leadership and Administration, Albany, NY 12203-1419. Offers MS Ed. Evening/weekend programs available. *Degree requirements:* For master's, capstone seminar. *Entrance requirements:* For master's, resume, one letter of recommendation.

Columbia College, Graduate Programs, Department of Education, Columbia, SC 29203-5998. Offers divergent learning (M Ed); higher education administration (M Ed). *Accreditation:* NCATE. Part-time and evening/weekend programs available. Postbaccalaureate distance learning degree programs offered. *Faculty:* 3 full-time (1 woman), 18 part-time/adjunct (10 women). *Students:* 113 full-time (96 women), 2 part-time (1 woman); includes 50 minority (46 Black or African American, non-Hispanic/Latino; 2 American Indian or Alaska Native, non-Hispanic/Latino; 2 Asian, non-Hispanic/Latino). Average age 27. 108 applicants, 81% accepted, 77 enrolled. In 2013, 106 master's awarded. *Degree requirements:* For master's, thesis. *Entrance requirements:* For master's, GRE General Test, MAT, 2 recommendations, current South Carolina teaching certificate, minimum GPA of 3.2. *Application deadline:* For fall admission, 8/22 for domestic students. Application fee: $50. *Expenses:* Contact institution. *Financial support:* Available to part-time students. Application deadline: 7/1; applicants required to submit FAFSA. *Unit head:* Dr. Chris Burkett, Chair, 803-786-3782, Fax: 803-786-3034, E-mail: chrisburkett@colacoll.edu. *Application contact:* Carolyn Emeneker, Director of Graduate School and Evening College Admissions, 803-786-3766, Fax: 803-786-3674, E-mail: emeneker@colacoll.edu.

Columbia International University, Columbia Graduate School, Columbia, SC 29230-3122. Offers Bible teaching (MABT); Christian higher education leadership (Ed D); Christian school educational leadership (Ed D); counseling (MACN); curriculum and instruction (M Ed), including Christian school guidance, English as a second language, learning disabilities, school technology; early childhood and elementary education (MAT); educational administration (M Ed); teaching English as a foreign language (Certificate); teaching English as a foreign language and intercultural studies (MATF). Part-time and evening/weekend programs available. *Degree requirements:* For master's, internships, professional project. *Entrance requirements:* For master's, Minnesota Multiphasic Personality Inventory, MAT, minimum GPA of 2.7. Additional exam requirements/recommendations for international students: Required—TOEFL. Electronic applications accepted.

Columbus State University, Graduate Studies, College of Education and Health Professions, Department of Counseling, Foundations, and Leadership, Columbus, GA 31907-5645. Offers community counseling (MS); curriculum and leadership (Ed D); educational leadership (M Ed, Ed S); higher education (M Ed); school counseling (M Ed, Ed S). *Accreditation:* ACA; NCATE. Part-time and evening/weekend programs available. Postbaccalaureate distance learning degree programs offered (minimal on-campus study). *Faculty:* 13 full-time (5 women), 11 part-time/adjunct (7 women). *Students:* 94 full-time (64 women), 120 part-time (96 women); includes 95 minority (78 Black or

Higher Education

African American, non-Hispanic/Latino; 1 American Indian or Alaska Native, non-Hispanic/Latino; 2 Asian, non-Hispanic/Latino; 9 Hispanic/Latino; 5 Two or more races, non-Hispanic/Latino). Average age 35. 139 applicants, 58% accepted, 49 enrolled. In 2013, 44 master's, 4 doctorates, 14 other advanced degrees awarded. *Degree requirements:* For master's, thesis, exit exam; for doctorate, comprehensive exam, thesis/dissertation; for Ed S, thesis or alternative. *Entrance requirements:* For master's, GRE General Test, minimum undergraduate GPA of 2.75; for doctorate, GRE General Test, minimum graduate GPA of 3.5, four years of professional service; for Ed S, GRE General Test, minimum undergraduate GPA of 2.75, graduate 3.0. Additional exam requirements/recommendations for international students: Required—TOEFL (minimum score 550 paper-based; 79 iBT). *Application deadline:* For fall admission, 6/30 for domestic and international students; for spring admission, 11/1 for domestic and international students; for summer admission, 3/1 for domestic and international students. Applications are processed on a rolling basis. Application fee: $40. Electronic applications accepted. *Expenses:* Tuition, state resident: full-time $4572; part-time $382 per credit hour. Tuition, nonresident: full-time $18,292; part-time $1526 per credit hour. *Required fees:* $1800; $196 per credit hour. Tuition and fees vary according to campus/location and program. *Financial support:* In 2013–14, 143 students received support, including 9 research assistantships with partial tuition reimbursements available (averaging $3,000 per year); career-related internships or fieldwork, Federal Work-Study, institutionally sponsored loans, scholarships/grants, tuition waivers (partial), and unspecified assistantships also available. Support available to part-time students. Financial award application deadline: 5/1; financial award applicants required to submit FAFSA. *Unit head:* Dr. Michael L. Baltimore, Department Chair, 706-569-3013, Fax: 706-569-3134, E-mail: baltimore_michael@columbusstate.edu. *Application contact:* Kristin Williams, Director of International and Graduate Recruitment, 706-507-8848, Fax: 706-568-5091, E-mail: williams_kristin@columbusstate.edu.
Website: http://cfl.columbusstate.edu/.

Dallas Baptist University, Gary Cook School of Leadership, Program in Education in Higher Education, Dallas, TX 75211-9299. Offers M Ed, MA/MA. Part-time and evening/weekend programs available. *Entrance requirements:* For master's, GRE General Test, minimum GPA of 3.0. Additional exam requirements/recommendations for international students: Required—TOEFL, IELTS. *Application deadline:* Applications are processed on a rolling basis. Application fee: $25. Electronic applications accepted. *Expenses: Tuition:* Full-time $13,410; part-time $745 per credit hour. *Required fees:* $300; $150 per semester. Tuition and fees vary according to degree level. *Financial support:* Federal Work-Study, institutionally sponsored loans, scholarships/grants, and tuition waivers (full and partial) available. Support available to part-time students. Financial award applicants required to submit FAFSA. *Faculty research:* Enrollment management, portfolio assessment, servant leadership. *Unit head:* Mamo Ishida, Director, 214-333-5812, E-mail: graduate@dbu.edu. *Application contact:* Kit P. Montgomery, Director of Graduate Programs, 214-333-5242, Fax: 214-333-5579, E-mail: graduate@dbu.edu.
Website: http://www3.dbu.edu/leadership/hied/.

Dallas Baptist University, Professional Development Program, Dallas, TX 75211-9299. Offers counseling (MA); criminal justice (MA); English as a second language (MA); higher education (MA); interdisciplinary (MA); leadership studies (MA); missions (MA); professional life coaching (MA); training and development (MA). Part-time and evening/weekend programs available. *Entrance requirements:* For master's, minimum GPA of 3.0. Additional exam requirements/recommendations for international students: Required—TOEFL, IELTS. Application fee: $25. *Expenses: Tuition:* Full-time $13,410; part-time $745 per credit hour. *Required fees:* $300; $150 per semester. Tuition and fees vary according to degree level. *Financial support:* Federal Work-Study, institutionally sponsored loans, scholarships/grants, and tuition waivers (full and partial) available. Support available to part-time students. Financial award applicants required to submit FAFSA. *Unit head:* Eric Wyatt, Director, 214-333-6830, E-mail: graduate@dbu.edu. *Application contact:* Kit P. Montgomery, Director of Graduate Programs, 214-333-5242, Fax: 214-333-5579, E-mail: graduate@dbu.edu.
Website: http://www3.dbu.edu/graduate/mapd.asp.

Delta State University, Graduate Programs, College of Education, Thad Cochran Center for Rural School Leadership and Research, Program in Professional Studies, Cleveland, MS 38733-0001. Offers counselor education (Ed D); educational leadership (Ed D); elementary education (Ed D); higher education (Ed D). Part-time and evening/weekend programs available. *Students:* 3 full-time (all women), 90 part-time (58 women); includes 31 minority (all Black or African American, non-Hispanic/Latino), 1 international. Average age 38. 44 applicants, 95% accepted, 28 enrolled. In 2013, 2 doctorates awarded. *Degree requirements:* For doctorate, thesis/dissertation. *Entrance requirements:* For doctorate, GRE General Test. *Application deadline:* For fall admission, 8/1 priority date for domestic students; for spring admission, 12/1 priority date for domestic students. Applications are processed on a rolling basis. Application fee: $0. *Expenses:* Tuition, state resident: full-time $3006; part-time $334 per credit hour. Tuition, nonresident: full-time $3006; part-time $334 per credit hour. *Financial support:* Research assistantships, career-related internships or fieldwork, Federal Work-Study, and institutionally sponsored loans available. Support available to part-time students. Financial award application deadline: 6/1. *Unit head:* Dr. Dan McFall, Interim Chair, 662-846-4395, Fax: 662-846-4402. *Application contact:* Dr. Albert Nylander, Dean of Graduate Studies, 662-846-4875, Fax: 662-846-4313, E-mail: grad-info@deltastate.edu.

Drexel University, Goodwin College of Professional Studies, School of Education, Philadelphia, PA 19104-2875. Offers educational administration (MS); educational improvement and transformation (MS); educational leadership and management (Ed D); educational leadership development and learning technologies (PhD); global and international education (MS); higher education (MS); human resources development (MS); learning technologies (MS); mathematics, learning and teaching (MS); special education (MS); teaching, learning and curriculum (MS). Part-time and evening/weekend programs available. Postbaccalaureate distance learning degree programs offered (no on-campus study). *Degree requirements:* For doctorate, thesis/dissertation. *Entrance requirements:* For doctorate, GRE or GMAT. Additional exam requirements/recommendations for international students: Required—TOEFL, IELTS. Electronic applications accepted. Application fee is waived when completed online. *Expenses:* Contact institution. *Faculty research:* Leadership development, mathematics education, literacy, autism, educational technology.

East Carolina University, Graduate School, College of Education, Department of Higher, Adult, and Counselor Education, Greenville, NC 27858-4353. Offers adult education (MA Ed); counselor education (MS); higher education administration (Ed D). *Accreditation:* NCATE. Part-time and evening/weekend programs available. *Degree requirements:* For master's, comprehensive exam, thesis optional. *Entrance requirements:* For master's, GRE General Test or MAT, interview, minimum GPA of 2.5, bachelor's degree in related field, teaching license (MA Ed). Additional exam requirements/recommendations for international students: Required—TOEFL. *Expenses:* Tuition, state resident: full-time $4223. Tuition, nonresident: full-time $16,540. *Required fees:* $2184.

Eastern Kentucky University, The Graduate School, College of Education, Department of Curriculum and Instruction, Program in Secondary and Higher Education, Richmond, KY 40475-3102. Offers secondary education (MA Ed), including agricultural education, art education, biological sciences education, business education, English education, geography education, history education, home economics education, industrial education, mathematical sciences education, physical education, school health education. *Accreditation:* NCATE. Part-time programs available. *Entrance requirements:* For master's, GRE General Test, minimum GPA of 2.5.

East Tennessee State University, School of Graduate Studies, College of Education, Department of Counseling and Human Services, Johnson City, TN 37614. Offers counseling (MA), including community agency counseling, higher education counseling, marriage and family therapy, school counseling. *Accreditation:* ACA; NCATE. Part-time programs available. *Faculty:* 33 full-time (22 women), 19 part-time/adjunct (13 women). *Students:* 64 full-time (51 women), 7 part-time (4 women); includes 4 minority (1 Black or African American, non-Hispanic/Latino; 1 Hispanic/Latino; 2 Two or more races, non-Hispanic/Latino), 2 international. Average age 28. 86 applicants, 42% accepted, 27 enrolled. In 2013, 48 master's awarded. Terminal master's awarded for partial completion of doctoral program. *Degree requirements:* For master's, comprehensive exam, thesis optional, internship, student teaching, culminating experience. *Entrance requirements:* For master's, GRE General Test, minimum GPA of 3.0. Additional exam requirements/recommendations for international students: Required—TOEFL (minimum score 550 paper-based; 79 iBT). *Application deadline:* For fall admission, 2/1 for domestic and international students. Application fee: $35 ($45 for international students). Electronic applications accepted. *Expenses:* Tuition, state resident: full-time $7900; part-time $395 per credit hour. Tuition, nonresident: full-time $21,960; part-time $1098 per credit hour. *Required fees:* $1345; $84 per credit hour. *Financial support:* In 2013–14, 54 students received support, including 18 research assistantships with full tuition reimbursements available (averaging $6,000 per year), 5 teaching assistantships with full tuition reimbursements available (averaging $6,000 per year); career-related internships or fieldwork, institutionally sponsored loans, scholarships/grants, traineeships, and unspecified assistantships also available. Financial award application deadline: 7/1; financial award applicants required to submit FAFSA. *Faculty research:* Intervention and assistance with at-risk and under-served youth and high conflict families; service and social justice; women and girls' issues in counseling; counseling competence with LGBTQ individuals; counselor education and supervision. *Unit head:* Dr. Janna Scarborough, Interim Chair, 423-439-7692, E-mail: scarboro@etsu.edu. *Application contact:* Fiona Goodyear, Graduate Specialist, 423-439-6148, Fax: 423-439-5624, E-mail: goodyear@etsu.edu.
Website: http://www.etsu.edu/coe/chs/default.aspx.

Florida Atlantic University, College of Education, Department of Educational Leadership and Research Methodology, Boca Raton, FL 33431-0991. Offers adult and community education (M Ed, PhD, Ed S); educational leadership (M Ed, PhD, Ed S); higher education (M Ed, PhD); K-12 school leadership (M Ed, PhD, Ed S). *Accreditation:* NCATE. Part-time and evening/weekend programs available. Postbaccalaureate distance learning degree programs offered (minimal on-campus study). *Faculty:* 19 full-time (9 women), 16 part-time/adjunct (7 women). *Students:* 97 full-time (72 women), 227 part-time (150 women); includes 140 minority (83 Black or African American, non-Hispanic/Latino; 8 Asian, non-Hispanic/Latino; 41 Hispanic/Latino; 8 Two or more races, non-Hispanic/Latino), 2 international. Average age 37. 180 applicants, 50% accepted, 74 enrolled. In 2013, 80 master's, 11 doctorates, 19 other advanced degrees awarded. *Degree requirements:* For doctorate, comprehensive exam, thesis/dissertation, departmental qualifying exam; for Ed S, departmental qualifying exam. *Entrance requirements:* For master's, GRE General Test, minimum GPA of 3.0 during previous 2 years; for doctorate, GRE General Test, minimum GPA of 3.5; for Ed S, GRE General Test. Additional exam requirements/recommendations for international students: Required—TOEFL (minimum score 500 paper-based; 61 iBT), IELTS (minimum score 6). *Application deadline:* For fall admission, 7/1 for domestic students, 2/15 for international students; for spring admission, 9/15 for domestic students, 7/15 for international students. Applications are processed on a rolling basis. Application fee: $30. Electronic applications accepted. *Expenses:* Tuition, state resident: full-time $6660; part-time $370 per credit hour. Tuition, nonresident: full-time $18,450; part-time $1025 per credit hour. Tuition and fees vary according to course load. *Financial support:* Fellowships, research assistantships, teaching assistantships, career-related internships or fieldwork, and tuition waivers (partial) available. *Faculty research:* Self-directed learning, school reform issues, legal issues, mentoring, school leadership. *Unit head:* Dr. Robert E. Shockley, Chair, 561-297-3550, Fax: 561-297-3618, E-mail: shockley@fau.edu. *Application contact:* Kathy DuBois, Senior Secretary, 561-297-3550, Fax: 561-297-3618, E-mail: edleadership@fau.edu.
Website: http://www.coe.fau.edu/academicdepartments/el/.

Florida International University, College of Education, Department of Leadership and Professional Studies, Miami, FL 33199. Offers adult education and human resource development (MS, Ed D); counseling (MS), including rehabilitation counseling, school counseling; counselor education (MS), including clinical mental health counseling; educational administration and supervision (Ed D); educational leadership (MS, Certificate, Ed S); higher education (Ed D); higher education administration (MS); recreation and sport management (MS), including recreation and sport management, recreational therapy; school psychology (Ed S); urban education (MS), including instruction in urban settings, learning technologies, multicultural/bilingual, multicultural/TESOL, urban education. Part-time and evening/weekend programs available. *Degree requirements:* For doctorate, thesis/dissertation. *Entrance requirements:* For master's, minimum GPA of 3.0; for doctorate and other advanced degree, GRE General Test. Additional exam requirements/recommendations for international students: Required—TOEFL (minimum score 550 paper-based; 80 iBT), IELTS (minimum score 6.3). Electronic applications accepted.

Florida State University, The Graduate School, College of Education, Department of Educational Leadership and Policy Studies, Program in Higher Education, Tallahassee, FL 32306. Offers MS, PhD, Ed S. *Faculty:* 10 full-time (5 women), 4 part-time/adjunct (2 women). *Students:* 67 full-time (44 women), 31 part-time (16 women); includes 29 minority (15 Black or African American, non-Hispanic/Latino; 11 Hispanic/Latino; 3 Two or more races, non-Hispanic/Latino), 2 international. Average age 30. 145 applicants, 48% accepted, 33 enrolled. In 2013, 39 master's, 6 doctorates awarded. Terminal master's awarded for partial completion of doctoral program. *Degree requirements:* For master's and Ed S, comprehensive exam, thesis optional; for doctorate, comprehensive exam, thesis/dissertation. *Entrance requirements:* For master's, GRE General Test, minimum GPA of 3.0; for doctorate and Ed S, GRE General Test, minimum graduate GPA of 3.0. Additional exam requirements/recommendations for international students: Required—TOEFL (minimum score 550 paper-based; 80 iBT). *Application deadline:* For fall admission, 7/1 for domestic and international students; for winter admission, 11/1 for domestic and international students; for spring admission, 3/1 for domestic and international students. Application fee: $30. Electronic applications accepted. *Expenses:* Tuition, state resident: part-time $403.51 per credit hour. Tuition, nonresident: part-time $1004.85 per credit hour. *Required fees:* $75.81 per credit hour. One-time fee: $20 part-time. Tuition and fees vary according to course load, campus/location and student level. *Financial support:* Fellowships with full and partial tuition reimbursements, research assistantships with full and partial tuition reimbursements, teaching assistantships with full and partial tuition reimbursements, career-related internships or fieldwork,

scholarships/grants, health care benefits, and unspecified assistantships available. Financial award applicants required to submit FAFSA. *Faculty research:* Higher education laws, public policy, organizational theory. *Unit head:* Dr. Shouping Hu, Associate Professor/Coordinator, 850-644-6777, Fax: 850-644-1258, E-mail: shu@fsu.edu. *Application contact:* Linda J. Lyons, Academic Support Assistant, 850-644-7077, Fax: 850-644-1258, E-mail: ljlyons@fsu.edu.
Website: http://www.coe.fsu.edu/Academic-Programs/Departments/Educational-Leadership-and-Policy-Studies-ELPS/Academic-Programs/Degree-Programs/Higher-Education.

Geneva College, Master of Arts in Higher Education Program, Beaver Falls, PA 15010-3599. Offers campus ministry (MA); college teaching (MA); educational leadership (MA); student affairs administration (MA). Part-time and evening/weekend programs available. Postbaccalaureate distance learning degree programs offered (minimal on-campus study). *Faculty:* 4 full-time (0 women). *Students:* 29 full-time (19 women), 43 part-time (23 women); includes 4 minority (3 Black or African American, non-Hispanic/Latino; 1 Hispanic/Latino). Average age 26. 46 applicants, 100% accepted, 28 enrolled. In 2013, 23 master's awarded. *Degree requirements:* For master's, 36 hours (27 in core courses) including a capstone research project. *Entrance requirements:* For master's, minimum GPA of 3.0, writing sample, 3 letters of recommendation, essay on motivation for participation in the HED program. Additional exam requirements/recommendations for international students: Required—TOEFL. *Application deadline:* For fall admission, 9/1 priority date for domestic students; for winter admission, 1/2 priority date for domestic students; for spring admission, 3/11 priority date for domestic students. Applications are processed on a rolling basis. Electronic applications accepted. *Expenses:* Contact institution. *Financial support:* In 2013–14, 59 students received support. Unspecified assistantships available. Financial award application deadline: 8/1; financial award applicants required to submit FAFSA. *Faculty research:* Student development, learning theories, church-related higher education, assessment, organizational culture. *Unit head:* Dr. Keith Martel, Program Director, 724-847-6884, Fax: 724-847-6107, E-mail: hed@geneva.edu. *Application contact:* Jerryn S. Carson, Program Coordinator, 724-847-6510, Fax: 724-847-6696, E-mail: hed@geneva.edu.
Website: http://www.geneva.edu/page/higher_ed.

George Fox University, College of Education, Educational Foundations and Leadership Program, Newberg, OR 97132-2697. Offers continuing administrator license (Certificate); curriculum and instruction (M Ed); educational leadership (M Ed, Ed D); ESOL (Certificate); higher education (M Ed); initial administrator license (Certificate); instructional leadership (Ed S); library media (M Ed, Certificate); literacy (M Ed); reading (M Ed); secondary education (M Ed). *Accreditation:* NCATE. Part-time and evening/weekend programs available. Postbaccalaureate distance learning degree programs offered (minimal on-campus study). *Faculty:* 7 full-time (3 women), 5 part-time/adjunct (4 women). *Students:* 194 part-time (128 women); includes 15 minority (1 Black or African American, non-Hispanic/Latino; 1 American Indian or Alaska Native, non-Hispanic/Latino; 3 Asian, non-Hispanic/Latino; 6 Hispanic/Latino; 1 Native Hawaiian or other Pacific Islander, non-Hispanic/Latino; 3 Two or more races, non-Hispanic/Latino), 2 international. Average age 42. 46 applicants, 85% accepted, 39 enrolled. In 2013, 15 master's, 16 doctorates, 106 Certificates awarded. *Degree requirements:* For master's, thesis (for some programs); for doctorate, comprehensive exam, thesis/dissertation, project. *Entrance requirements:* For master's, minimum undergraduate GPA of 3.0 during previous 2 years of course work, resume, 3 professional recommendations on university forms, official transcripts; for doctorate, GRE, master's degree with minimum GPA of 3.25, 3 years of relevant professional experience, interview, personal essay, scholarly work, 3 professional recommendations on university forms along with 3 written letters of recommendation, official transcripts. Additional exam requirements/recommendations for international students: Required—TOEFL (minimum score 577 paper-based; 90 iBT). *Application deadline:* For fall admission, 7/15 for domestic and international students; for winter admission, 11/1 for domestic and international students; for spring admission, 4/1 for domestic and international students. Applications are processed on a rolling basis. Application fee: $40. Electronic applications accepted. *Expenses:* Contact institution. *Financial support:* Career-related internships or fieldwork available. Financial award applicants required to submit FAFSA. *Unit head:* Dr. Scot Headley, Professor/Chair, 503-554-2836, E-mail: sheadley@georgefox.edu. *Application contact:* Kipp Wilfong, Graduate Admissions Counselor, 800-631-0921, Fax: 503-554-3110, E-mail: kwilfong@georgefox.edu.
Website: http://www.georgefox.edu/education/index.html.

George Mason University, College of Humanities and Social Sciences, Higher Education Program, Fairfax, VA 22030. Offers college teaching (Certificate); community college education (DA Ed); higher education administration (Certificate). *Faculty:* 4 full-time (all women), 1 (woman) part-time/adjunct. *Students:* 1 (woman) full-time, 44 part-time (28 women); includes 11 minority (7 Black or African American, non-Hispanic/Latino; 2 Asian, non-Hispanic/Latino; 2 Hispanic/Latino), 1 international. Average age 44. 12 applicants, 50% accepted, 5 enrolled. In 2013, 6 doctorates, 5 Certificates awarded. *Degree requirements:* For doctorate, thesis/dissertation, internship. *Entrance requirements:* For doctorate, GRE, 3 letters of recommendation; writing sample; resume; master's degree; expanded goals statement; official transcripts; for Certificate, official transcripts; expanded goals statement; 3 letters of recommendation; resume. Additional exam requirements/recommendations for international students: Required—TOEFL (minimum score 570 paper-based; 88 iBT), IELTS (minimum score 6.5), PTE. *Application deadline:* For fall admission, 4/15 priority date for domestic students; for spring admission, 11/1 priority date for domestic students. Application fee: $65 ($80 for international students). Electronic applications accepted. *Expenses:* Tuition, state resident: full-time $9350; part-time $390 per credit. Tuition, nonresident: full-time $25,754; part-time $1073 per credit. *Required fees:* $2688; $112 per credit. *Financial support:* In 2013–14, 1 student received support, including 1 teaching assistantship (averaging $20,000 per year); career-related internships or fieldwork, Federal Work-Study, scholarships/grants, unspecified assistantships, and health care benefits (for full-time research or teaching assistantship recipients) also available. Support available to part-time students. Financial award application deadline: 3/1; financial award applicants required to submit FAFSA. *Faculty research:* Leadership, the scholarship of teaching, learning, and assessment; ethical leadership; assessment; information technology; diversity. *Total annual research expenditures:* $984. *Unit head:* Jan Arminio, Director, 703-993-2064, Fax: 703-993-2307, E-mail: jarminio@gmu.edu. *Application contact:* Helen C. Zhao, Administrative Coordinator, 703-993-2310, Fax: 703-993-2307, E-mail: hzhao2@gmu.edu.
Website: http://highered.gmu.edu/.

George Mason University, College of Humanities and Social Sciences, Interdisciplinary Studies Program, Fairfax, VA 22030. Offers community college teaching (MAIS); computational social science (MAIS); energy and sustainability (MAIS); film and video studies (MAIS); folklore studies (MAIS); higher education administration (MAIS); neuroethics (MAIS); religion, culture and values (MAIS); social entrepreneurship (MAIS); war and military in society (MAIS); women and gender studies (MAIS). *Faculty:* 10 full-time (3 women), 7 part-time/adjunct (3 women). *Students:* 31 full-time (17 women), 79 part-time (50 women); includes 30 minority (17 Black or African American, non-Hispanic/Latino; 4 Asian, non-Hispanic/Latino; 6 Hispanic/Latino; 3 Two or more races, non-Hispanic/Latino), 3 international. Average age 33. 78 applicants, 59% accepted, 25 enrolled. In 2013, 32 master's awarded. *Degree requirements:* For master's, project or thesis. *Entrance requirements:* For master's, 3 letters of recommendation; writing sample; official transcript; resume. Additional exam requirements/recommendations for international students: Required—TOEFL (minimum score 570 paper-based; 88 iBT), IELTS (minimum score 6.5), PTE. *Application deadline:* For fall admission, 3/1 priority date for domestic students; for spring admission, 10/15 for domestic students. Application fee: $65 ($80 for international students). Electronic applications accepted. *Expenses:* Tuition, state resident: full-time $9350; part-time $390 per credit. Tuition, nonresident: full-time $25,754; part-time $1073 per credit. *Required fees:* $2688; $112 per credit. *Financial support:* In 2013–14, 8 students received support, including 3 research assistantships with full and partial tuition reimbursements available (averaging $10,238 per year), 5 teaching assistantships with full and partial tuition reimbursements available (averaging $7,655 per year); career-related internships or fieldwork, Federal Work-Study, scholarships/grants, unspecified assistantships, and health care benefits (for full-time research or teaching assistantship recipients) also available. Support available to part-time students. Financial award application deadline: 3/1; financial award applicants required to submit FAFSA. *Faculty research:* Combined English and folklore, religious and cultural studies (Christianity and Muslim society). *Unit head:* Jan Arminio, Interim Director, 703-993-2064, Fax: 703-993-2307, E-mail: jarminio@gmu.edu. *Application contact:* Becky Durham, Administrative Coordinator, 703-993-8762, Fax: 703-993-5585, E-mail: rdurham4@gmu.edu.
Website: http://mais.gmu.edu.

The George Washington University, Graduate School of Education and Human Development, Department of Educational Leadership, Program in Higher Education Administration, Washington, DC 20052. Offers MA Ed, Ed D, Ed S. *Accreditation:* NCATE. *Students:* 24 full-time (20 women), 91 part-time (61 women); includes 35 minority (19 Black or African American, non-Hispanic/Latino; 7 Asian, non-Hispanic/Latino; 8 Hispanic/Latino; 1 Two or more races, non-Hispanic/Latino), 1 international. Average age 33. 141 applicants, 71% accepted, 7 enrolled. In 2013, 29 master's, 14 doctorates, 1 other advanced degree awarded. *Degree requirements:* For master's and Ed S, comprehensive exam; for doctorate, comprehensive exam, thesis/dissertation. *Entrance requirements:* For master's, GRE General Test or MAT, minimum GPA of 2.75; for doctorate, GRE General Test or MAT, interview, minimum GPA of 3.3; for Ed S, GRE General Test or MAT, minimum GPA of 3.3. *Application deadline:* For fall admission, 1/15 priority date for domestic students; for spring admission, 10/1 for domestic students. Applications are processed on a rolling basis. Application fee: $75. *Financial support:* In 2013–14, 17 students received support. Fellowships, research assistantships, career-related internships or fieldwork, Federal Work-Study, and tuition waivers (partial) available. Financial award application deadline: 1/15; financial award applicants required to submit FAFSA. *Faculty research:* Technology in higher education administration. *Unit head:* Virginia Roach, Chair, 202-994-3094, E-mail: vroach@gwu.edu. *Application contact:* Sarah Lang, Director of Graduate Admissions, 202-994-1447, Fax: 202-994-7207, E-mail: slang@gwu.edu.

Georgia Southern University, Jack N. Averitt College of Graduate Studies, College of Education, Department of Leadership, Technology, and Human Development, Program in Higher Education, Statesboro, GA 30460. Offers M Ed. *Accreditation:* NCATE. Part-time and evening/weekend programs available. *Students:* 49 full-time (28 women), 99 part-time (79 women); includes 66 minority (57 Black or African American, non-Hispanic/Latino; 1 American Indian or Alaska Native, non-Hispanic/Latino; 1 Asian, non-Hispanic/Latino; 3 Hispanic/Latino; 4 Two or more races, non-Hispanic/Latino), 1 international. Average age 31. 46 applicants, 96% accepted, 37 enrolled. In 2013, 51 master's awarded. *Degree requirements:* For master's, portfolio, practicum, transition point assessments. *Entrance requirements:* For master's, GRE General Test or MAT, minimum GPA of 2.5. Additional exam requirements/recommendations for international students: Required—TOEFL (minimum score 550 paper-based; 80 iBT), IELTS (minimum score 6). *Application deadline:* For fall admission, 3/1 priority date for domestic and international students; for spring admission, 10/1 priority date for domestic students, 10/1 for international students. Applications are processed on a rolling basis. Application fee: $50. Electronic applications accepted. *Expenses:* Tuition, state resident: full-time $7068; part-time $270 per semester hour. Tuition, nonresident: full-time $26,446; part-time $1077 per semester hour. *Required fees:* $2092. *Financial support:* In 2013–14, 16 students received support, including research assistantships with partial tuition reimbursements available (averaging $7,200 per year), teaching assistantships with partial tuition reimbursements available (averaging $7,200 per year); career-related internships or fieldwork, Federal Work-Study, scholarships/grants, tuition waivers (partial), and unspecified assistantships also available. Support available to part-time students. Financial award application deadline: 4/15; financial award applicants required to submit FAFSA. *Faculty research:* Global issues in higher education, leadership and identity development in higher education. *Unit head:* Dr. Daniel Calhoun, Program Coordinator, 912-478-1428, Fax: 912-478-7140, E-mail: dwcalhoun@georgiasouthern.edu. *Application contact:* Amanda Gilliland, Coordinator for Graduate Student Recruitment, 912-478-5384, Fax: 912-478-0740, E-mail: gradadmissions@georgiasouthern.edu.
Website: http://coe.georgiasouthern.edu/edld/m-ed/.

Grambling State University, School of Graduate Studies and Research, College of Education, Department of Educational Leadership, Grambling, LA 71245. Offers developmental education (MS, Ed D, PMC), including curriculum and instructional design (Ed D), English (MS), guidance and counseling (MS), higher education administration and management (Ed D), mathematics (MS), reading (MS), science (MS), student development and personnel services (Ed D); educational leadership (M Ed). Part-time and evening/weekend programs available. *Faculty:* 10 full-time (7 women). *Students:* 19 full-time (13 women), 89 part-time (70 women); includes 83 minority (82 Black or African American, non-Hispanic/Latino; 1 Hispanic/Latino), 6 international. Average age 40. In 2013, 13 master's, 6 doctorates, 1 other advanced degree awarded. *Degree requirements:* For master's, comprehensive exam, thesis (for some programs); for doctorate, comprehensive exam, thesis/dissertation. *Entrance requirements:* For master's, GRE, minimum GPA of 2.5 on last degree; for doctorate, GRE (minimum score 1000, 500 on Verbal), master's degree, minimum GPA of 3.0 on last degree. Additional exam requirements/recommendations for international students: Required—TOEFL (minimum score 500 paper-based; 62 iBT). *Application deadline:* For fall admission, 7/1 for domestic and international students; for spring admission, 12/1 for domestic and international students; for summer admission, 5/1 for domestic and international students. Applications are processed on a rolling basis. Application fee: $20 ($30 for international students). Electronic applications accepted. *Financial support:* Research assistantships, health care benefits, tuition waivers (full), and unspecified assistantships available. Financial award application deadline: 5/31; financial award applicants required to submit FAFSA. *Unit head:* Dr. Olatunde Ogunyemi, Department Head, 318-274-2549, Fax: 318-274-6249, E-mail: ogunyemio@gram.edu. *Application contact:* Brenda Cooper, Administrative Assistant III, 318-274-2238, Fax: 318-274-6249, E-mail: cooper@gram.edu.
Website: http://www.gram.edu/academics/majors/education/departments/leadership/.

Grand Canyon University, College of Doctoral Studies, Phoenix, AZ 85017-1097. Offers business administration (DBA); general psychology (PhD), including cognition and instruction, industrial and organizational psychology; organizational leadership

(Ed D, PhD), including behavioral health (PhD), education and effective schools (PhD), higher education (PhD), instructional leadership (PhD), organizational development (Ed D). *Degree requirements:* For doctorate, comprehensive exam, thesis/dissertation. *Entrance requirements:* For doctorate, minimum GPA of 3.4 on earned advanced degree from regionally-accredited institution; transcripts; goals statement.

Grand Valley State University, College of Education, Program in College Student Affairs Leadership, Allendale, MI 49401-9403. Offers M Ed. Part-time programs available. *Entrance requirements:* For master's, GRE General Test or minimum GPA of 3.0. *Faculty research:* Adult learners, diversity and multiculturalism.

Grand Valley State University, College of Education, Program in Higher Education, Allendale, MI 49401-9403. Offers M Ed.

Grand Valley State University, College of Education, Programs in General Education, Allendale, MI 49401-9403. Offers adult and higher education (M Ed); early childhood education (M Ed); educational differentiation (M Ed); educational leadership (M Ed); educational technology integration (M Ed); elementary education (M Ed); middle level education (M Ed); school library media services (M Ed); secondary level education (M Ed); teaching English to speakers of other languages (M Ed). Part-time and evening/weekend programs available. Postbaccalaureate distance learning degree programs offered (minimal on-campus study). *Degree requirements:* For master's, thesis. *Entrance requirements:* For master's, GRE General Test or minimum GPA of 3.0. Additional exam requirements/recommendations for international students: Required—TOEFL. Electronic applications accepted. *Faculty research:* Effectiveness of technology in education, parental involvement, effective teaching, effective schools research.

Harvard University, Harvard Graduate School of Education, Doctoral Program in Education, Cambridge, MA 02138. Offers culture, communities and education (Ed D); education policy, leadership and instructional practice (Ed D); higher education (Ed D); human development and education (Ed D); quantitative policy analysis in education (Ed D). *Faculty:* 68 full-time (34 women), 77 part-time/adjunct (41 women). *Students:* 221 full-time (148 women), 8 part-time (4 women); includes 70 minority (28 Black or African American, non-Hispanic/Latino; 22 Asian, non-Hispanic/Latino; 14 Hispanic/Latino; 1 Native Hawaiian or other Pacific Islander, non-Hispanic/Latino; 5 Two or more races, non-Hispanic/Latino), 26 international. Average age 34. 472 applicants, 8% accepted, 25 enrolled. In 2013, 50 doctorates awarded. Terminal master's awarded for partial completion of doctoral program. *Degree requirements:* For doctorate, thesis/dissertation. *Entrance requirements:* For doctorate, GRE General Test, statement of purpose, 3 letters of recommendation, resume, official transcripts. Additional exam requirements/recommendations for international students: Required—TOEFL (minimum score 613 paper-based; 104 iBT), TWE (minimum score 5). *Application deadline:* For fall admission, 12/2 for domestic and international students. Application fee: $85. Electronic applications accepted. *Expenses:* Contact institution. *Financial support:* In 2013–14, 168 students received support, including 66 fellowships with full and partial tuition reimbursements available (averaging $15,034 per year), 48 research assistantships (averaging $11,714 per year), 190 teaching assistantships (averaging $6,097 per year); career-related internships or fieldwork, Federal Work-Study, institutionally sponsored loans, scholarships/grants, health care benefits, tuition waivers (full and partial), and unspecified assistantships also available. Support available to part-time students. Financial award application deadline: 2/1; financial award applicants required to submit FAFSA. *Faculty research:* Learning and development, educational leadership and organizations, education policy analysis. *Total annual research expenditures:* $34.3 million. *Unit head:* Dr. Barbara Selmo, Assistant Dean, 617-496-4406. *Application contact:* Information Contact, 617-495-3414, Fax: 617-496-3577, E-mail: gseadmissions@harvard.edu.
Website: http://gse.harvard.edu/.

Hofstra University, School of Education, Programs in Educational Policy and Leadership, Hempstead, NY 11549. Offers educational and policy leadership (MS Ed, Ed D), including K-12 (MS Ed), K-12/higher education (Ed D); educational policy and leadership (Advanced Certificate), including school district business leader; foundations of education (MA, Advanced Certificate); higher education leadership and policy studies (MS Ed).

Illinois State University, Graduate School, College of Education, Department of Curriculum and Instruction, Normal, IL 61790-2200. Offers curriculum and instruction (MS, MS Ed, Ed D); educational policies (Ed D); postsecondary education (Ed D); reading (MS Ed); supervision (Ed D). *Accreditation:* NCATE. *Degree requirements:* For master's, variable foreign language requirement, thesis or alternative; for doctorate, variable foreign language requirement, thesis/dissertation, 2 terms of residency, internship. *Entrance requirements:* For master's, GRE General Test, minimum GPA of 3.0 in last 60 hours of course work; for doctorate, GRE General Test. *Faculty research:* In-service and pre-service teacher education for teachers of English language learners; teachers for all children: developing a model for alternative, bilingual elementary certification for paraprofessionals in Illinois; Illinois Geographic Alliance, Connections Project.

Indiana State University, College of Graduate and Professional Studies, College of Education, Department of Educational Leadership, Administration, and Foundations, Terre Haute, IN 47809. Offers educational administration (PhD); leadership in higher education (PhD); school administration (Ed S); school administration and supervision (M Ed); student affairs in higher education (MS). *Accreditation:* NCATE. Part-time and evening/weekend programs available. Terminal master's awarded for partial completion of doctoral program. *Degree requirements:* For master's, thesis; for doctorate, thesis/dissertation. *Entrance requirements:* For master's, GRE General Test, minimum undergraduate GPA of 2.5; for doctorate, GRE General Test, minimum undergraduate GPA of 3.5; for Ed S, GRE General Test, minimum graduate GPA of 3.25. Electronic applications accepted.

Indiana University Bloomington, School of Education, Department of Educational Leadership and Policy Studies, Bloomington, IN 47405-7000. Offers education policy studies (PhD); educational leadership (MS, Ed D, Ed S); higher education (MS, Ed D, PhD); history and philosophy of education (MS); history of education (PhD); international and comparative education (MS, PhD); philosophy of education (PhD); student affairs administration (MS). *Accreditation:* NCATE. Part-time and evening/weekend programs available. *Degree requirements:* For master's, thesis optional; for doctorate, comprehensive exam, thesis/dissertation; for Ed S, comprehensive exam or project. *Entrance requirements:* For master's, doctorate, and Ed S, GRE General Test. Additional exam requirements/recommendations for international students: Required—TOEFL (minimum score 79 iBT). Electronic applications accepted. *Faculty research:* Student engagement at higher education institutions in the nation, Reading First professional development initiative, state finance policy on financial access to higher education, school reform, special needs studies.

Indiana University of Pennsylvania, School of Graduate Studies and Research, College of Education and Educational Technology, Department of Student Affairs in Higher Education, Indiana, PA 15705-1087. Offers MA. *Accreditation:* NCATE. Part-time programs available. *Faculty:* 4 full-time (2 women). *Students:* 57 full-time (45 women), 7 part-time (2 women); includes 8 minority (5 Black or African American, non-Hispanic/Latino; 1 Asian, non-Hispanic/Latino; 2 Hispanic/Latino). Average age 24. 137 applicants, 54% accepted, 26 enrolled. In 2013, 30 master's awarded. *Degree requirements:* For master's, comprehensive exam, thesis optional. *Entrance requirements:* For master's, resume, interview, 2 letters of recommendation, writing sample, minimum GPA of 2.8. Additional exam requirements/recommendations for international students: Required—TOEFL (minimum score 540 paper-based). *Application deadline:* For fall admission, 1/15 priority date for domestic students. Application fee: $50. Electronic applications accepted. *Expenses:* Tuition, state resident: full-time $3978; part-time $442 per credit. Tuition, nonresident: full-time $5967; part-time $663 per credit. *Required fees:* $2080; $115.55 per credit. $93 per semester. Tuition and fees vary according to degree level and program. *Financial support:* In 2013–14, 23 research assistantships with full and partial tuition reimbursements (averaging $5,216 per year) were awarded; fellowships, career-related internships or fieldwork, Federal Work-Study, scholarships/grants, and unspecified assistantships also available. Support available to part-time students. Financial award application deadline: 4/15; financial award applicants required to submit FAFSA. *Unit head:* Dr. John Wesley Lowery, Chairperson, 724-357-4535, E-mail: jlowery@iup.edu. *Application contact:* Paula Stossel, Assistant Dean for Administration, 724-357-4511, Fax: 724-357-4862, E-mail: graduate-admissions@iup.edu.
Website: http://www.iup.edu/sahe.

Indiana University–Purdue University Indianapolis, School of Education, Indianapolis, IN 46202-2896. Offers computer education (Certificate); curriculum and instruction (MS); early childhood (MS); educational leadership (MS, Certificate); English as a second language (Certificate); higher education and student affairs (MS); kindergarten (Certificate); language education (MS); reading (Certificate); school counseling (MS); special education (MS, Certificate). Part-time and evening/weekend programs available. *Faculty:* 41 full-time, 80 part-time/adjunct. *Students:* 113 full-time (78 women), 263 part-time (200 women); includes 88 minority (51 Black or African American, non-Hispanic/Latino; 1 American Indian or Alaska Native, non-Hispanic/Latino; 10 Asian, non-Hispanic/Latino; 19 Hispanic/Latino; 7 Two or more races, non-Hispanic/Latino), 5 international. Average age 33. 93 applicants, 54% accepted, 40 enrolled. In 2013, 179 master's awarded. *Degree requirements:* For master's, thesis optional. *Entrance requirements:* For master's, GRE General Test, minimum GPA of 3.0. Additional exam requirements/recommendations for international students: Required—TOEFL. *Application deadline:* For fall admission, 5/1 priority date for domestic students; for spring admission, 11/1 for domestic students. Application fee: $55 ($65 for international students). *Financial support:* Fellowships, research assistantships with partial tuition reimbursements, teaching assistantships, Federal Work-Study, institutionally sponsored loans, scholarships/grants, and tuition waivers (partial) available. Support available to part-time students. *Faculty research:* Teachers in the process of change, learning cycles, children's concepts of science. *Total annual research expenditures:* $614,458. *Unit head:* Dr. Pat Rogan, Executive Associate Dean, 317-274-6862, E-mail: progan@iupui.edu. *Application contact:* Donnella Dillon, Graduate Admissions Coordinator, 317-274-0645, E-mail: dmdillon@iupui.edu.
Website: http://education.iupui.edu/.

Indiana Wesleyan University, Graduate School, College of Arts and Sciences, Marion, IN 46953. Offers addictions counseling (MS); clinical mental health counseling (MS); community counseling (MS); marriage and family therapy (MS); school counseling (MS); student development counseling and administration (MS). *Accreditation:* ACA. Part-time programs available. *Degree requirements:* For master's, thesis or alternative. *Entrance requirements:* For master's, GRE General Test. Additional exam requirements/recommendations for international students: Required—TOEFL. Electronic applications accepted. *Expenses:* Contact institution. *Faculty research:* Community counseling, multicultural counseling, addictions.

Inter American University of Puerto Rico, Metropolitan Campus, Graduate Programs, Program in Higher Education Administration, San Juan, PR 00919-1293. Offers MA. *Degree requirements:* For master's, comprehensive exam. *Entrance requirements:* For master's, GRE or EXADEP, interview. Electronic applications accepted.

Iowa State University of Science and Technology, Department of Educational Leadership and Policy Studies, Ames, IA 50011. Offers counselor education (M Ed, MS); educational administration (M Ed, MS); educational leadership (PhD); higher education (M Ed, MS); organizational learning and human resource development (M Ed, MS); research and evaluation (MS); student affairs (MS). *Degree requirements:* For master's, thesis or alternative; for doctorate, thesis/dissertation. *Entrance requirements:* For master's and doctorate, GRE General Test. Additional exam requirements/recommendations for international students: Required—TOEFL (minimum score 560 paper-based; 83 iBT), IELTS (minimum score 6.5). Electronic applications accepted.

John Brown University, Graduate Business Programs, Siloam Springs, AR 72761-2121. Offers global continuous improvement (MBA); higher education leadership (MS); international community development leadership (MS); leadership and ethics (MBA, MS). *Accreditation:* ACBSP. Part-time and evening/weekend programs available. Postbaccalaureate distance learning degree programs offered (minimal on-campus study). *Faculty:* 6 full-time (1 woman), 29 part-time/adjunct (8 women). *Students:* 23 full-time (13 women), 210 part-time (102 women); includes 41 minority (14 Black or African American, non-Hispanic/Latino; 5 American Indian or Alaska Native, non-Hispanic/Latino; 3 Asian, non-Hispanic/Latino; 11 Hispanic/Latino; 8 Two or more races, non-Hispanic/Latino), 3 international. Average age 34. 121 applicants, 98% accepted, 99 enrolled. *Entrance requirements:* For master's, MAT, GMAT or GRE if undergraduate GPA is less than 3.0, recommendation forms from three people, 200-word essay describing professional plans and reason for seeking acceptance. Additional exam requirements/recommendations for international students: Required—TOEFL (minimum score 550 paper-based; 70 iBT). *Application deadline:* Applications are processed on a rolling basis. Application fee: $35 ($100 for international students). Electronic applications accepted. *Expenses: Tuition:* Part-time $515 per credit hour. *Financial support:* Fellowships with full tuition reimbursements, scholarships/grants, and unspecified assistantships available. Financial award applicants required to submit FAFSA. *Unit head:* Dr. Joe Walenciak, Program Director, 479-524-7431, E-mail: jwalenci@jbu.edu. *Application contact:* Brent Young, Graduate Business Representative, 479-524-7450, E-mail: byoung@jbu.edu.
Website: http://www.jbu.edu/grad/business/.

Johnson University, Graduate and Professional Programs, Knoxville, TN 37998-1001. Offers educational technology (MA); intercultural studies (MA); leadership studies (PhD); marriage and family therapy/professional counseling (MA); New Testament (MA); school counseling (MA); teacher education (MA). *Degree requirements:* For master's, variable foreign language requirement, comprehensive exam, thesis (for some programs), internship (500 client contact hours). *Entrance requirements:* For master's, interview, minimum GPA of 3.0, 20 credits of course work in psychology, 15 credits of course work in Bible. Additional exam requirements/recommendations for international students: Required—TOEFL.

Jones International University, School of Education, Centennial, CO 80112. Offers adult education (M Ed); corporate training and knowledge management (M Ed); curriculum and instruction (M Ed), including elementary teacher licensure, secondary teacher licensure; e-learning technology and design (M Ed); educational leadership and

administration (M Ed); educational leadership and administration: principal and administrator licensure (M Ed); elementary curriculum instruction and assessment (M Ed); higher education leadership and administration (M Ed); K-12 instructional technology (M Ed); K-12 instructional technology: teacher licensure (M Ed); secondary curriculum instruction and assessment (M Ed); technology and design (M Ed). Part-time and evening/weekend programs available. Postbaccalaureate distance learning degree programs offered (no on-campus study). *Entrance requirements:* For master's, minimum cumulative GPA of 2.5. Additional exam requirements/recommendations for international students: Recommended—TOEFL (minimum score 550 paper-based). Electronic applications accepted.

Kansas State University, Graduate School, College of Education, Department of Special Education, Counseling and Student Affairs, Manhattan, KS 66506. Offers academic advising (MS); counseling and student development (MS, Ed D, PhD), including college student development (MS), counselor education and supervision (PhD), school counseling (MS), student affairs in higher education (PhD); special education (MS, Ed D). *Accreditation:* ACA; NCATE. Part-time programs available. *Faculty:* 18 full-time (8 women), 15 part-time/adjunct (5 women). *Students:* 117 full-time (80 women), 327 part-time (257 women); includes 83 minority (42 Black or African American, non-Hispanic/Latino; 2 American Indian or Alaska Native, non-Hispanic/Latino; 9 Asian, non-Hispanic/Latino; 23 Hispanic/Latino; 1 Native Hawaiian or other Pacific Islander, non-Hispanic/Latino; 6 Two or more races, non-Hispanic/Latino), 9 international. Average age 33. 247 applicants, 69% accepted, 117 enrolled. In 2013, 117 master's, 7 doctorates awarded. *Degree requirements:* For master's, comprehensive exam; for doctorate, comprehensive exam, thesis/dissertation. *Entrance requirements:* For master's, minimum undergraduate GPA of 3.0; for doctorate, GRE General Test, minimum GPA of 3.0 in last 60 hours. Additional exam requirements/recommendations for international students: Required—TOEFL. *Application deadline:* For fall admission, 2/1 priority date for domestic and international students; for spring admission, 8/1 priority date for domestic and international students. Applications are processed on a rolling basis. Application fee: $50 ($75 for international students). Electronic applications accepted. *Financial support:* In 2013–14, 3 teaching assistantships (averaging $18,090 per year) were awarded; career-related internships or fieldwork, institutionally sponsored loans, and scholarships/grants also available. Financial award application deadline: 3/1; financial award applicants required to submit FAFSA. *Faculty research:* Counseling supervision, academic advising, career development, student development, universal design for learning, autism, learning disabilities. *Unit head:* Kenneth Hughey, Head, 785-532-6445, Fax: 785-532-7304, E-mail: khughey@ksu.edu. *Application contact:* Dona Deam, Application Contact, 785-532-5595, Fax: 785-532-7304, E-mail: ddeam@ksu.edu.
Website: http://www.coe.k-state.edu/departments/secsa/.

Kaplan University, Davenport Campus, School of Higher Education Studies, Davenport, IA 52807-2095. Offers college administration and leadership (MS); college teaching and learning (MS); student services (MS). Part-time and evening/weekend programs available. Postbaccalaureate distance learning degree programs offered (no on-campus study). *Entrance requirements:* Additional exam requirements/recommendations for international students: Required—TOEFL (minimum score 550 paper-based; 80 iBT).

Kent State University, Graduate School of Education, Health, and Human Services, School of Foundations, Leadership and Administration, Program in Higher Education, Kent, OH 44242-0001. Offers PhD, Ed S. *Accreditation:* NCATE. Part-time and evening/weekend programs available. *Faculty:* 5 full-time (3 women), 3 part-time/adjunct (2 women). *Students:* 27 full-time (17 women), 22 part-time (15 women); includes 6 minority (5 Black or African American, non-Hispanic/Latino; 1 Asian, non-Hispanic/Latino), 1 international. 23 applicants, 26% accepted. In 2013, 2 doctorates awarded. *Degree requirements:* For doctorate, comprehensive exam, thesis/dissertation. *Entrance requirements:* For doctorate, GRE General Test, 2 letters of reference, resume, interview, goals statement. Additional exam requirements/recommendations for international students: Required—TOEFL (minimum score 550 paper-based; 80 iBT). *Application deadline:* Applications are processed on a rolling basis. Application fee: $30 ($60 for international students). Electronic applications accepted. *Financial support:* In 2013–14, 2 research assistantships with full tuition reimbursements (averaging $12,000 per year), 1 teaching assistantship with full tuition reimbursement (averaging $12,000 per year) were awarded; career-related internships or fieldwork, Federal Work-Study, institutionally sponsored loans, scholarships/grants, health care benefits, and unspecified assistantships also available. Support available to part-time students. Financial award application deadline: 4/1; financial award applicants required to submit FAFSA. *Faculty research:* Leadership. *Unit head:* Dr. Mark Kretovics, Coordinator, 330-672-0642, E-mail: mkretov1@kent.edu. *Application contact:* Nancy Miller, Academic Program Director, Office of Graduate Student Services, 330-672-2576, Fax: 330-672-9162, E-mail: ogs@kent.edu.

Kent State University, Graduate School of Education, Health, and Human Services, School of Foundations, Leadership and Administration, Program in Higher Education and Student Personnel, Kent, OH 44242-0001. Offers M Ed. *Accreditation:* NCATE. Part-time and evening/weekend programs available. *Faculty:* 5 full-time (3 women), 3 part-time/adjunct (2 women). *Students:* 82 full-time (60 women), 23 part-time (20 women); includes 19 minority (10 Black or African American, non-Hispanic/Latino; 1 American Indian or Alaska Native, non-Hispanic/Latino; 1 Asian, non-Hispanic/Latino; 2 Hispanic/Latino; 5 Native Hawaiian or other Pacific Islander, non-Hispanic/Latino), 2 international. 182 applicants, 15% accepted. In 2013, 35 master's awarded. *Entrance requirements:* For master's, GRE if undergraduate GPA is below 3.0, resume, interview, 2 letters of recommendation, goals statement. Additional exam requirements/recommendations for international students: Required—TOEFL (minimum score 550 paper-based; 80 iBT). *Application deadline:* Applications are processed on a rolling basis. Application fee: $30 ($60 for international students). Electronic applications accepted. *Financial support:* In 2013–14, 2 research assistantships with full tuition reimbursements (averaging $8,500 per year) were awarded; teaching assistantships with full tuition reimbursements, Federal Work-Study, scholarships/grants, and unspecified assistantships also available. Financial award application deadline: 4/1; financial award applicants required to submit FAFSA. *Faculty research:* History/sociology of higher education, organization and administration in higher education. *Unit head:* Dr. Mark Kretovics, Coordinator, 330-672-0642, E-mail: mkretov1@kent.edu. *Application contact:* Nancy Miller, Academic Program Director, Office of Graduate Student Services, 330-672-2576, Fax: 330-672-9162, E-mail: ogs@kent.edu.

Lee University, Program in Education, Cleveland, TN 37320-3450. Offers college student development (MS); curriculum and instruction (M Ed, Ed S); educational leadership (M Ed, Ed S); elementary education (MAT); higher education administration (MS); middle grades (MAT); secondary education (MAT); special education (M Ed); special education (secondary) (MAT). Part-time programs available. *Faculty:* 14 full-time (7 women), 6 part-time/adjunct (3 women). *Students:* 30 full-time (23 women), 62 part-time (37 women); includes 8 minority (3 Black or African American, non-Hispanic/Latino; 1 American Indian or Alaska Native, non-Hispanic/Latino; 2 Asian, non-Hispanic/Latino; 2 Hispanic/Latino). Average age 30. 40 applicants, 100% accepted, 30 enrolled. In 2013, 117 master's, 2 other advanced degrees awarded. *Degree requirements:* For

master's, variable foreign language requirement, comprehensive exam, thesis, internship. *Entrance requirements:* For master's, MAT or GRE General Test, minimum GPA of 2.75, 3 letters of recommendation, interview, writing sample, official transcripts. Additional exam requirements/recommendations for international students: Required—TOEFL (minimum score 450 paper-based). *Application deadline:* For fall admission, 4/1 priority date for domestic and international students; for spring admission, 10/1 priority date for domestic and international students. Applications are processed on a rolling basis. Application fee: $25. *Expenses: Tuition:* Full-time $9900; part-time $550 per credit hour. *Required fees:* $35 per term. One-time fee: $25. *Financial support:* In 2013–14, 47 students received support, including 1 teaching assistantship (averaging $1,500 per year); career-related internships or fieldwork, Federal Work-Study, institutionally sponsored loans, scholarships/grants, and unspecified assistantships also available. Financial award application deadline: 3/1; financial award applicants required to submit FAFSA. *Unit head:* Dr. Gary Riggins, Director, 423-614-8193. *Application contact:* Vicki Glasscock, Graduate Admissions Director, 423-614-8059, E-mail: vglasscock@leeuniversity.edu.
Website: http://www.leeuniversity.edu/academics/graduate/education.

Lewis University, College of Arts and Sciences, Program in Organizational Leadership, Romeoville, IL 60446. Offers coaching (MA); higher education/student services (MA); non-for-profit management (MA); organizational management (MA); public administration (MA); training and development (MA). Part-time and evening/weekend programs available. Postbaccalaureate distance learning degree programs offered (no on-campus study). *Students:* 24 full-time (21 women), 200 part-time (152 women); includes 87 minority (60 Black or African American, non-Hispanic/Latino; 2 American Indian or Alaska Native, non-Hispanic/Latino; 4 Asian, non-Hispanic/Latino; 20 Hispanic/Latino; 1 Two or more races, non-Hispanic/Latino), 1 international. Average age 36. *Entrance requirements:* For master's, bachelor's degree, at least 24 years of age, minimum of 3 years of work experience, minimum GPA of 3.0, letter of recommendation. Additional exam requirements/recommendations for international students: Required—TOEFL (minimum score 550 paper-based; 80 iBT). *Application deadline:* For fall admission, 5/1 priority date for international students; for spring admission, 11/15 priority date for international students. Applications are processed on a rolling basis. Application fee: $40. Electronic applications accepted. *Financial support:* Tuition waivers and unspecified assistantships available. Financial award application deadline: 5/1; financial award applicants required to submit FAFSA. *Unit head:* Dr. Keith Lavine, Chair of Organizational Leadership, 815-838-0500, E-mail: lavineke@lewisu.edu. *Application contact:* Julie Branchaw, Assistant Director, Graduate and Adult Admission, 815-836-5574, Fax: 815-836-5578, E-mail: branchju@lewisu.edu.

Lincoln Memorial University, Carter and Moyers School of Education, Harrogate, TN 37752-1901. Offers administration and supervision (M Ed, Ed S); counseling and guidance (M Ed); curriculum and instruction (M Ed, Ed D, Ed S); English (M Ed); executive leadership (Ed D); higher education administration (Ed D); human resource development (Ed D); leadership and administration (Ed D). Part-time and evening/weekend programs available. Postbaccalaureate distance learning degree programs offered. *Degree requirements:* For master's, comprehensive exam, thesis optional; for Ed S, comprehensive exam. *Entrance requirements:* For master's, PRAXIS, NTE, GRE, MAT, letters of recommendation; for Ed S, graduate transcripts. Additional exam requirements/recommendations for international students: Recommended—TOEFL. *Faculty research:* Brain compatible teaching and learning; poverty in Appalachia; leadership for change; ethics, moral responsibility and social justice; human and organizational learning.

Louisiana State University and Agricultural & Mechanical College, Graduate School, College of Human Sciences and Education, Department of Educational Theory, Policy and Practice, Baton Rouge, LA 70803. Offers counseling (M Ed, MA, Ed S); educational administration (M Ed, MA, PhD, Ed S); educational technology (MA); elementary education (M Ed, MAT); higher education (PhD); research methodology (PhD); secondary education (M Ed, MAT). PhD programs offered jointly with Louisiana State University in Shreveport. *Accreditation:* ACA (one or more programs are accredited); NCATE. Part-time and evening/weekend programs available. *Faculty:* 39 full-time (22 women). *Students:* 185 full-time (136 women), 177 part-time (140 women); includes 110 minority (90 Black or African American, non-Hispanic/Latino; 1 American Indian or Alaska Native, non-Hispanic/Latino; 5 Asian, non-Hispanic/Latino; 9 Hispanic/Latino; 5 Two or more races, non-Hispanic/Latino), 5 international. Average age 31. 167 applicants, 66% accepted, 76 enrolled. In 2013, 134 master's, 23 doctorates, 17 other advanced degrees awarded. Terminal master's awarded for partial completion of doctoral program. *Degree requirements:* For doctorate, thesis/dissertation; for Ed S, thesis optional. *Entrance requirements:* For master's and doctorate, GRE General Test, minimum GPA of 3.0. Additional exam requirements/recommendations for international students: Required—TOEFL (minimum score 550 paper-based; 79 iBT), IELTS (minimum score 6.5), or PTE (minimum score 59). *Application deadline:* For fall admission, 1/25 priority date for domestic students, 5/15 for international students; for spring admission, 10/15 for international students. Applications are processed on a rolling basis. Application fee: $50 ($70 for international students). Electronic applications accepted. *Financial support:* In 2013–14, 253 students received support, including 5 fellowships (averaging $32,204 per year), 27 research assistantships with full and partial tuition reimbursements available (averaging $10,199 per year), 68 teaching assistantships with full and partial tuition reimbursements available (averaging $12,316 per year); career-related internships or fieldwork, Federal Work-Study, institutionally sponsored loans, health care benefits, and unspecified assistantships also available. Support available to part-time students. Financial award applicants required to submit FAFSA. *Faculty research:* Literary, curriculum studies, science education, K-12 leadership, higher education. *Total annual research expenditures:* $735,835. *Unit head:* Dr. Earl Cheek, Jr., Chair, 225-578-1258, Fax: 225-578-2267, E-mail: echeek@lsu.edu. *Application contact:* Dr. Kristin Gansle, Graduate Coordinator, 225-578-6780, Fax: 225-578-2267, E-mail: kgansle@lsu.edu.

Loyola University Chicago, School of Education, Program in Higher Education, Chicago, IL 60660. Offers M Ed, PhD. PhD offered through the Graduate School. *Accreditation:* NCATE. Part-time programs available. Postbaccalaureate distance learning degree programs offered (minimal on-campus study). *Faculty:* 5 full-time (2 women), 9 part-time/adjunct (3 women). *Students:* 134. Average age 38. 255 applicants, 63% accepted, 57 enrolled. In 2013, 49 master's, 3 doctorates awarded. *Degree requirements:* For master's, comprehensive exam; for doctorate, comprehensive exam, thesis/dissertation. *Entrance requirements:* For master's, letters of recommendation, minimum GPA of 3.0, resume, transcripts; for doctorate, GMAT, GRE General Test, or MAT, 5 years of higher education work experience, interview. Additional exam requirements/recommendations for international students: Required—TOEFL (minimum score 550 paper-based; 79 iBT). *Application deadline:* For fall admission, 12/1 for domestic and international students; for spring admission, 11/1 for domestic and international students. Applications are processed on a rolling basis. Application fee: $50. Electronic applications accepted. Application fee is waived when completed online. *Expenses: Tuition:* Full-time $16,740; part-time $930 per credit. *Required fees:* $135 per semester. *Financial support:* In 2013–14, 13 fellowships with partial tuition reimbursements, 12 research assistantships with full tuition reimbursements (averaging $12,000 per year), 15 teaching assistantships with full tuition reimbursements

(averaging $12,000 per year) were awarded; career-related internships or fieldwork, institutionally sponsored loans, scholarships/grants, traineeships, health care benefits, and unspecified assistantships also available. Support available to part-time students. Financial award application deadline: 2/1; financial award applicants required to submit FAFSA. *Faculty research:* Church-affiliated higher education, enrollment management, academic programs, program evaluation/quality. *Unit head:* Dr. Mark Engberg, Director, 312-915-7401, Fax: 312-915-6660, E-mail: mengber@luc.edu. *Application contact:* Marie Rosin-Dittmar, Information Contact, 312-915-6800, E-mail: schleduc@luc.edu.

Maryville University of Saint Louis, School of Education, St. Louis, MO 63141-7299. Offers art education (MA Ed); early childhood education (MA Ed); educational leadership (Ed D); educational leadership: principal certification (MA Ed); elementary education (MA Ed); gifted education (MA Ed); higher education leadership (Ed D); literacy specialist (MA Ed); middle grades education (MA Ed); secondary teaching and inquiry (MA Ed); teacher as leader (MA Ed); teacher leadership (Ed D). *Accreditation:* NCATE. Part-time and evening/weekend programs available. *Faculty:* 10 full-time (6 women), 17 part-time/adjunct (13 women). *Students:* 21 full-time (17 women), 238 part-time (167 women); includes 64 minority (54 Black or African American, non-Hispanic/Latino; 2 Asian, non-Hispanic/Latino; 4 Hispanic/Latino; 4 Two or more races, non-Hispanic/Latino), 2 international. Average age 39. In 2013, 61 master's, 40 doctorates awarded. *Degree requirements:* For master's, thesis, project. *Entrance requirements:* For master's, minimum cumulative GPA of 3.0, 3 professional recommendations, essays, interview with program faculty; for doctorate, minimum GPA of 3.0, 3 professional recommendations, essay, interview, on-site writing sample. Additional exam requirements/recommendations for international students: Required—TOEFL (minimum score 550 paper-based). *Application deadline:* Applications are processed on a rolling basis. Application fee: $40 ($60 for international students). Electronic applications accepted. Application fee is waived when completed online. *Expenses: Tuition:* Full-time $23,812; part-time $728 per credit hour. *Required fees:* $395 per year. Tuition and fees vary according to course load, degree level and program. *Financial support:* Career-related internships or fieldwork, Federal Work-Study, tuition waivers (partial), and professional educator discounts available. Financial award application deadline: 3/1; financial award applicants required to submit FAFSA. *Faculty research:* Collaboration with public schools, pre-service program development, mathematics, diversity, literacy. *Unit head:* Dr. Cathy Bear, Dean, 314-529-9692, Fax: 314-529-9921, E-mail: cbear@maryville.edu. *Application contact:* Holly Stanwich, Graduate Admissions Coordinator, 314-529-9542, Fax: 314-529-9921, E-mail: teachered@maryville.edu.
Website: http://www.maryville.edu/ed/graduate-programs/.

Marywood University, Academic Affairs, Reap College of Education and Human Development, Department of Education, Program in Higher Education Administration, Scranton, PA 18509-1598. Offers MS. Part-time and evening/weekend programs available. *Entrance requirements:* Additional exam requirements/recommendations for international students: Required—TOEFL (minimum score 550 paper-based; 79 iBT). *Application deadline:* For fall admission, 4/1 priority date for domestic students, 3/31 priority date for international students; for spring admission, 11/1 priority date for domestic students, 8/31 priority date for international students. Applications are processed on a rolling basis. Application fee: $30. Electronic applications accepted. *Expenses: Tuition:* Part-time $775 per credit. Tuition and fees vary according to degree level. *Financial support:* Research assistantships with tuition reimbursements, career-related internships or fieldwork, scholarships/grants, and unspecified assistantships available. Support available to part-time students. Financial award application deadline: 6/30; financial award applicants required to submit FAFSA. *Faculty research:* Integrated thematic instruction. *Unit head:* Dr. Patricia S. Arter, Chairperson, 570-348-6211 Ext. 2511, E-mail: psarter@marywood.edu. *Application contact:* Tammy Manka, Assistant Director of Graduate Admissions, 570-348-6211 Ext. 2322, E-mail: tmanka@marywood.edu.
Website: http://www.marywood.edu/education/graduate-programs/ms_higher_education_administration.html.

Marywood University, Academic Affairs, Reap College of Education and Human Development, Doctoral Program in Human Development, Emphasis in Higher Education Administration, Scranton, PA 18509-1598. Offers PhD. *Entrance requirements:* Additional exam requirements/recommendations for international students: Required—TOEFL (minimum score 550 paper-based; 79 iBT). *Application deadline:* For fall admission, 1/30 for domestic and international students. Application fee: $35. Electronic applications accepted. *Expenses:* Contact institution. *Financial support:* Career-related internships or fieldwork, scholarships/grants, and unspecified assistantships available. Support available to part-time students. Financial award application deadline: 6/30; financial award applicants required to submit FAFSA. *Unit head:* Dr. Tonya Nicole Saddler, Coordinator, 570-348-6270, E-mail: saddlert@marywood.edu. *Application contact:* Tammy Manka, Assistant Director of Graduate Admissions, 570-348-6211 Ext. 2322, E-mail: tmanka@marywood.edu.
Website: http://www.marywood.edu/phd/specializations.html.

McKendree University, Graduate Programs, Programs in Education, Lebanon, IL 62254-1299. Offers curriculum design and instruction (Ed D, Ed S); educational administration and leadership (MA Ed); educational studies (MA Ed); higher education administrative services (MA Ed); music education (MA Ed); reading (MA Ed); special education (MA Ed); teacher leadership (MA Ed); teaching certification (MA Ed). *Accreditation:* NCATE. Part-time and evening/weekend programs available. Postbaccalaureate distance learning degree programs offered (no on-campus study). *Entrance requirements:* For master's, official transcripts from all institutions previously attended, minimum GPA of 3.0, resume, references; for doctorate, GRE (within the past 5 years), master's degree in education and Ed S, or the equivalent, from regionally-accredited institution; official transcripts from all institutions previously attended; curriculum vitae/resume; essay/personal statement; two years of teaching/professional experience; for Ed S, GRE (within the past 5 years), master's degree in education from regionally-accredited institution of higher education; official transcripts from all institutions previously attended; curriculum vitae/resume; essay/personal statement; two years of teaching/professional experience. Additional exam requirements/recommendations for international students: Required—TOEFL. Electronic applications accepted.

Mercer University, Graduate Studies, Cecil B. Day Campus, Tift College of Education (Atlanta), Macon, GA 31207-0003. Offers curriculum and instruction (PhD); early childhood education (M Ed, MAT, Ed S); educational leadership (PhD, Ed S); higher education leadership (M Ed); independent and charter school leadership (M Ed); middle grades education (M Ed, MAT); reading education (M Ed); school counseling (Ed S); secondary education (M Ed, MAT); teacher leadership (Ed S). *Accreditation:* NCATE. Part-time and evening/weekend programs available. *Faculty:* 40 full-time (20 women), 9 part-time/adjunct (4 women). *Students:* 240 full-time (197 women), 382 part-time (320 women); includes 343 minority (315 Black or African American, non-Hispanic/Latino; 4 American Indian or Alaska Native, non-Hispanic/Latino; 9 Asian, non-Hispanic/Latino; 9 Hispanic/Latino; 1 Native Hawaiian or other Pacific Islander, non-Hispanic/Latino; 5 Two or more races, non-Hispanic/Latino), 4 international. Average age 36. In 2013, 233 master's, 24 doctorates, 47 other advanced degrees awarded. *Degree requirements:* For master's and Ed S, research project; for doctorate, comprehensive exam, thesis/dissertation. *Entrance requirements:* For master's, GRE or MAT, minimum undergraduate GPA of 2.75; for doctorate, GRE; for Ed S, GRE or MAT, minimum GPA of 3.25; for EDS degrees in educational leadership and teacher leadership: 3 years of certified teaching experience. Additional exam requirements/recommendations for international students: Required—TOEFL. *Application deadline:* For fall admission, 8/1 for domestic and international students; for spring admission, 12/1 for domestic and international students; for summer admission, 5/1 for domestic and international students. Applications are processed on a rolling basis. Application fee: $25. *Expenses:* Contact institution. *Financial support:* Federal Work-Study available. Support available to part-time students. Financial award application deadline: 5/1. *Faculty research:* Educational technology, multicultural and minority issues in education, educational leadership (P-12 and higher education), school discipline and school bullying, standards-based mathematics education. *Unit head:* Dr. Paige L. Tompkins, Interim Dean, 478-301-5397, Fax: 478-301-2280, E-mail: tompkins_pl@mercer.edu. *Application contact:* Dr. Allison Gilmore, Associate Dean for Graduate Teacher Education, 678-547-6333, Fax: 678-547-6055, E-mail: gilmore_a@mercer.edu.
Website: http://www.mercer.edu/education/.

Mercer University, Graduate Studies, Macon Campus, Tift College of Education (Macon), Macon, GA 31207-0003. Offers curriculum and instruction (PhD); education leadership (PhD), including P-12; educational leadership (Ed S); higher education (M Ed); teacher leadership (Ed S). *Accreditation:* NCATE. Part-time and evening/weekend programs available. Postbaccalaureate distance learning degree programs offered (minimal on-campus study). *Faculty:* 15 full-time (6 women), 2 part-time/adjunct (1 woman). *Students:* 39 full-time (20 women), 59 part-time (47 women); includes 41 minority (38 Black or African American, non-Hispanic/Latino; 1 Asian, non-Hispanic/Latino; 2 Hispanic/Latino), 2 international. Average age 35. In 2013, 7 master's, 18 doctorates awarded. *Degree requirements:* For master's, research project report; for doctorate, comprehensive exam, thesis/dissertation. *Entrance requirements:* For master's, GRE or MAT, minimum GPA of 2.75; for doctorate, GRE, minimum GPA of 3.5; interview; writing sample; 3 recommendations; for Ed S, GRE or MAT, minimum GPA of 3.5 (for Ed S in teacher leadership), 3.0 (for Ed S in educational leadership). Additional exam requirements/recommendations for international students: Required—TOEFL. *Application deadline:* For fall admission, 8/1 for domestic and international students; for spring admission, 12/1 for domestic and international students. Applications are processed on a rolling basis. Application fee: $35. *Expenses:* Contact institution. *Financial support:* Federal Work-Study and institutionally sponsored loans available. Support available to part-time students. Financial award application deadline: 5/1. *Faculty research:* Teacher effectiveness, specific learning disabilities, inclusion. *Unit head:* Dr. Paige L. Tompkins, Interim Dean, 478-301-5397, Fax: 478-301-2280, E-mail: tompkins_pl@mercer.edu. *Application contact:* Tracey M. Wofford, Associate Director of Admissions, 678-547-6422, Fax: 678-547-6367, E-mail: wofford_tm@mercer.edu.
Website: http://education.mercer.edu/graduate/.

Mercyhurst University, Graduate Studies, Program in Organizational Leadership, Erie, PA 16546. Offers accounting (MS); entrepreneurship (MS); higher education administration (MS); human resources (MS); nonprofit management (MS); organizational leadership (Certificate); sports leadership (MS). Part-time and evening/weekend programs available. *Degree requirements:* For master's, thesis. *Entrance requirements:* For master's, GRE General Test or MAT, interview, resume, essay, three professional references, transcripts. Additional exam requirements/recommendations for international students: Required—TOEFL. Electronic applications accepted. *Faculty research:* Leadership training, organizational communication, leadership pedagogy.

Merrimack College, School of Education, North Andover, MA 01845-5800. Offers community engagement (M Ed), including community organizations, higher education, K-12 education; early childhood education (M Ed); elementary education (M Ed); English as a second language (PreK-6) (M Ed); English language learners (M Ed); general studies (M Ed); higher education (M Ed), including leadership and organizational development, student affairs; middle (M Ed); moderate disabilities (PreK-8) (M Ed); secondary (M Ed); teacher leadership (CAGS), including instructional leadership, reading specialist. Part-time and evening/weekend programs available. *Faculty:* 4 full-time (all women), 23 part-time/adjunct (15 women). *Students:* 127 full-time (104 women), 61 part-time (52 women); includes 3 minority (1 Asian, non-Hispanic/Latino; 2 Hispanic/Latino), 2 international. Average age 25. 403 applicants, 47% accepted, 138 enrolled. In 2013, 140 master's awarded. *Degree requirements:* For master's, practicum, portfolio, and state test (for licensure track); capstone (for higher education and community engagement tracks). *Entrance requirements:* For master's, MTEL (Massachusetts Tests for Educator Licensure), official transcripts from other colleges, resume, personal statement, 2 letters of recommendation, additional essay requirements for fellowships. Additional exam requirements/recommendations for international students: Required—TOEFL (minimum score 84 iBT), IELTS (minimum score 6.5). *Application deadline:* For fall admission, 8/15 for domestic and international students; for winter admission, 12/1 for domestic students, 11/15 for international students; for spring admission, 1/10 for domestic and international students; for summer admission, 5/10 for domestic and international students. Applications are processed on a rolling basis. Application fee: $0. Electronic applications accepted. Tuition and fees vary according to course load and program. *Financial support:* In 2013–14, 91 fellowships with full tuition reimbursements were awarded; career-related internships or fieldwork, scholarships/grants, and health care benefits also available. Support available to part-time students. Financial award applicants required to submit FAFSA. *Faculty research:* Expressive language, civic engagement, family life education, reading genres, the psychological process of aging. *Application contact:* Kristen English, Interim Director of Graduate Admission, 978-837-5073, E-mail: englishkr@merrimack.edu.
Website: http://www.merrimack.edu/academics/graduate/education/.

Messiah College, Program in Higher Education, Mechanicsburg, PA 17055. Offers college athletics management (MA); self-designed concentration (MA); student affairs (MA). Part-time programs available. Electronic applications accepted. *Expenses: Tuition:* Part-time $595 per credit hour. *Required fees:* $30 per course. *Faculty research:* College athletics management, assessment and student learning outcomes, the life and legacy of Ernest L. Boyer, common learning, student affairs practice.

Miami University, College of Education, Health and Society, Department of Educational Leadership, Oxford, OH 45056. Offers educational administration (Ed D, PhD); school leadership (M Ed); student affairs in higher education (MS, PhD). *Accreditation:* NCATE. Part-time and evening/weekend programs available. *Students:* 99 full-time (65 women), 90 part-time (61 women); includes 44 minority (29 Black or African American, non-Hispanic/Latino; 2 Asian, non-Hispanic/Latino; 9 Hispanic/Latino; 4 Two or more races, non-Hispanic/Latino), 8 international. Average age 34. In 2013, 82 master's, 10 doctorates awarded. *Entrance requirements:* Additional exam requirements/recommendations for international students: Required—TOEFL (minimum score 550 paper-based). Application fee: $50. Electronic applications accepted. *Expenses:* Tuition, state resident: full-time $12,634; part-time $526 per credit hour. Tuition, nonresident: full-time $27,892; part-time $1162 per credit hour. Part-time tuition and fees vary according to course load, campus/location and program. *Financial support:* Research assistantships with full and partial tuition reimbursements, teaching assistantships with partial tuition reimbursements, career-related internships or

fieldwork, Federal Work-Study, scholarships/grants, health care benefits, tuition waivers (partial), and unspecified assistantships available. Financial award application deadline: 2/15; financial award applicants required to submit FAFSA. *Unit head:* Dr. Kathleen Knight Abowitz, Chair, 513-529-6825, E-mail: knightk2@miamioh.edu. *Application contact:* Dr. Thomas Poetter, Professor and Director of Graduate Studies, 513-529-6853, E-mail: poettets@miamioh.edu.
Website: http://www.MiamiOH.edu/EDL.

Michigan State University, The Graduate School, College of Education, Department of Educational Administration, East Lansing, MI 48824. Offers higher, adult and lifelong education (MA, PhD); K–12 educational administration (MA, PhD, Ed S); student affairs administration (MA). Part-time programs available. *Entrance requirements:* Additional exam requirements/recommendations for international students: Required—TOEFL. Electronic applications accepted.

Minnesota State University Mankato, College of Graduate Studies, College of Social and Behavioral Sciences, Department of Sociology and Corrections, Mankato, MN 56001. Offers sociology (MA); sociology: college teaching (MA); sociology: corrections (MS); sociology: human services planning and administration (MS). Part-time programs available. *Students:* 15 full-time (13 women), 16 part-time (10 women). *Degree requirements:* For master's, comprehensive exam, thesis or alternative. *Entrance requirements:* For master's, minimum GPA of 3.0 during previous 2 years, 3 letters of reference, resume. Additional exam requirements/recommendations for international students: Required—TOEFL. *Application deadline:* For fall admission, 7/1 priority date for domestic students; for spring admission, 11/1 for domestic students. Applications are processed on a rolling basis. Application fee: $40. Electronic applications accepted. *Financial support:* Research assistantships with full tuition reimbursements, teaching assistantships with full tuition reimbursements, career-related internships or fieldwork, Federal Work-Study, institutionally sponsored loans, and unspecified assistantships available. Support available to part-time students. Financial award application deadline: 3/15; financial award applicants required to submit FAFSA. *Faculty research:* Women's suffrage movements. *Unit head:* Dr. Barbara Carson, Chairperson, 507-389-1562. *Application contact:* 507-389-2321, E-mail: grad@mnsu.edu.
Website: http://sbs.mnsu.edu/soccorr/.

Mississippi College, Graduate School, School of Education, Department of Teacher Education and Leadership, Clinton, MS 39058. Offers art (M Ed); biological science (M Ed); business education (M Ed); computer science (M Ed); dyslexia therapy (M Ed); educational leadership (M Ed, Ed D, Ed S); elementary education (M Ed, Ed S); English (M Ed); higher education administration (MS); mathematics (M Ed); secondary education (M Ed); social studies (history) (M Ed); teaching arts (M Ed). Part-time programs available. Postbaccalaureate distance learning degree programs offered (no on-campus study). *Degree requirements:* For master's, comprehensive exam, thesis optional. *Entrance requirements:* For master's, NTE. Additional exam requirements/recommendations for international students: Recommended—TOEFL, IELTS. Electronic applications accepted.

Mississippi College, Graduate School, School of Education, Program in Higher Education Administration, Clinton, MS 39058. Offers MS. Part-time programs available. Postbaccalaureate distance learning degree programs offered (no on-campus study). *Degree requirements:* For master's, comprehensive exam, thesis optional. *Entrance requirements:* For master's, GRE or GMAT, minimum GPA of 3.0. Additional exam requirements/recommendations for international students: Recommended—TOEFL, IELTS.

Mississippi State University, College of Education, Department of Counseling and Educational Psychology, Mississippi State, MS 39762. Offers college/postsecondary student counseling and personnel services (PhD); counselor education (MS), including clinical mental health, college counseling, rehabilitation, school counseling, student affairs in higher education; counselor education/student counseling and guidance services (PhD); education (Ed S), including counselor education, school psychology (PhD, Ed S); educational psychology (MS, PhD), including general education psychology (MS), general educational psychology (PhD), psychometry (MS), school psychology (PhD, Ed S). *Accreditation:* ACA (one or more programs are accredited); APA; CORE (one or more programs are accredited); NCATE. Part-time programs available. Postbaccalaureate distance learning degree programs offered (minimal on-campus study). *Faculty:* 17 full-time (13 women). *Students:* 137 full-time (104 women), 81 part-time (73 women); includes 57 minority (47 Black or African American, non-Hispanic/Latino; 4 American Indian or Alaska Native, non-Hispanic/Latino; 3 Asian, non-Hispanic/Latino; 1 Hispanic/Latino; 2 Two or more races, non-Hispanic/Latino), 5 international. Average age 32. 287 applicants, 36% accepted, 72 enrolled. In 2013, 70 master's, 3 doctorates, 4 other advanced degrees awarded. Terminal master's awarded for partial completion of doctoral program. *Degree requirements:* For master's, comprehensive exam, thesis optional; for doctorate, thesis/dissertation, comprehensive oral and written exam. *Entrance requirements:* For master's, GRE (taken within the last five years), BS with minimum GPA of 2.75 on last 60 hours; for doctorate, GRE, MS from CACREP- or CORE-accredited program in counseling; for Ed S, GRE, MS in counseling or related field, minimum GPA of 3.3 on all graduate work. Additional exam requirements/recommendations for international students: Required—TOEFL (minimum score 550 paper-based; 79 iBT); Recommended—IELTS (minimum score 6.5). *Application deadline:* For fall admission, 2/1 priority date for domestic and international students. Applications are processed on a rolling basis. Application fee: $60. Electronic applications accepted. *Financial support:* In 2013–14, 1 research assistantship (averaging $10,800 per year), 11 teaching assistantships with full tuition reimbursements (averaging $8,401 per year) were awarded; career-related internships or fieldwork, Federal Work-Study, institutionally sponsored loans, and unspecified assistantships also available. Financial award application deadline: 2/1; financial award applicants required to submit FAFSA. *Faculty research:* HIV/AIDS in college population, substance abuse in youth and college students, ADHD and conduct disorders in youth, assessment and identification of early childhood disabilities, assessment and vocational transition of the disabled. *Unit head:* Dr. Daniel Wong, Professor/Head, 662-325-7928, Fax: 662-325-3263, E-mail: dwong@colled.msstate.edu. *Application contact:* Dr. Charles Palmer, Graduate Coordinator, Counselor Education, 662-325-7917, Fax: 662-325-3263, E-mail: cpalmer@colled.msstate.edu.
Website: http://www.cep.msstate.edu/.

Missouri State University, Graduate College, College of Education, Department of Counseling, Leadership, and Special Education, Program in Student Affairs in Higher Education, Springfield, MO 65897. Offers MS. Part-time programs available. *Students:* 38 full-time (26 women), 6 part-time (all women); includes 8 minority (4 Black or African American, non-Hispanic/Latino; 2 Hispanic/Latino; 2 Two or more races, non-Hispanic/Latino). Average age 27. 26 applicants, 100% accepted, 14 enrolled. In 2013, 22 master's awarded. *Degree requirements:* For master's, comprehensive exam, thesis or alternative. *Entrance requirements:* For master's, statement of purpose; three references. Additional exam requirements/recommendations for international students: Required—TOEFL (minimum score 550 paper-based; 79 iBT). *Application deadline:* For fall admission, 7/20 priority date for domestic students, 5/1 for international students; for spring admission, 12/20 priority date for domestic students, 9/1 for international students. Applications are processed on a rolling basis. Application fee: $35 ($50 for international students). Electronic applications accepted. *Expenses:* Tuition, state resident: full-time $4500; part-time $250 per credit hour. Tuition, nonresident: full-time $9018; part-time $501 per credit hour. *Required fees:* $361 per semester. Tuition and fees vary according to course level, course load and program. *Financial support:* Federal Work-Study, institutionally sponsored loans, scholarships/grants, and unspecified assistantships available. Financial award application deadline: 3/31; financial award applicants required to submit FAFSA. *Unit head:* Dr. Gilbert Brown, Program Director, 417-836-4428, E-mail: gilbertbrown@missouristate.edu. *Application contact:* Misty Stewart, Coordinator of Graduate Recruitment, 417-836-6079, Fax: 417-836-6200, E-mail: mistystewart@missouristate.edu.
Website: http://education.missouristate.edu/edadmin/MSEDSA.htm.

Montana State University, College of Graduate Studies, College of Education, Health, and Human Development, Department of Education, Bozeman, MT 59717. Offers adult and higher education (Ed D); curriculum and instruction (M Ed, Ed D), including professional educator (M Ed), technology education (M Ed); education (M Ed), including adult and higher education, educational leadership, school counseling; educational leadership (Ed D, Ed S). *Accreditation:* Teacher Education Accreditation Council. Part-time programs available. Postbaccalaureate distance learning degree programs offered (minimal on-campus study). *Degree requirements:* For master's, comprehensive exam; for doctorate, comprehensive exam, thesis/dissertation. *Entrance requirements:* For master's, GRE, 3 letters of reference, essays, BA transcripts; for doctorate, GRE, MAT, 3 letters of reference, essay, BA and M Ed transcripts; for Ed S, PRAXIS. Additional exam requirements/recommendations for international students: Required—TOEFL (minimum score 550 paper-based). Electronic applications accepted. *Faculty research:* Critical literacy; standards-based education; school Improvement, organizational change, leadership in rural education, leadership in Indian education; student Learning; multicultural/culturally responsive education for social justice Native American indigenous education, community-centered education teacher preparation.

Morehead State University, Graduate Programs, College of Education, Department of Foundational and Graduate Studies in Education, Morehead, KY 40351. Offers adult and higher education (MA, Ed S); certified professional counselor (Ed S); counseling P-12 (MA); curriculum and instruction (Ed S); educational technology (MA Ed); instructional leadership (Ed S); school administration (MA); school counseling (Ed S); teacher leader business and marketing content (MA Ed); teacher leader business and marketing technology (MA Ed); teacher leader educational technology (MA Ed); teacher leader English (MA Ed); teacher leader gifted education (MA Ed); teacher leader IECE certification (MA Ed); teacher leader interdisciplinary education P-5 (MA Ed); teacher leader middle grades (MA Ed); teacher leader non IECE certification (MA Ed); teacher leader reading/writing - non-certification (MA Ed); teacher leader reading/writing certification (MA Ed); teacher leader school communication - certification (MA Ed); teacher leader school communication - non-certification (MA Ed); teacher leader social studies (MA Ed); teacher leader special education (MA Ed). *Accreditation:* NCATE. Part-time and evening/weekend programs available. *Degree requirements:* For master's, thesis optional, oral and/or written comprehensive exams; for Ed S, thesis, oral exam. *Entrance requirements:* For master's, GRE General Test, minimum overall undergraduate GPA of 2.5; for Ed S, GRE General Test, interview, master's degree, minimum GPA of 3.5, work experience. Additional exam requirements/recommendations for international students: Required—TOEFL (minimum score 500 paper-based). Electronic applications accepted. *Faculty research:* Character education, school accountability, computer applications for school administrators.

Morgan State University, School of Graduate Studies, School of Education and Urban Studies, Department of Advanced Studies, Leadership and Policy, Program in Community College Leadership, Baltimore, MD 21251. Offers Ed D. *Accreditation:* NCATE. Part-time and evening/weekend programs available. *Degree requirements:* For doctorate, comprehensive exam, thesis/dissertation. *Entrance requirements:* For doctorate, GRE General Test or MAT. Additional exam requirements/recommendations for international students: Required—TOEFL (minimum score 550 paper-based). *Faculty research:* Multicultural education, cooperative learning, psychology of cognition.

Morgan State University, School of Graduate Studies, School of Education and Urban Studies, Department of Advanced Studies, Leadership and Policy, Program in Higher Education Administration, Baltimore, MD 21251. Offers higher education (PhD); higher education administration (MA). *Degree requirements:* For doctorate, comprehensive exam, thesis/dissertation. *Entrance requirements:* For doctorate, GRE General Test or MAT, minimum GPA of 3.0.

New England College, Program in Education, Henniker, NH 03242-3293. Offers higher education administration (MS, Ed D); K-12 leadership (Ed D); literacy and language arts (M Ed); meeting the needs of all learners/special education (M Ed); teacher leadership/school reform (M Ed). Part-time and evening/weekend programs available.

New York University, Steinhardt School of Culture, Education, and Human Development, Department of Administration, Leadership, and Technology, Program in Higher Education, New York, NY 10003. Offers higher education (Ed D, PhD); higher education and student affairs (MA). *Accreditation:* Teacher Education Accreditation Council. Part-time programs available. *Faculty:* 8 full-time (5 women). *Students:* 17 full-time (13 women), 136 part-time (41 women); includes 64 minority (20 Black or African American, non-Hispanic/Latino; 1 American Indian or Alaska Native, non-Hispanic/Latino; 18 Asian, non-Hispanic/Latino; 22 Hispanic/Latino; 3 Two or more races, non-Hispanic/Latino), 7 international. Average age 35. 268 applicants, 22% accepted, 51 enrolled. In 2013, 27 master's, 10 doctorates awarded. *Degree requirements:* For master's, thesis (for some programs); for doctorate, thesis/dissertation. *Entrance requirements:* For master's, interview, 2 letters of recommendation; for doctorate, GRE General Test, interview. Additional exam requirements/recommendations for international students: Required—TOEFL (minimum score 100 iBT). *Application deadline:* For fall admission, 12/1 priority date for domestic and international students; for spring admission, 10/1 for domestic and international students. Applications are processed on a rolling basis. Application fee: $75. Electronic applications accepted. *Expenses: Tuition:* Full-time $35,856; part-time $1494 per unit. *Required fees:* $1408; $64 per unit. $473 per term. Tuition and fees vary according to course load and program. *Financial support:* Fellowships with full and partial tuition reimbursements, career-related internships or fieldwork, Federal Work-Study, institutionally sponsored loans, scholarships/grants, tuition waivers (partial), and unspecified assistantships available. Support available to part-time students. Financial award application deadline: 2/1; financial award applicants required to submit FAFSA. *Faculty research:* Organizational theory and culture, systemic change, leadership development, access, equity and diversity. *Unit head:* Prof. Ann Marcus, Director, 212-998-5005, Fax: 212-995-4041, E-mail: alm1@nyu.edu. *Application contact:* 212-998-5030, Fax: 212-995-4328, E-mail: steinhardt.gradadmissions@nyu.edu.
Website: http://steinhardt.nyu.edu/alt/highered.

North Carolina State University, Graduate School, College of Education, Department of Adult and Higher Education, Program in Higher Education Administration, Raleigh, NC 27695. Offers M Ed, MS, Ed D. *Degree requirements:* For master's, thesis (for some programs); for doctorate, thesis/dissertation. *Entrance requirements:* For master's and doctorate, GRE General Test or MAT, minimum GPA of 3.0 in major. Electronic applications accepted.

Higher Education

North Dakota State University, College of Graduate and Interdisciplinary Studies, Program in College Teaching, Fargo, ND 58108. Offers Certificate. In 2013, 5 Certificates awarded. *Entrance requirements:* For degree, minimum cumulative GPA of 3.0. Application fee: $35. Electronic applications accepted. *Unit head:* Dr. Donald Schwert, Director, 701-231-7496, Fax: 701-231-5924, E-mail: donald.schwert@ndsu.edu. *Application contact:* Sonya Goergen, Marketing, Recruitment, and Public Relations Coordinator, 701-231-7033, Fax: 701-231-6524.
Website: http://www.ndsu.edu/gradschool/programs/college_teaching/.

Northeastern University, School of Education, Boston, MA 02115-5096. Offers curriculum, teaching, learning, and leadership (Ed D); elementary licensure (MAT); higher education administration (MAT, Ed D); Jewish education leadership (Ed D); learning and instruction (M Ed); organizational leadership studies (Ed D); secondary licensure (MAT); special education (M Ed). Part-time and evening/weekend programs available.

Northern Arizona University, Graduate College, College of Education, Department of Educational Leadership, Flagstaff , AZ 86011. Offers community college/higher education (M Ed); educational foundations (M Ed); educational leadership (M Ed, Ed D); principal (Certificate); principal K-12 (M Ed); school leadership K-12 (M Ed); superintendent (Certificate). Part-time programs available. *Faculty:* 22 full-time (9 women). *Students:* 159 full-time (103 women), 528 part-time (331 women); includes 199 minority (36 Black or African American, non-Hispanic/Latino; 20 American Indian or Alaska Native, non-Hispanic/Latino; 11 Asian, non-Hispanic/Latino; 115 Hispanic/Latino; 1 Native Hawaiian or other Pacific Islander, non-Hispanic/Latino; 16 Two or more races, non-Hispanic/Latino). Average age 38. 211 applicants, 97% accepted, 148 enrolled. In 2013, 269 master's, 20 doctorates, 47 Certificates awarded. *Degree requirements:* For master's, comprehensive exam, thesis (for some programs); for doctorate, comprehensive exam, thesis/dissertation. *Entrance requirements:* For master's, minimum GPA of 3.0; for doctorate, GRE or MAT, minimum GPA of 3.5. Additional exam requirements/recommendations for international students: Required—TOEFL (minimum score 550 paper-based; 80 iBT), IELTS (minimum score 7). *Application deadline:* For fall admission, 3/1 priority date for international students; for spring admission, 9/15 priority date for international students. Applications are processed on a rolling basis. Application fee: $65. Electronic applications accepted. *Financial support:* In 2013–14, 1 research assistantship with full tuition reimbursement (averaging $12,000 per year) was awarded. Financial award applicants required to submit FAFSA. *Unit head:* Dr. Michael Schwanenberger, Chair, 928-523-4212, Fax: 928-523-1929, E-mail: michael.schwanenberger@nau.edu. *Application contact:* Jennifer Offutt, Administrative Assistant, 928-523-5098, Fax: 928-523-1929, E-mail: jennifer.offutt@nau.edu.
Website: http://nau.edu/coe/ed-leadership/.

Northern Illinois University, Graduate School, College of Education, Department of Counseling, Adult and Higher Education, De Kalb, IL 60115-2854. Offers adult and higher education (MS Ed, Ed D); counseling (MS Ed, Ed D). *Accreditation:* ACA. Part-time and evening/weekend programs available. *Faculty:* 19 full-time (11 women), 2 part-time/adjunct (1 woman). *Students:* 121 full-time (94 women), 252 part-time (182 women); includes 149 minority (102 Black or African American, non-Hispanic/Latino; 1 American Indian or Alaska Native, non-Hispanic/Latino; 11 Asian, non-Hispanic/Latino; 28 Hispanic/Latino; 7 Two or more races, non-Hispanic/Latino), 9 international. Average age 36. 115 applicants, 48% accepted, 37 enrolled. In 2013, 73 master's, 19 doctorates awarded. Terminal master's awarded for partial completion of doctoral program. *Degree requirements:* For master's, comprehensive exam, thesis optional; for doctorate, thesis/dissertation, candidacy exam, dissertation defense. *Entrance requirements:* For master's, GRE General Test or MAT, minimum undergraduate GPA of 2.75, interview (for counseling); for doctorate, GRE General Test, minimum undergraduate GPA of 2.75, 3.2 graduate, interview (for counseling). Additional exam requirements/recommendations for international students: Required—TOEFL (minimum score 550 paper-based). *Application deadline:* For fall admission, 6/1 for domestic students, 5/1 for international students; for spring admission, 11/1 for domestic students, 10/1 for international students. Applications are processed on a rolling basis. Application fee: $40. Electronic applications accepted. *Financial support:* In 2013–14, 13 research assistantships with full tuition reimbursements, 2 teaching assistantships with full tuition reimbursements were awarded; fellowships with full tuition reimbursements, career-related internships or fieldwork, Federal Work-Study, scholarships/grants, tuition waivers (full), and staff assistantships also available. Support available to part-time students. Financial award applicants required to submit FAFSA. *Unit head:* Dr. Suzanne Degges-White, Interim Chair, 815-753-1448, E-mail: cahe@niu.edu. *Application contact:* Graduate School Office, 815-753-0395, E-mail: gradsch@niu.edu.
Website: http://www.cedu.niu.edu/cahe/index.html.

Oakland University, Graduate Study and Lifelong Learning, School of Education and Human Services, Department of Educational Leadership, Rochester, MI 48309-4401. Offers educational leadership (M Ed, PhD); higher education (Certificate); higher education administration (Certificate); school administration (Ed S). *Faculty:* 11 full-time (all women), 4 part-time/adjunct (2 women). *Students:* 22 full-time (15 women), 216 part-time (143 women); includes 43 minority (37 Black or African American, non-Hispanic/Latino; 1 American Indian or Alaska Native, non-Hispanic/Latino; 1 Asian, non-Hispanic/Latino; 4 Hispanic/Latino), 1 international. Average age 39. 149 applicants, 90% accepted, 118 enrolled. In 2013, 27 master's, 138 other advanced degrees awarded. *Entrance requirements:* Additional exam requirements/recommendations for international students: Required—TOEFL (minimum score 550 paper-based). *Application deadline:* For fall admission, 7/15 for domestic students, 5/1 priority date for international students; for winter admission, 9/1 priority date for international students. Application fee: $0. *Financial support:* Federal Work-Study, institutionally sponsored loans, and tuition waivers (full) available. Financial award application deadline: 3/1; financial award applicants required to submit FAFSA. *Faculty research:* Grizzlies Response: Awareness and suicide prevention at Oakland University. *Total annual research expenditures:* $56,687. *Unit head:* Dr. William G. Keane, Chair, 248-370-3070, Fax: 248-370-4605. *Application contact:* Christina J. Grabowski, Associate Director of Graduate Study and Lifelong Learning, 248-370-3167, Fax: 248-370-4114, E-mail: grabowsk@oakland.edu.

Ohio University, Graduate College, Gladys W. and David H. Patton College of Education and Human Services, Department of Counseling and Higher Education, Athens, OH 45701-2979. Offers college student personnel (M Ed); community/agency counseling (M Ed); counselor education (PhD); higher education (PhD); rehabilitation counseling (M Ed); school counseling (M Ed). *Accreditation:* ACA; CORE. Part-time and evening/weekend programs available. *Degree requirements:* For master's, comprehensive exam (for some programs), thesis or alternative; for doctorate, comprehensive exam, thesis/dissertation. *Entrance requirements:* For master's, GRE General Test or MAT (if GPA less than 2.9), 3 letters of reference; for doctorate, GRE General Test, work experience, minimum GPA of 3.4. Additional exam requirements/recommendations for international students: Required—TOEFL (minimum score 550 paper-based; 80 iBT) or IELTS (minimum score 6.5). Electronic applications accepted. *Faculty research:* Youth violence, gender studies, student affairs, chemical dependency, disabilities issues.

Oklahoma State University, College of Education, School of Educational Studies, Stillwater, OK 74078. Offers higher education (Ed D). Part-time programs available. *Faculty:* 23 full-time (11 women), 28 part-time/adjunct (6 women). *Students:* 45 full-time (18 women), 211 part-time (124 women); includes 49 minority (7 Black or African American, non-Hispanic/Latino; 17 American Indian or Alaska Native, non-Hispanic/Latino; 3 Asian, non-Hispanic/Latino; 14 Hispanic/Latino; 8 Two or more races, non-Hispanic/Latino), 14 international. Average age 39. 154 applicants, 44% accepted, 52 enrolled. In 2013, 11 master's, 6 doctorates awarded. *Degree requirements:* For master's, thesis (for some programs); for doctorate, comprehensive exam, thesis/dissertation. *Entrance requirements:* For master's and doctorate, GRE or GMAT. Additional exam requirements/recommendations for international students: Required—TOEFL (minimum score 550 paper-based; 79 iBT). *Application deadline:* For fall admission, 3/1 priority date for international students; for spring admission, 8/1 priority date for international students. Applications are processed on a rolling basis. Application fee: $40 ($75 for international students). Electronic applications accepted. *Expenses:* Tuition, state resident: full-time $4272; part-time $178 per credit hour. Tuition, nonresident: full-time $17,472; part-time $709 per credit hour. *Required fees:* $2413.20; $100.55 per credit hour. One-time fee: $50 full-time. Part-time tuition and fees vary according to course load and campus/location. *Financial support:* In 2013–14, 11 research assistantships (averaging $10,069 per year), 6 teaching assistantships (averaging $11,500 per year) were awarded; career-related internships or fieldwork, Federal Work-Study, scholarships/grants, health care benefits, tuition waivers (partial), and unspecified assistantships also available. Support available to part-time students. Financial award application deadline: 3/1; financial award applicants required to submit FAFSA. *Unit head:* Dr. Jesse Mendez, Head, 405-744-9447, Fax: 405-744-7758, E-mail: jesse.perez.mendez@okstate.edu.
Website: http://education.okstate.edu/ses.

Old Dominion University, Darden College of Education, Doctoral Program in Higher Education, Norfolk, VA 23529. Offers PhD. Part-time programs available. Postbaccalaureate distance learning degree programs offered (minimal on-campus study). *Faculty:* 3 full-time (0 women), 8 part-time/adjunct (2 women). *Students:* 6 full-time (all women), 22 part-time (11 women); includes 11 minority (8 Black or African American, non-Hispanic/Latino; 1 Asian, non-Hispanic/Latino; 1 Hispanic/Latino; 1 Two or more races, non-Hispanic/Latino). Average age 38. 13 applicants, 54% accepted, 5 enrolled. In 2013, 2 doctorates awarded. *Degree requirements:* For doctorate, comprehensive exam, thesis/dissertation. *Entrance requirements:* For doctorate, GRE, master's degree, minimum graduate GPA of 3.5. Additional exam requirements/recommendations for international students: Required—TOEFL. *Application deadline:* For spring admission, 2/1 for domestic and international students. Application fee: $50. Electronic applications accepted. *Expenses:* Tuition, state resident: full-time $9888; part-time $412 per credit. Tuition, nonresident: full-time $25,152; part-time $1048 per credit. *Required fees:* $59 per semester. One-time fee: $50. *Financial support:* In 2013–14, 2 fellowships with tuition reimbursements (averaging $15,000 per year), research assistantships with full tuition reimbursements (averaging $15,000 per year), 6 teaching assistantships with full tuition reimbursements (averaging $15,000 per year) were awarded; career-related internships or fieldwork, tuition waivers (full), and unspecified assistantships also available. Financial award application deadline: 2/1. *Faculty research:* Law leadership, student development, research administration, international higher education administration, academic integrity, leadership. *Unit head:* Dr. Chris Glass, Graduate Program Director, 757-683-4118, E-mail: cglass@odu.edu. *Application contact:* William Heffelfinger, Director of Graduate Admissions, 757-683-5554, Fax: 757-683-3255, E-mail: gradadmit@odu.edu.

Old Dominion University, Darden College of Education, Programs in Higher Education, Norfolk, VA 23529. Offers educational leadership (MS Ed, Ed S), including higher education. Part-time programs available. *Faculty:* 3 full-time (0 women), 8 part-time/adjunct (2 women). *Students:* 31 full-time (25 women), 14 part-time (9 women); includes 18 minority (14 Black or African American, non-Hispanic/Latino; 3 Hispanic/Latino; 1 Two or more races, non-Hispanic/Latino). Average age 29. 59 applicants, 64% accepted, 18 enrolled. In 2013, 25 master's, 2 Ed Ss awarded. *Degree requirements:* For master's, comprehensive exam. *Entrance requirements:* For master's, GRE, minimum undergraduate GPA of 2.8; for Ed S, GRE, 2 letters of reference, minimum GPA of 3.5, master's degree. Additional exam requirements/recommendations for international students: Required—TOEFL. *Application deadline:* For fall admission, 3/1 priority date for domestic and international students; for winter admission, 10/1 for domestic and international students; for spring admission, 3/1 for domestic and international students. Applications are processed on a rolling basis. Application fee: $50. Electronic applications accepted. *Expenses:* Tuition, state resident: full-time $9888; part-time $412 per credit. Tuition, nonresident: full-time $25,152; part-time $1048 per credit. *Required fees:* $59 per semester. One-time fee: $50. *Financial support:* Research assistantships with partial tuition reimbursements, career-related internships or fieldwork, scholarships/grants, and unspecified assistantships available. *Faculty research:* Law leadership, student development, research administration, international higher education administration. *Unit head:* Dr. Chris Glass, Graduate Program Director, 757-683-4118, E-mail: hied@odu.edu. *Application contact:* William Heffelfinger, Director of Graduate Admissions, 757-683-5554, Fax: 757-683-3255, E-mail: gradadmit@odu.edu.
Website: http://education.odu.edu/efl/academics/highered/msed/msed_international_2.shtml.

Oral Roberts University, School of Education, Tulsa, OK 74171. Offers Christian school administration (K-12) (MA Ed, Ed D); Christian school curriculum development (MA Ed); college and higher education administration (Ed D); public school administration (K-12) (MA Ed, Ed D); public school teaching (MA Ed). *Accreditation:* NCATE. Part-time programs available. Postbaccalaureate distance learning degree programs offered (minimal on-campus study). *Degree requirements:* For master's, comprehensive exam, thesis optional; for doctorate, comprehensive exam, thesis/dissertation. *Entrance requirements:* For master's, GRE General Test or MAT, minimum GPA of 3.0; for doctorate, minimum GPA of 3.0. Additional exam requirements/recommendations for international students: Required—TOEFL (minimum score 500 paper-based). *Expenses:* Contact institution. *Faculty research:* Teacher effectiveness, college success in high achieving African-Americans, professional development practices.

Penn State University Park, Graduate School, College of Education, Department of Education Policy Studies, State College, PA 16802. Offers college student affairs (M Ed); educational leadership (M Ed, D Ed, PhD, Certificate); educational theory and policy (MA, PhD); higher education (M Ed, D Ed, PhD). *Accreditation:* NCATE. *Unit head:* Dr. David H. Monk, Dean, 814-865-2523, Fax: 814-865-0555, E-mail: dhm6@psu.edu. *Application contact:* Cynthia E. Nicosia, Director, Graduate Enrollment Services, 814-865-1834, Fax: 814-863-4627, E-mail: cey1@psu.edu.
Website: http://www.ed.psu.edu/educ/eps/.

Phillips Theological Seminary, Programs in Theology, Tulsa, OK 74116. Offers administration of church agencies (M Div); campus ministry (M Div); church-related social work (M Div); college and seminary teaching (M Div); global mission work (M Div); institutional chaplaincy (M Div); ministerial vocations in Christian education (M Div);

ministry (D Min), including parish ministry, pastoral counseling, practices of ministry; ministry and culture (MAMC), including Christian education, congregational leadership, history and practice of Christian spirituality, theology, ethics, and culture; ministry of music (M Div); pastoral care and counseling (M Div); pastoral ministry (M Div); theological studies (MTS). *Accreditation:* ATS. Part-time programs available. Postbaccalaureate distance learning degree programs offered (minimal on-campus study). *Degree requirements:* For master's, thesis (for some programs); for doctorate, thesis/dissertation. *Entrance requirements:* For master's, minimum GPA of 2.5; for doctorate, M Div, minimum GPA of 3.0. *Faculty research:* Biblical studies, historical studies, theology and culture, practical theology, theology and film.

Pittsburg State University, Graduate School, College of Education, Department of Special Services and Leadership Studies, Pittsburg, KS 66762. Offers community college and higher education (Ed S); educational leadership (MS), including educational technology; educational technology (MS); general school administration (Ed S); special education (MS), including behavioral disorders, learning disabilities, mentally retarded. *Degree requirements:* For master's, thesis or alternative. *Entrance requirements:* For master's, GRE General Test or MAT.

Plymouth State University, College of Graduate Studies, Graduate Studies in Education, Certificate of Advanced Graduate Studies Programs, Plymouth, NH 03264-1595. Offers clinical mental health counseling (CAGS); educational leadership (CAGS); higher education (CAGS); school psychology (CAGS). Part-time and evening/weekend programs available.

Plymouth State University, College of Graduate Studies, Graduate Studies in Education, Program in Higher Education, Plymouth, NH 03264-1595. Offers Ed D.

Portland State University, Graduate Studies, School of Education, Department of Educational Policy, Foundations, and Administrative Studies, Portland, OR 97207-0751. Offers educational leadership (MA, MS, Ed D); postsecondary, adult and continuing education (Ed D). *Accreditation:* NCATE. Part-time and evening/weekend programs available. *Faculty:* 14 full-time (9 women), 9 part-time/adjunct (5 women). *Students:* 231 full-time (154 women), 382 part-time (256 women); includes 139 minority (22 Black or African American, non-Hispanic/Latino; 8 American Indian or Alaska Native, non-Hispanic/Latino; 24 Asian, non-Hispanic/Latino; 59 Hispanic/Latino; 3 Native Hawaiian or other Pacific Islander, non-Hispanic/Latino; 23 Two or more races, non-Hispanic/Latino), 11 international. Average age 38. 210 applicants, 60% accepted, 125 enrolled. In 2013, 79 master's, 13 doctorates awarded. *Degree requirements:* For master's, thesis or alternative, written exam or research project; for doctorate, comprehensive exam, thesis/dissertation. *Entrance requirements:* For master's, California Basic Educational Skills Test, minimum GPA of 3.0 in upper-division course work or 2.75 overall; for doctorate, GRE General Test or MAT. Additional exam requirements/recommendations for international students: Required—TOEFL (minimum score 550 paper-based). *Application deadline:* For fall admission, 4/1 for domestic and international students; for winter admission, 9/1 for domestic and international students; for spring admission, 11/1 for domestic and international students. Applications are processed on a rolling basis. Application fee: $50. *Expenses:* Tuition, state resident: full-time $9207; part-time $341 per credit. Tuition, nonresident: full-time $14,391; part-time $533 per credit. *Required fees:* $1263; $22 per credit. $98 per quarter. One-time fee: $150. Tuition and fees vary according to program. *Financial support:* Career-related internships or fieldwork, Federal Work-Study, and institutionally sponsored loans available. Support available to part-time students. Financial award application deadline: 3/1; financial award applicants required to submit FAFSA. *Faculty research:* Leadership development and research, principals and urban schools, accelerated schools, cooperative learning, family involvement in schools. *Total annual research expenditures:* $43,200. *Unit head:* Candyce Reynolds, Chair, 503-725-4657, Fax: 503-725-8475, E-mail: reynoldsc@pdx.edu. *Application contact:* Mindy Friend, Department Assistant, 503-725-4716, Fax: 503-725-8475, E-mail: mfriend@pdx.edu.
Website: http://www.ed.pdx.edu/epfa/.

Purdue University, Graduate School, College of Education, Department of Educational Studies, West Lafayette, IN 47907. Offers administration (MS Ed, PhD, Ed S); counseling and development (MS Ed, PhD); education of the gifted (MS Ed); educational psychology (MS Ed, PhD); foundations of education (MS Ed, PhD); higher education administration (MS Ed, PhD); special education (MS Ed, PhD). *Accreditation:* ACA (one or more programs are accredited); NCATE (one or more programs are accredited). Part-time and evening/weekend programs available. *Faculty:* 21 full-time (17 women), 7 part-time/adjunct (4 women). *Students:* 102 full-time (73 women), 45 part-time (27 women); includes 23 minority (10 Black or African American, non-Hispanic/Latino; 5 Asian, non-Hispanic/Latino; 5 Hispanic/Latino; 3 Two or more races, non-Hispanic/Latino), 32 international. Average age 35. 165 applicants, 40% accepted, 33 enrolled. In 2013, 26 master's, 21 doctorates awarded. *Degree requirements:* For master's, thesis optional; for doctorate, thesis/dissertation, oral and written exams; for Ed S, oral presentation, project. *Entrance requirements:* For master's, GRE General Test (except for special education if undergraduate GPA is higher than a 3.0), minimum undergraduate GPA of 3.0; for doctorate and Ed S, GRE General Test (minimum combined score of 1000, 300 for new scoring), minimum undergraduate GPA of 3.0. Additional exam requirements/recommendations for international students: Required—TOEFL (minimum score 550 paper-based; 77 iBT), TWE (minimum score 5). *Application deadline:* Applications are processed on a rolling basis. Application fee: $60 ($75 for international students). Electronic applications accepted. *Financial support:* Fellowships with full tuition reimbursements, research assistantships with full tuition reimbursements, teaching assistantships with full tuition reimbursements, career-related internships or fieldwork, and tuition waivers (full) available. Support available to part-time students. Financial award application deadline: 3/1; financial award applicants required to submit FAFSA. *Faculty research:* Motivation, learning disabilities, school learning, group processes, cognitive development. *Unit head:* Dr. Ala Samrapungavan, Head, 765-494-9170, Fax: 765-496-1228, E-mail: ala@purdue.edu. *Application contact:* Cindy Blankenship, Graduate Contact, 765-494-2345, Fax: 765-494-5832, E-mail: prater0@purdue.edu.
Website: http://www.edst.purdue.edu/.

Regent University, Graduate School, School of Education, Virginia Beach, VA 23464-9800. Offers adult education (Ed D, PhD); advanced educational leadership (Ed D, PhD); career switcher with licensure (M Ed), including alternative licensure; character education (Ed D, PhD); Christian education leadership (Ed D); Christian school administration (M Ed); curriculum and instruction (M Ed); distance education (Ed D, PhD); educational leadership (M Ed); educational leadership - special education (Ed S); educational psychology (Ed D); elementary education (M Ed); higher education (Ed D, PhD); higher education leadership and management (Ed D); K-12 school leadership (Ed D, PhD); leadership in mathematics education (M Ed); reading specialist (M Ed); special education (M Ed, Ed D, PhD); student affairs (M Ed); TESOL (M Ed), including adult education, PreK-12. *Accreditation:* Teacher Education Accreditation Council. Part-time and evening/weekend programs available. Postbaccalaureate distance learning degree programs offered (minimal on-campus study). *Faculty:* 25 full-time (12 women), 50 part-time/adjunct (31 women). *Students:* 100 full-time (78 women), 754 part-time (614 women); includes 225 minority (191 Black or African American, non-Hispanic/Latino; 1 American Indian or Alaska Native, non-Hispanic/Latino; 7 Asian, non-Hispanic/

Latino; 26 Hispanic/Latino), 16 international. Average age 39. 487 applicants, 63% accepted, 233 enrolled. In 2013, 202 master's, 19 doctorates awarded. *Degree requirements:* For master's, thesis or alternative; for doctorate, comprehensive exam, thesis/dissertation. *Entrance requirements:* For master's, MAT, minimum undergraduate GPA of 2.75, writing sample, resume, recommendations, interview; for doctorate, GRE, writing sample, 3 years of relevant professional experience, master's-level paper, copies of published work, resume, transcripts, interview, recommendations. Additional exam requirements/recommendations for international students: Required—TOEFL (minimum score 577 paper-based). *Application deadline:* For fall admission, 4/1 priority date for domestic students; for spring admission, 10/15 priority date for domestic students. Applications are processed on a rolling basis. Application fee: $50. Electronic applications accepted. Tuition and fees vary according to course load and degree level. *Financial support:* Fellowships, career-related internships or fieldwork, scholarships/grants, tuition waivers (full and partial), and unspecified assistantships available. Support available to part-time students. Financial award application deadline: 4/1; financial award applicants required to submit FAFSA. *Faculty research:* Character development and discipline for children, education leadership development, diversity in schools, classroom management, technology in education settings. *Unit head:* Dr. Alan Arroyo, Dean, 757-352-4261, Fax: 757-352-4318, E-mail: alanarr@regent.edu. *Application contact:* Matthew Chadwick, Director of Enrollment Support Services, 800-373-5504, Fax: 757-352-4381, E-mail: admissions@regent.edu.
Website: http://www.regent.edu/education/.

Regis College, Department of Education, Weston, MA 02493. Offers elementary teacher (MAT); higher education leadership (Ed D); reading (MAT); special education (MAT). Part-time and evening/weekend programs available. *Degree requirements:* For master's, thesis. *Entrance requirements:* For master's, GRE or MAT. Additional exam requirements/recommendations for international students: Required—TOEFL. Electronic applications accepted. *Faculty research:* Reflective teaching, gender-based education, integrated teaching.

Robert Morris University Illinois, Morris Graduate School of Management, Chicago, IL 60605. Offers accounting (MBA); accounting/finance (MBA); business analytics (MIS); design and media (MM); educational technology (MM); health care administration (MM); higher education administration (MM); human resource management (MBA); information security (MIS); information systems (MIS); law enforcement administration (MM); management (MBA); management/finance (MBA); management/human resource management (MBA); mobile computing (MIS); sports administration (MM). Part-time and evening/weekend programs available. *Faculty:* 12 full-time (5 women), 18 part-time/adjunct (4 women). *Students:* 240 full-time (128 women), 195 part-time (127 women); includes 242 minority (147 Black or African American, non-Hispanic/Latino; 2 American Indian or Alaska Native, non-Hispanic/Latino; 24 Asian, non-Hispanic/Latino; 63 Hispanic/Latino; 1 Native Hawaiian or other Pacific Islander, non-Hispanic/Latino; 5 Two or more races, non-Hispanic/Latino), 26 international. Average age 33. 210 applicants, 63% accepted, 116 enrolled. In 2013, 278 master's awarded. *Entrance requirements:* For master's, official transcripts, two letters of recommendation. Additional exam requirements/recommendations for international students: Required—TOEFL (minimum score 550 paper-based). *Application deadline:* Applications are processed on a rolling basis. Application fee: $20 ($100 for international students). Electronic applications accepted. *Expenses: Tuition:* Full-time $14,400; part-time $2400 per course. *Financial support:* In 2013–14, 488 students received support. Federal Work-Study and scholarships/grants available. Support available to part-time students. Financial award applicants required to submit FAFSA. *Unit head:* Kayed Akkawi, Dean for Morris Graduate School of Management, 312-935-6050, Fax: 312-935-6020, E-mail: kakkawi@robertmorris.edu. *Application contact:* Fernando Villeda, Dean of Graduate Enrollment, 312-935-6050, Fax: 312-935-6020, E-mail: fvilleda@robertmorris.edu.

Rowan University, Graduate School, College of Education, Department of Special Educational Services/Instruction, Program in Higher Education Administration, Glassboro, NJ 08028-1701. Offers MA. *Accreditation:* NCATE. Part-time and evening/weekend programs available. *Faculty:* 4 full-time (2 women), 3 part-time/adjunct (1 woman). *Students:* 22 full-time (17 women), 12 part-time (10 women); includes 8 minority (4 Black or African American, non-Hispanic/Latino; 2 Asian, non-Hispanic/Latino; 2 Hispanic/Latino), 2 international. Average age 28. 30 applicants, 97% accepted, 15 enrolled. In 2013, 13 master's awarded. *Degree requirements:* For master's, comprehensive exam, thesis. *Entrance requirements:* For master's, GRE General Test, minimum GPA of 2.8, 2 years of teaching experience. Additional exam requirements/recommendations for international students: Required—TOEFL. *Application deadline:* For fall admission, 6/1 for domestic students; for spring admission, 12/1 for domestic students; for summer admission, 2/15 for domestic students. Applications are processed on a rolling basis. Application fee: $65. Electronic applications accepted. *Expenses: Tuition, area resident:* Part-time $638 per credit. Tuition, state resident: full-time $5742. *Required fees:* $142 per credit. Tuition and fees vary according to course level and program. *Financial support:* Career-related internships or fieldwork, scholarships/grants, health care benefits, and unspecified assistantships available. Support available to part-time students. *Unit head:* Dr. Horacio Sosa, Dean, College of Graduate and Continuing Education, 856-256-4747, Fax: 856-256-5638, E-mail: sosa@rowan.edu. *Application contact:* Admissions and Enrollment Services, 856-256-5435, Fax: 856-256-5637, E-mail: cgceadmissions@rowan.edu.

St. Cloud State University, School of Graduate Studies, School of Education, Department of Educational Leadership and Higher Education, Program in Higher Education Administration, St. Cloud, MN 56301-4498. Offers MS, Ed D.

Saint Louis University, Graduate Education, College of Education and Public Service and Graduate Education, Department of Educational Leadership and Higher Education, St. Louis, MO 63103-2097. Offers Catholic school leadership (MA); educational administration (MA, Ed D, PhD, Ed S); higher education (MA, Ed D, PhD); student personnel administration (MA). *Accreditation:* NCATE. Part-time programs available. *Degree requirements:* For master's, comprehensive written and oral exam; for doctorate, comprehensive exam, thesis/dissertation, preliminary oral and written exams. *Entrance requirements:* For master's, GRE General Test, MAT, LSAT, GMAT or MCAT, letters of recommendation, resume; for doctorate and Ed S, GRE General Test, LSAT, GMAT or MCAT, letters of recommendation, resumé, goal statement, transcripts. Additional exam requirements/recommendations for international students: Required—TOEFL (minimum score 525 paper-based). Electronic applications accepted. *Faculty research:* Superintendent of schools, school finance, school facilities, student personal administration, building leadership.

Saint Peter's University, Graduate Programs in Education, Program in Higher Education, Jersey City, NJ 07306-5997. Offers Ed D. *Degree requirements:* For doctorate, comprehensive exam, thesis/dissertation, qualifying examination, internship. *Entrance requirements:* For doctorate, GRE or MAT (taken within the last 5 years), official transcripts from all previously attended postsecondary institutions; bachelor's degree; master's degree; three letters of recommendation; essay; current resume; personal interview.

Salem State University, School of Graduate Studies, Program in Higher Education in Student Affairs, Salem, MA 01970-5353. Offers M Ed. Part-time and evening/weekend programs available. *Students:* 21 full-time (16 women), 39 part-time (25 women);

includes 21 minority (9 Black or African American, non-Hispanic/Latino; 3 Asian, non-Hispanic/Latino; 8 Hispanic/Latino; 1 Two or more races, non-Hispanic/Latino). 39 applicants, 92% accepted, 22 enrolled. In 2013, 4 degrees awarded. *Entrance requirements:* For master's, GRE or MAT. Additional exam requirements/recommendations for international students: Required—TOEFL (minimum score 550 paper-based; 80 iBT) or IELTS (minimum score 5.5). *Application deadline:* For fall admission, 5/1 for domestic students. Application fee: $50. *Financial support:* Career-related internships or fieldwork, Federal Work-Study, scholarships/grants, and unspecified assistantships available. Support available to part-time students. Financial award application deadline: 5/1; financial award applicants required to submit FAFSA. *Application contact:* Dr. Lee A. Brossoit, Assistant Dean of Graduate Admissions, 978-542-6675, Fax: 978-542-7215, E-mail: lbrossoit@salemstate.edu.
Website: http://www.salemstate.edu/academics/schools/12569.php.

Sam Houston State University, College of Education and Applied Science, Department of Educational Leadership and Counseling, Huntsville, TX 77341. Offers administration (M Ed); clinical mental health counseling (MA); counselor education (PhD); developmental education administration (Ed D); educational leadership (Ed D); higher education administration (MA); instructional leadership (M Ed, MA); school counseling (M Ed). Part-time and evening/weekend programs available. Postbaccalaureate distance learning degree programs offered (no on-campus study). *Faculty:* 29 full-time (16 women). *Students:* 220 full-time (178 women), 463 part-time (374 women); includes 265 minority (128 Black or African American, non-Hispanic/Latino; 3 American Indian or Alaska Native, non-Hispanic/Latino; 6 Asian, non-Hispanic/Latino; 115 Hispanic/Latino; 13 Two or more races, non-Hispanic/Latino), 24 international. Average age 35. 294 applicants, 96% accepted, 130 enrolled. In 2013, 166 master's, 32 doctorates awarded. *Degree requirements:* For master's, comprehensive exam, thesis (for some programs); for doctorate, comprehensive exam, thesis/dissertation. *Entrance requirements:* For master's, GRE General Test. Additional exam requirements/recommendations for international students: Required—TOEFL (minimum score 550 paper-based; 79 iBT). *Application deadline:* For fall admission, 8/1 for domestic students, 6/25 for international students; for spring admission, 12/1 for domestic students, 11/12 for international students. Applications are processed on a rolling basis. Application fee: $45 ($75 for international students). Electronic applications accepted. *Financial support:* In 2013–14, 7 research assistantships (averaging $9,335 per year), 3 teaching assistantships (averaging $6,183 per year) were awarded; career-related internships or fieldwork, Federal Work-Study, institutionally sponsored loans, scholarships/grants, tuition waivers (partial), and unspecified assistantships also available. Support available to part-time students. Financial award application deadline: 5/31; financial award applicants required to submit FAFSA. *Unit head:* Dr. Stacey Edmonson, Chair, 936-294-1752, Fax: 936-294-3886, E-mail: edu_sle01@shsu.edu. *Application contact:* Dr. Barbara Polnick, Advisor, 936-294-3859, E-mail: bpolnick@shsu.edu.
Website: http://www.shsu.edu/~edu_elc/.

San Diego State University, Graduate and Research Affairs, College of Education, Department of Administration, Rehabilitation and Post-Secondary Education, San Diego, CA 92182. Offers educational leadership in post-secondary education (MA); rehabilitation counseling (MS), including deafness. Evening/weekend programs available. Postbaccalaureate distance learning degree programs offered. *Degree requirements:* For master's, comprehensive exam (for some programs), thesis (for some programs). *Entrance requirements:* For master's, GRE General Test, letters of reference. Additional exam requirements/recommendations for international students: Required—TOEFL. Electronic applications accepted. *Faculty research:* Rehabilitation in cultural diversity, distance learning technology.

San Jose State University, Graduate Studies and Research, Connie L. Lurie College of Education, Department of Educational Leadership, San Jose, CA 95192-0001. Offers educational administration (K-12) (MA); higher education administration (MA). *Accreditation:* NCATE. *Degree requirements:* For master's, thesis or alternative. Electronic applications accepted.

Seton Hall University, College of Education and Human Services, Department of Education Leadership, Management and Policy, Program in Higher Education Administration, South Orange, NJ 07079-2697. Offers Ed D, PhD. *Accreditation:* NCATE. Part-time and evening/weekend programs available. *Faculty:* 12 full-time (4 women), 1 part-time/adjunct (0 women). *Students:* 20 full-time (12 women), 73 part-time (45 women); includes 24 minority (15 Black or African American, non-Hispanic/Latino; 9 Hispanic/Latino), 9 international. Average age 41. 26 applicants, 81% accepted, 16 enrolled. In 2013, 7 degrees awarded. *Degree requirements:* For doctorate, comprehensive exam, thesis/dissertation, internship. *Entrance requirements:* For doctorate, GRE or MAT, interview, minimum GPA of 3.5. Additional exam requirements/recommendations for international students: Required—TOEFL. *Application deadline:* For fall admission, 2/1 priority date for domestic students; for spring admission, 10/1 for domestic students. Applications are processed on a rolling basis. Application fee: $75. *Financial support:* In 2013–14, 7 research assistantships with tuition reimbursements (averaging $5,000 per year) were awarded. Financial award application deadline: 2/1. *Unit head:* Dr. Michael Osnato, Chair, 973-275-2446, E-mail: osnatomi@shu.edu. *Application contact:* Diana Minakakis, Associate Dean, 973-275-2824, Fax: 973-275-2187, E-mail: diana.minakakis@shu.edu.
Website: http://www.shu.edu/academics/education/edd-higher-ed/index.cfm.

Shippensburg University of Pennsylvania, School of Graduate Studies, College of Arts and Sciences, Department of Sociology and Anthropology, Shippensburg, PA 17257-2299. Offers organizational development and leadership (MS), including business, communications, environmental management, higher education structure and policy, historical administration, individual and organizational development, management information systems, public organizations, social structures and organizations. Part-time and evening/weekend programs available. *Faculty:* 4 full-time (all women). *Students:* 19 full-time (11 women), 40 part-time (23 women); includes 7 minority (all Black or African American, non-Hispanic/Latino), 4 international. Average age 32. 63 applicants, 49% accepted, 19 enrolled. In 2013, 24 master's awarded. *Degree requirements:* For master's, capstone experience including internship. *Entrance requirements:* For master's, interview (if GPA less than 2.75), resume, personal goals statement. Additional exam requirements/recommendations for international students: Required—TOEFL (minimum score 580 paper-based); Recommended—IELTS (minimum score 6). *Application deadline:* For fall admission, 4/30 for international students; for spring admission, 9/30 for international students. Applications are processed on a rolling basis. Application fee: $45. Electronic applications accepted. *Expenses:* Tuition, area resident: Part-time $442 per credit. Tuition, state resident: part-time $442 per credit. Tuition, nonresident: part-time $663 per credit. *Required fees:* $127 per credit. *Financial support:* In 2013–14, 10 research assistantships with full tuition reimbursements (averaging $5,000 per year) were awarded; career-related internships or fieldwork, scholarships/grants, unspecified assistantships, and resident hall director and student payroll positions also available. Support available to part-time students. Financial award applicants required to submit FAFSA. *Unit head:* Dr. Barbara Denison, Program Coordinator, 717-477-1735, Fax: 717-477-4011, E-mail: bjdeni@

ship.edu. *Application contact:* Jeremy R. Goshorn, Assistant Dean of Graduate Admissions, 717-477-1231, Fax: 717-477-4016, E-mail: jrgoshorn@ship.edu.
Website: http://www.ship.edu/odl/.

Siena Heights University, Graduate College, Adrian, MI 49221-1796. Offers clinical mental health counseling (MA); education leadership (Specialist); leadership (MA), including health care, higher education leadership, organizational; teacher education (MA), including early childhood, early childhood: Montessori-based, education leadership: principal, elementary education, K-12 reading, leadership: higher education, secondary education, K-12 reading, special education, K-12 cognitive impairment, special education, K-12 learning disabled. Part-time and evening/weekend programs available. *Faculty:* 37. *Students:* 9 full-time (7 women), 251 part-time (179 women). In 2013, 32 master's awarded. *Degree requirements:* For master's, thesis, presentation. *Entrance requirements:* For master's, minimum GPA of 3.0, current resume, essay, all post-secondary transcripts, 3 letters of reference, conviction disclosure form; copy of teaching certificate (for some education programs); for Specialist, master's degree, minimum GPA of 3.0, current resume, essay, all post-secondary transcripts, 3 letters of reference, conviction disclosure form; copy of teaching certificate (for some education programs). *Application deadline:* Applications are processed on a rolling basis. Application fee: $50. *Expenses: Tuition:* Part-time $535 per semester hour. *Required fees:* $130 per semester. *Financial support:* Career-related internships or fieldwork, Federal Work-Study, and resident assistantships available. Financial award application deadline: 9/1; financial award applicants required to submit FAFSA. *Unit head:* Dr. Linda S. Pettit, Dean, Graduate College, 517-264-7661, Fax: 517-264-7714, E-mail: lpettit@sienahts.edu.
Website: http://www.sienaheights.edu.

Slippery Rock University of Pennsylvania, Graduate Studies (Recruitment), College of Education, Department of Counseling and Development, Slippery Rock, PA 16057-1383. Offers community counseling (MA), including addiction, adult, child/adolescent, older adult, youth; school counseling (M Ed); student affairs (MA), including higher education; student affairs in higher education (MA), including college counseling. *Accreditation:* ACA (one or more programs are accredited); NCATE. Part-time and evening/weekend programs available. *Faculty:* 9 full-time (5 women). *Students:* 85 full-time (69 women), 26 part-time (21 women); includes 9 minority (7 Black or African American, non-Hispanic/Latino; 1 American Indian or Alaska Native, non-Hispanic/Latino; 1 Hispanic/Latino). Average age 28. 137 applicants, 49% accepted, 51 enrolled. In 2013, 45 master's awarded. *Degree requirements:* For master's, comprehensive exam, thesis (for some programs). *Entrance requirements:* For master's, GRE General Test, MAT, minimum GPA of 2.75 or 3.0 (depending on program), personal statement, three letters of recommendation, interview. Additional exam requirements/recommendations for international students: Required—TOEFL (minimum score 550 paper-based; 80 iBT). *Application deadline:* For fall admission, 1/15 priority date for domestic and international students. Application fee: $25 ($30 for international students). Electronic applications accepted. *Expenses:* Tuition, state resident: full-time $7956; part-time $442 per credit. Tuition, nonresident: full-time $11,934; part-time $663 per credit. *Required fees:* $2896; $148 per credit. Tuition and fees vary according to degree level and program. *Financial support:* Career-related internships or fieldwork, Federal Work-Study, institutionally sponsored loans, scholarships/grants, tuition waivers (partial), and unspecified assistantships available. Support available to part-time students. Financial award application deadline: 5/1; financial award applicants required to submit FAFSA. *Unit head:* Dr. Donald Strano, Graduate Coordinator, 724-738-2035, Fax: 724-738-4859, E-mail: donald.strano@sru.edu. *Application contact:* Brandi Weber-Mortimer, Director of Graduate Admissions, 724-738-2051, Fax: 724-738-2146, E-mail: graduate.admissions@sru.edu.

Southeast Missouri State University, School of Graduate Studies, Department of Educational Leadership and Counseling, Program in Educational Administration, Cape Girardeau, MO 63701-4799. Offers educational administration (Ed S); educational leadership development (Ed S); elementary administration and supervision (MA); higher education administration (MA); school administration (MA); secondary administration and supervision (MA); teacher leadership (MA). *Accreditation:* NCATE. Part-time and evening/weekend programs available. *Faculty:* 6 full-time (3 women), 4 part-time/adjunct (1 woman). *Students:* 48 full-time (27 women), 181 part-time (118 women); includes 18 minority (11 Black or African American, non-Hispanic/Latino; 1 American Indian or Alaska Native, non-Hispanic/Latino; 2 Asian, non-Hispanic/Latino; 3 Hispanic/Latino; 1 Two or more races, non-Hispanic/Latino), 2 international. Average age 34. 83 applicants, 100% accepted, 83 enrolled. In 2013, 88 master's, 28 other advanced degrees awarded. *Degree requirements:* For master's and Ed S, comprehensive exam, thesis or alternative, paper. *Entrance requirements:* For master's, minimum undergraduate GPA of 2.75, valid teacher certification; for Ed S, minimum graduate GPA of 3.5; master's degree; valid teaching certificate. Additional exam requirements/recommendations for international students: Required—TOEFL (minimum score 550 paper-based; 79 iBT), IELTS (minimum score 6), PTE (minimum score 53). *Application deadline:* For fall admission, 8/1 for domestic students, 6/1 for international students; for spring admission, 11/21 for domestic students, 10/1 for international students; for summer admission, 5/15 for domestic students. Applications are processed on a rolling basis. Application fee: $30 ($40 for international students). Electronic applications accepted. *Expenses:* Tuition, state resident: full-time $5139; part-time $285.50 per credit hour. Tuition, nonresident: full-time $9099; part-time $505.50 per credit hour. *Financial support:* In 2013–14, 25 students received support. Career-related internships or fieldwork, Federal Work-Study, scholarships/grants, traineeships, tuition waivers (full), and unspecified assistantships available. Financial award application deadline: 6/30; financial award applicants required to submit FAFSA. *Faculty research:* Learning and the technology push, administration and student success, ethics of leaders. *Unit head:* Dr. Ruth Ann Williams, Professor/Interim Chair, Department of Educational Leadership and Counseling, 573-651-2417, E-mail: raroberts@semo.edu. *Application contact:* Alisa Aleen McFerron, Assistant Director of Admissions for Operations, 573-651-5937, E-mail: amcferron@semo.edu.
Website: http://www4.semo.edu/edadmin/admin.

Southern Baptist Theological Seminary, School of Church Ministries, Louisville, KY 40280-0004. Offers Biblical counseling (M Div, MA); children's and family ministry (M Div, MA); Christian education (MA); Christian worship (PhD); church ministries (M Div); church music (MCM); college ministry (M Div, MA); discipleship and family ministry (M Div, MA); education (Ed D); family ministry (D Min, PhD); higher education (PhD); leadership (M Div, MA, D Min, PhD); ministry (D Ed Min); missions and ethnodoxology (M Div); women's leadership (M Div, MA); worship leadership (M Div, MA); worship leadership and church ministry (MA); youth and family ministry (M Div, MA). Part-time programs available. Postbaccalaureate distance learning degree programs offered (minimal on-campus study). *Degree requirements:* For doctorate, thesis/dissertation. *Entrance requirements:* For doctorate, GRE General Test, interview, M Div or MACE. Additional exam requirements/recommendations for international students: Required—TWE. *Faculty research:* Gerontology, creative teaching methods, faith development in children, faith development in youth, transformational learning.

Southern Illinois University Carbondale, Graduate School, College of Education and Human Services, Department of Educational Administration and Higher Education,

Program in Higher Education, Carbondale, IL 62901-4701. Offers MS Ed. *Accreditation:* NCATE. Part-time programs available. *Faculty:* 9 full-time (3 women). *Students:* 25 full-time (12 women), 4 part-time (1 woman); includes 6 minority (4 Black or African American, non-Hispanic/Latino; 2 Hispanic/Latino). Average age 26. 20 applicants, 60% accepted, 8 enrolled. In 2013, 18 master's awarded. *Degree requirements:* For master's, thesis. *Entrance requirements:* For master's, GRE General Test or MAT, minimum GPA of 2.7. Additional exam requirements/recommendations for international students: Required—TOEFL. *Application deadline:* For fall admission, 5/15 for domestic students; for spring admission, 9/15 for domestic students. Applications are processed on a rolling basis. Application fee: $50. *Financial support:* In 2013–14, 15 students received support. Fellowships with full tuition reimbursements available, research assistantships with full tuition reimbursements available, teaching assistantships with full tuition reimbursements available, Federal Work-Study, institutionally sponsored loans, tuition waivers (full), and unspecified assistantships available. Support available to part-time students. Financial award application deadline: 4/1. *Faculty research:* Student affairs administration, international education, community college teaching. *Unit head:* Dr. Saran Donahoo, Associate Professor, 618-536-4434, Fax: 618-453-4338, E-mail: donahoo@siu.edu. *Application contact:* Cyndie Kessler-Criswell, Administrative Assistant, 618-453-6082, E-mail: criswell@siu.edu.

Southern Illinois University Edwardsville, Graduate School, College of Arts and Sciences, Department of Mathematics and Statistics, Program in Postsecondary Mathematics Education, Edwardsville, IL 62026. Offers MS. Part-time programs available. *Students:* 4 part-time (0 women). 2 applicants, 50% accepted. In 2013, 2 master's awarded. *Degree requirements:* For master's, thesis (for some programs), special project. *Entrance requirements:* Additional exam requirements/recommendations for international students: Required—TOEFL (minimum score 550 paper-based, 79 iBT), IELTS (minimum score 6.5), Michigan Test of English Language Proficiency or PTE. *Application deadline:* For fall admission, 7/18 for domestic students, 6/1 for international students; for spring admission, 12/12 for domestic students, 10/1 for international students; for summer admission, 4/24 for domestic students, 3/1 for international students. Applications are processed on a rolling basis. Application fee: $30. Electronic applications accepted. *Expenses:* Tuition, state resident: full-time $3551. Tuition, nonresident: full-time $8378. *Financial support:* Institutionally sponsored loans, scholarships/grants, and unspecified assistantships available. Financial award application deadline: 3/1; financial award applicants required to submit FAFSA. *Unit head:* Dr. Myung Sin Song, Program Director, 618-650-2580, E-mail: msong@siue.edu. *Application contact:* Melissa K. Mace, Assistant Director of Graduate and International Recruitment, 618-650-2756, Fax: 618-650-3618, E-mail: mmace@siue.edu.
Website: http://www.siue.edu/artsandsciences/math/.

Stony Brook University, State University of New York, School of Professional Development, Stony Brook, NY 11794. Offers biology (MAT); chemistry (MAT); coaching (Graduate Certificate); earth science (MAT); educational computing (Graduate Certificate); educational leadership (Advanced Certificate); English (MAT); environmental management (Graduate Certificate); French (MAT); German (MAT); higher education administration (MA, Certificate); human resource management (MS, Graduate Certificate); industrial management (Graduate Certificate); information systems management (Graduate Certificate); Italian (MAT); liberal studies (MA); mathematics (MAT); operations research (Graduate Certificate); physics (MAT); school district business leadership (Advanced Certificate); social science and the professions (MPS), including environmental management, human resource management; social studies (MAT); Spanish (MAT). Part-time and evening/weekend programs available. Postbaccalaureate distance learning degree programs offered. *Faculty:* 2 full-time (1 woman), 70 part-time/adjunct (30 women). *Students:* 241 full-time (135 women), 954 part-time (673 women); includes 209 minority (65 Black or African American, non-Hispanic/Latino; 2 American Indian or Alaska Native, non-Hispanic/Latino; 32 Asian, non-Hispanic/Latino; 104 Hispanic/Latino; 6 Two or more races, non-Hispanic/Latino), 7 international. Average age 28. 353 applicants, 92% accepted, 248 enrolled. In 2013, 312 master's, 131 other advanced degrees awarded. *Degree requirements:* For master's, one foreign language, thesis or alternative. *Application deadline:* For fall admission, 1/15 for domestic students; for spring admission, 10/1 for domestic students. Applications are processed on a rolling basis. Application fee: $100. *Expenses:* Tuition, state resident: full-time $9870; part-time $411 per credit. Tuition, nonresident: full-time $18,350; part-time $765 per credit. *Financial support:* Fellowships, research assistantships, teaching assistantships, and career-related internships or fieldwork available. Support available to part-time students. *Unit head:* Dr. Thomas Sexton, Interim Dean, 631-632-7181, Fax: 631-632-9046, E-mail: thomas.sexton@stonybrook.edu. *Application contact:* 631-632-7050 Ext. 1, E-mail: spd@stonybrook.edu.
Website: http://www.stonybrook.edu/spd/.

Syracuse University, College of Arts and Sciences, Program in College Science Teaching, Syracuse, NY 13244. Offers PhD. Part-time programs available. *Students:* 4 full-time (2 women), 3 part-time (2 women). Average age 39. 5 applicants, 60% accepted, 1 enrolled. In 2013, 1 doctorate awarded. *Degree requirements:* For doctorate, comprehensive exam, thesis/dissertation. *Entrance requirements:* For doctorate, GRE General Test, GRE Subject Test. Additional exam requirements/recommendations for international students: Required—TOEFL (minimum score 100 iBT). *Application deadline:* For fall admission, 2/1 priority date for domestic and international students. Applications are processed on a rolling basis. Application fee: $75. Electronic applications accepted. *Financial support:* Fellowships with full tuition reimbursements, research assistantships with full and partial tuition reimbursements, and teaching assistantships with full and partial tuition reimbursements available. Financial award application deadline: 1/1; financial award applicants required to submit FAFSA. *Unit head:* Dr. George M. Langford, Dean, 315-443-2201, E-mail: dean@cas.syr.edu. *Application contact:* Cynthia Daley, Information Contact, 315-443-2586, E-mail: cyndaley@syr.edu.
Website: http://sciteach.syr.edu/.

Syracuse University, School of Education, Program in Higher Education, Syracuse, NY 13244. Offers MS, PhD. Part-time programs available. *Students:* 31 full-time (24 women), 28 part-time (18 women); includes 18 minority (8 Black or African American, non-Hispanic/Latino; 1 American Indian or Alaska Native, non-Hispanic/Latino; 3 Asian, non-Hispanic/Latino; 6 Hispanic/Latino). Average age 30. 100 applicants, 71% accepted, 19 enrolled. In 2013, 22 master's awarded. *Degree requirements:* For master's, thesis or alternative; for doctorate, comprehensive exam, thesis/dissertation. *Entrance requirements:* For master's, resume; for doctorate, GRE, resume, interview, writing sample, 3-5 years of experience in higher education administration. Additional exam requirements/recommendations for international students: Required—TOEFL (minimum score 100 iBT). *Application deadline:* For fall admission, 1/15 priority date for domestic and international students; for spring admission, 10/15 priority date for domestic and international students. Applications are processed on a rolling basis. Application fee: $75. Electronic applications accepted. *Financial support:* Fellowships with full tuition reimbursements, research assistantships with full and partial tuition reimbursements, and teaching assistantships with full and partial tuition reimbursements available. Financial award application deadline: 1/1. *Faculty research:* Faculty evaluation, teaching portfolios, student culture, college student personnel development, organizational culture. *Unit head:* Dr. Catherine Engstrom, Chair, 315-443-4763, E-mail: cmengstr@syr.edu. *Application contact:* Laurie Deyo, Graduate Recruiter, School of Education, 315-443-2505, E-mail: e-gradrcrt@syr.edu.
Website: http://soeweb.syr.edu/highered/HIGHEREDU/.

Taylor University, Master of Arts in Higher Education and Student Development Program, Upland, IN 46989-1001. Offers MA. *Accreditation:* NCATE. Part-time programs available. *Degree requirements:* For master's, thesis.

Teachers College, Columbia University, Graduate Faculty of Education, Department of Organization and Leadership, Program in Higher Education, New York, NY 10027-6696. Offers Ed M, MA, Ed D. *Accreditation:* NCATE. *Faculty:* 4 full-time, 12 part-time/adjunct. *Students:* 23 full-time (16 women), 64 part-time (44 women); includes 43 minority (12 Black or African American, non-Hispanic/Latino; 10 Asian, non-Hispanic/Latino; 16 Hispanic/Latino; 5 Two or more races, non-Hispanic/Latino), 1 international. Average age 30. 140 applicants, 61% accepted, 13 enrolled. In 2013, 54 master's, 4 doctorates awarded. *Degree requirements:* For master's, culminating essay/integrative paper; for doctorate, comprehensive exam, thesis/dissertation. *Entrance requirements:* For doctorate, master's degree, 2 years of professional experience. *Application deadline:* For fall admission, 1/15 priority date for domestic students. Application fee: $65. Electronic applications accepted. *Financial support:* Career-related internships or fieldwork, Federal Work-Study, institutionally sponsored loans, and tuition waivers (full and partial) available. Support available to part-time students. Financial award application deadline: 2/1. *Faculty research:* Educational leadership, general management issues, finance and planning, organizational analysis and development, higher education issues. *Unit head:* Prof. Anna Neumann, Program Coordinator, 212-678-3272, E-mail: an350@columbia.edu. *Application contact:* Debbie Lesperance, Assistant Director of Admission, 212-678-3710, Fax: 212-678-4171.
Website: http://www.tc.columbia.edu/o&ldept/highered/.

Temple University, College of Education, Department of Psychological Studies in Education, Department of Educational Leadership and Policy Studies, Philadelphia, PA 19122-6096. Offers educational leadership (Ed D), including higher education, K-12. Part-time and evening/weekend programs available. *Faculty:* 7 full-time (3 women). *Students:* 10 full-time (7 women), 66 part-time (42 women); includes 20 minority (15 Black or African American, non-Hispanic/Latino; 1 American Indian or Alaska Native, non-Hispanic/Latino; 1 Asian, non-Hispanic/Latino; 3 Hispanic/Latino), 24 international. 58 applicants, 69% accepted, 24 enrolled. In 2013, 6 master's awarded. Terminal master's awarded for partial completion of doctoral program. *Degree requirements:* For master's, comprehensive exam, thesis or alternative, internship; for doctorate, thesis/dissertation, preliminary exam. *Entrance requirements:* For master's, GRE General Test or MAT, minimum undergraduate GPA of 3.0, 2 letters of recommendation, goal statement, resume; for doctorate, GRE General Test or MAT, minimum undergraduate GPA of 3.0, 3 letters of recommendation, goal statement, resume. Additional exam requirements/recommendations for international students: Required—TOEFL (minimum score 550 paper-based; 79 iBT). *Application deadline:* For fall admission, 1/5 for domestic students, 10/7 for international students; for spring admission, 11/1 for domestic students, 11/3 for international students. Application fee: $60. Electronic applications accepted. *Financial support:* In 2013–14, 2 students received support, including 1 research assistantship with full tuition reimbursement available (averaging $20,333 per year), 1 teaching assistantship with full tuition reimbursement available (averaging $17,046 per year); career-related internships or fieldwork, Federal Work-Study, scholarships/grants, health care benefits, and unspecified assistantships also available. Financial award application deadline: 1/15; financial award applicants required to submit FAFSA. *Faculty research:* School leadership, educational policy, educational accountability, democratic leadership, equity and access. *Unit head:* Dr. Joan Shapiro, Professor, 215-204-6645, E-mail: joan.shapiro@temple.edu. *Application contact:* Felicia Neuber, Enrollment Management, 215-204-8011, E-mail: educate@temple.edu.
Website: http://education.temple.edu/leadership.

Texas A&M University–Commerce, Graduate School, College of Education and Human Services, Department of Educational Leadership, Commerce, TX 75429-3011. Offers educational administration (M Ed, Ed D); educational technology (M Ed, MS); higher education (MS, Ed D); training and development (MS). Part-time programs available. Terminal master's awarded for partial completion of doctoral program. *Degree requirements:* For master's, comprehensive exam, thesis (for some programs); for doctorate, thesis/dissertation, departmental qualifying exam. *Entrance requirements:* For master's, GRE General Test; for doctorate, GRE General Test, writing skills exam, interview. Electronic applications accepted. *Expenses:* Tuition, state resident: full-time $3630; part-time $2420 per year. Tuition, nonresident: full-time $9948; part-time $6632.16 per year. *Required fees:* $1006 per year. Tuition and fees vary according to course load. *Faculty research:* Property tax reform, politics of education, administrative stress.

Texas A&M University–Kingsville, College of Graduate Studies, College of Education, Department of Education, Program in Higher Education Administration Leadership, Kingsville, TX 78363. Offers PhD. Program offered jointly with Texas A&M University. *Faculty:* 10 full-time (8 women), 9 part-time/adjunct (5 women). *Students:* 19 full-time (11 women), 58 part-time (40 women); includes 57 minority (2 Black or African American, non-Hispanic/Latino; 1 Asian, non-Hispanic/Latino; 54 Hispanic/Latino). Average age 42. 5 applicants, 80% accepted, 1 enrolled. In 2013, 11 doctorates awarded. *Degree requirements:* For doctorate, one foreign language, comprehensive exam, thesis/dissertation. *Entrance requirements:* For doctorate, GRE General Test, MAT, minimum GPA of 3.25. *Application deadline:* For fall admission, 6/1 for domestic students; for spring admission, 11/15 for domestic students. Applications are processed on a rolling basis. Application fee: $35 ($50 for international students). *Financial support:* Application deadline: 5/15. *Unit head:* Dr. Travis Polk, Chair, 361-593-3204. *Application contact:* Dr. Alberto M. Olivares, Dean, College of Graduate Studies, 361-593-2808, Fax: 361-593-3412, E-mail: a-olivares@tamuk.edu.

Texas Christian University, College of Education, Doctorate of Educational Leadership in Higher Education Program, Fort Worth, TX 76129-0002. Offers Ed D. Part-time and evening/weekend programs available. *Students:* 1 full-time (0 women), 14 part-time (7 women); includes 4 minority (1 Black or African American, non-Hispanic/Latino; 1 Asian, non-Hispanic/Latino; 2 Hispanic/Latino). Average age 37. 12 applicants, 83% accepted, 6 enrolled. *Degree requirements:* For doctorate, comprehensive exam, thesis/dissertation, field-based experience, dissertation/capstone experience. *Entrance requirements:* For doctorate, GRE or MAT. Additional exam requirements/recommendations for international students: Required—TOEFL (minimum score 550 paper-based; 80 iBT). *Application deadline:* For winter admission, 2/1 for domestic and international students. Electronic applications accepted. *Expenses: Tuition:* Part-time $1270 per credit hour. Tuition and fees vary according to course load and program. *Financial support:* Teaching assistantships with full tuition reimbursements, career-related internships or fieldwork, scholarships/grants, and unspecified assistantships available. Financial award application deadline: 2/1; financial award applicants required to submit FAFSA. *Unit head:* Dr. Jan Lacina, Associate Dean, 817-257-6786, E-mail: j.lacina@tcu.edu. *Application contact:* Lori Kimball, Administrative Program Specialist, 817-257-7661, E-mail: l.kimball@tcu.edu.
Website: http://www.coe.tcu.edu/graduate-students-graduate-programs.asp.

Higher Education

Texas Christian University, College of Education, Ed D in Educational Leadership Program, Fort Worth, TX 76129-0002. Offers educational leadership (Ed D); higher education (Ed D). Part-time and evening/weekend programs available. *Students:* 3 full-time (all women), 18 part-time (10 women); includes 5 minority (2 Black or African American, non-Hispanic/Latino; 1 Asian, non-Hispanic/Latino; 2 Hispanic/Latino), 1 international. Average age 36. 8 applicants, 75% accepted, 4 enrolled. In 2013, 10 doctorates awarded. *Degree requirements:* For doctorate, comprehensive exam, thesis/dissertation. *Entrance requirements:* For doctorate, GRE or MAT. Additional exam requirements/recommendations for international students: Required—TOEFL (minimum score 550 paper-based; 80 iBT). *Application deadline:* For winter admission, 2/1 for domestic and international students. Application fee: $60. Electronic applications accepted. *Expenses: Tuition:* Part-time $1270 per credit hour. Tuition and fees vary according to course load and program. *Financial support:* Teaching assistantships with full tuition reimbursements, career-related internships or fieldwork, scholarships/grants, and unspecified assistantships available. Financial award application deadline: 2/1; financial award applicants required to submit FAFSA. *Unit head:* Dr. Jan Lacina, Associate Dean, 817-257-6786, E-mail: j.lacina@tcu.edu. *Application contact:* Lori Kimball, Administrative Program Specialist, 817-257-7661, E-mail: l.kimball@tcu.edu. Website: http://www.coe.tcu.edu/graduate-students-graduate-programs.asp.

Texas Southern University, College of Education, Department of Educational Administration and Foundation, Houston, TX 77004-4584. Offers educational administration (M Ed, Ed D). Part-time and evening/weekend programs available. *Faculty:* 12 full-time (5 women), 5 part-time/adjunct (4 women). *Students:* 46 full-time (30 women), 56 part-time (37 women); includes 98 minority (96 Black or African American, non-Hispanic/Latino; 1 Asian, non-Hispanic/Latino; 1 Hispanic/Latino), 1 international. Average age 39. 45 applicants, 64% accepted, 23 enrolled. In 2013, 8 master's, 4 doctorates awarded. *Degree requirements:* For master's, comprehensive exam; for doctorate, comprehensive exam, thesis/dissertation. *Entrance requirements:* For master's, GRE General Test, minimum GPA of 2.5; for doctorate, GRE General Test or MAT, master's degree, minimum B+ average. Additional exam requirements/recommendations for international students: Required—TOEFL. *Application deadline:* For fall admission, 7/1 for domestic and international students; for spring admission, 11/1 for domestic and international students. Applications are processed on a rolling basis. Application fee: $50 ($75 for international students). Electronic applications accepted. *Financial support:* Fellowships, research assistantships, teaching assistantships, scholarships/grants, and unspecified assistantships available. Support available to part-time students. Financial award application deadline: 5/1. *Unit head:* Dr. Danita Bailey-Perry, Interim Chair, 713-313-4418, E-mail: bailey_dm@tsu.edu. *Application contact:* Dr. Gregory Maddox, Dean of the Graduate School, 713-313-7011 Ext. 4410, Fax: 713-639-1876, E-mail: maddox_gh@tsu.edu. Website: http://www.tsu.edu/academics/colleges__schools/College_of_Education/Departments/default.php.

Texas State University, Graduate School, College of Education, Department of Counseling, Leadership, Adult Education, and School Psychology, Program of Student Affairs in Higher Education, San Marcos, TX 78666. Offers M Ed. *Accreditation:* ACA. Part-time and evening/weekend programs available. *Faculty:* 4 full-time (2 women), 2 part-time/adjunct (1 woman). *Students:* 34 full-time (24 women), 3 part-time (all women); includes 19 minority (6 Black or African American, non-Hispanic/Latino; 13 Hispanic/Latino), 1 international. Average age 24. 50 applicants, 48% accepted, 18 enrolled. In 2013, 22 master's awarded. *Degree requirements:* For master's, comprehensive exam, thesis (for some programs). *Entrance requirements:* For master's, GRE General Test, minimum GPA of 3.0 in last 60 hours of course work. Additional exam requirements/recommendations for international students: Required—TOEFL (minimum score 550 paper-based; 78 iBT). *Application deadline:* For fall admission, 4/15 for domestic students, 3/15 for international students; for spring admission, 10/1 for domestic and international students. Applications are processed on a rolling basis. Application fee: $40 ($90 for international students). Electronic applications accepted. *Expenses:* Tuition, state resident: full-time $6663; part-time $278 per credit hour. Tuition, nonresident: full-time $15,159; part-time $632 per credit hour. *Required fees:* $1872; $54 per credit hour. $306 per term. Tuition and fees vary according to course load. *Financial support:* In 2013–14, 25 students received support, including 33 research assistantships (averaging $11,663 per year); teaching assistantships, career-related internships or fieldwork, Federal Work-Study, and institutionally sponsored loans also available. Support available to part-time students. Financial award application deadline: 4/1; financial award applicants required to submit FAFSA. *Unit head:* Dr. Paige Haber-Curran, Graduate Advisor, 512-245-7628, Fax: 512-245-8872, E-mail: ph31@txstate.edu. *Application contact:* Dr. Andrea Golato, Dean of Graduate School, 512-245-2581, Fax: 512-245-8365, E-mail: gradcollege@txstate.edu. Website: http://www.txstate.edu/clas/Student-Affairs/student-affairs-in-higher-ed2.html.

Texas Tech University, Graduate School, College of Education, Department of Educational Psychology and Leadership, Lubbock, TX 79409-1071. Offers counselor education (M Ed, PhD); educational leadership (M Ed, Ed D); educational psychology (M Ed, PhD); higher education (M Ed, Ed D); higher education research (PhD); instructional technology (M Ed, Ed D); special education (M Ed, Ed D, PhD). *Accreditation:* ACA; NCATE. Part-time and evening/weekend programs available. Postbaccalaureate distance learning degree programs offered (minimal on-campus study). *Faculty:* 42 full-time (20 women). *Students:* 220 full-time (171 women), 549 part-time (404 women); includes 219 minority (73 Black or African American, non-Hispanic/Latino; 5 American Indian or Alaska Native, non-Hispanic/Latino; 6 Asian, non-Hispanic/Latino; 122 Hispanic/Latino; 13 Two or more races, non-Hispanic/Latino), 48 international. Average age 36. 437 applicants, 72% accepted, 215 enrolled. In 2013, 137 master's, 38 doctorates awarded. Terminal master's awarded for partial completion of doctoral program. *Degree requirements:* For master's, comprehensive exam, thesis optional; for doctorate, comprehensive exam, thesis/dissertation. *Entrance requirements:* For master's, GRE (for some programs); for doctorate, GRE. Additional exam requirements/recommendations for international students: Required—TOEFL (minimum score 550 paper-based; 79 iBT). *Application deadline:* For fall admission, 6/1 priority date for domestic students, 1/15 priority date for international students; for spring admission, 9/1 priority date for domestic students, 6/15 priority date for international students. Applications are processed on a rolling basis. Application fee: $60. Electronic applications accepted. *Expenses:* Tuition, state resident: full-time $6062; part-time $252.57 per credit hour. Tuition, nonresident: full-time $14,558; part-time $606.57 per credit hour. *Required fees:* $2655; $35 per credit hour. $907.50 per semester. Tuition and fees vary according to course load. *Financial support:* In 2013–14, 188 students received support, including 179 fellowships (averaging $2,580 per year), 39 research assistantships (averaging $4,550 per year), 8 teaching assistantships (averaging $4,647 per year); scholarships/grants and unspecified assistantships also available. Support available to part-time students. Financial award application deadline: 1/3; financial award applicants required to submit FAFSA. *Faculty research:* Cognitive, motivational, and developmental processes in learning; counseling education; instructional technology; generic special education and sensory impairment; community college administration; K-12 school administration. *Total annual research expenditures:* $708,063. *Unit head:* Dr. Fred Hartmeister, Chair, 806-834-0248, Fax: 806-742-2179,

E-mail: fred.hartmeister@ttu.edu. *Application contact:* Pam Smith, Admissions Advisor, 806-834-2969, Fax: 806-742-2179, E-mail: pam.smith@ttu.edu. Website: http://www.educ.ttu.edu/.

Trident University International, College of Education, Program in Education, Cypress, CA 90630. Offers adult education (MA Ed); aviation education (MA Ed); children's literacy development (MA Ed); e-learning (MA Ed); early childhood education (MA Ed); enrollment management (MA Ed); higher education (MA Ed); teaching and instruction (MA Ed); training and development (MA Ed). Part-time and evening/weekend programs available. Postbaccalaureate distance learning degree programs offered (no on-campus study). *Degree requirements:* For master's, capstone project with integrative paper. *Entrance requirements:* For master's, minimum GPA of 2.5 (students with GPA 3.0 or greater may transfer up to 30% of graduate level credits). Additional exam requirements/recommendations for international students: Required—TOEFL (minimum score 525 paper-based). Electronic applications accepted.

Trident University International, College of Education, Program in Educational Leadership, Cypress, CA 90630. Offers e-learning leadership (MA Ed, PhD); educational leadership (MA Ed); higher education leadership (PhD); K-12 leadership (PhD). Part-time and evening/weekend programs available. Postbaccalaureate distance learning degree programs offered (no on-campus study). *Degree requirements:* For doctorate, comprehensive exam, thesis/dissertation, defense of dissertation. *Entrance requirements:* For master's, minimum GPA of 2.5 (students with GPA 3.0 or greater may transfer up to 30% of graduate level credits); for doctorate, minimum GPA of 3.4, course work in research methods or statistics. Additional exam requirements/recommendations for international students: Required—TOEFL. Electronic applications accepted.

Troy University, Graduate School, College of Education, Program in Postsecondary Education, Troy, AL 36082. Offers adult education (M Ed); biology (M Ed); criminal justice (M Ed); English (M Ed); foundations of education (M Ed); general science (M Ed); higher education administration (M Ed); history (M Ed); instructional technology (M Ed); mathematics (M Ed); music industry (M Ed); physical fitness (M Ed); political science (M Ed); public administration (M Ed); social science (M Ed); teaching English (M Ed). *Accreditation:* NCATE. Part-time and evening/weekend programs available. *Faculty:* 30 full-time (11 women), 8 part-time/adjunct (1 woman). *Students:* 17 full-time (13 women), 106 part-time (84 women); includes 55 minority (45 Black or African American, non-Hispanic/Latino; 3 Asian, non-Hispanic/Latino; 2 Hispanic/Latino; 5 Two or more races, non-Hispanic/Latino). Average age 34. 109 applicants, 83% accepted, 5 enrolled. In 2013, 130 master's awarded. *Degree requirements:* For master's, comprehensive exam (for some programs), thesis (for some programs), thesis or comprehensive exam. *Entrance requirements:* For master's, GRE (minimum score of 850 on old exam or 290 on new exam), GMAT (minimum score of 380), or MAT (minimum score of 385), bachelor's degree; minimum undergraduate GPA of 2.5 or 3.0 on last 30 semester hours, letter of recommendation. Additional exam requirements/recommendations for international students: Required—TOEFL (minimum score 523 paper-based; 70 iBT), IELTS (minimum score 6). *Application deadline:* Applications are processed on a rolling basis. Application fee: $50. Electronic applications accepted. *Expenses:* Tuition, state resident: full-time $6084; part-time $338 per credit hour. Tuition, nonresident: full-time $12,168; part-time $676 per credit hour. *Required fees:* $630; $35 per credit hour. $50 per semester. *Financial support:* Available to part-time students. Applicants required to submit FAFSA. *Unit head:* Dr. Jan Oliver, Associate Professor, 334-670-3444, Fax: 334-670-3474, E-mail: oliver@troy.edu. *Application contact:* Brenda K. Campbell, Director of Graduate Admissions, 334-670-3178, Fax: 334-670-3733, E-mail: bcamp@troy.edu.

Union Institute & University, Doctor of Education Program, Cincinnati, OH 45206-1925. Offers educational leadership (Ed D); higher education (Ed D). M Ed offered online and in Vermont and Florida, Ed S in Florida; Ed D program is offered online with limited residency in Ohio. Postbaccalaureate distance learning degree programs offered (minimal on-campus study). *Degree requirements:* For doctorate, comprehensive exam, thesis/dissertation, electronic portfolio. *Entrance requirements:* For doctorate, master's degree from regionally-accredited institution, letters of recommendation, essay. *Faculty research:* Adult education, higher education, social responsibility in education, educational technology.

Union University, School of Education, Jackson, TN 38305-3697. Offers education (M Ed, MA Ed); education administration generalist (Ed S); educational leadership (Ed D); educational supervision (Ed S); higher education (Ed D). M Ed also available at Germantown campus. *Accreditation:* NCATE. Part-time and evening/weekend programs available. *Degree requirements:* For master's, thesis (for some programs), capstone research course; for doctorate, comprehensive exam, thesis/dissertation; for Ed S, thesis or alternative. *Entrance requirements:* For master's, MAT, PRAXIS II or GRE, minimum GPA of 3.0, teaching license, writing sample; for doctorate, GRE, minimum graduate GPA of 3.2, writing sample; for Ed S, PRAXIS II, minimum graduate GPA of 3.2, writing sample. *Faculty research:* Mathematics education, direct instruction, language disorders and special education, brain compatible learning, empathy and school leadership.

United States University, School of Education, Cypress, CA 90630. Offers administration (MA Ed); early childhood education (MA Ed); general (MA Ed); higher education administration (MA Ed); Spanish language education (MA Ed); special education (MA Ed). *Degree requirements:* For master's, portfolio. *Entrance requirements:* For master's, minimum undergraduate GPA of 2.5. Additional exam requirements/recommendations for international students: Required—TOEFL (minimum score 500 paper-based; 61 iBT).

Universidad Central del Este, Graduate School, San Pedro de Macoris, Dominican Republic. Offers environmental engineering (ME); financial management (M Ad); higher education (M Ed), including higher education management, higher education pedagogy; human resources (M Ad). *Entrance requirements:* For master's, letters of recommendation.

Université de Sherbrooke, Faculty of Education, Program in Postsecondary Education Training, Sherbrooke, QC J1K 2R1, Canada. Offers M Ed, Diploma. *Degree requirements:* For master's, thesis.

University at Buffalo, the State University of New York, Graduate School, Graduate School of Education, Department of Educational Leadership and Policy, Buffalo, NY 14260. Offers education studies (Ed M); educational administration (Ed M, Ed D, PhD); educational culture, policy and society (PhD); higher education administration (Ed M, PhD); school building leadership (Certificate); school business and human resource administration (Certificate); school district business leadership (Certificate); school district leadership (Certificate). Part-time and evening/weekend programs available. *Faculty:* 13 full-time (7 women), 8 part-time/adjunct (all women). *Students:* 65 full-time (40 women), 139 part-time (83 women); includes 40 minority (24 Black or African American, non-Hispanic/Latino; 6 Asian, non-Hispanic/Latino; 10 Hispanic/Latino), 15 international. Average age 35. 159 applicants, 71% accepted, 65 enrolled. In 2013, 44 master's, 14 doctorates, 19 other advanced degrees awarded. *Degree requirements:* For master's, comprehensive exam (for some programs), thesis optional; for doctorate, comprehensive exam, thesis/dissertation. *Entrance requirements:* For master's, interview, letters of reference; for doctorate, GRE General Test or MAT, writing sample, letters of reference. Additional exam requirements/recommendations for international

students: Required—TOEFL (minimum score 550 paper-based; 79 iBT). *Application deadline:* For fall admission, 2/1 priority date for domestic students, 2/1 for international students; for spring admission, 11/15 priority date for domestic students, 10/1 for international students. Applications are processed on a rolling basis. Application fee: $50. Electronic applications accepted. *Financial support:* In 2013–14, 20 fellowships (averaging $6,639 per year), 6 research assistantships with tuition reimbursements (averaging $10,500 per year) were awarded; career-related internships or fieldwork, Federal Work-Study, institutionally sponsored loans, scholarships/grants, health care benefits, tuition waivers, and unspecified assistantships also available. Financial award application deadline: 3/15; financial award applicants required to submit FAFSA. *Faculty research:* College access and choice, school leadership preparation and practice, public policy, curriculum and pedagogy, comparative and international education. *Total annual research expenditures:* $455,347. *Unit head:* Dr. Janina C. Brutt-Griffler, Chair, 716-645-2471, Fax: 716-645-2481, E-mail: bruttg@buffalo.edu. *Application contact:* Ryan Taugrin, Admission and Student Services Coordinator, 716-645-2110, Fax: 716-645-7937, E-mail: ryantaug@buffalo.edu.
Website: http://gse.buffalo.edu/elp.

The University of Akron, Graduate School, College of Education, Department of Educational Foundations and Leadership, Program in Higher Education Administration, Akron, OH 44325. Offers MA, MS. *Accreditation:* NCATE. *Students:* 39 full-time (27 women), 17 part-time (14 women); includes 10 minority (8 Black or African American, non-Hispanic/Latino; 1 Hispanic/Latino; 1 Two or more races, non-Hispanic/Latino), 7 international. Average age 28. 42 applicants, 86% accepted, 19 enrolled. In 2013, 22 master's awarded. *Degree requirements:* For master's, comprehensive exam. *Entrance requirements:* For master's, GRE, minimum GPA of 2.75, declaration of intent that includes statement of professional goals and reasons for choosing the field of higher education administration and The University of Akron. Additional exam requirements/recommendations for international students: Required—TOEFL (minimum score 550 paper-based; 79 iBT). *Application deadline:* Applications are processed on a rolling basis. Application fee: $40 ($60 for international students). Electronic applications accepted. *Expenses:* Tuition, state resident: full-time $7430; part-time $412.80 per credit hour. Tuition, nonresident: full-time $12,722; part-time $706.80 per credit hour. *Required fees:* $53 per credit hour. $12 per semester. Tuition and fees vary according to course load and program. *Financial support:* Fellowships, research assistantships, and teaching assistantships available. *Unit head:* Dr. Sharon Kruse, Coordinator, 330-972-8177, E-mail: skruse@uakron.edu.

The University of Alabama, Graduate School, College of Education, Department of Educational Leadership, Policy, and Technology Studies, Higher Education Administration Program, Tuscaloosa, AL 35487. Offers MA, Ed D, PhD. Evening/weekend programs available. *Students:* 46 full-time (22 women), 114 part-time (61 women); includes 33 minority (23 Black or African American, non-Hispanic/Latino; 1 American Indian or Alaska Native, non-Hispanic/Latino; 1 Asian, non-Hispanic/Latino; 4 Hispanic/Latino; 4 Two or more races, non-Hispanic/Latino), 1 international. Average age 38. 73 applicants, 63% accepted, 27 enrolled. In 2013, 11 master's, 12 doctorates awarded. Terminal master's awarded for partial completion of doctoral program. *Degree requirements:* For master's, comprehensive exam; for doctorate, comprehensive exam, thesis/dissertation. *Entrance requirements:* For master's, GRE, MAT or GMAT; for doctorate, GRE or MAT. Additional exam requirements/recommendations for international students: Required—TOEFL. *Application deadline:* For fall admission, 2/15 for domestic and international students. Application fee: $50 ($60 for international students). Electronic applications accepted. *Expenses:* Tuition, state resident: full-time $9450. Tuition, nonresident: full-time $23,950. *Financial support:* In 2013–14, 5 students received support, including 2 research assistantships with full tuition reimbursements available (averaging $11,900 per year); career-related internships or fieldwork, scholarships/grants, and unspecified assistantships also available. *Faculty research:* College teaching and learning, faculty-administration relations, community colleges, organizational change, student affairs. *Unit head:* Dr. Nathaniel Bray, Coordinator and Associate Professor, 205-348-1159, Fax: 205-348-2161, E-mail: nbray@bamaed.ua.edu. *Application contact:* Donna Smith, Administrative Assistant, 205-348-6871, Fax: 205-348-2161, E-mail: dbsmith@bamaed.ua.edu.

The University of Arizona, College of Education, Department of Educational Policy Studies and Practice, Program in Higher Education, Tucson, AZ 85721. Offers MA, PhD. Part-time programs available. *Faculty:* 10 full-time (5 women). *Students:* 55 full-time (38 women), 38 part-time (23 women); includes 41 minority (4 Black or African American, non-Hispanic/Latino; 1 American Indian or Alaska Native, non-Hispanic/Latino; 1 Asian, non-Hispanic/Latino; 21 Hispanic/Latino; 14 Two or more races, non-Hispanic/Latino), 2 international. Average age 34. 93 applicants, 35% accepted, 19 enrolled. In 2013, 20 master's, 5 doctorates awarded. Terminal master's awarded for partial completion of doctoral program. *Degree requirements:* For master's, comprehensive exam, thesis; for doctorate, comprehensive exam, thesis/dissertation. *Entrance requirements:* For master's, GRE General Test or MAT, minimum undergraduate GPA of 3.0; for doctorate, GRE General Test or MAT, minimum undergraduate GPA of 3.0, graduate 3.5. Additional exam requirements/recommendations for international students: Required—TOEFL (minimum score 550 paper-based; 79 iBT). *Application deadline:* For fall admission, 1/15 for domestic and international students. Applications are processed on a rolling basis. Application fee: $75. Electronic applications accepted. *Expenses:* Tuition, state resident: full-time $11,526. Tuition, nonresident: full-time $27,398. *Financial support:* In 2013–14, 7 research assistantships with full tuition reimbursements (averaging $15,794 per year), 4 teaching assistantships with full tuition reimbursements (averaging $9,253 per year) were awarded; career-related internships or fieldwork, scholarships/grants, health care benefits, tuition waivers (partial), and unspecified assistantships also available. Financial award application deadline: 4/30. *Faculty research:* Technology transfer, higher education policy, finance, curricular change. *Unit head:* Dr. Gary Rhoades, Professor and Department Head, 520-626-7313, Fax: 520-621-1875, E-mail: grhoades@email.arizona.edu. *Application contact:* Margo Sallet, Graduate Program Coordinator, 520-626-7313, Fax: 520-621-1875, E-mail: msallet@email.arizona.edu.
Website: http://grad.arizona.edu/live/programs/description/76.

University of Arkansas, Graduate School, College of Education and Health Professions, Department of Rehabilitation, Human Resources and Communication Disorders, Program in Higher Education, Fayetteville, AR 72701-1201. Offers M Ed, Ed D, Ed S. *Accreditation:* NCATE. Part-time and evening/weekend programs available. *Degree requirements:* For master's, thesis optional; for doctorate, thesis/dissertation. *Entrance requirements:* For master's, GRE General Test, MAT or minimum GPA of 3.0; for doctorate, GRE General Test or MAT. Electronic applications accepted.

University of Arkansas at Little Rock, Graduate School, College of Education, Department of Educational Leadership, Program in Higher Education Administration, Little Rock, AR 72204-1099. Offers Ed D. *Degree requirements:* For doctorate, comprehensive exam, oral defense of dissertation, residency. *Entrance requirements:* For doctorate, GRE General Test or MAT, interview, minimum graduate GPA of 3.0, teaching certificate, work experience. *Expenses:* Tuition, state resident: full-time $5690; part-time $284.50 per credit hour. Tuition, nonresident: full-time $13,030; part-time $651.50 per credit hour. *Required fees:* $1121; $672 per term. One-time fee: $40 full-time.

The University of British Columbia, Faculty of Education, Department of Educational Studies, Vancouver, BC V6T 1Z1, Canada. Offers adult education (M Ed, MA); adult learning and global change (M Ed); educational administration (M Ed, MA); educational leadership and policy (Ed D); educational studies (PhD); higher education (M Ed, MA); society, culture and politics in education (M Ed, MA). Part-time and evening/weekend programs available. Terminal master's awarded for partial completion of doctoral program. *Degree requirements:* For master's, thesis; for doctorate, comprehensive exam, thesis/dissertation, master's thesis. *Entrance requirements:* For master's, minimum B+ average, 4-year undergraduate degree, field-related experience; for doctorate, minimum B+ average, 4-year undergraduate degree, master's degree, field-related experience. Additional exam requirements/recommendations for international students: Required—TOEFL (minimum score 600 paper-based; 100 iBT) or IELTS (minimum score 6.5). Electronic applications accepted. *Expenses: Tuition, area resident:* Full-time $8000 Canadian dollars. *Faculty research:* Educational leadership educational administration adult education politics in education, global change and adult learning.

University of California, Riverside, Graduate Division, Graduate School of Education, Riverside, CA 92521-0102. Offers autism (M Ed); diversity and equity (M Ed); education specialist (Credential); education, society and culture (MA, PhD); educational psychology (MA, PhD); general education (M Ed); higher education administration and policy (M Ed, PhD); multiple subject (Credential); reading (M Ed); school psychology (PhD); single subject (Credential); special education (M Ed, MA, PhD); TESOL (M Ed). *Faculty:* 22 full-time (11 women), 14 part-time/adjunct (10 women). *Students:* 218 full-time (148 women); includes 95 minority (10 Black or African American, non-Hispanic/Latino; 30 Asian, non-Hispanic/Latino; 49 Hispanic/Latino; 6 Two or more races, non-Hispanic/Latino), 12 international. Average age 31. 236 applicants, 66% accepted, 78 enrolled. In 2013, 66 master's, 13 doctorates, 86 other advanced degrees awarded. Terminal master's awarded for partial completion of doctoral program. *Degree requirements:* For master's, thesis optional, comprehensive exams or thesis (MA), case study or analytical report (M Ed); for doctorate, thesis/dissertation, written and oral qualifying exams, college teaching practicum. *Entrance requirements:* For master's, GRE General Test (for MA); CBEST and CSET (for M Ed in general education only), UCR Extension TESOL certificate (for M Ed with TESOL emphasis only); for doctorate, GRE General Test, writing sample; for Credential, CBEST, CSET. Additional exam requirements/recommendations for international students: Required—TOEFL (minimum score 550 paper-based; 80 iBT), IELTS (minimum score 7). *Application deadline:* For fall admission, 9/1 for domestic students, 5/1 for international students; for winter admission, 11/15 for domestic students, 7/1 for international students; for spring admission, 3/1 for domestic students, 10/1 for international students. Applications are processed on a rolling basis. Application fee: $80 ($100 for international students). Electronic applications accepted. *Financial support:* In 2013–14, 58 students received support, including 31 fellowships with full tuition reimbursements available, 11 research assistantships with full tuition reimbursements available (averaging $14,691 per year), 5 teaching assistantships with full tuition reimbursements available (averaging $17,655 per year); career-related internships or fieldwork, Federal Work-Study, institutionally sponsored loans, scholarships/grants, and unspecified assistantships also available. Financial award application deadline: 1/5. *Faculty research:* Responsiveness to intervention, faculty core, response to intervention of English language learners, advanced modeling techniques, study on social capital, trust, and motivation. *Total annual research expenditures:* $1.9 million. *Unit head:* Prof. Douglas Mitchell, Interim Dean and Professor, 951-827-5802, Fax: 951-827-3942, E-mail: douglas.mitchell@ucr.edu. *Application contact:* Prof. Michael Orosco, Assistant Professor and Graduate Advisor of Admissions, 951-827-6362, Fax: 951-827-3291, E-mail: edgrad@ucr.edu.
Website: http://www.education.ucr.edu/.

University of Central Florida, College of Education and Human Performance, Department of Educational and Human Sciences, Program in Educational Leadership, Orlando, FL 32816. Offers educational leadership (MA, Ed D), including community college education (MA), higher education (Ed D), student personnel (MA). Part-time and evening/weekend programs available. *Students:* 108 full-time (79 women), 259 part-time (180 women); includes 105 minority (43 Black or African American, non-Hispanic/Latino; 1 American Indian or Alaska Native, non-Hispanic/Latino; 8 Asian, non-Hispanic/Latino; 49 Hispanic/Latino; 4 Two or more races, non-Hispanic/Latino), 1 international. Average age 33. 218 applicants, 82% accepted, 117 enrolled. In 2013, 42 master's, 22 doctorates awarded. *Degree requirements:* For master's, thesis or alternative; for doctorate, thesis/dissertation, candidacy exam. *Entrance requirements:* For master's, GRE General Test; for doctorate, GRE General Test, GRE Subject Test, minimum GPA of 3.0, resume. Additional exam requirements/recommendations for international students: Required—TOEFL. *Application deadline:* For fall admission, 2/20 priority date for domestic students; for spring admission, 9/20 priority date for domestic students. Application fee: $30. Electronic applications accepted. *Financial support:* In 2013–14, 14 students received support, including 2 fellowships with partial tuition reimbursements available (averaging $2,800 per year), 12 research assistantships with partial tuition reimbursements available (averaging $6,700 per year), 1 teaching assistantship with partial tuition reimbursement available (averaging $6,600 per year); career-related internships or fieldwork, Federal Work-Study, institutionally sponsored loans, tuition waivers (partial), and unspecified assistantships also available. Financial award application deadline: 3/1; financial award applicants required to submit FAFSA. *Unit head:* Dr. Kenneth Murray, Program Coordinator, 407-832-1468, E-mail: kenneth.murray@ucf.edu. *Application contact:* Barbara Rodriguez Lamas, Director, Admissions and Student Services, 407-823-2766, Fax: 407-823-6442, E-mail: gradadmissions@ucf.edu.
Website: http://education.ucf.edu/departments.cfm.

University of Central Florida, College of Education and Human Performance, Education Doctoral Programs, Orlando, FL 32816. Offers communication sciences and disorders (PhD); counselor education (PhD); early childhood education (PhD); education (Ed D); elementary education (PhD); exceptional education (PhD); exercise physiology (PhD); higher education (PhD); hospitality education (PhD); instructional technology (PhD); mathematics education (PhD); reading education (PhD); science education (PhD); social science education (PhD); TESOL (PhD). *Students:* 137 full-time (94 women), 86 part-time (64 women); includes 45 minority (24 Black or African American, non-Hispanic/Latino; 5 Asian, non-Hispanic/Latino; 13 Hispanic/Latino; 3 Two or more races, non-Hispanic/Latino), 22 international. Average age 39. 132 applicants, 54% accepted, 54 enrolled. In 2013, 38 doctorates awarded. Application fee: $30. Electronic applications accepted. *Financial support:* In 2013–14, 84 students received support, including 38 fellowships with partial tuition reimbursements available (averaging $6,600 per year), 41 research assistantships with partial tuition reimbursements available (averaging $7,800 per year), 53 teaching assistantships with partial tuition reimbursements available (averaging $7,700 per year). *Unit head:* Dr. Edward Robinson, Director of Doctoral Programs, 407-823-6106, E-mail: edward.robinson@ucf.edu. *Application contact:* Barbara Rodriguez Lamas, Associate Director, Admissions

and Student Services, 407-823-2766, Fax: 407-823-6442, E-mail: gradadmissions@ucf.edu.
Website: http://education.ucf.edu/departments.cfm.

University of Central Oklahoma, The Jackson College of Graduate Studies, College of Education and Professional Studies, Department of Adult Education and Safety Science, Edmond, OK 73034-5209. Offers adult and higher education (M Ed), including adult and higher education, interdisciplinary studies, student personnel, training. Part-time programs available. *Faculty:* 7 full-time (4 women), 12 part-time/adjunct (5 women). *Students:* 37 full-time (23 women), 91 part-time (57 women); includes 50 minority (24 Black or African American, non-Hispanic/Latino; 3 American Indian or Alaska Native, non-Hispanic/Latino; 5 Asian, non-Hispanic/Latino; 12 Hispanic/Latino; 6 Two or more races, non-Hispanic/Latino), 5 international. Average age 36. 59 applicants, 78% accepted, 28 enrolled. In 2013, 17 master's awarded. *Degree requirements:* For master's, comprehensive exam (for some programs), thesis (for some programs). *Entrance requirements:* For master's, GRE General Test. Additional exam requirements/recommendations for international students: Required—TOEFL (minimum score 550 paper-based; 79 iBT), IELTS (minimum score 6.5). *Application deadline:* For fall admission, 7/1 for international students; for spring admission, 11/1 for international students. Applications are processed on a rolling basis. Application fee: $50. Electronic applications accepted. *Expenses:* Tuition, state resident: full-time $4137; part-time $206.85 per credit hour. Tuition, nonresident: full-time $10,359; part-time $517.95 per credit hour. *Required fees:* $481. Tuition and fees vary according to course load and program. *Financial support:* In 2013–14, 31 students received support, including 2 research assistantships with partial tuition reimbursements available (averaging $2,958 per year), 1 teaching assistantship with partial tuition reimbursement available (averaging $15,382 per year); career-related internships or fieldwork, scholarships/grants, tuition waivers (partial), and unspecified assistantships also available. Financial award application deadline: 3/31; financial award applicants required to submit FAFSA. *Faculty research:* Violence in the workplace/schools, aging issues, trade and industrial education. *Unit head:* Dr. Candy Sebert, Chair, 405-974-5780, Fax: 405-974-3822. *Application contact:* Dr. Richard Bernard, Dean, Graduate College, 405-974-3493, Fax: 405-974-3852, E-mail: gradcoll@uco.edu.

University of Connecticut, Graduate School, Neag School of Education, Department of Educational Leadership, Field of Higher Education and Student Affairs, Storrs, CT 06269. Offers MA. *Accreditation:* NCATE. *Degree requirements:* For master's, comprehensive exam, thesis or alternative. *Entrance requirements:* Additional exam requirements/recommendations for international students: Required—TOEFL (minimum score 550 paper-based). Electronic applications accepted.

University of Delaware, College of Education and Human Development, School of Education, Newark, DE 19716. Offers education (PhD); educational leadership (Ed D); higher education (M Ed); instruction (MI); reading (M Ed); school leadership (M Ed); school psychology (MA, Ed S); teaching English as a second language (TESL) (MA). *Accreditation:* NCATE. Part-time and evening/weekend programs available. Terminal master's awarded for partial completion of doctoral program. *Degree requirements:* For master's, comprehensive exam (for some programs), thesis (for some programs); for doctorate, comprehensive exam (for some programs), thesis/dissertation. *Entrance requirements:* For master's and doctorate, GRE, 3 letters of recommendation. Additional exam requirements/recommendations for international students: Required—TOEFL (minimum score 600 paper-based). Electronic applications accepted. *Faculty research:* Teacher education; curriculum theory and development; community based education models, educational leadership.

University of Denver, Morgridge College of Education, Denver, CO 80208. Offers child, family and school psychology (MA, PhD, Ed S); counseling psychology (MA, PhD); curriculum and instruction (MA, Ed D, PhD); curriculum instruction and teaching (Certificate); early childhood special education (MA); educational leadership and policy studies (MA, Ed D, PhD, Certificate); higher education (MA, Ed D, PhD); law librarianship (Certificate); library and information science (MLIS); research methods and statistics (MA, PhD). *Accreditation:* ALA; APA (one or more programs are accredited). Part-time and evening/weekend programs available. Postbaccalaureate distance learning degree programs offered (no on-campus study). *Faculty:* 35 full-time (21 women), 63 part-time/adjunct (43 women). *Students:* 435 full-time (332 women), 414 part-time (297 women); includes 194 minority (45 Black or African American, non-Hispanic/Latino; 9 American Indian or Alaska Native, non-Hispanic/Latino; 16 Asian, non-Hispanic/Latino; 96 Hispanic/Latino; 2 Native Hawaiian or other Pacific Islander, non-Hispanic/Latino; 26 Two or more races, non-Hispanic/Latino), 14 international. Average age 32. 672 applicants, 61% accepted, 193 enrolled. In 2013, 248 master's, 30 doctorates, 130 other advanced degrees awarded. Terminal master's awarded for partial completion of doctoral program. *Degree requirements:* For master's, comprehensive exam; for doctorate, 2 foreign languages, comprehensive exam, thesis/dissertation. *Entrance requirements:* For master's and doctorate, GRE General Test or GMAT. Additional exam requirements/recommendations for international students: Required—TOEFL (minimum score 550 paper-based; 80 iBT). *Application deadline:* Applications are processed on a rolling basis. Application fee: $65. Electronic applications accepted. *Financial support:* In 2013–14, 706 students received support, including 54 research assistantships with full and partial tuition reimbursements available (averaging $15,599 per year), 77 teaching assistantships with full and partial tuition reimbursements available (averaging $12,804 per year); career-related internships or fieldwork, Federal Work-Study, institutionally sponsored loans, scholarships/grants, and unspecified assistantships also available. Support available to part-time students. Financial award application deadline: 2/15; financial award applicants required to submit FAFSA. *Faculty research:* Principal and teacher preparation, development and assessments, gifted education, service-learning, early childhood, mathematics education, access to higher education. *Total annual research expenditures:* $6.3 million. *Unit head:* Dr. Karen Riley, Interim Dean, 303-871-3665, E-mail: karen.riley@du.edu. *Application contact:* Jodi Dye, Assistant Director of Admissions, 303-871-2510, E-mail: jodi.dye@du.edu.
Website: http://morgridge.du.edu/.

University of Florida, Graduate School, College of Education, School of Human Development and Organizational Studies in Education, Gainesville, FL 32611. Offers counseling and counselor education (Ed D, PhD), including counseling and counselor education, marriage and family counseling, mental health counseling, school counseling and guidance; educational leadership (M Ed, MAE, Ed D, PhD, Ed S), including educational leadership (Ed D, PhD), educational policy (Ed D, PhD); higher education administration (Ed D, PhD, Ed S), including education policy (Ed D), educational policy (Ed D, PhD), higher education administration (Ed D, PhD); marriage and family counseling (M Ed, MAE, Ed S); mental health counseling (M Ed, MAE, Ed S); research and evaluation methodology (M Ed, MAE, Ed D, PhD, Ed S); school counseling and guidance (M Ed, MAE, Ed S); student personnel in higher education (M Ed, MAE, Ed S). *Accreditation:* ACA (one or more programs are accredited); NCATE. Part-time programs available. Postbaccalaureate distance learning degree programs offered. *Faculty:* 20 full-time (11 women), 4 part-time/adjunct (1 woman). *Students:* 291 full-time (232 women), 212 part-time (157 women); includes 145 minority (71 Black or African American, non-Hispanic/Latino; 3 American Indian or Alaska Native, non-Hispanic/Latino; 11 Asian, non-Hispanic/Latino; 60 Hispanic/Latino), 38 international. Average age 31. 271 applicants, 42% accepted, 75 enrolled. In 2013, 71 master's, 31 doctorates, 62 other advanced degrees awarded. Terminal master's awarded for partial completion of doctoral program. *Degree requirements:* For master's, thesis optional; for doctorate, comprehensive exam, thesis/dissertation. *Entrance requirements:* For master's and doctorate, GRE General Test, minimum GPA of 3.0 (undergraduate), 3.5 (graduate); for Ed S, GRE General Test. Additional exam requirements/recommendations for international students: Required—TOEFL (minimum score 550 paper-based; 80 iBT), IELTS (minimum score 6). *Application deadline:* Applications are processed on a rolling basis. Application fee: $30. Electronic applications accepted. *Expenses:* Tuition, state resident: full-time $12,640. Tuition, nonresident: full-time $30,000. *Financial support:* In 2013–14, 85 students received support, including 6 fellowships (averaging $12,190 per year), 48 research assistantships (averaging $15,155 per year), 50 teaching assistantships (averaging $9,080 per year); career-related internships or fieldwork and unspecified assistantships also available. Financial award applicants required to submit FAFSA. *Unit head:* Glenn E. Good, PhD, Dean and Professor, 352-273-4135, Fax: 352-846-2697, E-mail: ggood@ufl.edu. *Application contact:* Thomasenia L. Adams, PhD, Professor and Associate Dean, 352-273-4119, Fax: 352-846-2697, E-mail: tla@coe.ufl.edu.
Website: http://education.ufl.edu/hdose/.

University of Georgia, College of Education, Program in Higher Education, Athens, GA 30602. Offers PhD. *Accreditation:* NCATE. *Degree requirements:* For doctorate, thesis/dissertation. *Entrance requirements:* For doctorate, GRE General Test. Electronic applications accepted.

University of Houston, College of Education, Department of Educational Leadership and Cultural Studies, Houston, TX 77204. Offers administration and supervision (M Ed, Ed D); higher education (M Ed); historical, social, and cultural foundations of education (M Ed). *Accreditation:* NCATE. Part-time and evening/weekend programs available. *Degree requirements:* For master's, comprehensive exam or thesis; for doctorate, comprehensive exam, thesis/dissertation. *Entrance requirements:* For master's, GRE General Test, minimum cumulative GPA of 2.6, 3 letters of recommendation, resume/vitae, goal statement; for doctorate, GRE General Test, minimum cumulative GPA of 2.6, 3 letters of recommendation, resume/vitae, goal statement, writing sample, interview. Additional exam requirements/recommendations for international students: Required—TOEFL (minimum score 550 paper-based; 79 iBT). Electronic applications accepted. *Faculty research:* Change, supervision, multiculturalism, evaluation, policy.

University of Houston, College of Education, Department of Educational Psychology, Houston, TX 77204. Offers administration and supervision - higher education (M Ed); counseling (M Ed); counseling psychology (PhD); educational psychology (M Ed); school psychology (PhD); school psychology and individual differences (PhD); special education (M Ed). *Accreditation:* NCATE. Part-time and evening/weekend programs available. Postbaccalaureate distance learning degree programs offered (no on-campus study). *Degree requirements:* For master's, comprehensive exam or thesis; for doctorate, comprehensive exam, thesis/dissertation. *Entrance requirements:* For master's, GRE, transcripts, 3 letters of recommendation, curriculum vita, goal statement; for doctorate, GRE, transcripts, 3 letters of recommendation, curriculum vita, goal statement, writing sample, interview. Additional exam requirements/recommendations for international students: Required—TOEFL (minimum score 550 paper-based; 79 iBT), IELTS (minimum score 6.5). Electronic applications accepted. *Faculty research:* Evidence-based assessment and intervention, multicultural issues in psychology, social and cultural context of learning, systemic barriers to college, motivational aspects of self-regulated learning.

University of Houston–Victoria, School of Education and Human Development, Victoria, TX 77901-4450. Offers administration and supervision (M Ed); adult and higher education (M Ed); counseling (M Ed); curriculum and instruction (M Ed); special education (M Ed). Part-time and evening/weekend programs available. Postbaccalaureate distance learning degree programs offered (minimal on-campus study). *Faculty:* 22 full-time (19 women). *Students:* 56 full-time (52 women), 325 part-time (274 women); includes 211 minority (113 Black or African American, non-Hispanic/Latino; 2 American Indian or Alaska Native, non-Hispanic/Latino; 16 Asian, non-Hispanic/Latino; 68 Hispanic/Latino; 12 Two or more races, non-Hispanic/Latino), 3 international. *Degree requirements:* For master's, comprehensive exam, project or thesis. *Entrance requirements:* For master's, GRE General Test. Additional exam requirements/recommendations for international students: Required—TOEFL. *Application deadline:* For fall admission, 6/1 for international students; for spring admission, 10/1 for international students. Applications are processed on a rolling basis. Application fee: $0. Electronic applications accepted. *Expenses:* Tuition, state resident: full-time $4534; part-time $251 per credit hour. Tuition, nonresident: full-time $10,906; part-time $606 per contact hour. *Required fees:* $68 per semester hour. Tuition and fees vary according to course load. *Financial support:* In 2013–14, research assistantships with partial tuition reimbursements (averaging $2,000 per year), teaching assistantships with partial tuition reimbursements (averaging $2,000 per year) were awarded; Federal Work-Study, scholarships/grants, and unspecified assistantships also available. Support available to part-time students. Financial award application deadline: 4/15; financial award applicants required to submit FAFSA. *Faculty research:* Reading and language arts education, evaluation and diagnosis of special children's abilities. *Unit head:* Freddie W. Litton, Dean, 361-570-4260, Fax: 361-580-5580. *Application contact:* Sandy Hybner, Senior Recruitment Coordinator, 361-570-4252, Fax: 361-580-5580, E-mail: hybners@uhv.edu.
Website: http://www.uhv.edu/edu/.

The University of Iowa, Graduate College, College of Education, Department of Educational Policy and Leadership Studies, Program in Higher Education and Student Affairs, Iowa City, IA 52242-1316. Offers MA, PhD. *Degree requirements:* For master's, exam; for doctorate, comprehensive exam, thesis/dissertation. *Entrance requirements:* For master's and doctorate, GRE General Test, minimum GPA of 3.0. Additional exam requirements/recommendations for international students: Required—TOEFL (minimum score 550 paper-based; 81 iBT). Electronic applications accepted.

The University of Kansas, Graduate Studies, School of Education, Department of Educational Leadership and Policy Studies, Education Leadership and Policy Program, Lawrence, KS 66045-3101. Offers educational administration (Ed D, PhD); foundations (PhD); higher education (Ed D, PhD); policy studies (PhD). Part-time and evening/weekend programs available. *Faculty:* 15. *Students:* 106 full-time (63 women), 46 part-time (19 women); includes 32 minority (10 Black or African American, non-Hispanic/Latino; 4 American Indian or Alaska Native, non-Hispanic/Latino; 6 Asian, non-Hispanic/Latino; 7 Hispanic/Latino; 5 Two or more races, non-Hispanic/Latino), 27 international. Average age 37. 63 applicants, 71% accepted, 32 enrolled. In 2013, 31 doctorates awarded. *Degree requirements:* For doctorate, comprehensive exam, thesis/dissertation. *Entrance requirements:* For doctorate, GRE General Test, minimum graduate GPA of 3.5. Additional exam requirements/recommendations for international students: Required—TOEFL (minimum score 570 paper-based; 80 iBT). *Application deadline:* For fall admission, 7/1 for domestic and international students; for spring admission, 11/1 for domestic and international students. Applications are processed on a rolling basis. Application fee: $55 ($65 for international students). Electronic

applications accepted. *Financial support:* Fellowships, research assistantships with full and partial tuition reimbursements, teaching assistantships with full and partial tuition reimbursements, scholarships/grants, and unspecified assistantships available. Financial award application deadline: 3/15. *Faculty research:* Historical and philosophical issues in education, education policy and leadership, higher education faculty, research on college students, education technology. *Unit head:* Dr. Susan Twombly, Chair, 785-864-9721, Fax: 785-864-4697, E-mail: stwombly@ku.edu. *Application contact:* Denise Brubaker, Admissions Coordinator, 785-864-7973, Fax: 785-864-4697, E-mail: brubaker@ku.edu.
Website: http://elps.soe.ku.edu/.

The University of Kansas, Graduate Studies, School of Education, Department of Educational Leadership and Policy Studies, Program in Higher Education Administration, Lawrence, KS 66045-3101. Offers higher education (MS Ed). Part-time and evening/weekend programs available. *Faculty:* 15. *Students:* 53 full-time (33 women), 16 part-time (12 women); includes 19 minority (8 Black or African American, non-Hispanic/Latino; 2 American Indian or Alaska Native, non-Hispanic/Latino; 1 Asian, non-Hispanic/Latino; 6 Hispanic/Latino; 2 Two or more races, non-Hispanic/Latino), 3 international. Average age 25. 90 applicants, 68% accepted, 33 enrolled. In 2013, 26 master's awarded. *Degree requirements:* For master's, comprehensive exam. *Entrance requirements:* For master's, minimum GPA of 3.0. Additional exam requirements/recommendations for international students: Required—TOEFL (minimum score 570 paper-based; 80 iBT). *Application deadline:* For fall admission, 2/1 priority date for domestic and international students. Application fee: $55 ($65 for international students). Electronic applications accepted. *Financial support:* Fellowships, career-related internships or fieldwork, and scholarships/grants available. Financial award application deadline: 2/1; financial award applicants required to submit FAFSA. *Faculty research:* Higher education policy, faculty issues, research on college students, financial aid, access to higher education. *Unit head:* Dr. Susan Twombly, Chair, 785-864-9721, Fax: 785-864-4697, E-mail: stwombly@ku.edu. *Application contact:* Denise Brubaker, Admissions Coordinator, 785-864-7973, Fax: 785-864-4697, E-mail: brubaker@ku.edu.
Website: http://kuhighered.wix.com/ku-hesa.

University of Kentucky, Graduate School, College of Education, Department of Educational Policy Studies and Evaluation, Lexington, KY 40506-0032. Offers educational policy studies and evaluation (Ed D); higher education (MS Ed, PhD); social and philosophical studies (MS Ed). *Accreditation:* NCATE. Terminal master's awarded for partial completion of doctoral program. *Degree requirements:* For master's, comprehensive exam, thesis optional; for doctorate, comprehensive exam, thesis/dissertation. *Entrance requirements:* For master's, GRE General Test, minimum undergraduate GPA of 2.75; for doctorate, GRE General Test, minimum graduate GPA of 3.0. Additional exam requirements/recommendations for international students: Required—TOEFL (minimum score 550 paper-based). Electronic applications accepted. *Faculty research:* Studies in higher education; comparative and international education; evaluation of educational programs, policies, and reform; student, teacher, and faculty cultures; gender and education.

University of Louisville, Graduate School, College of Education and Human Development, Department of Leadership, Foundations and Human Resource Education, Louisville, KY 40292-0001. Offers educational leadership and organizational development (Ed D, PhD); higher education (MA); human resource education (MS); P-12 educational administration (M Ed, Ed S). *Accreditation:* NCATE. Part-time and evening/weekend programs available. Postbaccalaureate distance learning degree programs offered. *Students:* 68 full-time (44 women), 319 part-time (227 women); includes 80 minority (61 Black or African American, non-Hispanic/Latino; 5 Asian, non-Hispanic/Latino; 9 Hispanic/Latino; 1 Native Hawaiian or other Pacific Islander, non-Hispanic/Latino; 4 Two or more races, non-Hispanic/Latino), 27 international. Average age 36. 219 applicants, 76% accepted, 136 enrolled. In 2013, 19 master's, 5 doctorates, 4 other advanced degrees awarded. *Degree requirements:* For doctorate, comprehensive exam, thesis/dissertation. *Entrance requirements:* For master's, doctorate, and Ed S, GRE General Test. Additional exam requirements/recommendations for international students: Required—TOEFL (minimum score 560 paper-based; 83 iBT). *Application deadline:* For fall admission, 5/1 priority date for international students; for winter admission, 11/1 priority date for international students; for summer admission, 1/1 priority date for international students. Applications are processed on a rolling basis. Application fee: $60. Electronic applications accepted. *Expenses:* Tuition, state resident: full-time $10,788; part-time $599 per credit hour. Tuition, nonresident: full-time $22,446; part-time $1247 per credit hour. *Required fees:* $196. Tuition and fees vary according to program and reciprocity agreements. *Financial support:* Fellowships, research assistantships, teaching assistantships, career-related internships or fieldwork, Federal Work-Study, scholarships/grants, health care benefits, and unspecified assistantships available. Financial award application deadline: 6/1; financial award applicants required to submit FAFSA. *Faculty research:* Evaluation of methods and programs to improve elementary and secondary education; research on organizational and human resource development; student access, retention and success in post-secondary education; educational policy analysis; multivariate quantitative research methods. *Unit head:* Dr. Gaetane Jean-Marie, Chair, 502-852-0634, Fax: 502-852-1164, E-mail: g0jean01@louisville.edu. *Application contact:* Libby Leggett, Director, Graduate Admissions, 502-852-3101, Fax: 502-852-6536, E-mail: gradadm@louisville.edu.
Website: http://www.louisville.edu/education/departments/elfh.

University of Maine, Graduate School, College of Education and Human Development, Department of Educational Leadership, Higher Education, and Human Development, Orono, ME 04469. Offers educational leadership (M Ed, Ed D, CAS); higher education (M Ed, MA, MS, Ed D, PhD, CAS); human development (MS). Part-time programs available. *Students:* 56 full-time (21 women), 73 part-time (41 women); includes 7 minority (2 Black or African American, non-Hispanic/Latino; 1 American Indian or Alaska Native, non-Hispanic/Latino; 2 Asian, non-Hispanic/Latino; 2 Hispanic/Latino), 4 international. Average age 39. 64 applicants, 63% accepted, 27 enrolled. In 2013, 20 master's, 6 other advanced degrees awarded. *Degree requirements:* For master's, thesis (for some programs); for doctorate, comprehensive exam, thesis/dissertation. *Entrance requirements:* For master's, GRE General Test, MAT; for doctorate, GRE. Additional exam requirements/recommendations for international students: Required—TOEFL. *Application deadline:* For fall admission, 2/1 priority date for domestic students. Applications are processed on a rolling basis. Application fee: $65. Electronic applications accepted. *Expenses:* Tuition, state resident: full-time $7524. Tuition, nonresident: full-time $23,112. *Required fees:* $1970. *Financial support:* In 2013–14, 26 students received support, including 1 research assistantship (averaging $18,000 per year), 3 teaching assistantships (averaging $14,600 per year); career-related internships or fieldwork, Federal Work-Study, institutionally sponsored loans, tuition waivers (full and partial), and unspecified assistantships also available. Financial award application deadline: 3/1. *Faculty research:* Leadership formation, school organization, collective efficacy and collaborative climate of high schools, change process in high schools, principalship; equity policy; gender and education; doctoral student development, retention, and attrition; faculty development and socialization; sexuality education and curriculum development; family/domestic violence; friendship/kin relationships; early childhood education; support for families with members with disabilities. *Unit head:* Dr. Janet Spector, Coordinator, 207-581-3162, Fax: 207-581-3120. *Application contact:* Scott G. Delcourt, Associate Dean of the Graduate School, 207-581-3291, Fax: 207-581-3232, E-mail: graduate@maine.edu.
Website: http://www.umaine.edu/edhd/.

University of Manitoba, Faculty of Graduate Studies, Faculty of Education, Department of Educational Administration, Foundations and Psychology, Winnipeg, MB R3T 2N2, Canada. Offers adult and post-secondary education (M Ed); educational administration (M Ed); guidance and counseling (M Ed); inclusive special education (M Ed); social foundations of education (M Ed). *Degree requirements:* For master's, thesis or alternative.

University of Mary, School of Education and Behavioral Sciences, Department of Education, Bismarck, ND 58504-9652. Offers college teaching (M Ed); curriculum, instruction and assessment (M Ed); early childhood education (M Ed); early childhood special education (M Ed); elementary administration (M Ed); emotional disorders (M Ed); learning disabilities (M Ed); reading (M Ed); secondary administration (M Ed); special education strategist (M Ed). Part-time programs available. *Degree requirements:* For master's, portfolio or thesis. *Entrance requirements:* For master's, interview, letters of reference, minimum GPA of 2.5. Additional exam requirements/recommendations for international students: Required—TOEFL (minimum score 500 paper-based; 71 iBT). Electronic applications accepted. *Faculty research:* Innovative pedagogy in higher education, technology in education, content standards, children of poverty, children with diverse learning needs.

University of Mary Hardin-Baylor, Graduate Studies in Education, Belton, TX 76513. Offers administration of intervention programs (M Ed); curriculum and instruction (M Ed); educational administration (M Ed, Ed D), including higher education (Ed D), leadership in nursing education (Ed D), P-12 (Ed D). Part-time and evening/weekend programs available. *Faculty:* 13 full-time (10 women), 6 part-time/adjunct (2 women). *Students:* 46 full-time (33 women), 61 part-time (40 women); includes 35 minority (15 Black or African American, non-Hispanic/Latino; 1 American Indian or Alaska Native, non-Hispanic/Latino; 19 Hispanic/Latino), 1 international. Average age 38. 72 applicants, 88% accepted, 47 enrolled. In 2013, 13 master's, 30 doctorates awarded. *Degree requirements:* For master's, comprehensive exam; for doctorate, thesis/dissertation. *Entrance requirements:* For master's, minimum GPA of 3.0, interview; for doctorate, minimum GPA of 3.5, interview, essay, resume, employment verification, employer letter of support, 3 letters of recommendation. Additional exam requirements/recommendations for international students: Required—TOEFL (minimum score 550 paper-based; 80 iBT), IELTS (minimum score 6). *Application deadline:* For fall admission, 6/1 for domestic students, 6/15 priority date for international students; for spring admission, 11/1 for domestic students, 10/15 priority date for international students. Applications are processed on a rolling basis. Application fee: $35 ($135 for international students). Electronic applications accepted. *Expenses: Tuition:* Full-time $14,130; part-time $785 per credit hour. *Required fees:* $1350; $75 per credit hour. $50 per term. *Financial support:* Federal Work-Study and scholarships (for some active duty military personnel only) available. Support available to part-time students. Financial award application deadline: 6/1; financial award applicants required to submit FAFSA. *Unit head:* Dr. Marlene Zipperlen, Dean, College of Education/Director, Doctor of Education Program, 254-295-4572, Fax: 254-295-4480, E-mail: mzipperlen@umhb.edu. *Application contact:* Melissa Ford, Director of Graduate Admissions, 254-295-4020, Fax: 254-295-5038, E-mail: mford@umhb.edu.
Website: http://graduate.umhb.edu/education/.

University of Massachusetts Amherst, Graduate School, College of Education, Program in Education, Amherst, MA 01003. Offers bilingual/English as a second language/multicultural education (M Ed, Ed S); child study and early education (M Ed); children, families and schools (Ed D, Ed S); early childhood and elementary teacher education (M Ed); educational leadership (M Ed); educational policy and leadership (Ed D); higher education (M Ed); international education (M Ed); language, literacy and culture (Ed D); learning, media and technology (M Ed, Ed S); mathematics, science, and learning technologies (Ed D); psychometric methods, educational statistics and research methods (Ed D); reading and writing (M Ed); school counselor education (M Ed, Ed S); school psychology (Ed S); science education (Ed S); secondary teacher education (M Ed); social justice education (M Ed, Ed D, Ed S); special education (M Ed, Ed D, Ed S); teacher education and school improvement (Ed D, Ed S). *Accreditation:* NCATE. Part-time programs available. Postbaccalaureate distance learning degree programs offered (minimal on-campus study). *Faculty:* 95 full-time (55 women). *Students:* 357 full-time (240 women), 264 part-time (194 women); includes 114 minority (41 Black or African American, non-Hispanic/Latino; 4 American Indian or Alaska Native, non-Hispanic/Latino; 10 Asian, non-Hispanic/Latino; 47 Hispanic/Latino; 12 Two or more races, non-Hispanic/Latino), 100 international. Average age 34. 761 applicants, 51% accepted, 200 enrolled. In 2013, 186 master's, 31 doctorates, 22 other advanced degrees awarded. Terminal master's awarded for partial completion of doctoral program. *Degree requirements:* For doctorate, comprehensive exam, thesis/dissertation. *Entrance requirements:* Additional exam requirements/recommendations for international students: Required—TOEFL (minimum score 550 paper-based; 80 iBT), IELTS (minimum score 6.5). *Application deadline:* For fall admission, 1/15 for domestic and international students. Applications are processed on a rolling basis. Application fee: $75. Electronic applications accepted. *Financial support:* Fellowships with full and partial tuition reimbursements, research assistantships with full and partial tuition reimbursements, teaching assistantships with full and partial tuition reimbursements, career-related internships or fieldwork, Federal Work-Study, scholarships/grants, traineeships, health care benefits, tuition waivers (full and partial), and unspecified assistantships available. Support available to part-time students. Financial award application deadline: 1/15; financial award applicants required to submit FAFSA. *Unit head:* Dr. Linda L. Griffin, Graduate Program Director, 413-545-6984, Fax: 413-545-1523. *Application contact:* Lindsay DeSantis, Supervisor of Admissions, 413-545-0722, Fax: 413-577-0010, E-mail: gradadm@grad.umass.edu.
Website: http://www.umass.edu/education/.

University of Massachusetts Amherst, Graduate School, Interdisciplinary Programs, Dual Degree Program in Education and Public Policy and Administration, Amherst, MA 01003. Offers MPPA/M Ed. *Entrance requirements:* Additional exam requirements/recommendations for international students: Required—TOEFL (minimum score 550 paper-based; 80 iBT), IELTS (minimum score 6.5). *Application deadline:* For fall admission, 2/1 for domestic and international students. Applications are processed on a rolling basis. Application fee: $75. Electronic applications accepted. *Financial support:* Career-related internships or fieldwork, Federal Work-Study, scholarships/grants, traineeships, health care benefits, tuition waivers, and unspecified assistantships available. Support available to part-time students. Financial award application deadline: 2/1. *Unit head:* Dr. Kathryn McDermott, Professor, 413-545-3162, E-mail: szoller@pubpol.umass.edu. *Application contact:* Lindsay DeSantis, Supervisor of Admissions, 413-545-0722, Fax: 413-577-0010, E-mail: gradadm@grad.umass.edu.
Website: http://www.masspolicy.org/acad_mppa_ed.html.

University of Massachusetts Boston, Office of Graduate Studies, Graduate College of Education, School Organization, Curriculum and Instruction Department, Boston, MA 02125-3393. Offers education (M Ed, Ed D), including elementary and secondary

education/certification (M Ed), higher education administration (Ed D), teacher certification (M Ed), urban school leadership (Ed D); educational administration (M Ed, CAGS); special education (M Ed). *Degree requirements:* For master's and CAGS, comprehensive exam; for doctorate, comprehensive exam, thesis/dissertation. *Entrance requirements:* For master's, GRE General Test or MAT; for doctorate, GRE General Test or MAT, minimum GPA of 2.75; for CAGS, minimum GPA of 2.75.

University of Massachusetts Boston, Office of Graduate Studies, Graduate College of Education, School Organization, Curriculum and Instruction Department, Program in Education, Track in Higher Education Administration, Boston, MA 02125-3393. Offers Ed D. Part-time and evening/weekend programs available. *Degree requirements:* For doctorate, comprehensive exam, thesis/dissertation. *Entrance requirements:* For doctorate, GRE General Test or MAT, minimum GPA of 2.75. *Faculty research:* Women, higher education and professionalization, school reform, urban classroom, higher education policy.

University of Memphis, Graduate School, College of Education, Department of Leadership, Memphis, TN 38152. Offers adult education (Ed D); educational leadership (Ed D); higher education (Ed D); leadership (MS); policy studies (Ed D); school administration and supervision (MS). *Accreditation:* NCATE. Part-time and evening/weekend programs available. Postbaccalaureate distance learning degree programs offered (minimal on-campus study). *Faculty:* 12 full-time (4 women), 2 part-time/adjunct (0 women). *Students:* 12 full-time (8 women), 138 part-time (87 women); includes 86 minority (79 Black or African American, non-Hispanic/Latino; 1 Asian, non-Hispanic/Latino; 1 Hispanic/Latino; 5 Two or more races, non-Hispanic/Latino), 1 international. Average age 40. 65 applicants, 66% accepted, 10 enrolled. In 2013, 12 master's, 13 doctorates awarded. *Degree requirements:* For master's, comprehensive exam, thesis optional; for doctorate, comprehensive exam, thesis/dissertation. *Entrance requirements:* For master's and doctorate, GRE. *Application deadline:* For fall admission, 4/1 for domestic students; for spring admission, 10/1 for domestic students. Application fee: $35 ($60 for international students). Electronic applications accepted. *Financial support:* In 2013–14, 70 students received support. Research assistantships with full tuition reimbursements available, teaching assistantships, Federal Work-Study, scholarships/grants, and unspecified assistantships available. Financial award application deadline: 2/15; financial award applicants required to submit FAFSA. *Faculty research:* School improvement, social justice, online learning, adult learning, diversity. *Unit head:* Katrina Mayer, Interim Chair, 901-678-2466, E-mail: kmeyer@memphis.edu. *Application contact:* Larry McNeal, Professor, School Administration and Supervision Programs, 901-678-2369, E-mail: lmcneal1@memphis.edu.
Website: http://www.memphis.edu/lead.

University of Miami, Graduate School, School of Education and Human Development, Department of Educational and Psychological Studies, Program in Higher Education Administration, Coral Gables, FL 33124. Offers enrollment management (MS Ed, Certificate); higher education leadership (Ed D); student life and development (MS Ed, Certificate). Part-time and evening/weekend programs available. *Faculty:* 2 full-time (both women), 9 part-time/adjunct (3 women). *Students:* 32 full-time (18 women), 22 part-time (12 women); includes 28 minority (10 Black or African American, non-Hispanic/Latino; 2 Asian, non-Hispanic/Latino; 15 Hispanic/Latino; 1 Two or more races, non-Hispanic/Latino), 7 international. Average age 34. 42 applicants, 31% accepted, 13 enrolled. In 2013, 2 master's, 1 doctorate awarded. Terminal master's awarded for partial completion of doctoral program. *Degree requirements:* For master's, comprehensive exam; for doctorate, thesis/dissertation, qualifying exam. *Entrance requirements:* For master's and doctorate, GRE General Test. Additional exam requirements/recommendations for international students: Required—TOEFL (minimum score 550 paper-based; 80 iBT); Recommended—IELTS (minimum score 6.5). *Application deadline:* Applications are processed on a rolling basis. Application fee: $65. Electronic applications accepted. *Financial support:* In 2013–14, 48 students received support. Institutionally sponsored loans and scholarships/grants available. Support available to part-time students. Financial award application deadline: 3/1; financial award applicants required to submit FAFSA. *Unit head:* Dr. Carol Anne Pekoo, Lecturer/Director, 305-284-5013, Fax: 305-284-3003, E-mail: cphekoo@miami.edu. *Application contact:* Lois Heffernan, Graduate Admissions Coordinator, 305-284-2167, Fax: 305-284-9395, E-mail: lheffernan@miami.edu.
Website: http://www.education.miami.edu/program/Programs.asp?Program_ID=148&Src=Graduate.

University of Minnesota, Twin Cities Campus, Graduate School, College of Education and Human Development, Department of Organizational Leadership, Policy and Development, Program in Higher Education, Minneapolis, MN 55455-0213. Offers MA, PhD. *Students:* 47 full-time (29 women), 103 part-time (67 women); includes 31 minority (13 Black or African American, non-Hispanic/Latino; 3 American Indian or Alaska Native, non-Hispanic/Latino; 9 Asian, non-Hispanic/Latino; 6 Hispanic/Latino), 8 international. Average age 38. 37 applicants, 84% accepted, 2 enrolled. In 2013, 11 master's, 19 doctorates awarded. Application fee: $75 ($95 for international students). *Unit head:* Dr. Rebecca Ropers-Huilman, Chair, 612-624-1006, Fax: 612-624-3377, E-mail: ropers@umn.edu. *Application contact:* Dr. Jennifer Engler, Assistant Dean, 612-626-2887, Fax: 612-626-7496, E-mail: engle009@umn.edu.
Website: http://www.cehd.umn.edu/EdPA/HigherEd/.

University of Minnesota, Twin Cities Campus, Graduate School, College of Education and Human Development, Department of Postsecondary Teaching and Learning, Minneapolis, MN 55455-0213. Offers multicultural college teaching and learning (MA). *Faculty:* 20 full-time (11 women). *Students:* 6 full-time (2 women), 8 part-time (5 women); includes 9 minority (4 Black or African American, non-Hispanic/Latino; 1 American Indian or Alaska Native, non-Hispanic/Latino; 1 Asian, non-Hispanic/Latino; 3 Hispanic/Latino), 1 international. Average age 35. 19 applicants, 84% accepted, 10 enrolled. In 2013, 7 master's awarded. Application fee: $75 ($95 for international students). *Financial support:* In 2013–14, 5 research assistantships (averaging $8,153 per year), 3 teaching assistantships (averaging $9,058 per year) were awarded. *Faculty research:* Diversity and equity in postsecondary education, teaching and learning in higher education, instructional design for diverse learning environments, developmental education, multicultural education, first-generation college students. *Total annual research expenditures:* $148,917. *Unit head:* Dr. Amy Lee, Chair, 612-625-0884, E-mail: amylee@umn.edu. *Application contact:* Dr. Jennifer Engler, Assistant Dean for Student Services, 612-626-2887, Fax: 612-626-7496, E-mail: engle009@umn.edu.
Website: http://www.cehd.umn.edu/PSTL/.

University of Mississippi, Graduate School, School of Education, Department of Leadership and Counselor Education, Oxford, MS 38677. Offers counselor education (M Ed, PhD); educational leadership (M Ed, PhD, Ed S); higher education/student personnel (MA, PhD); play therapy (Ed S). *Accreditation:* ACA; NCATE. *Faculty:* 13 full-time (6 women), 9 part-time/adjunct (6 women). *Students:* 155 full-time (123 women), 181 part-time (127 women); includes 136 minority (116 Black or African American, non-Hispanic/Latino; 3 American Indian or Alaska Native, non-Hispanic/Latino; 8 Hispanic/Latino; 9 Two or more races, non-Hispanic/Latino), 6 international. In 2013, 104 master's, 9 doctorates awarded. *Degree requirements:* For doctorate, thesis/dissertation. *Entrance requirements:* For master's, GRE General Test, minimum GPA of 3.0; for doctorate, GRE General Test. Additional exam requirements/recommendations for international students: Required—TOEFL. *Application deadline:* For fall admission, 4/1 for domestic students; for spring admission, 10/1 for domestic students. Applications are processed on a rolling basis. Application fee: $40. Electronic applications accepted. *Financial support:* Scholarships/grants available. Financial award application deadline: 3/1; financial award applicants required to submit FAFSA. *Unit head:* Dr. Timothy Letzring, Chair, 662-915-7069, Fax: 662-915-7230. *Application contact:* Dr. Christy M. Wyandt, Associate Dean, 662-915-7474, Fax: 662-915-7577, E-mail: cwyandt@olemiss.edu.
Website: http://education.olemiss.edu/dco/leadership_counselor_education.html.

University of Missouri, Graduate School, College of Education, Department of Educational Leadership and Policy Analysis, Columbia, MO 65211. Offers education administration (M Ed, MA, Ed D, PhD, Ed S); higher and adult education (M Ed, MA, Ed D, PhD, Ed S). Part-time programs available. *Faculty:* 15 full-time (8 women), 5 part-time/adjunct (4 women). *Students:* 118 full-time (67 women), 273 part-time (158 women); includes 52 minority (30 Black or African American, non-Hispanic/Latino; 1 American Indian or Alaska Native, non-Hispanic/Latino; 4 Asian, non-Hispanic/Latino; 10 Hispanic/Latino; 7 Two or more races, non-Hispanic/Latino), 18 international. Average age 37. 233 applicants, 62% accepted, 120 enrolled. In 2013, 35 master's, 70 doctorates, 31 other advanced degrees awarded. *Degree requirements:* For doctorate, variable foreign language requirement, comprehensive exam (for some programs), thesis/dissertation. *Entrance requirements:* For master's, doctorate, and Ed S, minimum GPA of 3.0. Additional exam requirements/recommendations for international students: Required—TOEFL (minimum score 500 paper-based; 61 iBT), IELTS (minimum score 5.5). *Application deadline:* For fall admission, 1/15 priority date for domestic and international students; for winter admission, 9/15 priority date for domestic and international students; for spring admission, 10/15 for domestic students. Applications are processed on a rolling basis. Application fee: $55 ($75 for international students). Electronic applications accepted. *Financial support:* Fellowships with full tuition reimbursements, research assistantships with full tuition reimbursements, teaching assistantships with full tuition reimbursements, institutionally sponsored loans, scholarships/grants, health care benefits, and unspecified assistantships available. *Faculty research:* Administrative communication and behavior, middle schools leadership, administration of special education. *Unit head:* Dr. Jeni Hart, Associate Division Director, 573-882-4225, E-mail: hartjl@missouri.edu. *Application contact:* Betty Kissane, Office Support Assistant IV, 573-882-8221, E-mail: kissaneb@missouri.edu.
Website: http://elpa.missouri.edu/.

University of Missouri–Kansas City, School of Education, Kansas City, MO 64110-2499. Offers administration (Ed D); counseling and guidance (MA, Ed S), including mental health counseling (Ed S), school counseling (Ed S); counseling psychology (PhD); curriculum and instruction (MA, Ed S), including language and literacy (Ed S); education (PhD), including higher education administration, PK-12 education administration; educational administration (MA, Ed S), including advanced principal (Ed S), beginning principal (Ed S), district-level administration (Ed S); reading education (MA, Ed S); special education (MA). PhD in education offered through the School of Graduate Studies. *Accreditation:* NCATE. Part-time and evening/weekend programs available. *Faculty:* 44 full-time (34 women), 60 part-time/adjunct (45 women). *Students:* 206 full-time (145 women), 394 part-time (291 women); includes 154 minority (99 Black or African American, non-Hispanic/Latino; 13 Asian, non-Hispanic/Latino; 30 Hispanic/Latino; 1 Native Hawaiian or other Pacific Islander, non-Hispanic/Latino; 11 Two or more races, non-Hispanic/Latino), 16 international. Average age 32. 401 applicants, 48% accepted, 188 enrolled. In 2013, 156 master's, 9 doctorates, 24 other advanced degrees awarded. *Degree requirements:* For doctorate, thesis/dissertation, internship, practicum. *Entrance requirements:* For master's, GRE, minimum GPA of 2.75, 2 letters of reference, written statement of purpose; for doctorate, GRE, minimum GPA of 3.0; for Ed S, minimum GPA of 3.0. Additional exam requirements/recommendations for international students: Required—TOEFL (minimum score 550 paper-based; 80 iBT). *Application deadline:* For fall admission, 4/1 priority date for domestic and international students; for spring admission, 11/1 priority date for domestic and international students. Applications are processed on a rolling basis. Application fee: $45 ($50 for international students). *Expenses:* Tuition, state resident: full-time $6073; part-time $337.40 per credit hour. Tuition, nonresident: full-time $15,680; part-time $871.10 per credit hour. *Required fees:* $97.59 per credit hour. Full-time tuition and fees vary according to program. *Financial support:* In 2013–14, 12 research assistantships with partial tuition reimbursements (averaging $11,140 per year) were awarded; career-related internships or fieldwork, Federal Work-Study, institutionally sponsored loans, and tuition waivers (full and partial) also available. Support available to part-time students. Financial award application deadline: 3/1; financial award applicants required to submit FAFSA. *Faculty research:* Urban education, inquiry-based field study, theories of counseling and psychotherapy, school literacy, educational technology. *Unit head:* Dr. Wanda Blanchett, Dean, 816-235-2234, Fax: 816-235-5270, E-mail: education@umkc.edu. *Application contact:* Erica Hernandez-Scott, Student Recruiter, 816-235-1295, Fax: 816-235-5270, E-mail: hernandeze@umkc.edu.
Website: http://education.umkc.edu.

University of Missouri–St. Louis, College of Education, Division of Educational Leadership and Policy Studies, St. Louis, MO 63121. Offers adult and higher education (M Ed), including adult education, higher education; educational administration (M Ed, Ed S), including community education (M Ed), elementary education (M Ed), secondary education (M Ed); institutional research (Certificate). *Accreditation:* NCATE. Part-time and evening/weekend programs available. *Faculty:* 13 full-time (8 women), 5 part-time/adjunct (2 women). *Students:* 17 full-time (13 women), 154 part-time (114 women); includes 77 minority (75 Black or African American, non-Hispanic/Latino; 1 Asian, non-Hispanic/Latino; 1 Hispanic/Latino), 7 international. Average age 35. 120 applicants, 68% accepted, 40 enrolled. In 2013, 63 master's, 28 Certificates awarded. *Degree requirements:* For master's, comprehensive exam (for some programs); for other advanced degree, comprehensive exam (for some programs), thesis or alternative. *Entrance requirements:* Additional exam requirements/recommendations for international students: Recommended—TOEFL (minimum score 550 paper-based; 79 iBT), IELTS (minimum score 6.5). *Application deadline:* For fall admission, 7/1 priority date for domestic and international students; for spring admission, 12/1 priority date for domestic and international students. Applications are processed on a rolling basis. Application fee: $50 ($40 for international students). Electronic applications accepted. *Expenses:* Tuition, state resident: full-time $7364; part-time $409.10 per credit hour. Tuition, nonresident: full-time $19,162; part-time $1008.50 per credit hour. *Financial support:* In 2013–14, 1 research assistantship with full and partial tuition reimbursement (averaging $12,000 per year), teaching assistantships with full and partial tuition reimbursements (averaging $8,470 per year) were awarded. Financial award application deadline: 4/1; financial award applicants required to submit FAFSA. *Faculty research:* Educational policy research; philosophy of education; higher, adult, and vocational education; school initiatives, change, and reform. *Unit head:* Dr. E. Kathleen Sullivan Brown, Chair, 514-516-5944. *Application contact:* 314-516-5458, Fax: 314-516-6996, E-mail: gradadm@umsl.edu.
Website: http://coe.umsl.edu/web/divisions/elaps/index.html.

University of Missouri–St. Louis, College of Education, Interdisciplinary Doctoral Programs, St. Louis, MO 63121. Offers adult and higher education (Ed D); counseling

(PhD); counselor education (Ed D); educational administration (Ed D); educational leadership and policy studies (PhD); educational psychology (PhD); teaching-learning processes (Ed D, PhD). *Faculty:* 72 full-time (33 women). *Students:* 58 full-time (46 women), 240 part-time (154 women); includes 106 minority (86 Black or African American, non-Hispanic/Latino; 4 American Indian or Alaska Native, non-Hispanic/Latino; 6 Asian, non-Hispanic/Latino; 8 Hispanic/Latino; 2 Two or more races, non-Hispanic/Latino), 9 international. Average age 42. 67 applicants, 58% accepted, 24 enrolled. In 2013, 24 doctorates awarded. *Degree requirements:* For doctorate, thesis/dissertation. *Entrance requirements:* For doctorate, GRE General Test, 3 letters of recommendation; personal interview. Additional exam requirements/recommendations for international students: Recommended—TOEFL (minimum score 550 paper-based; 79 iBT), IELTS (minimum score 6.5). *Application deadline:* For fall admission, 3/1 for domestic and international students; for spring admission, 10/1 for domestic and international students. Application fee: $50 ($40 for international students). Electronic applications accepted. *Expenses:* Tuition, state resident: full-time $7364; part-time $409.10 per credit hour. Tuition, nonresident: full-time $19,162; part-time $1008.50 per credit hour. *Financial support:* In 2013–14, 13 research assistantships (averaging $12,240 per year), 9 teaching assistantships (averaging $12,240 per year) were awarded. Financial award application deadline: 4/1; financial award applicants required to submit FAFSA. *Faculty research:* Higher education law and policy, gender and higher education, student retention, lifelong learning orientation, school counselor's role in violence prevention. *Unit head:* Dr. Kathleen Haywood, Director of Graduate Studies, 314-516-5483, Fax: 314-516-5227, E-mail: kathleen_haywood@umsl.edu. *Application contact:* 314-516-5458, Fax: 314-516-6996, E-mail: gradadm@umsl.edu.

University of Nevada, Las Vegas, Graduate College, College of Education, Department of Educational Psychology and Higher Education, Las Vegas, NV 89154-3002. Offers educational leadership (Ed D, PhD); educational psychology (MS, PhD, Ed S), including learning and technology (PhD); higher education (M Ed, PhD, Certificate); PhD/JD. Part-time and evening/weekend programs available. *Faculty:* 19 full-time (12 women), 4 part-time/adjunct (2 women). *Students:* 56 full-time (44 women), 79 part-time (58 women); includes 40 minority (12 Black or African American, non-Hispanic/Latino; 1 American Indian or Alaska Native, non-Hispanic/Latino; 7 Asian, non-Hispanic/Latino; 10 Hispanic/Latino; 2 Native Hawaiian or other Pacific Islander, non-Hispanic/Latino; 8 Two or more races, non-Hispanic/Latino), 2 international. Average age 35. 67 applicants, 64% accepted, 28 enrolled. In 2013, 22 master's, 36 doctorates, 10 other advanced degrees awarded. *Degree requirements:* For master's, comprehensive exam (for some programs), thesis (for some programs); for doctorate, comprehensive exam (for some programs), thesis/dissertation; for other advanced degree, comprehensive exam, thesis. *Entrance requirements:* For master's, GMAT or GRE General Test; for doctorate, GRE General Test, writing exam; for other advanced degree, GRE General Test. Additional exam requirements/recommendations for international students: Required—TOEFL (minimum score 550 paper-based; 80 iBT), IELTS (minimum score 7). *Application deadline:* For fall admission, 4/15 for domestic students, 5/1 for international students; for spring admission, 10/1 for international students. Application fee: $60 ($95 for international students). Electronic applications accepted. *Expenses:* Tuition, state resident: full-time $4752; part-time $264 per credit. Tuition, nonresident: full-time $18,662; part-time $554.50 per credit. *International tuition:* $18,952 full-time. *Required fees:* $532; $12 per credit. $266 per semester. One-time fee: $35. Tuition and fees vary according to course load and program. *Financial support:* In 2013–14, 48 students received support, including 39 research assistantships with partial tuition reimbursements available (averaging $11,046 per year), 9 teaching assistantships with partial tuition reimbursements available (averaging $10,922 per year); institutionally sponsored loans, scholarships/grants, health care benefits, and unspecified assistantships also available. Financial award application deadline: 3/1. *Faculty research:* Innovation and change in educational settings; educational policy, finance, and marketing; psycho-educational assessment; student retention, persistence, development, language, and culture; statistical modeling, program evaluation, qualitative and quantitative research methods. *Total annual research expenditures:* $158,645. *Unit head:* Dr. LeAnn Putney, Chair/Professor, 702-895-4879, Fax: 702-895-3492, E-mail: leann.putney@unlv.edu. *Application contact:* Graduate College Admissions Evaluator, 702-895-3320, Fax: 702-895-4180, E-mail: gradcollege@unlv.edu.
Website: http://education.unlv.edu/ephe/.

University of New Hampshire, Graduate School, Interdisciplinary Programs, Program in College Teaching, Durham, NH 03824. Offers MST, Postbaccalaureate Certificate. Program offered in summer only. Part-time programs available. *Students:* 1 applicant. In 2013, 2 master's, 1 other advanced degree awarded. *Entrance requirements:* Additional exam requirements/recommendations for international students: Required—TOEFL (minimum score 550 paper-based; 80 iBT). *Application deadline:* For fall admission, 6/1 priority date for domestic students, 4/1 for international students; for spring admission, 12/1 for domestic students. Applications are processed on a rolling basis. Application fee: $65. Electronic applications accepted. *Expenses:* Tuition, state resident: full-time $13,500; part-time $750 per credit hour. Tuition, nonresident: full-time $26,200; part-time $1100 per credit hour. *Required fees:* $1741; $435.25 per term. Tuition and fees vary according to course level, course load, campus/location and program. *Financial support:* Fellowships, research assistantships, and teaching assistantships available. Financial award application deadline: 2/15. *Unit head:* Dr. Harry J. Richards, Dean, 603-862-3005, Fax: 603-862-0275, E-mail: harry.richards@unh.edu. *Application contact:* Sharon Andrews, Administrative Assistant, 603-862-3005, E-mail: college.teaching@unh.edu.
Website: http://www.unh.edu/teaching-excellence/Academic_prog_in_coll_teach/index.html.

University of New Haven, Graduate School, College of Business, Program in Sports Management, West Haven, CT 06516-1916. Offers collegiate athletic administration (MS); facility management (MS); management of sports industries (Certificate); sports management (MS). Part-time and evening/weekend programs available. *Students:* 18 full-time (8 women), 8 part-time (0 women); includes 2 minority (1 Black or African American, non-Hispanic/Latino; 1 Asian, non-Hispanic/Latino), 8 international. 24 applicants, 83% accepted, 10 enrolled. In 2013, 11 master's awarded. *Entrance requirements:* For master's, GMAT. Additional exam requirements/recommendations for international students: Required—TOEFL (minimum score 80 iBT), IELTS, PTE (minimum score 53). *Application deadline:* For fall admission, 5/31 for international students; for winter admission, 10/15 for international students; for spring admission, 1/15 for international students. Applications are processed on a rolling basis. Application fee: $75. Electronic applications accepted. Application fee is waived when completed online. *Expenses: Tuition:* Full-time $21,600; part-time $800 per credit hour. *Required fees:* $45 per trimester. *Financial support:* Research assistantships with partial tuition reimbursements, teaching assistantships with partial tuition reimbursements, career-related internships or fieldwork, Federal Work-Study, scholarships/grants, and unspecified assistantships available. Support available to part-time students. Financial award applicants required to submit FAFSA. *Unit head:* Prof. Gil B. Fried, Chair, 203-932-7081, E-mail: gfried@newhaven.edu. *Application contact:* Eloise Gormley, Director of Graduate Admissions, 203-932-7440, E-mail: gradinfo@newhaven.edu.
Website: http://www.newhaven.edu/6851/.

University of New Mexico, School of Medicine, Program in Biomedical Sciences, Program in University Science Teaching, Albuquerque, NM 87131-2039. Offers Certificate. In 2013, 1 Certificate awarded. *Unit head:* Dr. Sherry Rogers, Program Director, 505-272-0007, E-mail: srogers@salud.unm.edu. *Application contact:* Dr. Angela Wandinger-Ness, Coordinator, 505-272-1459, Fax: 505-272-8738, E-mail: awandinger@salud.unm.edu.

The University of North Carolina at Greensboro, Graduate School, School of Education, Department of Curriculum and Instruction, Program in Curriculum and Teaching, Greensboro, NC 27412-5001. Offers higher education (PhD); teacher education and development (PhD). *Accreditation:* NCATE. *Degree requirements:* For doctorate, comprehensive exam, thesis/dissertation. *Entrance requirements:* For doctorate, GRE General Test. Additional exam requirements/recommendations for international students: Required—TOEFL. Electronic applications accepted.

University of Northern Colorado, Graduate School, College of Education and Behavioral Sciences, Department of Leadership, Policy and Development: Higher Education and P-12 Education, Program in Higher Education and Student Affairs Leadership, Greeley, CO 80639. Offers PhD. Part-time programs available. *Entrance requirements:* For doctorate, GRE General Test, transcripts, 3 letters of recommendation. Electronic applications accepted.

University of Northern Iowa, Graduate College, College of Education, Department of Educational Leadership and Postsecondary Education, MAE Program in Postsecondary Education: Student Affairs, Cedar Falls, IA 50614. Offers MAE. *Students:* 20 full-time (14 women), 7 part-time (6 women); includes 4 minority (1 Black or African American, non-Hispanic/Latino; 1 Asian, non-Hispanic/Latino; 2 Hispanic/Latino). 66 applicants, 42% accepted, 13 enrolled. In 2013, 17 master's awarded. *Degree requirements:* For master's, comprehensive exam, thesis or alternative. *Entrance requirements:* For master's, minimum GPA of 3.0. Additional exam requirements/recommendations for international students: Required—TOEFL (minimum score 500 paper-based; 61 iBT). *Application deadline:* For fall admission, 8/1 priority date for domestic students. Applications are processed on a rolling basis. Application fee: $50 ($70 for international students). Electronic applications accepted. *Financial support:* Career-related internships or fieldwork, Federal Work-Study, scholarships/grants, and tuition waivers (full) available. Financial award application deadline: 2/1. *Unit head:* Dr. Michael Waggoner, Coordinator, 319-273-2605, Fax: 319-273-5175, E-mail: mike.waggoner@uni.edu. *Application contact:* Laurie S. Russell, Record Analyst, 319-273-2623, Fax: 319-273-2885, E-mail: laurie.russell@uni.edu.
Website: http://www.uni.edu/coe/departments/educational-leadership-postsecondary-education/postsecondary-education.

University of North Texas, Robert B. Toulouse School of Graduate Studies, Denton, TN 76203-5017. Offers accounting (MS, PhD); applied anthropology (MA, MS); applied behavior analysis (Certificate); applied technology and performance improvement (M Ed, MS, PhD); art education (MA, PhD); art history (MA); art museum education (Certificate); arts leadership (Certificate); audiology (Au D); behavior analysis (MS); biochemistry and molecular biology (MS, PhD); biology (MA, MS, PhD); business (PhD); business computer information systems (PhD); chemistry (MS, PhD); clinical psychology (PhD); communication studies (MA, MS); computer engineering (MS); computer science (MS); computer science and engineering (PhD); counseling (M Ed, MS, PhD), including clinical mental health counseling (MS), college and university counseling (M Ed, MS), elementary school counseling (M Ed, MS), secondary school counseling (M Ed, MS); counseling psychology (PhD); creative writing (MA); criminal justice (MS); curriculum and instruction (M Ed, PhD), including curriculum studies (PhD), early childhood studies (PhD), language and literacy studies (PhD); decision sciences (MBA); design (MA, MFA), including fashion design (MFA), innovation studies, interior design (MFA); early childhood studies (MS); economics (MS); educational leadership (M Ed, Ed D, PhD); educational psychology (MS), including family studies, gifted and talented (MS, PhD), human development, learning and cognition, research, measurement and evaluation; educational research (PhD), including gifted and talented (MS, PhD), human development and family studies, psychological aspects of sports and exercise, research, measurement and statistics; electrical engineering (MS); emergency management (MPA); engineering systems (MS); English (MA, PhD); environmental science (MS, PhD); experimental psychology (PhD); finance (MBA, MS, PhD); financial management (MPA); French (MA); health psychology and behavioral medicine (PhD); health services management (MBA); higher education (M Ed, Ed D, PhD); history (MA, MS, PhD), including European history (PhD), military history (PhD), United States history (PhD); hospitality management (MS); human resources management (MPA); information science (MS, PhD); information technologies (MBA); information technology and decision sciences (MS); interdisciplinary studies (MA, MS); international sustainable tourism (MS); jazz studies (MM); journalism (MA, MJ, Graduate Certificate), including interactive and virtual digital communication (Graduate Certificate), narrative journalism (Graduate Certificate), public relations (Graduate Certificate); kinesiology (MS); learning technologies (MS, PhD); library science (MS); local government management (MPA); logistics and supply chain management (MBA, PhD); long-term care, senior housing, and aging services (MA, MS); management science (PhD); marketing (MBA, PhD); materials science and engineering (MS, PhD); mathematics (MA, PhD); merchandising (MS); music (MA, MM Ed, PhD), including ethnomusicology (MA), music education (MM Ed, PhD), music theory (MA, PhD), musicology (MA, PhD), performance (MA); nonprofit management (MPA); operations and supply chain management (MBA); performance (MM, DMA); philosophy (MA, PhD); physics (MS, PhD); political science (MA, MS, PhD); public administration and management (PhD), including emergency management, nonprofit management, public financial management, urban management; radio, television and film (MA, MFA); recreation, event and sport management (MS); rehabilitation counseling (MS, Certificate); sociology (MA, MS, PhD); Spanish (MA); special education (M Ed, PhD), including autism intervention (PhD), emotional/behavioral disorders (PhD), mild/moderate disabilities (PhD); speech-language pathology (MA, MS); strategic management (MBA); studio art (MFA); taxation (MS); teaching (M Ed); MBA/MS; MS/MPH; MSES/MBA. Part-time and evening/weekend programs available. Postbaccalaureate distance learning degree programs offered. *Faculty:* 661 full-time (213 women), 240 part-time/adjunct (144 women). *Students:* 3,106 full-time (1,620 women), 3,543 part-time (2,221 women); includes 1,740 minority (533 Black or African American, non-Hispanic/Latino; 15 American Indian or Alaska Native, non-Hispanic/Latino; 286 Asian, non-Hispanic/Latino; 746 Hispanic/Latino; 3 Native Hawaiian or other Pacific Islander, non-Hispanic/Latino; 157 Two or more races, non-Hispanic/Latino), 1,145 international. Average age 32. 6,289 applicants, 43% accepted, 1751 enrolled. In 2013, 1,778 master's, 239 doctorates, 10 other advanced degrees awarded. Terminal master's awarded for partial completion of doctoral program. *Degree requirements:* For master's, variable foreign language requirement, comprehensive exam (for some programs), thesis (for some programs); for doctorate, variable foreign language requirement, comprehensive exam (for some programs), thesis/dissertation; for other advanced degree, variable foreign language requirement, comprehensive exam (for some programs). *Entrance requirements:* For master's and doctorate, GRE, GMAT. Additional exam requirements/recommendations for international students: Required—TOEFL (minimum score 550 paper-based; 79 iBT). *Application deadline:* For fall admission, 7/15 for domestic students, 3/15 for international students; for spring admission, 11/15 for domestic students, 9/15 for

international students; for summer admission, 5/1 for domestic students. Applications are processed on a rolling basis. Application fee: $60. Electronic applications accepted. *Financial support:* Fellowships with partial tuition reimbursements, research assistantships with partial tuition reimbursements, teaching assistantships, career-related internships or fieldwork, Federal Work-Study, institutionally sponsored loans, scholarships/grants, health care benefits, and library assistantships available. Support available to part-time students. Financial award applicants required to submit FAFSA. *Unit head:* Mark Wardell, Dean, 940-565-2383, E-mail: mark.wardell@unt.edu. *Application contact:* Toulouse School of Graduate Studies, 940-565-2383, Fax: 940-565-2141, E-mail: gradsch@unt.edu.
Website: http://tsgs.unt.edu/.

University of Oklahoma, Jeannine Rainbolt College of Education, Department of Educational Leadership and Policy Studies, Program in Adult and Higher Education, Norman, OK 73019. Offers M Ed, PhD. *Accreditation:* NCATE. Part-time and evening/weekend programs available. *Students:* 140 full-time (72 women), 74 part-time (49 women); includes 65 minority (31 Black or African American, non-Hispanic/Latino; 13 American Indian or Alaska Native, non-Hispanic/Latino; 2 Asian, non-Hispanic/Latino; 10 Hispanic/Latino; 9 Two or more races, non-Hispanic/Latino), 5 international. Average age 29. 122 applicants, 71% accepted, 62 enrolled. In 2013, 69 master's, 3 doctorates awarded. *Degree requirements:* For master's, comprehensive exam; for doctorate, variable foreign language requirement, thesis/dissertation. *Entrance requirements:* For master's, minimum GPA of 3.0 in last 60 hours of undergraduate course work; for doctorate, GRE General Test, resume, 3 letters of reference, scholarly writing sample. Additional exam requirements/recommendations for international students: Required—TOEFL (minimum score 79 iBT). *Application deadline:* For fall admission, 2/1 for domestic and international students; for spring admission, 10/1 for domestic and international students; for summer admission, 4/1 for domestic and international students. Application fee: $50 ($100 for international students). Electronic applications accepted. *Expenses:* Tuition, state resident: full-time $4205; part-time $175.20 per credit hour. Tuition, nonresident: full-time $16,205; part-time $675.20 per credit hour. *Required fees:* $2745; $103.85 per credit hour. $126.50 per semester. *Financial support:* In 2013–14, 179 students received support. Unspecified assistantships available. Financial award application deadline: 6/1; financial award applicants required to submit FAFSA. *Faculty research:* Student-athlete development, equity in higher education, e-learning, student identity, diversity issues. *Unit head:* Dr. David Tan, Chair, 405-325-5986, Fax: 405-325-2403, E-mail: dtan@ou.edu. *Application contact:* Geri Evans, Graduate Programs Representative, 405-325-5978, Fax: 405-325-2403, E-mail: gevans@ou.edu.
Website: http://www.ou.edu/education/elps.

University of Oklahoma, Jeannine Rainbolt College of Education, Department of General Education, Norman, OK 73019. Offers college teaching (Graduate Certificate). Part-time and evening/weekend programs available. *Students:* 22 full-time (19 women), 8 part-time (4 women); includes 8 minority (2 Black or African American, non-Hispanic/Latino; 1 American Indian or Alaska Native, non-Hispanic/Latino; 1 Asian, non-Hispanic/Latino; 1 Hispanic/Latino; 3 Two or more races, non-Hispanic/Latino), 1 international. Average age 29. 19 applicants, 100% accepted, 18 enrolled. *Entrance requirements:* Additional exam requirements/recommendations for international students: Required—TOEFL (minimum score 79 iBT). *Application deadline:* For fall admission, 4/1 for domestic and international students; for spring admission, 9/1 for domestic and international students; for summer admission, 2/1 for domestic and international students. Application fee: $50 ($100 for international students). Electronic applications accepted. *Expenses:* Tuition, state resident: full-time $4205; part-time $175.20 per credit hour. Tuition, nonresident: full-time $16,205; part-time $675.20 per credit hour. *Required fees:* $2745; $103.85 per credit hour. $126.50 per semester. *Financial support:* Application deadline: 6/1; applicants required to submit FAFSA. *Unit head:* Dr. Gregg Garn, Dean, 405-325-1081, Fax: 405-325-7390, E-mail: garn@ou.edu. *Application contact:* Dr. Sherry Cox, Assistant Dean, 405-325-2238, Fax: 405-325-7620, E-mail: scox@ou.edu.
Website: http://education.ou.edu.

University of Pennsylvania, Graduate School of Education, Division of Higher Education, Executive Doctorate Program in Higher Education Management, Philadelphia, PA 19104. Offers Ed D. *Students:* 26 full-time (11 women), 20 part-time (11 women); includes 20 minority (15 Black or African American, non-Hispanic/Latino; 1 American Indian or Alaska Native, non-Hispanic/Latino; 3 Hispanic/Latino; 1 Two or more races, non-Hispanic/Latino), 2 international. 97 applicants, 29% accepted, 28 enrolled. In 2013, 21 doctorates awarded. *Unit head:* Dr. Andrew Porter, Dean, 215-898-7014. *Application contact:* 215-898-6415, Fax: 215-746-6884, E-mail: admissions@gse.upenn.edu.
Website: http://www.gse.upenn.edu/execdoc.

University of Pennsylvania, Graduate School of Education, Division of Higher Education, Program in Higher Education, Philadelphia, PA 19104. Offers MS Ed, Ed D, PhD. *Students:* 66 full-time (45 women), 28 part-time (19 women); includes 33 minority (14 Black or African American, non-Hispanic/Latino; 8 Asian, non-Hispanic/Latino; 7 Hispanic/Latino; 4 Two or more races, non-Hispanic/Latino), 6 international. 268 applicants, 41% accepted, 59 enrolled. In 2013, 53 master's, 5 doctorates awarded. *Degree requirements:* For doctorate, thesis/dissertation (for some programs). *Financial support:* Research assistantships available. *Unit head:* Dr. Andrew Porter, Dean, 215-898-7014. *Application contact:* 215-898-6415, Fax: 215-746-6884, E-mail: admissions@gse.upenn.edu.
Website: http://www.gse.upenn.edu.

University of Phoenix–Bay Area Campus, College of Education, San Jose, CA 95134-1805. Offers administration and supervision (MA Ed); adult education and training (MA Ed); early childhood education (MA Ed); education (Ed S); educational leadership (Ed D); elementary teacher education (MA Ed); higher education administration (PhD); secondary teacher education (MA Ed); special education (MA Ed); teacher leadership (MA Ed). Evening/weekend programs available. Postbaccalaureate distance learning degree programs offered (no on-campus study). *Degree requirements:* For master's, thesis (for some programs). *Entrance requirements:* For master's, minimum undergraduate GPA of 2.5, 3 years of work experience. Additional exam requirements/recommendations for international students: Required—TOEFL (minimum score 550 paper-based; 79 iBT). Electronic applications accepted.

University of Phoenix–Madison Campus, College of Education, Madison, WI 53718-2416. Offers education (Ed S); educational leadership (Ed D); educational leadership: curriculum and instruction (Ed D); higher education administration (PhD).

University of Phoenix–Online Campus, School of Advanced Studies, Phoenix, AZ 85034-7209. Offers business administration (DBA); education (Ed S); educational leadership (Ed D), including curriculum and instruction, education technology, educational leadership; health administration (DHA); higher education administration (PhD); industrial/organizational psychology (PhD); nursing (PhD); organizational leadership (DM), including information systems and technology, organizational leadership. Evening/weekend programs available. Postbaccalaureate distance learning degree programs offered. *Degree requirements:* For doctorate, thesis/dissertation. *Entrance requirements:* Additional exam requirements/recommendations for international students: Required—TOEFL, TOEIC (Test of English as an International Communication), Berlitz Online English Proficiency Exam, PTE, or IELTS. Electronic applications accepted. *Expenses:* Contact institution.

University of Phoenix–Washington D.C. Campus, College of Education, Washington, DC 20001. Offers administration and supervision (MA Ed); adult education and training (MA Ed); computer education (MA Ed); curriculum and instruction (MA Ed, Ed D); early childhood education (MA Ed); education (Ed S); educational leadership (Ed D); educational technology (Ed D); elementary teacher education (MA Ed); English and language arts education (MA Ed); English as a second language (MA Ed); higher education administration (PhD); mathematics education (MA Ed); secondary teacher education (MA Ed); special education (MA Ed); teacher leadership (MA Ed).

University of Pittsburgh, School of Education, Department of Administrative and Policy Studies, Program in Higher Education Management, Pittsburgh, PA 15260. Offers higher education (M Ed, Ed D, PhD). Part-time and evening/weekend programs available. *Students:* 34 full-time (23 women), 75 part-time (50 women); includes 16 minority (11 Black or African American, non-Hispanic/Latino; 1 Asian, non-Hispanic/Latino; 3 Hispanic/Latino; 1 Two or more races, non-Hispanic/Latino), 15 international. Average age 35. 60 applicants, 68% accepted, 23 enrolled. In 2013, 29 master's, 5 doctorates awarded. *Degree requirements:* For master's, thesis; for doctorate, thesis/dissertation. *Entrance requirements:* For doctorate, GRE General Test. Additional exam requirements/recommendations for international students: Required—TOEFL (minimum score 80 iBT). *Application deadline:* For fall admission, 2/1 priority date for domestic and international students; for spring admission, 11/1 priority date for domestic students, 7/1 priority date for international students. Applications are processed on a rolling basis. Application fee: $50. Electronic applications accepted. *Expenses:* Tuition, state resident: full-time $19,964; part-time $807 per credit. Tuition, nonresident: full-time $32,686; part-time $1337 per credit. *Required fees:* $740; $200. Tuition and fees vary according to program. *Financial support:* Fellowships, Federal Work-Study, institutionally sponsored loans, scholarships/grants, health care benefits, tuition waivers (partial), and unspecified assistantships available. Support available to part-time students. Financial award application deadline: 3/15; financial award applicants required to submit FAFSA. *Unit head:* Dr. Mary Margaret Kerr, Chair, 412-648-7205, Fax: 412-648-1784, E-mail: mmkerr@pitt.edu. *Application contact:* Norma Ann Yocco, Enrollment Manager, 412-648-2230, Fax: 412-648-1899, E-mail: soeinfo@pitt.edu.
Website: http://www.education.pitt.edu/.

University of Rochester, Margaret Warner Graduate School of Education and Human Development, Doctoral Programs in Education, Rochester, NY 14627. Offers counseling (Ed D); educational administration (Ed D); educational policy and theory (PhD); higher education (PhD); human development in educational context (PhD); teaching, curriculum, and change (PhD). *Expenses: Tuition:* Full-time $44,580; part-time $1394 per credit hour. *Required fees:* $492.

University of Rochester, Margaret Warner Graduate School of Education and Human Development, Master's Program in Higher Education, Rochester, NY 14627. Offers higher education (MS); higher education student affairs (MS). *Expenses: Tuition:* Full-time $44,580; part-time $1394 per credit hour. *Required fees:* $492.

University of St. Francis, College of Education, Joliet, IL 60435-6169. Offers educational leadership (MS, Ed D); elementary education (M Ed); higher education (MS); reading (MS); secondary education (M Ed), including English education, math education, science education, social studies education, visual arts education; special education (M Ed); teaching and learning (MS). *Accreditation:* NCATE. Part-time and evening/weekend programs available. Postbaccalaureate distance learning degree programs offered (no on-campus study). *Faculty:* 10 full-time (8 women), 34 part-time/adjunct (25 women). *Students:* 14 full-time (13 women), 250 part-time (183 women); includes 34 minority (20 Black or African American, non-Hispanic/Latino; 1 American Indian or Alaska Native, non-Hispanic/Latino; 13 Hispanic/Latino), 1 international. Average age 36. 133 applicants, 62% accepted, 71 enrolled. In 2013, 147 master's awarded. *Degree requirements:* For doctorate, thesis/dissertation. *Entrance requirements:* For doctorate, master's degree, IL Type 75 or Principal's endorsement, interview, minimum undergraduate GPA of 3.0, professional portfolio, letter of recommendation. Additional exam requirements/recommendations for international students: Required—TOEFL (minimum score 550 paper-based; 79 iBT), IELTS (minimum score 6.5). *Application deadline:* Applications are processed on a rolling basis. Application fee: $30. Electronic applications accepted. Application fee is waived when completed online. *Expenses:* Contact institution. *Financial support:* In 2013–14, 10 students received support. Scholarships/grants, tuition waivers (partial), and unspecified assistantships available. Support available to part-time students. Financial award applicants required to submit FAFSA. *Unit head:* Dr. John Gambro, Dean, 815-740-3829, Fax: 815-740-2264, E-mail: jgambro@stfrancis.edu. *Application contact:* Sandra Sloka, Director of Admissions for Graduate and Degree Completion Programs, 800-735-7500, Fax: 815-740-3431, E-mail: ssloka@stfrancis.edu.
Website: http://www.stfrancis.edu/academics/college-of-education/.

University of San Diego, School of Leadership and Education Sciences, Department of Leadership Studies, San Diego, CA 92110-2492. Offers higher education leadership (MA); leadership studies (MA, PhD); nonprofit leadership and management (MA, Certificate). Part-time and evening/weekend programs available. *Faculty:* 10 full-time (6 women), 25 part-time/adjunct (17 women). *Students:* 25 full-time (17 women), 193 part-time (134 women); includes 115 minority (13 Black or African American, non-Hispanic/Latino; 2 American Indian or Alaska Native, non-Hispanic/Latino; 22 Asian, non-Hispanic/Latino; 23 Hispanic/Latino; 18 Native Hawaiian or other Pacific Islander, non-Hispanic/Latino; 37 Two or more races, non-Hispanic/Latino), 16 international. Average age 35. 254 applicants, 58% accepted, 85 enrolled. In 2013, 63 master's, 11 doctorates awarded. *Degree requirements:* For master's, thesis (for some programs), international experience; for doctorate, comprehensive exam, thesis/dissertation, international experience. *Entrance requirements:* For master's, minimum GPA of 3.0, interview; for doctorate, GRE, master's degree, minimum GPA of 3.5 (recommended), interview, resume. Additional exam requirements/recommendations for international students: Required—TOEFL (minimum score 580 paper-based; 83 iBT), TWE. *Application deadline:* For fall admission, 12/1 for domestic and international students. Application fee: $45. Electronic applications accepted. *Expenses: Tuition:* Full-time $23,580; part-time $1310 per credit. *Required fees:* $350. *Financial support:* In 2013–14, 160 students received support. Career-related internships or fieldwork, Federal Work-Study, institutionally sponsored loans, unspecified assistantships, and stipends available. Support available to part-time students. Financial award application deadline: 4/1; financial award applicants required to submit FAFSA. *Faculty research:* Higher education administration policy and relations, organizational leadership, nonprofits and philanthropy, student affairs leadership. *Unit head:* Dr. Afsaneh Nahavandi, Graduate Program Director, 619-260-4181, E-mail: anahavandi@sandiego.edu. *Application contact:* Monica Mahon, Associate Director of Graduate Admissions, 619-260-4524, Fax: 619-260-4158, E-mail: grads@sandiego.edu.
Website: http://www.sandiego.edu/soles/departments/leadership-studies/.

University of South Carolina, The Graduate School, College of Education, Department of Educational Leadership and Policies, Program in Higher Education and Student Affairs, Columbia, SC 29208. Offers M Ed. *Accreditation:* NCATE. Part-time programs

available. *Degree requirements:* For master's, comprehensive exam, thesis (for some programs). *Entrance requirements:* For master's, GRE General Test or MAT, letters of reference. Electronic applications accepted. *Faculty research:* Minorities in higher education, community college transfer problem, federal role in educational research.

University of Southern California, Graduate School, Rossier School of Education, Doctor of Education Programs, Los Angeles, CA 90089. Offers educational psychology (Ed D); higher education administration (Ed D); K-12 leadership in urban school settings (Ed D); teacher education in multicultural societies (Ed D). Part-time and evening/weekend programs available. *Degree requirements:* For doctorate, thesis/dissertation. *Entrance requirements:* For doctorate, GRE. Additional exam requirements/recommendations for international students: Required—TOEFL (minimum score 100 iBT). Electronic applications accepted. *Faculty research:* Data-driven decision-making in K-12 schools and districts; examination of college and university leadership and management in U. S. and Asia; studies in facilitating student learning; organizational change and the role of leaders; leadership, diversity, learning and accountability.

University of Southern California, Graduate School, Rossier School of Education, Doctor of Philosophy in Education Programs, Los Angeles, CA 90089. Offers educational psychology (PhD); higher education administration and policy (PhD); K-12 policy and practice (PhD). *Degree requirements:* For doctorate, thesis/dissertation, 63 units; qualifying exam; dissertation proposal and defense. *Entrance requirements:* For doctorate, GRE. Additional exam requirements/recommendations for international students: Required—TOEFL (minimum score 100 iBT). Electronic applications accepted. *Faculty research:* Diversity in higher education, organizational change, educational psychology, policy and politics of educational reform, economics of education and education policy.

University of Southern Maine, College of Management and Human Service, School of Education and Human Development, Program in Adult Education, Portland, ME 04104-9300. Offers adult and higher education (MS); adult learning (CAS). *Accreditation:* Teacher Education Accreditation Council. Part-time and evening/weekend programs available. Postbaccalaureate distance learning degree programs offered (minimal on-campus study). *Faculty:* 3 full-time (1 woman), 2 part-time/adjunct (1 woman). *Students:* 4 full-time (3 women), 37 part-time (33 women); includes 1 minority (Hispanic/Latino). Average age 42. 16 applicants, 69% accepted, 9 enrolled. In 2013, 16 master's, 2 other advanced degrees awarded. *Degree requirements:* For master's and CAS, thesis or alternative. *Entrance requirements:* For master's, interview; for CAS, master's degree. Additional exam requirements/recommendations for international students: Required—TOEFL (minimum score 550 paper-based; 79 iBT). *Application deadline:* For fall admission, 5/1 priority date for domestic students; for spring admission, 10/15 priority date for domestic students. Applications are processed on a rolling basis. Application fee: $65. Electronic applications accepted. *Expenses:* Tuition, state resident: part-time $380 per credit. Tuition, nonresident: part-time $1026 per credit. Part-time tuition and fees vary according to program. *Financial support:* Research assistantships, career-related internships or fieldwork, Federal Work-Study, institutionally sponsored loans, scholarships/grants, and unspecified assistantships available. Support available to part-time students. Financial award application deadline: 3/1; financial award applicants required to submit FAFSA. *Faculty research:* Older learners, lifelong learning institutes, teaching and learning in later age. *Unit head:* Dr. E. Michael Brady, Program Coordinator, 207-780-5312, E-mail: mbrady@usm.maine.edu. *Application contact:* Mary Sloan, Assistant Dean of Graduate Studies and Director of Graduate Admissions, 207-780-4812, Fax: 207-780-4969, E-mail: gradstudies@usm.maine.edu.
Website: http://usm.maine.edu/adult-education.

University of Southern Mississippi, Graduate School, College of Education and Psychology, Department of Educational Studies and Research, Hattiesburg, MS 39406-0001. Offers adult education (Graduate Certificate); community college leadership (Graduate Certificate); counseling and personnel services (college) (M Ed); education (PhD, Ed S), including adult education, research, evaluation and statistics (PhD); education (Ed D), including educational administration, educational research; education: educational leadership and research (Ed S), including higher education administration; educational administration and supervision (M Ed); higher education administration (Ed D, PhD); institutional research (Graduate Certificate). *Faculty:* 7 full-time (1 woman), 5 part-time/adjunct (1 woman). *Students:* 32 full-time (21 women), 103 part-time (70 women); includes 44 minority (39 Black or African American, non-Hispanic/Latino; 2 Hispanic/Latino; 3 Two or more races, non-Hispanic/Latino), 4 international. Average age 36. 36 applicants, 72% accepted, 15 enrolled. In 2013, 18 master's, 9 doctorates, 7 other advanced degrees awarded. *Degree requirements:* For master's and other advanced degree, comprehensive exam, thesis (for some programs); for doctorate, comprehensive exam, thesis/dissertation. *Entrance requirements:* For master's, doctorate, and other advanced degree, GRE General Test, minimum GPA of 2.75. Additional exam requirements/recommendations for international students: Required—TOEFL. *Application deadline:* For fall admission, 2/1 for domestic students, 3/1 for international students. Applications are processed on a rolling basis. Application fee: $35. *Financial support:* Career-related internships or fieldwork, Federal Work-Study, and institutionally sponsored loans available. Financial award application deadline: 3/15; financial award applicants required to submit FAFSA. *Total annual research expenditures:* $88,500. *Unit head:* Dr. Thomas V. O'Brien, Chair, 601-266-6093, E-mail: thomas.obrien@usm.edu. *Application contact:* Shonna Breland, Manager of Graduate Admissions, 601-266-6563, Fax: 601-266-5138.
Website: http://www.usm.edu/cep/esr/.

University of South Florida, College of Education, Department of Adult, Career and Higher Education, Tampa, FL 33620-9951. Offers adult education (MA, Ed D, PhD, Ed S); career and technical education (MA); career and workforce education (PhD); higher education/community college teaching (MA, Ed D, PhD); vocational education (Ed S). Part-time programs available. Postbaccalaureate distance learning degree programs offered (minimal on-campus study). *Degree requirements:* For master's, comprehensive exam; for doctorate, comprehensive exam, thesis/dissertation, philosophies of inquiry; multiple research methods; for Ed S, comprehensive exam, thesis. *Entrance requirements:* For master's, minimum GPA of 3.0 in last 60 hours of course work; for doctorate and Ed S, GRE General Test, GRE Writing Test. Additional exam requirements/recommendations for international students: Required—TOEFL (minimum score 500 paper-based; 91 iBT). Electronic applications accepted. *Faculty research:* Community college leadership; integration of academic, career and technical education; competency-based education; continuing education administration; adult learning and development.

University of South Florida, University College/Distance Education, Tampa, FL 33620-9951. *Unit head:* Kathy Barnes, Interdisciplinary Programs Coordinator, 813-974-8031, Fax: 813-974-7061, E-mail: barnesk@usf.edu. *Application contact:* Karen Tylinski, Metro Initiatives, 813-974-9943, Fax: 813-974-7061, E-mail: ktylinsk@usf.edu.
Website: http://uc.usf.edu/.

The University of Texas at Arlington, Graduate School, College of Education and Health Professions, Department of Educational Leadership and Policy Studies, Arlington, TX 76019. Offers dual language (M Ed); education leadership and policy studies (PhD); higher education (M Ed); principal certification (M Ed). Part-time and evening/weekend programs available. Postbaccalaureate distance learning degree programs offered (no on-campus study). *Degree requirements:* For master's, 2 field-based practica; for doctorate, comprehensive exam, thesis/dissertation, 2 research-based practica. *Entrance requirements:* For master's, GRE, 3 references forms, minimum undergraduate GPA of 3.0 in the last 60 hours of course work; for doctorate, GRE, resume, statement of intent, 3 reference forms, applicable master's degree. *Faculty research:* Lived realities of students of color in K-16 contexts, K-16 faculty, K-16 policy and law, K-16 student access, K-16 student success.

The University of Texas at San Antonio, College of Education and Human Development, Department of Educational Leadership and Policy Studies, San Antonio, TX 78249-0617. Offers educational leadership (Ed D); educational leadership and policy studies (M Ed), including educational leadership, higher education administration. Part-time programs available. *Faculty:* 22 full-time (10 women), 16 part-time/adjunct (11 women). *Students:* 62 full-time (43 women), 265 part-time (189 women); includes 216 minority (22 Black or African American, non-Hispanic/Latino; 1 American Indian or Alaska Native, non-Hispanic/Latino; 4 Asian, non-Hispanic/Latino; 183 Hispanic/Latino; 6 Two or more races, non-Hispanic/Latino), 3 international. Average age 36. 129 applicants, 86% accepted, 69 enrolled. In 2013, 129 master's, 9 doctorates awarded. *Degree requirements:* For master's, comprehensive exam, thesis or alternative; for doctorate, comprehensive exam, thesis/dissertation. *Entrance requirements:* For master's, transcripts, statement of purpose, resume or curriculum vitae; for doctorate, GRE General Test, minimum GPA of 3.5 in a master's program, resume, three letters of recommendation, statement of purpose. Additional exam requirements/recommendations for international students: Required—TOEFL (minimum score 550 paper-based; 79 iBT), IELTS (minimum score 6.5). *Application deadline:* For fall admission, 7/1 for domestic students, 4/1 for international students; for spring admission, 11/1 for domestic students, 9/1 for international students. Application fee: $45 ($80 for international students). *Expenses:* Tuition, state resident: full-time $4671. Tuition, nonresident: full-time $8708. *International tuition:* $17,415 full-time. *Required fees:* $1924.60. Tuition and fees vary according to course load and degree level. *Financial support:* In 2013–14, 6 students received support, including 6 fellowships with full and partial tuition reimbursements available (averaging $40,000 per year). Financial award application deadline: 2/1. *Faculty research:* Urban and international school leadership, student success, college access, higher education policy, multiculturalism, minority student achievement. *Unit head:* Dr. Bruce G. Barnett, Department Chair, 210-458-5413, Fax: 210-458-5848, E-mail: bruce.barnett@utsa.edu. *Application contact:* Elisha Reynolds, Student Development Specialist, 210-458-6620, Fax: 210-458-5848, E-mail: elisha.reynolds@utsa.edu.
Website: http://education.utsa.edu/educational_leadership_and_policy_studies/.

University of the Incarnate Word, School of Graduate Studies and Research, Dreeben School of Education, Programs in Education, San Antonio, TX 78209-6397. Offers adult education (M Ed, MA); cross-cultural education (M Ed, MA); early childhood literacy (M Ed, MA); general education (M Ed, MA); higher education (PhD); instructional technology (M Ed, MA); international education and entrepreneurship (PhD); kinesiology (M Ed, MA); literacy (M Ed, MA); organizational leadership (PhD); organizational learning and learning (M Ed, MA); reading (M Ed, MA); special education (M Ed, MA); teacher leadership (M Ed, MA). Part-time and evening/weekend programs available. *Faculty:* 17 full-time (9 women), 6 part-time/adjunct (all women). *Students:* 23 full-time (13 women), 187 part-time (122 women); includes 114 minority (24 Black or African American, non-Hispanic/Latino; 1 American Indian or Alaska Native, non-Hispanic/Latino; 3 Asian, non-Hispanic/Latino; 85 Hispanic/Latino; 1 Two or more races, non-Hispanic/Latino), 30 international. Average age 41. 52 applicants, 67% accepted, 25 enrolled. In 2013, 12 master's, 14 doctorates awarded. *Degree requirements:* For master's, capstone; for doctorate, thesis/dissertation, qualifying exam. *Entrance requirements:* For master's, baccalaureate degree; minimum foundation GPA of 2.5; interview; for doctorate, master's degree; interview; supervised writing sample. Additional exam requirements/recommendations for international students: Required—TOEFL (minimum score 560 paper-based; 83 iBT). *Application deadline:* Applications are processed on a rolling basis. Application fee: $20. Electronic applications accepted. *Expenses: Tuition:* Part-time $815 per credit hour. *Required fees:* $86 per credit hour. One-time fee: $40 part-time. Tuition and fees vary according to degree level and program. *Financial support:* In 2013–14, 5 research assistantships were awarded; Federal Work-Study and scholarships/grants also available. Financial award applicants required to submit FAFSA. *Unit head:* Dr. Denise Staudt, Dean, Dreeben School of Education, 210-829-2762, E-mail: staudt@uiwtx.edu. *Application contact:* Andrea Cyterski-Acosta, Dean of Enrollment, 210-829-6005, Fax: 210-829-3921, E-mail: admis@uiwtx.edu.
Website: http://www.uiw.edu/education/index.htm.

The University of Toledo, College of Graduate Studies, College of Social Justice and Human Service, Department of School Psychology, Higher Education and Counselor Education, Toledo, OH 43606-3390. Offers counselor education (MA, PhD); higher education (ME, PhD, Certificate); school psychology (MA, Ed S). Part-time programs available. *Faculty:* 63. *Students:* 49 full-time (42 women), 174 part-time (111 women); includes 52 minority (35 Black or African American, non-Hispanic/Latino; 7 Asian, non-Hispanic/Latino; 10 Hispanic/Latino), 6 international. Average age 37. 103 applicants, 59% accepted, 42 enrolled. In 2013, 60 master's, 20 doctorates awarded. *Degree requirements:* For master's, comprehensive exam, thesis or alternative; for doctorate, comprehensive exam, thesis/dissertation; for other advanced degree, thesis optional. *Entrance requirements:* For master's, doctorate, and other advanced degree, minimum cumulative GPA of 2.7 for all previous academic work, letters of recommendation. Additional exam requirements/recommendations for international students: Required—TOEFL (minimum score 550 paper-based; 80 iBT). *Application deadline:* For fall admission, 1/15 priority date for domestic and international students. Applications are processed on a rolling basis. Application fee: $45 ($75 for international students). Electronic applications accepted. *Financial support:* In 2013–14, 1 research assistantship with full and partial tuition reimbursement (averaging $12,000 per year), 19 teaching assistantships with full and partial tuition reimbursements (averaging $9,841 per year) were awarded; career-related internships or fieldwork, Federal Work-Study, institutionally sponsored loans, scholarships/grants, tuition waivers (full and partial), unspecified assistantships, and administrative assistantships also available. *Unit head:* Dr. John Laux, Chair, 419-530-4705, E-mail: martin.laux@utoledo.edu. *Application contact:* Graduate School Office, 419-530-4723, Fax: 419-530-4724, E-mail: grdsch@utnet.utoledo.edu.
Website: http://www.utoledo.edu/csjhs/depts/sphece/index.html.

University of Utah, Graduate School, College of Education, Department of Educational Leadership and Policy, Salt Lake City, UT 84112. Offers educational leadership and policy (Ed D, PhD); K-12 administrative licensure (M Ed); K-12 teacher instructional leadership (M Ed); student affairs (M Ed); MPA/PhD. Part-time and evening/weekend programs available. *Faculty:* 10 full-time (7 women), 4 part-time/adjunct (3 women). *Students:* 55 full-time (38 women), 65 part-time (40 women); includes 33 minority (5 Black or African American, non-Hispanic/Latino; 1 American Indian or Alaska Native, non-Hispanic/Latino; 3 Asian, non-Hispanic/Latino; 21 Hispanic/Latino; 3 Two or more races, non-Hispanic/Latino), 3 international. Average age 35. 123 applicants, 45% accepted, 51 enrolled. In 2013, 33 master's, 5 doctorates awarded. *Degree requirements:* For master's, comprehensive exam (for some programs), internship; for

doctorate, thesis/dissertation, qualifying exam. *Entrance requirements:* For master's, minimum undergraduate GPA of 3.0, valid bachelor's degree, 3 years' teaching or leadership experience, Level 1 or 2 UT educator's license (for K-12 programs only); for doctorate, GRE General Test (taken with five years of applying), minimum undergraduate GPA of 3.0, valid master's degree. Additional exam requirements/recommendations for international students: Required—TOEFL (minimum score 500 paper-based). *Application deadline:* For fall and winter admission, 2/1 for domestic and international students; for summer admission, 1/15 for domestic and international students. Application fee: $55 ($65 for international students). Electronic applications accepted. *Expenses:* Tuition, state resident: full-time $5259. Tuition, nonresident: full-time $18,569. *Required fees:* $841. Tuition and fees vary according to course load. *Financial support:* In 2013–14, 86 students received support, including 7 fellowships (averaging $2,000 per year), research assistantships with full tuition reimbursements available (averaging $13,000 per year), 86 teaching assistantships with full tuition reimbursements available (averaging $13,000 per year); career-related internships or fieldwork, scholarships/grants, health care benefits, and unspecified assistantships also available. Financial award application deadline: 2/1. *Faculty research:* Education accountability, college student diversity, K-12 educational administration and school leadership, student affairs, higher education. *Total annual research expenditures:* $55,000. *Unit head:* Dr. Andrea Rorrer, Chair, 801-581-4207, Fax: 801-585-6756, E-mail: andrea.rorrer@utah.edu. *Application contact:* Marilynn S. Howard, Academic Coordinator, 801-581-6714, Fax: 801-585-6756, E-mail: marilynn.howard@utah.edu.
Website: http://elp.utah.edu/.

University of Virginia, Curry School of Education, Department of Leadership, Foundations and Policy, Program in Higher Education, Charlottesville, VA 22903. Offers higher education (Ed S); student affairs practice (M Ed). *Students:* 30 full-time (22 women), 17 part-time (6 women); includes 7 minority (3 Black or African American, non-Hispanic/Latino; 2 Asian, non-Hispanic/Latino; 2 Hispanic/Latino), 1 international. Average age 30. 14 applicants, 57% accepted, 6 enrolled. In 2013, 28 master's awarded. *Entrance requirements:* For master's, doctorate, and Ed S, GRE General Test, 2 letters of recommendation. Additional exam requirements/recommendations for international students: Required—TOEFL (minimum score 600 paper-based; 90 iBT), IELTS (minimum score 7). *Application deadline:* Applications are processed on a rolling basis. Application fee: $60. Electronic applications accepted. *Expenses:* Tuition, state resident: part-time $334 per credit hour. Tuition, nonresident: part-time $1224 per credit hour. *Financial support:* Fellowships, research assistantships, and teaching assistantships available. Financial award applicants required to submit FAFSA. *Unit head:* Karen Kurotsuchi Inkelas, Associate Professor and Director, 434-243-1943, E-mail: highered@virginia.edu. *Application contact:* Assistant to the Chair.
Website: http://curry.virginia.edu/academics/areas-of-study/higher-education.

University of Virginia, Curry School of Education, Program in Education, Charlottesville, VA 22903. Offers administration and supervision (PhD); applied developmental science (PhD); counselor education (PhD); curriculum and instruction (PhD); early childhood special education (MT); education evaluation (PhD); educational psychology (PhD); educational research (PhD); elementary education (MT); English education (MT, PhD); foreign language education (MT); higher education (PhD); instructional technology (PhD); kinesiology (MT, PhD); math education (PhD); reading education (PhD); research, statistics and evaluation (PhD); school psychology (PhD); science education (PhD); social studies education (MT, PhD); special education (PhD); world languages education (MT). *Students:* 474 full-time (379 women), 35 part-time (19 women); includes 89 minority (30 Black or African American, non-Hispanic/Latino; 1 American Indian or Alaska Native, non-Hispanic/Latino; 26 Asian, non-Hispanic/Latino; 19 Hispanic/Latino; 13 Two or more races, non-Hispanic/Latino), 21 international. Average age 26. 312 applicants, 49% accepted, 80 enrolled. In 2013, 137 master's, 38 doctorates awarded. *Degree requirements:* For master's, comprehensive exam (for some programs), field project; for doctorate, comprehensive exam, thesis/dissertation. *Entrance requirements:* For doctorate, GRE General Test. Additional exam requirements/recommendations for international students: Required—TOEFL (minimum score 600 paper-based; 90 iBT), IELTS (minimum score 7). *Application deadline:* Applications are processed on a rolling basis. Application fee: $60. Electronic applications accepted. *Expenses:* Tuition, state resident: part-time $334 per credit hour. Tuition, nonresident: part-time $1224 per credit hour. *Financial support:* Fellowships, research assistantships, and teaching assistantships available. Financial award application deadline: 1/5; financial award applicants required to submit FAFSA. *Unit head:* Robert C. Pianta, Dean, 434-924-3334, E-mail: pianta@virginia.edu. *Application contact:* Office of Admissions and Student Services, 434-924-0742, E-mail: curry-admissions@virginia.edu.
Website: http://curry.virginia.edu/teacher-education.

University of Washington, Graduate School, College of Education, Seattle, WA 98195. Offers curriculum and instruction (M Ed, Ed D, PhD), including educational technology, general curriculum (Ed D, PhD), language, literacy, and culture, mathematics education, multicultural education, reading and language arts education (Ed D), science education, social studies education, teaching and curriculum (M Ed); educational leadership and policy studies (M Ed, Ed D, PhD), including administration (Ed D), educational policy, organization, and leadership (M Ed, PhD), higher education, leadership for learning (Ed D), social and cultural foundations of education (M Ed, PhD); educational psychology (M Ed, PhD), including educational psychology (PhD), human development and cognition (M Ed), learning sciences, measurement, statistics and research design (M Ed), school psychology (M Ed); instructional leadership (M Ed); intercollegiate athletic leadership (M Ed); special education (M Ed, Ed D, PhD), including early childhood special education (M Ed), emotional and behavioral disabilities (M Ed), learning disabilities (M Ed), low-incidence disabilities (M Ed), severe disabilities (M Ed), special education (Ed D, PhD); teacher education (MIT). *Accreditation:* APA. Part-time and evening/weekend programs available. *Degree requirements:* For master's, thesis optional; for doctorate, thesis/dissertation. *Entrance requirements:* For master's and doctorate, GRE General Test, minimum GPA of 3.0. Additional exam requirements/recommendations for international students: Required—TOEFL. Electronic applications accepted. *Faculty research:* School restructuring/effective schools, special education interventions, literacy and writing, technology, school partnerships, teacher preparation.

University of Wisconsin–La Crosse, Graduate Studies, College of Liberal Studies, Department of Student Affairs Administration in Higher Education, La Crosse, WI 54601-3742. Offers MS Ed. Part-time programs available. Postbaccalaureate distance learning degree programs offered (no on-campus study). *Faculty:* 2 full-time (1 woman). *Students:* 49 full-time (35 women), 46 part-time (36 women); includes 18 minority (5 Black or African American, non-Hispanic/Latino; 1 American Indian or Alaska Native, non-Hispanic/Latino; 4 Asian, non-Hispanic/Latino; 4 Hispanic/Latino; 4 Two or more races, non-Hispanic/Latino), 1 international. Average age 27. 136 applicants, 40% accepted, 48 enrolled. In 2013, 48 master's awarded. *Degree requirements:* For master's, comprehensive exam (for some programs), thesis optional, electronic portfolio, applied research project. *Entrance requirements:* For master's, interview, writing sample, references, experience in the field. Additional exam requirements/recommendations for international students: Required—TOEFL (minimum score 550 paper-based; 79 iBT). *Application deadline:* For fall admission, 2/1 priority date for domestic and international students. Electronic applications accepted. *Financial support:* Research assistantships with partial tuition reimbursements, Federal Work-Study, scholarships/grants, and health care benefits available. Support available to part-time students. Financial award application deadline: 3/15; financial award applicants required to submit FAFSA. *Unit head:* Dr. Jodie Rindt, Director, 608-785-6450, E-mail: rindt.jodi@uwlax.edu. *Application contact:* Corey Sjoquist, Director of Admissions, 608-785-8939, E-mail: admissions@uwlax.edu.
Website: http://www.uwlax.edu/saa/.

University of Wisconsin–Madison, Graduate School, School of Education, Department of Educational Leadership and Policy Analysis, Madison, WI 53706-1380. Offers administration (Certificate); educational policy (MS, PhD); global higher education (MS). *Degree requirements:* For doctorate, thesis/dissertation. *Entrance requirements:* For master's and doctorate, GRE General Test. *Application deadline:* For fall admission, 1/15 for domestic and international students. Application fee: $56. Electronic applications accepted. *Expenses:* Tuition, state resident: full-time $10,728; part-time $790 per credit. Tuition, nonresident: full-time $24,054; part-time $1623 per credit. *Required fees:* $1130; $119 per credit. *Financial support:* Fellowships with full tuition reimbursements, research assistantships with full tuition reimbursements, teaching assistantships with full tuition reimbursements, and project assistantships available. *Unit head:* Dr. Eric Camburn, Chair, 608-262-3106, E-mail: elpa@education.wisc.edu. *Application contact:* 608-262-2433, Fax: 608-262-5134, E-mail: gradadmiss@mail.bascom.wisc.edu.
Website: http://www.education.wisc.edu/elpa.

University of Wisconsin–Milwaukee, Graduate School, School of Education, Department of Administrative Leadership, Milwaukee, WI 53201-0413. Offers administrative leadership and supervision in education (MS); specialist in administrative leadership (Certificate); teaching and learning in higher education (Certificate). Part-time programs available. *Faculty:* 9 full-time (6 women), 1 part-time/adjunct (0 women). *Students:* 27 full-time (22 women), 147 part-time (100 women); includes 43 minority (24 Black or African American, non-Hispanic/Latino; 1 American Indian or Alaska Native, non-Hispanic/Latino; 4 Asian, non-Hispanic/Latino; 5 Hispanic/Latino; 9 Two or more races, non-Hispanic/Latino), 2 international. Average age 34. 112 applicants, 72% accepted, 52 enrolled. In 2013, 52 master's awarded. *Degree requirements:* For master's, comprehensive exam, thesis or alternative. *Entrance requirements:* For master's, GRE General Test. Additional exam requirements/recommendations for international students: Required—TOEFL (minimum score 550 paper-based; 79 iBT), IELTS (minimum score 6.5). *Application deadline:* For fall admission, 1/1 priority date for domestic students; for spring admission, 9/1 for domestic students. Applications are processed on a rolling basis. Application fee: $56 ($96 for international students). Electronic applications accepted. *Financial support:* In 2013–14, 2 fellowships were awarded; research assistantships, teaching assistantships, career-related internships or fieldwork, health care benefits, unspecified assistantships, and project assistantships also available. Support available to part-time students. Financial award application deadline: 4/15; financial award applicants required to submit FAFSA. *Unit head:* Larry Martin, Department Chair, 414-229-5754, Fax: 414-229-5300, E-mail: lmartin@uwm.edu. *Application contact:* General Information Contact, 414-229-4982, Fax: 414-229-6967, E-mail: gradschool@uwm.edu.
Website: http://www.uwm.edu/Dept/Ad_Ldsp/.

University of Wisconsin–Whitewater, School of Graduate Studies, College of Education and Professional Studies, Department of Counselor Education, Whitewater, WI 53190-1790. Offers community counseling (MS Ed); higher education (MS Ed); school counseling (MS Ed). *Accreditation:* ACA; NCATE. Part-time and evening/weekend programs available. *Degree requirements:* For master's, thesis or alternative. *Entrance requirements:* For master's, resume, 2 letters of reference, goal statement, autobiography. Additional exam requirements/recommendations for international students: Required—TOEFL (minimum score 550 paper-based; 80 iBT), IELTS (minimum score 6). Electronic applications accepted. *Faculty research:* Alcohol and other drugs, counseling effectiveness, teacher mentoring.

Upper Iowa University, Online Master's Programs, Fayette, IA 52142-1857. Offers accounting (MBA); corporate financial management (MBA); global business (MBA); health and human services (MPA); higher education administration (MHEA); homeland security (MPA); human resources management (MBA); justice administration (MPA); organizational development (MBA); public personnel management (MPA); quality management (MBA). MBA also available at Madison, WI campus. Part-time programs available. Postbaccalaureate distance learning degree programs offered (no on-campus study). *Degree requirements:* For master's, research project. *Entrance requirements:* For master's, GMAT, GRE, or minimum GPA of 2.7 during last 60 hours. Additional exam requirements/recommendations for international students: Required—TOEFL (minimum score 570 paper-based). Electronic applications accepted. *Faculty research:* Total quality management, CQI, teams, organization culture and climate, management.

Valdosta State University, Program in Educational Leadership, Valdosta, GA 31698. Offers higher education (M Ed); information technology (M Ed, Ed S); leadership (M Ed, Ed D, Ed S). *Accreditation:* NCATE. *Faculty:* 15 full-time (6 women). *Students:* 70 full-time (36 women), 94 part-time (64 women); includes 44 minority (37 Black or African American, non-Hispanic/Latino; 1 American Indian or Alaska Native, non-Hispanic/Latino; 2 Hispanic/Latino; 4 Two or more races, non-Hispanic/Latino), 4 international. Average age 28. 80 applicants, 94% accepted, 69 enrolled. In 2013, 36 master's, 17 doctorates awarded. *Degree requirements:* For master's, thesis (for some programs), comprehensive written and/or oral exams; for doctorate, thesis/dissertation, comprehensive written and/or oral exams; for Ed S, thesis. *Entrance requirements:* For master's and Ed S, GRE General Test or MAT; for doctorate, GRE General Test, minimum GPA of 3.5. Additional exam requirements/recommendations for international students: Required—TOEFL (minimum score 523 paper-based). *Application deadline:* For fall admission, 7/1 for domestic and international students; for spring admission, 11/15 for domestic and international students. Applications are processed on a rolling basis. Application fee: $35. Electronic applications accepted. *Expenses:* Tuition, state resident: full-time $4140; part-time $230 per credit hour. Tuition, nonresident: full-time $14,904; part-time $828 per credit hour. *Required fees:* $995 per semester. Tuition and fees vary according to course load. *Financial support:* In 2013–14, 3 students received support, including 4 research assistantships with full tuition reimbursements available (averaging $3,652 per year); institutionally sponsored loans, scholarships/grants, and unspecified assistantships also available. Support available to part-time students. Financial award application deadline: 7/1; financial award applicants required to submit FAFSA. *Faculty research:* Mentoring in higher education, contemporary issues in higher education. *Unit head:* Dr. Leon Pate, Interim Department Head, 229-333-5633, E-mail: jlpate@valdosta.edu. *Application contact:* Rebecca Petrella, Coordinator of Graduate Programs, 229-333-5694, Fax: 229-245-3853, E-mail: rlwaters@valdosta.edu.
Website: http://www.valdosta.edu/academics/graduate-school/our-programs/leadership.php.

Vanderbilt University, Peabody College, Department of Leadership, Policy, and Organizations, Nashville, TN 37240-1001. Offers education policy (MPP); educational leadership and policy (Ed D); higher education (M Ed); higher education, leadership and policy (Ed D); international education policy and management (M Ed); leadership and organizational performance (M Ed). Part-time and evening/weekend programs available.

Faculty: 30 full-time (13 women), 13 part-time/adjunct (6 women). *Students:* 183 full-time (128 women), 92 part-time (49 women); includes 59 minority (32 Black or African American, non-Hispanic/Latino; 8 Asian, non-Hispanic/Latino; 14 Hispanic/Latino; 5 Two or more races, non-Hispanic/Latino), 21 international. Average age 28. 464 applicants, 62% accepted, 123 enrolled. In 2013, 91 master's, 24 doctorates awarded. *Degree requirements:* For master's, comprehensive exam, thesis optional; for doctorate, thesis/dissertation, qualifying exams, residency. *Entrance requirements:* For master's and doctorate, GRE General Test. Additional exam requirements/recommendations for international students: Required—TOEFL (minimum score 550 paper-based; 80 iBT). *Application deadline:* For fall admission, 12/31 priority date for domestic and international students; for spring admission, 11/1 priority date for domestic and international students. Applications are processed on a rolling basis. Application fee: $0. Electronic applications accepted. *Financial support:* Fellowships with full and partial tuition reimbursements, research assistantships with full and partial tuition reimbursements, teaching assistantships with full and partial tuition reimbursements, Federal Work-Study, institutionally sponsored loans, scholarships/grants, tuition waivers (partial), and unspecified assistantships available. Support available to part-time students. Financial award application deadline: 1/15; financial award applicants required to submit FAFSA. *Faculty research:* Higher education, educational leadership, education policy, economics of education, education accountability, school choice. *Unit head:* Dr. Ellen B. Goldring, Chair, 615-322-8000, Fax: 615-343-7094, E-mail: ellen.b.goldring@vanderbilt.edu. *Application contact:* Rosie Moody, Educational Coordinator, 615-322-8019, Fax: 615-343-7094, E-mail: rosie.moody@vanderbilt.edu.

Virginia Polytechnic Institute and State University, Graduate School, College of Liberal Arts and Human Sciences, Blacksburg, VA 24061. Offers career and technical education (MS Ed, Ed D, PhD, Ed S); communication (MA); counselor education (MA Ed, Ed D, PhD, Ed S); creative writing (MFA); curriculum and instruction (MA Ed, Ed D, PhD, Ed S); educational leadership and policy studies (MA Ed, Ed D, PhD, Ed S); educational research and evaluation (PhD); English (MA); foreign languages, cultures, and literatures (MA); higher education and student affairs (MA Ed); history (MA); human development (MS, PhD); material culture and public humanities (MA); philosophy (MA); political science (MA); rhetoric and writing (PhD); science and technology studies (MS, PhD); social, political, ethical, and cultural thought (PhD); sociology (MS, PhD); theater arts (MFA). *Faculty:* 410 full-time (211 women), 6 part-time/adjunct (5 women). *Students:* 688 full-time (464 women), 576 part-time (372 women); includes 243 minority (144 Black or African American, non-Hispanic/Latino; 3 American Indian or Alaska Native, non-Hispanic/Latino; 29 Asian, non-Hispanic/Latino; 48 Hispanic/Latino; 1 Native Hawaiian or other Pacific Islander, non-Hispanic/Latino; 18 Two or more races, non-Hispanic/Latino), 84 international. Average age 34. 1,054 applicants, 48% accepted, 374 enrolled. In 2013, 314 master's, 74 doctorates, 14 other advanced degrees awarded. *Degree requirements:* For master's, comprehensive exam (for some programs), thesis (for some programs); for doctorate, comprehensive exam (for some programs), thesis/dissertation (for some programs). *Entrance requirements:* For master's and doctorate, GRE/GMAT (may vary by department). Additional exam requirements/recommendations for international students: Required—TOEFL (minimum score 550 paper-based). *Application deadline:* For fall admission, 8/1 for domestic students, 4/1 for international students; for spring admission, 1/1 for domestic students, 9/1 for international students. Applications are processed on a rolling basis. Application fee: $75. Electronic applications accepted. *Expenses: Tuition:* State resident: full-time $11,185; part-time $621.50 per credit hour. Tuition, nonresident: full-time $22,146; part-time $1230.25 per credit hour. *Required fees:* $2442; $449.25 per semester. Tuition and fees vary according to course load, campus/location and program. *Financial support:* In 2013–14, 19 research assistantships with full tuition reimbursements (averaging $17,115 per year), 205 teaching assistantships with full tuition reimbursements (averaging $14,433 per year) were awarded. Financial award application deadline: 3/1; financial award applicants required to submit FAFSA. *Total annual research expenditures:* $6.8 million. *Unit head:* Joan Hirt, Interim Dean, 540-231-6779, Fax: 540-231-7157, E-mail: jbhirt@vt.edu. *Application contact:* Melissa Elliott, Executive Assistant, 540-231-6779, Fax: 540-231-7157, E-mail: elliott1@vt.edu. Website: http://www.clahs.vt.edu/.

Walden University, Graduate Programs, Richard W. Riley College of Education and Leadership, Minneapolis, MN 55401. *Accreditation:* NCATE. Part-time and evening/weekend programs available. Postbaccalaureate distance learning degree programs offered (minimal on-campus study). *Faculty:* 23 full-time (15 women), 830 part-time/adjunct (569 women). *Students:* 8,671 full-time (7,197 women), 2,122 part-time (1,735 women); includes 4,734 minority (3,802 Black or African American, non-Hispanic/Latino; 50 American Indian or Alaska Native, non-Hispanic/Latino; 136 Asian, non-Hispanic/Latino; 539 Hispanic/Latino; 35 Native Hawaiian or other Pacific Islander, non-Hispanic/Latino; 172 Two or more races, non-Hispanic/Latino), 73 international. Average age 40. 2,646 applicants, 96% accepted, 2074 enrolled. In 2013, 2,214 master's, 354 doctorates, 479 other advanced degrees awarded. *Degree requirements:* For doctorate, thesis/dissertation (for some programs), residency; for other advanced degree, residency (for some programs). *Entrance requirements:* For master's, bachelor's degree or higher; minimum GPA of 2.5; official transcripts; goal statement (for some programs); access to computer and Internet; for doctorate, master's degree or higher; three years of related professional or academic experience (preferred); minimum GPA of 3.0; goal statement and current resume (select programs); official transcripts; access to computer and Internet; for other advanced degree, relevant work experience; access to computer and Internet. Additional exam requirements/recommendations for international students: Required—TOEFL (minimum score 550 paper-based; 79 iBT), IELTS (minimum score 6.5), Michigan English Language Assessment Battery (minimum score 82), or PTE. *Application deadline:* Applications are processed on a rolling basis. Application fee: $0. Electronic applications accepted. *Expenses: Tuition:* Full-time $11,813.55; part-time $500 per credit. *Required fees:* $618.76. *Financial support:* In 2013–14, 1 fellowship was awarded; Federal Work-Study, scholarships/grants, unspecified assistantships, and family tuition reduction, active duty/veteran tuition reduction, group tuition reduction, interest-free payment plans, employee tuition reduction also available. Support available to part-time students. Financial award applicants required to submit FAFSA. *Unit head:* Dr. Kate Steffens, Dean, 800-925-3368. *Application contact:* Jennifer Hall, Vice President of Enrollment Management, 866-4-WALDEN, E-mail: info@waldenu.edu. Website: http://www.waldenu.edu/colleges-schools/riley-college-of-education/.

Walsh University, Graduate Studies, Program in Counseling and Human Development, North Canton, OH 44720-3396. Offers clinical mental health counseling (MA); school counseling (MA); student affairs in higher education (MA). *Accreditation:* ACA. Part-time and evening/weekend programs available. *Faculty:* 5 full-time (all women), 6 part-time/adjunct (2 women). *Students:* 38 full-time (27 women), 47 part-time (41 women); includes 3 minority (2 Black or African American, non-Hispanic/Latino; 1 Hispanic/Latino), 2 international. Average age 28. 94 applicants, 37% accepted, 26 enrolled. In 2013, 21 master's awarded. *Degree requirements:* For master's, comprehensive exam, internship, practicum. *Entrance requirements:* For master's, GRE (minimum score of 145 verbal and 146 quantitative) or MAT (minimum score of 397), interview, minimum GPA of 3.0, writing sample, reference forms, notarized affidavit of good moral conduct. Additional exam requirements/recommendations for international students: Required—TOEFL (minimum score 500 paper-based; 61 iBT). *Application deadline:* For fall

admission, 7/15 priority date for domestic students. Applications are processed on a rolling basis. Application fee: $25. Electronic applications accepted. *Expenses: Tuition:* Full-time $10,890; part-time $605 per credit hour. *Required fees:* $100; $100. *Financial support:* In 2013–14, 73 students received support, including 3 research assistantships with partial tuition reimbursements available (averaging $8,065 per year), 11 teaching assistantships with partial tuition reimbursements available (averaging $5,610 per year); scholarships/grants, tuition waivers (full and partial), and unspecified assistantships also available. Support available to part-time students. Financial award application deadline: 12/31. *Faculty research:* Clinical training and supervision of clinical mental health counselors, supervision of school counselors, cross-cultural training in counselor education, outcomes in adventure-based therapies with children, counseling for intimate partner violence and relational issues, refugee mental health and trauma, career counseling for refugees using ecological and social learning models, integration of neuroscience and culture in clinical mental health counseling. *Unit head:* Dr. Linda Barclay, Program Director, 330-490-7264, Fax: 330-490-7323, E-mail: lbarclay@walsh.edu. *Application contact:* Audra Dice, Graduate and Transfer Admissions Counselor, 330-490-7181, Fax: 330-244-4925, E-mail: adice@walsh.edu. Website: http://www.walsh.edu/counseling-graduate-program.

Wayland Baptist University, Graduate Programs, Program in Education, Plainview, TX 79072-6998. Offers education administration (M Ed); education diagnostics (M Ed); education literacy (M Ed); elementary certification (M Ed); English (M Ed); English as a second language (M Ed); higher education administration (M Ed); human resources (M Ed); instructional leadership (M Ed); instructional technology (M Ed); science education (M Ed); secondary certification (M Ed); social studies (M Ed); special education (M Ed). Part-time and evening/weekend programs available. Postbaccalaureate distance learning degree programs offered (no on-campus study). *Faculty:* 33 full-time (17 women), 28 part-time/adjunct (17 women). *Students:* 22 full-time (15 women), 316 part-time (189 women); includes 130 minority (48 Black or African American, non-Hispanic/Latino; 3 American Indian or Alaska Native, non-Hispanic/Latino; 71 Hispanic/Latino; 1 Native Hawaiian or other Pacific Islander, non-Hispanic/Latino; 7 Two or more races, non-Hispanic/Latino). Average age 39. 80 applicants, 96% accepted, 44 enrolled. In 2013, 170 master's awarded. *Degree requirements:* For master's, comprehensive exam, capstone course. *Entrance requirements:* For master's, GRE, GMAT or MAT. Additional exam requirements/recommendations for international students: Required—TOEFL (minimum score 500 paper-based; 61 iBT). *Application deadline:* Applications are processed on a rolling basis. Application fee: $50. Electronic applications accepted. *Expenses: Tuition:* Full-time $8190; part-time $455 per credit hour. *Required fees:* $970; $455 per credit hour. $485 per semester. *Financial support:* Federal Work-Study, institutionally sponsored loans, and scholarships/grants available. Support available to part-time students. Financial award application deadline: 5/1; financial award applicants required to submit FAFSA. *Unit head:* Dr. Jim Todd, Chairman, 806-291-1045, Fax: 806-291-1951. *Application contact:* Amanda Stanton, Coordinator of Graduate Studies, 806-291-3423, Fax: 806-291-1950, E-mail: stanton@wbu.edu.

Wayne State University, College of Education, Division of Administrative and Organizational Studies, Detroit, MI 48202. Offers college and university teaching (Certificate); educational administration and supervision (Ed S); educational leadership (M Ed); educational leadership and policy studies (Ed D, PhD); educational technology (Certificate); instructional technology (M Ed, Ed D, PhD, Ed S); online teaching (Certificate); secondary curriculum and instruction (Ed S); special education administration (Ed S). Part-time programs available. Postbaccalaureate distance learning degree programs offered. *Students:* 96 full-time (68 women), 207 part-time (137 women); includes 133 minority (115 Black or African American, non-Hispanic/Latino; 4 American Indian or Alaska Native, non-Hispanic/Latino; 2 Asian, non-Hispanic/Latino; 8 Hispanic/Latino; 4 Two or more races, non-Hispanic/Latino), 14 international. Average age 39. 127 applicants, 50% accepted, 42 enrolled. In 2013, 47 master's, 15 doctorates, 41 other advanced degrees awarded. *Degree requirements:* For doctorate, thesis/dissertation. *Entrance requirements:* For master's, baccalaureate degree from accredited U.S. institution or equivalent from college or university of government-recognized standing; minimum undergraduate GPA of 2.75 in upper-division coursework; for doctorate, GRE or MAT, interview; autobiography or curriculum vitae; references; master's degree; minimum undergraduate GPA of 3.0, graduate 3.75; 3 years of relevant experience; foundational course work; for other advanced degree, master's degree from accredited institution, minimum upper-division GPA of 2.6 or 3.4 master's, fulfillment of the special requirements of the area of concentration, 3 years of teaching experience (except for instructional technology). Additional exam requirements/recommendations for international students: Required—TOEFL (minimum score 550 paper-based; 79 iBT), Michigan English Language Assessment Battery (minimum score 85); Recommended—IELTS (minimum score 6.5), TWE (minimum score 5.5). *Application deadline:* For fall admission, 6/1 priority date for domestic students, 5/1 priority date for international students; for winter admission, 10/1 priority date for domestic students, 9/1 priority date for international students; for spring admission, 2/1 priority date for domestic students, 1/1 priority date for international students. Applications are processed on a rolling basis. Application fee: $0. Electronic applications accepted. *Expenses: Tuition:* state resident: part-time $554.15 per credit. Tuition, nonresident: part-time $1200.35 per credit. *Required fees:* $42.15 per credit. $268.30 per semester. Tuition and fees vary according to course load and program. *Financial support:* In 2013–14, 48 students received support, including 3 fellowships with tuition reimbursements available (averaging $15,541 per year), 4 research assistantships with tuition reimbursements available (averaging $16,508 per year); career-related internships or fieldwork, Federal Work-Study, scholarships/grants, health care benefits, and unspecified assistantships also available. Support available to part-time students. Financial award application deadline: 3/31; financial award applicants required to submit FAFSA. *Faculty research:* Total quality management, participatory management, administering educational technology, school improvement, principalship. *Total annual research expenditures:* $6,888. *Unit head:* Dr. William Hill, Assistant Dean, 313-577-9316, E-mail: william_e_hill@wayne.edu. *Application contact:* Janice Green, Assistant Dean, 313-577-1605, E-mail: jwgreen@wayne.edu. Website: http://coe.wayne.edu/aos/index.php.

West Chester University of Pennsylvania, College of Education, Department of Counselor Education, West Chester, PA 19383. Offers counseling (Teaching Certificate); elementary school counseling (M Ed); higher education counseling (MS); higher education counseling/student affairs (Certificate); secondary school counseling (M Ed). *Accreditation:* ACA; NCATE. Part-time and evening/weekend programs available. *Faculty:* 10 full-time (6 women), 7 part-time/adjunct (5 women). *Students:* 116 full-time (100 women), 110 part-time (93 women); includes 36 minority (19 Black or African American, non-Hispanic/Latino; 2 American Indian or Alaska Native, non-Hispanic/Latino; 2 Asian, non-Hispanic/Latino; 7 Hispanic/Latino; 6 Two or more races, non-Hispanic/Latino). Average age 28. 145 applicants, 76% accepted, 59 enrolled. In 2013, 83 master's awarded. *Degree requirements:* For master's, comprehensive exam. *Entrance requirements:* For master's, minimum GPA of 3.0, three letters of reference. Additional exam requirements/recommendations for international students: Required—TOEFL (minimum score 550 paper-based; 80 iBT). *Application deadline:* For fall admission, 4/15 priority date for domestic students, 3/15 for international students; for

spring admission, 10/15 priority date for domestic students, 9/1 for international students. Applications are processed on a rolling basis. Application fee: $45. Electronic applications accepted. *Expenses:* Tuition, state resident: full-time $7956; part-time $442 per credit. Tuition, nonresident: full-time $11,934; part-time $663 per credit. *Required fees:* $2134.20; $106.24 per credit. Tuition and fees vary according to campus/location and program. *Financial support:* Unspecified assistantships available. Support available to part-time students. Financial award application deadline: 2/15; financial award applicants required to submit FAFSA. *Faculty research:* Teacher and student cognition, adolescent cognitive development, college counseling, motivational interviewing. *Unit head:* Dr. Kathryn (Tina) Alessandria, Chair, 610-436-2559, Fax: 610-425-7432, E-mail: kalessandria@wcupa.edu. *Application contact:* Dr. Eric W. Owens, Graduate Coordinator, 610-436-2559, Fax: 610-425-7432, E-mail: eowens@wcupa.edu.
Website: http://www.wcupa.edu/_academics/sch_sed.counseling&edpsych/.

Western Carolina University, Graduate School, College of Education and Allied Professions, School of Teaching and Learning, Cullowhee, NC 28723. Offers community college and higher education (MA Ed), including community college administration, community college teaching; comprehensive education (MA Ed, MAT); educational leadership (MA Ed, MSA, Ed D, Ed S), including educational leadership (MSA, Ed D, Ed S), educational supervision (MA Ed); teaching (MA Ed, MAT), including comprehensive education (MA Ed), physical education (MA Ed), teaching (MAT). *Accreditation:* NCATE. Part-time and evening/weekend programs available. Postbaccalaureate distance learning degree programs offered. *Degree requirements:* For master's, comprehensive exam; for doctorate, comprehensive exam, thesis/ dissertation. *Entrance requirements:* For master's, GRE, appropriate undergraduate degree, 3 letters of recommendation; for doctorate, GRE General Test, minimum graduate GPA of 3.5, appropriate master's degree; for other advanced degree, GRE General Test, minimum graduate GPA of 3.5, work experience, appropriate master's degree. Additional exam requirements/recommendations for international students: Required—TOEFL (minimum score 550 paper-based; 79 iBT). *Faculty research:* Educational leadership, special education, rural education, organizational theory and practice, interinstitutional partnership, program evaluation.

Western Governors University, Teachers College, Salt Lake City, UT 84107. Offers curriculum and instruction (MS); educational leadership (MS); educational studies (MA); educational studies (5-12) (MA), including mathematics; elementary education (K-8) (MAT, Postbaccalaureate Certificate); elementary education (PreK-8) (MAT); English language learning (K-12) (MA); instructional design (MAT); learning and technology (M Ed, MA); management and innovation (M Ed); mathematics (5-12) (MAT, Postbaccalaureate Certificate); mathematics (5-9) (MAT, Postbaccalaureate Certificate); mathematics education (5-12) (MA); mathematics education (5-9) (MA); mathematics education (K-6) (MA); measurement and evaluation (M Ed); science (5-12) (Postbaccalaureate Certificate); science (5-9) (MAT, Postbaccalaureate Certificate); science education (5-12) (MA), including biology, chemistry, geology, physics; science education (5-9) (MA); social science (5-12) (MAT, Postbaccalaureate Certificate); special education (MAT, MS). *Accreditation:* NCATE. Evening/weekend programs available. Postbaccalaureate distance learning degree programs offered (no on-campus study). *Degree requirements:* For master's, capstone project. *Entrance requirements:* For master's and Postbaccalaureate Certificate, Readiness Assessment, transcripts. Additional exam requirements/recommendations for international students: Required—TOEFL (minimum score 450 paper-based; 80 iBT). Electronic applications accepted. *Expenses:* Contact institution.

Western Kentucky University, Graduate Studies, College of Education and Behavioral Sciences, Department of Counseling and Student Affairs, Bowling Green, KY 42101. Offers counseling (MA Ed), including marriage and family therapy, mental health counseling; school counseling (P-12) (MA Ed); student affairs in higher education (MA Ed). *Accreditation:* ACA; NCATE. Part-time and evening/weekend programs available. *Degree requirements:* For master's, comprehensive exam, thesis optional. *Entrance requirements:* For master's, GRE General Test. Additional exam requirements/ recommendations for international students: Required—TOEFL (minimum score 555 paper-based; 79 iBT). *Faculty research:* Counselor education, research for residential workers.

Western Washington University, Graduate School, Woodring College of Education, Department of Educational Leadership, Program in Continuing and College Education, Bellingham, WA 98225-5996. Offers M Ed. Part-time and evening/weekend programs available. Postbaccalaureate distance learning degree programs offered (minimal on-campus study). *Degree requirements:* For master's, comprehensive exam, thesis optional. *Entrance requirements:* For master's, GRE General Test or MAT, minimum GPA of 3.0 in last 60 semester hours or last 90 quarter hours. Additional exam requirements/recommendations for international students: Required—TOEFL (minimum score 567 paper-based). Electronic applications accepted. *Faculty research:* Transfer of learning, postsecondary faculty development, action research as professional development, literacy education in community colleges, adult education in the Middle East, distance learning tools for graduate students.

West Virginia University, College of Human Resources and Education, Department of Curriculum and Instruction/Literacy Studies, Program in Secondary Education, Morgantown, WV 26506. Offers higher education curriculum and teaching (MA); secondary education (MA). Students enter program as undergraduates. *Accreditation:* NCATE. Part-time programs available. *Degree requirements:* For master's, thesis optional, content exams. *Entrance requirements:* For master's, minimum GPA of 2.75. Additional exam requirements/recommendations for international students: Required—TOEFL. Electronic applications accepted. *Faculty research:* Teacher education, school reform, curriculum development, education technology.

West Virginia University, College of Human Resources and Education, Department of Educational Leadership Studies, Morgantown, WV 26506. Offers educational leadership (Ed D); higher education administration (MA); public school administration (MA). *Accreditation:* NCATE. Part-time programs available. *Degree requirements:* For master's, content exams; for doctorate, comprehensive exam, thesis/dissertation. *Entrance requirements:* For master's, minimum GPA of 2.75 or MA Degree or MAT of 4107; for doctorate, GRE General Test or MAT, minimum GPA of 3.25. Additional exam requirements/recommendations for international students: Required—TOEFL. Electronic applications accepted. *Faculty research:* Evaluation, collective bargaining, educational law, international higher education, superintendency.

Wilkes University, College of Graduate and Professional Studies, School of Education, Wilkes-Barre, PA 18766-0002. Offers art and science of teaching (MS Ed); classroom technology (MS Ed); early childhood literacy (MS Ed); educational development and strategies (MS Ed); educational leadership (MS Ed); educational technology (Ed D); higher education administration (Ed D); instructional media (MS Ed); instructional technology (MS Ed); international school leadership (MS Ed); K-12 administration (Ed D); middle level education (MS Ed); online teaching (MS Ed); reading (MS Ed); school business leadership (MS Ed); secondary education (MS Ed), including biology, chemistry, English, history, mathematics; special education (MS Ed); teaching English as a second language (MS Ed); twenty-first century teaching and learning (MS Ed). Part-time and evening/weekend programs available. Postbaccalaureate distance learning degree programs offered (minimal on-campus study). *Students:* 46 full-time (37 women), 1,410 part-time (1,039 women); includes 67 minority (12 Black or African American, non-Hispanic/Latino; 2 American Indian or Alaska Native, non-Hispanic/ Latino; 11 Asian, non-Hispanic/Latino; 28 Hispanic/Latino; 1 Native Hawaiian or other Pacific Islander, non-Hispanic/Latino; 13 Two or more races, non-Hispanic/Latino), 6 international. Average age 34. In 2013, 852 master's, 10 doctorates awarded. *Entrance requirements:* Additional exam requirements/recommendations for international students: Required—TOEFL (minimum score 550 paper-based; 79 iBT). *Application deadline:* Applications are processed on a rolling basis. Application fee: $45. Electronic applications accepted. *Expenses:* Contact institution. *Financial support:* Federal Work-Study and unspecified assistantships available. Financial award application deadline: 3/ 1; financial award applicants required to submit FAFSA. *Unit head:* Dr. Rhonda Waskiewicz, Interim Dean, Education, 570-408-4332, Fax: 570-408-7872, E-mail: rhonda.waskiewicz@wilkes.edu. *Application contact:* Joanne Thomas, Interim Director of Graduate Education, 570-408-4234, Fax: 570-408-7846, E-mail: joanne.thomas1@wilkes.edu.
Website: http://www.wilkes.edu/pages/383.asp.

Wilmington University, College of Education, New Castle, DE 19720-6491. Offers applied technology in education (M Ed); career and technical education (M Ed); educational leadership (Ed D); elementary and secondary school counseling (M Ed); elementary studies (M Ed); ESOL literacy (M Ed); higher education leadership (Ed D); instruction: gifted and talented (M Ed); instruction: teacher of reading (M Ed); instruction: teaching and learning (M Ed); organizational leadership (Ed D); school leadership (M Ed); secondary education (MAT); special education (M Ed). *Accreditation:* NCATE. Part-time and evening/weekend programs available. *Entrance requirements:* For master's, 2 letters of recommendation, interview. Additional exam requirements/ recommendations for international students: Required—TOEFL (minimum score 500 paper-based). Electronic applications accepted.

Wright State University, School of Graduate Studies, College of Education and Human Services, Department of Educational Leadership, Program in Advanced Educational Leadership, Dayton, OH 45435. Offers advanced curriculum and instruction (Ed S); higher education-adult education (Ed S); superintendent (Ed S). *Accreditation:* NCATE. *Degree requirements:* For Ed S, thesis. *Entrance requirements:* For degree, GRE General Test, MAT. Additional exam requirements/recommendations for international students: Required—TOEFL.

Wright State University, School of Graduate Studies, College of Education and Human Services, Department of Educational Leadership, Programs in Educational Leadership, Dayton, OH 45435. Offers curriculum and instruction: teacher leader (MA); educational administrative specialist: teacher leader (M Ed); educational administrative specialist: vocational education administration (M Ed, MA); student affairs in higher education-administration (M Ed, MA). *Accreditation:* NCATE. *Degree requirements:* For master's, thesis (for some programs). *Entrance requirements:* For master's, GRE General Test, MAT. Additional exam requirements/recommendations for international students: Required—TOEFL.

Middle School Education

Alaska Pacific University, Graduate Programs, Education Department, Program in Teaching, Anchorage, AK 99508-4672. Offers teaching (K-8) (MAT). *Degree requirements:* For master's, research project. *Entrance requirements:* For master's, GRE or MAT, PRAXIS, minimum GPA of 3.0.

Albany State University, College of Education, Albany, GA 31705-2717. Offers early childhood education (M Ed); education specialist (Ed S); educational leadership and administration (M Ed); health, physical education and recreation (M Ed); middle grades education (M Ed); school counseling (M Ed); special education (M Ed). *Accreditation:* NCATE. Part-time and evening/weekend programs available. Postbaccalaureate distance learning degree programs offered (minimal on-campus study). *Degree requirements:* For master's, comprehensive exam, internship, GACE Content Exam. *Entrance requirements:* For master's, GRE or MAT. Electronic applications accepted. *Faculty research:* GACE preparation, STEM (science, technology, engineering, and mathematics), technology education, special education, professional teacher development, health implications liberation philosophy, NET-Q, learning community, disabled or at-risk students.

American International College, School of Graduate and Adult Education, Department of Education, Springfield, MA 01109-3189. Offers early childhood education (M Ed, CAGS); educational leadership and supervision (Ed D); elementary education (M Ed, CAGS); middle/secondary education (M Ed, CAGS); moderate disabilities (M Ed, CAGS); reading (M Ed, CAGS); school adjustment counseling (MA, CAGS); school guidance counseling (MA, CAGS); school leadership preparation (M Ed, CAGS); teaching and learning (Ed D). Evening/weekend programs available. *Faculty:* 11 full-time (9 women), 235 part-time/adjunct. *Students:* 1,530 full-time (1,219 women), 184 part-time (143 women); includes 100 minority (58 Black or African American, non-Hispanic/Latino; 3 American Indian or Alaska Native, non-Hispanic/Latino; 14 Asian, non-Hispanic/Latino; 6 Hispanic/Latino; 19 Two or more races, non-Hispanic/Latino). Average age 36. 695 applicants, 82% accepted, 508 enrolled. In 2013, 449 master's, 17 doctorates, 135 other advanced degrees awarded. Terminal master's awarded for partial completion of doctoral program. *Degree requirements:* For master's, comprehensive exam (for some programs), thesis (for some programs), practicum/ culminating experience; for doctorate, comprehensive exam (for some programs), thesis/dissertation; for CAGS, practicum/culminating experience. *Entrance requirements:* For master's, graduate of accredited four-year college with minimum B-average in undergraduate course work; for doctorate, master's degree, minimum GPA of 3.0; for CAGS, M Ed or master's degree in field related to licensure from accredited institution. Additional exam requirements/recommendations for international students:

Required—TOEFL or IELTS. *Application deadline:* For fall admission, 7/1 for domestic and international students; for spring admission, 12/1 for domestic and international students. Applications are processed on a rolling basis. Application fee: $50. Electronic applications accepted. *Expenses: Tuition:* Full-time $14,040; part-time $780 per credit. Tuition and fees vary according to course load, degree level and program. *Financial support:* Career-related internships or fieldwork available. Financial award applicants required to submit FAFSA. *Unit head:* Esta Sobey, Associate Dean, 413-205-3453, Fax: 413-205-3943, E-mail: esta.sobey@aic.edu. *Application contact:* Kaitlyn Rickard, Director of XCP Admissions, 413-205-3090, Fax: 413-205-3911, E-mail: kaitlyn.rickard@aic.edu.
Website: http://www.aic.edu/academics.

Appalachian State University, Cratis D. Williams Graduate School, Department of Curriculum and Instruction, Boone, NC 28608. Offers curriculum specialist (MA); educational media (MA); elementary education (MA); middle grades education (MA), including language arts, mathematics, science, social studies. *Accreditation:* NCATE. Part-time and evening/weekend programs available. Postbaccalaureate distance learning degree programs offered (no on-campus study). *Degree requirements:* For master's, comprehensive exam, thesis or alternative. *Entrance requirements:* For master's, GRE General Test or MAT, 3 letters of recommendation. Additional exam requirements/recommendations for international students: Required—TOEFL (minimum score 570 paper-based; 79 iBT), IELTS (minimum score 6.5). Electronic applications accepted. *Faculty research:* Media literacy, elementary teaching, curriculum development, online learning environments.

Arkansas State University, Graduate School, College of Education and Behavioral Science, School of Teacher Education and Leadership, Jonesboro, AR 72467. Offers community college administration (SCCT); curriculum and instruction (MSE); early childhood education (MAT, MSE); early childhood services (MS); educational leadership (MSE, Ed D, PhD, Ed S); educational theory and practice (MSE); middle level education (MAT, MSE); reading (MSE, Ed S); special education - gifted, talented, and creative (MSE); special education - instructional specialist grades 4-12 (MSE); special education - instructional specialist grades P-4 (MSE). *Accreditation:* NCATE. Part-time programs available. Postbaccalaureate distance learning degree programs offered. *Faculty:* 28 full-time (16 women). *Students:* 77 full-time (68 women), 1,934 part-time (1,449 women); includes 361 minority (290 Black or African American, non-Hispanic/Latino; 11 American Indian or Alaska Native, non-Hispanic/Latino; 3 Asian, non-Hispanic/Latino; 26 Hispanic/Latino; 1 Native Hawaiian or other Pacific Islander, non-Hispanic/Latino; 30 Two or more races, non-Hispanic/Latino), 5 international. Average age 36. 1,627 applicants, 71% accepted, 770 enrolled. In 2013, 1,182 master's, 12 doctorates, 76 other advanced degrees awarded. *Degree requirements:* For master's, comprehensive exam, thesis or alternative; for doctorate, comprehensive exam, thesis/dissertation; for other advanced degree, comprehensive exam. *Entrance requirements:* For master's, GRE General Test or MAT, appropriate bachelor's degree, official transcripts, immunization records, letters of reference, interview; for doctorate, GRE General Test or MAT, interview, master's degree, letters of reference, official transcript, personal statement, writing sample, immunization records; for other advanced degree, GRE General Test or MAT, interview, master's degree, official transcript, immunization records, letters of reference, 3 years of teaching experience, teaching license. Additional exam requirements/recommendations for international students: Required—TOEFL (minimum score 550 paper-based; 79 iBT), IELTS (minimum score 6), PTE (minimum score 56). *Application deadline:* For fall admission, 7/1 for domestic and international students; for spring admission, 11/15 for domestic students, 11/14 for international students. Applications are processed on a rolling basis. Electronic applications accepted. *Expenses:* Tuition, state resident: full-time $4284; part-time $238 per credit hour. Tuition, nonresident: full-time $8568; part-time $476 per credit hour. *International tuition:* $9268 full-time. *Required fees:* $1098; $61 per credit hour. $25 per term. Tuition and fees vary according to course load and program. *Financial support:* In 2013–14, 20 students received support. Fellowships, teaching assistantships, career-related internships or fieldwork, scholarships/grants, and unspecified assistantships available. Financial award application deadline: 7/1; financial award applicants required to submit FAFSA. *Unit head:* Dr. Annette Hux, Interim Chair, 870-972-3059, Fax: 870-972-3344, E-mail: ahux@astate.edu. *Application contact:* Vickey Ring, Graduate Admissions Coordinator, 870-972-3029, Fax: 870-972-3857, E-mail: vickeyring@astate.edu.
Website: http://www.astate.edu/college/education/departments/school-of-teacher-education-and-leadership/index.dot.

Averett University, Master in Education Program, Danville, VA 24541-3692. Offers administration and supervision (M Ed); art (M Ed); biology (M Ed); chemistry (M Ed); curriculum and instruction (M Ed); early childhood (M Ed); English (M Ed); mathematics (M Ed); middle grades (M Ed); physical science (M Ed); reading specialist (M Ed); science (M Ed); special education (M Ed); special education learning disability (M Ed). Program offered on Danville Campus only. Part-time and evening/weekend programs available. *Faculty:* 4 full-time (3 women), 13 part-time/adjunct (8 women). *Students:* 43 full-time (35 women), 44 part-time (35 women); includes 7 minority (all Black or African American, non-Hispanic/Latino). *Degree requirements:* For master's, 30-credit core curriculum, minimum GPA of 3.0 throughout program, completion of degree requirements within six years from start of program. *Entrance requirements:* For master's, PRAXIS I, GRE, or MAT; writing proficiency test, minimum cumulative GPA of 3.0 over the last 60 hours of undergraduate study toward a baccalaureate degree, three letters of recommendation, Virginia teaching license (or eligibility). Additional exam requirements/recommendations for international students: Required—TOEFL (minimum score 600 paper-based; 100 iBT). *Application deadline:* Applications are processed on a rolling basis. Application fee: $100. *Expenses:* Contact institution. *Financial support:* Career-related internships or fieldwork, Federal Work-Study, and scholarships/grants available. Financial award application deadline: 4/1; financial award applicants required to submit FAFSA. *Unit head:* Wilfred Lawrence, Department Chair of Education, 434-791-5752, E-mail: priedel@averett.edu. *Application contact:* Christy Pack, Executive Director of Enrollment, 804-887-8612, E-mail: dpack@averett.edu.
Website: http://www.averett.edu/adultprograms/degrees/MEDtrad.php.

Bellarmine University, Annsley Frazier Thornton School of Education, Louisville, KY 40205-0671. Offers education and social change (PhD); elementary education (MA Ed, MAT); learning and behavior disorders (MA Ed, MAT); middle grades education (MA Ed, MAT); principalship (Ed S); reading and writing (MA Ed); secondary education (MAT); teacher leadership (MA Ed). *Accreditation:* NCATE. Part-time and evening/weekend programs available. *Faculty:* 13 full-time (7 women), 14 part-time/adjunct (9 women). *Students:* 60 full-time (47 women), 191 part-time (140 women); includes 35 minority (22 Black or African American, non-Hispanic/Latino; 1 American Indian or Alaska Native, non-Hispanic/Latino; 3 Asian, non-Hispanic/Latino; 5 Hispanic/Latino; 4 Two or more races, non-Hispanic/Latino). Average age 33. In 2013, 108 master's awarded. *Degree requirements:* For master's, comprehensive exam, thesis (for some programs); for doctorate, comprehensive exam, thesis/dissertation. *Entrance requirements:* For master's, GRE, baccalaureate degree from accredited institution; minimum overall GPA of 2.75, 3.0 in major; letters of recommendation; valid Kentucky provisional or professional certificate; for doctorate, GRE, minimum GPA of 3.5 in all graduate coursework; baccalaureate and master's degrees in education (MA, MS) or fields directly relevant to education; three letters of recommendation; two essays (no more than 1000 words each); interview. Additional exam requirements/recommendations for international students: Required—TOEFL (minimum score 550 paper-based; 80 iBT). *Application deadline:* Applications are processed on a rolling basis. Application fee: $25. *Expenses:* Contact institution. *Financial support:* Scholarships/grants available. Financial award applicants required to submit FAFSA. *Faculty research:* Literacy, service-learning, dispositions, educational technology, special education. *Unit head:* Dr. Robert Cooter, Dean, 502-272-8191, Fax: 502-272-8189, E-mail: rcooter@bellarmine.edu. *Application contact:* Theresa Klapheke, Administrative Director of Graduate Programs, 502-272-8271, Fax: 502-272-8002, E-mail: tklapheke@bellarmine.edu.
Website: http://www.bellarmine.edu/education/graduate.

Berry College, Graduate Programs, Graduate Programs in Education, Program in Middle Grades Education and Reading, Mount Berry, GA 30149-0159. Offers middle grades education (M Ed, MAT); reading (M Ed). *Accreditation:* NCATE. Part-time programs available. *Faculty:* 10 part-time/adjunct (6 women). *Students:* 1 (woman) full-time, 6 part-time (5 women). Average age 30. In 2013, 6 master's awarded. *Degree requirements:* For master's, thesis, portfolio, oral exams. *Entrance requirements:* For master's, GRE General Test or MAT, minimum GPA of 2.5. Additional exam requirements/recommendations for international students: Required—TOEFL (minimum score 550 paper-based). *Application deadline:* For fall admission, 7/25 for domestic students, 5/1 for international students; for spring admission, 12/1 for domestic students, 10/1 for international students. Applications are processed on a rolling basis. Application fee: $25 ($30 for international students). Electronic applications accepted. *Expenses:* Contact institution. *Financial support:* In 2013–14, 4 students received support, including 2 research assistantships with full tuition reimbursements available (averaging $1,158 per year); scholarships/grants, tuition waivers (partial), and unspecified assistantships also available. Support available to part-time students. Financial award application deadline: 3/1; financial award applicants required to submit FAFSA. *Unit head:* Dr. Jacqueline McDowell, Dean, 706-236-1717, Fax: 706-238-5827, E-mail: jmcdowell@berry.edu. *Application contact:* Brett Kennedy, Assistant Vice President of Enrollment Management, 706-236-2215, Fax: 706-290-2178, E-mail: admissions@berry.edu.
Website: http://www.berry.edu/academics/education/graduate/.

Bloomsburg University of Pennsylvania, School of Graduate Studies, College of Education, Department of Early Childhood and Adolescent Education, Program in Middle Level Education Grades 4-8, Bloomsburg, PA 17815-1301. Offers language arts (M Ed); math (M Ed); science (M Ed); social studies (M Ed). *Accreditation:* NCATE. *Faculty:* 14 full-time (6 women), 3 part-time/adjunct (2 women). In 2013, 2 master's awarded. *Degree requirements:* For master's, thesis optional, student teaching. *Entrance requirements:* For master's, MAT, GRE, or PRAXIS, minimum QPA of 3.0, teaching certificate, U.S. citizenship, related undergraduate coursework, professional liability insurance, recent TB test. Additional exam requirements/recommendations for international students: Required—TOEFL (minimum score 550 paper-based). *Application deadline:* Applications are processed on a rolling basis. Application fee: $35 ($60 for international students). Electronic applications accepted. *Expenses:* Tuition, state resident: full-time $7956; part-time $442 per credit. Tuition, nonresident: full-time $11,934; part-time $663 per credit. *Required fees:* $95.50 per credit. $55 per semester. Tuition and fees vary according to course load. *Financial support:* Unspecified assistantships available. *Unit head:* Dr. Tegan Kotarski, College of Education Graduate Coordinator, 570-389-3883, Fax: 570-389-5049, E-mail: tkotarsk@bloomu.edu. *Application contact:* Jennifer Richard, Administrative Assistant, 570-389-4015, Fax: 570-389-3054, E-mail: jrichard@bloomu.edu.
Website: http://www.bloomu.edu/gradschool/middle-level-education.

Brenau University, Sydney O. Smith Graduate School, School of Education, Gainesville, GA 30501. Offers early childhood (Ed S); early childhood education (M Ed, MAT); middle grades (Ed S); middle grades education (M Ed, MAT); secondary education (MAT); special education (M Ed, MAT). *Accreditation:* NCATE. Part-time and evening/weekend programs available. Postbaccalaureate distance learning degree programs offered (no on-campus study). *Degree requirements:* For master's, thesis optional, comprehensive exam or applied research project, effective portfolio; for Ed S, thesis, applied research project. *Entrance requirements:* For master's, GRE, MAT, interview, minimum GPA of 3.0, 3 references, writing samples; for Ed S, GRE, MAT, master's degree, minimum GPA of 3.0, writing sample, letters of reference. Additional exam requirements/recommendations for international students: Required—TOEFL (minimum score 500 paper-based; 61 iBT); Recommended—IELTS (minimum score 5). Electronic applications accepted. *Expenses:* Contact institution.

Brooklyn College of the City University of New York, Division of Graduate Studies, School of Education, Program in Middle Childhood Education (Math), Brooklyn, NY 11210-2889. Offers MS Ed. *Entrance requirements:* For master's, LAST, 2 letters of recommendation, essay, resume. Additional exam requirements/recommendations for international students: Required—TOEFL (minimum score 500 paper-based; 61 iBT). Electronic applications accepted.

Brooklyn College of the City University of New York, Division of Graduate Studies, School of Education, Program in Middle Childhood Education (Science), Brooklyn, NY 11210-2889. Offers biology (MA); chemistry (MA); earth science (MA); general science (MA); physics (MA). Part-time and evening/weekend programs available. *Entrance requirements:* For master's, LAST, interview, previous course work in education and mathematics, resume, 2 letters of recommendation, essay. Additional exam requirements/recommendations for international students: Required—TOEFL (minimum score 500 paper-based; 61 iBT). Electronic applications accepted. *Faculty research:* Geometric thinking, mastery of basic facts, problem-solving strategies, history of mathematics.

California Lutheran University, Graduate Studies, Graduate School of Education, Thousand Oaks, CA 91360-2787. Offers counseling and guidance (MS), including college student personnel, counseling and guidance; educational leadership (MA, Ed D), including educational leadership (K-12) (Ed D), higher education leadership (Ed D); special education (MS); teacher leadership (M Ed); teaching (M Ed). *Accreditation:* NCATE. Part-time and evening/weekend programs available. *Faculty:* 18 full-time (14 women), 28 part-time/adjunct (20 women). *Students:* 327 full-time (260 women), 96 part-time (77 women); includes 150 minority (7 Black or African American, non-Hispanic/Latino; 20 Asian, non-Hispanic/Latino; 112 Hispanic/Latino; 11 Two or more races, non-Hispanic/Latino), 1 international. Average age 33. 123 applicants, 85% accepted, 80 enrolled. In 2013, 117 master's, 9 doctorates awarded. *Entrance requirements:* For master's, GRE General Test, interview, minimum GPA of 3.0. *Application deadline:* For fall admission, 7/1 priority date for domestic students; for spring admission, 11/1 priority date for domestic students; for summer admission, 4/1 priority date for domestic students. Applications are processed on a rolling basis. Application fee: $50. *Unit head:* Dr. Robert Fraisse, Dean, 805-493-3421. *Application contact:* 805-493-3325, Fax: 805-493-3861, E-mail: clugrad@callutheran.edu.

California State University, Bakersfield, Division of Graduate Studies, School of Natural Sciences, Mathematics, and Engineering, Program in Teaching Mathematics, Bakersfield, CA 93311. Offers MA. *Entrance requirements:* For master's, minimum GPA of 2.5 for last 90 quarter units. *Unit head:* Dr. Joseph Fiedler, Head, 661-654-2058, Fax:

661-664-2039. *Application contact:* Debbie Blowers, Assistant Director of Admissions, 661-664-3381, E-mail: dblowers@csub.edu.

Cambridge College, School of Education, Cambridge, MA 02138-5304. Offers autism specialist (M Ed); autism/behavior analyst (M Ed); behavior analyst (Post-Master's Certificate); behavioral management (M Ed); early childhood teacher (M Ed); education specialist in curriculum and instruction (CAGS); educational leadership (Ed D); elementary teacher (M Ed); English as a second language (M Ed, Certificate); general science (M Ed); health education (Post-Master's Certificate); health/family and consumer sciences (M Ed); history (M Ed); individualized (M Ed); information technology literacy (M Ed); instructional technology (M Ed); interdisciplinary studies (M Ed); library teacher (M Ed); literacy education (M Ed); mathematics (M Ed); mathematics specialist (Certificate); middle school mathematics and science (M Ed); school administration (M Ed, CAGS); school guidance counselor (M Ed); school nurse education (M Ed); school social worker/school adjustment counselor (M Ed); special education administrator (CAGS); special education/moderate disabilities (M Ed); teaching skills and methodologies (M Ed). Part-time and evening/weekend programs available. Postbaccalaureate distance learning degree programs offered (minimal on-campus study). *Degree requirements:* For master's, thesis, internship/practicum (licensure program only); for doctorate, thesis/dissertation; for other advanced degree, thesis. *Entrance requirements:* For master's, interview, resume, documentation of licensure, 2 professional references; for doctorate, official transcripts, interview, resume, documentation of licensure (if any), written personal statement/essay, portfolio of scholarly and professional work, qualifying assessment, 2 professional references, health insurance, immunizations form; for other advanced degree, official transcripts, interview, resume, documentation of licensure (if any), written personal statement/ essay, 2 professional references, health insurance, immunizations form. Additional exam requirements/recommendations for international students: Required—TOEFL (minimum score 550 paper-based; 79 iBT), Michigan English Language Assessment Battery (minimum score 85); Recommended—IELTS (minimum score 6). Electronic applications accepted. *Expenses:* Contact institution. *Faculty research:* Adult education, accelerated learning, mathematics education, brain compatible learning, special education and law.

Campbell University, Graduate and Professional Programs, School of Education, Buies Creek, NC 27506. Offers administration (MSA); community counseling (MA); elementary education (M Ed); English education (M Ed); interdisciplinary studies (M Ed); mathematics education (M Ed); middle grades education (M Ed); physical education (M Ed); school counseling (M Ed); secondary education (M Ed); social science education (M Ed). *Accreditation:* NCATE. Part-time and evening/weekend programs available. *Degree requirements:* For master's, comprehensive exam. *Entrance requirements:* For master's, GRE General Test, minimum GPA of 2.7. *Faculty research:* Spiritual values and wellness issues in counseling, stress and professional burnout among counselors, thinking strategies, leadership, adaptive technology.

Canisius College, Graduate Division, School of Education and Human Services, Department of Teacher Education, Buffalo, NY 14208-1098. Offers adolescence education (MS Ed); childhood education (MS Ed); general education (MS Ed); special education (MS), including adolescence special education, advanced special education, childhood education grade 1-6, childhood special education. Part-time and evening/ weekend programs available. Postbaccalaureate distance learning degree programs offered (minimal on-campus study). *Faculty:* 23 full-time (18 women), 10 part-time/ adjunct (4 women). *Students:* 87 full-time (58 women), 32 part-time (27 women); includes 8 minority (4 Black or African American, non-Hispanic/Latino; 3 Asian, non-Hispanic/Latino; 1 Two or more races, non-Hispanic/Latino), 14 international. Average age 29. 73 applicants, 68% accepted, 23 enrolled. In 2013, 135 master's awarded. *Degree requirements:* For master's, research project or thesis, project internship. *Entrance requirements:* For master's, GRE if cumulative GPA is less than 2.7, transcripts, letters of recommendation. Additional exam requirements/recommendations for international students: Required—TOEFL (minimum score 550 paper-based, 80 iBT), IELTS (minimum score 6.5), or CAEL (minimum score 70). *Application deadline:* Applications are processed on a rolling basis. Application fee: $25. Electronic applications accepted. Application fee is waived when completed online. *Expenses: Tuition:* Part-time $750 per credit hour. *Financial support:* Career-related internships or fieldwork, Federal Work-Study, scholarships/grants, tuition waivers (partial), and unspecified assistantships available. Support available to part-time students. Financial award application deadline: 4/30; financial award applicants required to submit FAFSA. *Unit head:* Dr. Julie Henry, Chair/Professor, 716-888-3729, E-mail: henry1@ canisius.edu. *Application contact:* Julie A. Zulewski, Director of Graduate Admissions, 716-555-2548, Fax: 716-888-3195, E-mail: zulewskj@canisius.edu.
Website: http://www.canisius.edu/academics/graduate/.

Capella University, School of Education, Doctoral Programs in Education, Minneapolis, MN 55402. Offers curriculum and instruction (PhD); educational leadership and management (Ed D); instructional design for online learning (PhD); K-12 studies in education (PhD); leadership for higher education (PhD); leadership in educational administration (PhD); postsecondary and adult education (PhD); professional studies in education (PhD); reading and literacy (Ed D); special education leadership (PhD); training and performance improvement (PhD).

Capella University, School of Education, Master's Programs in Education, Minneapolis, MN 55402. Offers adult education (MS); curriculum and instruction (MS); early childhood education (MS); enrollment management (MS); higher education leadership and management (MS); instructional design for online learning (MS); integrative studies (MS); K-12 studies in education (MS); leadership in educational administration (MS); reading and literacy (MS); special education teaching (MS).

Chestnut Hill College, School of Graduate Studies, Department of Education, Program in Middle Education, Philadelphia, PA 19118-2693. Offers elementary/middle education (M Ed, CAS). Part-time and evening/weekend programs available. *Faculty:* 10 full-time (7 women), 48 part-time/adjunct (34 women). *Students:* 13 full-time (11 women), 96 part-time (78 women); includes 30 minority (22 Black or African American, non-Hispanic/ Latino; 1 American Indian or Alaska Native, non-Hispanic/Latino; 1 Asian, non-Hispanic/ Latino; 4 Hispanic/Latino; 2 Two or more races, non-Hispanic/Latino). Average age 31. 28 applicants, 100% accepted. In 2013, 51 master's, 11 CASs awarded. *Degree requirements:* For master's, thesis optional. *Entrance requirements:* For master's, PRAXIS I or proof of teaching certification, letters of recommendation, writing sample, 6 graduate credits with minimum B grade if undergraduate GPA less than 3.0. Additional exam requirements/recommendations for international students: Required—TOEFL (minimum score 500 paper-based), IELTS (mnimum score 6.0), or TWE (minimum score 22). *Application deadline:* For fall admission, 7/1 for domestic and international students; for spring admission, 11/1 for domestic and international students; for summer admission, 4/1 for domestic and international students. Applications are processed on a rolling basis. *Expenses:* Contact institution. *Financial support:* Unspecified assistantships available. *Faculty research:* Inclusive education, cultural issues in education. *Unit head:* Dr. Debra Chiaradonna, Chair, Department of Education, 215-248-7147, Fax: 215-248-7155, E-mail: chiaradonnad@chc.edu. *Application contact:* Jayne Mashett, Director of Admissions, School of Graduate Studies, 215-248-7020, Fax: 215-248-7161, E-mail: gradadmissions@chc.edu.
Website: http://www.chc.edu/Graduate/Programs/Masters/Education/.

Chicago State University, School of Graduate and Professional Studies, College of Education, Department of Reading, Elementary Education, Library Information and Media Studies, Program in Middle School Education, Chicago, IL 60628. Offers MAT.

City College of the City University of New York, Graduate School, School of Education, Department of Secondary Education, New York, NY 10031-9198. Offers adolescent mathematics education (MA, AC); English education (MA); middle school mathematics education (MS); science education (MA); social studies education (AC). *Accreditation:* NCATE. *Entrance requirements:* For master's, Liberal Arts and Sciences Test (LAST), Content Specialty Test (CST). Additional exam requirements/ recommendations for international students: Required—TOEFL.

Clemson University, Graduate School, College of Health, Education, and Human Development, Eugene T. Moore School of Education, Program in Middle Grades Education, Clemson, SC 29634. Offers MAT. *Students:* 25 full-time (14 women), 14 part-time (9 women); includes 3 minority (2 Black or African American, non-Hispanic/Latino; 1 Two or more races, non-Hispanic/Latino), 1 international. Average age 33. 12 applicants, 67% accepted, 8 enrolled. In 2013, 36 master's awarded. *Degree requirements:* For master's, student teaching. *Entrance requirements:* For master's, PRAXIS II. Additional exam requirements/recommendations for international students: Required—TOEFL; Recommended—IELTS. *Application deadline:* Applications are processed on a rolling basis. Application fee: $70 ($80 for international students). Electronic applications accepted. *Expenses:* Contact institution. *Financial support:* In 2013–14, 6 students received support, including 1 teaching assistantship with partial tuition reimbursement available (averaging $6,812 per year); research assistantships with partial tuition reimbursements available, institutionally sponsored loans, scholarships/grants, health care benefits, and unspecified assistantships also available. *Faculty research:* Language arts in the middle school, equity and social justice pedagogies in mathematics education, acquisition of scientific discourse. *Unit head:* Dr. Michael J. Padilla, Director/Associate Dean, 864-656-4444, Fax: 864-656-0311, E-mail: padilla@clemson.edu. *Application contact:* Dr. David Fleming, Graduate Coordinator, 864-656-1881, Fax: 864-656-0311, E-mail: dflemin@clemson.edu.
Website: http://www.grad.clemson.edu/programs/Middle-Level-Education/.

Cleveland State University, College of Graduate Studies, College of Education and Human Services, Department of Teacher Education, Cleveland, OH 44115. Offers art education (M Ed); early childhood education (M Ed); foreign language education (M Ed); mathematics and science education (M Ed); middle childhood education (M Ed); special education (M Ed), including mild/moderate disabilities, moderate/intensive disabilities; teaching English to speakers of other languages (M Ed). Part-time and evening/ weekend programs available. *Faculty:* 20 full-time (12 women), 26 part-time/adjunct (20 women). *Students:* 108 full-time (78 women), 311 part-time (252 women); includes 103 minority (80 Black or African American, non-Hispanic/Latino; 2 Asian, non-Hispanic/ Latino; 10 Hispanic/Latino; 1 Native Hawaiian or other Pacific Islander, non-Hispanic/ Latino; 10 Two or more races, non-Hispanic/Latino), 52 international. Average age 32. 177 applicants, 55% accepted, 68 enrolled. In 2013, 192 master's awarded. *Degree requirements:* For master's, comprehensive exam (for some programs), thesis or alternative. *Entrance requirements:* For master's, GRE General Test or MAT, minimum GPA of 2.75. Additional exam requirements/recommendations for international students: Required—TOEFL (minimum score 525 paper-based), IELTS (minimum score 6). *Application deadline:* For fall admission, 7/15 priority date for domestic students. Applications are processed on a rolling basis. Application fee: $30. *Expenses:* Tuition, state resident: full-time $8335; part-time $521 per credit hour. Tuition, nonresident: full-time $15,670; part-time $979 per credit hour. *Required fees:* $50; $25 per semester. *Financial support:* In 2013–14, 12 research assistantships with full tuition reimbursements (averaging $3,480 per year) were awarded; tuition waivers (partial) and unspecified assistantships also available. *Faculty research:* Early literacy, professional development in reading, reading recovery, dual language, induction programs. *Total annual research expenditures:* $6.2 million. *Unit head:* Dr. Clifford T. Bennett, Chairperson, 216-523-7105, Fax: 216-687-5379, E-mail: c.t.bennett@csuohio.edu. *Application contact:* Deborah L. Brown, Interim Assistant Director, Graduate Admissions, 216-523-7572, E-mail: d.l.brown@csuohio.edu.
Website: http://www.csuohio.edu/cehs/departments/TE/te_dept.html.

The College at Brockport, State University of New York, School of Education and Human Services, Department of Education and Human Development, Program in Adolescence Education, Brockport, NY 14420-2997. Offers adolescence biology education (MS Ed); adolescence chemistry education (MS Ed); adolescence earth science education (MS Ed); adolescence English education (MS Ed); adolescence mathematics education (MS Ed); adolescence physics education (MS Ed); adolescence social studies education (MS Ed). *Accreditation:* NCATE. Part-time programs available. *Students:* 13 full-time (7 women), 47 part-time (28 women); includes 3 minority (1 Black or African American, non-Hispanic/Latino; 1 American Indian or Alaska Native, non-Hispanic/Latino; 1 Asian, non-Hispanic/Latino). 26 applicants, 88% accepted, 14 enrolled. In 2013, 27 master's awarded. *Degree requirements:* For master's, thesis or alternative. *Entrance requirements:* For master's, minimum GPA of 3.0, letters of recommendation; statement of objectives, current resume. Additional exam requirements/recommendations for international students: Required—TOEFL (minimum score 550 paper-based; 79 iBT), IELTS (minimum score 6.5). *Application deadline:* For fall admission, 3/15 priority date for domestic and international students; for spring admission, 10/15 priority date for domestic and international students; for summer admission, 3/15 priority date for domestic students, 3/13 priority date for international students. Application fee: $80. Electronic applications accepted. *Expenses:* Tuition, state resident: full-time $9870. Tuition, nonresident: full-time $18,350. *Required fees:* $1848. *Financial support:* Federal Work-Study, scholarships/grants, and unspecified assistantships available. Support available to part-time students. Financial award application deadline: 3/15; financial award applicants required to submit FAFSA. *Unit head:* Dr. Don Halquist, Chairperson, 585-395-5550, Fax: 585-395-2172, E-mail: dhalquis@brockport.edu. *Application contact:* Michael Harrison, Coordinator of Certification and Graduate Advisement, 585-395-2326, Fax: 585-395-2172, E-mail: mharriso@brockport.edu.
Website: http://www.brockport.edu/ehd/.

The College at Brockport, State University of New York, School of Education and Human Services, Department of Education and Human Development, Program in Adolescence Inclusive Generalist Education, Brockport, NY 14420-2997. Offers English (MS Ed); mathematics (MS Ed); science (MS Ed); social studies (MS Ed). *Students:* 30 full-time (18 women), 24 part-time (17 women); includes 6 minority (3 Black or African American, non-Hispanic/Latino; 2 Hispanic/Latino; 1 Two or more races, non-Hispanic/ Latino). 16 applicants, 75% accepted, 8 enrolled. In 2013, 15 master's awarded. *Degree requirements:* For master's, thesis or alternative. *Entrance requirements:* For master's, minimum GPA of 3.0, letters of recommendation, statement of objectives, academic major (or equivalent) in program discipline; current resume. Additional exam requirements/recommendations for international students: Required—TOEFL (minimum score 550 paper-based; 79 iBT), IELTS (minimum score 6.5). *Application deadline:* For

fall admission, 3/15 priority date for domestic and international students; for spring admission, 10/15 priority date for domestic and international students; for summer admission, 3/15 for domestic and international students. Application fee: $80. Electronic applications accepted. *Expenses:* Tuition, state resident: full-time $9870. Tuition, nonresident: full-time $18,350. *Required fees:* $1848. *Financial support:* Federal Work-Study, scholarships/grants, and unspecified assistantships available. Support available to part-time students. Financial award application deadline: 3/15; financial award applicants required to submit FAFSA. *Unit head:* Dr. Don Halquist, Chairperson, 585-395-2205, Fax: 585-395-2171, E-mail: dhalquis@brockport.edu. *Application contact:* Michael Harrison, Coordinator of Certification and Graduate Advisement, 585-395-2326, Fax: 585-395-2172, E-mail: mharriso@brockport.edu.
Website: http://www.brockport.edu/ehd/.

College of Mount Saint Vincent, School of Professional and Continuing Studies, Department of Teacher Education, Riverdale, NY 10471-1093. Offers instructional technology and global perspectives (Certificate); middle level education (Certificate); multicultural studies (Certificate); urban and multicultural education (MS Ed). *Accreditation:* Teacher Education Accreditation Council. Part-time programs available. *Degree requirements:* For master's, comprehensive exam. *Entrance requirements:* For master's, interview, New York teaching certificate. Additional exam requirements/recommendations for international students: Required—TOEFL.

Columbus State University, Graduate Studies, College of Education and Health Professions, Department of Teacher Education, Columbus, GA 31907-5645. Offers accomplished teaching (M Ed); early childhood education (M Ed, MAT, Ed S); middle grades education (M Ed, MAT, Ed S); school library media (M Ed, MAT); secondary education (M Ed, MAT, Ed S), including English/language arts (M Ed, Ed S), general science (M Ed), mathematics (M Ed, Ed S), science (Ed S), social science (M Ed, Ed S); special education (M Ed, MAT, Ed S), including general curriculum (M Ed, MAT); teacher leadership (M Ed). *Accreditation:* NCATE. Part-time and evening/weekend programs available. Postbaccalaureate distance learning degree programs offered (minimal on-campus study). *Faculty:* 17 full-time (12 women), 31 part-time/adjunct (28 women). *Students:* 59 full-time (48 women), 190 part-time (150 women); includes 85 minority (68 Black or African American, non-Hispanic/Latino; 1 American Indian or Alaska Native, non-Hispanic/Latino; 6 Asian, non-Hispanic/Latino; 4 Hispanic/Latino; 6 Two or more races, non-Hispanic/Latino), 2 international. Average age 34. 132 applicants, 58% accepted, 50 enrolled. In 2013, 86 master's, 26 other advanced degrees awarded. *Degree requirements:* For master's, thesis, exit exam; for Ed S, thesis or alternative. *Entrance requirements:* For master's, GRE General Test, minimum undergraduate GPA of 2.75; for Ed S, GRE General Test, minimum undergraduate GPA of 2.75, graduate 3.0. Additional exam requirements/recommendations for international students: Required—TOEFL (minimum score 550 paper-based; 79 iBT). *Application deadline:* For fall admission, 6/30 for domestic students, 5/1 for international students; for spring admission, 11/1 for domestic and international students; for summer admission, 3/1 for domestic and international students. Applications are processed on a rolling basis. Application fee: $40. Electronic applications accepted. *Expenses:* Tuition, state resident: full-time $4572; part-time $382 per credit hour. Tuition, nonresident: full-time $18,292; part-time $1526 per credit hour. *Required fees:* $1800; $196 per credit hour. Tuition and fees vary according to campus/location and program. *Financial support:* In 2013–14, 173 students received support, including 12 research assistantships with partial tuition reimbursements available (averaging $3,000 per year); career-related internships or fieldwork, Federal Work-Study, institutionally sponsored loans, scholarships/grants, tuition waivers (partial), and unspecified assistantships also available. Support available to part-time students. Financial award application deadline: 5/1; financial award applicants required to submit FAFSA. *Unit head:* Dr. Deirdre Greer, Department Chair, 706-507-8034, Fax: 706-568-3134, E-mail: greer_deirdre@columbusstate.edu. *Application contact:* Kristin Williams, Director of International and Graduate Recruitment, 706-507-8848, Fax: 706-568-5091, E-mail: williams_kristin@columbusstate.edu.
Website: http://te.columbusstate.edu/.

Converse College, School of Education and Graduate Studies, Program in Middle Level Education, Spartanburg, SC 29302-0006. Offers language arts/English (MAT); mathematics (MAT); middle level education (M Ed); science (MAT); social studies (MAT).

Daemen College, Education Department, Amherst, NY 14226-3592. Offers adolescence education (MS); childhood education (MS); childhood special education (MS); childhood special-alternative certification (MS); early childhood special-alternative certification (MS). Part-time programs available. *Degree requirements:* For master's, thesis optional, research thesis in lieu of comprehensive exam; completion of degree within 5 years. *Entrance requirements:* For master's, 2 letters of recommendation (professional and character), proof of initial certificate of license for professional programs, resume. Additional exam requirements/recommendations for international students: Required—TOEFL (minimum score 500 paper-based; 63 iBT), IELTS (minimum score 5.5). Electronic applications accepted. *Faculty research:* Transition for students with disabilities, early childhood special education, traumatic brain injury (TBI), reading assessment.

Dowling College, Graduate Programs in Education, Oakdale, NY 11769-1999. Offers adolescence education with middle childhood extension (MS); childhood and early childhood education (MS); childhood and gifted education (MS); childhood education (1-6) (MS); computers in education (AC); early childhood education (B-2) (MS); educational administration (Ed D); educational technology leadership (MS); educational technology specialist (AC); gifted education (AC); literacy education (MS, AC), including 5-12 (MS), B-12 (MS); literacy education (MS), including B-6; school building leader (AC); school district business leader (MBA, AC); school district leader (AC); special education (MS), including autism, severe disabilities; sport management (MS). *Accreditation:* NCATE. Part-time and evening/weekend programs available. Postbaccalaureate distance learning degree programs offered (minimal on-campus study). *Faculty:* 44 full-time (24 women), 17 part-time/adjunct (8 women). *Students:* 183 full-time (124 women), 314 part-time (231 women); includes 51 minority (19 Black or African American, non-Hispanic/Latino; 1 American Indian or Alaska Native, non-Hispanic/Latino; 3 Asian, non-Hispanic/Latino; 26 Hispanic/Latino; 2 Native Hawaiian or other Pacific Islander, non-Hispanic/Latino). Average age 32. 174 applicants, 80% accepted, 82 enrolled. In 2013, 198 master's, 33 doctorates, 48 other advanced degrees awarded. *Degree requirements:* For master's and AC, comprehensive exam; for doctorate, thesis/dissertation. *Entrance requirements:* For master's, minimum GPA of 3.0; for doctorate, GRE, master's degree; for AC, teaching certificate. Additional exam requirements/recommendations for international students: Required—TOEFL (minimum score 550 paper-based). *Application deadline:* For fall admission, 9/1 priority date for domestic students; for winter admission, 1/1 priority date for domestic students; for spring admission, 2/1 priority date for domestic students. Applications are processed on a rolling basis. Application fee: $50. Electronic applications accepted. *Expenses: Tuition:* Full-time $22,731; part-time $1029 per credit. *Required fees:* $956; $956. *Financial support:* Career-related internships or fieldwork and Federal Work-Study available. Support available to part-time students. Financial award application deadline: 6/30; financial award applicants required to submit FAFSA. *Faculty research:* Natural readers, Korean styles and learning strategies, mothers of children with disabilities, computers in instruction, cultural background and organizational roadblocks to problem solving. *Unit head:* Dr. Robert Manley, Dean, 631-244-3447, E-mail: manleyr@dowling.edu. *Application contact:* Mary Boullianne, Director of Admissions, 631-244-3274, Fax: 631-244-1059, E-mail: boulliam@dowling.edu.

Drury University, Graduate Programs in Education, Springfield, MO 65802. Offers elementary education (M Ed); gifted education (M Ed); human services (M Ed); instructional mathematics K-8 (M Ed); instructional technology (M Ed); middle school teaching (M Ed); secondary education (M Ed); special education (M Ed); special reading (M Ed). *Accreditation:* NCATE. Part-time and evening/weekend programs available. *Degree requirements:* For master's, thesis. *Entrance requirements:* For master's, GRE or MAT, minimum GPA of 2.75. Additional exam requirements/recommendations for international students: Required—TOEFL. Electronic applications accepted. *Faculty research:* Cultural enrichment, research skills, parental involvement relating to reading skills, reading strategies for mainstreaming children.

Duquesne University, School of Education, Department of Instruction and Leadership, Program in Middle Level (4-8) Education, Pittsburgh, PA 15282-0001. Offers MS Ed. Part-time and evening/weekend programs available. *Faculty:* 2 full-time (both women). *Students:* 4 full-time (2 women); includes 1 minority (Two or more races, non-Hispanic/Latino). Average age 30. 9 applicants, 22% accepted, 2 enrolled. *Entrance requirements:* For master's, bachelor's degree. Additional exam requirements/recommendations for international students: Required—TOEFL (minimum score 550 paper-based). *Application deadline:* Applications are processed on a rolling basis. Electronic applications accepted. Application fee is waived when completed online. *Expenses: Tuition:* Full-time $18,162; part-time $1009 per credit. *Required fees:* $1728; $96 per credit. Tuition and fees vary according to program. *Financial support:* Research assistantships with tuition reimbursements available. *Unit head:* Dr. Alexandra Santau, Associate Professor and Program Director, 412-396-4516, Fax: 412-396-5388, E-mail: santaua@duq.edu. *Application contact:* Michael Dolinger, Director of Student and Academic Services, 412-396-6647, Fax: 412-396-5585, E-mail: dolingerm@duq.edu.
Website: http://www.duq.edu/academics/schools/education/graduate-programs-education/ms-middle-level-4-8.

East Carolina University, Graduate School, College of Education, Department of Business and Information Technologies Education, Greenville, NC 27858-4353. Offers business education (MA Ed); elementary education (MAT); English education (MAT); family and consumer science (MAT); health education (MAT); Hispanic studies (MAT); history education (MAT); marketing education (MA Ed); middle grades education (MAT); music education (MAT); physical education (MAT); science education (MAT); special education (MAT), including general curriculum; vocation education (MS). *Accreditation:* NCATE. Part-time and evening/weekend programs available. Postbaccalaureate distance learning degree programs offered (no on-campus study). *Degree requirements:* For master's, comprehensive exam, thesis optional. *Entrance requirements:* For master's, GRE or MAT, minimum GPA of 2.5, bachelor's degree in related field, teaching license (MA Ed). Additional exam requirements/recommendations for international students: Required—TOEFL. *Expenses:* Tuition, state resident: full-time $4223. Tuition, nonresident: full-time $16,540. *Required fees:* $2184.

East Carolina University, Graduate School, College of Education, Department of Curriculum and Instruction, Greenville, NC 27858-4353. Offers assistive technology (Certificate); autism (Certificate); deaf/blindness (Certificate); elementary education (MA Ed); English education (MA Ed); history (MA Ed); middle grade education (MA Ed); reading education (MA Ed); special education (MA Ed); teaching (MAT). Part-time programs available. Postbaccalaureate distance learning degree programs offered. *Degree requirements:* For master's, comprehensive exam, thesis optional. *Entrance requirements:* For master's, GRE General Test or MAT, interview, bachelor's degree in related field, minimum GPA of 2.5, teaching license. Additional exam requirements/recommendations for international students: Required—TOEFL. *Expenses:* Tuition, state resident: full-time $4223. Tuition, nonresident: full-time $16,540. *Required fees:* $2184.

Eastern Illinois University, Graduate School, College of Education and Professional Studies, Department of Early Childhood, Elementary and Middle Level Education, Charleston, IL 61920-3099. Offers elementary education (MS Ed). *Accreditation:* NCATE. Part-time programs available. *Degree requirements:* For master's, comprehensive exam. *Expenses: Tuition, area resident:* Part-time $283 per credit hour. Tuition, state resident: part-time $283 per credit hour. Tuition, nonresident: part-time $679 per credit hour.

Eastern Michigan University, Graduate School, College of Education, Department of Teacher Education, Programs in K–12 Education, Ypsilanti, MI 48197. Offers curriculum and instruction (MA); elementary education (MA); K-12 education (MA); middle school education (MA); secondary school education (MA). *Accreditation:* NCATE. Part-time and evening/weekend programs available. Postbaccalaureate distance learning degree programs offered (minimal on-campus study). *Students:* 11 full-time (4 women), 46 part-time (31 women); includes 8 minority (4 Black or African American, non-Hispanic/Latino; 1 American Indian or Alaska Native, non-Hispanic/Latino; 3 Hispanic/Latino). Average age 36. 41 applicants, 78% accepted, 20 enrolled. In 2013, 5 master's awarded. *Entrance requirements:* For master's, GRE. Additional exam requirements/recommendations for international students: Required—TOEFL. *Application deadline:* Applications are processed on a rolling basis. Application fee: $35. *Expenses:* Tuition, state resident: full-time $12,300; part-time $466 per credit hour. Tuition, nonresident: full-time $23,159; part-time $918 per credit hour. *Required fees:* $71 per credit hour. $46 per semester. One-time fee: $100. Tuition and fees vary according to course level and degree level. *Financial support:* Fellowships, research assistantships with full tuition reimbursements, teaching assistantships with full tuition reimbursements, career-related internships or fieldwork, Federal Work-Study, institutionally sponsored loans, scholarships/grants, tuition waivers (partial), and unspecified assistantships available. Support available to part-time students. Financial award applicants required to submit FAFSA. *Unit head:* Dr. Martha Kinney-Sedgwick, Interim Department Head, 734-487-3260, Fax: 734-487-2101, E-mail: mkinneys@emich.edu. *Application contact:* Dr. Ethan Lowenstein, Coordinator, 734-487-3260, Fax: 734-487-2101, E-mail: elowste@emich.edu.

Eastern Nazarene College, Adult and Graduate Studies, Division of Teacher Education, Quincy, MA 02170. Offers administration (M Ed); early childhood education (M Ed, Certificate); elementary education (M Ed, Certificate); English as a second language (Certificate); instructional enrichment and development (Certificate); middle school education (M Ed, Certificate); moderate special needs education (Certificate); principal (Certificate); program development and supervision (Certificate); secondary education (M Ed, Certificate); special education administrator (Certificate); special needs (M Ed); supervisor (Certificate); teacher of reading (M Ed, Certificate). M Ed also available through weekend program for administration, special needs, and teacher of reading only. Part-time and evening/weekend programs available. *Entrance requirements:* Additional exam requirements/recommendations for international students: Required—TOEFL (minimum score 550 paper-based).

Middle School Education

Eastern University, Graduate Education Programs, St. Davids, PA 19087-3696. Offers ESL program specialist (K-12) (Certificate); general supervisor (PreK-12) (Certificate); health and physical education (K-12) (Certificate); middle level (4-8) (Certificate); multicultural education (M Ed); pre K-4 (Certificate); pre K-4 with special education (Certificate); reading (M Ed); reading specialist (K-12) (Certificate); reading supervisor (K-12) (Certificate); school health services (M Ed); school health supervisor (Certificate); school nurse (Certificate); school principalship (K-12) (Certificate); secondary biology education (7-12) (Certificate); secondary chemistry education (7-12) (Certificate); secondary communication education (7-12) (Certificate); secondary education (7-12) (Certificate); secondary English education (7-12) (Certificate); secondary math education (7-12) (Certificate); secondary social studies education (7-12) (Certificate); special education (M Ed); special education (7-12) (Certificate); special education (Pre K-8) (Certificate); special education supervisor (N-12) (Certificate); TESOL (M Ed); world language (Certificate), including French, Mandarin Chinese, Spanish. Part-time and evening/weekend programs available. Postbaccalaureate distance learning degree programs offered (no on-campus study). *Faculty:* 22 full-time (11 women), 26 part-time/adjunct (18 women). *Students:* 77 full-time (58 women), 223 part-time (149 women); includes 112 minority (81 Black or African American, non-Hispanic/Latino; 1 American Indian or Alaska Native, non-Hispanic/Latino; 9 Asian, non-Hispanic/Latino; 18 Hispanic/Latino; 1 Native Hawaiian or other Pacific Islander, non-Hispanic/Latino; 2 Two or more races, non-Hispanic/Latino), 7 international. Average age 34. 94 applicants, 100% accepted, 81 enrolled. In 2013, 120 master's awarded. *Entrance requirements:* For master's, minimum GPA of 2.5 (for M Ed); for Certificate, minimum GPA of 3.0 for certifications. Additional exam requirements/recommendations for international students: Required—TOEFL. *Application deadline:* For fall admission, 8/14 for domestic students; for spring admission, 12/20 for domestic students. Applications are processed on a rolling basis. Application fee: $35. Application fee is waived when completed online. *Expenses: Tuition:* Full-time $15,600; part-time $650 per credit. *Required fees:* $27.50 per semester. One-time fee: $50. Tuition and fees vary according to course load, degree level and program. *Financial support:* In 2013–14, 84 students received support, including 6 research assistantships with partial tuition reimbursements available (averaging $7,710 per year); scholarships/grants and unspecified assistantships also available. Financial award application deadline: 3/15; financial award applicants required to submit FAFSA. *Unit head:* Harry Gutelius, Associate Dean, 610-341-1729. *Application contact:* Michael Perpiglia, Associate Director of Enrollment, 610-341-5947, Fax: 484-581-1276, E-mail: mperpigl@eastern.edu.
Website: http://www.eastern.edu/academics/programs/loeb-school-education-0/graduateprograms.

East Tennessee State University, School of Graduate Studies, College of Education, Department of Curriculum and Instruction, Johnson City, TN 37614. Offers educational media and educational technology (M Ed), including educational communications and technology, school library media; elementary education (M Ed); reading (MA), including reading education, storytelling; school library professional (Post-Master's Certificate); secondary education (M Ed), including classroom technology, secondary education (M Ed, MAT); storytelling (Postbaccalaureate Certificate); teacher education with multiple levels (MAT), including elementary education, middle grades education, secondary education (M Ed, MAT). *Accreditation:* NCATE. Part-time and evening/weekend programs available. Postbaccalaureate distance learning degree programs offered (no on-campus study). *Faculty:* 25 full-time (18 women), 12 part-time/adjunct (8 women). *Students:* 66 full-time (50 women), 97 part-time (85 women); includes 5 minority (3 Black or African American, non-Hispanic/Latino; 2 Two or more races, non-Hispanic/Latino), 2 international. Average age 31. 144 applicants, 57% accepted, 70 enrolled. In 2013, 83 master's, 5 other advanced degrees awarded. *Degree requirements:* For master's, comprehensive exam, thesis optional, student teaching, practicum; for other advanced degree, field work (school library); culminating experience (storytelling). *Entrance requirements:* For master's, GRE, SAT, ACT, PRAXIS, minimum GPA of 3.0; for other advanced degree, master's degree, TN teaching license (for school library professional Post-Master's Certificate); three letters of recommendation (for storytelling Postbaccalaureate Certificate). Additional exam requirements/recommendations for international students: Required—TOEFL (minimum score 550 paper-based; 79 iBT). *Application deadline:* For fall admission, 6/1 for domestic students, 4/30 for international students; for spring admission, 11/1 for domestic students, 4/30 for international students. Application fee: $35 ($45 for international students). Electronic applications accepted. *Expenses:* Tuition, state resident: full-time $7900; part-time $395 per credit hour. Tuition, nonresident: full-time $21,960; part-time $1098 per credit hour. *Required fees:* $1345; $84 per credit hour. *Financial support:* In 2013–14, 43 students received support, including 6 research assistantships with full tuition reimbursements available (averaging $6,000 per year), 10 teaching assistantships with full tuition reimbursements available (averaging $6,000 per year); career-related internships or fieldwork, institutionally sponsored loans, scholarships/grants, and unspecified assistantships also available. Financial award application deadline: 7/1; financial award applicants required to submit FAFSA. *Faculty research:* Critical thinking; curriculum development in reading, math, and science education; cultural diversity; cognitive processes; effective teaching strategies. *Unit head:* Dr. Rhona Hurwitz, Chair, 423-439-7598, Fax: 423-439-8362, E-mail: hurwitz@etsu.edu. *Application contact:* Fiona Goodyear, Graduate Specialist, 423-439-6148, Fax: 423-439-5624, E-mail: goodyear@etsu.edu.
Website: http://www.etsu.edu/coe/cuai/.

Edinboro University of Pennsylvania, School of Education, Department of Elementary, Middle and Secondary Education, Edinboro, PA 16444. Offers elementary education (M Ed); middle/secondary instruction (M Ed). Part-time and evening/weekend programs available. *Degree requirements:* For master's, comprehensive exam, thesis or alternative, project. *Entrance requirements:* For master's, GRE or MAT, minimum QPA of 2.5. Electronic applications accepted.

Emory University, Laney Graduate School, Division of Educational Studies, Atlanta, GA 30322-1100. Offers educational studies (MA, PhD); middle grades teaching (MAT); secondary teaching (MAT). *Accreditation:* NCATE. Terminal master's awarded for partial completion of doctoral program. *Degree requirements:* For master's, thesis; for doctorate, comprehensive exam, thesis/dissertation. *Entrance requirements:* For master's and doctorate, GRE General Test, minimum GPA of 3.0. Additional exam requirements/recommendations for international students: Required—TOEFL. Electronic applications accepted. *Faculty research:* Educational policy, educational measurement, urban and multicultural education, mathematics and science education, comparative education.

Fayetteville State University, Graduate School, Programs in Middle Grades, Secondary and Special Education and Elementary Education, Fayetteville, NC 28301-4298. Offers biology (MA Ed); elementary education (MA Ed); history (MA Ed); mathematics (MA Ed); middle grades (MA Ed); political science (MA Ed); reading (MA Ed); sociology (MA Ed); special education (MA Ed), including behavioral-emotional handicaps, mentally handicapped, specific training disability. *Accreditation:* NCATE. Part-time and evening/weekend programs available. *Faculty:* 12 full-time (8 women), 4 part-time/adjunct (3 women). *Students:* 25 full-time (22 women), 49 part-time (45 women); includes 51 minority (48 Black or African American, non-Hispanic/Latino; 1 American Indian or Alaska Native, non-Hispanic/Latino; 2 Hispanic/Latino). Average age

35. 5 applicants, 100% accepted, 5 enrolled. In 2013, 29 master's awarded. *Degree requirements:* For master's, comprehensive exam, internship. *Application deadline:* For fall admission, 4/15 for domestic students; for spring admission, 10/15 for domestic students. Applications are processed on a rolling basis. Application fee: $40. Electronic applications accepted. *Faculty research:* Students with disabilities and selected leadership behaviors, new vision for professional development, gifted and talented students, emotional and behavioral disabilities, professional development for high school biology teachers. *Unit head:* Dr. Kimberly Smith-Burton, Interim Chair, 910-672-1182, E-mail: cbarringerbrown@uncfsu.edu. *Application contact:* Katrina Hoffman, Graduate Admission Officer, 910-672-1374, Fax: 910-672-1470, E-mail: khoffma1@uncfsu.edu.

Fitchburg State University, Division of Graduate and Continuing Education, Program in Middle School Education, Fitchburg, MA 01420-2697. Offers M Ed. *Accreditation:* NCATE. Part-time and evening/weekend programs available. *Entrance requirements:* Additional exam requirements/recommendations for international students: Required—TOEFL (minimum score 550 paper-based; 79 iBT). Electronic applications accepted.

Gardner-Webb University, Graduate School, School of Education, Program in Middle Grades Education, Boiling Springs, NC 28017. Offers MA. *Accreditation:* NCATE. Part-time and evening/weekend programs available. *Students:* 48 full-time (41 women), 25 part-time (22 women); includes 16 minority (all Black or African American, non-Hispanic/Latino). Average age 35. 42 applicants, 48% accepted, 13 enrolled. In 2013, 4 master's awarded. *Degree requirements:* For master's, comprehensive exam. *Entrance requirements:* For master's, GRE General Test or NTE, PRAXIS, minimum GPA of 2.5. *Application deadline:* For fall admission, 8/1 priority date for domestic students. Applications are processed on a rolling basis. Application fee: $40. Electronic applications accepted. *Expenses: Tuition:* Full-time $7200; part-time $400 per credit hour. Tuition and fees vary according to course load and program. *Financial support:* Unspecified assistantships available. *Unit head:* Dr. Alan D. Eury, Chair, 704-406-4402, Fax: 704-406-3921, E-mail: dsimmons@gardner-webb.edu. *Application contact:* Office of Graduate Admissions, 877-498-4723, Fax: 704-406-3895, E-mail: gradinfo@gardner-webb.edu.

Georgia College & State University, Graduate School, The John H. Lounsbury College of Education, Program in Middle Grades Education, Milledgeville, GA 31061. Offers M Ed. *Accreditation:* NCATE. Part-time and evening/weekend programs available. In 2013, 7 master's awarded. *Degree requirements:* For master's, comprehensive exam, portfolio presentation, complete program within 6 years, minimum GPA of 3.0. *Entrance requirements:* For master's, on-site writing assessment, 2 letters of recommendation, level 4 teaching certificate. Additional exam requirements/recommendations for international students: Recommended—TOEFL (minimum score 550 paper-based; 79 iBT). *Application deadline:* For fall admission, 7/1 priority date for domestic students, 4/1 priority date for international students; for spring admission, 11/15 priority date for domestic students, 9/1 priority date for international students. Applications are processed on a rolling basis. Application fee: $40. Electronic applications accepted. *Financial support:* Career-related internships or fieldwork and Federal Work-Study available. Support available to part-time students. Financial award applicants required to submit FAFSA. *Application contact:* Shanda Brand, Graduate Admission Advisor, 478-445-1383, E-mail: shanda.brand@gcsu.edu.

Georgia Southern University, Jack N. Averitt College of Graduate Studies, College of Education, Department of Teaching and Learning, Program in Middle Grades Education, Statesboro, GA 30460. Offers M Ed, MAT, Ed S. *Accreditation:* NCATE. Part-time and evening/weekend programs available. *Students:* 8 full-time (6 women), 28 part-time (22 women); includes 10 minority (8 Black or African American, non-Hispanic/Latino; 2 Two or more races, non-Hispanic/Latino). Average age 34. 23 applicants, 61% accepted, 8 enrolled. In 2013, 7 master's awarded. *Degree requirements:* For master's, portfolio, transition point assessments, exit assessment. *Entrance requirements:* For master's, GRE General Test or MAT; GACE Basic Skills and Content Assessments (for MAT), minimum cumulative GPA of 2.5. Additional exam requirements/recommendations for international students: Required—TOEFL (minimum score 550 paper-based; 80 iBT), IELTS (minimum score 6). *Application deadline:* For fall admission, 3/1 priority date for domestic and international students; for spring admission, 10/1 priority date for domestic students, 10/1 for international students. Applications are processed on a rolling basis. Application fee: $50. Electronic applications accepted. *Expenses:* Tuition, state resident: full-time $7068; part-time $270 per semester hour. Tuition, nonresident: full-time $26,446; part-time $1077 per semester hour. *Required fees:* $2092. *Financial support:* In 2013–14, 1 student received support. Career-related internships or fieldwork, Federal Work-Study, and tuition waivers (partial) available. Support available to part-time students. Financial award application deadline: 4/15; financial award applicants required to submit FAFSA. *Faculty research:* Gender, technology applications, early and young adolescent literature, content subjects and literacy, integrated curriculum, content subject learning. *Unit head:* Dr. Greg Chamblee, Program Coordinator, 912-478-5701, Fax: 912-478-0026, E-mail: gchamblee@georgiasouthern.edu. *Application contact:* Amanda Gilliland, Coordinator for Graduate Student Recruitment, 912-478-5384, Fax: 912-478-0740, E-mail: gradadmissions@georgiasouthern.edu.
Website: http://coe.georgiasouthern.edu/ger/.

Georgia Southwestern State University, Graduate Studies, School of Education, Americus, GA 31709-4693. Offers early childhood education (M Ed, Ed S); health and physical education (M Ed); middle grades education (M Ed, Ed S); reading (M Ed); secondary education (M Ed); special education (M Ed). *Accreditation:* NCATE. *Degree requirements:* For master's, comprehensive exam. *Entrance requirements:* For master's, GRE General Test or MAT, minimum GPA of 2.5; for Ed S, GRE General Test or MAT, minimum graduate GPA of 3.25, M Ed from accredited college or university, 3 years teaching experience. Electronic applications accepted.

Georgia State University, College of Education, Department of Middle-Secondary Education and Instructional Technology, Atlanta, GA 30302-3083. Offers English education (M Ed, MAT); English speakers of other languages (MAT); instructional design and technology (MS); instructional technology (PhD), including alternative instructional delivery systems, consulting, instructional design, management, research; mathematics education (M Ed, MAT); middle level education (MAT); reading, language and literacy education (M Ed), including reading instruction; science education (MAT), including biology, broad field science, chemistry, earth science, physics; social studies education (M Ed, MAT), including economics (MAT), geography (MAT), history (MAT), political science (MAT); teaching and learning (PhD), including language and literacy, mathematics education, music education, science education, social studies, teaching and teacher education. *Accreditation:* NCATE. Part-time and evening/weekend programs available. Postbaccalaureate distance learning degree programs offered (minimal on-campus study). *Faculty:* 27 full-time (19 women). *Students:* 181 full-time (113 women), 203 part-time (145 women); includes 161 minority (127 Black or African American, non-Hispanic/Latino; 1 American Indian or Alaska Native, non-Hispanic/Latino; 10 Asian, non-Hispanic/Latino; 11 Hispanic/Latino; 1 Native Hawaiian or other Pacific Islander, non-Hispanic/Latino; 11 Two or more races, non-Hispanic/Latino), 9 international. Average age 36. 2 applicants, 50% accepted, 1 enrolled. In 2013, 213 master's, 17 doctorates awarded. *Degree requirements:* For master's, comprehensive

exam (for some programs), thesis or alternative, exit portfolio; for doctorate, comprehensive exam, thesis/dissertation. *Entrance requirements:* For master's, GRE; GACE I (for initial teacher preparation degree programs), baccalaureate degree or equivalent, resume, goals statement, two letters of recommendation, minimum undergraduate GPA of 2.5; proof of initial teacher certification in the content area (for M Ed); for doctorate, GRE, resume, goals statement, writing sample, two letters of recommendation, minimum graduate GPA of 3.3, interview. Additional exam requirements/recommendations for international students: Required—TOEFL (minimum score 550 paper-based; 79 iBT) or IELTS (minimum score 6.5). *Application deadline:* For fall admission, 1/15 priority date for domestic and international students; for spring admission, 10/1 for domestic and international students. Application fee: $50. Electronic applications accepted. *Expenses: Tuition, area resident:* Full-time $4176; part-time $348 per credit hour. Tuition, state resident: full-time $14,544; part-time $1212 per credit hour. Tuition, nonresident: full-time $14,544; part-time $1212 per credit hour. Tuition and fees vary according to course load and program. *Financial support:* In 2013–14, fellowships with full tuition reimbursements (averaging $19,667 per year), research assistantships with full tuition reimbursements (averaging $5,436 per year), teaching assistantships with full tuition reimbursements (averaging $2,779 per year) were awarded; career-related internships or fieldwork, Federal Work-Study, scholarships/grants, health care benefits, tuition waivers (full and partial), and unspecified assistantships also available. Financial award application deadline: 3/15. *Faculty research:* Teacher education in language and literacy, mathematics, science, and social studies in urban middle and secondary school settings; learning technologies in school, community, and corporate settings; multicultural education and education for social justice; urban education; international education. *Unit head:* Dr. Dana L. Fox, Chair, 404-413-8060, Fax: 404-413-8063, E-mail: dfox@gsu.edu. *Application contact:* Bobbie Turner, Administrative Coordinator I, 404-413-8405, Fax: 404-413-8063, E-mail: bnturner@gsu.edu.
Website: http://msit.gsu.edu/msit_programs.htm.

Grand Valley State University, College of Education, Programs in General Education, Allendale, MI 49401-9403. Offers adult and higher education (M Ed); early childhood education (M Ed); educational differentiation (M Ed); educational leadership (M Ed); educational technology integration (M Ed); elementary education (M Ed); middle level education (M Ed); school library media services (M Ed); secondary level education (M Ed); teaching English to speakers of other languages (M Ed). Part-time and evening/weekend programs available. Postbaccalaureate distance learning degree programs offered (minimal on-campus study). *Degree requirements:* For master's, thesis. *Entrance requirements:* For master's, GRE General Test or minimum GPA of 3.0. Additional exam requirements/recommendations for international students: Required—TOEFL. Electronic applications accepted. *Faculty research:* Effectiveness of technology in education, parental involvement, effective teaching, effective schools research.

Hampton University, Graduate College, College of Education and Continuing Studies, Program in Teaching, Hampton, VA 23668. Offers early childhood education (MT); middle school education (MT); music education (MT); secondary education (MT); special education (MT). *Entrance requirements:* For master's, GRE General Test.

Hebrew College, Shoolman Graduate School of Jewish Education, Newton Centre, MA 02459. Offers early childhood Jewish education (Certificate); Jewish day school education (Certificate); Jewish education (MJ Ed); Jewish family education (Certificate); Jewish special education (Certificate); Jewish youth education, informal education and camping (Certificate). Part-time and evening/weekend programs available. Postbaccalaureate distance learning degree programs offered. *Degree requirements:* For master's, one foreign language. *Entrance requirements:* For master's, GRE, interview. Additional exam requirements/recommendations for international students: Required—TOEFL.

Henderson State University, Graduate Studies, Teachers College, Department of Advanced Instructional Studies, Arkadelphia, AR 71999-0001. Offers early childhood (P-4) (MSE); education (MAT); English as a second language (Graduate Certificate); instructional facilitator (Graduate Certificate); middle school (MSE); reading (MSE); special education (MSE). *Accreditation:* NCATE. Part-time programs available. *Faculty:* 7 full-time (3 women), 2 part-time/adjunct (both women). *Students:* 1 (woman) full-time, 99 part-time (88 women); includes 20 minority (13 Black or African American, non-Hispanic/Latino; 1 American Indian or Alaska Native, non-Hispanic/Latino; 5 Hispanic/Latino; 1 Two or more races, non-Hispanic/Latino), 1 international. Average age 36. 7 applicants, 100% accepted, 7 enrolled. In 2013, 45 master's awarded. *Entrance requirements:* For master's, GRE General Test or MAT, minimum GPA of 2.7, teacher certification. Additional exam requirements/recommendations for international students: Required—TOEFL (minimum score 600 paper-based); Recommended—IELTS (minimum score 6.5). *Application deadline:* For fall admission, 8/1 priority date for domestic students, 6/30 priority date for international students; for spring admission, 1/1 priority date for domestic students, 11/30 priority date for international students. Applications are processed on a rolling basis. Application fee: $25 ($75 for international students). *Expenses:* Tuition, state resident: full-time $4284; part-time $238 per credit hour. Tuition, nonresident: full-time $8802; part-time $489 per credit hour. Tuition and fees vary according to course load and campus/location. *Financial support:* In 2013–14, 1 teaching assistantship with partial tuition reimbursement (averaging $4,000 per year) was awarded; scholarships/grants and unspecified assistantships also available. *Unit head:* Dr. Gary Smithey, Chairperson, 870-230-5361, Fax: 870-230-5455, E-mail: smitheg@hsu.edu. *Application contact:* Dr. Ken Taylor, Graduate Dean, 870-230-5126, Fax: 870-230-5479, E-mail: taylorke@hsu.edu.

Hofstra University, School of Education, Programs in Teaching - K-12, Hempstead, NY 11549. Offers bilingual education (MA, Advanced Certificate); family and consumer sciences (MS Ed); fine arts and music education (Advanced Certificate); fine arts education (MA, MS Ed); middle childhood extensions (Advanced Certificate), including grades 5-6 or 7-9; music education (MA, MS Ed); teaching languages other than English and TESOL (MS Ed); TESOL (MS Ed, Advanced Certificate); wind conducting (MA).

Holy Family University, Graduate School, School of Education, Master of Education Programs, Philadelphia, PA 19114. Offers early elementary education (PreK-Grade 4) (M Ed); education leadership (M Ed); general education (M Ed); middle level education (Grades 4-8) (M Ed); reading specialist (M Ed); secondary education (Grades 7-12) (M Ed); special education (M Ed); TESOL and literacy (M Ed). *Expenses: Tuition:* Full-time $12,060. *Required fees:* $250. Tuition and fees vary according to degree level. *Unit head:* Dr. Leonard Soroka, Dean, 267-341-3565, Fax: 215-824-2438, E-mail: lsoroka@holyfamily.edu. *Application contact:* Gidget Marie Montelibano, Associate Director of Graduate Admissions, 267-341-3358, Fax: 215-637-1478, E-mail: gmontelibano@holyfamily.edu.

Hood College, Graduate School, Program in Secondary Mathematics Education, Frederick, MD 21701-8575. Offers mathematics education (MS), including high school, middle school; secondary mathematics education (Certificate). Part-time and evening/weekend programs available. *Faculty:* 2 full-time (1 woman), 1 part-time/adjunct (0 women). *Students:* 1 full-time (0 women), 45 part-time (35 women); includes 1 minority (Hispanic/Latino). Average age 33. 9 applicants, 100% accepted, 8 enrolled. In 2013, 14 master's, 1 other advanced degree awarded. *Degree requirements:* For master's, capstone/research project. *Entrance requirements:* For master's, minimum GPA of 2.75.

Additional exam requirements/recommendations for international students: Required—TOEFL (minimum score 575 paper-based; 89 iBT), IELTS (minimum score 6.5). *Application deadline:* For fall admission, 7/15 priority date for domestic students, 7/15 for international students; for spring admission, 12/1 priority date for domestic students, 12/1 for international students. Applications are processed on a rolling basis. Application fee: $35. Electronic applications accepted. Application fee is waived when completed online. *Expenses: Tuition:* Part-time $405 per credit. *Required fees:* $100 per semester. *Financial support:* Tuition waivers (partial) and unspecified assistantships available. Financial award applicants required to submit FAFSA. *Unit head:* Dr. Betty Mayfield, Chairperson, 301-696-3763, E-mail: mayfield@hood.edu. *Application contact:* Dr. Maria Green Cowles, Dean of Graduate School, 301-696-3811, Fax: 301-696-3597, E-mail: gofurther@hood.edu.
Website: http://www.hood.edu/graduate.

James Madison University, The Graduate School, College of Education, Middle, Secondary, and Mathematics Education Department, Harrisonburg, VA 22807. Offers middle education (MAT); secondary education (MAT). *Students:* Average age 27. *Entrance requirements:* Additional exam requirements/recommendations for international students: Required—TOEFL. *Application deadline:* For fall admission, 5/1 for domestic students; for spring admission, 9/1 for domestic students. Application fee: $55. *Financial support:* Unspecified assistantships available. Financial award application deadline: 3/1; financial award applicants required to submit FAFSA. *Unit head:* Dr. Steven L. Purcell, Academic Unit Head, 540-568-6793. *Application contact:* Lynette M. Bible, Director of Graduate Admissions, 540-568-6395, Fax: 540-568-7860, E-mail: biblelm@jmu.edu.

John Carroll University, Graduate School, Department of Education and Allied Studies, Program in School Based Middle Childhood Education, University Heights, OH 44118-4581. Offers M Ed. *Accreditation:* NCATE. *Degree requirements:* For master's, comprehensive exam. *Entrance requirements:* For master's, GRE General Test or MAT, minimum GPA of 2.75, interview. Additional exam requirements/recommendations for international students: Required—TOEFL. Electronic applications accepted.

John Carroll University, Graduate School, Program in Integrated Science, University Heights, OH 44118-4581. Offers MA. Part-time programs available. *Degree requirements:* For master's, thesis optional. *Entrance requirements:* For master's, minimum GPA of 2.5, teachers license. Electronic applications accepted.

Kansas State University, Graduate School, College of Education, Department of Curriculum and Instruction, Manhattan, KS 66506. Offers career and technical education (Ed D, PhD); curriculum studies (Ed D, PhD); digital teaching and learning (MS); educational computing, design and online learning (MS); educational technology (Ed D, PhD); elementary/middle level curriculum and instruction (MS); English as a second language (MS); language/diversity education (Ed D, PhD); literacy education (Ed D, PhD); mathematics education (Ed D, PhD); middle level/secondary curriculum and instruction (MS); reading and language arts (MS); reading specialist endorsement (MS); science education (Ed D, PhD); social science education (Ed D, PhD); teacher education (Ed D, PhD); teacher leader/school improvement (MS, Ed D). *Accreditation:* NCATE. Part-time programs available. Postbaccalaureate distance learning degree programs offered (minimal on-campus study). *Faculty:* 18 full-time (13 women), 7 part-time/adjunct (4 women). *Students:* 39 full-time (23 women), 122 part-time (94 women); includes 19 minority (3 Black or African American, non-Hispanic/Latino; 2 Asian, non-Hispanic/Latino; 12 Hispanic/Latino; 2 Two or more races, non-Hispanic/Latino), 12 international. Average age 36. 80 applicants, 50% accepted, 34 enrolled. In 2013, 40 master's, 13 doctorates awarded. *Degree requirements:* For master's, comprehensive exam, portfolio, project, report or thesis; for doctorate, comprehensive exam, thesis/dissertation, preliminary exam. *Entrance requirements:* For master's, minimum GPA of 3.0, letters of recommendation; for doctorate, GRE, minimum GPA of 3.0, letters of recommendation, evidence of scholarly writing. Additional exam requirements/recommendations for international students: Required—TOEFL (minimum score 550 paper-based; 80 iBT). *Application deadline:* For fall admission, 3/1 priority date for domestic students, 2/1 priority date for international students; for spring admission, 10/1 priority date for domestic students, 8/1 priority date for international students. Applications are processed on a rolling basis. Application fee: $50 ($75 for international students). Electronic applications accepted. *Financial support:* In 2013–14, 1 research assistantship (averaging $16,900 per year), 8 teaching assistantships (averaging $12,466 per year) were awarded; career-related internships or fieldwork, institutionally sponsored loans, and scholarships/grants also available. Support available to part-time students. Financial award application deadline: 3/1; financial award applicants required to submit FAFSA. *Faculty research:* Literacy and technology, critical race theory and diversity, achievement gaps, school improvement, teacher education. *Total annual research expenditures:* $543,677. *Unit head:* Dr. Todd Goodson, Chair, 785-532-5904, Fax: 785-532-7304, E-mail: tgoodson@ksu.edu. *Application contact:* Dona Deam, Application Contact, 785-532-5595, Fax: 785-532-7304, E-mail: ddeam@ksu.edu.
Website: http://www.coe.k-state.edu/departments/edci/.

Kennesaw State University, Leland and Clarice C. Bagwell College of Education, Program in Graduate Education, Kennesaw, GA 30144-5591. Offers educational leadership (M Ed); educational leadership technology (M Ed); elementary and early childhood education (M Ed); instructional technology (M Ed); middle grades education (M Ed); reading (M Ed); secondary education (M Ed); special education (M Ed); teaching English to speakers of other languages (M Ed). *Accreditation:* NCATE. Part-time programs available. *Students:* 65 full-time (60 women), 229 part-time (158 women); includes 66 minority (46 Black or African American, non-Hispanic/Latino; 6 Asian, non-Hispanic/Latino; 9 Hispanic/Latino; 5 Two or more races, non-Hispanic/Latino), 1 international. Average age 34. 56 applicants, 86% accepted, 43 enrolled. In 2013, 109 master's awarded. *Degree requirements:* For master's, thesis or alternative. *Entrance requirements:* For master's, GRE General Test, T-4 state certification, minimum GPA of 2.75. Additional exam requirements/recommendations for international students: Required—TOEFL (minimum score 550 paper-based; 80 iBT), IELTS (minimum score 6.5). *Application deadline:* For fall admission, 7/1 for domestic and international students; for spring admission, 10/1 for domestic and international students; for summer admission, 4/15 for domestic and international students. Applications are processed on a rolling basis. Application fee: $60. Electronic applications accepted. *Expenses:* Tuition, state resident: full-time $4806; part-time $267 per semester hour. Tuition, nonresident: full-time $17,298; part-time $961 per semester hour. *Required fees:* $1834; $784.50 per semester. *Financial support:* In 2013–14, 10 research assistantships with tuition reimbursements (averaging $8,000 per year) were awarded; Federal Work-Study and unspecified assistantships also available. Support available to part-time students. Financial award application deadline: 4/1; financial award applicants required to submit FAFSA. *Unit head:* Melinda Ross, Administrative Coordinator for Graduate Programs in Education, 770-423-6043, E-mail: graded@kennesaw.edu. *Application contact:* Melinda Ross, Admissions Counselor, 770-423-6043, Fax: 770-423-6885, E-mail: ksugrad@kennesaw.edu.
Website: http://www.kennesaw.edu/education/grad/.

Kent State University, Graduate School of Education, Health, and Human Services, School of Teaching, Learning and Curriculum Studies, Program in Junior High/Middle School, Kent, OH 44242-0001. Offers M Ed, MA. Part-time programs available. *Faculty:*

5 full-time (4 women), 1 (woman) part-time/adjunct. *Students:* 4 full-time (3 women), 2 part-time (1 woman). 10 applicants, 20% accepted. In 2013, 6 master's awarded. *Degree requirements:* For master's, thesis (for some programs). *Entrance requirements:* For master's, 2 letters of reference, goals statement. Additional exam requirements/recommendations for international students: Required—TOEFL (minimum score 550 paper-based; 80 iBT). *Application deadline:* Applications are processed on a rolling basis. Application fee: $30 ($60 for international students). Electronic applications accepted. *Financial support:* Research assistantships with full tuition reimbursements, Federal Work-Study, scholarships/grants, and unspecified assistantships available. Financial award applicants required to submit FAFSA. *Faculty research:* Middle school reform, teacher action research. *Unit head:* Dr. Bette Brooks, Coordinator, 330-672-0536, E-mail: ebrooks@kent.edu. *Application contact:* Nancy Miller, Academic Program Director, Office of Graduate Student Services, 330-672-2576, Fax: 330-672-9162, E-mail: ogs@kent.edu.
Website: http://www.kent.edu/ehhs/mced/.

LaGrange College, Graduate Programs, Department of Education, LaGrange, GA 30240-2999. Offers curriculum and instruction (M Ed, Ed S); middle grades (MAT); secondary education (MAT). Part-time and evening/weekend programs available. *Degree requirements:* For master's, comprehensive exam. *Entrance requirements:* For master's, GRE, MAT, minimum GPA of 2.5. Additional exam requirements/recommendations for international students: Required—TOEFL (minimum score 550 paper-based).

La Salle University, School of Arts and Sciences, Program in Education, Philadelphia, PA 19141-1199. Offers American studies (MA); autism spectrum disorders (MA, Certificate); bilingual/bicultural studies (MA); classroom management (MA, Certificate); dual early childhood and special education (MA); dual middle-level science and math and special education secondary education (MA); education (MA); English (MA); English as a second language (Certificate); instructional coach (Certificate); instructional leadership (MA); reading specialist (MA, Certificate); secondary education (MA); special education (MA, Certificate). Part-time and evening/weekend programs available. *Faculty:* 5 full-time (4 women), 16 part-time/adjunct (10 women). *Students:* 18 full-time (13 women), 137 part-time (112 women); includes 33 minority (24 Black or African American, non-Hispanic/Latino; 9 Hispanic/Latino), 4 international. Average age 32. 47 applicants, 96% accepted, 28 enrolled. In 2013, 58 master's, 20 other advanced degrees awarded. *Degree requirements:* For master's, comprehensive exam. *Entrance requirements:* For master's and Certificate, MAT or GRE, 2 letters of recommendation. Additional exam requirements/recommendations for international students: Required—TOEFL. *Application deadline:* For fall admission, 8/15 priority date for domestic students, 7/15 for international students; for spring admission, 12/15 priority date for domestic students, 11/15 for international students; for summer admission, 4/15 priority date for domestic students, 3/15 for international students. Applications are processed on a rolling basis. Application fee: $35. Electronic applications accepted. Application fee is waived when completed online. *Expenses:* Contact institution. *Financial support:* In 2013–14, 28 students received support. Career-related internships or fieldwork, Federal Work-Study, and scholarships/grants available. Support available to part-time students. Financial award application deadline: 8/31; financial award applicants required to submit FAFSA. *Unit head:* Dr. Greer Richardson, Interim Director, 215-951-1806, Fax: 215-951-1843, E-mail: graded@lasalle.edu. *Application contact:* Paul J. Reilly, Assistant Vice President, Enrollment Services, 215-951-1946, Fax: 215-951-1462, E-mail: reilly@lasalle.edu.
Website: http://www.lasalle.edu/grad/index.php?section-education&page-index.

Lee University, Program in Education, Cleveland, TN 37320-3450. Offers college student development (MS); curriculum and instruction (M Ed, Ed S); educational leadership (M Ed, Ed S); elementary education (MAT); higher education administration (MS); middle grades (MAT); secondary education (MAT); special education (M Ed); special education (secondary) (MAT). Part-time programs available. *Faculty:* 14 full-time (7 women), 6 part-time/adjunct (3 women). *Students:* 30 full-time (23 women), 62 part-time (37 women); includes 8 minority (3 Black or African American, non-Hispanic/Latino; 1 American Indian or Alaska Native, non-Hispanic/Latino; 2 Asian, non-Hispanic/Latino; 2 Hispanic/Latino). Average age 30. 40 applicants, 100% accepted, 30 enrolled. In 2013, 117 master's, 2 other advanced degrees awarded. *Degree requirements:* For master's, variable foreign language requirement, comprehensive exam, thesis, internship. *Entrance requirements:* For master's, MAT or GRE General Test, minimum GPA of 2.75, 3 letters of recommendation, interview, writing sample, official transcripts. Additional exam requirements/recommendations for international students: Required—TOEFL (minimum score 450 paper-based). *Application deadline:* For fall admission, 4/1 priority date for domestic and international students; for spring admission, 10/1 priority date for domestic and international students. Applications are processed on a rolling basis. Application fee: $25. *Expenses: Tuition:* Full-time $9900; part-time $550 per credit hour. *Required fees:* $35 per term. One-time fee: $25. *Financial support:* In 2013–14, 47 students received support, including 1 teaching assistantship (averaging $1,500 per year); career-related internships or fieldwork, Federal Work-Study, institutionally sponsored loans, scholarships/grants, and unspecified assistantships also available. Financial award application deadline: 3/1; financial award applicants required to submit FAFSA. *Unit head:* Dr. Gary Riggins, Director, 423-614-8193. *Application contact:* Vicki Glasscock, Graduate Admissions Director, 423-614-8059, E-mail: vglasscock@leeuniversity.edu.
Website: http://www.leeuniversity.edu/academics/graduate/education.

Le Moyne College, Department of Education, Syracuse, NY 13214. Offers adolescent education (MS Ed, MST); adolescent education/special education (MS Ed, MST); adolescent English (MST), including grades 7-12 (MS Ed, MST); adolescent English/special education (MST), including grades 7-12 (MS Ed, MST); adolescent foreign language (MST), including grades 7-12 (MS Ed, MST); adolescent history (MST), including grades 7-12 (MS Ed, MST); childhood education (MS Ed); childhood education/special education (MS Ed); elementary education (MS Ed); general education (MS Ed); inclusive childhood education (MST); literacy education (MS Ed), including birth to grade 6, grades 5-12; school building leader (MS Ed); school building leadership (CAS); school district business leader (MS Ed, CAS); school district leader (MS Ed); school district leadership (CAS); secondary education (MS Ed); special education (MS Ed); students with disabilities-generalist (MS Ed), including grades 7-12 (MS Ed, MST); teaching English to speakers of other languages (MS Ed); urban studies (MS Ed). *Accreditation:* Teacher Education Accreditation Council. Part-time and evening/weekend programs available. *Faculty:* 8 full-time (5 women), 61 part-time/adjunct (38 women). *Students:* 24 full-time (20 women), 178 part-time (133 women); includes 22 minority (12 Black or African American, non-Hispanic/Latino; 1 American Indian or Alaska Native, non-Hispanic/Latino; 3 Asian, non-Hispanic/Latino; 6 Hispanic/Latino), 1 international. Average age 31. 248 applicants, 90% accepted, 86 enrolled. In 2013, 158 master's, 37 CASs awarded. *Degree requirements:* For master's, thesis. *Entrance requirements:* For master's, GRE General Test, bachelor's degree, 2 letters of recommendation, written statement, transcripts. Additional exam requirements/recommendations for international students: Required—TOEFL (minimum score 550 paper-based; 79 iBT). *Application deadline:* For fall admission, 4/1 priority date for domestic and international students; for spring admission, 10/1 priority date for domestic and international students; for summer admission, 3/1 priority date for domestic and international students. Applications are processed on a rolling basis. Application fee: $50. *Expenses:* Contact institution. *Financial support:* In 2013–14, 26 students received support. Career-related internships or fieldwork and health care benefits available. Support available to part-time students. Financial award applicants required to submit FAFSA. *Faculty research:* Minority teachers, special education, multiculturalism, literacy, technology, media literacy learning, autism, school district organization, service-learning, higher level problem solving, teacher leadership. *Unit head:* Dr. Suzanne L. Gilmour, Chair, Department of Education/Director of Graduate Education Programs, 315-445-4376, Fax: 315-445-4744, E-mail: gilmous@lemoyne.edu. *Application contact:* Kristen P. Trapasso, Senior Director of Enrollment Management, 315-445-4265, Fax: 315-445-6092, E-mail: trapaskp@lemoyne.edu.
Website: http://www.lemoyne.edu/education.

Lesley University, School of Education, Cambridge, MA 02138-2790. Offers arts, community, and education (M Ed); autism studies (Certificate); curriculum and instruction (M Ed, CAGS); early childhood education (M Ed); ecological teaching and learning (MS); educational studies (PhD), including adult learning, educational leadership, individually designed; elementary education (M Ed); emergent technologies for educators (Certificate); ESLArts: language learning through the arts (M Ed); high school education (M Ed); individually designed (M Ed); integrated teaching through the arts (M Ed); literacy for K-8 classroom teachers (M Ed); mathematics education (M Ed); middle school education (M Ed); moderate disabilities (M Ed); online learning (Certificate); reading (CAGS); science in education (M Ed); severe disabilities (M Ed); special needs (CAGS); specialist teacher of reading (M Ed); teacher of visual art (M Ed); technology in education (M Ed, CAGS). *Accreditation:* Teacher Education Accreditation Council. Part-time and evening/weekend programs available. Postbaccalaureate distance learning degree programs offered (no on-campus study). *Faculty:* 40 full-time (30 women), 104 part-time/adjunct (77 women). *Students:* 453 full-time (381 women), 1,672 part-time (1,435 women); includes 284 minority (139 Black or African American, non-Hispanic/Latino; 11 American Indian or Alaska Native, non-Hispanic/Latino; 38 Asian, non-Hispanic/Latino; 58 Hispanic/Latino; 5 Native Hawaiian or other Pacific Islander, non-Hispanic/Latino; 33 Two or more races, non-Hispanic/Latino), 22 international. Average age 35. In 2013, 1,137 master's, 18 doctorates, 51 other advanced degrees awarded. *Degree requirements:* For master's, practicum; for doctorate, thesis/dissertation. *Entrance requirements:* For master's, Massachusetts Tests for Educator Licensure (MTEL), transcripts, statement of purpose, recommendations; interview (for special education); for doctorate, GRE General Test, transcripts, statement of purpose, recommendations, interview, master's degree, resume; for other advanced degree, interview, master's degree. Additional exam requirements/recommendations for international students: Required—TOEFL (minimum score 550 paper-based; 80 iBT). *Application deadline:* Applications are processed on a rolling basis. Application fee: $50. Electronic applications accepted. *Expenses: Tuition:* Part-time $900 per credit. *Financial support:* In 2013–14, 15 fellowships (averaging $3,600 per year) were awarded; career-related internships or fieldwork, Federal Work-Study, scholarships/grants, tuition waivers, and unspecified assistantships also available. Financial award application deadline: 4/15; financial award applicants required to submit FAFSA. *Faculty research:* Assessment in literacy, mathematics and science; autism spectrum disorders; instructional technology and online learning; multicultural education and English language learners. *Unit head:* Dr. Jack Gillette, Dean, 617-349-8401, Fax: 617-349-8607, E-mail: jgillett@lesley.edu. *Application contact:* Martha Sheehan, Director of Admissions, 888-LESLEYU, Fax: 617-349-8313, E-mail: info@lesley.edu.
Website: http://www.lesley.edu/soe.html.

Lewis & Clark College, Graduate School of Education and Counseling, Department of Teacher Education, Program in Middle Level/High School Education, Portland, OR 97219-7899. Offers MAT. *Accreditation:* NCATE. *Entrance requirements:* For master's, prior experience working with children and/or youth; minimum undergraduate GPA of 2.75. Additional exam requirements/recommendations for international students: Required—TOEFL (minimum score 575 paper-based). Electronic applications accepted. *Faculty research:* Classroom management, classroom assessment, science education, classroom ethnography, moral development.

Liberty University, School of Education, Lynchburg, VA 24515. Offers administration and supervision (M Ed); curriculum and instruction (Ed D, Ed S); early childhood education (M Ed); educational leadership (Ed D, Ed S); educational technology and online instruction (M Ed); elementary education (M Ed, MAT); English (M Ed); gifted education (M Ed); history (M Ed); leadership (M Ed); math specialist (M Ed); middle grades (M Ed, MAT); outdoor adventure sport (MS); reading specialist (M Ed); school counseling (M Ed); secondary education (MAT); special education (M Ed, MAT); sport management (MS), including administration, outdoor recreation, sport management, tourism; sports administration (MS); student service (M Ed); teaching and learning (M Ed); tourism (MS). *Accreditation:* NCATE. Part-time programs available. Postbaccalaureate distance learning degree programs offered (minimal on-campus study). *Students:* 2,241 full-time (1,639 women), 4,413 part-time (3,240 women); includes 2,052 minority (1,588 Black or African American, non-Hispanic/Latino; 37 American Indian or Alaska Native, non-Hispanic/Latino; 67 Asian, non-Hispanic/Latino; 173 Hispanic/Latino; 37 Native Hawaiian or other Pacific Islander, non-Hispanic/Latino; 150 Two or more races, non-Hispanic/Latino), 15 international. Average age 37. 6,185 applicants, 43% accepted, 1603 enrolled. In 2013, 1,256 master's, 117 doctorates, 470 other advanced degrees awarded. *Degree requirements:* For doctorate, comprehensive exam, thesis/dissertation. *Entrance requirements:* For master's, GRE General Test or MAT (if taken in or before 1999), 2 letters of recommendation, minimum undergraduate GPA of 3.0, curriculum vitae; for doctorate and Ed S, GRE General Test or MAT (if taken before 1999), minimum master's GPA of 3.0, 3 years of teaching experience. Additional exam requirements/recommendations for international students: Required—TOEFL (minimum score 600 paper-based; 100 iBT). *Application deadline:* For fall admission, 6/1 for domestic students; for spring admission, 11/1 for domestic students. Applications are processed on a rolling basis. Application fee: $50. Electronic applications accepted. *Expenses:* Contact institution. *Financial support:* Federal Work-Study and tuition waivers (partial) available. *Faculty research:* Self-determination, character education, bibliotherapy, learning styles, distance education. *Unit head:* Dr. Karen L. Parker, Dean, 434-582-2195, Fax: 434-582-2468, E-mail: kparker@liberty.edu. *Application contact:* Jay Bridge, Director of Graduate Admissions, 800-424-9595, Fax: 800-628-7977, E-mail: gradadmissions@liberty.edu.
Website: http://www.liberty.edu/academics/education/graduate/.

Long Island University–LIU Post, School of Education, Department of Curriculum and Instruction, Brookville, NY 11548-1300. Offers adolescence education (MS); adolescence education: biology (MS); adolescence education: earth science (MS); adolescence education: English (MS); adolescence education: mathematics (MS); adolescence education: social studies (MS); adolescence education: Spanish (MS); art education (MS); bilingual education (MS); childhood education (MS); early childhood education (MS); middle childhood education (MS); music education (MS); teaching English to speakers of other languages (MS). Part-time and evening/weekend programs available. *Degree requirements:* For master's, comprehensive exam or thesis, student teaching. *Entrance requirements:* For master's, minimum GPA of 2.75 in major, 2.5

overall. Electronic applications accepted. *Faculty research:* Ethics and education, teaching strategies.

Longwood University, College of Graduate and Professional Studies, College of Education and Human Services, Farmville, VA 23909. Offers education (MS), including algebra and middle school math, counselor education, elementary and middle school math, elementary education, elementary education initial licensure, health and physical education, school librarianship, special education general curriculum, special education initial licensure; social work and communication sciences and disorders (MS). *Accreditation:* NCATE. Part-time and evening/weekend programs available. *Faculty:* 28 full-time (15 women), 9 part-time/adjunct (7 women). *Students:* 86 full-time (80 women), 187 part-time (173 women); includes 38 minority (26 Black or African American, non-Hispanic/Latino; 1 Asian, non-Hispanic/Latino; 5 Hispanic/Latino; 1 Native Hawaiian or other Pacific Islander, non-Hispanic/Latino; 5 Two or more races, non-Hispanic/Latino). 98 applicants, 89% accepted, 85 enrolled. In 2013, 132 master's awarded. *Degree requirements:* For master's, comprehensive exam (for some programs), thesis optional, professional portfolio, internship, clinical experience, or practicum. *Entrance requirements:* For master's, bachelor's degree from regionally-accredited institution, 2 recommendations, 500-word personal essay, official transcripts, minimum GPA of 2.75, valid teaching license (for some programs), passing Praxis I scores for initial teaching licensure programs. Additional exam requirements/recommendations for international students: Required—TOEFL (minimum score 570 paper-based), IELTS (minimum score 6.5). *Application deadline:* For fall admission, 5/1 priority date for domestic students; for spring admission, 10/1 priority date for domestic students; for summer admission, 2/1 priority date for domestic students. Applications are processed on a rolling basis. Application fee: $50. Electronic applications accepted. *Expenses:* Tuition, state resident: full-time $7506; part-time $327 per credit hour. Tuition, nonresident: full-time $17,100; part-time $837 per credit hour. Tuition and fees vary according to course load and campus/location. *Financial support:* Career-related internships or fieldwork and Federal Work-Study available. Financial award applicants required to submit FAFSA. *Unit head:* Dr. Peggy L. Tarpley, Chair of the Department of Education and Special Education, 434-395-2337, E-mail: tarpleypl@longwood.edu. *Application contact:* College of Graduate and Professional Studies, 434-395-2380, Fax: 434-395-2750, E-mail: graduate@longwood.edu.
Website: http://www.longwood.edu/cehs/.

Loyola University Maryland, Graduate Programs, School of Education, Master of Arts in Teaching Program, Baltimore, MD 21210-2699. Offers elementary/middle education (MAT); secondary education (MAT); secondary education: biology (MAT); secondary education: chemistries (MAT); secondary education: earth science (MAT); secondary education: English (MAT); secondary education: mathematics (MAT); secondary education: physics (MAT). Part-time programs available. *Entrance requirements:* For master's, essay, 2 letters of recommendation, resume, transcipt. Additional exam requirements/recommendations for international students: Required—TOEFL (minimum score 550 paper-based).

Loyola University Maryland, Graduate Programs, School of Education, Program in Special Education, Baltimore, MD 21210-2699. Offers early childhood education (M Ed, CAS); elementary/middle education (M Ed, CAS); secondary education (M Ed, CAS). *Accreditation:* NCATE. Part-time programs available. *Entrance requirements:* For master's, transcript, essay, letter of recommendation. Additional exam requirements/recommendations for international students: Required—TOEFL (minimum score 550 paper-based). Electronic applications accepted.

Manhattanville College, School of Education, Program in Middle Childhood/Adolescence Education (Grades 5-12), Purchase, NY 10577-2132. Offers biology (MAT); biology and special education (MPS); chemistry (MAT); chemistry and special education (MPS); English (MAT); English and special education (MPS); literacy and special education (MPS); literacy specialist (MPS); math and special education (MPS); mathematics (MAT); physics (MAT); social studies (MAT); social studies and special education (MPS); special education (MPS); teaching languages other than English (MAT), including French, Italian, Latin, Spanish. Part-time and evening/weekend programs available. *Degree requirements:* For master's, comprehensive exam or research project, field experience. *Entrance requirements:* For master's, minimum undergraduate GPA of 3.0, 2 letters of recommendation. Additional exam requirements/recommendations for international students: Required—TOEFL. Electronic applications accepted.

Mary Baldwin College, Graduate Studies, Program in Teaching, Staunton, VA 24401-3610. Offers elementary education (MAT); middle grades education (MAT). *Accreditation:* Teacher Education Accreditation Council.

Maryville University of Saint Louis, School of Education, St. Louis, MO 63141-7299. Offers art education (MA Ed); early childhood education (MA Ed); educational leadership (Ed D); educational leadership: principal certification (MA Ed); elementary education (MA Ed); gifted education (MA Ed); higher education leadership (Ed D); literacy specialist (MA Ed); middle grades education (MA Ed); secondary teaching and inquiry (MA Ed); teacher as leader (MA Ed); teacher leadership (Ed D). *Accreditation:* NCATE. Part-time and evening/weekend programs available. *Faculty:* 10 full-time (6 women), 17 part-time/adjunct (13 women). *Students:* 21 full-time (17 women), 238 part-time (167 women); includes 64 minority (54 Black or African American, non-Hispanic/Latino; 2 Asian, non-Hispanic/Latino; 4 Hispanic/Latino; 4 Two or more races, non-Hispanic/Latino), 2 international. Average age 39. In 2013, 61 master's, 40 doctorates awarded. *Degree requirements:* For master's, thesis, project. *Entrance requirements:* For master's, minimum cumulative GPA of 3.0, 3 professional recommendations, essays, interview with program faculty; for doctorate, minimum GPA of 3.0, 3 professional recommendations, essay, interview, on-site writing sample. Additional exam requirements/recommendations for international students: Required—TOEFL (minimum score 550 paper-based). *Application deadline:* Applications are processed on a rolling basis. Application fee: $40 ($60 for international students). Electronic applications accepted. Application fee is waived when completed online. *Expenses: Tuition:* Full-time $23,812; part-time $728 per credit hour. *Required fees:* $395 per year. Tuition and fees vary according to course load, degree level and program. *Financial support:* Career-related internships or fieldwork, Federal Work-Study, tuition waivers (partial), and professional educator discounts available. Financial award application deadline: 3/1; financial award applicants required to submit FAFSA. *Faculty research:* Collaboration with public schools, pre-service program development, mathematics, diversity, literacy. *Unit head:* Dr. Cathy Bear, Dean, 314-529-9692, Fax: 314-529-9921, E-mail: cbear@maryville.edu. *Application contact:* Holly Stanwich, Graduate Admissions Coordinator, 314-529-9542, Fax: 314-529-9921, E-mail: teachered@maryville.edu.
Website: http://www.maryville.edu/ed/graduate-programs/.

McNeese State University, Doré School of Graduate Studies, Burton College of Education, Office of Student Teaching and Professional Education Services, Program in Middle School Education Grades 4-8, Lake Charles, LA 70609. Offers Postbaccalaureate Certificate. *Entrance requirements:* For degree, PRAXIS, 2 letters of recommendation, autobiography.

Mercer University, Graduate Studies, Cecil B. Day Campus, Tift College of Education (Atlanta), Macon, GA 31207-0003. Offers curriculum and instruction (PhD); early childhood education (M Ed, MAT, Ed S); educational leadership (PhD, Ed S); higher education leadership (M Ed); independent and charter school leadership (M Ed); middle grades education (M Ed, MAT); reading education (M Ed); school counseling (Ed S); secondary education (M Ed, MAT); teacher leadership (Ed S). *Accreditation:* NCATE. Part-time and evening/weekend programs available. *Faculty:* 40 full-time (20 women), 9 part-time/adjunct (4 women). *Students:* 240 full-time (197 women), 382 part-time (320 women); includes 343 minority (315 Black or African American, non-Hispanic/Latino; 4 American Indian or Alaska Native, non-Hispanic/Latino; 9 Asian, non-Hispanic/Latino; 9 Hispanic/Latino; 1 Native Hawaiian or other Pacific Islander, non-Hispanic/Latino; 5 Two or more races, non-Hispanic/Latino), 4 international. Average age 36. In 2013, 233 master's, 24 doctorates, 47 other advanced degrees awarded. *Degree requirements:* For master's and Ed S, research project; for doctorate, comprehensive exam, thesis/dissertation. *Entrance requirements:* For master's, GRE or MAT, minimum undergraduate GPA of 2.75; for doctorate, GRE; for Ed S, GRE or MAT, minimum GPA of 3.25; for EDS degrees in educational leadership and teacher leadership: 3 years of certified teaching experience. Additional exam requirements/recommendations for international students: Required—TOEFL. *Application deadline:* For fall admission, 8/1 for domestic and international students; for spring admission, 12/1 for domestic and international students; for summer admission, 5/1 for domestic and international students. Applications are processed on a rolling basis. Application fee: $25. *Expenses:* Contact institution. *Financial support:* Federal Work-Study available. Support available to part-time students. Financial award application deadline: 5/1. *Faculty research:* Educational technology, multicultural and minority issues in education, educational leadership (P-12 and higher education), school discipline and school bullying, standards-based mathematics education. *Unit head:* Dr. Paige L. Tompkins, Interim Dean, 478-301-5397, Fax: 478-301-2280, E-mail: tompkins_pl@mercer.edu. *Application contact:* Dr. Allison Gilmore, Associate Dean for Graduate Teacher Education, 678-547-6333, Fax: 678-547-6055, E-mail: gilmore_a@mercer.edu.
Website: http://www.mercer.edu/education/.

Merrimack College, School of Education, North Andover, MA 01845-5800. Offers community engagement (M Ed), including community organizations, higher education, K-12 education; early childhood education (M Ed); elementary education (M Ed); English as a second language (PreK-6) (M Ed); English language learners (M Ed); general studies (M Ed); higher education (M Ed), including leadership and organizational development, student affairs; middle (M Ed); moderate disabilities (PreK-8) (M Ed); secondary (M Ed); teacher leadership (CAGS), including instructional leadership, reading specialist. Part-time and evening/weekend programs available. *Faculty:* 4 full-time (all women), 23 part-time/adjunct (15 women). *Students:* 127 full-time (104 women), 61 part-time (52 women); includes 3 minority (1 Asian, non-Hispanic/Latino; 2 Hispanic/Latino), 2 international. Average age 25. 403 applicants, 47% accepted, 138 enrolled. In 2013, 140 master's awarded. *Degree requirements:* For master's, practicum, portfolio, and state test (for licensure track); capstone (for higher education and community engagement tracks). *Entrance requirements:* For master's, MTEL (Massachusetts Tests for Educator Licensure), official transcripts from other colleges, resume, personal statement, 2 letters of recommendation, additional essay requirements for fellowships. Additional exam requirements/recommendations for international students: Required—TOEFL (minimum score 84 iBT), IELTS (minimum score 6.5). *Application deadline:* For fall admission, 8/15 for domestic and international students; for winter admission, 12/1 for domestic students, 11/15 for international students; for spring admission, 1/10 for domestic and international students; for summer admission, 5/10 for domestic and international students. Applications are processed on a rolling basis. Application fee: $0. Electronic applications accepted. Tuition and fees vary according to course load and program. *Financial support:* In 2013–14, 91 fellowships with full tuition reimbursements were awarded; career-related internships or fieldwork, scholarships/grants, and health care benefits also available. Support available to part-time students. Financial award applicants required to submit FAFSA. *Faculty research:* Expressive language, civic engagement, family life education, reading genres, the psychological process of aging. *Application contact:* Kristen English, Interim Director of Graduate Admission, 978-837-5073, E-mail: englishkr@merrimack.edu.
Website: http://www.merrimack.edu/academics/graduate/education/.

Miami University, College of Education, Health and Society, Department of Teacher Education, Oxford, OH 45056. Offers adolescent education (M Ed); elementary education (M Ed, MAT); reading education (M Ed); secondary education (MAT). Part-time and evening/weekend programs available. *Students:* 31 full-time (21 women), 26 part-time (23 women); includes 8 minority (3 Black or African American, non-Hispanic/Latino; 1 Asian, non-Hispanic/Latino; 2 Hispanic/Latino; 2 Two or more races, non-Hispanic/Latino), 2 international. Average age 31. In 2013, 31 master's awarded. *Entrance requirements:* Additional exam requirements/recommendations for international students: Recommended—TOEFL (minimum score 80 iBT), IELTS (minimum score 6.5), TSE (minimum score 54). *Application deadline:* Applications are processed on a rolling basis. Application fee: $50. Electronic applications accepted. *Expenses:* Tuition, state resident: full-time $12,634; part-time $526 per credit hour. Tuition, nonresident: full-time $27,892; part-time $1162 per credit hour. Part-time tuition and fees vary according to course load, campus/location and program. *Financial support:* Research assistantships with full tuition reimbursements, teaching assistantships with full tuition reimbursements, career-related internships or fieldwork, Federal Work-Study, scholarships/grants, health care benefits, tuition waivers, and unspecified assistantships available. Financial award application deadline: 2/15. *Unit head:* Dr. Paula Saine, Interim Co-Chair, 513-529-6443, Fax: 513-529-4931, E-mail: sainep@miamioh.edu. *Application contact:* Linda Dennett, Program Associate, 513-529-5708, E-mail: dennetlg@miamioh.edu.
Website: http://www.MiamiOH.edu/edt.

Middle Tennessee State University, College of Graduate Studies, College of Education, Department of Elementary and Special Education, Major in Curriculum and Instruction, Murfreesboro, TN 37132. Offers early childhood education (M Ed); elementary education (M Ed, Ed S); middle school education (M Ed). *Accreditation:* NCATE. Part-time and evening/weekend programs available. Postbaccalaureate distance learning degree programs offered. *Faculty:* 14 full-time (9 women), 7 part-time/adjunct (all women). *Degree requirements:* For master's, comprehensive exam; for Ed S, comprehensive exam, thesis or alternative. *Entrance requirements:* For master's and Ed S, GRE, MAT or PRAXIS. Additional exam requirements/recommendations for international students: Required—TOEFL (minimum score 525 paper-based; 71 iBT) or IELTS (minimum score 6). *Application deadline:* For fall admission, 8/1 priority date for domestic students. Applications are processed on a rolling basis. Application fee: $25. Electronic applications accepted. *Financial support:* Tuition waivers available. Support available to part-time students. Financial award application deadline: 5/1. *Unit head:* Dr. Kathleen Burriss, Interim Chair, 615-898-2680, Fax: 615-898-5309, E-mail: kathleen.burriss@mtsu.edu. *Application contact:* Dr. Michael D. Allen, Vice Provost for Research and Dean, 615-898-2840, Fax: 615-904-8020, E-mail: michael.allen@mtsu.edu.

Mississippi State University, College of Education, Department of Curriculum, Instruction and Special Education, Mississippi State, MS 39762. Offers curriculum and instruction (PhD), including early childhood education (MS, PhD), elementary education (PhD, Ed S), general curriculum and instruction, reading education, secondary

education (PhD, Ed S), special education (PhD, Ed S); education (Ed S), including elementary education (PhD, Ed S), secondary education (PhD, Ed S), special education (PhD, Ed S); elementary education (MS), including early childhood education (MS, PhD), general elementary education, middle level education; middle level alternate route (MAT); secondary education (MS); secondary teacher alternate route (MAT); special education (MS). *Accreditation:* NCATE. Part-time and evening/weekend programs available. *Faculty:* 11 full-time (9 women). *Students:* 58 full-time (40 women), 143 part-time (100 women); includes 62 minority (56 Black or African American, non-Hispanic/Latino; 2 American Indian or Alaska Native, non-Hispanic/Latino; 3 Hispanic/Latino; 1 Two or more races, non-Hispanic/Latino). Average age 33. 181 applicants, 32% accepted, 52 enrolled. In 2013, 44 master's, 1 doctorate, 7 other advanced degrees awarded. *Degree requirements:* For master's, comprehensive exam; for doctorate, thesis/dissertation; for Ed S, comprehensive exam, thesis or alternative. *Entrance requirements:* For master's, GRE, minimum GPA of 2.75 in junior and senior year, eligibility for initial teacher certification; for doctorate, GRE, minimum GPA of 3.4 on previous graduate work; for Ed S, GRE, minimum GPA of 3.2 on master's degree. Additional exam requirements/recommendations for international students: Required—TOEFL (minimum score 550 paper-based; 79 iBT); Recommended—IELTS (minimum score 6.5). *Application deadline:* For fall admission, 3/1 priority date for domestic students, 5/1 for international students; for spring admission, 9/1 priority date for domestic students, 9/1 for international students. Applications are processed on a rolling basis. Application fee: $60. Electronic applications accepted. *Financial support:* In 2013–14, 7 research assistantships with full and partial tuition reimbursements (averaging $9,623 per year), 2 teaching assistantships (averaging $11,382 per year) were awarded; Federal Work-Study, institutionally sponsored loans, scholarships/grants, and unspecified assistantships also available. Financial award application deadline: 4/1; financial award applicants required to submit FAFSA. *Faculty research:* Early childhood education, reading, rural schools, multicultural education, use of technology in instruction. *Unit head:* Dr. Devon Brenner, Professor and Interim Head, 662-325-7119, Fax: 662-325-7857, E-mail: devon@ra.msstate.edu. *Application contact:* Dr. Dana Franz, Graduate Coordinator, 662-325-3703, Fax: 662-325-7857, E-mail: tstevonson@colled.msstate.edu.
Website: http://www.cise.msstate.edu/.

Morehead State University, Graduate Programs, College of Education, Department of Curriculum and Instruction, Morehead, KY 40351. Offers curriculum and instruction (Ed S); elementary education (MA Ed), including elementary education, international education, middle school education, reading; secondary education (MA Ed); special education (MA Ed); teaching (MAT). Part-time and evening/weekend programs available. *Degree requirements:* For master's, comprehensive exam, thesis optional; for Ed S, thesis, oral exam. *Entrance requirements:* For master's, GRE General Test, minimum GPA of 2.75, teaching certificate; for Ed S, GRE General Test, interview, master's degree, minimum GPA of 3.5, work experience. Additional exam requirements/recommendations for international students: Required—TOEFL (minimum score 500 paper-based). Electronic applications accepted. *Faculty research:* Communicative competence of learning-disabled students, teaching social studies in elementary schools, ungraded primary school organization, study skills.

Morehead State University, Graduate Programs, College of Education, Department of Foundational and Graduate Studies in Education, Morehead, KY 40351. Offers adult and higher education (MA, Ed S); certified professional counselor (Ed S); counseling P-12 (MA); curriculum and instruction (Ed S); educational technology (MA Ed); instructional leadership (Ed S); school administration (MA); school counseling (Ed S); teacher leader business and marketing content (MA Ed); teacher leader business and marketing technology (MA Ed); teacher leader educational technology (MA Ed); teacher leader English (MA Ed); teacher leader gifted education (MA Ed); teacher leader IECE certification (MA Ed); teacher leader interdisciplinary education P-5 (MA Ed); teacher leader middle grades (MA Ed); teacher leader non IECE certification (MA Ed); teacher leader reading/writing - non-certification (MA Ed); teacher leader reading/writing certification (MA Ed); teacher leader school communication - certification (MA Ed); teacher leader school communication - non-certification (MA Ed); teacher leader social studies (MA Ed); teacher leader special education (MA Ed). *Accreditation:* NCATE. Part-time and evening/weekend programs available. *Degree requirements:* For master's, thesis optional, oral and/or written comprehensive exams; for Ed S, thesis, oral exam. *Entrance requirements:* For master's, GRE General Test, minimum overall undergraduate GPA of 2.5; for Ed S, GRE General Test, interview, master's degree, minimum GPA of 3.5, work experience. Additional exam requirements/recommendations for international students: Required—TOEFL (minimum score 500 paper-based). Electronic applications accepted. *Faculty research:* Character education, school accountability, computer applications for school administrators.

Morehead State University, Graduate Programs, College of Education, Department of Middle Grades and Secondary Education, Morehead, KY 40351. Offers business and marketing education (MAT); English/language arts 5-9 (MAT); French (MAT); health P-12 (MAT); mathematics 5-9 (MAT); physical education P-12 (MAT); science 5-9 (MAT); secondary biology (MAT); secondary chemistry (MAT); secondary earth science (MAT); secondary English (MAT); secondary math (MAT); secondary physics (MAT); secondary social studies (MAT); social studies 5-9 (MAT); Spanish (MAT). Part-time and evening/weekend programs available. *Degree requirements:* For master's, portfolio. *Entrance requirements:* For master's, GRE or PRAXIS II content exam, minimum overall undergraduate GPA of 2.5. Additional exam requirements/recommendations for international students: Required—TOEFL (minimum score 500 paper-based). Electronic applications accepted.

Morgan State University, School of Graduate Studies, School of Education and Urban Studies, MAT Program, Baltimore, MD 21251. Offers elementary education (MAT); high school education (MAT); middle school education (MAT). Part-time programs available. *Degree requirements:* For master's, comprehensive exam. *Entrance requirements:* For master's, GRE General Test or MAT. *Faculty research:* Multicultural education, cooperative learning, psychology of cognition.

Mount St. Joseph University, Graduate Education Program, Cincinnati, OH 45233-1670. Offers adolescent to young adult education (MA); dyslexia (Certificate); inclusive early childhood education (MA); instructional leadership (MA); middle childhood education (MA); multicultural special education (MA); Pre-K special needs (Certificate); principal licensure (MA); reading (Certificate); reading science (MA). *Accreditation:* Teacher Education Accreditation Council. Part-time and evening/weekend programs available. *Faculty:* 10 full-time (7 women), 7 part-time/adjunct (6 women). *Students:* 28 full-time (25 women), 95 part-time (76 women); includes 27 minority (19 Black or African American, non-Hispanic/Latino; 6 Hispanic/Latino; 2 Two or more races, non-Hispanic/Latino). Average age 36. 73 applicants, 44% accepted, 30 enrolled. In 2013, 69 master's awarded. *Degree requirements:* For master's, research project, student teaching, clinical and field-based experiences. *Entrance requirements:* For master's, GRE, PRAXIS II in teaching content area (math or science), 2 letters of recommendation, interview, resume. Additional exam requirements/recommendations for international students: Required—TOEFL (minimum score 560 paper-based; 83 iBT). *Application deadline:* Applications are processed on a rolling basis. Application fee: $50. Electronic applications accepted. *Expenses: Tuition:* Full-time $18,400; part-time $575 per credit hour. *Required fees:* $450; $450 per year. Part-time tuition and fees vary according to course load, degree level and program. *Financial support:* Scholarships/grants available. Financial award applicants required to submit FAFSA. *Faculty research:* Foreign and second language learning problems/reading disabilities/hyperlexia, multicultural/bilingual special education, alternative educator licensure, science education, pedagogical content knowledge. *Unit head:* Dr. Mary West, Chair, 513-244-3263, Fax: 513-244-4867, E-mail: mary_west@mail.msj.edu. *Application contact:* Mary Brigham, Assistant Director of Graduate Recruitment, 513-244-4233, Fax: 513-244-4629, E-mail: mary_brigham@mail.msj.edu.
Website: http://www.msj.edu/academics/graduate-programs/master-of-arts-initial-teacher-licensure-programs/.

Mount Saint Mary College, Division of Education, Newburgh, NY 12550-3494. Offers adolescence and special education (MS Ed); adolescence education (MS Ed); childhood and special education (MS Ed); childhood education (MS Ed); literacy (5-12) (Advanced Certificate); literacy (birth-6) (Advanced Certificate); literacy and special education (MS Ed); literacy/childhood (MS Ed); middle school (5-6) (MS Ed); middle school (7-9) (MS Ed); special education (1-6) (MS Ed); special education (7-12) (MS Ed). *Accreditation:* NCATE. Part-time and evening/weekend programs available. *Faculty:* 11 full-time (9 women), 9 part-time/adjunct (4 women). *Students:* 29 full-time (19 women), 142 part-time (117 women); includes 22 minority (5 Black or African American, non-Hispanic/Latino; 16 Hispanic/Latino; 1 Two or more races, non-Hispanic/Latino). Average age 29. 51 applicants, 65% accepted, 27 enrolled. In 2013, 72 master's awarded. *Application deadline:* Applications are processed on a rolling basis. Application fee: $45. Application fee is waived when completed online. *Expenses: Tuition:* Full-time $13,356; part-time $742 per credit. *Required fees:* $70 per semester. *Financial support:* In 2013–14, 69 students received support. Unspecified assistantships available. Financial award application deadline: 4/15; financial award applicants required to submit FAFSA. *Faculty research:* Learning and teaching styles, computers in special education, language development. *Unit head:* Dr. William Swart, Graduate Coordinator, 845-569-3149, Fax: 845-569-3535, E-mail: william.swart@msmc.edu. *Application contact:* Lisa Gallina, Director of Admissions for Graduate Programs and Adult Degree Completion, 845-569-3166, Fax: 845-569-3450, E-mail: lisa.gallina@msmc.edu.
Website: http://www.msmc.edu/Academics/Graduate_Programs/Master_of_Science_in_Education.

Mount Saint Vincent University, Graduate Programs, Faculty of Education, Program in Curriculum Studies, Halifax, NS B3M 2J6, Canada. Offers education of young adolescents (M Ed, MA Ed, MA-R); general studies (M Ed, MA Ed, MA-R); teaching English as a second language (M Ed, MA Ed, MA-R). Part-time and evening/weekend programs available. Postbaccalaureate distance learning degree programs offered (minimal on-campus study). *Degree requirements:* For master's, thesis (for some programs). *Entrance requirements:* For master's, bachelor's degree in related field, minimum B average, 1 year of teaching experience. Electronic applications accepted. *Faculty research:* Science education, cultural studies, international education, curriculum development.

Murray State University, College of Education, Department of Adolescent, Career and Special Education, Program in Middle School Education, Murray, KY 42071. Offers MA Ed, Ed S. *Accreditation:* NCATE. *Degree requirements:* For master's, comprehensive exam, thesis optional. *Entrance requirements:* Additional exam requirements/recommendations for international students: Required—TOEFL.

Nazareth College of Rochester, Graduate Studies, Department of Education, Program in Inclusive Education-Adolescence Level, Rochester, NY 14618-3790. Offers MS Ed. *Accreditation:* Teacher Education Accreditation Council. *Entrance requirements:* For master's, minimum GPA of 3.0.

New York Institute of Technology, School of Education, Department of Education, Old Westbury, NY 11568-8000. Offers adolescence education: mathematics (MS); adolescence education: science (MS); childhood education (MS); science, technology, engineering, and math education (Advanced Certificate); teaching 21st century skills (Advanced Certificate). Part-time and evening/weekend programs available. Postbaccalaureate distance learning degree programs offered (minimal on-campus study). *Faculty:* 1 (woman) full-time, 6 part-time/adjunct (3 women). *Students:* 13 full-time (11 women), 21 part-time (19 women); includes 7 minority (2 Black or African American, non-Hispanic/Latino; 3 Asian, non-Hispanic/Latino; 1 Hispanic/Latino; 1 Two or more races, non-Hispanic/Latino), 1 international. Average age 31. 32 applicants, 75% accepted, 13 enrolled. In 2013, 6 master's, 58 other advanced degrees awarded. *Entrance requirements:* Additional exam requirements/recommendations for international students: Required—TOEFL (minimum score 550 paper-based; 79 iBT), IELTS (minimum score 6). *Application deadline:* For fall admission, 7/1 priority date for domestic students, 6/1 for international students; for spring admission, 12/1 priority date for domestic students, 12/1 for international students. Applications are processed on a rolling basis. Application fee: $50. Electronic applications accepted. *Expenses: Tuition:* Full-time $18,900; part-time $1050 per credit. *Financial support:* Research assistantships with partial tuition reimbursements, career-related internships or fieldwork, scholarships/grants, health care benefits, tuition waivers (full and partial), and unspecified assistantships available. Support available to part-time students. Financial award applicants required to submit FAFSA. *Faculty research:* Evolving definition of new literacies and its impact on teaching and learning (twenty-first century skills), new literacies practices in teacher education, teachers' professional development, English language and literacy learning through mobile learning, teaching reading to culturally and linguistically diverse children. *Unit head:* Dr. Hui-Yin Hsu, Associate Professor, 516-686-1322, Fax: 516-686-7655, E-mail: hhsu02@nyit.edu. *Application contact:* Alice Dolitsky, Director, Graduate Admissions, 516-686-7520, Fax: 516-686-1116, E-mail: nyitgrad@nyit.edu.
Website: http://www.nyit.edu/education/departments.

New York University, Steinhardt School of Culture, Education, and Human Development, Department of Teaching and Learning, Program in Literacy Education, New York, NY 10012-1019. Offers grades 5-12 (MA). *Accreditation:* Teacher Education Accreditation Council. Part-time programs available. *Faculty:* 1 (woman) full-time. *Students:* 8 full-time (5 women), 7 part-time (all women); includes 3 minority (1 Black or African American, non-Hispanic/Latino; 1 Asian, non-Hispanic/Latino; 1 Hispanic/Latino), 2 international. Average age 26. 52 applicants, 94% accepted, 11 enrolled. In 2013, 17 master's awarded. *Degree requirements:* For master's, thesis (for some programs), fieldwork. *Entrance requirements:* For master's, teacher certification. Additional exam requirements/recommendations for international students: Required—TOEFL (minimum score 100 iBT). *Application deadline:* For fall admission, 2/1 priority date for domestic and international students. Applications are processed on a rolling basis. Application fee: $75. Electronic applications accepted. *Expenses: Tuition:* Full-time $35,856; part-time $1494 per unit. *Required fees:* $1408; $64 per unit. $473 per term. Tuition and fees vary according to course load and program. *Financial support:* Career-related internships or fieldwork, Federal Work-Study, institutionally sponsored loans, scholarships/grants, and tuition waivers (partial) available. Support available to part-time students. Financial award application deadline: 2/1; financial award applicants required to submit FAFSA. *Faculty research:* Early literacy intervention and

development, psycho and sociolinguistics, multicultural education, literacy assessment and instruction. *Unit head:* Prof. Kay Stahl, Director, 212-998-5204, Fax: 212-995-4049, E-mail: kay.stahl@nyu.edu. *Application contact:* Office of Graduate Admissions, 212-998-5030, Fax: 212-995-4328, E-mail: steinhardt.gradadmissions@nyu.edu. Website: http://steinhardt.nyu.edu/teachlearn/literacy.

Niagara University, Graduate Division of Education, Concentration in Teacher Education, Niagara Falls, NY 14109. Offers early childhood and childhood education (MS Ed, Certificate); middle and adolescence education (MS Ed, Certificate); special education (grades 1-12) (MS Ed, Certificate); teaching English to speakers of other languages (MS Ed). *Accreditation:* NCATE. *Students:* 168 full-time (130 women), 40 part-time (28 women); includes 11 minority (4 Black or African American, non-Hispanic/Latino; 1 Asian, non-Hispanic/Latino; 5 Hispanic/Latino; 1 Native Hawaiian or other Pacific Islander, non-Hispanic/Latino), 101 international. Average age 27. In 2013, 131 master's, 1 Certificate awarded. *Entrance requirements:* For master's, GRE General Test or MAT. Additional exam requirements/recommendations for international students: Required—TOEFL (minimum score 550 paper-based, 79 iBT) or IELTS (minimum score 6). *Application deadline:* For fall admission, 8/1 for domestic students. Applications are processed on a rolling basis. Application fee: $30. *Expenses:* Contact institution. *Financial support:* Research assistantships with full and partial tuition reimbursements, teaching assistantships with full and partial tuition reimbursements, career-related internships or fieldwork, Federal Work-Study, scholarships/grants, and unspecified assistantships available. Financial award application deadline: 4/15; financial award applicants required to submit FAFSA. *Unit head:* Dr. Chandra Foote, Chair, 716-286-8549. *Application contact:* Dr. Debra A. Colley, Dean of Education, 716-286-8560, Fax: 716-286-8561, E-mail: dcolley@niagara.edu. Website: http://www.niagara.edu/teacher-education.

North Carolina Central University, School of Education, Department of Curriculum, Instruction and Professional Studies, Durham, NC 27707-3129. Offers curriculum and instruction (MA), including elementary education, middle grades education. *Accreditation:* NCATE. Part-time and evening/weekend programs available. *Degree requirements:* For master's, comprehensive exam, thesis or alternative. *Entrance requirements:* For master's, minimum GPA of 3.0 in major, 2.5 overall. Additional exam requirements/recommendations for international students: Required—TOEFL. *Faculty research:* Simulation of decision-making behavior of school boards.

North Carolina State University, Graduate School, College of Education, Department of Curriculum and Instruction, Program in Middle Grades Education, Raleigh, NC 27695. Offers M Ed, MS. *Accreditation:* NCATE. *Degree requirements:* For master's, thesis optional. *Entrance requirements:* For master's, GRE General Test or MAT, minimum GPA of 3.0 in major.

Northwestern State University of Louisiana, Graduate Studies and Research, College of Education and Human Development, Program in Middle School Education, Natchitoches, LA 71497. Offers MAT. *Degree requirements:* For master's, comprehensive exam, thesis or alternative. *Entrance requirements:* For master's, GRE General Test, minimum undergraduate GPA of 2.5. Additional exam requirements/recommendations for international students: Required—TOEFL. Electronic applications accepted.

Northwest Missouri State University, Graduate School, College of Education and Human Services, Department of Professional Education, Program in Teaching: Middle School, Maryville, MO 64468-6001. Offers MS Ed. *Accreditation:* NCATE. *Degree requirements:* For master's, comprehensive exam. *Entrance requirements:* For master's, GRE General Test, minimum undergraduate GPA of 2.75, teaching certificate, writing sample. Additional exam requirements/recommendations for international students: Required—TOEFL.

The Ohio State University at Lima, Graduate Programs, Lima, OH 45804. Offers early childhood education (M Ed); education (MA); middle childhood education (M Ed); social work (MSW). Part-time programs available. *Faculty:* 37. *Students:* 8 full-time (6 women), 8 part-time (7 women). Average age 31. Terminal master's awarded for partial completion of doctoral program. *Degree requirements:* For master's, comprehensive exam (for some programs), thesis (for some programs). *Entrance requirements:* For master's, GRE, minimum GPA of 3.0. Additional exam requirements/recommendations for international students: Required—TOEFL (minimum score 550 paper-based, 79 iBT), IELTS (minimum score 7), or Michigan English Language Assessment Battery (minimum score 82). *Application deadline:* For fall admission, 6/1 for domestic and international students; for spring admission, 10/15 for domestic and international students. Applications are processed on a rolling basis. Application fee: $60 ($70 for international students). Electronic applications accepted. *Financial support:* Application deadline: 2/15. *Unit head:* Dr. Gregory Rose, Interim Dean and Director, 419-995-8481, E-mail: rose.9@osu.edu. *Application contact:* Graduate Admissions, 614-292-9444, Fax: 614-292-3895, E-mail: gradadmissions@osu.edu.

The Ohio State University at Marion, Graduate Programs, Marion, OH 43302-5695. Offers early childhood education (pre-K to grade 3) (M Ed); education - teaching and learning (MA); middle childhood education (grades 4-9) (M Ed). Part-time programs available. *Faculty:* 38. *Students:* 17 full-time (13 women); includes 1 minority (Asian, non-Hispanic/Latino). Average age 27. *Degree requirements:* For master's, comprehensive exam (for some programs), thesis (for some programs). *Entrance requirements:* For master's, GRE, minimum undergraduate GPA of 3.0. Additional exam requirements/recommendations for international students: Required—TOEFL (minimum score 550 paper-based, 79 iBT), IELTS (minimum score 7) or Michigan English Language Assessment Battery (minimum score 82). *Application deadline:* For fall admission, 6/1 for domestic students, 6/1 priority date for international students; for spring admission, 10/15 for domestic students, 10/15 priority date for international students. Applications are processed on a rolling basis. Application fee: $60 ($70 for international students). Electronic applications accepted. *Financial support:* Application deadline: 2/15; applicants required to submit FAFSA. *Unit head:* Dr. Gregory S. Rose, Dean/Director, 740-725-6218, E-mail: rose.9@osu.edu. *Application contact:* Graduate Admissions, 614-292-9444, Fax: 614-292-3895, E-mail: gradadmissions@osu.edu.

The Ohio State University–Mansfield Campus, Graduate Programs, Mansfield, OH 44906-1599. Offers early childhood education (M Ed); education (MA); middle childhood education (M Ed); social work (MSW). Part-time programs available. *Faculty:* 40. *Students:* 18 full-time (17 women), 30 part-time (29 women). Average age 31. *Degree requirements:* For master's, comprehensive exam (for some programs), thesis (for some programs). *Entrance requirements:* For master's, GRE, minimum GPA of 3.0. Additional exam requirements/recommendations for international students: Required—TOEFL (minimum 550 paper-based, 79 iBT), IELTS (minimum score 7) or Michigan English Language Assessment Battery (minimum score 82). *Application deadline:* For fall admission, 6/1 for domestic and international students; for spring admission, 10/15 for domestic and international students. Applications are processed on a rolling basis. Application fee: $60 ($70 for international students). Electronic applications accepted. *Financial support:* Teaching assistantships with full tuition reimbursements, Federal Work-Study, and scholarships/grants available. Support available to part-time students. Financial award application deadline: 2/15. *Unit head:* Dr. Stephen M. Gavazzi, Dean and Director, 419-755-4221, Fax: 419-755-4241, E-mail: gavazzi.1@osu.edu.

Application contact: Graduate Admissions, 614-292-9444, Fax: 614-292-3895, E-mail: gradadmissions@osu.edu.

The Ohio State University–Newark Campus, Graduate Programs, Newark, OH 43055-1797. Offers early/middle childhood education (M Ed); education - teaching and learning (MA); social work (MSW). Part-time programs available. *Faculty:* 53. *Students:* 10 full-time (9 women), 27 part-time (24 women); includes 3 minority (1 Black or African American, non-Hispanic/Latino; 2 Hispanic/Latino). Average age 35. Terminal master's awarded for partial completion of doctoral program. *Degree requirements:* For master's, comprehensive exam (for some programs), thesis (for some programs). *Entrance requirements:* For master's, GRE, minimum GPA of 3.0. Additional exam requirements/recommendations for international students: Required—TOEFL (minimum score 550 paper-based, 79 iBT), IELTS (minimum score 7), or Michigan English Language Assessment Battery (minimum score 82). *Application deadline:* For fall admission, 6/1 for domestic and international students; for spring admission, 10/15 for domestic students, 2/1 for international students. Applications are processed on a rolling basis. Application fee: $60 ($70 for international students). Electronic applications accepted. *Financial support:* Application deadline: 2/15. *Unit head:* Dr. William L. MacDonald, Dean/Director, 740-366-9333 Ext. 330, E-mail: macdonald.24@osu.edu. *Application contact:* Graduate Admissions, 614-292-9444, Fax: 614-292-3985, E-mail: gradadmissions@osu.edu.

Ohio University, Graduate College, Gladys W. and David H. Patton College of Education and Human Services, Department of Teacher Education, Athens, OH 45701-2979. Offers adolescent to young adult education (M Ed); curriculum and instruction (M Ed, PhD); early childhood/special education (M Ed); intervention specialist/mild-moderate needs (M Ed); intervention specialist/moderate-intensive needs (M Ed); mathematics education (PhD); middle childhood education (M Ed); reading education (M Ed); social studies education (PhD). Part-time and evening/weekend programs available. *Degree requirements:* For master's, thesis or alternative; for doctorate, comprehensive exam, thesis/dissertation. *Entrance requirements:* For master's, GRE General Test or MAT (if GPA is below 2.9); for doctorate, GRE General Test, minimum GPA of 3.4, work experience. Additional exam requirements/recommendations for international students: Required—TOEFL (minimum score 550 paper-based; 80 iBT) or IELTS (minimum score 6.5). Electronic applications accepted. *Faculty research:* Cognition literacy, character education, teacher's education reform, disabilities.

Old Dominion University, Darden College of Education, Program in Elementary/Middle Education, Norfolk, VA 23529. Offers elementary education (MS Ed); instructional technology (MS Ed); library science (MS Ed); middle school education (MS Ed). *Accreditation:* NCATE. Part-time and evening/weekend programs available. Postbaccalaureate distance learning degree programs offered (no on-campus study). *Faculty:* 20 full-time (15 women), 31 part-time/adjunct (26 women). *Students:* 157 full-time (152 women), 91 part-time (77 women); includes 46 minority (17 Black or African American, non-Hispanic/Latino; 3 Asian, non-Hispanic/Latino; 17 Hispanic/Latino; 1 Native Hawaiian or other Pacific Islander, non-Hispanic/Latino; 8 Two or more races, non-Hispanic/Latino), 1 international. Average age 31. 291 applicants, 50% accepted, 123 enrolled. In 2013, 142 master's awarded. *Degree requirements:* For master's, comprehensive exam. *Entrance requirements:* For master's, GRE General Test or MAT; PRAXIS I, SAT or ACT, minimum GPA of 2.8. Additional exam requirements/recommendations for international students: Required—TOEFL (minimum score 600 paper-based). *Application deadline:* For fall admission, 6/1 priority date for domestic students; for winter admission, 11/1 priority date for domestic students; for spring admission, 3/1 priority date for domestic students. Applications are processed on a rolling basis. Application fee: $50. Electronic applications accepted. *Expenses:* Tuition, state resident: full-time $9888; part-time $412 per credit. Tuition, nonresident: full-time $25,152; part-time $1048 per credit. *Required fees:* $59 per semester. One-time fee: $50. *Financial support:* In 2013–14, 180 students received support. Application deadline: 2/15; applicants required to submit FAFSA. *Faculty research:* Education pre-K to 6, school librarianship. *Unit head:* Dr. Charlene Fleener, Graduate Program Director, 757-683-3284, Fax: 757-683-5862, E-mail: cfleener@odu.edu. *Application contact:* William Heffelfinger, Director of Graduate Admissions, 757-683-5554, Fax: 757-683-3255, E-mail: gradadmit@odu.edu. Website: http://education.odu.edu/eci/.

Our Lady of the Lake University of San Antonio, School of Professional Studies, Program in Intermediate Education, San Antonio, TX 78207-4689. Offers math/science education (M Ed); professional studies (M Ed). Part-time and evening/weekend programs available. *Faculty:* 6 full-time (4 women), 3 part-time/adjunct (all women). *Students:* 1 (woman) full-time; minority (Black or African American, non-Hispanic/Latino). Average age 50. 1 applicant, 100% accepted. In 2013, 1 master's awarded. *Degree requirements:* For master's, comprehensive exam. *Entrance requirements:* For master's, GRE General Test or MAT. Additional exam requirements/recommendations for international students: Required—TOEFL. *Application deadline:* For fall admission, 4/1 priority date for domestic and international students; for spring admission, 11/1 priority date for domestic and international students; for summer admission, 2/1 priority date for domestic and international students. Applications are processed on a rolling basis. Application fee: $25 ($50 for international students). Electronic applications accepted. *Expenses:* Tuition: Full-time $9120; part-time $760 per credit. *Required fees:* $698; $334 per trimester. Tuition and fees vary according to course load, degree level, campus/location and program. *Financial support:* Research assistantships, teaching assistantships, career-related internships or fieldwork, Federal Work-Study, institutionally sponsored loans, scholarships/grants, and tuition waivers (partial) available. Support available to part-time students. Financial award application deadline: 4/15. *Faculty research:* Professional educator to understand and meet the comprehensive needs of a diverse student population, life-long learners, innovative practices. *Unit head:* Dr. Jerrie Jackson, 210-434-6711 Ext. 2698, E-mail: jjackson@lake.ollusa.edu. *Application contact:* Graduate Admission, 210-431-3961, Fax: 210-431-4013, E-mail: gradadm@lake.ollusa.edu. Website: http://www.ollusa.edu/s/1190/ollu-3-column-noads.aspx?sid=1190&gid=1&pgid=3855.

Pacific University, College of Education, Forest Grove, OR 97116-1797. Offers early childhood education (MAT); education (MAE); elementary education (MAT); high school education (MAT); middle school education (MAT); special education (MAT); visual function in learning (M Ed). *Accreditation:* NCATE. Part-time and evening/weekend programs available. *Degree requirements:* For master's, research project. *Entrance requirements:* For master's, California Basic Educational Skills Test, PRAXIS II, minimum undergraduate GPA of 2.75, 3.0 graduate. Additional exam requirements/recommendations for international students: Required—TOEFL. Electronic applications accepted. *Expenses:* Contact institution. *Faculty research:* Defining a culturally competent classroom, technology in the k-12 classroom, Socratic seminars, social studies education.

Piedmont College, School of Education, Demorest, GA 30535-0010. Offers art education (MAT); early childhood education (MA, MAT); instructional technology (MAT); middle grades education (MA, MAT); music education (MAT); secondary education (MA, MAT); special education (MA, MAT); teacher leadership (Ed S). Part-time and evening/weekend programs available. *Students:* 312 full-time (242 women), 694 part-time (563

women); includes 153 minority (103 Black or African American, non-Hispanic/Latino; 3 American Indian or Alaska Native, non-Hispanic/Latino; 17 Asian, non-Hispanic/Latino; 19 Hispanic/Latino; 11 Two or more races, non-Hispanic/Latino), 1 international. Average age 37. 165 applicants, 72% accepted, 118 enrolled. In 2013, 333 master's, 15 doctorates, 457 other advanced degrees awarded. *Degree requirements:* For master's, thesis, field experience in the classroom teaching; for doctorate, thesis/dissertation. *Entrance requirements:* For master's, GRE General Test, MAT, minimum undergraduate GPA of 2.5; for Ed S, minimum graduate GPA of 3.5, valid teaching certificate. Additional exam requirements/recommendations for international students: Required—TOEFL (minimum score 550 paper-based). *Application deadline:* For fall admission, 7/15 for domestic students; for spring admission, 12/1 for domestic students. Applications are processed on a rolling basis. Electronic applications accepted. *Expenses: Tuition:* Full-time $7992; part-time $444 per credit hour. *Financial support:* Career-related internships or fieldwork, Federal Work-Study, and unspecified assistantships available. Support available to part-time students. Financial award applicants required to submit FAFSA. *Unit head:* Dr. Don Gnecco, Dean, 706-778-3000 Ext. 1201, Fax: 706-776-9608, E-mail: dgnecco@piedmont.edu. *Application contact:* Kathleen Anderson, Director of Graduate Enrollment Management, 706-778-8500 Ext. 1181, Fax: 706-778-0150, E-mail: kanderson@piedmont.edu.

Quinnipiac University, School of Education, Program in Secondary Education, Hamden, CT 06518-1940. Offers biology (MAT); English (MAT); history/social studies (MAT); mathematics (MAT); Spanish (MAT). *Accreditation:* NCATE. *Faculty:* 14 full-time (7 women), 46 part-time/adjunct (27 women). *Students:* 44 full-time (37 women), 1 (woman) part-time; includes 2 minority (both Hispanic/Latino). 45 applicants, 93% accepted, 32 enrolled. In 2013, 32 master's awarded. *Entrance requirements:* For master's, PRAXIS I, minimum GPA of 2.67, interview. *Application deadline:* For fall admission, 4/1 priority date for domestic students. Applications are processed on a rolling basis. Application fee: $45. Electronic applications accepted. *Expenses: Tuition:* Part-time $920 per credit. *Required fees:* $37 per credit. *Financial support:* Career-related internships or fieldwork, tuition waivers (full and partial), and unspecified assistantships available. Support available to part-time students. Financial award application deadline: 6/1; financial award applicants required to submit FAFSA. *Faculty research:* Multicultural and urban education/leadership, challenges of teaching diverse learners, scholarship of teaching and learning, technology and teaching, humor and education. *Unit head:* Mordechai Gordon, Program Director, E-mail: mordechai.gordon@quinnipiac.edu. *Application contact:* Office of Graduate Admissions, 800-462-1944, Fax: 203-582-3443, E-mail: graduate@quinnipiac.edu.
Website: http://www.quinnipiac.edu/gradeducation.

Roberts Wesleyan College, Department of Teacher Education, Rochester, NY 14624-1997. Offers adolescence education (M Ed); childhood and special education (M Ed); literacy education (M Ed); special education online (M Ed). Part-time and evening/weekend programs available. *Faculty:* 10 full-time (7 women), 12 part-time/adjunct (6 women). *Students:* 37 full-time (29 women), 10 part-time (6 women); includes 16 minority (15 Black or African American, non-Hispanic/Latino; 1 Hispanic/Latino). Average age 33. 72 applicants, 63% accepted, 34 enrolled. In 2013, 20 master's awarded. *Degree requirements:* For master's, thesis. *Application deadline:* For fall admission, 6/1 for domestic and international students; for spring admission, 11/1 for domestic and international students; for summer admission, 3/1 for domestic and international students. Applications are processed on a rolling basis. Electronic applications accepted. Application fee is waived when completed online. *Expenses: Tuition:* Full-time $12,816; part-time $712 per credit hour. One-time fee: $300. Tuition and fees vary according to course load and program. *Financial support:* In 2013–14, 7 students received support. Career-related internships or fieldwork available. Financial award application deadline: 9/1; financial award applicants required to submit FAFSA. *Unit head:* Dr. Sharon Harris-Ewing, Chair, 585-594-6935, E-mail: harrisewing_sharon@roberts.edu. *Application contact:* Paul Ziegler, Director of Marketing and Recruitment for Teacher Education, 585-594-6146, Fax: 585-594-6108, E-mail: ziegler_paul@roberts.edu.
Website: https://www.roberts.edu/department-of-teacher-education.aspx.

Rowan University, Graduate School, College of Liberal Arts and Sciences, Department of Mathematics, Program in Middle Grades Math Education, Glassboro, NJ 08028-1701. Offers CGS. *Faculty:* 1 (woman) full-time. *Students:* 27 part-time (24 women); includes 6 minority (4 Black or African American, non-Hispanic/Latino; 1 Hispanic/Latino; 1 Two or more races, non-Hispanic/Latino). Average age 42. 3 applicants, 100% accepted, 3 enrolled. *Application deadline:* For fall admission, 8/1 for domestic and international students; for spring admission, 11/1 for domestic and international students; for summer admission, 4/1 for domestic and international students. Application fee: $65. *Expenses: Tuition, area resident:* Part-time $638 per credit. Tuition, state resident: full-time $5742. *Required fees:* $142 per credit. Tuition and fees vary according to course level and program. *Unit head:* Dr. Horacio Sosa, Dean, College of Graduate and Continuing Education, 856-256-4747, Fax: 856-256-5638, E-mail: sosa@rowan.edu. *Application contact:* Admissions and Enrollment Services, 856-256-5145, Fax: 856-256-5637, E-mail: cgceadmissions@rowan.edu.

Saginaw Valley State University, College of Education, Program in Middle School Classroom Teaching, University Center, MI 48710. Offers MAT. *Accreditation:* NCATE. Part-time and evening/weekend programs available. *Students:* 4 part-time (all women). Average age 34. In 2013, 5 master's awarded. *Degree requirements:* For master's, capstone course. *Entrance requirements:* For master's, minimum GPA of 3.0, teaching certificate. Additional exam requirements/recommendations for international students: Required—TOEFL (minimum score 550 paper-based; 79 iBT). *Application deadline:* For fall admission, 7/15 for international students; for winter admission, 11/15 for international students; for spring admission, 4/15 for international students. Applications are processed on a rolling basis. Application fee: $30 ($80 for international students). Electronic applications accepted. *Expenses:* Tuition, state resident: full-time $8933; part-time $496.30 per credit hour. Tuition, nonresident: full-time $16,806; part-time $933.65 per credit hour. *Required fees:* $263; $14.60 per credit hour. Tuition and fees vary according to degree level. *Financial support:* Federal Work-Study and scholarships/grants available. Support available to part-time students. Financial award applicants required to submit FAFSA. *Unit head:* Dr. Mary Harmon, Dean, 989-964-7107, Fax: 989-964-4563, E-mail: coeconnect@svsu.edu. *Application contact:* Jenna Briggs, Director, Graduate and International Programs, 989-964-6096, Fax: 989-964-2788, E-mail: gradadm@svsu.edu.

Saginaw Valley State University, College of Education, Program in Natural Science Teaching, University Center, MI 48710. Offers elementary school (MAT); middle school (MAT); secondary school (MAT). *Accreditation:* NCATE. Part-time and evening/weekend programs available. *Students:* 1 (woman) part-time. Average age 43. In 2013, 8 master's awarded. *Degree requirements:* For master's, capstone course. *Entrance requirements:* For master's, minimum GPA of 3.0, teaching certificate. Additional exam requirements/recommendations for international students: Required—TOEFL (minimum score 550 paper-based; 79 iBT). *Application deadline:* For fall admission, 7/15 for international students; for winter admission, 11/15 for international students; for spring admission, 4/15 for international students. Applications are processed on a rolling basis. Application fee: $30 ($80 for international students). Electronic applications accepted. *Expenses:* Tuition, state resident: full-time $8933; part-time $496.30 per credit hour. Tuition, nonresident: full-time $16,806; part-time $933.65 per credit hour. *Required fees:* $263; $14.60 per credit hour. Tuition and fees vary according to degree level. *Financial support:* Federal Work-Study and scholarships/grants available. Support available to part-time students. Financial award applicants required to submit FAFSA. *Unit head:* Dr. Mary Harmon, Dean, 989-964-7107, Fax: 989-964-4563, E-mail: coeconnect@svsu.edu. *Application contact:* Jenna Briggs, Director, Graduate and International Admissions, 989-964-6096, Fax: 989-964-2788, E-mail: gradadm@svsu.edu.

St. Bonaventure University, School of Graduate Studies, School of Education, Adolescence Education Program, St. Bonaventure, NY 14778-2284. Offers MS Ed. *Faculty:* 2 full-time (1 woman), 2 part-time/adjunct (1 woman). *Students:* 5 full-time (1 woman); includes 1 minority (Two or more races, non-Hispanic/Latino). Average age 23. In 2013, 6 master's awarded. *Degree requirements:* For master's, comprehensive exam, electronic portfolio, completion of student teaching. *Entrance requirements:* For master's, undergraduate degree in teachable content area; minimum GPA of 3.0, personal interview, writing sample, two letters of recommendation (ability to do graduate work, observation of work with children). Additional exam requirements/recommendations for international students: Required—TOEFL (minimum score 550 paper-based; 79 iBT). *Application deadline:* For fall admission, 3/15 priority date for domestic students, 2/1 priority date for international students; for spring admission, 11/1 for domestic students. Applications are processed on a rolling basis. Application fee: $0. Electronic applications accepted. *Financial support:* In 2013–14, 1 research assistantship was awarded; Federal Work-Study, scholarships/grants, health care benefits, tuition waivers (partial), and unspecified assistantships also available. Support available to part-time students. Financial award application deadline: 4/15; financial award applicants required to submit FAFSA. *Unit head:* Dr. Paula Kenneson, Director, 716-375-2177, Fax: 716-375-2360, E-mail: pkenneso@sbu.edu. *Application contact:* Bruce Campbell, Director of Graduate Admissions, 716-375-2429, Fax: 716-375-4015, E-mail: gradsch@sbu.edu.
Website: http://www.sbu.edu/academics/schools/education/graduate-degrees-certificates/msed-in-adolescence-education.

St. Bonaventure University, School of Graduate Studies, School of Education, Literacy Programs, St. Bonaventure, NY 14778-2284. Offers adolescent literacy 5-12 (MS Ed); childhood literacy B-6 (MS Ed). Program offered in Olean and Buffalo Center (Hamburg, NY). *Accreditation:* NCATE. Part-time and evening/weekend programs available. *Faculty:* 2 full-time (both women), 1 (woman) part-time/adjunct. *Students:* 14 full-time (13 women), 14 part-time (13 women). Average age 29. 19 applicants, 100% accepted, 13 enrolled. In 2013, 27 master's awarded. *Degree requirements:* For master's, comprehensive exam, thesis optional, literacy coaching internship, portfolio. *Entrance requirements:* For master's, interview, writing sample, minimum undergraduate GPA of 3.0, two letters of recommendation, teaching certificate in matching area, transcripts. Additional exam requirements/recommendations for international students: Required—TOEFL (minimum score 550 paper-based; 80 iBT). *Application deadline:* For fall admission, 6/15 priority date for domestic students, 2/1 for international students; for spring admission, 11/15 priority date for domestic students, 7/1 for international students. Applications are processed on a rolling basis. Application fee: $0. Electronic applications accepted. *Financial support:* In 2013–14, 4 research assistantships with full and partial tuition reimbursements were awarded; Federal Work-Study, scholarships/grants, health care benefits, and unspecified assistantships also available. Support available to part-time students. Financial award application deadline: 4/15; financial award applicants required to submit FAFSA. *Unit head:* Dr. Karen M. Wieland, Program Director, 716-375-2369, Fax: 716-375-2360, E-mail: kwieland@sbu.edu. *Application contact:* Bruce Campbell, Director of Graduate Admissions, 716-375-2429, Fax: 716-375-4015, E-mail: gradsch@sbu.edu.
Website: http://www.sbu.edu/academics/schools/education/graduate-degrees-certificates/msed-in-childhood-literacy.

St. John Fisher College, Ralph C. Wilson Jr. School of Education, Program in Adolescence Education and Special Education, Rochester, NY 14618-3597. Offers adolescence education: English with special education (MS Ed); adolescence education: French with special education (MS Ed); adolescence education: social studies with special education (MS Ed); adolescence education: Spanish with special education (MS Ed). Part-time and evening/weekend programs available. *Faculty:* 4 full-time (2 women), 4 part-time/adjunct (all women). *Students:* 20 full-time (10 women), 27 part-time (21 women); includes 4 minority (1 Black or African American, non-Hispanic/Latino; 1 Asian, non-Hispanic/Latino; 1 Hispanic/Latino; 1 Two or more races, non-Hispanic/Latino). Average age 27. 45 applicants, 89% accepted, 28 enrolled. In 2013, 28 master's awarded. *Degree requirements:* For master's, field experiences, student teaching, LAST. *Entrance requirements:* For master's, 2 letters of recommendation, personal statement, current resume. Additional exam requirements/recommendations for international students: Required—TOEFL (minimum score 575 paper-based; 80 iBT). *Application deadline:* Applications are processed on a rolling basis. Application fee: $30. Electronic applications accepted. *Expenses: Tuition:* Part-time $795 per credit hour. *Required fees:* $10 per credit hour. Tuition and fees vary according to course load, degree level and program. *Financial support:* In 2013–14, 11 students received support. Scholarships/grants available. Financial award applicants required to submit FAFSA. *Faculty research:* Arts and humanities, urban schools, constructivist learning, at-risk students, mentoring. *Unit head:* Dr. Susan Schultz, Program Director, 585-385-7296, E-mail: sschultz@sjfc.edu. *Application contact:* Jose Perales, Director of Graduate Admissions, 585-385-8067, E-mail: jperales@sjfc.edu.
Website: http://www.sjfc.edu/academics/education/departments/ms-special-ed/options/initial-adolescence.dot.

St. John's University, The School of Education, Department of Curriculum and Instruction, Queens, NY 11439. Offers adolescent education (MS Ed, Certificate); childhood education (MS Ed); early childhood education (MS Ed); middle school education (Certificate). Part-time and evening/weekend programs available. *Students:* 55 full-time (34 women), 271 part-time (186 women); includes 130 minority (48 Black or African American, non-Hispanic/Latino; 25 Asian, non-Hispanic/Latino; 52 Hispanic/Latino; 1 Native Hawaiian or other Pacific Islander, non-Hispanic/Latino; 4 Two or more races, non-Hispanic/Latino), 5 international. Average age 29. 171 applicants, 88% accepted, 77 enrolled. In 2013, 134 master's awarded. *Degree requirements:* For master's, comprehensive exam. *Entrance requirements:* For master's, minimum GPA of 3.0, 2 letters of recommendation, qualification for the New York State provisional (initial) teaching certificate, transcript, personal statement. Additional exam requirements/recommendations for international students: Required—TOEFL (minimum score 600 paper-based; 100 iBT), IELTS (minimum score 5.5). *Application deadline:* For fall admission, 8/17 for domestic students, 5/1 priority date for international students; for spring admission, 1/5 for domestic students, 11/1 priority date for international students. Applications are processed on a rolling basis. Application fee: $70. Electronic applications accepted. *Expenses: Tuition:* Full-time $19,800; part-time $1100 per credit. *Required fees:* $170 per semester. *Financial support:* Research assistantships available. *Faculty research:* Student learning and satisfaction in online courses, online collaboration needs, female education in south and east Asia, e-portfolio assessment, pedagogical practices in mathematics education. *Unit head:* Dr. Judith McVarish, Chair, 718-990-2334, E-mail: mcvarisj@stjohns.edu. *Application contact:* Dr. Kelly K. Ronayne,

Associate Dean for Graduate Admissions, 718-990-2304, Fax: 718-990-2343, E-mail: graded@stjohns.edu.
Website: http://www.stjohns.edu/academics/schools-and-colleges/school-education/curriculum-and-instruction.

Saint Joseph's University, College of Arts and Sciences, Department of Education, Philadelphia, PA 19131-1395. Offers curriculum supervisor (Certificate); educational leadership (MS, Ed D); elementary education (MS, Certificate); elementary/middle school education (Certificate); instructional technology (MS, Certificate); principal certification (Certificate); professional education (MS); reading specialist (MS, Certificate); reading supervisor (Certificate); secondary education (MS, Certificate); special education (MS, Certificate); superintendent's letter of eligibility (Certificate); supervisor of special education (Certificate). Part-time and evening/weekend programs available. Postbaccalaureate distance learning degree programs offered (no on-campus study). *Faculty:* 32 full-time (25 women), 75 part-time/adjunct (53 women). *Students:* 91 full-time (81 women), 858 part-time (656 women); includes 133 minority (96 Black or African American, non-Hispanic/Latino; 3 American Indian or Alaska Native, non-Hispanic/Latino; 9 Asian, non-Hispanic/Latino; 20 Hispanic/Latino; 5 Native Hawaiian or other Pacific Islander, non-Hispanic/Latino), 16 international. Average age 31. 359 applicants, 77% accepted, 203 enrolled. In 2013, 363 master's, 9 doctorates, 1 other advanced degree awarded. *Entrance requirements:* For master's, 2 letters of recommendation, minimum GPA of 3.0, official transcripts, personal statement; for doctorate, GRE, master's degree from accredited institution, minimum graduate GPA of 3.5, computer competence, commitment to participate in cohort, interview with program director. Additional exam requirements/recommendations for international students: Required—TOEFL (minimum score 550 paper-based; 79 iBT), IELTS (minimum score 6.5). *Application deadline:* For fall admission, 7/15 priority date for domestic students, 4/15 for international students; for winter admission, 11/15 for domestic students, 1/15 for international students; for spring admission, 11/15 priority date for domestic students, 10/15 for international students. Applications are processed on a rolling basis. Application fee: $35. Electronic applications accepted. *Expenses:* Contact institution. *Financial support:* Unspecified assistantships available. Financial award applicants required to submit FAFSA. *Faculty research:* Factors predicting early mathematics skills for low income children, early child care and development, preschool quality. *Total annual research expenditures:* $229,264. *Unit head:* Dr. John Vacca, Associate Dean, Education, 610-660-3131, E-mail: gradstudies@sju.edu. *Application contact:* Elisabeth Woodward, Director of Marketing and Admissions, Graduate Arts and Sciences, 610-660-3131, Fax: 610-660-3230, E-mail: gradstudies@sju.edu.
Website: http://sju.edu/int/academics/cas/grad/education/index.html.

Saint Peter's University, Graduate Programs in Education, Program in Teaching, Jersey City, NJ 07306-5997. Offers 6-8 middle school education (MA Ed, Certificate); K-12 secondary education (MA Ed, Certificate); K-5 elementary education (MA Ed, Certificate). Part-time and evening/weekend programs available. *Degree requirements:* For master's, comprehensive exam. *Entrance requirements:* For master's, GRE or MAT. Additional exam requirements/recommendations for international students: Required—TOEFL. Electronic applications accepted.

St. Thomas Aquinas College, Division of Teacher Education, Sparkill, NY 10976. Offers adolescence education (MST); childhood and special education (MST); childhood education (MST); educational leadership (MS Ed); reading (MS Ed, PMC); special education (MS Ed, PMC); teaching (MS Ed), including elementary education, middle school education, secondary education. *Accreditation:* NCATE. Part-time and evening/weekend programs available. *Degree requirements:* For master's, comprehensive exam, comprehensive professional portfolio; for PMC, action research project. *Entrance requirements:* For master's, New York State Qualifying Exam, GRE General Test or minimum GPA of 3.0, teaching certificate; for PMC, GRE General Test or minimum GPA of 3.0. Electronic applications accepted. *Faculty research:* Computer applications in education, adolescent special education students, literacy development, inclusive practices for special education students.

Salem College, Department of Education, Winston-Salem, NC 27101. Offers art education (MAT); elementary education (M Ed, MAT); language and literacy (M Ed); middle school education (MAT); school counseling (M Ed); second language studies (MAT); secondary education (MAT); special education (M Ed, MAT). *Accreditation:* NCATE. Part-time and evening/weekend programs available. Postbaccalaureate distance learning degree programs offered (minimal on-campus study). *Degree requirements:* For master's, practicum (MAT), project (M Ed), oral and written comprehensive exams. *Entrance requirements:* For master's, minimum GPA of 2.5. *Faculty research:* Content area reading strategies, literacy development, brain compatible instruction.

Salem State University, School of Graduate Studies, Program in Middle School Education, Salem, MA 01970-5353. Offers humanities (M Ed); math/science (MAT). Part-time and evening/weekend programs available. *Students:* 1 (woman) full-time, 9 part-time (6 women). 1 applicant, 100% accepted, 1 enrolled. In 2013, 9 master's awarded. *Entrance requirements:* For master's, GRE or MAT. Additional exam requirements/recommendations for international students: Required—TOEFL (minimum score 550 paper-based; 80 iBT) or IELTS (minimum score 5.5). *Application deadline:* For fall admission, 5/1 for domestic students; for spring admission, 10/1 for domestic students. Applications are processed on a rolling basis. Application fee: $50. *Financial support:* Career-related internships or fieldwork, Federal Work-Study, scholarships/grants, and unspecified assistantships available. Support available to part-time students. Financial award application deadline: 5/1; financial award applicants required to submit FAFSA. *Application contact:* Dr. Lee A. Brossoit, Assistant Dean of Graduate Admissions, 978-542-6675, Fax: 978-542-7215, E-mail: lbrossoit@salemstate.edu.
Website: http://www.salemstate.edu/academics/schools/12610.php.

Salem State University, School of Graduate Studies, Program in Middle School General Science, Salem, MA 01970-5353. Offers MAT. Part-time and evening/weekend programs available. *Students:* 2 full-time (both women), 3 part-time (all women). 2 applicants, 100% accepted, 2 enrolled. In 2013, 3 master's awarded. *Entrance requirements:* For master's, GRE or MAT. Additional exam requirements/recommendations for international students: Required—TOEFL (minimum score 550 paper-based; 80 iBT) or IELTS (minimum score 5.5). *Application deadline:* For fall admission, 5/1 for domestic students; for spring admission, 10/1 for domestic students. Applications are processed on a rolling basis. Application fee: $50. *Financial support:* Career-related internships or fieldwork, Federal Work-Study, scholarships/grants, and unspecified assistantships available. Support available to part-time students. Financial award application deadline: 5/1; financial award applicants required to submit FAFSA. *Application contact:* Dr. Lee A. Brossoit, Assistant Dean of Graduate Admissions, 978-542-6675, Fax: 978-542-7215, E-mail: lbrossoit@salemstate.edu.
Website: http://www.salemstate.edu/academics/schools/12196.php.

Salem State University, School of Graduate Studies, Program in Middle School Math, Salem, MA 01970-5353. Offers MAT. Part-time and evening/weekend programs available. *Students:* 1 full-time (0 women), 31 part-time (20 women); includes 1 minority (Two or more races, non-Hispanic/Latino). 10 applicants, 100% accepted, 8 enrolled. In 2013, 11 master's awarded. *Entrance requirements:* For master's, GRE or MAT. Additional exam requirements/recommendations for international students: Required—

TOEFL (minimum score 550 paper-based; 80 iBT) or IELTS (minimum score 5.5). *Application deadline:* For fall admission, 5/1 for domestic students; for spring admission, 10/1 for domestic students. Applications are processed on a rolling basis. Application fee: $50. *Financial support:* Career-related internships or fieldwork, Federal Work-Study, scholarships/grants, and unspecified assistantships available. Support available to part-time students. Financial award application deadline: 5/1; financial award applicants required to submit FAFSA. *Application contact:* Dr. Lee A. Brossoit, Assistant Dean of Graduate Admissions, 978-542-6675, Fax: 978-542-7215, E-mail: lbrossoit@salemstate.edu.
Website: http://www.salemstate.edu/academics/schools/5616.php.

Seton Hill University, Program in Elementary Education/Middle Level Education, Greensburg, PA 15601. Offers MA, Certificate. Part-time and evening/weekend programs available. Postbaccalaureate distance learning degree programs offered (minimal on-campus study). *Faculty:* 7 full-time (6 women), 6 part-time/adjunct (3 women). *Students:* 4 full-time (3 women), 3 part-time (2 women). Average age 29. 5 applicants, 80% accepted, 4 enrolled. In 2013, 1 master's awarded. *Entrance requirements:* For master's, teacher's certification, 3 letters of recommendation, personal statement, transcripts, resume. Additional exam requirements/recommendations for international students: Required—TOEFL (minimum score 600 paper-based; 100 iBT), IELTS (minimum score 6.5). *Application deadline:* Applications are processed on a rolling basis. Application fee: $0. Electronic applications accepted. *Expenses: Tuition:* Full-time $14,220; part-time $790 per credit. *Required fees:* $700; $34 per credit. $50 per semester. *Financial support:* Scholarships/grants and tuition discounts available. Financial award application deadline: 8/15. *Faculty research:* Autism spectrum disorder, assessment rubrics, brain-based teaching and learning, administration in public education, early intervention, STEM. *Unit head:* Dr. Audrey Quinlan, Director, 724-830-4734, E-mail: quinlan@setonhill.edu. *Application contact:* Laurel Komarny, Program Counselor, 724-838-4209, E-mail: lkomarny@setonhill.edu.
Website: http://www.setonhill.edu/academics/graduate_programs/elementary_middle_level_education.

Shippensburg University of Pennsylvania, School of Graduate Studies, College of Education and Human Services, Department of Teacher Education, Shippensburg, PA 17257-2299. Offers curriculum and instruction (M Ed), including biology, early childhood education, elementary education, geography/earth science, history, mathematics, middle level education, modern languages; reading (M Ed). *Accreditation:* NCATE. Part-time and evening/weekend programs available. *Faculty:* 13 full-time (9 women), 2 part-time/adjunct (both women). *Students:* 6 full-time (all women), 72 part-time (61 women); includes 5 minority (1 Black or African American, non-Hispanic/Latino; 1 Asian, non-Hispanic/Latino; 2 Hispanic/Latino; 1 Two or more races, non-Hispanic/Latino), 1 international. Average age 30. 55 applicants, 60% accepted, 24 enrolled. In 2013, 63 master's awarded. *Degree requirements:* For master's, comprehensive exam (for some programs), thesis optional, practicum or internship; capstone seminar (for some programs). *Entrance requirements:* For master's, MAT or GRE (if GPA less than 2.75), interview, 3 letters of reference, questionnaire of teaching background and future goals. Additional exam requirements/recommendations for international students: Required—TOEFL (minimum score 580 paper-based); Recommended—IELTS (minimum score 6). *Application deadline:* For fall admission, 4/1 priority date for domestic students, 4/30 for international students; for spring admission, 9/1 priority date for domestic students, 9/30 for international students. Applications are processed on a rolling basis. Application fee: $45. Electronic applications accepted. *Expenses: Tuition, area resident:* Part-time $442 per credit. Tuition, state resident: part-time $442 per credit. Tuition, nonresident: part-time $663 per credit. *Required fees:* $127 per credit. *Financial support:* In 2013–14, 4 research assistantships with full tuition reimbursements (averaging $5,000 per year) were awarded; career-related internships or fieldwork, scholarships/grants, unspecified assistantships, and resident hall director and student payroll positions also available. Support available to part-time students. Financial award application deadline: 3/1; financial award applicants required to submit FAFSA. *Unit head:* Dr. Christine A. Royce, Chairperson, 717-477-1688, Fax: 717-477-4046, E-mail: caroyc@ship.edu. *Application contact:* Jeremy R. Goshorn, Assistant Dean of Graduate Admissions, 717-477-1231, Fax: 717-477-4016, E-mail: jrgoshorn@ship.edu.
Website: http://www.ship.edu/teacher/.

Smith College, Graduate and Special Programs, Department of Education and Child Study, Northampton, MA 01063. Offers education of the deaf (MED); elementary education (MAT); middle school education (MAT); secondary education (MAT), including biological sciences education, chemistry education, English education, French education, geology education, government education, history education, mathematics education, physics education, Spanish education. Part-time programs available. *Faculty:* 6 full-time (4 women), 3 part-time/adjunct (2 women). *Students:* 23 full-time (20 women), 6 part-time (all women); includes 1 minority (Asian, non-Hispanic/Latino), 2 international. Average age 30. 58 applicants, 76% accepted, 31 enrolled. In 2013, 35 master's awarded. *Entrance requirements:* Additional exam requirements/recommendations for international students: Required—TOEFL (minimum score 595 paper-based; 97 iBT). *Application deadline:* For fall admission, 4/1 for domestic students, 1/15 for international students; for spring admission, 12/1 for domestic students. Application fee: $60. *Expenses: Tuition:* Full-time $32,160; part-time $1340 per credit. *Financial support:* In 2013–14, 26 students received support, including 6 fellowships with full tuition reimbursements available; career-related internships or fieldwork, institutionally sponsored loans, and scholarships/grants also available. Support available to part-time students. Financial award application deadline: 1/15; financial award applicants required to submit CSS PROFILE or FAFSA. *Unit head:* Susan Etheredge, Chair, 413-585-3256, Fax: 413-585-3268, E-mail: sethered@smith.edu. *Application contact:* Ruth Morgan, Administrative Assistant, 413-585-3050, Fax: 413-585-3054, E-mail: gradstdy@smith.edu.

Southeast Missouri State University, School of Graduate Studies, Department of Middle and Secondary Education, Cape Girardeau, MO 63701-4799. Offers secondary education (MA), including education studies, education technology. *Accreditation:* NCATE. Part-time programs available. *Faculty:* 5 full-time (3 women), 1 (woman) part-time/adjunct. *Students:* 6 full-time (4 women), 42 part-time (30 women); includes 4 minority (all Black or African American, non-Hispanic/Latino). Average age 30. 28 applicants, 100% accepted, 28 enrolled. In 2013, 8 master's awarded. *Degree requirements:* For master's, comprehensive exam, research paper. *Entrance requirements:* For master's, minimum undergraduate GPA of 2.75. Additional exam requirements/recommendations for international students: Required—TOEFL (minimum score 550 paper-based; 79 iBT), IELTS (minimum score 6), PTE (minimum score 53). *Application deadline:* For fall admission, 8/1 for domestic students, 6/1 for international students; for spring admission, 11/21 for domestic students, 10/1 for international students; for summer admission, 5/15 for domestic students. Applications are processed on a rolling basis. Application fee: $30 ($40 for international students). Electronic applications accepted. *Expenses:* Tuition, state resident: full-time $5139; part-time $285.50 per credit hour. Tuition, nonresident: full-time $9099; part-time $505.50 per credit hour. *Financial support:* In 2013–14, 7 students received support. Career-related internships or fieldwork, Federal Work-Study, scholarships/grants, traineeships, tuition waivers (full), and unspecified assistantships available. Financial award application deadline: 6/30; financial award applicants required to submit FAFSA. *Faculty research:*

Middle School Education

Pedagogy of teaching, multicultural education, reading and writing strategies, use of technology in the classroom. *Unit head:* Dr. Simin L. Cwick, Middle and Secondary Education Department Chair, 573-651-5965, E-mail: scwick@semo.edu. *Application contact:* Alisa Aleen McFerron, Assistant Director of Admissions for Operations, 573-651-5937, E-mail: amcferron@semo.edu.
Website: http://www5.semo.edu/middleandsec/.

Spalding University, Graduate Studies, College of Education, Programs in Education, Louisville, KY 40203-2188. Offers art teacher education (MAT); business teacher education (MAT); elementary school education (MAT); foreign language (MAT); general education (MA Ed); high school education (MAT); middle school education (MAT); school administration (MA Ed); secondary education (MAT); special education (learning and behavioral disorders) (MAT); student guidance counselor (MA); teacher education and professional development (MAT). *Accreditation:* NCATE. Part-time and evening/weekend programs available. *Faculty:* 12 full-time (11 women), 6 part-time/adjunct (4 women). *Students:* 92 full-time (63 women), 36 part-time (29 women); includes 43 minority (41 Black or African American, non-Hispanic/Latino; 2 Two or more races, non-Hispanic/Latino). Average age 35. 77 applicants, 48% accepted, 30 enrolled. In 2013, 81 master's awarded. *Degree requirements:* For master's, portfolio, final project, clinical experience. *Entrance requirements:* For master's, GRE General Test or MAT, interview, letters of recommendation, resume. Additional exam requirements/recommendations for international students: Required—TOEFL (minimum score 535 paper-based). *Application deadline:* Applications are processed on a rolling basis. Application fee: $30. Electronic applications accepted. *Expenses: Tuition:* Full-time $21,450. *Required fees:* $810. Tuition and fees vary according to course load, degree level, program and student level. *Financial support:* Scholarships/grants, traineeships, and unspecified assistantships available. Financial award application deadline: 3/30; financial award applicants required to submit FAFSA. *Faculty research:* Instructional technology, achievement gap, classroom management, assessment. *Unit head:* Dr. Beverly Keepers, Dean, 502-588-7121, Fax: 502-585-7123, E-mail: bkeepers@spalding.edu. *Application contact:* Bonnie Caughron, Administrative Assistant, College of Education, 502-873-4262, E-mail: bcaughron@spalding.edu.

State University of New York at Oswego, Graduate Studies, School of Education, Department of Curriculum and Instruction, Oswego, NY 13126. Offers adolescence education (MST); art education (MAT); childhood education (MST); elementary education (MS Ed); literacy education (MS Ed); secondary education (MS Ed); special education (MS Ed). Part-time and evening/weekend programs available. *Degree requirements:* For master's, comprehensive exam (for some programs), thesis optional. *Entrance requirements:* For master's, GRE General Test, minimum GPA of 2.7, provisional teaching certificate. Additional exam requirements/recommendations for international students: Required—TOEFL (minimum score 560 paper-based). *Faculty research:* Classroom applications for microcomputers; classroom questioning, wait-time, and achievement; values clarification and academic achievement.

State University of New York College at Old Westbury, Program in Adolescent Education, Old Westbury, NY 11568-0210. Offers biology (MAT, MS); chemistry (MAT, MS); English language arts (MAT, MS); math (MAT, MS); social studies (MAT, MS); Spanish (MAT, MS). Part-time and evening/weekend programs available. *Faculty:* 19 full-time (11 women), 6 part-time/adjunct (1 woman). *Students:* 33 full-time (20 women), 33 part-time (19 women); includes 16 minority (2 Black or African American, non-Hispanic/Latino; 4 Asian, non-Hispanic/Latino; 9 Hispanic/Latino; 1 Two or more races, non-Hispanic/Latino). 25 applicants, 84% accepted, 19 enrolled. In 2013, 29 master's awarded. *Entrance requirements:* For master's, Liberal Arts and Sciences Test, undergraduate degree with at least 30 semester hours of appropriate coursework as defined by the respective discipline; minimum cumulative undergraduate GPA of 3.0; two letters of recommendation (one from an academic source); essay. Additional exam requirements/recommendations for international students: Required—TOEFL (minimum score 550 paper-based); Recommended—IELTS. *Expenses:* Tuition, state resident: full-time $9370; part-time $390 per credit. Tuition, nonresident: full-time $16,680; part-time $695 per credit. *Required fees:* $45.85 per credit. $47 per term. *Application contact:* Philip D'Angelo, Graduate Admissions Office, 516-876-3073, E-mail: enroll@oldwestbury.edu.

State University of New York College at Oneonta, Graduate Education, Division of Education, Department of Secondary Education, Oneonta, NY 13820-4015. Offers adolescence education (MS Ed). *Accreditation:* NCATE. Part-time and evening/weekend programs available. *Students:* 3 full-time (2 women), 4 part-time (3 women). Average age 27. 7 applicants, 100% accepted, 7 enrolled. *Entrance requirements:* For master's, GRE General Test. *Application deadline:* For fall admission, 3/25 priority date for domestic students; for spring admission, 10/1 priority date for domestic students. Applications are processed on a rolling basis. Application fee: $50. *Unit head:* Dr. Dennis Banks, Chair, 607-436-3391, Fax: 607-436-2554, E-mail: banksdn@oneonta.edu. *Application contact:* Patrick J. Mente, Director of Graduate Studies, 607-436-2523, Fax: 607-436-3084, E-mail: gradstudies@oneonta.edu.

State University of New York College at Potsdam, School of Education and Professional Studies, Program in Special Education, Potsdam, NY 13676. Offers adolescence (grades 7-12) (MS Ed); childhood (grades 1-6) (MS Ed); early childhood (birth-grade 2) (MS Ed). *Accreditation:* NCATE. Part-time programs available. *Degree requirements:* For master's, culminating experience. *Entrance requirements:* For master's, minimum GPA of 3.0 in last 60 hours of course work. Additional exam requirements/recommendations for international students: Required—TOEFL (minimum score 550 paper-based; 80 iBT), IELTS (minimum score 6). Electronic applications accepted.

Temple University, College of Education, Department of Curriculum, Instruction, and Technology in Education, Program in Middle Grades Education, Philadelphia, PA 19122-6096. Offers math and language arts (Ed M); math and science (Ed M); science and language arts (Ed M).

Tennessee Technological University, College of Graduate Studies, College of Education, Department of Exercise Science, Physical Education and Wellness, Cookeville, TN 38505. Offers adapted physical education (MA); elementary/middle school physical education (MA); lifetime wellness (MA); sport management (MA). *Accreditation:* NCATE. Part-time programs available. Postbaccalaureate distance learning degree programs offered (no on-campus study). *Faculty:* 7 full-time (0 women). *Students:* 10 full-time (0 women), 38 part-time (11 women); includes 5 minority (all Black or African American, non-Hispanic/Latino). Average age 27. 38 applicants, 58% accepted, 20 enrolled. In 2013, 23 master's awarded. *Degree requirements:* For master's, comprehensive exam, thesis or alternative. *Entrance requirements:* For master's, MAT or GRE. Additional exam requirements/recommendations for international students: Required—TOEFL (minimum score 527 paper-based; 71 iBT), IELTS (minimum score 5.5), PTE (minimum score 48), or TOEIC (Test of English as an International Communication). *Application deadline:* For fall admission, 8/1 for domestic students, 5/1 for international students; for spring admission, 12/1 for domestic students, 10/1 for international students. Applications are processed on a rolling basis. Application fee: $35 ($40 for international students). Electronic applications accepted. *Expenses:* Tuition, state resident: full-time $9347; part-time $465 per credit hour. Tuition, nonresident: full-time $23,635; part-time $1152 per credit hour. *Financial support:* In

2013–14, fellowships (averaging $8,000 per year), 3 research assistantships (averaging $4,000 per year), 4 teaching assistantships (averaging $4,000 per year) were awarded; career-related internships or fieldwork also available. Financial award application deadline: 4/1. *Unit head:* Dr. John Steven Smith, Interim Chairperson, 931-372-3467, Fax: 931-372-6319, E-mail: jssmith@tntech.edu. *Application contact:* Shelia K. Kendrick, Coordinator of Graduate Studies, 931-372-3808, Fax: 931-372-3497, E-mail: skendrick@tntech.edu.

Texas Christian University, College of Education, Program in Middle School Education (Four-One Option), Fort Worth, TX 76129-0002. Offers M Ed. Part-time and evening/weekend programs available. *Students:* 2 full-time (both women). 2 applicants, 100% accepted, 1 enrolled. In 2013, 6 master's awarded. *Degree requirements:* For master's, comprehensive exam, thesis. *Entrance requirements:* Additional exam requirements/recommendations for international students: Required—TOEFL (minimum score 550 paper-based; 80 iBT). *Application deadline:* For fall admission, 11/16 for domestic and international students; for spring admission, 3/1 for domestic and international students. Application fee: $60. Electronic applications accepted. *Expenses: Tuition:* Part-time $1270 per credit hour. Tuition and fees vary according to course load and program. *Financial support:* Teaching assistantships with full tuition reimbursements, career-related internships or fieldwork, scholarships/grants, and unspecified assistantships available. Financial award application deadline: 3/1; financial award applicants required to submit FAFSA. *Unit head:* Dr. Jan Lacina, Associate Dean, 817-257-6786, E-mail: j.lacina@tcu.edu. *Application contact:* Lori Kimball, Academic Program Specialist, 817-257-7661, E-mail: l.kimball@tcu.edu.
Website: http://www.coe.tcu.edu/graduate-students-graduate-programs.asp.

Tufts University, Graduate School of Arts and Sciences, Department of Education, Program in Education, Medford, MA 02155. Offers educational studies (MA); elementary education (MAT); middle and secondary education (MA, MAT); museum education (MA); secondary education (MA); STEM education (MS, PhD). *Faculty:* 13 full-time, 9 part-time/adjunct. *Students:* 85 full-time (72 women); includes 19 minority (4 Black or African American, non-Hispanic/Latino; 1 American Indian or Alaska Native, non-Hispanic/Latino; 3 Asian, non-Hispanic/Latino; 7 Hispanic/Latino; 4 Two or more races, non-Hispanic/Latino), 5 international. Average age 27. 154 applicants, 69% accepted, 50 enrolled. In 2013, 84 master's awarded. *Degree requirements:* For master's, thesis optional; for doctorate, thesis/dissertation. *Entrance requirements:* For master's and doctorate, GRE General Test. Additional exam requirements/recommendations for international students: Required—TOEFL (minimum score 550 paper-based; 80 iBT), IELTS (minimum score 6.5). *Application deadline:* For fall admission, 1/2 for domestic and international students; for spring admission, 10/15 for domestic students, 9/15 for international students. Applications are processed on a rolling basis. Application fee: $75. Electronic applications accepted. *Financial support:* Teaching assistantships with full and partial tuition reimbursements, Federal Work-Study, scholarships/grants, and tuition waivers (full and partial) available. Support available to part-time students. Financial award application deadline: 1/2. *Unit head:* Hammer David, Chair, 617-627-3244, Fax: 617-627-3901. *Application contact:* Patricia Romeo, Information Contact, 617-627-3244.

Union College, Graduate Programs, Department of Education, Program in Middle Grades, Barbourville, KY 40906-1499. Offers MA. *Degree requirements:* For master's, thesis optional. *Entrance requirements:* For master's, GRE General Test, NTE.

Union Graduate College, School of Education, Schenectady, NY 12308-3107. Offers biology (MAT); chemistry (MAT); Chinese (MAT); earth science (MAT); English (MA, MAT); English and history (MA); French (MAT); general science (MAT); German (MAT); history (MA); Latin (MAT); life sciences (MS); mathematics (MAT); mathematics and computer technology (MS); mentoring and teacher leadership (AC); middle childhood extension (AC); national board certification and teacher leadership (AC); physical sciences (MS); physics (MAT); social studies (MAT); Spanish (MAT); technology (MAT). *Accreditation:* Teacher Education Accreditation Council. *Faculty:* 3 full-time (1 woman), 56 part-time/adjunct (34 women). *Students:* 32 full-time (16 women), 27 part-time (22 women); includes 15 minority (1 Black or African American, non-Hispanic/Latino; 4 Asian, non-Hispanic/Latino; 6 Hispanic/Latino; 4 Two or more races, non-Hispanic/Latino), 1 international. Average age 32. In 2013, 25 master's, 11 other advanced degrees awarded. *Degree requirements:* For master's, thesis or project. *Entrance requirements:* For master's, minimum GPA of 3.0, letters of recommendation. Additional exam requirements/recommendations for international students: Required—TOEFL (minimum score 550 paper-based). *Application deadline:* Applications are processed on a rolling basis. Application fee: $60. Electronic applications accepted. *Expenses:* Contact institution. *Financial support:* Career-related internships or fieldwork, Federal Work-Study, scholarships/grants, health care benefits, and tuition waivers (partial) available. Support available to part-time students. Financial award applicants required to submit FAFSA. *Faculty research:* Transformative learning, science education, National Board Certification, teacher leadership, teacher quality. *Unit head:* Dr. Lynn Gelzheiser, Dean, 518-631-9870, Fax: 518-631-9901. *Application contact:* Nicki Foley, Assistant, 518-631-9871, Fax: 518-631-9903, E-mail: foleyn@uniongraduatecollege.edu.

The University of Arizona, College of Science, Department of Mathematics, Program in Middle School Mathematics Teaching Leadership, Tucson, AZ 85721. Offers MA. Part-time programs available. *Students:* 18 full-time (14 women), 8 part-time (all women); includes 13 minority (1 Asian, non-Hispanic/Latino; 8 Hispanic/Latino; 1 Native Hawaiian or other Pacific Islander, non-Hispanic/Latino; 3 Two or more races, non-Hispanic/Latino). Average age 44. In 2013, 12 master's awarded. *Degree requirements:* For master's, thesis, internships, colloquium, business courses. *Entrance requirements:* For master's, GRE, minimum GPA of 3.0, statement of purpose. Additional exam requirements/recommendations for international students: Required—TOEFL (minimum score 550 paper-based). Application fee: $75. *Expenses:* Tuition, state resident: full-time $11,526. Tuition, nonresident: full-time $27,398. *Financial support:* Research assistantships, teaching assistantships, career-related internships or fieldwork, Federal Work-Study, scholarships/grants, health care benefits, and unspecified assistantships available. *Faculty research:* Algebra, coding theory, graph theory, combinatorics, probability. *Unit head:* William McCallum, Head, 520-621-2068, E-mail: stovall@math.arizona.edu. *Application contact:* Teresa Stoval, 520-626-6145, E-mail: stovall@math.arizona.edu.
Website: http://math.arizona.edu/.

University of Arkansas, Graduate School, College of Education and Health Professions, Department of Curriculum and Instruction, Fayetteville, AR 72701-1201. Offers childhood education (MAT); curriculum and instruction (PhD); educational leadership (M Ed, Ed D, Ed S); educational statistics and research methods (MS, PhD); educational technology (M Ed); middle-level education (MAT); secondary education (M Ed, MAT, Ed S); special education (M Ed, MAT). *Accreditation:* NCATE. *Degree requirements:* For doctorate, thesis/dissertation. *Entrance requirements:* For doctorate, GRE General Test or MAT. Electronic applications accepted.

University of Arkansas at Little Rock, Graduate School, College of Education, Department of Teacher Education, Program in Middle Childhood Education, Little Rock, AR 72204-1099. Offers M Ed. *Expenses:* Tuition, state resident: full-time $5690; part-time $284.50 per credit hour. Tuition, nonresident: full-time $13,030; part-time $651.50 per credit hour. *Required fees:* $1121; $672 per term. One-time fee: $40 full-time.

University of Bridgeport, School of Education, Department of Education, Bridgeport, CT 06604. Offers education (MS); educational management (Ed D, Diploma), including intermediate administrator or supervisor (Diploma), leadership (Ed D); elementary education (MS, Diploma), including early childhood education, elementary education; middle school education (MS); music education (MS); remedial reading and language arts (Diploma); secondary education (MS, Diploma), including computer specialist (Diploma), international education (Diploma), reading specialist, secondary education. Part-time and evening/weekend programs available. *Faculty:* 12 full-time (5 women), 108 part-time/adjunct (60 women). *Students:* 155 full-time (108 women), 139 part-time (98 women); includes 48 minority (22 Black or African American, non-Hispanic/Latino; 9 Asian, non-Hispanic/Latino; 15 Hispanic/Latino; 2 Two or more races, non-Hispanic/Latino), 2 international. Average age 30. 306 applicants, 55% accepted, 107 enrolled. In 2013, 153 master's, 16 other advanced degrees awarded. *Degree requirements:* For master's, final exam, final project, or thesis; for doctorate, comprehensive exam, thesis/dissertation; for Diploma, thesis or alternative, final project. *Entrance requirements:* For master's, minimum undergraduate QPA of 2.67; for doctorate, GRE, MAT; for Diploma, GRE General Test or MAT, minimum graduate QPA of 3.0. Additional exam requirements/recommendations for international students: Recommended—TOEFL (minimum score 550 paper-based; 80 iBT), IELTS (minimum score 6.5). *Application deadline:* For fall admission, 8/1 priority date for domestic and international students; for spring admission, 12/1 priority date for domestic and international students. Applications are processed on a rolling basis. Application fee: $50. Electronic applications accepted. *Expenses:* Contact institution. *Financial support:* In 2013–14, 120 students received support. Fellowships, research assistantships, teaching assistantships, career-related internships or fieldwork, Federal Work-Study, and institutionally sponsored loans available. Support available to part-time students. Financial award application deadline: 6/1; financial award applicants required to submit FAFSA. *Faculty research:* Self-concept, internship assessment, stress and situational development, follow-up of graduation, trend analysis. *Unit head:* Dr. Allen P. Cook, Dean, 203-576-4192, Fax: 203-576-4200, E-mail: acook@bridgeport.edu. *Application contact:* Leanne Proctor, Director of Graduate Admissions, 203-576-4552, Fax: 203-576-4941, E-mail: admit@bridgeport.edu.

University of Central Florida, College of Education and Human Performance, School of Teaching, Learning, and Leadership, Program in Mathematics Education, Orlando, FL 32816. Offers teacher education (MAT), including mathematics education, middle school mathematics; teacher leadership (M Ed). *Accreditation:* NCATE. Part-time and evening/weekend programs available. *Students:* 3 full-time (1 woman), 35 part-time (22 women); includes 12 minority (2 Black or African American, non-Hispanic/Latino; 3 Asian, non-Hispanic/Latino; 7 Hispanic/Latino). Average age 24. 11 applicants, 64% accepted, 3 enrolled. In 2013, 23 master's awarded. *Entrance requirements:* For master's, GRE General Test. Additional exam requirements/recommendations for international students: Required—TOEFL. *Application deadline:* For fall admission, 7/15 for domestic students; for spring admission, 12/1 for domestic students. Application fee: $30. Electronic applications accepted. *Financial support:* In 2013–14, 1 student received support. Fellowships, research assistantships, teaching assistantships, career-related internships or fieldwork, Federal Work-Study, institutionally sponsored loans, tuition waivers (partial), and unspecified assistantships available. Financial award application deadline: 3/1; financial award applicants required to submit FAFSA. *Unit head:* Dr. Erhan Seluk Haciomeroglu, Program Coordinator, 407-823-4336, E-mail: erhan.haciomeroglu@ucf.edu. *Application contact:* Barbara Rodriguez Lamas, Director, Admissions and Student Support, 407-823-2766, Fax: 407-823-6442, E-mail: gradadmissions@ucf.edu.

University of Dayton, Department of Teacher Education, Dayton, OH 45469-1300. Offers adolescence to young adult education (MS Ed); early childhood education (MS Ed); early childhood leadership and advocacy (MS Ed); interdisciplinary education studies (MS Ed); intervention specialist education, mild/moderate (MS Ed); literacy (MS Ed); middle childhood education (MS Ed); multi-age education (MS Ed); music education (MS Ed); teacher as leader (MS Ed); technology enhanced learning (MS Ed). Part-time and evening/weekend programs available. Postbaccalaureate distance learning degree programs offered (no on-campus study). *Faculty:* 19 full-time (13 women), 21 part-time/adjunct (18 women). *Students:* 69 full-time (57 women), 86 part-time (75 women); includes 16 minority (10 Black or African American, non-Hispanic/Latino; 2 Asian, non-Hispanic/Latino; 4 Hispanic/Latino), 10 international. Average age 31. 140 applicants, 54% accepted, 39 enrolled. In 2013, 93 master's awarded. *Degree requirements:* For master's, variable foreign language requirement, comprehensive exam (for some programs), thesis. *Entrance requirements:* For master's, GRE or MAT, minimum GPA of 2.75. Additional exam requirements/recommendations for international students: Required—TOEFL (minimum score 550 paper-based; 80 iBT), IELTS (minimum score 6.5). *Application deadline:* For fall admission, 3/1 for domestic students, 5/1 for international students; for winter admission, 7/1 for international students; for spring admission, 11/1 for international students. Applications are processed on a rolling basis. Application fee: $0 ($50 for international students). Electronic applications accepted. *Expenses:* Contact institution. *Financial support:* In 2013–14, 61 students received support, including 5 research assistantships with full tuition reimbursements available (averaging $8,720 per year), 3 teaching assistantships with full tuition reimbursements available (averaging $8,720 per year); career-related internships or fieldwork, institutionally sponsored loans, scholarships/grants, traineeships, health care benefits, and unspecified assistantships also available. Support available to part-time students. Financial award application deadline: 3/1; financial award applicants required to submit FAFSA. *Faculty research:* Diversity, literacy, art representation by young children, preservice teacher preparation. *Unit head:* Dr. Connie L. Bowman, Chair, 937-229-3305, E-mail: cbowman1@udayton.edu. *Application contact:* Gina Seiter, Graduate Program Advisor, 937-229-3103, E-mail: gseiter1@udayton.edu.

University of Georgia, College of Education, Department of Elementary and Social Studies Education, Athens, GA 30602. Offers early childhood education (M Ed, MAT, PhD, Ed S), including child and family development (MAT); elementary education (PhD); middle school education (M Ed, PhD, Ed S); social studies education (M Ed, Ed D, PhD, Ed S). *Entrance requirements:* For master's and Ed S, GRE General Test or MAT; for doctorate, GRE General Test. Electronic applications accepted.

University of Houston–Downtown, College of Public Service, Department of Urban Education, Houston, TX 77002. Offers curriculum and instruction (MAT); elementary (EC-6) generalist certification (MAT); elementary/middle school (4-8) generalist certification (MAT); secondary education certification (MAT). Part-time and evening/weekend programs available. Postbaccalaureate distance learning degree programs offered. *Faculty:* 7 full-time (3 women). *Students:* 4 full-time (3 women), 28 part-time (19 women); includes 22 minority (14 Black or African American, non-Hispanic/Latino; 1 Asian, non-Hispanic/Latino; 6 Hispanic/Latino; 1 Two or more races, non-Hispanic/Latino). Average age 36. 31 applicants, 87% accepted, 27 enrolled. In 2013, 10 master's awarded. *Degree requirements:* For master's, capstone course with completed project, position paper, grant proposal, empirical study, curriculum development/revision, or advanced technology project presented at annual Graduate Project Exhibition. *Entrance requirements:* For master's, GRE, personal statement, 3 recommendation forms. Additional exam requirements/recommendations for international students: Required—TOEFL (minimum score 550 paper-based; 80 iBT). *Application deadline:* For fall

admission, 7/15 for domestic and international students; for spring admission, 11/15 for domestic and international students. Application fee: $35 ($60 for international students). Electronic applications accepted. *Expenses:* Tuition, state resident: full-time $4212; part-time $234 per credit hour. Tuition, nonresident: full-time $9684; part-time $538 per credit hour. *Required fees:* $1074. Tuition and fees vary according to program. *Financial support:* Scholarships/grants available. Financial award applicants required to submit FAFSA. *Unit head:* Dr. Viola Garcia, Department Chair, 713-221-8165, Fax: 713-226-5294, E-mail: garciav@uhd.edu. *Application contact:* Ceshia Love, Assistant Director of Graduate Admissions, 713-221-8093, Fax: 713-223-7408, E-mail: gradadmissions@uhd.edu.
Website: http://www.uhd.edu/academic/colleges/publicservice/urbaned/.

University of Kentucky, Graduate School, College of Education, Department of Curriculum and Instruction, Lexington, KY 40506-0032. Offers curriculum and instruction (Ed D); elementary education (MA Ed); instructional system design (MS Ed); literacy (MA Ed); middle school education (MA Ed, MS Ed); secondary education (MA Ed, MS Ed). *Accreditation:* NCATE. *Degree requirements:* For master's, comprehensive exam, thesis optional; for doctorate, comprehensive exam, thesis/dissertation. *Entrance requirements:* For master's, GRE General Test, minimum undergraduate GPA of 2.75; for doctorate, GRE General Test, minimum graduate GPA of 3.0. Additional exam requirements/recommendations for international students: Required—TOEFL (minimum score 550 paper-based). Electronic applications accepted. *Faculty research:* Educational reform, multicultural education, classroom instructional practices, performance based assessment, primary school programs.

University of Louisiana at Monroe, Graduate School, College of Arts, Education, and Sciences, School of Education, Program in Curriculum and Instruction, Monroe, LA 71209-0001. Offers art education (M Ed); biology education (M Ed); chemistry education (M Ed); curriculum and instruction (Ed D); early childhood education (M Ed); earth science education (M Ed); educational leadership (M Ed); elementary education (1-5) (M Ed); English as a second language (M Ed); English education (M Ed); family and consumer education (M Ed); French education (M Ed); history education (M Ed); math education (M Ed); middle school education (M Ed); music education (M Ed); reading education (K-12) (M Ed); Spanish education (M Ed); special education - academically gifted (M Ed); special education - early intervention (M Ed); special education - educational diagnostician (M Ed); special education - mild/moderate disabilities (M Ed); speech education (M Ed). *Accreditation:* NCATE. *Degree requirements:* For master's, comprehensive exam (for some programs), thesis; for doctorate, thesis/dissertation, internships. *Entrance requirements:* For master's, GRE General Test; for doctorate, GRE General Test, minimum undergraduate GPA of 2.75, graduate 3.25. Additional exam requirements/recommendations for international students: Required—TOEFL (minimum score 500 paper-based; 61 iBT). *Application deadline:* For fall admission, 8/24 priority date for domestic students, 7/1 for international students; for winter admission, 12/14 priority date for domestic students; for spring admission, 1/19 for domestic students, 11/1 for international students. Applications are processed on a rolling basis. Application fee: $20 ($30 for international students). Electronic applications accepted. *Expenses:* Tuition, state resident: full-time $6607. Tuition, nonresident: full-time $17,179. Full-time tuition and fees vary according to program. *Financial support:* Research assistantships, career-related internships or fieldwork, Federal Work-Study, and unspecified assistantships available. Financial award application deadline: 4/1; financial award applicants required to submit FAFSA. *Unit head:* Dr. Dorothy Schween, Director, 318-342-1268, Fax: 318-342-3131, E-mail: schween@ulm.edu. *Application contact:* Dr. Dorothy Schween, Director, 318-342-1268, Fax: 318-342-3131, E-mail: schween@ulm.edu.

University of Louisiana at Monroe, Graduate School, College of Arts, Education, and Sciences, School of Education, Program in Multiple Levels Grades K-12, Monroe, LA 71209-0001. Offers MAT. *Degree requirements:* For master's, thesis optional. *Entrance requirements:* For master's, GRE, PRAXIS, minimum GPA of 2.5. Additional exam requirements/recommendations for international students: Required—TOEFL (minimum score 500 paper-based; 61 iBT). *Application deadline:* For fall admission, 8/24 priority date for domestic students, 7/1 for international students; for winter admission, 12/14 priority date for domestic students; for spring admission, 1/19 priority date for domestic students, 11/1 for international students. Applications are processed on a rolling basis. Electronic applications accepted. *Expenses:* Tuition, state resident: full-time $6607. Tuition, nonresident: full-time $17,179. Full-time tuition and fees vary according to program. *Financial support:* Career-related internships or fieldwork, Federal Work-Study, and unspecified assistantships available. Financial award application deadline: 4/1; financial award applicants required to submit FAFSA. *Unit head:* Dr. Dorothy Schween, Director, 318-342-1268, E-mail: schween@ulm.edu. *Application contact:* Dr. Dorothy Schween, Director, 318-342-1268, E-mail: schween@ulm.edu.

University of Louisville, Graduate School, College of Education and Human Development, Department of Teaching and Learning, Louisville, KY 40292-0001. Offers art education (MAT); curriculum and instruction (PhD); early elementary education (MAT); instructional technology (M Ed); interdisciplinary early childhood education (MAT); middle school education (MAT); music education (MAT); secondary education (MAT); special education (MAT); teacher leadership (M Ed). Part-time and evening/weekend programs available. *Students:* 137 full-time (93 women), 208 part-time (131 women); includes 44 minority (25 Black or African American, non-Hispanic/Latino; 1 American Indian or Alaska Native, non-Hispanic/Latino; 3 Asian, non-Hispanic/Latino; 12 Hispanic/Latino; 3 Two or more races, non-Hispanic/Latino), 2 international. Average age 32. 150 applicants, 51% accepted, 54 enrolled. In 2013, 127 master's, 5 doctorates awarded. *Degree requirements:* For doctorate, comprehensive exam, thesis/dissertation. *Entrance requirements:* For master's, GRE General Test, PRAXIS II (for some programs); for doctorate, GRE General Test. Additional exam requirements/recommendations for international students: Required—TOEFL (minimum score 560 paper-based; 83 iBT). *Application deadline:* For fall admission, 5/1 priority date for international students; for spring admission, 11/1 priority date for international students; for summer admission, 4/1 priority date for international students. Application fee: $60. Electronic applications accepted. *Expenses:* Tuition, state resident: full-time $10,788; part-time $599 per credit hour. Tuition, nonresident: full-time $22,446; part-time $1247 per credit hour. *Required fees:* $196. Tuition and fees vary according to program and reciprocity agreements. *Financial support:* Fellowships, research assistantships, teaching assistantships, career-related internships or fieldwork, Federal Work-Study, scholarships/grants, and unspecified assistantships available. Financial award application deadline: 6/1; financial award applicants required to submit FAFSA. *Faculty research:* Mathematics teacher education and ongoing professional development in pedagogy and content knowledge; development of literacy, including early literacy in science and mathematics and literacy development for English language learners; immersive visualizations for promoting STEM education from nanoscience to cosmic scales; evidence-based practices for students with disabilities; urban education, including teacher response to intervention systems in schools and cross-cultural competence. *Unit head:* Dr. Ann E. Larson, Acting Chair, 502-852-6431, Fax: 502-852-1497, E-mail: ann@louisville.edu. *Application contact:* Libby Leggett, Director, Graduate Admissions, 502-852-3101, Fax: 502-852-6536, E-mail: gradadm@louisville.edu.
Website: http://louisville.edu/delphi.

Middle School Education

University of Massachusetts Dartmouth, Graduate School, College of Arts and Sciences, School of Education, Program in Teaching and Learning, North Dartmouth, MA 02747-2300. Offers middle school education (Postbaccalaureate Certificate); secondary school education (Postbaccalaureate Certificate). Part-time programs available. *Faculty:* 3 full-time (2 women), 9 part-time/adjunct (4 women). *Students:* 9 full-time (4 women), 136 part-time (94 women); includes 14 minority (2 Black or African American, non-Hispanic/Latino; 6 Hispanic/Latino; 6 Two or more races, non-Hispanic/Latino). Average age 35. 69 applicants, 94% accepted, 55 enrolled. In 2013, 13 Postbaccalaureate Certificates awarded. *Entrance requirements:* For degree, MTEL, statement of purpose (minimum of 300 words), resume, 2 letters of recommendation, official transcripts. Additional exam requirements/recommendations for international students: Required—TOEFL (minimum score 533 paper-based; 72 iBT). *Application deadline:* For fall admission, 7/15 priority date for domestic students, 6/15 priority date for international students; for spring admission, 12/15 priority date for domestic students, 11/15 priority date for international students. Applications are processed on a rolling basis. Application fee: $60. Electronic applications accepted. *Expenses:* Tuition, state resident: full-time $2071; part-time $86.29 per credit. Tuition, nonresident: full-time $8099; part-time $337.46 per credit. Tuition and fees vary according to course load and reciprocity agreements. *Financial support:* Federal Work-Study available. Support available to part-time students. Financial award application deadline: 3/1; financial award applicants required to submit FAFSA. *Faculty research:* Reading/special education, education reform, English education, literacy, language arts K-12. *Total annual research expenditures:* $1.1 million. *Unit head:* Traci Almeida, Graduate Program Director, 508-999-8098, Fax: 508-910-9055, E-mail: talmeida@umassd.edu. *Application contact:* Steven Briggs, Director of Marketing and Recruitment for Graduate Studies, 508-999-8604, Fax: 508-999-8183, E-mail: graduate@umassd.edu.
Website: http://www.umassd.edu/cas/schoolofeducation/stemeducationandteacherdevelopment.

University of Memphis, Graduate School, College of Education, Department of Instruction and Curriculum Leadership, Memphis, TN 38152. Offers early childhood education (MAT, MS, Ed D); elementary education (MAT); instruction and curriculum (MS, Ed D); instruction design and technology (MS, Ed D); middle grades education (MAT); reading (MS, Ed D); secondary education (MAT); special education (MAT, MS, Ed D). *Accreditation:* NCATE (one or more programs are accredited). Part-time programs available. *Faculty:* 30 full-time (18 women), 16 part-time/adjunct (10 women). *Students:* 55 full-time (44 women), 370 part-time (300 women); includes 169 minority (153 Black or African American, non-Hispanic/Latino; 5 American Indian or Alaska Native, non-Hispanic/Latino; 1 Asian, non-Hispanic/Latino; 6 Hispanic/Latino; 4 Two or more races, non-Hispanic/Latino), 7 international. Average age 35. 181 applicants, 84% accepted, 21 enrolled. In 2013, 137 master's, 10 doctorates awarded. Terminal master's awarded for partial completion of doctoral program. *Degree requirements:* For master's, comprehensive exam, thesis or alternative; for doctorate, comprehensive exam, thesis/dissertation. *Entrance requirements:* For master's, GRE General Test, minimum GPA of 2.5; for doctorate, GRE General Test, GRE Subject Test, 2 years of teaching experience. *Application deadline:* For fall admission, 8/1 for domestic students; for spring admission, 12/1 for domestic students. Applications are processed on a rolling basis. Application fee: $35 ($60 for international students). Electronic applications accepted. *Financial support:* In 2013–14, 635 students received support. Research assistantships with full tuition reimbursements available, teaching assistantships with full tuition reimbursements available, career-related internships or fieldwork, Federal Work-Study, institutionally sponsored loans, scholarships/grants, traineeships, and unspecified assistantships available. Support available to part-time students. Financial award application deadline: 2/15; financial award applicants required to submit FAFSA. *Faculty research:* Effective urban teachers, preparation and retention of urban teachers, technology utilization in schools, field-based teacher preparation programs, effective use of online instruction. *Unit head:* Dr. Sandra Cooley-Nichols, Interim Chair, 901-678-2365. *Application contact:* Dr. Sally Blake, Director of Graduate Studies, 901-678-4861.
Website: http://www.memphis.edu/icl/.

University of Missouri–St. Louis, College of Education, Division of Teaching and Learning, St. Louis, MO 63121. Offers autism studies (Certificate); elementary education (M Ed), including early childhood, general, reading; secondary education (M Ed), including curriculum and instruction, general, middle level education, reading, teaching English to speakers of other languages (TESOL); secondary school teaching (Certificate); special education (M Ed), including autism and developmental disabilities, cross-categorical disabilities, early childhood; teaching English to speakers of other languages (Certificate). Part-time and evening/weekend programs available. *Faculty:* 20 full-time (11 women), 1 (woman) part-time/adjunct. *Students:* 42 full-time (33 women), 578 part-time (442 women); includes 152 minority (101 Black or African American, non-Hispanic/Latino; 1 American Indian or Alaska Native, non-Hispanic/Latino; 20 Asian, non-Hispanic/Latino; 23 Hispanic/Latino; 7 Two or more races, non-Hispanic/Latino), 19 international. Average age 29. 245 applicants, 97% accepted, 166 enrolled. In 2013, 219 master's, 14 Certificates awarded. *Degree requirements:* For master's, comprehensive exam. *Entrance requirements:* Additional exam requirements/recommendations for international students: Recommended—TOEFL (minimum score 550 paper-based; 79 iBT), IELTS (minimum score 6.5). *Application deadline:* For fall admission, 7/1 priority date for domestic and international students; for spring admission, 12/1 priority date for domestic and international students. Application fee: $50 ($40 for international students). Electronic applications accepted. *Expenses:* Tuition, state resident: full-time $7364; part-time $409.10 per credit hour. Tuition, nonresident: full-time $19,162; part-time $1008.50 per credit hour. *Financial support:* Application deadline: 4/1; applicants required to submit FAFSA. *Unit head:* Dr. Patricia Kopetz, Chair, 314-516-5791. *Application contact:* 314-516-5458, Fax: 314-516-6996, E-mail: gadadm@umsl.edu.
Website: http://coe.umsl.edu/web/divisions/teach-learn/index.html.

The University of North Carolina at Charlotte, The Graduate School, College of Education, Department of Middle, Secondary and K-12 Education, Charlotte, NC 28223-0001. Offers curriculum and instruction (PhD); English education (MA); mathematics education (MA); middle grades education (MAT); secondary education (MAT); teaching English as a second language (M Ed). *Faculty:* 19 full-time (11 women), 7 part-time/adjunct (3 women). *Students:* 16 full-time (14 women), 30 part-time (24 women); includes 8 minority (6 Black or African American, non-Hispanic/Latino; 1 Hispanic/Latino; 1 Two or more races, non-Hispanic/Latino). Average age 32. 23 applicants, 87% accepted, 19 enrolled. In 2013, 21 master's awarded. *Degree requirements:* For master's, thesis. *Entrance requirements:* For master's, GRE or MAT. Additional exam requirements/recommendations for international students: Required—TOEFL (minimum score 557 paper-based; 83 iBT). *Application deadline:* For fall admission, 5/1 priority date for domestic students, 5/1 for international students; for spring admission, 10/1 priority date for domestic students, 10/1 for international students. Applications are processed on a rolling basis. Application fee: $75. Electronic applications accepted. *Expenses:* Tuition, state resident: full-time $3522. Tuition, nonresident: full-time $16,051. *Required fees:* $2585. Tuition and fees vary according to course load and program. *Financial support:* In 2013–14, 6 students received support, including 1 fellowship (averaging $50,000 per year), 3 research assistantships (averaging $5,400 per year), 2 teaching assistantships (averaging $9,500 per year); career-related internships or fieldwork, institutionally sponsored loans, scholarships/grants, and unspecified assistantships also available. Support available to part-time students. Financial award application deadline: 4/1; financial award applicants required to submit FAFSA. *Total annual research expenditures:* $98,589. *Unit head:* Dr. Warren DiBiase, Chair, 704-687-8881, Fax: 704-687-6430, E-mail: wjdibias@uncc.edu. *Application contact:* Kathy B. Giddings, Director of Graduate Admissions, 704-687-5503, Fax: 704-687-1668, E-mail: gradadm@uncc.edu.
Website: http://education.uncc.edu/mdsk.

The University of North Carolina at Charlotte, The Graduate School, College of Education, Interdisciplinary Education Programs, Charlotte, NC 28223-0001. Offers art education (MAT); dance education (MAT); elementary education (MAT); English as a second language (MAT); foreign language education (MAT); middle grades education (MAT); music education (MAT); secondary education (MAT); special education (MAT); teacher certification (Graduate Certificate); teaching (Graduate Certificate); theater education (MAT). Part-time programs available. *Students:* 206 full-time (165 women), 791 part-time (628 women); includes 342 minority (247 Black or African American, non-Hispanic/Latino; 16 Asian, non-Hispanic/Latino; 62 Hispanic/Latino; 17 Two or more races, non-Hispanic/Latino), 14 international. Average age 32. 564 applicants, 91% accepted, 414 enrolled. In 2013, 145 master's, 271 other advanced degrees awarded. Terminal master's awarded for partial completion of doctoral program. *Degree requirements:* For master's, thesis. *Entrance requirements:* For master's, GRE or MAT. Additional exam requirements/recommendations for international students: Required—TOEFL (minimum score 550 paper-based; 83 iBT). *Application deadline:* For fall admission, 5/1 priority date for domestic and international students; for spring admission, 10/1 priority date for domestic and international students. Applications are processed on a rolling basis. Application fee: $75. Electronic applications accepted. *Expenses:* Tuition, state resident: full-time $3522. Tuition, nonresident: full-time $16,051. *Required fees:* $2585. Tuition and fees vary according to course load and program. *Total annual research expenditures:* $43,031. *Unit head:* Dr. Warren DiBiase, Chair, 704-687-8881, Fax: 704-687-4705, E-mail: wjdibias@uncc.edu. *Application contact:* Kathy B. Giddings, Director of Graduate Admissions, 704-687-5503, Fax: 704-687-1668, E-mail: gradadm@uncc.edu.
Website: http://education.uncc.edu/academic-programs.

The University of North Carolina at Greensboro, Graduate School, School of Education, Department of Curriculum and Instruction, Greensboro, NC 27412-5001. Offers college teaching and adult learning (Certificate); curriculum and instruction (M Ed), including chemistry education, elementary education, English as a second language, French education, instructional technology, mathematics education, middle grades education, reading education, science education, social studies education, Spanish education; curriculum and teaching (PhD), including higher education, teacher education and development; English as a second language (Certificate); higher education (M Ed); supervision (M Ed). *Accreditation:* NCATE. Part-time programs available. *Degree requirements:* For doctorate, thesis/dissertation. *Entrance requirements:* For master's and doctorate, GRE General Test. Additional exam requirements/recommendations for international students: Required—TOEFL. Electronic applications accepted. *Faculty research:* Community college literacy program, middle school mathematics/computer mathematics.

The University of North Carolina at Pembroke, Graduate Studies, School of Education, Program in Middle Grades Education, Pembroke, NC 28372-1510. Offers MA Ed, MAT. *Accreditation:* NCATE. Part-time and evening/weekend programs available. *Degree requirements:* For master's, thesis optional. *Entrance requirements:* For master's, GRE General Test or MAT, minimum GPA of 3.0 in major, 2.5 overall. Additional exam requirements/recommendations for international students: Required—TOEFL.

The University of North Carolina Wilmington, Watson College of Education, Department of Early Childhood, Elementary, Middle, Literacy and Special Education, Wilmington, NC 28403-3297. Offers MAT. *Accreditation:* NCATE. Part-time and evening/weekend programs available. *Faculty:* 21 full-time (17 women). *Students:* 47 full-time (36 women), 13 part-time (11 women); includes 9 minority (5 Black or African American, non-Hispanic/Latino; 2 Hispanic/Latino; 2 Two or more races, non-Hispanic/Latino), 3 international. Average age 31. 36 applicants, 97% accepted, 33 enrolled. In 2013, 24 master's awarded. *Degree requirements:* For master's, comprehensive exam. *Entrance requirements:* For master's, GRE General Test, MAT, minimum B average in upper-division undergraduate course work. *Application deadline:* For fall admission, 6/1 for domestic students. Applications are processed on a rolling basis. Application fee: $60. *Expenses:* Tuition, state resident: full-time $4163. Tuition, nonresident: full-time $16,098. *Financial support:* Career-related internships or fieldwork, Federal Work-Study, and unspecified assistantships available. Support available to part-time students. Financial award application deadline: 3/15. *Unit head:* Dr. Tracy Hargrove, Chair, 910-962-3240, Fax: 910-962-3988, E-mail: hargrovet@uncw.edu. *Application contact:* Dr. Ron Vetter, Dean, Graduate School, 910-962-3224, Fax: 910-962-3787, E-mail: vetterr@uncw.edu.

University of Northern Iowa, Graduate College, College of Humanities, Arts and Sciences, Department of Mathematics, Program in Mathematics for the Middle Grades, Cedar Falls, IA 50614. Offers MA. *Students:* 11 part-time (all women). 1 applicant, 100% accepted. In 2013, 1 master's awarded. Application fee: $50 ($70 for international students). *Unit head:* Dr. Brian Townsend, Coordinator, 319-273-2397, Fax: 319-273-2546, E-mail: brian.townsend@uni.edu. *Application contact:* Laurie S. Russell, Record Analyst, 319-273-2623, Fax: 319-273-2885, E-mail: laurie.russell@uni.edu.

University of North Georgia, School of Education, Dahlonega, GA 30597. Offers art education (MAT); early childhood education (M Ed); English education (MAT); history education (MAT); math education (MAT); middle grades education (M Ed, MAT); physical education (MS); school leadership (Ed S); secondary education (M Ed), including English education, history education, mathematics education, physical education; teacher education (MAT). *Accreditation:* NCATE. Part-time and evening/weekend programs available. Postbaccalaureate distance learning degree programs offered (no on-campus study). *Degree requirements:* For master's, comprehensive exam, thesis optional. *Entrance requirements:* For master's, GRE or MAT, GACE, minimum GPA of 2.75; for Ed S, GRE General Test or MAT, 3 years of teaching experience, master's degree, minimum graduate GPA of 3.25, leadership position in the school. Additional exam requirements/recommendations for international students: Required—TOEFL (minimum score 550 paper-based; 79 iBT), IELTS (minimum score 6.5). Electronic applications accepted. *Faculty research:* Identification of professional development school structures supporting P-12 student achievement, impact of diverse field placement settings in teacher belief development among preservice teachers, use of inquiry methodology in social studies teaching with English language learners, use of instructional differentiation in the middle grades classroom, effects of international school placements on preservice teacher beliefs and attitudes.

University of Phoenix–Online Campus, College of Education, Phoenix, AZ 85034-7209. Offers administration and supervision (MAEd, Certificate); adult education and training (MAEd); curriculum and instruction (MAEd), including computer education, curriculum and instruction, English as a second language, language arts, mathematics, reading; early childhood education (MAEd); educational studies (MAEd); elementary teacher education (MAEd), including early childhood, elementary teacher education,

high school middle level, middle level; principal licensure (Certificate); secondary teacher education (MAEd); special education (MAEd, Certificate); teacher education (MAEd), including middle level generalist; teacher education middle level mathematics (MAEd), including middle level mathematics; teacher education middle level science (MAEd), including middle level science; teacher education secondary mathematics (MAEd); teacher education secondary science (MAEd); teacher leadership (MAEd); teachers of English learners (Certificate); transition to teaching (Certificate), including elementary education, secondary education. *Accreditation:* Teacher Education Accreditation Council. Evening/weekend programs available. Postbaccalaureate distance learning degree programs offered. *Entrance requirements:* Additional exam requirements/recommendations for international students: Required—TOEFL, TOEIC (Test of English as an International Communication), Berlitz Online English Proficiency Exam, PTE, or IELTS. Electronic applications accepted. *Expenses:* Contact institution.

University of Phoenix–Oregon Campus, College of Education, Tigard, OR 97223. Offers curriculum and instruction (MA Ed); early childhood education (MA Ed); elementary education (MA Ed), including early childhood specialization, middle level specialization; secondary education (MA Ed). Evening/weekend programs available. *Degree requirements:* For master's, thesis (for some programs). *Entrance requirements:* For master's, minimum undergraduate GPA of 2.5, 3 years work experience. Additional exam requirements/recommendations for international students: Required—TOEFL (minimum score 550 paper-based; 79 iBT). Electronic applications accepted.

University of South Florida–St. Petersburg Campus, College of Education, St. Petersburg, FL 33701. Offers educational leadership development (M Ed); elementary education (MA), including math/science; English education (MA); middle grades STEM education (MS); reading education (MA). Part-time programs available. *Degree requirements:* For master's, comprehensive exam, practicum, internship, comprehensive portfolio. *Entrance requirements:* For master's, State of Florida General Knowledge Test (GKT), Florida Teaching Certificate (for non-initial certification programs), letters of recommendation. Additional exam requirements/recommendations for international students: Required—TOEFL (minimum score 550 paper-based; 79 iBT); Recommended—IELTS. Electronic applications accepted.

University of the Cumberlands, Graduate Programs in Education, Williamsburg, KY 40769-1372. Offers all grades (P-12) (M Ed); business and marketing (MA Ed, MAT); counselor education and supervision (Ed D); director of pupil personnel (Certificate); director of special education (Certificate); educational administration and supervision (Ed S); educational leadership (Ed D); elementary education (MA Ed, MAT); instructional leadership - principalship (MA Ed); instructional leadership - school principal (Certificate); middle school education (MA Ed, MAT); reading and writing (MA Ed); school counseling (MA Ed); school superintendent (Certificate); secondary education (MA Ed, MAT); special education (MAT); supervisor of instruction (Certificate); teacher leader (MA Ed). Part-time and evening/weekend programs available. Postbaccalaureate distance learning degree programs offered. *Degree requirements:* For master's, comprehensive exam. Electronic applications accepted.

The University of Toledo, College of Graduate Studies, Judith Herb College of Education, Department of Curriculum and Instruction, Toledo, OH 43606-3390. Offers art education (ME); career and technical education (ME); career-technical education (Ed S); curriculum and instruction (ME, PhD, Ed S); early childhood education (PhD, Ed S); education and biology (MES); education and chemistry (MES); education and economics (MAE); education and English (MAE); education and French (MAE); education and geography (MAE); education and geology (MES); education and German (MAE); education and history (MAE); education and mathematics (MAE, MES); education and physics (MES); education and political science (MAE); education and sociology (MAE); education and Spanish (MAE); educational media (PhD); educational technology (ME); educational technology: virtual educator (Certificate); elementary education (PhD); English as a second language (MAE); gifted and talented (PhD); middle childhood education licensure (ME); music education (MME); secondary education (PhD); secondary education licensure (ME); special education (PhD, Ed S). *Accreditation:* NCATE. Part-time and evening/weekend programs available. *Faculty:* 41. *Students:* 53 full-time (30 women), 154 part-time (111 women); includes 21 minority (16 Black or African American, non-Hispanic/Latino; 4 Hispanic/Latino; 1 Two or more races, non-Hispanic/Latino), 21 international. Average age 34. 82 applicants, 79% accepted, 47 enrolled. In 2013, 80 master's, 5 doctorates awarded. *Degree requirements:* For master's, comprehensive exam, thesis or alternative; for doctorate, comprehensive exam, thesis/dissertation; for other advanced degree, thesis optional. *Entrance requirements:* For master's, doctorate, and other advanced degree, minimum cumulative GPA of 2.7 for all previous academic work, letters of recommendation. Additional exam requirements/recommendations for international students: Required—TOEFL (minimum score 550 paper-based; 80 iBT). *Application deadline:* For fall admission, 1/15 priority date for domestic and international students. Applications are processed on a rolling basis. Application fee: $45 ($75 for international students). Electronic applications accepted. *Financial support:* In 2013–14, 5 research assistantships with full and partial tuition reimbursements (averaging $13,200 per year), 11 teaching assistantships with full and partial tuition reimbursements (averaging $8,809 per year) were awarded; career-related internships or fieldwork, Federal Work-Study, institutionally sponsored loans, scholarships/grants, tuition waivers (full and partial), unspecified assistantships, and administrative assistantships also available. Support available to part-time students. *Unit head:* Dr. Joan Kaderavek, Chair, 419-530-5373, E-mail: eigh.chiarelott@utoledo.edu. *Application contact:* Graduate School Office, 419-530-4723, Fax: 419-530-4724, E-mail: grdsch@utnet.utoledo.edu.
Website: http://www.utoledo.edu/eduhshs/.

University of Washington, Bothell, Program in Education, Bothell, WA 98011-8246. Offers education (M Ed); leadership development for educators (M Ed); secondary/middle level endorsement (M Ed). Part-time and evening/weekend programs available. *Degree requirements:* For master's, thesis. *Entrance requirements:* Additional exam requirements/recommendations for international students: Required—TOEFL. Electronic applications accepted. *Faculty research:* Multicultural education in citizenship education, intercultural education, knowledge and practice in the principalship, educational public policy, national board certification for teachers, teacher learning in literacy, technology and its impact on teaching and learning of mathematics, reading assessments, professional development in literacy education and mobility, digital media, education and class.

University of West Florida, College of Professional Studies, Department of Research and Advanced Studies, Pensacola, FL 32514-5750. Offers administration (MSA), including acquisition and contract administration, biomedical/pharmaceutical, criminal justice administration, database administration, education leadership, healthcare administration, human performance technology, leadership, nursing administration, public administration, software engineering and administration; college student personnel administration (M Ed), including college personnel administration, guidance and counseling; curriculum and instruction (M Ed, Ed S); educational leadership (M Ed); middle and secondary level education and ESOL (M Ed). Part-time and evening/weekend programs available. *Entrance requirements:* For master's, GRE or MAT, official transcripts; minimum undergraduate GPA of 3.0; letter of intent; three letters of recommendation; resume. Additional exam requirements/recommendations for international students: Required—TOEFL (minimum score 550 paper-based).

University of Wisconsin–Milwaukee, Graduate School, School of Education, Department of Curriculum and Instruction, Milwaukee, WI 53201-0413. Offers curriculum planning and instruction improvement (MS); early childhood education (MS); elementary education (MS); junior high/middle school education (MS); reading education (MS); secondary education (MS); teaching in an urban setting (MS). Part-time programs available. *Faculty:* 18 full-time (13 women). *Students:* 17 full-time (10 women), 46 part-time (42 women); includes 15 minority (7 Black or African American, non-Hispanic/Latino; 1 Asian, non-Hispanic/Latino; 7 Two or more races, non-Hispanic/Latino), 1 international. Average age 32. 35 applicants, 69% accepted, 11 enrolled. In 2013, 31 master's awarded. *Degree requirements:* For master's, thesis or alternative. *Entrance requirements:* Additional exam requirements/recommendations for international students: Required—TOEFL (minimum score 550 paper-based; 79 iBT), IELTS (minimum score 6.5). *Application deadline:* For fall admission, 1/1 priority date for domestic students; for spring admission, 9/1 for domestic students. Applications are processed on a rolling basis. Application fee: $56 ($96 for international students). Electronic applications accepted. *Financial support:* In 2013–14, 1 fellowship was awarded; research assistantships, teaching assistantships, career-related internships or fieldwork, health care benefits, unspecified assistantships, and project assistantships also available. Support available to part-time students. Financial award application deadline: 4/15; financial award applicants required to submit FAFSA. *Unit head:* Raquel Oxford, Department Chair, 414-229-4884, Fax: 414-229-5571, E-mail: roxford@uwm.edu. *Application contact:* General Information Contact, 414-229-4982, Fax: 414-229-6967, E-mail: gradschool@uwm.edu.
Website: http://www.uwm.edu/SOE/.

University of Wisconsin–Platteville, School of Graduate Studies, College of Liberal Arts and Education, School of Education, Platteville, WI 53818-3099. Offers adult education (MSE); elementary education (MSE); English education (MSE); middle school education (MSE); secondary education (MSE). *Accreditation:* NCATE. Part-time programs available. *Faculty:* 5 full-time (3 women), 13 part-time/adjunct (7 women). *Students:* 90 full-time (70 women), 30 part-time (16 women); includes 25 minority (21 Black or African American, non-Hispanic/Latino; 1 American Indian or Alaska Native, non-Hispanic/Latino; 2 Asian, non-Hispanic/Latino; 1 Hispanic/Latino), 3 international. 45 applicants, 96% accepted, 38 enrolled. In 2013, 82 master's awarded. *Degree requirements:* For master's, comprehensive exam, thesis or alternative. *Entrance requirements:* Additional exam requirements/recommendations for international students: Required—TOEFL (minimum score 500 paper-based; 61 iBT), IELTS (minimum score 6). *Application deadline:* For fall admission, 7/1 priority date for domestic students; for spring admission, 11/1 for domestic students. Applications are processed on a rolling basis. Application fee: $56. Electronic applications accepted. *Financial support:* Research assistantships with partial tuition reimbursements, career-related internships or fieldwork, Federal Work-Study, institutionally sponsored loans, scholarships/grants, and unspecified assistantships available. Support available to part-time students. Financial award applicants required to submit FAFSA. *Unit head:* Dr. Karen Stinson, Director, 608-342-1131, Fax: 608-342-1133, E-mail: stinsonk@uwplatt.edu. *Application contact:* Dee Dunbar, School of Graduate Studies, 608-342-1322, Fax: 608-342-1389, E-mail: dunbard@uwplatt.edu.
Website: http://www.uwplatt.edu/.

Ursuline College, School of Graduate Studies, Program in Education, Pepper Pike, OH 44124-4398. Offers art education (MA); early childhood education (MA); language arts education (MA); life science education (MA); math education (MA); middle school education (MA); social studies education (MA); special education (MA). *Accreditation:* NCATE. *Faculty:* 4 full-time (all women), 7 part-time/adjunct (5 women). *Students:* 18 full-time (16 women), 7 part-time (all women); includes 8 minority (4 Black or African American, non-Hispanic/Latino; 2 Asian, non-Hispanic/Latino; 2 Hispanic/Latino). Average age 34. 1 applicant, 100% accepted, 1 enrolled. In 2013, 25 master's awarded. *Degree requirements:* For master's, comprehensive exam. *Entrance requirements:* For master's, minimum undergraduate GPA of 3.0. Additional exam requirements/recommendations for international students: Required—TOEFL (minimum score 500 paper-based). *Application deadline:* For fall admission, 8/1 priority date for domestic students. Applications are processed on a rolling basis. Application fee: $25. *Expenses:* Contact institution. *Financial support:* In 2013–14, 1 student received support. Federal Work-Study available. Financial award application deadline: 3/1. *Unit head:* Dr. Edna West, Director, Master's Apprentice Program, 440-646-6134, Fax: 440-646-8328, E-mail: ewest@ursuline.edu. *Application contact:* Stephanie Pratt, Graduate Admission Coordinator, 440-646-8119, Fax: 440-684-6138, E-mail: graduateadmissions@ursuline.edu.

Wagner College, Division of Graduate Studies, Department of Education, Program in Secondary Education/Special Education, Staten Island, NY 10301-4495. Offers language arts (MS Ed); languages other than English (MS Ed); mathematics and technology (MS Ed); science and technology (MS Ed); social studies (MS Ed). Part-time and evening/weekend programs available. *Degree requirements:* For master's, thesis (for some programs). *Entrance requirements:* For master's, minimum GPA of 3.0, interview, recommendations. Electronic applications accepted. *Expenses: Tuition:* Full-time $17,496; part-time $972 per credit. Tuition and fees vary according to course load.

Walden University, Graduate Programs, Richard W. Riley College of Education and Leadership, Minneapolis, MN 55401. *Accreditation:* NCATE. Part-time and evening/weekend programs available. Postbaccalaureate distance learning degree programs offered (minimal on-campus study). *Faculty:* 23 full-time (15 women), 830 part-time/adjunct (569 women). *Students:* 8,671 full-time (7,197 women), 2,122 part-time (1,735 women); includes 4,734 minority (3,802 Black or African American, non-Hispanic/Latino; 50 American Indian or Alaska Native, non-Hispanic/Latino; 136 Asian, non-Hispanic/Latino; 539 Hispanic/Latino; 35 Native Hawaiian or other Pacific Islander, non-Hispanic/Latino; 172 Two or more races, non-Hispanic/Latino), 73 international. Average age 40. 2,646 applicants, 96% accepted, 2074 enrolled. In 2013, 2,214 master's, 354 doctorates, 479 other advanced degrees awarded. *Degree requirements:* For doctorate, thesis/dissertation (for some programs), residency; for other advanced degree, residency (for some programs). *Entrance requirements:* For master's, bachelor's degree or higher; minimum GPA of 2.5; official transcripts; goal statement (for some programs); access to computer and Internet; for doctorate, master's degree or higher; three years of related professional or academic experience (preferred); minimum GPA of 3.0; goal statement and current resume (select programs); official transcripts; access to computer and Internet; for other advanced degree, relevant work experience; access to computer and Internet. Additional exam requirements/recommendations for international students: Required—TOEFL (minimum score 550 paper-based; 79 iBT), IELTS (minimum score 6.5), Michigan English Language Assessment Battery (minimum score 82), or PTE. *Application deadline:* Applications are processed on a rolling basis. Application fee: $0. Electronic applications accepted. *Expenses: Tuition:* Full-time $11,813.55; part-time $500 per credit. *Required fees:* $618.76. *Financial support:* In 2013–14, 1 fellowship was awarded; Federal Work-Study, scholarships/grants, unspecified assistantships, and family tuition reduction, active duty/veteran tuition reduction, group tuition reduction, interest-free payment plans, employee tuition reduction also available. Support available

to part-time students. Financial award applicants required to submit FAFSA. *Unit head:* Dr. Kate Steffens, Dean, 800-925-3368. *Application contact:* Jennifer Hall, Vice President of Enrollment Management, 866-4-WALDEN, E-mail: info@waldenu.edu. Website: http://www.waldenu.edu/colleges-schools/riley-college-of-education/.

Webster University, School of Education, Department of Communication Arts, Reading and Early Childhood, St. Louis, MO 63119-3194. Offers early childhood education (MAT); elementary education (MAT); middle school education (MAT). *Entrance requirements:* For master's, minimum GPA of 2.5. Additional exam requirements/recommendations for international students: Required—TOEFL. *Expenses: Tuition:* Full-time $11,610; part-time $645 per credit hour. Tuition and fees vary according to campus/location and program.

West Chester University of Pennsylvania, College of Education, Department of Early and Middle Grades, West Chester, PA 19383. Offers applied studies in teaching and learning (M Ed); early childhood education (M Ed, Teaching Certificate); early grades preparation (Teaching Certificate); elementary education (Teaching Certificate); middle grades preparation (Teaching Certificate). *Accreditation:* NCATE. Part-time and evening/weekend programs available. *Faculty:* 5 full-time (all women), 1 part-time/adjunct (0 women). *Students:* 26 full-time (17 women), 68 part-time (58 women); includes 11 minority (7 Black or African American, non-Hispanic/Latino; 1 American Indian or Alaska Native, non-Hispanic/Latino; 1 Asian, non-Hispanic/Latino; 2 Hispanic/Latino), 3 international. Average age 31. 41 applicants, 83% accepted, 8 enrolled. In 2013, 17 master's, 3 other advanced degrees awarded. *Degree requirements:* For master's, teacher research project, portfolio. *Entrance requirements:* For master's, minimum GPA of 3.0, teacher certification (for applied studies in teaching and learning track), one year of full-time teaching experience; for Teaching Certificate, math, social studies, or science concentration exams (for middle grades preparation), minimum GPA of 3.0. Additional exam requirements/recommendations for international students: Required—TOEFL (minimum score 550 paper-based; 80 iBT). *Application deadline:* For fall admission, 4/15 priority date for domestic students, 3/15 for international students; for spring admission, 10/15 priority date for domestic students. Applications are processed on a rolling basis. Application fee: $45. Electronic applications accepted. *Expenses:* Tuition, state resident: full-time $7956; part-time $442 per credit. Tuition, nonresident: full-time $11,934; part-time $663 per credit. *Required fees:* $2134.20; $106.24 per credit. Tuition and fees vary according to campus/location and program. *Financial support:* Unspecified assistantships available. Support available to part-time students. Financial award application deadline: 2/15; financial award applicants required to submit FAFSA. *Faculty research:* Cooperative learning, creative expression and critical thinking, teacher research, learning styles, middle school education. *Unit head:* Dr. Heather Leaman, Chair, 610-436-2944, Fax: 610-436-3102, E-mail: hleaman@wcupa.edu. *Application contact:* Dr. Connie DiLucchio, Graduate Coordinator, 610-436-3323, Fax: 610-436-3102, E-mail: cdilucchio@wcupa.edu.

Western Kentucky University, Graduate Studies, College of Education and Behavioral Sciences, School of Teacher Education, Bowling Green, KY 42101. Offers elementary education (MAE, Ed S); exceptional education: learning and behavioral disorders (MAE); exceptional education: moderate and severe disabilities (MAE); instructional design (MS); interdisciplinary early childhood education (MAE); library media education (MS); literacy education (MAE); middle grades education (MAE); secondary education (MAE, Ed S). Part-time and evening/weekend programs available. Postbaccalaureate distance learning degree programs offered (minimal on-campus study). *Degree requirements:* For master's, comprehensive exam. *Entrance requirements:* For master's, GRE General Test. Additional exam requirements/recommendations for international students: Required—TOEFL (minimum score 555 paper-based; 79 iBT). *Faculty research:* Teacher preparation in moderate/severe disabilities.

Widener University, School of Human Service Professions, Center for Education, Chester, PA 19013-5792. Offers adult education (M Ed); counseling in higher education (M Ed); counselor education (M Ed); early childhood education (M Ed); educational foundations (M Ed); educational leadership (M Ed); educational psychology (M Ed); elementary education (M Ed); English and language arts (M Ed); health education (M Ed); higher education leadership (Ed D); home and school visitor (M Ed); human sexuality (M Ed, PhD); mathematics education (M Ed); middle school education (M Ed); principalship (M Ed); reading and language arts (Ed D); reading education (M Ed); school administration (Ed D); science education (M Ed); social studies education (M Ed); special education (M Ed); technology education (M Ed). *Accreditation:* NCATE. Part-time and evening/weekend programs available. *Faculty:* 34 full-time (22 women), 37 part-time/adjunct (14 women). *Students:* 64 full-time (44 women), 209 part-time (146 women); includes 49 minority (39 Black or African American, non-Hispanic/Latino; 1 American Indian or Alaska Native, non-Hispanic/Latino; 4 Asian, non-Hispanic/Latino; 4 Hispanic/Latino; 1 Two or more races, non-Hispanic/Latino), 8 international. Average age 39. 139 applicants, 88% accepted. In 2013, 168 master's, 31 doctorates awarded. Terminal master's awarded for partial completion of doctoral program. *Degree requirements:* For doctorate, thesis/dissertation. *Entrance requirements:* For master's, minimum GPA of 2.5; for doctorate, GRE or MAT, minimum GPA of 2.0 (undergraduate), 3.5 (graduate). *Application deadline:* Applications are processed on a rolling basis. Application fee: $25 ($300 for international students). Electronic applications accepted. *Expenses:* Contact institution. *Financial support:* Career-related internships or fieldwork, tuition waivers (full and partial), and unspecified assistantships available. Support available to part-time students. Financial award application deadline: 5/1. *Faculty research:* Reading and cognition, adult education, technology education, educational leadership, special education. *Unit head:* Dr. Michael W. LeDoux, Associate Dean, 610-499-4294, Fax: 610-499-4623, E-mail: mwledoux@widener.edu. *Application contact:* Dr. Roberta Nolan, Director of Graduate Admissions, 610-499-4125, E-mail: rdnolan@widener.edu.

Wilkes University, College of Graduate and Professional Studies, School of Education, Wilkes-Barre, PA 18766-0002. Offers art and science of teaching (MS Ed); classroom technology (MS Ed); early childhood literacy (MS Ed); educational development and strategies (MS Ed); educational leadership (MS Ed); educational technology (Ed D); higher education administration (Ed D); instructional media (MS Ed); instructional technology (MS Ed); international school leadership (MS Ed); K-12 administration (Ed D); middle level education (MS Ed); online teaching (MS Ed); reading (MS Ed); school business leadership (MS Ed); secondary education (MS Ed), including biology, chemistry, English, history, mathematics; special education (MS Ed); teaching English as a second language (MS Ed); twenty-first century teaching and learning (MS Ed). Part-time and evening/weekend programs available. Postbaccalaureate distance learning degree programs offered (minimal on-campus study). *Students:* 46 full-time (37 women), 1,410 part-time (1,039 women); includes 67 minority (12 Black or African American, non-Hispanic/Latino; 2 American Indian or Alaska Native, non-Hispanic/Latino; 11 Asian, non-Hispanic/Latino; 28 Hispanic/Latino; 1 Native Hawaiian or other Pacific Islander, non-Hispanic/Latino; 13 Two or more races, non-Hispanic/Latino), 6 international. Average age 34. In 2013, 852 master's, 10 doctorates awarded. *Entrance requirements:* Additional exam requirements/recommendations for international students: Required—TOEFL (minimum score 550 paper-based; 79 iBT). *Application deadline:* Applications are processed on a rolling basis. Application fee: $45. Electronic applications accepted. *Expenses:* Contact institution. *Financial support:* Federal Work-Study and unspecified assistantships available. Financial award application deadline: 3/1; financial award applicants required to submit FAFSA. *Unit head:* Dr. Rhonda Waskiewicz, Interim Dean, Education, 570-408-4332, Fax: 570-408-7872, E-mail: rhonda.waskiewicz@wilkes.edu. *Application contact:* Joanne Thomas, Interim Director of Graduate Education, 570-408-4234, Fax: 570-408-7846, E-mail: joanne.thomas1@wilkes.edu.
Website: http://www.wilkes.edu/pages/383.asp.

Winthrop University, College of Education, Program in Middle Level Education, Rock Hill, SC 29733. Offers M Ed. *Entrance requirements:* For master's, minimum GPA of 3.0, South Carolina Class III Teaching Certificate, 2 letters of recommendation. Electronic applications accepted.

Worcester State University, Graduate Studies, Department of Education, Program in Middle School Education, Worcester, MA 01602-2597. Offers M Ed, Postbaccalaureate Certificate. Part-time programs available. *Faculty:* 14 full-time (11 women), 22 part-time/adjunct (10 women). *Students:* 3 full-time (2 women), 28 part-time (20 women); includes 1 minority (Hispanic/Latino). Average age 34. 25 applicants, 84% accepted, 10 enrolled. In 2013, 1 master's awarded. *Degree requirements:* For master's, comprehensive exam (for some programs), thesis optional. *Entrance requirements:* For master's, GRE General Test or MAT. Additional exam requirements/recommendations for international students: Required—TOEFL (minimum score 500 paper-based; 61 iBT). *Application deadline:* For fall admission, 6/15 for domestic and international students; for spring admission, 4/1 for domestic and international students. Applications are processed on a rolling basis. Application fee: $40. Electronic applications accepted. *Expenses: Tuition, area resident:* Part-time $150 per credit. Tuition, state resident: part-time $150 per credit. Tuition, nonresident: part-time $150 per credit. *Required fees:* $114.50 per credit. *Financial support:* Career-related internships or fieldwork, scholarships/grants, and unspecified assistantships available. Financial award application deadline: 3/1; financial award applicants required to submit FAFSA. *Unit head:* Dr. Sara Young, Coordinator, 508-929-8246, E-mail: syoung3@worcester.edu. *Application contact:* Sara Grady, Assistant Dean of Graduate and Continuing Education, 508-929-8787, Fax: 508-929-8100, E-mail: sara.grady@worcester.edu.

Wright State University, School of Graduate Studies, College of Education and Human Services, Department of Teacher Education, Dayton, OH 45435. Offers adolescent young adult (M Ed, MA); classroom teacher education (M Ed, MA); early childhood education (M Ed, MA); intervention specialist (M Ed, MA), including gifted educational needs, mild to moderate educational needs, moderate to intensive educational needs; middle childhood education (M Ed, MA); multi-age (M Ed, MA); workforce education (M Ed, MA), including career, technology and vocational education, computer/technology education, library/media, vocational education. *Accreditation:* NCATE. *Entrance requirements:* For master's, GRE General Test, MAT, PRAXIS II. Additional exam requirements/recommendations for international students: Required—TOEFL. *Faculty research:* Reading recovery, early kindergarten birthdays, international children's literature, discipline models, university and public schools cooperation.

Youngstown State University, Graduate School, Beeghly College of Education, Department of Teacher Education, Program in Early Childhood Education, Youngstown, OH 44555-0001. Offers MS Ed. *Accreditation:* NCATE. Part-time and evening/weekend programs available. *Degree requirements:* For master's, comprehensive exam. *Entrance requirements:* For master's, GRE, MAT, or teaching certificate; minimum GPA of 2.7. Additional exam requirements/recommendations for international students: Required—TOEFL.

Youngstown State University, Graduate School, Beeghly College of Education, Department of Teacher Education, Program in Middle Childhood Education, Youngstown, OH 44555-0001. Offers MS Ed. *Accreditation:* NCATE. Part-time and evening/weekend programs available. *Degree requirements:* For master's, comprehensive exam, thesis optional. *Entrance requirements:* For master's, GRE, MAT, or teaching certificate; minimum GPA of 2.7. Additional exam requirements/recommendations for international students: Required—TOEFL. *Faculty research:* Critical reflectivity, gender issues in classroom instruction, collaborative research and analysis, literacy methodology.

Secondary Education

Acacia University, American Graduate School of Education, Tempe, AZ 85284. Offers educational administration (M Ed); elementary education (MA); English as a second language (M Ed); secondary education (MA); special education (M Ed).

Adelphi University, Ruth S. Ammon School of Education, Program in Adolescent Education, Garden City, NY 11530-0701. Offers MA. Part-time and evening/weekend programs available. *Students:* 57 full-time (41 women), 9 part-time (8 women); includes 14 minority (7 Black or African American, non-Hispanic/Latino; 2 Asian, non-Hispanic/Latino; 4 Hispanic/Latino; 1 Two or more races, non-Hispanic/Latino). Average age 26. In 2013, 35 master's awarded. *Entrance requirements:* For master's, 2 letters of recommendation, resume. Additional exam requirements/recommendations for international students: Required—TOEFL (minimum score 550 paper-based; 80 iBT). *Application deadline:* For fall admission, 4/1 for international students; for spring admission, 11/1 for international students. Applications are processed on a rolling basis. Application fee: $50. Electronic applications accepted. *Expenses: Tuition:* Full-time $32,530; part-time $1010 per credit. *Required fees:* $1150. Tuition and fees vary according to degree level and program. *Financial support:* Fellowships, research assistantships with partial tuition reimbursements, teaching assistantships, career-related internships or fieldwork, Federal Work-Study, institutionally sponsored loans, tuition waivers (full), and unspecified assistantships available. Support available to part-time students. Financial award application deadline: 2/15; financial award applicants required to submit FAFSA. *Faculty research:* Methods to enhance the development of teaching dispositions, ethical and moral issues in education. *Unit head:* Dr. Robert

Linne, Director, 516-877-4411, E-mail: linne@adelphi.edu. *Application contact:* Christine Murphy, Director of Admissions, 516-877-3050, Fax: 516-877-3039, E-mail: graduateadmissions@adelphi.edu.

Alabama Agricultural and Mechanical University, School of Graduate Studies, School of Education, Area in Secondary Education, Huntsville, AL 35811. Offers education (M Ed, Ed S); higher administration (MS). *Accreditation:* NCATE. Evening/weekend programs available. *Degree requirements:* For master's, comprehensive exam; for Ed S, thesis. *Entrance requirements:* For master's, GRE General Test. Additional exam requirements/recommendations for international students: Required—TOEFL (minimum score 500 paper-based; 61 iBT). Electronic applications accepted. *Faculty research:* World peace through education, computer-assisted instruction.

Alabama State University, College of Education, Department of Curriculum and Instruction, Montgomery, AL 36101-0271. Offers early childhood education (M Ed, Ed S); elementary education (M Ed, Ed S); secondary education (M Ed, Ed S), including biology education, English language arts education (M Ed), history education, math education, music education (M Ed), reading education (M Ed), social science education; special education (M Ed). Part-time programs available. *Faculty:* 11 full-time (8 women), 13 part-time/adjunct (10 women). *Students:* 32 full-time (19 women), 162 part-time (136 women); includes 189 minority (187 Black or African American, non-Hispanic/Latino; 1 Hispanic/Latino; 1 Two or more races, non-Hispanic/Latino). Average age 33. 99 applicants, 45% accepted, 34 enrolled. In 2013, 74 master's, 20 Ed Ss awarded. *Degree requirements:* For master's, comprehensive exam, thesis optional; for Ed S, comprehensive exam, thesis. *Entrance requirements:* For master's, GRE General Test, MAT, writing competency test; for Ed S, writing competency test, GRE, MAT. Additional exam requirements/recommendations for international students: Required—TOEFL (minimum score 500 paper-based). *Application deadline:* For fall admission, 7/15 for domestic students; for spring admission, 12/15 for domestic students. Applications are processed on a rolling basis. Application fee: $25. *Expenses:* Tuition, state resident: full-time $7958; part-time $343 per credit hour. Tuition, nonresident: full-time $14,132; part-time $686 per credit hour. *Required fees:* $446 per term. One-time fee: $1784 full-time; $892 part-time. Tuition and fees vary according to course load. *Financial support:* In 2013–14, research assistantships (averaging $9,450 per year) were awarded. *Unit head:* Dr. Joyce Johnson, Acting Chairperson, 334-229-4485, Fax: 334-229-5603, E-mail: jjohnson@alasu.edu. *Application contact:* Dr. William Person, Dean of Graduate Studies, 334-229-4274, Fax: 334-229-4928, E-mail: wperson@alasu.edu. Website: http://www.alasu.edu/academics/colleges—departments/college-of-education/curriculum—instruction/index.aspx.

Alcorn State University, School of Graduate Studies, School of Psychology and Education, Alcorn State, MS 39096-7500. Offers agricultural education (MS Ed); elementary education (MS Ed, Ed S); guidance and counseling (MS Ed); industrial education (MS Ed); secondary education (MS Ed), including health and physical education; special education (MS Ed). *Accreditation:* NCATE. *Degree requirements:* For master's, thesis optional.

American International College, School of Graduate and Adult Education, Department of Education, Springfield, MA 01109-3189. Offers early childhood education (M Ed, CAGS); educational leadership and supervision (Ed D); elementary education (M Ed, CAGS); middle/secondary education (M Ed, CAGS); moderate disabilities (M Ed, CAGS); reading (M Ed, CAGS); school adjustment counseling (MA, CAGS); school guidance counseling (MA, CAGS); school leadership preparation (M Ed, CAGS); teaching and learning (Ed D). Evening/weekend programs available. *Faculty:* 11 full-time (9 women), 235 part-time/adjunct. *Students:* 1,530 full-time (1,219 women), 184 part-time (143 women); includes 100 minority (58 Black or African American, non-Hispanic/Latino; 3 American Indian or Alaska Native, non-Hispanic/Latino; 14 Asian, non-Hispanic/Latino; 6 Hispanic/Latino; 19 Two or more races, non-Hispanic/Latino). Average age 36. 695 applicants, 82% accepted, 508 enrolled. In 2013, 449 master's, 17 doctorates, 135 other advanced degrees awarded. Terminal master's awarded for partial completion of doctoral program. *Degree requirements:* For master's, comprehensive exam (for some programs), thesis (for some programs), practicum/culminating experience; for doctorate, comprehensive exam (for some programs), thesis/dissertation; for CAGS, practicum/culminating experience. *Entrance requirements:* For master's, graduate of accredited four-year college with minimum B-average in undergraduate course work; for doctorate, master's degree, minimum GPA of 3.0; for CAGS, M Ed or master's degree in field related to licensure from accredited institution. Additional exam requirements/recommendations for international students: Required—TOEFL or IELTS. *Application deadline:* For fall admission, 7/1 for domestic and international students; for spring admission, 12/1 for domestic and international students. Applications are processed on a rolling basis. Application fee: $50. Electronic applications accepted. *Expenses:* Tuition: Full-time $14,040; part-time $780 per credit. Tuition and fees vary according to course load, degree level and program. *Financial support:* Career-related internships or fieldwork available. Financial award applicants required to submit FAFSA. *Unit head:* Esta Sobey, Associate Dean, 413-205-3453, Fax: 413-205-3943, E-mail: esta.sobey@aic.edu. *Application contact:* Kaitlyn Rickard, Director of XCP Admissions, 413-205-3090, Fax: 413-205-3911, E-mail: kaitlyn.rickard@aic.edu.
Website: http://www.aic.edu/academics.

American Public University System, AMU/APU Graduate Programs, Charles Town, WV 25414. Offers accounting (MBA, MS); criminal justice (MA), including business administration, emergency and disaster management, general (MA, MS); educational leadership (M Ed); emergency and disaster management (MA); entrepreneurship (MBA); environmental policy and management (MS), including environmental planning, environmental sustainability, fish and wildlife management, general (MA, MS); global environmental management; finance (MBA); general (MBA); global business management (MBA); history (MA), including American history, ancient and classical history, European history, global history, public history; homeland security (MA), including business administration, counter-terrorism studies, criminal justice, cyber, emergency management and public health, intelligence studies, transportation security; homeland security resource allocation (MBA); humanities (MA); information technology (MS), including digital forensics, enterprise software development, information assurance and security, IT project management; information technology management (MBA); intelligence studies (MA), including criminal intelligence, cyber, general (MA, MS), homeland security, intelligence analysis, intelligence collection, intelligence management, intelligence operations, terrorism studies; international relations and conflict resolution (MA), including comparative and security issues, conflict resolution, international and transnational security issues, peacekeeping; legal studies (MA); management (MA), including defense management, general (MA, MS), human resource management, organizational leadership, public administration; marketing (MBA); military history (MA), including American military history, American Revolution, civil war, war since 1945, World War II; military studies (MA), including joint warfare, strategic leadership; national security studies (MA), including general (MA, MS), homeland security, regional security studies, security and intelligence analysis, terrorism studies; nonprofit management (MBA); political science (MA), including American politics and government, comparative government and development, general (MA, MS), international relations, public policy; psychology (MA), including general (MA, MS),

maritime engineering management, reverse logistics management; public administration (MPA), including disaster management, environmental policy, health policy, human resources, national security, organizational management, security management; public health (MPH); reverse logistics management (MA); school counseling (M Ed); security management (MA); space studies (MS), including aerospace science, general (MA, MS), planetary science; sports and health sciences (MS); teaching (M Ed), including curriculum and instruction for elementary teachers, elementary reading, English language learners, instructional leadership, online learning, special education; transportation and logistics management (MA), including general (MA, MS), maritime engineering management, reverse logistics management. Programs offered via distance learning only. Part-time and evening/weekend programs available. Postbaccalaureate distance learning degree programs offered (no on-campus study). *Faculty:* 432 full-time (242 women), 1,722 part-time/adjunct (829 women). *Students:* 511 full-time (241 women), 10,947 part-time (4,294 women); includes 3,760 minority (2,058 Black or African American, non-Hispanic/Latino; 88 American Indian or Alaska Native, non-Hispanic/Latino; 293 Asian, non-Hispanic/Latino; 876 Hispanic/Latino; 91 Native Hawaiian or other Pacific Islander, non-Hispanic/Latino; 354 Two or more races, non-Hispanic/Latino; 134 international. Average age 36. In 2013, 3,323 master's awarded. *Degree requirements:* For master's, comprehensive exam or practicum. *Entrance requirements:* For master's, official transcript showing earned bachelor's degree from institution accredited by recognized accrediting body. Additional exam requirements/recommendations for international students: Required—TOEFL (minimum score 550 paper-based), IELTS (minimum score 6.5). *Application deadline:* Applications are processed on a rolling basis. Application fee: $0. Electronic applications accepted. *Expenses:* Tuition: Part-time $325 per semester hour. *Financial support:* Applicants required to submit FAFSA. *Faculty research:* Military history, criminal justice, management performance, national security. *Unit head:* Dr. Karan Powell, Executive Vice President and Provost, 877-468-6268, Fax: 304-724-3780. *Application contact:* Terry Grant, Vice President of Enrollment Management, 877-468-6268, Fax: 304-724-3780, E-mail: info@apus.edu.
Website: http://www.apus.edu.

American University, College of Arts and Sciences, Washington, DC 20016-8012. Offers addiction and addictive behavior (Certificate); anthropology (PhD); applied microeconomics (Certificate); applied statistics (Certificate); art history (MA); arts management (MA, Certificate); Asian studies (Certificate); audio production (Certificate); audio technology (MA); behavior, cognition, and neuroscience (PhD); bilingual education (MA, Certificate); biology (MA, MS); chemistry (MS); clinical psychology (PhD); computer science (MS, Certificate); creative writing (MFA); curriculum and instruction (M Ed, Certificate); economics (MA, PhD); environmental assessment (Certificate); environmental science (MS); ethics, peace, and global affairs (MA); gender analysis in economics (Certificate); health promotion management (MS); history (MA, PhD); international arts management (Certificate); international economic relations (Certificate); international economics (MA); international training and education (MA); literature (MA); mathematics (MA); North American studies (Certificate); nutrition education (MS, Certificate); philosophy (MA); professional science: biotechnology (MS); professional science: environmental assessment (MS); professional science: quantitative analysis (MS); psychobiology of healing (Certificate); psychology (MA); psychology: general (PhD); public anthropology (MA, Certificate); public sociology (Certificate); social research (Certificate); sociology (MA); Spanish: Latin American studies (MA); special education: learning disabilities (MA); statistics (MS); studio art (MFA); teaching (MAT); teaching English as a foreign language (MA); teaching: early childhood (Certificate); teaching: elementary (Certificate); teaching: ESOL (Certificate); teaching: secondary (Certificate); technology in arts management (Certificate); TESOL (MA); translation: French (Certificate); translation: Russian (Certificate); translation: Spanish (Certificate); women's, gender, and sexuality studies (Certificate). Part-time and evening/weekend programs available. Postbaccalaureate distance learning degree programs offered (no on-campus study). *Faculty:* 358 full-time (187 women), 254 part-time/adjunct (127 women). *Students:* 627 full-time (411 women), 416 part-time (300 women); includes 206 minority (91 Black or African American, non-Hispanic/Latino; 5 American Indian or Alaska Native, non-Hispanic/Latino; 32 Asian, non-Hispanic/Latino; 64 Hispanic/Latino; 1 Native Hawaiian or other Pacific Islander, non-Hispanic/Latino; 13 Two or more races, non-Hispanic/Latino), 124 international. Average age 29. 1,672 applicants, 52% accepted, 361 enrolled. In 2013, 382 master's, 38 doctorates, 33 other advanced degrees awarded. Terminal master's awarded for partial completion of doctoral program. *Degree requirements:* For master's, comprehensive exam (for some programs), thesis (for some programs); for doctorate, comprehensive exam (for some programs), thesis/dissertation. *Entrance requirements:* For master's, GRE, minimum GPA of 3.0 in last 60 credit hours, letter of recommendation, statement of purpose, resume, unofficial transcript; for doctorate, GRE, minimum GPA of 3.0 for all graduate work, letter of recommendation, statement of purpose, resume, unofficial transcript. Additional exam requirements/recommendations for international students: Required—TOEFL (minimum score 600 paper-based; 100 iBT), IELTS (minimum score 7). *Application deadline:* For fall admission, 2/1 for domestic students; for spring admission, 10/1 for domestic students. Applications are processed on a rolling basis. Application fee: $55. Electronic applications accepted. *Expenses:* Tuition: Full-time $25,920; part-time $1482 per credit hour. *Required fees:* $430. Tuition and fees vary according to course load and program. *Financial support:* Fellowships, research assistantships with full and partial tuition reimbursements, teaching assistantships with full and partial tuition reimbursements, career-related internships or fieldwork, Federal Work-Study, institutionally sponsored loans, scholarships/grants, traineeships, tuition waivers (full and partial), and unspecified assistantships available. Support available to part-time students. Financial award applicants required to submit FAFSA. *Unit head:* Dr. Peter Starr, Dean, 202-885-2446, Fax: 202-885-2429, E-mail: pstarr@american.edu. *Application contact:* Kathleen Clowery, Associate Director, Graduate Enrollment Management, 202-885-3621, Fax: 202-885-1505, E-mail: clowery@american.edu. Website: http://www.american.edu/cas/.

Andrews University, School of Graduate Studies, School of Education, Department of Teaching, Learning, and Curriculum, Berrien Springs, MI 49104. Offers curriculum and instruction (MA, Ed D, PhD, Ed S); elementary education (MAT); secondary education (MAT), including biology, education, English, English as a second language, French, history, physics; teacher education (MAT). *Faculty:* 7 full-time (4 women). *Students:* 16 full-time (11 women), 26 part-time (22 women); includes 14 minority (11 Black or African American, non-Hispanic/Latino; 1 Asian, non-Hispanic/Latino; 1 Hispanic/Latino; 1 Two or more races, non-Hispanic/Latino), 13 international. Average age 40. 33 applicants, 42% accepted, 3 enrolled. In 2013, 7 master's, 1 doctorate, 1 other advanced degree awarded. *Entrance requirements:* For master's, GRE Subject Test. Additional exam requirements/recommendations for international students: Required—TOEFL (minimum score 550 paper-based). *Application deadline:* For fall admission, 8/15 for domestic students. Applications are processed on a rolling basis. Application fee: $40. *Unit head:* Dr. Lee C. Davidson, Chair, 269-471-6364. *Application contact:* Monica Wringer, Supervisor of Graduate Admission, 800-253-2874, Fax: 269-471-6321, E-mail: graduate@andrews.edu.

Arcadia University, Graduate Studies, School of Education, Glenside, PA 19038-3295. Offers art education (M Ed); computer education (CAS); curriculum (CAS); curriculum

studies (M Ed); early childhood education (M Ed, CAS), including individualized (M Ed), master teacher (M Ed), research in child development (M Ed); educational leadership (M Ed, Ed D, CAS); elementary education (M Ed, CAS); English education (MA Ed); environmental education (MA Ed, CAS); history education (MA Ed); instructional technology (M Ed); language arts (M Ed, CAS); library science (M Ed); mathematics education (M Ed, MA Ed, CAS); music education (MA Ed); psychology (MA Ed); reading (M Ed, CAS); science education (M Ed, CAS); secondary education (M Ed, CAS); special education (M Ed, Ed D, CAS); theater arts (MA Ed); written communication (MA Ed). *Accreditation:* NASAD. Part-time and evening/weekend programs available. Postbaccalaureate distance learning degree programs offered (minimal on-campus study). Electronic applications accepted. *Expenses:* Contact institution.

Argosy University, Atlanta, College of Education, Atlanta, GA 30328. Offers educational leadership (MAEd, Ed D, Ed S), including higher education administration (Ed D), K-12 education (Ed D); teaching and learning (MAEd, Ed D, Ed S), including education technology (Ed D), higher education (Ed D), K-12 education (Ed D).

Argosy University, Chicago, College of Education, Chicago, IL 60601. Offers adult education and training (MA Ed); community college executive leadership (Ed D); educational leadership (MA Ed, Ed D, Ed S), including district leadership (Ed D), higher education administration (Ed D), K-12 education (Ed D); instructional leadership (Ed D, Ed S), including higher education (Ed D), K-12 education (Ed D). Postbaccalaureate distance learning degree programs offered (minimal on-campus study).

Argosy University, Hawai`i, College of Education, Honolulu, HI 96813. Offers adult education and training (MAEd); educational leadership (Ed D), including higher education administration, K-12 education; instructional leadership (Ed D), including higher education, K-12 education; school psychology (MA).

Argosy University, Inland Empire, College of Education, Ontario, CA 91761. Offers community college executive leadership (Ed D); educational leadership (MA Ed, Ed D), including higher education administration (Ed D), K-12 education (Ed D); instructional leadership (MA Ed, Ed D), including higher education (Ed D), K-12 education (Ed D), multiple subject teacher preparation (MA Ed), single subject teacher preparation (MA Ed).

Argosy University, Los Angeles, College of Education, Santa Monica, CA 90045. Offers community college executive leadership (Ed D); educational leadership (MA Ed, Ed D), including higher education administration (Ed D), K-12 education (Ed D); instructional leadership (MA Ed, Ed D), including higher education (Ed D), K-12 education (Ed D), multiple subject teacher preparation (MA Ed), single subject teacher preparation (MA Ed).

Argosy University, Nashville, College of Education, Program in Educational Leadership, Nashville, TN 37214. Offers educational leadership (MA Ed, Ed S); higher education administration (Ed D); K-12 education (Ed D).

Argosy University, Nashville, College of Education, Program in Instructional Leadership, Nashville, TN 37214. Offers education technology (Ed D); higher education administration (Ed D); instructional leadership (MA Ed, Ed S); K-12 education (Ed D).

Argosy University, Orange County, College of Education, Orange, CA 92868. Offers community college executive leadership (Ed D); educational leadership (MA Ed, Ed D), including higher education administration (Ed D), K-12 education (Ed D); instructional leadership (MA Ed, Ed D), including education technology (Ed D), higher education (Ed D), K-12 education (Ed D), multiple subject teacher preparation (MA Ed), single subject teacher preparation (MA Ed).

Argosy University, Phoenix, College of Education, Phoenix, AZ 85021. Offers adult education and training (MA Ed); advanced educational administration (Ed D, Ed S); community college executive leadership (Ed D); educational administration (MA Ed); educational leadership (MA Ed, Ed D, Ed S), including education technology (Ed D), higher education administration (Ed D), K-12 education (Ed D); higher and postsecondary education (MA Ed); initial educational administration (Ed D, Ed S); school psychology (MA); teaching and learning (MA Ed, Ed D, Ed S), including education technology (Ed D), higher education (Ed D), K-12 education (Ed D).

Argosy University, San Diego, College of Education, San Diego, CA 92108. Offers community college executive leadership (Ed D); educational leadership (MA Ed, Ed D), including higher education administration (Ed D), K-12 education (Ed D); instructional leadership (MA Ed, Ed D), including higher education (Ed D), K-12 education (Ed D).

Argosy University, San Francisco Bay Area, College of Education, Alameda, CA 94501. Offers community college executive leadership (Ed D); educational leadership (MA Ed, Ed D), including education technology (Ed D), higher education administration (Ed D), K-12 education (Ed D); instructional leadership (MA Ed, Ed D), including education technology (Ed D), higher education (Ed D), K-12 education (Ed D), multiple subject teacher preparation (MA Ed), single subject teacher preparation (MA Ed).

Argosy University, Sarasota, College of Education, Sarasota, FL 34235. Offers community college executive leadership (Ed D); educational leadership (MA Ed, Ed D, Ed S), including higher education administration (Ed D), K-12 education (Ed D); school counseling (MA, Ed S); school psychology (MA); teaching and learning (MA Ed, Ed D, Ed S), including education technology (Ed D), higher education (Ed D), K-12 education (Ed D).

Argosy University, Schaumburg, College of Education, Schaumburg, IL 60173-5403. Offers community college executive leadership (Ed D); educational leadership (MA Ed, Ed D, Ed S), including district leadership (Ed D), higher education administration (Ed D), K-12 education (Ed D); instructional leadership (Ed D, Ed S), including higher education (Ed D), K-12 education (Ed D).

Argosy University, Seattle, College of Education, Seattle, WA 98121. Offers adult education and training (MA Ed); community college executive leadership (Ed D); educational leadership (MA Ed, Ed D), including higher education administration (Ed D), K-12 education (Ed D); higher and postsecondary education (MA Ed); instructional leadership (MA Ed, Ed D), including education technology (Ed D), higher education (Ed D), K-12 education (Ed D).

Argosy University, Tampa, College of Education, Tampa, FL 33607. Offers community college executive leadership (Ed D); educational leadership (MA Ed, Ed D, Ed S), including higher education administration (Ed D), K-12 education (Ed D); school counseling (MA); teaching and learning (MA Ed, Ed D, Ed S), including higher education (Ed D), K-12 education (Ed D).

Argosy University, Twin Cities, College of Education, Eagan, MN 55121. Offers advanced educational administration (Ed D, Ed S); educational leadership (MA Ed, Ed D, Ed S), including higher education administration (Ed D), K-12 education (Ed D); higher and postsecondary education (MA Ed); initial educational administration (Ed D, Ed S); instructional leadership (MA Ed, Ed D, Ed S), including education technology (Ed D), higher education (Ed D), K-12 education (Ed D).

Argosy University, Washington DC, College of Education, Arlington, VA 22209. Offers community college executive leadership (Ed D); educational leadership (MA Ed, Ed D, Ed S), including higher education administration (Ed D), K-12 education (Ed D); instructional leadership (MA Ed, Ed D, Ed S), including higher education (Ed D), K-12 education (Ed D).

Arizona State University at the Tempe campus, Mary Lou Fulton Teachers College, Program in Curriculum and Instruction, Phoenix, AZ 85069. Offers curriculum and instruction (M Ed, MA, PhD); elementary education (M Ed); physical education (MPE); secondary education (M Ed). Part-time and evening/weekend programs available. Postbaccalaureate distance learning degree programs offered (minimal on-campus study). Terminal master's awarded for partial completion of doctoral program. *Degree requirements:* For master's, thesis or alternative, applied project, interactive Program of Study (iPOS) submitted before completing 50 percent of required credit hours; for doctorate, comprehensive exam, thesis/dissertation, interactive Program of Study (iPOS) submitted before completing 50 percent of required credit hours. *Entrance requirements:* For master's, GRE or GMAT (for some programs), minimum GPA of 3.0 or equivalent in last 2 years of work leading to bachelor's degree, 3 letters of recommendation, personal statement describing research and career goals, curriculum vitae or resume, IVP fingerprint clearance card (for those seeking Arizona certification); for doctorate, GRE or GMAT (depending on program), minimum GPA of 3.0 or equivalent in last 2 years of work leading to bachelor's degree, 3 letters of recommendation, personal statement describing research and career goals, curriculum vitae or resume. Additional exam requirements/recommendations for international students: Required—TOEFL, IELTS, or PTE. Electronic applications accepted. *Expenses:* Contact institution. *Faculty research:* Early childhood, media and computers, elementary education, secondary education, English education, bilingual education, language and literacy, science education, engineering education, exercise and wellness education.

Armstrong State University, School of Graduate Studies, Department of Adolescent and Adult Education, Savannah, GA 31419-1997. Offers adolescent and adult education (Certificate); adult education and community leadership (M Ed); curriculum and instruction (M Ed); secondary education (MAT). Part-time and evening/weekend programs available. Postbaccalaureate distance learning degree programs offered (minimal on-campus study). *Faculty:* 10 full-time (8 women), 2 part-time/adjunct (1 woman). *Students:* 35 full-time (29 women), 80 part-time (57 women); includes 34 minority (31 Black or African American, non-Hispanic/Latino; 1 Asian, non-Hispanic/Latino; 2 Hispanic/Latino). Average age 34. 61 applicants, 79% accepted, 43 enrolled. In 2013, 59 master's awarded. *Degree requirements:* For master's, comprehensive exam (for some programs), thesis (for some programs). *Entrance requirements:* For master's, GRE, MAT, minimum GPA of 2.5 and disposition statement (for MAT), 3.0 and clear certification (for M Ed). Additional exam requirements/recommendations for international students: Required—TOEFL (minimum score 523 paper-based). *Application deadline:* For fall admission, 6/30 priority date for domestic students, 5/1 priority date for international students; for spring admission, 11/15 priority date for domestic students, 9/15 priority date for international students; for summer admission, 4/15 priority date for domestic students, 9/15 for international students. Applications are processed on a rolling basis. Application fee: $30. Electronic applications accepted. *Expenses:* Tuition, state resident: part-time $201 per credit hour. Tuition, nonresident: part-time $745 per credit hour. *Required fees:* $310 per semester. Tuition and fees vary according to course load, campus/location and program. *Financial support:* In 2013–14, research assistantships with full tuition reimbursements (averaging $5,000 per year) were awarded; career-related internships or fieldwork, Federal Work-Study, scholarships/grants, and unspecified assistantships also available. Support available to part-time students. Financial award application deadline: 3/15; financial award applicants required to submit FAFSA. *Faculty research:* Women's issues, education pedagogy, reading, heat of body metabolism, geographic education. *Unit head:* Dr. Patrick Thomas, Interim Department Head, 912-344-2562, Fax: 912-344-3496, E-mail: patrick.thomas@armstrong.edu. *Application contact:* Jill Bell, Director, Graduate Enrollment Services, 912-344-2798, Fax: 912-344-3488, E-mail: graduate@armstrong.edu.
Website: http://www.armstrong.edu/Education/adolescent_adult_education2/aaed_welcome.

Auburn University, Graduate School, College of Education, Department of Curriculum and Teaching, Auburn University, AL 36849. Offers business education (M Ed, MS, PhD); early childhood education (M Ed, MS, PhD, Ed S); elementary education (M Ed, MS, PhD, Ed S); foreign languages (M Ed, MS); music education (M Ed, MS, PhD, Ed S); postsecondary education (PhD); reading education (PhD, Ed S); secondary education (M Ed, MS, PhD, Ed S), including English language arts, mathematics, science, social studies. *Accreditation:* NASM (one or more programs are accredited); NCATE. Part-time programs available. *Faculty:* 29 full-time (21 women), 4 part-time/adjunct (all women). *Students:* 61 full-time (40 women), 153 part-time (108 women); includes 37 minority (32 Black or African American, non-Hispanic/Latino; 2 Asian, non-Hispanic/Latino; 3 Hispanic/Latino), 1 international. Average age 34. 150 applicants, 59% accepted, 74 enrolled. In 2013, 70 master's, 6 doctorates, 26 other advanced degrees awarded. *Degree requirements:* For master's, thesis (for some programs); for doctorate, thesis/dissertation; for Ed S, field project. *Entrance requirements:* For master's, doctorate, and Ed S, GRE General Test. *Application deadline:* For fall admission, 7/7 for domestic students; for spring admission, 11/24 for domestic students. Applications are processed on a rolling basis. Application fee: $50 ($60 for international students). Electronic applications accepted. *Expenses:* Tuition, state resident: full-time $8262; part-time $459 per credit hour. Tuition, nonresident: full-time $24,786; part-time $1377 per credit hour. Tuition and fees vary according to degree level and program. *Financial support:* Fellowships, teaching assistantships, career-related internships or fieldwork, and Federal Work-Study available. Support available to part-time students. Financial award application deadline: 3/15; financial award applicants required to submit FAFSA. *Faculty research:* Emerging literacy, reading attitudes, music for at-risk youth, portfolio assessment. *Unit head:* Dr. Kimberly Walls, Head, 334-844-4434. *Application contact:* Dr. George Flowers, Dean of the Graduate School, 334-844-2125.
Website: http://education.auburn.edu/academic_departments/curr/.

Auburn University at Montgomery, School of Education, Department of Foundations, Technology, and Secondary Education, Montgomery, AL 36124-4023. Offers instructional technology (M Ed); secondary education (M Ed, Ed S), including art education (M Ed), biology (M Ed), English language arts (M Ed), general science (M Ed), history (M Ed), mathematics (M Ed), social science (M Ed). *Accreditation:* NCATE. Part-time and evening/weekend programs available. *Faculty:* 6 full-time (2 women), 1 (woman) part-time/adjunct. *Students:* 47 full-time (22 women), 77 part-time (48 women); includes 30 minority (29 Black or African American, non-Hispanic/Latino; 1 Asian, non-Hispanic/Latino), 1 international. Average age 30. In 2013, 86 master's awarded. *Degree requirements:* For master's and Ed S, comprehensive exam, thesis optional. *Entrance requirements:* For master's, GRE General Test or MAT, certification, BS in teaching; for Ed S, GRE General Test or MAT, certification. *Application deadline:* Applications are processed on a rolling basis. Electronic applications accepted. *Expenses:* Tuition, state resident: full-time $5994; part-time $333 per credit hour. Tuition, nonresident: full-time $17,982; part-time $999 per credit hour. *Financial support:* Teaching assistantships, career-related internships or fieldwork, and scholarships/grants available. Support available to part-time students. Financial award application deadline: 3/1; financial award applicants required to submit FAFSA. *Unit head:* Dr. Sheila Austin, Dean, 334-244-3425, Fax: 334-244-3102, E-mail: saustin1@aum.edu.

Application contact: Dr. Rhonda Morton, Associate Dean/Graduate Coordinator, 334-244-3287, Fax: 334-244-3978, E-mail: rmorton@aum.edu.
Website: http://www.education.aum.edu/departments/foundations-technology-and-secondary-education.

Austin Peay State University, College of Graduate Studies, College of Education, Department of Educational Specialties, Clarksville, TN 37044. Offers administration and supervision (Ed S); curriculum and instruction (MA Ed); education leadership (MA Ed); elementary education (Ed S); secondary education (Ed S); special education (MA Ed). Part-time and evening/weekend programs available. Postbaccalaureate distance learning degree programs offered. *Faculty:* 8 full-time (5 women), 4 part-time/adjunct (3 women). *Students:* 6 full-time (5 women), 87 part-time (73 women); includes 10 minority (5 Black or African American, non-Hispanic/Latino; 1 American Indian or Alaska Native, non-Hispanic/Latino; 1 Asian, non-Hispanic/Latino; 1 Hispanic/Latino; 2 Two or more races, non-Hispanic/Latino). Average age 35. 11 applicants, 82% accepted, 6 enrolled. In 2013, 37 master's, 6 Ed Ss awarded. *Degree requirements:* For master's, comprehensive exam, thesis optional. *Entrance requirements:* For master's, GRE General Test, 3 letters of recommendation, minimum undergraduate GPA of 2.75. Additional exam requirements/recommendations for international students: Required—TOEFL (minimum score 500 paper-based). *Application deadline:* For fall admission, 8/5 priority date for domestic students. Applications are processed on a rolling basis. Application fee: $25. Electronic applications accepted. *Expenses:* Tuition, state resident: full-time $7500; part-time $375 per credit hour. Tuition, nonresident: full-time $20,800; part-time $1040 per credit hour. *Required fees:* $1284; $64.20 per credit hour. *Financial support:* Career-related internships or fieldwork, Federal Work-Study, institutionally sponsored loans, scholarships/grants, and unspecified assistantships available. Support available to part-time students. Financial award application deadline: 3/1; financial award applicants required to submit FAFSA. *Unit head:* Dr. Moniqueka Gold, Chair, 931-221-7696, Fax: 931-221-1292, E-mail: goldm@apsu.edu. *Application contact:* June D. Lee, Graduate Coordinator, 800-859-4723, Fax: 931-221-7641, E-mail: gradadmissions@apsu.edu.

Austin Peay State University, College of Graduate Studies, College of Education, Department of Teaching and Learning, Clarksville, TN 37044. Offers elementary education K-6 (MAT); reading (MA Ed); secondary education 7-12 (MAT); special education K-12 (MAT). Part-time and evening/weekend programs available. Postbaccalaureate distance learning degree programs offered. *Faculty:* 7 full-time (4 women), 5 part-time/adjunct (all women). *Students:* 70 full-time (59 women), 77 part-time (55 women); includes 23 minority (10 Black or African American, non-Hispanic/Latino; 2 Asian, non-Hispanic/Latino; 5 Hispanic/Latino; 6 Two or more races, non-Hispanic/Latino). Average age 33. 50 applicants, 90% accepted, 37 enrolled. In 2013, 60 master's awarded. *Degree requirements:* For master's, comprehensive exam, thesis optional. *Entrance requirements:* For master's, GRE General Test, 3 letters of recommendation, minimum undergraduate GPA of 2.75. Additional exam requirements/recommendations for international students: Required—TOEFL (minimum score 500 paper-based). *Application deadline:* For fall admission, 8/5 priority date for domestic students. Applications are processed on a rolling basis. Application fee: $25. Electronic applications accepted. *Expenses:* Tuition, state resident: full-time $7500; part-time $375 per credit hour. Tuition, nonresident: full-time $20,800; part-time $1040 per credit hour. *Required fees:* $1284; $64.20 per credit hour. *Financial support:* Career-related internships or fieldwork, Federal Work-Study, institutionally sponsored loans, scholarships/grants, and unspecified assistantships available. Support available to part-time students. Financial award application deadline: 3/1; financial award applicants required to submit FAFSA. *Unit head:* Dr. Rebecca McMahan, Chair, 931-221-7513, Fax: 931-221-1292, E-mail: mcmahanb@apsu.edu. *Application contact:* June D. Lee, Graduate Coordinator, 800-859-4723, Fax: 931-221-7641, E-mail: gradadmissions@apsu.edu.

Ball State University, Graduate School, Teachers College, Department of Educational Studies, Program in Secondary Education, Muncie, IN 47306-1099. Offers MA. *Accreditation:* NCATE. *Students:* 8 full-time (5 women), 17 part-time (11 women); includes 2 minority (1 Black or African American, non-Hispanic/Latino; 1 Asian, non-Hispanic/Latino), 1 international. Average age 30. 21 applicants, 57% accepted, 7 enrolled. In 2013, 29 master's awarded. Application fee: $50. *Financial support:* In 2013–14, 3 students received support. Application deadline: 3/1. *Unit head:* Dr. Jayne Beilke, Head, 785-285-5460, Fax: 785-285-5489, E-mail: jbeilke@bsu.edu. *Application contact:* Dr. Robert Morris, Associate Provost for Research and Dean of the Graduate School, 765-285-1300, E-mail: rmorris@bsu.edu.

Belhaven University, School of Education, Jackson, MS 39202-1789. Offers educational technology (M Ed); elementary education (M Ed, MAT); reading literacy (M Ed); secondary education (M Ed, MAT). Part-time and evening/weekend programs available. Postbaccalaureate distance learning degree programs offered (no on-campus study). *Faculty:* 7 full-time (6 women), 15 part-time/adjunct (10 women). *Students:* 1 full-time (0 women), 406 part-time (311 women); includes 254 minority (250 Black or African American, non-Hispanic/Latino; 2 Hispanic/Latino; 2 Two or more races, non-Hispanic/Latino). Average age 36. 273 applicants, 67% accepted, 162 enrolled. In 2013, 24 master's awarded. *Degree requirements:* For master's, comprehensive exam, portfolio. *Entrance requirements:* For master's, PRAXIS I and II, minimum GPA of 2.8. *Application deadline:* Applications are processed on a rolling basis. Application fee: $25. Electronic applications accepted. *Financial support:* Federal Work-Study, scholarships/grants, tuition waivers (full), and unspecified assistantships available. Support available to part-time students. Financial award applicants required to submit FAFSA. *Unit head:* Dr. David Hand, Dean, 601-965-7020, E-mail: dhand@belhaven.edu. *Application contact:* Amanda Slaughter, Assistant Vice President for Adult and Graduate Enrollment and Student Services, 601-968-8727, Fax: 601-968-5953, E-mail: gradadmission@belhaven.edu.
Website: http://graduateed.belhaven.edu.

Bellarmine University, Annsley Frazier Thornton School of Education, Louisville, KY 40205-0671. Offers education and social change (PhD); elementary education (MA Ed, MAT); learning and behavior disorders (MA Ed, MAT); middle grades education (MA Ed, MAT); principalship (Ed S); reading and writing (MA Ed); secondary education (MAT); teacher leadership (MA Ed). *Accreditation:* NCATE. Part-time and evening/weekend programs available. *Faculty:* 13 full-time (7 women), 14 part-time/adjunct (9 women). *Students:* 60 full-time (47 women), 191 part-time (140 women); includes 35 minority (22 Black or African American, non-Hispanic/Latino; 1 American Indian or Alaska Native, non-Hispanic/Latino; 3 Asian, non-Hispanic/Latino; 5 Hispanic/Latino; 4 Two or more races, non-Hispanic/Latino). Average age 33. In 2013, 108 master's awarded. *Degree requirements:* For master's, comprehensive exam, thesis (for some programs); for doctorate, comprehensive exam, thesis/dissertation. *Entrance requirements:* For master's, GRE, baccalaureate degree from accredited institution; minimum overall GPA of 2.75, 3.0 in major; letters of recommendation; valid Kentucky provisional or professional certificate; for doctorate, GRE, minimum GPA of 3.5 in all graduate coursework; baccalaureate and master's degrees in education (MA, MS) or fields directly relevant to education; three letters of recommendation; two essays (no more than 1000 words each); interview. Additional exam requirements/recommendations for international students: Required—TOEFL (minimum score 550 paper-based; 80 iBT). *Application deadline:* Applications are processed on a rolling basis. Application fee: $25. *Expenses:* Contact institution. *Financial support:* Scholarships/grants available. Financial award applicants required to submit FAFSA. *Faculty research:* Literacy, service-learning, dispositions, educational technology, special education. *Unit head:* Dr. Robert Cooter, Dean, 502-272-8191, Fax: 502-272-8189, E-mail: rcooter@bellarmine.edu. *Application contact:* Theresa Klapheke, Administrative Director of Graduate Programs, 502-272-8271, Fax: 502-272-8002, E-mail: tklapheke@bellarmine.edu.
Website: http://www.bellarmine.edu/education/graduate.

Benedictine University, Graduate Programs, Program in Education, Lisle, IL 60532-0900. Offers curriculum and instruction and collaborative teaching (M Ed); elementary education (MA Ed); leadership and administration (M Ed); reading and literacy (M Ed); secondary education (MA Ed); special education (MA Ed). Part-time and evening/weekend programs available. *Students:* 6 full-time (all women), 124 part-time (106 women); includes 14 minority (8 Black or African American, non-Hispanic/Latino; 1 American Indian or Alaska Native, non-Hispanic/Latino; 2 Asian, non-Hispanic/Latino; 3 Hispanic/Latino). 21 applicants, 62% accepted, 8 enrolled. In 2013, 120 master's awarded. *Degree requirements:* For master's, comprehensive exam, thesis (for some programs). *Entrance requirements:* For master's, GRE or MAT. Additional exam requirements/recommendations for international students: Required—TOEFL (minimum score 550 paper-based). *Application deadline:* For fall admission, 9/1 for domestic students; for winter admission, 12/1 for domestic students; for spring admission, 2/15 for domestic students. Applications are processed on a rolling basis. Application fee: $40. Electronic applications accepted. *Expenses:* Contact institution. *Financial support:* Career-related internships or fieldwork and health care benefits available. Support available to part-time students. *Unit head:* MeShelda Jackson, Director, 630-829-6282, E-mail: mjackson@ben.edu. *Application contact:* Kari Gibbons, Associate Vice President, Enrollment Center, 630-829-6200, Fax: 630-829-6584, E-mail: kgibbons@ben.edu.

Berry College, Graduate Programs, Graduate Programs in Education, Program in Secondary Education, Mount Berry, GA 30149-0159. Offers M Ed, MAT. *Faculty:* 8 part-time/adjunct (4 women). *Students:* 1 (woman) full-time, 9 part-time (6 women). Average age 31. In 2013, 9 master's awarded. *Degree requirements:* For master's, thesis, portfolio, oral exams. *Entrance requirements:* For master's, GRE General Test or MAT, minimum GPA of 2.5. Additional exam requirements/recommendations for international students: Required—TOEFL (minimum score 550 paper-based). *Application deadline:* For fall admission, 7/25 for domestic students, 5/1 for international students; for spring admission, 12/1 for domestic students, 10/1 for international students. Applications are processed on a rolling basis. Application fee: $25 ($30 for international students). Electronic applications accepted. *Expenses:* Contact institution. *Financial support:* In 2013–14, 5 students received support, including 3 research assistantships with full tuition reimbursements available (averaging $4,889 per year); scholarships/grants, tuition waivers (partial), and unspecified assistantships also available. Support available to part-time students. Financial award application deadline: 3/1; financial award applicants required to submit FAFSA. *Unit head:* Dr. Jacqueline McDowell, Dean, Charter School of Education and Human Sciences, 706-236-1717, Fax: 706-238-5827, E-mail: jmcdowell@berry.edu. *Application contact:* Brett Kennedy, Assistant Vice President of Enrollment Management, 706-236-2215, Fax: 706-290-2178, E-mail: admissions@berry.edu.
Website: http://www.berry.edu/academics/education/graduate/.

Bethel University, Graduate School, St. Paul, MN 55112-6999. Offers autism spectrum disorders (Certificate); business administration (MBA); communication (MA); counseling psychology (MA); educational leadership (Ed D); gerontology (MA); international baccalaureate education (Certificate); K-12 education (MA); literacy education (MA, Certificate); nurse educator (Certificate); nurse leader (Certificate); nurse-midwifery (MS); nursing (MS); physician assistant (MS); postsecondary teaching (Certificate); special education (MA); strategic leadership (MA); teaching (MA). Part-time and evening/weekend programs available. Postbaccalaureate distance learning degree programs offered (no on-campus study). *Faculty:* 13 full-time (7 women), 89 part-time/adjunct (43 women). *Students:* 692 full-time (457 women), 573 part-time (371 women); includes 170 minority (86 Black or African American, non-Hispanic/Latino; 1 American Indian or Alaska Native, non-Hispanic/Latino; 49 Asian, non-Hispanic/Latino; 20 Hispanic/Latino; 1 Native Hawaiian or other Pacific Islander, non-Hispanic/Latino; 13 Two or more races, non-Hispanic/Latino), 21 international. Average age 37. In 2013, 166 master's, 9 doctorates, 11 other advanced degrees awarded. *Degree requirements:* For master's, comprehensive exam (for some programs), thesis (for some programs); for doctorate, comprehensive exam, thesis/dissertation. *Entrance requirements:* Additional exam requirements/recommendations for international students: Required—TOEFL (minimum score 550 paper-based; 80 iBT). *Application deadline:* Applications are processed on a rolling basis. Electronic applications accepted. Tuition and fees vary according to course load, degree level and program. *Financial support:* Teaching assistantships, career-related internships or fieldwork, and scholarships/grants available. Support available to part-time students. Financial award applicants required to submit FAFSA. *Unit head:* Dick Crombie, Vice-President/Dean, 651-635-8000, Fax: 651-635-8004, E-mail: gs@bethel.edu. *Application contact:* Director of Admissions, 651-635-8000, Fax: 651-635-8004, E-mail: gs@bethel.edu.
Website: http://gs.bethel.edu/.

Binghamton University, State University of New York, Graduate School, School of Education, Program in Adolescence Education, Vestal, NY 13850. Offers biology education (MAT, MS Ed); chemistry education (MAT, MS Ed); earth science education (MAT, MS Ed); English education (MAT, MS Ed); French education (MAT, MS Ed); literacy education (MS Ed); mathematical sciences education (MAT, MS Ed); physics (MAT, MS Ed); social studies (MAT, MS Ed); Spanish education (MAT, MS Ed). *Accreditation:* Teacher Education Accreditation Council. Part-time and evening/weekend programs available. *Students:* 48 full-time (29 women), 5 part-time (3 women); includes 7 minority (2 Black or African American, non-Hispanic/Latino; 3 Asian, non-Hispanic/Latino; 2 Hispanic/Latino), 1 international. Average age 26. 37 applicants, 86% accepted, 21 enrolled. In 2013, 34 master's awarded. *Entrance requirements:* For master's, GRE General Test. Additional exam requirements/recommendations for international students: Required—TOEFL (minimum score 550 paper-based; 80 iBT). *Application deadline:* For fall admission, 2/1 priority date for domestic and international students; for spring admission, 10/15 priority date for domestic and international students. Applications are processed on a rolling basis. Application fee: $75. Electronic applications accepted. *Financial support:* In 2013–14, 7 students received support, including 1 fellowship with partial tuition reimbursement available (averaging $4,500 per year); career-related internships or fieldwork, Federal Work-Study, institutionally sponsored loans, scholarships/grants, health care benefits, tuition waivers (full), and unspecified assistantships also available. Financial award application deadline: 2/15; financial award applicants required to submit FAFSA. *Unit head:* Dr. S. G. Grant, Dean of School of Education, 607-777-7329, E-mail: sggrant@binghamton.edu. *Application contact:* Kishan Zuber, Recruiting and Admissions Coordinator, 607-777-2151, Fax: 607-777-2501, E-mail: kzuber@binghamton.edu.

Secondary Education

Bloomsburg University of Pennsylvania, School of Graduate Studies, College of Education, Department of Educational Studies and Secondary Education, Program in School Counseling and Student Affairs, Bloomsburg, PA 17815-1301. Offers college student affairs (M Ed); elementary school (M Ed); secondary school (M Ed). *Faculty:* 5 full-time (3 women), 5 part-time/adjunct (2 women). *Students:* 8 full-time (6 women), 59 part-time (40 women); includes 16 minority (10 Black or African American, non-Hispanic/Latino; 4 Hispanic/Latino; 2 Two or more races, non-Hispanic/Latino), 1 international. Average age 25. 48 applicants, 79% accepted, 30 enrolled. *Degree requirements:* For master's, practicum. *Entrance requirements:* For master's, 3 letters of recommendation, resume, minimum QPA of 3.0, personal statement, interview. Additional exam requirements/recommendations for international students: Required—TOEFL. Application fee: $35 ($60 for international students). Electronic applications accepted. *Expenses:* Tuition, state resident: full-time $7956; part-time $442 per credit. Tuition, nonresident: full-time $11,934; part-time $663 per credit. *Required fees:* $95.50 per credit. $55 per semester. Tuition and fees vary according to course load. *Unit head:* Dr. Tegan Kotarski, College of Education Graduate Coordinator, 570-389-3883, Fax: 570-389-5049, E-mail: tkotarsk@bloomu.edu. *Application contact:* Jennifer Richard, Administrative Assistant, 570-389-4015, Fax: 570-389-3054, E-mail: jrichard@bloomu.edu.
Website: http://www.bloomu.edu/gradschool/counseling-student-affairs.

Bob Jones University, Graduate Programs, Greenville, SC 29614. Offers accountancy (MS); Bible (MA); Bible translation (MA); Biblical studies (Certificate); broadcast management (MS); business administration (MBA); church history (MA, PhD); church ministries (MA); church music (MM); cinema and video production (MA); counseling (MS); curriculum and instruction (Ed D); divinity (M Div); dramatic production (MA); educational leadership (MS, Ed D, Ed S); elementary education (M Ed, MAT); English (M Ed, MA, MAT); fine arts (MA); graphic design (MA); history (M Ed, MA); illustration (MA); interpretative speech (MA); mathematics (M Ed, MAT); medical missions (Certificate); ministry (MM, D Min); multi-categorical special education (M Ed, MAT); music (M Ed); New Testament interpretation (PhD); Old Testament interpretation (PhD); orchestral instrument performance (MM); organ performance (MM); pastoral studies (MA); personnel services (MS, Ed S); piano pedagogy (MM); piano performance (MM); platform arts (MA); radio and television broadcasting (MS); rhetoric and public address (MA); secondary education (M Ed); studio art (MA); teaching Bible (MA); theology (MA, PhD); voice performance (MM); youth ministries (MA); M Div/MM.

Boston College, Lynch Graduate School of Education, Program in Secondary Education, Chestnut Hill, MA 02467-3800. Offers M Ed, MAT, MST. *Accreditation:* Teacher Education Accreditation Council. Part-time and evening/weekend programs available. *Students:* 31 full-time (20 women), 5 part-time (all women). 151 applicants, 67% accepted, 36 enrolled. In 2013, 36 master's awarded. *Degree requirements:* For master's, comprehensive exam. *Entrance requirements:* For master's, GRE General Test or MAT. Additional exam requirements/recommendations for international students: Required—TOEFL (minimum score 100 iBT). *Application deadline:* For fall admission, 12/1 priority date for domestic students, 12/1 for international students; for spring admission, 11/1 for domestic and international students. Application fee: $65. Electronic applications accepted. *Financial support:* Fellowships with full and partial tuition reimbursements, research assistantships with full and partial tuition reimbursements, teaching assistantships with full and partial tuition reimbursements, career-related internships or fieldwork, Federal Work-Study, institutionally sponsored loans, scholarships/grants, traineeships, health care benefits, tuition waivers (full and partial), and unspecified assistantships available. Support available to part-time students. Financial award applicants required to submit FAFSA. *Faculty research:* School reform, urban science education, teacher research, critical literacy, poverty and achievement. *Unit head:* Dr. Alec Peck, Chairperson, 617-552-4214, Fax: 617-552-0398. *Application contact:* Domenic Lomanno, Director, Graduate Admission and Financial Aid, 617-552-4214, Fax: 617-552-0398, E-mail: lomanno@bc.edu.

Bowie State University, Graduate Programs, Program in Secondary Education, Bowie, MD 20715-9465. Offers M Ed. *Accreditation:* NCATE. Part-time and evening/weekend programs available. *Degree requirements:* For master's, comprehensive exam, thesis optional, research paper. *Entrance requirements:* For master's, minimum undergraduate GPA of 3.0, bachelor's degree in education, teaching certificate, teaching experience. Electronic applications accepted. *Expenses:* Tuition, state resident: full-time $8665. Tuition, nonresident: full-time $16,007. *Required fees:* $1927.

Brandeis University, Graduate School of Arts and Sciences, Teaching Program, Waltham, MA 02454-9110. Offers Jewish day school (MAT); public elementary education (MAT); secondary education (MAT), including Bible, biology, chemistry, Chinese, English, history, math, physics. *Degree requirements:* For master's, internship; research project. *Entrance requirements:* For master's, GRE General Test or MAT, official transcript(s), 3 letters of recommendation, resume, statement of purpose. Additional exam requirements/recommendations for international students: Required—TOEFL (minimum score 600 paper-based; 100 iBT), PTE (minimum score 68); Recommended—IELTS (minimum score 7). Electronic applications accepted. *Expenses:* Contact institution. *Faculty research:* Teacher education, education, teaching, elementary education, secondary education, Jewish education, English, history, biology, chemistry, physics, math, Chinese, Bible/Tanakh.

Brenau University, Sydney O. Smith Graduate School, School of Education, Gainesville, GA 30501. Offers early childhood (Ed S); early childhood education (M Ed, MAT); middle grades (Ed S); middle grades education (M Ed, MAT); secondary education (MAT); special education (M Ed, MAT). *Accreditation:* NCATE. Part-time and evening/weekend programs available. Postbaccalaureate distance learning degree programs offered (no on-campus study). *Degree requirements:* For master's, thesis optional, comprehensive exam or applied research project, effective portfolio; for Ed S, thesis, applied research project. *Entrance requirements:* For master's, GRE, MAT, interview, minimum GPA of 3.0, 3 references, writing samples; for Ed S, GRE, MAT, master's degree, minimum GPA of 3.0, writing sample, letters of reference. Additional exam requirements/recommendations for international students: Required—TOEFL (minimum score 500 paper-based; 61 iBT); Recommended—IELTS (minimum score 5). Electronic applications accepted. *Expenses:* Contact institution.

Bridgewater State University, School of Graduate Studies, School of Education and Allied Studies, Department of Secondary Education and Professional Programs, Program in Secondary Education, Bridgewater, MA 02325-0001. Offers MAT. *Accreditation:* NCATE. Part-time and evening/weekend programs available. *Entrance requirements:* For master's, GRE General Test.

Brooklyn College of the City University of New York, Division of Graduate Studies, School of Education, Program in Adolescence Education and Special Subjects, Brooklyn, NY 11210-2889. Offers adolescence science education (MAT); art teacher (MA); biology teacher (MA); chemistry teacher (MA); earth science teacher (MAT); English teacher (MA); French teacher (MA); health and nutrition sciences: health teacher (MS Ed); mathematics teacher (MA); music education (CAS); music teacher (MA); physical education teacher (MS Ed); physics teacher (MA); social studies teacher (MA); Spanish teacher (MA). Part-time and evening/weekend programs available. *Degree requirements:* For master's, comprehensive exam (for some programs), thesis (for some programs). *Entrance requirements:* For master's, LAST, previous course work

in education, resume, 2 letters of recommendation, essay. Additional exam requirements/recommendations for international students: Required—TOEFL (minimum score 500 paper-based; 61 iBT). Electronic applications accepted. *Faculty research:* Interdisciplinary education, semiotics, discourse analysis, autobiography, teacher identity.

Brown University, Graduate School, Department of Education, Program in Teaching, Providence, RI 02912. Offers elementary education (MAT); English (MAT); history/social studies (MAT); science (MAT); secondary education (MAT). *Degree requirements:* For master's, student teaching, portfolio. *Entrance requirements:* For master's, GRE General Test, transcript, personal statement, 3 letters of recommendation, interview, writing sample (English applicants only). Additional exam requirements/recommendations for international students: Required—TOEFL (minimum score 577 paper-based). Electronic applications accepted. *Faculty research:* Literacy, English language learners, diversity, special education, biodiversity.

California State University, Bakersfield, Division of Graduate Studies, School of Natural Sciences, Mathematics, and Engineering, Program in Teaching Mathematics, Bakersfield, CA 93311. Offers MA. *Entrance requirements:* For master's, minimum GPA of 2.5 for last 90 quarter units. *Unit head:* Dr. Joseph Fiedler, Head, 661-654-2058, Fax: 661-664-2039. *Application contact:* Debbie Blowers, Assistant Director of Admissions, 661-664-3381, E-mail: dblowers@csub.edu.

California State University, Fullerton, Graduate Studies, College of Education, Department of Secondary Education, Fullerton, CA 92834-9480. Offers secondary education (MS); teaching foundational mathematics (MS). Part-time programs available. *Students:* 5 full-time (3 women), 42 part-time (26 women); includes 29 minority (2 Black or African American, non-Hispanic/Latino; 9 Asian, non-Hispanic/Latino; 18 Hispanic/Latino). Average age 32. 28 applicants, 71% accepted, 18 enrolled. In 2013, 20 master's awarded. Application fee: $55. *Financial support:* Career-related internships or fieldwork, Federal Work-Study, institutionally sponsored loans, and scholarships/grants available. Support available to part-time students. Financial award application deadline: 3/1; financial award applicants required to submit FAFSA. *Unit head:* Dr. Grace Cho, Chair, 657-278-3283, E-mail: gcho@fullerton.edu. *Application contact:* Admissions/Applications, 657-278-2371.

California State University, Long Beach, Graduate Studies, College of Education, Department of Teacher Education, Long Beach, CA 90840. Offers elementary education (MA); secondary education (MA). Part-time and evening/weekend programs available. *Degree requirements:* For master's, comprehensive exam or thesis. *Entrance requirements:* For master's, GRE General Test, minimum GPA of 2.75. Electronic applications accepted. *Faculty research:* Teacher stress and burnout, new teacher induction.

California State University, Long Beach, Graduate Studies, College of Natural Sciences and Mathematics, Department of Mathematics and Statistics, Long Beach, CA 90840. Offers mathematics (MS), including applied mathematics, applied statistics, mathematics education for secondary school teachers. Part-time programs available. *Degree requirements:* For master's, comprehensive exam or thesis. Electronic applications accepted. *Faculty research:* Algebra, functional analysis, partial differential equations, operator theory, numerical analysis.

California State University, Los Angeles, Graduate Studies, Charter College of Education, Division of Curriculum and Instruction, Los Angeles, CA 90032-8530. Offers elementary teaching (MA); reading (MA); secondary teaching (MA). Part-time and evening/weekend programs available. *Faculty:* 4 full-time (2 women), 12 part-time/adjunct (8 women). *Students:* 144 full-time (104 women), 119 part-time (91 women); includes 188 minority (13 Black or African American, non-Hispanic/Latino; 39 Asian, non-Hispanic/Latino; 130 Hispanic/Latino; 6 Two or more races, non-Hispanic/Latino), 12 international. Average age 33. 78 applicants, 73% accepted, 41 enrolled. In 2013, 87 master's awarded. *Entrance requirements:* For master's, minimum GPA of 2.75 in last 90 units of course work, teaching certificate. Additional exam requirements/recommendations for international students: Required—TOEFL (minimum score 500 paper-based). *Application deadline:* For fall admission, 5/1 for domestic and international students. Applications are processed on a rolling basis. Application fee: $55. Electronic applications accepted. *Financial support:* Federal Work-Study available. Support available to part-time students. Financial award application deadline: 3/1. *Faculty research:* Media, language arts, mathematics, computers, drug-free schools. *Unit head:* Dr. Gay Yuen, Acting Chair, 323-343-4350, Fax: 323-343-5458, E-mail: gyuen@calstatela.edu. *Application contact:* Dr. Larry Fritz, Dean of Graduate Studies, 323-343-3827, Fax: 323-343-5653, E-mail: lfritz@calstatela.edu.
Website: http://www.calstatela.edu/academic/ccoe/index_edci.htm.

California State University, Northridge, Graduate Studies, College of Education, Department of Secondary Education, Northridge, CA 91330. Offers educational technology (MA); English education (MA); mathematics education (MA); secondary science education (MA); teaching and learning (MA). *Accreditation:* NCATE. Part-time programs available. *Degree requirements:* For master's, thesis optional. *Entrance requirements:* For master's, GRE General Test or minimum GPA of 3.0. Additional exam requirements/recommendations for international students: Required—TOEFL.

California State University, San Bernardino, Graduate Studies, College of Education, San Bernardino, CA 92407-2397. Offers bilingual/cross-cultural education (MA); curriculum and instruction (MA); educational administration (MA); educational leadership and curriculum (Ed D); educational psychology and counseling (MA, MS), including correctional and alternative education (MA), counseling and guidance (MS), rehabilitation counseling (MA); English as a second language (MA); general education (MA); history and English for secondary teachers (MA); instructional technology (MA); reading (MA); secondary education (MA); special education and rehabilitation counseling (MA), including rehabilitation counseling, special education; teaching of science (MA); vocational and career education (MA). *Accreditation:* NCATE. Part-time and evening/weekend programs available. *Students:* 217 full-time (172 women), 353 part-time (263 women); includes 283 minority (41 Black or African American, non-Hispanic/Latino; 1 American Indian or Alaska Native, non-Hispanic/Latino; 21 Asian, non-Hispanic/Latino; 204 Hispanic/Latino; 1 Native Hawaiian or other Pacific Islander, non-Hispanic/Latino; 15 Two or more races, non-Hispanic/Latino), 35 international. Average age 34. 349 applicants, 76% accepted, 207 enrolled. In 2013, 215 master's awarded. *Degree requirements:* For master's, comprehensive exam (for some programs), thesis (for some programs), advancement to candidacy. *Entrance requirements:* For master's, minimum GPA of 3.0 in education. *Application deadline:* For fall admission, 8/31 priority date for domestic students. Application fee: $55. *Financial support:* Career-related internships or fieldwork and Federal Work-Study available. Support available to part-time students. *Faculty research:* Multicultural education, brain-based learning, science education, social studies/global education. *Unit head:* Dr. Jay Fiene, Dean, 909-537-5600, Fax: 909-537-7011, E-mail: jfiene@csusb.edu. *Application contact:* Dr. Jeffrey Thompson, Dean of Graduate Studies, 909-537-5808, E-mail: jthompso@csusb.edu.

California State University, Stanislaus, College of Education, Program in Education (MA), Turlock, CA 95382. Offers curriculum and instruction (MA), including education technology, elementary education, multilingual education, physical education, reading,

secondary education, special education; school administration (MA); school counseling (MA). Part-time and evening/weekend programs available. *Degree requirements:* For master's, comprehensive exam (for some programs), thesis (for some programs). *Entrance requirements:* For master's, MAT, GRE, or CBEST (varies by concentration), 3 letters of recommendation, personal statement. Additional exam requirements/recommendations for international students: Required—TOEFL (minimum score 550 paper-based). Electronic applications accepted. *Faculty research:* Children's perspectives on historical events, method elementary schools dual language education, K-12 reading programs.

California State University, Stanislaus, College of Humanities and Social Sciences, Program in History (MA), Turlock, CA 95382. Offers history (MA); international relations (MA); secondary school teachers (MA). Part-time programs available. *Degree requirements:* For master's, comprehensive exam, thesis or alternative. *Entrance requirements:* For master's, GRE, minimum GPA of 3.0, personal statement. Additional exam requirements/recommendations for international students: Required—TOEFL (minimum score 575 paper-based). Electronic applications accepted. *Faculty research:* History of Ancient Greece, history and ecology of the Central Valley, acculturation and gender.

California University of Pennsylvania, School of Graduate Studies and Research, College of Education and Human Services, Department of Secondary Education and Administrative Leadership, California, PA 15419-1394. Offers MAT. Part-time and evening/weekend programs available. Postbaccalaureate distance learning degree programs offered (no on-campus study). *Degree requirements:* For master's, comprehensive exam, thesis. *Entrance requirements:* For master's, PRAXIS, minimum GPA of 3.0, clearances. Additional exam requirements/recommendations for international students: Required—TOEFL (minimum score 550 paper-based; 80 iBT). Electronic applications accepted. *Faculty research:* The effectiveness of online instruction, student-centered instruction strategies in secondary education, computer technology in education, environmental education, multi-media in education.

Campbell University, Graduate and Professional Programs, School of Education, Buies Creek, NC 27506. Offers administration (MSA); community counseling (MA); elementary education (M Ed); English education (M Ed); interdisciplinary studies (M Ed); mathematics education (M Ed); middle grades education (M Ed); physical education (M Ed); school counseling (M Ed); secondary education (M Ed); social science education (M Ed). *Accreditation:* NCATE. Part-time and evening/weekend programs available. *Degree requirements:* For master's, comprehensive exam. *Entrance requirements:* For master's, GRE General Test, minimum GPA of 2.7. *Faculty research:* Spiritual values and wellness issues in counseling, stress and professional burnout among counselors, thinking strategies, leadership, adaptive technology.

Canisius College, Graduate Division, School of Education and Human Services, Department of Graduate Education and Leadership, Buffalo, NY 14208-1098. Offers business and marketing education (MS Ed); college student personnel (MS Ed); deaf education (MS Ed); deaf/adolescent education, grades 7-12 (MS Ed); deaf/childhood education, grades 1-6 (MS Ed); differentiated instruction (MS Ed); education administration (MS); educational administration (MS Ed); educational technologies (Certificate); gifted education extension (Certificate); literacy (MS Ed); reading (Certificate); school building leadership (MS Ed, Certificate); school district leadership (Certificate); teacher leader (Certificate); TESOL (MS Ed). *Accreditation:* NCATE. Part-time and evening/weekend programs available. Postbaccalaureate distance learning degree programs offered (minimal on-campus study). *Faculty:* 6 full-time (5 women), 33 part-time/adjunct (20 women). *Students:* 134 full-time (106 women), 267 part-time (213 women); includes 36 minority (22 Black or African American, non-Hispanic/Latino; 1 American Indian or Alaska Native, non-Hispanic/Latino; 3 Asian, non-Hispanic/Latino; 8 Hispanic/Latino; 2 Two or more races, non-Hispanic/Latino), 2 international. Average age 30. 282 applicants, 80% accepted, 120 enrolled. In 2013, 178 master's awarded. *Entrance requirements:* For master's, GRE if cumulative GPA less than 2.7, transcripts, two letters of recommendation. Additional exam requirements/recommendations for international students: Required—TOEFL (minimum score 550 paper-based, 80 iBT), IELTS (minimum score 6.5), or CAEL (minimum score 70). *Application deadline:* Applications are processed on a rolling basis. Application fee: $25. Electronic applications accepted. Application fee is waived when completed online. *Expenses: Tuition:* Part-time $750 per credit hour. *Financial support:* Career-related internships or fieldwork, Federal Work-Study, scholarships/grants, tuition waivers (partial), and unspecified assistantships available. Support available to part-time students. Financial award application deadline: 4/30; financial award applicants required to submit FAFSA. *Faculty research:* Asperger's disease, autism, private higher education, reading strategies. *Unit head:* Dr. Rosemary K. Murray, Chair/Associate Professor of Graduate Education and Leadership, 716-888-3723, E-mail: murray1@canisius.edu. *Application contact:* Julie A. Zulewski, Director of Graduate Admissions, 716-888-2548, Fax: 716-888-3195, E-mail: zulewskj@canisius.edu.
Website: http://www.canisius.edu/graduate/.

Carlow University, School of Education, Program in Education, Pittsburgh, PA 15213-3165. Offers art education (M Ed); early childhood education (M Ed); secondary education (M Ed); special education (M Ed). Part-time and evening/weekend programs available. *Students:* 42 full-time (37 women), 36 part-time (34 women); includes 9 minority (6 Black or African American, non-Hispanic/Latino; 1 Asian, non-Hispanic/Latino; 2 Two or more races, non-Hispanic/Latino). Average age 31. 27 applicants, 100% accepted, 19 enrolled. In 2013, 17 master's awarded. *Entrance requirements:* For master's, resume, 3 letters of recommendation, minimum GPA of 3.0, interview. Additional exam requirements/recommendations for international students: Required—TOEFL. *Application deadline:* For fall admission, 6/15 priority date for domestic and international students; for spring admission, 11/15 priority date for domestic and international students. Applications are processed on a rolling basis. Application fee: $20. Electronic applications accepted. Application fee is waived when completed online. *Expenses: Tuition:* Full-time $9523; part-time $744 per credit. Tuition and fees vary according to course load, degree level and program. *Financial support:* Applicants required to submit FAFSA. *Unit head:* Dr. Marilyn Llewellyn, Dean, 412-578-6011, Fax: 412-578-0816, E-mail: llewellynmj@carlow.edu. *Application contact:* Jo Danhires, Administrative Assistant, Admissions, 412-578-6089, Fax: 412-578-6321, E-mail: gradstudies@carlow.edu.
Website: http://www.carlow.edu.

Carson-Newman University, Graduate Program in Education, Jefferson City, TN 37760. Offers curriculum and instruction (M Ed); educational leadership (M Ed); elementary education (MAT); school counseling (MS); secondary education (MAT); teaching English as a second language (MATESL). *Accreditation:* NCATE. Part-time and evening/weekend programs available. *Faculty:* 5 full-time (2 women), 10 part-time/adjunct (3 women). *Students:* 25 full-time (12 women), 100 part-time (70 women); includes 8 minority (4 Black or African American, non-Hispanic/Latino; 1 Asian, non-Hispanic/Latino; 1 Hispanic/Latino; 2 Two or more races, non-Hispanic/Latino), 1 international. Average age 32. In 2013, 34 master's awarded. *Degree requirements:* For master's, thesis or alternative. *Entrance requirements:* For master's, NTE, minimum GPA of 3.0 in major, 2.5 overall. *Application deadline:* For fall admission, 7/15 priority date for domestic students. Applications are processed on a rolling basis. Application fee: $25 ($50 for international students). *Expenses: Tuition:* Part-time $390 per credit hour. *Financial support:* Federal Work-Study and unspecified assistantships available. Financial award application deadline: 4/1; financial award applicants required to submit FAFSA. *Unit head:* Dr. Sharon Teets, Chair, 865-471-3461. *Application contact:* Graduate Admissions and Services Adviser, 865-471-3460, Fax: 865-471-3875.

The Catholic University of America, School of Arts and Sciences, Department of Education, Washington, DC 20064. Offers Catholic educational leadership and policy studies (PhD); Catholic school leadership (MA); education (Certificate); educational psychology (PhD); secondary education (MA); special education (MA). *Accreditation:* NCATE. Part-time programs available. *Faculty:* 9 full-time (8 women), 4 part-time/adjunct (all women). *Students:* 9 full-time (6 women), 44 part-time (37 women); includes 8 minority (3 Black or African American, non-Hispanic/Latino; 3 Hispanic/Latino; 2 Two or more races, non-Hispanic/Latino), 2 international. Average age 34. 53 applicants, 53% accepted, 17 enrolled. In 2013, 18 master's, 2 doctorates awarded. *Degree requirements:* For master's, comprehensive exam, thesis or alternative; for doctorate, comprehensive exam, thesis/dissertation; for Certificate, action research project. *Entrance requirements:* For master's and doctorate, GRE General Test or MAT, statement of purpose, official copies of academic transcripts, three letters of recommendation, interview; for Certificate, PRAXIS I, statement of purpose, official copies of academic transcripts, three letters of recommendation, interview. Additional exam requirements/recommendations for international students: Required—TOEFL (minimum score 580 paper-based). *Application deadline:* For fall admission, 8/1 priority date for domestic students, 7/15 for international students; for spring admission, 12/1 priority date for domestic students, 10/15 for international students. Applications are processed on a rolling basis. Application fee: $55. Electronic applications accepted. *Expenses: Tuition:* Full-time $38,500; part-time $1490 per credit hour. *Required fees:* $400; $1525 per credit hour. One-time fee: $425. Tuition and fees vary according to program. *Financial support:* Fellowships, research assistantships, teaching assistantships, Federal Work-Study, scholarships/grants, tuition waivers (full and partial), and unspecified assistantships available. Financial award application deadline: 2/1; financial award applicants required to submit FAFSA. *Faculty research:* Special education, early childhood education, educational psychology, Catholic school administration, leadership and policy studies, counseling, curriculum and instruction. *Total annual research expenditures:* $65,883. *Unit head:* Dr. Merylann J. Schuttloffel, Chair, 202-319-5805, Fax: 202-319-5815, E-mail: schuttloffel@cua.edu. *Application contact:* Andrew Woodall, Director of Graduate Admissions, 202-319-5057, Fax: 202-319-6533, E-mail: cua-admissions@cua.edu.
Website: http://education.cua.edu/.

Centenary College of Louisiana, Graduate Programs, Department of Education, Shreveport, LA 71104. Offers administration (M Ed); elementary education (MAT); secondary education (MAT); supervision of instruction (M Ed). Part-time and evening/weekend programs available. *Degree requirements:* For master's, comprehensive exam. *Entrance requirements:* For master's, GRE General Test (M Ed), PRAXIS I and PRAXIS II (MAT), teacher certification (M Ed), minimum GPA of 2.5. *Expenses:* Contact institution. *Faculty research:* Teachers as advocates for teachers, portfolio assessment, disabled readers.

Central Connecticut State University, School of Graduate Studies, School of Education and Professional Studies, Department of Teacher Education, Program in Educational Foundations Policy/Secondary Education, New Britain, CT 06050-4010. Offers MS. Part-time and evening/weekend programs available. *Students:* 2 part-time (both women). Average age 43. *Degree requirements:* For master's, comprehensive exam, thesis or alternative. *Entrance requirements:* For master's, minimum undergraduate GPA of 2.7. Additional exam requirements/recommendations for international students: Required—TOEFL (minimum score 550 paper-based; 79 iBT). *Application deadline:* For fall admission, 6/1 for domestic students, 5/1 for international students; for spring admission, 11/1 for domestic and international students. Applications are processed on a rolling basis. Application fee: $50. Electronic applications accepted. Part-time tuition and fees vary according to degree level. *Unit head:* Dr. Aram Ayalon, Chair, 860-832-2415, E-mail: casellar@ccsu.edu. *Application contact:* Patricia Gardner, Associate Director of Graduate Studies, 860-832-2350, Fax: 860-832-2362, E-mail: graduateadmissions@ccsu.edu.

Central Michigan University, College of Graduate Studies, College of Education and Human Services, Department of Teacher Education and Professional Development, Mount Pleasant, MI 48859. Offers educational technology (MA, Graduate Certificate); elementary education (MA), including classroom teaching, early childhood; reading and literacy K-12 (MA); secondary education (MA). Part-time and evening/weekend programs available. *Degree requirements:* For master's, thesis or alternative. Electronic applications accepted. *Faculty research:* Integrating literacy across the curriculum, science teaching and aesthetic learning in science, diversity education, educational technology, educational psychology and child development.

Central Michigan University, College of Graduate Studies, College of Science and Technology, Department of Chemistry, Mount Pleasant, MI 48859. Offers chemistry (MS); teaching chemistry (MA), including teaching college chemistry, teaching high school chemistry. Part-time programs available. *Degree requirements:* For master's, comprehensive exam, thesis or alternative. *Entrance requirements:* For master's, GRE. Electronic applications accepted. *Faculty research:* Analytical and organic-inorganic chemistry, biochemistry, catalysis, dendrimer and polymer studies, nanotechnology.

Chadron State College, School of Professional and Graduate Studies, Department of Education, Chadron, NE 69337. Offers business (MA Ed); community counseling (MA Ed); educational administration (MS Ed, Sp Ed); elementary education (MS Ed); history (MA Ed); language and literature (MA Ed); secondary administration (MS Ed); secondary education (MS Ed). *Accreditation:* NCATE. Part-time and evening/weekend programs available. Postbaccalaureate distance learning degree programs offered. *Degree requirements:* For master's, thesis optional. *Entrance requirements:* For master's, GRE General Test, GRE Writing Test, minimum GPA of 2.75 or 12 graduate hours at CSC with minimum GPA of 3.25. Additional exam requirements/recommendations for international students: Required—TOEFL. Electronic applications accepted. *Faculty research:* Rural education, technology, mental health.

Chaminade University of Honolulu, Graduate Services, Program in Education, Honolulu, HI 96816-1578. Offers child development (M Ed); early childhood education (M Ed); educational leadership (M Ed); elementary education (MAT); instructional leadership (M Ed); Montessori education (M Ed); secondary education (MAT), including English, math, science, social studies; special education (MAT). Part-time and evening/weekend programs available. Postbaccalaureate distance learning degree programs offered (minimal on-campus study). *Degree requirements:* For master's, thesis or alternative. *Entrance requirements:* For master's, PRAXIS (for MAT only), minimum GPA of 2.75, 3 letters of recommendation. Additional exam requirements/recommendations for international students: Required—TOEFL (minimum score 550 paper-based). Electronic applications accepted. *Faculty research:* Peace and curriculum education.

Chapman University, College of Educational Studies, Orange, CA 92866. Offers communication sciences and disorders (MS); counseling (MA), including school

counseling (MA, Credential); education (PhD), including cultural and curricular studies, disability studies, leadership studies, school psychology (PhD, Credential); educational psychology (MA); leadership development (MA); pupil personnel services (Credential), including school counseling (MA, Credential), school psychology (PhD, Credential); school psychology (Ed S); single subject (Credential); special education (MA, Credential), including mild/moderate (Credential), moderate/severe (Credential); speech language pathology (Credential); teaching (MA), including elementary education, secondary education. *Accreditation:* Teacher Education Accreditation Council. Part-time and evening/weekend programs available. *Faculty:* 29 full-time (18 women), 56 part-time/adjunct (38 women). *Students:* 251 full-time (208 women), 194 part-time (150 women); includes 185 minority (13 Black or African American, non-Hispanic/Latino; 61 Asian, non-Hispanic/Latino; 97 Hispanic/Latino; 1 Native Hawaiian or other Pacific Islander, non-Hispanic/Latino; 13 Two or more races, non-Hispanic/Latino), 7 international. Average age 29. 580 applicants, 42% accepted, 166 enrolled. In 2013, 140 master's, 10 doctorates awarded. *Entrance requirements:* Additional exam requirements/recommendations for international students: Required—TOEFL (minimum score 550 paper-based; 80 iBT). *Application deadline:* Applications are processed on a rolling basis. Application fee: $60. Electronic applications accepted. Tuition and fees vary according to program. *Financial support:* Fellowships and scholarships/grants available. Financial award application deadline: 6/30; financial award applicants required to submit FAFSA. *Unit head:* Dr. Don Cardinal, Dean, 714-997-6781, E-mail: cardinal@chapman.edu. *Application contact:* Admissions Coordinator, 714-997-6714.
Website: http://www.chapman.edu/CES/.

Chatham University, Program in Education, Pittsburgh, PA 15232-2826. Offers early childhood education (MAT); elementary education (MAT); environmental education (K-12) (MAT); secondary art (MAT); secondary biology education (MAT); secondary chemistry education (MAT); secondary English education (MAT); secondary math education (MAT); secondary physics education (MAT); secondary social studies education (MAT); special education (MAT). *Faculty:* 1 (woman) full-time, 5 part-time/adjunct (4 women). *Students:* 19 full-time (15 women), 4 part-time (all women); includes 2 minority (1 Black or African American, non-Hispanic/Latino; 1 Asian, non-Hispanic/Latino), 2 international. Average age 28. 22 applicants, 73% accepted, 6 enrolled. In 2013, 20 master's awarded. *Degree requirements:* For master's, thesis, teaching experience. *Entrance requirements:* For master's, minimum GPA of 3.0, sample of written work, recommendation letters. Additional exam requirements/recommendations for international students: Required—TOEFL (minimum score 600 paper-based; 100 iBT), IELTS (minimum score 7), TWE. *Application deadline:* For fall admission, 4/1 priority date for domestic and international students; for spring admission, 11/1 priority date for domestic students, 10/1 priority date for international students. Applications are processed on a rolling basis. Application fee: $45. Electronic applications accepted. Application fee is waived when completed online. *Expenses: Tuition:* Full-time $14,886; part-time $827 per credit hour. One-time fee: $396 full-time. *Financial support:* Career-related internships or fieldwork available. Financial award applicants required to submit FAFSA. *Faculty research:* Gifted education, environmental education, technology in education, writing as learning, class size and achievement. *Unit head:* Dr. Edward Donovan, Director of Education Programs, 412-365-2773, E-mail: edonovan@chatham.edu. *Application contact:* Katie Noel, Assistant Director of Graduate Admission, 412-365-2758, Fax: 412-365-1609, E-mail: gradadmissions@chatham.edu.
Website: http://www.chatham.edu/mat.

Chestnut Hill College, School of Graduate Studies, Department of Education, Program in Secondary Education, Philadelphia, PA 19118-2693. Offers instructional design and e-learning (M Ed); secondary education (CAS). Part-time and evening/weekend programs available. *Faculty:* 10 full-time (7 women), 48 part-time/adjunct (34 women). *Students:* 18 full-time (14 women), 51 part-time (31 women); includes 23 minority (15 Black or African American, non-Hispanic/Latino; 4 Asian, non-Hispanic/Latino; 4 Hispanic/Latino), 1 international. Average age 32. 36 applicants, 100% accepted. In 2013, 33 master's, 19 CASs awarded. *Degree requirements:* For master's, thesis optional. *Entrance requirements:* For master's, PRAXIS I or proof of teaching certification, letters of recommendation; writing sample; 6 graduate credits with minimum B grade if undergraduate GPA less than 3.0. Additional exam requirements/recommendations for international students: Required—TOEFL (minimum score 500 paper-based), IELTS (mnimum score 6.0), or TWE (minimum score 22). *Application deadline:* For fall admission, 7/1 for domestic and international students; for spring admission, 11/1 for domestic and international students; for summer admission, 4/1 for domestic and international students. Applications are processed on a rolling basis. *Expenses:* Contact institution. *Financial support:* Unspecified assistantships available. *Faculty research:* Science teaching. *Unit head:* Dr. Debra Chiaradonna, Chair, Department of Education, 215-248-7147, Fax: 215-248-7155, E-mail: chiaradonnad@chc.edu. *Application contact:* Jayne Mashett, Director of Admissions, School of Graduate Studies, 215-248-7020, Fax: 215-248-7161, E-mail: gradadmissions@chc.edu.
Website: http://www.chc.edu/Graduate/Programs/Masters/Education/.

Chicago State University, School of Graduate and Professional Studies, College of Education, Department of Technology and Education, Chicago, IL 60628. Offers secondary education (MAT); technology and education (MS Ed). Postbaccalaureate distance learning degree programs offered. *Degree requirements:* For master's, thesis optional. *Entrance requirements:* For master's, minimum GPA of 2.75.

Christopher Newport University, Graduate Studies, Department of Teacher Preparation, Newport News, VA 23606-3072. Offers art (PK-12) (MAT); biology (6-12) (MAT); chemistry (6-12) (MAT); computer science (6-12) (MAT); elementary (PK-6) (MAT); English (6-12) (MAT); English as second language (PK-12) (MAT); French (PK-12) (MAT); history and social science (6-12) (MAT); mathematics (6-12) (MAT); music (PK-12) (MAT), including choral, instrumental; physics (6-12) (MAT); Spanish (PK-12) (MAT). Part-time programs available. *Faculty:* 15 full-time (7 women), 14 part-time/adjunct (13 women). *Students:* 74 full-time (64 women), 2 part-time (both women); includes 6 minority (4 Hispanic/Latino; 2 Two or more races, non-Hispanic/Latino). Average age 23. 90 applicants, 100% accepted, 67 enrolled. In 2013, 96 master's awarded. *Degree requirements:* For master's, comprehensive exam, thesis or alternative. *Entrance requirements:* For master's, PRAXIS I, minimum GPA of 3.0. Additional exam requirements/recommendations for international students: Required—TOEFL (minimum score 580 paper-based; 92 iBT). *Application deadline:* For fall admission, 4/1 for international students; for spring admission, 10/15 for domestic students, 10/1 for international students; for summer admission, 1/15 for domestic students, 3/1 for international students. Applications are processed on a rolling basis. Application fee: $50. Electronic applications accepted. *Expenses: Tuition, area resident:* Part-time $498 per credit hour. Tuition, state resident: part-time $498 per credit hour. Tuition, nonresident: part-time $899 per credit hour. *Financial support:* In 2013–14, 3 students received support, including 3 research assistantships with full tuition reimbursements available (averaging $2,000 per year); career-related internships or fieldwork, Federal Work-Study, and unspecified assistantships also available. Financial award application deadline: 3/1; financial award applicants required to submit FAFSA. *Faculty research:* Early literacy development, instructional innovations, professional teaching standards, multicultural issues, aesthetic education. *Total annual research expenditures:* $24,000. *Unit head:* Dr. Marsha Sprague, Director, 757-594-7388, Fax: 757-594-7803, E-mail: msprague@cnu.edu. *Application contact:* Lyn Sawyer, Associate Director, Graduate Admissions, 757-594-7544, Fax: 757-594-7649, E-mail: gradstdy@cnu.edu.

The Citadel, The Military College of South Carolina, Citadel Graduate College, School of Education, Program in Guidance and Counseling, Charleston, SC 29409. Offers elementary/secondary school counseling (M Ed); student affairs and college counseling (M Ed). *Accreditation:* ACA; NCATE. Part-time and evening/weekend programs available. *Faculty:* 10 full-time (6 women), 8 part-time/adjunct (3 women). *Students:* 15 full-time (14 women), 40 part-time (35 women); includes 13 minority (12 Black or African American, non-Hispanic/Latino; 1 Two or more races, non-Hispanic/Latino). Average age 30. In 2013, 27 master's awarded. *Degree requirements:* For master's, comprehensive exam, practicum or internship. *Entrance requirements:* For master's, GRE (minimum score 290; 900 on old scoring system) or MAT (minimum score 396), minimum undergraduate GPA of 3.0, 3 letters of reference, group interview. Additional exam requirements/recommendations for international students: Required—TOEFL (minimum score 550 paper-based; 79 iBT). *Application deadline:* For fall admission, 6/1 for domestic students; for spring admission, 10/1 for domestic students. Application fee: $30. Electronic applications accepted. *Expenses: Tuition, area resident:* Part-time $525 per credit hour. Tuition, state resident: part-time $525 per credit hour. Tuition, nonresident: part-time $865 per credit hour. *Financial support:* Career-related internships or fieldwork, health care benefits, and unspecified assistantships available. Support available to part-time students. Financial award application deadline: 7/1; financial award applicants required to submit FAFSA. *Unit head:* Dr. George T. Williams, Director, 843-953-2205, Fax: 843-953-7258, E-mail: williamsg@citadel.edu. *Application contact:* Dr. Robert H. McNamara, Associate Provost, The Citadel Graduate College, 843-953-5089, Fax: 843-953-7630, E-mail: cgc@citadel.edu.
Website: http://www.citadel.edu/education/counselor.html.

The Citadel, The Military College of South Carolina, Citadel Graduate College, School of Education, Program in Secondary Education, Charleston, SC 29409. Offers biology (MAT); English language arts (MAT); mathematics (MAT); mathematics education (MAE); physical education (MAT); social studies (MAT). *Accreditation:* NCATE. Part-time and evening/weekend programs available. *Faculty:* 10 full-time (6 women), 8 part-time/adjunct (3 women). *Students:* 14 full-time (9 women), 56 part-time (31 women); includes 9 minority (8 Black or African American, non-Hispanic/Latino; 1 Hispanic/Latino). Average age 30. In 2013, 24 master's awarded. *Degree requirements:* For master's, comprehensive exam, internship. *Entrance requirements:* For master's, GRE (minimum score 290; 900 on old scoring system) or MAT (minimum score 396), minimum undergraduate GPA of 2.5. Additional exam requirements/recommendations for international students: Required—TOEFL (minimum score 550 paper-based). *Application deadline:* Applications are processed on a rolling basis. Application fee: $30. Electronic applications accepted. *Expenses: Tuition, area resident:* Part-time $525 per credit hour. Tuition, state resident: part-time $525 per credit hour. Tuition, nonresident: part-time $865 per credit hour. *Financial support:* Career-related internships or fieldwork, health care benefits, and unspecified assistantships available. Support available to part-time students. Financial award application deadline: 7/1; financial award applicants required to submit FAFSA. *Unit head:* Dr. Kathryn A. Richardson-Jones, Coordinator, 843-953-3163, Fax: 843-953-7258, E-mail: kathryn.jones@citadel.edu. *Application contact:* Dr. Robert H. McNamara, Associate Provost, The Citadel Graduate College, 843-953-5089, Fax: 843-953-7630, E-mail: cgc@citadel.edu.
Website: http://www.citadel.edu/education/teacher-education/mat-master-of-arts-in-teaching.html.

City College of the City University of New York, Graduate School, School of Education, Department of Secondary Education, New York, NY 10031-9198. Offers adolescent mathematics education (MA, AC); English education (MA); middle school mathematics education (MS); science education (MA); social studies education (AC). *Accreditation:* NCATE. *Entrance requirements:* For master's, Liberal Arts and Sciences Test (LAST), Content Specialty Test (CST). Additional exam requirements/recommendations for international students: Required—TOEFL.

Clemson University, Graduate School, College of Health, Education, and Human Development, Eugene T. Moore School of Education, Program in Secondary Education: Math and Science, Clemson, SC 29634. Offers MAT. *Accreditation:* NCATE. *Students:* 18 full-time (13 women); includes 1 minority (Black or African American, non-Hispanic/Latino). Average age 27. 4 applicants, 50% accepted, 1 enrolled. In 2013, 11 master's awarded. *Degree requirements:* For master's, digital portfolio. *Entrance requirements:* For master's, PRAXIS II. Additional exam requirements/recommendations for international students: Required—TOEFL; Recommended—IELTS. *Application deadline:* For fall admission, 4/1 for domestic students. Applications are processed on a rolling basis. Application fee: $70 ($80 for international students). Electronic applications accepted. *Expenses:* Contact institution. *Financial support:* In 2013–14, 4 students received support, including 12 fellowships with partial tuition reimbursements available (averaging $3,599 per year); institutionally sponsored loans, scholarships/grants, health care benefits, and unspecified assistantships also available. Financial award application deadline: 6/1; financial award applicants required to submit FAFSA. *Faculty research:* Science education, math education. *Unit head:* Dr. Michael J. Padilla, Director/Associate Dean, 864-656-4444, Fax: 864-656-0311, E-mail: padilla@clemson.edu. *Application contact:* Dr. David Fleming, Graduate Coordinator, 864-656-1881, Fax: 864-656-0311, E-mail: dflemin@clemson.edu.
Website: http://www.clemson.edu/hehd/departments/education/academics/graduate/MAT/secondary.html.

Colgate University, Master of Arts in Teaching Program, Hamilton, NY 13346-1386. Offers MAT. *Accreditation:* Teacher Education Accreditation Council. *Degree requirements:* For master's, special project or thesis. *Entrance requirements:* For master's, GRE General Test. *Faculty research:* Culturally-responsive teaching, comparative education, moral development in education, politics in education, educational psychology.

The College of New Jersey, Graduate Studies, School of Education, Department of Educational Administration and Secondary Education, Program in Secondary Education, Ewing, NJ 08628. Offers MAT. *Degree requirements:* For master's, comprehensive exam. *Entrance requirements:* For master's, GRE, minimum GPA of 3.0 in field or 2.75 overall. Additional exam requirements/recommendations for international students: Required—TOEFL. Electronic applications accepted.

College of St. Joseph, Graduate Programs, Division of Education, Program in Secondary Education, Rutland, VT 05701-3899. Offers English (M Ed); social studies (M Ed). Part-time and evening/weekend programs available. *Degree requirements:* For master's, comprehensive exam. *Entrance requirements:* For master's, PRAXIS I, official college transcripts; 2 letters of reference; minimum GPA of 3.0 (initial licensure) or 2.7 (nonlicensure); interview. Additional exam requirements/recommendations for international students: Required—TOEFL (minimum score 550 paper-based). Electronic applications accepted.

The College of Saint Rose, Graduate Studies, School of Education, Department of Special Education and Inclusive Education, Albany, NY 12203-1419. Offers birth-grade 2 special education (MS Ed); grades 1-6 special education (MS Ed); grades 1-6 special

education and childhood education (MS Ed); grades 7-12 adolescence education and special education (MS Ed); grades 7-12 special education (MS Ed); professional special education (MS Ed). *Accreditation:* NCATE. Part-time and evening/weekend programs available. *Degree requirements:* For master's, comprehensive exam (for some programs), thesis or alternative, research project. *Entrance requirements:* For master's, minimum undergraduate GPA of 3.0. Additional exam requirements/recommendations for international students: Required—TOEFL (minimum score 550 paper-based). Electronic applications accepted.

The College of Saint Rose, Graduate Studies, School of Education, Department of Teacher Education, Albany, NY 12203-1419. Offers adolescence education (MS Ed); childhood education (MS Ed); curriculum and instruction (MS Ed); early childhood education (MS Ed). Part-time and evening/weekend programs available. *Entrance requirements:* For master's, minimum undergraduate GPA of 3.0. Additional exam requirements/recommendations for international students: Required—TOEFL (minimum score 550 paper-based). Electronic applications accepted.

College of Staten Island of the City University of New York, Graduate Programs, School of Education, Program in Adolescence Education, Staten Island, NY 10314-6600. Offers MS Ed. Part-time and evening/weekend programs available. *Faculty:* 13 full-time (6 women), 6 part-time/adjunct (2 women). *Students:* 22 full-time (15 women), 129 part-time (84 women). Average age 29. 66 applicants, 71% accepted, 40 enrolled. In 2013, 52 master's awarded. *Degree requirements:* For master's, 2 foreign languages, thesis, fieldwork, 2 foreign language courses at the undergraduate level. *Entrance requirements:* For master's, relevant bachelor's degree, essay, letters of recommendation. Additional exam requirements/recommendations for international students: Required—TOEFL (minimum score 550 paper-based; 79 iBT), IELTS (minimum score 6.5). *Application deadline:* For fall admission, 4/25 for domestic and international students; for spring admission, 11/15 for domestic and international students. Applications are processed on a rolling basis. Application fee: $125. Electronic applications accepted. *Expenses:* Tuition, state resident: full-time $9240; part-time $385 per credit hour. Tuition, nonresident: full-time $17,040; part-time $710 per credit hour. *Required fees:* $428; $128 per term. *Financial support:* In 2013–14, 1 student received support. Career-related internships or fieldwork, Federal Work-Study, and scholarships/grants available. Support available to part-time students. Financial award applicants required to submit FAFSA. *Unit head:* Dr. Kenneth Gold, Coordinator, 718-982-3737, Fax: 718-982-3743, E-mail: kenneth.gold@csi.cuny.edu. *Application contact:* Sasha Spence, Assistant Director for Graduate Admissions, 718-982-2019, Fax: 718-982-2500, E-mail: sasha.spence@csi.cuny.edu.
Website: http://www.csi.cuny.edu/catalog/graduate/graduate-programs-in-education.htm#o2608.

The College of William and Mary, School of Education, Program in Curriculum and Instruction, Williamsburg, VA 23187-8795. Offers elementary education (MA Ed); gifted education (MA Ed); literacy leadership (MA Ed); math specialist (MA Ed); secondary education (MA Ed), including English education, mathematics education, modern foreign languages education, science education, social studies education; special education (MA Ed), including collaborating master educator, general curriculum. *Accreditation:* NCATE. Part-time programs available. *Faculty:* 15 full-time (10 women), 44 part-time/adjunct (38 women). *Students:* 66 full-time (55 women), 27 part-time (26 women); includes 17 minority (4 Black or African American, non-Hispanic/Latino; 1 American Indian or Alaska Native, non-Hispanic/Latino; 3 Asian, non-Hispanic/Latino; 5 Hispanic/Latino; 4 Two or more races, non-Hispanic/Latino). Average age 28. 179 applicants, 72% accepted, 92 enrolled. In 2013, 76 master's awarded. *Degree requirements:* For master's, project. *Entrance requirements:* For master's, GRE or MAT, minimum GPA of 2.5. Additional exam requirements/recommendations for international students: Required—TOEFL, IELTS. *Application deadline:* For fall admission, 1/15 for domestic and international students; for spring admission, 10/1 for domestic and international students. Application fee: $50. Electronic applications accepted. *Expenses:* Tuition, state resident: full-time $7120; part-time $405 per credit hour. Tuition, nonresident: full-time $21,639; part-time $1050 per credit hour. *Required fees:* $4764. *Financial support:* In 2013–14, 49 students received support, including 6 research assistantships with full and partial tuition reimbursements available (averaging $8,269 per year); career-related internships or fieldwork, Federal Work-Study, institutionally sponsored loans, scholarships/grants, and unspecified assistantships also available. Financial award application deadline: 1/15; financial award applicants required to submit FAFSA. *Faculty research:* National Council of Teachers of Mathematics standards, counseling, self-concept and self-esteem, special education, curriculum development. *Unit head:* Dr. Mark Hofer, Area Coordinator, 757-221-1713, E-mail: mjhofe@wm.edu. *Application contact:* Dorothy Smith Osborne, Assistant Dean for Academic Programs and Student Services, 757-221-2317, Fax: 757-221-2293, E-mail: dsosbo@wm.edu.
Website: http://education.wm.edu.

The Colorado College, Education Department, Program in Secondary Education, Colorado Springs, CO 80903-3294. Offers art teaching (K-12) (MAT); English teaching (MAT); foreign language teaching (MAT); mathematics teaching (MAT); music teaching (MAT); science teaching (MAT); social studies teaching (MAT). *Degree requirements:* For master's, thesis, internship. Electronic applications accepted.

Columbus State University, Graduate Studies, College of Education and Health Professions, Department of Teacher Education, Columbus, GA 31907-5645. Offers accomplished teaching (M Ed); early childhood education (M Ed, MAT, Ed S); middle grades education (M Ed, MAT, Ed S); school library media (M Ed, MAT); secondary education (M Ed, MAT, Ed S), including English/language arts (M Ed, Ed S), general science (M Ed), mathematics (M Ed, Ed S), science (Ed S), social science (M Ed, Ed S); special education (M Ed, MAT, Ed S), including general curriculum (M Ed, MAT); teacher leadership (M Ed). *Accreditation:* NCATE. Part-time and evening/weekend programs available. Postbaccalaureate distance learning degree programs offered (minimal on-campus study). *Faculty:* 17 full-time (12 women), 31 part-time/adjunct (28 women). *Students:* 59 full-time (48 women), 190 part-time (150 women); includes 85 minority (68 Black or African American, non-Hispanic/Latino; 1 American Indian or Alaska Native, non-Hispanic/Latino; 6 Asian, non-Hispanic/Latino; 4 Hispanic/Latino; 6 Two or more races, non-Hispanic/Latino), 2 international. Average age 34. 132 applicants, 58% accepted, 50 enrolled. In 2013, 86 master's, 26 other advanced degrees awarded. *Degree requirements:* For master's, thesis, exit exam; for Ed S, thesis or alternative. *Entrance requirements:* For master's, GRE General Test, minimum undergraduate GPA of 2.75; for Ed S, GRE General Test, minimum undergraduate GPA of 2.75, graduate 3.0. Additional exam requirements/recommendations for international students: Required—TOEFL (minimum score 550 paper-based; 79 iBT). *Application deadline:* For fall admission, 6/30 for domestic students, 5/1 for international students; for spring admission, 11/1 for domestic and international students; for summer admission, 3/1 for domestic and international students. Applications are processed on a rolling basis. Application fee: $40. Electronic applications accepted. *Expenses:* Tuition, state resident: full-time $4572; part-time $382 per credit hour. Tuition, nonresident: full-time $18,292; part-time $1526 per credit hour. *Required fees:* $1800; $196 per credit hour. Tuition and fees vary according to campus/location and program. *Financial support:* In 2013–14, 173 students received support, including 12 research assistantships with partial tuition reimbursements available (averaging $3,000 per year); career-related internships or fieldwork, Federal Work-Study, institutionally sponsored loans, scholarships/grants, tuition waivers (partial), and unspecified assistantships also available. Support available to part-time students. Financial award application deadline: 5/1; financial award applicants required to submit FAFSA. *Unit head:* Dr. Deirdre Greer, Department Chair, 706-507-8034, Fax: 706-568-3134, E-mail: greer_deirdre@columbusstate.edu. *Application contact:* Kristin Williams, Director of International and Graduate Recruitment, 706-507-8848, Fax: 706-568-5091, E-mail: williams_kristin@columbusstate.edu.
Website: http://te.columbusstate.edu/.

Concordia University, College of Education, Portland, OR 97211-6099. Offers career and technical education (M Ed); curriculum and instruction (M Ed), including adolescent literacy, career and technical education, e-learning/technology education, early childhood education, English for speakers of other languages, English language development, environmental education, mathematics, methods and curriculum, reading, science, teacher leadership, the inclusive classroom; early childhood (MAT); education leadership (Ed D); educational administration (M Ed); elementary education (MAT); secondary education (MAT); special education (M Ed); teacher leadership (Ed D). Part-time programs available. Postbaccalaureate distance learning degree programs offered (no on-campus study). *Degree requirements:* For master's, comprehensive exam, work samples/portfolio. *Entrance requirements:* For master's, California Basic Educational Skills Test or PRAXIS I, minimum undergraduate GPA of 2.8, graduate 3.0; 2 letters of recommendation. Additional exam requirements/recommendations for international students: Required—TOEFL (minimum score 525 paper-based). Electronic applications accepted. *Faculty research:* Learner-centered classroom, brain-based learning, future of online learning.

Concordia University Chicago, College of Education, Program in Teaching, River Forest, IL 60305-1499. Offers early childhood education (MAT); elementary education (MAT); secondary education (MAT). *Degree requirements:* For master's, thesis or alternative. *Entrance requirements:* For master's, minimum GPA of 2.9. Additional exam requirements/recommendations for international students: Required—TOEFL (minimum score 550 paper-based). Electronic applications accepted.

Concordia University, Nebraska, Graduate Programs in Education, Program in Educational Administration, Seward, NE 68434-1556. Offers elementary and secondary education (M Ed); elementary education (M Ed); secondary education (M Ed). *Accreditation:* NCATE. Part-time programs available. *Degree requirements:* For master's, thesis or alternative. *Entrance requirements:* For master's, GRE, MAT, or NTE, BS in education or equivalent, minimum GPA of 3.0.

Converse College, School of Education and Graduate Studies, Program in Secondary Education, Spartanburg, SC 29302-0006. Offers biology (MAT); chemistry (MAT); English (M Ed, MAT); mathematics (M Ed, MAT); natural sciences (M Ed); social sciences (M Ed, MAT). Part-time programs available. *Degree requirements:* For master's, capstone paper. *Entrance requirements:* For master's, NTE or PRAXIS II (M Ed), minimum GPA of 2.75, 2 recommendations. Electronic applications accepted.

Cornell University, Graduate School, Graduate Fields of Agriculture and Life Sciences, Field of Education, Ithaca, NY 14853-0001. Offers adult and extension education (MPS, MS, PhD); learning, teaching, and social policy (MPS, MS, PhD); mathematics 7-12 (MS). *Faculty:* 21 full-time (8 women). *Students:* 14 full-time (9 women); includes 2 minority (1 Asian, non-Hispanic/Latino; 1 Hispanic/Latino), 1 international. Average age 32. 20 applicants, 20% accepted, 2 enrolled. In 2013, 17 master's, 4 doctorates awarded. Terminal master's awarded for partial completion of doctoral program. *Degree requirements:* For master's, thesis (MS); for doctorate, comprehensive exam, thesis/dissertation. *Entrance requirements:* For master's and doctorate, GRE General Test, sample of written work (recommended), 2 letters of recommendation. Additional exam requirements/recommendations for international students: Required—TOEFL (minimum score 550 paper-based; 77 iBT). *Application deadline:* For fall admission, 2/15 for domestic students. Application fee: $95. Electronic applications accepted. *Financial support:* In 2013–14, 4 students received support, including 3 fellowships with full tuition reimbursements available, 1 research assistantship with full tuition reimbursement available; teaching assistantships with full tuition reimbursements available, institutionally sponsored loans, scholarships/grants, health care benefits, tuition waivers (full and partial), and unspecified assistantships also available. Financial award applicants required to submit FAFSA. *Faculty research:* Moral development and professional ethics, public issues education and community development, socio/political issues in public education, teacher education and curriculum in agricultural science and mathematics, extension research. *Unit head:* Director of Graduate Studies, 607-255-4278, Fax: 607-255-7905. *Application contact:* Graduate Field Assistant, 607-255-4278, Fax: 607-255-7905, E-mail: rh22@cornell.edu.
Website: http://www.gradschool.cornell.edu/fields.php?id-80&a-2.

Creighton University, Graduate School, College of Arts and Sciences, Department of Education, Program in Teaching, Omaha, NE 68178-0001. Offers elementary teaching (M Ed); secondary teaching (M Ed). Part-time and evening/weekend programs available. *Faculty:* 12 full-time (6 women). *Students:* 16 full-time (14 women), 18 part-time (11 women); includes 2 minority (both Black or African American, non-Hispanic/Latino). Average age 25. In 2013, 13 master's awarded. *Entrance requirements:* For master's, 3 letters of recommendation, 2 writing samples. Additional exam requirements/recommendations for international students: Required—TOEFL (minimum score 550 paper-based; 80 iBT). *Application deadline:* For fall admission, 7/1 priority date for domestic students, 3/1 priority date for international students; for winter admission, 12/1 priority date for domestic students, 6/1 priority date for international students; for spring admission, 3/1 priority date for domestic and international students; for summer admission, 3/1 for domestic and international students. Application fee: $50. Electronic applications accepted. *Expenses: Tuition:* Full-time $13,608; part-time $756 per credit hour. *Required fees:* $149 per semester. Tuition and fees vary according to course load, campus/location, program, reciprocity agreements and student's religious affiliation. *Financial support:* Scholarships/grants and tuition waivers (partial) available. Support available to part-time students. Financial award applicants required to submit FAFSA. *Unit head:* Dr. Lynn Olson, Director, 402-280-2554, E-mail: lolson@creighton.edu. *Application contact:* Valerie Mattix, Senior Program Coordinator, 402-280-2425, Fax: 402-280-2423, E-mail: valeriemattix@creighton.edu.

Dakota Wesleyan University, Program in Education, Mitchell, SD 57301-4398. Offers curriculum and instruction (MA Ed); educational policy and administration (MA Ed); preK-12 principal certification (MA Ed); secondary certification (MA Ed). Part-time and evening/weekend programs available. *Degree requirements:* For master's, comprehensive exam, thesis optional, electronic portfolio. *Entrance requirements:* For master's, minimum GPA of 2.7, elementary statistics course, statement of purpose, official transcripts, resume, three letters of recommendation. Additional exam requirements/recommendations for international students: Required—TOEFL (minimum score 500 paper-based), IELTS (minimum score 6.5). Electronic applications accepted. *Faculty research:* Math, political policy, technology in the classroom.

Dallas Baptist University, Dorothy M. Bush College of Education, Teaching Program, Dallas, TX 75211-9299. Offers distance learning (MAT); early childhood (MAT); elementary (MAT); English as a second language (MAT); Montessori (MAT);

multisensory (MAT); secondary (MAT). Part-time and evening/weekend programs available. *Entrance requirements:* For master's, GRE General Test, minimum GPA of 3.0. Additional exam requirements/recommendations for international students: Required—TOEFL, IELTS. *Application deadline:* Applications are processed on a rolling basis. Application fee: $25. Electronic applications accepted. *Expenses: Tuition:* Full-time $13,410; part-time $745 per credit hour. *Required fees:* $300; $150 per semester. Tuition and fees vary according to degree level. *Financial support:* Federal Work-Study, institutionally sponsored loans, scholarships/grants, and tuition waivers (full and partial) available. Support available to part-time students. Financial award applicants required to submit FAFSA. *Unit head:* Dr. Carolyn Spain, Director, 214-333-5217, E-mail: graduate@dbu.edu. *Application contact:* Kit P. Montgomery, Director of Graduate Programs, 214-333-5242, Fax: 214-333-5579, E-mail: graduate@dbu.edu.
Website: http://www3.dbu.edu/graduate/mat.asp.

Defiance College, Program in Education, Defiance, OH 43512-1610. Offers adolescent and young adult licensure (MA); mild and moderate intervention specialist (MA). Part-time programs available. *Degree requirements:* For master's, thesis (for some programs). *Entrance requirements:* For master's, teaching certificate.

Delta State University, Graduate Programs, College of Arts and Sciences, Division of Languages and Literature, Cleveland, MS 38733-0001. Offers secondary education (M Ed), including English. Part-time programs available. *Faculty:* 8 full-time (2 women). *Students:* 10 full-time (7 women), 11 part-time (7 women); includes 3 minority (all Black or African American, non-Hispanic/Latino). Average age 30. 15 applicants, 100% accepted, 9 enrolled. *Degree requirements:* For master's, thesis or alternative. *Application deadline:* For fall admission, 8/1 priority date for domestic students; for spring admission, 12/1 priority date for domestic students. Applications are processed on a rolling basis. Application fee: $0. *Expenses:* Tuition, state resident: full-time $3006; part-time $334 per credit hour. Tuition, nonresident: full-time $3006; part-time $334 per credit hour. *Financial support:* In 2013–14, research assistantships (averaging $4,000 per year) were awarded; career-related internships or fieldwork, Federal Work-Study, and institutionally sponsored loans also available. Support available to part-time students. Financial award application deadline: 6/1. *Unit head:* Dr. Bill Hays, Chair, 662-846-4060, Fax: 662-846-4016. *Application contact:* Dr. Beverly Moon, Dean of Graduate Studies, 662-846-4873, Fax: 662-846-4313, E-mail: grad-info@deltastate.edu.
Website: http://www.deltastate.edu/pages/2000.asp.

Delta State University, Graduate Programs, College of Arts and Sciences, Division of Social Sciences and History, Program in Social Science Secondary Education, Cleveland, MS 38733-0001. Offers secondary education (M Ed), including social science. Part-time programs available. *Students:* 8 part-time (3 women); includes 2 minority (both Black or African American, non-Hispanic/Latino). Average age 34. 5 applicants, 100% accepted, 4 enrolled. In 2013, 12 master's awarded. *Degree requirements:* For master's, thesis or alternative. *Application deadline:* For fall admission, 8/1 priority date for domestic students; for spring admission, 12/1 priority date for domestic students. Applications are processed on a rolling basis. Application fee: $0. *Expenses:* Tuition, state resident: full-time $3006; part-time $334 per credit hour. Tuition, nonresident: full-time $3006; part-time $334 per credit hour. *Financial support:* Research assistantships, career-related internships or fieldwork, Federal Work-Study, and institutionally sponsored loans available. Support available to part-time students. Financial award application deadline: 6/1. *Unit head:* Dr. Paulette Miekle, Chair, 662-846-4065, Fax: 662-846-4016, E-mail: pmeikleyaw@deltastate.edu. *Application contact:* Dr. Beverly Moon, Dean of Graduate Studies, 662-846-4873, Fax: 662-846-4313, E-mail: grad-info@deltastate.edu.
Website: http://www.deltastate.edu/pages/4450.asp.

Delta State University, Graduate Programs, College of Education, Division of Teacher Education, Cleveland, MS 38733-0001. Offers elementary education (M Ed, MAT, Ed S); secondary education (MAT); special education (M Ed). *Accreditation:* NCATE. Part-time and evening/weekend programs available. *Faculty:* 13 full-time (9 women), 7 part-time/adjunct (4 women). *Students:* 17 full-time (13 women), 356 part-time (285 women); includes 172 minority (168 Black or African American, non-Hispanic/Latino; 3 Hispanic/Latino; 1 Two or more races, non-Hispanic/Latino), 3 international. Average age 35. 147 applicants, 95% accepted, 101 enrolled. In 2013, 120 master's, 13 other advanced degrees awarded. *Degree requirements:* For master's, thesis optional. *Entrance requirements:* For master's, GRE General Test; for Ed S, master's degree, teaching certificate. *Application deadline:* For fall admission, 8/1 priority date for domestic students; for spring admission, 12/1 priority date for domestic students. Applications are processed on a rolling basis. Application fee: $0. Electronic applications accepted. *Expenses:* Tuition, state resident: full-time $3006; part-time $334 per credit hour. Tuition, nonresident: full-time $3006; part-time $334 per credit hour. *Financial support:* In 2013–14, research assistantships (averaging $6,000 per year) were awarded; career-related internships or fieldwork, Federal Work-Study, and institutionally sponsored loans also available. Support available to part-time students. Financial award application deadline: 6/1. *Faculty research:* Thinking skills, writing across the curriculum, mathematics/science education. *Unit head:* Dr. Jenetta Waddell, Chairperson, 662-846-4370, Fax: 662-846-4402. *Application contact:* Dr. Albert Nylander, Dean of Graduate Studies, 662-846-4875, Fax: 662-846-4313, E-mail: grad-info@deltastate.edu.
Website: http://www.deltastate.edu/pages/568.asp.

DePaul University, College of Education, Chicago, IL 60614. Offers bilingual bicultural education (M Ed, MA); counseling (M Ed, MA), including clinical mental health counseling, college student development, school counseling; curriculum studies (M Ed, MA, Ed D); early childhood education (M Ed, MA, Ed D); educating adults (MA); educational leadership (M Ed, MA, Ed D), including administration and supervision (M Ed, MA), principal preparation (M Ed, MA); elementary education (MA); mathematics education (MA); mathematics for teaching (MS); middle school mathematics education (MS); reading specialist (M Ed, MA); secondary education (M Ed); social and cultural foundations in education (MA); special education (M Ed, MA); world languages education (M Ed, MA). Part-time and evening/weekend programs available. Postbaccalaureate distance learning degree programs offered (no on-campus study). *Faculty:* 61 full-time (35 women), 59 part-time/adjunct (43 women). *Students:* 628 full-time (486 women), 324 part-time (243 women); includes 304 minority (144 Black or African American, non-Hispanic/Latino; 1 American Indian or Alaska Native, non-Hispanic/Latino; 38 Asian, non-Hispanic/Latino; 98 Hispanic/Latino; 23 Two or more races, non-Hispanic/Latino), 24 international. Average age 30. In 2013, 465 master's, 4 doctorates awarded. *Degree requirements:* For doctorate, thesis/dissertation. *Application deadline:* For fall admission, 8/15 for domestic students; for winter admission, 12/1 for domestic students; for spring admission, 3/1 for domestic students. Applications are processed on a rolling basis. Application fee: $40. Electronic applications accepted. Tuition and fees vary according to course level, course load and degree level. *Financial support:* Application deadline: 12/31; applicants required to submit FAFSA. *Unit head:* Dr. Paul Zionts, Dean, 773-325-7581, Fax: 773-325-7713, E-mail: pzionts@depaul.edu. *Application contact:* Farrah Dalal, Assistant Director, 773-325-2465, Fax: 773-325-2270, E-mail: fdalal@depaul.edu.
Website: http://education.depaul.edu.

DeSales University, Graduate Division, Division of Liberal Arts and Social Sciences, Program in Education, Center Valley, PA 18034-9568. Offers early childhood education Pre K-4 (M Ed); instructional technology for K-12 (M Ed); interdisciplinary (M Ed); secondary education (M Ed); special education (M Ed); teaching English to speakers of other languages (M Ed). Part-time and evening/weekend programs available. Postbaccalaureate distance learning degree programs offered (no on-campus study). *Degree requirements:* For master's, thesis project. *Entrance requirements:* Additional exam requirements/recommendations for international students: Required—TOEFL. *Application deadline:* Applications are processed on a rolling basis. Electronic applications accepted. *Expenses: Tuition:* Part-time $790 per credit. *Financial support:* Application deadline: 5/1. *Unit head:* Dr. Judith Rance-Roney, Chair, 610-282-1100 Ext. 1323, E-mail: judith.rance-roney@desales.edu. *Application contact:* Abigail Wernicki, Director of Graduate Admissions, 610-282-1100 Ext. 1768, E-mail: gradadmissions@desales.edu.

Drury University, Graduate Programs in Education, Springfield, MO 65802. Offers elementary education (M Ed); gifted education (M Ed); human services (M Ed); instructional mathematics K-8 (M Ed); instructional technology (M Ed); middle school teaching (M Ed); secondary education (M Ed); special education (M Ed); special reading (M Ed). *Accreditation:* NCATE. Part-time and evening/weekend programs available. *Degree requirements:* For master's, thesis. *Entrance requirements:* For master's, GRE or MAT, minimum GPA of 2.75. Additional exam requirements/recommendations for international students: Required—TOEFL. Electronic applications accepted. *Faculty research:* Cultural enrichment, research skills, parental involvement relating to reading skills, reading strategies for mainstreaming children.

Duquesne University, School of Education, Department of Instruction and Leadership, Program in Secondary Education, Pittsburgh, PA 15282-0001. Offers biology (MS Ed); chemistry (MS Ed); English (MS Ed); K-12 education (MS Ed), including Latin; mathematics (MS Ed); physics (MS Ed); social studies (MS Ed). Part-time and evening/weekend programs available. *Faculty:* 4 full-time (2 women). *Students:* 44 full-time (23 women), 3 part-time (2 women); includes 7 minority (6 Black or African American, non-Hispanic/Latino; 1 Two or more races, non-Hispanic/Latino), 1 international. Average age 27. 43 applicants, 35% accepted, 15 enrolled. In 2013, 28 master's awarded. *Degree requirements:* For master's, thesis optional. *Entrance requirements:* For master's, letters of recommendation, letter of intent, interview, bachelor's degree. Additional exam requirements/recommendations for international students: Required—TOEFL (minimum score 550 paper-based), IELTS (minimum score 7). *Application deadline:* For fall admission, 9/1 for domestic students; for spring admission, 1/1 for domestic students. Applications are processed on a rolling basis. Application fee: $0. Electronic applications accepted. Application fee is waived when completed online. *Expenses: Tuition:* Full-time $18,162; part-time $1009 per credit. *Required fees:* $1728; $96 per credit. Tuition and fees vary according to program. *Financial support:* Research assistantships and Federal Work-Study available. Support available to part-time students. *Unit head:* Dr. Melissa Boston, Associate Professor and Director, 412-396-6109, E-mail: bostonm@duq.edu. *Application contact:* Michael Dolinger, Director of Student and Academic Services, 412-396-6647, Fax: 412-396-5585, E-mail: dolingerm@duq.edu.
Website: http://www.duq.edu/academics/schools/education/graduate-programs-education/ms-ed-secondary-education.

D'Youville College, Department of Education, Buffalo, NY 14201-1084. Offers educational leadership (Ed D); elementary education (MS Ed, Teaching Certificate); secondary education (MS Ed, Teaching Certificate); special education (MS Ed). Part-time and evening/weekend programs available. *Students:* 96 full-time (68 women), 91 part-time (60 women); includes 14 minority (9 Black or African American, non-Hispanic/Latino; 1 American Indian or Alaska Native, non-Hispanic/Latino; 4 Hispanic/Latino), 90 international. Average age 32. 383 applicants, 48% accepted, 104 enrolled. In 2013, 128 master's awarded. *Degree requirements:* For master's, one foreign language, comprehensive exam, project or thesis. *Entrance requirements:* For master's, GRE (if GPA less than 2.75), minimum GPA of 3.0. Additional exam requirements/recommendations for international students: Required—TOEFL (minimum score 500 paper-based). *Application deadline:* For fall admission, 5/1 priority date for international students; for spring admission, 9/1 priority date for international students. Applications are processed on a rolling basis. Application fee: $25. Electronic applications accepted. *Financial support:* Career-related internships or fieldwork, Federal Work-Study, institutionally sponsored loans, scholarships/grants, tuition waivers (full and partial), and unspecified assistantships available. Support available to part-time students. Financial award application deadline: 3/1; financial award applicants required to submit FAFSA. *Faculty research:* Developmental disabilities, multiculturalism, early childhood education. *Unit head:* Dr. Hilary Lochte, Chair, 716-829-8110, Fax: 716-829-7660. *Application contact:* Mark Pavone, Graduate Admissions Director, 716-829-8400, Fax: 716-829-7900, E-mail: graduateadmissions@dyc.edu.

Eastern Connecticut State University, School of Education and Professional Studies/Graduate Division, Program in Secondary Education, Willimantic, CT 06226-2295. Offers MS. *Accreditation:* NCATE. Part-time and evening/weekend programs available. *Degree requirements:* For master's, comprehensive exam or thesis. *Entrance requirements:* For master's, PRAXIS I and II, minimum GPA of 2.7. Additional exam requirements/recommendations for international students: Required—TOEFL (minimum score 550 paper-based).

Eastern Kentucky University, The Graduate School, College of Education, Department of Curriculum and Instruction, Program in Secondary and Higher Education, Richmond, KY 40475-3102. Offers secondary education (MA Ed), including agricultural education, art education, biological sciences education, business education, English education, geography education, history education, home economics education, industrial education, mathematical sciences education, physical education, school health education. *Accreditation:* NCATE. Part-time programs available. *Entrance requirements:* For master's, GRE General Test, minimum GPA of 2.5.

Eastern Michigan University, Graduate School, College of Education, Department of Teacher Education, Programs in K–12 Education, Ypsilanti, MI 48197. Offers curriculum and instruction (MA); elementary education (MA); K-12 education (MA); middle school education (MA); secondary school education (MA). *Accreditation:* NCATE. Part-time and evening/weekend programs available. Postbaccalaureate distance learning degree programs offered (minimal on-campus study). *Students:* 11 full-time (4 women), 46 part-time (31 women); includes 8 minority (4 Black or African American, non-Hispanic/Latino; 1 American Indian or Alaska Native, non-Hispanic/Latino; 3 Hispanic/Latino). Average age 36. 41 applicants, 78% accepted, 20 enrolled. In 2013, 5 master's awarded. *Entrance requirements:* For master's, GRE. Additional exam requirements/recommendations for international students: Required—TOEFL. *Application deadline:* Applications are processed on a rolling basis. Application fee: $35. *Expenses:* Tuition, state resident: full-time $12,300; part-time $466 per credit hour. Tuition, nonresident: full-time $23,159; part-time $918 per credit hour. *Required fees:* $71 per credit hour. $46 per semester. One-time fee: $100. Tuition and fees vary according to course level and degree level. *Financial support:* Fellowships, research assistantships with full tuition reimbursements, teaching assistantships with full tuition reimbursements, career-related internships or fieldwork, Federal Work-Study, institutionally sponsored loans, scholarships/grants, tuition waivers (partial), and unspecified assistantships available. Support available to part-time students. Financial award applicants required to submit

FAFSA. *Unit head:* Dr. Martha Kinney-Sedgwick, Interim Department Head, 734-487-3260, Fax: 734-487-2101, E-mail: mkinneys@emich.edu. *Application contact:* Dr. Ethan Lowenstein, Coordinator, 734-487-3260, Fax: 734-487-2101, E-mail: elowste@emich.edu.

Eastern Nazarene College, Adult and Graduate Studies, Division of Teacher Education, Quincy, MA 02170. Offers administration (M Ed); early childhood education (M Ed, Certificate); elementary education (M Ed, Certificate); English as a second language (Certificate); instructional enrichment and development (Certificate); middle school education (M Ed, Certificate); moderate special needs education (Certificate); principal (Certificate); program development and supervision (Certificate); secondary education (M Ed, Certificate); special education administrator (Certificate); special needs (M Ed); supervisor (Certificate); teacher of reading (M Ed, Certificate). M Ed also available through weekend program for administration, special needs, and teacher of reading only. Part-time and evening/weekend programs available. *Entrance requirements:* Additional exam requirements/recommendations for international students: Required—TOEFL (minimum score 550 paper-based).

Eastern New Mexico University, Graduate School, College of Education and Technology, Department of Educational Studies, Portales, NM 88130. Offers counseling (MA); education (M Ed), including educational administration, secondary education; school counseling (M Ed); special education (M Sp Ed), including early childhood special education, general. *Accreditation:* NCATE. Part-time and evening/weekend programs available. Postbaccalaureate distance learning degree programs offered (minimal on-campus study). *Degree requirements:* For master's, comprehensive exam, thesis optional. *Entrance requirements:* For master's, minimum GPA of 3.0, letter of recommendation, photocopy of teaching license, writing assessment, Level II teaching license (for M Ed in educational administration). Additional exam requirements/recommendations for international students: Required—TOEFL (minimum score 550 paper-based; 79 iBT), IELTS (minimum score 6). Electronic applications accepted.

Eastern Oregon University, Program in Secondary Education, La Grande, OR 97850-2899. Offers MAT. Part-time programs available. Postbaccalaureate distance learning degree programs offered (minimal on-campus study). *Degree requirements:* For master's, thesis. *Entrance requirements:* For master's, NTE.

Eastern University, Graduate Education Programs, St. Davids, PA 19087-3696. Offers ESL program specialist (K-12) (Certificate); general supervisor (PreK-12) (Certificate); health and physical education (K-12) (Certificate); middle level (4-8) (Certificate); multicultural education (M Ed); pre K-4 (Certificate); pre K-4 with special education (Certificate); reading (M Ed); reading specialist (K-12) (Certificate); reading supervisor (K-12) (Certificate); school health services (M Ed); school health supervisor (Certificate); school nurse (Certificate); school principalship (K-12) (Certificate); secondary biology education (7-12) (Certificate); secondary chemistry education (7-12) (Certificate); secondary communication education (7-12) (Certificate); secondary education (7-12) (Certificate); secondary English education (7-12) (Certificate); secondary math education (7-12) (Certificate); secondary social studies education (7-12) (Certificate); special education (M Ed); special education (7-12) (Certificate); special education (Pre K-8) (Certificate); special education supervisor (N-12) (Certificate); TESOL (M Ed); world language (Certificate), including French, Mandarin Chinese, Spanish. Part-time and evening/weekend programs available. Postbaccalaureate distance learning degree programs offered (no on-campus study). *Faculty:* 22 full-time (11 women), 26 part-time/adjunct (18 women). *Students:* 77 full-time (58 women), 223 part-time (149 women); includes 112 minority (81 Black or African American, non-Hispanic/Latino; 1 American Indian or Alaska Native, non-Hispanic/Latino; 9 Asian, non-Hispanic/Latino; 18 Hispanic/Latino; 1 Native Hawaiian or other Pacific Islander, non-Hispanic/Latino; 2 Two or more races, non-Hispanic/Latino), 7 international. Average age 34. 94 applicants, 100% accepted, 81 enrolled. In 2013, 120 master's awarded. *Entrance requirements:* For master's, minimum GPA of 2.5 (for M Ed); for Certificate, minimum GPA of 3.0 for certifications. Additional exam requirements/recommendations for international students: Required—TOEFL. *Application deadline:* For fall admission, 8/14 for domestic students; for spring admission, 12/20 for domestic students. Applications are processed on a rolling basis. Application fee: $35. Application fee is waived when completed online. *Expenses: Tuition:* Full-time $15,600; part-time $650 per credit. *Required fees:* $27.50 per semester. One-time fee: $50. Tuition and fees vary according to course load, degree level and program. *Financial support:* In 2013–14, 84 students received support, including 6 research assistantships with partial tuition reimbursements available (averaging $7,710 per year); scholarships/grants and unspecified assistantships also available. Financial award application deadline: 3/15; financial award applicants required to submit FAFSA. *Unit head:* Harry Gutelius, Associate Dean, 610-341-1729. *Application contact:* Michael Perpiglia, Associate Director of Enrollment, 610-341-5947, Fax: 484-581-1276, E-mail: mperpigl@eastern.edu.
Website: http://www.eastern.edu/academics/programs/loeb-school-education-0/graduateprograms.

Eastern Washington University, Graduate Studies, College of Arts, Letters and Education, Department of Education, Cheney, WA 99004-2431. Offers adult education (M Ed); curriculum development (M Ed); early childhood education (M Ed); education (M Ed); elementary teaching (M Ed); literacy (M Ed); secondary teaching (M Ed); teaching K-8 (M Ed). Part-time programs available. *Faculty:* 29 full-time (20 women), 22 part-time/adjunct (12 women). *Students:* 43 full-time (27 women), 28 part-time (17 women); includes 10 minority (2 Black or African American, non-Hispanic/Latino; 1 American Indian or Alaska Native, non-Hispanic/Latino; 4 Asian, non-Hispanic/Latino; 3 Hispanic/Latino). Average age 38. 33 applicants, 30% accepted, 8 enrolled. In 2013, 50 master's awarded. *Degree requirements:* For master's, comprehensive exam. *Entrance requirements:* For master's, minimum GPA of 3.0. *Application deadline:* For fall admission, 4/1 priority date for domestic students; for spring admission, 1/15 for domestic students. Applications are processed on a rolling basis. Application fee: $50. *Financial support:* In 2013–14, 2 teaching assistantships with partial tuition reimbursements (averaging $7,000 per year) were awarded; career-related internships or fieldwork, Federal Work-Study, institutionally sponsored loans, scholarships/grants, health care benefits, tuition waivers (partial), and unspecified assistantships also available. Support available to part-time students. Financial award application deadline: 2/1; financial award applicants required to submit FAFSA. *Unit head:* Dr. Kevin Pyatt, Assistant Professor, Science and Technology, 509-359-2831, E-mail: kpyatt@ewu.edu. *Application contact:* Dr. Robin Showalter, Graduate Program Coordinator, 509-359-6492, E-mail: rshowalter@ewu.edu.
Website: http://www.ewu.edu/CALE/Programs/Education.xml.

East Stroudsburg University of Pennsylvania, Graduate College, College of Education, Department of Professional and Secondary Education, East Stroudsburg, PA 18301-2999. Offers M Ed. *Accreditation:* NCATE. Part-time and evening/weekend programs available. Postbaccalaureate distance learning degree programs offered. *Faculty:* 4 full-time (1 woman), 5 part-time/adjunct (2 women). *Students:* 22 full-time (9 women), 87 part-time (51 women); includes 16 minority (4 Black or African American, non-Hispanic/Latino; 1 American Indian or Alaska Native, non-Hispanic/Latino; 1 Asian, non-Hispanic/Latino; 10 Hispanic/Latino), 1 international. Average age 37. 57 applicants, 65% accepted, 29 enrolled. In 2013, 22 master's awarded. *Degree requirements:* For master's, independent research problem or comprehensive assessment portfolio. *Entrance requirements:* For master's, PRAXIS/teacher certification, letter of recommendation, Pennsylvania Department of Education requirements. Additional exam requirements/recommendations for international students: Required—TOEFL (minimum score 560 paper-based; 83 iBT) or IELTS. *Application deadline:* For fall admission, 7/31 priority date for domestic students, 5/30 priority date for international students; for spring admission, 11/30 for domestic students, 10/31 for international students. Applications are processed on a rolling basis. Application fee: $50. Electronic applications accepted. *Expenses:* Tuition, state resident: full-time $7956; part-time $442 per credit. Tuition, nonresident: full-time $11,934; part-time $663 per credit. *Required fees:* $2129; $118 per credit. *Financial support:* Research assistantships with full and partial tuition reimbursements, career-related internships or fieldwork, Federal Work-Study, and institutionally sponsored loans available. Financial award application deadline: 3/1; financial award applicants required to submit FAFSA. *Unit head:* Dr. Jeffrey T. Scheetz, Graduate Coordinator, 570-422-3361, Fax: 570-422-3506, E-mail: jscheetz@po-box.esu.edu. *Application contact:* Kevin Quintero, Graduate Admissions Coordinator, 570-422-3536, Fax: 570-422-2711, E-mail: kquintero@esu.edu.
Website: http://www.esu.edu/psed/.

East Tennessee State University, School of Graduate Studies, College of Education, Department of Curriculum and Instruction, Johnson City, TN 37614. Offers educational media and educational technology (M Ed), including educational communications and technology, school library media; elementary education (M Ed); reading (MA), including reading education, storytelling; school library professional (Post-Master's Certificate); secondary education (M Ed), including classroom technology, secondary education (M Ed, MAT); storytelling (Postbaccalaureate Certificate); teacher education with multiple levels (MAT), including elementary education, middle grades education, secondary education (M Ed, MAT). *Accreditation:* NCATE. Part-time and evening/weekend programs available. Postbaccalaureate distance learning degree programs offered (no on-campus study). *Faculty:* 25 full-time (18 women), 12 part-time/adjunct (8 women). *Students:* 66 full-time (50 women), 97 part-time (85 women); includes 5 minority (3 Black or African American, non-Hispanic/Latino; 2 Two or more races, non-Hispanic/Latino), 2 international. Average age 31. 144 applicants, 57% accepted, 70 enrolled. In 2013, 83 master's, 5 other advanced degrees awarded. *Degree requirements:* For master's, comprehensive exam, thesis optional, student teaching, practicum; for other advanced degree, field work (school library); culminating experience (storytelling). *Entrance requirements:* For master's, GRE, SAT, ACT, PRAXIS, minimum GPA of 3.0; for other advanced degree, master's degree, TN teaching license (for school library professional Post-Master's Certificate); three letters of recommendation (for storytelling Postbaccalaureate Certificate). Additional exam requirements/recommendations for international students: Required—TOEFL (minimum score 550 paper-based; 79 iBT). *Application deadline:* For fall admission, 6/1 for domestic students, 4/30 for international students; for spring admission, 11/1 for domestic students, 4/30 for international students. Application fee: $35 ($45 for international students). Electronic applications accepted. *Expenses:* Tuition, state resident: full-time $7900; part-time $395 per credit hour. Tuition, nonresident: full-time $21,960; part-time $1098 per credit hour. *Required fees:* $1345; $84 per credit hour. *Financial support:* In 2013–14, 43 students received support, including 6 research assistantships with full tuition reimbursements available (averaging $6,000 per year), 10 teaching assistantships with full tuition reimbursements available (averaging $6,000 per year); career-related internships or fieldwork, institutionally sponsored loans, scholarships/grants, and unspecified assistantships also available. Financial award application deadline: 7/1; financial award applicants required to submit FAFSA. *Faculty research:* Critical thinking; curriculum development in reading, math, and science education; cultural diversity; cognitive processes; effective teaching strategies. *Unit head:* Dr. Rhona Hurwitz, Chair, 423-439-7598, Fax: 423-439-8362, E-mail: hurwitz@etsu.edu. *Application contact:* Fiona Goodyear, Graduate Specialist, 423-439-6148, Fax: 423-439-5624, E-mail: goodyear@etsu.edu.
Website: http://www.etsu.edu/coe/cuai/.

Edinboro University of Pennsylvania, School of Education, Department of Elementary, Middle and Secondary Education, Edinboro, PA 16444. Offers elementary education (M Ed); middle/secondary instruction (M Ed). Part-time and evening/weekend programs available. *Degree requirements:* For master's, comprehensive exam, thesis or alternative, project. *Entrance requirements:* For master's, GRE or MAT, minimum QPA of 2.5. Electronic applications accepted.

Elms College, Division of Education, Chicopee, MA 01013-2839. Offers early childhood education (MAT); education (M Ed, CAGS); elementary education (MAT); English as a second language (MAT); reading (MAT); secondary education (MAT), including biology education, English education, Spanish education; special education (MAT). Part-time and evening/weekend programs available. *Degree requirements:* For master's, thesis (for some programs). *Entrance requirements:* For master's, Massachusetts Educators Certification Test, minimum GPA of 3.0; for CAGS, master's degree in education. Additional exam requirements/recommendations for international students: Required—TOEFL.

Emmanuel College, Graduate Studies, Graduate Programs in Education, Boston, MA 02115. Offers educational leadership (CAGS); elementary education (MAT); school administration (M Ed); secondary education (MAT). Part-time and evening/weekend programs available. *Faculty:* 3 full-time (all women), 10 part-time/adjunct (7 women). *Students:* 11 full-time (7 women), 22 part-time (13 women); includes 4 minority (3 Black or African American, non-Hispanic/Latino; 1 Native Hawaiian or other Pacific Islander, non-Hispanic/Latino). Average age 30. In 2013, 15 master's, 1 other advanced degree awarded. *Degree requirements:* For master's, 36 credits, including 6-credit practicum. *Entrance requirements:* For master's and CAGS, transcripts from all regionally-accredited institutions attended (showing proof of bachelor's degree completion), 2 letters of recommendation, essay, resume, interview. Additional exam requirements/recommendations for international students: Required—TOEFL (minimum score 600 paper-based; 106 iBT) or IELTS (minimum score 6.5). *Application deadline:* For fall admission, 7/31 priority date for domestic students; for spring admission, 11/30 priority date for domestic students. Applications are processed on a rolling basis. Application fee: $0. Electronic applications accepted. *Financial support:* Applicants required to submit FAFSA. *Unit head:* Sandy Robbins, Dean of Enrollment, 617-735-9700, Fax: 617-507-0434, E-mail: graduatestudies@emmanuel.edu. *Application contact:* Enrollment Counselor, 617-735-9700, Fax: 617-507-0434, E-mail: graduatestudies@emmanuel.edu.
Website: http://www.emmanuel.edu/graduate-studies-nursing/academics/education.html.

Emory University, Laney Graduate School, Division of Educational Studies, Atlanta, GA 30322-1100. Offers educational studies (MA, PhD); middle grades teaching (MAT); secondary teaching (MAT). *Accreditation:* NCATE. Terminal master's awarded for partial completion of doctoral program. *Degree requirements:* For master's, thesis; for doctorate, comprehensive exam, thesis/dissertation. *Entrance requirements:* For master's and doctorate, GRE General Test, minimum GPA of 3.0. Additional exam requirements/recommendations for international students: Required—TOEFL. Electronic applications accepted. *Faculty research:* Educational policy, educational

measurement, urban and multicultural education, mathematics and science education, comparative education.

Endicott College, Van Loan School of Graduate and Professional Studies, Program in Secondary Education, Beverly, MA 01915-2096. Offers M Ed. Part-time and evening/weekend programs available. Postbaccalaureate distance learning degree programs offered. *Faculty:* 8 part-time/adjunct (1 woman). *Students:* 47 full-time (29 women), 14 part-time (8 women); includes 3 minority (2 Asian, non-Hispanic/Latino; 1 Hispanic/Latino), 1 international. Average age 33. 49 applicants, 82% accepted, 38 enrolled. In 2013, 35 master's awarded. *Entrance requirements:* For master's, Massachusetts Tests for Educator Licensure (MTEL) Communication and Literacy Test, Massachusetts Tests for Educator Licensure (MTEL) Subject Matter Test (English, history, political science/philosophy, humanities, mathematics, biology, chemistry, earth science, physics, general science, mathematics/science), MAT or GRE, bachelor's degree from accredited college, transcript. Additional exam requirements/recommendations for international students: Required—TOEFL. *Application deadline:* Applications are processed on a rolling basis. Application fee: $50. Electronic applications accepted. *Financial support:* Applicants required to submit FAFSA. *Unit head:* Dr. John D. MacLean, Jr., Director, 978-232-2408, E-mail: jmaclean@endicott.edu. *Application contact:* Dr. Mary Huegel, Vice President and Dean of the School of Graduate and Professional Studies, 978-232-2084, Fax: 978-232-3000, E-mail: mhuegel@endicott.edu.

Evangel University, Department of Education, Springfield, MO 65802. Offers educational leadership (M Ed); reading education (M Ed); secondary teaching (M Ed); teaching (MA). *Accreditation:* NCATE. Part-time and evening/weekend programs available. *Faculty:* 7 full-time (4 women), 5 part-time/adjunct (4 women). *Students:* 5 full-time (3 women), 37 part-time (28 women); includes 4 minority (3 Hispanic/Latino; 1 Two or more races, non-Hispanic/Latino). Average age 32. 17 applicants, 65% accepted, 11 enrolled. In 2013, 22 master's awarded. *Degree requirements:* For master's, comprehensive exam, thesis optional. *Entrance requirements:* For master's, PRAXIS II (preferred) or GRE. Additional exam requirements/recommendations for international students: Required—TOEFL (minimum score 550 paper-based). *Application deadline:* For fall admission, 7/15 priority date for domestic students, 8/1 for international students; for spring admission, 11/15 priority date for domestic students, 12/1 for international students. Applications are processed on a rolling basis. Application fee: $25. Electronic applications accepted. *Financial support:* In 2013–14, 13 students received support. Career-related internships or fieldwork and scholarships/grants available. Support available to part-time students. Financial award application deadline: 3/1; financial award applicants required to submit FAFSA. *Unit head:* Dr. Matt Stringer, Program Coordinator, 417-865-2815 Ext. 8563, E-mail: stringerm@evangel.edu. *Application contact:* Karen Benitez, Admissions Representative, Graduate Studies, 417-865-2811 Ext. 7227, Fax: 417-865-9599, E-mail: benitezk@evangel.edu.
Website: http://www.evangel.edu/academics/graduate-studies/graduate-programs.

Fairfield University, Graduate School of Education and Allied Professions, Fairfield, CT 06824-5195. Offers applied behavior analysis (ATC); applied psychology (MA); clinical mental health counseling (MA, CAS); early childhood studies (ATC); educational technology (MA); elementary education (MA, CAS); family studies (MA); integration of spirituality and religion in counseling (ATC); marriage and family therapy (MA); school counseling (MA, CAS); school psychology (MA, CAS); school-based marriage and family therapy (ATC); secondary education (MA); special education (MA, CAS); substance abuse counseling (ATC); teaching (Certificate); teaching and foundations (MA, CAS); TESOL, world languages, and bilingual education (MA, CAS). *Accreditation:* NCATE. Part-time and evening/weekend programs available. *Faculty:* 24 full-time (21 women), 39 part-time/adjunct (27 women). *Students:* 154 full-time (130 women), 307 part-time (248 women); includes 75 minority (14 Black or African American, non-Hispanic/Latino; 1 American Indian or Alaska Native, non-Hispanic/Latino; 10 Asian, non-Hispanic/Latino; 44 Hispanic/Latino; 6 Two or more races, non-Hispanic/Latino), 13 international. Average age 34. 263 applicants, 41% accepted, 91 enrolled. In 2013, 149 master's, 21 other advanced degrees awarded. *Degree requirements:* For master's, comprehensive exam. *Entrance requirements:* For master's, PRAXIS I (for certification programs), minimum GPA of 3.0, 2 recommendations, resume. Additional exam requirements/recommendations for international students: Required—TOEFL (minimum score 550 paper-based; 84 iBT) or IELTS (minimum score 7.5). *Application deadline:* For fall admission, 2/15 for international students; for spring admission, 10/1 for international students. Application fee: $60. Electronic applications accepted. *Expenses: Tuition:* Part-time $675 per credit hour. Tuition and fees vary according to program. *Financial support:* In 2013–14, 55 students received support. Career-related internships or fieldwork and unspecified assistantships available. Financial award applicants required to submit FAFSA. *Faculty research:* Literacy, adolescent psychology, special education, teaching development, mentoring for professional development, multicultural education. *Total annual research expenditures:* $325,000. *Unit head:* Dr. Robert D. Hannafin, Dean, 203-254-4250, Fax: 203-254-4241, E-mail: rhannafin@fairfield.edu. *Application contact:* Marianne Gumpper, Director of Graduate and Continuing Studies Admission, 203-254-4184, Fax: 203-254-4073, E-mail: gradadmis@fairfield.edu.
Website: http://www.fairfield.edu/academics/schoolscollegescenters/graduateschoolofeducationalliedprofessions/graduateprograms/.

Fayetteville State University, Graduate School, Programs in Middle Grades, Secondary and Special Education and Elementary Education, Fayetteville, NC 28301-4298. Offers biology (MA Ed); elementary education (MA Ed); history (MA Ed); mathematics (MA Ed); middle grades (MA Ed); political science (MA Ed); reading (MA Ed); sociology (MA Ed); special education (MA Ed), including behavioral-emotional handicaps, mentally handicapped, specific training disability. *Accreditation:* NCATE. Part-time and evening/weekend programs available. *Faculty:* 12 full-time (8 women), 4 part-time/adjunct (3 women). *Students:* 25 full-time (22 women), 49 part-time (45 women); includes 51 minority (48 Black or African American, non-Hispanic/Latino; 1 American Indian or Alaska Native, non-Hispanic/Latino; 2 Hispanic/Latino). Average age 35. 5 applicants, 100% accepted, 5 enrolled. In 2013, 29 master's awarded. *Degree requirements:* For master's, comprehensive exam, internship. *Application deadline:* For fall admission, 4/15 for domestic students; for spring admission, 10/15 for domestic students. Applications are processed on a rolling basis. Application fee: $40. Electronic applications accepted. *Faculty research:* Students with disabilities and selected leadership behaviors, new vision for professional development, gifted and talented students, emotional and behavioral disabilities, professional development for high school biology teachers. *Unit head:* Dr. Kimberly Smith-Burton, Interim Chair, 910-672-1182, E-mail: cbarringerbrown@uncfsu.edu. *Application contact:* Katrina Hoffman, Graduate Admission Officer, 910-672-1374, Fax: 910-672-1470, E-mail: khoffma1@uncfsu.edu.

Fitchburg State University, Division of Graduate and Continuing Education, Program in Secondary Education, Fitchburg, MA 01420-2697. Offers M Ed. *Accreditation:* NCATE. Part-time and evening/weekend programs available. *Entrance requirements:* Additional exam requirements/recommendations for international students: Required—TOEFL (minimum score 550 paper-based; 79 iBT). Electronic applications accepted.

Florida Agricultural and Mechanical University, Division of Graduate Studies, Research, and Continuing Education, College of Education, Program in Secondary Education and Foundation, Tallahassee, FL 32307-3200. Offers biology (M Ed); chemistry (MS Ed); English (MS Ed); history (MS Ed); math (MS Ed); physics (MS Ed). *Accreditation:* NCATE. *Degree requirements:* For master's, thesis (for some programs). *Entrance requirements:* For master's, GRE General Test, minimum GPA of 3.0. Additional exam requirements/recommendations for international students: Required—TOEFL.

Florida State University, The Graduate School, College of Arts and Sciences, Department of Biological Science, Masters in Science Teaching Program, Tallahassee, FL 32306. Offers community college science teaching (MST); secondary science teaching (MST). *Faculty:* 2 full-time (both women). *Students:* 4 full-time (2 women). Average age 27. 3 applicants, 67% accepted, 2 enrolled. In 2013, 4 master's awarded. *Degree requirements:* For master's, thesis or alternative, teacher work sample (action research). *Entrance requirements:* For master's, GRE. *Application deadline:* For fall admission, 7/1 for domestic students; for spring admission, 11/1 for domestic students; for summer admission, 3/1 for domestic students. Application fee: $30. Electronic applications accepted. *Expenses:* Tuition, state resident: part-time $403.51 per credit hour. Tuition, nonresident: part-time $1004.85 per credit hour. *Required fees:* $75.81 per credit hour. One-time fee: $20 part-time. Tuition and fees vary according to course load, campus/location and student level. *Faculty research:* Science and mathematics education, science and mathematics teacher preparation. *Total annual research expenditures:* $500,000. *Unit head:* Dr. Don R. Levitan, Chairman and Professor, Department of Biological Science, 850-644-4424, Fax: 850-645-8447, E-mail: levitan@bio.fsu.edu. *Application contact:* Erica M. Staehling, Director, Master's in Science Teaching Program, 850-644-1142, Fax: 850-644-0643, E-mail: staehling@bio.fsu.edu.
Website: http://bio.fsu.edu/osta/tpp.php.

Fordham University, Graduate School of Education, Division of Curriculum and Teaching, New York, NY 10023. Offers adult education (MS, MSE); bilingual teacher education (MSE); curriculum and teaching (MSE); early childhood education (MSE); elementary education (MST); language, literacy, and learning (PhD); reading education (MSE, Adv C); secondary education (MAT, MSE); special education (MSE, Adv C); teaching English as a second language (MSE). *Accreditation:* NCATE. *Degree requirements:* For doctorate, thesis/dissertation; for Adv C, thesis. *Entrance requirements:* For doctorate, MAT, GRE General Test.

Francis Marion University, Graduate Programs, School of Education, Florence, SC 29502-0547. Offers early childhood education (M Ed); elementary education (M Ed); learning disabilities (M Ed, MAT); remedial education (M Ed); secondary education (M Ed). *Accreditation:* NCATE. Part-time programs available. *Faculty:* 17 full-time (12 women). *Students:* 5 full-time (3 women), 79 part-time (63 women); includes 33 minority (all Black or African American, non-Hispanic/Latino). Average age 34. 327 applicants, 42% accepted, 135 enrolled. In 2013, 45 master's awarded. *Degree requirements:* For master's, comprehensive exam. *Entrance requirements:* For master's, GRE General Test, MAT, NTE, or PRAXIS II. *Application deadline:* For fall admission, 3/15 priority date for domestic students; for spring admission, 10/15 priority date for domestic students. Application fee: $33. *Expenses:* Tuition, state resident: full-time $9184; part-time $459.20 per credit hour. Tuition, nonresident: full-time $18,368; part-time $918.40 per credit hour. *Required fees:* $13.50 per credit hour. $92 per semester. Tuition and fees vary according to program. *Financial support:* In 2013–14, 2 research assistantships (averaging $6,000 per year) were awarded; scholarships/grants and unspecified assistantships also available. Support available to part-time students. Financial award application deadline: 3/1; financial award applicants required to submit FAFSA. *Faculty research:* Identification and alternate assessment of at-risk students. *Unit head:* Dr. Shirley Carr Bausmith, Dean, 843-661-1460, Fax: 843-661-4647. *Application contact:* Rannie Gamble, Administrative Manager, 843-661-1286, Fax: 843-661-4688, E-mail: rgamble@fmarion.edu.

Frostburg State University, Graduate School, College of Education, Department of Educational Professions, Program in Curriculum and Instruction, Frostburg, MD 21532-1099. Offers educational technology (M Ed); elementary education (M Ed); secondary education (M Ed). Part-time and evening/weekend programs available. *Degree requirements:* For master's, thesis or alternative. *Entrance requirements:* For master's, teaching certificate. Additional exam requirements/recommendations for international students: Required—TOEFL. Electronic applications accepted. *Expenses: Tuition, area resident:* Part-time $340 per credit hour. Tuition, state resident: part-time $340 per credit hour. Tuition, nonresident: part-time $437 per credit hour.

Frostburg State University, Graduate School, College of Education, Department of Educational Professions, Program in Secondary Teaching, Frostburg, MD 21532-1099. Offers MAT. *Entrance requirements:* For master's, PRAXIS I, entry portfolio. Additional exam requirements/recommendations for international students: Required—TOEFL. *Expenses: Tuition, area resident:* Part-time $340 per credit hour. Tuition, state resident: part-time $340 per credit hour. Tuition, nonresident: part-time $437 per credit hour.

Gallaudet University, The Graduate School, Washington, DC 20002-3625. Offers ASL/English bilingual early childhood education: birth to 5 (Certificate); audiology (Au D); clinical psychology (PhD); critical studies in the education of deaf learners (PhD); deaf and hard of hearing infants, toddlers, and their families (Certificate); deaf education (Ed S); deaf education: advanced studies (MA); deaf education: special programs (MA); deaf history (Certificate); deaf studies (MA, Certificate); educating deaf students with disabilities (Certificate); education: teacher preparation (MA), including deaf education, early childhood education and deaf education, elementary education and deaf education, secondary education and deaf education; educational neuroscience (PhD); hearing, speech and language sciences (MS, PhD); international development (MA); interpretation (MA, PhD), including combined interpreting practice and research (MA), interpreting research (MA); linguistics (MA, PhD); mental health counseling (MA); peer mentoring (Certificate); public administration (MPA); school counseling (MA); school psychology (Psy S); sign language teaching (MA); social work (MSW); speech-language pathology (MS). Part-time programs available. *Faculty:* 55 full-time (37 women). *Students:* 361 full-time (279 women), 108 part-time (73 women); includes 98 minority (39 Black or African American, non-Hispanic/Latino; 1 American Indian or Alaska Native, non-Hispanic/Latino; 12 Asian, non-Hispanic/Latino; 36 Hispanic/Latino; 1 Native Hawaiian or other Pacific Islander, non-Hispanic/Latino; 9 Two or more races, non-Hispanic/Latino), 31 international. Average age 30. 602 applicants, 49% accepted, 177 enrolled. In 2013, 140 master's, 32 doctorates, 11 other advanced degrees awarded. Terminal master's awarded for partial completion of doctoral program. *Degree requirements:* For master's, comprehensive exam (for some programs), thesis optional; for doctorate, comprehensive exam, thesis/dissertation. *Entrance requirements:* For master's and doctorate, GRE General Test or MAT, letters of recommendation, interviews, goals statement, ASL proficiency interview, written English competency. Additional exam requirements/recommendations for international students: Required—TOEFL. *Application deadline:* For fall admission, 2/15 for domestic students. Applications are processed on a rolling basis. Application fee: $75. Electronic applications accepted. *Expenses: Tuition:* Full-time $14,774; part-time $821 per credit. *Required fees:* $198 per semester. *Financial support:* In 2013–14, 325 students received support. Fellowships, research assistantships, teaching assistantships, career-related internships or fieldwork, Federal Work-Study, scholarships/grants, tuition waivers (partial), and unspecified assistantships available. Support available to part-time

students. Financial award applicants required to submit FAFSA. *Faculty research:* Bimodal bilingualism development, cochlear implants, telecommunications access, cancer genetics, linguistics, visual language and visual learning, advancement of avatar and robotics translation, algal productivity and physiology in the Anacostia River. *Unit head:* Dr. Carol J. Erting, Dean, Research, Graduate School, Continuing Studies, and International Programs, 202-651-5520, Fax: 202-651-5027, E-mail: carol.erting@gallaudet.edu. *Application contact:* Wednesday Luria, Coordinator of Prospective Graduate Student Services, 202-651-5400, Fax: 202-651-5295, E-mail: graduate.school@gallaudet.edu.
Website: http://www.gallaudet.edu/x26696.xml.

George Fox University, College of Education, Educational Foundations and Leadership Program, Newberg, OR 97132-2697. Offers continuing administrator license (Certificate); curriculum and instruction (M Ed); educational leadership (M Ed, Ed D); ESOL (Certificate); higher education (M Ed); initial administrator license (Certificate); instructional leadership (Ed S); library media (M Ed, Certificate); literacy (M Ed); reading (M Ed); secondary education (M Ed). *Accreditation:* NCATE. Part-time and evening/weekend programs available. Postbaccalaureate distance learning degree programs offered (minimal on-campus study). *Faculty:* 7 full-time (3 women), 5 part-time/adjunct (4 women). *Students:* 194 part-time (128 women); includes 15 minority (1 Black or African American, non-Hispanic/Latino; 1 American Indian or Alaska Native, non-Hispanic/Latino; 3 Asian, non-Hispanic/Latino; 6 Hispanic/Latino; 1 Native Hawaiian or other Pacific Islander, non-Hispanic/Latino; 3 Two or more races, non-Hispanic/Latino), 2 international. Average age 42. 46 applicants, 85% accepted, 39 enrolled. In 2013, 15 master's, 16 doctorates, 106 Certificates awarded. *Degree requirements:* For master's, thesis (for some programs); for doctorate, comprehensive exam, thesis/dissertation, project. *Entrance requirements:* For master's, minimum undergraduate GPA of 3.0 during previous 2 years of course work, resume, 3 professional recommendations on university forms, official transcripts; for doctorate, GRE, master's degree with minimum GPA of 3.25, 3 years of relevant professional experience, interview, personal essay, scholarly work, 3 professional recommendations on university forms along with 3 written letters of recommendation, official transcripts. Additional exam requirements/recommendations for international students: Required—TOEFL (minimum score 577 paper-based; 90 iBT). *Application deadline:* For fall admission, 7/15 for domestic and international students; for winter admission, 11/1 for domestic and international students; for spring admission, 4/1 for domestic and international students. Applications are processed on a rolling basis. Application fee: $40. Electronic applications accepted. *Expenses:* Contact institution. *Financial support:* Career-related internships or fieldwork available. Financial award applicants required to submit FAFSA. *Unit head:* Dr. Scot Headley, Professor/Chair, 503-554-2836, E-mail: sheadley@georgefox.edu. *Application contact:* Kipp Wilfong, Graduate Admissions Counselor, 800-631-0921, Fax: 503-554-3110, E-mail: kwilfong@georgefox.edu.
Website: http://www.georgefox.edu/education/index.html.

The George Washington University, Graduate School of Education and Human Development, Department of Curriculum and Pedagogy, Program in Secondary Education, Washington, DC 20052. Offers M Ed. Program also offered in Arlington and Ashburn, VA. *Accreditation:* NCATE. *Students:* 14 full-time (12 women), 29 part-time (19 women); includes 11 minority (3 Black or African American, non-Hispanic/Latino; 2 Asian, non-Hispanic/Latino; 6 Hispanic/Latino), 3 international. Average age 32. 42 applicants, 93% accepted, 25 enrolled. In 2013, 23 master's awarded. *Degree requirements:* For master's, comprehensive exam. *Entrance requirements:* For master's, GRE General Test or MAT, interview, minimum GPA of 2.75. *Application deadline:* For fall admission, 1/15 priority date for domestic students; for spring admission, 10/1 for domestic students. Applications are processed on a rolling basis. Application fee: $75. *Financial support:* Fellowships, career-related internships or fieldwork, Federal Work-Study, tuition waivers (full and partial), and stipends available. Financial award application deadline: 1/15; financial award applicants required to submit FAFSA. *Unit head:* Prof. Curtis Pyke, Chair, 202-994-4516, E-mail: cpyke@gwu.edu. *Application contact:* Sarah Lang, Director of Graduate Admissions, 202-994-1447, Fax: 202-994-7207, E-mail: slang@gwu.edu.

Georgia College & State University, Graduate School, The John H. Lounsbury College of Education, Program in Secondary Education, Milledgeville, GA 31061. Offers M Ed, MAT, Ed S. *Students:* 49 full-time (30 women), 9 part-time (6 women); includes 5 minority (3 Black or African American, non-Hispanic/Latino; 1 Asian, non-Hispanic/Latino; 1 Native Hawaiian or other Pacific Islander, non-Hispanic/Latino). Average age 27. In 2013, 70 master's awarded. *Degree requirements:* For master's, comprehensive exam, minimum GPA of 3.0, complete program within 4 years; for Ed S, minimum GPA of 3.0, complete program within 4 years. *Entrance requirements:* For master's, writing assessment, 2 recommendations, transcripts, minimum GPA of 2.5, proof of immunization; for Ed S, 2 recommendations, transcripts, minimum GPA of 3.25, T5 certification, two years of teaching experience. Additional exam requirements/recommendations for international students: Recommended—TOEFL (minimum score 550 paper-based; 79 iBT). *Application deadline:* For fall admission, 7/1 for domestic students; for spring admission, 11/15 for domestic students. Applications are processed on a rolling basis. Application fee: $40. Electronic applications accepted. *Financial support:* In 2013–14, 6 research assistantships were awarded. Financial award applicants required to submit FAFSA. *Application contact:* Shanda Brand, Graduate Admission Advisor, 478-445-1383, Fax: 478-445-6582, E-mail: shanda.brand@gcsu.edu.

Georgia Regents University, The Graduate School, College of Education, Program in Teaching/Learning, Augusta, GA 30912. Offers MAT, Ed S. *Degree requirements:* For master's, thesis, portfolio. *Entrance requirements:* For master's, GRE, MAT, minimum GPA of 2.5.

Georgia Southern University, Jack N. Averitt College of Graduate Studies, College of Education, Department of Teaching and Learning, Program in P-12 Education, Statesboro, GA 30460. Offers MAT. *Students:* 4 full-time (all women); includes 3 minority (all Hispanic/Latino). Average age 28. 5 applicants, 100% accepted. In 2013, 2 master's awarded. *Expenses:* Tuition, state resident: full-time $7068; part-time $270 per semester hour. Tuition, nonresident: full-time $26,446; part-time $1077 per semester hour. *Required fees:* $2092. *Financial support:* In 2013–14, 4 students received support. *Unit head:* Dr. Greg Chamblee, Program Coordinator, 912-478-5783, Fax: 912-478-0026, E-mail: gchamblee@georgiasouthern.edu. *Application contact:* Amanda Gilliland, Coordinator for Graduate Student Recruitment, 912-478-5384, Fax: 912-478-0740, E-mail: gradschool@georgiasouthern.edu.

Georgia Southern University, Jack N. Averitt College of Graduate Studies, College of Education, Department of Teaching and Learning, Program in Secondary Education, Statesboro, GA 30460. Offers M Ed, MAT, Ed S. Part-time and evening/weekend programs available. *Students:* 31 full-time (21 women), 36 part-time (26 women); includes 11 minority (7 Black or African American, non-Hispanic/Latino; 1 Asian, non-Hispanic/Latino; 2 Hispanic/Latino; 1 Two or more races, non-Hispanic/Latino). Average age 29. 34 applicants, 71% accepted, 16 enrolled. In 2013, 4 master's, 1 other advanced degree awarded. *Degree requirements:* For master's, portfolio, transition point assessments, exit assessment. *Entrance requirements:* For master's, GRE General Test or MAT, minimum cumulative GPA of 2.5. Additional exam requirements/

recommendations for international students: Required—TOEFL (minimum score 550 paper-based; 80 iBT), IELTS (minimum score 6). *Application deadline:* For fall admission, 3/1 priority date for domestic and international students; for spring admission, 10/1 priority date for domestic students, 10/1 for international students. Applications are processed on a rolling basis. Application fee: $50. Electronic applications accepted. *Expenses:* Tuition, state resident: full-time $7068; part-time $270 per semester hour. Tuition, nonresident: full-time $26,446; part-time $1077 per semester hour. *Required fees:* $2092. *Financial support:* In 2013–14, 7 students received support, including research assistantships with partial tuition reimbursements available (averaging $7,200 per year), teaching assistantships with partial tuition reimbursements available (averaging $7,200 per year); career-related internships or fieldwork, Federal Work-Study, and tuition waivers (partial) also available. Support available to part-time students. Financial award application deadline: 4/15; financial award applicants required to submit FAFSA. *Faculty research:* Social studies education, mathematics education, science education, language arts education, dispositions. *Unit head:* Dr. Missy Bennett, Coordinator, 912-478-0356, Fax: 912-478-0026, E-mail: mbennett@georgiasouthern.edu. *Application contact:* Amanda Gilliland, Coordinator for Graduate Student Recruitment, 912-478-5384, Fax: 912-478-0740, E-mail: gradadmissions@georgiasouthern.edu.
Website: http://coe.georgiasouthern.edu/ger/.

Georgia Southwestern State University, Graduate Studies, School of Education, Americus, GA 31709-4693. Offers early childhood education (M Ed, Ed S); health and physical education (M Ed); middle grades education (M Ed, Ed S); reading (M Ed); secondary education (M Ed); special education (M Ed). *Accreditation:* NCATE. *Degree requirements:* For master's, comprehensive exam. *Entrance requirements:* For master's, GRE General Test or MAT, minimum GPA of 2.5; for Ed S, GRE General Test or MAT, minimum graduate GPA of 3.25, M Ed from accredited college or university, 3 years teaching experience. Electronic applications accepted.

Georgia State University, College of Education, Department of Middle-Secondary Education and Instructional Technology, Atlanta, GA 30302-3083. Offers English education (M Ed, MAT); English speakers of other languages (MAT); instructional design and technology (MS); instructional technology (PhD), including alternative instructional delivery systems, consulting, instructional design, management, research; mathematics education (M Ed, MAT); middle level education (MAT); reading, language and literacy education (M Ed), including reading instruction; science education (MAT), including biology, broad field science, chemistry, earth science, physics; social studies education (M Ed, MAT), including economics (MAT), geography (MAT), history (MAT), political science (MAT); teaching and learning (PhD), including language and literacy, mathematics education, music education, science education, social studies, teaching and teacher education. *Accreditation:* NCATE. Part-time and evening/weekend programs available. Postbaccalaureate distance learning degree programs offered (minimal on-campus study). *Faculty:* 27 full-time (19 women). *Students:* 181 full-time (113 women), 203 part-time (145 women); includes 161 minority (127 Black or African American, non-Hispanic/Latino; 1 American Indian or Alaska Native, non-Hispanic/Latino; 10 Asian, non-Hispanic/Latino; 11 Hispanic/Latino; 1 Native Hawaiian or other Pacific Islander, non-Hispanic/Latino; 11 Two or more races, non-Hispanic/Latino), 9 international. Average age 36. 2 applicants, 50% accepted, 1 enrolled. In 2013, 213 master's, 17 doctorates awarded. *Degree requirements:* For master's, comprehensive exam (for some programs), thesis or alternative, exit portfolio; for doctorate, comprehensive exam, thesis/dissertation. *Entrance requirements:* For master's, GRE; GACE I (for initial teacher preparation degree programs), baccalaureate degree or equivalent, resume, goals statement, two letters of recommendation, minimum undergraduate GPA of 2.5; proof of initial teacher certification in the content area (for M Ed); for doctorate, GRE, resume, goals statement, writing sample, two letters of recommendation, minimum graduate GPA of 3.3, interview. Additional exam requirements/recommendations for international students: Required—TOEFL (minimum score 550 paper-based; 79 iBT) or IELTS (minimum score 6.5). *Application deadline:* For fall admission, 1/15 priority date for domestic and international students; for spring admission, 10/1 for domestic and international students. Application fee: $50. Electronic applications accepted. *Expenses: Tuition, area resident:* Full-time $4176; part-time $348 per credit hour. Tuition, state resident: full-time $14,544; part-time $1212 per credit hour. Tuition, nonresident: full-time $14,544; part-time $1212 per credit hour. Tuition and fees vary according to course load and program. *Financial support:* In 2013–14, fellowships with full tuition reimbursements (averaging $19,667 per year), research assistantships with full tuition reimbursements (averaging $5,436 per year), teaching assistantships with full tuition reimbursements (averaging $2,779 per year) were awarded; career-related internships or fieldwork, Federal Work-Study, scholarships/grants, health care benefits, tuition waivers (full and partial), and unspecified assistantships also available. Financial award application deadline: 3/15. *Faculty research:* Teacher education in language and literacy, mathematics, science, and social studies in urban middle and secondary school settings; learning technologies in school, community, and corporate settings; multicultural education and education for social justice; urban education; international education. *Unit head:* Dr. Dana L. Fox, Chair, 404-413-8060, Fax: 404-413-8063, E-mail: dfox@gsu.edu. *Application contact:* Bobbie Turner, Administrative Coordinator I, 404-413-8405, Fax: 404-413-8063, E-mail: bnturner@gsu.edu.
Website: http://msit.gsu.edu/msit_programs.htm.

Grand Canyon University, College of Education, Phoenix, AZ 85017-1097. Offers curriculum and instruction (M Ed); education administration (M Ed); elementary education (M Ed); secondary education (M Ed); special education (M Ed); teaching (MA). Part-time and evening/weekend programs available. Postbaccalaureate distance learning degree programs offered (no on-campus study). *Degree requirements:* For master's, publishable research paper (M Ed), e-portfolio. *Entrance requirements:* For master's, undergraduate degree from accredited, GCU-approved college, university, or program with minimum GPA 2.8. Additional exam requirements/recommendations for international students: Required—TOEFL (minimum score 550 paper-based; 79 iBT), IELTS (minimum score 6). Electronic applications accepted.

Grand Valley State University, College of Education, Programs in General Education, Allendale, MI 49401-9403. Offers adult and higher education (M Ed); early childhood education (M Ed); educational differentiation (M Ed); educational leadership (M Ed); educational technology integration (M Ed); elementary education (M Ed); middle level education (M Ed); school library media services (M Ed); secondary level education (M Ed); teaching English to speakers of other languages (M Ed). Part-time and evening/weekend programs available. Postbaccalaureate distance learning degree programs offered (minimal on-campus study). *Degree requirements:* For master's, thesis. *Entrance requirements:* For master's, GRE General Test or minimum GPA of 3.0. Additional exam requirements/recommendations for international students: Required—TOEFL. Electronic applications accepted. *Faculty research:* Effectiveness of technology in education, parental involvement, effective teaching, effective schools research.

Greenville College, Program in Education, Greenville, IL 62246-0159. Offers education (MAT); elementary education (MAE); secondary education (MAE). *Degree requirements:* For master's, thesis (for some programs). *Entrance requirements:* For

master's, GRE, Illinois Basic Skills Test, teacher certification. Electronic applications accepted.

Hampton University, Graduate College, College of Education and Continuing Studies, Program in Teaching, Hampton, VA 23668. Offers early childhood education (MT); middle school education (MT); music education (MT); secondary education (MT); special education (MT). *Entrance requirements:* For master's, GRE General Test.

Harding University, Cannon-Clary College of Education, Searcy, AR 72149-0001. Offers advanced studies in teaching and learning (M Ed); art (MSE); behavioral science (MSE); counseling (MS, Ed S); early childhood special education (M Ed, MSE); education (MSE); educational leadership (M Ed, Ed S); elementary education (M Ed); English (MSE); French (MSE); history/social science (MSE); kinesiology (MSE); math (MSE); reading (M Ed); secondary education (M Ed); Spanish (MSE); teaching (MAT); teaching English as a second language (MSE). *Accreditation:* NCATE. Part-time and evening/weekend programs available. *Faculty:* 13 full-time (5 women), 42 part-time/adjunct (24 women). *Students:* 154 full-time (119 women), 393 part-time (270 women); includes 108 minority (81 Black or African American, non-Hispanic/Latino; 5 American Indian or Alaska Native, non-Hispanic/Latino; 5 Asian, non-Hispanic/Latino; 9 Hispanic/Latino; 8 Two or more races, non-Hispanic/Latino), 15 international. Average age 36. 187 applicants, 79% accepted, 135 enrolled. In 2013, 138 master's, 17 other advanced degrees awarded. *Degree requirements:* For master's, comprehensive exam (for some programs), thesis optional, portfolio(s); for Ed S, comprehensive exam, portfolio, project. *Entrance requirements:* For master's, GRE, MAT, PRAXIS; for Ed S, MAT or GRE. Additional exam requirements/recommendations for international students: Required—TOEFL (minimum score 550 paper-based; 79 iBT). *Application deadline:* For fall admission, 8/1 for domestic and international students; for spring admission, 1/1 for domestic and international students. Applications are processed on a rolling basis. Application fee: $35. *Expenses: Tuition:* Full-time $11,574; part-time $643 per credit hour. *Required fees:* $432; $24 per credit hour. Tuition and fees vary according to course load, degree level and program. *Financial support:* In 2013–14, 36 students received support. Unspecified assistantships available. *Faculty research:* Reading, comprehension, school violence, educational technology, behavior, college choice, differentiated instruction, brain-based teaching. *Unit head:* Dr. Clara Carroll, Chair, 501-279-4501, Fax: 501-279-4083, E-mail: ccarroll@harding.edu. *Application contact:* Information Contact, 501-279-4315, E-mail: gradstudiesedu@harding.edu.
Website: http://www.harding.edu/education.

Hawai`i Pacific University, College of Humanities and Social Sciences, Program in Secondary Education, Honolulu, HI 96813. Offers M Ed. Part-time and evening/weekend programs available. *Faculty:* 4 full-time (2 women), 4 part-time/adjunct (3 women). *Students:* 43 full-time (27 women), 4 part-time (3 women); includes 31 minority (9 Asian, non-Hispanic/Latino; 7 Hispanic/Latino; 1 Native Hawaiian or other Pacific Islander, non-Hispanic/Latino; 14 Two or more races, non-Hispanic/Latino). Average age 30. 13 applicants, 85% accepted, 10 enrolled. In 2013, 22 master's awarded. *Degree requirements:* For master's, thesis. *Entrance requirements:* For master's, PRAXIS I and II. Additional exam requirements/recommendations for international students: Recommended—TOEFL (minimum score 550 paper-based; 80 iBT), TWE (minimum score 5). *Application deadline:* For fall admission, 2/15 priority date for domestic students; for spring admission, 10/15 priority date for domestic students. Applications are processed on a rolling basis. Application fee: $50. Electronic applications accepted. *Financial support:* In 2013–14, 18 students received support. Career-related internships or fieldwork, Federal Work-Study, scholarships/grants, tuition waivers, and unspecified assistantships available. Financial award application deadline: 3/1. *Unit head:* Dr. Valentina Abordonado, Program Chair, 808-544-1143, Fax: 808-544-0841, E-mail: vabordonado@hpu.edu. *Application contact:* Rumi Yoshida, Associate Director of Graduate Admissions, 808-543-8035, Fax: 808-544-0280, E-mail: grad@hpu.edu.
Website: http://www.hpu.edu/CHSS/Education/MEDSE/index.html.

High Point University, Norcross Graduate School, High Point, NC 27262-3598. Offers business administration (MBA); educational leadership (M Ed); elementary education (M Ed); history (MA); nonprofit management (MA); secondary math (M Ed); special education (M Ed); strategic communication (MA); teaching elementary education k-6 (MAT); teaching secondary mathematics 9-12 (MAT). *Accreditation:* NCATE. Part-time and evening/weekend programs available. *Degree requirements:* For master's, comprehensive exam (for some programs), thesis (for some programs). *Entrance requirements:* For master's, GMAT (MBA), GRE, MAT, minimum GPA of 3.0. Additional exam requirements/recommendations for international students: Required—TOEFL (minimum score 550 paper-based). Electronic applications accepted.

Hofstra University, School of Education, Programs in Educational Policy and Leadership, Hempstead, NY 11549. Offers educational and policy leadership (MS Ed, Ed D), including K-12 (MS Ed), K-12/higher education (Ed D); educational policy and leadership (Advanced Certificate), including school district business leader; foundations of education (MA, Advanced Certificate); higher education leadership and policy studies (MS Ed).

Hofstra University, School of Education, Programs in Literacy, Hempstead, NY 11549. Offers advanced literacy studies (PD), including birth-grade 6 (MA, MS Ed, PD); advanced literary studies (PD), including grades 5-12 (MA, PD); birth-grade 6 (MS Ed, Advanced Certificate); grades 5-12 (Advanced Certificate); literacy studies (Ed D, PhD); special education (MS Ed), including birth-grade 2, birth-grade 6 (MA, MS Ed, PD); teaching of writing (MA), including birth-grade 6 (MA, MS Ed, PD), grades 5-12 (MA, PD).

Hofstra University, School of Education, Programs in Special Education, Hempstead, NY 11549. Offers applied behavior analysis (Advanced Certificate); early childhood special education (MS Ed, Advanced Certificate); gifted education (Advanced Certificate); inclusive early childhood special education (MS Ed); inclusive elementary special education (MS Ed); inclusive secondary special education (MS Ed); secondary education generalist (MS Ed), including students with disabilities 7-12; special education (MA, MS Ed, Advanced Certificate, PD); special education assessment and diagnosis (Advanced Certificate); special education generalist (MS Ed), including extension in secondary education; teaching students with severe or multiple disabilities (Advanced Certificate).

Hofstra University, School of Education, Programs in Teaching - Secondary Education, Hempstead, NY 11549. Offers business education (MS Ed); education technology (Advanced Certificate); English education (MA, MS Ed); foreign language and TESOL (MS Ed); foreign language education (MA, MS Ed), including French, German, Russian, Spanish; mathematics education (MA, MS Ed); science education (MA, MS Ed), including biology, chemistry, earth science, geology, physics; secondary education (Advanced Certificate); social studies education (MA, MS Ed); technology for learning (MA).

Holy Family University, Graduate School, School of Education, Master of Education Programs, Philadelphia, PA 19114. Offers early elementary education (PreK-Grade 4) (M Ed); education leadership (M Ed); general education (M Ed); middle level education (Grades 4-8) (M Ed); reading specialist (M Ed); secondary education (Grades 7-12) (M Ed); special education (M Ed); TESOL and literacy (M Ed). *Expenses: Tuition:* Full-time $12,060. *Required fees:* $250. Tuition and fees vary according to degree level. *Unit head:* Dr. Leonard Soroka, Dean, 267-341-3565, Fax: 215-824-2438, E-mail: lsoroka@holyfamily.edu. *Application contact:* Gidget Marie Montelibano, Associate Director of Graduate Admissions, 267-341-3358, Fax: 215-637-1478, E-mail: gmontelibano@holyfamily.edu.

Hood College, Graduate School, Department of Education, Frederick, MD 21701-8575. Offers curriculum and instruction (MS), including early childhood education, elementary education, elementary school science and mathematics, secondary education, special education; educational leadership (MS, Certificate); reading specialization (MS); STEM (Certificate). *Accreditation:* NCATE. Part-time and evening/weekend programs available. *Faculty:* 4 full-time (3 women), 33 part-time/adjunct (25 women). *Students:* 1 (woman) full-time, 340 part-time (282 women); includes 59 minority (31 Black or African American, non-Hispanic/Latino; 1 American Indian or Alaska Native, non-Hispanic/Latino; 10 Asian, non-Hispanic/Latino; 13 Hispanic/Latino; 4 Two or more races, non-Hispanic/Latino). Average age 33. 97 applicants, 99% accepted, 86 enrolled. In 2013, 64 master's, 40 other advanced degrees awarded. *Degree requirements:* For master's, action research project, portfolio (reading). *Entrance requirements:* For master's, minimum GPA of 2.75, teaching certification. Additional exam requirements/recommendations for international students: Required—TOEFL (minimum score 575 paper-based; 89 iBT), IELTS (minimum score 6.5). *Application deadline:* For fall admission, 7/15 priority date for domestic students, 7/15 for international students; for spring admission, 12/1 priority date for domestic students, 12/1 for international students. Applications are processed on a rolling basis. Application fee: $35. Electronic applications accepted. Application fee is waived when completed online. *Expenses: Tuition:* Part-time $405 per credit. *Required fees:* $100 per semester. *Financial support:* In 2013–14, 1 student received support. Tuition waivers (partial) and unspecified assistantships available. Financial award applicants required to submit FAFSA. *Faculty research:* Leadership, action research, brain research, learning styles. *Unit head:* Dr. Ellen Koitz, Chairperson, 301-696-3466, Fax: 301-696-3597, E-mail: koitz@hood.edu. *Application contact:* Dr. Maria Green Cowles, Dean of Graduate School, 301-696-3811, Fax: 301-696-3597, E-mail: gofurther@hood.edu.
Website: http://www.hood.edu/academics/education/index.html.

Hood College, Graduate School, Program in Secondary Mathematics Education, Frederick, MD 21701-8575. Offers mathematics education (MS), including high school, middle school; secondary mathematics education (Certificate). Part-time and evening/weekend programs available. *Faculty:* 2 full-time (1 woman), 1 part-time/adjunct (0 women). *Students:* 1 full-time (0 women), 45 part-time (35 women); includes 1 minority (Hispanic/Latino). Average age 33. 9 applicants, 100% accepted, 8 enrolled. In 2013, 14 master's, 1 other advanced degree awarded. *Degree requirements:* For master's, capstone/research project. *Entrance requirements:* For master's, minimum GPA of 2.75. Additional exam requirements/recommendations for international students: Required—TOEFL (minimum score 575 paper-based; 89 iBT), IELTS (minimum score 6.5). *Application deadline:* For fall admission, 7/15 priority date for domestic students, 7/15 for international students; for spring admission, 12/1 priority date for domestic students, 12/1 for international students. Applications are processed on a rolling basis. Application fee: $35. Electronic applications accepted. Application fee is waived when completed online. *Expenses: Tuition:* Part-time $405 per credit. *Required fees:* $100 per semester. *Financial support:* Tuition waivers (partial) and unspecified assistantships available. Financial award applicants required to submit FAFSA. *Unit head:* Dr. Betty Mayfield, Chairperson, 301-696-3763, E-mail: mayfield@hood.edu. *Application contact:* Dr. Maria Green Cowles, Dean of Graduate School, 301-696-3811, Fax: 301-696-3597, E-mail: gofurther@hood.edu.
Website: http://www.hood.edu/graduate.

Hope International University, School of Graduate and Professional Studies, Program in Education, Fullerton, CA 92831-3138. Offers education administration (MA); elementary education (ME); secondary education (ME). Part-time and evening/weekend programs available. *Degree requirements:* For master's, comprehensive exam (for some programs), thesis. *Entrance requirements:* For master's, minimum GPA of 3.0, 2 references. Additional exam requirements/recommendations for international students: Required—TOEFL (minimum score 550 paper-based; 86 iBT); Recommended—IELTS (minimum score 6.5). Electronic applications accepted. *Expenses:* Contact institution. *Faculty research:* Distance education.

Howard University, School of Education, Department of Curriculum and Instruction, Program in Secondary Education, Washington, DC 20059-0002. Offers M Ed. *Accreditation:* NCATE. *Faculty:* 4 full-time (3 women), 1 (woman) part-time/adjunct. *Students:* 13 part-time (11 women); all minorities (12 Black or African American, non-Hispanic/Latino; 1 Asian, non-Hispanic/Latino). Average age 32. In 2013, 5 master's awarded. *Degree requirements:* For master's, comprehensive exam, thesis (for some programs), expository writing exam, internships, practicum. *Entrance requirements:* For master's, PRAXIS I, GRE, minimum GPA of 2.7. Additional exam requirements/recommendations for international students: Required—TOEFL (minimum score 550 paper-based; 79 iBT). *Application deadline:* For fall admission, 2/15 priority date for domestic students; for spring admission, 11/1 for domestic students. Applications are processed on a rolling basis. Application fee: $45. Electronic applications accepted. *Financial support:* In 2013–14, 3 students received support, including 3 fellowships with full and partial tuition reimbursements available (averaging $15,000 per year); teaching assistantships, career-related internships or fieldwork, Federal Work-Study, institutionally sponsored loans, scholarships/grants, tuition waivers (full and partial), and unspecified assistantships also available. Financial award application deadline: 2/15; financial award applicants required to submit FAFSA. *Unit head:* Dr. Kenneth Anderson, Chair, Department of Curriculum and Instruction, 202-806-5300, Fax: 202-806-5297, E-mail: kenneth.anderson@howard.edu. *Application contact:* June L. Harris, Administrative Assistant, Department of Curriculum and Instruction, 202-806-7343, Fax: 202-806-5297, E-mail: jlharris@howard.edu.

Hunter College of the City University of New York, Graduate School, School of Arts and Sciences, Department of Mathematics and Statistics, New York, NY 10065-5085. Offers applied mathematics (MA); mathematics for secondary education (MA); pure mathematics (MA). Part-time and evening/weekend programs available. *Faculty:* 10 full-time (2 women), 2 part-time/adjunct (1 woman). *Students:* 6 full-time (all women), 70 part-time (37 women); includes 39 minority (4 Black or African American, non-Hispanic/Latino; 1 American Indian or Alaska Native, non-Hispanic/Latino; 26 Asian, non-Hispanic/Latino; 8 Hispanic/Latino), 3 international. Average age 31. 54 applicants, 41% accepted, 13 enrolled. In 2013, 28 master's awarded. *Degree requirements:* For master's, one foreign language, comprehensive exam, thesis (for some programs). *Entrance requirements:* For master's, GRE General Test, 24 credits in mathematics. Additional exam requirements/recommendations for international students: Required—TOEFL. *Application deadline:* For fall admission, 4/1 for domestic students, 2/1 for international students; for spring admission, 11/1 for domestic students, 9/1 for international students. Application fee: $125. *Financial support:* Federal Work-Study, institutionally sponsored loans, scholarships/grants, and tuition waivers (partial) available. Support available to part-time students. *Faculty research:* Data analysis, dynamical systems, computer graphics, topology, statistical decision theory. *Unit head:* Robert Thompson, Chair, 212-772-5300, Fax: 212-772-4858, E-mail: robert.thompson@

hunter.cuny.edu. *Application contact:* Ada Peluso, Director for Graduate Admissions, 212-772-4632, Fax: 212-772-4858, E-mail: peluso@math.hunter.cuny.edu.
Website: http://math.hunter.cuny.edu/.

Hunter College of the City University of New York, Graduate School, School of Education, Programs in Secondary Education, New York, NY 10065-5085. Offers biology education (MA); chemistry education (MA); earth science (MA); English education (MA); French education (MA); Italian education (MA); mathematics education (MA); physics education (MA); social studies education (MA); Spanish education (MA). *Accreditation:* NCATE. *Faculty:* 18 full-time (6 women), 120 part-time/adjunct (54 women). *Students:* 24 full-time (13 women), 183 part-time (110 women); includes 67 minority (24 Black or African American, non-Hispanic/Latino; 1 American Indian or Alaska Native, non-Hispanic/Latino; 14 Asian, non-Hispanic/Latino; 28 Hispanic/Latino), 8 international. Average age 32. 141 applicants, 66% accepted, 60 enrolled. In 2013, 121 master's awarded. *Degree requirements:* For master's, thesis. *Entrance requirements:* Additional exam requirements/recommendations for international students: Required—TOEFL. *Application deadline:* For fall admission, 4/1 for domestic students, 2/1 for international students; for spring admission, 11/1 for domestic students, 9/1 for international students. Applications are processed on a rolling basis. Application fee: $125. *Financial support:* Fellowships and tuition waivers (full and partial) available. Support available to part-time students. *Unit head:* Dr. Kenney Robinson, Director of Adolescent Education Clinical Experiences, 212-772-4038, E-mail: krobi@hunter.cuny.edu. *Application contact:* Milena Solo, Director for Graduate Admissions, 212-772-4482, E-mail: milena.solo@hunter.cuny.edu.
Website: http://www.hunter.cuny.edu/school-of-education/programs/graduate/adolescent.

Idaho State University, Office of Graduate Studies, College of Education, Department of Educational Foundations, Pocatello, ID 83209-8059. Offers child and family studies (M Ed); curriculum leadership (M Ed); education (M Ed); educational administration (M Ed); educational foundations (5th Year Certificate); elementary education (M Ed), including K-12 education, literacy, secondary education. Part-time programs available. *Degree requirements:* For master's, comprehensive exam, thesis optional, oral exam, written exam; for 5th Year Certificate, comprehensive exam, thesis (for some programs), oral exam, written exam. *Entrance requirements:* For master's, GRE General Test or MAT, minimum undergraduate GPA of 3.0; for 5th Year Certificate, GRE General Test, minimum undergraduate GPA of 3.0, master's degree. Additional exam requirements/recommendations for international students: Required—TOEFL (minimum score 550 paper-based; 80 iBT). Electronic applications accepted. *Faculty research:* Child and families studies; business education; special education; math, science, and technology education.

Immaculata University, College of Graduate Studies, Program in Educational Leadership and Administration, Immaculata, PA 19345. Offers educational leadership and administration (MA, Ed D); elementary education (Certificate); school principal (Certificate); school superintendent (Certificate); secondary education (Certificate); special education (Certificate). Part-time and evening/weekend programs available. *Degree requirements:* For master's, comprehensive exam, thesis optional; for doctorate, comprehensive exam, thesis/dissertation. *Entrance requirements:* For master's, GRE or MAT, minimum GPA of 3.0; for doctorate, GRE General Test or MAT, minimum GPA of 3.5. Additional exam requirements/recommendations for international students: Required—TOEFL. Electronic applications accepted. *Faculty research:* Cooperative learning, school-based management, whole language, performance assessment.

Indiana University Bloomington, School of Education, Department of Curriculum and Instruction, Bloomington, IN 47405-7000. Offers art education (MS, Ed D, PhD); curriculum studies (Ed D, PhD); elementary education (MS, Ed D, PhD, Ed S); mathematics education (MS, Ed D, PhD); science education (MS, Ed D, PhD); secondary education (MS, Ed D, PhD); social studies education (MS, PhD); special education (PhD, Ed S). *Accreditation:* NCATE. Part-time and evening/weekend programs available. Terminal master's awarded for partial completion of doctoral program. *Degree requirements:* For doctorate, thesis/dissertation; for Ed S, comprehensive exam or project. *Entrance requirements:* For master's, doctorate, and Ed S, GRE General Test. Electronic applications accepted.

Indiana University Northwest, School of Education, Gary, IN 46408-1197. Offers educational leadership (MS Ed); elementary education (MS Ed); secondary education (MS Ed). *Accreditation:* NCATE. Part-time and evening/weekend programs available. *Faculty:* 5 full-time (2 women). *Students:* 19 full-time (17 women), 119 part-time (98 women); includes 79 minority (63 Black or African American, non-Hispanic/Latino; 3 Asian, non-Hispanic/Latino; 12 Hispanic/Latino; 1 Two or more races, non-Hispanic/Latino), 1 international. Average age 37. 25 applicants, 92% accepted, 16 enrolled. In 2013, 69 master's awarded. *Entrance requirements:* For master's, GRE General Test or MAT, minimum GPA of 3.0. *Application deadline:* For fall admission, 7/15 priority date for domestic students; for spring admission, 11/15 for domestic students. *Unit head:* Dr. Stanley E. Wigle, Dean, 219-980-6989, E-mail: swigle@iun.edu. *Application contact:* Admissions Counselor, 219-980-6760, Fax: 219-980-7103.
Website: http://www.iun.edu/education/degrees/masters.htm.

Indiana University–Purdue University Fort Wayne, College of Education and Public Policy, Department of Educational Studies, Fort Wayne, IN 46805-1499. Offers elementary education (MS Ed); secondary education (MS Ed). *Accreditation:* NCATE. Part-time programs available. *Faculty:* 13 full-time (6 women). *Students:* 5 part-time (2 women); includes 1 minority (Hispanic/Latino). Average age 40. 2 applicants, 100% accepted, 2 enrolled. In 2013, 20 master's awarded. *Entrance requirements:* For master's, minimum GPA of 2.5, three professional letters of recommendation. Additional exam requirements/recommendations for international students: Required—TOEFL (minimum score 550 paper-based; 79 iBT). *Application deadline:* For fall admission, 4/1 priority date for domestic and international students. Applications are processed on a rolling basis. Application fee: $55. *Financial support:* In 2013–14, 1 teaching assistantship with partial tuition reimbursement (averaging $13,322 per year) was awarded; scholarships/grants also available. Support available to part-time students. Financial award application deadline: 3/1; financial award applicants required to submit FAFSA. *Faculty research:* Student course evaluation (SET) in higher education, North Korea's food shortage. *Unit head:* Dr. Terri Swim, Chair, 260-481-6442, Fax: 260-481-5408, E-mail: swimt@ipfw.edu. *Application contact:* Vicky L. Schmidt, Graduate Recorder, 260-481-6450, Fax: 260-481-5408, E-mail: schmidt@ipfw.edu.
Website: http://www.ipfw.edu/education.

Indiana University South Bend, School of Education, South Bend, IN 46634-7111. Offers counseling and human services (MS Ed); elementary and secondary education leadership (MS Ed); elementary education (MS Ed); secondary education (MS Ed); special education (MAT, MS Ed). *Accreditation:* NCATE. Part-time and evening/weekend programs available. *Faculty:* 21 full-time (11 women), 9 part-time/adjunct (3 women). *Students:* 12 full-time (8 women), 103 part-time (85 women); includes 18 minority (8 Black or African American, non-Hispanic/Latino; 1 Asian, non-Hispanic/Latino; 5 Hispanic/Latino; 4 Two or more races, non-Hispanic/Latino), 3 international. Average age 36. 24 applicants, 63% accepted, 9 enrolled. In 2013, 41 master's awarded. *Degree requirements:* For master's, thesis or alternative, exit project. *Entrance requirements:* For master's, letters of recommendation, GRE or minimum GPA of 3.0. Additional exam requirements/recommendations for international students: Required—TOEFL. *Application deadline:* For fall admission, 7/1 for domestic students; for spring admission, 11/1 for domestic students. Applications are processed on a rolling basis. Electronic applications accepted. *Financial support:* Career-related internships or fieldwork available. Support available to part-time students. Financial award application deadline: 3/1; financial award applicants required to submit FAFSA. *Faculty research:* Professional dispositions, early childhood literacy, online learning, program assessments, problem-based learning. *Unit head:* Dr. Marvin Lynn, Dean, 574-520-4339. *Application contact:* Yvonne Walker, Student Services Representative, 574-520-4185, E-mail: ydwalker@iusb.edu.
Website: http://www.iusb.edu/~edud/.

Indiana University Southeast, School of Education, New Albany, IN 47150-6405. Offers counselor education (MS Ed); elementary education (MS Ed); secondary education (MS Ed). *Accreditation:* NCATE. Part-time and evening/weekend programs available. *Students:* 23 full-time (21 women), 324 part-time (248 women); includes 44 minority (34 Black or African American, non-Hispanic/Latino; 1 American Indian or Alaska Native, non-Hispanic/Latino; 1 Asian, non-Hispanic/Latino; 5 Hispanic/Latino; 3 Two or more races, non-Hispanic/Latino). Average age 33. 36 applicants, 81% accepted, 25 enrolled. In 2013, 147 master's awarded. *Entrance requirements:* For master's, minimum undergraduate GPA of 2.5, graduate 3.0. *Application deadline:* Applications are processed on a rolling basis. *Financial support:* Career-related internships or fieldwork, Federal Work-Study, and institutionally sponsored loans available. Support available to part-time students. Financial award applicants required to submit FAFSA. *Faculty research:* Learning styles, technology, constructivism, group process, innovative math strategies. *Unit head:* Dr. Gloria Murray, Dean, 812-941-2169, Fax: 812-941-2667, E-mail: soeinfo@ius.edu. *Application contact:* Admissions Counselor, 812-941-2212, Fax: 812-941-2595, E-mail: admissions@ius.edu.
Website: http://www.ius.edu/education/.

Instituto Tecnologico de Santo Domingo, Graduate School, Area of Humanities and Social Sciences, Santo Domingo, Dominican Republic. Offers accounting (Certificate); adult education (Certificate); applied linguistics (MA); economics (MA); education (M Ed); educational psychology (MA, Certificate); gender and development (MA, Certificate); humanistic studies (MA); international marketing management (Certificate); international relations in the Caribbean basin (Certificate); intervention systems in family therapy (MA); linguistic and literary communication (Certificate); pedagogical support (MA); social science education (M Ed); sustainable human development (MA); terminal illness and death psychology (Certificate); youth and adult education (M Ed).

Iona College, School of Arts and Science, Department of Education, New Rochelle, NY 10801-1890. Offers adolescence education: biology (MS Ed, MST); adolescence education: English (MS Ed, MST); adolescence education: Italian (MS Ed, MST); adolescence education: mathematics (MS Ed, MST); adolescence education: social studies (MS Ed, MST); adolescence education: Spanish (MS Ed, MST); adolescence special education 5-12 (MST); adolescence special education and literacy (MS Ed); childhood and special education (MST); childhood education (MST); early childhood and childhood (MST); educational leadership (MS Ed); literacy education: birth-grade 6 (MS Ed). *Accreditation:* NCATE. Part-time and evening/weekend programs available. *Faculty:* 11 full-time (9 women), 7 part-time/adjunct (6 women). *Students:* 34 full-time (25 women), 61 part-time (47 women); includes 5 minority (2 Asian, non-Hispanic/Latino; 3 Hispanic/Latino), 1 international. Average age 25. 27 applicants, 93% accepted, 16 enrolled. In 2013, 54 master's awarded. *Degree requirements:* For master's, thesis or alternative. *Entrance requirements:* For master's, minimum GPA of 3.0, NY State teaching certificate (for all MS Ed programs). Additional exam requirements/recommendations for international students: Required—TOEFL (minimum score 550 paper-based; 80 iBT), IELTS (minimum score 6.5). *Application deadline:* For fall admission, 8/1 priority date for domestic students, 5/1 priority date for international students; for spring admission, 1/1 priority date for domestic students, 9/1 priority date for international students. Applications are processed on a rolling basis. Application fee: $50. Electronic applications accepted. *Expenses: Tuition:* Part-time $948 per credit. *Required fees:* $235 per term. *Financial support:* In 2013–14, 84 students received support. Unspecified assistantships available. Support available to part-time students. Financial award application deadline: 4/15; financial award applicants required to submit FAFSA. *Faculty research:* Reading/writing, educational technology, administration, early literacy assessment, literacy development. *Unit head:* Margaret Smith, PhD, Chair, 914-633-2210, Fax: 914-633-2608, E-mail: msmith@iona.edu. *Application contact:* Veronica Jarek-Prinz, Director, Graduate Admissions, 914-633-2420, Fax: 914-633-2277, E-mail: vjarekprinz@iona.edu.
Website: http://www.iona.edu/Academics/School-of-Arts-Science/Departments/Education/Graduate-Programs.aspx.

Ithaca College, School of Humanities and Sciences, Program in Adolescence Education, Ithaca, NY 14850. Offers biology 7-12 (MAT); chemistry 7-12 (MAT); English 7-12 (MAT); French 7-12 (MAT); math 7-12 (MAT); physics 7-12 (MAT); social studies 7-12 (MAT); Spanish (MAT). Part-time programs available. *Faculty:* 31 full-time (11 women). *Students:* 12 full-time (4 women); includes 1 minority (Hispanic/Latino). Average age 24. 27 applicants, 81% accepted, 12 enrolled. In 2013, 7 master's awarded. *Degree requirements:* For master's, thesis or alternative, student teaching. *Entrance requirements:* For master's, minimum GPA of 3.0. Additional exam requirements/recommendations for international students: Required—TOEFL (minimum score 550 paper-based; 80 iBT). *Application deadline:* For fall admission, 2/15 priority date for domestic and international students; for spring admission, 12/1 for domestic and international students. Applications are processed on a rolling basis. Application fee: $40. Electronic applications accepted. *Expenses:* Contact institution. *Financial support:* In 2013–14, 7 students received support, including 7 teaching assistantships (averaging $9,781 per year); career-related internships or fieldwork, Federal Work-Study, scholarships/grants, and unspecified assistantships also available. Support available to part-time students. Financial award application deadline: 2/15; financial award applicants required to submit CSS PROFILE or FAFSA. *Faculty research:* Teacher preparation (elementary and secondary education), equity and social justice in education, language and literacy, multicultural education/sociocultural studies, reflective practice and teacher research. *Unit head:* Dr. Linda Hanrahan, Chair, 607-274-3143, Fax: 607-274-1263, E-mail: gps@ithaca.edu. *Application contact:* Gerard Turbide, Director, Office of Admission, 607-274-3143, Fax: 607-274-1263, E-mail: gps@ithaca.edu.
Website: http://www.ithaca.edu/gradprograms/education/programs/aded.

Jackson State University, Graduate School, College of Education and Human Development, Department of Educational Leadership, Jackson, MS 39217. Offers education administration (Ed S); educational administration (MS Ed, PhD); secondary education (MS Ed, Ed S), including educational technology (MS Ed). *Accreditation:* NCATE. Part-time and evening/weekend programs available. *Degree requirements:* For master's, comprehensive exam, thesis or alternative; for doctorate, comprehensive exam, thesis/dissertation; for Ed S, comprehensive exam, thesis. *Entrance requirements:* For master's, GRE General Test; for doctorate, MAT, GRE, teaching experience. Additional exam requirements/recommendations for international students: Required—TOEFL (minimum score 520 paper-based; 67 iBT).

Secondary Education

Jacksonville State University, College of Graduate Studies and Continuing Education, College of Education and Professional Studies, Program in Secondary Education, Jacksonville, AL 36265-1602. Offers MS Ed. *Accreditation:* NCATE. Part-time and evening/weekend programs available. *Degree requirements:* For master's, comprehensive exam, thesis (for some programs). *Entrance requirements:* For master's, GRE General Test or MAT. Additional exam requirements/recommendations for international students: Required—TOEFL (minimum score 61 iBT). Electronic applications accepted.

James Madison University, The Graduate School, College of Education, Middle, Secondary, and Mathematics Education Department, Harrisonburg, VA 22807. Offers middle education (MAT); secondary education (MAT). *Students:* Average age 27. *Entrance requirements:* Additional exam requirements/recommendations for international students: Required—TOEFL. *Application deadline:* For fall admission, 5/1 for domestic students; for spring admission, 9/1 for domestic students. Application fee: $55. *Financial support:* Unspecified assistantships available. Financial award application deadline: 3/1; financial award applicants required to submit FAFSA. *Unit head:* Dr. Steven L. Purcell, Academic Unit Head, 540-568-6793. *Application contact:* Lynette M. Bible, Director of Graduate Admissions, 540-568-6395, Fax: 540-568-7860, E-mail: biblelm@jmu.edu.

John Carroll University, Graduate School, Department of Education and Allied Studies, Program in School Based Adolescent-Young Adult Education, University Heights, OH 44118-4581. Offers M Ed. *Degree requirements:* For master's, comprehensive exam. *Entrance requirements:* For master's, GRE General Test or MAT, minimum GPA of 2.75, interview. Electronic applications accepted.

Johns Hopkins University, School of Education, Master's Programs in Education, Baltimore, MD 21218-2699. Offers counseling (MS), including mental health counseling, school counseling; education (MS), including educational studies, gifted education, reading, school administration and supervision, technology for educators; elementary education (MAT); health professions (M Ed); intelligence analysis (MS); management (MS); secondary education (MAT); special education (MS), including early childhood special education, general special education studies, mild to moderate disabilities, severe disabilities. Part-time and evening/weekend programs available. Postbaccalaureate distance learning degree programs offered (no on-campus study). *Students:* 183 full-time (123 women), 1,001 part-time (757 women); includes 380 minority (160 Black or African American, non-Hispanic/Latino; 4 American Indian or Alaska Native, non-Hispanic/Latino; 91 Asian, non-Hispanic/Latino; 78 Hispanic/Latino; 4 Native Hawaiian or other Pacific Islander, non-Hispanic/Latino; 43 Two or more races, non-Hispanic/Latino), 28 international. Average age 28. 508 applicants, 90% accepted, 337 enrolled. In 2013, 565 degrees awarded. *Degree requirements:* For master's, comprehensive exam (for some programs), portfolio, capstone project and/or internship; PRAXIS II (for teacher preparation programs that lead to licensure). *Entrance requirements:* For master's, GRE (for full-time programs only); PRAXIS I or equivalent (for teacher preparation programs that lead to licensure), bachelor's degree from regionally- or nationally-accredited institution, minimum GPA of 3.0 in all previous programs of study, official transcripts from all post-secondary institutions attended, essay, curriculum vitae/resume, minimum of two letters of recommendation. Additional exam requirements/recommendations for international students: Required—TOEFL (minimum score 600 paper-based; 100 iBT) or IELTS (minimum score 7). *Application deadline:* For fall admission, 4/1 for domestic and international students; for spring admission, 10/1 for domestic and international students; for summer admission, 2/1 for domestic and international students. Application fee: $80. Electronic applications accepted. *Financial support:* Application deadline: 6/1; applicants required to submit FAFSA. *Unit head:* Dr. David A. Andrews, Dean, 410-516-7820, Fax: 410-516-6697, E-mail: davidandrews@jhu.edu. *Application contact:* Catherine Wilson, Associate Director of Admissions, 410-516-9797, Fax: 410-516-9799, E-mail: soe.info@jhu.edu.

Johnson & Wales University, MAT Program in Teacher Education, Providence, RI 02903-3703. Offers business education and secondary special education (MAT); elementary education and elementary special education (MAT); elementary education and elementary/secondary special education (MAT); elementary education and secondary special education (MAT); food service education (MAT). Part-time and evening/weekend programs available. *Entrance requirements:* For master's, MAT, minimum GPA of 2.75. Additional exam requirements/recommendations for international students: Required—TOEFL (minimum score 550 paper-based) or IELTS (recommended). *Faculty research:* Secondary education, student teaching, educational reform, evaluation procedures.

Johnson State College, Graduate Program in Education, Johnson, VT 05656. Offers applied behavior analysis (MA Ed), including applied behavior analysis; curriculum and instruction (MA Ed); literacy (MA Ed); secondary education (MA Ed); special education (MA Ed). Part-time programs available. *Faculty:* 3 full-time (1 woman), 6 part-time/adjunct (5 women). *Students:* 6 full-time (5 women), 69 part-time (52 women). Average age 28. In 2013, 44 master's awarded. *Degree requirements:* For master's, comprehensive exam, thesis or alternative. *Entrance requirements:* For master's, interview. Additional exam requirements/recommendations for international students: Required—TOEFL. *Application deadline:* For fall admission, 4/1 priority date for domestic students, 1/15 priority date for international students; for spring admission, 11/1 for domestic students, 8/15 priority date for international students. Applications are processed on a rolling basis. Electronic applications accepted. *Expenses:* Tuition, state resident: full-time $11,448; part-time $477 per credit. Tuition, nonresident: full-time $24,720; part-time $1030 per credit. Tuition and fees vary according to reciprocity agreements. *Financial support:* Unspecified assistantships available. Financial award application deadline: 3/1; financial award applicants required to submit FAFSA. *Application contact:* Catherine H. Higley, Administrative Assistant, 800-635-2356 Ext. 1244, Fax: 802-635-1248, E-mail: catherine.higley@jsc.edu.

Jones International University, School of Education, Centennial, CO 80112. Offers adult education (M Ed); corporate training and knowledge management (M Ed); curriculum and instruction (M Ed), including elementary teacher licensure, secondary teacher licensure; e-learning technology and design (M Ed); educational leadership and administration (M Ed); educational leadership and administration: principal and administrator licensure (M Ed); elementary curriculum instruction and assessment (M Ed); higher education leadership and administration (M Ed); K-12 instructional technology (M Ed); K-12 instructional technology: teacher licensure (M Ed); secondary curriculum instruction and assessment (M Ed); technology and design (M Ed). Part-time and evening/weekend programs available. Postbaccalaureate distance learning degree programs offered (no on-campus study). *Entrance requirements:* For master's, minimum cumulative GPA of 2.5. Additional exam requirements/recommendations for international students: Recommended—TOEFL (minimum score 550 paper-based). Electronic applications accepted.

Kansas State University, Graduate School, College of Education, Department of Curriculum and Instruction, Manhattan, KS 66506. Offers career and technical education (Ed D, PhD); curriculum studies (Ed D, PhD); digital teaching and learning (MS); educational computing, design and online learning (MS); educational technology (Ed D, PhD); elementary/middle level curriculum and instruction (MS); English as a second language (MS); language/diversity education (Ed D, PhD); literacy education (Ed D, PhD); mathematics education (Ed D, PhD); middle level/secondary curriculum and instruction (MS); reading and language arts (MS); reading specialist endorsement (MS); science education (Ed D, PhD); social science education (Ed D, PhD); teacher education (Ed D, PhD); teacher leader/school improvement (MS, Ed D). *Accreditation:* NCATE. Part-time programs available. Postbaccalaureate distance learning degree programs offered (minimal on-campus study). *Faculty:* 18 full-time (13 women), 7 part-time/adjunct (4 women). *Students:* 39 full-time (23 women), 122 part-time (94 women); includes 19 minority (3 Black or African American, non-Hispanic/Latino; 2 Asian, non-Hispanic/Latino; 12 Hispanic/Latino; 2 Two or more races, non-Hispanic/Latino), 12 international. Average age 36. 80 applicants, 50% accepted, 34 enrolled. In 2013, 40 master's, 13 doctorates awarded. *Degree requirements:* For master's, comprehensive exam, portfolio, project, report or thesis; for doctorate, comprehensive exam, thesis/dissertation, preliminary exam. *Entrance requirements:* For master's, minimum GPA of 3.0, letters of recommendation; for doctorate, GRE, minimum GPA of 3.0, letters of recommendation, evidence of scholarly writing. Additional exam requirements/recommendations for international students: Required—TOEFL (minimum score 550 paper-based; 80 iBT). *Application deadline:* For fall admission, 3/1 priority date for domestic students, 2/1 priority date for international students; for spring admission, 10/1 priority date for domestic students, 8/1 priority date for international students. Applications are processed on a rolling basis. Application fee: $50 ($75 for international students). Electronic applications accepted. *Financial support:* In 2013–14, 1 research assistantship (averaging $16,900 per year), 8 teaching assistantships (averaging $12,466 per year) were awarded; career-related internships or fieldwork, institutionally sponsored loans, and scholarships/grants also available. Support available to part-time students. Financial award application deadline: 3/1; financial award applicants required to submit FAFSA. *Faculty research:* Literacy and technology, critical race theory and diversity, achievement gaps, school improvement, teacher education. *Total annual research expenditures:* $543,677. *Unit head:* Dr. Todd Goodson, Chair, 785-532-5904, Fax: 785-532-7304, E-mail: tgoodson@ksu.edu. *Application contact:* Dona Deam, Application Contact, 785-532-5595, Fax: 785-532-7304, E-mail: ddeam@ksu.edu. Website: http://www.coe.k-state.edu/departments/edci/.

Kaplan University, Davenport Campus, School of Teacher Education, Davenport, IA 52807-2095. Offers education (M Ed); secondary education (M Ed); teaching and learning (MA); teaching literacy and language: grades 6-12 (MA); teaching literacy and language: grades K-6 (MA); teaching mathematics: grades 6-8 (MA); teaching mathematics: grades 9-12 (MA); teaching mathematics: grades K-5 (MA); teaching science: grades 6-12 (MA); teaching science: grades K-6 (MA); teaching students with special needs (MA); teaching with technology (MA). Part-time and evening/weekend programs available. Postbaccalaureate distance learning degree programs offered (no on-campus study). *Entrance requirements:* Additional exam requirements/recommendations for international students: Required—TOEFL (minimum score 550 paper-based; 80 iBT).

Kennesaw State University, Leland and Clarice C. Bagwell College of Education, Program in Graduate Education, Kennesaw, GA 30144-5591. Offers educational leadership (M Ed); educational leadership technology (M Ed); elementary and early childhood education (M Ed); instructional technology (M Ed); middle grades education (M Ed); reading (M Ed); secondary education (M Ed); special education (M Ed); teaching English to speakers of other languages (M Ed). *Accreditation:* NCATE. Part-time programs available. *Students:* 65 full-time (60 women), 229 part-time (158 women); includes 66 minority (46 Black or African American, non-Hispanic/Latino; 6 Asian, non-Hispanic/Latino; 9 Hispanic/Latino; 5 Two or more races, non-Hispanic/Latino), 1 international. Average age 34. 56 applicants, 86% accepted, 43 enrolled. In 2013, 109 master's awarded. *Degree requirements:* For master's, thesis or alternative. *Entrance requirements:* For master's, GRE General Test, T-4 state certification, minimum GPA of 2.75. Additional exam requirements/recommendations for international students: Required—TOEFL (minimum score 550 paper-based; 80 iBT), IELTS (minimum score 6.5). *Application deadline:* For fall admission, 7/1 for domestic and international students; for spring admission, 10/1 for domestic and international students; for summer admission, 4/15 for domestic and international students. Applications are processed on a rolling basis. Application fee: $60. Electronic applications accepted. *Expenses:* Tuition, state resident: full-time $4806; part-time $267 per semester hour. Tuition, nonresident: full-time $17,298; part-time $961 per semester hour. Required fees: $1834; $784.50 per semester. *Financial support:* In 2013–14, 10 research assistantships with tuition reimbursements (averaging $8,000 per year) were awarded; Federal Work-Study and unspecified assistantships also available. Support available to part-time students. Financial award application deadline: 4/1; financial award applicants required to submit FAFSA. *Unit head:* Melinda Ross, Administrative Coordinator for Graduate Programs in Education, 770-423-6043, E-mail: graded@kennesaw.edu. *Application contact:* Melinda Ross, Admissions Counselor, 770-423-6043, Fax: 770-423-6885, E-mail: ksugrad@kennesaw.edu. Website: http://www.kennesaw.edu/education/grad/.

Kennesaw State University, Leland and Clarice C. Bagwell College of Education, Program in Teaching, Kennesaw, GA 30144-5591. Offers art education (MAT); biology (MAT); chemistry (MAT); foreign language education (Chinese and Spanish) (MAT); physics (MAT); secondary English (MAT); secondary mathematics (MAT); special education (MAT); teaching English to speakers of other languages (MAT). Part-time and evening/weekend programs available. *Students:* 82 full-time (59 women), 16 part-time (12 women); includes 28 minority (14 Black or African American, non-Hispanic/Latino; 4 Asian, non-Hispanic/Latino; 7 Hispanic/Latino; 1 Native Hawaiian or other Pacific Islander, non-Hispanic/Latino; 2 Two or more races, non-Hispanic/Latino), 3 international. Average age 35. 28 applicants, 68% accepted, 15 enrolled. In 2013, 54 master's awarded. *Entrance requirements:* For master's, GRE, GACE I (state certificate exam), minimum GPA of 2.75, 2 recommendations, resume. Additional exam requirements/recommendations for international students: Required—TOEFL (minimum score 550 paper-based; 80 iBT), IELTS (minimum score 6). *Application deadline:* For fall admission, 6/1 for domestic and international students; for spring admission, 3/1 for domestic and international students; for summer admission, 4/15 for domestic and international students. Applications are processed on a rolling basis. Application fee: $60. Electronic applications accepted. *Expenses:* Tuition, state resident: full-time $4806; part-time $267 per semester hour. Tuition, nonresident: full-time $17,298; part-time $961 per semester hour. Required fees: $1834; $784.50 per semester. *Financial support:* In 2013–14, 2 research assistantships with tuition reimbursements (averaging $8,000 per year) were awarded; unspecified assistantships also available. Financial award application deadline: 4/1; financial award applicants required to submit FAFSA. *Unit head:* Dr. Jillian Ford, Director, 770-499-3093, E-mail: graded@kennesaw.edu. *Application contact:* Melinda Ross, Admissions Counselor, 770-423-6122, Fax: 770-423-6885, E-mail: ksugrad@kennesaw.edu. Website: http://www.kennesaw.edu.

Kent State University, Graduate School of Education, Health, and Human Services, School of Teaching, Learning and Curriculum Studies, Program in Secondary Education, Kent, OH 44242-0001. Offers MAT. *Accreditation:* NCATE. *Faculty:* 5 full-time (3 women). *Students:* 17 full-time (11 women); includes 2 minority (1 Asian, non-Hispanic/Latino; 1 Hispanic/Latino). 44 applicants, 39% accepted. In 2013, 26 master's awarded. *Entrance requirements:* For master's, GRE General Test, 2 letters of

reference, moral character form. Additional exam requirements/recommendations for international students: Required—TOEFL (minimum score 550 paper-based; 80 iBT). Application fee: $30 ($60 for international students). Electronic applications accepted. *Financial support:* Research assistantships with full tuition reimbursements, career-related internships or fieldwork, Federal Work-Study, institutionally sponsored loans, scholarships/grants, health care benefits, and unspecified assistantships available. Support available to part-time students. Financial award application deadline: 4/1; financial award applicants required to submit FAFSA. *Faculty research:* Creativity in science, women in science, teaching of writing, curriculum theory, mathematical reasoning. *Unit head:* Dr. Janice Hutchison, Coordinator, 330-672-0629, E-mail: jhutchi1@kent.edu. *Application contact:* Nancy Miller, Academic Program Director, Office of Graduate Student Services, 330-672-2576, Fax: 330-672-9162, E-mail: ogs@kent.edu.
Website: http://www.kent.edu/ehhs/aded/.

Kutztown University of Pennsylvania, College of Education, Program in Secondary Education, Kutztown, PA 19530-0730. Offers biology (M Ed); curriculum and instruction (M Ed); English (M Ed); mathematics (M Ed); social studies (M Ed). *Accreditation:* NCATE. Part-time and evening/weekend programs available. *Faculty:* 6 full-time (2 women). *Students:* 34 full-time (17 women), 46 part-time (34 women); includes 4 minority (1 Asian, non-Hispanic/Latino; 3 Hispanic/Latino). Average age 31. 50 applicants, 70% accepted, 26 enrolled. In 2013, 31 master's awarded. *Degree requirements:* For master's, comprehensive exam, thesis optional. *Entrance requirements:* For master's, GRE General Test. Additional exam requirements/recommendations for international students: Required—TOEFL (minimum score 550 paper-based; 79 iBT). *Application deadline:* For fall admission, 8/1 priority date for domestic and international students; for spring admission, 12/1 priority date for domestic and international students. Applications are processed on a rolling basis. Application fee: $35. Electronic applications accepted. *Expenses: Tuition, area resident:* Part-time $442 per credit. Tuition, state resident: part-time $442 per credit. Tuition, nonresident: part-time $663 per credit. *Required fees:* $80 per credit. *Financial support:* Career-related internships or fieldwork, Federal Work-Study, scholarships/grants, and unspecified assistantships available. Financial award application deadline: 3/1; financial award applicants required to submit FAFSA. *Unit head:* Dr. Theresa Stahler, Chairperson, 610-683-4259, Fax: 610-683-1338, E-mail: stahler@kutztown.edu. *Application contact:* Kelly Hish, Admissions Clerk, 610-683-4200, Fax: 610-683-1393, E-mail: graduate@kutztown.edu.

LaGrange College, Graduate Programs, Department of Education, LaGrange, GA 30240-2999. Offers curriculum and instruction (M Ed, Ed S); middle grades (MAT); secondary education (MAT). Part-time and evening/weekend programs available. *Degree requirements:* For master's, comprehensive exam. *Entrance requirements:* For master's, GRE, MAT, minimum GPA of 2.5. Additional exam requirements/recommendations for international students: Required—TOEFL (minimum score 550 paper-based).

Lake Forest College, Master of Arts in Teaching Program, Lake Forest, IL 60045. Offers elementary education (MAT); K-12 French (MAT); K-12 music (MAT); K-12 Spanish (MAT); K-12 visual art (MAT); secondary biology (MAT); secondary chemistry (MAT); secondary English (MAT); secondary history (MAT); secondary mathematics (MAT). *Degree requirements:* For master's, comprehensive exam, portfolio. *Entrance requirements:* For master's, GRE.

Lancaster Bible College, Graduate School, Lancaster, PA 17601-5036. Offers adult ministries (MA); Bible (MA); children and family ministry (MA); church planting (MA); consulting resource teacher (M Ed); elementary school counseling (M Ed); leadership (PhD); leadership studies (MA); marriage and family counseling (MA); mental health counseling (MA); pastoral studies (MA); secondary school counseling (M Ed); sports ministry (MA); student ministry (MA); town and country ministry (MA). Part-time and evening/weekend programs available. *Degree requirements:* For master's, comprehensive exam (for some programs), thesis (for some programs). *Entrance requirements:* For master's, bachelor's degree with a minimum of 30 credits of course work in Bible, minimum undergraduate GPA of 3.0, interview. Additional exam requirements/recommendations for international students: Required—TOEFL.

La Salle University, School of Arts and Sciences, Program in Education, Philadelphia, PA 19141-1199. Offers American studies (MA); autism spectrum disorders (MA, Certificate); bilingual/bicultural studies (MA); classroom management (MA, Certificate); dual early childhood and special education (MA); dual middle-level science and math and special education secondary education (MA); education (MA); English (MA); English as a second language (Certificate); instructional coach (Certificate); instructional leadership (MA); reading specialist (MA, Certificate); secondary education (MA); special education (MA, Certificate). Part-time and evening/weekend programs available. *Faculty:* 5 full-time (4 women), 16 part-time/adjunct (10 women). *Students:* 18 full-time (13 women), 137 part-time (112 women); includes 33 minority (24 Black or African American, non-Hispanic/Latino; 9 Hispanic/Latino), 4 international. Average age 32. 47 applicants, 96% accepted, 28 enrolled. In 2013, 58 master's, 20 other advanced degrees awarded. *Degree requirements:* For master's, comprehensive exam. *Entrance requirements:* For master's and Certificate, MAT or GRE, 2 letters of recommendation. Additional exam requirements/recommendations for international students: Required—TOEFL. *Application deadline:* For fall admission, 8/15 priority date for domestic students, 7/15 for international students; for spring admission, 12/15 priority date for domestic students, 11/15 for international students; for summer admission, 4/15 priority date for domestic students, 3/15 for international students. Applications are processed on a rolling basis. Application fee: $35. Electronic applications accepted. Application fee is waived when completed online. *Expenses:* Contact institution. *Financial support:* In 2013–14, 28 students received support. Career-related internships or fieldwork, Federal Work-Study, and scholarships/grants available. Support available to part-time students. Financial award application deadline: 8/31; financial award applicants required to submit FAFSA. *Unit head:* Dr. Greer Richardson, Interim Director, 215-951-1806, Fax: 215-951-1843, E-mail: graded@lasalle.edu. *Application contact:* Paul J. Reilly, Assistant Vice President, Enrollment Services, 215-951-1946, Fax: 215-951-1462, E-mail: reilly@lasalle.edu.
Website: http://www.lasalle.edu/grad/index.php?section-education&page-index.

Lee University, Program in Education, Cleveland, TN 37320-3450. Offers college student development (MS); curriculum and instruction (M Ed, Ed S); educational leadership (M Ed, Ed S); elementary education (MAT); higher education administration (MS); middle grades (MAT); secondary education (MAT); special education (M Ed); special education (secondary) (MAT). Part-time programs available. *Faculty:* 14 full-time (7 women), 6 part-time/adjunct (3 women). *Students:* 30 full-time (23 women), 62 part-time (37 women); includes 8 minority (3 Black or African American, non-Hispanic/Latino; 1 American Indian or Alaska Native, non-Hispanic/Latino; 2 Asian, non-Hispanic/Latino; 2 Hispanic/Latino). Average age 30. 40 applicants, 100% accepted, 30 enrolled. In 2013, 117 master's, 2 other advanced degrees awarded. *Degree requirements:* For master's, variable foreign language requirement, comprehensive exam, thesis, internship. *Entrance requirements:* For master's, MAT or GRE General Test, minimum GPA of 2.75, 3 letters of recommendation, interview, writing sample, official transcripts. Additional exam requirements/recommendations for international students: Required—TOEFL (minimum score 450 paper-based). *Application deadline:* For fall admission, 4/1 priority date for domestic and international students; for spring admission, 10/1 priority date for domestic and international students. Applications are processed on a rolling basis. Application fee: $25. *Expenses: Tuition:* Full-time $9900; part-time $550 per credit hour. *Required fees:* $35 per term. One-time fee: $25. *Financial support:* In 2013–14, 47 students received support, including 1 teaching assistantship (averaging $1,500 per year); career-related internships or fieldwork, Federal Work-Study, institutionally sponsored loans, scholarships/grants, and unspecified assistantships also available. Financial award application deadline: 3/1; financial award applicants required to submit FAFSA. *Unit head:* Dr. Gary Riggins, Director, 423-614-8193. *Application contact:* Vicki Glasscock, Graduate Admissions Director, 423-614-8059, E-mail: vglasscock@leeuniversity.edu.
Website: http://www.leeuniversity.edu/academics/graduate/education.

Le Moyne College, Department of Education, Syracuse, NY 13214. Offers adolescent education (MS Ed, MST); adolescent education/special education (MS Ed, MST); adolescent English (MST), including grades 7-12 (MS Ed, MST); adolescent English/special education (MST), including grades 7-12 (MS Ed, MST); adolescent foreign language (MST), including grades 7-12 (MS Ed, MST); adolescent history (MST), including grades 7-12 (MS Ed, MST); childhood education (MS Ed); childhood education/special education (MS Ed); elementary education (MS Ed); general education (MS Ed); inclusive childhood education (MST); literacy education (MS Ed), including birth to grade 6, grades 5-12; school building leader (MS Ed); school building leadership (CAS); school district business leader (MS Ed, CAS); school district leader (MS Ed); school district leadership (CAS); secondary education (MS Ed); special education (MS Ed); students with disabilities-generalist (MS Ed), including grades 7-12 (MS Ed, MST); teaching English to speakers of other languages (MS Ed); urban studies (MS Ed). *Accreditation:* Teacher Education Accreditation Council. Part-time and evening/weekend programs available. *Faculty:* 8 full-time (5 women), 61 part-time/adjunct (38 women). *Students:* 24 full-time (20 women), 178 part-time (133 women); includes 22 minority (12 Black or African American, non-Hispanic/Latino; 1 American Indian or Alaska Native, non-Hispanic/Latino; 3 Asian, non-Hispanic/Latino; 6 Hispanic/Latino), 1 international. Average age 31. 248 applicants, 90% accepted, 86 enrolled. In 2013, 158 master's, 37 CASs awarded. *Degree requirements:* For master's, thesis. *Entrance requirements:* For master's, GRE General Test, bachelor's degree, 2 letters of recommendation, written statement, transcripts. Additional exam requirements/recommendations for international students: Required—TOEFL (minimum score 550 paper-based; 79 iBT). *Application deadline:* For fall admission, 4/1 priority date for domestic and international students; for spring admission, 10/1 priority date for domestic and international students; for summer admission, 3/1 priority date for domestic and international students. Applications are processed on a rolling basis. Application fee: $50. *Expenses:* Contact institution. *Financial support:* In 2013–14, 26 students received support. Career-related internships or fieldwork and health care benefits available. Support available to part-time students. Financial award applicants required to submit FAFSA. *Faculty research:* Minority teachers, special education, multiculturalism, literacy, technology, media literacy learning, autism, school district organization, service-learning, higher level problem solving, teacher leadership. *Unit head:* Dr. Suzanne L. Gilmour, Chair, Department of Education/Director of Graduate Education Programs, 315-445-4376, Fax: 315-445-4744, E-mail: gilmous@lemoyne.edu. *Application contact:* Kristen P. Trapasso, Senior Director of Enrollment Management, 315-445-4265, Fax: 315-445-6092, E-mail: trapaskp@lemoyne.edu.
Website: http://www.lemoyne.edu/education.

Lesley University, School of Education, Cambridge, MA 02138-2790. Offers arts, community, and education (M Ed); autism studies (Certificate); curriculum and instruction (M Ed, CAGS); early childhood education (M Ed); ecological teaching and learning (MS); educational studies (PhD), including adult learning, educational leadership, individually designed; elementary education (M Ed); emergent technologies for educators (Certificate); ESLArts: language learning through the arts (M Ed); high school education (M Ed); individually designed (M Ed); integrated teaching through the arts (M Ed); literacy for K-8 classroom teachers (M Ed); mathematics education (M Ed); middle school education (M Ed); moderate disabilities (M Ed); online learning (Certificate); reading (CAGS); science in education (M Ed); severe disabilities (M Ed); special needs (CAGS); specialist teacher of reading (M Ed); teacher of visual art (M Ed); technology in education (M Ed, CAGS). *Accreditation:* Teacher Education Accreditation Council. Part-time and evening/weekend programs available. Postbaccalaureate distance learning degree programs offered (no on-campus study). *Faculty:* 40 full-time (30 women), 104 part-time/adjunct (77 women). *Students:* 453 full-time (381 women), 1,672 part-time (1,435 women); includes 284 minority (139 Black or African American, non-Hispanic/Latino; 11 American Indian or Alaska Native, non-Hispanic/Latino; 38 Asian, non-Hispanic/Latino; 58 Hispanic/Latino; 5 Native Hawaiian or other Pacific Islander, non-Hispanic/Latino; 33 Two or more races, non-Hispanic/Latino), 22 international. Average age 35. In 2013, 1,137 master's, 18 doctorates, 51 other advanced degrees awarded. *Degree requirements:* For master's, practicum; for doctorate, thesis/dissertation. *Entrance requirements:* For master's, Massachusetts Tests for Educator Licensure (MTEL), transcripts, statement of purpose, recommendations; interview (for special education); for doctorate, GRE General Test, transcripts, statement of purpose, recommendations, interview, master's degree, resume; for other advanced degree, interview, master's degree. Additional exam requirements/recommendations for international students: Required—TOEFL (minimum score 550 paper-based; 80 iBT). *Application deadline:* Applications are processed on a rolling basis. Application fee: $50. Electronic applications accepted. *Expenses: Tuition:* Part-time $900 per credit. *Financial support:* In 2013–14, 15 fellowships (averaging $3,600 per year) were awarded; career-related internships or fieldwork, Federal Work-Study, scholarships/grants, tuition waivers, and unspecified assistantships also available. Financial award application deadline: 4/15; financial award applicants required to submit FAFSA. *Faculty research:* Assessment in literacy, mathematics and science; autism spectrum disorders; instructional technology and online learning; multicultural education and English language learners. *Unit head:* Dr. Jack Gillette, Dean, 617-349-8401, Fax: 617-349-8607, E-mail: jgillett@lesley.edu. *Application contact:* Martha Sheehan, Director of Admissions, 888-LESLEYU, Fax: 617-349-8313, E-mail: info@lesley.edu.
Website: http://www.lesley.edu/soe.html.

Lewis & Clark College, Graduate School of Education and Counseling, Department of Teacher Education, Program in Middle Level/High School Education, Portland, OR 97219-7899. Offers MAT. *Accreditation:* NCATE. *Entrance requirements:* For master's, prior experience working with children and/or youth; minimum undergraduate GPA of 2.75. Additional exam requirements/recommendations for international students: Required—TOEFL (minimum score 575 paper-based). Electronic applications accepted. *Faculty research:* Classroom management, classroom assessment, science education, classroom ethnography, moral development.

Lewis University, College of Education, Program in Secondary Education, Romeoville, IL 60446. Offers biology (MA); chemistry (MA); English (MA); history (MA); math (MA); physics (MA); psychology and social science (MA). Part-time programs available. *Students:* 15 full-time (6 women), 15 part-time (9 women); includes 6 minority (2 Black or African American, non-Hispanic/Latino; 1 Asian, non-Hispanic/Latino; 3 Hispanic/

Latino). Average age 30. *Entrance requirements:* For master's, departmental qualifying exam, writing exam, minimum GPA of 2.75, 2 letters of recommendation, interview. Additional exam requirements/recommendations for international students: Required—TOEFL (minimum score 550 paper-based; 80 iBT). *Application deadline:* For fall admission, 5/1 priority date for international students; for spring admission, 11/15 priority date for international students. Applications are processed on a rolling basis. Application fee: $40. Electronic applications accepted. *Financial support:* Federal Work-Study, scholarships/grants, and unspecified assistantships available. Financial award application deadline: 5/1; financial award applicants required to submit FAFSA. *Unit head:* Dr. Dorene Huvaere, Program Director, 815-838-0500 Ext. 5885, E-mail: huvaersdo@lewisu.edu. *Application contact:* Fran Welsh, Secretary, 815-838-0500 Ext. 5880, E-mail: welshfr@lewisu.edu.

Liberty University, School of Education, Lynchburg, VA 24515. Offers administration and supervision (M Ed); curriculum and instruction (Ed D, Ed S); early childhood education (M Ed); educational leadership (Ed D, Ed S); educational technology and online instruction (M Ed); elementary education (M Ed, MAT); English (M Ed); gifted education (M Ed); history (M Ed); leadership (M Ed); math specialist (M Ed); middle grades (M Ed, MAT); outdoor adventure sport (MS); reading specialist (M Ed); school counseling (M Ed); secondary education (MAT); special education (M Ed, MAT); sport management (MS), including administration, outdoor recreation, sport management, tourism; sports administration (MS); student service (M Ed); teaching and learning (M Ed); tourism (MS). *Accreditation:* NCATE. Part-time programs available. Postbaccalaureate distance learning degree programs offered (minimal on-campus study). *Students:* 2,241 full-time (1,639 women), 4,413 part-time (3,240 women); includes 2,052 minority (1,588 Black or African American, non-Hispanic/Latino; 37 American Indian or Alaska Native, non-Hispanic/Latino; 67 Asian, non-Hispanic/Latino; 173 Hispanic/Latino; 37 Native Hawaiian or other Pacific Islander, non-Hispanic/Latino; 150 Two or more races, non-Hispanic/Latino), 15 international. Average age 37. 6,185 applicants, 43% accepted, 1603 enrolled. In 2013, 1,256 master's, 117 doctorates, 470 other advanced degrees awarded. *Degree requirements:* For doctorate, comprehensive exam, thesis/dissertation. *Entrance requirements:* For master's, GRE General Test or MAT (if taken in or before 1999), 2 letters of recommendation, minimum undergraduate GPA of 3.0, curriculum vitae; for doctorate and Ed S, GRE General Test or MAT (if taken before 1999), minimum master's GPA of 3.0, 3 years of teaching experience. Additional exam requirements/recommendations for international students: Required—TOEFL (minimum score 600 paper-based; 100 iBT). *Application deadline:* For fall admission, 6/1 for domestic students; for spring admission, 11/1 for domestic students. Applications are processed on a rolling basis. Application fee: $50. Electronic applications accepted. *Expenses:* Contact institution. *Financial support:* Federal Work-Study and tuition waivers (partial) available. *Faculty research:* Self-determination, character education, bibliotherapy, learning styles, distance education. *Unit head:* Dr. Karen L. Parker, Dean, 434-582-2195, Fax: 434-582-2468, E-mail: kparker@liberty.edu. *Application contact:* Jay Bridge, Director of Graduate Admissions, 800-424-9595, Fax: 800-628-7977, E-mail: gradadmissions@liberty.edu.
Website: http://www.liberty.edu/academics/education/graduate/.

Lincoln University, Graduate Studies, Jefferson City, MO 65101. Offers business administration (MBA), including accounting, entrepreneurship, management, public administration and policy; educational leadership (Ed S), including elementary leadership, secondary leadership, superintendency; guidance and counseling (M Ed), including community/agency counseling, elementary school, secondary school; history (MA); school administration and supervision (M Ed), including elementary school administration, secondary school administration, special education administration; school teaching (M Ed), including elementary school teaching, secondary school teaching; sociology (MA); sociology/criminal justice (MA). Part-time and evening/weekend programs available. Postbaccalaureate distance learning degree programs offered (minimal on-campus study). *Students:* 42 full-time (29 women), 109 part-time (66 women); includes 51 minority (37 Black or African American, non-Hispanic/Latino; 10 American Indian or Alaska Native, non-Hispanic/Latino; 1 Asian, non-Hispanic/Latino; 2 Hispanic/Latino; 1 Two or more races, non-Hispanic/Latino), 10 international. Average age 33. 84 applicants, 76% accepted, 51 enrolled. In 2013, 73 master's, 6 other advanced degrees awarded. *Degree requirements:* For master's and Ed S, comprehensive exam, thesis optional. *Entrance requirements:* For master's and Ed S, GRE, MAT or GMAT, minimum GPA of 2.75 in major, 2.5 overall; 3 letters of recommendation; minimum C average in English composition; personal statement of purpose. Additional exam requirements/recommendations for international students: Required—TOEFL (minimum score 500 paper-based; 61 iBT). *Application deadline:* For fall admission, 8/1 priority date for domestic and international students; for spring admission, 12/1 priority date for domestic and international students; for summer admission, 5/1 priority date for domestic and international students. Applications are processed on a rolling basis. Application fee: $30. *Expenses:* Tuition, state resident: full-time $6840; part-time $285 per credit hour. Tuition, nonresident: full-time $12,720; part-time $530 per credit hour. *Required fees:* $587; $587 per year. Tuition and fees vary according to course load. *Financial support:* Federal Work-Study and scholarships/grants available. Support available to part-time students. Financial award application deadline: 3/1; financial award applicants required to submit FAFSA. *Unit head:* Dr. Linda S. Bickel, Dean, 573-681-5247, Fax: 573-681-5106, E-mail: gradschool@lincolnu.edu. *Application contact:* Irasema Steck, Administrative Assistant, 573-681-5247, Fax: 573-681-5106, E-mail: gradschool@lincolnu.edu.
Website: http://www.lincolnu.edu/web/graduate-studies/graduate-studies.

Long Island University–Hudson at Rockland, Graduate School, Program in Curriculum and Instruction, Orangeburg, NY 10962. Offers adolescence education (MS Ed); childhood education (MS Ed). Part-time and evening/weekend programs available. *Degree requirements:* For master's, LAST and CST exams. *Entrance requirements:* For master's, college transcripts, letters of recommendation, personal statement.

Long Island University–Hudson at Westchester, Programs in Education-Teaching, Program in Special Education and Secondary Education, Purchase, NY 10577. Offers MS Ed, Advanced Certificate. Part-time and evening/weekend programs available.

Long Island University–LIU Post, College of Liberal Arts and Sciences, Department of English, Brookville, NY 11548-1300. Offers English (MA); English for adolescence education (MS). Part-time and evening/weekend programs available. *Degree requirements:* For master's, comprehensive exam (for some programs), thesis (for some programs). *Entrance requirements:* For master's, minimum GPA of 3.5 in major, 3.0 overall; 21 credits of English. Electronic applications accepted. *Faculty research:* English Renaissance, Sinclair Lewis: The Early Years, puppetry archives, Irish-American Experiences: literature of memory, Henry James's anxiety of Poe's influence.

Louisiana State University and Agricultural & Mechanical College, Graduate School, College of Human Sciences and Education, Department of Educational Theory, Policy and Practice, Baton Rouge, LA 70803. Offers counseling (M Ed, MA, Ed S); educational administration (M Ed, MA, PhD, Ed S); educational technology (MA); elementary education (M Ed, MAT); higher education (PhD); research methodology (PhD); secondary education (M Ed, MAT). PhD programs offered jointly with Louisiana State University in Shreveport. *Accreditation:* ACA (one or more programs are accredited); NCATE. Part-time and evening/weekend programs available. *Faculty:* 39 full-time (22 women). *Students:* 185 full-time (136 women), 177 part-time (140 women); includes 110 minority (90 Black or African American, non-Hispanic/Latino; 1 American Indian or Alaska Native, non-Hispanic/Latino; 5 Asian, non-Hispanic/Latino; 9 Hispanic/Latino; 5 Two or more races, non-Hispanic/Latino), 5 international. Average age 31. 167 applicants, 66% accepted, 76 enrolled. In 2013, 134 master's, 23 doctorates, 17 other advanced degrees awarded. Terminal master's awarded for partial completion of doctoral program. *Degree requirements:* For doctorate, thesis/dissertation; for Ed S, thesis optional. *Entrance requirements:* For master's and doctorate, GRE General Test, minimum GPA of 3.0. Additional exam requirements/recommendations for international students: Required—TOEFL (minimum score 550 paper-based; 79 IBT), IELTS (minimum score 6.5), or PTE (minimum score 59). *Application deadline:* For fall admission, 1/25 priority date for domestic students, 5/15 for international students; for spring admission, 10/15 for international students. Applications are processed on a rolling basis. Application fee: $50 ($70 for international students). Electronic applications accepted. *Financial support:* In 2013–14, 253 students received support, including 5 fellowships (averaging $32,204 per year), 27 research assistantships with full and partial tuition reimbursements available (averaging $10,199 per year), 68 teaching assistantships with full and partial tuition reimbursements available (averaging $12,316 per year); career-related internships or fieldwork, Federal Work-Study, institutionally sponsored loans, health care benefits, and unspecified assistantships also available. Support available to part-time students. Financial award applicants required to submit FAFSA. *Faculty research:* Literary, curriculum studies, science education, K-12 leadership, higher education. *Total annual research expenditures:* $735,835. *Unit head:* Dr. Earl Cheek, Jr., Chair, 225-578-1258, Fax: 225-578-2267, E-mail: echeek@lsu.edu. *Application contact:* Dr. Kristin Gansle, Graduate Coordinator, 225-578-6780, Fax: 225-578-2267, E-mail: kgansle@lsu.edu.

Loyola Marymount University, School of Education, Department of Elementary and Secondary Education, Program in Secondary Education, Los Angeles, CA 90045. Offers MA. Part-time programs available. *Faculty:* 5 full-time (4 women), 19 part-time/adjunct (11 women). *Students:* 95 full-time (55 women), 15 part-time (9 women); includes 52 minority (4 Black or African American, non-Hispanic/Latino; 1 American Indian or Alaska Native, non-Hispanic/Latino; 16 Asian, non-Hispanic/Latino; 27 Hispanic/Latino; 4 Two or more races, non-Hispanic/Latino), 2 international. Average age 30. 83 applicants, 60% accepted, 50 enrolled. In 2013, 56 master's awarded. *Degree requirements:* For master's, comprehensive exam. *Entrance requirements:* For master's, CBEST, CSET, 3 letters of recommendation. Additional exam requirements/recommendations for international students: Required—TOEFL (minimum score 600 paper-based; 100 iBT). *Application deadline:* For fall admission, 6/15 for domestic students; for spring admission, 11/15 for domestic students. Application fee: $50. Electronic applications accepted. *Financial support:* In 2013–14, 71 students received support. Scholarships/grants and unspecified assistantships available. Support available to part-time students. Financial award application deadline: 6/30; financial award applicants required to submit FAFSA. *Unit head:* Dr. Irene Oliver, Chair, 310-338-7302, E-mail: ioliver@lmu.edu. *Application contact:* Chake H. Kouyoumjian, Director, Graduate Admissions, 310-338-2721, E-mail: ckouyoum@lmu.edu.
Website: http://soe.lmu.edu/admissions/programs/tcp/secondaryeducation/.

Loyola University Chicago, School of Education, Program in Teaching and Learning, Chicago, IL 60660. Offers behavior intervention specialist (M Ed); elementary education (M Ed); English as a second language (Certificate); English language teaching and learning (M Ed); math education (M Ed); reading specialist (M Ed); reading teacher endorsement (Certificate); school technology (M Ed); science education (M Ed); secondary education (M Ed); special education (M Ed). *Accreditation:* NCATE. *Faculty:* 23 full-time (16 women), 49 part-time/adjunct (42 women). *Students:* 109. Average age 28. 104 applicants, 71% accepted, 44 enrolled. In 2013, 39 master's awarded. *Degree requirements:* For master's, comprehensive exam. *Entrance requirements:* For master's, Illinois Basic Skills Test, 3 letters of recommendation, minimum GPA of 3.0, resume. Additional exam requirements/recommendations for international students: Required—TOEFL (minimum score 550 paper-based; 79 iBT). *Application deadline:* For fall admission, 7/1 priority date for domestic and international students; for spring admission, 11/1 priority date for domestic and international students; for summer admission, 4/1 for domestic and international students. Applications are processed on a rolling basis. Application fee: $50. Electronic applications accepted. Application fee is waived when completed online. *Expenses:* Tuition: Full-time $16,740; part-time $930 per credit. *Required fees:* $135 per semester. *Financial support:* In 2013–14, 58 fellowships with partial tuition reimbursements were awarded; research assistantships, teaching assistantships, institutionally sponsored loans, scholarships/grants, and unspecified assistantships also available. Support available to part-time students. Financial award application deadline: 2/1; financial award applicants required to submit FAFSA. *Faculty research:* Positive behavior support, school reform, school improvement. *Unit head:* Dr. Ann Marie Ryan, Director, 312-915-7027, E-mail: aryan3@luc.edu. *Application contact:* Marie Rosin-Dittmar, Information Contact, 312-915-6800, E-mail: schleduc@luc.edu.

Loyola University Maryland, Graduate Programs, School of Education, Master of Arts in Teaching Program, Baltimore, MD 21210-2699. Offers elementary/middle education (MAT); secondary education (MAT); secondary education: biology (MAT); secondary education: chemistries (MAT); secondary education: earth science (MAT); secondary education: English (MAT); secondary education: mathematics (MAT); secondary education: physics (MAT). Part-time programs available. *Entrance requirements:* For master's, essay, 2 letters of recommendation, resume, transcipt. Additional exam requirements/recommendations for international students: Required—TOEFL (minimum score 550 paper-based).

Loyola University Maryland, Graduate Programs, School of Education, Program in Special Education, Baltimore, MD 21210-2699. Offers early childhood education (M Ed, CAS); elementary/middle education (M Ed, CAS); secondary education (M Ed, CAS). *Accreditation:* NCATE. Part-time programs available. *Entrance requirements:* For master's, transcript, essay, letter of recommendation. Additional exam requirements/recommendations for international students: Required—TOEFL (minimum score 550 paper-based). Electronic applications accepted.

Maharishi University of Management, Graduate Studies, Department of Education, Fairfield, IA 52557. Offers teaching elementary education (MA); teaching secondary education (MA). *Degree requirements:* For master's, thesis or alternative. *Entrance requirements:* For master's, GRE, minimum GPA of 3.0. Additional exam requirements/recommendations for international students: Required—TOEFL. *Faculty research:* Unified field-based approach to education, moral climate, scientific study of teaching.

Manhattanville College, School of Education, Program in Middle Childhood/Adolescence Education (Grades 5-12), Purchase, NY 10577-2132. Offers biology (MAT); biology and special education (MPS); chemistry (MAT); chemistry and special education (MPS); English (MAT); English and special education (MPS); literacy and special education (MPS); literacy specialist (MPS); math and special education (MPS); mathematics (MAT); physics (MAT); social studies (MAT); social studies and special education (MPS); special education (MPS); teaching languages other than English (MAT), including French, Italian, Latin, Spanish. Part-time and evening/weekend

programs available. *Degree requirements:* For master's, comprehensive exam or research project, field experience. *Entrance requirements:* For master's, minimum undergraduate GPA of 3.0, 2 letters of recommendation. Additional exam requirements/recommendations for international students: Required—TOEFL. Electronic applications accepted.

Mansfield University of Pennsylvania, Graduate Studies, Department of Education and Special Education, Mansfield, PA 16933. Offers elementary education (M Ed); secondary education (MS); special education (M Ed). *Accreditation:* NCATE (one or more programs are accredited). Part-time and evening/weekend programs available. Postbaccalaureate distance learning degree programs offered (no on-campus study). *Degree requirements:* For master's, comprehensive exam, thesis optional. *Entrance requirements:* For master's, minimum GPA of 3.0. Additional exam requirements/recommendations for international students: Required—TOEFL (minimum score 550 paper-based). Electronic applications accepted.

Marquette University, Graduate School, College of Education, Department of Educational Policy and Leadership, Milwaukee, WI 53201-1881. Offers college student personnel administration (M Ed); curriculum and instruction (MA); education (MA); educational administration (M Ed); educational policy and foundations (MA); elementary education (Certificate); literacy (MA); principal (Certificate); reading specialist (Certificate); reading teacher (Certificate); secondary education (Certificate); superintendent (Certificate). Part-time and evening/weekend programs available. *Faculty:* 15 full-time (10 women), 3 part-time/adjunct (2 women). *Students:* 39 full-time (31 women), 107 part-time (70 women); includes 19 minority (7 Black or African American, non-Hispanic/Latino; 2 American Indian or Alaska Native, non-Hispanic/Latino; 3 Asian, non-Hispanic/Latino; 6 Hispanic/Latino; 1 Two or more races, non-Hispanic/Latino), 2 international. Average age 30. 144 applicants, 74% accepted, 67 enrolled. In 2013, 48 master's, 4 doctorates, 12 other advanced degrees awarded. Terminal master's awarded for partial completion of doctoral program. *Degree requirements:* For master's, comprehensive exam, thesis (for some programs); for doctorate, thesis/dissertation, qualifying exam, supporting minor. *Entrance requirements:* For master's, GRE General Test or MAT, official transcripts from all current and previous colleges/universities except Marquette, three letters of recommendation, statement of purpose; for doctorate, GRE General Test, MAT, sample of written work, official transcripts from all current and previous colleges/universities except Marquette, three letters of recommendation, statement of purpose, resume/curriculum vitae; for Certificate, GRE General Test or MAT, master's degree. Additional exam requirements/recommendations for international students: Required—TOEFL (minimum score 530 paper-based). *Application deadline:* For fall admission, 1/15 for domestic and international students. Application fee: $50. *Expenses:* Contact institution. *Financial support:* In 2013–14, 130 students received support, including 1 fellowship with full tuition reimbursement available (averaging $18,780 per year), 5 research assistantships with full tuition reimbursements available (averaging $13,404 per year); health care benefits, tuition waivers (partial), and unspecified assistantships also available. Support available to part-time students. Financial award application deadline: 2/15. *Faculty research:* Leadership; social justice in education; development of lifelong learners; race, class, and schooling in historical perspective; urban teacher education. *Unit head:* Dr. Ellen Eckman, Chair, 414-288-1561, E-mail: ellen.eckman@marquette.edu. *Application contact:* Dr. Sharon Chubbuck, Associate Professor, 414-288-5895.

Marshall University, Academic Affairs Division, College of Education and Professional Development, Program in Secondary Education, Huntington, WV 25755. Offers MA. *Accreditation:* NCATE. Part-time and evening/weekend programs available. *Students:* 4 full-time (2 women), 46 part-time (37 women); includes 2 minority (1 Black or African American, non-Hispanic/Latino; 1 Two or more races, non-Hispanic/Latino). Average age 32. In 2013, 28 master's awarded. *Degree requirements:* For master's, thesis optional, comprehensive or oral assessment. *Entrance requirements:* For master's, GRE General Test or MAT. Application fee: $40. *Financial support:* Federal Work-Study, tuition waivers (full), and unspecified assistantships available. Support available to part-time students. Financial award applicants required to submit FAFSA. *Unit head:* Dr. Lisa Heaton, Director, 304-746-2026, E-mail: heaton@marshall.edu. *Application contact:* Information Contact, Graduate Admissions, 304-746-1900, Fax: 304-746-1902, E-mail: services@marshall.edu.

Marygrove College, Graduate Division, Sage Program, Detroit, MI 48221-2599. Offers M Ed. *Entrance requirements:* For master's, Michigan Teacher Test for Certification.

Marymount University, School of Education and Human Services, Program in Education, Arlington, VA 22207-4299. Offers counselor education and supervision (Ed D); elementary education (M Ed); English as a second language (M Ed); professional studies (M Ed); secondary education (M Ed); special education: general curriculum (M Ed). *Accreditation:* NCATE. Part-time and evening/weekend programs available. *Faculty:* 8 full-time (6 women), 13 part-time/adjunct (9 women). *Students:* 76 full-time (67 women), 83 part-time (70 women); includes 30 minority (12 Black or African American, non-Hispanic/Latino; 2 American Indian or Alaska Native, non-Hispanic/Latino; 9 Asian, non-Hispanic/Latino; 6 Hispanic/Latino; 1 Two or more races, non-Hispanic/Latino), 12 international. Average age 31. 63 applicants, 95% accepted, 44 enrolled. In 2013, 88 master's awarded. *Degree requirements:* For master's, thesis or alternative; for doctorate, thesis/dissertation. *Entrance requirements:* For master's, GRE or MAT and PRAXIS I or SAT/ACT and VCLA, 2 letters of recommendation, resume, interview. Additional exam requirements/recommendations for international students: Required—TOEFL (minimum score 600 paper-based; 96 iBT), IELTS (minimum score 6.5). *Application deadline:* For fall admission, 7/1 for international students. Applications are processed on a rolling basis. Application fee: $40. Electronic applications accepted. *Expenses: Tuition:* Part-time $850 per credit. *Required fees:* $10 per credit. One-time fee: $200 part-time. Tuition and fees vary according to program. *Financial support:* In 2013–14, 41 students received support, including 4 research assistantships with full and partial tuition reimbursements available, 1 teaching assistantship with full and partial tuition reimbursement available; career-related internships or fieldwork, Federal Work-Study, scholarships/grants, and unspecified assistantships also available. Support available to part-time students. Financial award applicants required to submit FAFSA. *Unit head:* Dr. Lisa Turissini, Chair, 703-526-1668, Fax: 703-284-1631, E-mail: lisa.turissini@marymount.edu. *Application contact:* Francesca Reed, Director, Graduate Admissions, 703-284-5901, Fax: 703-527-3815, E-mail: grad.admissions@marymount.edu.
Website: http://www.marymount.edu/academics/schools/sehs/grad.aspx.

Maryville University of Saint Louis, School of Education, St. Louis, MO 63141-7299. Offers art education (MA Ed); early childhood education (MA Ed); educational leadership (Ed D); educational leadership: principal certification (MA Ed); elementary education (MA Ed); gifted education (MA Ed); higher education leadership (Ed D); literacy specialist (MA Ed); middle grades education (MA Ed); secondary teaching and inquiry (MA Ed); teacher as leader (MA Ed); teacher leadership (Ed D). *Accreditation:* NCATE. Part-time and evening/weekend programs available. *Faculty:* 10 full-time (6 women), 17 part-time/adjunct (13 women). *Students:* 21 full-time (17 women), 238 part-time (167 women); includes 64 minority (54 Black or African American, non-Hispanic/Latino; 2 Asian, non-Hispanic/Latino; 4 Hispanic/Latino; 4 Two or more races, non-Hispanic/Latino), 2 international. Average age 39. In 2013, 61 master's, 40 doctorates awarded. *Degree requirements:* For master's, thesis, project. *Entrance requirements:* For master's, minimum cumulative GPA of 3.0, 3 professional recommendations, essays, interview with program faculty; for doctorate, minimum GPA of 3.0, 3 professional recommendations, essay, interview, on-site writing sample. Additional exam requirements/recommendations for international students: Required—TOEFL (minimum score 550 paper-based). *Application deadline:* Applications are processed on a rolling basis. Application fee: $40 ($60 for international students). Electronic applications accepted. Application fee is waived when completed online. *Expenses: Tuition:* Full-time $23,812; part-time $728 per credit hour. *Required fees:* $395 per year. Tuition and fees vary according to course load, degree level and program. *Financial support:* Career-related internships or fieldwork, Federal Work-Study, tuition waivers (partial), and professional educator discounts available. Financial award application deadline: 3/1; financial award applicants required to submit FAFSA. *Faculty research:* Collaboration with public schools, pre-service program development, mathematics, diversity, literacy. *Unit head:* Dr. Cathy Bear, Dean, 314-529-9692, Fax: 314-529-9921, E-mail: cbear@maryville.edu. *Application contact:* Holly Stanwich, Graduate Admissions Coordinator, 314-529-9542, Fax: 314-529-9921, E-mail: teachered@maryville.edu.
Website: http://www.maryville.edu/ed/graduate-programs/.

Marywood University, Academic Affairs, Reap College of Education and Human Development, Department of Education, Program in Secondary/K-12 Education, Scranton, PA 18509-1598. Offers MAT. *Entrance requirements:* Additional exam requirements/recommendations for international students: Required—TOEFL (minimum score 550 paper-based; 79 iBT). *Application deadline:* For fall admission, 4/1 priority date for domestic students, 3/31 priority date for international students; for spring admission, 11/1 priority date for domestic students, 8/31 priority date for international students. Applications are processed on a rolling basis. Application fee: $35. Electronic applications accepted. *Expenses: Tuition:* Part-time $775 per credit. Tuition and fees vary according to degree level. *Financial support:* Career-related internships or fieldwork, scholarships/grants, and unspecified assistantships available. Support available to part-time students. Financial award application deadline: 6/30; financial award applicants required to submit FAFSA. *Unit head:* Dr. Patricia S. Arter, Chairperson, 570-348-6211 Ext. 2511, E-mail: psarter@marywood.edu. *Application contact:* Tammy Manka, Assistant Director of Graduate Admissions, 570-348-6211 Ext. 2322, E-mail: tmanka@marywood.edu.
Website: http://www.marywood.edu/education/graduate-programs/mat-secondary-ed.html.

McDaniel College, Graduate and Professional Studies, Program in Elementary and Secondary Education, Westminster, MD 21157-4390. Offers elementary education (MS); secondary education (MS). *Accreditation:* NCATE. Part-time and evening/weekend programs available. *Degree requirements:* For master's, comprehensive exam (for some programs), thesis optional. *Entrance requirements:* For master's, GRE General Test, MAT, or NTE/PRAXIS I, 3 letters of reference. Additional exam requirements/recommendations for international students: Required—TOEFL.

McNeese State University, Doré School of Graduate Studies, Burton College of Education, Office of Graduate Education Programs, Program in Curriculum and Instruction, Lake Charles, LA 70609. Offers early childhood education (M Ed); elementary education (M Ed); reading (M Ed); secondary education (M Ed). Evening/weekend programs available. *Entrance requirements:* For master's, GRE, teaching certificate.

McNeese State University, Doré School of Graduate Studies, Burton College of Education, Office of Graduate Education Programs, Program in Secondary Education, Lake Charles, LA 70609. Offers MAT. Evening/weekend programs available. *Degree requirements:* For master's, comprehensive exam, field experiences. *Entrance requirements:* For master's, GRE General Test, PRAXIS I and II, autobiography, two letters of recommendation.

McNeese State University, Doré School of Graduate Studies, Burton College of Education, Office of Student Teaching and Professional Education Services, Program in Secondary Education Grades 6-12, Lake Charles, LA 70609. Offers Postbaccalaureate Certificate. *Entrance requirements:* For degree, PRAXIS, 2 letters of recommendation, autobiography.

Medaille College, Program in Education, Buffalo, NY 14214-2695. Offers adolescent education (MS Ed); curriculum and instruction (MS Ed); education preparation (MS Ed); literacy (MS Ed); special education (MS). *Accreditation:* Teacher Education Accreditation Council. Part-time and evening/weekend programs available. *Faculty:* 12 full-time (9 women), 28 part-time/adjunct (19 women). *Students:* 159 full-time (123 women), 25 part-time (22 women); includes 8 minority (5 Black or African American, non-Hispanic/Latino; 3 Hispanic/Latino), 88 international. Average age 29. 209 applicants, 96% accepted, 61 enrolled. In 2013, 253 master's awarded. *Degree requirements:* For master's, comprehensive exam (for some programs), thesis or alternative. *Entrance requirements:* For master's, minimum undergraduate GPA of 2.7. Additional exam requirements/recommendations for international students: Required—TOEFL (minimum score 550 paper-based). *Application deadline:* For fall admission, 8/15 priority date for domestic students; for spring admission, 1/15 priority date for domestic students. Applications are processed on a rolling basis. Application fee: $35. Electronic applications accepted. *Financial support:* Federal Work-Study available. Financial award applicants required to submit FAFSA. *Faculty research:* Curriculum planning, truancy, tracking minority students, curriculum design, mentoring students. *Unit head:* Dr. Illana Lane, Dean, School of Education, 716-880-2553, E-mail: ilane@medaille.edu. *Application contact:* E-mail: sageadmissions@medaille.edu.
Website: http://www.medaille.edu.

Mercer University, Graduate Studies, Cecil B. Day Campus, Tift College of Education (Atlanta), Macon, GA 31207-0003. Offers curriculum and instruction (PhD); early childhood education (M Ed, MAT, Ed S); educational leadership (PhD, Ed S); higher education leadership (M Ed); independent and charter school leadership (M Ed); middle grades education (M Ed, MAT); reading education (M Ed); school counseling (Ed S); secondary education (M Ed, MAT); teacher leadership (Ed S). *Accreditation:* NCATE. Part-time and evening/weekend programs available. *Faculty:* 40 full-time (20 women), 9 part-time/adjunct (4 women). *Students:* 240 full-time (197 women), 382 part-time (320 women); includes 343 minority (315 Black or African American, non-Hispanic/Latino; 4 American Indian or Alaska Native, non-Hispanic/Latino; 9 Asian, non-Hispanic/Latino; 9 Hispanic/Latino; 1 Native Hawaiian or other Pacific Islander, non-Hispanic/Latino; 5 Two or more races, non-Hispanic/Latino), 4 international. Average age 36. In 2013, 233 master's, 24 doctorates, 47 other advanced degrees awarded. *Degree requirements:* For master's and Ed S, research project; for doctorate, comprehensive exam, thesis/dissertation. *Entrance requirements:* For master's, GRE or MAT, minimum undergraduate GPA of 2.75; for doctorate, GRE; for Ed S, GRE or MAT, minimum GPA of 3.25; for EDS degrees in educational leadership and teacher leadership: 3 years of certified teaching experience. Additional exam requirements/recommendations for international students: Required—TOEFL. *Application deadline:* For fall admission, 8/1 for domestic and international students; for spring admission, 12/1 for domestic and international students; for summer admission, 5/1 for domestic and international students. Applications are processed on a rolling basis. Application fee: $25. *Expenses:*

Contact institution. *Financial support:* Federal Work-Study available. Support available to part-time students. Financial award application deadline: 5/1. *Faculty research:* Educational technology, multicultural and minority issues in education, educational leadership (P-12 and higher education), school discipline and school bullying, standards-based mathematics education. *Unit head:* Dr. Paige L. Tompkins, Interim Dean, 478-301-5397, Fax: 478-301-2280, E-mail: tompkins_pl@mercer.edu. *Application contact:* Dr. Allison Gilmore, Associate Dean for Graduate Teacher Education, 678-547-6333, Fax: 678-547-6055, E-mail: gilmore_a@mercer.edu.
Website: http://www.mercer.edu/education/.

Mercy College, School of Education, Program in Adolescence Education, Dobbs Ferry, NY 10522-1189. Offers MS. Part-time and evening/weekend programs available. Postbaccalaureate distance learning degree programs offered (no on-campus study). *Students:* 49 full-time (31 women), 96 part-time (56 women); includes 67 minority (34 Black or African American, non-Hispanic/Latino; 1 Asian, non-Hispanic/Latino; 30 Hispanic/Latino; 2 Two or more races, non-Hispanic/Latino). Average age 32. 92 applicants, 59% accepted, 37 enrolled. In 2013, 13 master's awarded. *Degree requirements:* For master's, comprehensive exam (for some programs), thesis (for some programs). *Entrance requirements:* For master's, resume, undergraduate transcript. Additional exam requirements/recommendations for international students: Required—TOEFL (minimum score 600 paper-based; 100 iBT), IELTS (minimum score 8). *Application deadline:* For fall admission, 8/1 for international students. Applications are processed on a rolling basis. Application fee: $40. Electronic applications accepted. *Expenses: Tuition:* Full-time $19,344; part-time $806 per credit. *Required fees:* $580; $806 per credit. $145 per term. Tuition and fees vary according to course load, degree level and program. *Financial support:* Career-related internships or fieldwork, Federal Work-Study, scholarships/grants, and unspecified assistantships available. Support available to part-time students. Financial award applicants required to submit FAFSA. *Unit head:* Dr. Alfred S. Posamentier, Dean for the School of Education, 914-674-7350, Fax: 914-674-7352, E-mail: apeiser@mercy.edu. *Application contact:* Allison Gurdineer, Senior Director of Admissions, 877-637-2946, Fax: 914-674-7382, E-mail: admissions@mercy.edu.
Website: https://www.mercy.edu/academics/school-of-education/department-of-middle-childhood-adolescence-education/.

Mercyhurst University, Graduate Studies, Program in Secondary Education: Pedagogy and Practice, Erie, PA 16546. Offers MS. Part-time and evening/weekend programs available. *Entrance requirements:* For master's, GRE or PRAXIS I, resume, essay, three professional references, transcripts. Additional exam requirements/recommendations for international students: Required—TOEFL.

Merrimack College, School of Education, North Andover, MA 01845-5800. Offers community engagement (M Ed), including community organizations, higher education, K-12 education; early childhood education (M Ed); elementary education (M Ed); English as a second language (PreK-6) (M Ed); English language learners (M Ed); general studies (M Ed); higher education (M Ed), including leadership and organizational development, student affairs; middle (M Ed); moderate disabilities (PreK-8) (M Ed); secondary (M Ed); teacher leadership (CAGS), including instructional leadership, reading specialist. Part-time and evening/weekend programs available. *Faculty:* 4 full-time (all women), 23 part-time/adjunct (15 women). *Students:* 127 full-time (104 women), 61 part-time (52 women); includes 3 minority (1 Asian, non-Hispanic/Latino; 2 Hispanic/Latino), 2 international. Average age 25. 403 applicants, 47% accepted, 138 enrolled. In 2013, 140 master's awarded. *Degree requirements:* For master's, practicum, portfolio, and state test (for licensure track); capstone (for higher education and community engagement tracks). *Entrance requirements:* For master's, MTEL (Massachusetts Tests for Educator Licensure), official transcripts from other colleges, resume, personal statement, 2 letters of recommendation, additional essay requirements for fellowships. Additional exam requirements/recommendations for international students: Required—TOEFL (minimum score 84 iBT), IELTS (minimum score 6.5). *Application deadline:* For fall admission, 8/15 for domestic and international students; for winter admission, 12/1 for domestic students, 11/15 for international students; for spring admission, 1/10 for domestic and international students; for summer admission, 5/10 for domestic and international students. Applications are processed on a rolling basis. Application fee: $0. Electronic applications accepted. Tuition and fees vary according to course load and program. *Financial support:* In 2013–14, 91 fellowships with full tuition reimbursements were awarded; career-related internships or fieldwork, scholarships/grants, and health care benefits also available. Support available to part-time students. Financial award applicants required to submit FAFSA. *Faculty research:* Expressive language, civic engagement, family life education, reading genres, the psychological process of aging. *Application contact:* Kristen English, Interim Director of Graduate Admission, 978-837-5073, E-mail: englishkr@merrimack.edu.
Website: http://www.merrimack.edu/academics/graduate/education/.

Miami University, College of Education, Health and Society, Department of Teacher Education, Oxford, OH 45056. Offers adolescent education (M Ed); elementary education (M Ed, MAT); reading education (M Ed); secondary education (MAT). Part-time and evening/weekend programs available. *Students:* 31 full-time (21 women), 26 part-time (23 women); includes 8 minority (3 Black or African American, non-Hispanic/Latino; 1 Asian, non-Hispanic/Latino; 2 Hispanic/Latino; 2 Two or more races, non-Hispanic/Latino), 2 international. Average age 31. In 2013, 31 master's awarded. *Entrance requirements:* Additional exam requirements/recommendations for international students: Recommended—TOEFL (minimum score 80 iBT), IELTS (minimum score 6.5), TSE (minimum score 54). *Application deadline:* Applications are processed on a rolling basis. Application fee: $50. Electronic applications accepted. *Expenses:* Tuition, state resident: full-time $12,634; part-time $526 per credit hour. Tuition, nonresident: full-time $27,892; part-time $1162 per credit hour. Part-time tuition and fees vary according to course load, campus/location and program. *Financial support:* Research assistantships with full tuition reimbursements, teaching assistantships with full tuition reimbursements, career-related internships or fieldwork, Federal Work-Study, scholarships/grants, health care benefits, tuition waivers, and unspecified assistantships available. Financial award application deadline: 2/15. *Unit head:* Dr. Paula Saine, Interim Co-Chair, 513-529-6443, Fax: 513-529-4931, E-mail: sainep@miamioh.edu. *Application contact:* Linda Dennett, Program Associate, 513-529-5708, E-mail: dennetlg@miamioh.edu.
Website: http://www.MiamiOH.edu/edt.

Middle Tennessee State University, College of Graduate Studies, College of Education, Department of Educational Leadership, Program in Curriculum and Instruction, Murfreesboro, TN 37132. Offers curriculum and instruction (M Ed, Ed S); English as a second language (M Ed, Ed S); secondary education (M Ed); technology and curriculum design (Ed S). *Accreditation:* NCATE. Part-time and evening/weekend programs available. Postbaccalaureate distance learning degree programs offered. *Faculty:* 22 full-time (11 women), 22 part-time/adjunct (12 women). *Degree requirements:* For master's, comprehensive exam; for Ed S, comprehensive exam, thesis or alternative. *Entrance requirements:* For master's and Ed S, GRE, MAT or PRAXIS. Additional exam requirements/recommendations for international students: Required—TOEFL (minimum score 525 paper-based; 71 iBT) or IELTS (minimum score 6). *Application deadline:* For fall admission, 6/1 for domestic and international students. Applications are processed on a rolling basis. Application fee: $25 ($30 for international students). Electronic applications accepted. *Financial support:* Tuition waivers available. Support available to part-time students. Financial award application deadline: 5/1. *Unit head:* Dr. James Huffman, Chair, 615-898-2331, Fax: 615-898-2859, E-mail: jim.huffman@mtsu.edu. *Application contact:* Dr. Michael D. Allen, Vice Provost for Research and Dean, 615-898-2840, Fax: 615-904-8020, E-mail: michael.allen@mtsu.edu.

Mills College, Graduate Studies, School of Education, Oakland, CA 94613-1000. Offers child life in hospitals (MA); early childhood education (MA); education (MA), including art education, curriculum and instruction, elementary education, English education, foreign language education, mathematics education, science education, secondary education, social studies education, teaching; educational leadership (MA, Ed D). Part-time and evening/weekend programs available. *Faculty:* 10 full-time (7 women), 13 part-time/adjunct (10 women). *Students:* 154 full-time (136 women), 54 part-time (47 women); includes 96 minority (32 Black or African American, non-Hispanic/Latino; 1 American Indian or Alaska Native, non-Hispanic/Latino; 23 Asian, non-Hispanic/Latino; 27 Hispanic/Latino; 1 Native Hawaiian or other Pacific Islander, non-Hispanic/Latino; 12 Two or more races, non-Hispanic/Latino), 2 international. Average age 25. 222 applicants, 89% accepted, 110 enrolled. In 2013, 96 master's, 38 doctorates awarded. Terminal master's awarded for partial completion of doctoral program. *Degree requirements:* For master's, comprehensive exam, thesis (for some programs); for doctorate, thesis/dissertation. *Entrance requirements:* For master's, statement of purpose, official transcript, 3 recommendations. Additional exam requirements/recommendations for international students: Required—TOEFL (minimum score 550 paper-based; 80 iBT) or IELTS (minimum score 6). *Application deadline:* For fall admission, 12/31 priority date for domestic students, 12/15 for international students; for spring admission, 11/1 priority date for domestic students, 10/1 for international students. Applications are processed on a rolling basis. Application fee: $50. Electronic applications accepted. *Expenses: Tuition:* Full-time $29,860. *Required fees:* $1134. Part-time tuition and fees vary according to course load, degree level and program. *Financial support:* In 2013–14, 130 students received support, including 130 fellowships with full and partial tuition reimbursements available (averaging $7,565 per year); career-related internships or fieldwork and scholarships/grants also available. Support available to part-time students. Financial award application deadline: 2/1; financial award applicants required to submit FAFSA. *Faculty research:* Early childhood education, teacher preparation, educational leadership. *Total annual research expenditures:* $3.5 million. *Unit head:* Dr. Katherine Schultz, Department Head, 510-430-3384, Fax: 510-430-2159, E-mail: kschultz@mills.edu. *Application contact:* Shrim Bathey, Director of Graduate Admission, 510-430-3309, Fax: 510-430-2159, E-mail: grad-admission@mills.edu.
Website: http://www.mills.edu/education.

Minnesota State University Mankato, College of Graduate Studies, College of Education, Department of Educational Studies: K–12 and Secondary Programs, Mankato, MN 56001. Offers curriculum and instruction (SP); educational technology (MS); library media education (MS, Certificate); teacher licensure (MAT); teaching and learning (MS, Certificate). *Accreditation:* NCATE. *Students:* 53 full-time (35 women), 107 part-time (73 women). *Degree requirements:* For master's, comprehensive exam, thesis or alternative; for other advanced degree, comprehensive exam, thesis. *Entrance requirements:* For master's, GRE General Test or MAT, minimum GPA of 3.0 during previous 2 years; for other advanced degree, GRE, minimum GPA of 3.0. Additional exam requirements/recommendations for international students: Required—TOEFL. *Application deadline:* For fall admission, 7/1 priority date for domestic students, 5/1 for international students; for spring admission, 11/1 for domestic students, 10/1 for international students. Applications are processed on a rolling basis. Application fee: $40. Electronic applications accepted. *Financial support:* Application deadline: 3/15. *Unit head:* Dr. Kitty Foord, Chairperson, 507-389-1965. *Application contact:* 507-389-2321, E-mail: grad@mnsu.edu.
Website: http://ed.mnsu.edu/ksp/.

Mississippi College, Graduate School, School of Education, Department of Teacher Education and Leadership, Clinton, MS 39058. Offers art (M Ed); biological science (M Ed); business education (M Ed); computer science (M Ed); dyslexia therapy (M Ed); educational leadership (M Ed, Ed D, Ed S); elementary education (M Ed, Ed S); English (M Ed); higher education administration (MS); mathematics (M Ed); secondary education (M Ed); social studies (history) (M Ed); teaching arts (M Ed). Part-time programs available. Postbaccalaureate distance learning degree programs offered (no on-campus study). *Degree requirements:* For master's, comprehensive exam, thesis optional. *Entrance requirements:* For master's, NTE. Additional exam requirements/recommendations for international students: Recommended—TOEFL, IELTS. Electronic applications accepted.

Mississippi State University, College of Education, Department of Curriculum, Instruction and Special Education, Mississippi State, MS 39762. Offers curriculum and instruction (PhD), including early childhood education (MS, PhD), elementary education (PhD, Ed S), general curriculum and instruction, reading education, secondary education (PhD, Ed S), special education (PhD, Ed S); education (Ed S), including elementary education (PhD, Ed S), secondary education (PhD, Ed S), special education (PhD, Ed S); elementary education (MS), including early childhood education (MS, PhD), general elementary education, middle level education; middle level alternate route (MAT); secondary education (MS); secondary teacher alternate route (MAT); special education (MS). *Accreditation:* NCATE. Part-time and evening/weekend programs available. *Faculty:* 11 full-time (9 women). *Students:* 58 full-time (40 women), 143 part-time (100 women); includes 62 minority (56 Black or African American, non-Hispanic/Latino; 2 American Indian or Alaska Native, non-Hispanic/Latino; 3 Hispanic/Latino; 1 Two or more races, non-Hispanic/Latino). Average age 33. 181 applicants, 32% accepted, 52 enrolled. In 2013, 44 master's, 1 doctorate, 7 other advanced degrees awarded. *Degree requirements:* For master's, comprehensive exam; for doctorate, thesis/dissertation; for Ed S, comprehensive exam, thesis or alternative. *Entrance requirements:* For master's, GRE, minimum GPA of 2.75 in junior and senior year, eligibility for initial teacher certification; for doctorate, GRE, minimum GPA of 3.4 on previous graduate work; for Ed S, GRE, minimum GPA of 3.2 on master's degree. Additional exam requirements/recommendations for international students: Required—TOEFL (minimum score 550 paper-based; 79 iBT); Recommended—IELTS (minimum score 6.5). *Application deadline:* For fall admission, 3/1 priority date for domestic students, 5/1 for international students; for spring admission, 9/1 priority date for domestic students, 9/1 for international students. Applications are processed on a rolling basis. Application fee: $60. Electronic applications accepted. *Financial support:* In 2013–14, 7 research assistantships with full and partial tuition reimbursements (averaging $9,623 per year), 2 teaching assistantships (averaging $11,382 per year) were awarded; Federal Work-Study, institutionally sponsored loans, scholarships/grants, and unspecified assistantships also available. Financial award application deadline: 4/1; financial award applicants required to submit FAFSA. *Faculty research:* Early childhood education, reading, rural schools, multicultural education, use of technology in instruction. *Unit head:* Dr. Devon Brenner, Professor and Interim Head, 662-325-7119, Fax: 662-325-7857, E-mail: devon@ra.msstate.edu. *Application contact:*

Dr. Dana Franz, Graduate Coordinator, 662-325-3703, Fax: 662-325-7857, E-mail: tstevonson@colled.msstate.edu.
Website: http://www.cise.msstate.edu/.

Mississippi State University, College of Education, Department of Leadership and Foundations, Mississippi State, MS 39762. Offers community college education (MAT); community college leadership (PhD); education (Ed S), including school administration; elementary, middle and secondary education administration (PhD); school administration (MS); workforce education leadership (MS). MS in workforce educational leadership held jointly with Alcorn State University. *Faculty:* 9 full-time (3 women). *Students:* 50 full-time (26 women), 156 part-time (100 women); includes 104 minority (99 Black or African American, non-Hispanic/Latino; 1 American Indian or Alaska Native, non-Hispanic/Latino; 1 Asian, non-Hispanic/Latino; 1 Hispanic/Latino; 1 Native Hawaiian or other Pacific Islander, non-Hispanic/Latino; 1 Two or more races, non-Hispanic/Latino). Average age 39. 121 applicants, 32% accepted, 33 enrolled. In 2013, 47 master's, 15 doctorates, 7 other advanced degrees awarded. *Degree requirements:* For master's and Ed S, comprehensive exam, thesis; for doctorate, comprehensive exam, thesis/dissertation. *Entrance requirements:* For master's, GRE, minimum GPA of 2.75 in junior and senior courses; for doctorate, GRE, minimum GPA of 3.4 on previous graduate work; for Ed S, GRE, minimum GPA of 3.2, master's degree. Additional exam requirements/recommendations for international students: Required—TOEFL (minimum score 550 paper-based; 79 iBT); Recommended—IELTS (minimum score 6.5). *Application deadline:* For fall admission, 7/1 for domestic students, 5/1 for international students; for spring admission, 11/1 for domestic students, 9/1 for international students. Application fee: $60. *Financial support:* In 2013–14, 3 research assistantships with full tuition reimbursements (averaging $12,400 per year), 1 teaching assistantship with full tuition reimbursement (averaging $10,194 per year) were awarded; Federal Work-Study, institutionally sponsored loans, and unspecified assistantships also available. Financial award application deadline: 4/1; financial award applicants required to submit FAFSA. *Unit head:* Dr. David Morse, Interim Department Head and Professor, 662-325-0969, Fax: 662-325-0975, E-mail: dmorse@colled.msstate.edu.
Website: http://www.leadershipandfoundations.msstate.edu/.

Missouri State University, Graduate College, College of Arts and Letters, Department of English, Springfield, MO 65897. Offers English and writing (MA); secondary education (MS Ed), including English. Part-time and evening/weekend programs available. *Faculty:* 22 full-time (14 women), 4 part-time/adjunct (1 woman). *Students:* 55 full-time (39 women), 47 part-time (32 women); includes 6 minority (1 Asian, non-Hispanic/Latino; 3 Hispanic/Latino; 2 Two or more races, non-Hispanic/Latino), 7 international. Average age 28. 51 applicants, 92% accepted, 32 enrolled. In 2013, 32 master's awarded. *Degree requirements:* For master's, one foreign language, comprehensive exam, thesis or alternative. *Entrance requirements:* For master's, GRE (MA), minimum GPA of 3.0 (MA), 9-12 teacher certification (MS Ed). Additional exam requirements/recommendations for international students: Required—TOEFL (minimum score 550 paper-based; 79 iBT). *Application deadline:* For fall admission, 7/20 for domestic students, 5/1 for international students; for spring admission, 12/20 for domestic students, 9/1 for international students. Applications are processed on a rolling basis. Application fee: $35 ($50 for international students). Electronic applications accepted. *Expenses:* Tuition, state resident: full-time $4500; part-time $250 per credit hour. Tuition, nonresident: full-time $9018; part-time $501 per credit hour. *Required fees:* $361 per semester. Tuition and fees vary according to course level, course load and program. *Financial support:* In 2013–14, 3 research assistantships with full tuition reimbursements (averaging $8,324 per year), 33 teaching assistantships with full tuition reimbursements (averaging $8,324 per year) were awarded; Federal Work-Study, institutionally sponsored loans, scholarships/grants, and unspecified assistantships also available. Support available to part-time students. Financial award application deadline: 3/31; financial award applicants required to submit FAFSA. *Faculty research:* Renaissance literature, William Blake, autobiography, Georgian theatre, TESOL. *Unit head:* Dr. W. D. Blackmon, Head, 417-836-5107, Fax: 417-836-6940, E-mail: english@missouristate.edu. *Application contact:* Misty Stewart, Coordinator of Graduate Recruitment, 417-836-5331, Fax: 417-836-6888, E-mail: mistystewart@missouristate.edu.
Website: http://english.missouristate.edu/.

Missouri State University, Graduate College, College of Arts and Letters, Department of Music, Springfield, MO 65897. Offers music (MM), including conducting, music education, music pedagogy, music theory and composition, performance; secondary education (MS Ed), including music. *Accreditation:* NASM. Part-time programs available. *Faculty:* 28 full-time (10 women), 1 (woman) part-time/adjunct. *Students:* 21 full-time (10 women), 12 part-time (8 women); includes 3 minority (1 Black or African American, non-Hispanic/Latino; 2 Hispanic/Latino), 6 international. Average age 27. 30 applicants, 83% accepted, 13 enrolled. In 2013, 17 master's awarded. *Degree requirements:* For master's, comprehensive exam, thesis or alternative. *Entrance requirements:* For master's, GRE, interview/audition (MM), 9-12 teaching certification (MS Ed). Additional exam requirements/recommendations for international students: Required—TOEFL (minimum score 550 paper-based; 79 iBT). *Application deadline:* For fall admission, 7/20 for domestic students, 5/1 for international students; for spring admission, 12/20 for domestic students, 9/1 for international students. Applications are processed on a rolling basis. Application fee: $35 ($50 for international students). Electronic applications accepted. *Expenses:* Tuition, state resident: full-time $4500; part-time $250 per credit hour. Tuition, nonresident: full-time $9018; part-time $501 per credit hour. *Required fees:* $361 per semester. Tuition and fees vary according to course level, course load and program. *Financial support:* In 2013–14, 5 teaching assistantships with full tuition reimbursements (averaging $8,324 per year) were awarded; Federal Work-Study, institutionally sponsored loans, scholarships/grants, tuition waivers (partial), and unspecified assistantships also available. Financial award application deadline: 3/31; financial award applicants required to submit FAFSA. *Faculty research:* Bulgarian violin literature, Ozarks fiddle music, carillon, nineteenth-century piano. *Unit head:* Dr. Julie Combs, Head, 417-836-5648, Fax: 417-836-7665, E-mail: music@missouristate.edu. *Application contact:* Misty Stewart, Coordinator of Graduate Recruitment, 417-836-6079, Fax: 417-836-6200, E-mail: mistystewart@missouristate.edu.
Website: http://www.missouristate.edu/music/.

Missouri State University, Graduate College, College of Arts and Letters, Department of Theatre and Dance, Springfield, MO 65897. Offers secondary education (MS Ed), including speech and theatre; theatre (MA). *Accreditation:* NAST. Part-time programs available. *Faculty:* 9 full-time (5 women). *Students:* 1 full-time (0 women), 9 part-time (6 women). Average age 28. 9 applicants, 67% accepted, 6 enrolled. In 2013, 5 master's awarded. *Degree requirements:* For master's, comprehensive exam, thesis or alternative. *Entrance requirements:* For master's, minimum GPA of 3.0 (MA), 9-12 teaching certification (MS Ed). Additional exam requirements/recommendations for international students: Required—TOEFL (minimum score 550 paper-based; 79 iBT). *Application deadline:* For fall admission, 7/20 for domestic students, 5/1 for international students; for spring admission, 12/20 for domestic students, 9/1 for international students. Applications are processed on a rolling basis. Application fee: $35 ($50 for international students). Electronic applications accepted. *Expenses:* Tuition, state resident: full-time $4500; part-time $250 per credit hour. Tuition, nonresident: full-time $9018; part-time $501 per credit hour. *Required fees:* $361 per semester. Tuition and fees vary according to course level, course load and program. *Financial support:* In 2013–14, 2 teaching assistantships with full tuition reimbursements (averaging $8,324 per year) were awarded; Federal Work-Study, institutionally sponsored loans, scholarships/grants, and unspecified assistantships also available. Financial award application deadline: 3/31; financial award applicants required to submit FAFSA. *Unit head:* Dr. Christopher Herr, Interim Department Head, 417-836-4400, Fax: 417-836-4234, E-mail: theatreanddance@missouristate.edu. *Application contact:* Misty Stewart, Coordinator of Admissions and Recruitment, 417-836-6079, Fax: 417-836-6200, E-mail: mistystewart@missouristate.edu.
Website: http://theatreanddance.missouristate.edu/.

Missouri State University, Graduate College, College of Business Administration, Department of Computer Information Systems, Springfield, MO 65897. Offers computer information systems (MS); secondary education (MS Ed), including business. Part-time and evening/weekend programs available. Postbaccalaureate distance learning degree programs offered (no on-campus study). *Faculty:* 13 full-time (2 women), 6 part-time/adjunct (0 women). *Students:* 22 full-time (3 women); includes 4 minority (2 Black or African American, non-Hispanic/Latino; 1 Hispanic/Latino; 1 Two or more races, non-Hispanic/Latino), 21 international. Average age 38. 20 applicants, 70% accepted, 12 enrolled. In 2013, 15 master's awarded. *Degree requirements:* For master's, thesis optional. *Entrance requirements:* For master's, GMAT, 3 years of work experience in computer information systems, minimum GPA of 2.75 (MS), 9-12 teaching certification (MS Ed). Additional exam requirements/recommendations for international students: Required—TOEFL (minimum score 550 paper-based; 79 iBT). *Application deadline:* For fall admission, 7/20 priority date for domestic students, 5/1 for international students; for spring admission, 12/20 priority date for domestic students, 9/1 for international students. Applications are processed on a rolling basis. Application fee: $35 ($50 for international students). Electronic applications accepted. *Expenses:* Contact institution. *Financial support:* Federal Work-Study, institutionally sponsored loans, scholarships/grants, and unspecified assistantships available. Support available to part-time students. Financial award application deadline: 3/31; financial award applicants required to submit FAFSA. *Faculty research:* Decision support systems, algorithms in Visual Basic, end-user satisfaction, information security. *Unit head:* Dr. Jerry Chin, Head, 417-836-4131, Fax: 417-836-6907, E-mail: jerrychin@missouristate.edu. *Application contact:* Misty Stewart, Coordinator of Graduate Admissions and Recruitment, 417-836-6079, Fax: 417-836-6200, E-mail: mistystewart@missouristate.edu.
Website: http://cis.missouristate.edu/.

Missouri State University, Graduate College, College of Education, Department of Counseling, Leadership, and Special Education, Program in Counseling, Springfield, MO 65897. Offers counseling and assessment (Ed S); elementary school counseling (MS); mental health counseling (MS); secondary school counseling (MS). Part-time and evening/weekend programs available. *Students:* 51 full-time (44 women), 66 part-time (54 women); includes 11 minority (2 Black or African American, non-Hispanic/Latino; 1 American Indian or Alaska Native, non-Hispanic/Latino; 1 Asian, non-Hispanic/Latino; 4 Hispanic/Latino; 3 Two or more races, non-Hispanic/Latino), 4 international. Average age 33. 59 applicants, 51% accepted, 16 enrolled. In 2013, 39 master's awarded. *Degree requirements:* For master's, comprehensive exam, thesis or alternative. *Entrance requirements:* For master's, GRE or MAT, minimum GPA of 2.75. Additional exam requirements/recommendations for international students: Required—TOEFL (minimum score 550 paper-based; 79 iBT). *Application deadline:* For fall admission, 2/1 priority date for domestic students, 1/1 priority date for international students; for spring admission, 10/1 priority date for domestic students, 9/1 priority date for international students. Application fee: $35 ($50 for international students). Electronic applications accepted. *Expenses:* Tuition, state resident: full-time $4500; part-time $250 per credit hour. Tuition, nonresident: full-time $9018; part-time $501 per credit hour. *Required fees:* $361 per semester. Tuition and fees vary according to course level, course load and program. *Financial support:* Federal Work-Study, institutionally sponsored loans, scholarships/grants, and unspecified assistantships available. Financial award application deadline: 3/31; financial award applicants required to submit FAFSA. *Unit head:* Dr. Jeffrey Cornelius-White, Program Coordinator, 417-836-6517, Fax: 417-836-4918, E-mail: jcornelius-white@missouristate.edu. *Application contact:* Misty Stewart, Coordinator of Admissions and Recruitment, 417-836-6079, Fax: 417-836-6200, E-mail: mistystewart@missouristate.edu.
Website: http://education.missouristate.edu/clse/.

Missouri State University, Graduate College, College of Education, Department of Counseling, Leadership, and Special Education, Program in Educational Administration, Springfield, MO 65897. Offers educational administration (MS Ed, Ed S); elementary education (MS Ed); elementary principal (Ed S); secondary education (MS Ed); secondary principal (Ed S); superintendent (Ed S). Part-time and evening/weekend programs available. *Students:* 30 full-time (22 women), 88 part-time (56 women); includes 7 minority (1 Black or African American, non-Hispanic/Latino; 1 American Indian or Alaska Native, non-Hispanic/Latino; 3 Hispanic/Latino; 2 Two or more races, non-Hispanic/Latino), 2 international. Average age 35. 49 applicants, 100% accepted, 44 enrolled. In 2013, 57 master's, 16 Ed Ss awarded. *Degree requirements:* For master's and Ed S, comprehensive exam, thesis or alternative. *Entrance requirements:* For master's, minimum GPA of 2.75; for Ed S, GRE General Test, MAT, minimum GPA of 2.75. Additional exam requirements/recommendations for international students: Required—TOEFL (minimum score 550 paper-based; 79 iBT). *Application deadline:* For fall admission, 7/20 priority date for domestic students, 5/1 for international students; for spring admission, 12/20 priority date for domestic students, 9/1 for international students. Applications are processed on a rolling basis. Application fee: $35 ($50 for international students). Electronic applications accepted. *Expenses:* Tuition, state resident: full-time $4500; part-time $250 per credit hour. Tuition, nonresident: full-time $9018; part-time $501 per credit hour. *Required fees:* $361 per semester. Tuition and fees vary according to course level, course load and program. *Financial support:* Career-related internships or fieldwork, Federal Work-Study, institutionally sponsored loans, scholarships/grants, and unspecified assistantships available. Financial award application deadline: 3/31; financial award applicants required to submit FAFSA. *Unit head:* Dr. Kim Finch, Program Coordinator, 417-836-5192, Fax: 417-836-4918, E-mail: kimfinch@missouristate.edu. *Application contact:* Misty Stewart, Coordinator of Admissions and Recruitment, 417-836-6079, Fax: 417-836-6200, E-mail: mistystewart@missouristate.edu.
Website: http://education.missouristate.edu/edadmin/.

Missouri State University, Graduate College, College of Education, Department of Reading, Foundations, and Technology, Master of Arts in Teaching Program, Springfield, MO 65897. Offers MAT. Part-time programs available. *Students:* 27 full-time (20 women), 64 part-time (43 women); includes 9 minority (2 American Indian or Alaska Native, non-Hispanic/Latino; 2 Asian, non-Hispanic/Latino; 4 Hispanic/Latino; 1 Two or more races, non-Hispanic/Latino), 1 international. Average age 35. 17 applicants, 94% accepted, 14 enrolled. In 2013, 25 master's awarded. *Degree requirements:* For master's, comprehensive exam, project. *Entrance requirements:* For master's, PRAXIS II. Additional exam requirements/recommendations for international students: Required—TOEFL (minimum score 550 paper-based; 79 iBT). *Application deadline:* For fall admission, 2/15 priority date for domestic and international students. Application fee:

$35 ($50 for international students). Electronic applications accepted. *Expenses:* Tuition, state resident: full-time $4500; part-time $250 per credit hour. Tuition, nonresident: full-time $9018; part-time $501 per credit hour. *Required fees:* $361 per semester. Tuition and fees vary according to course level, course load and program. *Financial support:* Federal Work-Study, institutionally sponsored loans, scholarships/grants, tuition waivers (full), and unspecified assistantships available. Financial award application deadline: 3/31; financial award applicants required to submit FAFSA. *Unit head:* Dr. Fred Groves, Program Coordinator, 417-836-3170, E-mail: fredgroves@missouristate.edu. *Application contact:* Misty Stewart, Coordinator of Admissions and Recruitment, 417-836-6079, Fax: 417-836-6200, E-mail: mistystewart@missouristate.edu.

Missouri State University, Graduate College, College of Health and Human Services, Department of Kinesiology, Springfield, MO 65897. Offers health promotion and wellness management (MS); secondary education (MS Ed), including physical education. Part-time programs available. *Faculty:* 14 full-time (6 women). *Students:* 14 full-time (6 women), 17 part-time (10 women); includes 1 minority (Hispanic/Latino), 7 international. Average age 28. 15 applicants, 93% accepted, 7 enrolled. In 2013, 7 master's awarded. *Degree requirements:* For master's, comprehensive exam, thesis or alternative. *Entrance requirements:* For master's, GRE (MS), minimum GPA of 2.8 (MS); 9-12 teaching certification (MS Ed). Additional exam requirements/recommendations for international students: Required—TOEFL (minimum score 550 paper-based; 79 iBT). *Application deadline:* For fall admission, 7/20 priority date for domestic students, 5/1 for international students; for spring admission, 12/20 priority date for domestic students, 9/1 for international students. Applications are processed on a rolling basis. Application fee: $35 ($50 for international students). Electronic applications accepted. *Expenses:* Tuition, state resident: full-time $4500; part-time $250 per credit hour. Tuition, nonresident: full-time $9018; part-time $501 per credit hour. *Required fees:* $361 per semester. Tuition and fees vary according to course level, course load and program. *Financial support:* In 2013–14, 7 teaching assistantships with full tuition reimbursements (averaging $9,097 per year) were awarded; Federal Work-Study, institutionally sponsored loans, scholarships/grants, and unspecified assistantships also available. Financial award application deadline: 3/31; financial award applicants required to submit FAFSA. *Unit head:* Dr. Sarah McCallister, Acting Head, 417-836-6582, Fax: 417-836-5371, E-mail: sarahmccallister@missouristate.edu. *Application contact:* Misty Stewart, Coordinator of Graduate Admissions and Recruitment, 417-836-6079, Fax: 417-836-6200, E-mail: mistystewart@missouristate.edu.
Website: http://www.missouristate.edu/kinesiology/.

Missouri State University, Graduate College, College of Humanities and Public Affairs, Department of History, Springfield, MO 65897. Offers history (MA); secondary education (MS Ed), including history, social science. Part-time programs available. *Faculty:* 20 full-time (7 women). *Students:* 12 full-time (4 women), 38 part-time (17 women); includes 3 minority (1 American Indian or Alaska Native, non-Hispanic/Latino; 1 Hispanic/Latino; 1 Two or more races, non-Hispanic/Latino). Average age 31. 17 applicants, 94% accepted, 8 enrolled. In 2013, 9 master's awarded. *Degree requirements:* For master's, comprehensive exam, thesis or alternative. *Entrance requirements:* For master's, minimum GPA of 2.75, 24 hours of undergraduate course work in history (MA), 9-12 teaching certification (MS Ed). Additional exam requirements/recommendations for international students: Required—TOEFL (minimum score 550 paper-based; 79 iBT). *Application deadline:* For fall admission, 7/20 priority date for domestic students, 5/1 for international students; for spring admission, 12/20 priority date for domestic students, 9/1 for international students. Applications are processed on a rolling basis. Application fee: $35 ($50 for international students). Electronic applications accepted. *Expenses:* Tuition, state resident: full-time $4500; part-time $250 per credit hour. Tuition, nonresident: full-time $9018; part-time $501 per credit hour. *Required fees:* $361 per semester. Tuition and fees vary according to course level, course load and program. *Financial support:* Federal Work-Study, scholarships/grants, and unspecified assistantships available. Support available to part-time students. Financial award application deadline: 3/31; financial award applicants required to submit FAFSA. *Faculty research:* U.S. history, Native American history, Latin American history, women's history, ancient Near East. *Unit head:* Dr. Kathleen Kennedy, Head, 417-836-5511, Fax: 417-836-5523, E-mail: history@missouristate.edu. *Application contact:* Misty Stewart, Coordinator of Graduate Recruitment, 417-836-6079, Fax: 417-836-6200, E-mail: mistystewart@missouristate.edu.
Website: http://history.missouristate.edu/.

Missouri State University, Graduate College, College of Natural and Applied Sciences, Department of Biology, Springfield, MO 65897. Offers biology (MS); natural and applied science (MNAS), including biology (MNAS, MS Ed); secondary education (MS Ed), including biology (MNAS, MS Ed). *Faculty:* 16 full-time (4 women), 8 part-time/adjunct (2 women). *Students:* 17 full-time (10 women), 28 part-time (15 women), 3 international. Average age 28. 27 applicants, 48% accepted, 12 enrolled. In 2013, 18 master's awarded. *Degree requirements:* For master's, comprehensive exam, thesis or alternative. *Entrance requirements:* For master's, GRE (MS, MNAS), 24 hours of course work in biology (MS); minimum GPA of 3.0 (MS, MNAS), 9-12 teacher certification (MS Ed). Additional exam requirements/recommendations for international students: Required—TOEFL (minimum score 550 paper-based; 79 iBT). *Application deadline:* For fall admission, 7/20 priority date for domestic students, 5/1 for international students; for spring admission, 12/20 priority date for domestic students, 9/1 for international students. Applications are processed on a rolling basis. Application fee: $35 ($50 for international students). Electronic applications accepted. *Expenses:* Tuition, state resident: full-time $4500; part-time $250 per credit hour. Tuition, nonresident: full-time $9018; part-time $501 per credit hour. *Required fees:* $361 per semester. Tuition and fees vary according to course level, course load and program. *Financial support:* In 2013–14, 18 research assistantships with full tuition reimbursements (averaging $10,128 per year), 18 teaching assistantships with full tuition reimbursements (averaging $9,226 per year) were awarded; Federal Work-Study, institutionally sponsored loans, scholarships/grants, and unspecified assistantships also available. Financial award application deadline: 3/31; financial award applicants required to submit FAFSA. *Faculty research:* Hibernation physiology of bats, behavioral ecology of salamanders, mussel conservation, plant evolution and systematics, cellular/molecular mechanisms involved in migraine pathology. *Unit head:* Dr. S. Alicia Mathis, Head, 417-836-5126, Fax: 417-836-6934, E-mail: biology@missouristate.edu. *Application contact:* Misty Stewart, Coordinator of Graduate Recruitment, 417-836-6079, Fax: 417-836-6200, E-mail: mistystewart@missouristate.edu.
Website: http://biology.missouristate.edu/.

Missouri State University, Graduate College, College of Natural and Applied Sciences, Department of Chemistry, Springfield, MO 65897. Offers chemistry (MS); natural and applied science (MNAS), including chemistry (MNAS, MS Ed); secondary education (MS Ed), including chemistry (MNAS, MS Ed). Part-time programs available. *Faculty:* 15 full-time (3 women). *Students:* 10 full-time (5 women), 13 part-time (3 women), 7 international. Average age 31. 9 applicants, 56% accepted, 3 enrolled. In 2013, 5 master's awarded. *Degree requirements:* For master's, comprehensive exam, thesis. *Entrance requirements:* For master's, GRE General Test (MS, MNAS), minimum undergraduate GPA of 3.0 (MS and MNAS), 9-12 teacher certification (MS Ed). Additional exam requirements/recommendations for international students: Required—TOEFL (minimum score 550 paper-based; 79 iBT). *Application deadline:* For fall admission, 7/20 priority date for domestic students, 5/1 for international students; for spring admission, 12/20 priority date for domestic students, 9/1 for international students. Applications are processed on a rolling basis. Application fee: $35 ($50 for international students). Electronic applications accepted. *Expenses:* Tuition, state resident: full-time $4500; part-time $250 per credit hour. Tuition, nonresident: full-time $9018; part-time $501 per credit hour. *Required fees:* $361 per semester. Tuition and fees vary according to course level, course load and program. *Financial support:* In 2013–14, 4 research assistantships with full tuition reimbursements (averaging $10,128 per year), 20 teaching assistantships with full tuition reimbursements (averaging $8,324 per year) were awarded; Federal Work-Study, institutionally sponsored loans, scholarships/grants, and unspecified assistantships also available. Financial award application deadline: 3/31; financial award applicants required to submit FAFSA. *Faculty research:* Polyethylene glycol derivatives, electrochemiluminescence of environmental systems, enzymology, environmental organic pollutants, DNA repair via NMR. *Unit head:* Dr. Alan Schick, Department Head, 417-836-5506, Fax: 417-836-5507, E-mail: chemistry@missouristate.edu. *Application contact:* Misty Stewart, Coordinator of Graduate Recruitment, 417-836-6079, Fax: 417-836-6200, E-mail: mistystewart@missouristate.edu.
Website: http://chemistry.missouristate.edu/.

Missouri State University, Graduate College, College of Natural and Applied Sciences, Department of Geography, Geology, and Planning, Springfield, MO 65897. Offers geospatial sciences (MS, MS Ed), including earth science (MS Ed), geology (MS), human geography and planning (MS), physical geography (MS Ed); natural and applied science (MNAS), including geography, geology and planning; secondary education (MS Ed), including geography. *Accreditation:* ACSP. Part-time and evening/weekend programs available. *Faculty:* 18 full-time (4 women). *Students:* 15 full-time (11 women), 15 part-time (10 women), 2 international. Average age 31. 18 applicants, 100% accepted, 10 enrolled. In 2013, 8 master's awarded. *Degree requirements:* For master's, comprehensive exam, thesis (for some programs). *Entrance requirements:* For master's, GRE General Test (MS, MNAS), minimum undergraduate GPA of 3.0 (MS, MNAS), 9-12 teacher certification (MS Ed). Additional exam requirements/recommendations for international students: Required—TOEFL (minimum score 550 paper-based; 79 iBT). *Application deadline:* For fall admission, 7/20 priority date for domestic students, 5/1 for international students; for spring admission, 12/20 priority date for domestic students, 9/1 for international students. Applications are processed on a rolling basis. Application fee: $35 ($50 for international students). Electronic applications accepted. *Expenses:* Tuition, state resident: full-time $4500; part-time $250 per credit hour. Tuition, nonresident: full-time $9018; part-time $501 per credit hour. *Required fees:* $361 per semester. Tuition and fees vary according to course level, course load and program. *Financial support:* In 2013–14, 9 research assistantships with full tuition reimbursements (averaging $10,128 per year), 16 teaching assistantships with full tuition reimbursements (averaging $8,324 per year) were awarded; career-related internships or fieldwork, Federal Work-Study, institutionally sponsored loans, scholarships/grants, and unspecified assistantships also available. Financial award application deadline: 3/31; financial award applicants required to submit FAFSA. *Faculty research:* Stratigraphy and ancient meteorite impacts, environmental geochemistry of karst, hyperspectral image processing, water quality, small town planning. *Unit head:* Dr. Thomas Plymate, Head, 417-836-5800, Fax: 417-836-6934, E-mail: tomplymate@missouristate.edu. *Application contact:* Misty Stewart, Coordinator of Graduate Recruitment, 417-836-6079, Fax: 417-836-6200, E-mail: mistystewart@missouristate.edu.
Website: http://geosciences.missouristate.edu/.

Missouri State University, Graduate College, College of Natural and Applied Sciences, Department of Mathematics, Springfield, MO 65897. Offers mathematics (MS); natural and applied science (MNAS), including mathematics (MNAS, MS Ed); secondary education (MS Ed), including mathematics (MNAS, MS Ed). Part-time programs available. *Faculty:* 22 full-time (4 women). *Students:* 19 full-time (10 women), 13 part-time (7 women), 6 international. Average age 27. 18 applicants, 100% accepted, 9 enrolled. In 2013, 9 master's awarded. *Degree requirements:* For master's, comprehensive exam, thesis or alternative. *Entrance requirements:* For master's, GRE (MS, MNAS), minimum undergraduate GPA of 3.0 (MS, MNAS), 9-12 teacher certification (MS Ed). Additional exam requirements/recommendations for international students: Required—TOEFL (minimum score 550 paper-based; 79 iBT). *Application deadline:* For fall admission, 7/20 priority date for domestic students, 5/1 for international students; for spring admission, 12/20 priority date for domestic students, 9/1 for international students. Applications are processed on a rolling basis. Application fee: $35 ($50 for international students). Electronic applications accepted. *Expenses:* Tuition, state resident: full-time $4500; part-time $250 per credit hour. Tuition, nonresident: full-time $9018; part-time $501 per credit hour. *Required fees:* $361 per semester. Tuition and fees vary according to course level, course load and program. *Financial support:* In 2013–14, 1 research assistantship with full tuition reimbursement (averaging $10,128 per year), 13 teaching assistantships with full tuition reimbursements (averaging $9,226 per year) were awarded; Federal Work-Study, institutionally sponsored loans, scholarships/grants, and unspecified assistantships also available. Financial award application deadline: 3/31; financial award applicants required to submit FAFSA. *Faculty research:* Harmonic analysis, commutative algebra, number theory, K-theory, probability. *Unit head:* Dr. William Bray, Department Head, 417-836-5112, Fax: 417-836-6966, E-mail: mathematics@missouristate.edu. *Application contact:* Misty Stewart, Coordinator of Graduate Recruitment, 417-836-6079, Fax: 417-836-6200, E-mail: mistystewart@missouristate.edu.
Website: http://math.missouristate.edu/.

Missouri State University, Graduate College, College of Natural and Applied Sciences, Department of Physics, Astronomy, and Materials Science, Springfield, MO 65897. Offers materials science (MS); physics, astronomy, and materials science (MNAS); secondary education (MS Ed), including physics. Part-time programs available. *Faculty:* 11 full-time (0 women). *Students:* 13 full-time (1 woman), 6 part-time (0 women); includes 1 minority (Hispanic/Latino), 14 international. Average age 29. 15 applicants, 73% accepted, 7 enrolled. In 2013, 9 master's awarded. *Degree requirements:* For master's, comprehensive exam, thesis. *Entrance requirements:* For master's, GRE (MS, MNAS), minimum undergraduate GPA of 3.0 (MS and MNAS), 9-12 teaching certification (MS Ed). Additional exam requirements/recommendations for international students: Required—TOEFL (minimum score 550 paper-based; 79 iBT). *Application deadline:* For fall admission, 7/20 priority date for domestic students, 5/1 for international students; for spring admission, 12/20 priority date for domestic students, 9/1 for international students. Applications are processed on a rolling basis. Application fee: $35 ($50 for international students). Electronic applications accepted. *Expenses:* Tuition, state resident: full-time $4500; part-time $250 per credit hour. Tuition, nonresident: full-time $9018; part-time $501 per credit hour. *Required fees:* $361 per semester. Tuition and fees vary according to course level, course load and program. *Financial support:* In 2013–14, 1 research assistantship with full tuition reimbursement (averaging $10,128 per year), 10 teaching assistantships with full tuition reimbursements (averaging $10,128 per year) were awarded; Federal Work-Study, institutionally sponsored loans, scholarships/grants, and unspecified assistantships also

available. Financial award application deadline: 3/31; financial award applicants required to submit FAFSA. *Faculty research:* Nanocomposites, ferroelectricity, infrared focal plane array sensors, biosensors, pulsating stars. *Unit head:* Dr. David Cornelison, Department Head, 417-836-4467, Fax: 417-836-6226, E-mail: physics@missouristate.edu. *Application contact:* Misty Stewart, Coordinator of Graduate Recruitment, 417-836-6079, Fax: 417-836-6200, E-mail: mistystewart@missouristate.edu.
Website: http://physics.missouristate.edu/.

Missouri State University, Graduate College, William H. Darr School of Agriculture, Springfield, MO 65897. Offers natural and applied science (MNAS), including agriculture (MNAS, MS Ed); plant science (MS); secondary education (MS Ed), including agriculture (MNAS, MS Ed). Part-time programs available. *Faculty:* 16 full-time (4 women), 1 part-time/adjunct (0 women). *Students:* 16 full-time (11 women), 21 part-time (8 women); includes 2 minority (1 Black or African American, non-Hispanic/Latino; 1 Asian, non-Hispanic/Latino), 2 international. Average age 29. 14 applicants, 86% accepted, 9 enrolled. In 2013, 19 master's awarded. *Degree requirements:* For master's, comprehensive exam, thesis or alternative. *Entrance requirements:* For master's, GRE (MS in plant science, MNAS), 9-12 teacher certification (MS Ed), minimum GPA of 3.0 (MS plant science, MNAS). Additional exam requirements/recommendations for international students: Required—TOEFL (minimum score 550 paper-based; 79 iBT). *Application deadline:* For fall admission, 7/20 priority date for domestic students, 5/1 for international students; for spring admission, 12/20 priority date for domestic students, 9/1 for international students. Applications are processed on a rolling basis. Application fee: $35 ($50 for international students). Electronic applications accepted. *Expenses:* Tuition, state resident: full-time $4500; part-time $250 per credit hour. Tuition, nonresident: full-time $9018; part-time $501 per credit hour. *Required fees:* $361 per semester. Tuition and fees vary according to course level, course load and program. *Financial support:* In 2013–14, 3 research assistantships with full tuition reimbursements (averaging $9,526 per year), 2 teaching assistantships with full tuition reimbursements (averaging $10,128 per year) were awarded; Federal Work-Study, institutionally sponsored loans, scholarships/grants, and unspecified assistantships also available. Financial award application deadline: 3/31; financial award applicants required to submit FAFSA. *Faculty research:* Grapevine biotechnology, agricultural marketing, Asian elephant reproduction, poultry science, integrated pest management. *Unit head:* Dr. W. Anson Elliott, Head, 417-836-5638, E-mail: ansonelliot@missouristate.edu. *Application contact:* Misty Stewart, Coordinator of Graduate Recruitment, 417-836-6079, Fax: 417-836-6200, E-mail: mistystewart@missouristate.edu.
Website: http://ag.missouristate.edu/.

Monmouth University, The Graduate School, School of Education, West Long Branch, NJ 07764-1898. Offers applied behavioral analysis (Certificate); autism (Certificate); initial certification (MAT), including elementary level, K-12, secondary level; principal (MS Ed); principal/school administrator (MS Ed); reading specialist (MS Ed); school counseling (MS Ed); special education (MS Ed), including autism, learning disabilities teacher consultant, teacher of students with disabilities, teaching in inclusive settings; speech-language pathology (MS Ed); student affairs and college counseling (MS Ed); teaching English to speakers of other languages (TESOL) (Certificate). *Accreditation:* NCATE. Part-time and evening/weekend programs available. *Faculty:* 15 full-time (11 women), 19 part-time/adjunct (17 women). *Students:* 125 full-time (97 women), 168 part-time (146 women); includes 38 minority (12 Black or African American, non-Hispanic/Latino; 5 Asian, non-Hispanic/Latino; 16 Hispanic/Latino; 5 Two or more races, non-Hispanic/Latino). Average age 28. 176 applicants, 90% accepted, 112 enrolled. In 2013, 147 master's awarded. *Entrance requirements:* For master's, GRE within last 5 years (for MS Ed in speech-language pathology), minimum GPA of 3.0 in major; 2 letters of recommendation (for some programs), resume, personal statement or essay (depending on degree program). Additional exam requirements/recommendations for international students: Required—TOEFL (minimum score 550 paper-based; 79 iBT), IELTS (minimum score 6), Michigan English Language Assessment Battery (minimum score 77). *Application deadline:* For fall admission, 7/15 priority date for domestic students, 7/1 for international students; for spring admission, 11/15 priority date for domestic students, 11/1 for international students. Applications are processed on a rolling basis. Application fee: $50. Electronic applications accepted. *Expenses: Tuition:* Part-time $1004 per credit hour. *Required fees:* $157 per semester. *Financial support:* In 2013–14, 191 students received support, including 159 fellowships (averaging $2,786 per year), 30 research assistantships (averaging $8,755 per year); career-related internships or fieldwork, scholarships/grants, and unspecified assistantships also available. Support available to part-time students. Financial award applicants required to submit FAFSA. *Faculty research:* Multicultural literacy, science and mathematics teaching strategies, teacher as reflective practitioner, children with disabilities. *Unit head:* Dr. Jason Barr, Program Director, 732-263-5238, Fax: 732-263-5277, E-mail: jbarr@monmouth.edu. *Application contact:* Lauren Vento-Cifelli, Associate Vice President of Undergraduate and Graduate Admission, 732-571-3452, Fax: 732-263-5123, E-mail: gradadm@monmouth.edu.
Website: http://www.monmouth.edu/academics/schools/education/default.asp.

Morehead State University, Graduate Programs, College of Education, Department of Curriculum and Instruction, Morehead, KY 40351. Offers curriculum and instruction (Ed S); elementary education (MA Ed), including elementary education, international education, middle school education, reading; secondary education (MA Ed); special education (MA Ed); teaching (MAT). Part-time and evening/weekend programs available. *Degree requirements:* For master's, comprehensive exam, thesis optional; for Ed S, thesis, oral exam. *Entrance requirements:* For master's, GRE General Test, minimum GPA of 2.75, teaching certificate; for Ed S, GRE General Test, interview, master's degree, minimum GPA of 3.5, work experience. Additional exam requirements/recommendations for international students: Required—TOEFL (minimum score 500 paper-based). Electronic applications accepted. *Faculty research:* Communicative competence of learning-disabled students, teaching social studies in elementary schools, ungraded primary school organization, study skills.

Morehead State University, Graduate Programs, College of Education, Department of Middle Grades and Secondary Education, Morehead, KY 40351. Offers business and marketing education (MAT); English/language arts 5-9 (MAT); French (MAT); health P-12 (MAT); mathematics 5-9 (MAT); physical education P-12 (MAT); science 5-9 (MAT); secondary biology (MAT); secondary chemistry (MAT); secondary earth science (MAT); secondary English (MAT); secondary math (MAT); secondary physics (MAT); secondary social studies (MAT); social studies 5-9 (MAT); Spanish (MAT). Part-time and evening/weekend programs available. *Degree requirements:* For master's, portfolio. *Entrance requirements:* For master's, GRE or PRAXIS II content exam, minimum overall undergraduate GPA of 2.5. Additional exam requirements/recommendations for international students: Required—TOEFL (minimum score 500 paper-based). Electronic applications accepted.

Morgan State University, School of Graduate Studies, School of Education and Urban Studies, MAT Program, Baltimore, MD 21251. Offers elementary education (MAT); high school education (MAT); middle school education (MAT). Part-time programs available. *Degree requirements:* For master's, comprehensive exam. *Entrance requirements:* For master's, GRE General Test or MAT. *Faculty research:* Multicultural education, cooperative learning, psychology of cognition.

Mount St. Joseph University, Graduate Education Program, Cincinnati, OH 45233-1670. Offers adolescent to young adult education (MA); dyslexia (Certificate); inclusive early childhood education (MA); instructional leadership (MA); middle childhood education (MA); multicultural special education (MA); Pre-K special needs (Certificate); principal licensure (MA); reading (Certificate); reading science (MA). *Accreditation:* Teacher Education Accreditation Council. Part-time and evening/weekend programs available. *Faculty:* 10 full-time (7 women), 7 part-time/adjunct (6 women). *Students:* 28 full-time (25 women), 95 part-time (76 women); includes 27 minority (19 Black or African American, non-Hispanic/Latino; 6 Hispanic/Latino; 2 Two or more races, non-Hispanic/Latino). Average age 36. 73 applicants, 44% accepted, 30 enrolled. In 2013, 69 master's awarded. *Degree requirements:* For master's, research project, student teaching, clinical and field-based experiences. *Entrance requirements:* For master's, GRE, PRAXIS II in teaching content area (math or science), 2 letters of recommendation, interview, resume. Additional exam requirements/recommendations for international students: Required—TOEFL (minimum score 560 paper-based; 83 iBT). *Application deadline:* Applications are processed on a rolling basis. Application fee: $50. Electronic applications accepted. *Expenses: Tuition:* Full-time $18,400; part-time $575 per credit hour. *Required fees:* $450; $450 per year. Part-time tuition and fees vary according to course load, degree level and program. *Financial support:* Scholarships/grants available. Financial award applicants required to submit FAFSA. *Faculty research:* Foreign and second language learning problems/reading disabilities/hyperlexia, multicultural/bilingual special education, alternative educator licensure, science education, pedagogical content knowledge. *Unit head:* Dr. Mary West, Chair, 513-244-3263, Fax: 513-244-4867, E-mail: mary_west@mail.msj.edu. *Application contact:* Mary Brigham, Assistant Director of Graduate Recruitment, 513-244-4233, Fax: 513-244-4629, E-mail: mary_brigham@mail.msj.edu.
Website: http://www.msj.edu/academics/graduate-programs/master-of-arts-initial-teacher-licensure-programs/.

Mount Saint Mary College, Division of Education, Newburgh, NY 12550-3494. Offers adolescence and special education (MS Ed); adolescence education (MS Ed); childhood and special education (MS Ed); childhood education (MS Ed); literacy (5-12) (Advanced Certificate); literacy (birth-6) (Advanced Certificate); literacy and special education (MS Ed); literacy/childhood (MS Ed); middle school (5-6) (MS Ed); middle school (7-9) (MS Ed); special education (1-6) (MS Ed); special education (7-12) (MS Ed). *Accreditation:* NCATE. Part-time and evening/weekend programs available. *Faculty:* 11 full-time (9 women), 9 part-time/adjunct (4 women). *Students:* 29 full-time (19 women), 142 part-time (117 women); includes 22 minority (5 Black or African American, non-Hispanic/Latino; 16 Hispanic/Latino; 1 Two or more races, non-Hispanic/Latino). Average age 29. 51 applicants, 65% accepted, 27 enrolled. In 2013, 72 master's awarded. *Application deadline:* Applications are processed on a rolling basis. Application fee: $45. Application fee is waived when completed online. *Expenses: Tuition:* Full-time $13,356; part-time $742 per credit. *Required fees:* $70 per semester. *Financial support:* In 2013–14, 69 students received support. Unspecified assistantships available. Financial award application deadline: 4/15; financial award applicants required to submit FAFSA. *Faculty research:* Learning and teaching styles, computers in special education, language development. *Unit head:* Dr. William Swart, Graduate Coordinator, 845-569-3149, Fax: 845-569-3535, E-mail: william.swart@msmc.edu. *Application contact:* Lisa Gallina, Director of Admissions for Graduate Programs and Adult Degree Completion, 845-569-3166, Fax: 845-569-3450, E-mail: lisa.gallina@msmc.edu.
Website: http://www.msmc.edu/Academics/Graduate_Programs/Master_of_Science_in_Education.

Murray State University, College of Education, Department of Adolescent, Career and Special Education, Program in Secondary Education, Murray, KY 42071. Offers MA Ed, Ed S. *Accreditation:* NCATE. Part-time programs available. *Degree requirements:* For master's, comprehensive exam, thesis optional; for Ed S, comprehensive exam. *Entrance requirements:* Additional exam requirements/recommendations for international students: Required—TOEFL.

National Louis University, National College of Education, Chicago, IL 60603. Offers administration and supervision (M Ed, Ed D, CAS, Ed S); curriculum and instruction (M Ed, MS Ed, CAS); early childhood administration (M Ed, CAS); early childhood education (M Ed, MAT, MS Ed, CAS); education (Ed D); educational psychology/human learning and development (M Ed, MS Ed, CAS, Ed S); elementary education (MAT); interdisciplinary curriculum and instruction (M Ed); mathematics education (M Ed, MS Ed, CAS); reading and language (M Ed, MS Ed, CAS); school psychology (M Ed, Ed S); science education (M Ed, MS Ed, CAS); secondary education (MAT); special education (M Ed, MAT, CAS); technology in education (M Ed, CAS). *Accreditation:* NCATE. Part-time and evening/weekend programs available. *Degree requirements:* For doctorate, comprehensive exam, thesis/dissertation. *Entrance requirements:* For master's, MAT or GRE, minimum GPA of 3.0; for doctorate, GRE General Test, minimum GPA of 3.25, interview, resume, writing sample, 4 recommendations. Additional exam requirements/recommendations for international students: Required—TOEFL (minimum score 550 paper-based; 79 iBT).

New Jersey City University, Graduate Studies and Continuing Education, Debra Cannon Partridge Wolfe College of Education, Department of Elementary and Secondary Education, Jersey City, NJ 07305-1597. Offers elementary education (MAT); secondary education (MAT). Part-time and evening/weekend programs available. *Faculty:* 16 full-time (14 women), 8 part-time/adjunct (4 women). *Students:* 14 full-time (12 women), 23 part-time (11 women); includes 15 minority (6 Black or African American, non-Hispanic/Latino; 2 Asian, non-Hispanic/Latino; 7 Hispanic/Latino). Average age 33. In 2013, 21 master's awarded. *Entrance requirements:* Additional exam requirements/recommendations for international students: Required—TOEFL (minimum score 61 iBT). *Application deadline:* For fall admission, 8/1 priority date for domestic students; for spring admission, 12/1 for domestic students. Applications are processed on a rolling basis. Application fee: $0. *Expenses: Tuition, area resident:* Part-time $527.90 per credit. Tuition, nonresident: part-time $947.75 per credit. *Financial support:* Teaching assistantships, career-related internships or fieldwork, and unspecified assistantships available. *Unit head:* Dr. Althea Hall, Coordinator, 201-200-2101, E-mail: ahall@njcu.edu. *Application contact:* Dr. William Bajor, Dean of Graduate Studies, 201-200-3409, Fax: 201-200-3411, E-mail: wbajor@njcu.edu.

New York Institute of Technology, School of Education, Department of Education, Old Westbury, NY 11568-8000. Offers adolescence education: mathematics (MS); adolescence education: science (MS); childhood education (MS); science, technology, engineering, and math education (Advanced Certificate); teaching 21st century skills (Advanced Certificate). Part-time and evening/weekend programs available. Postbaccalaureate distance learning degree programs offered (minimal on-campus study). *Faculty:* 1 (woman) full-time, 6 part-time/adjunct (3 women). *Students:* 13 full-time (11 women), 21 part-time (19 women); includes 7 minority (2 Black or African American, non-Hispanic/Latino; 3 Asian, non-Hispanic/Latino; 1 Hispanic/Latino; 1 Two or more races, non-Hispanic/Latino), 1 international. Average age 31. 32 applicants, 75% accepted, 13 enrolled. In 2013, 6 master's, 58 other advanced degrees awarded. *Entrance requirements:* Additional exam requirements/recommendations for international students: Required—TOEFL (minimum score 550 paper-based; 79 iBT),

IELTS (minimum score 6). *Application deadline:* For fall admission, 7/1 priority date for domestic students, 6/1 for international students; for spring admission, 12/1 priority date for domestic students, 12/1 for international students. Applications are processed on a rolling basis. Application fee: $50. Electronic applications accepted. *Expenses: Tuition:* Full-time $18,900; part-time $1050 per credit. *Financial support:* Research assistantships with partial tuition reimbursements, career-related internships or fieldwork, scholarships/grants, health care benefits, tuition waivers (full and partial), and unspecified assistantships available. Support available to part-time students. Financial award applicants required to submit FAFSA. *Faculty research:* Evolving definition of new literacies and its impact on teaching and learning (twenty-first century skills), new literacies practices in teacher education, teachers' professional development, English language and literacy learning through mobile learning, teaching reading to culturally and linguistically diverse children. *Unit head:* Dr. Hui-Yin Hsu, Associate Professor, 516-686-1322, Fax: 516-686-7655, E-mail: hhsu02@nyit.edu. *Application contact:* Alice Dolitsky, Director, Graduate Admissions, 516-686-7520, Fax: 516-686-1116, E-mail: nyitgrad@nyit.edu.
Website: http://www.nyit.edu/education/departments.

New York University, Steinhardt School of Culture, Education, and Human Development, Department of Art and Art Professions, Program in Art Education, New York, NY 10003-5799. Offers art, education, and community practice (MA); teaching art and social studies (MA); teaching art, all grades (MA). *Accreditation:* Teacher Education Accreditation Council. Part-time programs available. *Faculty:* 2 full-time (1 woman). *Students:* 10 full-time (9 women), 12 part-time (9 women); includes 10 minority (1 Black or African American, non-Hispanic/Latino; 4 American Indian or Alaska Native, non-Hispanic/Latino; 3 Asian, non-Hispanic/Latino; 2 Hispanic/Latino), 4 international. Average age 35. 34 applicants, 94% accepted, 12 enrolled. In 2013, 14 master's awarded. *Degree requirements:* For master's, thesis (for some programs). *Entrance requirements:* For master's, portfolio. Additional exam requirements/recommendations for international students: Required—TOEFL (minimum score 100 iBT). *Application deadline:* For fall admission, 11/16 priority date for domestic and international students. Applications are processed on a rolling basis. Application fee: $75. Electronic applications accepted. *Expenses: Tuition:* Full-time $35,856; part-time $1494 per unit. *Required fees:* $1408; $64 per unit. $473 per term. Tuition and fees vary according to course load and program. *Financial support:* Career-related internships or fieldwork, Federal Work-Study, and tuition waivers (partial) available. Support available to part-time students. Financial award application deadline: 2/1; financial award applicants required to submit FAFSA. *Faculty research:* Multicultural aesthetic inquiry, urban art education, feminism, equity and social justice. *Unit head:* Prof. Dipti Desai, Director, 212-998-9022, Fax: 212-995-4320, E-mail: dd25@nyu.edu. *Application contact:* 212-998-5030, Fax: 212-995-4328, E-mail: steinhardt.gradadmissions@nyu.edu.
Website: http://steinhardt.nyu.edu/art/education.

New York University, Steinhardt School of Culture, Education, and Human Development, Department of Music and Performing Arts Professions, Program in Educational Theatre, New York, NY 10012. Offers educational theatre (Ed D, Advanced Certificate); educational theatre and English 7-12: dual certificate (MA); educational theatre and social studies 7-12: dual certificate (MA); educational theatre in colleges and communities (MA, PhD); educational theatre, all grades (MA). Part-time programs available. *Faculty:* 5 full-time (2 women). *Students:* 51 full-time (34 women), 36 part-time (24 women); includes 20 minority (10 Black or African American, non-Hispanic/Latino; 1 Asian, non-Hispanic/Latino; 7 Hispanic/Latino; 2 Two or more races, non-Hispanic/Latino), 5 international. Average age 28. 66 applicants, 80% accepted, 25 enrolled. In 2013, 51 master's, 1 doctorate awarded. *Degree requirements:* For master's, thesis (for some programs); for doctorate, thesis/dissertation. *Entrance requirements:* For master's, audition; for doctorate, GRE General Test, interview; for Advanced Certificate, master's degree. Additional exam requirements/recommendations for international students: Required—TOEFL (minimum score 100 iBT). *Application deadline:* For fall admission, 12/1 priority date for domestic and international students; for spring admission, 10/1 for domestic and international students. Applications are processed on a rolling basis. Application fee: $75. Electronic applications accepted. *Expenses: Tuition:* Full-time $35,856; part-time $1494 per unit. *Required fees:* $1408; $64 per unit. $473 per term. Tuition and fees vary according to course load and program. *Financial support:* Teaching assistantships with partial tuition reimbursements, career-related internships or fieldwork, Federal Work-Study, institutionally sponsored loans, and scholarships/grants available. Support available to part-time students. Financial award application deadline: 2/1; financial award applicants required to submit FAFSA. *Faculty research:* Theatre for young audiences, drama in education, applied theatre, arts education assessment, reflective praxis. *Unit head:* Prof. David Montgomery, Director, 212-998-5869, Fax: 212-995-4043, E-mail: dm635@nyu.edu. *Application contact:* 212-998-5030, Fax: 212-995-4328, E-mail: steinhardt.gradadmissions@nyu.edu.
Website: http://steinhardt.nyu.edu/music/edtheatre.

New York University, Steinhardt School of Culture, Education, and Human Development, Department of Teaching and Learning, Clinically Rich Integrated Science Program (CRISP), New York, NY 10003. Offers biology (MA), including teaching biology grades 7-12; chemistry (MA), including teaching chemistry grades 7-12; physics (MA), including teaching physics grades 7-12. Part-time and evening/weekend programs available. *Faculty:* 4 full-time (3 women). *Students:* 22 full-time (14 women), 1 part-time (0 women); includes 8 minority (3 Black or African American, non-Hispanic/Latino; 3 Asian, non-Hispanic/Latino; 2 Hispanic/Latino), 2 international. Average age 27. 42 applicants, 64% accepted, 19 enrolled. In 2013, 9 master's awarded. *Degree requirements:* For master's, thesis (for some programs). *Entrance requirements:* Additional exam requirements/recommendations for international students: Required—TOEFL (minimum score 100 iBT). *Application deadline:* For fall admission, 2/1 priority date for domestic and international students; for spring admission, 10/1 for domestic and international students. Applications are processed on a rolling basis. Application fee: $75. Electronic applications accepted. *Expenses: Tuition:* Full-time $35,856; part-time $1494 per unit. *Required fees:* $1408; $64 per unit. $473 per term. Tuition and fees vary according to course load and program. *Financial support:* Career-related internships or fieldwork, Federal Work-Study, institutionally sponsored loans, scholarships/grants, and tuition waivers (partial) available. Support available to part-time students. Financial award application deadline: 2/1; financial award applicants required to submit FAFSA. *Faculty research:* Science curriculum development, gender and ethnicity, technology use, history and philosophy of school science, science in urban schools. *Unit head:* Dr. Pamela Fraser-Abder, Director, 212-998-5870, Fax: 212-995-4049. *Application contact:* 212-998-5030, Fax: 212-995-4328, E-mail: steinhardt.gradadmissions@nyu.edu.
Website: http://steinhardt.nyu.edu/teachlearn/crisp.

New York University, Steinhardt School of Culture, Education, and Human Development, Department of Teaching and Learning, Program in Literacy Education, New York, NY 10012-1019. Offers grades 5-12 (MA). *Accreditation:* Teacher Education Accreditation Council. Part-time programs available. *Faculty:* 1 (woman) full-time. *Students:* 8 full-time (5 women), 7 part-time (all women); includes 3 minority (1 Black or African American, non-Hispanic/Latino; 1 Asian, non-Hispanic/Latino; 1 Hispanic/Latino), 2 international. Average age 26. 52 applicants, 94% accepted, 11 enrolled. In 2013, 17 master's awarded. *Degree requirements:* For master's, thesis (for some programs), fieldwork. *Entrance requirements:* For master's, teacher certification. Additional exam requirements/recommendations for international students: Required—TOEFL (minimum score 100 iBT). *Application deadline:* For fall admission, 2/1 priority date for domestic and international students. Applications are processed on a rolling basis. Application fee: $75. Electronic applications accepted. *Expenses: Tuition:* Full-time $35,856; part-time $1494 per unit. *Required fees:* $1408; $64 per unit. $473 per term. Tuition and fees vary according to course load and program. *Financial support:* Career-related internships or fieldwork, Federal Work-Study, institutionally sponsored loans, scholarships/grants, and tuition waivers (partial) available. Support available to part-time students. Financial award application deadline: 2/1; financial award applicants required to submit FAFSA. *Faculty research:* Early literacy intervention and development, psycho and sociolinguistics, multicultural education, literacy assessment and instruction. *Unit head:* Prof. Kay Stahl, Director, 212-998-5204, Fax: 212-995-4049, E-mail: kay.stahl@nyu.edu. *Application contact:* Office of Graduate Admissions, 212-998-5030, Fax: 212-995-4328, E-mail: steinhardt.gradadmissions@nyu.edu.
Website: http://steinhardt.nyu.edu/teachlearn/literacy.

New York University, Steinhardt School of Culture, Education, and Human Development, Department of Teaching and Learning, Program in Multilingual/Multicultural Studies, New York, NY 10003. Offers bilingual education (MA, PhD, Advanced Certificate); foreign language education (MA, Advanced Certificate); foreign language education (7-12) and TESOL (K-12) (MA); teaching English to speakers of other languages (MA, PhD, Advanced Certificate); teaching foreign languages, 7-12 (MA), including Chinese, French, Italian, Japanese, Spanish; teaching foreign languages, college and adult (MA); teaching French as a foreign language and TESOL (MA); teaching Spanish as a foreign language and TESOL (MA). *Accreditation:* Teacher Education Accreditation Council. Part-time and evening/weekend programs available. *Faculty:* 5 full-time (4 women). *Students:* 134 full-time (112 women), 77 part-time (68 women); includes 43 minority (6 Black or African American, non-Hispanic/Latino; 18 Asian, non-Hispanic/Latino; 15 Hispanic/Latino; 4 Two or more races, non-Hispanic/Latino), 113 international. Average age 31. 501 applicants, 39% accepted, 68 enrolled. In 2013, 91 master's, 3 doctorates, 7 other advanced degrees awarded. *Degree requirements:* For master's, thesis (for some programs); for doctorate, thesis/dissertation. *Entrance requirements:* For doctorate, GRE General Test, interview; for Advanced Certificate, master's degree. Additional exam requirements/recommendations for international students: Required—TOEFL (minimum score 100 iBT). *Application deadline:* For fall admission, 12/1 priority date for domestic and international students; for spring admission, 10/1 for domestic and international students. Applications are processed on a rolling basis. Application fee: $75. Electronic applications accepted. *Expenses: Tuition:* Full-time $35,856; part-time $1494 per unit. *Required fees:* $1408; $64 per unit. $473 per term. Tuition and fees vary according to course load and program. *Financial support:* Fellowships with full and partial tuition reimbursements, career-related internships or fieldwork, Federal Work-Study, institutionally sponsored loans, scholarships/grants, and tuition waivers (partial) available. Support available to part-time students. Financial award application deadline: 2/1; financial award applicants required to submit FAFSA. *Faculty research:* Second language acquisition, cross-cultural communication, technology-enhanced language learning, language variation, action learning. *Unit head:* Prof. Shondel Nero, Director, 212-998-5757, E-mail: shondel.nero@nyu.edu. *Application contact:* 212-998-5030, Fax: 212-995-4328, E-mail: steinhardt.gradadmissions@nyu.edu.
Website: http://steinhardt.nyu.edu/teachlearn/mms.

New York University, Steinhardt School of Culture, Education, and Human Development, Department of Teaching and Learning, Program in Social Studies Education, New York, NY 10003. Offers history, social studies, and global education (PhD); teaching art and social studies 7-12 (MA); teaching social studies 7-12 (MA). *Accreditation:* Teacher Education Accreditation Council. Part-time and evening/weekend programs available. *Faculty:* 3 full-time (2 women). *Students:* 5 full-time (3 women), 5 part-time (2 women); includes 4 minority (all Hispanic/Latino). Average age 27. 48 applicants, 88% accepted, 6 enrolled. In 2013, 23 master's awarded. *Degree requirements:* For master's, thesis (for some programs). *Entrance requirements:* Additional exam requirements/recommendations for international students: Required—TOEFL (minimum score 100 iBT). *Application deadline:* For fall admission, 2/1 priority date for domestic and international students; for spring admission, 10/1 for domestic and international students. Applications are processed on a rolling basis. Application fee: $75. Electronic applications accepted. *Expenses: Tuition:* Full-time $35,856; part-time $1494 per unit. *Required fees:* $1408; $64 per unit. $473 per term. Tuition and fees vary according to course load and program. *Financial support:* Career-related internships or fieldwork, Federal Work-Study, institutionally sponsored loans, scholarships/grants, and tuition waivers (partial) available. Support available to part-time students. Financial award application deadline: 2/1; financial award applicants required to submit FAFSA. *Faculty research:* Social studies education reform, ethnography and oral history, civic education, labor history and social studies curriculum, material culture. *Unit head:* 212-998-5460, Fax: 212-995-4049. *Application contact:* 212-998-5030, Fax: 212-995-4328, E-mail: steinhardt.gradadmissions@nyu.edu.
Website: http://steinhardt.nyu.edu/teachlearn/social_studies.

Niagara University, Graduate Division of Education, Concentration in Teacher Education, Niagara Falls, NY 14109. Offers early childhood and childhood education (MS Ed, Certificate); middle and adolescence education (MS Ed, Certificate); special education (grades 1-12) (MS Ed, Certificate); teaching English to speakers of other languages (MS Ed). *Accreditation:* NCATE. *Students:* 168 full-time (130 women), 40 part-time (28 women); includes 11 minority (4 Black or African American, non-Hispanic/Latino; 1 Asian, non-Hispanic/Latino; 5 Hispanic/Latino; 1 Native Hawaiian or other Pacific Islander, non-Hispanic/Latino), 101 international. Average age 27. In 2013, 131 master's, 1 Certificate awarded. *Entrance requirements:* For master's, GRE General Test or MAT. Additional exam requirements/recommendations for international students: Required—TOEFL (minimum score 550 paper-based, 79 iBT) or IELTS (minimum score 6). *Application deadline:* For fall admission, 8/1 for domestic students. Applications are processed on a rolling basis. Application fee: $30. *Expenses:* Contact institution. *Financial support:* Research assistantships with full and partial tuition reimbursements, teaching assistantships with full and partial tuition reimbursements, career-related internships or fieldwork, Federal Work-Study, scholarships/grants, and unspecified assistantships available. Financial award application deadline: 4/15; financial award applicants required to submit FAFSA. *Unit head:* Dr. Chandra Foote, Chair, 716-286-8549. *Application contact:* Dr. Debra A. Colley, Dean of Education, 716-286-8560, Fax: 716-286-8561, E-mail: dcolley@niagara.edu.
Website: http://www.niagara.edu/teacher-education.

Norfolk State University, School of Graduate Studies, School of Education, Department of Secondary Education and School Leadership, Norfolk, VA 23504. Offers principal preparation (MA); secondary education (MAT); urban education/administration (MA), including teaching. *Accreditation:* NCATE. Part-time programs available. *Faculty:* 3 full-time, 1 part-time/adjunct. *Students:* 89 full-time (71 women), 73 part-time (49 women); includes 143 minority (137 Black or African American, non-Hispanic/Latino; 1 Asian, non-Hispanic/Latino; 3 Hispanic/Latino; 2 Two or more races, non-Hispanic/Latino), 2 international. Average age 32. In 2013, 94 master's awarded. *Entrance requirements:* For master's, GRE General Test, PRAXIS I, minimum GPA of 3.0 in major, 2.5 overall. Additional exam requirements/recommendations for international

students: Required—TOEFL (minimum score 500 paper-based). *Application deadline:* For fall admission, 3/1 for domestic and international students; for spring admission, 10/1 for domestic and international students. Application fee: $30. *Financial support:* Fellowships and career-related internships or fieldwork available. *Unit head:* Dr. Margaret Knight, Acting Head, 757-823-8715, Fax: 757-823-8757, E-mail: mknight@nsu.edu. *Application contact:* Karen Fauntleroy, Education Specialist, 757-823-8178, Fax: 757-823-8757, E-mail: kfauntleroy@nsu.edu.

North Carolina Agricultural and Technical State University, School of Graduate Studies, College of Arts and Sciences, Department of Mathematics, Greensboro, NC 27411. Offers applied mathematics (MS), including secondary education. *Accreditation:* NCATE. Part-time and evening/weekend programs available. *Degree requirements:* For master's, comprehensive exam, thesis or alternative, qualifying exam. *Entrance requirements:* For master's, GRE General Test, minimum GPA of 3.0.

North Carolina State University, Graduate School, College of Education, Department of Curriculum and Instruction, Program in Secondary English Education, Raleigh, NC 27695. Offers M Ed, MS Ed. *Degree requirements:* For master's, thesis optional.

Northeastern Illinois University, College of Graduate Studies and Research, College of Arts and Sciences, Program in Mathematics, Chicago, IL 60625-4699. Offers MS. Part-time and evening/weekend programs available. *Degree requirements:* For master's, comprehensive exam, thesis optional, project. *Entrance requirements:* For master's, minimum GPA of 2.75, 6 undergraduate courses in mathematics. Additional exam requirements/recommendations for international students: Required—TOEFL (minimum score 550 paper-based; 79 iBT). Electronic applications accepted. *Faculty research:* Numerical analysis, mathematical biology, operations research, statistics, geometry and mathematics of finance.

Northeastern Illinois University, College of Graduate Studies and Research, College of Education, MAT Program in Language Arts - Secondary Education, Chicago, IL 60625-4699. Offers MAT.

Northeastern Illinois University, College of Graduate Studies and Research, College of Education, MSI Program in Language Arts - Secondary Education, Chicago, IL 60625-4699. Offers MSI.

Northeastern University, School of Education, Boston, MA 02115-5096. Offers curriculum, teaching, learning, and leadership (Ed D); elementary licensure (MAT); higher education administration (MAT, Ed D); Jewish education leadership (Ed D); learning and instruction (M Ed); organizational leadership studies (Ed D); secondary licensure (MAT); special education (M Ed). Part-time and evening/weekend programs available.

Northern Arizona University, Graduate College, College of Education, Department of Teaching and Learning, Flagstaff , AZ 86011. Offers early childhood education (M Ed); elementary education (M Ed); secondary education (M Ed). Part-time programs available. *Faculty:* 33 full-time (26 women), 3 part-time/adjunct (all women). *Students:* 146 full-time (119 women), 188 part-time (169 women); includes 91 minority (5 Black or African American, non-Hispanic/Latino; 16 American Indian or Alaska Native, non-Hispanic/Latino; 1 Asian, non-Hispanic/Latino; 65 Hispanic/Latino; 4 Two or more races, non-Hispanic/Latino), 2 international. Average age 35. 114 applicants, 94% accepted, 67 enrolled. In 2013, 205 master's awarded. *Degree requirements:* For master's, comprehensive exam (for some programs), thesis (for some programs). *Entrance requirements:* For master's, minimum GPA of 3.0. Additional exam requirements/recommendations for international students: Required—TOEFL (minimum score 550 paper-based; 80 iBT), IELTS (minimum score 7). *Application deadline:* For fall admission, 3/1 priority date for international students; for spring admission, 9/15 priority date for international students. Applications are processed on a rolling basis. Application fee: $65. Electronic applications accepted. *Financial support:* In 2013–14, 6 teaching assistantships with full tuition reimbursements (averaging $9,698 per year) were awarded; Federal Work-Study, scholarships/grants, health care benefits, tuition waivers (full and partial), and unspecified assistantships also available. Financial award applicants required to submit FAFSA. *Unit head:* Dr. Pamela Powell, Chair, 928-523-5644, Fax: 928-523-1929, E-mail: pamela.powell@nau.edu. *Application contact:* Kay Quillen, Administrative Assistant, 928-523-9316, Fax: 928-523-1929, E-mail: kay.quillen@nau.edu.
Website: http://nau.edu/coe/teaching-and-learning/.

Northern Illinois University, Graduate School, College of Education, Department of Special and Early Education, De Kalb, IL 60115-2854. Offers curriculum and instruction (MS Ed, Ed D), including curriculum leadership (Ed D), elementary education (Ed D), secondary education (Ed D); early childhood education (MS Ed); elementary education (MS Ed); special education (MS Ed). Part-time and evening/weekend programs available. *Faculty:* 22 full-time (14 women), 2 part-time/adjunct (both women). *Students:* 52 full-time (41 women), 168 part-time (137 women); includes 29 minority (11 Black or African American, non-Hispanic/Latino; 7 Asian, non-Hispanic/Latino; 6 Hispanic/Latino; 5 Two or more races, non-Hispanic/Latino), 3 international. Average age 36. 38 applicants, 63% accepted, 18 enrolled. In 2013, 59 master's, 15 doctorates awarded. *Degree requirements:* For master's, comprehensive exam, thesis optional; for doctorate, thesis/dissertation, candidacy exam, dissertation defense. *Entrance requirements:* For master's, GRE General Test or MAT, minimum undergraduate GPA of 2.75; for doctorate, GRE General Test or MAT, minimum undergraduate GPA of 2.75, graduate 3.2. Additional exam requirements/recommendations for international students: Required—TOEFL (minimum score 550 paper-based). *Application deadline:* For fall admission, 6/1 for domestic students, 5/1 for international students; for spring admission, 11/1 for domestic students, 10/1 for international students. Applications are processed on a rolling basis. Application fee: $40. Electronic applications accepted. *Financial support:* In 2013–14, 24 research assistantships with full tuition reimbursements were awarded; fellowships with full tuition reimbursements, teaching assistantships with full tuition reimbursements, career-related internships or fieldwork, Federal Work-Study, scholarships/grants, tuition waivers (full), and unspecified assistantships also available. Support available to part-time students. Financial award applicants required to submit FAFSA. *Faculty research:* Teacher certification, stress reduction during student teaching, teaching history, portfolios in student teaching. *Unit head:* Dr. Barbara Schwartz-Bechet, Interim Chair, 815-753-1619, E-mail: seed@niu.edu. *Application contact:* Gail Myers, Clerk, Graduate Advising, 815-753-0381, E-mail: gmyers@niu.edu.
Website: http://www.cedu.niu.edu/seed/.

Northern Michigan University, College of Graduate Studies, College of Health Sciences and Professional Studies, School of Education, Leadership and Public Service, Program in Secondary Education, Marquette, MI 49855-5301. Offers MAE. Part-time programs available. *Students:* 2 full-time (0 women), 16 part-time (10 women); includes 2 minority (both American Indian or Alaska Native, non-Hispanic/Latino). In 2013, 9 master's awarded. *Degree requirements:* For master's, thesis or alternative. *Entrance requirements:* For master's, minimum GPA of 3.0. *Application deadline:* For fall admission, 7/1 priority date for domestic students; for spring admission, 11/1 for domestic students. Applications are processed on a rolling basis. Application fee: $25. *Expenses:* Tuition, state resident: part-time $427 per credit. Tuition, nonresident: part-time $614.50 per credit. *Required fees:* $325 per semester. Tuition and fees vary according to course load and program. *Financial support:* Teaching assistantships, Federal Work-Study, and institutionally sponsored loans available. Support available to part-time students. Financial award application deadline: 3/1. *Faculty research:* Supervision and improvement of instruction. *Unit head:* Rodney Clarken, Associate Dean, 906-227-1880, E-mail: rclarken@nmu.edu. *Application contact:* Nancy E. Carter, Coordinator, 906-227-1625.

Northwestern Oklahoma State University, School of Professional Studies, Program in Secondary Education, Alva, OK 73717-2799. Offers M Ed. *Accreditation:* NCATE. Part-time programs available. *Degree requirements:* For master's, thesis optional, portfolio. *Entrance requirements:* For master's, GRE General Test or MAT, minimum GPA of 2.75. *Faculty research:* Teacher education, professional school models of pedagogy, competency exams for teachers, teacher accreditation/certification.

Northwestern State University of Louisiana, Graduate Studies and Research, College of Education and Human Development, Program in Secondary Education, Natchitoches, LA 71497. Offers MAT. *Degree requirements:* For master's, comprehensive exam, thesis or alternative. *Entrance requirements:* For master's, GRE General Test, minimum undergraduate GPA of 2.5. Additional exam requirements/recommendations for international students: Required—TOEFL. Electronic applications accepted.

Northwestern State University of Louisiana, Graduate Studies and Research, College of Education and Human Development, Programs in Educational Leadership and Instruction, Natchitoches, LA 71497. Offers counseling (Ed S); educational leadership (M Ed, Ed S); educational technology (Ed S); elementary teaching (Ed S); reading (Ed S); secondary teaching (Ed S); special education (Ed S). *Accreditation:* NASAD. *Degree requirements:* For master's, comprehensive exam, thesis (for some programs). *Entrance requirements:* For master's and Ed S, GRE General Test. Additional exam requirements/recommendations for international students: Required—TOEFL. Electronic applications accepted.

Northwestern University, The Graduate School, School of Education and Social Policy, Education and Social Policy Program, Evanston, IL 60035. Offers elementary teaching (MS); secondary teaching (MS); teacher leadership (MS). Part-time and evening/weekend programs available. *Degree requirements:* For master's, research project. *Entrance requirements:* For master's, GRE General Test, Illinois State Board of Education Basic Skills Exam (secondary and elementary), bachelor's degree. Additional exam requirements/recommendations for international students: Recommended—TOEFL. Electronic applications accepted. *Faculty research:* Cultural context and literacy, philosophy of education and interpretive discussion, productivity, enhancing research and teaching, motivation, new and junior faculty issues, professional development for K-12 teachers to improve math and science teaching, female/underrepresented students/faculty in STEM disciplines.

Northwest Missouri State University, Graduate School, College of Education and Human Services, Department of Professional Education, Program in Educational Leadership, Maryville, MO 64468-6001. Offers educational leadership: elementary (MS Ed); educational leadership: K-12 (MS Ed); educational leadership: secondary (MS Ed); elementary principalship (Ed S); secondary principalship (Ed S); superintendency (Ed S). *Accreditation:* NCATE. Part-time programs available. *Degree requirements:* For master's, comprehensive exam; for Ed S, comprehensive exam, thesis. *Entrance requirements:* For master's, GRE General Test, minimum undergraduate GPA of 2.75, teaching certificate, writing sample; for Ed S, minimum graduate GPA of 3.25. Additional exam requirements/recommendations for international students: Required—TOEFL (minimum score 550 paper-based).

Northwest Missouri State University, Graduate School, College of Education and Human Services, Program in Secondary Individualized Prescribed Programs, Maryville, MO 64468-6001. Offers teaching secondary (MS Ed). *Entrance requirements:* Additional exam requirements/recommendations for international students: Required—TOEFL (minimum score 550 paper-based).

Oakland University, Graduate Study and Lifelong Learning, School of Education and Human Services, Department of Teacher Development and Educational Studies, Rochester, MI 48309-4401. Offers education studies (M Ed); secondary education (MAT). *Faculty:* 6 full-time (3 women), 17 part-time/adjunct (11 women). *Students:* 85 full-time (71 women), 151 part-time (99 women); includes 42 minority (24 Black or African American, non-Hispanic/Latino; 2 American Indian or Alaska Native, non-Hispanic/Latino; 9 Asian, non-Hispanic/Latino; 7 Hispanic/Latino), 3 international. Average age 30. 175 applicants, 47% accepted, 76 enrolled. In 2013, 69 master's awarded. *Entrance requirements:* For master's, minimum GPA of 3.0 for unconditional admission. *Application deadline:* For fall admission, 3/1 for domestic students. Application fee: $35. Electronic applications accepted. *Financial support:* Federal Work-Study, institutionally sponsored loans, and tuition waivers (full) available. Financial award application deadline: 3/1; financial award applicants required to submit FAFSA. *Total annual research expenditures:* $182,162. *Unit head:* Dr. Dyanne M. Tracy, Chair, 248-370-3064, Fax: 248-370-4605, E-mail: dtracy@oakland.edu. *Application contact:* Christina J. Grabowski, Associate Director of Graduate Study and Lifelong Learning, 248-370-3167, Fax: 248-370-4114, E-mail: grabowsk@oakland.edu.

Occidental College, Graduate Studies, Department of Education, Los Angeles, CA 90041-3314. Offers elementary education (MAT), including liberal studies; secondary education (MAT), including English and comparative literary studies, history, life science, mathematics, physical science, social science, Spanish. Part-time programs available. *Degree requirements:* For master's, comprehensive exam, synthesis paper. *Entrance requirements:* For master's, GRE General Test, minimum GPA of 3.0. Additional exam requirements/recommendations for international students: Required—TOEFL (minimum score 625 paper-based). *Expenses:* Contact institution. *Faculty research:* Preparing teacher-leaders, curriculum development.

Ohio University, Graduate College, Gladys W. and David H. Patton College of Education and Human Services, Department of Teacher Education, Athens, OH 45701-2979. Offers adolescent to young adult education (M Ed); curriculum and instruction (M Ed, PhD); early childhood/special education (M Ed); intervention specialist/mild-moderate needs (M Ed); intervention specialist/moderate-intensive needs (M Ed); mathematics education (PhD); middle childhood education (M Ed); reading education (M Ed); social studies education (PhD). Part-time and evening/weekend programs available. *Degree requirements:* For master's, thesis or alternative; for doctorate, comprehensive exam, thesis/dissertation. *Entrance requirements:* For master's, GRE General Test or MAT (if GPA is below 2.9); for doctorate, GRE General Test, minimum GPA of 3.4, work experience. Additional exam requirements/recommendations for international students: Required—TOEFL (minimum score 550 paper-based; 80 iBT) or IELTS (minimum score 6.5). Electronic applications accepted. *Faculty research:* Cognition literacy, character education, teacher's education reform, disabilities.

Old Dominion University, Darden College of Education, Programs in Secondary Education, Norfolk, VA 23529. Offers biology (MS Ed); chemistry (MS Ed); English (MS Ed); instructional technology (MS Ed); library science (MS Ed); secondary education (MS Ed). *Accreditation:* NCATE. Part-time and evening/weekend programs available. Postbaccalaureate distance learning degree programs offered (minimal on-campus study). *Faculty:* 13 full-time (7 women), 10 part-time/adjunct (7 women).

Students: 74 full-time (56 women), 78 part-time (49 women); includes 25 minority (13 Black or African American, non-Hispanic/Latino; 6 Hispanic/Latino; 6 Two or more races, non-Hispanic/Latino). Average age 32. 75 applicants, 71% accepted, 53 enrolled. In 2013, 79 master's awarded. *Degree requirements:* For master's, comprehensive exam, thesis. *Entrance requirements:* For master's, GRE General Test or MAT, PRAXIS I (for licensure), minimum GPA of 2.8, teaching certificate. Additional exam requirements/recommendations for international students: Required—TOEFL. *Application deadline:* For fall admission, 6/1 for domestic and international students; for winter admission, 11/1 for domestic and international students; for spring admission, 3/1 for domestic and international students. Applications are processed on a rolling basis. Application fee: $50. Electronic applications accepted. *Expenses:* Tuition, state resident: full-time $9888; part-time $412 per credit. Tuition, nonresident: full-time $25,152; part-time $1048 per credit. *Required fees:* $59 per semester. One-time fee: $50. *Financial support:* In 2013–14, 56 students received support, including fellowships (averaging $15,000 per year), research assistantships with tuition reimbursements available (averaging $9,000 per year), teaching assistantships with tuition reimbursements available (averaging $15,000 per year). Financial award application deadline: 2/15; financial award applicants required to submit FAFSA. *Faculty research:* Use of technology, writing project for teachers, geography teaching, reading. *Unit head:* Dr. Robert Lucking, Graduate Program Director, 757-683-5545, Fax: 757-683-5862, E-mail: rlucking@odu.edu. *Application contact:* William Heffelfinger, Director of Graduate Admissions, 757-683-5554, Fax: 757-683-3255, E-mail: gradadmit@odu.edu. Website: http://education.odu.edu/eci/secondary/.

Olivet Nazarene University, Graduate School, Division of Education, Program in Secondary Education, Bourbonnais, IL 60914. Offers MAT. *Accreditation:* NCATE. Evening/weekend programs available. *Degree requirements:* For master's, thesis or alternative.

Our Lady of the Lake University of San Antonio, School of Professional Studies, Program in Secondary Education, San Antonio, TX 78207-4689. Offers M Ed. Part-time and evening/weekend programs available. *Faculty:* 6 full-time (4 women), 3 part-time/adjunct (all women). *Students:* 3 full-time (2 women); includes 2 minority (1 Black or African American, non-Hispanic/Latino; 1 Hispanic/Latino). Average age 34. 3 applicants, 100% accepted, 1 enrolled. In 2013, 5 master's awarded. *Degree requirements:* For master's, comprehensive exam, thesis optional. *Entrance requirements:* For master's, GRE General Test or MAT. Additional exam requirements/recommendations for international students: Required—TOEFL. *Application deadline:* For fall admission, 4/1 priority date for domestic and international students; for spring admission, 11/1 priority date for domestic and international students; for summer admission, 2/1 priority date for domestic and international students. Applications are processed on a rolling basis. Application fee: $25 ($50 for international students). Electronic applications accepted. *Expenses:* Tuition: Full-time $9120; part-time $760 per credit. *Required fees:* $698; $334 per trimester. Tuition and fees vary according to course load, degree level, campus/location and program. *Financial support:* Research assistantships, teaching assistantships, career-related internships or fieldwork, Federal Work-Study, institutionally sponsored loans, scholarships/grants, and tuition waivers (partial) available. Support available to part-time students. Financial award application deadline: 4/15. *Faculty research:* Professional educator to understand and meet the comprehensive needs of a diverse student population, life-long learners, innovative practices. *Unit head:* Dr. Jerrie Jackson, 210-434-6711 Ext. 2698, E-mail: jjackson@lake.ollusa.edu. *Application contact:* Graduate Admission, 210-431-3961, Fax: 210-431-4013, E-mail: gradadm@lake.ollusa.edu.

Pacific Union College, Education Department, Angwin, CA 94508-9707. Offers education (M Ed); elementary teaching (MAT); secondary teaching (MAT). Part-time programs available. *Faculty:* 3 full-time (1 woman), 3 part-time/adjunct (all women). *Students:* 3 full-time (2 women), 11 part-time (7 women); includes 4 minority (1 Black or African American, non-Hispanic/Latino; 2 Asian, non-Hispanic/Latino; 1 Hispanic/Latino). Average age 35. In 2013, 2 master's awarded. *Degree requirements:* For master's, thesis, action research project, field experiences. *Entrance requirements:* For master's, GRE (for M Ed), two interviews, teaching credential, letters of recommendation, essay. *Application deadline:* Applications are processed on a rolling basis. Application fee: $0. *Expenses:* Tuition: Full-time $26,550; part-time $770 per quarter hour. *Required fees:* $930. Full-time tuition and fees vary according to course load and student's religious affiliation. Part-time tuition and fees vary according to class time and student's religious affiliation. *Financial support:* In 2013–14, 2 students received support. Scholarships/grants available. Support available to part-time students. *Faculty research:* Choice theory. *Unit head:* Prof. Thomas Lee, Chair, 707-965-6646, Fax: 707-965-6645, E-mail: tdlee@puc.edu. *Application contact:* Marsha Crow, Assistant Chair/Accreditation and Certification Specialist/Credential Analyst, 707-965-6643, Fax: 707-965-6645, E-mail: mcrow@puc.edu. Website: http://www.puc.edu/academics/departments/education/.

Pacific University, College of Education, Forest Grove, OR 97116-1797. Offers early childhood education (MAT); education (MAE); elementary education (MAT); high school education (MAT); middle school education (MAT); special education (MAT); visual function in learning (M Ed). *Accreditation:* NCATE. Part-time and evening/weekend programs available. *Degree requirements:* For master's, research project. *Entrance requirements:* For master's, California Basic Educational Skills Test, PRAXIS II, minimum undergraduate GPA of 2.75, 3.0 graduate. Additional exam requirements/recommendations for international students: Required—TOEFL. Electronic applications accepted. *Expenses:* Contact institution. *Faculty research:* Defining a culturally competent classroom, technology in the k-12 classroom, Socratic seminars, social studies education.

Piedmont College, School of Education, Demorest, GA 30535-0010. Offers art education (MAT); early childhood education (MA, MAT); instructional technology (MAT); middle grades education (MA, MAT); music education (MAT); secondary education (MA, MAT); special education (MA, MAT); teacher leadership (Ed S). Part-time and evening/weekend programs available. *Students:* 312 full-time (242 women), 694 part-time (563 women); includes 153 minority (103 Black or African American, non-Hispanic/Latino; 3 American Indian or Alaska Native, non-Hispanic/Latino; 17 Asian, non-Hispanic/Latino; 19 Hispanic/Latino; 11 Two or more races, non-Hispanic/Latino), 1 international. Average age 37. 165 applicants, 72% accepted, 118 enrolled. In 2013, 333 master's, 15 doctorates, 457 other advanced degrees awarded. *Degree requirements:* For master's, thesis, field experience in the classroom teaching; for doctorate, thesis/dissertation. *Entrance requirements:* For master's, GRE General Test, MAT, minimum undergraduate GPA of 2.5; for Ed S, minimum graduate GPA of 3.5, valid teaching certificate. Additional exam requirements/recommendations for international students: Required—TOEFL (minimum score 550 paper-based). *Application deadline:* For fall admission, 7/15 for domestic students; for spring admission, 12/1 for domestic students. Applications are processed on a rolling basis. Electronic applications accepted. *Expenses: Tuition:* Full-time $7992; part-time $444 per credit hour. *Financial support:* Career-related internships or fieldwork, Federal Work-Study, and unspecified assistantships available. Support available to part-time students. Financial award applicants required to submit FAFSA. *Unit head:* Dr. Don Gnecco, Dean, 706-778-3000 Ext. 1201, Fax: 706-776-9608, E-mail: dgnecco@piedmont.edu. *Application contact:* Kathleen Anderson,

Director of Graduate Enrollment Management, 706-778-8500 Ext. 1181, Fax: 706-778-0150, E-mail: kanderson@piedmont.edu.

Pittsburg State University, Graduate School, College of Education, Department of Curriculum and Instruction, Pittsburg, KS 66762. Offers classroom reading teacher (MS); early childhood education (MS); elementary education (MS); reading (MS); reading specialist (MS); secondary education (MS); teaching (MAT). *Accreditation:* NCATE. *Degree requirements:* For master's, thesis or alternative. *Entrance requirements:* For master's, GRE or MAT.

Plymouth State University, College of Graduate Studies, Graduate Studies in Education, Program in Secondary Education, Plymouth, NH 03264-1595. Offers curriculum and instruction (M Ed); language education (M Ed); library media (M Ed); physical education (M Ed); social studies education (M Ed); special education (M Ed). Part-time and evening/weekend programs available. *Entrance requirements:* For master's, MAT.

Portland State University, Graduate Studies, School of Education, Department of Curriculum and Instruction, Portland, OR 97207-0751. Offers early childhood education (MA, MS); education (M Ed, MA, MS); educational leadership: curriculum and instruction (Ed D); educational media/school librarianship (MA, MS); elementary education (M Ed, MAT, MST); reading (MA, MS); secondary education (M Ed, MAT, MST). *Accreditation:* NCATE. Part-time programs available. *Faculty:* 22 full-time (15 women), 28 part-time/adjunct (20 women). *Students:* 29 full-time (23 women), 162 part-time (123 women); includes 26 minority (3 Black or African American, non-Hispanic/Latino; 6 Asian, non-Hispanic/Latino; 13 Hispanic/Latino; 4 Two or more races, non-Hispanic/Latino), 6 international. Average age 36. 145 applicants, 69% accepted, 93 enrolled. In 2013, 257 master's, 5 doctorates awarded. *Degree requirements:* For master's, comprehensive exam, thesis or alternative; for doctorate, thesis/dissertation. *Entrance requirements:* For master's, California Basic Educational Skills Test, minimum GPA of 3.0 in upper-division course work or 2.75 overall. Additional exam requirements/recommendations for international students: Required—TOEFL (minimum score 550 paper-based). *Application deadline:* For fall admission, 4/1 for domestic and international students; for winter admission, 9/1 for domestic and international students; for spring admission, 11/1 for domestic and international students. Applications are processed on a rolling basis. Application fee: $50. *Expenses:* Tuition, state resident: full-time $9207; part-time $341 per credit. Tuition, nonresident: full-time $14,391; part-time $533 per credit. *Required fees:* $1263; $22 per credit. $98 per quarter. One-time fee: $150. Tuition and fees vary according to program. *Financial support:* In 2013–14, 1 research assistantship with full tuition reimbursement (averaging $6,248 per year), 2 teaching assistantships with full tuition reimbursements (averaging $7,755 per year) were awarded; career-related internships or fieldwork, Federal Work-Study, and institutionally sponsored loans also available. Support available to part-time students. Financial award application deadline: 3/1; financial award applicants required to submit FAFSA. *Faculty research:* Early literacy, characteristics of successful teachers of at-risk students, participation of women/minorities in technology courses, selection of cooperating teachers. *Total annual research expenditures:* $1 million. *Unit head:* Christine Chaille, Head, 503-725-4753, Fax: 203-725-8475, E-mail: chaillec@pdx.edu. *Application contact:* Jake Fernandez, Department Assistant, 503-725-4756, Fax: 503-725-8475, E-mail: jifern@pdx.edu. Website: http://www.ed.pdx.edu/ci/.

Prescott College, Graduate Programs, Program in Education, Prescott, AZ 86301. Offers early childhood education (MA); early childhood special education (MA); education (MA); elementary education (MA); environmental education leadership and administration (MA); equine-assisted learning (MA); school guidance counseling (MA); secondary education (MA); special education: learning disabilities (MA); special education: mental retardation (MA); special education: serious emotional disabilities (MA); student-directed independent study (MA); sustainability education (PhD). Part-time programs available. Postbaccalaureate distance learning degree programs offered (minimal on-campus study). *Degree requirements:* For master's, thesis, fieldwork or internship, practicum; for doctorate, thesis/dissertation. *Entrance requirements:* For master's, 2 letters of recommendation, resume; for doctorate, 3 letters of recommendation, resume, official transcripts, personal statement, program proposal. Additional exam requirements/recommendations for international students: Required—TOEFL (minimum score 500 paper-based). Electronic applications accepted.

Providence College, Program in Special Education, Providence, RI 02918. Offers special education (M Ed), including elementary teaching, secondary teaching. Part-time and evening/weekend programs available. *Faculty:* 9 part-time/adjunct (5 women). *Students:* 7 full-time (5 women), 18 part-time (15 women). Average age 29. 3 applicants, 33% accepted. In 2013, 15 master's awarded. *Degree requirements:* For master's, comprehensive exam. *Entrance requirements:* For master's, GRE General Test. Additional exam requirements/recommendations for international students: Required—TOEFL (minimum score 550 paper-based; 80 iBT). *Application deadline:* For fall admission, 8/1 priority date for domestic and international students; for spring admission, 12/1 priority date for domestic and international students. Applications are processed on a rolling basis. Application fee: $55. *Expenses: Tuition:* Part-time $432 per credit. *Required fees:* $432 per credit. *Financial support:* Career-related internships or fieldwork and unspecified assistantships available. Support available to part-time students. Financial award application deadline: 8/1; financial award applicants required to submit FAFSA. *Unit head:* Barbara Vigeant, Director, 401-865-2912, Fax: 401-865-1147, E-mail: bvigeant@providence.edu. *Application contact:* Rev. Mark D. Nowel, Dean of Undergraduate and Graduate Studies, 401-865-2649, Fax: 401-865-1496, E-mail: mnowel@providence.edu. Website: http://www.providence.edu/professional-studies/graduate-degrees/Pages/master-education-specialed.aspx.

Providence College, Programs in Administration, Providence, RI 02918. Offers elementary administration (M Ed); secondary administration (M Ed). Part-time and evening/weekend programs available. *Faculty:* 14 part-time/adjunct (6 women). *Students:* 5 full-time (1 woman), 50 part-time (31 women). Average age 37. 9 applicants, 100% accepted, 8 enrolled. In 2013, 33 master's awarded. *Degree requirements:* For master's, comprehensive exam, portfolio. *Entrance requirements:* For master's, GRE General Test. Additional exam requirements/recommendations for international students: Required—TOEFL (minimum score 550 paper-based; 80 iBT). *Application deadline:* For fall admission, 8/1 priority date for domestic and international students; for spring admission, 12/1 priority date for domestic and international students. Applications are processed on a rolling basis. Application fee: $55. *Expenses: Tuition:* Part-time $432 per credit. *Required fees:* $432 per credit. *Financial support:* Career-related internships or fieldwork, institutionally sponsored loans, and unspecified assistantships available. Support available to part-time students. Financial award application deadline: 8/1; financial award applicants required to submit FAFSA. *Unit head:* Francis J. Leary, Director, 401-865-2881, E-mail: fleary@providence.edu. *Application contact:* Rev. Mark D. Nowel, Dean of Undergraduate and Graduate Studies, 401-865-2649, Fax: 401-865-1496, E-mail: mnowel@providence.edu. Website: http://www.providence.edu/professional-studies/graduate-degrees/Pages/master-education-administration.aspx.

Providence College, Providence Alliance for Catholic Teachers (PACT) Program, Providence, RI 02918. Offers secondary education (M Ed). *Faculty:* 2 full-time (0

women), 19 part-time/adjunct (9 women). *Students:* 22 full-time (14 women). Average age 23. In 2013, 14 master's awarded. *Degree requirements:* For master's, comprehensive exam. *Entrance requirements:* For master's, GRE/MAT/PRAXIS. Additional exam requirements/recommendations for international students: Required—TOEFL (minimum score 550 paper-based; 80 iBT). *Application deadline:* For fall admission, 2/14 priority date for domestic students, 3/1 priority date for international students. Applications are processed on a rolling basis. Application fee: $55. *Expenses: Tuition:* Part-time $432 per credit. *Required fees:* $432 per credit. *Financial support:* Application deadline: 8/1; applicants required to submit FAFSA. *Unit head:* Br. Patrick Carey, Director, 401-865-2657, Fax: 401-865-1657, E-mail: pcarey@providence.edu. *Application contact:* Rev. Mark D. Nowel, Dean of Undergraduate and Graduate Studies, 401-865-2649, Fax: 401-865-1496, E-mail: mnowel@providence.edu.
Website: http://www.providence.edu/pact/Pages/default.aspx.

Queens College of the City University of New York, Division of Graduate Studies, Division of Education, Department of Secondary Education, Flushing, NY 11367-1597. Offers art (MS Ed); biology (MS Ed, AC); chemistry (MS Ed, AC); earth sciences (MS Ed, AC); English (MS Ed, AC); French (MS Ed, AC); Italian (MS Ed, AC); mathematics (MS Ed, AC); music (MS Ed, AC); physics (MS Ed, AC); social studies (MS Ed, AC); Spanish (MS Ed, AC). Part-time and evening/weekend programs available. *Degree requirements:* For master's, research project; for AC, thesis optional. *Entrance requirements:* For master's, minimum GPA of 3.0. Additional exam requirements/recommendations for international students: Required—TOEFL.

Quinnipiac University, School of Education, Program in Secondary Education, Hamden, CT 06518-1940. Offers biology (MAT); English (MAT); history/social studies (MAT); mathematics (MAT); Spanish (MAT). *Accreditation:* NCATE. *Faculty:* 14 full-time (7 women), 46 part-time/adjunct (27 women). *Students:* 44 full-time (37 women), 1 (woman) part-time; includes 2 minority (both Hispanic/Latino). 45 applicants, 93% accepted, 32 enrolled. In 2013, 32 master's awarded. *Entrance requirements:* For master's, PRAXIS I, minimum GPA of 2.67, interview. *Application deadline:* For fall admission, 4/1 priority date for domestic students. Applications are processed on a rolling basis. Application fee: $45. Electronic applications accepted. *Expenses: Tuition:* Part-time $920 per credit. *Required fees:* $37 per credit. *Financial support:* Career-related internships or fieldwork, tuition waivers (full and partial), and unspecified assistantships available. Support available to part-time students. Financial award application deadline: 6/1; financial award applicants required to submit FAFSA. *Faculty research:* Multicultural and urban education/leadership, challenges of teaching diverse learners, scholarship of teaching and learning, technology and teaching, humor and education. *Unit head:* Mordechai Gordon, Program Director, E-mail: mordechai.gordon@quinnipiac.edu. *Application contact:* Office of Graduate Admissions, 800-462-1944, Fax: 203-582-3443, E-mail: graduate@quinnipiac.edu.
Website: http://www.quinnipiac.edu/gradeducation.

Rhode Island College, School of Graduate Studies, Feinstein School of Education and Human Development, Department of Educational Studies, Providence, RI 02908-1991. Offers advanced studies in teaching and learning (M Ed); English (MAT); French (MAT); history (MAT); math (MAT); secondary education (MAT); Spanish (MAT); teaching English as a second language (M Ed). *Accreditation:* NCATE. Part-time and evening/weekend programs available. *Faculty:* 10 full-time (6 women), 7 part-time/adjunct (all women). *Students:* 4 full-time (3 women), 61 part-time (54 women); includes 2 minority (both Hispanic/Latino). Average age 37. In 2013, 27 master's awarded. *Degree requirements:* For master's, capstone or comprehensive assessment. *Entrance requirements:* For master's, GRE or MAT (for most programs), minimum undergraduate GPA of 3.0; baccalaureate degree in English, French, history, math or Spanish; evaluation of content area knowledge; 3 letters of recommendation; interview. Additional exam requirements/recommendations for international students: Recommended—TOEFL (minimum score 550 paper-based; 79 iBT). *Application deadline:* For fall admission, 3/1 for domestic students; for spring admission, 11/1 for domestic students. Applications are processed on a rolling basis. Application fee: $50. *Expenses:* Tuition, state resident: full-time $8928; part-time $372 per credit hour. Tuition, nonresident: full-time $17,376; part-time $724 per credit hour. *Required fees:* $602; $22 per credit. $72 per term. *Financial support:* In 2013–14, 2 teaching assistantships with full tuition reimbursements (averaging $2,250 per year) were awarded; career-related internships or fieldwork, Federal Work-Study, scholarships/grants, health care benefits, and unspecified assistantships also available. Support available to part-time students. Financial award application deadline: 5/15; financial award applicants required to submit FAFSA. *Faculty research:* School administration, school/college articulation. *Unit head:* Dr. Paul Tiskus, Chair, 401-456-8170. *Application contact:* Graduate Studies, 401-456-8700.
Website: http://www.ric.edu/educationalStudies/.

Roberts Wesleyan College, Department of Teacher Education, Rochester, NY 14624-1997. Offers adolescence education (M Ed); childhood and special education (M Ed); literacy education (M Ed); special education online (M Ed). Part-time and evening/weekend programs available. *Faculty:* 10 full-time (7 women), 12 part-time/adjunct (6 women). *Students:* 37 full-time (29 women), 10 part-time (6 women); includes 16 minority (15 Black or African American, non-Hispanic/Latino; 1 Hispanic/Latino). Average age 33. 72 applicants, 63% accepted, 34 enrolled. In 2013, 20 master's awarded. *Degree requirements:* For master's, thesis. *Application deadline:* For fall admission, 6/1 for domestic and international students; for spring admission, 11/1 for domestic and international students; for summer admission, 3/1 for domestic and international students. Applications are processed on a rolling basis. Electronic applications accepted. Application fee is waived when completed online. *Expenses: Tuition:* Full-time $12,816; part-time $712 per credit hour. One-time fee: $300. Tuition and fees vary according to course load and program. *Financial support:* In 2013–14, 7 students received support. Career-related internships or fieldwork available. Financial award application deadline: 9/1; financial award applicants required to submit FAFSA. *Unit head:* Dr. Sharon Harris-Ewing, Chair, 585-594-6935, E-mail: harrisewing_sharon@roberts.edu. *Application contact:* Paul Ziegler, Director of Marketing and Recruitment for Teacher Education, 585-594-6146, Fax: 585-594-6108, E-mail: ziegler_paul@roberts.edu.
Website: https://www.roberts.edu/department-of-teacher-education.aspx.

Rochester Institute of Technology, Graduate Enrollment Services, National Technical Institute for the Deaf, Department of Research and Teacher Education, Rochester, NY 14623-5603. Offers MS. *Accreditation:* Teacher Education Accreditation Council. *Students:* 40 full-time (29 women), 1 part-time (0 women); includes 3 minority (1 American Indian or Alaska Native, non-Hispanic/Latino; 1 Hispanic/Latino; 1 Two or more races, non-Hispanic/Latino), 5 international. Average age 29. 38 applicants, 42% accepted, 16 enrolled. In 2013, 17 master's awarded. *Degree requirements:* For master's, thesis or alternative. *Entrance requirements:* For master's, minimum GPA of 3.0. Additional exam requirements/recommendations for international students: Required—TOEFL (minimum score 550 paper-based; 79 iBT) or IELTS (minimum score 6.5). *Application deadline:* For fall admission, 2/15 priority date for domestic and international students. Applications are processed on a rolling basis. Application fee: $60. Electronic applications accepted. *Expenses: Tuition:* Full-time $37,236; part-time $1552 per credit hour. *Required fees:* $250. *Financial support:* Fellowships with full and partial tuition reimbursements, research assistantships with partial tuition reimbursements, teaching assistantships with partial tuition reimbursements, career-related internships or fieldwork, institutionally sponsored loans, scholarships/grants, and unspecified assistantships available. Support available to part-time students. Financial award applicants required to submit FAFSA. *Faculty research:* Applied research on the effective use of access and support services to enhance learning for deaf and hard-of-hearing students in the mainstreamed classroom, STEM research and instruction. *Unit head:* Gerald Bateman, Director, 585-475-6480, Fax: 585-475-2525, E-mail: gcbnmp@rit.edu. *Application contact:* Diane Ellison, Assistant Vice President, Graduate Enrollment Services, 585-475-2229, Fax: 585-475-7164, E-mail: gradinfo@rit.edu.
Website: http://www.ntid.rit.edu/research/department/.

Rockford University, Graduate Studies, Department of Education, Program in Secondary Education, Rockford, IL 61108-2393. Offers MAT. Part-time and evening/weekend programs available. *Degree requirements:* For master's, thesis optional. *Entrance requirements:* For master's, GRE General Test, basic skills test (for students seeking certification), 3 letters of recommendation. Additional exam requirements/recommendations for international students: Required—TOEFL (minimum score 550 paper-based; 79 iBT). Electronic applications accepted.

Roosevelt University, Graduate Division, College of Education, Department of Secondary Education, Chicago, IL 60605. Offers MA.

Rowan University, Graduate School, College of Education, Department of Teacher Education, Program in Secondary Education, Glassboro, NJ 08028-1701. Offers MST. *Faculty:* 3 full-time (1 woman), 5 part-time/adjunct (2 women). *Students:* 18 full-time (8 women); includes 1 minority (Asian, non-Hispanic/Latino). Average age 26. In 2013, 10 master's awarded. *Expenses: Tuition, area resident:* Part-time $638 per credit. Tuition, state resident: full-time $5742. *Required fees:* $142 per credit. Tuition and fees vary according to course level and program. *Unit head:* Dr. Horacio Sosa, Dean, College of Graduate and Continuing Education, 856-256-4747, Fax: 856-256-5638, E-mail: sosa@rowan.edu. *Application contact:* Admissions and Enrollment Services, 856-256-5435, Fax: 856-256-5637, E-mail: cgceadmissions@rowan.edu.

Sacred Heart University, Graduate Programs, Isabelle Farrington College of Education, Fairfield, CT 06825-1000. Offers administration (CAS); educational technology (MAT); elementary education (MAT); leadership/literacy (CAS), including literacy; reading (CAS); secondary education (MAT); teaching (CAS). Part-time and evening/weekend programs available. *Faculty:* 23 full-time (13 women), 32 part-time/adjunct (14 women). *Students:* 210 full-time (155 women), 603 part-time (451 women); includes 86 minority (38 Black or African American, non-Hispanic/Latino; 1 American Indian or Alaska Native, non-Hispanic/Latino; 6 Asian, non-Hispanic/Latino; 35 Hispanic/Latino; 6 Two or more races, non-Hispanic/Latino). Average age 35. 278 applicants, 95% accepted, 227 enrolled. In 2013, 262 master's, 72 other advanced degrees awarded. *Degree requirements:* For master's, comprehensive exam (for some programs), thesis (for some programs). *Entrance requirements:* For master's, PRAXIS (teacher certification/MAT), minimum GPA of 2.75; for CAS, PRAXIS I, minimum GPA of 2.75. Additional exam requirements/recommendations for international students: Required—PTE; Recommended—TOEFL (minimum score 570 paper-based; 80 iBT), IELTS (minimum score 6.5). *Application deadline:* Applications are processed on a rolling basis. Application fee: $60. Electronic applications accepted. *Expenses:* Contact institution. *Financial support:* Teaching assistantships with partial tuition reimbursements, career-related internships or fieldwork, institutionally sponsored loans, traineeships, tuition waivers (partial), and unspecified assistantships available. Support available to part-time students. Financial award applicants required to submit FAFSA. *Faculty research:* Reading education, learning theory, teacher preparation, education of underachievers. *Unit head:* Dr. Jim Carl, Dean, 203-396-8454, Fax: 203-365-7513, E-mail: carlj@sacredheart.edu. *Application contact:* Kathy Dilks, Executive Director of Graduate Admissions, 203-365-7619, Fax: 203-365-4732, E-mail: gradstudies@sacredheart.edu.
Website: http://www.sacredheart.edu/academics/isabellefarringtoncollegeofeducation/.

Saginaw Valley State University, College of Education, Program in Natural Science Teaching, University Center, MI 48710. Offers elementary school (MAT); middle school (MAT); secondary school (MAT). *Accreditation:* NCATE. Part-time and evening/weekend programs available. *Students:* 1 (woman) part-time. Average age 43. In 2013, 8 master's awarded. *Degree requirements:* For master's, capstone course. *Entrance requirements:* For master's, minimum GPA of 3.0, teaching certificate. Additional exam requirements/recommendations for international students: Required—TOEFL (minimum score 550 paper-based; 79 iBT). *Application deadline:* For fall admission, 7/15 for international students; for winter admission, 11/15 for international students; for spring admission, 4/15 for international students. Applications are processed on a rolling basis. Application fee: $30 ($80 for international students). Electronic applications accepted. *Expenses:* Tuition, state resident: full-time $8933; part-time $496.30 per credit hour. Tuition, nonresident: full-time $16,806; part-time $933.65 per credit hour. *Required fees:* $263; $14.60 per credit hour. Tuition and fees vary according to degree level. *Financial support:* Federal Work-Study and scholarships/grants available. Support available to part-time students. Financial award applicants required to submit FAFSA. *Unit head:* Dr. Mary Harmon, Dean, 989-964-7107, Fax: 989-964-4563, E-mail: coeconnect@svsu.edu. *Application contact:* Jenna Briggs, Director, Graduate and International Admissions, 989-964-6096, Fax: 989-964-2788, E-mail: gradadm@svsu.edu.

Saginaw Valley State University, College of Education, Program in Secondary Classroom Teaching, University Center, MI 48710. Offers MAT. *Accreditation:* NCATE. Part-time and evening/weekend programs available. *Students:* 15 part-time (8 women); includes 2 minority (1 Black or African American, non-Hispanic/Latino; 1 Hispanic/Latino). Average age 33. In 2013, 12 master's awarded. *Degree requirements:* For master's, capstone course. *Entrance requirements:* For master's, minimum GPA of 3.0, teaching certificate. Additional exam requirements/recommendations for international students: Required—TOEFL (minimum score 550 paper-based; 79 iBT). *Application deadline:* For fall admission, 7/15 for international students; for winter admission, 11/15 for international students; for spring admission, 4/15 for international students. Applications are processed on a rolling basis. Application fee: $30 ($80 for international students). Electronic applications accepted. *Expenses:* Tuition, state resident: full-time $8933; part-time $496.30 per credit hour. Tuition, nonresident: full-time $16,806; part-time $933.65 per credit hour. *Required fees:* $263; $14.60 per credit hour. Tuition and fees vary according to degree level. *Financial support:* Federal Work-Study and scholarships/grants available. Support available to part-time students. Financial award applicants required to submit FAFSA. *Unit head:* Dr. Mary Harmon, Dean, 989-964-7107, Fax: 989-964-4563, E-mail: coeconnect@svsu.edu. *Application contact:* Jenna Briggs, Director, Graduate and International Admissions, 989-964-6096, Fax: 989-964-2788, E-mail: gradadm@svsu.edu.

St. Bonaventure University, School of Graduate Studies, School of Education, Literacy Programs, St. Bonaventure, NY 14778-2284. Offers adolescent literacy 5-12 (MS Ed); childhood literacy B-6 (MS Ed). Program offered in Olean and Buffalo Center (Hamburg, NY). *Accreditation:* NCATE. Part-time and evening/weekend programs available. *Faculty:* 2 full-time (both women), 1 (woman) part-time/adjunct. *Students:* 14 full-time (13 women), 14 part-time (13 women). Average age 29. 19 applicants, 100% accepted, 13 enrolled. In 2013, 27 master's awarded. *Degree requirements:* For master's,

Secondary Education

comprehensive exam, thesis optional, literacy coaching internship, portfolio. *Entrance requirements:* For master's, interview, writing sample, minimum undergraduate GPA of 3.0, two letters of recommendation, teaching certificate in matching area, transcripts. Additional exam requirements/recommendations for international students: Required—TOEFL (minimum score 550 paper-based; 80 iBT). *Application deadline:* For fall admission, 6/15 priority date for domestic students, 2/1 for international students; for spring admission, 11/15 priority date for domestic students, 7/1 for international students. Applications are processed on a rolling basis. Application fee: $0. Electronic applications accepted. *Financial support:* In 2013–14, 4 research assistantships with full and partial tuition reimbursements were awarded; Federal Work-Study, scholarships/grants, health care benefits, and unspecified assistantships also available. Support available to part-time students. Financial award application deadline: 4/15; financial award applicants required to submit FAFSA. *Unit head:* Dr. Karen M. Wieland, Program Director, 716-375-2369, Fax: 716-375-2360, E-mail: kwieland@sbu.edu. *Application contact:* Bruce Campbell, Director of Graduate Admissions, 716-375-2429, Fax: 716-375-4015, E-mail: gradsch@sbu.edu.
Website: http://www.sbu.edu/academics/schools/education/graduate-degrees-certificates/msed-in-childhood-literacy.

St. John's University, The School of Education, Department of Curriculum and Instruction, Program in Adolescent Education, Queens, NY 11439. Offers MS Ed, Certificate. Part-time and evening/weekend programs available. *Students:* 28 full-time (10 women), 214 part-time (132 women); includes 91 minority (34 Black or African American, non-Hispanic/Latino; 17 Asian, non-Hispanic/Latino; 36 Hispanic/Latino; 4 Two or more races, non-Hispanic/Latino), 2 international. Average age 29. 99 applicants, 91% accepted, 57 enrolled. In 2013, 89 master's awarded. *Degree requirements:* For master's, variable foreign language requirement, comprehensive exam. *Entrance requirements:* For master's, minimum GPA of 3.0, 2 letters of recommendation, qualification for the New York State provisional (initial) teaching certificate, transcript, personal statement. Additional exam requirements/recommendations for international students: Required—TOEFL (minimum score 600 paper-based; 100 iBT), IELTS (minimum score 5.5). *Application deadline:* For fall admission, 8/17 for domestic students, 5/1 priority date for international students; for spring admission, 1/5 for domestic students, 11/1 priority date for international students. Applications are processed on a rolling basis. Application fee: $70. Electronic applications accepted. *Expenses: Tuition:* Full-time $19,800; part-time $1100 per credit. *Required fees:* $170 per semester. *Financial support:* Research assistantships, career-related internships or fieldwork, and scholarships/grants available. Support available to part-time students. Financial award application deadline: 3/1; financial award applicants required to submit FAFSA. *Faculty research:* Investigating self-efficacy in literacy learning, using problem solving as an approach for math learning. *Unit head:* Dr. Judith McVarish, Chair, 718-990-2334, E-mail: mcvarisj@stjohns.edu. *Application contact:* Dr. Kelly K. Ronayne, Associate Dean for Graduate Admissions, 718-990-2304, Fax: 718-990-2343, E-mail: graded@stjohns.edu.

Saint Joseph's University, College of Arts and Sciences, Department of Education, Philadelphia, PA 19131-1395. Offers curriculum supervisor (Certificate); educational leadership (MS, Ed D); elementary education (MS, Certificate); elementary/middle school education (Certificate); instructional technology (MS, Certificate); principal certification (Certificate); professional education (MS); reading specialist (MS, Certificate); reading supervisor (Certificate); secondary education (MS, Certificate); special education (MS, Certificate); superintendent's letter of eligibility (Certificate); supervisor of special education (Certificate). Part-time and evening/weekend programs available. Postbaccalaureate distance learning degree programs offered (no on-campus study). *Faculty:* 32 full-time (25 women), 75 part-time/adjunct (53 women). *Students:* 91 full-time (81 women), 858 part-time (656 women); includes 133 minority (96 Black or African American, non-Hispanic/Latino; 3 American Indian or Alaska Native, non-Hispanic/Latino; 9 Asian, non-Hispanic/Latino; 20 Hispanic/Latino; 5 Native Hawaiian or other Pacific Islander, non-Hispanic/Latino), 16 international. Average age 31. 359 applicants, 77% accepted, 203 enrolled. In 2013, 363 master's, 9 doctorates, 1 other advanced degree awarded. *Entrance requirements:* For master's, 2 letters of recommendation, minimum GPA of 3.0, official transcripts, personal statement; for doctorate, GRE, master's degree from accredited institution, minimum graduate GPA of 3.5, computer competence, commitment to participate in cohort, interview with program director. Additional exam requirements/recommendations for international students: Required—TOEFL (minimum score 550 paper-based; 79 iBT), IELTS (minimum score 6.5). *Application deadline:* For fall admission, 7/15 priority date for domestic students, 4/15 for international students; for winter admission, 11/15 for domestic students, 1/15 for international students; for spring admission, 11/15 priority date for domestic students, 10/15 for international students. Applications are processed on a rolling basis. Application fee: $35. Electronic applications accepted. *Expenses:* Contact institution. *Financial support:* Unspecified assistantships available. Financial award applicants required to submit FAFSA. *Faculty research:* Factors predicting early mathematics skills for low income children, early child care and development, preschool quality. *Total annual research expenditures:* $229,264. *Unit head:* Dr. John Vacca, Associate Dean, Education, 610-660-3131, E-mail: gradstudies@sju.edu. *Application contact:* Elisabeth Woodward, Director of Marketing and Admissions, Graduate Arts and Sciences, 610-660-3131, Fax: 610-660-3230, E-mail: gradstudies@sju.edu.
Website: http://sju.edu/int/academics/cas/grad/education/index.html.

Saint Mary's University of Minnesota, Schools of Graduate and Professional Programs, Graduate School of Education, Instruction Program, Winona, MN 55987-1399. Offers MA, Certificate. *Unit head:* Kellie Schmitz, Director, 507-457-6619, E-mail: kschmitz@smumn.edu. *Application contact:* Russell Kreager, Director of Admissions for Graduate and Professional Programs, 612-728-5207, Fax: 612-728-5121, E-mail: rkreager@smumn.edu.
Website: http://www.smumn.edu/graduate-home/areas-of-study/graduate-school-of-education/ma-in-instruction.

Saint Peter's University, Graduate Programs in Education, Program in Teaching, Jersey City, NJ 07306-5997. Offers 6-8 middle school education (MA Ed, Certificate); K-12 secondary education (MA Ed, Certificate); K-5 elementary education (MA Ed, Certificate). Part-time and evening/weekend programs available. *Degree requirements:* For master's, comprehensive exam. *Entrance requirements:* For master's, GRE or MAT. Additional exam requirements/recommendations for international students: Required—TOEFL. Electronic applications accepted.

St. Thomas Aquinas College, Division of Teacher Education, Sparkill, NY 10976. Offers adolescence education (MST); childhood and special education (MST); childhood education (MST); educational leadership (MS Ed); reading (MS Ed, PMC); special education (MS Ed, PMC); teaching (MS Ed), including elementary education, middle school education, secondary education. *Accreditation:* NCATE. Part-time and evening/weekend programs available. *Degree requirements:* For master's, comprehensive exam, comprehensive professional portfolio; for PMC, action research project. *Entrance requirements:* For master's, New York State Qualifying Exam, GRE General Test or minimum GPA of 3.0, teaching certificate; for PMC, GRE General Test or minimum GPA of 3.0. Electronic applications accepted. *Faculty research:* Computer applications in

education, adolescent special education students, literacy development, inclusive practices for special education students.

Saint Xavier University, Graduate Studies, School of Education, Chicago, IL 60655-3105. Offers counseling (MA); curriculum and instruction (MA); early childhood education (MA); educational administration (MA); elementary education (MA); individualized studies (MA), including educational technology, English as a second language (ESL), ISTEM (integrative science, technology, engineering, and math), science education; music education (MA); reading (MA); secondary education (MA); Spanish education (MA); special education (MA); teaching and leadership (MA). *Accreditation:* NCATE. Part-time and evening/weekend programs available. *Degree requirements:* For master's, thesis or project. *Entrance requirements:* For master's, minimum GPA of 3.0. *Expenses:* Contact institution.

Salem College, Department of Education, Winston-Salem, NC 27101. Offers art education (MAT); elementary education (M Ed, MAT); language and literacy (M Ed); middle school education (MAT); school counseling (M Ed); second language studies (MAT); secondary education (MAT); special education (M Ed, MAT). *Accreditation:* NCATE. Part-time and evening/weekend programs available. Postbaccalaureate distance learning degree programs offered (minimal on-campus study). *Degree requirements:* For master's, practicum (MAT), project (M Ed), oral and written comprehensive exams. *Entrance requirements:* For master's, minimum GPA of 2.5. *Faculty research:* Content area reading strategies, literacy development, brain compatible instruction.

Salem State University, School of Graduate Studies, Program in Secondary Education, Salem, MA 01970-5353. Offers M Ed. Part-time and evening/weekend programs available. *Students:* 8 part-time (4 women). 1 applicant, 100% accepted, 1 enrolled. In 2013, 7 master's awarded. *Entrance requirements:* For master's, GRE or MAT. Additional exam requirements/recommendations for international students: Required—TOEFL (minimum score 550 paper-based; 80 iBT) or IELTS (minimum score 5.5). *Application deadline:* For fall admission, 5/1 for domestic students; for spring admission, 10/1 for domestic students. Applications are processed on a rolling basis. Application fee: $50. *Financial support:* Career-related internships or fieldwork, Federal Work-Study, scholarships/grants, and unspecified assistantships available. Support available to part-time students. Financial award application deadline: 5/1; financial award applicants required to submit FAFSA. *Application contact:* Dr. Lee A. Brossoit, Assistant Dean of Graduate Admissions, 978-542-6675, Fax: 978-542-7215, E-mail: lbrossoit@salemstate.edu.
Website: http://www.salemstate.edu/academics/schools/1619.php.

Salem State University, School of Graduate Studies, Program in Spanish, Salem, MA 01970-5353. Offers MAT. Part-time and evening/weekend programs available. *Students:* 2 full-time (1 woman), 17 part-time (15 women); includes 6 minority (all Hispanic/Latino). 2 applicants, 50% accepted, 1 enrolled. In 2013, 6 master's awarded. *Entrance requirements:* For master's, GRE or MAT. Additional exam requirements/recommendations for international students: Required—TOEFL (minimum score 550 paper-based; 80 iBT) or IELTS (minimum score 5.5). *Application deadline:* For fall admission, 5/1 for domestic students; for spring admission, 10/1 for domestic students. Applications are processed on a rolling basis. Application fee: $50. *Financial support:* Career-related internships or fieldwork, Federal Work-Study, scholarships/grants, and unspecified assistantships available. Support available to part-time students. Financial award application deadline: 5/1; financial award applicants required to submit FAFSA. *Application contact:* Dr. Lee A. Brossoit, Assistant Dean of Graduate Admissions, 978-542-6675, Fax: 978-542-7215, E-mail: lbrossoit@salemstate.edu.
Website: http://www.salemstate.edu/academics/schools/6646.php.

Salisbury University, Department of Education Specialties, Program in Secondary Education, Salisbury, MD 21801-6837. Offers MAT. Part-time programs available. *Faculty:* 7 full-time (3 women), 3 part-time/adjunct (1 woman). *Students:* 10 full-time (6 women), 19 part-time (14 women); includes 2 minority (1 Black or African American, non-Hispanic/Latino; 1 Two or more races, non-Hispanic/Latino), 1 international. Average age 30. 3 applicants. In 2013, 17 master's awarded. *Degree requirements:* For master's, comprehensive exam. *Entrance requirements:* For master's, PRAXIS I or Maryland State Department of Education equivalent, minimum undergraduate GPA of 3.0 or prior graduate degree, 3 recommendations, interview, written approval from content major advisor and education advisor, completion of prerequisite courses with minimum C grade. Additional exam requirements/recommendations for international students: Required—TOEFL (minimum score 550 paper-based; 79 iBT), IELTS (minimum score 6.5). *Application deadline:* For fall admission, 10/1 for domestic and international students; for winter admission, 10/1 for domestic students. Application fee: $50. Electronic applications accepted. *Expenses: Tuition, area resident:* Part-time $342 per credit hour. Tuition, state resident: part-time $342 per credit hour. Tuition, nonresident: part-time $631 per credit hour. *Required fees:* $76 per credit hour. Tuition and fees vary according to program. *Financial support:* In 2013–14, 1 student received support, including 2 teaching assistantships with full tuition reimbursements available (averaging $5,750 per year); career-related internships or fieldwork, institutionally sponsored loans, scholarships/grants, and unspecified assistantships also available. Support available to part-time students. Financial award application deadline: 3/1; financial award applicants required to submit FAFSA. *Faculty research:* Online learning, mobile technology. *Unit head:* Dr. Nancy Michelson, Chair of Department of Education Specialties, 410-544-2430, E-mail: nlmichelson@salisbury.edu. *Application contact:* Claire Williams, Program Management Specialist, 410-543-622, E-mail: clwilliams@salisbury.edu.
Website: http://www.salisbury.edu/educationspecialties/secondary.html.

Samford University, Orlean Bullard Beeson School of Education, Birmingham, AL 35229. Offers early childhood/elementary education (MS Ed); educational leadership (MS Ed, Ed D); gifted education (MS Ed); instructional leadership (MS Ed, Ed S); secondary collaboration (MS Ed); M Div/MS Ed. *Accreditation:* NCATE. Part-time and evening/weekend programs available. *Faculty:* 10 full-time (5 women), 16 part-time/adjunct (15 women). *Students:* 40 full-time (25 women), 210 part-time (156 women); includes 39 minority (33 Black or African American, non-Hispanic/Latino; 3 American Indian or Alaska Native, non-Hispanic/Latino; 2 Asian, non-Hispanic/Latino; 1 Hispanic/Latino), 4 international. Average age 38. 81 applicants, 89% accepted, 70 enrolled. In 2013, 94 master's, 21 doctorates, 16 other advanced degrees awarded. *Degree requirements:* For master's and Ed S, comprehensive exam; for doctorate, comprehensive exam, thesis/dissertation. *Entrance requirements:* For master's, GRE (minimum score of 295) or MAT (minimum score of 396); waived if previously completed a graduate degree, writing sample, statement of purpose, 3 letters of recommendation, 2 original copies of all transcripts, minimum GPA of 2.75, teaching certificate; for doctorate, minimum GPA of 3.7, professional resume, writing sample, 3 letters of recommendation, 1 original copy of all transcripts; for Ed S, master's degree, teaching certificate, minimum GPA of 3.25, 3 letters of recommendation, 2 original copies of all transcripts, writing sample, statement of purpose. Additional exam requirements/recommendations for international students: Required—TOEFL (minimum score 90 iBT), IELTS (minimum score 7). *Application deadline:* For fall admission, 7/30 for domestic and international students; for winter admission, 4/5 for domestic students; for spring admission, 12/5 for domestic and international students; for summer admission,

4/18 for domestic and international students. Applications are processed on a rolling basis. Application fee: $35. Electronic applications accepted. *Expenses: Tuition:* Full-time $11,552; part-time $722 per credit. *Required fees:* $500; $250 per term. *Financial support:* In 2013–14, 162 students received support. Research assistantships, career-related internships or fieldwork, Federal Work-Study, scholarships/grants, and tuition waivers (partial) available. Support available to part-time students. Financial award applicants required to submit FAFSA. *Faculty research:* Research on gifted/high ability students (K-12), school law, the characteristics of beginning teachers, the nature of school reform, school culture, quality improvement in education, K-12 student achievement, reading research, classroom management, reading intervention, schema theory. *Unit head:* Dr. Maurice Persall, Chair, Department of Educational Leadership, 205-726-2019, E-mail: jmpersal@samford.edu. *Application contact:* Brooke Gilreath Karr, Graduate Admissions Coordinator, 205-729-2783, Fax: 205-726-4233, E-mail: kbgilrea@samford.edu.
Website: http://www.samford.edu/education/.

San Diego State University, Graduate and Research Affairs, College of Education, School of Teacher Education, Program in Secondary Curriculum and Instruction, San Diego, CA 92182. Offers MA. *Accreditation:* NCATE. *Entrance requirements:* For master's, GRE General Test, letters of reference. Additional exam requirements/recommendations for international students: Required—TOEFL. Electronic applications accepted.

San Francisco State University, Division of Graduate Studies, College of Education, Department of Secondary Education, San Francisco, CA 94132-1722. Offers MA. *Accreditation:* NCATE. *Unit head:* Dr. Nathan Avani, Chair and Graduate Coordinator, 415-338-7649, E-mail: natalio@sfsu.edu. *Application contact:* Gary Gin, Assistant to the Chair, 415-338-1201, E-mail: ggin@sfsu.edu.
Website: http://coe.sfsu.edu/sed.

San Jose State University, Graduate Studies and Research, Connie L. Lurie College of Education, Department of Secondary Education, San Jose, CA 95192-0001. Offers Certificate. *Accreditation:* NCATE. Evening/weekend programs available. Electronic applications accepted.

Seattle Pacific University, Master of Arts in Teaching Program, Seattle, WA 98119-1997. Offers MAT. *Accreditation:* NCATE. Part-time and evening/weekend programs available. *Students:* 77 full-time (23 women), 64 part-time (16 women); includes 17 minority (2 Black or African American, non-Hispanic/Latino; 8 Asian, non-Hispanic/Latino; 6 Hispanic/Latino; 1 Two or more races, non-Hispanic/Latino). Average age 30. 88 applicants, 45% accepted, 40 enrolled. In 2013, 73 master's awarded. *Degree requirements:* For master's, field experience, internship. *Entrance requirements:* For master's, GRE or MAT, WEST-B, WEST-E, official transcript(s) from each college/university attended, resume, personal statement (one to two pages), two to four letters of recommendation, endorsement verification form, moral character and personal fitness policy form. *Application deadline:* For fall admission, 3/15 for domestic students. Application fee: $50. Electronic applications accepted. *Expenses:* Contact institution. *Financial support:* Scholarships/grants available. Financial award applicants required to submit FAFSA. *Unit head:* Dr. David W. Denton, Chair, 206-281-2504, Fax: 206-281-2756, E-mail: dentod@spu.edu. *Application contact:* The Graduate Center, 206-281-2091.
Website: http://spu.edu/academics/school-of-education/graduate-programs/masters-programs/masters-of-arts-in-teaching.

Siena Heights University, Graduate College, Adrian, MI 49221-1796. Offers clinical mental health counseling (MA); education leadership (Specialist); leadership (MA), including health care, higher education leadership, organizational; teacher education (MA), including early childhood, early childhood: Montessori-based, education leadership: principal, elementary education, K-12 reading, leadership: higher education, secondary education, K-12 reading, special education, K-12 cognitive impairment, special education, K-12 learning disabled. Part-time and evening/weekend programs available. *Faculty:* 37. *Students:* 9 full-time (7 women), 251 part-time (179 women). In 2013, 32 master's awarded. *Degree requirements:* For master's, thesis, presentation. *Entrance requirements:* For master's, minimum GPA of 3.0, current resume, essay, all post-secondary transcripts, 3 letters of reference, conviction disclosure form; copy of teaching certificate (for some education programs); for Specialist, master's degree, minimum GPA of 3.0, current resume, essay, all post-secondary transcripts, 3 letters of reference, conviction disclosure form; copy of teaching certificate (for some education programs). *Application deadline:* Applications are processed on a rolling basis. Application fee: $50. *Expenses: Tuition:* Part-time $535 per semester hour. *Required fees:* $130 per semester. *Financial support:* Career-related internships or fieldwork, Federal Work-Study, and resident assistantships available. Financial award application deadline: 9/1; financial award applicants required to submit FAFSA. *Unit head:* Dr. Linda S. Pettit, Dean, Graduate College, 517-264-7661, Fax: 517-264-7714, E-mail: lpettit@sienahts.edu.
Website: http://www.sienaheights.edu.

Sierra Nevada College, Teacher Education Program, Incline Village, NV 89451. Offers advanced teaching and leadership (M Ed); elementary education (MAT); secondary education (MAT). Part-time and evening/weekend programs available. Postbaccalaureate distance learning degree programs offered (minimal on-campus study). *Degree requirements:* For master's, comprehensive exam, thesis, PRAXIS I and II. *Entrance requirements:* For master's, 2 letters of recommendation, minimum GPA of 3.0. Electronic applications accepted.

Simmons College, School of Social Work, Boston, MA 02115. Offers assistive technology (MS Ed, Ed S); behavior analysis (MS, PhD, Ed S); education (MA, CAGS); language and literacy (MS Ed, Ed S); social work (MSW, PhD); special education (MS Ed), including moderate disabilities, severe disabilities; teaching (MAT), including elementary education, general education, high school education; teaching English as a second language (MA, CAGS); urban leadership (MSW); MSW/MBA. *Accreditation:* CSWE (one or more programs are accredited). Part-time programs available. Postbaccalaureate distance learning degree programs offered (no on-campus study). *Students:* 519 full-time (454 women), 703 part-time (604 women); includes 192 minority (61 Black or African American, non-Hispanic/Latino; 1 American Indian or Alaska Native, non-Hispanic/Latino; 35 Asian, non-Hispanic/Latino; 71 Hispanic/Latino; 2 Native Hawaiian or other Pacific Islander, non-Hispanic/Latino; 22 Two or more races, non-Hispanic/Latino), 16 international. 952 applicants, 66% accepted, 353 enrolled. In 2013, 159 master's, 2 doctorates awarded. Terminal master's awarded for partial completion of doctoral program. *Degree requirements:* For master's, thesis (for some programs); for doctorate, comprehensive exam (for some programs), thesis/dissertation (for some programs). *Entrance requirements:* For master's, GRE, MAT, MTEL (for different programs); for doctorate, GRE, BCBA Analyst Exam. Additional exam requirements/recommendations for international students: Required—TOEFL (minimum score 600 paper-based; 100 iBT). *Application deadline:* Applications are processed on a rolling basis. Application fee: $45. Electronic applications accepted. *Financial support:* Teaching assistantships and scholarships/grants available. *Unit head:* Dr. Stefan Krug, Dean, 617-521-3924. *Application contact:* Carlos D. Frontado, Director of Admissions, 617-521-3920, Fax: 617-521-3980, E-mail: ssw@simmons.edu.
Website: http://www.simmons.edu/ssw/.

Simpson College, Department of Education, Indianola, IA 50125-1297. Offers secondary education (MAT). *Degree requirements:* For master's, PRAXIS II, electronic portfolio. *Entrance requirements:* For master's, bachelor's degree; minimum cumulative GPA of 2.75, 3.0 in major; 3 letters of recommendation.

Slippery Rock University of Pennsylvania, Graduate Studies (Recruitment), College of Education, Department of Secondary Education/Foundations of Education, Slippery Rock, PA 16057-1383. Offers educational leadership (M Ed); secondary education (M Ed), including English, math/science, social studies/history. *Accreditation:* NCATE. Part-time and evening/weekend programs available. *Faculty:* 12 full-time (5 women). *Students:* 48 full-time (24 women), 10 part-time (6 women). Average age 27. 50 applicants, 84% accepted, 29 enrolled. In 2013, 28 master's awarded. *Degree requirements:* For master's, comprehensive exam, thesis (for some programs). *Entrance requirements:* For master's, GRE General Test, MAT, minimum GPA of 2.8 or 3.0 (depending on program); copy of teaching certification and two letters of recommendation (for some programs). Additional exam requirements/recommendations for international students: Required—TOEFL (minimum score 550 paper-based; 80 iBT). *Application deadline:* For fall admission, 3/1 priority date for domestic students, 5/1 priority date for international students; for spring admission, 10/1 priority date for domestic students, 9/1 priority date for international students. Applications are processed on a rolling basis. Application fee: $25 ($30 for international students). Electronic applications accepted. *Expenses:* Tuition, state resident: full-time $7956; part-time $442 per credit. Tuition, nonresident: full-time $11,934; part-time $663 per credit. *Required fees:* $2896; $148 per credit. Tuition and fees vary according to degree level and program. *Financial support:* Career-related internships or fieldwork, Federal Work-Study, institutionally sponsored loans, scholarships/grants, tuition waivers (partial), and unspecified assistantships available. Support available to part-time students. Financial award application deadline: 5/1; financial award applicants required to submit FAFSA. *Unit head:* Dr. Jeffrey Lehman, Graduate Coordinator, 724-738-2311, Fax: 724-738-4987, E-mail: jeffrey.lehman@sru.edu. *Application contact:* Brandi Weber-Mortimer, Interim Director of Graduate Studies, 724-738-2051, Fax: 724-738-2146, E-mail: graduate.admissions@sru.edu.

Smith College, Graduate and Special Programs, Department of Education and Child Study, Program in Secondary Education, Northampton, MA 01063. Offers biological sciences education (MAT); chemistry education (MAT); English education (MAT); French education (MAT); geology education (MAT); government education (MAT); history education (MAT); mathematics education (MAT); physics education (MAT); Spanish education (MAT). Part-time programs available. *Faculty:* 6 full-time (4 women), 3 part-time/adjunct (2 women). *Students:* 4 full-time (3 women), 1 (woman) part-time, 2 international. Average age 33. 12 applicants, 92% accepted, 4 enrolled. In 2013, 6 master's awarded. *Entrance requirements:* Additional exam requirements/recommendations for international students: Required—TOEFL (minimum score 595 paper-based; 97 iBT). *Application deadline:* For fall admission, 4/1 for domestic students, 1/15 priority date for international students; for spring admission, 12/1 for domestic students. Application fee: $60. *Expenses: Tuition:* Full-time $32,160; part-time $1340 per credit. *Financial support:* In 2013–14, 5 students received support, including 2 fellowships with full tuition reimbursements available; career-related internships or fieldwork, institutionally sponsored loans, and scholarships/grants also available. Support available to part-time students. Financial award application deadline: 1/15; financial award applicants required to submit CSS PROFILE or FAFSA. *Unit head:* Rosetta Cohen, Graduate Student Advisor, 413-585-3266, E-mail: rcohen@smith.edu. *Application contact:* Ruth Morgan, Administrative Assistant, 413-585-3050, Fax: 413-585-3054, E-mail: gradstdy@smith.edu.
Website: http://www.smith.edu/educ/.

South Carolina State University, School of Graduate and Professional Studies, Department of Education, Orangeburg, SC 29117-0001. Offers early childhood and special education (M Ed); early childhood education (MAT); elementary education (M Ed, MAT); general science (MAT); mathematics (MAT); secondary education (M Ed), including biology education, business education, counselor education, English education, home economics education, industrial education, mathematics education, science education, social studies education; special education (M Ed), including emotionally handicapped, learning disabilities, mentally handicapped. *Accreditation:* NCATE. Part-time and evening/weekend programs available. *Faculty:* 9 full-time (3 women), 4 part-time/adjunct (3 women). *Students:* 32 full-time (26 women), 33 part-time (26 women); includes 63 minority (61 Black or African American, non-Hispanic/Latino; 2 Asian, non-Hispanic/Latino). Average age 31. 21 applicants, 100% accepted, 21 enrolled. In 2013, 15 master's awarded. *Degree requirements:* For master's, thesis optional, departmental qualifying exam. *Entrance requirements:* For master's, GRE General Test, NTE, interview, teaching certificate. *Application deadline:* For fall admission, 6/15 priority date for domestic students, 6/15 for international students; for spring admission, 11/1 for domestic and international students. Applications are processed on a rolling basis. Application fee: $25. Electronic applications accepted. *Expenses:* Tuition, state resident: full-time $8906; part-time $543 per credit hour. Tuition, nonresident: full-time $18,040; part-time $1051 per credit hour. *Financial support:* Fellowships, career-related internships or fieldwork, Federal Work-Study, and institutionally sponsored loans available. Financial award application deadline: 6/1. *Faculty research:* Critical thinking, child abuse, stress, test-taking skills, conflict resolution, mainstreaming. *Unit head:* Dr. Margaret Evelyn Fields, Interim Chair, 803-536-7098, Fax: 803-516-4568, E-mail: efields@scsu.edu. *Application contact:* Curtis Foskey, Coordinator of Graduate Studies, 803-536-8419, Fax: 803-536-8812, E-mail: cfoskey@scsu.edu.

Southeast Missouri State University, School of Graduate Studies, Department of Educational Leadership and Counseling, Program in Educational Administration, Cape Girardeau, MO 63701-4799. Offers educational administration (Ed S); educational leadership development (Ed S); elementary administration and supervision (MA); higher education administration (MA); school administration (MA); secondary administration and supervision (MA); teacher leadership (MA). *Accreditation:* NCATE. Part-time and evening/weekend programs available. *Faculty:* 6 full-time (3 women), 4 part-time/adjunct (1 woman). *Students:* 48 full-time (27 women), 181 part-time (118 women); includes 18 minority (11 Black or African American, non-Hispanic/Latino; 1 American Indian or Alaska Native, non-Hispanic/Latino; 2 Asian, non-Hispanic/Latino; 3 Hispanic/Latino; 1 Two or more races, non-Hispanic/Latino), 2 international. Average age 34. 83 applicants, 100% accepted, 83 enrolled. In 2013, 88 master's, 28 other advanced degrees awarded. *Degree requirements:* For master's and Ed S, comprehensive exam, thesis or alternative, paper. *Entrance requirements:* For master's, minimum undergraduate GPA of 2.75, valid teacher certification; for Ed S, minimum graduate GPA of 3.5; master's degree; valid teaching certificate. Additional exam requirements/recommendations for international students: Required—TOEFL (minimum score 550 paper-based; 79 iBT), IELTS (minimum score 6), PTE (minimum score 53). *Application deadline:* For fall admission, 8/1 for domestic students, 6/1 for international students; for spring admission, 11/21 for domestic students, 10/1 for international students; for summer admission, 5/15 for domestic students. Applications are processed on a rolling basis. Application fee: $30 ($40 for international students). Electronic applications accepted. *Expenses:* Tuition, state resident: full-time $5139; part-time $285.50 per credit hour. Tuition, nonresident: full-time $9099; part-time $505.50 per credit hour.

Financial support: In 2013–14, 25 students received support. Career-related internships or fieldwork, Federal Work-Study, scholarships/grants, traineeships, tuition waivers (full), and unspecified assistantships available. Financial award application deadline: 6/30; financial award applicants required to submit FAFSA. *Faculty research:* Learning and the technology push, administration and student success, ethics of leaders. *Unit head:* Dr. Ruth Ann Williams, Professor/Interim Chair, Department of Educational Leadership and Counseling, 573-651-2417, E-mail: raroberts@semo.edu. *Application contact:* Alisa Aleen McFerron, Assistant Director of Admissions for Operations, 573-651-5937, E-mail: amcferron@semo.edu.
Website: http://www4.semo.edu/edadmin/admin.

Southeast Missouri State University, School of Graduate Studies, Department of Middle and Secondary Education, Cape Girardeau, MO 63701-4799. Offers secondary education (MA), including education studies, education technology. *Accreditation:* NCATE. Part-time programs available. *Faculty:* 5 full-time (3 women), 1 (woman) part-time/adjunct. *Students:* 6 full-time (4 women), 42 part-time (30 women); includes 4 minority (all Black or African American, non-Hispanic/Latino). Average age 30. 28 applicants, 100% accepted, 28 enrolled. In 2013, 8 master's awarded. *Degree requirements:* For master's, comprehensive exam, research paper. *Entrance requirements:* For master's, minimum undergraduate GPA of 2.75. Additional exam requirements/recommendations for international students: Required—TOEFL (minimum score 550 paper-based; 79 iBT), IELTS (minimum score 6), PTE (minimum score 53). *Application deadline:* For fall admission, 8/1 for domestic students, 6/1 for international students; for spring admission, 11/21 for domestic students, 10/1 for international students; for summer admission, 5/15 for domestic students. Applications are processed on a rolling basis. Application fee: $30 ($40 for international students). Electronic applications accepted. *Expenses:* Tuition, state resident: full-time $5139; part-time $285.50 per credit hour. Tuition, nonresident: full-time $9099; part-time $505.50 per credit hour. *Financial support:* In 2013–14, 7 students received support. Career-related internships or fieldwork, Federal Work-Study, scholarships/grants, traineeships, tuition waivers (full), and unspecified assistantships available. Financial award application deadline: 6/30; financial award applicants required to submit FAFSA. *Faculty research:* Pedagogy of teaching, multicultural education, reading and writing strategies, use of technology in the classroom. *Unit head:* Dr. Simin L. Cwick, Middle and Secondary Education Department Chair, 573-651-5965, E-mail: scwick@semo.edu. *Application contact:* Alisa Aleen McFerron, Assistant Director of Admissions for Operations, 573-651-5937, E-mail: amcferron@semo.edu.
Website: http://www5.semo.edu/middleandsec/.

Southern Arkansas University–Magnolia, Graduate Programs, Magnolia, AR 71753. Offers agriculture (MS); business administration (MBA); computer and information sciences (MS); education (M Ed), including counseling and development, curriculum and instruction, educational administration and supervision, elementary education, reading, secondary education, TESOL; kinesiology (M Ed); library media and information specialist (M Ed); mental health and clinical counseling (MS); public administration (MPA); school counseling (M Ed); teaching (MAT). *Accreditation:* NCATE. Part-time and evening/weekend programs available. Postbaccalaureate distance learning degree programs offered. *Faculty:* 34 full-time (15 women), 8 part-time/adjunct (5 women). *Students:* 48 full-time (22 women), 269 part-time (167 women); includes 85 minority (78 Black or African American, non-Hispanic/Latino; 2 Asian, non-Hispanic/Latino; 2 Hispanic/Latino; 1 Native Hawaiian or other Pacific Islander, non-Hispanic/Latino; 2 Two or more races, non-Hispanic/Latino), 5 international. Average age 33. 149 applicants, 73% accepted, 109 enrolled. In 2013, 149 master's awarded. *Degree requirements:* For master's, comprehensive exam (for some programs), thesis optional. *Entrance requirements:* For master's, GRE, MAT or GMAT, minimum GPA of 2.5. Additional exam requirements/recommendations for international students: Required—TOEFL, IELTS. *Application deadline:* For fall admission, 7/10 for domestic and international students; for winter admission, 12/1 for domestic and international students; for spring admission, 12/1 for domestic and international students; for summer admission, 4/1 for domestic students. Applications are processed on a rolling basis. Application fee: $25 ($50 for international students). Electronic applications accepted. *Expenses:* Tuition, state resident: part-time $254 per credit hour. Tuition, nonresident: part-time $370 per credit hour. *Required fees:* $136 per credit hour. $259 per semester. Tuition and fees vary according to course load and program. *Financial support:* Career-related internships or fieldwork, Federal Work-Study, scholarships/grants, tuition waivers (full), and unspecified assistantships available. Financial award applicants required to submit FAFSA. *Faculty research:* Alternative certification for teachers, supervision of instruction, instructional leadership, counseling. *Unit head:* Dr. Kim Bloss, Dean, School of Graduate Studies, 870-235-4150, Fax: 870-235-5227, E-mail: kkbloss@saumag.edu. *Application contact:* Shrijana Malaka, Admissions Specialist, 870-235-4150, Fax: 870-235-5227, E-mail: smalakar@saumag.edu.
Website: http://www.saumag.edu/graduate.

Southern New Hampshire University, School of Education, Manchester, NH 03106-1045. Offers business education (M Ed); child development (M Ed); curriculum and instruction (M Ed), including education leadership, reading, special education, technology integration; education (M Ed); educational leadership (M Ed, Ed D); educational studies (M Ed); elementary education (M Ed); English (MAT); English for speakers of other languages (M Ed); reading and writing specialist (M Ed); school business administration (Certificate); secondary education (M Ed); special education (M Ed); technology integration specialist (M Ed). Part-time and evening/weekend programs available. Postbaccalaureate distance learning degree programs offered (no on-campus study). *Degree requirements:* For master's, comprehensive exam (for some programs), thesis or alternative. *Entrance requirements:* For master's, PRAXIS I, minimum GPA of 2.75. Additional exam requirements/recommendations for international students: Required—TOEFL (minimum score 550 paper-based). Electronic applications accepted. *Expenses:* Contact institution.

Southern Oregon University, Graduate Studies, School of Education, Ashland, OR 97520. Offers elementary education (MA Ed, MS Ed), including classroom teacher, early childhood, handicapped learner, reading, supervision; secondary education (MA Ed, MS Ed), including classroom teacher, handicapped learner, reading, supervision; teaching (MAT). Postbaccalaureate distance learning degree programs offered (minimal on-campus study). *Faculty:* 23 full-time (16 women), 21 part-time/adjunct (20 women). *Students:* 92 full-time (68 women), 118 part-time (88 women); includes 19 minority (1 Black or African American, non-Hispanic/Latino; 1 American Indian or Alaska Native, non-Hispanic/Latino; 2 Asian, non-Hispanic/Latino; 10 Hispanic/Latino; 5 Two or more races, non-Hispanic/Latino), 5 international. Average age 36. 22 applicants, 59% accepted, 12 enrolled. In 2013, 127 master's awarded. *Degree requirements:* For master's, thesis optional. *Entrance requirements:* For master's, GRE General Test, minimum cumulative GPA of 3.0 in the last 90 quarter credits (60 semester credits) of undergraduate coursework. Additional exam requirements/recommendations for international students: Required—TOEFL (minimum score 540 paper-based; 76 iBT), IELTS (minimum score 6), ELPT (minimum score 964) or ELS (minimum score 112). *Application deadline:* For fall admission, 7/31 priority date for domestic and international students; for winter admission, 11/15 priority date for domestic and international students; for spring admission, 1/7 priority date for domestic and international students. Applications are processed on a rolling basis. Application fee: $50. Electronic applications accepted. *Expenses:* Tuition, state resident: full-time $13,635; part-time $378.72 per credit hour. Tuition, nonresident: full-time $17,042; part-time $473.40 per credit hour. *Required fees:* $408 per quarter. *Financial support:* Research assistantships with partial tuition reimbursements, career-related internships or fieldwork, institutionally sponsored loans, scholarships/grants, and unspecified assistantships available. *Unit head:* Dr. Gerry McCain, Graduate Program Coordinator, 541-552-6934, E-mail: mccaing@sou.edu. *Application contact:* Kelly Moutsatson, Director of Admissions, 541-552-6411, Fax: 541-552-8403, E-mail: admissions@sou.edu.
Website: http://www.sou.edu/education/.

Southern University and Agricultural and Mechanical College, Graduate School, College of Education, Department of Curriculum and Instruction, Baton Rouge, LA 70813. Offers elementary education (M Ed); media (M Ed); secondary education (M Ed). *Degree requirements:* For master's, comprehensive exam, thesis optional. *Entrance requirements:* For master's, GMAT or GRE General Test. Additional exam requirements/recommendations for international students: Required—TOEFL (minimum score 525 paper-based).

Southwestern Assemblies of God University, Thomas F. Harrison School of Graduate Studies, Program in Education, Waxahachie, TX 75165-5735. Offers Christian school administration (MS); curriculum development (MS); early education administration (M Ed); middle and secondary education (M Ed). *Degree requirements:* For master's, comprehensive written and oral exams. *Entrance requirements:* For master's, GRE General Test, minimum GPA of 2.5. Electronic applications accepted.

Southwestern Oklahoma State University, College of Professional and Graduate Studies, School of Behavioral Sciences and Education, Weatherford, OK 73096-3098. Offers community counseling (M Ed); early childhood education (M Ed); educational administration (M Ed); elementary education (M Ed); health sciences and microbiology (M Ed); kinesiology (M Ed); parks and recreation management (M Ed); school counseling (M Ed); school psychology (MS); school psychometry (M Ed); secondary education (M Ed); special education (M Ed). *Accreditation:* NCATE. Part-time and evening/weekend programs available. Postbaccalaureate distance learning degree programs offered (minimal on-campus study). *Degree requirements:* For master's, exam. *Entrance requirements:* For master's, GRE General Test or minimum undergraduate GPA of 3.0. Additional exam requirements/recommendations for international students: Required—TOEFL.

Spalding University, Graduate Studies, College of Education, Programs in Education, Louisville, KY 40203-2188. Offers art teacher education (MAT); business teacher education (MAT); elementary school education (MAT); foreign language (MAT); general education (MA Ed); high school education (MAT); middle school education (MAT); school administration (MA Ed); secondary education (MAT); special education (learning and behavioral disorders) (MAT); student guidance counselor (MA); teacher education and professional development (MAT). *Accreditation:* NCATE. Part-time and evening/weekend programs available. *Faculty:* 12 full-time (11 women), 6 part-time/adjunct (4 women). *Students:* 92 full-time (63 women), 36 part-time (29 women); includes 43 minority (41 Black or African American, non-Hispanic/Latino; 2 Two or more races, non-Hispanic/Latino). Average age 35. 77 applicants, 48% accepted, 30 enrolled. In 2013, 81 master's awarded. *Degree requirements:* For master's, portfolio, final project, clinical experience. *Entrance requirements:* For master's, GRE General Test or MAT, interview, letters of recommendation, resume. Additional exam requirements/recommendations for international students: Required—TOEFL (minimum score 535 paper-based). *Application deadline:* Applications are processed on a rolling basis. Application fee: $30. Electronic applications accepted. *Expenses: Tuition:* Full-time $21,450. *Required fees:* $810. Tuition and fees vary according to course load, degree level, program and student level. *Financial support:* Scholarships/grants, traineeships, and unspecified assistantships available. Financial award application deadline: 3/30; financial award applicants required to submit FAFSA. *Faculty research:* Instructional technology, achievement gap, classroom management, assessment. *Unit head:* Dr. Beverly Keepers, Dean, 502-588-7121, Fax: 502-585-7123, E-mail: bkeepers@spalding.edu. *Application contact:* Bonnie Caughron, Administrative Assistant, College of Education, 502-873-4262, E-mail: bcaughron@spalding.edu.

Springfield College, Graduate Programs, Program in Education, Springfield, MA 01109-3797. Offers counseling and secondary education (M Ed, MS); early childhood education (M Ed, MS); education (M Ed, MS); educational administration (M Ed, MS); educational studies (M Ed, MS); elementary education (M Ed, MS); secondary education (M Ed, MS); special education (M Ed, MS). Part-time and evening/weekend programs available. *Faculty:* 6 full-time. *Students:* 47 full-time. 45 applicants, 87% accepted, 35 enrolled. In 2013, 15 master's awarded. *Entrance requirements:* Additional exam requirements/recommendations for international students: Required—TOEFL (minimum score 550 paper-based); Recommended—IELTS (minimum score 6). *Application deadline:* For fall admission, 1/15 for domestic and international students; for winter admission, 11/1 for domestic and international students; for spring admission, 11/1 for domestic and international students. Applications are processed on a rolling basis. Application fee: $50. Electronic applications accepted. *Expenses: Tuition:* Full-time $13,620; part-time $908 per credit. *Financial support:* Fellowships with partial tuition reimbursements, teaching assistantships with partial tuition reimbursements, career-related internships or fieldwork, Federal Work-Study, institutionally sponsored loans, and unspecified assistantships available. Financial award application deadline: 3/1; financial award applicants required to submit FAFSA. *Unit head:* Jennifer Johnston, Program Coordinator, 413-748-3348, E-mail: jjohnston@springfieldcollege.edu. *Application contact:* Evelyn Cohen, Associate Director of Graduate Admissions, 413-748-3479, Fax: 413-748-3694, E-mail: ecohen@springfieldcollege.edu.

Spring Hill College, Graduate Programs, Program in Education, Mobile, AL 36608-1791. Offers early childhood education (MAT, MS Ed); educational theory (MS Ed); elementary education (MAT, MS Ed); secondary education (MAT, MS Ed). Part-time programs available. *Faculty:* 3 full-time (all women). *Students:* 2 full-time (both women), 17 part-time (14 women); includes 2 minority (both Black or African American, non-Hispanic/Latino). Average age 32. In 2013, 7 master's awarded. *Degree requirements:* For master's, comprehensive exam, completion of program within 6 calendar years of entrance into graduate studies at Spring Hill; documentation of course field assignments (MS) or completion of internship (MAT). *Entrance requirements:* For master's, GRE, MAT, or PRAXIS (varies by program), bachelor's degree with minimum undergraduate GPA of 3.0; class B certificate (MS) or minimum number of hours in specific fields (MAT). Additional exam requirements/recommendations for international students: Required—TOEFL (minimum score 550 paper-based; 80 iBT), IELTS (minimum score 6.5), CPE or CAE (minimum score C), Michigan English Language Assessment Battery (minimum score 90). *Application deadline:* For fall admission, 8/1 priority date for domestic and international students; for spring admission, 12/1 priority date for domestic and international students. Applications are processed on a rolling basis. Application fee: $25 ($35 for international students). Electronic applications accepted. *Expenses:* Contact institution. *Financial support:* Applicants required to submit FAFSA. *Unit head:* Dr. Lori P. Aultman, Chair of Teacher Education, 251-380-3473, Fax: 251-460-2184, E-mail: laultman@shc.edu. *Application contact:* Donna B. Tarasavage, Associate

Director, Academic Affairs, 251-380-3067, Fax: 251-460-2182, E-mail: dtarasavage@shc.edu.
Website: http://www.shc.edu/page/teacher-education.

Stanford University, School of Education, Teacher Education Program, Stanford, CA 94305-9991. Offers elementary (MAE); secondary (MAE). *Degree requirements:* For master's, thesis. *Entrance requirements:* For master's, GRE General Test. Electronic applications accepted. *Expenses: Tuition:* Full-time $42,690; part-time $949 per credit. *Required fees:* $185.

State University of New York at Fredonia, Graduate Studies, College of Education, Program in Secondary Education, Fredonia, NY 14063-1136. Offers MS Ed. *Accreditation:* NCATE. Part-time and evening/weekend programs available. *Degree requirements:* For master's, thesis optional. *Expenses:* Tuition, state resident: full-time $7398; part-time $411 per credit hour. Tuition, nonresident: full-time $13,770; part-time $765 per credit hour. *Required fees:* $1143.90; $63.55 per credit hour. Tuition and fees vary according to course load.

State University of New York at New Paltz, Graduate School, School of Education, Department of Educational Studies, Program in Special Education, New Paltz, NY 12561. Offers adolescence special education (7-12) (MS Ed); adolescence special education and literacy education (MS Ed); childhood special education (1-6) (MS Ed); childhood special education and literacy education (MS Ed); early childhood special education (B-2) (MS Ed). *Accreditation:* NCATE. Part-time and evening/weekend programs available. *Faculty:* 6 full-time (4 women), 9 part-time/adjunct (all women). *Students:* 42 full-time (35 women), 35 part-time (24 women); includes 11 minority (1 Asian, non-Hispanic/Latino; 8 Hispanic/Latino; 2 Two or more races, non-Hispanic/Latino). Average age 27. 63 applicants, 73% accepted, 24 enrolled. In 2013, 43 master's awarded. *Degree requirements:* For master's, portfolio. *Entrance requirements:* For master's, minimum GPA of 3.0 (3.2 for special education and literacy programs), New York state teaching certificate. Additional exam requirements/recommendations for international students: Required—TOEFL (minimum score 550 paper-based; 80 iBT), IELTS (minimum score 6.5). *Application deadline:* For fall admission, 3/15 priority date for domestic students, 3/15 for international students; for spring admission, 11/1 for domestic and international students. Application fee: $50. Electronic applications accepted. *Expenses:* Tuition, state resident: full-time $9870; part-time $411 per credit. Tuition, nonresident: full-time $18,350; part-time $765 per credit. *Required fees:* $1213. Tuition and fees vary according to program. *Financial support:* Application deadline: 8/1. *Unit head:* Dr. Jane Sileo, Coordinator, 845-257-2835, E-mail: sileoj@newpaltz.edu. *Application contact:* Caroline Murphy, Graduate Admissions Advisor, 845-257-3285, E-mail: gradschool@newpaltz.edu.
Website: http://www.newpaltz.edu/edstudies/special_ed.html.

State University of New York at New Paltz, Graduate School, School of Education, Department of Secondary Education, New Paltz, NY 12561. Offers adolescence education: biology (MAT, MS Ed); adolescence education: chemistry (MAT, MS Ed); adolescence education: earth science (MAT, MS Ed); adolescence education: English (MAT, MS Ed); adolescence education: French (MAT, MS Ed); adolescence education: social studies (MAT, MS Ed); adolescence education: Spanish (MAT, MS Ed); second language education (MS Ed, AC), including second language education (MS Ed), teaching English language learners (AC). *Accreditation:* NCATE. Part-time and evening/weekend programs available. *Faculty:* 10 full-time (8 women), 15 part-time/adjunct (10 women). *Students:* 73 full-time (47 women), 52 part-time (39 women); includes 27 minority (2 Black or African American, non-Hispanic/Latino; 6 Asian, non-Hispanic/Latino; 16 Hispanic/Latino; 3 Two or more races, non-Hispanic/Latino), 1 international. Average age 29. 81 applicants, 84% accepted, 51 enrolled. In 2013, 85 master's awarded. *Degree requirements:* For master's, comprehensive exam (for some programs), portfolio. *Entrance requirements:* For master's, minimum GPA of 3.0, New York state teaching certificate (MS Ed). Additional exam requirements/recommendations for international students: Required—TOEFL (minimum score 550 paper-based; 80 iBT), IELTS (minimum score 6.5). *Application deadline:* For fall admission, 3/1 priority date for domestic students, 3/1 for international students; for spring admission, 10/1 priority date for domestic students, 10/1 for international students. Application fee: $50. Electronic applications accepted. *Expenses:* Tuition, state resident: full-time $9870; part-time $411 per credit. Tuition, nonresident: full-time $18,350; part-time $765 per credit. *Required fees:* $1213. Tuition and fees vary according to program. *Financial support:* Application deadline: 8/1. *Unit head:* Dr. Laura Dull, Chair, 845-257-2850, E-mail: dulll@newpaltz.edu. *Application contact:* Caroline Murphy, Graduate Admissions Advisor, 845-257-3285, Fax: 845-257-3284, E-mail: gradschool@newpaltz.edu.
Website: http://www.newpaltz.edu/secondaryed/.

State University of New York at Oswego, Graduate Studies, School of Education, Department of Curriculum and Instruction, Oswego, NY 13126. Offers adolescence education (MST); art education (MAT); childhood education (MST); elementary education (MS Ed); literacy education (MS Ed); secondary education (MS Ed); special education (MS Ed). Part-time and evening/weekend programs available. *Degree requirements:* For master's, comprehensive exam (for some programs), thesis optional. *Entrance requirements:* For master's, GRE General Test, minimum GPA of 2.7, provisional teaching certificate. Additional exam requirements/recommendations for international students: Required—TOEFL (minimum score 560 paper-based). *Faculty research:* Classroom applications for microcomputers; classroom questioning, wait-time, and achievement; values clarification and academic achievement.

State University of New York at Plattsburgh, Division of Education, Health, and Human Services, Program in Teacher Education: Adolescence, Plattsburgh, NY 12901-2681. Offers adolescence education (MST); biology 7-12 (MST); chemistry 7-12 (MST); earth science 7-12 (MST); English 7-12 (MST); French 7-12 (MST); mathematics 7-12 (MST); physics 7-12 (MST); social studies 7-12 (MST); Spanish 7-12 (MST). *Accreditation:* Teacher Education Accreditation Council. Part-time and evening/weekend programs available. *Students:* 75 full-time (47 women), 5 part-time (3 women); includes 10 minority (1 Black or African American, non-Hispanic/Latino; 4 Asian, non-Hispanic/Latino; 5 Hispanic/Latino), 1 international. Average age 25. *Entrance requirements:* For master's, minimum GPA of 2.75. Additional exam requirements/recommendations for international students: Required—TOEFL. *Application deadline:* For fall admission, 2/15 priority date for domestic students. Applications are processed on a rolling basis. Application fee: $75. *Financial support:* Application deadline: 4/15; applicants required to submit FAFSA. *Unit head:* Dr. Robert Ackland, Coordinator, 518-564-5131, E-mail: acklanrt@plattsburgh.edu. *Application contact:* Betsy Kane, Director, Graduate Admissions, 518-564-4723, Fax: 518-564-4722, E-mail: bkane002@plattsburgh.edu.

State University of New York College at Cortland, Graduate Studies, School of Arts and Sciences, Programs in Adolescence Education, Cortland, NY 13045. Offers biology (MAT, MS Ed); chemistry (MAT, MS Ed); earth science (MAT, MS Ed); English (MAT, MS Ed); mathematics (MAT, MS Ed); physics (MAT, MS Ed); physics and mathematics (MS Ed); social studies (MS Ed), including geography, history. *Accreditation:* NCATE. Part-time and evening/weekend programs available. *Degree requirements:* For master's, one foreign language, comprehensive exam (for some programs), thesis (for some programs). *Entrance requirements:* For master's, GRE General Test. *Expenses:* Tuition, state resident: full-time $9870; part-time $411 per credit hour. Tuition, nonresident: full-time $18,350; part-time $765 per credit hour. *Required fees:* $1458; $65 per credit hour.

State University of New York College at Geneseo, Graduate Studies, School of Education, Program in Adolescence Education, Geneseo, NY 14454-1401. Offers MS Ed. Part-time and evening/weekend programs available. *Faculty:* 5 full-time (2 women). *Students:* 1 full-time (0 women), 7 part-time (5 women). Average age 26. 4 applicants, 100% accepted. In 2013, 8 master's awarded. *Degree requirements:* For master's, thesis optional. *Application deadline:* For fall admission, 3/1 priority date for domestic students; for spring admission, 10/1 for domestic students. Application fee: $50. *Expenses:* Tuition, state resident: full-time $8790; part-time $411 per credit hour. Tuition, nonresident: full-time $18,350; part-time $765 per credit hour. *Required fees:* $795; $32.90 per credit hour. *Financial support:* In 2013–14, 1 student received support. Scholarships/grants, health care benefits, tuition waivers (full), and unspecified assistantships available. Support available to part-time students. Financial award application deadline: 4/1; financial award applicants required to submit FAFSA. *Unit head:* Dr. Anjoo Sikka, Dean of School of Education, 585-245-5151, Fax: 585-245-5220, E-mail: sikka@geneseo.edu. *Application contact:* Tracy Peterson, Director of Student Success, 585-245-5443, Fax: 585-245-5220, E-mail: peterson@geneseo.edu.

State University of New York College at Oneonta, Graduate Education, Division of Education, Department of Secondary Education, Oneonta, NY 13820-4015. Offers adolescence education (MS Ed). *Accreditation:* NCATE. Part-time and evening/weekend programs available. *Students:* 3 full-time (2 women), 4 part-time (3 women). Average age 27. 7 applicants, 100% accepted, 7 enrolled. *Entrance requirements:* For master's, GRE General Test. *Application deadline:* For fall admission, 3/25 priority date for domestic students; for spring admission, 10/1 priority date for domestic students. Applications are processed on a rolling basis. Application fee: $50. *Unit head:* Dr. Dennis Banks, Chair, 607-436-3391, Fax: 607-436-2554, E-mail: banksdn@oneonta.edu. *Application contact:* Patrick J. Mente, Director of Graduate Studies, 607-436-2523, Fax: 607-436-3084, E-mail: gradstudies@oneonta.edu.

State University of New York College at Potsdam, School of Education and Professional Studies, Program in Secondary Education, Potsdam, NY 13676. Offers English education (MST); mathematics education (MST); science education (MST), including biology, chemistry, earth science, physics; social studies education (MST). *Accreditation:* NCATE. *Degree requirements:* For master's, culminating experience. *Entrance requirements:* For master's, minimum GPA of 2.75 in last 60 hours of course work (3.0 for English program). Additional exam requirements/recommendations for international students: Required—TOEFL (minimum score 550 paper-based; 80 iBT), IELTS (minimum score 6). Electronic applications accepted.

Stephen F. Austin State University, Graduate School, College of Education, Department of Secondary Education and Educational Leadership, Nacogdoches, TX 75962. Offers educational leadership (Ed D); secondary education (M Ed). *Accreditation:* NCATE. *Degree requirements:* For master's, comprehensive exam; for doctorate, thesis/dissertation. *Entrance requirements:* For master's, GRE General Test; for doctorate, GRE General Test, interview, writing sample. Additional exam requirements/recommendations for international students: Required—TOEFL. Electronic applications accepted.

Sul Ross State University, Rio Grande College of Sul Ross State University, Alpine, TX 79832. Offers business administration (MBA); teacher education (M Ed), including bilingual education, counseling, educational diagnostics, elementary education, general education, reading, school administration, secondary education. Part-time and evening/weekend programs available. Postbaccalaureate distance learning degree programs offered (no on-campus study). *Degree requirements:* For master's, comprehensive exam, thesis optional, minimum GPA of 3.0. *Entrance requirements:* For master's, GMAT or GRE General Test, minimum GPA of 2.5 in last 60 hours of undergraduate work. Additional exam requirements/recommendations for international students: Required—TOEFL.

Syracuse University, School of Education, Program in Mathematics Education, Syracuse, NY 13244. Offers mathematics education (PhD); teacher preparation 7-12 (MS). Part-time programs available. *Students:* 9 full-time (5 women), 3 part-time (2 women); includes 3 minority (2 Black or African American, non-Hispanic/Latino; 1 Hispanic/Latino), 4 international. Average age 32. 12 applicants, 67% accepted, 4 enrolled. In 2013, 1 master's, 1 doctorate awarded. *Degree requirements:* For master's, thesis or alternative; for doctorate, comprehensive exam, thesis/dissertation. *Entrance requirements:* For master's, GRE (for assistantship applicants); for doctorate, GRE, MS. Additional exam requirements/recommendations for international students: Required—TOEFL (minimum score 100 iBT). *Application deadline:* For fall admission, 1/15 priority date for domestic and international students; for spring admission, 10/15 for domestic students, 10/15 priority date for international students. Applications are processed on a rolling basis. Application fee: $75. Electronic applications accepted. *Financial support:* Fellowships with full tuition reimbursements and teaching assistantships with full and partial tuition reimbursements available. Financial award application deadline: 1/1. *Unit head:* Dr. Joanna Masingila, Chair, 315-443-1483, E-mail: jomasing@syr.edu. *Application contact:* Laurie Deyo, Graduate Recruiter, School of Education, 315-443-2505, E-mail: e-gradrcrt@syr.edu.
Website: http://soe.syr.edu/.

Tarleton State University, College of Graduate Studies, College of Education, Department of Psychology and Counseling, Stephenville, TX 76402. Offers counseling and psychology (M Ed), including counseling, counseling psychology, educational psychology; educational administration (M Ed); secondary education (Certificate); special education (Certificate). Part-time and evening/weekend programs available. Postbaccalaureate distance learning degree programs offered (minimal on-campus study). *Faculty:* 8 full-time (6 women), 14 part-time/adjunct (7 women). *Students:* 60 full-time (48 women), 183 part-time (157 women); includes 63 minority (21 Black or African American, non-Hispanic/Latino; 3 Asian, non-Hispanic/Latino; 30 Hispanic/Latino; 9 Two or more races, non-Hispanic/Latino). Average age 34. 78 applicants, 81% accepted, 47 enrolled. In 2013, 76 master's awarded. *Degree requirements:* For master's, comprehensive exam, thesis optional. *Entrance requirements:* For master's, GRE General Test, minimum GPA of 3.0. Additional exam requirements/recommendations for international students: Required—TOEFL (minimum score 550 paper-based; 80 iBT). *Application deadline:* For fall admission, 8/15 priority date for domestic students; for spring admission, 1/7 for domestic students. Applications are processed on a rolling basis. Application fee: $30 ($130 for international students). Electronic applications accepted. *Expenses:* Tuition, state resident: full-time $3312; part-time $184 per credit hour. Tuition, nonresident: full-time $9144; part-time $508 per credit hour. *Required fees:* $1916. Tuition and fees vary according to course load and campus/location. *Financial support:* Research assistantships, teaching assistantships, career-related internships or fieldwork, Federal Work-Study, institutionally sponsored loans, and tuition waivers (partial) available. Support available to part-time students. Financial award application deadline: 5/1; financial award applicants required to submit FAFSA. *Unit head:* Dr. Bob Newby, Department Head, 254-968-9813, Fax: 254-968-1991, E-mail: newby@tarleton.edu. *Application contact:* Information Contact, 254-968-9104, Fax: 254-968-9670, E-mail: gradoffice@tarleton.edu.
Website: http://www.tarleton.edu/COEWEB/pc/.

Secondary Education

Temple University, College of Education, Department of Curriculum, Instruction, and Technology in Education, Program in Secondary Education, Philadelphia, PA 19122-6096. Offers English (Ed M); math (Ed M); social studies (Ed M).

Temple University, College of Education, Department of Psychological Studies in Education, Department of Educational Leadership and Policy Studies, Philadelphia, PA 19122-6096. Offers educational leadership (Ed D), including higher education, K-12. Part-time and evening/weekend programs available. *Faculty:* 7 full-time (3 women). *Students:* 10 full-time (7 women), 66 part-time (42 women); includes 20 minority (15 Black or African American, non-Hispanic/Latino; 1 American Indian or Alaska Native, non-Hispanic/Latino; 1 Asian, non-Hispanic/Latino; 3 Hispanic/Latino), 24 international. 58 applicants, 69% accepted, 24 enrolled. In 2013, 6 master's awarded. Terminal master's awarded for partial completion of doctoral program. *Degree requirements:* For master's, comprehensive exam, thesis or alternative, internship; for doctorate, thesis/dissertation, preliminary exam. *Entrance requirements:* For master's, GRE General Test or MAT, minimum undergraduate GPA of 3.0, 2 letters of recommendation, goal statement, resume; for doctorate, GRE General Test or MAT, minimum undergraduate GPA of 3.0, 3 letters of recommendation, goal statement, resume. Additional exam requirements/recommendations for international students: Required—TOEFL (minimum score 550 paper-based; 79 iBT). *Application deadline:* For fall admission, 1/5 for domestic students, 10/7 for international students; for spring admission, 11/1 for domestic students, 11/3 for international students. Application fee: $60. Electronic applications accepted. *Financial support:* In 2013–14, 2 students received support, including 1 research assistantship with full tuition reimbursement available (averaging $20,333 per year), 1 teaching assistantship with full tuition reimbursement available (averaging $17,046 per year); career-related internships or fieldwork, Federal Work-Study, scholarships/grants, health care benefits, and unspecified assistantships also available. Financial award application deadline: 1/15; financial award applicants required to submit FAFSA. *Faculty research:* School leadership, educational policy, educational accountability, democratic leadership, equity and access. *Unit head:* Dr. Joan Shapiro, Professor, 215-204-6645, E-mail: joan.shapiro@temple.edu. *Application contact:* Felicia Neuber, Enrollment Management, 215-204-8011, E-mail: educate@temple.edu.
Website: http://education.temple.edu/leadership.

Tennessee Technological University, College of Graduate Studies, College of Education, Department of Curriculum and Instruction, Program in Secondary Education, Cookeville, TN 38505. Offers MA, Ed S. *Accreditation:* NCATE. Part-time and evening/weekend programs available. *Faculty:* 7 full-time (0 women). *Students:* 19 full-time (11 women), 36 part-time (27 women); includes 11 minority (6 Black or African American, non-Hispanic/Latino; 1 American Indian or Alaska Native, non-Hispanic/Latino; 2 Asian, non-Hispanic/Latino; 2 Hispanic/Latino). Average age 27. 28 applicants, 89% accepted, 18 enrolled. In 2013, 12 master's, 4 other advanced degrees awarded. *Degree requirements:* For master's and Ed S, comprehensive exam, thesis or alternative. *Entrance requirements:* For master's and Ed S, MAT or GRE. Additional exam requirements/recommendations for international students: Required—TOEFL (minimum score 527 paper-based; 71 iBT), IELTS (minimum score 5.5), PTE (minimum score 48), or TOEIC (Test of English as an International Communication). *Application deadline:* For fall admission, 8/1 for domestic students, 5/1 for international students; for spring admission, 12/1 for domestic students, 10/1 for international students. Applications are processed on a rolling basis. Application fee: $35 ($40 for international students). Electronic applications accepted. *Expenses:* Tuition, state resident: full-time $9347; part-time $465 per credit hour. Tuition, nonresident: full-time $23,635; part-time $1152 per credit hour. *Financial support:* In 2013–14, 1 fellowship (averaging $8,000 per year), 1 research assistantship (averaging $4,000 per year), 1 teaching assistantship (averaging $4,000 per year) were awarded; career-related internships or fieldwork also available. Financial award application deadline: 4/1. *Unit head:* Dr. Jeremy Wendt, Interim Chairperson, 931-372-3181, Fax: 931-372-6270, E-mail: jwendt@tntech.edu. *Application contact:* Shelia K. Kendrick, Coordinator of Graduate Studies, 931-372-3808, Fax: 931-372-3497, E-mail: skendrick@tntech.edu.

Texas A&M University–Commerce, Graduate School, College of Education and Human Services, Department of Curriculum and Instruction, Commerce, TX 75429-3011. Offers bilingual/ESL education (M Ed, MS); early childhood education (M Ed, MS); elementary education (M Ed, MS); reading (M Ed, MS); secondary education (M Ed, MS); supervision, curriculum and instruction: elementary education (Ed D). MS and M Ed programs in early childhood education offered jointly with Texas Woman's University and University of North Texas. Part-time programs available. Terminal master's awarded for partial completion of doctoral program. *Degree requirements:* For master's, comprehensive exam, thesis (for some programs); for doctorate, 2 foreign languages, thesis/dissertation, departmental qualifying exam. *Entrance requirements:* For master's and doctorate, GRE General Test. Electronic applications accepted. *Expenses:* Tuition, state resident: full-time $3630; part-time $2420 per year. Tuition, nonresident: full-time $9948; part-time $6632.16 per year. *Required fees:* $1006 per year. Tuition and fees vary according to course load. *Faculty research:* Literacy and learning, early childhood, preservice teacher education, technology.

Texas A&M University–Corpus Christi, Graduate Studies and Research, College of Education, Program in Secondary Education, Corpus Christi, TX 78412-5503. Offers MS. Part-time and evening/weekend programs available. *Degree requirements:* For master's, comprehensive exam, thesis (for some programs). *Entrance requirements:* For master's, GRE General Test. Additional exam requirements/recommendations for international students: Required—TOEFL. Electronic applications accepted.

Texas Christian University, College of Education, Program in Secondary Education (Four-One Option), Fort Worth, TX 76129-0002. Offers M Ed. Part-time and evening/weekend programs available. *Students:* 3 full-time (all women). 7 applicants, 100% accepted, 3 enrolled. In 2013, 1 master's awarded. *Degree requirements:* For master's, oral exam. *Entrance requirements:* Additional exam requirements/recommendations for international students: Required—TOEFL (minimum score 550 paper-based; 80 iBT). *Application deadline:* For fall admission, 11/16 for domestic and international students; for spring admission, 3/1 for domestic and international students. Application fee: $60. Electronic applications accepted. *Expenses: Tuition:* Part-time $1270 per credit hour. Tuition and fees vary according to course load and program. *Financial support:* Teaching assistantships with full tuition reimbursements, career-related internships or fieldwork, scholarships/grants, and unspecified assistantships available. Financial award application deadline: 3/1; financial award applicants required to submit FAFSA. *Unit head:* Dr. Jan Lacina, Associate Dean, 817-257-6786, E-mail: j.lacina@tcu.edu. *Application contact:* Lori Kimball, Administrative Program Specialist, 817-257-7661, E-mail: l.kimball@tcu.edu.
Website: http://www.coe.tcu.edu/graduate-students-graduate-programs.asp.

Texas Southern University, College of Education, Area of Curriculum and Instruction, Houston, TX 77004-4584. Offers bilingual education (M Ed); curriculum and instruction (Ed D); secondary education (M Ed). Part-time and evening/weekend programs available. *Faculty:* 2 full-time (1 woman), 8 part-time/adjunct (all women). *Students:* 18 full-time (17 women), 38 part-time (32 women); includes 55 minority (53 Black or African American, non-Hispanic/Latino; 2 Hispanic/Latino), 1 international. Average age 36. 27 applicants, 22% accepted, 5 enrolled. In 2013, 7 master's, 2 doctorates awarded. *Degree requirements:* For master's, comprehensive exam; for doctorate, comprehensive exam, thesis/dissertation. *Entrance requirements:* For master's, GRE General Test, minimum GPA of 2.5; for doctorate, GRE General Test or MAT, master's degree, minimum B+ average. Additional exam requirements/recommendations for international students: Required—TOEFL. *Application deadline:* For fall admission, 7/1 for domestic and international students; for spring admission, 11/1 for domestic and international students. Applications are processed on a rolling basis. Application fee: $50 ($75 for international students). Electronic applications accepted. *Financial support:* Fellowships, teaching assistantships, scholarships/grants, and unspecified assistantships available. Support available to part-time students. Financial award application deadline: 5/1. *Unit head:* Dr. Ingrid Haynes-Mays, Interim Chair, 713-313-7179, Fax: 713-313-7496, E-mail: haynesmaysi@tsu.edu. *Application contact:* Dr. Gregory Maddox, Dean of the Graduate School, 713-313-7011 Ext. 4410, Fax: 713-639-1876, E-mail: maddox_gh@tsu.edu.
Website: http://www.tsu.edu/academics/colleges__schools/College_of_Education/Departments/default.php.

Texas State University, Graduate School, College of Education, Department of Curriculum and Instruction, Program in Secondary Education, San Marcos, TX 78666. Offers M Ed, MA. Part-time and evening/weekend programs available. *Faculty:* 29 full-time (22 women), 6 part-time/adjunct (4 women). *Students:* 60 full-time (39 women), 46 part-time (32 women); includes 32 minority (11 Black or African American, non-Hispanic/Latino; 2 Asian, non-Hispanic/Latino; 18 Hispanic/Latino; 1 Two or more races, non-Hispanic/Latino), 1 international. Average age 33. 58 applicants, 78% accepted, 24 enrolled. In 2013, 61 master's awarded. *Degree requirements:* For master's, comprehensive exam, thesis (for some programs). *Entrance requirements:* For master's, GRE General Test, minimum GPA of 2.75 in last 60 hours of course work, teaching experience. Additional exam requirements/recommendations for international students: Required—TOEFL (minimum score 550 paper-based; 78 iBT). *Application deadline:* For fall admission, 6/15 priority date for domestic students, 6/1 for international students; for spring admission, 10/15 priority date for domestic students, 10/1 for international students. Applications are processed on a rolling basis. Application fee: $40 ($90 for international students). Electronic applications accepted. *Expenses:* Tuition, state resident: full-time $6663; part-time $278 per credit hour. Tuition, nonresident: full-time $15,159; part-time $632 per credit hour. *Required fees:* $1872; $54 per credit hour. $306 per term. Tuition and fees vary according to course load. *Financial support:* In 2013–14, 80 students received support, including 8 research assistantships (averaging $26,226 per year), 3 teaching assistantships (averaging $11,280 per year); career-related internships or fieldwork, Federal Work-Study, and institutionally sponsored loans also available. Support available to part-time students. Financial award application deadline: 4/1; financial award applicants required to submit FAFSA. *Faculty research:* Gifted and talented education, general secondary education, induction of first-year teachers. *Unit head:* Dr. Gene Martin, Graduate Advisor, 512-245-2157, Fax: 512-245-7911, E-mail: gm01@txstate.edu. *Application contact:* Dr. Andrea Golato, Dean of Graduate School, 512-245-2581, Fax: 512-245-8365, E-mail: gradcollege@txstate.edu.
Website: http://www.education.txstate.edu/ci/degrees-programs/graduate/secondary-education.html.

Texas Tech University, Graduate School, College of Education, Department of Curriculum and Instruction, Lubbock, TX 79409-1071. Offers bilingual education (M Ed); curriculum and instruction (M Ed, PhD); elementary education (M Ed); language/literacy education (M Ed); multidisciplinary science (MS); secondary education (M Ed). *Accreditation:* NCATE. Part-time programs available. Postbaccalaureate distance learning degree programs offered (minimal on-campus study). *Faculty:* 27 full-time (21 women). *Students:* 49 full-time (40 women), 194 part-time (149 women); includes 74 minority (13 Black or African American, non-Hispanic/Latino; 6 Asian, non-Hispanic/Latino; 50 Hispanic/Latino; 5 Two or more races, non-Hispanic/Latino), 20 international. Average age 38. 105 applicants, 66% accepted, 46 enrolled. In 2013, 48 master's, 14 doctorates awarded. *Degree requirements:* For master's, comprehensive exam (for some programs), thesis optional; for doctorate, comprehensive exam, thesis/dissertation. *Entrance requirements:* For master's, bachelor's degree; resume; letter of intent; academic writing sample; 2 letters of recommendation; for doctorate, GRE, master's degree; resume; letter of intent; academic writing sample; 3 letters of recommendation. Additional exam requirements/recommendations for international students: Required—TOEFL (minimum score 550 paper-based; 79 iBT). *Application deadline:* For fall admission, 6/1 priority date for domestic students, 1/15 priority date for international students; for spring admission, 9/1 priority date for domestic students, 6/15 priority date for international students. Applications are processed on a rolling basis. Application fee: $60. Electronic applications accepted. *Expenses:* Tuition, state resident: full-time $6062; part-time $252.57 per credit hour. Tuition, nonresident: full-time $14,558; part-time $606.57 per credit hour. *Required fees:* $2655; $35 per credit hour. $907.50 per semester. Tuition and fees vary according to course load. *Financial support:* In 2013–14, 94 students received support, including 89 fellowships (averaging $2,276 per year), 14 research assistantships (averaging $5,226 per year), 6 teaching assistantships (averaging $4,517 per year); career-related internships or fieldwork, Federal Work-Study, institutionally sponsored loans, scholarships/grants, traineeships, health care benefits, and unspecified assistantships also available. Support available to part-time students. Financial award application deadline: 2/1; financial award applicants required to submit FAFSA. *Faculty research:* Teacher education, curriculum studies, bilingual education, science and math education, language and literacy education. *Total annual research expenditures:* $413,968. *Unit head:* Dr. Margaret Ann Price, Department Chair, Curriculum and Instruction, 806-834-4347, E-mail: peggie.price@ttu.edu. *Application contact:* Stephenie A. Jones, Administrative Assistant, 806-834-2751, Fax: 806-742-2179, E-mail: stephenie.a.jones@ttu.edu.
Website: http://www.educ.ttu.edu.

Towson University, Program in Secondary Education, Towson, MD 21252-0001. Offers M Ed. *Accreditation:* NCATE. Part-time and evening/weekend programs available. *Students:* 12 part-time (11 women); includes 1 minority (Black or African American, non-Hispanic/Latino), 1 international. *Degree requirements:* For master's, thesis optional. *Entrance requirements:* For master's, Maryland teaching certification or permission of program director, minimum GPA of 3.0. *Application deadline:* Applications are processed on a rolling basis. Application fee: $45. Electronic applications accepted. *Financial support:* Application deadline: 4/1. *Unit head:* Dr. Todd Kenreich, Graduate Program Director, 410-704-5897, E-mail: tkenreich@towson.edu. *Application contact:* Alicia Arkell-Kleis, Information Contact, 410-704-6004, E-mail: grads@towson.edu.
Website: http://grad.towson.edu/program/master/sced-med/.

Trevecca Nazarene University, Graduate Education Program, Nashville, TN 37210-2877. Offers curriculum, assessment, and instruction K-12 (M Ed); educational leadership (M Ed); English language learners (PreK-12) (M Ed); leadership and professional practice (Ed D); library and information science (MLI Sc); teacher leader (M Ed); teaching (MAE, MAT), including teaching 7-12 (MAT), teaching K-6 (MAT); visual impairments special education (M Ed). *Accreditation:* NCATE. Part-time and evening/weekend programs available. Postbaccalaureate distance learning degree programs offered. *Faculty:* 19 full-time (17 women), 14 part-time/adjunct (5 women). *Students:* 186 full-time (137 women), 134 part-time (94 women); includes 93 minority (87 Black or African American, non-Hispanic/Latino; 1 American Indian or Alaska Native, non-Hispanic/Latino; 2 Asian, non-Hispanic/Latino; 1 Hispanic/Latino; 1 Native Hawaiian

or other Pacific Islander, non-Hispanic/Latino; 1 Two or more races, non-Hispanic/Latino), 2 international. In 2013, 201 master's, 40 doctorates awarded. *Degree requirements:* For master's, comprehensive exam, exit assessment/e-portfolio; for doctorate, thesis/dissertation, proposal study, symposium presentation. *Entrance requirements:* For master's, GRE with minimum score of 378 or MAT with minimum score of 290, ACT with minimum score of 22 or SAT with minimum score of 1020 (for MAT programs only); PRAXIS (for MAT and MAE programs), minimum GPA of 2.7, official transcript from regionally accredited institution, 3+ years successful teaching experience (Teacher Leader and Education Leadership majors), technology pre-assessment written requirements (some majors); for doctorate, GRE or MAT, minimum GPA of 3.4, official transcript from regionally-accredited institution, resume, writing sample, interview, reference forms. Additional exam requirements/recommendations for international students: Required—TOEFL (minimum score 550 paper-based). *Application deadline:* Applications are processed on a rolling basis. *Expenses:* Contact institution. *Financial support:* Applicants required to submit FAFSA. *Unit head:* Dr. Suzie Harris, Dean, School of Education/Director of Graduate Education Programs, 615-248-1201, Fax: 615-248-1597, E-mail: admissions_ged@trevecca.edu. *Application contact:* 615-248-1529, E-mail: cll@trevecca.edu.
Website: http://www.trevecca.edu/academics/schools-colleges/education/.

Trinity Washington University, School of Education, Washington, DC 20017-1094. Offers clinical mental health counseling (MA); early childhood education (MAT); educating for change (M Ed); educational administration (MSA); elementary education (MAT); reading (M Ed); school counseling (MA); secondary education (MAT), including English, social studies; special education (MAT). *Accreditation:* NCATE. Part-time and evening/weekend programs available. *Degree requirements:* For master's, thesis (for some programs), capstone project(s). *Entrance requirements:* For master's, PRAXIS I, minimum GPA of 2.8. Additional exam requirements/recommendations for international students: Required—TOEFL (minimum score 550 paper-based). *Application deadline:* For fall admission, 4/1 priority date for domestic students; for winter admission, 11/1 priority date for domestic students; for spring admission, 11/1 priority date for domestic students. Applications are processed on a rolling basis. Application fee: $40. *Expenses: Tuition:* Part-time $715 per credit. *Financial support:* Career-related internships or fieldwork, health care benefits, and unspecified assistantships available. Support available to part-time students. Financial award application deadline: 4/1; financial award applicants required to submit FAFSA. *Faculty research:* Technology, literacy, special education, organizations, inclusion models. *Unit head:* Dr. Janet Stocks, Dean, 202-884-9380, Fax: 202-884-9506, E-mail: stocksj@trinitydc.edu. *Application contact:* Erika Davis, Director of Admissions for School of Education, 202-884-9400, Fax: 202-884-9229, E-mail: daviser@trinitydc.edu.
Website: http://www.trinitydc.edu/education/.

Troy University, Graduate School, College of Education, Program in Secondary Education, Troy, AL 36082. Offers 5th year biology (MS); 5th year computer science (MS); 5th year history (MS); 5th year language arts (MS); 5th year mathematics (MS); 5th year social science (MS); traditional biology (MS); traditional computer science (MS); traditional history (MS); traditional language arts (MS); traditional mathematics (MS); traditional social science (MS). *Accreditation:* NCATE. Part-time and evening/weekend programs available. *Faculty:* 2 full-time (1 woman). *Students:* 10 full-time (9 women), 21 part-time (14 women); includes 8 minority (6 Black or African American, non-Hispanic/Latino; 2 Hispanic/Latino). Average age 29. 15 applicants, 87% accepted, 6 enrolled. In 2013, 12 master's awarded. *Degree requirements:* For master's, comprehensive exam, thesis. *Entrance requirements:* For master's, GRE (minimum score of 850 on old exam or 290 on new exam), GMAT (minimum score of 380), or MAT (minimum score of 385), bachelor's degree; minimum undergraduate GPA of 2.5 or 3.0 on last 30 semester hours, letter of recommendation. Additional exam requirements/recommendations for international students: Required—TOEFL (minimum score 523 paper-based; 70 iBT), IELTS (minimum score 6). *Application deadline:* Applications are processed on a rolling basis. Application fee: $50. Electronic applications accepted. *Expenses:* Tuition, state resident: full-time $6084; part-time $338 per credit hour. Tuition, nonresident: full-time $12,168; part-time $676 per credit hour. *Required fees:* $630; $35 per credit hour. $50 per semester. *Financial support:* Career-related internships or fieldwork available. Support available to part-time students. Financial award applicants required to submit FAFSA. *Unit head:* Dr. Jan Oliver, Associate Professor, 334-670-3444, Fax: 334-670-3548, E-mail: oliver@troy.edu. *Application contact:* Brenda K. Campbell, Director of Graduate Admissions, 334-670-3178, Fax: 334-670-3733, E-mail: bcamp@troy.edu.

Tufts University, Graduate School of Arts and Sciences, Department of Education, Program in Education, Medford, MA 02155. Offers educational studies (MA); elementary education (MAT); middle and secondary education (MA, MAT); museum education (MA); secondary education (MA); STEM education (MS, PhD). *Faculty:* 13 full-time, 9 part-time/adjunct. *Students:* 85 full-time (72 women); includes 19 minority (4 Black or African American, non-Hispanic/Latino; 1 American Indian or Alaska Native, non-Hispanic/Latino; 3 Asian, non-Hispanic/Latino; 7 Hispanic/Latino; 4 Two or more races, non-Hispanic/Latino), 5 international. Average age 27. 154 applicants, 69% accepted, 50 enrolled. In 2013, 84 master's awarded. *Degree requirements:* For master's, thesis optional; for doctorate, thesis/dissertation. *Entrance requirements:* For master's and doctorate, GRE General Test. Additional exam requirements/recommendations for international students: Required—TOEFL (minimum score 550 paper-based; 80 iBT), IELTS (minimum score 6.5). *Application deadline:* For fall admission, 1/2 for domestic and international students; for spring admission, 10/15 for domestic students, 9/15 for international students. Applications are processed on a rolling basis. Application fee: $75. Electronic applications accepted. *Financial support:* Teaching assistantships with full and partial tuition reimbursements, Federal Work-Study, scholarships/grants, and tuition waivers (full and partial) available. Support available to part-time students. Financial award application deadline: 1/2. *Unit head:* Hammer David, Chair, 617-627-3244, Fax: 617-627-3901. *Application contact:* Patricia Romeo, Information Contact, 617-627-3244.

Union College, Graduate Programs, Department of Education, Program in Secondary Education, Barbourville, KY 40906-1499. Offers MA. *Degree requirements:* For master's, thesis optional. *Entrance requirements:* For master's, GRE General Test, NTE.

Universidad Metropolitana, School of Education, Program in Teaching of Physical Education, San Juan, PR 00928-1150. Offers teaching of adult physical education (M Ed); teaching of elementary physical education (M Ed); teaching of secondary physical education (M Ed). *Degree requirements:* For master's, thesis or alternative. *Entrance requirements:* For master's, EXADEP, interview. Electronic applications accepted.

The University of Akron, Graduate School, College of Education, Department of Curricular and Instructional Studies, Program in Secondary Education, Akron, OH 44325. Offers MA, MS, PhD. *Accreditation:* NCATE. *Students:* 27 full-time (20 women), 64 part-time (44 women); includes 14 minority (5 Black or African American, non-Hispanic/Latino; 5 Asian, non-Hispanic/Latino; 4 Hispanic/Latino), 9 international. Average age 40. 13 applicants, 46% accepted, 6 enrolled. In 2013, 26 master's, 3 doctorates awarded. *Degree requirements:* For master's, comprehensive exam, portfolio; for doctorate, variable foreign language requirement, comprehensive exam,

thesis/dissertation, written and oral exams. *Entrance requirements:* For master's, minimum GPA of 2.75, valid teaching license; for doctorate, MAT or GRE, minimum GPA of 3.5, three letters of recommendation, statement of purpose indicating career goals and research interest, controlled department writing sample, completion of Agreement to Advise Form, current curriculum vitae, at least three years of teaching experience. Additional exam requirements/recommendations for international students: Required—TOEFL (minimum score 550 paper-based; 79 iBT). *Application deadline:* For fall admission, 3/1 for domestic and international students; for spring admission, 10/1 for domestic and international students. Applications are processed on a rolling basis. Application fee: $40 ($60 for international students). Electronic applications accepted. *Expenses:* Tuition, state resident: full-time $7430; part-time $412.80 per credit hour. Tuition, nonresident: full-time $12,722; part-time $706.80 per credit hour. *Required fees:* $53 per credit hour. $12 per semester. Tuition and fees vary according to course load and program. *Unit head:* Dr. Sandra Coyner, Interim Chair, 330-972-5822, E-mail: scoyner@uakron.edu.

The University of Alabama, Graduate School, College of Education, Department of Curriculum and Instruction, Tuscaloosa, AL 35487. Offers elementary education (MA, Ed D, PhD, Ed S); secondary education (MA, Ed D, PhD, Ed S). Part-time and evening/weekend programs available. Postbaccalaureate distance learning degree programs offered (no on-campus study). *Faculty:* 20 full-time (15 women), 2 part-time/adjunct (both women). *Students:* 78 full-time (59 women), 102 part-time (81 women); includes 22 minority (18 Black or African American, non-Hispanic/Latino; 1 Hispanic/Latino; 3 Two or more races, non-Hispanic/Latino), 6 international. Average age 33. 71 applicants, 62% accepted, 33 enrolled. In 2013, 107 master's, 13 doctorates, 9 other advanced degrees awarded. *Degree requirements:* For master's, comprehensive exam, thesis (for some programs); for doctorate, comprehensive exam, thesis/dissertation; for Ed S, comprehensive exam, thesis optional. *Entrance requirements:* For master's, doctorate, and Ed S, MAT and/or GRE. Additional exam requirements/recommendations for international students: Recommended—TOEFL (minimum score 550 paper-based), IELTS (minimum score 6.5). *Application deadline:* For fall admission, 7/1 priority date for domestic students, 1/15 priority date for international students; for spring admission, 11/1 priority date for domestic students, 6/1 priority date for international students; for summer admission, 3/1 priority date for domestic and international students. Applications are processed on a rolling basis. Application fee: $50 ($60 for international students). Electronic applications accepted. *Expenses:* Tuition, state resident: full-time $9450. Tuition, nonresident: full-time $23,950. *Financial support:* In 2013–14, 14 students received support, including 10 research assistantships with tuition reimbursements available (averaging $9,844 per year), 4 teaching assistantships with tuition reimbursements available (averaging $9,844 per year); institutionally sponsored loans, traineeships, and unspecified assistantships also available. Financial award applicants required to submit FAFSA. *Faculty research:* Teacher education, diversity, integration of curriculum, technology, pedagogical content knowledge. *Total annual research expenditures:* $141,733. *Unit head:* Dr. Cynthia Sunal, Chair, 205-348-8264, Fax: 205-348-9863, E-mail: cvsunal@bamaed.ua.edu. *Application contact:* Dr. Kathy S. Wetzel, Assistant Dean for Student Services, 205-348-1154, Fax: 205-348-0080, E-mail: kwetzel@bamaed.ua.edu.
Website: http://courseleaf.ua.edu/education/curriculumandinstruction/.

The University of Alabama at Birmingham, School of Education, Program in High School Education, Birmingham, AL 35294. Offers MA Ed. *Accreditation:* NCATE. *Degree requirements:* For master's, thesis optional. *Entrance requirements:* For master's, GRE General Test, MAT, or NTE, minimum GPA of 3.0. Electronic applications accepted.

University of Alaska Fairbanks, School of Education, Program in Education, Fairbanks, AK 99775. Offers curriculum and instruction (M Ed); education (M Ed, Graduate Certificate); elementary education (M Ed); language and literacy (M Ed); reading (M Ed); secondary education (M Ed); special education (M Ed). *Faculty:* 23 full-time (14 women), 1 part-time/adjunct (0 women). *Students:* 37 full-time (26 women), 78 part-time (54 women); includes 15 minority (6 American Indian or Alaska Native, non-Hispanic/Latino; 6 Hispanic/Latino; 3 Two or more races, non-Hispanic/Latino), 2 international. Average age 34. 37 applicants, 68% accepted, 19 enrolled. In 2013, 39 master's, 28 other advanced degrees awarded. *Degree requirements:* For master's, comprehensive exam, thesis, oral defense. *Entrance requirements:* Additional exam requirements/recommendations for international students: Required—TOEFL (minimum score 550 paper-based; 80 iBT). *Application deadline:* For fall admission, 5/1 for domestic students, 3/1 for international students; for spring admission, 10/15 for domestic students, 8/1 for international students. Applications are processed on a rolling basis. Application fee: $60. Electronic applications accepted. *Expenses:* Tuition, state resident: full-time $7254; part-time $403 per credit. Tuition, nonresident: full-time $14,814; part-time $823 per credit. Tuition and fees vary according to course level, course load and reciprocity agreements. *Financial support:* In 2013–14, 1 teaching assistantship with tuition reimbursement (averaging $11,011 per year) was awarded; fellowships with tuition reimbursements, research assistantships with tuition reimbursements, career-related internships or fieldwork, Federal Work-Study, scholarships/grants, health care benefits, and unspecified assistantships also available. Support available to part-time students. Financial award application deadline: 6/1; financial award applicants required to submit FAFSA. *Unit head:* Allan Morotti, Interim Dean, 907-474-7341, Fax: 907-474-5451, E-mail: uaf-soe-school@alaska.edu. *Application contact:* Libby Eddy, Director of Admissions, 907-474-7500, Fax: 907-474-7097, E-mail: admissions@uaf.edu.
Website: https://sites.google.com/a/alaska.edu/soe-graduate/.

University of Alaska Southeast, Graduate Programs, Program in Education, Juneau, AK 99801. Offers early childhood education (M Ed, MAT); educational technology (M Ed); elementary education (MAT); reading (M Ed); secondary education (MAT). *Accreditation:* NCATE. Part-time and evening/weekend programs available. Postbaccalaureate distance learning degree programs offered (minimal on-campus study). *Degree requirements:* For master's, comprehensive exam or project, portfolio. *Entrance requirements:* For master's, PRAXIS, minimum GPA of 3.0, writing sample, letters of recommendation. Electronic applications accepted. *Faculty research:* Applied classroom research, culturally responsive practices, action research, teaching effectiveness.

University of Alberta, Faculty of Graduate Studies and Research, Department of Secondary Education, Edmonton, AB T6G 2E1, Canada. Offers M Ed, Ed D, PhD. Part-time programs available. *Degree requirements:* For master's, thesis or alternative, 1 year of residency; for doctorate, thesis/dissertation, 2 years of residency (PhD), 1 year of residency (Ed D). *Entrance requirements:* For master's, teaching certificate, 2 years of teaching experience; for doctorate, master's degree. *Faculty research:* Curriculum studies, teacher education, subject area specializations.

The University of Arizona, College of Education, Department of Teaching, Learning and Sociocultural Studies, Program in Teaching and Teacher Education, Tucson, AZ 85721. Offers M Ed, MA, PhD. Part-time and evening/weekend programs available. *Faculty:* 24 full-time (19 women), 1 (woman) part-time/adjunct. *Students:* 90 full-time (61 women), 37 part-time (24 women); includes 31 minority (3 Black or African American, non-Hispanic/Latino; 2 Asian, non-Hispanic/Latino; 18 Hispanic/Latino; 8 Two or more

races, non-Hispanic/Latino), 7 international. Average age 36. 111 applicants, 71% accepted, 57 enrolled. In 2013, 70 master's, 3 doctorates awarded. *Degree requirements:* For master's, thesis optional; for doctorate, comprehensive exam, thesis/dissertation. *Entrance requirements:* For master's, writing sample, 1 year of teaching experience, 3 letters of recommendation; for doctorate, GRE General Test (minimum score 1000), minimum GPA of 3.5, 2 years of teaching experience, 3 letters of recommendation, writing sample. Additional exam requirements/recommendations for international students: Required—TOEFL (minimum score 550 paper-based; 79 iBT). *Application deadline:* For fall admission, 2/1 for domestic students, 12/1 for international students; for spring admission, 10/1 for domestic students, 6/1 for international students. Applications are processed on a rolling basis. Application fee: $75. Electronic applications accepted. *Expenses:* Tuition, state resident: full-time $11,526. Tuition, nonresident: full-time $27,398. *Financial support:* In 2013–14, 19 research assistantships with full tuition reimbursements (averaging $19,534 per year), 25 teaching assistantships with full tuition reimbursements (averaging $16,157 per year) were awarded; career-related internships or fieldwork, scholarships/grants, health care benefits, tuition waivers (full and partial), and unspecified assistantships also available. Financial award application deadline: 4/15. *Faculty research:* Staff development, science education, environmental education, math education. *Total annual research expenditures:* $1.7 million. *Unit head:* Dr. Bruce Johnson, Department Head, 520-621-7820, E-mail: brucej@email.arizona.edu. *Application contact:* Information Contact, 520-621-6993, E-mail: ttegrad@email.arizona.edu.
Website: https://www.coe.arizona.edu/tls/degrees_programs.

University of Arkansas, Graduate School, College of Education and Health Professions, Department of Curriculum and Instruction, Program in Secondary Education, Fayetteville, AR 72701-1201. Offers M Ed, MAT, Ed S. *Accreditation:* NCATE. Electronic applications accepted. *Faculty research:* Mathematics.

University of Arkansas at Little Rock, Graduate School, College of Education, Department of Teacher Education, Program in Secondary Education, Little Rock, AR 72204-1099. Offers M Ed. *Accreditation:* NCATE. Part-time programs available. *Degree requirements:* For master's, comprehensive exam. *Entrance requirements:* For master's, interview, minimum GPA of 2.75, GRE General Test or teaching certificate. *Expenses:* Tuition, state resident: full-time $5690; part-time $284.50 per credit hour. Tuition, nonresident: full-time $13,030; part-time $651.50 per credit hour. *Required fees:* $1121; $672 per term. One-time fee: $40 full-time.

University of Arkansas at Pine Bluff, School of Education, Pine Bluff, AR 71601-2799. Offers early childhood education (M Ed); secondary education (M Ed), including English education, mathematics education, physical education, science education, social studies education; teaching (MAT). *Accreditation:* NCATE. Part-time and evening/weekend programs available. *Degree requirements:* For master's, comprehensive exam. *Entrance requirements:* For master's, GRE, minimum GPA of 2.75, NTE or Standard Arkansas Teaching Certificate. *Faculty research:* Teacher certification, accreditation, assessment, standards, portfolio development, rehabilitation, technology.

University of Bridgeport, School of Education, Department of Education, Bridgeport, CT 06604. Offers education (MS); educational management (Ed D, Diploma), including intermediate administrator or supervisor (Diploma), leadership (Ed D); elementary education (MS, Diploma), including early childhood education, elementary education; middle school education (MS); music education (MS); remedial reading and language arts (Diploma); secondary education (MS, Diploma), including computer specialist (Diploma), international education (Diploma), reading specialist, secondary education. Part-time and evening/weekend programs available. *Faculty:* 12 full-time (5 women), 108 part-time/adjunct (60 women). *Students:* 155 full-time (108 women), 139 part-time (98 women); includes 48 minority (22 Black or African American, non-Hispanic/Latino; 9 Asian, non-Hispanic/Latino; 15 Hispanic/Latino; 2 Two or more races, non-Hispanic/Latino), 2 international. Average age 30. 306 applicants, 55% accepted, 107 enrolled. In 2013, 153 master's, 16 other advanced degrees awarded. *Degree requirements:* For master's, final exam, final project, or thesis; for doctorate, comprehensive exam, thesis/dissertation; for Diploma, thesis or alternative, final project. *Entrance requirements:* For master's, minimum undergraduate QPA of 2.67; for doctorate, GRE, MAT; for Diploma, GRE General Test or MAT, minimum graduate QPA of 3.0. Additional exam requirements/recommendations for international students: Recommended—TOEFL (minimum score 550 paper-based; 80 iBT), IELTS (minimum score 6.5). *Application deadline:* For fall admission, 8/1 priority date for domestic and international students; for spring admission, 12/1 priority date for domestic and international students. Applications are processed on a rolling basis. Application fee: $50. Electronic applications accepted. *Expenses:* Contact institution. *Financial support:* In 2013–14, 120 students received support. Fellowships, research assistantships, teaching assistantships, career-related internships or fieldwork, Federal Work-Study, and institutionally sponsored loans available. Support available to part-time students. Financial award application deadline: 6/1; financial award applicants required to submit FAFSA. *Faculty research:* Self-concept, internship assessment, stress and situational development, follow-up of graduation, trend analysis. *Unit head:* Dr. Allen P. Cook, Dean, 203-576-4192, Fax: 203-576-4200, E-mail: acook@bridgeport.edu. *Application contact:* Leanne Proctor, Director of Graduate Admissions, 203-576-4552, Fax: 203-576-4941, E-mail: admit@bridgeport.edu.

University of California, Irvine, Department of Education, Irvine, CA 92697. Offers educational administration (Ed D); educational administration and leadership (Ed D); elementary and secondary education (MAT). Part-time and evening/weekend programs available. *Students:* 254 full-time (194 women), 4 part-time (3 women); includes 125 minority (1 Black or African American, non-Hispanic/Latino; 69 Asian, non-Hispanic/Latino; 41 Hispanic/Latino; 2 Native Hawaiian or other Pacific Islander, non-Hispanic/Latino; 12 Two or more races, non-Hispanic/Latino), 11 international. Average age 28. 506 applicants, 70% accepted, 200 enrolled. In 2013, 133 master's, 17 doctorates awarded. *Degree requirements:* For doctorate, thesis/dissertation. *Entrance requirements:* For master's, GRE, minimum GPA of 3.0; for doctorate, GRE General Test, minimum GPA of 3.0. Additional exam requirements/recommendations for international students: Required—TOEFL (minimum score 550 paper-based). *Application deadline:* For fall admission, 1/2 priority date for domestic students, 1/2 for international students. Application fee: $80 ($100 for international students). Electronic applications accepted. *Financial support:* Fellowships, research assistantships with full tuition reimbursements, institutionally sponsored loans, traineeships, health care benefits, and unspecified assistantships available. Financial award application deadline: 3/1; financial award applicants required to submit FAFSA. *Faculty research:* Education technology, learning theory, social theory, cultural diversity, postmodernism. *Unit head:* Deborah L. Vandell, Dean, 949-824-8026, Fax: 949-824-3968, E-mail: dvandell@uci.edu. *Application contact:* Judi Conroy, Director of Student Services, 949-824-7465, Fax: 949-824-9103, E-mail: jconroy@uci.edu.
Website: http://www.gse.uci.edu/.

University of Central Oklahoma, The Jackson College of Graduate Studies, College of Education and Professional Studies, Department of Educational Sciences, Foundations and Research, Edmond, OK 73034-5209. Offers secondary education (M Ed). Part-time programs available. *Faculty:* 5 full-time (2 women), 7 part-time/adjunct (4 women). *Students:* 26 full-time (16 women), 59 part-time (39 women); includes 18 minority (5

Black or African American, non-Hispanic/Latino; 3 American Indian or Alaska Native, non-Hispanic/Latino; 3 Hispanic/Latino; 1 Native Hawaiian or other Pacific Islander, non-Hispanic/Latino; 6 Two or more races, non-Hispanic/Latino), 1 international. Average age 31. 29 applicants, 86% accepted, 24 enrolled. In 2013, 19 master's awarded. *Degree requirements:* For master's, comprehensive exam (for some programs). *Entrance requirements:* For master's, GRE General Test. Additional exam requirements/recommendations for international students: Required—TOEFL (minimum score 550 paper-based; 79 iBT); Recommended—IELTS (minimum score 6.5). *Application deadline:* For fall admission, 7/1 for international students; for spring admission, 11/1 for international students. Applications are processed on a rolling basis. Application fee: $50. Electronic applications accepted. *Expenses:* Tuition, state resident: full-time $4137; part-time $206.85 per credit hour. Tuition, nonresident: full-time $10,359; part-time $517.95 per credit hour. *Required fees:* $481. Tuition and fees vary according to course load and program. *Financial support:* In 2013–14, 17 students received support, including 2 research assistantships with partial tuition reimbursements available (averaging $5,915 per year); teaching assistantships with partial tuition reimbursements available, career-related internships or fieldwork, scholarships/grants, tuition waivers (partial), and unspecified assistantships also available. Financial award application deadline: 3/31; financial award applicants required to submit FAFSA. *Faculty research:* At-risk youth. *Unit head:* Dr. Diane Jackson, Chair, 405-974-5327, Fax: 405-974-3851, E-mail: djackson@uco.edu. *Application contact:* Dr. Richard Bernard, Dean, Jackson College of Graduate Studies, 405-974-3493, Fax: 405-974-3852, E-mail: gradcoll@uco.edu.
Website: http://www.uco.edu/ceps/dept/pte/.

University of Cincinnati, Graduate School, College of Education, Criminal Justice, and Human Services, Division of Teacher Education, Program in Secondary Education, Cincinnati, OH 45221. Offers M Ed. *Accreditation:* NCATE. Part-time programs available. *Degree requirements:* For master's, thesis or alternative. *Entrance requirements:* For master's, GRE General Test. Additional exam requirements/recommendations for international students: Required—TOEFL (minimum score 550 paper-based), TWE (minimum score 4.5), OEPT. Electronic applications accepted.

University of Colorado Denver, School of Education and Human Development, Information and Learning Technologies Program, Denver, CO 80217-3364. Offers e-learning design and implementation (MA); instructional design and adult learning (MA); K-12 teaching (MA). Part-time and evening/weekend programs available. Postbaccalaureate distance learning degree programs offered (no on-campus study). *Students:* 60 full-time (49 women), 59 part-time (43 women); includes 16 minority (2 Black or African American, non-Hispanic/Latino; 3 Asian, non-Hispanic/Latino; 10 Hispanic/Latino; 1 Two or more races, non-Hispanic/Latino), 1 international. Average age 38. 32 applicants, 88% accepted, 23 enrolled. In 2013, 47 master's awarded. *Degree requirements:* For master's, comprehensive exam (for some programs), comprehensive exam or online portfolio; 30 credit hours. *Entrance requirements:* For master's, GRE or MAT (if GPA is below 2.75), resume, statement of intent, three letters of recommendation. Additional exam requirements/recommendations for international students: Required—TOEFL (minimum score 537 paper-based; 75 iBT); Recommended—IELTS (minimum score 6.5). *Application deadline:* For fall admission, 5/15 for domestic students, 5/1 for international students; for spring admission, 11/15 for domestic students, 11/1 for international students. Application fee: $50 ($75 for international students). *Expenses:* Contact institution. *Financial support:* In 2013–14, 2 students received support. Fellowships, research assistantships, teaching assistantships, Federal Work-Study, institutionally sponsored loans, scholarships/grants, and traineeships available. Financial award application deadline: 4/1; financial award applicants required to submit FAFSA. *Faculty research:* Technology for educational management, instructional design foundations, e-Learning, educational design. *Unit head:* Brent Wilson, Professor, 303-315-4963, E-mail: brent.wilson@ucdenver.edu. *Application contact:* Hans Broers, Academic Advisor, 303-315-6351, Fax: 303-315-6311, E-mail: hans.broers@ucdenver.edu.
Website: http://www.ucdenver.edu/academics/colleges/SchoolOfEducation/Academics/MASTERS/ILT/Pages/default.aspx.

University of Colorado Denver, School of Education and Human Development, Teacher Education Programs, Denver, CO 80217. Offers elementary linguistically diverse education (MA); elementary math and science education (MA); elementary math education (MA); elementary reading and writing (MA); elementary science education (MA); secondary English education (MA); secondary linguistically diverse education (MA); secondary math education (MA); secondary reading and writing (MA); secondary science education (MA); special education (MA). *Accreditation:* NCATE. Part-time and evening/weekend programs available. *Students:* 269 full-time (208 women), 141 part-time (111 women); includes 55 minority (4 Black or African American, non-Hispanic/Latino; 1 American Indian or Alaska Native, non-Hispanic/Latino; 10 Asian, non-Hispanic/Latino; 39 Hispanic/Latino; 1 Two or more races, non-Hispanic/Latino), 7 international. Average age 31. 97 applicants, 81% accepted, 62 enrolled. In 2013, 180 master's awarded. *Degree requirements:* For master's, comprehensive exam. *Entrance requirements:* For master's, GRE or MAT (for those with GPA below 2.75), transcripts, resume, letters of recommendation. Additional exam requirements/recommendations for international students: Required—TOEFL (minimum score 537 paper-based; 75 iBT); Recommended—IELTS (minimum score 6.5). *Application deadline:* For fall admission, 4/15 priority date for domestic students, 4/1 for international students; for spring admission, 9/15 priority date for domestic students, 9/1 for international students. Applications are processed on a rolling basis. Application fee: $50 ($75 for international students). Electronic applications accepted. *Expenses:* Contact institution. *Financial support:* In 2013–14, 42 students received support. Fellowships, research assistantships, teaching assistantships, Federal Work-Study, institutionally sponsored loans, scholarships/grants, and traineeships available. Financial award application deadline: 4/1; financial award applicants required to submit FAFSA. *Faculty research:* Linguistically diverse education/ESL, elementary reading and writing, elementary teacher education, secondary teacher education, special education. *Unit head:* Cindy Gutierrez, Director, 303-315-4982, E-mail: cindy.gutierrez@ucdenver.edu. *Application contact:* Lori Sisneros, Student Services Center, 303-315-4979, E-mail: education@ucdenver.edu.
Website: http://www.ucdenver.edu/academics/colleges/SchoolOfEducation/Academics/MASTERS/Pages/default.aspx.

University of Connecticut, Graduate School, Neag School of Education, Department of Curriculum and Instruction, Program in Secondary Education, Storrs, CT 06269. Offers MA, PhD, Post-Master's Certificate. *Accreditation:* NCATE. Terminal master's awarded for partial completion of doctoral program. *Degree requirements:* For master's, comprehensive exam, thesis or alternative; for doctorate, thesis/dissertation. *Entrance requirements:* For doctorate, GRE General Test. Additional exam requirements/recommendations for international students: Required—TOEFL (minimum score 550 paper-based). Electronic applications accepted.

University of Dayton, Department of Teacher Education, Dayton, OH 45469-1300. Offers adolescence to young adult education (MS Ed); early childhood education (MS Ed); early childhood leadership and advocacy (MS Ed); interdisciplinary education studies (MS Ed); intervention specialist education, mild/moderate (MS Ed); literacy

(MS Ed); middle childhood education (MS Ed); multi-age education (MS Ed); music education (MS Ed); teacher as leader (MS Ed); technology enhanced learning (MS Ed). Part-time and evening/weekend programs available. Postbaccalaureate distance learning degree programs offered (no on-campus study). *Faculty:* 19 full-time (13 women), 21 part-time/adjunct (18 women). *Students:* 69 full-time (57 women), 86 part-time (75 women); includes 16 minority (10 Black or African American, non-Hispanic/Latino; 2 Asian, non-Hispanic/Latino; 4 Hispanic/Latino), 10 international. Average age 31. 140 applicants, 54% accepted, 39 enrolled. In 2013, 93 master's awarded. *Degree requirements:* For master's, variable foreign language requirement, comprehensive exam (for some programs), thesis. *Entrance requirements:* For master's, GRE or MAT, minimum GPA of 2.75. Additional exam requirements/recommendations for international students: Required—TOEFL (minimum score 550 paper-based; 80 iBT), IELTS (minimum score 6.5). *Application deadline:* For fall admission, 3/1 for domestic students, 5/1 for international students; for winter admission, 7/1 for international students; for spring admission, 11/1 for international students. Applications are processed on a rolling basis. Application fee: $0 ($50 for international students). Electronic applications accepted. *Expenses:* Contact institution. *Financial support:* In 2013–14, 61 students received support, including 5 research assistantships with full tuition reimbursements available (averaging $8,720 per year), 3 teaching assistantships with full tuition reimbursements available (averaging $8,720 per year); career-related internships or fieldwork, institutionally sponsored loans, scholarships/grants, traineeships, health care benefits, and unspecified assistantships also available. Support available to part-time students. Financial award application deadline: 3/1; financial award applicants required to submit FAFSA. *Faculty research:* Diversity, literacy, art representation by young children, preservice teacher preparation. *Unit head:* Dr. Connie L. Bowman, Chair, 937-229-3305, E-mail: cbowman1@udayton.edu. *Application contact:* Gina Seiter, Graduate Program Advisor, 937-229-3103, E-mail: gseiter1@udayton.edu.

University of Great Falls, Graduate Studies, Secondary Teaching Program, Great Falls, MT 59405. Offers MAT. Part-time programs available. Postbaccalaureate distance learning degree programs offered (no on-campus study). *Degree requirements:* For master's, comprehensive exam, thesis optional, extensive portfolio. *Entrance requirements:* For master's, GRE General Test or MAT, bachelor's degree in teaching, teaching certificate, interview, 3 letters of recommendation, minimum undergraduate GPA of 3.0. Additional exam requirements/recommendations for international students: Required—TOEFL (minimum score 500 paper-based). Electronic applications accepted. *Faculty research:* Gifted, curriculum design, administration.

University of Guam, Office of Graduate Studies, School of Education, Program in Secondary Education, Mangilao, GU 96923. Offers M Ed. *Degree requirements:* For master's, thesis, comprehensive oral and written exams. *Entrance requirements:* For master's, GRE General Test. Additional exam requirements/recommendations for international students: Required—TOEFL.

University of Houston–Downtown, College of Public Service, Department of Urban Education, Houston, TX 77002. Offers curriculum and instruction (MAT); elementary (EC-6) generalist certification (MAT); elementary/middle school (4-8) generalist certification (MAT); secondary education certification (MAT). Part-time and evening/weekend programs available. Postbaccalaureate distance learning degree programs offered. *Faculty:* 7 full-time (3 women). *Students:* 4 full-time (3 women), 28 part-time (19 women); includes 22 minority (14 Black or African American, non-Hispanic/Latino; 1 Asian, non-Hispanic/Latino; 6 Hispanic/Latino; 1 Two or more races, non-Hispanic/Latino). Average age 36. 31 applicants, 87% accepted, 27 enrolled. In 2013, 10 master's awarded. *Degree requirements:* For master's, capstone course with completed project, position paper, grant proposal, empirical study, curriculum development/revision, or advanced technology project presented at annual Graduate Project Exhibition. *Entrance requirements:* For master's, GRE, personal statement, 3 recommendation forms. Additional exam requirements/recommendations for international students: Required—TOEFL (minimum score 550 paper-based; 80 iBT). *Application deadline:* For fall admission, 7/15 for domestic and international students; for spring admission, 11/15 for domestic and international students. Application fee: $35 ($60 for international students). Electronic applications accepted. *Expenses:* Tuition, state resident: full-time $4212; part-time $234 per credit hour. Tuition, nonresident: full-time $9684; part-time $538 per credit hour. *Required fees:* $1074. Tuition and fees vary according to program. *Financial support:* Scholarships/grants available. Financial award applicants required to submit FAFSA. *Unit head:* Dr. Viola Garcia, Department Chair, 713-221-8165, Fax: 713-226-5294, E-mail: garciav@uhd.edu. *Application contact:* Ceshia Love, Assistant Director of Graduate Admissions, 713-221-8093, Fax: 713-223-7408, E-mail: gradadmissions@uhd.edu.
Website: http://www.uhd.edu/academic/colleges/publicservice/urbaned/.

University of Illinois at Chicago, Graduate College, College of Education, Department of Curriculum and Instruction, Chicago, IL 60607-7128. Offers curriculum studies (PhD); educational studies (M Ed); elementary education (M Ed); instructional leadership (M Ed); literacy, language and culture (M Ed, PhD); science education (M Ed); secondary education (M Ed). Part-time and evening/weekend programs available. *Faculty:* 20 full-time (10 women), 10 part-time/adjunct (8 women). *Students:* 124 full-time (89 women), 155 part-time (117 women); includes 117 minority (51 Black or African American, non-Hispanic/Latino; 19 Asian, non-Hispanic/Latino; 43 Hispanic/Latino; 4 Two or more races, non-Hispanic/Latino), 11 international. Average age 32. 154 applicants, 70% accepted, 74 enrolled. In 2013, 108 master's, 16 doctorates awarded. *Degree requirements:* For doctorate, thesis/dissertation. *Entrance requirements:* For master's, minimum GPA of 2.75; for doctorate, GRE General Test, minimum GPA of 2.75. Additional exam requirements/recommendations for international students: Required—TOEFL. *Application deadline:* For fall admission, 1/9 for domestic and international students; for spring admission, 10/1 for domestic and international students. Applications are processed on a rolling basis. Application fee: $40 ($50 for international students). Electronic applications accepted. *Expenses:* Tuition, state resident: full-time $11,066; part-time $3689 per term. Tuition, nonresident: full-time $23,064; part-time $7688 per term. *Required fees:* $3004; $1190 per term. Tuition and fees vary according to course level and program. *Financial support:* In 2013–14, 101 students received support, including 4 fellowships with full tuition reimbursements available; research assistantships with full tuition reimbursements available, teaching assistantships with full tuition reimbursements available, career-related internships or fieldwork, Federal Work-Study, institutionally sponsored loans, traineeships, tuition waivers (full), and unspecified assistantships also available. Support available to part-time students. Financial award application deadline: 3/1; financial award applicants required to submit FAFSA. *Faculty research:* Curriculum theory, curriculum development, research on teaching, curriculum and context, reading/literacy. *Total annual research expenditures:* $70,000. *Unit head:* Prof. Alfred Tatum, Associate Professor/Director/Chair, 312-413-3883, Fax: 312-996-8134, E-mail: atatum1@uic.edu.
Website: http://education.uic.edu.

University of Indianapolis, Graduate Programs, School of Education, Indianapolis, IN 46227-3697. Offers art education (MAT); biology (MAT); chemistry (MAT); curriculum and instruction (MA); earth sciences (MAT); education (MA, MAT); educational leadership (MA); elementary education (MA); English (MAT); French (MAT); math (MAT); physical education (MAT); physics (MAT); secondary education (MA), including art education, education, English education, social studies education; social studies (MAT); Spanish (MAT). *Accreditation:* NCATE. Part-time and evening/weekend programs available. *Faculty:* 5 full-time (4 women), 2 part-time/adjunct (1 woman). *Students:* 19 full-time (9 women), 54 part-time (27 women); includes 13 minority (5 Black or African American, non-Hispanic/Latino; 1 Asian, non-Hispanic/Latino; 5 Hispanic/Latino; 2 Two or more races, non-Hispanic/Latino), 1 international. Average age 32. In 2013, 52 master's awarded. *Entrance requirements:* For master's, GRE Subject Test, PRAXIS I, minimum GPA of 2.5, 3 letters of recommendation, interview. Additional exam requirements/recommendations for international students: Required—TOEFL (minimum score 550 paper-based). *Application deadline:* Applications are processed on a rolling basis. Application fee: $50. *Expenses:* Tuition: Full-time $5436; part-time $810 per credit hour. *Financial support:* Federal Work-Study available. Financial award application deadline: 5/1; financial award applicants required to submit FAFSA. *Faculty research:* Assessment of teacher education, perceptions of prospective teachers by parents. *Unit head:* Dr. Kathy Moran, Dean, 317-788-3285, Fax: 317-788-3300, E-mail: kmoran@uindy.edu. *Application contact:* Jeni Kirby, Administrative Assistant, Teacher Education, 317-788-2113, E-mail: kirbyj@uindy.edu.
Website: http://education.uindy.edu/.

The University of Iowa, Graduate College, College of Education, Department of Teaching and Learning, Program in Education, Iowa City, IA 52242-1316. Offers art education (MA); developmental reading (MA); elementary education (MA); English education (MA, MAT); foreign and second language education (MAT); foreign language education (MA); foreign language/ESL education (PhD); language, literacy and culture (PhD); mathematics education (MA, MAT, PhD); music education (MM, PhD); science education (MA); secondary education (MA); social studies (MA, PhD). *Degree requirements:* For master's, thesis optional, exam; for doctorate, comprehensive exam, thesis/dissertation. *Entrance requirements:* For master's and doctorate, GRE General Test, minimum GPA of 3.0. Additional exam requirements/recommendations for international students: Required—TOEFL (minimum score 550 paper-based; 81 iBT). Electronic applications accepted.

University of Kentucky, Graduate School, College of Education, Department of Curriculum and Instruction, Lexington, KY 40506-0032. Offers curriculum and instruction (Ed D); elementary education (MA Ed); instructional system design (MS Ed); literacy (MA Ed); middle school education (MA Ed, MS Ed); secondary education (MA Ed, MS Ed). *Accreditation:* NCATE. *Degree requirements:* For master's, comprehensive exam, thesis optional; for doctorate, comprehensive exam, thesis/dissertation. *Entrance requirements:* For master's, GRE General Test, minimum undergraduate GPA of 2.75; for doctorate, GRE General Test, minimum graduate GPA of 3.0. Additional exam requirements/recommendations for international students: Required—TOEFL (minimum score 550 paper-based). Electronic applications accepted. *Faculty research:* Educational reform, multicultural education, classroom instructional practices, performance based assessment, primary school programs.

University of La Verne, Regional and Online Campuses, Graduate Programs, Central Coast/Vandenberg Air Force Base Campuses, La Verne, CA 91750-4443. Offers business administration for experienced professionals (MBA), including health services management, information technology; education (special emphasis) (M Ed); educational counseling (MS); educational leadership (M Ed); multiple subject (elementary) (Credential); preliminary administrative services (Credential); pupil personnel services (Credential); single subject (secondary) (Credential). Part-time programs available. *Faculty:* 11 part-time/adjunct (2 women). *Students:* 17 full-time (7 women), 34 part-time (22 women); includes 15 minority (1 Black or African American, non-Hispanic/Latino; 1 American Indian or Alaska Native, non-Hispanic/Latino; 1 Asian, non-Hispanic/Latino; 10 Hispanic/Latino; 2 Two or more races, non-Hispanic/Latino). Average age 38. In 2013, 25 master's awarded. *Application deadline:* Applications are processed on a rolling basis. Application fee: $50. *Expenses:* Contact institution. *Financial support:* Institutionally sponsored loans available. Financial award application deadline: 3/2; financial award applicants required to submit FAFSA. *Unit head:* Kitt Vincent, Director, Central Coast Campus, 805-788-6202, Fax: 805-788-6201, E-mail: kvincent@laverne.edu. *Application contact:* Gene Teal, Admissions, 805-788-6205, Fax: 805-788-6201, E-mail: eteal@laverne.edu.
Website: http://www.laverne.edu/locations.

University of La Verne, Regional and Online Campuses, Graduate Programs, High Desert Campus, Victorville, CA 92392. Offers business administration for experienced professionals (MBA); educational counseling (MS); educational leadership (M Ed); multiple subject (elementary) (Credential); preliminary administrative services (Credential); pupil personnel services (Credential); single subject (secondary) (Credential). *Faculty:* 3 part-time/adjunct (0 women). *Students:* 10 full-time (6 women), 17 part-time (12 women); includes 14 minority (3 Black or African American, non-Hispanic/Latino; 3 Asian, non-Hispanic/Latino; 6 Hispanic/Latino; 1 Native Hawaiian or other Pacific Islander, non-Hispanic/Latino; 1 Two or more races, non-Hispanic/Latino). Average age 38. In 2013, 6 master's awarded. *Application deadline:* Applications are processed on a rolling basis. Application fee: $50. *Expenses:* Contact institution. *Financial support:* Application deadline: 3/2; applicants required to submit FAFSA. *Unit head:* Juli Roberts, Regional Campus Director, 760-955-6448, Fax: 760-843-9505, E-mail: jroberts@laverne.edu. *Application contact:* Donald Parker, Associate Director of Admissions, 760-955-6477, E-mail: dparker@laverne.edu.
Website: http://www.laverne.edu/locations/victorville/.

University of La Verne, Regional and Online Campuses, Graduate Programs, Kern County Campus, Bakersfield, CA 93301. Offers business administration for experienced professionals (MBA-EP); education (special emphasis) (M Ed); educational counseling (MS); educational leadership (M Ed); health administration (MHA); leadership and management (MS); mild/moderate education specialist preliminary (Credential); multiple subject (elementary) (Credential); organizational leadership (Ed D); preliminary administrative services (Credential); single subject (secondary) (Credential); special education studies (MS). Part-time and evening/weekend programs available. *Faculty:* 2 part-time/adjunct (1 woman). *Students:* 1 (woman) full-time, 5 part-time (3 women); includes 4 minority (3 Hispanic/Latino; 1 Two or more races, non-Hispanic/Latino). Average age 36. In 2013, 4 master's awarded. *Application deadline:* Applications are processed on a rolling basis. Application fee: $50. *Expenses:* Contact institution. *Financial support:* Institutionally sponsored loans available. Financial award application deadline: 3/2; financial award applicants required to submit FAFSA. *Unit head:* Nora Dominguez, Regional Campus Director, 661-861-6802, E-mail: ndominguez@laverne.edu. *Application contact:* Regina Benavides, Associate Director of Admissions, 661-861-6807, E-mail: rbenavides@laverne.edu.
Website: http://laverne.edu/locations/bakersfield/.

University of La Verne, Regional and Online Campuses, Graduate Programs, Ventura County/Point Mugu Naval Air Station Campuses, Oxnard, CA 93036. Offers business administration for experienced professionals (MS); educational counseling (MS); educational leadership (M Ed); leadership and management (MS); multiple subject (elementary) (Credential); pupil personnel services (Credential); single subject (secondary) (Credential). Part-time and evening/weekend programs available. *Faculty:* 12 part-time/adjunct (2 women). *Students:* 34 full-time (13 women), 37 part-time (20 women); includes 39 minority (3 Black or African American, non-Hispanic/Latino; 2

American Indian or Alaska Native, non-Hispanic/Latino; 3 Asian, non-Hispanic/Latino; 29 Hispanic/Latino; 2 Two or more races, non-Hispanic/Latino). Average age 38. In 2013, 31 master's awarded. Application fee: $50. *Expenses:* Contact institution. *Financial support:* Institutionally sponsored loans available. Financial award application deadline: 3/2; financial award applicants required to submit FAFSA. *Unit head:* Jamie Dempsey, Director, Point Mugu, 661-986-6902, E-mail: jdempsey@laverne.edu. *Application contact:* Kevin Laack, Regional Campus Director, Ventura, 805-981-6022, E-mail: klaack@laverne.edu.
Website: http://laverne.edu/locations/oxnard/.

University of Louisiana at Monroe, Graduate School, College of Arts, Education, and Sciences, School of Education, Program in Secondary Education 6-12, Monroe, LA 71209-0001. Offers MAT. *Accreditation:* NCATE. Part-time and evening/weekend programs available. *Entrance requirements:* For master's, GRE General Test, PRAXIS, minimum GPA of 2.5. Additional exam requirements/recommendations for international students: Required—TOEFL (minimum score 500 paper-based; 61 iBT). *Application deadline:* For fall admission, 8/24 priority date for domestic students, 7/1 for international students; for winter admission, 12/14 priority date for domestic students; for spring admission, 1/19 for domestic students, 11/1 for international students. Applications are processed on a rolling basis. Application fee: $20 ($30 for international students). Electronic applications accepted. *Expenses:* Tuition, state resident: full-time $6607. Tuition, nonresident: full-time $17,179. Full-time tuition and fees vary according to program. *Financial support:* Career-related internships or fieldwork, Federal Work-Study, and unspecified assistantships available. Financial award application deadline: 4/1; financial award applicants required to submit FAFSA. *Unit head:* Dr. Dorothy Schween, Director, 318-342-1268, E-mail: schween@ulm.edu. *Application contact:* Dr. Dorothy Schween, Director, 318-342-1268, E-mail: schween@ulm.edu.

University of Louisville, Graduate School, College of Education and Human Development, Department of Teaching and Learning, Louisville, KY 40292-0001. Offers art education (MAT); curriculum and instruction (PhD); early elementary education (MAT); instructional technology (M Ed); interdisciplinary early childhood education (MAT); middle school education (MAT); music education (MAT); secondary education (MAT); special education (MAT); teacher leadership (M Ed). Part-time and evening/weekend programs available. *Students:* 137 full-time (93 women), 208 part-time (131 women); includes 44 minority (25 Black or African American, non-Hispanic/Latino; 1 American Indian or Alaska Native, non-Hispanic/Latino; 3 Asian, non-Hispanic/Latino; 12 Hispanic/Latino; 3 Two or more races, non-Hispanic/Latino), 2 international. Average age 32. 150 applicants, 51% accepted, 54 enrolled. In 2013, 127 master's, 5 doctorates awarded. *Degree requirements:* For doctorate, comprehensive exam, thesis/dissertation. *Entrance requirements:* For master's, GRE General Test, PRAXIS II (for some programs); for doctorate, GRE General Test. Additional exam requirements/recommendations for international students: Required—TOEFL (minimum score 560 paper-based; 83 iBT). *Application deadline:* For fall admission, 5/1 priority date for international students; for spring admission, 11/1 priority date for international students; for summer admission, 4/1 priority date for international students. Application fee: $60. Electronic applications accepted. *Expenses:* Tuition, state resident: full-time $10,788; part-time $599 per credit hour. Tuition, nonresident: full-time $22,446; part-time $1247 per credit hour. *Required fees:* $196. Tuition and fees vary according to program and reciprocity agreements. *Financial support:* Fellowships, research assistantships, teaching assistantships, career-related internships or fieldwork, Federal Work-Study, scholarships/grants, and unspecified assistantships available. Financial award application deadline: 6/1; financial award applicants required to submit FAFSA. *Faculty research:* Mathematics teacher education and ongoing professional development in pedagogy and content knowledge; development of literacy, including early literacy in science and mathematics and literacy development for English language learners; immersive visualizations for promoting STEM education from nanoscience to cosmic scales; evidence-based practices for students with disabilities; urban education, including teacher response to intervention systems in schools and cross-cultural competence. *Unit head:* Dr. Ann E. Larson, Acting Chair, 502-852-6431, Fax: 502-852-1497, E-mail: ann@louisville.edu. *Application contact:* Libby Leggett, Director, Graduate Admissions, 502-852-3101, Fax: 502-852-6536, E-mail: gradadm@louisville.edu.
Website: http://louisville.edu/delphi.

University of Maine, Graduate School, College of Education and Human Development, Department of Teacher and Counselor Education, Orono, ME 04469. Offers counselor education (M Ed, MA, MS, CAS); early childhood teacher (CGS); education (PhD), including counselor education, literacy education, prevention and intervention studies; elementary education (M Ed, CAS); individualized education (M Ed); literacy education (M Ed, MS, CAS); response to intervention for behavior (CGS); secondary education (M Ed, MAT, CAS); social studies education (M Ed); special education (M Ed, CAS); teacher consultant in writing (CGS). Part-time programs available. *Students:* 147 full-time (118 women), 15 part-time (2 women); includes 8 minority (4 Black or African American, non-Hispanic/Latino; 2 American Indian or Alaska Native, non-Hispanic/Latino; 1 Hispanic/Latino; 1 Two or more races, non-Hispanic/Latino), 3 international. Average age 37. 100 applicants, 58% accepted, 50 enrolled. In 2013, 83 master's, 5 doctorates, 17 other advanced degrees awarded. *Degree requirements:* For master's, thesis (for some programs); for doctorate, comprehensive exam, thesis/dissertation. *Entrance requirements:* For master's, GRE General Test, MAT. Additional exam requirements/recommendations for international students: Required—TOEFL. *Application deadline:* For fall admission, 2/1 priority date for domestic students. Applications are processed on a rolling basis. Application fee: $65. Electronic applications accepted. *Expenses:* Tuition, state resident: full-time $7524. Tuition, nonresident: full-time $23,112. *Required fees:* $1970. *Financial support:* In 2013–14, 46 students received support, including 1 research assistantship (averaging $14,600 per year), 11 teaching assistantships (averaging $14,600 per year). Financial award application deadline: 3/1. *Unit head:* Dr. Janet Spector, Coordinator, 207-581-2459. *Application contact:* Scott G. Delcourt, Associate Dean of the Graduate School, 207-581-3291, Fax: 207-581-3232, E-mail: graduate@maine.edu.
Website: http://umaine.edu/edhd/.

University of Mary Hardin-Baylor, Graduate Studies in Education, Belton, TX 76513. Offers administration of intervention programs (M Ed); curriculum and instruction (M Ed); educational administration (M Ed, Ed D), including higher education (Ed D), leadership in nursing education (Ed D), P-12 (Ed D). Part-time and evening/weekend programs available. *Faculty:* 13 full-time (10 women), 6 part-time/adjunct (2 women). *Students:* 46 full-time (33 women), 61 part-time (40 women); includes 35 minority (15 Black or African American, non-Hispanic/Latino; 1 American Indian or Alaska Native, non-Hispanic/Latino; 19 Hispanic/Latino), 1 international. Average age 38. 72 applicants, 88% accepted, 47 enrolled. In 2013, 13 master's, 30 doctorates awarded. *Degree requirements:* For master's, comprehensive exam; for doctorate, thesis/dissertation. *Entrance requirements:* For master's, minimum GPA of 3.0, interview; for doctorate, minimum GPA of 3.5, interview, essay, resume, employment verification, employer letter of support, 3 letters of recommendation. Additional exam requirements/recommendations for international students: Required—TOEFL (minimum score 550 paper-based; 80 iBT), IELTS (minimum score 6). *Application deadline:* For fall admission, 6/1 for domestic students, 6/15 priority date for international students; for spring admission, 11/1 for domestic students, 10/15 priority date for international students. Applications are processed on a rolling basis. Application fee: $35 ($135 for international students). Electronic applications accepted. *Expenses: Tuition:* Full-time $14,130; part-time $785 per credit hour. *Required fees:* $1350; $75 per credit hour. $50 per term. *Financial support:* Federal Work-Study and scholarships (for some active duty military personnel only) available. Support available to part-time students. Financial award application deadline: 6/1; financial award applicants required to submit FAFSA. *Unit head:* Dr. Marlene Zipperlen, Dean, College of Education/Director, Doctor of Education Program, 254-295-4572, Fax: 254-295-4480, E-mail: mzipperlen@umhb.edu. *Application contact:* Melissa Ford, Director of Graduate Admissions, 254-295-4020, Fax: 254-295-5038, E-mail: mford@umhb.edu.
Website: http://graduate.umhb.edu/education/.

University of Maryland, Baltimore County, Graduate School, College of Arts, Humanities and Social Sciences, Department of Education, Program in Teaching, Baltimore, MD 21250. Offers early childhood education (MAT); elementary education (MAT); secondary education (MAT), including art, biology, chemistry, dance, earth/space science, English, foreign language, mathematics, music, physics, social studies, theatre. Part-time and evening/weekend programs available. *Faculty:* 24 full-time (18 women), 25 part-time/adjunct (19 women). *Students:* 49 full-time (34 women), 35 part-time (23 women); includes 19 minority (9 Black or African American, non-Hispanic/Latino; 3 Asian, non-Hispanic/Latino; 6 Hispanic/Latino; 1 Two or more races, non-Hispanic/Latino). Average age 30. 40 applicants, 95% accepted, 35 enrolled. In 2013, 106 master's awarded. *Degree requirements:* For master's, comprehensive exam (for some programs), thesis (for some programs). *Entrance requirements:* For master's, PRAXIS I or SAT (minimum score of 1000), minimum GPA of 3.0. Additional exam requirements/recommendations for international students: Required—TOEFL. *Application deadline:* For fall admission, 6/1 for domestic students; for spring admission, 11/1 for domestic students. Applications are processed on a rolling basis. Application fee: $50. Electronic applications accepted. One-time fee: $200 full-time. *Financial support:* In 2013–14, 6 students received support, including teaching assistantships with full and partial tuition reimbursements available (averaging $12,000 per year); career-related internships or fieldwork, Federal Work-Study, scholarships/grants, tuition waivers, and unspecified assistantships also available. Financial award application deadline: 3/1. *Faculty research:* STEM teacher education, culturally sensitive pedagogy, ESOL/bilingual education, early childhood education, language, literacy and culture. *Unit head:* Dr. Susan M. Blunck, Graduate Program Director, 410-455-2869, Fax: 410-455-3986, E-mail: blunck@umbc.edu. *Application contact:* Dr. Susan M. Blunck, Graduate Program Director, 410-455-2869, Fax: 410-455-3986, E-mail: blunck@umbc.edu.
Website: http://www.umbc.edu/education/.

University of Maryland, College Park, Academic Affairs, College of Education, Department of Teaching, Learning, Policy and Leadership, College Park, MD 20742. Offers reading (M Ed, MA, PhD, CAGS); secondary education (M Ed, MA, Ed D, PhD, CAGS); teaching English to speakers of other languages (M Ed). *Accreditation:* NCATE. Part-time and evening/weekend programs available. Postbaccalaureate distance learning degree programs offered (no on-campus study). *Faculty:* 63 full-time (43 women), 20 part-time/adjunct (13 women). *Students:* 283 full-time (209 women), 188 part-time (151 women); includes 158 minority (58 Black or African American, non-Hispanic/Latino; 53 Asian, non-Hispanic/Latino; 23 Hispanic/Latino; 1 Native Hawaiian or other Pacific Islander, non-Hispanic/Latino; 23 Two or more races, non-Hispanic/Latino), 52 international. 482 applicants, 44% accepted, 126 enrolled. In 2013, 211 master's, 42 doctorates awarded. *Degree requirements:* For master's, comprehensive exam, seminar paper; for doctorate, comprehensive exam, thesis/dissertation, published paper, oral exam. *Entrance requirements:* For master's, GRE General Test or MAT, minimum GPA of 3.0, 3 letters of recommendation; for doctorate, GRE General Test or MAT, minimum undergraduate GPA of 3.0, graduate 3.5; 3 letters of recommendation. *Application deadline:* For fall admission, 2/1 priority date for domestic students, 9/1 priority date for international students; for spring admission, 9/1 for domestic students, 8/1 for international students. Applications are processed on a rolling basis. Application fee: $75. Electronic applications accepted. *Expenses:* Tuition, state resident: full-time $10,314; part-time $573 per credit hour. Tuition, nonresident: full-time $22,248; part-time $1236 per credit. *Required fees:* $1446; $403.15 per semester. Tuition and fees vary according to program. *Financial support:* In 2013–14, 11 fellowships with full and partial tuition reimbursements (averaging $22,271 per year), 7 research assistantships with tuition reimbursements (averaging $18,573 per year), 85 teaching assistantships with tuition reimbursements (averaging $17,609 per year) were awarded; Federal Work-Study and scholarships/grants also available. Support available to part-time students. Financial award applicants required to submit FAFSA. *Faculty research:* Teacher preparation, curriculum study, in-service education. *Total annual research expenditures:* $3.9 million. *Unit head:* Francine Hultgren, Interim Chair, 301-405-3117, E-mail: fh@umd.edu. *Application contact:* Dr. Charles A. Caramello, Dean of Graduate School, 301-405-0358, Fax: 301-314-9305, E-mail: ccaramel@umd.edu.

University of Massachusetts Amherst, Graduate School, College of Education, Program in Education, Amherst, MA 01003. Offers bilingual/English as a second language/multicultural education (M Ed, Ed S); child study and early education (M Ed); children, families and schools (Ed D, Ed S); early childhood and elementary teacher education (M Ed); educational leadership (M Ed); educational policy and leadership (Ed D); higher education (M Ed); international education (M Ed); language, literacy and culture (Ed D); learning, media and technology (M Ed, Ed S); mathematics, science, and learning technologies (Ed D); psychometric methods, educational statistics and research methods (Ed D); reading and writing (M Ed); school counselor education (M Ed, Ed S); school psychology (Ed S); science education (Ed S); secondary teacher education (M Ed); social justice education (M Ed, Ed D, Ed S); special education (M Ed, Ed D, Ed S); teacher education and school improvement (Ed D, Ed S). *Accreditation:* NCATE. Part-time programs available. Postbaccalaureate distance learning degree programs offered (minimal on-campus study). *Faculty:* 95 full-time (55 women). *Students:* 357 full-time (240 women), 264 part-time (194 women); includes 114 minority (41 Black or African American, non-Hispanic/Latino; 4 American Indian or Alaska Native, non-Hispanic/Latino; 10 Asian, non-Hispanic/Latino; 47 Hispanic/Latino; 12 Two or more races, non-Hispanic/Latino), 100 international. Average age 34. 761 applicants, 51% accepted, 200 enrolled. In 2013, 186 master's, 31 doctorates, 22 other advanced degrees awarded. Terminal master's awarded for partial completion of doctoral program. *Degree requirements:* For doctorate, comprehensive exam, thesis/dissertation. *Entrance requirements:* Additional exam requirements/recommendations for international students: Required—TOEFL (minimum score 550 paper-based; 80 iBT), IELTS (minimum score 6.5). *Application deadline:* For fall admission, 1/15 for domestic and international students. Applications are processed on a rolling basis. Application fee: $75. Electronic applications accepted. *Financial support:* Fellowships with full and partial tuition reimbursements, research assistantships with full and partial tuition reimbursements, teaching assistantships with full and partial tuition reimbursements, career-related internships or fieldwork, Federal Work-Study, scholarships/grants, traineeships, health care benefits, tuition waivers (full and partial), and unspecified assistantships available. Support available to part-time students. Financial award application deadline: 1/15; financial award applicants required to submit FAFSA. *Unit head:* Dr. Linda L. Griffin, Graduate Program Director, 413-545-6984, Fax: 413-545-

1523. *Application contact:* Lindsay DeSantis, Supervisor of Admissions, 413-545-0722, Fax: 413-577-0010, E-mail: gradadm@grad.umass.edu.
Website: http://www.umass.edu/education/.

University of Massachusetts Boston, Office of Graduate Studies, Graduate College of Education, School Organization, Curriculum and Instruction Department, Boston, MA 02125-3393. Offers education (M Ed, Ed D), including elementary and secondary education/certification (M Ed), higher education administration (Ed D), teacher certification (M Ed), urban school leadership (Ed D); educational administration (M Ed, CAGS); special education (M Ed). *Degree requirements:* For master's and CAGS, comprehensive exam; for doctorate, comprehensive exam, thesis/dissertation. *Entrance requirements:* For master's, GRE General Test or MAT; for doctorate, GRE General Test or MAT, minimum GPA of 2.75; for CAGS, minimum GPA of 2.75.

University of Massachusetts Boston, Office of Graduate Studies, Graduate College of Education, School Organization, Curriculum and Instruction Department, Program in Education, Track in Elementary and Secondary Education/Certification, Boston, MA 02125-3393. Offers M Ed. Part-time and evening/weekend programs available. *Degree requirements:* For master's, comprehensive exam, thesis optional, practicum. *Entrance requirements:* For master's, GRE General Test or MAT, minimum GPA of 3.0, 2 years of teaching experience. *Faculty research:* Anti-bias education, inclusionary curriculum and instruction, creativity and learning, science, technology and society, teaching of reading.

University of Massachusetts Dartmouth, Graduate School, College of Arts and Sciences, School of Education, Program in Teaching and Learning, North Dartmouth, MA 02747-2300. Offers middle school education (Postbaccalaureate Certificate); secondary school education (Postbaccalaureate Certificate). Part-time programs available. *Faculty:* 3 full-time (2 women), 9 part-time/adjunct (4 women). *Students:* 9 full-time (4 women), 136 part-time (94 women); includes 14 minority (2 Black or African American, non-Hispanic/Latino; 6 Hispanic/Latino; 6 Two or more races, non-Hispanic/Latino). Average age 35. 69 applicants, 94% accepted, 55 enrolled. In 2013, 13 Postbaccalaureate Certificates awarded. *Entrance requirements:* For degree, MTEL, statement of purpose (minimum of 300 words), resume, 2 letters of recommendation, official transcripts. Additional exam requirements/recommendations for international students: Required—TOEFL (minimum score 533 paper-based; 72 iBT). *Application deadline:* For fall admission, 7/15 priority date for domestic students, 6/15 priority date for international students; for spring admission, 12/15 priority date for domestic students, 11/15 priority date for international students. Applications are processed on a rolling basis. Application fee: $60. Electronic applications accepted. *Expenses:* Tuition, state resident: full-time $2071; part-time $86.29 per credit. Tuition, nonresident: full-time $8099; part-time $337.46 per credit. Tuition and fees vary according to course load and reciprocity agreements. *Financial support:* Federal Work-Study available. Support available to part-time students. Financial award application deadline: 3/1; financial award applicants required to submit FAFSA. *Faculty research:* Reading/special education, education reform, English education, literacy, language arts K-12. *Total annual research expenditures:* $1.1 million. *Unit head:* Traci Almeida, Graduate Program Director, 508-999-8098, Fax: 508-910-9055, E-mail: talmeida@umassd.edu. *Application contact:* Steven Briggs, Director of Marketing and Recruitment for Graduate Studies, 508-999-8604, Fax: 508-999-8183, E-mail: graduate@umassd.edu.
Website: http://www.umassd.edu/cas/schoolofeducation/stemeducationandteacherdevelopment.

University of Memphis, Graduate School, College of Education, Department of Instruction and Curriculum Leadership, Memphis, TN 38152. Offers early childhood education (MAT, MS, Ed D); elementary education (MAT); instruction and curriculum (MS, Ed D); instruction design and technology (MS, Ed D); middle grades education (MAT); reading (MS, Ed D); secondary education (MAT); special education (MAT, MS, Ed D). *Accreditation:* NCATE (one or more programs are accredited). Part-time programs available. *Faculty:* 30 full-time (18 women), 16 part-time/adjunct (10 women). *Students:* 55 full-time (44 women), 370 part-time (300 women); includes 169 minority (153 Black or African American, non-Hispanic/Latino; 5 American Indian or Alaska Native, non-Hispanic/Latino; 1 Asian, non-Hispanic/Latino; 6 Hispanic/Latino; 4 Two or more races, non-Hispanic/Latino), 7 international. Average age 35. 181 applicants, 84% accepted, 21 enrolled. In 2013, 137 master's, 10 doctorates awarded. Terminal master's awarded for partial completion of doctoral program. *Degree requirements:* For master's, comprehensive exam, thesis or alternative; for doctorate, comprehensive exam, thesis/dissertation. *Entrance requirements:* For master's, GRE General Test, minimum GPA of 2.5; for doctorate, GRE General Test, GRE Subject Test, 2 years of teaching experience. *Application deadline:* For fall admission, 8/1 for domestic students; for spring admission, 12/1 for domestic students. Applications are processed on a rolling basis. Application fee: $35 ($60 for international students). Electronic applications accepted. *Financial support:* In 2013–14, 635 students received support. Research assistantships with full tuition reimbursements available, teaching assistantships with full tuition reimbursements available, career-related internships or fieldwork, Federal Work-Study, institutionally sponsored loans, scholarships/grants, traineeships, and unspecified assistantships available. Support available to part-time students. Financial award application deadline: 2/15; financial award applicants required to submit FAFSA. *Faculty research:* Effective urban teachers, preparation and retention of urban teachers, technology utilization in schools, field-based teacher preparation programs, effective use of online instruction. *Unit head:* Dr. Sandra Cooley-Nichols, Interim Chair, 901-678-2365. *Application contact:* Dr. Sally Blake, Director of Graduate Studies, 901-678-4861.
Website: http://www.memphis.edu/icl/.

University of Michigan–Flint, School of Education and Human Services, Flint, MI 48502-1950. Offers early childhood education (MA); education (MA, Ed D), including education (MA), educational leadership (Ed D), elementary education with teaching certification (MA), literacy (K-12) (MA), technology in education (MA); education specialist (Ed S), including curriculum and instruction, education leadership; secondary education (MA); special education (MA). Part-time programs available. *Faculty:* 9 full-time (6 women), 12 part-time/adjunct (7 women). *Students:* 31 full-time (20 women), 206 part-time (153 women); includes 35 minority (31 Black or African American, non-Hispanic/Latino; 1 American Indian or Alaska Native, non-Hispanic/Latino; 1 Asian, non-Hispanic/Latino; 2 Hispanic/Latino), 1 international. Average age 36. 135 applicants, 80% accepted, 91 enrolled. In 2013, 99 master's awarded. *Entrance requirements:* For master's, BS with minimum GPA of 3.0. Additional exam requirements/recommendations for international students: Required—TOEFL (minimum score 560 paper-based; 84 iBT), IELTS (minimum score 6.5). *Application deadline:* For fall admission, 8/1 priority date for domestic students, 5/1 priority date for international students; for winter admission, 11/15 priority date for domestic students, 9/1 priority date for international students; for spring admission, 3/15 priority date for domestic students, 1/1 priority date for international students. Application fee: $55. Electronic applications accepted. *Expenses:* Contact institution. *Financial support:* Federal Work-Study, scholarships/grants, and unspecified assistantships available. Support available to part-time students. Financial award application deadline: 3/1; financial award applicants required to submit FAFSA. *Unit head:* Dr. Bob Barnett, Interim Dean, 810-766-6878, Fax: 810-766-6891, E-mail: rbarnett@umflint.edu. *Application contact:* Bradley T. Maki, Director of Graduate Admissions, 810-762-3171, Fax: 810-766-6789, E-mail: bmaki@umflint.edu.
Website: http://www.umflint.edu/sehs/.

University of Mississippi, Graduate School, School of Education, Department of Teacher Education, Oxford, MS 38677. Offers curriculum and instruction (MA); elementary education (M Ed, Ed D, Ed S); literacy education (M Ed); secondary education (M Ed, PhD, Ed S); special education (M Ed, PhD, Ed S). *Accreditation:* NCATE. *Faculty:* 42 full-time (29 women), 25 part-time/adjunct (22 women). *Students:* 70 full-time (59 women), 194 part-time (156 women); includes 67 minority (60 Black or African American, non-Hispanic/Latino; 1 Asian, non-Hispanic/Latino; 4 Hispanic/Latino; 2 Two or more races, non-Hispanic/Latino), 1 international. In 2013, 122 master's, 1 doctorate awarded. *Degree requirements:* For master's, thesis (for some programs); for doctorate, one foreign language, thesis/dissertation. *Entrance requirements:* For master's, GRE General Test, minimum GPA of 3.0; for doctorate, GRE General Test. Additional exam requirements/recommendations for international students: Required—TOEFL. *Application deadline:* For fall admission, 7/1 for domestic students; for spring admission, 10/1 for domestic students. Applications are processed on a rolling basis. Application fee: $40. *Financial support:* Scholarships/grants available. Financial award application deadline: 3/1; financial award applicants required to submit FAFSA. *Unit head:* Dr. Susan McClelland, Interim Chair, 662-915-7350. *Application contact:* Dr. Christy M. Wyandt, Associate Dean, 662-915-7474, Fax: 662-915-7577, E-mail: cwyandt@olemiss.edu.
Website: http://education.olemiss.edu/dco/teacher_education.html.

University of Missouri–St. Louis, College of Education, Division of Counseling, St. Louis, MO 63121. Offers clinical mental health counseling (M Ed); elementary school counseling (M Ed); secondary school counseling (M Ed). *Accreditation:* ACA; NCATE. Part-time and evening/weekend programs available. *Faculty:* 6 full-time (3 women), 19 part-time/adjunct (13 women). *Students:* 65 full-time (53 women), 131 part-time (108 women); includes 46 minority (32 Black or African American, non-Hispanic/Latino; 1 American Indian or Alaska Native, non-Hispanic/Latino; 3 Asian, non-Hispanic/Latino; 6 Hispanic/Latino; 4 Two or more races, non-Hispanic/Latino), 2 international. Average age 32. 73 applicants, 73% accepted, 37 enrolled. In 2013, 54 master's awarded. *Degree requirements:* For master's, comprehensive exam. *Entrance requirements:* For master's, 3 letters of recommendation. Additional exam requirements/recommendations for international students: Recommended—TOEFL (minimum score 550 paper-based; 79 iBT), IELTS (minimum score 6.5). *Application deadline:* For fall admission, 6/1 for domestic and international students; for spring admission, 10/1 for domestic and international students. Application fee: $50 ($40 for international students). Electronic applications accepted. *Expenses:* Tuition, state resident: full-time $7364; part-time $409.10 per credit hour. Tuition, nonresident: full-time $19,162; part-time $1008.50 per credit hour. *Financial support:* In 2013–14, 1 research assistantship with full and partial tuition reimbursement (averaging $12,500 per year), 2 teaching assistantships with full and partial tuition reimbursements (averaging $8,470 per year) were awarded. Financial award application deadline: 4/1; financial award applicants required to submit FAFSA. *Faculty research:* Vocational interests, self-concept, decision-making factors, developmental differences. *Unit head:* Dr. Mark Pope, Chair, 314-516-5782. *Application contact:* 314-516-5458, Fax: 314-516-6996, E-mail: gradadm@umsl.edu.

University of Missouri–St. Louis, College of Education, Division of Teaching and Learning, St. Louis, MO 63121. Offers autism studies (Certificate); elementary education (M Ed), including early childhood, general, reading; secondary education (M Ed), including curriculum and instruction, general, middle level education, reading, teaching English to speakers of other languages (TESOL); secondary school teaching (Certificate); special education (M Ed), including autism and developmental disabilities, cross-categorical disabilities, early childhood; teaching English to speakers of other languages (Certificate). Part-time and evening/weekend programs available. *Faculty:* 20 full-time (11 women), 1 (woman) part-time/adjunct. *Students:* 42 full-time (33 women), 578 part-time (442 women); includes 152 minority (101 Black or African American, non-Hispanic/Latino; 1 American Indian or Alaska Native, non-Hispanic/Latino; 20 Asian, non-Hispanic/Latino; 23 Hispanic/Latino; 7 Two or more races, non-Hispanic/Latino), 19 international. Average age 29. 245 applicants, 97% accepted, 166 enrolled. In 2013, 219 master's, 14 Certificates awarded. *Degree requirements:* For master's, comprehensive exam. *Entrance requirements:* Additional exam requirements/recommendations for international students: Recommended—TOEFL (minimum score 550 paper-based; 79 iBT), IELTS (minimum score 6.5). *Application deadline:* For fall admission, 7/1 priority date for domestic and international students; for spring admission, 12/1 priority date for domestic and international students. Application fee: $50 ($40 for international students). Electronic applications accepted. *Expenses:* Tuition, state resident: full-time $7364; part-time $409.10 per credit hour. Tuition, nonresident: full-time $19,162; part-time $1008.50 per credit hour. *Financial support:* Application deadline: 4/1; applicants required to submit FAFSA. *Unit head:* Dr. Patricia Kopetz, Chair, 314-516-5791. *Application contact:* 314-516-5458, Fax: 314-516-6996, E-mail: gadadm@umsl.edu.
Website: http://coe.umsl.edu/web/divisions/teach-learn/index.html.

University of Montevallo, College of Education, Program in Secondary/High School Education, Montevallo, AL 35115. Offers M Ed. *Accreditation:* NCATE. *Students:* 39 full-time (27 women), 72 part-time (41 women); includes 14 minority (13 Black or African American, non-Hispanic/Latino; 1 American Indian or Alaska Native, non-Hispanic/Latino). In 2013, 59 master's awarded. *Degree requirements:* For master's, comprehensive exam. *Entrance requirements:* For master's, GRE General Test, MAT, minimum undergraduate GPA of 2.5. Additional exam requirements/recommendations for international students: Required—TOEFL (minimum score 550 paper-based). *Application deadline:* For fall admission, 7/15 for domestic students; for spring admission, 11/15 for domestic students. Application fee: $25. *Financial support:* Federal Work-Study, scholarships/grants, and unspecified assistantships available. *Unit head:* Dr. Anna E. McEwan, Dean, 205-665-6360, E-mail: mcewanae@montevallo.edu. *Application contact:* Kevin Thornthwaite, Director, Graduate Admissions and Records, 205-665-6350, E-mail: graduate@montevallo.edu.
Website: http://www.montevallo.edu/education/college-of-education/traditional-masters-degrees/elementary-secondary-p-12-education/.

University of Nebraska at Kearney, Graduate Programs, College of Education, Department of Teacher Education, Kearney, NE 68849-0001. Offers curriculum and instruction (MA Ed), including early childhood education, elementary education, English as a second language, instructional effectiveness, reading/special education, secondary education; instructional technology (MS Ed), including information technology, instructional technology, school librarian; reading PK-12 (MA Ed); special education (MA Ed), including advanced practitioner, gifted, mild/moderate. Part-time and evening/weekend programs available. *Degree requirements:* For master's, comprehensive exam, thesis optional. *Entrance requirements:* For master's, portfolio or GRE. Additional exam requirements/recommendations for international students: Required—TOEFL (minimum score 550 paper-based). Electronic applications accepted.

University of Nebraska at Omaha, Graduate Studies, College of Education, Department of Teacher Education, Program in Secondary Education, Omaha, NE 68182. Offers MA, MS. *Accreditation:* NCATE. Part-time and evening/weekend programs available. *Faculty:* 8 full-time (6 women). *Students:* 13 full-time (7 women), 87

part-time (60 women); includes 10 minority (1 Asian, non-Hispanic/Latino; 6 Hispanic/Latino; 3 Two or more races, non-Hispanic/Latino), 2 international. Average age 35. 17 applicants, 71% accepted, 8 enrolled. In 2013, 31 master's awarded. *Degree requirements:* For master's, comprehensive exam, thesis (for some programs). *Entrance requirements:* For master's, minimum GPA of 3.0, transcripts. Additional exam requirements/recommendations for international students: Required—TOEFL, IELTS, PTE. *Application deadline:* For fall admission, 8/1 priority date for domestic students; for spring admission, 12/1 priority date for domestic students; for summer admission, 6/1 for domestic students. Applications are processed on a rolling basis. Application fee: $45. Electronic applications accepted. *Financial support:* In 2013–14, 2 students received support, including 2 research assistantships with tuition reimbursements available; fellowships, teaching assistantships with tuition reimbursements available, Federal Work-Study, institutionally sponsored loans, scholarships/grants, tuition waivers (full), and unspecified assistantships also available. Support available to part-time students. Financial award application deadline: 3/1. *Unit head:* Dr. Sarah Edwards, Advisor, 402-554-3512. *Application contact:* Dr. Wilma Kuhlman, Graduate Program Chair, 402-554-3926, E-mail: graduate@unomaha.edu.

University of Nevada, Reno, Graduate School, College of Education, Department of Curriculum, Teaching and Learning, Program in Secondary Education, Reno, NV 89557. Offers M Ed, MA, MS. *Degree requirements:* For master's, thesis optional. *Entrance requirements:* For master's, GRE General Test, minimum GPA of 2.75. Additional exam requirements/recommendations for international students: Required—TOEFL (minimum score 500 paper-based; 61 iBT), IELTS (minimum score 6). Electronic applications accepted. *Faculty research:* Educational trends, pedagogy.

University of New Hampshire, Graduate School, College of Liberal Arts, Department of Education, Program in Secondary Education, Durham, NH 03824. Offers M Ed, MAT. Part-time programs available. *Faculty:* 32 full-time. *Students:* 37 full-time (21 women), 61 part-time (31 women); includes 6 minority (3 Hispanic/Latino; 3 Native Hawaiian or other Pacific Islander, non-Hispanic/Latino). Average age 24. 46 applicants, 83% accepted, 27 enrolled. In 2013, 91 master's awarded. *Degree requirements:* For master's, thesis or alternative. *Entrance requirements:* For master's, GRE General Test. Additional exam requirements/recommendations for international students: Required—TOEFL (minimum score 550 paper-based; 80 iBT). *Application deadline:* For fall admission, 6/1 priority date for domestic students, 4/1 for international students; for spring admission, 12/1 for domestic students. Applications are processed on a rolling basis. Application fee: $65. Electronic applications accepted. *Expenses:* Tuition, state resident: full-time $13,500; part-time $750 per credit hour. Tuition, nonresident: full-time $26,200; part-time $1100 per credit hour. *Required fees:* $1741; $435.25 per term. Tuition and fees vary according to course level, course load, campus/location and program. *Financial support:* In 2013–14, 2 students received support, including 2 teaching assistantships; fellowships, research assistantships, career-related internships or fieldwork, Federal Work-Study, scholarships/grants, and tuition waivers (full and partial) also available. Support available to part-time students. Financial award application deadline: 2/15. *Faculty research:* Pre-service teacher education. *Unit head:* Dr. Mike Middleton, Chairperson, 603-862-7054, E-mail: education.department@unh.edu. *Application contact:* Lisa Wilder, Administrative Assistant, 603-862-2381, E-mail: education.department@unh.edu.
Website: http://www.unh.edu/education.

University of New Mexico, Graduate School, College of Education, Department of Teacher Education, Educational Leadership and Policy, Program in Secondary Education, Albuquerque, NM 87131-2039. Offers mathematics, science, and educational technology education (MA). Part-time programs available. *Faculty:* 10 full-time (7 women). *Students:* 31 full-time (20 women), 60 part-time (40 women); includes 26 minority (1 Black or African American, non-Hispanic/Latino; 3 American Indian or Alaska Native, non-Hispanic/Latino; 3 Asian, non-Hispanic/Latino; 17 Hispanic/Latino; 2 Two or more races, non-Hispanic/Latino). Average age 30. 57 applicants, 65% accepted, 35 enrolled. In 2013, 42 master's awarded. *Degree requirements:* For master's, comprehensive exam, thesis optional. *Entrance requirements:* For master's, minimum overall GPA of 3.0, some experience working with students, NMTA or teacher's licensure, 3 letters of reference, letter of intent. Additional exam requirements/recommendations for international students: Required—TOEFL (minimum score 550 paper-based). *Application deadline:* For fall admission, 2/1 for domestic students; for spring admission, 10/1 for domestic students. Application fee: $50. Electronic applications accepted. *Financial support:* In 2013–14, 74 students received support, including 2 teaching assistantships with partial tuition reimbursements available (averaging $8,713 per year); career-related internships or fieldwork, scholarships/grants, and unspecified assistantships also available. Financial award application deadline: 4/15. *Faculty research:* Secondary education, teacher education, reflective practice, teacher leadership, student learning. *Unit head:* Dr. Cheryl Torrez, Chair, 505-277-0911, Fax: 505-277-0455, E-mail: ted@unm.edu. *Application contact:* Robert Romero, Administrative Assistant, 505-277-0513, Fax: 505-277-0455, E-mail: ted@unm.edu.
Website: http://ted.unm.edu.

University of North Alabama, College of Education, Department of Health, Physical Education, and Recreation, Florence, AL 35632-0001. Offers health and human performance (MS), including exercise science, kinesiology, wellness and health promotion; secondary education (MA Ed), including physical education (P-12). Part-time and evening/weekend programs available. *Faculty:* 5 full-time (2 women). *Students:* 21 full-time (11 women), 7 part-time (2 women); includes 3 minority (2 Black or African American, non-Hispanic/Latino; 1 Two or more races, non-Hispanic/Latino), 3 international. Average age 27. 30 applicants, 90% accepted, 22 enrolled. In 2013, 3 master's awarded. *Degree requirements:* For master's, comprehensive exam (for some programs), thesis optional. *Entrance requirements:* For master's, MAT or GRE, 3 letters of recommendation, essay. Additional exam requirements/recommendations for international students: Required—TOEFL (minimum score 550 paper-based; 79 iBT), IELTS (minimum score 6). *Application deadline:* For fall admission, 7/1 for domestic and international students; for spring admission, 12/1 for domestic and international students. Applications are processed on a rolling basis. Application fee: $25 ($50 for international students). Electronic applications accepted. *Expenses:* Tuition, state resident: full-time $4968; part-time $3312 per year. Tuition, nonresident: full-time $9936; part-time $6624 per year. *Required fees:* $970; $60.33 per credit. $362 per semester. *Financial support:* Application deadline: 4/1; applicants required to submit FAFSA. *Unit head:* Dr. Thomas E. Coates, Chair, 256-765-4377. *Application contact:* Russ Darracott, Graduate Admissions Counselor, 256-765-4447, E-mail: erdarracott@una.edu.
Website: http://www.una.edu/hper/docs/HPERThesisGuideliens.pdf.

University of North Alabama, College of Education, Department of Secondary Education, Program in Secondary Education, Florence, AL 35632-0001. Offers MA Ed. *Accreditation:* NCATE. Part-time and evening/weekend programs available. *Faculty:* 5 full-time (3 women). *Students:* 47 full-time (35 women), 45 part-time (31 women); includes 9 minority (6 Black or African American, non-Hispanic/Latino; 2 Hispanic/Latino; 1 Two or more races, non-Hispanic/Latino), 4 international. Average age 29. 68 applicants, 76% accepted, 22 enrolled. In 2013, 33 master's awarded. *Degree requirements:* For master's, comprehensive exam. *Entrance requirements:* For master's, GRE, MAT, or NTE, minimum GPA of 2.5, Alabama Class B Certificate or equivalent, teaching experience. Additional exam requirements/recommendations for international students: Required—TOEFL (minimum score 550 paper-based; 79 iBT), IELTS (minimum score 6). *Application deadline:* For fall admission, 7/1 priority date for domestic students, 7/1 for international students; for spring admission, 12/1 for domestic and international students. Applications are processed on a rolling basis. Application fee: $25 ($50 for international students). Electronic applications accepted. *Expenses:* Tuition, state resident: full-time $4968; part-time $3312 per year. Tuition, nonresident: full-time $9936; part-time $6624 per year. *Required fees:* $970; $60.33 per credit. $362 per semester. *Financial support:* Federal Work-Study available. Support available to part-time students. Financial award application deadline: 4/1; financial award applicants required to submit FAFSA. *Unit head:* Dr. Beth H. Sewell, Chair, 256-765-4447, E-mail: bsewell@una.edu. *Application contact:* Russ Darracott, Graduate Admissions Counselor, 256-765-4447, E-mail: erdarracott@una.edu.

The University of North Carolina at Chapel Hill, Graduate School, School of Education, Program in Secondary Education, Chapel Hill, NC 27599. Offers English (Grades 9-12) (MAT); English as a second language (MAT); French (Grades K-12) (MAT); German (Grades K-12) (MAT); Japanese (Grades K-12) (MAT); Latin (Grades 9-12) (MAT); mathematics (Grades 9-12) (MAT); music (Grades K-12) (MAT); science (Grades 9-12) (MAT); social studies (Grades 9-12) (MAT); Spanish (Grades K-12) (MAT). *Accreditation:* NCATE. *Degree requirements:* For master's, comprehensive exam. *Entrance requirements:* For master's, GRE General Test, minimum GPA of 3.0 during last 2 years of undergraduate course work. Additional exam requirements/recommendations for international students: Required—TOEFL (minimum score 550 paper-based). Electronic applications accepted.

The University of North Carolina at Charlotte, The Graduate School, College of Education, Department of Middle, Secondary and K-12 Education, Charlotte, NC 28223-0001. Offers curriculum and instruction (PhD); English education (MA); mathematics education (MA); middle grades education (MAT); secondary education (MAT); teaching English as a second language (M Ed). *Faculty:* 19 full-time (11 women), 7 part-time/adjunct (3 women). *Students:* 16 full-time (14 women), 30 part-time (24 women); includes 8 minority (6 Black or African American, non-Hispanic/Latino; 1 Hispanic/Latino; 1 Two or more races, non-Hispanic/Latino). Average age 32. 23 applicants, 87% accepted, 19 enrolled. In 2013, 21 master's awarded. *Degree requirements:* For master's, thesis. *Entrance requirements:* For master's, GRE or MAT. Additional exam requirements/recommendations for international students: Required—TOEFL (minimum score 557 paper-based; 83 iBT). *Application deadline:* For fall admission, 5/1 priority date for domestic students, 5/1 for international students; for spring admission, 10/1 priority date for domestic students, 10/1 for international students. Applications are processed on a rolling basis. Application fee: $75. Electronic applications accepted. *Expenses:* Tuition, state resident: full-time $3522. Tuition, nonresident: full-time $16,051. *Required fees:* $2585. Tuition and fees vary according to course load and program. *Financial support:* In 2013–14, 6 students received support, including 1 fellowship (averaging $50,000 per year), 3 research assistantships (averaging $5,400 per year), 2 teaching assistantships (averaging $9,500 per year); career-related internships or fieldwork, institutionally sponsored loans, scholarships/grants, and unspecified assistantships also available. Support available to part-time students. Financial award application deadline: 4/1; financial award applicants required to submit FAFSA. *Total annual research expenditures:* $98,589. *Unit head:* Dr. Warren DiBiase, Chair, 704-687-8881, Fax: 704-687-6430, E-mail: wjdibias@uncc.edu. *Application contact:* Kathy B. Giddings, Director of Graduate Admissions, 704-687-5503, Fax: 704-687-1668, E-mail: gradadm@uncc.edu.
Website: http://education.uncc.edu/mdsk.

The University of North Carolina at Charlotte, The Graduate School, College of Education, Interdisciplinary Education Programs, Charlotte, NC 28223-0001. Offers art education (MAT); dance education (MAT); elementary education (MAT); English as a second language (MAT); foreign language education (MAT); middle grades education (MAT); music education (MAT); secondary education (MAT); special education (MAT); teacher certification (Graduate Certificate); teaching (Graduate Certificate); theater education (MAT). Part-time programs available. *Students:* 206 full-time (165 women), 791 part-time (628 women); includes 342 minority (247 Black or African American, non-Hispanic/Latino; 16 Asian, non-Hispanic/Latino; 62 Hispanic/Latino; 17 Two or more races, non-Hispanic/Latino), 14 international. Average age 32. 564 applicants, 91% accepted, 414 enrolled. In 2013, 145 master's, 271 other advanced degrees awarded. Terminal master's awarded for partial completion of doctoral program. *Degree requirements:* For master's, thesis. *Entrance requirements:* For master's, GRE or MAT. Additional exam requirements/recommendations for international students: Required—TOEFL (minimum score 550 paper-based; 83 iBT). *Application deadline:* For fall admission, 5/1 priority date for domestic and international students; for spring admission, 10/1 priority date for domestic and international students. Applications are processed on a rolling basis. Application fee: $75. Electronic applications accepted. *Expenses:* Tuition, state resident: full-time $3522. Tuition, nonresident: full-time $16,051. *Required fees:* $2585. Tuition and fees vary according to course load and program. *Total annual research expenditures:* $43,031. *Unit head:* Dr. Warren DiBiase, Chair, 704-687-8881, Fax: 704-687-4705, E-mail: wjdibias@uncc.edu. *Application contact:* Kathy B. Giddings, Director of Graduate Admissions, 704-687-5503, Fax: 704-687-1668, E-mail: gradadm@uncc.edu.
Website: http://education.uncc.edu/academic-programs.

The University of North Carolina Wilmington, Watson College of Education, Department of Instructional Technology, Foundations and Secondary Education, Wilmington, NC 28403-3297. Offers instructional technology (MS); secondary education (M Ed). *Faculty:* 17 full-time (10 women). *Students:* 55 full-time (44 women), 127 part-time (99 women); includes 29 minority (23 Black or African American, non-Hispanic/Latino; 1 American Indian or Alaska Native, non-Hispanic/Latino; 2 Hispanic/Latino; 3 Two or more races, non-Hispanic/Latino). Average age 31. 21 applicants, 95% accepted, 14 enrolled. In 2013, 12 master's awarded. *Degree requirements:* For master's, comprehensive exam, thesis or alternative. *Entrance requirements:* Additional exam requirements/recommendations for international students: Required—TOEFL (minimum score 550 paper-based; 79 iBT), IELTS (minimum score 6.5). *Application deadline:* For fall admission, 6/1 for domestic students. Applications are processed on a rolling basis. Application fee: $60. *Expenses:* Tuition, state resident: full-time $4163. Tuition, nonresident: full-time $16,098. *Financial support:* In 2013–14, teaching assistantships with full and partial tuition reimbursements (averaging $9,000 per year) were awarded. *Unit head:* Dr. Vance Durrington, Chair, 910-962-7539, E-mail: durringtonv@uncw.edu. *Application contact:* Dr. Mahnaz Moallem, Graduate Coordinator, 910-962-4183, E-mail: moallemm@uncw.edu.

University of North Dakota, Graduate School, College of Education and Human Development, Teaching and Learning Program, Grand Forks, ND 58202. Offers elementary education (Ed D, PhD); measurement and statistics (Ed D, PhD); secondary education (Ed D, PhD); special education (Ed D, PhD). *Accreditation:* NCATE. Postbaccalaureate distance learning degree programs offered (minimal on-campus study). *Degree requirements:* For doctorate, comprehensive exam, thesis/dissertation,

final exam. *Entrance requirements:* For doctorate, minimum GPA of 3.5. Additional exam requirements/recommendations for international students: Required—TOEFL (minimum score 550 paper-based; 79 iBT), IELTS (minimum score 6.5). Electronic applications accepted.

University of Northern Iowa, Graduate College, College of Humanities, Arts and Sciences, Department of Mathematics, Program in Mathematics, Cedar Falls, IA 50614. Offers community college teaching (MA); mathematics (MA); secondary teaching (MA). *Students:* 5 full-time (1 woman), 23 part-time (13 women); includes 1 minority (Black or African American, non-Hispanic/Latino). 8 applicants, 50% accepted, 2 enrolled. In 2013, 4 master's awarded. Application fee: $50 ($70 for international students). *Unit head:* Dr. Michael Prophet, Coordinator, 319-273-2104, Fax: 319-273-2546, E-mail: mike.prophet@uni.edu. *Application contact:* Laurie S. Russell, Record Analyst, 319-273-2623, Fax: 319-273-2885, E-mail: laurie.russell@uni.edu.

University of North Florida, College of Education and Human Services, Department of Foundations and Secondary Education, Jacksonville, FL 32224. Offers adult learning (M Ed); professional education (M Ed). *Accreditation:* NCATE. Part-time and evening/weekend programs available. *Faculty:* 12 full-time (5 women). *Students:* 1 (woman) full-time, 13 part-time (10 women); includes 4 minority (2 Black or African American, non-Hispanic/Latino; 1 Asian, non-Hispanic/Latino; 1 Hispanic/Latino). Average age 33. 13 applicants, 69% accepted, 7 enrolled. In 2013, 2 master's awarded. *Entrance requirements:* For master's, GRE General Test, minimum GPA of 3.0 in last 60 hours, interview, 3 letters of recommendation. Additional exam requirements/recommendations for international students: Required—TOEFL (minimum score 500 paper-based; 61 iBT). *Application deadline:* For fall admission, 7/1 priority date for domestic students, 5/1 for international students; for spring admission, 11/1 priority date for domestic students, 10/1 for international students. Application fee: $30. Electronic applications accepted. *Expenses:* Tuition, state resident: full-time $9794; part-time $408.10 per credit hour. Tuition, nonresident: full-time $22,383; part-time $932.61 per credit hour. *Required fees:* $2020; $84.20 per credit hour. Tuition and fees vary according to course load and program. *Financial support:* In 2013–14, 11 students received support, including 1 research assistantship (averaging $4,264 per year); teaching assistantships, career-related internships or fieldwork, Federal Work-Study, and tuition waivers (partial) also available. Support available to part-time students. Financial award application deadline: 4/1; financial award applicants required to submit FAFSA. *Faculty research:* Using children's literature to enhance metalinguistic awareness, education, oral language diagnosis of middle-schoolers, science inquiry teaching and learning. *Total annual research expenditures:* $821. *Unit head:* Dr. Jeffery Cornett, Chair, 904-620-2610, Fax: 904-620-1821, E-mail: jcornett@unf.edu. *Application contact:* Dr. Amanda Pascale, Director, The Graduate School, 904-620-1360, Fax: 904-620-1362, E-mail: graduateschool@unf.edu.
Website: http://www.unf.edu/coehs/fse/.

University of North Georgia, School of Education, Dahlonega, GA 30597. Offers art education (MAT); early childhood education (M Ed); English education (MAT); history education (MAT); math education (MAT); middle grades education (M Ed, MAT); physical education (MS); school leadership (Ed S); secondary education (M Ed), including English education, history education, mathematics education, physical education; teacher education (MAT). *Accreditation:* NCATE. Part-time and evening/weekend programs available. Postbaccalaureate distance learning degree programs offered (no on-campus study). *Degree requirements:* For master's, comprehensive exam, thesis optional. *Entrance requirements:* For master's, GRE or MAT, GACE, minimum GPA of 2.75; for Ed S, GRE General Test or MAT, 3 years of teaching experience, master's degree, minimum graduate GPA of 3.25, leadership position in the school. Additional exam requirements/recommendations for international students: Required—TOEFL (minimum score 550 paper-based; 79 iBT), IELTS (minimum score 6.5). Electronic applications accepted. *Faculty research:* Identification of professional development school structures supporting P-12 student achievement, impact of diverse field placement settings in teacher belief development among preservice teachers, use of inquiry methodology in social studies teaching with English language learners, use of instructional differentiation in the middle grades classroom, effects of international school placements on preservice teacher beliefs and attitudes.

University of Oklahoma, Jeannine Rainbolt College of Education, Department of Instructional Leadership and Academic Curriculum, Norman, OK 73072. Offers communication, culture and pedagogy for Hispanic populations in educational settings (Graduate Certificate); instructional leadership and academic curriculum (M Ed, PhD), including bilingual education (PhD), early childhood education, elementary education, English education, instructional leadership, mathematics education, reading education, science education, science, technology, engineering and mathematics education (M Ed), secondary education, social studies education, teacher education (M Ed), world language education (M Ed). *Accreditation:* NCATE. Part-time and evening/weekend programs available. Postbaccalaureate distance learning degree programs offered (no on-campus study). *Faculty:* 22 full-time (15 women), 1 (woman) part-time/adjunct. *Students:* 64 full-time (49 women), 103 part-time (81 women); includes 33 minority (8 Black or African American, non-Hispanic/Latino; 9 American Indian or Alaska Native, non-Hispanic/Latino; 5 Asian, non-Hispanic/Latino; 4 Hispanic/Latino; 1 Native Hawaiian or other Pacific Islander, non-Hispanic/Latino; 6 Two or more races, non-Hispanic/Latino), 10 international. Average age 34. 50 applicants, 84% accepted, 36 enrolled. In 2013, 26 master's, 11 doctorates awarded. Terminal master's awarded for partial completion of doctoral program. *Degree requirements:* For master's, comprehensive exam (for some programs), thesis (for some programs); for doctorate, comprehensive exam, thesis/dissertation. *Entrance requirements:* For master's, essay; for doctorate, GRE, 3 recommendation letters; autobiography, statement of objectives; essay on chosen major; transcripts; writing sample. Additional exam requirements/recommendations for international students: Required—TOEFL (minimum score 79 iBT). *Application deadline:* For fall admission, 4/30 for domestic and international students; for spring admission, 10/31 for domestic and international students; for summer admission, 3/15 for domestic and international students. Applications are processed on a rolling basis. Application fee: $50 ($100 for international students). Electronic applications accepted. *Expenses:* Tuition, state resident: full-time $4205; part-time $175.20 per credit hour. Tuition, nonresident: full-time $16,205; part-time $675.20 per credit hour. *Required fees:* $2745; $103.85 per credit hour. $126.50 per semester. *Financial support:* In 2013–14, 98 students received support, including 10 research assistantships with partial tuition reimbursements available (averaging $10,671 per year), 7 teaching assistantships with partial tuition reimbursements available (averaging $10,753 per year); Federal Work-Study, institutionally sponsored loans, scholarships/grants, and unspecified assistantships also available. Support available to part-time students. Financial award application deadline: 6/1; financial award applicants required to submit FAFSA. *Total annual research expenditures:* $1 million. *Unit head:* Dr. Stacy Reeder, Chair/Graduate Liaison, 405-325-1498, Fax: 405-325-4061, E-mail: reeder@ou.edu. *Application contact:* Lynn Crussel, Graduate Programs Officer, 405-325-1498, Fax: 405-325-4061, E-mail: lcrussel@ou.edu.
Website: http://education.ou.edu/departments/ilac.

University of Pennsylvania, Graduate School of Education, Division of Teaching, Learning, and Leadership, Teacher Education Program, Philadelphia, PA 19104. Offers elementary education (MS Ed); secondary education (MS Ed). *Students:* 59 full-time (42 women); includes 15 minority (2 Black or African American, non-Hispanic/Latino; 10 Asian, non-Hispanic/Latino; 2 Hispanic/Latino; 1 Two or more races, non-Hispanic/Latino), 1 international. 157 applicants, 70% accepted, 66 enrolled. In 2013, 80 master's awarded. *Degree requirements:* For master's, comprehensive exam or portfolio. *Entrance requirements:* For master's, GRE General Test, MAT. *Application deadline:* For fall admission, 12/15 priority date for domestic students. Applications are processed on a rolling basis. Application fee: $70. Electronic applications accepted. *Expenses:* Contact institution. *Financial support:* Fellowships available. Financial award applicants required to submit FAFSA. *Unit head:* Dr. Andrew Porter, Dean, 215-898-7014. *Application contact:* Maureen Cotterill, Program Manager, 215-898-7364, E-mail: maureenc@gse.upenn.edu.
Website: http://www.gse.upenn.edu/tll.

University of Phoenix–Bay Area Campus, College of Education, San Jose, CA 95134-1805. Offers administration and supervision (MA Ed); adult education and training (MA Ed); early childhood education (MA Ed); education (Ed S); educational leadership (Ed D); elementary teacher education (MA Ed); higher education administration (PhD); secondary teacher education (MA Ed); special education (MA Ed); teacher leadership (MA Ed). Evening/weekend programs available. Postbaccalaureate distance learning degree programs offered (no on-campus study). *Degree requirements:* For master's, thesis (for some programs). *Entrance requirements:* For master's, minimum undergraduate GPA of 2.5, 3 years of work experience. Additional exam requirements/recommendations for international students: Required—TOEFL (minimum score 550 paper-based; 79 iBT). Electronic applications accepted.

University of Phoenix–Central Valley Campus, College of Education, Fresno, CA 93720-1562. Offers curriculum and instruction (MA Ed); curriculum and instruction-computer education (MA Ed); elementary teacher education (MA Ed); secondary teacher education (MA Ed).

University of Phoenix–Chattanooga Campus, College of Education, Chattanooga, TN 37421-3707. Offers administration and supervision (MA Ed); curriculum and instruction (MA Ed); elementary teacher education (MA Ed); secondary teacher education (MA Ed).

University of Phoenix–Denver Campus, College of Education, Lone Tree, CO 80124-5453. Offers administration and supervision (MAEd); curriculum instruction (MAEd); elementary teacher education (MAEd); school counseling (MSC); secondary teacher education (MAEd). Evening/weekend programs available. *Degree requirements:* For master's, thesis (for some programs). *Entrance requirements:* For master's, minimum undergraduate GPA of 2.5, 3 years work experience. Additional exam requirements/recommendations for international students: Required—TOEFL (minimum score 550 paper-based; 79 iBT). Electronic applications accepted.

University of Phoenix–Hawaii Campus, College of Education, Honolulu, HI 96813-4317. Offers administration and supervision (MA Ed); curriculum and instruction (MA Ed); elementary education (MA Ed); secondary education (MA Ed); special education (MA Ed); teacher education for elementary licensure (MA Ed). Evening/weekend programs available. *Degree requirements:* For master's, thesis (for some programs). *Entrance requirements:* For master's, minimum undergraduate GPA of 2.5, 3 years of work experience. Additional exam requirements/recommendations for international students: Required—TOEFL (minimum score 550 paper-based; 79 iBT). Electronic applications accepted.

University of Phoenix–Idaho Campus, College of Education, Meridian, ID 83642-5114. Offers administration and supervision (MA Ed); curriculum and instruction (MA Ed); elementary teacher education (MA Ed); secondary teacher education (MA Ed). Evening/weekend programs available. *Degree requirements:* For master's, thesis (for some programs). *Entrance requirements:* For master's, minimum undergraduate GPA of 2.5, 3 years of work experience. Additional exam requirements/recommendations for international students: Required—TOEFL (minimum score 550 paper-based). Electronic applications accepted.

University of Phoenix–Indianapolis Campus, College of Education, Indianapolis, IN 46250-932. Offers elementary teacher education (MA Ed); secondary teacher education (MA Ed).

University of Phoenix–Memphis Campus, College of Education, Cordova, TN 38018. Offers administration and supervision (MA Ed); curriculum and instruction (MA Ed); elementary teacher education (MA Ed); secondary teacher education (MA Ed).

University of Phoenix–Nashville Campus, College of Education, Nashville, TN 37214-5048. Offers administration and supervision (MA Ed); curriculum and instruction (MA Ed); elementary teacher education (MA Ed); secondary teacher education (MA Ed). Evening/weekend programs available. *Degree requirements:* For master's, thesis (for some programs). *Entrance requirements:* For master's, minimum undergraduate GPA of 2.5, 3 years work experience. Additional exam requirements/recommendations for international students: Required—TOEFL (minimum score 500 paper-based; 79 iBT). Electronic applications accepted.

University of Phoenix–New Mexico Campus, College of Education, Albuquerque, NM 87113-1570. Offers administration and supervision (MAEd); curriculum and instruction (MAEd); elementary teacher education (MAEd); school counseling (MSC); secondary teacher education (MAEd). Evening/weekend programs available. *Degree requirements:* For master's, thesis (for some programs). *Entrance requirements:* For master's, minimum undergraduate GPA of 2.5, 3 years of work experience. Additional exam requirements/recommendations for international students: Required—TOEFL (minimum score 550 paper-based; 79 iBT). Electronic applications accepted.

University of Phoenix–North Florida Campus, College of Education, Jacksonville, FL 32216-0959. Offers administration and supervision (MA Ed); curriculum and instruction (MA Ed), including computer education, mathematics education; early childhood education (MA Ed); elementary teacher education (MA Ed); secondary teacher education (MA Ed). Evening/weekend programs available. *Degree requirements:* For master's, thesis (for some programs). *Entrance requirements:* For master's, 3 years of work experience, minimum undergraduate GPA of 2.5. Additional exam requirements/recommendations for international students: Required—TOEFL (minimum score 550 paper-based; 49 iBT). Electronic applications accepted.

University of Phoenix–Omaha Campus, College of Education, Omaha, NE 68154-5240. Offers administration and supervision (MA Ed); curriculum and instruction (MA Ed), including adult education, computer education, curriculum and instruction, English and language arts education, English as a second language, mathematics education; elementary teacher education (MA Ed); secondary teacher education (MA Ed); special education (MA Ed).

University of Phoenix–Online Campus, College of Education, Phoenix, AZ 85034-7209. Offers administration and supervision (MAEd, Certificate); adult education and training (MAEd); curriculum and instruction (MAEd), including computer education, curriculum and instruction, English as a second language, language arts, mathematics, reading; early childhood education (MAEd); educational studies (MAEd); elementary teacher education (MAEd), including early childhood, elementary teacher education, high school middle level, middle level; principal licensure (Certificate); secondary

teacher education (MAEd); special education (MAEd, Certificate); teacher education (MAEd), including middle level generalist; teacher education middle level mathematics (MAEd), including middle level mathematics; teacher education middle level science (MAEd), including middle level science; teacher education secondary mathematics (MAEd); teacher education secondary science (MAEd); teacher leadership (MAEd); teachers of English learners (Certificate); transition to teaching (Certificate), including elementary education, secondary education. *Accreditation:* Teacher Education Accreditation Council. Evening/weekend programs available. Postbaccalaureate distance learning degree programs offered. *Entrance requirements:* Additional exam requirements/recommendations for international students: Required—TOEFL, TOEIC (Test of English as an International Communication), Berlitz Online English Proficiency Exam, PTE, or IELTS. Electronic applications accepted. *Expenses:* Contact institution.

University of Phoenix–Oregon Campus, College of Education, Tigard, OR 97223. Offers curriculum and instruction (MA Ed); early childhood education (MA Ed); elementary education (MA Ed), including early childhood specialization, middle level specialization; secondary education (MA Ed). Evening/weekend programs available. *Degree requirements:* For master's, thesis (for some programs). *Entrance requirements:* For master's, minimum undergraduate GPA of 2.5, 3 years work experience. Additional exam requirements/recommendations for international students: Required—TOEFL (minimum score 550 paper-based; 79 iBT). Electronic applications accepted.

University of Phoenix–Phoenix Campus, College of Education, Tempe, AZ 85282-2371. Offers administration and supervision (MA Ed); adult education and training (MA Ed); curriculum and instruction reading (MA Ed); early childhood education (MA Ed); education studies (MA Ed); elementary teacher education (MA Ed); secondary teacher education (MA Ed); special education (MA Ed); teacher leadership (MA Ed). Evening/weekend programs available. Postbaccalaureate distance learning degree programs offered. *Entrance requirements:* Additional exam requirements/recommendations for international students: Required—TOEFL, TOEIC (Test of English as an International Communication), Berlitz Online English Proficiency Exam, PTE, or IELTS. Electronic applications accepted. *Expenses:* Contact institution.

University of Phoenix–Sacramento Valley Campus, College of Education, Sacramento, CA 95833-3632. Offers adult education (MA Ed); curriculum instruction (MA Ed); elementary teacher education (MA Ed); secondary teacher education (MA Ed); teacher education (Certificate). Evening/weekend programs available. *Degree requirements:* For master's, thesis (for some programs). *Entrance requirements:* For master's, 3 years of work experience, minimum undergraduate GPA of 2.5. Additional exam requirements/recommendations for international students: Required—TOEFL (minimum score 550 paper-based; 79 iBT). Electronic applications accepted.

University of Phoenix–San Diego Campus, College of Education, San Diego, CA 92123. Offers curriculum and instruction (MA Ed), including computer education, curriculum and instruction, English as a second language; elementary teacher education (MA Ed); secondary teacher education (MA Ed). Evening/weekend programs available. *Degree requirements:* For master's, thesis (for some programs). *Entrance requirements:* For master's, 3 years of work experience, minimum undergraduate GPA of 3.0. Additional exam requirements/recommendations for international students: Required—TOEFL (minimum score 550 paper-based; 79 iBT). Electronic applications accepted.

University of Phoenix–Southern Arizona Campus, College of Education, Tucson, AZ 85711. Offers administration and supervision (MA Ed); adult education and training (MA Ed); curriculum instruction (MA Ed); educational counseling (MA Ed); elementary teacher education (MA Ed); school counseling (MSC); secondary teacher education (MA Ed); special education (MA Ed, Certificate). Evening/weekend programs available. *Degree requirements:* For master's, thesis (for some programs). *Entrance requirements:* For master's, minimum undergraduate GPA of 2.5, 3 years of work experience. Additional exam requirements/recommendations for international students: Required—TOEFL (minimum score 550 paper-based; 79 iBT). Electronic applications accepted.

University of Phoenix–Southern California Campus, College of Education, Costa Mesa, CA 92626. Offers administration and supervision (MA Ed, Certificate); adult education and training (MA Ed); educational studies (MA Ed); elementary teacher education (MA Ed); secondary teacher education (MA Ed); teacher leadership (MA Ed); teachers of English learners (Certificate). Evening/weekend programs available. Postbaccalaureate distance learning degree programs offered. *Entrance requirements:* Additional exam requirements/recommendations for international students: Required—TOEFL, TOEIC (Test of English as an International Communication), Berlitz Online English Proficiency Exam, PTE, or IELTS. Electronic applications accepted. *Expenses:* Contact institution.

University of Phoenix–Southern Colorado Campus, College of Education, Colorado Springs, CO 80903. Offers administration and supervision (MA Ed); curriculum and instruction (MA Ed); elementary teacher education (MA Ed); principal licensure certification (Certificate); school counseling (MSC); secondary teacher education (MA Ed). Evening/weekend programs available. *Degree requirements:* For master's, thesis (for some programs). *Entrance requirements:* For master's, minimum undergraduate GPA of 2.5, 3 years of work experience. Additional exam requirements/recommendations for international students: Required—TOEFL (minimum score 550 paper-based; 79 iBT). Electronic applications accepted.

University of Phoenix–South Florida Campus, College of Education, Miramar, FL 33030. Offers administration and supervision (MA Ed); curriculum and instruction (MA Ed), including computer education, curriculum and instruction, mathematics education; early childhood education (MA Ed); elementary teacher education (MA Ed); secondary teacher education (MA Ed). Evening/weekend programs available. *Degree requirements:* For master's, thesis (for some programs). *Entrance requirements:* For master's, 3 years of work experience, minimum undergraduate GPA of 2.5. Additional exam requirements/recommendations for international students: Required—TOEFL (minimum score 550 paper-based; 79 iBT). Electronic applications accepted.

University of Phoenix–Utah Campus, College of Education, Salt Lake City, UT 84123-4617. Offers administration and supervision (MA Ed); curriculum and instruction (MA Ed); elementary teacher education (MA Ed); school counseling (MSC); secondary teacher education (MA Ed); special education (MA Ed). Evening/weekend programs available. *Degree requirements:* For master's, thesis (for some programs). *Entrance requirements:* For master's, minimum undergraduate GPA of 2.5, 3 years work experience. Additional exam requirements/recommendations for international students: Required—TOEFL (minimum score 550 paper-based; 79 iBT). Electronic applications accepted.

University of Phoenix–Washington D.C. Campus, College of Education, Washington, DC 20001. Offers administration and supervision (MA Ed); adult education and training (MA Ed); computer education (MA Ed); curriculum and instruction (MA Ed, Ed D); early childhood education (MA Ed); education (Ed S); educational leadership (Ed D); educational technology (Ed D); elementary teacher education (MA Ed); English and language arts education (MA Ed); English as a second language (MA Ed); higher education administration (PhD); mathematics education (MA Ed); secondary teacher education (MA Ed); special education (MA Ed); teacher leadership (MA Ed).

University of Phoenix–West Florida Campus, College of Education, Temple Terrace, FL 33637. Offers administration and supervision (MA Ed); curriculum and instruction (MA Ed), including computer education, curriculum and instruction, mathematics education; curriculum and technology (MA Ed); early childhood education (MA Ed); elementary teacher education (MA Ed); secondary teacher education (MA Ed). Evening/weekend programs available. *Degree requirements:* For master's, thesis (for some programs). *Entrance requirements:* For master's, 3 years of work experience, minimum undergraduate GPA of 2.5. Additional exam requirements/recommendations for international students: Required—TOEFL (minimum score 550 paper-based; 79 iBT).

University of Pittsburgh, School of Education, Department of Instruction and Learning, Program in Secondary Education, Pittsburgh, PA 15260. Offers English/communications education (M Ed, MAT); foreign languages education (M Ed, MAT); mathematics education (M Ed, MAT, Ed D); science education (M Ed, MAT, Ed D); secondary education (PhD); social studies education (M Ed, MAT). Part-time and evening/weekend programs available. *Students:* 116 full-time (78 women), 47 part-time (36 women); includes 16 minority (4 Black or African American, non-Hispanic/Latino; 3 Asian, non-Hispanic/Latino; 5 Hispanic/Latino; 4 Two or more races, non-Hispanic/Latino), 29 international. Average age 30. 279 applicants, 66% accepted, 91 enrolled. In 2013, 113 master's, 8 doctorates awarded. *Degree requirements:* For master's, thesis; for doctorate, thesis/dissertation. *Entrance requirements:* For master's, PRAXIS I; for doctorate, GRE General Test. Additional exam requirements/recommendations for international students: Required—TOEFL. *Application deadline:* For fall admission, 2/1 priority date for domestic students; for spring admission, 11/15 priority date for domestic students. Applications are processed on a rolling basis. Application fee: $50. Electronic applications accepted. *Expenses:* Tuition, state resident: full-time $19,964; part-time $807 per credit. Tuition, nonresident: full-time $32,686; part-time $1337 per credit. *Required fees:* $740; $200. Tuition and fees vary according to program. *Financial support:* Fellowships, teaching assistantships, career-related internships or fieldwork, Federal Work-Study, tuition waivers (partial), and unspecified assistantships available. Support available to part-time students. Financial award application deadline: 3/15; financial award applicants required to submit FAFSA. *Unit head:* Dr. Richard Donato, Chairman, 412-624-7248, Fax: 412-648-7081, E-mail: donato@pitt.edu. *Application contact:* Marianne L. Budziszewski, Director of Admissions and Enrollment Services, 412-648-2230, Fax: 412-648-1899, E-mail: soeinfo@pitt.edu.
Website: http://www.education.pitt.edu/.

University of Puget Sound, Graduate Studies, School of Education, Program in Teaching, Tacoma, WA 98416. Offers elementary education (MAT); secondary education (MAT). *Accreditation:* NASM. *Degree requirements:* For master's, capstone course. *Entrance requirements:* For master's, GRE General Test, WEST-B, WEST-E in content area, minimum baccalaureate GPA of 3.0. Additional exam requirements/recommendations for international students: Required—TOEFL (minimum score 550 paper-based; 90 iBT). Electronic applications accepted. *Expenses:* Contact institution. *Faculty research:* Mathematics education, professional development, social studies education, gender studies.

University of Rhode Island, Graduate School, College of Human Science and Services, School of Education, Kingston, RI 02881. Offers adult education (MA); education (PhD); elementary education (MA); music education (MM); reading education (MA); secondary education (MA); special education (MA); MS/PhD. *Accreditation:* NCATE. Part-time and evening/weekend programs available. *Faculty:* 16 full-time (9 women). *Students:* 64 full-time (48 women), 91 part-time (68 women); includes 17 minority (8 Black or African American, non-Hispanic/Latino; 2 American Indian or Alaska Native, non-Hispanic/Latino; 2 Asian, non-Hispanic/Latino; 3 Hispanic/Latino; 2 Two or more races, non-Hispanic/Latino), 6 international. In 2013, 47 master's, 11 doctorates awarded. *Degree requirements:* For master's, comprehensive exam (for some programs), thesis optional; for doctorate, comprehensive exam, thesis/dissertation. *Entrance requirements:* For master's, 2 letters of recommendation; interview (for special education applicants); for doctorate, GRE, 3 letters of recommendation, resume. Additional exam requirements/recommendations for international students: Required—TOEFL (minimum score 600 paper-based; 100 iBT). *Application deadline:* For fall admission, 1/31 for domestic and international students. Application fee: $65. Electronic applications accepted. *Expenses:* Tuition, state resident: full-time $11,532; part-time $641 per credit. Tuition, nonresident: full-time $23,606; part-time $1311 per credit. *Required fees:* $1388; $36 per credit. $35 per semester. One-time fee: $130. *Financial support:* In 2013–14, 2 research assistantships with full and partial tuition reimbursements (averaging $11,883 per year), 4 teaching assistantships with full and partial tuition reimbursements (averaging $8,488 per year) were awarded; career-related internships or fieldwork also available. Financial award application deadline: 1/31; financial award applicants required to submit FAFSA. *Total annual research expenditures:* $1.1 million. *Unit head:* Dr. David Byrd, Director, 401-874-5484, Fax: 401-874-5471, E-mail: dbyrd@uri.edu. *Application contact:* Graduate Admissions, 401-874-2872, E-mail: gradadm@etal.uri.edu.
Website: http://www.uri.edu/hss/education/.

University of St. Francis, College of Education, Joliet, IL 60435-6169. Offers educational leadership (MS, Ed D); elementary education (M Ed); higher education (MS); reading (MS); secondary education (M Ed), including English education, math education, science education, social studies education, visual arts education; special education (M Ed); teaching and learning (MS). *Accreditation:* NCATE. Part-time and evening/weekend programs available. Postbaccalaureate distance learning degree programs offered (no on-campus study). *Faculty:* 10 full-time (8 women), 34 part-time/adjunct (25 women). *Students:* 14 full-time (13 women), 250 part-time (183 women); includes 34 minority (20 Black or African American, non-Hispanic/Latino; 1 American Indian or Alaska Native, non-Hispanic/Latino; 13 Hispanic/Latino), 1 international. Average age 36. 133 applicants, 62% accepted, 71 enrolled. In 2013, 147 master's awarded. *Degree requirements:* For doctorate, thesis/dissertation. *Entrance requirements:* For doctorate, master's degree, IL Type 75 or Principal's endorsement, interview, minimum undergraduate GPA of 3.0, professional portfolio, letter of recommendation. Additional exam requirements/recommendations for international students: Required—TOEFL (minimum score 550 paper-based; 79 iBT), IELTS (minimum score 6.5). *Application deadline:* Applications are processed on a rolling basis. Application fee: $30. Electronic applications accepted. Application fee is waived when completed online. *Expenses:* Contact institution. *Financial support:* In 2013–14, 10 students received support. Scholarships/grants, tuition waivers (partial), and unspecified assistantships available. Support available to part-time students. Financial award applicants required to submit FAFSA. *Unit head:* Dr. John Gambro, Dean, 815-740-3829, Fax: 815-740-2264, E-mail: jgambro@stfrancis.edu. *Application contact:* Sandra Sloka, Director of Admissions for Graduate and Degree Completion Programs, 800-735-7500, Fax: 815-740-3431, E-mail: ssloka@stfrancis.edu.
Website: http://www.stfrancis.edu/academics/college-of-education/.

University of St. Thomas, Graduate Studies, School of Education, Department of Teacher Education, St. Paul, MN 55105-1096. Offers curriculum and instruction (MA), including elementary, individualized, K-12, secondary; elementary education (MA); English as a second language (MA); math education (Certificate); multicultural education (Certificate); reading (MA, Certificate), including elementary (MA), K-12 (MA).

Accreditation: NCATE. Part-time and evening/weekend programs available. *Entrance requirements:* For master's, minimum GPA of 3.0 or MAT. Additional exam requirements/recommendations for international students: Required—TOEFL (minimum score 550 paper-based; 80 iBT). *Application deadline:* For fall admission, 6/1 for domestic students; for spring admission, 11/1 for domestic students. Applications are processed on a rolling basis. Application fee: $50. *Financial support:* Fellowships, research assistantships, institutionally sponsored loans, and scholarships/grants available. Support available to part-time students. Financial award applicants required to submit FAFSA. *Unit head:* Dr. Jan L. H. Frank, Chair, 651-962-4446, Fax: 651-962-4169, E-mail: jlhfrank@stthomas.edu. *Application contact:* Rosemary R. Barreto, Department Assistant, 651-962-4420, Fax: 651-962-4169, E-mail: barr7879@stthomas.edu.

University of St. Thomas, School of Education, Houston, TX 77006-4696. Offers all level education (M Ed); bilingual/dual language (M Ed); Catholic school teaching (M Ed); Catholic/private school leadership (M Ed); counselor education (M Ed); curriculum and instruction (M Ed); educational leadership (M Ed); elementary teaching (M Ed); English as a second language (M Ed); exceptionality/educational diagnostician (M Ed); exceptionality/special education (M Ed); generalist (M Ed); reading (M Ed); secondary teaching (M Ed). *Accreditation:* Teacher Education Accreditation Council. Part-time and evening/weekend programs available. Postbaccalaureate distance learning degree programs offered (no on-campus study). *Faculty:* 40 full-time (26 women), 43 part-time/adjunct (31 women). *Students:* 27 full-time (20 women), 1,091 part-time (981 women); includes 691 minority (247 Black or African American, non-Hispanic/Latino; 1 American Indian or Alaska Native, non-Hispanic/Latino; 44 Asian, non-Hispanic/Latino; 379 Hispanic/Latino; 2 Native Hawaiian or other Pacific Islander, non-Hispanic/Latino; 18 Two or more races, non-Hispanic/Latino), 28 international. Average age 36. 858 applicants, 83% accepted, 458 enrolled. In 2013, 454 master's awarded. *Degree requirements:* For master's, thesis, field experience. *Entrance requirements:* For master's, GRE or MAT if GPA is below 3.0, bachelor's degree; minimum GPA of 2.75 in bachelor's degree or last 60 credit hours; official transcripts from all institutions; goal statement of 250-300 words; 1 reference. Additional exam requirements/recommendations for international students: Required—TOEFL. *Application deadline:* Applications are processed on a rolling basis. Application fee: $35. Electronic applications accepted. *Expenses:* Contact institution. *Financial support:* In 2013–14, 41 students received support. Federal Work-Study, scholarships/grants, and state work-study, institutional employment available. Support available to part-time students. Financial award application deadline: 4/15; financial award applicants required to submit FAFSA. *Faculty research:* Leadership, diversity, personality traits, second language acquisition. *Unit head:* Dr. Robert LeBlanc, Dean, 713-525-3540, Fax: 713-525-3871, E-mail: education@stthom.edu. *Application contact:* Rita Paredes, Administrative Assistant, 713-525-3442, Fax: 713-525-3871, E-mail: rparede@stthom.edu.
Website: http://www.stthom.edu/Academics/School_of_Education/Index.aqf.

The University of Scranton, College of Graduate and Continuing Education, Department of Education, Program in Secondary Education, Scranton, PA 18510. Offers MS. *Accreditation:* NCATE. Part-time and evening/weekend programs available. *Students:* 13 full-time (6 women), 2 part-time (1 woman); includes 2 minority (1 Asian, non-Hispanic/Latino; 1 Hispanic/Latino), 1 international. Average age 28. 20 applicants, 90% accepted. In 2013, 16 master's awarded. *Degree requirements:* For master's, comprehensive exam, capstone experience. *Entrance requirements:* For master's, minimum GPA of 3.0. Additional exam requirements/recommendations for international students: Required—TOEFL (minimum score 500 paper-based), IELTS (minimum score 6). *Application deadline:* Applications are processed on a rolling basis. Application fee: $0. *Financial support:* Teaching assistantships, career-related internships or fieldwork, Federal Work-Study, and unspecified assistantships available. Support available to part-time students. Financial award application deadline: 3/1. *Unit head:* Dr. Art Chambers, Director, 570-941-4668, Fax: 570-941-5515, E-mail: chambersa2@scranton.edu. *Application contact:* Joseph M. Roback, Director of Admissions, 570-941-4385, Fax: 570-941-5928, E-mail: robackj2@scranton.edu.

University of South Alabama, Graduate School, College of Education, Department of Leadership and Teacher Education, Mobile, AL 36688-0002. Offers early childhood education (M Ed); educational administration (Ed S); educational leadership (M Ed); elementary education (M Ed); reading education (M Ed); science education (M Ed); secondary education (M Ed); special education (M Ed, Ed S). *Accreditation:* NCATE. Part-time programs available. *Faculty:* 17 full-time (11 women), 4 part-time/adjunct (all women). *Students:* 136 full-time (103 women), 78 part-time (67 women); includes 45 minority (40 Black or African American, non-Hispanic/Latino; 2 Asian, non-Hispanic/Latino; 1 Hispanic/Latino; 2 Two or more races, non-Hispanic/Latino). 90 applicants, 53% accepted, 45 enrolled. In 2013, 69 master's awarded. *Degree requirements:* For master's, comprehensive exam. *Entrance requirements:* For master's, GRE General Test or MAT, minimum GPA of 3.0. *Application deadline:* For fall admission, 7/15 priority date for domestic students, 6/15 priority date for international students; for spring admission, 12/1 priority date for domestic students, 11/1 priority date for international students. Applications are processed on a rolling basis. Application fee: $35. *Expenses:* Tuition, state resident: full-time $8976; part-time $374 per credit hour. Tuition, nonresident: full-time $17,952; part-time $748 per credit hour. *Financial support:* Research assistantships and career-related internships or fieldwork available. Support available to part-time students. Financial award application deadline: 4/1. *Unit head:* Dr. Harold Dodge, Jr., Chair, 251-380-2894. *Application contact:* Dr. Abigail Baxter, Director of Graduate Studies, 251-380-2738, Fax: 251-380-2748, E-mail: abaxter@southalabama.edu.
Website: http://www.southalabama.edu/coe/lted.

University of South Carolina, The Graduate School, College of Education, Department of Instruction and Teacher Education, Program in Secondary Education, Columbia, SC 29208. Offers art education (IMA, MAT); business education (IMA, MAT); English (MAT); foreign language (MAT); health education (MAT); mathematics (MAT); science (IMA, MAT); secondary (Ed D); secondary education (MT, PhD); social studies (MAT); theatre and speech (MAT). IMA and MT offered jointly with the subject areas. *Accreditation:* NCATE. *Degree requirements:* For master's, comprehensive exam, thesis (for some programs), foreign language (MA); for doctorate, one foreign language, comprehensive exam, thesis/dissertation. *Entrance requirements:* For master's, GRE General Test or MAT, teaching certificate (IMA, M Ed), interview; for doctorate, GRE General Test or MAT, interview. *Faculty research:* Middle school programs, professional development, school collaboration.

The University of South Dakota, Graduate School, School of Education, Division of Curriculum and Instruction, Program in Secondary Education, Vermillion, SD 57069-2390. Offers MA. *Accreditation:* NCATE. Part-time programs available. Postbaccalaureate distance learning degree programs offered. *Degree requirements:* For master's, comprehensive exam, thesis or alternative. *Entrance requirements:* For master's, GRE General Test, MAT, minimum GPA of 2.7. Additional exam requirements/recommendations for international students: Required—TOEFL (minimum score 550 paper-based; 79 iBT). Electronic applications accepted.

University of Southern Indiana, Graduate Studies, College of Science, Engineering, and Education, Department of Teacher Education, Program in Secondary Education, Evansville, IN 47712-3590. Offers MS. *Accreditation:* NCATE. Part-time and evening/weekend programs available. *Faculty:* 13 full-time (7 women), 3 part-time/adjunct (1 woman). *Students:* 2 full-time (both women), 36 part-time (27 women), 7 international. Average age 34. 12 applicants, 75% accepted, 8 enrolled. In 2013, 20 master's awarded. *Entrance requirements:* For master's, GRE General Test, NTE or PRAXIS II, minimum GPA of 3.0, teaching license. Additional exam requirements/recommendations for international students: Required—TOEFL (minimum score 550 paper-based; 79 iBT), IELTS (minimum score 6). *Application deadline:* For fall admission, 7/1 priority date for domestic students, 1/1 priority date for international students. Applications are processed on a rolling basis. Application fee: $40. Electronic applications accepted. *Expenses:* Tuition, state resident: full-time $5567; part-time $309 per credit hour. Tuition, nonresident: full-time $10,977; part-time $610 per credit. *Required fees:* $23 per semester. *Financial support:* In 2013–14, 10 students received support. Federal Work-Study, institutionally sponsored loans, scholarships/grants, tuition waivers (full and partial), and unspecified assistantships available. Financial award application deadline: 3/1; financial award applicants required to submit FAFSA. *Unit head:* Dr. Vella Goebel, Coordinator, 812-461-5306, E-mail: vgoebel@usi.edu. *Application contact:* Dr. Mayola Rowser, Interim Director, Graduate Studies, 812-465-7016, Fax: 812-464-1956, E-mail: mrowser@usi.edu.
Website: http://www.usi.edu/science/teacher-education/programs/mse.

University of Southern Mississippi, Graduate School, College of Education and Psychology, Department of Curriculum, Instruction, and Special Education, Hattiesburg, MS 39406-0001. Offers elementary education (M Ed, PhD, Ed S); instructional technology (MS, PhD); secondary education (MAT); special education (M Ed, PhD, Ed S). Part-time programs available. *Faculty:* 23 full-time (17 women), 3 part-time/adjunct (2 women). *Students:* 20 full-time (19 women), 59 part-time (49 women); includes 18 minority (14 Black or African American, non-Hispanic/Latino; 3 Hispanic/Latino; 1 Two or more races, non-Hispanic/Latino). Average age 36. 21 applicants, 95% accepted, 17 enrolled. In 2013, 22 master's, 3 doctorates, 13 other advanced degrees awarded. *Degree requirements:* For master's and Ed S, comprehensive exam, thesis (for some programs); for doctorate, comprehensive exam, thesis/dissertation. *Entrance requirements:* For master's, GRE General Test, MAT, minimum GPA of 3.0; for doctorate, GRE General Test, minimum GPA of 3.5; for Ed S, GRE General Test, MAT, minimum GPA of 3.25. Additional exam requirements/recommendations for international students: Required—TOEFL, IELTS. *Application deadline:* For fall admission, 3/1 priority date for domestic students, 3/1 for international students; for spring admission, 1/10 priority date for domestic and international students. Applications are processed on a rolling basis. Application fee: $50. *Financial support:* In 2013–14, 9 research assistantships with tuition reimbursements (averaging $18,316 per year), 2 teaching assistantships with full tuition reimbursements (averaging $8,500 per year) were awarded; Federal Work-Study, institutionally sponsored loans, scholarships/grants, health care benefits, tuition waivers (partial), and unspecified assistantships also available. Financial award application deadline: 3/15; financial award applicants required to submit FAFSA. *Faculty research:* Mathematical problem solving, integrative curriculum, writing process, teacher education models. *Total annual research expenditures:* $100,000. *Unit head:* Dr. Ravic P. Ringlaben, Chair, 601-266-4547, Fax: 601-266-4175. *Application contact:* David Daves, Director of Graduate Studies, 601-266-6005, Fax: 601-266-4548.
Website: http://www.usm.edu/graduateschool/table.php.

University of South Florida, College of Education, Department of Secondary Education, Tampa, FL 33620-9951. Offers English education (M Ed, MA, MAT, PhD); foreign language education/ESOL (M Ed, MA, MAT); instructional technology (M Ed, PhD, Ed S); mathematics education (M Ed, MA, MAT, PhD, Ed S); science education (M Ed, MA, MAT, PhD); second language acquisition/instructional technology (PhD); secondary education (M Ed, PhD); secondary education/TESOL (M Ed); social science education (M Ed, MA, MAT); teaching and learning in the content area (PhD). *Accreditation:* NCATE. Part-time and evening/weekend programs available. *Degree requirements:* For master's, variable foreign language requirement, comprehensive exam, project (for some programs); for doctorate, variable foreign language requirement, comprehensive exam, thesis/dissertation, philosophies of inquiry; multiple research methods. *Entrance requirements:* For master's, GRE General Test or General Knowledge Test, minimum GPA of 3.0; for doctorate, GRE General Test, minimum GPA of 3.5; for Ed S, GRE General Test. Additional exam requirements/recommendations for international students: Required—TOEFL (minimum score 550 paper-based; 79 iBT). Electronic applications accepted. *Faculty research:* English language learners/multicultural, social science education, mathematics education, science education, instructional technology.

University of South Florida, University College/Distance Education, Tampa, FL 33620-9951. *Unit head:* Kathy Barnes, Interdisciplinary Programs Coordinator, 813-974-8031, Fax: 813-974-7061, E-mail: barnesk@usf.edu. *Application contact:* Karen Tylinski, Metro Initiatives, 813-974-9943, Fax: 813-974-7061, E-mail: ktylinsk@usf.edu.
Website: http://uc.usf.edu/.

The University of Tennessee, Graduate School, College of Education, Health and Human Sciences, Program in Education, Knoxville, TN 37996. Offers art education (MS); counseling education (PhD); cultural studies in education (PhD); curriculum (MS, Ed S); curriculum, educational research and evaluation (Ed D, PhD); early childhood education (PhD); early childhood special education (MS); education of deaf and hard of hearing (MS); educational administration and policy studies (Ed D, PhD); educational administration and supervision (Ed S); educational psychology (Ed D, PhD); elementary education (MS, Ed S); elementary teaching (MS); English education (MS, Ed S); exercise science (PhD); foreign language/ESL education (MS, Ed S); instructional technology (MS, Ed D, PhD, Ed S); literacy, language and ESL education (PhD); literacy, language education, and ESL education (Ed D); mathematics education (MS, Ed S); modified and comprehensive special education (MS); reading education (MS, Ed S); school counseling (Ed S); school psychology (PhD, Ed S); science education (MS, Ed S); secondary teaching (MS); social foundations (MS); social science education (MS, Ed S); socio-cultural foundations of sports and education (PhD); special education (Ed S); teacher education (Ed D, PhD). *Accreditation:* NCATE. Part-time and evening/weekend programs available. *Degree requirements:* For master's and Ed S, thesis optional; for doctorate, variable foreign language requirement, thesis/dissertation. *Entrance requirements:* For master's, minimum GPA of 2.7; for doctorate and Ed S, GRE General Test, minimum GPA of 2.7. Additional exam requirements/recommendations for international students: Required—TOEFL. Electronic applications accepted. *Expenses:* Tuition, state resident: full-time $9540; part-time $531 per credit hour. Tuition, nonresident: full-time $27,728; part-time $1542 per credit hour. *Required fees:* $1404; $67 per credit hour.

The University of Tennessee at Chattanooga, Graduate School, College of Health, Education and Professional Studies, School of Education, Chattanooga, TN 37403. Offers counseling (M Ed), including community counseling, school counseling; education (M Ed, Post-Master's Certificate), including elementary education (M Ed), school leadership, secondary education (M Ed), special education (M Ed); educational specialist (Ed S), including educational technology, school psychology; learning and leadership (Ed D), including educational leadership. *Accreditation:* ACA; NCATE. Part-

Secondary Education

time and evening/weekend programs available. Postbaccalaureate distance learning degree programs offered (no on-campus study). *Faculty:* 24 full-time (17 women), 6 part-time/adjunct (4 women). *Students:* 107 full-time (86 women), 263 part-time (192 women); includes 71 minority (46 Black or African American, non-Hispanic/Latino; 2 American Indian or Alaska Native, non-Hispanic/Latino; 5 Asian, non-Hispanic/Latino; 11 Hispanic/Latino; 7 Two or more races, non-Hispanic/Latino), 2 international. Average age 34. 121 applicants, 83% accepted, 67 enrolled. In 2013, 125 master's, 10 doctorates, 3 other advanced degrees awarded. *Degree requirements:* For master's, comprehensive exam, thesis optional, culminating experience; for doctorate, comprehensive exam, thesis/dissertation; for other advanced degree, internship. *Entrance requirements:* For master's, GRE General Test, PPST 1, teaching certificate; for doctorate, GRE General Test, master's degree, two years of practical work experience in organizational environment; for other advanced degree, GRE General Test, letters of reference. Additional exam requirements/recommendations for international students: Required—TOEFL (minimum score 550 paper-based; 79 iBT), IELTS (minimum score 6). *Application deadline:* For fall admission, 6/13 for domestic students, 6/1 for international students; for spring admission, 10/15 for domestic students, 10/1 for international students. Applications are processed on a rolling basis. Application fee: $30 ($35 for international students). Electronic applications accepted. *Financial support:* In 2013–14, 20 research assistantships with tuition reimbursements (averaging $6,340 per year), 4 teaching assistantships with tuition reimbursements (averaging $7,234 per year) were awarded; career-related internships or fieldwork, institutionally sponsored loans, scholarships/grants, and unspecified assistantships also available. Support available to part-time students. Financial award applicants required to submit FAFSA. *Faculty research:* School counseling, community counseling, elementary and secondary education, school leadership and administration. *Total annual research expenditures:* $967,880. *Unit head:* Dr. Linda Johnston, Director, 423-425-4122, Fax: 423-425-5380, E-mail: linda-johnston@utc.edu. *Application contact:* Dr. J. Randy Walker, Interim Dean of Graduate Studies, 423-425-4478, Fax: 423-425-5223, E-mail: randy-walker@utc.edu.
Website: http://www.utc.edu/school-education/abouttheschool/gradprograms.php.

The University of Tennessee at Martin, Graduate Programs, College of Education, Health and Behavioral Sciences, Program in Teaching, Martin, TN 38238-1000. Offers curriculum and instruction (MS Ed), including 7-12, K-6; initial licensure (MS Ed), including elementary, secondary; initial licensure K-12 (MS Ed), including physical education, special education; interdisciplinary (MS Ed). Part-time programs available. *Students:* 20 full-time (14 women), 88 part-time (65 women); includes 9 minority (8 Black or African American, non-Hispanic/Latino; 1 Two or more races, non-Hispanic/Latino). 78 applicants, 64% accepted, 33 enrolled. In 2013, 32 master's awarded. *Degree requirements:* For master's, comprehensive exam. *Entrance requirements:* For master's, GRE General Test, minimum GPA of 2.5. Additional exam requirements/recommendations for international students: Required—TOEFL (minimum score 525 paper-based; 71 iBT). *Application deadline:* For fall admission, 7/29 priority date for domestic students, 7/29 for international students; for spring admission, 12/12 priority date for domestic students, 12/12 for international students. Applications are processed on a rolling basis. Application fee: $30 ($130 for international students). Electronic applications accepted. *Financial support:* Research assistantships with full tuition reimbursements, teaching assistantships with full tuition reimbursements, career-related internships or fieldwork, scholarships/grants, and unspecified assistantships available. Financial award application deadline: 3/1. *Faculty research:* Special education, science/math/technology, school reform, reading. *Unit head:* Dr. Gail Stephens, Interim Dean, 731-881-7127, Fax: 731-881-7975, E-mail: gstephe6@utm.edu. *Application contact:* Jolene L. Cunningham, Student Services Specialist, 731-881-7012, Fax: 731-881-7499, E-mail: jcunningham@utm.edu.

The University of Texas–Pan American, College of Education, Department of Curriculum and Instruction: Elementary and Secondary, Edinburg, TX 78539. Offers bilingual education (M Ed); early childhood education (M Ed); elementary education (M Ed); reading (M Ed); secondary education (M Ed). Part-time programs available. *Degree requirements:* For master's, comprehensive exam, thesis optional. *Entrance requirements:* For master's, GRE. Additional exam requirements/recommendations for international students: Required—TOEFL, IELTS. *Expenses:* Tuition, state resident: full-time $5986; part-time $333 per credit hour. Tuition, nonresident: full-time $12,358; part-time $687 per credit hour. *Required fees:* $782. Tuition and fees vary according to program. *Faculty research:* Dual language instruction, literacy and technology, teacher education in diverse populations, mathematics and science education.

University of the Cumberlands, Graduate Programs in Education, Williamsburg, KY 40769-1372. Offers all grades (P-12) (M Ed); business and marketing (MA Ed, MAT); counselor education and supervision (Ed D); director of pupil personnel (Certificate); director of special education (Certificate); educational administration and supervision (Ed S); educational leadership (Ed D); elementary education (MA Ed, MAT); instructional leadership - principalship (MA Ed); instructional leadership - school principal (Certificate); middle school education (MA Ed, MAT); reading and writing (MA Ed); school counseling (MA Ed); school superintendent (Certificate); secondary education (MA Ed, MAT); special education (MAT); supervisor of instruction (Certificate); teacher leader (MA Ed). Part-time and evening/weekend programs available. Postbaccalaureate distance learning degree programs offered. *Degree requirements:* For master's, comprehensive exam. Electronic applications accepted.

University of the Incarnate Word, School of Graduate Studies and Research, Dreeben School of Education, Program in Teaching, San Antonio, TX 78209-6397. Offers all-level teaching (MAT); elementary teaching (MAT); secondary teaching (MAT). Part-time and evening/weekend programs available. *Faculty:* 17 full-time (9 women), 6 part-time/adjunct (all women). *Students:* 1 full-time (0 women), 45 part-time (40 women); includes 28 minority (1 Black or African American, non-Hispanic/Latino; 26 Hispanic/Latino; 1 Two or more races, non-Hispanic/Latino). Average age 26. 17 applicants, 88% accepted, 8 enrolled. In 2013, 6 master's awarded. *Degree requirements:* For master's, internship. *Entrance requirements:* For master's, GRE, Texas Higher Education Assessment test (THEA), interview. Additional exam requirements/recommendations for international students: Required—TOEFL (minimum score 560 paper-based; 83 iBT). *Application deadline:* Applications are processed on a rolling basis. Application fee: $20. Electronic applications accepted. *Expenses:* Tuition: Part-time $815 per credit hour. *Required fees:* $86 per credit hour. One-time fee: $40 part-time. Tuition and fees vary according to degree level and program. *Financial support:* Federal Work-Study and scholarships/grants available. Financial award applicants required to submit FAFSA. *Unit head:* Dr. Elda Martinez, Director of Teacher Education, 210-832-3297, Fax: 210-829-3134, E-mail: eemartin@uiwtx.edu. *Application contact:* Andrea Cyterski-Acosta, Dean of Enrollment, 210-829-6005, Fax: 210-829-3921, E-mail: admis@uiwtx.edu.
Website: http://www.uiw.edu/education/graduate.html.

The University of Toledo, College of Graduate Studies, Judith Herb College of Education, Department of Curriculum and Instruction, Toledo, OH 43606-3390. Offers art education (ME); career and technical education (ME); career-technical education (Ed S); curriculum and instruction (ME, PhD, Ed S); early childhood education (PhD, Ed S); education and biology (MES); education and chemistry (MES); education and economics (MAE); education and English (MAE); education and French (MAE); education and geography (MAE); education and geology (MES); education and German (MAE); education and history (MAE); education and mathematics (MAE, MES); education and physics (MES); education and political science (MAE); education and sociology (MAE); education and Spanish (MAE); educational media (PhD); educational technology (ME); educational technology: virtual educator (Certificate); elementary education (PhD); English as a second language (MAE); gifted and talented (PhD); middle childhood education licensure (ME); music education (MME); secondary education (PhD); secondary education licensure (ME); special education (PhD, Ed S). *Accreditation:* NCATE. Part-time and evening/weekend programs available. *Faculty:* 41. *Students:* 53 full-time (30 women), 154 part-time (111 women); includes 21 minority (16 Black or African American, non-Hispanic/Latino; 4 Hispanic/Latino; 1 Two or more races, non-Hispanic/Latino), 21 international. Average age 34. 82 applicants, 79% accepted, 47 enrolled. In 2013, 80 master's, 5 doctorates awarded. *Degree requirements:* For master's, comprehensive exam, thesis or alternative; for doctorate, comprehensive exam, thesis/dissertation; for other advanced degree, thesis optional. *Entrance requirements:* For master's, doctorate, and other advanced degree, minimum cumulative GPA of 2.7 for all previous academic work, letters of recommendation. Additional exam requirements/recommendations for international students: Required—TOEFL (minimum score 550 paper-based; 80 iBT). *Application deadline:* For fall admission, 1/15 priority date for domestic and international students. Applications are processed on a rolling basis. Application fee: $45 ($75 for international students). Electronic applications accepted. *Financial support:* In 2013–14, 5 research assistantships with full and partial tuition reimbursements (averaging $13,200 per year), 11 teaching assistantships with full and partial tuition reimbursements (averaging $8,809 per year) were awarded; career-related internships or fieldwork, Federal Work-Study, institutionally sponsored loans, scholarships/grants, tuition waivers (full and partial), unspecified assistantships, and administrative assistantships also available. Support available to part-time students. *Unit head:* Dr. Joan Kaderavek, Chair, 419-530-5373, E-mail: eigh.chiarelott@utoledo.edu. *Application contact:* Graduate School Office, 419-530-4723, Fax: 419-530-4724, E-mail: grdsch@utnet.utoledo.edu.
Website: http://www.utoledo.edu/eduhshs/.

The University of Tulsa, Graduate School, College of Arts and Sciences, School of Urban Education, Program in Education, Tulsa, OK 74104-3189. Offers education (MA); elementary certification (M Ed); secondary certification (M Ed). Part-time programs available. *Faculty:* 7 full-time (3 women). *Students:* 4 full-time (1 woman), 1 part-time (0 women), 1 international. Average age 30. 5 applicants, 80% accepted, 3 enrolled. In 2013, 10 master's awarded. *Degree requirements:* For master's, thesis optional. *Entrance requirements:* For master's, GRE General Test. Additional exam requirements/recommendations for international students: Required—TOEFL (minimum score 577 paper-based; 91 iBT), IELTS (minimum score 6.5). *Application deadline:* Applications are processed on a rolling basis. Application fee: $40. Electronic applications accepted. *Expenses:* Tuition: Full-time $19,566; part-time $1087 per credit hour. *Required fees:* $1690; $5 per credit hour. $160 per semester. Tuition and fees vary according to course load. *Financial support:* In 2013–14, 5 students received support, including 5 teaching assistantships with full and partial tuition reimbursements available (averaging $12,310 per year); fellowships with full and partial tuition reimbursements available, research assistantships with full and partial tuition reimbursements available, Federal Work-Study, scholarships/grants, health care benefits, tuition waivers (full and partial), and unspecified assistantships also available. Support available to part-time students. Financial award application deadline: 2/1; financial award applicants required to submit FAFSA. *Faculty research:* Elementary and secondary education; educational foundations; language, discourse and development. *Unit head:* Dr. Kara Gae Neal, Chair, 918-631-2541, Fax: 918-631-2238, E-mail: karagae-neal@utulsa.edu. *Application contact:* Dr. David Brown, Advisor, 918-631-2719, Fax: 918-631-2133, E-mail: david-brown@utulsa.edu.

University of Utah, Graduate School, College of Education, Department of Educational Leadership and Policy, Salt Lake City, UT 84112. Offers educational leadership and policy (Ed D, PhD); K-12 administrative licensure (M Ed); K-12 teacher instructional leadership (M Ed); student affairs (M Ed); MPA/PhD. Part-time and evening/weekend programs available. *Faculty:* 10 full-time (7 women), 4 part-time/adjunct (3 women). *Students:* 55 full-time (38 women), 65 part-time (40 women); includes 33 minority (5 Black or African American, non-Hispanic/Latino; 1 American Indian or Alaska Native, non-Hispanic/Latino; 3 Asian, non-Hispanic/Latino; 21 Hispanic/Latino; 3 Two or more races, non-Hispanic/Latino), 3 international. Average age 35. 123 applicants, 45% accepted, 51 enrolled. In 2013, 33 master's, 5 doctorates awarded. *Degree requirements:* For master's, comprehensive exam (for some programs), internship; for doctorate, thesis/dissertation, qualifying exam. *Entrance requirements:* For master's, minimum undergraduate GPA of 3.0, valid bachelor's degree, 3 years' teaching or leadership experience, Level 1 or 2 UT educator's license (for K-12 programs only); for doctorate, GRE General Test (taken with five years of applying), minimum undergraduate GPA of 3.0, valid master's degree. Additional exam requirements/recommendations for international students: Required—TOEFL (minimum score 500 paper-based). *Application deadline:* For fall and winter admission, 2/1 for domestic and international students; for summer admission, 1/15 for domestic and international students. Application fee: $55 ($65 for international students). Electronic applications accepted. *Expenses:* Tuition, state resident: full-time $5259. Tuition, nonresident: full-time $18,569. *Required fees:* $841. Tuition and fees vary according to course load. *Financial support:* In 2013–14, 86 students received support, including 7 fellowships (averaging $2,000 per year), research assistantships with full tuition reimbursements available (averaging $13,000 per year), 86 teaching assistantships with full tuition reimbursements available (averaging $13,000 per year); career-related internships or fieldwork, scholarships/grants, health care benefits, and unspecified assistantships also available. Financial award application deadline: 2/1. *Faculty research:* Education accountability, college student diversity, K-12 educational administration and school leadership, student affairs, higher education. *Total annual research expenditures:* $55,000. *Unit head:* Dr. Andrea Rorrer, Chair, 801-581-4207, Fax: 801-585-6756, E-mail: andrea.rorrer@utah.edu. *Application contact:* Marilynn S. Howard, Academic Coordinator, 801-581-6714, Fax: 801-585-6756, E-mail: marilynn.howard@utah.edu.
Website: http://elp.utah.edu/.

University of Washington, Bothell, Program in Education, Bothell, WA 98011-8246. Offers education (M Ed); leadership development for educators (M Ed); secondary/middle level endorsement (M Ed). Part-time and evening/weekend programs available. *Degree requirements:* For master's, thesis. *Entrance requirements:* Additional exam requirements/recommendations for international students: Required—TOEFL. Electronic applications accepted. *Faculty research:* Multicultural education in citizenship education, intercultural education, knowledge and practice in the principalship, educational public policy, national board certification for teachers, teacher learning in literacy, technology and its impact on teaching and learning of mathematics, reading assessments, professional development in literacy education and mobility, digital media, education and class.

The University of West Alabama, School of Graduate Studies, College of Education, Departments of Instructional Leadership and Support/Curriculum and Instruction, Program in Secondary Education, Livingston, AL 35470. Offers biology (MAT); English language arts (MAT); history (MAT); mathematics (MAT); physical education (MAT);

science (MAT); secondary education (M Ed); social science (MAT). Part-time and evening/weekend programs available. Postbaccalaureate distance learning degree programs offered (no on-campus study). *Faculty:* 20 full-time (4 women), 5 part-time/adjunct (2 women). *Students:* 210 (139 women); includes 86 minority (80 Black or African American, non-Hispanic/Latino; 2 Asian, non-Hispanic/Latino; 2 Hispanic/Latino; 2 Two or more races, non-Hispanic/Latino). 115 applicants, 86% accepted, 72 enrolled. In 2013, 61 master's awarded. *Degree requirements:* For master's, comprehensive exam, thesis optional. *Entrance requirements:* For master's, GRE General Test, MAT, minimum GPA of 2.75. Additional exam requirements/recommendations for international students: Required—TOEFL (minimum score 500 paper-based; 61 iBT). *Application deadline:* For fall admission, 8/12 priority date for domestic students; for spring admission, 3/24 for domestic students. Applications are processed on a rolling basis. Application fee: $25 ($50 for international students). Electronic applications accepted. Tuition and fees vary according to course load. *Financial support:* Teaching assistantships, career-related internships or fieldwork, Federal Work-Study, scholarships/grants, and unspecified assistantships available. Support available to part-time students. Financial award application deadline: 3/1; financial award applicants required to submit FAFSA. *Faculty research:* Integrated arts in the curriculum, moral development of children. *Unit head:* Dr. Esther Howard, Chair of Curriculum and Instruction, 205-652-3428, Fax: 205-652-3706, E-mail: ehoward@uwa.edu. *Application contact:* Dr. Kathy Chandler, Dean of Graduate Studies, 205-652-3421, Fax: 205-652-3706, E-mail: kchandler@uwa.edu.
Website: http://www.uwa.edu/highschool612.aspx.

University of West Florida, College of Professional Studies, Department of Research and Advanced Studies, Pensacola, FL 32514-5750. Offers administration (MSA), including acquisition and contract administration, biomedical/pharmaceutical, criminal justice administration, database administration, education leadership, healthcare administration, human performance technology, leadership, nursing administration, public administration, software engineering and administration; college student personnel administration (M Ed), including college personnel administration, guidance and counseling; curriculum and instruction (M Ed, Ed S); educational leadership (M Ed); middle and secondary level education and ESOL (M Ed). Part-time and evening/weekend programs available. *Entrance requirements:* For master's, GRE or MAT, official transcripts; minimum undergraduate GPA of 3.0; letter of intent; three letters of recommendation; resume. Additional exam requirements/recommendations for international students: Required—TOEFL (minimum score 550 paper-based).

University of Wisconsin–Eau Claire, College of Education and Human Sciences, Program in Secondary Education, Eau Claire, WI 54702-4004. Offers professional development (ME-PD), including library science, professional development. Part-time programs available. Postbaccalaureate distance learning degree programs offered (minimal on-campus study). *Faculty:* 5 full-time (3 women), 1 (woman) part-time/adjunct. *Students:* 1 full-time (0 women), 17 part-time (13 women); includes 1 minority (Black or African American, non-Hispanic/Latino), 1 international. Average age 31. 6 applicants, 83% accepted, 3 enrolled. In 2013, 8 master's awarded. *Degree requirements:* For master's, comprehensive exam, thesis, research paper, portfolio or written exam; oral exam. *Entrance requirements:* For master's, certification to teach, minimum GPA of 2.75. Additional exam requirements/recommendations for international students: Required—TOEFL (minimum score 79 iBT). *Application deadline:* For fall admission, 7/1 priority date for domestic students, 6/1 priority date for international students; for spring admission, 12/1 priority date for domestic students, 11/1 priority date for international students. Applications are processed on a rolling basis. Application fee: $56. *Expenses:* Tuition, state resident: full-time $7640; part-time $424.47 per credit. Tuition, nonresident: full-time $16,771; part-time $931.74 per credit. *Required fees:* $1146; $63.65 per credit. *Financial support:* In 2013–14, 1 student received support. Federal Work-Study and unspecified assistantships available. Financial award application deadline: 3/1; financial award applicants required to submit FAFSA. *Unit head:* Dr. Rose Battalio, Interim Chair, 715-836-2013, Fax: 715-836-4868, E-mail: battalrl@uwec.edu. *Application contact:* Nancy Amdahl, Graduate Dean Assistant, 715-836-2721, Fax: 715-836-2902, E-mail: graduate@uwec.edu.
Website: http://www.uwec.edu/ES/programs/graduateprograms.htm.

University of Wisconsin–La Crosse, Graduate Studies, College of Liberal Studies, Department of Educational Studies, La Crosse, WI 54601-3742. Offers professional development (ME-PD), including elementary education, K-12, professional development, secondary education; professional development learning community (ME-PD). Part-time programs available. *Faculty:* 6 full-time (4 women), 4 part-time/adjunct (all women). *Students:* 2 full-time (1 woman), 27 part-time (24 women); includes 2 minority (both Asian, non-Hispanic/Latino). Average age 30. 21 applicants, 100% accepted, 21 enrolled. In 2013, 61 master's awarded. *Entrance requirements:* Additional exam requirements/recommendations for international students: Required—TOEFL (minimum score 550 paper-based; 79 iBT). *Application deadline:* Applications are processed on a rolling basis. Electronic applications accepted. *Financial support:* Research assistantships, Federal Work-Study, scholarships/grants, health care benefits, and tuition waivers (partial) available. Support available to part-time students. Financial award application deadline: 3/15; financial award applicants required to submit FAFSA. *Unit head:* Dr. Carol Angell, E-mail: cangell@uwlax.edu. *Application contact:* Corey Sjoquist, Director of Admissions, 608-785-8939, E-mail: admissions@uwlax.edu.
Website: http://www.uwlax.edu/educational-studies/.

University of Wisconsin–Milwaukee, Graduate School, School of Education, Department of Curriculum and Instruction, Milwaukee, WI 53201-0413. Offers curriculum planning and instruction improvement (MS); early childhood education (MS); elementary education (MS); junior high/middle school education (MS); reading education (MS); secondary education (MS); teaching in an urban setting (MS). Part-time programs available. *Faculty:* 18 full-time (13 women). *Students:* 17 full-time (10 women), 46 part-time (42 women); includes 15 minority (7 Black or African American, non-Hispanic/Latino; 1 Asian, non-Hispanic/Latino; 7 Two or more races, non-Hispanic/Latino), 1 international. Average age 32. 35 applicants, 69% accepted, 11 enrolled. In 2013, 31 master's awarded. *Degree requirements:* For master's, thesis or alternative. *Entrance requirements:* Additional exam requirements/recommendations for international students: Required—TOEFL (minimum score 550 paper-based; 79 iBT), IELTS (minimum score 6.5). *Application deadline:* For fall admission, 1/1 priority date for domestic students; for spring admission, 9/1 for domestic students. Applications are processed on a rolling basis. Application fee: $56 ($96 for international students). Electronic applications accepted. *Financial support:* In 2013–14, 1 fellowship was awarded; research assistantships, teaching assistantships, career-related internships or fieldwork, health care benefits, unspecified assistantships, and project assistantships also available. Support available to part-time students. Financial award application deadline: 4/15; financial award applicants required to submit FAFSA. *Unit head:* Raquel Oxford, Department Chair, 414-229-4884, Fax: 414-229-5571, E-mail: roxford@uwm.edu. *Application contact:* General Information Contact, 414-229-4982, Fax: 414-229-6967, E-mail: gradschool@uwm.edu.
Website: http://www.uwm.edu/SOE/.

University of Wisconsin–Platteville, School of Graduate Studies, College of Liberal Arts and Education, School of Education, Platteville, WI 53818-3099. Offers adult education (MSE); elementary education (MSE); English education (MSE); middle school education (MSE); secondary education (MSE). *Accreditation:* NCATE. Part-time programs available. *Faculty:* 5 full-time (3 women), 13 part-time/adjunct (7 women). *Students:* 90 full-time (70 women), 30 part-time (16 women); includes 25 minority (21 Black or African American, non-Hispanic/Latino; 1 American Indian or Alaska Native, non-Hispanic/Latino; 2 Asian, non-Hispanic/Latino; 1 Hispanic/Latino; 3 international. 45 applicants, 96% accepted, 38 enrolled. In 2013, 82 master's awarded. *Degree requirements:* For master's, comprehensive exam, thesis or alternative. *Entrance requirements:* Additional exam requirements/recommendations for international students: Required—TOEFL (minimum score 500 paper-based; 61 iBT), IELTS (minimum score 6). *Application deadline:* For fall admission, 7/1 priority date for domestic students; for spring admission, 11/1 for domestic students. Applications are processed on a rolling basis. Application fee: $56. Electronic applications accepted. *Financial support:* Research assistantships with partial tuition reimbursements, career-related internships or fieldwork, Federal Work-Study, institutionally sponsored loans, scholarships/grants, and unspecified assistantships available. Support available to part-time students. Financial award applicants required to submit FAFSA. *Unit head:* Dr. Karen Stinson, Director, 608-342-1131, Fax: 608-342-1133, E-mail: stinsonk@uwplatt.edu. *Application contact:* Dee Dunbar, School of Graduate Studies, 608-342-1322, Fax: 608-342-1389, E-mail: dunbard@uwplatt.edu.
Website: http://www.uwplatt.edu/.

University of Wisconsin–Stevens Point, College of Fine Arts and Communication, Department of Music, Stevens Point, WI 54481-3897. Offers elementary/secondary (MM Ed); studio pedagogy (MM Ed); Suzuki talent education (MM Ed). *Accreditation:* NASM. Part-time programs available. *Degree requirements:* For master's, thesis or alternative. *Entrance requirements:* For master's, teaching certificate. *Faculty research:* Music education, music composition, music performance.

Utah State University, School of Graduate Studies, Emma Eccles Jones College of Education and Human Services, Program in Secondary Education, Logan, UT 84322. Offers M Ed, MA, MS. Part-time and evening/weekend programs available. *Degree requirements:* For master's, thesis (for some programs). *Entrance requirements:* For master's, GRE General Test or MAT, minimum GPA of 3.0, 1 year teaching, teaching license, letters of recommendation. Additional exam requirements/recommendations for international students: Required—TOEFL. Electronic applications accepted. *Faculty research:* Character education, science education, reading/writing skills, mathematics education, pre-service teacher education.

Vanderbilt University, Peabody College, Department of Teaching and Learning, Nashville, TN 37240-1001. Offers elementary education (M Ed); English language learners (M Ed); learning and instruction (M Ed); learning, diversity, and urban studies (M Ed); reading education (M Ed); secondary education (M Ed). *Accreditation:* NCATE. *Faculty:* 35 full-time (25 women), 20 part-time/adjunct (14 women). *Students:* 103 full-time (74 women), 44 part-time (39 women); includes 22 minority (8 Black or African American, non-Hispanic/Latino; 5 Asian, non-Hispanic/Latino; 5 Hispanic/Latino; 1 Native Hawaiian or other Pacific Islander, non-Hispanic/Latino; 3 Two or more races, non-Hispanic/Latino), 21 international. Average age 25. 264 applicants, 73% accepted, 57 enrolled. In 2013, 95 master's awarded. *Degree requirements:* For master's, comprehensive exam, thesis optional. *Entrance requirements:* For master's, GRE General Test, MAT. Additional exam requirements/recommendations for international students: Required—TOEFL (minimum score 550 paper-based; 80 iBT). *Application deadline:* For fall admission, 12/31 priority date for domestic and international students; for spring admission, 11/1 priority date for domestic and international students. Applications are processed on a rolling basis. Application fee: $0. Electronic applications accepted. *Financial support:* Fellowships with full and partial tuition reimbursements, research assistantships with full and partial tuition reimbursements, teaching assistantships with full and partial tuition reimbursements, Federal Work-Study, institutionally sponsored loans, scholarships/grants, tuition waivers (partial), and unspecified assistantships available. Support available to part-time students. Financial award application deadline: 1/15; financial award applicants required to submit FAFSA. *Faculty research:* Learning environments for mathematics of space and motion, visual programming tools for children's learning of basic science concepts, pathways for elementary and middle school children's learning about measurement and statistics, early reading intervention, professional development for ambitious mathematics teaching. *Unit head:* Dr. Rogers Hall, Chair, 615-322-8100, Fax: 615-322-8999, E-mail: rogers.hall@vanderbilt.edu. *Application contact:* Angela Saylor, Educational Coordinator, 615-322-8092, Fax: 615-322-8999, E-mail: angela.saylor@vanderbilt.edu.

Villanova University, Graduate School of Liberal Arts and Sciences, Department of Education and Counseling, Program in Education plus Teacher Certification, Villanova, PA 19085-1699. Offers MA. Part-time and evening/weekend programs available. *Students:* 9 full-time (5 women), 1 part-time (0 women); includes 2 minority (1 Black or African American, non-Hispanic/Latino; 1 Asian, non-Hispanic/Latino). Average age 26. In 2013, 15 master's awarded. *Degree requirements:* For master's, comprehensive exam. *Entrance requirements:* For master's, GRE or MAT, minimum GPA of 3.0. *Application deadline:* Applications are processed on a rolling basis. Application fee: $50. Electronic applications accepted. *Financial support:* Career-related internships or fieldwork and Federal Work-Study available. Financial award applicants required to submit FAFSA. *Unit head:* Dr. Edward Fierros, Coordinator, 610-519-4620. *Application contact:* Dean, Graduate School of Liberal Arts and Sciences.

Virginia Commonwealth University, Graduate School, School of Education, Program in Teaching and Learning, Richmond, VA 23284-9005. Offers early and elementary education (MT); health and physical education (MT); secondary 6-12 education (MT); secondary education (Certificate). *Accreditation:* NCATE. Part-time programs available. *Entrance requirements:* For master's, GRE General Test or MAT. Additional exam requirements/recommendations for international students: Required—TOEFL (minimum score 600 paper-based; 100 iBT). Electronic applications accepted.

Wagner College, Division of Graduate Studies, Department of Education, Program in Secondary Education/Special Education, Staten Island, NY 10301-4495. Offers language arts (MS Ed); languages other than English (MS Ed); mathematics and technology (MS Ed); science and technology (MS Ed); social studies (MS Ed). Part-time and evening/weekend programs available. *Degree requirements:* For master's, thesis (for some programs). *Entrance requirements:* For master's, minimum GPA of 3.0, interview, recommendations. Electronic applications accepted. *Expenses:* Tuition: Full-time $17,496; part-time $972 per credit. Tuition and fees vary according to course load.

Wake Forest University, Graduate School of Arts and Sciences, Department of Education, Winston-Salem, NC 27109. Offers secondary education (MA Ed). *Accreditation:* ACA; NCATE. *Faculty:* 6 full-time (2 women). *Students:* 20 full-time (12 women); includes 2 minority (1 Black or African American, non-Hispanic/Latino; 1 Asian, non-Hispanic/Latino). Average age 24. 35 applicants, 69% accepted, 20 enrolled. In 2013, 14 master's awarded. *Degree requirements:* For master's, thesis optional. *Entrance requirements:* For master's, GRE General Test. Additional exam requirements/recommendations for international students: Required—TOEFL (minimum score 550 paper-based). *Application deadline:* For fall admission, 1/15 for domestic students, 1/15 priority date for international students. Application fee: $75. Electronic applications accepted. *Expenses:* Contact institution. *Financial support:* In 2013–14, 20 students

received support, including 20 fellowships with full tuition reimbursements available (averaging $48,000 per year); teaching assistantships with full tuition reimbursements available, scholarships/grants, and tuition waivers (full) also available. Financial award application deadline: 2/15. *Faculty research:* Teaching and learning. *Unit head:* Dr. Woodrow Hood, Chair, 336-758-5348, Fax: 336-758-4591, E-mail: hoodwb@wfu.edu. *Application contact:* Dr. Leah McCoy, Program Director, 336-758-5498, Fax: 336-758-4591, E-mail: mccoy@wfu.edu.
Website: http://college.wfu.edu/education/graduate-program/overview-of-graduate-programs/.

Washington State University, Graduate School, College of Education, Department of Teaching and Learning, Program in Teaching, Pullman, WA 99164. Offers elementary education (MIT), including K-8; secondary education (MIT). *Degree requirements:* For master's, comprehensive exam, written and oral exam. *Entrance requirements:* For master's, WEST-B; WEST-E, minimum GPA of 3.0, letters of recommendation, letter of intent, current resume, writing sample, transcripts. Additional exam requirements/recommendations for international students: Required—TOEFL (minimum score 550 paper-based; 80 iBT). Electronic applications accepted.

Washington State University Spokane, Graduate Programs, Education Department, Spokane, WA 99210. Offers curriculum and instruction (Ed M); educational leadership (Ed M, MA); principal (Certificate); program administrator (Certificate); superintendent (Certificate); teaching (MIT), including elementary, secondary. *Degree requirements:* For master's, comprehensive exam (for some programs), thesis (for some programs). *Entrance requirements:* For master's, GRE or GMAT, minimum GPA of 3.0, 3 letters of recommendation, resume. Additional exam requirements/recommendations for international students: Required—TOEFL (minimum score 550 paper-based).

Washington State University Tri-Cities, Graduate Programs, Program in Education, Richland, WA 99352-1671. Offers educational leadership (Ed M, Ed D); literacy (Ed M); secondary certification (Ed M); teaching (MIT). Part-time programs available. *Degree requirements:* For master's, comprehensive exam, thesis or alternative; for doctorate, comprehensive exam, thesis/dissertation. *Entrance requirements:* For master's, GRE, minimum GPA of 3.0, Working with Youth form, Character and Fitness form, 3 letters of recommendation. Additional exam requirements/recommendations for international students: Required—TOEFL. Electronic applications accepted. *Faculty research:* Multicultural counseling, socio-cultural influences in schools, diverse learners, teacher education, K-12 educational leadership.

Washington University in St. Louis, Graduate School of Arts and Sciences, Department of Education, Program in Secondary Education, St. Louis, MO 63130-4899. Offers MAT. *Degree requirements:* For master's, thesis or alternative. *Entrance requirements:* For master's, GRE General Test or MAT. *Application deadline:* For fall admission, 1/15 priority date for domestic students. Applications are processed on a rolling basis. Application fee: $35. Electronic applications accepted. *Financial support:* Career-related internships or fieldwork available. Financial award application deadline: 1/15. *Unit head:* Dr. William Tate, Chair, 314-935-6730.

Wayland Baptist University, Graduate Programs, Program in Education, Plainview, TX 79072-6998. Offers education administration (M Ed); education diagnostics (M Ed); education literacy (M Ed); elementary certification (M Ed); English (M Ed); English as a second language (M Ed); higher education administration (M Ed); human resources (M Ed); instructional leadership (M Ed); instructional technology (M Ed); science education (M Ed); secondary certification (M Ed); social studies (M Ed); special education (M Ed). Part-time and evening/weekend programs available. Postbaccalaureate distance learning degree programs offered (no on-campus study). *Faculty:* 33 full-time (17 women), 28 part-time/adjunct (17 women). *Students:* 22 full-time (15 women), 316 part-time (189 women); includes 130 minority (48 Black or African American, non-Hispanic/Latino; 3 American Indian or Alaska Native, non-Hispanic/Latino; 71 Hispanic/Latino; 1 Native Hawaiian or other Pacific Islander, non-Hispanic/Latino; 7 Two or more races, non-Hispanic/Latino). Average age 39. 80 applicants, 96% accepted, 44 enrolled. In 2013, 170 master's awarded. *Degree requirements:* For master's, comprehensive exam, capstone course. *Entrance requirements:* For master's, GRE, GMAT or MAT. Additional exam requirements/recommendations for international students: Required—TOEFL (minimum score 500 paper-based; 61 iBT). *Application deadline:* Applications are processed on a rolling basis. Application fee: $50. Electronic applications accepted. *Expenses: Tuition:* Full-time $8190; part-time $455 per credit hour. *Required fees:* $970; $455 per credit hour. $485 per semester. *Financial support:* Federal Work-Study, institutionally sponsored loans, and scholarships/grants available. Support available to part-time students. Financial award application deadline: 5/1; financial award applicants required to submit FAFSA. *Unit head:* Dr. Jim Todd, Chairman, 806-291-1045, Fax: 806-291-1951. *Application contact:* Amanda Stanton, Coordinator of Graduate Studies, 806-291-3423, Fax: 806-291-1950, E-mail: stanton@wbu.edu.

Wayne State University, College of Education, Division of Administrative and Organizational Studies, Detroit, MI 48202. Offers college and university teaching (Certificate); educational administration and supervision (Ed S); educational leadership (M Ed); educational leadership and policy studies (Ed D, PhD); educational technology (Certificate); instructional technology (M Ed, Ed D, PhD, Ed S); online teaching (Certificate); secondary curriculum and instruction (Ed S); special education administration (Ed S). Part-time programs available. Postbaccalaureate distance learning degree programs offered. *Students:* 96 full-time (68 women), 207 part-time (137 women); includes 133 minority (115 Black or African American, non-Hispanic/Latino; 4 American Indian or Alaska Native, non-Hispanic/Latino; 2 Asian, non-Hispanic/Latino; 8 Hispanic/Latino; 4 Two or more races, non-Hispanic/Latino), 14 international. Average age 39. 127 applicants, 50% accepted, 42 enrolled. In 2013, 47 master's, 15 doctorates, 41 other advanced degrees awarded. *Degree requirements:* For doctorate, thesis/dissertation. *Entrance requirements:* For master's, baccalaureate degree from accredited U.S. institution or equivalent from college or university of government-recognized standing; minimum undergraduate GPA of 2.75 in upper-division coursework; for doctorate, GRE or MAT, interview; autobiography or curriculum vitae; references; master's degree; minimum undergraduate GPA of 3.0, graduate 3.75; 3 years of relevant experience; foundational course work; for other advanced degree, master's degree from accredited institution, minimum upper-division GPA of 2.6 or 3.4 master's, fulfillment of the special requirements of the area of concentration, 3 years of teaching experience (except for instructional technology). Additional exam requirements/recommendations for international students: Required—TOEFL (minimum score 550 paper-based; 79 iBT), Michigan English Language Assessment Battery (minimum score 85); Recommended—IELTS (minimum score 6.5), TWE (minimum score 5.5). *Application deadline:* For fall admission, 6/1 priority date for domestic students, 5/1 priority date for international students; for winter admission, 10/1 priority date for domestic students, 9/1 priority date for international students; for spring admission, 2/1 priority date for domestic students, 1/1 priority date for international students. Applications are processed on a rolling basis. Application fee: $0. Electronic applications accepted. *Expenses:* Tuition, state resident: part-time $554.15 per credit. Tuition, nonresident: part-time $1200.35 per credit. *Required fees:* $42.15 per credit. $268.30 per semester. Tuition and fees vary according to course load and program. *Financial support:* In 2013–14, 48 students received support, including 3 fellowships with tuition reimbursements available (averaging $15,541 per year), 4 research assistantships with tuition reimbursements available (averaging $16,508 per year); career-related internships or fieldwork, Federal Work-Study, scholarships/grants, health care benefits, and unspecified assistantships also available. Support available to part-time students. Financial award application deadline: 3/31; financial award applicants required to submit FAFSA. *Faculty research:* Total quality management, participatory management, administering educational technology, school improvement, principalship. *Total annual research expenditures:* $6,888. *Unit head:* Dr. William Hill, Assistant Dean, 313-577-9316, E-mail: william_e_hill@wayne.edu. *Application contact:* Janice Green, Assistant Dean, 313-577-1605, E-mail: jwgreen@wayne.edu.
Website: http://coe.wayne.edu/aos/index.php.

Wayne State University, College of Education, Division of Kinesiology, Health and Sports Studies, Detroit, MI 48202. Offers adapted physical education (Certificate); coaching (Certificate); elementary physical education (Certificate); exercise and sport science (M Ed); health education (M Ed, Certificate); kinesiology (M Ed, PhD), including exercise and sport science (PhD), physical education pedagogy (PhD); physical education (M Ed); secondary physical education (Certificate); sports administration (MA); wellness clinician/research (M Ed). Part-time programs available. *Students:* 42 full-time (27 women), 78 part-time (38 women); includes 43 minority (35 Black or African American, non-Hispanic/Latino; 1 Asian, non-Hispanic/Latino; 5 Hispanic/Latino; 2 Two or more races, non-Hispanic/Latino), 5 international. Average age 30. 120 applicants, 48% accepted, 30 enrolled. In 2013, 32 master's awarded. *Degree requirements:* For master's, thesis (for some programs); for doctorate, thesis/dissertation. *Entrance requirements:* For master's and doctorate, minimum undergraduate GPA of 3.0, undergraduate degree directly relating to the field of specialization being applied for, or undergraduate degree accompanied by extensive educational background in a closely-related field. Additional exam requirements/recommendations for international students: Required—TOEFL (minimum score 79 iBT), TWE (minimum score 5.5), Michigan English Language Assessment Battery (minimum score 85); Recommended—IELTS (minimum score 6.5). *Application deadline:* For fall admission, 6/1 priority date for domestic students, 5/1 priority date for international students; for winter admission, 10/1 priority date for domestic students, 9/1 priority date for international students; for spring admission, 2/1 priority date for domestic students, 1/1 priority date for international students. Applications are processed on a rolling basis. Application fee: $0. Electronic applications accepted. *Expenses:* Tuition, state resident: part-time $554.15 per credit. Tuition, nonresident: part-time $1200.35 per credit. *Required fees:* $42.15 per credit. $268.30 per semester. Tuition and fees vary according to course load and program. *Financial support:* In 2013–14, 22 students received support, including 4 fellowships with tuition reimbursements available (averaging $13,050 per year), 5 research assistantships with tuition reimbursements available (averaging $16,508 per year); career-related internships or fieldwork, Federal Work-Study, scholarships/grants, health care benefits, and unspecified assistantships also available. Support available to part-time students. Financial award application deadline: 3/31; financial award applicants required to submit FAFSA. *Faculty research:* Exercise and sport science, nutrition and physical activity interventions, school and community health, obesity prevention. *Total annual research expenditures:* $1.3 million. *Unit head:* Dr. Nate McCaughtry, Assistant Dean, Division of Kinesiology, Health and Sport Studies/Director, Center for School Health, 313-577-0014, Fax: 313-577-5002, E-mail: aj4391@wayne.edu. *Application contact:* Janice Green, Assistant Dean, 313-577-1605, E-mail: jwgreen@wayne.edu.
Website: http://coe.wayne.edu/kinesiology/index.php.

Wayne State University, College of Education, Division of Teacher Education, Detroit, MI 48202. Offers art education (M Ed), including art therapy; autism spectrum disorders (Certificate); bilingual/bicultural education (M Ed, Certificate); career and technical education (M Ed, Certificate); cognitive impairment (Certificate); curriculum and instruction (Ed D, PhD, Ed S), including art education (PhD), bilingual education (Ed D, Ed S), bilingual-bicultural education (PhD), career and technical education (MAT, Ed D, PhD, Ed S), early childhood education (MAT, Ed D, PhD, Ed S), elementary education, English as a second language (MAT, Ed D, Ed S), English education (MAT, Ed D, PhD, Ed S), foreign language education (MAT, PhD), K-12 curriculum, mathematics education (MAT, Ed D, PhD, Ed S), science education (MAT, Ed D, PhD, Ed S), secondary education, social studies education (MAT, Ed S), social studies education: secondary (Ed D, PhD); early childhood education (M Ed, Certificate); elementary education (M Ed, MAT), including children's literature (MAT), early childhood education (MAT, Ed D, PhD, Ed S), general elementary education (MAT); elementary or secondary education (MAT), including bilingual/bicultural education, English as a second language (MAT, Ed D, Ed S), mathematics education (MAT, Ed D, PhD, Ed S), science education (MAT, Ed D, PhD, Ed S), social studies education (MAT, Ed S); emotionally impaired (Certificate); English as a second language (Certificate); English education (M Ed), including secondary; foreign language education (M Ed); K-12 reading specialist (Certificate); learning disabilities (Certificate); mathematics education (M Ed), including secondary; reading (M Ed, Ed S); reading, language and literature (Ed D); science education (M Ed), including secondary; secondary education (MAT), including art education (K-12), career and technical education (MAT, Ed D, PhD, Ed S), English education (MAT, Ed D, PhD, Ed S), foreign language education (MAT, PhD), kinesiology; social studies education (M Ed), including secondary; special education (M Ed, MAT, Ed D, PhD, Ed S); visual arts education (Certificate). Part-time programs available. *Faculty:* 36 full-time (25 women), 55 part-time/adjunct (43 women). *Students:* 218 full-time (163 women), 448 part-time (344 women); includes 218 minority (177 Black or African American, non-Hispanic/Latino; 2 American Indian or Alaska Native, non-Hispanic/Latino; 11 Asian, non-Hispanic/Latino; 19 Hispanic/Latino; 1 Native Hawaiian or other Pacific Islander, non-Hispanic/Latino; 8 Two or more races, non-Hispanic/Latino), 10 international. Average age 37. 258 applicants, 30% accepted, 52 enrolled. In 2013, 183 master's, 10 doctorates, 35 other advanced degrees awarded. *Degree requirements:* For master's, thesis, essay or project (for some M Ed programs), professional field experience (for MAT programs); for doctorate, thesis/dissertation. *Entrance requirements:* For master's, Michigan Basic Skills Test (MA in teaching), admission to the graduate school, verification of participation in group work with children and Michigan State Police Criminal Background check; for doctorate, minimum undergraduate GPA of 3.0, graduate 3.5; interview, curriculum vitae; references. Additional exam requirements/recommendations for international students: Required—TOEFL (minimum score 550 paper-based; 79 iBT), TWE (minimum score 5.5), Michigan English Language Assessment Battery (minimum score 85); Recommended—IELTS (minimum score 6.5). *Application deadline:* For fall admission, 6/1 priority date for domestic students, 5/1 priority date for international students; for winter admission, 10/1 priority date for domestic students, 9/1 priority date for international students; for spring admission, 2/1 priority date for domestic students, 1/1 priority date for international students. Applications are processed on a rolling basis. Application fee: $0. Electronic applications accepted. *Expenses:* Tuition, state resident: part-time $554.15 per credit. Tuition, nonresident: part-time $1200.35 per credit. *Required fees:* $42.15 per credit. $268.30 per semester. Tuition and fees vary according to course load and program. *Financial support:* In 2013–14, 83 students received support, including 1 fellowship (averaging $16,842 per year), 1 research assistantship with tuition reimbursement available (averaging $21,229 per year); career-related internships or fieldwork, Federal Work-Study, scholarships/grants, health care benefits, and unspecified assistantships

also available. Support available to part-time students. Financial award application deadline: 3/31; financial award applicants required to submit FAFSA. *Faculty research:* Improving students' skill achievement in mathematics; improving elementary children's understanding of informational text; teachers' use of their pedagogical and mathematical knowledge in the interactive work of teaching; the intersection of identity construction in teaching and learning; identifying effective methods of literacy instruction and assessments for bilingual students in elementary language arts classrooms. *Total annual research expenditures:* $368,105. *Unit head:* Dr. Kathleen Crawford-McKinney, Assistant Dean, 313-577-0122. *Application contact:* Janice Green, Assistant Dean, 313-577-1605, E-mail: jwgreen@wayne.edu.
Website: http://coe.wayne.edu/ted/index.php.

West Chester University of Pennsylvania, College of Education, Department of Professional and Secondary Education, West Chester, PA 19383. Offers education for sustainability (Certificate); educational technology (Certificate); entrepreneurial education (Certificate); secondary education (M Ed). Part-time programs available. *Faculty:* 9 full-time (4 women). *Students:* 1 (woman) full-time, 20 part-time (14 women); includes 2 minority (1 Black or African American, non-Hispanic/Latino; 1 Two or more races, non-Hispanic/Latino). Average age 29. 19 applicants, 89% accepted, 12 enrolled. In 2013, 15 master's, 3 Certificates awarded. *Degree requirements:* For master's, comprehensive exam, thesis (for some programs), 36 credits. *Entrance requirements:* For master's, GRE or MAT, teaching certification (strongly recommended); for Certificate, minimum GPA of 3.0. Additional exam requirements/recommendations for international students: Required—TOEFL (minimum score 550 paper-based; 80 iBT). *Application deadline:* For fall admission, 4/15 priority date for domestic students, 3/15 for international students; for spring admission, 10/15 priority date for domestic students, 9/1 for international students. Applications are processed on a rolling basis. Application fee: $45. Electronic applications accepted. *Expenses:* Tuition, state resident: full-time $7956; part-time $442 per credit. Tuition, nonresident: full-time $11,934; part-time $663 per credit. *Required fees:* $2134.20; $106.24 per credit. Tuition and fees vary according to campus/location and program. *Financial support:* Unspecified assistantships available. Support available to part-time students. Financial award application deadline: 2/15; financial award applicants required to submit FAFSA. *Faculty research:* Technology integration: preparing our teachers for the twenty-first century, critical pedagogy. *Unit head:* Dr. John Elmore, Chair, 610-436-6934, Fax: 610-436-3102, E-mail: jelmore@wcupa.edu. *Application contact:* Dr. Rob Haworth, Graduate Coordinator, 610-436-2246, Fax: 610-436-3102, E-mail: rhaworth@wcupa.edu.
Website: http://www.wcupa.edu/_academics/sch_sed.prof&seced/.

West Chester University of Pennsylvania, College of Education, Department of Special Education, West Chester, PA 19383. Offers autism (Certificate); special education (M Ed); special education 7-12 (Certificate); special education PK-8 (Certificate); universal design for learning and assistive technology (Certificate). Programs available in traditional, distance, and blended formats. *Accreditation:* NCATE. Part-time programs available. Postbaccalaureate distance learning degree programs offered (no on-campus study). *Faculty:* 4 full-time (all women), 3 part-time/adjunct (2 women). *Students:* 7 full-time (6 women), 106 part-time (91 women); includes 7 minority (5 Black or African American, non-Hispanic/Latino; 1 Asian, non-Hispanic/Latino; 1 Hispanic/Latino), 1 international. Average age 29. 83 applicants, 89% accepted, 42 enrolled. In 2013, 30 master's, 2 Certificates awarded. *Degree requirements:* For master's, thesis optional, minimum GPA of 3.0, action research; for Certificate, minimum GPA of 3.0; modified student teaching. *Entrance requirements:* For master's, GRE if GPA below 3.0, two letters of recommendation; for Certificate, minimum GPA of 2.8 on last 48 credits or 3.0 overall undergraduate. Additional exam requirements/recommendations for international students: Required—TOEFL (minimum score 550 paper-based; 80 iBT). *Application deadline:* For fall admission, 4/15 priority date for domestic students, 3/15 for international students; for spring admission, 10/15 priority date for domestic students, 9/1 for international students. Applications are processed on a rolling basis. Application fee: $45. Electronic applications accepted. *Expenses:* Tuition, state resident: full-time $7956; part-time $442 per credit. Tuition, nonresident: full-time $11,934; part-time $663 per credit. *Required fees:* $2134.20; $106.24 per credit. Tuition and fees vary according to campus/location and program. *Financial support:* Unspecified assistantships available. Support available to part-time students. Financial award application deadline: 2/15; financial award applicants required to submit FAFSA. *Unit head:* Dr. Donna Wandry, Chair, 610-436-3431, Fax: 610-436-3102, E-mail: dwandry@wcupa.edu. *Application contact:* Dr. Vicki McGinley, Graduate Coordinator, 610-436-2867, E-mail: vmcginley@wcupa.edu.
Website: http://www.wcupa.edu/_academics/sch_sed.earlyspecialed/.

Western Connecticut State University, Division of Graduate Studies, School of Professional Studies, Department of Education and Educational Psychology, Program in Secondary Education, Danbury, CT 06810-6885. Offers biology (MAT); mathematics (MAT). Part-time programs available. *Entrance requirements:* For master's, PRAXIS I Pre-Professional Skills Tests, PRAXIS II subject assessment(s), minimum combined undergraduate GPA of 2.8 or MAT (minimum score in 35th percentile). Additional exam requirements/recommendations for international students: Recommended—TOEFL (minimum score 550 paper-based; 79 iBT), IELTS (minimum score 6). *Faculty research:* Differentiated instruction, the transition of teacher learning, teacher retention, relationship building through the evaluation process and leadership development, culture development, differentiated instruction, scheduling, transitioning teacher learning and curriculum.

Western Kentucky University, Graduate Studies, College of Education and Behavioral Sciences, School of Teacher Education, Bowling Green, KY 42101. Offers elementary education (MAE, Ed S); exceptional education: learning and behavioral disorders (MAE); exceptional education: moderate and severe disabilities (MAE); instructional design (MS); interdisciplinary early childhood education (MAE); library media education (MS); literacy education (MAE); middle grades education (MAE); secondary education (MAE, Ed S). Part-time and evening/weekend programs available. Postbaccalaureate distance learning degree programs offered (minimal on-campus study). *Degree requirements:* For master's, comprehensive exam. *Entrance requirements:* For master's, GRE General Test. Additional exam requirements/recommendations for international students: Required—TOEFL (minimum score 555 paper-based; 79 iBT). *Faculty research:* Teacher preparation in moderate/severe disabilities.

Western New Mexico University, Graduate Division, School of Education, Silver City, NM 88062-0680. Offers bilingual education (MAT); counseling (MA); educational leadership (MA); elementary education (MAT); reading (MAT); school psychology (MA); secondary education (MAT); special education (MAT); TESOL (teaching English to speakers of other languages) (MAT). *Accreditation:* NCATE. *Degree requirements:* For master's, comprehensive exam. *Entrance requirements:* For master's, GRE General Test, GRE Subject Test, minimum GPA of 3.2 in last 64 hours of undergraduate study. Additional exam requirements/recommendations for international students: Required—TOEFL (minimum score 550 paper-based). Electronic applications accepted.

Western Oregon University, Graduate Programs, College of Education, Division of Teacher Education, Program in Secondary Education, Monmouth, OR 97361-1394. Offers bilingual education (MS Ed); health (MS Ed); humanities (MAT, MS Ed); initial licensure (MAT); mathematics (MAT, MS Ed); science (MAT, MS Ed); social science

(MAT, MS Ed). *Accreditation:* NCATE. Part-time and evening/weekend programs available. *Degree requirements:* For master's, thesis optional, written exam. *Entrance requirements:* For master's, minimum GPA of 3.0, teaching license. Additional exam requirements/recommendations for international students: Required—TOEFL (minimum score 550 paper-based; 79 iBT), IELTS (minimum score 6.5). *Faculty research:* Literacy, science in primary grades, geography education, retention, teacher burnout.

Western Washington University, Graduate School, Woodring College of Education, Department of Secondary Education, Bellingham, WA 98225-5996. Offers MIT. *Accreditation:* NCATE. Part-time programs available. *Degree requirements:* For master's, comprehensive exam, thesis optional. *Entrance requirements:* For master's, GRE General Test or MAT, minimum GPA of 3.0 in last 60 semester hours or last 90 quarter hours, secondary teaching certification. Additional exam requirements/recommendations for international students: Required—TOEFL (minimum score 567 paper-based). Electronic applications accepted. *Faculty research:* Service learning, controversial issues in classroom, trauma-sensitive teaching-learning, measuring a teacher's "withitness".

Westfield State University, Division of Graduate and Continuing Education, Department of Education, Program in Secondary Education, Westfield, MA 01086. Offers M Ed. *Accreditation:* NCATE. Part-time and evening/weekend programs available. *Degree requirements:* For master's, comprehensive exam, practicum. *Entrance requirements:* For master's, GRE General Test or MAT, minimum undergraduate GPA of 2.7.

West Virginia University, College of Human Resources and Education, Department of Curriculum and Instruction/Literacy Studies, Program in Secondary Education, Morgantown, WV 26506. Offers higher education curriculum and teaching (MA); secondary education (MA). Students enter program as undergraduates. *Accreditation:* NCATE. Part-time programs available. *Degree requirements:* For master's, thesis optional, content exams. *Entrance requirements:* For master's, minimum GPA of 2.75. Additional exam requirements/recommendations for international students: Required—TOEFL. Electronic applications accepted. *Faculty research:* Teacher education, school reform, curriculum development, education technology.

West Virginia University, Eberly College of Arts and Sciences, Department of Mathematics, Morgantown, WV 26506. Offers applied mathematics (MS, PhD); discrete mathematics (PhD); interdisciplinary mathematics (MS); mathematics for secondary education (MS); pure mathematics (MS). Part-time programs available. Terminal master's awarded for partial completion of doctoral program. *Degree requirements:* For master's, comprehensive exam (for some programs), thesis optional; for doctorate, one foreign language, comprehensive exam, thesis/dissertation. *Entrance requirements:* For master's, GRE Subject Test (recommended), minimum GPA of 2.5; for doctorate, GRE Subject Test (recommended), master's degree in mathematics. Additional exam requirements/recommendations for international students: Required—TOEFL (paper-based 550) or IELTS (6). *Faculty research:* Combinatorics and graph theory, differential equations, applied and computational mathematics.

Wheaton College, Graduate School, Department of Education, Wheaton, IL 60187-5593. Offers elementary education (MAT); secondary education (MAT). *Accreditation:* NCATE. *Degree requirements:* For master's, thesis or alternative. *Entrance requirements:* For master's, GRE General Test or MAT. Additional exam requirements/recommendations for international students: Required—TOEFL (minimum score 550 paper-based; 80 iBT), IELTS (minimum score 6.5). Electronic applications accepted.

Whittier College, Graduate Programs, Department of Education and Child Development, Program in Secondary Education, Whittier, CA 90608-0634. Offers MA Ed. Part-time and evening/weekend programs available. *Degree requirements:* For master's, thesis. *Entrance requirements:* For master's, GRE General Test, MAT.

Whitworth University, School of Education, Graduate Studies in Education, Spokane, WA 99251-0001. Offers administration (M Ed); counseling (M Ed), including school counselors, social agency/church setting; elementary education (M Ed); gifted and talented (MAT); secondary education (M Ed); special education (MAT); teaching (MIT). *Accreditation:* NCATE. Part-time and evening/weekend programs available. *Degree requirements:* For master's, comprehensive exam, thesis (for some programs). *Entrance requirements:* For master's, GRE General Test, MAT. Additional exam requirements/recommendations for international students: Required—TOEFL. *Faculty research:* Rural program development, mainstreaming, special needs learners.

Wilkes University, College of Graduate and Professional Studies, School of Education, Wilkes-Barre, PA 18766-0002. Offers art and science of teaching (MS Ed); classroom technology (MS Ed); early childhood literacy (MS Ed); educational development and strategies (MS Ed); educational leadership (MS Ed); educational technology (Ed D); higher education administration (Ed D); instructional media (MS Ed); instructional technology (MS Ed); international school leadership (MS Ed); K-12 administration (Ed D); middle level education (MS Ed); online teaching (MS Ed); reading (MS Ed); school business leadership (MS Ed); secondary education (MS Ed), including biology, chemistry, English, history, mathematics; special education (MS Ed); teaching English as a second language (MS Ed); twenty-first century teaching and learning (MS Ed). Part-time and evening/weekend programs available. Postbaccalaureate distance learning degree programs offered (minimal on-campus study). *Students:* 46 full-time (37 women), 1,410 part-time (1,039 women); includes 67 minority (12 Black or African American, non-Hispanic/Latino; 2 American Indian or Alaska Native, non-Hispanic/Latino; 11 Asian, non-Hispanic/Latino; 28 Hispanic/Latino; 1 Native Hawaiian or other Pacific Islander, non-Hispanic/Latino; 13 Two or more races, non-Hispanic/Latino), 6 international. Average age 34. In 2013, 852 master's, 10 doctorates awarded. *Entrance requirements:* Additional exam requirements/recommendations for international students: Required—TOEFL (minimum score 550 paper-based; 79 iBT). *Application deadline:* Applications are processed on a rolling basis. Application fee: $45. Electronic applications accepted. *Expenses:* Contact institution. *Financial support:* Federal Work-Study and unspecified assistantships available. Financial award application deadline: 3/1; financial award applicants required to submit FAFSA. *Unit head:* Dr. Rhonda Waskiewicz, Interim Dean, Education, 570-408-4332, Fax: 570-408-7872, E-mail: rhonda.waskiewicz@wilkes.edu. *Application contact:* Joanne Thomas, Interim Director of Graduate Education, 570-408-4234, Fax: 570-408-7846, E-mail: joanne.thomas1@wilkes.edu.
Website: http://www.wilkes.edu/pages/383.asp.

William Carey University, School of Education, Hattiesburg, MS 39401-5499. Offers art education (M Ed); art of teaching (M Ed); elementary education (M Ed, Ed S); English education (M Ed); gifted education (M Ed); history and social science (M Ed); mild/moderate disabilities (M Ed); secondary education (M Ed). *Accreditation:* NCATE. Part-time programs available. *Degree requirements:* For master's, comprehensive exam. *Entrance requirements:* For master's, GRE, MAT, minimum GPA of 2.5, Class A teacher's license. Additional exam requirements/recommendations for international students: Required—TOEFL (minimum score 550 paper-based).

Wilmington University, College of Education, New Castle, DE 19720-6491. Offers applied technology in education (M Ed); career and technical education (M Ed); educational leadership (Ed D); elementary and secondary school counseling (M Ed); elementary studies (M Ed); ESOL literacy (M Ed); higher education leadership (Ed D);

Secondary Education

instruction: gifted and talented (M Ed); instruction: teacher of reading (M Ed); instruction: teaching and learning (M Ed); organizational leadership (Ed D); school leadership (M Ed); secondary education (MAT); special education (M Ed). *Accreditation:* NCATE. Part-time and evening/weekend programs available. *Entrance requirements:* For master's, 2 letters of recommendation, interview. Additional exam requirements/ recommendations for international students: Required—TOEFL (minimum score 500 paper-based). Electronic applications accepted.

Wilson College, Program in Education, Chambersburg, PA 17201-1285. Offers M Ed. Evening/weekend programs available. *Degree requirements:* For master's, project. *Entrance requirements:* For master's, PRAXIS, minimum undergraduate cumulative GPA of 3.0, 2 letters of recommendation, current certification for eligibility to teach in grades K-12, resume, personal interview. Electronic applications accepted.

Winthrop University, College of Education, Program in Secondary Education, Rock Hill, SC 29733. Offers M Ed, MAT. *Accreditation:* NCATE. Part-time programs available. *Entrance requirements:* For master's, PRAXIS, minimum GPA of 3.0, South Carolina Class III Teaching Certificate. Electronic applications accepted.

Worcester State University, Graduate Studies, Department of Education, Program in Secondary Education, Worcester, MA 01602-2597. Offers M Ed. Part-time programs available. *Faculty:* 14 full-time (11 women), 22 part-time/adjunct (10 women). *Students:* 6 full-time (3 women), 56 part-time (32 women); includes 7 minority (1 Asian, non-Hispanic/Latino; 6 Hispanic/Latino), 1 international. Average age 34. 46 applicants, 70% accepted, 10 enrolled. In 2013, 6 master's awarded. *Degree requirements:* For master's, comprehensive exam (for some programs), thesis optional. *Entrance requirements:* For master's, GRE General Test or MAT, initial license in middle school education or secondary school license from Commonwealth of Massachusetts; evidence of course in adolescent developmental psychology with minimum grade of B or CLEP exam in human growth and development (minimum score of 50). Additional exam requirements/ recommendations for international students: Required—TOEFL (minimum score 500 paper-based; 61 iBT). *Application deadline:* For fall admission, 6/15 for domestic and international students; for spring admission, 4/1 for domestic and international students. Applications are processed on a rolling basis. Application fee: $40. Electronic applications accepted. *Expenses: Tuition, area resident:* Part-time $150 per credit. Tuition, state resident: part-time $150 per credit. Tuition, nonresident: part-time $150 per credit. *Required fees:* $114.50 per credit. *Financial support:* Career-related internships or fieldwork, scholarships/grants, and unspecified assistantships available.

Financial award application deadline: 3/1; financial award applicants required to submit FAFSA. *Unit head:* Dr. Sara Young, Coordinator, 508-929-8246, E-mail: syoung3@ worcester.edu. *Application contact:* Sara Grady, Assistant Dean of Continuing Education, 508-929-8787, Fax: 508-929-8100, E-mail: sara.grady@worcester.edu.

Wright State University, School of Graduate Studies, College of Education and Human Services, Department of Teacher Education, Programs in Classroom Teacher Education, Dayton, OH 45435. Offers M Ed, MA. *Accreditation:* NCATE. *Degree requirements:* For master's, thesis (for some programs). *Entrance requirements:* For master's, GRE General Test, MAT, PRAXIS II. Additional exam requirements/ recommendations for international students: Required—TOEFL.

Xavier University, College of Social Sciences, Health and Education, School of Education, Department of Secondary and Special Education, Program in Secondary Education, Cincinnati, OH 45207. Offers M Ed. Part-time and evening/weekend programs available. *Faculty:* 4 full-time (1 woman), 1 (woman) part-time/adjunct. *Students:* 45 full-time (22 women), 35 part-time (20 women); includes 13 minority (3 Black or African American, non-Hispanic/Latino; 5 Asian, non-Hispanic/Latino; 4 Hispanic/Latino; 1 Two or more races, non-Hispanic/Latino). Average age 30. 17 applicants, 100% accepted, 14 enrolled. In 2013, 35 master's awarded. *Degree requirements:* For master's, comprehensive exam, thesis. *Entrance requirements:* For master's, MAT. *Expenses: Tuition:* Part-time $594 per credit hour. *Required fees:* $3 per semester. *Financial support:* In 2013–14, 76 students received support. Applicants required to submit FAFSA. *Unit head:* Dr. Michael Flick, Chair, Department of Secondary and Special Education, 513-745-3225, Fax: 513-745-3410, E-mail: flick@ xavier.edu. *Application contact:* Jeff Hutton, Director, 513-745-3702, Fax: 513-745-3410, E-mail: hutton@xavier.edu.
Website: http://www.xavier.edu/education/secondary-special-education/index.cfm.

Youngstown State University, Graduate School, Beeghly College of Education, Department of Teacher Education, Program in Middle Childhood Education, Youngstown, OH 44555-0001. Offers MS Ed. *Accreditation:* NCATE. Part-time and evening/weekend programs available. *Degree requirements:* For master's, comprehensive exam, thesis optional. *Entrance requirements:* For master's, GRE, MAT, or teaching certificate; minimum GPA of 2.7. Additional exam requirements/ recommendations for international students: Required—TOEFL. *Faculty research:* Critical reflectivity, gender issues in classroom instruction, collaborative research and analysis, literacy methodology.

Section 25
Special Focus

This section contains a directory of institutions offering graduate work in a special focus of education. Additional information about programs listed in the directory may be obtained by writing directly to the dean of a graduate school or chair of a department at the address given in the directory.

For programs offering related work, see also in this book *Administration, Instruction, and Theory; Education; Instructional Levels; Leisure Studies and Recreation; Physical Education and Kinesiology;* and *Subject Areas.* In other guides in this series:

Graduate Programs in the Humanities, Arts & Social Sciences
See *Psychology and Counseling (School Psychology)* and *Public, Regional, and Industrial Affairs (Urban Studies)*

Graduate Programs in the Biological/Biomedical Sciences and Health-Related Medical Professions
See *Health-Related Professions*

CONTENTS

Program Directories

Education of Students with Severe/Multiple Disabilities	1128
Education of the Gifted	1129
English as a Second Language	1136
Multilingual and Multicultural Education	1165
Special Education	1179
Urban Education	1241

Education of Students with Severe/Multiple Disabilities

Cleveland State University, College of Graduate Studies, College of Education and Human Services, Department of Teacher Education, Cleveland, OH 44115. Offers art education (M Ed); early childhood education (M Ed); foreign language education (M Ed); mathematics and science education (M Ed); middle childhood education (M Ed); special education (M Ed), including mild/moderate disabilities, moderate/intensive disabilities; teaching English to speakers of other languages (M Ed). Part-time and evening/weekend programs available. *Faculty:* 20 full-time (12 women), 26 part-time/adjunct (20 women). *Students:* 108 full-time (78 women), 311 part-time (252 women); includes 103 minority (80 Black or African American, non-Hispanic/Latino; 2 Asian, non-Hispanic/Latino; 10 Hispanic/Latino; 1 Native Hawaiian or other Pacific Islander, non-Hispanic/Latino; 10 Two or more races, non-Hispanic/Latino), 52 international. Average age 32. 177 applicants, 55% accepted, 68 enrolled. In 2013, 192 master's awarded. *Degree requirements:* For master's, comprehensive exam (for some programs), thesis or alternative. *Entrance requirements:* For master's, GRE General Test or MAT, minimum GPA of 2.75. Additional exam requirements/recommendations for international students: Required—TOEFL (minimum score 525 paper-based), IELTS (minimum score 6). *Application deadline:* For fall admission, 7/15 priority date for domestic students. Applications are processed on a rolling basis. Application fee: $30. *Expenses:* Tuition, state resident: full-time $8335; part-time $521 per credit hour. Tuition, nonresident: full-time $15,670; part-time $979 per credit hour. *Required fees:* $50; $25 per semester. *Financial support:* In 2013–14, 12 research assistantships with full tuition reimbursements (averaging $3,480 per year) were awarded; tuition waivers (partial) and unspecified assistantships also available. *Faculty research:* Early literacy, professional development in reading, reading recovery, dual language, induction programs. *Total annual research expenditures:* $6.2 million. *Unit head:* Dr. Clifford T. Bennett, Chairperson, 216-523-7105, Fax: 216-687-5379, E-mail: c.t.bennett@csuohio.edu. *Application contact:* Deborah L. Brown, Interim Assistant Director, Graduate Admissions, 216-523-7572, E-mail: d.l.brown@csuohio.edu.
Website: http://www.csuohio.edu/cehs/departments/TE/te_dept.html.

Georgia State University, College of Education, Department of Educational Psychology and Special Education, Program in Multiple and Severe Disabilities, Atlanta, GA 30302-3083. Offers early childhood special education general curriculum (M Ed); special education adapted curriculum (intellectual disability) (M Ed); special education deaf education (M Ed); special education general/adapted (autism spectrum disorders) (M Ed); special education physical and health disabilities (orthopedic impairments) (M Ed). *Accreditation:* NCATE. Part-time programs available. *Students:* Average age 0. *Degree requirements:* For master's, variable foreign language requirement, comprehensive exam, thesis (for some programs). *Entrance requirements:* For master's, GRE. Additional exam requirements/recommendations for international students: Required—TOEFL (minimum score 550 paper-based; 79 iBT) or IELTS (minimum score 6.5). *Application deadline:* For fall admission, 6/1 for domestic and international students; for winter admission, 11/1 for domestic and international students; for spring admission, 5/1 for domestic and international students. Application fee: $50. Electronic applications accepted. *Expenses:* Tuition, area resident: Full-time $4176; part-time $348 per credit hour. Tuition, state resident: full-time $14,544; part-time $1212 per credit hour. Tuition, nonresident: full-time $14,544; part-time $1212 per credit hour. Tuition and fees vary according to course load and program. *Financial support:* In 2013–14, fellowships with full tuition reimbursements (averaging $25,000 per year), research assistantships with full tuition reimbursements (averaging $2,000 per year) were awarded; teaching assistantships with full tuition reimbursements, scholarships/grants, health care benefits, and unspecified assistantships also available. *Faculty research:* Literacy, language, behavioral supports. *Unit head:* Dr. Kathryn Wolff Heller, Professor, 404-413-8040, E-mail: kheller@gsu.edu. *Application contact:* Sandy Vaughn, Senior Administrative Coordinator, 404-413-8318, Fax: 404-413-8043, E-mail: svaughn@gsu.edu.
Website: http://education.gsu.edu/EPSE/4637.html.

Hunter College of the City University of New York, Graduate School, School of Education, Department of Special Education, New York, NY 10065-5085. Offers blind or visually impaired (MS Ed); deaf or hard of hearing (MS Ed); severe/multiple disabilities (MS Ed); special education (MS Ed). *Accreditation:* NCATE. *Faculty:* 7 full-time (5 women), 71 part-time/adjunct (59 women). *Students:* 43 full-time (38 women), 478 part-time (389 women); includes 143 minority (43 Black or African American, non-Hispanic/Latino; 1 American Indian or Alaska Native, non-Hispanic/Latino; 34 Asian, non-Hispanic/Latino; 65 Hispanic/Latino). Average age 27. 44 applicants, 91% accepted, 28 enrolled. In 2013, 331 master's awarded. *Degree requirements:* For master's, comprehensive exam, thesis, student teaching practica, clinical teaching lab courses, New York State Teacher Certification Exams. *Entrance requirements:* For master's, minimum GPA of 2.8. Additional exam requirements/recommendations for international students: Required—TOEFL, TWE. *Application deadline:* For fall admission, 4/1 for domestic students, 2/1 for international students; for spring admission, 11/1 for domestic students, 9/1 for international students. Applications are processed on a rolling basis. Application fee: $50. *Financial support:* Career-related internships or fieldwork, Federal Work-Study, institutionally sponsored loans, and tuition waivers (partial) available. Support available to part-time students. *Faculty research:* Mathematics learning disabilities; street behavior; assessment; bilingual special education; families, diversity, and disabilities. *Unit head:* Prof. David Connor, Chairperson, 212-772-4700, E-mail: dconnor@hunter.cuny.edu. *Application contact:* Milena Solo, Director for Graduate Admissions, 212-772-4480, E-mail: admissions@hunter.cuny.edu.
Website: http://www.hunter.cuny.edu/school-of-education/programs/graduate/special-education.

Minot State University, Graduate School, Program in Special Education, Minot, ND 58707-0002. Offers education of the deaf (MS); learning disabilities (MS); special education strategist (MS), including early childhood special education, severe multiple handicaps. *Accreditation:* NCATE. *Degree requirements:* For master's, comprehensive exam (for some programs), thesis (for some programs). *Entrance requirements:* For master's, GRE General Test or minimum GPA of 3.0. Additional exam requirements/recommendations for international students: Required—TOEFL. *Faculty research:* Special education team diagnostic unit; individual diagnostic assessments of mentally retarded, learning-disabled, hearing-impaired, and speech-impaired youth; educational programming for the hearing impaired.

Norfolk State University, School of Graduate Studies, School of Education, Department of Special Education, Program in Severe Disabilities, Norfolk, VA 23504. Offers MA. *Accreditation:* NCATE. Part-time programs available. *Students:* 10 full-time (8 women), 8 part-time (7 women); includes 12 minority (all Black or African American, non-Hispanic/Latino). Average age 37. In 2013, 3 master's awarded. *Degree requirements:* For master's, thesis or alternative. *Entrance requirements:* For master's, GRE, minimum GPA of 3.0 in major, 2.5 overall. *Application deadline:* For fall admission, 3/1 for domestic students; for spring admission, 10/1 for domestic students. Application fee: $30. *Financial support:* In 2013–14, 2 fellowships were awarded; career-related internships or fieldwork also available. *Unit head:* Dr. Helen Bessant-Byrd, Program Coordinator, 757-823-8733, Fax: 757-823-2053, E-mail: hbyrd@nsu.edu. *Application contact:* Dr. Helen Bessant-Byrd, Program Coordinator, 757-823-8733, Fax: 757-823-2053, E-mail: hbyrd@nsu.edu.

Syracuse University, School of Education, Program in Inclusive Special Education: Severe/Multiple Disabilities, Syracuse, NY 13244. Offers MS. Part-time programs available. *Students:* 3 full-time (all women), 4 part-time (2 women); includes 1 minority (Asian, non-Hispanic/Latino). Average age 28. 5 applicants, 100% accepted, 3 enrolled. In 2013, 5 master's awarded. *Entrance requirements:* For master's, New York state initial certification in students with disabilities (Birth-2, 1-6, 5-9, or 7-12), interview. Additional exam requirements/recommendations for international students: Required—TOEFL (minimum score 100 iBT). *Application deadline:* For fall admission, 1/15 priority date for domestic and international students; for spring admission, 10/15 priority date for domestic and international students. Applications are processed on a rolling basis. Application fee: $75. Electronic applications accepted. *Financial support:* Fellowships with full tuition reimbursements and teaching assistantships with full and partial tuition reimbursements available. Financial award application deadline: 1/1. *Unit head:* Dr. Gail Ensher, Program Coordinator, 315-443-9650, E-mail: glensher@syr.edu. *Application contact:* Laurie Deyo, Graduate Recruiter, School of Education, 315-443-2505, E-mail: e-gradrcrt@syr.edu.
Website: http://soeweb.syr.edu/.

Teachers College, Columbia University, Graduate Faculty of Education, Department of Health and Behavioral Studies, Program in Severe or Multiple Disabilities, New York, NY 10027-6696. Offers MA. *Faculty:* 7 full-time, 13 part-time/adjunct. *Students:* 5 full-time (all women), 4 part-time (all women); includes 3 minority (all Asian, non-Hispanic/Latino). Average age 25. 12 applicants, 92% accepted, 6 enrolled. In 2013, 7 master's awarded. *Degree requirements:* For master's, integrative project. *Entrance requirements:* For master's, minimum GPA of 3.0, evidence of New York State initial teacher certification in one of the required areas. *Application deadline:* For fall admission, 1/15 priority date for domestic students; for spring admission, 11/1 for domestic students. Applications are processed on a rolling basis. Application fee: $65. Electronic applications accepted. *Financial support:* Career-related internships or fieldwork, Federal Work-Study, institutionally sponsored loans, and tuition waivers (partial) available. Support available to part-time students. Financial award application deadline: 2/1; financial award applicants required to submit FAFSA. *Faculty research:* Reading and spelling disorders, workplace literacy, reading and writing among children and adults. *Unit head:* Prof. Hsu-Min Chiang, Program Coordinator, 212-678-8346, E-mail: chiang@tc.edu. *Application contact:* Peter Shon, Assistant Director of Admission, 212-678-3305, Fax: 212-678-4171, E-mail: shon@exchange.tc.columbia.edu.
Website: http://www.tc.edu/hbs/specialed/.

University of Illinois at Urbana–Champaign, Graduate College, College of Education, Department of Special Education, Champaign, IL 61820. Offers Ed M, MS, Ed D, PhD, CAS. Part-time programs available. Postbaccalaureate distance learning degree programs offered. *Students:* 58 (51 women). Application fee: $75 ($90 for international students). *Unit head:* Michaelene Ostrosky, Interim Head, 217-333-0260, Fax: 217-333-6555, E-mail: ostrosky@illinois.edu. *Application contact:* Evelyn Grady, Manager I, 217-333-2267, Fax: 217-333-6555, E-mail: egrady@illinois.edu.
Website: http://education.illinois.edu/SPED/.

West Virginia University, College of Human Resources and Education, Department of Special Education, Morgantown, WV 26506. Offers autism spectrum disorder (5-adult) (MA); autism spectrum disorder (K-6) (MA); early intervention/early childhood special education (MA); gifted education (1-12) (MA); low vision (PreK-adult) (MA); multicategorical special education (5-adult) (MA); multicategorical special education (K-6) (MA); severe/multiple disabilities (K-adult) (MA); special education (MA, Ed D); vision impairments (PreK-adult) (MA). *Accreditation:* NCATE. Part-time and evening/weekend programs available. Postbaccalaureate distance learning degree programs offered (no on-campus study). *Degree requirements:* For master's, thesis optional; for doctorate, comprehensive exam, thesis/dissertation. *Entrance requirements:* For master's, minimum GPA of 2.75 passing scores on PRAXIS PPST; for doctorate, GRE General Test or MAT. Additional exam requirements/recommendations for international students: Required—TOEFL.

Education of the Gifted

Arkansas State University, Graduate School, College of Education and Behavioral Science, School of Teacher Education and Leadership, Jonesboro, AR 72467. Offers community college administration (SCCT); curriculum and instruction (MSE); early childhood education (MAT, MSE); early childhood services (MS); educational leadership (MSE, Ed D, PhD, Ed S); educational theory and practice (MSE); middle level education (MAT, MSE); reading (MSE, Ed S); special education - gifted, talented, and creative (MSE); special education - instructional specialist grades 4-12 (MSE); special education - instructional specialist grades P-4 (MSE). *Accreditation:* NCATE. Part-time programs available. Postbaccalaureate distance learning degree programs offered. *Faculty:* 28 full-time (16 women). *Students:* 77 full-time (68 women), 1,934 part-time (1,449 women); includes 361 minority (290 Black or African American, non-Hispanic/Latino; 11 American Indian or Alaska Native, non-Hispanic/Latino; 3 Asian, non-Hispanic/Latino; 26 Hispanic/Latino; 1 Native Hawaiian or other Pacific Islander, non-Hispanic/Latino; 30 Two or more races, non-Hispanic/Latino), 5 international. Average age 36. 1,627 applicants, 71% accepted, 770 enrolled. In 2013, 1,182 master's, 12 doctorates, 76 other advanced degrees awarded. *Degree requirements:* For master's, comprehensive exam, thesis or alternative; for doctorate, comprehensive exam, thesis/dissertation; for other advanced degree, comprehensive exam. *Entrance requirements:* For master's, GRE General Test or MAT, appropriate bachelor's degree, official transcripts, immunization records, letters of reference, interview; for doctorate, GRE General Test or MAT, interview, master's degree, letters of reference, official transcript, personal statement, writing sample, immunization records; for other advanced degree, GRE General Test or MAT, interview, master's degree, official transcript, immunization records, letters of reference, 3 years of teaching experience, teaching license. Additional exam requirements/recommendations for international students: Required—TOEFL (minimum score 550 paper-based; 79 iBT), IELTS (minimum score 6), PTE (minimum score 56). *Application deadline:* For fall admission, 7/1 for domestic and international students; for spring admission, 11/15 for domestic students, 11/14 for international students. Applications are processed on a rolling basis. Electronic applications accepted. *Expenses:* Tuition, state resident: full-time $4284; part-time $238 per credit hour. Tuition, nonresident: full-time $8568; part-time $476 per credit hour. *International tuition:* $9268 full-time. *Required fees:* $1098; $61 per credit hour. $25 per term. Tuition and fees vary according to course load and program. *Financial support:* In 2013–14, 20 students received support. Fellowships, teaching assistantships, career-related internships or fieldwork, scholarships/grants, and unspecified assistantships available. Financial award application deadline: 7/1; financial award applicants required to submit FAFSA. *Unit head:* Dr. Annette Hux, Interim Chair, 870-972-3059, Fax: 870-972-3344, E-mail: ahux@astate.edu. *Application contact:* Vickey Ring, Graduate Admissions Coordinator, 870-972-3029, Fax: 870-972-3857, E-mail: vickeyring@astate.edu.
Website: http://www.astate.edu/college/education/departments/school-of-teacher-education-and-leadership/index.dot.

Ashland University, Dwight Schar College of Education, Department of Inclusive Services and Exceptional Learners, Ashland, OH 44805-3702. Offers intervention specialist, mild/moderate (M Ed); intervention specialist, moderate/intensive (M Ed); talented and gifted (M Ed). Part-time and evening/weekend programs available. *Degree requirements:* For master's, thesis or alternative, internship, practicum, inquiry seminar. *Entrance requirements:* Additional exam requirements/recommendations for international students: Required—TOEFL. Electronic applications accepted.

Barry University, School of Education, Program in Curriculum and Instruction, Miami Shores, FL 33161-6695. Offers accomplished teacher (Ed S); culture, language and literacy (TESOL) (PhD); curriculum evaluation and research (PhD); early childhood (Ed S); early childhood education (PhD); elementary (Ed S); elementary education (PhD); ESOL (Ed S); gifted (Ed S); Montessori (Ed S); PKP/elementary (Ed S); reading (Ed S); reading, language and cognition (PhD). *Entrance requirements:* For doctorate, GRE, minimum GPA of 3.25.

Barry University, School of Education, Program in Exceptional Student Education, Miami Shores, FL 33161-6695. Offers MS, Ed S. Part-time and evening/weekend programs available. *Degree requirements:* For master's, comprehensive exam; for Ed S, practicum. *Entrance requirements:* For master's, GRE General Test or MAT, minimum GPA of 3.0; for Ed S, GRE General Test, minimum GPA of 3.0. Electronic applications accepted.

Barry University, School of Education, Program in Leadership and Education, Miami Shores, FL 33161-6695. Offers educational technology (PhD); exceptional student education (PhD); higher education administration (PhD); human resource development (PhD); leadership (PhD). Part-time and evening/weekend programs available. *Degree requirements:* For doctorate, thesis/dissertation. *Entrance requirements:* For doctorate, GRE General Test, minimum GPA of 3.25. Electronic applications accepted.

Bowling Green State University, Graduate College, College of Education and Human Development, School of Education and Intervention Services, Intervention Services Division, Program in Special Education, Bowling Green, OH 43403. Offers assistive technology (M Ed); early childhood intervention (M Ed); gifted education (M Ed); hearing impaired intervention (M Ed); mild/moderate intervention (M Ed); moderate/intensive intervention (M Ed). *Accreditation:* NCATE. Part-time programs available. *Degree requirements:* For master's, thesis or alternative. *Entrance requirements:* For master's, GRE General Test. Additional exam requirements/recommendations for international students: Required—TOEFL. Electronic applications accepted. *Faculty research:* Reading and special populations, deafness, early childhood, gifted and talented, behavior disorders.

Canisius College, Graduate Division, School of Education and Human Services, Department of Graduate Education and Leadership, Buffalo, NY 14208-1098. Offers business and marketing education (MS Ed); college student personnel (MS Ed); deaf education (MS Ed); deaf/adolescent education, grades 7-12 (MS Ed); deaf/childhood education, grades 1-6 (MS Ed); differentiated instruction (MS Ed); education administration (MS); educational administration (MS Ed); educational technologies (Certificate); gifted education extension (Certificate); literacy (MS Ed); reading (Certificate); school building leadership (MS Ed, Certificate); school district leadership (Certificate); teacher leader (Certificate); TESOL (MS Ed). *Accreditation:* NCATE. Part-time and evening/weekend programs available. Postbaccalaureate distance learning degree programs offered (minimal on-campus study). *Faculty:* 6 full-time (5 women), 33 part-time/adjunct (20 women). *Students:* 134 full-time (106 women), 267 part-time (213 women); includes 36 minority (22 Black or African American, non-Hispanic/Latino; 1 American Indian or Alaska Native, non-Hispanic/Latino; 3 Asian, non-Hispanic/Latino; 8 Hispanic/Latino; 2 Two or more races, non-Hispanic/Latino), 2 international. Average age 30. 282 applicants, 80% accepted, 120 enrolled. In 2013, 178 master's awarded. *Entrance requirements:* For master's, GRE if cumulative GPA less than 2.7, transcripts, two letters of recommendation. Additional exam requirements/recommendations for

international students: Required—TOEFL (minimum score 550 paper-based, 80 iBT), IELTS (minimum score 6.5), or CAEL (minimum score 70). *Application deadline:* Applications are processed on a rolling basis. Application fee: $25. Electronic applications accepted. Application fee is waived when completed online. *Expenses:* Tuition: Part-time $750 per credit hour. *Financial support:* Career-related internships or fieldwork, Federal Work-Study, scholarships/grants, tuition waivers (partial), and unspecified assistantships available. Support available to part-time students. Financial award application deadline: 4/30; financial award applicants required to submit FAFSA. *Faculty research:* Asperger's disease, autism, private higher education, reading strategies. *Unit head:* Dr. Rosemary K. Murray, Chair/Associate Professor of Graduate Education and Leadership, 716-888-3723, E-mail: murray1@canisius.edu. *Application contact:* Julie A. Zulewski, Director of Graduate Admissions, 716-888-2548, Fax: 716-888-3195, E-mail: zulewskj@canisius.edu.
Website: http://www.canisius.edu/graduate/.

Carlos Albizu University, Miami Campus, Graduate Programs, Miami, FL 33172-2209. Offers clinical psychology (Psy D); entrepreneurship (MBA); exceptional student education (MS); human services (PhD); industrial/organizational psychology (MS); marriage and family therapy (MS); mental health counseling (MS); nonprofit management (MBA); organizational management (MBA); psychology (MS); school counseling (MS); teaching English as a second language (MS). *Accreditation:* APA. Part-time and evening/weekend programs available. *Faculty:* 26 full-time (20 women), 34 part-time/adjunct (16 women). *Students:* 416 full-time (335 women), 281 part-time (237 women); includes 604 minority (57 Black or African American, non-Hispanic/Latino; 1 American Indian or Alaska Native, non-Hispanic/Latino; 13 Asian, non-Hispanic/Latino; 533 Hispanic/Latino), 14 international. Average age 36. 176 applicants, 59% accepted, 96 enrolled. In 2013, 176 master's, 37 doctorates awarded. Terminal master's awarded for partial completion of doctoral program. *Degree requirements:* For master's, one foreign language, comprehensive exam, integrative project (MBA), research project (exceptional student education, teaching English as a second language); for doctorate, one foreign language, comprehensive exam, internship, project. *Entrance requirements:* For master's, 3 letters of recommendation, interview, minimum GPA of 3.0, resume, statement of purpose, official transcripts; for doctorate, 3 letters of recommendation, minimum GPA of 3.0, resume, interview, statement of purpose, official transcripts. Additional exam requirements/recommendations for international students: Required—Michigan Test of English Language Proficiency. *Application deadline:* For fall admission, 4/1 priority date for domestic students, 5/1 priority date for international students; for spring admission, 11/1 priority date for domestic students, 9/1 priority date for international students. Applications are processed on a rolling basis. Application fee: $50. Electronic applications accepted. *Expenses: Tuition:* Full-time $9360; part-time $520 per credit. *Required fees:* $298 per term. Tuition and fees vary according to course load, degree level and program. *Financial support:* In 2013–14, 62 students received support. Federal Work-Study, scholarships/grants, and tuition discounts available. Financial award application deadline: 6/1; financial award applicants required to submit FAFSA. *Faculty research:* Psychotherapy, forensic psychology, neuropsychology, marketing strategy, entrepreneurship, special education. *Unit head:* Peter M. Rubio, Interim Chancellor, 305-593-1223 Ext. 3120, Fax: 305-592-7930, E-mail: prubio@albizu.edu. *Application contact:* Vanessa Almendarez, Administrative Assistant, 305-593-1223 Ext. 3137, Fax: 305-593-1854, E-mail: valmendarez@albizu.edu.

Carthage College, Division of Teacher Education, Kenosha, WI 53140. Offers classroom guidance and counseling (M Ed); creative arts (M Ed); gifted and talented children (M Ed); language arts (M Ed); modern language (M Ed); natural sciences (M Ed); reading (M Ed, Certificate); social sciences (M Ed); teacher leadership (M Ed). Part-time and evening/weekend programs available. *Degree requirements:* For master's, thesis optional. *Entrance requirements:* For master's, MAT, minimum B average, letters of reference.

The College of New Rochelle, Graduate School, Division of Education, Program in Creative Teaching and Learning, New Rochelle, NY 10805-2308. Offers MS Ed, Certificate. Part-time programs available. *Degree requirements:* For master's, practicum. *Entrance requirements:* For master's, interview, minimum GPA of 3.0 in field, 2.7 overall. *Expenses: Tuition:* Part-time $894 per credit. *Required fees:* $300 per semester. One-time fee: $200. Tuition and fees vary according to course load.

The College of William and Mary, School of Education, Program in Curriculum and Instruction, Williamsburg, VA 23187-8795. Offers elementary education (MA Ed); gifted education (MA Ed); literacy leadership (MA Ed); math specialist (MA Ed); secondary education (MA Ed), including English education, mathematics education, modern foreign languages education, science education, social studies education; special education (MA Ed), including collaborating master educator, general curriculum. *Accreditation:* NCATE. Part-time programs available. *Faculty:* 15 full-time (10 women), 44 part-time/adjunct (38 women). *Students:* 66 full-time (55 women), 27 part-time (26 women); includes 17 minority (4 Black or African American, non-Hispanic/Latino; 1 American Indian or Alaska Native, non-Hispanic/Latino; 3 Asian, non-Hispanic/Latino; 5 Hispanic/Latino; 4 Two or more races, non-Hispanic/Latino). Average age 28. 179 applicants, 72% accepted, 92 enrolled. In 2013, 76 master's awarded. *Degree requirements:* For master's, project. *Entrance requirements:* For master's, GRE or MAT, minimum GPA of 2.5. Additional exam requirements/recommendations for international students: Required—TOEFL, IELTS. *Application deadline:* For fall admission, 1/15 for domestic and international students; for spring admission, 10/1 for domestic and international students. Application fee: $50. Electronic applications accepted. *Expenses:* Tuition, state resident: full-time $7120; part-time $405 per credit hour. Tuition, nonresident: full-time $21,639; part-time $1050 per credit hour. *Required fees:* $4764. *Financial support:* In 2013–14, 49 students received support, including 6 research assistantships with full and partial tuition reimbursements available (averaging $8,269 per year); career-related internships or fieldwork, Federal Work-Study, institutionally sponsored loans, scholarships/grants, and unspecified assistantships also available. Financial award application deadline: 1/15; financial award applicants required to submit FAFSA. *Faculty research:* National Council of Teachers of Mathematics standards, counseling, self-concept and self-esteem, special education, curriculum development. *Unit head:* Dr. Mark Hofer, Area Coordinator, 757-221-1713, E-mail: mjhofe@wm.edu. *Application contact:* Dorothy Smith Osborne, Assistant Dean for Academic Programs and Student Services, 757-221-2317, Fax: 757-221-2293, E-mail: dsosbo@wm.edu.
Website: http://education.wm.edu.

Converse College, School of Education and Graduate Studies, Program in Gifted Education, Spartanburg, SC 29302-0006. Offers M Ed. Part-time programs available. *Degree requirements:* For master's, capstone paper. *Entrance requirements:* For master's, NTE or PRAXIS II, minimum GPA of 2.75, teaching certificate, 2 recommendations. Electronic applications accepted. *Faculty research:* Identification of gifted minorities, arts in gifted education.

Education of the Gifted

Dowling College, Graduate Programs in Education, Oakdale, NY 11769-1999. Offers adolescence education with middle childhood extension (MS); childhood and early childhood education (MS); childhood and gifted education (MS); childhood education (1-6) (MS); computers in education (AC); early childhood education (B-2) (MS); educational administration (Ed D); educational technology leadership (MS); educational technology specialist (AC); gifted education (AC); literacy education (MS, AC), including 5-12 (MS), B-12 (MS); literacy education (MS), including B-6; school building leader (AC); school district business leader (MBA, AC); school district leader (AC); special education (MS), including autism, severe disabilities; sport management (MS). *Accreditation:* NCATE. Part-time and evening/weekend programs available. Postbaccalaureate distance learning degree programs offered (minimal on-campus study). *Faculty:* 44 full-time (24 women), 17 part-time/adjunct (8 women). *Students:* 183 full-time (124 women), 314 part-time (231 women); includes 51 minority (19 Black or African American, non-Hispanic/Latino; 1 American Indian or Alaska Native, non-Hispanic/Latino; 3 Asian, non-Hispanic/Latino; 26 Hispanic/Latino; 2 Native Hawaiian or other Pacific Islander, non-Hispanic/Latino). Average age 32. 174 applicants, 80% accepted, 82 enrolled. In 2013, 198 master's, 33 doctorates, 48 other advanced degrees awarded. *Degree requirements:* For master's and AC, comprehensive exam; for doctorate, thesis/dissertation. *Entrance requirements:* For master's, minimum GPA of 3.0; for doctorate, GRE, master's degree; for AC, teaching certificate. Additional exam requirements/recommendations for international students: Required—TOEFL (minimum score 550 paper-based). *Application deadline:* For fall admission, 9/1 priority date for domestic students; for winter admission, 1/1 priority date for domestic students; for spring admission, 2/1 priority date for domestic students. Applications are processed on a rolling basis. Application fee: $50. Electronic applications accepted. *Expenses: Tuition:* Full-time $22,731; part-time $1029 per credit. *Required fees:* $956; $956. *Financial support:* Career-related internships or fieldwork and Federal Work-Study available. Support available to part-time students. Financial award application deadline: 6/30; financial award applicants required to submit FAFSA. *Faculty research:* Natural readers, Korean styles and learning strategies, mothers of children with disabilities, computers in instruction, cultural background and organizational roadblocks to problem solving. *Unit head:* Dr. Robert Manley, Dean, 631-244-3447, E-mail: manleyr@dowling.edu. *Application contact:* Mary Boullianne, Director of Admissions, 631-244-3274, Fax: 631-244-1059, E-mail: boulliam@dowling.edu.

Drury University, Graduate Programs in Education, Springfield, MO 65802. Offers elementary education (M Ed); gifted education (M Ed); human services (M Ed); instructional mathematics K-8 (M Ed); instructional technology (M Ed); middle school teaching (M Ed); secondary education (M Ed); special education (M Ed); special reading (M Ed). *Accreditation:* NCATE. Part-time and evening/weekend programs available. *Degree requirements:* For master's, thesis. *Entrance requirements:* For master's, GRE or MAT, minimum GPA of 2.75. Additional exam requirements/recommendations for international students: Required—TOEFL. Electronic applications accepted. *Faculty research:* Cultural enrichment, research skills, parental involvement relating to reading skills, reading strategies for mainstreaming children.

Elon University, Program in Education, Elon, NC 27244-2010. Offers elementary education (M Ed); gifted education (M Ed); special education (M Ed). *Accreditation:* NCATE. Part-time programs available. *Faculty:* 16 full-time (13 women), 3 part-time/adjunct (2 women). *Students:* 62 part-time (53 women); includes 11 minority (5 Black or African American, non-Hispanic/Latino; 1 Asian, non-Hispanic/Latino; 5 Hispanic/Latino). Average age 33. 35 applicants, 94% accepted, 29 enrolled. *Entrance requirements:* For master's, GRE, MAT. Additional exam requirements/recommendations for international students: Required—TOEFL (minimum score 550 paper-based; 79 iBT). *Application deadline:* For winter admission, 6/1 priority date for domestic students. Applications are processed on a rolling basis. Application fee: $50. Electronic applications accepted. *Expenses:* Contact institution. *Financial support:* In 2013–14, 5 students received support. Federal Work-Study and scholarships/grants available. Support available to part-time students. Financial award application deadline: 6/1; financial award applicants required to submit FAFSA. *Faculty research:* Teaching reading to low-achieving second and third graders, pre- and post-student teaching attitudes, children's writing, whole language methodology, critical creative thinking. *Unit head:* Dr. Angela Owusu-Ansah, Director and Associate Dean of Education, 336-278-5885, Fax: 336-278-5919, E-mail: aansah@elon.edu. *Application contact:* Art Fadde, Director of Graduate Admissions, 800-334-8448 Ext. 3, Fax: 336-278-7699, E-mail: afadde@elon.edu.
Website: http://www.elon.edu/med/.

Emporia State University, Program in Special Education, Emporia, KS 66801-5415. Offers behavior disorders (MS); gifted, talented, and creative (MS); interrelated special education (MS); learning disabilities (MS); mental retardation (MS). *Accreditation:* NCATE. Part-time programs available. *Faculty:* 7 full-time (5 women). *Students:* 7 full-time (6 women), 182 part-time (129 women); includes 9 minority (4 Black or African American, non-Hispanic/Latino; 3 Hispanic/Latino; 2 Two or more races, non-Hispanic/Latino). 69 applicants, 78% accepted, 35 enrolled. In 2013, 38 master's awarded. *Degree requirements:* For master's, comprehensive exam or thesis, practicum. *Entrance requirements:* For master's, GRE General Test or MAT, essay exam, appropriate bachelor's degree, teacher certification, letters of recommendation. Additional exam requirements/recommendations for international students: Required—TOEFL (minimum score 520 paper-based; 68 iBT). *Application deadline:* For fall admission, 8/15 priority date for domestic students. Applications are processed on a rolling basis. Application fee: $30 ($75 for international students). Electronic applications accepted. *Expenses: Tuition, area resident:* Part-time $220 per credit hour. Tuition, state resident: part-time $220 per credit hour. Tuition, nonresident: part-time $685 per credit hour. *Required fees:* $73 per credit hour. *Financial support:* Federal Work-Study, institutionally sponsored loans, health care benefits, and unspecified assistantships available. Financial award application deadline: 3/15; financial award applicants required to submit FAFSA. *Unit head:* Dr. Jean Morrow, Chair, 620-341-5317, E-mail: jmorrow@emporia.edu. *Application contact:* Mary Sewell, Admissions Coordinator, 800-950-GRAD, Fax: 620-341-5909, E-mail: msewell@emporia.edu.
Website: http://www.emporia.edu/elecse/sped/.

Hampton University, Graduate College, College of Education and Continuing Studies, Program in Gifted Education, Hampton, VA 23668. Offers MA. *Accreditation:* NCATE. Part-time and evening/weekend programs available. *Entrance requirements:* For master's, GRE General Test.

Hardin-Simmons University, Graduate School, Irvin School of Education, Department of Educational Studies, Program in Gifted Education, Abilene, TX 79698-0001. Offers M Ed. Part-time programs available. *Faculty:* 2 full-time (both women), 1 (woman) part-time/adjunct. *Students:* 26 part-time (25 women); includes 6 minority (1 Black or African American, non-Hispanic/Latino; 1 Asian, non-Hispanic/Latino; 3 Hispanic/Latino; 1 Two or more races, non-Hispanic/Latino). Average age 41. 8 applicants, 100% accepted, 8 enrolled. In 2013, 7 master's awarded. *Degree requirements:* For master's, comprehensive exam. *Entrance requirements:* For master's, minimum undergraduate GPA of 3.0 in major, 2.7 overall. Additional exam requirements/recommendations for international students: Required—TOEFL (minimum score 550 paper-based; 75 iBT). *Application deadline:* For fall admission, 8/15 priority date for domestic students, 4/1 for international students; for spring admission, 1/5 priority date for domestic students, 9/1 for international students. Applications are processed on a rolling basis. Application fee: $50. *Expenses: Tuition:* Full-time $13,410; part-time $745 per credit hour. *Required fees:* $325; $110 per semester. Tuition and fees vary according to program. *Financial support:* In 2013–14, 6 students received support, including 2 fellowships (averaging $1,650 per year); scholarships/grants also available. Support available to part-time students. Financial award application deadline: 6/30; financial award applicants required to submit FAFSA. *Faculty research:* Experiences of gifted learners in college, use of authentic assessment, brain research and how it works in learning, theories of multiple intelligence beyond Howard Gardner. *Unit head:* Dr. Mary Christopher, Director, 325-670-1510, Fax: 325-670-1397, E-mail: mchris@hsutx.edu. *Application contact:* Dr. Nancy Kucinski, Dean of Graduate Studies, 325-670-1298, Fax: 325-670-1564, E-mail: gradoff@hsutx.edu.
Website: http://www.hsutx.edu/academics/irvin/graduate/gifted.

Hofstra University, School of Education, Programs in Special Education, Hempstead, NY 11549. Offers applied behavior analysis (Advanced Certificate); early childhood special education (MS Ed, Advanced Certificate); gifted education (Advanced Certificate); inclusive early childhood special education (MS Ed); inclusive elementary special education (MS Ed); inclusive secondary special education (MS Ed); secondary education generalist (MS Ed), including students with disabilities 7-12; special education (MA, MS Ed, Advanced Certificate, PD); special education assessment and diagnosis (Advanced Certificate); special education generalist (MS Ed), including extension in secondary education; teaching students with severe or multiple disabilities (Advanced Certificate).

Johns Hopkins University, School of Education, Certificate Programs in Education, Baltimore, MD 21218-2699. Offers advanced methods for differentiated instruction and inclusive education (Certificate); applied behavior analysis (Certificate); counseling (CAGS); data-based decision making and organizational improvement (Certificate); early intervention/preschool special education specialist (Certificate); education leadership for independent schools (Certificate); education of students with autism and other pervasive developmental disorders (Certificate); evidence-based teaching in the health professions (Certificate); gifted education (Certificate); K-8 mathematics lead-teacher (Certificate); K-8 STEM education lead-teacher (Certificate); leadership for school, family, and community collaboration (Certificate); leadership in technology integration (Certificate); mental health counseling (Certificate); mind, brain, and teaching (Certificate); school administration and supervision (Certificate); urban education (Certificate). Part-time and evening/weekend programs available. Postbaccalaureate distance learning degree programs offered (no on-campus study). *Students:* 7 full-time (4 women), 216 part-time (169 women); includes 66 minority (35 Black or African American, non-Hispanic/Latino; 17 Asian, non-Hispanic/Latino; 6 Hispanic/Latino; 8 Two or more races, non-Hispanic/Latino), 6 international. Average age 35. 257 applicants, 81% accepted, 62 enrolled. In 2013, 202 CAGSs awarded. *Entrance requirements:* For degree, bachelor's degree from regionally- or nationally-accredited institution (master's for some programs), minimum GPA of 3.0 in all previous programs of study, official transcripts from all post-secondary institutions attended, essay, curriculum vitae/resume, minimum of two letters of recommendation. Additional exam requirements/recommendations for international students: Required—TOEFL (minimum score 600 paper-based; 100 iBT) or IELTS (minimum score 7). *Application deadline:* For fall admission, 4/1 for domestic students; for spring admission, 10/1 for domestic students; for summer admission, 2/1 for domestic students. Application fee: $80. Electronic applications accepted. *Financial support:* Application deadline: 6/1; applicants required to submit FAFSA. *Unit head:* Dr. David A. Andrews, Dean, 410-516-7820, Fax: 410-516-6697, E-mail: davidandrews@jhu.edu. *Application contact:* Catherine Wilson, Associate Director of Admissions, 410-516-9797, Fax: 410-516-9799, E-mail: soe.info@jhu.edu.

Johns Hopkins University, School of Education, Master's Programs in Education, Baltimore, MD 21218-2699. Offers counseling (MS), including mental health counseling, school counseling; education (MS), including educational studies, gifted education, reading, school administration and supervision, technology for educators; elementary education (MAT); health professions (M Ed); intelligence analysis (MS); management (MS); secondary education (MAT); special education (MS), including early childhood special education, general special education studies, mild to moderate disabilities, severe disabilities. Part-time and evening/weekend programs available. Postbaccalaureate distance learning degree programs offered (no on-campus study). *Students:* 183 full-time (123 women), 1,001 part-time (757 women); includes 380 minority (160 Black or African American, non-Hispanic/Latino; 4 American Indian or Alaska Native, non-Hispanic/Latino; 91 Asian, non-Hispanic/Latino; 78 Hispanic/Latino; 4 Native Hawaiian or other Pacific Islander, non-Hispanic/Latino; 43 Two or more races, non-Hispanic/Latino), 28 international. Average age 28. 508 applicants, 90% accepted, 337 enrolled. In 2013, 565 degrees awarded. *Degree requirements:* For master's, comprehensive exam (for some programs), portfolio, capstone project and/or internship; PRAXIS II (for teacher preparation programs that lead to licensure). *Entrance requirements:* For master's, GRE (for full-time programs only); PRAXIS I or equivalent (for teacher preparation programs that lead to licensure), bachelor's degree from regionally- or nationally-accredited institution, minimum GPA of 3.0 in all previous programs of study, official transcripts from all post-secondary institutions attended, essay, curriculum vitae/resume, minimum of two letters of recommendation. Additional exam requirements/recommendations for international students: Required—TOEFL (minimum score 600 paper-based; 100 iBT) or IELTS (minimum score 7). *Application deadline:* For fall admission, 4/1 for domestic and international students; for spring admission, 10/1 for domestic and international students; for summer admission, 2/1 for domestic and international students. Application fee: $80. Electronic applications accepted. *Financial support:* Application deadline: 6/1; applicants required to submit FAFSA. *Unit head:* Dr. David A. Andrews, Dean, 410-516-7820, Fax: 410-516-6697, E-mail: davidandrews@jhu.edu. *Application contact:* Catherine Wilson, Associate Director of Admissions, 410-516-9797, Fax: 410-516-9799, E-mail: soe.info@jhu.edu.

Kent State University, Graduate School of Education, Health, and Human Services, School of Lifespan Development and Educational Sciences, Program in Special Education, Kent, OH 44242-0001. Offers deaf education (M Ed); early childhood education (M Ed); educational interpreter K-12 (M Ed); general special education (M Ed); gifted education (M Ed); mild/moderate intervention (M Ed); special education (PhD, Ed S); transition to work (M Ed). *Accreditation:* NCATE. *Faculty:* 11 full-time (6 women), 12 part-time/adjunct (all women). *Students:* 75 full-time (61 women), 59 part-time (50 women); includes 15 minority (12 Black or African American, non-Hispanic/Latino; 1 Asian, non-Hispanic/Latino; 2 Native Hawaiian or other Pacific Islander, non-Hispanic/Latino), 8 international. 80 applicants, 35% accepted. In 2013, 44 master's, 4 doctorates awarded. *Degree requirements:* For doctorate, comprehensive exam, thesis/dissertation. *Entrance requirements:* For master's, minimum undergraduate GPA of 2.75, moral character form, 2 letters of reference, goals statement; for doctorate and Ed S, GRE General Test, goals statement, 2 letters of reference, interview, resume. Additional exam requirements/recommendations for international students: Required—TOEFL (minimum score 550 paper-based; 80 iBT). *Application deadline:* Applications are processed on a rolling basis. Application fee: $30 ($60 for international students). Electronic applications accepted. *Financial support:* In 2013–14, 6 research assistantships with full tuition reimbursements (averaging $9,667 per year), 1 teaching

assistantship with full tuition reimbursement (averaging $12,000 per year) were awarded; career-related internships or fieldwork, Federal Work-Study, institutionally sponsored loans, scholarships/grants, health care benefits, and unspecified assistantships also available. Support available to part-time students. Financial award application deadline: 4/1; financial award applicants required to submit FAFSA. *Faculty research:* Social/emotional needs of gifted, inclusion transition services, early intervention/ecobehavioral assessments, applied behavioral analysis. *Unit head:* Sonya Wisdom, Coordinator, 330-672-0578, E-mail: swisdom@kent.edu. *Application contact:* Nancy Miller, Academic Program Director, Office of Graduate Student Services, 330-672-2576, Fax: 330-672-9162, E-mail: ogs@kent.edu.
Website: http://www.kent.edu/ehhs/sped/.

Liberty University, School of Education, Lynchburg, VA 24515. Offers administration and supervision (M Ed); curriculum and instruction (Ed D, Ed S); early childhood education (M Ed); educational leadership (Ed D, Ed S); educational technology and online instruction (M Ed); elementary education (M Ed, MAT); English (M Ed); gifted education (M Ed); history (M Ed); leadership (M Ed); math specialist (M Ed); middle grades (M Ed, MAT); outdoor adventure sport (MS); reading specialist (M Ed); school counseling (M Ed); secondary education (MAT); special education (M Ed, MAT); sport management (MS), including administration, outdoor recreation, sport management, tourism; sports administration (MS); student service (M Ed); teaching and learning (M Ed); tourism (MS). *Accreditation:* NCATE. Part-time programs available. Postbaccalaureate distance learning degree programs offered (minimal on-campus study). *Students:* 2,241 full-time (1,639 women), 4,413 part-time (3,240 women); includes 2,052 minority (1,588 Black or African American, non-Hispanic/Latino; 37 American Indian or Alaska Native, non-Hispanic/Latino; 67 Asian, non-Hispanic/Latino; 173 Hispanic/Latino; 37 Native Hawaiian or other Pacific Islander, non-Hispanic/Latino; 150 Two or more races, non-Hispanic/Latino), 15 international. Average age 37. 6,185 applicants, 43% accepted, 1603 enrolled. In 2013, 1,256 master's, 117 doctorates, 470 other advanced degrees awarded. *Degree requirements:* For doctorate, comprehensive exam, thesis/dissertation. *Entrance requirements:* For master's, GRE General Test or MAT (if taken in or before 1999), 2 letters of recommendation, minimum undergraduate GPA of 3.0, curriculum vitae; for doctorate and Ed S, GRE General Test or MAT (if taken before 1999), minimum master's GPA of 3.0, 3 years of teaching experience. Additional exam requirements/recommendations for international students: Required—TOEFL (minimum score 600 paper-based; 100 iBT). *Application deadline:* For fall admission, 6/1 for domestic students; for spring admission, 11/1 for domestic students. Applications are processed on a rolling basis. Application fee: $50. Electronic applications accepted. *Expenses:* Contact institution. *Financial support:* Federal Work-Study and tuition waivers (partial) available. *Faculty research:* Self-determination, character education, bibliotherapy, learning styles, distance education. *Unit head:* Dr. Karen L. Parker, Dean, 434-582-2195, Fax: 434-582-2468, E-mail: kparker@liberty.edu. *Application contact:* Jay Bridge, Director of Graduate Admissions, 800-424-9595, Fax: 800-628-7977, E-mail: gradadmissions@liberty.edu.
Website: http://www.liberty.edu/academics/education/graduate/.

Lynn University, Donald E. and Helen L. Ross College of Education, Boca Raton, FL 33431-5598. Offers educational leadership (M Ed, Ed D); exceptional student education (M Ed). Part-time and evening/weekend programs available. *Faculty:* 2 full-time (both women), 6 part-time/adjunct (5 women). *Students:* 28 full-time (24 women), 54 part-time (28 women); includes 9 minority (8 Black or African American, non-Hispanic/Latino; 1 Hispanic/Latino), 8 international. Average age 36. 31 applicants, 97% accepted, 25 enrolled. In 2013, 29 master's, 7 doctorates awarded. *Degree requirements:* For master's, thesis (for some programs); for doctorate, thesis/dissertation, qualifying paper. *Entrance requirements:* For master's, bachelor's degree from accredited institution, minimum undergraduate GPA of 3.0, resume, 2 letters of recommendation, statement of professional goals; for doctorate, master's degree from accredited institution, minimum GPA of 3.5, resume, 2 letters of recommendation, professional practice statement, interview and presentation. Additional exam requirements/recommendations for international students: Required—TOEFL (minimum score 550 paper-based). *Application deadline:* Applications are processed on a rolling basis. Application fee: $45. Electronic applications accepted. *Expenses: Tuition:* Full-time $23,760; part-time $660 per credit. *Required fees:* $300; $50 per term. Tuition and fees vary according to degree level and program. *Financial support:* Career-related internships or fieldwork, Federal Work-Study, institutionally sponsored loans, scholarships/grants, tuition waivers (partial), and unspecified assistantships available. Support available to part-time students. Financial award application deadline: 8/1; financial award applicants required to submit FAFSA. *Faculty research:* Non-traditional education, innovative curricula, multicultural education, simulation games. *Unit head:* Dr. Gregg Cox, Dean of College, 561-237-7210, E-mail: gcox@lynn.edu. *Application contact:* Steven Pruitt, Director of Graduate and Undergraduate Evening Admission, 561-237-7834, Fax: 561-237-7100, E-mail: spruitt@lynn.edu.
Website: http://www.lynn.edu/academics/colleges/education.

Maryville University of Saint Louis, School of Education, St. Louis, MO 63141-7299. Offers art education (MA Ed); early childhood education (MA Ed); educational leadership (Ed D); educational leadership: principal certification (MA Ed); elementary education (MA Ed); gifted education (MA Ed); higher education leadership (Ed D); literacy specialist (MA Ed); middle grades education (MA Ed); secondary teaching and inquiry (MA Ed); teacher as leader (MA Ed); teacher leadership (Ed D). *Accreditation:* NCATE. Part-time and evening/weekend programs available. *Faculty:* 10 full-time (6 women), 17 part-time/adjunct (13 women). *Students:* 21 full-time (17 women), 238 part-time (167 women); includes 64 minority (54 Black or African American, non-Hispanic/Latino; 2 Asian, non-Hispanic/Latino; 4 Hispanic/Latino; 4 Two or more races, non-Hispanic/Latino), 2 international. Average age 39. In 2013, 61 master's, 40 doctorates awarded. *Degree requirements:* For master's, thesis, project. *Entrance requirements:* For master's, minimum cumulative GPA of 3.0, 3 professional recommendations, essays, interview with program faculty; for doctorate, minimum GPA of 3.0, 3 professional recommendations, essay, interview, on-site writing sample. Additional exam requirements/recommendations for international students: Required—TOEFL (minimum score 550 paper-based). *Application deadline:* Applications are processed on a rolling basis. Application fee: $40 ($60 for international students). Electronic applications accepted. Application fee is waived when completed online. *Expenses: Tuition:* Full-time $23,812; part-time $728 per credit hour. *Required fees:* $395 per year. Tuition and fees vary according to course load, degree level and program. *Financial support:* Career-related internships or fieldwork, Federal Work-Study, tuition waivers (partial), and professional educator discounts available. Financial award application deadline: 3/1; financial award applicants required to submit FAFSA. *Faculty research:* Collaboration with public schools, pre-service program development, mathematics, diversity, literacy. *Unit head:* Dr. Cathy Bear, Dean, 314-529-9692, Fax: 314-529-9921, E-mail: cbear@maryville.edu. *Application contact:* Holly Stanwich, Graduate Admissions Coordinator, 314-529-9542, Fax: 314-529-9921, E-mail: teachered@maryville.edu.
Website: http://www.maryville.edu/ed/graduate-programs/.

Millersville University of Pennsylvania, College of Graduate and Professional Studies, School of Education, Department of Elementary and Early Childhood Education, Program in Gifted Education, Millersville, PA 17551-0302. Offers M Ed. Part-time and evening/weekend programs available. *Faculty:* 17 full-time (11 women), 18 part-time/adjunct (15 women). *Students:* 1 (woman) full-time, 7 part-time (4 women). Average age 28. 2 applicants, 100% accepted, 2 enrolled. In 2013, 2 master's awarded. *Degree requirements:* For master's, thesis optional. *Entrance requirements:* For master's, GRE or MAT, 3 letters of recommendation, copy of teaching certificate, goal statement, official transcripts. Additional exam requirements/recommendations for international students: Required—TOEFL (minimum score 550 paper-based, 79 iBT) or IELTS (minimum score 6). *Application deadline:* For fall admission, 1/15 priority date for domestic and international students; for winter admission, 10/1 priority date for domestic and international students; for spring admission, 10/1 priority date for domestic and international students. Applications are processed on a rolling basis. Application fee: $40. Electronic applications accepted. *Expenses:* Tuition, state resident: full-time $7956; part-time $442 per credit. Tuition, nonresident: full-time $11,934; part-time $663 per credit. *Required fees:* $2196; $122 per credit. Tuition and fees vary according to course load. *Financial support:* In 2013–14, 1 student received support, including 1 research assistantship with full tuition reimbursement available (averaging $2,700 per year); institutionally sponsored loans and unspecified assistantships also available. Support available to part-time students. Financial award application deadline: 3/15; financial award applicants required to submit FAFSA. *Faculty research:* Under-identified and under-served populations (African-American, Native American, Latin American, low SES and twice exceptional), on-traditional educational options for gifted learners (focusing on trends in home schooling and cyber schooling), role of curriculum and technology and how they guide instruction of gifted students who are being educated at home (in both hybrid and full-time delivery models). *Unit head:* Dr. Kimberly S. Heilshorn, Coordinator, 717-871-5146, Fax: 717-871-5462, E-mail: kimberly.heilshorn@millersville.edu. *Application contact:* Dr. Victor S. DeSantis, Dean of College of Graduate and Professional Studies/Associate Provost for Civic and Community Engagement, 717-872-3099, Fax: 717-872-3453, E-mail: victor.desantis@millersville.edu.
Website: http://www.millersville.edu/academics/educ/eled/graduate.php.

Mississippi University for Women, Graduate School, College of Education and Human Sciences, Columbus, MS 39701-9998. Offers differentiated instruction (M Ed); educational leadership (M Ed); gifted studies (M Ed); reading/literacy (M Ed); teaching (MAT). *Accreditation:* ASHA; NCATE. Part-time programs available. *Degree requirements:* For master's, comprehensive exam, thesis optional. *Entrance requirements:* For master's, GRE General Test or NTE (M Ed in gifted education or MS in speech/language pathology), MAT (M Ed in instructional management), minimum QPA of 3.0.

Morehead State University, Graduate Programs, College of Education, Department of Foundational and Graduate Studies in Education, Morehead, KY 40351. Offers adult and higher education (MA, Ed S); certified professional counselor (Ed S); counseling P-12 (MA); curriculum and instruction (Ed S); educational technology (MA Ed); instructional leadership (Ed S); school administration (MA); school counseling (Ed S); teacher leader business and marketing content (MA Ed); teacher leader business and marketing technology (MA Ed); teacher leader educational technology (MA Ed); teacher leader English (MA Ed); teacher leader gifted education (MA Ed); teacher leader IECE certification (MA Ed); teacher leader interdisciplinary education P-5 (MA Ed); teacher leader middle grades (MA Ed); teacher leader non IECE certification (MA Ed); teacher leader reading/writing - non-certification (MA Ed); teacher leader reading/writing certification (MA Ed); teacher leader school communication - certification (MA Ed); teacher leader school communication - non-certification (MA Ed); teacher leader social studies (MA Ed); teacher leader special education (MA Ed). *Accreditation:* NCATE. Part-time and evening/weekend programs available. *Degree requirements:* For master's, thesis optional, oral and/or written comprehensive exams; for Ed S, thesis, oral exam. *Entrance requirements:* For master's, GRE General Test, minimum overall undergraduate GPA of 2.5; for Ed S, GRE General Test, interview, master's degree, minimum GPA of 3.5, work experience. Additional exam requirements/recommendations for international students: Required—TOEFL (minimum score 500 paper-based). Electronic applications accepted. *Faculty research:* Character education, school accountability, computer applications for school administrators.

Northeastern Illinois University, College of Graduate Studies and Research, College of Education, Program in Gifted Education, Chicago, IL 60625-4699. Offers MA. Part-time and evening/weekend programs available. *Degree requirements:* For master's, comprehensive exam, thesis or alternative. *Entrance requirements:* For master's, teaching certificate or previous course work in history or philosophy of education, minimum GPA of 2.75. Additional exam requirements/recommendations for international students: Required—TOEFL (minimum score 550 paper-based; 79 iBT). Electronic applications accepted. *Faculty research:* Effect of inclusion in public school gifted programs, social and emotional needs of gifted children, problem-based learning strategies.

Purdue University, Graduate School, College of Education, Department of Educational Studies, West Lafayette, IN 47907. Offers administration (MS Ed, PhD, Ed S); counseling and development (MS Ed, PhD); education of the gifted (MS Ed); educational psychology (MS Ed, PhD); foundations of education (MS Ed, PhD); higher education administration (MS Ed, PhD); special education (MS Ed, PhD). *Accreditation:* ACA (one or more programs are accredited); NCATE (one or more programs are accredited). Part-time and evening/weekend programs available. *Faculty:* 21 full-time (17 women), 7 part-time/adjunct (4 women). *Students:* 102 full-time (73 women), 45 part-time (27 women); includes 23 minority (10 Black or African American, non-Hispanic/Latino; 5 Asian, non-Hispanic/Latino; 5 Hispanic/Latino; 3 Two or more races, non-Hispanic/Latino), 32 international. Average age 35. 165 applicants, 40% accepted, 33 enrolled. In 2013, 26 master's, 21 doctorates awarded. *Degree requirements:* For master's, thesis optional; for doctorate, thesis/dissertation, oral and written exams; for Ed S, oral presentation, project. *Entrance requirements:* For master's, GRE General Test (except for special education if undergraduate GPA is higher than a 3.0), minimum undergraduate GPA of 3.0; for doctorate and Ed S, GRE General Test (minimum combined score of 1000, 300 for new scoring), minimum undergraduate GPA of 3.0. Additional exam requirements/recommendations for international students: Required—TOEFL (minimum score 550 paper-based; 77 iBT), TWE (minimum score 5). *Application deadline:* Applications are processed on a rolling basis. Application fee: $60 ($75 for international students). Electronic applications accepted. *Financial support:* Fellowships with full tuition reimbursements, research assistantships with full tuition reimbursements, teaching assistantships with full tuition reimbursements, career-related internships or fieldwork, and tuition waivers (full) available. Support available to part-time students. Financial award application deadline: 3/1; financial award applicants required to submit FAFSA. *Faculty research:* Motivation, learning disabilities, school learning, group processes, cognitive development. *Unit head:* Dr. Ala Samrapungavan, Head, 765-494-9170, Fax: 765-496-1228, E-mail: ala@purdue.edu. *Application contact:* Cindy Blankenship, Graduate Contact, 765-494-2345, Fax: 765-494-5832, E-mail: prater0@purdue.edu.
Website: http://www.edst.purdue.edu/.

Regis University, College for Professional Studies, School of Education, Education Division, Denver, CO 80221-1099. Offers adult learning, training, and development (M Ed, Certificate); autism education (Certificate); curriculum, instruction, and assessment (M Ed); educational leadership (M Ed); gifted and talented education

(M Ed); gifted/talented education (Certificate); initial licensure (M Ed); instructional technology (M Ed, Certificate); literacy (Certificate); reading (M Ed); school executive leadership (Certificate); space studies (M Ed). Program also offered in Henderson and Las Vegas (Summerlin), NV. *Accreditation:* Teacher Education Accreditation Council. Part-time and evening/weekend programs available. Postbaccalaureate distance learning degree programs offered (no on-campus study). *Degree requirements:* For master's, thesis. *Entrance requirements:* For master's, resume, minimum GPA of 2.75, criminal background check. Additional exam requirements/recommendations for international students: Required—TOEFL, TWE (minimum score 5). *Application deadline:* For fall admission, 7/23 priority date for domestic students; for winter admission, 9/17 priority date for domestic students; for spring admission, 12/3 priority date for domestic students. Applications are processed on a rolling basis. Application fee: $75. Electronic applications accepted. *Expenses:* Contact institution. *Financial support:* Federal Work-Study and scholarships/grants available. *Faculty research:* Issues of equity in the middle school classroom, professional learning communities, school reform, sociolinguistic and discursive obstacles to student integration, inclusive language arts curriculum. *Unit head:* Dr. Janna L. Oakes, Dean, 303-458-4302. *Application contact:* Information Contact, 303-458-4300, Fax: 303-964-5274, E-mail: masters@regis.edu.

St. Bonaventure University, School of Graduate Studies, School of Education, Differentiated Instruction Program, St. Bonaventure, NY 14778-2284. Offers gifted education (MS Ed, Adv C); gifted education and students with disabilities (MS Ed). Program offered in Olean and Buffalo Center (Hamburg, NY). Part-time and evening/weekend programs available. *Faculty:* 3 full-time (all women), 2 part-time/adjunct (both women). *Students:* 27 full-time (25 women), 19 part-time (17 women). Average age 25. 21 applicants, 100% accepted, 14 enrolled. In 2013, 18 master's awarded. *Degree requirements:* For master's, comprehensive exam, internship, portfolio; for Adv C, practicum, portfolio. *Entrance requirements:* For master's, teaching certification, interview, two letters of recommendation, writing sample, transcripts; for Adv C, teaching certification, master's degree, interview, references (ability to do graduate work, success as a teacher), writing sample. Additional exam requirements/recommendations for international students: Required—TOEFL (minimum score 550 paper-based; 79 iBT). *Application deadline:* For fall admission, 6/15 priority date for domestic students, 2/1 priority date for international students; for spring admission, 11/15 priority date for domestic students, 7/1 priority date for international students. Applications are processed on a rolling basis. Application fee: $0. Electronic applications accepted. *Financial support:* In 2013–14, 3 research assistantships with full and partial tuition reimbursements were awarded; Federal Work-Study, scholarships/grants, health care benefits, tuition waivers (partial), and unspecified assistantships also available. Support available to part-time students. Financial award application deadline: 4/15; financial award applicants required to submit FAFSA. *Unit head:* Dr. Rene' Garrison, Director, 716-375-4078, Fax: 716-375-2360, E-mail: rgarriso@sbu.edu. *Application contact:* Bruce Campbell, Director of Graduate Admissions, 716-375-2429, Fax: 716-375-4015, E-mail: gradsch@sbu.edu.
Website: http://www.sbu.edu/academics/schools/education/graduate-degrees-certificates/msed-in-differentiated-instruction-gifted.

St. John's University, The School of Education, Division of Administrative and Instructional Leadership, Queens, NY 11439. Offers educational administration and supervision (Ed D), including administration and supervision; gifted education (Certificate); instructional leadership (Ed D, Adv C); school building leadership (MS Ed, Adv C); school building leadership/school district leadership (Adv C); school district leadership (Adv C). Part-time and evening/weekend programs available. Postbaccalaureate distance learning degree programs offered. *Students:* 21 full-time (15 women), 365 part-time (248 women); includes 111 minority (63 Black or African American, non-Hispanic/Latino; 8 Asian, non-Hispanic/Latino; 40 Hispanic/Latino), 13 international. Average age 40. 199 applicants, 91% accepted, 110 enrolled. In 2013, 63 master's, 40 doctorates, 23 Adv Cs awarded. *Degree requirements:* For master's, comprehensive exam; for doctorate, thesis/dissertation. *Entrance requirements:* For master's, GRE, personal statement, official transcript, minimum GPA of 3.0, 2 letters of recommendation, NYC permanent teaching certificate, 3 years of teaching, bachelor's degree; for doctorate, GRE General Test, interview, personal statement, official transcript, minimum GPA of 3.2, 2 letters of recommendation; for other advanced degree, New York teaching certificate, minimum GPA of 3.2, 2 letters of recommendation. Additional exam requirements/recommendations for international students: Required—TOEFL (minimum score 600 paper-based; 100 iBT), IELTS (minimum score 5.5). *Application deadline:* For fall admission, 8/17 for domestic students, 5/1 priority date for international students; for spring admission, 1/5 for domestic students, 11/1 priority date for international students. Applications are processed on a rolling basis. Application fee: $70. Electronic applications accepted. *Expenses: Tuition:* Full-time $19,800; part-time $1100 per credit. *Required fees:* $170 per semester. *Financial support:* Fellowships, research assistantships, career-related internships or fieldwork, and scholarships/grants available. Support available to part-time students. Financial award application deadline: 3/1; financial award applicants required to submit FAFSA. *Faculty research:* Mathematics learning disabilities and difficulties with learning disabled or English language learner students, identification of mathematical giftedness in students who are English language learners, effects of parental participation and parenting behaviors on the science and mathematics academic achievement of school-age students, school administrators' accountability in response to N.Y. state and federal regulations and reforms, use of twenty-first century technology in today's schools. *Unit head:* Dr. Rene Parmar, Chair, 718-990-5915, E-mail: parmarr@stjohns.edu. *Application contact:* Dr. Kelly K. Ronayne, Associate Dean for Graduate Admissions, 718-990-2304, Fax: 718-990-2343, E-mail: graded@stjohns.edu.
Website: http://www.stjohns.edu/academics/schools-and-colleges/school-education/administrative-and-instructional-leadership.

Saint Leo University, Graduate Studies in Education, Saint Leo, FL 33574-6665. Offers educational leadership (M Ed); exceptional student education (M Ed); instructional design (MS); instructional leadership (M Ed); reading (M Ed). Part-time and evening/weekend programs available. Postbaccalaureate distance learning degree programs offered (minimal on-campus study). *Faculty:* 10 full-time (8 women), 31 part-time/adjunct (23 women). *Students:* 680 full-time (554 women), 4 part-time (all women); includes 83 minority (51 Black or African American, non-Hispanic/Latino; 2 Asian, non-Hispanic/Latino; 27 Hispanic/Latino; 3 Two or more races, non-Hispanic/Latino), 4 international. Average age 36. In 2013, 295 master's awarded. *Degree requirements:* For master's, comprehensive exam, appropriate State of Florida certification tests. *Entrance requirements:* For master's, GRE (minimum score of 1000) or MAT (minimum score of 410) if undergraduate GPA for last 60 hours of coursework was below 3.0 (for M Ed), bachelor's degree with minimum GPA of 3.0 for last 60 hours of coursework from regionally-accredited college or university, 2 recommendations, resume, statement of professional goals, copy of valid teaching certificate (for M Ed). Additional exam requirements/recommendations for international students: Required—TOEFL (minimum score 550 paper-based; 80 iBT). *Application deadline:* For fall admission, 7/1 priority date for domestic students, 7/1 for international students; for winter admission, 7/1 for international students; for spring admission, 11/1 priority date for domestic students. Applications are processed on a rolling basis. Application fee: $80. Electronic applications accepted. *Expenses:* Contact institution. *Financial support:* In 2013–14, 618 students received support. Career-related internships or fieldwork, Federal Work-Study, scholarships/grants, and health care benefits available. Financial award application deadline: 3/1; financial award applicants required to submit FAFSA. *Faculty research:* The role of the school leader in data analysis of student achievement, teacher recruitment, teacher effectiveness. *Unit head:* Dr. Sharyn Disabato, Director of Graduate Education, 352-588-8309, Fax: 352-588-8861, E-mail: med@saintleo.edu. *Application contact:* Joshua Stagner, Director of Graduate Admission, 800-707-8846, Fax: 352-588-7873, E-mail: grad.admissions@saintleo.edu.
Website: http://www.saintleo.edu/admissions/graduate.aspx.

Saint Mary's University of Minnesota, Schools of Graduate and Professional Programs, Graduate School of Education, Education Program, Winona, MN 55987-1399. Offers culturally responsive teaching (Certificate); education (MA); gifted and talented instruction (Certificate). *Unit head:* Lynn Albee, Director, 612-728-5179, Fax: 612-728-5128, E-mail: lgalbe02@smumn.edu. *Application contact:* Russell Kreager, Director of Admissions for Graduate and Professional Programs, 612-728-5207, Fax: 612-728-5121, E-mail: rkreager@smumn.edu.
Website: http://www.smumn.edu/graduate-home/areas-of-study/graduate-school-of-education/ma-in-education.

St. Thomas University, School of Leadership Studies, Institute for Education, Miami Gardens, FL 33054-6459. Offers earth/space science (Certificate); educational administration (MS, Certificate); educational leadership (Ed D); elementary education (MS); ESOL (Certificate); gifted education (Certificate); instructional technology (MS, Certificate); professional/studies (Certificate); reading (MS, Certificate); special education (MS). Part-time and evening/weekend programs available. *Degree requirements:* For master's, comprehensive exam; for doctorate, comprehensive exam, thesis/dissertation. *Entrance requirements:* For master's, interview, minimum GPA of 3.0 or GRE; for doctorate, GRE or MAT. Additional exam requirements/recommendations for international students: Required—TOEFL (minimum score 550 paper-based; 79 iBT). Electronic applications accepted.

Samford University, Orlean Bullard Beeson School of Education, Birmingham, AL 35229. Offers early childhood/elementary education (MS Ed); educational leadership (MS Ed, Ed D); gifted education (MS Ed); instructional leadership (MS Ed, Ed S); secondary collaboration (MS Ed); M Div/MS Ed. *Accreditation:* NCATE. Part-time and evening/weekend programs available. *Faculty:* 10 full-time (5 women), 16 part-time/adjunct (15 women). *Students:* 40 full-time (25 women), 210 part-time (156 women); includes 39 minority (33 Black or African American, non-Hispanic/Latino; 3 American Indian or Alaska Native, non-Hispanic/Latino; 2 Asian, non-Hispanic/Latino; 1 Hispanic/Latino), 4 international. Average age 38. 81 applicants, 89% accepted, 70 enrolled. In 2013, 94 master's, 21 doctorates, 16 other advanced degrees awarded. *Degree requirements:* For master's and Ed S, comprehensive exam; for doctorate, comprehensive exam, thesis/dissertation. *Entrance requirements:* For master's, GRE (minimum score of 295) or MAT (minimum score of 396); waived if previously completed a graduate degree, writing sample, statement of purpose, 3 letters of recommendation, 2 original copies of all transcripts, minimum GPA of 2.75, teaching certificate; for doctorate, minimum GPA of 3.7, professional resume, writing sample, 3 letters of recommendation, 1 original copy of all transcripts; for Ed S, master's degree, teaching certificate, minimum GPA of 3.25, 3 letters of recommendation, 2 original copies of all transcripts, writing sample, statement of purpose. Additional exam requirements/recommendations for international students: Required—TOEFL (minimum score 90 iBT), IELTS (minimum score 7). *Application deadline:* For fall admission, 7/30 for domestic and international students; for winter admission, 4/5 for domestic students; for spring admission, 12/5 for domestic and international students; for summer admission, 4/18 for domestic and international students. Applications are processed on a rolling basis. Application fee: $35. Electronic applications accepted. *Expenses: Tuition:* Full-time $11,552; part-time $722 per credit. *Required fees:* $500; $250 per term. *Financial support:* In 2013–14, 162 students received support. Research assistantships, career-related internships or fieldwork, Federal Work-Study, scholarships/grants, and tuition waivers (partial) available. Support available to part-time students. Financial award applicants required to submit FAFSA. *Faculty research:* Research on gifted/high ability students (K-12), school law, the characteristics of beginning teachers, the nature of school reform, school culture, quality improvement in education, K-12 student achievement, reading research, classroom management, reading intervention, schema theory. *Unit head:* Dr. Maurice Persall, Chair, Department of Educational Leadership, 205-726-2019, E-mail: jmpersal@samford.edu. *Application contact:* Brooke Gilreath Karr, Graduate Admissions Coordinator, 205-729-2783, Fax: 205-726-4233, E-mail: kbgilrea@samford.edu.
Website: http://www.samford.edu/education/.

Southern Methodist University, Annette Caldwell Simmons School of Education and Human Development, Department of Teaching and Learning, Dallas, TX 75275. Offers bilingual/ESL education (MBE); education (M Ed, PhD); gifted education (MBE); reading and writing (M Ed); special education (M Ed). Part-time and evening/weekend programs available. Terminal master's awarded for partial completion of doctoral program. *Degree requirements:* For master's, comprehensive exam, minimum GPA of 3.0; for doctorate, thesis/dissertation, qualifying exams, major area paper, evidence of teaching competency, dissemination of research (e.g., conference presentation), professional portfolio. *Entrance requirements:* For master's, minimum GPA of 3.0 or GRE, 3 letters of recommendation; for doctorate, GRE, minimum GPA of 3.3, 3 years of full-time teaching, 3 letters of recommendation, interview. Additional exam requirements/recommendations for international students: Required—TOEFL. Electronic applications accepted. *Faculty research:* Reading intervention, mathematics intervention, bilingual education, new literacies.

Teachers College, Columbia University, Graduate Faculty of Education, Department of Curriculum and Teaching, Program in Giftedness, New York, NY 10027. Offers MA, Ed D. Part-time programs available. *Faculty:* 1 full-time, 2 part-time/adjunct. *Students:* 4 full-time (all women), 5 part-time (all women); includes 4 minority (1 Black or African American, non-Hispanic/Latino; 3 Asian, non-Hispanic/Latino). Average age 26. 4 applicants, 100% accepted, 3 enrolled. In 2013, 4 master's awarded. Terminal master's awarded for partial completion of doctoral program. *Degree requirements:* For master's, culminating project; for doctorate, thesis/dissertation. *Entrance requirements:* For doctorate, GRE General Test or MAT. *Application deadline:* For fall admission, 1/15 priority date for domestic students; for spring admission, 11/1 for domestic students. Application fee: $65. Electronic applications accepted. *Financial support:* Research assistantships, career-related internships or fieldwork, Federal Work-Study, institutionally sponsored loans, and tuition waivers (full and partial) available. Support available to part-time students. Financial award application deadline: 2/1; financial award applicants required to submit FAFSA. *Faculty research:* Urban and economically disadvantaged gifted children, identification issues with regard to gifted and early childhood giftedness. *Unit head:* Prof. James Borland, Program Coordinator, 212-678-3801, E-mail: borland@tc.edu. *Application contact:* Peter Shon, Assistant Director of

Admission, 212-678-3305, Fax: 212-678-4171, E-mail: shon@exchange.tc.columbia.edu.
Website: http://www.tc.edu/c%26t/GiftedEd/.

Tennessee Technological University, College of Graduate Studies, College of Education, Department of Curriculum and Instruction, Program in Exceptional Learning, Cookeville, TN 38505. Offers applied behavior analysis (PhD); literacy (PhD); program planning and evaluation (PhD); STEM education (PhD). Part-time and evening/weekend programs available. *Students:* 14 full-time (12 women), 22 part-time (16 women); includes 2 minority (1 Black or African American, non-Hispanic/Latino; 1 Two or more races, non-Hispanic/Latino), 1 international. 15 applicants, 47% accepted, 6 enrolled. In 2013, 1 doctorate awarded. *Degree requirements:* For doctorate, comprehensive exam, thesis/dissertation. *Entrance requirements:* For doctorate, GRE, minimum GPA of 3.0. Additional exam requirements/recommendations for international students: Required—TOEFL (minimum score 550 paper-based; 79 iBT), IELTS (minimum score 5.5), PTE (minimum score 53), or TOEIC (Test of English as an International Communication). *Application deadline:* For fall admission, 8/1 for domestic students, 5/1 for international students; for spring admission, 12/1 for domestic students, 10/1 for international students. Applications are processed on a rolling basis. Application fee: $35 ($40 for international students). Electronic applications accepted. *Expenses:* Tuition, state resident: full-time $9347; part-time $465 per credit hour. Tuition, nonresident: full-time $23,635; part-time $1152 per credit hour. *Financial support:* In 2013–14, 4 fellowships (averaging $8,000 per year), 10 research assistantships (averaging $12,000 per year), 1 teaching assistantship (averaging $12,000 per year) were awarded. Financial award application deadline: 4/1. *Unit head:* Dr. Lisa Zagumny, Director, 931-372-3078, Fax: 931-372-3517, E-mail: lzagumny@tntech.edu. *Application contact:* Shelia K. Kendrick, Coordinator of Graduate Studies, 931-372-3808, Fax: 931-372-3497, E-mail: skendrick@tntech.edu.
Website: https://www.tntech.edu/education/elphd/.

Troy University, Graduate School, College of Education, Program in Teacher Education-Multiple Levels, Troy, AL 36082. Offers art education (MS); gifted education (MS); instrumental (MS); physical education (MS); reading specialist (MS); vocal/choral (MS). Part-time and evening/weekend programs available. *Faculty:* 8 full-time (4 women). *Students:* 2 full-time (both women), 17 part-time (15 women); includes 3 minority (all Black or African American, non-Hispanic/Latino). Average age 30. 9 applicants, 89% accepted, 4 enrolled. In 2013, 19 master's awarded. *Degree requirements:* For master's, comprehensive exam, thesis. *Entrance requirements:* For master's, GRE (minimum score of 850 on old exam or 290 on new exam), GMAT (minimum score of 380), or MAT (minimum score of 385), bachelor's degree; minimum undergraduate GPA of 2.5 or 3.0 on last 30 semester hours, letter of recommendation. Additional exam requirements/recommendations for international students: Required—TOEFL (minimum score 523 paper-based; 70 iBT), IELTS (minimum score 6). *Application deadline:* Applications are processed on a rolling basis. Application fee: $50. Electronic applications accepted. *Expenses:* Tuition, state resident: full-time $6084; part-time $338 per credit hour. Tuition, nonresident: full-time $12,168; part-time $676 per credit hour. *Required fees:* $630; $35 per credit hour. $50 per semester. *Financial support:* Available to part-time students. Applicants required to submit FAFSA. *Unit head:* Dr. Charlotte S. Minnick, Director, Teacher Education, 334-670-3544, Fax: 334-670-3548, E-mail: csminnick@troy.edu. *Application contact:* Brenda K. Campbell, Director of Graduate Admissions, 334-670-3178, Fax: 334-670-3733, E-mail: bcamp@troy.edu.

University at Buffalo, the State University of New York, Graduate School, Graduate School of Education, Department of Learning and Instruction, Buffalo, NY 14260. Offers biology education (Ed M, Certificate); chemistry education (Ed M, Certificate); childhood education (Ed M); childhood education with bilingual extension (Ed M); curriculum, instruction and the science of learning (PhD); early childhood education (Ed M); early childhood education with bilingual extension (birth-grade 2) (Ed M); earth science education (Ed M, Certificate); education studies (Ed M); educational technology and new literacies (Certificate); elementary education (Ed D); English education (Ed M, Certificate); English for speakers of other languages (Ed M); foreign and second language education (PhD); French education (Ed M, Certificate); German education (Ed M, Certificate); gifted education (Certificate); Latin education (Ed M, Certificate); literacy specialist (Ed M); literacy teaching and learning (Certificate); mathematics education (Ed M, Certificate); music education (Ed M, Certificate); physics education (Ed M, Certificate); science and the public (Ed M); social studies education (Ed M, Certificate); Spanish education (Ed M, Certificate); special education (PhD); teaching English to speakers of other languages (Ed M). Part-time and evening/weekend programs available. Postbaccalaureate distance learning degree programs offered (no on-campus study). *Faculty:* 31 full-time (23 women), 64 part-time/adjunct (53 women). *Students:* 275 full-time (215 women), 293 part-time (205 women); includes 35 minority (16 Black or African American, non-Hispanic/Latino; 5 American Indian or Alaska Native, non-Hispanic/Latino; 11 Asian, non-Hispanic/Latino; 3 Hispanic/Latino), 97 international. Average age 30. 544 applicants, 81% accepted, 246 enrolled. In 2013, 222 master's, 17 doctorates, 35 other advanced degrees awarded. *Degree requirements:* For master's, comprehensive exam; for doctorate, thesis/dissertation, research analysis exam, research experience component. *Entrance requirements:* For master's, content test in science and math, letters of reference; for doctorate, GRE General Test or MAT, interview, writing sample, letters of recommendation. Additional exam requirements/recommendations for international students: Required—TOEFL (minimum score 600 paper-based; 96 iBT). *Application deadline:* For fall admission, 2/1 priority date for domestic and international students; for spring admission, 11/15 priority date for domestic students, 10/1 for international students. Applications are processed on a rolling basis. Application fee: $50. Electronic applications accepted. *Financial support:* In 2013–14, 50 fellowships (averaging $8,589 per year), 31 research assistantships with tuition reimbursements (averaging $11,406 per year) were awarded; teaching assistantships, career-related internships or fieldwork, Federal Work-Study, institutionally sponsored loans, scholarships/grants, tuition waivers, and unspecified assistantships also available. Financial award application deadline: 2/28; financial award applicants required to submit FAFSA. *Faculty research:* Science assessment, foreign language teaching and learning, early learning, new literacies, gender and education. *Total annual research expenditures:* $1.7 million. *Unit head:* Dr. Suzanne Miller, Chair, 716-645-2455, Fax: 716-645-3161, E-mail: smiller@buffalo.edu. *Application contact:* Cathy Dimino, Admissions Assistant, 716-645-2110, Fax: 716-645-7937, E-mail: cadimino@buffalo.edu.
Website: http://gse.buffalo.edu/lai.

The University of Alabama, Graduate School, College of Education, Department of Special Education and Multiple Abilities, Tuscaloosa, AL 35487. Offers collaborative special education (M Ed, Ed S); early intervention (M Ed, Ed S); gifted and talented education (M Ed, Ed S); multiple abilities (M Ed); special education (Ed D, PhD). Part-time and evening/weekend programs available. *Faculty:* 12 full-time (8 women). *Students:* 23 full-time (all women), 43 part-time (37 women); includes 11 minority (7 Black or African American, non-Hispanic/Latino; 1 American Indian or Alaska Native, non-Hispanic/Latino; 2 Asian, non-Hispanic/Latino; 1 Two or more races, non-Hispanic/Latino). Average age 34. 33 applicants, 67% accepted, 16 enrolled. In 2013, 20 master's, 2 doctorates, 3 other advanced degrees awarded. Terminal master's awarded for partial completion of doctoral program. *Degree requirements:* For master's, comprehensive exam, thesis optional; for doctorate, one foreign language, comprehensive exam, thesis/dissertation. *Entrance requirements:* For master's, GRE or MAT, minimum undergraduate GPA of 3.0, teaching certificate, 3 letters of recommendation; for doctorate, GRE or MAT, 3 years of teaching experience, minimum undergraduate GPA of 3.25. Additional exam requirements/recommendations for international students: Required—TOEFL. *Application deadline:* For fall admission, 7/1 for domestic students; for spring admission, 11/1 for domestic students. Applications are processed on a rolling basis. Application fee: $50 ($60 for international students). Electronic applications accepted. *Expenses:* Tuition, state resident: full-time $9450. Tuition, nonresident: full-time $23,950. *Financial support:* In 2013–14, 8 students received support, including 4 research assistantships with tuition reimbursements available (averaging $9,000 per year); 4 teaching assistantships with tuition reimbursements available (averaging $9,000 per year); health care benefits and unspecified assistantships also available. Financial award application deadline: 7/1; financial award applicants required to submit FAFSA. *Faculty research:* Gifted education, mild disabilities, early intervention, severe disabilities. *Unit head:* James A. Siders, Associate Professor and Head, 205-348-5577, Fax: 205-348-6782, E-mail: jsiders@bama.ua.edu. *Application contact:* April Zark, Office Support, 205-348-6093, Fax: 205-348-6782, E-mail: azark@bamaed.ua.edu.
Website: http://education.ua.edu/departments/spema/.

University of Arkansas at Little Rock, Graduate School, College of Education, Department of Teacher Education, Program in Teaching the Gifted and Talented, Little Rock, AR 72204-1099. Offers M Ed. *Accreditation:* NCATE. Part-time and evening/weekend programs available. *Degree requirements:* For master's, comprehensive exam. *Entrance requirements:* For master's, interview, minimum GPA of 2.75, GRE General Test or teaching certificate. *Expenses:* Tuition, state resident: full-time $5690; part-time $284.50 per credit hour. Tuition, nonresident: full-time $13,030; part-time $651.50 per credit hour. *Required fees:* $1121; $672 per term. One-time fee: $40 full-time.

University of Central Arkansas, Graduate School, College of Education, Department of Early Childhood and Special Education, Conway, AR 72035-0001. Offers gifted and talented education (Graduate Certificate); instructional facilitator (Graduate Certificate); reading education (MSE); special education (MSE, Graduate Certificate), including collaborative instructional specialist (ages 0-8) (MSE), collaborative instructional specialist (grades 4-12) (MSE), special education instructional specialist grades 4-12 (Graduate Certificate), special education instructional specialist P-4 (Graduate Certificate). Part-time and evening/weekend programs available. Postbaccalaureate distance learning degree programs offered (minimal on-campus study). *Degree requirements:* For master's, comprehensive exam, thesis optional. *Entrance requirements:* For master's, GRE General Test, minimum GPA of 2.7. Additional exam requirements/recommendations for international students: Required—TOEFL (minimum score 550 paper-based; 80 iBT). Electronic applications accepted.

University of Central Arkansas, Graduate School, College of Education, Department of Leadership Studies, Conway, AR 72035-0001. Offers college student personnel (MS); district-level administration (PMC); educational leadership - district level (Ed S); instructional technology (MS); library media and information technology (MS); school counseling (MS); school leadership (MS); school-based leadership adult education program administration (PMC); school-based leadership building administration (PMC); school-based leadership curriculum administration (PMC); school-based leadership gifted and talented program administration (PMC); school-based leadership special education program administration (PMC). *Accreditation:* NCATE. Part-time and evening/weekend programs available. Postbaccalaureate distance learning degree programs offered (minimal on-campus study). *Degree requirements:* For master's and other advanced degree, comprehensive exam. *Entrance requirements:* For master's, GRE. Additional exam requirements/recommendations for international students: Required—TOEFL (minimum score 80 iBT). Electronic applications accepted. *Expenses:* Contact institution.

University of Central Florida, College of Education and Human Performance, School of Teaching, Learning, and Leadership, Applied Learning and Instruction Program, Orlando, FL 32816. Offers applied learning and instruction (MA); community college education (Certificate); gifted education (Certificate); global and comparative education (Certificate); initial teacher professional preparation (Certificate); urban education (Certificate). *Accreditation:* NCATE. Part-time and evening/weekend programs available. *Students:* 11 full-time (9 women), 80 part-time (62 women); includes 27 minority (10 Black or African American, non-Hispanic/Latino; 2 Asian, non-Hispanic/Latino; 13 Hispanic/Latino; 2 Two or more races, non-Hispanic/Latino). Average age 33. 61 applicants, 70% accepted, 29 enrolled. In 2013, 19 master's, 26 other advanced degrees awarded. *Degree requirements:* For Certificate, thesis or alternative, final exam. *Entrance requirements:* For degree, GRE General Test, minimum GPA of 3.0, resume. Additional exam requirements/recommendations for international students: Required—TOEFL. *Application deadline:* For fall admission, 2/20 for domestic students; for spring admission, 9/20 for domestic students. Application fee: $30. Electronic applications accepted. *Financial support:* In 2013–14, 3 students received support, including 1 research assistantship with partial tuition reimbursement available (averaging $8,100 per year), 2 teaching assistantships with partial tuition reimbursements available (averaging $6,900 per year); fellowships, career-related internships or fieldwork, Federal Work-Study, institutionally sponsored loans, and unspecified assistantships also available. Financial award application deadline: 3/1; financial award applicants required to submit FAFSA. *Unit head:* Dr. Bobby Hoffman, Program Coordinator, 407-823-1770, E-mail: bobby.hoffman@ucf.edu. *Application contact:* Barbara Rodriguez Lamas, Director, Admissions and Student Services, 407-823-2766, Fax: 407-823-6442, E-mail: gradadmissions@ucf.edu.
Website: http://education.ucf.edu/departments.cfm.

University of Connecticut, Graduate School, Neag School of Education, Department of Educational Psychology, Program in Gifted and Talented Education, Storrs, CT 06269. Offers MA, PhD, Post-Master's Certificate. *Accreditation:* NCATE. Terminal master's awarded for partial completion of doctoral program. *Degree requirements:* For master's, comprehensive exam, thesis or alternative; for doctorate, thesis/dissertation. *Entrance requirements:* For master's and doctorate, GRE General Test. Additional exam requirements/recommendations for international students: Required—TOEFL (minimum score 550 paper-based). Electronic applications accepted.

University of Louisiana at Lafayette, College of Education, Graduate Studies and Research in Education, Program in Education of the Gifted, Lafayette, LA 70504. Offers M Ed. *Accreditation:* NCATE. *Degree requirements:* For master's, thesis or alternative. *Entrance requirements:* For master's, GRE General Test, teaching certificate. Additional exam requirements/recommendations for international students: Required—TOEFL (minimum score 550 paper-based). Electronic applications accepted.

University of Louisiana at Monroe, Graduate School, College of Arts, Education, and Sciences, School of Education, Program in Curriculum and Instruction, Monroe, LA 71209-0001. Offers art education (M Ed); biology education (M Ed); chemistry education (M Ed); curriculum and instruction (Ed D); early childhood education (M Ed); earth science education (M Ed); educational leadership (M Ed); elementary education (1-5)

Education of the Gifted

(M Ed); English as a second language (M Ed); English education (M Ed); family and consumer education (M Ed); French education (M Ed); history education (M Ed); math education (M Ed); middle school education (M Ed); music education (M Ed); reading education (K-12) (M Ed); Spanish education (M Ed); special education - academically gifted (M Ed); special education - early intervention (M Ed); special education - educational diagnostician (M Ed); special education - mild/moderate disabilities (M Ed); speech education (M Ed). *Accreditation:* NCATE. *Degree requirements:* For master's, comprehensive exam (for some programs), thesis; for doctorate, thesis/dissertation, internships. *Entrance requirements:* For master's, GRE General Test; for doctorate, GRE General Test, minimum undergraduate GPA of 2.75, graduate 3.25. Additional exam requirements/recommendations for international students: Required—TOEFL (minimum score 500 paper-based; 61 iBT). *Application deadline:* For fall admission, 8/24 priority date for domestic students, 7/1 for international students; for winter admission, 12/14 priority date for domestic students; for spring admission, 1/19 for domestic students, 11/1 for international students. Applications are processed on a rolling basis. Application fee: $20 ($30 for international students). Electronic applications accepted. *Expenses:* Tuition, state resident: full-time $6607. Tuition, nonresident: full-time $17,179. Full-time tuition and fees vary according to program. *Financial support:* Research assistantships, career-related internships or fieldwork, Federal Work-Study, and unspecified assistantships available. Financial award application deadline: 4/1; financial award applicants required to submit FAFSA. *Unit head:* Dr. Dorothy Schween, Director, 318-342-1268, Fax: 318-342-3131, E-mail: schween@ulm.edu. *Application contact:* Dr. Dorothy Schween, Director, 318-342-1268, Fax: 318-342-3131, E-mail: schween@ulm.edu.

University of Minnesota, Twin Cities Campus, Graduate School, College of Education and Human Development, Department of Educational Psychology, Minneapolis, MN 55455-0213. Offers counseling and student personnel psychology (MA, PhD, Ed S); early childhood education (M Ed, MA, PhD); educational psychology (PhD); psychological foundations of education (MA, PhD, Ed S); school psychology (MA, PhD, Ed S); special education (M Ed, MA, PhD, Ed S); talent development and gifted education (Certificate). *Accreditation:* APA (one or more programs are accredited). *Faculty:* 31 full-time (15 women). *Students:* 276 full-time (215 women), 1,982 part-time (65 women); includes 47 minority (12 Black or African American, non-Hispanic/Latino; 4 American Indian or Alaska Native, non-Hispanic/Latino; 16 Asian, non-Hispanic/Latino; 15 Hispanic/Latino), 45 international. Average age 29. 342 applicants, 47% accepted, 97 enrolled. In 2013, 109 master's, 26 doctorates, 30 other advanced degrees awarded. Application fee: $75 ($95 for international students). *Financial support:* In 2013–14, 5 fellowships (averaging $21,623 per year), 62 research assistantships (averaging $10,081 per year), 31 teaching assistantships (averaging $7,120 per year) were awarded. *Faculty research:* Learning, cognitive and social processes; multicultural education and counseling; measurement and statistical processes; performance assessment; instructional design/strategies for students with special needs. *Total annual research expenditures:* $3.5 million. *Unit head:* Geoff Maruyama, Chair, 612-625-5861, Fax: 612-624-8241, E-mail: geoff@umn.edu. *Application contact:* Dr. Jennifer Engler, Assistant Dean, 612-626-2887, Fax: 612-626-7496, E-mail: engle009@umn.edu.
Website: http://www.cehd.umn.edu/EdPsych.

University of Missouri, Graduate School, College of Education, Department of Special Education, Columbia, MO 65211. Offers administration and supervision of special education (PhD); behavior disorders (M Ed, PhD); curriculum development of exceptional students (M Ed, PhD); early childhood special education (M Ed, PhD); general special education (M Ed, MA, PhD); learning and instruction (M Ed); learning disabilities (M Ed, PhD); mental retardation (M Ed, PhD). Part-time and evening/weekend programs available. Postbaccalaureate distance learning degree programs offered (no on-campus study). *Faculty:* 11 full-time (8 women), 1 (woman) part-time/adjunct. *Students:* 21 full-time (19 women), 43 part-time (37 women); includes 4 minority (2 Black or African American, non-Hispanic/Latino; 1 Hispanic/Latino; 1 Two or more races, non-Hispanic/Latino), 2 international. Average age 32. 42 applicants, 64% accepted, 23 enrolled. In 2013, 28 master's, 6 doctorates awarded. *Degree requirements:* For master's, comprehensive exam, thesis or alternative; for doctorate, comprehensive exam, thesis/dissertation. *Entrance requirements:* For master's and doctorate, GRE General Test, letters of recommendation. Additional exam requirements/recommendations for international students: Required—TOEFL (minimum score 500 paper-based; 61 iBT). *Application deadline:* For fall admission, 1/15 priority date for domestic and international students; for winter admission, 11/1 priority date for domestic and international students; for spring admission, 4/1 priority date for domestic and international students. Application fee: $55 ($75 for international students). Electronic applications accepted. *Financial support:* Fellowships with full and partial tuition reimbursements, research assistantships with full and partial tuition reimbursements, teaching assistantships with full and partial tuition reimbursements, career-related internships or fieldwork, scholarships/grants, health care benefits, and unspecified assistantships available. *Faculty research:* Positive behavior support, applied behavior analysis, attention deficit disorder, pre-linguistic development, school discipline. *Total annual research expenditures:* $1.4 million. *Unit head:* Dr. Mike Pullis, Department Chair, 573-882-8192, E-mail: pullism@missouri.edu. *Application contact:* Recruitment Coordinator, 573-884-3742, E-mail: mucoesped@missouri.edu.
Website: http://education.missouri.edu/SPED/.

University of Nebraska at Kearney, Graduate Programs, College of Education, Department of Teacher Education, Kearney, NE 68849-0001. Offers curriculum and instruction (MA Ed), including early childhood education, elementary education, English as a second language, instructional effectiveness, reading/special education, secondary education; instructional technology (MS Ed), including information technology, instructional technology, school librarian; reading PK-12 (MA Ed); special education (MA Ed), including advanced practitioner, gifted, mild/moderate. Part-time and evening/weekend programs available. *Degree requirements:* For master's, comprehensive exam, thesis optional. *Entrance requirements:* For master's, portfolio or GRE. Additional exam requirements/recommendations for international students: Required—TOEFL (minimum score 550 paper-based). Electronic applications accepted.

The University of North Carolina at Charlotte, The Graduate School, College of Education, Department of Special Education and Child Development, Charlotte, NC 28223-0001. Offers academically gifted (Graduate Certificate); child and family studies (M Ed); special education (M Ed, PhD), including academically or intellectually gifted (M Ed), behavioral - emotional handicaps (M Ed), cross-categorical disabilities (M Ed), learning disabilities (M Ed), mental handicaps (M Ed), severe and profound handicaps (M Ed). Part-time programs available. *Faculty:* 24 full-time (17 women), 13 part-time/adjunct (12 women). *Students:* 17 full-time (16 women), 100 part-time (88 women); includes 12 minority (9 Black or African American, non-Hispanic/Latino; 2 Asian, non-Hispanic/Latino; 1 Hispanic/Latino), 1 international. Average age 36. 79 applicants, 90% accepted, 55 enrolled. In 2013, 9 master's, 6 doctorates, 38 other advanced degrees awarded. Terminal master's awarded for partial completion of doctoral program. *Degree requirements:* For master's, thesis or alternative; for doctorate, comprehensive exam, thesis/dissertation, portfolio, qualifying exam. *Entrance requirements:* For master's, GRE or MAT; for doctorate, GRE or MAT, 3 letters of reference, resume or curriculum vitae, minimum GPA of 3.5, master's degree in special education or related field, 3 years of teaching experience. Additional exam requirements/recommendations for international students: Required—TOEFL (minimum score 557 paper-based; 83 iBT). *Application deadline:* For fall admission, 5/1 priority date for domestic students, 5/1 for international students; for spring admission, 10/1 priority date for domestic students, 10/1 for international students. Application fee: $75. Electronic applications accepted. *Expenses:* Tuition, state resident: full-time $3522. Tuition, nonresident: full-time $16,051. *Required fees:* $2585. Tuition and fees vary according to course load and program. *Financial support:* In 2013–14, 10 students received support, including 9 research assistantships (averaging $10,581 per year), 1 teaching assistantship (averaging $9,364 per year). Financial award application deadline: 4/1; financial award applicants required to submit FAFSA. *Faculty research:* Transition to adulthood and self-determination, teaching reading and other academic skills to students with disabilities, alternate assessment, early intervention, preschool education. *Unit head:* Dr. Mary Lynne Calhoun, Dean, 704-687-8722, Fax: 704-687-2916. *Application contact:* Kathy B. Giddings, Director of Graduate Admissions, 704-687-5503, Fax: 704-687-1668, E-mail: gradadm@uncc.edu.
Website: http://education.uncc.edu/spcd/sped/special_ed.htm.

University of Northern Colorado, Graduate School, College of Education and Behavioral Sciences, School of Special Education, Greeley, CO 80639. Offers deaf/hard of hearing (MA); early childhood special education (MA); gifted and talented (MA); special education (MA, Ed D); visual impairment (MA). Part-time and evening/weekend programs available. Postbaccalaureate distance learning degree programs offered (no on-campus study). *Degree requirements:* For master's, comprehensive exam, thesis or alternative; for doctorate, comprehensive exam, thesis/dissertation. *Entrance requirements:* For master's, letters of recommendation, interview; for doctorate, GRE General Test, resume. Electronic applications accepted.

University of North Texas, Robert B. Toulouse School of Graduate Studies, Denton, TN 76203-5017. Offers accounting (MS, PhD); applied anthropology (MA, MS); applied behavior analysis (Certificate); applied technology and performance improvement (M Ed, MS, PhD); art education (MA, PhD); art history (MA); art museum education (Certificate); arts leadership (Certificate); audiology (Au D); behavior analysis (MS); biochemistry and molecular biology (MS, PhD); biology (MA, MS, PhD); business (PhD); business computer information systems (PhD); chemistry (MS, PhD); clinical psychology (PhD); communication studies (MA, MS); computer engineering (MS); computer science (MS); computer science and engineering (PhD); counseling (M Ed, MS, PhD), including clinical mental health counseling (MS), college and university counseling (M Ed, MS), elementary school counseling (M Ed, MS), secondary school counseling (M Ed, MS); counseling psychology (PhD); creative writing (MA); criminal justice (MS); curriculum and instruction (M Ed, PhD), including curriculum studies (PhD), early childhood studies (PhD), language and literacy studies (PhD); decision sciences (MBA); design (MA, MFA), including fashion design (MFA), innovation studies, interior design (MFA); early childhood studies (MS); economics (MS); educational leadership (M Ed, Ed D, PhD); educational psychology (MS), including family studies, gifted and talented (MS, PhD), human development, learning and cognition, research, measurement and evaluation; educational research (PhD), including gifted and talented (MS, PhD), human development and family studies, psychological aspects of sports and exercise, research, measurement and statistics; electrical engineering (MS); emergency management (MPA); engineering systems (MS); English (MA, PhD); environmental science (MS, PhD); experimental psychology (PhD); finance (MBA, MS, PhD); financial management (MPA); French (MA); health psychology and behavioral medicine (PhD); health services management (MBA); higher education (M Ed, Ed D, PhD); history (MA, MS, PhD), including European history (PhD), military history (PhD), United States history (PhD); hospitality management (MS); human resources management (MPA); information science (MS, PhD); information technologies (MBA); information technology and decision sciences (MS); interdisciplinary studies (MA, MS); international sustainable tourism (MS); jazz studies (MM); journalism (MA, MJ, Graduate Certificate), including interactive and virtual digital communication (Graduate Certificate), narrative journalism (Graduate Certificate), public relations (Graduate Certificate); kinesiology (MS); learning technologies (MS, PhD); library science (MS); local government management (MPA); logistics and supply chain management (MBA, PhD); long-term care, senior housing, and aging services (MA, MS); management science (PhD); marketing (MBA, PhD); materials science and engineering (MS, PhD); mathematics (MA, PhD); merchandising (MS); music (MA, MM Ed, PhD), including ethnomusicology (MA), music education (MM Ed, PhD), music theory (MA, PhD), musicology (MA, PhD), performance (MA); nonprofit management (MPA); operations and supply chain management (MBA); performance (MM, DMA); philosophy (MA, PhD); physics (MS, PhD); political science (MA, MS, PhD); public administration and management (PhD), including emergency management, nonprofit management, public financial management, urban management; radio, television and film (MA, MFA); recreation, event and sport management (MS); rehabilitation counseling (MS, Certificate); sociology (MA, MS, PhD); Spanish (MA); special education (M Ed, PhD), including autism intervention (PhD), emotional/behavioral disorders (PhD), mild/moderate disabilities (PhD); speech-language pathology (MA, MS); strategic management (MBA); studio art (MFA); taxation (MS); teaching (M Ed); MBA/MS; MS/MPH; MSES/MBA. Part-time and evening/weekend programs available. Postbaccalaureate distance learning degree programs offered. *Faculty:* 661 full-time (213 women), 240 part-time/adjunct (144 women). *Students:* 3,106 full-time (1,620 women), 3,543 part-time (2,221 women); includes 1,740 minority (533 Black or African American, non-Hispanic/Latino; 15 American Indian or Alaska Native, non-Hispanic/Latino; 286 Asian, non-Hispanic/Latino; 746 Hispanic/Latino; 3 Native Hawaiian or other Pacific Islander, non-Hispanic/Latino; 157 Two or more races, non-Hispanic/Latino), 1,145 international. Average age 32. 6,289 applicants, 43% accepted, 1751 enrolled. In 2013, 1,778 master's, 239 doctorates, 10 other advanced degrees awarded. Terminal master's awarded for partial completion of doctoral program. *Degree requirements:* For master's, variable foreign language requirement, comprehensive exam (for some programs), thesis (for some programs); for doctorate, variable foreign language requirement, comprehensive exam (for some programs), thesis/dissertation; for other advanced degree, variable foreign language requirement, comprehensive exam (for some programs). *Entrance requirements:* For master's and doctorate, GRE, GMAT. Additional exam requirements/recommendations for international students: Required—TOEFL (minimum score 550 paper-based; 79 iBT). *Application deadline:* For fall admission, 7/15 for domestic students, 3/15 for international students; for spring admission, 11/15 for domestic students, 9/15 for international students; for summer admission, 5/1 for domestic students. Applications are processed on a rolling basis. Application fee: $60. Electronic applications accepted. *Financial support:* Fellowships with partial tuition reimbursements, research assistantships with partial tuition reimbursements, teaching assistantships, career-related internships or fieldwork, Federal Work-Study, institutionally sponsored loans, scholarships/grants, health care benefits, and library assistantships available. Support available to part-time students. Financial award applicants required to submit FAFSA. *Unit head:* Mark Wardell, Dean, 940-565-2383, E-mail: mark.wardell@unt.edu. *Application contact:* Toulouse School of Graduate Studies, 940-565-2383, Fax: 940-565-2141, E-mail: gradsch@unt.edu.
Website: http://tsgs.unt.edu/.

University of Southern Maine, College of Management and Human Service, School of Education and Human Development, Program in Special Education, Portland, ME 04104-9300. Offers abilities and disabilities (MS); gifted and talented (MS); gifted and talented education (Certificate); teaching all students (Certificate); teaching students with mild to moderate disabilities (MS); youth with moderate to severe disabilities (Certificate). *Accreditation:* Teacher Education Accreditation Council. Part-time and evening/weekend programs available. *Faculty:* 7 full-time (4 women), 2 part-time/adjunct (both women). *Students:* 5 full-time (4 women), 33 part-time (31 women); includes 1 minority (Black or African American, non-Hispanic/Latino). Average age 34. 18 applicants, 89% accepted, 12 enrolled. In 2013, 13 master's, 1 other advanced degree awarded. *Degree requirements:* For master's, thesis or alternative, portfolio. *Entrance requirements:* For master's, proof of teacher certification. Additional exam requirements/recommendations for international students: Required—TOEFL (minimum score 550 paper-based; 79 iBT). *Application deadline:* For fall admission, 5/1 priority date for domestic students; for spring admission, 10/15 priority date for domestic students. Applications are processed on a rolling basis. Application fee: $65. Electronic applications accepted. *Expenses:* Tuition, state resident: part-time $380 per credit. Tuition, nonresident: part-time $1026 per credit. Part-time tuition and fees vary according to program. *Financial support:* Research assistantships, career-related internships or fieldwork, Federal Work-Study, institutionally sponsored loans, scholarships/grants, and unspecified assistantships available. Support available to part-time students. Financial award application deadline: 3/1; financial award applicants required to submit FAFSA. *Faculty research:* Special education, gifted and talented education, diversity education, positive behavioral interventions and supports. *Unit head:* Julie Alexandrin, Program Coordinator, 207-228-8320, E-mail: jalexandrin@usm.maine.edu. *Application contact:* Mary Sloan, Assistant Dean of Graduate Studies and Director of Graduate Admissions, 207-780-4386, Fax: 207-780-4969, E-mail: gradstudies@usm.maine.edu.
Website: http://www.usm.maine.edu/sehd/.

University of South Florida, College of Education, Department of Special Education, Tampa, FL 33620-9951. Offers autism spectrum disorders and severe intellectual disabilities (MA); behavior disorders (MA); exceptional student education (MA, MAT); gifted education (MA); mental retardation (MA); special education (PhD); specific learning disabilities (MA). *Accreditation:* NCATE. Part-time and evening/weekend programs available. *Degree requirements:* For master's, comprehensive exam; for doctorate, comprehensive exam, thesis/dissertation, philosophies of inquiry; multiple research methods. *Entrance requirements:* For master's, GRE General Test (if undergraduate GPA less than 3.0), minimum GPA of 3.0 in last 60 hours of course work; for doctorate, GRE General Test, minimum GPA of 3.0 undergraduate, 3.5 graduate; interview. Additional exam requirements/recommendations for international students: Required—TOEFL (minimum score 500 paper-based). Electronic applications accepted. *Faculty research:* Instruction methods for students with learning and behavioral disabilities; teacher preparation, experiential learning, and participatory action research; public policy research; personal preparation for transitional services; case-based instruction, partnerships and mentor development; inclusion and voices of teachers and students with disabilities; narrative ethics and philosophies of research.

The University of Texas–Pan American, College of Education, Department of Educational Psychology, Edinburg, TX 78539. Offers educational diagnostician (M Ed); gifted education (M Ed); guidance and counseling (M Ed); school psychology (MA); special education (M Ed). Part-time and evening/weekend programs available. *Degree requirements:* For master's, comprehensive exam (for some programs), thesis (for some programs). *Entrance requirements:* For master's, GRE General Test, interview. *Expenses:* Tuition, state resident: full-time $5986; part-time $333 per credit hour. Tuition, nonresident: full-time $12,358; part-time $687 per credit hour. *Required fees:* $782. Tuition and fees vary according to program. *Faculty research:* Reading instruction, assessment practice, behavior interventions consultation, mental retardation.

The University of Toledo, College of Graduate Studies, Judith Herb College of Education, Department of Curriculum and Instruction, Toledo, OH 43606-3390. Offers art education (ME); career and technical education (ME); career-technical education (Ed S); curriculum and instruction (ME, PhD, Ed S); early childhood education (PhD, Ed S); education and biology (MES); education and chemistry (MES); education and economics (MAE); education and English (MAE); education and French (MAE); education and geography (MAE); education and geology (MES); education and German (MAE); education and history (MAE); education and mathematics (MAE, MES); education and physics (MES); education and political science (MAE); education and sociology (MAE); education and Spanish (MAE); educational media (PhD); educational technology (ME); educational technology: virtual educator (Certificate); elementary education (PhD); English as a second language (MAE); gifted and talented (PhD); middle childhood education licensure (ME); music education (MME); secondary education (PhD); secondary education licensure (ME); special education (PhD, Ed S). *Accreditation:* NCATE. Part-time and evening/weekend programs available. *Faculty:* 41. *Students:* 53 full-time (30 women), 154 part-time (111 women); includes 21 minority (16 Black or African American, non-Hispanic/Latino; 4 Hispanic/Latino; 1 Two or more races, non-Hispanic/Latino), 21 international. Average age 34. 82 applicants, 79% accepted, 47 enrolled. In 2013, 80 master's, 5 doctorates awarded. *Degree requirements:* For master's, comprehensive exam, thesis or alternative; for doctorate, comprehensive exam, thesis/dissertation; for other advanced degree, thesis optional. *Entrance requirements:* For master's, doctorate, and other advanced degree, minimum cumulative GPA of 2.7 for all previous academic work, letters of recommendation. Additional exam requirements/recommendations for international students: Required—TOEFL (minimum score 550 paper-based; 80 iBT). *Application deadline:* For fall admission, 1/15 priority date for domestic and international students. Applications are processed on a rolling basis. Application fee: $45 ($75 for international students). Electronic applications accepted. *Financial support:* In 2013–14, 5 research assistantships with full and partial tuition reimbursements (averaging $13,200 per year), 11 teaching assistantships with full and partial tuition reimbursements (averaging $8,809 per year) were awarded; career-related internships or fieldwork, Federal Work-Study, institutionally sponsored loans, scholarships/grants, tuition waivers (full and partial), unspecified assistantships, and administrative assistantships also available. Support available to part-time students. *Unit head:* Dr. Joan Kaderavek, Chair, 419-530-5373, E-mail: eigh.chiarelott@utoledo.edu. *Application contact:* Graduate School Office, 419-530-4723, Fax: 419-530-4724, E-mail: grdsch@utnet.utoledo.edu.
Website: http://www.utoledo.edu/eduhshs/.

University of Virginia, Curry School of Education, Department of Leadership, Foundations and Policy, Program in Educational Psychology, Charlottesville, VA 22903. Offers applied developmental science (M Ed); educational evaluation (M Ed); educational psychology (M Ed, Ed D, Ed S); educational research (Ed D); gifted education (M Ed); instructional technology (M Ed, Ed S); research statistics and evaluation (Ed D); school psychology (Ed D). *Students:* 21 full-time (14 women), 12 part-time (9 women); includes 9 minority (4 Black or African American, non-Hispanic/Latino; 2 Asian, non-Hispanic/Latino; 3 Hispanic/Latino), 2 international. Average age 32. 67 applicants, 78% accepted, 27 enrolled. In 2013, 42 master's, 1 doctorate awarded. *Degree requirements:* For master's, comprehensive exam. *Entrance requirements:* For master's and doctorate, GRE General Test, 2 letters of recommendation. Additional exam requirements/recommendations for international students: Required—TOEFL (minimum score 600 paper-based; 90 iBT), IELTS (minimum score 7). *Application deadline:* Applications are processed on a rolling basis. Application fee: $60. Electronic applications accepted. *Expenses:* Tuition, state resident: part-time $334 per credit hour. Tuition, nonresident: part-time $1224 per credit hour. *Financial support:* Fellowships, research assistantships, and teaching assistantships available. Financial award application deadline: 1/5; financial award applicants required to submit FAFSA. *Unit head:* Leslie Booren, Managing Director, 434-243-2021, E-mail: booren@virginia.edu.
Website: http://curry.virginia.edu/academics/areas-of-study/educational-psychology.

University of Wisconsin–Whitewater, School of Graduate Studies, College of Education and Professional Studies, Department of Curriculum and Instruction, Whitewater, WI 53190-1790. Offers professional development (MS), including bilingual education, challenging advanced learners, curriculum and instruction, educational leadership, health, human performance and recreation, health, physical education and coaching, information technologies and libraries, reading. *Accreditation:* NCATE. Part-time and evening/weekend programs available. Postbaccalaureate distance learning degree programs offered. *Degree requirements:* For master's, thesis or integrated project. *Entrance requirements:* Additional exam requirements/recommendations for international students: Required—TOEFL (minimum score 550 paper-based; 80 iBT), IELTS (minimum score 6). Electronic applications accepted. *Faculty research:* Hybrid of exercise physiology and psychology; gender equity; education, pedagogy, and technology; comprehensive school health education.

Western Washington University, Graduate School, Woodring College of Education, Department of Special Education, Bellingham, WA 98225-5996. Offers M Ed. *Accreditation:* NCATE. Part-time programs available. *Degree requirements:* For master's, comprehensive exam, thesis optional. *Entrance requirements:* For master's, GRE General Test or MAT, minimum GPA of 3.0 in last 60 semester hours or last 90 quarter hours. Additional exam requirements/recommendations for international students: Required—TOEFL (minimum score 567 paper-based). Electronic applications accepted. *Faculty research:* Applied behavioral analysis, controversial practices, infant/toddler social-emotional interventions, reflective practices in teacher education.

West Virginia University, College of Human Resources and Education, Department of Special Education, Morgantown, WV 26506. Offers autism spectrum disorder (5-adult) (MA); autism spectrum disorder (K-6) (MA); early intervention/early childhood special education (MA); gifted education (1-12) (MA); low vision (PreK-adult) (MA); multicategorical special education (5-adult) (MA); multicategorical special education (K-6) (MA); severe/multiple disabilities (K-adult) (MA); special education (MA, Ed D); vision impairments (PreK-adult) (MA). *Accreditation:* NCATE. Part-time and evening/weekend programs available. Postbaccalaureate distance learning degree programs offered (no on-campus study). *Degree requirements:* For master's, thesis optional; for doctorate, comprehensive exam, thesis/dissertation. *Entrance requirements:* For master's, minimum GPA of 2.75 passing scores on PRAXIS PPST; for doctorate, GRE General Test or MAT. Additional exam requirements/recommendations for international students: Required—TOEFL.

Whitworth University, School of Education, Graduate Studies in Education, Program in Gifted and Talented, Spokane, WA 99251-0001. Offers MAT. *Accreditation:* NCATE. Part-time and evening/weekend programs available. *Degree requirements:* For master's, comprehensive exam, thesis (for some programs). *Entrance requirements:* For master's, GRE General Test, MAT.

Wichita State University, Graduate School, College of Education, Department of Curriculum and Instruction, Wichita, KS 67260. Offers curriculum and instruction (M Ed); special education (M Ed), including adaptive, early childhood unified (M Ed, MAT), functional, gifted; teaching (MAT), including curriculum and instruction, early childhood unified (M Ed, MAT). *Accreditation:* NCATE. Part-time and evening/weekend programs available. *Entrance requirements:* For master's, MAT, minimum GPA of 2.75. *Unit head:* Dr. Janice Ewing, Chairperson, 316-978-3322, E-mail: janice.ewing@wichita.edu. *Application contact:* Jordan Oleson, Admission Coordinator, 316-978-3095, Fax: 316-978-3253, E-mail: jordan.oleson@wichita.edu.

William Carey University, School of Education, Hattiesburg, MS 39401-5499. Offers art education (M Ed); art of teaching (M Ed); elementary education (M Ed, Ed S); English education (M Ed); gifted education (M Ed); history and social science (M Ed); mild/moderate disabilities (M Ed); secondary education (M Ed). *Accreditation:* NCATE. Part-time programs available. *Degree requirements:* For master's, comprehensive exam. *Entrance requirements:* For master's, GRE, MAT, minimum GPA of 2.5, Class A teacher's license. Additional exam requirements/recommendations for international students: Required—TOEFL (minimum score 550 paper-based).

Wilmington University, College of Education, New Castle, DE 19720-6491. Offers applied technology in education (M Ed); career and technical education (M Ed); educational leadership (Ed D); elementary and secondary school counseling (M Ed); elementary studies (M Ed); ESOL literacy (M Ed); higher education leadership (Ed D); instruction: gifted and talented (M Ed); instruction: teacher of reading (M Ed); instruction: teaching and learning (M Ed); organizational leadership (Ed D); school leadership (M Ed); secondary education (MAT); special education (M Ed). *Accreditation:* NCATE. Part-time and evening/weekend programs available. *Entrance requirements:* For master's, 2 letters of recommendation, interview. Additional exam requirements/recommendations for international students: Required—TOEFL (minimum score 500 paper-based). Electronic applications accepted.

Wright State University, School of Graduate Studies, College of Education and Human Services, Department of Teacher Education, Programs in Intervention Specialist, Dayton, OH 45435. Offers gifted educational needs (M Ed, MA); mild to moderate educational needs (M Ed, MA); moderate to intensive educational needs (M Ed, MA). *Accreditation:* NCATE. *Degree requirements:* For master's, thesis (for some programs). *Entrance requirements:* For master's, GRE General Test, MAT. Additional exam requirements/recommendations for international students: Required—TOEFL.

Youngstown State University, Graduate School, Beeghly College of Education, Department of Teacher Education, Program in Special Education, Youngstown, OH 44555-0001. Offers gifted and talented education (MS Ed); special education (MS Ed). *Accreditation:* NCATE. Part-time and evening/weekend programs available. *Degree requirements:* For master's, comprehensive exam. *Entrance requirements:* For master's, GRE, MAT, or teaching certificate; interview; minimum GPA of 2.7. Additional exam requirements/recommendations for international students: Required—TOEFL. *Faculty research:* Learning disabilities, learning styles, developing self-esteem and social skills of severe behaviorally handicapped students, inclusion.

English as a Second Language

Acacia University, American Graduate School of Education, Tempe, AZ 85284. Offers educational administration (M Ed); elementary education (MA); English as a second language (M Ed); secondary education (MA); special education (M Ed).

Adelphi University, Ruth S. Ammon School of Education, Program in Teaching English to Speakers of Other Languages, Garden City, NY 11530-0701. Offers MA, Certificate. Part-time and evening/weekend programs available. *Students:* 18 full-time (17 women), 19 part-time (all women); includes 16 minority (1 Black or African American, non-Hispanic/Latino; 4 Asian, non-Hispanic/Latino; 10 Hispanic/Latino; 1 Two or more races, non-Hispanic/Latino), 5 international. Average age 28. In 2013, 21 master's, 5 other advanced degrees awarded. *Entrance requirements:* For master's, 2 letters of recommendation, resume. Additional exam requirements/recommendations for international students: Required—TOEFL (minimum score 550 paper-based; 80 iBT). *Application deadline:* For fall admission, 4/1 priority date for domestic students; for spring admission, 11/1 priority date for domestic students. Applications are processed on a rolling basis. Application fee: $50. Electronic applications accepted. *Expenses: Tuition:* Full-time $32,530; part-time $1010 per credit. *Required fees:* $1150. Tuition and fees vary according to degree level and program. *Financial support:* Fellowships, research assistantships with partial tuition reimbursements, teaching assistantships, career-related internships or fieldwork, Federal Work-Study, institutionally sponsored loans, tuition waivers (full), and unspecified assistantships available. Support available to part-time students. Financial award application deadline: 2/15; financial award applicants required to submit FAFSA. *Faculty research:* Theories of language acquisition, English as a second language in the content areas, apprenticeship in English as a second language instruction. *Unit head:* Eva Roca, Director, 516-877-4072, E-mail: rocaz@adelphi.edu. *Application contact:* Christine Murphy, Director of Admissions, 516-877-3050, Fax: 516-877-3039, E-mail: graduateadmissions@adelphi.edu.

Albright College, Graduate Division, Reading, PA 19612-5234. Offers early childhood education (MS); elementary education (MS); English as a second language (MA); general education (MA); special education (MS). Part-time and evening/weekend programs available. *Degree requirements:* For master's, thesis. *Entrance requirements:* For master's, GRE General Test or MAT, minimum undergraduate GPA of 3.0, 2 letters of recommendation, interview. Additional exam requirements/recommendations for international students: Recommended—TOEFL (minimum score 525 paper-based). Electronic applications accepted.

Alliant International University–San Diego, Shirley M. Hufstedler School of Education, Program in Teaching English to Speakers of Other Languages, San Diego, CA 92131-1799. Offers MA, Ed D, Certificate. Part-time programs available. *Faculty:* 4 full-time (2 women), 4 part-time/adjunct (3 women). *Students:* 19 full-time (14 women), 27 part-time (20 women); includes 10 minority (3 Black or African American, non-Hispanic/Latino; 2 Asian, non-Hispanic/Latino; 5 Hispanic/Latino), 22 international. Average age 38. 32 applicants, 81% accepted, 16 enrolled. In 2013, 27 master's, 5 doctorates, 1 other advanced degree awarded. *Degree requirements:* For doctorate, thesis/dissertation. *Entrance requirements:* For master's, minimum GPA of 2.5, letters of recommendation; for doctorate, minimum GPA of 3.0, letters of recommendation. Additional exam requirements/recommendations for international students: Required—TOEFL (minimum score 575 paper-based; 83 iBT), TWE (minimum score 5). *Application deadline:* For fall admission, 4/15 priority date for domestic and international students; for spring admission, 10/3 priority date for domestic students, 11/3 priority date for international students. Applications are processed on a rolling basis. Application fee: $65. Electronic applications accepted. *Financial support:* Federal Work-Study, institutionally sponsored loans, and scholarships/grants available. Financial award applicants required to submit FAFSA. *Faculty research:* Global education, psycho-linguistics, bilingualism and education, curriculum and instruction. *Unit head:* Dr. Mary Ellen Butler-Pascoe, Systemwide Program Director for International Teacher Education, 858-635-4791, Fax: 858-635-4739, E-mail: admissions@alliant.edu. *Application contact:* Alliant International University Central Contact Center, 866-U-ALLIANT, Fax: 858-635-4555, E-mail: admissions@alliant.edu.
Website: http://www.alliant.edu/hsoe.

Alliant International University–San Francisco, Shirley M. Hufstedler School of Education, Teacher Education Programs, San Francisco, CA 94133-1221. Offers auditory oral education (Certificate); CLAD (Certificate); education specialist: mild/moderate disabilities (Credential); preliminary multiple subject (Credential); preliminary single subject (Credential); professional clear multiple subject (Credential); professional clear single subject (Credential); special education (MA); teaching (MA); TESOL (Certificate). Part-time and evening/weekend programs available. *Faculty:* 6 full-time (4 women), 10 part-time/adjunct (8 women). *Students:* 16 full-time (10 women), 135 part-time (97 women); includes 22 minority (6 Black or African American, non-Hispanic/Latino; 6 Asian, non-Hispanic/Latino; 8 Hispanic/Latino; 2 Two or more races, non-Hispanic/Latino). Average age 41. 172 applicants, 94% accepted, 142 enrolled. In 2013, 11 master's, 167 other advanced degrees awarded. *Degree requirements:* For master's, thesis. *Entrance requirements:* For degree, California Basic Educational Skills Test, minimum GPA of 2.5. Additional exam requirements/recommendations for international students: Required—TOEFL (minimum score 550 paper-based), TWE (minimum score 5). *Application deadline:* For fall admission, 7/1 priority date for domestic and international students; for spring admission, 12/1 priority date for domestic and international students. Applications are processed on a rolling basis. Application fee: $55. Electronic applications accepted. *Financial support:* Career-related internships or fieldwork, Federal Work-Study, institutionally sponsored loans, and scholarships/grants available. Financial award application deadline: 2/15; financial award applicants required to submit FAFSA. *Faculty research:* Curriculum development, first year teachers, cross-cultural issues in teaching, biliteracy. *Unit head:* Dr. Debra Reeves-Gutierrez, Program Director, 415-955-2084, Fax: 415-955-2179, E-mail: admissions@alliant.edu. *Application contact:* Alliant International University Central Contact Center, 866-U-ALLIANT, Fax: 858-635-4555, E-mail: admissions@alliant.edu.
Website: http://www.alliant.edu/.

American College of Education, Graduate Programs, Chicago, IL 60606. Offers curriculum and instruction (M Ed), including bilingual, ESL; educational leadership (M Ed); educational technology (M Ed).

American Public University System, AMU/APU Graduate Programs, Charles Town, WV 25414. Offers accounting (MBA, MS); criminal justice (MA), including business administration, emergency and disaster management, general (MA, MS); educational leadership (M Ed); emergency and disaster management (MA); entrepreneurship (MBA); environmental policy and management (MS), including environmental planning, environmental sustainability, fish and wildlife management, general (MA, MS), global environmental management; finance (MBA); general (MBA); global business

management (MBA); history (MA), including American history, ancient and classical history, European history, global history, public history; homeland security (MA), including business administration, counter-terrorism studies, criminal justice, cyber, emergency management and public health, intelligence studies, transportation security; homeland security resource allocation (MBA); humanities (MA); information technology (MS), including digital forensics, enterprise software development, information assurance and security, IT project management; information technology management (MBA); intelligence studies (MA), including criminal intelligence, cyber, general (MA, MS), homeland security, intelligence analysis, intelligence collection, intelligence management, intelligence operations, terrorism studies; international relations and conflict resolution (MA), including comparative and security issues, conflict resolution, international and transnational security issues, peacekeeping; legal studies (MA); management (MA), including defense management, general (MA, MS), human resource management, organizational leadership, public administration; marketing (MBA); military history (MA), including American military history, American Revolution, civil war, war since 1945, World War II; military studies (MA), including joint warfare, strategic leadership; national security studies (MA), including general (MA, MS), homeland security, regional security studies, security and intelligence analysis, terrorism studies; nonprofit management (MBA); political science (MA), including American politics and government, comparative government and development, general (MA, MS), international relations, public policy; psychology (MA), including general (MA, MS), maritime engineering management, reverse logistics management; public administration (MPA), including disaster management, environmental policy, health policy, human resources, national security, organizational management, security management; public health (MPH); reverse logistics management (MA); school counseling (M Ed); security management (MA); space studies (MS), including aerospace science, general (MA, MS), planetary science; sports and health sciences (MS); teaching (M Ed), including curriculum and instruction for elementary teachers, elementary reading, English language learners, instructional leadership, online learning, special education; transportation and logistics management (MA), including general (MA, MS), maritime engineering management, reverse logistics management. Programs offered via distance learning only. Part-time and evening/weekend programs available. Postbaccalaureate distance learning degree programs offered (no on-campus study). *Faculty:* 432 full-time (242 women), 1,722 part-time/adjunct (829 women). *Students:* 511 full-time (241 women), 10,947 part-time (4,294 women); includes 3,760 minority (2,058 Black or African American, non-Hispanic/Latino; 88 American Indian or Alaska Native, non-Hispanic/Latino; 293 Asian, non-Hispanic/Latino; 876 Hispanic/Latino; 91 Native Hawaiian or other Pacific Islander, non-Hispanic/Latino; 354 Two or more races, non-Hispanic/Latino), 134 international. Average age 36. In 2013, 3,323 master's awarded. *Degree requirements:* For master's, comprehensive exam or practicum. *Entrance requirements:* For master's, official transcript showing earned bachelor's degree from institution accredited by recognized accrediting body. Additional exam requirements/recommendations for international students: Required—TOEFL (minimum score 550 paper-based), IELTS (minimum score 6.5). *Application deadline:* Applications are processed on a rolling basis. Application fee: $0. Electronic applications accepted. *Expenses: Tuition:* Part-time $325 per semester hour. *Financial support:* Applicants required to submit FAFSA. *Faculty research:* Military history, criminal justice, management performance, national security. *Unit head:* Dr. Karan Powell, Executive Vice President and Provost, 877-468-6268, Fax: 304-724-3780. *Application contact:* Terry Grant, Vice President of Enrollment Management, 877-468-6268, Fax: 304-724-3780, E-mail: info@apus.edu.
Website: http://www.apus.edu.

American University, College of Arts and Sciences, Washington, DC 20016-8012. Offers addiction and addictive behavior (Certificate); anthropology (PhD); applied microeconomics (Certificate); applied statistics (Certificate); art history (MA); arts management (MA, Certificate); Asian studies (Certificate); audio production (Certificate); audio technology (MA); behavior, cognition, and neuroscience (PhD); bilingual education (MA, Certificate); biology (MA, MS); chemistry (MS); clinical psychology (PhD); computer science (MS, Certificate); creative writing (MFA); curriculum and instruction (M Ed, Certificate); economics (MA, PhD); environmental assessment (Certificate); environmental science (MS); ethics, peace, and global affairs (MA); gender analysis in economics (Certificate); health promotion management (MS); history (MA, PhD); international arts management (Certificate); international economic relations (Certificate); international economics (MA); international training and education (MA); literature (MA); mathematics (MA); North American studies (Certificate); nutrition education (MS, Certificate); philosophy (MA); professional science: biotechnology (MS); professional science: environmental assessment (MS); professional science: quantitative analysis (MS); psychobiology of healing (Certificate); psychology (MA); psychology: general (PhD); public anthropology (MA, Certificate); public sociology (Certificate); social research (Certificate); sociology (MA); Spanish: Latin American studies (MA); special education: learning disabilities (MA); statistics (MS); studio art (MFA); teaching (MAT); teaching English as a foreign language (MA); teaching: early childhood (Certificate); teaching: elementary (Certificate); teaching: ESOL (Certificate); teaching: secondary (Certificate); technology in arts management (Certificate); TESOL (MA); translation: French (Certificate); translation: Russian (Certificate); translation: Spanish (Certificate); women's, gender, and sexuality studies (Certificate). Part-time and evening/weekend programs available. Postbaccalaureate distance learning degree programs offered (no on-campus study). *Faculty:* 358 full-time (187 women), 254 part-time/adjunct (127 women). *Students:* 627 full-time (411 women), 416 part-time (300 women); includes 206 minority (91 Black or African American, non-Hispanic/Latino; 5 American Indian or Alaska Native, non-Hispanic/Latino; 32 Asian, non-Hispanic/Latino; 64 Hispanic/Latino; 1 Native Hawaiian or other Pacific Islander, non-Hispanic/Latino; 13 Two or more races, non-Hispanic/Latino), 124 international. Average age 29. 1,672 applicants, 52% accepted, 361 enrolled. In 2013, 382 master's, 38 doctorates, 33 other advanced degrees awarded. Terminal master's awarded for partial completion of doctoral program. *Degree requirements:* For master's, comprehensive exam (for some programs), thesis (for some programs); for doctorate, comprehensive exam (for some programs), thesis/dissertation. *Entrance requirements:* For master's, GRE, minimum GPA of 3.0 in last 60 credit hours, letter of recommendation, statement of purpose, resume, unofficial transcript; for doctorate, GRE, minimum GPA of 3.0 for all graduate work, letter of recommendation, statement of purpose, resume, unofficial transcript. Additional exam requirements/recommendations for international students: Required—TOEFL (minimum score 600 paper-based; 100 iBT), IELTS (minimum score 7). *Application deadline:* For fall admission, 2/1 for domestic students; for spring admission, 10/1 for domestic students. Applications are processed on a rolling basis. Application fee: $55. Electronic applications accepted. *Expenses: Tuition:* Full-time $25,920; part-time $1482 per credit hour. *Required fees:* $430. Tuition and fees vary according to course load and program. *Financial support:* Fellowships, research assistantships with

full and partial tuition reimbursements, teaching assistantships with full and partial tuition reimbursements, career-related internships or fieldwork, Federal Work-Study, institutionally sponsored loans, scholarships/grants, traineeships, tuition waivers (full and partial), and unspecified assistantships available. Support available to part-time students. Financial award applicants required to submit FAFSA. *Unit head:* Dr. Peter Starr, Dean, 202-885-2446, Fax: 202-885-2429, E-mail: pstarr@american.edu. *Application contact:* Kathleen Clowery, Associate Director, Graduate Enrollment Management, 202-885-3621, Fax: 202-885-1505, E-mail: clowery@american.edu. Website: http://www.american.edu/cas/.

The American University in Cairo, School of Humanities and Social Sciences, English Language Institute, Cairo, Egypt. Offers teaching English as a foreign language (MA, Diploma). Part-time programs available. *Degree requirements:* For master's, one foreign language, thesis optional. *Entrance requirements:* Additional exam requirements/recommendations for international students: Required—English entrance exam and/or TOEFL. Electronic applications accepted. Tuition and fees vary according to course level, course load and program. *Faculty research:* Teacher education, social linguistics, teaching methodology pragmatics.

American University of Armenia, Graduate Programs, Yerevan, Armenia. Offers business administration (MBA); computer and information science (MS), including business management, design and manufacturing, energy (ME, MS), industrial engineering and systems management; economics (MS); industrial engineering and systems management (ME), including business, computer aided design/manufacturing, energy (ME, MS), information technology; law (LL M); political science and international affairs (MPSIA); public health (MPH); teaching English as a foreign language (MA). Part-time and evening/weekend programs available. *Faculty:* 30 full-time (10 women), 42 part-time/adjunct (13 women). *Students:* 398 full-time (272 women), 138 part-time (84 women). Average age 24. 351 applicants, 77% accepted, 247 enrolled. In 2013, 215 master's awarded. *Degree requirements:* For master's, thesis (for some programs), capstone/project. *Entrance requirements:* For master's, GRE, GMAT, or LSAT. Additional exam requirements/recommendations for international students: Recommended—TOEFL (minimum score 79 iBT), IELTS (minimum score 6.5). *Application deadline:* For fall admission, 3/31 for domestic and international students; for spring admission, 12/20 for domestic and international students. Applications are processed on a rolling basis. Application fee: $30 ($70 for international students). *Expenses: Tuition:* Full-time $2683; part-time $122 per credit. Full-time tuition and fees vary according to program. *Financial support:* In 2013–14, 199 students received support. Teaching assistantships with partial tuition reimbursements available, career-related internships or fieldwork, institutionally sponsored loans, scholarships/grants, unspecified assistantships, and tuition assistance, institutionally-sponsored work study available. Support available to part-time students. Financial award application deadline: 6/30. *Faculty research:* Microfinance, finance (rural/development, international, corporate), firm life cycle theory, TESOL, language proficiency testing, public policy, administrative law, economic development, cryptography, artificial intelligence, energy efficiency/renewable energy, computer-aided design/manufacturing, health financing, tuberculosis control, mother/child health, preventive ophthalmology, post-earthquake psychopathological investigations, tobacco control, environmental health risk assessments. *Total annual research expenditures:* $465,763. *Unit head:* Dr. Dennis Leavens, Provost, 374 10512526, E-mail: provost@aua.am. *Application contact:* Karine Satamyan, Admissions Coordinator, 374-10324040, E-mail: grad@aua.am. Website: http://www.aua.am.

American University of Sharjah, Graduate Programs, Sharjah, United Arab Emirates. Offers accounting (MS); business (EMBA, MBA); chemical engineering (MS Ch E); civil engineering (MSCE); computer engineering (MS); electrical engineering (MSEE); engineering systems management (MS); mathematics (MS); mechanical engineering (MSME); mechatronics engineering (MS); teaching English to speakers of other languages (MA); translation and interpreting (MA); urban planning (MUP). Part-time and evening/weekend programs available. *Faculty:* 59 full-time (4 women), 5 part-time/adjunct (1 woman). *Students:* 127 full-time (50 women), 342 part-time (148 women). Average age 27. 184 applicants, 83% accepted, 92 enrolled. In 2013, 97 master's awarded. *Degree requirements:* For master's, thesis (for some programs). *Entrance requirements:* For master's, GMAT (for MBA). Additional exam requirements/recommendations for international students: Required—TOEFL (minimum score 550 paper-based; 80 iBT), TWE (minimum score 5); Recommended—IELTS (minimum score 6.5). *Application deadline:* For fall admission, 8/28 priority date for domestic students, 8/14 priority date for international students; for spring admission, 1/22 priority date for domestic students, 1/8 for international students; for summer admission, 5/21 for domestic and international students. Applications are processed on a rolling basis. Application fee: $350. Electronic applications accepted. *Expenses: Tuition:* Full-time 69,660 United Arab Emirates dirhams; part-time 3870 United Arab Emirates dirhams per credit. Tuition and fees vary according to course load and program. *Financial support:* In 2013–14, 63 students received support, including 28 research assistantships with full and partial tuition reimbursements available, 35 teaching assistantships with full and partial tuition reimbursements available; scholarships/grants also available. *Faculty research:* Water pollution, management and waste water treatment, energy and sustainability, air pollution, Islamic finance, family business and small and medium enterprises. *Unit head:* Rami Mahfouz, Director of Enrollment Services, 971-6515-1030, E-mail: mahfouzr@aus.edu. *Application contact:* Mona A. Mabrouk, Graduate Admissions/Office of Enrollment Management, 971-65151012, E-mail: graduateadmission@aus.edu. Website: http://www.aus.edu/programs/graduate/.

Anaheim University, Program in Teaching English to Speakers of Other Languages, Anaheim, CA 92806-5150. Offers MA, Ed D, Certificate, Diploma. Postbaccalaureate distance learning degree programs offered (no on-campus study).

Andrews University, School of Graduate Studies, School of Education, Department of Teaching, Learning, and Curriculum, Berrien Springs, MI 49104. Offers curriculum and instruction (MA, Ed D, PhD, Ed S); elementary education (MAT); secondary education (MAT), including biology, education, English, English as a second language, French, history, physics; teacher education (MAT). *Faculty:* 7 full-time (4 women). *Students:* 16 full-time (11 women), 26 part-time (22 women); includes 14 minority (11 Black or African American, non-Hispanic/Latino; 1 Asian, non-Hispanic/Latino; 1 Hispanic/Latino; 1 Two or more races, non-Hispanic/Latino), 13 international. Average age 40. 33 applicants, 42% accepted, 3 enrolled. In 2013, 7 master's, 1 doctorate, 1 other advanced degree awarded. *Entrance requirements:* For master's, GRE Subject Test. Additional exam requirements/recommendations for international students: Required—TOEFL (minimum score 550 paper-based). *Application deadline:* For fall admission, 8/15 for domestic students. Applications are processed on a rolling basis. Application fee: $40. *Unit head:* Dr. Lee C. Davidson, Chair, 269-471-6364. *Application contact:* Monica Wringer, Supervisor of Graduate Admission, 800-253-2874, Fax: 269-471-6321, E-mail: graduate@andrews.edu.

Arizona State University at the Tempe campus, College of Liberal Arts and Sciences, Department of English, Tempe, AZ 85287-0302. Offers applied linguistics (PhD); creative writing (MFA); English (MA, PhD), including comparative literature (MA), linguistics (MA), literature, rhetoric and composition (MA), rhetoric/composition and

linguistics (PhD); linguistics (Graduate Certificate); teaching English to speakers of other languages (MTESOL). Terminal master's awarded for partial completion of doctoral program. *Degree requirements:* For master's, variable foreign language requirement, comprehensive exam (for some programs), thesis (for some programs), interactive Program of Study (iPOS) submitted before completing 50 percent of required credit hours; for doctorate, variable foreign language requirement, comprehensive exam, thesis/dissertation, interactive Program of Study (iPOS) submitted before completing 50 percent of required credit hours. *Entrance requirements:* For master's and doctorate, GRE, minimum GPA of 3.0 or equivalent in last 2 years of work leading to bachelor's degree. Additional exam requirements/recommendations for international students: Required—TOEFL (minimum score 80 iBT), TOEFL, IELTS, or PTE. Electronic applications accepted.

Arkansas Tech University, College of Arts and Humanities, Russellville, AR 72801. Offers English (M Ed, MA); history (MA); liberal arts (MLA); multi-media journalism (MA); psychology (MS); Spanish (MA); teaching English as a second language (MA). Part-time programs available. *Students:* 64 full-time (45 women), 81 part-time (62 women); includes 22 minority (3 Black or African American, non-Hispanic/Latino; 2 American Indian or Alaska Native, non-Hispanic/Latino; 2 Asian, non-Hispanic/Latino; 12 Hispanic/Latino; 3 Two or more races, non-Hispanic/Latino), 36 international. Average age 29. In 2013, 67 master's awarded. *Degree requirements:* For master's, comprehensive exam (for some programs), thesis (for some programs), project. *Entrance requirements:* For master's, GRE General Test or GMAT. Additional exam requirements/recommendations for international students: Required—TOEFL (minimum score 550 paper-based; 79 iBT), IELTS (minimum score 6). *Application deadline:* For fall admission, 3/1 priority date for domestic students, 5/1 priority date for international students; for spring admission, 10/1 priority date for domestic and international students. Applications are processed on a rolling basis. Application fee: $25 ($75 for international students). Electronic applications accepted. *Expenses:* Tuition, state resident: full-time $5976; part-time $249 per credit hour. Tuition, nonresident: full-time $11,952; part-time $498 per credit hour. *Required fees:* $411 per semester. Tuition and fees vary according to course load. *Financial support:* In 2013–14, research assistantships with full tuition reimbursements (averaging $4,800 per year), teaching assistantships with full tuition reimbursements (averaging $4,800 per year) were awarded; career-related internships or fieldwork, Federal Work-Study, scholarships/grants, health care benefits, and unspecified assistantships also available. Support available to part-time students. Financial award application deadline: 4/15; financial award applicants required to submit FAFSA. *Unit head:* Dr. Jeffrey Woods, Dean, 479-968-0274, Fax: 479-964-0812, E-mail: jwoods@atu.edu. *Application contact:* Dr. Mary B. Gunter, Dean of Graduate College, 479-968-0398, Fax: 479-964-0542, E-mail: gradcollege@atu.edu. Website: http://www.atu.edu/humanities/.

Asbury University, School of Graduate and Professional Studies, Wilmore, KY 40390-1198. Offers biology: alternative certificate (MA Ed); chemistry: alternative certificate (MA Ed); English (MA Ed); English as a second language (MA Ed); ESL (MA Ed); French (MA Ed); Latin: alternative certificate (MA Ed); mathematics: alternative certificate (MA Ed); reading/writing endorsement (MA Ed); social studies (MA Ed); social work (MSW), including child and family services; Spanish (MA Ed); special education (MA Ed); special education: alternative certificate (MA Ed); teacher as leader endorsement (MA Ed). *Accreditation:* NCATE. Part-time programs available. *Degree requirements:* For master's, action research project, portfolio. *Entrance requirements:* For master's, PRAXIS/NTE, minimum GPA of 2.75, letters of recommendation. Additional exam requirements/recommendations for international students: Required—TOEFL (minimum score 550 paper-based). Electronic applications accepted.

Avila University, School of Education, Kansas City, MO 64145-1698. Offers English for speakers of other languages (Advanced Certificate); teaching and learning (MA); TESL (MA). Part-time and evening/weekend programs available. *Faculty:* 5 full-time (4 women), 5 part-time/adjunct (3 women). *Students:* 123 full-time (86 women), 17 part-time (13 women); includes 12 minority (6 Black or African American, non-Hispanic/Latino; 2 American Indian or Alaska Native, non-Hispanic/Latino; 1 Hispanic/Latino; 3 Two or more races, non-Hispanic/Latino), 3 international. Average age 34. 45 applicants, 64% accepted, 28 enrolled. In 2013, 46 master's awarded. *Entrance requirements:* For master's, minimum GPA of 3.0, writing sample, recommendation, interview; for Advanced Certificate, foreign language. Additional exam requirements/recommendations for international students: Required—TOEFL (minimum score 580 paper-based; 92 iBT). *Application deadline:* Applications are processed on a rolling basis. Electronic applications accepted. *Expenses:* Contact institution. *Financial support:* In 2013–14, 9 students received support, including 1 research assistantship; career-related internships or fieldwork also available. Support available to part-time students. Financial award applicants required to submit FAFSA. *Unit head:* Deana Angotti, Director of Graduate Education, 816-501-2446, Fax: 816-501-2915, E-mail: deana.angotti@avila.edu. *Application contact:* Margaret Longstreet, Office Manager, 816-501-2464, E-mail: margaret.longstreet@avila.edu.

Azusa Pacific University, College of Liberal Arts and Sciences, Program in Teaching English to Speakers of Other Languages, Azusa, CA 91702-7000. Offers MA.

Ball State University, Graduate School, College of Sciences and Humanities, Department of English, Muncie, IN 47306-1099. Offers English (MA, PhD), including composition, creative writing (MA), general (MA), literature; linguistics (MA, PhD), including applied linguistics (PhD), linguistics (MA); linguistics and teaching English to speakers of other languages (MA); teaching English to speakers of other languages (MA). *Faculty:* 20 full-time (12 women), 1 (woman) part-time/adjunct. *Students:* 35 full-time (22 women), 45 part-time (24 women); includes 2 minority (1 Hispanic/Latino; 1 Two or more races, non-Hispanic/Latino), 24 international. Average age 27. 87 applicants, 49% accepted, 23 enrolled. In 2013, 18 master's, 8 doctorates awarded. *Degree requirements:* For doctorate, variable foreign language requirement, thesis/dissertation. *Entrance requirements:* For master's, GRE General Test, writing sample; for doctorate, GRE General Test, GRE Subject Test, minimum graduate GPA of 3.2, writing sample. Application fee: $25 ($35 for international students). *Financial support:* In 2013–14, 58 students received support, including 34 teaching assistantships with full tuition reimbursements available (averaging $15,470 per year); fellowships, career-related internships or fieldwork, and unspecified assistantships also available. Financial award application deadline: 3/1. *Faculty research:* American literature; literary editing; medieval, Renaissance, and eighteenth century British literature; rhetoric. *Unit head:* Dr. Elizabeth Riddle, Chairperson, 765-285-8580, Fax: 765-285-3765, E-mail: emriddle@bsu.edu. *Application contact:* Dr. Jill Christman, Assistant Chair, 765-285-8415, E-mail: jcchristman@bsu.edu. Website: http://www.bsu.edu/english/.

Baptist Bible College of Pennsylvania, Graduate Studies, Clarks Summit, PA 18411-1297. Offers Bible (MA); counseling (MA, MS); curriculum and instruction (M Ed); educational administration (M Ed); intercultural studies (MA); literature (MA); missions (MA); organizational leadership (MA); reading specialist (M Ed); secondary English/communications (M Ed); social entrepreneurship (MA); worldview studies (MA). MA in missions program available only for Association of Baptists for World Evangelism missionary personnel. Part-time and evening/weekend programs available. Postbaccalaureate distance learning degree programs offered (no on-campus study).

English as a Second Language

Entrance requirements: Additional exam requirements/recommendations for international students: Required—TOEFL (minimum score 500 paper-based).

Barry University, School of Education, Program in Curriculum and Instruction, Miami Shores, FL 33161-6695. Offers accomplished teacher (Ed S); culture, language and literacy (TESOL) (PhD); curriculum evaluation and research (PhD); early childhood (Ed S); early childhood education (PhD); elementary (Ed S); elementary education (PhD); ESOL (Ed S); gifted (Ed S); Montessori (Ed S); PKP/elementary (Ed S); reading (Ed S); reading, language and cognition (PhD). *Entrance requirements:* For doctorate, GRE, minimum GPA of 3.25.

Barry University, School of Education, Program in Technology and TESOL, Miami Shores, FL 33161-6695. Offers MS, Ed S.

Barry University, School of Education, Program in TESOL, Miami Shores, FL 33161-6695. Offers TESOL (MS); TESOL international (MS). *Entrance requirements:* For master's, GRE or MAT.

Biola University, Cook School of Intercultural Studies, La Mirada, CA 90639-0001. Offers anthropology (MA); applied linguistics (MA); intercultural education (PhD); intercultural studies (MA, PhD); linguistics (Certificate); linguistics and Biblical languages (MA); missions (MA); teaching English to speakers of other languages (MA, Certificate). Part-time programs available. *Faculty:* 21. *Students:* 77 full-time (43 women), 124 part-time (69 women); includes 57 minority (4 Black or African American, non-Hispanic/Latino; 1 American Indian or Alaska Native, non-Hispanic/Latino; 49 Asian, non-Hispanic/Latino; 3 Two or more races, non-Hispanic/Latino), 25 international. In 2013, 34 master's, 14 doctorates awarded. *Entrance requirements:* For master's, minimum undergraduate GPA of 3.0; for doctorate, master's degree or equivalent, 3 years of cross-cultural experience, minimum graduate GPA of 3.3. Additional exam requirements/recommendations for international students: Required—TOEFL. *Application deadline:* For fall admission, 7/1 for domestic students, 6/1 for international students; for spring admission, 12/1 for domestic students. Applications are processed on a rolling basis. Application fee: $55. Electronic applications accepted. *Financial support:* Scholarships/grants available. Support available to part-time students. Financial award applicants required to submit FAFSA. *Faculty research:* Linguistics, anthropology, intercultural studies, teaching English to speakers of other languages. *Unit head:* Dr. F. Douglas Pennoyer, Dean, 562-903-4844. *Application contact:* Graduate Admissions Office, 562-903-4752, E-mail: graduate.admissions@biola.edu. Website: http://cook.biola.edu.

Biola University, School of Education, La Mirada, CA 90639-0001. Offers apologetics (MA Ed); curriculum and instruction (MA Ed, MAT, Certificate); early childhood (MA Ed, MAT); history and philosophy of science (MA Ed, MAT); linguistics and inter-cultural studies (MAT); linguistics and international studies (MA Ed); multiple subject (MAT); single subject (MAT); special education (MA Ed, MAT, Certificate); TESOL (MA Ed, MAT). Part-time and evening/weekend programs available. Postbaccalaureate distance learning degree programs offered (no on-campus study). *Faculty:* 14. *Students:* 51 full-time (38 women), 101 part-time (83 women); includes 47 minority (8 Black or African American, non-Hispanic/Latino; 1 American Indian or Alaska Native, non-Hispanic/Latino; 32 Asian, non-Hispanic/Latino; 6 Two or more races, non-Hispanic/Latino), 4 international. In 2013, 33 master's awarded. *Entrance requirements:* For master's, CBEST, CSET. Additional exam requirements/recommendations for international students: Required—TOEFL (minimum score 100 iBT). *Application deadline:* For fall admission, 7/1 for domestic students, 6/1 for international students; for spring admission, 12/1 for domestic students; for summer admission, 5/1 for domestic students. Applications are processed on a rolling basis. Application fee: $55. Electronic applications accepted. *Financial support:* Scholarships/grants available. Support available to part-time students. Financial award applicants required to submit FAFSA. *Faculty research:* Early childhood education, elementary education, special education, curriculum development, teacher preparation. *Unit head:* Dr. June Hetzel, Dean, 562-903-4715. *Application contact:* Graduate Admissions Office, 562-903-4752, E-mail: graduate.admissions@biola.edu.
Website: http://education.biola.edu/.

Bishop's University, School of Education, Sherbrooke, QC J1M 0C8, Canada. Offers advanced studies in education (Diploma); education (M Ed, MA); teaching English as a second language (Certificate). Part-time programs available. Postbaccalaureate distance learning degree programs offered (minimal on-campus study). *Degree requirements:* For master's, thesis (for some programs). *Entrance requirements:* For master's, teaching license, 2 years of teaching experience. *Faculty research:* Integration of special needs students, multigrade classes/small schools, leadership in organizational development, second language acquisition.

Boricua College, Program in TESOL Education (K-12), New York, NY 10032-1560. Offers MS. Evening/weekend programs available. *Degree requirements:* For master's, thesis. *Entrance requirements:* For master's, interview by the faculty.

Brigham Young University, Graduate Studies, College of Humanities, Department of Linguistics and English Language, Provo, UT 84602. Offers linguistics (MA); teaching English as a second language (MA). Part-time programs available. *Faculty:* 22 full-time (5 women), 1 part-time/adjunct (0 women). *Students:* 37 full-time (21 women), 23 part-time (16 women); includes 1 minority (Hispanic/Latino), 12 international. Average age 29. 33 applicants, 94% accepted, 20 enrolled. In 2013, 25 master's awarded. *Degree requirements:* For master's, 2 foreign languages, thesis. *Entrance requirements:* For master's, GRE General Test, minimum GPA of 3.6 in last 60 hours of course work. Additional exam requirements/recommendations for international students: Required—TOEFL (minimum score 580 paper-based; 90 iBT), TWE. *Application deadline:* 1/15 for domestic and international students. Application fee: $50. Electronic applications accepted. *Expenses: Tuition:* Full-time $6130; part-time $340 per credit hour. Tuition and fees vary according to program and student's religious affiliation. *Financial support:* In 2013–14, 23 research assistantships with partial tuition reimbursements (averaging $2,058 per year), 8 teaching assistantships with partial tuition reimbursements (averaging $2,746 per year) were awarded; fellowships with partial tuition reimbursements, career-related internships or fieldwork, institutionally sponsored loans, scholarships/grants, tuition waivers (partial), unspecified assistantships, and student instructorships also available. Support available to part-time students. Financial award application deadline: 5/1. *Faculty research:* Teaching English to speakers of other languages, second language acquisition, computational linguistics, semiotics and semantics, computer-assisted language instruction, forensic linguistics. *Total annual research expenditures:* $30,559. *Unit head:* Dr. Diane Strong-Krause, Chair, 801-422-3970, Fax: 801-422-3970, E-mail: diane_strong-krause@byu.edu. *Application contact:* LoriAnne Spear, Secretary, 801-422-9010, Fax: 801-422-9010, E-mail: lorianne_spear@byu.edu.
Website: http://linguistics.byu.edu/.

Brock University, Faculty of Graduate Studies, Faculty of Humanities, Program in Applied Linguistics, St. Catharines, ON L2S 3A1, Canada. Offers MA. Part-time programs available. *Degree requirements:* For master's, thesis optional. *Entrance requirements:* For master's, honours degree with a background in English, English linguistics, teaching English as a second language, or a comparable field. Additional exam requirements/recommendations for international students: Required—TOEFL (minimum score 630 paper-based; 109 iBT), IELTS (minimum score 8), TWE (minimum score 5.5). Electronic applications accepted. *Expenses:* Contact institution. *Faculty research:* Metalinguistic ability in subsequent language learning, language teaching methodology, forensic linguistics, philosophy of education, culturally appropriate pedagogy.

Brown University, Graduate School, Department of Portuguese and Brazilian Studies, Providence, RI 02912. Offers Brazilian studies (AM); English as a second language and cross-cultural studies (AM); Portuguese and Brazilian studies (AM, PhD); Portuguese bilingual education and cross-cultural studies (AM). *Degree requirements:* For doctorate, thesis/dissertation.

Buena Vista University, School of Education, Storm Lake, IA 50588. Offers curriculum and instruction (M Ed), including effective teaching, TESL; school guidance and counseling (MS Ed). Program offered in summer only. Part-time and evening/weekend programs available. Postbaccalaureate distance learning degree programs offered (minimal on-campus study). *Degree requirements:* For master's, thesis, fieldwork/practicum, capstone portfolio. *Entrance requirements:* For master's, Analytical Writing Assessment (in-house), minimum undergraduate GPA of 2.75. Electronic applications accepted. *Faculty research:* Reading, curriculum, educational psychology, special education.

California Baptist University, Program in Education, Riverside, CA 92504-3206. Offers educational leadership for faith-based institutions (MS); educational leadership for public institutions (MS); educational technology (MS); instructional computer applications (MS); international education (MS); leadership and adult learning (MS); leadership and organizational studies (MS); reading (MS); school counseling (MS); school psychology (MS); science education (MS); special education in mild/moderate disabilities (MS); special education in moderate/severe disabilities (MS); teaching (MS); teaching and learning (MS); TESOL (teachers of English to speakers of other languages) (MS). Part-time and evening/weekend programs available. Postbaccalaureate distance learning degree programs offered (minimal on-campus study). *Faculty:* 18 full-time (9 women), 8 part-time/adjunct (5 women). *Students:* 158 full-time (127 women), 228 part-time (179 women); includes 159 minority (27 Black or African American, non-Hispanic/Latino; 4 American Indian or Alaska Native, non-Hispanic/Latino; 13 Asian, non-Hispanic/Latino; 107 Hispanic/Latino; 1 Native Hawaiian or other Pacific Islander, non-Hispanic/Latino; 7 Two or more races, non-Hispanic/Latino), 2 international. Average age 33. 298 applicants, 74% accepted, 113 enrolled. In 2013, 70 master's awarded. *Degree requirements:* For master's, comprehensive exam, project, or thesis. *Entrance requirements:* For master's, minimum undergraduate GPA of 3.0; 18 semester units of prerequisite course work in education; three recommendations; 500-word essay; interview. Additional exam requirements/recommendations for international students: Required—TOEFL (minimum score 80 iBT). *Application deadline:* For fall admission, 8/1 priority date for domestic students, 7/1 for international students; for spring admission, 12/1 priority date for domestic students, 11/1 for international students. Applications are processed on a rolling basis. Application fee: $45. Electronic applications accepted. *Expenses:* Contact institution. *Financial support:* Institutionally sponsored loans available. Financial award applicants required to submit CSS PROFILE or FAFSA. *Faculty research:* Leadership development, complexity theory, faith and learning, special education, social and philosophical contexts of education. *Unit head:* Dr. John Shoup, Dean, School of Education, 951-343-4205, Fax: 951-343-4516, E-mail: jshoup@calbaptist.edu. *Application contact:* Dr. Kathryn Norwood, Director, Master of Science Program in Education, 951-343-4760, E-mail: knorwood@calbaptist.edu.
Website: http://www.calbaptist.edu/mastersined/.

California Baptist University, Program in English, Riverside, CA 92504-3206. Offers English pedagogy (MA); literature (MA); teaching English to speakers of other languages (TESOL) (MA). Part-time and evening/weekend programs available. *Faculty:* 8 full-time (5 women), 1 (woman) part-time/adjunct. *Students:* 1 (woman) full-time, 21 part-time (17 women); includes 5 minority (1 Black or African American, non-Hispanic/Latino; 1 Asian, non-Hispanic/Latino; 3 Hispanic/Latino), 1 international. Average age 31. 8 applicants, 75% accepted, 3 enrolled. In 2013, 7 master's awarded. *Degree requirements:* For master's, comprehensive exam, research thesis, or project. *Entrance requirements:* For master's, minimum undergraduate GPA of 3.0; 18 semester hours of course work in English beyond freshman level; three recommendations; essay; demonstration of writing; interview. Additional exam requirements/recommendations for international students: Required—TOEFL (minimum score 80 iBT). *Application deadline:* For fall admission, 8/1 priority date for domestic students, 7/1 for international students; for spring admission, 12/1 priority date for domestic students, 11/1 for international students. Applications are processed on a rolling basis. Application fee: $45. Electronic applications accepted. *Expenses:* Contact institution. *Financial support:* Institutionally sponsored loans available. Financial award applicants required to submit CSS PROFILE or FAFSA. *Faculty research:* Classical mythology and folklore, multicultural literature, genre studies, science fiction and fantasy literature, intercultural rhetoric. *Unit head:* Dr. Gayne Anacker, Dean, College of Arts and Sciences, 951-343-4682, E-mail: ganacker@calbaptist.edu. *Application contact:* Dr. Jennifer Newton, Director, Master of Arts Program in English, 951-343-4276, Fax: 951-343-4661, E-mail: jnewton@calbaptist.edu.
Website: http://www.calbaptist.edu/maenglish/.

California State University, Chico, Office of Graduate Studies, College of Communication and Education, School of Education, Teaching English Learners and Special Education Advising Patterns Program, Chico, CA 95929-0722. Offers special education (MA); teaching English learners (MA). Part-time and evening/weekend programs available. *Degree requirements:* For master's, comprehensive exam, thesis or project. *Entrance requirements:* Additional exam requirements/recommendations for international students: Required—TOEFL (minimum score 550 paper-based; 80 iBT), IELTS (minimum score 6.5), PTE (minimum score 59). Electronic applications accepted.

California State University, Dominguez Hills, College of Arts and Humanities, Department of English, Carson, CA 90747-0001. Offers English (MA); rhetoric and composition (Certificate); teaching English as a second language (Certificate). Part-time and evening/weekend programs available. *Faculty:* 9 full-time (3 women). *Students:* 29 full-time (19 women), 58 part-time (37 women); includes 47 minority (8 Black or African American, non-Hispanic/Latino; 2 American Indian or Alaska Native, non-Hispanic/Latino; 13 Asian, non-Hispanic/Latino; 22 Hispanic/Latino; 2 Two or more races, non-Hispanic/Latino), 6 international. Average age 37. 42 applicants, 83% accepted, 22 enrolled. In 2013, 18 master's awarded. *Degree requirements:* For master's, comprehensive exam (for some programs), thesis or alternative. *Entrance requirements:* For master's, minimum GPA of 3.0 in last 60 units. Additional exam requirements/recommendations for international students: Required—TOEFL (minimum score 550 paper-based). *Application deadline:* Applications are processed on a rolling basis. Application fee: $55. Electronic applications accepted. *Expenses:* Tuition, state resident: full-time $6738. Tuition, nonresident: full-time $13,434. *Required fees:* $622. *Faculty research:* Gender studies, transnationalism, discourse analysis, visual culture, Shakespeare. *Unit head:* Dr. Cyril E. Zoerner, Chair, 310-243-3322, E-mail: ezoerner@csudh.edu. *Application contact:* Brandy McLelland, Director of Student Information Services and Registrar, 310-243-3645, E-mail: bmclelland@csudh.edu.
Website: http://cah.csudh.edu/english/.

California State University, East Bay, Office of Academic Programs and Graduate Studies, College of Letters, Arts, and Social Sciences, Department of English, Hayward, CA 94542-3000. Offers creative writing (MA); literary studies (MA); teaching English to speakers of other languages (MA). Part-time programs available. *Degree requirements:* For master's, one foreign language, comprehensive exam, thesis optional. *Entrance requirements:* For master's, minimum GPA of 3.0 in field; 2 letters of recommendation; academic or professional writing sample; preferred teaching experience and some degree of bilingualism (for TESOL). Additional exam requirements/recommendations for international students: Required—TOEFL (minimum score 550 paper-based); Recommended—IELTS (minimum score 6.5). Electronic applications accepted.

California State University, Fresno, Division of Graduate Studies, College of Arts and Humanities, Department of Linguistics, Fresno, CA 93740-8027. Offers linguistics (MA), including Teaching English as a second language. Part-time and evening/weekend programs available. *Degree requirements:* For master's, comprehensive exam. *Entrance requirements:* For master's, GRE General Test, minimum GPA of 3.0. Additional exam requirements/recommendations for international students: Required—TOEFL. Electronic applications accepted. *Faculty research:* Communication systems, bilingual education, animal communication, conflict resolution, literacy programs.

California State University, Fullerton, Graduate Studies, College of Humanities and Social Sciences, Department of Modern Languages and Literatures, Fullerton, CA 92834-9480. Offers French (MA); German (MA); Spanish (MA); teaching English to speakers of other languages (MS). Part-time programs available. *Students:* 56 full-time (35 women), 59 part-time (48 women); includes 66 minority (15 Asian, non-Hispanic/Latino; 50 Hispanic/Latino; 1 Two or more races, non-Hispanic/Latino), 20 international. Average age 31. 97 applicants, 69% accepted, 45 enrolled. In 2013, 43 master's awarded. *Degree requirements:* For master's, comprehensive exam, thesis or alternative. *Entrance requirements:* For master's, minimum GPA of 2.5 in last 60 hours of course work, undergraduate major in a language. Application fee: $55. *Financial support:* Career-related internships or fieldwork, Federal Work-Study, institutionally sponsored loans, and scholarships/grants available. Support available to part-time students. Financial award application deadline: 3/1; financial award applicants required to submit FAFSA. *Unit head:* Dr. Reyes Fidalgo, Chair, 657-278-4563. *Application contact:* Admissions/Applications, 657-278-2371.

California State University, Long Beach, Graduate Studies, College of Liberal Arts, Department of Linguistics, Long Beach, CA 90840. Offers general linguistics (MA); language and culture (MA); special concentration (MA); teaching English to speakers of other languages (MA). Part-time and evening/weekend programs available. *Degree requirements:* For master's, one foreign language, comprehensive exam, thesis optional. Electronic applications accepted. *Faculty research:* Pedagogy of language instruction, role of language in society, Khmer language instruction.

California State University, Sacramento, Office of Graduate Studies, College of Arts and Letters, Department of English, Sacramento, CA 95819. Offers composition (MA); creative writing (MA); literature (MA); teaching English to speakers of other languages (MA). Part-time programs available. *Degree requirements:* For master's, thesis, project, or comprehensive exam; TESOL exam; writing proficiency exam. *Entrance requirements:* For master's, portfolio (creative writing); minimum GPA of 3.0 in English, 2.75 overall during previous 2 years. Additional exam requirements/recommendations for international students: Required—TOEFL. *Application deadline:* For fall admission, 2/15 for domestic students, 3/1 for international students; for spring admission, 9/30 for international students. Applications are processed on a rolling basis. Application fee: $55. Electronic applications accepted. *Financial support:* Research assistantships, teaching assistantships, career-related internships or fieldwork, and Federal Work-Study available. Support available to part-time students. Financial award application deadline: 3/1; financial award applicants required to submit FAFSA. *Faculty research:* Teaching composition, remedial writing. *Unit head:* David Toise, Chair, 916-278-6586, E-mail: dwtoise@csus.edu. *Application contact:* Jose Martinez, Graduate Admissions Supervisor, 916-278-7871, E-mail: martinj@skymail.csus.edu.
Website: http://www.csus.edu/engl.

California State University, San Bernardino, Graduate Studies, College of Education, San Bernardino, CA 92407-2397. Offers bilingual/cross-cultural education (MA); curriculum and instruction (MA); educational administration (MA); educational leadership and curriculum (Ed D); educational psychology and counseling (MA, MS), including correctional and alternative education (MA), counseling and guidance (MS), rehabilitation counseling (MA); English as a second language (MA); general education (MA); history and English for secondary teachers (MA); instructional technology (MA); reading (MA); secondary education (MA); special education and rehabilitation counseling (MA), including rehabilitation counseling, special education; teaching of science (MA); vocational and career education (MA). *Accreditation:* NCATE. Part-time and evening/weekend programs available. *Students:* 217 full-time (172 women), 353 part-time (263 women); includes 283 minority (41 Black or African American, non-Hispanic/Latino; 1 American Indian or Alaska Native, non-Hispanic/Latino; 21 Asian, non-Hispanic/Latino; 204 Hispanic/Latino; 1 Native Hawaiian or other Pacific Islander, non-Hispanic/Latino; 15 Two or more races, non-Hispanic/Latino), 35 international. Average age 34. 349 applicants, 76% accepted, 207 enrolled. In 2013, 215 master's awarded. *Degree requirements:* For master's, comprehensive exam (for some programs), thesis (for some programs), advancement to candidacy. *Entrance requirements:* For master's, minimum GPA of 3.0 in education. *Application deadline:* For fall admission, 8/31 priority date for domestic students. Application fee: $55. *Financial support:* Career-related internships or fieldwork and Federal Work-Study available. Support available to part-time students. *Faculty research:* Multicultural education, brain-based learning, science education, social studies/global education. *Unit head:* Dr. Jay Fiene, Dean, 909-537-5600, Fax: 909-537-7011, E-mail: jfiene@csusb.edu. *Application contact:* Dr. Jeffrey Thompson, Dean of Graduate Studies, 909-537-5808, E-mail: jthompso@csusb.edu.

California State University, Stanislaus, College of Humanities and Social Sciences, Program in English (MA), Turlock, CA 95382. Offers literature (Certificate); rhetoric and teaching writing (MA); teaching English to speakers of other languages (MA). Part-time programs available. *Degree requirements:* For master's, comprehensive exam, thesis or alternative. *Entrance requirements:* For master's, GRE, minimum GPA of 3.0, 2 letters of reference, personal statement. Additional exam requirements/recommendations for international students: Required—TOEFL (minimum score 575 paper-based), TWE (minimum score 4). Electronic applications accepted. *Faculty research:* Transnational literacies, Renaissance and medieval literature, abolition writings and slave narratives, qualitative writing.

Cambridge College, School of Education, Cambridge, MA 02138-5304. Offers autism specialist (M Ed); autism/behavior analyst (M Ed); behavior analyst (Post-Master's Certificate); behavioral management (M Ed); early childhood teacher (M Ed); education specialist in curriculum and instruction (CAGS); educational leadership (Ed D); elementary teacher (M Ed); English as a second language (M Ed, Certificate); general science (M Ed); health education (Post-Master's Certificate); health/family and consumer sciences (M Ed); history (M Ed); individualized (M Ed); information technology literacy (M Ed); instructional technology (M Ed); interdisciplinary studies (M Ed); library teacher (M Ed); literacy education (M Ed); mathematics (M Ed); mathematics specialist (Certificate); middle school mathematics and science (M Ed); school administration (M Ed, CAGS); school guidance counselor (M Ed); school nurse education (M Ed); school social worker/school adjustment counselor (M Ed); special education administrator (CAGS); special education/moderate disabilities (M Ed); teaching skills and methodologies (M Ed). Part-time and evening/weekend programs available. Postbaccalaureate distance learning degree programs offered (minimal on-campus study). *Degree requirements:* For master's, thesis, internship/practicum (licensure program only); for doctorate, thesis/dissertation; for other advanced degree, thesis. *Entrance requirements:* For master's, interview, resume, documentation of licensure, 2 professional references; for doctorate, official transcripts, interview, resume, documentation of licensure (if any), written personal statement/essay, portfolio of scholarly and professional work, qualifying assessment, 2 professional references, health insurance, immunizations form; for other advanced degree, official transcripts, interview, resume, documentation of licensure (if any), written personal statement/essay, 2 professional references, health insurance, immunizations form. Additional exam requirements/recommendations for international students: Required—TOEFL (minimum score 550 paper-based; 79 iBT), Michigan English Language Assessment Battery (minimum score 85); Recommended—IELTS (minimum score 6). Electronic applications accepted. *Expenses:* Contact institution. *Faculty research:* Adult education, accelerated learning, mathematics education, brain compatible learning, special education and law.

Canisius College, Graduate Division, School of Education and Human Services, Department of Graduate Education and Leadership, Buffalo, NY 14208-1098. Offers business and marketing education (MS Ed); college student personnel (MS Ed); deaf education (MS Ed); deaf/adolescent education, grades 7-12 (MS Ed); deaf/childhood education, grades 1-6 (MS Ed); differentiated instruction (MS Ed); education administration (MS); educational administration (MS); educational technologies (Certificate); gifted education extension (Certificate); literacy (MS Ed); reading (Certificate); school building leadership (MS Ed, Certificate); school district leadership (Certificate); teacher leader (Certificate); TESOL (MS Ed). *Accreditation:* NCATE. Part-time and evening/weekend programs available. Postbaccalaureate distance learning degree programs offered (minimal on-campus study). *Faculty:* 6 full-time (5 women), 33 part-time/adjunct (20 women). *Students:* 134 full-time (106 women), 267 part-time (213 women); includes 36 minority (22 Black or African American, non-Hispanic/Latino; 1 American Indian or Alaska Native, non-Hispanic/Latino; 3 Asian, non-Hispanic/Latino; 8 Hispanic/Latino; 2 Two or more races, non-Hispanic/Latino), 2 international. Average age 30. 282 applicants, 80% accepted, 120 enrolled. In 2013, 178 master's awarded. *Entrance requirements:* For master's, GRE if cumulative GPA less than 2.7, transcripts, two letters of recommendation. Additional exam requirements/recommendations for international students: Required—TOEFL (minimum score 550 paper-based, 80 iBT), IELTS (minimum score 6.5), or CAEL (minimum score 70). *Application deadline:* Applications are processed on a rolling basis. Application fee: $25. Electronic applications accepted. Application fee is waived when completed online. *Expenses: Tuition:* Part-time $750 per credit hour. *Financial support:* Career-related internships or fieldwork, Federal Work-Study, scholarships/grants, tuition waivers (partial), and unspecified assistantships available. Support available to part-time students. Financial award application deadline: 4/30; financial award applicants required to submit FAFSA. *Faculty research:* Asperger's disease, autism, private higher education, reading strategies. *Unit head:* Dr. Rosemary K. Murray, Chair/Associate Professor of Graduate Education and Leadership, 716-888-3723, E-mail: murray1@canisius.edu. *Application contact:* Julie A. Zulewski, Director of Graduate Admissions, 716-888-2548, Fax: 716-888-3195, E-mail: zulewskj@canisius.edu.
Website: http://www.canisius.edu/graduate/.

Cardinal Stritch University, College of Education, Department of Literacy, Milwaukee, WI 53217-3985. Offers literacy/English as a second language (MA); reading/language arts (MA); reading/learning disability (MA). *Accreditation:* NCATE. Part-time and evening/weekend programs available. *Degree requirements:* For master's, comprehensive exam, thesis, faculty recommendation, research project. *Entrance requirements:* For master's, letters of recommendation (2), minimum GPA of 2.75.

Carlos Albizu University, Miami Campus, Graduate Programs, Miami, FL 33172-2209. Offers clinical psychology (Psy D); entrepreneurship (MBA); exceptional student education (MS); human services (PhD); industrial/organizational psychology (MS); marriage and family therapy (MS); mental health counseling (MS); nonprofit management (MBA); organizational management (MBA); psychology (MS); school counseling (MS); teaching English as a second language (MS). *Accreditation:* APA. Part-time and evening/weekend programs available. *Faculty:* 26 full-time (20 women), 34 part-time/adjunct (16 women). *Students:* 416 full-time (335 women), 281 part-time (237 women); includes 604 minority (57 Black or African American, non-Hispanic/Latino; 1 American Indian or Alaska Native, non-Hispanic/Latino; 13 Asian, non-Hispanic/Latino; 533 Hispanic/Latino), 14 international. Average age 36. 176 applicants, 59% accepted, 96 enrolled. In 2013, 176 master's, 37 doctorates awarded. Terminal master's awarded for partial completion of doctoral program. *Degree requirements:* For master's, one foreign language, comprehensive exam, integrative project (MBA), research project (exceptional student education, teaching English as a second language); for doctorate, one foreign language, comprehensive exam, internship, project. *Entrance requirements:* For master's, 3 letters of recommendation, interview, minimum GPA of 3.0, resume, statement of purpose, official transcripts; for doctorate, 3 letters of recommendation, minimum GPA of 3.0, resume, interview, statement of purpose, official transcripts. Additional exam requirements/recommendations for international students: Required—Michigan Test of English Language Proficiency. *Application deadline:* For fall admission, 4/1 priority date for domestic students, 5/1 priority date for international students; for spring admission, 11/1 priority date for domestic students, 9/1 priority date for international students. Applications are processed on a rolling basis. Application fee: $50. Electronic applications accepted. *Expenses: Tuition:* Full-time $9360; part-time $520 per credit. *Required fees:* $298 per term. Tuition and fees vary according to course load, degree level and program. *Financial support:* In 2013–14, 62 students received support. Federal Work-Study, scholarships/grants, and tuition discounts available. Financial award application deadline: 6/1; financial award applicants required to submit FAFSA. *Faculty research:* Psychotherapy, forensic psychology, neuropsychology, marketing strategy, entrepreneurship, special education. *Unit head:* Peter M. Rubio, Interim Chancellor, 305-593-1223 Ext. 3120, Fax: 305-592-7930, E-mail: prubio@albizu.edu. *Application contact:* Vanessa Almendarez, Administrative Assistant, 305-593-1223 Ext. 3137, Fax: 305-593-1854, E-mail: valmendarez@albizu.edu.

Carson-Newman University, Graduate Program in Education, Jefferson City, TN 37760. Offers curriculum and instruction (M Ed); educational leadership (M Ed); elementary education (MAT); school counseling (MS); secondary education (MAT); teaching English as a second language (MATESL). *Accreditation:* NCATE. Part-time and evening/weekend programs available. *Faculty:* 5 full-time (2 women), 10 part-time/adjunct (3 women). *Students:* 25 full-time (12 women), 100 part-time (70 women); includes 8 minority (4 Black or African American, non-Hispanic/Latino; 1 Asian, non-Hispanic/Latino; 1 Hispanic/Latino; 2 Two or more races, non-Hispanic/Latino), 1 international. Average age 32. In 2013, 34 master's awarded. *Degree requirements:* For master's, thesis or alternative. *Entrance requirements:* For master's, NTE, minimum GPA of 3.0 in major, 2.5 overall. *Application deadline:* For fall admission, 7/15 priority

date for domestic students. Applications are processed on a rolling basis. Application fee: $25 ($50 for international students). *Expenses: Tuition:* Part-time $390 per credit hour. *Financial support:* Federal Work-Study and unspecified assistantships available. Financial award application deadline: 4/1; financial award applicants required to submit FAFSA. *Unit head:* Dr. Sharon Teets, Chair, 865-471-3461. *Application contact:* Graduate Admissions and Services Adviser, 865-471-3460, Fax: 865-471-3875.

Carson-Newman University, Program in Teaching English as a Second Language, Jefferson City, TN 37760. Offers MAT. *Expenses: Tuition:* Part-time $390 per credit hour.

Central Connecticut State University, School of Graduate Studies, School of Arts and Sciences, Department of English, Program in Teaching English to Speakers of Other Languages, New Britain, CT 06050-4010. Offers MS, Certificate. Part-time and evening/weekend programs available. *Students:* 16 full-time (12 women), 26 part-time (24 women); includes 6 minority (2 Asian, non-Hispanic/Latino; 2 Hispanic/Latino; 2 Two or more races, non-Hispanic/Latino), 2 international. Average age 47. 24 applicants, 92% accepted, 16 enrolled. In 2013, 7 master's, 1 other advanced degree awarded. *Degree requirements:* For master's, comprehensive exam, thesis or alternative; for Certificate, qualifying exam. *Entrance requirements:* For master's, minimum undergraduate GPA of 3.0, essay, letters of recommendation. Additional exam requirements/recommendations for international students: Required—TOEFL (minimum score 550 paper-based; 79 iBT). *Application deadline:* For fall admission, 6/1 for domestic students, 5/1 for international students; for spring admission, 11/1 for domestic and international students. Applications are processed on a rolling basis. Application fee: $50. Electronic applications accepted. Part-time tuition and fees vary according to degree level. *Faculty research:* Phonology, general linguistics, second language writing, East Asian languages, English language structure. *Unit head:* Dr. Stephen Cohen, Chair, 860-832-2795, E-mail: cohens@mail.ccsu.edu. *Application contact:* Patricia Gardner, Associate Director of Graduate Studies, 860-832-2350, Fax: 860-832-2362, E-mail: graduateadmissions@ccsu.edu.

Central Michigan University, College of Graduate Studies, College of Humanities and Social and Behavioral Sciences, Department of English Language and Literature, Mount Pleasant, MI 48859. Offers English composition and communication (MA); English language and literature (MA), including children's and young adult literature, creative writing, English language and literature; TESOL: teaching English to speakers of other languages (MA). Part-time and evening/weekend programs available. *Degree requirements:* For master's, thesis or alternative. Electronic applications accepted. *Faculty research:* Composition theory, science fiction history and bibliography, children's and young adult literature, nineteenth century American literature, applied linguistics.

Central Washington University, Graduate Studies and Research, College of Arts and Humanities, Department of English, Ellensburg, WA 98926. Offers English (MA); teaching English as a second language (MA). Part-time programs available. *Degree requirements:* For master's, thesis or alternative. *Entrance requirements:* For master's, GRE General Test, minimum GPA of 3.0, writing sample. Additional exam requirements/recommendations for international students: Required—TOEFL (minimum score 550 paper-based; 79 iBT) or IELTS (minimum score 6.5). Electronic applications accepted.

Christopher Newport University, Graduate Studies, Department of Teacher Preparation, Newport News, VA 23606-3072. Offers art (PK-12) (MAT); biology (6-12) (MAT); chemistry (6-12) (MAT); computer science (6-12) (MAT); elementary (PK-6) (MAT); English (6-12) (MAT); English as second language (PK-12) (MAT); French (PK-12) (MAT); history and social science (6-12) (MAT); mathematics (6-12) (MAT); music (PK-12) (MAT), including choral, instrumental; physics (6-12) (MAT); Spanish (PK-12) (MAT). Part-time programs available. *Faculty:* 15 full-time (7 women), 14 part-time/adjunct (13 women). *Students:* 74 full-time (64 women), 2 part-time (both women); includes 6 minority (4 Hispanic/Latino; 2 Two or more races, non-Hispanic/Latino). Average age 23. 90 applicants, 100% accepted, 67 enrolled. In 2013, 96 master's awarded. *Degree requirements:* For master's, comprehensive exam, thesis or alternative. *Entrance requirements:* For master's, PRAXIS I, minimum GPA of 3.0. Additional exam requirements/recommendations for international students: Required—TOEFL (minimum score 580 paper-based; 92 iBT). *Application deadline:* For fall admission, 4/1 for international students; for spring admission, 10/15 for domestic students, 10/1 for international students; for summer admission, 1/15 for domestic students, 3/1 for international students. Applications are processed on a rolling basis. Application fee: $50. Electronic applications accepted. *Expenses: Tuition, area resident:* Part-time $498 per credit hour. Tuition, state resident: part-time $498 per credit hour. Tuition, nonresident: part-time $899 per credit hour. *Financial support:* In 2013–14, 3 students received support, including 3 research assistantships with full tuition reimbursements available (averaging $2,000 per year); career-related internships or fieldwork, Federal Work-Study, and unspecified assistantships also available. Financial award application deadline: 3/1; financial award applicants required to submit FAFSA. *Faculty research:* Early literacy development, instructional innovations, professional teaching standards, multicultural issues, aesthetic education. *Total annual research expenditures:* $24,000. *Unit head:* Dr. Marsha Sprague, Director, 757-594-7388, Fax: 757-594-7803, E-mail: msprague@cnu.edu. *Application contact:* Lyn Sawyer, Associate Director, Graduate Admissions, 757-594-7544, Fax: 757-594-7649, E-mail: gradstdy@cnu.edu.

Cleveland State University, College of Graduate Studies, College of Education and Human Services, Department of Teacher Education, Cleveland, OH 44115. Offers art education (M Ed); early childhood education (M Ed); foreign language education (M Ed); mathematics and science education (M Ed); middle childhood education (M Ed); special education (M Ed), including mild/moderate disabilities, moderate/intensive disabilities; teaching English to speakers of other languages (M Ed). Part-time and evening/weekend programs available. *Faculty:* 20 full-time (12 women), 26 part-time/adjunct (20 women). *Students:* 108 full-time (78 women), 311 part-time (252 women); includes 103 minority (80 Black or African American, non-Hispanic/Latino; 2 Asian, non-Hispanic/Latino; 10 Hispanic/Latino; 1 Native Hawaiian or other Pacific Islander, non-Hispanic/Latino; 10 Two or more races, non-Hispanic/Latino), 52 international. Average age 32. 177 applicants, 55% accepted, 68 enrolled. In 2013, 192 master's awarded. *Degree requirements:* For master's, comprehensive exam (for some programs), thesis or alternative. *Entrance requirements:* For master's, GRE General Test or MAT, minimum GPA of 2.75. Additional exam requirements/recommendations for international students: Required—TOEFL (minimum score 525 paper-based), IELTS (minimum score 6). *Application deadline:* For fall admission, 7/15 priority date for domestic students. Applications are processed on a rolling basis. Application fee: $30. *Expenses: Tuition, state resident: full-time $8335; part-time $521 per credit hour. Tuition, nonresident: full-time $15,670; part-time $979 per credit hour. Required fees: $50; $25 per semester. *Financial support:* In 2013–14, 12 research assistantships with full tuition reimbursements (averaging $3,480 per year) were awarded; tuition waivers (partial) and unspecified assistantships also available. *Faculty research:* Early literacy, professional development in reading, reading recovery, dual language, induction programs. *Total annual research expenditures:* $6.2 million. *Unit head:* Dr. Clifford T. Bennett, Chairperson, 216-523-7105, Fax: 216-687-5379, E-mail: c.t.bennett@csuohio.edu.

Application contact: Deborah L. Brown, Interim Assistant Director, Graduate Admissions, 216-523-7572, E-mail: d.l.brown@csuohio.edu. Website: http://www.csuohio.edu/cehs/departments/TE/te_dept.html.

College of Charleston, Graduate School, School of Education, Health, and Human Performance, Program in English to Speakers of Other Languages, Charleston, SC 29424-0001. Offers Certificate. Part-time programs available. Postbaccalaureate distance learning degree programs offered (minimal on-campus study). *Entrance requirements:* Additional exam requirements/recommendations for international students: Required—TOEFL (minimum score 81 iBT). Electronic applications accepted.

The College of New Jersey, Graduate Studies, School of Education, Department of Special Education, Language and Literacy, Program in Teaching English as a Second Language, Ewing, NJ 08628. Offers English as a second language (M Ed); teaching English as a second language (Certificate). *Accreditation:* NCATE. Part-time programs available. *Degree requirements:* For master's, comprehensive exam. *Entrance requirements:* For master's, GRE General Test, minimum GPA of 3.0 in field or 2.75 overall. Additional exam requirements/recommendations for international students: Required—TOEFL. Electronic applications accepted.

The College of New Rochelle, Graduate School, Division of Education, Program in Teaching English as a Second Language and Multilingual/Multicultural Education, New Rochelle, NY 10805-2308. Offers bilingual education (Certificate); teaching English as a second language (MS Ed). Part-time and evening/weekend programs available. *Degree requirements:* For master's, practicum. *Entrance requirements:* For master's, interview, minimum GPA of 3.0 in field, 2.7 overall. *Expenses: Tuition:* Part-time $894 per credit. *Required fees:* $300 per semester. One-time fee: $200. Tuition and fees vary according to course load.

College of Saint Mary, Program in Education, Omaha, NE 68106. Offers assessment leadership (MSE); English as a second language (MSE). Part-time programs available. *Entrance requirements:* For master's, technology competency test or equivalent, minimum cumulative GPA of 3.0, teaching certificate, 2 letters of reference, resume.

Colorado Mesa University, Center for Teacher Education, Grand Junction, CO 81501-3122. Offers educational leadership (MAEd); English for speakers of other languages (MAEd). *Accreditation:* NCATE. Part-time programs available. Postbaccalaureate distance learning degree programs offered (minimal on-campus study). *Degree requirements:* For master's, comprehensive exam, capstone presentation. *Entrance requirements:* For master's, GRE, 2 professional letters of recommendation. Additional exam requirements/recommendations for international students: Required—TOEFL (minimum score 550 paper-based). Electronic applications accepted.

Columbia International University, Columbia Graduate School, Columbia, SC 29230-3122. Offers Bible teaching (MABT); Christian higher education leadership (Ed D); Christian school educational leadership (Ed D); counseling (MACN); curriculum and instruction (M Ed), including Christian school guidance, English as a second language, learning disabilities, school technology; early childhood and elementary education (MAT); educational administration (M Ed); teaching English as a foreign language (Certificate); teaching English as a foreign language and intercultural studies (MATF). Part-time and evening/weekend programs available. *Degree requirements:* For master's, internships, professional project. *Entrance requirements:* For master's, Minnesota Multiphasic Personality Inventory, MAT, minimum GPA of 2.7. Additional exam requirements/recommendations for international students: Required—TOEFL. Electronic applications accepted.

Columbus State University, Graduate Studies, College of Letters and Sciences, Columbus, GA 31907-5645. Offers earth and space science (MS), including environmental science; history and geography (MA), including history; political science (MPA), including public administration; public safety administration (MS); teaching English as a second language (Certificate). Part-time and evening/weekend programs available. Postbaccalaureate distance learning degree programs offered (no on-campus study). *Faculty:* 12 full-time (2 women), 12 part-time/adjunct (2 women). *Students:* 93 full-time (48 women), 203 part-time (89 women); includes 138 minority (121 Black or African American, non-Hispanic/Latino; 2 American Indian or Alaska Native, non-Hispanic/Latino; 4 Asian, non-Hispanic/Latino; 6 Hispanic/Latino; 5 Two or more races, non-Hispanic/Latino), 2 international. Average age 37. 197 applicants, 64% accepted, 99 enrolled. In 2013, 120 master's awarded. *Entrance requirements:* For master's, GRE General Test. Additional exam requirements/recommendations for international students: Required—TOEFL (minimum score 550 paper-based; 79 iBT). *Application deadline:* For fall admission, 6/30 for domestic students, 5/1 for international students; for spring admission, 11/1 for domestic students, 4/1 for international students; for summer admission, 3/1 for domestic and international students. Applications are processed on a rolling basis. Application fee: $40. Electronic applications accepted. *Expenses:* Tuition, state resident: full-time $4572; part-time $382 per credit hour. Tuition, nonresident: full-time $18,292; part-time $1526 per credit hour. *Required fees:* $1800; $196 per credit hour. Tuition and fees vary according to campus/location and program. *Financial support:* In 2013–14, 141 students received support, including 22 research assistantships with tuition reimbursements available (averaging $3,000 per year); career-related internships or fieldwork, Federal Work-Study, institutionally sponsored loans, scholarships/grants, tuition waivers (partial), and unspecified assistantships also available. Support available to part-time students. Financial award application deadline: 5/1; financial award applicants required to submit FAFSA. *Unit head:* Dr. James Pat McHenry, Interim Dean, 706-568-2056, E-mail: lanoue_david@colstate.edu. *Application contact:* Kristin Williams, Director of International and Graduate Recruitment, 706-507-8848, Fax: 706-568-5091, E-mail: williams_kristin@columbusstate.edu.
Website: http://cols.columbusstate.edu/.

Concordia University, College of Education, Portland, OR 97211-6099. Offers career and technical education (M Ed); curriculum and instruction (M Ed), including adolescent literacy, career and technical education, e-learning/technology education, early childhood education, English for speakers of other languages, English language development, environmental education, mathematics, methods and curriculum, reading, science, teacher leadership, the inclusive classroom; early childhood (MAT); education leadership (Ed D); educational administration (M Ed); elementary education (MAT); secondary education (MAT); special education (M Ed); teacher leadership (Ed D). Part-time programs available. Postbaccalaureate distance learning degree programs offered (no on-campus study). *Degree requirements:* For master's, comprehensive exam, work samples/portfolio. *Entrance requirements:* For master's, California Basic Educational Skills Test or PRAXIS I, minimum undergraduate GPA of 2.8, graduate 3.0; 2 letters of recommendation. Additional exam requirements/recommendations for international students: Required—TOEFL (minimum score 525 paper-based). Electronic applications accepted. *Faculty research:* Learner-centered classroom, brain-based learning, future of online learning.

Concordia University, School of Graduate Studies, Faculty of Arts and Science, Department of Education, Program in Applied Linguistics, Montréal, QC H3G 1M8, Canada. Offers applied linguistics (MA); teaching English as a second language (Certificate).

Cornerstone University, Graduate Programs, Grand Rapids, MI 49525-5897. Offers business administration (MBA); education (MA Ed); management (MSM); teaching English to speakers of other languages (MA, Graduate Certificate). Programs also offered at Holland, Kalamazoo, and Troy, MI campuses. Part-time programs available. Postbaccalaureate distance learning degree programs offered. *Degree requirements:* For master's, comprehensive exam (for some programs), thesis (for some programs). *Entrance requirements:* For master's, minimum GPA of 2.5, 2 letters of reference. Additional exam requirements/recommendations for international students: Required—TOEFL (minimum score 575 paper-based). Electronic applications accepted.

Dallas Baptist University, Dorothy M. Bush College of Education, Program in Reading and English as a Second Language, Dallas, TX 75211-9299. Offers bilingual education (M Ed); English as a second language (M Ed); master reading teacher (M Ed); reading specialist (M Ed). Part-time and evening/weekend programs available. *Entrance requirements:* For master's, GRE General Test, minimum GPA of 3.0. Additional exam requirements/recommendations for international students: Required—TOEFL, IELTS. Application fee: $25. *Expenses: Tuition:* Full-time $13,410; part-time $745 per credit hour. *Required fees:* $300; $150 per semester. Tuition and fees vary according to degree level. *Financial support:* Federal Work-Study, institutionally sponsored loans, scholarships/grants, and tuition waivers (full and partial) available. Support available to part-time students. Financial award applicants required to submit FAFSA. *Unit head:* Amie Sarker, Director, 214-333-5200, Fax: 214-333-5551, E-mail: graduate@dbu.edu. *Application contact:* Kit P. Montgomery, Director of Graduate Programs, 214-333-5242, Fax: 214-333-5579, E-mail: graduate@dbu.edu.
Website: http://www3.dbu.edu/graduate/english_reading.asp.

Dallas Baptist University, Dorothy M. Bush College of Education, Teaching Program, Dallas, TX 75211-9299. Offers distance learning (MAT); early childhood (MAT); elementary (MAT); English as a second language (MAT); Montessori (MAT); multisensory (MAT); secondary (MAT). Part-time and evening/weekend programs available. *Entrance requirements:* For master's, GRE General Test, minimum GPA of 3.0. Additional exam requirements/recommendations for international students: Required—TOEFL, IELTS. *Application deadline:* Applications are processed on a rolling basis. Application fee: $25. Electronic applications accepted. *Expenses: Tuition:* Full-time $13,410; part-time $745 per credit hour. *Required fees:* $300; $150 per semester. Tuition and fees vary according to degree level. *Financial support:* Federal Work-Study, institutionally sponsored loans, scholarships/grants, and tuition waivers (full and partial) available. Support available to part-time students. Financial award applicants required to submit FAFSA. *Unit head:* Dr. Carolyn Spain, Director, 214-333-5217, E-mail: graduate@dbu.edu. *Application contact:* Kit P. Montgomery, Director of Graduate Programs, 214-333-5242, Fax: 214-333-5579, E-mail: graduate@dbu.edu.
Website: http://www3.dbu.edu/graduate/mat.asp.

Dallas Baptist University, Gary Cook School of Leadership, Program in Global Leadership, Dallas, TX 75211-9299. Offers business communication (MA); East Asian studies (MA); ESL (MA); general studies (MA); global leadership (MA); global studies (MA); international business (MA); leading the nonprofit organization (MA); missions (MA); small group ministry (MA); MA/MA. Part-time and evening/weekend programs available. *Entrance requirements:* For master's, minimum GPA of 3.0. Additional exam requirements/recommendations for international students: Required—TOEFL, IELTS. Application fee: $25. *Expenses: Tuition:* Full-time $13,410; part-time $745 per credit hour. *Required fees:* $300; $150 per semester. Tuition and fees vary according to degree level. *Financial support:* Federal Work-Study, institutionally sponsored loans, scholarships/grants, and tuition waivers (full and partial) available. Support available to part-time students. Financial award applicants required to submit FAFSA. *Unit head:* Dr. Bob Garrett, Director, 214-333-5508, Fax: 214-333-5689, E-mail: graduate@dbu.edu. *Application contact:* Kit P. Montgomery, Director of Graduate Programs, 214-333-5242, Fax: 214-333-5579, E-mail: graduate@dbu.edu.
Website: http://www3.dbu.edu/leadership/globalleadership.asp.

Dallas Baptist University, Liberal Arts Program, Dallas, TX 75211-9299. Offers arts (MLA); Christian ministry (MLA); East Asian studies (MLA); English (MLA); English as a second language (MLA); fine arts (MLA); history (MLA); missions (MLA); political science (MLA). Part-time and evening/weekend programs available. *Entrance requirements:* For master's, minimum GPA of 3.0. Additional exam requirements/recommendations for international students: Required—TOEFL. *Application deadline:* Applications are processed on a rolling basis. Application fee: $25. Electronic applications accepted. *Expenses: Tuition:* Full-time $13,410; part-time $745 per credit hour. *Required fees:* $300; $150 per semester. Tuition and fees vary according to degree level. *Financial support:* Federal Work-Study, institutionally sponsored loans, scholarships/grants, and tuition waivers (full and partial) available. Support available to part-time students. Financial award applicants required to submit FAFSA. *Faculty research:* Milton and seventeenth century Puritans, inter-Biblical years, nineteenth century literature, Latin American and Texas history. *Unit head:* Angela Fogle, Director, 214-333-6830, Fax: 214-333-5558, E-mail: graduate@dbu.edu. *Application contact:* Kit P. Montgomery, Director of Graduate Programs, 214-333-5242, Fax: 214-333-5579, E-mail: graduate@dbu.edu.
Website: http://www3.dbu.edu/graduate/mla.asp.

Dallas Baptist University, Professional Development Program, Dallas, TX 75211-9299. Offers counseling (MA); criminal justice (MA); English as a second language (MA); higher education (MA); interdisciplinary (MA); leadership studies (MA); missions (MA); professional life coaching (MA); training and development (MA). Part-time and evening/weekend programs available. *Entrance requirements:* For master's, minimum GPA of 3.0. Additional exam requirements/recommendations for international students: Required—TOEFL, IELTS. Application fee: $25. *Expenses: Tuition:* Full-time $13,410; part-time $745 per credit hour. *Required fees:* $300; $150 per semester. Tuition and fees vary according to degree level. *Financial support:* Federal Work-Study, institutionally sponsored loans, scholarships/grants, and tuition waivers (full and partial) available. Support available to part-time students. Financial award applicants required to submit FAFSA. *Unit head:* Eric Wyatt, Director, 214-333-6830, E-mail: graduate@dbu.edu. *Application contact:* Kit P. Montgomery, Director of Graduate Programs, 214-333-5242, Fax: 214-333-5579, E-mail: graduate@dbu.edu.
Website: http://www3.dbu.edu/graduate/mapd.asp.

DeSales University, Graduate Division, Division of Liberal Arts and Social Sciences, Program in Education, Center Valley, PA 18034-9568. Offers early childhood education Pre K-4 (M Ed); instructional technology for K-12 (M Ed); interdisciplinary (M Ed); secondary education (M Ed); special education (M Ed); teaching English to speakers of other languages (M Ed). Part-time and evening/weekend programs available. Postbaccalaureate distance learning degree programs offered (no on-campus study). *Degree requirements:* For master's, thesis project. *Entrance requirements:* Additional exam requirements/recommendations for international students: Required—TOEFL. *Application deadline:* Applications are processed on a rolling basis. Electronic applications accepted. *Expenses: Tuition:* Part-time $790 per credit. *Financial support:* Application deadline: 5/1. *Unit head:* Dr. Judith Rance-Roney, Chair, 610-282-1100 Ext. 1323, E-mail: judith.rance-roney@desales.edu. *Application contact:* Abigail Wernicki, Director of Graduate Admissions, 610-282-1100 Ext. 1768, E-mail: gradadmissions@desales.edu.

Dominican University, School of Education, River Forest, IL 60305-1099. Offers curriculum and instruction (MA Ed); early childhood education (MS); education (MAT); educational administration (MA); elementary education (MA Ed); English as a second language (MA Ed); reading (MA Ed); special education (MS). Part-time and evening/weekend programs available. Postbaccalaureate distance learning degree programs offered (no on-campus study). *Faculty:* 19 full-time (14 women), 51 part-time/adjunct (42 women). *Students:* 18 full-time (13 women), 334 part-time (274 women); includes 76 minority (26 Black or African American, non-Hispanic/Latino; 9 Asian, non-Hispanic/Latino; 41 Hispanic/Latino). Average age 32. 119 applicants, 77% accepted, 70 enrolled. In 2013, 246 master's awarded. *Entrance requirements:* For master's, Illinois Test of Basic Skills. Additional exam requirements/recommendations for international students: Required—TOEFL (minimum score 550 paper-based; 79 iBT). *Application deadline:* Applications are processed on a rolling basis. Application fee: $25. *Expenses:* Contact institution. *Financial support:* In 2013–14, 97 students received support. Career-related internships or fieldwork, scholarships/grants, and tuition waivers (partial) available. Support available to part-time students. Financial award application deadline: 8/15; financial award applicants required to submit FAFSA. *Faculty research:* Governance of private education institutions, reading and language arts, inclusion, organizational planning, leadership and vision. *Unit head:* Dr. Colleen Reardon, Dean, 718-524-6643, Fax: 708-524-6665, E-mail: creardon@dom.edu. *Application contact:* Keven Hansen, Coordinator of Recruitment and Admissions, 708-524-6921, Fax: 708-524-6665, E-mail: educate@dom.edu.
Website: http://educate.dom.edu/.

Duquesne University, School of Education, Department of Instruction and Leadership, Program in English as a Second Language, Pittsburgh, PA 15282-0001. Offers MS Ed. Part-time and evening/weekend programs available. *Faculty:* 3 full-time (1 woman). *Students:* 22 full-time (18 women), 4 part-time (3 women); includes 3 minority (2 Black or African American, non-Hispanic/Latino; 1 Asian, non-Hispanic/Latino), 16 international. Average age 28. 45 applicants, 47% accepted, 9 enrolled. In 2013, 12 master's awarded. *Degree requirements:* For master's, thesis optional. *Entrance requirements:* For master's, bachelor's degree. Additional exam requirements/recommendations for international students: Required—TOEFL (minimum score 550 paper-based), IELTS (minimum score 7). *Application deadline:* For fall admission, 9/1 for domestic students; for spring admission, 1/1 for domestic students. Applications are processed on a rolling basis. Electronic applications accepted. Application fee is waived when completed online. *Expenses: Tuition:* Full-time $18,162; part-time $1009 per credit. *Required fees:* $1728; $96 per credit. Tuition and fees vary according to program. *Unit head:* Dr. Nihat Polat, Associate Professor and Director, 412-396-4464, Fax: 412-396-1997, E-mail: polatn@duq.edu. *Application contact:* Michael Dolinger, Director of Student and Academic Services, 412-396-6647, Fax: 412-396-5585, E-mail: dolingerm@duq.edu.
Website: http://www.duq.edu/academics/schools/education/graduate-programs-education/english-second-language.

East Carolina University, Graduate School, Thomas Harriot College of Arts and Sciences, Department of English, Greenville, NC 27858-4353. Offers creative writing (MA); discourses and cultures (PhD); English studies (MA); linguistics (MA); literature (MA); multicultural and transnational literatures (MA, Certificate); professional communication (Certificate); rhetoric and composition (MA); rhetoric, writing studies and pedagogy (PhD); teaching English to speakers of other languages (MA, Certificate); technical and professional communication (MA, PhD). Part-time and evening/weekend programs available. *Degree requirements:* For master's, one foreign language, comprehensive exam, thesis optional. *Entrance requirements:* For master's, GRE General Test, MAT (MA Ed). Additional exam requirements/recommendations for international students: Required—TOEFL. *Expenses:* Tuition, state resident: full-time $4223. Tuition, nonresident: full-time $16,540. *Required fees:* $2184.

Eastern Michigan University, Graduate School, College of Arts and Sciences, Department of World Languages, Program in Teaching English to Speakers of Other Languages, Ypsilanti, MI 48197. Offers MA, Graduate Certificate. Part-time and evening/weekend programs available. Postbaccalaureate distance learning degree programs offered (minimal on-campus study). *Students:* 5 full-time (4 women), 35 part-time (27 women); includes 6 minority (3 Black or African American, non-Hispanic/Latino; 2 Asian, non-Hispanic/Latino; 1 Hispanic/Latino), 5 international. Average age 35. 41 applicants, 51% accepted, 13 enrolled. In 2013, 14 master's, 7 other advanced degrees awarded. *Degree requirements:* For master's, one foreign language. *Entrance requirements:* Additional exam requirements/recommendations for international students: Required—TOEFL. *Application deadline:* Applications are processed on a rolling basis. Application fee: $35. *Expenses:* Tuition, state resident: full-time $12,300; part-time $466 per credit hour. Tuition, nonresident: full-time $23,159; part-time $918 per credit hour. *Required fees:* $71 per credit hour. $46 per semester. One-time fee: $100. Tuition and fees vary according to course level and degree level. *Financial support:* Fellowships, research assistantships with full tuition reimbursements, teaching assistantships with full tuition reimbursements, career-related internships or fieldwork, Federal Work-Study, institutionally sponsored loans, scholarships/grants, tuition waivers (partial), and unspecified assistantships available. Support available to part-time students. Financial award applicants required to submit FAFSA. *Unit head:* Dr. Rosemary Weston-Gil, Department Head, 734-487-0130, Fax: 734-487-3411, E-mail: rweston3@emich.edu. *Application contact:* Dr. Alexander (Jeff) Popko, Program Advisor, 734-487-3347, Fax: 734-487-3411, E-mail: apopko@emich.edu.

Eastern Nazarene College, Adult and Graduate Studies, Division of Teacher Education, Quincy, MA 02170. Offers administration (M Ed); early childhood education (M Ed, Certificate); elementary education (M Ed, Certificate); English as a second language (Certificate); instructional enrichment and development (Certificate); middle school education (M Ed, Certificate); moderate special needs education (Certificate); principal (Certificate); program development and supervision (Certificate); secondary education (M Ed, Certificate); special education administrator (Certificate); special needs (M Ed); supervisor (Certificate); teacher of reading (M Ed, Certificate). M Ed also available through weekend program for administration, special needs, and teacher of reading only. Part-time and evening/weekend programs available. *Entrance requirements:* Additional exam requirements/recommendations for international students: Required—TOEFL (minimum score 550 paper-based).

Eastern New Mexico University, Graduate School, College of Education and Technology, Department of Curriculum and Instruction, Portales, NM 88130. Offers bilingual education (M Ed); educational technology (M Ed); elementary education (M Ed); English as a second language (M Ed); pedagogy and learning (M Ed); professional technical education (M Ed); reading/literacy (M Ed). Part-time programs available. Postbaccalaureate distance learning degree programs offered (minimal on-campus study). *Degree requirements:* For master's, comprehensive exam, thesis optional. *Entrance requirements:* For master's, minimum GPA of 3.0, photocopy of teaching license, writing assessment, letter of recommendation. Additional exam requirements/recommendations for international students: Required—TOEFL (minimum score 550 paper-based; 79 iBT), IELTS (minimum score 6). Electronic applications accepted.

Eastern University, Graduate Education Programs, St. Davids, PA 19087-3696. Offers ESL program specialist (K-12) (Certificate); general supervisor (PreK-12) (Certificate);

health and physical education (K-12) (Certificate); middle level (4-8) (Certificate); multicultural education (M Ed); pre K-4 (Certificate); pre K-4 with special education (Certificate); reading (M Ed); reading specialist (K-12) (Certificate); reading supervisor (K-12) (Certificate); school health services (M Ed); school health supervisor (Certificate); school nurse (Certificate); school principalship (K-12) (Certificate); secondary biology education (7-12) (Certificate); secondary chemistry education (7-12) (Certificate); secondary communication education (7-12) (Certificate); secondary education (7-12) (Certificate); secondary English education (7-12) (Certificate); secondary math education (7-12) (Certificate); secondary social studies education (7-12) (Certificate); special education (M Ed); special education (7-12) (Certificate); special education (Pre K-8) (Certificate); special education supervisor (N-12) (Certificate); TESOL (M Ed); world language (Certificate), including French, Mandarin Chinese, Spanish. Part-time and evening/weekend programs available. Postbaccalaureate distance learning degree programs offered (no on-campus study). *Faculty:* 22 full-time (11 women), 26 part-time/adjunct (18 women). *Students:* 77 full-time (58 women), 223 part-time (149 women); includes 112 minority (81 Black or African American, non-Hispanic/Latino; 1 American Indian or Alaska Native, non-Hispanic/Latino; 9 Asian, non-Hispanic/Latino; 18 Hispanic/Latino; 1 Native Hawaiian or other Pacific Islander, non-Hispanic/Latino; 2 Two or more races, non-Hispanic/Latino), 7 international. Average age 34. 94 applicants, 100% accepted, 81 enrolled. In 2013, 120 master's awarded. *Entrance requirements:* For master's, minimum GPA of 2.5 (for M Ed); for Certificate, minimum GPA of 3.0 for certifications. Additional exam requirements/recommendations for international students: Required—TOEFL. *Application deadline:* For fall admission, 8/14 for domestic students; for spring admission, 12/20 for domestic students. Applications are processed on a rolling basis. Application fee: $35. Application fee is waived when completed online. *Expenses: Tuition:* Full-time $15,600; part-time $650 per credit. *Required fees:* $27.50 per semester. One-time fee: $50. Tuition and fees vary according to course load, degree level and program. *Financial support:* In 2013–14, 84 students received support, including 6 research assistantships with partial tuition reimbursements available (averaging $7,710 per year); scholarships/grants and unspecified assistantships also available. Financial award application deadline: 3/15; financial award applicants required to submit FAFSA. *Unit head:* Harry Gutelius, Associate Dean, 610-341-1729. *Application contact:* Michael Perpiglia, Associate Director of Enrollment, 610-341-5947, Fax: 484-581-1276, E-mail: mperpigl@eastern.edu.
Website: http://www.eastern.edu/academics/programs/loeb-school-education-0/graduateprograms.

Eastern Washington University, Graduate Studies, College of Arts, Letters and Education, Department of English, Cheney, WA 99004-2431. Offers literature (MA); rhetoric, composition, and technical communication (MA); teaching English as a second language (MA). *Students:* 19 full-time (9 women), 4 part-time (2 women); includes 4 minority (1 Black or African American, non-Hispanic/Latino; 1 American Indian or Alaska Native, non-Hispanic/Latino; 1 Asian, non-Hispanic/Latino; 1 Hispanic/Latino). 26 applicants, 38% accepted, 7 enrolled. In 2013, 20 master's awarded. *Degree requirements:* For master's, comprehensive exam, thesis or alternative. *Entrance requirements:* For master's, GRE General Test, minimum GPA of 3.0. *Application deadline:* For fall admission, 4/1 priority date for domestic students; for spring admission, 1/15 for domestic students. Applications are processed on a rolling basis. Application fee: $50. *Financial support:* In 2013–14, 25 teaching assistantships with partial tuition reimbursements (averaging $7,000 per year) were awarded; career-related internships or fieldwork, Federal Work-Study, institutionally sponsored loans, scholarships/grants, health care benefits, tuition waivers (partial), and unspecified assistantships also available. Support available to part-time students. Financial award application deadline: 2/1; financial award applicants required to submit FAFSA. *Unit head:* Dr. Teena Carnegie, Chair, 509-359-2400, E-mail: tcarnegie@ewu.edu. *Application contact:* Julie Marr, Advisor/Recruiter for Graduate Studies, 509-359-2491, E-mail: gradprograms@ewu.edu.
Website: http://www.ewu.edu/CALE/Programs/English.xml.

East Tennessee State University, School of Graduate Studies, College of Arts and Sciences, Department of Literature and Language, Johnson City, TN 37614. Offers English (MA); teaching English to speakers of other languages (Postbaccalaureate Certificate). Part-time and evening/weekend programs available. *Faculty:* 29 full-time (14 women). *Students:* 19 full-time (11 women), 8 part-time (6 women); includes 6 minority (3 Black or African American, non-Hispanic/Latino; 1 American Indian or Alaska Native, non-Hispanic/Latino; 2 Two or more races, non-Hispanic/Latino), 2 international. Average age 30. 32 applicants, 75% accepted, 21 enrolled. In 2013, 8 master's, 8 other advanced degrees awarded. *Degree requirements:* For master's, comprehensive exam, thesis optional. *Entrance requirements:* For master's, GRE General Test, minimum undergraduate GPA of 3.0 in English, writing samples. Additional exam requirements/recommendations for international students: Required—TOEFL (minimum score 550 paper-based; 79 iBT). *Application deadline:* For fall admission, 6/1 for domestic students, 4/30 for international students; for spring admission, 11/1 for domestic students, 9/30 for international students. Application fee: $35 ($45 for international students). Electronic applications accepted. *Expenses:* Tuition, state resident: full-time $7900; part-time $395 per credit hour. Tuition, nonresident: full-time $21,960; part-time $1098 per credit hour. *Required fees:* $1345; $84 per credit hour. *Financial support:* In 2013–14, 17 students received support, including 8 research assistantships with full tuition reimbursements available (averaging $7,000 per year), 7 teaching assistantships with full tuition reimbursements available (averaging $7,000 per year); career-related internships or fieldwork, institutionally sponsored loans, scholarships/grants, and unspecified assistantships also available. Financial award application deadline: 7/1; financial award applicants required to submit FAFSA. *Faculty research:* Linguistics and dialectology, English education, critical literary theory, literary biography, environmental literature, modern and ancient languages. *Unit head:* Dr. Judith B. Slagle, Chair, 423-439-4339, Fax: 423-439-7193, E-mail: slagle@etsu.edu. *Application contact:* Kimberly Brockman, Graduate Specialist, 423-439-6165, Fax: 423-439-5624, E-mail: brockmank@etsu.edu.
Website: http://www.etsu.edu/cas/litlang/.

Edgewood College, Program in Education, Madison, WI 53711-1997. Offers adult learning (MA Ed); bilingual teaching and learning (MA Ed); director of instruction (Certificate); director of special education and pupil services (Certificate); education (MA Ed); educational administration (MA Ed); educational leadership (Ed D); professional studies (MA Ed); program coordinator (Certificate); reading administration (MA Ed); school business administration (Certificate); school principalship K-12 (Certificate); special education (MA Ed); sustainability leadership (MA Ed); teaching and learning (MA Ed); teaching English to speakers of other languages (TESOL) (MA Ed). *Accreditation:* NCATE (one or more programs are accredited). Part-time and evening/weekend programs available. *Students:* 159 full-time (95 women), 164 part-time (121 women); includes 61 minority (19 Black or African American, non-Hispanic/Latino; 9 Asian, non-Hispanic/Latino; 25 Hispanic/Latino; 8 Two or more races, non-Hispanic/Latino), 27 international. Average age 36. In 2013, 51 master's, 22 doctorates awarded. *Degree requirements:* For master's, practicum, research project; for doctorate, comprehensive exam, thesis/dissertation. *Entrance requirements:* For master's, minimum GPA of 2.75, 2 letters of recommendation, personal statement; for doctorate, resume, letter of intent, 2 letters of recommendation, interview, writing sample. Additional exam requirements/recommendations for international students: Required—TOEFL (minimum score 525 paper-based; 72 iBT). *Application deadline:* For fall admission, 8/15 for domestic students, 5/1 for international students; for spring admission, 1/8 for domestic students, 11/1 for international students. Applications are processed on a rolling basis. Application fee: $30. Electronic applications accepted. *Unit head:* Dr. Timothy Slekar, Dean, E-mail: tslekar@edgewood.edu. *Application contact:* Joann Eastman, Admissions Counselor, 608-663-3250, Fax: 608-663-2214, E-mail: gps@edgewood.edu.
Website: http://www.edgewood.edu/Academics/School-of-Education.

Elms College, Division of Education, Chicopee, MA 01013-2839. Offers early childhood education (MAT); education (M Ed, CAGS); elementary education (MAT); English as a second language (MAT); reading (MAT); secondary education (MAT), including biology education, English education, Spanish education; special education (MAT). Part-time and evening/weekend programs available. *Degree requirements:* For master's, thesis (for some programs). *Entrance requirements:* For master's, Massachusetts Educators Certification Test, minimum GPA of 3.0; for CAGS, master's degree in education. Additional exam requirements/recommendations for international students: Required—TOEFL.

Emporia State University, Program in Teaching English to Speakers of Other Languages, Emporia, KS 66801-5415. Offers MA. Part-time programs available. *Students:* 2 full-time (both women), 25 part-time (22 women), 3 international. 18 applicants, 50% accepted, 3 enrolled. In 2013, 7 master's awarded. *Degree requirements:* For master's, comprehensive exam, thesis optional. *Entrance requirements:* For master's, minimum undergraduate GPA of 2.75 over last 60 hours. Additional exam requirements/recommendations for international students: Required—TOEFL (minimum score 520 paper-based; 68 iBT). *Application deadline:* For fall admission, 8/15 priority date for domestic students. Applications are processed on a rolling basis. Application fee: $30 ($75 for international students). Electronic applications accepted. *Expenses: Tuition, area resident:* Part-time $220 per credit hour. Tuition, state resident: part-time $220 per credit hour. Tuition, nonresident: part-time $685 per credit hour. *Required fees:* $73 per credit hour. *Financial support:* Federal Work-Study, institutionally sponsored loans, health care benefits, and unspecified assistantships available. Financial award application deadline: 2/15. *Unit head:* Dr. Abdelilah Salim Sehlaoui, Associate Professor, 620-341-5237, E-mail: asehlaou@emporia.edu. *Application contact:* Mary Sewell, Admissions Coordinator, 800-950-GRAD, Fax: 620-341-5909, E-mail: msewell@emporia.edu.

Erikson Institute, Academic Programs, Chicago, IL 60654. Offers administration (Certificate); bilingual/ESL (Certificate); child development (MS); early childhood education (MS); infant mental health (Certificate); infant studies (Certificate); MS/MSW. MS/MSW offered jointly with Loyola University Chicago. Part-time and evening/weekend programs available. *Degree requirements:* For master's, comprehensive exam, internship; for Certificate, internship. *Entrance requirements:* For master's and Certificate, minimum GPA of 2.75. Additional exam requirements/recommendations for international students: Required—TOEFL. *Faculty research:* Assessment strategies from early childhood through elementary years; language, literacy, and the arts in children's development; inclusive special education; parent-child relationships; cognitive development.

Fairfield University, Graduate School of Education and Allied Professions, Fairfield, CT 06824-5195. Offers applied behavior analysis (ATC); applied psychology (MA); clinical mental health counseling (MA, CAS); early childhood studies (ATC); educational technology (MA); elementary education (MA, CAS); family studies (MA); integration of spirituality and religion in counseling (ATC); marriage and family therapy (MA); school counseling (MA, CAS); school psychology (MA, CAS); school-based marriage and family therapy (ATC); secondary education (MA); special education (MA, CAS); substance abuse counseling (ATC); teaching (Certificate); teaching and foundations (MA, CAS); TESOL, world languages, and bilingual education (MA, CAS). *Accreditation:* NCATE. Part-time and evening/weekend programs available. *Faculty:* 24 full-time (21 women), 39 part-time/adjunct (27 women). *Students:* 154 full-time (130 women), 307 part-time (248 women); includes 75 minority (14 Black or African American, non-Hispanic/Latino; 1 American Indian or Alaska Native, non-Hispanic/Latino; 10 Asian, non-Hispanic/Latino; 44 Hispanic/Latino; 6 Two or more races, non-Hispanic/Latino), 13 international. Average age 34. 263 applicants, 41% accepted, 91 enrolled. In 2013, 149 master's, 21 other advanced degrees awarded. *Degree requirements:* For master's, comprehensive exam. *Entrance requirements:* For master's, PRAXIS I (for certification programs), minimum GPA of 3.0, 2 recommendations, resume. Additional exam requirements/recommendations for international students: Required—TOEFL (minimum score 550 paper-based; 84 iBT) or IELTS (minimum score 7.5). *Application deadline:* For fall admission, 2/15 for international students; for spring admission, 10/1 for international students. Application fee: $60. Electronic applications accepted. *Expenses: Tuition:* Part-time $675 per credit hour. Tuition and fees vary according to program. *Financial support:* In 2013–14, 55 students received support. Career-related internships or fieldwork and unspecified assistantships available. Financial award applicants required to submit FAFSA. *Faculty research:* Literacy, adolescent psychology, special education, teaching development, mentoring for professional development, multicultural education. *Total annual research expenditures:* $325,000. *Unit head:* Dr. Robert D. Hannafin, Dean, 203-254-4250, Fax: 203-254-4241, E-mail: rhannafin@fairfield.edu. *Application contact:* Marianne Gumpper, Director of Graduate and Continuing Studies Admission, 203-254-4184, Fax: 203-254-4073, E-mail: gradadmis@fairfield.edu.
Website: http://www.fairfield.edu/academics/schoolscollegescenters/graduateschoolofeducationalliedprofessions/graduateprograms/.

Florida Atlantic University, College of Education, Department of Curriculum, Culture, and Educational Inquiry, Boca Raton, FL 33431-0991. Offers curriculum and instruction (M Ed, PhD, Ed S); early childhood education (M Ed); multicultural education (M Ed); TESOL and bilingual education (MA). Part-time and evening/weekend programs available. *Faculty:* 9 full-time (8 women), 3 part-time/adjunct (all women). *Students:* 17 full-time (14 women), 119 part-time (93 women); includes 41 minority (18 Black or African American, non-Hispanic/Latino; 4 Asian, non-Hispanic/Latino; 18 Hispanic/Latino; 1 Two or more races, non-Hispanic/Latino), 5 international. Average age 36. 49 applicants, 39% accepted, 13 enrolled. In 2013, 31 master's, 2 other advanced degrees awarded. *Entrance requirements:* Additional exam requirements/recommendations for international students: Required—TOEFL (minimum score 500 paper-based; 61 iBT), IELTS (minimum score 6). *Application deadline:* For fall admission, 7/1 for domestic students, 2/15 for international students; for spring admission, 11/1 for domestic students, 7/15 for international students. Application fee: $30. *Expenses:* Tuition, state resident: full-time $6660; part-time $370 per credit hour. Tuition, nonresident: full-time $18,450; part-time $1025 per credit hour. Tuition and fees vary according to course load. *Faculty research:* Multicultural education, early intervention strategies, family literacy, religious diversity in schools, early childhood curriculum. *Unit head:* Dr. Emery Hyslop-Margison, Interim Chair, 561-297-3965, E-mail: ehyslopmargison@fau.edu. *Application contact:* Dr. Eliah Watlington, Associate Dean, 561-296-8520, Fax: 261-297-2991, E-mail: ewatling@fau.edu.
Website: http://www.coe.fau.edu/academicdepartments/ccei/.

Florida International University, College of Education, Department of Leadership and Professional Studies, Miami, FL 33199. Offers adult education and human resource development (MS, Ed D); counseling (MS), including rehabilitation counseling, school counseling; counselor education (MS), including clinical mental health counseling; educational administration and supervision (Ed D); educational leadership (MS, Certificate, Ed S); higher education (Ed D); higher education administration (MS); recreation and sport management (MS), including recreation and sport management, recreational therapy; school psychology (Ed S); urban education (MS), including instruction in urban settings, learning technologies, multicultural/bilingual, multicultural/ TESOL, urban education. Part-time and evening/weekend programs available. *Degree requirements:* For doctorate, thesis/dissertation. *Entrance requirements:* For master's, minimum GPA of 3.0; for doctorate and other advanced degree, GRE General Test. Additional exam requirements/recommendations for international students: Required— TOEFL (minimum score 550 paper-based; 80 iBT), IELTS (minimum score 6.3). Electronic applications accepted.

Florida International University, College of Education, Department of Teaching and Learning, Miami, FL 33199. Offers art education (MA, MS); curriculum and instruction (MS, Ed D, PhD, Ed S), including curriculum development (MS), elementary education (MS), English education (MS), learning technologies (MS), mathematics education (MS), modern language education (MS), physical education (MS), science education (MS), social studies education (MS), special education (MS); early childhood education (MS); exceptional student education (Ed D); foreign language education (MS), including foreign language education, teaching English to speakers of other languages (TESOL); international/intercultural education (MS); language, literacy and culture (PhD); mathematics, science, and learning technologies (PhD); physical education (MS), including sport and fitness; reading education (MS). Part-time and evening/weekend programs available. *Degree requirements:* For doctorate, comprehensive exam, thesis/ dissertation. *Entrance requirements:* For master's, GRE General Test, Florida General Knowledge Test or Florida College Level Academic Skills Test; for doctorate and Ed S, GRE General Test. Additional exam requirements/recommendations for international students: Required—TOEFL (minimum score 550 paper-based; 80 iBT), IELTS (minimum score 6.3). Electronic applications accepted.

Fordham University, Graduate School of Education, Division of Curriculum and Teaching, New York, NY 10023. Offers adult education (MS, MSE); bilingual teacher education (MSE); curriculum and teaching (MSE); early childhood education (MSE); elementary education (MST); language, literacy, and learning (PhD); reading education (MSE, Adv C); secondary education (MAT, MSE); special education (MSE, Adv C); teaching English as a second language (MSE). *Accreditation:* NCATE. *Degree requirements:* For doctorate, thesis/dissertation; for Adv C, thesis. *Entrance requirements:* For doctorate, MAT, GRE General Test.

Framingham State University, Continuing Education, Program in the Teaching of English as a Second Language, Framingham, MA 01701-9101. Offers M Ed.

Fresno Pacific University, Graduate Programs, School of Education, Division of Language, Literacy, and Culture, Program in Reading, Fresno, CA 93702-4709. Offers reading (Certificate); reading/English as a second language (MA Ed); reading/language arts (MA Ed). Part-time and evening/weekend programs available. *Faculty:* 1 (woman) full-time. *Students:* 1 part-time. Average age 40. In 2013, 2 master's awarded. *Degree requirements:* For master's, thesis or alternative. *Entrance requirements:* Additional exam requirements/recommendations for international students: Required—TOEFL (minimum score 550 paper-based). *Application deadline:* For fall admission, 7/15 for domestic and international students; for spring admission, 11/15 for domestic and international students. Applications are processed on a rolling basis. Application fee: $90. Electronic applications accepted. *Expenses: Tuition:* Full-time $8910; part-time $495 per unit. *Required fees:* $270. Tuition and fees vary according to course load and program. *Financial support:* Scholarships/grants and tuition waivers (full and partial) available. Support available to part-time students. Financial award applicants required to submit FAFSA. *Unit head:* Jo Ellen Misakian, Program Director, 559-453-2291, Fax: 559-453-7168, E-mail: jmisakian@fresno.edu. *Application contact:* Jon Endicott, Director of Graduate Admissions, 559-453-2016.

Fresno Pacific University, Graduate Programs, School of Education, Division of Language, Literacy, and Culture, Program in Teaching English to Speakers of Other Languages, Fresno, CA 93702-4709. Offers MA. Part-time and evening/weekend programs available. *Students:* Average age 31. 1 applicant. In 2013, 1 master's awarded. *Degree requirements:* For master's, thesis. *Entrance requirements:* For master's, GMAT, MAT, GRE, interview, 2 writing samples. Additional exam requirements/recommendations for international students: Required—TOEFL (minimum score 550 paper-based). *Application deadline:* For fall admission, 7/15 for domestic and international students; for spring admission, 11/15 for domestic and international students. Applications are processed on a rolling basis. Application fee: $90. Electronic applications accepted. *Expenses: Tuition:* Full-time $8910; part-time $495 per unit. *Required fees:* $270. Tuition and fees vary according to course load and program. *Financial support:* In 2013–14, 5 students received support. Scholarships/grants and tuition waivers (full and partial) available. Support available to part-time students. Financial award applicants required to submit FAFSA. *Unit head:* Sandra Mercuri, Director, 559-453-7100, Fax: 559-453-2001, E-mail: smercuri@fresno.edu. *Application contact:* Jon Endicott, Director of Graduate Admissions, 559-453-2016.

Furman University, Graduate Division, Department of Education, Greenville, SC 29613. Offers curriculum and instruction (MA); early childhood education (MA); educational leadership (Ed S); English as a second language (MA); literacy (MA); school leadership (MA); special education (MA). *Accreditation:* NCATE. Part-time programs available. Postbaccalaureate distance learning degree programs offered (minimal on-campus study). *Degree requirements:* For master's, comprehensive exam (for some programs), thesis or alternative. *Entrance requirements:* For master's, PRAXIS II. *Faculty research:* Literacy, pedagogy and practice, social justice, advanced leadership, achievement in high poverty schools.

Gannon University, School of Graduate Studies, College of Humanities, Education, and Social Sciences, School of Education, Program in English as a Second Language, Erie, PA 16541-0001. Offers Certificate. Part-time and evening/weekend programs available. *Students:* 2 part-time (both women). Average age 41. 2 applicants. *Degree requirements:* For Certificate, comprehensive exam, practicum. *Entrance requirements:* For degree, valid instructional certificate, minimum GPA of 3.0. Additional exam requirements/recommendations for international students: Required—TOEFL (minimum score 79 iBT). *Application deadline:* Applications are processed on a rolling basis. Application fee: $25. Electronic applications accepted. *Expenses:* Contact institution. *Financial support:* Application deadline: 7/1; applicants required to submit FAFSA. *Unit head:* Dr. Robin Quick, Director, 814-871-5399, E-mail: quick003@gannon.edu. *Application contact:* Kara Morgan, Director of Graduate Admissions, 814-871-5831, Fax: 814-871-5827, E-mail: graduate@gannon.edu.

George Fox University, College of Education, Educational Foundations and Leadership Program, Newberg, OR 97132-2697. Offers continuing administrator license (Certificate); curriculum and instruction (M Ed); educational leadership (M Ed, Ed D); ESOL (Certificate); higher education (M Ed); initial administrator license (Certificate);

instructional leadership (Ed S); library media (M Ed, Certificate); literacy (M Ed); reading (M Ed); secondary education (M Ed). *Accreditation:* NCATE. Part-time and evening/weekend programs available. Postbaccalaureate distance learning degree programs offered (minimal on-campus study). *Faculty:* 7 full-time (3 women), 5 part-time/adjunct (4 women). *Students:* 194 part-time (128 women); includes 15 minority (1 Black or African American, non-Hispanic/Latino; 1 American Indian or Alaska Native, non-Hispanic/ Latino; 3 Asian, non-Hispanic/Latino; 6 Hispanic/Latino; 1 Native Hawaiian or other Pacific Islander, non-Hispanic/Latino; 3 Two or more races, non-Hispanic/Latino), 2 international. Average age 42. 46 applicants, 85% accepted, 39 enrolled. In 2013, 15 master's, 16 doctorates, 106 Certificates awarded. *Degree requirements:* For master's, thesis (for some programs); for doctorate, comprehensive exam, thesis/dissertation, project. *Entrance requirements:* For master's, minimum undergraduate GPA of 3.0 during previous 2 years of course work, resume, 3 professional recommendations on university forms, official transcripts; for doctorate, GRE, master's degree with minimum GPA of 3.25, 3 years of relevant professional experience, interview, personal essay, scholarly work, 3 professional recommendations on university forms along with 3 written letters of recommendation, official transcripts. Additional exam requirements/ recommendations for international students: Required—TOEFL (minimum score 577 paper-based; 90 iBT). *Application deadline:* For fall admission, 7/15 for domestic and international students; for winter admission, 11/1 for domestic and international students; for spring admission, 4/1 for domestic and international students. Applications are processed on a rolling basis. Application fee: $40. Electronic applications accepted. *Expenses:* Contact institution. *Financial support:* Career-related internships or fieldwork available. Financial award applicants required to submit FAFSA. *Unit head:* Dr. Scot Headley, Professor/Chair, 503-554-2836, E-mail: sheadley@georgefox.edu. *Application contact:* Kipp Wilfong, Graduate Admissions Counselor, 800-631-0921, Fax: 503-554-3110, E-mail: kwilfong@georgefox.edu.
Website: http://www.georgefox.edu/education/index.html.

George Fox University, College of Education, Master of Arts in Teaching Program, Newberg, OR 97132-2697. Offers teaching (MAT); teaching plus ESOL (MAT); teaching plus ESOL/bilingual (MAT); teaching plus reading (MAT); teaching plus special education (MAT). Program offered in Oregon and Idaho. Part-time and evening/weekend programs available. *Faculty:* 11 full-time (9 women), 24 part-time/adjunct (16 women). *Students:* 64 full-time (44 women), 20 part-time (14 women); includes 11 minority (1 Black or African American, non-Hispanic/Latino; 2 Asian, non-Hispanic/Latino; 1 Hispanic/Latino; 2 Native Hawaiian or other Pacific Islander, non-Hispanic/Latino; 5 Two or more races, non-Hispanic/Latino), 1 international. Average age 30. 28 applicants, 100% accepted, 18 enrolled. In 2013, 116 master's awarded. *Entrance requirements:* For master's, CBEST, PRAXIS PPST, or EAS, bachelor's degree with minimum GPA of 3.0 in last two years of course work from regionally-accredited college or university, official transcripts. Additional exam requirements/recommendations for international students: Required—TOEFL (minimum score 577 paper-based; 90 iBT), IELTS (minimum score 7). *Application deadline:* For fall admission, 6/1 for domestic and international students; for winter admission, 10/1 for domestic and international students; for spring admission, 2/1 for domestic and international students. Applications are processed on a rolling basis. Application fee: $40. Electronic applications accepted. *Expenses:* Contact institution. *Financial support:* In 2013–14, 20 students received support. Scholarships/grants available. Financial award application deadline: 2/1; financial award applicants required to submit FAFSA. *Application contact:* Kipp Wilfong, Graduate Admissions Counselor, 800-631-0921, Fax: 503-554-3110, E-mail: mat@georgefox.edu.
Website: http://www.georgefox.edu/soe/mat/.

George Mason University, College of Humanities and Social Sciences, Department of English, Fairfax, VA 22030. Offers creative writing (MFA); English (MA); folklore studies (Certificate); linguistics (PhD); professional writing and rhetoric (Certificate); teaching English as a second language (Certificate); writing and rhetoric (PhD). *Faculty:* 78 full-time (44 women), 30 part-time/adjunct (21 women). *Students:* 112 full-time (74 women), 130 part-time (96 women); includes 41 minority (12 Black or African American, non-Hispanic/Latino; 12 Asian, non-Hispanic/Latino; 11 Hispanic/Latino; 6 Two or more races, non-Hispanic/Latino), 12 international. Average age 32. 278 applicants, 66% accepted, 78 enrolled. In 2013, 88 master's, 17 other advanced degrees awarded. *Degree requirements:* For master's, thesis (for some programs), proficiency in a foreign language by course work or translation test; for doctorate, thesis/dissertation, 2 graduating papers. *Entrance requirements:* For master's, official transcripts; expanded goals statement; writing sample; portfolio; 2 letters of recommendation; for doctorate, GRE, expanded goals statement; 3 letters of recommendation; writing sample; introductory course in linguistics; official transcripts; for Certificate, official transcripts; expanded goals statement; 3 letters of recommendation; portfolio and writing sample (for professional writing and rhetoric); resume and writing sample (for folklore). Additional exam requirements/recommendations for international students: Required— TOEFL (minimum score 570 paper-based; 88 iBT), IELTS (minimum score 6.5), PTE. *Application deadline:* For fall admission, 3/15 priority date for domestic students; for spring admission, 10/15 priority date for domestic students. Application fee: $65 ($80 for international students). Electronic applications accepted. *Expenses:* Tuition, state resident: full-time $9350; part-time $390 per credit. Tuition, nonresident: full-time $25,754; part-time $1073 per credit. *Required fees:* $2688; $112 per credit. *Financial support:* In 2013–14, 69 students received support, including 8 fellowships (averaging $1,394 per year), 8 research assistantships with full and partial tuition reimbursements available (averaging $14,854 per year), 57 teaching assistantships with full and partial tuition reimbursements available (averaging $11,694 per year); career-related internships or fieldwork, Federal Work-Study, scholarships/grants, unspecified assistantships, and health care benefits (for full-time research or teaching assistantship recipients) also available. Support available to part-time students. Financial award application deadline: 3/1; financial award applicants required to submit FAFSA. *Faculty research:* Literature, professional writing and editing, writing of fiction or poetry. *Total annual research expenditures:* $65,931. *Unit head:* Debra Lattanzi-Shutika, Chair, 703-993-1170, Fax: 703-993-1161, E-mail: dshutika@gmu.edu. *Application contact:* Diane Swain, Graduate Program Admissions, 703-993-1185, Fax: 703-993-1161, E-mail: dswain6@gmu.edu.
Website: http://english.gmu.edu.

Georgetown University, Graduate School of Arts and Sciences, Department of Linguistics, Washington, DC 20057. Offers bilingual education (Certificate); language and communication (MA); linguistics (MS, PhD), including applied linguistics, computational linguistics, sociolinguistics, theoretical linguistics; teaching English as a second language (MAT, Certificate); teaching English as a second language and bilingual education (MAT). Terminal master's awarded for partial completion of doctoral program. *Degree requirements:* For master's, one foreign language, comprehensive exam, optional research project; for doctorate, 2 foreign languages, comprehensive exam, thesis/dissertation. *Entrance requirements:* For master's and doctorate, 18 undergraduate credits in a foreign language. Additional exam requirements/ recommendations for international students: Required—TOEFL.

Georgia State University, College of Education, Department of Middle-Secondary Education and Instructional Technology, Atlanta, GA 30302-3083. Offers English education (M Ed, MAT); English speakers of other languages (MAT); instructional

design and technology (MS); instructional technology (PhD), including alternative instructional delivery systems, consulting, instructional design, management, research; mathematics education (M Ed, MAT); middle level education (MAT); reading, language and literacy education (M Ed), including reading instruction; science education (MAT), including biology, broad field science, chemistry, earth science, physics; social studies education (M Ed, MAT), including economics (MAT), geography (MAT), history (MAT), political science (MAT); teaching and learning (PhD), including language and literacy, mathematics education, music education, science education, social studies, teaching and teacher education. *Accreditation:* NCATE. Part-time and evening/weekend programs available. Postbaccalaureate distance learning degree programs offered (minimal on-campus study). *Faculty:* 27 full-time (19 women). *Students:* 181 full-time (113 women), 203 part-time (145 women); includes 161 minority (127 Black or African American, non-Hispanic/Latino; 1 American Indian or Alaska Native, non-Hispanic/Latino; 10 Asian, non-Hispanic/Latino; 11 Hispanic/Latino; 1 Native Hawaiian or other Pacific Islander, non-Hispanic/Latino; 11 Two or more races, non-Hispanic/Latino), 9 international. Average age 36. 2 applicants, 50% accepted, 1 enrolled. In 2013, 213 master's, 17 doctorates awarded. *Degree requirements:* For master's, comprehensive exam (for some programs), thesis or alternative, exit portfolio; for doctorate, comprehensive exam, thesis/dissertation. *Entrance requirements:* For master's, GRE; GACE I (for initial teacher preparation degree programs), baccalaureate degree or equivalent, resume, goals statement, two letters of recommendation, minimum undergraduate GPA of 2.5; proof of initial teacher certification in the content area (for M Ed); for doctorate, GRE, resume, goals statement, writing sample, two letters of recommendation, minimum graduate GPA of 3.3, interview. Additional exam requirements/recommendations for international students: Required—TOEFL (minimum score 550 paper-based; 79 iBT) or IELTS (minimum score 6.5). *Application deadline:* For fall admission, 1/15 priority date for domestic and international students; for spring admission, 10/1 for domestic and international students. Application fee: $50. Electronic applications accepted. *Expenses: Tuition, area resident:* Full-time $4176; part-time $348 per credit hour. Tuition, state resident: full-time $14,544; part-time $1212 per credit hour. Tuition, nonresident: full-time $14,544; part-time $1212 per credit hour. Tuition and fees vary according to course load and program. *Financial support:* In 2013–14, fellowships with full tuition reimbursements (averaging $19,667 per year), research assistantships with full tuition reimbursements (averaging $5,436 per year), teaching assistantships with full tuition reimbursements (averaging $2,779 per year) were awarded; career-related internships or fieldwork, Federal Work-Study, scholarships/grants, health care benefits, tuition waivers (full and partial), and unspecified assistantships also available. Financial award application deadline: 3/15. *Faculty research:* Teacher education in language and literacy, mathematics, science, and social studies in urban middle and secondary school settings; learning technologies in school, community, and corporate settings; multicultural education and education for social justice; urban education; international education. *Unit head:* Dr. Dana L. Fox, Chair, 404-413-8060, Fax: 404-413-8063, E-mail: dfox@gsu.edu. *Application contact:* Bobbie Turner, Administrative Coordinator I, 404-413-8405, Fax: 404-413-8063, E-mail: bnturner@gsu.edu.
Website: http://msit.gsu.edu/msit_programs.htm.

Gonzaga University, Program in Teaching English as a Second Language, Spokane, WA 99258. Offers MATESL. Part-time programs available. *Faculty:* 1 (woman) full-time, 2 part-time/adjunct (both women). *Students:* 3 full-time (2 women), 24 part-time (17 women); includes 1 minority (Black or African American, non-Hispanic/Latino), 11 international. Average age 35. 22 applicants, 64% accepted, 8 enrolled. In 2013, 18 master's awarded. *Entrance requirements:* Additional exam requirements/recommendations for international students: Recommended—TOEFL (minimum score 550 paper-based; 80 iBT), IELTS (minimum score 6.5). *Application deadline:* Applications are processed on a rolling basis. Application fee: $40. Electronic applications accepted. *Expenses:* Contact institution. *Financial support:* Applicants required to submit FAFSA. *Unit head:* Dr. Mary Jeannot, Chairperson, 509-324-6559. *Application contact:* Julie McCulloh, Dean of Admissions, 509-323-6592, Fax: 509-323-5780, E-mail: mcculloh@gu.gonzaga.edu.

Gordon College, Graduate Education Program, Wenham, MA 01984-1899. Offers education (M Ed); educational leadership (Ed S); English as a second language (ESL) (Ed S); mathematics specialist (Ed S); reading (Ed S). Part-time and evening/weekend programs available. *Faculty:* 1 (woman) full-time, 45 part-time/adjunct (27 women). *Students:* 106 full-time (86 women), 281 part-time (230 women); includes 30 minority (4 Black or African American, non-Hispanic/Latino; 7 Asian, non-Hispanic/Latino; 17 Hispanic/Latino; 2 Two or more races, non-Hispanic/Latino), 5 international. In 2013, 52 master's awarded. *Degree requirements:* For master's and Ed S, action research or clinical experience (for some programs). *Entrance requirements:* For master's, GRE or MAT, references, minimum undergraduate GPA of 3.0; for Ed S, references, minimum undergraduate GPA of 3.0. Additional exam requirements/recommendations for international students: Required—TOEFL (minimum score 550 paper-based, 80 iBT) or IELTS (minimum score 6.5). *Application deadline:* Applications are processed on a rolling basis. Application fee: $50. *Expenses: Tuition:* Part-time $325 per credit. *Required fees:* $50 per term. One-time fee: $50. Tuition and fees vary according to program. *Financial support:* Applicants required to submit FAFSA. *Faculty research:* Reading, early childhood development, English language learners. *Unit head:* Dr. Janet Arndt, Director of Graduate Studies, 978-867-4355, Fax: 978-867-4663. *Application contact:* Julie Lenocker, Program Administrator, 978-867-4322, Fax: 978-867-4663, E-mail: graduate-education@gordon.edu.
Website: http://www.gordon.edu/graduate.

Grand Valley State University, College of Education, Programs in General Education, Allendale, MI 49401-9403. Offers adult and higher education (M Ed); early childhood education (M Ed); educational differentiation (M Ed); educational leadership (M Ed); educational technology integration (M Ed); elementary education (M Ed); middle level education (M Ed); school library media services (M Ed); secondary level education (M Ed); teaching English to speakers of other languages (M Ed). Part-time and evening/weekend programs available. Postbaccalaureate distance learning degree programs offered (minimal on-campus study). *Degree requirements:* For master's, thesis. *Entrance requirements:* For master's, GRE General Test or minimum GPA of 3.0. Additional exam requirements/recommendations for international students: Required—TOEFL. Electronic applications accepted. *Faculty research:* Effectiveness of technology in education, parental involvement, effective teaching, effective schools research.

Greensboro College, Program in Teaching English to Speakers of Other Languages, Greensboro, NC 27401-1875. Offers MA. *Accreditation:* NCATE. Part-time and evening/weekend programs available. *Degree requirements:* For master's, thesis, portfolio. *Entrance requirements:* For master's, GRE or MAT, 2 letters of reference. Additional exam requirements/recommendations for international students: Required—TOEFL (minimum score 550 paper-based). Electronic applications accepted.

Hamline University, School of Education, St. Paul, MN 55104-1284. Offers education (MA Ed, Ed D); English as a second language (MA); literacy education (MA); natural science and environmental education (MA Ed); teaching (MAT). *Accreditation:* NCATE (one or more programs are accredited). Part-time and evening/weekend programs available. Postbaccalaureate distance learning degree programs offered (no on-campus study). *Faculty:* 19 full-time (14 women), 44 part-time/adjunct (38 women). *Students:* 107 full-time (75 women), 997 part-time (744 women); includes 71 minority (23 Black or African American, non-Hispanic/Latino; 4 American Indian or Alaska Native, non-Hispanic/Latino; 17 Asian, non-Hispanic/Latino; 21 Hispanic/Latino; 6 Two or more races, non-Hispanic/Latino), 10 international. Average age 33. 395 applicants, 74% accepted, 224 enrolled. In 2013, 221 master's, 13 doctorates awarded. *Degree requirements:* For master's, foreign language (for MA in English as a second language only); thesis or capstone project; for doctorate, comprehensive exam, thesis/dissertation. *Entrance requirements:* For master's, written essay, official transcripts, 2 letters of recommendation, minimum GPA of 3.0 from bachelor's work; for doctorate, personal statement, master's degree with minimum GPA of 3.0, 3 letters of recommendation, writing sample, interview. Additional exam requirements/recommendations for international students: Required—TOEFL (minimum score 550 paper-based; 80 iBT), TOEFL (625 paper-based, 107 iBT) or IELTS (minimum 7.5) for MA in ESL. *Application deadline:* Applications are processed on a rolling basis. Application fee: $0 ($100 for international students). Electronic applications accepted. *Financial support:* Career-related internships or fieldwork, Federal Work-Study, and scholarships/grants available. Support available to part-time students. Financial award applicants required to submit FAFSA. *Faculty research:* Adult basic education, service-learning, teacher dispositions, diversity, technology. *Unit head:* Dr. Nancy Sorenson, Dean, 651-523-2600, Fax: 651-523-2489, E-mail: nsorenson01@hamline.edu. *Application contact:* Shawn Skoog, Director of Graduate Recruitment and Admission, 651-523-2900, Fax: 651-523-3058, E-mail: sskoog03@hamline.edu.
Website: http://www.hamline.edu/education.

Harding University, Cannon-Clary College of Education, Searcy, AR 72149-0001. Offers advanced studies in teaching and learning (M Ed); art (MSE); behavioral science (MSE); counseling (MS, Ed S); early childhood special education (M Ed, MSE); education (MSE); educational leadership (M Ed, Ed S); elementary education (M Ed); English (MSE); French (MSE); history/social science (MSE); kinesiology (MSE); math (MSE); reading (M Ed); secondary education (M Ed); Spanish (MSE); teaching (MAT); teaching English as a second language (MSE). *Accreditation:* NCATE. Part-time and evening/weekend programs available. *Faculty:* 13 full-time (5 women), 42 part-time/adjunct (24 women). *Students:* 154 full-time (119 women), 393 part-time (270 women); includes 108 minority (81 Black or African American, non-Hispanic/Latino; 5 American Indian or Alaska Native, non-Hispanic/Latino; 5 Asian, non-Hispanic/Latino; 9 Hispanic/Latino; 8 Two or more races, non-Hispanic/Latino), 15 international. Average age 36. 187 applicants, 79% accepted, 135 enrolled. In 2013, 138 master's, 17 other advanced degrees awarded. *Degree requirements:* For master's, comprehensive exam (for some programs), thesis optional, portfolio(s); for Ed S, comprehensive exam, portfolio, project. *Entrance requirements:* For master's, GRE, MAT, PRAXIS; for Ed S, MAT or GRE. Additional exam requirements/recommendations for international students: Required—TOEFL (minimum score 550 paper-based; 79 iBT). *Application deadline:* For fall admission, 8/1 for domestic and international students; for spring admission, 1/1 for domestic and international students. Applications are processed on a rolling basis. Application fee: $35. *Expenses: Tuition:* Full-time $11,574; part-time $643 per credit hour. *Required fees:* $432; $24 per credit hour. Tuition and fees vary according to course load, degree level and program. *Financial support:* In 2013–14, 36 students received support. Unspecified assistantships available. *Faculty research:* Reading, comprehension, school violence, educational technology, behavior, college choice, differentiated instruction, brain-based teaching. *Unit head:* Dr. Clara Carroll, Chair, 501-279-4501, Fax: 501-279-4083, E-mail: ccarroll@harding.edu. *Application contact:* Information Contact, 501-279-4315, E-mail: gradstudiesedu@harding.edu.
Website: http://www.harding.edu/education.

Hawai`i Pacific University, College of Humanities and Social Sciences, Program in Teaching English to Speakers of Other Languages, Honolulu, HI 96813. Offers MA. Part-time and evening/weekend programs available. *Faculty:* 5 full-time (2 women). *Students:* 30 full-time (20 women), 6 part-time (3 women); includes 21 minority (1 Black or African American, non-Hispanic/Latino; 11 Asian, non-Hispanic/Latino; 3 Hispanic/Latino; 6 Two or more races, non-Hispanic/Latino). Average age 31. 31 applicants, 84% accepted, 14 enrolled. In 2013, 24 master's awarded. *Entrance requirements:* Additional exam requirements/recommendations for international students: Recommended—TOEFL (minimum score 550 paper-based; 80 iBT), TWE (minimum score 5). *Application deadline:* For fall admission, 2/15 priority date for domestic students; for spring admission, 10/15 priority date for domestic students. Applications are processed on a rolling basis. Application fee: $50. Electronic applications accepted. *Financial support:* In 2013–14, 11 students received support. Career-related internships or fieldwork, Federal Work-Study, scholarships/grants, tuition waivers, and unspecified assistantships available. Financial award application deadline: 3/1; financial award applicants required to submit FAFSA. *Unit head:* Dr. Charles Boyer, Department Chair, 808-356-5208, E-mail: cboyer@hpu.edu. *Application contact:* Rumi Yoshida, Associate Director of Graduate Admissions, 808-543-8034, Fax: 808-544-0280, E-mail: grad@hpu.edu.
Website: http://www.hpu.edu/CHSS/LangLing/TESOL/MATESOL/MATESOL.html.

Henderson State University, Graduate Studies, Teachers College, Department of Advanced Instructional Studies, Arkadelphia, AR 71999-0001. Offers early childhood (P-4) (MSE); education (MAT); English as a second language (Graduate Certificate); instructional facilitator (Graduate Certificate); middle school (MSE); reading (MSE); special education (MSE). *Accreditation:* NCATE. Part-time programs available. *Faculty:* 7 full-time (3 women), 2 part-time/adjunct (both women). *Students:* 1 (woman) full-time, 99 part-time (88 women); includes 20 minority (13 Black or African American, non-Hispanic/Latino; 1 American Indian or Alaska Native, non-Hispanic/Latino; 5 Hispanic/Latino; 1 Two or more races, non-Hispanic/Latino), 1 international. Average age 36. 7 applicants, 100% accepted, 7 enrolled. In 2013, 45 master's awarded. *Entrance requirements:* For master's, GRE General Test or MAT, minimum GPA of 2.7, teacher certification. Additional exam requirements/recommendations for international students: Required—TOEFL (minimum score 600 paper-based); Recommended—IELTS (minimum score 6.5). *Application deadline:* For fall admission, 8/1 priority date for domestic students, 6/30 priority date for international students; for spring admission, 1/1 priority date for domestic students, 11/30 priority date for international students. Applications are processed on a rolling basis. Application fee: $25 ($75 for international students). *Expenses:* Tuition, state resident: full-time $4284; part-time $238 per credit hour. Tuition, nonresident: full-time $8802; part-time $489 per credit hour. Tuition and fees vary according to course load and campus/location. *Financial support:* In 2013–14, 1 teaching assistantship with partial tuition reimbursement (averaging $4,000 per year) was awarded; scholarships/grants and unspecified assistantships also available. *Unit head:* Dr. Gary Smithey, Chairperson, 870-230-5361, Fax: 870-230-5455, E-mail: smitheg@hsu.edu. *Application contact:* Dr. Ken Taylor, Graduate Dean, 870-230-5126, Fax: 870-230-5479, E-mail: taylorke@hsu.edu.

Heritage University, Graduate Programs in Education, Program in Professional Studies, Toppenish, WA 98948-9599. Offers bilingual education/ESL (M Ed); biology (M Ed); English and literature (M Ed); reading/literacy (M Ed); special education (M Ed). Part-time and evening/weekend programs available. *Degree requirements:* For master's, comprehensive exam (for some programs), thesis (for some programs).

Hofstra University, College of Liberal Arts and Sciences, Programs in Forensic and Applied Linguistics, Hempstead, NY 11549. Offers applied linguistics (TESOL) (MA); linguistics (MA), including forensic linguistics.

Hofstra University, School of Education, Programs in Teaching - K-12, Hempstead, NY 11549. Offers bilingual education (MA, Advanced Certificate); family and consumer sciences (MS Ed); fine arts and music education (Advanced Certificate); fine arts education (MA, MS Ed); middle childhood extensions (Advanced Certificate), including grades 5-6 or 7-9; music education (MA, MS Ed); teaching languages other than English and TESOL (MS Ed); TESOL (MS Ed, Advanced Certificate); wind conducting (MA).

Hofstra University, School of Education, Programs in Teaching - Secondary Education, Hempstead, NY 11549. Offers business education (MS Ed); education technology (Advanced Certificate); English education (MA, MS Ed); foreign language and TESOL (MS Ed); foreign language education (MA, MS Ed), including French, German, Russian, Spanish; mathematics education (MA, MS Ed); science education (MA, MS Ed), including biology, chemistry, earth science, geology, physics; secondary education (Advanced Certificate); social studies education (MA, MS Ed); technology for learning (MA).

Holy Family University, Graduate School, School of Education, Master of Education Programs, Philadelphia, PA 19114. Offers early elementary education (PreK-Grade 4) (M Ed); education leadership (M Ed); general education (M Ed); middle level education (Grades 4-8) (M Ed); reading specialist (M Ed); secondary education (Grades 7-12) (M Ed); special education (M Ed); TESOL and literacy (M Ed). *Expenses: Tuition:* Full-time $12,060. *Required fees:* $250. Tuition and fees vary according to degree level. *Unit head:* Dr. Leonard Soroka, Dean, 267-341-3565, Fax: 215-824-2438, E-mail: lsoroka@holyfamily.edu. *Application contact:* Gidget Marie Montelibano, Associate Director of Graduate Admissions, 267-341-3358, Fax: 215-637-1478, E-mail: gmontelibano@holyfamily.edu.

Holy Names University, Graduate Division, Department of Education, Oakland, CA 94619-1699. Offers educational therapy (Certificate); mild/moderate disabilities (Ed S); multiple subject teaching (Credential); single subject teaching (Credential); teaching English as a second language (TESL) (M Ed); urban education: educational therapy (M Ed); urban education: K-12 education (M Ed); urban education: special education (M Ed). Part-time programs available. *Faculty:* 4 full-time, 14 part-time/adjunct. *Students:* 25 full-time (19 women), 127 part-time (93 women); includes 74 minority (37 Black or African American, non-Hispanic/Latino; 7 Asian, non-Hispanic/Latino; 28 Hispanic/Latino; 1 Native Hawaiian or other Pacific Islander, non-Hispanic/Latino; 1 Two or more races, non-Hispanic/Latino), 2 international. Average age 35. 72 applicants, 75% accepted, 37 enrolled. In 2013, 15 master's, 22 Certificates awarded. *Degree requirements:* For master's, comprehensive exam, research paper, thesis or project. *Entrance requirements:* For master's, minimum undergraduate GPA of 2.6 overall, 3.0 in major, personal statement, two recommendations, interview. Additional exam requirements/recommendations for international students: Required—TOEFL (minimum score 550 paper-based; 79 iBT). *Application deadline:* For fall admission, 8/1 priority date for domestic students, 7/15 for international students; for spring admission, 12/1 priority date for domestic students, 12/1 for international students; for summer admission, 5/1 priority date for domestic students, 5/1 for international students. Applications are processed on a rolling basis. Application fee: $65. Electronic applications accepted. Application fee is waived when completed online. *Expenses: Tuition:* Part-time $866 per unit. *Financial support:* Career-related internships or fieldwork, Federal Work-Study, scholarships/grants, and unspecified assistantships available. Support available to part-time students. Financial award application deadline: 3/2; financial award applicants required to submit FAFSA. *Faculty research:* Cognitive development, language development, learning handicaps. *Unit head:* Dr. Kimberly Mayfiel, 510-436-1396, Fax: 510-436-1325, E-mail: mayfield@hnu.edu. *Application contact:* Graduate Admission, 800-430-1321, Fax: 510-436-1325, E-mail: graduateadmissions@hnu.edu.
Website: http://www.hnu.edu/academics/graduatePrograms/education.html.

Houston Baptist University, College of Education and Behavioral Sciences, Programs in Education, Houston, TX 77074-3298. Offers bilingual education (M Ed); counselor education (M Ed); curriculum and instruction (M Ed); educational administration (M Ed); educational diagnostician (M Ed); reading education (M Ed). Part-time programs available. Postbaccalaureate distance learning degree programs offered (no on-campus study). *Entrance requirements:* For master's, GRE General Test or MAT. Additional exam requirements/recommendations for international students: Required—TOEFL (minimum score 550 paper-based).

Humboldt State University, Academic Programs, College of Arts, Humanities, and Social Sciences, Department of English, Arcata, CA 95521-8299. Offers English (MA), including composition studies and pedagogy, literary and cultural studies, teaching English as a second language. *Students:* 16 full-time (10 women), 3 part-time (all women); includes 4 minority (3 Hispanic/Latino; 1 Two or more races, non-Hispanic/Latino). Average age 29. 7 applicants, 86% accepted, 3 enrolled. *Degree requirements:* For master's, variable foreign language requirement, thesis or alternative, qualifying exam. *Entrance requirements:* For master's, GRE, minimum GPA of 3.0, 3 letters of recommendation, sample of writing. Additional exam requirements/recommendations for international students: Required—TOEFL (minimum score 500 paper-based). *Application deadline:* For fall admission, 3/1 for domestic students; for spring admission, 11/1 for domestic students. Applications are processed on a rolling basis. Application fee: $55. *Financial support:* Teaching assistantships, career-related internships or fieldwork, Federal Work-Study, and institutionally sponsored loans available. Financial award application deadline: 3/1; financial award applicants required to submit FAFSA. *Faculty research:* Teaching of writing, literature. *Unit head:* Dr. Nikola Hobbel, Graduate Coordinator, 707-826-3758, Fax: 707-826-5939, E-mail: nh16@humboldt.edu. *Application contact:* Fax: 707-826-6190.
Website: http://www.humboldt.edu/english/.

Hunter College of the City University of New York, Graduate School, School of Education, Department of Curriculum and Teaching, Program in Teaching English as a Second Language, New York, NY 10065-5085. Offers MA. *Accreditation:* NCATE. *Faculty:* 11 full-time (5 women), 19 part-time/adjunct (12 women). *Students:* 37 full-time (28 women), 217 part-time (179 women); includes 91 minority (16 Black or African American, non-Hispanic/Latino; 1 American Indian or Alaska Native, non-Hispanic/Latino; 40 Asian, non-Hispanic/Latino; 34 Hispanic/Latino), 8 international. Average age 32. 162 applicants, 59% accepted, 65 enrolled. In 2013, 70 master's awarded. *Degree requirements:* For master's, one foreign language, thesis, comprehensive exam or essay, New York state teacher certification exams. *Entrance requirements:* For master's, minimum GPA of 2.8, 2 letters of recommendation, interview. Additional exam requirements/recommendations for international students: Required—TOEFL (minimum score 600 paper-based), TWE (minimum score 5). *Application deadline:* For fall admission, 4/1 for domestic students, 2/1 for international students; for spring admission, 11/1 for domestic students, 9/1 for international students. Applications are processed on a rolling basis. Application fee: $125. *Financial support:* Federal Work-Study, scholarships/grants, and tuition waivers (partial) available. Support available to part-time students. *Unit head:* Dr. Anne Ediger, Coordinator, 212-777-4665, E-mail: aediger@hunter.cuny.edu. *Application contact:* Milena Solo, Director for Graduate Admissions, 212-772-4480, E-mail: admissions@hunter.cuny.edu.
Website: http://www.hunter.cuny.edu/school-of-education/programs/graduate/tesol.

Idaho State University, Office of Graduate Studies, College of Arts and Letters, Department of English, Pocatello, ID 83209-8056. Offers English (MA, DA); English and the teaching of English (PhD); TESOL (Post-Master's Certificate). Part-time programs available. *Degree requirements:* For master's, one foreign language, comprehensive exam, thesis optional; for doctorate, one foreign language, comprehensive exam, thesis/dissertation, 2 papers, 2 teaching internships; for Post-Master's Certificate, 6 credits of elective linguistics, practicum. *Entrance requirements:* For master's, GRE General Test (minimum 50th percentile verbal), general literature exam, minimum GPA of 3.0, 3 letters of recommendation, 5-page writing sample; for doctorate, GRE General Test, GRE Subject Test, minimum GPA of 3.5, writing examples, 3 letters of recommendation, master's degree in English; for Post-Master's Certificate, GRE (minimum 35th percentile on verbal section), bachelor's degree, minimum undergraduate GPA of 3.0 in last 2 years, 3 letters of recommendation, knowledge of second language. Additional exam requirements/recommendations for international students: Required—TOEFL (minimum score 550 paper-based; 80 iBT). Electronic applications accepted. *Faculty research:* American literature, Renaissance literature, composition and rhetoric, Intermountain West studies, ethics.

Indiana State University, College of Graduate and Professional Studies, College of Arts and Sciences, Department of Languages, Literatures, and Linguistics, Terre Haute, IN 47809. Offers linguistics/teaching English as a second language (MA); TESL/TEFL (CAS). *Faculty:* 7 full-time (4 women), 2 part-time/adjunct (1 woman). *Students:* 26 full-time (20 women), 8 part-time (7 women); includes 6 minority (2 Asian, non-Hispanic/Latino; 4 Hispanic/Latino), 19 international. Average age 32. 26 applicants, 92% accepted, 8 enrolled. In 2013, 20 master's awarded. *Degree requirements:* For master's, comprehensive exam. *Application deadline:* For fall admission, 7/1 priority date for domestic students; for spring admission, 11/1 priority date for domestic students. Applications are processed on a rolling basis. Application fee: $35. Electronic applications accepted. *Financial support:* In 2013–14, 8 teaching assistantships (averaging $7,000 per year) were awarded; research assistantships with partial tuition reimbursements and tuition waivers (partial) also available. Financial award application deadline: 3/1; financial award applicants required to submit FAFSA. *Unit head:* Dr. Ronald W. Dunbar, Chairperson, 812-237-2368. *Application contact:* Information Contact, 812-237-2366.

Indiana University Bloomington, University Graduate School, College of Arts and Sciences, Department of Second Language Studies, Bloomington, IN 47405-7000. Offers second language studies (MA, PhD); TESOL and applied linguistics (MA). *Faculty:* 1 (woman) full-time. *Students:* 34 full-time (22 women), 2 part-time (0 women); includes 2 minority (1 Hispanic/Latino; 1 Two or more races, non-Hispanic/Latino), 12 international. Average age 31. 115 applicants, 37% accepted, 9 enrolled. In 2013, 12 master's, 1 doctorate awarded. *Entrance requirements:* Additional exam requirements/recommendations for international students: Required—TOEFL (minimum score 100 iBT). *Application deadline:* For fall admission, 1/15 for domestic students, 12/1 for international students. Application fee: $55 ($65 for international students). *Financial support:* In 2013–14, 3 fellowships with tuition reimbursements (averaging $18,300 per year), 14 teaching assistantships with tuition reimbursements (averaging $15,750 per year) were awarded. *Unit head:* Kathleen Bardovi-Harlig, Chair, 812-855-7951, E-mail: bardovi@indiana.edu. *Application contact:* Regina Skeans, Graduate Secretary, 812-855-7951, E-mail: rskeans@indiana.edu.
Website: http://www.indiana.edu/~dsls/.

Indiana University of Pennsylvania, School of Graduate Studies and Research, College of Humanities and Social Sciences, Department of English, Program in Composition and Teaching English to Speakers of Other Languages, Indiana, PA 15705-1087. Offers PhD. Part-time programs available. *Faculty:* 30 full-time (15 women). *Students:* 23 full-time (17 women), 104 part-time (73 women); includes 10 minority (5 Black or African American, non-Hispanic/Latino; 3 Asian, non-Hispanic/Latino; 1 Hispanic/Latino; 1 Two or more races, non-Hispanic/Latino), 33 international. Average age 39. 190 applicants, 18% accepted, 17 enrolled. In 2013, 25 doctorates awarded. *Degree requirements:* For doctorate, one foreign language, comprehensive exam, thesis/dissertation. *Entrance requirements:* For doctorate, 2 letters of recommendation. Additional exam requirements/recommendations for international students: Required—TOEFL (minimum score 600 paper-based). *Application deadline:* For fall admission, 2/1 priority date for domestic students; for summer admission, 11/1 priority date for domestic students. Applications are processed on a rolling basis. Application fee: $50. Electronic applications accepted. *Expenses:* Tuition, state resident: full-time $3978; part-time $442 per credit. Tuition, nonresident: full-time $5967; part-time $663 per credit. *Required fees:* $2080; $115.55 per credit. $93 per semester. Tuition and fees vary according to degree level and program. *Financial support:* In 2013–14, 15 fellowships with full tuition reimbursements (averaging $392 per year), 15 research assistantships with full and partial tuition reimbursements (averaging $6,710 per year), 6 teaching assistantships with partial tuition reimbursements (averaging $22,848 per year) were awarded; career-related internships or fieldwork, Federal Work-Study, scholarships/grants, and unspecified assistantships also available. Support available to part-time students. Financial award application deadline: 4/15; financial award applicants required to submit FAFSA. *Unit head:* Dr. Sharon Deckert, Graduate Coordinator, 724-357-2261, E-mail: sharon.deckert@iup.edu. *Application contact:* Paula Stossel, Assistant Dean for Administration, 724-357-4511, Fax: 724-357-4862, E-mail: graduate-admissions@iup.edu.
Website: http://www.iup.edu/upper.aspx?id-49407.

Indiana University of Pennsylvania, School of Graduate Studies and Research, College of Humanities and Social Sciences, Department of English, Program in English: TESOL, Indiana, PA 15705-1087. Offers MA. Part-time programs available. *Faculty:* 30 full-time (15 women). *Students:* 24 full-time (20 women), 2 part-time (both women); includes 1 minority (Hispanic/Latino), 17 international. Average age 27. 75 applicants, 33% accepted, 12 enrolled. In 2013, 23 master's awarded. *Degree requirements:* For master's, thesis optional. *Entrance requirements:* For master's, two letters of recommendation. Additional exam requirements/recommendations for international students: Required—TOEFL (minimum score 580 paper-based). *Application deadline:* Applications are processed on a rolling basis. Application fee: $50. Electronic applications accepted. *Expenses:* Tuition, state resident: full-time $3978; part-time $442 per credit. Tuition, nonresident: full-time $5967; part-time $663 per credit. *Required fees:* $2080; $115.55 per credit. $93 per semester. Tuition and fees vary according to degree level and program. *Financial support:* In 2013–14, 1 fellowship with full tuition reimbursement (averaging $1,000 per year), 6 research assistantships with full and partial tuition reimbursements (averaging $2,544 per year) were awarded; Federal Work-Study, scholarships/grants, and unspecified assistantships also available. Financial award application deadline: 4/15; financial award applicants required to submit FAFSA. *Unit head:* Dr. Gloria Park, Director, 724-357-3095, E-mail: gloria.park@iup.edu. *Application contact:* Paula Stossel, Assistant Dean, 724-357-2222, Fax: 724-357-4862, E-mail: graduate-admissions@iup.edu.
Website: http://www.iup.edu/upper.aspx?id-91110.

English as a Second Language

Indiana University–Purdue University Fort Wayne, College of Arts and Sciences, Department of English and Linguistics, Fort Wayne, IN 46805-1499. Offers English (MA, MAT); TENL (teaching English as a new language) (Certificate). Part-time programs available. *Faculty:* 22 full-time (9 women), 1 (woman) part-time/adjunct. *Students:* 8 full-time (7 women), 18 part-time (13 women); includes 2 minority (both Two or more races, non-Hispanic/Latino), 1 international. Average age 30. 5 applicants, 100% accepted, 3 enrolled. In 2013, 16 master's awarded. *Degree requirements:* For master's, one foreign language, thesis (for some programs), teaching certificate (MAT). *Entrance requirements:* For master's, GRE General Test, minimum GPA of 3.0, major or minor in English, 3 letters of recommendation; for Certificate, bachelor's degree with minimum GPA of 2.5. Additional exam requirements/recommendations for international students: Required—TOEFL (minimum score 600 paper-based; 79 iBT). *Application deadline:* For fall admission, 8/1 for domestic students; for spring admission, 10/15 for domestic students. Applications are processed on a rolling basis. Application fee: $50. *Financial support:* In 2013–14, 9 teaching assistantships with partial tuition reimbursements (averaging $13,322 per year) were awarded; career-related internships or fieldwork, scholarships/grants, and unspecified assistantships also available. Support available to part-time students. Financial award application deadline: 3/1; financial award applicants required to submit FAFSA. *Faculty research:* Feminism to post-feminism, Shanghai telephone service, customer-employee interaction. *Total annual research expenditures:* $97,110. *Unit head:* Dr. Hardin Aasand, Chair/Professor, 260-481-6750, Fax: 260-481-6985, E-mail: aasandh@ipfw.edu. *Application contact:* Dr. Lewis Roberts, Graduate Program Director, 260-481-6754, Fax: 260-481-6985, E-mail: robertlc@ipfw.edu. Website: http://www.ipfw.edu/english.

Indiana University–Purdue University Indianapolis, School of Education, Indianapolis, IN 46202-2896. Offers computer education (Certificate); curriculum and instruction (MS); early childhood (MS); educational leadership (MS, Certificate); English as a second language (Certificate); higher education and student affairs (MS); kindergarten (Certificate); language education (MS); reading (Certificate); school counseling (MS); special education (MS, Certificate). Part-time and evening/weekend programs available. *Faculty:* 41 full-time, 80 part-time/adjunct. *Students:* 113 full-time (78 women), 263 part-time (200 women); includes 88 minority (51 Black or African American, non-Hispanic/Latino; 1 American Indian or Alaska Native, non-Hispanic/Latino; 10 Asian, non-Hispanic/Latino; 19 Hispanic/Latino; 7 Two or more races, non-Hispanic/Latino), 5 international. Average age 33. 93 applicants, 54% accepted, 40 enrolled. In 2013, 179 master's awarded. *Degree requirements:* For master's, thesis optional. *Entrance requirements:* For master's, GRE General Test, minimum GPA of 3.0. Additional exam requirements/recommendations for international students: Required—TOEFL. *Application deadline:* For fall admission, 5/1 priority date for domestic students; for spring admission, 11/1 for domestic students. Application fee: $55 ($65 for international students). *Financial support:* Fellowships, research assistantships with partial tuition reimbursements, teaching assistantships, Federal Work-Study, institutionally sponsored loans, scholarships/grants, and tuition waivers (partial) available. Support available to part-time students. *Faculty research:* Teachers in the process of change, learning cycles, children's concepts of science. *Total annual research expenditures:* $614,458. *Unit head:* Dr. Pat Rogan, Executive Associate Dean, 317-274-6862, E-mail: progan@iupui.edu. *Application contact:* Donnella Dillon, Graduate Admissions Coordinator, 317-274-0645, E-mail: dmdillon@iupui.edu. Website: http://education.iupui.edu/.

Indiana University–Purdue University Indianapolis, School of Liberal Arts, Department of English, Indianapolis, IN 46202-2896. Offers English (MA); teaching English to speakers of other languages (TESOL) (Certificate); teaching writing (Certificate). *Faculty:* 22 full-time (11 women). *Students:* 17 full-time (10 women), 19 part-time (14 women); includes 6 minority (1 Black or African American, non-Hispanic/Latino; 1 Native Hawaiian or other Pacific Islander, non-Hispanic/Latino; 4 Two or more races, non-Hispanic/Latino), 1 international. Average age 32. 29 applicants, 79% accepted, 16 enrolled. In 2013, 15 master's, 4 other advanced degrees awarded. *Entrance requirements:* For master's, GRE. Additional exam requirements/recommendations for international students: Required—TOEFL. *Application deadline:* For fall admission, 1/15 priority date for domestic and international students; for spring admission, 10/15 priority date for domestic and international students. Application fee: $55 ($65 for international students). *Financial support:* In 2013–14, 5 research assistantships (averaging $9,500 per year) were awarded; fellowships, teaching assistantships, and career-related internships or fieldwork also available. *Unit head:* Dr. Robert Rebein, Chair, 317-274-1405, E-mail: rrebein@iupui.edu. *Application contact:* Dr. Robert Rebein, Director of Graduate Studies in English, 317-274-1405, Fax: 317-278-1287, E-mail: rrebein@iupui.edu. Website: http://liberalarts.iupui.edu/english/.

Inter American University of Puerto Rico, Arecibo Campus, Programs in Education, Arecibo, PR 00614-4050. Offers administration and educational supervision (MA Ed); counseling and guidance (MA Ed); curriculum and teaching (MA Ed), including biology education, English as a second language, history education, math education, Spanish; elementary education (MA Ed). *Degree requirements:* For master's, comprehensive exam, thesis optional. *Entrance requirements:* For master's, GRE, EXADEP, bachelor's degree in education or teaching license (administration and supervision) or courses in education and psychology (counseling and guidance), minimum GPA of 2.5 in last 60 credits.

Inter American University of Puerto Rico, Barranquitas Campus, Program in Education, Barranquitas, PR 00794. Offers curriculum and teaching (M Ed), including biology education, English as a second language, history education, mathematics education, Spanish; educational leadership and management (MA); elementary education (M Ed); information and library service technology (M Ed); special education (MA). *Degree requirements:* For master's, comprehensive exam, thesis optional. *Entrance requirements:* For master's, EXADEP, letter of recommendation. Electronic applications accepted.

Inter American University of Puerto Rico, Metropolitan Campus, Graduate Programs, Program in Teaching English as a Second Language, San Juan, PR 00919-1293. Offers MA. Part-time and evening/weekend programs available. *Degree requirements:* For master's, comprehensive exam, thesis or alternative. *Entrance requirements:* For master's, GRE General Test or EXADEP, interview, minimum GPA of 2.5. Electronic applications accepted.

Inter American University of Puerto Rico, Ponce Campus, Graduate School, Mercedita, PR 00715-1602. Offers accounting (MBA); biology (M Ed); chemistry (M Ed); criminal justice (MA); elementary education (M Ed); English as a Second Language (M Ed); finance (MBA); history (M Ed); human resources (MBA); marketing (MBA); mathematics (M Ed); Spanish (M Ed). *Entrance requirements:* For master's, minimum GPA of 2.5.

Inter American University of Puerto Rico, San Germán Campus, Graduate Studies Center, Program in Teaching English as a Second Language, San Germán, PR 00683-5008. Offers MA. Part-time and evening/weekend programs available. *Faculty:* 4 full-time (2 women). *Students:* 18 full-time (14 women), 11 part-time (9 women); includes 27 minority (all Hispanic/Latino). Average age 31. 6 applicants, 100% accepted, 6 enrolled. In 2013, 12 master's awarded. *Degree requirements:* For master's, comprehensive

exam. *Entrance requirements:* For master's, GRE General Test or EXADEP, minimum GPA of 3.0. *Application deadline:* For fall admission, 4/30 priority date for domestic students; for spring admission, 11/15 for domestic students. Applications are processed on a rolling basis. Application fee: $31. *Expenses: Tuition:* Full-time $2424; part-time $202 per credit hour. *Required fees:* $260 per semester. Tuition and fees vary according to course level, course load, degree level and program. *Financial support:* Teaching assistantships and unspecified assistantships available. *Unit head:* Dr. Elba T. Irizarry, Director of Graduate Studies Center, 787-264-1912 Ext. 7357, Fax: 787-892-6350, E-mail: elbat@sg.inter.edu. *Application contact:* Dr. Carol Moe, Coordinator, 787-264-1912 Ext. 7539, E-mail: carolmoe@yahoo.com. Website: http://www.sg.inter.edu/tesl/.

Iowa State University of Science and Technology, Program in Teaching English as a Second Language/Applied Linguistics, Ames, IA 50011. Offers MA. *Entrance requirements:* For master's, GRE, official academic transcripts, resume, three letters of recommendation, statement of personal goals, writing sample. Additional exam requirements/recommendations for international students: Required—TOEFL (minimum score 600 paper-based; 100 iBT), IELTS (minimum score 7). Electronic applications accepted.

Kansas State University, Graduate School, College of Arts and Sciences, Department of Modern Languages, Manhattan, KS 66506. Offers French (MA); German (MA); Spanish (MA); teaching English as a foreign language (MA). Part-time and evening/weekend programs available. Postbaccalaureate distance learning degree programs offered (minimal on-campus study). *Faculty:* 14 full-time (9 women), 3 part-time/adjunct (1 woman). *Students:* 20 full-time (14 women), 10 part-time (9 women); includes 8 minority (6 Hispanic/Latino; 2 Two or more races, non-Hispanic/Latino), 4 international. Average age 30. 19 applicants, 53% accepted, 7 enrolled. In 2013, 13 master's awarded. *Degree requirements:* For master's, thesis optional. *Entrance requirements:* For master's, teaching certificate. Additional exam requirements/recommendations for international students: Required—TOEFL (minimum score 560 paper-based; 83 iBT), TOEFL (minimum iBT speaking portion score of 26). *Application deadline:* For fall admission, 3/1 priority date for domestic students, 2/1 priority date for international students; for spring admission, 12/1 priority date for domestic students, 8/1 priority date for international students. Applications are processed on a rolling basis. Application fee: $50 ($75 for international students). Electronic applications accepted. *Financial support:* In 2013–14, 18 teaching assistantships with full tuition reimbursements (averaging $10,938 per year) were awarded; Federal Work-Study, institutionally sponsored loans, scholarships/grants, and health care benefits also available. Support available to part-time students. Financial award application deadline: 3/1; financial award applicants required to submit FAFSA. *Faculty research:* Second language acquisitions; U.S. Latino literature; Francophone literature; German, French, Spanish, and Spanish-American literature from the Middle Ages to the modern era; teaching English as a foreign language; linguistics. *Unit head:* Dr. Salvador A. Oropesa, Head, 785-532-6760, Fax: 785-532-7004, E-mail: oropesa@ksu.edu. *Application contact:* Dr. Claire Dehon, Coordinator, 785-532-1929, Fax: 785-532-7004, E-mail: dehoncl@ksu.edu. Website: http://www.k-state.edu/mlangs/.

Kansas State University, Graduate School, College of Education, Department of Curriculum and Instruction, Manhattan, KS 66506. Offers career and technical education (Ed D, PhD); curriculum studies (Ed D, PhD); digital teaching and learning (MS); educational computing, design and online learning (MS); educational technology (Ed D, PhD); elementary/middle level curriculum and instruction (MS); English as a second language (MS); language/diversity education (Ed D, PhD); literacy education (Ed D, PhD); mathematics education (Ed D, PhD); middle level/secondary curriculum and instruction (MS); reading and language arts (MS); reading specialist endorsement (MS); science education (Ed D, PhD); social science education (Ed D, PhD); teacher education (Ed D, PhD); teacher leader/school improvement (MS, Ed D). *Accreditation:* NCATE. Part-time programs available. Postbaccalaureate distance learning degree programs offered (minimal on-campus study). *Faculty:* 18 full-time (13 women), 7 part-time/adjunct (4 women). *Students:* 39 full-time (23 women), 122 part-time (94 women); includes 19 minority (3 Black or African American, non-Hispanic/Latino; 2 Asian, non-Hispanic/Latino; 12 Hispanic/Latino; 2 Two or more races, non-Hispanic/Latino), 12 international. Average age 36. 80 applicants, 50% accepted, 34 enrolled. In 2013, 40 master's, 13 doctorates awarded. *Degree requirements:* For master's, comprehensive exam, portfolio, project, report or thesis; for doctorate, comprehensive exam, thesis/dissertation, preliminary exam. *Entrance requirements:* For master's, minimum GPA of 3.0, letters of recommendation; for doctorate, GRE, minimum GPA of 3.0, letters of recommendation, evidence of scholarly writing. Additional exam requirements/recommendations for international students: Required—TOEFL (minimum score 550 paper-based; 80 iBT). *Application deadline:* For fall admission, 3/1 priority date for domestic students, 2/1 priority date for international students; for spring admission, 10/1 priority date for domestic students, 8/1 priority date for international students. Applications are processed on a rolling basis. Application fee: $50 ($75 for international students). Electronic applications accepted. *Financial support:* In 2013–14, 1 research assistantship (averaging $16,900 per year), 8 teaching assistantships (averaging $12,466 per year) were awarded; career-related internships or fieldwork, institutionally sponsored loans, and scholarships/grants also available. Support available to part-time students. Financial award application deadline: 3/1; financial award applicants required to submit FAFSA. *Faculty research:* Literacy and technology, critical race theory and diversity, achievement gaps, school improvement, teacher education. *Total annual research expenditures:* $543,677. *Unit head:* Dr. Todd Goodson, Chair, 785-532-5904, Fax: 785-532-7304, E-mail: tgoodson@ksu.edu. *Application contact:* Dona Deam, Application Contact, 785-532-5595, Fax: 785-532-7304, E-mail: ddeam@ksu.edu. Website: http://www.coe.k-state.edu/departments/edci/.

Kean University, College of Education, Program in Instruction and Curriculum, Union, NJ 07083. Offers bilingual/bicultural education (MA); classroom instruction (MA); earth science (MA); mathematics/science/computer education (MA); teaching (MA); teaching English as a second language (MA); world languages (Spanish) (MA). *Accreditation:* NCATE. Part-time programs available. *Faculty:* 22 full-time (12 women). *Students:* 16 full-time (10 women), 100 part-time (72 women); includes 57 minority (8 Black or African American, non-Hispanic/Latino; 3 Asian, non-Hispanic/Latino; 45 Hispanic/Latino; 1 Two or more races, non-Hispanic/Latino). Average age 35. 56 applicants, 100% accepted, 38 enrolled. In 2013, 42 master's awarded. *Degree requirements:* For master's, comprehensive exam, thesis (for some programs), two-semester advanced seminar. *Entrance requirements:* For master's, GRE General Test or MAT, PRAXIS, minimum GPA of 3.0, personal statement, professional resume/curriculum vitae, commitment to working with children, certification (for some programs). Additional exam requirements/recommendations for international students: Required—TOEFL (minimum score 550 paper-based; 79 iBT). *Application deadline:* For fall admission, 6/1 for domestic and international students; for spring admission, 12/1 for domestic and international students. Applications are processed on a rolling basis. Application fee: $75 ($150 for international students). Electronic applications accepted. *Expenses:* Tuition, state resident: full-time $12,099; part-time $589 per credit. Tuition, nonresident: full-time $16,399; part-time $722 per credit. *Required fees:* $3050; $139 per credit. Part-time tuition and fees vary according to course level, course load, degree level and program. *Financial support:* In 2013–14, 6 research assistantships with full tuition

reimbursements (averaging $3,713 per year) were awarded; unspecified assistantships also available. Financial award applicants required to submit FAFSA. *Unit head:* Dr. Gail Verdi, Program Coordinator, 908-737-3908, E-mail: gverdi@kean.edu. *Application contact:* Ann-Marie Kay, Assistant Director for Graduate Admissions, 908-737-5922, Fax: 908-737-5925, E-mail: akay@kean.edu.
Website: http://grad.kean.edu/masters-programs/bilingualbicultural-education-instruction-and-curriculum.

Kennesaw State University, Leland and Clarice C. Bagwell College of Education, Program in Graduate Education, Kennesaw, GA 30144-5591. Offers educational leadership (M Ed); educational leadership technology (M Ed); elementary and early childhood education (M Ed); instructional technology (M Ed); middle grades education (M Ed); reading (M Ed); secondary education (M Ed); special education (M Ed); teaching English to speakers of other languages (M Ed). *Accreditation:* NCATE. Part-time programs available. *Students:* 65 full-time (60 women), 229 part-time (158 women); includes 66 minority (46 Black or African American, non-Hispanic/Latino; 6 Asian, non-Hispanic/Latino; 9 Hispanic/Latino; 5 Two or more races, non-Hispanic/Latino), 1 international. Average age 34. 56 applicants, 86% accepted, 43 enrolled. In 2013, 109 master's awarded. *Degree requirements:* For master's, thesis or alternative. *Entrance requirements:* For master's, GRE General Test, T-4 state certification, minimum GPA of 2.75. Additional exam requirements/recommendations for international students: Required—TOEFL (minimum score 550 paper-based; 80 iBT), IELTS (minimum score 6.5). *Application deadline:* For fall admission, 7/1 for domestic and international students; for spring admission, 10/1 for domestic and international students; for summer admission, 4/15 for domestic and international students. Applications are processed on a rolling basis. Application fee: $60. Electronic applications accepted. *Expenses:* Tuition, state resident: full-time $4806; part-time $267 per semester hour. Tuition, nonresident: full-time $17,298; part-time $961 per semester hour. *Required fees:* $1834; $784.50 per semester. *Financial support:* In 2013–14, 10 research assistantships with tuition reimbursements (averaging $8,000 per year) were awarded; Federal Work-Study and unspecified assistantships also available. Support available to part-time students. Financial award application deadline: 4/1; financial award applicants required to submit FAFSA. *Unit head:* Melinda Ross, Administrative Coordinator for Graduate Programs in Education, 770-423-6043, E-mail: graded@kennesaw.edu. *Application contact:* Melinda Ross, Admissions Counselor, 770-423-6043, Fax: 770-423-6885, E-mail: ksugrad@kennesaw.edu.
Website: http://www.kennesaw.edu/education/grad/.

Kennesaw State University, Leland and Clarice C. Bagwell College of Education, Program in Teaching, Kennesaw, GA 30144-5591. Offers art education (MAT); biology (MAT); chemistry (MAT); foreign language education (Chinese and Spanish) (MAT); physics (MAT); secondary English (MAT); secondary mathematics (MAT); special education (MAT); teaching English to speakers of other languages (MAT). Part-time and evening/weekend programs available. *Students:* 82 full-time (59 women), 16 part-time (12 women); includes 28 minority (14 Black or African American, non-Hispanic/Latino; 4 Asian, non-Hispanic/Latino; 7 Hispanic/Latino; 1 Native Hawaiian or other Pacific Islander, non-Hispanic/Latino; 2 Two or more races, non-Hispanic/Latino), 3 international. Average age 35. 28 applicants, 68% accepted, 15 enrolled. In 2013, 54 master's awarded. *Entrance requirements:* For master's, GRE, GACE I (state certificate exam), minimum GPA of 2.75, 2 recommendations, resume. Additional exam requirements/recommendations for international students: Required—TOEFL (minimum score 550 paper-based; 80 iBT), IELTS (minimum score 6). *Application deadline:* For fall admission, 6/1 for domestic and international students; for spring admission, 3/1 for domestic and international students; for summer admission, 4/15 for domestic and international students. Applications are processed on a rolling basis. Application fee: $60. Electronic applications accepted. *Expenses:* Tuition, state resident: full-time $4806; part-time $267 per semester hour. Tuition, nonresident: full-time $17,298; part-time $961 per semester hour. *Required fees:* $1834; $784.50 per semester. *Financial support:* In 2013–14, 2 research assistantships with tuition reimbursements (averaging $8,000 per year) were awarded; unspecified assistantships also available. Financial award application deadline: 4/1; financial award applicants required to submit FAFSA. *Unit head:* Dr. Jillian Ford, Director, 770-499-3093, E-mail: graded@kennesaw.edu. *Application contact:* Melinda Ross, Admissions Counselor, 770-423-6122, Fax: 770-423-6885, E-mail: ksugrad@kennesaw.edu.
Website: http://www.kennesaw.edu.

Kent State University, College of Arts and Sciences, Department of English, Kent, OH 44242-0001. Offers comparative literature (MA); creative writing (MFA); English (PhD); English for teachers (MA); literature and writing (MA); rhetoric and composition (PhD); teaching English as a second language (MA). MFA program offered jointly with Cleveland State University, The University of Akron, and Youngstown State University. Part-time programs available. Terminal master's awarded for partial completion of doctoral program. *Degree requirements:* For master's, one foreign language, thesis optional; for doctorate, one foreign language, thesis/dissertation, qualifying exams. *Entrance requirements:* For master's and doctorate, GRE General Test, writing sample, letters of recommendation. Additional exam requirements/recommendations for international students: Required—TOEFL (minimum score 600 paper-based). Electronic applications accepted. *Faculty research:* British and American literature, textual editing, rhetoric and composition, cultural studies, linguistic and critical theories.

Langston University, School of Education and Behavioral Sciences, Langston, OK 73050. Offers bilingual/multicultural (M Ed); elementary education (M Ed); English as a second language (M Ed); rehabilitation counseling (M Sc); urban education (M Ed). *Accreditation:* CORE; NCATE (one or more programs are accredited). Part-time programs available. *Degree requirements:* For master's, comprehensive exam, thesis optional. *Entrance requirements:* For master's, GRE, writing skills test, minimum GPA of 2.5, 3 letters of recommendation. Additional exam requirements/recommendations for international students: Required—TOEFL, TWE. *Faculty research:* Bilingual/multicultural education, financing post-secondary education.

La Salle University, School of Arts and Sciences, Hispanic Institute, Philadelphia, PA 19141-1199. Offers bilingual/bicultural studies (MA); ESL specialist (Certificate); interpretation in English-Spanish/Spanish-English (Certificate); teaching English to speakers of other languages (MA); translation and interpretation (MA); translation English/Spanish-Spanish/English (Certificate). Part-time and evening/weekend programs available. *Faculty:* 2 full-time (both women), 7 part-time/adjunct (4 women). *Students:* 3 full-time (all women), 66 part-time (50 women); includes 23 minority (11 Black or African American, non-Hispanic/Latino; 1 American Indian or Alaska Native, non-Hispanic/Latino; 11 Hispanic/Latino). Average age 36. 22 applicants, 100% accepted, 18 enrolled. In 2013, 4 master's, 5 other advanced degrees awarded. *Degree requirements:* For master's, one foreign language, project or thesis. *Entrance requirements:* For master's, GRE, MAT, or GMAT, professional resume; two letters of recommendation; for Certificate, GRE, MAT, or GMAT, professional resume; two letters of recommendation; evidence of an advanced level in Spanish. Additional exam requirements/recommendations for international students: Required—TOEFL. *Application deadline:* For fall admission, 8/15 priority date for domestic students, 7/15 for international students; for spring admission, 12/15 priority date for domestic students, 11/15 for international students; for summer admission, 4/15 priority date for domestic

students, 3/15 for international students. Applications are processed on a rolling basis. Application fee: $35. Electronic applications accepted. Application fee is waived when completed online. *Expenses:* Contact institution. *Financial support:* In 2013–14, 13 students received support. Federal Work-Study and scholarships/grants available. Support available to part-time students. Financial award application deadline: 8/31; financial award applicants required to submit FAFSA. *Faculty research:* Puerto Rican literature, cross-cultural communication, English as a second language methodology, Spanish language. *Unit head:* Dr. Carmen Lamas, Director, 215-951-1209, Fax: 215-991-3506, E-mail: lamas@lasalle.edu. *Application contact:* Paul J. Reilly, Assistant Vice President, Enrollment Services, 215-951-1946, Fax: 215-951-1462, E-mail: reilly@lasalle.edu.
Website: http://www.lasalle.edu/grad/index.php?section-hispanic&page-index.

La Salle University, School of Arts and Sciences, Program in Education, Philadelphia, PA 19141-1199. Offers American studies (MA); autism spectrum disorders (MA, Certificate); bilingual/bicultural studies (MA); classroom management (MA, Certificate); dual early childhood and special education (MA); dual middle-level science and math and special education secondary education (MA); education (MA); English (MA); English as a second language (Certificate); instructional coach (Certificate); instructional leadership (MA); reading specialist (MA, Certificate); secondary education (MA); special education (MA, Certificate). Part-time and evening/weekend programs available. *Faculty:* 5 full-time (4 women), 16 part-time/adjunct (10 women). *Students:* 18 full-time (13 women), 137 part-time (112 women); includes 33 minority (24 Black or African American, non-Hispanic/Latino; 9 Hispanic/Latino), 4 international. Average age 32. 47 applicants, 96% accepted, 28 enrolled. In 2013, 58 master's, 20 other advanced degrees awarded. *Degree requirements:* For master's, comprehensive exam. *Entrance requirements:* For master's and Certificate, MAT or GRE, 2 letters of recommendation. Additional exam requirements/recommendations for international students: Required—TOEFL. *Application deadline:* For fall admission, 8/15 priority date for domestic students, 7/15 for international students; for spring admission, 12/15 priority date for domestic students, 11/15 for international students; for summer admission, 4/15 priority date for domestic students, 3/15 for international students. Applications are processed on a rolling basis. Application fee: $35. Electronic applications accepted. Application fee is waived when completed online. *Expenses:* Contact institution. *Financial support:* In 2013–14, 28 students received support. Career-related internships or fieldwork, Federal Work-Study, and scholarships/grants available. Support available to part-time students. Financial award application deadline: 8/31; financial award applicants required to submit FAFSA. *Unit head:* Dr. Greer Richardson, Interim Director, 215-951-1806, Fax: 215-951-1843, E-mail: graded@lasalle.edu. *Application contact:* Paul J. Reilly, Assistant Vice President, Enrollment Services, 215-951-1946, Fax: 215-951-1462, E-mail: reilly@lasalle.edu.
Website: http://www.lasalle.edu/grad/index.php?section-education&page-index.

Lehigh University, College of Education, Program in Comparative and International Education, Bethlehem, PA 18015. Offers comparative and international education (MA, PhD); globalization and educational change (M Ed); international counseling (Certificate); international development in education (Certificate); special education (Certificate); technology use in schools (Certificate); TESOL (Certificate). Part-time and evening/weekend programs available. Postbaccalaureate distance learning degree programs offered (minimal on-campus study). *Faculty:* 4 full-time (2 women). *Students:* 20 full-time (18 women), 26 part-time (17 women); includes 3 minority (2 Asian, non-Hispanic/Latino; 1 Hispanic/Latino), 14 international. Average age 33. 59 applicants, 63% accepted, 10 enrolled. In 2013, 17 master's awarded. Terminal master's awarded for partial completion of doctoral program. *Degree requirements:* For master's, thesis (MA); for doctorate, comprehensive exam, thesis/dissertation. *Entrance requirements:* For master's, 2 letters of recommendation; for doctorate, GRE, transcripts, 2 letters of recommendation, essay, and TOEFL if International applicant. Additional exam requirements/recommendations for international students: Required—TOEFL (minimum score 600 paper-based; 93 iBT). *Application deadline:* For fall and spring admission, 2/1 for domestic and international students. Application fee: $65. Electronic applications accepted. *Financial support:* Application deadline: 3/15. *Faculty research:* Comparative education, rural education, gender equity in education, post-socialist education transformation, educational borrowing, comparing education systems, education policy and globalization, family-school relationships, China, international testing, social inequities. *Unit head:* Dr. Iveta Silova, Program Director and Associate Professor, 610-758-5750, Fax: 610-758-6223, E-mail: ism207@lehigh.edu. *Application contact:* Sharon Y. Warden, Coordinator, 610-758-3256, Fax: 610-758-6223, E-mail: sy00@lehigh.edu.
Website: http://www.lehigh.edu/education/cie.

Lehman College of the City University of New York, Division of Education, Department of Middle and High School Education, Program in Teaching English to Speakers of Other Languages, Bronx, NY 10468-1589. Offers MS Ed. *Accreditation:* NCATE. *Degree requirements:* For master's, thesis. *Entrance requirements:* For master's, minimum GPA of 3.0.

Le Moyne College, Department of Education, Syracuse, NY 13214. Offers adolescent education (MS Ed, MST); adolescent education/special education (MS Ed, MST); adolescent English (MST), including grades 7-12 (MS Ed, MST); adolescent English/special education (MST), including grades 7-12 (MS Ed, MST); adolescent foreign language (MST), including grades 7-12 (MS Ed, MST); adolescent history (MST), including grades 7-12 (MS Ed, MST); childhood education (MS Ed); childhood education/special education (MS Ed); elementary education (MS Ed); general education (MS Ed); inclusive childhood education (MST); literacy education (MS Ed), including birth to grade 6, grades 5-12; school building leader (MS Ed); school building leadership (CAS); school district business leader (MS Ed, CAS); school district leader (MS Ed); school district leadership (CAS); secondary education (MS Ed); special education (MS Ed); students with disabilities-generalist (MS Ed), including grades 7-12 (MS Ed, MST); teaching English to speakers of other languages (MS Ed); urban studies (MS Ed). *Accreditation:* Teacher Education Accreditation Council. Part-time and evening/weekend programs available. *Faculty:* 8 full-time (5 women), 61 part-time/adjunct (38 women). *Students:* 24 full-time (20 women), 178 part-time (133 women); includes 22 minority (12 Black or African American, non-Hispanic/Latino; 1 American Indian or Alaska Native, non-Hispanic/Latino; 3 Asian, non-Hispanic/Latino; 6 Hispanic/Latino), 1 international. Average age 31. 248 applicants, 90% accepted, 86 enrolled. In 2013, 158 master's, 37 CASs awarded. *Degree requirements:* For master's, thesis. *Entrance requirements:* For master's, GRE General Test, bachelor's degree, 2 letters of recommendation, written statement, transcripts. Additional exam requirements/recommendations for international students: Required—TOEFL (minimum score 550 paper-based; 79 iBT). *Application deadline:* For fall admission, 4/1 priority date for domestic and international students; for spring admission, 10/1 priority date for domestic and international students; for summer admission, 3/1 priority date for domestic and international students. Applications are processed on a rolling basis. Application fee: $50. *Expenses:* Contact institution. *Financial support:* In 2013–14, 26 students received support. Career-related internships or fieldwork and health care benefits available. Support available to part-time students. Financial award applicants required to submit FAFSA. *Faculty research:* Minority teachers, special education, multiculturalism, literacy, technology, media literacy learning, autism, school district organization, service-learning, higher level problem solving, teacher leadership. *Unit head:* Dr. Suzanne L. Gilmour, Chair, Department of

Education/Director of Graduate Education Programs, 315-445-4376, Fax: 315-445-4744, E-mail: gilmous@lemoyne.edu. *Application contact:* Kristen P. Trapasso, Senior Director of Enrollment Management, 315-445-4265, Fax: 315-445-6092, E-mail: trapaskp@lemoyne.edu.
Website: http://www.lemoyne.edu/education.

Lesley University, School of Education, Cambridge, MA 02138-2790. Offers arts, community, and education (M Ed); autism studies (Certificate); curriculum and instruction (M Ed, CAGS); early childhood education (M Ed); ecological teaching and learning (MS); educational studies (PhD), including adult learning, educational leadership, individually designed; elementary education (M Ed); emergent technologies for educators (Certificate); ESLArts: language learning through the arts (M Ed); high school education (M Ed); individually designed (M Ed); integrated teaching through the arts (M Ed); literacy for K-8 classroom teachers (M Ed); mathematics education (M Ed); middle school education (M Ed); moderate disabilities (M Ed); online learning (Certificate); reading (CAGS); science in education (M Ed); severe disabilities (M Ed); special needs (CAGS); specialist teacher of reading (M Ed); teacher of visual art (M Ed); technology in education (M Ed, CAGS). *Accreditation:* Teacher Education Accreditation Council. Part-time and evening/weekend programs available. Postbaccalaureate distance learning degree programs offered (no on-campus study). *Faculty:* 40 full-time (30 women), 104 part-time/adjunct (77 women). *Students:* 453 full-time (381 women), 1,672 part-time (1,435 women); includes 284 minority (139 Black or African American, non-Hispanic/Latino; 11 American Indian or Alaska Native, non-Hispanic/Latino; 38 Asian, non-Hispanic/Latino; 58 Hispanic/Latino; 5 Native Hawaiian or other Pacific Islander, non-Hispanic/Latino; 33 Two or more races, non-Hispanic/Latino), 22 international. Average age 35. In 2013, 1,137 master's, 18 doctorates, 51 other advanced degrees awarded. *Degree requirements:* For master's, practicum; for doctorate, thesis/dissertation. *Entrance requirements:* For master's, Massachusetts Tests for Educator Licensure (MTEL), transcripts, statement of purpose, recommendations; interview (for special education); for doctorate, GRE General Test, transcripts, statement of purpose, recommendations, interview, master's degree, resume; for other advanced degree, interview, master's degree. Additional exam requirements/recommendations for international students: Required—TOEFL (minimum score 550 paper-based; 80 iBT). *Application deadline:* Applications are processed on a rolling basis. Application fee: $50. Electronic applications accepted. *Expenses: Tuition:* Part-time $900 per credit. *Financial support:* In 2013–14, 15 fellowships (averaging $3,600 per year) were awarded; career-related internships or fieldwork, Federal Work-Study, scholarships/grants, tuition waivers, and unspecified assistantships also available. Financial award application deadline: 4/15; financial award applicants required to submit FAFSA. *Faculty research:* Assessment in literacy, mathematics and science; autism spectrum disorders; instructional technology and online learning; multicultural education and English language learners. *Unit head:* Dr. Jack Gillette, Dean, 617-349-8401, Fax: 617-349-8607, E-mail: jgillett@lesley.edu. *Application contact:* Martha Sheehan, Director of Admissions, 888-LESLEYU, Fax: 617-349-8313, E-mail: info@lesley.edu.
Website: http://www.lesley.edu/soe.html.

Lewis University, College of Education, Program in English as a Second Language, Romeoville, IL 60446. Offers M Ed. Part-time and evening/weekend programs available. *Students:* 3 full-time (all women), 78 part-time (68 women); includes 11 minority (3 Black or African American, non-Hispanic/Latino; 7 Hispanic/Latino; 1 Two or more races, non-Hispanic/Latino). Average age 35. *Entrance requirements:* For master's, departmental qualifying exam, writing exam, minimum GPA of 2.75, 2 letters of recommendation, interview. Additional exam requirements/recommendations for international students: Required—TOEFL (minimum score 550 paper-based; 80 iBT). *Application deadline:* For fall admission, 5/1 priority date for international students; for spring admission, 11/15 priority date for international students. Application fee: $40. *Financial support:* Federal Work-Study, scholarships/grants, and unspecified assistantships available. Financial award application deadline: 5/1; financial award applicants required to submit FAFSA. *Unit head:* Dr. Barbara Mackey, Program Director, 815-838-0500 Ext. 5962, E-mail: mackeyba@lewisu.edu. *Application contact:* Linda Campbell, Graduate Admission Counselor, 815-838-0500 Ext. 5704, E-mail: campbeli@lewisu.edu.

Lindenwood University, Graduate Programs, School of Education, St. Charles, MO 63301-1695. Offers education (MA); educational administration (MA, Ed D, Ed S); human performance (MS); instructional leadership (Ed D, Ed S); library media (MA); professional counseling (MA); school administration (Ed S); school counseling (MA); teaching (MA); teaching English to speakers of other languages (MA). Part-time and evening/weekend programs available. Postbaccalaureate distance learning degree programs offered (no on-campus study). *Faculty:* 50 full-time (33 women), 228 part-time/adjunct (136 women). *Students:* 454 full-time (352 women), 1,772 part-time (1,351 women); includes 637 minority (545 Black or African American, non-Hispanic/Latino; 9 American Indian or Alaska Native, non-Hispanic/Latino; 9 Asian, non-Hispanic/Latino; 42 Hispanic/Latino; 32 Two or more races, non-Hispanic/Latino), 32 international. Average age 36. 644 applicants, 71% accepted, 401 enrolled. In 2013, 564 master's, 35 doctorates, 83 other advanced degrees awarded. *Degree requirements:* For master's, thesis (for some programs), minimum GPA of 3.0; for doctorate, thesis/dissertation, minimum GPA of 3.0; for Ed S, comprehensive exam, project, minimum GPA of 3.0. *Entrance requirements:* For master's, interview, minimum GPA of 3.0, writing sample, letter of recommendation; for doctorate, GRE, minimum graduate GPA of 3.4, resume, interview, writing sample, 4 letters of recommendation; for Ed S, master's degree in education, relevant work experience. Additional exam requirements/recommendations for international students: Required—TOEFL (minimum score 550 paper-based; 80 iBT). *Application deadline:* For fall admission, 8/26 priority date for domestic and international students; for spring admission, 1/27 priority date for domestic and international students. Applications are processed on a rolling basis. Application fee: $30 ($100 for international students). Electronic applications accepted. *Expenses: Tuition:* Full-time $14,800; part-time $428 per credit hour. *Required fees:* $350. Tuition and fees vary according to course level and course load. *Financial support:* In 2013–14, 385 students received support. Career-related internships or fieldwork, Federal Work-Study, institutionally sponsored loans, scholarships/grants, tuition waivers (partial), and unspecified assistantships available. Financial award application deadline: 6/30; financial award applicants required to submit FAFSA. *Unit head:* Dr. Cynthia Bice, Dean, 636-949-4618, Fax: 636-949-4197, E-mail: cbice@lindenwood.edu. *Application contact:* Brett Barger, Dean of Evening Admissions and Extension Campuses, 636-949-4934, Fax: 636-949-4109, E-mail: adultadmissions@lindenwood.edu.

Lindenwood University, Graduate Programs, School of Humanities, St. Charles, MO 63301-1695. Offers teaching English to speakers of other languages (MA). Part-time programs available. *Faculty:* 4 full-time (3 women), 2 part-time/adjunct (both women). *Students:* 4 full-time (3 women), 5 part-time (all women); includes 7 minority (all Black or African American, non-Hispanic/Latino), 2 international. Average age 36. 4 applicants, 25% accepted, 1 enrolled. In 2013, 15 master's awarded. *Degree requirements:* For master's, minimum cumulative GPA of 3.0. *Entrance requirements:* For master's, minimum GPA of 2.5, 2 letters of recommendation. Additional exam requirements/recommendations for international students: Required—TOEFL (minimum score 550 paper-based; 80 iBT). *Application deadline:* For fall admission, 8/26 priority date for domestic and international students; for spring admission, 1/27 priority date for domestic and international students. Applications are processed on a rolling basis. Application fee: $30 ($100 for international students). Electronic applications accepted. *Expenses: Tuition:* Full-time $14,800; part-time $428 per credit hour. *Required fees:* $350. Tuition and fees vary according to course level and course load. *Financial support:* In 2013–14, 5 students received support. Career-related internships or fieldwork, institutionally sponsored loans, scholarships/grants, tuition waivers (partial), and unspecified assistantships available. Financial award application deadline: 6/30; financial award applicants required to submit FAFSA. *Unit head:* Dr. Michael Whaley, Dean of Humanities, 636-949-4561, E-mail: mwhaley@lindenwood.edu. *Application contact:* Brett Barger, Dean of Evening Admissions and Extension Campuses, 636-949-4934, Fax: 636-949-4109, E-mail: adultadmissions@lindenwood.edu.

Long Island University–Hudson at Westchester, Programs in Education-Teaching, Program in Second Language, TESOL, Bilingual Education, Purchase, NY 10577. Offers MS Ed, Advanced Certificate. Part-time and evening/weekend programs available.

Long Island University–LIU Brooklyn, School of Education, Department of Teaching and Learning, Program in Teaching English to Speakers of Other Languages, Brooklyn, NY 11201-8423. Offers MS Ed. Part-time and evening/weekend programs available. *Degree requirements:* For master's, thesis optional. *Entrance requirements:* For master's, 2 letters of recommendation. Additional exam requirements/recommendations for international students: Required—TOEFL (minimum score 500 paper-based). Electronic applications accepted.

Long Island University–LIU Post, School of Education, Department of Curriculum and Instruction, Brookville, NY 11548-1300. Offers adolescence education (MS); adolescence education: biology (MS); adolescence education: earth science (MS); adolescence education: English (MS); adolescence education: mathematics (MS); adolescence education: social studies (MS); adolescence education: Spanish (MS); art education (MS); bilingual education (MS); childhood education (MS); early childhood education (MS); middle childhood education (MS); music education (MS); teaching English to speakers of other languages (MS). Part-time and evening/weekend programs available. *Degree requirements:* For master's, comprehensive exam or thesis, student teaching. *Entrance requirements:* For master's, minimum GPA of 2.75 in major, 2.5 overall. Electronic applications accepted. *Faculty research:* Ethics and education, teaching strategies.

Loyola University Chicago, School of Education, Program in Teaching and Learning, Chicago, IL 60660. Offers behavior intervention specialist (M Ed); elementary education (M Ed); English as a second language (Certificate); English language teaching and learning (M Ed); math education (M Ed); reading specialist (M Ed); reading teacher endorsement (Certificate); school technology (M Ed); science education (M Ed); secondary education (M Ed); special education (M Ed). *Accreditation:* NCATE. *Faculty:* 23 full-time (16 women), 49 part-time/adjunct (42 women). *Students:* 109. Average age 28. 104 applicants, 71% accepted, 44 enrolled. In 2013, 39 master's awarded. *Degree requirements:* For master's, comprehensive exam. *Entrance requirements:* For master's, Illinois Basic Skills Test, 3 letters of recommendation, minimum GPA of 3.0, resume. Additional exam requirements/recommendations for international students: Required—TOEFL (minimum score 550 paper-based; 79 iBT). *Application deadline:* For fall admission, 7/1 priority date for domestic and international students; for spring admission, 11/1 priority date for domestic and international students; for summer admission, 4/1 for domestic and international students. Applications are processed on a rolling basis. Application fee: $50. Electronic applications accepted. Application fee is waived when completed online. *Expenses: Tuition:* Full-time $16,740; part-time $930 per credit. *Required fees:* $135 per semester. *Financial support:* In 2013–14, 58 fellowships with partial tuition reimbursements were awarded; research assistantships, teaching assistantships, institutionally sponsored loans, scholarships/grants, and unspecified assistantships also available. Support available to part-time students. Financial award application deadline: 2/1; financial award applicants required to submit FAFSA. *Faculty research:* Positive behavior support, school reform, school improvement. *Unit head:* Dr. Ann Marie Ryan, Director, 312-915-7027, E-mail: aryan3@luc.edu. *Application contact:* Marie Rosin-Dittmar, Information Contact, 312-915-6800, E-mail: schleduc@luc.edu.

Madonna University, Program in Teaching English to Speakers of Other Languages, Livonia, MI 48150-1173. Offers MATESOL. Part-time and evening/weekend programs available. *Degree requirements:* For master's, one foreign language, thesis or alternative. Electronic applications accepted.

Manhattanville College, School of Education, Program in Teaching English to Speakers of Other Languages, Purchase, NY 10577-2132. Offers teaching English as a second language (MPS). Part-time and evening/weekend programs available. *Degree requirements:* For master's, comprehensive exam or research project, field experience. *Entrance requirements:* For master's, minimum undergraduate GPA of 3.0. Additional exam requirements/recommendations for international students: Required—TOEFL. Electronic applications accepted.

Marlboro College, Graduate and Professional Studies, Program in Teaching English to Speakers of Other Languages, Brattleboro, VT 05301. Offers MAT. Postbaccalaureate distance learning degree programs offered (minimal on-campus study). *Faculty:* 1 (woman) full-time, 4 part-time/adjunct (2 women). *Students:* 14 part-time (8 women); includes 2 minority (both Asian, non-Hispanic/Latino). Average age 44. *Degree requirements:* For master's, 32 credits, final learning portfolio. *Entrance requirements:* For master's, 2 letters of recommendation, letter of intent, transcripts, interview. Additional exam requirements/recommendations for international students: Required—TOEFL (minimum score 577 paper-based, 90 iBT) or IELTS (minimum score 7). *Application deadline:* For spring admission, 3/1 priority date for domestic students, 3/1 for international students. Applications are processed on a rolling basis. Application fee: $0. Electronic applications accepted. *Expenses: Tuition:* Part-time $685 per credit. Tuition and fees vary according to course load and program. *Financial support:* Applicants required to submit FAFSA. *Unit head:* Beverley Burkett, Degree Chair, 802-451-7514, Fax: 802-258-9201, E-mail: bburkett@gradschool.marlboro.edu. *Application contact:* Matthew Livingston, Director of Graduate Admissions, 802-258-9209, Fax: 802-258-9201, E-mail: mlivingston@marlboro.edu.
Website: https://www.marlboro.edu/academics/graduate/tesol.

Marymount University, School of Education and Human Services, Program in Education, Arlington, VA 22207-4299. Offers counselor education and supervision (Ed D); elementary education (M Ed); English as a second language (M Ed); professional studies (M Ed); secondary education (M Ed); special education: general curriculum (M Ed). *Accreditation:* NCATE. Part-time and evening/weekend programs available. *Faculty:* 8 full-time (6 women), 13 part-time/adjunct (9 women). *Students:* 76 full-time (67 women), 83 part-time (70 women); includes 30 minority (12 Black or African American, non-Hispanic/Latino; 2 American Indian or Alaska Native, non-Hispanic/Latino; 9 Asian, non-Hispanic/Latino; 6 Hispanic/Latino; 1 Two or more races, non-Hispanic/Latino), 12 international. Average age 31. 63 applicants, 95% accepted, 44 enrolled. In 2013, 88 master's awarded. *Degree requirements:* For master's, thesis or alternative; for doctorate, thesis/dissertation. *Entrance requirements:* For master's, GRE or MAT and PRAXIS I or SAT/ACT and VCLA, 2 letters of recommendation, resume,

interview. Additional exam requirements/recommendations for international students: Required—TOEFL (minimum score 600 paper-based; 96 iBT), IELTS (minimum score 6.5). *Application deadline:* For fall admission, 7/1 for international students. Applications are processed on a rolling basis. Application fee: $40. Electronic applications accepted. *Expenses: Tuition:* Part-time $850 per credit. *Required fees:* $10 per credit. One-time fee: $200 part-time. Tuition and fees vary according to program. *Financial support:* In 2013–14, 41 students received support, including 4 research assistantships with full and partial tuition reimbursements available, 1 teaching assistantship with full and partial tuition reimbursement available; career-related internships or fieldwork, Federal Work-Study, scholarships/grants, and unspecified assistantships also available. Support available to part-time students. Financial award applicants required to submit FAFSA. *Unit head:* Dr. Lisa Turissini, Chair, 703-526-1668, Fax: 703-284-1631, E-mail: lisa.turissini@marymount.edu. *Application contact:* Francesca Reed, Director, Graduate Admissions, 703-284-5901, Fax: 703-527-3815, E-mail: grad.admissions@marymount.edu.
Website: http://www.marymount.edu/academics/schools/sehs/grad.aspx.

McDaniel College, Graduate and Professional Studies, TESOL Program, Westminster, MD 21157-4390. Offers MS. Postbaccalaureate distance learning degree programs offered (no on-campus study). *Entrance requirements:* For master's, PRAXIS I, bachelor's degree from accredited institution with minimum cumulative GPA of 2.75; statement of intent; three references.

Mercy College, School of Education, Program in Teaching English to Speakers of Other Languages (TESOL), Dobbs Ferry, NY 10522-1189. Offers MS, Advanced Certificate. Part-time and evening/weekend programs available. Postbaccalaureate distance learning degree programs offered (no on-campus study). *Students:* 22 full-time (20 women), 63 part-time (60 women); includes 62 minority (9 Black or African American, non-Hispanic/Latino; 1 Asian, non-Hispanic/Latino; 48 Hispanic/Latino; 4 Two or more races, non-Hispanic/Latino). Average age 32. 76 applicants, 78% accepted, 22 enrolled. In 2013, 17 master's, 5 other advanced degrees awarded. *Degree requirements:* For master's, comprehensive exam (for some programs). *Entrance requirements:* For master's, resume, interview, undergraduate transcript. Additional exam requirements/recommendations for international students: Required—TOEFL (minimum score 600 paper-based; 100 iBT), IELTS (minimum score 8). *Application deadline:* For fall admission, 8/1 for international students. Applications are processed on a rolling basis. Application fee: $40. Electronic applications accepted. *Expenses: Tuition:* Full-time $19,344; part-time $806 per credit. *Required fees:* $580; $806 per credit. $145 per term. Tuition and fees vary according to course load, degree level and program. *Financial support:* Career-related internships or fieldwork, Federal Work-Study, scholarships/grants, and unspecified assistantships available. Support available to part-time students. Financial award applicants required to submit FAFSA. *Unit head:* Dr. Alfred S. Posamentier, Dean for the School of Education, 914-674-7350, E-mail: aposamentier@mercy.edu. *Application contact:* Allison Gurdineer, Senior Director of Admissions, 877-637-2946, Fax: 914-674-7382, E-mail: admissions@mercy.edu.
Website: https://www.mercy.edu/academics/school-of-education/department-of-literacy-and-multilingual-studies/ms-in-teaching-english-to-speakers-of-other-langua.

Merrimack College, School of Education, North Andover, MA 01845-5800. Offers community engagement (M Ed), including community organizations, higher education, K-12 education; early childhood education (M Ed); elementary education (M Ed); English as a second language (PreK-6) (M Ed); English language learners (M Ed); general studies (M Ed); higher education (M Ed), including leadership and organizational development, student affairs; middle (M Ed); moderate disabilities (PreK-8) (M Ed); secondary (M Ed); teacher leadership (CAGS), including instructional leadership, reading specialist. Part-time and evening/weekend programs available. *Faculty:* 4 full-time (all women), 23 part-time/adjunct (15 women). *Students:* 127 full-time (104 women), 61 part-time (52 women); includes 3 minority (1 Asian, non-Hispanic/Latino; 2 Hispanic/Latino), 2 international. Average age 25. 403 applicants, 47% accepted, 138 enrolled. In 2013, 140 master's awarded. *Degree requirements:* For master's, practicum, portfolio, and state test (for licensure track); capstone (for higher education and community engagement tracks). *Entrance requirements:* For master's, MTEL (Massachusetts Tests for Educator Licensure), official transcripts from other colleges, resume, personal statement, 2 letters of recommendation, additional essay requirements for fellowships. Additional exam requirements/recommendations for international students: Required—TOEFL (minimum score 84 iBT), IELTS (minimum score 6.5). *Application deadline:* For fall admission, 8/15 for domestic and international students; for winter admission, 12/1 for domestic students, 11/15 for international students; for spring admission, 1/10 for domestic and international students; for summer admission, 5/10 for domestic and international students. Applications are processed on a rolling basis. Application fee: $0. Electronic applications accepted. Tuition and fees vary according to course load and program. *Financial support:* In 2013–14, 91 fellowships with full tuition reimbursements were awarded; career-related internships or fieldwork, scholarships/grants, and health care benefits also available. Support available to part-time students. Financial award applicants required to submit FAFSA. *Faculty research:* Expressive language, civic engagement, family life education, reading genres, the psychological process of aging. *Application contact:* Kristen English, Interim Director of Graduate Admission, 978-837-5073, E-mail: englishkr@merrimack.edu.
Website: http://www.merrimack.edu/academics/graduate/education/.

Messiah College, Program in Education, Mechanicsburg, PA 17055. Offers curriculum and instruction (M Ed); special education (M Ed); teaching English to speakers of other languages (M Ed). Part-time programs available. Postbaccalaureate distance learning degree programs offered (no on-campus study). Electronic applications accepted. *Expenses: Tuition:* Part-time $595 per credit hour. *Required fees:* $30 per course. *Faculty research:* Socio-cultural perspectives on education, TESOL, autism, special education.

Michigan State University, The Graduate School, College of Arts and Letters, Department of Linguistics and Germanic, Slavic, Asian, and African Languages, East Lansing, MI 48824. Offers German studies (MA, PhD); linguistics (MA, PhD); teaching English to speakers of other languages (MA). Part-time and evening/weekend programs available. *Entrance requirements:* For master's, GRE General Test, minimum GPA of 3.2 in last 2 undergraduate years, 2 years of college-level foreign language, 3 letters of recommendation, portfolio (German studies); for doctorate, GRE General Test, minimum graduate GPA of 3.5, 3 letters of recommendation, master's degree or sufficient graduate course work in linguistics or language of study, master's thesis or major research paper. Additional exam requirements/recommendations for international students: Required—TOEFL. Electronic applications accepted.

MidAmerica Nazarene University, Graduate Studies in Education, Olathe, KS 66062-1899. Offers ESOL (M Ed); professional teaching (M Ed); special education (MA); technology enhanced teaching (M Ed). *Accreditation:* NCATE. Part-time and evening/weekend programs available. Postbaccalaureate distance learning degree programs offered (no on-campus study). *Degree requirements:* For master's, thesis or alternative, creative project, technology leadership practicum. *Entrance requirements:* For master's, minimum undergraduate GPA of 2.8, 2 years of teaching experience. *Expenses:* Contact institution.

Middle Tennessee State University, College of Graduate Studies, College of Education, Department of Educational Leadership, Program in Curriculum and Instruction, Murfreesboro, TN 37132. Offers curriculum and instruction (M Ed, Ed S); English as a second language (M Ed, Ed S); secondary education (M Ed); technology and curriculum design (Ed S). *Accreditation:* NCATE. Part-time and evening/weekend programs available. Postbaccalaureate distance learning degree programs offered. *Faculty:* 22 full-time (11 women), 22 part-time/adjunct (12 women). *Degree requirements:* For master's, comprehensive exam; for Ed S, comprehensive exam, thesis or alternative. *Entrance requirements:* For master's and Ed S, GRE, MAT or PRAXIS. Additional exam requirements/recommendations for international students: Required—TOEFL (minimum score 525 paper-based; 71 iBT) or IELTS (minimum score 6). *Application deadline:* For fall admission, 6/1 for domestic and international students. Applications are processed on a rolling basis. Application fee: $25 ($30 for international students). Electronic applications accepted. *Financial support:* Tuition waivers available. Support available to part-time students. Financial award application deadline: 5/1. *Unit head:* Dr. James Huffman, Chair, 615-898-2331, Fax: 615-898-2859, E-mail: jim.huffman@mtsu.edu. *Application contact:* Dr. Michael D. Allen, Vice Provost for Research and Dean, 615-898-2840, Fax: 615-904-8020, E-mail: michael.allen@mtsu.edu.

Midwestern State University, Graduate School, West College of Education, Programs in Educational Leadership and Technology, Wichita Falls, TX 76308. Offers bilingual education/English language learners (M Ed); educational leadership (M Ed); educational technology (M Ed). Part-time and evening/weekend programs available. *Degree requirements:* For master's, comprehensive exam. *Entrance requirements:* For master's, GRE General Test or MAT. Additional exam requirements/recommendations for international students: Required—TOEFL (minimum score 550 paper-based). *Application deadline:* For fall admission, 7/1 priority date for domestic students, 4/1 for international students; for spring admission, 11/1 priority date for domestic students, 8/1 for international students. Applications are processed on a rolling basis. Application fee: $35 ($50 for international students). Electronic applications accepted. *Expenses:* Tuition, state resident: full-time $3627; part-time $201.50 per credit hour. Tuition, nonresident: full-time $10,899; part-time $605.50 per credit hour. *Required fees:* $1357. *Financial support:* Career-related internships or fieldwork, Federal Work-Study, institutionally sponsored loans, scholarships/grants, tuition waivers (partial), and unspecified assistantships available. Support available to part-time students. Financial award application deadline: 3/1; financial award applicants required to submit FAFSA. *Faculty research:* Role of the principal in the twenty-first century, culturally proficient leadership, human diversity, immigration, teacher collaboration. *Unit head:* Dr. Pamela Whitehouse, Graduate Coordinator, 940-397-4139, Fax: 940-397-4694, E-mail: pamela.whitehouse@mwsu.edu. *Application contact:* Dr. Pamela Whitehouse, Graduate Coordinator, 940-397-4139, Fax: 940-397-4694, E-mail: pamela.whitehouse@mwsu.edu.
Website: http://www.mwsu.edu/academics/education/.

Millersville University of Pennsylvania, College of Graduate and Professional Studies, School of Education, Department of Elementary and Early Childhood Education, Program in Language and Literacy Education, Millersville, PA 17551-0302. Offers ESL (M Ed); language and literacy education (M Ed). *Accreditation:* NCATE. Part-time and evening/weekend programs available. *Faculty:* 17 full-time (11 women), 18 part-time/adjunct (15 women). *Students:* 1 (woman) full-time, 58 part-time (52 women); includes 2 minority (1 Black or African American, non-Hispanic/Latino; 1 Hispanic/Latino). Average age 29. 12 applicants, 100% accepted, 11 enrolled. In 2013, 41 master's awarded. *Degree requirements:* For master's, thesis optional. *Entrance requirements:* For master's, GRE or MAT, 3 letters of recommendation, copy of teaching certificate, goal statement, official transcripts. Additional exam requirements/recommendations for international students: Required—TOEFL (minimum score 550 paper-based, 79 iBT) or IELTS (minimum score 6). *Application deadline:* For fall admission, 1/15 priority date for domestic and international students; for winter admission, 10/1 priority date for domestic and international students; for spring admission, 10/1 priority date for domestic and international students. Applications are processed on a rolling basis. Application fee: $40. Electronic applications accepted. *Expenses:* Tuition, state resident: full-time $7956; part-time $442 per credit. Tuition, nonresident: full-time $11,934; part-time $663 per credit. *Required fees:* $2196; $122 per credit. Tuition and fees vary according to course load. *Financial support:* In 2013–14, 3 students received support, including 3 research assistantships with full tuition reimbursements available (averaging $4,367 per year); institutionally sponsored loans and unspecified assistantships also available. Support available to part-time students. Financial award application deadline: 3/15; financial award applicants required to submit FAFSA. *Faculty research:* Academic vocabulary, new literacies, literacy coaching, trends and issues in multicultural children's literature, graphic novels and emergent readers, transgender characters in young adult literature. *Unit head:* Dr. Judith K. Wenrich, Coordinator, 717-872-3395, Fax: 717-871-5462, E-mail: judith.wenrich@millersville.edu. *Application contact:* Dr. Victor S. DeSantis, Dean of College of Graduate and Professional Studies/Associate Provost for Civic and Community Engagement, 717-872-3099, Fax: 717-872-3453, E-mail: victor.desantis@millersville.edu.
Website: http://www.millersville.edu/academics/educ/eled/graduate.php.

Minnesota State University Mankato, College of Graduate Studies, College of Arts and Humanities, Department of English, Mankato, MN 56001. Offers creative writing (MFA); English (MAT); English studies (MA); teaching English as a second language (MA, Certificate); technical communication (MA, Certificate). Part-time programs available. *Students:* 46 full-time (29 women), 136 part-time (87 women). *Degree requirements:* For master's, one foreign language, comprehensive exam, thesis or alternative. *Entrance requirements:* For master's, minimum GPA of 3.0 during previous 2 years, writing sample (MFA). Additional exam requirements/recommendations for international students: Required—TOEFL (minimum score 500 paper-based; 61 iBT). *Application deadline:* For fall admission, 7/1 for domestic students, 5/1 for international students. Applications are processed on a rolling basis. Application fee: $40. Electronic applications accepted. *Financial support:* Research assistantships with full tuition reimbursements, teaching assistantships with full tuition reimbursements, career-related internships or fieldwork, Federal Work-Study, and unspecified assistantships available. Financial award application deadline: 3/15; financial award applicants required to submit FAFSA. *Faculty research:* Keats and Christianity. *Unit head:* Dr. John Banschbach, Chairperson, 507-389-2117. *Application contact:* 507-389-2321, E-mail: grad@mnsu.edu.
Website: http://english.mnsu.edu/.

Mississippi College, Graduate School, College of Arts and Sciences, School of Humanities and Social Sciences, Department of Modern Languages, Clinton, MS 39058. Offers teaching English to speakers of other languages (MA, MS). Part-time programs available. *Degree requirements:* For master's, thesis (for some programs). *Entrance requirements:* For master's, GRE or NTE. Additional exam requirements/recommendations for international students: Recommended—TOEFL, IELTS. Electronic applications accepted.

Missouri Western State University, Program in Assessment, St. Joseph, MO 64507-2294. Offers autism spectrum disorders (MAS, Graduate Certificate); TESOL (MAS,

Graduate Certificate); writing (MAS). Part-time programs available. *Students:* 6 full-time (4 women), 44 part-time (42 women); includes 4 minority (2 Black or African American, non-Hispanic/Latino; 1 Asian, non-Hispanic/Latino; 1 Hispanic/Latino), 1 international. Average age 36. 2 applicants, 50% accepted, 1 enrolled. In 2013, 9 master's, 7 other advanced degrees awarded. *Entrance requirements:* For master's, minimum GPA of 2.75. Additional exam requirements/recommendations for international students: Recommended—TOEFL (minimum score 500 paper-based; 61 iBT), IELTS (minimum score 5.5). *Application deadline:* For fall admission, 7/15 for domestic students, 6/15 for international students; for spring admission, 10/1 for domestic students, 10/15 for international students. Applications are processed on a rolling basis. Application fee: $45 ($50 for international students). Electronic applications accepted. *Expenses:* Tuition, state resident: full-time $6019; part-time $300.96 per credit hour. Tuition, nonresident: full-time $11,194; part-time $559.71 per credit hour. *Required fees:* $542; $99 per credit hour. $176 per semester. Tuition and fees vary according to course load and program. *Financial support:* Scholarships/grants and unspecified assistantships available. Support available to part-time students. *Unit head:* Dr. Susan Bashinski, Coordinator, 816-271-5629, E-mail: sbashinski@missouriwestern.edu. *Application contact:* Dr. Benjamin D. Caldwell, Dean of the Graduate School, 816-271-4394, Fax: 816-271-4525, E-mail: graduate@missouriwestern.edu.
Website: https://www.missouriwestern.edu/masa/.

Monmouth University, The Graduate School, School of Education, West Long Branch, NJ 07764-1898. Offers applied behavioral analysis (Certificate); autism (Certificate); initial certification (MAT), including elementary level, K-12, secondary level; principal (MS Ed); principal/school administrator (MS Ed); reading specialist (MS Ed); school counseling (MS Ed); special education (MS Ed), including autism, learning disabilities teacher consultant, teacher of students with disabilities, teaching in inclusive settings; speech-language pathology (MS Ed); student affairs and college counseling (MS Ed); teaching English to speakers of other languages (TESOL) (Certificate). *Accreditation:* NCATE. Part-time and evening/weekend programs available. *Faculty:* 15 full-time (11 women), 19 part-time/adjunct (17 women). *Students:* 125 full-time (97 women), 168 part-time (146 women); includes 38 minority (12 Black or African American, non-Hispanic/Latino; 5 Asian, non-Hispanic/Latino; 16 Hispanic/Latino; 5 Two or more races, non-Hispanic/Latino). Average age 28. 176 applicants, 90% accepted, 112 enrolled. In 2013, 147 master's awarded. *Entrance requirements:* For master's, GRE within last 5 years (for MS Ed in speech-language pathology), minimum GPA of 3.0 in major; 2 letters of recommendation (for some programs), resume, personal statement or essay (depending on degree program). Additional exam requirements/recommendations for international students: Required—TOEFL (minimum score 550 paper-based; 79 iBT), IELTS (minimum score 6), Michigan English Language Assessment Battery (minimum score 77). *Application deadline:* For fall admission, 7/15 priority date for domestic students, 7/1 for international students; for spring admission, 11/15 priority date for domestic students, 11/1 for international students. Applications are processed on a rolling basis. Application fee: $50. Electronic applications accepted. *Expenses: Tuition:* Part-time $1004 per credit hour. *Required fees:* $157 per semester. *Financial support:* In 2013–14, 191 students received support, including 159 fellowships (averaging $2,786 per year), 30 research assistantships (averaging $8,755 per year); career-related internships or fieldwork, scholarships/grants, and unspecified assistantships also available. Support available to part-time students. Financial award applicants required to submit FAFSA. *Faculty research:* Multicultural literacy, science and mathematics teaching strategies, teacher as reflective practitioner, children with disabilities. *Unit head:* Dr. Jason Barr, Program Director, 732-263-5238, Fax: 732-263-5277, E-mail: jbarr@monmouth.edu. *Application contact:* Lauren Vento-Cifelli, Associate Vice President of Undergraduate and Graduate Admission, 732-571-3452, Fax: 732-263-5123, E-mail: gradadm@monmouth.edu.
Website: http://www.monmouth.edu/academics/schools/education/default.asp.

Montclair State University, The Graduate School, College of Education and Human Services, Department of Secondary and Special Education, Program in Teaching in Subject Area, Montclair, NJ 07043-1624. Offers art (MAT); biology (MAT); chemistry (MAT); earth science (MAT); English (MAT); French (MAT); health and physical education (MAT); health education (MAT); mathematics (MAT); music (MAT); physical education (MAT); physical science (MAT); social studies (MAT); Spanish (MAT); teacher of English as a second language (MAT). *Degree requirements:* For master's, comprehensive exam, thesis or alternative. *Entrance requirements:* For master's, GRE General Test, interview, 2 letters of recommendation. Additional exam requirements/recommendations for international students: Required—TOEFL (minimum score 83 iBT), IELTS (minimum score 6.5). Electronic applications accepted.

Montclair State University, The Graduate School, College of Humanities and Social Sciences, Department of Linguistics, Program in Teaching English as a Second Language, Montclair, NJ 07043-1624. Offers MAT. *Degree requirements:* For master's, comprehensive exam. *Entrance requirements:* For master's, GRE General Test, 2 letters of recommendation, essay. Additional exam requirements/recommendations for international students: Required—TOEFL (minimum score 83 iBT), IELTS (minimum score 6.5). Electronic applications accepted. *Faculty research:* Cultural factors in bilingualism, emergent technologies in language learning.

Montclair State University, The Graduate School, College of Humanities and Social Sciences, Department of Linguistics, Teaching English to Speakers of Other Languages Certificate Program, Montclair, NJ 07043-1624. Offers Certificate. Part-time and evening/weekend programs available. *Degree requirements:* For Certificate, comprehensive exam. *Entrance requirements:* For degree, 2 letters of recommendation, essay. Additional exam requirements/recommendations for international students: Required—TOEFL (minimum score 83 iBT), IELTS (minimum score 6.5). Electronic applications accepted. *Faculty research:* Language learning and technology research, interlanguage, bilingual pragmatics.

Monterey Institute of International Studies, Graduate School of Translation, Interpretation and Language Education, Program in Teaching English to Speakers of Other Languages, Monterey, CA 93940-2691. Offers MATESOL. *Degree requirements:* For master's, portfolio, oral defense. *Entrance requirements:* For master's, minimum GPA of 3.0. Additional exam requirements/recommendations for international students: Required—TOEFL (minimum score 600 paper-based; 100 iBT). Electronic applications accepted. *Expenses: Tuition:* Full-time $34,970; part-time $1665 per credit. *Required fees:* $28 per semester.

Mount Saint Vincent University, Graduate Programs, Faculty of Education, Program in Curriculum Studies, Halifax, NS B3M 2J6, Canada. Offers education of young adolescents (M Ed, MA Ed, MA-R); general studies (M Ed, MA Ed, MA-R); teaching English as a second language (M Ed, MA Ed, MA-R). Part-time and evening/weekend programs available. Postbaccalaureate distance learning degree programs offered (minimal on-campus study). *Degree requirements:* For master's, thesis (for some programs). *Entrance requirements:* For master's, bachelor's degree in related field, minimum B average, 1 year of teaching experience. Electronic applications accepted. *Faculty research:* Science education, cultural studies, international education, curriculum development.

Multnomah University, Multnomah Bible College Graduate Degree Programs, Portland, OR 97220-5898. Offers counseling (MA); global development and justice (MA); teaching (MA); TESOL (MA). *Faculty:* 6 full-time (4 women), 23 part-time/adjunct (11 women). *Students:* 124 full-time (84 women), 21 part-time (12 women); includes 16 minority (4 Black or African American, non-Hispanic/Latino; 1 Asian, non-Hispanic/Latino; 7 Hispanic/Latino; 4 Two or more races, non-Hispanic/Latino), 1 international. Average age 30. 103 applicants, 94% accepted, 53 enrolled. In 2013, 49 master's awarded. *Degree requirements:* For master's, variable foreign language requirement, comprehensive exam (for some programs), thesis (for some programs). *Entrance requirements:* For master's, CBEST or WEST-B (for MAT), interview; references (4 for teaching); writing sample (for counseling). Additional exam requirements/recommendations for international students: Required—TOEFL (minimum score 550 paper-based). *Application deadline:* For fall admission, 8/1 for domestic students, 12/1 for international students; for spring admission, 12/1 for domestic and international students. Application fee: $40. *Expenses: Tuition:* Full-time $7360; part-time $460 per credit hour. *Financial support:* Career-related internships or fieldwork and scholarships/grants available. Support available to part-time students. Financial award application deadline: 7/1; financial award applicants required to submit FAFSA. *Unit head:* Dr. Rex Koivisto, Academic Dean, 503-251-6401. *Application contact:* Stephanie Pollard, Admissions Counselor, 503-251-5166, Fax: 503-254-1268, E-mail: admiss@multnomah.edu.

Murray State University, College of Humanities and Fine Arts, Department of English and Philosophy, Program in Teaching English to Speakers of Other Languages, Murray, KY 42071. Offers MA. Part-time programs available. Postbaccalaureate distance learning degree programs offered (no on-campus study). *Degree requirements:* For master's, one foreign language, comprehensive exam, 12 hours for portfolio. *Entrance requirements:* For master's, minimum GPA of 2.25. Additional exam requirements/recommendations for international students: Required—TOEFL (minimum score 525 paper-based), IELTS (minimum score 5.5). *Faculty research:* Methods, integrated skills, intercultural communication, assessment.

Nazareth College of Rochester, Graduate Studies, Department of Education, Program in Teaching English to Speakers of Other Languages, Rochester, NY 14618-3790. Offers MS Ed. *Accreditation:* Teacher Education Accreditation Council. *Entrance requirements:* For master's, minimum GPA of 3.0.

New Jersey City University, Graduate Studies and Continuing Education, Debra Cannon Partridge Wolfe College of Education, Department of Educational Leadership, Jersey City, NJ 07305-1597. Offers basics and urban studies (MA); bilingual/bicultural education and English as a second language (MA); educational administration and supervision (MA). Part-time and evening/weekend programs available. *Faculty:* 9 full-time (7 women), 7 part-time/adjunct (4 women). *Students:* 25 full-time (17 women), 206 part-time (155 women); includes 121 minority (17 Black or African American, non-Hispanic/Latino; 7 Asian, non-Hispanic/Latino; 97 Hispanic/Latino), 2 international. Average age 37. In 2013, 71 master's awarded. *Entrance requirements:* Additional exam requirements/recommendations for international students: Required—TOEFL (minimum score 61 iBT). *Application deadline:* For fall admission, 8/1 priority date for domestic students; for spring admission, 12/1 for domestic students. Applications are processed on a rolling basis. Application fee: $0. *Expenses: Tuition, area resident:* Part-time $527.90 per credit. Tuition, nonresident: part-time $947.75 per credit. *Financial support:* Fellowships, teaching assistantships, career-related internships or fieldwork, and unspecified assistantships available. *Unit head:* Dr. Catherine Rogers, Chairperson, 201-200-3012, E-mail: cshevey@njcu.edu. *Application contact:* Dr. William Bajor, Dean of Graduate Studies, 201-200-3409, Fax: 201-200-3411, E-mail: wbajor@njcu.edu.

Newman University, Master of Education Program, Wichita, KS 67213-2097. Offers building leadership (MS Ed); curriculum and instruction (MS Ed), including English as a second language, reading specialist; organizational leadership (MS Ed). *Accreditation:* NCATE. Part-time and evening/weekend programs available. Postbaccalaureate distance learning degree programs offered (no on-campus study). *Faculty:* 3 full-time (1 woman), 22 part-time/adjunct (all women). *Students:* 19 full-time (15 women), 498 part-time (407 women); includes 66 minority (19 Black or African American, non-Hispanic/Latino; 5 American Indian or Alaska Native, non-Hispanic/Latino; 10 Asian, non-Hispanic/Latino; 27 Hispanic/Latino; 1 Native Hawaiian or other Pacific Islander, non-Hispanic/Latino; 4 Two or more races, non-Hispanic/Latino). Average age 37. 67 applicants, 73% accepted, 35 enrolled. In 2013, 53 master's awarded. *Degree requirements:* For master's, thesis optional. *Entrance requirements:* For master's, 3 years' full-time teaching experience, minimum GPA of 3.0, writing sample, 2 letters of recommendation, evidence of teaching certification. Additional exam requirements/recommendations for international students: Required—TOEFL (minimum score 600 paper-based; 100 iBT). *Application deadline:* For fall admission, 8/15 priority date for domestic students, 7/15 priority date for international students; for spring admission, 1/10 priority date for domestic students, 11/15 priority date for international students. Applications are processed on a rolling basis. Application fee: $25 ($40 for international students). Electronic applications accepted. *Expenses:* Contact institution. *Financial support:* Application deadline: 8/15; applicants required to submit FAFSA. *Unit head:* Dr. Gina Marx, Director of Graduate Education, 316-942-4291 Ext. 2416, Fax: 316-942-4483, E-mail: marxg@newmanu.edu. *Application contact:* Linda Kay Sabala, Director of Graduate Admissions, 316-942-4291 Ext. 2230, Fax: 316-942-4483, E-mail: sabalal@newmanu.edu.
Website: http://www.newmanu.edu/studynu/graduate/master-science-education.

The New School, The New School for Public Engagement, Program in Teaching English to Speakers of Other Languages, New York, NY 10011. Offers MA. Part-time and evening/weekend programs available. Postbaccalaureate distance learning degree programs offered (no on-campus study). *Entrance requirements:* Additional exam requirements/recommendations for international students: Required—TOEFL (minimum score 600 paper-based; 100 iBT), IELTS (minimum score 7), TWE. Electronic applications accepted.

New York University, Steinhardt School of Culture, Education, and Human Development, Department of Teaching and Learning, Program in Multilingual/Multicultural Studies, New York, NY 10003. Offers bilingual education (MA, PhD, Advanced Certificate); foreign language education (MA, Advanced Certificate); foreign language education (7-12) and TESOL (K-12) (MA); teaching English to speakers of other languages (MA, PhD, Advanced Certificate); teaching foreign languages, 7-12 (MA), including Chinese, French, Italian, Japanese, Spanish; teaching foreign languages, college and adult (MA); teaching French as a foreign language and TESOL (MA); teaching Spanish as a foreign language and TESOL (MA). *Accreditation:* Teacher Education Accreditation Council. Part-time and evening/weekend programs available. *Faculty:* 5 full-time (4 women). *Students:* 134 full-time (112 women), 77 part-time (68 women); includes 43 minority (6 Black or African American, non-Hispanic/Latino; 18 Asian, non-Hispanic/Latino; 15 Hispanic/Latino; 4 Two or more races, non-Hispanic/Latino), 113 international. Average age 31. 501 applicants, 39% accepted, 68 enrolled. In 2013, 91 master's, 3 doctorates, 7 other advanced degrees awarded. *Degree requirements:* For master's, thesis (for some programs); for doctorate, thesis/dissertation. *Entrance requirements:* For doctorate, GRE General Test, interview; for Advanced Certificate, master's degree. Additional exam requirements/recommendations for international students: Required—TOEFL (minimum score 100 iBT). *Application deadline:* For fall admission, 12/1 priority date for domestic and international students;

for spring admission, 10/1 for domestic and international students. Applications are processed on a rolling basis. Application fee: $75. Electronic applications accepted. *Expenses:* Tuition: Full-time $35,856; part-time $1494 per unit. *Required fees:* $1408; $64 per unit. $473 per term. Tuition and fees vary according to course load and program. *Financial support:* Fellowships with full and partial tuition reimbursements, career-related internships or fieldwork, Federal Work-Study, institutionally sponsored loans, scholarships/grants, and tuition waivers (partial) available. Support available to part-time students. Financial award application deadline: 2/1; financial award applicants required to submit FAFSA. *Faculty research:* Second language acquisition, cross-cultural communication, technology-enhanced language learning, language variation, action learning. *Unit head:* Prof. Shondel Nero, Director, 212-998-5757, E-mail: shondel.nero@nyu.edu. *Application contact:* 212-998-5030, Fax: 212-995-4328, E-mail: steinhardt.gradadmissions@nyu.edu.
Website: http://steinhardt.nyu.edu/teachlearn/mms.

Niagara University, Graduate Division of Education, Concentration in Teacher Education, Niagara Falls, NY 14109. Offers early childhood and childhood education (MS Ed, Certificate); middle and adolescence education (MS Ed, Certificate); special education (grades 1-12) (MS Ed, Certificate); teaching English to speakers of other languages (MS Ed). *Accreditation:* NCATE. *Students:* 168 full-time (130 women), 40 part-time (28 women); includes 11 minority (4 Black or African American, non-Hispanic/Latino; 1 Asian, non-Hispanic/Latino; 5 Hispanic/Latino; 1 Native Hawaiian or other Pacific Islander, non-Hispanic/Latino), 101 international. Average age 27. In 2013, 131 master's, 1 Certificate awarded. *Entrance requirements:* For master's, GRE General Test or MAT. Additional exam requirements/recommendations for international students: Required—TOEFL (minimum score 550 paper-based, 79 iBT) or IELTS (minimum score 6). *Application deadline:* For fall admission, 8/1 for domestic students. Applications are processed on a rolling basis. Application fee: $30. *Expenses:* Contact institution. *Financial support:* Research assistantships with full and partial tuition reimbursements, teaching assistantships with full and partial tuition reimbursements, career-related internships or fieldwork, Federal Work-Study, scholarships/grants, and unspecified assistantships available. Financial award application deadline: 4/15; financial award applicants required to submit FAFSA. *Unit head:* Dr. Chandra Foote, Chair, 716-286-8549. *Application contact:* Dr. Debra A. Colley, Dean of Education, 716-286-8560, Fax: 716-286-8561, E-mail: dcolley@niagara.edu.
Website: http://www.niagara.edu/teacher-education.

Northeastern Illinois University, College of Graduate Studies and Research, College of Arts and Sciences, Program in Linguistics, Chicago, IL 60625-4699. Offers linguistics (MA); TESL (MA). Part-time and evening/weekend programs available. *Degree requirements:* For master's, one foreign language, comprehensive exam, thesis optional. *Entrance requirements:* For master's, 9 undergraduate hours in a foreign language or equivalent, minimum GPA of 2.75. Additional exam requirements/recommendations for international students: Required—TOEFL (minimum score 550 paper-based; 79 iBT). Electronic applications accepted. *Faculty research:* Acquisition of literacy, Mayan language, Rotuman language, English as a second language methodology, Farsi language.

Northeastern Illinois University, College of Graduate Studies and Research, College of Arts and Sciences, Program in Teaching English as a Second/Foreign Language, Chicago, IL 60625-4699. Offers MA.

Northern Arizona University, Graduate College, College of Arts and Letters, Department of English, Flagstaff, AZ 86011. Offers applied linguistics (PhD); English (MA, MFA), including creative writing (MFA), general English studies (MA), literature (MA), rhetoric and the teaching of writing (MA), secondary English education (MA); professional writing (Certificate); teaching English as a second language (MA, Certificate). Part-time programs available. *Faculty:* 62 full-time (43 women), 15 part-time/adjunct (9 women). *Students:* 168 full-time (120 women), 133 part-time (100 women); includes 52 minority (12 Black or African American, non-Hispanic/Latino; 4 American Indian or Alaska Native, non-Hispanic/Latino; 5 Asian, non-Hispanic/Latino; 22 Hispanic/Latino; 9 Two or more races, non-Hispanic/Latino), 37 international. Average age 33. 230 applicants, 69% accepted, 92 enrolled. In 2013, 117 master's, 3 doctorates, 16 other advanced degrees awarded. *Degree requirements:* For master's, comprehensive exam (for some programs), thesis (for some programs), departmental qualifying exam; for doctorate, comprehensive exam, thesis/dissertation, departmental qualifying exam. *Entrance requirements:* For master's, minimum GPA of 3.0 or GRE; for doctorate, GRE General Test. Additional exam requirements/recommendations for international students: Required—TOEFL (minimum score 550 paper-based; 80 iBT), IELTS (minimum score 7), TOEFL (minimum score 600 paper-based; 100 iBT) for PhD; TOEFL (minimum score 570 paper-based; 89 iBT) for MA. *Application deadline:* For fall admission, 4/15 priority date for domestic students, 2/15 priority date for international students; for spring admission, 11/15 priority date for domestic and international students. Applications are processed on a rolling basis. Application fee: $65. Electronic applications accepted. *Financial support:* In 2013–14, 73 teaching assistantships with full tuition reimbursements (averaging $13,500 per year) were awarded; Federal Work-Study, scholarships/grants, health care benefits, tuition waivers (full and partial), and unspecified assistantships also available. Financial award applicants required to submit FAFSA. *Unit head:* Dr. John Rothfork, Chair, 928-523-0559, Fax: 928-523-4911, E-mail: john.rothfork@nau.edu. *Application contact:* Yvette Loeffler-Schmelzle, Secretary, 928-523-6842, Fax: 928-523-4911, E-mail: yvette.schmelzle@nau.edu.
Website: http://nau.edu/cal/english/.

Northern Arizona University, Graduate College, College of Education, Department of Educational Specialties, Flagstaff, AZ 86011. Offers autism spectrum disorders (Certificate); bilingual/multicultural education (M Ed), including bilingual education, ESL education; career and technical education (M Ed, Certificate); early childhood special education (M Ed); educational technology (M Ed, Certificate); special education (M Ed). *Faculty:* 32 full-time (21 women), 4 part-time/adjunct (all women). *Students:* 68 full-time (48 women), 158 part-time (119 women); includes 93 minority (6 Black or African American, non-Hispanic/Latino; 29 American Indian or Alaska Native, non-Hispanic/Latino; 4 Asian, non-Hispanic/Latino; 53 Hispanic/Latino; 1 Native Hawaiian or other Pacific Islander, non-Hispanic/Latino), 6 international. Average age 37. 66 applicants, 95% accepted, 38 enrolled. In 2013, 121 master's, 3 Certificates awarded. *Degree requirements:* For master's, comprehensive exam (for some programs), thesis (for some programs). *Entrance requirements:* For master's, minimum GPA of 3.0. Additional exam requirements/recommendations for international students: Required—TOEFL (minimum score 550 paper-based; 80 iBT), IELTS (minimum score 7). *Application deadline:* For fall admission, 3/1 for international students; for spring admission, 9/15 for international students. Applications are processed on a rolling basis. Application fee: $65. Electronic applications accepted. *Financial support:* In 2013–14, 9 teaching assistantships with full tuition reimbursements (averaging $9,698 per year) were awarded. Financial award applicants required to submit FAFSA. *Unit head:* Dr. Laura Sujo-Montes, Chair, 928-523-0892, Fax: 928-523-1929, E-mail: laura.sujo-montes@nau.edu. *Application contact:* Laura Cook, Coordinator, 928-523-5342, Fax: 928-523-8950, E-mail: laura.cook@nau.edu.
Website: http://nau.edu/coe/ed-specialties/.

Northern Michigan University, College of Graduate Studies, College of Arts and Sciences, Department of English, Marquette, MI 49855-5301. Offers creative writing (MFA); literature (MA); pedagogy (MA); teaching English to speakers of other languages (Graduate Certificate); theater (MA); writing (MA). Part-time and evening/weekend programs available. *Faculty:* 38. *Students:* 53 full-time (30 women), 10 part-time (9 women); includes 9 minority (2 American Indian or Alaska Native, non-Hispanic/Latino; 1 Asian, non-Hispanic/Latino; 3 Hispanic/Latino; 3 Two or more races, non-Hispanic/Latino). Average age 31. 119 applicants, 42% accepted, 28 enrolled. In 2013, 31 master's awarded. *Degree requirements:* For master's, capstone project: thesis, practicum or portfolio (for MA); thesis (for MFA); for Graduate Certificate, one foreign language. *Entrance requirements:* For master's, minimum GPA of 3.0, bachelor's degree in English or minimum of 30 credit hours in undergraduate English; for Graduate Certificate, bachelor's degree. Additional exam requirements/recommendations for international students: Required—TOEFL (minimum score 550 paper-based; 79 iBT), IELTS (minimum score 6.5). *Application deadline:* For fall admission, 7/1 for domestic students; for winter admission, 2/1 for domestic students; for spring admission, 3/17 for domestic students. Applications are processed on a rolling basis. Application fee: $50. Electronic applications accepted. *Expenses:* Tuition, state resident: part-time $427 per credit. Tuition, nonresident: part-time $614.50 per credit. *Required fees:* $325 per semester. Tuition and fees vary according to course load and program. *Financial support:* In 2013–14, 4 research assistantships with full tuition reimbursements (averaging $8,898 per year), 40 teaching assistantships with full tuition reimbursements (averaging $8,898 per year) were awarded; Federal Work-Study, institutionally sponsored loans, and unspecified assistantships also available. Support available to part-time students. Financial award application deadline: 3/1. *Faculty research:* Modern Arabic literature, British literature (medieval to contemporary), postcolonial literature, Native and African-American literature, creative writing, critical theory, pedagogy. *Unit head:* Prof. Ray Ventre, PhD, Head of English Department/Professor, 906-227-2222, E-mail: rventre@nmu.edu. *Application contact:* Prof. Russell Prather, PhD, Director of MA Program/Professor, 906-227-2857, E-mail: rprather@nmu.edu.
Website: http://www.nmu.edu/english/.

Northwest Missouri State University, Graduate School, College of Education and Human Services, Department of Professional Education, Maryville, MO 64468-6001. Offers educational leadership (MS Ed, Ed S), including educational leadership: elementary (MS Ed), educational leadership: K-12 (MS Ed), educational leadership: secondary (MS Ed), elementary principalship (Ed S), secondary principalship (Ed S), superintendency (Ed S); English language learners (Certificate); reading (MS Ed); special education (MS Ed); teaching: early childhood (MS Ed); teaching: elementary self contained (MS Ed); teaching: English language learners (MS Ed); teaching: middle school (MS Ed). *Accreditation:* NCATE. Part-time programs available. *Degree requirements:* For master's, comprehensive exam. *Entrance requirements:* For master's, GRE General Test, minimum undergraduate GPA of 2.75, teaching certificate, writing sample. Additional exam requirements/recommendations for international students: Required—TOEFL (minimum score 550 paper-based). Electronic applications accepted.

Notre Dame de Namur University, Division of Academic Affairs, College of Arts and Sciences, Program in English, Belmont, CA 94002-1908. Offers English (MA); teaching English to speakers of other languages (Certificate). Part-time programs available. *Degree requirements:* For master's, thesis. *Entrance requirements:* For master's, minimum GPA of 2.5, writing sample. Additional exam requirements/recommendations for international students: Required—TOEFL (minimum score 550 paper-based; 79 iBT). Electronic applications accepted.

Notre Dame of Maryland University, Graduate Studies, Program in Teaching English to Speakers of Other Languages, Baltimore, MD 21210-2476. Offers MA. *Accreditation:* NCATE. Part-time and evening/weekend programs available. *Entrance requirements:* Additional exam requirements/recommendations for international students: Required—TOEFL (minimum score 500 paper-based; 61 iBT). Electronic applications accepted.

Nyack College, School of Education, Nyack, NY 10960-3698. Offers childhood education (MS); childhood special education (MS); TESOL (MAT, MS). Part-time programs available. Postbaccalaureate distance learning degree programs offered (no on-campus study). *Students:* 37 full-time (31 women), 14 part-time (10 women); includes 34 minority (22 Black or African American, non-Hispanic/Latino; 3 Asian, non-Hispanic/Latino; 9 Hispanic/Latino), 2 international. Average age 34. In 2013, 11 master's awarded. *Degree requirements:* For master's, comprehensive exam, clinical experience. *Entrance requirements:* For master's, LAST (Liberal Arts and Sciences Test), transcripts, autobiography and statement on reasons for pursuing graduate study in education, recommendations, 6 credits of language, evidence of computer literacy, introductory course in psychology. Additional exam requirements/recommendations for international students: Required—TOEFL (minimum score 550 paper-based). *Application deadline:* Applications are processed on a rolling basis. Application fee: $30. Electronic applications accepted. *Expenses:* Contact institution. *Financial support:* Scholarships/grants available. Financial award applicants required to submit FAFSA. *Unit head:* Dr. JoAnn Looney, Dean, 845-675-4538, Fax: 845-358-0874. *Application contact:* Traci Piescki, Director of Admissions, 800-541-6891, Fax: 845-348-3912, E-mail: admissions.grad@nyack.edu.
Website: http://www.nyack.edu/edu.

Oakland University, Graduate Study and Lifelong Learning, College of Arts and Sciences, Department of Linguistics, Rochester, MI 48309-4401. Offers linguistics (MA); teaching English as a second language (Certificate). Part-time and evening/weekend programs available. *Faculty:* 6 full-time (3 women), 1 (woman) part-time/adjunct. *Students:* 15 full-time (10 women), 15 part-time (10 women); includes 2 minority (1 Black or African American, non-Hispanic/Latino; 1 Asian, non-Hispanic/Latino), 8 international. Average age 34. 36 applicants, 31% accepted, 10 enrolled. In 2013, 3 master's awarded. *Entrance requirements:* For master's, minimum GPA of 3.0 for unconditional admission. Additional exam requirements/recommendations for international students: Required—TOEFL (minimum score 550 paper-based). *Application deadline:* For fall admission, 7/15 priority date for domestic students, 5/1 for international students; for winter admission, 12/1 priority date for domestic students, 9/1 for international students; for spring admission, 3/15 priority date for domestic students. Application fee: $35. *Financial support:* Federal Work-Study, institutionally sponsored loans, and tuition waivers (full) available. Financial award application deadline: 3/1; financial award applicants required to submit FAFSA. *Unit head:* Dr. Sam Rosenthall, Chair, 248-370-2163, Fax: 248-370-3144, E-mail: srosenth@oakland.edu. *Application contact:* Katherine Z. Rowley, Associate Director of Graduate Study and Lifelong Learning, 248-370-3167, Fax: 248-370-4114, E-mail: kzrowley@oakland.edu.

Ohio Dominican University, Graduate Programs, Division of Education, Columbus, OH 43219-2099. Offers curriculum and instruction (M Ed); educational leadership (M Ed); teaching English to speakers of other languages (MA). *Accreditation:* NCATE. Part-time and evening/weekend programs available. Postbaccalaureate distance learning degree programs offered. *Degree requirements:* For master's, thesis or alternative. *Entrance requirements:* For master's, minimum undergraduate GPA of 3.0, teaching certificate, teaching experience, 3 letters of recommendation. Additional exam

requirements/recommendations for international students: Required—TOEFL (minimum score 550 paper-based), IELTS (minimum score 6.5).

Oklahoma City University, Petree College of Arts and Sciences, Program in Teaching English to Speakers of Other Languages, Oklahoma City, OK 73106-1402. Offers MA. Part-time and evening/weekend programs available. *Students:* 71 full-time (61 women), 29 part-time (17 women); includes 2 minority (1 Black or African American, non-Hispanic/Latino; 1 Two or more races, non-Hispanic/Latino), 92 international. Average age 32. 62 applicants, 71% accepted, 11 enrolled. In 2013, 42 master's awarded. *Degree requirements:* For master's, comprehensive exam, thesis optional. *Entrance requirements:* For master's, bachelor's degree from accredited institution, minimum GPA of 3.0, essay, recommendation letters. Additional exam requirements/recommendations for international students: Required—TOEFL (minimum score 550 paper-based; 80 iBT). *Application deadline:* Applications are processed on a rolling basis. Application fee: $50. Electronic applications accepted. *Expenses: Tuition:* Full-time $16,848; part-time $936 per credit hour. Tuition and fees vary according to course load, degree level and program. *Financial support:* Career-related internships or fieldwork, Federal Work-Study, institutionally sponsored loans, scholarships/grants, and tuition waivers available. Support available to part-time students. Financial award application deadline: 6/1; financial award applicants required to submit FAFSA. *Faculty research:* Second language acquisition, second writing language. *Unit head:* Dr. Robert Griffin, Acting Director, 405-208-5941, Fax: 405-208-6012, E-mail: rgriffin@okcu.edu. *Application contact:* Heidi Puckett, Director, Graduate Admissions, 800-633-7242, Fax: 405-208-5916, E-mail: gadmissions@okcu.edu.
Website: http://www.okcu.edu/petree/graduate/tesol/.

Our Lady of the Lake University of San Antonio, School of Professional Studies, Program in Curriculum and Instruction, San Antonio, TX 78207-4689. Offers bilingual education (M Ed); early childhood education (M Ed); English as a second language (M Ed); integrated math teaching (M Ed); integrated science teaching (M Ed); reading specialist (M Ed). Part-time and evening/weekend programs available. *Faculty:* 6 full-time (4 women), 3 part-time/adjunct (all women). *Students:* 4 full-time (all women), 84 part-time (72 women); includes 52 minority (2 Black or African American, non-Hispanic/Latino; 2 Asian, non-Hispanic/Latino; 48 Hispanic/Latino). Average age 40. 9 applicants, 56% accepted, 1 enrolled. In 2013, 8 master's awarded. *Degree requirements:* For master's, comprehensive exam. *Entrance requirements:* For master's, GRE General Test or MAT. Additional exam requirements/recommendations for international students: Required—TOEFL. *Application deadline:* For fall admission, 4/1 priority date for domestic and international students; for spring admission, 11/1 priority date for domestic and international students; for summer admission, 2/1 priority date for domestic students, 4/1 priority date for international students. Applications are processed on a rolling basis. Application fee: $25 ($50 for international students). Electronic applications accepted. *Expenses: Tuition:* Full-time $9120; part-time $760 per credit. *Required fees:* $698; $334 per trimester. Tuition and fees vary according to course load, degree level, campus/location and program. *Financial support:* Research assistantships, teaching assistantships, career-related internships or fieldwork, Federal Work-Study, institutionally sponsored loans, scholarships/grants, and tuition waivers (partial) available. Support available to part-time students. Financial award application deadline: 4/1. *Faculty research:* Professional educator to understand and meet the comprehensive needs of a diverse student population, life-long learners, innovative practices. *Unit head:* Dr. Jerrie Jackson, 210-434-6711 Ext. 2698, E-mail: jjackson@lake.ollusa.edu. *Application contact:* Graduate Admission, 210-431-3961, Fax: 210-431-4013, E-mail: gradadm@lake.ollusa.edu.
Website: http://www.ollusa.edu/s/1190/ollu-3-column-noads.aspx?sid=1190&gid=1&pgid=4173.

Penn State University Park, Graduate School, College of the Liberal Arts, Department of Applied Linguistics, State College, PA 16802. Offers applied linguistics (PhD); teaching English as a second language (MA). *Unit head:* Dr. Susan Welch, Dean, 814-865-7691, Fax: 814-863-2085, E-mail: swelch@psu.edu. *Application contact:* Cynthia E. Nicosia, Director, Graduate Enrollment Services, 814-865-1834, Fax: 814-863-4627, E-mail: cey1@psu.edu.
Website: http://aplng.la.psu.edu/.

Pontifical Catholic University of Puerto Rico, College of Education, Program in English as a Second Language, Ponce, PR 00717-0777. Offers M Ed. *Degree requirements:* For master's, comprehensive exam, thesis (for some programs). *Entrance requirements:* For master's, GRE, 2 letters of recommendation, interview, minimum GPA of 2.75.

Portland State University, Graduate Studies, College of Liberal Arts and Sciences, Department of Applied Linguistics, Portland, OR 97207-0751. Offers teaching English to speakers of other languages (MA). Part-time programs available. *Faculty:* 10 full-time (6 women), 3 part-time/adjunct (2 women). *Students:* 30 full-time (20 women), 41 part-time (25 women); includes 7 minority (4 Asian, non-Hispanic/Latino; 1 Hispanic/Latino; 2 Two or more races, non-Hispanic/Latino), 8 international. Average age 33. 85 applicants, 71% accepted, 26 enrolled. In 2013, 18 master's awarded. *Degree requirements:* For master's, one foreign language, comprehensive exam, thesis. *Entrance requirements:* For master's, minimum GPA of 3.0 in upper-division course work or 2.75 overall, proficiency in at least 1 foreign language. Additional exam requirements/recommendations for international students: Required—TOEFL (minimum score 600 paper-based). *Application deadline:* For fall admission, 2/1 priority date for domestic students, 2/1 for international students. Applications are processed on a rolling basis. Application fee: $50. *Expenses:* Tuition, state resident: full-time $9207; part-time $341 per credit. Tuition, nonresident: full-time $14,391; part-time $533 per credit. *Required fees:* $1263; $22 per credit. $98 per quarter. One-time fee: $150. Tuition and fees vary according to program. *Financial support:* In 2013–14, 1 research assistantship with full tuition reimbursement (averaging $6,292 per year), 1 teaching assistantship with full tuition reimbursement (averaging $5,778 per year) were awarded; career-related internships or fieldwork, Federal Work-Study, scholarships/grants, tuition waivers (partial), and unspecified assistantships also available. Support available to part-time students. Financial award application deadline: 3/1; financial award applicants required to submit FAFSA. *Faculty research:* Sociolinguistics, linguistics and cognitive science, language proficiency testing, lexical phrases and language teaching, teaching English as a second language methodology. *Total annual research expenditures:* $1.6 million. *Unit head:* Dr. Susan Conrad, Acting Chair, 503-725-8727, Fax: 503-725-4139, E-mail: conrads@pdx.edu. *Application contact:* Ylai Martinez, Office Coordinator, 503-725-4098, Fax: 503-725-4139, E-mail: ylai.martinez@pdx.edu.
Website: http://www.ling.pdx.edu/.

Post University, Program in Education, Waterbury, CT 06723-2540. Offers education (M Ed); higher education administration (M Ed); instructional design and technology (M Ed); online teaching (M Ed); teaching and learning (M Ed); TESOL (teaching English to speakers of other languages) (M Ed). Postbaccalaureate distance learning degree programs offered.

Providence University College & Theological Seminary, Theological Seminary, Otterburne, MB R0A 1G0, Canada. Offers children's ministry (Certificate); Christian studies (MA, Certificate); counseling (MA); cross-cultural discipleship (Certificate); divinity (M Div); educational studies (MA), including counseling psychology, educational ministries, student development, teaching English to speakers of other languages, training teachers of English to speakers of other languages; global studies (MA); lay counseling (Diploma); ministry (D Min); teaching English to speakers of other languages (Certificate); theological studies (MA); training teacher of English to speakers of other languages (Certificate); youth ministry (Certificate). *Accreditation:* ATS. Part-time programs available. *Degree requirements:* For master's, variable foreign language requirement, thesis (for some programs); for doctorate, thesis/dissertation. *Entrance requirements:* Additional exam requirements/recommendations for international students: Recommended—TOEFL (minimum score 550 paper-based). *Faculty research:* Studies in Isaiah, theology of sin.

Queens College of the City University of New York, Division of Graduate Studies, Arts and Humanities Division, Department of Linguistics and Communication Disorders, Program in Teaching English to Speakers of Other Languages, Flushing, NY 11367-1597. Offers MS Ed. Part-time and evening/weekend programs available. *Degree requirements:* For master's, thesis optional. *Entrance requirements:* For master's, minimum GPA of 3.0. Additional exam requirements/recommendations for international students: Required—TOEFL.

Quincy University, Program in Education, Quincy, IL 62301-2699. Offers curriculum and instruction (MS Ed), including bilingual/English as a second language; leadership (MS Ed); reading education (MS Ed); special education (MS Ed); teacher leader (MS Ed). Part-time and evening/weekend programs available. Postbaccalaureate distance learning degree programs offered (minimal on-campus study). *Students:* 62 full-time (39 women), 97 part-time (68 women); includes 43 minority (29 Black or African American, non-Hispanic/Latino; 1 American Indian or Alaska Native, non-Hispanic/Latino; 4 Asian, non-Hispanic/Latino; 9 Hispanic/Latino). In 2013, 105 master's awarded. *Degree requirements:* For master's, comprehensive exam (for some programs), thesis optional. *Entrance requirements:* For master's, MAT or GRE. Additional exam requirements/recommendations for international students: Required—TOEFL (minimum score 550 paper-based; 79 iBT). *Application deadline:* Applications are processed on a rolling basis. Application fee: $25. Electronic applications accepted. *Expenses: Tuition:* Full-time $9600; part-time $400 per semester hour. *Required fees:* $720; $30 per semester hour. Tuition and fees vary according to course load and program. *Financial support:* Applicants required to submit FAFSA. *Unit head:* Dr. Kristen R. Anguiano, Director, 217-228-5432 Ext. 3119, E-mail: anguikr@quincy.edu. *Application contact:* Office of Admissions, 217-228-5210, Fax: 217-228-5479, E-mail: admissions@quincy.edu.
Website: http://www.quincy.edu/academics/graduate-programs/education.

Regent University, Graduate School, School of Education, Virginia Beach, VA 23464-9800. Offers adult education (Ed D, PhD); advanced educational leadership (Ed D, PhD); career switcher with licensure (M Ed), including alternative licensure; character education (Ed D, PhD); Christian education leadership (Ed D); Christian school administration (M Ed); curriculum and instruction (M Ed); distance education (Ed D, PhD); educational leadership (M Ed); educational leadership - special education (Ed S); educational psychology (Ed D); elementary education (M Ed); higher education (Ed D, PhD); higher education leadership and management (Ed D); K-12 school leadership (Ed D, PhD); leadership in mathematics education (M Ed); reading specialist (M Ed); special education (M Ed, Ed D, PhD); student affairs (M Ed); TESOL (M Ed), including adult education, PreK-12. *Accreditation:* Teacher Education Accreditation Council. Part-time and evening/weekend programs available. Postbaccalaureate distance learning degree programs offered (minimal on-campus study). *Faculty:* 25 full-time (12 women), 50 part-time/adjunct (31 women). *Students:* 100 full-time (78 women), 754 part-time (614 women); includes 225 minority (191 Black or African American, non-Hispanic/Latino; 1 American Indian or Alaska Native, non-Hispanic/Latino; 7 Asian, non-Hispanic/Latino; 26 Hispanic/Latino), 16 international. Average age 39. 487 applicants, 63% accepted, 233 enrolled. In 2013, 202 master's, 19 doctorates awarded. *Degree requirements:* For master's, thesis or alternative; for doctorate, comprehensive exam, thesis/dissertation. *Entrance requirements:* For master's, MAT, minimum undergraduate GPA of 2.75, writing sample, resume, recommendations, interview; for doctorate, GRE, writing sample, 3 years of relevant professional experience, master's-level paper, copies of published work, resume, transcripts, interview, recommendations. Additional exam requirements/recommendations for international students: Required—TOEFL (minimum score 577 paper-based). *Application deadline:* For fall admission, 4/1 priority date for domestic students; for spring admission, 10/15 priority date for domestic students. Applications are processed on a rolling basis. Application fee: $50. Electronic applications accepted. Tuition and fees vary according to course load and degree level. *Financial support:* Fellowships, career-related internships or fieldwork, scholarships/grants, tuition waivers (full and partial), and unspecified assistantships available. Support available to part-time students. Financial award application deadline: 4/1; financial award applicants required to submit FAFSA. *Faculty research:* Character development and discipline for children, education leadership development, diversity in schools, classroom management, technology in education settings. *Unit head:* Dr. Alan Arroyo, Dean, 757-352-4261, Fax: 757-352-4318, E-mail: alanarr@regent.edu. *Application contact:* Matthew Chadwick, Director of Enrollment Support Services, 800-373-5504, Fax: 757-352-4381, E-mail: admissions@regent.edu.
Website: http://www.regent.edu/education/.

Rhode Island College, School of Graduate Studies, Feinstein School of Education and Human Development, Department of Educational Studies, Providence, RI 02908-1991. Offers advanced studies in teaching and learning (M Ed); English (MAT); French (MAT); history (MAT); math (MAT); secondary education (MAT); Spanish (MAT); teaching English as a second language (M Ed). *Accreditation:* NCATE. Part-time and evening/weekend programs available. *Faculty:* 10 full-time (6 women), 7 part-time/adjunct (all women). *Students:* 4 full-time (3 women), 61 part-time (54 women); includes 2 minority (both Hispanic/Latino). Average age 37. In 2013, 27 master's awarded. *Degree requirements:* For master's, capstone or comprehensive assessment. *Entrance requirements:* For master's, GRE or MAT (for most programs), minimum undergraduate GPA of 3.0; baccalaureate degree in English, French, history, math or Spanish; evaluation of content area knowledge; 3 letters of recommendation; interview. Additional exam requirements/recommendations for international students: Recommended—TOEFL (minimum score 550 paper-based; 79 iBT). *Application deadline:* For fall admission, 3/1 for domestic students; for spring admission, 11/1 for domestic students. Applications are processed on a rolling basis. Application fee: $50. *Expenses:* Tuition, state resident: full-time $8928; part-time $372 per credit hour. Tuition, nonresident: full-time $17,376; part-time $724 per credit hour. *Required fees:* $602; $22 per credit. $72 per term. *Financial support:* In 2013–14, 2 teaching assistantships with full tuition reimbursements (averaging $2,250 per year) were awarded; career-related internships or fieldwork, Federal Work-Study, scholarships/grants, health care benefits, and unspecified assistantships also available. Support available to part-time students. Financial award application deadline: 5/15; financial award applicants required to submit FAFSA. *Faculty research:* School administration, school/college articulation. *Unit head:* Dr. Paul Tiskus, Chair, 401-456-8170. *Application contact:* Graduate Studies, 401-456-8700.
Website: http://www.ric.edu/educationalStudies/.

Rider University, Department of Graduate Education, Leadership and Counseling, Teacher Certification Program, Lawrenceville, NJ 08648-3001. Offers business education (Certificate); elementary education (Certificate); English as a second language (Certificate); English education (Certificate); mathematics education (Certificate); preschool to grade 3 (Certificate); science education (Certificate); social studies education (Certificate); world languages (Certificate), including French, German, Spanish. Part-time programs available. *Degree requirements:* For Certificate, internship, professional portfolio. *Entrance requirements:* For degree, PRAXIS, resume. Additional exam requirements/recommendations for international students: Required—TOEFL (minimum score 550 paper-based). Electronic applications accepted. *Faculty research:* Conceptual foundations for optimal development of creativity; creative theory, cognitive processes in mathematics learning, teacher collaboration.

Rowan University, Graduate School, College of Education, Department of Teacher Education, Program in ESL Education, Glassboro, NJ 08028-1701. Offers CGS. *Faculty:* 1 (woman) full-time, 1 (woman) part-time/adjunct. *Students:* 3 full-time (all women), 40 part-time (38 women); includes 9 minority (all Hispanic/Latino). Average age 36. 36 applicants, 100% accepted, 20 enrolled. Application fee: $65. *Expenses: Tuition, area resident:* Part-time $638 per credit. Tuition, state resident: full-time $5742. *Required fees:* $142 per credit. Tuition and fees vary according to course level and program. *Unit head:* Dr. Horacio Sosa, Dean, College of Graduate and Continuing Education, 856-256-4747, Fax: 856-256-5638, E-mail: sosa@rowan.edu. *Application contact:* Admissions and Enrollment Services, 856-256-5145, Fax: 856-256-5637, E-mail: cgceadmissions@rowan.edu.

Rutgers, The State University of New Jersey, New Brunswick, Graduate School of Education, Department of Learning and Teaching, Program in Language Education, Piscataway, NJ 08854-8097. Offers English as a second language education (Ed M); language education (Ed M, Ed D). Part-time programs available. Terminal master's awarded for partial completion of doctoral program. *Degree requirements:* For master's, comprehensive exam; for doctorate, thesis/dissertation, concept paper, qualifying exam. *Entrance requirements:* For master's, GRE General Test, minimum GPA of 3.0; for doctorate, GRE General Test, minimum GPA of 3.5. Additional exam requirements/recommendations for international students: Required—TOEFL. Electronic applications accepted. *Faculty research:* Linguistics, sociolinguistics, cross-cultural/international communication.

Sacred Heart University, Graduate Programs, Isabelle Farrington College of Education, Department of Teacher Education, Fairfield, CT 06825-1000. Offers administration (CAS); advanced educational studies for teachers (CAS); educational technology (Certificate); teaching (MAT); TESOL (MAT); Web development (Certificate). *Faculty:* 14 full-time (7 women), 15 part-time/adjunct (8 women). *Students:* 210 full-time (155 women), 517 part-time (376 women); includes 78 minority (36 Black or African American, non-Hispanic/Latino; 1 American Indian or Alaska Native, non-Hispanic/Latino; 5 Asian, non-Hispanic/Latino; 31 Hispanic/Latino; 5 Two or more races, non-Hispanic/Latino). Average age 34. 90 applicants, 90% accepted, 75 enrolled. In 2013, 262 master's, 60 other advanced degrees awarded. *Entrance requirements:* For master's, bachelor's degree, copy of official teaching certificate, background check. Additional exam requirements/recommendations for international students: Required—PTE; Recommended—TOEFL (minimum score 570 paper-based; 80 iBT), IELTS (minimum score 6.5). *Application deadline:* Applications are processed on a rolling basis. Application fee: $60. Electronic applications accepted. *Expenses: Tuition:* Full-time $22,775; part-time $617 per credit. *Financial support:* Applicants required to submit FAFSA. *Unit head:* Dr. Jim Carl, Dean, 203-371-7800, Fax: 203-365-7513, E-mail: carlj@sacredheart.edu. *Application contact:* Kathy Dilks, Executive Director of Graduate Admissions, 203-365-7619, Fax: 203-365-4732, E-mail: gradstudies@sacredheart.edu. Website: http://www.sacredheart.edu/academics/isabellefarringtoncollegeofeducation/.

St. Cloud State University, School of Graduate Studies, College of Liberal Arts, Department of English, St. Cloud, MN 56301-4498. Offers English (MA, MS); teaching English as a second language (MA). Part-time programs available. *Degree requirements:* For master's, thesis or alternative. *Entrance requirements:* For master's, GRE General Test, minimum GPA of 2.75. Additional exam requirements/recommendations for international students: Required—Michigan English Language Assessment Battery; Recommended—TOEFL (minimum score 550 paper-based), IELTS (minimum score 6.5). Electronic applications accepted.

St. John's University, The School of Education, Department of Human Services and Counseling, Programs in Bilingual Education/Teaching English to Speakers of Other Languages, Queens, NY 11439. Offers MS Ed, Adv C. Part-time and evening/weekend programs available. Postbaccalaureate distance learning degree programs offered. *Students:* 86 full-time (74 women), 125 part-time (115 women); includes 59 minority (12 Black or African American, non-Hispanic/Latino; 7 Asian, non-Hispanic/Latino; 37 Hispanic/Latino; 3 Two or more races, non-Hispanic/Latino), 54 international. Average age 30. 160 applicants, 93% accepted, 71 enrolled. In 2013, 69 master's, 17 Adv Cs awarded. *Degree requirements:* For master's, comprehensive exam, fieldwork. *Entrance requirements:* For master's, minimum GPA of 3.0, eligibility for teacher certification, 2 letters of recommendation, bachelor's degree; for Adv C, New York State initial teaching certification or eligibility. Additional exam requirements/recommendations for international students: Required—TOEFL (minimum score 600 paper-based; 100 iBT), IELTS (minimum score 5.5). *Application deadline:* For fall admission, 8/17 for domestic students, 5/1 priority date for international students; for spring admission, 1/5 for domestic students, 11/1 priority date for international students. Applications are processed on a rolling basis. Application fee: $70. Electronic applications accepted. *Expenses: Tuition:* Full-time $19,800; part-time $1100 per credit. *Required fees:* $170 per semester. *Financial support:* Research assistantships, career-related internships or fieldwork, and scholarships/grants available. Support available to part-time students. Financial award application deadline: 3/1; financial award applicants required to submit FAFSA. *Faculty research:* Second language learning and academic achievement, heritage language education, assessing the progress of English language learners toward English acquisition, dual language acquisition, study of English Creoles and dialects of other Englishes. *Unit head:* Dr. E. Francine Guastello, Chair, 718-990-1475, E-mail: guastelf@stjohns.edu. *Application contact:* Dr. Kelly K. Ronayne, Associate Dean of Graduate Admissions, 718-990-2304, Fax: 718-990-2343, E-mail: graded@stjohns.edu.

Saint Martin's University, Office of Graduate Studies, College of Education, Lacey, WA 98503. Offers administration (M Ed); English as a second language (M Ed); guidance and counseling (M Ed); reading (M Ed); special education (M Ed); teaching (MIT). *Accreditation:* Teacher Education Accreditation Council. Part-time and evening/weekend programs available. *Faculty:* 10 full-time (6 women), 15 part-time/adjunct (12 women). *Students:* 57 full-time (35 women), 52 part-time (38 women); includes 20 minority (7 Black or African American, non-Hispanic/Latino; 1 American Indian or Alaska Native, non-Hispanic/Latino; 2 Asian, non-Hispanic/Latino; 6 Hispanic/Latino; 1 Native Hawaiian or other Pacific Islander, non-Hispanic/Latino; 3 Two or more races, non-Hispanic/Latino). Average age 35. 63 applicants, 25% accepted, 13 enrolled. In 2013, 12 master's awarded. *Degree requirements:* For master's, comprehensive exam (for some programs), thesis or alternative, project or comprehensives. *Entrance requirements:* For master's, GRE General Test or MAT, three letters of recommendations; curriculum vitae. Additional exam requirements/recommendations for international students: Required—TOEFL (minimum score 550 paper-based; 79 iBT); Recommended—IELTS (minimum score 6.5). *Application deadline:* For fall admission, 4/1 priority date for domestic and international students; for spring admission, 11/1 priority date for domestic and international students. Applications are processed on a rolling basis. Application fee: $50. Electronic applications accepted. *Expenses: Tuition:* Part-time $990 per credit hour. Tuition and fees vary according to course level and program. *Financial support:* Career-related internships or fieldwork, Federal Work-Study, institutionally sponsored loans, and unspecified assistantships available. Support available to part-time students. Financial award application deadline: 3/1; financial award applicants required to submit FAFSA. *Faculty research:* Reader's theatre and reader/writer workshops, curriculum and assessment integration, gender and equity, classroom evaluations, organizational leadership. *Unit head:* Dr. Joyce Westgard, Dean, College of Education and Professional Psychology, 360-438-4509, Fax: 360-438-4486, E-mail: westgard@stmartin.edu. *Application contact:* Marie C. Boisvert, Administrative Assistant, 360-412-6145, E-mail: gradstudies@stmartin.edu. Website: http://www.stmartin.edu/gradstudies.

Saint Michael's College, Graduate Programs, Program in Teaching English as a Second Language, Colchester, VT 05439. Offers MATESL, Certificate. Part-time and evening/weekend programs available. *Degree requirements:* For master's, one foreign language, comprehensive exam (for some programs), thesis or alternative, capstone paper or portfolio. *Entrance requirements:* For master's, minimum GPA of 3.0. Additional exam requirements/recommendations for international students: Required—TOEFL (minimum score 550 paper-based; 80 iBT); Recommended—IELTS. *Faculty research:* Language teaching methodology, discourse analysis, second language acquisition, language assessment, sociolinguistics, K–12 English as a second language for children.

St. Thomas University, School of Leadership Studies, Institute for Education, Miami Gardens, FL 33054-6459. Offers earth/space science (Certificate); educational administration (MS, Certificate); educational leadership (Ed D); elementary education (MS); ESOL (Certificate); gifted education (Certificate); instructional technology (MS, Certificate); professional/studies (Certificate); reading (MS, Certificate); special education (MS). Part-time and evening/weekend programs available. *Degree requirements:* For master's, comprehensive exam; for doctorate, comprehensive exam, thesis/dissertation. *Entrance requirements:* For master's, interview, minimum GPA of 3.0 or GRE; for doctorate, GRE or MAT. Additional exam requirements/recommendations for international students: Required—TOEFL (minimum score 550 paper-based; 79 iBT). Electronic applications accepted.

Saint Xavier University, Graduate Studies, School of Education, Chicago, IL 60655-3105. Offers counseling (MA); curriculum and instruction (MA); early childhood education (MA); educational administration (MA); elementary education (MA); individualized studies (MA), including educational technology, English as a second language (ESL), ISTEM (integrative science, technology, engineering, and math), science education; music education (MA); reading (MA); secondary education (MA); Spanish education (MA); special education (MA); teaching and leadership (MA). *Accreditation:* NCATE. Part-time and evening/weekend programs available. *Degree requirements:* For master's, thesis or project. *Entrance requirements:* For master's, minimum GPA of 3.0. *Expenses:* Contact institution.

Salem College, Department of Education, Winston-Salem, NC 27101. Offers art education (MAT); elementary education (M Ed, MAT); language and literacy (M Ed); middle school education (MAT); school counseling (M Ed); second language studies (MAT); secondary education (MAT); special education (M Ed, MAT). *Accreditation:* NCATE. Part-time and evening/weekend programs available. Postbaccalaureate distance learning degree programs offered (minimal on-campus study). *Degree requirements:* For master's, practicum (MAT), project (M Ed), oral and written comprehensive exams. *Entrance requirements:* For master's, minimum GPA of 2.5. *Faculty research:* Content area reading strategies, literacy development, brain compatible instruction.

Salem State University, School of Graduate Studies, Program in Teaching English as a Second Language, Salem, MA 01970-5353. Offers MAT. Part-time and evening/weekend programs available. *Students:* 7 full-time (all women), 26 part-time (19 women); includes 2 minority (1 Asian, non-Hispanic/Latino; 1 Native Hawaiian or other Pacific Islander, non-Hispanic/Latino), 6 international. 13 applicants, 100% accepted, 9 enrolled. In 2013, 18 master's awarded. *Entrance requirements:* Additional exam requirements/recommendations for international students: Required—TOEFL (minimum score 550 paper-based; 80 iBT) or IELTS (minimum score 5.5). *Application deadline:* For fall admission, 5/1 for domestic students; for spring admission, 10/1 for domestic students. Applications are processed on a rolling basis. Application fee: $50. *Financial support:* Career-related internships or fieldwork, Federal Work-Study, scholarships/grants, and unspecified assistantships available. Support available to part-time students. Financial award application deadline: 5/1; financial award applicants required to submit FAFSA. *Application contact:* Dr. Lee A. Brossoit, Assistant Dean of Graduate Admissions, 978-542-6675, Fax: 978-542-7215, E-mail: lbrossoit@salemstate.edu. Website: http://www.salemstate.edu/academics/schools/17138.php.

Salisbury University, Program in English, Salisbury, MD 21801-6837. Offers composition, language and rhetoric (MA); English (MA); literature (MA); teaching English to speakers of other languages (MA). Part-time and evening/weekend programs available. *Faculty:* 13 full-time (5 women), 1 part-time/adjunct (0 women). *Students:* 17 full-time (13 women), 26 part-time (22 women); includes 6 minority (4 Black or African American, non-Hispanic/Latino; 2 Hispanic/Latino), 1 international. Average age 31. 18 applicants, 72% accepted, 13 enrolled. In 2013, 21 master's awarded. *Degree requirements:* For master's, comprehensive exam (for some programs), thesis optional. *Entrance requirements:* For master's, GRE, MAT or PRAXIS, minimum GPA of 3.0, 2 letters of recommendation, personal statement. Additional exam requirements/recommendations for international students: Required—TOEFL (minimum score 550 paper-based; 79 iBT), IELTS (minimum score 6.5). *Application deadline:* For fall admission, 8/1 priority date for domestic and international students; for spring admission, 1/1 priority date for domestic and international students. Applications are processed on a rolling basis. Application fee: $50. Electronic applications accepted. *Expenses: Tuition, area resident:* Part-time $342 per credit hour. Tuition, state resident: part-time $342 per credit hour. Tuition, nonresident: part-time $631 per credit hour. *Required fees:* $76 per credit hour. Tuition and fees vary according to program. *Financial support:* In 2013–14, 15 teaching assistantships with full tuition reimbursements (averaging $10,033 per year) were awarded; career-related internships or fieldwork, institutionally sponsored loans, and unspecified assistantships also available. Support available to part-time students. Financial award application deadline: 3/1; financial award applicants required to submit FAFSA. *Faculty research:* Literature, rhetoric and composition, linguistics, film, creative writing. *Unit head:* Dr. Elizabeth Curtin, Chair of Department of English, 410-548-5594, Fax: -, E-mail: ehcurtin@salisbury.edu. *Application contact:* Clacie Hubbard, Program Management Specialist, 410-543-6445, E-mail: cdhubbard@salisbury.edu. Website: http://www.salisbury.edu/english/grad.

San Diego State University, Graduate and Research Affairs, College of Arts and Letters, Department of Linguistics and Oriental Languages, San Diego, CA 92182.

English as a Second Language

Offers applied linguistics and English as a second language (CAL); computational linguistics (MA); English as a second language/applied linguistics (MA); general linguistics (MA). *Degree requirements:* For master's, one foreign language, comprehensive exam, thesis optional. *Entrance requirements:* For master's, GRE General Test, 2 letters of recommendation. Additional exam requirements/recommendations for international students: Required—TOEFL (minimum score 570 paper-based). Electronic applications accepted. *Faculty research:* Cross-cultural linguistic studies of semantics.

San Francisco State University, Division of Graduate Studies, College of Liberal and Creative Arts, Department of English Language and Literature, Program in Teaching English to Speakers of Other Languages, San Francisco, CA 94132-1722. Offers MA. Part-time programs available. *Degree requirements:* For master's, comprehensive exam (for some programs), thesis (for some programs). *Application deadline:* Applications are processed on a rolling basis. Electronic applications accepted. *Unit head:* Dr. Sugie Goen-Salter, Chair, 415-338-2264, E-mail: english@sfsu.edu. *Application contact:* Prof. Maricel Santos, Professor and Graduate Coordinator, 415-338-7445, E-mail: mgsantos@sfsu.edu.
Website: http://matesol.sfsu.edu/.

San Jose State University, Graduate Studies and Research, College of Humanities and the Arts, Department of Linguistics and Language Development, San Jose, CA 95192-0001. Offers computational linguistics (Certificate); linguistics (MA); teaching English to speakers of other languages (MA, Certificate). *Entrance requirements:* Additional exam requirements/recommendations for international students: Required—TOEFL (minimum score 570 paper-based). Electronic applications accepted.

Seattle Pacific University, MA in Teaching English to Speakers of Other Languages Program, Seattle, WA 98119-1997. Offers K-12 certification (MA); teaching English to speakers of other languages (MA). Part-time programs available. *Students:* 4 full-time (2 women), 14 part-time (10 women); includes 1 minority (Asian, non-Hispanic/Latino), 5 international. Average age 32. 17 applicants, 18% accepted, 3 enrolled. In 2013, 11 master's awarded. *Degree requirements:* For master's, one foreign language, practicum. *Entrance requirements:* For master's, GRE (minimum score of 155 verbal/500 old scoring, 3.5 analytical writing) or MAT (minimum score of 400), bachelor's degree; letters of recommendation; official copies of transcripts; minimum GPA of 3.0; personal statement; essay; resume. Additional exam requirements/recommendations for international students: Required—TOEFL (minimum score 600 paper-based). *Application deadline:* For fall admission, 8/1 priority date for domestic students; for winter admission, 12/1 for domestic students; for spring admission, 3/1 for domestic students; for summer admission, 5/1 for domestic students. Applications are processed on a rolling basis. Application fee: $50. Electronic applications accepted. *Expenses:* Contact institution. *Financial support:* Career-related internships or fieldwork available. Financial award applicants required to submit FAFSA. *Faculty research:* Second language acquisition. *Unit head:* Dr. Kathryn Bartholomew, Program Director, 206-281-3533, Fax: 206-281-2500, E-mail: kbarthol@spu.edu. *Application contact:* 206-281-2091.
Website: http://www.spu.edu/depts/tesol/.

Seattle University, College of Education, Program in Teaching English to Speakers of Other Languages, Seattle, WA 98122-1090. Offers M Ed, MA, Certificate. *Accreditation:* NCATE. Part-time programs available. *Faculty:* 2 full-time (1 woman). *Students:* 7 full-time (5 women), 45 part-time (31 women); includes 12 minority (4 Black or African American, non-Hispanic/Latino; 5 Asian, non-Hispanic/Latino; 2 Hispanic/Latino; 1 Native Hawaiian or other Pacific Islander, non-Hispanic/Latino), 5 international. Average age 35. 31 applicants, 68% accepted, 9 enrolled. In 2013, 19 master's awarded. *Degree requirements:* For master's, comprehensive exam, thesis, internship. *Entrance requirements:* For master's, GRE, MAT, or minimum GPA of 3.0. Additional exam requirements/recommendations for international students: Required—TOEFL. *Application deadline:* For fall admission, 8/20 priority date for domestic students; for winter admission, 11/20 for domestic students; for spring admission, 2/20 for domestic students. Applications are processed on a rolling basis. Application fee: $55. *Financial support:* Career-related internships or fieldwork and Federal Work-Study available. Support available to part-time students. Financial award applicants required to submit FAFSA. *Unit head:* Dr. Jian Yang, Coordinator, 209-296-5908, E-mail: tesol@seattleu.edu. *Application contact:* Janet Shandley, Associate Dean of Graduate Admissions, 206-296-5900, Fax: 206-298-5656, E-mail: grad_admissions@seattleu.edu.
Website: http://www.seattleu.edu/coe/tesol/Default.aspx?id=11242.

Simmons College, School of Social Work, Boston, MA 02115. Offers assistive technology (MS Ed, Ed S); behavior analysis (MS, PhD, Ed S); education (MA, CAGS); language and literacy (MS Ed, Ed S); social work (MSW, PhD); special education (MS Ed), including moderate disabilities, severe disabilities; teaching (MAT), including elementary education, general education, high school education; teaching English as a second language (MA, CAGS); urban leadership (MSW); MSW/MBA. *Accreditation:* CSWE (one or more programs are accredited). Part-time programs available. Postbaccalaureate distance learning degree programs offered (no on-campus study). *Students:* 519 full-time (454 women), 703 part-time (604 women); includes 192 minority (61 Black or African American, non-Hispanic/Latino; 1 American Indian or Alaska Native, non-Hispanic/Latino; 35 Asian, non-Hispanic/Latino; 71 Hispanic/Latino; 2 Native Hawaiian or other Pacific Islander, non-Hispanic/Latino; 22 Two or more races, non-Hispanic/Latino), 16 international. 952 applicants, 66% accepted, 353 enrolled. In 2013, 159 master's, 2 doctorates awarded. Terminal master's awarded for partial completion of doctoral program. *Degree requirements:* For master's, thesis (for some programs); for doctorate, comprehensive exam (for some programs), thesis/dissertation (for some programs). *Entrance requirements:* For master's, GRE, MAT, MTEL (for different programs); for doctorate, GRE, BCBA Analyst Exam. Additional exam requirements/recommendations for international students: Required—TOEFL (minimum score 600 paper-based; 100 iBT). *Application deadline:* Applications are processed on a rolling basis. Application fee: $45. Electronic applications accepted. *Financial support:* Teaching assistantships and scholarships/grants available. *Unit head:* Dr. Stefan Krug, Dean, 617-521-3924. *Application contact:* Carlos D. Frontado, Director of Admissions, 617-521-3920, Fax: 617-521-3980, E-mail: ssw@simmons.edu.
Website: http://www.simmons.edu/ssw/.

Simon Fraser University, Office of Graduate Studies, Faculty of Education, Program in Teaching English as a Second/Foreign Language, Burnaby, BC V5A 1S6, Canada. Offers M Ed. Part-time and evening/weekend programs available. *Degree requirements:* For master's, comprehensive exam. *Entrance requirements:* For master's, minimum GPA of 3.0 (on scale of 4.33), or 3.33 based on last 60 credits of undergraduate courses. Additional exam requirements/recommendations for international students: Recommended—TOEFL (minimum score 580 paper-based; 93 iBT), IELTS (minimum score 7), TWE (minimum score 5). Electronic applications accepted. *Expenses:* Tuition, area resident: Full-time $5084 Canadian dollars. *Required fees:* $840 Canadian dollars. *Faculty research:* Internationalization of higher education, international student experiences, language practices and language ideology in the globalized political economy, integration of immigrants, minorities and international students in educational

settings, critical and psychoanalytical perspectives on second language learning, pedagogy, and curriculum.

SIT Graduate Institute, Graduate Programs, Programs in Language Teacher Education, Brattleboro, VT 05302-0676. Offers TESOL (MAT). *Degree requirements:* For master's, one foreign language, thesis, teaching practice. *Entrance requirements:* For master's, 4 letters of reference. Additional exam requirements/recommendations for international students: Required—TOEFL. *Faculty research:* Teaching English to speakers of other languages (TESOL).

Soka University of America, Graduate School, Aliso Viejo, CA 92656. Offers teaching Japanese as a foreign language (Certificate). Evening/weekend programs available. *Entrance requirements:* For degree, bachelor's degree with minimum GPA of 3.0, proficiency in Japanese. Additional exam requirements/recommendations for international students: Required—TOEFL (minimum score 600 paper-based; 100 iBT).

Southeast Missouri State University, School of Graduate Studies, Department of English, Cape Girardeau, MO 63701-4799. Offers English (MA), including English studies, professional writing; teaching English to speakers of other languages (MA). Part-time and evening/weekend programs available. Postbaccalaureate distance learning degree programs offered (no on-campus study). *Faculty:* 13 full-time (8 women), 1 part-time/adjunct (0 women). *Students:* 41 full-time (32 women), 45 part-time (39 women); includes 4 minority (2 Black or African American, non-Hispanic/Latino; 1 Hispanic/Latino; 1 Two or more races, non-Hispanic/Latino), 16 international. Average age 32. 43 applicants, 98% accepted, 34 enrolled. In 2013, 39 master's awarded. *Degree requirements:* For master's, paper and comprehensive exam or thesis and oral defense. *Entrance requirements:* For master's, minimum undergraduate GPA of 2.5; 24 undergraduate credit hours in field (for English); bachelor's degree from accredited university (for teaching English to speakers of other languages). Additional exam requirements/recommendations for international students: Required—TOEFL (minimum score 550 paper-based; 79 iBT), IELTS (minimum score 6), PTE (minimum score 53). *Application deadline:* For fall admission, 8/1 for domestic students, 6/1 for international students; for spring admission, 11/21 for domestic students, 10/1 for international students; for summer admission, 5/15 for domestic students. Applications are processed on a rolling basis. Application fee: $30 ($40 for international students). Electronic applications accepted. *Expenses:* Tuition, state resident: full-time $5139; part-time $285.50 per credit hour. Tuition, nonresident: full-time $9099; part-time $505.50 per credit hour. *Financial support:* In 2013–14, 34 students received support, including 13 teaching assistantships with full tuition reimbursements available (averaging $8,144 per year); career-related internships or fieldwork, Federal Work-Study, scholarships/grants, traineeships, tuition waivers (full), and unspecified assistantships also available. Financial award application deadline: 6/30; financial award applicants required to submit FAFSA. *Faculty research:* Literature, creative writing, technical writing, secondary English education, linguistics. *Unit head:* Dr. Carol Scates, Department of English Chair, 573-651-2156, Fax: 573-651-5188, E-mail: cscates@semo.edu. *Application contact:* Gail Amick, Administrative Secretary, 573-651-2049, Fax: 573-651-2001, E-mail: gamick@semo.edu.
Website: http://www.semo.edu/english/.

Southern Arkansas University–Magnolia, Graduate Programs, Magnolia, AR 71753. Offers agriculture (MS); business administration (MBA); computer and information sciences (MS); education (M Ed), including counseling and development, curriculum and instruction, educational administration and supervision, elementary education, reading, secondary education, TESOL; kinesiology (M Ed); library media and information specialist (M Ed); mental health and clinical counseling (MS); public administration (MPA); school counseling (M Ed); teaching (MAT). *Accreditation:* NCATE. Part-time and evening/weekend programs available. Postbaccalaureate distance learning degree programs offered. *Faculty:* 34 full-time (15 women), 8 part-time/adjunct (5 women). *Students:* 48 full-time (22 women), 269 part-time (167 women); includes 85 minority (78 Black or African American, non-Hispanic/Latino; 2 Asian, non-Hispanic/Latino; 2 Hispanic/Latino; 1 Native Hawaiian or other Pacific Islander, non-Hispanic/Latino; 2 Two or more races, non-Hispanic/Latino), 5 international. Average age 33. 149 applicants, 73% accepted, 109 enrolled. In 2013, 149 master's awarded. *Degree requirements:* For master's, comprehensive exam (for some programs), thesis optional. *Entrance requirements:* For master's, GRE, MAT or GMAT, minimum GPA of 2.5. Additional exam requirements/recommendations for international students: Required—TOEFL, IELTS. *Application deadline:* For fall admission, 7/10 for domestic and international students; for winter admission, 12/1 for domestic and international students; for spring admission, 12/1 for domestic and international students; for summer admission, 4/1 for domestic students. Applications are processed on a rolling basis. Application fee: $25 ($50 for international students). Electronic applications accepted. *Expenses:* Tuition, state resident: part-time $254 per credit hour. Tuition, nonresident: part-time $370 per credit hour. *Required fees:* $136 per credit hour. $259 per semester. Tuition and fees vary according to course load and program. *Financial support:* Career-related internships or fieldwork, Federal Work-Study, scholarships/grants, tuition waivers (full), and unspecified assistantships available. Financial award applicants required to submit FAFSA. *Faculty research:* Alternative certification for teachers, supervision of instruction, instructional leadership, counseling. *Unit head:* Dr. Kim Bloss, Dean, School of Graduate Studies, 870-235-4150, Fax: 870-235-5227, E-mail: kkbloss@saumag.edu. *Application contact:* Shrijana Malaka, Admissions Specialist, 870-235-4150, Fax: 870-235-5227, E-mail: smalakar@saumag.edu.
Website: http://www.saumag.edu/graduate.

Southern Connecticut State University, School of Graduate Studies, School of Arts and Sciences, Department of World Languages and Literatures, New Haven, CT 06515-1355. Offers multicultural-bilingual education/teaching English to speakers of other languages (MS); romance languages (MA). Part-time and evening/weekend programs available. *Degree requirements:* For master's, one foreign language, thesis or alternative. *Entrance requirements:* For master's, interview, minimum undergraduate GPA of 2.7. Electronic applications accepted.

Southern Illinois University Carbondale, Graduate School, College of Liberal Arts, Department of Applied Linguistics, Program in Teaching English to Speakers of Other Languages, Carbondale, IL 62901-4701. Offers MA. *Students:* 53 full-time (37 women), 8 part-time (4 women); includes 2 minority (both Asian, non-Hispanic/Latino), 33 international. 62 applicants, 63% accepted, 22 enrolled. In 2013, 27 master's awarded. Application fee: $50. *Unit head:* Dr. Elizabeth Klaver, Chair, 618-453-8331, E-mail: etklaver@siu.edu. *Application contact:* Diane Korando, Office Specialist, 618-536-3385, E-mail: ling@siu.edu.

Southern Illinois University Edwardsville, Graduate School, College of Arts and Sciences, Department of English Language and Literature, Program in Teaching English as a Second Language, Edwardsville, IL 62026-0001. Offers MA, Postbaccalaureate Certificate. Part-time and evening/weekend programs available. *Students:* 4 full-time (3 women), 9 part-time (7 women); includes 4 minority (1 Black or African American, non-Hispanic/Latino; 1 Asian, non-Hispanic/Latino; 2 Hispanic/Latino), 3 international. 11 applicants, 73% accepted. In 2013, 10 master's awarded. *Degree requirements:* For master's, one foreign language, thesis (for some programs), final exam. *Entrance requirements:* Additional exam requirements/recommendations for international students: Required—TOEFL (minimum score 550 paper-based, 79 iBT), IELTS

(minimum score 6.5), Michigan Test of English Language Proficiency or PTE. *Application deadline:* For fall admission, 7/18 for domestic students, 6/1 for international students; for spring admission, 12/12 for domestic students, 10/1 for international students; for summer admission, 4/24 for domestic students, 3/1 for international students. Applications are processed on a rolling basis. Application fee: $30. Electronic applications accepted. *Expenses:* Tuition, state resident: full-time $3551. Tuition, nonresident: full-time $8378. *Financial support:* Fellowships with full tuition reimbursements, research assistantships with full tuition reimbursements, teaching assistantships with full tuition reimbursements, scholarships/grants, and unspecified assistantships available. Financial award application deadline: 3/1; financial award applicants required to submit FAFSA. *Unit head:* Dr. Jessica DeSpain, Program Director, 618-650-2151, E-mail: jdespai@siue.edu. *Application contact:* Melissa K. Mace, Assistant Director of Graduate and International Recruitment, 618-650-2756, Fax: 618-650-3618, E-mail: mmace@siue.edu.
Website: http://www.siue.edu/ENGLISH/TESL/index.html.

Southern New Hampshire University, School of Arts and Sciences, Manchester, NH 03106-1045. Offers community mental health (Graduate Certificate); community mental health and mental health counseling (MS); fiction and nonfiction (MFA); teaching English as a foreign language (MS). Part-time and evening/weekend programs available. *Degree requirements:* For master's, one foreign language, thesis. *Entrance requirements:* For master's, minimum GPA of 2.75 (for MS in teaching English as a foreign language), 3.0 (for MFA). Additional exam requirements/recommendations for international students: Required—TOEFL (minimum score 550 paper-based; 79 iBT), IELTS (minimum score 6.5), TWE (minimum score 5). Electronic applications accepted. *Expenses:* Contact institution. *Faculty research:* Action research, state of the art practice in behavioral health services, wraparound approaches to working with youth, learning styles.

Southern New Hampshire University, School of Education, Manchester, NH 03106-1045. Offers business education (M Ed); child development (M Ed); curriculum and instruction (M Ed), including education leadership, reading, special education, technology integration; education (M Ed); educational leadership (M Ed, Ed D); educational studies (M Ed); elementary education (M Ed); English (MAT); English for speakers of other languages (M Ed); reading and writing specialist (M Ed); school business administration (Certificate); secondary education (M Ed); special education (M Ed); technology integration specialist (M Ed). Part-time and evening/weekend programs available. Postbaccalaureate distance learning degree programs offered (no on-campus study). *Degree requirements:* For master's, comprehensive exam (for some programs), thesis or alternative. *Entrance requirements:* For master's, PRAXIS I, minimum GPA of 2.75. Additional exam requirements/recommendations for international students: Required—TOEFL (minimum score 550 paper-based). Electronic applications accepted. *Expenses:* Contact institution.

Southwest Minnesota State University, Department of Education, Marshall, MN 56258. Offers ESL (MS); math (MS); reading (MS); special education (MS), including developmental disabilities, early childhood education, emotional behavioral disorders, learning disabilities; teaching, learning and leadership (MS). Part-time and evening/weekend programs available. Postbaccalaureate distance learning degree programs offered (no on-campus study). *Entrance requirements:* Additional exam requirements/recommendations for international students: Required—TOEFL or IELTS; Recommended—TOEFL (minimum score 550 paper-based; 80 iBT), IELTS.

State University of New York at Fredonia, Graduate Studies, College of Education, Program in Teaching English to Speakers of Other Languages, Fredonia, NY 14063-1136. Offers MS Ed. *Expenses:* Tuition, state resident: full-time $7398; part-time $411 per credit hour. Tuition, nonresident: full-time $13,770; part-time $765 per credit hour. *Required fees:* $1143.90; $63.55 per credit hour. Tuition and fees vary according to course load.

State University of New York at New Paltz, Graduate School, School of Education, Department of Secondary Education, Program in Second Language Education, New Paltz, NY 12561. Offers second language education (MS Ed); teaching English language learners (AC). *Accreditation:* NCATE. Part-time and evening/weekend programs available. *Students:* 22 full-time (18 women), 30 part-time (26 women); includes 14 minority (1 Black or African American, non-Hispanic/Latino; 1 Asian, non-Hispanic/Latino; 12 Hispanic/Latino), 1 international. Average age 30. 31 applicants, 90% accepted, 22 enrolled. In 2013, 23 master's awarded. *Degree requirements:* For master's, practicum. *Entrance requirements:* For master's, minimum GPA of 3.0, 12 credits of a foreign language. Additional exam requirements/recommendations for international students: Required—TOEFL (minimum score 575 paper-based; 90 iBT), IELTS (minimum score 7). *Application deadline:* For fall admission, 4/15 priority date for domestic and international students. Application fee: $50. Electronic applications accepted. *Expenses:* Tuition, state resident: full-time $9870; part-time $411 per credit. Tuition, nonresident: full-time $18,350; part-time $765 per credit. *Required fees:* $1213. Tuition and fees vary according to program. *Financial support:* Application deadline: 8/1. *Unit head:* Prof. Vern Todd, Coordinator, 845-257-2818, E-mail: toddv@newpaltz.edu. *Application contact:* Caroline Murphy, Graduate Admissions Advisor, 845-257-3285, Fax: 845-257-3284, E-mail: gradschool@newpaltz.edu.
Website: http://www.newpaltz.edu/secondaryed/sec_ed_msed_2nd_lang_ed.html.

State University of New York College at Cortland, Graduate Studies, School of Arts and Sciences, Department of Second Language Education, Cortland, NY 13045. Offers ESL (MS Ed); French (MS Ed); Spanish (MS Ed). *Accreditation:* NCATE. *Expenses:* Tuition, state resident: full-time $9870; part-time $411 per credit hour. Tuition, nonresident: full-time $18,350; part-time $765 per credit hour. *Required fees:* $1458; $65 per credit hour.

Stony Brook University, State University of New York, Graduate School, College of Arts and Sciences, Department of Linguistics, Program in Teaching English to Speakers of Other Languages, Stony Brook, NY 11794. Offers MA. *Accreditation:* NCATE. *Students:* 30 full-time (28 women), 8 part-time (all women); includes 7 minority (2 Asian, non-Hispanic/Latino; 4 Hispanic/Latino; 1 Native Hawaiian or other Pacific Islander, non-Hispanic/Latino), 8 international. Average age 30. 68 applicants, 53% accepted, 15 enrolled. In 2013, 23 master's awarded. *Application deadline:* For fall admission, 1/15 for domestic students; for spring admission, 10/1 for domestic students. Application fee: $100. *Expenses:* Tuition, state resident: full-time $9870; part-time $411 per credit. Tuition, nonresident: full-time $18,350; part-time $765 per credit. *Financial support:* Fellowships, research assistantships, and teaching assistantships available. *Unit head:* Dr. Richard Larson, Chair, 631-632-7774, E-mail: richard.larson@stonybrook.edu. *Application contact:* Michelle Carbone, Coordinator, 631-632-7774, Fax: 631-632-9789, E-mail: michelle.carbone@stonybrook.edu.
Website: https://linguistics.stonybrook.edu/programs/graduate/ma.

Syracuse University, College of Arts and Sciences, Program in Language Teaching: TESOL/TLOTE, Syracuse, NY 13244. Offers CAS. Part-time programs available. *Students:* 2 part-time (1 woman). Average age 38. 17 applicants, 76% accepted, 1 enrolled. In 2013, 15 CASs awarded. *Entrance requirements:* Additional exam requirements/recommendations for international students: Required—TOEFL (minimum score 100 iBT). *Application deadline:* For fall admission, 1/10 priority date for domestic and international students. Applications are processed on a rolling basis. Electronic applications accepted. *Unit head:* Dr. Amanda Brown, Graduate Director, 315-443-2244, E-mail: abrown08@syr.edu. *Application contact:* Dr. Amanda Brown, Assistant Professor, 315-443-2244, E-mail: abrown08@syr.edu.
Website: http://lang.syr.edu/.

Syracuse University, School of Education, Program in Teaching English Language Learners, Syracuse, NY 13244. Offers MS. Part-time programs available. *Students:* 3 full-time (all women), 1 (woman) part-time. Average age 26. 8 applicants, 100% accepted, 3 enrolled. In 2013, 9 master's awarded. *Entrance requirements:* For master's, New York State Teacher Certification or eligibility. Additional exam requirements/recommendations for international students: Required—TOEFL (minimum score 100 iBT). *Application deadline:* For fall admission, 1/15 priority date for domestic and international students. Application fee: $75. Electronic applications accepted. *Financial support:* Fellowships with full tuition reimbursements, teaching assistantships with full and partial tuition reimbursements, and tuition waivers available. Financial award application deadline: 1/1; financial award applicants required to submit FAFSA. *Unit head:* Dr. Zaline Roy-Campbell, Program Coordinator, 315-443-8194, E-mail: zmroycam@syr.edu. *Application contact:* Laurie Deyo, Graduate Recruiter, School of Education, 315-443-2505, E-mail: e-gradrcrt@syr.edu.
Website: http://soeweb.syr.edu/.

Taylor College and Seminary, Graduate and Professional Programs, Edmonton, AB T6J 4T3, Canada. Offers Christian studies (Diploma); intercultural studies (MA, Diploma), including intercultural studies (Diploma), TESOL; theology (M Div, MTS). *Accreditation:* ATS. Part-time programs available. Postbaccalaureate distance learning degree programs offered (minimal on-campus study). *Degree requirements:* For master's, thesis optional. *Entrance requirements:* Additional exam requirements/recommendations for international students: Required—TOEFL (minimum score 550 paper-based; 80 iBT), IELTS (minimum score 6.5). *Faculty research:* Biblical studies, administration and organization, world religions, ethics, missiology.

Teachers College, Columbia University, Graduate Faculty of Education, Department of Arts and Humanities, Program in Teaching English to Speakers of Other Languages, New York, NY 10027-6696. Offers Ed M, MA, Ed D. *Accreditation:* NCATE. Part-time programs available. *Faculty:* 9 full-time, 9 part-time/adjunct. *Students:* 39 full-time (35 women), 92 part-time (75 women); includes 41 minority (2 Black or African American, non-Hispanic/Latino; 29 Asian, non-Hispanic/Latino; 8 Hispanic/Latino; 2 Two or more races, non-Hispanic/Latino), 42 international. Average age 30. 327 applicants, 39% accepted, 56 enrolled. In 2013, 68 master's, 2 doctorates awarded. *Degree requirements:* For master's, project; for doctorate, comprehensive exam, thesis/dissertation. *Entrance requirements:* For master's, MA in related field (for Ed M); for doctorate, MA in teaching English to speakers of other languages. Additional exam requirements/recommendations for international students: Required—TOEFL (minimum score 102 iBT), IELTS (minimum score 7). *Application deadline:* For fall admission, 1/15 priority date for domestic students; for spring admission, 11/15 for domestic students. Application fee: $65. Electronic applications accepted. *Financial support:* Career-related internships or fieldwork, Federal Work-Study, institutionally sponsored loans, and tuition waivers (full and partial) available. Support available to part-time students. Financial award application deadline: 2/1. *Faculty research:* Classroom-centered research, electronic media, K-12 English as a second language, second language acquisition. *Unit head:* Prof. ZhaoHong Han, Program Coordinator, 212-678-4051, E-mail: zhh2@columbia.edu. *Application contact:* Thomas P. Rock, Director of Admissions, 212-678-3083, Fax: 212-678-4171, E-mail: rock@tc.edu.

Temple University, College of Education, Department of Curriculum, Instruction, and Technology in Education, Program in Teaching English to Speakers of Other Languages (TESOL), Philadelphia, PA 19122-6096. Offers MS Ed. *Degree requirements:* For master's, comprehensive exam. *Entrance requirements:* For master's, MAT or GRE, official transcripts, two professional letters of recommendation, professional goal statement, professional resume. Additional exam requirements/recommendations for international students: Required—TOEFL or IELTS.

Texas A&M University–Commerce, Graduate School, College of Education and Human Services, Department of Curriculum and Instruction, Commerce, TX 75429-3011. Offers bilingual/ESL education (M Ed, MS); early childhood education (M Ed, MS); elementary education (M Ed, MS); reading (M Ed, MS); secondary education (M Ed, MS); supervision, curriculum and instruction: elementary education (Ed D). MS and M Ed programs in early childhood education offered jointly with Texas Woman's University and University of North Texas. Part-time programs available. Terminal master's awarded for partial completion of doctoral program. *Degree requirements:* For master's, comprehensive exam, thesis (for some programs); for doctorate, 2 foreign languages, thesis/dissertation, departmental qualifying exam. *Entrance requirements:* For master's and doctorate, GRE General Test. Electronic applications accepted. *Expenses:* Tuition, state resident: full-time $3630; part-time $2420 per year. Tuition, nonresident: full-time $9948; part-time $6632.16 per year. *Required fees:* $1006 per year. Tuition and fees vary according to course load. *Faculty research:* Literacy and learning, early childhood, preservice teacher education, technology.

Texas A&M University–Kingsville, College of Graduate Studies, College of Education, Department of Education, Program in English as a Second Language, Kingsville, TX 78363. Offers M Ed. *Faculty:* 9 full-time (5 women), 4 part-time/adjunct (2 women). In 2013, 3 master's awarded. *Degree requirements:* For master's, comprehensive exam. *Entrance requirements:* For master's, GRE General Test, MAT, minimum GPA of 3.0. *Application deadline:* For fall admission, 6/1 for domestic students; for spring admission, 11/15 for domestic students. Applications are processed on a rolling basis. Application fee: $35 ($50 for international students). *Financial support:* Application deadline: 5/15. *Unit head:* Dr. Travis Polk, Chair, 361-593-3204. *Application contact:* Dr. Alberto M. Olivares, Dean, College of Graduate Studies, 361-593-2808, Fax: 361-593-3412, E-mail: a-olivares@tamuk.edu.

Touro College, Graduate School of Education, New York, NY 10010. Offers education and special education (MS); education biology (MS); instructional technology (MS); mathematics education (MS); school leadership (MS); teaching English to speakers of other languages (MS); teaching literacy (MS). Part-time and evening/weekend programs available. Postbaccalaureate distance learning degree programs offered (no on-campus study). *Faculty:* 75 full-time, 131 part-time/adjunct. *Students:* 327 full-time (272 women), 2,454 part-time (2,103 women); includes 840 minority (333 Black or African American, non-Hispanic/Latino; 4 American Indian or Alaska Native, non-Hispanic/Latino; 139 Asian, non-Hispanic/Latino; 334 Hispanic/Latino; 8 Native Hawaiian or other Pacific Islander, non-Hispanic/Latino; 22 Two or more races, non-Hispanic/Latino), 4 international. 1,422 applicants, 50% accepted, 675 enrolled. In 2013, 6 master's awarded. *Entrance requirements:* Additional exam requirements/recommendations for international students: Required—TOEFL (minimum score 83 iBT), IELTS (minimum score 6.5). *Application deadline:* For fall admission, 8/26 for domestic students, 7/15 for international students; for spring admission, 12/31 for domestic students, 12/15 for international students. Applications are processed on a rolling basis. Application fee: $50. *Financial support:* Federal Work-Study available. Financial award applicants required to submit FAFSA. *Faculty research:* Equity assistance, language development, scholar communications, Latin American studies and cultural sensitivity, behavior

management techniques and strategies in special education. *Unit head:* Dr. LaMar Miller, Dean, 212-463-0400 Ext. 5561, Fax: 212-462-4889, E-mail: lpmiller@touro.edu. *Application contact:* Natalie Arroyo, Admissions, 212-463-0400.

Trevecca Nazarene University, Graduate Education Program, Nashville, TN 37210-2877. Offers curriculum, assessment, and instruction K-12 (M Ed); educational leadership (M Ed); English language learners (PreK-12) (M Ed); leadership and professional practice (Ed D); library and information science (MLI Sc); teacher leader (M Ed); teaching (MAE, MAT), including teaching 7-12 (MAT), teaching K-6 (MAT); visual impairments special education (M Ed). *Accreditation:* NCATE. Part-time and evening/weekend programs available. Postbaccalaureate distance learning degree programs offered. *Faculty:* 19 full-time (17 women), 14 part-time/adjunct (5 women). *Students:* 186 full-time (137 women), 134 part-time (94 women); includes 93 minority (87 Black or African American, non-Hispanic/Latino; 1 American Indian or Alaska Native, non-Hispanic/Latino; 2 Asian, non-Hispanic/Latino; 1 Hispanic/Latino; 1 Native Hawaiian or other Pacific Islander, non-Hispanic/Latino; 1 Two or more races, non-Hispanic/Latino), 2 international. In 2013, 201 master's, 40 doctorates awarded. *Degree requirements:* For master's, comprehensive exam, exit assessment/e-portfolio; for doctorate, thesis/dissertation, proposal study, symposium presentation. *Entrance requirements:* For master's, GRE with minimum score of 378 or MAT with minimum score of 290, ACT with minimum score of 22 or SAT with minimum score of 1020 (for MAT programs only); PRAXIS (for MAT and MAE programs), minimum GPA of 2.7, official transcript from regionally accredited institution, 3+ years successful teaching experience (Teacher Leader and Education Leadership majors), technology pre-assessment written requirements (some majors); for doctorate, GRE or MAT, minimum GPA of 3.4, official transcript from regionally-accredited institution, resume, writing sample, interview, reference forms. Additional exam requirements/recommendations for international students: Required—TOEFL (minimum score 550 paper-based). *Application deadline:* Applications are processed on a rolling basis. *Expenses:* Contact institution. *Financial support:* Applicants required to submit FAFSA. *Unit head:* Dr. Suzie Harris, Dean, School of Education/Director of Graduate Education Programs, 615-248-1201, Fax: 615-248-1597, E-mail: admissions_ged@trevecca.edu. *Application contact:* 615-248-1529, E-mail: cll@trevecca.edu.
Website: http://www.trevecca.edu/academics/schools-colleges/education/.

Trinity Western University, School of Graduate Studies, Program in Teaching English to Speakers of Other Languages (TESOL), Langley, BC V2Y 1Y1, Canada. Offers MA. Part-time programs available. Postbaccalaureate distance learning degree programs offered (minimal on-campus study). *Degree requirements:* For master's, project. *Entrance requirements:* For master's, minimum GPA of 3.0. Additional exam requirements/recommendations for international students: Required—TOEFL (minimum score 600 paper-based). *Faculty research:* ESL methodology, second language acquisition, computer assisted language learning.

Universidad del Este, Graduate School, Carolina, PR 00984. Offers accounting (MBA); adult education (M Ed); agribusiness (MBA); criminal justice and criminology (MA); curriculum and instruction - early education (M Ed); curriculum and instruction - elementary (M Ed); curriculum and instruction - English (M Ed); curriculum and instruction - Spanish (M Ed); human resources (MBA); information security management (MBA); information technology and Web business development (MBA); management (MBA); public policy (MPA); social work (MA), including clinical social work; special education (M Ed); strategic leadership (MBA). *Students:* 464 full-time (322 women), 669 part-time (499 women); all minorities (all Hispanic/Latino). Average age 35. 693 applicants, 61% accepted, 332 enrolled. In 2013, 228 master's awarded. *Unit head:* Jose R. Clintron, Dean, 787-257-7373 Ext. 3007, E-mail: ue_jcintron@suagm.edu. *Application contact:* Clotilde Santiago, Director of Admissions, 787-257-7373 Ext. 3400, E-mail: ue_csantiago@suagm.edu.

Universidad del Turabo, Graduate Programs, Programs in Education, Program in Teaching English as a Second Language, Gurabo, PR 00778-3030. Offers M Ed. *Entrance requirements:* For master's, GRE, EXADEP, interview.

University at Buffalo, the State University of New York, Graduate School, Graduate School of Education, Department of Learning and Instruction, Buffalo, NY 14260. Offers biology education (Ed M, Certificate); chemistry education (Ed M, Certificate); childhood education (Ed M); childhood education with bilingual extension (Ed M); curriculum, instruction and the science of learning (PhD); early childhood education (Ed M); early childhood education with bilingual extension (birth-grade 2) (Ed M); earth science education (Ed M, Certificate); education studies (Ed M); educational technology and new literacies (Certificate); elementary education (Ed D); English education (Ed M, Certificate); English for speakers of other languages (Ed M); foreign and second language education (PhD); French education (Ed M, Certificate); German education (Ed M, Certificate); gifted education (Certificate); Latin education (Ed M, Certificate); literacy specialist (Ed M); literacy teaching and learning (Certificate); mathematics education (Ed M, Certificate); music education (Ed M, Certificate); physics education (Ed M, Certificate); science and the public (Ed M); social studies education (Ed M, Certificate); Spanish education (Ed M, Certificate); special education (PhD); teaching English to speakers of other languages (Ed M). Part-time and evening/weekend programs available. Postbaccalaureate distance learning degree programs offered (no on-campus study). *Faculty:* 31 full-time (23 women), 64 part-time/adjunct (53 women). *Students:* 275 full-time (215 women), 293 part-time (205 women); includes 35 minority (16 Black or African American, non-Hispanic/Latino; 5 American Indian or Alaska Native, non-Hispanic/Latino; 11 Asian, non-Hispanic/Latino; 3 Hispanic/Latino), 97 international. Average age 30. 544 applicants, 81% accepted, 246 enrolled. In 2013, 222 master's, 17 doctorates, 35 other advanced degrees awarded. *Degree requirements:* For master's, comprehensive exam; for doctorate, thesis/dissertation, research analysis exam, research experience component. *Entrance requirements:* For master's, content test in science and math, letters of reference; for doctorate, GRE General Test or MAT, interview, writing sample, letters of recommendation. Additional exam requirements/recommendations for international students: Required—TOEFL (minimum score 600 paper-based; 96 iBT). *Application deadline:* For fall admission, 2/1 priority date for domestic and international students; for spring admission, 11/15 priority date for domestic students, 10/1 for international students. Applications are processed on a rolling basis. Application fee: $50. Electronic applications accepted. *Financial support:* In 2013–14, 50 fellowships (averaging $8,589 per year), 31 research assistantships with tuition reimbursements (averaging $11,406 per year) were awarded; teaching assistantships, career-related internships or fieldwork, Federal Work-Study, institutionally sponsored loans, scholarships/grants, tuition waivers, and unspecified assistantships also available. Financial award application deadline: 2/28; financial award applicants required to submit FAFSA. *Faculty research:* Science assessment, foreign language teaching and learning, early learning, new literacies, gender and education. *Total annual research expenditures:* $1.7 million. *Unit head:* Dr. Suzanne Miller, Chair, 716-645-2455, Fax: 716-645-3161, E-mail: smiller@buffalo.edu. *Application contact:* Cathy Dimino, Admissions Assistant, 716-645-2110, Fax: 716-645-7937, E-mail: cadimino@buffalo.edu.
Website: http://gse.buffalo.edu/lai.

The University of Alabama, Graduate School, College of Arts and Sciences, Department of English, Tuscaloosa, AL 35487. Offers applied linguistics (PhD); composition and rhetoric (PhD); creative writing (MFA), including fiction, poetry; literature (MA, PhD); rhetoric and composition (MA); teaching English as a second language (MATESOL). *Faculty:* 31 full-time (15 women). *Students:* 58 full-time (43 women), 75 part-time (44 women); includes 18 minority (8 Black or African American, non-Hispanic/Latino; 2 Asian, non-Hispanic/Latino; 4 Hispanic/Latino; 1 Native Hawaiian or other Pacific Islander, non-Hispanic/Latino; 3 Two or more races, non-Hispanic/Latino), 10 international. Average age 27. 339 applicants, 16% accepted, 40 enrolled. In 2013, 31 master's, 3 doctorates awarded. *Degree requirements:* For master's, one foreign language, comprehensive exam, thesis optional; for doctorate, 2 foreign languages, comprehensive exam, thesis/dissertation. *Entrance requirements:* For master's, GRE with minimum score of 300 (except for MFA), minimum GPA of 3.0, critical writing sample; for doctorate, GRE (minimum score of 300), minimum GPA of 3.5 on master's or equivalent graduate work, critical writing sample. Additional exam requirements/recommendations for international students: Required—TOEFL (minimum score 100 iBT). *Application deadline:* For fall admission, 12/31 priority date for domestic and international students. Application fee: $50 ($60 for international students). Electronic applications accepted. *Expenses:* Tuition, state resident: full-time $9450. Tuition, nonresident: full-time $23,950. *Financial support:* In 2013–14, 11 fellowships with full tuition reimbursements (averaging $15,000 per year), 1 research assistantship with full tuition reimbursement (averaging $12,366 per year), 110 teaching assistantships with full tuition reimbursements (averaging $12,366 per year) were awarded; career-related internships or fieldwork, scholarships/grants, health care benefits, and unspecified assistantships also available. Financial award application deadline: 12/31. *Faculty research:* American literature, British literature, composition/rhetoric, applied linguistics, creative writing. *Unit head:* Dr. Catherine E. Davies, Department Chair, 205-348-9525, Fax: 205-348-1388, E-mail: cdavies@as.ua.edu. *Application contact:* Jennifer Fuqua, Senior Office Assistant, 205-348-0766, Fax: 205-348-1388, E-mail: jfuqua@as.ua.edu.

The University of Alabama at Birmingham, School of Education, Program in English as a Second Language, Birmingham, AL 35294. Offers MA Ed. *Entrance requirements:* For master's, MAT (minimum score of 388 scaled, 35 raw) or GRE (minimum 2960 on current test).

University of Alberta, Faculty of Graduate Studies and Research, Department of Educational Psychology, Edmonton, AB T6G 2E1, Canada. Offers counseling psychology (M Ed, PhD); educational psychology (M Ed, PhD); instructional technology (M Ed); school counseling (M Ed); school psychology (M Ed, PhD); special education (M Ed, PhD); special education-deafness studies (M Ed); teaching English as a second language (M Ed). Part-time programs available. *Degree requirements:* For master's, thesis optional; for doctorate, comprehensive exam, thesis/dissertation. *Entrance requirements:* For master's and doctorate, minimum GPA of 3.0. Additional exam requirements/recommendations for international students: Required—TOEFL. *Faculty research:* Human learning, development and assessment.

The University of Arizona, College of Humanities, Department of English, English Language/Linguistics Program, Tucson, AZ 85721. Offers English (MA, PhD); ESL (MA). *Faculty:* 45 full-time (17 women), 3 part-time/adjunct (1 woman). *Students:* 83 full-time (45 women), 6 part-time (2 women); includes 13 minority (1 Black or African American, non-Hispanic/Latino; 1 American Indian or Alaska Native, non-Hispanic/Latino; 1 Asian, non-Hispanic/Latino; 5 Hispanic/Latino; 5 Two or more races, non-Hispanic/Latino), 13 international. Average age 33. 65 applicants, 23% accepted, 9 enrolled. In 2013, 6 master's, 3 doctorates awarded. *Entrance requirements:* Additional exam requirements/recommendations for international students: Required—TOEFL (minimum score 550 paper-based; 79 iBT); Recommended—IELTS (minimum score 7). *Application deadline:* For fall admission, 1/15 priority date for domestic students, 1/15 for international students. Application fee: $75. Electronic applications accepted. *Expenses:* Tuition, state resident: full-time $11,526. Tuition, nonresident: full-time $27,398. *Financial support:* In 2013–14, 1 research assistantship with full tuition reimbursement (averaging $11,258 per year), 128 teaching assistantships with full tuition reimbursements (averaging $20,796 per year) were awarded. *Total annual research expenditures:* $164,565. *Unit head:* Dr. Lawrence J. Evers, Interim Department Head, 520-621-3287, E-mail: levers@email.arizona.edu. *Application contact:* Marcia Marma, Graduate Secretary, 520-621-1358, Fax: 520-621-7397, E-mail: mmarma@u.arizona.edu.

The University of Arizona, Graduate Interdisciplinary Programs, Graduate Interdisciplinary Program in Second Language Acquisition and Teaching, Tucson, AZ 85721. Offers PhD. *Students:* 71 full-time (40 women), 8 part-time (5 women); includes 13 minority (2 Black or African American, non-Hispanic/Latino; 2 Asian, non-Hispanic/Latino; 4 Hispanic/Latino; 5 Two or more races, non-Hispanic/Latino), 29 international. Average age 36. 87 applicants, 15% accepted, 5 enrolled. In 2013, 4 doctorates awarded. *Degree requirements:* For doctorate, one foreign language, comprehensive exam, thesis/dissertation. *Entrance requirements:* For doctorate, GRE, 3 letters of recommendation, writing sample. Additional exam requirements/recommendations for international students: Required—TOEFL (minimum score 550 paper-based; 79 iBT); Recommended—TWE. *Application deadline:* For fall admission, 2/1 for domestic students, 1/15 for international students. Applications are processed on a rolling basis. Application fee: $75. Electronic applications accepted. *Expenses:* Tuition, state resident: full-time $11,526. Tuition, nonresident: full-time $27,398. *Financial support:* Scholarships/grants, health care benefits, tuition waivers (full and partial), and unspecified assistantships available. Financial award application deadline: 2/1; financial award applicants required to submit FAFSA. *Unit head:* Dr. Robert Ariew, Chair, 520-621-7391, E-mail: gidp-slat@email.arizona.edu. *Application contact:* Shaun O'Connor, Senior Program Coordinator, 520-621-7391, E-mail: gidp-slat@email.arizona.edu.
Website: http://slat.arizona.edu/.

University of Arkansas at Little Rock, Graduate School, College of Arts, Humanities, and Social Science, Department of International and Second Language Studies, Little Rock, AR 72204-1099. Offers second languages (MA). *Expenses:* Tuition, state resident: full-time $5690; part-time $284.50 per credit hour. Tuition, nonresident: full-time $13,030; part-time $651.50 per credit hour. *Required fees:* $1121; $672 per term. One-time fee: $40 full-time.

The University of British Columbia, Faculty of Education, Program in Language and Literacy Education, Vancouver, BC V6T 1Z1, Canada. Offers library education (M Ed); literacy education (M Ed, MA, PhD); modern language education (M Ed, MA, PhD); teaching English as a second language (M Ed, MA, PhD). Part-time and evening/weekend programs available. *Degree requirements:* For master's, thesis (MA); for doctorate, thesis/dissertation. *Entrance requirements:* For master's and doctorate, minimum B+ average in last 2 years with minimum 2 courses at A standing. Additional exam requirements/recommendations for international students: Required—TOEFL (minimum score 580 paper-based; 92 iBT), TWE (minimum score 5). Electronic applications accepted. *Expenses: Tuition, area resident:* Full-time $8000 Canadian dollars. *Faculty research:* Language and literacy development, second language acquisition, Asia Pacific language curriculum, children's literature, whole language instruction.

University of California, Berkeley, UC Berkeley Extension, Certificate Programs in Education, Berkeley, CA 94720-1500. Offers college admissions and career planning (Certificate); teaching English as a second language (Certificate).

University of California, Los Angeles, Graduate Division, College of Letters and Science, Department of Applied Linguistics and Teaching English as a Second Language, Los Angeles, CA 90095. Offers applied linguistics (PhD); applied linguistics and teaching English as a second language (MA); teaching English as a second language (Certificate). *Degree requirements:* For master's, one foreign language, thesis; for doctorate, one foreign language, thesis/dissertation, oral and written qualifying exams. *Entrance requirements:* For master's and doctorate, bachelor's degree; minimum undergraduate GPA of 3.0 (or its equivalent if letter grade system not used). Additional exam requirements/recommendations for international students: Required—TOEFL. Electronic applications accepted.

University of California, Riverside, Graduate Division, Graduate School of Education, Riverside, CA 92521-0102. Offers autism (M Ed); diversity and equity (M Ed); education specialist (Credential); education, society and culture (MA, PhD); educational psychology (MA, PhD); general education (M Ed); higher education administration and policy (M Ed, PhD); multiple subject (Credential); reading (M Ed); school psychology (PhD); single subject (Credential); special education (M Ed, MA, PhD); TESOL (M Ed). *Faculty:* 22 full-time (11 women), 14 part-time/adjunct (10 women). *Students:* 218 full-time (148 women); includes 95 minority (10 Black or African American, non-Hispanic/Latino; 30 Asian, non-Hispanic/Latino; 49 Hispanic/Latino; 6 Two or more races, non-Hispanic/Latino), 12 international. Average age 31. 236 applicants, 66% accepted, 78 enrolled. In 2013, 66 master's, 13 doctorates, 86 other advanced degrees awarded. Terminal master's awarded for partial completion of doctoral program. *Degree requirements:* For master's, thesis optional, comprehensive exams or thesis (MA), case study or analytical report (M Ed); for doctorate, thesis/dissertation, written and oral qualifying exams, college teaching practicum. *Entrance requirements:* For master's, GRE General Test (for MA); CBEST and CSET (for M Ed in general education only), UCR Extension TESOL certificate (for M Ed with TESOL emphasis only); for doctorate, GRE General Test, writing sample; for Credential, CBEST, CSET. Additional exam requirements/recommendations for international students: Required—TOEFL (minimum score 550 paper-based; 80 iBT), IELTS (minimum score 7). *Application deadline:* For fall admission, 9/1 for domestic students, 5/1 for international students; for winter admission, 11/15 for domestic students, 7/1 for international students; for spring admission, 3/1 for domestic students, 10/1 for international students. Applications are processed on a rolling basis. Application fee: $80 ($100 for international students). Electronic applications accepted. *Financial support:* In 2013–14, 58 students received support, including 31 fellowships with full tuition reimbursements available, 11 research assistantships with full tuition reimbursements available (averaging $14,691 per year), 5 teaching assistantships with full tuition reimbursements available (averaging $17,655 per year); career-related internships or fieldwork, Federal Work-Study, institutionally sponsored loans, scholarships/grants, and unspecified assistantships also available. Financial award application deadline: 1/5. *Faculty research:* Responsiveness to intervention, faculty core, response to intervention of English language learners, advanced modeling techniques, study on social capital, trust, and motivation. *Total annual research expenditures:* $1.9 million. *Unit head:* Prof. Douglas Mitchell, Interim Dean and Professor, 951-827-5802, Fax: 951-827-3942, E-mail: douglas.mitchell@ucr.edu. *Application contact:* Prof. Michael Orosco, Assistant Professor and Graduate Advisor of Admissions, 951-827-6362, Fax: 951-827-3291, E-mail: edgrad@ucr.edu. Website: http://www.education.ucr.edu/.

University of Central Florida, College of Arts and Humanities, Department of Modern Languages and Literatures, Program in Teaching English to Speakers of Other Languages, Orlando, FL 32816. Offers ESOL endorsement K-12 (Certificate); teaching English as a foreign language (Certificate); teaching English to speakers of other languages (MA). *Accreditation:* NCATE. Part-time and evening/weekend programs available. *Students:* 25 full-time (18 women), 32 part-time (23 women); includes 17 minority (1 Black or African American, non-Hispanic/Latino; 3 Asian, non-Hispanic/Latino; 13 Hispanic/Latino), 4 international. Average age 33. 39 applicants, 82% accepted, 23 enrolled. In 2013, 21 master's, 29 other advanced degrees awarded. *Degree requirements:* For master's, comprehensive exam, thesis or alternative. *Entrance requirements:* For master's, GRE General Test, minimum GPA of 3.0 in last 60 hours. Additional exam requirements/recommendations for international students: Required—TOEFL. *Application deadline:* For fall admission, 6/15 for domestic students; for spring admission, 11/1 for domestic students. Application fee: $30. Electronic applications accepted. *Financial support:* In 2013–14, 2 students received support, including 2 fellowships (averaging $4,000 per year), 2 teaching assistantships with partial tuition reimbursements available (averaging $8,200 per year); career-related internships or fieldwork, Federal Work-Study, institutionally sponsored loans, tuition waivers (partial), and unspecified assistantships also available. Financial award application deadline: 3/1; financial award applicants required to submit FAFSA. *Unit head:* Dr. Kerry Purmensky, Program Coordinator, 407-823-0110, E-mail: kerry.purmensky@ucf.edu. *Application contact:* Barbara Rodriguez Lamas, Director, Admissions and Student Services, 407-823-2766, Fax: 407-823-6442, E-mail: gradadmissions@ucf.edu.
Website: http://mll.cah.ucf.edu/graduate/index.php#TESOL.

University of Central Florida, College of Education and Human Performance, Education Doctoral Programs, Orlando, FL 32816. Offers communication sciences and disorders (PhD); counselor education (PhD); early childhood education (PhD); education (Ed D); elementary education (PhD); exceptional education (PhD); exercise physiology (PhD); higher education (PhD); hospitality education (PhD); instructional technology (PhD); mathematics education (PhD); reading education (PhD); science education (PhD); social science education (PhD); TESOL (PhD). *Students:* 137 full-time (94 women), 86 part-time (64 women); includes 45 minority (24 Black or African American, non-Hispanic/Latino; 5 Asian, non-Hispanic/Latino; 13 Hispanic/Latino; 3 Two or more races, non-Hispanic/Latino), 22 international. Average age 39. 132 applicants, 54% accepted, 54 enrolled. In 2013, 38 doctorates awarded. Application fee: $30. Electronic applications accepted. *Financial support:* In 2013–14, 84 students received support, including 38 fellowships with partial tuition reimbursements available (averaging $6,600 per year), 41 research assistantships with partial tuition reimbursements available (averaging $7,800 per year), 53 teaching assistantships with partial tuition reimbursements available (averaging $7,700 per year). *Unit head:* Dr. Edward Robinson, Director of Doctoral Programs, 407-823-6106, E-mail: edward.robinson@ucf.edu. *Application contact:* Barbara Rodriguez Lamas, Associate Director, Admissions and Student Services, 407-823-2766, Fax: 407-823-6442, E-mail: gradadmissions@ucf.edu.
Website: http://education.ucf.edu/departments.cfm.

University of Central Missouri, The Graduate School, Warrensburg, MO 6409. Offers accountancy (MA); accounting (MBA); applied mathematics (MS); aviation safety (MA); biology (MS); business administration (MBA); career and technical education leadership (MS); college student personnel administration (MS); communication (MA); computer science (MS); counseling (MS); criminal justice (MS); educational leadership (Ed D); educational technology (MS); elementary and early childhood education (MSE); English (MA); environmental studies (MA); finance (MBA); history (MA); human services/educational technology (Ed S); human services/learning resources (Ed S); human services/professional counseling (Ed S); industrial hygiene (MS); industrial management (MS); information systems (MBA); information technology (MS); kinesiology (MS); library science and information services (MS); literacy education (MSE); marketing (MBA); mathematics (MS); music (MA); occupational safety management (MS); psychology (MS); rural family nursing (MS); school administration (MSE); social gerontology (MS); sociology (MA); special education (MSE); speech language pathology (MS); superintendency (Ed S); teaching (MAT); teaching English as a second language (MA); technology (MS); technology management (PhD); theatre (MA). Part-time programs available. *Faculty:* 233. *Students:* 890 full-time (396 women), 1,486 part-time (1,001 women); includes 192 minority (97 Black or African American, non-Hispanic/Latino; 9 American Indian or Alaska Native, non-Hispanic/Latino; 32 Asian, non-Hispanic/Latino; 40 Hispanic/Latino; 3 Native Hawaiian or other Pacific Islander, non-Hispanic/Latino; 11 Two or more races, non-Hispanic/Latino), 539 international. Average age 31. 1,953 applicants, 75% accepted. In 2013, 719 master's, 58 other advanced degrees awarded. *Degree requirements:* For master's and Ed S, comprehensive exam (for some programs), thesis (for some programs). *Entrance requirements:* Additional exam requirements/recommendations for international students: Required—TOEFL (minimum score 550 paper-based; 79 iBT). *Application deadline:* For fall admission, 6/1 for domestic students; for spring admission, 10/1 for domestic and international students. Applications are processed on a rolling basis. Application fee: $30 ($75 for international students). Electronic applications accepted. *Expenses:* Tuition, state resident: full-time $7326; part-time $276.25 per credit hour. Tuition, nonresident: full-time $13,956; part-time $552.50 per credit hour. *Required fees:* $29 per credit hour. *Financial support:* In 2013–14, 118 students received support, including 271 research assistantships with full and partial tuition reimbursements available (averaging $7,500 per year), 109 teaching assistantships with full and partial tuition reimbursements available (averaging $7,500 per year); career-related internships or fieldwork, Federal Work-Study, scholarships/grants, and administrative and laboratory assistantships also available. Support available to part-time students. Financial award application deadline: 3/1; financial award applicants required to submit FAFSA. *Unit head:* Dr. Joseph Vaughn, Assistant Provost for Research/Dean, 660-543-4092, Fax: 660-543-4778, E-mail: vaughn@ucmo.edu. *Application contact:* Brittany Lawrence, Graduate Student Services Coordinator, 660-543-4621, Fax: 660-543-4778, E-mail: gradinfo@ucmo.edu. Website: http://www.ucmo.edu/graduate/.

University of Central Oklahoma, The Jackson College of Graduate Studies, College of Education and Professional Studies, Department of Curriculum and Instruction, Edmond, OK 73034-5209. Offers bilingual education/teaching English as a second language (M Ed); early childhood education (M Ed); elementary education (M Ed). Part-time programs available. *Faculty:* 8 full-time (6 women), 10 part-time/adjunct (8 women). *Students:* 50 full-time (46 women), 68 part-time (61 women); includes 21 minority (7 Black or African American, non-Hispanic/Latino; 1 American Indian or Alaska Native, non-Hispanic/Latino; 3 Asian, non-Hispanic/Latino; 8 Hispanic/Latino; 2 Two or more races, non-Hispanic/Latino), 51 international. Average age 34. 55 applicants, 91% accepted, 25 enrolled. In 2013, 65 master's awarded. *Degree requirements:* For master's, comprehensive exam (for some programs), thesis optional. *Entrance requirements:* For master's, GRE General Test. Additional exam requirements/recommendations for international students: Required—TOEFL (minimum score 550 paper-based; 79 iBT), IELTS (minimum score 6.5). *Application deadline:* For fall admission, 7/1 for international students; for spring admission, 11/1 for international students. Applications are processed on a rolling basis. Application fee: $50. Electronic applications accepted. *Expenses:* Tuition, state resident: full-time $4137; part-time $206.85 per credit hour. Tuition, nonresident: full-time $10,359; part-time $517.95 per credit hour. *Required fees:* $481. Tuition and fees vary according to course load and program. *Financial support:* In 2013–14, 26 students received support, including research assistantships with partial tuition reimbursements available (averaging $5,454 per year), teaching assistantships with partial tuition reimbursements available (averaging $9,478 per year); Federal Work-Study, scholarships/grants, tuition waivers (partial), and unspecified assistantships also available. Financial award application deadline: 3/31; financial award applicants required to submit FAFSA. *Faculty research:* Tourette's syndrome, bilingual education, science education, language development/disorders. *Unit head:* Dr. Paulette Shreck, Chair, 405-974-5721, Fax: 405-974-3858, E-mail: pshreck@uco.edu. *Application contact:* Dr. Richard Bernard, Dean, Graduate College, 405-974-3493, Fax: 405-974-3852, E-mail: gradcoll@uco.edu.

University of Cincinnati, Graduate School, College of Education, Criminal Justice, and Human Services, Division of Teacher Education, Program in Teaching English as a Second Language, Cincinnati, OH 45221. Offers M Ed, Ed D, Certificate. *Entrance requirements:* For master's and doctorate, GRE General Test. Additional exam requirements/recommendations for international students: Required—TOEFL (minimum score 550 paper-based), TWE (minimum score 5), Test of Spoken English (minimum score: 50).

University of Delaware, College of Education and Human Development, School of Education, Newark, DE 19716. Offers education (PhD); educational leadership (Ed D); higher education (M Ed); instruction (MI); reading (M Ed); school leadership (M Ed); school psychology (MA, Ed S); teaching English as a second language (TESL) (MA). *Accreditation:* NCATE. Part-time and evening/weekend programs available. Terminal master's awarded for partial completion of doctoral program. *Degree requirements:* For master's, comprehensive exam (for some programs), thesis (for some programs); for doctorate, comprehensive exam (for some programs), thesis/dissertation. *Entrance requirements:* For master's and doctorate, GRE, 3 letters of recommendation. Additional exam requirements/recommendations for international students: Required—TOEFL (minimum score 600 paper-based). Electronic applications accepted. *Faculty research:* Teacher education; curriculum theory and development; community based education models, educational leadership.

The University of Findlay, Office of Graduate Admissions, Findlay, OH 45840-3653. Offers athletic training (MAT); business (MBA), including health care management, hospitality management, organizational leadership, public management; education (MA Ed), including administration, children's literature, early childhood, human resource development, reading, science, special education, technology; environmental, safety and health management (MSEM); health informatics (MS); occupational therapy (MOT); pharmacy (Pharm D); physical therapy (DPT); physician assistant (MPA); rhetoric and writing (MA); teaching English to speakers of other languages (TESOL) and bilingual education (MA). Part-time and evening/weekend programs available. Postbaccalaureate distance learning degree programs offered (no on-campus study). *Faculty:* 209 full-time (98 women), 69 part-time/adjunct (38 women). *Students:* 551 full-time (332 women), 457 part-time (276 women); includes 77 minority (37 Black or African American, non-Hispanic/Latino; 1 American Indian or Alaska Native, non-Hispanic/Latino; 15 Asian, non-Hispanic/Latino; 23 Hispanic/Latino; 1 Native Hawaiian or other Pacific Islander, non-Hispanic/Latino), 135 international. Average age 28. 637 applicants, 66% accepted, 241 enrolled. In 2013, 267 master's, 91 doctorates awarded. *Degree requirements:* For master's, thesis, cumulative project, capstone project. *Entrance requirements:* For master's, GRE/GMAT, bachelor's degree from accredited institution, minimum undergraduate GPA of 2.5 in last 64 hours of course work; for doctorate, GRE, minimum

cumulative GPA of 3.0. Additional exam requirements/recommendations for international students: Required—TOEFL (minimum score 80 iBT). *Application deadline:* Applications are processed on a rolling basis. Application fee: $25. Electronic applications accepted. *Expenses: Required fees:* $146 per semester. Tuition and fees vary according to degree level and program. *Financial support:* In 2013–14, 11 research assistantships with full and partial tuition reimbursements (averaging $4,000 per year), 10 teaching assistantships with full and partial tuition reimbursements (averaging $3,600 per year) were awarded; career-related internships or fieldwork, Federal Work-Study, health care benefits, and unspecified assistantships also available. Financial award application deadline: 4/1; financial award applicants required to submit FAFSA. *Unit head:* Christopher M. Harris, Director of Admissions, 419-434-4347, E-mail: harrisc1@findlay.edu. *Application contact:* Emily Ickes, Graduate Admissions Counselor, 419-434-6933, Fax: 419-434-4898, E-mail: ickese@findlay.edu.
Website: http://www.findlay.edu/admissions/graduate/Pages/default.aspx.

University of Florida, Graduate School, College of Liberal Arts and Sciences, Department of Linguistics, Gainesville, FL 32611. Offers linguistics (MA, PhD); teaching English as a second language (Certificate). Part-time programs available. *Faculty:* 14 full-time (11 women), 7 part-time/adjunct (4 women). *Students:* 48 full-time (27 women), 5 part-time (1 woman); includes 3 minority (1 American Indian or Alaska Native, non-Hispanic/Latino; 1 Asian, non-Hispanic/Latino; 1 Hispanic/Latino), 35 international. Average age 31. 101 applicants, 28% accepted, 11 enrolled. In 2013, 8 master's, 5 doctorates awarded. Terminal master's awarded for partial completion of doctoral program. *Degree requirements:* For master's, one foreign language, comprehensive exam, thesis (for some programs); for doctorate, 2 foreign languages, comprehensive exam, thesis/dissertation. *Entrance requirements:* For master's and doctorate, GRE General Test, minimum GPA of 3.0. Additional exam requirements/recommendations for international students: Required—TOEFL (minimum score 550 paper-based; 80 iBT), IELTS (minimum score 6). *Application deadline:* For fall admission, 12/15 priority date for domestic students, 12/15 for international students. Applications are processed on a rolling basis. Application fee: $30. Electronic applications accepted. *Expenses:* Tuition, state resident: full-time $12,640. Tuition, nonresident: full-time $30,000. *Financial support:* In 2013–14, 27 students received support, including 5 fellowships with tuition reimbursements available (averaging $21,020 per year), 5 research assistantships (averaging $14,305 per year), 23 teaching assistantships with tuition reimbursements available (averaging $10,270 per year); institutionally sponsored loans and unspecified assistantships also available. Financial award application deadline: 12/15; financial award applicants required to submit FAFSA. *Faculty research:* Theoretical, applied, and descriptive linguistics. *Unit head:* Fiona McLaughlin, PhD, Chair, 352-392-4829, Fax: 352-392-8480, E-mail: fmcl@ufl.edu. *Application contact:* Eric Potsdam, PhD, Graduate Coordinator, 352-294-7456, Fax: 352-392-8480, E-mail: potsdam@ufl.edu.
Website: http://lin.ufl.edu/.

University of Guam, Office of Graduate Studies, School of Education, Program in Teaching English to Speakers of Other Languages, Mangilao, GU 96923. Offers M Ed. *Degree requirements:* For master's, comprehensive oral and written exams, special project or thesis. *Entrance requirements:* For master's, GRE General Test. Additional exam requirements/recommendations for international students: Required—TOEFL.

University of Hawaii at Manoa, Graduate Division, College of Languages, Linguistics and Literature, Department of Second Language Studies, Honolulu, HI 96822. Offers English as a second language (MA, Graduate Certificate); second language acquisition (PhD). Part-time programs available. *Degree requirements:* For master's, 2 foreign languages, thesis optional; for doctorate, 2 foreign languages, comprehensive exam, thesis/dissertation. *Entrance requirements:* For master's, GRE General Test, minimum GPA of 3.0; for doctorate, GRE General Test, MA, scholarly publications. Additional exam requirements/recommendations for international students: Required—TOEFL (minimum score 600 paper-based; 100 iBT), IELTS (minimum score 7). *Faculty research:* Second language use, second language analysis, second language pedagogy and testing, second language learning, qualitative and quantitative research methods for second languages.

University of Idaho, College of Graduate Studies, College of Letters, Arts and Social Sciences, Department of English, Moscow, ID 83844-1102. Offers creative writing (MFA); English (MA, MAT); teaching English as a second language (MA). *Faculty:* 16 full-time. *Students:* 69 full-time, 9 part-time. Average age 31. In 2013, 36 master's awarded. *Entrance requirements:* For master's, minimum GPA of 2.8. Additional exam requirements/recommendations for international students: Required—TOEFL (minimum score 550 paper-based). *Application deadline:* For fall admission, 8/1 for domestic students; for spring admission, 12/15 for domestic students. Applications are processed on a rolling basis. Application fee: $60. Electronic applications accepted. *Expenses:* Tuition, state resident: full-time $5596; part-time $363 per credit hour. Tuition, nonresident: full-time $18,672; part-time $1089 per credit hour. *Financial support:* Research assistantships and teaching assistantships available. Financial award applicants required to submit FAFSA. *Unit head:* Dr. Gary Wiliams, Chair, 208-883-6156, E-mail: englishdept@uidaho.edu. *Application contact:* Stephanie Thomas, Graduate Recruitment Coordinator, 208-885-4001, Fax: 208-885-4406, E-mail: gadms@uidaho.edu.
Website: http://www.uidaho.edu/class/english.

University of Illinois at Chicago, Graduate College, College of Liberal Arts and Sciences, School of Literatures, Cultural Studies and Linguistics, Department of Linguistics, Chicago, IL 60607-7128. Offers teaching English to speakers of other languages/applied linguistics (MA). Part-time programs available. *Faculty:* 8 full-time (6 women). *Students:* 26 full-time (15 women), 1 (woman) part-time; includes 4 minority (1 Asian, non-Hispanic/Latino; 2 Hispanic/Latino; 1 Two or more races, non-Hispanic/Latino), 3 international. Average age 32. 64 applicants, 59% accepted, 13 enrolled. In 2013, 20 master's awarded. *Degree requirements:* For master's, one foreign language, comprehensive exam, thesis (for some programs). *Entrance requirements:* For master's, minimum GPA of 3.0. Additional exam requirements/recommendations for international students: Required—TOEFL. *Application deadline:* For fall admission, 5/15 for domestic students, 2/15 for international students. Applications are processed on a rolling basis. Application fee: $40 ($50 for international students). Electronic applications accepted. *Expenses:* Tuition, state resident: full-time $11,066; part-time $3689 per term. Tuition, nonresident: full-time $23,064; part-time $7688 per term. *Required fees:* $3004; $1190 per term. Tuition and fees vary according to course level and program. *Financial support:* Fellowships, research assistantships, teaching assistantships, career-related internships or fieldwork, Federal Work-Study, institutionally sponsored loans, and tuition waivers (full) available. Financial award application deadline: 3/1; financial award applicants required to submit FAFSA. *Faculty research:* Second language acquisition, methodology of second language teaching, lexicography, language, sex and gender. *Unit head:* Prof. Jessica Williams, Department Head/Professor of Linguistics/Director of Graduate Studies, 312-996-0259, Fax: 312-413-1005, E-mail: jessicaw@uic.edu.
Website: http://lcsl.las.uic.edu/linguistics.

University of Illinois at Springfield, Graduate Programs, College of Education and Human Services, Department of Educational Leadership, Springfield, IL 62703-5407. Offers chief school business official endorsement (CAS); educational leadership (MA, CAS); English as a second language (Graduate Certificate); legal aspects of education (Graduate Certificate); school superintendent endorsement (CAS); teacher leadership (MA). Part-time and evening/weekend programs available. Postbaccalaureate distance learning degree programs offered (no on-campus study). *Faculty:* 7 full-time (2 women), 13 part-time/adjunct (8 women). *Students:* 7 full-time (all women), 139 part-time (95 women); includes 14 minority (11 Black or African American, non-Hispanic/Latino; 1 American Indian or Alaska Native, non-Hispanic/Latino; 1 Hispanic/Latino; 1 Two or more races, non-Hispanic/Latino). Average age 35. 47 applicants, 53% accepted, 24 enrolled. In 2013, 62 master's, 8 other advanced degrees awarded. *Degree requirements:* For master's, project or thesis, capstone course (for teacher leadership option). *Entrance requirements:* For master's, minimum undergraduate GPA of 3.0. Additional exam requirements/recommendations for international students: Required—TOEFL (minimum score 500 paper-based; 61 iBT). *Application deadline:* Applications are processed on a rolling basis. Application fee: $60 ($75 for international students). Electronic applications accepted. *Expenses:* Tuition, state resident: full-time $7440. Tuition, nonresident: full-time $15,744. *Required fees:* $2985.60. *Financial support:* In 2013–14, fellowships with full tuition reimbursements (averaging $9,900 per year), research assistantships with full tuition reimbursements (averaging $9,550 per year), teaching assistantships with full tuition reimbursements (averaging $9,700 per year) were awarded; career-related internships or fieldwork, Federal Work-Study, scholarships/grants, health care benefits, and unspecified assistantships also available. Support available to part-time students. Financial award application deadline: 11/15; financial award applicants required to submit FAFSA. *Unit head:* Dr. Scott Day, Program Administrator, 217-206-7520, Fax: 217-206-6775, E-mail: day.scott@uis.edu. *Application contact:* Dr. Lynn Pardie, Office of Graduate Studies, 800-252-8533, Fax: 217-206-7623, E-mail: lpard1@uis.edu.
Website: http://www.uis.edu/edl/.

University of Illinois at Urbana–Champaign, Graduate College, College of Liberal Arts and Sciences, School of Literatures, Cultures and Linguistics, Department of Linguistics, Champaign, IL 61820. Offers linguistics (MA, PhD); teaching of English as a second language (MA). *Students:* 100 (69 women). Application fee: $75 ($90 for international students). *Unit head:* Hye Suk James Yoon, Acting Head, 217-244-3340, E-mail: jyoon@illinois.edu. *Application contact:* Lynn Stanke, Office Support Specialist, 217-333-6269, Fax: 217-244-3050, E-mail: stanke@illinois.edu.
Website: http://www.linguistics.illinois.edu/.

University of Illinois at Urbana–Champaign, Graduate College, College of Liberal Arts and Sciences, School of Literatures, Cultures and Linguistics, Program in Second Language Acquisition and Teacher Education, Champaign, IL 61820. Offers PhD. *Unit head:* Jean-Philippe Mathy, Director, 217-244-2718, Fax: 217-244-8430, E-mail: jmathy@illinois.edu. *Application contact:* Lynn Stanke, Office Support Specialist, 217-333-6269, Fax: 217-244-3050, E-mail: stanke@illinois.edu.
Website: http://www.slate.illinois.edu/.

The University of Iowa, Graduate College, College of Education, Department of Teaching and Learning, Program in Education, Iowa City, IA 52242-1316. Offers art education (MA); developmental reading (MA); elementary education (MA); English education (MA, MAT); foreign and second language education (MAT); foreign language education (MA); foreign language/ESL education (PhD); language, literacy and culture (PhD); mathematics education (MA, MAT, PhD); music education (MM, PhD); science education (MA); secondary education (MA); social studies (MA, PhD). *Degree requirements:* For master's, thesis optional, exam; for doctorate, comprehensive exam, thesis/dissertation. *Entrance requirements:* For master's and doctorate, GRE General Test, minimum GPA of 3.0. Additional exam requirements/recommendations for international students: Required—TOEFL (minimum score 550 paper-based; 81 iBT). Electronic applications accepted.

University of Louisiana at Monroe, Graduate School, College of Arts, Education, and Sciences, School of Education, Program in Curriculum and Instruction, Monroe, LA 71209-0001. Offers art education (M Ed); biology education (M Ed); chemistry education (M Ed); curriculum and instruction (Ed D); early childhood education (M Ed); earth science education (M Ed); educational leadership (M Ed); elementary education (1-5) (M Ed); English as a second language (M Ed); English education (M Ed); family and consumer education (M Ed); French education (M Ed); history education (M Ed); math education (M Ed); middle school education (M Ed); music education (M Ed); reading education (K-12) (M Ed); Spanish education (M Ed); special education - academically gifted (M Ed); special education - early intervention (M Ed); special education - educational diagnostician (M Ed); special education - mild/moderate disabilities (M Ed); speech education (M Ed). *Accreditation:* NCATE. *Degree requirements:* For master's, comprehensive exam (for some programs), thesis; for doctorate, thesis/dissertation, internships. *Entrance requirements:* For master's, GRE General Test; for doctorate, GRE General Test, minimum undergraduate GPA of 2.75, graduate 3.25. Additional exam requirements/recommendations for international students: Required—TOEFL (minimum score 500 paper-based; 61 iBT). *Application deadline:* For fall admission, 8/24 priority date for domestic students, 7/1 for international students; for winter admission, 12/14 priority date for domestic students; for spring admission, 1/19 for domestic students, 11/1 for international students. Applications are processed on a rolling basis. Application fee: $20 ($30 for international students). Electronic applications accepted. *Expenses:* Tuition, state resident: full-time $6607. Tuition, nonresident: full-time $17,179. Full-time tuition and fees vary according to program. *Financial support:* Research assistantships, career-related internships or fieldwork, Federal Work-Study, and unspecified assistantships available. Financial award application deadline: 4/1; financial award applicants required to submit FAFSA. *Unit head:* Dr. Dorothy Schween, Director, 318-342-1268, Fax: 318-342-3131, E-mail: schween@ulm.edu. *Application contact:* Dr. Dorothy Schween, Director, 318-342-1268, Fax: 318-342-3131, E-mail: schween@ulm.edu.

The University of Manchester, School of Languages, Linguistics and Cultures, Manchester, United Kingdom. Offers Arab world studies (PhD); Chinese studies (M Phil, PhD); East Asian studies (M Phil, PhD); English language (PhD); French studies (M Phil, PhD); German studies (M Phil, PhD); interpreting studies (PhD); Italian studies (M Phil, PhD); Japanese studies (M Phil, PhD); Latin American cultural studies (M Phil, PhD); linguistics (M Phil, PhD); Middle Eastern studies (M Phil, PhD); Polish studies (M Phil, PhD); Portuguese studies (M Phil, PhD); Russian studies (M Phil, PhD); Spanish studies (M Phil, PhD); translation and intercultural studies (M Phil, PhD).

University of Manitoba, Faculty of Graduate Studies, Faculty of Education, Department of Curriculum, Teaching and Learning, Winnipeg, MB R3T 2N2, Canada. Offers language and literacy (M Ed); second language education (M Ed); studies in curriculum, teaching and learning (M Ed). *Degree requirements:* For master's, thesis or alternative.

University of Maryland, Baltimore County, Graduate School, College of Arts, Humanities and Social Sciences, Department of Education, Program in Teaching English to Speakers of Other Languages, Baltimore, MD 21250. Offers MA, Postbaccalaureate Certificate. Part-time and evening/weekend programs available. Postbaccalaureate distance learning degree programs offered (no on-campus study). *Faculty:* 3 full-time (2 women), 13 part-time/adjunct (9 women). *Students:* 27 full-time (22 women), 67 part-time (55 women); includes 11 minority (4 Black or African American, non-Hispanic/Latino; 5 Asian, non-Hispanic/Latino; 2 Hispanic/Latino), 10 international. Average age 36. 74 applicants, 70% accepted, 38 enrolled. In 2013, 22

master's, 23 other advanced degrees awarded. *Degree requirements:* For master's, comprehensive exam, thesis optional, internship (for certification). *Entrance requirements:* For master's, GRE (minimum score 500 verbal or 150 on the new version), 3 letters of reference. Additional exam requirements/recommendations for international students: Required—TOEFL (minimum score 550 paper-based; 80 iBT). *Application deadline:* For fall admission, 4/15 priority date for domestic students, 3/1 priority date for international students; for spring admission, 10/31 priority date for domestic and international students. Application fee: $50. Electronic applications accepted. One-time fee: $200 full-time. *Financial support:* In 2013–14, 14 students received support, including 2 research assistantships with full tuition reimbursements available (averaging $12,000 per year); career-related internships or fieldwork, Federal Work-Study, scholarships/grants, and unspecified assistantships also available. *Faculty research:* Adult education, bilingual language learning, online instruction, English grammar, cross-culture communication. *Unit head:* Dr. John Nelson, Co-Director, 410-455-2379, E-mail: jnelson@umbc.edu. *Application contact:* Anna Smoot, Graduate Assistant, 410-455-3061, E-mail: esol@umbc.edu.
Website: http://www.umbc.edu/education/.

University of Maryland, College Park, Academic Affairs, College of Education, Department of Teaching, Learning, Policy and Leadership, College Park, MD 20742. Offers reading (M Ed, MA, PhD, CAGS); secondary education (M Ed, MA, Ed D, PhD, CAGS); teaching English to speakers of other languages (M Ed). *Accreditation:* NCATE. Part-time and evening/weekend programs available. Postbaccalaureate distance learning degree programs offered (no on-campus study). *Faculty:* 63 full-time (43 women), 20 part-time/adjunct (13 women). *Students:* 283 full-time (209 women), 188 part-time (151 women); includes 158 minority (58 Black or African American, non-Hispanic/Latino; 53 Asian, non-Hispanic/Latino; 23 Hispanic/Latino; 1 Native Hawaiian or other Pacific Islander, non-Hispanic/Latino; 23 Two or more races, non-Hispanic/Latino), 52 international. 482 applicants, 44% accepted, 126 enrolled. In 2013, 211 master's, 42 doctorates awarded. *Degree requirements:* For master's, comprehensive exam, seminar paper; for doctorate, comprehensive exam, thesis/dissertation, published paper, oral exam. *Entrance requirements:* For master's, GRE General Test or MAT, minimum GPA of 3.0, 3 letters of recommendation; for doctorate, GRE General Test or MAT, minimum undergraduate GPA of 3.0, graduate 3.5; 3 letters of recommendation. *Application deadline:* For fall admission, 2/1 priority date for domestic students, 9/1 priority date for international students; for spring admission, 9/1 for domestic students, 8/1 for international students. Applications are processed on a rolling basis. Application fee: $75. Electronic applications accepted. *Expenses:* Tuition, state resident: full-time $10,314; part-time $573 per credit hour. Tuition, nonresident: full-time $22,248; part-time $1236 per credit. *Required fees:* $1446; $403.15 per semester. Tuition and fees vary according to program. *Financial support:* In 2013–14, 11 fellowships with full and partial tuition reimbursements (averaging $22,271 per year), 7 research assistantships with tuition reimbursements (averaging $18,573 per year), 85 teaching assistantships with tuition reimbursements (averaging $17,609 per year) were awarded; Federal Work-Study and scholarships/grants also available. Support available to part-time students. Financial award applicants required to submit FAFSA. *Faculty research:* Teacher preparation, curriculum study, in-service education. *Total annual research expenditures:* $3.9 million. *Unit head:* Francine Hultgren, Interim Chair, 301-405-3117, E-mail: fh@umd.edu. *Application contact:* Dr. Charles A. Caramello, Dean of Graduate School, 301-405-0358, Fax: 301-314-9305, E-mail: ccaramel@umd.edu.

University of Massachusetts Amherst, Graduate School, College of Education, Program in Education, Amherst, MA 01003. Offers bilingual/English as a second language/multicultural education (M Ed, Ed S); child study and early education (M Ed); children, families and schools (Ed D, Ed S); early childhood and elementary teacher education (M Ed); educational leadership (M Ed); educational policy and leadership (Ed D); higher education (M Ed); international education (M Ed); language, literacy and culture (Ed D); learning, media and technology (M Ed, Ed S); mathematics, science, and learning technologies (Ed D); psychometric methods, educational statistics and research methods (Ed D); reading and writing (M Ed); school counselor education (M Ed, Ed S); school psychology (Ed S); science education (Ed S); secondary teacher education (M Ed); social justice education (M Ed, Ed D, Ed S); special education (M Ed, Ed D, Ed S); teacher education and school improvement (Ed D, Ed S). *Accreditation:* NCATE. Part-time programs available. Postbaccalaureate distance learning degree programs offered (minimal on-campus study). *Faculty:* 95 full-time (55 women). *Students:* 357 full-time (240 women), 264 part-time (194 women); includes 114 minority (41 Black or African American, non-Hispanic/Latino; 4 American Indian or Alaska Native, non-Hispanic/Latino; 10 Asian, non-Hispanic/Latino; 47 Hispanic/Latino; 12 Two or more races, non-Hispanic/Latino), 100 international. Average age 34. 761 applicants, 51% accepted, 200 enrolled. In 2013, 186 master's, 31 doctorates, 22 other advanced degrees awarded. Terminal master's awarded for partial completion of doctoral program. *Degree requirements:* For doctorate, comprehensive exam, thesis/dissertation. *Entrance requirements:* Additional exam requirements/recommendations for international students: Required—TOEFL (minimum score 550 paper-based; 80 iBT), IELTS (minimum score 6.5). *Application deadline:* For fall admission, 1/15 for domestic and international students. Applications are processed on a rolling basis. Application fee: $75. Electronic applications accepted. *Financial support:* Fellowships with full and partial tuition reimbursements, research assistantships with full and partial tuition reimbursements, teaching assistantships with full and partial tuition reimbursements, career-related internships or fieldwork, Federal Work-Study, scholarships/grants, traineeships, health care benefits, tuition waivers (full and partial), and unspecified assistantships available. Support available to part-time students. Financial award application deadline: 1/15; financial award applicants required to submit FAFSA. *Unit head:* Dr. Linda L. Griffin, Graduate Program Director, 413-545-6984, Fax: 413-545-1523. *Application contact:* Lindsay DeSantis, Supervisor of Admissions, 413-545-0722, Fax: 413-577-0010, E-mail: gradadm@grad.umass.edu.
Website: http://www.umass.edu/education/.

University of Massachusetts Boston, Office of Graduate Studies, College of Liberal Arts, Program in Applied Linguistics, Boston, MA 02125-3393. Offers bilingual education (MA); English as a second language (MA); foreign language pedagogy (MA). Part-time and evening/weekend programs available. *Degree requirements:* For master's, one foreign language, comprehensive exam. *Entrance requirements:* For master's, minimum GPA of 2.75. *Faculty research:* Multicultural theory and curriculum development, foreign language pedagogy, language and culture, applied psycholinguistics, bilingual education.

University of Memphis, Graduate School, College of Arts and Sciences, Department of English, Memphis, TN 38152. Offers African-American literature (Graduate Certificate); applied linguistics (PhD); composition studies (PhD); creative writing (MFA); English as a second language (MA); linguistics (MA); literary and cultural studies (PhD), including African-American literature; literature (MA); professional writing (MA, PhD); teaching English as a second language (Graduate Certificate). Part-time and evening/weekend programs available. Postbaccalaureate distance learning degree programs offered (no on-campus study). *Faculty:* 28 full-time (12 women), 2 part-time/adjunct (1 woman). *Students:* 89 full-time (45 women), 85 part-time (57 women); includes 35 minority (23 Black or African American, non-Hispanic/Latino; 6 Asian, non-Hispanic/Latino; 5 Hispanic/Latino; 1 Two or more races, non-Hispanic/Latino), 17 international. Average

age 35. 114 applicants, 71% accepted, 19 enrolled. In 2013, 38 master's, 4 doctorates, 21 other advanced degrees awarded. Terminal master's awarded for partial completion of doctoral program. *Degree requirements:* For master's, one foreign language, comprehensive exam, thesis optional; for doctorate, 2 foreign languages, comprehensive exam, thesis/dissertation. *Entrance requirements:* For master's and doctorate, GRE. Additional exam requirements/recommendations for international students: Required—TOEFL. *Application deadline:* For fall admission, 7/1 for domestic students; for spring admission, 10/15 for domestic students. Applications are processed on a rolling basis. Application fee: $35 ($60 for international students). Electronic applications accepted. *Financial support:* In 2013–14, 123 students received support. Research assistantships with full tuition reimbursements available, teaching assistantships with full tuition reimbursements available, Federal Work-Study, scholarships/grants, and unspecified assistantships available. Financial award application deadline: 2/15; financial award applicants required to submit FAFSA. *Faculty research:* Applied linguistics, British and American literature, professional writing, composition studies. *Unit head:* Dr. Henry A. Kurtz, Dean, 901-678-3067, Fax: 901-678-4831, E-mail: hkurtz@memphis.edu. *Application contact:* Dr. Verner D. Mitchell, Director, Graduate Studies, 901-678-3099, Fax: 901-678-2226, E-mail: vdmtchll@memphis.edu.
Website: http://www.memphis.edu/english.

University of Minnesota, Twin Cities Campus, Graduate School, College of Education and Human Development, Department of Curriculum and Instruction, Program in Teaching, Minneapolis, MN 55455-0213. Offers Chinese (M Ed); earth science (M Ed); elementary special education (M Ed); English (M Ed); English as a second language (M Ed); French (M Ed); German (M Ed); Hebrew (M Ed); Japanese (M Ed); life sciences (M Ed); mathematics (M Ed); middle school science (M Ed); science (M Ed); second languages and cultures (M Ed); social studies (M Ed); Spanish (M Ed). *Students:* 220 full-time (154 women), 83 part-time (60 women); includes 43 minority (10 Black or African American, non-Hispanic/Latino; 26 Asian, non-Hispanic/Latino; 7 Hispanic/Latino), 4 international. Average age 27. 261 applicants, 87% accepted, 222 enrolled. In 2013, 561 master's awarded. Application fee: $75 ($95 for international students). *Unit head:* Dr. Nina Asher, Chair, 612-624-1357, Fax: 612-624-8277, E-mail: nasher@umn.edu. *Application contact:* Dr. Jennifer Engler, Assistant Dean, 612-626-2887, Fax: 612-626-7496, E-mail: engle009@umn.edu.
Website: http://www.cehd.umn.edu/ci/.

University of Minnesota, Twin Cities Campus, Graduate School, College of Liberal Arts, Institute of Linguistics, English as a Second Language, and Slavic Languages and Literatures (ILES), English as a Second Language Program, Minneapolis, MN 55455-0213. Offers MA. *Degree requirements:* For master's, one foreign language, comprehensive exam, thesis. *Entrance requirements:* For master's, GRE, 3 letters of recommendation. Additional exam requirements/recommendations for international students: Required—TOEFL (minimum score 600 paper-based). Electronic applications accepted. *Faculty research:* Second language acquisitions, communication strategies, English for specific purposes, literacy, speech act, proymatics in general, language assessment, discourse analysis, research methods.

University of Missouri–St. Louis, College of Education, Division of Teaching and Learning, St. Louis, MO 63121. Offers autism studies (Certificate); elementary education (M Ed), including early childhood, general, reading; secondary education (M Ed), including curriculum and instruction, general, middle level education, reading, teaching English to speakers of other languages (TESOL); secondary school teaching (Certificate); special education (M Ed), including autism and developmental disabilities, cross-categorical disabilities, early childhood; teaching English to speakers of other languages (Certificate). Part-time and evening/weekend programs available. *Faculty:* 20 full-time (11 women), 1 (woman) part-time/adjunct. *Students:* 42 full-time (33 women), 578 part-time (442 women); includes 152 minority (101 Black or African American, non-Hispanic/Latino; 1 American Indian or Alaska Native, non-Hispanic/Latino; 20 Asian, non-Hispanic/Latino; 23 Hispanic/Latino; 7 Two or more races, non-Hispanic/Latino), 19 international. Average age 29. 245 applicants, 97% accepted, 166 enrolled. In 2013, 219 master's, 14 Certificates awarded. *Degree requirements:* For master's, comprehensive exam. *Entrance requirements:* Additional exam requirements/recommendations for international students: Recommended—TOEFL (minimum score 550 paper-based; 79 iBT), IELTS (minimum score 6.5). *Application deadline:* For fall admission, 7/1 priority date for domestic and international students; for spring admission, 12/1 priority date for domestic and international students. Application fee: $50 ($40 for international students). Electronic applications accepted. *Expenses:* Tuition, state resident: full-time $7364; part-time $409.10 per credit hour. Tuition, nonresident: full-time $19,162; part-time $1008.50 per credit hour. *Financial support:* Application deadline: 4/1; applicants required to submit FAFSA. *Unit head:* Dr. Patricia Kopetz, Chair, 314-516-5791. *Application contact:* 314-516-5458, Fax: 314-516-6996, E-mail: gadadm@umsl.edu.
Website: http://coe.umsl.edu/web/divisions/teach-learn/index.html.

University of Nebraska at Kearney, Graduate Programs, College of Education, Department of Teacher Education, Kearney, NE 68849-0001. Offers curriculum and instruction (MA Ed), including early childhood education, elementary education, English as a second language, instructional effectiveness, reading/special education, secondary education; instructional technology (MS Ed), including information technology, instructional technology, school librarian; reading PK-12 (MA Ed); special education (MA Ed), including advanced practitioner, gifted, mild/moderate. Part-time and evening/weekend programs available. *Degree requirements:* For master's, comprehensive exam, thesis optional. *Entrance requirements:* For master's, portfolio or GRE. Additional exam requirements/recommendations for international students: Required—TOEFL (minimum score 550 paper-based). Electronic applications accepted.

University of Nebraska at Omaha, Graduate Studies, College of Arts and Sciences, Department of English, Omaha, NE 68182. Offers advanced writing (Certificate); English (MA); teaching English to speakers of other languages (Certificate). Part-time and evening/weekend programs available. *Faculty:* 19 full-time (10 women). *Students:* 10 full-time (5 women), 54 part-time (39 women); includes 5 minority (1 Black or African American, non-Hispanic/Latino; 1 Asian, non-Hispanic/Latino; 2 Hispanic/Latino; 1 Two or more races, non-Hispanic/Latino). Average age 34. 33 applicants, 85% accepted, 17 enrolled. In 2013, 30 master's, 11 other advanced degrees awarded. *Degree requirements:* For master's, comprehensive exam, thesis (for some programs). *Entrance requirements:* For master's, GRE or MAT, minimum GPA of 3.0, transcripts, 3 letters of recommendation, statement of purpose, writing sample; for Certificate, minimum GPA of 3.0, transcripts, statement of purpose. Additional exam requirements/recommendations for international students: Required—TOEFL, IELTS, PTE. *Application deadline:* For fall admission, 8/1 priority date for domestic students; for spring admission, 12/1 priority date for domestic students. Applications are processed on a rolling basis. Application fee: $45. Electronic applications accepted. *Financial support:* In 2013–14, 16 students received support, including 16 teaching assistantships with tuition reimbursements available; fellowships, Federal Work-Study, institutionally sponsored loans, scholarships/grants, tuition waivers (partial), and unspecified assistantships also available. Support available to part-time students. Financial award application deadline: 3/1; financial award applicants required to submit FAFSA. *Unit head:* Dr. Robert Darcy,

Chairperson, 402-554-2635. *Application contact:* Dr. Tracy Bridgeford, Graduate Program Chair, 402-554-3312, E-mail: graduate@unomaha.edu.

University of Nevada, Reno, Graduate School, College of Education, Department of Educational Specialties, Program in Teaching English to Speakers of Other Languages, Reno, NV 89557. Offers MA. Terminal master's awarded for partial completion of doctoral program. *Degree requirements:* For master's, thesis optional. *Entrance requirements:* For master's, minimum GPA of 2.75. Additional exam requirements/recommendations for international students: Required—TOEFL (minimum score 500 paper-based; 61 iBT), IELTS (minimum score 6). Electronic applications accepted. *Faculty research:* Bilingualism, multicultural education.

University of New Mexico, Graduate School, College of Education, Department of Language, Literacy and Sociocultural Studies, Program in Language, Literacy and Sociocultural Studies, Albuquerque, NM 87131. Offers American Indian education (MA); bilingual education (MA, PhD); educational linguistics (PhD); educational thought and sociocultural studies (MA, PhD); literacy/language arts (MA, PhD); social studies (MA); TESOL (MA, PhD). *Faculty:* 10 full-time (6 women), 3 part-time/adjunct (1 woman). *Students:* 63 full-time (48 women), 117 part-time (105 women); includes 96 minority (8 Black or African American, non-Hispanic/Latino; 16 American Indian or Alaska Native, non-Hispanic/Latino; 6 Asian, non-Hispanic/Latino; 62 Hispanic/Latino; 4 Two or more races, non-Hispanic/Latino), 20 international. Average age 39. 67 applicants, 63% accepted, 30 enrolled. In 2013, 30 master's, 8 doctorates awarded. *Degree requirements:* For master's, comprehensive exam, thesis optional; for doctorate, comprehensive exam, thesis/dissertation, research skills. *Entrance requirements:* For master's, letter of intent, 3 letters of recommendation, resume, BA/BS, department demographic form, transcripts; for doctorate, writing sample, letter of intent, 3 letters of recommendation, resume, BA/BS, MA, department demographic form, transcripts. Additional exam requirements/recommendations for international students: Required—TOEFL. *Application deadline:* For fall admission, 12/1 for domestic and international students; for spring admission, 9/15 for domestic and international students. Application fee: $50. Electronic applications accepted. *Financial support:* In 2013–14, 7 students received support, including 7 fellowships (averaging $3,170 per year), 1,318 teaching assistantships with tuition reimbursements available (averaging $3,789 per year); research assistantships, career-related internships or fieldwork, institutionally sponsored loans, scholarships/grants, and unspecified assistantships also available. Support available to part-time students. Financial award application deadline: 3/1; financial award applicants required to submit FAFSA. *Faculty research:* School reform, professional development, history of education, Native American education, politics of education, feminism and issues of sexual identity, critical race theory, bilingualism, literacy reading, adolescent literature, second language acquisition, critical theory and schooling, indigenous languages. *Unit head:* Dr. Lois M. Meyer, Chair, 505-277-7244, Fax: 505-277-8362, E-mail: lsmeyer@unm.edu. *Application contact:* Debra Schaffer, Administrative Assistant, 505-277-0437, Fax: 505-277-8362, E-mail: schaffer@unm.edu.
Website: http://coe.unm.edu/departments/department-of-language-literacy-and-sociocultural-studies/llss-program.html.

The University of North Carolina at Chapel Hill, Graduate School, School of Education, Program in Secondary Education, Chapel Hill, NC 27599. Offers English (Grades 9-12) (MAT); English as a second language (MAT); French (Grades K-12) (MAT); German (Grades K-12) (MAT); Japanese (Grades K-12) (MAT); Latin (Grades 9-12) (MAT); mathematics (Grades 9-12) (MAT); music (Grades K-12) (MAT); science (Grades 9-12) (MAT); social studies (Grades 9-12) (MAT); Spanish (Grades K-12) (MAT). *Accreditation:* NCATE. *Degree requirements:* For master's, comprehensive exam. *Entrance requirements:* For master's, GRE General Test, minimum GPA of 3.0 during last 2 years of undergraduate course work. Additional exam requirements/recommendations for international students: Required—TOEFL (minimum score 550 paper-based). Electronic applications accepted.

The University of North Carolina at Charlotte, The Graduate School, College of Education, Interdisciplinary Education Programs, Charlotte, NC 28223-0001. Offers art education (MAT); dance education (MAT); elementary education (MAT); English as a second language (MAT); foreign language education (MAT); middle grades education (MAT); music education (MAT); secondary education (MAT); special education (MAT); teacher certification (Graduate Certificate); teaching (Graduate Certificate); theater education (MAT). Part-time programs available. *Students:* 206 full-time (165 women), 791 part-time (628 women); includes 342 minority (247 Black or African American, non-Hispanic/Latino; 16 Asian, non-Hispanic/Latino; 62 Hispanic/Latino; 17 Two or more races, non-Hispanic/Latino), 14 international. Average age 32. 564 applicants, 91% accepted, 414 enrolled. In 2013, 145 master's, 271 other advanced degrees awarded. Terminal master's awarded for partial completion of doctoral program. *Degree requirements:* For master's, thesis. *Entrance requirements:* For master's, GRE or MAT. Additional exam requirements/recommendations for international students: Required—TOEFL (minimum score 550 paper-based; 83 iBT). *Application deadline:* For fall admission, 5/1 priority date for domestic and international students; for spring admission, 10/1 priority date for domestic and international students. Applications are processed on a rolling basis. Application fee: $75. Electronic applications accepted. *Expenses:* Tuition, state resident: full-time $3522. Tuition, nonresident: full-time $16,051. *Required fees:* $2585. Tuition and fees vary according to course load and program. *Total annual research expenditures:* $43,031. *Unit head:* Dr. Warren DiBiase, Chair, 704-687-8881, Fax: 704-687-4705, E-mail: wjdibias@uncc.edu. *Application contact:* Kathy B. Giddings, Director of Graduate Admissions, 704-687-5503, Fax: 704-687-1668, E-mail: gradadm@uncc.edu.
Website: http://education.uncc.edu/academic-programs.

The University of North Carolina at Greensboro, Graduate School, School of Education, Department of Curriculum and Instruction, Greensboro, NC 27412-5001. Offers college teaching and adult learning (Certificate); curriculum and instruction (M Ed), including chemistry education, elementary education, English as a second language, French education, instructional technology, mathematics education, middle grades education, reading education, science education, social studies education, Spanish education; curriculum and teaching (PhD), including higher education, teacher education and development; English as a second language (Certificate); higher education (M Ed); supervision (M Ed). *Accreditation:* NCATE. Part-time programs available. *Degree requirements:* For doctorate, thesis/dissertation. *Entrance requirements:* For master's and doctorate, GRE General Test. Additional exam requirements/recommendations for international students: Required—TOEFL. Electronic applications accepted. *Faculty research:* Community college literacy program, middle school mathematics/computer mathematics.

University of Northern Iowa, Graduate College, College of Humanities, Arts and Sciences, Department of Languages and Literatures, Program in Teaching English to Speakers of Other Languages, Cedar Falls, IA 50614. Offers MA. *Students:* 10 full-time (7 women), 29 part-time (21 women); includes 4 minority (2 Asian, non-Hispanic/Latino; 1 Hispanic/Latino; 1 Two or more races, non-Hispanic/Latino), 6 international. 24 applicants, 67% accepted, 12 enrolled. In 2013, 5 master's awarded. *Degree requirements:* For master's, comprehensive exam, thesis or research paper. Application fee: $50 ($70 for international students). *Unit head:* Dr. Joyce Milambiling, Coordinator, 319-273-6099, Fax: 319-273-5807, E-mail: joyce.milambiling@uni.edu. *Application contact:* Laurie S. Russell, Record Analyst, 319-273-2623, Fax: 319-273-2885, E-mail: laurie.russell@uni.edu.

University of North Florida, College of Education and Human Services, Department of Childhood Education, Jacksonville, FL 32224. Offers literacy K-12 (M Ed); professional education - elementary education (M Ed); TESOL K-12 (M Ed). *Accreditation:* NCATE. Part-time and evening/weekend programs available. *Faculty:* 10 full-time (8 women). *Students:* 11 full-time (10 women), 24 part-time (18 women); includes 6 minority (1 Black or African American, non-Hispanic/Latino; 1 Asian, non-Hispanic/Latino; 4 Hispanic/Latino), 1 international. Average age 33. 24 applicants, 79% accepted, 10 enrolled. In 2013, 21 master's awarded. *Entrance requirements:* For master's, GRE General Test, minimum GPA of 3.0 in last 60 hours, 3 letters of recommendation, interview. Additional exam requirements/recommendations for international students: Required—TOEFL (minimum score 500 paper-based). *Application deadline:* For fall admission, 7/1 priority date for domestic students, 5/1 for international students; for spring admission, 11/1 priority date for domestic students, 10/1 for international students. Application fee: $30. Electronic applications accepted. *Expenses:* Tuition, state resident: full-time $9794; part-time $408.10 per credit hour. Tuition, nonresident: full-time $22,383; part-time $932.61 per credit hour. *Required fees:* $2020; $84.20 per credit hour. Tuition and fees vary according to course load and program. *Financial support:* In 2013–14, 8 students received support, including 2 research assistantships (averaging $5,183 per year); Federal Work-Study, tuition waivers (partial), and unspecified assistantships also available. Support available to part-time students. Financial award application deadline: 4/1; financial award applicants required to submit FAFSA. *Faculty research:* The social context of and processes in learning, inter-disciplinary instruction, cross-cultural conflict resolution, the Vygotskian perspective on literacy diagnosis and instruction, performance poetry and teaching the language arts through drama. *Total annual research expenditures:* $2,158. *Unit head:* Dr. John Venn, Chair, 904-620-5352, Fax: 904-620-1025, E-mail: j.venn@unf.edu. *Application contact:* Dr. Amanda Pascale, Director, The Graduate School, 904-620-1360, Fax: 904-620-1362, E-mail: graduateschool@unf.edu.
Website: http://www.unf.edu/coehs/celt/.

University of Pennsylvania, Graduate School of Education, Division of Educational Linguistics, Program in Teaching English to Speakers of Other Languages, Philadelphia, PA 19104. Offers MS Ed, PhD. Part-time programs available. Postbaccalaureate distance learning degree programs offered (minimal on-campus study). *Students:* 141 full-time (124 women), 14 part-time (12 women); includes 6 minority (5 Asian, non-Hispanic/Latino; 1 Two or more races, non-Hispanic/Latino), 140 international. 357 applicants, 39% accepted, 79 enrolled. In 2013, 70 master's awarded. Terminal master's awarded for partial completion of doctoral program. *Degree requirements:* For master's, comprehensive exam, thesis (for some programs). *Entrance requirements:* For master's, GRE General Test or MAT. Additional exam requirements/recommendations for international students: Required—TOEFL. *Application deadline:* For fall admission, 12/15 priority date for domestic students. Applications are processed on a rolling basis. Application fee: $70. Electronic applications accepted. *Expenses:* Contact institution. *Financial support:* Fellowships, research assistantships, institutionally sponsored loans, scholarships/grants, traineeships, health care benefits, and unspecified assistantships available. *Faculty research:* Second language acquisition, social linguistics, English as a second language. *Unit head:* Dr. Andrew Porter, Dean, 215-898-7014. *Application contact:* 215-898-6415, Fax: 215-746-6884, E-mail: admissions@gse.upenn.edu.
Website: http://www.gse.upenn.edu/elx/tesol.

University of Phoenix–Omaha Campus, College of Education, Omaha, NE 68154-5240. Offers administration and supervision (MA Ed); curriculum and instruction (MA Ed), including adult education, computer education, curriculum and instruction, English and language arts education, English as a second language, mathematics education; elementary teacher education (MA Ed); secondary teacher education (MA Ed); special education (MA Ed).

University of Phoenix–Online Campus, College of Education, Phoenix, AZ 85034-7209. Offers administration and supervision (MAEd, Certificate); adult education and training (MAEd); curriculum and instruction (MAEd), including computer education, curriculum and instruction, English as a second language, language arts, mathematics, reading; early childhood education (MAEd); educational studies (MAEd); elementary teacher education (MAEd), including early childhood, elementary teacher education, high school middle level, middle level; principal licensure (Certificate); secondary teacher education (MAEd); special education (MAEd, Certificate); teacher education (MAEd), including middle level generalist; teacher education middle level mathematics (MAEd), including middle level mathematics; teacher education middle level science (MAEd), including middle level science; teacher education secondary mathematics (MAEd); teacher education secondary science (MAEd); teacher leadership (MAEd); teachers of English learners (Certificate); transition to teaching (Certificate), including elementary education, secondary education. *Accreditation:* Teacher Education Accreditation Council. Evening/weekend programs available. Postbaccalaureate distance learning degree programs offered. *Entrance requirements:* Additional exam requirements/recommendations for international students: Required—TOEFL, TOEIC (Test of English as an International Communication), Berlitz Online English Proficiency Exam, PTE, or IELTS. Electronic applications accepted. *Expenses:* Contact institution.

University of Phoenix–San Diego Campus, College of Education, San Diego, CA 92123. Offers curriculum and instruction (MA Ed), including computer education, curriculum and instruction, English as a second language; elementary teacher education (MA Ed); secondary teacher education (MA Ed). Evening/weekend programs available. *Degree requirements:* For master's, thesis (for some programs). *Entrance requirements:* For master's, 3 years of work experience, minimum undergraduate GPA of 3.0. Additional exam requirements/recommendations for international students: Required—TOEFL (minimum score 550 paper-based; 79 iBT). Electronic applications accepted.

University of Phoenix–Southern California Campus, College of Education, Costa Mesa, CA 92626. Offers administration and supervision (MA Ed, Certificate); adult education and training (MA Ed); educational studies (MA Ed); elementary teacher education (MA Ed); secondary teacher education (MA Ed); teacher leadership (MA Ed); teachers of English learners (Certificate). Evening/weekend programs available. Postbaccalaureate distance learning degree programs offered. *Entrance requirements:* Additional exam requirements/recommendations for international students: Required—TOEFL, TOEIC (Test of English as an International Communication), Berlitz Online English Proficiency Exam, PTE, or IELTS. Electronic applications accepted. *Expenses:* Contact institution.

University of Phoenix–Springfield Campus, College of Education, Springfield, MO 65804-7211. Offers administration and supervision (MA Ed); curriculum and instruction (MA Ed), including computer education, curriculum and instruction, English and language arts education, English as a second language, mathematics education; English and language arts education (MA Ed).

University of Phoenix–Washington D.C. Campus, College of Education, Washington, DC 20001. Offers administration and supervision (MA Ed); adult education and training (MA Ed); computer education (MA Ed); curriculum and instruction (MA Ed, Ed D); early

childhood education (MA Ed); education (Ed S); educational leadership (Ed D); educational technology (Ed D); elementary teacher education (MA Ed); English and language arts education (MA Ed); English as a second language (MA Ed); higher education administration (PhD); mathematics education (MA Ed); secondary teacher education (MA Ed); special education (MA Ed); teacher leadership (MA Ed).

University of Pittsburgh, Dietrich School of Arts and Sciences, TESOL Certificate Program, Pittsburgh, PA 15260. Offers Certificate. Part-time programs available. *Faculty:* 9 full-time (4 women). *Students:* 8 full-time (all women), 7 part-time (5 women), 4 international. Average age 30. 7 applicants, 71% accepted, 5 enrolled. *Entrance requirements:* Additional exam requirements/recommendations for international students: Required—TOEFL (minimum score 600 paper-based; 100 iBT), IELTS (minimum score 7.5). *Application deadline:* For spring admission, 3/15 for domestic and international students. Application fee: $50. *Expenses:* Tuition, state resident: full-time $19,964; part-time $807 per credit. Tuition, nonresident: full-time $32,686; part-time $1337 per credit. *Required fees:* $740; $200. Tuition and fees vary according to program. *Faculty research:* Language contact, second language acquisition, applied linguistics, sociolinguistics. *Unit head:* Dr. Shelome Gooden, Chair, 412-624-5922, Fax: 412-624-5520, E-mail: sgooden@pitt.edu. *Application contact:* Dr. Dawn E. McCormick, Lecturer/Associate Director, 412-624-5902, Fax: 412-624-6130, E-mail: mccormic@pitt.edu.
Website: http://www.linguistics.pitt.edu/tesol/.

University of Portland, School of Education, Portland, OR 97203-5798. Offers education (MA, MAT); educational leadership (M Ed); English for speakers of other languages (M Ed); initial administrator licensure (M Ed); neuroeducation (Ed D); organizational leadership and development (Ed D); reading (M Ed); special education (M Ed). M Ed also available through the Graduate Outreach Program for teachers residing in the Oregon and Washington state areas. *Accreditation:* NCATE. Part-time and evening/weekend programs available. *Faculty:* 17 full-time (10 women), 12 part-time/adjunct (4 women). *Students:* 47 full-time (29 women), 214 part-time (155 women); includes 25 minority (1 Black or African American, non-Hispanic/Latino; 1 American Indian or Alaska Native, non-Hispanic/Latino; 8 Asian, non-Hispanic/Latino; 6 Hispanic/Latino; 6 Native Hawaiian or other Pacific Islander, non-Hispanic/Latino; 3 Two or more races, non-Hispanic/Latino), 63 international. Average age 32. In 2013, 96 master's awarded. *Entrance requirements:* For master's, minimum GPA of 3.0, teaching certificate, letters of recommendation, resume, statement of goals, official transcripts. Additional exam requirements/recommendations for international students: Required—TOEFL (minimum score 550 paper-based; 80 iBT), IELTS (minimum score 7). *Application deadline:* For fall admission, 7/15 priority date for domestic and international students; for spring admission, 12/15 priority date for domestic and international students. Applications are processed on a rolling basis. Application fee: $50. *Expenses: Tuition:* Part-time $1025 per credit hour. Tuition and fees vary according to program. *Financial support:* Federal Work-Study and scholarships/grants available. Support available to part-time students. Financial award application deadline: 3/1; financial award applicants required to submit FAFSA. *Faculty research:* Multicultural education, supervision/leadership. *Unit head:* Dr. Bruce Weitzel, Associate Dean, 503-943-7135, E-mail: soed@up.edu. *Application contact:* Dr. Matt Baasten, Assistant to the Provost and Dean of the Graduate School, 503-943-7107, Fax: 503-943-7315, E-mail: baasten@up.edu.
Website: http://education.up.edu/default.aspx?cid-4318&pid-5590.

University of Puerto Rico, Río Piedras Campus, College of Education, Program in Teaching English as a Second Language, San Juan, PR 00931-3300. Offers M Ed. Part-time programs available. *Degree requirements:* For master's, thesis. *Entrance requirements:* For master's, PAEG or GRE, minimum GPA of 3.0, letter of recommendation. *Faculty research:* Second language acquisition, bilingual education.

University of St. Thomas, Graduate Studies, School of Education, Department of Teacher Education, St. Paul, MN 55105-1096. Offers curriculum and instruction (MA), including elementary, individualized, K-12, secondary; elementary education (MA); English as a second language (MA); math education (Certificate); multicultural education (Certificate); reading (MA, Certificate), including elementary (MA), K-12 (MA). *Accreditation:* NCATE. Part-time and evening/weekend programs available. *Entrance requirements:* For master's, minimum GPA of 3.0 or MAT. Additional exam requirements/recommendations for international students: Required—TOEFL (minimum score 550 paper-based; 80 iBT). *Application deadline:* For fall admission, 6/1 for domestic students; for spring admission, 11/1 for domestic students. Applications are processed on a rolling basis. Application fee: $50. *Financial support:* Fellowships, research assistantships, institutionally sponsored loans, and scholarships/grants available. Support available to part-time students. Financial award applicants required to submit FAFSA. *Unit head:* Dr. Jan L. H. Frank, Chair, 651-962-4446, Fax: 651-962-4169, E-mail: jlhfrank@stthomas.edu. *Application contact:* Rosemary R. Barreto, Department Assistant, 651-962-4420, Fax: 651-962-4169, E-mail: barr7879@stthomas.edu.

University of St. Thomas, School of Education, Houston, TX 77006-4696. Offers all level education (M Ed); bilingual/dual language (M Ed); Catholic school teaching (M Ed); Catholic/private school leadership (M Ed); counselor education (M Ed); curriculum and instruction (M Ed); educational leadership (M Ed); elementary teaching (M Ed); English as a second language (M Ed); exceptionality/educational diagnostician (M Ed); exceptionality/special education (M Ed); generalist (M Ed); reading (M Ed); secondary teaching (M Ed). *Accreditation:* Teacher Education Accreditation Council. Part-time and evening/weekend programs available. Postbaccalaureate distance learning degree programs offered (no on-campus study). *Faculty:* 40 full-time (26 women), 43 part-time/adjunct (31 women). *Students:* 27 full-time (20 women), 1,091 part-time (981 women); includes 691 minority (247 Black or African American, non-Hispanic/Latino; 1 American Indian or Alaska Native, non-Hispanic/Latino; 44 Asian, non-Hispanic/Latino; 379 Hispanic/Latino; 2 Native Hawaiian or other Pacific Islander, non-Hispanic/Latino; 18 Two or more races, non-Hispanic/Latino), 28 international. Average age 36. 858 applicants, 83% accepted, 458 enrolled. In 2013, 454 master's awarded. *Degree requirements:* For master's, thesis, field experience. *Entrance requirements:* For master's, GRE or MAT if GPA is below 3.0, bachelor's degree; minimum GPA of 2.75 in bachelor's degree or last 60 credit hours; official transcripts from all institutions; goal statement of 250-300 words; 1 reference. Additional exam requirements/recommendations for international students: Required—TOEFL. *Application deadline:* Applications are processed on a rolling basis. Application fee: $35. Electronic applications accepted. *Expenses:* Contact institution. *Financial support:* In 2013–14, 41 students received support. Federal Work-Study, scholarships/grants, and state work-study, institutional employment available. Support available to part-time students. Financial award application deadline: 4/15; financial award applicants required to submit FAFSA. *Faculty research:* Leadership, diversity, personality traits, second language acquisition. *Unit head:* Dr. Robert LeBlanc, Dean, 713-525-3540, Fax: 713-525-3871, E-mail: education@stthom.edu. *Application contact:* Rita Paredes, Administrative Assistant, 713-525-3442, Fax: 713-525-3871, E-mail: rparede@stthom.edu.
Website: http://www.stthom.edu/Academics/School_of_Education/Index.aqf.

University of San Diego, School of Leadership and Education Sciences, Department of Learning and Teaching, San Diego, CA 92110-2492. Offers curriculum and instruction (M Ed); special education (M Ed); special education with deaf and hard of hearing (M Ed); teaching (MAT); TESOL, literacy and culture (M Ed). Part-time and evening/weekend programs available. *Faculty:* 10 full-time (6 women), 46 part-time/adjunct (38 women). *Students:* 132 full-time (100 women), 52 part-time (43 women); includes 141 minority (1 Black or African American, non-Hispanic/Latino; 16 American Indian or Alaska Native, non-Hispanic/Latino; 30 Asian, non-Hispanic/Latino; 79 Hispanic/Latino; 1 Native Hawaiian or other Pacific Islander, non-Hispanic/Latino; 14 Two or more races, non-Hispanic/Latino), 4 international. Average age 29. 253 applicants, 85% accepted, 108 enrolled. In 2013, 94 master's awarded. *Degree requirements:* For master's, thesis (for some programs), international experience. *Entrance requirements:* For master's, California Basic Educational Skills Test, minimum GPA of 3.0. Additional exam requirements/recommendations for international students: Required—TOEFL (minimum score 580 paper-based; 83 iBT), TWE. *Application deadline:* For fall admission, 3/1 priority date for domestic and international students; for spring admission, 10/15 priority date for domestic and international students. Applications are processed on a rolling basis. Application fee: $45. Electronic applications accepted. *Expenses: Tuition:* Full-time $23,580; part-time $1310 per credit. *Required fees:* $350. *Financial support:* In 2013–14, 52 students received support. Career-related internships or fieldwork, Federal Work-Study, institutionally sponsored loans, and stipends available. Support available to part-time students. Financial award application deadline: 4/1; financial award applicants required to submit FAFSA. *Faculty research:* Action research methodology, cultural studies, instructional theories and practices, second language acquisition, school reform. *Unit head:* Dr. Heather Lattimer, Director, 619-260-7616, Fax: 619-260-8159, E-mail: hlattimer@sandiego.edu. *Application contact:* Monica Mahon, Associate Director of Graduate Admissions, 619-260-4524, Fax: 619-260-4158, E-mail: grads@sandiego.edu.
Website: http://www.sandiego.edu/soles/departments/learning-and-teaching/.

University of San Francisco, School of Education, Department of International and Multicultural Education, San Francisco, CA 94117-1080. Offers human rights education (MA); international and multicultural education (MA, Ed D); multicultural literature for children and young adults (MA); teaching English to speakers of other languages (MA). Evening/weekend programs available. *Faculty:* 2 full-time (both women), 9 part-time/adjunct (5 women). *Students:* 132 full-time (99 women), 62 part-time (53 women); includes 90 minority (12 Black or African American, non-Hispanic/Latino; 26 Asian, non-Hispanic/Latino; 39 Hispanic/Latino; 1 Native Hawaiian or other Pacific Islander, non-Hispanic/Latino; 12 Two or more races, non-Hispanic/Latino), 30 international. Average age 35. 202 applicants, 80% accepted, 60 enrolled. In 2013, 41 master's, 10 doctorates awarded. *Degree requirements:* For doctorate, thesis/dissertation. *Application deadline:* For fall admission, 3/1 priority date for domestic students, 3/1 for international students; for spring admission, 10/15 priority date for domestic and international students. Applications are processed on a rolling basis. Application fee: $55 ($65 for international students). Electronic applications accepted. *Expenses: Tuition:* Full-time $21,150; part-time $1175 per unit. Tuition and fees vary according to course load, campus/location and program. *Financial support:* In 2013–14, 18 students received support. Fellowships, research assistantships, and teaching assistantships available. Financial award application deadline: 3/2; financial award applicants required to submit FAFSA. *Unit head:* Dr. Katz Susan, Chair, 415-422-6878. *Application contact:* Amy Fogliani, Associate Director of Graduate Outreach, 415-422-5467, E-mail: schoolofeducation@usfca.edu.

University of South Africa, College of Human Sciences, Pretoria, South Africa. Offers adult education (M Ed); African languages (MA, PhD); African politics (MA, PhD); Afrikaans (MA, PhD); ancient history (MA, PhD); ancient Near Eastern studies (MA, PhD); anthropology (MA, PhD); applied linguistics (MA); Arabic (MA, PhD); archaeology (MA); art history (MA); Biblical archaeology (MA); Biblical studies (M Th, D Th, PhD); Christian spirituality (M Th, D Th); church history (M Th, D Th); classical studies (MA, PhD); clinical psychology (MA); communication (MA, PhD); comparative education (M Ed, Ed D); consulting psychology (D Admin, D Com, PhD); curriculum studies (M Ed, Ed D); development studies (M Admin, MA, D Admin, PhD); didactics (M Ed, Ed D); education (M Tech); education management (M Ed, Ed D); educational psychology (M Ed); English (MA); environmental education (M Ed); French (MA, PhD); German (MA, PhD); Greek (MA); guidance and counseling (M Ed); health studies (MA, PhD), including health sciences education (MA), health services management (MA), medical and surgical nursing science (critical care general) (MA), midwifery and neonatal nursing science (MA), trauma and emergency care (MA); history (MA, PhD); history of education (Ed D); inclusive education (M Ed, Ed D); information and communications technology policy and regulation (MA); information science (MA, MIS, PhD); international politics (MA, PhD); Islamic studies (MA, PhD); Italian (MA, PhD); Judaica (MA, PhD); linguistics (MA, PhD); mathematical education (M Ed); mathematics education (MA); missiology (M Th, D Th); modern Hebrew (MA, PhD); musicology (MA, MMus, D Mus, PhD); natural science education (M Ed); New Testament (M Th, D Th); Old Testament (D Th); pastoral therapy (M Th, D Th); philosophy (MA); philosophy of education (M Ed, Ed D); politics (MA, PhD); Portuguese (MA, PhD); practical theology (M Th, D Th); psychology (MA, MS, PhD); psychology of education (M Ed, Ed D); public health (MA); religious studies (MA, D Th, PhD); Romance languages (MA); Russian (MA, PhD); Semitic languages (MA, PhD); social behavior studies in HIV/AIDS (MA); social science (mental health) (MA); social science in development studies (MA); social science in psychology (MA); social science in social work (MA); social science in sociology (MA); social work (MSW, DSW, PhD); socio-education (M Ed, Ed D); sociolinguistics (MA); sociology (MA, PhD); Spanish (MA, PhD); systematic theology (M Th, D Th); TESOL (teaching English to speakers of other languages) (MA); theological ethics (M Th, D Th); theory of literature (MA, PhD); urban ministries (D Th); urban ministry (M Th).

University of South Carolina, The Graduate School, College of Arts and Sciences, Linguistics Program, Columbia, SC 29208. Offers linguistics (MA, PhD); teaching English to speakers of other languages (Certificate). Part-time programs available. Terminal master's awarded for partial completion of doctoral program. *Degree requirements:* For master's, one foreign language, comprehensive exam, thesis optional; for doctorate, 3 foreign languages, comprehensive exam, thesis/dissertation. *Entrance requirements:* For master's and Certificate, GRE General Test, minimum GPA of 3.0; for doctorate, GRE General Test, minimum GPA of 3.5. Additional exam requirements/recommendations for international students: Required—TOEFL. Electronic applications accepted. *Faculty research:* Second language acquisition, sociolinguistics, syntax, historical linguistics and phonology.

University of Southern California, Graduate School, Rossier School of Education, Master's Programs in Education, Los Angeles, CA 90089-4038. Offers educational counseling (ME); marriage, family and child counseling (MMFT); postsecondary administration and student affairs [PASA] (ME); school counseling (ME); teaching (online) (MAT); teaching and teaching credential (MAT); teaching English to speakers of other languages (MAT). Part-time and evening/weekend programs available. Postbaccalaureate distance learning degree programs offered (no on-campus study). *Degree requirements:* For master's, thesis optional. *Entrance requirements:* For master's, GRE (for all programs except MAT). Additional exam requirements/recommendations for international students: Required—TOEFL (minimum score 100 iBT). Electronic applications accepted. *Faculty research:* College access and equity, preparing teachers for culturally diverse populations, sociocultural basis of learning as

mediated by instruction with focus on reading and literacy in English learners, social and political aspects of teaching and learning English, school counselor development and training.

University of Southern Maine, College of Management and Human Service, School of Education and Human Development, Program in Literacy Education, Portland, ME 04104-9300. Offers applied literacy (MS Ed); English as a second language (MS Ed, CAS, Certificate); literacy (CAS); literacy education (MS Ed, Certificate). *Accreditation:* Teacher Education Accreditation Council. Part-time and evening/weekend programs available. *Faculty:* 15 full-time (9 women), 11 part-time/adjunct (8 women). *Students:* 5 full-time (all women), 51 part-time (47 women); includes 2 minority (1 Hispanic/Latino; 1 Two or more races, non-Hispanic/Latino), 1 international. Average age 38. 18 applicants, 89% accepted, 8 enrolled. In 2013, 19 master's, 20 CASs awarded. *Degree requirements:* For master's, comprehensive exam, thesis or alternative; for other advanced degree, thesis or alternative. *Entrance requirements:* For master's, teacher certification; for other advanced degree, master's degree. Additional exam requirements/recommendations for international students: Required—TOEFL (minimum score 550 paper-based; 79 iBT). *Application deadline:* For fall admission, 5/1 priority date for domestic students; for spring admission, 10/15 priority date for domestic students. Applications are processed on a rolling basis. Application fee: $65. Electronic applications accepted. *Expenses:* Tuition, state resident: part-time $380 per credit. Tuition, nonresident: part-time $1026 per credit. Part-time tuition and fees vary according to program. *Financial support:* Research assistantships, career-related internships or fieldwork, Federal Work-Study, institutionally sponsored loans, scholarships/grants, and unspecified assistantships available. Support available to part-time students. Financial award application deadline: 3/1; financial award applicants required to submit FAFSA. *Faculty research:* Teacher research in literacy, multiliteracies, learning to teach culturally and linguistically diverse students, motivation to read. *Unit head:* Dr. Andrea Stairs, Program Director, 207-780-5971, E-mail: astairs@usm.maine.edu. *Application contact:* Mary Sloan, Assistant Dean of Graduate Studies and Director of Graduate Admissions, 207-780-4812, E-mail: gradstudies@usm.maine.edu.
Website: http://usm.maine.edu/literacy-education/msed-literacy-education.

University of South Florida, College of Arts and Sciences, Department of World Languages, Tampa, FL 33620-9951. Offers applied linguistics: English as a second language (MA); French (MA); second language acquisition and instructional technology (PhD); Spanish (MA). Part-time and evening/weekend programs available. *Faculty:* 21 full-time (14 women). *Students:* 40 full-time (22 women), 18 part-time (12 women); includes 32 minority (5 Black or African American, non-Hispanic/Latino; 1 Asian, non-Hispanic/Latino; 26 Hispanic/Latino), 8 international. Average age 32. 41 applicants, 73% accepted, 19 enrolled. In 2013, 20 master's awarded. *Degree requirements:* For master's, one foreign language, comprehensive exam, thesis optional; for doctorate, one foreign language, comprehensive exam, thesis/dissertation. *Entrance requirements:* For master's, GRE General Test (minimum preferred scores of 430 verbal and 4 in analytic writing on old scoring, except for French program), minimum undergraduate GPA of 3.0; two-page statement of purpose (written in Spanish for Spanish program); oral interview (for Spanish and French programs); writing sample (for French program); 2-3 letters of recommendation; for doctorate, GRE General Test (minimum preferred scores of 500 verbal and 4 in analytical writing on old scoring), minimum GPA of 3.5 or international equivalent; master's degree or equivalent academic level; statement of purpose; current curriculum vitae; three letters of recommendation; personal interview with graduate faculty; evidence of research experience or scholarly promise. Additional exam requirements/recommendations for international students: Required—TOEFL (minimum score 600 paper-based; 80 iBT) or IELTS (minimum score 6.5) for MA; TOEFL (minimum score 550 paper-based; 80 iBT) or IELTS (minimum score 6.5) for PhD. *Application deadline:* For fall admission, 2/15 for domestic students, 1/2 for international students; for spring admission, 10/15 for domestic students, 6/1 for international students. Application fee: $30. Electronic applications accepted. *Financial support:* In 2013–14, 43 students received support, including 43 teaching assistantships with full and partial tuition reimbursements available (averaging $10,152 per year); tuition waivers (partial) and unspecified assistantships also available. Financial award application deadline: 6/30. *Faculty research:* Second language acquisition, instructional technology, foreign language education, ESOL, distance learning. *Total annual research expenditures:* $87,194. *Unit head:* Dr. Stephan Schindler, Chair and Professor, 813-974-2548, Fax: 813-905-9937, E-mail: skschindler@.usf.edu. *Application contact:* Patricia Garcia, Academic Program Specialist, 813-974-2548, Fax: 813-905-9937, E-mail: pgarcia@usf.edu.
Website: http://languages.usf.edu/.

University of South Florida, College of Education, Department of Secondary Education, Tampa, FL 33620-9951. Offers English education (M Ed, MA, MAT, PhD); foreign language education/ESOL (M Ed, MA, MAT); instructional technology (M Ed, PhD, Ed S); mathematics education (M Ed, MA, MAT, PhD, Ed S); science education (M Ed, MA, MAT, PhD); second language acquisition/instructional technology (PhD); secondary education (M Ed, PhD); secondary education/TESOL (M Ed); social science education (M Ed, MA, MAT); teaching and learning in the content area (PhD). *Accreditation:* NCATE. Part-time and evening/weekend programs available. *Degree requirements:* For master's, variable foreign language requirement, comprehensive exam, project (for some programs); for doctorate, variable foreign language requirement, comprehensive exam, thesis/dissertation, philosophies of inquiry; multiple research methods. *Entrance requirements:* For master's, GRE General Test or General Knowledge Test, minimum GPA of 3.0; for doctorate, GRE General Test, minimum GPA of 3.5; for Ed S, GRE General Test. Additional exam requirements/recommendations for international students: Required—TOEFL (minimum score 550 paper-based; 79 iBT). Electronic applications accepted. *Faculty research:* English language learners/multicultural, social science education, mathematics education, science education, instructional technology.

University of South Florida, University College/Distance Education, Tampa, FL 33620-9951. *Unit head:* Kathy Barnes, Interdisciplinary Programs Coordinator, 813-974-8031, Fax: 813-974-7061, E-mail: barnesk@usf.edu. *Application contact:* Karen Tylinski, Metro Initiatives, 813-974-9943, Fax: 813-974-7061, E-mail: ktylinsk@usf.edu.
Website: http://uc.usf.edu/.

University of South Florida Sarasota-Manatee, College of Education, Sarasota, FL 34243. Offers education (MA); educational leadership (M Ed), including curriculum leadership, K-12, non-public/charter school leadership; English education (MA); teaching K-6 with ESOL endorsement (MAT). Part-time and evening/weekend programs available. *Faculty:* 7 full-time (all women), 5 part-time/adjunct (3 women). *Students:* 11 full-time (9 women), 43 part-time (33 women); includes 6 minority (2 Black or African American, non-Hispanic/Latino; 2 Hispanic/Latino; 1 Native Hawaiian or other Pacific Islander, non-Hispanic/Latino; 1 Two or more races, non-Hispanic/Latino). Average age 33. 46 applicants, 39% accepted, 15 enrolled. In 2013, 33 master's awarded. *Degree requirements:* For master's, comprehensive exam (for some programs). *Entrance requirements:* For master's, GRE (within last 5 years) or minimum GPA of 3.0, letters of recommendation. Additional exam requirements/recommendations for international students: Required—TOEFL (minimum score 550 paper-based; 79 iBT), IELTS (minimum score 6.5). *Application deadline:* For fall admission, 3/1 priority date for domestic students, 3/1 for international students; for spring admission, 10/1 priority date for domestic students, 10/1 for international students. Applications are processed on a rolling basis. Application fee: $30. Electronic applications accepted. *Expenses:* Tuition, state resident: full-time $10,029; part-time $418 per credit. Tuition, nonresident: full-time $20,727; part-time $863 per credit. *Required fees:* $10; $5. Tuition and fees vary according to program. *Financial support:* In 2013–14, 10 students received support. Career-related internships or fieldwork, institutionally sponsored loans, scholarships/grants, health care benefits, and unspecified assistantships available. Support available to part-time students. Financial award application deadline: 3/1; financial award applicants required to submit FAFSA. *Faculty research:* Child development, student achievement, inter-generational studies, equitable implementation of educational policy, linguistics and its applications. *Unit head:* Dr. Terry A. Osborn, Dean, 941-359-4531, Fax: 941-359-4778, E-mail: terryosborn@sar.usf.edu. *Application contact:* Andy Telatovich, Director, Admissions, 941-359-4330, Fax: 941-359-4585, E-mail: atelatovich@sar.usf.edu.
Website: http://usfsm.edu/college-of-education/.

The University of Tennessee, Graduate School, College of Education, Health and Human Sciences, Program in Education, Knoxville, TN 37996. Offers art education (MS); counseling education (PhD); cultural studies in education (PhD); curriculum (MS, Ed S); curriculum, educational research and evaluation (Ed D, PhD); early childhood education (PhD); early childhood special education (MS); education of deaf and hard of hearing (MS); educational administration and policy studies (Ed D, PhD); educational administration and supervision (Ed S); educational psychology (Ed D, PhD); elementary education (MS, Ed S); elementary teaching (MS); English education (MS, Ed S); exercise science (PhD); foreign language/ESL education (MS, Ed S); instructional technology (MS, Ed D, PhD, Ed S); literacy, language and ESL education (PhD); literacy, language education, and ESL education (Ed D); mathematics education (MS, Ed S); modified and comprehensive special education (MS); reading education (MS, Ed S); school counseling (Ed S); school psychology (PhD, Ed S); science education (MS, Ed S); secondary teaching (MS); social foundations (MS); social science education (MS, Ed S); socio-cultural foundations of sports and education (PhD); special education (Ed S); teacher education (Ed D, PhD). *Accreditation:* NCATE. Part-time and evening/weekend programs available. *Degree requirements:* For master's and Ed S, thesis optional; for doctorate, variable foreign language requirement, thesis/dissertation. *Entrance requirements:* For master's, minimum GPA of 2.7; for doctorate and Ed S, GRE General Test, minimum GPA of 2.7. Additional exam requirements/recommendations for international students: Required—TOEFL. Electronic applications accepted. *Expenses:* Tuition, state resident: full-time $9540; part-time $531 per credit hour. Tuition, nonresident: full-time $27,728; part-time $1542 per credit hour. *Required fees:* $1404; $67 per credit hour.

The University of Texas at Arlington, Graduate School, College of Liberal Arts, Department of Linguistics and TESOL, Program in Teaching English to Speakers of Other Languages, Arlington, TX 76019. Offers MA. *Accreditation:* NCATE. Part-time and evening/weekend programs available. *Degree requirements:* For master's, comprehensive exam (for some programs), thesis optional. *Entrance requirements:* For master's, GRE General Test, minimum undergraduate GPA of 3.0, 6 credits of undergraduate foundation courses, the equivalent of 2 years of university level foreign language study. Additional exam requirements/recommendations for international students: Required—TOEFL (minimum score 550 paper-based). Electronic applications accepted.

The University of Texas at El Paso, Graduate School, College of Liberal Arts, Department of Languages and Linguistics, El Paso, TX 79968-0001. Offers linguistics (MA); Spanish (MA); teaching English to speakers of other languages (Certificate). Part-time and evening/weekend programs available. *Degree requirements:* For master's, thesis optional. *Entrance requirements:* For master's, GRE General Test, departmental exam, minimum GPA of 3.0, letters of recommendation. Additional exam requirements/recommendations for international students: Required—TOEFL; Recommended—IELTS. Electronic applications accepted.

The University of Texas at San Antonio, College of Education and Human Development, Department of Bicultural and Bilingual Studies, San Antonio, TX 78249-0617. Offers bicultural/bilingual studies (MA), including bicultural studies, bicultural/bilingual education; culture, literacy, and language (PhD); teaching English as a second language (MA). Part-time and evening/weekend programs available. *Faculty:* 17 full-time (11 women), 1 (woman) part-time/adjunct. *Students:* 49 full-time (42 women), 122 part-time (97 women); includes 105 minority (3 Black or African American, non-Hispanic/Latino; 7 Asian, non-Hispanic/Latino; 91 Hispanic/Latino; 4 Two or more races, non-Hispanic/Latino), 23 international. Average age 36. 59 applicants, 88% accepted, 26 enrolled. In 2013, 52 master's, 2 doctorates awarded. *Degree requirements:* For master's, one foreign language, comprehensive exam, thesis optional; for doctorate, one foreign language, comprehensive exam, thesis/dissertation. *Entrance requirements:* For master's, GRE General Test if GPA is less than 3.0 for last 60 hours, bachelor's degree with 18 credit hours in field of study or in another appropriate field of study; for doctorate, GRE General Test, resume or curriculum vitae, 3 letters of recommendation, statement of purpose. Additional exam requirements/recommendations for international students: Required—TOEFL (minimum score 550 paper-based; 79 iBT), IELTS (minimum score 6.5). *Application deadline:* For fall admission, 7/1 for domestic students, 4/1 for international students; for spring admission, 11/1 for domestic students, 9/1 for international students. Applications are processed on a rolling basis. Application fee: $45 ($80 for international students). Electronic applications accepted. *Expenses:* Tuition, state resident: full-time $4671. Tuition, nonresident: full-time $8708. *International tuition:* $17,415 full-time. *Required fees:* $1924.60. Tuition and fees vary according to course load and degree level. *Financial support:* In 2013–14, 19 students received support, including 7 fellowships with full tuition reimbursements available (averaging $27,315 per year), 9 research assistantships with full tuition reimbursements available (averaging $13,618 per year), 7 teaching assistantships with full tuition reimbursements available (averaging $11,000 per year). Financial award applicants required to submit FAFSA. *Faculty research:* Bilingualism and biliteracy development, second language teaching and learning, language minority education, Mexican American studies, transnationalism and immigration. *Unit head:* Dr. Belinda Bustos Flores, Chair, 210-458-4426, Fax: 210-458-5962, E-mail: belinda.flores@utsa.edu. *Application contact:* Armando Trujillo, Assistant Dean of the Graduate School, 210-458-5576, Fax: 210-458-5576, E-mail: armando.trujillo@utsa.edu.
Website: http://education.utsa.edu/bicultural-bilingual_studies.

The University of Texas of the Permian Basin, Office of Graduate Studies, School of Education, Program in Bilingual/English as a Second Language Education, Odessa, TX 79762-0001. Offers MA. *Degree requirements:* For master's, comprehensive exam (for some programs), thesis (for some programs). *Entrance requirements:* For master's, GRE General Test. Additional exam requirements/recommendations for international students: Required—TOEFL (minimum score 550 paper-based).

The University of Texas–Pan American, College of Arts and Humanities, Department of English, Program in English as a Second Language, Edinburg, TX 78539. Offers MA. Part-time and evening/weekend programs available. *Degree requirements:* For

master's, comprehensive exam, thesis optional. *Entrance requirements:* For master's, GRE General Test, minimum GPA of 3.0. *Expenses:* Tuition, state resident: full-time $5986; part-time $333 per credit hour. Tuition, nonresident: full-time $12,358; part-time $687 per credit hour. *Required fees:* $782. Tuition and fees vary according to program. *Faculty research:* Oral versus literary culture discourse analysis, language shift among Hispanics.

University of the Southwest, Graduate Programs, Hobbs, NM 88240-9129. Offers business administration (MBA); curriculum and instruction (MSE); curriculum and instruction: bilingual (MSE); curriculum and instruction: TESOL (MSE); early childhood education (MSE); educational administration (MSE); mental health counseling (MSE); school counseling (MSE); special education (MSE); sports management (MBA). Part-time and evening/weekend programs available. Postbaccalaureate distance learning degree programs offered (no on-campus study). *Degree requirements:* For master's, comprehensive exam, thesis (for some programs). *Entrance requirements:* Additional exam requirements/recommendations for international students: Recommended—TOEFL. Electronic applications accepted.

The University of Toledo, College of Graduate Studies, College of Language, Literature and Social Sciences, Department of English Language and Literature, Toledo, OH 43606-3390. Offers English as a second language (MA); teaching of writing (Certificate). Part-time programs available. *Faculty:* 15. *Students:* 30 full-time (20 women), 10 part-time (7 women); includes 8 minority (3 Black or African American, non-Hispanic/Latino; 2 Asian, non-Hispanic/Latino; 1 Hispanic/Latino; 2 Two or more races, non-Hispanic/Latino), 2 international. Average age 32. 24 applicants, 71% accepted, 14 enrolled. In 2013, 15 master's, 3 other advanced degrees awarded. *Degree requirements:* For master's, thesis. *Entrance requirements:* For master's, GRE if GPA is less than 3.0, minimum cumulative point-hour ratio of 2.7 for all previous academic work, three letters of recommendation, transcripts from all prior institutions attended, critical essay; for Certificate, statement of purpose, transcripts from all prior institutions attended, 2 letters of recommendation. Additional exam requirements/recommendations for international students: Required—TOEFL (minimum score 550 paper-based; 80 iBT). *Application deadline:* For fall admission, 1/15 priority date for domestic and international students. Applications are processed on a rolling basis. Application fee: $45 ($75 for international students). Electronic applications accepted. *Financial support:* In 2013–14, 33 teaching assistantships with full and partial tuition reimbursements (averaging $7,514 per year) were awarded; Federal Work-Study, institutionally sponsored loans, scholarships/grants, tuition waivers (full), unspecified assistantships, and administrative assistantships also available. Support available to part-time students. Financial award applicants required to submit FAFSA. *Faculty research:* Literary criticism, linguistics, creative writing, folklore and cultural studies. *Unit head:* Dr. Sara Lundquist, Chair, 419-530-2506, Fax: 419-530-2590, E-mail: sara.lundquist@utoledo.edu. *Application contact:* Graduate School Office, 419-530-4723, Fax: 419-530-4724, E-mail: grdsch@utnet.utoledo.edu.
Website: http://www.utoledo.edu/llss/.

The University of Toledo, College of Graduate Studies, Judith Herb College of Education, Department of Curriculum and Instruction, Toledo, OH 43606-3390. Offers art education (ME); career and technical education (ME); career-technical education (Ed S); curriculum and instruction (ME, PhD, Ed S); early childhood education (PhD, Ed S); education and biology (MES); education and chemistry (MES); education and economics (MAE); education and English (MAE); education and French (MAE); education and geography (MAE); education and geology (MES); education and German (MAE); education and history (MAE); education and mathematics (MAE, MES); education and physics (MES); education and political science (MAE); education and sociology (MAE); education and Spanish (MAE); educational media (PhD); educational technology (ME); educational technology: virtual educator (Certificate); elementary education (PhD); English as a second language (MAE); gifted and talented (PhD); middle childhood education licensure (ME); music education (MME); secondary education (PhD); secondary education licensure (ME); special education (PhD, Ed S). *Accreditation:* NCATE. Part-time and evening/weekend programs available. *Faculty:* 41. *Students:* 53 full-time (30 women), 154 part-time (111 women); includes 21 minority (16 Black or African American, non-Hispanic/Latino; 4 Hispanic/Latino; 1 Two or more races, non-Hispanic/Latino), 21 international. Average age 34. 82 applicants, 79% accepted, 47 enrolled. In 2013, 80 master's, 5 doctorates awarded. *Degree requirements:* For master's, comprehensive exam, thesis or alternative; for doctorate, comprehensive exam, thesis/dissertation; for other advanced degree, thesis optional. *Entrance requirements:* For master's, doctorate, and other advanced degree, minimum cumulative GPA of 2.7 for all previous academic work, letters of recommendation. Additional exam requirements/recommendations for international students: Required—TOEFL (minimum score 550 paper-based; 80 iBT). *Application deadline:* For fall admission, 1/15 priority date for domestic and international students. Applications are processed on a rolling basis. Application fee: $45 ($75 for international students). Electronic applications accepted. *Financial support:* In 2013–14, 5 research assistantships with full and partial tuition reimbursements (averaging $13,200 per year), 11 teaching assistantships with full and partial tuition reimbursements (averaging $8,809 per year) were awarded; career-related internships or fieldwork, Federal Work-Study, institutionally sponsored loans, scholarships/grants, tuition waivers (full and partial), unspecified assistantships, and administrative assistantships also available. Support available to part-time students. *Unit head:* Dr. Joan Kaderavek, Chair, 419-530-5373, E-mail: eigh.chiarelott@utoledo.edu. *Application contact:* Graduate School Office, 419-530-4723, Fax: 419-530-4724, E-mail: grdsch@utnet.utoledo.edu.
Website: http://www.utoledo.edu/eduhshs/.

University of Washington, Graduate School, College of Arts and Sciences, Department of English, Seattle, WA 98195. Offers creative writing (MFA); English as a second language (MAT); English literature and language (MA, MAT, PhD). Part-time programs available. Terminal master's awarded for partial completion of doctoral program. *Degree requirements:* For master's, one foreign language, thesis (for some programs); for doctorate, one foreign language, thesis/dissertation. *Entrance requirements:* For master's, GRE General Test, GRE Subject Test (MA and MAT in English), minimum GPA of 3.0; for doctorate, GRE General Test, GRE Subject Test. Additional exam requirements/recommendations for international students: Required—TOEFL. Electronic applications accepted. *Faculty research:* English and American literature, critical theory, creative writing, language theory.

University of Wisconsin–Milwaukee, Graduate School, College of Letters and Sciences, Department of Linguistics, Milwaukee, WI 53201-0413. Offers linguistics (MA, PhD); TESOL (Graduate Certificate). *Faculty:* 7 full-time (2 women). *Students:* 22 full-time (16 women), 3 part-time (all women); includes 5 minority (3 Asian, non-Hispanic/Latino; 1 Hispanic/Latino; 1 Two or more races, non-Hispanic/Latino), 11 international. Average age 34. 49 applicants, 33% accepted, 8 enrolled. *Unit head:* Hamid Ouali, Department Chair, 414-229-1113, E-mail: ouali@uwm.edu. *Application contact:* General Information Contact, 414-229-4982, Fax: 414-229-6967, E-mail: gradschool@uwm.edu.
Website: http://www4.uwm.edu/letsci/linguistics/.

University of Wisconsin–River Falls, Outreach and Graduate Studies, College of Arts and Science, Program in Teaching English to Speakers of Other Languages, River Falls, WI 54022. Offers MA.

Utah Valley University, Program in Education, Orem, UT 84058-5999. Offers educational technology (M Ed); elementary mathematics (M Ed); English as a second language (M Ed); models of instruction (M Ed). *Accreditation:* Teacher Education Accreditation Council. Part-time programs available. *Faculty:* 4 full-time (2 women). *Students:* 107 part-time (76 women); includes 2 minority (1 Asian, non-Hispanic/Latino; 1 Hispanic/Latino). Average age 33. *Degree requirements:* For master's, project. *Entrance requirements:* For master's, GRE, 3 letters of recommendation, interview. Additional exam requirements/recommendations for international students: Required—TOEFL (minimum score 83 iBT). *Application deadline:* For fall admission, 3/31 for domestic and international students. Application fee: $45 ($100 for international students). Electronic applications accepted. *Expenses:* Tuition, state resident: full-time $8520; part-time $355 per credit. Tuition, nonresident: full-time $21,232; part-time $885 per credit. *Required fees:* $700; $350 per semester. Tuition and fees vary according to program. *Financial support:* Application deadline: 5/1; applicants required to submit FAFSA. *Unit head:* Parker Fewson, Dean, School of Education, 801-863-8006. *Application contact:* Mary Sowder, Coordinator of Graduate Studies, 801-863-6723.

Valley City State University, Online Master of Education Program, Valley City, ND 58072. Offers elementary education (M Ed); English education (M Ed); library and information technologies (M Ed); teaching and technology (M Ed); teaching English language learners (ELL) (M Ed); technology education (M Ed). *Accreditation:* NCATE. Part-time and evening/weekend programs available. Postbaccalaureate distance learning degree programs offered (no on-campus study). *Faculty:* 21 full-time (14 women), 7 part-time/adjunct (all women). *Students:* 2 full-time (both women), 151 part-time (102 women); includes 10 minority (1 Black or African American, non-Hispanic/Latino; 3 Asian, non-Hispanic/Latino; 2 Hispanic/Latino; 4 Two or more races, non-Hispanic/Latino), 1 international. Average age 34. 27 applicants, 93% accepted, 21 enrolled. In 2013, 45 master's awarded. *Degree requirements:* For master's, action research report, comprehensive portfolio. *Entrance requirements:* For master's, GRE, MAT, PRAXIS II or National Teaching Board for Professional Standards (if GPA is less than 3.0). Additional exam requirements/recommendations for international students: Required—TOEFL (minimum score 525 paper-based; 71 iBT); Recommended—IELTS (minimum score 5.5). *Application deadline:* For fall admission, 7/19 priority date for domestic and international students; for spring admission, 12/13 priority date for domestic and international students; for summer admission, 5/9 priority date for domestic and international students. Applications are processed on a rolling basis. Application fee: $35. Electronic applications accepted. *Expenses:* Contact institution. *Financial support:* In 2013–14, 24 students received support. Scholarships/grants and tuition waivers (full and partial) available. Financial award application deadline: 5/15; financial award applicants required to submit FAFSA. *Faculty research:* Academically at-risk students in higher education, communication pedagogy and technology, gender communication, computer-mediated communication, creativity in music, STEM education in K-12. *Total annual research expenditures:* $26,000. *Unit head:* Dr. Gary Thompson, Dean, 701-845-7197, E-mail: gary.thompson@vcsu.edu. *Application contact:* Misty Lindgren, Graduate Studies, 701-845-7303, Fax: 701-845-7190, E-mail: misty.lindgren@vcsu.edu.
Website: http://www.vcsu.edu/graduate.

Valparaiso University, Graduate School, Program in English Studies and Communication, Valparaiso, IN 46383. Offers English studies and communication (MA); teaching English to speakers of other languages (TESOL) (MA, Certificate). Part-time and evening/weekend programs available. *Students:* 14 full-time (5 women), 8 part-time (6 women); includes 3 minority (1 Black or African American, non-Hispanic/Latino; 1 Hispanic/Latino; 1 Two or more races, non-Hispanic/Latino), 13 international. Average age 29. In 2013, 6 master's, 1 other advanced degree awarded. *Entrance requirements:* For master's, minimum GPA of 3.0. Additional exam requirements/recommendations for international students: Required—TOEFL (minimum score 550 paper-based; 80 iBT), IELTS (minimum score 6). *Application deadline:* Applications are processed on a rolling basis. Application fee: $30 ($50 for international students). Electronic applications accepted. *Expenses:* *Tuition:* Full-time $10,350; part-time $575 per credit hour. *Required fees:* $378; $101 per term. Tuition and fees vary according to course load and program. *Financial support:* Available to part-time students. Applicants required to submit FAFSA. *Unit head:* Dr. Jennifer A. Ziegler, Dean, Graduate School and Continuing Education, 219-464-5313, Fax: 219-464-5381, E-mail: jennifer.ziegler@valpo.edu. *Application contact:* Jessica Choquette, Graduate Admissions Specialist, 219-464-5313, Fax: 219-464-5381, E-mail: jessica.choquette@valpo.edu.
Website: http://www.valpo.edu/grad/esc/.

Virginia International University, School of English Language Studies, Fairfax, VA 22030. Offers teaching English to speakers of other languages (MA, Graduate Certificate). Part-time programs available. *Entrance requirements:* For master's and Graduate Certificate, bachelor's degree. Additional exam requirements/recommendations for international students: Required—TOEFL (minimum score 550 paper-based; 80 iBT), IELTS (minimum score 6). Electronic applications accepted.

Walden University, Graduate Programs, Richard W. Riley College of Education and Leadership, Minneapolis, MN 55401. *Accreditation:* NCATE. Part-time and evening/weekend programs available. Postbaccalaureate distance learning degree programs offered (minimal on-campus study). *Faculty:* 23 full-time (15 women), 830 part-time/adjunct (569 women). *Students:* 8,671 full-time (7,197 women), 2,122 part-time (1,735 women); includes 4,734 minority (3,802 Black or African American, non-Hispanic/Latino; 50 American Indian or Alaska Native, non-Hispanic/Latino; 136 Asian, non-Hispanic/Latino; 539 Hispanic/Latino; 35 Native Hawaiian or other Pacific Islander, non-Hispanic/Latino; 172 Two or more races, non-Hispanic/Latino), 73 international. Average age 40. 2,646 applicants, 96% accepted, 2074 enrolled. In 2013, 2,214 master's, 354 doctorates, 479 other advanced degrees awarded. *Degree requirements:* For doctorate, thesis/dissertation (for some programs), residency; for other advanced degree, residency (for some programs). *Entrance requirements:* For master's, bachelor's degree or higher; minimum GPA of 2.5; official transcripts; goal statement (for some programs); access to computer and Internet; for doctorate, master's degree or higher; three years of related professional or academic experience (preferred); minimum GPA of 3.0; goal statement and current resume (select programs); official transcripts; access to computer and Internet; for other advanced degree, relevant work experience; access to computer and Internet. Additional exam requirements/recommendations for international students: Required—TOEFL (minimum score 550 paper-based; 79 iBT), IELTS (minimum score 6.5), Michigan English Language Assessment Battery (minimum score 82), or PTE. *Application deadline:* Applications are processed on a rolling basis. Application fee: $0. Electronic applications accepted. *Expenses:* *Tuition:* Full-time $11,813.55; part-time $500 per credit. *Required fees:* $618.76. *Financial support:* In 2013–14, 1 fellowship was awarded; Federal Work-Study, scholarships/grants, unspecified assistantships, and family tuition reduction, active duty/veteran tuition reduction, group tuition reduction, interest-free payment plans, employee tuition reduction also available. Support available to part-time students. Financial award applicants required to submit FAFSA. *Unit head:* Dr. Kate Steffens, Dean, 800-925-3368. *Application contact:* Jennifer Hall, Vice President of Enrollment Management, 866-4-WALDEN, E-mail: info@waldenu.edu.
Website: http://www.waldenu.edu/colleges-schools/riley-college-of-education/.

English as a Second Language

Washington State University, Graduate School, College of Education, Department of Teaching and Learning, Pullman, WA 99164. Offers cultural studies and social thought in education (PhD); curriculum and instruction (Ed M, MA); English language learners (Ed M, MA); language, literacy and technology (PhD); literacy education (Ed M, MA); mathematics and science education (PhD); special education (Ed M, MA, PhD); teacher leadership (Ed D); teaching (MIT), including elementary education, secondary education. *Degree requirements:* For master's, comprehensive exam (for some programs), thesis (for some programs), oral or written exam; for doctorate, comprehensive exam, thesis/dissertation, oral and written exam. *Entrance requirements:* For master's, GRE General Test, minimum GPA of 3.0, 3 letters of recommendation, letter of intent, transcripts, resume/curriculum vitae; for doctorate, GRE General Test, minimum GPA of 3.0, 3 letters of recommendation, letter of intent, transcripts, writing sample, resume/curriculum vitae. Additional exam requirements/recommendations for international students: Required—TOEFL (minimum score 550 paper-based; 80 iBT). Electronic applications accepted.

Wayland Baptist University, Graduate Programs, Program in Education, Plainview, TX 79072-6998. Offers education administration (M Ed); education diagnostics (M Ed); education literacy (M Ed); elementary certification (M Ed); English (M Ed); English as a second language (M Ed); higher education administration (M Ed); human resources (M Ed); instructional leadership (M Ed); instructional technology (M Ed); science education (M Ed); secondary certification (M Ed); social studies (M Ed); special education (M Ed). Part-time and evening/weekend programs available. Postbaccalaureate distance learning degree programs offered (no on-campus study). *Faculty:* 33 full-time (17 women), 28 part-time/adjunct (17 women). *Students:* 22 full-time (15 women), 316 part-time (189 women); includes 130 minority (48 Black or African American, non-Hispanic/Latino; 3 American Indian or Alaska Native, non-Hispanic/Latino; 71 Hispanic/Latino; 1 Native Hawaiian or other Pacific Islander, non-Hispanic/Latino; 7 Two or more races, non-Hispanic/Latino). Average age 39. 80 applicants, 96% accepted, 44 enrolled. In 2013, 170 master's awarded. *Degree requirements:* For master's, comprehensive exam, capstone course. *Entrance requirements:* For master's, GRE, GMAT or MAT. Additional exam requirements/recommendations for international students: Required—TOEFL (minimum score 500 paper-based; 61 iBT). *Application deadline:* Applications are processed on a rolling basis. Application fee: $50. Electronic applications accepted. *Expenses: Tuition:* Full-time $8190; part-time $455 per credit hour. *Required fees:* $970; $455 per credit hour. $485 per semester. *Financial support:* Federal Work-Study, institutionally sponsored loans, and scholarships/grants available. Support available to part-time students. Financial award application deadline: 5/1; financial award applicants required to submit FAFSA. *Unit head:* Dr. Jim Todd, Chairman, 806-291-1045, Fax: 806-291-1951. *Application contact:* Amanda Stanton, Coordinator of Graduate Studies, 806-291-3423, Fax: 806-291-1950, E-mail: stanton@wbu.edu.

Wayne State College, School of Education and Counseling, Department of Educational Foundations and Leadership, Program in Curriculum and Instruction, Wayne, NE 68787. Offers alternative education (MSE); business and information technology education (MSE); communication arts education (MSE); early childhood education (MSE); elementary education (MSE); English as a second language (MSE); English education (MSE); family and consumer sciences education (MSE); industrial technology and vocational education (MSE); learning communities (MSE); mathematics education (MSE); music education (MSE); science education (MSE); social science education (MSE). *Accreditation:* NCATE. Part-time and evening/weekend programs available. *Degree requirements:* For master's, comprehensive exam, thesis optional. *Entrance requirements:* For master's, GRE General Test. Additional exam requirements/recommendations for international students: Required—TOEFL (minimum score 550 paper-based).

Wayne State University, College of Education, Division of Teacher Education, Detroit, MI 48202. Offers art education (M Ed), including art therapy; autism spectrum disorders (Certificate); bilingual/bicultural education (M Ed, Certificate); career and technical education (M Ed, Certificate); cognitive impairment (Certificate); curriculum and instruction (Ed D, PhD, Ed S), including art education (PhD), bilingual education (Ed D, Ed S), bilingual-bicultural education (PhD), career and technical education (MAT, Ed D, PhD, Ed S), early childhood education (MAT, Ed D, PhD, Ed S), elementary education, English as a second language (MAT, Ed D, Ed S), English education (MAT, Ed D, PhD, Ed S), foreign language education (MAT, PhD), K-12 curriculum, mathematics education (MAT, Ed D, PhD, Ed S), science education (MAT, Ed D, PhD, Ed S), secondary education, social studies education (MAT, Ed S), social studies education: secondary (Ed D, PhD); early childhood education (M Ed, Certificate); elementary education (M Ed, MAT), including children's literature (MAT), early childhood education (MAT, Ed D, PhD, Ed S), general elementary education (MAT); elementary or secondary education (MAT), including bilingual/bicultural education, English as a second language (MAT, Ed D, Ed S), mathematics education (MAT, Ed D, PhD, Ed S), science education (MAT, Ed D, PhD, Ed S), social studies education (MAT, Ed S); emotionally impaired (Certificate); English as a second language (Certificate); English education (M Ed), including secondary; foreign language education (M Ed); K-12 reading specialist (Certificate); learning disabilities (Certificate); mathematics education (M Ed), including secondary; reading (M Ed, Ed S); reading, language and literature (Ed D); science education (M Ed), including secondary; secondary education (MAT), including art education (K-12), career and technical education (MAT, Ed D, PhD, Ed S), English education (MAT, Ed D, PhD, Ed S), foreign language education (MAT, PhD), kinesiology; social studies education (M Ed), including secondary; special education (M Ed, MAT, Ed D, PhD, Ed S); visual arts education (Certificate). Part-time programs available. *Faculty:* 36 full-time (25 women), 55 part-time/adjunct (43 women). *Students:* 218 full-time (163 women), 448 part-time (344 women); includes 218 minority (177 Black or African American, non-Hispanic/Latino; 2 American Indian or Alaska Native, non-Hispanic/Latino; 11 Asian, non-Hispanic/Latino; 19 Hispanic/Latino; 1 Native Hawaiian or other Pacific Islander, non-Hispanic/Latino; 8 Two or more races, non-Hispanic/Latino), 10 international. Average age 37. 258 applicants, 30% accepted, 52 enrolled. In 2013, 183 master's, 10 doctorates, 35 other advanced degrees awarded. *Degree requirements:* For master's, thesis, essay or project (for some M Ed programs), professional field experience (for MAT programs); for doctorate, thesis/dissertation. *Entrance requirements:* For master's, Michigan Basic Skills Test (MA in teaching), admission to the graduate school, verification of participation in group work with children and Michigan State Police Criminal Background check; for doctorate, minimum undergraduate GPA of 3.0, graduate 3.5; interview, curriculum vitae; references. Additional exam requirements/recommendations for international students: Required—TOEFL (minimum score 550 paper-based; 79 iBT), TWE (minimum score 5.5), Michigan English Language Assessment Battery (minimum score 85); Recommended—IELTS (minimum score 6.5). *Application deadline:* For fall admission, 6/1 priority date for domestic students, 5/1 priority date for international students; for winter admission, 10/1 priority date for domestic students, 9/1 priority date for international students; for spring admission, 2/1 priority date for domestic students, 1/1 priority date for international students. Applications are processed on a rolling basis. Application fee: $0. Electronic applications accepted. *Expenses: Tuition,* state resident: part-time $554.15 per credit. Tuition, nonresident: part-time $1200.35 per credit. *Required fees:* $42.15 per credit. $268.30 per semester. Tuition and fees vary according to course load and program.

Financial support: In 2013–14, 83 students received support, including 1 fellowship (averaging $16,842 per year), 1 research assistantship with tuition reimbursement available (averaging $21,229 per year); career-related internships or fieldwork, Federal Work-Study, scholarships/grants, health care benefits, and unspecified assistantships also available. Support available to part-time students. Financial award application deadline: 3/31; financial award applicants required to submit FAFSA. *Faculty research:* Improving students' skill achievement in mathematics; improving elementary children's understanding of informational text; teachers' use of their pedagogical and mathematical knowledge in the interactive work of teaching; the intersection of identity construction in teaching and learning; identifying effective methods of literacy instruction and assessments for bilingual students in elementary language arts classrooms. *Total annual research expenditures:* $368,105. *Unit head:* Dr. Kathleen Crawford-McKinney, Assistant Dean, 313-577-0122. *Application contact:* Janice Green, Assistant Dean, 313-577-1605, E-mail: jwgreen@wayne.edu.
Website: http://coe.wayne.edu/ted/index.php.

West Chester University of Pennsylvania, College of Arts and Sciences, Department of English, West Chester, PA 19383. Offers English (MA, Teaching Certificate); TESL (Certificate); TESOL (MA). Part-time and evening/weekend programs available. *Faculty:* 21 full-time (8 women). *Students:* 41 full-time (26 women), 52 part-time (41 women); includes 11 minority (5 Black or African American, non-Hispanic/Latino; 4 Hispanic/Latino; 2 Two or more races, non-Hispanic/Latino), 2 international. Average age 29. 44 applicants, 91% accepted, 23 enrolled. In 2013, 34 master's, 3 other advanced degrees awarded. *Degree requirements:* For master's, thesis optional, capstone experience (for English). *Entrance requirements:* For master's, minimum GPA of 2.8 and writing sample; two letters of recommendation, goals statement, and official transcripts (for English); three letters of recommendation and interview (for TESL); for other advanced degree, goals statement (for Certificate). Additional exam requirements/recommendations for international students: Required—TOEFL (minimum score 550 paper-based; 80 iBT). *Application deadline:* For fall admission, 4/15 priority date for domestic students, 3/15 for international students; for spring admission, 10/15 priority date for domestic students, 9/1 for international students. Applications are processed on a rolling basis. Application fee: $45. Electronic applications accepted. *Expenses:* Tuition, state resident: full-time $7956; part-time $442 per credit. Tuition, nonresident: full-time $11,934; part-time $663 per credit. *Required fees:* $2134.20; $106.24 per credit. Tuition and fees vary according to campus/location and program. *Financial support:* Unspecified assistantships available. Support available to part-time students. Financial award application deadline: 2/15; financial award applicants required to submit FAFSA. *Faculty research:* Critical theory, cultural studies, literature, composition, rhetoric, second language acquisition and teaching, second language writing, phonology, language teacher development. *Unit head:* Dr. Vicki Tischio, Chair, 610-436-2822, Fax: 610-738-0516, E-mail: vtischio@wcupa.edu. *Application contact:* Dr. Eric Dodson-Robinson, Interim Graduate Coordinator, 610-738-0499, Fax: 610-738-0516, E-mail: edodsonrobinson@wcupa.edu.
Website: http://www.wcupa.edu/_academics/sch_cas.eng/.

Western Carolina University, Graduate School, College of Arts and Sciences, Department of English, Cullowhee, NC 28723. Offers English (MA); teaching English as a second language or foreign language (MA). Part-time and evening/weekend programs available. *Degree requirements:* For master's, one foreign language, comprehensive exam, thesis (for some programs). *Entrance requirements:* For master's, GRE General Test, appropriate undergraduate degree, writing sample, 3 letters of recommendation. Additional exam requirements/recommendations for international students: Required—TOEFL (minimum score 550 paper-based; 79 iBT). *Faculty research:* Teaching English to speakers of other languages (TESOL), language assessment, applied linguistics, poetry, folk and fairy tales, post World War II British literature, Appalachian and southern literature.

Western Connecticut State University, Division of Graduate Studies, School of Arts and Sciences, Department of English, Danbury, CT 06810-6885. Offers English (MA); literature (MA); TESOL (MA); writing (MA). Part-time programs available. *Degree requirements:* For master's, thesis (for writing option), completion of program in 6 years. *Entrance requirements:* For master's, minimum GPA of 2.5, writing sample. Additional exam requirements/recommendations for international students: Recommended—TOEFL (minimum score 550 paper-based; 79 iBT), IELTS (minimum score 6). *Faculty research:* Developing inquiry in teachers and students, encouraging talent development, analyzing program development and assessment techniques, developing student learning outcomes, encouraging teachers as researchers, assessing the impact of computer technologies.

Western Illinois University, School of Graduate Studies, College of Education and Human Services, Department of Educational and Interdisciplinary Studies, Program in Educational and Interdisciplinary Studies, Macomb, IL 61455-1390. Offers educational and interdisciplinary studies (MS Ed); teaching English to speakers of other languages (Certificate). *Accreditation:* NCATE. Part-time programs available. *Students:* 13 full-time (11 women), 36 part-time (28 women); includes 11 minority (3 Black or African American, non-Hispanic/Latino; 1 Asian, non-Hispanic/Latino; 6 Hispanic/Latino; 1 Two or more races, non-Hispanic/Latino), 2 international. Average age 34. In 2013, 16 master's, 5 Certificates awarded. *Degree requirements:* For master's, thesis or alternative. *Entrance requirements:* For master's, minimum GPA of 2.75, interview. Additional exam requirements/recommendations for international students: Required—TOEFL (minimum score 550 paper-based; 80 iBT). *Application deadline:* Applications are processed on a rolling basis. Application fee: $30. Electronic applications accepted. *Financial support:* In 2013–14, 9 students received support, including 5 research assistantships with full tuition reimbursements available (averaging $7,544 per year), 4 teaching assistantships with full tuition reimbursements available (averaging $8,688 per year). Financial award applicants required to submit FAFSA. *Unit head:* Dr. Gloria Delany-Barmann, Chairperson, 309-298-1183. *Application contact:* Dr. Nancy Parsons, Associate Provost and Director of Graduate Studies, 309-298-1806, Fax: 309-298-2345, E-mail: grad-office@wiu.edu.
Website: http://wiu.edu/eis.

Western Kentucky University, Graduate Studies, Potter College of Arts and Letters, Department of English, Bowling Green, KY 42101. Offers education (MA); English (MA Ed); literature (MA), including American literature, British literature, literary theory, women writers, world literature; teaching English as a second language (MA); writing (MA). Part-time and evening/weekend programs available. *Degree requirements:* For master's, comprehensive exam, thesis optional, final exam. *Entrance requirements:* For master's, GRE General Test, minimum GPA of 2.75. Additional exam requirements/recommendations for international students: Required—TOEFL (minimum score 555 paper-based; 79 iBT). *Faculty research:* Improving writing, linking teacher knowledge and performance, Victorian women writers, Kentucky women writers, Kentucky poets.

Western New Mexico University, Graduate Division, School of Education, Silver City, NM 88062-0680. Offers bilingual education (MAT); counseling (MA); educational leadership (MA); elementary education (MAT); reading (MAT); school psychology (MA); secondary education (MAT); special education (MAT); TESOL (teaching English to speakers of other languages) (MAT). *Accreditation:* NCATE. *Degree requirements:* For master's, comprehensive exam. *Entrance requirements:* For master's, GRE General Test, GRE Subject Test, minimum GPA of 3.2 in last 64 hours of undergraduate study.

Additional exam requirements/recommendations for international students: Required—TOEFL (minimum score 550 paper-based). Electronic applications accepted.

West Virginia University, Eberly College of Arts and Sciences, Department of Foreign Languages, Morgantown, WV 26506. Offers French (MA); linguistics (MA); Spanish (MA); teaching English to speakers of other languages (MA). Part-time programs available. *Degree requirements:* For master's, one foreign language, comprehensive exam (for some programs), thesis optional. *Entrance requirements:* For master's, minimum GPA of 3.0. Electronic applications accepted. *Faculty research:* French, German, and Spanish literature; foreign language pedagogy; English as a second language; cultural studies; linguistics.

Wheaton College, Graduate School, Department of Intercultural Studies, Wheaton, IL 60187-5593. Offers evangelism and leadership (MA); intercultural studies (MA); intercultural studies/teaching English as a second language (MA); missions (MA); teaching English as a second language (Certificate). Part-time programs available. *Degree requirements:* For master's, thesis or alternative. *Entrance requirements:* For master's, GRE General Test, MAT. Additional exam requirements/recommendations for international students: Required—TOEFL (minimum score 550 paper-based; 80 iBT), IELTS (minimum score 6.5), TOEFL (minimum score 600 paper-based; 90 iBT) or IELTS (minimum score 7.5) for MA in TESOL. Electronic applications accepted.

Wilkes University, College of Graduate and Professional Studies, School of Education, Wilkes-Barre, PA 18766-0002. Offers art and science of teaching (MS Ed); classroom technology (MS Ed); early childhood literacy (MS Ed); educational development and strategies (MS Ed); educational leadership (MS Ed); educational technology (Ed D); higher education administration (Ed D); instructional media (MS Ed); instructional technology (MS Ed); international school leadership (MS Ed); K-12 administration (Ed D); middle level education (MS Ed); online teaching (MS Ed); reading (MS Ed); school business leadership (MS Ed); secondary education (MS Ed), including biology, chemistry, English, history, mathematics; special education (MS Ed); teaching English as a second language (MS Ed); twenty-first century teaching and learning (MS Ed). Part-time and evening/weekend programs available. Postbaccalaureate distance learning degree programs offered (minimal on-campus study). *Students:* 46 full-time (37 women), 1,410 part-time (1,039 women); includes 67 minority (12 Black or African American, non-Hispanic/Latino; 2 American Indian or Alaska Native, non-Hispanic/Latino; 11 Asian, non-Hispanic/Latino; 28 Hispanic/Latino; 1 Native Hawaiian or other Pacific Islander, non-Hispanic/Latino; 13 Two or more races, non-Hispanic/Latino), 6 international. Average age 34. In 2013, 852 master's, 10 doctorates awarded. *Entrance requirements:* Additional exam requirements/recommendations for international students: Required—TOEFL (minimum score 550 paper-based; 79 iBT). *Application deadline:* Applications are processed on a rolling basis. Application fee: $45. Electronic applications accepted. *Expenses:* Contact institution. *Financial support:* Federal Work-Study and unspecified assistantships available. Financial award application deadline: 3/1; financial award applicants required to submit FAFSA. *Unit head:* Dr. Rhonda Waskiewicz, Interim Dean, Education, 570-408-4332, Fax: 570-408-7872, E-mail: rhonda.waskiewicz@wilkes.edu. *Application contact:* Joanne Thomas, Interim Director of Graduate Education, 570-408-4234, Fax: 570-408-7846, E-mail: joanne.thomas1@wilkes.edu.
Website: http://www.wilkes.edu/pages/383.asp.

Wilmington University, College of Education, New Castle, DE 19720-6491. Offers applied technology in education (M Ed); career and technical education (M Ed); educational leadership (Ed D); elementary and secondary school counseling (M Ed); elementary studies (M Ed); ESOL literacy (M Ed); higher education leadership (Ed D); instruction: gifted and talented (M Ed); instruction: teacher of reading (M Ed); instruction: teaching and learning (M Ed); organizational leadership (Ed D); school leadership (M Ed); secondary education (MAT); special education (M Ed). *Accreditation:* NCATE. Part-time and evening/weekend programs available. *Entrance requirements:* For master's, 2 letters of recommendation, interview. Additional exam requirements/recommendations for international students: Required—TOEFL (minimum score 500 paper-based). Electronic applications accepted.

Worcester State University, Graduate Studies, Department of Education, Program in English as a Second Language, Worcester, MA 01602-2597. Offers M Ed. *Faculty:* 14 full-time (11 women), 22 part-time/adjunct (10 women). *Students:* 2 full-time (both women), 5 part-time (4 women); includes 1 minority (Hispanic/Latino). Average age 42. 4 applicants. *Degree requirements:* For master's, one foreign language. *Entrance requirements:* For master's, GRE or MAT, bachelor's degree from accredited institution with minimum cumulative GPA of 2.75, current teaching license in ESL at initial or professional level, essay, official transcripts, two letters of recommendation. Additional exam requirements/recommendations for international students: Required—TOEFL (minimum score 500 paper-based; 61 iBT). *Application deadline:* For fall admission, 6/15 for domestic and international students; for spring admission, 4/1 for domestic and international students. Applications are processed on a rolling basis. Electronic applications accepted. *Expenses: Tuition, area resident:* Part-time $150 per credit. Tuition, state resident: part-time $150 per credit. Tuition, nonresident: part-time $150 per credit. *Required fees:* $114.50 per credit. *Unit head:* Dr. Margarita Perez, Coordinator, 508-929-8609, E-mail: mperez@worcester.edu. *Application contact:* Sara Grady, Assistant Dean of Graduate and Continuing Education, 508-929-8787, Fax: 508-929-8100, E-mail: sara.grady@worcester.edu.

Wright State University, School of Graduate Studies, College of Liberal Arts, Department of English Language and Literatures, Dayton, OH 45435. Offers composition and rhetoric (MA); English (MA); literature (MA); teaching English to speakers of other languages (MA). *Degree requirements:* For master's, thesis optional, portfolio. *Entrance requirements:* For master's, 20 hours in upper-level English. Additional exam requirements/recommendations for international students: Required—TOEFL. *Faculty research:* American literature, world literature in English, applied linguistics, writing theory and pedagogy.

Multilingual and Multicultural Education

Alliant International University–San Francisco, Shirley M. Hufstedler School of Education, Teacher Education Programs, San Francisco, CA 94133-1221. Offers auditory oral education (Certificate); CLAD (Certificate); education specialist: mild/moderate disabilities (Credential); preliminary multiple subject (Credential); preliminary single subject (Credential); professional clear multiple subject (Credential); professional clear single subject (Credential); special education (MA); teaching (MA); TESOL (Certificate). Part-time and evening/weekend programs available. *Faculty:* 6 full-time (4 women), 10 part-time/adjunct (8 women). *Students:* 16 full-time (10 women), 135 part-time (97 women); includes 22 minority (6 Black or African American, non-Hispanic/Latino; 6 Asian, non-Hispanic/Latino; 8 Hispanic/Latino; 2 Two or more races, non-Hispanic/Latino). Average age 41. 172 applicants, 94% accepted, 142 enrolled. In 2013, 11 master's, 167 other advanced degrees awarded. *Degree requirements:* For master's, thesis. *Entrance requirements:* For degree, California Basic Educational Skills Test, minimum GPA of 2.5. Additional exam requirements/recommendations for international students: Required—TOEFL (minimum score 550 paper-based), TWE (minimum score 5). *Application deadline:* For fall admission, 7/1 priority date for domestic and international students; for spring admission, 12/1 priority date for domestic and international students. Applications are processed on a rolling basis. Application fee: $55. Electronic applications accepted. *Financial support:* Career-related internships or fieldwork, Federal Work-Study, institutionally sponsored loans, and scholarships/grants available. Financial award application deadline: 2/15; financial award applicants required to submit FAFSA. *Faculty research:* Curriculum development, first year teachers, cross-cultural issues in teaching, biliteracy. *Unit head:* Dr. Debra Reeves-Gutierrez, Program Director, 415-955-2084, Fax: 415-955-2179, E-mail: admissions@alliant.edu. *Application contact:* Alliant International University Central Contact Center, 866-U-ALLIANT, Fax: 858-635-4555, E-mail: admissions@alliant.edu.
Website: http://www.alliant.edu/.

American College of Education, Graduate Programs, Chicago, IL 60606. Offers curriculum and instruction (M Ed), including bilingual, ESL; educational leadership (M Ed); educational technology (M Ed).

American University, College of Arts and Sciences, Washington, DC 20016-8012. Offers addiction and addictive behavior (Certificate); anthropology (PhD); applied microeconomics (Certificate); applied statistics (Certificate); art history (MA); arts management (MA, Certificate); Asian studies (Certificate); audio production (Certificate); audio technology (MA); behavior, cognition, and neuroscience (PhD); bilingual education (MA, Certificate); biology (MA, MS); chemistry (MS); clinical psychology (PhD); computer science (MS, Certificate); creative writing (MFA); curriculum and instruction (M Ed, Certificate); economics (MA, PhD); environmental assessment (Certificate); environmental science (MS); ethics, peace, and global affairs (MA); gender analysis in economics (Certificate); health promotion management (MS); history (MA, PhD); international arts management (Certificate); international economic relations (Certificate); international economics (MA); international training and education (MA); literature (MA); mathematics (MA); North American studies (Certificate); nutrition education (MS, Certificate); philosophy (MA); professional science: biotechnology (MS); professional science: environmental assessment (MS); professional science: quantitative analysis (MS); psychobiology of healing (Certificate); psychology (MA); psychology: general (PhD); public anthropology (MA, Certificate); public sociology (Certificate); social research (Certificate); sociology (MA); Spanish: Latin American studies (MA); special education: learning disabilities (MA); statistics (MS); studio art (MFA); teaching (MAT); teaching English as a foreign language (MA); teaching: early childhood (Certificate); teaching: elementary (Certificate); teaching: ESOL (Certificate); teaching: secondary (Certificate); technology in arts management (Certificate); TESOL (MA); translation: French (Certificate); translation: Russian (Certificate); translation: Spanish (Certificate); women's, gender, and sexuality studies (Certificate). Part-time and evening/weekend programs available. Postbaccalaureate distance learning degree programs offered (no on-campus study). *Faculty:* 358 full-time (187 women), 254 part-time/adjunct (127 women). *Students:* 627 full-time (411 women), 416 part-time (300 women); includes 206 minority (91 Black or African American, non-Hispanic/Latino; 5 American Indian or Alaska Native, non-Hispanic/Latino; 32 Asian, non-Hispanic/Latino; 64 Hispanic/Latino; 1 Native Hawaiian or other Pacific Islander, non-Hispanic/Latino; 13 Two or more races, non-Hispanic/Latino), 124 international. Average age 29. 1,672 applicants, 52% accepted, 361 enrolled. In 2013, 382 master's, 38 doctorates, 33 other advanced degrees awarded. Terminal master's awarded for partial completion of doctoral program. *Degree requirements:* For master's, comprehensive exam (for some programs), thesis (for some programs); for doctorate, comprehensive exam (for some programs), thesis/dissertation. *Entrance requirements:* For master's, GRE, minimum GPA of 3.0 in last 60 credit hours, letter of recommendation, statement of purpose, resume, unofficial transcript; for doctorate, GRE, minimum GPA of 3.0 for all graduate work, letter of recommendation, statement of purpose, resume, unofficial transcript. Additional exam requirements/recommendations for international students: Required—TOEFL (minimum score 600 paper-based; 100 iBT), IELTS (minimum score 7). *Application deadline:* For fall admission, 2/1 for domestic students; for spring admission, 10/1 for domestic students. Applications are processed on a rolling basis. Application fee: $55. Electronic applications accepted. *Expenses: Tuition:* Full-time $25,920; part-time $1482 per credit hour. *Required fees:* $430. Tuition and fees vary according to course load and program. *Financial support:* Fellowships, research assistantships with full and partial tuition reimbursements, teaching assistantships with full and partial tuition reimbursements, career-related internships or fieldwork, Federal Work-Study, institutionally sponsored loans, scholarships/grants, traineeships, tuition waivers (full and partial), and unspecified assistantships available. Support available to part-time students. Financial award applicants required to submit FAFSA. *Unit head:* Dr. Peter Starr, Dean, 202-885-2446, Fax: 202-885-2429, E-mail: pstarr@american.edu. *Application contact:* Kathleen Clowery, Associate Director, Graduate Enrollment Management, 202-885-3621, Fax: 202-885-1505, E-mail: clowery@american.edu.
Website: http://www.american.edu/cas/.

Azusa Pacific University, School of Education, Department of Foundations and Transdisciplinary Studies, Program in Curriculum and Instruction in Multicultural Contexts, Azusa, CA 91702-7000. Offers MA Ed. *Accreditation:* NCATE. Part-time and evening/weekend programs available. *Degree requirements:* For master's, core exams, oral presentation. *Entrance requirements:* For master's, 12 units of course work in education, minimum GPA of 3.0. *Faculty research:* Diversity in teacher education programs, teacher morale, student perception of school, case study instruction.

Bank Street College of Education, Graduate School, Program in Bilingual Education, New York, NY 10025. Offers bilingual childhood special education (Ed M); bilingual early childhood general education (MS Ed); bilingual early childhood special and general education (MS Ed); bilingual early childhood special education (Ed M, MS Ed); bilingual elementary/childhood general education (MS Ed); bilingual elementary/childhood special and general education (MS Ed); bilingual elementary/childhood special education (MS Ed). *Degree requirements:* For master's, thesis. *Entrance requirements:* For master's, interview, fluency in Spanish and English, essays. Additional exam requirements/recommendations for international students: Required—TOEFL (minimum score 600 paper-based; 100 iBT), IELTS (minimum score 7). Electronic applications

accepted. *Faculty research:* Dual language education, language immersion, bilingual education in the urban classroom, community and school partnerships.

Belhaven University, School of Education, Jackson, MS 39202-1789. Offers educational technology (M Ed); elementary education (M Ed, MAT); reading literacy (M Ed); secondary education (M Ed, MAT). Part-time and evening/weekend programs available. Postbaccalaureate distance learning degree programs offered (no on-campus study). *Faculty:* 7 full-time (6 women), 15 part-time/adjunct (10 women). *Students:* 1 full-time (0 women), 406 part-time (311 women); includes 254 minority (250 Black or African American, non-Hispanic/Latino; 2 Hispanic/Latino; 2 Two or more races, non-Hispanic/Latino). Average age 36. 273 applicants, 67% accepted, 162 enrolled. In 2013, 24 master's awarded. *Degree requirements:* For master's, comprehensive exam, portfolio. *Entrance requirements:* For master's, PRAXIS I and II, minimum GPA of 2.8. *Application deadline:* Applications are processed on a rolling basis. Application fee: $25. Electronic applications accepted. *Financial support:* Federal Work-Study, scholarships/grants, tuition waivers (full), and unspecified assistantships available. Support available to part-time students. Financial award applicants required to submit FAFSA. *Unit head:* Dr. David Hand, Dean, 601-965-7020, E-mail: dhand@belhaven.edu. *Application contact:* Amanda Slaughter, Assistant Vice President for Adult and Graduate Enrollment and Student Services, 601-968-8727, Fax: 601-968-5953, E-mail: gradadmission@belhaven.edu.
Website: http://graduateed.belhaven.edu.

Bennington College, Graduate Programs, MA in Teaching a Second Language Program, Bennington, VT 05201. Offers education (MATSL); foreign language education (MATSL); French (MATSL); Spanish (MATSL). Part-time programs available. *Degree requirements:* For master's, one foreign language, 2 major projects and presentations. *Entrance requirements:* For master's, Oral Proficiency Interview (OPI). Additional exam requirements/recommendations for international students: Required—TOEFL (minimum score 577 paper-based; 91 iBT). *Expenses:* Contact institution. *Faculty research:* Acquisition, evaluation, assessment, conceptual teaching and learning, content-driven communication, applied linguistics.

Biola University, School of Education, La Mirada, CA 90639-0001. Offers apologetics (MA Ed); curriculum and instruction (MA Ed, MAT, Certificate); early childhood (MA Ed, MAT); history and philosophy of science (MA Ed, MAT); linguistics and inter-cultural studies (MAT); linguistics and international studies (MA Ed); multiple subject (MAT); single subject (MAT); special education (MA Ed, MAT, Certificate); TESOL (MA Ed, MAT). Part-time and evening/weekend programs available. Postbaccalaureate distance learning degree programs offered (no on-campus study). *Faculty:* 14. *Students:* 51 full-time (38 women), 101 part-time (83 women); includes 47 minority (8 Black or African American, non-Hispanic/Latino; 1 American Indian or Alaska Native, non-Hispanic/Latino; 32 Asian, non-Hispanic/Latino; 6 Two or more races, non-Hispanic/Latino), 4 international. In 2013, 33 master's awarded. *Entrance requirements:* For master's, CBEST, CSET. Additional exam requirements/recommendations for international students: Required—TOEFL (minimum score 100 iBT). *Application deadline:* For fall admission, 7/1 for domestic students, 6/1 for international students; for spring admission, 12/1 for domestic students; for summer admission, 5/1 for domestic students. Applications are processed on a rolling basis. Application fee: $55. Electronic applications accepted. *Financial support:* Scholarships/grants available. Support available to part-time students. Financial award applicants required to submit FAFSA. *Faculty research:* Early childhood education, elementary education, special education, curriculum development, teacher preparation. *Unit head:* Dr. June Hetzel, Dean, 562-903-4715. *Application contact:* Graduate Admissions Office, 562-903-4752, E-mail: graduate.admissions@biola.edu.
Website: http://education.biola.edu/.

Brooklyn College of the City University of New York, Division of Graduate Studies, School of Education, Program in Childhood Education, Brooklyn, NY 11210-2889. Offers bilingual education (MS Ed); liberal arts (MS Ed); mathematics (MS Ed); science/environmental education (MS Ed). Part-time and evening/weekend programs available. *Entrance requirements:* For master's, LAST, interview, previous course work in education, writing sample, resume, 2 letters of recommendation. Additional exam requirements/recommendations for international students: Required—TOEFL (minimum score 500 paper-based; 61 iBT). Electronic applications accepted. *Faculty research:* Emotional intelligence, multiculturalism, arts immersion, the Holocaust.

Brown University, Graduate School, Department of Portuguese and Brazilian Studies, Providence, RI 02912. Offers Brazilian studies (AM); English as a second language and cross-cultural studies (AM); Portuguese and Brazilian studies (AM, PhD); Portuguese bilingual education and cross-cultural studies (AM). *Degree requirements:* For doctorate, thesis/dissertation.

Buffalo State College, State University of New York, The Graduate School, Faculty of Applied Science and Education, Department of Exceptional Education, Program in Teaching Bilingual Exceptional Individuals, Buffalo, NY 14222-1095. Offers MS Ed. *Accreditation:* NCATE. Part-time and evening/weekend programs available. *Degree requirements:* For master's, project. *Entrance requirements:* For master's, minimum GPA of 2.5. Additional exam requirements/recommendations for international students: Required—TOEFL (minimum score 550 paper-based).

California State University, Dominguez Hills, College of Education, Division of Graduate Education, Program in Multicultural Education, Carson, CA 90747-0001. Offers MA. Part-time and evening/weekend programs available. *Faculty:* 1 (woman) full-time. *Students:* 10 full-time (6 women), 30 part-time (24 women); includes 29 minority (10 Black or African American, non-Hispanic/Latino; 4 Asian, non-Hispanic/Latino; 15 Hispanic/Latino), 1 international. Average age 38. 14 applicants, 100% accepted, 11 enrolled. In 2013, 16 master's awarded. *Degree requirements:* For master's, comprehensive exam. *Entrance requirements:* For master's, minimum GPA of 2.75. *Application deadline:* For fall admission, 8/1 for domestic students; for spring admission, 10/1 for domestic students. Applications are processed on a rolling basis. Application fee: $55. *Expenses:* Tuition, state resident: full-time $6738. Tuition, nonresident: full-time $13,434. *Required fees:* $622. *Faculty research:* English learning, intercultural communications. *Unit head:* Dr. Maximilian Contreras, Chairperson, 310-343-3918 Ext. 3524, E-mail: mcontreras@csudh.edu. *Application contact:* Admissions Office, 310-243-3530.
Website: http://www4.csudh.edu/coe/programs/grad-prgs/multicultural-education/index.

California State University, Fullerton, Graduate Studies, College of Education, Department of Elementary and Bilingual Education, Fullerton, CA 92834-9480. Offers bilingual/bicultural education (MS); educational technology (MS); elementary curriculum and instruction (MS). *Accreditation:* NCATE. Part-time programs available. *Students:* 140 full-time (118 women), 97 part-time (89 women); includes 101 minority (3 Black or African American, non-Hispanic/Latino; 31 Asian, non-Hispanic/Latino; 61 Hispanic/Latino; 6 Two or more races, non-Hispanic/Latino). Average age 30. 184 applicants, 68% accepted, 99 enrolled. In 2013, 102 master's awarded. *Degree requirements:* For master's, comprehensive exam, project or thesis. *Entrance requirements:* For master's, minimum GPA of 2.5, teaching certificate. Application fee: $55. *Financial support:* Career-related internships or fieldwork, Federal Work-Study, institutionally sponsored loans, and scholarships/grants available. Support available to part-time students. Financial award application deadline: 3/1; financial award applicants required to submit FAFSA. *Faculty research:* Teacher training and tracking, model for improvement of teaching. *Unit head:* Lisa Kirtman, Chair, 657-278-4731. *Application contact:* Admissions/Applications, 657-278-2371.

California State University, Northridge, Graduate Studies, College of Education, Department of Elementary Education, Northridge, CA 91330. Offers curriculum and instruction (MA); language and literacy (MA); multilingual/multicultural education (MA); teaching and learning (MA). *Accreditation:* NCATE. Part-time and evening/weekend programs available. *Degree requirements:* For master's, comprehensive exam. *Entrance requirements:* For master's, GRE General Test or minimum GPA of 3.0. Additional exam requirements/recommendations for international students: Required—TOEFL.

California State University, Sacramento, Office of Graduate Studies, College of Education, Department of Bilingual/Multicultural Education, Sacramento, CA 95819. Offers MA. Part-time programs available. *Degree requirements:* For master's, thesis or alternative. *Entrance requirements:* For master's, minimum GPA of 2.5. Additional exam requirements/recommendations for international students: Required—TOEFL. *Application deadline:* For fall admission, 3/1 for domestic and international students; for spring admission, 9/15 for domestic students, 9/30 for international students. Applications are processed on a rolling basis. Application fee: $55. Electronic applications accepted. *Financial support:* Career-related internships or fieldwork and Federal Work-Study available. Support available to part-time students. Financial award application deadline: 3/1; financial award applicants required to submit FAFSA. *Unit head:* Susan Heredia, Chair, 916-278-6807, E-mail: heredias@csus.edu. *Application contact:* Jose Martinez, Graduate Admissions Supervisor, 916-278-7871, E-mail: martinj@skymail.csus.edu.
Website: http://www.edweb.csus.edu/bmed.

California State University, San Bernardino, Graduate Studies, College of Education, Program in Bilingual/Cross-Cultural Education, San Bernardino, CA 92407-2397. Offers MA. *Accreditation:* NCATE. *Students:* 2 part-time (both women); both minorities (both Hispanic/Latino). Average age 42. 1 applicant. In 2013, 1 master's awarded. *Unit head:* Dr. Jay Fiene, Dean, 909-537-7621, E-mail: jfiene@csusb.edu. *Application contact:* Dr. Jeffrey Thompson, Dean of Graduate Studies, 909-537-5058, E-mail: jthompso@csusb.edu.

California State University, Stanislaus, College of Education, Program in Education (MA), Turlock, CA 95382. Offers curriculum and instruction (MA), including education technology, elementary education, multilingual education, physical education, reading, secondary education, special education; school administration (MA); school counseling (MA). Part-time and evening/weekend programs available. *Degree requirements:* For master's, comprehensive exam (for some programs), thesis (for some programs). *Entrance requirements:* For master's, MAT, GRE, or CBEST (varies by concentration), 3 letters of recommendation, personal statement. Additional exam requirements/recommendations for international students: Required—TOEFL (minimum score 550 paper-based). Electronic applications accepted. *Faculty research:* Children's perspectives on historical events, method elementary schools dual language education, K-12 reading programs.

Chicago State University, School of Graduate and Professional Studies, College of Education, Department of Special Education, Early Childhood Education and Bilingual Education, Program in Bilingual Education, Chicago, IL 60628. Offers M Ed. *Accreditation:* NCATE. *Degree requirements:* For master's, comprehensive exam, thesis optional. *Entrance requirements:* For master's, minimum GPA of 2.75.

City College of the City University of New York, Graduate School, School of Education, Program in Bilingual Education, New York, NY 10031-9198. Offers MS. *Accreditation:* NCATE. Part-time programs available. *Degree requirements:* For master's, thesis. *Entrance requirements:* For master's, Liberal Arts and Sciences Test (LAST), Content Specialty Test (CST). Additional exam requirements/recommendations for international students: Required—TOEFL.

The College at Brockport, State University of New York, School of Education and Human Services, Department of Education and Human Development, Program in Bilingual Education, Brockport, NY 14420-2997. Offers MS Ed, AGC. *Accreditation:* NCATE. Part-time programs available. *Students:* 9 part-time (8 women); includes 5 minority (all Hispanic/Latino). *Degree requirements:* For master's, thesis or alternative. *Entrance requirements:* For master's, minimum GPA of 3.0, letters of recommendation, statement of objectives, demonstrated proficiency in Spanish at the advanced level, appropriate provisional or initial teaching certificate; for AGC, minimum GPA of 3.0, appropriate New York state teaching certification, demonstrated proficiency in Spanish at the advanced level. Additional exam requirements/recommendations for international students: Required—TOEFL (minimum score 550 paper-based; 79 iBT), IELTS (minimum score 6.5). *Application deadline:* For fall admission, 3/15 priority date for domestic and international students; for spring admission, 10/15 priority date for domestic and international students. Application fee: $80. Electronic applications accepted. *Expenses:* Tuition, state resident: full-time $9870. Tuition, nonresident: full-time $18,350. *Required fees:* $1848. *Financial support:* Federal Work-Study, scholarships/grants, and unspecified assistantships available. Support available to part-time students. Financial award application deadline: 3/15; financial award applicants required to submit FAFSA. *Unit head:* Dr. Don Halquist, Chairperson, 585-395-5550, Fax: 585-395-2172, E-mail: dhalquis@brockport.edu. *Application contact:* Michael Harrison, Coordinator of Certification and Graduate Advisement, 585-395-2326, Fax: 585-395-2172, E-mail: mharriso@brockport.edu.
Website: http://www.brockport.edu/ehd.

College of Mount Saint Vincent, School of Professional and Continuing Studies, Department of Teacher Education, Riverdale, NY 10471-1093. Offers instructional technology and global perspectives (Certificate); middle level education (Certificate); multicultural studies (Certificate); urban and multicultural education (MS Ed). *Accreditation:* Teacher Education Accreditation Council. Part-time programs available. *Degree requirements:* For master's, comprehensive exam. *Entrance requirements:* For master's, interview, New York teaching certificate. Additional exam requirements/recommendations for international students: Required—TOEFL.

The College of New Rochelle, Graduate School, Division of Education, Program in Teaching English as a Second Language and Multilingual/Multicultural Education, New Rochelle, NY 10805-2308. Offers bilingual education (Certificate); teaching English as a second language (MS Ed). Part-time and evening/weekend programs available. *Degree requirements:* For master's, practicum. *Entrance requirements:* For master's, interview, minimum GPA of 3.0 in field, 2.7 overall. *Expenses: Tuition:* Part-time $894 per credit. *Required fees:* $300 per semester. One-time fee: $200. Tuition and fees vary according to course load.

Columbia International University, Columbia Graduate School, Columbia, SC 29230-3122. Offers Bible teaching (MABT); Christian higher education leadership (Ed D); Christian school educational leadership (Ed D); counseling (MACN); curriculum and instruction (M Ed), including Christian school guidance, English as a second language, learning disabilities, school technology; early childhood and elementary education (MAT); educational administration (M Ed); teaching English as a foreign language

(Certificate); teaching English as a foreign language and intercultural studies (MATF). Part-time and evening/weekend programs available. *Degree requirements:* For master's, internships, professional project. *Entrance requirements:* For master's, Minnesota Multiphasic Personality Inventory, MAT, minimum GPA of 2.7. Additional exam requirements/recommendations for international students: Required—TOEFL. Electronic applications accepted.

Dallas Baptist University, Dorothy M. Bush College of Education, Program in Reading and English as a Second Language, Dallas, TX 75211-9299. Offers bilingual education (M Ed); English as a second language (M Ed); master reading teacher (M Ed); reading specialist (M Ed). Part-time and evening/weekend programs available. *Entrance requirements:* For master's, GRE General Test, minimum GPA of 3.0. Additional exam requirements/recommendations for international students: Required—TOEFL, IELTS. Application fee: $25. *Expenses: Tuition:* Full-time $13,410; part-time $745 per credit hour. *Required fees:* $300; $150 per semester. Tuition and fees vary according to degree level. *Financial support:* Federal Work-Study, institutionally sponsored loans, scholarships/grants, and tuition waivers (full and partial) available. Support available to part-time students. Financial award applicants required to submit FAFSA. *Unit head:* Amie Sarker, Director, 214-333-5200, Fax: 214-333-5551, E-mail: graduate@dbu.edu. *Application contact:* Kit P. Montgomery, Director of Graduate Programs, 214-333-5242, Fax: 214-333-5579, E-mail: graduate@dbu.edu. Website: http://www3.dbu.edu/graduate/english_reading.asp.

DePaul University, College of Education, Chicago, IL 60614. Offers bilingual bicultural education (M Ed, MA); counseling (M Ed, MA), including clinical mental health counseling, college student development, school counseling; curriculum studies (M Ed, MA, Ed D); early childhood education (M Ed, MA, Ed D); educating adults (MA); educational leadership (M Ed, MA, Ed D), including administration and supervision (M Ed, MA), principal preparation (M Ed, MA); elementary education (MA); mathematics education (MA); mathematics for teaching (MS); middle school mathematics education (MS); reading specialist (M Ed, MA); secondary education (M Ed); social and cultural foundations in education (MA); special education (M Ed, MA); world languages education (M Ed, MA). Part-time and evening/weekend programs available. Postbaccalaureate distance learning degree programs offered (no on-campus study). *Faculty:* 61 full-time (35 women), 59 part-time/adjunct (43 women). *Students:* 628 full-time (486 women), 324 part-time (243 women); includes 304 minority (144 Black or African American, non-Hispanic/Latino; 1 American Indian or Alaska Native, non-Hispanic/Latino; 38 Asian, non-Hispanic/Latino; 98 Hispanic/Latino; 23 Two or more races, non-Hispanic/Latino), 24 international. Average age 30. In 2013, 465 master's, 4 doctorates awarded. *Degree requirements:* For doctorate, thesis/dissertation. *Application deadline:* For fall admission, 8/15 for domestic students; for winter admission, 12/1 for domestic students; for spring admission, 3/1 for domestic students. Applications are processed on a rolling basis. Application fee: $40. Electronic applications accepted. Tuition and fees vary according to course level, course load and degree level. *Financial support:* Application deadline: 12/31; applicants required to submit FAFSA. *Unit head:* Dr. Paul Zionts, Dean, 773-325-7581, Fax: 773-325-7713, E-mail: pzionts@depaul.edu. *Application contact:* Farrah Dalal, Assistant Director, 773-325-2465, Fax: 773-325-2270, E-mail: fdalal@depaul.edu. Website: http://education.depaul.edu.

Eastern Michigan University, Graduate School, College of Education, Department of Teacher Education, Ypsilanti, MI 48197. Offers curriculum and instruction (MA); early childhood education (MA); educational media and technology (MA, Graduate Certificate); educational psychology and assessment (MA, Graduate Certificate), including educational assessment (Graduate Certificate), educational psychology (MA); educational studies (PhD); K-12 education (MA), including curriculum and instruction, elementary education, K-12 education, middle school education, secondary school education; reading (MA); social foundations (MA); urban/diversity education (MA). Part-time and evening/weekend programs available. Postbaccalaureate distance learning degree programs offered (minimal on-campus study). *Faculty:* 38 full-time (30 women). *Students:* 28 full-time (17 women), 378 part-time (320 women); includes 79 minority (54 Black or African American, non-Hispanic/Latino; 3 American Indian or Alaska Native, non-Hispanic/Latino; 10 Asian, non-Hispanic/Latino; 8 Hispanic/Latino; 4 Two or more races, non-Hispanic/Latino), 10 international. Average age 35. 172 applicants, 72% accepted, 76 enrolled. In 2013, 121 master's, 3 doctorates, 510 other advanced degrees awarded. *Entrance requirements:* For master's, GRE. Additional exam requirements/recommendations for international students: Required—TOEFL. *Application deadline:* Applications are processed on a rolling basis. Application fee: $35. *Expenses:* Tuition, state resident: full-time $12,300; part-time $466 per credit hour. Tuition, nonresident: full-time $23,159; part-time $918 per credit hour. *Required fees:* $71 per credit hour. $46 per semester. One-time fee: $100. Tuition and fees vary according to course level and degree level. *Financial support:* Fellowships, research assistantships with full tuition reimbursements, teaching assistantships with full tuition reimbursements, career-related internships or fieldwork, Federal Work-Study, institutionally sponsored loans, scholarships/grants, tuition waivers (partial), and unspecified assistantships available. Support available to part-time students. Financial award applicants required to submit FAFSA. *Unit head:* Dr. Martha Kinney-Sedgwick, Interim Department Head, 734-487-3260, Fax: 734-487-2101, E-mail: mkinneys@emich.edu. *Application contact:* Dr. Anne Bednar, Advisor, 734-487-3260, Fax: 734-487-2101, E-mail: anne.bednar@emich.edu. Website: http://www.emich.edu/coe/ted/.

Eastern New Mexico University, Graduate School, College of Education and Technology, Department of Curriculum and Instruction, Portales, NM 88130. Offers bilingual education (M Ed); educational technology (M Ed); elementary education (M Ed); English as a second language (M Ed); pedagogy and learning (M Ed); professional technical education (M Ed); reading/literacy (M Ed). Part-time programs available. Postbaccalaureate distance learning degree programs offered (minimal on-campus study). *Degree requirements:* For master's, comprehensive exam, thesis optional. *Entrance requirements:* For master's, minimum GPA of 3.0, photocopy of teaching license, writing assessment, letter of recommendation. Additional exam requirements/recommendations for international students: Required—TOEFL (minimum score 550 paper-based; 79 iBT), IELTS (minimum score 6). Electronic applications accepted.

Eastern University, Graduate Education Programs, St. Davids, PA 19087-3696. Offers ESL program specialist (K-12) (Certificate); general supervisor (PreK-12) (Certificate); health and physical education (K-12) (Certificate); middle level (4-8) (Certificate); multicultural education (M Ed); pre K-4 (Certificate); pre K-4 with special education (Certificate); reading (M Ed); reading specialist (K-12) (Certificate); reading supervisor (K-12) (Certificate); school health services (M Ed); school health supervisor (Certificate); school nurse (Certificate); school principalship (K-12) (Certificate); secondary biology education (7-12) (Certificate); secondary chemistry education (7-12) (Certificate); secondary communication education (7-12) (Certificate); secondary education (7-12) (Certificate); secondary English education (7-12) (Certificate); secondary math education (7-12) (Certificate); secondary social studies education (7-12) (Certificate); special education (M Ed); special education (7-12) (Certificate); special education (Pre K-8) (Certificate); special education supervisor (N-12) (Certificate); TESOL (M Ed); world language (Certificate), including French, Mandarin Chinese, Spanish. Part-time

and evening/weekend programs available. Postbaccalaureate distance learning degree programs offered (no on-campus study). *Faculty:* 22 full-time (11 women), 26 part-time/adjunct (18 women). *Students:* 77 full-time (58 women), 223 part-time (149 women); includes 112 minority (81 Black or African American, non-Hispanic/Latino; 1 American Indian or Alaska Native, non-Hispanic/Latino; 9 Asian, non-Hispanic/Latino; 18 Hispanic/Latino; 1 Native Hawaiian or other Pacific Islander, non-Hispanic/Latino; 2 Two or more races, non-Hispanic/Latino), 7 international. Average age 34. 94 applicants, 100% accepted, 81 enrolled. In 2013, 120 master's awarded. *Entrance requirements:* For master's, minimum GPA of 2.5 (for M Ed); for Certificate, minimum GPA of 3.0 for certifications. Additional exam requirements/recommendations for international students: Required—TOEFL. *Application deadline:* For fall admission, 8/14 for domestic students; for spring admission, 12/20 for domestic students. Applications are processed on a rolling basis. Application fee: $35. Application fee is waived when completed online. *Expenses: Tuition:* Full-time $15,600; part-time $650 per credit. *Required fees:* $27.50 per semester. One-time fee: $50. Tuition and fees vary according to course load, degree level and program. *Financial support:* In 2013–14, 84 students received support, including 6 research assistantships with partial tuition reimbursements available (averaging $7,710 per year); scholarships/grants and unspecified assistantships also available. Financial award application deadline: 3/15; financial award applicants required to submit FAFSA. *Unit head:* Harry Gutelius, Associate Dean, 610-341-1729. *Application contact:* Michael Perpiglia, Associate Director of Enrollment, 610-341-5947, Fax: 484-581-1276, E-mail: mperpigl@eastern.edu. Website: http://www.eastern.edu/academics/programs/loeb-school-education-0/graduateprograms.

Edgewood College, Program in Education, Madison, WI 53711-1997. Offers adult learning (MA Ed); bilingual teaching and learning (MA Ed); director of instruction (Certificate); director of special education and pupil services (Certificate); education (MA Ed); educational administration (MA Ed); educational leadership (Ed D); professional studies (MA Ed); program coordinator (Certificate); reading administration (MA Ed); school business administration (Certificate); school principalship K-12 (Certificate); special education (MA Ed); sustainability leadership (MA Ed); teaching and learning (MA Ed); teaching English to speakers of other languages (TESOL) (MA Ed). *Accreditation:* NCATE (one or more programs are accredited). Part-time and evening/weekend programs available. *Students:* 159 full-time (95 women), 164 part-time (121 women); includes 61 minority (19 Black or African American, non-Hispanic/Latino; 9 Asian, non-Hispanic/Latino; 25 Hispanic/Latino; 8 Two or more races, non-Hispanic/Latino), 27 international. Average age 36. In 2013, 51 master's, 22 doctorates awarded. *Degree requirements:* For master's, practicum, research project; for doctorate, comprehensive exam, thesis/dissertation. *Entrance requirements:* For master's, minimum GPA of 2.75, 2 letters of recommendation, personal statement; for doctorate, resume, letter of intent, 2 letters of recommendation, interview, writing sample. Additional exam requirements/recommendations for international students: Required—TOEFL (minimum score 525 paper-based; 72 iBT). *Application deadline:* For fall admission, 8/15 for domestic students, 5/1 for international students; for spring admission, 1/8 for domestic students, 11/1 for international students. Applications are processed on a rolling basis. Application fee: $30. Electronic applications accepted. *Unit head:* Dr. Timothy Slekar, Dean, E-mail: tslekar@edgewood.edu. *Application contact:* Joann Eastman, Admissions Counselor, 608-663-3250, Fax: 608-663-2214, E-mail: gps@edgewood.edu. Website: http://www.edgewood.edu/Academics/School-of-Education.

Fairfield University, Graduate School of Education and Allied Professions, Fairfield, CT 06824-5195. Offers applied behavior analysis (ATC); applied psychology (MA); clinical mental health counseling (MA, CAS); early childhood studies (ATC); educational technology (MA); elementary education (MA, CAS); family studies (MA); integration of spirituality and religion in counseling (ATC); marriage and family therapy (MA); school counseling (MA, CAS); school psychology (MA, CAS); school-based marriage and family therapy (ATC); secondary education (MA); special education (MA, CAS); substance abuse counseling (ATC); teaching (Certificate); teaching and foundations (MA, CAS); TESOL, world languages, and bilingual education (MA, CAS). *Accreditation:* NCATE. Part-time and evening/weekend programs available. *Faculty:* 24 full-time (21 women), 39 part-time/adjunct (27 women). *Students:* 154 full-time (130 women), 307 part-time (248 women); includes 75 minority (14 Black or African American, non-Hispanic/Latino; 1 American Indian or Alaska Native, non-Hispanic/Latino; 10 Asian, non-Hispanic/Latino; 44 Hispanic/Latino; 6 Two or more races, non-Hispanic/Latino), 13 international. Average age 34. 263 applicants, 41% accepted, 91 enrolled. In 2013, 149 master's, 21 other advanced degrees awarded. *Degree requirements:* For master's, comprehensive exam. *Entrance requirements:* For master's, PRAXIS I (for certification programs), minimum GPA of 3.0, 2 recommendations, resume. Additional exam requirements/recommendations for international students: Required—TOEFL (minimum score 550 paper-based; 84 iBT) or IELTS (minimum score 7.5). *Application deadline:* For fall admission, 2/15 for international students; for spring admission, 10/1 for international students. Application fee: $60. Electronic applications accepted. *Expenses: Tuition:* Part-time $675 per credit hour. Tuition and fees vary according to program. *Financial support:* In 2013–14, 55 students received support. Career-related internships or fieldwork and unspecified assistantships available. Financial award applicants required to submit FAFSA. *Faculty research:* Literacy, adolescent psychology, special education, teaching development, mentoring for professional development, multicultural education. *Total annual research expenditures:* $325,000. *Unit head:* Dr. Robert D. Hannafin, Dean, 203-254-4250, Fax: 203-254-4241, E-mail: rhannafin@fairfield.edu. *Application contact:* Marianne Gumpper, Director of Graduate and Continuing Studies Admission, 203-254-4184, Fax: 203-254-4073, E-mail: gradadmis@fairfield.edu. Website: http://www.fairfield.edu/academics/schoolscollegescenters/graduateschoolofeducationalliedprofessions/graduateprograms/.

Fairleigh Dickinson University, Metropolitan Campus, University College: Arts, Sciences, and Professional Studies, Peter Sammartino School of Education, Program in Multilingual Education, Teaneck, NJ 07666-1914. Offers MA. *Accreditation:* Teacher Education Accreditation Council.

Florida Atlantic University, College of Education, Department of Curriculum, Culture, and Educational Inquiry, Boca Raton, FL 33431-0991. Offers curriculum and instruction (M Ed, PhD, Ed S); early childhood education (M Ed); multicultural education (M Ed); TESOL and bilingual education (MA). Part-time and evening/weekend programs available. *Faculty:* 9 full-time (8 women), 3 part-time/adjunct (all women). *Students:* 17 full-time (14 women), 119 part-time (93 women); includes 41 minority (18 Black or African American, non-Hispanic/Latino; 4 Asian, non-Hispanic/Latino; 18 Hispanic/Latino; 1 Two or more races, non-Hispanic/Latino), 5 international. Average age 36. 49 applicants, 39% accepted, 13 enrolled. In 2013, 31 master's, 2 other advanced degrees awarded. *Entrance requirements:* Additional exam requirements/recommendations for international students: Required—TOEFL (minimum score 500 paper-based; 61 iBT), IELTS (minimum score 6). *Application deadline:* For fall admission, 7/1 for domestic students, 2/15 for international students; for spring admission, 11/1 for domestic students, 7/15 for international students. Application fee: $30. *Expenses:* Tuition, state resident: full-time $6660; part-time $370 per credit hour. Tuition, nonresident: full-time $18,450; part-time $1025 per credit hour. Tuition and fees vary according to course load. *Faculty research:* Multicultural education, early intervention strategies, family literacy,

religious diversity in schools, early childhood curriculum. *Unit head:* Dr. Emery Hyslop-Margison, Interim Chair, 561-297-3965, E-mail: ehyslopmargison@fau.edu. *Application contact:* Dr. Eliah Watlington, Associate Dean, 561-296-8520, Fax: 261-297-2991, E-mail: ewatling@fau.edu.
Website: http://www.coe.fau.edu/academicdepartments/ccei/.

Florida Atlantic University, College of Education, Department of Teaching and Learning, Boca Raton, FL 33431-0991. Offers curriculum and instruction (M Ed), including art, biology, chemistry, English, French, German, mathematics, music, physics, Pre-K and primary education, reading, social sciences, Spanish; elementary education (M Ed); environmental education (M Ed); reading education (M Ed); social foundations of education (M Ed), including educational psychology, educational technology, multilingual education. *Accreditation:* NCATE. Part-time and evening/weekend programs available. *Faculty:* 16 full-time (12 women), 1 (woman) part-time/adjunct. *Students:* 56 full-time (46 women), 96 part-time (78 women); includes 39 minority (10 Black or African American, non-Hispanic/Latino; 6 Asian, non-Hispanic/Latino; 20 Hispanic/Latino; 3 Two or more races, non-Hispanic/Latino), 4 international. Average age 32. 101 applicants, 54% accepted, 42 enrolled. In 2013, 64 master's awarded. *Entrance requirements:* For master's, GRE General Test, minimum GPA of 3.0 in last 2 years of undergraduate course work. Additional exam requirements/recommendations for international students: Required—TOEFL (minimum score 500 paper-based; 61 iBT), IELTS (minimum score 6). *Application deadline:* For fall admission, 7/1 for domestic students, 2/15 for international students; for spring admission, 11/1 for domestic students, 7/15 for international students. Applications are processed on a rolling basis. Application fee: $30. *Expenses:* Tuition, state resident: full-time $6660; part-time $370 per credit hour. Tuition, nonresident: full-time $18,450; part-time $1025 per credit hour. Tuition and fees vary according to course load. *Financial support:* Fellowships with partial tuition reimbursements, research assistantships with partial tuition reimbursements, teaching assistantships with partial tuition reimbursements, career-related internships or fieldwork, scholarships/grants, and unspecified assistantships available. *Faculty research:* Technology, teaching English to speakers of other languages, math teaching, electronic portfolio assessment, global perspectives through social studies. *Unit head:* Dr. Barbara Ridener, Chairperson, 561-297-3588. *Application contact:* Dr. Eliah Watlington, Associate Dean, 561-296-8520, Fax: 261-297-2991, E-mail: ewatling@fau.edu.
Website: http://www.coe.fau.edu/academicdepartments/tl/.

Florida International University, College of Education, Department of Leadership and Professional Studies, Miami, FL 33199. Offers adult education and human resource development (MS, Ed D); counseling (MS), including rehabilitation counseling, school counseling; counselor education (MS), including clinical mental health counseling; educational administration and supervision (Ed D); educational leadership (MS, Certificate, Ed S); higher education (Ed D); higher education administration (MS); recreation and sport management (MS), including recreation and sport management, recreational therapy; school psychology (Ed S); urban education (MS), including instruction in urban settings, learning technologies, multicultural/bilingual, multicultural/TESOL, urban education. Part-time and evening/weekend programs available. *Degree requirements:* For doctorate, thesis/dissertation. *Entrance requirements:* For master's, minimum GPA of 3.0; for doctorate and other advanced degree, GRE General Test. Additional exam requirements/recommendations for international students: Required—TOEFL (minimum score 550 paper-based; 80 iBT), IELTS (minimum score 6.3). Electronic applications accepted.

Fordham University, Graduate School of Education, Division of Curriculum and Teaching, New York, NY 10023. Offers adult education (MS, MSE); bilingual teacher education (MSE); curriculum and teaching (MSE); early childhood education (MSE); elementary education (MST); language, literacy, and learning (PhD); reading education (MSE, Adv C); secondary education (MAT, MSE); special education (MSE, Adv C); teaching English as a second language (MSE). *Accreditation:* NCATE. *Degree requirements:* For doctorate, thesis/dissertation; for Adv C, thesis. *Entrance requirements:* For doctorate, MAT, GRE General Test.

Gallaudet University, The Graduate School, Washington, DC 20002-3625. Offers ASL/English bilingual early childhood education: birth to 5 (Certificate); audiology (Au D); clinical psychology (PhD); critical studies in the education of deaf learners (PhD); deaf and hard of hearing infants, toddlers, and their families (Certificate); deaf education (Ed S); deaf education: advanced studies (MA); deaf education: special programs (MA); deaf history (Certificate); deaf studies (MA, Certificate); educating deaf students with disabilities (Certificate); education: teacher preparation (MA), including deaf education, early childhood education and deaf education, elementary education and deaf education, secondary education and deaf education; educational neuroscience (PhD); hearing, speech and language sciences (MS, PhD); international development (MA); interpretation (MA, PhD), including combined interpreting practice and research (MA), interpreting research (MA); linguistics (MA, PhD); mental health counseling (MA); peer mentoring (Certificate); public administration (MPA); school counseling (MA); school psychology (Psy S); sign language teaching (MA); social work (MSW); speech-language pathology (MS). Part-time programs available. *Faculty:* 55 full-time (37 women). *Students:* 361 full-time (279 women), 108 part-time (73 women); includes 98 minority (39 Black or African American, non-Hispanic/Latino; 1 American Indian or Alaska Native, non-Hispanic/Latino; 12 Asian, non-Hispanic/Latino; 36 Hispanic/Latino; 1 Native Hawaiian or other Pacific Islander, non-Hispanic/Latino; 9 Two or more races, non-Hispanic/Latino), 31 international. Average age 30. 602 applicants, 49% accepted, 177 enrolled. In 2013, 140 master's, 32 doctorates, 11 other advanced degrees awarded. Terminal master's awarded for partial completion of doctoral program. *Degree requirements:* For master's, comprehensive exam (for some programs), thesis optional; for doctorate, comprehensive exam, thesis/dissertation. *Entrance requirements:* For master's and doctorate, GRE General Test or MAT, letters of recommendation, interviews, goals statement, ASL proficiency interview, written English competency. Additional exam requirements/recommendations for international students: Required—TOEFL. *Application deadline:* For fall admission, 2/15 for domestic students. Applications are processed on a rolling basis. Application fee: $75. Electronic applications accepted. *Expenses: Tuition:* Full-time $14,774; part-time $821 per credit. *Required fees:* $198 per semester. *Financial support:* In 2013–14, 325 students received support. Fellowships, research assistantships, teaching assistantships, career-related internships or fieldwork, Federal Work-Study, scholarships/grants, tuition waivers (partial), and unspecified assistantships available. Support available to part-time students. Financial award applicants required to submit FAFSA. *Faculty research:* Bimodal bilingualism development, cochlear implants, telecommunications access, cancer genetics, linguistics, visual language and visual learning, advancement of avatar and robotics translation, algal productivity and physiology in the Anacostia River. *Unit head:* Dr. Carol J. Erting, Dean, Research, Graduate School, Continuing Studies, and International Programs, 202-651-5520, Fax: 202-651-5027, E-mail: carol.erting@gallaudet.edu. *Application contact:* Wednesday Luria, Coordinator of Prospective Graduate Student Services, 202-651-5400, Fax: 202-651-5295, E-mail: graduate.school@gallaudet.edu.
Website: http://www.gallaudet.edu/x26696.xml.

George Fox University, College of Education, Master of Arts in Teaching Program, Newberg, OR 97132-2697. Offers teaching (MAT); teaching plus ESOL (MAT); teaching plus ESOL/bilingual (MAT); teaching plus reading (MAT); teaching plus special education (MAT). Program offered in Oregon and Idaho. Part-time and evening/weekend programs available. *Faculty:* 11 full-time (9 women), 24 part-time/adjunct (16 women). *Students:* 64 full-time (44 women), 20 part-time (14 women); includes 11 minority (1 Black or African American, non-Hispanic/Latino; 2 Asian, non-Hispanic/Latino; 1 Hispanic/Latino; 2 Native Hawaiian or other Pacific Islander, non-Hispanic/Latino; 5 Two or more races, non-Hispanic/Latino), 1 international. Average age 30. 28 applicants, 100% accepted, 18 enrolled. In 2013, 116 master's awarded. *Entrance requirements:* For master's, CBEST, PRAXIS PPST, or EAS, bachelor's degree with minimum GPA of 3.0 in last two years of course work from regionally-accredited college or university, official transcripts. Additional exam requirements/recommendations for international students: Required—TOEFL (minimum score 577 paper-based; 90 iBT), IELTS (minimum score 7). *Application deadline:* For fall admission, 6/1 for domestic and international students; for winter admission, 10/1 for domestic and international students; for spring admission, 2/1 for domestic and international students. Applications are processed on a rolling basis. Application fee: $40. Electronic applications accepted. *Expenses:* Contact institution. *Financial support:* In 2013–14, 20 students received support. Scholarships/grants available. Financial award application deadline: 2/1; financial award applicants required to submit FAFSA. *Application contact:* Kipp Wilfong, Graduate Admissions Counselor, 800-631-0921, Fax: 503-554-3110, E-mail: mat@georgefox.edu.
Website: http://www.georgefox.edu/soe/mat/.

Georgetown University, Graduate School of Arts and Sciences, Department of Linguistics, Washington, DC 20057. Offers bilingual education (Certificate); language and communication (MA); linguistics (MS, PhD), including applied linguistics, computational linguistics, sociolinguistics, theoretical linguistics; teaching English as a second language (MAT, Certificate); teaching English as a second language and bilingual education (MAT). Terminal master's awarded for partial completion of doctoral program. *Degree requirements:* For master's, one foreign language, comprehensive exam, optional research project; for doctorate, 2 foreign languages, comprehensive exam, thesis/dissertation. *Entrance requirements:* For master's and doctorate, 18 undergraduate credits in a foreign language. Additional exam requirements/recommendations for international students: Required—TOEFL.

The George Washington University, Graduate School of Education and Human Development, Department of Counseling and Human Development, Program in Counseling Culturally and Linguistically Diverse Persons, Washington, DC 20052. Offers Graduate Certificate. *Students:* 1 (woman) part-time. Average age 32. 4 applicants, 100% accepted. In 2013, 1 Graduate Certificate awarded. *Unit head:* Dr. Pat Schwallie-Giddis, Chair, 202-994-6856, E-mail: drpat@gwu.edu. *Application contact:* Sarah Lang, Director of Graduate Admissions, 202-994-1447, Fax: 202-994-7207, E-mail: slang@gwu.edu.

The George Washington University, Graduate School of Education and Human Development, Department of Special Education and Disability Studies, Program in Bilingual Special Education, Washington, DC 20052. Offers MA Ed, Certificate. *Students:* 5 full-time (all women), 31 part-time (all women); includes 16 minority (7 Black or African American, non-Hispanic/Latino; 5 Asian, non-Hispanic/Latino; 4 Hispanic/Latino), 5 international. Average age 34. 41 applicants, 100% accepted, 28 enrolled. In 2013, 9 master's, 51 Certificates awarded. *Unit head:* Prof. Curtis Pyke, Chair, 202-994-4516, E-mail: cpyke@gwu.edu. *Application contact:* Sarah Lang, Director of Graduate Admissions, 202-994-1447, Fax: 202-994-7207, E-mail: slang@gwu.edu.

Graduate Institute of Applied Linguistics, Graduate Programs, Dallas, TX 75236. Offers applied linguistics (MA, Certificate); language development (MA). Part-time programs available. *Degree requirements:* For master's, one foreign language, comprehensive exam (for some programs), thesis (for some programs). *Entrance requirements:* For master's, GRE. Additional exam requirements/recommendations for international students: Required—TOEFL (minimum score 577 paper-based; 90 iBT). Electronic applications accepted. *Faculty research:* Minority languages, endangered languages, language documentation.

Harvard University, Harvard Graduate School of Education, Doctoral Program in Education, Cambridge, MA 02138. Offers culture, communities and education (Ed D); education policy, leadership and instructional practice (Ed D); higher education (Ed D); human development and education (Ed D); quantitative policy analysis in education (Ed D). *Faculty:* 68 full-time (34 women), 77 part-time/adjunct (41 women). *Students:* 221 full-time (148 women), 8 part-time (4 women); includes 70 minority (28 Black or African American, non-Hispanic/Latino; 22 Asian, non-Hispanic/Latino; 14 Hispanic/Latino; 1 Native Hawaiian or other Pacific Islander, non-Hispanic/Latino; 5 Two or more races, non-Hispanic/Latino), 26 international. Average age 34. 472 applicants, 8% accepted, 25 enrolled. In 2013, 50 doctorates awarded. Terminal master's awarded for partial completion of doctoral program. *Degree requirements:* For doctorate, thesis/dissertation. *Entrance requirements:* For doctorate, GRE General Test, statement of purpose, 3 letters of recommendation, resume, official transcripts. Additional exam requirements/recommendations for international students: Required—TOEFL (minimum score 613 paper-based; 104 iBT), TWE (minimum score 5). *Application deadline:* For fall admission, 12/2 for domestic and international students. Application fee: $85. Electronic applications accepted. *Expenses:* Contact institution. *Financial support:* In 2013–14, 168 students received support, including 66 fellowships with full and partial tuition reimbursements available (averaging $15,034 per year), 48 research assistantships (averaging $11,714 per year), 190 teaching assistantships (averaging $6,097 per year); career-related internships or fieldwork, Federal Work-Study, institutionally sponsored loans, scholarships/grants, health care benefits, tuition waivers (full and partial), and unspecified assistantships also available. Support available to part-time students. Financial award application deadline: 2/1; financial award applicants required to submit FAFSA. *Faculty research:* Learning and development, educational leadership and organizations, education policy analysis. *Total annual research expenditures:* $34.3 million. *Unit head:* Dr. Barbara Selmo, Assistant Dean, 617-496-4406. *Application contact:* Information Contact, 617-495-3414, Fax: 617-496-3577, E-mail: gseadmissions@harvard.edu.
Website: http://gse.harvard.edu/.

Heritage University, Graduate Programs in Education, Program in Professional Studies, Toppenish, WA 98948-9599. Offers bilingual education/ESL (M Ed); biology (M Ed); English and literature (M Ed); reading/literacy (M Ed); special education (M Ed). Part-time and evening/weekend programs available. *Degree requirements:* For master's, comprehensive exam (for some programs), thesis (for some programs).

Hofstra University, School of Education, Programs in Teaching - Elementary and Early Childhood Education, Hempstead, NY 11549. Offers early childhood and childhood education (MS Ed); early childhood education (MA, MS Ed); educational technology (MA); elementary education (MS Ed); literacy (MA); math specialist (Advanced Certificate); math, science, technology (MA); multiculturalism (MA).

Hofstra University, School of Education, Programs in Teaching - K-12, Hempstead, NY 11549. Offers bilingual education (MA, Advanced Certificate); family and consumer

sciences (MS Ed); fine arts and music education (Advanced Certificate); fine arts education (MA, MS Ed); middle childhood extensions (Advanced Certificate), including grades 5-6 or 7-9; music education (MA, MS Ed); teaching languages other than English and TESOL (MS Ed); TESOL (MS Ed, Advanced Certificate); wind conducting (MA).

Howard University, School of Communications, Department of Communication and Culture, Washington, DC 20059-0002. Offers intercultural communication (MA, PhD); organizational communication (MA, PhD). Offered through the Graduate School of Arts and Sciences. Part-time programs available. Terminal master's awarded for partial completion of doctoral program. *Degree requirements:* For master's, comprehensive exam or thesis; for doctorate, one foreign language, comprehensive exam, thesis/dissertation. *Entrance requirements:* For master's, English proficiency exam, GRE General Test, minimum GPA of 3.0; for doctorate, English proficiency exam, GRE General Test, master's degree in related field, minimum GPA of 3.5. Additional exam requirements/recommendations for international students: Required—TOEFL. *Faculty research:* Media effects, black discourse, development communication, African-American organizations.

Hunter College of the City University of New York, Graduate School, School of Education, Department of Curriculum and Teaching, Program in Bilingual Education, New York, NY 10065-5085. Offers MS. *Accreditation:* NCATE. *Faculty:* 1 full-time (0 women), 6 part-time/adjunct (5 women). *Students:* 33 part-time (24 women); includes 20 minority (2 Black or African American, non-Hispanic/Latino; 1 Asian, non-Hispanic/Latino; 17 Hispanic/Latino). Average age 30. 18 applicants, 56% accepted, 5 enrolled. *Degree requirements:* For master's, one foreign language, thesis, research seminar, student teaching experience or practicum, New York State Teacher Certification Exams. *Entrance requirements:* For master's, interview, minimum GPA of 2.8, writing sample in English and Spanish. Additional exam requirements/recommendations for international students: Required—TOEFL, TWE. *Application deadline:* For fall admission, 4/1 for domestic students, 2/1 for international students; for spring admission, 11/1 for domestic students, 9/1 for international students. Applications are processed on a rolling basis. Application fee: $125. *Financial support:* Federal Work-Study, scholarships/grants, and tuition waivers (partial) available. Support available to part-time students. *Faculty research:* Teacher effectiveness, language development, Spanish language and linguistics and multicultural education. *Unit head:* Prof. Anne Ebe, Program Coordinator, 212-772-4693, E-mail: aebe@hunter.cuny.edu. *Application contact:* Milena Solo, Director for Graduate Admissions, 212-772-4482, E-mail: admissions@hunter.cuny.edu. Website: http://www.hunter.cuny.edu/school-of-education/programs/graduate/bilingual.

Hunter College of the City University of New York, Graduate School, School of Education, Department of Educational Foundations and Counseling Programs, Programs in School Counselor, New York, NY 10065-5085. Offers school counseling (MS Ed); school counseling with bilingual extension (MS Ed). *Accreditation:* ACA; NCATE. *Faculty:* 7 full-time (4 women), 17 part-time/adjunct (9 women). *Students:* 42 full-time (33 women), 81 part-time (74 women); includes 52 minority (14 Black or African American, non-Hispanic/Latino; 10 Asian, non-Hispanic/Latino; 28 Hispanic/Latino), 2 international. Average age 29. 227 applicants, 23% accepted, 16 enrolled. In 2013, 33 master's awarded. *Degree requirements:* For master's, thesis, internship, practicum, research seminar. *Entrance requirements:* For master's, interview, minimum GPA of 2.7. Additional exam requirements/recommendations for international students: Required—TOEFL, TWE. *Application deadline:* For fall admission, 4/1 for domestic students, 2/1 for international students; for spring admission, 11/1 for domestic students, 9/1 for international students. Applications are processed on a rolling basis. Application fee: $125. *Financial support:* Federal Work-Study and tuition waivers (partial) available. Support available to part-time students. *Unit head:* Dr. Tamara Buckley, Coordinator, 212-772-4758, E-mail: tamara.buckley@hunter.cuny.edu. *Application contact:* Milena Solo, Director for Graduate Admissions, 212-772-4480, E-mail: admissions@hunter.cuny.edu. Website: http://www.hunter.cuny.edu/school-of-education/programs/graduate/counseling.

Immaculata University, College of Graduate Studies, Program in Cultural and Linguistic Diversity, Immaculata, PA 19345. Offers MA. Part-time and evening/weekend programs available. *Degree requirements:* For master's, one foreign language, comprehensive exam, thesis optional, professional experience. *Entrance requirements:* For master's, GRE or MAT, proficiency in Spanish or Asian language, minimum GPA of 3.0. Additional exam requirements/recommendations for international students: Required—TOEFL, IELTS. Electronic applications accepted. *Faculty research:* Cognitive learning, Caribbean literature and culture, English as a second language, teaching English to speakers of other languages.

Indiana State University, College of Graduate and Professional Studies, College of Arts and Sciences, Department of Languages, Literatures, and Linguistics, Terre Haute, IN 47809. Offers linguistics/teaching English as a second language (MA); TESL/TEFL (CAS). *Faculty:* 7 full-time (4 women), 2 part-time/adjunct (1 woman). *Students:* 26 full-time (20 women), 8 part-time (7 women); includes 6 minority (2 Asian, non-Hispanic/Latino; 4 Hispanic/Latino), 19 international. Average age 32. 26 applicants, 92% accepted, 8 enrolled. In 2013, 20 master's awarded. *Degree requirements:* For master's, comprehensive exam. *Application deadline:* For fall admission, 7/1 priority date for domestic students; for spring admission, 11/1 priority date for domestic students. Applications are processed on a rolling basis. Application fee: $35. Electronic applications accepted. *Financial support:* In 2013–14, 8 teaching assistantships (averaging $7,000 per year) were awarded; research assistantships with partial tuition reimbursements and tuition waivers (partial) also available. Financial award application deadline: 3/1; financial award applicants required to submit FAFSA. *Unit head:* Dr. Ronald W. Dunbar, Chairperson, 812-237-2368. *Application contact:* Information Contact, 812-237-2366.

Indiana University Bloomington, University Graduate School, College of Arts and Sciences, Department of Second Language Studies, Bloomington, IN 47405-7000. Offers second language studies (MA, PhD); TESOL and applied linguistics (MA). *Faculty:* 1 (woman) full-time. *Students:* 34 full-time (22 women), 2 part-time (0 women); includes 2 minority (1 Hispanic/Latino; 1 Two or more races, non-Hispanic/Latino), 12 international. Average age 31. 115 applicants, 37% accepted, 9 enrolled. In 2013, 12 master's, 1 doctorate awarded. *Entrance requirements:* Additional exam requirements/recommendations for international students: Required—TOEFL (minimum score 100 iBT). *Application deadline:* For fall admission, 1/15 for domestic students, 12/1 for international students. Application fee: $55 ($65 for international students). *Financial support:* In 2013–14, 3 fellowships with tuition reimbursements (averaging $18,300 per year), 14 teaching assistantships with tuition reimbursements (averaging $15,750 per year) were awarded. *Unit head:* Kathleen Bardovi-Harlig, Chair, 812-855-7951, E-mail: bardovi@indiana.edu. *Application contact:* Regina Skeans, Graduate Secretary, 812-855-7951, E-mail: rskeans@indiana.edu. Website: http://www.indiana.edu/~dsls/.

Kean University, College of Education, Program in Instruction and Curriculum, Union, NJ 07083. Offers bilingual/bicultural education (MA); classroom instruction (MA); earth science (MA); mathematics/science/computer education (MA); teaching (MA); teaching English as a second language (MA); world languages (Spanish) (MA). *Accreditation:* NCATE. Part-time programs available. *Faculty:* 22 full-time (12 women). *Students:* 16

full-time (10 women), 100 part-time (72 women); includes 57 minority (8 Black or African American, non-Hispanic/Latino; 3 Asian, non-Hispanic/Latino; 45 Hispanic/Latino; 1 Two or more races, non-Hispanic/Latino). Average age 35. 56 applicants, 100% accepted, 38 enrolled. In 2013, 42 master's awarded. *Degree requirements:* For master's, comprehensive exam, thesis (for some programs), two-semester advanced seminar. *Entrance requirements:* For master's, GRE General Test or MAT, PRAXIS, minimum GPA of 3.0, personal statement, professional resume/curriculum vitae, commitment to working with children, certification (for some programs). Additional exam requirements/recommendations for international students: Required—TOEFL (minimum score 550 paper-based; 79 iBT). *Application deadline:* For fall admission, 6/1 for domestic and international students; for spring admission, 12/1 for domestic and international students. Applications are processed on a rolling basis. Application fee: $75 ($150 for international students). Electronic applications accepted. *Expenses:* Tuition, state resident: full-time $12,099; part-time $589 per credit. Tuition, nonresident: full-time $16,399; part-time $722 per credit. *Required fees:* $3050; $139 per credit. Part-time tuition and fees vary according to course level, course load, degree level and program. *Financial support:* In 2013–14, 6 research assistantships with full tuition reimbursements (averaging $3,713 per year) were awarded; unspecified assistantships also available. Financial award applicants required to submit FAFSA. *Unit head:* Dr. Gail Verdi, Program Coordinator, 908-737-3908, E-mail: gverdi@kean.edu. *Application contact:* Ann-Marie Kay, Assistant Director for Graduate Admissions, 908-737-5922, Fax: 908-737-5925, E-mail: akay@kean.edu. Website: http://grad.kean.edu/masters-programs/bilingualbicultural-education-instruction-and-curriculum.

Langston University, School of Education and Behavioral Sciences, Langston, OK 73050. Offers bilingual/multicultural (M Ed); elementary education (M Ed); English as a second language (M Ed); rehabilitation counseling (M Sc); urban education (M Ed). *Accreditation:* CORE; NCATE (one or more programs are accredited). Part-time programs available. *Degree requirements:* For master's, comprehensive exam, thesis optional. *Entrance requirements:* For master's, GRE, writing skills test, minimum GPA of 2.5, 3 letters of recommendation. Additional exam requirements/recommendations for international students: Required—TOEFL, TWE. *Faculty research:* Bilingual/multicultural education, financing post-secondary education.

La Salle University, School of Arts and Sciences, Hispanic Institute, Philadelphia, PA 19141-1199. Offers bilingual/bicultural studies (MA); ESL specialist (Certificate); interpretation in English-Spanish/Spanish-English (Certificate); teaching English to speakers of other languages (MA); translation and interpretation (MA); translation English/Spanish-Spanish/English (Certificate). Part-time and evening/weekend programs available. *Faculty:* 2 full-time (both women), 7 part-time/adjunct (4 women). *Students:* 3 full-time (all women), 66 part-time (50 women); includes 23 minority (11 Black or African American, non-Hispanic/Latino; 1 American Indian or Alaska Native, non-Hispanic/Latino; 11 Hispanic/Latino). Average age 36. 22 applicants, 100% accepted, 18 enrolled. In 2013, 4 master's, 5 other advanced degrees awarded. *Degree requirements:* For master's, one foreign language, project or thesis. *Entrance requirements:* For master's, GRE, MAT, or GMAT, professional resume; two letters of recommendation; for Certificate, GRE, MAT, or GMAT, professional resume; two letters of recommendation; evidence of an advanced level in Spanish. Additional exam requirements/recommendations for international students: Required—TOEFL. *Application deadline:* For fall admission, 8/15 priority date for domestic students, 7/15 for international students; for spring admission, 12/15 priority date for domestic students, 11/15 for international students; for summer admission, 4/15 priority date for domestic students, 3/15 for international students. Applications are processed on a rolling basis. Application fee: $35. Electronic applications accepted. Application fee is waived when completed online. *Expenses:* Contact institution. *Financial support:* In 2013–14, 13 students received support. Federal Work-Study and scholarships/grants available. Support available to part-time students. Financial award application deadline: 8/31; financial award applicants required to submit FAFSA. *Faculty research:* Puerto Rican literature, cross-cultural communication, English as a second language methodology, Spanish language. *Unit head:* Dr. Carmen Lamas, Director, 215-951-1209, Fax: 215-991-3506, E-mail: lamas@lasalle.edu. *Application contact:* Paul J. Reilly, Assistant Vice President, Enrollment Services, 215-951-1946, Fax: 215-951-1462, E-mail: reilly@lasalle.edu. Website: http://www.lasalle.edu/grad/index.php?section-hispanic&page-index.

La Salle University, School of Arts and Sciences, Program in Education, Philadelphia, PA 19141-1199. Offers American studies (MA); autism spectrum disorders (MA, Certificate); bilingual/bicultural studies (MA); classroom management (MA, Certificate); dual early childhood and special education (MA); dual middle-level science and math and special education secondary education (MA); education (MA); English (MA); English as a second language (Certificate); instructional coach (Certificate); instructional leadership (MA); reading specialist (MA, Certificate); secondary education (MA); special education (MA, Certificate). Part-time and evening/weekend programs available. *Faculty:* 5 full-time (4 women), 16 part-time/adjunct (10 women). *Students:* 18 full-time (13 women), 137 part-time (112 women); includes 33 minority (24 Black or African American, non-Hispanic/Latino; 9 Hispanic/Latino), 4 international. Average age 32. 47 applicants, 96% accepted, 28 enrolled. In 2013, 58 master's, 20 other advanced degrees awarded. *Degree requirements:* For master's, comprehensive exam. *Entrance requirements:* For master's and Certificate, MAT or GRE, 2 letters of recommendation. Additional exam requirements/recommendations for international students: Required—TOEFL. *Application deadline:* For fall admission, 8/15 priority date for domestic students, 7/15 for international students; for spring admission, 12/15 priority date for domestic students, 11/15 for international students; for summer admission, 4/15 priority date for domestic students, 3/15 for international students. Applications are processed on a rolling basis. Application fee: $35. Electronic applications accepted. Application fee is waived when completed online. *Expenses:* Contact institution. *Financial support:* In 2013–14, 28 students received support. Career-related internships or fieldwork, Federal Work-Study, and scholarships/grants available. Support available to part-time students. Financial award application deadline: 8/31; financial award applicants required to submit FAFSA. *Unit head:* Dr. Greer Richardson, Interim Director, 215-951-1806, Fax: 215-951-1843, E-mail: graded@lasalle.edu. *Application contact:* Paul J. Reilly, Assistant Vice President, Enrollment Services, 215-951-1946, Fax: 215-951-1462, E-mail: reilly@lasalle.edu. Website: http://www.lasalle.edu/grad/index.php?section-education&page-index.

Lehman College of the City University of New York, Division of Education, Department of Specialized Services in Education, Bronx, NY 10468-1589. Offers guidance and counseling (MS Ed); reading teacher (MS Ed); teachers of special education (MS Ed), including bilingual special education, early special education, emotional handicaps, learning disabilities, mental retardation. Part-time and evening/weekend programs available. *Faculty research:* Battered women, whole language classrooms, parent education, mainstreaming.

Lehman College of the City University of New York, Division of Education, Department of Specialized Services in Education, Teachers of Special Education Program, Option in Bilingual Special Education, Bronx, NY 10468-1589. Offers MS Ed. *Accreditation:* NCATE. *Entrance requirements:* For master's, minimum GPA of 3.0.

Long Island University–Hudson at Westchester, Programs in Education-Teaching, Program in Second Language, TESOL, Bilingual Education, Purchase, NY 10577. Offers MS Ed, Advanced Certificate. Part-time and evening/weekend programs available.

Long Island University–LIU Brooklyn, School of Education, Department of Teaching and Learning, Program in Bilingual Education, Brooklyn, NY 11201-8423. Offers MS Ed. Part-time and evening/weekend programs available. *Degree requirements:* For master's, one foreign language, thesis optional. *Entrance requirements:* For master's, 2 letters of recommendation. Additional exam requirements/recommendations for international students: Required—TOEFL (minimum score 500 paper-based). Electronic applications accepted.

Long Island University–LIU Post, School of Education, Department of Curriculum and Instruction, Brookville, NY 11548-1300. Offers adolescence education (MS); adolescence education: biology (MS); adolescence education: earth science (MS); adolescence education: English (MS); adolescence education: mathematics (MS); adolescence education: social studies (MS); adolescence education: Spanish (MS); art education (MS); bilingual education (MS); childhood education (MS); early childhood education (MS); middle childhood education (MS); music education (MS); teaching English to speakers of other languages (MS). Part-time and evening/weekend programs available. *Degree requirements:* For master's, comprehensive exam or thesis, student teaching. *Entrance requirements:* For master's, minimum GPA of 2.75 in major, 2.5 overall. Electronic applications accepted. *Faculty research:* Ethics and education, teaching strategies.

Loyola Marymount University, School of Education, Department of Language and Culture in Education, Program in Bilingual Elementary Education, Los Angeles, CA 90045. Offers MA. Part-time and evening/weekend programs available. *Faculty:* 6 full-time (5 women). *Students:* 26 full-time (all women), 1 (woman) part-time; includes 23 minority (7 Asian, non-Hispanic/Latino; 16 Hispanic/Latino), 4 international. Average age 28. 16 applicants, 81% accepted, 14 enrolled. In 2013, 2 master's awarded. *Degree requirements:* For master's, comprehensive exam. *Entrance requirements:* For master's, CBEST, CSET, 3 letters of recommendation. Additional exam requirements/recommendations for international students: Required—TOEFL (minimum score 600 paper-based; 100 iBT). *Application deadline:* For fall admission, 6/15 for domestic students; for spring admission, 11/15 for domestic students. Application fee: $50. Electronic applications accepted. *Financial support:* In 2013–14, 21 students received support, including 2 research assistantships (averaging $680 per year); scholarships/grants and unspecified assistantships also available. Support available to part-time students. Financial award application deadline: 6/30; financial award applicants required to submit FAFSA. *Unit head:* Dr. Magaly Lavadenz, Program Director, 310-338-2924, E-mail: mlavaden@lmu.edu. *Application contact:* Chake H. Kouyoumjian, Director, Graduate Admissions, 310-338-2721, Fax: 310-338-6086, E-mail: ckouyoum@lmu.edu.
Website: http://soe.lmu.edu/admissions/programs/bilingualeducation/bilingualelementaryeducation/.

Loyola Marymount University, School of Education, Department of Language and Culture in Education, Program in Bilingual Secondary Education, Los Angeles, CA 90064. Offers MA. Part-time and evening/weekend programs available. *Faculty:* 6 full-time (5 women). *Students:* 8 full-time (7 women), 2 part-time (both women); includes 7 minority (1 Black or African American, non-Hispanic/Latino; 6 Hispanic/Latino), 2 international. Average age 26. 9 applicants, 100% accepted, 4 enrolled. In 2013, 7 master's awarded. *Degree requirements:* For master's, comprehensive exam. *Entrance requirements:* For master's, CBEST, CSET, 3 letters of recommendation. Additional exam requirements/recommendations for international students: Required—TOEFL (minimum score 600 paper-based; 100 iBT). *Application deadline:* For fall admission, 6/15 for domestic students; for spring admission, 11/15 for domestic students. Application fee: $50. Electronic applications accepted. *Financial support:* In 2013–14, 7 students received support, including 1 research assistantship (averaging $2,880 per year); scholarships/grants and unspecified assistantships also available. Support available to part-time students. Financial award application deadline: 6/30; financial award applicants required to submit FAFSA. *Unit head:* Dr. Olga Moraga, Program Director, 310-338-3778, E-mail: olga.moraga@lmu.edu. *Application contact:* Chake H. Kouyoumjian, Director, Graduate Admissions, 310-338-2721, E-mail: ckouyoum@lmu.edu.
Website: http://soe.lmu.edu/admissions/programs/bilingualeducation/bilingualsecondaryeducation/.

Manhattan College, Graduate Programs, School of Education and Health, Program in Special Education, Riverdale, NY 10471. Offers adolescent special education generalist in English, math or social studies (MS Ed); autism spectrum disorder (Certificate); bilingual special education (Professional Diploma); dual childhood/special education (MS Ed); special education (MS Ed). Part-time and evening/weekend programs available. *Faculty:* 8 full-time (5 women), 16 part-time/adjunct (12 women). *Students:* 30 full-time (28 women), 68 part-time (61 women). Average age 24. 86 applicants, 94% accepted, 76 enrolled. In 2013, 37 master's awarded. *Degree requirements:* For master's, thesis, internship (if not certified). *Entrance requirements:* For master's, minimum GPA of 3.0. Additional exam requirements/recommendations for international students: Required—TOEFL (minimum score 550 paper-based). *Application deadline:* For fall admission, 8/10 priority date for domestic students; for spring admission, 1/7 priority date for domestic students. Applications are processed on a rolling basis. Application fee: $60. *Expenses:* Contact institution. *Financial support:* Federal Work-Study, scholarships/grants, and unspecified assistantships available. Financial award application deadline: 2/1. *Unit head:* Dr. Elizabeth Mary Kosky, Director of Childhood/Adolescent Special Education Programs, 718-862-7969, Fax: 718-862-7816, E-mail: elizabeth.kosky@manhattan.edu. *Application contact:* William Bisset, Information Contact, 718-862-8000, E-mail: william.bisset@manhattan.edu.
Website: http://www.manhattan.edu/academics/education/special-education-dept.

Mercyhurst University, Graduate Studies, Program in Special Education, Erie, PA 16546. Offers bilingual/bicultural special education (MS); educational leadership (Certificate); special education (MS). Part-time and evening/weekend programs available. *Degree requirements:* For master's, thesis optional. *Entrance requirements:* For master's, GRE or PRAXIS I, interview, resume, essay, three professional references, transcripts. Additional exam requirements/recommendations for international students: Required—TOEFL. Electronic applications accepted. *Faculty research:* College-age learning disabled program, teacher preparation/collaboration, applied behavior analysis, special education policy issues.

Midwestern State University, Graduate School, West College of Education, Programs in Educational Leadership and Technology, Wichita Falls, TX 76308. Offers bilingual education/English language learners (M Ed); educational leadership (M Ed); educational technology (M Ed). Part-time and evening/weekend programs available. *Degree requirements:* For master's, comprehensive exam. *Entrance requirements:* For master's, GRE General Test or MAT. Additional exam requirements/recommendations for international students: Required—TOEFL (minimum score 550 paper-based). *Application deadline:* For fall admission, 7/1 priority date for domestic students, 4/1 for international students; for spring admission, 11/1 priority date for domestic students, 8/1 for international students. Applications are processed on a rolling basis. Application fee: $35 ($50 for international students). Electronic applications accepted. *Expenses:* Tuition, state resident: full-time $3627; part-time $201.50 per credit hour. Tuition, nonresident: full-time $10,899; part-time $605.50 per credit hour. *Required fees:* $1357. *Financial support:* Career-related internships or fieldwork, Federal Work-Study, institutionally sponsored loans, scholarships/grants, tuition waivers (partial), and unspecified assistantships available. Support available to part-time students. Financial award application deadline: 3/1; financial award applicants required to submit FAFSA. *Faculty research:* Role of the principal in the twenty-first century, culturally proficient leadership, human diversity, immigration, teacher collaboration. *Unit head:* Dr. Pamela Whitehouse, Graduate Coordinator, 940-397-4139, Fax: 940-397-4694, E-mail: pamela.whitehouse@mwsu.edu. *Application contact:* Dr. Pamela Whitehouse, Graduate Coordinator, 940-397-4139, Fax: 940-397-4694, E-mail: pamela.whitehouse@mwsu.edu.
Website: http://www.mwsu.edu/academics/education/.

Minnesota State University Mankato, College of Graduate Studies, College of Social and Behavioral Sciences, Department of Ethnic Studies, Mankato, MN 56001. Offers MS, Certificate. *Students:* 6 full-time (all women), 11 part-time (5 women). *Application deadline:* For fall admission, 7/1 for domestic students, 5/1 for international students; for winter admission, 11/1 for domestic students; for spring admission, 10/1 for international students. Applications are processed on a rolling basis. Electronic applications accepted. *Unit head:* Dr. Hanh Huy Phan, Graduate Coordinator, 507-389-1185. *Application contact:* 507-389-2321, E-mail: grad@mnsu.edu.
Website: http://sbs.mnsu.edu/ethnic/.

Mount St. Joseph University, Graduate Education Program, Cincinnati, OH 45233-1670. Offers adolescent to young adult education (MA); dyslexia (Certificate); inclusive early childhood education (MA); instructional leadership (MA); middle childhood education (MA); multicultural special education (MA); Pre-K special needs (Certificate); principal licensure (MA); reading (Certificate); reading science (MA). *Accreditation:* Teacher Education Accreditation Council. Part-time and evening/weekend programs available. *Faculty:* 10 full-time (7 women), 7 part-time/adjunct (6 women). *Students:* 28 full-time (25 women), 95 part-time (76 women); includes 27 minority (19 Black or African American, non-Hispanic/Latino; 6 Hispanic/Latino; 2 Two or more races, non-Hispanic/Latino). Average age 36. 73 applicants, 44% accepted, 30 enrolled. In 2013, 69 master's awarded. *Degree requirements:* For master's, research project, student teaching, clinical and field-based experiences. *Entrance requirements:* For master's, GRE, PRAXIS II in teaching content area (math or science), 2 letters of recommendation, interview, resume. Additional exam requirements/recommendations for international students: Required—TOEFL (minimum score 560 paper-based; 83 iBT). *Application deadline:* Applications are processed on a rolling basis. Application fee: $50. Electronic applications accepted. *Expenses: Tuition:* Full-time $18,400; part-time $575 per credit hour. *Required fees:* $450; $450 per year. Part-time tuition and fees vary according to course load, degree level and program. *Financial support:* Scholarships/grants available. Financial award applicants required to submit FAFSA. *Faculty research:* Foreign and second language learning problems/reading disabilities/hyperlexia, multicultural/bilingual special education, alternative educator licensure, science education, pedagogical content knowledge. *Unit head:* Dr. Mary West, Chair, 513-244-3263, Fax: 513-244-4867, E-mail: mary_west@mail.msj.edu. *Application contact:* Mary Brigham, Assistant Director of Graduate Recruitment, 513-244-4233, Fax: 513-244-4629, E-mail: mary_brigham@mail.msj.edu.
Website: http://www.msj.edu/academics/graduate-programs/master-of-arts-initial-teacher-licensure-programs/.

New Jersey City University, Graduate Studies and Continuing Education, Debra Cannon Partridge Wolfe College of Education, Department of Educational Leadership, Jersey City, NJ 07305-1597. Offers basics and urban studies (MA); bilingual/bicultural education and English as a second language (MA); educational administration and supervision (MA). Part-time and evening/weekend programs available. *Faculty:* 9 full-time (7 women), 7 part-time/adjunct (4 women). *Students:* 25 full-time (17 women), 206 part-time (155 women); includes 121 minority (17 Black or African American, non-Hispanic/Latino; 7 Asian, non-Hispanic/Latino; 97 Hispanic/Latino), 2 international. Average age 37. In 2013, 71 master's awarded. *Entrance requirements:* Additional exam requirements/recommendations for international students: Required—TOEFL (minimum score 61 iBT). *Application deadline:* For fall admission, 8/1 priority date for domestic students; for spring admission, 12/1 for domestic students. Applications are processed on a rolling basis. Application fee: $0. *Expenses: Tuition, area resident:* Part-time $527.90 per credit. Tuition, nonresident: part-time $947.75 per credit. *Financial support:* Fellowships, teaching assistantships, career-related internships or fieldwork, and unspecified assistantships available. *Unit head:* Dr. Catherine Rogers, Chairperson, 201-200-3012, E-mail: cshevey@njcu.edu. *Application contact:* Dr. William Bajor, Dean of Graduate Studies, 201-200-3409, Fax: 201-200-3411, E-mail: wbajor@njcu.edu.

New Mexico State University, Graduate School, College of Education, Department of Special Education and Communication Disorders, Las Cruces, NM 88003-8001. Offers bilingual/multicultural special education (Ed D, PhD); communication disorders (MA); special education (MA, Ed D, PhD). *Accreditation:* ASHA (one or more programs are accredited); NCATE. Part-time and evening/weekend programs available. Postbaccalaureate distance learning degree programs offered. *Faculty:* 15 full-time (13 women), 2 part-time/adjunct (1 woman). *Students:* 87 full-time (80 women), 53 part-time (40 women); includes 75 minority (3 Asian, non-Hispanic/Latino; 68 Hispanic/Latino; 4 Two or more races, non-Hispanic/Latino), 6 international. Average age 33. 157 applicants, 27% accepted, 35 enrolled. In 2013, 47 master's, 3 doctorates awarded. *Degree requirements:* For master's, comprehensive exam, thesis optional; for doctorate, comprehensive exam, thesis/dissertation. *Entrance requirements:* For master's, GRE General Test or MAT. Additional exam requirements/recommendations for international students: Required—TOEFL (minimum score 550 paper-based; 79 iBT), IELTS (minimum score 6.5). *Application deadline:* For fall admission, 2/1 priority date for domestic students. Applications are processed on a rolling basis. Application fee: $40 ($50 for international students). Electronic applications accepted. *Expenses:* Tuition, state resident: full-time $5398; part-time $224.90 per credit. Tuition, nonresident: full-time $18,821; part-time $784.20 per credit. *Required fees:* $1310; $54.60 per credit. *Financial support:* In 2013–14, 65 students received support, including 1 research assistantship (averaging $18,261 per year), 25 teaching assistantships (averaging $8,389 per year); career-related internships or fieldwork, Federal Work-Study, health care benefits, and unspecified assistantships also available. Support available to part-time students. Financial award application deadline: 3/1; financial award applicants required to submit FAFSA. *Faculty research:* Multicultural special education, multicultural communication disorders, mild disability, multicultural assessment, deaf education, early childhood, bilingual special education. *Total annual research expenditures:* $289,421. *Unit head:* Dr. Eric Joseph Lopez, Interim Department Head, 575-646-2402, Fax: 575-646-7712, E-mail: leric@nmsu.edu. *Application contact:* Coordinator, 575-646-2736, Fax: 575-646-7721, E-mail: gradinfo@nmsu.edu.
Website: http://education.nmsu.edu/spedcd/.

New York University, Steinhardt School of Culture, Education, and Human Development, Department of Humanities and Social Sciences in the Professions,

Program in Sociology of Education, New York, NY 10003. Offers education policy (MA); social and cultural studies of education (MA); sociology of education (PhD). Part-time programs available. *Faculty:* 14 full-time (7 women). *Students:* 32 full-time (29 women), 30 part-time (24 women); includes 21 minority (7 Black or African American, non-Hispanic/Latino; 6 Asian, non-Hispanic/Latino; 5 Hispanic/Latino; 3 Two or more races, non-Hispanic/Latino), 18 international. Average age 28. 102 applicants, 43% accepted, 9 enrolled. In 2013, 6 master's, 1 doctorate awarded. *Degree requirements:* For master's, thesis (for some programs); for doctorate, thesis/dissertation. *Entrance requirements:* For master's, letters of recommendation; for doctorate, GRE General Test, interview. Additional exam requirements/recommendations for international students: Required—TOEFL (minimum score 100 iBT). *Application deadline:* For fall admission, 12/1 priority date for domestic and international students; for spring admission, 11/1 for domestic and international students. Applications are processed on a rolling basis. Application fee: $75. Electronic applications accepted. *Expenses: Tuition:* Full-time $35,856; part-time $1494 per unit. *Required fees:* $1408; $64 per unit. $473 per term. Tuition and fees vary according to course load and program. *Financial support:* Fellowships with full and partial tuition reimbursements, Federal Work-Study, institutionally sponsored loans, scholarships/grants, and tuition waivers (partial) available. Support available to part-time students. Financial award application deadline: 2/1; financial award applicants required to submit FAFSA. *Faculty research:* Legal and institutional environments of schools; social inequality; high school reform and achievement; urban schooling, economics and education, educational policy. *Unit head:* Prof. Lisa Stulberg, Program Director, 212-992-9373, Fax: 212-995-4832, E-mail: lisa.stulberg@nyu.edu. *Application contact:* 212-998-5030, Fax: 212-995-4328, E-mail: steinhardt.gradadmissions@nyu.edu.
Website: http://steinhardt.nyu.edu/humsocsci/sociology.

New York University, Steinhardt School of Culture, Education, and Human Development, Department of Teaching and Learning, Program in Multilingual/Multicultural Studies, New York, NY 10003. Offers bilingual education (MA, PhD, Advanced Certificate); foreign language education (MA, Advanced Certificate); foreign language education (7-12) and TESOL (K-12) (MA); teaching English to speakers of other languages (MA, PhD, Advanced Certificate); teaching foreign languages, 7-12 (MA), including Chinese, French, Italian, Japanese, Spanish; teaching foreign languages, college and adult (MA); teaching French as a foreign language and TESOL (MA); teaching Spanish as a foreign language and TESOL (MA). *Accreditation:* Teacher Education Accreditation Council. Part-time and evening/weekend programs available. *Faculty:* 5 full-time (4 women). *Students:* 134 full-time (112 women), 77 part-time (68 women); includes 43 minority (6 Black or African American, non-Hispanic/Latino; 18 Asian, non-Hispanic/Latino; 15 Hispanic/Latino; 4 Two or more races, non-Hispanic/Latino), 113 international. Average age 31. 501 applicants, 39% accepted, 68 enrolled. In 2013, 91 master's, 3 doctorates, 7 other advanced degrees awarded. *Degree requirements:* For master's, thesis (for some programs); for doctorate, thesis/dissertation. *Entrance requirements:* For doctorate, GRE General Test, interview; for Advanced Certificate, master's degree. Additional exam requirements/recommendations for international students: Required—TOEFL (minimum score 100 iBT). *Application deadline:* For fall admission, 12/1 priority date for domestic and international students; for spring admission, 10/1 for domestic and international students. Applications are processed on a rolling basis. Application fee: $75. Electronic applications accepted. *Expenses: Tuition:* Full-time $35,856; part-time $1494 per unit. *Required fees:* $1408; $64 per unit. $473 per term. Tuition and fees vary according to course load and program. *Financial support:* Fellowships with full and partial tuition reimbursements, career-related internships or fieldwork, Federal Work-Study, institutionally sponsored loans, scholarships/grants, and tuition waivers (partial) available. Support available to part-time students. Financial award application deadline: 2/1; financial award applicants required to submit FAFSA. *Faculty research:* Second language acquisition, cross-cultural communication, technology-enhanced language learning, language variation, action learning. *Unit head:* Prof. Shondel Nero, Director, 212-998-5757, E-mail: shondel.nero@nyu.edu. *Application contact:* 212-998-5030, Fax: 212-995-4328, E-mail: steinhardt.gradadmissions@nyu.edu.
Website: http://steinhardt.nyu.edu/teachlearn/mms.

Northeastern Illinois University, College of Graduate Studies and Research, College of Education, MAT Program in Bicultural/Bilingual Education, Chicago, IL 60625-4699. Offers MAT. *Degree requirements:* For master's, research paper. *Entrance requirements:* For master's, GRE, Illinois Basic Skills Test, bachelor's degree, minimum undergraduate GPA of 2.75.

Northeastern Illinois University, College of Graduate Studies and Research, College of Education, Program in Bilingual/Bicultural Education, Chicago, IL 60625-4699. Offers MAT, MSI. *Entrance requirements:* For master's, GRE, minimum GPA of 2.75. Additional exam requirements/recommendations for international students: Required—TOEFL (minimum score 550 paper-based; 79 iBT). Electronic applications accepted. *Faculty research:* Bilingual teacher preparation, linguistics and phonetics, Middle Eastern languages and cultures, TOEFL.

Northern Arizona University, Graduate College, College of Education, Department of Educational Specialties, Flagstaff, AZ 86011. Offers autism spectrum disorders (Certificate); bilingual/multicultural education (M Ed), including bilingual education, ESL education; career and technical education (M Ed, Certificate); early childhood special education (M Ed); educational technology (M Ed, Certificate); special education (M Ed). *Faculty:* 32 full-time (21 women), 4 part-time/adjunct (all women). *Students:* 68 full-time (48 women), 158 part-time (119 women); includes 93 minority (6 Black or African American, non-Hispanic/Latino; 29 American Indian or Alaska Native, non-Hispanic/Latino; 4 Asian, non-Hispanic/Latino; 53 Hispanic/Latino; 1 Native Hawaiian or other Pacific Islander, non-Hispanic/Latino), 6 international. Average age 37. 66 applicants, 95% accepted, 38 enrolled. In 2013, 121 master's, 3 Certificates awarded. *Degree requirements:* For master's, comprehensive exam (for some programs), thesis (for some programs). *Entrance requirements:* For master's, minimum GPA of 3.0. Additional exam requirements/recommendations for international students: Required—TOEFL (minimum score 550 paper-based; 80 iBT), IELTS (minimum score 7). *Application deadline:* For fall admission, 3/1 for international students; for spring admission, 9/15 for international students. Applications are processed on a rolling basis. Application fee: $65. Electronic applications accepted. *Financial support:* In 2013–14, 9 teaching assistantships with full tuition reimbursements (averaging $9,698 per year) were awarded. Financial award applicants required to submit FAFSA. *Unit head:* Dr. Laura Sujo-Montes, Chair, 928-523-0892, Fax: 928-523-1929, E-mail: laura.sujo-montes@nau.edu. *Application contact:* Laura Cook, Coordinator, 928-523-5342, Fax: 928-523-8950, E-mail: laura.cook@nau.edu.
Website: http://nau.edu/coe/ed-specialties/.

Ohio University, Graduate College, Gladys W. and David H. Patton College of Education and Human Services, Department of Educational Studies, Athens, OH 45701-2979. Offers computer education and technology (M Ed); cultural studies (M Ed); educational administration (M Ed, Ed D); educational research and evaluation (M Ed, PhD); instructional technology (PhD). Part-time and evening/weekend programs available. Postbaccalaureate distance learning degree programs offered (minimal on-campus study). *Degree requirements:* For master's, thesis or alternative; for doctorate, comprehensive exam, thesis/dissertation. *Entrance requirements:* For master's, GRE General Test (if GPA less than 2.9); for doctorate, GRE General Test, GRE Subject Test, minimum GPA of 2.9, work experience, 3 letters of reference, autobiography. Additional exam requirements/recommendations for international students: Required—TOEFL (minimum score 550 paper-based; 80 iBT) or IELTS (minimum score 6.5). Electronic applications accepted. *Faculty research:* Race, class and gender; computer programs; development and organization theory; evaluation/development of instruments, leadership.

Our Lady of the Lake University of San Antonio, School of Professional Studies, Program in Curriculum and Instruction, San Antonio, TX 78207-4689. Offers bilingual education (M Ed); early childhood education (M Ed); English as a second language (M Ed); integrated math teaching (M Ed); integrated science teaching (M Ed); reading specialist (M Ed). Part-time and evening/weekend programs available. *Faculty:* 6 full-time (4 women), 3 part-time/adjunct (all women). *Students:* 4 full-time (all women), 84 part-time (72 women); includes 52 minority (2 Black or African American, non-Hispanic/Latino; 2 Asian, non-Hispanic/Latino; 48 Hispanic/Latino). Average age 40. 9 applicants, 56% accepted, 1 enrolled. In 2013, 8 master's awarded. *Degree requirements:* For master's, comprehensive exam. *Entrance requirements:* For master's, GRE General Test or MAT. Additional exam requirements/recommendations for international students: Required—TOEFL. *Application deadline:* For fall admission, 4/1 priority date for domestic and international students; for spring admission, 11/1 priority date for domestic and international students; for summer admission, 2/1 priority date for domestic students, 4/1 priority date for international students. Applications are processed on a rolling basis. Application fee: $25 ($50 for international students). Electronic applications accepted. *Expenses: Tuition:* Full-time $9120; part-time $760 per credit. *Required fees:* $698; $334 per trimester. Tuition and fees vary according to course load, degree level, campus/location and program. *Financial support:* Research assistantships, teaching assistantships, career-related internships or fieldwork, Federal Work-Study, institutionally sponsored loans, scholarships/grants, and tuition waivers (partial) available. Support available to part-time students. Financial award application deadline: 4/1. *Faculty research:* Professional educator to understand and meet the comprehensive needs of a diverse student population, life-long learners, innovative practices. *Unit head:* Dr. Jerrie Jackson, 210-434-6711 Ext. 2698, E-mail: jjackson@lake.ollusa.edu. *Application contact:* Graduate Admission, 210-431-3961, Fax: 210-431-4013, E-mail: gradadm@lake.ollusa.edu.
Website: http://www.ollusa.edu/s/1190/ollu-3-column-noads.aspx?sid=1190&gid=1&pgid=4173.

Queens College of the City University of New York, Division of Graduate Studies, Division of Education, Department of Elementary and Early Childhood Education, Flushing, NY 11367-1597. Offers bilingual education (MS Ed); childhood education (MA); early childhood education (MA); elementary education (MS Ed, AC); literacy (MS Ed). Part-time and evening/weekend programs available. *Degree requirements:* For master's, research project; for AC, thesis optional. *Entrance requirements:* For master's, minimum GPA of 3.0. Additional exam requirements/recommendations for international students: Required—TOEFL.

Quincy University, Program in Education, Quincy, IL 62301-2699. Offers curriculum and instruction (MS Ed), including bilingual/English as a second language; leadership (MS Ed); reading education (MS Ed); special education (MS Ed); teacher leader (MS Ed). Part-time and evening/weekend programs available. Postbaccalaureate distance learning degree programs offered (minimal on-campus study). *Students:* 62 full-time (39 women), 97 part-time (68 women); includes 43 minority (29 Black or African American, non-Hispanic/Latino; 1 American Indian or Alaska Native, non-Hispanic/Latino; 4 Asian, non-Hispanic/Latino; 9 Hispanic/Latino). In 2013, 105 master's awarded. *Degree requirements:* For master's, comprehensive exam (for some programs), thesis optional. *Entrance requirements:* For master's, MAT or GRE. Additional exam requirements/recommendations for international students: Required—TOEFL (minimum score 550 paper-based; 79 iBT). *Application deadline:* Applications are processed on a rolling basis. Application fee: $25. Electronic applications accepted. *Expenses: Tuition:* Full-time $9600; part-time $400 per semester hour. *Required fees:* $720; $30 per semester hour. Tuition and fees vary according to course load and program. *Financial support:* Applicants required to submit FAFSA. *Unit head:* Dr. Kristen R. Anguiano, Director, 217-228-5432 Ext. 3119, E-mail: anguikr@quincy.edu. *Application contact:* Office of Admissions, 217-228-5210, Fax: 217-228-5479, E-mail: admissions@quincy.edu.
Website: http://www.quincy.edu/academics/graduate-programs/education.

Rowan University, Graduate School, College of Education, Department of Teacher Education, Glassboro, NJ 08028-1701. Offers bilingual/bicultural education (CGS); collaborative teaching (MST); educational technology (CGS); elementary education (MST); elementary school teaching (MA); ESL education (CGS); foreign language education (MST); music education (MA); science teaching (MST); secondary education (MST); subject matter teaching (MA); teacher leadership (M Ed); teaching and learning (CGS); theatre education (MST). *Accreditation:* NCATE. Part-time and evening/weekend programs available. *Faculty:* 7 full-time (5 women), 1 (woman) part-time/adjunct. *Students:* 35 full-time (22 women), 78 part-time (66 women); includes 23 minority (4 Black or African American, non-Hispanic/Latino; 3 Asian, non-Hispanic/Latino; 16 Hispanic/Latino). Average age 28. 58 applicants, 100% accepted, 37 enrolled. In 2013, 12 master's awarded. *Degree requirements:* For master's, comprehensive exam, thesis. *Entrance requirements:* For master's, GRE General Test, PRAXIS I, PRAXIS II, interview, minimum GPA of 2.8. Additional exam requirements/recommendations for international students: Required—TOEFL. *Application deadline:* For spring admission, 2/15 priority date for domestic students. Applications are processed on a rolling basis. Application fee: $65. Electronic applications accepted. *Expenses: Tuition, area resident:* Part-time $638 per credit. Tuition, state resident: full-time $5742. *Required fees:* $142 per credit. Tuition and fees vary according to course level and program. *Financial support:* Career-related internships or fieldwork, scholarships/grants, health care benefits, and unspecified assistantships available. Support available to part-time students. *Unit head:* Dr. Horacio Sosa, Dean, College of Graduate and Continuing Education, 856-256-4747, Fax: 856-256-5638, E-mail: sosa@rowan.edu. *Application contact:* Karen Haynes, Graduate Coordinator, 856-256-4052, Fax: 856-256-4436, E-mail: haynes@rowan.edu.

Rutgers, The State University of New Jersey, New Brunswick, Graduate School-New Brunswick, Program in Spanish, Piscataway, NJ 08854-8097. Offers bilingualism and second language acquisition (MA, PhD); Spanish (MA, MAT, PhD); Spanish literature (MA, PhD); translation (MA). Part-time programs available. *Degree requirements:* For master's, comprehensive exam (for some programs), thesis (for some programs); for doctorate, 2 foreign languages, comprehensive exam, thesis/dissertation. *Entrance requirements:* For master's and doctorate, GRE General Test. Additional exam requirements/recommendations for international students: Required—TOEFL. Electronic applications accepted. *Faculty research:* Hispanic literature, Luso-Brazilian literature, Spanish linguistics, Spanish translation.

St. John's University, The School of Education, Department of Human Services and Counseling, Program in School Counseling with Bilingual Extension, Queens, NY 11439. Offers MS Ed. Part-time and evening/weekend programs available. *Students:* 3

full-time (2 women), 1 (woman) part-time; includes 3 minority (1 Asian, non-Hispanic/Latino; 2 Hispanic/Latino). Average age 30. 4 applicants, 100% accepted, 1 enrolled. In 2013, 14 master's awarded. *Degree requirements:* For master's, comprehensive exam. *Entrance requirements:* For master's, GRE, New York State Bilingual Assessment (BEA), bachelor's degree from an accredited college or university, minimum GPA of 3.0, 2 letters of recommendation, interview, minimum of 18 credits in behavioral or social science. Additional exam requirements/recommendations for international students: Required—TOEFL (minimum score 600 paper-based; 100 iBT), IELTS (minimum score 5.5). *Application deadline:* For fall admission, 4/1 for domestic students, 4/1 priority date for international students; for spring admission, 11/1 for domestic students, 11/1 priority date for international students. Applications are processed on a rolling basis. Application fee: $70. Electronic applications accepted. *Expenses: Tuition:* Full-time $19,800; part-time $1100 per credit. *Required fees:* $170 per semester. *Financial support:* Research assistantships, career-related internships or fieldwork, and scholarships/grants available. Support available to part-time students. Financial award application deadline: 3/1; financial award applicants required to submit FAFSA. *Faculty research:* Cross-cultural comparisons of predictors of active coping. *Unit head:* Dr. E. Francine Guastello, Chair, 718-990-1475, E-mail: guastelf@stjohns.edu. *Application contact:* Dr. Kelly K. Ronayne, Associate Dean for Graduate Admissions, 718-990-2304, Fax: 718-990-2343, E-mail: graded@stjohns.edu.

St. John's University, The School of Education, Department of Human Services and Counseling, Programs in Bilingual Education/Teaching English to Speakers of Other Languages, Queens, NY 11439. Offers MS Ed, Adv C. Part-time and evening/weekend programs available. Postbaccalaureate distance learning degree programs offered. *Students:* 86 full-time (74 women), 125 part-time (115 women); includes 59 minority (12 Black or African American, non-Hispanic/Latino; 7 Asian, non-Hispanic/Latino; 37 Hispanic/Latino; 3 Two or more races, non-Hispanic/Latino), 54 international. Average age 30. 160 applicants, 93% accepted, 71 enrolled. In 2013, 69 master's, 17 Adv Cs awarded. *Degree requirements:* For master's, comprehensive exam, fieldwork. *Entrance requirements:* For master's, minimum GPA of 3.0, eligibility for teacher certification, 2 letters of recommendation, bachelor's degree; for Adv C, New York State initial teaching certification or eligibility. Additional exam requirements/recommendations for international students: Required—TOEFL (minimum score 600 paper-based; 100 iBT), IELTS (minimum score 5.5). *Application deadline:* For fall admission, 8/17 for domestic students, 5/1 priority date for international students; for spring admission, 1/5 for domestic students, 11/1 priority date for international students. Applications are processed on a rolling basis. Application fee: $70. Electronic applications accepted. *Expenses: Tuition:* Full-time $19,800; part-time $1100 per credit. *Required fees:* $170 per semester. *Financial support:* Research assistantships, career-related internships or fieldwork, and scholarships/grants available. Support available to part-time students. Financial award application deadline: 3/1; financial award applicants required to submit FAFSA. *Faculty research:* Second language learning and academic achievement, heritage language education, assessing the progress of English language learners toward English acquisition, dual language acquisition, study of English Creoles and dialects of other Englishes. *Unit head:* Dr. E. Francine Guastello, Chair, 718-990-1475, E-mail: guastelf@stjohns.edu. *Application contact:* Dr. Kelly K. Ronayne, Associate Dean of Graduate Admissions, 718-990-2304, Fax: 718-990-2343, E-mail: graded@stjohns.edu.

Saint Mary's University of Minnesota, Schools of Graduate and Professional Programs, Graduate School of Education, Education Program, Winona, MN 55987-1399. Offers culturally responsive teaching (Certificate); education (MA); gifted and talented instruction (Certificate). *Unit head:* Lynn Albee, Director, 612-728-5179, Fax: 612-728-5128, E-mail: lgalbe02@smumn.edu. *Application contact:* Russell Kreager, Director of Admissions for Graduate and Professional Programs, 612-728-5207, Fax: 612-728-5121, E-mail: rkreager@smumn.edu.
Website: http://www.smumn.edu/graduate-home/areas-of-study/graduate-school-of-education/ma-in-education.

San Diego State University, Graduate and Research Affairs, College of Education, Department of Policy Studies in Language and Cross Cultural Education, San Diego, CA 92182. Offers multi-cultural emphasis (PhD); policy studies in language and cross cultural education (MA). *Accreditation:* NCATE. *Entrance requirements:* For master's, GRE General Test, letters of reference; for doctorate, GRE General Test, 3 letters of reference, resumé. Additional exam requirements/recommendations for international students: Required—TOEFL. Electronic applications accepted.

Southern Connecticut State University, School of Graduate Studies, School of Arts and Sciences, Department of World Languages and Literatures, New Haven, CT 06515-1355. Offers multicultural-bilingual education/teaching English to speakers of other languages (MS); romance languages (MA). Part-time and evening/weekend programs available. *Degree requirements:* For master's, one foreign language, thesis or alternative. *Entrance requirements:* For master's, interview, minimum undergraduate GPA of 2.7. Electronic applications accepted.

Southern Methodist University, Annette Caldwell Simmons School of Education and Human Development, Department of Teaching and Learning, Dallas, TX 75275. Offers bilingual/ESL education (MBE); education (M Ed, PhD); gifted education (MBE); reading and writing (M Ed); special education (M Ed). Part-time and evening/weekend programs available. Terminal master's awarded for partial completion of doctoral program. *Degree requirements:* For master's, comprehensive exam, minimum GPA of 3.0; for doctorate, thesis/dissertation, qualifying exams, major area paper, evidence of teaching competency, dissemination of research (e.g., conference presentation), professional portfolio. *Entrance requirements:* For master's, minimum GPA of 3.0 or GRE, 3 letters of recommendation; for doctorate, GRE, minimum GPA of 3.3, 3 years of full-time teaching, 3 letters of recommendation, interview. Additional exam requirements/recommendations for international students: Required—TOEFL. Electronic applications accepted. *Faculty research:* Reading intervention, mathematics intervention, bilingual education, new literacies.

State University of New York at New Paltz, Graduate School, School of Education, Department of Educational Studies, Program in Humanistic/Multicultural Education, New Paltz, NY 12561. Offers humanistic/multicultural education (MPS); multicultural education (AC). *Accreditation:* NCATE. Part-time and evening/weekend programs available. *Faculty:* 8 full-time (6 women), 8 part-time/adjunct (all women). *Students:* 12 full-time (7 women), 27 part-time (18 women); includes 11 minority (2 Black or African American, non-Hispanic/Latino; 9 Hispanic/Latino). Average age 31. 12 applicants, 100% accepted, 11 enrolled. In 2013, 20 master's awarded. *Degree requirements:* For master's, portfolio. *Entrance requirements:* For master's, minimum GPA of 3.0. Additional exam requirements/recommendations for international students: Required—TOEFL (minimum score 550 paper-based; 80 iBT), IELTS (minimum score 6.5). *Application deadline:* For fall admission, 3/15 priority date for domestic students, 3/15 for international students; for spring admission, 10/15 for domestic and international students. Application fee: $50. Electronic applications accepted. *Expenses:* Tuition, state resident: full-time $9870; part-time $411 per credit. Tuition, nonresident: full-time $18,350; part-time $765 per credit. *Required fees:* $1213. Tuition and fees vary according to program. *Financial support:* Application deadline: 8/1. *Unit head:* Dr. Nancy Schniedewind, Coordinator, 845-257-2827, E-mail: schniedn@newpaltz.edu. *Application contact:* Caroline Murphy, Graduate Admissions Advisor, 845-257-3285, E-mail: gradschool@newpaltz.edu.
Website: http://www.newpaltz.edu/edstudies/humanistic.html.

State University of New York College at Geneseo, Graduate Studies, School of Education, Program in Childhood Multicultural Education (1-6), Geneseo, NY 14454-1401. Offers MS Ed. Part-time and evening/weekend programs available. *Faculty:* 5 full-time (4 women). *Students:* 5 part-time (2 women); includes 1 minority (Hispanic/Latino). Average age 26. In 2013, 2 master's awarded. *Degree requirements:* For master's, thesis optional, culminating experience. *Application deadline:* For fall admission, 3/1 for domestic students; for spring admission, 10/1 for domestic students. Application fee: $50. *Expenses:* Tuition, state resident: full-time $8790; part-time $411 per credit hour. Tuition, nonresident: full-time $18,350; part-time $765 per credit hour. *Required fees:* $795; $32.90 per credit hour. *Financial support:* Scholarships/grants, health care benefits, tuition waivers (full), and unspecified assistantships available. Support available to part-time students. Financial award application deadline: 4/1; financial award applicants required to submit FAFSA. *Unit head:* Dr. Anjoo Sikka, Dean of the School of Education, 585-245-5151, Fax: 585-245-5220, E-mail: sikka@geneseo.edu. *Application contact:* Tracy Peterson, Director of Student Success, 585-245-5443, Fax: 585-245-5220, E-mail: peterson@geneseo.edu.

Sul Ross State University, Rio Grande College of Sul Ross State University, Alpine, TX 79832. Offers business administration (MBA); teacher education (M Ed), including bilingual education, counseling, educational diagnostics, elementary education, general education, reading, school administration, secondary education. Part-time and evening/weekend programs available. Postbaccalaureate distance learning degree programs offered (no on-campus study). *Degree requirements:* For master's, comprehensive exam, thesis optional, minimum GPA of 3.0. *Entrance requirements:* For master's, GMAT or GRE General Test, minimum GPA of 2.5 in last 60 hours of undergraduate work. Additional exam requirements/recommendations for international students: Required—TOEFL.

Teachers College, Columbia University, Graduate Faculty of Education, Department of Arts and Humanities, Program in Bilingual and Bicultural Education, New York, NY 10027-6696. Offers MA. *Accreditation:* NCATE. Part-time programs available. *Faculty:* 3 full-time, 4 part-time/adjunct. *Students:* 10 full-time (9 women), 40 part-time (37 women); includes 20 minority (2 Black or African American, non-Hispanic/Latino; 5 Asian, non-Hispanic/Latino; 12 Hispanic/Latino; 1 Two or more races, non-Hispanic/Latino), 16 international. Average age 27. 55 applicants, 64% accepted, 17 enrolled. In 2013, 22 master's awarded. *Degree requirements:* For master's, one foreign language. *Application deadline:* For fall admission, 1/15 priority date for domestic students. Application fee: $65. *Financial support:* Research assistantships, career-related internships or fieldwork, Federal Work-Study, institutionally sponsored loans, scholarships/grants, and tuition waivers (full and partial) available. Support available to part-time students. Financial award application deadline: 2/1. *Faculty research:* Cross-cultural research in bilingual and bicultural school settings, diversity and teacher education. *Unit head:* Prof. Patricia Martinez-Alvarez, 212-678-3758, E-mail: pmartinez@tc.columbia.edu. *Application contact:* Deanna Ghozati, Associate Director of Admission, 212-678-3710, Fax: 212-678-4171, E-mail: tcinfo@tc.edu.

Texas A&M University, College of Education and Human Development, Department of Educational Psychology, College Station, TX 77843. Offers bilingual education (M Ed, MS); counseling psychology (PhD); educational psychology (M Ed, MS, PhD); educational technology (M Ed); school psychology (PhD); special education (M Ed, MS). *Accreditation:* APA (one or more programs are accredited). Part-time and evening/weekend programs available. Postbaccalaureate distance learning degree programs offered (no on-campus study). *Faculty:* 41. *Students:* 148 full-time (122 women), 143 part-time (124 women); includes 97 minority (15 Black or African American, non-Hispanic/Latino; 11 Asian, non-Hispanic/Latino; 66 Hispanic/Latino; 5 Two or more races, non-Hispanic/Latino), 49 international. Average age 31. 249 applicants, 52% accepted, 83 enrolled. In 2013, 43 master's, 22 doctorates awarded. *Degree requirements:* For master's, thesis optional; for doctorate, thesis/dissertation. *Entrance requirements:* For master's and doctorate, GRE General Test. Additional exam requirements/recommendations for international students: Required—TOEFL. Application fee: $50 ($75 for international students). Electronic applications accepted. *Expenses:* Tuition, state resident: full-time $4078; part-time $226.55 per credit hour. Tuition, nonresident: full-time $10,450; part-time $580.55 per credit hour. *Required fees:* $2328; $278.50 per credit hour. $642.45 per semester. *Financial support:* In 2013–14, fellowships (averaging $12,000 per year), research assistantships (averaging $9,000 per year), teaching assistantships (averaging $9,000 per year) were awarded; career-related internships or fieldwork, institutionally sponsored loans, scholarships/grants, and unspecified assistantships also available. Financial award applicants required to submit FAFSA. *Unit head:* Dr. Cathy Watson, Head, 979-845-1394, E-mail: cwatson@tamu.edu. *Application contact:* Christy Porter, Senior Academic Advisor, 979-845-1874, E-mail: csporter@tamu.edu.
Website: http://epsy.tamu.edu.

Texas A&M University–Commerce, Graduate School, College of Education and Human Services, Department of Curriculum and Instruction, Commerce, TX 75429-3011. Offers bilingual/ESL education (M Ed, MS); early childhood education (M Ed, MS); elementary education (M Ed, MS); reading (M Ed, MS); secondary education (M Ed, MS); supervision, curriculum and instruction: elementary education (Ed D). MS and M Ed programs in early childhood education offered jointly with Texas Woman's University and University of North Texas. Part-time programs available. Terminal master's awarded for partial completion of doctoral program. *Degree requirements:* For master's, comprehensive exam, thesis (for some programs); for doctorate, 2 foreign languages, thesis/dissertation, departmental qualifying exam. *Entrance requirements:* For master's and doctorate, GRE General Test. Electronic applications accepted. *Expenses:* Tuition, state resident: full-time $3630; part-time $2420 per year. Tuition, nonresident: full-time $9948; part-time $6632.16 per year. *Required fees:* $1006 per year. Tuition and fees vary according to course load. *Faculty research:* Literacy and learning, early childhood, preservice teacher education, technology.

Texas A&M University–San Antonio, Department of Curriculum and Kinesiology, San Antonio, TX 78224. Offers bilingual education (MA); early childhood education (M Ed); kinesiology (MS); reading (MS); special education (M Ed), including educational diagnostician, instructional specialist. Part-time and evening/weekend programs available. *Degree requirements:* For master's, comprehensive exam, thesis or alternative. *Entrance requirements:* For master's, MAT. Additional exam requirements/recommendations for international students: Required—TOEFL (minimum score 550 paper-based; 80 iBT), IELTS (minimum score 6). Electronic applications accepted.

Texas Southern University, College of Education, Area of Curriculum and Instruction, Houston, TX 77004-4584. Offers bilingual education (M Ed); curriculum and instruction (Ed D); secondary education (M Ed). Part-time and evening/weekend programs available. *Faculty:* 2 full-time (1 woman), 8 part-time/adjunct (all women). *Students:* 18 full-time (17 women), 38 part-time (32 women); includes 55 minority (53 Black or African American, non-Hispanic/Latino; 2 Hispanic/Latino), 1 international. Average age 36. 27 applicants, 22% accepted, 5 enrolled. In 2013, 7 master's, 2 doctorates awarded. *Degree requirements:* For master's, comprehensive exam; for doctorate,

comprehensive exam, thesis/dissertation. *Entrance requirements:* For master's, GRE General Test, minimum GPA of 2.5; for doctorate, GRE General Test or MAT, master's degree, minimum B+ average. Additional exam requirements/recommendations for international students: Required—TOEFL. *Application deadline:* For fall admission, 7/1 for domestic and international students; for spring admission, 11/1 for domestic and international students. Applications are processed on a rolling basis. Application fee: $50 ($75 for international students). Electronic applications accepted. *Financial support:* Fellowships, teaching assistantships, scholarships/grants, and unspecified assistantships available. Support available to part-time students. Financial award application deadline: 5/1. *Unit head:* Dr. Ingrid Haynes-Mays, Interim Chair, 713-313-7179, Fax: 713-313-7496, E-mail: haynesmaysi@tsu.edu. *Application contact:* Dr. Gregory Maddox, Dean of the Graduate School, 713-313-7011 Ext. 4410, Fax: 713-639-1876, E-mail: maddox_gh@tsu.edu.
Website: http://www.tsu.edu/academics/colleges__schools/College_of_Education/Departments/default.php.

Texas State University, Graduate School, College of Education, Department of Curriculum and Instruction, Program in Elementary Education-Bilingual/Bicultural, San Marcos, TX 78666. Offers M Ed, MA. Part-time programs available. *Faculty:* 5 full-time (all women). *Students:* 6 full-time (all women), 13 part-time (11 women); includes 16 minority (all Hispanic/Latino), 1 international. Average age 34. 14 applicants, 79% accepted, 7 enrolled. In 2013, 5 master's awarded. *Degree requirements:* For master's, comprehensive exam, thesis optional. *Entrance requirements:* For master's, minimum GPA of 2.75 in last 60 hours of course work, teaching experience. Additional exam requirements/recommendations for international students: Required—TOEFL (minimum score 550 paper-based; 78 iBT). *Application deadline:* For fall admission, 6/15 priority date for domestic students, 6/1 for international students; for spring admission, 10/15 priority date for domestic students, 10/1 for international students. Applications are processed on a rolling basis. Application fee: $40 ($90 for international students). Electronic applications accepted. *Expenses:* Tuition, state resident: full-time $6663; part-time $278 per credit hour. Tuition, nonresident: full-time $15,159; part-time $632 per credit hour. Required fees: $1872; $54 per credit hour. $306 per term. Tuition and fees vary according to course load. *Financial support:* In 2013–14, 15 students received support, including 2 teaching assistantships (averaging $11,280 per year); research assistantships, career-related internships or fieldwork, Federal Work-Study, institutionally sponsored loans, and unspecified assistantships also available. Support available to part-time students. Financial award application deadline: 4/1; financial award applicants required to submit FAFSA. *Unit head:* Dr. Roxanne Cuellar Allsup, Graduate Advisor, 512-245-7486, Fax: 512-245-7911, E-mail: ra17@txstate.edu. *Application contact:* Dr. Andrea Golato, Dean of Graduate School, 512-245-2581, Fax: 512-245-8365, E-mail: gradcollege@txstate.edu.
Website: http://www.education.txstate.edu/ci/degrees-programs/graduate/elementary-education.html.

Texas Tech University, Graduate School, College of Education, Department of Curriculum and Instruction, Lubbock, TX 79409-1071. Offers bilingual education (M Ed); curriculum and instruction (M Ed, PhD); elementary education (M Ed); language/literacy education (M Ed); multidisciplinary science (MS); secondary education (M Ed). *Accreditation:* NCATE. Part-time programs available. Postbaccalaureate distance learning degree programs offered (minimal on-campus study). *Faculty:* 27 full-time (21 women). *Students:* 49 full-time (40 women), 194 part-time (149 women); includes 74 minority (13 Black or African American, non-Hispanic/Latino; 6 Asian, non-Hispanic/Latino; 50 Hispanic/Latino; 5 Two or more races, non-Hispanic/Latino), 20 international. Average age 38. 105 applicants, 66% accepted, 46 enrolled. In 2013, 48 master's, 14 doctorates awarded. *Degree requirements:* For master's, comprehensive exam (for some programs), thesis optional; for doctorate, comprehensive exam, thesis/dissertation. *Entrance requirements:* For master's, bachelor's degree; resume; letter of intent; academic writing sample; 2 letters of recommendation; for doctorate, GRE, master's degree; resume; letter of intent; academic writing sample; 3 letters of recommendation. Additional exam requirements/recommendations for international students: Required—TOEFL (minimum score 550 paper-based; 79 iBT). *Application deadline:* For fall admission, 6/1 priority date for domestic students, 1/15 priority date for international students; for spring admission, 9/1 priority date for domestic students, 6/15 priority date for international students. Applications are processed on a rolling basis. Application fee: $60. Electronic applications accepted. *Expenses:* Tuition, state resident: full-time $6062; part-time $252.57 per credit hour. Tuition, nonresident: full-time $14,558; part-time $606.57 per credit hour. Required fees: $2655; $35 per credit hour. $907.50 per semester. Tuition and fees vary according to course load. *Financial support:* In 2013–14, 94 students received support, including 89 fellowships (averaging $2,276 per year), 14 research assistantships (averaging $5,226 per year), 6 teaching assistantships (averaging $4,517 per year); career-related internships or fieldwork, Federal Work-Study, institutionally sponsored loans, scholarships/grants, traineeships, health care benefits, and unspecified assistantships also available. Support available to part-time students. Financial award application deadline: 2/1; financial award applicants required to submit FAFSA. *Faculty research:* Teacher education, curriculum studies, bilingual education, science and math education, language and literacy education. *Total annual research expenditures:* $413,968. *Unit head:* Dr. Margaret Ann Price, Department Chair, Curriculum and Instruction, 806-834-4347, E-mail: peggie.price@ttu.edu. *Application contact:* Stephenie A. Jones, Administrative Assistant, 806-834-2751, Fax: 806-742-2179, E-mail: stephenie.a.jones@ttu.edu.
Website: http://www.educ.ttu.edu.

University at Buffalo, the State University of New York, Graduate School, Graduate School of Education, Department of Learning and Instruction, Buffalo, NY 14260. Offers biology education (Ed M, Certificate); chemistry education (Ed M, Certificate); childhood education (Ed M); childhood education with bilingual extension (Ed M); curriculum, instruction and the science of learning (PhD); early childhood education (Ed M); early childhood education with bilingual extension (birth-grade 2) (Ed M); earth science education (Ed M, Certificate); education studies (Ed M); educational technology and new literacies (Certificate); elementary education (Ed D); English education (Ed M, Certificate); English for speakers of other languages (Ed M); foreign and second language education (PhD); French education (Ed M, Certificate); German education (Ed M, Certificate); gifted education (Certificate); Latin education (Ed M, Certificate); literacy specialist (Ed M); literacy teaching and learning (Certificate); mathematics education (Ed M, Certificate); music education (Ed M, Certificate); physics education (Ed M, Certificate); science and the public (Ed M); social studies education (Ed M, Certificate); Spanish education (Ed M, Certificate); special education (PhD); teaching English to speakers of other languages (Ed M). Part-time and evening/weekend programs available. Postbaccalaureate distance learning degree programs offered (no on-campus study). *Faculty:* 31 full-time (23 women), 64 part-time/adjunct (53 women). *Students:* 275 full-time (215 women), 293 part-time (205 women); includes 35 minority (16 Black or African American, non-Hispanic/Latino; 5 American Indian or Alaska Native, non-Hispanic/Latino; 11 Asian, non-Hispanic/Latino; 3 Hispanic/Latino), 97 international. Average age 30. 544 applicants, 81% accepted, 246 enrolled. In 2013, 222 master's, 17 doctorates, 35 other advanced degrees awarded. *Degree requirements:* For master's, comprehensive exam; for doctorate, thesis/dissertation, research analysis exam, research experience component. *Entrance requirements:* For master's, content test in

science and math, letters of reference; for doctorate, GRE General Test or MAT, interview, writing sample, letters of recommendation. Additional exam requirements/recommendations for international students: Required—TOEFL (minimum score 600 paper-based; 96 iBT). *Application deadline:* For fall admission, 2/1 priority date for domestic and international students; for spring admission, 11/15 priority date for domestic students, 10/1 for international students. Applications are processed on a rolling basis. Application fee: $50. Electronic applications accepted. *Financial support:* In 2013–14, 50 fellowships (averaging $8,589 per year), 31 research assistantships with tuition reimbursements (averaging $11,406 per year) were awarded; teaching assistantships, career-related internships or fieldwork, Federal Work-Study, institutionally sponsored loans, scholarships/grants, tuition waivers, and unspecified assistantships also available. Financial award application deadline: 2/28; financial award applicants required to submit FAFSA. *Faculty research:* Science assessment, foreign language teaching and learning, early learning, new literacies, gender and education. *Total annual research expenditures:* $1.7 million. *Unit head:* Dr. Suzanne Miller, Chair, 716-645-2455, Fax: 716-645-3161, E-mail: smiller@buffalo.edu. *Application contact:* Cathy Dimino, Admissions Assistant, 716-645-2110, Fax: 716-645-7937, E-mail: cadimino@buffalo.edu.
Website: http://gse.buffalo.edu/lai.

University of Alaska Fairbanks, College of Liberal Arts, Department of Cross-Cultural Studies, Fairbanks, AK 99775-6300. Offers MA. *Faculty:* 2 full-time (both women). *Students:* 1 (woman) full-time, 4 part-time (3 women); includes 2 minority (1 American Indian or Alaska Native, non-Hispanic/Latino; 1 Native Hawaiian or other Pacific Islander, non-Hispanic/Latino). Average age 33. 2 applicants, 50% accepted, 1 enrolled. In 2013, 2 master's awarded. *Degree requirements:* For master's, comprehensive exam. *Entrance requirements:* Additional exam requirements/recommendations for international students: Required—TOEFL (minimum score 550 paper-based; 80 iBT). *Application deadline:* For fall admission, 6/1 for domestic students, 3/1 for international students; for spring admission, 10/15 for domestic students, 9/1 for international students. Applications are processed on a rolling basis. Application fee: $60. Electronic applications accepted. *Expenses:* Tuition, state resident: full-time $7254; part-time $403 per credit. Tuition, nonresident: full-time $14,814; part-time $823 per credit. Tuition and fees vary according to course level, course load and reciprocity agreements. *Financial support:* Fellowships with tuition reimbursements, research assistantships with tuition reimbursements, teaching assistantships with tuition reimbursements, Federal Work-Study, scholarships/grants, health care benefits, and unspecified assistantships available. Support available to part-time students. Financial award application deadline: 7/1; financial award applicants required to submit FAFSA. *Faculty research:* Alaska native literature, oral traditions, history, law and policy; Alaska native cultures, art, Native American religion and philosophy. *Total annual research expenditures:* $1,000. *Unit head:* Raymond Barnhardt, Director of the Center for Cross-Cultural Studies, 907-474-1902, Fax: 907-474-1957, E-mail: fycxcs@uaf.edu. *Application contact:* Libby Eddy, Registrar and Director of Admissions, 907-474-7500, Fax: 907-474-7097, E-mail: admissions@uaf.edu.
Website: http://www.uaf.edu/cxcs.

University of Alaska Fairbanks, College of Liberal Arts, Program in Linguistics, Fairbanks, AK 99775-6280. Offers applied linguistics (MA), including language documentation, second language acquisition teacher education. Part-time programs available. *Faculty:* 1 (woman) full-time. *Students:* 3 full-time (1 woman), 15 part-time (14 women); includes 10 minority (6 American Indian or Alaska Native, non-Hispanic/Latino; 4 Two or more races, non-Hispanic/Latino). Average age 35. 6 applicants, 67% accepted, 4 enrolled. In 2013, 3 master's awarded. *Degree requirements:* For master's, comprehensive exam, thesis or alternative. *Entrance requirements:* Additional exam requirements/recommendations for international students: Required—TOEFL (minimum score 550 paper-based; 80 iBT). *Application deadline:* For fall admission, 6/1 for domestic students, 3/1 for international students; for spring admission, 10/15 for domestic students, 9/1 for international students. Application fee: $60. *Expenses:* Tuition, state resident: full-time $7254; part-time $403 per credit. Tuition, nonresident: full-time $14,814; part-time $823 per credit. Tuition and fees vary according to course level, course load and reciprocity agreements. *Financial support:* In 2013–14, 1 research assistantship with tuition reimbursement (averaging $12,143 per year), 1 teaching assistantship with tuition reimbursement (averaging $11,955 per year) were awarded; fellowships with tuition reimbursements, career-related internships or fieldwork, Federal Work-Study, scholarships/grants, health care benefits, and unspecified assistantships also available. Support available to part-time students. Financial award application deadline: 7/1; financial award applicants required to submit FAFSA. *Faculty research:* Second language acquisition/teaching, Inupiaq, Athabaskan languages, language maintenance and shift, phonology, morphology. *Total annual research expenditures:* $29,000. *Unit head:* Dr. Siri Tuttle, Program Head, 907-474-7876, Fax: 907-474-6586, E-mail: fyling@uaf.edu. *Application contact:* Libby Eddy, Registrar and Director of Admissions, 907-474-7500, Fax: 907-474-7097, E-mail: admissions@uaf.edu.
Website: http://www.uaf.edu/linguist/.

University of Alaska Fairbanks, School of Education, Fairbanks, AK 99775. Offers counseling (M Ed), including counseling; education (M Ed, Graduate Certificate), including cross-cultural education (M Ed), curriculum and instruction (M Ed), education (M Ed), elementary education (M Ed), language and literacy (M Ed), reading (M Ed), secondary education (M Ed), special education (M Ed); guidance and counseling (M Ed). *Accreditation:* NCATE. Postbaccalaureate distance learning degree programs offered. *Faculty:* 23 full-time (14 women), 1 part-time/adjunct (0 women). *Students:* 59 full-time (45 women), 116 part-time (85 women); includes 24 minority (2 Black or African American, non-Hispanic/Latino; 10 American Indian or Alaska Native, non-Hispanic/Latino; 7 Hispanic/Latino; 1 Native Hawaiian or other Pacific Islander, non-Hispanic/Latino; 4 Two or more races, non-Hispanic/Latino), 2 international. Average age 35. 77 applicants, 62% accepted, 40 enrolled. In 2013, 56 master's, 32 other advanced degrees awarded. *Degree requirements:* For master's, comprehensive exam, thesis or alternative, student teaching. *Entrance requirements:* For master's, GRE General Test, PRAXIS I, PRAXIS II, writing sample, evidence of technology competence, criminal background check. Additional exam requirements/recommendations for international students: Required—TOEFL (minimum score 550 paper-based; 80 iBT). *Application deadline:* For fall admission, 3/1 for domestic and international students; for spring admission, 10/15 for domestic students, 9/1 for international students. Application fee: $60. Electronic applications accepted. *Expenses:* Tuition, state resident: full-time $7254; part-time $403 per credit. Tuition, nonresident: full-time $14,814; part-time $823 per credit. Tuition and fees vary according to course level, course load and reciprocity agreements. *Financial support:* In 2013–14, 4 teaching assistantships with tuition reimbursements (averaging $10,932 per year) were awarded; fellowships with tuition reimbursements, research assistantships with tuition reimbursements, career-related internships or fieldwork, Federal Work-Study, scholarships/grants, health care benefits, and unspecified assistantships also available. Support available to part-time students. Financial award application deadline: 2/15; financial award applicants required to submit FAFSA. *Faculty research:* Native ways of knowing, classroom research in methods of literacy instruction, multiple intelligence theory, geometry concept development, mathematics and science curriculum development. *Total annual research expenditures:*

$244,000. *Unit head:* Allan Morotti, Dean, 907-474-7341, Fax: 907-474-5451, E-mail: uaf-soe-school@alaska.edu. *Application contact:* Libby Eddy, Registrar and Director of Admissions, 907-474-7500, Fax: 907-474-7097, E-mail: admissions@uaf.edu.
Website: https://sites.google.com/a/alaska.edu/soe-home/.

University of Alberta, Faculty of Graduate Studies and Research, Facultè Saint Jean, Edmonton, AB T6G 2E1, Canada. Offers M Ed. Part-time and evening/weekend programs available. Postbaccalaureate distance learning degree programs offered (minimal on-campus study). *Degree requirements:* For master's, thesis (for some programs). *Entrance requirements:* For master's, proficiency in French, 2 years of teaching experience. *Faculty research:* First and second language acquisition, first and second language learning through subject matter, cultural transmission.

The University of Arizona, College of Education, Department of Teaching, Learning and Sociocultural Studies, Tucson, AZ 85721. Offers bilingual education (M Ed); bilingual/multicultural education (MA); language, reading and culture (MA, Ed D, PhD, Ed S); teaching and teacher education (M Ed, MA, PhD). Part-time programs available. *Faculty:* 24 full-time (19 women), 1 (woman) part-time/adjunct. *Students:* 167 full-time (122 women), 82 part-time (59 women); includes 82 minority (9 Black or African American, non-Hispanic/Latino; 4 American Indian or Alaska Native, non-Hispanic/Latino; 5 Asian, non-Hispanic/Latino; 47 Hispanic/Latino; 17 Two or more races, non-Hispanic/Latino), 26 international. Average age 37. 152 applicants, 66% accepted, 67 enrolled. In 2013, 84 master's, 12 doctorates awarded. Terminal master's awarded for partial completion of doctoral program. *Degree requirements:* For master's, thesis optional, thesis (MA); for doctorate, comprehensive exam, thesis/dissertation; for Ed S, thesis optional. *Entrance requirements:* For master's, 2 letters of recommendation, resume; for doctorate, GRE or MAT, 2 letters of recommendation, resume; for Ed S, GRE, MAT. Additional exam requirements/recommendations for international students: Required—TOEFL (minimum score 550 paper-based; 79 iBT). *Application deadline:* For fall admission, 2/1 for domestic and international students. Application fee: $75. Electronic applications accepted. *Expenses:* Tuition, state resident: full-time $11,526. Tuition, nonresident: full-time $27,398. *Financial support:* In 2013–14, 19 research assistantships with full tuition reimbursements (averaging $19,534 per year), 25 teaching assistantships with full tuition reimbursements (averaging $16,157 per year) were awarded; career-related internships or fieldwork, scholarships/grants, health care benefits, tuition waivers (full and partial), and unspecified assistantships also available. Financial award application deadline: 3/7; financial award applicants required to submit FAFSA. *Faculty research:* Reading, Native American education, language policy, children's literature, bilingual/bicultural literacy. *Total annual research expenditures:* $1.7 million. *Unit head:* Dr. Bruce Johnson, Department Head, 520-626-8700, Fax: 520-621-1853, E-mail: brucej@email.arizona.edu. *Application contact:* Information Contact, 520-621-1311, Fax: 520-621-1853, E-mail: lrcinfo@email.arizona.edu.
Website: https://www.coe.arizona.edu/tls.

University of Calgary, Faculty of Graduate Studies, Werklund School of Education, Graduate Division of Educational Research, Calgary, AB T2N 1N4, Canada. Offers adult learning (M Ed, MA, Ed D, PhD); curriculum and learning (M Ed, MA, Ed D, PhD); educational leadership (M Ed, MA, Ed D, PhD); languages and diversity (M Ed, MA, Ed D, PhD); learning sciences (M Ed, MA, Ed D, PhD). Ed D in educational leadership offered via distance delivery. Part-time and evening/weekend programs available. Postbaccalaureate distance learning degree programs offered (minimal on-campus study). *Degree requirements:* For master's, thesis (for some programs); for doctorate, thesis/dissertation, candidacy exam. *Entrance requirements:* For master's, minimum GPA of 3.0, 3 letters of reference; for doctorate, minimum GPA of 3.5, 3 letters of reference. Additional exam requirements/recommendations for international students: Required—TOEFL, IELTS. Electronic applications accepted. *Faculty research:* Curriculum, leadership, technology, contexts, gifted, second language teaching, work place and adult learning.

University of California, Riverside, Graduate Division, Graduate School of Education, Riverside, CA 92521-0102. Offers autism (M Ed); diversity and equity (M Ed); education specialist (Credential); education, society and culture (MA, PhD); educational psychology (MA, PhD); general education (M Ed); higher education administration and policy (M Ed, PhD); multiple subject (Credential); reading (M Ed); school psychology (PhD); single subject (Credential); special education (M Ed, MA, PhD); TESOL (M Ed). *Faculty:* 22 full-time (11 women), 14 part-time/adjunct (10 women). *Students:* 218 full-time (148 women); includes 95 minority (10 Black or African American, non-Hispanic/Latino; 30 Asian, non-Hispanic/Latino; 49 Hispanic/Latino; 6 Two or more races, non-Hispanic/Latino), 12 international. Average age 31. 236 applicants, 66% accepted, 78 enrolled. In 2013, 66 master's, 13 doctorates, 86 other advanced degrees awarded. Terminal master's awarded for partial completion of doctoral program. *Degree requirements:* For master's, thesis optional, comprehensive exams or thesis (MA), case study or analytical report (M Ed); for doctorate, thesis/dissertation, written and oral qualifying exams, college teaching practicum. *Entrance requirements:* For master's, GRE General Test (for MA); CBEST and CSET (for M Ed in general education only), UCR Extension TESOL certificate (for M Ed with TESOL emphasis only); for doctorate, GRE General Test, writing sample; for Credential, CBEST, CSET. Additional exam requirements/recommendations for international students: Required—TOEFL (minimum score 550 paper-based; 80 iBT), IELTS (minimum score 7). *Application deadline:* For fall admission, 9/1 for domestic students, 5/1 for international students; for winter admission, 11/15 for domestic students, 7/1 for international students; for spring admission, 3/1 for domestic students, 10/1 for international students. Applications are processed on a rolling basis. Application fee: $80 ($100 for international students). Electronic applications accepted. *Financial support:* In 2013–14, 58 students received support, including 31 fellowships with full tuition reimbursements available, 11 research assistantships with full tuition reimbursements available (averaging $14,691 per year), 5 teaching assistantships with full tuition reimbursements available (averaging $17,655 per year); career-related internships or fieldwork, Federal Work-Study, institutionally sponsored loans, scholarships/grants, and unspecified assistantships also available. Financial award application deadline: 1/5. *Faculty research:* Responsiveness to intervention, faculty core, response to intervention of English language learners, advanced modeling techniques, study on social capital, trust, and motivation. *Total annual research expenditures:* $1.9 million. *Unit head:* Prof. Douglas Mitchell, Interim Dean and Professor, 951-827-5802, Fax: 951-827-3942, E-mail: douglas.mitchell@ucr.edu. *Application contact:* Prof. Michael Orosco, Assistant Professor and Graduate Advisor of Admissions, 951-827-6362, Fax: 951-827-3291, E-mail: edgrad@ucr.edu.
Website: http://www.education.ucr.edu/.

University of California, San Diego, Office of Graduate Studies, Program in Education Studies, La Jolla, CA 92093. Offers education (M Ed); educational leadership (Ed D); teaching and learning (M Ed, MA, Ed D), including bilingual education (M Ed), curriculum design (MA). Ed D offered jointly with California State University, San Marcos. *Students:* 66 full-time (46 women), 66 part-time (54 women); includes 66 minority (11 Black or African American, non-Hispanic/Latino; 6 American Indian or Alaska Native, non-Hispanic/Latino; 29 Asian, non-Hispanic/Latino; 20 Hispanic/Latino), 1 international. 91 applicants, 87% accepted, 64 enrolled. In 2013, 78 master's, 15 doctorates awarded. *Degree requirements:* For master's, thesis (for some programs), student teaching; for doctorate, thesis/dissertation. *Entrance requirements:* For master's, GRE General Test; CBEST and appropriate CSET exam (for select tracks), current teaching or educational assignment (for select tracks); for doctorate, GRE General Test, current teaching or educational assignment (for select tracks). Additional exam requirements/recommendations for international students: Required—TOEFL, IELTS. *Application deadline:* For fall admission, 2/4 for domestic students; for winter admission, 8/1 for domestic students; for summer admission, 2/4 for domestic students. Application fee: $80 ($100 for international students). Electronic applications accepted. *Expenses:* Tuition, state resident: full-time $11,220; part-time $1870 per quarter. Tuition, nonresident: full-time $26,322; part-time $4387 per quarter. *Required fees:* $519.50 per quarter. Part-time tuition and fees vary according to course load and program. *Financial support:* Fellowships and scholarships/grants available. Financial award applicants required to submit FAFSA. *Faculty research:* Language, culture and literacy development of deaf/hard of hearing children; equity issues in education; educational reform; evaluation, assessment, and research methodologies; distributed learning. *Unit head:* Alan J. Daly, Chair, 858-822-6472, E-mail: ajdaly@ucsd.edu. *Application contact:* Giselle Van Luit, Graduate Coordinator, 858-534-2958, E-mail: edsinfo@ucsd.edu.

University of Colorado Boulder, Graduate School, School of Education, Division of Social Multicultural and Bilingual Foundations, Boulder, CO 80309. Offers MA, PhD. *Accreditation:* NCATE. *Students:* 43 full-time (34 women), 128 part-time (109 women); includes 62 minority (3 Black or African American, non-Hispanic/Latino; 1 American Indian or Alaska Native, non-Hispanic/Latino; 3 Asian, non-Hispanic/Latino; 54 Hispanic/Latino; 1 Native Hawaiian or other Pacific Islander, non-Hispanic/Latino), 6 international. Average age 36. 47 applicants, 64% accepted, 24 enrolled. In 2013, 96 master's, 3 doctorates awarded. Terminal master's awarded for partial completion of doctoral program. *Degree requirements:* For master's, comprehensive exam, thesis or alternative; for doctorate, one foreign language, comprehensive exam, thesis/dissertation. *Entrance requirements:* For master's, GRE General Test or MAT, minimum undergraduate GPA of 2.75; for doctorate, GRE General Test. *Application deadline:* For fall admission, 2/1 for domestic students, 12/1 for international students; for spring admission, 9/1 for domestic and international students. Application fee: $50 ($60 for international students). Electronic applications accepted. *Financial support:* In 2013–14, 145 students received support, including 4 fellowships (averaging $8,616 per year), 20 research assistantships with full and partial tuition reimbursements available (averaging $34,375 per year), 5 teaching assistantships with full and partial tuition reimbursements available (averaging $12,627 per year); institutionally sponsored loans, scholarships/grants, health care benefits, and unspecified assistantships also available. Financial award applicants required to submit FAFSA. *Faculty research:* Bilingual education, inclusion.
Website: http://www.colorado.edu/education/.

University of Colorado Denver, School of Education and Human Development, Teacher Education Programs, Denver, CO 80217. Offers elementary linguistically diverse education (MA); elementary math and science education (MA); elementary math education (MA); elementary reading and writing (MA); elementary science education (MA); secondary English education (MA); secondary linguistically diverse education (MA); secondary math education (MA); secondary reading and writing (MA); secondary science education (MA); special education (MA). *Accreditation:* NCATE. Part-time and evening/weekend programs available. *Students:* 269 full-time (208 women), 141 part-time (111 women); includes 55 minority (4 Black or African American, non-Hispanic/Latino; 1 American Indian or Alaska Native, non-Hispanic/Latino; 10 Asian, non-Hispanic/Latino; 39 Hispanic/Latino; 1 Two or more races, non-Hispanic/Latino), 7 international. Average age 31. 97 applicants, 81% accepted, 62 enrolled. In 2013, 180 master's awarded. *Degree requirements:* For master's, comprehensive exam. *Entrance requirements:* For master's, GRE or MAT (for those with GPA below 2.75), transcripts, resume, letters of recommendation. Additional exam requirements/recommendations for international students: Required—TOEFL (minimum score 537 paper-based; 75 iBT); Recommended—IELTS (minimum score 6.5). *Application deadline:* For fall admission, 4/15 priority date for domestic students, 4/1 for international students; for spring admission, 9/15 priority date for domestic students, 9/1 for international students. Applications are processed on a rolling basis. Application fee: $50 ($75 for international students). Electronic applications accepted. *Expenses:* Contact institution. *Financial support:* In 2013–14, 42 students received support. Fellowships, research assistantships, teaching assistantships, Federal Work-Study, institutionally sponsored loans, scholarships/grants, and traineeships available. Financial award application deadline: 4/1; financial award applicants required to submit FAFSA. *Faculty research:* Linguistically diverse education/ESL, elementary reading and writing, elementary teacher education, secondary teacher education, special education. *Unit head:* Cindy Gutierrez, Director, 303-315-4982, E-mail: cindy.gutierrez@ucdenver.edu. *Application contact:* Lori Sisneros, Student Services Center, 303-315-4979, E-mail: education@ucdenver.edu.
Website: http://www.ucdenver.edu/academics/colleges/SchoolOfEducation/Academics/MASTERS/Pages/default.aspx.

University of Connecticut, Graduate School, Neag School of Education, Department of Curriculum and Instruction, Program in Bilingual and Bicultural Education, Storrs, CT 06269. Offers MA, PhD, Post-Master's Certificate. *Accreditation:* NCATE. Terminal master's awarded for partial completion of doctoral program. *Degree requirements:* For master's, comprehensive exam; for doctorate, thesis/dissertation. *Entrance requirements:* For doctorate, GRE General Test. Additional exam requirements/recommendations for international students: Required—TOEFL (minimum score 550 paper-based). Electronic applications accepted.

University of Delaware, College of Education and Human Development, School of Education, Newark, DE 19716. Offers education (PhD); educational leadership (Ed D); higher education (M Ed); instruction (MI); reading (M Ed); school leadership (M Ed); school psychology (MA, Ed S); teaching English as a second language (TESL) (MA). *Accreditation:* NCATE. Part-time and evening/weekend programs available. Terminal master's awarded for partial completion of doctoral program. *Degree requirements:* For master's, comprehensive exam (for some programs), thesis (for some programs); for doctorate, comprehensive exam (for some programs), thesis/dissertation. *Entrance requirements:* For master's and doctorate, GRE, 3 letters of recommendation. Additional exam requirements/recommendations for international students: Required—TOEFL (minimum score 600 paper-based). Electronic applications accepted. *Faculty research:* Teacher education; curriculum theory and development; community based education models, educational leadership.

The University of Findlay, Office of Graduate Admissions, Findlay, OH 45840-3653. Offers athletic training (MAT); business (MBA), including health care management, hospitality management, organizational leadership, public management; education (MA Ed), including administration, children's literature, early childhood, human resource development, reading, science, special education, technology; environmental, safety and health management (MSEM); health informatics (MS); occupational therapy (MOT); pharmacy (Pharm D); physical therapy (DPT); physician assistant (MPA); rhetoric and writing (MA); teaching English to speakers of other languages (TESOL) and bilingual education (MA). Part-time and evening/weekend programs available. Postbaccalaureate distance learning degree programs offered (no on-campus study). *Faculty:* 209 full-time

(98 women), 69 part-time/adjunct (38 women). *Students:* 551 full-time (332 women), 457 part-time (276 women); includes 77 minority (37 Black or African American, non-Hispanic/Latino; 1 American Indian or Alaska Native, non-Hispanic/Latino; 15 Asian, non-Hispanic/Latino; 23 Hispanic/Latino; 1 Native Hawaiian or other Pacific Islander, non-Hispanic/Latino), 135 international. Average age 28. 637 applicants, 66% accepted, 241 enrolled. In 2013, 267 master's, 91 doctorates awarded. *Degree requirements:* For master's, thesis, cumulative project, capstone project. *Entrance requirements:* For master's, GRE/GMAT, bachelor's degree from accredited institution, minimum undergraduate GPA of 2.5 in last 64 hours of course work; for doctorate, GRE, minimum cumulative GPA of 3.0. Additional exam requirements/recommendations for international students: Required—TOEFL (minimum score 80 iBT). *Application deadline:* Applications are processed on a rolling basis. Application fee: $25. Electronic applications accepted. *Expenses: Required fees:* $146 per semester. Tuition and fees vary according to degree level and program. *Financial support:* In 2013–14, 11 research assistantships with full and partial tuition reimbursements (averaging $4,000 per year), 10 teaching assistantships with full and partial tuition reimbursements (averaging $3,600 per year) were awarded; career-related internships or fieldwork, Federal Work-Study, health care benefits, and unspecified assistantships also available. Financial award application deadline: 4/1; financial award applicants required to submit FAFSA. *Unit head:* Christopher M. Harris, Director of Admissions, 419-434-4347, E-mail: harrisc1@findlay.edu. *Application contact:* Emily Ickes, Graduate Admissions Counselor, 419-434-6933, Fax: 419-434-4898, E-mail: ickese@findlay.edu.
Website: http://www.findlay.edu/admissions/graduate/Pages/default.aspx.

University of Florida, Graduate School, College of Education, School of Teaching and Learning, Gainesville, FL 32611. Offers curriculum and instruction (M Ed, MAE, Ed D, PhD, Ed S), including bilingual/ESOL specialization; elementary education (M Ed, MAE); English education (M Ed, MAE); mathematics education (M Ed, MAE); reading education (M Ed, MAE); science education (M Ed, MAE); social studies education (M Ed, MAE). *Accreditation:* NCATE. Part-time and evening/weekend programs available. Postbaccalaureate distance learning degree programs offered (no on-campus study). *Faculty:* 24 full-time (17 women), 12 part-time/adjunct (7 women). *Students:* 201 full-time (162 women), 325 part-time (255 women); includes 124 minority (36 Black or African American, non-Hispanic/Latino; 4 American Indian or Alaska Native, non-Hispanic/Latino; 10 Asian, non-Hispanic/Latino; 74 Hispanic/Latino), 47 international. Average age 34. 220 applicants, 55% accepted, 64 enrolled. In 2013, 215 master's, 15 doctorates, 14 other advanced degrees awarded. Terminal master's awarded for partial completion of doctoral program. *Degree requirements:* For master's, comprehensive exam (for some programs), thesis (for some programs); for doctorate, comprehensive exam (for some programs), thesis/dissertation (for some programs). *Entrance requirements:* For master's and doctorate, GRE General Test, minimum GPA of 3.0; for Ed S, GRE General Test. Additional exam requirements/recommendations for international students: Required—TOEFL (minimum score 550 paper-based; 80 iBT), IELTS (minimum score 6). *Application deadline:* For fall admission, 2/15 for domestic students, 12/1 for international students; for spring admission, 9/15 for domestic students, 3/1 for international students. Applications are processed on a rolling basis. Application fee: $30. Electronic applications accepted. *Expenses:* Tuition, state resident: full-time $12,640. Tuition, nonresident: full-time $30,000. *Financial support:* In 2013–14, 52 students received support, including 3 fellowships (averaging $2,365 per year), 20 research assistantships (averaging $11,715 per year), 58 teaching assistantships (averaging $8,410 per year); career-related internships or fieldwork and unspecified assistantships also available. Financial award applicants required to submit FAFSA. *Faculty research:* Early childhood, child and adolescents, diverse learners, race/ethnicity issues, teacher education, professional development, language and literacy development, policy development. *Unit head:* Elizabeth Bondy, PhD, Interim Director and Professor, 352-273-4242, Fax: 352-392-9193, E-mail: bondy@coe.ufl.edu. *Application contact:* Sevan Terzian, Graduate Coordinator, 352-273-4216, Fax: 352-392-9193, E-mail: sterzian@coe.ufl.edu.
Website: http://education.ufl.edu/school-teaching-learning/.

University of Houston–Clear Lake, School of Education, Program in Foundations and Professional Studies, Houston, TX 77058-1002. Offers counseling (MS); instructional technology (MS); multicultural studies (MS). Part-time and evening/weekend programs available. *Degree requirements:* For master's, thesis optional. *Entrance requirements:* For master's, GRE or minimum GPA of 3.0 in last 60 hours. Additional exam requirements/recommendations for international students: Required—TOEFL (minimum score 550 paper-based). Electronic applications accepted.

University of Illinois at Chicago, Graduate College, College of Education, Department of Curriculum and Instruction, Chicago, IL 60607-7128. Offers curriculum studies (PhD); educational studies (M Ed); elementary education (M Ed); instructional leadership (M Ed); literacy, language and culture (M Ed, PhD); science education (M Ed); secondary education (M Ed). Part-time and evening/weekend programs available. *Faculty:* 20 full-time (10 women), 10 part-time/adjunct (8 women). *Students:* 124 full-time (89 women), 155 part-time (117 women); includes 117 minority (51 Black or African American, non-Hispanic/Latino; 19 Asian, non-Hispanic/Latino; 43 Hispanic/Latino; 4 Two or more races, non-Hispanic/Latino), 11 international. Average age 32. 154 applicants, 70% accepted, 74 enrolled. In 2013, 108 master's, 16 doctorates awarded. *Degree requirements:* For doctorate, thesis/dissertation. *Entrance requirements:* For master's, minimum GPA of 2.75; for doctorate, GRE General Test, minimum GPA of 2.75. Additional exam requirements/recommendations for international students: Required—TOEFL. *Application deadline:* For fall admission, 1/9 for domestic and international students; for spring admission, 10/1 for domestic and international students. Applications are processed on a rolling basis. Application fee: $40 ($50 for international students). Electronic applications accepted. *Expenses:* Tuition, state resident: full-time $11,066; part-time $3689 per term. Tuition, nonresident: full-time $23,064; part-time $7688 per term. *Required fees:* $3004; $1190 per term. Tuition and fees vary according to course level and program. *Financial support:* In 2013–14, 101 students received support, including 4 fellowships with full tuition reimbursements available; research assistantships with full tuition reimbursements available, teaching assistantships with full tuition reimbursements available, career-related internships or fieldwork, Federal Work-Study, institutionally sponsored loans, traineeships, tuition waivers (full), and unspecified assistantships also available. Support available to part-time students. Financial award application deadline: 3/1; financial award applicants required to submit FAFSA. *Faculty research:* Curriculum theory, curriculum development, research on teaching, curriculum and context, reading/literacy. *Total annual research expenditures:* $70,000. *Unit head:* Prof. Alfred Tatum, Associate Professor/Director/Chair, 312-413-3883, Fax: 312-996-8134, E-mail: atatum1@uic.edu.
Website: http://education.uic.edu.

University of Maryland, Baltimore County, Graduate School, College of Arts, Humanities and Social Sciences, Department of Modern Languages and Linguistics, Program in Intercultural Communication, Baltimore, MD 21250. Offers MA. Part-time and evening/weekend programs available. *Faculty:* 17 full-time (9 women), 2 part-time/adjunct (1 woman). *Students:* 24 full-time (20 women), 9 part-time (all women); includes 5 minority (3 Black or African American, non-Hispanic/Latino; 2 Hispanic/Latino), 11 international. 15 applicants, 80% accepted, 10 enrolled. In 2013, 12 master's awarded. *Degree requirements:* For master's, one foreign language, comprehensive exam (for some programs), thesis (for some programs). *Entrance requirements:* For master's, GRE General Test, minimum GPA of 3.0, 3 letters of recommendation, self-evaluation and statement of support, resume. Additional exam requirements/recommendations for international students: Required—TOEFL (minimum score 550 paper-based; 80 iBT). *Application deadline:* For fall admission, 1/31 for domestic and international students. Application fee: $50. Electronic applications accepted. One-time fee: $200 full-time. *Financial support:* In 2013–14, 8 students received support, including 6 teaching assistantships with full tuition reimbursements available (averaging $11,324 per year); Federal Work-Study, scholarships/grants, and tuition waivers (partial) also available. Financial award application deadline: 1/31; financial award applicants required to submit FAFSA. *Faculty research:* Comparative television research-cross-cultural; cultural studies; social developments in Latin America; intercultural communication; French civilization and cultural studies; language, gender and sexuality; sociolinguistics; African linguistics; immigrants in U.S. and Latin American societies. *Unit head:* Dr. Denis Provencher, Director, 410-455-2109 Ext. 52636, Fax: 410-455-2636, E-mail: provench@umbc.edu. *Application contact:* Dr. Denis Provencher, Director, 410-455-2109 Ext. 52636, Fax: 410-455-1025, E-mail: provench@umbc.edu.
Website: http://www.umbc.edu/mll/incc/.

University of Maryland, Baltimore County, Graduate School, College of Arts, Humanities and Social Sciences, Program in Language, Literacy, and Culture, Baltimore, MD 21250. Offers PhD. Part-time and evening/weekend programs available. *Faculty:* 4 full-time (3 women). *Students:* 35 full-time (22 women), 24 part-time (19 women); includes 14 minority (10 Black or African American, non-Hispanic/Latino; 1 Asian, non-Hispanic/Latino; 1 Hispanic/Latino; 2 Two or more races, non-Hispanic/Latino), 13 international. Average age 35. 39 applicants, 28% accepted, 10 enrolled. In 2013, 7 doctorates awarded. *Degree requirements:* For doctorate, comprehensive exam, thesis/dissertation. *Entrance requirements:* For doctorate, research writing sample; resume or curriculum vitae; master's degree. Additional exam requirements/recommendations for international students: Required—TOEFL (minimum score 80 iBT). *Application deadline:* For fall admission, 12/1 for domestic and international students. Application fee: $50. Electronic applications accepted. One-time fee: $200 full-time. *Financial support:* In 2013–14, 14 research assistantships with full and partial tuition reimbursements, 2 teaching assistantships with full and partial tuition reimbursements were awarded; health care benefits and unspecified assistantships also available. Financial award application deadline: 12/1. *Faculty research:* Educational equity, identity, intercultural communication, technology and communication. *Unit head:* Dr. Craig Saper, Director, 410-455-2376, Fax: 410-455-8947, E-mail: csaper@umbc.edu. *Application contact:* Liz Steenrod, Administrative Assistant, 410-455-2376, Fax: 410-455-8947, E-mail: llc@umbc.edu.
Website: http://llc.umbc.edu.

University of Massachusetts Amherst, Graduate School, College of Education, Program in Education, Amherst, MA 01003. Offers bilingual/English as a second language/multicultural education (M Ed, Ed S); child study and early education (M Ed); children, families and schools (Ed D, Ed S); early childhood and elementary teacher education (M Ed); educational leadership (M Ed); educational policy and leadership (Ed D); higher education (M Ed); international education (M Ed); language, literacy and culture (Ed D); learning, media and technology (M Ed, Ed S); mathematics, science, and learning technologies (Ed D); psychometric methods, educational statistics and research methods (Ed D); reading and writing (M Ed); school counselor education (M Ed, Ed S); school psychology (Ed S); science education (Ed S); secondary teacher education (M Ed); social justice education (M Ed, Ed D, Ed S); special education (M Ed, Ed D, Ed S); teacher education and school improvement (Ed D, Ed S). *Accreditation:* NCATE. Part-time programs available. Postbaccalaureate distance learning degree programs offered (minimal on-campus study). *Faculty:* 95 full-time (55 women). *Students:* 357 full-time (240 women), 264 part-time (194 women); includes 114 minority (41 Black or African American, non-Hispanic/Latino; 4 American Indian or Alaska Native, non-Hispanic/Latino; 10 Asian, non-Hispanic/Latino; 47 Hispanic/Latino; 12 Two or more races, non-Hispanic/Latino), 100 international. Average age 34. 761 applicants, 51% accepted, 200 enrolled. In 2013, 186 master's, 31 doctorates, 22 other advanced degrees awarded. Terminal master's awarded for partial completion of doctoral program. *Degree requirements:* For doctorate, comprehensive exam, thesis/dissertation. *Entrance requirements:* Additional exam requirements/recommendations for international students: Required—TOEFL (minimum score 550 paper-based; 80 iBT), IELTS (minimum score 6.5). *Application deadline:* For fall admission, 1/15 for domestic and international students. Applications are processed on a rolling basis. Application fee: $75. Electronic applications accepted. *Financial support:* Fellowships with full and partial tuition reimbursements, research assistantships with full and partial tuition reimbursements, teaching assistantships with full and partial tuition reimbursements, career-related internships or fieldwork, Federal Work-Study, scholarships/grants, traineeships, health care benefits, tuition waivers (full and partial), and unspecified assistantships available. Support available to part-time students. Financial award application deadline: 1/15; financial award applicants required to submit FAFSA. *Unit head:* Dr. Linda L. Griffin, Graduate Program Director, 413-545-6984, Fax: 413-545-1523. *Application contact:* Lindsay DeSantis, Supervisor of Admissions, 413-545-0722, Fax: 413-577-0010, E-mail: gradadm@grad.umass.edu.
Website: http://www.umass.edu/education/.

University of Massachusetts Boston, Office of Graduate Studies, College of Liberal Arts, Program in Applied Linguistics, Boston, MA 02125-3393. Offers bilingual education (MA); English as a second language (MA); foreign language pedagogy (MA). Part-time and evening/weekend programs available. *Degree requirements:* For master's, one foreign language, comprehensive exam. *Entrance requirements:* For master's, minimum GPA of 2.75. *Faculty research:* Multicultural theory and curriculum development, foreign language pedagogy, language and culture, applied psycholinguistics, bilingual education.

University of Miami, Graduate School, School of Education and Human Development, Department of Teaching and Learning, Program in Teaching and Learning, Coral Gables, FL 33124. Offers language and literacy learning in multilingual settings (PhD); science, technology, engineering and mathematics (PhD); special education (PhD). *Faculty:* 14 full-time (10 women), 9 part-time/adjunct (all women). *Students:* 24 full-time (21 women); includes 11 minority (3 Black or African American, non-Hispanic/Latino; 7 Hispanic/Latino; 1 Two or more races, non-Hispanic/Latino), 5 international. Average age 32. 29 applicants, 21% accepted, 5 enrolled. In 2013, 2 doctorates awarded. *Degree requirements:* For doctorate, thesis/dissertation, qualifying exam, electronic portfolio. *Entrance requirements:* For doctorate, GRE General Test. Additional exam requirements/recommendations for international students: Required—TOEFL (minimum score 550 paper-based; 80 iBT); Recommended—IELTS (minimum score 6.5). *Application deadline:* For fall admission, 2/15 for domestic students, 10/1 for international students. Application fee: $65. Electronic applications accepted. *Financial support:* In 2013–14, 24 students received support, including 11 research assistantships with full and partial tuition reimbursements available (averaging $18,900 per year), 8 teaching assistantships with full and partial tuition reimbursements available (averaging $18,900 per year). Financial award application deadline: 3/1; financial award applicants required to submit FAFSA. *Faculty research:* Teacher education, multicultural education, special education, second language acquisition, math and science education.

Unit head: Dr. Elizabeth Harry, Department Chairperson and Program Director, 305-284-4961, Fax: 305-284-6998, E-mail: bharry@miami.edu. *Application contact:* Lois Heffernan, Graduate Admission Coordinator, 305-284-2167, Fax: 305-284-9395, E-mail: lheffernan@miami.edu.

University of Minnesota, Twin Cities Campus, Graduate School, College of Education and Human Development, Department of Curriculum and Instruction, Program in Teaching, Minneapolis, MN 55455-0213. Offers Chinese (M Ed); earth science (M Ed); elementary special education (M Ed); English (M Ed); English as a second language (M Ed); French (M Ed); German (M Ed); Hebrew (M Ed); Japanese (M Ed); life sciences (M Ed); mathematics (M Ed); middle school science (M Ed); science (M Ed); second languages and cultures (M Ed); social studies (M Ed); Spanish (M Ed). *Students:* 220 full-time (154 women), 83 part-time (60 women); includes 43 minority (10 Black or African American, non-Hispanic/Latino; 26 Asian, non-Hispanic/Latino; 7 Hispanic/Latino), 4 international. Average age 27. 261 applicants, 87% accepted, 222 enrolled. In 2013, 561 master's awarded. Application fee: $75 ($95 for international students). *Unit head:* Dr. Nina Asher, Chair, 612-624-1357, Fax: 612-624-8277, E-mail: nasher@umn.edu. *Application contact:* Dr. Jennifer Engler, Assistant Dean, 612-626-2887, Fax: 612-626-7496, E-mail: engle009@umn.edu.
Website: http://www.cehd.umn.edu/ci/.

University of Minnesota, Twin Cities Campus, Graduate School, College of Education and Human Development, Department of Postsecondary Teaching and Learning, Minneapolis, MN 55455-0213. Offers multicultural college teaching and learning (MA). *Faculty:* 20 full-time (11 women). *Students:* 6 full-time (2 women), 8 part-time (5 women); includes 9 minority (4 Black or African American, non-Hispanic/Latino; 1 American Indian or Alaska Native, non-Hispanic/Latino; 1 Asian, non-Hispanic/Latino; 3 Hispanic/Latino), 1 international. Average age 35. 19 applicants, 84% accepted, 10 enrolled. In 2013, 7 master's awarded. Application fee: $75 ($95 for international students). *Financial support:* In 2013–14, 5 research assistantships (averaging $8,153 per year), 3 teaching assistantships (averaging $9,058 per year) were awarded. *Faculty research:* Diversity and equity in postsecondary education, teaching and learning in higher education, instructional design for diverse learning environments, developmental education, multicultural education, first-generation college students. *Total annual research expenditures:* $148,917. *Unit head:* Dr. Amy Lee, Chair, 612-625-0884, E-mail: amylee@umn.edu. *Application contact:* Dr. Jennifer Engler, Assistant Dean for Student Services, 612-626-2887, Fax: 612-626-7496, E-mail: engle009@umn.edu.
Website: http://www.cehd.umn.edu/PSTL/.

University of New Mexico, Graduate School, College of Education, Department of Language, Literacy and Sociocultural Studies, Program in Language, Literacy and Sociocultural Studies, Albuquerque, NM 87131. Offers American Indian education (MA); bilingual education (MA, PhD); educational linguistics (PhD); educational thought and sociocultural studies (MA, PhD); literacy/language arts (MA, PhD); social studies (MA); TESOL (MA, PhD). *Faculty:* 10 full-time (6 women), 3 part-time/adjunct (1 woman). *Students:* 63 full-time (48 women), 117 part-time (105 women); includes 96 minority (8 Black or African American, non-Hispanic/Latino; 16 American Indian or Alaska Native, non-Hispanic/Latino; 6 Asian, non-Hispanic/Latino; 62 Hispanic/Latino; 4 Two or more races, non-Hispanic/Latino), 20 international. Average age 39. 67 applicants, 63% accepted, 30 enrolled. In 2013, 30 master's, 8 doctorates awarded. *Degree requirements:* For master's, comprehensive exam, thesis optional; for doctorate, comprehensive exam, thesis/dissertation, research skills. *Entrance requirements:* For master's, letter of intent, 3 letters of recommendation, resume, BA/BS, department demographic form, transcripts; for doctorate, writing sample, letter of intent, 3 letters of recommendation, resume, BA/BS, MA, department demographic form, transcripts. Additional exam requirements/recommendations for international students: Required—TOEFL. *Application deadline:* For fall admission, 12/1 for domestic and international students; for spring admission, 9/15 for domestic and international students. Application fee: $50. Electronic applications accepted. *Financial support:* In 2013–14, 7 students received support, including 7 fellowships (averaging $3,170 per year), 1,318 teaching assistantships with tuition reimbursements available (averaging $3,789 per year); research assistantships, career-related internships or fieldwork, institutionally sponsored loans, scholarships/grants, and unspecified assistantships also available. Support available to part-time students. Financial award application deadline: 3/1; financial award applicants required to submit FAFSA. *Faculty research:* School reform, professional development, history of education, Native American education, politics of education, feminism and issues of sexual identity, critical race theory, bilingualism, literacy reading, adolescent literature, second language acquisition, critical theory and schooling, indigenous languages. *Unit head:* Dr. Lois M. Meyer, Chair, 505-277-7244, Fax: 505-277-8362, E-mail: lsmeyer@unm.edu. *Application contact:* Debra Schaffer, Administrative Assistant, 505-277-0437, Fax: 505-277-8362, E-mail: schaffer@unm.edu.
Website: http://coe.unm.edu/departments/department-of-language-literacy-and-sociocultural-studies/llss-program.html.

University of New Mexico, Graduate School, College of Education, Department of Teacher Education, Educational Leadership and Policy, Program in Multicultural Teacher and Childhood Education, Albuquerque, NM 87131-2039. Offers Ed D, PhD. *Accreditation:* NCATE. Part-time programs available. *Faculty:* 16 full-time (14 women). *Students:* 4 full-time (3 women), 11 part-time (8 women); includes 8 minority (all Hispanic/Latino). Average age 49. 1 applicant, 100% accepted. In 2013, 2 doctorates awarded. *Degree requirements:* For doctorate, comprehensive exam, thesis/dissertation. *Entrance requirements:* For doctorate, GRE, master's degree, minimum GPA of 3.0, 3 years of teaching experience, 3-5 letters of reference, 1 letter of intent, professional writing sample. Additional exam requirements/recommendations for international students: Required—TOEFL (minimum score 550 paper-based). *Application deadline:* For fall admission, 1/15 priority date for domestic students, 1/15 for international students; for spring admission, 10/30 for domestic and international students. Application fee: $50. Electronic applications accepted. *Financial support:* In 2013–14, 10 students received support, including 2 research assistantships (averaging $22,000 per year), 3 teaching assistantships with partial tuition reimbursements available (averaging $8,628 per year); fellowships, scholarships/grants, and unspecified assistantships also available. Financial award application deadline: 3/1; financial award applicants required to submit FAFSA. *Faculty research:* Teacher education, clinical preparation, reflective practice, science education, mathematics education, social justice, technology education, media literacy. *Unit head:* Dr. Cheryl Torrez, Department Chair, 505-277-9611, Fax: 505-277-0455, E-mail: ted@unm.edu. *Application contact:* Robert Romero, Program Coordinator, 505-277-0513, Fax: 505-277-0455, E-mail: ted@unm.edu.
Website: http://coe.unm.edu/departments/teacher-ed/grad-degrees-certs/mctc-edd-phd.html.

The University of North Carolina at Greensboro, Graduate School, School of Education, Department of Educational Leadership and Cultural Foundations, Greensboro, NC 27412-5001. Offers curriculum and teaching (PhD), including cultural studies; educational leadership (Ed D, Ed S); school administration (MSA). *Accreditation:* NCATE. *Degree requirements:* For doctorate, thesis/dissertation. *Entrance requirements:* For master's, doctorate, and Ed S, GRE General Test. Additional exam requirements/recommendations for international students: Required—TOEFL. Electronic applications accepted.

University of Oklahoma, Jeannine Rainbolt College of Education, Department of Instructional Leadership and Academic Curriculum, Norman, OK 73072. Offers communication, culture and pedagogy for Hispanic populations in educational settings (Graduate Certificate); instructional leadership and academic curriculum (M Ed, PhD), including bilingual education (PhD), early childhood education, elementary education, English education, instructional leadership, mathematics education, reading education, science education, science, technology, engineering and mathematics education (M Ed), secondary education, social studies education, teacher education (M Ed), world language education (M Ed). *Accreditation:* NCATE. Part-time and evening/weekend programs available. Postbaccalaureate distance learning degree programs offered (no on-campus study). *Faculty:* 22 full-time (15 women), 1 (woman) part-time/adjunct. *Students:* 64 full-time (49 women), 103 part-time (81 women); includes 33 minority (8 Black or African American, non-Hispanic/Latino; 9 American Indian or Alaska Native, non-Hispanic/Latino; 5 Asian, non-Hispanic/Latino; 4 Hispanic/Latino; 1 Native Hawaiian or other Pacific Islander, non-Hispanic/Latino; 6 Two or more races, non-Hispanic/Latino), 10 international. Average age 34. 50 applicants, 84% accepted, 36 enrolled. In 2013, 26 master's, 11 doctorates awarded. Terminal master's awarded for partial completion of doctoral program. *Degree requirements:* For master's, comprehensive exam (for some programs), thesis (for some programs); for doctorate, comprehensive exam, thesis/dissertation. *Entrance requirements:* For master's, essay; for doctorate, GRE, 3 recommendation letters; autobiography, statement of objectives; essay on chosen major; transcripts; writing sample. Additional exam requirements/recommendations for international students: Required—TOEFL (minimum score 79 iBT). *Application deadline:* For fall admission, 4/30 for domestic and international students; for spring admission, 10/31 for domestic and international students; for summer admission, 3/15 for domestic and international students. Applications are processed on a rolling basis. Application fee: $50 ($100 for international students). Electronic applications accepted. *Expenses:* Tuition, state resident: full-time $4205; part-time $175.20 per credit hour. Tuition, nonresident: full-time $16,205; part-time $675.20 per credit hour. *Required fees:* $2745; $103.85 per credit hour. $126.50 per semester. *Financial support:* In 2013–14, 98 students received support, including 10 research assistantships with partial tuition reimbursements available (averaging $10,671 per year), 7 teaching assistantships with partial tuition reimbursements available (averaging $10,753 per year); Federal Work-Study, institutionally sponsored loans, scholarships/grants, and unspecified assistantships also available. Support available to part-time students. Financial award application deadline: 6/1; financial award applicants required to submit FAFSA. *Total annual research expenditures:* $1 million. *Unit head:* Dr. Stacy Reeder, Chair/Graduate Liaison, 405-325-1498, Fax: 405-325-4061, E-mail: reeder@ou.edu. *Application contact:* Lynn Crussel, Graduate Programs Officer, 405-325-1498, Fax: 405-325-4061, E-mail: lcrussel@ou.edu.
Website: http://education.ou.edu/departments/ilac.

University of Pennsylvania, Graduate School of Education, Division of Educational Linguistics, Program in Intercultural Communication, Philadelphia, PA 19104. Offers MS Ed. Part-time programs available. *Students:* 31 full-time (30 women), 6 part-time (all women); includes 6 minority (1 Black or African American, non-Hispanic/Latino; 3 Asian, non-Hispanic/Latino; 2 Hispanic/Latino), 24 international. 73 applicants, 44% accepted, 15 enrolled. In 2013, 17 master's awarded. *Degree requirements:* For master's, comprehensive exam, thesis. *Entrance requirements:* For master's, GRE General Test or MAT. *Application deadline:* For fall admission, 12/15 priority date for domestic students. Applications are processed on a rolling basis. Application fee: $70. Electronic applications accepted. *Expenses:* Contact institution. *Financial support:* Career-related internships or fieldwork, Federal Work-Study, and institutionally sponsored loans available. Support available to part-time students. Financial award applicants required to submit FAFSA. *Faculty research:* Anthropology of education, history of education, bicultural education, identity and gender education. *Unit head:* Dr. Andrew Porter, Dean, 215-898-7014. *Application contact:* 215-898-6415, Fax: 215-746-6884, E-mail: admissions@gse.upenn.edu.
Website: http://www.gse.upenn.edu.

University of St. Thomas, Graduate Studies, School of Education, Department of Teacher Education, St. Paul, MN 55105-1096. Offers curriculum and instruction (MA), including elementary, individualized, K-12, secondary; elementary education (MA); English as a second language (MA); math education (Certificate); multicultural education (Certificate); reading (MA, Certificate), including elementary (MA), K-12 (MA). *Accreditation:* NCATE. Part-time and evening/weekend programs available. *Entrance requirements:* For master's, minimum GPA of 3.0 or MAT. Additional exam requirements/recommendations for international students: Required—TOEFL (minimum score 550 paper-based; 80 iBT). *Application deadline:* For fall admission, 6/1 for domestic students; for spring admission, 11/1 for domestic students. Applications are processed on a rolling basis. Application fee: $50. *Financial support:* Fellowships, research assistantships, institutionally sponsored loans, and scholarships/grants available. Support available to part-time students. Financial award applicants required to submit FAFSA. *Unit head:* Dr. Jan L. H. Frank, Chair, 651-962-4446, Fax: 651-962-4169, E-mail: jlhfrank@stthomas.edu. *Application contact:* Rosemary R. Barreto, Department Assistant, 651-962-4420, Fax: 651-962-4169, E-mail: barr7879@stthomas.edu.

University of St. Thomas, School of Education, Houston, TX 77006-4696. Offers all level education (M Ed); bilingual/dual language (M Ed); Catholic school teaching (M Ed); Catholic/private school leadership (M Ed); counselor education (M Ed); curriculum and instruction (M Ed); educational leadership (M Ed); elementary teaching (M Ed); English as a second language (M Ed); exceptionality/educational diagnostician (M Ed); exceptionality/special education (M Ed); generalist (M Ed); reading (M Ed); secondary teaching (M Ed). *Accreditation:* Teacher Education Accreditation Council. Part-time and evening/weekend programs available. Postbaccalaureate distance learning degree programs offered (no on-campus study). *Faculty:* 40 full-time (26 women), 43 part-time/adjunct (31 women). *Students:* 27 full-time (20 women), 1,091 part-time (981 women); includes 691 minority (247 Black or African American, non-Hispanic/Latino; 1 American Indian or Alaska Native, non-Hispanic/Latino; 44 Asian, non-Hispanic/Latino; 379 Hispanic/Latino; 2 Native Hawaiian or other Pacific Islander, non-Hispanic/Latino; 18 Two or more races, non-Hispanic/Latino), 28 international. Average age 36. 858 applicants, 83% accepted, 458 enrolled. In 2013, 454 master's awarded. *Degree requirements:* For master's, thesis, field experience. *Entrance requirements:* For master's, GRE or MAT if GPA is below 3.0, bachelor's degree; minimum GPA of 2.75 in bachelor's degree or last 60 credit hours; official transcripts from all institutions; goal statement of 250-300 words; 1 reference. Additional exam requirements/recommendations for international students: Required—TOEFL. *Application deadline:* Applications are processed on a rolling basis. Application fee: $35. Electronic applications accepted. *Expenses:* Contact institution. *Financial support:* In 2013–14, 41 students received support. Federal Work-Study, scholarships/grants, and state work-study, institutional employment available. Support available to part-time students. Financial award application deadline: 4/15; financial award applicants required to submit FAFSA. *Faculty research:* Leadership, diversity, personality traits, second language acquisition. *Unit head:* Dr. Robert LeBlanc, Dean, 713-525-3540, Fax: 713-525-3871,

E-mail: education@stthom.edu. *Application contact:* Rita Paredes, Administrative Assistant, 713-525-3442, Fax: 713-525-3871, E-mail: rparede@stthom.edu.
Website: http://www.stthom.edu/Academics/School_of_Education/Index.aqf.

University of San Francisco, School of Education, Department of International and Multicultural Education, San Francisco, CA 94117-1080. Offers human rights education (MA); international and multicultural education (MA, Ed D); multicultural literature for children and young adults (MA); teaching English to speakers of other languages (MA). Evening/weekend programs available. *Faculty:* 2 full-time (both women), 9 part-time/adjunct (5 women). *Students:* 132 full-time (99 women), 62 part-time (53 women); includes 90 minority (12 Black or African American, non-Hispanic/Latino; 26 Asian, non-Hispanic/Latino; 39 Hispanic/Latino; 1 Native Hawaiian or other Pacific Islander, non-Hispanic/Latino; 12 Two or more races, non-Hispanic/Latino), 30 international. Average age 35. 202 applicants, 80% accepted, 60 enrolled. In 2013, 41 master's, 10 doctorates awarded. *Degree requirements:* For doctorate, thesis/dissertation. *Application deadline:* For fall admission, 3/1 priority date for domestic students, 3/1 for international students; for spring admission, 10/15 priority date for domestic and international students. Applications are processed on a rolling basis. Application fee: $55 ($65 for international students). Electronic applications accepted. *Expenses: Tuition:* Full-time $21,150; part-time $1175 per unit. Tuition and fees vary according to course load, campus/location and program. *Financial support:* In 2013–14, 18 students received support. Fellowships, research assistantships, and teaching assistantships available. Financial award application deadline: 3/2; financial award applicants required to submit FAFSA. *Unit head:* Dr. Katz Susan, Chair, 415-422-6878. *Application contact:* Amy Fogliani, Associate Director of Graduate Outreach, 415-422-5467, E-mail: schoolofeducation@usfca.edu.

University of Southern California, Graduate School, Rossier School of Education, Doctor of Education Programs, Los Angeles, CA 90089. Offers educational psychology (Ed D); higher education administration (Ed D); K-12 leadership in urban school settings (Ed D); teacher education in multicultural societies (Ed D). Part-time and evening/weekend programs available. *Degree requirements:* For doctorate, thesis/dissertation. *Entrance requirements:* For doctorate, GRE. Additional exam requirements/recommendations for international students: Required—TOEFL (minimum score 100 iBT). Electronic applications accepted. *Faculty research:* Data-driven decision-making in K-12 schools and districts; examination of college and university leadership and management in U. S. and Asia; studies in facilitating student learning; organizational change and the role of leaders; leadership, diversity, learning and accountability.

The University of Tennessee, Graduate School, College of Education, Health and Human Sciences, Program in Education, Knoxville, TN 37996. Offers art education (MS); counseling education (PhD); cultural studies in education (PhD); curriculum (MS, Ed S); curriculum, educational research and evaluation (Ed D, PhD); early childhood education (PhD); early childhood special education (MS); education of deaf and hard of hearing (MS); educational administration and policy studies (Ed D, PhD); educational administration and supervision (Ed S); educational psychology (Ed D, PhD); elementary education (MS, Ed S); elementary teaching (MS); English education (MS, Ed S); exercise science (PhD); foreign language/ESL education (MS, Ed S); instructional technology (MS, Ed D, PhD, Ed S); literacy, language and ESL education (PhD); literacy, language education, and ESL education (Ed D); mathematics education (MS, Ed S); modified and comprehensive special education (MS); reading education (MS, Ed S); school counseling (Ed S); school psychology (PhD, Ed S); science education (MS, Ed S); secondary teaching (MS); social foundations (MS); social science education (MS, Ed S); socio-cultural foundations of sports and education (PhD); special education (Ed S); teacher education (Ed D, PhD). *Accreditation:* NCATE. Part-time and evening/weekend programs available. *Degree requirements:* For master's and Ed S, thesis optional; for doctorate, variable foreign language requirement, thesis/dissertation. *Entrance requirements:* For master's, minimum GPA of 2.7; for doctorate and Ed S, GRE General Test, minimum GPA of 2.7. Additional exam requirements/recommendations for international students: Required—TOEFL. Electronic applications accepted. *Expenses:* Tuition, state resident: full-time $9540; part-time $531 per credit hour. Tuition, nonresident: full-time $27,728; part-time $1542 per credit hour. *Required fees:* $1404; $67 per credit hour.

The University of Texas at Arlington, Graduate School, College of Education and Health Professions, Department of Educational Leadership and Policy Studies, Arlington, TX 76019. Offers dual language (M Ed); education leadership and policy studies (PhD); higher education (M Ed); principal certification (M Ed). Part-time and evening/weekend programs available. Postbaccalaureate distance learning degree programs offered (no on-campus study). *Degree requirements:* For master's, 2 field-based practica; for doctorate, comprehensive exam, thesis/dissertation, 2 research-based practica. *Entrance requirements:* For master's, GRE, 3 references forms, minimum undergraduate GPA of 3.0 in the last 60 hours of course work; for doctorate, GRE, resume, statement of intent, 3 reference forms, applicable master's degree. *Faculty research:* Lived realities of students of color in K-16 contexts, K-16 faculty, K-16 policy and law, K-16 student access, K-16 student success.

The University of Texas at Austin, Graduate School, College of Education, Department of Curriculum and Instruction, Austin, TX 78712-1111. Offers bilingual/bicultural education (M Ed, MA, PhD); cultural studies in education (M Ed, MA, PhD); early childhood education (M Ed, MA, PhD); language and literacy studies (M Ed, PhD); learning technologies (M Ed, MA, PhD); physical education (M Ed, MA, PhD). Terminal master's awarded for partial completion of doctoral program. *Degree requirements:* For doctorate, thesis/dissertation. *Entrance requirements:* For master's and doctorate, GRE General Test. Electronic applications accepted.

The University of Texas at Austin, Graduate School, College of Education, Department of Special Education, Austin, TX 78712-1111. Offers autism and developmental disabilities (Ed D, PhD); autism and developmental disability (M Ed, MA); early childhood special education (M Ed, MA, Ed D, PhD); learning disabilities (Ed D, PhD); learning disabilities/behavior disorders (M Ed, MA); multicultural special education (M Ed, MA, Ed D, PhD); rehabilitation counselor (M Ed); rehabilitation counselor education (Ed D, PhD); special education administration (Ed D, PhD). *Accreditation:* CORE. Part-time and evening/weekend programs available. Postbaccalaureate distance learning degree programs offered (no on-campus study). *Degree requirements:* For master's, thesis or alternative; for doctorate, thesis/dissertation. *Entrance requirements:* For master's and doctorate, GRE General Test. *Faculty research:* Anchored instruction, reading disabilities, multicultural/bilingual.

The University of Texas at Brownsville, Graduate Studies, College of Education, Brownsville, TX 78520-4991. Offers bilingual education (M Ed); counseling and guidance (M Ed); curriculum and instruction (M Ed); early childhood education (M Ed); educational leadership (M Ed); educational technology (M Ed); exercise science (MS); special education (M Ed). Part-time and evening/weekend programs available. Postbaccalaureate distance learning degree programs offered (no on-campus study). *Faculty:* 51 full-time (28 women). *Students:* 60 full-time (43 women), 496 part-time (363 women); includes 467 minority (4 Black or African American, non-Hispanic/Latino; 1 American Indian or Alaska Native, non-Hispanic/Latino; 10 Asian, non-Hispanic/Latino; 451 Hispanic/Latino; 1 Native Hawaiian or other Pacific Islander, non-Hispanic/Latino), 12 international. 161 applicants, 67% accepted, 81 enrolled. In 2013, 142 master's awarded. *Degree requirements:* For master's, comprehensive exam (for some programs), thesis optional, electronic portfolio. *Entrance requirements:* For master's, GRE General Test, curriculum vitae or resume, teaching certificate. Additional exam requirements/recommendations for international students: Required—TOEFL (minimum score 550 paper-based; 77 iBT). *Application deadline:* For fall admission, 7/1 priority date for domestic students, 7/1 for international students; for spring admission, 12/1 priority date for domestic students, 12/1 for international students. Applications are processed on a rolling basis. Application fee: $30. Electronic applications accepted. *Expenses:* Tuition, state resident: full-time $3444; part-time $1148 per semester. Tuition, nonresident: full-time $9816. *Required fees:* $1018; $221 per credit hour. $401 per semester. *Financial support:* In 2013–14, 136 students received support, including 6 research assistantships (averaging $10,000 per year); career-related internships or fieldwork, Federal Work-Study, scholarships/grants, tuition waivers (partial), and unspecified assistantships also available. Support available to part-time students. Financial award application deadline: 3/1; financial award applicants required to submit FAFSA. *Unit head:* Dr. Miguel Angel Escotet, Dean, 956-882-7220, Fax: 956-882-7431, E-mail: miguel.escotet@utb.edu. *Application contact:* Mari E. Stevens, Graduate Studies Specialist, 956-882-6587, Fax: 956-882-7279, E-mail: mari.stevens@utb.edu.
Website: http://www.utb.edu/vpaa/coe/Pages/default.aspx.

The University of Texas at El Paso, Graduate School, College of Liberal Arts, Department of English, El Paso, TX 79968-0001. Offers bilingual professional writing (Certificate); English and American literature (MA); rhetoric and composition (PhD); rhetoric and writing studies (MA); teaching English (MAT). Part-time and evening/weekend programs available. *Degree requirements:* For master's, thesis optional. *Entrance requirements:* For master's, GRE General Test, minimum GPA of 3.0. Additional exam requirements/recommendations for international students: Required—TOEFL. Electronic applications accepted. *Faculty research:* Literature, creative writing, literary theory.

The University of Texas at San Antonio, College of Education and Human Development, Department of Bicultural and Bilingual Studies, San Antonio, TX 78249-0617. Offers bicultural/bilingual studies (MA), including bicultural studies, bicultural/bilingual education; culture, literacy, and language (PhD); teaching English as a second language (MA). Part-time and evening/weekend programs available. *Faculty:* 17 full-time (11 women), 1 (woman) part-time/adjunct. *Students:* 49 full-time (42 women), 122 part-time (97 women); includes 105 minority (3 Black or African American, non-Hispanic/Latino; 7 Asian, non-Hispanic/Latino; 91 Hispanic/Latino; 4 Two or more races, non-Hispanic/Latino), 23 international. Average age 36. 59 applicants, 88% accepted, 26 enrolled. In 2013, 52 master's, 2 doctorates awarded. *Degree requirements:* For master's, one foreign language, comprehensive exam, thesis optional; for doctorate, one foreign language, comprehensive exam, thesis/dissertation. *Entrance requirements:* For master's, GRE General Test if GPA is less than 3.0 for last 60 hours, bachelor's degree with 18 credit hours in field of study or in another appropriate field of study; for doctorate, GRE General Test, resume or curriculum vitae, 3 letters of recommendation, statement of purpose. Additional exam requirements/recommendations for international students: Required—TOEFL (minimum score 550 paper-based; 79 iBT), IELTS (minimum score 6.5). *Application deadline:* For fall admission, 7/1 for domestic students, 4/1 for international students; for spring admission, 11/1 for domestic students, 9/1 for international students. Applications are processed on a rolling basis. Application fee: $45 ($80 for international students). Electronic applications accepted. *Expenses:* Tuition, state resident: full-time $4671. Tuition, nonresident: full-time $8708. *International tuition:* $17,415 full-time. *Required fees:* $1924.60. Tuition and fees vary according to course load and degree level. *Financial support:* In 2013–14, 19 students received support, including 7 fellowships with full tuition reimbursements available (averaging $27,315 per year), 9 research assistantships with full tuition reimbursements available (averaging $13,618 per year), 7 teaching assistantships with full tuition reimbursements available (averaging $11,000 per year). Financial award applicants required to submit FAFSA. *Faculty research:* Bilingualism and biliteracy development, second language teaching and learning, language minority education, Mexican American studies, transnationalism and immigration. *Unit head:* Dr. Belinda Bustos Flores, Chair, 210-458-4426, Fax: 210-458-5962, E-mail: belinda.flores@utsa.edu. *Application contact:* Armando Trujillo, Assistant Dean of the Graduate School, 210-458-5576, Fax: 210-458-5576, E-mail: armando.trujillo@utsa.edu.
Website: http://education.utsa.edu/bicultural-bilingual_studies.

The University of Texas–Pan American, College of Education, Department of Curriculum and Instruction: Elementary and Secondary, Edinburg, TX 78539. Offers bilingual education (M Ed); early childhood education (M Ed); elementary education (M Ed); reading (M Ed); secondary education (M Ed). Part-time programs available. *Degree requirements:* For master's, comprehensive exam, thesis optional. *Entrance requirements:* For master's, GRE. Additional exam requirements/recommendations for international students: Required—TOEFL, IELTS. *Expenses:* Tuition, state resident: full-time $5986; part-time $333 per credit hour. Tuition, nonresident: full-time $12,358; part-time $687 per credit hour. *Required fees:* $782. Tuition and fees vary according to program. *Faculty research:* Dual language instruction, literacy and technology, teacher education in diverse populations, mathematics and science education.

University of the Incarnate Word, School of Graduate Studies and Research, Dreeben School of Education, Programs in Education, San Antonio, TX 78209-6397. Offers adult education (M Ed, MA); cross-cultural education (M Ed, MA); early childhood literacy (M Ed, MA); general education (M Ed, MA); higher education (PhD); instructional technology (M Ed, MA); international education and entrepreneurship (PhD); kinesiology (M Ed, MA); literacy (M Ed, MA); organizational leadership (PhD); organizational learning and learning (M Ed, MA); reading (M Ed, MA); special education (M Ed, MA); teacher leadership (M Ed, MA). Part-time and evening/weekend programs available. *Faculty:* 17 full-time (9 women), 6 part-time/adjunct (all women). *Students:* 23 full-time (13 women), 187 part-time (122 women); includes 114 minority (24 Black or African American, non-Hispanic/Latino; 1 American Indian or Alaska Native, non-Hispanic/Latino; 3 Asian, non-Hispanic/Latino; 85 Hispanic/Latino; 1 Two or more races, non-Hispanic/Latino), 30 international. Average age 41. 52 applicants, 67% accepted, 25 enrolled. In 2013, 12 master's, 14 doctorates awarded. *Degree requirements:* For master's, capstone; for doctorate, thesis/dissertation, qualifying exam. *Entrance requirements:* For master's, baccalaureate degree; minimum foundation GPA of 2.5; interview; for doctorate, master's degree; interview; supervised writing sample. Additional exam requirements/recommendations for international students: Required—TOEFL (minimum score 560 paper-based; 83 iBT). *Application deadline:* Applications are processed on a rolling basis. Application fee: $20. Electronic applications accepted. *Expenses: Tuition:* Part-time $815 per credit hour. *Required fees:* $86 per credit hour. One-time fee: $40 part-time. Tuition and fees vary according to degree level and program. *Financial support:* In 2013–14, 5 research assistantships were awarded; Federal Work-Study and scholarships/grants also available. Financial award applicants required to submit FAFSA. *Unit head:* Dr. Denise Staudt, Dean, Dreeben School of Education, 210-829-2762, E-mail: staudt@uiwtx.edu. *Application contact:* Andrea Cyterski-Acosta, Dean of Enrollment, 210-829-6005, Fax: 210-829-3921, E-mail: admis@uiwtx.edu.
Website: http://www.uiw.edu/education/index.htm.

Multilingual and Multicultural Education

University of the Southwest, Graduate Programs, Hobbs, NM 88240-9129. Offers business administration (MBA); curriculum and instruction (MSE); curriculum and instruction: bilingual (MSE); curriculum and instruction: TESOL (MSE); early childhood education (MSE); educational administration (MSE); mental health counseling (MSE); school counseling (MSE); special education (MSE); sports management (MBA). Part-time and evening/weekend programs available. Postbaccalaureate distance learning degree programs offered (no on-campus study). *Degree requirements:* For master's, comprehensive exam, thesis (for some programs). *Entrance requirements:* Additional exam requirements/recommendations for international students: Recommended—TOEFL. Electronic applications accepted.

University of Washington, Graduate School, College of Education, Seattle, WA 98195. Offers curriculum and instruction (M Ed, Ed D, PhD), including educational technology, general curriculum (Ed D, PhD), language, literacy, and culture, mathematics education, multicultural education, reading and language arts education (Ed D); science education, social studies education, teaching and curriculum (M Ed); educational leadership and policy studies (M Ed, Ed D, PhD), including administration (Ed D), educational policy, organization, and leadership (M Ed, PhD), higher education, leadership for learning (Ed D), social and cultural foundations of education (M Ed, PhD); educational psychology (M Ed, PhD), including educational psychology (PhD), human development and cognition (M Ed), learning sciences, measurement, statistics and research design (M Ed), school psychology (M Ed); instructional leadership (M Ed); intercollegiate athletic leadership (M Ed); special education (M Ed, Ed D, PhD), including early childhood special education (M Ed), emotional and behavioral disabilities (M Ed), learning disabilities (M Ed), low-incidence disabilities (M Ed), severe disabilities (M Ed), special education (Ed D, PhD); teacher education (MIT). *Accreditation:* APA. Part-time and evening/weekend programs available. *Degree requirements:* For master's, thesis optional; for doctorate, thesis/dissertation. *Entrance requirements:* For master's and doctorate, GRE General Test, minimum GPA of 3.0. Additional exam requirements/recommendations for international students: Required—TOEFL. Electronic applications accepted. *Faculty research:* School restructuring/effective schools, special education interventions, literacy and writing, technology, school partnerships, teacher preparation.

University of West Florida, College of Professional Studies, Ed D Programs, Specialization in Curriculum and Instruction: Curriculum and Diversity Studies, Pensacola, FL 32514-5750. Offers Ed D. Part-time and evening/weekend programs available. *Degree requirements:* For doctorate, comprehensive exam, thesis/dissertation. *Entrance requirements:* For doctorate, GRE, MAT, or GMAT, letter of intent; writing sample; three letters of recommendation; two completed disposition assessment forms; written statement of goals; interview with admissions committee. Additional exam requirements/recommendations for international students: Required—TOEFL (minimum score 550 paper-based).

University of Wisconsin–Milwaukee, Graduate School, School of Education, Urban Education Doctoral Program, Milwaukee, WI 53201-0413. Offers adult, continuing and higher education leadership (PhD); curriculum and instruction (PhD); educational administration (PhD); exceptional education (PhD); multicultural studies (PhD); social foundations of education (PhD). *Students:* 51 full-time (37 women), 40 part-time (25 women); includes 32 minority (16 Black or African American, non-Hispanic/Latino; 1 American Indian or Alaska Native, non-Hispanic/Latino; 3 Asian, non-Hispanic/Latino; 5 Hispanic/Latino; 7 Two or more races, non-Hispanic/Latino), 3 international. Average age 41. 25 applicants, 44% accepted, 4 enrolled. In 2013, 11 doctorates awarded. *Degree requirements:* For doctorate, comprehensive exam, thesis/dissertation. *Entrance requirements:* For doctorate, GRE General Test, minimum undergraduate GPA of 2.85, graduate 3.5. Additional exam requirements/recommendations for international students: Required—TOEFL (minimum score 550 paper-based; 79 iBT), IELTS (minimum score 6.5). *Application deadline:* For fall admission, 1/1 priority date for domestic students; for spring admission, 9/1 for domestic students. Applications are processed on a rolling basis. Application fee: $56 ($96 for international students). Electronic applications accepted. *Financial support:* In 2013–14, 11 fellowships, 1 teaching assistantship were awarded; research assistantships, career-related internships or fieldwork, health care benefits, unspecified assistantships, and project assistantships also available. Support available to part-time students. Financial award application deadline: 4/15; financial award applicants required to submit FAFSA. *Unit head:* Raji Swaminathan, Representative, 414-229-6740, Fax: 414-229-2920, E-mail: swaminar@uwm.edu. *Application contact:* General Information Contact, 414-229-4982, Fax: 414-229-6967, E-mail: gradschool@uwm.edu.
Website: http://www4.uwm.edu/soe/academics/urban_ed/.

University of Wisconsin–Whitewater, School of Graduate Studies, College of Education and Professional Studies, Department of Curriculum and Instruction, Whitewater, WI 53190-1790. Offers professional development (MS), including bilingual education, challenging advanced learners, curriculum and instruction, educational leadership, health, human performance and recreation, health, physical education and coaching, information technologies and libraries, reading. *Accreditation:* NCATE. Part-time and evening/weekend programs available. Postbaccalaureate distance learning degree programs offered. *Degree requirements:* For master's, thesis or integrated project. *Entrance requirements:* Additional exam requirements/recommendations for international students: Required—TOEFL (minimum score 550 paper-based; 80 iBT), IELTS (minimum score 6). Electronic applications accepted. *Faculty research:* Hybrid of exercise physiology and psychology; gender equity; education, pedagogy, and technology; comprehensive school health education.

Utah State University, School of Graduate Studies, College of Humanities, Arts and Social Sciences, Department of Languages, Philosophy, and Speech Communication, Logan, UT 84322. Offers second language teaching (MSLT). *Entrance requirements:* For master's, GRE General Test or MAT, minimum GPA of 3.0. Additional exam requirements/recommendations for international students: Required—TOEFL.

Vanderbilt University, Graduate School, Program in Learning, Teaching and Diversity, Nashville, TN 37240-1001. Offers MS, PhD. *Faculty:* 15 full-time (6 women), 2 part-time/adjunct (1 woman). *Students:* 42 full-time (27 women), 2 part-time (1 woman); includes 8 minority (3 Black or African American, non-Hispanic/Latino; 2 Asian, non-Hispanic/Latino; 1 Hispanic/Latino; 2 Two or more races, non-Hispanic/Latino), 3 international. Average age 32. 133 applicants, 5% accepted, 6 enrolled. In 2013, 10 doctorates awarded. *Degree requirements:* For doctorate, comprehensive exam, thesis/dissertation. *Entrance requirements:* For doctorate, GRE General Test. Additional exam requirements/recommendations for international students: Required—TOEFL (minimum score 570 paper-based; 88 iBT). *Application deadline:* For fall admission, 12/31 for domestic and international students. Electronic applications accepted. *Financial support:* Fellowships with full and partial tuition reimbursements, research assistantships with full tuition reimbursements, teaching assistantships with full tuition reimbursements, Federal Work-Study, institutionally sponsored loans, scholarships/grants, traineeships, and health care benefits available. Financial award application deadline: 1/15; financial award applicants required to submit CSS PROFILE or FAFSA. *Faculty research:* New pedagogies for math, science, and language; the support of English language learners; the uses of new technology and media in the classroom; middle school mathematics and the institutional setting of teaching. *Unit head:* Dr. Clifford Hofwolt, Director of Graduate Studies, 615-322-8227, Fax: 615-322-8014, E-mail: clifford.hofwolt@vanderbilt.edu.

Application contact: Angela Saylor, Administrative Assistant, 615-322-8092, Fax: 615-322-8014, E-mail: angela.saylor@vanderbilt.edu.
Website: http://peabody.vanderbilt.edu/departments/tl/index.php.

Vanderbilt University, Peabody College, Department of Teaching and Learning, Nashville, TN 37240-1001. Offers elementary education (M Ed); English language learners (M Ed); learning and instruction (M Ed); learning, diversity, and urban studies (M Ed); reading education (M Ed); secondary education (M Ed). *Accreditation:* NCATE. *Faculty:* 35 full-time (25 women), 20 part-time/adjunct (14 women). *Students:* 103 full-time (74 women), 44 part-time (39 women); includes 22 minority (8 Black or African American, non-Hispanic/Latino; 5 Asian, non-Hispanic/Latino; 5 Hispanic/Latino; 1 Native Hawaiian or other Pacific Islander, non-Hispanic/Latino; 3 Two or more races, non-Hispanic/Latino), 21 international. Average age 25. 264 applicants, 73% accepted, 57 enrolled. In 2013, 95 master's awarded. *Degree requirements:* For master's, comprehensive exam, thesis optional. *Entrance requirements:* For master's, GRE General Test, MAT. Additional exam requirements/recommendations for international students: Required—TOEFL (minimum score 550 paper-based; 80 iBT). *Application deadline:* For fall admission, 12/31 priority date for domestic and international students; for spring admission, 11/1 priority date for domestic and international students. Applications are processed on a rolling basis. Application fee: $0. Electronic applications accepted. *Financial support:* Fellowships with full and partial tuition reimbursements, research assistantships with full and partial tuition reimbursements, teaching assistantships with full and partial tuition reimbursements, Federal Work-Study, institutionally sponsored loans, scholarships/grants, tuition waivers (partial), and unspecified assistantships available. Support available to part-time students. Financial award application deadline: 1/15; financial award applicants required to submit FAFSA. *Faculty research:* Learning environments for mathematics of space and motion, visual programming tools for children's learning of basic science concepts, pathways for elementary and middle school children's learning about measurement and statistics, early reading intervention, professional development for ambitious mathematics teaching. *Unit head:* Dr. Rogers Hall, Chair, 615-322-8100, Fax: 615-322-8999, E-mail: rogers.hall@vanderbilt.edu. *Application contact:* Angela Saylor, Educational Coordinator, 615-322-8092, Fax: 615-322-8999, E-mail: angela.saylor@vanderbilt.edu.

Walden University, Graduate Programs, Richard W. Riley College of Education and Leadership, Minneapolis, MN 55401. *Accreditation:* NCATE. Part-time and evening/weekend programs available. Postbaccalaureate distance learning degree programs offered (minimal on-campus study). *Faculty:* 23 full-time (15 women), 830 part-time/adjunct (569 women). *Students:* 8,671 full-time (7,197 women), 2,122 part-time (1,735 women); includes 4,734 minority (3,802 Black or African American, non-Hispanic/Latino; 50 American Indian or Alaska Native, non-Hispanic/Latino; 136 Asian, non-Hispanic/Latino; 539 Hispanic/Latino; 35 Native Hawaiian or other Pacific Islander, non-Hispanic/Latino; 172 Two or more races, non-Hispanic/Latino), 73 international. Average age 40. 2,646 applicants, 96% accepted, 2074 enrolled. In 2013, 2,214 master's, 354 doctorates, 479 other advanced degrees awarded. *Degree requirements:* For doctorate, thesis/dissertation (for some programs), residency; for other advanced degree, residency (for some programs). *Entrance requirements:* For master's, bachelor's degree or higher; minimum GPA of 2.5; official transcripts; goal statement (for some programs); access to computer and Internet; for doctorate, master's degree or higher; three years of related professional or academic experience (preferred); minimum GPA of 3.0; goal statement and current resume (select programs); official transcripts; access to computer and Internet; for other advanced degree, relevant work experience; access to computer and Internet. Additional exam requirements/recommendations for international students: Required—TOEFL (minimum score 550 paper-based; 79 iBT), IELTS (minimum score 6.5), Michigan English Language Assessment Battery (minimum score 82), or PTE. *Application deadline:* Applications are processed on a rolling basis. Application fee: $0. Electronic applications accepted. *Expenses:* Tuition: Full-time $11,813.55; part-time $500 per credit. *Required fees:* $618.76. *Financial support:* In 2013–14, 1 fellowship was awarded; Federal Work-Study, scholarships/grants, unspecified assistantships, and family tuition reduction, active duty/veteran tuition reduction, group tuition reduction, interest-free payment plans, employee tuition reduction also available. Support available to part-time students. Financial award applicants required to submit FAFSA. *Unit head:* Dr. Kate Steffens, Dean, 800-925-3368. *Application contact:* Jennifer Hall, Vice President of Enrollment Management, 866-4-WALDEN, E-mail: info@waldenu.edu. Website: http://www.waldenu.edu/colleges-schools/riley-college-of-education/.

Washington State University, Graduate School, College of Education, Department of Teaching and Learning, Program in English Language Learners, Pullman, WA 99164. Offers Ed M, MA. *Degree requirements:* For master's, comprehensive exam (for some programs), thesis (for some programs), written or oral exam. *Entrance requirements:* For master's, minimum GPA of 3.0, letters of recommendation, transcripts, resume/curriculum vitae, personal statement. Additional exam requirements/recommendations for international students: Required—TOEFL (minimum score 550 paper-based; 80 iBT). Electronic applications accepted. *Faculty research:* Language and education in culturally and linguistically diverse settings using ethnographic and sociolinguistic perspective; English language teacher education; teacher racial and cultural identity; the intersections of language, race, and gender in learning.

Washington State University, Graduate School, The Edward R. Murrow College of Communication, Pullman, WA 99164-2520. Offers communication and technology (MA, PhD); health communication and promotion (MA, PhD); intercultural communication (PhD); media processes and effects (PhD); political communication (MA, PhD); science communication (MA, PhD); strategic communication (MA). *Degree requirements:* For master's, comprehensive exam (for some programs), thesis optional, oral exam; for doctorate, comprehensive exam, thesis/dissertation. *Entrance requirements:* For master's, GRE General Test, minimum GPA of 3.25, 3 letters of recommendation; for doctorate, GRE General Test, minimum undergraduate GPA of 3.25, graduate 3.5; MA in communication; 3 letters of recommendation. Additional exam requirements/recommendations for international students: Required—TOEFL (minimum score 580 paper-based). Electronic applications accepted. *Faculty research:* Communication technology, health communication, science communication, political communication, intercultural communication.

Wayne State University, College of Education, Division of Teacher Education, Detroit, MI 48202. Offers art education (M Ed), including art therapy; autism spectrum disorders (Certificate); bilingual/bicultural education (M Ed, Certificate); career and technical education (M Ed, Certificate); cognitive impairment (Certificate); curriculum and instruction (Ed D, PhD, Ed S), including art education (PhD), bilingual education (Ed D, Ed S), bilingual-bicultural education (PhD), career and technical education (MAT, Ed D, PhD, Ed S), early childhood education (MAT, Ed D, PhD, Ed S), elementary education, English as a second language (MAT, Ed D, Ed S), English education (MAT, Ed D, PhD, Ed S), foreign language education (MAT, PhD), K-12 curriculum, mathematics education (MAT, Ed D, PhD, Ed S), science education (MAT, Ed D, PhD, Ed S), secondary education, social studies education (MAT, Ed S), social studies education: secondary (Ed D, PhD); early childhood education (M Ed, Certificate); elementary education (M Ed, MAT), including children's literature (MAT), early childhood education (MAT, Ed D, PhD, Ed S), general elementary education (MAT); elementary or secondary education (MAT), including bilingual/bicultural education, English as a second language (MAT, Ed D,

Ed S), mathematics education (MAT, Ed D, PhD, Ed S), science education (MAT, Ed D, PhD, Ed S), social studies education (MAT, Ed S); emotionally impaired (Certificate); English as a second language (Certificate); English education (M Ed), including secondary; foreign language education (M Ed); K-12 reading specialist (Certificate); learning disabilities (Certificate); mathematics education (M Ed), including secondary; reading (M Ed, Ed S); reading, language and literature (Ed D); science education (M Ed), including secondary; secondary education (MAT), including art education (K-12), career and technical education (MAT, Ed D, PhD, Ed S), English education (MAT, Ed D, PhD, Ed S), foreign language education (MAT, PhD), kinesiology; social studies education (M Ed), including secondary; special education (M Ed, MAT, Ed D, PhD, Ed S); visual arts education (Certificate). Part-time programs available. *Faculty:* 36 full-time (25 women), 55 part-time/adjunct (43 women). *Students:* 218 full-time (163 women), 448 part-time (344 women); includes 218 minority (177 Black or African American, non-Hispanic/Latino; 2 American Indian or Alaska Native, non-Hispanic/Latino; 11 Asian, non-Hispanic/Latino; 19 Hispanic/Latino; 1 Native Hawaiian or other Pacific Islander, non-Hispanic/Latino; 8 Two or more races, non-Hispanic/Latino), 10 international. Average age 37. 258 applicants, 30% accepted, 52 enrolled. In 2013, 183 master's, 10 doctorates, 35 other advanced degrees awarded. *Degree requirements:* For master's, thesis, essay or project (for some M Ed programs), professional field experience (for MAT programs); for doctorate, thesis/dissertation. *Entrance requirements:* For master's, Michigan Basic Skills Test (MA in teaching), admission to the graduate school, verification of participation in group work with children and Michigan State Police Criminal Background check; for doctorate, minimum undergraduate GPA of 3.0, graduate 3.5; interview, curriculum vitae; references. Additional exam requirements/recommendations for international students: Required—TOEFL (minimum score 550 paper-based; 79 iBT), TWE (minimum score 5.5), Michigan English Language Assessment Battery (minimum score 85); Recommended—IELTS (minimum score 6.5). *Application deadline:* For fall admission, 6/1 priority date for domestic students, 5/1 priority date for international students; for winter admission, 10/1 priority date for domestic students, 9/1 priority date for international students; for spring admission, 2/1 priority date for domestic students, 1/1 priority date for international students. Applications are processed on a rolling basis. Application fee: $0. Electronic applications accepted. *Expenses:* Tuition, state resident: part-time $554.15 per credit. Tuition, nonresident: part-time $1200.35 per credit. *Required fees:* $42.15 per credit. $268.30 per semester. Tuition and fees vary according to course load and program. *Financial support:* In 2013–14, 83 students received support, including 1 fellowship (averaging $16,842 per year), 1 research assistantship with tuition reimbursement available (averaging $21,229 per year); career-related internships or fieldwork, Federal Work-Study, scholarships/grants, health care benefits, and unspecified assistantships also available. Support available to part-time students. Financial award application deadline: 3/31; financial award applicants required to submit FAFSA. *Faculty research:* Improving students' skill achievement in mathematics; improving elementary children's understanding of informational text; teachers' use of their pedagogical and mathematical knowledge in the interactive work of teaching; the intersection of identity construction in teaching and learning; identifying effective methods of literacy instruction and assessments for bilingual students in elementary language arts classrooms. *Total annual research expenditures:* $368,105. *Unit head:* Dr. Kathleen Crawford-McKinney, Assistant Dean, 313-577-0122. *Application contact:* Janice Green, Assistant Dean, 313-577-1605, E-mail: jwgreen@wayne.edu.
Website: http://coe.wayne.edu/ted/index.php.

Western New Mexico University, Graduate Division, School of Education, Silver City, NM 88062-0680. Offers bilingual education (MAT); counseling (MA); educational leadership (MA); elementary education (MAT); reading (MAT); school psychology (MA); secondary education (MAT); special education (MAT); TESOL (teaching English to speakers of other languages) (MAT). *Accreditation:* NCATE. *Degree requirements:* For master's, comprehensive exam. *Entrance requirements:* For master's, GRE General Test, GRE Subject Test, minimum GPA of 3.2 in last 64 hours of undergraduate study. Additional exam requirements/recommendations for international students: Required—TOEFL (minimum score 550 paper-based). Electronic applications accepted.

Western Oregon University, Graduate Programs, College of Education, Division of Teacher Education, Program in Secondary Education, Monmouth, OR 97361-1394. Offers bilingual education (MS Ed); health (MS Ed); humanities (MAT, MS Ed); initial licensure (MAT); mathematics (MAT, MS Ed); science (MAT, MS Ed); social science (MAT, MS Ed). *Accreditation:* NCATE. Part-time and evening/weekend programs available. *Degree requirements:* For master's, thesis optional, written exam. *Entrance requirements:* For master's, minimum GPA of 3.0, teaching license. Additional exam requirements/recommendations for international students: Required—TOEFL (minimum score 550 paper-based; 79 iBT), IELTS (minimum score 6.5). *Faculty research:* Literacy, science in primary grades, geography education, retention, teacher burnout.

Xavier University, College of Social Sciences, Health and Education, School of Education, Department of Childhood Education and Literacy, Program in Children's Multicultural Literature, Cincinnati, OH 45207. Offers M Ed. Part-time programs available. *Faculty:* 2 part-time/adjunct (1 woman). In 2013, 4 master's awarded. *Degree requirements:* For master's, comprehensive exam, thesis, research project. *Entrance requirements:* For master's, GRE or MAT. Additional exam requirements/recommendations for international students: Required—TOEFL (minimum score 550 paper-based; 79 iBT). *Application deadline:* Applications are processed on a rolling basis. Application fee: $35. Electronic applications accepted. *Expenses: Tuition:* Part-time $594 per credit hour. *Required fees:* $3 per semester. *Financial support:* Tuition waivers (partial) and unspecified assistantships available. Financial award applicants required to submit FAFSA. *Faculty research:* First-year teacher retention, teaching efficacy of science educators, adolescents' literacy practices, family resiliency, preparing culturally responsive teachers. *Unit head:* Dr. Cynthia Hayes Geer, Chair, 513-745-3262, Fax: 513-745-3504, E-mail: geer@xavier.edu. *Application contact:* Roger Bosse, Director of Graduate Studies, 513-745-3357, Fax: 513-745-1048, E-mail: bosse@xavier.edu.
Website: http://www.xavier.edu/multicultural-literature/.

Special Education

Acacia University, American Graduate School of Education, Tempe, AZ 85284. Offers educational administration (M Ed); elementary education (MA); English as a second language (M Ed); secondary education (MA); special education (M Ed).

Acadia University, Faculty of Professional Studies, School of Education, Program in Inclusive Education, Wolfville, NS B4P 2R6, Canada. Offers M Ed. Part-time programs available. *Degree requirements:* For master's, thesis optional. *Entrance requirements:* For master's, bachelor's degree in education, minimum B average in undergraduate course work, course work in special education. Additional exam requirements/recommendations for international students: Required—TOEFL (minimum score 580 paper-based; 93 iBT), IELTS (minimum score 6.5). *Faculty research:* Technology and human interaction, inclusive education and community, accommodating diversity, program evaluation.

Adams State University, The Graduate School, Department of Teacher Education, Program in Special Education, Alamosa, CO 81101. Offers MA. *Accreditation:* Teacher Education Accreditation Council. Part-time programs available. Postbaccalaureate distance learning degree programs offered. *Degree requirements:* For master's, practicum, qualifying exam. *Entrance requirements:* For master's, GRE General Test or MAT, minimum undergraduate GPA of 3.0.

Adelphi University, Ruth S. Ammon School of Education, Program in Special Education, Garden City, NY 11530-0701. Offers MS, Certificate. Part-time and evening/weekend programs available. *Students:* 54 full-time (50 women), 68 part-time (62 women); includes 45 minority (22 Black or African American, non-Hispanic/Latino; 4 Asian, non-Hispanic/Latino; 15 Hispanic/Latino; 2 Native Hawaiian or other Pacific Islander, non-Hispanic/Latino; 2 Two or more races, non-Hispanic/Latino), 2 international. Average age 30. In 2013, 81 master's, 76 other advanced degrees awarded. *Entrance requirements:* For master's, 2 letters of recommendation, resume detailing paid/volunteer experience and organizational membership. Additional exam requirements/recommendations for international students: Required—TOEFL (minimum score 550 paper-based; 80 iBT). *Application deadline:* For fall admission, 4/1 for international students; for spring admission, 11/1 for international students. Electronic applications accepted. *Expenses: Tuition:* Full-time $32,530; part-time $1010 per credit. *Required fees:* $1150. Tuition and fees vary according to degree level and program. *Financial support:* Fellowships, research assistantships with partial tuition reimbursements, teaching assistantships, career-related internships or fieldwork, Federal Work-Study, institutionally sponsored loans, tuition waivers (full), and unspecified assistantships available. Support available to part-time students. Financial award application deadline: 2/15; financial award applicants required to submit FAFSA. *Unit head:* Dr. Anne Mungai, Director, 516-877-4096, E-mail: mungai@adelphi.edu. *Application contact:* Christine Murphy, Director of Admissions, 516-877-3050, Fax: 516-877-3039, E-mail: graduateadmissions@adelphi.edu.

Alabama Agricultural and Mechanical University, School of Graduate Studies, School of Education, Department of Counseling and Special Education, Huntsville, AL 35811. Offers communicative disorders (M Ed, MS); psychology and counseling (MS, Ed S), including clinical psychology (MS), counseling and guidance, counseling psychology (MS), personnel management (MS), psychometry (MS), school psychology (MS); special education (M Ed, MS). *Accreditation:* CORE; NCATE. Part-time and evening/weekend programs available. *Degree requirements:* For master's, comprehensive exam. *Entrance requirements:* For master's, GRE General Test. Additional exam requirements/recommendations for international students: Required—TOEFL (minimum score 500 paper-based; 61 iBT). *Faculty research:* Increasing numbers of minorities in special education and speech-language pathology.

Alabama State University, College of Education, Department of Curriculum and Instruction, Montgomery, AL 36101-0271. Offers early childhood education (M Ed, Ed S); elementary education (M Ed, Ed S); secondary education (M Ed, Ed S), including biology education, English language arts education (M Ed), history education, math education, music education (M Ed), reading education (M Ed), social science education; special education (M Ed). Part-time programs available. *Faculty:* 11 full-time (8 women), 13 part-time/adjunct (10 women). *Students:* 32 full-time (19 women), 162 part-time (136 women); includes 189 minority (187 Black or African American, non-Hispanic/Latino; 1 Hispanic/Latino; 1 Two or more races, non-Hispanic/Latino). Average age 33. 99 applicants, 45% accepted, 34 enrolled. In 2013, 74 master's, 20 Ed Ss awarded. *Degree requirements:* For master's, comprehensive exam, thesis optional; for Ed S, comprehensive exam, thesis. *Entrance requirements:* For master's, GRE General Test, MAT, writing competency test; for Ed S, writing competency test, GRE, MAT. Additional exam requirements/recommendations for international students: Required—TOEFL (minimum score 500 paper-based). *Application deadline:* For fall admission, 7/15 for domestic students; for spring admission, 12/15 for domestic students. Applications are processed on a rolling basis. Application fee: $25. *Expenses:* Tuition, state resident: full-time $7958; part-time $343 per credit hour. Tuition, nonresident: full-time $14,132; part-time $686 per credit hour. *Required fees:* $446 per term. One-time fee: $1784 full-time; $892 part-time. Tuition and fees vary according to course load. *Financial support:* In 2013–14, research assistantships (averaging $9,450 per year) were awarded. *Unit head:* Dr. Joyce Johnson, Acting Chairperson, 334-229-4485, Fax: 334-229-5603, E-mail: jjohnson@alasu.edu. *Application contact:* Dr. William Person, Dean of Graduate Studies, 334-229-4274, Fax: 334-229-4928, E-mail: wperson@alasu.edu.
Website: http://www.alasu.edu/academics/colleges—departments/college-of-education/curriculum—instruction/index.aspx.

Albany State University, College of Education, Albany, GA 31705-2717. Offers early childhood education (M Ed); education specialist (Ed S); educational leadership and administration (M Ed); health, physical education and recreation (M Ed); middle grades education (M Ed); school counseling (M Ed); special education (M Ed). *Accreditation:* NCATE. Part-time and evening/weekend programs available. Postbaccalaureate distance learning degree programs offered (minimal on-campus study). *Degree requirements:* For master's, comprehensive exam, internship, GACE Content Exam. *Entrance requirements:* For master's, GRE or MAT. Electronic applications accepted. *Faculty research:* GACE preparation, STEM (science, technology, engineering, and mathematics), technology education, special education, professional teacher development, health implications liberation philosophy, NET-Q, learning community, disabled or at-risk students.

Albright College, Graduate Division, Reading, PA 19612-5234. Offers early childhood education (MS); elementary education (MS); English as a second language (MA); general education (MA); special education (MS). Part-time and evening/weekend programs available. *Degree requirements:* For master's, thesis. *Entrance requirements:* For master's, GRE General Test or MAT, minimum undergraduate GPA of 3.0, 2 letters of recommendation, interview. Additional exam requirements/recommendations for international students: Recommended—TOEFL (minimum score 525 paper-based). Electronic applications accepted.

Special Education

Alcorn State University, School of Graduate Studies, School of Psychology and Education, Alcorn State, MS 39096-7500. Offers agricultural education (MS Ed); elementary education (MS Ed, Ed S); guidance and counseling (MS Ed); industrial education (MS Ed); secondary education (MS Ed), including health and physical education; special education (MS Ed). *Accreditation:* NCATE. *Degree requirements:* For master's, thesis optional.

Alliant International University–San Francisco, Shirley M. Hufstedler School of Education, Teacher Education Programs, San Francisco, CA 94133-1221. Offers auditory oral education (Certificate); CLAD (Certificate); education specialist: mild/moderate disabilities (Credential); preliminary multiple subject (Credential); preliminary single subject (Credential); professional clear multiple subject (Credential); professional clear single subject (Credential); special education (MA); teaching (MA); TESOL (Certificate). Part-time and evening/weekend programs available. *Faculty:* 6 full-time (4 women), 10 part-time/adjunct (8 women). *Students:* 16 full-time (10 women), 135 part-time (97 women); includes 22 minority (6 Black or African American, non-Hispanic/Latino; 6 Asian, non-Hispanic/Latino; 8 Hispanic/Latino; 2 Two or more races, non-Hispanic/Latino). Average age 41. 172 applicants, 94% accepted, 142 enrolled. In 2013, 11 master's, 167 other advanced degrees awarded. *Degree requirements:* For master's, thesis. *Entrance requirements:* For degree, California Basic Educational Skills Test, minimum GPA of 2.5. Additional exam requirements/recommendations for international students: Required—TOEFL (minimum score 550 paper-based), TWE (minimum score 5). *Application deadline:* For fall admission, 7/1 priority date for domestic and international students; for spring admission, 12/1 priority date for domestic and international students. Applications are processed on a rolling basis. Application fee: $55. Electronic applications accepted. *Financial support:* Career-related internships or fieldwork, Federal Work-Study, institutionally sponsored loans, and scholarships/grants available. Financial award application deadline: 2/15; financial award applicants required to submit FAFSA. *Faculty research:* Curriculum development, first year teachers, cross-cultural issues in teaching, biliteracy. *Unit head:* Dr. Debra Reeves-Gutierrez, Program Director, 415-955-2084, Fax: 415-955-2179, E-mail: admissions@alliant.edu. *Application contact:* Alliant International University Central Contact Center, 866-U-ALLIANT, Fax: 858-635-4555, E-mail: admissions@alliant.edu. Website: http://www.alliant.edu/.

American International College, School of Graduate and Adult Education, Department of Education, Springfield, MA 01109-3189. Offers early childhood education (M Ed, CAGS); educational leadership and supervision (Ed D); elementary education (M Ed, CAGS); middle/secondary education (M Ed, CAGS); moderate disabilities (M Ed, CAGS); reading (M Ed, CAGS); school adjustment counseling (MA, CAGS); school guidance counseling (MA, CAGS); school leadership preparation (M Ed, CAGS); teaching and learning (Ed D). Evening/weekend programs available. *Faculty:* 11 full-time (9 women), 235 part-time/adjunct. *Students:* 1,530 full-time (1,219 women), 184 part-time (143 women); includes 100 minority (58 Black or African American, non-Hispanic/Latino; 3 American Indian or Alaska Native, non-Hispanic/Latino; 14 Asian, non-Hispanic/Latino; 6 Hispanic/Latino; 19 Two or more races, non-Hispanic/Latino). Average age 36. 695 applicants, 82% accepted, 508 enrolled. In 2013, 449 master's, 17 doctorates, 135 other advanced degrees awarded. Terminal master's awarded for partial completion of doctoral program. *Degree requirements:* For master's, comprehensive exam (for some programs), thesis (for some programs), practicum/culminating experience; for doctorate, comprehensive exam (for some programs), thesis/dissertation; for CAGS, practicum/culminating experience. *Entrance requirements:* For master's, graduate of accredited four-year college with minimum B-average in undergraduate course work; for doctorate, master's degree, minimum GPA of 3.0; for CAGS, M Ed or master's degree in field related to licensure from accredited institution. Additional exam requirements/recommendations for international students: Required—TOEFL or IELTS. *Application deadline:* For fall admission, 7/1 for domestic and international students; for spring admission, 12/1 for domestic and international students. Applications are processed on a rolling basis. Application fee: $50. Electronic applications accepted. *Expenses: Tuition:* Full-time $14,040; part-time $780 per credit. Tuition and fees vary according to course load, degree level and program. *Financial support:* Career-related internships or fieldwork available. Financial award applicants required to submit FAFSA. *Unit head:* Esta Sobey, Associate Dean, 413-205-3453, Fax: 413-205-3943, E-mail: esta.sobey@aic.edu. *Application contact:* Kaitlyn Rickard, Director of XCP Admissions, 413-205-3090, Fax: 413-205-3911, E-mail: kaitlyn.rickard@aic.edu. Website: http://www.aic.edu/academics.

American Public University System, AMU/APU Graduate Programs, Charles Town, WV 25414. Offers accounting (MBA, MS); criminal justice (MA), including business administration, emergency and disaster management, general (MA, MS); educational leadership (M Ed); emergency and disaster management (MA); entrepreneurship (MBA); environmental policy and management (MS), including environmental planning, environmental sustainability, fish and wildlife management, general (MA, MS), global environmental management; finance (MBA); general (MBA); global business management (MBA); history (MA), including American history, ancient and classical history, European history, global history, public history; homeland security (MA), including business administration, counter-terrorism studies, criminal justice, cyber, emergency management and public health, intelligence studies, transportation security; homeland security resource allocation (MBA); humanities (MA); information technology (MS), including digital forensics, enterprise software development, information assurance and security, IT project management; information technology management (MBA); intelligence studies (MA), including criminal intelligence, cyber, general (MA, MS), homeland security, intelligence analysis, intelligence collection, intelligence management, intelligence operations, terrorism studies; international relations and conflict resolution (MA), including comparative and security issues, conflict resolution, international and transnational security issues, peacekeeping; legal studies (MA); management (MA), including defense management, general (MA, MS), human resource management, organizational leadership, public administration; marketing (MBA); military history (MA), including American military history, American Revolution, civil war, war since 1945, World War II; military studies (MA), including joint warfare, strategic leadership; national security studies (MA), including general (MA, MS), homeland security, regional security studies, security and intelligence analysis, terrorism studies; nonprofit management (MBA); political science (MA), including American politics and government, comparative government and development, general (MA, MS), international relations, public policy; psychology (MA), including general (MA, MS), maritime engineering management, reverse logistics management; public administration (MPA), including disaster management, environmental policy, health policy, human resources, national security, organizational management, security management; public health (MPH); reverse logistics management (MA); school counseling (M Ed); security management (MA); space studies (MS), including aerospace science, general (MA, MS), planetary science; sports and health sciences (MS); teaching (M Ed), including curriculum and instruction for elementary teachers, elementary reading, English language learners, instructional leadership, online learning, special education; transportation and logistics management (MA), including general (MA, MS), maritime engineering management, reverse logistics management. Programs offered via distance learning only. Part-time and evening/weekend programs available. Postbaccalaureate distance learning degree programs offered (no on-campus study). *Faculty:* 432 full-time (242 women), 1,722 part-time/adjunct (829 women). *Students:* 511 full-time (241 women), 10,947 part-time (4,294 women); includes 3,760 minority (2,058 Black or African American, non-Hispanic/Latino; 88 American Indian or Alaska Native, non-Hispanic/Latino; 293 Asian, non-Hispanic/Latino; 876 Hispanic/Latino; 91 Native Hawaiian or other Pacific Islander, non-Hispanic/Latino; 354 Two or more races, non-Hispanic/Latino; 134 international. Average age 36. In 2013, 3,323 master's awarded. *Degree requirements:* For master's, comprehensive exam or practicum. *Entrance requirements:* For master's, official transcript showing earned bachelor's degree from institution accredited by recognized accrediting body. Additional exam requirements/recommendations for international students: Required—TOEFL (minimum score 550 paper-based), IELTS (minimum score 6.5). *Application deadline:* Applications are processed on a rolling basis. Application fee: $0. Electronic applications accepted. *Expenses: Tuition:* Part-time $325 per semester hour. *Financial support:* Applicants required to submit FAFSA. *Faculty research:* Military history, criminal justice, management performance, national security. *Unit head:* Dr. Karan Powell, Executive Vice President and Provost, 877-468-6268, Fax: 304-724-3780. *Application contact:* Terry Grant, Vice President of Enrollment Management, 877-468-6268, Fax: 304-724-3780, E-mail: info@apus.edu. Website: http://www.apus.edu.

American University, College of Arts and Sciences, Washington, DC 20016-8012. Offers addiction and addictive behavior (Certificate); anthropology (PhD); applied microeconomics (Certificate); applied statistics (Certificate); art history (MA); arts management (MA, Certificate); Asian studies (Certificate); audio production (Certificate); audio technology (MA); behavior, cognition, and neuroscience (PhD); bilingual education (MA, Certificate); biology (MA, MS); chemistry (MS); clinical psychology (PhD); computer science (MS, Certificate); creative writing (MFA); curriculum and instruction (M Ed, Certificate); economics (MA, PhD); environmental assessment (Certificate); environmental science (MS); ethics, peace, and global affairs (MA); gender analysis in economics (Certificate); health promotion management (MS); history (MA, PhD); international arts management (Certificate); international economic relations (Certificate); international economics (MA); international training and education (MA); literature (MA); mathematics (MA); North American studies (Certificate); nutrition education (MS, Certificate); philosophy (MA); professional science: biotechnology (MS); professional science: environmental assessment (MS); professional science: quantitative analysis (MS); psychobiology of healing (Certificate); psychology (MA); psychology: general (PhD); public anthropology (MA, Certificate); public sociology (Certificate); social research (Certificate); sociology (MA); Spanish: Latin American studies (MA); special education: learning disabilities (MA); statistics (MS); studio art (MFA); teaching (MAT); teaching English as a foreign language (MA); teaching: early childhood (Certificate); teaching: elementary (Certificate); teaching: ESOL (Certificate); teaching: secondary (Certificate); technology in arts management (Certificate); TESOL (MA); translation: French (Certificate); translation: Russian (Certificate); translation: Spanish (Certificate); women's, gender, and sexuality studies (Certificate). Part-time and evening/weekend programs available. Postbaccalaureate distance learning degree programs offered (no on-campus study). *Faculty:* 358 full-time (187 women), 254 part-time/adjunct (127 women). *Students:* 627 full-time (411 women), 416 part-time (300 women); includes 206 minority (91 Black or African American, non-Hispanic/Latino; 5 American Indian or Alaska Native, non-Hispanic/Latino; 32 Asian, non-Hispanic/Latino; 64 Hispanic/Latino; 1 Native Hawaiian or other Pacific Islander, non-Hispanic/Latino; 13 Two or more races, non-Hispanic/Latino), 124 international. Average age 29. 1,672 applicants, 52% accepted, 361 enrolled. In 2013, 382 master's, 38 doctorates, 33 other advanced degrees awarded. Terminal master's awarded for partial completion of doctoral program. *Degree requirements:* For master's, comprehensive exam (for some programs), thesis (for some programs); for doctorate, comprehensive exam (for some programs), thesis/dissertation. *Entrance requirements:* For master's, GRE, minimum GPA of 3.0 in last 60 credit hours, letter of recommendation, statement of purpose, resume, unofficial transcript; for doctorate, GRE, minimum GPA of 3.0 for all graduate work, letter of recommendation, statement of purpose, resume, unofficial transcript. Additional exam requirements/recommendations for international students: Required—TOEFL (minimum score 600 paper-based; 100 iBT), IELTS (minimum score 7). *Application deadline:* For fall admission, 2/1 for domestic students; for spring admission, 10/1 for domestic students. Applications are processed on a rolling basis. Application fee: $55. Electronic applications accepted. *Expenses: Tuition:* Full-time $25,920; part-time $1482 per credit hour. *Required fees:* $430. Tuition and fees vary according to course load and program. *Financial support:* Fellowships, research assistantships with full and partial tuition reimbursements, teaching assistantships with full and partial tuition reimbursements, career-related internships or fieldwork, Federal Work-Study, institutionally sponsored loans, scholarships/grants, traineeships, tuition waivers (full and partial), and unspecified assistantships available. Support available to part-time students. Financial award applicants required to submit FAFSA. *Unit head:* Dr. Peter Starr, Dean, 202-885-2446, Fax: 202-885-2429, E-mail: pstarr@american.edu. *Application contact:* Kathleen Clowery, Associate Director, Graduate Enrollment Management, 202-885-3621, Fax: 202-885-1505, E-mail: clowery@american.edu. Website: http://www.american.edu/cas/.

American University of Puerto Rico, Program in Education, Bayamón, PR 00960-2037. Offers art education (M Ed); elementary education 4-6 (M Ed); elementary education K-3 (M Ed); general science education (M Ed); physical education (M Ed); special education (M Ed). *Faculty:* 17 part-time/adjunct (7 women). *Students:* 55 full-time (42 women), 105 part-time (96 women); all minorities (all Hispanic/Latino). Average age 33. 120 applicants, 99% accepted, 81 enrolled. In 2013, 52 master's awarded. *Entrance requirements:* For master's, EXADEP, GRE, or MAT, 2 letters of recommendation, minimum GPA of 2.5. *Application deadline:* For fall admission, 8/1 for domestic students; for winter admission, 10/18 for domestic students; for spring admission, 3/15 for domestic students. Applications are processed on a rolling basis. Application fee: $25. *Expenses: Tuition:* Part-time $240 per credit. Tuition and fees vary according to course load. *Unit head:* Dr. Jose A. Ramirez-Figueroa, Education and Technology Department Director/Chancellor, 787-620-2040 Ext. 2010, Fax: 787-620-2958, E-mail: jramirez@aupr.edu. *Application contact:* Keren I. Llanos-Figueroa, Information Contact, 787-620-2040 Ext. 2021, Fax: 787-785-7377, E-mail: oficnaadmisiones@aupr.edu.

Andrews University, School of Graduate Studies, School of Education, Department of Graduate Psychology and Counseling, Program in Special Education, Berrien Springs, MI 49104. Offers MS. *Students:* 1 (woman) full-time, 2 part-time (both women); includes 1 minority (Hispanic/Latino), 2 international. Average age 34. 2 applicants, 50% accepted. In 2013, 3 master's awarded. *Entrance requirements:* Additional exam requirements/recommendations for international students: Required—TOEFL (minimum score 550 paper-based). Application fee: $40. *Unit head:* Dr. Nona Elmendorf-Steele, Dean, 269-471-6468. *Application contact:* Monica Wringer, Supervisor of Graduate Admission, 800-253-2874, Fax: 269-471-6321, E-mail: graduate@andrews.edu.

Angelo State University, College of Graduate Studies, College of Education, Department of Teacher Education, Program in Special Education, San Angelo, TX 76909. Offers M Ed. Part-time and evening/weekend programs available. *Degree requirements:* For master's, comprehensive exam. *Entrance requirements:* Additional

exam requirements/recommendations for international students: Required—TOEFL or IELTS. Electronic applications accepted.

Antioch University New England, Graduate School, Department of Applied Psychology, Program in Autism Spectrum Disorders, Keene, NH 03431-3552. Offers applied behavior analysis (Certificate); applied behavior analysis internship (Certificate); autism spectrum disorders (Certificate). *Entrance requirements:* Additional exam requirements/recommendations for international students: Required—TOEFL (minimum score 550 paper-based).

Antioch University New England, Graduate School, Department of Education, Experienced Educators Program, Keene, NH 03431-3552. Offers foundations of education (M Ed), including applied behavioral analysis, autism spectrum disorders, educating for sustainability, next-generation learning using technology, problem-based learning using critical skills, teacher leadership; principal certification (PMC). *Degree requirements:* For master's, thesis, practicum. *Entrance requirements:* For master's, previous course work and work experience in education. Additional exam requirements/recommendations for international students: Required—TOEFL (minimum score 550 paper-based). Electronic applications accepted. *Expenses:* Contact institution. *Faculty research:* Classroom action research, school restructuring, problem-based learning, brain-based learning.

Antioch University New England, Graduate School, Department of Education, Integrated Learning Program, Keene, NH 03431-3552. Offers early childhood education (M Ed); elementary education (M Ed), including arts and humanities, science and environmental education; special education (M Ed). *Degree requirements:* For master's, internship. *Entrance requirements:* For master's, previous course work or work experience in education. Additional exam requirements/recommendations for international students: Required—TOEFL (minimum score 550 paper-based). Electronic applications accepted. *Expenses:* Contact institution. *Faculty research:* Problem-based learning, place-based education, mathematics education, democratic classrooms, art education.

Appalachian State University, Cratis D. Williams Graduate School, Department of Reading Education and Special Education, Boone, NC 28608. Offers reading education (MA); special education (MA). *Accreditation:* ASHA. Part-time and evening/weekend programs available. Postbaccalaureate distance learning degree programs offered (no on-campus study). *Degree requirements:* For master's, comprehensive exam, thesis optional. *Entrance requirements:* For master's, GRE General Test or MAT, 3 letters of recommendation. Additional exam requirements/recommendations for international students: Required—TOEFL (minimum score 570 paper-based; 79 iBT), IELTS (minimum score 6.5). Electronic applications accepted. *Faculty research:* Special education, language arts, reading.

Arcadia University, Graduate Studies, School of Education, Glenside, PA 19038-3295. Offers art education (M Ed); computer education (CAS); curriculum (CAS); curriculum studies (M Ed); early childhood education (M Ed, CAS), including individualized (M Ed), master teacher (M Ed), research in child development (M Ed); educational leadership (M Ed, Ed D, CAS); elementary education (M Ed, CAS); English education (MA Ed); environmental education (MA Ed, CAS); history education (MA Ed); instructional technology (M Ed); language arts (M Ed, CAS); library science (M Ed); mathematics education (M Ed, MA Ed, CAS); music education (MA Ed); psychology (MA Ed); reading (M Ed, CAS); science education (M Ed, CAS); secondary education (M Ed, CAS); special education (M Ed, Ed D, CAS); theater arts (MA Ed); written communication (MA Ed). *Accreditation:* NASAD. Part-time and evening/weekend programs available. Postbaccalaureate distance learning degree programs offered (minimal on-campus study). Electronic applications accepted. *Expenses:* Contact institution.

Arizona State University at the Tempe campus, Mary Lou Fulton Teachers College, Program in Special Education, Phoenix, AZ 85069. Offers autism spectrum disorder (Graduate Certificate); special education (M Ed, MA). Postbaccalaureate distance learning degree programs offered (minimal on-campus study). *Degree requirements:* For master's, thesis or alternative, applied project, student teaching, interactive Program of Study (iPOS) submitted before completing 50 percent of required credit hours. *Entrance requirements:* For master's, Arizona Educator Proficiency Assessments (AEPA), minimum GPA of 3.0 or equivalent in last 2 years of work leading to bachelor's degree, 3 letters of recommendation, personal statement, resume, IVP fingerprint clearance card (for those seeking Arizona certification). Additional exam requirements/recommendations for international students: Required—TOEFL (minimum score 80 iBT), TOEFL, IELTS, or PTE. Electronic applications accepted.

Arkansas State University, Graduate School, College of Education and Behavioral Science, School of Teacher Education and Leadership, Jonesboro, AR 72467. Offers community college administration (SCCT); curriculum and instruction (MSE); early childhood education (MAT, MSE); early childhood services (MS); educational leadership (MSE, Ed D, PhD, Ed S); educational theory and practice (MSE); middle level education (MAT, MSE); reading (MSE, Ed S); special education - gifted, talented, and creative (MSE); special education - instructional specialist grades 4-12 (MSE); special education - instructional specialist grades P-4 (MSE). *Accreditation:* NCATE. Part-time programs available. Postbaccalaureate distance learning degree programs offered. *Faculty:* 28 full-time (16 women). *Students:* 77 full-time (68 women), 1,934 part-time (1,449 women); includes 361 minority (290 Black or African American, non-Hispanic/Latino; 11 American Indian or Alaska Native, non-Hispanic/Latino; 3 Asian, non-Hispanic/Latino; 26 Hispanic/Latino; 1 Native Hawaiian or other Pacific Islander, non-Hispanic/Latino; 30 Two or more races, non-Hispanic/Latino), 5 international. Average age 36. 1,627 applicants, 71% accepted, 770 enrolled. In 2013, 1,182 master's, 12 doctorates, 76 other advanced degrees awarded. *Degree requirements:* For master's, comprehensive exam, thesis or alternative; for doctorate, comprehensive exam, thesis/dissertation; for other advanced degree, comprehensive exam. *Entrance requirements:* For master's, GRE General Test or MAT, appropriate bachelor's degree, official transcripts, immunization records, letters of reference, interview; for doctorate, GRE General Test or MAT, interview, master's degree, letters of reference, official transcript, personal statement, writing sample, immunization records; for other advanced degree, GRE General Test or MAT, interview, master's degree, official transcript, immunization records, letters of reference, 3 years of teaching experience, teaching license. Additional exam requirements/recommendations for international students: Required—TOEFL (minimum score 550 paper-based; 79 iBT), IELTS (minimum score 6), PTE (minimum score 56). *Application deadline:* For fall admission, 7/1 for domestic and international students; for spring admission, 11/15 for domestic students, 11/14 for international students. Applications are processed on a rolling basis. Electronic applications accepted. *Expenses:* Tuition, state resident: full-time $4284; part-time $238 per credit hour. Tuition, nonresident: full-time $8568; part-time $476 per credit hour. *International tuition:* $9268 full-time. *Required fees:* $1098; $61 per credit hour. $25 per term. Tuition and fees vary according to course load and program. *Financial support:* In 2013–14, 20 students received support. Fellowships, teaching assistantships, career-related internships or fieldwork, scholarships/grants, and unspecified assistantships available. Financial award application deadline: 7/1; financial award applicants required to submit FAFSA. *Unit head:* Dr. Annette Hux, Interim Chair, 870-972-3059, Fax: 870-972-3344, E-mail: ahux@astate.edu. *Application contact:* Vickey Ring, Graduate Admissions Coordinator, 870-972-3029, Fax: 870-972-3857, E-mail: vickeyring@astate.edu.
Website: http://www.astate.edu/college/education/departments/school-of-teacher-education-and-leadership/index.dot.

Armstrong State University, School of Graduate Studies, Department of Childhood and Exceptional Student Education, Savannah, GA 31419-1997. Offers early childhood education (M Ed, MAT); reading endorsement (Certificate); special education (M Ed, MAT). *Accreditation:* NCATE. Part-time and evening/weekend programs available. Postbaccalaureate distance learning degree programs offered (minimal on-campus study). *Faculty:* 12 full-time (9 women), 4 part-time/adjunct (0 women). *Students:* 26 full-time (22 women), 208 part-time (186 women); includes 74 minority (66 Black or African American, non-Hispanic/Latino; 1 Asian, non-Hispanic/Latino; 5 Hispanic/Latino; 2 Two or more races, non-Hispanic/Latino), 1 international. Average age 33. 107 applicants, 70% accepted, 69 enrolled. In 2013, 122 master's, 64 other advanced degrees awarded. *Degree requirements:* For master's, comprehensive exam. *Entrance requirements:* For master's, GRE General Test or MAT. Additional exam requirements/recommendations for international students: Required—TOEFL (minimum score 523 paper-based). *Application deadline:* For fall admission, 6/30 priority date for domestic students, 5/1 priority date for international students; for spring admission, 11/15 priority date for domestic students, 9/15 priority date for international students; for summer admission, 4/15 priority date for domestic students, 9/15 for international students. Applications are processed on a rolling basis. Application fee: $30. Electronic applications accepted. *Expenses:* Tuition, state resident: part-time $201 per credit hour. Tuition, nonresident: part-time $745 per credit hour. *Required fees:* $310 per semester. Tuition and fees vary according to course load, campus/location and program. *Financial support:* In 2013–14, research assistantships with full tuition reimbursements (averaging $5,000 per year) were awarded; career-related internships or fieldwork, Federal Work-Study, scholarships/grants, and unspecified assistantships also available. Support available to part-time students. Financial award application deadline: 3/15; financial award applicants required to submit FAFSA. *Faculty research:* Literacy, instructional design, poetry, working with local schools. *Unit head:* Dr. John Hobe, Department Head, 912-344-2564, Fax: 912-344-3443, E-mail: john.hobe@armstrong.edu. *Application contact:* Jill Bell, Director, Graduate Enrollment Services, 912-344-2798, Fax: 912-344-3488, E-mail: graduate@armstrong.edu.
Website: http://www.armstrong.edu/Education/childhood_exceptional_education2/ceed_welcome.

Asbury University, School of Graduate and Professional Studies, Wilmore, KY 40390-1198. Offers biology: alternative certificate (MA Ed); chemistry: alternative certificate (MA Ed); English (MA Ed); English as a second language (MA Ed); ESL (MA Ed); French (MA Ed); Latin: alternative certificate (MA Ed); mathematics: alternative certificate (MA Ed); reading/writing endorsement (MA Ed); social studies (MA Ed); social work (MSW), including child and family services; Spanish (MA Ed); special education (MA Ed); special education: alternative certificate (MA Ed); teacher as leader endorsement (MA Ed). *Accreditation:* NCATE. Part-time programs available. *Degree requirements:* For master's, action research project, portfolio. *Entrance requirements:* For master's, PRAXIS/NTE, minimum GPA of 2.75, letters of recommendation. Additional exam requirements/recommendations for international students: Required—TOEFL (minimum score 550 paper-based). Electronic applications accepted.

Ashland University, Dwight Schar College of Education, Department of Inclusive Services and Exceptional Learners, Ashland, OH 44805-3702. Offers intervention specialist, mild/moderate (M Ed); intervention specialist, moderate/intensive (M Ed); talented and gifted (M Ed). Part-time and evening/weekend programs available. *Degree requirements:* For master's, thesis or alternative, internship, practicum, inquiry seminar. *Entrance requirements:* Additional exam requirements/recommendations for international students: Required—TOEFL. Electronic applications accepted.

Assumption College, Graduate Studies, Special Education Program, Worcester, MA 01609-1296. Offers positive behavior support (CAGS); special education (MA). Part-time and evening/weekend programs available. *Faculty:* 3 full-time (all women), 3 part-time/adjunct (all women). *Students:* 11 full-time (10 women), 40 part-time (35 women); includes 2 minority (both Hispanic/Latino). Average age 27. 19 applicants, 74% accepted, 13 enrolled. In 2013, 15 master's, 5 other advanced degrees awarded. *Degree requirements:* For master's, comprehensive exam, internship, practicum. *Entrance requirements:* For master's and CAGS, 3 letters of recommendation, resume, essay. Additional exam requirements/recommendations for international students: Required—TOEFL (minimum score 540 paper-based; 76 iBT), IELTS (minimum score 6). *Application deadline:* For fall admission, 10/1 for domestic and international students; for winter admission, 2/1 for domestic and international students; for spring admission, 4/1 for domestic and international students. Applications are processed on a rolling basis. Application fee: $30. Electronic applications accepted. *Expenses: Tuition:* Full-time $10,098; part-time $561 per credit. *Required fees:* $20 per term. Full-time tuition and fees vary according to course load and program. *Financial support:* In 2013–14, 5 students received support. Tuition waivers (full and partial), unspecified assistantships, and institutional discounts available. Financial award application deadline: 5/1; financial award applicants required to submit FAFSA. *Unit head:* Dr. Nanho Vander Hart, Director, 508-767-7380, Fax: 508-767-7263, E-mail: nvanderh@assumption.edu. *Application contact:* Laura Lawrence, Graduate Programs Operations Manager, 508-767-7387, Fax: 508-767-7030, E-mail: graduate@assumption.edu.
Website: http://graduate.assumption.edu/special-education/masterofarts.

Auburn University, Graduate School, College of Education, Department of Special Education, Rehabilitation, Counseling and School Psychology, Auburn University, AL 36849. Offers collaborative teacher special education (M Ed, MS); early childhood special education (M Ed, MS); rehabilitation counseling (M Ed, MS, PhD). *Accreditation:* CORE; NCATE. Part-time programs available. *Faculty:* 18 full-time (14 women), 8 part-time/adjunct (7 women). *Students:* 142 full-time (118 women), 80 part-time (64 women); includes 57 minority (53 Black or African American, non-Hispanic/Latino; 1 American Indian or Alaska Native, non-Hispanic/Latino; 2 Asian, non-Hispanic/Latino; 1 Hispanic/Latino). Average age 30. 239 applicants, 42% accepted, 83 enrolled. In 2013, 59 master's, 10 doctorates awarded. *Degree requirements:* For master's, thesis (for some programs); for doctorate, thesis/dissertation. *Entrance requirements:* For master's, GRE General Test; for doctorate, GRE General Test, interview. *Application deadline:* For fall admission, 7/7 for domestic students; for spring admission, 11/24 for domestic students. Applications are processed on a rolling basis. Application fee: $50 ($60 for international students). Electronic applications accepted. *Expenses:* Tuition, state resident: full-time $8262; part-time $459 per credit hour. Tuition, nonresident: full-time $24,786; part-time $1377 per credit hour. Tuition and fees vary according to degree level and program. *Financial support:* Research assistantships, teaching assistantships, and Federal Work-Study available. Support available to part-time students. Financial award application deadline: 3/15; financial award applicants required to submit FAFSA. *Faculty research:* Emotional conflict/behavior disorders, gifted and talented, learning disabilities, mental retardation, multi-handicapped. *Unit head:* Dr. E. Davis Martin, Jr., Head, 334-844-7676. *Application contact:* Dr. George Flowers, Dean of the Graduate School, 334-844-2125.

Auburn University at Montgomery, School of Education, Department of Counselor, Leadership, and Special Education, Montgomery, AL 36124-4023. Offers counseling

education (M Ed, Ed S), including counseling and development (Ed S), school counseling (Ed S); early childhood special education (M Ed); instructional leadership (Ed S); special education (Ed S); special education/collaborative teacher (M Ed). *Accreditation:* ACA; NCATE. Part-time and evening/weekend programs available. *Faculty:* 6 full-time (5 women), 2 part-time/adjunct (1 woman). *Students:* 15 full-time (11 women), 55 part-time (42 women); includes 32 minority (31 Black or African American, non-Hispanic/Latino; 1 Hispanic/Latino). Average age 33. In 2013, 22 master's awarded. *Degree requirements:* For master's and Ed S, comprehensive exam. *Entrance requirements:* For master's, GRE General Test or MAT, certification, BS in teaching; for Ed S, GRE General Test or MAT, certification. *Application deadline:* Applications are processed on a rolling basis. Electronic applications accepted. *Expenses:* Tuition, state resident: full-time $5994; part-time $333 per credit hour. Tuition, nonresident: full-time $17,982; part-time $999 per credit hour. *Financial support:* Career-related internships or fieldwork and scholarships/grants available. Support available to part-time students. Financial award application deadline: 3/1; financial award applicants required to submit FAFSA. *Unit head:* Dr. Sheila Austin, Dean, 334-244-3425, Fax: 334-244-3102, E-mail: saustin1@aum.edu. *Application contact:* Dr. Rhonda Morton, Associate Dean/Graduate Coordinator, 334-244-3287, Fax: 334-244-3978, E-mail: rmorton@aum.edu.
Website: http://www.aum.edu/Education.

Augustana College, MA in Education Program, Sioux Falls, SD 57197. Offers instructional strategies (MA); reading (MA); special populations (MA); technology (MA). *Accreditation:* NCATE. Part-time and evening/weekend programs available. Postbaccalaureate distance learning degree programs offered (no on-campus study). *Faculty:* 9 full-time (6 women). *Students:* 48 part-time (40 women). Average age 33. 55 applicants, 100% accepted, 49 enrolled. In 2013, 14 master's awarded. *Degree requirements:* For master's, thesis. *Entrance requirements:* For master's, appropriate bachelor's degree, minimum GPA of 3.0, teaching certificate. Additional exam requirements/recommendations for international students: Required—TOEFL (minimum score 550 paper-based). *Application deadline:* For spring admission, 4/1 priority date for domestic and international students. Applications are processed on a rolling basis. Application fee: $50. Electronic applications accepted. *Expenses:* Contact institution. *Financial support:* Application deadline: 3/1; applicants required to submit FAFSA. *Unit head:* Dr. Sheryl Feinstein, MA in Education Program Director, 605-274-5211, E-mail: sheryl.feinstein@augie.edu. *Application contact:* Nancy Wright, Graduate Coordinator, 605-274-4043, Fax: 605-274-4450, E-mail: graduate@augie.edu.
Website: http://www.augie.edu/academics/graduate-education/master-arts-education.

Aurora University, College of Education, Aurora, IL 60506-4892. Offers curriculum and instruction (MA, Ed D); early childhood and special education (MA); education (MAT), including elementary certification; education and administration (Ed D); educational leadership (MEL); educational technology (MATL); reading instruction (MA); special education (MA). *Accreditation:* NCATE. Part-time and evening/weekend programs available. *Degree requirements:* For doctorate, comprehensive exam, thesis/dissertation. *Entrance requirements:* For master's, 2 years of teaching experience, valid teaching certificate. Additional exam requirements/recommendations for international students: Required—TOEFL (minimum score 550 paper-based). Electronic applications accepted. *Expenses:* Contact institution.

Austin Peay State University, College of Graduate Studies, College of Education, Department of Educational Specialties, Clarksville, TN 37044. Offers administration and supervision (Ed S); curriculum and instruction (MA Ed); education leadership (MA Ed); elementary education (Ed S); secondary education (Ed S); special education (MA Ed). Part-time and evening/weekend programs available. Postbaccalaureate distance learning degree programs offered. *Faculty:* 8 full-time (5 women), 4 part-time/adjunct (3 women). *Students:* 6 full-time (5 women), 87 part-time (73 women); includes 10 minority (5 Black or African American, non-Hispanic/Latino; 1 American Indian or Alaska Native, non-Hispanic/Latino; 1 Asian, non-Hispanic/Latino; 1 Hispanic/Latino; 2 Two or more races, non-Hispanic/Latino). Average age 35. 11 applicants, 82% accepted, 6 enrolled. In 2013, 37 master's, 6 Ed Ss awarded. *Degree requirements:* For master's, comprehensive exam, thesis optional. *Entrance requirements:* For master's, GRE General Test, 3 letters of recommendation, minimum undergraduate GPA of 2.75. Additional exam requirements/recommendations for international students: Required—TOEFL (minimum score 500 paper-based). *Application deadline:* For fall admission, 8/5 priority date for domestic students. Applications are processed on a rolling basis. Application fee: $25. Electronic applications accepted. *Expenses:* Tuition, state resident: full-time $7500; part-time $375 per credit hour. Tuition, nonresident: full-time $20,800; part-time $1040 per credit hour. *Required fees:* $1284; $64.20 per credit hour. *Financial support:* Career-related internships or fieldwork, Federal Work-Study, institutionally sponsored loans, scholarships/grants, and unspecified assistantships available. Support available to part-time students. Financial award application deadline: 3/1; financial award applicants required to submit FAFSA. *Unit head:* Dr. Moniqueka Gold, Chair, 931-221-7696, Fax: 931-221-1292, E-mail: goldm@apsu.edu. *Application contact:* June D. Lee, Graduate Coordinator, 800-859-4723, Fax: 931-221-7641, E-mail: gradadmissions@apsu.edu.

Austin Peay State University, College of Graduate Studies, College of Education, Department of Teaching and Learning, Clarksville, TN 37044. Offers elementary education K-6 (MAT); reading (MA Ed); secondary education 7-12 (MAT); special education K-12 (MAT). Part-time and evening/weekend programs available. Postbaccalaureate distance learning degree programs offered. *Faculty:* 7 full-time (4 women), 5 part-time/adjunct (all women). *Students:* 70 full-time (59 women), 77 part-time (55 women); includes 23 minority (10 Black or African American, non-Hispanic/Latino; 2 Asian, non-Hispanic/Latino; 5 Hispanic/Latino; 6 Two or more races, non-Hispanic/Latino). Average age 33. 50 applicants, 90% accepted, 37 enrolled. In 2013, 60 master's awarded. *Degree requirements:* For master's, comprehensive exam, thesis optional. *Entrance requirements:* For master's, GRE General Test, 3 letters of recommendation, minimum undergraduate GPA of 2.75. Additional exam requirements/recommendations for international students: Required—TOEFL (minimum score 500 paper-based). *Application deadline:* For fall admission, 8/5 priority date for domestic students. Applications are processed on a rolling basis. Application fee: $25. Electronic applications accepted. *Expenses:* Tuition, state resident: full-time $7500; part-time $375 per credit hour. Tuition, nonresident: full-time $20,800; part-time $1040 per credit hour. *Required fees:* $1284; $64.20 per credit hour. *Financial support:* Career-related internships or fieldwork, Federal Work-Study, institutionally sponsored loans, scholarships/grants, and unspecified assistantships available. Support available to part-time students. Financial award application deadline: 3/1; financial award applicants required to submit FAFSA. *Unit head:* Dr. Rebecca McMahan, Chair, 931-221-7513, Fax: 931-221-1292, E-mail: mcmahanb@apsu.edu. *Application contact:* June D. Lee, Graduate Coordinator, 800-859-4723, Fax: 931-221-7641, E-mail: gradadmissions@apsu.edu.

Averett University, Master in Education Program, Danville, VA 24541-3692. Offers administration and supervision (M Ed); art (M Ed); biology (M Ed); chemistry (M Ed); curriculum and instruction (M Ed); early childhood (M Ed); English (M Ed); mathematics (M Ed); middle grades (M Ed); physical science (M Ed); reading specialist (M Ed); science (M Ed); special education (M Ed); special education learning disability (M Ed). Program offered on Danville Campus only. Part-time and evening/weekend programs available. *Faculty:* 4 full-time (3 women), 13 part-time/adjunct (8 women). *Students:* 43 full-time (35 women), 44 part-time (35 women); includes 7 minority (all Black or African American, non-Hispanic/Latino). *Degree requirements:* For master's, 30-credit core curriculum, minimum GPA of 3.0 throughout program, completion of degree requirements within six years from start of program. *Entrance requirements:* For master's, PRAXIS I, GRE, or MAT; writing proficiency test, minimum cumulative GPA of 3.0 over the last 60 hours of undergraduate study toward a baccalaureate degree, three letters of recommendation, Virginia teaching license (or eligibility). Additional exam requirements/recommendations for international students: Required—TOEFL (minimum score 600 paper-based; 100 iBT). *Application deadline:* Applications are processed on a rolling basis. Application fee: $100. *Expenses:* Contact institution. *Financial support:* Career-related internships or fieldwork, Federal Work-Study, and scholarships/grants available. Financial award application deadline: 4/1; financial award applicants required to submit FAFSA. *Unit head:* Wilfred Lawrence, Department Chair of Education, 434-791-5752, E-mail: priedel@averett.edu. *Application contact:* Christy Pack, Executive Director of Enrollment, 804-887-8612, E-mail: dpack@averett.edu.
Website: http://www.averett.edu/adultprograms/degrees/MEDtrad.php.

Azusa Pacific University, School of Education, Department of Special Education, Program in Special Education, Azusa, CA 91702-7000. Offers MA Ed. *Accreditation:* NCATE. Part-time and evening/weekend programs available. *Degree requirements:* For master's, core exams, oral presentations. *Entrance requirements:* For master's, 12 units of course work in education, minimum GPA of 3.0.

Azusa Pacific University, School of Education, Department of Special Education, Program in Special Education and Educational Technology, Azusa, CA 91702-7000. Offers M Ed.

Baldwin Wallace University, Graduate Programs, Division of Education, Specialization in Mild/Moderate Educational Needs, Berea, OH 44017-2088. Offers MA Ed. *Accreditation:* NCATE. Part-time and evening/weekend programs available. Postbaccalaureate distance learning degree programs offered (no on-campus study). *Faculty:* 2 full-time (1 woman), 5 part-time/adjunct (2 women). *Students:* 31 full-time (26 women), 20 part-time (17 women); includes 6 minority (4 Black or African American, non-Hispanic/Latino; 2 Hispanic/Latino). Average age 32. 25 applicants, 60% accepted, 9 enrolled. In 2013, 30 master's awarded. *Degree requirements:* For master's, comprehensive exam, capstone practicum. *Entrance requirements:* For master's, bachelor's degree in field, MAT or minimum GPA of 2.75. Additional exam requirements/recommendations for international students: Required—TOEFL (minimum score 523 paper-based; 70 iBT). *Application deadline:* For fall admission, 8/15 priority date for domestic students; for spring admission, 12/15 priority date for domestic students. Applications are processed on a rolling basis. Application fee: $25. Electronic applications accepted. Application fee is waived when completed online. *Expenses:* Contact institution. *Financial support:* Career-related internships or fieldwork available. Support available to part-time students. Financial award application deadline: 5/1; financial award applicants required to submit FAFSA. *Faculty research:* Adult adjustment of individuals formerly identified as having mild/moderate special education needs, professional development of special educators, teacher beliefs and special education, classroom assessment practices. *Unit head:* Dr. Karen Kaye, Chair, 440-826-2168, Fax: 440-826-3779, E-mail: kkaye@bw.edu. *Application contact:* Winifred W. Gerhardt, Director of Admission, Adult and Graduate Programs, 440-826-2222, Fax: 440-826-3830, E-mail: admission@bw.edu.
Website: http://www.bw.edu/academics/mae/needs.

Ball State University, Graduate School, Teachers College, Department of Special Education, Muncie, IN 47306-1099. Offers applied behavior analysis (MA); special education (MA, MAE, Ed D, Ed S). *Accreditation:* NCATE. *Faculty:* 19 full-time (14 women), 23 part-time/adjunct (19 women). *Students:* 255 full-time (218 women), 770 part-time (696 women); includes 71 minority (38 Black or African American, non-Hispanic/Latino; 4 American Indian or Alaska Native, non-Hispanic/Latino; 11 Asian, non-Hispanic/Latino; 13 Hispanic/Latino; 2 Native Hawaiian or other Pacific Islander, non-Hispanic/Latino; 3 Two or more races, non-Hispanic/Latino), 47 international. Average age 33. 93 applicants, 68% accepted, 6 enrolled. In 2013, 263 master's, 2 doctorates, 145 other advanced degrees awarded. *Degree requirements:* For doctorate, thesis/dissertation; for Ed S, thesis. *Entrance requirements:* For doctorate, GRE General Test, interview, minimum graduate GPA of 3.2; for Ed S, GRE General Test. Application fee: $50. *Financial support:* In 2013–14, 6 students received support, including 4 research assistantships with full tuition reimbursements available (averaging $10,394 per year), 19 teaching assistantships with full tuition reimbursements available (averaging $9,706 per year); career-related internships or fieldwork also available. Financial award application deadline: 3/1. *Faculty research:* Language development and utilization in the handicapped (preschool through adult). *Unit head:* Dr. John Merbler, Chairperson, 765-285-5700, Fax: 765-285-4280, E-mail: jmerbler@bsu.edu. *Application contact:* Dr. Robert Morris, Associate Provost for Research and Dean of the Graduate School, 765-285-1300, E-mail: rmorris@bsu.edu.
Website: http://www.bsu.edu/teachers/departments/sped/.

Bank Street College of Education, Graduate School, Program in Infant and Family Development and Early Intervention, New York, NY 10025. Offers infant and family development (MS Ed); infant and family early childhood special and general education (MS Ed); infant and family/early childhood special education (Ed M). *Degree requirements:* For master's, thesis. *Entrance requirements:* For master's, interview, essays. Additional exam requirements/recommendations for international students: Required—TOEFL (minimum score 600 paper-based; 100 iBT), IELTS (minimum score 7). Electronic applications accepted. *Faculty research:* Early intervention, early attachment practice in infant and toddler childcare, parenting skills in adolescents.

Bank Street College of Education, Graduate School, Program in Special Education, New York, NY 10025. Offers early childhood special and general education (MS Ed); early childhood special education (Ed M, MS Ed); elementary/childhood special and general education (MS Ed); elementary/childhood special education (MS Ed); elementary/childhood special education certification (Ed M). *Degree requirements:* For master's, thesis. *Entrance requirements:* For master's, interview, essays. Additional exam requirements/recommendations for international students: Required—TOEFL (minimum score 600 paper-based; 100 iBT), IELTS (minimum score 7). Electronic applications accepted. *Faculty research:* Teaching students with disabilities, inclusion, observation and assessment, early intervention, neurodevelopmental assessment, equity and social justice in education.

Barry University, School of Education, Program in Education for Teachers of Students with Hearing Impairments, Miami Shores, FL 33161-6695. Offers MS.

Barry University, School of Education, Program in Exceptional Student Education, Miami Shores, FL 33161-6695. Offers MS, Ed S. Part-time and evening/weekend programs available. *Degree requirements:* For master's, comprehensive exam; for Ed S, practicum. *Entrance requirements:* For master's, GRE General Test or MAT, minimum GPA of 3.0; for Ed S, GRE General Test, minimum GPA of 3.0. Electronic applications accepted.

Barry University, School of Education, Program in Leadership and Education, Miami Shores, FL 33161-6695. Offers educational technology (PhD); exceptional student

education (PhD); higher education administration (PhD); human resource development (PhD); leadership (PhD). Part-time and evening/weekend programs available. *Degree requirements:* For doctorate, thesis/dissertation. *Entrance requirements:* For doctorate, GRE General Test, minimum GPA of 3.25. Electronic applications accepted.

Bayamón Central University, Graduate Programs, Program in Education, Bayamón, PR 00960-1725. Offers administration and supervision (MA Ed); commercial education (MA Ed); elementary education (K–3) (MA Ed); family counseling (Graduate Certificate); guidance and counseling (MA Ed); pre-elementary teacher (MA Ed); rehabilitation counseling (MA Ed); special education (MA Ed), including attention deficit disorder, education of the autistic, learning disabilities. Part-time and evening/weekend programs available. *Degree requirements:* For master's, comprehensive exam. *Entrance requirements:* For master's, EXADEP, bachelor's degree in education or related field.

Baylor University, Graduate School, School of Education, Department of Educational Psychology, Waco, TX 76798-7301. Offers applied behavior analysis (MS Ed); educational psychology (MA, PhD); exceptionalities (PhD); learning and development (PhD); measurement (PhD); school psychology (Ed S). *Accreditation:* NCATE. *Faculty:* 12 full-time (7 women), 2 part-time/adjunct (1 woman). *Students:* 36 full-time (30 women), 6 part-time (all women); includes 8 minority (1 Black or African American, non-Hispanic/Latino; 3 Asian, non-Hispanic/Latino; 4 Hispanic/Latino), 2 international. Average age 29. 40 applicants, 38% accepted, 12 enrolled. In 2013, 4 master's, 8 doctorates, 8 other advanced degrees awarded. *Degree requirements:* For master's, thesis optional; for doctorate, comprehensive exam, thesis/dissertation; for Ed S, comprehensive exam, thesis or alternative. *Entrance requirements:* For master's, minimum GPA of 3.0; for doctorate, GRE General Test, master's degree; for Ed S, GRE General Test. Additional exam requirements/recommendations for international students: Required—TOEFL. *Application deadline:* For fall admission, 2/1 priority date for domestic and international students. Application fee: $50. Electronic applications accepted. *Expenses: Tuition:* Full-time $25,866; part-time $1437 per credit hour. *Required fees:* $2736; $152 per credit hour. Tuition and fees vary according to course load and program. *Financial support:* In 2013–14, 42 students received support, including 20 fellowships with full and partial tuition reimbursements available, 22 research assistantships with full and partial tuition reimbursements available; career-related internships or fieldwork, Federal Work-Study, institutionally sponsored loans, scholarships/grants, health care benefits, tuition waivers (full and partial), unspecified assistantships, and stipends also available. Financial award application deadline: 2/1; financial award applicants required to submit FAFSA. *Faculty research:* Individual differences, quantitative methods, gifted and talented, special education, school psychology, autism, applied behavior analysis, learning, human development. *Total annual research expenditures:* $248,000. *Unit head:* Dr. Marley W. Watkins, Professor and Chairman, 254-710-4234, Fax: 254-710-3987, E-mail: marley_watkins@baylor.edu. *Application contact:* Lisa Rowe, Office Manager, 254-710-3112, Fax: 254-710-3112, E-mail: lisa_rowe@baylor.edu.
Website: http://www.baylor.edu/soe/EDP/.

Bay Path College, Program in Special Education, Longmeadow, MA 01106-2292. Offers applied behavior analysis (MS Ed); moderate disabilities 5-12 (MS Ed); moderate disabilities PreK-8 (MS Ed); non-licensure (MS Ed); severe disabilities PreK-12 (MS Ed); special education (MS Ed, Ed S). Part-time and evening/weekend programs available. Postbaccalaureate distance learning degree programs offered. *Students:* 46 full-time (43 women), 224 part-time (210 women); includes 29 minority (12 Black or African American, non-Hispanic/Latino; 3 Asian, non-Hispanic/Latino; 11 Hispanic/Latino; 2 Native Hawaiian or other Pacific Islander, non-Hispanic/Latino; 1 Two or more races, non-Hispanic/Latino). Average age 34. 106 applicants, 79% accepted, 71 enrolled. In 2013, 95 master's, 5 Ed Ss awarded. *Degree requirements:* For master's, six 3-credit courses and one 12-credit practicum for a total of 30 credits. *Application deadline:* Applications are processed on a rolling basis. Application fee: $45. Electronic applications accepted. Application fee is waived when completed online. *Expenses:* Contact institution. *Financial support:* In 2013–14, 4 students received support. Scholarships/grants available. Financial award applicants required to submit FAFSA. *Unit head:* Dr. Liz Fleming, Director/Founding Dean, 413-565-1332. *Application contact:* Lisa Adams, Director of Graduate Admissions, 413-565-1317, Fax: 413-565-1250, E-mail: ladams@baypath.edu.
Website: http://graduate.baypath.edu/Graduate-Programs/Programs-On-Campus/MS-Programs/Education-Special-Education.

Bellarmine University, Annsley Frazier Thornton School of Education, Louisville, KY 40205-0671. Offers education and social change (PhD); elementary education (MA Ed, MAT); learning and behavior disorders (MA Ed, MAT); middle grades education (MA Ed, MAT); principalship (Ed S); reading and writing (MA Ed); secondary education (MAT); teacher leadership (MA Ed). *Accreditation:* NCATE. Part-time and evening/weekend programs available. *Faculty:* 13 full-time (7 women), 14 part-time/adjunct (9 women). *Students:* 60 full-time (47 women), 191 part-time (140 women); includes 35 minority (22 Black or African American, non-Hispanic/Latino; 1 American Indian or Alaska Native, non-Hispanic/Latino; 3 Asian, non-Hispanic/Latino; 5 Hispanic/Latino; 4 Two or more races, non-Hispanic/Latino). Average age 33. In 2013, 108 master's awarded. *Degree requirements:* For master's, comprehensive exam, thesis (for some programs); for doctorate, comprehensive exam, thesis/dissertation. *Entrance requirements:* For master's, GRE, baccalaureate degree from accredited institution; minimum overall GPA of 2.75, 3.0 in major; letters of recommendation; valid Kentucky provisional or professional certificate; for doctorate, GRE, minimum GPA of 3.5 in all graduate coursework; baccalaureate and master's degrees in education (MA, MS) or fields directly relevant to education; three letters of recommendation; two essays (no more than 1000 words each); interview. Additional exam requirements/recommendations for international students: Required—TOEFL (minimum score 550 paper-based; 80 iBT). *Application deadline:* Applications are processed on a rolling basis. Application fee: $25. *Expenses:* Contact institution. *Financial support:* Scholarships/grants available. Financial award applicants required to submit FAFSA. *Faculty research:* Literacy, service-learning, dispositions, educational technology, special education. *Unit head:* Dr. Robert Cooter, Dean, 502-272-8191, Fax: 502-272-8189, E-mail: rcooter@bellarmine.edu. *Application contact:* Theresa Klapheke, Administrative Director of Graduate Programs, 502-272-8271, Fax: 502-272-8002, E-mail: tklapheke@bellarmine.edu.
Website: http://www.bellarmine.edu/education/graduate.

Belmont University, College of Arts and Sciences, Nashville, TN 37212-3757. Offers education (M Ed); English (MA); special education (MA); sport administration (MSA); teaching (MAT). Part-time and evening/weekend programs available. *Faculty:* 29 full-time (21 women), 24 part-time/adjunct (12 women). *Students:* 144 full-time (97 women), 63 part-time (49 women); includes 26 minority (9 Black or African American, non-Hispanic/Latino; 1 Asian, non-Hispanic/Latino; 8 Hispanic/Latino; 8 Two or more races, non-Hispanic/Latino), 3 international. Average age 29. 201 applicants, 57% accepted, 81 enrolled. *Degree requirements:* For master's, comprehensive exam (for some programs), thesis (for some programs). *Entrance requirements:* For master's, GRE, GMAT, MAT. Additional exam requirements/recommendations for international students: Required—TOEFL. *Application deadline:* For fall admission, 8/1 for domestic students; for spring admission, 12/1 for domestic students. Applications are processed on a rolling basis. Application fee: $50. Electronic applications accepted. *Expenses:* Contact institution. *Financial support:* In 2013–14, 50 students received support. Fellowships with partial tuition reimbursements available, teaching assistantships with partial tuition reimbursements available, Federal Work-Study, institutionally sponsored loans, scholarships/grants, tuition waivers (partial), and unspecified assistantships available. Financial award application deadline: 4/15; financial award applicants required to submit FAFSA. *Unit head:* Dr. Bryce Sullivan, Dean, 615-460-6437, Fax: 615-385-5084, E-mail: bryce.sullivan@belmont.edu. *Application contact:* David Mee, Dean of Enrollment Services, 615-460-6785, Fax: 615-460-5434, E-mail: david.mee@belmont.edu.

Bemidji State University, School of Graduate Studies, Bemidji, MN 56601. Offers biology (MS); education (MS); English (MA, MS); environmental studies (MS); mathematics (MS); mathematics (elementary and middle level education) (MS); special education (M Sp Ed, MS). Part-time programs available. Postbaccalaureate distance learning degree programs offered (no on-campus study). *Faculty:* 117 full-time (53 women), 20 part-time/adjunct (15 women). *Students:* 30 full-time (17 women), 157 part-time (108 women); includes 16 minority (2 Black or African American, non-Hispanic/Latino; 4 American Indian or Alaska Native, non-Hispanic/Latino; 2 Asian, non-Hispanic/Latino; 1 Hispanic/Latino; 7 Two or more races, non-Hispanic/Latino), 1 international. Average age 35. 73 applicants, 93% accepted, 38 enrolled. In 2013, 49 master's awarded. *Degree requirements:* For master's, comprehensive exam, thesis (for some programs). *Entrance requirements:* For master's, GRE; GMAT, letters of recommendation, letters of interest. Additional exam requirements/recommendations for international students: Required—TOEFL (minimum score 550 paper-based; 80 iBT). *Application deadline:* Applications are processed on a rolling basis. Application fee: $20. Electronic applications accepted. *Expenses:* Tuition, state resident: full-time $6941; part-time $365 per credit. Tuition, nonresident: full-time $6941; part-time $365 per credit. *Required fees:* $16 per credit. Tuition and fees vary according to program and reciprocity agreements. *Financial support:* In 2013–14, 131 students received support, including 18 research assistantships with partial tuition reimbursements available (averaging $12,889 per year), 23 teaching assistantships with partial tuition reimbursements available (averaging $12,889 per year); scholarships/grants and unspecified assistantships also available. Financial award application deadline: 3/31; financial award applicants required to submit FAFSA. *Faculty research:* Human performance, sport, and health: physical education teacher education, continuum models, spiritual health, intellectual health, resiliency, health priorities; psychology: health psychology, college student drinking behavior, micro-aggressions, infant cognition, false memories, leadership assessment; biology: structure and dynamics of forest communities, aquatic and riverine ecology, interaction between animal populations and aquatic environments, cellular motility. *Unit head:* Dr. James Barta, Interim Dean of Health Sciences and Human Ecology, 218-755-3874, Fax: 218-755-2258, E-mail: jbarta@bemidjistate.edu. *Application contact:* Joan Miller, Director, School of Graduate Studies, 218-755-2027, Fax: 218-755-2258, E-mail: jmiller@bemidjistate.edu.
Website: http://www.bemidjistate.edu/academics/graduate_studies/.

Benedictine University, Graduate Programs, Program in Education, Lisle, IL 60532-0900. Offers curriculum and instruction and collaborative teaching (M Ed); elementary education (MA Ed); leadership and administration (M Ed); reading and literacy (M Ed); secondary education (MA Ed); special education (MA Ed). Part-time and evening/weekend programs available. *Students:* 6 full-time (all women), 124 part-time (106 women); includes 14 minority (8 Black or African American, non-Hispanic/Latino; 1 American Indian or Alaska Native, non-Hispanic/Latino; 2 Asian, non-Hispanic/Latino; 3 Hispanic/Latino). 21 applicants, 62% accepted, 8 enrolled. In 2013, 120 master's awarded. *Degree requirements:* For master's, comprehensive exam, thesis (for some programs). *Entrance requirements:* For master's, GRE or MAT. Additional exam requirements/recommendations for international students: Required—TOEFL (minimum score 550 paper-based). *Application deadline:* For fall admission, 9/1 for domestic students; for winter admission, 12/1 for domestic students; for spring admission, 2/15 for domestic students. Applications are processed on a rolling basis. Application fee: $40. Electronic applications accepted. *Expenses:* Contact institution. *Financial support:* Career-related internships or fieldwork and health care benefits available. Support available to part-time students. *Unit head:* MeShelda Jackson, Director, 630-829-6282, E-mail: mjackson@ben.edu. *Application contact:* Kari Gibbons, Associate Vice President, Enrollment Center, 630-829-6200, Fax: 630-829-6584, E-mail: kgibbons@ben.edu.

Bethel University, Graduate School, St. Paul, MN 55112-6999. Offers autism spectrum disorders (Certificate); business administration (MBA); communication (MA); counseling psychology (MA); educational leadership (Ed D); gerontology (MA); international baccalaureate education (Certificate); K-12 education (MA); literacy education (MA, Certificate); nurse educator (Certificate); nurse leader (Certificate); nurse-midwifery (MS); nursing (MS); physician assistant (MS); postsecondary teaching (Certificate); special education (MA); strategic leadership (MA); teaching (MA). Part-time and evening/weekend programs available. Postbaccalaureate distance learning degree programs offered (no on-campus study). *Faculty:* 13 full-time (7 women), 89 part-time/adjunct (43 women). *Students:* 692 full-time (457 women), 573 part-time (371 women); includes 170 minority (86 Black or African American, non-Hispanic/Latino; 1 American Indian or Alaska Native, non-Hispanic/Latino; 49 Asian, non-Hispanic/Latino; 20 Hispanic/Latino; 1 Native Hawaiian or other Pacific Islander, non-Hispanic/Latino; 13 Two or more races, non-Hispanic/Latino), 21 international. Average age 37. In 2013, 166 master's, 9 doctorates, 11 other advanced degrees awarded. *Degree requirements:* For master's, comprehensive exam (for some programs), thesis (for some programs); for doctorate, comprehensive exam, thesis/dissertation. *Entrance requirements:* Additional exam requirements/recommendations for international students: Required—TOEFL (minimum score 550 paper-based; 80 iBT). *Application deadline:* Applications are processed on a rolling basis. Electronic applications accepted. Tuition and fees vary according to course load, degree level and program. *Financial support:* Teaching assistantships, career-related internships or fieldwork, and scholarships/grants available. Support available to part-time students. Financial award applicants required to submit FAFSA. *Unit head:* Dick Crombie, Vice-President/Dean, 651-635-8000, Fax: 651-635-8004, E-mail: gs@bethel.edu. *Application contact:* Director of Admissions, 651-635-8000, Fax: 651-635-8004, E-mail: gs@bethel.edu.
Website: http://gs.bethel.edu/.

Binghamton University, State University of New York, Graduate School, School of Education, Program in Special Education, Vestal, NY 13850. Offers MS Ed. *Accreditation:* Teacher Education Accreditation Council. Part-time and evening/weekend programs available. *Students:* 24 full-time (21 women), 23 part-time (21 women); includes 3 minority (2 Asian, non-Hispanic/Latino; 1 Hispanic/Latino). Average age 27. 44 applicants, 82% accepted, 24 enrolled. In 2013, 31 master's awarded. *Entrance requirements:* For master's, GRE General Test. Additional exam requirements/recommendations for international students: Required—TOEFL (minimum score 550 paper-based; 80 iBT). *Application deadline:* For fall admission, 2/1 priority date for domestic and international students; for spring admission, 10/15 priority date for domestic and international students. Applications are processed on a rolling basis. Application fee: $75. Electronic applications accepted. *Financial support:* In 2013–14, 4

students received support. Career-related internships or fieldwork, Federal Work-Study, institutionally sponsored loans, and unspecified assistantships available. Support available to part-time students. Financial award application deadline: 2/15; financial award applicants required to submit FAFSA. *Unit head:* Dr. S. G. Grant, Dean of the Graduate School of Education, 607-777-7329, E-mail: sggrant@binghamton.edu. *Application contact:* Kishan Zuber, Recruiting and Admissions Coordinator, 607-777-2151, Fax: 607-777-2501, E-mail: kzuber@binghamton.edu.

Biola University, School of Education, La Mirada, CA 90639-0001. Offers apologetics (MA Ed); curriculum and instruction (MA Ed, MAT, Certificate); early childhood (MA Ed, MAT); history and philosophy of science (MA Ed, MAT); linguistics and inter-cultural studies (MAT); linguistics and international studies (MA Ed); multiple subject (MAT); single subject (MAT); special education (MA Ed, MAT, Certificate); TESOL (MA Ed, MAT). Part-time and evening/weekend programs available. Postbaccalaureate distance learning degree programs offered (no on-campus study). *Faculty:* 14. *Students:* 51 full-time (38 women), 101 part-time (83 women); includes 47 minority (8 Black or African American, non-Hispanic/Latino; 1 American Indian or Alaska Native, non-Hispanic/Latino; 32 Asian, non-Hispanic/Latino; 6 Two or more races, non-Hispanic/Latino), 4 international. In 2013, 33 master's awarded. *Entrance requirements:* For master's, CBEST, CSET. Additional exam requirements/recommendations for international students: Required—TOEFL (minimum score 100 iBT). *Application deadline:* For fall admission, 7/1 for domestic students, 6/1 for international students; for spring admission, 12/1 for domestic students; for summer admission, 5/1 for domestic students. Applications are processed on a rolling basis. Application fee: $55. Electronic applications accepted. *Financial support:* Scholarships/grants available. Support available to part-time students. Financial award applicants required to submit FAFSA. *Faculty research:* Early childhood education, elementary education, special education, curriculum development, teacher preparation. *Unit head:* Dr. June Hetzel, Dean, 562-903-4715. *Application contact:* Graduate Admissions Office, 562-903-4752, E-mail: graduate.admissions@biola.edu.
Website: http://education.biola.edu/.

Bloomsburg University of Pennsylvania, School of Graduate Studies, College of Education, Department of Exceptionality Programs, Program in Special Education, Bloomsburg, PA 17815-1301. Offers M Ed, MS, Certificate. *Accreditation:* NCATE. *Faculty:* 9 full-time (5 women), 3 part-time/adjunct (all women). *Students:* 32 full-time (31 women), 13 part-time (12 women). Average age 31. 43 applicants, 88% accepted, 14 enrolled. In 2013, 34 master's awarded. *Degree requirements:* For master's, thesis, minimum QPA of 3.0, practicum. *Entrance requirements:* For master's, teaching certificate, minimum QPA of 2.8, letter of intent, 2 letters of recommendation, interview, professional liability insurance, recent TB screening. Additional exam requirements/recommendations for international students: Required—TOEFL (minimum score 550 paper-based). *Application deadline:* Applications are processed on a rolling basis. Application fee: $35 ($60 for international students). Electronic applications accepted. *Expenses:* Tuition, state resident: full-time $7956; part-time $442 per credit. Tuition, nonresident: full-time $11,934; part-time $663 per credit. *Required fees:* $95.50 per credit. $55 per semester. Tuition and fees vary according to course load. *Financial support:* Unspecified assistantships available. *Unit head:* Dr. Tegan Kotarski, College of Education Graduate Coordinator, 570-389-3883, Fax: 570-389-5049, E-mail: tkotarsk@bloomu.edu. *Application contact:* Jennifer Richard, Administrative Assistant, 570-389-4015, Fax: 570-389-3054, E-mail: jrichard@bloomu.edu.
Website: http://www.bloomu.edu/gradschool/special-education.

Bob Jones University, Graduate Programs, Greenville, SC 29614. Offers accountancy (MS); Bible (MA); Bible translation (MA); Biblical studies (Certificate); broadcast management (MS); business administration (MBA); church history (MA, PhD); church ministries (MA); church music (MM); cinema and video production (MA); counseling (MS); curriculum and instruction (Ed D); divinity (M Div); dramatic production (MA); educational leadership (MS, Ed D, Ed S); elementary education (M Ed, MAT); English (M Ed, MA, MAT); fine arts (MA); graphic design (MA); history (M Ed, MA); illustration (MA); interpretative speech (MA); mathematics (M Ed, MAT); medical missions (Certificate); ministry (MM, D Min); multi-categorical special education (M Ed, MAT); music (M Ed); New Testament interpretation (PhD); Old Testament interpretation (PhD); orchestral instrument performance (MM); organ performance (MM); pastoral studies (MA); personnel services (MS, Ed S); piano pedagogy (MM); piano performance (MM); platform arts (MA); radio and television broadcasting (MS); rhetoric and public address (MA); secondary education (M Ed); studio art (MA); teaching Bible (MA); theology (MA, PhD); voice performance (MM); youth ministries (MA); M Div/MM.

Boise State University, College of Education, Department of Special Education, Boise, ID 83725-0399. Offers M Ed, MA. *Accreditation:* NCATE. *Degree requirements:* For master's, thesis optional. *Entrance requirements:* For master's, minimum GPA of 3.0. Electronic applications accepted.

Boston College, Lynch Graduate School of Education, Program in Special Needs: Moderate Disabilities, Chestnut Hill, MA 02467-3800. Offers M Ed, CAES. *Accreditation:* Teacher Education Accreditation Council. Part-time and evening/weekend programs available. *Students:* 10 full-time (all women), 17 part-time (16 women). 65 applicants, 71% accepted, 27 enrolled. In 2013, 21 master's awarded. *Degree requirements:* For master's and CAES, comprehensive exam. *Entrance requirements:* For master's, GRE General Test or MAT, general licensure at the elementary or secondary level; for CAES, GRE General Test or MAT. Additional exam requirements/recommendations for international students: Required—TOEFL (minimum score 100 iBT). *Application deadline:* For fall admission, 12/1 priority date for domestic and international students; for spring admission, 11/1 for domestic and international students. Application fee: $65. Electronic applications accepted. *Financial support:* Fellowships with full and partial tuition reimbursements, research assistantships with full and partial tuition reimbursements, teaching assistantships with full and partial tuition reimbursements, career-related internships or fieldwork, Federal Work-Study, scholarships/grants, traineeships, health care benefits, and unspecified assistantships available. Support available to part-time students. Financial award applicants required to submit FAFSA. *Faculty research:* Learning disabilities, emotional behavior difficulties, Universal Design for Learning. *Unit head:* Dr. Alec Peck, Chairperson, 617-552-4214, Fax: 617-552-0398. *Application contact:* Domenic Lomanno, Director, Graduate Admission and Financial Aid, 617-552-4214, Fax: 617-552-0398, E-mail: lomanno@bc.edu.

Boston College, Lynch Graduate School of Education, Program in Special Needs: Severe Disabilities, Chestnut Hill, MA 02467-3800. Offers M Ed, CAES. *Accreditation:* Teacher Education Accreditation Council. Part-time and evening/weekend programs available. *Students:* 7 full-time (5 women), 5 part-time (4 women). 19 applicants, 95% accepted, 12 enrolled. In 2013, 17 master's awarded. *Degree requirements:* For master's, comprehensive exam. *Entrance requirements:* For master's, GRE General Test or MAT. Additional exam requirements/recommendations for international students: Required—TOEFL (minimum score 100 iBT). *Application deadline:* For fall admission, 12/1 priority date for domestic and international students; for spring admission, 11/1 for domestic and international students. Application fee: $65. Electronic applications accepted. *Financial support:* Fellowships with full and partial tuition reimbursements, research assistantships with full and partial tuition reimbursements, teaching assistantships with full and partial tuition reimbursements, career-related internships or fieldwork, Federal Work-Study, scholarships/grants, traineeships, health care benefits, tuition waivers (full and partial), and unspecified assistantships available. Support available to part-time students. Financial award applicants required to submit FAFSA. *Faculty research:* Communication and language in learners with severe and multiple disabilities, assistive technology. *Unit head:* Dr. Alec Peck, Chairperson, 617-552-4214, Fax: 617-552-0398. *Application contact:* Domenic Lomanno, Director, Graduate Admission and Financial Aid, 617-552-4214, Fax: 617-552-0398, E-mail: lomanno@bc.edu.

Bowie State University, Graduate Programs, Program in Special Education, Bowie, MD 20715-9465. Offers M Ed. *Accreditation:* NCATE. Part-time and evening/weekend programs available. *Degree requirements:* For master's, comprehensive exam, thesis optional, research paper. *Entrance requirements:* For master's, teaching experience, 3 professional letters of recommendation. Electronic applications accepted. *Expenses:* Tuition, state resident: full-time $8665. Tuition, nonresident: full-time $16,007. *Required fees:* $1927.

Bowling Green State University, Graduate College, College of Education and Human Development, School of Education and Intervention Services, Intervention Services Division, Program in Special Education, Bowling Green, OH 43403. Offers assistive technology (M Ed); early childhood intervention (M Ed); gifted education (M Ed); hearing impaired intervention (M Ed); mild/moderate intervention (M Ed); moderate/intensive intervention (M Ed). *Accreditation:* NCATE. Part-time programs available. *Degree requirements:* For master's, thesis or alternative. *Entrance requirements:* For master's, GRE General Test. Additional exam requirements/recommendations for international students: Required—TOEFL. Electronic applications accepted. *Faculty research:* Reading and special populations, deafness, early childhood, gifted and talented, behavior disorders.

Brandman University, School of Education, Irvine, CA 92618. Offers education (MA); educational leadership (MA); school counseling (MA); special education (MA); teaching (MA).

Brandon University, Faculty of Education, Brandon, MB R7A 6A9, Canada. Offers curriculum and instruction (M Ed, Diploma); educational administration (M Ed, Diploma); guidance and counseling (M Ed, Diploma); special education (M Ed, Diploma). *Degree requirements:* For master's, thesis. *Entrance requirements:* For master's, minimum GPA of 3.0, teaching certificate or equivalent. Additional exam requirements/recommendations for international students: Required—TOEFL. *Faculty research:* Comparative education, environmental studies, parent/school council.

Brenau University, Sydney O. Smith Graduate School, School of Education, Gainesville, GA 30501. Offers early childhood (Ed S); early childhood education (M Ed, MAT); middle grades (Ed S); middle grades education (M Ed, MAT); secondary education (MAT); special education (M Ed, MAT). *Accreditation:* NCATE. Part-time and evening/weekend programs available. Postbaccalaureate distance learning degree programs offered (no on-campus study). *Degree requirements:* For master's, thesis optional, comprehensive exam or applied research project, effective portfolio; for Ed S, thesis, applied research project. *Entrance requirements:* For master's, GRE, MAT, interview, minimum GPA of 3.0, 3 references, writing samples; for Ed S, GRE, MAT, master's degree, minimum GPA of 3.0, writing sample, letters of reference. Additional exam requirements/recommendations for international students: Required—TOEFL (minimum score 500 paper-based; 61 iBT); Recommended—IELTS (minimum score 5). Electronic applications accepted. *Expenses:* Contact institution.

Bridgewater State University, School of Graduate Studies, School of Education and Allied Studies, Department of Special Education and Communication Disorders, Bridgewater, MA 02325-0001. Offers special education (M Ed). *Accreditation:* NCATE. Part-time and evening/weekend programs available. *Entrance requirements:* For master's, GRE General Test or Massachusetts Test for Educator Licensure.

Brigham Young University, Graduate Studies, David O. McKay School of Education, Department of Counseling Psychology and Special Education, Provo, UT 84602-1001. Offers counseling psychology (PhD); school psychology (Ed S); special education (MS). Part-time and evening/weekend programs available. *Faculty:* 14 full-time (5 women), 9 part-time/adjunct (3 women). *Students:* 69 full-time (47 women), 13 part-time (11 women); includes 14 minority (2 Black or African American, non-Hispanic/Latino; 2 American Indian or Alaska Native, non-Hispanic/Latino; 2 Asian, non-Hispanic/Latino; 7 Hispanic/Latino; 1 Native Hawaiian or other Pacific Islander, non-Hispanic/Latino), 3 international. Average age 29. 64 applicants, 36% accepted, 23 enrolled. In 2013, 2 master's, 7 doctorates, 11 other advanced degrees awarded. *Degree requirements:* For master's and Ed S, comprehensive exam, thesis; for doctorate, comprehensive exam, thesis/dissertation. *Entrance requirements:* For master's, GRE General Test or MAT, minimum GPA of 3.0 in last 60 hours of undergraduate coursework; for doctorate and Ed S, GRE General Test, minimum GPA of 3.0 in last 60 hours of undergraduate coursework. Additional exam requirements/recommendations for international students: Required—TOEFL (minimum score 580 paper-based; 85 iBT), IELTS (minimum score 7). *Application deadline:* For fall admission, 1/15 for domestic and international students. Application fee: $50. Electronic applications accepted. *Expenses: Tuition:* Full-time $6130; part-time $340 per credit hour. Tuition and fees vary according to program and student's religious affiliation. *Financial support:* In 2013–14, 53 students received support, including 43 research assistantships with partial tuition reimbursements available (averaging $8,160 per year), 2 teaching assistantships with partial tuition reimbursements available (averaging $5,320 per year); institutionally sponsored loans and tuition waivers (partial) also available. Financial award application deadline: 7/1. *Faculty research:* Positive behavioral support in schools, spirituality in psychotherapy, multicultural psychology, gender issues in education, crisis management in schools. *Unit head:* Dr. Timothy B. Smith, Professor and Development Chair, 801-422-3857, Fax: 801-422-0198. *Application contact:* Diane E. Hancock, Department Secretary, 801-422-3859, Fax: 801-422-0198, E-mail: diane_hancock@byu.edu.
Website: http://education.byu.edu/cpse/.

Brooklyn College of the City University of New York, Division of Graduate Studies, School of Education, Program in Special Education, Brooklyn, NY 11210-2889. Offers teacher of students with disabilities (MS Ed), including birth-grade 2, grades 1-6, grades 5-9. Part-time programs available. *Entrance requirements:* For master's, LAST, interview; previous course work in education and psychology; minimum GPA of 3.0 in education, 2.8 overall; resume, 2 letters of recommendation; essay. Additional exam requirements/recommendations for international students: Required—TOEFL (minimum score 500 paper-based; 61 iBT). Electronic applications accepted. *Faculty research:* School reform, conflict resolution, curriculum for inclusive settings, urban issues in special education.

Buffalo State College, State University of New York, The Graduate School, Faculty of Applied Science and Education, Department of Exceptional Education, Programs in Special Education, Buffalo, NY 14222-1095. Offers special education (MS Ed); special education: adolescents (MS Ed); special education: childhood (MS Ed); special education: early childhood (MS Ed). *Accreditation:* NCATE. Part-time and evening/weekend programs available. *Degree requirements:* For master's, thesis or project. *Entrance requirements:* For master's, minimum GPA of 2.5. Additional exam

requirements/recommendations for international students: Required—TOEFL (minimum score 550 paper-based).

Caldwell University, Graduate Studies, Division of Education, Caldwell, NJ 07006-6195. Offers curriculum and instruction (MA); education (Postbaccalaureate Certificate); educational administration (MA); learning disabilities teacher-consultant (Post-Master's Certificate); literacy instruction (MA); principal (Post-Master's Certificate); reading specialist (Post-Master's Certificate); special education (MA), including special education, teaching of students with disabilities, teaching of students with disabilities and learning disabilities teacher-consultant; superintendent (Post-Master's Certificate); supervisor (Post-Master's Certificate). Part-time and evening/weekend programs available. *Faculty:* 11 full-time (7 women), 12 part-time/adjunct (6 women). *Students:* 42 full-time (31 women), 255 part-time (219 women); includes 40 minority (14 Black or African American, non-Hispanic/Latino; 5 Asian, non-Hispanic/Latino; 18 Hispanic/Latino; 1 Native Hawaiian or other Pacific Islander, non-Hispanic/Latino; 2 Two or more races, non-Hispanic/Latino). Average age 37. 140 applicants, 71% accepted, 83 enrolled. In 2013, 63 master's awarded. *Degree requirements:* For master's, comprehensive exam (for some programs). *Entrance requirements:* For master's, PRAXIS, 3 years of work experience, prior teaching certification. Additional exam requirements/recommendations for international students: Required—TOEFL (minimum score 580 paper-based). *Application deadline:* Applications are processed on a rolling basis. Application fee: $40. Electronic applications accepted. *Financial support:* Career-related internships or fieldwork available. Financial award applicants required to submit FAFSA. *Faculty research:* Curriculum and instruction, secondary education, special education, education and technology. *Unit head:* Dr. Janice Stewart, Division Associate Dean, 973-618-3626, E-mail: jstewart@caldwell.edu. *Application contact:* Vilma Mueller, Director of Graduate Studies, 973-618-3544, E-mail: graduate@caldwell.edu.

California Baptist University, Program in Education, Riverside, CA 92504-3206. Offers educational leadership for faith-based institutions (MS); educational leadership for public institutions (MS); educational technology (MS); instructional computer applications (MS); international education (MS); leadership and adult learning (MS); leadership and organizational studies (MS); reading (MS); school counseling (MS); school psychology (MS); science education (MS); special education in mild/moderate disabilities (MS); special education in moderate/severe disabilities (MS); teaching (MS); teaching and learning (MS); TESOL (teachers of English to speakers of other languages) (MS). Part-time and evening/weekend programs available. Postbaccalaureate distance learning degree programs offered (minimal on-campus study). *Faculty:* 18 full-time (9 women), 8 part-time/adjunct (5 women). *Students:* 158 full-time (127 women), 228 part-time (179 women); includes 159 minority (27 Black or African American, non-Hispanic/Latino; 4 American Indian or Alaska Native, non-Hispanic/Latino; 13 Asian, non-Hispanic/Latino; 107 Hispanic/Latino; 1 Native Hawaiian or other Pacific Islander, non-Hispanic/Latino; 7 Two or more races, non-Hispanic/Latino), 2 international. Average age 33. 298 applicants, 74% accepted, 113 enrolled. In 2013, 70 master's awarded. *Degree requirements:* For master's, comprehensive exam, project, or thesis. *Entrance requirements:* For master's, minimum undergraduate GPA of 3.0; 18 semester units of prerequisite course work in education; three recommendations; 500-word essay; interview. Additional exam requirements/recommendations for international students: Required—TOEFL (minimum score 80 iBT). *Application deadline:* For fall admission, 8/1 priority date for domestic students, 7/1 for international students; for spring admission, 12/1 priority date for domestic students, 11/1 for international students. Applications are processed on a rolling basis. Application fee: $45. Electronic applications accepted. *Expenses:* Contact institution. *Financial support:* Institutionally sponsored loans available. Financial award applicants required to submit CSS PROFILE or FAFSA. *Faculty research:* Leadership development, complexity theory, faith and learning, special education, social and philosophical contexts of education. *Unit head:* Dr. John Shoup, Dean, School of Education, 951-343-4205, Fax: 951-343-4516, E-mail: jshoup@calbaptist.edu. *Application contact:* Dr. Kathryn Norwood, Director, Master of Science Program in Education, 951-343-4760, E-mail: knorwood@calbaptist.edu. Website: http://www.calbaptist.edu/mastersined/.

California Lutheran University, Graduate Studies, Graduate School of Education, Thousand Oaks, CA 91360-2787. Offers counseling and guidance (MS), including college student personnel, counseling and guidance; educational leadership (MA, Ed D); including educational leadership (K-12) (Ed D), higher education leadership (Ed D); special education (MS); teacher leadership (M Ed); teaching (M Ed). *Accreditation:* NCATE. Part-time and evening/weekend programs available. *Faculty:* 18 full-time (14 women), 28 part-time/adjunct (20 women). *Students:* 327 full-time (260 women), 96 part-time (77 women); includes 150 minority (7 Black or African American, non-Hispanic/Latino; 20 Asian, non-Hispanic/Latino; 112 Hispanic/Latino; 11 Two or more races, non-Hispanic/Latino), 1 international. Average age 33. 123 applicants, 85% accepted, 80 enrolled. In 2013, 117 master's, 9 doctorates awarded. *Entrance requirements:* For master's, GRE General Test, interview, minimum GPA of 3.0. *Application deadline:* For fall admission, 7/1 priority date for domestic students; for spring admission, 11/1 priority date for domestic students; for summer admission, 4/1 priority date for domestic students. Applications are processed on a rolling basis. Application fee: $50. *Unit head:* Dr. Robert Fraisse, Dean, 805-493-3421. *Application contact:* 805-493-3325, Fax: 805-493-3861, E-mail: clugrad@callutheran.edu.

California State Polytechnic University, Pomona, Academic Affairs, College of Education and Integrative Studies, Master's Programs in Education, Pomona, CA 91768-2557. Offers curriculum and instruction (MA); educational leadership (MA); educational multimedia (MA); special education (MA). *Students:* 39 full-time (26 women), 140 part-time (96 women); includes 91 minority (9 Black or African American, non-Hispanic/Latino; 1 American Indian or Alaska Native, non-Hispanic/Latino; 24 Asian, non-Hispanic/Latino; 53 Hispanic/Latino; 3 Native Hawaiian or other Pacific Islander, non-Hispanic/Latino; 1 Two or more races, non-Hispanic/Latino), 3 international. Average age 35. 64 applicants, 64% accepted, 25 enrolled. In 2013, 74 master's awarded. Application fee: $55. *Expenses:* Tuition, state resident: full-time $6738. Tuition, nonresident: full-time $12,690. *Required fees:* $878; $248 per credit hour. *Unit head:* Dr. Peggy Kelly, Dean, 909-869-2307, E-mail: pkelly@csupomona.edu. *Application contact:* Dr. Dorothy MacNevin, Co-Chair, Graduate Education Department, 909-869-2311, Fax: 909-869-4822, E-mail: dmacnevin@csupomona.edu.

California State University, Bakersfield, Division of Graduate Studies, School of Social Sciences and Education, Program in Special Education, Bakersfield, CA 93311. Offers MA. *Accreditation:* NCATE. *Degree requirements:* For master's, thesis or alternative, project or culminating exam. *Entrance requirements:* For master's, 3 letters of recommendation, minimum GPA of 2.67, interview. *Application deadline:* Applications are processed on a rolling basis. Application fee: $55. *Unit head:* Dr. Louis Wildman, Department Chair, 661-654-3047, Fax: 661-654-3029, E-mail: lwildman@csub.edu. *Application contact:* Debbie Blowers, Assistant Director of Admissions, 661-664-3381, E-mail: dblowers@csub.edu. Website: http://www.csub.edu/specialed/index.html.

California State University, Chico, Office of Graduate Studies, College of Communication and Education, School of Education, Teaching English Learners and Special Education Advising Patterns Program, Chico, CA 95929-0722. Offers special education (MA); teaching English learners (MA). Part-time and evening/weekend

programs available. *Degree requirements:* For master's, comprehensive exam, thesis or project. *Entrance requirements:* Additional exam requirements/recommendations for international students: Required—TOEFL (minimum score 550 paper-based; 80 iBT), IELTS (minimum score 6.5), PTE (minimum score 59). Electronic applications accepted.

California State University, Dominguez Hills, College of Education, Division of Teacher Education, Program in Special Education, Carson, CA 90747-0001. Offers early childhood (MA); mild/moderate (MA); moderate/severe (MA). Part-time and evening/weekend programs available. *Faculty:* 8 full-time (7 women), 7 part-time/adjunct (all women). *Students:* 35 full-time (27 women), 138 part-time (107 women); includes 108 minority (22 Black or African American, non-Hispanic/Latino; 15 Asian, non-Hispanic/Latino; 65 Hispanic/Latino; 1 Native Hawaiian or other Pacific Islander, non-Hispanic/Latino; 5 Two or more races, non-Hispanic/Latino), 1 international. Average age 37. 11 applicants, 36% accepted, 1 enrolled. In 2013, 34 master's awarded. *Degree requirements:* For master's, comprehensive exam, thesis or alternative. *Entrance requirements:* For master's, minimum GPA of 2.75 in last 60 units, 3 letters of recommendation. *Application deadline:* For fall admission, 6/1 for domestic students. Applications are processed on a rolling basis. Application fee: $55. *Expenses:* Tuition, state resident: full-time $6738. Tuition, nonresident: full-time $13,434. *Required fees:* $622. *Unit head:* Dr. Anthony Normore, Chair, 310-243-3925, E-mail: anormore@csudh.edu. *Application contact:* Admissions Office, 310-243-3530. Website: http://www4.csudh.edu/coe/programs/special-education/index.

California State University, East Bay, Office of Academic Programs and Graduate Studies, College of Education and Allied Studies, Department of Educational Psychology, Special Education Program, Hayward, CA 94542-3000. Offers mild-moderate disabilities (MS); moderate-severe disabilities (MS). *Accreditation:* NCATE. *Degree requirements:* For master's, project or thesis. *Entrance requirements:* For master's, GRE or MAT, interview, minimum GPA of 2.5 during previous 2 years of course work. Additional exam requirements/recommendations for international students: Required—TOEFL (minimum score 550 paper-based). Electronic applications accepted.

California State University, Fresno, Division of Graduate Studies, School of Education and Human Development, Department of Counseling and Special Education, Program in Special Education, Fresno, CA 93740-8027. Offers MA. *Accreditation:* NCATE. Part-time and evening/weekend programs available. *Degree requirements:* For master's, thesis or alternative. *Entrance requirements:* For master's, GRE General Test, MAT, minimum GPA of 3.0. Additional exam requirements/recommendations for international students: Required—TOEFL. Electronic applications accepted.

California State University, Fullerton, Graduate Studies, College of Education, Department of Special Education, Fullerton, CA 92834-9480. Offers MS. *Accreditation:* NCATE. Part-time programs available. *Students:* 15 full-time (all women), 85 part-time (79 women); includes 49 minority (2 Black or African American, non-Hispanic/Latino; 11 Asian, non-Hispanic/Latino; 33 Hispanic/Latino; 3 Two or more races, non-Hispanic/Latino), 1 international. Average age 32. 51 applicants, 45% accepted, 23 enrolled. In 2013, 40 master's awarded. *Degree requirements:* For master's, comprehensive exam, project or thesis. *Entrance requirements:* For master's, minimum GPA of 2.75. Application fee: $55. *Financial support:* Career-related internships or fieldwork, Federal Work-Study, institutionally sponsored loans, and scholarships/grants available. Support available to part-time students. Financial award application deadline: 3/1; financial award applicants required to submit FAFSA. *Unit head:* Dr. Melinda Pierson, Chair, 657-278-4711. *Application contact:* Admissions/Applications, 657-278-2371.

California State University, Long Beach, Graduate Studies, College of Education, Department of Advanced Studies in Education and Counseling, Master of Science in Special Education Program, Long Beach, CA 90840. Offers MS. *Accreditation:* NCATE. *Degree requirements:* For master's, comprehensive exam or thesis. *Entrance requirements:* For master's, GRE General Test, minimum GPA of 2.75. Electronic applications accepted.

California State University, Los Angeles, Graduate Studies, Charter College of Education, Division of Special Education and Counseling, Los Angeles, CA 90032-8530. Offers counseling (MS), including applied behavior analysis, community college counseling, rehabilitation counseling, school counseling, school psychology; special education (MA, PhD). *Accreditation:* ACA. Part-time and evening/weekend programs available. *Faculty:* 18 full-time (11 women), 18 part-time/adjunct (12 women). *Students:* 299 full-time (237 women), 278 part-time (211 women); includes 389 minority (32 Black or African American, non-Hispanic/Latino; 1 American Indian or Alaska Native, non-Hispanic/Latino; 53 Asian, non-Hispanic/Latino; 280 Hispanic/Latino; 8 Native Hawaiian or other Pacific Islander, non-Hispanic/Latino; 15 Two or more races, non-Hispanic/Latino), 26 international. Average age 33. 274 applicants, 42% accepted, 100 enrolled. In 2013, 154 master's awarded. *Entrance requirements:* For master's, minimum GPA of 2.75 in last 90 units of course work, teaching certificate. Additional exam requirements/recommendations for international students: Required—TOEFL (minimum score 500 paper-based). *Application deadline:* For fall admission, 5/1 for domestic and international students. Applications are processed on a rolling basis. Application fee: $55. Electronic applications accepted. *Financial support:* Career-related internships or fieldwork and Federal Work-Study available. Support available to part-time students. Financial award application deadline: 3/1. *Unit head:* Dr. Andrea Zetlin, Acting Chair, 323-343-4400, Fax: 323-343-5605, E-mail: azetlin@calstatela.edu. *Application contact:* Dr. Larry Fritz, Dean of Graduate Studies, 323-343-3820, Fax: 323-343-5653, E-mail: lfritz@calstatela.edu. Website: http://www.calstatela.edu/academic/ccoe/index_edsp.htm.

California State University, Northridge, Graduate Studies, College of Education, Department of Special Education, Northridge, CA 91330. Offers early childhood special education (MA); education of the deaf and hard of hearing (MA); educational therapy (MA); mild/moderate disabilities (MA); moderate/severe disabilities (MA). *Accreditation:* NCATE. *Entrance requirements:* For master's, GRE General Test (if cumulative undergraduate GPA less than 3.0). Additional exam requirements/recommendations for international students: Required—TOEFL. *Faculty research:* Teacher training, classroom aide training.

California State University, Sacramento, Office of Graduate Studies, College of Education, Department of Special Education, Rehabilitation, and School Psychology, Sacramento, CA 95819. Offers school psychology (MA); special education (MA); vocational rehabilitation (MS). *Accreditation:* CORE. Part-time programs available. *Entrance requirements:* For master's, minimum GPA of 2.5. Additional exam requirements/recommendations for international students: Required—TOEFL. *Application deadline:* For fall admission, 3/1 for domestic and international students; for spring admission, 9/15 for domestic students, 9/30 for international students. Applications are processed on a rolling basis. Application fee: $55. Electronic applications accepted. *Financial support:* Career-related internships or fieldwork and Federal Work-Study available. Support available to part-time students. Financial award application deadline: 3/1; financial award applicants required to submit FAFSA. *Faculty research:* Reading and learning disabilities; vocational rehabilitation counseling issues and implementation; school-based crisis intervention; posttraumatic stress disorder; attention-deficit/hyperactivity disorder; school-based suicide prevention, intervention, and postvention; autism spectrum disorders; special education technology, strategies

and assessment. *Unit head:* Bruce A. Ostertag, Chair, 916-278-5541, E-mail: ostertag@csus.edu. *Application contact:* Jose Martinez, Graduate Admissions Coordinator, 916-278-7871, E-mail: martinj@skymail.csus.edu.
Website: http://www.edweb.csus.edu/eds.

California State University, San Bernardino, Graduate Studies, College of Education, Programs in Special Education and Rehabilitation Counseling, San Bernardino, CA 92407-2397. Offers rehabilitation counseling (MA); special education (MA). *Accreditation:* CORE; NCATE. Part-time and evening/weekend programs available. *Students:* 47 full-time (42 women), 113 part-time (93 women); includes 87 minority (20 Black or African American, non-Hispanic/Latino; 1 American Indian or Alaska Native, non-Hispanic/Latino; 6 Asian, non-Hispanic/Latino; 50 Hispanic/Latino; 10 Two or more races, non-Hispanic/Latino), 1 international. Average age 37. 91 applicants, 82% accepted, 61 enrolled. In 2013, 74 master's awarded. *Degree requirements:* For master's, thesis or alternative, advancement to candidacy. *Entrance requirements:* For master's, minimum GPA of 3.0 in education. *Application deadline:* For fall admission, 8/31 priority date for domestic students. Application fee: $55. *Financial support:* Career-related internships or fieldwork and Federal Work-Study available. Support available to part-time students. *Unit head:* Patty Imbiorski, Coordinator, 909-537-7737, E-mail: imbiorsk@csusb.edu. *Application contact:* Dr. Jeffrey Thompson, Dean of Graduate Studies, 909-537-5058, E-mail: jthompso@csusb.edu.

California State University, San Marcos, School of Education, San Marcos, CA 92096-0001. Offers educational administration (MA); educational leadership (Ed D); general education (MA); literacy education (MA); special education (MA). *Accreditation:* NCATE (one or more programs are accredited). Part-time and evening/weekend programs available. *Degree requirements:* For master's, thesis. *Entrance requirements:* For master's, minimum GPA of 3.0, teaching credentials, 1 year of teaching experience. Tuition and fees vary according to program. *Faculty research:* Multicultural literature, art as knowledge, poetry and second language acquisition, restructuring K–12 education and improving the training of K–8 science teachers.

California State University, Stanislaus, College of Education, Program in Education (MA), Turlock, CA 95382. Offers curriculum and instruction (MA), including education technology, elementary education, multilingual education, physical education, reading, secondary education, special education; school administration (MA); school counseling (MA). Part-time and evening/weekend programs available. *Degree requirements:* For master's, comprehensive exam (for some programs), thesis (for some programs). *Entrance requirements:* For master's, MAT, GRE, or CBEST (varies by concentration), 3 letters of recommendation, personal statement. Additional exam requirements/recommendations for international students: Required—TOEFL (minimum score 550 paper-based). Electronic applications accepted. *Faculty research:* Children's perspectives on historical events, method elementary schools dual language education, K-12 reading programs.

California University of Pennsylvania, School of Graduate Studies and Research, College of Education and Human Services, Department of Special Education, California, PA 15419-1394. Offers mentally and/or physically handicapped education (M Ed). *Accreditation:* NCATE. Part-time and evening/weekend programs available. *Degree requirements:* For master's, comprehensive exam, thesis optional. *Entrance requirements:* For master's, MAT, PRAXIS. Additional exam requirements/recommendations for international students: Required—TOEFL (minimum score 550 paper-based; 80 iBT). Electronic applications accepted. *Faculty research:* Case-based instruction, electronic performance support tools, students with disabilities, teacher preparation, No Child Left Behind.

Calvin College, Graduate Programs in Education, Grand Rapids, MI 49546-4388. Offers curriculum and instruction (M Ed); educational leadership (M Ed); learning disabilities (M Ed); literacy (M Ed). Part-time programs available. *Faculty:* 12 full-time (5 women). *Students:* 9 full-time (7 women), 133 part-time (87 women); includes 12 minority (3 Black or African American, non-Hispanic/Latino; 3 Asian, non-Hispanic/Latino; 3 Hispanic/Latino; 3 Two or more races, non-Hispanic/Latino), 20 international. Average age 29. 15 applicants, 87% accepted, 13 enrolled. In 2013, 27 master's awarded. *Degree requirements:* For master's, thesis or seminar. *Entrance requirements:* For master's, teaching certificate. Additional exam requirements/recommendations for international students: Required—TOEFL (minimum score 550 paper-based; 80 iBT). *Application deadline:* For fall admission, 8/1 priority date for domestic students, 5/1 priority date for international students; for spring admission, 1/1 priority date for domestic students, 12/1 priority date for international students; for summer admission, 5/18 for domestic students. Applications are processed on a rolling basis. Application fee: $0. Electronic applications accepted. *Financial support:* Federal Work-Study, scholarships/grants, and tuition waivers (full and partial) available. Financial award application deadline: 4/3; financial award applicants required to submit FAFSA. *Faculty research:* Literacy, racialized gender and gendered identity, teacher learning, learning disabilities identification, leadership. *Unit head:* Dr. David Smith, Graduate Program Director, 616-526-6158, Fax: 616-526-6505, E-mail: dsmith@calvin.edu. *Application contact:* Cindi Hoekstra, Program Coordinator, 616-526-6158, Fax: 616-526-6505, E-mail: choekstr@calvin.edu.
Website: http://www.calvin.edu/academic/graduate_studies.

Cambridge College, School of Education, Cambridge, MA 02138-5304. Offers autism specialist (M Ed); autism/behavior analyst (M Ed); behavior analyst (Post-Master's Certificate); behavioral management (M Ed); early childhood teacher (M Ed); education specialist in curriculum and instruction (CAGS); educational leadership (Ed D); elementary teacher (M Ed); English as a second language (M Ed, Certificate); general science (M Ed); health education (Post-Master's Certificate); health/family and consumer sciences (M Ed); history (M Ed); individualized (M Ed); information technology literacy (M Ed); instructional technology (M Ed); interdisciplinary studies (M Ed); library teacher (M Ed); literacy education (M Ed); mathematics (M Ed); mathematics specialist (Certificate); middle school mathematics and science (M Ed); school administration (M Ed, CAGS); school guidance counselor (M Ed); school nurse education (M Ed); school social worker/school adjustment counselor (M Ed); special education administrator (CAGS); special education/moderate disabilities (M Ed); teaching skills and methodologies (M Ed). Part-time and evening/weekend programs available. Postbaccalaureate distance learning degree programs offered (minimal on-campus study). *Degree requirements:* For master's, thesis, internship/practicum (licensure program only); for doctorate, thesis/dissertation; for other advanced degree, thesis. *Entrance requirements:* For master's, interview, resume, documentation of licensure, 2 professional references; for doctorate, official transcripts, interview, resume, documentation of licensure (if any), written personal statement/essay, portfolio of scholarly and professional work, qualifying assessment, 2 professional references, health insurance, immunizations form; for other advanced degree, official transcripts, interview, resume, documentation of licensure (if any); written personal statement/essay, 2 professional references, health insurance, immunizations form. Additional exam requirements/recommendations for international students: Required—TOEFL (minimum score 550 paper-based; 79 iBT), Michigan English Language Assessment Battery (minimum score 85); Recommended—IELTS (minimum score 6). Electronic applications accepted. *Expenses:* Contact institution. *Faculty research:* Adult education, accelerated learning, mathematics education, brain compatible learning, special education and law.

Campbellsville University, School of Education, Campbellsville, KY 42718-2799. Offers curriculum and instruction (MAE); special education (MASE). *Accreditation:* NCATE. Part-time and evening/weekend programs available. Postbaccalaureate distance learning degree programs offered (minimal on-campus study). *Degree requirements:* For master's, thesis, research paper. *Entrance requirements:* For master's, GRE or PRAXIS, minimum undergraduate GPA of 2.75, teaching certificate, professional growth plan, letters of recommendation, disposition assessment, interview. Electronic applications accepted. *Faculty research:* Professional development, curriculum development, school governance, assessment, special education.

Canisius College, Graduate Division, School of Education and Human Services, Department of Graduate Education and Leadership, Buffalo, NY 14208-1098. Offers business and marketing education (MS Ed); college student personnel (MS Ed); deaf education (MS Ed); deaf/adolescent education, grades 7-12 (MS Ed); deaf/childhood education, grades 1-6 (MS Ed); differentiated instruction (MS Ed); education administration (MS); educational administration (MS Ed); educational technologies (Certificate); gifted education extension (Certificate); literacy (MS Ed); reading (Certificate); school building leadership (MS Ed, Certificate); school district leadership (Certificate); teacher leader (Certificate); TESOL (MS Ed). *Accreditation:* NCATE. Part-time and evening/weekend programs available. Postbaccalaureate distance learning degree programs offered (minimal on-campus study). *Faculty:* 6 full-time (5 women), 33 part-time/adjunct (20 women). *Students:* 134 full-time (106 women), 267 part-time (213 women); includes 36 minority (22 Black or African American, non-Hispanic/Latino; 1 American Indian or Alaska Native, non-Hispanic/Latino; 3 Asian, non-Hispanic/Latino; 8 Hispanic/Latino; 2 Two or more races, non-Hispanic/Latino), 2 international. Average age 30. 282 applicants, 80% accepted, 120 enrolled. In 2013, 178 master's awarded. *Entrance requirements:* For master's, GRE if cumulative GPA less than 2.7, transcripts, two letters of recommendation. Additional exam requirements/recommendations for international students: Required—TOEFL (minimum score 550 paper-based, 80 iBT), IELTS (minimum score 6.5), or CAEL (minimum score 70). *Application deadline:* Applications are processed on a rolling basis. Application fee: $25. Electronic applications accepted. Application fee is waived when completed online. *Expenses:* *Tuition:* Part-time $750 per credit hour. *Financial support:* Career-related internships or fieldwork, Federal Work-Study, scholarships/grants, tuition waivers (partial), and unspecified assistantships available. Support available to part-time students. Financial award application deadline: 4/30; financial award applicants required to submit FAFSA. *Faculty research:* Asperger's disease, autism, private higher education, reading strategies. *Unit head:* Dr. Rosemary K. Murray, Chair/Associate Professor of Graduate Education and Leadership, 716-888-3723, E-mail: murray1@canisius.edu. *Application contact:* Julie A. Zulewski, Director of Graduate Admissions, 716-888-2548, Fax: 716-888-3195, E-mail: zulewskj@canisius.edu.
Website: http://www.canisius.edu/graduate/.

Canisius College, Graduate Division, School of Education and Human Services, Department of Teacher Education, Buffalo, NY 14208-1098. Offers adolescence education (MS Ed); childhood education (MS Ed); general education (MS Ed); special education (MS), including adolescence special education, advanced special education, childhood education grade 1-6, childhood special education. Part-time and evening/weekend programs available. Postbaccalaureate distance learning degree programs offered (minimal on-campus study). *Faculty:* 23 full-time (18 women), 10 part-time/adjunct (4 women). *Students:* 87 full-time (58 women), 32 part-time (27 women); includes 8 minority (4 Black or African American, non-Hispanic/Latino; 3 Asian, non-Hispanic/Latino; 1 Two or more races, non-Hispanic/Latino), 14 international. Average age 29. 73 applicants, 68% accepted, 23 enrolled. In 2013, 135 master's awarded. *Degree requirements:* For master's, research project or thesis, project internship. *Entrance requirements:* For master's, GRE if cumulative GPA is less than 2.7, transcripts, letters of recommendation. Additional exam requirements/recommendations for international students: Required—TOEFL (minimum score 550 paper-based, 80 iBT), IELTS (minimum score 6.5), or CAEL (minimum score 70). *Application deadline:* Applications are processed on a rolling basis. Application fee: $25. Electronic applications accepted. Application fee is waived when completed online. *Expenses:* *Tuition:* Part-time $750 per credit hour. *Financial support:* Career-related internships or fieldwork, Federal Work-Study, scholarships/grants, tuition waivers (partial), and unspecified assistantships available. Support available to part-time students. Financial award application deadline: 4/30; financial award applicants required to submit FAFSA. *Unit head:* Dr. Julie Henry, Chair/Professor, 716-888-3729, E-mail: henry1@canisius.edu. *Application contact:* Julie A. Zulewski, Director of Graduate Admissions, 716-555-2548, Fax: 716-888-3195, E-mail: zulewskj@canisius.edu.
Website: http://www.canisius.edu/academics/graduate/.

Capella University, School of Education, Doctoral Programs in Education, Minneapolis, MN 55402. Offers curriculum and instruction (PhD); educational leadership and management (Ed D); instructional design for online learning (PhD); K-12 studies in education (PhD); leadership for higher education (PhD); leadership in educational administration (PhD); postsecondary and adult education (PhD); professional studies in education (PhD); reading and literacy (Ed D); special education leadership (PhD); training and performance improvement (PhD).

Capella University, School of Education, Master's Programs in Education, Minneapolis, MN 55402. Offers adult education (MS); curriculum and instruction (MS); early childhood education (MS); enrollment management (MS); higher education leadership and management (MS); instructional design for online learning (MS); integrative studies (MS); K-12 studies in education (MS); leadership in educational administration (MS); reading and literacy (MS); special education teaching (MS).

Cardinal Stritch University, College of Education, Department of Literacy, Milwaukee, WI 53217-3985. Offers literacy/English as a second language (MA); reading/language arts (MA); reading/learning disability (MA). *Accreditation:* NCATE. Part-time and evening/weekend programs available. *Degree requirements:* For master's, comprehensive exam, thesis, faculty recommendation, research project. *Entrance requirements:* For master's, letters of recommendation (2), minimum GPA of 2.75.

Cardinal Stritch University, College of Education, Department of Special Education, Milwaukee, WI 53217-3985. Offers MA. *Accreditation:* NCATE. Part-time and evening/weekend programs available. *Degree requirements:* For master's, comprehensive exam, thesis, practica. *Entrance requirements:* For master's, letters of recommendation (2), minimum GPA of 2.75.

Caribbean University, Graduate School, Bayamón, PR 00960-0493. Offers administration and supervision (MA Ed); criminal justice (MA); curriculum and instruction (MA Ed, PhD), including elementary education (MA Ed), English education (MA Ed), history education (MA Ed), mathematics education (MA Ed), primary education (MA Ed), science education (MA Ed), Spanish education (MA Ed); educational technology in instructional systems (MA Ed); gerontology (MSN); human resources (MBA); museology, archiving and art history (MA Ed); neonatal pediatrics (MSN); physical education (MA Ed); special education (MA Ed). *Entrance requirements:* For master's, interview, minimum GPA of 2.5.

Carlos Albizu University, Miami Campus, Graduate Programs, Miami, FL 33172-2209. Offers clinical psychology (Psy D); entrepreneurship (MBA); exceptional student education (MS); human services (PhD); industrial/organizational psychology (MS); marriage and family therapy (MS); mental health counseling (MS); nonprofit management (MBA); organizational management (MBA); psychology (MS); school counseling (MS); teaching English as a second language (MS). *Accreditation:* APA. Part-time and evening/weekend programs available. *Faculty:* 26 full-time (20 women), 34 part-time/adjunct (16 women). *Students:* 416 full-time (335 women), 281 part-time (237 women); includes 604 minority (57 Black or African American, non-Hispanic/Latino; 1 American Indian or Alaska Native, non-Hispanic/Latino; 13 Asian, non-Hispanic/Latino; 533 Hispanic/Latino), 14 international. Average age 36. 176 applicants, 59% accepted, 96 enrolled. In 2013, 176 master's, 37 doctorates awarded. Terminal master's awarded for partial completion of doctoral program. *Degree requirements:* For master's, one foreign language, comprehensive exam, integrative project (MBA), research project (exceptional student education, teaching English as a second language); for doctorate, one foreign language, comprehensive exam, internship, project. *Entrance requirements:* For master's, 3 letters of recommendation, interview, minimum GPA of 3.0, resume, statement of purpose, official transcripts; for doctorate, 3 letters of recommendation, minimum GPA of 3.0, resume, interview, statement of purpose, official transcripts. Additional exam requirements/recommendations for international students: Required—Michigan Test of English Language Proficiency. *Application deadline:* For fall admission, 4/1 priority date for domestic students, 5/1 priority date for international students; for spring admission, 11/1 priority date for domestic students, 9/1 priority date for international students. Applications are processed on a rolling basis. Application fee: $50. Electronic applications accepted. *Expenses: Tuition:* Full-time $9360; part-time $520 per credit. *Required fees:* $298 per term. Tuition and fees vary according to course load, degree level and program. *Financial support:* In 2013–14, 62 students received support. Federal Work-Study, scholarships/grants, and tuition discounts available. Financial award application deadline: 6/1; financial award applicants required to submit FAFSA. *Faculty research:* Psychotherapy, forensic psychology, neuropsychology, marketing strategy, entrepreneurship, special education. *Unit head:* Peter M. Rubio, Interim Chancellor, 305-593-1223 Ext. 3120, Fax: 305-592-7930, E-mail: prubio@albizu.edu. *Application contact:* Vanessa Almendarez, Administrative Assistant, 305-593-1223 Ext. 3137, Fax: 305-593-1854, E-mail: valmendarez@albizu.edu.

Carlow University, School of Education, Program in Education, Pittsburgh, PA 15213-3165. Offers art education (M Ed); early childhood education (M Ed); secondary education (M Ed); special education (M Ed). Part-time and evening/weekend programs available. *Students:* 42 full-time (37 women), 36 part-time (34 women); includes 9 minority (6 Black or African American, non-Hispanic/Latino; 1 Asian, non-Hispanic/Latino; 2 Two or more races, non-Hispanic/Latino). Average age 31. 27 applicants, 100% accepted, 19 enrolled. In 2013, 17 master's awarded. *Entrance requirements:* For master's, resume, 3 letters of recommendation, minimum GPA of 3.0, interview. Additional exam requirements/recommendations for international students: Required—TOEFL. *Application deadline:* For fall admission, 6/15 priority date for domestic and international students; for spring admission, 11/15 priority date for domestic and international students. Applications are processed on a rolling basis. Application fee: $20. Electronic applications accepted. Application fee is waived when completed online. *Expenses: Tuition:* Full-time $9523; part-time $744 per credit. Tuition and fees vary according to course load, degree level and program. *Financial support:* Applicants required to submit FAFSA. *Unit head:* Dr. Marilyn Llewellyn, Dean, 412-578-6011, Fax: 412-578-0816, E-mail: llewellynmj@carlow.edu. *Application contact:* Jo Danhires, Administrative Assistant, Admissions, 412-578-6089, Fax: 412-578-6321, E-mail: gradstudies@carlow.edu.
Website: http://www.carlow.edu.

Castleton State College, Division of Graduate Studies, Department of Education, Program in Special Education, Castleton, VT 05735. Offers MA Ed, CAGS. Part-time and evening/weekend programs available. *Degree requirements:* For master's, thesis or alternative; for CAGS, publishable paper. *Entrance requirements:* For master's, GRE General Test, MAT, interview, minimum undergraduate GPA of 3.0; for CAGS, educational research, master's degree, minimum undergraduate GPA of 3.0.

The Catholic University of America, School of Arts and Sciences, Department of Education, Washington, DC 20064. Offers Catholic educational leadership and policy studies (PhD); Catholic school leadership (MA); education (Certificate); educational psychology (PhD); secondary education (MA); special education (MA). *Accreditation:* NCATE. Part-time programs available. *Faculty:* 9 full-time (8 women), 4 part-time/adjunct (all women). *Students:* 9 full-time (6 women), 44 part-time (37 women); includes 8 minority (3 Black or African American, non-Hispanic/Latino; 3 Hispanic/Latino; 2 Two or more races, non-Hispanic/Latino), 2 international. Average age 34. 53 applicants, 53% accepted, 17 enrolled. In 2013, 18 master's, 2 doctorates awarded. *Degree requirements:* For master's, comprehensive exam, thesis or alternative; for doctorate, comprehensive exam, thesis/dissertation; for Certificate, action research project. *Entrance requirements:* For master's and doctorate, GRE General Test or MAT, statement of purpose, official copies of academic transcripts, three letters of recommendation, interview; for Certificate, PRAXIS I, statement of purpose, official copies of academic transcripts, three letters of recommendation, interview. Additional exam requirements/recommendations for international students: Required—TOEFL (minimum score 580 paper-based). *Application deadline:* For fall admission, 8/1 priority date for domestic students, 7/15 for international students; for spring admission, 12/1 priority date for domestic students, 10/15 for international students. Applications are processed on a rolling basis. Application fee: $55. Electronic applications accepted. *Expenses: Tuition:* Full-time $38,500; part-time $1490 per credit hour. *Required fees:* $400; $1525 per credit hour. One-time fee: $425. Tuition and fees vary according to program. *Financial support:* Fellowships, research assistantships, teaching assistantships, Federal Work-Study, scholarships/grants, tuition waivers (full and partial), and unspecified assistantships available. Financial award application deadline: 2/1; financial award applicants required to submit FAFSA. *Faculty research:* Special education, early childhood education, educational psychology, Catholic school administration, leadership and policy studies, counseling, curriculum and instruction. *Total annual research expenditures:* $65,883. *Unit head:* Dr. Merylann J. Schuttloffel, Chair, 202-319-5805, Fax: 202-319-5815, E-mail: schuttloffel@cua.edu. *Application contact:* Andrew Woodall, Director of Graduate Admissions, 202-319-5057, Fax: 202-319-6533, E-mail: cua-admissions@cua.edu.
Website: http://education.cua.edu/.

Centenary College, Program in Education, Hackettstown, NJ 07840-2100. Offers educational leadership (MA); instructional leadership (MA); special education (MA). *Accreditation:* Teacher Education Accreditation Council. Part-time and evening/weekend programs available. Postbaccalaureate distance learning degree programs offered (minimal on-campus study). *Degree requirements:* For master's, thesis. *Entrance requirements:* For master's, interview, minimum undergraduate GPA of 2.8.

Central Connecticut State University, School of Graduate Studies, School of Education and Professional Studies, Department of Special Education, New Britain, CT 06050-4010. Offers special education (Certificate); special education for special educators (MS); special education for teachers certified in areas other than education (MS). Part-time and evening/weekend programs available. *Faculty:* 6 full-time (2 women), 7 part-time/adjunct (4 women). *Students:* 24 full-time (18 women), 146 part-time (116 women); includes 15 minority (7 Black or African American, non-Hispanic/Latino; 1 Asian, non-Hispanic/Latino; 2 Hispanic/Latino; 5 Two or more races, non-Hispanic/Latino). Average age 31. 63 applicants, 78% accepted, 34 enrolled. In 2013, 48 master's, 8 other advanced degrees awarded. *Degree requirements:* For master's, comprehensive exam, thesis or alternative; for Certificate, qualifying exam. *Entrance requirements:* For master's, minimum undergraduate GPA of 2.7, teacher certification. Additional exam requirements/recommendations for international students: Required—TOEFL (minimum score 550 paper-based; 79 iBT). *Application deadline:* For fall admission, 6/1 for domestic students, 5/1 for international students; for spring admission, 11/1 for domestic and international students. Applications are processed on a rolling basis. Application fee: $50. Electronic applications accepted. Part-time tuition and fees vary according to degree level. *Financial support:* In 2013–14, 2 students received support. Career-related internships or fieldwork, Federal Work-Study, scholarships/grants, and unspecified assistantships available. Support available to part-time students. Financial award application deadline: 3/1; financial award applicants required to submit FAFSA. *Faculty research:* Learning disabilities/language development, consulting teacher practice, occupational/special education, teaching emotionally disturbed students. *Unit head:* Dr. Mitchell Beck, Chair, 860-832-2400, E-mail: beckm@ccsu.edu. *Application contact:* Patricia Gardner, Associate Director of Graduate Studies, 860-832-2350, Fax: 860-832-2362, E-mail: graduateadmissions@ccsu.edu.
Website: http://www.ccsu.edu/page.cfm?p=14477.

Central Michigan University, College of Graduate Studies, College of Education and Human Services, Department of Counseling and Special Education, Program in Special Education, Mount Pleasant, MI 48859. Offers autism (Graduate Certificate); special education (MA), including the master teacher. *Accreditation:* Teacher Education Accreditation Council. Part-time programs available. *Degree requirements:* For master's, comprehensive exam (for some programs), thesis or alternative. *Entrance requirements:* For master's, Michigan elementary or secondary provisional, permanent, or life certificate or special education endorsement. Electronic applications accepted. *Faculty research:* Mainstreaming, learning disabled, attention and organization disorders.

Central Washington University, Graduate Studies and Research, College of Education and Professional Studies, Department of Language, Literacy and Special Education, Program in Special Education, Ellensburg, WA 98926. Offers M Ed. Part-time programs available. *Degree requirements:* For master's, thesis or alternative. *Entrance requirements:* For master's, minimum GPA of 3.0. Additional exam requirements/recommendations for international students: Required—TOEFL (minimum score 550 paper-based; 79 iBT), IELTS (minimum score 6.5).

Chaminade University of Honolulu, Graduate Services, Program in Education, Honolulu, HI 96816-1578. Offers child development (M Ed); early childhood education (M Ed); educational leadership (M Ed); elementary education (MAT); instructional leadership (M Ed); Montessori education (M Ed); secondary education (MAT), including English, math, science, social studies; special education (MAT). Part-time and evening/weekend programs available. Postbaccalaureate distance learning degree programs offered (minimal on-campus study). *Degree requirements:* For master's, thesis or alternative. *Entrance requirements:* For master's, PRAXIS (for MAT only), minimum GPA of 2.75, 3 letters of recommendation. Additional exam requirements/recommendations for international students: Required—TOEFL (minimum score 550 paper-based). Electronic applications accepted. *Faculty research:* Peace and curriculum education.

Chapman University, College of Educational Studies, Orange, CA 92866. Offers communication sciences and disorders (MS); counseling (MA), including school counseling (MA, Credential); education (PhD), including cultural and curricular studies, disability studies, leadership studies, school psychology (PhD, Credential); educational psychology (MA); leadership development (MA); pupil personnel services (Credential), including school counseling (MA, Credential), school psychology (PhD, Credential); school psychology (Ed S); single subject (Credential); special education (MA, Credential), including mild/moderate (Credential), moderate/severe (Credential); speech language pathology (Credential); teaching (MA), including elementary education, secondary education. *Accreditation:* Teacher Education Accreditation Council. Part-time and evening/weekend programs available. *Faculty:* 29 full-time (18 women), 56 part-time/adjunct (38 women). *Students:* 251 full-time (208 women), 194 part-time (150 women); includes 185 minority (13 Black or African American, non-Hispanic/Latino; 61 Asian, non-Hispanic/Latino; 97 Hispanic/Latino; 1 Native Hawaiian or other Pacific Islander, non-Hispanic/Latino; 13 Two or more races, non-Hispanic/Latino), 7 international. Average age 29. 580 applicants, 42% accepted, 166 enrolled. In 2013, 140 master's, 10 doctorates awarded. *Entrance requirements:* Additional exam requirements/recommendations for international students: Required—TOEFL (minimum score 550 paper-based; 80 iBT). *Application deadline:* Applications are processed on a rolling basis. Application fee: $60. Electronic applications accepted. Tuition and fees vary according to program. *Financial support:* Fellowships and scholarships/grants available. Financial award application deadline: 6/30; financial award applicants required to submit FAFSA. *Unit head:* Dr. Don Cardinal, Dean, 714-997-6781, E-mail: cardinal@chapman.edu. *Application contact:* Admissions Coordinator, 714-997-6714.
Website: http://www.chapman.edu/CES/.

Chatham University, Program in Education, Pittsburgh, PA 15232-2826. Offers early childhood education (MAT); elementary education (MAT); environmental education (K-12) (MAT); secondary art (MAT); secondary biology education (MAT); secondary chemistry education (MAT); secondary English education (MAT); secondary math education (MAT); secondary physics education (MAT); secondary social studies education (MAT); special education (MAT). *Faculty:* 1 (woman) full-time, 5 part-time/adjunct (4 women). *Students:* 19 full-time (15 women), 4 part-time (all women); includes 2 minority (1 Black or African American, non-Hispanic/Latino; 1 Asian, non-Hispanic/Latino), 2 international. Average age 28. 22 applicants, 73% accepted, 6 enrolled. In 2013, 20 master's awarded. *Degree requirements:* For master's, thesis, teaching experience. *Entrance requirements:* For master's, minimum GPA of 3.0, sample of written work, recommendation letters. Additional exam requirements/recommendations for international students: Required—TOEFL (minimum score 600 paper-based; 100 iBT), IELTS (minimum score 7), TWE. *Application deadline:* For fall admission, 4/1 priority date for domestic and international students; for spring admission, 11/1 priority date for domestic students, 10/1 priority date for international students. Applications are processed on a rolling basis. Application fee: $45. Electronic applications accepted. Application fee is waived when completed online. *Expenses: Tuition:* Full-time $14,886; part-time $827 per credit hour. One-time fee: $396 full-time. *Financial support:* Career-related internships or fieldwork available. Financial award applicants required to submit FAFSA. *Faculty research:* Gifted education, environmental education, technology in education, writing as learning, class size and achievement. *Unit head:* Dr. Edward Donovan, Director of Education Programs, 412-365-2773, E-mail: edonovan@

chatham.edu. *Application contact:* Katie Noel, Assistant Director of Graduate Admission, 412-365-2758, Fax: 412-365-1609, E-mail: gradadmissions@chatham.edu.
Website: http://www.chatham.edu/mat.

Chestnut Hill College, School of Graduate Studies, Department of Education, Program in Special Education, Philadelphia, PA 19118-2693. Offers M Ed, CAS. Part-time and evening/weekend programs available. *Faculty:* 10 full-time (7 women), 48 part-time/adjunct (34 women). *Students:* 13 full-time (11 women), 96 part-time (78 women); includes 5 minority (2 Black or African American, non-Hispanic/Latino; 1 Asian, non-Hispanic/Latino; 1 Hispanic/Latino; 1 Two or more races, non-Hispanic/Latino). Average age 31. 1 applicant, 100% accepted. In 2013, 1 master's, 35 CASs awarded. *Degree requirements:* For master's, thesis optional. *Entrance requirements:* For master's, PRAXIS I or proof of teaching certification, letters of recommendation, writing sample, 6 graduate credits with minimum B grade if undergraduate GPA less than 3.0. Additional exam requirements/recommendations for international students: Required—TOEFL (minimum score 500 paper-based), IELTS (minimum score 6), or TWE (minimum score 22). *Application deadline:* For fall admission, 7/1 for domestic and international students; for spring admission, 11/1 for domestic and international students; for summer admission, 4/1 for domestic and international students. Applications are processed on a rolling basis. *Expenses: Tuition:* Full-time $10,800; part-time $625 per credit. One-time fee: $425 full-time. Tuition and fees vary according to degree level and program. *Financial support:* Unspecified assistantships available. *Faculty research:* Inclusive education, cultural issues in education. *Unit head:* Dr. Debra Chiaradonna, Chair, Department of Education, 215-248-7147, Fax: 215-248-7155, E-mail: chiaradonnad@chc.edu. *Application contact:* Jayne Mashett, Director of Admissions, School of Graduate Studies, 215-248-7020, Fax: 215-248-7161, E-mail: gradadmissions@chc.edu.

Chestnut Hill College, School of Graduate Studies, Division of Psychology, Program in Clinical and Counseling Psychology, Philadelphia, PA 19118-2693. Offers addictions treatment (MA, MS, CAS); child and adolescent therapy (MA, MS, CAS); marriage and family therapy (MA, MS, CAS); trauma studies (MA, MS, CAS); treatment of autism spectrum disorders (MA, MS, CAS). Part-time and evening/weekend programs available. *Faculty:* 7 full-time (5 women), 28 part-time/adjunct (20 women). *Students:* 111 full-time (93 women), 146 part-time (113 women); includes 35 minority (22 Black or African American, non-Hispanic/Latino; 1 Asian, non-Hispanic/Latino; 9 Hispanic/Latino; 3 Two or more races, non-Hispanic/Latino), 5 international. Average age 32. 151 applicants, 95% accepted. In 2013, 84 master's, 6 other advanced degrees awarded. *Degree requirements:* For master's, thesis optional, practica. *Entrance requirements:* For master's, GRE General Test, writing sample, letters of recommendation. Additional exam requirements/recommendations for international students: Required—TOEFL (minimum score 500 paper-based), IELTS (mnimum score 6.0), or TWE (minimum score 22). *Application deadline:* For fall admission, 7/1 for domestic and international students; for spring admission, 11/1 for domestic and international students; for summer admission, 4/1 for domestic and international students. Applications are processed on a rolling basis. *Expenses:* Contact institution. *Financial support:* Unspecified assistantships available. *Faculty research:* Play therapy, eating disorders, addictions, group psychology and group therapy, health psychology. *Unit head:* Dr. Cheryll Rothery, Chair, Psychology Division, 215-248-7023, Fax: 215-248-3619, E-mail: rotheryc@chc.edu. *Application contact:* Jayne Mashett, Director of Admissions, School of Graduate Studies, 215-248-7020, Fax: 215-248-7161, E-mail: gradadmissions@chc.edu.
Website: http://www.chc.edu/Graduate/Programs/.

Cheyney University of Pennsylvania, Graduate Programs, Program in Special Education, Cheyney, PA 19319. Offers M Ed. Part-time and evening/weekend programs available. *Degree requirements:* For master's, thesis. *Entrance requirements:* For master's, GRE General Test, MAT, minimum GPA of 2.75. Electronic applications accepted.

Chicago State University, School of Graduate and Professional Studies, College of Education, Department of Special Education, Early Childhood Education and Bilingual Education, Program in Special Education, Chicago, IL 60628. Offers M Ed. *Accreditation:* NCATE. *Degree requirements:* For master's, thesis optional. *Entrance requirements:* For master's, minimum GPA of 2.75. *Faculty research:* Assistive technology, teacher efficiency.

City College of the City University of New York, Graduate School, School of Education, Department of Leadership and Special Education, New York, NY 10031-9198. Offers bilingual special education (MS Ed); educational leadership (MS, AC); teacher of students with disabilities in childhood education (MS Ed); teacher of students with disabilities in middle childhood education (MS Ed). *Degree requirements:* For master's, thesis, research paper. *Entrance requirements:* For master's, Liberal Arts and Sciences Test (LAST), Content Specialty Test (CST), interview; minimum GPA of 3.0 in major, 2.5 overall. Additional exam requirements/recommendations for international students: Required—TOEFL. *Faculty research:* Dynamics of organizational change, impact of laws on educational policy, leadership development in schools.

City College of the City University of New York, Graduate School, School of Education, Program in Teaching Students with Disabilities, New York, NY 10031-9198. Offers MA. *Accreditation:* NCATE. *Degree requirements:* For master's, thesis. *Entrance requirements:* For master's, Liberal Arts and Sciences Test (LAST), Content Specialty Test (CST). Additional exam requirements/recommendations for international students: Required—TOEFL.

City University of Seattle, Graduate Division, Albright School of Education, Bellevue, WA 98005. Offers administrator certification (Certificate); curriculum and instruction (M Ed); educational leadership (Ed D); elementary education (MIT); guidance and counseling (M Ed); higher education leadership (Ed D); leadership (M Ed); leadership and school counseling (M Ed); organizational leadership (Ed D); reading and literacy (M Ed); special education (MIT); superintendent certification (Certificate). Part-time and evening/weekend programs available. Postbaccalaureate distance learning degree programs offered (no on-campus study). *Degree requirements:* For master's, comprehensive exam (for some programs), thesis (for some programs); for doctorate, comprehensive exam, thesis/dissertation. *Entrance requirements:* Additional exam requirements/recommendations for international students: Required—TOEFL (minimum score 567 paper-based; 87 iBT); Recommended—IELTS. Electronic applications accepted. *Expenses:* Contact institution.

Claremont Graduate University, Graduate Programs, School of Educational Studies, Claremont, CA 91711-6160. Offers Africana education (Certificate); education and policy (MA, PhD); higher education/student affairs (MA, PhD); human development (MA, PhD); public school administration (MA, PhD); quantitative evaluation (MA, PhD); special education (MA, PhD); teacher education (MA); teaching and learning (MA, PhD); urban leadership (PhD); MBA/PhD. PhD program offered jointly with San Diego State University. Part-time programs available. *Faculty:* 16 full-time (9 women), 1 part-time/adjunct (0 women). *Students:* 224 full-time (158 women), 221 part-time (151 women); includes 229 minority (52 Black or African American, non-Hispanic/Latino; 3 American Indian or Alaska Native, non-Hispanic/Latino; 43 Asian, non-Hispanic/Latino; 113 Hispanic/Latino; 1 Native Hawaiian or other Pacific Islander, non-Hispanic/Latino; 17 Two or more races, non-Hispanic/Latino), 15 international. Average age 39. In 2013, 51 master's, 33 doctorates, 5 other advanced degrees awarded. Terminal master's awarded for partial completion of doctoral program. *Entrance requirements:* For master's and doctorate, GRE General Test. Additional exam requirements/recommendations for international students: Required—TOEFL (minimum score 550 paper-based; 80 iBT). *Application deadline:* For fall admission, 4/1 priority date for domestic and international students. Applications are processed on a rolling basis. Application fee: $80. Electronic applications accepted. *Expenses: Tuition:* Full-time $40,560; part-time $1690 per credit. *Required fees:* $275 per semester. Tuition and fees vary according to program. *Financial support:* Fellowships, research assistantships, Federal Work-Study, institutionally sponsored loans, and scholarships/grants available. Support available to part-time students. Financial award application deadline: 2/15; financial award applicants required to submit FAFSA. *Faculty research:* Education administration, K-12 and higher education, multicultural education, education policy, diversity in higher education, faculty issues. *Unit head:* Scott Thomas, Dean, 909-621-8075, Fax: 909-621-8734, E-mail: scott.thomas@cgu.edu. *Application contact:* Julia Wendt, Director of Central Recruitment, 909-607-3689, Fax: 909-607-7285, E-mail: admiss@cgu.edu.
Website: http://www.cgu.edu/pages/267.asp.

Clarion University of Pennsylvania, Office of Transfer, Adult and Graduate Admissions, Master of Education Program, Clarion, PA 16214. Offers curriculum and instruction (M Ed); early childhood (M Ed); math education (M Ed); reading (M Ed); science education (M Ed); special education (M Ed); technology (M Ed). *Accreditation:* NCATE. Part-time programs available. Postbaccalaureate distance learning degree programs offered (no on-campus study). *Faculty:* 17 full-time (10 women). *Students:* 231 full-time (191 women), 535 part-time (448 women); includes 39 minority (12 Black or African American, non-Hispanic/Latino; 8 Asian, non-Hispanic/Latino; 11 Hispanic/Latino; 1 Native Hawaiian or other Pacific Islander, non-Hispanic/Latino; 7 Two or more races, non-Hispanic/Latino). Average age 31. 28 applicants, 75% accepted, 18 enrolled. In 2013, 99 master's awarded. *Degree requirements:* For master's, comprehensive exam, thesis, or portfolio. *Entrance requirements:* For master's, minimum QPA of 3.0. Additional exam requirements/recommendations for international students: Required—TOEFL (minimum score 550 paper-based; 80 iBT), IELTS (minimum score 7). *Application deadline:* For fall admission, 8/1 for domestic students, 4/15 for international students; for spring admission, 8/1 for domestic students, 9/15 for international students. Applications are processed on a rolling basis. Application fee: $40. Electronic applications accepted. *Expenses:* Tuition, state resident: part-time $442 per credit. Tuition, nonresident: part-time $451 per credit. *Required fees:* $142.40 per semester. One-time fee: $150 part-time. *Financial support:* In 2013–14, 8 research assistantships with full and partial tuition reimbursements (averaging $9,420 per year) were awarded; career-related internships or fieldwork also available. Support available to part-time students. Financial award application deadline: 3/1. *Unit head:* Ray Puller, Interim Dean, 814-393-2146, Fax: 514-393-2446, E-mail: rpuller@clarion.edu. *Application contact:* Susan Staub, Assistant Director, Graduate Programs, 814-393-2337, Fax: 814-393-2722, E-mail: gradstudies@clarion.edu.
Website: http://www.clarion.edu/25887/.

Clarion University of Pennsylvania, Office of Transfer, Adult and Graduate Admissions, On-Campus Master's Programs, Clarion, PA 16214. Offers rehabilitative sciences (MS); special education (MS); speech language pathology (MS). *Accreditation:* ASHA. Part-time programs available. Postbaccalaureate distance learning degree programs offered (no on-campus study). *Faculty:* 23 full-time (16 women). *Students:* 113 full-time (97 women), 42 part-time (33 women); includes 4 minority (2 Black or African American, non-Hispanic/Latino; 1 American Indian or Alaska Native, non-Hispanic/Latino; 1 Hispanic/Latino). Average age 24. 297 applicants, 18% accepted, 44 enrolled. In 2013, 68 master's awarded. *Degree requirements:* For master's, comprehensive exam (for some programs), thesis or alternative. *Entrance requirements:* For master's, GRE, minimum QPA of 3.0. Additional exam requirements/recommendations for international students: Required—TOEFL (minimum score 600 paper-based; 89 iBT), IELTS (minimum score 7.5). *Application deadline:* For fall admission, 1/31 for domestic and international students. Applications are processed on a rolling basis. Application fee: $40. Electronic applications accepted. *Expenses:* Tuition, state resident: part-time $442 per credit. Tuition, nonresident: part-time $451 per credit. *Required fees:* $142.40 per semester. One-time fee: $150 part-time. *Financial support:* In 2013–14, 21 research assistantships with full and partial tuition reimbursements (averaging $9,240 per year) were awarded; career-related internships or fieldwork also available. Support available to part-time students. Financial award application deadline: 3/1. *Unit head:* Dr. Colleen McAleer, Chair, 814-393-2581, Fax: 814-393-2206, E-mail: cmcaleer@clarion.edu. *Application contact:* Michelle Ritzler, Assistant Director, Graduate Programs, 814-393-2337, Fax: 814-393-2722, E-mail: gradstudies@clarion.edu.
Website: http://www.clarion.edu/991/.

Clark Atlanta University, School of Education, Department of Curriculum, Atlanta, GA 30314. Offers special education general curriculum (MA); teaching math and science (MAT). Part-time programs available. *Faculty:* 2 full-time (1 woman), 1 (woman) part-time/adjunct. *Students:* 9 full-time (8 women), 3 part-time (1 woman); includes 11 minority (all Black or African American, non-Hispanic/Latino). Average age 28. 8 applicants, 88% accepted, 7 enrolled. In 2013, 4 master's awarded. *Degree requirements:* For master's, one foreign language, comprehensive exam. *Entrance requirements:* For master's, GRE General Test, minimum undergraduate GPA of 2.6. Additional exam requirements/recommendations for international students: Required—TOEFL (minimum score 500 paper-based; 61 iBT). *Application deadline:* For fall admission, 4/1 for domestic and international students; for spring admission, 11/1 for domestic and international students. Applications are processed on a rolling basis. Application fee: $40 ($55 for international students). *Expenses: Tuition:* Full-time $14,616; part-time $812 per credit hour. *Required fees:* $706; $353 per semester. *Financial support:* Career-related internships or fieldwork, Federal Work-Study, scholarships/grants, and unspecified assistantships available. Support available to part-time students. Financial award application deadline: 4/30; financial award applicants required to submit FAFSA. *Unit head:* Dr. Doris Terrell, Chairperson, 404-880-6336, E-mail: dterrell@cau.edu. *Application contact:* Michelle Clark-Davis, Graduate Program Admissions, 404-880-6605, E-mail: cauadmissions@cau.edu.
Website: http://www.cau.edu/School_of_Education_curriculum_dept.aspx.

Clarke University, Program in Education, Dubuque, IA 52001-3198. Offers early childhood/special education (MAE); educational administration: elementary and secondary (MAE); educational media: elementary and secondary (MAE); multi-categorical resource k-12 (MAE); multidisciplinary studies (MAE); reading: elementary (MAE); technology in education (MAE). Part-time and evening/weekend programs available. Postbaccalaureate distance learning degree programs offered (minimal on-campus study). *Faculty:* 10 full-time (9 women), 1 (woman) part-time/adjunct. *Students:* 5 full-time (3 women), 27 part-time (24 women); includes 2 minority (1 Black or African American, non-Hispanic/Latino; 1 American Indian or Alaska Native, non-Hispanic/Latino). In 2013, 11 master's awarded. *Degree requirements:* For master's, comprehensive exam, thesis optional. *Entrance requirements:* For master's, GRE General Test or MAT, minimum GPA of 2.75. *Application deadline:* Applications are processed on a rolling basis. Application fee: $25. Electronic applications accepted.

Expenses: Tuition: Part-time $660 per credit. *Required fees:* $15 per credit. *Financial support:* Career-related internships or fieldwork available. Financial award applicants required to submit FAFSA. *Unit head:* Dr. Michele Slover, Chair, 319-588-6397, Fax: 319-584-8604. *Application contact:* Kara Shroeder, Information Contact, 563-588-6354, Fax: 563-588-6789, E-mail: graduate@clarke.edu.

Clemson University, Graduate School, College of Health, Education, and Human Development, Eugene T. Moore School of Education, Program in Special Education, Clemson, SC 29634. Offers M Ed. *Accreditation:* NCATE. Part-time and evening/weekend programs available. *Degree requirements:* For master's, comprehensive exam. *Entrance requirements:* For master's, GRE General Test, minimum GPA of 3.0, teaching certificate, two letters of recommendation. Additional exam requirements/recommendations for international students: Required—TOEFL; Recommended—IELTS. *Application deadline:* Applications are processed on a rolling basis. Application fee: $70 ($80 for international students). Electronic applications accepted. *Expenses:* Contact institution. *Financial support:* Fellowships with full and partial tuition reimbursements, research assistantships with partial tuition reimbursements, teaching assistantships with partial tuition reimbursements, institutionally sponsored loans, health care benefits, and unspecified assistantships available. Financial award application deadline: 6/1; financial award applicants required to submit FAFSA. *Faculty research:* Instructional interventions in reading for individuals with learning disabilities, legal and policy issues in special education, Response to Intervention (RTI), behavior management, student progress monitoring. *Unit head:* Antonis Katsiyannis, Coordinator, 864-656-5114, Fax: 864-656-0311, E-mail: antonis@clemson.edu. *Application contact:* Dr. David Fleming, Graduate Coordinator, 864-656-1881, Fax: 864-656-0311, E-mail: dflemin@clemson.edu.
Website: http://www.clemson.edu/hehd/departments/education/index.html.

Cleveland State University, College of Graduate Studies, College of Education and Human Services, Department of Teacher Education, Cleveland, OH 44115. Offers art education (M Ed); early childhood education (M Ed); foreign language education (M Ed); mathematics and science education (M Ed); middle childhood education (M Ed); special education (M Ed), including mild/moderate disabilities, moderate/intensive disabilities; teaching English to speakers of other languages (M Ed). Part-time and evening/weekend programs available. *Faculty:* 20 full-time (12 women), 26 part-time/adjunct (20 women). *Students:* 108 full-time (78 women), 311 part-time (252 women); includes 103 minority (80 Black or African American, non-Hispanic/Latino; 2 Asian, non-Hispanic/Latino; 10 Hispanic/Latino; 1 Native Hawaiian or other Pacific Islander, non-Hispanic/Latino; 10 Two or more races, non-Hispanic/Latino), 52 international. Average age 32. 177 applicants, 55% accepted, 68 enrolled. In 2013, 192 master's awarded. *Degree requirements:* For master's, comprehensive exam (for some programs), thesis or alternative. *Entrance requirements:* For master's, GRE General Test or MAT, minimum GPA of 2.75. Additional exam requirements/recommendations for international students: Required—TOEFL (minimum score 525 paper-based), IELTS (minimum score 6). *Application deadline:* For fall admission, 7/15 priority date for domestic students. Applications are processed on a rolling basis. Application fee: $30. *Expenses:* Tuition, state resident: full-time $8335; part-time $521 per credit hour. Tuition, nonresident: full-time $15,670; part-time $979 per credit hour. *Required fees:* $50; $25 per semester. *Financial support:* In 2013–14, 12 research assistantships with full tuition reimbursements (averaging $3,480 per year) were awarded; tuition waivers (partial) and unspecified assistantships also available. *Faculty research:* Early literacy, professional development in reading, reading recovery, dual language, induction programs. *Total annual research expenditures:* $6.2 million. *Unit head:* Dr. Clifford T. Bennett, Chairperson, 216-523-7105, Fax: 216-687-5379, E-mail: c.t.bennett@csuohio.edu. *Application contact:* Deborah L. Brown, Interim Assistant Director, Graduate Admissions, 216-523-7572, E-mail: d.l.brown@csuohio.edu.
Website: http://www.csuohio.edu/cehs/departments/TE/te_dept.html.

College of Charleston, Graduate School, School of Education, Health, and Human Performance, Department of Foundations, Secondary, and Special Education, Program in Special Education, Charleston, SC 29424-0001. Offers MAT. Part-time and evening/weekend programs available. *Entrance requirements:* For master's, GRE, minimum GPA of 2.5, 2 letters of recommendation. Additional exam requirements/recommendations for international students: Required—TOEFL (minimum score 81 iBT). Electronic applications accepted.

The College of New Jersey, Graduate Studies, School of Education, Department of Special Education, Language and Literacy, Program in Special Education, Ewing, NJ 08628. Offers M Ed, MAT. *Accreditation:* NCATE. Part-time programs available. *Degree requirements:* For master's, comprehensive exam. *Entrance requirements:* For master's, GRE General Test, minimum GPA of 3.0 in field or 2.75 overall. Additional exam requirements/recommendations for international students: Required—TOEFL. Electronic applications accepted.

The College of New Jersey, Graduate Studies, School of Education, Department of Special Education, Language and Literacy, Program in Special Education with Learning Disabilities, Ewing, NJ 08628. Offers Certificate. *Accreditation:* NCATE. Part-time programs available. *Entrance requirements:* Additional exam requirements/recommendations for international students: Required—TOEFL. Electronic applications accepted.

The College of New Rochelle, Graduate School, Division of Education, Program in Special Education, New Rochelle, NY 10805-2308. Offers MS Ed. Part-time programs available. *Degree requirements:* For master's, practicum. *Entrance requirements:* For master's, interview, minimum GPA of 3.0 in field, 2.7 overall. *Expenses: Tuition:* Part-time $894 per credit. *Required fees:* $300 per semester. One-time fee: $200. Tuition and fees vary according to course load.

College of Saint Elizabeth, Department of Educational Leadership, Morristown, NJ 07960-6989. Offers accelerated certification for teaching (Certificate); assistive technology (Certificate); educational leadership (MA, Ed D); special education (MA). Part-time programs available. *Faculty:* 5 full-time (0 women), 21 part-time/adjunct (9 women). *Students:* 67 full-time (44 women), 146 part-time (117 women); includes 52 minority (36 Black or African American, non-Hispanic/Latino; 2 Asian, non-Hispanic/Latino; 12 Hispanic/Latino; 1 Native Hawaiian or other Pacific Islander, non-Hispanic/Latino; 1 Two or more races, non-Hispanic/Latino), 1 international. Average age 38. In 2013, 55 master's, 14 doctorates, 42 other advanced degrees awarded. *Degree requirements:* For master's, thesis or alternative; for doctorate, thesis/dissertation. *Entrance requirements:* For master's, personal written statement, interview, minimum undergraduate GPA of 3.0; for doctorate, master's degree. Additional exam requirements/recommendations for international students: Required—TOEFL. *Application deadline:* For fall admission, 6/30 priority date for domestic students; for spring admission, 11/30 for domestic students. Applications are processed on a rolling basis. Application fee: $35. Electronic applications accepted. *Expenses: Tuition:* Full-time $19,152; part-time $1064 per credit. *Financial support:* Career-related internships or fieldwork, tuition waivers (partial), and unspecified assistantships available. Support available to part-time students. Financial award application deadline: 3/15; financial award applicants required to submit FAFSA. *Faculty research:* Developmental stages for teaching and human services professionals, effectiveness of humanities core curriculum. *Unit head:* Dr. Joseph Ciccone, Associate Professor/Course of Study Coordinator, 973-290-4383, Fax: 973-290-4389, E-mail: jciccone@cse.edu. *Application contact:* Deborah S. Cobo, Associate Director for Graduate Admissions, 973-290-4194, Fax: 973-290-4710, E-mail: dscobo@cse.edu.
Website: http://www.cse.edu/academics/catalog/academic-programs/education.dot?tabID=tabMinor&divID=catalogMinor#maeducation.

College of St. Joseph, Graduate Programs, Division of Education, Program in Special Education, Rutland, VT 05701-3899. Offers M Ed. Part-time and evening/weekend programs available. *Degree requirements:* For master's, comprehensive exam. *Entrance requirements:* For master's, PRAXIS I (for initial licensure), official college transcripts; 2 letters of reference; minimum GPA of 3.0 (initial licensure) or 2.7 (nonlicensure); interview. Additional exam requirements/recommendations for international students: Required—TOEFL (minimum score 550 paper-based). Electronic applications accepted. *Faculty research:* Co-teaching, Response to Intervention (RTI).

The College of Saint Rose, Graduate Studies, School of Education, Department of Special Education and Inclusive Education, Albany, NY 12203-1419. Offers birth-grade 2 special education (MS Ed); grades 1-6 special education (MS Ed); grades 1-6 special education and childhood education (MS Ed); grades 7-12 adolescence education and special education (MS Ed); grades 7-12 special education (MS Ed); professional special education (MS Ed). *Accreditation:* NCATE. Part-time and evening/weekend programs available. *Degree requirements:* For master's, comprehensive exam (for some programs), thesis or alternative, research project. *Entrance requirements:* For master's, minimum undergraduate GPA of 3.0. Additional exam requirements/recommendations for international students: Required—TOEFL (minimum score 550 paper-based). Electronic applications accepted.

College of Staten Island of the City University of New York, Graduate Programs, Program in Autism Spectrum Disorder, Staten Island, NY 10314-6600. Offers Advanced Certificate. *Faculty:* 1 (woman) full-time. *Students:* 5 part-time (all women). Average age 27. 8 applicants, 63% accepted, 5 enrolled. *Degree requirements:* For Advanced Certificate, 12 credits. *Entrance requirements:* Additional exam requirements/recommendations for international students: Required—TOEFL (minimum score 550 paper-based; 79 iBT), IELTS (minimum score 6.5). *Application deadline:* For fall admission, 4/1 priority date for domestic and international students; for spring admission, 11/19 priority date for domestic students, 11/9 priority date for international students. Applications are processed on a rolling basis. Application fee: $125. Electronic applications accepted. *Expenses:* Tuition, state resident: full-time $9240; part-time $385 per credit hour. Tuition, nonresident: full-time $17,040; part-time $710 per credit hour. *Required fees:* $428; $128 per term. *Financial support:* Federal Work-Study available. Support available to part-time students. Financial award applicants required to submit FAFSA. *Unit head:* Dr. Kristen Gillespie, Graduate Program Coordinator, 718-982-4121, Fax: 718-982-4114, E-mail: kristen.gillespie@csi.cuny.edu. *Application contact:* Sasha Spence, Assistant Director for Graduate Recruitment and Admissions, 718-982-2019, Fax: 718-982-2500, E-mail: sasha.spence@csi.cuny.edu.

College of Staten Island of the City University of New York, Graduate Programs, School of Education, Program in Special Education, Staten Island, NY 10314-6600. Offers MS Ed. Part-time and evening/weekend programs available. *Faculty:* 5 full-time (all women), 10 part-time/adjunct (6 women). *Students:* 18 full-time, 194 part-time. Average age 28. 104 applicants, 71% accepted, 53 enrolled. In 2013, 89 master's awarded. *Degree requirements:* For master's, 2 foreign languages, thesis, fieldwork. *Entrance requirements:* For master's, baaccalaureate degree in liberal arts and science major or 36 approved credits in liberal arts and sciences concentration, one year of college-level foreign language, minimum overall GPA of 3.0, two letters of recommendation, one- or two-page personal statement. Additional exam requirements/recommendations for international students: Required—TOEFL (minimum score 550 paper-based; 79 iBT), IELTS (minimum score 6.5). *Application deadline:* For fall admission, 4/25 for domestic and international students; for spring admission, 11/15 for domestic and international students. Applications are processed on a rolling basis. Application fee: $125. Electronic applications accepted. *Expenses:* Tuition, state resident: full-time $9240; part-time $385 per credit hour. Tuition, nonresident: full-time $17,040; part-time $710 per credit hour. *Required fees:* $428; $128 per term. *Financial support:* In 2013–14, 3 students received support. Career-related internships or fieldwork, Federal Work-Study, and scholarships/grants available. Support available to part-time students. Financial award applicants required to submit FAFSA. *Unit head:* Dr. Nelly Tournaki, Graduate Program Coordinator, 718-982-3728, Fax: 718-982-3743, E-mail: nelly.tournaki@csi.cuny.edu. *Application contact:* Sasha Spence, Assistant Director for Graduate Admissions, 718-982-2019, Fax: 718-982-2500, E-mail: sasha.spence@.csi.cuny.edu.
Website: http://csivc.csi.cuny.edu/education/files/.

The College of William and Mary, School of Education, Program in Curriculum and Instruction, Williamsburg, VA 23187-8795. Offers elementary education (MA Ed); gifted education (MA Ed); literacy leadership (MA Ed); math specialist (MA Ed); secondary education (MA Ed), including English education, mathematics education, modern foreign languages education, science education, social studies education; special education (MA Ed), including collaborating master educator, general curriculum. *Accreditation:* NCATE. Part-time programs available. *Faculty:* 15 full-time (10 women), 44 part-time/adjunct (38 women). *Students:* 66 full-time (55 women), 27 part-time (26 women); includes 17 minority (4 Black or African American, non-Hispanic/Latino; 1 American Indian or Alaska Native, non-Hispanic/Latino; 3 Asian, non-Hispanic/Latino; 5 Hispanic/Latino; 4 Two or more races, non-Hispanic/Latino). Average age 28. 179 applicants, 72% accepted, 92 enrolled. In 2013, 76 master's awarded. *Degree requirements:* For master's, project. *Entrance requirements:* For master's, GRE or MAT, minimum GPA of 2.5. Additional exam requirements/recommendations for international students: Required—TOEFL, IELTS. *Application deadline:* For fall admission, 1/15 for domestic and international students; for spring admission, 10/1 for domestic and international students. Application fee: $50. Electronic applications accepted. *Expenses:* Tuition, state resident: full-time $7120; part-time $405 per credit hour. Tuition, nonresident: full-time $21,639; part-time $1050 per credit hour. *Required fees:* $4764. *Financial support:* In 2013–14, 49 students received support, including 6 research assistantships with full and partial tuition reimbursements available (averaging $8,269 per year); career-related internships or fieldwork, Federal Work-Study, institutionally sponsored loans, scholarships/grants, and unspecified assistantships also available. Financial award application deadline: 1/15; financial award applicants required to submit FAFSA. *Faculty research:* National Council of Teachers of Mathematics standards, counseling, self-concept and self-esteem, special education, curriculum development. *Unit head:* Dr. Mark Hofer, Area Coordinator, 757-221-1713, E-mail: mjhofe@wm.edu. *Application contact:* Dorothy Smith Osborne, Assistant Dean for Academic Programs and Student Services, 757-221-2317, Fax: 757-221-2293, E-mail: dsosbo@wm.edu.
Website: http://education.wm.edu.

Colorado Christian University, Program in Curriculum and Instruction, Lakewood, CO 80226. Offers corporate education (MACI); early childhood educator (MACI); elementary educator (MACI); instructional technology (MACI); master educator (MACI); online course developer (MACI); online teaching and learning (MACI); special education generalist (MACI). Part-time and evening/weekend programs available. *Degree requirements:* For master's, thesis optional, practicum. *Entrance requirements:* For

master's, interviews, letters of recommendation. Additional exam requirements/ recommendations for international students: Required—TOEFL. Electronic applications accepted. *Expenses:* Contact institution.

Colorado State University–Pueblo, College of Education, Engineering and Professional Studies, Education Program, Pueblo, CO 81001-4901. Offers art education (M Ed); foreign language education (M Ed); health and physical education (M Ed); instructional technology (M Ed); linguistically diverse education (M Ed); music education (M Ed); special education (M Ed). *Accreditation:* Teacher Education Accreditation Council. Part-time programs available. *Degree requirements:* For master's, portfolio. *Entrance requirements:* For master's, 3 recommendations, teaching license. Additional exam requirements/recommendations for international students: Required—TOEFL (minimum score 500 paper-based). Electronic applications accepted. *Faculty research:* Portfolio assessment, math education, science education.

Columbia International University, Columbia Graduate School, Columbia, SC 29230-3122. Offers Bible teaching (MABT); Christian higher education leadership (Ed D); Christian school educational leadership (Ed D); counseling (MACN); curriculum and instruction (M Ed), including Christian school guidance, English as a second language, learning disabilities, school technology; early childhood and elementary education (MAT); educational administration (M Ed); teaching English as a foreign language (Certificate); teaching English as a foreign language and intercultural studies (MATF). Part-time and evening/weekend programs available. *Degree requirements:* For master's, internships, professional project. *Entrance requirements:* For master's, Minnesota Multiphasic Personality Inventory, MAT, minimum GPA of 2.7. Additional exam requirements/recommendations for international students: Required—TOEFL. Electronic applications accepted.

Columbus State University, Graduate Studies, College of Education and Health Professions, Department of Teacher Education, Columbus, GA 31907-5645. Offers accomplished teaching (M Ed); early childhood education (M Ed, MAT, Ed S); middle grades education (M Ed, MAT, Ed S); school library media (M Ed, MAT); secondary education (M Ed, MAT, Ed S), including English/language arts (M Ed, Ed S), general science (M Ed), mathematics (M Ed, Ed S), science (Ed S), social science (M Ed, Ed S); special education (M Ed, MAT, Ed S), including general curriculum (M Ed, MAT); teacher leadership (M Ed). *Accreditation:* NCATE. Part-time and evening/weekend programs available. Postbaccalaureate distance learning degree programs offered (minimal on-campus study). *Faculty:* 17 full-time (12 women), 31 part-time/adjunct (28 women). *Students:* 59 full-time (48 women), 190 part-time (150 women); includes 85 minority (68 Black or African American, non-Hispanic/Latino; 1 American Indian or Alaska Native, non-Hispanic/Latino; 6 Asian, non-Hispanic/Latino; 4 Hispanic/Latino; 6 Two or more races, non-Hispanic/Latino), 2 international. Average age 34. 132 applicants, 58% accepted, 50 enrolled. In 2013, 86 master's, 26 other advanced degrees awarded. *Degree requirements:* For master's, thesis, exit exam; for Ed S, thesis or alternative. *Entrance requirements:* For master's, GRE General Test, minimum undergraduate GPA of 2.75; for Ed S, GRE General Test, minimum undergraduate GPA of 2.75, graduate 3.0. Additional exam requirements/recommendations for international students: Required—TOEFL (minimum score 550 paper-based; 79 iBT). *Application deadline:* For fall admission, 6/30 for domestic students, 5/1 for international students; for spring admission, 11/1 for domestic and international students; for summer admission, 3/1 for domestic and international students. Applications are processed on a rolling basis. Application fee: $40. Electronic applications accepted. *Expenses:* Tuition, state resident: full-time $4572; part-time $382 per credit hour. Tuition, nonresident: full-time $18,292; part-time $1526 per credit hour. *Required fees:* $1800; $196 per credit hour. Tuition and fees vary according to campus/location and program. *Financial support:* In 2013–14, 173 students received support, including 12 research assistantships with partial tuition reimbursements available (averaging $3,000 per year); career-related internships or fieldwork, Federal Work-Study, institutionally sponsored loans, scholarships/grants, tuition waivers (partial), and unspecified assistantships also available. Support available to part-time students. Financial award application deadline: 5/1; financial award applicants required to submit FAFSA. *Unit head:* Dr. Deirdre Greer, Department Chair, 706-507-8034, Fax: 706-568-3134, E-mail: greer_deirdre@columbusstate.edu. *Application contact:* Kristin Williams, Director of International and Graduate Recruitment, 706-507-8848, Fax: 706-568-5091, E-mail: williams_kristin@columbusstate.edu.
Website: http://te.columbusstate.edu/.

Concordia College–New York, Program in Childhood Special Education, Bronxville, NY 10708-1998. Offers MS Ed.

Concordia University, College of Education, Portland, OR 97211-6099. Offers career and technical education (M Ed); curriculum and instruction (M Ed), including adolescent literacy, career and technical education, e-learning/technology education, early childhood education, English for speakers of other languages, English language development, environmental education, mathematics, methods and curriculum, reading, science, teacher leadership, the inclusive classroom; early childhood (MAT); education leadership (Ed D); educational administration (M Ed); elementary education (MAT); secondary education (MAT); special education (M Ed); teacher leadership (Ed D). Part-time programs available. Postbaccalaureate distance learning degree programs offered (no on-campus study). *Degree requirements:* For master's, comprehensive exam, work samples/portfolio. *Entrance requirements:* For master's, California Basic Educational Skills Test or PRAXIS I, minimum undergraduate GPA of 2.8, graduate 3.0; 2 letters of recommendation. Additional exam requirements/recommendations for international students: Required—TOEFL (minimum score 525 paper-based). Electronic applications accepted. *Faculty research:* Learner-centered classroom, brain-based learning, future of online learning.

Concordia University, St. Paul, College of Education and Science, St. Paul, MN 55104-5494. Offers curriculum and instruction (MA Ed), including K-12 reading; differentiated instruction (MA Ed); early childhood education (MA Ed); educational leadership (MA Ed); educational technology (MA Ed); exercise science (MA); family life education (MA); K-12 principal licensure (Ed S); K-12 reading (Certificate); special education (MA Ed, Certificate), including autism spectrum disorder (MA Ed), emotional and behavioral disorders (MA Ed), learning disabilities (MA Ed); sports management (MA); superintendent (Ed S). *Accreditation:* NCATE. Part-time and evening/weekend programs available. Postbaccalaureate distance learning degree programs offered (minimal on-campus study). *Faculty:* 12 full-time (7 women), 92 part-time/adjunct (49 women). *Students:* 915 full-time (659 women), 64 part-time (53 women); includes 99 minority (47 Black or African American, non-Hispanic/Latino; 5 American Indian or Alaska Native, non-Hispanic/Latino; 18 Asian, non-Hispanic/Latino; 15 Hispanic/Latino; 2 Native Hawaiian or other Pacific Islander, non-Hispanic/Latino; 12 Two or more races, non-Hispanic/Latino), 24 international. Average age 34. 664 applicants, 67% accepted, 411 enrolled. In 2013, 275 master's, 69 other advanced degrees awarded. *Degree requirements:* For master's, thesis (for some programs). *Entrance requirements:* For master's, official transcripts from regionally-accredited institution stating the conferral of a bachelor's degree with minimum cumulative GPA of 3.0; personal statement; professional resume; practitioner in field through work or volunteerism; resume. Additional exam requirements/recommendations for international students: Recommended—TOEFL (minimum score 547 paper-based; 78 iBT), IELTS (minimum score 6). *Application deadline:* For fall admission, 8/1 for domestic and international students; for spring admission, 12/1 for domestic and international students; for summer admission, 5/1 for domestic and international students. Applications are processed on a rolling basis. Application fee: $50. Electronic applications accepted. *Expenses: Tuition:* Full-time $6200; part-time $425 per credit. Tuition and fees vary according to degree level and program. *Financial support:* Applicants required to submit FAFSA. *Unit head:* Dr. Donald Helmstetter, Dean, 651-641-8227, Fax: 651-641-8807, E-mail: helmstetter@csp.edu. *Application contact:* Kimberly Craig, Director of Graduate and Cohort Admission, 651-603-6223, Fax: 651-603-6320, E-mail: craig@csp.edu.

Concordia University Wisconsin, Graduate Programs, Department of Education, Mequon, WI 53097-2402. Offers art education (MS Ed); curriculum and instruction (MS Ed); early childhood (MS Ed); educational administration (MS Ed); environmental education (MS Ed); family studies (MS Ed); reading (MS Ed); school counseling (MS Ed); special education (MS Ed). Part-time and evening/weekend programs available. Postbaccalaureate distance learning degree programs offered (minimal on-campus study). *Degree requirements:* For master's, comprehensive exam, thesis or alternative. *Entrance requirements:* For master's, minimum GPA of 3.0, teaching license. Additional exam requirements/recommendations for international students: Required—TOEFL. *Faculty research:* Motivation, developmental learning, learning styles.

Concord University, Graduate Studies, Athens, WV 24712-1000. Offers educational leadership and supervision (M Ed); geography (M Ed); health promotion (MA); reading specialist (M Ed); special education (M Ed); teaching (MAT). Part-time and evening/weekend programs available. Postbaccalaureate distance learning degree programs offered (no on-campus study). *Degree requirements:* For master's, thesis (for some programs). *Entrance requirements:* For master's, GRE or MAT, baccalaureate degree with minimum GPA of 2.5 from regionally-accredited institution; teaching license; 2 letters of recommendation; completed disposition assessment form. Electronic applications accepted.

Converse College, School of Education and Graduate Studies, Program in Special Education, Spartanburg, SC 29302-0006. Offers intellectual disabilities (MAT); learning disabilities (MAT); special education (M Ed). Part-time programs available. *Degree requirements:* For master's, capstone paper. *Entrance requirements:* For master's, NTE or PRAXIS II (M Ed), minimum GPA of 2.75, 2 recommendations. Electronic applications accepted.

Coppin State University, Division of Graduate Studies, Division of Education, Department of Special Education, Baltimore, MD 21216-3698. Offers M Ed. Part-time and evening/weekend programs available. *Degree requirements:* For master's, exit portfolio. *Entrance requirements:* For master's, PRAXIS I, minimum GPA of 3.0, interview, writing sample, resume, references. *Faculty research:* Survey of colleges and universities in Maryland with programs for the learning disabled.

Creighton University, Graduate School, College of Arts and Sciences, Department of Education, Program in Special Populations in Education, Omaha, NE 68178-0001. Offers MS. Part-time and evening/weekend programs available. *Students:* 2 part-time (both women). Average age 44. *Entrance requirements:* For master's, GRE, 3 letters of recommendation, resume. Additional exam requirements/recommendations for international students: Required—TOEFL (minimum score 550 paper-based; 80 iBT). *Application deadline:* For fall admission, 7/1 priority date for domestic students, 3/1 priority date for international students; for winter admission, 12/1 priority date for domestic students, 7/1 priority date for international students; for spring admission, 4/1 priority date for domestic students, 10/1 priority date for international students. Applications are processed on a rolling basis. Application fee: $50. Electronic applications accepted. *Expenses: Tuition:* Full-time $13,608; part-time $756 per credit hour. *Required fees:* $149 per semester. Tuition and fees vary according to course load, campus/location, program, reciprocity agreements and student's religious affiliation. *Financial support:* Scholarships/grants and tuition waivers (partial) available. Support available to part-time students. Financial award application deadline: 5/1; financial award applicants required to submit FAFSA. *Unit head:* Dr. Sharon Ishii-Jordan, Associate Professor of Education, 402-280-2553, E-mail: sharonishii-jordan@creighton.edu. *Application contact:* Valerie Mattix, Senior Program Coordinator, 402-280-2425, Fax: 402-280-2423, E-mail: valeriemattix@creighton.edu.

Curry College, Graduate Studies, Program in Education, Milton, MA 02186-9984. Offers elementary education (M Ed); foundations (non-license) (M Ed); reading (M Ed, Certificate); special education (M Ed). Part-time and evening/weekend programs available. *Degree requirements:* For master's, project or thesis. *Entrance requirements:* For master's, interview, recommendations, resume, written statement. Additional exam requirements/recommendations for international students: Required—TOEFL (minimum score 550 paper-based; 80 iBT). *Expenses:* Contact institution. *Faculty research:* Classroom trauma, therapeutic writing, inclusionary practices.

Daemen College, Education Department, Amherst, NY 14226-3592. Offers adolescence education (MS); childhood education (MS); childhood special education (MS); childhood special-alternative certification (MS); early childhood special-alternative certification (MS). Part-time programs available. *Degree requirements:* For master's, thesis optional, research thesis in lieu of comprehensive exam; completion of degree within 5 years. *Entrance requirements:* For master's, 2 letters of recommendation (professional and character), proof of initial certificate of license for professional programs, resume. Additional exam requirements/recommendations for international students: Required—TOEFL (minimum score 500 paper-based; 63 iBT), IELTS (minimum score 5.5). Electronic applications accepted. *Faculty research:* Transition for students with disabilities, early childhood special education, traumatic brain injury (TBI), reading assessment.

Dallas Baptist University, Dorothy M. Bush College of Education, Program in Special Education, Dallas, TX 75211-9299. Offers M Ed. *Degree requirements:* For master's, professional portfolio; exam or internship. *Expenses: Tuition:* Full-time $13,410; part-time $745 per credit hour. *Required fees:* $300; $150 per semester. Tuition and fees vary according to degree level. *Unit head:* Dr. Mary Beth Sanders, Director, 214-333-5413. *Application contact:* Kit P. Montgomery, Director of Graduate Programs, 214-333-5242, Fax: 214-333-5579, E-mail: graduate@dbu.edu.
Website: http://www3.dbu.edu/graduate/special_education.asp.

Defiance College, Program in Education, Defiance, OH 43512-1610. Offers adolescent and young adult licensure (MA); mild and moderate intervention specialist (MA). Part-time programs available. *Degree requirements:* For master's, thesis (for some programs). *Entrance requirements:* For master's, teaching certificate.

Delaware State University, Graduate Programs, College of Education, Health and Public Policy, Program in Special Education, Dover, DE 19901-2277. Offers MA. Part-time and evening/weekend programs available. *Degree requirements:* For master's, comprehensive exam, thesis optional. *Entrance requirements:* For master's, GRE General Test, minimum GPA of 3.0 in field, 2.75 overall. Additional exam requirements/recommendations for international students: Required—TOEFL (minimum score 550 paper-based). Electronic applications accepted. *Faculty research:* Curriculum and instruction, distributive education.

Delta State University, Graduate Programs, College of Education, Division of Teacher Education, Program in Special Education, Cleveland, MS 38733-0001. Offers M Ed. *Accreditation:* NCATE. Part-time and evening/weekend programs available. *Faculty:* 3 full-time (all women). *Students:* 1 full-time (0 women), 55 part-time (49 women); includes 44 minority (all Black or African American, non-Hispanic/Latino), 1 international. Average age 33. 35 applicants, 100% accepted, 24 enrolled. *Degree requirements:* For master's, thesis optional, practicum. *Application deadline:* For fall admission, 8/1 priority date for domestic students; for spring admission, 12/1 priority date for domestic students. Applications are processed on a rolling basis. Application fee: $0. *Expenses:* Tuition, state resident: full-time $3006; part-time $334 per credit hour. Tuition, nonresident: full-time $3006; part-time $334 per credit hour. *Financial support:* Research assistantships, career-related internships or fieldwork, Federal Work-Study, and institutionally sponsored loans available. Support available to part-time students. Financial award application deadline: 6/1. *Unit head:* Vicki Hartley, Head, 662-846-3000. *Application contact:* Dr. Albert Nylander, Dean of Graduate Studies, 662-846-4875, Fax: 662-846-4313, E-mail: grad-info@deltastate.edu.

DePaul University, College of Education, Chicago, IL 60614. Offers bilingual bicultural education (M Ed, MA); counseling (M Ed, MA), including clinical mental health counseling, college student development, school counseling; curriculum studies (M Ed, MA, Ed D); early childhood education (M Ed, MA, Ed D); educating adults (MA); educational leadership (M Ed, MA, Ed D), including administration and supervision (M Ed, MA), principal preparation (M Ed, MA); elementary education (MA); mathematics education (MA); mathematics for teaching (MS); middle school mathematics education (MS); reading specialist (M Ed, MA); secondary education (M Ed); social and cultural foundations in education (MA); special education (M Ed, MA); world languages education (M Ed, MA). Part-time and evening/weekend programs available. Postbaccalaureate distance learning degree programs offered (no on-campus study). *Faculty:* 61 full-time (35 women), 59 part-time/adjunct (43 women). *Students:* 628 full-time (486 women), 324 part-time (243 women); includes 304 minority (144 Black or African American, non-Hispanic/Latino; 1 American Indian or Alaska Native, non-Hispanic/Latino; 38 Asian, non-Hispanic/Latino; 98 Hispanic/Latino; 23 Two or more races, non-Hispanic/Latino), 24 international. Average age 30. In 2013, 465 master's, 4 doctorates awarded. *Degree requirements:* For doctorate, thesis/dissertation. *Application deadline:* For fall admission, 8/15 for domestic students; for winter admission, 12/1 for domestic students; for spring admission, 3/1 for domestic students. Applications are processed on a rolling basis. Application fee: $40. Electronic applications accepted. Tuition and fees vary according to course level, course load and degree level. *Financial support:* Application deadline: 12/31; applicants required to submit FAFSA. *Unit head:* Dr. Paul Zionts, Dean, 773-325-7581, Fax: 773-325-7713, E-mail: pzionts@depaul.edu. *Application contact:* Farrah Dalal, Assistant Director, 773-325-2465, Fax: 773-325-2270, E-mail: fdalal@depaul.edu.
Website: http://education.depaul.edu.

DeSales University, Graduate Division, Division of Liberal Arts and Social Sciences, Program in Education, Center Valley, PA 18034-9568. Offers early childhood education Pre K-4 (M Ed); instructional technology for K-12 (M Ed); interdisciplinary (M Ed); secondary education (M Ed); special education (M Ed); teaching English to speakers of other languages (M Ed). Part-time and evening/weekend programs available. Postbaccalaureate distance learning degree programs offered (no on-campus study). *Degree requirements:* For master's, thesis project. *Entrance requirements:* Additional exam requirements/recommendations for international students: Required—TOEFL. *Application deadline:* Applications are processed on a rolling basis. Electronic applications accepted. *Expenses: Tuition:* Part-time $790 per credit. *Financial support:* Application deadline: 5/1. *Unit head:* Dr. Judith Rance-Roney, Chair, 610-282-1100 Ext. 1323, E-mail: judith.rance-roney@desales.edu. *Application contact:* Abigail Wernicki, Director of Graduate Admissions, 610-282-1100 Ext. 1768, E-mail: gradadmissions@desales.edu.

Dominican College, Division of Teacher Education, Orangeburg, NY 10962-1210. Offers MS Ed. Part-time and evening/weekend programs available. Postbaccalaureate distance learning degree programs offered (minimal on-campus study). *Faculty:* 4 full-time (2 women), 4 part-time/adjunct (2 women). *Students:* 65 part-time (53 women). In 2013, 22 master's awarded. *Degree requirements:* For master's, comprehensive exam (for some programs). *Entrance requirements:* Additional exam requirements/recommendations for international students: Required—TOEFL. *Application deadline:* Applications are processed on a rolling basis. *Expenses: Tuition:* Part-time $815 per credit. *Required fees:* $180 per semester. *Financial support:* Application deadline: 2/15; applicants required to submit FAFSA. *Unit head:* Dr. Mike Kelly, Director, 845-848-4090, Fax: 845-359-7802, E-mail: mike.kelly@dc.edu. *Application contact:* Joyce Elbe, Director of Admissions, 845-848-7896 Ext. 15, Fax: 845-365-3150, E-mail: admissions@dc.edu.

Dominican University, School of Education, River Forest, IL 60305-1099. Offers curriculum and instruction (MA Ed); early childhood education (MS); education (MAT); educational administration (MA); elementary education (MA Ed); English as a second language (MA Ed); reading (MA Ed); special education (MS). Part-time and evening/weekend programs available. Postbaccalaureate distance learning degree programs offered (no on-campus study). *Faculty:* 19 full-time (14 women), 51 part-time/adjunct (42 women). *Students:* 18 full-time (13 women), 334 part-time (274 women); includes 76 minority (26 Black or African American, non-Hispanic/Latino; 9 Asian, non-Hispanic/Latino; 41 Hispanic/Latino). Average age 32. 119 applicants, 77% accepted, 70 enrolled. In 2013, 246 master's awarded. *Entrance requirements:* For master's, Illinois Test of Basic Skills. Additional exam requirements/recommendations for international students: Required—TOEFL (minimum score 550 paper-based; 79 iBT). *Application deadline:* Applications are processed on a rolling basis. Application fee: $25. *Expenses:* Contact institution. *Financial support:* In 2013–14, 97 students received support. Career-related internships or fieldwork, scholarships/grants, and tuition waivers (partial) available. Support available to part-time students. Financial award application deadline: 8/15; financial award applicants required to submit FAFSA. *Faculty research:* Governance of private education institutions, reading and language arts, inclusion, organizational planning, leadership and vision. *Unit head:* Dr. Colleen Reardon, Dean, 718-524-6643, Fax: 708-524-6665, E-mail: creardon@dom.edu. *Application contact:* Keven Hansen, Coordinator of Recruitment and Admissions, 708-524-6921, Fax: 708-524-6665, E-mail: educate@dom.edu.
Website: http://educate.dom.edu/.

Dominican University of California, School of Education and Counseling Psychology, Education Department, San Rafael, CA 94901-2298. Offers education (MS), including education specialist, interdisciplinary, multiple subject, single subject, special education. Part-time programs available. *Faculty:* 10 full-time (9 women), 22 part-time/adjunct (19 women). *Students:* 94 full-time (78 women), 66 part-time (54 women); includes 21 minority (4 Black or African American, non-Hispanic/Latino; 2 American Indian or Alaska Native, non-Hispanic/Latino; 4 Asian, non-Hispanic/Latino; 9 Hispanic/Latino; 1 Native Hawaiian or other Pacific Islander, non-Hispanic/Latino; 1 Two or more races, non-Hispanic/Latino), 5 international. Average age 34. 123 applicants, 69% accepted, 64 enrolled. *Unit head:* Dr. Nicola Pitchford. *Application contact:* Shana Friedman,

Admissions Counselor, 415-485-3246, Fax: 415-485-3214, E-mail: shana.friedman@dominican.edu.
Website: http://www.dominican.edu/academics/education/department-of-education/teaching-credentials/dual.

Dowling College, Graduate Programs in Education, Oakdale, NY 11769-1999. Offers adolescence education with middle childhood extension (MS); childhood and early childhood education (MS); childhood and gifted education (MS); childhood education (1-6) (MS); computers in education (AC); early childhood education (B-2) (MS); educational administration (Ed D); educational technology leadership (MS); educational technology specialist (AC); gifted education (AC); literacy education (MS, AC), including 5-12 (MS), B-12 (MS); literacy education (MS), including B-6; school building leader (AC); school district business leader (MBA, AC); school district leader (AC); special education (MS), including autism, severe disabilities; sport management (MS). *Accreditation:* NCATE. Part-time and evening/weekend programs available. Postbaccalaureate distance learning degree programs offered (minimal on-campus study). *Faculty:* 44 full-time (24 women), 17 part-time/adjunct (8 women). *Students:* 183 full-time (124 women), 314 part-time (231 women); includes 51 minority (19 Black or African American, non-Hispanic/Latino; 1 American Indian or Alaska Native, non-Hispanic/Latino; 3 Asian, non-Hispanic/Latino; 26 Hispanic/Latino; 2 Native Hawaiian or other Pacific Islander, non-Hispanic/Latino). Average age 32. 174 applicants, 80% accepted, 82 enrolled. In 2013, 198 master's, 33 doctorates, 48 other advanced degrees awarded. *Degree requirements:* For master's and AC, comprehensive exam; for doctorate, thesis/dissertation. *Entrance requirements:* For master's, minimum GPA of 3.0; for doctorate, GRE, master's degree; for AC, teaching certificate. Additional exam requirements/recommendations for international students: Required—TOEFL (minimum score 550 paper-based). *Application deadline:* For fall admission, 9/1 priority date for domestic students; for winter admission, 1/1 priority date for domestic students; for spring admission, 2/1 priority date for domestic students. Applications are processed on a rolling basis. Application fee: $50. Electronic applications accepted. *Expenses: Tuition:* Full-time $22,731; part-time $1029 per credit. *Required fees:* $956; $956. *Financial support:* Career-related internships or fieldwork and Federal Work-Study available. Support available to part-time students. Financial award application deadline: 6/30; financial award applicants required to submit FAFSA. *Faculty research:* Natural readers, Korean styles and learning strategies, mothers of children with disabilities, computers in instruction, cultural background and organizational roadblocks to problem solving. *Unit head:* Dr. Robert Manley, Dean, 631-244-3447, E-mail: manleyr@dowling.edu. *Application contact:* Mary Boullianne, Director of Admissions, 631-244-3274, Fax: 631-244-1059, E-mail: boulliam@dowling.edu.

Drexel University, Goodwin College of Professional Studies, School of Education, Philadelphia, PA 19104-2875. Offers educational administration (MS); educational improvement and transformation (MS); educational leadership and management (Ed D); educational leadership development and learning technologies (PhD); global and international education (MS); higher education (MS); human resources development (MS); learning technologies (MS); mathematics, learning and teaching (MS); special education (MS); teaching, learning and curriculum (MS). Part-time and evening/weekend programs available. Postbaccalaureate distance learning degree programs offered (no on-campus study). *Degree requirements:* For doctorate, thesis/dissertation. *Entrance requirements:* For doctorate, GRE or GMAT. Additional exam requirements/recommendations for international students: Required—TOEFL, IELTS. Electronic applications accepted. Application fee is waived when completed online. *Expenses:* Contact institution. *Faculty research:* Leadership development, mathematics education, literacy, autism, educational technology.

Drury University, Graduate Programs in Education, Springfield, MO 65802. Offers elementary education (M Ed); gifted education (M Ed); human services (M Ed); instructional mathematics K-8 (M Ed); instructional technology (M Ed); middle school teaching (M Ed); secondary education (M Ed); special education (M Ed); special reading (M Ed). *Accreditation:* NCATE. Part-time and evening/weekend programs available. *Degree requirements:* For master's, thesis. *Entrance requirements:* For master's, GRE or MAT, minimum GPA of 2.75. Additional exam requirements/recommendations for international students: Required—TOEFL. Electronic applications accepted. *Faculty research:* Cultural enrichment, research skills, parental involvement relating to reading skills, reading strategies for mainstreaming children.

Duquesne University, School of Education, Department of Counseling, Psychology, and Special Education, Program in Special Education, Pittsburgh, PA 15282-0001. Offers cognitive, behavior, physical/health disabilities (MS Ed); community and special education support (MS Ed). Part-time and evening/weekend programs available. *Faculty:* 7 full-time (6 women). *Students:* 14 full-time (12 women), 1 (woman) part-time; includes 1 minority (Black or African American, non-Hispanic/Latino), 2 international. Average age 26. 23 applicants, 30% accepted, 5 enrolled. In 2013, 16 master's awarded. *Degree requirements:* For master's, thesis optional. *Entrance requirements:* For master's, bachelor's degree. Additional exam requirements/recommendations for international students: Required—TOEFL (minimum score 550 paper-based), IELTS (minimum score 7). *Application deadline:* For fall admission, 9/1 for domestic students; for spring admission, 1/1 for domestic students. Applications are processed on a rolling basis. Application fee: $0. Electronic applications accepted. Application fee is waived when completed online. *Expenses: Tuition:* Full-time $18,162; part-time $1009 per credit. *Required fees:* $1728; $96 per credit. Tuition and fees vary according to program. *Financial support:* In 2013–14, 1 research assistantship was awarded. Support available to part-time students. *Unit head:* Dr. Morgan Chitiyo, Associate Professor, 412-396-4036, Fax: 412-396-1340, E-mail: chitiyom@duq.edu. *Application contact:* Michael Dolinger, Director of Student and Academic Services, 412-396-6647, Fax: 412-396-5585, E-mail: dolingerm@duq.edu.
Website: http://www.duq.edu/academics/schools/education/graduate-programs-education/msed-special-education.

D'Youville College, Department of Education, Buffalo, NY 14201-1084. Offers educational leadership (Ed D); elementary education (MS Ed, Teaching Certificate); secondary education (MS Ed, Teaching Certificate); special education (MS Ed). Part-time and evening/weekend programs available. *Students:* 96 full-time (68 women), 91 part-time (60 women); includes 14 minority (9 Black or African American, non-Hispanic/Latino; 1 American Indian or Alaska Native, non-Hispanic/Latino; 4 Hispanic/Latino), 90 international. Average age 32. 383 applicants, 48% accepted, 104 enrolled. In 2013, 128 master's awarded. *Degree requirements:* For master's, one foreign language, comprehensive exam, project or thesis. *Entrance requirements:* For master's, GRE (if GPA less than 2.75), minimum GPA of 3.0. Additional exam requirements/recommendations for international students: Required—TOEFL (minimum score 500 paper-based). *Application deadline:* For fall admission, 5/1 priority date for international students; for spring admission, 9/1 priority date for international students. Applications are processed on a rolling basis. Application fee: $25. Electronic applications accepted. *Financial support:* Career-related internships or fieldwork, Federal Work-Study, institutionally sponsored loans, scholarships/grants, tuition waivers (full and partial), and unspecified assistantships available. Support available to part-time students. Financial award application deadline: 3/1; financial award applicants required to submit FAFSA. *Faculty research:* Developmental disabilities, multiculturalism, early childhood

education. *Unit head:* Dr. Hilary Lochte, Chair, 716-829-8110, Fax: 716-829-7660. *Application contact:* Mark Pavone, Graduate Admissions Director, 716-829-8400, Fax: 716-829-7900, E-mail: graduateadmissions@dyc.edu.

East Carolina University, Graduate School, College of Education, Department of Business and Information Technologies Education, Greenville, NC 27858-4353. Offers business education (MA Ed); elementary education (MAT); English education (MAT); family and consumer science (MAT); health education (MAT); Hispanic studies (MAT); history education (MAT); marketing education (MA Ed); middle grades education (MAT); music education (MAT); physical education (MAT); science education (MAT); special education (MAT), including general curriculum; vocation education (MS). *Accreditation:* NCATE. Part-time and evening/weekend programs available. Postbaccalaureate distance learning degree programs offered (no on-campus study). *Degree requirements:* For master's, comprehensive exam, thesis optional. *Entrance requirements:* For master's, GRE or MAT, minimum GPA of 2.5, bachelor's degree in related field, teaching license (MA Ed). Additional exam requirements/recommendations for international students: Required—TOEFL. *Expenses:* Tuition, state resident: full-time $4223. Tuition, nonresident: full-time $16,540. *Required fees:* $2184.

East Carolina University, Graduate School, College of Education, Department of Curriculum and Instruction, Greenville, NC 27858-4353. Offers assistive technology (Certificate); autism (Certificate); deaf/blindness (Certificate); elementary education (MA Ed); English education (MA Ed); history (MA Ed); middle grade education (MA Ed); reading education (MA Ed); special education (MA Ed); teaching (MAT). Part-time programs available. Postbaccalaureate distance learning degree programs offered. *Degree requirements:* For master's, comprehensive exam, thesis optional. *Entrance requirements:* For master's, GRE General Test or MAT, interview, bachelor's degree in related field, minimum GPA of 2.5, teaching license. Additional exam requirements/ recommendations for international students: Required—TOEFL. *Expenses:* Tuition, state resident: full-time $4223. Tuition, nonresident: full-time $16,540. *Required fees:* $2184.

Eastern Illinois University, Graduate School, College of Education and Professional Studies, Department of Special Education, Charleston, IL 61920-3099. Offers MS Ed. *Accreditation:* NCATE. Part-time programs available. *Degree requirements:* For master's, comprehensive exam. *Entrance requirements:* For master's, GRE General Test or MAT. *Expenses: Tuition, area resident:* Part-time $283 per credit hour. Tuition, state resident: part-time $283 per credit hour. Tuition, nonresident: part-time $679 per credit hour.

Eastern Kentucky University, The Graduate School, College of Education, Department of Special Education, Richmond, KY 40475-3102. Offers communication disorders (MA Ed). *Accreditation:* NCATE. Part-time programs available. *Degree requirements:* For master's, comprehensive exam. *Entrance requirements:* For master's, GRE General Test, MAT, minimum GPA of 2.5. *Faculty research:* Personnel needs in communication disorders, education needs of people who stutter, attention of special ed teacher.

Eastern Michigan University, Graduate School, College of Education, Department of Special Education, Program in Autism Spectrum Disorders, Ypsilanti, MI 48197. Offers MA. *Students:* 7 full-time (5 women), 23 part-time (22 women); includes 2 minority (both Black or African American, non-Hispanic/Latino), 1 international. Average age 31. 12 applicants, 67% accepted, 4 enrolled. In 2013, 8 master's awarded. Application fee: $35. *Expenses:* Tuition, state resident: full-time $12,300; part-time $466 per credit hour. Tuition, nonresident: full-time $23,159; part-time $918 per credit hour. *Required fees:* $71 per credit hour. $46 per semester. One-time fee: $100. Tuition and fees vary according to course level and degree level. *Unit head:* Dr. Janet Fisher, Interim Department Head, 734-487-2716, Fax: 734-487-2473, E-mail: jfisher3@emich.edu. *Application contact:* Dr. Derrick Fries, Program Coordinator, 734-487-3300, Fax: 734-487-2473, E-mail: dfries@emich.edu.

Eastern Michigan University, Graduate School, College of Education, Department of Special Education, Program in Cognitive Impairment, Ypsilanti, MI 48197. Offers cognitive impairment (MA); mentally impaired (MA). *Students:* 22 full-time (19 women), 35 part-time (23 women); includes 10 minority (5 Black or African American, non-Hispanic/Latino; 3 Asian, non-Hispanic/Latino; 2 Hispanic/Latino). Average age 34. 14 applicants, 86% accepted, 6 enrolled. In 2013, 9 master's awarded. *Expenses:* Tuition, state resident: full-time $12,300; part-time $466 per credit hour. Tuition, nonresident: full-time $23,159; part-time $918 per credit hour. *Required fees:* $71 per credit hour. $46 per semester. One-time fee: $100. Tuition and fees vary according to course level and degree level. *Unit head:* Dr. Janet Fisher, Interim Department Head, 734-487-2716, Fax: 734-487-2473, E-mail: jfisher3@emich.edu. *Application contact:* Dr. Ann Orr, Advisor, 734-487-3300, Fax: 734-487-2473, E-mail: aorr@emich.edu.

Eastern Michigan University, Graduate School, College of Education, Department of Special Education, Program in Emotional Impairment, Ypsilanti, MI 48197. Offers MA. *Students:* 3 full-time (1 woman), 21 part-time (19 women); includes 7 minority (6 Black or African American, non-Hispanic/Latino; 1 Asian, non-Hispanic/Latino). Average age 31. 9 applicants, 89% accepted, 3 enrolled. In 2013, 7 master's awarded. Application fee: $35. *Expenses:* Tuition, state resident: full-time $12,300; part-time $466 per credit hour. Tuition, nonresident: full-time $23,159; part-time $918 per credit hour. *Required fees:* $71 per credit hour. $46 per semester. One-time fee: $100. Tuition and fees vary according to course level and degree level. *Unit head:* Dr. Janet Fisher, Interim Department Head, 734-487-2716, Fax: 734-487-2473, E-mail: jfisher3@emich.edu. *Application contact:* Dr. John Palladino, Coordinator, 734-487-3300, Fax: 734-487-2473, E-mail: jpalladi@emich.edu.

Eastern Michigan University, Graduate School, College of Education, Department of Special Education, Program in Hearing Impairment, Ypsilanti, MI 48197. Offers MA. *Students:* 2 full-time (both women); both minorities (both Black or African American, non-Hispanic/Latino). Average age 27. Application fee: $35. *Expenses:* Tuition, state resident: full-time $12,300; part-time $466 per credit hour. Tuition, nonresident: full-time $23,159; part-time $918 per credit hour. *Required fees:* $71 per credit hour. $46 per semester. One-time fee: $100. Tuition and fees vary according to course level and degree level. *Unit head:* Dr. Janet Fisher, Interim Department Head, 734-487-3300, Fax: 734-487-2473, E-mail: psmith16@emich.edu. *Application contact:* Linda Polter, Coordinator, 734-487-3300, Fax: 734-487-2473, E-mail: lpolter1@emich.edu.

Eastern Michigan University, Graduate School, College of Education, Department of Special Education, Program in Learning Disabilities, Ypsilanti, MI 48197. Offers MA. *Students:* 3 full-time (2 women), 32 part-time (28 women); includes 5 minority (3 Black or African American, non-Hispanic/Latino; 1 Hispanic/Latino; 1 Two or more races, non-Hispanic/Latino), 2 international. Average age 35. 15 applicants, 67% accepted, 3 enrolled. In 2013, 6 master's awarded. Application fee: $35. *Expenses:* Tuition, state resident: full-time $12,300; part-time $466 per credit hour. Tuition, nonresident: full-time $23,159; part-time $918 per credit hour. *Required fees:* $71 per credit hour. $46 per semester. One-time fee: $100. Tuition and fees vary according to course level and degree level. *Unit head:* Dr. Janet Fisher, Interim Department Head, 734-487-2716, Fax: 734-487-2473, E-mail: jfisher3@emich.edu. *Application contact:* Dr. Loreena Parks, Associate Professor, 734-487-3300, Fax: 734-487-2473, E-mail: lparks1@emich.edu.

Eastern Michigan University, Graduate School, College of Education, Department of Special Education, Program in Physical and Other Health Impairment, Ypsilanti, MI 48197. Offers MA. *Students:* 3 part-time (all women). Average age 27. 1 applicant, 100% accepted, 1 enrolled. In 2013, 1 master's awarded. Application fee: $35. *Expenses:* Tuition, state resident: full-time $12,300; part-time $466 per credit hour. Tuition, nonresident: full-time $23,159; part-time $918 per credit hour. *Required fees:* $71 per credit hour. $46 per semester. One-time fee: $100. Tuition and fees vary according to course level and degree level. *Unit head:* Dr. Janet Fisher, Interim Department Head, 734-487-2716, Fax: 734-487-2473, E-mail: jfisher3@emich.edu. *Application contact:* Dr. Jacquelyn McGinnis, Coordinator, 734-487-3300, Fax: 734-487-2473, E-mail: jmcginnis@emich.edu.

Eastern Michigan University, Graduate School, College of Education, Department of Special Education, Program in Visual Impairment, Ypsilanti, MI 48197. Offers MA. In 2013, 1 master's awarded. Application fee: $35. *Expenses:* Tuition, state resident: full-time $12,300; part-time $466 per credit hour. Tuition, nonresident: full-time $23,159; part-time $918 per credit hour. *Required fees:* $71 per credit hour. $46 per semester. One-time fee: $100. Tuition and fees vary according to course level and degree level. *Unit head:* Dr. Janet Fisher, Interim Department Head, 734-487-2716, Fax: 734-487-2473, E-mail: jfisher3@emich.edu. *Application contact:* Dr. Alicia Li, Advisor, 734-487-3300, Fax: 734-487-2473, E-mail: tli@emich.edu.

Eastern Michigan University, Graduate School, College of Education, Department of Special Education, Programs in Special Education, Ypsilanti, MI 48197. Offers administration and supervision (SPA); curriculum development (SPA); special education (MA). *Accreditation:* NCATE. Part-time and evening/weekend programs available. Postbaccalaureate distance learning degree programs offered (minimal on-campus study). *Students:* 1 (woman) full-time, 41 part-time (34 women); includes 5 minority (4 Black or African American, non-Hispanic/Latino; 1 Hispanic/Latino). Average age 42. 20 applicants, 75% accepted, 6 enrolled. In 2013, 5 master's, 6 other advanced degrees awarded. *Entrance requirements:* For master's, GRE General Test. Additional exam requirements/recommendations for international students: Required—TOEFL. *Application deadline:* Applications are processed on a rolling basis. Application fee: $35. *Expenses:* Tuition, state resident: full-time $12,300; part-time $466 per credit hour. Tuition, nonresident: full-time $23,159; part-time $918 per credit hour. *Required fees:* $71 per credit hour. $46 per semester. One-time fee: $100. Tuition and fees vary according to course level and degree level. *Financial support:* Fellowships, research assistantships with full tuition reimbursements, teaching assistantships with full tuition reimbursements, career-related internships or fieldwork, Federal Work-Study, institutionally sponsored loans, scholarships/grants, tuition waivers (partial), and unspecified assistantships available. Support available to part-time students. Financial award applicants required to submit FAFSA. *Unit head:* Dr. Janet Fisher, Interim Department Head, 734-487-2716, Fax: 734-487-2473, E-mail: jfisher3@emich.edu. *Application contact:* Dr. Steven Camron, Advisor, 734-487-3300, Fax: 734-487-2473, E-mail: scamron@emich.edu.

Eastern Nazarene College, Adult and Graduate Studies, Division of Teacher Education, Quincy, MA 02170. Offers administration (M Ed); early childhood education (M Ed, Certificate); elementary education (M Ed, Certificate); English as a second language (Certificate); instructional enrichment and development (Certificate); middle school education (M Ed, Certificate); moderate special needs education (Certificate); principal (Certificate); program development and supervision (Certificate); secondary education (M Ed, Certificate); special education administrator (Certificate); special needs (M Ed); supervisor (Certificate); teacher of reading (M Ed, Certificate). M Ed also available through weekend program for administration, special needs, and teacher of reading only. Part-time and evening/weekend programs available. *Entrance requirements:* Additional exam requirements/recommendations for international students: Required—TOEFL (minimum score 550 paper-based).

Eastern New Mexico University, Graduate School, College of Education and Technology, Department of Educational Studies, Program in Special Education, Portales, NM 88130. Offers early childhood special education (M Sp Ed); general (M Sp Ed). Part-time programs available. *Degree requirements:* For master's, comprehensive exam, thesis optional. *Entrance requirements:* For master's, minimum GPA of 3.0, letter of recommendation, photocopy of teaching license or confirmation of entrance into alternative licensure program, writing assessment, 2 letters of application, special education license or minimum 30 hours of undergraduate course work. Additional exam requirements/recommendations for international students: Required—TOEFL (minimum score 550 paper-based; 79 iBT), IELTS (minimum score 6). Electronic applications accepted.

Eastern University, Graduate Education Programs, St. Davids, PA 19087-3696. Offers ESL program specialist (K-12) (Certificate); general supervisor (PreK-12) (Certificate); health and physical education (K-12) (Certificate); middle level (4-8) (Certificate); multicultural education (M Ed); pre K-4 (Certificate); pre K-4 with special education (Certificate); reading (M Ed); reading specialist (K-12) (Certificate); reading supervisor (K-12) (Certificate); school health services (M Ed); school health supervisor (Certificate); school nurse (Certificate); school principalship (K-12) (Certificate); secondary biology education (7-12) (Certificate); secondary chemistry education (7-12) (Certificate); secondary communication education (7-12) (Certificate); secondary education (7-12) (Certificate); secondary English education (7-12) (Certificate); secondary math education (7-12) (Certificate); secondary social studies education (7-12) (Certificate); special education (M Ed); special education (7-12) (Certificate); special education (Pre K-8) (Certificate); special education supervisor (N-12) (Certificate); TESOL (M Ed); world language (Certificate), including French, Mandarin Chinese, Spanish. Part-time and evening/weekend programs available. Postbaccalaureate distance learning degree programs offered (no on-campus study). *Faculty:* 22 full-time (11 women), 26 part-time/ adjunct (18 women). *Students:* 77 full-time (58 women), 223 part-time (149 women); includes 112 minority (81 Black or African American, non-Hispanic/Latino; 1 American Indian or Alaska Native, non-Hispanic/Latino; 9 Asian, non-Hispanic/Latino; 18 Hispanic/ Latino; 1 Native Hawaiian or other Pacific Islander, non-Hispanic/Latino; 2 Two or more races, non-Hispanic/Latino), 7 international. Average age 34. 94 applicants, 100% accepted, 81 enrolled. In 2013, 120 master's awarded. *Entrance requirements:* For master's, minimum GPA of 2.5 (for M Ed); for Certificate, minimum GPA of 3.0 for certifications. Additional exam requirements/recommendations for international students: Required—TOEFL. *Application deadline:* For fall admission, 8/14 for domestic students; for spring admission, 12/20 for domestic students. Applications are processed on a rolling basis. Application fee: $35. Application fee is waived when completed online. *Expenses: Tuition:* Full-time $15,600; part-time $650 per credit. *Required fees:* $27.50 per semester. One-time fee: $50. Tuition and fees vary according to course load, degree level and program. *Financial support:* In 2013–14, 84 students received support, including 6 research assistantships with partial tuition reimbursements available (averaging $7,710 per year); scholarships/grants and unspecified assistantships also available. Financial award application deadline: 3/15; financial award applicants required to submit FAFSA. *Unit head:* Harry Gutelius, Associate Dean, 610-341-1729.

Application contact: Michael Perpiglia, Associate Director of Enrollment, 610-341-5947, Fax: 484-581-1276, E-mail: mperpigl@eastern.edu. Website: http://www.eastern.edu/academics/programs/loeb-school-education-0/graduateprograms.

Eastern Washington University, Graduate Studies, College of Arts, Letters and Education, Program in Special Education, Cheney, WA 99004-2431. Offers M Ed. *Degree requirements:* For master's, comprehensive exam, thesis or alternative. *Entrance requirements:* For master's, GRE General Test, minimum GPA of 3.0. *Application deadline:* Applications are processed on a rolling basis. Application fee: $50. *Financial support:* Teaching assistantships with partial tuition reimbursements, career-related internships or fieldwork, Federal Work-Study, institutionally sponsored loans, scholarships/grants, tuition waivers (partial), and unspecified assistantships available. Support available to part-time students. Financial award application deadline: 2/1; financial award applicants required to submit FAFSA. *Unit head:* Ronald C. Martella, Director, 509-359-6196, E-mail: rmartella@mail.ewu.edu. *Application contact:* Julie Marr, Advisor/Recruiter for Graduate Studies, 509-359-6656, E-mail: gradprograms@ewu.edu.

East Stroudsburg University of Pennsylvania, Graduate College, College of Education, Department of Special Education, East Stroudsburg, PA 18301-2999. Offers M Ed. Part-time and evening/weekend programs available. Postbaccalaureate distance learning degree programs offered. *Faculty:* 1 (woman) full-time, 2 part-time/adjunct (both women). *Students:* 1 (woman) full-time, 33 part-time (29 women); includes 3 minority (1 Black or African American, non-Hispanic/Latino; 1 Hispanic/Latino; 1 Two or more races, non-Hispanic/Latino). Average age 30. 44 applicants, 66% accepted, 19 enrolled. In 2013, 36 master's awarded. *Degree requirements:* For master's, comprehensive exam. *Entrance requirements:* For master's, PRAXIS/teacher certification, letter of recommendation, Pennsylvania Department of Education requirements. Additional exam requirements/recommendations for international students: Required—TOEFL (minimum score 560 paper-based; 83 iBT) or IELTS. *Application deadline:* For fall admission, 7/31 priority date for domestic students, 6/30 priority date for international students; for spring admission, 11/30 for domestic students, 10/31 for international students. Applications are processed on a rolling basis. Application fee: $50. Electronic applications accepted. *Expenses:* Tuition, state resident: full-time $7956; part-time $442 per credit. Tuition, nonresident: full-time $11,934; part-time $663 per credit. *Required fees:* $2129; $118 per credit. *Financial support:* Research assistantships with full and partial tuition reimbursements, career-related internships or fieldwork, Federal Work-Study, and institutionally sponsored loans available. Financial award application deadline: 3/1; financial award applicants required to submit FAFSA. *Unit head:* Dr. Teri Burcroff, Graduate Coordinator, 570-422-3558, Fax: 570-422-3506, E-mail: tburcroff@po-box.esu.edu. *Application contact:* Kevin Quintero, Graduate Admissions Coordinator, 570-422-3536, Fax: 570-422-2711, E-mail: kquintero@esu.edu.

East Tennessee State University, School of Graduate Studies, College of Education, Department of Teaching and Learning, Johnson City, TN 37614. Offers early childhood education (MA, PhD), including initial licensure PreK-3 (MA), master teacher (MA), researcher (MA); early childhood education emergent inquiry (Post-Master's Certificate); special education (M Ed), including advanced practitioner, early childhood special education, special education. Part-time programs available. *Faculty:* 8 full-time (7 women), 4 part-time/adjunct (3 women). *Students:* 45 full-time (43 women), 43 part-time (40 women); includes 5 minority (2 Black or African American, non-Hispanic/Latino; 1 Asian, non-Hispanic/Latino; 2 Hispanic/Latino), 4 international. Average age 36. 75 applicants, 64% accepted, 41 enrolled. *Entrance requirements:* For master's, PRAXIS I or Tennessee teaching license (for special education only), minimum GPA of 3.0 (or complete probationary period with no grade lower than B for first 9 graduate hours for early childhood education); for doctorate, GRE General Test, professional resume; master's degree in early childhood or related field; interview; for Post-Master's Certificate, bachelor's or master's degree in early childhood or related field; two years of experience working with young children (preferred). Additional exam requirements/recommendations for international students: Required—TOEFL (minimum score 550 paper-based; 79 iBT). *Application deadline:* For fall admission, 3/15 for domestic and international students. Application fee: $35 ($45 for international students). *Expenses:* Tuition, state resident: full-time $7900; part-time $395 per credit hour. Tuition, nonresident: full-time $21,960; part-time $1098 per credit hour. *Required fees:* $1345; $84 per credit hour. *Financial support:* In 2013-14, 31 students received support, including 5 fellowships with full tuition reimbursements available (averaging $18,000 per year), 7 research assistantships with full tuition reimbursements available (averaging $6,000 per year), 4 teaching assistantships with full tuition reimbursements available (averaging $6,000 per year); career-related internships or fieldwork, institutionally sponsored loans, scholarships/grants, and unspecified assistantships also available. Financial award application deadline: 7/1; financial award applicants required to submit FAFSA. *Faculty research:* Teaching students with significant disabilities, problem solving in toddlers, children and their development and learning, connecting classroom environment to student engagement in PreK-3, bilingual education in Ecuador, positive discipline/behavior support programs, early childhood relationships, international and comparative special education. *Unit head:* Dr. Pamela Evanshen, Chair, 423-439-7694, E-mail: evanshep@etsu.edu. *Application contact:* Fiona Goodyear, School of Graduate Studies, 423-439-6148, Fax: 423-439-5624, E-mail: goodyear@etsu.edu. Website: http://www.etsu.edu/coe/teachlearn/default.aspx.

Edgewood College, Program in Education, Madison, WI 53711-1997. Offers adult learning (MA Ed); bilingual teaching and learning (MA Ed); director of instruction (Certificate); director of special education and pupil services (Certificate); education (MA Ed); educational administration (MA Ed); educational leadership (Ed D); professional studies (MA Ed); program coordinator (Certificate); reading administration (MA Ed); school business administration (Certificate); school principalship K-12 (Certificate); special education (MA Ed); sustainability leadership (MA Ed); teaching and learning (MA Ed); teaching English to speakers of other languages (TESOL) (MA Ed). *Accreditation:* NCATE (one or more programs are accredited). Part-time and evening/weekend programs available. *Students:* 159 full-time (95 women), 164 part-time (121 women); includes 61 minority (19 Black or African American, non-Hispanic/Latino; 9 Asian, non-Hispanic/Latino; 25 Hispanic/Latino; 8 Two or more races, non-Hispanic/Latino), 27 international. Average age 36. In 2013, 51 master's, 22 doctorates awarded. *Degree requirements:* For master's, practicum, research project; for doctorate, comprehensive exam, thesis/dissertation. *Entrance requirements:* For master's, minimum GPA of 2.75, 2 letters of recommendation, personal statement; for doctorate, resume, letter of intent, 2 letters of recommendation, interview, writing sample. Additional exam requirements/recommendations for international students: Required—TOEFL (minimum score 525 paper-based; 72 iBT). *Application deadline:* For fall admission, 8/15 for domestic students, 5/1 for international students; for spring admission, 1/8 for domestic students, 11/1 for international students. Applications are processed on a rolling basis. Application fee: $30. Electronic applications accepted. *Unit head:* Dr. Timothy Slekar, Dean, E-mail: tslekar@edgewood.edu. *Application contact:* Joann Eastman, Admissions Counselor, 608-663-3250, Fax: 608-663-2214, E-mail: gps@edgewood.edu. Website: http://www.edgewood.edu/Academics/School-of-Education.

Edinboro University of Pennsylvania, School of Education, Department of Early Childhood and Special Education, Edinboro, PA 16444. Offers early childhood education (M Ed); special education (M Ed). Part-time and evening/weekend programs available. *Degree requirements:* For master's, thesis or alternative, competency exam. *Entrance requirements:* For master's, GRE or MAT, minimum QPA of 2.5. Electronic applications accepted.

Elmhurst College, Graduate Programs, Program in Early Childhood Special Education, Elmhurst, IL 60126-3296. Offers M Ed. Part-time and evening/weekend programs available. *Faculty:* 2 full-time (both women), 3 part-time/adjunct (all women). *Students:* 8 full-time (all women), 22 part-time (all women); includes 5 minority (2 Black or African American, non-Hispanic/Latino; 2 Hispanic/Latino; 1 Two or more races, non-Hispanic/Latino). Average age 28. 37 applicants, 51% accepted, 15 enrolled. In 2013, 10 master's awarded. *Entrance requirements:* For master's, 3 recommendations, resume, statement of purpose. Additional exam requirements/recommendations for international students: Required—TOEFL (minimum score 550 paper-based; 79 iBT). *Application deadline:* Applications are processed on a rolling basis. Application fee: $0. Electronic applications accepted. *Expenses:* Contact institution. *Financial support:* In 2013-14, 13 students received support. Federal Work-Study and scholarships/grants available. Support available to part-time students. Financial award application deadline: 6/1; financial award applicants required to submit FAFSA. *Application contact:* Timothy J. Panfil, Director of Enrollment Management, School for Professional Studies, 630-617-3300 Ext. 3256, Fax: 630-617-6471, E-mail: panfilt@elmhurst.edu.

Elms College, Division of Education, Chicopee, MA 01013-2839. Offers early childhood education (MAT); education (M Ed, CAGS); elementary education (MAT); English as a second language (MAT); reading (MAT); secondary education (MAT), including biology education, English education, Spanish education; special education (MAT). Part-time and evening/weekend programs available. *Degree requirements:* For master's, thesis (for some programs). *Entrance requirements:* For master's, Massachusetts Educators Certification Test, minimum GPA of 3.0; for CAGS, master's degree in education. Additional exam requirements/recommendations for international students: Required—TOEFL.

Elon University, Program in Education, Elon, NC 27244-2010. Offers elementary education (M Ed); gifted education (M Ed); special education (M Ed). *Accreditation:* NCATE. Part-time programs available. *Faculty:* 16 full-time (13 women), 3 part-time/adjunct (2 women). *Students:* 62 part-time (53 women); includes 11 minority (5 Black or African American, non-Hispanic/Latino; 1 Asian, non-Hispanic/Latino; 5 Hispanic/Latino). Average age 33. 35 applicants, 94% accepted, 29 enrolled. *Entrance requirements:* For master's, GRE, MAT. Additional exam requirements/recommendations for international students: Required—TOEFL (minimum score 550 paper-based; 79 iBT). *Application deadline:* For winter admission, 6/1 priority date for domestic students. Applications are processed on a rolling basis. Application fee: $50. Electronic applications accepted. *Expenses:* Contact institution. *Financial support:* In 2013-14, 5 students received support. Federal Work-Study and scholarships/grants available. Support available to part-time students. Financial award application deadline: 6/1; financial award applicants required to submit FAFSA. *Faculty research:* Teaching reading to low-achieving second and third graders, pre- and post-student teaching attitudes, children's writing, whole language methodology, critical creative thinking. *Unit head:* Dr. Angela Owusu-Ansah, Director and Associate Dean of Education, 336-278-5885, Fax: 336-278-5919, E-mail: aansah@elon.edu. *Application contact:* Art Fadde, Director of Graduate Admissions, 800-334-8448 Ext. 3, Fax: 336-278-7699, E-mail: afadde@elon.edu. Website: http://www.elon.edu/med/.

Emporia State University, Program in Early Childhood Education, Emporia, KS 66801-5415. Offers early childhood curriculum (MS); early childhood special education (MS). *Accreditation:* NCATE. Part-time programs available. Postbaccalaureate distance learning degree programs offered. *Faculty:* 31 full-time (24 women), 4 part-time/adjunct (2 women). *Students:* 3 full-time (all women), 69 part-time (68 women); includes 7 minority (2 Black or African American, non-Hispanic/Latino; 5 Hispanic/Latino), 1 international. 29 applicants, 93% accepted, 17 enrolled. In 2013, 7 master's awarded. *Degree requirements:* For master's, comprehensive exam or thesis, practicum. *Entrance requirements:* For master's, GRE General Test or MAT, essay exam, appropriate bachelor's degree, letters of recommendation. Additional exam requirements/recommendations for international students: Required—TOEFL (minimum score 520 paper-based; 68 iBT). *Application deadline:* For fall admission, 8/15 priority date for domestic students. Applications are processed on a rolling basis. Application fee: $30 ($75 for international students). Electronic applications accepted. *Expenses:* Tuition, area resident: Part-time $220 per credit hour. Tuition, state resident: part-time $220 per credit hour. Tuition, nonresident: part-time $685 per credit hour. *Required fees:* $73 per credit hour. *Financial support:* In 2013-14, 1 research assistantship with full tuition reimbursement (averaging $7,200 per year), 4 teaching assistantships with full tuition reimbursements (averaging $7,200 per year) were awarded; Federal Work-Study, institutionally sponsored loans, health care benefits, and unspecified assistantships also available. Financial award application deadline: 3/15; financial award applicants required to submit FAFSA. *Unit head:* Dr. Jean Morrow, Chair, 620-341-5766, E-mail: jmorrow@emporia.edu. *Application contact:* Mary Sewell, Admissions Coordinator, 800-950-GRAD, Fax: 620-341-5909, E-mail: msewell@emporia.edu.

Emporia State University, Program in Special Education, Emporia, KS 66801-5415. Offers behavior disorders (MS); gifted, talented, and creative (MS); interrelated special education (MS); learning disabilities (MS); mental retardation (MS). *Accreditation:* NCATE. Part-time programs available. *Faculty:* 7 full-time (5 women). *Students:* 7 full-time (6 women), 182 part-time (129 women); includes 9 minority (4 Black or African American, non-Hispanic/Latino; 3 Hispanic/Latino; 2 Two or more races, non-Hispanic/Latino). 69 applicants, 78% accepted, 35 enrolled. In 2013, 38 master's awarded. *Degree requirements:* For master's, comprehensive exam or thesis, practicum. *Entrance requirements:* For master's, GRE General Test or MAT, essay exam, appropriate bachelor's degree, teacher certification, letters of recommendation. Additional exam requirements/recommendations for international students: Required—TOEFL (minimum score 520 paper-based; 68 iBT). *Application deadline:* For fall admission, 8/15 priority date for domestic students. Applications are processed on a rolling basis. Application fee: $30 ($75 for international students). Electronic applications accepted. *Expenses:* Tuition, area resident: Part-time $220 per credit hour. Tuition, state resident: part-time $220 per credit hour. Tuition, nonresident: part-time $685 per credit hour. *Required fees:* $73 per credit hour. *Financial support:* Federal Work-Study, institutionally sponsored loans, health care benefits, and unspecified assistantships available. Financial award application deadline: 3/15; financial award applicants required to submit FAFSA. *Unit head:* Dr. Jean Morrow, Chair, 620-341-5317, E-mail: jmorrow@emporia.edu. *Application contact:* Mary Sewell, Admissions Coordinator, 800-950-GRAD, Fax: 620-341-5909, E-mail: msewell@emporia.edu. Website: http://www.emporia.edu/elecse/sped/.

Endicott College, Van Loan School of Graduate and Professional Studies, Program in Autism and Applied Behavior Analysis, Beverly, MA 01915-2096. Offers M Ed. Part-time and evening/weekend programs available. Postbaccalaureate distance learning degree programs offered. *Faculty:* 3 full-time (1 woman), 9 part-time/adjunct (6 women).

Students: 7 full-time (6 women), 70 part-time (61 women); includes 6 minority (2 Black or African American, non-Hispanic/Latino; 2 Asian, non-Hispanic/Latino; 1 Hispanic/Latino; 1 Two or more races, non-Hispanic/Latino), 2 international. Average age 31. 47 applicants, 68% accepted, 27 enrolled. In 2013, 4 master's awarded. *Degree requirements:* For master's, thesis. *Entrance requirements:* For master's, MAT or GRE. Additional exam requirements/recommendations for international students: Required—TOEFL. *Application deadline:* Applications are processed on a rolling basis. Electronic applications accepted. *Financial support:* Applicants required to submit FAFSA. *Unit head:* Dr. Mary Jane Weiss, Director, 978-232-2199, E-mail: mweiss@endicott.edu. *Application contact:* Dr. Mary Huegel, Vice President and Dean of the School of Graduate and Professional Studies, 978-232-2084, Fax: 978-232-3000, E-mail: mhuegel@endicott.edu.
Website: http://www.endicott.edu/GradProf/InstBehavStudies/GPSGradMEd/InstBehavStudiesAutismAppBehavAnalysis.aspx.

Endicott College, Van Loan School of Graduate and Professional Studies, Program in Special Needs and Special Needs/Applied Behavior Analysis, Beverly, MA 01915-2096. Offers M Ed. Part-time and evening/weekend programs available. *Faculty:* 2 full-time (0 women), 19 part-time/adjunct (13 women). *Students:* 44 full-time (37 women), 136 part-time (114 women); includes 9 minority (5 Black or African American, non-Hispanic/Latino; 4 Hispanic/Latino). Average age 31. 58 applicants, 64% accepted, 35 enrolled. In 2013, 56 master's awarded. *Degree requirements:* For master's, comprehensive exam, practicum. *Entrance requirements:* For master's, MAT or GRE, Massachusetts teaching certificate, letters of recommendation. Additional exam requirements/recommendations for international students: Required—TOEFL. *Application deadline:* Applications are processed on a rolling basis. Application fee: $50. Electronic applications accepted. *Financial support:* Career-related internships or fieldwork, Federal Work-Study, and institutionally sponsored loans available. Financial award applicants required to submit FAFSA. *Faculty research:* Literacy, parent education, inclusion, school reform, technology in education. *Unit head:* Dr. John D. MacLean, Jr., Director of Licensure Programs, 978-232-2408, E-mail: jmaclean@endicott.edu. *Application contact:* Vice President and Dean of the School of Graduate and Professional Studies.

Fairfield University, Graduate School of Education and Allied Professions, Fairfield, CT 06824-5195. Offers applied behavior analysis (ATC); applied psychology (MA); clinical mental health counseling (MA, CAS); early childhood studies (ATC); educational technology (MA); elementary education (MA, CAS); family studies (MA); integration of spirituality and religion in counseling (ATC); marriage and family therapy (MA); school counseling (MA, CAS); school psychology (MA, CAS); school-based marriage and family therapy (ATC); secondary education (MA); special education (MA, CAS); substance abuse counseling (ATC); teaching (Certificate); teaching and foundations (MA, CAS); TESOL, world languages, and bilingual education (MA, CAS). *Accreditation:* NCATE. Part-time and evening/weekend programs available. *Faculty:* 24 full-time (21 women), 39 part-time/adjunct (27 women). *Students:* 154 full-time (130 women), 307 part-time (248 women); includes 75 minority (14 Black or African American, non-Hispanic/Latino; 1 American Indian or Alaska Native, non-Hispanic/Latino; 10 Asian, non-Hispanic/Latino; 44 Hispanic/Latino; 6 Two or more races, non-Hispanic/Latino), 13 international. Average age 34. 263 applicants, 41% accepted, 91 enrolled. In 2013, 149 master's, 21 other advanced degrees awarded. *Degree requirements:* For master's, comprehensive exam. *Entrance requirements:* For master's, PRAXIS I (for certification programs), minimum GPA of 3.0, 2 recommendations, resume. Additional exam requirements/recommendations for international students: Required—TOEFL (minimum score 550 paper-based; 84 iBT) or IELTS (minimum score 7.5). *Application deadline:* For fall admission, 2/15 for international students; for spring admission, 10/1 for international students. Application fee: $60. Electronic applications accepted. *Expenses: Tuition:* Part-time $675 per credit hour. Tuition and fees vary according to program. *Financial support:* In 2013–14, 55 students received support. Career-related internships or fieldwork and unspecified assistantships available. Financial award applicants required to submit FAFSA. *Faculty research:* Literacy, adolescent psychology, special education, teaching development, mentoring for professional development, multicultural education. *Total annual research expenditures:* $325,000. *Unit head:* Dr. Robert D. Hannafin, Dean, 203-254-4250, Fax: 203-254-4241, E-mail: rhannafin@fairfield.edu. *Application contact:* Marianne Gumpper, Director of Graduate and Continuing Studies Admission, 203-254-4184, Fax: 203-254-4073, E-mail: gradadmis@fairfield.edu.
Website: http://www.fairfield.edu/academics/schoolscollegescenters/graduateschoolofeducationalliedprofessions/graduateprograms/.

Fairleigh Dickinson University, Metropolitan Campus, University College: Arts, Sciences, and Professional Studies, Peter Sammartino School of Education, Program in Learning Disabilities, Teaneck, NJ 07666-1914. Offers MA. *Accreditation:* Teacher Education Accreditation Council.

Fairmont State University, Programs in Education, Fairmont, WV 26554. Offers digital media, new literacies and learning (M Ed); education (MAT); exercise science, fitness and wellness (M Ed); online learning (M Ed); professional studies (M Ed); reading (M Ed); special education (M Ed). *Accreditation:* NCATE. Part-time and evening/weekend programs available. Postbaccalaureate distance learning degree programs offered. *Faculty:* 18 part-time/adjunct (11 women). *Students:* 75 full-time (55 women), 120 part-time (96 women); includes 11 minority (5 Black or African American, non-Hispanic/Latino; 2 American Indian or Alaska Native, non-Hispanic/Latino; 1 Asian, non-Hispanic/Latino; 1 Hispanic/Latino; 2 Two or more races, non-Hispanic/Latino), 1 international. Average age 32. 69 applicants, 86% accepted, 45 enrolled. In 2013, 82 master's awarded. *Entrance requirements:* For master's, GRE. Additional exam requirements/recommendations for international students: Required—TOEFL. *Application deadline:* For fall admission, 5/1 for domestic and international students. Applications are processed on a rolling basis. Application fee: $40. *Expenses:* Tuition, state resident: full-time $6404; part-time $349 per credit hour. Tuition, nonresident: full-time $13,694; part-time $754 per credit hour. Part-time tuition and fees vary according to course load. *Financial support:* In 2013–14, 30 students received support. *Unit head:* Dr. Carolyn Crislip-Tacy, Interim Dean, School of Education, 304-367-4143, Fax: 304-367-4599, E-mail: carolyn.crislip-tacy@fairmontstate.edu. *Application contact:* Jack Kirby, Director of Graduate Studies, 304-367-4101, E-mail: jack.kirby@fairmontstate.edu.
Website: http://www.fairmontstate.edu/graduatestudies/default.asp.

Ferris State University, College of Education and Human Services, School of Education, Big Rapids, MI 49307. Offers curriculum and instruction (M Ed), including reading, special education, subject area; educational leadership (MS); instructor (MSCTE); post-secondary administration (MSCTE); training and development (MSCTE). Part-time and evening/weekend programs available. Postbaccalaureate distance learning degree programs offered (minimal on-campus study). *Faculty:* 7 full-time (5 women), 9 part-time/adjunct (6 women). *Students:* 17 full-time (14 women), 88 part-time (53 women); includes 8 minority (3 Black or African American, non-Hispanic/Latino; 1 American Indian or Alaska Native, non-Hispanic/Latino; 1 Asian, non-Hispanic/Latino; 3 Two or more races, non-Hispanic/Latino), 12 international. Average age 35. 16 applicants, 63% accepted, 6 enrolled. In 2013, 31 master's awarded. *Degree requirements:* For master's, thesis, research paper or project. *Entrance requirements:* For master's, minimum undergraduate degree GPA of 3.0. Additional exam requirements/recommendations for international students: Required—TOEFL (minimum score 500 paper-based; 61 iBT), IELTS. *Application deadline:* For fall admission, 7/1 priority date for domestic and international students; for spring admission, 11/1 priority date for domestic and international students; for summer admission, 3/1 priority date for domestic and international students. Applications are processed on a rolling basis. Application fee: $30. Electronic applications accepted. Application fee is waived when completed online. *Financial support:* Career-related internships or fieldwork and scholarships/grants available. Support available to part-time students. Financial award applicants required to submit FAFSA. *Faculty research:* Suicide prevention, reading, women in education, special needs, administration. *Unit head:* Dr. James Powell, Director, 231-591-3512, Fax: 231-591-2043, E-mail: powelj20@ferris.edu. *Application contact:* Kimisue Worrall, Secretary, 231-591-5361, Fax: 231-591-2043.
Website: http://www.ferris.edu/education/education/.

Fitchburg State University, Division of Graduate and Continuing Education, Program in Special Education, Fitchburg, MA 01420-2697. Offers guided studies (M Ed); reading specialist (M Ed); teaching students with moderate disabilities (M Ed); teaching students with severe disabilities (M Ed). *Accreditation:* NCATE. Part-time and evening/weekend programs available. *Degree requirements:* For master's, internship. *Entrance requirements:* Additional exam requirements/recommendations for international students: Required—TOEFL (minimum score 550 paper-based; 79 iBT). Electronic applications accepted.

Florida Atlantic University, College of Education, Department of Exceptional Student Education, Boca Raton, FL 33431-0991. Offers M Ed, Ed D. *Accreditation:* NCATE. Part-time and evening/weekend programs available. *Faculty:* 8 full-time (4 women), 5 part-time/adjunct (3 women). *Students:* 6 full-time (5 women), 39 part-time (37 women); includes 9 minority (3 Black or African American, non-Hispanic/Latino; 1 Asian, non-Hispanic/Latino; 5 Hispanic/Latino). Average age 31. 18 applicants, 72% accepted, 11 enrolled. In 2013, 8 master's, 1 doctorate awarded. *Degree requirements:* For master's, thesis optional, internship; for doctorate, comprehensive exam, thesis/dissertation, internship. *Entrance requirements:* For master's, GRE General Test, minimum GPA of 3.0 during previous 2 years; for doctorate, GRE General Test, 3 years of teaching experience, interview. Additional exam requirements/recommendations for international students: Required—TOEFL (minimum score 500 paper-based; 61 iBT), IELTS (minimum score 6). *Application deadline:* For fall admission, 7/1 for domestic students, 2/15 for international students; for spring admission, 11/1 for domestic students, 7/15 for international students. Applications are processed on a rolling basis. Application fee: $30. Electronic applications accepted. *Expenses:* Tuition, state resident: full-time $6660; part-time $370 per credit hour. Tuition, nonresident: full-time $18,450; part-time $1025 per credit hour. Tuition and fees vary according to course load. *Financial support:* Fellowships with tuition reimbursements, research assistantships with tuition reimbursements, teaching assistantships with partial tuition reimbursements, career-related internships or fieldwork, Federal Work-Study, scholarships/grants, tuition waivers (partial), and unspecified assistantships available. Support available to part-time students. Financial award applicants required to submit FAFSA. *Faculty research:* Instructional design, assessment, educational reform, behavioral research, social integration. *Unit head:* Dr. Michael P. Brady, Chairperson, 561-297-3280, Fax: 561-297-2507, E-mail: mbrady@fau.edu. *Application contact:* Dr. Eliah Watlington, Associate Dean, 561-296-8520, Fax: 261-297-2991, E-mail: ewatling@fau.edu.
Website: http://www.coe.fau.edu/academicdepartments/ese/.

Florida Gulf Coast University, College of Education, Program in Special Education, Fort Myers, FL 33965-6565. Offers behavior disorders (MA); mental retardation (MA); specific learning disabilities (MA); varying exceptionalities (MA). Part-time and evening/weekend programs available. *Degree requirements:* For master's, thesis or alternative. *Entrance requirements:* For master's, GRE General Test, MAT, minimum GPA of 3.0. Additional exam requirements/recommendations for international students: Required—TOEFL (minimum score 550 paper-based). Electronic applications accepted. *Faculty research:* Inclusion, interacting with families, alternative certification.

Florida International University, College of Education, Department of Teaching and Learning, Miami, FL 33199. Offers art education (MA, MS); curriculum and instruction (MS, Ed D, PhD, Ed S), including curriculum development (MS), elementary education (MS), English education (MS), learning technologies (MS), mathematics education (MS), modern language education (MS), physical education (MS), science education (MS), social studies education (MS), special education (MS); early childhood education (MS); exceptional student education (Ed D); foreign language education (MS), including foreign language education, teaching English to speakers of other languages (TESOL); international/intercultural education (MS); language, literacy and culture (PhD); mathematics, science, and learning technologies (PhD); physical education (MS), including sport and fitness; reading education (MS). Part-time and evening/weekend programs available. *Degree requirements:* For doctorate, comprehensive exam, thesis/dissertation. *Entrance requirements:* For master's, GRE General Test, Florida General Knowledge Test or Florida College Level Academic Skills Test; for doctorate and Ed S, GRE General Test. Additional exam requirements/recommendations for international students: Required—TOEFL (minimum score 550 paper-based; 80 iBT), IELTS (minimum score 6.3). Electronic applications accepted.

Florida Memorial University, School of Education, Miami-Dade, FL 33054. Offers elementary education (MS); exceptional student education (MS); reading (MS). *Degree requirements:* For master's, comprehensive exam or thesis, field and clinical experiences, exit exam. *Entrance requirements:* For master's, GRE, CLAST, PRAXIS I, baccalaureate or graduate degree with minimum GPA of 3.0 in last 60 hours, 3 recommendations. Additional exam requirements/recommendations for international students: Recommended—TOEFL.

Florida State University, The Graduate School, College of Education, School of Teacher Education, Tallahassee, FL 32306. Offers curriculum and instruction (MS, MST, PhD, Ed S), including early childhood education (MS, PhD, Ed S), elementary education (MS, PhD, Ed S), English education (MS, PhD, Ed S), English teaching (MST), exceptional student education (MST), foreign and second language education (MS, PhD, Ed S), foreign and second language teaching (MST), math education (MS, PhD, Ed S), math teaching (MST), reading education and language arts (MS, PhD, Ed S), science education (MS, PhD, Ed S), social science education (MS, PhD, Ed S), social science teaching (MST), special education (MS, PhD, Ed S), special education studies (MST), visual disabilities (MS, Ed S). Part-time programs available. *Faculty:* 30 full-time (20 women), 22 part-time/adjunct (18 women). *Students:* 183 full-time (151 women), 92 part-time (80 women); includes 47 minority (20 Black or African American, non-Hispanic/Latino; 3 American Indian or Alaska Native, non-Hispanic/Latino; 1 Asian, non-Hispanic/Latino; 20 Hispanic/Latino; 3 Two or more races, non-Hispanic/Latino), 61 international. Average age 30. 199 applicants, 79% accepted, 86 enrolled. In 2013, 119 master's, 9 doctorates, 4 other advanced degrees awarded. *Degree requirements:* For master's and Ed S, comprehensive exam, thesis optional; for doctorate, comprehensive exam, thesis/dissertation, preliminary exam, prospectus defense. *Entrance requirements:* For master's, doctorate, and Ed S, GRE General Test, minimum GPA of 3.0. Additional exam requirements/recommendations for international students: Required—TOEFL (minimum score 550 paper-based; 80 iBT). *Application deadline:* For fall admission, 7/1 for domestic and international students; for winter admission, 10/1 for

domestic students, 11/1 for international students; for spring admission, 3/1 for domestic and international students. Applications are processed on a rolling basis. Application fee: $30. Electronic applications accepted. *Expenses:* Tuition, state resident: part-time $403.51 per credit hour. Tuition, nonresident: part-time $1004.85 per credit hour. *Required fees:* $75.81 per credit hour. One-time fee: $20 part-time. Tuition and fees vary according to course load, campus/location and student level. *Financial support:* In 2013–14, 113 students received support, including 55 research assistantships with full and partial tuition reimbursements available, 18 teaching assistantships with full and partial tuition reimbursements available; fellowships with full and partial tuition reimbursements available, career-related internships or fieldwork, scholarships/grants, health care benefits, and unspecified assistantships also available. Financial award application deadline: 1/15; financial award applicants required to submit FAFSA. *Faculty research:* Effective intervention and assessment strategies to improve reading skills; literacy teaching and learning through technology; understanding of student sense-making through instructions, especially STEM learning for all students; international education and consequences of globalization; support professional teacher development and adoption of effective/transformative practices. *Total annual research expenditures:* $1.3 million. *Unit head:* Dr. Sherry Southerland, Chair, 850-644-4880, Fax: 850-644-7736, E-mail: ssoutherland@admin.fsu.edu. *Application contact:* Dawn Matthews, Academic Support Assistant, 850-644-2122, Fax: 850-644-7736, E-mail: dmatthews@fsu.edu.
Website: http://www.coe.fsu.edu/STE.

Fontbonne University, Graduate Programs, Department of Communication Disorders and Deaf Education, Studies in Early Intervention in Deaf Education, St. Louis, MO 63105-3098. Offers MA. *Entrance requirements:* For master's, minimum GPA of 3.0. *Expenses: Tuition:* Full-time $11,646; part-time $647 per credit hour. *Required fees:* $324; $18 per credit hour. Tuition and fees vary according to course load and program.

Fordham University, Graduate School of Education, Division of Curriculum and Teaching, New York, NY 10023. Offers adult education (MS, MSE); bilingual teacher education (MSE); curriculum and teaching (MSE); early childhood education (MSE); elementary education (MST); language, literacy, and learning (PhD); reading education (MSE, Adv C); secondary education (MAT, MSE); special education (MSE, Adv C); teaching English as a second language (MSE). *Accreditation:* NCATE. *Degree requirements:* For doctorate, thesis/dissertation; for Adv C, thesis. *Entrance requirements:* For doctorate, MAT, GRE General Test.

Fort Hays State University, Graduate School, College of Education and Technology, Department of Special Education, Hays, KS 67601-4099. Offers MS. *Accreditation:* NCATE. *Degree requirements:* For master's, comprehensive exam, thesis optional. *Entrance requirements:* Additional exam requirements/recommendations for international students: Required—TOEFL (minimum score 550 paper-based). Electronic applications accepted. *Faculty research:* Severe behavior disorders, early childhood language, multicultural speech.

Framingham State University, Continuing Education, Program in Special Education, Framingham, MA 01701-9101. Offers M Ed. Part-time and evening/weekend programs available. *Entrance requirements:* For master's, MAT, interview.

Francis Marion University, Graduate Programs, School of Education, Florence, SC 29502-0547. Offers early childhood education (M Ed); elementary education (M Ed); learning disabilities (M Ed, MAT); remedial education (M Ed); secondary education (M Ed). *Accreditation:* NCATE. Part-time programs available. *Faculty:* 17 full-time (12 women). *Students:* 5 full-time (3 women), 79 part-time (63 women); includes 33 minority (all Black or African American, non-Hispanic/Latino). Average age 34. 327 applicants, 42% accepted, 135 enrolled. In 2013, 45 master's awarded. *Degree requirements:* For master's, comprehensive exam. *Entrance requirements:* For master's, GRE General Test, MAT, NTE, or PRAXIS II. *Application deadline:* For fall admission, 3/15 priority date for domestic students; for spring admission, 10/15 priority date for domestic students. Application fee: $33. *Expenses:* Tuition, state resident: full-time $9184; part-time $459.20 per credit hour. Tuition, nonresident: full-time $18,368; part-time $918.40 per credit hour. *Required fees:* $13.50 per credit hour. $92 per semester. Tuition and fees vary according to program. *Financial support:* In 2013–14, 2 research assistantships (averaging $6,000 per year) were awarded; scholarships/grants and unspecified assistantships also available. Support available to part-time students. Financial award application deadline: 3/1; financial award applicants required to submit FAFSA. *Faculty research:* Identification and alternate assessment of at-risk students. *Unit head:* Dr. Shirley Carr Bausmith, Dean, 843-661-1460, Fax: 843-661-4647. *Application contact:* Rannie Gamble, Administrative Manager, 843-661-1286, Fax: 843-661-4688, E-mail: rgamble@fmarion.edu.

Franklin Pierce University, Graduate Studies, Rindge, NH 03461-0060. Offers curriculum and instruction (M Ed); emerging network technologies (Graduate Certificate); energy and sustainability studies (MBA); health administration (MBA, Graduate Certificate); human resource management (MBA, Graduate Certificate); information technology (MBA); information technology management (MS); leadership (MBA, DA); nursing (MS); physical therapy (DPT); physician assistant studies (MPAS); special education (M Ed); sports management (MBA). *Accreditation:* APTA. Part-time programs available. Postbaccalaureate distance learning degree programs offered (no on-campus study). *Degree requirements:* For master's, concentrated original research projects; student teaching; fieldwork and/or internship; leadership project; PRAXIS I and II (for M Ed); for doctorate, concentrated original research projects, clinical fieldwork and/or internship, leadership project. *Entrance requirements:* For master's, minimum GPA of 2.5, 3 letters of recommendation; competencies in accounting, economics, statistics, and computer skills through life experience or undergraduate coursework (for MBA); certification/e-portfolio, minimum C grade in all education courses (for M Ed); license to practice as RN (for MS in nursing); for doctorate, GRE, BA/BS, 3 letters of recommendation, personal mission statement, interview, writing sample, minimum cumulative GPA of 2.8, master's degree (for DA); 80 hours of observation/work in PT settings, completion of anatomy, chemistry, physics, and statistics, minimum GPA of 3.0 (for DPT). Additional exam requirements/recommendations for international students: Required—TOEFL (minimum score 550 paper-based; 61 iBT). Electronic applications accepted. *Faculty research:* Evidence-based practice in sports physical therapy, human resource management in economic crisis, leadership in nursing, innovation in sports facility management, differentiated learning and understanding by design.

Freed-Hardeman University, Program in Education, Henderson, TN 38340-2399. Offers curriculum and instruction (M Ed); school counseling (M Ed), including administration and supervision, special education; school leadership (Ed S). *Accreditation:* NCATE. Part-time and evening/weekend programs available. *Degree requirements:* For master's, comprehensive exam, thesis optional; for Ed S, thesis. *Entrance requirements:* For master's, GRE General Test or NTE; for Ed S, 3 years of teaching experience. Additional exam requirements/recommendations for international students: Required—TOEFL (minimum score 500 paper-based).

Fresno Pacific University, Graduate Programs, School of Education, Division of Special Education, Fresno, CA 93702-4709. Offers autism (Certificate); special education (MA Ed). Part-time and evening/weekend programs available. *Faculty:* 5 full-time (4 women), 1 (woman) part-time/adjunct. *Students:* 18 full-time (16 women), 63 part-time (58 women); includes 24 minority (3 Black or African American, non-Hispanic/Latino; 1 American Indian or Alaska Native, non-Hispanic/Latino; 20 Hispanic/Latino), 1 international. Average age 35. In 2013, 8 master's awarded. *Degree requirements:* For master's, thesis or alternative. *Entrance requirements:* Additional exam requirements/recommendations for international students: Required—TOEFL (minimum score 550 paper-based). *Application deadline:* For fall admission, 7/15 for domestic and international students; for spring admission, 11/15 for domestic and international students. Applications are processed on a rolling basis. Application fee: $90. *Expenses: Tuition:* Full-time $8910; part-time $495 per unit. *Required fees:* $270. Tuition and fees vary according to course load and program. *Financial support:* Career-related internships or fieldwork, scholarships/grants, and tuition waivers (full and partial) available. Support available to part-time students. Financial award applicants required to submit FAFSA. *Unit head:* Dr. Julie M. Lane, 559-453-5682, E-mail: julie.lane@fresno.edu. *Application contact:* Amanda Krum-Stovall, Director of Graduate Admissions, 559-453-2016, E-mail: amanda.krum-stovall@fresno.edu.
Website: http://grad.fresno.edu/programs/special-education-program.

Frostburg State University, Graduate School, College of Education, Department of Educational Professions, Program in Special Education, Frostburg, MD 21532-1099. Offers M Ed. *Accreditation:* NCATE. Part-time and evening/weekend programs available. *Degree requirements:* For master's, thesis or alternative, PRAXIS II (special education section). *Entrance requirements:* For master's, teaching certificate. Additional exam requirements/recommendations for international students: Required—TOEFL. Electronic applications accepted. *Expenses: Tuition, area resident:* Part-time $340 per credit hour. Tuition, state resident: part-time $340 per credit hour. Tuition, nonresident: part-time $437 per credit hour.

Furman University, Graduate Division, Department of Education, Greenville, SC 29613. Offers curriculum and instruction (MA); early childhood education (MA); educational leadership (Ed S); English as a second language (MA); literacy (MA); school leadership (MA); special education (MA). *Accreditation:* NCATE. Part-time programs available. Postbaccalaureate distance learning degree programs offered (minimal on-campus study). *Degree requirements:* For master's, comprehensive exam (for some programs), thesis or alternative. *Entrance requirements:* For master's, PRAXIS II. *Faculty research:* Literacy, pedagogy and practice, social justice, advanced leadership, achievement in high poverty schools.

Gallaudet University, The Graduate School, Washington, DC 20002-3625. Offers ASL/English bilingual early childhood education: birth to 5 (Certificate); audiology (Au D); clinical psychology (PhD); critical studies in the education of deaf learners (PhD); deaf and hard of hearing infants, toddlers, and their families (Certificate); deaf education (Ed S); deaf education: advanced studies (MA); deaf education: special programs (MA); deaf history (Certificate); deaf studies (MA, Certificate); educating deaf students with disabilities (Certificate); education: teacher preparation (MA), including deaf education, early childhood education and deaf education, elementary education and deaf education, secondary education and deaf education; educational neuroscience (PhD); hearing, speech and language sciences (MS, PhD); international development (MA); interpretation (MA, PhD), including combined interpreting practice and research (MA), interpreting research (MA); linguistics (MA, PhD); mental health counseling (MA); peer mentoring (Certificate); public administration (MPA); school counseling (MA); school psychology (Psy S); sign language teaching (MA); social work (MSW); speech-language pathology (MS). Part-time programs available. *Faculty:* 55 full-time (37 women). *Students:* 361 full-time (279 women), 108 part-time (73 women); includes 98 minority (39 Black or African American, non-Hispanic/Latino; 1 American Indian or Alaska Native, non-Hispanic/Latino; 12 Asian, non-Hispanic/Latino; 36 Hispanic/Latino; 1 Native Hawaiian or other Pacific Islander, non-Hispanic/Latino; 9 Two or more races, non-Hispanic/Latino), 31 international. Average age 30. 602 applicants, 49% accepted, 177 enrolled. In 2013, 140 master's, 32 doctorates, 11 other advanced degrees awarded. Terminal master's awarded for partial completion of doctoral program. *Degree requirements:* For master's, comprehensive exam (for some programs), thesis optional; for doctorate, comprehensive exam, thesis/dissertation. *Entrance requirements:* For master's and doctorate, GRE General Test or MAT, letters of recommendation, interviews, goals statement, ASL proficiency interview, written English competency. Additional exam requirements/recommendations for international students: Required—TOEFL. *Application deadline:* For fall admission, 2/15 for domestic students. Applications are processed on a rolling basis. Application fee: $75. Electronic applications accepted. *Expenses: Tuition:* Full-time $14,774; part-time $821 per credit. *Required fees:* $198 per semester. *Financial support:* In 2013–14, 325 students received support. Fellowships, research assistantships, teaching assistantships, career-related internships or fieldwork, Federal Work-Study, scholarships/grants, tuition waivers (partial), and unspecified assistantships available. Support available to part-time students. Financial award applicants required to submit FAFSA. *Faculty research:* Bimodal bilingualism development, cochlear implants, telecommunications access, cancer genetics, linguistics, visual language and visual learning, advancement of avatar and robotics translation, algal productivity and physiology in the Anacostia River. *Unit head:* Dr. Carol J. Erting, Dean, Research, Graduate School, Continuing Studies, and International Programs, 202-651-5520, Fax: 202-651-5027, E-mail: carol.erting@gallaudet.edu. *Application contact:* Wednesday Luria, Coordinator of Prospective Graduate Student Services, 202-651-5400, Fax: 202-651-5295, E-mail: graduate.school@gallaudet.edu.
Website: http://www.gallaudet.edu/x26696.xml.

Gannon University, School of Graduate Studies, College of Humanities, Education, and Social Sciences, School of Education, Program in Special Education Supervisor, Erie, PA 16541-0001. Offers Certificate. Part-time and evening/weekend programs available. Postbaccalaureate distance learning degree programs offered. *Degree requirements:* For Certificate, internship. *Entrance requirements:* For degree, minimum GPA of 3.0, valid PA teaching certificate, 5 years of experience in field. Additional exam requirements/recommendations for international students: Required—TOEFL (minimum score 79 iBT). *Application deadline:* Applications are processed on a rolling basis. Application fee: $25. Electronic applications accepted. *Expenses:* Contact institution. *Financial support:* Career-related internships or fieldwork available. Financial award application deadline: 7/1; financial award applicants required to submit FAFSA. *Unit head:* Dr. Kathleen Kingston, Director, 814-871-5626, E-mail: kingston002@gannon.edu. *Application contact:* Kara Morgan, Assistant Director of Graduate Admissions, 814-871-5831, Fax: 814-871-5827, E-mail: graduate@gannon.edu.

Geneva College, Master of Education in Special Education Program, Beaver Falls, PA 15010-3599. Offers M Ed. Part-time and evening/weekend programs available. *Faculty:* 4 full-time (all women). *Students:* 1 full-time (0 women), 4 part-time (all women). Average age 32. In 2013, 4 master's awarded. *Entrance requirements:* For master's, resume, letters of recommendation, proof of certification, transcript. Additional exam requirements/recommendations for international students: Required—TOEFL. *Application deadline:* For fall admission, 8/1 priority date for domestic students; for spring admission, 12/1 priority date for domestic students. Applications are processed on a rolling basis. Application fee: $0. Electronic applications accepted. *Expenses:* Contact institution. *Financial support:* In 2013–14, 1 student received support. Scholarships/grants available. Financial award applicants required to submit FAFSA.

Special Education

Unit head: Dr. Karen Schmalz, Program Head, 724-847-6125, E-mail: kschmalz@geneva.edu. *Application contact:* Marina Frazier, Director of Graduate Enrollment, 724-847-6697, E-mail: speced@geneva.edu.
Website: http://www.geneva.edu/page/special_ed.

George Fox University, College of Education, Master of Arts in Teaching Program, Newberg, OR 97132-2697. Offers teaching (MAT); teaching plus ESOL (MAT); teaching plus ESOL/bilingual (MAT); teaching plus reading (MAT); teaching plus special education (MAT). Program offered in Oregon and Idaho. Part-time and evening/weekend programs available. *Faculty:* 11 full-time (9 women), 24 part-time/adjunct (16 women). *Students:* 64 full-time (44 women), 20 part-time (14 women); includes 11 minority (1 Black or African American, non-Hispanic/Latino; 2 Asian, non-Hispanic/Latino; 1 Hispanic/Latino; 2 Native Hawaiian or other Pacific Islander, non-Hispanic/Latino; 5 Two or more races, non-Hispanic/Latino), 1 international. Average age 30. 28 applicants, 100% accepted, 18 enrolled. In 2013, 116 master's awarded. *Entrance requirements:* For master's, CBEST, PRAXIS PPST, or EAS, bachelor's degree with minimum GPA of 3.0 in last two years of course work from regionally-accredited college or university, official transcripts. Additional exam requirements/recommendations for international students: Required—TOEFL (minimum score 577 paper-based; 90 iBT), IELTS (minimum score 7). *Application deadline:* For fall admission, 6/1 for domestic and international students; for winter admission, 10/1 for domestic and international students; for spring admission, 2/1 for domestic and international students. Applications are processed on a rolling basis. Application fee: $40. Electronic applications accepted. *Expenses:* Contact institution. *Financial support:* In 2013–14, 20 students received support. Scholarships/grants available. Financial award application deadline: 2/1; financial award applicants required to submit FAFSA. *Application contact:* Kipp Wilfong, Graduate Admissions Counselor, 800-631-0921, Fax: 503-554-3110, E-mail: mat@georgefox.edu.
Website: http://www.georgefox.edu/soe/mat/.

George Mason University, College of Education and Human Development, Program in Special Education, Fairfax, VA 22030. Offers M Ed. *Faculty:* 20 full-time (16 women), 66 part-time/adjunct (58 women). *Students:* 86 full-time (76 women), 435 part-time (366 women); includes 110 minority (43 Black or African American, non-Hispanic/Latino; 4 American Indian or Alaska Native, non-Hispanic/Latino; 17 Asian, non-Hispanic/Latino; 35 Hispanic/Latino; 11 Two or more races, non-Hispanic/Latino), 5 international. Average age 33. 237 applicants, 86% accepted, 158 enrolled. In 2013, 259 master's awarded. *Degree requirements:* For master's, professional portfolio. *Entrance requirements:* For master's, bachelor's degree from regionally-accredited institution with minimum GPA of 3.0, cumulative or in last 60 credits of undergraduate study (or PRAXIS I, SAT, ACT or VCLA); 2 official transcripts; 3 letters of recommendation with recommendation form. Additional exam requirements/recommendations for international students: Required—TOEFL (minimum score 575 paper-based; 88 iBT), IELTS (minimum score 6.5), PTE. *Application deadline:* For fall admission, 3/1 priority date for domestic students; for spring admission, 11/1 priority date for domestic students. Applications are processed on a rolling basis. Application fee: $65 ($80 for international students). Electronic applications accepted. *Expenses:* Tuition, state resident: full-time $9350; part-time $390 per credit. Tuition, nonresident: full-time $25,754; part-time $1073 per credit. *Required fees:* $2688; $112 per credit. *Financial support:* Career-related internships or fieldwork, Federal Work-Study, and scholarships/grants available. Financial award application deadline: 3/1; financial award applicants required to submit FAFSA. *Faculty research:* Adapted captions through interactive video, DEVISE Project (multi-sensory virtual learning environment), KIHd System Project (teachers utilizing Kellar Institute handheld data system and Literary Online). *Unit head:* Michael M. Behrmann, Director, 703-993-2051, Fax: 703-993-3681, E-mail: mbehrman@gmu.edu. *Application contact:* Jancy Templeton, Advisor, 703-993-2387, Fax: 703-993-3681, E-mail: jtemple1@gmu.edu.
Website: http://gse.gmu.edu/programs/sped/.

Georgetown College, Department of Education, Georgetown, KY 40324-1696. Offers reading and writing (MA Ed); special education (MA Ed); teaching (MA Ed). *Accreditation:* NCATE. Part-time programs available. *Degree requirements:* For master's, portfolio. *Entrance requirements:* For master's, teaching certificate, minimum GPA of 2.7 or GRE General Test.

The George Washington University, Graduate School of Education and Human Development, Department of Special Education and Disability Studies, Program in Bilingual Special Education, Washington, DC 20052. Offers MA Ed, Certificate. *Students:* 5 full-time (all women), 31 part-time (all women); includes 16 minority (7 Black or African American, non-Hispanic/Latino; 5 Asian, non-Hispanic/Latino; 4 Hispanic/Latino), 5 international. Average age 34. 41 applicants, 100% accepted, 28 enrolled. In 2013, 9 master's, 51 Certificates awarded. *Unit head:* Prof. Curtis Pyke, Chair, 202-994-4516, E-mail: cpyke@gwu.edu. *Application contact:* Sarah Lang, Director of Graduate Admissions, 202-994-1447, Fax: 202-994-7207, E-mail: slang@gwu.edu.

The George Washington University, Graduate School of Education and Human Development, Department of Special Education and Disability Studies, Program in Early Childhood Special Education, Washington, DC 20052. Offers MA Ed. *Accreditation:* NCATE. *Students:* 20 full-time (19 women), 14 part-time (12 women); includes 9 minority (6 Black or African American, non-Hispanic/Latino; 2 Asian, non-Hispanic/Latino; 1 Two or more races, non-Hispanic/Latino), 3 international. Average age 31. 43 applicants, 98% accepted, 11 enrolled. In 2013, 20 master's awarded. *Degree requirements:* For master's, comprehensive exam. *Entrance requirements:* For master's, GRE General Test or MAT, minimum GPA of 2.75. *Application deadline:* For fall admission, 1/15 priority date for domestic students; for spring admission, 10/1 for domestic students. Applications are processed on a rolling basis. Application fee: $75. *Financial support:* In 2013–14, 19 students received support. Fellowships, career-related internships or fieldwork, Federal Work-Study, and tuition waivers (full) available. Financial award application deadline: 1/15; financial award applicants required to submit FAFSA. *Faculty research:* Computer-assisted instruction and learning, disabled learner assessment of preschool, handicapped children. *Unit head:* Dr. Marian H. Jarrett, Faculty Coordinator, 202-994-1509, E-mail: mjarrett@gwu.edu. *Application contact:* Sarah Lang, Director of Graduate Admissions, 202-994-1447, Fax: 202-994-7207, E-mail: slang@gwu.edu.

The George Washington University, Graduate School of Education and Human Development, Department of Special Education and Disability Studies, Program in Secondary Special Education and Transition Services, Washington, DC 20052. Offers MA Ed. *Students:* 7 full-time (all women), 5 part-time (3 women); includes 8 minority (5 Black or African American, non-Hispanic/Latino; 1 Asian, non-Hispanic/Latino; 2 Two or more races, non-Hispanic/Latino). Average age 38. 17 applicants, 100% accepted, 8 enrolled. In 2013, 10 master's awarded. *Unit head:* Prof. Curtis Pyke, Chair, 202-994-4516, E-mail: cpyke@gwu.edu. *Application contact:* Sarah Lang, Director of Graduate Admissions, 202-994-1447, Fax: 202-994-7207, E-mail: slang@gwu.edu.
Website: http://gsehd.gwu.edu/programs/ssets/masters.

The George Washington University, Graduate School of Education and Human Development, Department of Special Education and Disability Studies, Program in Special Education, Washington, DC 20052. Offers Ed D, Ed S. *Accreditation:* NCATE. *Students:* 9 full-time (all women), 75 part-time (65 women); includes 39 minority (26 Black or African American, non-Hispanic/Latino; 5 Asian, non-Hispanic/Latino; 7 Hispanic/Latino; 1 Two or more races, non-Hispanic/Latino), 3 international. Average age 38. 31 applicants, 71% accepted, 16 enrolled. In 2013, 11 doctorates, 18 other advanced degrees awarded. *Degree requirements:* For doctorate, comprehensive exam, thesis/dissertation; for Ed S, comprehensive exam. *Entrance requirements:* For doctorate and Ed S, GRE General Test or MAT, interview, minimum GPA of 3.3. *Application deadline:* For fall admission, 1/15 priority date for domestic students; for spring admission, 10/1 for domestic students. Applications are processed on a rolling basis. Application fee: $75. *Financial support:* In 2013–14, 46 students received support. Fellowships, research assistantships, career-related internships or fieldwork, Federal Work-Study, and tuition waivers (partial) available. Financial award application deadline: 1/15; financial award applicants required to submit FAFSA. *Unit head:* Dr. Carol Kochhar, Faculty Coordinator, 202-994-6170, E-mail: kochhar@gwu.edu. *Application contact:* Sarah Lang, Director of Graduate Admissions, 202-994-1447, Fax: 202-994-7207, E-mail: slang@gwu.edu.

The George Washington University, Graduate School of Education and Human Development, Department of Special Education and Disability Studies, Program in Special Education for Children with Emotional and Behavioral Disabilities, Washington, DC 20052. Offers MA Ed. *Accreditation:* NCATE. *Students:* 12 full-time (9 women); includes 5 minority (all Black or African American, non-Hispanic/Latino). Average age 30. 21 applicants, 90% accepted, 12 enrolled. In 2013, 14 master's awarded. *Degree requirements:* For master's, comprehensive exam. *Entrance requirements:* For master's, GRE General Test or MAT, interview, minimum GPA of 2.75. *Application deadline:* For fall admission, 1/15 priority date for domestic students; for spring admission, 10/1 for domestic students. Applications are processed on a rolling basis. Application fee: $75. *Financial support:* In 2013–14, 14 students received support. Fellowships, career-related internships or fieldwork, and Federal Work-Study available. Financial award application deadline: 1/15; financial award applicants required to submit FAFSA. *Faculty research:* Action research on the act of teaching emotionally disturbed students, teacher training. *Unit head:* Elisabeth Rice, Program Coordinator, 202-994-1535, E-mail: ehess@gwu.edu. *Application contact:* Sarah Lang, Director of Admission, 202-994-1447, Fax: 202-994-7207, E-mail: slang@gwu.edu.

The George Washington University, Graduate School of Education and Human Development, Department of Special Education and Disability Studies, Program in Transition Special Education, Washington, DC 20052. Offers Certificate. *Accreditation:* NCATE. Evening/weekend programs available. *Students:* 8 part-time (all women); includes 2 minority (1 Black or African American, non-Hispanic/Latino; 1 Asian, non-Hispanic/Latino). Average age 39. 7 applicants, 100% accepted, 5 enrolled. In 2013, 4 Certificates awarded. *Degree requirements:* For Certificate, comprehensive exam. *Entrance requirements:* For degree, GRE General Test or MAT, interview, minimum GPA of 2.75. *Application deadline:* For fall admission, 1/15 priority date for domestic students; for spring admission, 10/1 for domestic students. Applications are processed on a rolling basis. Application fee: $75. *Financial support:* Fellowships, research assistantships, career-related internships or fieldwork, Federal Work-Study, tuition waivers (full and partial), and stipends available. Financial award application deadline: 1/15. *Faculty research:* Computer applications for transition, transition follow-up research, curriculum-based vocational assessment, traumatic brain injury. *Unit head:* Dr. Lynda West, Coordinator, 202-994-1533, E-mail: lwest@gwu.edu. *Application contact:* Sarah Lang, Director of Graduate Admissions, 202-994-1447, Fax: 202-994-7207, E-mail: slang@gwu.edu.

Georgia College & State University, Graduate School, The John H. Lounsbury College of Education, Program in Special Education, Milledgeville, GA 31061. Offers M Ed, MAT, Ed S. *Accreditation:* NCATE. Part-time and evening/weekend programs available. *Students:* 39 full-time (30 women), 14 part-time (13 women); includes 16 minority (all Black or African American, non-Hispanic/Latino). Average age 31. In 2013, 29 master's, 6 other advanced degrees awarded. *Degree requirements:* For master's, comprehensive exam. *Entrance requirements:* For master's, on-site writing exam; for Ed S, on-site writing exam, 2 years of teaching experience, minimum GPA of 3.25. Additional exam requirements/recommendations for international students: Required—TOEFL (minimum score 550 paper-based; 79 iBT). *Application deadline:* For fall admission, 7/1 priority date for domestic students; for spring admission, 11/15 priority date for domestic students. Applications are processed on a rolling basis. Electronic applications accepted. *Financial support:* In 2013–14, 3 research assistantships with full tuition reimbursements were awarded; career-related internships or fieldwork, Federal Work-Study, and unspecified assistantships also available. Support available to part-time students. *Application contact:* Shanda Brand, Graduate Admissions Advisor, 478-445-1383, E-mail: shanda.brand@gcsu.edu.

Georgia Regents University, The Graduate School, College of Education, Program in Special Education, Augusta, GA 30912. Offers M Ed, Ed S. *Accreditation:* NCATE. Part-time and evening/weekend programs available. *Degree requirements:* For master's, thesis, portfolio. *Entrance requirements:* For master's, GRE, MAT, minimum GPA of 2.5; for Ed S, GRE, MAT. *Faculty research:* Behavior disorders, gifted programs.

Georgia Southern University, Jack N. Averitt College of Graduate Studies, College of Education, Department of Teaching and Learning, Program in Special Education, Statesboro, GA 30460. Offers M Ed, MAT, Ed S. *Accreditation:* NCATE. Part-time and evening/weekend programs available. *Students:* 40 full-time (33 women), 36 part-time (30 women); includes 19 minority (15 Black or African American, non-Hispanic/Latino; 1 Asian, non-Hispanic/Latino; 1 Hispanic/Latino; 1 Native Hawaiian or other Pacific Islander, non-Hispanic/Latino; 1 Two or more races, non-Hispanic/Latino). Average age 32. 21 applicants, 62% accepted, 8 enrolled. In 2013, 12 master's awarded. *Degree requirements:* For master's, portfolio, transition point assessments, exit assessment. *Entrance requirements:* For master's, GRE General Test or MAT; GACE Basic Skills and Content Assessments (for MAT), minimum cumulative GPA of 2.5. Additional exam requirements/recommendations for international students: Required—TOEFL (minimum score 550 paper-based; 80 iBT), IELTS (minimum score 6). *Application deadline:* For fall admission, 3/1 priority date for domestic and international students; for spring admission, 10/1 priority date for domestic students, 10/1 for international students. Applications are processed on a rolling basis. Application fee: $50. Electronic applications accepted. *Expenses:* Tuition, state resident: full-time $7068; part-time $270 per semester hour. Tuition, nonresident: full-time $26,446; part-time $1077 per semester hour. *Required fees:* $2092. *Financial support:* In 2013–14, 2 students received support. Career-related internships or fieldwork, Federal Work-Study, scholarships/grants, tuition waivers (partial), and unspecified assistantships available. Support available to part-time students. Financial award application deadline: 4/15; financial award applicants required to submit FAFSA. *Faculty research:* Learning disorders, behavior disorders, education of the mentally retarded. *Unit head:* Dr. Eric Landers, Department Chair, 912-478-5203, Fax: 912-478-0026, E-mail: ericlanders@georgiasouthern.edu. *Application contact:* Amanda Gilliland, Coordinator for Graduate Student Recruitment, 912-478-5384, Fax: 912-478-0740, E-mail: gradadmissions@georgiasouthern.edu.

Georgia Southwestern State University, Graduate Studies, School of Education, Americus, GA 31709-4693. Offers early childhood education (M Ed, Ed S); health and physical education (M Ed); middle grades education (M Ed, Ed S); reading (M Ed);

secondary education (M Ed); special education (M Ed). *Accreditation:* NCATE. *Degree requirements:* For master's, comprehensive exam. *Entrance requirements:* For master's, GRE General Test or MAT, minimum GPA of 2.5; for Ed S, GRE General Test or MAT, minimum graduate GPA of 3.25, M Ed from accredited college or university, 3 years teaching experience. Electronic applications accepted.

Georgia State University, College of Education, Department of Educational Psychology and Special Education, Program in Behavior and Learning Disabilities, Atlanta, GA 30302-3083. Offers M Ed. *Accreditation:* NCATE. Part-time and evening/weekend programs available. *Students:* Average age 0. *Degree requirements:* For master's, comprehensive exam, minimum grade of B in each course in the teaching field/major. *Entrance requirements:* For master's, GRE (minimum scores at or above the 50th percentile), GACE Basics Skills Assessment, two official transcripts, minimum GPA of 3.0, certification in special education/T4 certificate, written statement of goals, resume, two letters of recommendation. Additional exam requirements/recommendations for international students: Required—TOEFL (minimum score 550 paper-based; 79 iBT) or IELTS (minimum score 6.5). *Application deadline:* For fall admission, 6/1 for domestic and international students; for winter admission, 11/1 for domestic and international students; for spring admission, 5/1 for domestic and international students. Application fee: $50. Electronic applications accepted. *Expenses: Tuition, area resident:* Full-time $4176; part-time $348 per credit hour. Tuition, state resident: full-time $14,544; part-time $1212 per credit hour. Tuition, nonresident: full-time $14,544; part-time $1212 per credit hour. Tuition and fees vary according to course load and program. *Financial support:* In 2013–14, fellowships with full tuition reimbursements (averaging $30,000 per year), research assistantships with full tuition reimbursements (averaging $2,000 per year) were awarded; teaching assistantships with full tuition reimbursements, scholarships/grants, health care benefits, and unspecified assistantships also available. *Faculty research:* Academic and behavioral supports for students with emotional/behavior disorders; academic interventions for learning disabilities; cultural, socioeconomic, and linguistic diversity; language and literacy development, disorders, and instruction, positive behavior supports. *Unit head:* Dr. Kristine Jolivette, Associate Professor, 404-413-8040, Fax: 404-413-8043, E-mail: kjolivette@gsu.edu. *Application contact:* Sandy Vaughn, Senior Administrative Coordinator, 404-413-8318, Fax: 404-413-8043, E-mail: svaughn@gsu.edu. Website: http://education.gsu.edu/EPSE/4622.html.

Georgia State University, College of Education, Department of Educational Psychology and Special Education, Program in Communication Disorders, Atlanta, GA 30302-3083. Offers M Ed. *Accreditation:* ASHA; NCATE. *Students:* Average age 0. *Entrance requirements:* For master's, GRE, minimum undergraduate GPA of 3.0. Additional exam requirements/recommendations for international students: Required—TOEFL (minimum score 550 paper-based; 79 iBT), IELTS (minimum score 6.5). *Application deadline:* For fall admission, 1/15 for domestic and international students. Application fee: $50. Electronic applications accepted. *Expenses: Tuition, area resident:* Full-time $4176; part-time $348 per credit hour. Tuition, state resident: full-time $14,544; part-time $1212 per credit hour. Tuition, nonresident: full-time $14,544; part-time $1212 per credit hour. Tuition and fees vary according to course load and program. *Faculty research:* Dialect, aphasia, motor speech disorders, child language development, high risk populations. *Unit head:* Dr. Jacqueline Sue Laures-Gore, Program Coordinator, 404-413-8299, E-mail: jlaures@gsu.edu. *Application contact:* Sandy Vaughn, Senior Administrative Coordinator, 404-413-8318, Fax: 404-413-8043, E-mail: svaughn@gsu.edu. Website: http://education.gsu.edu/EPSE/4717.html.

Georgia State University, College of Education, Department of Educational Psychology and Special Education, Program in Education of Students with Exceptionalities, Atlanta, GA 30302-3083. Offers autism spectrum disorders (PhD); behavior disorders (PhD); communication disorders (PhD); early childhood special education (PhD); learning disabilities (PhD); mental retardation (PhD); orthopedic impairments (PhD); sensory impairments (PhD). *Accreditation:* NCATE. Part-time and evening/weekend programs available. *Students:* Average age 0. *Degree requirements:* For doctorate, comprehensive exam, thesis/dissertation. *Entrance requirements:* Additional exam requirements/recommendations for international students: Required—TOEFL (minimum score 550 paper-based; 79 iBT) or IELTS (minimum score 6.5). *Application deadline:* For fall admission, 6/1 for domestic and international students; for winter admission, 11/1 for domestic and international students; for spring admission, 5/1 for domestic and international students. Application fee: $50. Electronic applications accepted. *Expenses: Tuition, area resident:* Full-time $4176; part-time $348 per credit hour. Tuition, state resident: full-time $14,544; part-time $1212 per credit hour. Tuition, nonresident: full-time $14,544; part-time $1212 per credit hour. Tuition and fees vary according to course load and program. *Financial support:* In 2013–14, fellowships with full tuition reimbursements (averaging $28,000 per year), research assistantships with full tuition reimbursements (averaging $2,000 per year) were awarded; scholarships/grants, health care benefits, and unspecified assistantships also available. *Faculty research:* Academic and behavioral supports for students with emotional/behavior disorders; academic interventions for learning disabilities; cultural, socioeconomic, and linguistic diversity; language and literacy development, disorders, and instruction. *Unit head:* Dr. Kristine Jolivette, Associate Professor, 404-413-8040, Fax: 404-413-8043, E-mail: kjolivette@gsu.edu. *Application contact:* Sandy Vaughn, Senior Administrative Coordinator, 404-413-8318, Fax: 404-413-8043, E-mail: svaughn@gsu.edu. Website: http://education.gsu.edu/EPSE/4922.html.

Georgia State University, College of Education, Department of Educational Psychology and Special Education, Program in Multiple and Severe Disabilities, Atlanta, GA 30302-3083. Offers early childhood special education general curriculum (M Ed); special education adapted curriculum (intellectual disability) (M Ed); special education deaf education (M Ed); special education general/adapted (autism spectrum disorders) (M Ed); special education physical and health disabilities (orthopedic impairments) (M Ed). *Accreditation:* NCATE. Part-time programs available. *Students:* Average age 0. *Degree requirements:* For master's, variable foreign language requirement, comprehensive exam, thesis (for some programs). *Entrance requirements:* For master's, GRE. Additional exam requirements/recommendations for international students: Required—TOEFL (minimum score 550 paper-based; 79 iBT) or IELTS (minimum score 6.5). *Application deadline:* For fall admission, 6/1 for domestic and international students; for winter admission, 11/1 for domestic and international students; for spring admission, 5/1 for domestic and international students. Application fee: $50. Electronic applications accepted. *Expenses: Tuition, area resident:* Full-time $4176; part-time $348 per credit hour. Tuition, state resident: full-time $14,544; part-time $1212 per credit hour. Tuition, nonresident: full-time $14,544; part-time $1212 per credit hour. Tuition and fees vary according to course load and program. *Financial support:* In 2013–14, fellowships with full tuition reimbursements (averaging $25,000 per year), research assistantships with full tuition reimbursements (averaging $2,000 per year) were awarded; teaching assistantships with full tuition reimbursements, scholarships/grants, health care benefits, and unspecified assistantships also available. *Faculty research:* Literacy, language, behavioral supports. *Unit head:* Dr. Kathryn Wolff Heller, Professor, 404-413-8040, E-mail: kheller@gsu.edu. *Application contact:* Sandy Vaughn, Senior

Administrative Coordinator, 404-413-8318, Fax: 404-413-8043, E-mail: svaughn@gsu.edu.
Website: http://education.gsu.edu/EPSE/4637.html.

Gonzaga University, School of Education, Program in Special Education, Spokane, WA 99258. Offers MES. *Accreditation:* NCATE. Part-time programs available. *Faculty:* 5 full-time (3 women), 1 (woman) part-time/adjunct. *Students:* 4 full-time (3 women), 5 part-time (all women), 2 international. Average age 32. 5 applicants, 20% accepted. In 2013, 11 master's awarded. *Degree requirements:* For master's, comprehensive exam. *Entrance requirements:* For master's, GRE General Test or MAT, minimum B average in undergraduate course work. Additional exam requirements/recommendations for international students: Required—TOEFL. *Application deadline:* For fall admission, 7/20 for domestic students; for spring admission, 11/1 for domestic students. Applications are processed on a rolling basis. Application fee: $50. Electronic applications accepted. *Expenses:* Contact institution. *Financial support:* Teaching assistantships available. Support available to part-time students. Financial award application deadline: 2/1; financial award applicants required to submit FAFSA. *Unit head:* Dr. Kimberly Weber, Department Chair, 509-313-3661, E-mail: weberk@gonzaga.edu. *Application contact:* Julie McCulloh, Dean of Admissions, 509-323-6592, Fax: 509-323-5780, E-mail: mcculloh@gu.gonzaga.edu.

Governors State University, College of Education, Program in Multi-Categorical Special Education, University Park, IL 60484. Offers MA. *Accreditation:* NCATE. Part-time and evening/weekend programs available. *Degree requirements:* For master's, comprehensive exam, practicum. *Entrance requirements:* For master's, minimum GPA of 2.75 in last 60 hours of undergraduate course work, 3.0 graduate.

Graceland University, Gleazer School of Education, Independence, MO 64050. Offers differentiated instruction (M Ed); literacy and instruction (M Ed); management in the inclusive classroom (M Ed); mild/moderate special education (M Ed); technology integration (M Ed). *Accreditation:* NCATE. Part-time and evening/weekend programs available. Postbaccalaureate distance learning degree programs offered (no on-campus study). *Faculty:* 12 full-time (11 women), 18 part-time/adjunct (14 women). *Students:* 139 full-time (119 women), 18 part-time (14 women); includes 8 minority (3 Black or African American, non-Hispanic/Latino; 1 Asian, non-Hispanic/Latino; 4 Hispanic/Latino). Average age 36. 36 applicants, 81% accepted, 24 enrolled. In 2013, 196 master's awarded. *Degree requirements:* For master's, action research project. *Entrance requirements:* For master's, minimum GPA of 3.0, teaching certificate, current teaching contract. *Application deadline:* For fall admission, 7/15 for domestic students; for winter admission, 10/15 for domestic students; for spring admission, 1/15 priority date for domestic students. Application fee: $50. Electronic applications accepted. *Expenses: Tuition:* Part-time $450 per semester hour. Tuition and fees vary according to course load, degree level, campus/location and program. *Financial support:* Institutionally sponsored loans and scholarships/grants available. Financial award application deadline: 12/15; financial award applicants required to submit FAFSA. *Unit head:* Dr. Scott Huddleston, Dean, 641-784-5000 Ext. 4744, E-mail: huddlest@graceland.edu. *Application contact:* Cathy Porter, Program Consultant, 816-423-4716, Fax: 816-833-2990, E-mail: cgporter@graceland.edu.
Website: http://www.graceland.edu/education.

Grambling State University, School of Graduate Studies and Research, College of Education, Department of Curriculum and Instruction, Grambling, LA 71245. Offers curriculum and instruction (MS); special education (M Ed). Part-time programs available. *Faculty:* 6 full-time (5 women). *Students:* 14 full-time (11 women), 48 part-time (43 women); includes 59 minority (58 Black or African American, non-Hispanic/Latino; 1 Hispanic/Latino), 2 international. Average age 35. In 2013, 29 master's awarded. *Degree requirements:* For master's, comprehensive exam, thesis (for some programs). *Entrance requirements:* Additional exam requirements/recommendations for international students: Required—TOEFL (minimum score 500 paper-based; 62 iBT). *Application deadline:* For fall admission, 7/1 for domestic and international students; for spring admission, 12/1 for domestic and international students; for summer admission, 5/1 for domestic and international students. *Financial support:* Application deadline: 5/31; applicants required to submit FAFSA. *Unit head:* Dr. Patricia P. Johnson, Interim Department Head, 318-274-2251, Fax: 318-274-3213, E-mail: johnsonp@gram.edu. *Application contact:* Katina S. Crowe-Fields, Special Assistant to Associate Vice President/Dean, 318-274-2158, Fax: 318-274-7373, E-mail: croweks@gram.edu. Website: http://www.gram.edu/academics/majors/education/departments/instruction/.

Grand Canyon University, College of Education, Phoenix, AZ 85017-1097. Offers curriculum and instruction (M Ed); education administration (M Ed); elementary education (M Ed); secondary education (M Ed); special education (M Ed); teaching (MA). Part-time and evening/weekend programs available. Postbaccalaureate distance learning degree programs offered (no on-campus study). *Degree requirements:* For master's, publishable research paper (M Ed), e-portfolio. *Entrance requirements:* For master's, undergraduate degree from accredited, GCU-approved college, university, or program with minimum GPA 2.8. Additional exam requirements/recommendations for international students: Required—TOEFL (minimum score 550 paper-based; 79 iBT), IELTS (minimum score 6). Electronic applications accepted.

Grand Valley State University, College of Education, Program in Special Education, Allendale, MI 49401-9403. Offers cognitive impairment (M Ed); early childhood developmental delay (M Ed); emotional impairment (M Ed); learning disabilities (M Ed); special education (M Ed). *Accreditation:* NCATE. Part-time and evening/weekend programs available. *Degree requirements:* For master's, thesis. *Entrance requirements:* For master's, GRE General Test or minimum GPA of 3.0. Additional exam requirements/recommendations for international students: Required—TOEFL. Electronic applications accepted. *Faculty research:* Evaluation of special education program effects, adaptive behavior assessment, language development, writing disorders, comparative effects of presentation methods.

Greensboro College, Program in Education, Greensboro, NC 27401-1875. Offers elementary education (M Ed); special education (M Ed). Part-time and evening/weekend programs available. *Degree requirements:* For master's, thesis. *Entrance requirements:* For master's, GRE, teacher license, 2 years of teaching experience, 2 letters of recommendation. Additional exam requirements/recommendations for international students: Required—TOEFL (minimum score 550 paper-based). Electronic applications accepted.

Gwynedd Mercy University, School of Education, Gwynedd Valley, PA 19437-0901. Offers educational administration (MS); master teacher (MS); reading (MS); school counseling (MS); special education (MS). Part-time and evening/weekend programs available. *Degree requirements:* For master's, thesis, internship, practicum. *Entrance requirements:* For master's, GRE or MAT; PRAXIS I, minimum GPA of 3.0. *Faculty research:* Learning and the brain, reading literacy, ethics and moral judgment, leadership, teaching and multicultural education.

Hampton University, Graduate College, College of Education and Continuing Studies, Program in Teaching, Hampton, VA 23668. Offers early childhood education (MT); middle school education (MT); music education (MT); secondary education (MT); special education (MT). *Entrance requirements:* For master's, GRE General Test.

Special Education

Harding University, Cannon-Clary College of Education, Searcy, AR 72149-0001. Offers advanced studies in teaching and learning (M Ed); art (MSE); behavioral science (MSE); counseling (MS, Ed S); early childhood special education (M Ed, MSE); education (MSE); educational leadership (M Ed, Ed S); elementary education (M Ed); English (MSE); French (MSE); history/social science (MSE); kinesiology (MSE); math (MSE); reading (M Ed); secondary education (M Ed); Spanish (MSE); teaching (MAT); teaching English as a second language (MSE). *Accreditation:* NCATE. Part-time and evening/weekend programs available. *Faculty:* 13 full-time (5 women), 42 part-time/adjunct (24 women). *Students:* 154 full-time (119 women), 393 part-time (270 women); includes 108 minority (81 Black or African American, non-Hispanic/Latino; 5 American Indian or Alaska Native, non-Hispanic/Latino; 5 Asian, non-Hispanic/Latino; 9 Hispanic/Latino; 8 Two or more races, non-Hispanic/Latino), 15 international. Average age 36. 187 applicants, 79% accepted, 135 enrolled. In 2013, 138 master's, 17 other advanced degrees awarded. *Degree requirements:* For master's, comprehensive exam (for some programs), thesis optional, portfolio(s); for Ed S, comprehensive exam, portfolio, project. *Entrance requirements:* For master's, GRE, MAT, PRAXIS; for Ed S, MAT or GRE. Additional exam requirements/recommendations for international students: Required—TOEFL (minimum score 550 paper-based; 79 iBT). *Application deadline:* For fall admission, 8/1 for domestic and international students; for spring admission, 1/1 for domestic and international students. Applications are processed on a rolling basis. Application fee: $35. *Expenses: Tuition:* Full-time $11,574; part-time $643 per credit hour. *Required fees:* $432; $24 per credit hour. Tuition and fees vary according to course load, degree level and program. *Financial support:* In 2013–14, 36 students received support. Unspecified assistantships available. *Faculty research:* Reading, comprehension, school violence, educational technology, behavior, college choice, differentiated instruction, brain-based teaching. *Unit head:* Dr. Clara Carroll, Chair, 501-279-4501, Fax: 501-279-4083, E-mail: ccarroll@harding.edu. *Application contact:* Information Contact, 501-279-4315, E-mail: gradstudiesedu@harding.edu.
Website: http://www.harding.edu/education.

Hebrew College, Shoolman Graduate School of Jewish Education, Newton Centre, MA 02459. Offers early childhood Jewish education (Certificate); Jewish day school education (Certificate); Jewish education (MJ Ed); Jewish family education (Certificate); Jewish special education (Certificate); Jewish youth education, informal education and camping (Certificate). Part-time and evening/weekend programs available. Postbaccalaureate distance learning degree programs offered. *Degree requirements:* For master's, one foreign language. *Entrance requirements:* For master's, GRE, interview. Additional exam requirements/recommendations for international students: Required—TOEFL.

Henderson State University, Graduate Studies, Teachers College, Department of Advanced Instructional Studies, Arkadelphia, AR 71999-0001. Offers early childhood (P-4) (MSE); education (MAT); English as a second language (Graduate Certificate); instructional facilitator (Graduate Certificate); middle school (MSE); reading (MSE); special education (MSE). *Accreditation:* NCATE. Part-time programs available. *Faculty:* 7 full-time (3 women), 2 part-time/adjunct (both women). *Students:* 1 (woman) full-time, 99 part-time (88 women); includes 20 minority (13 Black or African American, non-Hispanic/Latino; 1 American Indian or Alaska Native, non-Hispanic/Latino; 5 Hispanic/Latino; 1 Two or more races, non-Hispanic/Latino), 1 international. Average age 36. 7 applicants, 100% accepted, 7 enrolled. In 2013, 45 master's awarded. *Entrance requirements:* For master's, GRE General Test or MAT, minimum GPA of 2.7, teacher certification. Additional exam requirements/recommendations for international students: Required—TOEFL (minimum score 600 paper-based); Recommended—IELTS (minimum score 6.5). *Application deadline:* For fall admission, 8/1 priority date for domestic students, 6/30 priority date for international students; for spring admission, 1/1 priority date for domestic students, 11/30 priority date for international students. Applications are processed on a rolling basis. Application fee: $25 ($75 for international students). *Expenses:* Tuition, state resident: full-time $4284; part-time $238 per credit hour. Tuition, nonresident: full-time $8802; part-time $489 per credit hour. Tuition and fees vary according to course load and campus/location. *Financial support:* In 2013–14, 1 teaching assistantship with partial tuition reimbursement (averaging $4,000 per year) was awarded; scholarships/grants and unspecified assistantships also available. *Unit head:* Dr. Gary Smithey, Chairperson, 870-230-5361, Fax: 870-230-5455, E-mail: smitheg@hsu.edu. *Application contact:* Dr. Ken Taylor, Graduate Dean, 870-230-5126, Fax: 870-230-5479, E-mail: taylorke@hsu.edu.

Heritage University, Graduate Programs in Education, Program in Professional Studies, Toppenish, WA 98948-9599. Offers bilingual education/ESL (M Ed); biology (M Ed); English and literature (M Ed); reading/literacy (M Ed); special education (M Ed). Part-time and evening/weekend programs available. *Degree requirements:* For master's, comprehensive exam (for some programs), thesis (for some programs).

High Point University, Norcross Graduate School, High Point, NC 27262-3598. Offers business administration (MBA); educational leadership (M Ed); elementary education (M Ed); history (MA); nonprofit management (MA); secondary math (M Ed); special education (M Ed); strategic communication (MA); teaching elementary education k-6 (MAT); teaching secondary mathematics 9-12 (MAT). *Accreditation:* NCATE. Part-time and evening/weekend programs available. *Degree requirements:* For master's, comprehensive exam (for some programs), thesis (for some programs). *Entrance requirements:* For master's, GMAT (MBA), GRE, MAT, minimum GPA of 3.0. Additional exam requirements/recommendations for international students: Required—TOEFL (minimum score 550 paper-based). Electronic applications accepted.

Hofstra University, School of Education, Programs in Literacy, Hempstead, NY 11549. Offers advanced literacy studies (PD), including birth-grade 6 (MA, MS Ed, PD); advanced literary studies (PD), including grades 5-12 (MA, PD); birth-grade 6 (MS Ed, Advanced Certificate); grades 5-12 (Advanced Certificate); literacy studies (Ed D, PhD); special education (MS Ed), including birth-grade 2, birth-grade 6 (MA, MS Ed, PD); teaching of writing (MA), including birth-grade 6 (MA, MS Ed, PD), grades 5-12 (MA, PD).

Hofstra University, School of Education, Programs in Special Education, Hempstead, NY 11549. Offers applied behavior analysis (Advanced Certificate); early childhood special education (MS Ed, Advanced Certificate); gifted education (Advanced Certificate); inclusive early childhood special education (MS Ed); inclusive elementary special education (MS Ed); inclusive secondary special education (MS Ed); secondary education generalist (MS Ed), including students with disabilities 7-12; special education (MA, MS Ed, Advanced Certificate, PD); special education assessment and diagnosis (Advanced Certificate); special education generalist (MS Ed), including extension in secondary education; teaching students with severe or multiple disabilities (Advanced Certificate).

Holy Family University, Graduate School, School of Education, Master of Education Programs, Philadelphia, PA 19114. Offers early elementary education (PreK-Grade 4) (M Ed); education leadership (M Ed); general education (M Ed); middle level education (Grades 4-8) (M Ed); reading specialist (M Ed); secondary education (Grades 7-12) (M Ed); special education (M Ed); TESOL and literacy (M Ed). *Expenses: Tuition:* Full-time $12,060. *Required fees:* $250. Tuition and fees vary according to degree level. *Unit head:* Dr. Leonard Soroka, Dean, 267-341-3565, Fax: 215-824-2438, E-mail: lsoroka@holyfamily.edu. *Application contact:* Gidget Marie Montelibano, Associate Director of Graduate Admissions, 267-341-3358, Fax: 215-637-1478, E-mail: gmontelibano@holyfamily.edu.

Holy Names University, Graduate Division, Department of Education, Oakland, CA 94619-1699. Offers educational therapy (Certificate); mild/moderate disabilities (Ed S); multiple subject teaching (Credential); single subject teaching (Credential); teaching English as a second language (TESL) (M Ed); urban education: educational therapy (M Ed); urban education: K-12 education (M Ed); urban education: special education (M Ed). Part-time programs available. *Faculty:* 4 full-time, 14 part-time/adjunct. *Students:* 25 full-time (19 women), 127 part-time (93 women); includes 74 minority (37 Black or African American, non-Hispanic/Latino; 7 Asian, non-Hispanic/Latino; 28 Hispanic/Latino; 1 Native Hawaiian or other Pacific Islander, non-Hispanic/Latino; 1 Two or more races, non-Hispanic/Latino), 2 international. Average age 35. 72 applicants, 75% accepted, 37 enrolled. In 2013, 15 master's, 22 Certificates awarded. *Degree requirements:* For master's, comprehensive exam, research paper, thesis or project. *Entrance requirements:* For master's, minimum undergraduate GPA of 2.6 overall, 3.0 in major, personal statement, two recommendations, interview. Additional exam requirements/recommendations for international students: Required—TOEFL (minimum score 550 paper-based; 79 iBT). *Application deadline:* For fall admission, 8/1 priority date for domestic students, 7/15 for international students; for spring admission, 12/1 priority date for domestic students, 12/1 for international students; for summer admission, 5/1 priority date for domestic students, 5/1 for international students. Applications are processed on a rolling basis. Application fee: $65. Electronic applications accepted. Application fee is waived when completed online. *Expenses: Tuition:* Part-time $866 per unit. *Financial support:* Career-related internships or fieldwork, Federal Work-Study, scholarships/grants, and unspecified assistantships available. Support available to part-time students. Financial award application deadline: 3/2; financial award applicants required to submit FAFSA. *Faculty research:* Cognitive development, language development, learning handicaps. *Unit head:* Dr. Kimberly Mayfiel, 510-436-1396, Fax: 510-436-1325, E-mail: mayfield@hnu.edu. *Application contact:* Graduate Admission, 800-430-1321, Fax: 510-436-1325, E-mail: graduateadmissions@hnu.edu.
Website: http://www.hnu.edu/academics/graduatePrograms/education.html.

Hood College, Graduate School, Department of Education, Frederick, MD 21701-8575. Offers curriculum and instruction (MS), including early childhood education, elementary education, elementary school science and mathematics, secondary education, special education; educational leadership (MS, Certificate); reading specialization (MS); STEM (Certificate). *Accreditation:* NCATE. Part-time and evening/weekend programs available. *Faculty:* 4 full-time (3 women), 33 part-time/adjunct (25 women). *Students:* 1 (woman) full-time, 340 part-time (282 women); includes 59 minority (31 Black or African American, non-Hispanic/Latino; 1 American Indian or Alaska Native, non-Hispanic/Latino; 10 Asian, non-Hispanic/Latino; 13 Hispanic/Latino; 4 Two or more races, non-Hispanic/Latino). Average age 33. 97 applicants, 99% accepted, 86 enrolled. In 2013, 64 master's, 40 other advanced degrees awarded. *Degree requirements:* For master's, action research project, portfolio (reading). *Entrance requirements:* For master's, minimum GPA of 2.75, teaching certification. Additional exam requirements/recommendations for international students: Required—TOEFL (minimum score 575 paper-based; 89 iBT), IELTS (minimum score 6.5). *Application deadline:* For fall admission, 7/15 priority date for domestic students, 7/15 for international students; for spring admission, 12/1 priority date for domestic students, 12/1 for international students. Applications are processed on a rolling basis. Application fee: $35. Electronic applications accepted. Application fee is waived when completed online. *Expenses: Tuition:* Part-time $405 per credit. *Required fees:* $100 per semester. *Financial support:* In 2013–14, 1 student received support. Tuition waivers (partial) and unspecified assistantships available. Financial award applicants required to submit FAFSA. *Faculty research:* Leadership, action research, brain research, learning styles. *Unit head:* Dr. Ellen Koitz, Chairperson, 301-696-3466, Fax: 301-696-3597, E-mail: koitz@hood.edu. *Application contact:* Dr. Maria Green Cowles, Dean of Graduate School, 301-696-3811, Fax: 301-696-3597, E-mail: gofurther@hood.edu.
Website: http://www.hood.edu/academics/education/index.html.

Howard University, School of Education, Department of Curriculum and Instruction, Program in Special Education, Washington, DC 20059-0002. Offers M Ed. *Accreditation:* NCATE. Part-time programs available. *Faculty:* 2 full-time (1 woman), 1 part-time/adjunct (0 women). *Students:* 4 full-time (3 women), 6 part-time (3 women); all minorities (all Black or African American, non-Hispanic/Latino). Average age 32. 5 applicants, 60% accepted, 1 enrolled. In 2013, 6 master's awarded. *Degree requirements:* For master's, comprehensive exam, thesis (for some programs), expository writing exam, internships, practicum. *Entrance requirements:* For master's, minimum GPA of 2.7. Additional exam requirements/recommendations for international students: Required—TOEFL (minimum score 550 paper-based; 79 iBT). *Application deadline:* For fall admission, 2/15 priority date for domestic students; for spring admission, 11/1 for domestic students. Applications are processed on a rolling basis. Application fee: $45. Electronic applications accepted. *Financial support:* In 2013–14, 2 students received support, including 2 fellowships with full and partial tuition reimbursements available; career-related internships or fieldwork, Federal Work-Study, institutionally sponsored loans, scholarships/grants, tuition waivers (full and partial), and unspecified assistantships also available. Financial award application deadline: 3/15; financial award applicants required to submit FAFSA. *Unit head:* Dr. Kenneth Anderson, Chair, Department of Curriculum and Instruction, 202-806-5300, Fax: 202-806-5297, E-mail: kenneth.anderson@howard.edu. *Application contact:* June L. Harris, Administrative Assistant, Department of Curriculum and Instruction, 202-806-7343, Fax: 202-806-5297, E-mail: jlharris@howard.edu.

Hunter College of the City University of New York, Graduate School, School of Education, Department of Special Education, New York, NY 10065-5085. Offers blind or visually impaired (MS Ed); deaf or hard of hearing (MS Ed); severe/multiple disabilities (MS Ed); special education (MS Ed). *Accreditation:* NCATE. *Faculty:* 7 full-time (5 women), 71 part-time/adjunct (59 women). *Students:* 43 full-time (38 women), 478 part-time (389 women); includes 143 minority (43 Black or African American, non-Hispanic/Latino; 1 American Indian or Alaska Native, non-Hispanic/Latino; 34 Asian, non-Hispanic/Latino; 65 Hispanic/Latino). Average age 27. 44 applicants, 91% accepted, 28 enrolled. In 2013, 331 master's awarded. *Degree requirements:* For master's, comprehensive exam, thesis, student teaching practica, clinical teaching lab courses, New York State Teacher Certification Exams. *Entrance requirements:* For master's, minimum GPA of 2.8. Additional exam requirements/recommendations for international students: Required—TOEFL, TWE. *Application deadline:* For fall admission, 4/1 for domestic students, 2/1 for international students; for spring admission, 11/1 for domestic students, 9/1 for international students. Applications are processed on a rolling basis. Application fee: $50. *Financial support:* Career-related internships or fieldwork, Federal Work-Study, institutionally sponsored loans, and tuition waivers (partial) available. Support available to part-time students. *Faculty research:* Mathematics learning disabilities; street behavior; assessment; bilingual special education; families, diversity, and disabilities. *Unit head:* Prof. David Connor, Chairperson, 212-772-4700, E-mail:

dconnor@hunter.cuny.edu. *Application contact:* Milena Solo, Director for Graduate Admissions, 212-772-4480, E-mail: admissions@hunter.cuny.edu. Website: http://www.hunter.cuny.edu/school-of-education/programs/graduate/special-education.

Idaho State University, Office of Graduate Studies, College of Education, Department of School Psychology, Literacy, and Special Education, Pocatello, ID 83209-8059. Offers deaf education (M Ed); human exceptionality (M Ed); literacy (M Ed); school psychology (Ed S); special education (Ed S). Part-time programs available. *Degree requirements:* For master's, comprehensive exam, thesis (for some programs), oral thesis defense or written comprehensive exam and oral exam; for Ed S, comprehensive exam, thesis (for some programs), oral exam, specialist paper or portfolio. *Entrance requirements:* For master's, GRE or MAT, minimum undergraduate GPA of 3.0, bachelor's degree, professional experience in an educational context; for Ed S, GRE or MAT, master's degree in related field. Additional exam requirements/recommendations for international students: Required—TOEFL (minimum score 550 paper-based; 80 iBT). Electronic applications accepted. *Faculty research:* Literacy, school psychology, special education.

Idaho State University, Office of Graduate Studies, Kasiska College of Health Professions, Department of Communication Sciences and Disorders and Education of the Deaf, Pocatello, ID 83209-8116. Offers audiology (MS, Au D); communication sciences and disorders (Postbaccalaureate Certificate); communication sciences and disorders and education of the deaf (Certificate); deaf education (MS); speech language pathology (MS). *Accreditation:* ASHA (one or more programs are accredited). Part-time programs available. *Degree requirements:* For master's, thesis optional, written and oral comprehensive exams; for doctorate, comprehensive exam, thesis/dissertation optional, externship, 1 year full time clinical practicum, 3rd year spent in Boise. *Entrance requirements:* For master's, GRE General Test, minimum GPA of 3.0, 3 letters of recommendation; for doctorate, GRE General Test (at least 2 scores minimum 40th percentile), minimum GPA of 3.0, 3 letters of recommendation, bachelor's degree. Additional exam requirements/recommendations for international students: Required—TOEFL (minimum score 600 paper-based; 80 iBT). Electronic applications accepted. *Faculty research:* Neurogenic disorders, central auditory processing disorders, vestibular disorders, cochlear implants, language disorders, professional burnout, swallowing disorders.

Illinois State University, Graduate School, College of Education, Department of Special Education, Normal, IL 61790-2200. Offers MS, MS Ed, Ed D. *Accreditation:* NCATE. *Degree requirements:* For doctorate, thesis/dissertation, 2 terms of residency. *Entrance requirements:* For master's, GRE General Test, minimum GPA of 3.0 in last 60 hours; for doctorate, GRE General Test. *Faculty research:* Center for adult learning leadership, promoting a learning community, autism spectrum professional development and technical assistance project, preparing qualified personnel to provide early intervention for children who are deaf.

Immaculata University, College of Graduate Studies, Program in Educational Leadership and Administration, Immaculata, PA 19345. Offers educational leadership and administration (MA, Ed D); elementary education (Certificate); school principal (Certificate); school superintendent (Certificate); secondary education (Certificate); special education (Certificate). Part-time and evening/weekend programs available. *Degree requirements:* For master's, comprehensive exam, thesis optional; for doctorate, comprehensive exam, thesis/dissertation. *Entrance requirements:* For master's, GRE or MAT, minimum GPA of 3.0; for doctorate, GRE General Test or MAT, minimum GPA of 3.5. Additional exam requirements/recommendations for international students: Required—TOEFL. Electronic applications accepted. *Faculty research:* Cooperative learning, school-based management, whole language, performance assessment.

Indiana University Bloomington, School of Education, Department of Curriculum and Instruction, Bloomington, IN 47405-7000. Offers art education (MS, Ed D, PhD); curriculum studies (Ed D, PhD); elementary education (MS, Ed D, PhD, Ed S); mathematics education (MS, Ed D, PhD); science education (MS, Ed D, PhD); secondary education (MS, Ed D, PhD); social studies education (MS, PhD); special education (PhD, Ed S). *Accreditation:* NCATE. Part-time and evening/weekend programs available. Terminal master's awarded for partial completion of doctoral program. *Degree requirements:* For doctorate, thesis/dissertation; for Ed S, comprehensive exam or project. *Entrance requirements:* For master's, doctorate, and Ed S, GRE General Test. Electronic applications accepted.

Indiana University of Pennsylvania, School of Graduate Studies and Research, College of Education and Educational Technology, Department of Special Education and Clinical Services, Program in Education of Exceptional Persons, Indiana, PA 15705-1087. Offers M Ed. *Accreditation:* NCATE. Part-time programs available. *Faculty:* 9 full-time (8 women), 2 part-time/adjunct (both women). *Students:* 5 full-time (4 women), 11 part-time (8 women); includes 1 minority (Two or more races, non-Hispanic/Latino), 1 international. Average age 28. 19 applicants, 26% accepted, 4 enrolled. In 2013, 16 master's awarded. *Degree requirements:* For master's, comprehensive exam, thesis optional. *Entrance requirements:* For master's, 2 letters of recommendation. Additional exam requirements/recommendations for international students: Required—TOEFL (minimum score 540 paper-based). *Application deadline:* For fall admission, 3/1 for domestic students; for spring admission, 7/1 for domestic students. Applications are processed on a rolling basis. Application fee: $50. Electronic applications accepted. *Expenses:* Tuition, state resident: full-time $3978; part-time $442 per credit. Tuition, nonresident: full-time $5967; part-time $663 per credit. *Required fees:* $2080; $115.55 per credit. $93 per semester. Tuition and fees vary according to degree level and program. *Financial support:* In 2013–14, 4 research assistantships with full and partial tuition reimbursements (averaging $2,720 per year) were awarded; career-related internships or fieldwork, Federal Work-Study, scholarships/grants, and unspecified assistantships also available. Support available to part-time students. Financial award application deadline: 4/15; financial award applicants required to submit FAFSA. *Unit head:* Dr. Joan Migyanka, Graduate Coordinator, 724-357-5679, E-mail: j.migyanka@iup.edu. *Application contact:* Paula Stossel, Assistant Dean for Administration, 724-357-4511, Fax: 724-357-4862, E-mail: graduate-admissions@iup.edu. Website: http://www.iup.edu/grad/edex/default.aspx.

Indiana University–Purdue University Fort Wayne, College of Education and Public Policy, Department of Professional Studies, Fort Wayne, IN 46805-1499. Offers counselor education (MS Ed); couple and family counseling (MS Ed); educational leadership (MS Ed); school counseling (MS Ed); special education (MS Ed, Certificate). Part-time programs available. *Faculty:* 7 full-time (6 women). *Students:* 5 full-time (2 women), 100 part-time (80 women); includes 11 minority (8 Black or African American, non-Hispanic/Latino; 1 Asian, non-Hispanic/Latino; 2 Hispanic/Latino), 1 international. Average age 32. 14 applicants, 100% accepted, 9 enrolled. In 2013, 57 master's awarded. *Degree requirements:* For master's, comprehensive exam, practicum, internship, portfolio. *Entrance requirements:* For master's, minimum GPA of 2.5, three professional letters of recommendation. Additional exam requirements/recommendations for international students: Required—TOEFL (minimum score 550 paper-based; 79 iBT). *Application deadline:* For fall admission, 4/1 priority date for domestic and international students. Applications are processed on a rolling basis. Application fee: $55. *Financial support:* In 2013–14, 1 research assistantship with partial tuition reimbursement (averaging $13,322 per year), 1 teaching assistantship with partial tuition reimbursement (averaging $13,322 per year) were awarded; scholarships/grants also available. Support available to part-time students. Financial award application deadline: 3/1; financial award applicants required to submit FAFSA. *Faculty research:* Perceptions of children and early adolescents at-risk. *Unit head:* Dr. Jane Leatherman, Acting Chair, 260-481-5742, Fax: 260-481-5408, E-mail: leatherj@ipfw.edu. *Application contact:* Vicky L. Schmidt, Graduate Recorder, 260-481-6450, Fax: 260-481-5408, E-mail: schmidt@ipfw.edu. Website: http://new.ipfw.edu/education.

Indiana University–Purdue University Indianapolis, School of Education, Indianapolis, IN 46202-2896. Offers computer education (Certificate); curriculum and instruction (MS); early childhood (MS); educational leadership (MS, Certificate); English as a second language (Certificate); higher education and student affairs (MS); kindergarten (Certificate); language education (MS); reading (Certificate); school counseling (MS); special education (MS, Certificate). Part-time and evening/weekend programs available. *Faculty:* 41 full-time, 80 part-time/adjunct. *Students:* 113 full-time (78 women), 263 part-time (200 women); includes 88 minority (51 Black or African American, non-Hispanic/Latino; 1 American Indian or Alaska Native, non-Hispanic/Latino; 10 Asian, non-Hispanic/Latino; 19 Hispanic/Latino; 7 Two or more races, non-Hispanic/Latino), 5 international. Average age 33. 93 applicants, 54% accepted, 40 enrolled. In 2013, 179 master's awarded. *Degree requirements:* For master's, thesis optional. *Entrance requirements:* For master's, GRE General Test, minimum GPA of 3.0. Additional exam requirements/recommendations for international students: Required—TOEFL. *Application deadline:* For fall admission, 5/1 priority date for domestic students; for spring admission, 11/1 for domestic students. Application fee: $55 ($65 for international students). *Financial support:* Fellowships, research assistantships with partial tuition reimbursements, teaching assistantships, Federal Work-Study, institutionally sponsored loans, scholarships/grants, and tuition waivers (partial) available. Support available to part-time students. *Faculty research:* Teachers in the process of change, learning cycles, children's concepts of science. *Total annual research expenditures:* $614,458. *Unit head:* Dr. Pat Rogan, Executive Associate Dean, 317-274-6862, E-mail: progan@iupui.edu. *Application contact:* Donnella Dillon, Graduate Admissions Coordinator, 317-274-0645, E-mail: dmdillon@iupui.edu. Website: http://education.iupui.edu/.

Indiana University South Bend, School of Education, South Bend, IN 46634-7111. Offers counseling and human services (MS Ed); elementary and secondary education leadership (MS Ed); elementary education (MS Ed); secondary education (MS Ed); special education (MAT, MS Ed). *Accreditation:* NCATE. Part-time and evening/weekend programs available. *Faculty:* 21 full-time (11 women), 9 part-time/adjunct (3 women). *Students:* 12 full-time (8 women), 103 part-time (85 women); includes 18 minority (8 Black or African American, non-Hispanic/Latino; 1 Asian, non-Hispanic/Latino; 5 Hispanic/Latino; 4 Two or more races, non-Hispanic/Latino), 3 international. Average age 36. 24 applicants, 63% accepted, 9 enrolled. In 2013, 41 master's awarded. *Degree requirements:* For master's, thesis or alternative, exit project. *Entrance requirements:* For master's, letters of recommendation, GRE or minimum GPA of 3.0. Additional exam requirements/recommendations for international students: Required—TOEFL. *Application deadline:* For fall admission, 7/1 for domestic students; for spring admission, 11/1 for domestic students. Applications are processed on a rolling basis. Electronic applications accepted. *Financial support:* Career-related internships or fieldwork available. Support available to part-time students. Financial award application deadline: 3/1; financial award applicants required to submit FAFSA. *Faculty research:* Professional dispositions, early childhood literacy, online learning, program assessments, problem-based learning. *Unit head:* Dr. Marvin Lynn, Dean, 574-520-4339. *Application contact:* Yvonne Walker, Student Services Representative, 574-520-4185, E-mail: ydwalker@iusb.edu. Website: http://www.iusb.edu/~edud/.

Inter American University of Puerto Rico, Barranquitas Campus, Program in Education, Barranquitas, PR 00794. Offers curriculum and teaching (M Ed), including biology education, English as a second language, history education, mathematics education, Spanish; educational leadership and management (MA); elementary education (M Ed); information and library service technology (M Ed); special education (MA). *Degree requirements:* For master's, comprehensive exam, thesis optional. *Entrance requirements:* For master's, EXADEP, letter of recommendation. Electronic applications accepted.

Inter American University of Puerto Rico, Metropolitan Campus, Graduate Programs, Program in Special Education, San Juan, PR 00919-1293. Offers MA. *Degree requirements:* For master's, comprehensive exam. *Entrance requirements:* For master's, GRE or EXADEP, interview. Electronic applications accepted.

Inter American University of Puerto Rico, San Germán Campus, Graduate Studies Center, Program in Special Education, San Germán, PR 00683-5008. Offers MA. Part-time and evening/weekend programs available. *Faculty:* 8 full-time (6 women), 13 part-time/adjunct (7 women). *Students:* 27 full-time (25 women), 1 (woman) part-time; all minorities (all Hispanic/Latino). Average age 30. 13 applicants, 69% accepted, 9 enrolled. In 2013, 3 master's awarded. *Degree requirements:* For master's, comprehensive exam. *Entrance requirements:* For master's, GRE General Test or EXADEP, minimum GPA of 3.0. *Application deadline:* For fall admission, 4/30 priority date for domestic students; for spring admission, 11/15 for domestic students. Applications are processed on a rolling basis. Application fee: $31. *Expenses: Tuition:* Full-time $2424; part-time $202 per credit hour. *Required fees:* $260 per semester. Tuition and fees vary according to course level, course load, degree level and program. *Financial support:* Teaching assistantships available. *Unit head:* Dr. Elba T. Irizarry, Director of Graduate Studies Center, 787-264-1912 Ext. 7357, Fax: 787-892-6350, E-mail: elbat@sg.inter.edu. *Application contact:* Dr. Elba T. Irizarry, Director of Graduate Studies Center, 787-264-1912 Ext. 7357, Fax: 787-892-6350, E-mail: elbat@sg.inter.edu.

Iona College, School of Arts and Science, Department of Education, New Rochelle, NY 10801-1890. Offers adolescence education: biology (MS Ed, MST); adolescence education: English (MS Ed, MST); adolescence education: Italian (MS Ed, MST); adolescence education: mathematics (MS Ed, MST); adolescence education: social studies (MS Ed, MST); adolescence education: Spanish (MS Ed, MST); adolescence special education 5-12 (MST); adolescence special education and literacy (MS Ed); childhood and special education (MST); childhood education (MST); early childhood and childhood (MST); educational leadership (MS Ed); literacy education: birth-grade 6 (MS Ed). *Accreditation:* NCATE. Part-time and evening/weekend programs available. *Faculty:* 11 full-time (9 women), 7 part-time/adjunct (6 women). *Students:* 34 full-time (25 women), 61 part-time (47 women); includes 5 minority (2 Asian, non-Hispanic/Latino; 3 Hispanic/Latino), 1 international. Average age 25. 27 applicants, 93% accepted, 16 enrolled. In 2013, 54 master's awarded. *Degree requirements:* For master's, thesis or alternative. *Entrance requirements:* For master's, minimum GPA of 3.0, NY State teaching certificate (for all MS Ed programs). Additional exam requirements/recommendations for international students: Required—TOEFL (minimum score 550 paper-based; 80 iBT), IELTS (minimum score 6.5). *Application deadline:* For fall admission, 8/1 priority date for domestic students, 5/1 priority date for international

students; for spring admission, 1/1 priority date for domestic students, 9/1 priority date for international students. Applications are processed on a rolling basis. Application fee: $50. Electronic applications accepted. *Expenses: Tuition:* Part-time $948 per credit. *Required fees:* $235 per term. *Financial support:* In 2013–14, 84 students received support. Unspecified assistantships available. Support available to part-time students. Financial award application deadline: 4/15; financial award applicants required to submit FAFSA. *Faculty research:* Reading/writing, educational technology, administration, early literacy assessment, literacy development. *Unit head:* Margaret Smith, PhD, Chair, 914-633-2210, Fax: 914-633-2608, E-mail: msmith@iona.edu. *Application contact:* Veronica Jarek-Prinz, Director, Graduate Admissions, 914-633-2420, Fax: 914-633-2277, E-mail: vjarekprinz@iona.edu.
Website: http://www.iona.edu/Academics/School-of-Arts-Science/Departments/Education/Graduate-Programs.aspx.

Iowa State University of Science and Technology, Department of Curriculum and Instruction, Ames, IA 50011. Offers curriculum and instructional technology (M Ed, MS, PhD); elementary education (M Ed, MS); historical, philosophical, and comparative studies in education (M Ed, MS); special education (M Ed, MS, PhD). *Degree requirements:* For master's, thesis or alternative; for doctorate, thesis/dissertation. *Entrance requirements:* For master's and doctorate, GRE General Test. Additional exam requirements/recommendations for international students: Required—TOEFL (minimum score 560 paper-based; 83 iBT), IELTS (minimum score 6.5). Electronic applications accepted.

Jackson State University, Graduate School, College of Education and Human Development, Department of Special Education and Rehabilitative Services, Jackson, MS 39217. Offers special education (MS Ed, Ed S). *Accreditation:* NCATE. Evening/weekend programs available. *Degree requirements:* For master's, comprehensive exam, thesis or alternative. *Entrance requirements:* For master's, GRE General Test. Additional exam requirements/recommendations for international students: Required—TOEFL (minimum score 520 paper-based; 67 iBT).

Jacksonville State University, College of Graduate Studies and Continuing Education, College of Education and Professional Studies, Program in Special Education, Jacksonville, AL 36265-1602. Offers MS Ed. *Accreditation:* NCATE. *Degree requirements:* For master's, comprehensive exam, thesis (for some programs). *Entrance requirements:* For master's, GRE General Test or MAT. Additional exam requirements/recommendations for international students: Required—TOEFL (minimum score 61 iBT). Electronic applications accepted.

James Madison University, The Graduate School, College of Education, Exceptional Education Department, Program in Exceptional Education, Harrisonburg, VA 22807. Offers M Ed. *Accreditation:* NCATE. Part-time programs available. *Students:* 24 full-time (23 women), 18 part-time (15 women). Average age 27. In 2013, 30 master's awarded. *Entrance requirements:* For master's, GRE General Test or PRAXIS, minimum undergraduate GPA of 2.75, resume. Additional exam requirements/recommendations for international students: Required—TOEFL. *Application deadline:* For fall admission, 5/1 priority date for domestic students; for spring admission, 9/1 priority date for domestic students. Applications are processed on a rolling basis. Application fee: $55. Electronic applications accepted. *Financial support:* In 2013–14, 1 student received support. Federal Work-Study and 1 graduate assistantship (averaging $7530) available. Financial award application deadline: 3/1; financial award applicants required to submit FAFSA. *Unit head:* Dr. Laura Desportes, Academic Unit Head, 540-568-6193. *Application contact:* Lynette M. Bible, Director of Graduate Admissions, 540-568-6395, Fax: 540-568-7860, E-mail: biblelm@jmu.edu.

Johns Hopkins University, School of Education, Certificate Programs in Education, Baltimore, MD 21218-2699. Offers advanced methods for differentiated instruction and inclusive education (Certificate); applied behavior analysis (Certificate); counseling (CAGS); data-based decision making and organizational improvement (Certificate); early intervention/preschool special education specialist (Certificate); education leadership for independent schools (Certificate); education of students with autism and other pervasive developmental disorders (Certificate); evidence-based teaching in the health professions (Certificate); gifted education (Certificate); K-8 mathematics lead-teacher (Certificate); K-8 STEM education lead-teacher (Certificate); leadership for school, family, and community collaboration (Certificate); leadership in technology integration (Certificate); mental health counseling (Certificate); mind, brain, and teaching (Certificate); school administration and supervision (Certificate); urban education (Certificate). Part-time and evening/weekend programs available. Postbaccalaureate distance learning degree programs offered (no on-campus study). *Students:* 7 full-time (4 women), 216 part-time (169 women); includes 66 minority (35 Black or African American, non-Hispanic/Latino; 17 Asian, non-Hispanic/Latino; 6 Hispanic/Latino; 8 Two or more races, non-Hispanic/Latino), 6 international. Average age 35. 257 applicants, 81% accepted, 62 enrolled. In 2013, 202 CAGSs awarded. *Entrance requirements:* For degree, bachelor's degree from regionally- or nationally-accredited institution (master's for some programs), minimum GPA of 3.0 in all previous programs of study, official transcripts from all post-secondary institutions attended, essay, curriculum vitae/resume, minimum of two letters of recommendation. Additional exam requirements/recommendations for international students: Required—TOEFL (minimum score 600 paper-based; 100 iBT) or IELTS (minimum score 7). *Application deadline:* For fall admission, 4/1 for domestic students; for spring admission, 10/1 for domestic students; for summer admission, 2/1 for domestic students. Application fee: $80. Electronic applications accepted. *Financial support:* Application deadline: 6/1; applicants required to submit FAFSA. *Unit head:* Dr. David A. Andrews, Dean, 410-516-7820, Fax: 410-516-6697, E-mail: davidandrews@jhu.edu. *Application contact:* Catherine Wilson, Associate Director of Admissions, 410-516-9797, Fax: 410-516-9799, E-mail: soe.info@jhu.edu.

Johns Hopkins University, School of Education, Master's Programs in Education, Baltimore, MD 21218-2699. Offers counseling (MS), including mental health counseling, school counseling; education (MS), including educational studies, gifted education, reading, school administration and supervision, technology for educators; elementary education (MAT); health professions (M Ed); intelligence analysis (MS); management (MS); secondary education (MAT); special education (MS), including early childhood special education, general special education studies, mild to moderate disabilities, severe disabilities. Part-time and evening/weekend programs available. Postbaccalaureate distance learning degree programs offered (no on-campus study). *Students:* 183 full-time (123 women), 1,001 part-time (757 women); includes 380 minority (160 Black or African American, non-Hispanic/Latino; 4 American Indian or Alaska Native, non-Hispanic/Latino; 91 Asian, non-Hispanic/Latino; 78 Hispanic/Latino; 4 Native Hawaiian or other Pacific Islander, non-Hispanic/Latino; 43 Two or more races, non-Hispanic/Latino), 28 international. Average age 28. 508 applicants, 90% accepted, 337 enrolled. In 2013, 565 degrees awarded. *Degree requirements:* For master's, comprehensive exam (for some programs), portfolio, capstone project and/or internship; PRAXIS II (for teacher preparation programs that lead to licensure). *Entrance requirements:* For master's, GRE (for full-time programs only); PRAXIS I or equivalent (for teacher preparation programs that lead to licensure), bachelor's degree from regionally- or nationally-accredited institution, minimum GPA of 3.0 in all previous programs of study, official transcripts from all post-secondary institutions attended, essay, curriculum vitae/resume, minimum of two letters of recommendation. Additional exam requirements/recommendations for international students: Required—TOEFL (minimum score 600 paper-based; 100 iBT) or IELTS (minimum score 7). *Application deadline:* For fall admission, 4/1 for domestic and international students; for spring admission, 10/1 for domestic and international students; for summer admission, 2/1 for domestic and international students. Application fee: $80. Electronic applications accepted. *Financial support:* Application deadline: 6/1; applicants required to submit FAFSA. *Unit head:* Dr. David A. Andrews, Dean, 410-516-7820, Fax: 410-516-6697, E-mail: davidandrews@jhu.edu. *Application contact:* Catherine Wilson, Associate Director of Admissions, 410-516-9797, Fax: 410-516-9799, E-mail: soe.info@jhu.edu.

Johnson & Wales University, MAT Program in Teacher Education, Providence, RI 02903-3703. Offers business education and secondary special education (MAT); elementary education and elementary special education (MAT); elementary education and elementary/secondary special education (MAT); elementary education and secondary special education (MAT); food service education (MAT). Part-time and evening/weekend programs available. *Entrance requirements:* For master's, MAT, minimum GPA of 2.75. Additional exam requirements/recommendations for international students: Required—TOEFL (minimum score 550 paper-based) or IELTS (recommended). *Faculty research:* Secondary education, student teaching, educational reform, evaluation procedures.

Johnson State College, Graduate Program in Education, Johnson, VT 05656. Offers applied behavior analysis (MA Ed), including applied behavior analysis; curriculum and instruction (MA Ed); literacy (MA Ed); secondary education (MA Ed); special education (MA Ed). Part-time programs available. *Faculty:* 3 full-time (1 woman), 6 part-time/adjunct (5 women). *Students:* 6 full-time (5 women), 69 part-time (52 women). Average age 28. In 2013, 44 master's awarded. *Degree requirements:* For master's, comprehensive exam, thesis or alternative. *Entrance requirements:* For master's, interview. Additional exam requirements/recommendations for international students: Required—TOEFL. *Application deadline:* For fall admission, 4/1 priority date for domestic students, 1/15 priority date for international students; for spring admission, 11/1 for domestic students, 8/15 priority date for international students. Applications are processed on a rolling basis. Electronic applications accepted. *Expenses:* Tuition, state resident: full-time $11,448; part-time $477 per credit. Tuition, nonresident: full-time $24,720; part-time $1030 per credit. Tuition and fees vary according to reciprocity agreements. *Financial support:* Unspecified assistantships available. Financial award application deadline: 3/1; financial award applicants required to submit FAFSA. *Application contact:* Catherine H. Higley, Administrative Assistant, 800-635-2356 Ext. 1244, Fax: 802-635-1248, E-mail: catherine.higley@jsc.edu.

Kansas State University, Graduate School, College of Education, Department of Special Education, Counseling and Student Affairs, Manhattan, KS 66506. Offers academic advising (MS); counseling and student development (MS, Ed D, PhD), including college student development (MS), counselor education and supervision (PhD), school counseling (MS), student affairs in higher education (PhD); special education (MS, Ed D). *Accreditation:* ACA; NCATE. Part-time programs available. *Faculty:* 18 full-time (8 women), 15 part-time/adjunct (5 women). *Students:* 117 full-time (80 women), 327 part-time (257 women); includes 83 minority (42 Black or African American, non-Hispanic/Latino; 2 American Indian or Alaska Native, non-Hispanic/Latino; 9 Asian, non-Hispanic/Latino; 23 Hispanic/Latino; 1 Native Hawaiian or other Pacific Islander, non-Hispanic/Latino; 6 Two or more races, non-Hispanic/Latino), 9 international. Average age 33. 247 applicants, 69% accepted, 117 enrolled. In 2013, 117 master's, 7 doctorates awarded. *Degree requirements:* For master's, comprehensive exam; for doctorate, comprehensive exam, thesis/dissertation. *Entrance requirements:* For master's, minimum undergraduate GPA of 3.0; for doctorate, GRE General Test, minimum GPA of 3.0 in last 60 hours. Additional exam requirements/recommendations for international students: Required—TOEFL. *Application deadline:* For fall admission, 2/1 priority date for domestic and international students; for spring admission, 8/1 priority date for domestic and international students. Applications are processed on a rolling basis. Application fee: $50 ($75 for international students). Electronic applications accepted. *Financial support:* In 2013–14, 3 teaching assistantships (averaging $18,090 per year) were awarded; career-related internships or fieldwork, institutionally sponsored loans, and scholarships/grants also available. Financial award application deadline: 3/1; financial award applicants required to submit FAFSA. *Faculty research:* Counseling supervision, academic advising, career development, student development, universal design for learning, autism, learning disabilities. *Unit head:* Kenneth Hughey, Head, 785-532-6445, Fax: 785-532-7304, E-mail: khughey@ksu.edu. *Application contact:* Dona Deam, Application Contact, 785-532-5595, Fax: 785-532-7304, E-mail: ddeam@ksu.edu.
Website: http://www.coe.k-state.edu/departments/secsa/.

Kaplan University, Davenport Campus, School of Teacher Education, Davenport, IA 52807-2095. Offers education (M Ed); secondary education (M Ed); teaching and learning (MA); teaching literacy and language: grades 6-12 (MA); teaching literacy and language: grades K-6 (MA); teaching mathematics: grades 6-8 (MA); teaching mathematics: grades 9-12 (MA); teaching mathematics: grades K-5 (MA); teaching science: grades 6-12 (MA); teaching science: grades K-6 (MA); teaching students with special needs (MA); teaching with technology (MA). Part-time and evening/weekend programs available. Postbaccalaureate distance learning degree programs offered (no on-campus study). *Entrance requirements:* Additional exam requirements/recommendations for international students: Required—TOEFL (minimum score 550 paper-based; 80 iBT).

Kean University, College of Education, Program in Special Education, Union, NJ 07083. Offers high incidence disabilities (MA); low incidence disabilities (MA). *Accreditation:* NCATE. *Faculty:* 10 full-time (all women). *Students:* 20 full-time (18 women), 253 part-time (211 women); includes 81 minority (32 Black or African American, non-Hispanic/Latino; 2 American Indian or Alaska Native, non-Hispanic/Latino; 9 Asian, non-Hispanic/Latino; 35 Hispanic/Latino; 1 Native Hawaiian or other Pacific Islander, non-Hispanic/Latino; 2 Two or more races, non-Hispanic/Latino), 1 international. Average age 34. 106 applicants, 100% accepted, 75 enrolled. In 2013, 59 master's awarded. *Degree requirements:* For master's, comprehensive exam, thesis, portfolio, two semesters of advanced seminar. *Entrance requirements:* For master's, GRE General Test or MAT, minimum GPA of 3.0, teaching certificate, 2 letters of recommendation, interview, transcripts, writing sample. Additional exam requirements/recommendations for international students: Required—TOEFL (minimum score 550 paper-based; 79 iBT). *Application deadline:* For fall admission, 6/1 for domestic and international students; for spring admission, 12/1 for domestic and international students. Applications are processed on a rolling basis. Application fee: $75 ($150 for international students). Electronic applications accepted. *Expenses:* Tuition, state resident: full-time $12,099; part-time $589 per credit. Tuition, nonresident: full-time $16,399; part-time $722 per credit. *Required fees:* $3050; $139 per credit. Part-time tuition and fees vary according to course level, course load, degree level and program. *Financial support:* In 2013–14, 3 research assistantships with full tuition reimbursements (averaging $3,713 per year) were awarded; unspecified assistantships also available. Financial award applicants required to submit FAFSA. *Unit head:* Dr. Beverly Kling, Program Coordinator, 908-737-3845, E-mail: bkling@kean.edu.

Application contact: Ann-Marie Kay, Assistant Director of Graduate Admissions, 908-737-5922, Fax: 908-737-5925, E-mail: akay@kean.edu.
Website: http://grad.kean.edu/masters-programs/special-education-high-incidence-disabilities.

Keene State College, School of Professional and Graduate Studies, Keene, NH 03435. Offers curriculum and instruction (M Ed); education leadership (PMC); educational leadership (M Ed); safety and occupational health applied science (MS); school counselor (M Ed, PMC); special education (M Ed); teacher certification (Postbaccalaureate Certificate). *Accreditation:* NCATE. Part-time and evening/weekend programs available. *Faculty:* 8 full-time (5 women), 12 part-time/adjunct (6 women). *Students:* 39 full-time (33 women), 46 part-time (32 women); includes 8 minority (1 American Indian or Alaska Native, non-Hispanic/Latino; 2 Asian, non-Hispanic/Latino; 5 Hispanic/Latino). Average age 30. 46 applicants, 61% accepted, 13 enrolled. In 2013, 26 master's, 1 other advanced degree awarded. *Entrance requirements:* For master's, PRAXIS I, 3 references; official transcripts; minimum GPA of 2.5; interview. Additional exam requirements/recommendations for international students: Required—TOEFL (minimum score 550 paper-based; 61 iBT). *Application deadline:* For fall admission, 4/1 for domestic students; for spring admission, 12/1 for domestic students. Applications are processed on a rolling basis. Application fee: $50. Electronic applications accepted. *Expenses:* Tuition, state resident: full-time $10,410; part-time $480 per credit. Tuition, nonresident: full-time $17,795; part-time $530 per credit. *Required fees:* $2366; $94 per credit. Full-time tuition and fees vary according to course load. *Financial support:* Career-related internships or fieldwork, Federal Work-Study, institutionally sponsored loans, scholarships/grants, and unspecified assistantships available. Support available to part-time students. Financial award application deadline: 3/1; financial award applicants required to submit FAFSA. *Unit head:* Dr. Wayne Hartz, Interim Dean of Professional and Graduate Studies, 603-358-2220, E-mail: whartz@keene.edu. *Application contact:* Peggy Richmond, Director of Admissions, 603-358-2276, Fax: 603-358-2767, E-mail: admissions@keene.edu.
Website: http://www.keene.edu/gradstudies/.

Kennesaw State University, Leland and Clarice C. Bagwell College of Education, Program in Graduate Education, Kennesaw, GA 30144-5591. Offers educational leadership (M Ed); educational leadership technology (M Ed); elementary and early childhood education (M Ed); instructional technology (M Ed); middle grades education (M Ed); reading (M Ed); secondary education (M Ed); special education (M Ed); teaching English to speakers of other languages (M Ed). *Accreditation:* NCATE. Part-time programs available. *Students:* 65 full-time (60 women), 229 part-time (158 women); includes 66 minority (46 Black or African American, non-Hispanic/Latino; 6 Asian, non-Hispanic/Latino; 9 Hispanic/Latino; 5 Two or more races, non-Hispanic/Latino), 1 international. Average age 34. 56 applicants, 86% accepted, 43 enrolled. In 2013, 109 master's awarded. *Degree requirements:* For master's, thesis or alternative. *Entrance requirements:* For master's, GRE General Test, T-4 state certification, minimum GPA of 2.75. Additional exam requirements/recommendations for international students: Required—TOEFL (minimum score 550 paper-based; 80 iBT), IELTS (minimum score 6.5). *Application deadline:* For fall admission, 7/1 for domestic and international students; for spring admission, 10/1 for domestic and international students; for summer admission, 4/15 for domestic and international students. Applications are processed on a rolling basis. Application fee: $60. Electronic applications accepted. *Expenses:* Tuition, state resident: full-time $4806; part-time $267 per semester hour. Tuition, nonresident: full-time $17,298; part-time $961 per semester hour. *Required fees:* $1834; $784.50 per semester. *Financial support:* In 2013–14, 10 research assistantships with tuition reimbursements (averaging $8,000 per year) were awarded; Federal Work-Study and unspecified assistantships also available. Support available to part-time students. Financial award application deadline: 4/1; financial award applicants required to submit FAFSA. *Unit head:* Melinda Ross, Administrative Coordinator for Graduate Programs in Education, 770-423-6043, E-mail: graded@kennesaw.edu. *Application contact:* Melinda Ross, Admissions Counselor, 770-423-6043, Fax: 770-423-6885, E-mail: ksugrad@kennesaw.edu.
Website: http://www.kennesaw.edu/education/grad/.

Kennesaw State University, Leland and Clarice C. Bagwell College of Education, Program in Teaching, Kennesaw, GA 30144-5591. Offers art education (MAT); biology (MAT); chemistry (MAT); foreign language education (Chinese and Spanish) (MAT); physics (MAT); secondary English (MAT); secondary mathematics (MAT); special education (MAT); teaching English to speakers of other languages (MAT). Part-time and evening/weekend programs available. *Students:* 82 full-time (59 women), 16 part-time (12 women); includes 28 minority (14 Black or African American, non-Hispanic/Latino; 4 Asian, non-Hispanic/Latino; 7 Hispanic/Latino; 1 Native Hawaiian or other Pacific Islander, non-Hispanic/Latino; 2 Two or more races, non-Hispanic/Latino), 3 international. Average age 35. 28 applicants, 68% accepted, 15 enrolled. In 2013, 54 master's awarded. *Entrance requirements:* For master's, GRE, GACE I (state certificate exam), minimum GPA of 2.75, 2 recommendations, resume. Additional exam requirements/recommendations for international students: Required—TOEFL (minimum score 550 paper-based; 80 iBT), IELTS (minimum score 6). *Application deadline:* For fall admission, 6/1 for domestic and international students; for spring admission, 3/1 for domestic and international students; for summer admission, 4/15 for domestic and international students. Applications are processed on a rolling basis. Application fee: $60. Electronic applications accepted. *Expenses:* Tuition, state resident: full-time $4806; part-time $267 per semester hour. Tuition, nonresident: full-time $17,298; part-time $961 per semester hour. *Required fees:* $1834; $784.50 per semester. *Financial support:* In 2013–14, 2 research assistantships with tuition reimbursements (averaging $8,000 per year) were awarded; unspecified assistantships also available. Financial award application deadline: 4/1; financial award applicants required to submit FAFSA. *Unit head:* Dr. Jillian Ford, Director, 770-499-3093, E-mail: graded@kennesaw.edu. *Application contact:* Melinda Ross, Admissions Counselor, 770-423-6122, Fax: 770-423-6885, E-mail: ksugrad@kennesaw.edu.
Website: http://www.kennesaw.edu.

Kent State University, Graduate School of Education, Health, and Human Services, School of Lifespan Development and Educational Sciences, Program in Special Education, Kent, OH 44242-0001. Offers deaf education (M Ed); early childhood education (M Ed); educational interpreter K-12 (M Ed); general special education (M Ed); gifted education (M Ed); mild/moderate intervention (M Ed); special education (PhD, Ed S); transition to work (M Ed). *Accreditation:* NCATE. *Faculty:* 11 full-time (6 women), 12 part-time/adjunct (all women). *Students:* 75 full-time (61 women), 59 part-time (50 women); includes 15 minority (12 Black or African American, non-Hispanic/Latino; 1 Asian, non-Hispanic/Latino; 2 Native Hawaiian or other Pacific Islander, non-Hispanic/Latino), 8 international. 80 applicants, 35% accepted. In 2013, 44 master's, 4 doctorates awarded. *Degree requirements:* For doctorate, comprehensive exam, thesis/dissertation. *Entrance requirements:* For master's, minimum undergraduate GPA of 2.75, moral character form, 2 letters of reference, goals statement; for doctorate and Ed S, GRE General Test, goals statement, 2 letters of reference, interview, resume. Additional exam requirements/recommendations for international students: Required—TOEFL (minimum score 550 paper-based; 80 iBT). *Application deadline:* Applications are processed on a rolling basis. Application fee: $30 ($60 for international students). Electronic applications accepted. *Financial support:* In 2013–14, 6 research assistantships with full tuition reimbursements (averaging $9,667 per year), 1 teaching assistantship with full tuition reimbursement (averaging $12,000 per year) were awarded; career-related internships or fieldwork, Federal Work-Study, institutionally sponsored loans, scholarships/grants, health care benefits, and unspecified assistantships also available. Support available to part-time students. Financial award application deadline: 4/1; financial award applicants required to submit FAFSA. *Faculty research:* Social/emotional needs of gifted, inclusion transition services, early intervention/ecobehavioral assessments, applied behavioral analysis. *Unit head:* Sonya Wisdom, Coordinator, 330-672-0578, E-mail: swisdom@kent.edu. *Application contact:* Nancy Miller, Academic Program Director, Office of Graduate Student Services, 330-672-2576, Fax: 330-672-9162, E-mail: ogs@kent.edu.
Website: http://www.kent.edu/ehhs/sped/.

Kentucky State University, College of Professional Studies, Frankfort, KY 40601. Offers public administration (MPA), including human resource management, international development, management information systems, nonprofit management; special education (MA). Part-time and evening/weekend programs available. Postbaccalaureate distance learning degree programs offered (minimal on-campus study). *Degree requirements:* For master's, comprehensive exam, thesis optional. *Entrance requirements:* For master's, GMAT, GRE. Additional exam requirements/recommendations for international students: Required—TOEFL (minimum score 525 paper-based). Electronic applications accepted.

Lamar University, College of Graduate Studies, College of Education and Human Development, Department of Counseling and Special Populations, Beaumont, TX 77710. Offers counseling and development (M Ed); school counseling (M Ed); special education (M Ed); student affairs (Certificate).

Lamar University, College of Graduate Studies, College of Fine Arts and Communication, Department of Deaf Studies and Deaf Education, Beaumont, TX 77710. Offers MS, Ed D. *Accreditation:* ASHA. Part-time and evening/weekend programs available. *Degree requirements:* For master's, thesis optional; for doctorate, thesis/dissertation. *Entrance requirements:* For master's, GRE General Test, performance IQ score of 115 (for deaf students), minimum GPA of 2.5; for doctorate, GRE General Test, performance IQ score of 115 (for deaf students). Additional exam requirements/recommendations for international students: Required—TOEFL. *Faculty research:* Multicultural and deaf teacher training, central auditory processing, voice sign language.

Lancaster Bible College, Graduate School, Lancaster, PA 17601-5036. Offers adult ministries (MA); Bible (MA); children and family ministry (MA); church planting (MA); consulting resource teacher (M Ed); elementary school counseling (M Ed); leadership (PhD); leadership studies (MA); marriage and family counseling (MA); mental health counseling (MA); pastoral studies (MA); secondary school counseling (M Ed); sports ministry (MA); student ministry (MA); town and country ministry (MA). Part-time and evening/weekend programs available. *Degree requirements:* For master's, comprehensive exam (for some programs), thesis (for some programs). *Entrance requirements:* For master's, bachelor's degree with a minimum of 30 credits of course work in Bible, minimum undergraduate GPA of 3.0, interview. Additional exam requirements/recommendations for international students: Required—TOEFL.

La Salle University, School of Arts and Sciences, Program in Education, Philadelphia, PA 19141-1199. Offers American studies (MA); autism spectrum disorders (MA, Certificate); bilingual/bicultural studies (MA); classroom management (MA, Certificate); dual early childhood and special education (MA); dual middle-level science and math and special education secondary education (MA); education (MA); English (MA); English as a second language (Certificate); instructional coach (Certificate); instructional leadership (MA); reading specialist (MA, Certificate); secondary education (MA); special education (MA, Certificate). Part-time and evening/weekend programs available. *Faculty:* 5 full-time (4 women), 16 part-time/adjunct (10 women). *Students:* 18 full-time (13 women), 137 part-time (112 women); includes 33 minority (24 Black or African American, non-Hispanic/Latino; 9 Hispanic/Latino), 4 international. Average age 32. 47 applicants, 96% accepted, 28 enrolled. In 2013, 58 master's, 20 other advanced degrees awarded. *Degree requirements:* For master's, comprehensive exam. *Entrance requirements:* For master's and Certificate, MAT or GRE, 2 letters of recommendation. Additional exam requirements/recommendations for international students: Required—TOEFL. *Application deadline:* For fall admission, 8/15 priority date for domestic students, 7/15 for international students; for spring admission, 12/15 priority date for domestic students, 11/15 for international students; for summer admission, 4/15 priority date for domestic students, 3/15 for international students. Applications are processed on a rolling basis. Application fee: $35. Electronic applications accepted. Application fee is waived when completed online. *Expenses:* Contact institution. *Financial support:* In 2013–14, 28 students received support. Career-related internships or fieldwork, Federal Work-Study, and scholarships/grants available. Support available to part-time students. Financial award application deadline: 8/31; financial award applicants required to submit FAFSA. *Unit head:* Dr. Greer Richardson, Interim Director, 215-951-1806, Fax: 215-951-1843, E-mail: graded@lasalle.edu. *Application contact:* Paul J. Reilly, Assistant Vice President, Enrollment Services, 215-951-1946, Fax: 215-951-1462, E-mail: reilly@lasalle.edu.
Website: http://www.lasalle.edu/grad/index.php?section-education&page-index.

Lasell College, Graduate and Professional Studies in Education, Newton, MA 02466-2709. Offers elementary education (M Ed); special education (M Ed), including moderate disabilities. Part-time and evening/weekend programs available. Postbaccalaureate distance learning degree programs offered. *Faculty:* 2 full-time (both women), 5 part-time/adjunct (4 women). *Students:* 8 full-time (7 women), 23 part-time (22 women); includes 5 minority (4 Black or African American, non-Hispanic/Latino; 1 Hispanic/Latino). Average age 28. 25 applicants, 64% accepted, 15 enrolled. In 2013, 2 master's awarded. *Entrance requirements:* For master's, bachelor's degree from an accredited institution. Additional exam requirements/recommendations for international students: Required—TOEFL (minimum score 550 paper-based; 79 iBT), IELTS. *Application deadline:* For fall admission, 8/31 priority date for domestic students, 6/30 priority date for international students; for spring admission, 12/31 priority date for domestic students, 10/31 priority date for international students. Applications are processed on a rolling basis. Electronic applications accepted. *Expenses: Tuition:* Part-time $575 per credit. *Required fees:* $80 per semester. *Financial support:* Available to part-time students. Application deadline: 8/31; applicants required to submit FAFSA. *Unit head:* Dr. Joan Dolamore, Dean of Graduate and Professional Studies, 617-243-2485, Fax: 617-243-2450, E-mail: gradinfo@lasell.edu. *Application contact:* Adrienne Franciosi, Director of Graduate Admission, 617-243-2214, Fax: 617-243-2450, E-mail: gradinfo@lasell.edu.
Website: http://www.lasell.edu/Academics/Graduate-and-Professional-Studies/Master-of-Education.html.

Lee University, Program in Education, Cleveland, TN 37320-3450. Offers college student development (MS); curriculum and instruction (M Ed, Ed S); educational leadership (M Ed, Ed S); elementary education (MAT); higher education administration (MS); middle grades (MAT); secondary education (MAT); special education (M Ed); special education (secondary) (MAT). Part-time programs available. *Faculty:* 14 full-time (7 women), 6 part-time/adjunct (3 women). *Students:* 30 full-time (23 women), 62 part-

time (37 women); includes 8 minority (3 Black or African American, non-Hispanic/Latino; 1 American Indian or Alaska Native, non-Hispanic/Latino; 2 Asian, non-Hispanic/Latino; 2 Hispanic/Latino). Average age 30. 40 applicants, 100% accepted, 30 enrolled. In 2013, 117 master's, 2 other advanced degrees awarded. *Degree requirements:* For master's, variable foreign language requirement, comprehensive exam, thesis, internship. *Entrance requirements:* For master's, MAT or GRE General Test, minimum GPA of 2.75, 3 letters of recommendation, interview, writing sample, official transcripts. Additional exam requirements/recommendations for international students: Required—TOEFL (minimum score 450 paper-based). *Application deadline:* For fall admission, 4/1 priority date for domestic and international students; for spring admission, 10/1 priority date for domestic and international students. Applications are processed on a rolling basis. Application fee: $25. *Expenses: Tuition:* Full-time $9900; part-time $550 per credit hour. *Required fees:* $35 per term. One-time fee: $25. *Financial support:* In 2013–14, 47 students received support, including 1 teaching assistantship (averaging $1,500 per year); career-related internships or fieldwork, Federal Work-Study, institutionally sponsored loans, scholarships/grants, and unspecified assistantships also available. Financial award application deadline: 3/1; financial award applicants required to submit FAFSA. *Unit head:* Dr. Gary Riggins, Director, 423-614-8193. *Application contact:* Vicki Glasscock, Graduate Admissions Director, 423-614-8059, E-mail: vglasscock@leeuniversity.edu.
Website: http://www.leeuniversity.edu/academics/graduate/education.

Lehigh University, College of Education, Program in Comparative and International Education, Bethlehem, PA 18015. Offers comparative and international education (MA, PhD); globalization and educational change (M Ed); international counseling (Certificate); international development in education (Certificate); special education (Certificate); technology use in schools (Certificate); TESOL (Certificate). Part-time and evening/weekend programs available. Postbaccalaureate distance learning degree programs offered (minimal on-campus study). *Faculty:* 4 full-time (2 women). *Students:* 20 full-time (18 women), 26 part-time (17 women); includes 3 minority (2 Asian, non-Hispanic/Latino; 1 Hispanic/Latino), 14 international. Average age 33. 59 applicants, 63% accepted, 10 enrolled. In 2013, 17 master's awarded. Terminal master's awarded for partial completion of doctoral program. *Degree requirements:* For master's, thesis (MA); for doctorate, comprehensive exam, thesis/dissertation. *Entrance requirements:* For master's, 2 letters of recommendation; for doctorate, GRE, transcripts, 2 letters of recommendation, essay, and TOEFL if International applicant. Additional exam requirements/recommendations for international students: Required—TOEFL (minimum score 600 paper-based; 93 iBT). *Application deadline:* For fall and spring admission, 2/1 for domestic and international students. Application fee: $65. Electronic applications accepted. *Financial support:* Application deadline: 3/15. *Faculty research:* Comparative education, rural education, gender equity in education, post-socialist education transformation, educational borrowing, comparing education systems, education policy and globalization, family-school relationships, China, international testing, social inequities. *Unit head:* Dr. Iveta Silova, Program Director and Associate Professor, 610-758-5750, Fax: 610-758-6223, E-mail: ism207@lehigh.edu. *Application contact:* Sharon Y. Warden, Coordinator, 610-758-3256, Fax: 610-758-6223, E-mail: sy00@lehigh.edu.
Website: http://www.lehigh.edu/education/cie.

Lehigh University, College of Education, Program in Educational Leadership, Bethlehem, PA 18015. Offers educational leadership (M Ed, Ed D); K-12 principal (Certificate); superintendent of schools (Certificate); supervisor of curriculum and instruction (Certificate); supervisor of pupil services (Certificate); supervisor of special education (Certificate); MBA/M Ed. Part-time and evening/weekend programs available. Postbaccalaureate distance learning degree programs offered (minimal on-campus study). *Faculty:* 7 full-time (2 women), 7 part-time/adjunct (2 women). *Students:* 7 full-time (6 women), 114 part-time (54 women); includes 14 minority (8 Black or African American, non-Hispanic/Latino; 1 American Indian or Alaska Native, non-Hispanic/Latino; 5 Hispanic/Latino), 11 international. Average age 36. 66 applicants, 76% accepted, 17 enrolled. In 2013, 45 master's, 15 doctorates awarded. *Degree requirements:* For doctorate, comprehensive exam, thesis/dissertation. *Entrance requirements:* For master's and Certificate, minimum undergraduate GPA of 3.0; for doctorate, GRE General Test or MAT, minimum graduate GPA of 3.6, 2 letters of recommendation, essay, transcript. Additional exam requirements/recommendations for international students: Required—TOEFL (minimum score 600 paper-based; 93 iBT). *Application deadline:* For fall admission, 1/15 for domestic and international students; for spring admission, 11/1 for domestic and international students. Applications are processed on a rolling basis. Application fee: $65. Electronic applications accepted. *Financial support:* In 2013–14, 1 student received support. Fellowships with full and partial tuition reimbursements available, research assistantships with full and partial tuition reimbursements available, teaching assistantships with full and partial tuition reimbursements available, career-related internships or fieldwork, Federal Work-Study, institutionally sponsored loans, scholarships/grants, tuition waivers (full and partial), and unspecified assistantships available. Financial award application deadline: 1/31; financial award applicants required to submit FAFSA. *Faculty research:* School finance and law, supervision of instruction, middle-level education, organizational change, leadership preparation and development, international school leadership, urban school leadership, comparative education, social justice. *Unit head:* Dr. Floyd D. Beachum, Director, 610-758-5955, Fax: 610-758-3227, E-mail: fdb209@lehigh.edu. *Application contact:* Donna M. Johnson, Manager, Graduate Programs Admissions, 610-758-3231, Fax: 610-758-6223, E-mail: dmj4@lehigh.edu.
Website: http://coe.lehigh.edu/academics/disciplines/edl.

Lehigh University, College of Education, Program in Special Education, Bethlehem, PA 18015. Offers M Ed, PhD. Part-time and evening/weekend programs available. *Faculty:* 5 full-time (all women), 5 part-time/adjunct (all women). *Students:* 18 full-time (17 women), 39 part-time (30 women); includes 1 minority (Asian, non-Hispanic/Latino), 1 international. Average age 29. 36 applicants, 72% accepted, 10 enrolled. In 2013, 31 master's awarded. *Degree requirements:* For doctorate, comprehensive exam, thesis/dissertation. *Entrance requirements:* For master's, minimum GPA of 3.0, 2 letters of recommendation (academic), essay, transcripts; for doctorate, GRE General Test, minimum GPA of 3.0, 2 letters of recommendation (academic), essay, transcripts. Additional exam requirements/recommendations for international students: Required—TOEFL (minimum score 600 paper-based; 93 iBT). *Application deadline:* For fall admission, 2/1 for domestic and international students; for winter admission, 5/15 for domestic and international students. Application fee: $65. Electronic applications accepted. *Financial support:* In 2013–14, 7 research assistantships (averaging $13,600 per year) were awarded; unspecified assistantships also available. Financial award application deadline: 1/31. *Faculty research:* Special education, autism spectrum disorder, emotional and behavioral disorders, positive behavior support, early childhood special education. *Unit head:* Dr. Linda Bambara, Director, 610-758-3271, Fax: 610-758-6223, E-mail: lmb1@lehigh.edu. *Application contact:* Donna Johnson, Manager, Admissions and Recruitment, 610-758-3231, Fax: 610-758-3243, E-mail: dmj4@lehigh.edu.
Website: http://coe.lehigh.edu/academics/disciplines/sped.

Lehman College of the City University of New York, Division of Education, Department of Specialized Services in Education, Bronx, NY 10468-1589. Offers guidance and counseling (MS Ed); reading teacher (MS Ed); teachers of special education (MS Ed), including bilingual special education, early special education, emotional handicaps, learning disabilities, mental retardation. Part-time and evening/weekend programs available. *Faculty research:* Battered women, whole language classrooms, parent education, mainstreaming.

Lehman College of the City University of New York, Division of Education, Department of Specialized Services in Education, Teachers of Special Education Program, Option in Bilingual Special Education, Bronx, NY 10468-1589. Offers MS Ed. *Accreditation:* NCATE. *Entrance requirements:* For master's, minimum GPA of 3.0.

Lehman College of the City University of New York, Division of Education, Department of Specialized Services in Education, Teachers of Special Education Program, Option in Early Special Education, Bronx, NY 10468-1589. Offers MS Ed. *Accreditation:* NCATE. *Entrance requirements:* For master's, minimum GPA of 3.0.

Lehman College of the City University of New York, Division of Education, Department of Specialized Services in Education, Teachers of Special Education Program, Option in Emotional Handicaps, Bronx, NY 10468-1589. Offers MS Ed. *Accreditation:* NCATE. Part-time and evening/weekend programs available. *Entrance requirements:* For master's, minimum GPA of 2.7. *Faculty research:* Behavioral disorders, self-evaluation, applied behavior analysis.

Lehman College of the City University of New York, Division of Education, Department of Specialized Services in Education, Teachers of Special Education Program, Option in Learning Disabilities, Bronx, NY 10468-1589. Offers MS Ed. *Accreditation:* NCATE. Part-time and evening/weekend programs available. *Entrance requirements:* For master's, interview, minimum GPA of 2.7. *Faculty research:* Emergent literacy, language-based classrooms, primary and secondary social contexts of language and literacy, innovative in-service education models, adult literacy.

Lehman College of the City University of New York, Division of Education, Department of Specialized Services in Education, Teachers of Special Education Program, Option in Mental Retardation, Bronx, NY 10468-1589. Offers MS Ed. *Accreditation:* NCATE. Part-time and evening/weekend programs available. *Entrance requirements:* For master's, minimum GPA of 2.7. *Faculty research:* Conductive education, homeless infants and their families, infant stimulation, hospitalizing infants with AIDS, legislation PL99-457.

Le Moyne College, Department of Education, Syracuse, NY 13214. Offers adolescent education (MS Ed, MST); adolescent education/special education (MS Ed, MST); adolescent English (MST), including grades 7-12 (MS Ed, MST); adolescent English/special education (MST), including grades 7-12 (MS Ed, MST); adolescent foreign language (MST), including grades 7-12 (MS Ed, MST); adolescent history (MST), including grades 7-12 (MS Ed, MST); childhood education (MS Ed); childhood education/special education (MS Ed); elementary education (MS Ed); general education (MS Ed); inclusive childhood education (MST); literacy education (MS Ed), including birth to grade 6, grades 5-12; school building leader (MS Ed); school building leadership (CAS); school district business leader (MS Ed, CAS); school district leader (MS Ed); school district leadership (CAS); secondary education (MS Ed); special education (MS Ed); students with disabilities-generalist (MS Ed), including grades 7-12 (MS Ed, MST); teaching English to speakers of other languages (MS Ed); urban studies (MS Ed). *Accreditation:* Teacher Education Accreditation Council. Part-time and evening/weekend programs available. *Faculty:* 8 full-time (5 women), 61 part-time/adjunct (38 women). *Students:* 24 full-time (20 women), 178 part-time (133 women); includes 22 minority (12 Black or African American, non-Hispanic/Latino; 1 American Indian or Alaska Native, non-Hispanic/Latino; 3 Asian, non-Hispanic/Latino; 6 Hispanic/Latino), 1 international. Average age 31. 248 applicants, 90% accepted, 86 enrolled. In 2013, 158 master's, 37 CASs awarded. *Degree requirements:* For master's, thesis. *Entrance requirements:* For master's, GRE General Test, bachelor's degree, 2 letters of recommendation, written statement, transcripts. Additional exam requirements/recommendations for international students: Required—TOEFL (minimum score 550 paper-based; 79 iBT). *Application deadline:* For fall admission, 4/1 priority date for domestic and international students; for spring admission, 10/1 priority date for domestic and international students; for summer admission, 3/1 priority date for domestic and international students. Applications are processed on a rolling basis. Application fee: $50. *Expenses:* Contact institution. *Financial support:* In 2013–14, 26 students received support. Career-related internships or fieldwork and health care benefits available. Support available to part-time students. Financial award applicants required to submit FAFSA. *Faculty research:* Minority teachers, special education, multiculturalism, literacy, technology, media literacy learning, autism, school district organization, service-learning, higher level problem solving, teacher leadership. *Unit head:* Dr. Suzanne L. Gilmour, Chair, Department of Education/Director of Graduate Education Programs, 315-445-4376, Fax: 315-445-4744, E-mail: gilmous@lemoyne.edu. *Application contact:* Kristen P. Trapasso, Senior Director of Enrollment Management, 315-445-4265, Fax: 315-445-6092, E-mail: trapaskp@lemoyne.edu.
Website: http://www.lemoyne.edu/education.

Lesley University, School of Education, Cambridge, MA 02138-2790. Offers arts, community, and education (M Ed); autism studies (Certificate); curriculum and instruction (M Ed, CAGS); early childhood education (M Ed); ecological teaching and learning (MS); educational studies (PhD), including adult learning, educational leadership, individually designed; elementary education (M Ed); emergent technologies for educators (Certificate); ESLArts: language learning through the arts (M Ed); high school education (M Ed); individually designed (M Ed); integrated teaching through the arts (M Ed); literacy for K-8 classroom teachers (M Ed); mathematics education (M Ed); middle school education (M Ed); moderate disabilities (M Ed); online learning (Certificate); reading (CAGS); science in education (M Ed); severe disabilities (M Ed); special needs (CAGS); specialist teacher of reading (M Ed); teacher of visual art (M Ed); technology in education (M Ed, CAGS). *Accreditation:* Teacher Education Accreditation Council. Part-time and evening/weekend programs available. Postbaccalaureate distance learning degree programs offered (no on-campus study). *Faculty:* 40 full-time (30 women), 104 part-time/adjunct (77 women). *Students:* 453 full-time (381 women), 1,672 part-time (1,435 women); includes 284 minority (139 Black or African American, non-Hispanic/Latino; 11 American Indian or Alaska Native, non-Hispanic/Latino; 38 Asian, non-Hispanic/Latino; 58 Hispanic/Latino; 5 Native Hawaiian or other Pacific Islander, non-Hispanic/Latino; 33 Two or more races, non-Hispanic/Latino), 22 international. Average age 35. In 2013, 1,137 master's, 18 doctorates, 51 other advanced degrees awarded. *Degree requirements:* For master's, practicum; for doctorate, thesis/dissertation. *Entrance requirements:* For master's, Massachusetts Tests for Educator Licensure (MTEL), transcripts, statement of purpose, recommendations; interview (for special education); for doctorate, GRE General Test, transcripts, statement of purpose, recommendations, interview, master's degree, resume; for other advanced degree, interview, master's degree. Additional exam requirements/recommendations for international students: Required—TOEFL (minimum score 550 paper-based; 80 iBT). *Application deadline:* Applications are processed on a rolling basis. Application fee: $50. Electronic applications accepted. *Expenses: Tuition:* Part-time $900 per credit. *Financial support:* In 2013–14, 15 fellowships (averaging $3,600 per year) were awarded; career-related internships or fieldwork, Federal Work-Study, scholarships/grants, tuition waivers, and unspecified assistantships also available. Financial award application deadline: 4/15; financial award applicants required

to submit FAFSA. *Faculty research:* Assessment in literacy, mathematics and science; autism spectrum disorders; instructional technology and online learning; multicultural education and English language learners. *Unit head:* Dr. Jack Gillette, Dean, 617-349-8401, Fax: 617-349-8607, E-mail: jgillett@lesley.edu. *Application contact:* Martha Sheehan, Director of Admissions, 888-LESLEYU, Fax: 617-349-8313, E-mail: info@lesley.edu.
Website: http://www.lesley.edu/soe.html.

Lewis & Clark College, Graduate School of Education and Counseling, Department of Teacher Education, Program in Special Education, Portland, OR 97219-7899. Offers M Ed. *Accreditation:* NCATE. Part-time and evening/weekend programs available. *Entrance requirements:* For master's, minimum GPA of 2.75. Additional exam requirements/recommendations for international students: Required—TOEFL (minimum score 575 paper-based). Electronic applications accepted.

Lewis University, College of Education, Program in Special Education, Romeoville, IL 60446. Offers MA. *Students:* 25 full-time (22 women), 2 part-time (both women); includes 7 minority (3 Black or African American, non-Hispanic/Latino; 2 Asian, non-Hispanic/Latino; 1 Hispanic/Latino; 1 Two or more races, non-Hispanic/Latino). Average age 32. *Entrance requirements:* For master's, departmental qualifying exam, writing exam, minimum GPA of 2.75, 2 letters of recommendation, interview. Additional exam requirements/recommendations for international students: Required—TOEFL (minimum score 550 paper-based; 80 iBT). *Application deadline:* For fall admission, 5/1 priority date for international students; for spring admission, 11/15 priority date for international students. Applications are processed on a rolling basis. Application fee: $40. Electronic applications accepted. *Financial support:* Federal Work-Study, scholarships/grants, and unspecified assistantships available. Financial award application deadline: 5/1; financial award applicants required to submit FAFSA. *Unit head:* Dr. Christy Roberts, Director, 815-838-0500 Ext. 5317, E-mail: robertch@lewisu.edu. *Application contact:* Linda Campbell, Graduate Admission Counselor, 815-838-5704, E-mail: campbeli@lewisu.edu.

Liberty University, School of Education, Lynchburg, VA 24515. Offers administration and supervision (M Ed); curriculum and instruction (Ed D, Ed S); early childhood education (M Ed); educational leadership (Ed D, Ed S); educational technology and online instruction (M Ed); elementary education (M Ed, MAT); English (M Ed); gifted education (M Ed); history (M Ed); leadership (M Ed); math specialist (M Ed); middle grades (M Ed, MAT); outdoor adventure sport (MS); reading specialist (M Ed); school counseling (M Ed); secondary education (MAT); special education (M Ed, MAT); sport management (MS), including administration, outdoor recreation, sport management, tourism; sports administration (MS); student service (M Ed); teaching and learning (M Ed); tourism (MS). *Accreditation:* NCATE. Part-time programs available. Postbaccalaureate distance learning degree programs offered (minimal on-campus study). *Students:* 2,241 full-time (1,639 women), 4,413 part-time (3,240 women); includes 2,052 minority (1,588 Black or African American, non-Hispanic/Latino; 37 American Indian or Alaska Native, non-Hispanic/Latino; 67 Asian, non-Hispanic/Latino; 173 Hispanic/Latino; 37 Native Hawaiian or other Pacific Islander, non-Hispanic/Latino; 150 Two or more races, non-Hispanic/Latino), 15 international. Average age 37. 6,185 applicants, 43% accepted, 1603 enrolled. In 2013, 1,256 master's, 117 doctorates, 470 other advanced degrees awarded. *Degree requirements:* For doctorate, comprehensive exam, thesis/dissertation. *Entrance requirements:* For master's, GRE General Test or MAT (if taken in or before 1999), 2 letters of recommendation, minimum undergraduate GPA of 3.0, curriculum vitae; for doctorate and Ed S, GRE General Test or MAT (if taken before 1999), minimum master's GPA of 3.0, 3 years of teaching experience. Additional exam requirements/recommendations for international students: Required—TOEFL (minimum score 600 paper-based; 100 iBT). *Application deadline:* For fall admission, 6/1 for domestic students; for spring admission, 11/1 for domestic students. Applications are processed on a rolling basis. Application fee: $50. Electronic applications accepted. *Expenses:* Contact institution. *Financial support:* Federal Work-Study and tuition waivers (partial) available. *Faculty research:* Self-determination, character education, bibliotherapy, learning styles, distance education. *Unit head:* Dr. Karen L. Parker, Dean, 434-582-2195, Fax: 434-582-2468, E-mail: kparker@liberty.edu. *Application contact:* Jay Bridge, Director of Graduate Admissions, 800-424-9595, Fax: 800-628-7977, E-mail: gradadmissions@liberty.edu.
Website: http://www.liberty.edu/academics/education/graduate/.

Lincoln University, Graduate Studies, Jefferson City, MO 65101. Offers business administration (MBA), including accounting, entrepreneurship, management, public administration and policy; educational leadership (Ed S), including elementary leadership, secondary leadership, superintendency; guidance and counseling (M Ed), including community/agency counseling, elementary school, secondary school; history (MA); school administration and supervision (M Ed), including elementary school administration, secondary school administration, special education administration; school teaching (M Ed), including elementary school teaching, secondary school teaching; sociology (MA); sociology/criminal justice (MA). Part-time and evening/weekend programs available. Postbaccalaureate distance learning degree programs offered (minimal on-campus study). *Students:* 42 full-time (29 women), 109 part-time (66 women); includes 51 minority (37 Black or African American, non-Hispanic/Latino; 10 American Indian or Alaska Native, non-Hispanic/Latino; 1 Asian, non-Hispanic/Latino; 2 Hispanic/Latino; 1 Two or more races, non-Hispanic/Latino), 10 international. Average age 33. 84 applicants, 76% accepted, 51 enrolled. In 2013, 73 master's, 6 other advanced degrees awarded. *Degree requirements:* For master's and Ed S, comprehensive exam, thesis optional. *Entrance requirements:* For master's and Ed S, GRE, MAT or GMAT, minimum GPA of 2.75 in major, 2.5 overall; 3 letters of recommendation; minimum C average in English composition; personal statement of purpose. Additional exam requirements/recommendations for international students: Required—TOEFL (minimum score 500 paper-based; 61 iBT). *Application deadline:* For fall admission, 8/1 priority date for domestic and international students; for spring admission, 12/1 priority date for domestic and international students; for summer admission, 5/1 priority date for domestic and international students. Applications are processed on a rolling basis. Application fee: $30. *Expenses:* Tuition, state resident: full-time $6840; part-time $285 per credit hour. Tuition, nonresident: full-time $12,720; part-time $530 per credit hour. *Required fees:* $587; $587 per year. Tuition and fees vary according to course load. *Financial support:* Federal Work-Study and scholarships/grants available. Support available to part-time students. Financial award application deadline: 3/1; financial award applicants required to submit FAFSA. *Unit head:* Dr. Linda S. Bickel, Dean, 573-681-5247, Fax: 573-681-5106, E-mail: gradschool@lincolnu.edu. *Application contact:* Irasema Steck, Administrative Assistant, 573-681-5247, Fax: 573-681-5106, E-mail: gradschool@lincolnu.edu.
Website: http://www.lincolnu.edu/web/graduate-studies/graduate-studies.

Lipscomb University, Program in Education, Nashville, TN 37204-3951. Offers applied behavior analysis (Certificate); collaborative professional learning (M Ed, Ed S); educational leadership (M Ed, Ed S); English language learning (M Ed, Ed S); instructional coaching (Certificate); instructional practice (M Ed); learning organizations and strategic change (Ed D); math specialty (M Ed); reading specialty (M Ed, Ed S); special education (M Ed); teaching, learning, and leading (M Ed); technology integration (M Ed); technology integration specialist (Certificate). *Accreditation:* NCATE. Part-time

and evening/weekend programs available. Postbaccalaureate distance learning degree programs offered (no on-campus study). *Faculty:* 19 full-time (13 women), 28 part-time/adjunct (22 women). *Students:* 171 full-time (123 women), 509 part-time (429 women); includes 118 minority (91 Black or African American, non-Hispanic/Latino; 1 American Indian or Alaska Native, non-Hispanic/Latino; 4 Asian, non-Hispanic/Latino; 15 Hispanic/Latino; 1 Native Hawaiian or other Pacific Islander, non-Hispanic/Latino; 6 Two or more races, non-Hispanic/Latino). Average age 32. 237 applicants, 65% accepted, 150 enrolled. In 2013, 212 master's awarded. *Degree requirements:* For master's, comprehensive exam, portfolio, research project and presentation; for doctorate, practical capstone project in experiential setting. *Entrance requirements:* For master's, MAT (minimum 31) or GRE General Test (minimum 294), 2 reference letters, goals statement, writing sample, interview; for doctorate, MAT or GRE General Test, 3 reference letters, artifact of demonstrated academic excellence, written personal statements, interview. Additional exam requirements/recommendations for international students: Required—TOEFL (minimum score 570 paper-based). *Application deadline:* For fall admission, 8/29 priority date for domestic students; for spring admission, 1/15 priority date for domestic students. Applications are processed on a rolling basis. Application fee: $50 ($75 for international students). *Expenses: Tuition:* Full-time $15,570; part-time $865 per credit hour. Tuition and fees vary according to degree level and program. *Financial support:* Scholarships/grants and unspecified assistantships available. Financial award applicants required to submit FAFSA. *Faculty research:* Facilitative learning styles, leadership, student assessment, interactive multimedia inclusion, learning organizations and strategic change. *Unit head:* Dr. Deborah Boyd, Director of Graduate Studies, 615-966-6263, E-mail: deborah.boyd@lipscomb.edu. *Application contact:* Kristin Baese, Director of Enrollment and Outreach, 615-966-7628 Ext. 6081, Fax: 615-966-5173, E-mail: kristin.baese@lipscomb.edu.
Website: http://www.lipscomb.edu/education/graduate-programs.

Long Island University–Brentwood Campus, School of Education, Brentwood, NY 11717. Offers childhood education (MS); early childhood education (MS); literacy (MS); mental health counseling (MS); school counseling (MS); special education (MS). Part-time and evening/weekend programs available.

Long Island University–Hudson at Rockland, Graduate School, Programs in Special Education and Literacy, Orangeburg, NY 10962. Offers autism (MS Ed); childhood/literacy (MS Ed); childhood/special education (MS Ed); literacy (MS Ed); special education (MS Ed). Part-time programs available. *Entrance requirements:* For master's, college transcripts, two letters of recommendation, personal statement, resume.

Long Island University–Hudson at Westchester, Programs in Education-Teaching, Program in Special Education and Secondary Education, Purchase, NY 10577. Offers MS Ed, Advanced Certificate. Part-time and evening/weekend programs available.

Long Island University–LIU Brooklyn, School of Education, Department of Teaching and Learning, Program in Special Education, Brooklyn, NY 11201-8423. Offers MS Ed. Part-time and evening/weekend programs available. *Degree requirements:* For master's, thesis optional. *Entrance requirements:* For master's, 2 letters of recommendation. Additional exam requirements/recommendations for international students: Required—TOEFL (minimum score 500 paper-based). Electronic applications accepted.

Long Island University–LIU Post, School of Education, Department of Special Education and Literacy, Brookville, NY 11548-1300. Offers childhood education/literacy (MS); childhood education/special education (MS); literacy (MS Ed); special education (MS Ed). *Accreditation:* Teacher Education Accreditation Council. Part-time and evening/weekend programs available. *Degree requirements:* For master's, research project, comprehensive exam or thesis. *Entrance requirements:* For master's, interview, minimum GPA of 2.75 in major, 2.5 overall. Electronic applications accepted. *Faculty research:* Autism, mainstreaming, robotics and microcomputers in special education, transition from school to work.

Long Island University–Riverhead, Education Division, Program in Teaching Students with Disabilities, Riverhead, NY 11901. Offers MS Ed. *Degree requirements:* For master's, thesis. *Entrance requirements:* For master's, minimum GPA of 2.75, New York state teacher certification, interview, writing sample. Additional exam requirements/recommendations for international students: Required—TOEFL (minimum score 550 paper-based). Electronic applications accepted.

Longwood University, College of Graduate and Professional Studies, College of Education and Human Services, Farmville, VA 23909. Offers education (MS), including algebra and middle school math, counselor education, elementary and middle school math, elementary education, elementary education initial licensure, health and physical education, school librarianship, special education general curriculum, special education initial licensure; social work and communication sciences and disorders (MS). *Accreditation:* NCATE. Part-time and evening/weekend programs available. *Faculty:* 28 full-time (15 women), 9 part-time/adjunct (7 women). *Students:* 86 full-time (80 women), 187 part-time (173 women); includes 38 minority (26 Black or African American, non-Hispanic/Latino; 1 Asian, non-Hispanic/Latino; 5 Hispanic/Latino; 1 Native Hawaiian or other Pacific Islander, non-Hispanic/Latino; 5 Two or more races, non-Hispanic/Latino). 98 applicants, 89% accepted, 85 enrolled. In 2013, 132 master's awarded. *Degree requirements:* For master's, comprehensive exam (for some programs), thesis optional, professional portfolio, internship, clinical experience, or practicum. *Entrance requirements:* For master's, bachelor's degree from regionally-accredited institution, 2 recommendations, 500-word personal essay, official transcripts, minimum GPA of 2.75, valid teaching license (for some programs), passing Praxis I scores for initial teaching licensure programs. Additional exam requirements/recommendations for international students: Required—TOEFL (minimum score 570 paper-based), IELTS (minimum score 6.5). *Application deadline:* For fall admission, 5/1 priority date for domestic students; for spring admission, 10/1 priority date for domestic students; for summer admission, 2/1 priority date for domestic students. Applications are processed on a rolling basis. Application fee: $50. Electronic applications accepted. *Expenses:* Tuition, state resident: full-time $7506; part-time $327 per credit hour. Tuition, nonresident: full-time $17,100; part-time $837 per credit hour. Tuition and fees vary according to course load and campus/location. *Financial support:* Career-related internships or fieldwork and Federal Work-Study available. Financial award applicants required to submit FAFSA. *Unit head:* Dr. Peggy L. Tarpley, Chair of the Department of Education and Special Education, 434-395-2337, E-mail: tarpleypl@longwood.edu. *Application contact:* College of Graduate and Professional Studies, 434-395-2380, Fax: 434-395-2750, E-mail: graduate@longwood.edu.
Website: http://www.longwood.edu/cehs/.

Loras College, Graduate Division, Program in Education with an Emphasis in Special Education, Dubuque, IA 52004-0178. Offers instructional strategist I K-6 and 7-12 (MA). Part-time and evening/weekend programs available. *Degree requirements:* For master's, comprehensive exam, thesis optional. *Entrance requirements:* For master's, minimum cumulative undergraduate GPA of 3.0.

Louisiana Tech University, Graduate School, College of Education, Department of Curriculum, Instruction and Leadership, Ruston, LA 71272. Offers curriculum and instruction (M Ed, Ed D), including adult education (M Ed), early childhood (M Ed), English education (M Ed), mathematics education (M Ed), science education (M Ed),

social studies education (M Ed), special education (M Ed); educational leadership (M Ed, Ed D). *Accreditation:* NCATE. Part-time programs available. *Degree requirements:* For doctorate, thesis/dissertation. *Entrance requirements:* For master's and doctorate, GRE General Test. *Application deadline:* For fall admission, 7/29 for domestic students; for spring admission, 2/3 for domestic students. Application fee: $20 ($30 for international students). *Financial support:* Fellowships, research assistantships, and teaching assistantships available. Financial award application deadline: 2/1. *Unit head:* Dr. Pauline Leonard, Head, 318-257-4609, Fax: 318-257-2379. *Application contact:* Dr. John Harrison, Associate Dean of Graduate Studies, 318-257-3229, Fax: 318-257-2379, E-mail: johnharrison@latech.edu.
Website: http://www.latech.edu/education/cil/.

Loyola Marymount University, School of Education, Department of Educational Support Services, Program in Special Education, Los Angeles, CA 90045. Offers MA. Part-time and evening/weekend programs available. *Faculty:* 12 full-time (6 women), 35 part-time/adjunct (26 women). *Students:* 210 full-time (162 women), 2 part-time (both women); includes 127 minority (18 Black or African American, non-Hispanic/Latino; 25 Asian, non-Hispanic/Latino; 70 Hispanic/Latino; 14 Two or more races, non-Hispanic/Latino). Average age 26. 139 applicants, 94% accepted, 114 enrolled. In 2013, 31 master's awarded. *Degree requirements:* For master's, comprehensive exam. *Entrance requirements:* For master's, CBEST, CSET, 3 letters of recommendation. Additional exam requirements/recommendations for international students: Required—TOEFL (minimum score 600 paper-based; 100 iBT). *Application deadline:* For fall admission, 6/15 for domestic students; for spring admission, 11/15 for domestic students. Application fee: $50. Electronic applications accepted. *Financial support:* In 2013–14, 194 students received support, including 1 research assistantship (averaging $1,440 per year); scholarships/grants and unspecified assistantships also available. Support available to part-time students. Financial award application deadline: 6/30; financial award applicants required to submit FAFSA. *Total annual research expenditures:* $132,233. *Unit head:* Dr. Victoria Graf, Program Director, 310-338-7305, E-mail: vgraf@lmu.edu. *Application contact:* Chake H. Kouyoumjian, Graduate Admissions Director, 310-338-2721, E-mail: ckouyoum@lmu.edu.
Website: http://soe.lmu.edu/admissions/programs/sped/.

Loyola University Chicago, School of Education, Program in Teaching and Learning, Chicago, IL 60660. Offers behavior intervention specialist (M Ed); elementary education (M Ed); English as a second language (Certificate); English language teaching and learning (M Ed); math education (M Ed); reading specialist (M Ed); reading teacher endorsement (Certificate); school technology (M Ed); science education (M Ed); secondary education (M Ed); special education (M Ed). *Accreditation:* NCATE. *Faculty:* 23 full-time (16 women), 49 part-time/adjunct (42 women). *Students:* 109. Average age 28. 104 applicants, 71% accepted, 44 enrolled. In 2013, 39 master's awarded. *Degree requirements:* For master's, comprehensive exam. *Entrance requirements:* For master's, Illinois Basic Skills Test, 3 letters of recommendation, minimum GPA of 3.0, resume. Additional exam requirements/recommendations for international students: Required—TOEFL (minimum score 550 paper-based; 79 iBT). *Application deadline:* For fall admission, 7/1 priority date for domestic and international students; for spring admission, 11/1 priority date for domestic and international students; for summer admission, 4/1 for domestic and international students. Applications are processed on a rolling basis. Application fee: $50. Electronic applications accepted. Application fee is waived when completed online. *Expenses: Tuition:* Full-time $16,740; part-time $930 per credit. *Required fees:* $135 per semester. *Financial support:* In 2013–14, 58 fellowships with partial tuition reimbursements were awarded; research assistantships, teaching assistantships, institutionally sponsored loans, scholarships/grants, and unspecified assistantships also available. Support available to part-time students. Financial award application deadline: 2/1; financial award applicants required to submit FAFSA. *Faculty research:* Positive behavior support, school reform, school improvement. *Unit head:* Dr. Ann Marie Ryan, Director, 312-915-7027, E-mail: aryan3@luc.edu. *Application contact:* Marie Rosin-Dittmar, Information Contact, 312-915-6800, E-mail: schleduc@luc.edu.

Loyola University Maryland, Graduate Programs, School of Education, Program in Special Education, Baltimore, MD 21210-2699. Offers early childhood education (M Ed, CAS); elementary/middle education (M Ed, CAS); secondary education (M Ed, CAS). *Accreditation:* NCATE. Part-time programs available. *Entrance requirements:* For master's, transcript, essay, letter of recommendation. Additional exam requirements/recommendations for international students: Required—TOEFL (minimum score 550 paper-based). Electronic applications accepted.

Lynchburg College, Graduate Studies, School of Education and Human Development, M Ed Program in Special Education, Lynchburg, VA 24501-3199. Offers M Ed. Part-time and evening/weekend programs available. *Faculty:* 4 full-time (3 women), 2 part-time/adjunct (1 woman). *Students:* 16 full-time (12 women), 16 part-time (10 women); includes 2 minority (1 Black or African American, non-Hispanic/Latino; 1 Hispanic/Latino), 3 international. Average age 32. In 2013, 12 master's awarded. *Degree requirements:* For master's, comprehensive exam. *Entrance requirements:* For master's, GRE, minimum GPA of 3.0 (preferred), official transcripts (bachelor's, others as relevant), three letters of recommendation, career goals statement. Additional exam requirements/recommendations for international students: Required—TOEFL (minimum score 550 paper-based; 79 iBT), IELTS (minimum score 6.5). *Application deadline:* For fall admission, 7/31 for domestic students, 6/1 for international students; for spring admission, 11/30 for domestic students, 10/15 for international students. Applications are processed on a rolling basis. Application fee: $30. Electronic applications accepted. Application fee is waived when completed online. *Financial support:* Fellowships, research assistantships, Federal Work-Study, scholarships/grants, health care benefits, and unspecified assistantships available. Support available to part-time students. Financial award application deadline: 7/31; financial award applicants required to submit FAFSA. *Unit head:* Dr. Gena Barnhill, Associate Professor/Director of M Ed in Special Education, 434-544-8771, Fax: 434-544-8483, E-mail: barnhill@lynchburg.edu. *Application contact:* Anne Pingstock, Executive Assistant, Graduate Studies, 434-544-8383, Fax: 434-544-8483, E-mail: gradstudies@lynchburg.edu.
Website: http://www.lynchburg.edu/master-education-special-education.

Lyndon State College, Graduate Programs in Education, Department of Education, Lyndonville, VT 05851-0919. Offers curriculum and instruction (M Ed); reading specialist (M Ed); special education (M Ed); teaching and counseling (M Ed). Part-time and evening/weekend programs available. *Degree requirements:* For master's, exam or major field project. *Entrance requirements:* Additional exam requirements/recommendations for international students: Recommended—TOEFL (minimum score 500 paper-based).

Lynn University, Donald E. and Helen L. Ross College of Education, Boca Raton, FL 33431-5598. Offers educational leadership (M Ed, Ed D); exceptional student education (M Ed). Part-time and evening/weekend programs available. *Faculty:* 2 full-time (both women), 6 part-time/adjunct (5 women). *Students:* 28 full-time (24 women), 54 part-time (28 women); includes 9 minority (8 Black or African American, non-Hispanic/Latino; 1 Hispanic/Latino), 8 international. Average age 36. 31 applicants, 97% accepted, 25 enrolled. In 2013, 29 master's, 7 doctorates awarded. *Degree requirements:* For master's, thesis (for some programs); for doctorate, thesis/dissertation, qualifying paper. *Entrance requirements:* For master's, bachelor's degree from accredited institution, minimum undergraduate GPA of 3.0, resume, 2 letters of recommendation, statement of professional goals; for doctorate, master's degree from accredited institution, minimum GPA of 3.5, resume, 2 letters of recommendation, professional practice statement, interview and presentation. Additional exam requirements/recommendations for international students: Required—TOEFL (minimum score 550 paper-based). *Application deadline:* Applications are processed on a rolling basis. Application fee: $45. Electronic applications accepted. *Expenses: Tuition:* Full-time $23,760; part-time $660 per credit. *Required fees:* $300; $50 per term. Tuition and fees vary according to degree level and program. *Financial support:* Career-related internships or fieldwork, Federal Work-Study, institutionally sponsored loans, scholarships/grants, tuition waivers (partial), and unspecified assistantships available. Support available to part-time students. Financial award application deadline: 8/1; financial award applicants required to submit FAFSA. *Faculty research:* Non-traditional education, innovative curricula, multicultural education, simulation games. *Unit head:* Dr. Gregg Cox, Dean of College, 561-237-7210, E-mail: gcox@lynn.edu. *Application contact:* Steven Pruitt, Director of Graduate and Undergraduate Evening Admission, 561-237-7834, Fax: 561-237-7100, E-mail: spruitt@lynn.edu.
Website: http://www.lynn.edu/academics/colleges/education.

Madonna University, Programs in Education, Livonia, MI 48150-1173. Offers Catholic school leadership (MSA); educational leadership (MSA); learning disabilities (MAT); literacy education (MAT); teaching and learning (MAT). *Accreditation:* NCATE. Part-time and evening/weekend programs available. *Degree requirements:* For master's, thesis or alternative. Electronic applications accepted.

Malone University, Graduate Program in Education, Canton, OH 44709. Offers curriculum and instruction (MA); curriculum, instruction, and professional development (MA); educational leadership (principal license) (MA); intervention specialist (MA). Part-time and evening/weekend programs available. *Faculty:* 8 full-time (4 women), 12 part-time/adjunct (9 women). *Students:* 10 full-time (6 women), 59 part-time (44 women); includes 5 minority (2 Black or African American, non-Hispanic/Latino; 1 Hispanic/Latino; 2 Two or more races, non-Hispanic/Latino). Average age 32. In 2013, 13 master's awarded. *Degree requirements:* For master's, research project. *Entrance requirements:* For master's, minimum GPA of 3.0, teaching license. Additional exam requirements/recommendations for international students: Required—TOEFL (minimum score 550 paper-based; 79 iBT). *Application deadline:* Applications are processed on a rolling basis. *Financial support:* Tuition waivers (partial) available. Support available to part-time students. Financial award application deadline: 6/30. *Faculty research:* Educational leadership styles: Jesus as master teacher, assessment accommodations for English language learners, preparing culturally proficient teachers, using naturally occurring text in the classroom to meet the syntactic needs of students with learning disabilities, using tablet instructional technology to meet the needs of students with disabilities. *Unit head:* Dr. Moses B. Rumano, Director, 330-471-8349, Fax: 330-471-8563, E-mail: mrumano@malone.edu. *Application contact:* Dan DePasquale, Senior Recruiter, 330-471-8381, Fax: 330-471-8343, E-mail: depasquale@malone.edu.
Website: http://www.malone.edu/admissions/graduate/education/.

Manhattan College, Graduate Programs, School of Education and Health, Program in Special Education, Riverdale, NY 10471. Offers adolescent special education generalist in English, math or social studies (MS Ed); autism spectrum disorder (Certificate); bilingual special education (Professional Diploma); dual childhood/special education (MS Ed); special education (MS Ed). Part-time and evening/weekend programs available. *Faculty:* 8 full-time (5 women), 16 part-time/adjunct (12 women). *Students:* 30 full-time (28 women), 68 part-time (61 women). Average age 24. 86 applicants, 94% accepted, 76 enrolled. In 2013, 37 master's awarded. *Degree requirements:* For master's, thesis, internship (if not certified). *Entrance requirements:* For master's, minimum GPA of 3.0. Additional exam requirements/recommendations for international students: Required—TOEFL (minimum score 550 paper-based). *Application deadline:* For fall admission, 8/10 priority date for domestic students; for spring admission, 1/7 priority date for domestic students. Applications are processed on a rolling basis. Application fee: $60. *Expenses:* Contact institution. *Financial support:* Federal Work-Study, scholarships/grants, and unspecified assistantships available. Financial award application deadline: 2/1. *Unit head:* Dr. Elizabeth Mary Kosky, Director of Childhood/Adolescent Special Education Programs, 718-862-7969, Fax: 718-862-7816, E-mail: elizabeth.kosky@manhattan.edu. *Application contact:* William Bisset, Information Contact, 718-862-8000, E-mail: william.bisset@manhattan.edu.
Website: http://www.manhattan.edu/academics/education/special-education-dept.

Manhattanville College, School of Education, Program in Childhood Education, Purchase, NY 10577-2132. Offers childhood and special education (MPS); childhood education (MAT); special education childhood (MPS). Part-time and evening/weekend programs available. *Degree requirements:* For master's, comprehensive exam or research project, field experience. *Entrance requirements:* For master's, minimum undergraduate GPA of 3.0, 2 letters of recommendation. Additional exam requirements/recommendations for international students: Required—TOEFL.

Manhattanville College, School of Education, Program in Early Childhood Education, Purchase, NY 10577-2132. Offers childhood and early childhood education (MAT); early childhood and special education (birth-grade 2) (MPS); early childhood education (birth-grade 2) (MAT); special education (birth-grade 2) (MPS); special education (birth-grade 6) (MPS). Part-time and evening/weekend programs available. *Degree requirements:* For master's, comprehensive exam or research project, field experience. *Entrance requirements:* For master's, minimum undergraduate GPA of 3.0, 2 letters of recommendation. Additional exam requirements/recommendations for international students: Required—TOEFL. Electronic applications accepted.

Manhattanville College, School of Education, Program in Middle Childhood/Adolescence Education (Grades 5-12), Purchase, NY 10577-2132. Offers biology (MAT); biology and special education (MPS); chemistry (MAT); chemistry and special education (MPS); English (MAT); English and special education (MPS); literacy and special education (MPS); literacy specialist (MPS); math and special education (MPS); mathematics (MAT); physics (MAT); social studies (MAT); social studies and special education (MPS); special education (MPS); teaching languages other than English (MAT), including French, Italian, Latin, Spanish. Part-time and evening/weekend programs available. *Degree requirements:* For master's, comprehensive exam or research project, field experience. *Entrance requirements:* For master's, minimum undergraduate GPA of 3.0, 2 letters of recommendation. Additional exam requirements/recommendations for international students: Required—TOEFL. Electronic applications accepted.

Mansfield University of Pennsylvania, Graduate Studies, Department of Education and Special Education, Mansfield, PA 16933. Offers elementary education (M Ed); secondary education (MS); special education (M Ed). *Accreditation:* NCATE (one or more programs are accredited). Part-time and evening/weekend programs available. Postbaccalaureate distance learning degree programs offered (no on-campus study). *Degree requirements:* For master's, comprehensive exam, thesis optional. *Entrance requirements:* For master's, minimum GPA of 3.0. Additional exam requirements/recommendations for international students: Required—TOEFL (minimum score 550 paper-based). Electronic applications accepted.

Marshall University, Academic Affairs Division, College of Education and Professional Development, Program in Special Education, Huntington, WV 25755. Offers MA. *Accreditation:* NCATE. Part-time and evening/weekend programs available. *Students:* 62 full-time (51 women), 152 part-time (120 women); includes 10 minority (7 Black or African American, non-Hispanic/Latino; 2 Hispanic/Latino; 1 Two or more races, non-Hispanic/Latino), 4 international. Average age 35. In 2013, 64 master's awarded. *Degree requirements:* For master's, thesis optional, comprehensive or oral assessment, research project. *Entrance requirements:* For master's, GRE General Test or MAT, minimum GPA of 3.0. Application fee: $40. *Financial support:* Federal Work-Study, tuition waivers (full), and unspecified assistantships available. Support available to part-time students. Financial award applicants required to submit FAFSA. *Faculty research:* Teaching the severely handicapped, career/vocational education, education of the gifted. *Unit head:* Dr. Joyce Meikamp, Director, 304-746-1983, E-mail: jmeikamp@marshall.edu. *Application contact:* Information Contact, 304-746-1900, Fax: 304-746-1902, E-mail: services@marshall.edu.

Martin Luther College, Graduate Studies, New Ulm, MN 56073. Offers instruction (MS Ed); leadership (MS Ed); special education (MS Ed). Part-time programs available. Postbaccalaureate distance learning degree programs offered. *Degree requirements:* For master's, capstone project or comprehensive exam. *Entrance requirements:* For master's, undergraduate degree in education from an accredited college or university, minimum undergraduate GPA of 3.0. Electronic applications accepted.

Marymount University, School of Education and Human Services, Program in Education, Arlington, VA 22207-4299. Offers counselor education and supervision (Ed D); elementary education (M Ed); English as a second language (M Ed); professional studies (M Ed); secondary education (M Ed); special education: general curriculum (M Ed). *Accreditation:* NCATE. Part-time and evening/weekend programs available. *Faculty:* 8 full-time (6 women), 13 part-time/adjunct (9 women). *Students:* 76 full-time (67 women), 83 part-time (70 women); includes 30 minority (12 Black or African American, non-Hispanic/Latino; 2 American Indian or Alaska Native, non-Hispanic/Latino; 9 Asian, non-Hispanic/Latino; 6 Hispanic/Latino; 1 Two or more races, non-Hispanic/Latino), 12 international. Average age 31. 63 applicants, 95% accepted, 44 enrolled. In 2013, 88 master's awarded. *Degree requirements:* For master's, thesis or alternative; for doctorate, thesis/dissertation. *Entrance requirements:* For master's, GRE or MAT and PRAXIS I or SAT/ACT and VCLA, 2 letters of recommendation, resume, interview. Additional exam requirements/recommendations for international students: Required—TOEFL (minimum score 600 paper-based; 96 iBT), IELTS (minimum score 6.5). *Application deadline:* For fall admission, 7/1 for international students. Applications are processed on a rolling basis. Application fee: $40. Electronic applications accepted. *Expenses: Tuition:* Part-time $850 per credit. *Required fees:* $10 per credit. One-time fee: $200 part-time. Tuition and fees vary according to program. *Financial support:* In 2013–14, 41 students received support, including 4 research assistantships with full and partial tuition reimbursements available, 1 teaching assistantship with full and partial tuition reimbursement available; career-related internships or fieldwork, Federal Work-Study, scholarships/grants, and unspecified assistantships also available. Support available to part-time students. Financial award applicants required to submit FAFSA. *Unit head:* Dr. Lisa Turissini, Chair, 703-526-1668, Fax: 703-284-1631, E-mail: lisa.turissini@marymount.edu. *Application contact:* Francesca Reed, Director, Graduate Admissions, 703-284-5901, Fax: 703-527-3815, E-mail: grad.admissions@marymount.edu. Website: http://www.marymount.edu/academics/schools/sehs/grad.aspx.

Marywood University, Academic Affairs, Reap College of Education and Human Development, Department of Education, Program in Administration and Supervision of Special Education, Scranton, PA 18509-1598. Offers MS. *Accreditation:* NCATE. *Entrance requirements:* Additional exam requirements/recommendations for international students: Required—TOEFL (minimum score 550 paper-based; 79 iBT). *Application deadline:* For fall admission, 4/1 priority date for domestic students, 3/31 priority date for international students; for spring admission, 11/1 priority date for domestic students, 8/31 priority date for international students. Applications are processed on a rolling basis. Application fee: $35. Electronic applications accepted. *Expenses: Tuition:* Part-time $775 per credit. Tuition and fees vary according to degree level. *Financial support:* Career-related internships or fieldwork, scholarships/grants, and unspecified assistantships available. Support available to part-time students. Financial award application deadline: 6/30; financial award applicants required to submit FAFSA. *Unit head:* Dr. Patricia S. Arter, Director, 570-348-6211 Ext. 2511, E-mail: psarter@marywood.edu. *Application contact:* Tammy Manka, Associate Director of Graduate Admissions, 570-348-6211 Ext. 2322, E-mail: tmanka@marywood.edu. Website: http://www.marywood.edu/academics/gradcatalog/.

Marywood University, Academic Affairs, Reap College of Education and Human Development, Department of Education, Program in Special Education, Scranton, PA 18509-1598. Offers MS. *Accreditation:* NCATE. *Entrance requirements:* Additional exam requirements/recommendations for international students: Required—TOEFL (minimum score 550 paper-based; 79 iBT). *Application deadline:* For fall admission, 4/1 priority date for domestic students, 3/31 priority date for international students; for spring admission, 11/1 priority date for domestic students, 8/30 priority date for international students. Applications are processed on a rolling basis. Application fee: $35. Electronic applications accepted. *Expenses: Tuition:* Part-time $775 per credit. Tuition and fees vary according to degree level. *Financial support:* Career-related internships or fieldwork, scholarships/grants, and unspecified assistantships available. Support available to part-time students. Financial award application deadline: 6/30; financial award applicants required to submit FAFSA. *Unit head:* Dr. Patricia S. Arter, Director, 570-348-6211 Ext. 2511, E-mail: psarter@marywood.edu. *Application contact:* Tammy Manka, Associate Director of Graduate Admissions, 570-348-6211 Ext. 2322, E-mail: tmanka@marywood.edu. Website: http://www.marywood.edu/education/graduate-programs/ms-special-ed.html.

Massachusetts College of Liberal Arts, Graduate Programs, North Adams, MA 01247-4100. Offers business (MBA); educational administration (M Ed); educational leadership (CAGS); instruction and curriculum (M Ed); instructional technology (M Ed); physical education and health (M Ed); reading (M Ed); special education (M Ed). Part-time and evening/weekend programs available. *Degree requirements:* For master's, thesis. *Entrance requirements:* For master's, writing sample.

McDaniel College, Graduate and Professional Studies, Program in Deaf Education, Westminster, MD 21157-4390. Offers MS. *Accreditation:* NCATE. Part-time programs available. *Degree requirements:* For master's, comprehensive exam, thesis optional. *Entrance requirements:* For master's, American Sign Language Proficiency Interview (ASLPI). Additional exam requirements/recommendations for international students: Required—TOEFL. *Faculty research:* Mainstreaming of multihandicapped children.

McDaniel College, Graduate and Professional Studies, Program in Human Services Management, Westminster, MD 21157-4390. Offers MS. *Accreditation:* NCATE. Evening/weekend programs available. *Degree requirements:* For master's, internship. *Entrance requirements:* For master's, 3 letters of reference. Additional exam requirements/recommendations for international students: Required—TOEFL.

McDaniel College, Graduate and Professional Studies, Program in Special Education, Westminster, MD 21157-4390. Offers MS. *Accreditation:* NCATE. Part-time and evening/weekend programs available. *Degree requirements:* For master's, comprehensive exam, thesis optional. *Entrance requirements:* For master's, GRE General Test, MAT, or NTE/PRAXIS I, 3 letters of reference. Additional exam requirements/recommendations for international students: Required—TOEFL.

McKendree University, Graduate Programs, Programs in Education, Lebanon, IL 62254-1299. Offers curriculum design and instruction (Ed D, Ed S); educational administration and leadership (MA Ed); educational studies (MA Ed); higher education administrative services (MA Ed); music education (MA Ed); reading (MA Ed); special education (MA Ed); teacher leadership (MA Ed); teaching certification (MA Ed). *Accreditation:* NCATE. Part-time and evening/weekend programs available. Postbaccalaureate distance learning degree programs offered (no on-campus study). *Entrance requirements:* For master's, official transcripts from all institutions previously attended, minimum GPA of 3.0, resume, references; for doctorate, GRE (within the past 5 years), master's degree in education and Ed S, or the equivalent, from regionally-accredited institution; official transcripts from all institutions previously attended; curriculum vitae/resume; essay/personal statement; two years of teaching/professional experience; for Ed S, GRE (within the past 5 years), master's degree in education from regionally-accredited institution of higher education; official transcripts from all institutions previously attended; curriculum vitae/resume; essay/personal statement; two years of teaching/professional experience. Additional exam requirements/recommendations for international students: Required—TOEFL. Electronic applications accepted.

McNeese State University, Doré School of Graduate Studies, Burton College of Education, Office of Graduate Education Programs, Program in Special Education, Lake Charles, LA 70609. Offers advanced professional (M Ed); autism (M Ed); educational diagnostician (M Ed). *Entrance requirements:* For master's, GRE, teaching certificate.

McNeese State University, Doré School of Graduate Studies, Burton College of Education, Office of Graduate Education Programs, Program in Special Education - Mild/Moderate Grades 1-12, Lake Charles, LA 70609. Offers MAT. *Entrance requirements:* For master's, GRE, PRAXIS, 2 letters of recommendation; autobiography.

McNeese State University, Doré School of Graduate Studies, Burton College of Education, Office of Student Teaching and Professional Education Services, Program in Special Education Intervention Birth-5, Lake Charles, LA 70609. Offers Postbaccalaureate Certificate. *Entrance requirements:* For degree, PRAXIS, 2 letters of recommendation, autobiography.

McNeese State University, Doré School of Graduate Studies, Burton College of Education, Office of Student Teaching and Professional Education Services, Program in Special Education, Mild/Moderate for Elementary Education Grades 1-5, Lake Charles, LA 70609. Offers Postbaccalaureate Certificate. *Entrance requirements:* For degree, PRAXIS, 2 letters of recommendation, autobiography.

McNeese State University, Doré School of Graduate Studies, Burton College of Education, Office of Student Teaching and Professional Education Services, Program in Special Education, Mild/Moderate for Secondary Education Grades 6-12, Lake Charles, LA 70609. Offers Postbaccalaureate Certificate. *Entrance requirements:* For degree, PRAXIS, 2 letters of recommendation, autobiography.

Medaille College, Program in Education, Buffalo, NY 14214-2695. Offers adolescent education (MS Ed); curriculum and instruction (MS Ed); education preparation (MS Ed); literacy (MS Ed); special education (MS). *Accreditation:* Teacher Education Accreditation Council. Part-time and evening/weekend programs available. *Faculty:* 12 full-time (9 women), 28 part-time/adjunct (19 women). *Students:* 159 full-time (123 women), 25 part-time (22 women); includes 8 minority (5 Black or African American, non-Hispanic/Latino; 3 Hispanic/Latino), 88 international. Average age 29. 209 applicants, 96% accepted, 61 enrolled. In 2013, 253 master's awarded. *Degree requirements:* For master's, comprehensive exam (for some programs), thesis or alternative. *Entrance requirements:* For master's, minimum undergraduate GPA of 2.7. Additional exam requirements/recommendations for international students: Required—TOEFL (minimum score 550 paper-based). *Application deadline:* For fall admission, 8/15 priority date for domestic students; for spring admission, 1/15 priority date for domestic students. Applications are processed on a rolling basis. Application fee: $35. Electronic applications accepted. *Financial support:* Federal Work-Study available. Financial award applicants required to submit FAFSA. *Faculty research:* Curriculum planning, truancy, tracking minority students, curriculum design, mentoring students. *Unit head:* Dr. Illana Lane, Dean, School of Education, 716-880-2553, E-mail: ilane@medaille.edu. *Application contact:* E-mail: sageadmissions@medaille.edu. Website: http://www.medaille.edu.

Mercyhurst University, Graduate Studies, Program in Special Education, Erie, PA 16546. Offers bilingual/bicultural special education (MS); educational leadership (Certificate); special education (MS). Part-time and evening/weekend programs available. *Degree requirements:* For master's, thesis optional. *Entrance requirements:* For master's, GRE or PRAXIS I, interview, resume, essay, three professional references, transcripts. Additional exam requirements/recommendations for international students: Required—TOEFL. Electronic applications accepted. *Faculty research:* College-age learning disabled program, teacher preparation/collaboration, applied behavior analysis, special education policy issues.

Merrimack College, School of Education, North Andover, MA 01845-5800. Offers community engagement (M Ed), including community organizations, higher education, K-12 education; early childhood education (M Ed); elementary education (M Ed); English as a second language (PreK-6) (M Ed); English language learners (M Ed); general studies (M Ed); higher education (M Ed), including leadership and organizational development, student affairs; middle (M Ed); moderate disabilities (PreK-8) (M Ed); secondary (M Ed); teacher leadership (CAGS), including instructional leadership, reading specialist. Part-time and evening/weekend programs available. *Faculty:* 4 full-time (all women), 23 part-time/adjunct (15 women). *Students:* 127 full-time (104 women), 61 part-time (52 women); includes 3 minority (1 Asian, non-Hispanic/Latino; 2 Hispanic/Latino), 2 international. Average age 25. 403 applicants, 47% accepted, 138 enrolled. In 2013, 140 master's awarded. *Degree requirements:* For master's, practicum, portfolio, and state test (for licensure track); capstone (for higher education and community engagement tracks). *Entrance requirements:* For master's, MTEL (Massachusetts Tests for Educator Licensure), official transcripts from other colleges, resume, personal statement, 2 letters of recommendation, additional essay requirements for fellowships. Additional exam requirements/recommendations for international students: Required—TOEFL (minimum score 84 iBT), IELTS (minimum score 6.5). *Application deadline:* For fall admission, 8/15 for domestic and international students; for winter admission, 12/1 for domestic students, 11/15 for international students; for spring admission, 1/10 for domestic and international students; for summer admission, 5/10 for domestic and international students. Applications are processed on a rolling basis. Application fee: $0. Electronic applications accepted. Tuition and fees vary according to course load and program. *Financial support:* In 2013–14, 91 fellowships with full tuition reimbursements were awarded; career-related internships or fieldwork, scholarships/grants, and health care benefits also available. Support available

to part-time students. Financial award applicants required to submit FAFSA. *Faculty research:* Expressive language, civic engagement, family life education, reading genres, the psychological process of aging. *Application contact:* Kristen English, Interim Director of Graduate Admission, 978-837-5073, E-mail: englishkr@merrimack.edu.
Website: http://www.merrimack.edu/academics/graduate/education/.

Messiah College, Program in Education, Mechanicsburg, PA 17055. Offers curriculum and instruction (M Ed); special education (M Ed); teaching English to speakers of other languages (M Ed). Part-time programs available. Postbaccalaureate distance learning degree programs offered (no on-campus study). Electronic applications accepted. *Expenses: Tuition:* Part-time \$595 per credit hour. *Required fees:* \$30 per course. *Faculty research:* Socio-cultural perspectives on education, TESOL, autism, special education.

Metropolitan State University of Denver, School of Professional Studies, Denver, CO 80217-3362. Offers elementary education (MAT); special education (MAT).

Miami University, College of Education, Health and Society, Department of Educational Psychology, Oxford, OH 45056. Offers educational psychology (M Ed); instructional design and technology (M Ed, MA); school psychology (MS, Ed S); special education (M Ed, MA). *Accreditation:* NCATE. *Students:* 45 full-time (35 women), 41 part-time (31 women); includes 8 minority (1 Black or African American, non-Hispanic/Latino; 1 American Indian or Alaska Native, non-Hispanic/Latino; 5 Asian, non-Hispanic/Latino; 1 Two or more races, non-Hispanic/Latino), 18 international. Average age 27. In 2013, 79 master's awarded. *Entrance requirements:* For degree, GRE General Test or MAT. Additional exam requirements/recommendations for international students: Recommended—TOEFL (minimum score 80 iBT), IELTS (minimum score 6.5), TSE (minimum score 54). Application fee: \$50. Electronic applications accepted. *Expenses:* Tuition, state resident: full-time \$12,634; part-time \$526 per credit hour. Tuition, nonresident: full-time \$27,892; part-time \$1162 per credit hour. Part-time tuition and fees vary according to course load, campus/location and program. *Financial support:* Fellowships with full tuition reimbursements, research assistantships with full tuition reimbursements, teaching assistantships with full tuition reimbursements, career-related internships or fieldwork, Federal Work-Study, health care benefits, and unspecified assistantships available. Financial award application deadline: 2/15; financial award applicants required to submit FAFSA. *Unit head:* Dr. Susan Mosley-Howard, Chair, 513-529-6621, E-mail: edp@miamioh.edu. *Application contact:* 513-529-6621, E-mail: edp@miamioh.edu.
Website: http://www.MiamiOH.edu/EDP.

Michigan State University, The Graduate School, College of Education, Department of Counseling, Educational Psychology and Special Education, East Lansing, MI 48824. Offers counseling (MA); educational psychology and educational technology (PhD); educational technology (MA); measurement and quantitative methods (PhD); rehabilitation counseling (MA); rehabilitation counselor education (PhD); school psychology (MA, PhD, Ed S); special education (MA, PhD). *Accreditation:* APA (one or more programs are accredited); CORE (one or more programs are accredited). Part-time programs available. *Entrance requirements:* Additional exam requirements/recommendations for international students: Required—TOEFL. Electronic applications accepted.

MidAmerica Nazarene University, Graduate Studies in Education, Olathe, KS 66062-1899. Offers ESOL (M Ed); professional teaching (M Ed); special education (MA); technology enhanced teaching (M Ed). *Accreditation:* NCATE. Part-time and evening/weekend programs available. Postbaccalaureate distance learning degree programs offered (no on-campus study). *Degree requirements:* For master's, thesis or alternative, creative project, technology leadership practicum. *Entrance requirements:* For master's, minimum undergraduate GPA of 2.8, 2 years of teaching experience. *Expenses:* Contact institution.

Middle Tennessee State University, College of Graduate Studies, College of Education, Department of Elementary and Special Education, Major in Special Education, Murfreesboro, TN 37132. Offers M Ed. *Accreditation:* NCATE. Part-time and evening/weekend programs available. Postbaccalaureate distance learning degree programs offered. *Faculty:* 14 full-time (9 women), 7 part-time/adjunct (all women). *Students:* 7 full-time (4 women), 13 part-time (11 women); includes 4 minority (all Asian, non-Hispanic/Latino). 30 applicants, 43% accepted. In 2013, 17 master's awarded. *Degree requirements:* For master's, comprehensive exam. *Entrance requirements:* For master's, GRE, MAT or PRAXIS. Additional exam requirements/recommendations for international students: Required—TOEFL (minimum score 525 paper-based; 71 iBT) or IELTS (minimum score 6). *Application deadline:* For fall admission, 6/1 for domestic and international students. Applications are processed on a rolling basis. Application fee: \$25 (\$30 for international students). Electronic applications accepted. *Financial support:* Institutionally sponsored loans and tuition waivers available. Support available to part-time students. Financial award application deadline: 5/1. *Unit head:* Dr. Kathleen Burriss, Interim Chair, 615-898-2680, Fax: 615-898-5309, E-mail: kathleen.burriss@mtsu.edu. *Application contact:* Dr. Michael D. Allen, Vice Provost for Research and Dean, 615-898-2840, Fax: 615-904-8020, E-mail: michael.allen@mtsu.edu.

Midwestern State University, Graduate School, West College of Education, Program in Special Education, Wichita Falls, TX 76308. Offers M Ed. Part-time and evening/weekend programs available. *Degree requirements:* For master's, comprehensive exam. *Entrance requirements:* For master's, GRE General Test, MAT, or GMAT, Texas teacher certificate or equivalent GPA of 3.0 in previous education courses. Additional exam requirements/recommendations for international students: Required—TOEFL (minimum score 550 paper-based). *Application deadline:* For fall admission, 7/1 priority date for domestic students, 4/1 for international students; for spring admission, 11/1 priority date for domestic students, 8/1 for international students. Applications are processed on a rolling basis. Application fee: \$35 (\$50 for international students). Electronic applications accepted. *Expenses:* Tuition, state resident: full-time \$3627; part-time \$201.50 per credit hour. Tuition, nonresident: full-time \$10,899; part-time \$605.50 per credit hour. *Required fees:* \$1357. *Financial support:* Teaching assistantships with partial tuition reimbursements, career-related internships or fieldwork, Federal Work-Study, institutionally sponsored loans, scholarships/grants, tuition waivers (partial), and unspecified assistantships available. Support available to part-time students. Financial award application deadline: 3/1; financial award applicants required to submit FAFSA. *Faculty research:* Fragile-X syndrome, phenylketonuria and other causes of handicapping conditions, autism, social development of students with disabilities. *Unit head:* Dr. Michaelle Kitchen, Chair, 940-397-4141, Fax: 940-397-4694, E-mail: michaelle.kitchen@mwsu.edu. *Application contact:* Dr. Michaelle Kitchen, Chair, 940-397-4141, Fax: 940-397-4694, E-mail: michaelle.kitchen@mwsu.edu.
Website: http://www.mwsu.edu/academics/education/.

Millersville University of Pennsylvania, College of Graduate and Professional Studies, School of Education, Department of Educational Foundations, Program in Special Education, Millersville, PA 17551-0302. Offers M Ed. *Accreditation:* NCATE. Part-time and evening/weekend programs available. *Faculty:* 13 full-time (7 women), 18 part-time/adjunct (11 women). *Students:* 15 part-time (all women); includes 2 minority (1 Black or African American, non-Hispanic/Latino; 1 American Indian or Alaska Native, non-Hispanic/Latino). Average age 30. 3 applicants, 100% accepted, 3 enrolled. In

2013, 13 master's awarded. *Degree requirements:* For master's, thesis optional. *Entrance requirements:* For master's, GRE or MAT, 3 letters of recommendation, teaching certificate, official transcripts, goal statement. Additional exam requirements/recommendations for international students: Required—TOEFL (minimum score 550 paper-based, 79 iBT) or IELTS (minimum score 6). *Application deadline:* For fall admission, 1/15 priority date for domestic and international students; for winter admission, 10/1 priority date for domestic and international students; for spring admission, 10/1 priority date for domestic and international students. Applications are processed on a rolling basis. Application fee: \$40. Electronic applications accepted. *Expenses:* Tuition, state resident: full-time \$7956; part-time \$442 per credit. Tuition, nonresident: full-time \$11,934; part-time \$663 per credit. *Required fees:* \$2196; \$122 per credit. Tuition and fees vary according to course load. *Financial support:* In 2013–14, 1 student received support, including 1 research assistantship with full tuition reimbursement available (averaging \$2,500 per year); institutionally sponsored loans and unspecified assistantships also available. Support available to part-time students. Financial award application deadline: 3/15; financial award applicants required to submit FAFSA. *Faculty research:* Resilience among gifted students from different cultural, linguistic, and low socio-economic backgrounds; Reactive Attachment Disorder: A Quilting Method Approach; dysphagia in the PA school system; content and development of IEP for secondary English language learners; Professional Development School (PDS). *Unit head:* Dr. Ojoma Edeh Herr, Coordinator, 717-871-4772, Fax: 717-871-5754, E-mail: ojoma.edeh@millersville.edu. *Application contact:* Dr. Victor S. DeSantis, Dean of College of Graduate and Professional Studies/Associate Provost for Civic and Community Engagement, 717-872-3099, Fax: 717-872-3453, E-mail: victor.desantis@millersville.edu.
Website: http://www.millersville.edu/graduate/programs/masters/index.php.

Minnesota State University Mankato, College of Graduate Studies, College of Education, Department of Special Education, Mankato, MN 56001. Offers emotional/behavioral disorders (MS, Certificate); learning disabilities (MS, Certificate). *Accreditation:* NCATE. Part-time programs available. Postbaccalaureate distance learning degree programs offered. *Students:* 28 full-time (19 women), 110 part-time (83 women). *Degree requirements:* For master's, comprehensive exam, thesis or alternative. *Entrance requirements:* For master's, Council for Exceptional Children pre-program assessment, minimum GPA of 3.2 during previous 2 years. Additional exam requirements/recommendations for international students: Required—TOEFL. *Application deadline:* For fall admission, 7/1 priority date for domestic students; for spring admission, 11/1 for domestic students. Applications are processed on a rolling basis. Application fee: \$40. Electronic applications accepted. *Financial support:* Research assistantships, teaching assistantships with full tuition reimbursements, career-related internships or fieldwork, Federal Work-Study, and institutionally sponsored loans available. Support available to part-time students. Financial award application deadline: 3/15; financial award applicants required to submit FAFSA. *Unit head:* Dr. Karen Hurlbutt, Graduate Coordinator, 507-389-1122. *Application contact:* 507-389-2321, E-mail: grad@mnsu.edu.
Website: http://ed.mnsu.edu/sped/.

Minnesota State University Moorhead, Graduate Studies, College of Education and Human Services, Program in Special Education, Moorhead, MN 56563-0002. Offers MS. *Accreditation:* NCATE. Part-time and evening/weekend programs available. *Degree requirements:* For master's, comprehensive exam, final oral exam, project or thesis. *Entrance requirements:* For master's, MAT, 1 year teaching experience or bachelor's degree in education, minimum GPA of 3.0. Additional exam requirements/recommendations for international students: Required—TOEFL (minimum score 550 paper-based). Electronic applications accepted.

Minot State University, Graduate School, Program in Special Education, Minot, ND 58707-0002. Offers education of the deaf (MS); learning disabilities (MS); special education strategist (MS), including early childhood special education, severe multiple handicaps. *Accreditation:* NCATE. *Degree requirements:* For master's, comprehensive exam (for some programs), thesis (for some programs). *Entrance requirements:* For master's, GRE General Test or minimum GPA of 3.0. Additional exam requirements/recommendations for international students: Required—TOEFL. *Faculty research:* Special education team diagnostic unit; individual diagnostic assessments of mentally retarded, learning-disabled, hearing-impaired, and speech-impaired youth; educational programming for the hearing impaired.

Misericordia University, College of Professional Studies and Social Sciences, Program in Education, Dallas, PA 18612-1098. Offers instructional technology (MS); reading specialist (MS); special education (MS). Part-time and evening/weekend programs available. *Faculty:* 1 full-time (0 women), 12 part-time/adjunct (8 women). *Students:* 44 part-time (35 women); includes 1 minority (Hispanic/Latino). Average age 32. In 2013, 24 master's awarded. *Entrance requirements:* For master's, minimum undergraduate GPA of 3.0. Additional exam requirements/recommendations for international students: Required—TOEFL. *Application deadline:* Applications are processed on a rolling basis. Application fee: \$35. Electronic applications accepted. *Expenses:* Tuition: Full-time \$14,450; part-time \$680 per credit. Tuition and fees vary according to degree level. *Financial support:* In 2013–14, 11 students received support. Scholarships/grants available. Support available to part-time students. Financial award application deadline: 6/30; financial award applicants required to submit FAFSA. *Unit head:* Dr. Steven Broskoske, Associate Professor, Education Department, 570-674-6761, E-mail: sbroskos@misericordia.edu. *Application contact:* David Pasquini, Assistant Director of Admissions, 570-674-8183, Fax: 570-674-6232, E-mail: dpasquin@misericordia.edu.
Website: http://www.misericordia.edu/misericordia_pg.cfm?page_id=387&subcat_id=108.

Mississippi College, Graduate School, School of Education, Department of Teacher Education and Leadership, Clinton, MS 39058. Offers art (M Ed); biological science (M Ed); business education (M Ed); computer science (M Ed); dyslexia therapy (M Ed); educational leadership (M Ed, Ed D, Ed S); elementary education (M Ed, Ed S); English (M Ed); higher education administration (MS); mathematics (M Ed); secondary education (M Ed); social studies (history) (M Ed); teaching arts (M Ed). Part-time programs available. Postbaccalaureate distance learning degree programs offered (no on-campus study). *Degree requirements:* For master's, comprehensive exam, thesis optional. *Entrance requirements:* For master's, NTE. Additional exam requirements/recommendations for international students: Recommended—TOEFL, IELTS. Electronic applications accepted.

Mississippi State University, College of Education, Department of Curriculum, Instruction and Special Education, Mississippi State, MS 39762. Offers curriculum and instruction (PhD), including early childhood education (MS, PhD), elementary education (PhD, Ed S), general curriculum and instruction, reading education, secondary education (PhD, Ed S), special education (PhD, Ed S); education (Ed S), including elementary education (PhD, Ed S), secondary education (PhD, Ed S), special education (PhD, Ed S); elementary education (MS), including early childhood education (MS, PhD), general elementary education, middle level education; middle level alternate route (MAT); secondary education (MS); secondary teacher alternate route (MAT); special education (MS). *Accreditation:* NCATE. Part-time and evening/weekend programs

available. *Faculty:* 11 full-time (9 women). *Students:* 58 full-time (40 women), 143 part-time (100 women); includes 62 minority (56 Black or African American, non-Hispanic/Latino; 2 American Indian or Alaska Native, non-Hispanic/Latino; 3 Hispanic/Latino; 1 Two or more races, non-Hispanic/Latino). Average age 33. 181 applicants, 32% accepted, 52 enrolled. In 2013, 44 master's, 1 doctorate, 7 other advanced degrees awarded. *Degree requirements:* For master's, comprehensive exam; for doctorate, thesis/dissertation; for Ed S, comprehensive exam, thesis or alternative. *Entrance requirements:* For master's, GRE, minimum GPA of 2.75 in junior and senior year, eligibility for initial teacher certification; for doctorate, GRE, minimum GPA of 3.4 on previous graduate work; for Ed S, GRE, minimum GPA of 3.2 on master's degree. Additional exam requirements/recommendations for international students: Required—TOEFL (minimum score 550 paper-based; 79 iBT); Recommended—IELTS (minimum score 6.5). *Application deadline:* For fall admission, 3/1 priority date for domestic students, 5/1 for international students; for spring admission, 9/1 priority date for domestic students, 9/1 for international students. Applications are processed on a rolling basis. Application fee: $60. Electronic applications accepted. *Financial support:* In 2013–14, 7 research assistantships with full and partial tuition reimbursements (averaging $9,623 per year), 2 teaching assistantships (averaging $11,382 per year) were awarded; Federal Work-Study, institutionally sponsored loans, scholarships/grants, and unspecified assistantships also available. Financial award application deadline: 4/1; financial award applicants required to submit FAFSA. *Faculty research:* Early childhood education, reading, rural schools, multicultural education, use of technology in instruction. *Unit head:* Dr. Devon Brenner, Professor and Interim Head, 662-325-7119, Fax: 662-325-7857, E-mail: devon@ra.msstate.edu. *Application contact:* Dr. Dana Franz, Graduate Coordinator, 662-325-3703, Fax: 662-325-7857, E-mail: tstevonson@colled.msstate.edu.
Website: http://www.cise.msstate.edu/.

Missouri State University, Graduate College, College of Education, Department of Counseling, Leadership, and Special Education, Program in Special Education, Springfield, MO 65897. Offers alternative certification (MS Ed); autism spectrum disorder (MS Ed); blindness and low vision (MS Ed); orientation and mobility (MS Ed). Part-time and evening/weekend programs available. *Students:* 131 full-time (114 women), 120 part-time (101 women); includes 17 minority (7 Black or African American, non-Hispanic/Latino; 3 Asian, non-Hispanic/Latino; 2 Hispanic/Latino; 1 Native Hawaiian or other Pacific Islander, non-Hispanic/Latino; 4 Two or more races, non-Hispanic/Latino). Average age 35. 21 applicants, 95% accepted, 16 enrolled. In 2013, 27 master's awarded. *Degree requirements:* For master's, comprehensive exam, thesis or alternative. *Entrance requirements:* For master's, GRE or minimum GPA of 3.0, teaching certificate. Additional exam requirements/recommendations for international students: Required—TOEFL (minimum score 550 paper-based; 79 iBT). *Application deadline:* For fall admission, 7/20 for domestic students, 5/1 for international students; for spring admission, 12/20 for domestic students, 9/1 for international students. Applications are processed on a rolling basis. Application fee: $35 ($50 for international students). Electronic applications accepted. *Expenses:* Tuition, state resident: full-time $4500; part-time $250 per credit hour. Tuition, nonresident: full-time $9018; part-time $501 per credit hour. *Required fees:* $361 per semester. Tuition and fees vary according to course level, course load and program. *Financial support:* Federal Work-Study, institutionally sponsored loans, scholarships/grants, and unspecified assistantships available. Financial award application deadline: 3/31; financial award applicants required to submit FAFSA. *Unit head:* Dr. Tamara Arthaud, Department Head, 417-836-5449, Fax: 417-836-4918, E-mail: spe@missouristate.edu. *Application contact:* Misty Stewart, Coordinator of Graduate Recruitment, 417-836-6079, Fax: 417-836-6200, E-mail: mistystewart@missouristate.edu.
Website: http://education.missouristate.edu/sped/.

Missouri State University, Graduate College, College of Health and Human Services, Department of Communication Sciences and Disorders, Springfield, MO 65897. Offers audiology (Au D); communication sciences and disorders (MS), including education of deaf/hard of hearing, speech-language pathology. *Accreditation:* ASHA (one or more programs are accredited). *Faculty:* 18 full-time (15 women), 11 part-time/adjunct (2 women). *Students:* 101 full-time (91 women), 2 part-time (1 woman); includes 8 minority (2 Black or African American, non-Hispanic/Latino; 1 American Indian or Alaska Native, non-Hispanic/Latino; 2 Asian, non-Hispanic/Latino; 2 Hispanic/Latino; 1 Two or more races, non-Hispanic/Latino), 4 international. Average age 25. 20 applicants, 95% accepted, 19 enrolled. In 2013, 33 master's, 12 doctorates awarded. *Degree requirements:* For master's, comprehensive exam, thesis or alternative; for doctorate, comprehensive exam, thesis/dissertation or alternative, clinical externship. *Entrance requirements:* For master's and doctorate, GRE, minimum GPA of 3.0. Additional exam requirements/recommendations for international students: Required—TOEFL (minimum score 550 paper-based; 79 iBT). *Application deadline:* For fall admission, 2/1 for domestic and international students. Application fee: $35 ($50 for international students). Electronic applications accepted. *Expenses:* Tuition, state resident: full-time $4500; part-time $250 per credit hour. Tuition, nonresident: full-time $9018; part-time $501 per credit hour. *Required fees:* $361 per semester. Tuition and fees vary according to course level, course load and program. *Financial support:* In 2013–14, 3 research assistantships with full tuition reimbursements (averaging $8,324 per year) were awarded; career-related internships or fieldwork, Federal Work-Study, scholarships/grants, and unspecified assistantships also available. Support available to part-time students. Financial award application deadline: 3/31; financial award applicants required to submit FAFSA. *Faculty research:* Dysphagia, phonological intervention, elderly adult aural rehabilitation, vestibular disorders. *Unit head:* Dr. Letitia White, Head, 417-836-5368, Fax: 417-836-4242, E-mail: csd@missouristate.edu. *Application contact:* Misty Stewart, Coordinator of Graduate Recruitment, 417-836-6079, Fax: 417-836-6200, E-mail: mistystewart@missouristate.edu.
Website: http://www.missouristate.edu/CSD/.

Missouri Western State University, Program in Assessment, St. Joseph, MO 64507-2294. Offers autism spectrum disorders (MAS, Graduate Certificate); TESOL (MAS, Graduate Certificate); writing (MAS). Part-time programs available. *Students:* 6 full-time (4 women), 44 part-time (42 women); includes 4 minority (2 Black or African American, non-Hispanic/Latino; 1 Asian, non-Hispanic/Latino; 1 Hispanic/Latino), 1 international. Average age 36. 2 applicants, 50% accepted, 1 enrolled. In 2013, 9 master's, 7 other advanced degrees awarded. *Entrance requirements:* For master's, minimum GPA of 2.75. Additional exam requirements/recommendations for international students: Recommended—TOEFL (minimum score 500 paper-based; 61 iBT), IELTS (minimum score 5.5). *Application deadline:* For fall admission, 7/15 for domestic students, 6/15 for international students; for spring admission, 10/1 for domestic students, 10/15 for international students. Applications are processed on a rolling basis. Application fee: $45 ($50 for international students). Electronic applications accepted. *Expenses:* Tuition, state resident: full-time $6019; part-time $300.96 per credit hour. Tuition, nonresident: full-time $11,194; part-time $559.71 per credit hour. *Required fees:* $542; $99 per credit hour. $176 per semester. Tuition and fees vary according to course load and program. *Financial support:* Scholarships/grants and unspecified assistantships available. Support available to part-time students. *Unit head:* Dr. Susan Bashinski, Coordinator, 816-271-5629, E-mail: sbashinski@missouriwestern.edu. *Application contact:* Dr. Benjamin D. Caldwell, Dean of the Graduate School, 816-271-4394, Fax: 816-271-4525, E-mail: graduate@missouriwestern.edu.
Website: https://www.missouriwestern.edu/masa/.

Monmouth University, The Graduate School, School of Education, West Long Branch, NJ 07764-1898. Offers applied behavioral analysis (Certificate); autism (Certificate); initial certification (MAT), including elementary level, K-12, secondary level; principal (MS Ed); principal/school administrator (MS Ed); reading specialist (MS Ed); school counseling (MS Ed); special education (MS Ed), including autism, learning disabilities teacher consultant, teacher of students with disabilities, teaching in inclusive settings; speech-language pathology (MS Ed); student affairs and college counseling (MS Ed); teaching English to speakers of other languages (TESOL) (Certificate). *Accreditation:* NCATE. Part-time and evening/weekend programs available. *Faculty:* 15 full-time (11 women), 19 part-time/adjunct (17 women). *Students:* 125 full-time (97 women), 168 part-time (146 women); includes 38 minority (12 Black or African American, non-Hispanic/Latino; 5 Asian, non-Hispanic/Latino; 16 Hispanic/Latino; 5 Two or more races, non-Hispanic/Latino). Average age 28. 176 applicants, 90% accepted, 112 enrolled. In 2013, 147 master's awarded. *Entrance requirements:* For master's, GRE within last 5 years (for MS Ed in speech-language pathology), minimum GPA of 3.0 in major; 2 letters of recommendation (for some programs), resume, personal statement or essay (depending on degree program). Additional exam requirements/recommendations for international students: Required—TOEFL (minimum score 550 paper-based; 79 iBT), IELTS (minimum score 6), Michigan English Language Assessment Battery (minimum score 77). *Application deadline:* For fall admission, 7/15 priority date for domestic students, 7/1 for international students; for spring admission, 11/15 priority date for domestic students, 11/1 for international students. Applications are processed on a rolling basis. Application fee: $50. Electronic applications accepted. *Expenses: Tuition:* Part-time $1004 per credit hour. *Required fees:* $157 per semester. *Financial support:* In 2013–14, 191 students received support, including 159 fellowships (averaging $2,786 per year), 30 research assistantships (averaging $8,755 per year); career-related internships or fieldwork, scholarships/grants, and unspecified assistantships also available. Support available to part-time students. Financial award applicants required to submit FAFSA. *Faculty research:* Multicultural literacy, science and mathematics teaching strategies, teacher as reflective practitioner, children with disabilities. *Unit head:* Dr. Jason Barr, Program Director, 732-263-5238, Fax: 732-263-5277, E-mail: jbarr@monmouth.edu. *Application contact:* Lauren Vento-Cifelli, Associate Vice President of Undergraduate and Graduate Admission, 732-571-3452, Fax: 732-263-5123, E-mail: gradadm@monmouth.edu.
Website: http://www.monmouth.edu/academics/schools/education/default.asp.

Montana State University Billings, College of Education, Department of Educational Theory and Practice, Billings, MT 59101-0298. Offers educational technology (M Ed); general curriculum (M Ed); interdisciplinary studies (M Ed); reading (M Ed); school counseling (M Ed); special education (MS Sp Ed), including special education generalist; special education (MS Sp Ed), including advanced studies; teaching (Certificate). Part-time programs available. Postbaccalaureate distance learning degree programs offered (minimal on-campus study). *Degree requirements:* For master's, thesis optional. *Entrance requirements:* For master's, GRE General Test or MAT, minimum GPA of 3.0 (undergraduate), 3.25 (graduate). *Application deadline:* For fall admission, 7/15 for international students; for spring admission, 12/1 for international students. Applications are processed on a rolling basis. Application fee: $40. *Expenses:* Tuition, state resident: full-time $2653.75; part-time $1718 per semester. Tuition, nonresident: full-time $7015; part-time $4640 per semester. *Required fees:* $2445; $444 per credit. *Financial support:* Teaching assistantships with partial tuition reimbursements, career-related internships or fieldwork, Federal Work-Study, institutionally sponsored loans, scholarships/grants, tuition waivers (partial), and unspecified assistantships available. Support available to part-time students. Financial award application deadline: 5/1; financial award applicants required to submit FAFSA. *Unit head:* Dr. Ken Miller, Chair, 406-657-2034, E-mail: kmiller@msubillings.edu. *Application contact:* David M. Sullivan, Graduate Studies Counselor, 406-657-2053, Fax: 406-657-2299, E-mail: dsullivan@msubillings.edu.

Montana State University Billings, College of Education, Department of Special Education, Counseling, Reading and Early Childhood, Program in Special Education, Billings, MT 59101-0298. Offers advanced studies (MS Sp Ed); special education generalist (MS Sp Ed). *Accreditation:* NCATE. Part-time programs available. *Degree requirements:* For master's, thesis or professional paper and/or field experience. *Entrance requirements:* For master's, GRE General Test or MAT, minimum GPA of 3.0 (undergraduate), 3.25 (graduate). *Application deadline:* Applications are processed on a rolling basis. Application fee: $40. *Expenses:* Tuition, state resident: full-time $2653.75; part-time $1718 per semester. Tuition, nonresident: full-time $7015; part-time $4640 per semester. *Required fees:* $2445; $444 per credit. *Financial support:* Teaching assistantships, career-related internships or fieldwork, Federal Work-Study, institutionally sponsored loans, scholarships/grants, tuition waivers (partial), and unspecified assistantships available. Support available to part-time students. Financial award application deadline: 5/1; financial award applicants required to submit FAFSA. *Unit head:* Dr. Ken Miller, Chair, 406-657-2034, E-mail: kmiller@msubillings.edu. *Application contact:* David M. Sullivan, Graduate Studies Counselor, 406-657-2053, Fax: 406-657-2299, E-mail: dsullivan@msubillings.edu.

Montclair State University, The Graduate School, College of Education and Human Services, Department of Early Childhood, Elementary and Literacy Education, Program in Inclusive Early Childhood Education, Montclair, NJ 07043-1624. Offers M Ed. *Degree requirements:* For master's, comprehensive exam, thesis or alternative. *Entrance requirements:* For master's, GRE General Test, interview, 2 letters of recommendation. Additional exam requirements/recommendations for international students: Required—TOEFL (minimum score 83 iBT), IELTS (minimum score 6.5). Electronic applications accepted.

Montclair State University, The Graduate School, College of Education and Human Services, Department of Secondary and Special Education, Learning Disabilities Teacher-Consultant Post-Master's Certificate Program, Montclair, NJ 07043-1624. Offers Post-Master's Certificate. Part-time and evening/weekend programs available. *Entrance requirements:* Additional exam requirements/recommendations for international students: Required—TOEFL (minimum score 83 iBT), IELTS (minimum score 6.5). Electronic applications accepted.

Montclair State University, The Graduate School, College of Education and Human Services, Department of Secondary and Special Education, Master of Education Program in Special Education, Montclair, NJ 07043-1624. Offers M Ed. Part-time and evening/weekend programs available. *Degree requirements:* For master's, comprehensive exam, thesis or alternative. *Entrance requirements:* For master's, GRE General Test, interview, 2 letters of recommendation. Additional exam requirements/recommendations for international students: Required—TOEFL (minimum score 83 iBT), IELTS (minimum score 6.5). Electronic applications accepted.

Morehead State University, Graduate Programs, College of Education, Department of Curriculum and Instruction, Morehead, KY 40351. Offers curriculum and instruction (Ed S); elementary education (MA Ed), including elementary education, international education, middle school education, reading; secondary education (MA Ed); special education (MA Ed); teaching (MAT). Part-time and evening/weekend programs

available. *Degree requirements:* For master's, comprehensive exam, thesis optional; for Ed S, thesis, oral exam. *Entrance requirements:* For master's, GRE General Test, minimum GPA of 2.75, teaching certificate; for Ed S, GRE General Test, interview, master's degree, minimum GPA of 3.5, work experience. Additional exam requirements/recommendations for international students: Required—TOEFL (minimum score 500 paper-based). Electronic applications accepted. *Faculty research:* Communicative competence of learning-disabled students, teaching social studies in elementary schools, ungraded primary school organization, study skills.

Morehead State University, Graduate Programs, College of Education, Department of Early Childhood, Elementary and Special Education, Morehead, KY 40351. Offers learning and behavioral disorders P-12 (MAT); moderate and severe disabilities P-12 (MAT). Part-time and evening/weekend programs available. *Degree requirements:* For master's, thesis. *Entrance requirements:* For master's, GRE or PRAXIS II content exam, minimum overall undergraduate GPA of 2.5. Additional exam requirements/recommendations for international students: Required—TOEFL (minimum score 500 paper-based). Electronic applications accepted.

Morehead State University, Graduate Programs, College of Education, Department of Foundational and Graduate Studies in Education, Morehead, KY 40351. Offers adult and higher education (MA, Ed S); certified professional counselor (Ed S); counseling P-12 (MA); curriculum and instruction (Ed S); educational technology (MA Ed); instructional leadership (Ed S); school administration (MA); school counseling (Ed S); teacher leader business and marketing content (MA Ed); teacher leader business and marketing technology (MA Ed); teacher leader educational technology (MA Ed); teacher leader English (MA Ed); teacher leader gifted education (MA Ed); teacher leader IECE certification (MA Ed); teacher leader interdisciplinary education P-5 (MA Ed); teacher leader middle grades (MA Ed); teacher leader non IECE certification (MA Ed); teacher leader reading/writing - non-certification (MA Ed); teacher leader reading/writing certification (MA Ed); teacher leader school communication - certification (MA Ed); teacher leader school communication - non-certification (MA Ed); teacher leader social studies (MA Ed); teacher leader special education (MA Ed). *Accreditation:* NCATE. Part-time and evening/weekend programs available. *Degree requirements:* For master's, thesis optional, oral and/or written comprehensive exams; for Ed S, thesis, oral exam. *Entrance requirements:* For master's, GRE General Test, minimum overall undergraduate GPA of 2.5; for Ed S, GRE General Test, interview, master's degree, minimum GPA of 3.5, work experience. Additional exam requirements/recommendations for international students: Required—TOEFL (minimum score 500 paper-based). Electronic applications accepted. *Faculty research:* Character education, school accountability, computer applications for school administrators.

Morningside College, Graduate Division, Department of Education, Sioux City, IA 51106. Offers professional educator (MAT); special education: instructional strategist I: mild/moderate elementary (K-6) (MAT); special education: instructional strategist II-mild/moderate secondary (7-12) (MAT); special education: K-12 instructional strategist II-behavior disorders/learning disabilities (MAT); special education: K-12 instructional strategist II-mental disabilities (MAT). Part-time and evening/weekend programs available. *Entrance requirements:* For master's, MAT, writing sample.

Mount Mercy University, Program in Education, Cedar Rapids, IA 52402-4797. Offers reading (MA Ed); special education (MA Ed). *Entrance requirements:* For master's, minimum cumulative GPA of 3.0, 2 letters of recommendation, resume, valid teaching license. Additional exam requirements/recommendations for international students: Required—TOEFL (minimum score 570 paper-based; 88 iBT). Electronic applications accepted.

Mount St. Joseph University, Graduate Education Program, Cincinnati, OH 45233-1670. Offers adolescent to young adult education (MA); dyslexia (Certificate); inclusive early childhood education (MA); instructional leadership (MA); middle childhood education (MA); multicultural special education (MA); Pre-K special needs (Certificate); principal licensure (MA); reading (Certificate); reading science (MA). *Accreditation:* Teacher Education Accreditation Council. Part-time and evening/weekend programs available. *Faculty:* 10 full-time (7 women), 7 part-time/adjunct (6 women). *Students:* 28 full-time (25 women), 95 part-time (76 women); includes 27 minority (19 Black or African American, non-Hispanic/Latino; 6 Hispanic/Latino; 2 Two or more races, non-Hispanic/Latino). Average age 36. 73 applicants, 44% accepted, 30 enrolled. In 2013, 69 master's awarded. *Degree requirements:* For master's, research project, student teaching, clinical and field-based experiences. *Entrance requirements:* For master's, GRE, PRAXIS II in teaching content area (math or science), 2 letters of recommendation, interview, resume. Additional exam requirements/recommendations for international students: Required—TOEFL (minimum score 560 paper-based; 83 iBT). *Application deadline:* Applications are processed on a rolling basis. Application fee: $50. Electronic applications accepted. *Expenses: Tuition:* Full-time $18,400; part-time $575 per credit hour. *Required fees:* $450; $450 per year. Part-time tuition and fees vary according to course load, degree level and program. *Financial support:* Scholarships/grants available. Financial award applicants required to submit FAFSA. *Faculty research:* Foreign and second language learning problems/reading disabilities/hyperlexia, multicultural/bilingual special education, alternative educator licensure, science education, pedagogical content knowledge. *Unit head:* Dr. Mary West, Chair, 513-244-3263, Fax: 513-244-4867, E-mail: mary_west@mail.msj.edu. *Application contact:* Mary Brigham, Assistant Director of Graduate Recruitment, 513-244-4233, Fax: 513-244-4629, E-mail: mary_brigham@mail.msj.edu.
Website: http://www.msj.edu/academics/graduate-programs/master-of-arts-initial-teacher-licensure-programs/.

Mount Saint Mary College, Division of Education, Newburgh, NY 12550-3494. Offers adolescence and special education (MS Ed); adolescence education (MS Ed); childhood and special education (MS Ed); childhood education (MS Ed); literacy (5-12) (Advanced Certificate); literacy (birth-6) (Advanced Certificate); literacy and special education (MS Ed); literacy/childhood (MS Ed); middle school (5-6) (MS Ed); middle school (7-9) (MS Ed); special education (1-6) (MS Ed); special education (7-12) (MS Ed). *Accreditation:* NCATE. Part-time and evening/weekend programs available. *Faculty:* 11 full-time (9 women), 9 part-time/adjunct (4 women). *Students:* 29 full-time (19 women), 142 part-time (117 women); includes 22 minority (5 Black or African American, non-Hispanic/Latino; 16 Hispanic/Latino; 1 Two or more races, non-Hispanic/Latino). Average age 29. 51 applicants, 65% accepted, 27 enrolled. In 2013, 72 master's awarded. *Application deadline:* Applications are processed on a rolling basis. Application fee: $45. Application fee is waived when completed online. *Expenses: Tuition:* Full-time $13,356; part-time $742 per credit. *Required fees:* $70 per semester. *Financial support:* In 2013–14, 69 students received support. Unspecified assistantships available. Financial award application deadline: 4/15; financial award applicants required to submit FAFSA. *Faculty research:* Learning and teaching styles, computers in special education, language development. *Unit head:* Dr. William Swart, Graduate Coordinator, 845-569-3149, Fax: 845-569-3535, E-mail: william.swart@msmc.edu. *Application contact:* Lisa Gallina, Director of Admissions for Graduate Programs and Adult Degree Completion, 845-569-3166, Fax: 845-569-3450, E-mail: lisa.gallina@msmc.edu.
Website: http://www.msmc.edu/Academics/Graduate_Programs/Master_of_Science_in_Education.

Mount Saint Vincent University, Graduate Programs, Faculty of Education, Program in Educational Psychology, Halifax, NS B3M 2J6, Canada. Offers education of the blind or visually impaired (M Ed, MA Ed); education of the deaf or hard of hearing (M Ed, MA Ed); educational psychology (MA-R); human relations (M Ed, MA Ed). Part-time and evening/weekend programs available. Postbaccalaureate distance learning degree programs offered (minimal on-campus study). *Degree requirements:* For master's, thesis (for some programs). *Entrance requirements:* For master's, bachelor's degree in related field, 1 year of teaching experience. Electronic applications accepted. *Faculty research:* Personality measurement, values reasoning, aggression and sexuality, power and control, quantitative and qualitative research methodologies.

Murray State University, College of Education, Department of Adolescent, Career and Special Education, Program in Special Education, Murray, KY 42071. Offers advanced learning behavior disorders (MA Ed); learning disabilities (MA Ed); moderate/severe disorders (MA Ed). *Accreditation:* NCATE. Part-time and evening/weekend programs available. *Degree requirements:* For master's, thesis optional, portfolio. *Entrance requirements:* For master's, GRE General Test or MAT, teacher certification. Additional exam requirements/recommendations for international students: Required—TOEFL. *Faculty research:* Attention Deficit Hyperactivity Disorder, assistive technology.

National Louis University, National College of Education, Chicago, IL 60603. Offers administration and supervision (M Ed, Ed D, CAS, Ed S); curriculum and instruction (M Ed, MS Ed, CAS); early childhood administration (M Ed, CAS); early childhood education (M Ed, MAT, MS Ed, CAS); education (Ed D); educational psychology/human learning and development (M Ed, MS Ed, CAS, Ed S); elementary education (MAT); interdisciplinary curriculum and instruction (M Ed); mathematics education (M Ed, MS Ed, CAS); reading and language (M Ed, MS Ed, CAS); school psychology (M Ed, Ed S); science education (M Ed, MS Ed, CAS); secondary education (MAT); special education (M Ed, MAT, CAS); technology in education (M Ed, CAS). *Accreditation:* NCATE. Part-time and evening/weekend programs available. *Degree requirements:* For doctorate, comprehensive exam, thesis/dissertation. *Entrance requirements:* For master's, MAT or GRE, minimum GPA of 3.0; for doctorate, GRE General Test, minimum GPA of 3.25, interview, resume, writing sample, 4 recommendations. Additional exam requirements/recommendations for international students: Required—TOEFL (minimum score 550 paper-based; 79 iBT).

National University, Academic Affairs, School of Education, La Jolla, CA 92037-1011. Offers applied behavior analysis (Certificate); applied school leadership (MS); autism (Certificate); best practices (Certificate); e-teaching and learning (Certificate); early childhood education (Certificate); education (MA), including best practices (M Ed, MA), e-teaching and learning (M Ed, MA), education technology, teacher leadership (M Ed, MA), teaching and learning in a global society (M Ed, MA), teaching mathematics (M Ed, MA); education with preliminary multiple or single subject (M Ed), including best practices (M Ed, MA), e-teaching and learning (M Ed, MA), educational technology (M Ed, MA), teacher leadership (M Ed, MA), teaching and learning in a global society (M Ed, MA), teaching mathematics (M Ed, MA); educational administration (MS); educational and instructional technology (MS); educational counseling (MS); educational technology (Certificate); higher education administration (MS); innovative school leadership (MS); instructional leadership (MS); juvenile justice special education (MS); reading (Certificate); school psychology (MS); special education (MS), including deaf and hard-of-hearing, mild/moderate disabilities, moderate/severe disabilities; teacher leadership (Certificate); teaching (MA), including applied behavioral analysis, autism, best practices (M Ed, MA), e-teaching and learning (M Ed, MA), early childhood education, educational technology (M Ed, MA), reading, special education, teacher leadership (M Ed, MA), teaching and learning in a global society (M Ed, MA), teaching mathematics (M Ed, MA); teaching mathematics (Certificate). Part-time and evening/weekend programs available. Postbaccalaureate distance learning degree programs offered (no on-campus study). *Faculty:* 72 full-time (43 women), 287 part-time/adjunct (170 women). *Students:* 2,433 full-time (1,744 women), 2,017 part-time (1,371 women); includes 1,834 minority (358 Black or African American, non-Hispanic/Latino; 15 American Indian or Alaska Native, non-Hispanic/Latino; 250 Asian, non-Hispanic/Latino; 1,056 Hispanic/Latino; 29 Native Hawaiian or other Pacific Islander, non-Hispanic/Latino; 126 Two or more races, non-Hispanic/Latino), 1 international. Average age 34. 1,339 applicants, 100% accepted, 1035 enrolled. In 2013, 1,662 master's awarded. *Degree requirements:* For master's, thesis (for some programs). *Entrance requirements:* For master's, interview, minimum GPA of 2.5. Additional exam requirements/recommendations for international students: Required—TOEFL (minimum score 550 paper-based; 79 iBT), IELTS (minimum score 6). *Application deadline:* Applications are processed on a rolling basis. Application fee: $60 ($65 for international students). Electronic applications accepted. *Expenses: Tuition:* Full-time $13,824; part-time $1728 per course. One-time fee: $160. *Financial support:* Career-related internships or fieldwork, institutionally sponsored loans, scholarships/grants, and tuition waivers (partial) available. Support available to part-time students. Financial award application deadline: 6/30. *Faculty research:* Teacher education, special education, educational effectiveness, teaching abroad, school counseling. *Unit head:* School of Education, 800-628-8648, E-mail: soe@nu.edu. *Application contact:* Louis Cruz, Interim Vice President for Enrollment Services, 800-628-8648, E-mail: advisor@nu.edu.
Website: http://www.nu.edu/OurPrograms/SchoolOfEducation.html.

New England College, Program in Education, Henniker, NH 03242-3293. Offers higher education administration (MS, Ed D); K-12 leadership (Ed D); literacy and language arts (M Ed); meeting the needs of all learners/special education (M Ed); teacher leadership/school reform (M Ed). Part-time and evening/weekend programs available.

New Jersey City University, Graduate Studies and Continuing Education, Debra Cannon Partridge Wolfe College of Education, Department of Special Education, Jersey City, NJ 07305-1597. Offers MA. Part-time and evening/weekend programs available. *Faculty:* 7 full-time (4 women), 5 part-time/adjunct (4 women). *Students:* 50 full-time (41 women), 165 part-time (136 women); includes 91 minority (49 Black or African American, non-Hispanic/Latino; 11 Asian, non-Hispanic/Latino; 31 Hispanic/Latino). Average age 35. In 2013, 63 master's awarded. *Entrance requirements:* Additional exam requirements/recommendations for international students: Required—TOEFL (minimum score 61 iBT). *Application deadline:* For fall admission, 8/1 priority date for domestic students; for spring admission, 12/1 for domestic students. Applications are processed on a rolling basis. Application fee: $0. *Expenses: Tuition, area resident:* Part-time $527.90 per credit. Tuition, nonresident: part-time $947.75 per credit. *Financial support:* Unspecified assistantships available. *Faculty research:* Mainstreaming the handicapped child and the autistic child. *Unit head:* Dr. Tracy Amerman, Chairperson, 201-200-3023, E-mail: cfleres@njcu.edu. *Application contact:* Dr. William Bajor, Dean of Graduate Studies, 201-200-3409, Fax: 201-200-3411, E-mail: wbajor@njcu.edu.

New Mexico Highlands University, Graduate Studies, School of Education, Las Vegas, NM 87701. Offers curriculum and instruction (MA); educational leadership (MA); professional counseling (MA); special education (MA), including). Part-time programs available. *Faculty:* 25 full-time (12 women), 26 part-time/adjunct (22 women). *Students:* 139 full-time (106 women), 245 part-time (180 women); includes 207 minority (10 Black or African American, non-Hispanic/Latino; 20 American Indian or Alaska Native, non-Hispanic/Latino; 3 Asian, non-Hispanic/Latino; 172 Hispanic/Latino; 1 Native Hawaiian or other Pacific Islander, non-Hispanic/Latino; 1 Two or more races, non-Hispanic/

Latino), 17 international. Average age 39. 137 applicants, 99% accepted, 102 enrolled. In 2013, 112 master's awarded. *Degree requirements:* For master's, comprehensive exam, thesis or alternative. *Entrance requirements:* For master's, minimum undergraduate GPA of 3.0. Additional exam requirements/recommendations for international students: Required—TOEFL (minimum score 540 paper-based). *Application deadline:* For fall admission, 8/1 priority date for domestic students. Applications are processed on a rolling basis. Application fee: $15. *Expenses:* Tuition, state resident: full-time $4278; part-time $178 per credit hour. Tuition, nonresident: full-time $6716; part-time $281 per credit hour. One-time fee: $15. *Financial support:* Career-related internships or fieldwork, Federal Work-Study, institutionally sponsored loans, scholarships/grants, traineeships, tuition waivers (partial), and unspecified assistantships available. Support available to part-time students. Financial award application deadline: 3/1; financial award applicants required to submit FAFSA. *Faculty research:* Middle school curriculum, integrated computer applications for pre-service classroom teachers, adolescent literacy, narrative cognitive modes in New Mexico multicultural setting, math and math education. *Unit head:* Dr. Belinda Laumbach, Interim Dean, 505-454-3146, Fax: 505-454-8884, E-mail: laumbach_b@nmhu.edu. *Application contact:* Diane Trujillo, Administrative Assistant for Graduate Studies, 505-454-3266, Fax: 505-426-2117, E-mail: dtrujillo@nmhu.edu.

New Mexico State University, Graduate School, College of Education, Department of Special Education and Communication Disorders, Las Cruces, NM 88003-8001. Offers bilingual/multicultural special education (Ed D, PhD); communication disorders (MA); special education (MA, Ed D, PhD). *Accreditation:* ASHA (one or more programs are accredited); NCATE. Part-time and evening/weekend programs available. Postbaccalaureate distance learning degree programs offered. *Faculty:* 15 full-time (13 women), 2 part-time/adjunct (1 woman). *Students:* 87 full-time (80 women), 53 part-time (40 women); includes 75 minority (3 Asian, non-Hispanic/Latino; 68 Hispanic/Latino; 4 Two or more races, non-Hispanic/Latino), 6 international. Average age 33. 157 applicants, 27% accepted, 35 enrolled. In 2013, 47 master's, 3 doctorates awarded. *Degree requirements:* For master's, comprehensive exam, thesis optional; for doctorate, comprehensive exam, thesis/dissertation. *Entrance requirements:* For master's, GRE General Test or MAT. Additional exam requirements/recommendations for international students: Required—TOEFL (minimum score 550 paper-based; 79 iBT), IELTS (minimum score 6.5). *Application deadline:* For fall admission, 2/1 priority date for domestic students. Applications are processed on a rolling basis. Application fee: $40 ($50 for international students). Electronic applications accepted. *Expenses:* Tuition, state resident: full-time $5398; part-time $224.90 per credit. Tuition, nonresident: full-time $18,821; part-time $784.20 per credit. *Required fees:* $1310; $54.60 per credit. *Financial support:* In 2013–14, 65 students received support, including 1 research assistantship (averaging $18,261 per year), 25 teaching assistantships (averaging $8,389 per year); career-related internships or fieldwork, Federal Work-Study, health care benefits, and unspecified assistantships also available. Support available to part-time students. Financial award application deadline: 3/1; financial award applicants required to submit FAFSA. *Faculty research:* Multicultural special education, multicultural communication disorders, mild disability, multicultural assessment, deaf education, early childhood, bilingual special education. *Total annual research expenditures:* $289,421. *Unit head:* Dr. Eric Joseph Lopez, Interim Department Head, 575-646-2402, Fax: 575-646-7712, E-mail: leric@nmsu.edu. *Application contact:* Coordinator, 575-646-2736, Fax: 575-646-7721, E-mail: gradinfo@nmsu.edu.
Website: http://education.nmsu.edu/spedcd/.

New York University, Steinhardt School of Culture, Education, and Human Development, Department of Teaching and Learning, Program in Early Childhood and Childhood Education, New York, NY 10003. Offers childhood education (MA), including childhood education, special education; early childhood and childhood education (PhD); early childhood education (MA); early childhood education/early childhood special education (MA). *Accreditation:* Teacher Education Accreditation Council. Part-time programs available. *Faculty:* 10 full-time (all women). *Students:* 75 full-time (67 women), 27 part-time (26 women); includes 40 minority (6 Black or African American, non-Hispanic/Latino; 1 American Indian or Alaska Native, non-Hispanic/Latino; 18 Asian, non-Hispanic/Latino; 12 Hispanic/Latino; 3 Two or more races, non-Hispanic/Latino), 11 international. Average age 28. 122 applicants, 59% accepted, 14 enrolled. In 2013, 64 master's, 2 doctorates awarded. *Degree requirements:* For master's, thesis (for some programs); for doctorate, thesis/dissertation. *Entrance requirements:* For doctorate, GRE General Test, interview. Additional exam requirements/recommendations for international students: Required—TOEFL (minimum score 100 iBT). *Application deadline:* For fall admission, 12/1 priority date for domestic and international students; for spring admission, 11/1 for domestic and international students. Applications are processed on a rolling basis. Application fee: $75. Electronic applications accepted. *Expenses: Tuition:* Full-time $35,856; part-time $1494 per unit. *Required fees:* $1408; $64 per unit. $473 per term. Tuition and fees vary according to course load and program. *Financial support:* Fellowships with full and partial tuition reimbursements, career-related internships or fieldwork, Federal Work-Study, institutionally sponsored loans, scholarships/grants, tuition waivers (partial), and unspecified assistantships available. Support available to part-time students. Financial award application deadline: 2/1; financial award applicants required to submit FAFSA. *Faculty research:* Teacher evaluation and beliefs about teaching, early literacy development, language arts, child development and education, cultural differences. *Unit head:* 212-998-5460, Fax: 212-995-4049. *Application contact:* 212-998-5030, Fax: 212-995-4328, E-mail: steinhardt.gradadmissions@nyu.edu.
Website: http://steinhardt.nyu.edu/teachlearn/childhood.

New York University, Steinhardt School of Culture, Education, and Human Development, Department of Teaching and Learning, Program in Special Education, New York, NY 10012-1019. Offers childhood (MA); early childhood (MA). *Accreditation:* Teacher Education Accreditation Council. Part-time programs available. *Faculty:* 11 full-time (8 women). *Students:* 10 full-time (all women), 3 part-time (all women); includes 7 minority (2 Asian, non-Hispanic/Latino; 4 Hispanic/Latino; 1 Two or more races, non-Hispanic/Latino), 1 international. Average age 25. 132 applicants, 74% accepted, 34 enrolled. In 2013, 9 master's awarded. *Degree requirements:* For master's, thesis (for some programs). *Entrance requirements:* Additional exam requirements/recommendations for international students: Required—TOEFL (minimum score 100 iBT). *Application deadline:* For fall admission, 2/1 priority date for domestic and international students. Applications are processed on a rolling basis. Application fee: $75. Electronic applications accepted. *Expenses: Tuition:* Full-time $35,856; part-time $1494 per unit. *Required fees:* $1408; $64 per unit. $473 per term. Tuition and fees vary according to course load and program. *Financial support:* Career-related internships or fieldwork, Federal Work-Study, institutionally sponsored loans, scholarships/grants, tuition waivers (partial) available. Support available to part-time students. Financial award application deadline: 2/1; financial award applicants required to submit FAFSA. *Faculty research:* Special education referrals, attention deficit disorders in children, mainstreaming, curriculum-based assessment and program implementation, special education policy. *Unit head:* Prof. Joan Rosenberg, 212-998-5554, Fax: 212-995-4049, E-mail: joanrosenberg@nyu.edu. *Application contact:* 212-998-5030, Fax: 212-995-4328, E-mail: steinhardt.gradadmissions@nyu.edu.
Website: http://steinhardt.nyu.edu/teachlearn/special/ma.

Niagara University, Graduate Division of Education, Concentration in Teacher Education, Niagara Falls, NY 14109. Offers early childhood and childhood education (MS Ed, Certificate); middle and adolescence education (MS Ed, Certificate); special education (grades 1-12) (MS Ed, Certificate); teaching English to speakers of other languages (MS Ed). *Accreditation:* NCATE. *Students:* 168 full-time (130 women), 40 part-time (28 women); includes 11 minority (4 Black or African American, non-Hispanic/Latino; 1 Asian, non-Hispanic/Latino; 5 Hispanic/Latino; 1 Native Hawaiian or other Pacific Islander, non-Hispanic/Latino), 101 international. Average age 27. In 2013, 131 master's, 1 Certificate awarded. *Entrance requirements:* For master's, GRE General Test or MAT. Additional exam requirements/recommendations for international students: Required—TOEFL (minimum score 550 paper-based, 79 iBT) or IELTS (minimum score 6). *Application deadline:* For fall admission, 8/1 for domestic students. Applications are processed on a rolling basis. Application fee: $30. *Expenses:* Contact institution. *Financial support:* Research assistantships with full and partial tuition reimbursements, teaching assistantships with full and partial tuition reimbursements, career-related internships or fieldwork, Federal Work-Study, scholarships/grants, and unspecified assistantships available. Financial award application deadline: 4/15; financial award applicants required to submit FAFSA. *Unit head:* Dr. Chandra Foote, Chair, 716-286-8549. *Application contact:* Dr. Debra A. Colley, Dean of Education, 716-286-8560, Fax: 716-286-8561, E-mail: dcolley@niagara.edu.
Website: http://www.niagara.edu/teacher-education.

Norfolk State University, School of Graduate Studies, School of Education, Department of Special Education, Norfolk, VA 23504. Offers severe disabilities (MA). *Accreditation:* NCATE. Part-time programs available. *Students:* 10 full-time (8 women), 8 part-time (7 women); includes 15 minority (13 Black or African American, non-Hispanic/Latino; 2 Two or more races, non-Hispanic/Latino). Average age 37. In 2013, 3 master's awarded. *Degree requirements:* For master's, thesis or alternative. *Entrance requirements:* For master's, minimum GPA of 3.0 in major, 2.5 overall. *Application deadline:* For fall admission, 3/1 for domestic students; for spring admission, 10/1 for domestic students. Application fee: $30. *Financial support:* Fellowships, research assistantships with tuition reimbursements, teaching assistantships, and career-related internships or fieldwork available. Financial award applicants required to submit FAFSA. *Unit head:* Dr. June Harris, Head, 757-823-2272, E-mail: jlharris@nsu.edu. *Application contact:* Dr. Helen Bessant-Byrd, Program Coordinator, 757-823-8733, Fax: 757-823-2053, E-mail: hbyrd@nsu.edu.
Website: http://www.nsu.edu.

North Carolina Central University, School of Education, Special Education Program, Durham, NC 27707-3129. Offers M Ed, MAT. *Accreditation:* NCATE. Part-time and evening/weekend programs available. *Degree requirements:* For master's, comprehensive exam, thesis or alternative. *Entrance requirements:* For master's, GRE, minimum GPA of 3.0 in major, 2.5 overall. Additional exam requirements/recommendations for international students: Required—TOEFL. *Faculty research:* Vocational programs for special needs learners.

North Carolina State University, Graduate School, College of Education, Department of Curriculum and Instruction, Program in Special Education, Raleigh, NC 27695. Offers M Ed, MS. *Accreditation:* NCATE. *Degree requirements:* For master's, thesis optional. *Entrance requirements:* For master's, GRE General Test and MAT, minimum GPA of 3.0 in major. Electronic applications accepted. *Faculty research:* Nature of disabilities, intervention research.

Northeastern Illinois University, College of Graduate Studies and Research, College of Education, Program in Learning Behavior Specialist I, Chicago, IL 60625-4699. Offers MA. *Degree requirements:* For master's, internship. *Entrance requirements:* For master's, bachelor's degree, minimum GPA of 2.75, two professional letters of recommendation. Electronic applications accepted.

Northeastern Illinois University, College of Graduate Studies and Research, College of Education, Program in Learning Behavior Specialist II, Chicago, IL 60625-4699. Offers MS. *Entrance requirements:* For master's, Illinois Test of Basic Skills (or equivalent), bachelor's degree; minimum GPA of 2.75 undergraduate, 3.0 graduate; writing sample; interview. Electronic applications accepted.

Northeastern University, School of Education, Boston, MA 02115-5096. Offers curriculum, teaching, learning, and leadership (Ed D); elementary licensure (MAT); higher education administration (MAT, Ed D); Jewish education leadership (Ed D); learning and instruction (M Ed); organizational leadership studies (Ed D); secondary licensure (MAT); special education (M Ed). Part-time and evening/weekend programs available.

Northern Arizona University, Graduate College, College of Education, Department of Educational Specialties, Flagstaff, AZ 86011. Offers autism spectrum disorders (Certificate); bilingual/multicultural education (M Ed), including bilingual education, ESL education; career and technical education (M Ed, Certificate); early childhood special education (M Ed); educational technology (M Ed, Certificate); special education (M Ed). *Faculty:* 32 full-time (21 women), 4 part-time/adjunct (all women). *Students:* 68 full-time (48 women), 158 part-time (119 women); includes 93 minority (6 Black or African American, non-Hispanic/Latino; 29 American Indian or Alaska Native, non-Hispanic/Latino; 4 Asian, non-Hispanic/Latino; 53 Hispanic/Latino; 1 Native Hawaiian or other Pacific Islander, non-Hispanic/Latino), 6 international. Average age 37. 66 applicants, 95% accepted, 38 enrolled. In 2013, 121 master's, 3 Certificates awarded. *Degree requirements:* For master's, comprehensive exam (for some programs), thesis (for some programs). *Entrance requirements:* For master's, minimum GPA of 3.0. Additional exam requirements/recommendations for international students: Required—TOEFL (minimum score 550 paper-based; 80 iBT), IELTS (minimum score 7). *Application deadline:* For fall admission, 3/1 for international students; for spring admission, 9/15 for international students. Applications are processed on a rolling basis. Application fee: $65. Electronic applications accepted. *Financial support:* In 2013–14, 9 teaching assistantships with full tuition reimbursements (averaging $9,698 per year) were awarded. Financial award applicants required to submit FAFSA. *Unit head:* Dr. Laura Sujo-Montes, Chair, 928-523-0892, Fax: 928-523-1929, E-mail: laura.sujo-montes@nau.edu. *Application contact:* Laura Cook, Coordinator, 928-523-5342, Fax: 928-523-8950, E-mail: laura.cook@nau.edu.
Website: http://nau.edu/coe/ed-specialties/.

Northern Illinois University, Graduate School, College of Education, Department of Special and Early Education, De Kalb, IL 60115-2854. Offers curriculum and instruction (MS Ed, Ed D), including curriculum leadership (Ed D), elementary education (Ed D), secondary education (Ed D); early childhood education (MS Ed); elementary education (MS Ed); special education (MS Ed). Part-time and evening/weekend programs available. *Faculty:* 22 full-time (14 women), 2 part-time/adjunct (both women). *Students:* 52 full-time (41 women), 168 part-time (137 women); includes 29 minority (11 Black or African American, non-Hispanic/Latino; 7 Asian, non-Hispanic/Latino; 6 Hispanic/Latino; 5 Two or more races, non-Hispanic/Latino), 3 international. Average age 36. 38 applicants, 63% accepted, 18 enrolled. In 2013, 59 master's, 15 doctorates awarded. *Degree requirements:* For master's, comprehensive exam, thesis optional; for doctorate, thesis/dissertation, candidacy exam, dissertation defense. *Entrance requirements:* For master's, GRE General Test or MAT, minimum undergraduate GPA of 2.75; for

doctorate, GRE General Test or MAT, minimum undergraduate GPA of 2.75, graduate 3.2. Additional exam requirements/recommendations for international students: Required—TOEFL (minimum score 550 paper-based). *Application deadline:* For fall admission, 6/1 for domestic students, 5/1 for international students; for spring admission, 11/1 for domestic students, 10/1 for international students. Applications are processed on a rolling basis. Application fee: $40. Electronic applications accepted. *Financial support:* In 2013–14, 24 research assistantships with full tuition reimbursements were awarded; fellowships with full tuition reimbursements, teaching assistantships with full tuition reimbursements, career-related internships or fieldwork, Federal Work-Study, scholarships/grants, tuition waivers (full), and unspecified assistantships also available. Support available to part-time students. Financial award applicants required to submit FAFSA. *Faculty research:* Teacher certification, stress reduction during student teaching, teaching history, portfolios in student teaching. *Unit head:* Dr. Barbara Schwartz-Bechet, Interim Chair, 815-753-1619, E-mail: seed@niu.edu. *Application contact:* Gail Myers, Clerk, Graduate Advising, 815-753-0381, E-mail: gmyers@niu.edu.
Website: http://www.cedu.niu.edu/seed/.

Northern Kentucky University, Office of Graduate Programs, College of Education and Human Services, Program in Teaching, Highland Heights, KY 41099. Offers education (Certificate); special education (Certificate); teaching (MAT). Part-time programs available. *Faculty:* 4 full-time (1 woman), 2 part-time/adjunct (1 woman). *Students:* 6 full-time (4 women), 24 part-time (15 women); includes 1 minority (Black or African American, non-Hispanic/Latino), 1 international. Average age 41. 41 applicants, 39% accepted, 15 enrolled. In 2013, 18 master's awarded. *Degree requirements:* For master's, comprehensive exam, thesis optional, portfolio, student teaching or internship. *Entrance requirements:* For master's, GRE (minimum scores: verbal 150, quantitative reasoning 143, writing 4.0), PRAXIS II, minimum GPA of 2.75, criminal background check (state and federal), resume, interview, three letters of recommendation. Additional exam requirements/recommendations for international students: Required—TOEFL (minimum score 550 paper-based; 79 iBT); Recommended—IELTS (minimum score 6.5). *Application deadline:* For fall admission, 6/1 for domestic students, 6/1 priority date for international students; for spring admission, 10/1 priority date for international students. Application fee: $40. Electronic applications accepted. *Expenses:* Tuition, state resident: full-time $4446; part-time $494 per credit hour. Tuition, nonresident: full-time $6885; part-time $765 per credit hour. *Required fees:* $72 per semester. One-time fee: $125.50. Part-time tuition and fees vary according to course load, degree level, program and reciprocity agreements. *Financial support:* In 2013–14, 6 students received support. Unspecified assistantships available. Financial award applicants required to submit FAFSA. *Faculty research:* Middle grades students, secondary students, rural classrooms, urban classrooms, teacher preparation. *Unit head:* Dr. Lenore Kinne, Director, Teacher Education Program, 859-572-1503, E-mail: kinnel1@nku.edu. *Application contact:* Melissa Decker, Alternative Certification Coordinator, 859-572-6330, Fax: 859-572-1384, E-mail: deckerm@nku.edu.

Northern Michigan University, College of Graduate Studies, College of Health Sciences and Professional Studies, School of Education, Leadership and Public Service, Program in Learning Disabilities, Marquette, MI 49855-5301. Offers MAE. Part-time programs available. Postbaccalaureate distance learning degree programs offered. *Students:* 40 part-time (36 women); includes 1 minority (American Indian or Alaska Native, non-Hispanic/Latino). 9 applicants, 100% accepted. In 2013, 16 master's awarded. *Degree requirements:* For master's, thesis or alternative. *Entrance requirements:* For master's, GRE General Test, minimum GPA of 3.0. *Application deadline:* For fall admission, 7/1 priority date for domestic students; for spring admission, 11/1 for domestic students. Applications are processed on a rolling basis. Application fee: $25. *Expenses:* Tuition, state resident: part-time $427 per credit. Tuition, nonresident: part-time $614.50 per credit. *Required fees:* $325 per semester. Tuition and fees vary according to course load and program. *Financial support:* Federal Work-Study and institutionally sponsored loans available. Support available to part-time students. Financial award application deadline: 3/1. *Faculty research:* Interdisciplinary approaches to learning disabilities, neurological bases for cognitive processing of information. *Unit head:* Dr. Joseph Lubig, Associate Dean/Director of the School of Education, Leadership and Public Service, 906-227-1880, E-mail: jlubig@nmu.edu. *Application contact:* Nancy E. Carter, Certification Counselor, 906-227-1625, E-mail: ncarter@nmu.edu.

Northwestern State University of Louisiana, Graduate Studies and Research, College of Education and Human Development, Program in Special Education, Natchitoches, LA 71497. Offers M Ed, MAT. *Degree requirements:* For master's, comprehensive exam, thesis (for some programs). *Entrance requirements:* For master's, GRE General Test. Additional exam requirements/recommendations for international students: Required—TOEFL. Electronic applications accepted.

Northwestern State University of Louisiana, Graduate Studies and Research, College of Education and Human Development, Programs in Educational Leadership and Instruction, Natchitoches, LA 71497. Offers counseling (Ed S); educational leadership (M Ed, Ed S); educational technology (Ed S); elementary teaching (Ed S); reading (Ed S); secondary teaching (Ed S); special education (Ed S). *Accreditation:* NASAD. *Degree requirements:* For master's, comprehensive exam, thesis (for some programs). *Entrance requirements:* For master's and Ed S, GRE General Test. Additional exam requirements/recommendations for international students: Required—TOEFL. Electronic applications accepted.

Northwest Missouri State University, Graduate School, College of Education and Human Services, Department of Professional Education, Program in Special Education, Maryville, MO 64468-6001. Offers MS Ed. *Entrance requirements:* For master's, GRE General Test, minimum GPA of 2.75, teaching certificate. Additional exam requirements/recommendations for international students: Required—TOEFL (minimum score 550 paper-based).

Northwest Nazarene University, Graduate Studies, Program in Teacher Education, Nampa, ID 83686-5897. Offers curriculum and instruction (M Ed); educational leadership (M Ed, Ed D, Ed S); exceptional child (M Ed); reading education (M Ed). *Accreditation:* ACA (one or more programs are accredited); NCATE. Part-time programs available. Postbaccalaureate distance learning degree programs offered (no on-campus study). *Faculty:* 6 full-time (5 women), 29 part-time/adjunct (16 women). *Students:* 101 full-time (66 women), 98 part-time (74 women); includes 14 minority (1 Asian, non-Hispanic/Latino; 10 Hispanic/Latino; 3 Two or more races, non-Hispanic/Latino), 12 international. Average age 38. In 2013, 60 master's, 28 doctorates, 14 other advanced degrees awarded. *Degree requirements:* For master's, comprehensive exam (for some programs), action research project; for doctorate, thesis/dissertation; for Ed S, comprehensive exam (for some programs). *Entrance requirements:* For master's, minimum undergraduate GPA of 2.8 overall or 3.0 during final 30 semester credits, undergraduate degree; for doctorate, Ed S or equivalent; for Ed S, EDS - MEd required. Additional exam requirements/recommendations for international students: Recommended—TOEFL (minimum score 80 iBT). *Application deadline:* For fall admission, 9/1 for domestic students. Applications are processed on a rolling basis. Application fee: $50. *Expenses: Tuition:* Part-time $565 per credit. *Financial support:* In 2013–14, research assistantships (averaging $5,000 per year) were awarded. *Faculty research:* Action research, cooperative learning, accountability, institutional accreditation. *Unit head:* Dr. Paula Kellerer, Chair, 208-467-8729, Fax: 208-467-8562. *Application contact:* Lynette Kingsmore, Admissions Counselor, 208-467-8107, Fax: 208-467-8786, E-mail: lkingsmore@nnu.edu.
Website: http://www.nnu.edu/graded/.

Notre Dame College, Graduate Programs, South Euclid, OH 44121-4293. Offers mild/moderate needs (M Ed); reading (M Ed); security policy studies (MA, Graduate Certificate); technology (M Ed). Part-time and evening/weekend programs available. *Degree requirements:* For master's, thesis. *Entrance requirements:* For master's, GRE General Test, MAT, minimum undergraduate GPA of 2.75, valid teaching certificate, bachelor's degree in an education-related field from accredited college or university, official transcripts of most recent college work. *Faculty research:* Cognitive psychology, teaching critical thinking in the classroom.

Notre Dame de Namur University, Division of Academic Affairs, School of Education and Leadership, Program in Special Education, Belmont, CA 94002-1908. Offers preliminary education specialist credential (Certificate); special education (MA). Part-time and evening/weekend programs available. *Degree requirements:* For master's, thesis optional, capstone course. *Entrance requirements:* For master's, interview, minimum GPA of 2.5. Additional exam requirements/recommendations for international students: Required—TOEFL (minimum score 550 paper-based; 79 iBT). Electronic applications accepted.

Nyack College, School of Education, Nyack, NY 10960-3698. Offers childhood education (MS); childhood special education (MS); TESOL (MAT, MS). Part-time programs available. Postbaccalaureate distance learning degree programs offered (no on-campus study). *Students:* 37 full-time (31 women), 14 part-time (10 women); includes 34 minority (22 Black or African American, non-Hispanic/Latino; 3 Asian, non-Hispanic/Latino; 9 Hispanic/Latino), 2 international. Average age 34. In 2013, 11 master's awarded. *Degree requirements:* For master's, comprehensive exam, clinical experience. *Entrance requirements:* For master's, LAST (Liberal Arts and Sciences Test), transcripts, autobiography and statement on reasons for pursuing graduate study in education, recommendations, 6 credits of language, evidence of computer literacy, introductory course in psychology. Additional exam requirements/recommendations for international students: Required—TOEFL (minimum score 550 paper-based). *Application deadline:* Applications are processed on a rolling basis. Application fee: $30. Electronic applications accepted. *Expenses:* Contact institution. *Financial support:* Scholarships/grants available. Financial award applicants required to submit FAFSA. *Unit head:* Dr. JoAnn Looney, Dean, 845-675-4538, Fax: 845-358-0874. *Application contact:* Traci Piescki, Director of Admissions, 800-541-6891, Fax: 845-348-3912, E-mail: admissions.grad@nyack.edu.
Website: http://www.nyack.edu/edu.

Oakland University, Graduate Study and Lifelong Learning, School of Education and Human Services, Department of Human Development and Child Studies, Program in Special Education, Rochester, MI 48309-4401. Offers M Ed, Certificate. *Accreditation:* Teacher Education Accreditation Council. *Students:* 41 full-time (39 women), 148 part-time (130 women); includes 12 minority (6 Black or African American, non-Hispanic/Latino; 3 American Indian or Alaska Native, non-Hispanic/Latino; 1 Asian, non-Hispanic/Latino; 2 Hispanic/Latino), 4 international. Average age 34. 92 applicants, 99% accepted, 59 enrolled. In 2013, 71 master's awarded. *Entrance requirements:* For master's, minimum GPA of 3.0 for unconditional admission, interview. Additional exam requirements/recommendations for international students: Required—TOEFL (minimum score 550 paper-based). *Application deadline:* For fall admission, 7/1 for domestic students, 5/1 for international students; for winter admission, 11/1 for domestic students, 9/1 for international students; for spring admission, 3/1 for domestic students. Applications are processed on a rolling basis. Application fee: $35. Electronic applications accepted. *Financial support:* Career-related internships or fieldwork, Federal Work-Study, institutionally sponsored loans, and tuition waivers (full) available. Financial award application deadline: 3/1; financial award applicants required to submit FAFSA. *Unit head:* Dr. Sherri Oden, Coordinator, 248-370-3027, E-mail: oden@oakland.edu.

The Ohio State University, Graduate School, College of Arts and Sciences, Division of Social and Behavioral Sciences, Department of Psychology, Columbus, OH 43210. Offers behavioral neuroscience (PhD); clinical psychology (PhD); cognitive psychology (PhD); developmental psychology (PhD); intellectual and developmental disabilities psychology (PhD); quantitative psychology (PhD); social psychology (PhD). *Accreditation:* APA. *Faculty:* 57. *Students:* 145 full-time (87 women), 2 part-time (both women); includes 24 minority (7 Black or African American, non-Hispanic/Latino; 1 American Indian or Alaska Native, non-Hispanic/Latino; 6 Asian, non-Hispanic/Latino; 7 Hispanic/Latino; 3 Two or more races, non-Hispanic/Latino), 16 international. Average age 27. In 2013, 13 doctorates awarded. *Degree requirements:* For doctorate, thesis/dissertation. *Entrance requirements:* For doctorate, GRE General Test. Additional exam requirements/recommendations for international students: Required—TOEFL (minimum score 600 paper-based; 100 iBT); Recommended—IELTS (minimum score 8). *Application deadline:* For fall admission, 12/1 priority date for domestic students, 11/30 priority date for international students. Applications are processed on a rolling basis. Application fee: $60 ($70 for international students). Electronic applications accepted. *Financial support:* Fellowships with tuition reimbursements, research assistantships with tuition reimbursements, and teaching assistantships with tuition reimbursements available. *Unit head:* Dr. Richard Petty, Chair, 614-292-1640, E-mail: petty.1@osu.edu. *Application contact:* Graduate Admissions, 614-292-9444, Fax: 614-292-3895, E-mail: gradadmissions@osu.edu.
Website: http://www.psy.ohio-state.edu/.

Ohio University, Graduate College, Gladys W. and David H. Patton College of Education and Human Services, Department of Teacher Education, Athens, OH 45701-2979. Offers adolescent to young adult education (M Ed); curriculum and instruction (M Ed, PhD); early childhood/special education (M Ed); intervention specialist/mild-moderate needs (M Ed); intervention specialist/moderate-intensive needs (M Ed); mathematics education (PhD); middle childhood education (M Ed); reading education (M Ed); social studies education (PhD). Part-time and evening/weekend programs available. *Degree requirements:* For master's, thesis or alternative; for doctorate, comprehensive exam, thesis/dissertation. *Entrance requirements:* For master's, GRE General Test or MAT (if GPA is below 2.9); for doctorate, GRE General Test, minimum GPA of 3.4, work experience. Additional exam requirements/recommendations for international students: Required—TOEFL (minimum score 550 paper-based; 80 iBT) or IELTS (minimum score 6.5). Electronic applications accepted. *Faculty research:* Cognition literacy, character education, teacher's education reform, disabilities.

Old Dominion University, Darden College of Education, Program in Special Education, Norfolk, VA 23529. Offers MS Ed, PhD. *Accreditation:* NCATE. Part-time and evening/weekend programs available. Postbaccalaureate distance learning degree programs offered (no on-campus study). *Faculty:* 12 full-time (9 women), 13 part-time/adjunct (9 women). *Students:* 15 full-time (all women), 107 part-time (92 women); includes 20 minority (11 Black or African American, non-Hispanic/Latino; 2 Asian, non-Hispanic/Latino; 3 Hispanic/Latino; 4 Two or more races, non-Hispanic/Latino). Average age 32. 78 applicants, 85% accepted, 61 enrolled. In 2013, 37 master's awarded. *Degree*

requirements: For master's, comprehensive exam, thesis or alternative; for doctorate, comprehensive exam, thesis/dissertation. *Entrance requirements:* For master's, GRE General Test or MAT, PRAXIS I, Core Academic Skills for Educator Tests, minimum GPA of 2.8; for doctorate, GRE. Additional exam requirements/recommendations for international students: Recommended—TOEFL (minimum score 550 paper-based). *Application deadline:* For fall admission, 6/1 priority date for domestic and international students; for winter admission, 11/1 priority date for domestic and international students; for spring admission, 3/1 priority date for domestic and international students. Applications are processed on a rolling basis. Application fee: $50. Electronic applications accepted. *Expenses:* Tuition, state resident: full-time $9888; part-time $412 per credit. Tuition, nonresident: full-time $25,152; part-time $1048 per credit. *Required fees:* $59 per semester. One-time fee: $50. *Financial support:* In 2013–14, 70 students received support, including 1 fellowship (averaging $15,000 per year), 2 teaching assistantships with tuition reimbursements available (averaging $15,000 per year); research assistantships with tuition reimbursements available, career-related internships or fieldwork, scholarships/grants, tuition waivers (partial), and unspecified assistantships also available. Financial award application deadline: 2/15; financial award applicants required to submit FAFSA. *Faculty research:* Inclusion, autism spectrum disorder, functional behavioral assessment, infant and preschool handicapped, distance learning. *Total annual research expenditures:* $3.6 million. *Unit head:* Dr. Sabra Gear, Graduate Program Director, 757-683-4117, Fax: 757-683-4129, E-mail: sgear@odu.edu. *Application contact:* William Heffelfinger, Director of Graduate Admissions, 757-683-5554, Fax: 757-683-3255, E-mail: gradadmit@odu.edu.
Website: http://education.odu.edu/esse/academics/sped/speddeg.shtml.

Ottawa University, Graduate Studies-Arizona, Program in Education, Ottawa, KS 66067-3399. Offers community college counseling (MA); curriculum and instruction (MA); early childhood (MA); education intervention (MA); education leadership (MA); education technology (MA); Montessori early childhood education (MA); Montessori elementary education (MA); professional development (MA); school guidance counseling (MA); special education - cross categorical (MA). Programs offered in Mesa, Phoenix, Tempe and West Valley, AZ. *Accreditation:* NCATE. Part-time programs available. *Degree requirements:* For master's, thesis or alternative. *Entrance requirements:* For master's, minimum undergraduate GPA of 3.0, copy of current state certification or teaching license. Additional exam requirements/recommendations for international students: Required—TOEFL (minimum score 550 paper-based). Electronic applications accepted. *Expenses:* Contact institution.

Our Lady of the Lake University of San Antonio, School of Professional Studies, Program in Generic Special Education, San Antonio, TX 78207-4689. Offers elementary education (M Ed). Part-time and evening/weekend programs available. *Faculty:* 6 full-time (4 women), 3 part-time/adjunct (all women). *Students:* 9 full-time (7 women), 4 part-time (all women); includes 9 minority (1 Black or African American, non-Hispanic/Latino; 8 Hispanic/Latino). Average age 37. 10 applicants, 90% accepted, 5 enrolled. In 2013, 6 master's awarded. *Degree requirements:* For master's, comprehensive exam, thesis optional, examination for the Certification of Education in Texas. *Entrance requirements:* For master's, GRE General Test or MAT. Additional exam requirements/recommendations for international students: Required—TOEFL. *Application deadline:* For fall admission, 4/1 priority date for domestic and international students; for spring admission, 11/1 priority date for domestic and international students; for summer admission, 2/1 priority date for domestic and international students. Applications are processed on a rolling basis. Application fee: $25 ($50 for international students). Electronic applications accepted. *Expenses: Tuition:* Full-time $9120; part-time $760 per credit. *Required fees:* $698; $334 per trimester. Tuition and fees vary according to course load, degree level, campus/location and program. *Financial support:* Research assistantships, teaching assistantships, career-related internships or fieldwork, Federal Work-Study, institutionally sponsored loans, scholarships/grants, and tuition waivers (partial) available. Support available to part-time students. Financial award application deadline: 4/15. *Faculty research:* Professional educator to understand and meet the comprehensive needs of a diverse student population, life-long learners, innovative practices. *Unit head:* Dr. Jerrie Jackson, Coordinator, 210-434-6711 Ext. 2698, E-mail: jjackson@lake.ollusa.edu. *Application contact:* Graduate Admission, 210-434-6711 Ext. 3961, Fax: 210-431-4013, E-mail: gradadm@lake.ollusa.edu.
Website: http://www.ollusa.edu/s/1190/ollu-3-column-noads.aspx?sid=1190&gid=1&pgid=3855.

Pace University, School of Education, New York, NY 10038. Offers adolescent education (MST); childhood education (MST); early childhood development, learning and intervention (MST); educational leadership (MS Ed); educational technology studies (MS); inclusive adolescent education (MST); literacy (MS Ed); school business management (Certificate); special education (MS Ed). *Accreditation:* NCATE. Part-time and evening/weekend programs available. *Students:* 186 full-time (154 women), 441 part-time (315 women); includes 209 minority (89 Black or African American, non-Hispanic/Latino; 2 American Indian or Alaska Native, non-Hispanic/Latino; 30 Asian, non-Hispanic/Latino; 74 Hispanic/Latino; 1 Native Hawaiian or other Pacific Islander, non-Hispanic/Latino; 13 Two or more races, non-Hispanic/Latino), 7 international. Average age 29. 207 applicants, 71% accepted, 105 enrolled. In 2013, 296 master's, 25 other advanced degrees awarded. *Degree requirements:* For master's, internship. *Entrance requirements:* For master's, interview, teaching certificate. Additional exam requirements/recommendations for international students: Required—TOEFL. *Application deadline:* For fall admission, 8/1 priority date for domestic students, 6/1 for international students; for spring admission, 12/1 priority date for domestic students, 10/1 for international students. Applications are processed on a rolling basis. Application fee: $70. Electronic applications accepted. *Expenses:* Contact institution. *Financial support:* Research assistantships, career-related internships or fieldwork, and Federal Work-Study available. Support available to part-time students. Financial award applicants required to submit FAFSA. *Faculty research:* Teacher education, technology in education, STEM, literacy education, special education. *Total annual research expenditures:* $1.3 million. *Unit head:* Dr. Andrea M. Spencer, Dean, School of Education, 914-773-3341, E-mail: aspencer@pace.edu. *Application contact:* Susan Ford-Goldschein, Director of Graduate Admissions, 212-346-1660, Fax: 212-346-1585, E-mail: gradnyc@pace.edu.
Website: http://www.pace.edu/school-of-education.

Pacific University, College of Education, Forest Grove, OR 97116-1797. Offers early childhood education (MAT); education (MAE); elementary education (MAT); high school education (MAT); middle school education (MAT); special education (MAT); visual function in learning (M Ed). *Accreditation:* NCATE. Part-time and evening/weekend programs available. *Degree requirements:* For master's, research project. *Entrance requirements:* For master's, California Basic Educational Skills Test, PRAXIS II, minimum undergraduate GPA of 2.75, 3.0 graduate. Additional exam requirements/recommendations for international students: Required—TOEFL. Electronic applications accepted. *Expenses:* Contact institution. *Faculty research:* Defining a culturally competent classroom, technology in the k-12 classroom, Socratic seminars, social studies education.

Penn State University Park, Graduate School, College of Education, Department of Educational Psychology, Counseling and Special Education, State College, PA 16802. Offers counselor education (M Ed, D Ed, PhD, Certificate); educational psychology (MS, PhD, Certificate); school psychology (M Ed, MS, PhD, Certificate); special education (M Ed, MS, PhD, Certificate). *Unit head:* Dr. David H. Monk, Dean, 814-865-2523, Fax: 814-865-0555, E-mail: dhm6@psu.edu. *Application contact:* Cynthia E. Nicosia, Director, Graduate Enrollment Services, 814-865-1834, Fax: 814-863-4627, E-mail: cey1@psu.edu.
Website: http://www.ed.psu.edu/educ/epcse.

Piedmont College, School of Education, Demorest, GA 30535-0010. Offers art education (MAT); early childhood education (MA, MAT); instructional technology (MAT); middle grades education (MA, MAT); music education (MAT); secondary education (MA, MAT); special education (MA, MAT); teacher leadership (Ed S). Part-time and evening/weekend programs available. *Students:* 312 full-time (242 women), 694 part-time (563 women); includes 153 minority (103 Black or African American, non-Hispanic/Latino; 3 American Indian or Alaska Native, non-Hispanic/Latino; 17 Asian, non-Hispanic/Latino; 19 Hispanic/Latino; 11 Two or more races, non-Hispanic/Latino), 1 international. Average age 37. 165 applicants, 72% accepted, 118 enrolled. In 2013, 333 master's, 15 doctorates, 457 other advanced degrees awarded. *Degree requirements:* For master's, thesis, field experience in the classroom teaching; for doctorate, thesis/dissertation. *Entrance requirements:* For master's, GRE General Test, MAT, minimum undergraduate GPA of 2.5; for Ed S, minimum graduate GPA of 3.5, valid teaching certificate. Additional exam requirements/recommendations for international students: Required—TOEFL (minimum score 550 paper-based). *Application deadline:* For fall admission, 7/15 for domestic students; for spring admission, 12/1 for domestic students. Applications are processed on a rolling basis. Electronic applications accepted. *Expenses: Tuition:* Full-time $7992; part-time $444 per credit hour. *Financial support:* Career-related internships or fieldwork, Federal Work-Study, and unspecified assistantships available. Support available to part-time students. Financial award applicants required to submit FAFSA. *Unit head:* Dr. Don Gnecco, Dean, 706-778-3000 Ext. 1201, Fax: 706-776-9608, E-mail: dgnecco@piedmont.edu. *Application contact:* Kathleen Anderson, Director of Graduate Enrollment Management, 706-778-8500 Ext. 1181, Fax: 706-778-0150, E-mail: kanderson@piedmont.edu.

Pittsburg State University, Graduate School, College of Education, Department of Special Services and Leadership Studies, Program in Special Education, Pittsburg, KS 66762. Offers behavioral disorders (MS); learning disabilities (MS); mentally retarded (MS). *Accreditation:* NCATE. *Degree requirements:* For master's, thesis or alternative. *Entrance requirements:* For master's, GRE General Test or MAT.

Plymouth State University, College of Graduate Studies, Graduate Studies in Education, Program in Secondary Education, Plymouth, NH 03264-1595. Offers curriculum and instruction (M Ed); language education (M Ed); library media (M Ed); physical education (M Ed); social studies education (M Ed); special education (M Ed). Part-time and evening/weekend programs available. *Entrance requirements:* For master's, MAT.

Point Loma Nazarene University, School of Education, Program in Special Education, San Diego, CA 92106-2899. Offers MA. Part-time and evening/weekend programs available. *Students:* 11 full-time (10 women), 62 part-time (49 women); includes 23 minority (7 Black or African American, non-Hispanic/Latino; 1 American Indian or Alaska Native, non-Hispanic/Latino; 2 Asian, non-Hispanic/Latino; 11 Hispanic/Latino; 2 Two or more races, non-Hispanic/Latino). Average age 36. 20 applicants, 65% accepted, 13 enrolled. In 2013, 46 master's awarded. *Entrance requirements:* For master's, CBEST, letters of recommendation, essay, interview. Additional exam requirements/recommendations for international students: Required—TOEFL. *Application deadline:* For fall admission, 8/4 priority date for domestic students; for spring admission, 12/8 priority date for domestic students; for summer admission, 4/13 priority date for domestic students. Applications are processed on a rolling basis. Application fee: $50. Electronic applications accepted. *Expenses: Tuition:* Full-time $6900; part-time $567 per credit hour. *Financial support:* Applicants required to submit FAFSA. *Unit head:* Dr. Shirlee Gibbs, Special Education Coordinator, 619-849-2852, E-mail: shirleegibbs@pointloma.edu. *Application contact:* Laura Leinweber, Director of Graduate Admission, 866-692-4723, E-mail: lauraleinweber@pointloma.edu.
Website: http://www.pointloma.edu/discover/graduate-school-san-diego/san-diego-graduate-programs-masters-degree-san-diego/education.

Point Park University, School of Arts and Sciences, Department of Education, Pittsburgh, PA 15222-1984. Offers curriculum and instruction (MA); educational administration (MA); special education (M Ed); teaching and leadership (M Ed). Part-time and evening/weekend programs available. *Degree requirements:* For master's, comprehensive exam (for some programs), thesis or alternative. *Entrance requirements:* For master's, minimum GPA of 3.0, resume, 2 letters of recommendation. Additional exam requirements/recommendations for international students: Required—TOEFL. Electronic applications accepted.

Portland State University, Graduate Studies, School of Education, Department of Special Education and Counselor Education, Portland, OR 97207-0751. Offers counselor education (MA, MS); special and counselor education (Ed D); special education (MA, MS). *Accreditation:* ACA (one or more programs are accredited). Part-time and evening/weekend programs available. *Faculty:* 23 full-time (13 women), 79 part-time/adjunct (56 women). *Students:* 191 full-time (159 women), 128 part-time (91 women); includes 52 minority (3 Black or African American, non-Hispanic/Latino; 2 American Indian or Alaska Native, non-Hispanic/Latino; 12 Asian, non-Hispanic/Latino; 24 Hispanic/Latino; 1 Native Hawaiian or other Pacific Islander, non-Hispanic/Latino; 10 Two or more races, non-Hispanic/Latino), 6 international. Average age 35. 390 applicants, 34% accepted, 119 enrolled. In 2013, 149 master's awarded. *Degree requirements:* For master's, thesis or alternative. *Entrance requirements:* For master's, California Basic Educational Skills Test, minimum GPA of 3.0 in upper-division course work or 2.75 overall. Additional exam requirements/recommendations for international students: Required—TOEFL (minimum score 550 paper-based). *Application deadline:* For fall admission, 2/1 for domestic and international students. Application fee: $50. *Expenses:* Tuition, state resident: full-time $9207; part-time $341 per credit. Tuition, nonresident: full-time $14,391; part-time $533 per credit. *Required fees:* $1263; $22 per credit. $98 per quarter. One-time fee: $150. Tuition and fees vary according to program. *Financial support:* In 2013–14, 1 research assistantship with full tuition reimbursement (averaging $6,372 per year) was awarded; career-related internships or fieldwork, Federal Work-Study, and institutionally sponsored loans also available. Support available to part-time students. Financial award application deadline: 3/1; financial award applicants required to submit FAFSA. *Faculty research:* Transition of students with disabilities, functional curriculum, supported/inclusive education, leisure/recreation, autism. *Total annual research expenditures:* $1.2 million. *Unit head:* Rick Johnson, Chair, 503-725-9764, Fax: 503-725-5599, E-mail: johnsonp@pdx.edu. *Application contact:* Kris Smith, Admission Specialist, 503-725-4654, Fax: 503-725-5599, E-mail: kmsmith@pdx.edu.

Prairie View A&M University, College of Education, Department of Curriculum and Instruction, Prairie View, TX 77446-0519. Offers curriculum and instruction (M Ed, MS Ed); special education (M Ed, MS Ed). *Accreditation:* NCATE. Part-time and evening/weekend programs available. *Faculty:* 7 full-time (5 women), 5 part-time/adjunct (all women). *Students:* 15 full-time (12 women), 43 part-time (35 women); includes 53

minority (51 Black or African American, non-Hispanic/Latino; 1 Asian, non-Hispanic/Latino; 1 Hispanic/Latino). Average age 36. 57 applicants, 100% accepted, 21 enrolled. In 2013, 13 master's awarded. *Degree requirements:* For master's, thesis optional. *Entrance requirements:* For master's, GRE, minimum GPA of 2.5, 3 references. *Application deadline:* For fall admission, 7/1 priority date for domestic students, 7/1 for international students; for winter admission, 3/1 priority date for domestic students, 3/1 for international students; for spring admission, 11/1 priority date for domestic students, 11/1 for international students. Applications are processed on a rolling basis. Application fee: $50. Electronic applications accepted. *Expenses:* Tuition, state resident: full-time $3776; part-time $209.77 per credit hour. Tuition, nonresident: full-time $10,183; part-time $565.77 per credit hour. *Required fees:* $2037; $446.50 per credit hour. *Financial support:* In 2013–14, 1 research assistantship with tuition reimbursement (averaging $18,000 per year) was awarded; fellowships with tuition reimbursements, teaching assistantships, career-related internships or fieldwork, institutionally sponsored loans, scholarships/grants, health care benefits, tuition waivers (full and partial), and unspecified assistantships also available. Support available to part-time students. Financial award application deadline: 4/1. *Faculty research:* Metacognitive strategies, emotionally disturbed, language arts, teachers recruit, diversity, recruitment, retention, school collaboration. *Total annual research expenditures:* $25,000. *Unit head:* Dr. Edward Mason, Head, 936-261-3403, Fax: 936-261-3419, E-mail: elmason@pvamu.edu. *Application contact:* Head.

Pratt Institute, School of Art, Programs in Creative Arts Therapy, Brooklyn, NY 11205-3899. Offers art therapy and creativity development (MPS); art therapy-special education (MPS); dance/movement therapy (MS). *Accreditation:* NASAD (one or more programs are accredited). Part-time programs available. *Faculty:* 3 full-time (all women), 22 part-time/adjunct (19 women). *Students:* 107 full-time (102 women), 1 (woman) part-time; includes 36 minority (17 Black or African American, non-Hispanic/Latino; 8 Asian, non-Hispanic/Latino; 11 Hispanic/Latino), 6 international. Average age 29. 177 applicants, 41% accepted, 35 enrolled. In 2013, 45 master's awarded. *Degree requirements:* For master's, thesis. *Entrance requirements:* For master's, letters of recommendation, portfolio. Additional exam requirements/recommendations for international students: Required—TOEFL (minimum score 600 paper-based; 100 iBT). *Application deadline:* For fall admission, 1/5 for domestic and international students; for spring admission, 10/1 for domestic and international students. Applications are processed on a rolling basis. Application fee: $50 ($90 for international students). Electronic applications accepted. *Expenses: Tuition:* Full-time $26,478; part-time $1471 per credit. *Required fees:* $1830; $1050 per year. *Financial support:* Career-related internships or fieldwork, Federal Work-Study, institutionally sponsored loans, scholarships/grants, health care benefits, tuition waivers (full), and unspecified assistantships available. Support available to part-time students. Financial award application deadline: 2/1; financial award applicants required to submit FAFSA. *Faculty research:* Psychology and aesthetic interaction, art therapy and AIDS, art therapy and autism, art diagnosis. *Unit head:* Julie Miller, Chairperson, 718-636-3428, E-mail: jmiller2@pratt.edu. *Application contact:* Young Hah, Director of Graduate Admissions, 718-636-3683, Fax: 718-399-4242, E-mail: yhah@pratt.edu.
Website: https://www.pratt.edu/academics/art-design/art-grad/creative-arts-therapy/.

Prescott College, Graduate Programs, Program in Education, Prescott, AZ 86301. Offers early childhood education (MA); early childhood special education (MA); education (MA); elementary education (MA); environmental education leadership and administration (MA); equine-assisted learning (MA); school guidance counseling (MA); secondary education (MA); special education: learning disabilities (MA); special education: mental retardation (MA); special education: serious emotional disabilities (MA); student-directed independent study (MA); sustainability education (PhD). Part-time programs available. Postbaccalaureate distance learning degree programs offered (minimal on-campus study). *Degree requirements:* For master's, thesis, fieldwork or internship, practicum; for doctorate, thesis/dissertation. *Entrance requirements:* For master's, 2 letters of recommendation, resume; for doctorate, 3 letters of recommendation, resume, official transcripts, personal statement, program proposal. Additional exam requirements/recommendations for international students: Required—TOEFL (minimum score 500 paper-based). Electronic applications accepted.

Providence College, Program in Special Education, Providence, RI 02918. Offers special education (M Ed), including elementary teaching, secondary teaching. Part-time and evening/weekend programs available. *Faculty:* 9 part-time/adjunct (5 women). *Students:* 7 full-time (5 women), 18 part-time (15 women). Average age 29. 3 applicants, 33% accepted. In 2013, 15 master's awarded. *Degree requirements:* For master's, comprehensive exam. *Entrance requirements:* For master's, GRE General Test. Additional exam requirements/recommendations for international students: Required—TOEFL (minimum score 550 paper-based; 80 iBT). *Application deadline:* For fall admission, 8/1 priority date for domestic and international students; for spring admission, 12/1 priority date for domestic and international students. Applications are processed on a rolling basis. Application fee: $55. *Expenses: Tuition:* Part-time $432 per credit. *Required fees:* $432 per credit. *Financial support:* Career-related internships or fieldwork and unspecified assistantships available. Support available to part-time students. Financial award application deadline: 8/1; financial award applicants required to submit FAFSA. *Unit head:* Barbara Vigeant, Director, 401-865-2912, Fax: 401-865-1147, E-mail: bvigeant@providence.edu. *Application contact:* Rev. Mark D. Nowel, Dean of Undergraduate and Graduate Studies, 401-865-2649, Fax: 401-865-1496, E-mail: mnowel@providence.edu.
Website: http://www.providence.edu/professional-studies/graduate-degrees/Pages/master-education-specialed.aspx.

Purdue University, Graduate School, College of Education, Department of Educational Studies, West Lafayette, IN 47907. Offers administration (MS Ed, PhD, Ed S); counseling and development (MS Ed, PhD); education of the gifted (MS Ed); educational psychology (MS Ed, PhD); foundations of education (MS Ed, PhD); higher education administration (MS Ed, PhD); special education (MS Ed, PhD). *Accreditation:* ACA (one or more programs are accredited); NCATE (one or more programs are accredited). Part-time and evening/weekend programs available. *Faculty:* 21 full-time (17 women), 7 part-time/adjunct (4 women). *Students:* 102 full-time (73 women), 45 part-time (27 women); includes 23 minority (10 Black or African American, non-Hispanic/Latino; 5 Asian, non-Hispanic/Latino; 5 Hispanic/Latino; 3 Two or more races, non-Hispanic/Latino), 32 international. Average age 35. 165 applicants, 40% accepted, 33 enrolled. In 2013, 26 master's, 21 doctorates awarded. *Degree requirements:* For master's, thesis optional; for doctorate, thesis/dissertation, oral and written exams; for Ed S, oral presentation, project. *Entrance requirements:* For master's, GRE General Test (except for special education if undergraduate GPA is higher than a 3.0), minimum undergraduate GPA of 3.0; for doctorate and Ed S, GRE General Test (minimum combined score of 1000, 300 for new scoring), minimum undergraduate GPA of 3.0. Additional exam requirements/recommendations for international students: Required—TOEFL (minimum score 550 paper-based; 77 iBT), TWE (minimum score 5). *Application deadline:* Applications are processed on a rolling basis. Application fee: $60 ($75 for international students). Electronic applications accepted. *Financial support:* Fellowships with full tuition reimbursements, research assistantships with full tuition reimbursements, teaching assistantships with full tuition reimbursements, career-related internships or fieldwork, and tuition waivers (full) available. Support available to part-time students. Financial award application deadline: 3/1; financial award applicants required to submit FAFSA. *Faculty research:* Motivation, learning disabilities, school learning, group processes, cognitive development. *Unit head:* Dr. Ala Samrapungavan, Head, 765-494-9170, Fax: 765-496-1228, E-mail: ala@purdue.edu. *Application contact:* Cindy Blankenship, Graduate Contact, 765-494-2345, Fax: 765-494-5832, E-mail: prater0@purdue.edu.
Website: http://www.edst.purdue.edu/.

Purdue University Calumet, Graduate Studies Office, School of Education, Program in Special Education, Hammond, IN 46323-2094. Offers MS Ed.

Queens College of the City University of New York, Division of Graduate Studies, Division of Education, Department of Educational and Community Programs, Program in Special Education, Flushing, NY 11367-1597. Offers MS Ed. Part-time programs available. *Degree requirements:* For master's, research project. *Entrance requirements:* For master's, minimum GPA of 3.0. Additional exam requirements/recommendations for international students: Required—TOEFL.

Quincy University, Program in Education, Quincy, IL 62301-2699. Offers curriculum and instruction (MS Ed), including bilingual/English as a second language; leadership (MS Ed); reading education (MS Ed); special education (MS Ed); teacher leader (MS Ed). Part-time and evening/weekend programs available. Postbaccalaureate distance learning degree programs offered (minimal on-campus study). *Students:* 62 full-time (39 women), 97 part-time (68 women); includes 43 minority (29 Black or African American, non-Hispanic/Latino; 1 American Indian or Alaska Native, non-Hispanic/Latino; 4 Asian, non-Hispanic/Latino; 9 Hispanic/Latino). In 2013, 105 master's awarded. *Degree requirements:* For master's, comprehensive exam (for some programs), thesis optional. *Entrance requirements:* For master's, MAT or GRE. Additional exam requirements/recommendations for international students: Required—TOEFL (minimum score 550 paper-based; 79 iBT). *Application deadline:* Applications are processed on a rolling basis. Application fee: $25. Electronic applications accepted. *Expenses: Tuition:* Full-time $9600; part-time $400 per semester hour. *Required fees:* $720; $30 per semester hour. Tuition and fees vary according to course load and program. *Financial support:* Applicants required to submit FAFSA. *Unit head:* Dr. Kristen R. Anguiano, Director, 217-228-5432 Ext. 3119, E-mail: anguikr@quincy.edu. *Application contact:* Office of Admissions, 217-228-5210, Fax: 217-228-5479, E-mail: admissions@quincy.edu.
Website: http://www.quincy.edu/academics/graduate-programs/education.

Radford University, College of Graduate and Professional Studies, College of Education and Human Development, School of Teacher Education and Leadership, Program in Special Education, Radford, VA 24142. Offers adapted curriculum (MS); autism studies (Certificate); early childhood special education (MS); general curriculum (MS); hearing impairments (MS); visual impairment (MS). *Accreditation:* NCATE. Part-time and evening/weekend programs available. *Faculty:* 8 full-time (7 women), 5 part-time/adjunct (all women). *Students:* 27 full-time (22 women), 27 part-time (22 women). Average age 28. 21 applicants, 100% accepted, 18 enrolled. In 2013, 46 master's, 2 other advanced degrees awarded. *Degree requirements:* For master's, comprehensive exam. *Entrance requirements:* For master's, GRE, minimum GPA of 2.75, 3 letters of reference, resume, personal essay, official transcripts. Additional exam requirements/recommendations for international students: Required—TOEFL (minimum score 550 paper-based; 79 iBT). *Application deadline:* For fall admission, 2/15 for domestic students, 12/1 for international students; for spring admission, 7/1 for international students. Applications are processed on a rolling basis. Application fee: $50. Electronic applications accepted. *Expenses:* Tuition, state resident: full-time $6800; part-time $283 per credit hour. Tuition, nonresident: full-time $15,610; part-time $627 per credit hour. *Required fees:* $2944; $123 per credit hour. Tuition and fees vary according to program. *Financial support:* In 2013–14, 6 students received support, including 5 research assistantships (averaging $6,300 per year); career-related internships or fieldwork, Federal Work-Study, institutionally sponsored loans, scholarships/grants, and unspecified assistantships also available. Financial award application deadline: 3/1; financial award applicants required to submit FAFSA. *Faculty research:* Collaborative new visions for alignment in elementary, reading and special education teacher preparation; Project MERGE: Merging Expertise for Results in the General Education Curriculum. *Unit head:* Dr. Brenda Tyler, Coordinator, 540-831-5868, Fax: 540-831-5059, E-mail: ruspecialed@radford.edu. *Application contact:* Rebecca Conner, Director, Graduate Enrollment, 540-831-6296, Fax: 540-831-6061, E-mail: gradcollege@radford.edu.
Website: http://www.radford.edu/content/cehd/home/departments/STEL/programs/special-educationms.html.

Randolph College, Programs in Education, Lynchburg, VA 24503. Offers curriculum and instruction (MAT); special education-learning disabilities (M Ed, MAT). *Accreditation:* Teacher Education Accreditation Council. *Entrance requirements:* For master's, minimum GPA of 3.0 in prerequisite education coursework, 2.7 in major or field of interest (MAT); teaching license (M Ed); 2 recommendations; interview.

Regent University, Graduate School, School of Education, Virginia Beach, VA 23464-9800. Offers adult education (Ed D, PhD); advanced educational leadership (Ed D, PhD); career switcher with licensure (M Ed), including alternative licensure; character education (Ed D, PhD); Christian education leadership (Ed D); Christian school administration (M Ed); curriculum and instruction (M Ed); distance education (Ed D, PhD); educational leadership (M Ed); educational leadership - special education (Ed S); educational psychology (Ed D); elementary education (M Ed); higher education (Ed D, PhD); higher education leadership and management (Ed D); K-12 school leadership (Ed D, PhD); leadership in mathematics education (M Ed); reading specialist (M Ed); special education (M Ed, Ed D, PhD); student affairs (M Ed); TESOL (M Ed), including adult education, PreK-12. *Accreditation:* Teacher Education Accreditation Council. Part-time and evening/weekend programs available. Postbaccalaureate distance learning degree programs offered (minimal on-campus study). *Faculty:* 25 full-time (12 women), 50 part-time/adjunct (31 women). *Students:* 100 full-time (78 women), 754 part-time (614 women); includes 225 minority (191 Black or African American, non-Hispanic/Latino; 1 American Indian or Alaska Native, non-Hispanic/Latino; 7 Asian, non-Hispanic/Latino; 26 Hispanic/Latino), 16 international. Average age 39. 487 applicants, 63% accepted, 233 enrolled. In 2013, 202 master's, 19 doctorates awarded. *Degree requirements:* For master's, thesis or alternative; for doctorate, comprehensive exam, thesis/dissertation. *Entrance requirements:* For master's, MAT, minimum undergraduate GPA of 2.75, writing sample, resume, recommendations, interview; for doctorate, GRE, writing sample, 3 years of relevant professional experience, master's-level paper, copies of published work, resume, transcripts, interview, recommendations. Additional exam requirements/recommendations for international students: Required—TOEFL (minimum score 577 paper-based). *Application deadline:* For fall admission, 4/1 priority date for domestic students; for spring admission, 10/15 priority date for domestic students. Applications are processed on a rolling basis. Application fee: $50. Electronic applications accepted. Tuition and fees vary according to course load and degree level. *Financial support:* Fellowships, career-related internships or fieldwork, scholarships/grants, tuition waivers (full and partial), and unspecified assistantships available. Support available to part-time students. Financial award application deadline: 4/1; financial award applicants required to submit FAFSA. *Faculty research:* Character

development and discipline for children, education leadership development, diversity in schools, classroom management, technology in education settings. *Unit head:* Dr. Alan Arroyo, Dean, 757-352-4261, Fax: 757-352-4318, E-mail: alanarr@regent.edu. *Application contact:* Matthew Chadwick, Director of Enrollment Support Services, 800-373-5504, Fax: 757-352-4381, E-mail: admissions@regent.edu.
Website: http://www.regent.edu/education/.

Regis College, Department of Education, Weston, MA 02493. Offers elementary teacher (MAT); higher education leadership (Ed D); reading (MAT); special education (MAT). Part-time and evening/weekend programs available. *Degree requirements:* For master's, thesis. *Entrance requirements:* For master's, GRE or MAT. Additional exam requirements/recommendations for international students: Required—TOEFL. Electronic applications accepted. *Faculty research:* Reflective teaching, gender-based education, integrated teaching.

Regis University, College for Professional Studies, School of Education, Education Division, Denver, CO 80221-1099. Offers adult learning, training, and development (M Ed, Certificate); autism education (Certificate); curriculum, instruction, and assessment (M Ed); educational leadership (M Ed); gifted and talented education (M Ed); gifted/talented education (Certificate); initial licensure (M Ed); instructional technology (M Ed, Certificate); literacy (Certificate); reading (M Ed); school executive leadership (Certificate); space studies (M Ed). Program also offered in Henderson and Las Vegas (Summerlin), NV. *Accreditation:* Teacher Education Accreditation Council. Part-time and evening/weekend programs available. Postbaccalaureate distance learning degree programs offered (no on-campus study). *Degree requirements:* For master's, thesis. *Entrance requirements:* For master's, resume, minimum GPA of 2.75, criminal background check. Additional exam requirements/recommendations for international students: Required—TOEFL, TWE (minimum score 5). *Application deadline:* For fall admission, 7/23 priority date for domestic students; for winter admission, 9/17 priority date for domestic students; for spring admission, 12/3 priority date for domestic students. Applications are processed on a rolling basis. Application fee: $75. Electronic applications accepted. *Expenses:* Contact institution. *Financial support:* Federal Work-Study and scholarships/grants available. *Faculty research:* Issues of equity in the middle school classroom, professional learning communities, school reform, sociolinguistic and discursive obstacles to student integration, inclusive language arts curriculum. *Unit head:* Dr. Janna L. Oakes, Dean, 303-458-4302. *Application contact:* Information Contact, 303-458-4300, Fax: 303-964-5274, E-mail: masters@regis.edu.

Rhode Island College, School of Graduate Studies, Feinstein School of Education and Human Development, Department of Special Education, Providence, RI 02908-1991. Offers autism education (CGS); middle-secondary level special education (CGS); special education (M Ed). *Accreditation:* NCATE. Part-time and evening/weekend programs available. *Faculty:* 3 full-time (2 women), 9 part-time/adjunct (8 women). *Students:* 4 full-time (all women), 46 part-time (all women); includes 3 minority (1 Black or African American, non-Hispanic/Latino; 1 American Indian or Alaska Native, non-Hispanic/Latino; 1 Hispanic/Latino). Average age 30. In 2013, 20 master's awarded. *Degree requirements:* For master's, comprehensive assessment/assignment. *Entrance requirements:* For master's, GRE General Test or MAT, undergraduate transcripts; minimum undergraduate GPA of 3.0; 3 letters of recommendation; for CGS, GRE or MAT, master's degree or equivalent, teaching certificate, 3 letters of recommendation, interview. Additional exam requirements/recommendations for international students: Recommended—TOEFL (minimum score 550 paper-based; 79 iBT). *Application deadline:* For fall admission, 3/1 for domestic students; for spring admission, 11/1 for domestic students. Applications are processed on a rolling basis. Application fee: $50. *Expenses:* Tuition, state resident: full-time $8928; part-time $372 per credit hour. Tuition, nonresident: full-time $17,376; part-time $724 per credit hour. *Required fees:* $602; $22 per credit. $72 per term. *Financial support:* Teaching assistantships with full tuition reimbursements, career-related internships or fieldwork, Federal Work-Study, scholarships/grants, health care benefits, and unspecified assistantships available. Support available to part-time students. Financial award application deadline: 5/15; financial award applicants required to submit FAFSA. *Faculty research:* Early detection, handicapped infants. *Unit head:* Dr. Marie Lynch, Chair, 401-456-8763. *Application contact:* Graduate Studies, 401-456-8700.
Website: http://www.ric.edu/specialEducation/.

Rider University, Department of Graduate Education, Leadership and Counseling, Program in Special Education, Lawrenceville, NJ 08648-3001. Offers alternative route in special education (Certificate); special education (MA); teacher of students with disabilities (Certificate); teacher of the handicapped (Certificate). Part-time and evening/weekend programs available. *Degree requirements:* For master's, comprehensive exam. *Entrance requirements:* For master's, letters of reference, resume, NJ teaching license, interview. Additional exam requirements/recommendations for international students: Required—TOEFL (minimum score 550 paper-based). Electronic applications accepted. *Faculty research:* Collaboration/inclusive, practice, service learning, transition.

Rivier University, School of Graduate Studies, Department of Education, Nashua, NH 03060. Offers curriculum and instruction (M Ed); early childhood education (M Ed); educational administration (M Ed); educational studies (M Ed); elementary education (M Ed); elementary education and general special education (M Ed); emotional and behavioral disorders (M Ed); general social education (M Ed); leadership and learning (Ed D, CAGS); learning disabilities (M Ed); learning disabilities and reading (M Ed); mental health counseling (MA); reading (M Ed); school counseling (M Ed). Part-time and evening/weekend programs available. *Degree requirements:* For master's, comprehensive exam (for some programs), internships. *Entrance requirements:* For master's, GRE General Test or MAT.

Roberts Wesleyan College, Department of Teacher Education, Rochester, NY 14624-1997. Offers adolescence education (M Ed); childhood and special education (M Ed); literacy education (M Ed); special education online (M Ed). Part-time and evening/weekend programs available. *Faculty:* 10 full-time (7 women), 12 part-time/adjunct (6 women). *Students:* 37 full-time (29 women), 10 part-time (6 women); includes 16 minority (15 Black or African American, non-Hispanic/Latino; 1 Hispanic/Latino). Average age 33. 72 applicants, 63% accepted, 34 enrolled. In 2013, 20 master's awarded. *Degree requirements:* For master's, thesis. *Application deadline:* For fall admission, 6/1 for domestic and international students; for spring admission, 11/1 for domestic and international students; for summer admission, 3/1 for domestic and international students. Applications are processed on a rolling basis. Electronic applications accepted. Application fee is waived when completed online. *Expenses: Tuition:* Full-time $12,816; part-time $712 per credit hour. One-time fee: $300. Tuition and fees vary according to course load and program. *Financial support:* In 2013–14, 7 students received support. Career-related internships or fieldwork available. Financial award application deadline: 9/1; financial award applicants required to submit FAFSA. *Unit head:* Dr. Sharon Harris-Ewing, Chair, 585-594-6935, E-mail: harrisewing_sharon@roberts.edu. *Application contact:* Paul Ziegler, Director of Marketing and Recruitment for Teacher Education, 585-594-6146, Fax: 585-594-6108, E-mail: ziegler_paul@roberts.edu.
Website: https://www.roberts.edu/department-of-teacher-education.aspx.

Rochester Institute of Technology, Graduate Enrollment Services, National Technical Institute for the Deaf, Department of Research and Teacher Education, Rochester, NY 14623-5603. Offers MS. *Accreditation:* Teacher Education Accreditation Council. *Students:* 40 full-time (29 women), 1 part-time (0 women); includes 3 minority (1 American Indian or Alaska Native, non-Hispanic/Latino; 1 Hispanic/Latino; 1 Two or more races, non-Hispanic/Latino), 5 international. Average age 29. 38 applicants, 42% accepted, 16 enrolled. In 2013, 17 master's awarded. *Degree requirements:* For master's, thesis or alternative. *Entrance requirements:* For master's, minimum GPA of 3.0. Additional exam requirements/recommendations for international students: Required—TOEFL (minimum score 550 paper-based; 79 iBT) or IELTS (minimum score 6.5). *Application deadline:* For fall admission, 2/15 priority date for domestic and international students. Applications are processed on a rolling basis. Application fee: $60. Electronic applications accepted. *Expenses: Tuition:* Full-time $37,236; part-time $1552 per credit hour. *Required fees:* $250. *Financial support:* Fellowships with full and partial tuition reimbursements, research assistantships with partial tuition reimbursements, teaching assistantships with partial tuition reimbursements, career-related internships or fieldwork, institutionally sponsored loans, scholarships/grants, and unspecified assistantships available. Support available to part-time students. Financial award applicants required to submit FAFSA. *Faculty research:* Applied research on the effective use of access and support services to enhance learning for deaf and hard-of-hearing students in the mainstreamed classroom, STEM research and instruction. *Unit head:* Gerald Bateman, Director, 585-475-6480, Fax: 585-475-2525, E-mail: gcbnmp@rit.edu. *Application contact:* Diane Ellison, Assistant Vice President, Graduate Enrollment Services, 585-475-2229, Fax: 585-475-7164, E-mail: gradinfo@rit.edu.
Website: http://www.ntid.rit.edu/research/department/.

Rockford University, Graduate Studies, Department of Education, Program in Special Education, Rockford, IL 61108-2393. Offers MAT. Part-time and evening/weekend programs available. *Degree requirements:* For master's, thesis optional. *Entrance requirements:* For master's, GRE General Test, 3 letters of recommendation. Additional exam requirements/recommendations for international students: Required—TOEFL (minimum score 550 paper-based; 79 iBT). Electronic applications accepted.

Roosevelt University, Graduate Division, College of Education, Department of Teaching and Learning, Program in Special Education, Chicago, IL 60605. Offers MA.

Rowan University, Graduate School, College of Education, Department of Reading Education, Autism Spectrum Disorders Certificate of Graduate Study Program, Glassboro, NJ 08028-1701. Offers CGS. *Faculty:* 1 full-time (0 women). *Students:* 2 part-time (1 woman); includes 1 minority (Two or more races, non-Hispanic/Latino). Average age 22. 3 applicants, 67% accepted, 2 enrolled. *Application deadline:* For spring admission, 11/1 for domestic and international students; for summer admission, 4/1 for domestic and international students. Application fee: $65. *Expenses: Tuition, area resident:* Part-time $638 per credit. Tuition, state resident: full-time $5742. *Required fees:* $142 per credit. Tuition and fees vary according to course level and program. *Unit head:* Dr. S. Jay Kuder, Academic Advisor/Coordinator, 856-256-5659, E-mail: kuder@rowan.edu. *Application contact:* Admissions and Enrollment Services, 856-256-4747, Fax: 856-256-5637, E-mail: cgceadmissions@rowan.edu.

Rowan University, Graduate School, College of Education, Department of Reading Education, Program in Learning Disabilities, Glassboro, NJ 08028-1701. Offers MA. *Accreditation:* NCATE. Part-time and evening/weekend programs available. *Faculty:* 11 full-time (10 women). *Students:* 25 part-time (24 women); includes 2 minority (1 Black or African American, non-Hispanic/Latino; 1 Hispanic/Latino). Average age 35. 7 applicants, 86% accepted, 5 enrolled. In 2013, 8 master's awarded. *Degree requirements:* For master's, comprehensive exam, thesis. *Entrance requirements:* For master's, GRE General Test, minimum GPA of 2.8, 1 year of teaching experience. Additional exam requirements/recommendations for international students: Required—TOEFL. *Application deadline:* For fall admission, 8/1 for domestic and international students; for spring admission, 12/1 for domestic and international students; for summer admission, 4/15 for domestic and international students. Applications are processed on a rolling basis. Application fee: $65. Electronic applications accepted. *Expenses: Tuition, area resident:* Part-time $638 per credit. Tuition, state resident: full-time $5742. *Required fees:* $142 per credit. Tuition and fees vary according to course level and program. *Financial support:* Career-related internships or fieldwork, scholarships/grants, health care benefits, and unspecified assistantships available. Support available to part-time students. *Unit head:* Dr. Horacio Sosa, Dean, College of Graduate and Continuing Education, 856-256-4747, Fax: 856-256-5638, E-mail: sosa@rowan.edu. *Application contact:* Admissions and Enrollment Services, 856-256-5435, Fax: 856-256-5637, E-mail: cgceadmissions@rowan.edu.

Rowan University, Graduate School, College of Education, Department of Reading Education, Program in Special Education, Glassboro, NJ 08028-1701. Offers MA, CGS. *Accreditation:* NCATE. Part-time and evening/weekend programs available. *Faculty:* 3 full-time (2 women), 4 part-time/adjunct (3 women). *Students:* 2 full-time (1 woman), 32 part-time (28 women); includes 5 minority (4 Black or African American, non-Hispanic/Latino; 1 Hispanic/Latino). Average age 35. 8 applicants, 88% accepted, 5 enrolled. In 2013, 9 master's awarded. *Degree requirements:* For master's, comprehensive exam, thesis. *Entrance requirements:* For master's, GRE General Test, minimum GPA of 2.8. Additional exam requirements/recommendations for international students: Required—TOEFL. *Application deadline:* For fall admission, 6/1 for domestic and international students; for spring admission, 1/20 for domestic and international students; for summer admission, 4/1 for domestic and international students. Applications are processed on a rolling basis. Application fee: $65. Electronic applications accepted. *Expenses: Tuition, area resident:* Part-time $638 per credit. Tuition, state resident: full-time $5742. *Required fees:* $142 per credit. Tuition and fees vary according to course level and program. *Financial support:* Career-related internships or fieldwork, Federal Work-Study, scholarships/grants, health care benefits, and unspecified assistantships available. *Unit head:* Dr. Horacio Sosa, Dean, College of Graduate and Continuing Education, 856-256-4747, Fax: 856-256-5638, E-mail: sosa@rowan.edu. *Application contact:* Admissions and Enrollment Services, 856-256-5435, Fax: 856-256-5637, E-mail: cgceadmissions@rowan.edu.

Rowan University, Graduate School, College of Education, Department of Reading Education, Teacher of Students with Disabilities Post-Baccalaureate Certification Program, Glassboro, NJ 08028-1701. Offers Postbaccalaureate Certificate. Part-time programs available. Postbaccalaureate distance learning degree programs offered (no on-campus study). *Faculty:* 2 full-time (1 woman), 1 (woman) part-time/adjunct. *Students:* 55 part-time (41 women); includes 4 minority (2 Black or African American, non-Hispanic/Latino; 1 Asian, non-Hispanic/Latino; 1 Hispanic/Latino). Average age 38. 25 applicants, 100% accepted, 16 enrolled. *Entrance requirements:* For degree, official transcripts from all colleges attended; current professional resume; two letters of recommendation; minimum cumulative undergraduate GPA of 2.75; essay; BA or BS. *Application deadline:* For fall admission, 8/1 for domestic students. Application fee: $65. Electronic applications accepted. *Expenses: Tuition, area resident:* Part-time $638 per credit. Tuition, state resident: full-time $5742. *Required fees:* $142 per credit. Tuition and fees vary according to course level and program. *Unit head:* Dr. Horacio Sosa, Dean, College of Graduate and Continuing Education, 856-256-4747, Fax: 856-256-

5638, E-mail: sosa@rowan.edu. *Application contact:* Admissions and Enrollment Services, 856-256-4747, Fax: 856-256-5637, E-mail: cgceadmissions@rowan.edu.

Rutgers, The State University of New Jersey, New Brunswick, Graduate School of Education, Department of Educational Psychology, Program in Special Education, Piscataway, NJ 08854-8097. Offers Ed M, Ed D. Part-time and evening/weekend programs available. *Degree requirements:* For doctorate, thesis/dissertation, residency. *Entrance requirements:* For master's, GRE General Test, 3 letters of recommendation; for doctorate, GRE General Test, 3 letters of recommendation, master's degree. Additional exam requirements/recommendations for international students: Required—TOEFL (minimum score 550 paper-based; 83 iBT). Electronic applications accepted. *Faculty research:* Pre- and in-service teacher education, teacher development, inclusion, early identification and intervention of reading disabilities, special education law and social policy.

Sage Graduate School, Esteves School of Education, Program in Childhood Special Education, Troy, NY 12180-4115. Offers MS Ed. *Accreditation:* NCATE. Part-time and evening/weekend programs available. *Faculty:* 10 full-time (5 women), 33 part-time/adjunct (25 women). *Students:* 2 full-time (both women), 10 part-time (9 women); includes 2 minority (1 Black or African American, non-Hispanic/Latino; 1 Hispanic/Latino). Average age 24. 15 applicants, 53% accepted, 2 enrolled. In 2013, 4 master's awarded. *Degree requirements:* For master's, thesis optional. *Entrance requirements:* For master's, minimum GPA of 2.75, resume, 2 letters of recommendation, interview, assessment of writing skills. Additional exam requirements/recommendations for international students: Required—TOEFL (minimum score 550 paper-based). *Application deadline:* Applications are processed on a rolling basis. Application fee: $40. *Expenses: Tuition:* Full-time $11,880; part-time $660 per credit hour. *Financial support:* Fellowships, research assistantships, Federal Work-Study, scholarships/grants, and unspecified assistantships available. Support available to part-time students. Financial award application deadline: 3/1; financial award applicants required to submit FAFSA. *Faculty research:* Effective behavioral strategies for classroom instruction. *Unit head:* Dr. Lori Quigley, Dean, Esteves School of Education, 518-244-2326, Fax: 518-244-4571, E-mail: l.quigley@sage.edu. *Application contact:* Mary Grace Luibrand, Director, 518-244-4578, Fax: 518-244-4571, E-mail: luibrm@sage.edu.

Sage Graduate School, Esteves School of Education, Program in Literacy/Childhood Special Education, Troy, NY 12180-4115. Offers MS Ed. *Accreditation:* NCATE. Part-time and evening/weekend programs available. *Faculty:* 10 full-time (5 women), 2 part-time/adjunct (both women). *Students:* 3 full-time (all women), 14 part-time (13 women); includes 1 minority (Two or more races, non-Hispanic/Latino). Average age 25. 22 applicants, 64% accepted, 11 enrolled. In 2013, 6 master's awarded. *Entrance requirements:* For master's, assessment of writing skills, minimum GPA of 2.75, resume, 2 letters of recommendation, interview with advisor. Additional exam requirements/recommendations for international students: Required—TOEFL (minimum score 550 paper-based). *Application deadline:* Applications are processed on a rolling basis. Application fee: $40. *Expenses: Tuition:* Full-time $11,880; part-time $660 per credit hour. *Financial support:* Fellowships, research assistantships, Federal Work-Study, scholarships/grants, and unspecified assistantships available. Support available to part-time students. Financial award application deadline: 3/1; financial award applicants required to submit FAFSA. *Faculty research:* Commonalities in the roles of reading specialists and resource/consultant teachers. *Unit head:* Dr. Lori Quigley, Dean, Esteves School of Education, 518-244-2326, Fax: 518-244-4571, E-mail: l.quigley@sage.edu. *Application contact:* Mary Grace Luibrand, Director, 518-244-4578, Fax: 518-244-2334, E-mail: luibrm@sage.edu.

Sage Graduate School, Esteves School of Education, Program in Special Education, Troy, NY 12180-4115. Offers MS Ed. Part-time and evening/weekend programs available. *Faculty:* 10 full-time (5 women). *Students:* 2 full-time (both women), 12 part-time (11 women); includes 1 minority (Black or African American, non-Hispanic/Latino). Average age 28. 10 applicants, 30% accepted, 3 enrolled. In 2013, 16 master's awarded. *Entrance requirements:* For master's, minimum GPA of 2.75, resume, 2 letters of recommendation. Additional exam requirements/recommendations for international students: Required—TOEFL (minimum score 550 paper-based). *Application deadline:* Applications are processed on a rolling basis. Application fee: $40. *Expenses: Tuition:* Full-time $11,880; part-time $660 per credit hour. *Financial support:* Fellowships, research assistantships, Federal Work-Study, scholarships/grants, tuition waivers (partial), and unspecified assistantships available. Support available to part-time students. Financial award application deadline: 3/1; financial award applicants required to submit FAFSA. *Unit head:* Dr. Lori Quigley, Dean, Esteves School of Education, 518-244-2326, Fax: 518-244-4571, E-mail: l.quigley@sage.edu. *Application contact:* Mary Grace Luibrand, Professional Advisor for Special Education, 518-244-4578, Fax: 518-244-4571, E-mail: luibrm@sage.edu.

Saginaw Valley State University, College of Education, Program in Special Education, University Center, MI 48710. Offers MAT. Part-time and evening/weekend programs available. *Students:* 9 full-time (8 women), 139 part-time (112 women); includes 3 minority (1 Black or African American, non-Hispanic/Latino; 1 American Indian or Alaska Native, non-Hispanic/Latino; 1 Hispanic/Latino). Average age 34. 19 applicants, 100% accepted, 14 enrolled. In 2013, 65 master's awarded. *Degree requirements:* For master's, capstone course and practicum or thesis. *Entrance requirements:* For master's, minimum GPA of 3.0, teacher certification. Additional exam requirements/recommendations for international students: Required—TOEFL (minimum score 550 paper-based; 79 iBT). *Application deadline:* For fall admission, 7/15 for international students; for winter admission, 11/15 for international students; for spring admission, 4/15 for international students. Applications are processed on a rolling basis. Application fee: $30 ($80 for international students). Electronic applications accepted. *Expenses:* Tuition, state resident: full-time $8933; part-time $496.30 per credit hour. Tuition, nonresident: full-time $16,806; part-time $933.65 per credit hour. *Required fees:* $263; $14.60 per credit hour. Tuition and fees vary according to degree level. *Financial support:* Federal Work-Study and scholarships/grants available. Support available to part-time students. Financial award applicants required to submit FAFSA. *Unit head:* Dr. Mary Harmon, Dean, 989-964-7107, Fax: 989-964-4563, E-mail: coeconnect@svsu.edu. *Application contact:* Jenna Briggs, Director, Graduate and International Admissions, 989-964-6096, Fax: 989-964-2788, E-mail: gradadm@svsu.edu.

St. Ambrose University, College of Education and Health Sciences, Program in Education, Davenport, IA 52803-2898. Offers special education (M Ed); teaching (M Ed). *Accreditation:* Teacher Education Accreditation Council. Part-time and evening/weekend programs available. Postbaccalaureate distance learning degree programs offered (no on-campus study). *Degree requirements:* For master's, comprehensive exam. *Entrance requirements:* For master's, GRE General Test or MAT, minimum GPA of 2.75. Additional exam requirements/recommendations for international students: Required—TOEFL. Electronic applications accepted. *Faculty research:* Disabilities and postsecondary career avenues, self-determination.

St. Bonaventure University, School of Graduate Studies, School of Education, Differentiated Instruction Program, St. Bonaventure, NY 14778-2284. Offers gifted education (MS Ed, Adv C); gifted education and students with disabilities (MS Ed). Program offered in Olean and Buffalo Center (Hamburg, NY). Part-time and evening/weekend programs available. *Faculty:* 3 full-time (all women), 2 part-time/adjunct (both women). *Students:* 27 full-time (25 women), 19 part-time (17 women). Average age 25. 21 applicants, 100% accepted, 14 enrolled. In 2013, 18 master's awarded. *Degree requirements:* For master's, comprehensive exam, internship, portfolio; for Adv C, practicum, portfolio. *Entrance requirements:* For master's, teaching certification, interview, two letters of recommendation, writing sample, transcripts; for Adv C, teaching certification, master's degree, interview, references (ability to do graduate work, success as a teacher), writing sample. Additional exam requirements/recommendations for international students: Required—TOEFL (minimum score 550 paper-based; 79 iBT). *Application deadline:* For fall admission, 6/15 priority date for domestic students, 2/1 priority date for international students; for spring admission, 11/15 priority date for domestic students, 7/1 priority date for international students. Applications are processed on a rolling basis. Application fee: $0. Electronic applications accepted. *Financial support:* In 2013–14, 3 research assistantships with full and partial tuition reimbursements were awarded; Federal Work-Study, scholarships/grants, health care benefits, tuition waivers (partial), and unspecified assistantships also available. Support available to part-time students. Financial award application deadline: 4/15; financial award applicants required to submit FAFSA. *Unit head:* Dr. Rene' Garrison, Director, 716-375-4078, Fax: 716-375-2360, E-mail: rgarriso@sbu.edu. *Application contact:* Bruce Campbell, Director of Graduate Admissions, 716-375-2429, Fax: 716-375-4015, E-mail: gradsch@sbu.edu.
Website: http://www.sbu.edu/academics/schools/education/graduate-degrees-certificates/msed-in-differentiated-instruction-gifted.

St. Cloud State University, School of Graduate Studies, School of Education, Department of Special Education, St. Cloud, MN 56301-4498. Offers developmental/cognitive disabilities (MS); emotional/behavioral disorders (MS); gifted and talented (MS); learning disabilities (MS); special education (MS). *Accreditation:* NCATE. *Degree requirements:* For master's, thesis or alternative. *Entrance requirements:* For master's, GRE General Test, minimum GPA of 2.75. Additional exam requirements/recommendations for international students: Required—Michigan English Language Assessment Battery; Recommended—TOEFL (minimum score 550 paper-based), IELTS (minimum score 6.5). Electronic applications accepted.

St. John Fisher College, Ralph C. Wilson Jr. School of Education, Program in Adolescence Education and Special Education, Rochester, NY 14618-3597. Offers adolescence education: English with special education (MS Ed); adolescence education: French with special education (MS Ed); adolescence education: social studies with special education (MS Ed); adolescence education: Spanish with special education (MS Ed). Part-time and evening/weekend programs available. *Faculty:* 4 full-time (2 women), 4 part-time/adjunct (all women). *Students:* 20 full-time (10 women), 27 part-time (21 women); includes 4 minority (1 Black or African American, non-Hispanic/Latino; 1 Asian, non-Hispanic/Latino; 1 Hispanic/Latino; 1 Two or more races, non-Hispanic/Latino). Average age 27. 45 applicants, 89% accepted, 28 enrolled. In 2013, 28 master's awarded. *Degree requirements:* For master's, field experiences, student teaching, LAST. *Entrance requirements:* For master's, 2 letters of recommendation, personal statement, current resume. Additional exam requirements/recommendations for international students: Required—TOEFL (minimum score 575 paper-based; 80 iBT). *Application deadline:* Applications are processed on a rolling basis. Application fee: $30. Electronic applications accepted. *Expenses: Tuition:* Part-time $795 per credit hour. *Required fees:* $10 per credit hour. Tuition and fees vary according to course load, degree level and program. *Financial support:* In 2013–14, 11 students received support. Scholarships/grants available. Financial award applicants required to submit FAFSA. *Faculty research:* Arts and humanities, urban schools, constructivist learning, at-risk students, mentoring. *Unit head:* Dr. Susan Schultz, Program Director, 585-385-7296, E-mail: sschultz@sjfc.edu. *Application contact:* Jose Perales, Director of Graduate Admissions, 585-385-8067, E-mail: jperales@sjfc.edu.
Website: http://www.sjfc.edu/academics/education/departments/ms-special-ed/options/initial-adolescence.dot.

St. John Fisher College, Ralph C. Wilson Jr. School of Education, Program in Childhood Education/Special Education, Rochester, NY 14618-3597. Offers childhood education (MS); childhood education/special education (Certificate). Part-time and evening/weekend programs available. *Faculty:* 3 full-time (1 woman), 4 part-time/adjunct (all women). *Students:* 38 full-time (32 women), 6 part-time (5 women); includes 7 minority (2 Black or African American, non-Hispanic/Latino; 2 Asian, non-Hispanic/Latino; 3 Hispanic/Latino). Average age 29. 40 applicants, 90% accepted, 27 enrolled. In 2013, 12 master's awarded. *Degree requirements:* For master's, field experience, student teaching, LAST. *Entrance requirements:* For master's, 2 letters of recommendation, personal statement, current resume. Additional exam requirements/recommendations for international students: Required—TOEFL (minimum score 575 paper-based; 80 iBT). *Application deadline:* Applications are processed on a rolling basis. Application fee: $30. Electronic applications accepted. *Expenses: Tuition:* Part-time $795 per credit hour. *Required fees:* $10 per credit hour. Tuition and fees vary according to course load, degree level and program. *Financial support:* In 2013–14, 9 students received support. Scholarships/grants available. Financial award applicants required to submit FAFSA. *Faculty research:* Professional development, science assessment, multi-cultural, educational technology. *Unit head:* Dr. Susan Schultz, Program Director, 585-385-7296, E-mail: sschultz@sjfc.edu. *Application contact:* Jose Perales, Director of Graduate Admissions, 585-385-8067, E-mail: jperales@sjfc.edu.
Website: http://www.sjfc.edu/admissions/graduate/programs/childhood.dot.

St. John's University, The School of Education, Department of Human Services and Counseling, Literacy Program, Queens, NY 11439. Offers literacy (PhD); literacy B-6 or 5-12 (Adv C); teaching literacy 5-12 (MS Ed); teaching literacy B-12 (MS Ed); teaching literacy B-6 (MS Ed); teaching literacy B-6 and children with disabilities (MS Ed). Part-time and evening/weekend programs available. *Students:* 32 full-time (30 women), 89 part-time (84 women); includes 33 minority (13 Black or African American, non-Hispanic/Latino; 2 Asian, non-Hispanic/Latino; 17 Hispanic/Latino; 1 Two or more races, non-Hispanic/Latino), 1 international. Average age 30. 68 applicants, 94% accepted, 33 enrolled. In 2013, 33 master's, 4 doctorates, 3 other advanced degrees awarded. *Degree requirements:* For master's, comprehensive exam; for doctorate, thesis/dissertation, residency; for Adv C, 50-hour practicum, content specialty test in literacy. *Entrance requirements:* For master's, minimum GPA of 3.0, transcript, personal statement; for doctorate, MAT, GRE General Test (analytical), statement of goals, official transcripts showing conferral of degree, minimum GPA of 3.2, 2 letters of recommendation, resume, evidence of teaching experience, interview; for Adv C, master's degree, initial teaching certification, minimum GPA of 3.0. Additional exam requirements/recommendations for international students: Required—TOEFL (minimum score 600 paper-based; 100 iBT), IELTS (minimum score 5.5). *Application deadline:* For fall admission, 4/1 for domestic students, 4/1 priority date for international students; for spring admission, 11/1 priority date for international students. Applications are processed on a rolling basis. Application fee: $70. Electronic applications accepted. *Expenses: Tuition:* Full-time $19,800; part-time $1100 per credit. *Required fees:* $170 per semester. *Financial support:* Research assistantships, career-related internships or fieldwork, and scholarships/grants available. Support available to part-time students. Financial award application deadline: 3/1; financial award applicants required to submit FAFSA. *Faculty research:* Higher order reading comprehension development and instruction, children's literature theory and children's reading interests, critical

comprehension development, early writing development at the primary level, self-efficacy with textbook formats, out of school time program effects for at-risk students, teacher training effects for low performing parochial school students. *Unit head:* Dr. E Francine Guastello, Chair, 718-990-1475, E-mail: guastelf@stjohns.edu. *Application contact:* Dr. Kelly K. Ronayne, Associate Dean of Graduate Admissions, 718-990-2304, Fax: 718-990-2343, E-mail: graded@stjohns.edu.

St. John's University, The School of Education, Department of Human Services and Counseling, Program in Teaching Children with Disabilities in Childhood Education, Queens, NY 11439. Offers MS Ed, Adv C. Part-time and evening/weekend programs available. Postbaccalaureate distance learning degree programs offered. *Students:* 47 full-time (45 women), 211 part-time (146 women); includes 109 minority (55 Black or African American, non-Hispanic/Latino; 1 American Indian or Alaska Native, non-Hispanic/Latino; 14 Asian, non-Hispanic/Latino; 36 Hispanic/Latino; 3 Two or more races, non-Hispanic/Latino), 1 international. Average age 30. 183 applicants, 97% accepted, 130 enrolled. In 2013, 68 master's awarded. *Degree requirements:* For master's, comprehensive exam. *Entrance requirements:* For master's, bachelor's degree from accredited college or university, minimum GPA of 3.0, 2 letters of recommendation. Additional exam requirements/recommendations for international students: Required—TOEFL (minimum score 600 paper-based; 100 iBT), IELTS (minimum score 5.5). *Application deadline:* For fall admission, 8/17 for domestic students, 5/1 priority date for international students; for spring admission, 1/5 for domestic students, 11/1 priority date for international students. Applications are processed on a rolling basis. Application fee: $70. Electronic applications accepted. *Expenses: Tuition:* Full-time $19,800; part-time $1100 per credit. *Required fees:* $170 per semester. *Financial support:* Research assistantships available. *Faculty research:* Demographics in special education, literacy skill development in special populations, effects of distance learning in teacher training programs. *Unit head:* Dr. E. Francine Guastello, Chair, 718-990-1475, E-mail: guastelf@stjohns.edu. *Application contact:* Dr. Kelly K. Ronayne, Associate Dean for Graduate Admissions, 718-990-2304, Fax: 718-990-2343, E-mail: graded@stjohns.edu.

St. Joseph's College, Long Island Campus, Program in Infant/Toddler Early Childhood Special Education, Patchogue, NY 11772-2399. Offers MA. Part-time and evening/weekend programs available. *Degree requirements:* For master's, thesis, full-time practicum experience. *Entrance requirements:* For master's, 1 course in child development, 2 courses in special education, minimum undergraduate GPA of 3.0, New York state teaching certificate, interview. Additional exam requirements/recommendations for international students: Required—TOEFL (minimum score 550 paper-based).

St. Joseph's College, New York, Graduate Programs, Program in Education, Field of Infant/Toddler Early Childhood Special Education, Brooklyn, NY 11205-3688. Offers MA.

St. Joseph's College, New York, Graduate Programs, Program in Education, Field of Special Education, Brooklyn, NY 11205-3688. Offers severe and multiple disabilities (MA).

Saint Joseph's University, College of Arts and Sciences, Department of Education, Philadelphia, PA 19131-1395. Offers curriculum supervisor (Certificate); educational leadership (MS, Ed D); elementary education (MS, Certificate); elementary/middle school education (Certificate); instructional technology (MS, Certificate); principal certification (Certificate); professional education (MS); reading specialist (MS, Certificate); reading supervisor (Certificate); secondary education (MS, Certificate); special education (MS, Certificate); superintendent's letter of eligibility (Certificate); supervisor of special education (Certificate). Part-time and evening/weekend programs available. Postbaccalaureate distance learning degree programs offered (no on-campus study). *Faculty:* 32 full-time (25 women), 75 part-time/adjunct (53 women). *Students:* 91 full-time (81 women), 858 part-time (656 women); includes 133 minority (96 Black or African American, non-Hispanic/Latino; 3 American Indian or Alaska Native, non-Hispanic/Latino; 9 Asian, non-Hispanic/Latino; 20 Hispanic/Latino; 5 Native Hawaiian or other Pacific Islander, non-Hispanic/Latino), 16 international. Average age 31. 359 applicants, 77% accepted, 203 enrolled. In 2013, 363 master's, 9 doctorates, 1 other advanced degree awarded. *Entrance requirements:* For master's, 2 letters of recommendation, minimum GPA of 3.0, official transcripts, personal statement; for doctorate, GRE, master's degree from accredited institution, minimum graduate GPA of 3.5, computer competence, commitment to participate in cohort, interview with program director. Additional exam requirements/recommendations for international students: Required—TOEFL (minimum score 550 paper-based; 79 iBT), IELTS (minimum score 6.5). *Application deadline:* For fall admission, 7/15 priority date for domestic students, 4/15 for international students; for winter admission, 11/15 for domestic students, 1/15 for international students; for spring admission, 11/15 priority date for domestic students, 10/15 for international students. Applications are processed on a rolling basis. Application fee: $35. Electronic applications accepted. *Expenses:* Contact institution. *Financial support:* Unspecified assistantships available. Financial award applicants required to submit FAFSA. *Faculty research:* Factors predicting early mathematics skills for low income children, early child care and development, preschool quality. *Total annual research expenditures:* $229,264. *Unit head:* Dr. John Vacca, Associate Dean, Education, 610-660-3131, E-mail: gradstudies@sju.edu. *Application contact:* Elisabeth Woodward, Director of Marketing and Admissions, Graduate Arts and Sciences, 610-660-3131, Fax: 610-660-3230, E-mail: gradstudies@sju.edu. Website: http://sju.edu/int/academics/cas/grad/education/index.html.

Saint Louis University, Graduate Education, College of Education and Public Service, Department of Educational Studies, St. Louis, MO 63103-2097. Offers curriculum and instruction (MA, Ed D, PhD); educational foundations (MA, Ed D, PhD); special education (MA); teaching (MAT). *Accreditation:* NCATE. Part-time programs available. *Degree requirements:* For master's, comprehensive exam; for doctorate, comprehensive exam, thesis/dissertation, preliminary oral and written exams. *Entrance requirements:* For master's, GRE General Test or MAT, letters of recommendation, resume; for doctorate, GRE General Test, letters of recommendation, resumé, goal statement, transcripts. Additional exam requirements/recommendations for international students: Required—TOEFL (minimum score 525 paper-based). Electronic applications accepted. *Faculty research:* Teacher preparation, multicultural issues, children with special needs, qualitative research in education, inclusion.

Saint Martin's University, Office of Graduate Studies, College of Education, Lacey, WA 98503. Offers administration (M Ed); English as a second language (M Ed); guidance and counseling (M Ed); reading (M Ed); special education (M Ed); teaching (MIT). *Accreditation:* Teacher Education Accreditation Council. Part-time and evening/weekend programs available. *Faculty:* 10 full-time (6 women), 15 part-time/adjunct (12 women). *Students:* 57 full-time (35 women), 52 part-time (38 women); includes 20 minority (7 Black or African American, non-Hispanic/Latino; 1 American Indian or Alaska Native, non-Hispanic/Latino; 2 Asian, non-Hispanic/Latino; 6 Hispanic/Latino; 1 Native Hawaiian or other Pacific Islander, non-Hispanic/Latino; 3 Two or more races, non-Hispanic/Latino). Average age 35. 63 applicants, 25% accepted, 13 enrolled. In 2013, 12 master's awarded. *Degree requirements:* For master's, comprehensive exam (for some programs), thesis or alternative, project or comprehensives. *Entrance requirements:* For master's, GRE General Test or MAT, three letters of

recommendations; curriculum vitae. Additional exam requirements/recommendations for international students: Required—TOEFL (minimum score 550 paper-based; 79 iBT); Recommended—IELTS (minimum score 6.5). *Application deadline:* For fall admission, 4/1 priority date for domestic and international students; for spring admission, 11/1 priority date for domestic and international students. Applications are processed on a rolling basis. Application fee: $50. Electronic applications accepted. *Expenses: Tuition:* Part-time $990 per credit hour. Tuition and fees vary according to course level and program. *Financial support:* Career-related internships or fieldwork, Federal Work-Study, institutionally sponsored loans, and unspecified assistantships available. Support available to part-time students. Financial award application deadline: 3/1; financial award applicants required to submit FAFSA. *Faculty research:* Reader's theatre and reader/writer workshops, curriculum and assessment integration, gender and equity, classroom evaluations, organizational leadership. *Unit head:* Dr. Joyce Westgard, Dean, College of Education and Professional Psychology, 360-438-4509, Fax: 360-438-4486, E-mail: westgard@stmartin.edu. *Application contact:* Marie C. Boisvert, Administrative Assistant, 360-412-6145, E-mail: gradstudies@stmartin.edu. Website: http://www.stmartin.edu/gradstudies.

Saint Mary's College of California, Kalmanovitz School of Education, Program in Special Education, Moraga, CA 94575. Offers M Ed, MA. Part-time programs available. *Degree requirements:* For master's, thesis or alternative. *Entrance requirements:* For master's, writing proficiency exam, interview, minimum GPA of 3.0, teaching experience. *Faculty research:* Consultation model, impact of gifted model on special education.

Saint Mary's University of Minnesota, Schools of Graduate and Professional Programs, Graduate School of Education, Educational Administration Program, Winona, MN 55987-1399. Offers educational administration (Certificate, Ed S), including director of special education, K-12 principal, superintendent. *Unit head:* Dr. William Bjorum, Director, 612-728-5126, Fax: 612-728-5121, E-mail: wbjorum@smumn.edu. *Application contact:* Russell Kreager, Director of Admissions for Graduate and Professional Programs, 612-728-5207, Fax: 612-728-5121, E-mail: rkreager@smumn.edu. Website: http://www.smumn.edu/graduate-home/areas-of-study/graduate-school-of-education/eds-in-educational-administration-director-of-special-education-k-12-pr.

Saint Mary's University of Minnesota, Schools of Graduate and Professional Programs, Graduate School of Education, Special Education Program, Winona, MN 55987-1399. Offers behavioral disorders (Certificate); learning disabilities (Certificate); special education (MA). Part-time and evening/weekend programs available. Postbaccalaureate distance learning degree programs offered (no on-campus study). *Unit head:* Troy Gonzales, Director, 612-238-4565, E-mail: tgonzale@smumn.edu. *Application contact:* Russell Kreager, Director of Admission, 612-728-5207, E-mail: rkreager@smumn.edu. Website: http://www.smumn.edu/graduate-home/areas-of-study/graduate-school-of-education/ma-in-special-education.

Saint Michael's College, Graduate Programs, Program in Education, Colchester, VT 05439. Offers administration (M Ed, CAGS); arts in education (CAGS); curriculum and instruction (M Ed, CAGS); information technology (CAGS); reading (M Ed); special education (M Ed, CAGS); technology (M Ed). Part-time and evening/weekend programs available. *Degree requirements:* For master's, thesis. *Entrance requirements:* For master's, minimum GPA of 3.0. Electronic applications accepted. *Faculty research:* Integrative curriculum, moral and spiritual dimensions of education, learning styles, multiple intelligences, integrating technology into the curriculum.

Saint Peter's University, Graduate Programs in Education, Program in Special Education, Jersey City, NJ 07306-5997. Offers literacy (MA Ed). Part-time and evening/weekend programs available. *Degree requirements:* For master's, comprehensive exam. *Entrance requirements:* For master's, GRE or MAT. Additional exam requirements/recommendations for international students: Required—TOEFL. Electronic applications accepted.

St. Thomas Aquinas College, Division of Teacher Education, Sparkill, NY 10976. Offers adolescence education (MST); childhood and special education (MST); childhood education (MST); educational leadership (MS Ed); reading (MS Ed, PMC); special education (MS Ed, PMC); teaching (MS Ed), including elementary education, middle school education, secondary education. *Accreditation:* NCATE. Part-time and evening/weekend programs available. *Degree requirements:* For master's, comprehensive exam, comprehensive professional portfolio; for PMC, action research project. *Entrance requirements:* For master's, New York State Qualifying Exam, GRE General Test or minimum GPA of 3.0, teaching certificate; for PMC, GRE General Test or minimum GPA of 3.0. Electronic applications accepted. *Faculty research:* Computer applications in education, adolescent special education students, literacy development, inclusive practices for special education students.

St. Thomas University, School of Leadership Studies, Institute for Education, Miami Gardens, FL 33054-6459. Offers earth/space science (Certificate); educational administration (MS, Certificate); educational leadership (Ed D); elementary education (MS); ESOL (Certificate); gifted education (Certificate); instructional technology (MS, Certificate); professional/studies (Certificate); reading (MS, Certificate); special education (MS). Part-time and evening/weekend programs available. *Degree requirements:* For master's, comprehensive exam; for doctorate, comprehensive exam, thesis/dissertation. *Entrance requirements:* For master's, interview, minimum GPA of 3.0 or GRE; for doctorate, GRE or MAT. Additional exam requirements/recommendations for international students: Required—TOEFL (minimum score 550 paper-based; 79 iBT). Electronic applications accepted.

Saint Vincent College, Program in Education, Latrobe, PA 15650-2690. Offers curriculum and instruction (MS); educational media and technology (MS); environmental education (MS); school administration and supervision (MS); special education (MS). Part-time and evening/weekend programs available. *Degree requirements:* For master's, comprehensive exam. *Entrance requirements:* For master's, GRE (if undergraduate GPA less than 3.0). Additional exam requirements/recommendations for international students: Required—TOEFL (minimum score 550 paper-based). *Faculty research:* Assessment and instructional technology.

Saint Xavier University, Graduate Studies, School of Education, Chicago, IL 60655-3105. Offers counseling (MA); curriculum and instruction (MA); early childhood education (MA); educational administration (MA); elementary education (MA); individualized studies (MA), including educational technology, English as a second language (ESL), ISTEM (integrative science, technology, engineering, and math), science education; music education (MA); reading (MA); secondary education (MA); Spanish education (MA); special education (MA); teaching and leadership (MA). *Accreditation:* NCATE. Part-time and evening/weekend programs available. *Degree requirements:* For master's, thesis or project. *Entrance requirements:* For master's, minimum GPA of 3.0. *Expenses:* Contact institution.

Salem College, Department of Education, Winston-Salem, NC 27101. Offers art education (MAT); elementary education (M Ed, MAT); language and literacy (M Ed); middle school education (MAT); school counseling (M Ed); second language studies (MAT); secondary education (MAT); special education (M Ed, MAT). *Accreditation:* NCATE. Part-time and evening/weekend programs available. Postbaccalaureate distance learning degree programs offered (minimal on-campus study). *Degree*

requirements: For master's, practicum (MAT), project (M Ed), oral and written comprehensive exams. *Entrance requirements:* For master's, minimum GPA of 2.5. *Faculty research:* Content area reading strategies, literacy development, brain compatible instruction.

Salem State University, School of Graduate Studies, Program in Special Education, Salem, MA 01970-5353. Offers M Ed. *Accreditation:* NCATE. Part-time and evening/weekend programs available. *Students:* 15 full-time (14 women), 69 part-time (55 women); includes 3 minority (1 Black or African American, non-Hispanic/Latino; 1 Asian, non-Hispanic/Latino; 1 Hispanic/Latino). 29 applicants, 97% accepted, 19 enrolled. In 2013, 57 master's awarded. *Entrance requirements:* For master's, GRE, MAT. Additional exam requirements/recommendations for international students: Required—TOEFL (minimum score 550 paper-based; 80 iBT) or IELTS (minimum score 5.5). *Application deadline:* For fall admission, 5/1 for domestic students; for spring admission, 10/1 for domestic students. Applications are processed on a rolling basis. Application fee: $50. *Financial support:* Career-related internships or fieldwork, Federal Work-Study, scholarships/grants, and unspecified assistantships available. Support available to part-time students. Financial award application deadline: 5/1; financial award applicants required to submit FAFSA. *Application contact:* Dr. Lee A. Brossoit, Assistant Dean of Graduate Admissions, 978-542-6675, Fax: 978-542-7215, E-mail: lbrossoit@salemstate.edu.
Website: http://www.salemstate.edu/academics/schools/12667.php.

Salus University, College of Education and Rehabilitation, Elkins Park, PA 19027-1598. Offers education of children and youth with visual and multiple impairments (M Ed, Certificate); low vision rehabilitation (MS, Certificate); orientation and mobility therapy (MS, Certificate); vision rehabilitation therapy (MS, Certificate); OD/MS. Part-time programs available. Postbaccalaureate distance learning degree programs offered. *Entrance requirements:* For master's, GRE or MAT, letters of reference (3), interviews (2). Additional exam requirements/recommendations for international students: Required—TOEFL, TWE. *Expenses:* Contact institution. *Faculty research:* Knowledge utilization, technology transfer.

Sam Houston State University, College of Education and Applied Science, Department of Language, Literacy, and Special Populations, Huntsville, TX 77341. Offers international literacy (M Ed); reading (M Ed, Ed D); special education (M Ed, MA). Part-time and evening/weekend programs available. *Faculty:* 26 full-time (22 women). *Students:* 44 full-time (38 women), 195 part-time (182 women); includes 85 minority (32 Black or African American, non-Hispanic/Latino; 5 Asian, non-Hispanic/Latino; 43 Hispanic/Latino; 5 Two or more races, non-Hispanic/Latino), 12 international. Average age 38. 129 applicants, 89% accepted, 54 enrolled. In 2013, 37 master's, 5 doctorates awarded. *Degree requirements:* For master's, comprehensive exam (for some programs), thesis optional, portfolio; for doctorate, comprehensive exam, thesis/dissertation. *Entrance requirements:* For master's, GRE General Test, minimum GPA of 2.5; for doctorate, GRE General Test. Additional exam requirements/recommendations for international students: Required—TOEFL (minimum score 550 paper-based; 79 iBT), IELTS (minimum score 6.5). *Application deadline:* For fall admission, 8/1 for domestic students, 6/25 for international students; for spring admission, 12/1 for domestic students, 11/12 for international students. Applications are processed on a rolling basis. Application fee: $45 ($75 for international students). Electronic applications accepted. *Financial support:* In 2013–14, 7 research assistantships (averaging $11,999 per year), 4 teaching assistantships (averaging $13,348 per year) were awarded. Financial award application deadline: 5/31; financial award applicants required to submit FAFSA. *Unit head:* Dr. Melinda Miller, Chair, 936-294-1357, Fax: 936-294-1131, E-mail: mmiller@shsu.edu. *Application contact:* Molly Doughtie, Advisor, 936-294-1105, E-mail: edu_mxd@shsu.edu.
Website: http://www.shsu.edu/~edu_lls/.

San Diego State University, Graduate and Research Affairs, College of Education, Department of Administration, Rehabilitation and Post-Secondary Education, San Diego, CA 92182. Offers educational leadership in post-secondary education (MA); rehabilitation counseling (MS), including deafness. Evening/weekend programs available. Postbaccalaureate distance learning degree programs offered. *Degree requirements:* For master's, comprehensive exam (for some programs), thesis (for some programs). *Entrance requirements:* For master's, GRE General Test, letters of reference. Additional exam requirements/recommendations for international students: Required—TOEFL. Electronic applications accepted. *Faculty research:* Rehabilitation in cultural diversity, distance learning technology.

San Diego State University, Graduate and Research Affairs, College of Education, Department of Special Education, San Diego, CA 92182. Offers MA. *Accreditation:* NCATE. Evening/weekend programs available. *Entrance requirements:* For master's, GRE General Test, letters of reference. Additional exam requirements/recommendations for international students: Required—TOEFL. Electronic applications accepted.

San Francisco State University, Division of Graduate Studies, College of Education, Department of Special Education, Program in Orientation and Mobility, San Francisco, CA 94132-1722. Offers MA, Credential. *Unit head:* Dr. Sandra Rosen, Program Coordinator, 415-338-1245, E-mail: mobility@sfsu.edu. *Application contact:* Louise Guy, Office Coordinator, 415-338-1161, E-mail: lguy@sfsu.edu.
Website: http://online.sfsu.edu/~mobility/.

San Jose State University, Graduate Studies and Research, Connie L. Lurie College of Education, Department of Special Education, San Jose, CA 95192-0001. Offers MA. *Accreditation:* NCATE. Evening/weekend programs available. Electronic applications accepted.

Seattle University, College of Education, Program in Special Education, Seattle, WA 98122-1090. Offers M Ed, MA, Certificate. *Faculty:* 2 full-time (1 woman), 1 part-time/adjunct (0 women). *Students:* 3 full-time (2 women), 10 part-time (8 women); includes 1 minority (Two or more races, non-Hispanic/Latino). Average age 34. 4 applicants, 50% accepted, 1 enrolled. In 2013, 3 master's, 1 other advanced degree awarded. *Entrance requirements:* For master's, GRE, MAT or minimum GPA of 3.0, 1 year of K-12 teaching experience; for Certificate, master's degree, minimum GPA of 3.0, 1 year of K-12 teaching experience. *Application deadline:* For fall admission, 8/20 priority date for domestic students; for winter admission, 11/20 priority date for domestic students; for spring admission, 2/20 priority date for domestic students. *Financial support:* In 2013–14, 7 students received support. *Unit head:* Dr. Katherine Schlick Noe, Director, 206-296-5768, E-mail: kschlnoe@seattleu.edu. *Application contact:* Janet Shandley, Associate Dean of Graduate Admissions, 206-296-5900, Fax: 206-298-5656, E-mail: grad_admissions@seattleu.edu.
Website: http://www.seattleu.edu/coe/specialed/Default.aspx?id=11238.

Seton Hall University, College of Education and Human Services, Department of Educational Studies, South Orange, NJ 07079-2697. Offers instructional design (MA); school library media specialist (MA); special education (MA). Part-time and evening/weekend programs available. *Faculty:* 18 full-time (14 women). *Students:* 7 full-time (3 women), 53 part-time (39 women); includes 8 minority (3 Black or African American, non-Hispanic/Latino; 1 Asian, non-Hispanic/Latino; 4 Hispanic/Latino), 1 international. Average age 32. 39 applicants, 90% accepted, 27 enrolled. In 2013, 27 degrees awarded. *Entrance requirements:* For master's, GRE or MAT, PRAXIS (for certification candidates), minimum GPA of 2.75. *Application deadline:* For fall admission, 5/1 for domestic students; for spring admission, 10/1 for domestic students. Applications are processed on a rolling basis. Application fee: $50. *Financial support:* In 2013–14, 3 research assistantships with full tuition reimbursements (averaging $4,000 per year) were awarded; fellowships, career-related internships or fieldwork, institutionally sponsored loans, and unspecified assistantships also available. Financial award application deadline: 2/1. *Unit head:* Dr. Joseph Martinelli, Chair, 973-275-2733, E-mail: joseph.martinelli@shu.edu. *Application contact:* Diana Minakakis, Associate Dean, 973-275-2824, Fax: 973-275-2187, E-mail: diana.minakakis@shu.edu.
Website: http://www.shu.edu/academics/education/graduate-studies.cfm.

Seton Hill University, Program in Special Education, Greensburg, PA 15601. Offers autism (Certificate); special education (MA). Part-time and evening/weekend programs available. Postbaccalaureate distance learning degree programs offered (minimal on-campus study). *Faculty:* 7 full-time (6 women), 6 part-time/adjunct (3 women). *Students:* 5 full-time (3 women), 7 part-time (3 women); includes 1 minority (Black or African American, non-Hispanic/Latino). Average age 29. 11 applicants, 27% accepted, 2 enrolled. In 2013, 2 master's awarded. *Entrance requirements:* For master's, 3 letters of recommendation, copy of teacher's certification, transcripts, resume, letter of intent. Additional exam requirements/recommendations for international students: Required—TOEFL (minimum score 600 paper-based; 100 iBT), IELTS (minimum score 6.5). *Application deadline:* Applications are processed on a rolling basis. Application fee: $0. Electronic applications accepted. *Expenses: Tuition:* Full-time $14,220; part-time $790 per credit. *Required fees:* $700; $34 per credit. $50 per semester. *Financial support:* Scholarships/grants and tuition discounts available. Financial award application deadline: 8/15. *Faculty research:* Assessment rubrics, autism, brain-based teaching/learning, early intervention (special needs), STEM. *Unit head:* Jennifer Suppo, Director, 724-830-1032, E-mail: jsuppo@setonhill.edu. *Application contact:* Laurel Komarny, Program Counselor, 724-838-4209, E-mail: komarny@setonhill.edu.
Website: http://www.setonhill.edu/academics/graduate_programs/special_education.

Shippensburg University of Pennsylvania, School of Graduate Studies, College of Education and Human Services, Department of Educational Leadership and Special Education, Shippensburg, PA 17257-2299. Offers school administration principal K-12 (M Ed); special education (M Ed), including behavior disorders, comprehensive, learning disabilities, mental retardation/development disabilities. *Accreditation:* NCATE. Part-time and evening/weekend programs available. *Faculty:* 10 full-time (4 women), 1 (woman) part-time/adjunct. *Students:* 8 full-time (all women), 70 part-time (48 women); includes 1 minority (Two or more races, non-Hispanic/Latino), 3 international. Average age 30. 63 applicants, 68% accepted, 29 enrolled. In 2013, 53 master's awarded. *Degree requirements:* For master's, candidacy, thesis, or practicum. *Entrance requirements:* For master's, instructional or educational specialist certificate; 3 letters of reference; 2 years of successful teaching experience; interview and GRE or MAT (if GPA is less than 2.75); statement of purpose; writing sample; personal goals statement and resume. Additional exam requirements/recommendations for international students: Required—TOEFL (minimum score 580 paper-based); Recommended—IELTS (minimum score 6). *Application deadline:* For fall admission, 2/1 for domestic students, 4/30 for international students; for spring admission, 7/1 for domestic students, 9/30 for international students. Applications are processed on a rolling basis. Application fee: $45. Electronic applications accepted. *Expenses: Tuition, area resident:* Part-time $442 per credit. Tuition, state resident: part-time $442 per credit. Tuition, nonresident: part-time $663 per credit. *Required fees:* $127 per credit. *Financial support:* In 2013–14, 1 research assistantship with full tuition reimbursement (averaging $5,000 per year) was awarded; career-related internships or fieldwork, scholarships/grants, unspecified assistantships, and resident hall director and student payroll positions also available. Support available to part-time students. Financial award application deadline: 3/1; financial award applicants required to submit FAFSA. *Unit head:* Dr. Christopher L. Schwilk, Chairperson, 717-477-1591, Fax: 717-477-4026, E-mail: clschwi@ship.edu. *Application contact:* Jeremy R. Goshorn, Assistant Dean of Graduate Admissions, 717-477-1231, Fax: 717-477-4016, E-mail: jrgoshorn@ship.edu.
Website: http://www.ship.edu/else/.

Siena Heights University, Graduate College, Adrian, MI 49221-1796. Offers clinical mental health counseling (MA); education leadership (Specialist); leadership (MA), including health care, higher education leadership, organizational; teacher education (MA), including early childhood, early childhood: Montessori-based, education leadership: principal, elementary education, K-12 reading, leadership: higher education, secondary education, K-12 reading, special education, K-12 cognitive impairment, special education, K-12 learning disabled. Part-time and evening/weekend programs available. *Faculty:* 37. *Students:* 9 full-time (7 women), 251 part-time (179 women). In 2013, 32 master's awarded. *Degree requirements:* For master's, thesis, presentation. *Entrance requirements:* For master's, minimum GPA of 3.0, current resume, essay, all post-secondary transcripts, 3 letters of reference, conviction disclosure form; copy of teaching certificate (for some education programs); for Specialist, master's degree, minimum GPA of 3.0, current resume, essay, all post-secondary transcripts, 3 letters of reference, conviction disclosure form; copy of teaching certificate (for some education programs). *Application deadline:* Applications are processed on a rolling basis. Application fee: $50. *Expenses: Tuition:* Part-time $535 per semester hour. *Required fees:* $130 per semester. *Financial support:* Career-related internships or fieldwork, Federal Work-Study, and resident assistantships available. Financial award application deadline: 9/1; financial award applicants required to submit FAFSA. *Unit head:* Dr. Linda S. Pettit, Dean, Graduate College, 517-264-7661, Fax: 517-264-7714, E-mail: lpettit@sienahts.edu.
Website: http://www.sienaheights.edu.

Silver Lake College of the Holy Family, Division of Graduate Studies, Program in Special Education, Manitowoc, WI 54220-9319. Offers MASE. Part-time and evening/weekend programs available. *Faculty:* 3 full-time (all women), 3 part-time/adjunct (all women). *Students:* 8 part-time (6 women). Average age 30. 13 applicants, 92% accepted, 8 enrolled. In 2013, 2 master's awarded. *Entrance requirements:* For master's, minimum undergraduate GPA of 3.0, written essay, three letters of recommendation from professional educators. Additional exam requirements/recommendations for international students: Required—TOEFL. *Application deadline:* For fall admission, 8/1 for domestic students; for spring admission, 12/1 for domestic students. Applications are processed on a rolling basis. Application fee: $0. Electronic applications accepted. *Expenses: Tuition:* Part-time $500 per credit. *Financial support:* Federal Work-Study and scholarships/grants available. Support available to part-time students. Financial award application deadline: 6/30; financial award applicants required to submit FAFSA. *Unit head:* Sr. Mary Karen Oudeans, OSF, Director, 920-686-6157, Fax: 920-684-7082, E-mail: marykaren.oudeans@sl.edu. *Application contact:* Jamie Grant, Director of Admissions, 920-686-6206, Fax: 920-686-6322, E-mail: jamie.grant@sl.edu.
Website: https://www.sl.edu/adult-education/academics/graduate-program/special-education/.

Simmons College, School of Social Work, Boston, MA 02115. Offers assistive technology (MS Ed, Ed S); behavior analysis (MS, PhD, Ed S); education (MA, CAGS);

language and literacy (MS Ed, Ed S); social work (MSW, PhD); special education (MS Ed), including moderate disabilities, severe disabilities; teaching (MAT), including elementary education, general education, high school education; teaching English as a second language (MA, CAGS); urban leadership (MSW); MSW/MBA. *Accreditation:* CSWE (one or more programs are accredited). Part-time programs available. Postbaccalaureate distance learning degree programs offered (no on-campus study). *Students:* 519 full-time (454 women), 703 part-time (604 women); includes 192 minority (61 Black or African American, non-Hispanic/Latino; 1 American Indian or Alaska Native, non-Hispanic/Latino; 35 Asian, non-Hispanic/Latino; 71 Hispanic/Latino; 2 Native Hawaiian or other Pacific Islander, non-Hispanic/Latino; 22 Two or more races, non-Hispanic/Latino), 16 international. 952 applicants, 66% accepted, 353 enrolled. In 2013, 159 master's, 2 doctorates awarded. Terminal master's awarded for partial completion of doctoral program. *Degree requirements:* For master's, thesis (for some programs); for doctorate, comprehensive exam (for some programs), thesis/dissertation (for some programs). *Entrance requirements:* For master's, GRE, MAT, MTEL (for different programs); for doctorate, GRE, BCBA Analyst Exam. Additional exam requirements/recommendations for international students: Required—TOEFL (minimum score 600 paper-based; 100 iBT). *Application deadline:* Applications are processed on a rolling basis. Application fee: $45. Electronic applications accepted. *Financial support:* Teaching assistantships and scholarships/grants available. *Unit head:* Dr. Stefan Krug, Dean, 617-521-3924. *Application contact:* Carlos D. Frontado, Director of Admissions, 617-521-3920, Fax: 617-521-3980, E-mail: ssw@simmons.edu. Website: http://www.simmons.edu/ssw/.

Slippery Rock University of Pennsylvania, Graduate Studies (Recruitment), College of Education, Department of Special Education, Slippery Rock, PA 16057-1383. Offers autism (M Ed); birth to grade 8 (M Ed); grade 7 to grade 12 (M Ed); master teacher (M Ed); supervision (M Ed). *Accreditation:* NCATE. Part-time and evening/weekend programs available. Postbaccalaureate distance learning degree programs offered (no on-campus study). *Faculty:* 8 full-time (4 women). *Students:* 31 full-time (28 women), 154 part-time (130 women); includes 5 minority (2 Black or African American, non-Hispanic/Latino; 2 Asian, non-Hispanic/Latino; 1 Hispanic/Latino). Average age 29. 187 applicants, 90% accepted, 107 enrolled. In 2013, 81 master's awarded. *Degree requirements:* For master's, thesis optional. *Entrance requirements:* For master's, GRE General Test, MAT, minimum GPA of 3.0, official transcripts, teaching certification. Additional exam requirements/recommendations for international students: Required—TOEFL (minimum score 550 paper-based; 80 iBT). *Application deadline:* For fall admission, 3/1 priority date for domestic students, 5/1 priority date for international students; for spring admission, 10/1 priority date for domestic students, 9/1 priority date for international students. Applications are processed on a rolling basis. Application fee: $25 ($30 for international students). Electronic applications accepted. *Expenses:* Tuition, state resident: full-time $7956; part-time $442 per credit. Tuition, nonresident: full-time $11,934; part-time $663 per credit. *Required fees:* $2896; $148 per credit. Tuition and fees vary according to degree level and program. *Financial support:* Career-related internships or fieldwork, Federal Work-Study, institutionally sponsored loans, scholarships/grants, tuition waivers (partial), and unspecified assistantships available. Support available to part-time students. Financial award application deadline: 5/1; financial award applicants required to submit FAFSA. *Unit head:* Dr. Robert Isherwood, Graduate Coordinator, 724-738-2453, Fax: 724-738-4395, E-mail: robert.isherwood@sru.edu. *Application contact:* Brandi Weber-Mortimer, Director of Graduate Admissions, 724-738-2051, Fax: 724-738-2146, E-mail: graduate.admissions@sru.edu.

Smith College, Graduate and Special Programs, Department of Education and Child Study, Program in the Education of the Deaf, Northampton, MA 01063. Offers MED. Part-time programs available. *Students:* 11 full-time (all women), 3 part-time (all women). Average age 27. 16 applicants, 81% accepted, 12 enrolled. In 2013, 14 master's awarded. *Entrance requirements:* For master's, GRE General Test or MAT. Additional exam requirements/recommendations for international students: Required—TOEFL (minimum score 595 paper-based; 97 iBT). *Application deadline:* For fall admission, 4/1 for domestic students, 1/15 for international students. Applications are processed on a rolling basis. Application fee: $60. *Expenses: Tuition:* Full-time $32,160; part-time $1340 per credit. *Financial support:* In 2013–14, 14 students received support. Career-related internships or fieldwork, institutionally sponsored loans, scholarships/grants, and tuition waivers (full) available. Support available to part-time students. Financial award application deadline: 1/15; financial award applicants required to submit CSS PROFILE or FAFSA. *Unit head:* Danial Salvucci, Interim Director, 413-585-3255, Fax: 413-585-3268, E-mail: dsalvucc@smith.edu. *Application contact:* Ruth Morgan, Administrative Assistant, 413-585-3050, Fax: 413-585-3054, E-mail: gradstdy@smith.edu. Website: http://www.smith.edu/education/med.php.

Sonoma State University, School of Education, Rohnert Park, CA 94928. Offers curriculum, teaching, and learning (MA); early childhood education (MA); education (Ed D); educational administration (MA); multiple subject (Credential); reading and literacy (MA); single subject (Credential); special education (MA, Credential). *Accreditation:* NCATE. Part-time and evening/weekend programs available. *Faculty:* 11 full-time (9 women), 1 (woman) part-time/adjunct. *Students:* 162 full-time (119 women), 165 part-time (125 women); includes 61 minority (4 Black or African American, non-Hispanic/Latino; 1 American Indian or Alaska Native, non-Hispanic/Latino; 12 Asian, non-Hispanic/Latino; 29 Hispanic/Latino; 1 Native Hawaiian or other Pacific Islander, non-Hispanic/Latino; 14 Two or more races, non-Hispanic/Latino), 1 international. Average age 33. 314 applicants, 82% accepted, 75 enrolled. In 2013, 41 master's, 287 other advanced degrees awarded. *Degree requirements:* For master's, thesis or alternative. *Entrance requirements:* For master's, minimum GPA of 2.5. Additional exam requirements/recommendations for international students: Required—TOEFL (minimum score 500 paper-based). Application fee: $55. *Expenses:* Tuition, state resident: full-time $8500. Tuition, nonresident: full-time $12,964. *Required fees:* $1762. *Financial support:* In 2013–14, 1 research assistantship (averaging $1,876 per year) was awarded; fellowships, career-related internships or fieldwork, and Federal Work-Study also available. Support available to part-time students. Financial award application deadline: 3/2; financial award applicants required to submit FAFSA. *Unit head:* Dr. Carlos Ayala, Dean, 707-664-4412, E-mail: carlos.ayala@sonoma.edu. *Application contact:* Dr. Jennifer Mahdavi, Coordinator of Graduate Studies, 707-664-3311, E-mail: jennifer.mahdavi@sonoma.edu. Website: http://www.sonoma.edu/education/.

South Carolina State University, School of Graduate and Professional Studies, Department of Education, Orangeburg, SC 29117-0001. Offers early childhood and special education (M Ed); early childhood education (MAT); elementary education (M Ed, MAT); general science (MAT); mathematics (MAT); secondary education (M Ed), including biology education, business education, counselor education, English education, home economics education, industrial education, mathematics education, science education, social studies education; special education (M Ed), including emotionally handicapped, learning disabilities, mentally handicapped. *Accreditation:* NCATE. Part-time and evening/weekend programs available. *Faculty:* 9 full-time (3 women), 4 part-time/adjunct (3 women). *Students:* 32 full-time (26 women), 33 part-time (26 women); includes 63 minority (61 Black or African American, non-Hispanic/Latino; 2 Asian, non-Hispanic/Latino). Average age 31. 21 applicants, 100% accepted, 21

enrolled. In 2013, 15 master's awarded. *Degree requirements:* For master's, thesis optional, departmental qualifying exam. *Entrance requirements:* For master's, GRE General Test, NTE, interview, teaching certificate. *Application deadline:* For fall admission, 6/15 priority date for domestic students, 6/15 for international students; for spring admission, 11/1 for domestic and international students. Applications are processed on a rolling basis. Application fee: $25. Electronic applications accepted. *Expenses:* Tuition, state resident: full-time $8906; part-time $543 per credit hour. Tuition, nonresident: full-time $18,040; part-time $1051 per credit hour. *Financial support:* Fellowships, career-related internships or fieldwork, Federal Work-Study, and institutionally sponsored loans available. Financial award application deadline: 6/1. *Faculty research:* Critical thinking, child abuse, stress, test-taking skills, conflict resolution, mainstreaming. *Unit head:* Dr. Margaret Evelyn Fields, Interim Chair, 803-536-7098, Fax: 803-516-4568, E-mail: efields@scsu.edu. *Application contact:* Curtis Foskey, Coordinator of Graduate Studies, 803-536-8419, Fax: 803-536-8812, E-mail: cfoskey@scsu.edu.

Southeastern Louisiana University, College of Education, Department of Teaching and Learning, Hammond, LA 70402. Offers curriculum and instruction (M Ed); elementary education (MAT); special education (M Ed); special education: early interventionist (MAT). *Accreditation:* NCATE. Part-time and evening/weekend programs available. *Faculty:* 11 full-time (9 women). *Students:* 40 full-time (38 women), 191 part-time (165 women); includes 55 minority (35 Black or African American, non-Hispanic/Latino; 1 American Indian or Alaska Native, non-Hispanic/Latino; 4 Asian, non-Hispanic/Latino; 13 Hispanic/Latino; 2 Two or more races, non-Hispanic/Latino), 2 international. Average age 34. 35 applicants, 66% accepted, 20 enrolled. In 2013, 50 master's awarded. *Degree requirements:* For master's, comprehensive exam (for some programs), thesis (for some programs), action research project, oral defense of research project, portfolio, teaching certificate, minimum cumulative GPA of 3.0. *Entrance requirements:* For master's, GRE (verbal and quantitative), PRAXIS (MAT). Additional exam requirements/recommendations for international students: Required—TOEFL (minimum score 500 paper-based; 61 iBT). *Application deadline:* For fall admission, 7/15 priority date for domestic students, 6/1 priority date for international students; for spring admission, 12/1 priority date for domestic students, 10/1 priority date for international students. Applications are processed on a rolling basis. Application fee: $20 ($30 for international students). Electronic applications accepted. *Expenses:* Tuition, state resident: full-time $5047. Tuition, nonresident: full-time $17,066. *Required fees:* $1213. Tuition and fees vary according to degree level. *Financial support:* Career-related internships or fieldwork, Federal Work-Study, institutionally sponsored loans, scholarships/grants, and unspecified assistantships available. Support available to part-time students. Financial award application deadline: 5/1; financial award applicants required to submit FAFSA. *Faculty research:* ESL, dyslexia, pre-service teachers, inclusion, early childhood education. Total annual research expenditures: $45,104. *Unit head:* Dr. Cynthia Elliott, Interim Department Head, 985-549-2221, Fax: 985-549-5009, E-mail: celliott@selu.edu. *Application contact:* Sandra Meyers, Graduate Admissions Analyst, 985-549-5620, Fax: 985-549-5632, E-mail: admissions@selu.edu. Website: http://www.selu.edu/acad_research/depts/teach_lrn/index.html.

Southeast Missouri State University, School of Graduate Studies, Department of Elementary, Early and Special Education, Program in Exceptional Child Education, Cape Girardeau, MO 63701-4799. Offers MA. *Accreditation:* NCATE. Part-time and evening/weekend programs available. Postbaccalaureate distance learning degree programs offered (no on-campus study). *Faculty:* 12 full-time (10 women). *Students:* 3 full-time (all women), 31 part-time (30 women). Average age 34. 11 applicants, 100% accepted, 11 enrolled. In 2013, 8 master's awarded. *Degree requirements:* For master's, comprehensive exam, action research project. *Entrance requirements:* For master's, GRE General Test, MAT, or PRAXIS, minimum undergraduate GPA of 2.75; valid elementary or secondary teaching certificate. Additional exam requirements/recommendations for international students: Required—TOEFL (minimum score 550 paper-based; 79 iBT), IELTS (minimum score 6), PTE (minimum score 53). *Application deadline:* For fall admission, 8/1 for domestic students, 6/1 for international students; for spring admission, 11/21 for domestic students, 10/1 for international students; for summer admission, 5/15 for domestic students. Applications are processed on a rolling basis. Application fee: $30 ($40 for international students). Electronic applications accepted. *Expenses:* Tuition, state resident: full-time $5139; part-time $285.50 per credit hour. Tuition, nonresident: full-time $9099; part-time $505.50 per credit hour. *Financial support:* In 2013–14, 8 students received support. Career-related internships or fieldwork, Federal Work-Study, scholarships/grants, traineeships, tuition waivers (full), and unspecified assistantships available. Financial award application deadline: 6/30; financial award applicants required to submit FAFSA. *Unit head:* Dr. Julie Ray, Department of Elementary, Early, and Special Education Chair and Professor, 573-651-2444, E-mail: jaray@semo.edu. *Application contact:* Dr. Nancy Aguinaga, Associate Professor, 573-651-2122, E-mail: naguinaga@semo.edu. Website: http://www.semo.edu/eese/.

Southern Connecticut State University, School of Graduate Studies, School of Education, Program in Special Education, New Haven, CT 06515-1355. Offers MS Ed. Part-time and evening/weekend programs available. *Degree requirements:* For master's, thesis or alternative. *Entrance requirements:* For master's, interview. Electronic applications accepted.

Southern Illinois University Carbondale, Graduate School, College of Education and Human Services, Department of Educational Psychology and Special Education, Program in Special Education, Carbondale, IL 62901-4701. Offers MS Ed. *Accreditation:* NCATE. Part-time programs available. *Faculty:* 19 full-time (9 women), 7 part-time/adjunct (2 women). *Students:* 3 full-time (2 women), 13 part-time (11 women); includes 2 minority (both Black or African American, non-Hispanic/Latino), 2 international. Average age 28. 6 applicants, 33% accepted, 2 enrolled. In 2013, 3 master's awarded. *Degree requirements:* For master's, thesis. *Entrance requirements:* For master's, GRE General Test, minimum GPA of 2.7. Additional exam requirements/recommendations for international students: Required—TOEFL. *Application deadline:* Applications are processed on a rolling basis. Application fee: $50. *Financial support:* In 2013–14, 3 students received support. Fellowships with full tuition reimbursements available, research assistantships with full tuition reimbursements available, teaching assistantships with full tuition reimbursements available, career-related internships or fieldwork, Federal Work-Study, institutionally sponsored loans, tuition waivers (full), and unspecified assistantships available. Support available to part-time students. *Faculty research:* Applied and action research; scientific methods used to evaluate effectiveness of products and programs for the handicapped; scientific methods used to develop generalizations about instructional, motivational, and learning processes of the handicapped. *Unit head:* Dr. Todd Headrick, Chairperson, 618-536-1818, E-mail: headrick@siu.edu. *Application contact:* Brenda Prell, Administrative Clerk, 618-453-2311, E-mail: bprell@siu.edu.

Southern Illinois University Edwardsville, Graduate School, School of Education, Department of Special Education and Communication Disorders, Program in Special Education, Edwardsville, IL 62026. Offers MS Ed, Post-Master's Certificate. Part-time and evening/weekend programs available. *Students:* 3 full-time (all women), 41 part-time (37 women); includes 6 minority (4 Black or African American, non-Hispanic/Latino;

2 Two or more races, non-Hispanic/Latino), 2 international. 12 applicants, 92% accepted. In 2013, 17 master's awarded. *Degree requirements:* For master's, thesis or alternative, final project. *Entrance requirements:* Additional exam requirements/recommendations for international students: Required—TOEFL (minimum score 550 paper-based, 79 iBT), IELTS (minimum score 6.5), Michigan Test of English Language Proficiency or PTE. *Application deadline:* For fall admission, 7/18 for domestic students, 6/1 for international students; for spring admission, 12/12 for domestic students, 10/1 for international students; for summer admission, 4/24 for domestic students, 3/1 for international students. Applications are processed on a rolling basis. Application fee: $30. Electronic applications accepted. *Expenses:* Tuition, state resident: full-time $3551. Tuition, nonresident: full-time $8378. *Financial support:* In 2013–14, teaching assistantships (averaging $9,585 per year) were awarded; fellowships, research assistantships, institutionally sponsored loans, scholarships/grants, and unspecified assistantships also available. Financial award application deadline: 3/1; financial award applicants required to submit FAFSA. *Unit head:* Dr. Linda Forbringer, Director, 618-650-3488, E-mail: lforbri@siue.edu. *Application contact:* Melissa K. Mace, Assistant Director of Graduate and International Recruitment, 618-650-2756, Fax: 618-650-3618, E-mail: mmace@siue.edu.
Website: http://www.siue.edu/education/secd/.

Southern Methodist University, Annette Caldwell Simmons School of Education and Human Development, Department of Teaching and Learning, Dallas, TX 75275. Offers bilingual/ESL education (MBE); education (M Ed, PhD); gifted education (MBE); reading and writing (M Ed); special education (M Ed). Part-time and evening/weekend programs available. Terminal master's awarded for partial completion of doctoral program. *Degree requirements:* For master's, comprehensive exam, minimum GPA of 3.0; for doctorate, thesis/dissertation, qualifying exams, major area paper, evidence of teaching competency, dissemination of research (e.g., conference presentation), professional portfolio. *Entrance requirements:* For master's, minimum GPA of 3.0 or GRE, 3 letters of recommendation; for doctorate, GRE, minimum GPA of 3.3, 3 years of full-time teaching, 3 letters of recommendation, interview. Additional exam requirements/recommendations for international students: Required—TOEFL. Electronic applications accepted. *Faculty research:* Reading intervention, mathematics intervention, bilingual education, new literacies.

Southern New Hampshire University, School of Education, Manchester, NH 03106-1045. Offers business education (M Ed); child development (M Ed); curriculum and instruction (M Ed), including education leadership, reading, special education, technology integration; education (M Ed); educational leadership (M Ed, Ed D); educational studies (M Ed); elementary education (M Ed); English (MAT); English for speakers of other languages (M Ed); reading and writing specialist (M Ed); school business administration (Certificate); secondary education (M Ed); special education (M Ed); technology integration specialist (M Ed). Part-time and evening/weekend programs available. Postbaccalaureate distance learning degree programs offered (no on-campus study). *Degree requirements:* For master's, comprehensive exam (for some programs), thesis or alternative. *Entrance requirements:* For master's, PRAXIS I, minimum GPA of 2.75. Additional exam requirements/recommendations for international students: Required—TOEFL (minimum score 550 paper-based). Electronic applications accepted. *Expenses:* Contact institution.

Southern Oregon University, Graduate Studies, School of Education, Ashland, OR 97520. Offers elementary education (MA Ed, MS Ed), including classroom teacher, early childhood, handicapped learner, reading, supervision; secondary education (MA Ed, MS Ed), including classroom teacher, handicapped learner, reading, supervision; teaching (MAT). Postbaccalaureate distance learning degree programs offered (minimal on-campus study). *Faculty:* 23 full-time (16 women), 21 part-time/adjunct (20 women). *Students:* 92 full-time (68 women), 118 part-time (88 women); includes 19 minority (1 Black or African American, non-Hispanic/Latino; 1 American Indian or Alaska Native, non-Hispanic/Latino; 2 Asian, non-Hispanic/Latino; 10 Hispanic/Latino; 5 Two or more races, non-Hispanic/Latino), 5 international. Average age 36. 22 applicants, 59% accepted, 12 enrolled. In 2013, 127 master's awarded. *Degree requirements:* For master's, thesis optional. *Entrance requirements:* For master's, GRE General Test, minimum cumulative GPA of 3.0 in the last 90 quarter credits (60 semester credits) of undergraduate coursework. Additional exam requirements/recommendations for international students: Required—TOEFL (minimum score 540 paper-based; 76 iBT), IELTS (minimum score 6), ELPT (minimum score 964) or ELS (minimum score 112). *Application deadline:* For fall admission, 7/31 priority date for domestic and international students; for winter admission, 11/15 priority date for domestic and international students; for spring admission, 1/7 priority date for domestic and international students. Applications are processed on a rolling basis. Application fee: $50. Electronic applications accepted. *Expenses:* Tuition, state resident: full-time $13,635; part-time $378.72 per credit hour. Tuition, nonresident: full-time $17,042; part-time $473.40 per credit hour. *Required fees:* $408 per quarter. *Financial support:* Research assistantships with partial tuition reimbursements, career-related internships or fieldwork, institutionally sponsored loans, scholarships/grants, and unspecified assistantships available. *Unit head:* Dr. Gerry McCain, Graduate Program Coordinator, 541-552-6934, E-mail: mccaing@sou.edu. *Application contact:* Kelly Moutsatson, Director of Admissions, 541-552-6411, Fax: 541-552-8403, E-mail: admissions@sou.edu.
Website: http://www.sou.edu/education/.

Southern University and Agricultural and Mechanical College, Graduate School and College of Education, Department of Special Education, Baton Rouge, LA 70813. Offers M Ed, PhD. *Accreditation:* NCATE. Part-time and evening/weekend programs available. *Degree requirements:* For master's, comprehensive exam, thesis optional; for doctorate, thesis/dissertation, comprehensive qualifying exam, oral defense of dissertation. *Entrance requirements:* For master's, GMAT or GRE General Test, PRAXIS; for doctorate, GRE General Test, PRAXIS, letters of recommendation, 2 years experience (individuals with disabilities). Additional exam requirements/recommendations for international students: Required—TOEFL. *Faculty research:* Classroom discipline/management, minority students in gifted/special education, learning styles/brain hemisphericity, school violence and prevention, certifications for special education teachers.

Southwestern College, Education Programs, Winfield, KS 67156-2499. Offers curriculum and instruction (M Ed); education (Ed D); special education (M Ed); teaching (MA). *Accreditation:* NCATE. Part-time and evening/weekend programs available. Postbaccalaureate distance learning degree programs offered (minimal on-campus study). *Faculty:* 5 full-time (4 women), 22 part-time/adjunct (17 women). *Students:* 9 full-time (7 women), 145 part-time (105 women); includes 22 minority (6 Black or African American, non-Hispanic/Latino; 1 American Indian or Alaska Native, non-Hispanic/Latino; 1 Asian, non-Hispanic/Latino; 8 Hispanic/Latino; 6 Two or more races, non-Hispanic/Latino), 4 international. Average age 39. 127 applicants, 79% accepted, 68 enrolled. In 2013, 96 master's awarded. Terminal master's awarded for partial completion of doctoral program. *Degree requirements:* For master's, practicum, portfolio; for doctorate, thesis/dissertation, professional portfolio. *Entrance requirements:* For master's, baccalaureate degree, minimum GPA of 2.5, valid teaching certificate (for special education); for doctorate, baccalaureate degree with minimum GPA of 3.25, current teaching experience, and GRE; or master's degree with minimum GPA of 3.5. Additional exam requirements/recommendations for international students: Required—TOEFL (minimum score 550 paper-based). *Application deadline:* For fall admission, 8/1 for domestic students; for spring admission, 12/1 for domestic students. Applications are processed on a rolling basis. Application fee: $0. Electronic applications accepted. *Expenses:* Contact institution. *Financial support:* In 2013–14, 4 students received support. Federal Work-Study, tuition waivers (partial), and unspecified assistantships available. Financial award application deadline: 4/1; financial award applicants required to submit FAFSA. *Unit head:* Dr. Cameron Carlson, Dean of Education, 800-846-1543 Ext. 6115, Fax: 620-229-6341, E-mail: cameron.carlson@sckans.edu. *Application contact:* Marla Sexson, Vice President for Enrollment Management, 620-229-6364, Fax: 620-229-6344, E-mail: marla.sexson@sckans.edu.
Website: http://www.sckans.edu/graduate/education-med/.

Southwestern Oklahoma State University, College of Professional and Graduate Studies, School of Behavioral Sciences and Education, Specialization in Special Education, Weatherford, OK 73096-3098. Offers M Ed. M Ed distance learning degree program offered to Oklahoma residents only. *Accreditation:* NCATE. Part-time and evening/weekend programs available. *Degree requirements:* For master's, exam. *Entrance requirements:* For master's, GRE General Test or minimum undergraduate GPA of 3.0. Additional exam requirements/recommendations for international students: Required—TOEFL.

Southwest Minnesota State University, Department of Education, Marshall, MN 56258. Offers ESL (MS); math (MS); reading (MS); special education (MS), including developmental disabilities, early childhood education, emotional behavioral disorders, learning disabilities; teaching, learning and leadership (MS). Part-time and evening/weekend programs available. Postbaccalaureate distance learning degree programs offered (no on-campus study). *Entrance requirements:* Additional exam requirements/recommendations for international students: Required—TOEFL or IELTS; Recommended—TOEFL (minimum score 550 paper-based; 80 iBT), IELTS.

Spalding University, Graduate Studies, College of Education, Programs in Education, Louisville, KY 40203-2188. Offers art teacher education (MAT); business teacher education (MAT); elementary school education (MAT); foreign language (MAT); general education (MA Ed); high school education (MAT); middle school education (MAT); school administration (MA Ed); secondary education (MAT); special education (learning and behavioral disorders) (MAT); student guidance counselor (MA); teacher education and professional development (MAT). *Accreditation:* NCATE. Part-time and evening/weekend programs available. *Faculty:* 12 full-time (11 women), 6 part-time/adjunct (4 women). *Students:* 92 full-time (63 women), 36 part-time (29 women); includes 43 minority (41 Black or African American, non-Hispanic/Latino; 2 Two or more races, non-Hispanic/Latino). Average age 35. 77 applicants, 48% accepted, 30 enrolled. In 2013, 81 master's awarded. *Degree requirements:* For master's, portfolio, final project, clinical experience. *Entrance requirements:* For master's, GRE General Test or MAT, interview, letters of recommendation, resume. Additional exam requirements/recommendations for international students: Required—TOEFL (minimum score 535 paper-based). *Application deadline:* Applications are processed on a rolling basis. Application fee: $30. Electronic applications accepted. *Expenses: Tuition:* Full-time $21,450. *Required fees:* $810. Tuition and fees vary according to course load, degree level, program and student level. *Financial support:* Scholarships/grants, traineeships, and unspecified assistantships available. Financial award application deadline: 3/30; financial award applicants required to submit FAFSA. *Faculty research:* Instructional technology, achievement gap, classroom management, assessment. *Unit head:* Dr. Beverly Keepers, Dean, 502-588-7121, Fax: 502-585-7123, E-mail: bkeepers@spalding.edu. *Application contact:* Bonnie Caughron, Administrative Assistant, College of Education, 502-873-4262, E-mail: bcaughron@spalding.edu.

Spring Arbor University, School of Education, Spring Arbor, MI 49283-9799. Offers education (MAE); reading (MAR); special education (MSE). *Accreditation:* Teacher Education Accreditation Council. Part-time and evening/weekend programs available. Postbaccalaureate distance learning degree programs offered (minimal on-campus study). *Faculty:* 6 full-time (5 women), 13 part-time/adjunct (8 women). *Students:* 49 full-time (44 women), 175 part-time (141 women); includes 13 minority (10 Black or African American, non-Hispanic/Latino; 1 Asian, non-Hispanic/Latino; 2 Hispanic/Latino). Average age 36. In 2013, 54 master's awarded. *Degree requirements:* For master's, thesis. *Entrance requirements:* For master's, official transcripts from all institutions attended, including evidence of an earned bachelor's degree from regionally-accredited college or university with minimum cumulative GPA of 3.0 for the last two years of the bachelor's degree; two professional letters of recommendation. Additional exam requirements/recommendations for international students: Required—TOEFL (minimum score 600 paper-based). *Application deadline:* For fall admission, 9/1 priority date for domestic students; for winter admission, 2/1 priority date for domestic students; for spring admission, 2/1 priority date for domestic students. Applications are processed on a rolling basis. Application fee: $40. Electronic applications accepted. *Financial support:* Applicants required to submit FAFSA. *Unit head:* Dr. Linda Sherrill, Dean, 517-750-1200 Ext. 1562, Fax: 517-750-6629, E-mail: lsherril@arbor.edu. *Application contact:* James R. Weidman, Coordinator of Graduate Recruitment, 517-750-6523, Fax: 517-750-6629, E-mail: jimw@arbor.edu.
Website: http://www.arbor.edu/academics/school-of-education/.

Springfield College, Graduate Programs, Program in Education, Springfield, MA 01109-3797. Offers counseling and secondary education (M Ed, MS); early childhood education (M Ed, MS); education (M Ed, MS); educational administration (M Ed, MS); educational studies (M Ed, MS); elementary education (M Ed, MS); secondary education (M Ed, MS); special education (M Ed, MS). Part-time and evening/weekend programs available. *Faculty:* 6 full-time. *Students:* 47 full-time. 45 applicants, 87% accepted, 35 enrolled. In 2013, 15 master's awarded. *Entrance requirements:* Additional exam requirements/recommendations for international students: Required—TOEFL (minimum score 550 paper-based); Recommended—IELTS (minimum score 6). *Application deadline:* For fall admission, 1/15 for domestic and international students; for winter admission, 11/1 for domestic and international students; for spring admission, 11/1 for domestic and international students. Applications are processed on a rolling basis. Application fee: $50. Electronic applications accepted. *Expenses: Tuition:* Full-time $13,620; part-time $908 per credit. *Financial support:* Fellowships with partial tuition reimbursements, teaching assistantships with partial tuition reimbursements, career-related internships or fieldwork, Federal Work-Study, institutionally sponsored loans, and unspecified assistantships available. Financial award application deadline: 3/1; financial award applicants required to submit FAFSA. *Unit head:* Jennifer Johnston, Program Coordinator, 413-748-3348, E-mail: jjohnston@springfieldcollege.edu. *Application contact:* Evelyn Cohen, Associate Director of Graduate Admissions, 413-748-3479, Fax: 413-748-3694, E-mail: ecohen@springfieldcollege.edu.

State University of New York at New Paltz, Graduate School, School of Education, Department of Educational Studies, Program in Special Education, New Paltz, NY 12561. Offers adolescence special education (7-12) (MS Ed); adolescence special education and literacy education (MS Ed); childhood special education (1-6) (MS Ed); childhood special education and literacy education (MS Ed); early childhood special education (B-2) (MS Ed). *Accreditation:* NCATE. Part-time and evening/weekend

programs available. *Faculty:* 6 full-time (4 women), 9 part-time/adjunct (all women). *Students:* 42 full-time (35 women), 35 part-time (24 women); includes 11 minority (1 Asian, non-Hispanic/Latino; 8 Hispanic/Latino; 2 Two or more races, non-Hispanic/Latino). Average age 27. 63 applicants, 73% accepted, 24 enrolled. In 2013, 43 master's awarded. *Degree requirements:* For master's, portfolio. *Entrance requirements:* For master's, minimum GPA of 3.0 (3.2 for special education and literacy programs), New York state teaching certificate. Additional exam requirements/recommendations for international students: Required—TOEFL (minimum score 550 paper-based; 80 iBT), IELTS (minimum score 6.5). *Application deadline:* For fall admission, 3/15 priority date for domestic students, 3/15 for international students; for spring admission, 11/1 for domestic and international students. Application fee: $50. Electronic applications accepted. *Expenses:* Tuition, state resident: full-time $9870; part-time $411 per credit. Tuition, nonresident: full-time $18,350; part-time $765 per credit. *Required fees:* $1213. Tuition and fees vary according to program. *Financial support:* Application deadline: 8/1. *Unit head:* Dr. Jane Sileo, Coordinator, 845-257-2835, E-mail: sileoj@newpaltz.edu. *Application contact:* Caroline Murphy, Graduate Admissions Advisor, 845-257-3285, E-mail: gradschool@newpaltz.edu.
Website: http://www.newpaltz.edu/edstudies/special_ed.html.

State University of New York at New Paltz, Graduate School, School of Education, Department of Elementary Education, New Paltz, NY 12561. Offers childhood education 1-6 (MS Ed, MST), including childhood education 1-6 (MST), early childhood B-2 (MS Ed), mathematics, science and technology (MS Ed), reading/literacy (MS Ed); literacy education 5-12 (MS Ed); literacy education and childhood special education (MS Ed); literacy education B-6 (MS Ed). *Accreditation:* NCATE. Part-time and evening/weekend programs available. *Faculty:* 11 full-time (10 women), 9 part-time/adjunct (8 women). *Students:* 51 full-time (47 women), 128 part-time (117 women); includes 13 minority (2 Black or African American, non-Hispanic/Latino; 11 Hispanic/Latino). Average age 27. 103 applicants, 89% accepted, 57 enrolled. In 2013, 96 master's awarded. *Degree requirements:* For master's, comprehensive exam (for some programs), portfolio. *Entrance requirements:* For master's, GRE or MAT (for MST), minimum GPA of 3.0 (3.2 for literacy and special education), New York state teaching certificate (for MS Ed). Additional exam requirements/recommendations for international students: Required—TOEFL (minimum score 550 paper-based; 80 iBT), IELTS (minimum score 6.5). *Application deadline:* For fall admission, 4/1 for domestic and international students; for spring admission, 11/15 for domestic and international students. Application fee: $50. Electronic applications accepted. *Expenses:* Tuition, state resident: full-time $9870; part-time $411 per credit. Tuition, nonresident: full-time $18,350; part-time $765 per credit. *Required fees:* $1213. Tuition and fees vary according to program. *Financial support:* Application deadline: 8/1. *Faculty research:* Multi-sensory teaching methods, volunteer tutoring programs for struggling readers, school readiness and transition, math/science/technology, university-school partnerships. *Unit head:* Dr. Andrea Noel, Chair, 845-257-2860, E-mail: noela@newpaltz.edu. *Application contact:* Caroline Murphy, Graduate Admissions Advisor, 845-257-3285, Fax: 845-257-3284, E-mail: gradschool@newpaltz.edu.
Website: http://www.newpaltz.edu/elementaryed/.

State University of New York at Oswego, Graduate Studies, School of Education, Department of Curriculum and Instruction, Oswego, NY 13126. Offers adolescence education (MST); art education (MAT); childhood education (MST); elementary education (MS Ed); literacy education (MS Ed); secondary education (MS Ed); special education (MS Ed). Part-time and evening/weekend programs available. *Degree requirements:* For master's, comprehensive exam (for some programs), thesis optional. *Entrance requirements:* For master's, GRE General Test, minimum GPA of 2.7, provisional teaching certificate. Additional exam requirements/recommendations for international students: Required—TOEFL (minimum score 560 paper-based). *Faculty research:* Classroom applications for microcomputers; classroom questioning, wait-time, and achievement; values clarification and academic achievement.

State University of New York at Plattsburgh, Division of Education, Health, and Human Services, Program in Teacher Education: Special Education, Plattsburgh, NY 12901-2681. Offers birth to grade 2 (MS Ed); birth to grade 6 (MS Ed); grades 1 to 6 (MS Ed); grades 7 to 12 (MS Ed). *Accreditation:* Teacher Education Accreditation Council. Part-time and evening/weekend programs available. *Students:* 56 full-time (44 women), 9 part-time (7 women); includes 1 minority (Hispanic/Latino), 1 international. Average age 25. *Entrance requirements:* For master's, minimum GPA of 2.75. Additional exam requirements/recommendations for international students: Required—TOEFL. *Application deadline:* For fall admission, 2/15 priority date for domestic students; for spring admission, 10/15 priority date for domestic students. Applications are processed on a rolling basis. Application fee: $75. *Financial support:* Federal Work-Study available. Support available to part-time students. Financial award application deadline: 4/15; financial award applicants required to submit FAFSA. *Faculty research:* Inclusion behavior management technology, applied behavior analysis. *Unit head:* Dr. Heidi Schnackenberg, Coordinator, 518-564-5143, E-mail: schnachl@plattsburgh.edu. *Application contact:* Betsy Kane, Director, Graduate Admissions, 518-564-4723, Fax: 518-564-4722, E-mail: bkane002@plattsburgh.edu.

State University of New York College at Cortland, Graduate Studies, School of Education, Programs in Teaching Students with Disabilities, Cortland, NY 13045. Offers MS Ed. *Accreditation:* NCATE. Part-time and evening/weekend programs available. *Degree requirements:* For master's, one foreign language, comprehensive exam, thesis (for some programs). *Entrance requirements:* For master's, provisional certification. Additional exam requirements/recommendations for international students: Required—TOEFL. *Expenses:* Tuition, state resident: full-time $9870; part-time $411 per credit hour. Tuition, nonresident: full-time $18,350; part-time $765 per credit hour. *Required fees:* $1458; $65 per credit hour.

State University of New York College at Oneonta, Graduate Education, Division of Education, Oneonta, NY 13820-4015. Offers educational psychology and counseling (MS Ed, CAS), including school counselor K-12; educational technology specialist (MS Ed); elementary education and reading (MS Ed), including childhood education, literacy education; secondary education (MS Ed), including adolescence education; special education (MS Ed), including adolescence, childhood. *Accreditation:* NCATE. Part-time and evening/weekend programs available. *Entrance requirements:* For master's, GRE General Test.

State University of New York College at Potsdam, School of Education and Professional Studies, Program in Special Education, Potsdam, NY 13676. Offers adolescence (grades 7-12) (MS Ed); childhood (grades 1-6) (MS Ed); early childhood (birth-grade 2) (MS Ed). *Accreditation:* NCATE. Part-time programs available. *Degree requirements:* For master's, culminating experience. *Entrance requirements:* For master's, minimum GPA of 3.0 in last 60 hours of course work. Additional exam requirements/recommendations for international students: Required—TOEFL (minimum score 550 paper-based; 80 iBT), IELTS (minimum score 6). Electronic applications accepted.

Stephen F. Austin State University, Graduate School, College of Education, Department of Human Services, Nacogdoches, TX 75962. Offers counseling (MA); school psychology (MA); special education (M Ed); speech pathology (MS). *Accreditation:* ACA (one or more programs are accredited); ASHA (one or more programs are accredited); CORE; NCATE. *Degree requirements:* For master's, comprehensive exam, thesis (for some programs). *Entrance requirements:* For master's, GRE General Test, minimum GPA of 2.8. Additional exam requirements/recommendations for international students: Required—TOEFL.

Syracuse University, School of Education, Program in Early Childhood Special Education, Syracuse, NY 13244. Offers MS. Part-time programs available. *Students:* 19 full-time (18 women), 6 part-time (all women); includes 6 minority (2 Black or African American, non-Hispanic/Latino; 1 American Indian or Alaska Native, non-Hispanic/Latino; 1 Asian, non-Hispanic/Latino; 1 Hispanic/Latino; 1 Two or more races, non-Hispanic/Latino). Average age 29. 17 applicants, 65% accepted, 4 enrolled. In 2013, 13 master's awarded. *Entrance requirements:* For master's, interview. Additional exam requirements/recommendations for international students: Required—TOEFL (minimum score 100 iBT). *Application deadline:* For fall admission, 1/15 for domestic students, 1/15 priority date for international students; for spring admission, 10/15 priority date for domestic and international students. Applications are processed on a rolling basis. Application fee: $75. Electronic applications accepted. *Financial support:* Fellowships with full tuition reimbursements and teaching assistantships with full and partial tuition reimbursements available. Financial award application deadline: 1/1; financial award applicants required to submit FAFSA. *Unit head:* Dr. Gail Ensher, Director, 315-443-9650. *Application contact:* Laurie Deyo, Graduate Recruiter, School of Education, 315-443-2505, E-mail: e-gradrcrt@syr.edu.
Website: http://soeweb.syr.edu/.

Syracuse University, School of Education, Program in Inclusive Special Education 7-12 (Generalist), Syracuse, NY 13244. Offers MS. Part-time programs available. *Students:* 4 full-time (3 women); includes 1 minority (Hispanic/Latino). Average age 29. 7 applicants, 86% accepted. In 2013, 4 master's awarded. *Degree requirements:* For master's, thesis or alternative. *Entrance requirements:* For master's, certification or eligibility for certification in content area at secondary level (math, social studies, science, English or Spanish). Additional exam requirements/recommendations for international students: Required—TOEFL (minimum score 100 iBT). *Application deadline:* For fall admission, 1/15 priority date for domestic and international students; for spring admission, 10/15 priority date for domestic and international students. Applications are processed on a rolling basis. Application fee: $75. Electronic applications accepted. *Financial support:* Fellowships with full tuition reimbursements and teaching assistantships with full and partial tuition reimbursements available. Financial award application deadline: 1/1; financial award applicants required to submit FAFSA. *Unit head:* Dr. Christine Ashby, 315-443-8689, E-mail: ceashby@syr.edu. *Application contact:* Laurie Deyo, Graduate Recruiter, School of Education, 315-443-2505, E-mail: e-gradrcrt@syr.edu.
Website: http://soe.syr.edu/academic/teaching_and_leadership/graduate/masters/inclusive_special_education_grades_7_12/default.aspx.

Syracuse University, School of Education, Program in Inclusive Special Education (Grades 1-6), Syracuse, NY 13244. Offers MS. Part-time programs available. *Students:* 7 full-time (all women); includes 2 minority (1 Black or African American, non-Hispanic/Latino; 1 Two or more races, non-Hispanic/Latino). Average age 27. 7 applicants, 71% accepted, 4 enrolled. In 2013, 3 master's awarded. *Degree requirements:* For master's, thesis or alternative. *Entrance requirements:* For master's, provisional/initial certification. Additional exam requirements/recommendations for international students: Required—TOEFL (minimum score 100 iBT). *Application deadline:* For fall admission, 1/15 priority date for domestic and international students; for spring admission, 10/15 priority date for domestic and international students. Applications are processed on a rolling basis. Application fee: $75. Electronic applications accepted. *Financial support:* Fellowships with full tuition reimbursements and teaching assistantships with full and partial tuition reimbursements available. Financial award application deadline: 1/1; financial award applicants required to submit FAFSA. *Unit head:* Dr. Christine Ashby, Assistant Professor, 315-443-8689, E-mail: ceashby@syr.edu. *Application contact:* Laurie Deyo, Graduate Recruiter, School of Education, 315-443-2505, E-mail: e-gradrcrt@syr.edu.
Website: http://soeweb.syr.edu/.

Syracuse University, School of Education, Program in Inclusive Special Education: Severe/Multiple Disabilities, Syracuse, NY 13244. Offers MS. Part-time programs available. *Students:* 3 full-time (all women), 4 part-time (2 women); includes 1 minority (Asian, non-Hispanic/Latino). Average age 28. 5 applicants, 100% accepted, 3 enrolled. In 2013, 5 master's awarded. *Entrance requirements:* For master's, New York state initial certification in students with disabilities (Birth-2, 1-6, 5-9, or 7-12), interview. Additional exam requirements/recommendations for international students: Required—TOEFL (minimum score 100 iBT). *Application deadline:* For fall admission, 1/15 priority date for domestic and international students; for spring admission, 10/15 priority date for domestic and international students. Applications are processed on a rolling basis. Application fee: $75. Electronic applications accepted. *Financial support:* Fellowships with full tuition reimbursements and teaching assistantships with full and partial tuition reimbursements available. Financial award application deadline: 1/1. *Unit head:* Dr. Gail Ensher, Program Coordinator, 315-443-9650, E-mail: glensher@syr.edu. *Application contact:* Laurie Deyo, Graduate Recruiter, School of Education, 315-443-2505, E-mail: e-gradrcrt@syr.edu.
Website: http://soeweb.syr.edu/.

Syracuse University, School of Education, Program in Special Education, Syracuse, NY 13244. Offers PhD. Part-time programs available. *Students:* 17 full-time (15 women), 4 part-time (all women); includes 4 minority (1 Black or African American, non-Hispanic/Latino; 1 American Indian or Alaska Native, non-Hispanic/Latino; 1 Hispanic/Latino; 1 Native Hawaiian or other Pacific Islander, non-Hispanic/Latino), 5 international. Average age 36. 16 applicants, 38% accepted, 5 enrolled. In 2013, 3 doctorates awarded. *Degree requirements:* For doctorate, comprehensive exam, thesis/dissertation. *Entrance requirements:* For doctorate, GRE General Test, master's degree, interview, writing sample, disability experience (preferred). Additional exam requirements/recommendations for international students: Required—TOEFL (minimum score 100 iBT). *Application deadline:* For fall admission, 1/15 priority date for domestic and international students; for spring admission, 10/15 for domestic and international students. Applications are processed on a rolling basis. Application fee: $75. Electronic applications accepted. *Financial support:* Fellowships with full tuition reimbursements, research assistantships with full and partial tuition reimbursements, teaching assistantships with full and partial tuition reimbursements, and institutionally sponsored loans available. Financial award application deadline: 1/1. *Faculty research:* Aggression, inclusive education, autistic children, validation of social skills, cooperative learning in the heterogeneous classroom. *Unit head:* Dr. Beth Ferri, Program Director, 315-443-1269. *Application contact:* Laurie Deyo, Graduate Recruiter, School of Education, 315-443-2505, E-mail: e-gradrcrt@syr.edu.
Website: http://soeweb.syr.edu/.

Tarleton State University, College of Graduate Studies, College of Education, Department of Psychology and Counseling, Stephenville, TX 76402. Offers counseling and psychology (M Ed), including counseling, counseling psychology, educational psychology; educational administration (M Ed); secondary education (Certificate); special education (Certificate). Part-time and evening/weekend programs available. Postbaccalaureate distance learning degree programs offered (minimal on-campus

study). *Faculty:* 8 full-time (6 women), 14 part-time/adjunct (7 women). *Students:* 60 full-time (48 women), 183 part-time (157 women); includes 63 minority (21 Black or African American, non-Hispanic/Latino; 3 Asian, non-Hispanic/Latino; 30 Hispanic/Latino; 9 Two or more races, non-Hispanic/Latino). Average age 34. 78 applicants, 81% accepted, 47 enrolled. In 2013, 76 master's awarded. *Degree requirements:* For master's, comprehensive exam, thesis optional. *Entrance requirements:* For master's, GRE General Test, minimum GPA of 3.0. Additional exam requirements/recommendations for international students: Required—TOEFL (minimum score 550 paper-based; 80 iBT). *Application deadline:* For fall admission, 8/15 priority date for domestic students; for spring admission, 1/7 for domestic students. Applications are processed on a rolling basis. Application fee: $30 ($130 for international students). Electronic applications accepted. *Expenses:* Tuition, state resident: full-time $3312; part-time $184 per credit hour. Tuition, nonresident: full-time $9144; part-time $508 per credit hour. *Required fees:* $1916. Tuition and fees vary according to course load and campus/location. *Financial support:* Research assistantships, teaching assistantships, career-related internships or fieldwork, Federal Work-Study, institutionally sponsored loans, and tuition waivers (partial) available. Support available to part-time students. Financial award application deadline: 5/1; financial award applicants required to submit FAFSA. *Unit head:* Dr. Bob Newby, Department Head, 254-968-9813, Fax: 254-968-1991, E-mail: newby@tarleton.edu. *Application contact:* Information Contact, 254-968-9104, Fax: 254-968-9670, E-mail: gradoffice@tarleton.edu.
Website: http://www.tarleton.edu/COEWEB/pc/.

Teachers College, Columbia University, Graduate Faculty of Education, Department of Curriculum and Teaching, Program in Dual Certificate Childhood/Disabilities, New York, NY 10027-6696. Offers Certificate. *Students:* 7 full-time (4 women); includes 3 minority (all Asian, non-Hispanic/Latino). Average age 28. Application fee: $65. *Unit head:* Prof. Britt Hamre, Chair, 212-678-3695. *Application contact:* Elizabeth Puleio, Assistant Director of Admission, 212-678-3710, Fax: 212-678-4171, E-mail: tcinfo@tc.edu.

Teachers College, Columbia University, Graduate Faculty of Education, Department of Curriculum and Teaching, Program in Early Childhood Special Education, New York, NY 10027-6696. Offers Ed M, MA. *Accreditation:* NCATE. *Faculty:* 6 full-time, 3 part-time/adjunct. *Students:* 22 full-time (21 women), 51 part-time (49 women); includes 30 minority (3 Black or African American, non-Hispanic/Latino; 9 Asian, non-Hispanic/Latino; 10 Hispanic/Latino; 8 Two or more races, non-Hispanic/Latino), 6 international. Average age 26. 112 applicants, 66% accepted, 30 enrolled. In 2013, 34 master's awarded. *Degree requirements:* For master's, culminating project. *Application deadline:* For fall admission, 1/15 priority date for domestic students. Application fee: $65. Electronic applications accepted. *Financial support:* Research assistantships, teaching assistantships, career-related internships or fieldwork, Federal Work-Study, institutionally sponsored loans, and tuition waivers (full and partial) available. Support available to part-time students. Financial award application deadline: 2/1; financial award applicants required to submit FAFSA. *Faculty research:* Curriculum development, infants, urban education, visually-impaired infants. *Unit head:* Prof. Mariana Souto-Manning, Program Coordinator, 212-678-3970, E-mail: ms3983@columbia.edu. *Application contact:* Peter Shon, Assistant Director of Admission, 212-678-3305, Fax: 212-678-4171, E-mail: shon@exchange.tc.columbia.edu.

Teachers College, Columbia University, Graduate Faculty of Education, Department of Curriculum and Teaching, Program in Learning Disabilities, New York, NY 10027-6696. Offers Ed M, MA, Ed D. *Accreditation:* NCATE. *Students:* 11 full-time (8 women), 1 part-time (0 women); includes 7 minority (4 Black or African American, non-Hispanic/Latino; 1 Asian, non-Hispanic/Latino; 1 Hispanic/Latino; 1 Two or more races, non-Hispanic/Latino). Average age 38. *Degree requirements:* For doctorate, thesis/dissertation. *Entrance requirements:* For doctorate, GRE General Test or MAT. *Application deadline:* For fall admission, 5/15 for domestic students; for spring admission, 12/1 for domestic students. Application fee: $75. *Financial support:* Fellowships, teaching assistantships, career-related internships or fieldwork, Federal Work-Study, institutionally sponsored loans, and tuition waivers (full and partial) available. Support available to part-time students. Financial award application deadline: 2/1. *Faculty research:* Reading and mathematics disorders in students with learning disabilities, special education curriculum development. *Unit head:* Prof. Marjorie Siegel, Chair, 212-678-3765. *Application contact:* Peter Shon, Assistant Director of Admission, 212-678-3305, Fax: 212-678-4171, E-mail: shon@exchange.tc.columbia.edu.

Teachers College, Columbia University, Graduate Faculty of Education, Department of Health and Behavioral Studies, Program in Blind and Visual Impairment, New York, NY 10027-6696. Offers MA, Ed D. *Faculty:* 7 full-time, 13 part-time/adjunct. *Students:* 5 part-time (all women); includes 3 minority (1 Black or African American, non-Hispanic/Latino; 2 Hispanic/Latino). Average age 33. In 2013, 1 master's awarded. *Degree requirements:* For master's, comprehensive exam, integrative project; for doctorate, comprehensive exam, thesis/dissertation. *Entrance requirements:* For doctorate, writing sample. *Application deadline:* For fall admission, 1/15 priority date for domestic students; for spring admission, 11/1 for domestic students. Applications are processed on a rolling basis. Application fee: $65. Electronic applications accepted. *Financial support:* Career-related internships or fieldwork, Federal Work-Study, institutionally sponsored loans, and tuition waivers (full and partial) available. Support available to part-time students. Financial award application deadline: 2/1; financial award applicants required to submit FAFSA. *Faculty research:* Cross-modality transfer, issues in early childhood. *Unit head:* Prof. Peg Cummings, Program Coordinator, 212-678-3880, E-mail: cummins@tc.edu. *Application contact:* Elizabeth Puleio, Assistant Director of Admission, 212-678-3730, E-mail: eap2136@tc.columbia.edu.

Teachers College, Columbia University, Graduate Faculty of Education, Department of Health and Behavioral Studies, Program in Hearing Impairment, New York, NY 10027-6696. Offers MA, Ed D. *Faculty:* 7 full-time, 13 part-time/adjunct. *Students:* 11 full-time (all women), 12 part-time (11 women); includes 9 minority (3 Black or African American, non-Hispanic/Latino; 2 Asian, non-Hispanic/Latino; 2 Hispanic/Latino; 2 Two or more races, non-Hispanic/Latino), 1 international. Average age 25. 16 applicants, 81% accepted, 7 enrolled. In 2013, 26 master's awarded. *Degree requirements:* For master's, comprehensive exam (for some programs), project; for doctorate, thesis/dissertation. *Application deadline:* For fall admission, 1/15 priority date for domestic students; for spring admission, 11/1 for domestic students. Applications are processed on a rolling basis. Application fee: $65. Electronic applications accepted. *Financial support:* Fellowships, career-related internships or fieldwork, Federal Work-Study, institutionally sponsored loans, and tuition waivers (full and partial) available. Support available to part-time students. Financial award application deadline: 2/1; financial award applicants required to submit FAFSA. *Faculty research:* Language development, reading/writing, cognitive abilities, text analysis, auditory streaming. *Unit head:* Prof. Robert Kretschmer, Program Coordinator, 212-678-3867, E-mail: kretschmer@tc.edu. *Application contact:* Elizabeth Puleio, Assistant Director of Admission, 212-678-3710, Fax: 212-678-4171, E-mail: tcinfo@tc.edu.

Teachers College, Columbia University, Graduate Faculty of Education, Department of Health and Behavioral Studies, Program in Mental Retardation, New York, NY 10027. Offers MA, Ed D, PhD. Part-time programs available. *Faculty:* 7 full-time, 13 part-time/adjunct. *Students:* 22 full-time (20 women), 45 part-time (38 women); includes 10 minority (2 Black or African American, non-Hispanic/Latino; 4 Asian, non-Hispanic/Latino; 2 Hispanic/Latino; 2 Two or more races, non-Hispanic/Latino), 4 international. Average age 26. 65 applicants, 60% accepted, 22 enrolled. In 2013, 25 master's, 3 doctorates awarded. Terminal master's awarded for partial completion of doctoral program. *Degree requirements:* For master's, comprehensive exam, integrative project, student portfolio; for doctorate, comprehensive exam, thesis/dissertation, certification project. *Entrance requirements:* For master's, minimum GPA of 3.0; for doctorate, 2-3 years of successful teaching experience in special education, writing sample. Additional exam requirements/recommendations for international students: Required—TOEFL (minimum score 600 paper-based). *Application deadline:* For fall admission, 1/2 priority date for domestic students; for spring admission, 11/1 for domestic students. Applications are processed on a rolling basis. Application fee: $65. Electronic applications accepted. *Financial support:* Fellowships, research assistantships, teaching assistantships, career-related internships or fieldwork, Federal Work-Study, institutionally sponsored loans, and tuition waivers (full and partial) available. Support available to part-time students. Financial award application deadline: 2/1. *Faculty research:* Information processing, memory comprehension and problem-solving issues related to mental retardation, transition issues, cognition and comprehension. *Unit head:* Prof. Hsu-Min Chiang, Program Coordinator, 212-678-8346, E-mail: hchiang@tc.columbia.edu. *Application contact:* Peter Shon, Assistant Director of Admission, 212-678-3305, Fax: 212-678-4171, E-mail: shon@exchange.tc.columbia.edu.
Website: http://www.tc.columbia.edu/hbs/SpecialEd/.

Teachers College, Columbia University, Graduate Faculty of Education, Department of Health and Behavioral Studies, Program in Physical Disabilities, New York, NY 10027-6696. Offers Ed D, PhD. Part-time and evening/weekend programs available. *Faculty:* 7 full-time, 13 part-time/adjunct. *Students:* 3 part-time (all women); includes 1 minority (Asian, non-Hispanic/Latino). Average age 39. In 2013, 3 doctorates awarded. *Degree requirements:* For doctorate, comprehensive exam, thesis/dissertation. *Entrance requirements:* For doctorate, GRE General Test or MAT. Additional exam requirements/recommendations for international students: Required—TOEFL. *Application deadline:* For fall admission, 12/15 priority date for domestic students; for spring admission, 11/1 for domestic students. Applications are processed on a rolling basis. Application fee: $65. Electronic applications accepted. *Financial support:* Fellowships, teaching assistantships, career-related internships or fieldwork, Federal Work-Study, institutionally sponsored loans, and tuition waivers (full and partial) available. Support available to part-time students. Financial award application deadline: 2/1; financial award applicants required to submit FAFSA. *Faculty research:* Students with traumatic brain injury, health impairments, learning disabilities. *Unit head:* Prof. Robert Krestchner, Program Coordinator, 212-678-3867, E-mail: kretschmer@tc.edu. *Application contact:* Elizabeth Puleio, Assistant Director of Admission, 212-678-3710, Fax: 212-678-4171, E-mail: tcinfo@tc.edu.

Teachers College, Columbia University, Graduate Faculty of Education, Department of Health and Behavioral Studies, Program in Severe or Multiple Disabilities, New York, NY 10027-6696. Offers MA. *Faculty:* 7 full-time, 13 part-time/adjunct. *Students:* 5 full-time (all women), 4 part-time (all women); includes 3 minority (all Asian, non-Hispanic/Latino). Average age 25. 12 applicants, 92% accepted, 6 enrolled. In 2013, 7 master's awarded. *Degree requirements:* For master's, integrative project. *Entrance requirements:* For master's, minimum GPA of 3.0, evidence of New York State initial teacher certification in one of the required areas. *Application deadline:* For fall admission, 1/15 priority date for domestic students; for spring admission, 11/1 for domestic students. Applications are processed on a rolling basis. Application fee: $65. Electronic applications accepted. *Financial support:* Career-related internships or fieldwork, Federal Work-Study, institutionally sponsored loans, and tuition waivers (partial) available. Support available to part-time students. Financial award application deadline: 2/1; financial award applicants required to submit FAFSA. *Faculty research:* Reading and spelling disorders, workplace literacy, reading and writing among children and adults. *Unit head:* Prof. Hsu-Min Chiang, Program Coordinator, 212-678-8346, E-mail: chiang@tc.edu. *Application contact:* Peter Shon, Assistant Director of Admission, 212-678-3305, Fax: 212-678-4171, E-mail: shon@exchange.tc.columbia.edu.
Website: http://www.tc.edu/hbs/specialed/.

Teachers College, Columbia University, Graduate Faculty of Education, Department of Health and Behavioral Studies, Program in Special Education, New York, NY 10027. Offers Ed M, MA, Ed D. *Accreditation:* NCATE. Part-time and evening/weekend programs available. *Faculty:* 7 full-time, 13 part-time/adjunct. *Students:* 3 full-time (all women), 3 part-time (all women); includes 1 minority (Hispanic/Latino), 4 international. Average age 29. 4 applicants, 75% accepted, 3 enrolled. In 2013, 6 master's, 2 doctorates awarded. Terminal master's awarded for partial completion of doctoral program. *Degree requirements:* For doctorate, thesis/dissertation. *Entrance requirements:* For doctorate, writing sample. *Application deadline:* For fall admission, 1/2 for domestic students. Application fee: $65. Electronic applications accepted. *Financial support:* Career-related internships or fieldwork, Federal Work-Study, institutionally sponsored loans, and tuition waivers (full and partial) available. Support available to part-time students. Financial award application deadline: 2/1; financial award applicants required to submit FAFSA. *Faculty research:* Communication skills, academic skills (reading and math), behavior problems, cultural differences, transition support services and teacher preparation for individuals with autism; education of children, adolescents and adults with intellectual disabilities and autism; cognitive, motivational, and emotional aspects of decision-making; prevention of abuse and victimization. *Unit head:* Dr. Douglas Greer, Program Coordinator, 212-678-3880, E-mail: rdg13@columbia.edu. *Application contact:* Peter Shon, Assistant Director of Admission, 212-678-3305, Fax: 212-678-4171, E-mail: shon@exchange.tc.columbia.edu.
Website: http://www.tc.edu/hbs/specialed/.

Teachers College, Columbia University, Graduate Faculty of Education, Department of Health and Behavioral Studies, Program in Teaching of Sign Language, New York, NY 10027-6696. Offers MA. *Accreditation:* NCATE. *Faculty:* 7 full-time, 13 part-time/adjunct. *Students:* 5 part-time (4 women); includes 2 minority (both Hispanic/Latino). Average age 27. 1 applicant. In 2013, 3 master's awarded. *Degree requirements:* For master's, comprehensive exam, project. *Entrance requirements:* For master's, demonstrated proficiency in American Sign Language. *Application deadline:* For fall admission, 1/15 for domestic students; for spring admission, 11/1 for domestic students. Application fee: $65. *Financial support:* Applicants required to submit FAFSA. *Faculty research:* Teaching of the deaf and hard of hearing; linguistics of English and American Sign Language (ASL); literacy development; text structure; school psychology; auditory streaming; sociology, anthropology, and history of deaf community and culture; American Sign Language; second language acquisition, curriculum, and instruction; disability studies. *Unit head:* Prof. Russell S. Rosen, Program Coordinator, 212-678-3880, E-mail: rrosen@tc.edu. *Application contact:* Elizabeth Puleio, Assistant Director of Admission, 212-678-3710, Fax: 212-678-4171, E-mail: eap2136@tc.columbia.edu.
Website: http://www.tc.columbia.edu/hbs/ASL/index.asp.

Temple University, College of Education, Department of Psychological Studies in Education, Program in Special Education, Philadelphia, PA 19122-6096. Offers applied

behavioral analysis (MS Ed); applied behavioral analysis/autism spectrum disorders (Ed M); mild disabilities (Ed M); severe disabilities (Ed M); special education (PhD).

Tennessee State University, The School of Graduate Studies and Research, College of Education, Department of Teaching and Learning, Nashville, TN 37209-1561. Offers curriculum and instruction (M Ed, Ed D); elementary education (M Ed); special education (M Ed). *Accreditation:* NCATE. *Degree requirements:* For doctorate, thesis/dissertation. *Entrance requirements:* For master's, GRE General Test, GRE Subject Test, or MAT, minimum GPA of 2.5; for doctorate, GRE General Test, GRE Subject Test, or MAT, minimum GPA of 3.25. Electronic applications accepted. *Faculty research:* Multicultural education, teacher education reform, whole language, interactive video teaching, English as a second language.

Tennessee Technological University, College of Graduate Studies, College of Education, Department of Curriculum and Instruction, Program in Special Education, Cookeville, TN 38505. Offers MA, Ed S. *Accreditation:* NCATE. Part-time programs available. *Faculty:* 6 full-time (3 women). *Students:* 11 full-time (all women), 20 part-time (16 women); includes 2 minority (both Black or African American, non-Hispanic/Latino), 2 international. Average age 27. 17 applicants, 76% accepted, 6 enrolled. In 2013, 8 master's awarded. *Degree requirements:* For master's and Ed S, comprehensive exam, thesis or alternative. *Entrance requirements:* For master's and Ed S, MAT or GRE. Additional exam requirements/recommendations for international students: Required—TOEFL (minimum score 527 paper-based; 71 iBT), IELTS (minimum score 5.5), PTE (minimum score 48), or TOEIC (Test of English as an International Communication). *Application deadline:* For fall admission, 8/1 for domestic students, 5/1 for international students; for spring admission, 12/1 for domestic students, 10/1 for international students. Applications are processed on a rolling basis. Application fee: $35 ($40 for international students). Electronic applications accepted. *Expenses:* Tuition, state resident: full-time $9347; part-time $465 per credit hour. Tuition, nonresident: full-time $23,635; part-time $1152 per credit hour. *Financial support:* In 2013–14, fellowships (averaging $8,000 per year), research assistantships (averaging $5,000 per year), 2 teaching assistantships (averaging $4,000 per year) were awarded; career-related internships or fieldwork also available. Financial award application deadline: 4/1. *Unit head:* Dr. Jeremy Wendt, Interim Chairperson, 931-372-3181, Fax: 931-372-6270, E-mail: jwendt@tntech.edu. *Application contact:* Shelia K. Kendrick, Coordinator of Graduate Studies, 931-372-3808, Fax: 931-372-3497, E-mail: skendrick@tntech.edu.

Texas A&M International University, Office of Graduate Studies and Research, College of Education, Department of Professional Programs, Laredo, TX 78041-1900. Offers educational administration (MS Ed); generic special education (MS Ed); school counseling (MS). *Faculty:* 7 full-time (4 women), 4 part-time/adjunct (2 women). *Students:* 19 full-time (18 women), 137 part-time (104 women); includes 150 minority (2 Black or African American, non-Hispanic/Latino; 148 Hispanic/Latino), 1 international. Average age 33. 61 applicants, 75% accepted, 42 enrolled. In 2013, 87 master's awarded. *Entrance requirements:* Additional exam requirements/recommendations for international students: Required—TOEFL (minimum score 550 paper-based; 79 iBT). *Application deadline:* For fall admission, 4/30 priority date for domestic students, 4/30 for international students; for spring admission, 11/30 priority date for domestic students, 10/1 for international students. Application fee: $35 ($50 for international students). *Expenses:* Tuition, state resident: full-time $5184. *International tuition:* $11,556 full-time. *Financial support:* In 2013–14, 5 students received support, including 1 teaching assistantship; fellowships, research assistantships, Federal Work-Study, scholarships/grants, and unspecified assistantships also available. Financial award application deadline: 4/1. *Unit head:* Dr. Randel Brown, Chair, 956-326-2679, E-mail: brown@tamiu.edu. *Application contact:* Suzanne H. Alford, Director of Admissions, 956-326-3023, E-mail: graduateschool@tamiu.edu.
Website: http://www.tamiu.edu/coedu/DOPPPrograms.shtml.

Texas A&M University, College of Education and Human Development, Department of Educational Psychology, College Station, TX 77843. Offers bilingual education (M Ed, MS); counseling psychology (PhD); educational psychology (M Ed, MS, PhD); educational technology (M Ed); school psychology (PhD); special education (M Ed, MS). *Accreditation:* APA (one or more programs are accredited). Part-time and evening/weekend programs available. Postbaccalaureate distance learning degree programs offered (no on-campus study). *Faculty:* 41. *Students:* 148 full-time (122 women), 143 part-time (124 women); includes 97 minority (15 Black or African American, non-Hispanic/Latino; 11 Asian, non-Hispanic/Latino; 66 Hispanic/Latino; 5 Two or more races, non-Hispanic/Latino), 49 international. Average age 31. 249 applicants, 52% accepted, 83 enrolled. In 2013, 43 master's, 22 doctorates awarded. *Degree requirements:* For master's, thesis optional; for doctorate, thesis/dissertation. *Entrance requirements:* For master's and doctorate, GRE General Test. Additional exam requirements/recommendations for international students: Required—TOEFL. Application fee: $50 ($75 for international students). Electronic applications accepted. *Expenses:* Tuition, state resident: full-time $4078; part-time $226.55 per credit hour. Tuition, nonresident: full-time $10,450; part-time $580.55 per credit hour. *Required fees:* $2328; $278.50 per credit hour. $642.45 per semester. *Financial support:* In 2013–14, fellowships (averaging $12,000 per year), research assistantships (averaging $9,000 per year), teaching assistantships (averaging $9,000 per year) were awarded; career-related internships or fieldwork, institutionally sponsored loans, scholarships/grants, and unspecified assistantships also available. Financial award applicants required to submit FAFSA. *Unit head:* Dr. Cathy Watson, Head, 979-845-1394, E-mail: cwatson@tamu.edu. *Application contact:* Christy Porter, Senior Academic Advisor, 979-845-1874, E-mail: csporter@tamu.edu.
Website: http://epsy.tamu.edu.

Texas A&M University–Commerce, Graduate School, College of Education and Human Services, Department of Psychology and Special Education, Commerce, TX 75429-3011. Offers cognition and instruction (PhD); psychology (MA, MS); special education (M Ed, MA, MS). Part-time programs available. Terminal master's awarded for partial completion of doctoral program. *Degree requirements:* For master's, comprehensive exam, thesis (for some programs); for doctorate, thesis/dissertation, departmental qualifying exam. *Entrance requirements:* For master's, GRE General Test; for doctorate, GRE General Test, 3 letters of recommendation. Electronic applications accepted. *Expenses:* Tuition, state resident: full-time $3630; part-time $2420 per year. Tuition, nonresident: full-time $9948; part-time $6632.16 per year. *Required fees:* $1006 per year. Tuition and fees vary according to course load. *Faculty research:* Human learning, study skills, multicultural bilingual, diversity and special education, educationally handicapped.

Texas A&M University–Corpus Christi, Graduate Studies and Research, College of Education, Program in Special Education, Corpus Christi, TX 78412-5503. Offers MS. Part-time and evening/weekend programs available. *Degree requirements:* For master's, comprehensive exam, thesis (for some programs). *Entrance requirements:* For master's, GRE General Test. Additional exam requirements/recommendations for international students: Required—TOEFL. Electronic applications accepted.

Texas A&M University–Kingsville, College of Graduate Studies, College of Education, Department of Education, Program in Special Education, Kingsville, TX 78363. Offers M Ed. Part-time and evening/weekend programs available. *Faculty:* 9 full-time (5 women), 4 part-time/adjunct (2 women). *Students:* 4 full-time (all women), 3 part-time (2 women); includes 6 minority (all Hispanic/Latino). Average age 34. 5 applicants, 100% accepted, 4 enrolled. In 2013, 5 master's awarded. *Degree requirements:* For master's, comprehensive exam, mini-thesis. *Entrance requirements:* For master's, GRE General Test, MAT, minimum GPA of 3.0. *Application deadline:* For fall admission, 6/1 for domestic students; for spring admission, 11/15 for domestic students. Applications are processed on a rolling basis. Application fee: $35 ($50 for international students). *Financial support:* Federal Work-Study and institutionally sponsored loans available. Financial award application deadline: 5/15. *Faculty research:* Training for trainers of the disabled. *Unit head:* Dr. Grace Hopkins, Director, 361-593-2843, E-mail: g-hopkins1@tamuk.edu. *Application contact:* Dr. Alberto M. Olivares, Dean, College of Graduate Studies, 361-593-2808, Fax: 361-593-3412, E-mail: a-olivares@tamuk.edu.

Texas A&M University–San Antonio, Department of Curriculum and Kinesiology, San Antonio, TX 78224. Offers bilingual education (MA); early childhood education (M Ed); kinesiology (MS); reading (MS); special education (M Ed), including educational diagnostician, instructional specialist. Part-time and evening/weekend programs available. *Degree requirements:* For master's, comprehensive exam, thesis or alternative. *Entrance requirements:* For master's, MAT. Additional exam requirements/recommendations for international students: Required—TOEFL (minimum score 550 paper-based; 80 iBT), IELTS (minimum score 6). Electronic applications accepted.

Texas A&M University–Texarkana, Graduate Studies and Research, College of Education and Liberal Arts, Texarkana, TX 75505-5518. Offers adult education (MS); curriculum and instruction (M Ed); education (MS); educational administration (M Ed); English (MA); instructional technology (MS); interdisciplinary studies (MA, MS); special education (MS). Part-time and evening/weekend programs available. *Degree requirements:* For master's, comprehensive exam (for some programs), thesis optional. *Entrance requirements:* For master's, minimum GPA of 2.5 on last 60 hours of bachelor's degree. Additional exam requirements/recommendations for international students: Required—TOEFL. Electronic applications accepted.

Texas Christian University, College of Education, Program in Special Education, Fort Worth, TX 76129-0002. Offers M Ed. Part-time and evening/weekend programs available. *Students:* 3 full-time (all women), 1 (woman) part-time. 3 applicants, 33% accepted, 1 enrolled. In 2013, 2 master's awarded. *Degree requirements:* For master's, oral exam. *Entrance requirements:* Additional exam requirements/recommendations for international students: Required—TOEFL (minimum score 550 paper-based; 80 iBT). *Application deadline:* For fall admission, 11/16 for domestic and international students; for spring admission, 3/1 for domestic and international students. Application fee: $60. Electronic applications accepted. *Expenses: Tuition:* Part-time $1270 per credit hour. Tuition and fees vary according to course load and program. *Financial support:* Teaching assistantships with full tuition reimbursements, career-related internships or fieldwork, scholarships/grants, and unspecified assistantships available. Financial award application deadline: 3/1; financial award applicants required to submit FAFSA. *Unit head:* Dr. Jan Lacina, Associate Dean, 817-257-6786, E-mail: j.lacina@tcu.edu. *Application contact:* Lori Kimball, Administrative Program Specialist, 817-257-7661, E-mail: l.kimball@tcu.edu.
Website: http://www.education.tcu.edu/graduate-students-masters-in-special-education.asp.

Texas Christian University, College of Education, Program in Special Education (Four-One Option), Fort Worth, TX 76129-0002. Offers M Ed. Part-time and evening/weekend programs available. *Students:* 7 full-time (all women). 7 applicants, 86% accepted, 6 enrolled. In 2013, 4 master's awarded. *Degree requirements:* For master's, oral exam. *Entrance requirements:* Additional exam requirements/recommendations for international students: Required—TOEFL (minimum score 550 paper-based; 80 iBT). *Application deadline:* For fall admission, 11/16 for domestic and international students; for spring admission, 3/1 for domestic and international students. Application fee: $60. Electronic applications accepted. *Expenses: Tuition:* Part-time $1270 per credit hour. Tuition and fees vary according to course load and program. *Financial support:* Teaching assistantships with full tuition reimbursements, career-related internships or fieldwork, scholarships/grants, and unspecified assistantships available. Financial award application deadline: 3/1; financial award applicants required to submit FAFSA. *Unit head:* Dr. Jan Lacina, Associate Dean, 817-257-6786, E-mail: j.lacina@tcu.edu. *Application contact:* Lori Kimball, Administrative Program Specialist, 817-257-7661, E-mail: l.kimball@tcu.edu.
Website: http://www.coe.tcu.edu/graduate-students-graduate-programs.asp.

Texas State University, Graduate School, College of Education, Department of Curriculum and Instruction, Program in Special Education, San Marcos, TX 78666. Offers M Ed. Part-time programs available. *Faculty:* 8 full-time (5 women), 3 part-time/adjunct (all women). *Students:* 32 full-time (24 women), 36 part-time (32 women); includes 15 minority (3 Black or African American, non-Hispanic/Latino; 1 Asian, non-Hispanic/Latino; 11 Hispanic/Latino), 2 international. Average age 32. 46 applicants, 59% accepted, 17 enrolled. In 2013, 45 master's awarded. *Degree requirements:* For master's, comprehensive exam. *Entrance requirements:* For master's, GRE General Test, minimum GPA of 2.75 in last 60 hours of course work, teaching experience. Additional exam requirements/recommendations for international students: Required—TOEFL (minimum score 550 paper-based; 78 iBT). *Application deadline:* For fall admission, 6/15 priority date for domestic students, 6/1 for international students; for spring admission, 10/15 priority date for domestic students, 10/1 for international students. Applications are processed on a rolling basis. Application fee: $40 ($90 for international students). Electronic applications accepted. *Expenses:* Tuition, state resident: full-time $6663; part-time $278 per credit hour. Tuition, nonresident: full-time $15,159; part-time $632 per credit hour. *Required fees:* $1872; $54 per credit hour. $306 per term. Tuition and fees vary according to course load. *Financial support:* In 2013–14, 34 students received support, including 4 research assistantships (averaging $15,644 per year); fellowships, teaching assistantships, career-related internships or fieldwork, Federal Work-Study, and institutionally sponsored loans also available. Support available to part-time students. Financial award application deadline: 4/1; financial award applicants required to submit FAFSA. *Faculty research:* Educational diagnostics; generic, severely handicapped, emotionally disturbed, autistic education. *Unit head:* Dr. Larry J. Wheeler, Graduate Adviser, 512-245-2157, Fax: 512-245-7911, E-mail: lw06@txstate.edu. *Application contact:* Dr. Andrea Golato, Dean of Graduate School, 512-245-2581, Fax: 512-245-8365, E-mail: gradcollege@txstate.edu.
Website: http://www.education.txstate.edu/ci/degrees-programs/graduate.html.

Texas Tech University, Graduate School, College of Education, Department of Educational Psychology and Leadership, Lubbock, TX 79409-1071. Offers counselor education (M Ed, PhD); educational leadership (M Ed, Ed D); educational psychology (M Ed, PhD); higher education (M Ed, Ed D); higher education research (PhD); instructional technology (M Ed, Ed D); special education (M Ed, Ed D, PhD). *Accreditation:* ACA; NCATE. Part-time and evening/weekend programs available. Postbaccalaureate distance learning degree programs offered (minimal on-campus study). *Faculty:* 42 full-time (20 women). *Students:* 220 full-time (171 women), 549 part-time (404 women); includes 219 minority (73 Black or African American, non-Hispanic/Latino; 5 American Indian or Alaska Native, non-Hispanic/Latino; 6 Asian, non-Hispanic/Latino; 122 Hispanic/Latino; 13 Two or more races, non-Hispanic/Latino), 48 international. Average age 36. 437 applicants, 72% accepted, 215 enrolled. In 2013, 137

master's, 38 doctorates awarded. Terminal master's awarded for partial completion of doctoral program. *Degree requirements:* For master's, comprehensive exam, thesis optional; for doctorate, comprehensive exam, thesis/dissertation. *Entrance requirements:* For master's, GRE (for some programs); for doctorate, GRE. Additional exam requirements/recommendations for international students: Required—TOEFL (minimum score 550 paper-based; 79 iBT). *Application deadline:* For fall admission, 6/1 priority date for domestic students, 1/15 priority date for international students; for spring admission, 9/1 priority date for domestic students, 6/15 priority date for international students. Applications are processed on a rolling basis. Application fee: $60. Electronic applications accepted. *Expenses:* Tuition, state resident: full-time $6062; part-time $252.57 per credit hour. Tuition, nonresident: full-time $14,558; part-time $606.57 per credit hour. *Required fees:* $2655; $35 per credit hour. $907.50 per semester. Tuition and fees vary according to course load. *Financial support:* In 2013–14, 188 students received support, including 179 fellowships (averaging $2,580 per year), 39 research assistantships (averaging $4,550 per year), 8 teaching assistantships (averaging $4,647 per year); scholarships/grants and unspecified assistantships also available. Support available to part-time students. Financial award application deadline: 1/3; financial award applicants required to submit FAFSA. *Faculty research:* Cognitive, motivational, and developmental processes in learning; counseling education; instructional technology; generic special education and sensory impairment; community college administration; K-12 school administration. *Total annual research expenditures:* $708,063. *Unit head:* Dr. Fred Hartmeister, Chair, 806-834-0248, Fax: 806-742-2179, E-mail: fred.hartmeister@ttu.edu. *Application contact:* Pam Smith, Admissions Advisor, 806-834-2969, Fax: 806-742-2179, E-mail: pam.smith@ttu.edu.
Website: http://www.educ.ttu.edu/.

Texas Woman's University, Graduate School, College of Professional Education, Department of Teacher Education, Denton, TX 76201. Offers administration (M Ed, MA); special education (M Ed, MA, PhD), including educational diagnostician (M Ed, MA); teaching, learning, and curriculum (M Ed). Part-time programs available. *Faculty:* 16 full-time (13 women), 37 part-time/adjunct (29 women). *Students:* 15 full-time (all women), 135 part-time (120 women); includes 56 minority (26 Black or African American, non-Hispanic/Latino; 4 American Indian or Alaska Native, non-Hispanic/Latino; 1 Asian, non-Hispanic/Latino; 25 Hispanic/Latino), 3 international. Average age 37. 29 applicants, 69% accepted, 17 enrolled. In 2013, 51 master's, 1 doctorate awarded. Terminal master's awarded for partial completion of doctoral program. *Degree requirements:* For master's, comprehensive exam, thesis, professional paper (M Ed); for doctorate, comprehensive exam, thesis/dissertation. *Entrance requirements:* For master's, minimum GPA of 3.0 on last 60 undergraduate hours, 2 letters of reference, resume, copy of certifications, teacher service record, statement of intent; for doctorate, GRE General Test, minimum GPA of 3.0, 3 letters of reference, resume, copy of certifications, teacher service record, statement of intent. Additional exam requirements/recommendations for international students: Required—TOEFL (minimum score 550 paper-based; 79 iBT). *Application deadline:* For fall admission, 7/1 priority date for domestic students, 3/1 for international students; for spring admission, 11/1 priority date for domestic students, 7/1 for international students. Applications are processed on a rolling basis. Application fee: $50 ($75 for international students). Electronic applications accepted. *Expenses:* Tuition, state resident: full-time $4182; part-time $233.32 per credit hour. Tuition, nonresident: full-time $10,716; part-time $595.32 per credit hour. *Financial support:* In 2013–14, 42 students received support, including 8 research assistantships (averaging $12,942 per year); career-related internships or fieldwork, Federal Work-Study, institutionally sponsored loans, scholarships/grants, traineeships, health care benefits, and unspecified assistantships also available. Support available to part-time students. Financial award application deadline: 3/1; financial award applicants required to submit FAFSA. *Faculty research:* Language and literacy, classroom management, learning disabilities, staff and professional development, leadership preparation practice. *Unit head:* Dr. Jane Pemberton, Chair, 940-898-2271, Fax: 940-898-2270, E-mail: teachereducation@twu.edu. *Application contact:* Dr. Samuel Wheeler, Assistant Director of Admissions, 940-898-3188, Fax: 940-898-3081, E-mail: wheelersr@twu.edu.
Website: http://www.twu.edu/teacher-education/.

Touro College, Graduate School of Education, New York, NY 10010. Offers education and special education (MS); education biology (MS); instructional technology (MS); mathematics education (MS); school leadership (MS); teaching English to speakers of other languages (MS); teaching literacy (MS). Part-time and evening/weekend programs available. Postbaccalaureate distance learning degree programs offered (no on-campus study). *Faculty:* 75 full-time, 131 part-time/adjunct. *Students:* 327 full-time (272 women), 2,454 part-time (2,103 women); includes 840 minority (333 Black or African American, non-Hispanic/Latino; 4 American Indian or Alaska Native, non-Hispanic/Latino; 139 Asian, non-Hispanic/Latino; 334 Hispanic/Latino; 8 Native Hawaiian or other Pacific Islander, non-Hispanic/Latino; 22 Two or more races, non-Hispanic/Latino), 4 international. 1,422 applicants, 50% accepted, 675 enrolled. In 2013, 6 master's awarded. *Entrance requirements:* Additional exam requirements/recommendations for international students: Required—TOEFL (minimum score 83 iBT), IELTS (minimum score 6.5). *Application deadline:* For fall admission, 8/26 for domestic students, 7/15 for international students; for spring admission, 12/31 for domestic students, 12/15 for international students. Applications are processed on a rolling basis. Application fee: $50. *Financial support:* Federal Work-Study available. Financial award applicants required to submit FAFSA. *Faculty research:* Equity assistance, language development, scholar communications, Latin American studies and cultural sensitivity, behavior management techniques and strategies in special education. *Unit head:* Dr. LaMar Miller, Dean, 212-463-0400 Ext. 5561, Fax: 212-462-4889, E-mail: lpmiller@touro.edu. *Application contact:* Natalie Arroyo, Admissions, 212-463-0400.

Towson University, Program in Autism Studies, Towson, MD 21252-0001. Offers Postbaccalaureate Certificate. *Students:* 12 full-time (11 women), 31 part-time (28 women); includes 4 minority (3 Black or African American, non-Hispanic/Latino; 1 Hispanic/Latino), 1 international. *Entrance requirements:* For degree, bachelor's degree with minimum GPA of 3.0, 30 hours of human service activity as part of field experience, volunteer or paid work in the last five years, prerequisite courses or experience. *Application deadline:* Applications are processed on a rolling basis. Application fee: $45. Electronic applications accepted. *Unit head:* Dr. Connie Anderson, Graduate Program Director, 410-704-4640, E-mail: connieanderson@towson.edu. *Application contact:* Alicia Arkell-Kleis, Information Contact, 410-704-6004, E-mail: grads@towson.edu.
Website: http://grad.towson.edu/program/certificate/auts-pbc/.

Towson University, Program in Special Education, Towson, MD 21252-0001. Offers M Ed. *Accreditation:* NCATE. Part-time and evening/weekend programs available. *Students:* 7 full-time (6 women), 177 part-time (165 women); includes 16 minority (9 Black or African American, non-Hispanic/Latino; 1 American Indian or Alaska Native, non-Hispanic/Latino; 2 Asian, non-Hispanic/Latino; 4 Hispanic/Latino). *Degree requirements:* For master's, thesis optional. *Entrance requirements:* For master's, letter of recommendation, bachelor's degree, professional teacher certification, minimum GPA of 3.0. *Application deadline:* For fall admission, 2/15 for domestic and international students; for spring admission, 10/15 for domestic and international students. Applications are processed on a rolling basis. Application fee: $45. Electronic applications accepted. *Unit head:* Prof. Rosemary Rappa, Graduate Program Director, 410-704-3835, E-mail: rrappa@towson.edu. *Application contact:* Alicia Arkell-Kleis, Information Contact, 410-704-6004, E-mail: grads@towson.edu.
Website: http://grad.towson.edu/program/master/sped-med/.

Trevecca Nazarene University, Graduate Education Program, Nashville, TN 37210-2877. Offers curriculum, assessment, and instruction K-12 (M Ed); educational leadership (M Ed); English language learners (PreK-12) (M Ed); leadership and professional practice (Ed D); library and information science (MLI Sc); teacher leader (M Ed); teaching (MAE, MAT), including teaching 7-12 (MAT), teaching K-6 (MAT); visual impairments special education (M Ed). *Accreditation:* NCATE. Part-time and evening/weekend programs available. Postbaccalaureate distance learning degree programs offered. *Faculty:* 19 full-time (17 women), 14 part-time/adjunct (5 women). *Students:* 186 full-time (137 women), 134 part-time (94 women); includes 93 minority (87 Black or African American, non-Hispanic/Latino; 1 American Indian or Alaska Native, non-Hispanic/Latino; 2 Asian, non-Hispanic/Latino; 1 Hispanic/Latino; 1 Native Hawaiian or other Pacific Islander, non-Hispanic/Latino; 1 Two or more races, non-Hispanic/Latino), 2 international. In 2013, 201 master's, 40 doctorates awarded. *Degree requirements:* For master's, comprehensive exam, exit assessment/e-portfolio; for doctorate, thesis/dissertation, proposal study, symposium presentation. *Entrance requirements:* For master's, GRE with minimum score of 378 or MAT with minimum score of 290, ACT with minimum score of 22 or SAT with minimum score of 1020 (for MAT programs only); PRAXIS (for MAT and MAE programs), minimum GPA of 2.7, official transcript from regionally accredited institution, 3+ years successful teaching experience (Teacher Leader and Education Leadership majors), technology pre-assessment written requirements (some majors); for doctorate, GRE or MAT, minimum GPA of 3.4, official transcript from regionally-accredited institution, resume, writing sample, interview, reference forms. Additional exam requirements/recommendations for international students: Required—TOEFL (minimum score 550 paper-based). *Application deadline:* Applications are processed on a rolling basis. *Expenses:* Contact institution. *Financial support:* Applicants required to submit FAFSA. *Unit head:* Dr. Suzie Harris, Dean, School of Education/Director of Graduate Education Programs, 615-248-1201, Fax: 615-248-1597, E-mail: admissions_ged@trevecca.edu. *Application contact:* 615-248-1529, E-mail: cll@trevecca.edu.
Website: http://www.trevecca.edu/academics/schools-colleges/education/.

Trinity Baptist College, Graduate Programs, Jacksonville, FL 32221. Offers educational leadership (M Ed); ministry (MA); special education (M Ed). Postbaccalaureate distance learning degree programs offered. *Entrance requirements:* For master's, GRE (for M Ed), 2 letters of recommendation; minimum GPA of 2.5 (for M Min), 3.0 (for M Ed); computer proficiency.

Trinity Christian College, Program in Special Education, Palos Heights, IL 60463-0929. Offers MA. Evening/weekend programs available. *Degree requirements:* For master's, project. *Entrance requirements:* For master's, valid teaching license, official transcripts, two letters of recommendation. Electronic applications accepted.

Trinity Washington University, School of Education, Washington, DC 20017-1094. Offers clinical mental health counseling (MA); early childhood education (MAT); educating for change (M Ed); educational administration (MSA); elementary education (MAT); reading (M Ed); school counseling (MA); secondary education (MAT), including English, social studies; special education (MAT). *Accreditation:* NCATE. Part-time and evening/weekend programs available. *Degree requirements:* For master's, thesis (for some programs), capstone project(s). *Entrance requirements:* For master's, PRAXIS I, minimum GPA of 2.8. Additional exam requirements/recommendations for international students: Required—TOEFL (minimum score 550 paper-based). *Application deadline:* For fall admission, 4/1 priority date for domestic students; for winter admission, 11/1 priority date for domestic students; for spring admission, 11/1 priority date for domestic students. Applications are processed on a rolling basis. Application fee: $40. *Expenses:* *Tuition:* Part-time $715 per credit. *Financial support:* Career-related internships or fieldwork, health care benefits, and unspecified assistantships available. Support available to part-time students. Financial award application deadline: 4/1; financial award applicants required to submit FAFSA. *Faculty research:* Technology, literacy, special education, organizations, inclusion models. *Unit head:* Dr. Janet Stocks, Dean, 202-884-9380, Fax: 202-884-9506, E-mail: stocksj@trinitydc.edu. *Application contact:* Erika Davis, Director of Admissions for School of Education, 202-884-9400, Fax: 202-884-9229, E-mail: daviser@trinitydc.edu.
Website: http://www.trinitydc.edu/education/.

Union College, Graduate Programs, Department of Education, Program in Special Education, Barbourville, KY 40906-1499. Offers MA. *Degree requirements:* For master's, thesis optional. *Entrance requirements:* For master's, GRE General Test, NTE.

United States University, School of Education, Cypress, CA 90630. Offers administration (MA Ed); early childhood education (MA Ed); general (MA Ed); higher education administration (MA Ed); Spanish language education (MA Ed); special education (MA Ed). *Degree requirements:* For master's, portfolio. *Entrance requirements:* For master's, minimum undergraduate GPA of 2.5. Additional exam requirements/recommendations for international students: Required—TOEFL (minimum score 500 paper-based; 61 iBT).

Universidad del Este, Graduate School, Carolina, PR 00984. Offers accounting (MBA); adult education (M Ed); agribusiness (MBA); criminal justice and criminology (MA); curriculum and instruction - early education (M Ed); curriculum and instruction - elementary (M Ed); curriculum and instruction - English (M Ed); curriculum and instruction - Spanish (M Ed); human resources (MBA); information security management (MBA); information technology and Web business development (MBA); management (MBA); public policy (MPA); social work (MA), including clinical social work; special education (M Ed); strategic leadership (MBA). *Students:* 464 full-time (322 women), 669 part-time (499 women); all minorities (all Hispanic/Latino). Average age 35. 693 applicants, 61% accepted, 332 enrolled. In 2013, 228 master's awarded. *Unit head:* Jose R. Clintron, Dean, 787-257-7373 Ext. 3007, E-mail: ue_jcintron@suagm.edu. *Application contact:* Clotilde Santiago, Director of Admissions, 787-257-7373 Ext. 3400, E-mail: ue_csantiago@suagm.edu.

Universidad del Turabo, Graduate Programs, Programs in Education, Program in Special Education, Gurabo, PR 00778-3030. Offers M Ed. *Entrance requirements:* For master's, GRE, EXADEP, interview.

Universidad Iberoamericana, Graduate School, Santo Domingo D.N., Dominican Republic. Offers business administration (MBA, PMBA); constitutional law (LL M); dentistry (DMD); educational management (MA); integrated marketing communication (MA); psychopedagogical intervention (M Ed); real estate law (LL M); strategic management of human talent (MM).

Universidad Metropolitana, School of Education, Program in Special Education, San Juan, PR 00928-1150. Offers M Ed. *Degree requirements:* For master's, thesis or alternative. Electronic applications accepted.

Université de Sherbrooke, Faculty of Education, Program in Special Education, Sherbrooke, QC J1K 2R1, Canada. Offers M Ed, Diploma. Part-time and evening/weekend programs available. *Degree requirements:* For master's, thesis.

University at Albany, State University of New York, School of Education, Department of Educational and Counseling Psychology, Program in Special Education, Albany, NY 12222-0001. Offers MS. *Entrance requirements:* Additional exam requirements/recommendations for international students: Required—TOEFL (minimum score 550 paper-based). Electronic applications accepted.

University at Buffalo, the State University of New York, Graduate School, Graduate School of Education, Department of Learning and Instruction, Buffalo, NY 14260. Offers biology education (Ed M, Certificate); chemistry education (Ed M, Certificate); childhood education (Ed M); childhood education with bilingual extension (Ed M); curriculum, instruction and the science of learning (PhD); early childhood education (Ed M); early childhood education with bilingual extension (birth-grade 2) (Ed M); earth science education (Ed M, Certificate); education studies (Ed M); educational technology and new literacies (Certificate); elementary education (Ed D); English education (Ed M, Certificate); English for speakers of other languages (Ed M); foreign and second language education (PhD); French education (Ed M, Certificate); German education (Ed M, Certificate); gifted education (Certificate); Latin education (Ed M, Certificate); literacy specialist (Ed M); literacy teaching and learning (Certificate); mathematics education (Ed M, Certificate); music education (Ed M, Certificate); physics education (Ed M, Certificate); science and the public (Ed M); social studies education (Ed M, Certificate); Spanish education (Ed M, Certificate); special education (PhD); teaching English to speakers of other languages (Ed M). Part-time and evening/weekend programs available. Postbaccalaureate distance learning degree programs offered (no on-campus study). *Faculty:* 31 full-time (23 women), 64 part-time/adjunct (53 women). *Students:* 275 full-time (215 women), 293 part-time (205 women); includes 35 minority (16 Black or African American, non-Hispanic/Latino; 5 American Indian or Alaska Native, non-Hispanic/Latino; 11 Asian, non-Hispanic/Latino; 3 Hispanic/Latino), 97 international. Average age 30. 544 applicants, 81% accepted, 246 enrolled. In 2013, 222 master's, 17 doctorates, 35 other advanced degrees awarded. *Degree requirements:* For master's, comprehensive exam; for doctorate, thesis/dissertation, research analysis exam, research experience component. *Entrance requirements:* For master's, content test in science and math, letters of reference; for doctorate, GRE General Test or MAT, interview, writing sample, letters of recommendation. Additional exam requirements/recommendations for international students: Required—TOEFL (minimum score 600 paper-based; 96 iBT). *Application deadline:* For fall admission, 2/1 priority date for domestic and international students; for spring admission, 11/15 priority date for domestic students, 10/1 for international students. Applications are processed on a rolling basis. Application fee: $50. Electronic applications accepted. *Financial support:* In 2013–14, 50 fellowships (averaging $8,589 per year), 31 research assistantships with tuition reimbursements (averaging $11,406 per year) were awarded; teaching assistantships, career-related internships or fieldwork, Federal Work-Study, institutionally sponsored loans, scholarships/grants, tuition waivers, and unspecified assistantships also available. Financial award application deadline: 2/28; financial award applicants required to submit FAFSA. *Faculty research:* Science assessment, foreign language teaching and learning, early learning, new literacies, gender and education. *Total annual research expenditures:* $1.7 million. *Unit head:* Dr. Suzanne Miller, Chair, 716-645-2455, Fax: 716-645-3161, E-mail: smiller@buffalo.edu. *Application contact:* Cathy Dimino, Admissions Assistant, 716-645-2110, Fax: 716-645-7937, E-mail: cadimino@buffalo.edu.
Website: http://gse.buffalo.edu/lai.

The University of Akron, Graduate School, College of Education, Department of Curricular and Instructional Studies, Program in Special Education, Akron, OH 44325. Offers MA, MS. *Accreditation:* NCATE. *Students:* 49 full-time (39 women), 51 part-time (37 women); includes 12 minority (11 Black or African American, non-Hispanic/Latino; 1 Asian, non-Hispanic/Latino), 20 international. Average age 33. 22 applicants, 77% accepted, 17 enrolled. In 2013, 55 master's awarded. *Degree requirements:* For master's, comprehensive exam. *Entrance requirements:* For master's, minimum GPA of 2.75, valid teaching license. Additional exam requirements/recommendations for international students: Required—TOEFL (minimum score 550 paper-based; 79 iBT). *Application deadline:* Applications are processed on a rolling basis. Application fee: $40 ($60 for international students). Electronic applications accepted. *Expenses:* Tuition, state resident: full-time $7430; part-time $412.80 per credit hour. Tuition, nonresident: full-time $12,722; part-time $706.80 per credit hour. *Required fees:* $53 per credit hour. $12 per semester. Tuition and fees vary according to course load and program. *Unit head:* Dr. Sandra Coyner, Interim Chair, 330-972-5822, E-mail: scoyner@uakron.edu.

The University of Alabama, Graduate School, College of Education, Department of Special Education and Multiple Abilities, Tuscaloosa, AL 35487. Offers collaborative special education (M Ed, Ed S); early intervention (M Ed, Ed S); gifted and talented education (M Ed, Ed S); multiple abilities (M Ed); special education (Ed D, PhD). Part-time and evening/weekend programs available. *Faculty:* 12 full-time (8 women). *Students:* 23 full-time (all women), 43 part-time (37 women); includes 11 minority (7 Black or African American, non-Hispanic/Latino; 1 American Indian or Alaska Native, non-Hispanic/Latino; 2 Asian, non-Hispanic/Latino; 1 Two or more races, non-Hispanic/Latino). Average age 34. 33 applicants, 67% accepted, 16 enrolled. In 2013, 20 master's, 2 doctorates, 3 other advanced degrees awarded. Terminal master's awarded for partial completion of doctoral program. *Degree requirements:* For master's, comprehensive exam, thesis optional; for doctorate, one foreign language, comprehensive exam, thesis/dissertation. *Entrance requirements:* For master's, GRE or MAT, minimum undergraduate GPA of 3.0, teaching certificate, 3 letters of recommendation; for doctorate, GRE or MAT, 3 years of teaching experience, minimum undergraduate GPA of 3.25. Additional exam requirements/recommendations for international students: Required—TOEFL. *Application deadline:* For fall admission, 7/1 for domestic students; for spring admission, 11/1 for domestic students. Applications are processed on a rolling basis. Application fee: $50 ($60 for international students). Electronic applications accepted. *Expenses:* Tuition, state resident: full-time $9450. Tuition, nonresident: full-time $23,950. *Financial support:* In 2013–14, 8 students received support, including 4 research assistantships with tuition reimbursements available (averaging $9,000 per year), 4 teaching assistantships with tuition reimbursements available (averaging $9,000 per year); health care benefits and unspecified assistantships also available. Financial award application deadline: 7/1; financial award applicants required to submit FAFSA. *Faculty research:* Gifted education, mild disabilities, early intervention, severe disabilities. *Unit head:* James A. Siders, Associate Professor and Head, 205-348-5577, Fax: 205-348-6782, E-mail: jsiders@bama.ua.edu. *Application contact:* April Zark, Office Support, 205-348-6093, Fax: 205-348-6782, E-mail: azark@bamaed.ua.edu.
Website: http://education.ua.edu/departments/spema/.

The University of Alabama at Birmingham, School of Education, Program in Special Education, Birmingham, AL 35294. Offers MA Ed. *Accreditation:* NCATE. *Degree requirements:* For master's, thesis optional. *Entrance requirements:* For master's, GRE General Test or NTE, minimum GPA of 3.0. Electronic applications accepted.

University of Alaska Anchorage, College of Education, Program in Special Education, Anchorage, AK 99508. Offers early childhood special education (M Ed); special education (M Ed, Certificate). Part-time programs available. *Degree requirements:* For master's, comprehensive exam (for some programs), thesis or alternative. *Entrance requirements:* For master's, GRE or MAT, interview, minimum GPA of 2.75. Additional exam requirements/recommendations for international students: Required—TOEFL (minimum score 550 paper-based). *Faculty research:* Mild disabilities, substance abuse issues for educators, partnerships to improve at-risk youth, analysis of planning models for teachers in special education.

University of Alaska Fairbanks, School of Education, Program in Education, Fairbanks, AK 99775. Offers curriculum and instruction (M Ed); education (M Ed, Graduate Certificate); elementary education (M Ed); language and literacy (M Ed); reading (M Ed); secondary education (M Ed); special education (M Ed). *Faculty:* 23 full-time (14 women), 1 part-time/adjunct (0 women). *Students:* 37 full-time (26 women), 78 part-time (54 women); includes 15 minority (6 American Indian or Alaska Native, non-Hispanic/Latino; 6 Hispanic/Latino; 3 Two or more races, non-Hispanic/Latino), 2 international. Average age 34. 37 applicants, 68% accepted, 19 enrolled. In 2013, 39 master's, 28 other advanced degrees awarded. *Degree requirements:* For master's, comprehensive exam, thesis, oral defense. *Entrance requirements:* Additional exam requirements/recommendations for international students: Required—TOEFL (minimum score 550 paper-based; 80 iBT). *Application deadline:* For fall admission, 5/1 for domestic students, 3/1 for international students; for spring admission, 10/15 for domestic students, 8/1 for international students. Applications are processed on a rolling basis. Application fee: $60. Electronic applications accepted. *Expenses:* Tuition, state resident: full-time $7254; part-time $403 per credit. Tuition, nonresident: full-time $14,814; part-time $823 per credit. Tuition and fees vary according to course level, course load and reciprocity agreements. *Financial support:* In 2013–14, 1 teaching assistantship with tuition reimbursement (averaging $11,011 per year) was awarded; fellowships with tuition reimbursements, research assistantships with tuition reimbursements, career-related internships or fieldwork, Federal Work-Study, scholarships/grants, health care benefits, and unspecified assistantships also available. Support available to part-time students. Financial award application deadline: 6/1; financial award applicants required to submit FAFSA. *Unit head:* Allan Morotti, Interim Dean, 907-474-7341, Fax: 907-474-5451, E-mail: uaf-soe-school@alaska.edu. *Application contact:* Libby Eddy, Director of Admissions, 907-474-7500, Fax: 907-474-7097, E-mail: admissions@uaf.edu.
Website: https://sites.google.com/a/alaska.edu/soe-graduate/.

University of Alberta, Faculty of Graduate Studies and Research, Department of Educational Psychology, Edmonton, AB T6G 2E1, Canada. Offers counseling psychology (M Ed, PhD); educational psychology (M Ed, PhD); instructional technology (M Ed); school counseling (M Ed); school psychology (M Ed, PhD); special education (M Ed, PhD); special education-deafness studies (M Ed); teaching English as a second language (M Ed). Part-time programs available. *Degree requirements:* For master's, thesis optional; for doctorate, comprehensive exam, thesis/dissertation. *Entrance requirements:* For master's and doctorate, minimum GPA of 3.0. Additional exam requirements/recommendations for international students: Required—TOEFL. *Faculty research:* Human learning, development and assessment.

The University of Arizona, College of Education, Department of Disability and Psychoeducational Studies, Program in Special Education, Tucson, AZ 85721. Offers cross-categorical special education (MA); deaf and hard of hearing (MA); learning disabilities (MA); severe and multiple disabilities (MA); special education (Ed D, PhD); visual impairment (MA). Part-time programs available. *Faculty:* 15 full-time (8 women), 1 (woman) part-time/adjunct. *Students:* 43 full-time (35 women), 53 part-time (46 women); includes 17 minority (1 Black or African American, non-Hispanic/Latino; 2 Asian, non-Hispanic/Latino; 6 Hispanic/Latino; 8 Two or more races, non-Hispanic/Latino), 2 international. Average age 35. 68 applicants, 59% accepted, 28 enrolled. In 2013, 23 master's, 5 doctorates awarded. *Entrance requirements:* Additional exam requirements/recommendations for international students: Required—TOEFL (minimum score 550 paper-based; 79 iBT). Application fee: $75. Electronic applications accepted. *Expenses:* Tuition, state resident: full-time $11,526. Tuition, nonresident: full-time $27,398. *Financial support:* In 2013–14, 6 research assistantships (averaging $13,880 per year), 3 teaching assistantships (averaging $18,507 per year) were awarded. *Total annual research expenditures:* $3.1 million. *Unit head:* Dr. Linda R. Shaw, Department Head, 520-621-7822, Fax: 520-621-3821, E-mail: lshaw@email.arizona.edu. *Application contact:* Cecilia Carlon, Coordinator, 520-621-7822, Fax: 520-621-3821, E-mail: ccarlon@email.arizona.edu.

University of Arkansas, Graduate School, College of Education and Health Professions, Department of Curriculum and Instruction, Program in Special Education, Fayetteville, AR 72701-1201. Offers M Ed, MAT. *Accreditation:* NCATE. Part-time and evening/weekend programs available. Postbaccalaureate distance learning degree programs offered (no on-campus study). *Entrance requirements:* For master's, GRE General Test or MAT. Electronic applications accepted.

University of Arkansas at Little Rock, Graduate School, College of Education, Department of Counseling, Adult and Rehabilitation Education, Little Rock, AR 72204-1099. Offers adult education (M Ed); counselor education (M Ed), including school counseling; orientation and mobility of the blind (Graduate Certificate); rehabilitation counseling (MA, Graduate Certificate); rehabilitation of the blind (MA). *Accreditation:* CORE; NCATE. Part-time programs available. *Entrance requirements:* For master's, interview, minimum GPA of 2.75. *Expenses:* Tuition, state resident: full-time $5690; part-time $284.50 per credit hour. Tuition, nonresident: full-time $13,030; part-time $651.50 per credit hour. *Required fees:* $1121; $672 per term. One-time fee: $40 full-time. *Faculty research:* Low vision, orientation and mobility instruction.

University of Arkansas at Little Rock, Graduate School, College of Education, Department of Teacher Education, Program in Special Education, Little Rock, AR 72204-1099. Offers teaching deaf and hard of hearing (M Ed); teaching the visually impaired (M Ed). *Accreditation:* NCATE. Part-time and evening/weekend programs available. *Degree requirements:* For master's, comprehensive exam, portfolio or thesis. *Entrance requirements:* For master's, interview, minimum GPA of 2.75, GRE General Test or teaching certificate. *Expenses:* Tuition, state resident: full-time $5690; part-time $284.50 per credit hour. Tuition, nonresident: full-time $13,030; part-time $651.50 per credit hour. *Required fees:* $1121; $672 per term. One-time fee: $40 full-time.

The University of British Columbia, Faculty of Education, Department of Educational and Counseling Psychology, and Special Education, Vancouver, BC V6T 1Z1, Canada. Offers counseling psychology (M Ed, MA, PhD); development, learning and culture (PhD); guidance studies (Diploma); human development, learning and culture (M Ed, MA); measurement and evaluation and research methodology (M Ed); measurement, evaluation and research methodology (MA); measurement, evaluation, and research methodology (PhD); school psychology (M Ed, MA, PhD); special education (M Ed, MA, PhD, Diploma). Part-time programs available. *Degree requirements:* For master's, thesis (for some programs); for doctorate, comprehensive exam, thesis/dissertation. *Entrance requirements:* For master's, GRE General Test (counseling psychology MA); for doctorate, GRE General Test. Additional exam requirements/recommendations for international students: Required—TOEFL. Electronic applications accepted. *Expenses:* Tuition, area resident: Full-time $8000 Canadian dollars. *Faculty research:* Women, family, social problems, career transition, stress and coping problems.

Special Education

University of California, Berkeley, Graduate Division, School of Education, Program in Special Education, Berkeley, CA 94720-1500. Offers PhD. Applicants must apply to both the University of California, Berkeley and San Francisco State University; Program held jointly with San Francisco State University. *Degree requirements:* For doctorate, thesis/dissertation, oral qualifying exam. *Entrance requirements:* For doctorate, GRE General Test, minimum undergraduate GPA of 3.0 during last 2 years, 3 letters of recommendation. Electronic applications accepted.

University of California, Berkeley, Graduate Division, School of Education, Programs in Education, Berkeley, CA 94720-1500. Offers development in mathematics and science (MA); education in mathematics, science, and technology (MA, PhD); human development and education (MA, PhD); special education (PhD); MA/Credential; PhD/Credential; PhD/MA. Terminal master's awarded for partial completion of doctoral program. *Degree requirements:* For master's, exam or thesis; for doctorate, thesis/dissertation, oral qualifying exam. *Entrance requirements:* For master's and doctorate, GRE General Test, minimum GPA of 3.0 during last 2 years of undergraduate course work. Electronic applications accepted. *Faculty research:* Human development, social and moral educational psychology, developmental teacher preparation.

University of California, Los Angeles, Graduate Division, Graduate School of Education and Information Studies, Program in Special Education, Los Angeles, CA 90095. Offers PhD. Program offered jointly with California State University, Los Angeles. *Degree requirements:* For doctorate, thesis/dissertation, oral and written qualifying exams. *Entrance requirements:* For doctorate, GRE General Test, minimum undergraduate GPA of 3.0. Additional exam requirements/recommendations for international students: Required—TOEFL (minimum score 560 paper-based; 87 iBT). Electronic applications accepted.

University of California, Riverside, Graduate Division, Graduate School of Education, Riverside, CA 92521-0102. Offers autism (M Ed); diversity and equity (M Ed); education specialist (Credential); education, society and culture (MA, PhD); educational psychology (MA, PhD); general education (M Ed); higher education administration and policy (M Ed, PhD); multiple subject (Credential); reading (M Ed); school psychology (PhD); single subject (Credential); special education (M Ed, MA, PhD); TESOL (M Ed). *Faculty:* 22 full-time (11 women), 14 part-time/adjunct (10 women). *Students:* 218 full-time (148 women); includes 95 minority (10 Black or African American, non-Hispanic/Latino; 30 Asian, non-Hispanic/Latino; 49 Hispanic/Latino; 6 Two or more races, non-Hispanic/Latino), 12 international. Average age 31. 236 applicants, 66% accepted, 78 enrolled. In 2013, 66 master's, 13 doctorates, 86 other advanced degrees awarded. Terminal master's awarded for partial completion of doctoral program. *Degree requirements:* For master's, thesis optional, comprehensive exams or thesis (MA), case study or analytical report (M Ed); for doctorate, thesis/dissertation, written and oral qualifying exams, college teaching practicum. *Entrance requirements:* For master's, GRE General Test (for MA); CBEST and CSET (for M Ed in general education only), UCR Extension TESOL certificate (for M Ed with TESOL emphasis only); for doctorate, GRE General Test, writing sample; for Credential, CBEST, CSET. Additional exam requirements/recommendations for international students: Required—TOEFL (minimum score 550 paper-based; 80 iBT), IELTS (minimum score 7). *Application deadline:* For fall admission, 9/1 for domestic students, 5/1 for international students; for winter admission, 11/15 for domestic students, 7/1 for international students; for spring admission, 3/1 for domestic students, 10/1 for international students. Applications are processed on a rolling basis. Application fee: $80 ($100 for international students). Electronic applications accepted. *Financial support:* In 2013–14, 58 students received support, including 31 fellowships with full tuition reimbursements available, 11 research assistantships with full tuition reimbursements available (averaging $14,691 per year), 5 teaching assistantships with full tuition reimbursements available (averaging $17,655 per year); career-related internships or fieldwork, Federal Work-Study, institutionally sponsored loans, scholarships/grants, and unspecified assistantships also available. Financial award application deadline: 1/5. *Faculty research:* Responsiveness to intervention, faculty core, response to intervention of English language learners, advanced modeling techniques, study on social capital, trust, and motivation. *Total annual research expenditures:* $1.9 million. *Unit head:* Prof. Douglas Mitchell, Interim Dean and Professor, 951-827-5802, Fax: 951-827-3942, E-mail: douglas.mitchell@ucr.edu. *Application contact:* Prof. Michael Orosco, Assistant Professor and Graduate Advisor of Admissions, 951-827-6362, Fax: 951-827-3291, E-mail: edgrad@ucr.edu. Website: http://www.education.ucr.edu/.

University of Central Arkansas, Graduate School, College of Education, Department of Early Childhood and Special Education, Program in Special Education, Conway, AR 72035-0001. Offers collaborative instructional specialist (ages 0-8) (MSE); collaborative instructional specialist (grades 4-12) (MSE); special education instructional specialist grades 4-12 (Graduate Certificate); special education instructional specialist P-4 (Graduate Certificate). *Accreditation:* NCATE. Part-time and evening/weekend programs available. Postbaccalaureate distance learning degree programs offered (minimal on-campus study). *Degree requirements:* For master's, comprehensive exam, thesis optional. *Entrance requirements:* For master's, GRE General Test, minimum GPA of 2.7. Additional exam requirements/recommendations for international students: Required—TOEFL (minimum score 550 paper-based; 80 iBT).

University of Central Arkansas, Graduate School, College of Education, Department of Leadership Studies, Conway, AR 72035-0001. Offers college student personnel (MS); district-level administration (PMC); educational leadership - district level (Ed S); instructional technology (MS); library media and information technology (MS); school counseling (MS); school leadership (MS); school-based leadership adult education program administration (PMC); school-based leadership building administration (PMC); school-based leadership curriculum administration (PMC); school-based leadership gifted and talented program administration (PMC); school-based leadership special education program administration (PMC). *Accreditation:* NCATE. Part-time and evening/weekend programs available. Postbaccalaureate distance learning degree programs offered (minimal on-campus study). *Degree requirements:* For master's and other advanced degree, comprehensive exam. *Entrance requirements:* For master's, GRE. Additional exam requirements/recommendations for international students: Required—TOEFL (minimum score 80 iBT). Electronic applications accepted. *Expenses:* Contact institution.

University of Central Florida, College of Education and Human Performance, Department of Child, Family and Community Sciences, Program in Exceptional Student Education, Orlando, FL 32816. Offers autism spectrum disorders (Certificate); exceptional student education (M Ed); exceptional student education K-12 (MA); pre-kindergarten disabilities (Certificate); severe or profound disabilities (Certificate); special education (Certificate). *Accreditation:* NCATE. Part-time and evening/weekend programs available. *Students:* 13 full-time (all women), 114 part-time (106 women); includes 37 minority (16 Black or African American, non-Hispanic/Latino; 4 Asian, non-Hispanic/Latino; 17 Hispanic/Latino). Average age 32. 77 applicants, 86% accepted, 43 enrolled. In 2013, 53 master's, 41 other advanced degrees awarded. *Degree requirements:* For master's, thesis or alternative, research project. *Entrance requirements:* For master's, GRE General Test. Additional exam requirements/recommendations for international students: Required—TOEFL. *Application deadline:* For fall admission, 7/15 for domestic students; for spring admission, 12/1 for domestic

students. Application fee: $30. Electronic applications accepted. *Financial support:* Career-related internships or fieldwork, Federal Work-Study, institutionally sponsored loans, tuition waivers (partial), and unspecified assistantships available. Financial award application deadline: 3/1; financial award applicants required to submit FAFSA. *Unit head:* Dr. Mary Little, Program Coordinator, 407-823-3275, E-mail: mary.little@ucf.edu. *Application contact:* Barbara Rodriguez Lamas, Director, Admissions and Student Services, 407-823-2766, Fax: 407-823-6442, E-mail: gradadmissions@ucf.edu.

University of Central Florida, College of Education and Human Performance, Education Doctoral Programs, Orlando, FL 32816. Offers communication sciences and disorders (PhD); counselor education (PhD); early childhood education (PhD); education (Ed D); elementary education (PhD); exceptional education (PhD); exercise physiology (PhD); higher education (PhD); hospitality education (PhD); instructional technology (PhD); mathematics education (PhD); reading education (PhD); science education (PhD); social science education (PhD); TESOL (PhD). *Students:* 137 full-time (94 women), 86 part-time (64 women); includes 45 minority (24 Black or African American, non-Hispanic/Latino; 5 Asian, non-Hispanic/Latino; 13 Hispanic/Latino; 3 Two or more races, non-Hispanic/Latino), 22 international. Average age 39. 132 applicants, 54% accepted, 54 enrolled. In 2013, 38 doctorates awarded. Application fee: $30. Electronic applications accepted. *Financial support:* In 2013–14, 84 students received support, including 38 fellowships with partial tuition reimbursements available (averaging $6,600 per year), 41 research assistantships with partial tuition reimbursements available (averaging $7,800 per year), 53 teaching assistantships with partial tuition reimbursements available (averaging $7,700 per year). *Unit head:* Dr. Edward Robinson, Director of Doctoral Programs, 407-823-6106, E-mail: edward.robinson@ucf.edu. *Application contact:* Barbara Rodriguez Lamas, Associate Director, Admissions and Student Services, 407-823-2766, Fax: 407-823-6442, E-mail: gradadmissions@ucf.edu.
Website: http://education.ucf.edu/departments.cfm.

University of Central Missouri, The Graduate School, Warrensburg, MO 6409. Offers accountancy (MA); accounting (MBA); applied mathematics (MS); aviation safety (MA); biology (MS); business administration (MBA); career and technical education leadership (MS); college student personnel administration (MS); communication (MA); computer science (MS); counseling (MS); criminal justice (MS); educational leadership (Ed D); educational technology (MS); elementary and early childhood education (MSE); English (MA); environmental studies (MA); finance (MBA); history (MA); human services/educational technology (Ed S); human services/learning resources (Ed S); human services/professional counseling (Ed S); industrial hygiene (MS); industrial management (MS); information systems (MBA); information technology (MS); kinesiology (MS); library science and information services (MS); literacy education (MSE); marketing (MBA); mathematics (MS); music (MA); occupational safety management (MS); psychology (MS); rural family nursing (MS); school administration (MSE); social gerontology (MS); sociology (MA); special education (MSE); speech language pathology (MS); superintendency (Ed S); teaching (MAT); teaching English as a second language (MA); technology (MS); technology management (PhD); theatre (MA). Part-time programs available. *Faculty:* 233. *Students:* 890 full-time (396 women), 1,486 part-time (1,001 women); includes 192 minority (97 Black or African American, non-Hispanic/Latino; 9 American Indian or Alaska Native, non-Hispanic/Latino; 32 Asian, non-Hispanic/Latino; 40 Hispanic/Latino; 3 Native Hawaiian or other Pacific Islander, non-Hispanic/Latino; 11 Two or more races, non-Hispanic/Latino), 539 international. Average age 31. 1,953 applicants, 75% accepted. In 2013, 719 master's, 58 other advanced degrees awarded. *Degree requirements:* For master's and Ed S, comprehensive exam (for some programs), thesis (for some programs). *Entrance requirements:* Additional exam requirements/recommendations for international students: Required—TOEFL (minimum score 550 paper-based; 79 iBT). *Application deadline:* For fall admission, 6/1 for domestic students; for spring admission, 10/1 for domestic and international students. Applications are processed on a rolling basis. Application fee: $30 ($75 for international students). Electronic applications accepted. *Expenses:* Tuition, state resident: full-time $7326; part-time $276.25 per credit hour. Tuition, nonresident: full-time $13,956; part-time $552.50 per credit hour. *Required fees:* $29 per credit hour. *Financial support:* In 2013–14, 118 students received support, including 271 research assistantships with full and partial tuition reimbursements available (averaging $7,500 per year), 109 teaching assistantships with full and partial tuition reimbursements available (averaging $7,500 per year); career-related internships or fieldwork, Federal Work-Study, scholarships/grants, and administrative and laboratory assistantships also available. Support available to part-time students. Financial award application deadline: 3/1; financial award applicants required to submit FAFSA. *Unit head:* Dr. Joseph Vaughn, Assistant Provost for Research/Dean, 660-543-4092, Fax: 660-543-4778, E-mail: vaughn@ucmo.edu. *Application contact:* Brittany Lawrence, Graduate Student Services Coordinator, 660-543-4621, Fax: 660-543-4778, E-mail: gradinfo@ucmo.edu.
Website: http://www.ucmo.edu/graduate/.

University of Central Oklahoma, The Jackson College of Graduate Studies, College of Education and Professional Studies, Department of Advanced Professional and Special Services, Edmond, OK 73034-5209. Offers educational leadership (M Ed); library media education (M Ed); reading (M Ed); school counseling (M Ed); special education (M Ed), including mild/moderate disabilities, severe-profound/multiple disabilities, special education; speech-language pathology (MS). Part-time programs available. *Faculty:* 14 full-time (9 women), 16 part-time/adjunct (8 women). *Students:* 87 full-time (80 women), 298 part-time (251 women); includes 77 minority (32 Black or African American, non-Hispanic/Latino; 10 American Indian or Alaska Native, non-Hispanic/Latino; 2 Asian, non-Hispanic/Latino; 15 Hispanic/Latino; 18 Two or more races, non-Hispanic/Latino), 9 international. Average age 34. 147 applicants, 94% accepted, 89 enrolled. In 2013, 163 master's awarded. *Degree requirements:* For master's, comprehensive exam (for some programs), thesis (for some programs). *Entrance requirements:* For master's, GRE. Additional exam requirements/recommendations for international students: Required—TOEFL (minimum score 550 paper-based; 79 iBT), IELTS (minimum score 6.5). *Application deadline:* For fall admission, 7/1 for international students; for spring admission, 7/1 for international students. Applications are processed on a rolling basis. Application fee: $50. Electronic applications accepted. *Expenses:* Tuition, state resident: full-time $4137; part-time $206.85 per credit hour. Tuition, nonresident: full-time $10,359; part-time $517.95 per credit hour. *Required fees:* $481. Tuition and fees vary according to course load and program. *Financial support:* In 2013–14, 93 students received support, including 4 research assistantships with partial tuition reimbursements available (averaging $8,133 per year); teaching assistantships with partial tuition reimbursements available, career-related internships or fieldwork, scholarships/grants, tuition waivers (partial), and unspecified assistantships also available. Financial award application deadline: 3/31; financial award applicants required to submit FAFSA. *Faculty research:* Intellectual freedom, fair use copyright, technology integration, young adult literature, distance learning. *Unit head:* Dr. Patsy Couts, Chair, 405-974-3888, Fax: 405-974-3857, E-mail: pcouts@uco.edu. *Application contact:* Dr. Richard Bernard, Dean, Graduate College, 405-974-3493, Fax: 405-974-3852, E-mail: gradcoll@uco.edu.
Website: http://www.uco.edu/ceps/dept/apss/.

University of Cincinnati, Graduate School, College of Education, Criminal Justice, and Human Services, Division of Teacher Education, Program in Special Education, Cincinnati, OH 45221. Offers M Ed, Ed D. *Accreditation:* NCATE. Part-time programs

available. *Degree requirements:* For master's, thesis or alternative; for doctorate, thesis/dissertation. *Entrance requirements:* For master's, GRE General Test; for doctorate, GRE General Test, GRE Subject Test. Additional exam requirements/recommendations for international students: Required—TOEFL (minimum score 550 paper-based), TWE (minimum score 4.5), OEPT. Electronic applications accepted.

University of Colorado Colorado Springs, College of Education, Colorado Springs, CO 80933-7150. Offers counseling and human services (MA); curriculum and instruction (MA); educational administration (MA); educational leadership (MA, PhD); special education (MA). *Accreditation:* ACA; NCATE. Part-time and evening/weekend programs available. Postbaccalaureate distance learning degree programs offered (minimal on-campus study). *Faculty:* 25 full-time (17 women), 39 part-time/adjunct (29 women). *Students:* 220 full-time (146 women), 237 part-time (163 women); includes 86 minority (18 Black or African American, non-Hispanic/Latino; 3 American Indian or Alaska Native, non-Hispanic/Latino; 11 Asian, non-Hispanic/Latino; 46 Hispanic/Latino; 8 Two or more races, non-Hispanic/Latino), 16 international. Average age 35. 182 applicants, 88% accepted, 118 enrolled. In 2013, 140 master's, 8 doctorates awarded. *Degree requirements:* For master's, comprehensive exam, thesis or alternative, microcomputer proficiency; for doctorate, comprehensive exam, thesis/dissertation, research lab. *Entrance requirements:* For master's, GRE General Test. Additional exam requirements/recommendations for international students: Recommended—TOEFL. *Application deadline:* For fall admission, 2/28 priority date for domestic students, 2/28 for international students; for spring admission, 10/15 for domestic and international students. Applications are processed on a rolling basis. Application fee: $60 ($75 for international students). *Expenses:* Tuition, state resident: full-time $8882; part-time $1622 per course. Tuition, nonresident: full-time $17,435; part-time $3048 per course. One-time fee: $100. Tuition and fees vary according to course load, degree level, campus/location and program. *Financial support:* In 2013–14, 23 students received support, including 23 fellowships (averaging $1,577 per year); career-related internships or fieldwork, Federal Work-Study, and scholarships/grants also available. Support available to part-time students. Financial award application deadline: 3/1; financial award applicants required to submit FAFSA. *Faculty research:* Linguistically diverse education (LDE), educational policy, evidence-based reading and writing instruction, relational and social aggression, positive behavior supports (PBS), inclusive schooling, K-12 education policy. *Total annual research expenditures:* $136,574. *Unit head:* Dr. Mary Snyder, Dean, 719-255-3701, Fax: 719-262-4133, E-mail: msnyder3@uccs.edu. *Application contact:* Juliane Field, Director, 719-255-4526, Fax: 719-255-4110, E-mail: jfield@uccs.edu.
Website: http://www.uccs.edu/coe.

University of Colorado Denver, School of Education and Human Development, Early Childhood Education Program, Denver, CO 80217. Offers early childhood education (MA); special education (MA). *Accreditation:* NCATE. Part-time and evening/weekend programs available. Postbaccalaureate distance learning degree programs offered (no on-campus study). *Students:* 121 full-time (113 women), 42 part-time (41 women); includes 18 minority (1 Black or African American, non-Hispanic/Latino; 2 American Indian or Alaska Native, non-Hispanic/Latino; 3 Asian, non-Hispanic/Latino; 8 Hispanic/Latino; 4 Two or more races, non-Hispanic/Latino), 11 international. Average age 32. 71 applicants, 66% accepted, 28 enrolled. In 2013, 73 master's awarded. *Degree requirements:* For master's, comprehensive exam, fieldwork, practica, 40 credit hours. *Entrance requirements:* For master's, GRE or MAT (if GPA is below 2.75), minimum GPA of 2.75, resume, three letters of recommendation. Additional exam requirements/recommendations for international students: Required—TOEFL (minimum score 537 paper-based; 75 iBT); Recommended—IELTS (minimum score 6.5). *Application deadline:* For fall admission, 4/15 for domestic students, 4/1 for international students; for spring admission, 9/15 for domestic students, 9/1 for international students. Application fee: $50 ($75 for international students). Electronic applications accepted. *Expenses:* Contact institution. *Financial support:* In 2013–14, 3 students received support. Research assistantships, teaching assistantships, Federal Work-Study, institutionally sponsored loans, scholarships/grants, and traineeships available. Financial award application deadline: 4/1; financial award applicants required to submit FAFSA. *Faculty research:* Early childhood growth and development, faculty development, adult learning, gender and equity issues, research methodology. *Unit head:* Lori Ryan, Professor, 303-315-2578, E-mail: lori.ryan@ucdenver.edu. *Application contact:* Jason Clark, Director of Recruitment and Retention, 300-315-0183, E-mail: jason.clark@ucdenver.edu.
Website: http://www.ucdenver.edu/academics/colleges/SchoolOfEducation/Academics/MASTERS/ECE/Pages/EarlyChildhoodEducation.aspx.

University of Colorado Denver, School of Education and Human Development, Program in Educational Leadership and Innovation, Denver, CO 80217-3364. Offers educational studies and research (PhD), including administrative leadership and policy, early childhood special education, math education, research, assessment and evaluation, science education, urban ecologies. Part-time and evening/weekend programs available. *Students:* 16 full-time (12 women), 12 part-time (9 women); includes 6 minority (2 Black or African American, non-Hispanic/Latino; 3 Asian, non-Hispanic/Latino; 1 Hispanic/Latino), 1 international. Average age 39. 16 applicants, 31% accepted, 4 enrolled. In 2013, 10 doctorates awarded. *Degree requirements:* For doctorate, comprehensive exam, thesis/dissertation, 75 credit hours (for PhD). *Entrance requirements:* For doctorate, GRE or equivalent, resume or curriculum vitae, letters of recommendation, master's degree or equivalent, completion of basic or advanced statistics course with minimum B grade. Additional exam requirements/recommendations for international students: Required—TOEFL (minimum score 537 paper-based; 75 iBT); Recommended—IELTS (minimum score 6.5). *Application deadline:* For fall admission, 5/1 priority date for domestic students, 4/15 priority date for international students. Applications are processed on a rolling basis. Application fee: $50 ($75 for international students). Electronic applications accepted. *Expenses:* Contact institution. *Financial support:* In 2013–14, 19 students received support. Fellowships, research assistantships, teaching assistantships, Federal Work-Study, institutionally sponsored loans, scholarships/grants, and traineeships available. Financial award application deadline: 4/1; financial award applicants required to submit FAFSA. *Faculty research:* Administrative leadership and policy studies, early childhood education, research in diversity, paraprofessionals in education, urban schools lab. *Unit head:* Dr. Deanna Sands, Associate Dean, Research and Professional Development, 303-315-4931, E-mail: deanna.sands@ucdenver.edu. *Application contact:* Student Services Center, 303-315-6300, Fax: 303-315-6311, E-mail: education@ucdenver.edu.
Website: http://www.ucdenver.edu/academics/colleges/SchoolOfEducation/Academics/Doctorate/Pages/PhD.aspx.

University of Colorado Denver, School of Education and Human Development, Teacher Education Programs, Denver, CO 80217. Offers elementary linguistically diverse education (MA); elementary math and science education (MA); elementary math education (MA); elementary reading and writing (MA); elementary science education (MA); secondary English education (MA); secondary linguistically diverse education (MA); secondary math education (MA); secondary reading and writing (MA); secondary science education (MA); special education (MA). *Accreditation:* NCATE. Part-time and evening/weekend programs available. *Students:* 269 full-time (208 women), 141 part-time (111 women); includes 55 minority (4 Black or African American, non-Hispanic/

Latino; 1 American Indian or Alaska Native, non-Hispanic/Latino; 10 Asian, non-Hispanic/Latino; 39 Hispanic/Latino; 1 Two or more races, non-Hispanic/Latino), 7 international. Average age 31. 97 applicants, 81% accepted, 62 enrolled. In 2013, 180 master's awarded. *Degree requirements:* For master's, comprehensive exam. *Entrance requirements:* For master's, GRE or MAT (for those with GPA below 2.75), transcripts, resume, letters of recommendation. Additional exam requirements/recommendations for international students: Required—TOEFL (minimum score 537 paper-based; 75 iBT); Recommended—IELTS (minimum score 6.5). *Application deadline:* For fall admission, 4/15 priority date for domestic students, 4/1 for international students; for spring admission, 9/15 priority date for domestic students, 9/1 for international students. Applications are processed on a rolling basis. Application fee: $50 ($75 for international students). Electronic applications accepted. *Expenses:* Contact institution. *Financial support:* In 2013–14, 42 students received support. Fellowships, research assistantships, teaching assistantships, Federal Work-Study, institutionally sponsored loans, scholarships/grants, and traineeships available. Financial award application deadline: 4/1; financial award applicants required to submit FAFSA. *Faculty research:* Linguistically diverse education/ESL, elementary reading and writing, elementary teacher education, secondary teacher education, special education. *Unit head:* Cindy Gutierrez, Director, 303-315-4982, E-mail: cindy.gutierrez@ucdenver.edu. *Application contact:* Lori Sisneros, Student Services Center, 303-315-4979, E-mail: education@ucdenver.edu.
Website: http://www.ucdenver.edu/academics/colleges/SchoolOfEducation/Academics/MASTERS/Pages/default.aspx.

University of Connecticut, Graduate School, Neag School of Education, Department of Educational Psychology, Program in Special Education, Storrs, CT 06269. Offers MA, PhD, Post-Master's Certificate. *Accreditation:* NCATE. Terminal master's awarded for partial completion of doctoral program. *Degree requirements:* For master's, comprehensive exam, thesis or alternative; for doctorate, thesis/dissertation. *Entrance requirements:* For doctorate, GRE General Test. Additional exam requirements/recommendations for international students: Required—TOEFL (minimum score 550 paper-based). Electronic applications accepted.

University of Dayton, Department of Teacher Education, Dayton, OH 45469-1300. Offers adolescence to young adult education (MS Ed); early childhood education (MS Ed); early childhood leadership and advocacy (MS Ed); interdisciplinary education studies (MS Ed); intervention specialist education, mild/moderate (MS Ed); literacy (MS Ed); middle childhood education (MS Ed); multi-age education (MS Ed); music education (MS Ed); teacher as leader (MS Ed); technology enhanced learning (MS Ed). Part-time and evening/weekend programs available. Postbaccalaureate distance learning degree programs offered (no on-campus study). *Faculty:* 19 full-time (13 women), 21 part-time/adjunct (18 women). *Students:* 69 full-time (57 women), 86 part-time (75 women); includes 16 minority (10 Black or African American, non-Hispanic/Latino; 2 Asian, non-Hispanic/Latino; 4 Hispanic/Latino), 10 international. Average age 31. 140 applicants, 54% accepted, 39 enrolled. In 2013, 93 master's awarded. *Degree requirements:* For master's, variable foreign language requirement, comprehensive exam (for some programs), thesis. *Entrance requirements:* For master's, GRE or MAT, minimum GPA of 2.75. Additional exam requirements/recommendations for international students: Required—TOEFL (minimum score 550 paper-based; 80 iBT), IELTS (minimum score 6.5). *Application deadline:* For fall admission, 3/1 for domestic students, 5/1 for international students; for winter admission, 7/1 for international students; for spring admission, 11/1 for international students. Applications are processed on a rolling basis. Application fee: $0 ($50 for international students). Electronic applications accepted. *Expenses:* Contact institution. *Financial support:* In 2013–14, 61 students received support, including 5 research assistantships with full tuition reimbursements available (averaging $8,720 per year), 3 teaching assistantships with full tuition reimbursements available (averaging $8,720 per year); career-related internships or fieldwork, institutionally sponsored loans, scholarships/grants, traineeships, health care benefits, and unspecified assistantships also available. Support available to part-time students. Financial award application deadline: 3/1; financial award applicants required to submit FAFSA. *Faculty research:* Diversity, literacy, art representation by young children, preservice teacher preparation. *Unit head:* Dr. Connie L. Bowman, Chair, 937-229-3305, E-mail: cbowman1@udayton.edu. *Application contact:* Gina Seiter, Graduate Program Advisor, 937-229-3103, E-mail: gseiter1@udayton.edu.

University of Denver, Morgridge College of Education, Denver, CO 80208. Offers child, family and school psychology (MA, PhD, Ed S); counseling psychology (MA, PhD); curriculum and instruction (MA, Ed D, PhD); curriculum instruction and teaching (Certificate); early childhood special education (MA); educational leadership and policy studies (MA, Ed D, PhD, Certificate); higher education (MA, Ed D, PhD); law librarianship (Certificate); library and information science (MLIS); research methods and statistics (MA, PhD). *Accreditation:* ALA; APA (one or more programs are accredited). Part-time and evening/weekend programs available. Postbaccalaureate distance learning degree programs offered (no on-campus study). *Faculty:* 35 full-time (21 women), 63 part-time/adjunct (43 women). *Students:* 435 full-time (332 women), 414 part-time (297 women); includes 194 minority (45 Black or African American, non-Hispanic/Latino; 9 American Indian or Alaska Native, non-Hispanic/Latino; 16 Asian, non-Hispanic/Latino; 96 Hispanic/Latino; 2 Native Hawaiian or other Pacific Islander, non-Hispanic/Latino; 26 Two or more races, non-Hispanic/Latino), 14 international. Average age 32. 672 applicants, 61% accepted, 193 enrolled. In 2013, 248 master's, 30 doctorates, 130 other advanced degrees awarded. Terminal master's awarded for partial completion of doctoral program. *Degree requirements:* For master's, comprehensive exam; for doctorate, 2 foreign languages, comprehensive exam, thesis/dissertation. *Entrance requirements:* For master's and doctorate, GRE General Test or GMAT. Additional exam requirements/recommendations for international students: Required—TOEFL (minimum score 550 paper-based; 80 iBT). *Application deadline:* Applications are processed on a rolling basis. Application fee: $65. Electronic applications accepted. *Financial support:* In 2013–14, 706 students received support, including 54 research assistantships with full and partial tuition reimbursements available (averaging $15,599 per year), 77 teaching assistantships with full and partial tuition reimbursements available (averaging $12,804 per year); career-related internships or fieldwork, Federal Work-Study, institutionally sponsored loans, scholarships/grants, and unspecified assistantships also available. Support available to part-time students. Financial award application deadline: 2/15; financial award applicants required to submit FAFSA. *Faculty research:* Principal and teacher preparation, development and assessments, gifted education, service-learning, early childhood, mathematics education, access to higher education. *Total annual research expenditures:* $6.3 million. *Unit head:* Dr. Karen Riley, Interim Dean, 303-871-3665, E-mail: karen.riley@du.edu. *Application contact:* Jodi Dye, Assistant Director of Admissions, 303-871-2510, E-mail: jodi.dye@du.edu.
Website: http://morgridge.du.edu/.

University of Detroit Mercy, College of Liberal Arts and Education, Department of Education, Program in Special Education, Detroit, MI 48221. Offers emotionally impaired (MA); learning disabilities (MA). Part-time programs available. *Degree requirements:* For master's, thesis or alternative, practicum. *Entrance requirements:* For master's, minimum GPA of 2.75. *Faculty research:* Emerging roles of special education, inclusionary education, high potential underachievers in secondary schools.

Special Education

University of Florida, Graduate School, College of Education, Department of Special Education, School Psychology and Early Childhood Studies, Gainesville, FL 32611. Offers early childhood education (M Ed, MAE); school psychology (M Ed, MAE, Ed D, PhD, Ed S); special education (M Ed, MAE, Ed D, PhD, Ed S). *Accreditation:* NCATE. Part-time and evening/weekend programs available. Postbaccalaureate distance learning degree programs offered (no on-campus study). *Faculty:* 22 full-time (17 women), 1 (woman) part-time/adjunct. *Students:* 130 full-time (120 women), 41 part-time (34 women); includes 50 minority (19 Black or African American, non-Hispanic/Latino; 8 Asian, non-Hispanic/Latino; 23 Hispanic/Latino), 9 international. Average age 29. 114 applicants, 37% accepted, 18 enrolled. In 2013, 64 master's, 17 doctorates, 12 other advanced degrees awarded. *Degree requirements:* For master's, comprehensive exam (for some programs), thesis (MAE); for doctorate, comprehensive exam, thesis/dissertation. *Entrance requirements:* For master's and doctorate, GRE General Test, minimum GPA of 3.0; for Ed S, GRE General Test. Additional exam requirements/recommendations for international students: Required—TOEFL (minimum score 550 paper-based; 80 iBT), IELTS (minimum score 6). *Application deadline:* For fall admission, 11/1 priority date for domestic students. Applications are processed on a rolling basis. Application fee: $30. Electronic applications accepted. *Expenses:* Tuition, state resident: full-time $12,640. Tuition, nonresident: full-time $30,000. *Financial support:* In 2013–14, 55 students received support, including 45 research assistantships (averaging $15,225 per year), 27 teaching assistantships (averaging $9,655 per year); career-related internships or fieldwork and unspecified assistantships also available. Financial award application deadline: 11/15; financial award applicants required to submit FAFSA. *Faculty research:* Teacher quality/teacher education, early childhood, autism, instructional interventions in reading and mathematics, behavioral interventions. *Unit head:* Jean Crockett, PhD, Chair and Associate Professor, 352-273-4292, Fax: 352-392-2655, E-mail: crocketj@coe.ufl.edu. *Application contact:* Nancy L. Waldron, PhD, Professor and Graduate Coordinator, 352-273-4284, Fax: 352-392-2655, E-mail: waldron@coe.ufl.edu.
Website: http://education.ufl.edu/sespecs/.

University of Georgia, College of Education, Department of Communication Sciences and Special Education, Athens, GA 30602. Offers communication science and disorders (M Ed, MA, PhD, Ed S); special education (M Ed, Ed D, PhD, Ed S). *Accreditation:* ASHA (one or more programs are accredited). Terminal master's awarded for partial completion of doctoral program. *Degree requirements:* For master's, comprehensive exam (for some programs), thesis (for some programs); for doctorate, thesis/dissertation. *Entrance requirements:* For master's, doctorate, and Ed S, GRE General Test. Additional exam requirements/recommendations for international students: Required—TOEFL. Electronic applications accepted.

University of Guam, Office of Graduate Studies, School of Education, Program in Special Education, Mangilao, GU 96923. Offers M Ed. *Degree requirements:* For master's, comprehensive oral and written exams, special project or thesis. *Entrance requirements:* For master's, GRE General Test. Additional exam requirements/recommendations for international students: Required—TOEFL. *Faculty research:* Mainstreaming, multiculturalism.

University of Hawaii at Manoa, Graduate Division, College of Education, Department of Special Education, Honolulu, HI 96822. Offers M Ed. *Accreditation:* NCATE. Part-time programs available. *Degree requirements:* For master's, thesis optional. *Entrance requirements:* For master's, GRE General Test, interview, minimum GPA of 3.0. Additional exam requirements/recommendations for international students: Required—TOEFL (minimum score 580 paper-based; 92 iBT), IELTS (minimum score 5). *Faculty research:* Mild/moderate/severe disabilities, early childhood interventions, inclusion, transition.

University of Hawaii at Manoa, Graduate Division, College of Education, PhD in Education Program, Honolulu, HI 96822. Offers curriculum and instruction (PhD); educational administration (PhD); educational foundations (PhD); educational policy studies (PhD); educational technology (PhD); exceptionalities (PhD); kinesiology (PhD). Part-time and evening/weekend programs available. *Degree requirements:* For doctorate, thesis/dissertation. *Entrance requirements:* For doctorate, GRE General Test, sample of written work. Additional exam requirements/recommendations for international students: Required—TOEFL (minimum score 600 paper-based; 100 iBT), IELTS (minimum score 7).

University of Houston, College of Education, Department of Educational Psychology, Houston, TX 77204. Offers administration and supervision - higher education (M Ed); counseling (M Ed); counseling psychology (PhD); educational psychology (M Ed); school psychology (PhD); school psychology and individual differences (PhD); special education (M Ed). *Accreditation:* NCATE. Part-time and evening/weekend programs available. Postbaccalaureate distance learning degree programs offered (no on-campus study). *Degree requirements:* For master's, comprehensive exam or thesis; for doctorate, comprehensive exam, thesis/dissertation. *Entrance requirements:* For master's, GRE, transcripts, 3 letters of recommendation, curriculum vita, goal statement; for doctorate, GRE, transcripts, 3 letters of recommendation, curriculum vita, goal statement, writing sample, interview. Additional exam requirements/recommendations for international students: Required—TOEFL (minimum score 550 paper-based; 79 iBT), IELTS (minimum score 6.5). Electronic applications accepted. *Faculty research:* Evidence-based assessment and intervention, multicultural issues in psychology, social and cultural context of learning, systemic barriers to college, motivational aspects of self-regulated learning.

University of Houston–Victoria, School of Education and Human Development, Victoria, TX 77901-4450. Offers administration and supervision (M Ed); adult and higher education (M Ed); counseling (M Ed); curriculum and instruction (M Ed); special education (M Ed). Part-time and evening/weekend programs available. Postbaccalaureate distance learning degree programs offered (minimal on-campus study). *Faculty:* 22 full-time (19 women). *Students:* 56 full-time (52 women), 325 part-time (274 women); includes 211 minority (113 Black or African American, non-Hispanic/Latino; 2 American Indian or Alaska Native, non-Hispanic/Latino; 16 Asian, non-Hispanic/Latino; 68 Hispanic/Latino; 12 Two or more races, non-Hispanic/Latino), 3 international. *Degree requirements:* For master's, comprehensive exam, project or thesis. *Entrance requirements:* For master's, GRE General Test. Additional exam requirements/recommendations for international students: Required—TOEFL. *Application deadline:* For fall admission, 6/1 for international students; for spring admission, 10/1 for international students. Applications are processed on a rolling basis. Application fee: $0. Electronic applications accepted. *Expenses:* Tuition, state resident: full-time $4534; part-time $251 per credit hour. Tuition, nonresident: full-time $10,906; part-time $606 per contact hour. *Required fees:* $68 per semester hour. Tuition and fees vary according to course load. *Financial support:* In 2013–14, research assistantships with partial tuition reimbursements (averaging $2,000 per year), teaching assistantships with partial tuition reimbursements (averaging $2,000 per year) were awarded; Federal Work-Study, scholarships/grants, and unspecified assistantships also available. Support available to part-time students. Financial award application deadline: 4/15; financial award applicants required to submit FAFSA. *Faculty research:* Reading and language arts education, evaluation and diagnosis of special children's abilities. *Unit head:* Freddie W. Litton, Dean, 361-570-4260, Fax: 361-580-5580. *Application contact:* Sandy Hybner, Senior Recruitment Coordinator, 361-570-4252, Fax: 361-580-5580, E-mail: hybners@uhv.edu.
Website: http://www.uhv.edu/edu/.

University of Idaho, College of Graduate Studies, College of Education, Department of Leadership and Counseling, Boise, ID 83844-2282. Offers adult/organizational learning and leadership (MS, Ed S); educational leadership (M Ed, Ed S); rehabilitation counseling and human services (M Ed, MS); school counseling (M Ed, MS); special education (M Ed). *Faculty:* 13 full-time, 11 part-time/adjunct. *Students:* 58 full-time (39 women), 200 part-time (121 women). Average age 39. In 2013, 83 master's, 38 other advanced degrees awarded. *Entrance requirements:* Additional exam requirements/recommendations for international students: Required—TOEFL (minimum score 550 paper-based). *Application deadline:* Applications are processed on a rolling basis. Application fee: $60. Electronic applications accepted. *Expenses:* Tuition, state resident: full-time $5596; part-time $363 per credit hour. Tuition, nonresident: full-time $18,672; part-time $1089 per credit hour. *Financial support:* Applicants required to submit FAFSA. *Unit head:* Dr. Jeffrey Brooks, Chair, 208-364-4047, E-mail: mweitz@uidaho.edu. *Application contact:* Stephanie Thomas, Graduate Recruitment Coordinator, 208-885-4001, Fax: 208-885-4406, E-mail: gadms@uidaho.edu.
Website: http://www.uidaho.edu/ed/leadershipcounseling.

University of Illinois at Chicago, Graduate College, College of Education, Department of Special Education, Chicago, IL 60607-7128. Offers M Ed, PhD. Part-time programs available. *Faculty:* 9 full-time (7 women), 6 part-time/adjunct (5 women). *Students:* 26 full-time (20 women), 58 part-time (47 women); includes 26 minority (9 Black or African American, non-Hispanic/Latino; 2 Asian, non-Hispanic/Latino; 14 Hispanic/Latino; 1 Two or more races, non-Hispanic/Latino), 1 international. Average age 33. In 2013, 36 master's, 5 doctorates awarded. Terminal master's awarded for partial completion of doctoral program. *Degree requirements:* For doctorate, thesis/dissertation. *Entrance requirements:* For master's, minimum GPA of 2.75; for doctorate, GRE General Test, minimum GPA of 2.75. Additional exam requirements/recommendations for international students: Required—TOEFL. *Application deadline:* For fall admission, 1/9 for domestic and international students; for spring admission, 10/1 for domestic and international students. Applications are processed on a rolling basis. Application fee: $40 ($50 for international students). Electronic applications accepted. *Expenses:* Tuition, state resident: full-time $11,066; part-time $3689 per term. Tuition, nonresident: full-time $23,064; part-time $7688 per term. *Required fees:* $3004; $1190 per term. Tuition and fees vary according to course level and program. *Financial support:* In 2013–14, 17 students received support, including 1 fellowship with full tuition reimbursement available; research assistantships with full tuition reimbursements available, teaching assistantships with full tuition reimbursements available, career-related internships or fieldwork, Federal Work-Study, traineeships, tuition waivers (full), and unspecified assistantships also available. Support available to part-time students. Financial award application deadline: 3/1; financial award applicants required to submit FAFSA. *Faculty research:* Teaching and learning for special learners, individual differences. *Unit head:* Elizabeth Talbott, Chair, 312-413-8745, E-mail: etalbott@uic.edu. *Application contact:* Receptionist, 312-413-2550, E-mail: gradcoll@uic.edu.
Website: http://education.uic.edu/.

University of Illinois at Urbana–Champaign, Graduate College, College of Education, Department of Special Education, Champaign, IL 61820. Offers Ed M, MS, Ed D, PhD, CAS. Part-time programs available. Postbaccalaureate distance learning degree programs offered. *Students:* 58 (51 women). Application fee: $75 ($90 for international students). *Unit head:* Michaelene Ostrosky, Interim Head, 217-333-0260, Fax: 217-333-6555, E-mail: ostrosky@illinois.edu. *Application contact:* Evelyn Grady, Manager I, 217-333-2267, Fax: 217-333-6555, E-mail: egrady@illinois.edu.
Website: http://education.illinois.edu/SPED/.

The University of Iowa, Graduate College, College of Education, Department of Teaching and Learning, Program in Special Education, Iowa City, IA 52242-1316. Offers MA, PhD. *Degree requirements:* For master's, thesis optional, exam; for doctorate, comprehensive exam, thesis/dissertation. *Entrance requirements:* For master's and doctorate, GRE General Test, minimum GPA of 3.0. Additional exam requirements/recommendations for international students: Required—TOEFL (minimum score 550 paper-based; 81 iBT). Electronic applications accepted.

The University of Kansas, Graduate Studies, School of Education, Department of Special Education, Lawrence, KS 66045. Offers MS Ed, Ed D, PhD. *Accreditation:* NCATE. Part-time programs available. *Faculty:* 30. *Students:* 65 full-time (54 women), 115 part-time (101 women); includes 15 minority (4 Black or African American, non-Hispanic/Latino; 4 American Indian or Alaska Native, non-Hispanic/Latino; 5 Asian, non-Hispanic/Latino; 2 Two or more races, non-Hispanic/Latino), 16 international. Average age 35. 102 applicants, 78% accepted, 52 enrolled. In 2013, 61 master's, 12 doctorates awarded. *Degree requirements:* For master's, project, thesis or capstone; for doctorate, comprehensive exam, thesis/dissertation. *Entrance requirements:* For master's, minimum GPA of 3.0; for doctorate, GRE General Test, master's degree. Additional exam requirements/recommendations for international students: Required—TOEFL (minimum score 23 iBT). *Application deadline:* For fall admission, 3/15 for domestic and international students; for spring admission, 10/15 for domestic and international students. Application fee: $55 ($65 for international students). Electronic applications accepted. *Financial support:* Fellowships with full and partial tuition reimbursements, research assistantships with full and partial tuition reimbursements, teaching assistantships with full and partial tuition reimbursements, Federal Work-Study, scholarships/grants, and unspecified assistantships available. Support available to part-time students. Financial award applicants required to submit FAFSA. *Faculty research:* Autism spectrum disorders, learning disabilities research, leadership development, qualitative research and evaluation. *Unit head:* Elizabeth B. Kozleski, Chair, 785-864-0556, Fax: 785-864-4149, E-mail: elizabeth.kozleski@ku.edu. *Application contact:* Patti Wakolee, Academic Affairs, 785-864-4342, Fax: 785-864-4149, E-mail: pwakolee@ku.edu.
Website: http://specialedu.soe.ku.edu/.

University of Kentucky, Graduate School, College of Education, Department of Early Childhood, Special Education, and Rehabilitation Counseling, Lexington, KY 40506-0032. Offers early childhood (MS Ed); rehabilitation counseling (MRC); special education (MS Ed, Ed D). *Accreditation:* CORE; NCATE. Terminal master's awarded for partial completion of doctoral program. *Degree requirements:* For master's, comprehensive exam, thesis optional; for doctorate, comprehensive exam, thesis/dissertation. *Entrance requirements:* For master's, GRE General Test, minimum undergraduate GPA of 2.75; for doctorate, GRE General Test, minimum graduate GPA of 3.0. Additional exam requirements/recommendations for international students: Required—TOEFL (minimum score 550 paper-based). Electronic applications accepted. *Faculty research:* Applied behavior analysis applications in special education, single subject research design in classroom settings, transition research across life span, rural special education personnel.

University of La Verne, College of Education and Organizational Leadership, Program in Special Education, La Verne, CA 91750-4443. Offers mild/moderate education specialist (Credential); mild/moderate professional emphasis (MS). *Expenses: Tuition:* Part-time $690 per credit hour. *Required fees:* $30 per course. *Unit head:* Dr. Barbara

Poling, Interim Dean, College of Education and Organizational Leadership, 909-448-4380, E-mail: bpoling@laverne.edu. *Application contact:* Christy Ranells, Admissions Information Specialist, 909-448-4644, Fax: 909-392-2744, E-mail: cranells@laverne.edu.

University of La Verne, Regional and Online Campuses, Graduate Credential Program in Education, California Statewide Campus, La Verne, CA 91750-4443. Offers administration services (preliminary) (Credential); education specialist: mild/moderate (Credential); multiple subject teaching (Credential); pupil personnel services: school counseling (Credential); single subject teaching (Credential). *Accreditation:* NCATE. Part-time programs available. *Faculty:* 10 full-time (7 women), 1 (woman) part-time/adjunct. *Students:* 128 full-time (92 women), 49 part-time (43 women); includes 58 minority (6 Black or African American, non-Hispanic/Latino; 1 American Indian or Alaska Native, non-Hispanic/Latino; 3 Asian, non-Hispanic/Latino; 44 Hispanic/Latino; 4 Two or more races, non-Hispanic/Latino). Average age 32. In 2013, 24 Credentials awarded. *Entrance requirements:* For degree, California Basic Educational Skills Test, minimum undergraduate GPA of 2.75, 3 letters of recommendation, interview. *Application deadline:* Applications are processed on a rolling basis. Application fee: $50. *Expenses:* Contact institution. *Financial support:* Institutionally sponsored loans available. Financial award application deadline: 3/2; financial award applicants required to submit FAFSA. *Unit head:* Pam Bergovoy, Assistant Dean, Regional and Online Campuses/Director, Center for Educators, 909-448-4953, E-mail: pbergovoy@laverne.edu.
Website: http://www.laverne.edu/locations.

University of La Verne, Regional and Online Campuses, Graduate Programs, Kern County Campus, Bakersfield, CA 93301. Offers business administration for experienced professionals (MBA-EP); education (special emphasis) (M Ed); educational counseling (MS); educational leadership (M Ed); health administration (MHA); leadership and management (MS); mild/moderate education specialist preliminary (Credential); multiple subject (elementary) (Credential); organizational leadership (Ed D); preliminary administrative services (Credential); single subject (secondary) (Credential); special education studies (MS). Part-time and evening/weekend programs available. *Faculty:* 2 part-time/adjunct (1 woman). *Students:* 1 (woman) full-time, 5 part-time (3 women); includes 4 minority (3 Hispanic/Latino; 1 Two or more races, non-Hispanic/Latino). Average age 36. In 2013, 4 master's awarded. *Application deadline:* Applications are processed on a rolling basis. Application fee: $50. *Expenses:* Contact institution. *Financial support:* Institutionally sponsored loans available. Financial award application deadline: 3/2; financial award applicants required to submit FAFSA. *Unit head:* Nora Dominguez, Regional Campus Director, 661-861-6802, E-mail: ndominguez@laverne.edu. *Application contact:* Regina Benavides, Associate Director of Admissions, 661-861-6807, E-mail: rbenavides@laverne.edu.
Website: http://laverne.edu/locations/bakersfield/.

University of La Verne, Regional and Online Campuses, Master's Programs in Education, California Statewide Campus, La Verne, CA 91750-4443. Offers administration services (preliminary) (Credential); education specialist: mild/moderate (Credential); educational counseling (MS); educational leadership (M Ed); multiple subject teaching (Credential); pupil personnel services: school counseling (Credential); single subject teaching (Credential); special education studies (MS); special emphasis (M Ed). *Accreditation:* NCATE. *Faculty:* 6 full-time (2 women), 23 part-time/adjunct (16 women). *Students:* 109 full-time (88 women), 63 part-time (53 women); includes 94 minority (8 Black or African American, non-Hispanic/Latino; 6 Asian, non-Hispanic/Latino; 76 Hispanic/Latino; 4 Two or more races, non-Hispanic/Latino). Average age 33. In 2013, 76 master's awarded. *Entrance requirements:* For master's, California Basic Educational Skills Test, 3 letters of recommendation, teaching credential. *Application deadline:* Applications are processed on a rolling basis. Application fee: $50. *Expenses:* Contact institution. *Financial support:* Fellowships and institutionally sponsored loans available. Financial award application deadline: 3/2; financial award applicants required to submit FAFSA. *Unit head:* Pam Bergovoy, Assistant Dean, Regional and Online Campuses/Director, Center for Educators, 909-448-4953, E-mail: pbergovoy@laverne.edu.
Website: http://www.laverne.edu/locations.

University of Louisiana at Monroe, Graduate School, College of Arts, Education, and Sciences, School of Education, Program in Curriculum and Instruction, Monroe, LA 71209-0001. Offers art education (M Ed); biology education (M Ed); chemistry education (M Ed); curriculum and instruction (Ed D); early childhood education (M Ed); earth science education (M Ed); educational leadership (M Ed); elementary education (1-5) (M Ed); English as a second language (M Ed); English education (M Ed); family and consumer education (M Ed); French education (M Ed); history education (M Ed); math education (M Ed); middle school education (M Ed); music education (M Ed); reading education (K-12) (M Ed); Spanish education (M Ed); special education - academically gifted (M Ed); special education - early intervention (M Ed); special education - educational diagnostician (M Ed); special education - mild/moderate disabilities (M Ed); speech education (M Ed). *Accreditation:* NCATE. *Degree requirements:* For master's, comprehensive exam (for some programs), thesis; for doctorate, thesis/dissertation, internships. *Entrance requirements:* For master's, GRE General Test; for doctorate, GRE General Test, minimum undergraduate GPA of 2.75, graduate 3.25. Additional exam requirements/recommendations for international students: Required—TOEFL (minimum score 500 paper-based; 61 iBT). *Application deadline:* For fall admission, 8/24 priority date for domestic students, 7/1 for international students; for winter admission, 12/14 priority date for domestic students; for spring admission, 1/19 for domestic students, 11/1 for international students. Applications are processed on a rolling basis. Application fee: $20 ($30 for international students). Electronic applications accepted. *Expenses:* Tuition, state resident: full-time $6607. Tuition, nonresident: full-time $17,179. Full-time tuition and fees vary according to program. *Financial support:* Research assistantships, career-related internships or fieldwork, Federal Work-Study, and unspecified assistantships available. Financial award application deadline: 4/1; financial award applicants required to submit FAFSA. *Unit head:* Dr. Dorothy Schween, Director, 318-342-1268, Fax: 318-342-3131, E-mail: schween@ulm.edu. *Application contact:* Dr. Dorothy Schween, Director, 318-342-1268, Fax: 318-342-3131, E-mail: schween@ulm.edu.

University of Louisiana at Monroe, Graduate School, College of Arts, Education, and Sciences, School of Education, Program in Special Education, Monroe, LA 71209-0001. Offers MAT. *Accreditation:* NCATE. Part-time and evening/weekend programs available. *Entrance requirements:* For master's, GRE General Test, minimum GPA of 2.5. Additional exam requirements/recommendations for international students: Required—TOEFL (minimum score 500 paper-based; 61 iBT). *Application deadline:* For fall admission, 8/22 priority date for domestic students, 7/1 for international students; for winter admission, 12/12 priority date for domestic students; for spring admission, 1/17 for domestic students, 11/1 for international students. Applications are processed on a rolling basis. Application fee: $20 ($30 for international students). Electronic applications accepted. *Expenses:* Tuition, state resident: full-time $6607. Tuition, nonresident: full-time $17,179. Full-time tuition and fees vary according to program. *Financial support:* Research assistantships, career-related internships or fieldwork, Federal Work-Study, and unspecified assistantships available. Financial award application deadline: 4/1; financial award applicants required to submit FAFSA. *Unit head:* Dr. Dorothy Schween, Director, 318-342-1268, E-mail: schween@ulm.edu. *Application contact:* Dr. Dorothy Schween, Director, 318-342-1268, E-mail: schween@ulm.edu.

University of Louisville, Graduate School, College of Education and Human Development, Department of Teaching and Learning, Louisville, KY 40292-0001. Offers art education (MAT); curriculum and instruction (PhD); early elementary education (MAT); instructional technology (M Ed); interdisciplinary early childhood education (MAT); middle school education (MAT); music education (MAT); secondary education (MAT); special education (MAT); teacher leadership (M Ed). Part-time and evening/weekend programs available. *Students:* 137 full-time (93 women), 208 part-time (131 women); includes 44 minority (25 Black or African American, non-Hispanic/Latino; 1 American Indian or Alaska Native, non-Hispanic/Latino; 3 Asian, non-Hispanic/Latino; 12 Hispanic/Latino; 3 Two or more races, non-Hispanic/Latino), 2 international. Average age 32. 150 applicants, 51% accepted, 54 enrolled. In 2013, 127 master's, 5 doctorates awarded. *Degree requirements:* For doctorate, comprehensive exam, thesis/dissertation. *Entrance requirements:* For master's, GRE General Test, PRAXIS II (for some programs); for doctorate, GRE General Test. Additional exam requirements/recommendations for international students: Required—TOEFL (minimum score 560 paper-based; 83 iBT). *Application deadline:* For fall admission, 5/1 priority date for international students; for spring admission, 11/1 priority date for international students; for summer admission, 4/1 priority date for international students. Application fee: $60. Electronic applications accepted. *Expenses:* Tuition, state resident: full-time $10,788; part-time $599 per credit hour. Tuition, nonresident: full-time $22,446; part-time $1247 per credit hour. *Required fees:* $196. Tuition and fees vary according to program and reciprocity agreements. *Financial support:* Fellowships, research assistantships, teaching assistantships, career-related internships or fieldwork, Federal Work-Study, scholarships/grants, and unspecified assistantships available. Financial award application deadline: 6/1; financial award applicants required to submit FAFSA. *Faculty research:* Mathematics teacher education and ongoing professional development in pedagogy and content knowledge; development of literacy, including early literacy in science and mathematics and literacy development for English language learners; immersive visualizations for promoting STEM education from nanoscience to cosmic scales; evidence-based practices for students with disabilities; urban education, including teacher response to intervention systems in schools and cross-cultural competence. *Unit head:* Dr. Ann E. Larson, Acting Chair, 502-852-6431, Fax: 502-852-1497, E-mail: ann@louisville.edu. *Application contact:* Libby Leggett, Director, Graduate Admissions, 502-852-3101, Fax: 502-852-6536, E-mail: gradadm@louisville.edu.
Website: http://louisville.edu/delphi.

University of Maine, Graduate School, College of Education and Human Development, Department of Teacher and Counselor Education, Orono, ME 04469. Offers counselor education (M Ed, MA, MS, CAS); early childhood teacher (CGS); education (PhD), including counselor education, literacy education, prevention and intervention studies; elementary education (M Ed, CAS); individualized education (M Ed); literacy education (M Ed, MS, CAS); response to intervention for behavior (CGS); secondary education (M Ed, MAT, CAS); social studies education (M Ed); special education (M Ed, CAS); teacher consultant in writing (CGS). Part-time programs available. *Students:* 147 full-time (118 women), 15 part-time (2 women); includes 8 minority (4 Black or African American, non-Hispanic/Latino; 2 American Indian or Alaska Native, non-Hispanic/Latino; 1 Hispanic/Latino; 1 Two or more races, non-Hispanic/Latino), 3 international. Average age 37. 100 applicants, 58% accepted, 50 enrolled. In 2013, 83 master's, 5 doctorates, 17 other advanced degrees awarded. *Degree requirements:* For master's, thesis (for some programs); for doctorate, comprehensive exam, thesis/dissertation. *Entrance requirements:* For master's, GRE General Test, MAT. Additional exam requirements/recommendations for international students: Required—TOEFL. *Application deadline:* For fall admission, 2/1 priority date for domestic students. Applications are processed on a rolling basis. Application fee: $65. Electronic applications accepted. *Expenses:* Tuition, state resident: full-time $7524. Tuition, nonresident: full-time $23,112. *Required fees:* $1970. *Financial support:* In 2013–14, 46 students received support, including 1 research assistantship (averaging $14,600 per year), 11 teaching assistantships (averaging $14,600 per year). Financial award application deadline: 3/1. *Unit head:* Dr. Janet Spector, Coordinator, 207-581-2459. *Application contact:* Scott G. Delcourt, Associate Dean of the Graduate School, 207-581-3291, Fax: 207-581-3232, E-mail: graduate@maine.edu.
Website: http://umaine.edu/edhd/.

University of Manitoba, Faculty of Graduate Studies, Faculty of Education, Department of Educational Administration, Foundations and Psychology, Winnipeg, MB R3T 2N2, Canada. Offers adult and post-secondary education (M Ed); educational administration (M Ed); guidance and counseling (M Ed); inclusive special education (M Ed); social foundations of education (M Ed). *Degree requirements:* For master's, thesis or alternative.

University of Mary, School of Education and Behavioral Sciences, Department of Education, Bismarck, ND 58504-9652. Offers college teaching (M Ed); curriculum, instruction and assessment (M Ed); early childhood education (M Ed); early childhood special education (M Ed); elementary administration (M Ed); emotional disorders (M Ed); learning disabilities (M Ed); reading (M Ed); secondary administration (M Ed); special education strategist (M Ed). Part-time programs available. *Degree requirements:* For master's, portfolio or thesis. *Entrance requirements:* For master's, interview, letters of reference, minimum GPA of 2.5. Additional exam requirements/recommendations for international students: Required—TOEFL (minimum score 500 paper-based; 71 iBT). Electronic applications accepted. *Faculty research:* Innovative pedagogy in higher education, technology in education, content standards, children of poverty, children with diverse learning needs.

University of Maryland Eastern Shore, Graduate Programs, Department of Education, Program in Special Education, Princess Anne, MD 21853-1299. Offers M Ed. *Accreditation:* NCATE. *Degree requirements:* For master's, comprehensive exam, seminar paper, internship. *Entrance requirements:* For master's, PRAXIS I, interview, minimum GPA of 3.0. Additional exam requirements/recommendations for international students: Required—TOEFL (minimum score 80 iBT). Electronic applications accepted.

University of Massachusetts Amherst, Graduate School, College of Education, Program in Education, Amherst, MA 01003. Offers bilingual/English as a second language/multicultural education (M Ed, Ed S); child study and early education (M Ed); children, families and schools (Ed D, Ed S); early childhood and elementary teacher education (M Ed); educational leadership (M Ed); educational policy and leadership (Ed D); higher education (M Ed); international education (M Ed); language, literacy and culture (Ed D); learning, media and technology (M Ed, Ed S); mathematics, science, and learning technologies (Ed D); psychometric methods, educational statistics and research methods (Ed D); reading and writing (M Ed); school counselor education (M Ed, Ed S); school psychology (Ed S); science education (Ed S); secondary teacher education (M Ed); social justice education (M Ed, Ed D, Ed S); special education (M Ed, Ed D, Ed S); teacher education and school improvement (Ed D, Ed S). *Accreditation:* NCATE. Part-time programs available. Postbaccalaureate distance learning degree programs offered (minimal on-campus study). *Faculty:* 95 full-time (55 women). *Students:* 357 full-time (240 women), 264 part-time (194 women); includes 114 minority (41 Black or African American, non-Hispanic/Latino; 4 American Indian or Alaska Native,

non-Hispanic/Latino; 10 Asian, non-Hispanic/Latino; 47 Hispanic/Latino; 12 Two or more races, non-Hispanic/Latino), 100 international. Average age 34. 761 applicants, 51% accepted, 200 enrolled. In 2013, 186 master's, 31 doctorates, 22 other advanced degrees awarded. Terminal master's awarded for partial completion of doctoral program. *Degree requirements:* For doctorate, comprehensive exam, thesis/dissertation. *Entrance requirements:* Additional exam requirements/recommendations for international students: Required—TOEFL (minimum score 550 paper-based; 80 iBT), IELTS (minimum score 6.5). *Application deadline:* For fall admission, 1/15 for domestic and international students. Applications are processed on a rolling basis. Application fee: $75. Electronic applications accepted. *Financial support:* Fellowships with full and partial tuition reimbursements, research assistantships with full and partial tuition reimbursements, teaching assistantships with full and partial tuition reimbursements, career-related internships or fieldwork, Federal Work-Study, scholarships/grants, traineeships, health care benefits, tuition waivers (full and partial), and unspecified assistantships available. Support available to part-time students. Financial award application deadline: 1/15; financial award applicants required to submit FAFSA. *Unit head:* Dr. Linda L. Griffin, Graduate Program Director, 413-545-6984, Fax: 413-545-1523. *Application contact:* Lindsay DeSantis, Supervisor of Admissions, 413-545-0722, Fax: 413-577-0010, E-mail: gradadm@grad.umass.edu.
Website: http://www.umass.edu/education/.

University of Massachusetts Boston, Office of Graduate Studies, Graduate College of Education, School Organization, Curriculum and Instruction Department, Program in Special Education, Boston, MA 02125-3393. Offers M Ed. Part-time and evening/weekend programs available. *Degree requirements:* For master's, comprehensive exam, practicum. *Entrance requirements:* For master's, GRE General Test or MAT, minimum GPA of 2.75. *Faculty research:* Inclusionary learning, cross-cultural special needs, special education restructuring.

University of Memphis, Graduate School, College of Education, Department of Instruction and Curriculum Leadership, Memphis, TN 38152. Offers early childhood education (MAT, MS, Ed D); elementary education (MAT); instruction and curriculum (MS, Ed D); instruction design and technology (MS, Ed D); middle grades education (MAT); reading (MS, Ed D); secondary education (MAT); special education (MAT, MS, Ed D). *Accreditation:* NCATE (one or more programs are accredited). Part-time programs available. *Faculty:* 30 full-time (18 women), 16 part-time/adjunct (10 women). *Students:* 55 full-time (44 women), 370 part-time (300 women); includes 169 minority (153 Black or African American, non-Hispanic/Latino; 5 American Indian or Alaska Native, non-Hispanic/Latino; 1 Asian, non-Hispanic/Latino; 6 Hispanic/Latino; 4 Two or more races, non-Hispanic/Latino), 7 international. Average age 35. 181 applicants, 84% accepted, 21 enrolled. In 2013, 137 master's, 10 doctorates awarded. Terminal master's awarded for partial completion of doctoral program. *Degree requirements:* For master's, comprehensive exam, thesis or alternative; for doctorate, comprehensive exam, thesis/dissertation. *Entrance requirements:* For master's, GRE General Test, minimum GPA of 2.5; for doctorate, GRE General Test, GRE Subject Test, 2 years of teaching experience. *Application deadline:* For fall admission, 8/1 for domestic students; for spring admission, 12/1 for domestic students. Applications are processed on a rolling basis. Application fee: $35 ($60 for international students). Electronic applications accepted. *Financial support:* In 2013–14, 635 students received support. Research assistantships with full tuition reimbursements available, teaching assistantships with full tuition reimbursements available, career-related internships or fieldwork, Federal Work-Study, institutionally sponsored loans, scholarships/grants, traineeships, and unspecified assistantships available. Support available to part-time students. Financial award application deadline: 2/15; financial award applicants required to submit FAFSA. *Faculty research:* Effective urban teachers, preparation and retention of urban teachers, technology utilization in schools, field-based teacher preparation programs, effective use of online instruction. *Unit head:* Dr. Sandra Cooley-Nichols, Interim Chair, 901-678-2365. *Application contact:* Dr. Sally Blake, Director of Graduate Studies, 901-678-4861.
Website: http://www.memphis.edu/icl/.

University of Miami, Graduate School, School of Education and Human Development, Department of Teaching and Learning, Program in Early Childhood Special Education, Coral Gables, FL 33124. Offers MS Ed, Ed S. Part-time and evening/weekend programs available. *Faculty:* 4 full-time (3 women), 6 part-time/adjunct (all women). *Students:* 31 part-time (29 women); includes 22 minority (5 Black or African American, non-Hispanic/Latino; 1 Asian, non-Hispanic/Latino; 14 Hispanic/Latino; 2 Two or more races, non-Hispanic/Latino). Average age 35. 30 applicants, 70% accepted, 21 enrolled. In 2013, 1 master's awarded. *Degree requirements:* For master's, electronic portfolio. *Entrance requirements:* For master's, GRE General Test. Additional exam requirements/recommendations for international students: Required—TOEFL (minimum score 550 paper-based; 80 iBT); Recommended—IELTS (minimum score 6.5). *Application deadline:* For fall admission, 6/30 for domestic students. Application fee: $65. Electronic applications accepted. *Financial support:* In 2013–14, 30 students received support. Application deadline: 3/1; applicants required to submit FAFSA. *Unit head:* Dr. Elizabeth Harry, Department Chairperson and Program Director, 305-284-4961, Fax: 305-284-6998, E-mail: bharry@miami.edu. *Application contact:* Maria Papazian, Graduate Admissions Coordinator, 305-284-2963, Fax: 305-284-6998, E-mail: m.papazian@miami.edu.
Website: http://www.education.miami.edu/program/Programs.asp?Program_ID=43&Src=Graduate.

University of Miami, Graduate School, School of Education and Human Development, Department of Teaching and Learning, Program in Teaching and Learning, Coral Gables, FL 33124. Offers language and literacy learning in multilingual settings (PhD); science, technology, engineering and mathematics (PhD); special education (PhD). *Faculty:* 14 full-time (10 women), 9 part-time/adjunct (all women). *Students:* 24 full-time (21 women); includes 11 minority (3 Black or African American, non-Hispanic/Latino; 7 Hispanic/Latino; 1 Two or more races, non-Hispanic/Latino), 5 international. Average age 32. 29 applicants, 21% accepted, 5 enrolled. In 2013, 2 doctorates awarded. *Degree requirements:* For doctorate, thesis/dissertation, qualifying exam, electronic portfolio. *Entrance requirements:* For doctorate, GRE General Test. Additional exam requirements/recommendations for international students: Required—TOEFL (minimum score 550 paper-based; 80 iBT); Recommended—IELTS (minimum score 6.5). *Application deadline:* For fall admission, 2/15 for domestic students, 10/1 for international students. Application fee: $65. Electronic applications accepted. *Financial support:* In 2013–14, 24 students received support, including 11 research assistantships with full and partial tuition reimbursements available (averaging $18,900 per year), 8 teaching assistantships with full and partial tuition reimbursements available (averaging $18,900 per year). Financial award application deadline: 3/1; financial award applicants required to submit FAFSA. *Faculty research:* Teacher education, multicultural education, special education, second language acquisition, math and science education. *Unit head:* Dr. Elizabeth Harry, Department Chairperson and Program Director, 305-284-4961, Fax: 305-284-6998, E-mail: bharry@miami.edu. *Application contact:* Lois Heffernan, Graduate Admission Coordinator, 305-284-2167, Fax: 305-284-9395, E-mail: lheffernan@miami.edu.

University of Michigan–Dearborn, College of Education, Health, and Human Services, Programs in Special Education, Dearborn, MI 48126. Offers emotional impairments endorsement (M Ed); inclusion specialist (M Ed); learning disabilities endorsement (M Ed). *Accreditation:* Teacher Education Accreditation Council. Part-time and evening/weekend programs available. Postbaccalaureate distance learning degree programs offered (minimal on-campus study). *Faculty:* 2 full-time (both women), 5 part-time/adjunct (2 women). *Students:* 57 part-time (50 women); includes 6 minority (3 Black or African American, non-Hispanic/Latino; 3 Hispanic/Latino), 2 international. Average age 36. 13 applicants, 54% accepted, 6 enrolled. In 2013, 34 master's awarded. *Entrance requirements:* For master's, minimum GPA of 3.0, Michigan teaching certificate (for learning disabilities and emotional impairments endorsements); statement of purpose; 3 letters of recommendations. Additional exam requirements/recommendations for international students: Required—TOEFL (minimum score 560 paper-based; 84 iBT), IELTS (minimum score 6.5), TWE. *Application deadline:* For fall admission, 8/1 priority date for domestic students, 5/1 priority date for international students; for winter admission, 12/1 priority date for domestic students, 9/1 priority date for international students; for spring admission, 4/1 priority date for domestic students, 1/1 priority date for international students. Applications are processed on a rolling basis. Application fee: $60. Electronic applications accepted. *Expenses:* Tuition, state resident: full-time $11,838; part-time $686 per credit hour. Tuition, nonresident: full-time $20,926; part-time $1206 per credit hour. *Required fees:* $760; $286 per semester. Tuition and fees vary according to course load and program. *Financial support:* Career-related internships or fieldwork, Federal Work-Study, and scholarships/grants available. Support available to part-time students. Financial award application deadline: 4/1; financial award applicants required to submit FAFSA. *Unit head:* Dr. Kim Killu, Program Coordinator, 313-593-3240, Fax: 313-593-4748, E-mail: kimkillu@umich.edu. *Application contact:* Elizabeth Morden, Customer Service Assistant, 313-583-6333, Fax: 313-593-4748, E-mail: emorden@umich.edu.
Website: http://cehhs.umd.umich.edu/cehhs_medsped/.

University of Michigan–Flint, School of Education and Human Services, Department of Education, Flint, MI 48502-1950. Offers early childhood education (MA); educational technology (MA); elementary education with teaching certification (MA); literacy education (MA); special education (MA). Part-time programs available. *Faculty:* 14 full-time (12 women), 8 part-time/adjunct (4 women). *Students:* 27 full-time (24 women), 215 part-time (186 women); includes 22 minority (20 Black or African American, non-Hispanic/Latino; 2 American Indian or Alaska Native, non-Hispanic/Latino). Average age 35. 63 applicants, 86% accepted, 43 enrolled. In 2013, 91 master's awarded. *Entrance requirements:* For master's, BS with minimum GPA of 3.0. Additional exam requirements/recommendations for international students: Required—TOEFL (minimum score 560 paper-based; 84 iBT), IELTS (minimum score 6.5). *Application deadline:* For fall admission, 8/1 priority date for domestic students, 5/1 priority date for international students; for winter admission, 11/15 priority date for domestic students, 9/15 priority date for international students; for spring admission, 3/15 priority date for domestic students, 1/15 priority date for international students. Application fee: $55. *Expenses:* Contact institution. *Financial support:* Federal Work-Study, scholarships/grants, and unspecified assistantships available. Support available to part-time students. Financial award application deadline: 6/1; financial award applicants required to submit FAFSA. *Unit head:* Dr. Beverly Schumer, Director, 810-424-5215, E-mail: bschumer@umflint.edu. *Application contact:* Beulah Alexander, Executive Secretary, 810-766-6879, Fax: 810-766-6891, E-mail: beulaha@umflint.edu.
Website: http://www.umflint.edu/education/graduate-programs.

University of Minnesota, Twin Cities Campus, Graduate School, College of Education and Human Development, Department of Curriculum and Instruction, Program in Teaching, Minneapolis, MN 55455-0213. Offers Chinese (M Ed); earth science (M Ed); elementary special education (M Ed); English (M Ed); English as a second language (M Ed); French (M Ed); German (M Ed); Hebrew (M Ed); Japanese (M Ed); life sciences (M Ed); mathematics (M Ed); middle school science (M Ed); science (M Ed); second languages and cultures (M Ed); social studies (M Ed); Spanish (M Ed). *Students:* 220 full-time (154 women), 83 part-time (60 women); includes 43 minority (10 Black or African American, non-Hispanic/Latino; 26 Asian, non-Hispanic/Latino; 7 Hispanic/Latino), 4 international. Average age 27. 261 applicants, 87% accepted, 222 enrolled. In 2013, 561 master's awarded. Application fee: $75 ($95 for international students). *Unit head:* Dr. Nina Asher, Chair, 612-624-1357, Fax: 612-624-8277, E-mail: nasher@umn.edu. *Application contact:* Dr. Jennifer Engler, Assistant Dean, 612-626-2887, Fax: 612-626-7496, E-mail: engle009@umn.edu.
Website: http://www.cehd.umn.edu/ci/.

University of Minnesota, Twin Cities Campus, Graduate School, College of Education and Human Development, Department of Educational Psychology, Program in Special Education, Minneapolis, MN 55455-0213. Offers M Ed, MA, PhD, Ed S. *Students:* 94 full-time (76 women), 34 part-time (30 women); includes 11 minority (3 Black or African American, non-Hispanic/Latino; 1 American Indian or Alaska Native, non-Hispanic/Latino; 5 Asian, non-Hispanic/Latino; 2 Hispanic/Latino), 6 international. Average age 29. 120 applicants, 46% accepted, 48 enrolled. In 2013, 66 master's, 3 doctorates, 30 other advanced degrees awarded. Application fee: $75 ($95 for international students). *Unit head:* Geoff Maruyama, Chair, 612-625-5861, Fax: 612-624-8241, E-mail: geoff@umn.edu. *Application contact:* Dr. Jennifer Engler, Assistant Dean, 612-626-2887, Fax: 612-626-7496, E-mail: engle009@umn.edu.
Website: http://www.cehd.umn.edu/EdPsych/specialEd.

University of Mississippi, Graduate School, School of Education, Department of Teacher Education, Oxford, MS 38677. Offers curriculum and instruction (MA); elementary education (M Ed, Ed D, Ed S); literacy education (M Ed); secondary education (M Ed, PhD, Ed S); special education (M Ed, PhD, Ed S). *Accreditation:* NCATE. *Faculty:* 42 full-time (29 women), 25 part-time/adjunct (22 women). *Students:* 70 full-time (59 women), 194 part-time (156 women); includes 67 minority (60 Black or African American, non-Hispanic/Latino; 1 Asian, non-Hispanic/Latino; 4 Hispanic/Latino; 2 Two or more races, non-Hispanic/Latino), 1 international. In 2013, 122 master's, 1 doctorate awarded. *Degree requirements:* For master's, thesis (for some programs); for doctorate, one foreign language, thesis/dissertation. *Entrance requirements:* For master's, GRE General Test, minimum GPA of 3.0; for doctorate, GRE General Test. Additional exam requirements/recommendations for international students: Required—TOEFL. *Application deadline:* For fall admission, 7/1 for domestic students; for spring admission, 10/1 for domestic students. Applications are processed on a rolling basis. Application fee: $40. *Financial support:* Scholarships/grants available. Financial award application deadline: 3/1; financial award applicants required to submit FAFSA. *Unit head:* Dr. Susan McClelland, Interim Chair, 662-915-7350. *Application contact:* Dr. Christy M. Wyandt, Associate Dean, 662-915-7474, Fax: 662-915-7577, E-mail: cwyandt@olemiss.edu.
Website: http://education.olemiss.edu/dco/teacher_education.html.

University of Missouri, Graduate School, College of Education, Department of Special Education, Columbia, MO 65211. Offers administration and supervision of special education (PhD); behavior disorders (M Ed, PhD); curriculum development of exceptional students (M Ed, PhD); early childhood special education (M Ed, PhD); general special education (M Ed, MA, PhD); learning and instruction (M Ed); learning disabilities (M Ed, PhD); mental retardation (M Ed, PhD). Part-time and evening/weekend programs available. Postbaccalaureate distance learning degree programs

offered (no on-campus study). *Faculty:* 11 full-time (8 women), 1 (woman) part-time/adjunct. *Students:* 21 full-time (19 women), 43 part-time (37 women); includes 4 minority (2 Black or African American, non-Hispanic/Latino; 1 Hispanic/Latino; 1 Two or more races, non-Hispanic/Latino), 2 international. Average age 32. 42 applicants, 64% accepted, 23 enrolled. In 2013, 28 master's, 6 doctorates awarded. *Degree requirements:* For master's, comprehensive exam, thesis or alternative; for doctorate, comprehensive exam, thesis/dissertation. *Entrance requirements:* For master's and doctorate, GRE General Test, letters of recommendation. Additional exam requirements/recommendations for international students: Required—TOEFL (minimum score 500 paper-based; 61 iBT). *Application deadline:* For fall admission, 1/15 priority date for domestic and international students; for winter admission, 11/1 priority date for domestic and international students; for spring admission, 4/1 priority date for domestic and international students. Application fee: $55 ($75 for international students). Electronic applications accepted. *Financial support:* Fellowships with full and partial tuition reimbursements, research assistantships with full and partial tuition reimbursements, teaching assistantships with full and partial tuition reimbursements, career-related internships or fieldwork, scholarships/grants, health care benefits, and unspecified assistantships available. *Faculty research:* Positive behavior support, applied behavior analysis, attention deficit disorder, pre-linguistic development, school discipline. *Total annual research expenditures:* $1.4 million. *Unit head:* Dr. Mike Pullis, Department Chair, 573-882-8192, E-mail: pullism@missouri.edu. *Application contact:* Recruitment Coordinator, 573-884-3742, E-mail: mucoesped@missouri.edu.
Website: http://education.missouri.edu/SPED/.

University of Missouri–Kansas City, School of Education, Kansas City, MO 64110-2499. Offers administration (Ed D); counseling and guidance (MA, Ed S), including mental health counseling (Ed S), school counseling (Ed S); counseling psychology (PhD); curriculum and instruction (MA, Ed S), including language and literacy (Ed S); education (PhD), including higher education administration, PK-12 education administration; educational administration (MA, Ed S), including advanced principal (Ed S), beginning principal (Ed S), district-level administration (Ed S); reading education (MA, Ed S); special education (MA). PhD in education offered through the School of Graduate Studies. *Accreditation:* NCATE. Part-time and evening/weekend programs available. *Faculty:* 44 full-time (34 women), 60 part-time/adjunct (45 women). *Students:* 206 full-time (145 women), 394 part-time (291 women); includes 154 minority (99 Black or African American, non-Hispanic/Latino; 13 Asian, non-Hispanic/Latino; 30 Hispanic/Latino; 1 Native Hawaiian or other Pacific Islander, non-Hispanic/Latino; 11 Two or more races, non-Hispanic/Latino), 16 international. Average age 32. 401 applicants, 48% accepted, 188 enrolled. In 2013, 156 master's, 9 doctorates, 24 other advanced degrees awarded. *Degree requirements:* For doctorate, thesis/dissertation, internship, practicum. *Entrance requirements:* For master's, GRE, minimum GPA of 2.75, 2 letters of reference, written statement of purpose; for doctorate, GRE, minimum GPA of 3.0; for Ed S, minimum GPA of 3.0. Additional exam requirements/recommendations for international students: Required—TOEFL (minimum score 550 paper-based; 80 iBT). *Application deadline:* For fall admission, 4/1 priority date for domestic and international students; for spring admission, 11/1 priority date for domestic and international students. Applications are processed on a rolling basis. Application fee: $45 ($50 for international students). *Expenses:* Tuition, state resident: full-time $6073; part-time $337.40 per credit hour. Tuition, nonresident: full-time $15,680; part-time $871.10 per credit hour. *Required fees:* $97.59 per credit hour. Full-time tuition and fees vary according to program. *Financial support:* In 2013–14, 12 research assistantships with partial tuition reimbursements (averaging $11,140 per year) were awarded; career-related internships or fieldwork, Federal Work-Study, institutionally sponsored loans, and tuition waivers (full and partial) also available. Support available to part-time students. Financial award application deadline: 3/1; financial award applicants required to submit FAFSA. *Faculty research:* Urban education, inquiry-based field study, theories of counseling and psychotherapy, school literacy, educational technology. *Unit head:* Dr. Wanda Blanchett, Dean, 816-235-2234, Fax: 816-235-5270, E-mail: education@umkc.edu. *Application contact:* Erica Hernandez-Scott, Student Recruiter, 816-235-1295, Fax: 816-235-5270, E-mail: hernandeze@umkc.edu.
Website: http://education.umkc.edu.

University of Missouri–St. Louis, College of Education, Division of Teaching and Learning, St. Louis, MO 63121. Offers autism studies (Certificate); elementary education (M Ed), including early childhood, general, reading; secondary education (M Ed), including curriculum and instruction, general, middle level education, reading, teaching English to speakers of other languages (TESOL); secondary school teaching (Certificate); special education (M Ed), including autism and developmental disabilities, cross-categorical disabilities, early childhood; teaching English to speakers of other languages (Certificate). Part-time and evening/weekend programs available. *Faculty:* 20 full-time (11 women), 1 (woman) part-time/adjunct. *Students:* 42 full-time (33 women), 578 part-time (442 women); includes 152 minority (101 Black or African American, non-Hispanic/Latino; 1 American Indian or Alaska Native, non-Hispanic/Latino; 20 Asian, non-Hispanic/Latino; 23 Hispanic/Latino; 7 Two or more races, non-Hispanic/Latino), 19 international. Average age 29. 245 applicants, 97% accepted, 166 enrolled. In 2013, 219 master's, 14 Certificates awarded. *Degree requirements:* For master's, comprehensive exam. *Entrance requirements:* Additional exam requirements/recommendations for international students: Recommended—TOEFL (minimum score 550 paper-based; 79 iBT), IELTS (minimum score 6.5). *Application deadline:* For fall admission, 7/1 priority date for domestic and international students; for spring admission, 12/1 priority date for domestic and international students. Application fee: $50 ($40 for international students). Electronic applications accepted. *Expenses:* Tuition, state resident: full-time $7364; part-time $409.10 per credit hour. Tuition, nonresident: full-time $19,162; part-time $1008.50 per credit hour. *Financial support:* Application deadline: 4/1; applicants required to submit FAFSA. *Unit head:* Dr. Patricia Kopetz, Chair, 314-516-5791. *Application contact:* 314-516-5458, Fax: 314-516-6996, E-mail: gadadm@umsl.edu.
Website: http://coe.umsl.edu/web/divisions/teach-learn/index.html.

University of Nebraska at Kearney, Graduate Programs, College of Education, Department of Educational Administration, Kearney, NE 68849-0001. Offers curriculum supervisor of academic area (MA Ed); school principalship 7-12 (MA Ed); school principalship PK-8 (MA Ed); school superintendent (Ed S); supervisor of special education (MA Ed). *Accreditation:* NCATE. Part-time and evening/weekend programs available. *Degree requirements:* For master's, thesis optional; for Ed S, thesis. *Entrance requirements:* For master's, letters of recommendation, resume, letter of interest. Additional exam requirements/recommendations for international students: Required—TOEFL (minimum score 550 paper-based). Electronic applications accepted. *Faculty research:* Leadership and organizational behavior.

University of Nebraska at Kearney, Graduate Programs, College of Education, Department of Health, Physical Education, Recreation, and Leisure Studies, Kearney, NE 68849-0001. Offers general physical education (MA Ed), including recreation and leisure, sports administration; physical education exercise science (MA Ed); physical education master teacher (MA Ed), including pedagogy, special populations. Part-time and evening/weekend programs available. *Degree requirements:* For master's, comprehensive exam, thesis optional. *Entrance requirements:* For master's, GRE General Test, personal statement. Additional exam requirements/recommendations for international students: Required—TOEFL (minimum score 550 paper-based). Electronic applications accepted. *Faculty research:* Ergonomic aids, nutrition, motor development, sports pedagogy, applied behavior analysis.

University of Nebraska at Kearney, Graduate Programs, College of Education, Department of Teacher Education, Kearney, NE 68849-0001. Offers curriculum and instruction (MA Ed), including early childhood education, elementary education, English as a second language, instructional effectiveness, reading/special education, secondary education; instructional technology (MS Ed), including information technology, instructional technology, school librarian; reading PK-12 (MA Ed); special education (MA Ed), including advanced practitioner, gifted, mild/moderate. Part-time and evening/weekend programs available. *Degree requirements:* For master's, comprehensive exam, thesis optional. *Entrance requirements:* For master's, portfolio or GRE. Additional exam requirements/recommendations for international students: Required—TOEFL (minimum score 550 paper-based). Electronic applications accepted.

University of Nebraska at Omaha, Graduate Studies, College of Education, Department of Special Education and Communication Disorders, Omaha, NE 68182. Offers special education (MA, MS); speech-language pathology (MS). *Accreditation:* ASHA (one or more programs are accredited); NCATE. Part-time and evening/weekend programs available. *Faculty:* 12 full-time (8 women). *Students:* 36 full-time (33 women), 59 part-time (52 women); includes 9 minority (1 American Indian or Alaska Native, non-Hispanic/Latino; 1 Asian, non-Hispanic/Latino; 4 Hispanic/Latino; 3 Two or more races, non-Hispanic/Latino), 2 international. Average age 31. 183 applicants, 26% accepted, 21 enrolled. In 2013, 29 master's awarded. *Degree requirements:* For master's, comprehensive exam, thesis (for some programs). *Entrance requirements:* For master's, minimum GPA of 3.0, statement of purpose, 2 letters of recommendation, copy of teaching certificate. Additional exam requirements/recommendations for international students: Required—TOEFL, IELTS, PTE. *Application deadline:* For fall admission, 8/1 for domestic students; for spring admission, 12/1 for domestic students; for summer admission, 5/1 for domestic students. Applications are processed on a rolling basis. Application fee: $45. Electronic applications accepted. *Financial support:* In 2013–14, 6 students received support, including 4 research assistantships with tuition reimbursements available, 2 teaching assistantships with tuition reimbursements available; fellowships, career-related internships or fieldwork, Federal Work-Study, institutionally sponsored loans, scholarships/grants, tuition waivers (partial), and unspecified assistantships also available. Support available to part-time students. Financial award application deadline: 3/1; financial award applicants required to submit FAFSA. *Unit head:* Dr. Kristine Swain, Chairperson, 402-554-2201. *Application contact:* Dr. Philip Nordness, Graduate Program Chair, 402-554-3582, E-mail: graduate@unomaha.edu.

University of Nebraska–Lincoln, Graduate College, College of Education and Human Sciences, Department of Special Education and Communication Disorders, Program in Special Education, Lincoln, NE 68588. Offers M Ed, MA, Ed S. *Accreditation:* NCATE; Teacher Education Accreditation Council. *Degree requirements:* For master's, thesis optional. *Entrance requirements:* For master's, GRE. Additional exam requirements/recommendations for international students: Required—TOEFL (minimum score 500 paper-based). Electronic applications accepted.

University of Nebraska–Lincoln, Graduate College, College of Education and Human Sciences, Department of Teaching, Learning and Teacher Education, Lincoln, NE 68588. Offers adult and continuing education (MA); educational studies (Ed D, PhD), including special education (Ed D); teaching, learning and teacher education (M Ed, MA, MST, Ed D, PhD); vocational and adult education (M Ed, MA). *Accreditation:* NCATE. *Degree requirements:* For master's, thesis optional. *Entrance requirements:* Additional exam requirements/recommendations for international students: Required—TOEFL (minimum score 550 paper-based). Electronic applications accepted. *Faculty research:* Teacher education, instructional leadership, literacy education, technology, improvement of school curriculum.

University of Nevada, Las Vegas, Graduate College, College of Education, Department of Educational and Clinical Studies, Las Vegas, NV 89154-3066. Offers addiction studies (Advanced Certificate); counselor education (Ed D, Ed S), including clinical mental health (Ed D), school counseling (Ed S); mental health counseling (Advanced Certificate); rehabilitation counseling (Advanced Certificate); special education (MS, Ed D, PhD, Ed S), including early childhood education (Ed D), special education (Ed D). Part-time and evening/weekend programs available. *Faculty:* 16 full-time (7 women), 17 part-time/adjunct (16 women). *Students:* 161 full-time (136 women), 184 part-time (148 women); includes 153 minority (31 Black or African American, non-Hispanic/Latino; 13 Asian, non-Hispanic/Latino; 53 Hispanic/Latino; 3 Native Hawaiian or other Pacific Islander, non-Hispanic/Latino; 53 Two or more races, non-Hispanic/Latino), 14 international. Average age 33. 140 applicants, 84% accepted, 100 enrolled. In 2013, 133 master's, 11 doctorates, 2 other advanced degrees awarded. *Degree requirements:* For master's, comprehensive exam (for some programs), thesis (for some programs); for other advanced degree, thesis (for some programs). *Entrance requirements:* Additional exam requirements/recommendations for international students: Required—TOEFL (minimum score 550 paper-based; 80 iBT), IELTS (minimum score 7). *Application deadline:* For fall admission, 2/1 for domestic students, 5/1 for international students; for spring admission, 10/1 for domestic and international students. Application fee: $60 ($95 for international students). Electronic applications accepted. *Expenses:* Tuition, state resident: full-time $4752; part-time $264 per credit. Tuition, nonresident: full-time $18,662; part-time $554.50 per credit. *International tuition:* $18,952 full-time. *Required fees:* $532; $12 per credit. $266 per semester. One-time fee: $35. Tuition and fees vary according to course load and program. *Financial support:* In 2013–14, 35 students received support, including 27 research assistantships with partial tuition reimbursements available (averaging $9,213 per year), 8 teaching assistantships with partial tuition reimbursements available (averaging $11,438 per year); institutionally sponsored loans, scholarships/grants, health care benefits, and unspecified assistantships also available. Financial award application deadline: 3/1. *Faculty research:* Multicultural issues in counseling, academic interventions for students with disabilities, rough and tumble play in early childhood, inclusive strategies for students with disabilities, addictions. *Total annual research expenditures:* $343,782. *Unit head:* Dr. Thomas Pierce, Interim Chair/Associate Professor, 702-895-1104, Fax: 702-895-5550, E-mail: tom.pierce@unlv.edu. *Application contact:* Graduate College Admissions Evaluator, 702-895-3320, Fax: 702-895-4180, E-mail: gradcollege@unlv.edu.
Website: http://education.unlv.edu/ecs/.

University of Nevada, Reno, Graduate School, College of Education, Department of Curriculum, Teaching and Learning, Reno, NV 89557. Offers curriculum and instruction (PhD); curriculum, teaching and learning (Ed D, PhD); elementary education (M Ed, MA, MS); secondary education (M Ed, MA, MS); special education and disability studies (PhD). *Degree requirements:* For master's, thesis optional; for doctorate, thesis/dissertation. *Entrance requirements:* For master's, GRE General Test, minimum GPA of 2.75; for doctorate, GRE General Test, minimum GPA of 3.0. Additional exam requirements/recommendations for international students: Required—TOEFL (minimum score 500 paper-based; 61 iBT), IELTS (minimum score 6). Electronic applications accepted. *Faculty research:* Education, curricula, pedagogy.

University of Nevada, Reno, Graduate School, College of Education, Department of Educational Specialties, Program in Special Education, Reno, NV 89557. Offers M Ed,

MA, MS, Ed D, PhD. Terminal master's awarded for partial completion of doctoral program. *Degree requirements:* For master's, thesis optional; for doctorate, thesis/dissertation. *Entrance requirements:* For master's, minimum GPA of 2.75; for doctorate, GRE General Test, minimum GPA of 3.0. Additional exam requirements/recommendations for international students: Required—TOEFL (minimum score 500 paper-based; 61 iBT), IELTS (minimum score 6). Electronic applications accepted. *Faculty research:* Learning disabilities, equity and diversity in educational settings.

University of New England, College of Arts and Sciences, Program in Education, Biddeford, ME 04005-9526. Offers advanced educational leadership (CAGS); career and technical education (MS Ed, CAGS); curriculum and instruction strategies (CAGS); curriculum and instruction strategy (MS Ed); educational leadership (MS Ed, CAGS); inclusion education (MS Ed); leadership, ethics and change (CAGS); literacy K-12 (MS Ed, CAGS); teaching methodologies (MS Ed). Part-time and evening/weekend programs available. Postbaccalaureate distance learning degree programs offered (no on-campus study). *Faculty:* 5 full-time (4 women), 17 part-time/adjunct (9 women). *Students:* 295 full-time (228 women), 233 part-time (175 women); includes 26 minority (19 Black or African American, non-Hispanic/Latino; 2 American Indian or Alaska Native, non-Hispanic/Latino; 2 Asian, non-Hispanic/Latino; 2 Hispanic/Latino; 1 Two or more races, non-Hispanic/Latino). Average age 37. 289 applicants, 84% accepted, 189 enrolled. In 2013, 257 master's, 106 CAGSs awarded. *Degree requirements:* For master's, collaborative action research project, integrative seminar portfolio. *Entrance requirements:* For master's, teaching certificate, 2 years of teaching experience. *Application deadline:* For fall admission, 9/15 for domestic students; for spring admission, 1/15 for domestic students. Applications are processed on a rolling basis. Application fee: $40. Electronic applications accepted. *Financial support:* Application deadline: 5/1; applicants required to submit FAFSA. *Faculty research:* Distance learning, effective teaching, transition planning, adult learning. *Unit head:* Paulette St. Ours, Associate Dean, College of Arts and Sciences, 207-602-2400, E-mail: pstours@une.edu. *Application contact:* Dr. Cynthia Forrest, Vice President for Student Affairs, 207-221-4225, Fax: 207-523-1925, E-mail: gradadmissions@une.edu.
Website: http://www.une.edu/cas/education/msonline.cfm.

University of New Hampshire, Graduate School, College of Liberal Arts, Department of Education, Program in Early Childhood Education, Durham, NH 03824. Offers early childhood education (M Ed, Postbaccalaureate Certificate); special needs (M Ed). Part-time programs available. *Faculty:* 32 full-time. *Students:* 9 full-time (all women), 7 part-time (6 women); includes 2 minority (1 Black or African American, non-Hispanic/Latino; 1 Hispanic/Latino), 1 international. Average age 29. 13 applicants, 69% accepted, 8 enrolled. In 2013, 7 master's, 2 other advanced degrees awarded. *Degree requirements:* For master's, thesis or alternative. *Entrance requirements:* For master's, GRE General Test. Additional exam requirements/recommendations for international students: Required—TOEFL (minimum score 550 paper-based; 80 iBT). *Application deadline:* For fall admission, 2/1 priority date for domestic students, 2/1 for international students; for spring admission, 12/1 for domestic students. Applications are processed on a rolling basis. Application fee: $65. Electronic applications accepted. *Expenses:* Tuition, state resident: full-time $13,500; part-time $750 per credit hour. Tuition, nonresident: full-time $26,200; part-time $1100 per credit hour. *Required fees:* $1741; $435.25 per term. Tuition and fees vary according to course level, course load, campus/location and program. *Financial support:* In 2013–14, 8 students received support, including 1 teaching assistantship; fellowships, research assistantships, career-related internships or fieldwork, Federal Work-Study, scholarships/grants, and tuition waivers (full and partial) also available. Support available to part-time students. Financial award application deadline: 2/15. *Faculty research:* Young children with special needs. *Unit head:* Dr. Mike Middleton, Chairperson, 603-862-7054, E-mail: education.department@unh.edu. *Application contact:* Lisa Wilder, Administrative Assistant, 603-862-2381, E-mail: education.department@unh.edu.
Website: http://www.unh.edu/education.

University of New Hampshire, Graduate School, College of Liberal Arts, Department of Education, Program in Special Education, Durham, NH 03824. Offers M Ed, Postbaccalaureate Certificate. Part-time programs available. *Faculty:* 32 full-time. *Students:* 5 full-time (3 women), 4 part-time (3 women). Average age 26. 6 applicants, 33% accepted, 1 enrolled. In 2013, 10 master's awarded. *Degree requirements:* For master's, thesis or alternative. *Entrance requirements:* For master's, GRE General Test. Additional exam requirements/recommendations for international students: Required—TOEFL (minimum score 550 paper-based; 80 iBT). *Application deadline:* For fall admission, 6/1 priority date for domestic students, 4/1 for international students; for spring admission, 12/1 for domestic students. Applications are processed on a rolling basis. Application fee: $65. Electronic applications accepted. *Expenses:* Tuition, state resident: full-time $13,500; part-time $750 per credit hour. Tuition, nonresident: full-time $26,200; part-time $1100 per credit hour. *Required fees:* $1741; $435.25 per term. Tuition and fees vary according to course level, course load, campus/location and program. *Financial support:* In 2013–14, 2 students received support. Fellowships, research assistantships, teaching assistantships, career-related internships or fieldwork, Federal Work-Study, scholarships/grants, and tuition waivers (full and partial) available. Support available to part-time students. Financial award application deadline: 2/15. *Unit head:* Dr. Mike Middleton, Chairperson, 603-862-7054, E-mail: education.department@unh.edu. *Application contact:* Lisa Wilder, Administrative Assistant, 603-862-2381, E-mail: education.department@unh.edu.
Website: http://www.unh.edu/education.

University of New Mexico, Graduate School, College of Education, Department of Educational Specialties, Program in Intensive Social, Language and Behavioral Needs, Albuquerque, NM 87131-2039. Offers Graduate Certificate. Part-time and evening/weekend programs available. *Students:* 2 part-time (both women); includes 1 minority (Hispanic/Latino), 1 international. Average age 48. 1 applicant, 100% accepted. In 2013, 2 Graduate Certificates awarded. *Entrance requirements:* Additional exam requirements/recommendations for international students: Required—TOEFL (minimum score 550 paper-based). *Application deadline:* For fall admission, 3/31 priority date for domestic students, 3/1 for international students; for spring admission, 9/30 priority date for domestic students, 8/1 for international students. Applications are processed on a rolling basis. Application fee: $50. Electronic applications accepted. *Financial support:* In 2013–14, 1 student received support, including 1 fellowship (averaging $3,600 per year). Financial award application deadline: 3/1; financial award applicants required to submit FAFSA. *Unit head:* Prof. Ruth Luckasson, Chair, 505-266-6510, Fax: 505-277-6929, E-mail: ruthl@unm.edu. *Application contact:* Jo Sanchez, Information Contact, 505-277-5018, Fax: 505-277-8679, E-mail: jsanchez@unm.edu.
Website: http://coe.unm.edu.

University of New Mexico, Graduate School, College of Education, Department of Educational Specialties, Program in Special Education, Albuquerque, NM 87131. Offers learning and behavioral exceptionalities (MA); mental retardation and severe disabilities (MA); special education (Ed D, PhD, Ed S). *Accreditation:* NCATE. Part-time and evening/weekend programs available. *Faculty:* 10 full-time (all women), 12 part-time/adjunct (8 women). *Students:* 58 full-time (49 women), 82 part-time (62 women); includes 46 minority (3 Black or African American, non-Hispanic/Latino; 3 American Indian or Alaska Native, non-Hispanic/Latino; 1 Asian, non-Hispanic/Latino; 37 Hispanic/Latino; 2 Two or more races, non-Hispanic/Latino), 7 international. Average age 36. 43 applicants, 56% accepted, 20 enrolled. In 2013, 42 master's, 3 doctorates awarded. *Degree requirements:* For master's, comprehensive exam, thesis optional; for doctorate, comprehensive exam, thesis/dissertation, screening, proposal hearing. *Entrance requirements:* For master's, minimum GPA of 3.2; for doctorate, minimum GPA of 3.2, 2 years of relevant experience; for Ed S, special education degree, 2 years of teaching experience with people with disabilities, writing sample, minimum GPA of 3.2. *Application deadline:* For fall admission, 3/31 priority date for domestic students; for spring admission, 9/30 priority date for domestic students. Applications are processed on a rolling basis. Application fee: $50. Electronic applications accepted. *Financial support:* In 2013–14, 128 students received support, including 4 fellowships (averaging $1,132 per year), 5 research assistantships with tuition reimbursements available (averaging $3,200 per year), 11 teaching assistantships with tuition reimbursements available (averaging $4,168 per year); career-related internships or fieldwork, Federal Work-Study, scholarships/grants, traineeships, health care benefits, unspecified assistantships, and stipends also available. Support available to part-time students. Financial award application deadline: 3/1; financial award applicants required to submit FAFSA. *Faculty research:* Mathematics instruction, bilingual special education, inclusive education, autism, reading instruction for students with cognitive disabilities, alternative assessment, human rights and disability, applied behavior analysis, bilingualism, language and literacy, mathematics, science instruction, special education. *Unit head:* Prof. Ruth Luckasson, Chair, 505-277-6510, Fax: 505-277-6929, E-mail: luckasson@unm.edu. *Application contact:* Della Gallegos, Information Contact, 505-277-5018, Fax: 505-277-8679, E-mail: dgalle06@unm.edu.
Website: http://coe.unm.edu/departments/ed-specialties/special-education.html.

University of New Orleans, Graduate School, College of Education and Human Development, Department of Special Education, New Orleans, LA 70148. Offers M Ed, PhD. *Accreditation:* NCATE. Evening/weekend programs available. *Degree requirements:* For doctorate, variable foreign language requirement, thesis/dissertation. *Entrance requirements:* For master's, GRE General Test; for doctorate, GRE General Test, GRE Subject Test. Additional exam requirements/recommendations for international students: Required—TOEFL (minimum score 550 paper-based; 79 iBT). Electronic applications accepted. *Faculty research:* Inclusion, transition, early childhood, mild/moderate, severe/profound.

University of North Alabama, College of Education, Department of Elementary Education, Collaborative Teacher Special Education Program, Florence, AL 35632-0001. Offers MA Ed. *Accreditation:* NCATE. Part-time and evening/weekend programs available. *Faculty:* 6 full-time (all women). *Students:* 2 full-time (both women), 16 part-time (14 women); includes 1 minority (American Indian or Alaska Native, non-Hispanic/Latino). Average age 31. 12 applicants, 92% accepted, 4 enrolled. In 2013, 7 master's awarded. *Degree requirements:* For master's, comprehensive exam. *Entrance requirements:* For master's, GRE, MAT, or NTE, minimum GPA of 2.5, Alabama Class B Certificate or equivalent, teaching experience. Additional exam requirements/recommendations for international students: Required—TOEFL (minimum score 550 paper-based; 79 iBT), IELTS (minimum score 6). *Application deadline:* For fall admission, 7/1 priority date for domestic students, 7/1 for international students; for spring admission, 12/1 for domestic and international students. Applications are processed on a rolling basis. Application fee: $25 ($50 for international students). Electronic applications accepted. *Expenses:* Tuition, state resident: full-time $4968; part-time $3312 per year. Tuition, nonresident: full-time $9936; part-time $6624 per year. *Required fees:* $970; $60.33 per credit. $362 per semester. *Financial support:* Federal Work-Study available. Support available to part-time students. Financial award application deadline: 4/1; financial award applicants required to submit FAFSA. *Unit head:* Dr. Victoria W. Hulsey, Chair, 256-765-5024, E-mail: vwhulsey@una.edu. *Application contact:* Russ Draccott, Graduate Admissions Counselor, 256-765-4447, E-mail: erdarracott@una.edu.

The University of North Carolina at Charlotte, The Graduate School, College of Education, Department of Special Education and Child Development, Charlotte, NC 28223-0001. Offers academically gifted (Graduate Certificate); child and family studies (M Ed); special education (M Ed, PhD), including academically or intellectually gifted (M Ed), behavioral - emotional handicaps (M Ed), cross-categorical disabilities (M Ed), learning disabilities (M Ed), mental handicaps (M Ed), severe and profound handicaps (M Ed). Part-time programs available. *Faculty:* 24 full-time (17 women), 13 part-time/adjunct (12 women). *Students:* 17 full-time (16 women), 100 part-time (88 women); includes 12 minority (9 Black or African American, non-Hispanic/Latino; 2 Asian, non-Hispanic/Latino; 1 Hispanic/Latino), 1 international. Average age 36. 79 applicants, 90% accepted, 55 enrolled. In 2013, 9 master's, 6 doctorates, 38 other advanced degrees awarded. Terminal master's awarded for partial completion of doctoral program. *Degree requirements:* For master's, thesis or alternative; for doctorate, comprehensive exam, thesis/dissertation, portfolio, qualifying exam. *Entrance requirements:* For master's, GRE or MAT; for doctorate, GRE or MAT, 3 letters of reference, resume or curriculum vitae, minimum GPA of 3.5, master's degree in special education or related field, 3 years of teaching experience. Additional exam requirements/recommendations for international students: Required—TOEFL (minimum score 557 paper-based; 83 iBT). *Application deadline:* For fall admission, 5/1 priority date for domestic students, 5/1 for international students; for spring admission, 10/1 priority date for domestic students, 10/1 for international students. Application fee: $75. Electronic applications accepted. *Expenses:* Tuition, state resident: full-time $3522. Tuition, nonresident: full-time $16,051. *Required fees:* $2585. Tuition and fees vary according to course load and program. *Financial support:* In 2013–14, 10 students received support, including 9 research assistantships (averaging $10,581 per year), 1 teaching assistantship (averaging $9,364 per year). Financial award application deadline: 4/1; financial award applicants required to submit FAFSA. *Faculty research:* Transition to adulthood and self-determination, teaching reading and other academic skills to students with disabilities, alternate assessment, early intervention, preschool education. *Unit head:* Dr. Mary Lynne Calhoun, Dean, 704-687-8722, Fax: 704-687-2916. *Application contact:* Kathy B. Giddings, Director of Graduate Admissions, 704-687-5503, Fax: 704-687-1668, E-mail: gradadm@uncc.edu.
Website: http://education.uncc.edu/spcd/sped/special_ed.htm.

The University of North Carolina at Charlotte, The Graduate School, College of Education, Interdisciplinary Education Programs, Charlotte, NC 28223-0001. Offers art education (MAT); dance education (MAT); elementary education (MAT); English as a second language (MAT); foreign language education (MAT); middle grades education (MAT); music education (MAT); secondary education (MAT); special education (MAT); teacher certification (Graduate Certificate); teaching (Graduate Certificate); theater education (MAT). Part-time programs available. *Students:* 206 full-time (165 women), 791 part-time (628 women); includes 342 minority (247 Black or African American, non-Hispanic/Latino; 16 Asian, non-Hispanic/Latino; 62 Hispanic/Latino; 17 Two or more races, non-Hispanic/Latino), 14 international. Average age 32. 564 applicants, 91% accepted, 414 enrolled. In 2013, 145 master's, 271 other advanced degrees awarded. Terminal master's awarded for partial completion of doctoral program. *Degree requirements:* For master's, thesis. *Entrance requirements:* For master's, GRE or MAT. Additional exam requirements/recommendations for international students: Required—TOEFL (minimum score 550 paper-based; 83 iBT). *Application deadline:* For fall

admission, 5/1 priority date for domestic and international students; for spring admission, 10/1 priority date for domestic and international students. Applications are processed on a rolling basis. Application fee: $75. Electronic applications accepted. *Expenses:* Tuition, state resident: full-time $3522. Tuition, nonresident: full-time $16,051. *Required fees:* $2585. Tuition and fees vary according to course load and program. *Total annual research expenditures:* $43,031. *Unit head:* Dr. Warren DiBiase, Chair, 704-687-8881, Fax: 704-687-4705, E-mail: wjdibias@uncc.edu. *Application contact:* Kathy B. Giddings, Director of Graduate Admissions, 704-687-5503, Fax: 704-687-1668, E-mail: gradadm@uncc.edu.
Website: http://education.uncc.edu/academic-programs.

The University of North Carolina at Greensboro, Graduate School, School of Education, Department of Specialized Education Services, Greensboro, NC 27412-5001. Offers cross-categorical special education (M Ed); interdisciplinary studies in special education (M Ed); leadership early care and education (Certificate); special education (M Ed, PhD). *Degree requirements:* For master's, thesis or alternative. *Entrance requirements:* For master's, GRE General Test. Additional exam requirements/recommendations for international students: Required—TOEFL. Electronic applications accepted.

The University of North Carolina Wilmington, Watson College of Education, Department of Early Childhood, Elementary, Middle, Literacy and Special Education, Wilmington, NC 28403-3297. Offers MAT. *Accreditation:* NCATE. Part-time and evening/weekend programs available. *Faculty:* 21 full-time (17 women). *Students:* 47 full-time (36 women), 13 part-time (11 women); includes 9 minority (5 Black or African American, non-Hispanic/Latino; 2 Hispanic/Latino; 2 Two or more races, non-Hispanic/Latino), 3 international. Average age 31. 36 applicants, 97% accepted, 33 enrolled. In 2013, 24 master's awarded. *Degree requirements:* For master's, comprehensive exam. *Entrance requirements:* For master's, GRE General Test, MAT, minimum B average in upper-division undergraduate course work. *Application deadline:* For fall admission, 6/1 for domestic students. Applications are processed on a rolling basis. Application fee: $60. *Expenses:* Tuition, state resident: full-time $4163. Tuition, nonresident: full-time $16,098. *Financial support:* Career-related internships or fieldwork, Federal Work-Study, and unspecified assistantships available. Support available to part-time students. Financial award application deadline: 3/15. *Unit head:* Dr. Tracy Hargrove, Chair, 910-962-3240, Fax: 910-962-3988, E-mail: hargrovet@uncw.edu. *Application contact:* Dr. Ron Vetter, Dean, Graduate School, 910-962-3224, Fax: 910-962-3787, E-mail: vetterr@uncw.edu.

University of North Dakota, Graduate School, College of Education and Human Development, Program in Special Education, Grand Forks, ND 58202. Offers M Ed, MS. *Accreditation:* NCATE. Part-time programs available. Postbaccalaureate distance learning degree programs offered (minimal on-campus study). *Degree requirements:* For master's, comprehensive exam, thesis or alternative. *Entrance requirements:* For master's, minimum GPA of 3.0. Additional exam requirements/recommendations for international students: Required—TOEFL (minimum score 550 paper-based; 79 iBT), IELTS (minimum score 6.5). Electronic applications accepted. *Faculty research:* Visual, emotional, and mental disabilities; early childhood.

University of North Dakota, Graduate School, College of Education and Human Development, Teaching and Learning Program, Grand Forks, ND 58202. Offers elementary education (Ed D, PhD); measurement and statistics (Ed D, PhD); secondary education (Ed D, PhD); special education (Ed D, PhD). *Accreditation:* NCATE. Postbaccalaureate distance learning degree programs offered (minimal on-campus study). *Degree requirements:* For doctorate, comprehensive exam, thesis/dissertation, final exam. *Entrance requirements:* For doctorate, minimum GPA of 3.5. Additional exam requirements/recommendations for international students: Required—TOEFL (minimum score 550 paper-based; 79 iBT), IELTS (minimum score 6.5). Electronic applications accepted.

University of Northern Colorado, Graduate School, College of Education and Behavioral Sciences, School of Special Education, Greeley, CO 80639. Offers deaf/hard of hearing (MA); early childhood special education (MA); gifted and talented (MA); special education (MA, Ed D); visual impairment (MA). Part-time and evening/weekend programs available. Postbaccalaureate distance learning degree programs offered (no on-campus study). *Degree requirements:* For master's, comprehensive exam, thesis or alternative; for doctorate, comprehensive exam, thesis/dissertation. *Entrance requirements:* For master's, letters of recommendation, interview; for doctorate, GRE General Test, resume. Electronic applications accepted.

University of Northern Iowa, Graduate College, College of Education, Department of Special Education, Program in Special Education, Cedar Falls, IA 50614. Offers career/vocational programming and transition (MAE); consultation (MAE); field specialization (MAE); special education (Ed D). *Students:* 8 full-time (7 women), 19 part-time (18 women); includes 1 minority (Asian, non-Hispanic/Latino), 3 international. 15 applicants, 60% accepted, 5 enrolled. In 2013, 3 doctorates awarded. Application fee: $50 ($70 for international students). *Unit head:* Dr. Susan Etscheidt, Coordinator, 319-273-3279, Fax: 319-273-7852, E-mail: susan.etscheidt@uni.edu. *Application contact:* Laurie S. Russell, Record Analyst, 319-273-2623, Fax: 319-273-2885, E-mail: laurie.russell@uni.edu.

University of Northern Iowa, Graduate College, College of Education, Department of Special Education, Teacher of Students with Visual Impairments Program, Cedar Falls, IA 50614. Offers MAE. *Students:* 3 part-time (2 women). 1 applicant. In 2013, 2 master's awarded. Application fee: $50 ($70 for international students). *Unit head:* Dr. Susan Etscheidt, Coordinator, 319-273-3279, Fax: 319-273-7852, E-mail: susan.etscheidt@uni.edu. *Application contact:* Laurie S. Russell, Record Analyst, 319-273-2623, Fax: 319-273-2885, E-mail: laurie.russell@uni.edu.

University of North Florida, College of Education and Human Services, Department of Exceptional Student and Deaf Education, Jacksonville, FL 32224. Offers American Sign Language/English interpreting (M Ed); applied behavior analysis (M Ed); autism (M Ed); deaf education (M Ed); disability services (M Ed); exceptional student education (M Ed). *Accreditation:* NCATE. Part-time and evening/weekend programs available. *Faculty:* 11 full-time (9 women), 4 part-time/adjunct (all women). *Students:* 26 full-time (21 women), 52 part-time (44 women); includes 15 minority (9 Black or African American, non-Hispanic/Latino; 2 Asian, non-Hispanic/Latino; 3 Hispanic/Latino; 1 Two or more races, non-Hispanic/Latino), 2 international. Average age 32. 39 applicants, 51% accepted, 15 enrolled. In 2013, 51 master's awarded. *Entrance requirements:* For master's, GRE General Test, minimum GPA of 3.0 in last 60 hours, interview, 3 letters of recommendation. Additional exam requirements/recommendations for international students: Required—TOEFL (minimum score 500 paper-based). *Application deadline:* For fall admission, 7/1 priority date for domestic students, 5/1 for international students; for spring admission, 11/1 priority date for domestic students, 10/1 for international students. Application fee: $30. Electronic applications accepted. *Expenses:* Tuition, state resident: full-time $9794; part-time $408.10 per credit hour. Tuition, nonresident: full-time $22,383; part-time $932.61 per credit hour. *Required fees:* $2020; $84.20 per credit hour. Tuition and fees vary according to course load and program. *Financial support:* In 2013–14, 19 students received support, including 1 research assistantship (averaging $4,524 per year); teaching assistantships, career-related internships or

fieldwork, Federal Work-Study, scholarships/grants, tuition waivers (partial), and unspecified assistantships also available. Support available to part-time students. Financial award application deadline: 4/1; financial award applicants required to submit FAFSA. *Faculty research:* Transition, integrating technology into teacher education, written language development, professional school development, learning strategies. *Total annual research expenditures:* $816,202. *Unit head:* Dr. Karen Patterson, Chair, 904-620-2930, Fax: 904-620-3895, E-mail: karen.patterson@unf.edu. *Application contact:* Dr. Amanda Pascale, Director, The Graduate School, 904-620-1360, Fax: 904-620-1362, E-mail: graduateschool@unf.edu.
Website: http://www.unf.edu/coehs/edie/.

University of North Texas, Robert B. Toulouse School of Graduate Studies, Denton, TN 76203-5017. Offers accounting (MS, PhD); applied anthropology (MA, MS); applied behavior analysis (Certificate); applied technology and performance improvement (M Ed, MS, PhD); art education (MA, PhD); art history (MA); art museum education (Certificate); arts leadership (Certificate); audiology (Au D); behavior analysis (MS); biochemistry and molecular biology (MS, PhD); biology (MA, MS, PhD); business (PhD); business computer information systems (PhD); chemistry (MS, PhD); clinical psychology (PhD); communication studies (MA, MS); computer engineering (MS); computer science (MS); computer science and engineering (PhD); counseling (M Ed, MS, PhD), including clinical mental health counseling (MS), college and university counseling (M Ed, MS), elementary school counseling (M Ed, MS), secondary school counseling (M Ed, MS); counseling psychology (PhD); creative writing (MA); criminal justice (MS); curriculum and instruction (M Ed, PhD), including curriculum studies (PhD), early childhood studies (PhD), language and literacy studies (PhD); decision sciences (MBA); design (MA, MFA), including fashion design (MFA), innovation studies, interior design (MFA); early childhood studies (MS); economics (MS); educational leadership (M Ed, Ed D, PhD); educational psychology (MS), including family studies, gifted and talented (MS, PhD), human development, learning and cognition, research, measurement and evaluation; educational research (PhD), including gifted and talented (MS, PhD), human development and family studies, psychological aspects of sports and exercise, research, measurement and statistics; electrical engineering (MS); emergency management (MPA); engineering systems (MS); English (MA, PhD); environmental science (MS, PhD); experimental psychology (PhD); finance (MBA, MS, PhD); financial management (MPA); French (MA); health psychology and behavioral medicine (PhD); health services management (MBA); higher education (M Ed, Ed D, PhD); history (MA, MS, PhD), including European history (PhD), military history (PhD), United States history (PhD); hospitality management (MS); human resources management (MPA); information science (MS, PhD); information technologies (MBA); information technology and decision sciences (MS); interdisciplinary studies (MA, MS); international sustainable tourism (MS); jazz studies (MM); journalism (MA, MJ, Graduate Certificate), including interactive and virtual digital communication (Graduate Certificate), narrative journalism (Graduate Certificate), public relations (Graduate Certificate); kinesiology (MS); learning technologies (MS, PhD); library science (MS); local government management (MPA); logistics and supply chain management (MBA, PhD); long-term care, senior housing, and aging services (MA, MS); management science (PhD); marketing (MBA, PhD); materials science and engineering (MS, PhD); mathematics (MA, PhD); merchandising (MS); music (MA, MM Ed, PhD), including ethnomusicology (MA), music education (MM Ed, PhD), music theory (MA, PhD), musicology (MA, PhD), performance (MA); nonprofit management (MPA); operations and supply chain management (MBA); performance (MM, DMA); philosophy (MA, PhD); physics (MS, PhD); political science (MA, MS, PhD); public administration and management (PhD), including emergency management, nonprofit management, public financial management, urban management; radio, television and film (MA, MFA); recreation, event and sport management (MS); rehabilitation counseling (MS, Certificate); sociology (MA, MS, PhD); Spanish (MA); special education (M Ed, PhD), including autism intervention (PhD), emotional/behavioral disorders (PhD), mild/moderate disabilities (PhD); speech-language pathology (MA, MS); strategic management (MBA); studio art (MFA); taxation (MS); teaching (M Ed); MBA/MS; MS/MPH; MSES/MBA. Part-time and evening/weekend programs available. Postbaccalaureate distance learning degree programs offered. *Faculty:* 661 full-time (213 women), 240 part-time/adjunct (144 women). *Students:* 3,106 full-time (1,620 women), 3,543 part-time (2,221 women); includes 1,740 minority (533 Black or African American, non-Hispanic/Latino; 15 American Indian or Alaska Native, non-Hispanic/Latino; 286 Asian, non-Hispanic/Latino; 746 Hispanic/Latino; 3 Native Hawaiian or other Pacific Islander, non-Hispanic/Latino; 157 Two or more races, non-Hispanic/Latino), 1,145 international. Average age 32. 6,289 applicants, 43% accepted, 1751 enrolled. In 2013, 1,778 master's, 239 doctorates, 10 other advanced degrees awarded. Terminal master's awarded for partial completion of doctoral program. *Degree requirements:* For master's, variable foreign language requirement, comprehensive exam (for some programs), thesis (for some programs); for doctorate, variable foreign language requirement, comprehensive exam (for some programs), thesis/dissertation; for other advanced degree, variable foreign language requirement, comprehensive exam (for some programs). *Entrance requirements:* For master's and doctorate, GRE, GMAT. Additional exam requirements/recommendations for international students: Required—TOEFL (minimum score 550 paper-based; 79 iBT). *Application deadline:* For fall admission, 7/15 for domestic students, 3/15 for international students; for spring admission, 11/15 for domestic students, 9/15 for international students; for summer admission, 5/1 for domestic students. Applications are processed on a rolling basis. Application fee: $60. Electronic applications accepted. *Financial support:* Fellowships with partial tuition reimbursements, research assistantships with partial tuition reimbursements, teaching assistantships, career-related internships or fieldwork, Federal Work-Study, institutionally sponsored loans, scholarships/grants, health care benefits, and library assistantships available. Support available to part-time students. Financial award applicants required to submit FAFSA. *Unit head:* Mark Wardell, Dean, 940-565-2383, E-mail: mark.wardell@unt.edu. *Application contact:* Toulouse School of Graduate Studies, 940-565-2383, Fax: 940-565-2141, E-mail: gradsch@unt.edu.
Website: http://tsgs.unt.edu/.

University of Oklahoma, Jeannine Rainbolt College of Education, Department of Educational Psychology, Program in Special Education, Norman, OK 73019. Offers M Ed, PhD. *Accreditation:* NCATE. Part-time and evening/weekend programs available. *Students:* 12 full-time (11 women), 41 part-time (36 women); includes 14 minority (6 Black or African American, non-Hispanic/Latino; 3 American Indian or Alaska Native, non-Hispanic/Latino; 1 Asian, non-Hispanic/Latino; 1 Hispanic/Latino; 3 Two or more races, non-Hispanic/Latino), 3 international. Average age 38. 16 applicants, 38% accepted, 5 enrolled. In 2013, 2 master's, 2 doctorates awarded. *Degree requirements:* For master's, comprehensive exam, thesis optional; for doctorate, variable foreign language requirement, comprehensive exam, thesis/dissertation. *Entrance requirements:* For master's, minimum GPA of 3.0 in last degree conferred; for doctorate, GRE, minimum GPA of 3.0 in last degree conferred, minimum 2 years of special education teaching experience. Additional exam requirements/recommendations for international students: Required—TOEFL (minimum score 79 iBT). *Application deadline:* For fall admission, 3/1 for domestic and international students; for spring admission, 10/1 for domestic students, 9/1 for international students. Application fee: $50 ($100 for international students). Electronic applications accepted. *Expenses:* Tuition, state

Special Education

resident: full-time $4205; part-time $175.20 per credit hour. Tuition, nonresident: full-time $16,205; part-time $675.20 per credit hour. *Required fees:* $2745; $103.85 per credit hour. $126.50 per semester. *Financial support:* In 2013–14, 35 students received support. Career-related internships or fieldwork, Federal Work-Study, scholarships/grants, health care benefits, and unspecified assistantships available. Support available to part-time students. Financial award application deadline: 6/1; financial award applicants required to submit FAFSA. *Faculty research:* Intellectual and behavioral disabilities, transition, self-determination, early childhood special education, autism, technology, post-secondary outcomes, assessment. *Unit head:* Dr. David Lovett, Program Coordinator, 405-325-1507, Fax: 405-325-6655, E-mail: dlovett@ou.edu. *Application contact:* Shannon Vazquez, Graduate Programs Officer, 405-325-4525, Fax: 405-325-6655, E-mail: shannonv@ou.edu.
Website: http://www.ou.edu/content/education/edpy/special-education.html.

University of Oklahoma Health Sciences Center, Graduate College, College of Allied Health, Department of Communication Sciences and Disorders, Oklahoma City, OK 73190. Offers audiology (MS, Au D, PhD); communication sciences and disorders (Certificate), including reading, speech-language pathology; education of the deaf (MS); speech-language pathology (MS, PhD). *Accreditation:* ASHA (one or more programs are accredited). Part-time programs available. *Faculty:* 15 full-time (12 women). *Students:* 72 full-time (67 women), 5 part-time (4 women); includes 12 minority (3 Asian, non-Hispanic/Latino; 1 Hispanic/Latino; 8 Two or more races, non-Hispanic/Latino). Average age 26. 181 applicants, 45% accepted, 30 enrolled. In 2013, 19 master's, 3 doctorates awarded. Terminal master's awarded for partial completion of doctoral program. *Degree requirements:* For master's, comprehensive exam, thesis optional; for doctorate, one foreign language, comprehensive exam, thesis/dissertation. *Entrance requirements:* For master's and doctorate, GRE General Test, 3 letters of recommendation. Additional exam requirements/recommendations for international students: Required—TOEFL (minimum score 550 paper-based). *Application deadline:* For fall admission, 2/1 for domestic students. Applications are processed on a rolling basis. Application fee: $50. *Expenses:* Tuition, state resident: full-time $3504; part-time $175.20 per credit hour. Tuition, nonresident: full-time $13,504; part-time $675.20 per credit hour. *Required fees:* $1545; $52.70 per credit hour. $245.25 per semester. Tuition and fees vary according to course load. *Financial support:* In 2013–14, 8 research assistantships (averaging $16,000 per year) were awarded; fellowships, career-related internships or fieldwork, Federal Work-Study, institutionally sponsored loans, and traineeships also available. Support available to part-time students. *Faculty research:* Event-related potentials, cleft palate, fluency disorders, language disorders, hearing and speech science. *Unit head:* Dr. Stephen Painton, Chair, 405-271-4214, E-mail: stephen-painton@ouhsc.edu. *Application contact:* Dr. Sarah Buckingham, Graduate Liaison, 405-271-4214, Fax: 405-271-1153, E-mail: sarah-buckingham@ouhsc.edu.

University of Phoenix–Bay Area Campus, College of Education, San Jose, CA 95134-1805. Offers administration and supervision (MA Ed); adult education and training (MA Ed); early childhood education (MA Ed); education (Ed S); educational leadership (Ed D); elementary teacher education (MA Ed); higher education administration (PhD); secondary teacher education (MA Ed); special education (MA Ed); teacher leadership (MA Ed). Evening/weekend programs available. Postbaccalaureate distance learning degree programs offered (no on-campus study). *Degree requirements:* For master's, thesis (for some programs). *Entrance requirements:* For master's, minimum undergraduate GPA of 2.5, 3 years of work experience. Additional exam requirements/recommendations for international students: Required—TOEFL (minimum score 550 paper-based; 79 iBT). Electronic applications accepted.

University of Phoenix–Hawaii Campus, College of Education, Honolulu, HI 96813-4317. Offers administration and supervision (MA Ed); curriculum and instruction (MA Ed); elementary education (MA Ed); secondary education (MA Ed); special education (MA Ed); teacher education for elementary licensure (MA Ed). Evening/weekend programs available. *Degree requirements:* For master's, thesis (for some programs). *Entrance requirements:* For master's, minimum undergraduate GPA of 2.5, 3 years of work experience. Additional exam requirements/recommendations for international students: Required—TOEFL (minimum score 550 paper-based; 79 iBT). Electronic applications accepted.

University of Phoenix–Omaha Campus, College of Education, Omaha, NE 68154-5240. Offers administration and supervision (MA Ed); curriculum and instruction (MA Ed), including adult education, computer education, curriculum and instruction, English and language arts education, English as a second language, mathematics education; elementary teacher education (MA Ed); secondary teacher education (MA Ed); special education (MA Ed).

University of Phoenix–Online Campus, College of Education, Phoenix, AZ 85034-7209. Offers administration and supervision (MAEd, Certificate); adult education and training (MAEd); curriculum and instruction (MAEd), including computer education, curriculum and instruction, English as a second language, language arts, mathematics, reading; early childhood education (MAEd); educational studies (MAEd); elementary teacher education (MAEd), including early childhood, elementary teacher education, high school middle level, middle level; principal licensure (Certificate); secondary teacher education (MAEd); special education (MAEd, Certificate); teacher education (MAEd), including middle level generalist; teacher education middle level mathematics (MAEd), including middle level mathematics; teacher education middle level science (MAEd), including middle level science; teacher education secondary mathematics (MAEd); teacher education secondary science (MAEd); teacher leadership (MAEd); teachers of English learners (Certificate); transition to teaching (Certificate), including elementary education, secondary education. *Accreditation:* Teacher Education Accreditation Council. Evening/weekend programs available. Postbaccalaureate distance learning degree programs offered. *Entrance requirements:* Additional exam requirements/recommendations for international students: Required—TOEFL, TOEIC (Test of English as an International Communication), Berlitz Online English Proficiency Exam, PTE, or IELTS. Electronic applications accepted. *Expenses:* Contact institution.

University of Phoenix–Phoenix Campus, College of Education, Tempe, AZ 85282-2371. Offers administration and supervision (MA Ed); adult education and training (MA Ed); curriculum and instruction reading (MA Ed); early childhood education (MA Ed); education studies (MA Ed); elementary teacher education (MA Ed); secondary teacher education (MA Ed); special education (MA Ed); teacher leadership (MA Ed). Evening/weekend programs available. Postbaccalaureate distance learning degree programs offered. *Entrance requirements:* Additional exam requirements/recommendations for international students: Required—TOEFL, TOEIC (Test of English as an International Communication), Berlitz Online English Proficiency Exam, PTE, or IELTS. Electronic applications accepted. *Expenses:* Contact institution.

University of Phoenix–Southern Arizona Campus, College of Education, Tucson, AZ 85711. Offers administration and supervision (MA Ed); adult education and training (MA Ed); curriculum instruction (MA Ed); educational counseling (MA Ed); elementary teacher education (MA Ed); school counseling (MSC); secondary teacher education (MA Ed); special education (MA Ed, Certificate). Evening/weekend programs available. *Degree requirements:* For master's, thesis (for some programs). *Entrance requirements:* For master's, minimum undergraduate GPA of 2.5, 3 years of work experience.

Additional exam requirements/recommendations for international students: Required—TOEFL (minimum score 550 paper-based; 79 iBT). Electronic applications accepted.

University of Phoenix–Utah Campus, College of Education, Salt Lake City, UT 84123-4617. Offers administration and supervision (MA Ed); curriculum and instruction (MA Ed); elementary teacher education (MA Ed); school counseling (MSC); secondary teacher education (MA Ed); special education (MA Ed). Evening/weekend programs available. *Degree requirements:* For master's, thesis (for some programs). *Entrance requirements:* For master's, minimum undergraduate GPA of 2.5, 3 years work experience. Additional exam requirements/recommendations for international students: Required—TOEFL (minimum score 550 paper-based; 79 iBT). Electronic applications accepted.

University of Phoenix–Washington D.C. Campus, College of Education, Washington, DC 20001. Offers administration and supervision (MA Ed); adult education and training (MA Ed); computer education (MA Ed); curriculum and instruction (MA Ed, Ed D); early childhood education (MA Ed); education (Ed S); educational leadership (Ed D); educational technology (Ed D); elementary teacher education (MA Ed); English and language arts education (MA Ed); English as a second language (MA Ed); higher education administration (PhD); mathematics education (MA Ed); secondary teacher education (MA Ed); special education (MA Ed); teacher leadership (MA Ed).

University of Pittsburgh, School of Education, Department of Instruction and Learning, Program in Special Education, Pittsburgh, PA 15260. Offers applied behavior analysis (M Ed); combined studies in early childhood and special education (M Ed); early education of disabled students (M Ed); education of students with mental and physical disabilities (M Ed); general special education (M Ed); special education (Ed D, PhD); special education teacher preparation K-8 (M Ed); special education with academic instruction certification (M Ed); vision studies (M Ed). Part-time and evening/weekend programs available. *Students:* 72 full-time (66 women), 91 part-time (83 women); includes 8 minority (3 Black or African American, non-Hispanic/Latino; 1 Asian, non-Hispanic/Latino; 1 Hispanic/Latino; 3 Two or more races, non-Hispanic/Latino), 3 international. Average age 30. 91 applicants, 85% accepted, 56 enrolled. In 2013, 68 master's, 4 doctorates awarded. *Degree requirements:* For master's, thesis; for doctorate, thesis/dissertation. *Entrance requirements:* For master's, PRAXIS I; for doctorate, GRE General Test. Additional exam requirements/recommendations for international students: Required—TOEFL. *Application deadline:* For fall admission, 2/1 priority date for domestic students; for spring admission, 11/1 priority date for domestic students. Applications are processed on a rolling basis. Application fee: $50. *Expenses:* Tuition, state resident: full-time $19,964; part-time $807 per credit. Tuition, nonresident: full-time $32,686; part-time $1337 per credit. *Required fees:* $740; $200. Tuition and fees vary according to program. *Financial support:* Research assistantships, teaching assistantships, career-related internships or fieldwork, Federal Work-Study, and tuition waivers (partial) available. Support available to part-time students. Financial award application deadline: 3/15; financial award applicants required to submit FAFSA. *Unit head:* Dr. Richard Donato, Chairman, 412-624-7248, Fax: 412-648-7081, E-mail: donato@pitt.edu. *Application contact:* Norma Ann McMichael, Graduate Enrollment Manager, 412-648-2230, Fax: 412-648-1899, E-mail: soeinfo@pitt.edu.
Website: http://www.education.pitt.edu/AcademicDepartments/InstructionLearning/Programs/GeneralSpecialEducation.aspx.

University of Portland, School of Education, Portland, OR 97203-5798. Offers education (MA, MAT); educational leadership (M Ed); English for speakers of other languages (M Ed); initial administrator licensure (M Ed); neuroeducation (Ed D); organizational leadership and development (Ed D); reading (M Ed); special education (M Ed). M Ed also available through the Graduate Outreach Program for teachers residing in the Oregon and Washington state areas. *Accreditation:* NCATE. Part-time and evening/weekend programs available. *Faculty:* 17 full-time (10 women), 12 part-time/adjunct (4 women). *Students:* 47 full-time (29 women), 214 part-time (155 women); includes 25 minority (1 Black or African American, non-Hispanic/Latino; 1 American Indian or Alaska Native, non-Hispanic/Latino; 8 Asian, non-Hispanic/Latino; 6 Hispanic/Latino; 6 Native Hawaiian or other Pacific Islander, non-Hispanic/Latino; 3 Two or more races, non-Hispanic/Latino), 63 international. Average age 32. In 2013, 96 master's awarded. *Entrance requirements:* For master's, minimum GPA of 3.0, teaching certificate, letters of recommendation, resume, statement of goals, official transcripts. Additional exam requirements/recommendations for international students: Required—TOEFL (minimum score 550 paper-based; 80 iBT), IELTS (minimum score 7). *Application deadline:* For fall admission, 7/15 priority date for domestic and international students; for spring admission, 12/15 priority date for domestic and international students. Applications are processed on a rolling basis. Application fee: $50. *Expenses:* Tuition: Part-time $1025 per credit hour. Tuition and fees vary according to program. *Financial support:* Federal Work-Study and scholarships/grants available. Support available to part-time students. Financial award application deadline: 3/1; financial award applicants required to submit FAFSA. *Faculty research:* Multicultural education, supervision/leadership. *Unit head:* Dr. Bruce Weitzel, Associate Dean, 503-943-7135, E-mail: soed@up.edu. *Application contact:* Dr. Matt Baasten, Assistant to the Provost and Dean of the Graduate School, 503-943-7107, Fax: 503-943-7315, E-mail: baasten@up.edu.
Website: http://education.up.edu/default.aspx?cid-4318&pid-5590.

University of Puerto Rico, Medical Sciences Campus, Graduate School of Public Health, Department of Human Development, Program in Developmental Disabilities-Early Intervention, San Juan, PR 00936-5067. Offers Certificate. Part-time and evening/weekend programs available.

University of Puerto Rico, Río Piedras Campus, College of Education, Program in Special and Differentiated Education, San Juan, PR 00931-3300. Offers M Ed. *Degree requirements:* For master's, thesis. *Entrance requirements:* For master's, GRE or PAEG, interview, minimum GPA of 3.0, letter of recommendation.

University of Rhode Island, Graduate School, College of Human Science and Services, School of Education, Kingston, RI 02881. Offers adult education (MA); education (PhD); elementary education (MA); music education (MM); reading education (MA); secondary education (MA); special education (MA); MS/PhD. *Accreditation:* NCATE. Part-time and evening/weekend programs available. *Faculty:* 16 full-time (9 women). *Students:* 64 full-time (48 women), 91 part-time (68 women); includes 17 minority (8 Black or African American, non-Hispanic/Latino; 2 American Indian or Alaska Native, non-Hispanic/Latino; 2 Asian, non-Hispanic/Latino; 3 Hispanic/Latino; 2 Two or more races, non-Hispanic/Latino), 6 international. In 2013, 47 master's, 11 doctorates awarded. *Degree requirements:* For master's, comprehensive exam (for some programs), thesis optional; for doctorate, comprehensive exam, thesis/dissertation. *Entrance requirements:* For master's, 2 letters of recommendation; interview (for special education applicants); for doctorate, GRE, 3 letters of recommendation, resume. Additional exam requirements/recommendations for international students: Required—TOEFL (minimum score 600 paper-based; 100 iBT). *Application deadline:* For fall admission, 1/31 for domestic and international students. Application fee: $65. Electronic applications accepted. *Expenses:* Tuition, state resident: full-time $11,532; part-time $641 per credit. Tuition, nonresident: full-time $23,606; part-time $1311 per credit. *Required fees:* $1388; $36 per credit. $35 per semester. One-time fee: $130. *Financial support:* In 2013–14, 2 research assistantships with full and partial tuition

reimbursements (averaging $11,883 per year), 4 teaching assistantships with full and partial tuition reimbursements (averaging $8,488 per year) were awarded; career-related internships or fieldwork also available. Financial award application deadline: 1/31; financial award applicants required to submit FAFSA. *Total annual research expenditures:* $1.1 million. *Unit head:* Dr. David Byrd, Director, 401-874-5484, Fax: 401-874-5471, E-mail: dbyrd@uri.edu. *Application contact:* Graduate Admissions, 401-874-2872, E-mail: gradadm@etal.uri.edu.
Website: http://www.uri.edu/hss/education/.

University of Rio Grande, Graduate School, Rio Grande, OH 45674. Offers classroom teaching (M Ed), including fine arts, learning disabilities, mathematics, reading education. *Accreditation:* NCATE. Part-time and evening/weekend programs available. *Degree requirements:* For master's, final research project, portfolio. *Entrance requirements:* For master's, minimum GPA of 2.7 in major, 2.5 overall. Additional exam requirements/recommendations for international students: Required—TOEFL. *Faculty research:* Interagency collaboration, reading and mathematics, learning styles, college access, literacy.

University of St. Francis, College of Education, Joliet, IL 60435-6169. Offers educational leadership (MS, Ed D); elementary education (M Ed); higher education (MS); reading (MS); secondary education (M Ed), including English education, math education, science education, social studies education, visual arts education; special education (M Ed); teaching and learning (MS). *Accreditation:* NCATE. Part-time and evening/weekend programs available. Postbaccalaureate distance learning degree programs offered (no on-campus study). *Faculty:* 10 full-time (8 women), 34 part-time/adjunct (25 women). *Students:* 14 full-time (13 women), 250 part-time (183 women); includes 34 minority (20 Black or African American, non-Hispanic/Latino; 1 American Indian or Alaska Native, non-Hispanic/Latino; 13 Hispanic/Latino), 1 international. Average age 36. 133 applicants, 62% accepted, 71 enrolled. In 2013, 147 master's awarded. *Degree requirements:* For doctorate, thesis/dissertation. *Entrance requirements:* For doctorate, master's degree, IL Type 75 or Principal's endorsement, interview, minimum undergraduate GPA of 3.0, professional portfolio, letter of recommendation. Additional exam requirements/recommendations for international students: Required—TOEFL (minimum score 550 paper-based; 79 iBT), IELTS (minimum score 6.5). *Application deadline:* Applications are processed on a rolling basis. Application fee: $30. Electronic applications accepted. Application fee is waived when completed online. *Expenses:* Contact institution. *Financial support:* In 2013–14, 10 students received support. Scholarships/grants, tuition waivers (partial), and unspecified assistantships available. Support available to part-time students. Financial award applicants required to submit FAFSA. *Unit head:* Dr. John Gambro, Dean, 815-740-3829, Fax: 815-740-2264, E-mail: jgambro@stfrancis.edu. *Application contact:* Sandra Sloka, Director of Admissions for Graduate and Degree Completion Programs, 800-735-7500, Fax: 815-740-3431, E-mail: ssloka@stfrancis.edu.
Website: http://www.stfrancis.edu/academics/college-of-education/.

University of Saint Francis, Graduate School, Department of Education, Fort Wayne, IN 46808-3994. Offers 21st century interventions (Post Master's Certificate); special education (MS Ed), including intense intervention, mild intervention, special education. *Accreditation:* NCATE. Part-time and evening/weekend programs available. Postbaccalaureate distance learning degree programs offered (no on-campus study). *Faculty:* 2. *Students:* 3 full-time (1 woman), 14 part-time (13 women); includes 1 minority (Black or African American, non-Hispanic/Latino). Average age 31. 4 applicants, 100% accepted, 4 enrolled. In 2013, 6 master's awarded. *Degree requirements:* For master's, comprehensive exam. *Entrance requirements:* For master's, GRE or MAT if undergraduate GPA is less than 3.0, minimum undergraduate GPA of 2.8; standard teaching license and/or bachelor's degree from regionally-accredited institution (or CASA scores if no license). *Application deadline:* For fall admission, 7/1 priority date for domestic students; for spring admission, 11/1 priority date for domestic students. Applications are processed on a rolling basis. Application fee: $20. Application fee is waived when completed online. *Financial support:* Federal Work-Study, scholarships/grants, and unspecified assistantships available. Support available to part-time students. Financial award application deadline: 3/10; financial award applicants required to submit FAFSA. *Unit head:* Maureen McCon, Licensing Officer/Unit Assessment System (UAS) Coordinator, 260-399-7700 Ext. 8415, Fax: 260-399-8170, E-mail: mmccon@sf.edu. *Application contact:* James Cashdollar, Admissions Counselor, 260-399-7700 Ext. 6302, Fax: 260-399-8152, E-mail: jcashdollar@sf.edu.
Website: http://www.sf.edu/sf/education.

University of Saint Joseph, Department of Autism and Applied Behavior Analysis, West Hartford, CT 06117-2700. Offers applied behavior analysis (Postbaccalaureate Certificate); autism and applied behavior analysis (MS); autism spectrum disorders (Postbaccalaureate Certificate). Part-time and evening/weekend programs available. *Degree requirements:* For master's, thesis. Electronic applications accepted. Application fee is waived when completed online.

University of Saint Joseph, Department of Education, West Hartford, CT 06117-2700. Offers education (MA); special education (MA). Part-time and evening/weekend programs available. *Degree requirements:* For master's, comprehensive exam, thesis or alternative. *Entrance requirements:* For master's, 2 letters of recommendation. Electronic applications accepted. Application fee is waived when completed online.

University of Saint Mary, Graduate Programs, Program in Special Education, Leavenworth, KS 66048-5082. Offers MA. Part-time and evening/weekend programs available. *Expenses: Tuition:* Part-time $550 per credit hour.

University of St. Thomas, Graduate Studies, School of Education, Department of Special Education, St. Paul, MN 55105-1096. Offers autism spectrum disorders (MA, Certificate); developmental disabilities (MA); early childhood special education (MA); educational leadership (Ed S); emotional behavioral disorders (MA); gifted, creative, and talented education (MA); learning disabilities (MA); Orton-Gillingham reading (Certificate); special education (MA). *Accreditation:* NCATE. Part-time and evening/weekend programs available. *Degree requirements:* For master's, thesis; for other advanced degree, professional portfolio. *Entrance requirements:* For master's, minimum GPA of 3.0 or MAT; for other advanced degree, MAT or minimum GPA of 2.75. Additional exam requirements/recommendations for international students: Required—TOEFL (minimum score 550 paper-based; 80 iBT). *Application deadline:* For fall admission, 6/1 priority date for domestic students; for spring admission, 11/1 priority date for domestic students. Applications are processed on a rolling basis. Application fee: $50. *Financial support:* Fellowships, research assistantships, institutionally sponsored loans, and scholarships/grants available. Support available to part-time students. Financial award applicants required to submit FAFSA. *Faculty research:* Reading and math fluency, inclusion curriculum for developmental disorders, parent involvement in positive behavior supports, children's friendships, preschool inclusion. *Unit head:* Dr. Terri L. Vandercook, Chair, 651-962-4389, Fax: 651-962-4169, E-mail: tlvandercook@stthomas.edu. *Application contact:* Patricia L. Thomas, Department Assistant, 651-962-4980, Fax: 651-962-4169, E-mail: thom2319@stthomas.edu.

University of St. Thomas, School of Education, Houston, TX 77006-4696. Offers all level education (M Ed); bilingual/dual language (M Ed); Catholic school teaching (M Ed); Catholic/private school leadership (M Ed); counselor education (M Ed); curriculum and instruction (M Ed); educational leadership (M Ed); elementary teaching (M Ed); English as a second language (M Ed); exceptionality/educational diagnostician (M Ed); exceptionality/special education (M Ed); generalist (M Ed); reading (M Ed); secondary teaching (M Ed). *Accreditation:* Teacher Education Accreditation Council. Part-time and evening/weekend programs available. Postbaccalaureate distance learning degree programs offered (no on-campus study). *Faculty:* 40 full-time (26 women), 43 part-time/adjunct (31 women). *Students:* 27 full-time (20 women), 1,091 part-time (981 women); includes 691 minority (247 Black or African American, non-Hispanic/Latino; 1 American Indian or Alaska Native, non-Hispanic/Latino; 44 Asian, non-Hispanic/Latino; 379 Hispanic/Latino; 2 Native Hawaiian or other Pacific Islander, non-Hispanic/Latino; 18 Two or more races, non-Hispanic/Latino), 28 international. Average age 36. 858 applicants, 83% accepted, 458 enrolled. In 2013, 454 master's awarded. *Degree requirements:* For master's, thesis, field experience. *Entrance requirements:* For master's, GRE or MAT if GPA is below 3.0, bachelor's degree; minimum GPA of 2.75 in bachelor's degree or last 60 credit hours; official transcripts from all institutions; goal statement of 250-300 words; 1 reference. Additional exam requirements/recommendations for international students: Required—TOEFL. *Application deadline:* Applications are processed on a rolling basis. Application fee: $35. Electronic applications accepted. *Expenses:* Contact institution. *Financial support:* In 2013–14, 41 students received support. Federal Work-Study, scholarships/grants, and state work-study, institutional employment available. Support available to part-time students. Financial award application deadline: 4/15; financial award applicants required to submit FAFSA. *Faculty research:* Leadership, diversity, personality traits, second language acquisition. *Unit head:* Dr. Robert LeBlanc, Dean, 713-525-3540, Fax: 713-525-3871, E-mail: education@stthom.edu. *Application contact:* Rita Paredes, Administrative Assistant, 713-525-3442, Fax: 713-525-3871, E-mail: rparede@stthom.edu.
Website: http://www.stthom.edu/Academics/School_of_Education/Index.aqf.

University of San Diego, School of Leadership and Education Sciences, Department of Learning and Teaching, San Diego, CA 92110-2492. Offers curriculum and instruction (M Ed); special education (M Ed); special education with deaf and hard of hearing (M Ed); teaching (MAT); TESOL, literacy and culture (M Ed). Part-time and evening/weekend programs available. *Faculty:* 10 full-time (6 women), 46 part-time/adjunct (38 women). *Students:* 132 full-time (100 women), 52 part-time (43 women); includes 141 minority (1 Black or African American, non-Hispanic/Latino; 16 American Indian or Alaska Native, non-Hispanic/Latino; 30 Asian, non-Hispanic/Latino; 79 Hispanic/Latino; 1 Native Hawaiian or other Pacific Islander, non-Hispanic/Latino; 14 Two or more races, non-Hispanic/Latino), 4 international. Average age 29. 253 applicants, 85% accepted, 108 enrolled. In 2013, 94 master's awarded. *Degree requirements:* For master's, thesis (for some programs), international experience. *Entrance requirements:* For master's, California Basic Educational Skills Test, minimum GPA of 3.0. Additional exam requirements/recommendations for international students: Required—TOEFL (minimum score 580 paper-based; 83 iBT), TWE. *Application deadline:* For fall admission, 3/1 priority date for domestic and international students; for spring admission, 10/15 priority date for domestic and international students. Applications are processed on a rolling basis. Application fee: $45. Electronic applications accepted. *Expenses: Tuition:* Full-time $23,580; part-time $1310 per credit. *Required fees:* $350. *Financial support:* In 2013–14, 52 students received support. Career-related internships or fieldwork, Federal Work-Study, institutionally sponsored loans, and stipends available. Support available to part-time students. Financial award application deadline: 4/1; financial award applicants required to submit FAFSA. *Faculty research:* Action research methodology, cultural studies, instructional theories and practices, second language acquisition, school reform. *Unit head:* Dr. Heather Lattimer, Director, 619-260-7616, Fax: 619-260-8159, E-mail: hlattimer@sandiego.edu. *Application contact:* Monica Mahon, Associate Director of Graduate Admissions, 619-260-4524, Fax: 619-260-4158, E-mail: grads@sandiego.edu.
Website: http://www.sandiego.edu/soles/departments/learning-and-teaching/.

University of San Francisco, School of Education, Department of Learning and Instruction, San Francisco, CA 94117-1080. Offers digital technologies for teaching and learning (MA); learning and instruction (MA, Ed D); special education (MA, Ed D); teaching reading (MA). Part-time and evening/weekend programs available. *Faculty:* 7 full-time (4 women), 6 part-time/adjunct (4 women). *Students:* 76 full-time (59 women), 40 part-time (26 women); includes 35 minority (5 Black or African American, non-Hispanic/Latino; 2 American Indian or Alaska Native, non-Hispanic/Latino; 9 Asian, non-Hispanic/Latino; 16 Hispanic/Latino; 3 Two or more races, non-Hispanic/Latino), 5 international. Average age 39. 73 applicants, 86% accepted, 40 enrolled. In 2013, 14 master's, 7 doctorates awarded. *Degree requirements:* For doctorate, thesis/dissertation. *Application deadline:* For fall admission, 3/1 priority date for domestic and international students; for spring admission, 11/1 priority date for domestic and international students. Applications are processed on a rolling basis. Application fee: $55 ($65 for international students). Electronic applications accepted. *Expenses: Tuition:* Full-time $21,150; part-time $1175 per unit. Tuition and fees vary according to course load, campus/location and program. *Financial support:* In 2013–14, 14 students received support. Fellowships, research assistantships, and teaching assistantships available. Financial award application deadline: 3/2; financial award applicants required to submit FAFSA. *Unit head:* Dr. Patricia Busk, Chair, 415-422-6289. *Application contact:* Amy Fogliani, Associate Director of Graduate Outreach, 415-422-5467, E-mail: schoolofeducation@usfca.edu.

University of Saskatchewan, College of Graduate Studies and Research, College of Education, Department of Educational Psychology and Special Education, Saskatoon, SK S7N 5A2, Canada. Offers M Ed, PhD, Diploma. *Degree requirements:* For master's, thesis (for some programs); for doctorate, comprehensive exam (for some programs), thesis/dissertation. *Entrance requirements:* Additional exam requirements/recommendations for international students: Required—TOEFL (minimum score 80 iBT); Recommended—IELTS (minimum score 6.5). Electronic applications accepted. *Expenses: Tuition, area resident:* Full-time $3585 Canadian dollars; part-time $585 Canadian dollars per course. Tuition, nonresident: part-time $877 Canadian dollars per course. *International tuition:* $5377 Canadian dollars full-time. *Required fees:* $889.51 Canadian dollars.

University of South Alabama, Graduate School, College of Education, Department of Leadership and Teacher Education, Mobile, AL 36688-0002. Offers early childhood education (M Ed); educational administration (Ed S); educational leadership (M Ed); elementary education (M Ed); reading education (M Ed); science education (M Ed); secondary education (M Ed); special education (M Ed, Ed S). *Accreditation:* NCATE. Part-time programs available. *Faculty:* 17 full-time (11 women), 4 part-time/adjunct (all women). *Students:* 136 full-time (103 women), 78 part-time (67 women); includes 45 minority (40 Black or African American, non-Hispanic/Latino; 2 Asian, non-Hispanic/Latino; 1 Hispanic/Latino; 2 Two or more races, non-Hispanic/Latino). 90 applicants, 53% accepted, 45 enrolled. In 2013, 69 master's awarded. *Degree requirements:* For master's, comprehensive exam. *Entrance requirements:* For master's, GRE General Test or MAT, minimum GPA of 3.0. *Application deadline:* For fall admission, 7/15 priority date for domestic students, 6/15 priority date for international students; for spring admission, 12/1 priority date for domestic students, 11/1 priority date for international students. Applications are processed on a rolling basis. Application fee: $35. *Expenses:* Tuition, state resident: full-time $8976; part-time $374 per credit hour. Tuition,

nonresident: full-time $17,952; part-time $748 per credit hour. *Financial support:* Research assistantships and career-related internships or fieldwork available. Support available to part-time students. Financial award application deadline: 4/1. *Unit head:* Dr. Harold Dodge, Jr., Chair, 251-380-2894. *Application contact:* Dr. Abigail Baxter, Director of Graduate Studies, 251-380-2738, Fax: 251-380-2748, E-mail: abaxter@southalabama.edu.
Website: http://www.southalabama.edu/coe/lted.

University of South Carolina, The Graduate School, College of Education, Department of Educational Studies, Program in Special Education, Columbia, SC 29208. Offers M Ed, MAT, PhD. *Accreditation:* NCATE. Part-time programs available. *Degree requirements:* For master's, comprehensive exam; for doctorate, one foreign language, comprehensive exam, thesis/dissertation. *Entrance requirements:* For master's, GRE General Test, MAT, interview, sample of written work; for doctorate, GRE General Test or MAT, interview, sample of written work. *Faculty research:* Strategy training, transition, technology, rural special education, behavior management.

University of South Carolina Upstate, Graduate Programs, Spartanburg, SC 29303-4999. Offers early childhood education (M Ed); elementary education (M Ed); informatics (MS); special education: visual impairment (M Ed). *Accreditation:* NCATE. Part-time and evening/weekend programs available. *Faculty:* 8 full-time (6 women), 5 part-time/adjunct (4 women). *Students:* 10 full-time (4 women), 13 part-time (11 women); includes 8 minority (6 Black or African American, non-Hispanic/Latino; 2 Two or more races, non-Hispanic/Latino). Average age 33. In 2013, 11 master's awarded. *Degree requirements:* For master's, professional portfolio. *Entrance requirements:* For master's, GRE General Test or MAT, interview, minimum undergraduate GPA of 2.5, teaching certificate, 2 letters of recommendation. *Application deadline:* Applications are processed on a rolling basis. Application fee: $40. *Expenses:* Tuition, state resident: full-time $11,272; part-time $470 per semester hour. Tuition, nonresident: full-time $24,196; part-time $1008 per semester hour. Tuition and fees vary according to course load and program. *Financial support:* Institutionally sponsored loans and institutional work-study available. Financial award application deadline: 7/15; financial award applicants required to submit FAFSA. *Faculty research:* Promoting university diversity awareness, rough and tumble play, social justice education, American Indian literatures and cultures, diversity and multicultural education, science teaching strategy. *Unit head:* Dr. Tina Herzberg, Director of Graduate Programs, 864-503-5572, Fax: 864-503-5573, E-mail: rstevens@uscupstate.edu. *Application contact:* Donette Stewart, Associate Vice Chancellor for Enrollment Services, 864-503-5280, E-mail: dstewart@uscupstate.edu.
Website: http://www.uscupstate.edu/graduate/.

The University of South Dakota, Graduate School, School of Education, Division of Curriculum and Instruction, Program in Special Education, Vermillion, SD 57069-2390. Offers MA. *Accreditation:* NCATE. Part-time programs available. Postbaccalaureate distance learning degree programs offered. *Degree requirements:* For master's, comprehensive exam, thesis or alternative. *Entrance requirements:* For master's, GRE General Test, MAT, minimum GPA of 2.7. Additional exam requirements/recommendations for international students: Required—TOEFL (minimum score 550 paper-based; 79 iBT). Electronic applications accepted.

University of Southern Maine, College of Management and Human Service, School of Education and Human Development, Program in Special Education, Portland, ME 04104-9300. Offers abilities and disabilities (MS); gifted and talented (MS); gifted and talented education (Certificate); teaching all students (Certificate); teaching students with mild to moderate disabilities (MS); youth with moderate to severe disabilities (Certificate). *Accreditation:* Teacher Education Accreditation Council. Part-time and evening/weekend programs available. *Faculty:* 7 full-time (4 women), 2 part-time/adjunct (both women). *Students:* 5 full-time (4 women), 33 part-time (31 women); includes 1 minority (Black or African American, non-Hispanic/Latino). Average age 34. 18 applicants, 89% accepted, 12 enrolled. In 2013, 13 master's, 1 other advanced degree awarded. *Degree requirements:* For master's, thesis or alternative, portfolio. *Entrance requirements:* For master's, proof of teacher certification. Additional exam requirements/recommendations for international students: Required—TOEFL (minimum score 550 paper-based; 79 iBT). *Application deadline:* For fall admission, 5/1 priority date for domestic students; for spring admission, 10/15 priority date for domestic students. Applications are processed on a rolling basis. Application fee: $65. Electronic applications accepted. *Expenses:* Tuition, state resident: part-time $380 per credit. Tuition, nonresident: part-time $1026 per credit. Part-time tuition and fees vary according to program. *Financial support:* Research assistantships, career-related internships or fieldwork, Federal Work-Study, institutionally sponsored loans, scholarships/grants, and unspecified assistantships available. Support available to part-time students. Financial award application deadline: 3/1; financial award applicants required to submit FAFSA. *Faculty research:* Special education, gifted and talented education, diversity education, positive behavioral interventions and supports. *Unit head:* Julie Alexandrin, Program Coordinator, 207-228-8320, E-mail: jalexandrin@usm.maine.edu. *Application contact:* Mary Sloan, Assistant Dean of Graduate Studies and Director of Graduate Admissions, 207-780-4386, Fax: 207-780-4969, E-mail: gradstudies@usm.maine.edu.
Website: http://www.usm.maine.edu/sehd/.

University of Southern Mississippi, Graduate School, College of Education and Psychology, Department of Curriculum, Instruction, and Special Education, Hattiesburg, MS 39406-0001. Offers elementary education (M Ed, PhD, Ed S); instructional technology (MS, PhD); secondary education (MAT); special education (M Ed, PhD, Ed S). Part-time programs available. *Faculty:* 23 full-time (17 women), 3 part-time/adjunct (2 women). *Students:* 20 full-time (19 women), 59 part-time (49 women); includes 18 minority (14 Black or African American, non-Hispanic/Latino; 3 Hispanic/Latino; 1 Two or more races, non-Hispanic/Latino). Average age 36. 21 applicants, 95% accepted, 17 enrolled. In 2013, 22 master's, 3 doctorates, 13 other advanced degrees awarded. *Degree requirements:* For master's and Ed S, comprehensive exam, thesis (for some programs); for doctorate, comprehensive exam, thesis/dissertation. *Entrance requirements:* For master's, GRE General Test, MAT, minimum GPA of 3.0; for doctorate, GRE General Test, minimum GPA of 3.5; for Ed S, GRE General Test, MAT, minimum GPA of 3.25. Additional exam requirements/recommendations for international students: Required—TOEFL, IELTS. *Application deadline:* For fall admission, 3/1 priority date for domestic students, 3/1 for international students; for spring admission, 1/10 priority date for domestic and international students. Applications are processed on a rolling basis. Application fee: $50. *Financial support:* In 2013–14, 9 research assistantships with tuition reimbursements (averaging $18,316 per year), 2 teaching assistantships with full tuition reimbursements (averaging $8,500 per year) were awarded; Federal Work-Study, institutionally sponsored loans, scholarships/grants, health care benefits, tuition waivers (partial), and unspecified assistantships also available. Financial award application deadline: 3/15; financial award applicants required to submit FAFSA. *Faculty research:* Mathematical problem solving, integrative curriculum, writing process, teacher education models. *Total annual research expenditures:* $100,000. *Unit head:* Dr. Ravic P. Ringlaben, Chair, 601-266-4547, Fax: 601-266-4175. *Application contact:* David Daves, Director of Graduate Studies, 601-266-6005, Fax: 601-266-4548.
Website: http://www.usm.edu/graduateschool/table.php.

University of South Florida, College of Education, Department of Special Education, Tampa, FL 33620-9951. Offers autism spectrum disorders and severe intellectual disabilities (MA); behavior disorders (MA); exceptional student education (MA, MAT); gifted education (MA); mental retardation (MA); special education (PhD); specific learning disabilities (MA). *Accreditation:* NCATE. Part-time and evening/weekend programs available. *Degree requirements:* For master's, comprehensive exam; for doctorate, comprehensive exam, thesis/dissertation, philosophies of inquiry; multiple research methods. *Entrance requirements:* For master's, GRE General Test (if undergraduate GPA less than 3.0), minimum GPA of 3.0 in last 60 hours of course work; for doctorate, GRE General Test, minimum GPA of 3.0 undergraduate, 3.5 graduate; interview. Additional exam requirements/recommendations for international students: Required—TOEFL (minimum score 500 paper-based). Electronic applications accepted. *Faculty research:* Instruction methods for students with learning and behavioral disabilities; teacher preparation, experiential learning, and participatory action research; public policy research; personal preparation for transitional services; case-based instruction, partnerships and mentor development; inclusion and voices of teachers and students with disabilities; narrative ethics and philosophies of research.

University of South Florida, University College/Distance Education, Tampa, FL 33620-9951. *Unit head:* Kathy Barnes, Interdisciplinary Programs Coordinator, 813-974-8031, Fax: 813-974-7061, E-mail: barnesk@usf.edu. *Application contact:* Karen Tylinski, Metro Initiatives, 813-974-9943, Fax: 813-974-7061, E-mail: ktylinsk@usf.edu.
Website: http://uc.usf.edu/.

The University of Tennessee, Graduate School, College of Education, Health and Human Sciences, Program in Education, Knoxville, TN 37996. Offers art education (MS); counseling education (PhD); cultural studies in education (PhD); curriculum (MS, Ed S); curriculum, educational research and evaluation (Ed D, PhD); early childhood education (PhD); early childhood special education (MS); education of deaf and hard of hearing (MS); educational administration and policy studies (Ed D, PhD); educational administration and supervision (Ed S); educational psychology (Ed D, PhD); elementary education (MS, Ed S); elementary teaching (MS); English education (MS, Ed S); exercise science (PhD); foreign language/ESL education (MS, Ed S); instructional technology (MS, Ed D, PhD, Ed S); literacy, language and ESL education (PhD); literacy, language education, and ESL education (Ed D); mathematics education (MS, Ed S); modified and comprehensive special education (MS); reading education (MS, Ed S); school counseling (Ed S); school psychology (PhD, Ed S); science education (MS, Ed S); secondary teaching (MS); social foundations (MS); social science education (MS, Ed S); socio-cultural foundations of sports and education (PhD); special education (Ed S); teacher education (Ed D, PhD). *Accreditation:* NCATE. Part-time and evening/weekend programs available. *Degree requirements:* For master's and Ed S, thesis optional; for doctorate, variable foreign language requirement, thesis/dissertation. *Entrance requirements:* For master's, minimum GPA of 2.7; for doctorate and Ed S, GRE General Test, minimum GPA of 2.7. Additional exam requirements/recommendations for international students: Required—TOEFL. Electronic applications accepted. *Expenses:* Tuition, state resident: full-time $9540; part-time $531 per credit hour. Tuition, nonresident: full-time $27,728; part-time $1542 per credit hour. *Required fees:* $1404; $67 per credit hour.

The University of Tennessee at Chattanooga, Graduate School, College of Health, Education and Professional Studies, School of Education, Chattanooga, TN 37403. Offers counseling (M Ed), including community counseling, school counseling; education (M Ed, Post-Master's Certificate), including elementary education (M Ed), school leadership, secondary education (M Ed), special education (M Ed); educational specialist (Ed S), including educational technology, school psychology; learning and leadership (Ed D), including educational leadership. *Accreditation:* ACA; NCATE. Part-time and evening/weekend programs available. Postbaccalaureate distance learning degree programs offered (no on-campus study). *Faculty:* 24 full-time (17 women), 6 part-time/adjunct (4 women). *Students:* 107 full-time (86 women), 263 part-time (192 women); includes 71 minority (46 Black or African American, non-Hispanic/Latino; 2 American Indian or Alaska Native, non-Hispanic/Latino; 5 Asian, non-Hispanic/Latino; 11 Hispanic/Latino; 7 Two or more races, non-Hispanic/Latino), 2 international. Average age 34. 121 applicants, 83% accepted, 67 enrolled. In 2013, 125 master's, 10 doctorates, 3 other advanced degrees awarded. *Degree requirements:* For master's, comprehensive exam, thesis optional, culminating experience; for doctorate, comprehensive exam, thesis/dissertation; for other advanced degree, internship. *Entrance requirements:* For master's, GRE General Test, PPST 1, teaching certificate; for doctorate, GRE General Test, master's degree, two years of practical work experience in organizational environment; for other advanced degree, GRE General Test, letters of reference. Additional exam requirements/recommendations for international students: Required—TOEFL (minimum score 550 paper-based; 79 iBT), IELTS (minimum score 6). *Application deadline:* For fall admission, 6/13 for domestic students, 6/1 for international students; for spring admission, 10/15 for domestic students, 10/1 for international students. Applications are processed on a rolling basis. Application fee: $30 ($35 for international students). Electronic applications accepted. *Financial support:* In 2013–14, 20 research assistantships with tuition reimbursements (averaging $6,340 per year), 4 teaching assistantships with tuition reimbursements (averaging $7,234 per year) were awarded; career-related internships or fieldwork, institutionally sponsored loans, scholarships/grants, and unspecified assistantships also available. Support available to part-time students. Financial award applicants required to submit FAFSA. *Faculty research:* School counseling, community counseling, elementary and secondary education, school leadership and administration. *Total annual research expenditures:* $967,880. *Unit head:* Dr. Linda Johnston, Director, 423-425-4122, Fax: 423-425-5380, E-mail: linda-johnston@utc.edu. *Application contact:* Dr. J. Randy Walker, Interim Dean of Graduate Studies, 423-425-4478, Fax: 423-425-5223, E-mail: randy-walker@utc.edu.
Website: http://www.utc.edu/school-education/abouttheschool/gradprograms.php.

The University of Tennessee at Martin, Graduate Programs, College of Education, Health and Behavioral Sciences, Program in Teaching, Martin, TN 38238-1000. Offers curriculum and instruction (MS Ed), including 7-12, K-6; initial licensure (MS Ed), including elementary, secondary; initial licensure K-12 (MS Ed), including physical education, special education; interdisciplinary (MS Ed). Part-time programs available. *Students:* 20 full-time (14 women), 88 part-time (65 women); includes 9 minority (8 Black or African American, non-Hispanic/Latino; 1 Two or more races, non-Hispanic/Latino). 78 applicants, 64% accepted, 33 enrolled. In 2013, 32 master's awarded. *Degree requirements:* For master's, comprehensive exam. *Entrance requirements:* For master's, GRE General Test, minimum GPA of 2.5. Additional exam requirements/recommendations for international students: Required—TOEFL (minimum score 525 paper-based; 71 iBT). *Application deadline:* For fall admission, 7/29 priority date for domestic students, 7/29 for international students; for spring admission, 12/12 priority date for domestic students, 12/12 for international students. Applications are processed on a rolling basis. Application fee: $30 ($130 for international students). Electronic applications accepted. *Financial support:* Research assistantships with full tuition reimbursements, teaching assistantships with full tuition reimbursements, career-related internships or fieldwork, scholarships/grants, and unspecified assistantships available. Financial award application deadline: 3/1. *Faculty research:* Special education, science/math/technology, school reform, reading. *Unit head:* Dr. Gail Stephens, Interim Dean,

731-881-7127, Fax: 731-881-7975, E-mail: gstephe6@utm.edu. *Application contact:* Jolene L. Cunningham, Student Services Specialist, 731-881-7012, Fax: 731-881-7499, E-mail: jcunningham@utm.edu.

The University of Texas at Austin, Graduate School, College of Education, Department of Special Education, Austin, TX 78712-1111. Offers autism and developmental disabilities (Ed D, PhD); autism and developmental disability (M Ed, MA); early childhood special education (M Ed, MA, Ed D, PhD); learning disabilities (Ed D, PhD); learning disabilities/behavior disorders (M Ed, MA); multicultural special education (M Ed, MA, Ed D, PhD); rehabilitation counselor (M Ed); rehabilitation counselor education (Ed D, PhD); special education administration (Ed D, PhD). *Accreditation:* CORE. Part-time and evening/weekend programs available. Postbaccalaureate distance learning degree programs offered (no on-campus study). *Degree requirements:* For master's, thesis or alternative; for doctorate, thesis/dissertation. *Entrance requirements:* For master's and doctorate, GRE General Test. *Faculty research:* Anchored instruction, reading disabilities, multicultural/bilingual.

The University of Texas at Brownsville, Graduate Studies, College of Education, Brownsville, TX 78520-4991. Offers bilingual education (M Ed); counseling and guidance (M Ed); curriculum and instruction (M Ed); early childhood education (M Ed); educational leadership (M Ed); educational technology (M Ed); exercise science (MS); special education (M Ed). Part-time and evening/weekend programs available. Postbaccalaureate distance learning degree programs offered (no on-campus study). *Faculty:* 51 full-time (28 women). *Students:* 60 full-time (43 women), 496 part-time (363 women); includes 467 minority (4 Black or African American, non-Hispanic/Latino; 1 American Indian or Alaska Native, non-Hispanic/Latino; 10 Asian, non-Hispanic/Latino; 451 Hispanic/Latino; 1 Native Hawaiian or other Pacific Islander, non-Hispanic/Latino), 12 international. 161 applicants, 67% accepted, 81 enrolled. In 2013, 142 master's awarded. *Degree requirements:* For master's, comprehensive exam (for some programs), thesis optional, electronic portfolio. *Entrance requirements:* For master's, GRE General Test, curriculum vitae or resume, teaching certificate. Additional exam requirements/recommendations for international students: Required—TOEFL (minimum score 550 paper-based; 77 iBT). *Application deadline:* For fall admission, 7/1 priority date for domestic students, 7/1 for international students; for spring admission, 12/1 priority date for domestic students, 12/1 for international students. Applications are processed on a rolling basis. Application fee: $30. Electronic applications accepted. *Expenses:* Tuition, state resident: full-time $3444; part-time $1148 per semester. Tuition, nonresident: full-time $9816. *Required fees:* $1018; $221 per credit hour. $401 per semester. *Financial support:* In 2013–14, 136 students received support, including 6 research assistantships (averaging $10,000 per year); career-related internships or fieldwork, Federal Work-Study, scholarships/grants, tuition waivers (partial), and unspecified assistantships also available. Support available to part-time students. Financial award application deadline: 3/1; financial award applicants required to submit FAFSA. *Unit head:* Dr. Miguel Angel Escotet, Dean, 956-882-7220, Fax: 956-882-7431, E-mail: miguel.escotet@utb.edu. *Application contact:* Mari E. Stevens, Graduate Studies Specialist, 956-882-6587, Fax: 956-882-7279, E-mail: mari.stevens@utb.edu. Website: http://www.utb.edu/vpaa/coe/Pages/default.aspx.

The University of Texas at El Paso, Graduate School, College of Education, Department of Educational Psychology and Special Services, El Paso, TX 79968-0001. Offers educational diagnostics (M Ed); guidance and counseling (M Ed); special education (M Ed). Part-time and evening/weekend programs available. *Degree requirements:* For master's, thesis optional. *Entrance requirements:* For master's, minimum GPA of 3.0. Additional exam requirements/recommendations for international students: Required—TOEFL. Electronic applications accepted.

The University of Texas at San Antonio, College of Education and Human Development, Department of Interdisciplinary Learning and Teaching, San Antonio, TX 78249-0617. Offers education (MA), including curriculum and instruction, early childhood and elementary education, instructional technology, reading and literacy, special education; interdisciplinary learning and teaching (PhD). Part-time and evening/weekend programs available. *Faculty:* 22 full-time (16 women), 1 (woman) part-time/adjunct. *Students:* 109 full-time (80 women), 272 part-time (221 women); includes 209 minority (24 Black or African American, non-Hispanic/Latino; 3 American Indian or Alaska Native, non-Hispanic/Latino; 12 Asian, non-Hispanic/Latino; 166 Hispanic/Latino; 4 Two or more races, non-Hispanic/Latino), 40 international. Average age 33. 178 applicants, 87% accepted, 80 enrolled. In 2013, 136 master's, 7 doctorates awarded. *Degree requirements:* For master's, comprehensive exam, thesis optional, 36 hours of course work without thesis (33 with thesis); for doctorate, comprehensive exam, thesis/dissertation, minimum of 60 semester credit hours. *Entrance requirements:* For master's, bachelor's degree with minimum GPA of 3.0 in last 60 hours of coursework; 18 hours of undergraduate coursework in education or related field; for doctorate, GRE, transcripts from all colleges and universities attended, professional vitae demonstrating experience in work environment where education was primary professional emphasis, 3 letters of recommendation, statement of purpose, minimum GPA of 3.5. Additional exam requirements/recommendations for international students: Required—TOEFL (minimum score 550 paper-based; 79 iBT), IELTS (minimum score 6.5). *Application deadline:* For fall admission, 7/1 for domestic students, 4/1 for international students; for spring admission, 11/1 for domestic students, 9/1 for international students. Applications are processed on a rolling basis. Application fee: $45 ($80 for international students). Electronic applications accepted. *Expenses:* Tuition, state resident: full-time $4671. Tuition, nonresident: full-time $8708. *International tuition:* $17,415 full-time. *Required fees:* $1924.60. Tuition and fees vary according to course load and degree level. *Financial support:* In 2013–14, 7 fellowships with partial tuition reimbursements (averaging $27,000 per year) were awarded; career-related internships or fieldwork, Federal Work-Study, and scholarships/grants also available. Support available to part-time students. *Faculty research:* Explorations of science, learning and teaching, family involvement in early childhood, culturally-responsive literacy instruction in diverse settings, STEM education, autism spectrum disorder. *Total annual research expenditures:* $5.9 million. *Unit head:* Dr. Maria R. Cortez, Department Chair, 210-458-5969, Fax: 210-458-7281, E-mail: mari.cortez@utsa.edu. *Application contact:* Erin Doran, Student Development Specialist, 210-458-7443, Fax: 210-458-7281, E-mail: erin.doran@utsa.edu. Website: http://education.utsa.edu/interdisciplinary_learning_and_teaching/.

The University of Texas at Tyler, College of Education and Psychology, School of Education, Tyler, TX 75799-0001. Offers early childhood education (M Ed, MA); reading (M Ed, MA); special education (M Ed, MA). Part-time and evening/weekend programs available. *Degree requirements:* For master's, comprehensive exam, thesis (for some programs), research project. *Entrance requirements:* For master's, GRE General Test. Additional exam requirements/recommendations for international students: Required—TOEFL. Electronic applications accepted. *Faculty research:* Improving quality in childcare settings, play and creativity, teacher interactions, effects of modeling on early childhood teachers, biofeedback, literacy instruction.

The University of Texas Health Science Center at San Antonio, School of Medicine, San Antonio, TX 78229-3900. Offers deaf education and hearing (MS); medicine (MD); MPH/MD. *Accreditation:* LCME/AMA. *Faculty:* 838 full-time (348 women), 394 part-time/adjunct (142 women). *Students:* 876 full-time (420 women), 20 part-time (all women);

includes 392 minority (41 Black or African American, non-Hispanic/Latino; 152 Asian, non-Hispanic/Latino; 179 Hispanic/Latino; 20 Two or more races, non-Hispanic/Latino), 1 international. Average age 26. 4,100 applicants, 17% accepted, 220 enrolled. In 2013, 12 master's, 228 doctorates awarded. *Degree requirements:* For master's, comprehensive exam, practicum assignments. *Entrance requirements:* For master's, minimum GPA of 3.0, interview, 3 professional letters of recommendation; for doctorate, MCAT. *Application deadline:* For fall admission, 10/1 for domestic and international students. Applications are processed on a rolling basis. Application fee: $140. Electronic applications accepted. *Expenses:* Contact institution. *Financial support:* In 2013–14, 599 students received support. Federal Work-Study, institutionally sponsored loans, tuition waivers (full and partial), and stipends, department payments available. Financial award application deadline: 6/1; financial award applicants required to submit FAFSA. *Faculty research:* Geriatrics, diabetes, cancer, AIDS, obesity. *Total annual research expenditures:* $117.4 million. *Unit head:* Dr. Francisco Gonzalez-Scarano, Dean, 210-567-4432, Fax: 210-567-3435, E-mail: scarano@uthscsa.edu. *Application contact:* Dr. David J. Jones, Senior Associate Dean for Admissions, 210-567-6080, Fax: 210-567-6962, E-mail: jonesd@uthscsa.edu. Website: som.uthscsa.edu.

The University of Texas of the Permian Basin, Office of Graduate Studies, School of Education, Program in Special Education, Odessa, TX 79762-0001. Offers MA. *Degree requirements:* For master's, comprehensive exam (for some programs), thesis (for some programs). *Entrance requirements:* For master's, GRE General Test. Additional exam requirements/recommendations for international students: Required—TOEFL (minimum score 550 paper-based).

The University of Texas–Pan American, College of Education, Department of Educational Psychology, Edinburg, TX 78539. Offers educational diagnostician (M Ed); gifted education (M Ed); guidance and counseling (M Ed); school psychology (MA); special education (M Ed). Part-time and evening/weekend programs available. *Degree requirements:* For master's, comprehensive exam (for some programs), thesis (for some programs). *Entrance requirements:* For master's, GRE General Test, interview. *Expenses:* Tuition, state resident: full-time $5986; part-time $333 per credit hour. Tuition, nonresident: full-time $12,358; part-time $687 per credit hour. *Required fees:* $782. Tuition and fees vary according to program. *Faculty research:* Reading instruction, assessment practice, behavior interventions consultation, mental retardation.

University of the Cumberlands, Graduate Programs in Education, Williamsburg, KY 40769-1372. Offers all grades (P-12) (M Ed); business and marketing (MA Ed, MAT); counselor education and supervision (Ed D); director of pupil personnel (Certificate); director of special education (Certificate); educational administration and supervision (Ed S); educational leadership (Ed D); elementary education (MA Ed, MAT); instructional leadership - principalship (MA Ed); instructional leadership - school principal (Certificate); middle school education (MA Ed, MAT); reading and writing (MA Ed); school counseling (MA Ed); school superintendent (Certificate); secondary education (MA Ed, MAT); special education (MAT); supervisor of instruction (Certificate); teacher leader (MA Ed). Part-time and evening/weekend programs available. Postbaccalaureate distance learning degree programs offered. *Degree requirements:* For master's, comprehensive exam. Electronic applications accepted.

University of the District of Columbia, College of Arts and Sciences, Department of Education, Program in Special Education, Washington, DC 20008-1175. Offers MA. *Accreditation:* NCATE. Part-time programs available. *Expenses:* Tuition, area resident: Full-time $7883.28; part-time $437.96 per credit hour. Tuition, state resident: full-time $8923.14. Tuition, nonresident: full-time $15,163; part-time $842.40 per credit hour. *Required fees:* $620; $30 per credit hour.

University of the Incarnate Word, School of Graduate Studies and Research, Dreeben School of Education, Programs in Education, San Antonio, TX 78209-6397. Offers adult education (M Ed, MA); cross-cultural education (M Ed, MA); early childhood literacy (M Ed, MA); general education (M Ed, MA); higher education (PhD); instructional technology (M Ed, MA); international education and entrepreneurship (PhD); kinesiology (M Ed, MA); literacy (M Ed, MA); organizational leadership (PhD); organizational learning and learning (M Ed, MA); reading (M Ed, MA); special education (M Ed, MA); teacher leadership (M Ed, MA). Part-time and evening/weekend programs available. *Faculty:* 17 full-time (9 women), 6 part-time/adjunct (all women). *Students:* 23 full-time (13 women), 187 part-time (122 women); includes 114 minority (24 Black or African American, non-Hispanic/Latino; 1 American Indian or Alaska Native, non-Hispanic/Latino; 3 Asian, non-Hispanic/Latino; 85 Hispanic/Latino; 1 Two or more races, non-Hispanic/Latino), 30 international. Average age 41. 52 applicants, 67% accepted, 25 enrolled. In 2013, 12 master's, 14 doctorates awarded. *Degree requirements:* For master's, capstone; for doctorate, thesis/dissertation, qualifying exam. *Entrance requirements:* For master's, baccalaureate degree; minimum foundation GPA of 2.5; interview; for doctorate, master's degree; interview; supervised writing sample. Additional exam requirements/recommendations for international students: Required—TOEFL (minimum score 560 paper-based; 83 iBT). *Application deadline:* Applications are processed on a rolling basis. Application fee: $20. Electronic applications accepted. *Expenses:* Tuition: Part-time $815 per credit hour. *Required fees:* $86 per credit hour. One-time fee: $40 part-time. Tuition and fees vary according to degree level and program. *Financial support:* In 2013–14, 5 research assistantships were awarded; Federal Work-Study and scholarships/grants also available. Financial award applicants required to submit FAFSA. *Unit head:* Dr. Denise Staudt, Dean, Dreeben School of Education, 210-829-2762, E-mail: staudt@uiwtx.edu. *Application contact:* Andrea Cyterski-Acosta, Dean of Enrollment, 210-829-6005, Fax: 210-829-3921, E-mail: admis@uiwtx.edu. Website: http://www.uiw.edu/education/index.htm.

University of the Pacific, Gladys L. Benerd School of Education, Department of Curriculum and Instruction, Stockton, CA 95211-0197. Offers curriculum and instruction (M Ed, MA, Ed D); education (M Ed); special education (MA). *Accreditation:* NCATE. *Faculty:* 10 full-time (6 women), 3 part-time/adjunct (2 women). *Students:* 87 full-time (65 women), 139 part-time (103 women); includes 74 minority (18 Black or African American, non-Hispanic/Latino; 1 American Indian or Alaska Native, non-Hispanic/Latino; 18 Asian, non-Hispanic/Latino; 32 Hispanic/Latino; 1 Native Hawaiian or other Pacific Islander, non-Hispanic/Latino; 4 Two or more races, non-Hispanic/Latino), 23 international. Average age 30. 108 applicants, 81% accepted, 65 enrolled. In 2013, 111 master's, 5 doctorates awarded. *Degree requirements:* For master's, thesis (for some programs). *Entrance requirements:* For master's, GRE General Test. Additional exam requirements/recommendations for international students: Required—TOEFL (minimum score 475 paper-based). *Application deadline:* For fall admission, 3/1 priority date for domestic students; for spring admission, 10/1 priority date for domestic students. Applications are processed on a rolling basis. Application fee: $75. *Financial support:* In 2013–14, 7 teaching assistantships were awarded. Financial award application deadline: 3/1; financial award applicants required to submit FAFSA. *Unit head:* Dr. Marilyn Draheim, Chairperson, 209-946-2685, E-mail: mdraheim@pacific.edu. *Application contact:* Office of Graduate Admissions, 209-946-2344.

University of the Southwest, Graduate Programs, Hobbs, NM 88240-9129. Offers business administration (MBA); curriculum and instruction (MSE); curriculum and instruction: bilingual (MSE); curriculum and instruction: TESOL (MSE); early childhood

education (MSE); educational administration (MSE); mental health counseling (MSE); school counseling (MSE); special education (MSE); sports management (MBA). Part-time and evening/weekend programs available. Postbaccalaureate distance learning degree programs offered (no on-campus study). *Degree requirements:* For master's, comprehensive exam, thesis (for some programs). *Entrance requirements:* Additional exam requirements/recommendations for international students: Recommended—TOEFL. Electronic applications accepted.

The University of Toledo, College of Graduate Studies, Judith Herb College of Education, Department of Curriculum and Instruction, Toledo, OH 43606-3390. Offers art education (ME); career and technical education (ME); career-technical education (Ed S); curriculum and instruction (ME, PhD, Ed S); early childhood education (PhD, Ed S); education and biology (MES); education and chemistry (MES); education and economics (MAE); education and English (MAE); education and French (MAE); education and geography (MAE); education and geology (MES); education and German (MAE); education and history (MAE); education and mathematics (MAE, MES); education and physics (MES); education and political science (MAE); education and sociology (MAE); education and Spanish (MAE); educational media (PhD); educational technology (ME); educational technology: virtual educator (Certificate); elementary education (PhD); English as a second language (MAE); gifted and talented (PhD); middle childhood education licensure (ME); music education (MME); secondary education (PhD); secondary education licensure (ME); special education (PhD, Ed S). *Accreditation:* NCATE. Part-time and evening/weekend programs available. *Faculty:* 41. *Students:* 53 full-time (30 women), 154 part-time (111 women); includes 21 minority (16 Black or African American, non-Hispanic/Latino; 4 Hispanic/Latino; 1 Two or more races, non-Hispanic/Latino), 21 international. Average age 34. 82 applicants, 79% accepted, 47 enrolled. In 2013, 80 master's, 5 doctorates awarded. *Degree requirements:* For master's, comprehensive exam, thesis or alternative; for doctorate, comprehensive exam, thesis/dissertation; for other advanced degree, thesis optional. *Entrance requirements:* For master's, doctorate, and other advanced degree, minimum cumulative GPA of 2.7 for all previous academic work, letters of recommendation. Additional exam requirements/recommendations for international students: Required—TOEFL (minimum score 550 paper-based; 80 iBT). *Application deadline:* For fall admission, 1/15 priority date for domestic and international students. Applications are processed on a rolling basis. Application fee: $45 ($75 for international students). Electronic applications accepted. *Financial support:* In 2013–14, 5 research assistantships with full and partial tuition reimbursements (averaging $13,200 per year), 11 teaching assistantships with full and partial tuition reimbursements (averaging $8,809 per year) were awarded; career-related internships or fieldwork, Federal Work-Study, institutionally sponsored loans, scholarships/grants, tuition waivers (full and partial), unspecified assistantships, and administrative assistantships also available. Support available to part-time students. *Unit head:* Dr. Joan Kaderavek, Chair, 419-530-5373, E-mail: eigh.chiarelott@utoledo.edu. *Application contact:* Graduate School Office, 419-530-4723, Fax: 419-530-4724, E-mail: grdsch@utnet.utoledo.edu.
Website: http://www.utoledo.edu/eduhshs/.

The University of Toledo, College of Graduate Studies, Judith Herb College of Education, Department of Early Childhood, Physical and Special Education, Toledo, OH 43606-3390. Offers early childhood education (ME); physical education (ME); special education (ME). Part-time programs available. *Faculty:* 25. *Students:* 9 full-time (all women), 89 part-time (80 women); includes 16 minority (13 Black or African American, non-Hispanic/Latino; 3 Hispanic/Latino), 1 international. Average age 32. 28 applicants, 75% accepted, 16 enrolled. In 2013, 47 master's awarded. *Degree requirements:* For master's, thesis. *Entrance requirements:* For master's, minimum cumulative GPA of 2.7 for all previous academic work, letters of recommendation. Additional exam requirements/recommendations for international students: Required—TOEFL (minimum score 550 paper-based; 80 iBT). *Application deadline:* For fall admission, 1/15 priority date for domestic and international students. Applications are processed on a rolling basis. Application fee: $45 ($75 for international students). Electronic applications accepted. *Financial support:* In 2013–14, 3 teaching assistantships with full and partial tuition reimbursements (averaging $4,500 per year) were awarded; career-related internships or fieldwork, Federal Work-Study, institutionally sponsored loans, scholarships/grants, tuition waivers (full and partial), unspecified assistantships, and administrative assistantships also available. Support available to part-time students. *Unit head:* Dr. Richard Welsch, Chair, 419-530-7736, E-mail: richard.welsch@utoledo.edu. *Application contact:* Graduate School Office, 419-530-4723, Fax: 419-530-4724, E-mail: grdsch@utnet.utoledo.edu.
Website: http://www.utoledo.edu/eduhshs/.

University of Utah, Graduate School, College of Education, Department of Special Education, Salt Lake City, UT 84112. Offers deaf and hard of hearing (M Ed); deaf/blind (M Ed); early childhood hearing impairments (M Ed, MS); early childhood special education (M Ed, MS, PhD); early childhood vision impairments (M Ed, MS); hearing impairments (MS); mild/moderate (MS); mild/moderate disabilities (M Ed, MS, PhD); professional practice (M Ed); research in special education (MS); research without licensure (MS); severe (MS); severe disabilities (M Ed, MS, PhD); vision impairments (M Ed, MS). Part-time and evening/weekend programs available. Postbaccalaureate distance learning degree programs offered (no on-campus study). *Faculty:* 9 full-time (6 women), 8 part-time/adjunct (7 women). *Students:* 28 full-time (23 women), 12 part-time (10 women); includes 7 minority (2 Black or African American, non-Hispanic/Latino; 3 Hispanic/Latino; 1 Native Hawaiian or other Pacific Islander, non-Hispanic/Latino; 1 Two or more races, non-Hispanic/Latino), 1 international. Average age 33. 15 applicants, 93% accepted, 13 enrolled. In 2013, 36 master's, 4 doctorates awarded. Terminal master's awarded for partial completion of doctoral program. *Degree requirements:* For master's, comprehensive exam, thesis (for some programs), qualifying exam; for doctorate, thesis/dissertation, qualifying exam. *Entrance requirements:* For master's, GRE or Analytical Writing portion of GRE plus PRAXIS I, minimum GPA of 3.0; for doctorate, GRE General Test (minimum scores: Verbal 600; Quantitative 600; Analytical/Writing 4), minimum GPA of 3.0 (3.5 recommended). Additional exam requirements/recommendations for international students: Required—TOEFL (minimum score 600 paper-based; 100 iBT); Recommended—IELTS (minimum score 7). *Application deadline:* For fall admission, 3/1 for domestic and international students; for spring admission, 11/1 for domestic and international students. Application fee: $55 ($65 for international students). Electronic applications accepted. *Expenses:* Contact institution. *Financial support:* In 2013–14, 27 students received support, including 27 fellowships with full and partial tuition reimbursements available (averaging $5,015 per year), 4 teaching assistantships with full tuition reimbursements available (averaging $17,175 per year); research assistantships and career-related internships or fieldwork also available. Support available to part-time students. Financial award application deadline: 3/1; financial award applicants required to submit FAFSA. *Faculty research:* Inclusive education, positive behavior support, reading, instruction and intervention strategies. *Total annual research expenditures:* $5,926. *Unit head:* Dr. Robert E. O'Neill, Chair, 801-581-8121, Fax: 801-585-6476, E-mail: rob.oneill@utah.edu. *Application contact:* Patty Davis, Academic Advisor, 801-581-4764, Fax: 801-585-6476, E-mail: patty.davis@utah.edu.
Website: http://www.ed.utah.edu/sped/.

University of Vermont, Graduate College, College of Education and Social Services, Department of Education, Program in Special Education, Burlington, VT 05405. Offers M Ed. *Accreditation:* NCATE. *Students:* 36 (33 women); includes 2 minority (1 Black or African American, non-Hispanic/Latino; 1 Hispanic/Latino). 29 applicants, 66% accepted, 16 enrolled. In 2013, 28 master's awarded. *Degree requirements:* For master's, thesis or alternative. *Entrance requirements:* For master's, license (or eligible for licensure). Additional exam requirements/recommendations for international students: Required—TOEFL (minimum score 550 paper-based; 80 iBT). *Application deadline:* For fall admission, 2/15 priority date for domestic students, 2/15 for international students. Applications are processed on a rolling basis. Application fee: $65. Electronic applications accepted. *Financial support:* Research assistantships, teaching assistantships, and career-related internships or fieldwork available. Financial award application deadline: 3/1. *Unit head:* Katherine Shepherd, Coordinator, 802-656-2936.

University of Victoria, Faculty of Graduate Studies, Faculty of Education, Department of Educational Psychology and Leadership Studies, Victoria, BC V8W 2Y2, Canada. Offers aboriginal communities counseling (M Ed); counseling (M Ed, MA); educational psychology (M Ed, MA, PhD), including counseling psychology (M Ed, MA), leadership studies (PhD), learning and development (MA, PhD), measurement and evaluation, special education (M Ed, MA); leadership studies (M Ed, MA). Part-time programs available. *Degree requirements:* For master's, thesis (for some programs), comprehensive exam (M Ed); for doctorate, comprehensive exam, thesis/dissertation, candidacy exam. *Entrance requirements:* For master's, 2 years of work experience in a relevant field; for doctorate, GRE, 2 years of work experience in a relevant field, minimum B average. Additional exam requirements/recommendations for international students: Required—TOEFL (minimum score 575 paper-based), IELTS (minimum score 7). *Faculty research:* Learning and development (child, adolescent and adult), special education and exceptional children.

University of Virginia, Curry School of Education, Department of Curriculum, Instruction, and Special Education, Program in Special Education, Charlottesville, VA 22903. Offers M Ed, Ed D, Ed S. *Accreditation:* Teacher Education Accreditation Council. *Students:* 1 (woman) full-time, 1 (woman) part-time. Average age 34. 9 applicants, 78% accepted, 5 enrolled. In 2013, 14 master's awarded. *Entrance requirements:* For master's, doctorate, and Ed S, GRE General Test, 2 letters of recommendation. Additional exam requirements/recommendations for international students: Required—TOEFL (minimum score 600 paper-based; 90 iBT), IELTS (minimum score 7). *Application deadline:* Applications are processed on a rolling basis. Application fee: $60. Electronic applications accepted. *Expenses:* Tuition, state resident: part-time $334 per credit hour. Tuition, nonresident: part-time $1224 per credit hour. *Financial support:* Applicants required to submit FAFSA. *Unit head:* John Lloyd, Program Coordinator, 434-924-0759, E-mail: johnl@virginia.edu. *Application contact:* Karen Dwier, Information Contact, 434-924-0831, E-mail: kgd9g@virginia.edu.
Website: http://curry.virginia.edu/academics/areas-of-study/special-education.

University of Virginia, Curry School of Education, Program in Education, Charlottesville, VA 22903. Offers administration and supervision (PhD); applied developmental science (PhD); counselor education (PhD); curriculum and instruction (PhD); early childhood special education (MT); education evaluation (PhD); educational psychology (PhD); educational research (PhD); elementary education (MT); English education (MT, PhD); foreign language education (MT); higher education (PhD); instructional technology (PhD); kinesiology (MT, PhD); math education (PhD); reading education (PhD); research, statistics and evaluation (PhD); school psychology (PhD); science education (PhD); social studies education (MT, PhD); special education (PhD); world languages education (MT). *Students:* 474 full-time (379 women), 35 part-time (19 women); includes 89 minority (30 Black or African American, non-Hispanic/Latino; 1 American Indian or Alaska Native, non-Hispanic/Latino; 26 Asian, non-Hispanic/Latino; 19 Hispanic/Latino; 13 Two or more races, non-Hispanic/Latino), 21 international. Average age 26. 312 applicants, 49% accepted, 80 enrolled. In 2013, 137 master's, 38 doctorates awarded. *Degree requirements:* For master's, comprehensive exam (for some programs), field project; for doctorate, comprehensive exam, thesis/dissertation. *Entrance requirements:* For doctorate, GRE General Test. Additional exam requirements/recommendations for international students: Required—TOEFL (minimum score 600 paper-based; 90 iBT), IELTS (minimum score 7). *Application deadline:* Applications are processed on a rolling basis. Application fee: $60. Electronic applications accepted. *Expenses:* Tuition, state resident: part-time $334 per credit hour. Tuition, nonresident: part-time $1224 per credit hour. *Financial support:* Fellowships, research assistantships, and teaching assistantships available. Financial award application deadline: 1/5; financial award applicants required to submit FAFSA. *Unit head:* Robert C. Pianta, Dean, 434-924-3334, E-mail: pianta@virginia.edu. *Application contact:* Office of Admissions and Student Services, 434-924-0742, E-mail: curry-admissions@virginia.edu.
Website: http://curry.virginia.edu/teacher-education.

University of Washington, Graduate School, College of Education, Program in Special Education, Seattle, WA 98195. Offers early childhood special education (M Ed); emotional and behavioral disabilities (M Ed); learning disabilities (M Ed); low-incidence disabilities (M Ed); severe disabilities (M Ed); special education (Ed D, PhD). *Degree requirements:* For master's, thesis optional; for doctorate, thesis/dissertation. *Entrance requirements:* For master's and doctorate, GRE General Test, minimum GPA of 3.0. Additional exam requirements/recommendations for international students: Required—TOEFL.

University of Washington, Tacoma, Graduate Programs, Program in Education, Tacoma, WA 98402-3100. Offers education (M Ed); educational administration (principal or program administrator certification) (M Ed); elementary education teacher certification (M Ed); elementary education/special education teacher certification (M Ed); secondary science or math teacher certification (M Ed). Part-time and evening/weekend programs available. *Degree requirements:* For master's, culminating project. *Entrance requirements:* For master's, WEST-B, WEST-E (teacher certification programs only), official sealed transcript from every college/university attended, personal goal statement, letters of recommendation, copy of valid teaching certificate. Additional exam requirements/recommendations for international students: Required—TOEFL (minimum score 580 paper-based; 92 iBT). Electronic applications accepted. *Faculty research:* Global learning communities for English/Chinese languages, evaluation of mathematics and reading intervention programs, response to intervention, school-wide behavioral and emotional support, mathematics education and culturally responsive mathematics education.

The University of West Alabama, School of Graduate Studies, College of Education, Departments of Instructional Leadership and Support/Curriculum and Instruction, Program in Special Education, Livingston, AL 35470. Offers collaborative special education 6-12 (Ed S); collaborative special education K-6 (Ed S); special education (M Ed). *Accreditation:* NCATE. Part-time and evening/weekend programs available. Postbaccalaureate distance learning degree programs offered (no on-campus study). *Faculty:* 13 full-time (11 women), 33 part-time/adjunct (24 women). *Students:* 175 (157 women); includes 89 minority (85 Black or African American, non-Hispanic/Latino; 2 American Indian or Alaska Native, non-Hispanic/Latino; 1 Hispanic/Latino; 1 Two or

more races, non-Hispanic/Latino). 50 applicants, 92% accepted, 31 enrolled. In 2013, 31 master's, 16 Ed Ss awarded. *Degree requirements:* For master's, comprehensive exam, thesis optional. *Entrance requirements:* For master's, GRE General Test, MAT, minimum GPA of 2.75. Additional exam requirements/recommendations for international students: Required—TOEFL (minimum score 500 paper-based; 61 iBT). *Application deadline:* For fall admission, 8/12 priority date for domestic students; for spring admission, 3/24 for domestic students. Applications are processed on a rolling basis. Application fee: $25 ($50 for international students). Electronic applications accepted. Tuition and fees vary according to course load. *Financial support:* Teaching assistantships, career-related internships or fieldwork, Federal Work-Study, scholarships/grants, and unspecified assistantships available. Support available to part-time students. Financial award application deadline: 3/1; financial award applicants required to submit FAFSA. *Faculty research:* Learning strategies/reading; imagine, discuss, and decide; transition; at-risk students. *Unit head:* Dr. Esther Howard, Chair of Curriculum and Instruction, 205-652-3428, Fax: 205-652-3706, E-mail: ehoward@uwa.edu. *Application contact:* Dr. Kathy Chandler, Dean of Graduate Studies, 205-652-3421, Fax: 205-652-3706, E-mail: kchandler@uwa.edu.
Website: http://www.uwa.edu/medspecialeducation612.aspx.

The University of Western Ontario, Faculty of Graduate Studies, Social Sciences Division, Faculty of Education, Program in Educational Studies, London, ON N6A 5B8, Canada. Offers curriculum studies (M Ed); educational policy studies (M Ed); educational psychology/special education (M Ed). Part-time programs available. *Faculty research:* Reflective practice, gender and schooling, feminist pedagogy, narrative inquiry, second language, multiculturalism in Canada, education and law.

University of West Florida, College of Professional Studies, School of Education, Program in Curriculum and Instruction, Pensacola, FL 32514-5750. Offers curriculum and instruction: special education (M Ed); elementary education (M Ed); primary education (M Ed). Part-time and evening/weekend programs available. *Entrance requirements:* For master's, GRE (minimum score 450 verbal) or MAT (minimum score 396) if bachelor's GPA less than 3.0, state teaching certification; letter of intent; two professional references. Additional exam requirements/recommendations for international students: Required—TOEFL (minimum score 550 paper-based).

University of West Florida, College of Professional Studies, School of Education, Program in Exceptional Student Education, Pensacola, FL 32514-5750. Offers clinical teaching (MA), including emotionally handicapped, learning disabled, mentally handicapped; habilitative science (MA). *Accreditation:* NCATE. Part-time and evening/weekend programs available. Postbaccalaureate distance learning degree programs offered (no on-campus study). *Entrance requirements:* For master's, GRE (minimum score 450 verbal) or MAT (minimum score 396) if bachelor's GPA less than 3.0, state teaching certification; letter of intent; two professional references. Additional exam requirements/recommendations for international students: Required—TOEFL (minimum score 550 paper-based). *Faculty research:* Memory, semantic structure, remedial programming.

University of West Georgia, College of Education, Department of Learning and Teaching, Carrollton, GA 30118. Offers early childhood education (M Ed, Ed S); reading education (M Ed); special education (M Ed, Ed S). *Accreditation:* ACA; NCATE. Part-time and evening/weekend programs available. *Faculty:* 10 full-time (9 women), 3 part-time/adjunct (all women). *Students:* 50 full-time (44 women), 228 part-time (204 women); includes 112 minority (102 Black or African American, non-Hispanic/Latino; 6 Hispanic/Latino; 4 Two or more races, non-Hispanic/Latino), 2 international. Average age 34. 198 applicants, 57% accepted, 46 enrolled. In 2013, 73 master's, 31 Ed Ss awarded. *Degree requirements:* For master's and Ed S, comprehensive exam. *Entrance requirements:* For master's, undergraduate degree in early childhood, elementary (P-5), middle grades (4-8), special education; one year of teaching experience; minimum overall GPA of 2.7; clear and renewable level 4 teaching certificate; for Ed S, master's degree in early childhood or elementary education; minimum overall GPA of 3.0 in graduate work; level 5 teaching certificate. Additional exam requirements/recommendations for international students: Required—TOEFL (minimum score 523 paper-based; 69 iBT); Recommended—IELTS (minimum score 6). *Application deadline:* For fall admission, 7/21 for domestic students, 6/1 for international students; for spring admission, 1/30 for domestic students, 10/15 for international students. Applications are processed on a rolling basis. Application fee: $40. Electronic applications accepted. *Expenses:* Tuition, state resident: full-time $4600; part-time $192 per semester hour. Tuition, nonresident: full-time $17,880; part-time $745 per semester hour. *Required fees:* $1858; $46.34 per semester hour. $512 per semester. Tuition and fees vary according to course load, degree level, campus/location and program. *Financial support:* In 2013–14, 10 students received support, including 1 research assistantship with full tuition reimbursement available (averaging $2,963 per year); scholarships/grants and unspecified assistantships also available. Support available to part-time students. Financial award application deadline: 4/1; financial award applicants required to submit FAFSA. *Faculty research:* Early childhood education, social justice, action research. *Total annual research expenditures:* $274,000. *Unit head:* Dr. Donna Harkins, Chair, 678-839-6066, Fax: 678-839-6063, E-mail: dharkins@westga.edu. *Application contact:* Dr. Jill Drake, Coordinator, Early Childhood Education, 678-839-6080, Fax: 678-839-6063, E-mail: jdrake@westga.edu.
Website: http://www.westga.edu/coeelce.

University of Wisconsin–Eau Claire, College of Education and Human Sciences, Program in Special Education, Eau Claire, WI 54702-4004. Offers MSE. Part-time programs available. *Faculty:* 4 full-time (3 women). *Students:* 3 part-time (all women); includes 1 minority (Two or more races, non-Hispanic/Latino). Average age 29. In 2013, 5 master's awarded. *Degree requirements:* For master's, comprehensive exam, thesis, research paper, or written exam; oral exam. *Entrance requirements:* For master's, minimum GPA of 2.75. Additional exam requirements/recommendations for international students: Required—TOEFL (minimum score 79 iBT). *Application deadline:* For fall admission, 7/1 priority date for domestic students, 6/1 priority date for international students; for spring admission, 12/1 priority date for domestic students, 11/1 priority date for international students. Applications are processed on a rolling basis. Application fee: $56. *Expenses:* Tuition, state resident: full-time $7640; part-time $424.47 per credit. Tuition, nonresident: full-time $16,771; part-time $931.74 per credit. *Required fees:* $1146; $63.65 per credit. *Financial support:* Federal Work-Study and unspecified assistantships available. Financial award application deadline: 3/1; financial award applicants required to submit FAFSA. *Unit head:* Dr. Rose Battalio, Chair, 715-836-5352, Fax: 715-836-3162, E-mail: battalrl@uwec.edu. *Application contact:* Nancy Amdahl, Graduate Dean Assistant, 715-836-2721, Fax: 715-836-2902, E-mail: graduate@uwec.edu.
Website: http://www.uwec.edu/sped/.

University of Wisconsin–La Crosse, Graduate Studies, College of Science and Health, Department of Exercise and Sport Science, La Crosse, WI 54601-3742. Offers clinical exercise physiology (MS); human performance (MS), including applied sport science, human performance, strength and conditioning; physical education teaching (MS), including adapted physical education, adventure education, physical education teaching; special/adapted physical education (MS); sport administration (MS). Part-time and evening/weekend programs available. *Faculty:* 11 full-time (1 woman), 1 part-time/adjunct (0 women). *Students:* 45 full-time (17 women), 22 part-time (8 women); includes 4 minority (1 Black or African American, non-Hispanic/Latino; 1 American Indian or Alaska Native, non-Hispanic/Latino; 1 Asian, non-Hispanic/Latino; 1 Two or more races, non-Hispanic/Latino), 1 international. Average age 25. 107 applicants, 51% accepted, 41 enrolled. In 2013, 53 master's awarded. *Entrance requirements:* Additional exam requirements/recommendations for international students: Required—TOEFL (minimum score 550 paper-based; 79 iBT). Electronic applications accepted. *Financial support:* Research assistantships with partial tuition reimbursements, Federal Work-Study, scholarships/grants, health care benefits, and tuition waivers (partial) available. Support available to part-time students. Financial award application deadline: 3/15; financial award applicants required to submit FAFSA. *Unit head:* Mark Gibson, Chair, E-mail: mgibson@uwlax.edu. *Application contact:* Corey Sjoquist, Director of Admissions, 608-785-8939, E-mail: admissions@uwlax.edu.
Website: http://www.uwlax.edu/sah/ess/index.htm.

University of Wisconsin–Madison, Graduate School, School of Education, Department of Rehabilitation Psychology and Special Education, Program in Special Education, Madison, WI 53706-1380. Offers MA, MS, PhD. *Degree requirements:* For doctorate, thesis/dissertation. *Application deadline:* For fall admission, 3/15 for domestic and international students; for spring admission, 10/15 for domestic and international students. Application fee: $56. Electronic applications accepted. *Expenses:* Tuition, state resident: full-time $10,728; part-time $790 per credit. Tuition, nonresident: full-time $24,054; part-time $1623 per credit. *Required fees:* $1130; $119 per credit. *Financial support:* Fellowships with full tuition reimbursements, research assistantships with full tuition reimbursements, teaching assistantships with full tuition reimbursements, and project assistantships available. *Unit head:* Dr. Kimber Wilkerson, Chair, 608-263-5860, E-mail: klwilkerson@wisc.edu. *Application contact:* 608-262-2433, Fax: 608-262-5134, E-mail: gradadmiss@mail.bascom.wisc.edu.

University of Wisconsin–Milwaukee, Graduate School, School of Education, Department of Exceptional Education, Milwaukee, WI 53201-0413. Offers assistive technology and accessible design (Certificate); exceptional education (MS). Part-time programs available. *Faculty:* 11 full-time (9 women). *Students:* 7 full-time (6 women), 22 part-time (20 women); includes 4 minority (2 Black or African American, non-Hispanic/Latino; 1 Hispanic/Latino; 1 Two or more races, non-Hispanic/Latino). Average age 33. 11 applicants, 91% accepted, 8 enrolled. In 2013, 23 master's awarded. *Degree requirements:* For master's, thesis. *Entrance requirements:* Additional exam requirements/recommendations for international students: Required—TOEFL (minimum score 550 paper-based; 79 iBT), IELTS (minimum score 6.5). *Application deadline:* For fall admission, 1/1 priority date for domestic students; for spring admission, 9/1 for domestic students. Applications are processed on a rolling basis. Application fee: $56 ($96 for international students). Electronic applications accepted. *Financial support:* Fellowships, research assistantships, teaching assistantships, career-related internships or fieldwork, health care benefits, and unspecified assistantships available. Support available to part-time students. Financial award application deadline: 4/15; financial award applicants required to submit FAFSA. *Faculty research:* Emotional disturbance, hearing impairment, learning disabilities, mental retardation. *Unit head:* Elise Frattura, Department Chair, 414-229-3864, E-mail: frattura@uwm.edu. *Application contact:* General Information Contact, 414-229-4982, Fax: 414-229-6967, E-mail: gradschool@uwm.edu.
Website: http://www.uwm.edu/Dept/EXED/.

University of Wisconsin–Milwaukee, Graduate School, School of Education, Urban Education Doctoral Program, Milwaukee, WI 53201-0413. Offers adult, continuing and higher education leadership (PhD); curriculum and instruction (PhD); educational administration (PhD); exceptional education (PhD); multicultural studies (PhD); social foundations of education (PhD). *Students:* 51 full-time (37 women), 40 part-time (25 women); includes 32 minority (16 Black or African American, non-Hispanic/Latino; 1 American Indian or Alaska Native, non-Hispanic/Latino; 3 Asian, non-Hispanic/Latino; 5 Hispanic/Latino; 7 Two or more races, non-Hispanic/Latino), 3 international. Average age 41. 25 applicants, 44% accepted, 4 enrolled. In 2013, 11 doctorates awarded. *Degree requirements:* For doctorate, comprehensive exam, thesis/dissertation. *Entrance requirements:* For doctorate, GRE General Test, minimum undergraduate GPA of 2.85, graduate 3.5. Additional exam requirements/recommendations for international students: Required—TOEFL (minimum score 550 paper-based; 79 iBT), IELTS (minimum score 6.5). *Application deadline:* For fall admission, 1/1 priority date for domestic students; for spring admission, 9/1 for domestic students. Applications are processed on a rolling basis. Application fee: $56 ($96 for international students). Electronic applications accepted. *Financial support:* In 2013–14, 11 fellowships, 1 teaching assistantship were awarded; research assistantships, career-related internships or fieldwork, health care benefits, unspecified assistantships, and project assistantships also available. Support available to part-time students. Financial award application deadline: 4/15; financial award applicants required to submit FAFSA. *Unit head:* Raji Swaminathan, Representative, 414-229-6740, Fax: 414-229-2920, E-mail: swaminar@uwm.edu. *Application contact:* General Information Contact, 414-229-4982, Fax: 414-229-6967, E-mail: gradschool@uwm.edu.
Website: http://www4.uwm.edu/soe/academics/urban_ed/.

University of Wisconsin–Oshkosh, Graduate Studies, College of Education and Human Services, Department of Special Education, Oshkosh, WI 54901. Offers cross-categorical (MSE); early childhood: exceptional education needs (MSE); non-licensure (MSE). Part-time and evening/weekend programs available. *Degree requirements:* For master's, comprehensive exam (for some programs), thesis or alternative, field report. *Entrance requirements:* For master's, interview, minimum GPA of 3.0, teaching license, letters of recommendation. Additional exam requirements/recommendations for international students: Required—TOEFL (minimum score 550 paper-based; 79 iBT). Electronic applications accepted. *Faculty research:* Private agency contributions to the disabled, graduation requirements for exceptional education needs students, direct instruction in spelling for learning disabled, effects of behavioral parent training, secondary education programming issues.

University of Wisconsin–Stevens Point, College of Professional Studies, School of Education, Program in Education—General/Special, Stevens Point, WI 54481-3897. Offers MSE. Part-time programs available. *Degree requirements:* For master's, comprehensive exam, thesis or alternative. *Entrance requirements:* For master's, minimum undergraduate GPA of 3.0, 2 years teaching experience, letters of recommendation, teacher certification. *Faculty research:* Curriculum and instruction, early childhood special education, standards-based education.

University of Wisconsin–Superior, Graduate Division, Department of Teacher Education, Program in Special Education, Superior, WI 54880-4500. Offers emotional/behavior disabilities (MSE); learning disabilities (MSE). Part-time and evening/weekend programs available. Postbaccalaureate distance learning degree programs offered (minimal on-campus study). *Faculty:* 2 full-time (both women). *Students:* 11 full-time (6 women), 2 part-time (both women); includes 1 minority (Asian, non-Hispanic/Latino). Average age 34. 6 applicants, 83% accepted, 3 enrolled. In 2013, 12 master's awarded. *Degree requirements:* For master's, research project. *Entrance requirements:* For master's, minimum GPA of 2.75, teaching certificate. *Application deadline:* For fall admission, 4/1 priority date for domestic students; for spring admission, 10/15 priority

date for domestic students. Applications are processed on a rolling basis. Application fee: $56. Electronic applications accepted. *Expenses:* Tuition, state resident: full-time $4526; part-time $649.24 per credit. Tuition, nonresident: full-time $9091; part-time $1156.51 per credit. *Financial support:* Career-related internships or fieldwork, Federal Work-Study, institutionally sponsored loans, and tuition waivers (partial) available. Support available to part-time students. Financial award application deadline: 4/15; financial award applicants required to submit FAFSA. *Unit head:* Dr. Maryjane Burdge, Associate Professor, 715-394-8048, E-mail: mburdge@uwsuper.edu. *Application contact:* Suzie Finckler, Student Status Examiner, 715-394-8295, Fax: 715-394-8371, E-mail: gradstudy@uwsuper.edu.
Website: http://www.uwsuper.edu/.

University of Wisconsin–Whitewater, School of Graduate Studies, College of Education and Professional Studies, Department of Special Education, Whitewater, WI 53190-1790. Offers cross categorical licensure (MSE); professional development (MSE). *Accreditation:* NCATE. Part-time and evening/weekend programs available. Postbaccalaureate distance learning degree programs offered (no on-campus study). *Degree requirements:* For master's, thesis or alternative. *Entrance requirements:* Additional exam requirements/recommendations for international students: Required—TOEFL (minimum score 550 paper-based; 80 iBT), IELTS (minimum score 6). Electronic applications accepted. *Faculty research:* Language ability, cultural interaction with disability, juvenile corrections, early childhood programming and childcare issues.

University of Wyoming, College of Education, Program in Special Education, Laramie, WY 82071. Offers MA, PhD, Ed S. *Degree requirements:* For master's, comprehensive exam, thesis. *Entrance requirements:* For master's, GRE, 2 years teaching experience, 3 letters of recommendation, writing sample. *Faculty research:* Self-determination; transition; digital learning; severe disabilities; response to intervention.

Ursuline College, School of Graduate Studies, Program in Education, Pepper Pike, OH 44124-4398. Offers art education (MA); early childhood education (MA); language arts education (MA); life science education (MA); math education (MA); middle school education (MA); social studies education (MA); special education (MA). *Accreditation:* NCATE. *Faculty:* 4 full-time (all women), 7 part-time/adjunct (5 women). *Students:* 18 full-time (16 women), 7 part-time (all women); includes 8 minority (4 Black or African American, non-Hispanic/Latino; 2 Asian, non-Hispanic/Latino; 2 Hispanic/Latino). Average age 34. 1 applicant, 100% accepted, 1 enrolled. In 2013, 25 master's awarded. *Degree requirements:* For master's, comprehensive exam. *Entrance requirements:* For master's, minimum undergraduate GPA of 3.0. Additional exam requirements/recommendations for international students: Required—TOEFL (minimum score 500 paper-based). *Application deadline:* For fall admission, 8/1 priority date for domestic students. Applications are processed on a rolling basis. Application fee: $25. *Expenses:* Contact institution. *Financial support:* In 2013–14, 1 student received support. Federal Work-Study available. Financial award application deadline: 3/1. *Unit head:* Dr. Edna West, Director, Master's Apprentice Program, 440-646-6134, Fax: 440-646-8328, E-mail: ewest@ursuline.edu. *Application contact:* Stephanie Pratt, Graduate Admission Coordinator, 440-646-8119, Fax: 440-684-6138, E-mail: graduateadmissions@ursuline.edu.

Utah State University, School of Graduate Studies, Emma Eccles Jones College of Education and Human Services, Department of Special Education and Rehabilitation, Logan, UT 84322. Offers disability disciplines (PhD); rehabilitation counselor education (MRC); special education (M Ed, MS, Ed S). Part-time programs available. Postbaccalaureate distance learning degree programs offered (minimal on-campus study). *Degree requirements:* For master's, thesis (for some programs), internships (for some programs); for doctorate, comprehensive exam, thesis/dissertation. *Entrance requirements:* For master's and doctorate, GRE General Test, minimum GPA of 3.0. Additional exam requirements/recommendations for international students: Required—TOEFL (minimum score 550 paper-based). Electronic applications accepted. *Faculty research:* Applied behavior analysis, effective instructional practices, early childhood teacher training research, distance education, multicultural rehabilitation.

Valdosta State University, Department of Early Childhood and Special Education, Valdosta, GA 31698. Offers early childhood (M Ed); special education (M Ed, MAT, Ed S). *Accreditation:* ASHA (one or more programs are accredited); NCATE. Part-time and evening/weekend programs available. Postbaccalaureate distance learning degree programs offered (no on-campus study). *Faculty:* 9 full-time (8 women), 4 part-time/adjunct (all women). *Students:* 31 full-time (27 women), 13 part-time (10 women); includes 11 minority (8 Black or African American, non-Hispanic/Latino; 1 Asian, non-Hispanic/Latino; 1 Hispanic/Latino; 1 Two or more races, non-Hispanic/Latino). Average age 23. 13 applicants, 92% accepted, 12 enrolled. In 2013, 23 master's awarded. *Degree requirements:* For master's, thesis (for some programs), comprehensive written and/or oral exams; for Ed S, thesis. *Entrance requirements:* For master's, GRE General Test or MAT, minimum GPA of 2.5; for Ed S, GRE General Test or MAT, minimum GPA of 3.0. Additional exam requirements/recommendations for international students: Required—TOEFL (minimum score 523 paper-based). *Application deadline:* For fall and spring admission, 7/1 for domestic and international students. Applications are processed on a rolling basis. Application fee: $35. Electronic applications accepted. *Expenses:* Tuition, state resident: full-time $4140; part-time $230 per credit hour. Tuition, nonresident: full-time $14,904; part-time $828 per credit hour. *Required fees:* $995 per semester. Tuition and fees vary according to course load. *Financial support:* In 2013–14, 4 students received support, including 5 research assistantships with full tuition reimbursements available (averaging $3,252 per year); institutionally sponsored loans, scholarships/grants, and unspecified assistantships also available. Support available to part-time students. Financial award application deadline: 7/1; financial award applicants required to submit FAFSA. *Unit head:* Dr. Festus Obiakor, Head, 229-333-5929, E-mail: feobiakor@valdosta.edu. *Application contact:* Rebecca Petrella, Graduate Admissions Coordinator, 229-333-5694, Fax: 229-245-3853, E-mail: rlwaters@valdosta.edu.
Website: http://www.valdosta.edu/colleges/education/early-childhood-and-special-education/welcome.php.

Vanderbilt University, Peabody College, Department of Special Education, Nashville, TN 37240-1001. Offers M Ed. *Accreditation:* NCATE. *Faculty:* 25 full-time (16 women), 11 part-time/adjunct (9 women). *Students:* 83 full-time (77 women), 12 part-time (all women); includes 7 minority (1 Black or African American, non-Hispanic/Latino; 2 Asian, non-Hispanic/Latino; 4 Hispanic/Latino), 1 international. Average age 26. 88 applicants, 65% accepted, 45 enrolled. In 2013, 44 master's awarded. *Degree requirements:* For master's, comprehensive exam, thesis optional. *Entrance requirements:* For master's, GRE General Test, MAT. Additional exam requirements/recommendations for international students: Required—TOEFL (minimum score 550 paper-based; 80 iBT). *Application deadline:* For fall admission, 12/31 priority date for domestic and international students; for spring admission, 11/1 priority date for domestic and international students. Applications are processed on a rolling basis. Application fee: $0. Electronic applications accepted. *Financial support:* Fellowships with full and partial tuition reimbursements, research assistantships with full and partial tuition reimbursements, teaching assistantships with full and partial tuition reimbursements, Federal Work-Study, institutionally sponsored loans, scholarships/grants, traineeships, health care benefits, tuition waivers (partial), and unspecified assistantships available.

Support available to part-time students. Financial award application deadline: 1/15; financial award applicants required to submit CSS PROFILE or FAFSA. *Faculty research:* Early language and social skills development, learning and behavior disorders, autism and developmental/intellectual disabilities, low vision and blindness, giftedness and diversity. *Unit head:* Dr. Donald Compton, Chair, 615-322-8150, Fax: 615-343-1570, E-mail: donald.l.compton@vanderbilt.edu. *Application contact:* Alfred Brady, Admissions Coordinator, 615-322-8195, Fax: 615-343-1570, E-mail: alfred.l.brady@vanderbilt.edu.

Vanderbilt University, School of Medicine, Department of Hearing and Speech Sciences, Nashville, TN 37240-1001. Offers audiology (Au D, PhD); deaf education (MED); speech-language pathology (MS). *Degree requirements:* For master's, thesis optional; for doctorate, thesis/dissertation, final and qualifying exams. *Entrance requirements:* For master's and doctorate, GRE General Test. Additional exam requirements/recommendations for international students: Required—TOEFL. Electronic applications accepted. *Faculty research:* Child language.

Virginia Commonwealth University, Graduate School, School of Education, Doctoral Program in Education, Special Education and Disability Leadership Track, Richmond, VA 23284-9005. Offers PhD. *Entrance requirements:* For doctorate, GRE. Additional exam requirements/recommendations for international students: Required—TOEFL (minimum score 600 paper-based; 100 iBT). Electronic applications accepted.

Virginia Commonwealth University, Graduate School, School of Education, Program in Special Education, Richmond, VA 23284-9005. Offers autism spectrum disorders (Certificate); disability leadership (Certificate); early childhood (M Ed); general education (M Ed); severe disabilities (M Ed). *Accreditation:* NCATE. *Degree requirements:* For master's, comprehensive exam. *Entrance requirements:* For master's, GRE General Test or MAT. Additional exam requirements/recommendations for international students: Required—TOEFL (minimum score 600 paper-based; 100 iBT). Electronic applications accepted.

Wagner College, Division of Graduate Studies, Department of Education, Program in Childhood Education/Special Education, Staten Island, NY 10301-4495. Offers MS Ed. Part-time and evening/weekend programs available. *Degree requirements:* For master's, thesis (for some programs). *Entrance requirements:* For master's, minimum GPA of 3.0, interview, recommendations. Additional exam requirements/recommendations for international students: Required—TOEFL. Electronic applications accepted. *Expenses:* Tuition: Full-time $17,496; part-time $972 per credit. Tuition and fees vary according to course load.

Wagner College, Division of Graduate Studies, Department of Education, Program in Early Childhood Education/Special Education (Birth-Grade 2), Staten Island, NY 10301-4495. Offers MS Ed. Part-time and evening/weekend programs available. *Degree requirements:* For master's, thesis. *Entrance requirements:* For master's, minimum GPA of 3.0, valid initial NY State Certificate or equivalent, interview, recommendations. Electronic applications accepted. *Expenses:* Tuition: Full-time $17,496; part-time $972 per credit. Tuition and fees vary according to course load.

Wagner College, Division of Graduate Studies, Department of Education, Program in Secondary Education/Special Education, Staten Island, NY 10301-4495. Offers language arts (MS Ed); languages other than English (MS Ed); mathematics and technology (MS Ed); science and technology (MS Ed); social studies (MS Ed). Part-time and evening/weekend programs available. *Degree requirements:* For master's, thesis (for some programs). *Entrance requirements:* For master's, minimum GPA of 3.0, interview, recommendations. Electronic applications accepted. *Expenses:* Tuition: Full-time $17,496; part-time $972 per credit. Tuition and fees vary according to course load.

Walden University, Graduate Programs, Richard W. Riley College of Education and Leadership, Minneapolis, MN 55401. *Accreditation:* NCATE. Part-time and evening/weekend programs available. Postbaccalaureate distance learning degree programs offered (minimal on-campus study). *Faculty:* 23 full-time (15 women), 830 part-time/adjunct (569 women). *Students:* 8,671 full-time (7,197 women), 2,122 part-time (1,735 women); includes 4,734 minority (3,802 Black or African American, non-Hispanic/Latino; 50 American Indian or Alaska Native, non-Hispanic/Latino; 136 Asian, non-Hispanic/Latino; 539 Hispanic/Latino; 35 Native Hawaiian or other Pacific Islander, non-Hispanic/Latino; 172 Two or more races, non-Hispanic/Latino), 73 international. Average age 40. 2,646 applicants, 96% accepted, 2074 enrolled. In 2013, 2,214 master's, 354 doctorates, 479 other advanced degrees awarded. *Degree requirements:* For doctorate, thesis/dissertation (for some programs), residency; for other advanced degree, residency (for some programs). *Entrance requirements:* For master's, bachelor's degree or higher; minimum GPA of 2.5; official transcripts; goal statement (for some programs); access to computer and Internet; for doctorate, master's degree or higher; three years of related professional or academic experience (preferred); minimum GPA of 3.0; goal statement and current resume (select programs); official transcripts; access to computer and Internet; for other advanced degree, relevant work experience; access to computer and Internet. Additional exam requirements/recommendations for international students: Required—TOEFL (minimum score 550 paper-based; 79 iBT), IELTS (minimum score 6.5), Michigan English Language Assessment Battery (minimum score 82), or PTE. *Application deadline:* Applications are processed on a rolling basis. Application fee: $0. Electronic applications accepted. *Expenses:* Tuition: Full-time $11,813.55; part-time $500 per credit. *Required fees:* $618.76. *Financial support:* In 2013–14, 1 fellowship was awarded; Federal Work-Study, scholarships/grants, unspecified assistantships, and family tuition reduction, active duty/veteran tuition reduction, group tuition reduction, interest-free payment plans, employee tuition reduction also available. Support available to part-time students. Financial award applicants required to submit FAFSA. *Unit head:* Dr. Kate Steffens, Dean, 800-925-3368. *Application contact:* Jennifer Hall, Vice President of Enrollment Management, 866-4-WALDEN, E-mail: info@waldenu.edu.
Website: http://www.waldenu.edu/colleges-schools/riley-college-of-education/.

Walla Walla University, Graduate School, School of Education and Psychology, College Place, WA 99324-1198. Offers counseling psychology (MA); curriculum and instruction (M Ed, MA, MAT); educational leadership (M Ed, MA, MAT); literacy instruction (M Ed, MA, MAT); students at risk (M Ed, MA, MAT); teaching (MAT). Part-time programs available. *Entrance requirements:* For master's, GRE General Test, minimum GPA of 2.75. Additional exam requirements/recommendations for international students: Required—TOEFL (minimum score 550 paper-based; 79 iBT). Electronic applications accepted. *Faculty research:* Admissions/retention, instructional psychology, moral development, teaching of reading.

Washburn University, College of Arts and Sciences, Department of Education, Topeka, KS 66621. Offers curriculum and instruction (M Ed); educational leadership (M Ed); reading (M Ed); special education (M Ed). *Accreditation:* NCATE. Part-time programs available. *Faculty:* 7 full-time (5 women). *Students:* 32 part-time (21 women). Average age 33. In 2013, 9 master's awarded. *Degree requirements:* For master's, comprehensive exam, thesis or alternative, portfolio, comprehensive paper, or action research project. *Entrance requirements:* For master's, department exam, GRE General Test, or MAT, minimum GPA of 3.0 in graduate coursework or last 60 hours of undergraduate coursework. Additional exam requirements/recommendations for international students: Required—TOEFL (minimum score 80 iBT). *Application deadline:* For fall admission, 8/1 for domestic and international students; for spring admission, 11/

1 for domestic and international students. Applications are processed on a rolling basis. *Expenses:* Tuition, state resident: full-time $5850; part-time $325 per credit hour. Tuition, nonresident: full-time $11,916; part-time $662 per credit hour. *Required fees:* $86; $43 per semester. Tuition and fees vary according to program. *Financial support:* Federal Work-Study, institutionally sponsored loans, and scholarships/grants available. Support available to part-time students. Financial award applicants required to submit FAFSA. *Faculty research:* Reading/literature/literacy, foundations, special education, diversity, teaching and technology. *Unit head:* Dr. Donna Lalonde, Interim Chairperson, 785-670-1943, Fax: 785-670-1046, E-mail: donna.lalonde@washburn.edu. *Application contact:* Tara Porter, Licensure Officer, 785-670-1434, Fax: 785-670-1046, E-mail: tara.porter@washburn.edu.
Website: http://www.washburn.edu/academics/college-schools/arts-sciences/departments/education.

Washington State University, Graduate School, College of Education, Department of Teaching and Learning, Program in Special Education, Pullman, WA 99164. Offers Ed M, MA, PhD. Postbaccalaureate distance learning degree programs offered (no on-campus study). *Degree requirements:* For master's, comprehensive exam (for some programs), thesis (for some programs), oral or written exam; for doctorate, comprehensive exam, thesis/dissertation, oral and written exam. *Entrance requirements:* For master's, undergraduate degree from accredited four-year institution, minimum GPA of 3.0, 3 letters of recommendation, transcripts showing all college or university course work, statement of professional objectives, current curriculum vitae/resume; for doctorate, master's degree from accredited institution, minimum GPA of 3.0, 3 letters of recommendation, transcripts showing all college or university course work, statement of professional objectives, current curriculum vitae/resume. Additional exam requirements/recommendations for international students: Required—TOEFL (minimum score 550 paper-based; 80 iBT). Electronic applications accepted. *Faculty research:* Indigenous family involvement in education, early childhood special education, culturally responsive curriculum development and delivery, special education issues and policies.

Washington University in St. Louis, School of Medicine, Program in Audiology and Communication Sciences, Saint Louis, MO 63110. Offers audiology (Au D); deaf education (MS); speech and hearing sciences (PhD). *Accreditation:* ASHA (one or more programs are accredited). *Faculty:* 22 full-time (12 women), 18 part-time/adjunct (12 women). *Students:* 73 full-time (71 women). Average age 24. 136 applicants, 29% accepted, 27 enrolled. In 2013, 10 master's, 11 doctorates awarded. *Degree requirements:* For master's, comprehensive exam, thesis, independent study project, oral exam; for doctorate, comprehensive exam, thesis/dissertation, capstone project. *Entrance requirements:* For master's and doctorate, GRE General Test, minimum B average in previous college/university coursework (recommended). Additional exam requirements/recommendations for international students: Required—TOEFL (minimum score 100 iBT). *Application deadline:* For fall admission, 2/15 for domestic and international students. Application fee: $60 ($80 for international students). Electronic applications accepted. *Expenses:* Contact institution. *Financial support:* In 2013–14, 72 students received support, including 73 fellowships with full and partial tuition reimbursements available (averaging $15,000 per year), 6 teaching assistantships with partial tuition reimbursements available (averaging $1,000 per year); career-related internships or fieldwork, Federal Work-Study, institutionally sponsored loans, scholarships/grants, traineeships, health care benefits, tuition waivers (partial), and unspecified assistantships also available. Financial award application deadline: 2/15; financial award applicants required to submit FAFSA. *Faculty research:* Audiology, deaf education, speech and hearing sciences, sensory neuroscience. *Unit head:* Dr. William W. Clark, Program Director, 314-747-0104, Fax: 314-747-0105. *Application contact:* Elizabeth A. Elliott, Director, Finance and Student Academic Affairs, 314-747-0104, Fax: 314-747-0105, E-mail: elliottb@wustl.edu.
Website: http://pacs.wustl.edu/.

Wayland Baptist University, Graduate Programs, Program in Education, Plainview, TX 79072-6998. Offers education administration (M Ed); education diagnostics (M Ed); education literacy (M Ed); elementary certification (M Ed); English (M Ed); English as a second language (M Ed); higher education administration (M Ed); human resources (M Ed); instructional leadership (M Ed); instructional technology (M Ed); science education (M Ed); secondary certification (M Ed); social studies (M Ed); special education (M Ed). Part-time and evening/weekend programs available. Postbaccalaureate distance learning degree programs offered (no on-campus study). *Faculty:* 33 full-time (17 women), 28 part-time/adjunct (17 women). *Students:* 22 full-time (15 women), 316 part-time (189 women); includes 130 minority (48 Black or African American, non-Hispanic/Latino; 3 American Indian or Alaska Native, non-Hispanic/Latino; 71 Hispanic/Latino; 1 Native Hawaiian or other Pacific Islander, non-Hispanic/Latino; 7 Two or more races, non-Hispanic/Latino). Average age 39. 80 applicants, 96% accepted, 44 enrolled. In 2013, 170 master's awarded. *Degree requirements:* For master's, comprehensive exam, capstone course. *Entrance requirements:* For master's, GRE, GMAT or MAT. Additional exam requirements/recommendations for international students: Required—TOEFL (minimum score 500 paper-based; 61 iBT). *Application deadline:* Applications are processed on a rolling basis. Application fee: $50. Electronic applications accepted. *Expenses: Tuition:* Full-time $8190; part-time $455 per credit hour. *Required fees:* $970; $455 per credit hour. $485 per semester. *Financial support:* Federal Work-Study, institutionally sponsored loans, and scholarships/grants available. Support available to part-time students. Financial award application deadline: 5/1; financial award applicants required to submit FAFSA. *Unit head:* Dr. Jim Todd, Chairman, 806-291-1045, Fax: 806-291-1951. *Application contact:* Amanda Stanton, Coordinator of Graduate Studies, 806-291-3423, Fax: 806-291-1950, E-mail: stanton@wbu.edu.

Waynesburg University, Graduate and Professional Studies, Canonsburg, PA 15370. Offers business (MBA), including energy management, finance, health systems, human resources, leadership, market development; counseling (MA), including addictions counseling, clinical mental health; education (M Ed, MAT), including autism (M Ed), curriculum and instruction (M Ed), educational leadership (M Ed), online teaching (M Ed); nursing (MSN), including administration, education, informatics; nursing practice (DNP); special education (M Ed); technology (M Ed); MSN/MBA. *Accreditation:* AACN. Part-time and evening/weekend programs available. *Faculty:* 11 full-time (5 women), 136 part-time/adjunct (80 women). *Students:* 146 full-time (99 women), 419 part-time (268 women). In 2013, 290 master's, 7 doctorates awarded. *Degree requirements:* For doctorate, thesis/dissertation. *Entrance requirements:* Additional exam requirements/recommendations for international students: Required—TOEFL. *Application deadline:* For fall admission, 8/1 priority date for domestic students. Applications are processed on a rolling basis. Electronic applications accepted. *Financial support:* Available to part-time students. Application deadline: 5/1. *Unit head:* David Mariner, Dean, 724-743-4420, Fax: 724-743-4425, E-mail: dmariner@waynesburg.edu. *Application contact:* Dr. Michael Bednarski, Director of Enrollment, 724-743-4420, Fax: 724-743-4425, E-mail: mbednars@waynesburg.edu.
Website: http://www.waynesburg.edu/.

Wayne State College, School of Education and Counseling, Department of Counseling and Special Education, Program in Special Education, Wayne, NE 68787. Offers MSE. *Accreditation:* NCATE. Part-time and evening/weekend programs available. *Degree requirements:* For master's, comprehensive exam, thesis. *Entrance requirements:* For master's, GRE General Test, minimum GPA of 3.0. Additional exam requirements/recommendations for international students: Required—TOEFL (minimum score 550 paper-based). Electronic applications accepted.

Wayne State University, College of Education, Division of Administrative and Organizational Studies, Detroit, MI 48202. Offers college and university teaching (Certificate); educational administration and supervision (Ed S); educational leadership (M Ed); educational leadership and policy studies (Ed D, PhD); educational technology (Certificate); instructional technology (M Ed, Ed D, PhD, Ed S); online teaching (Certificate); secondary curriculum and instruction (Ed S); special education administration (Ed S). Part-time programs available. Postbaccalaureate distance learning degree programs offered. *Students:* 96 full-time (68 women), 207 part-time (137 women); includes 133 minority (115 Black or African American, non-Hispanic/Latino; 4 American Indian or Alaska Native, non-Hispanic/Latino; 2 Asian, non-Hispanic/Latino; 8 Hispanic/Latino; 4 Two or more races, non-Hispanic/Latino), 14 international. Average age 39. 127 applicants, 50% accepted, 42 enrolled. In 2013, 47 master's, 15 doctorates, 41 other advanced degrees awarded. *Degree requirements:* For doctorate, thesis/dissertation. *Entrance requirements:* For master's, baccalaureate degree from accredited U.S. institution or equivalent from college or university of government-recognized standing; minimum undergraduate GPA of 2.75 in upper-division coursework; for doctorate, GRE or MAT, interview; autobiography or curriculum vitae; references; master's degree; minimum undergraduate GPA of 3.0, graduate 3.75; 3 years of relevant experience; foundational course work; for other advanced degree, master's degree from accredited institution, minimum upper-division GPA of 2.6 or 3.4 master's, fulfillment of the special requirements of the area of concentration, 3 years of teaching experience (except for instructional technology). Additional exam requirements/recommendations for international students: Required—TOEFL (minimum score 550 paper-based; 79 iBT), Michigan English Language Assessment Battery (minimum score 85); Recommended—IELTS (minimum score 6.5), TWE (minimum score 5.5). *Application deadline:* For fall admission, 6/1 priority date for domestic students, 5/1 priority date for international students; for winter admission, 10/1 priority date for domestic students, 9/1 priority date for international students; for spring admission, 2/1 priority date for domestic students, 1/1 priority date for international students. Applications are processed on a rolling basis. Application fee: $0. Electronic applications accepted. *Expenses:* Tuition, state resident: part-time $554.15 per credit. Tuition, nonresident: part-time $1200.35 per credit. *Required fees:* $42.15 per credit. $268.30 per semester. Tuition and fees vary according to course load and program. *Financial support:* In 2013–14, 48 students received support, including 3 fellowships with tuition reimbursements available (averaging $15,541 per year), 4 research assistantships with tuition reimbursements available (averaging $16,508 per year); career-related internships or fieldwork, Federal Work-Study, scholarships/grants, health care benefits, and unspecified assistantships also available. Support available to part-time students. Financial award application deadline: 3/31; financial award applicants required to submit FAFSA. *Faculty research:* Total quality management, participatory management, administering educational technology, school improvement, principalship. *Total annual research expenditures:* $6,888. *Unit head:* Dr. William Hill, Assistant Dean, 313-577-9316, E-mail: william_e_hill@wayne.edu. *Application contact:* Janice Green, Assistant Dean, 313-577-1605, E-mail: jwgreen@wayne.edu.
Website: http://coe.wayne.edu/aos/index.php.

Wayne State University, College of Education, Division of Teacher Education, Detroit, MI 48202. Offers art education (M Ed), including art therapy; autism spectrum disorders (Certificate); bilingual/bicultural education (M Ed, Certificate); career and technical education (M Ed, Certificate); cognitive impairment (Certificate); curriculum and instruction (Ed D, PhD, Ed S), including art education (PhD), bilingual education (Ed D, Ed S), bilingual-bicultural education (PhD), career and technical education (MAT, Ed D, PhD, Ed S), early childhood education (MAT, Ed D, PhD, Ed S), elementary education, English as a second language (MAT, Ed D, Ed S), English education (MAT, Ed D, PhD, Ed S), foreign language education (MAT, PhD), K-12 curriculum, mathematics education (MAT, Ed D, PhD, Ed S), science education (MAT, Ed D, PhD, Ed S), secondary education, social studies education (MAT, Ed S), social studies education: secondary (Ed D, PhD); early childhood education (M Ed, Certificate); elementary education (M Ed, MAT), including children's literature (MAT), early childhood education (MAT, Ed D, PhD, Ed S), general elementary education (MAT); elementary or secondary education (MAT), including bilingual/bicultural education, English as a second language (MAT, Ed D, Ed S), mathematics education (MAT, Ed D, PhD, Ed S), science education (MAT, Ed D, PhD, Ed S), social studies education (MAT, Ed S); emotionally impaired (Certificate); English as a second language (Certificate); English education (M Ed), including secondary; foreign language education (M Ed); K-12 reading specialist (Certificate); learning disabilities (Certificate); mathematics education (M Ed), including secondary; reading (M Ed, Ed S); reading, language and literature (Ed D); science education (M Ed), including secondary; secondary education (MAT), including art education (K-12), career and technical education (MAT, Ed D, PhD, Ed S), English education (MAT, Ed D, PhD, Ed S), foreign language education (MAT, PhD), kinesiology; social studies education (M Ed), including secondary; special education (M Ed, MAT, Ed D, PhD, Ed S); visual arts education (Certificate). Part-time programs available. *Faculty:* 36 full-time (25 women), 55 part-time/adjunct (43 women). *Students:* 218 full-time (163 women), 448 part-time (344 women); includes 218 minority (177 Black or African American, non-Hispanic/Latino; 2 American Indian or Alaska Native, non-Hispanic/Latino; 11 Asian, non-Hispanic/Latino; 19 Hispanic/Latino; 1 Native Hawaiian or other Pacific Islander, non-Hispanic/Latino; 8 Two or more races, non-Hispanic/Latino), 10 international. Average age 37. 258 applicants, 30% accepted, 52 enrolled. In 2013, 183 master's, 10 doctorates, 35 other advanced degrees awarded. *Degree requirements:* For master's, thesis, essay or project (for some M Ed programs), professional field experience (for MAT programs); for doctorate, thesis/dissertation. *Entrance requirements:* For master's, Michigan Basic Skills Test (MA in teaching), admission to the graduate school, verification of participation in group work with children and Michigan State Police Criminal Background check; for doctorate, minimum undergraduate GPA of 3.0, graduate 3.5; interview, curriculum vitae; references. Additional exam requirements/recommendations for international students: Required—TOEFL (minimum score 550 paper-based; 79 iBT), TWE (minimum score 5.5), Michigan English Language Assessment Battery (minimum score 85); Recommended—IELTS (minimum score 6.5). *Application deadline:* For fall admission, 6/1 priority date for domestic students, 5/1 priority date for international students; for winter admission, 10/1 priority date for domestic students, 9/1 priority date for international students; for spring admission, 2/1 priority date for domestic students, 1/1 priority date for international students. Applications are processed on a rolling basis. Application fee: $0. Electronic applications accepted. *Expenses:* Tuition, state resident: part-time $554.15 per credit. Tuition, nonresident: part-time $1200.35 per credit. *Required fees:* $42.15 per credit. $268.30 per semester. Tuition and fees vary according to course load and program. *Financial support:* In 2013–14, 83 students received support, including 1 fellowship (averaging $16,842 per year), 1 research assistantship with tuition reimbursement available (averaging $21,229 per year); career-related internships or fieldwork, Federal Work-Study, scholarships/grants, health care benefits, and unspecified assistantships also available. Support available to part-time students. Financial award application

deadline: 3/31; financial award applicants required to submit FAFSA. *Faculty research:* Improving students' skill achievement in mathematics; improving elementary children's understanding of informational text; teachers' use of their pedagogical and mathematical knowledge in the interactive work of teaching; the intersection of identity construction in teaching and learning; identifying effective methods of literacy instruction and assessments for bilingual students in elementary language arts classrooms. *Total annual research expenditures:* $368,105. *Unit head:* Dr. Kathleen Crawford-McKinney, Assistant Dean, 313-577-0122. *Application contact:* Janice Green, Assistant Dean, 313-577-1605, E-mail: jwgreen@wayne.edu.
Website: http://coe.wayne.edu/ted/index.php.

Webster University, School of Education, Department of Multidisciplinary Studies, St. Louis, MO 63119-3194. Offers education leadership (Ed S); educational technology (MAT); educational technology leadership (Ed S); mathematics (MA); multidisciplinary studies (MAT); school psychology (Ed S); school systems, superintendency and leadership (Ed S); social science (MAT); special education (MA). Part-time programs available. *Entrance requirements:* For master's, minimum GPA of 2.5. Additional exam requirements/recommendations for international students: Required—TOEFL. *Expenses: Tuition:* Full-time $11,610; part-time $645 per credit hour. Tuition and fees vary according to campus/location and program.

West Chester University of Pennsylvania, College of Education, Department of Special Education, West Chester, PA 19383. Offers autism (Certificate); special education (M Ed); special education 7-12 (Certificate); special education PK-8 (Certificate); universal design for learning and assistive technology (Certificate). Programs available in traditional, distance, and blended formats. *Accreditation:* NCATE. Part-time programs available. Postbaccalaureate distance learning degree programs offered (no on-campus study). *Faculty:* 4 full-time (all women), 3 part-time/adjunct (2 women). *Students:* 7 full-time (6 women), 106 part-time (91 women); includes 7 minority (5 Black or African American, non-Hispanic/Latino; 1 Asian, non-Hispanic/Latino; 1 Hispanic/Latino), 1 international. Average age 29. 83 applicants, 89% accepted, 42 enrolled. In 2013, 30 master's, 2 Certificates awarded. *Degree requirements:* For master's, thesis optional, minimum GPA of 3.0, action research; for Certificate, minimum GPA of 3.0; modified student teaching. *Entrance requirements:* For master's, GRE if GPA below 3.0, two letters of recommendation; for Certificate, minimum GPA of 2.8 on last 48 credits or 3.0 overall undergraduate. Additional exam requirements/recommendations for international students: Required—TOEFL (minimum score 550 paper-based; 80 iBT). *Application deadline:* For fall admission, 4/15 priority date for domestic students, 3/15 for international students; for spring admission, 10/15 priority date for domestic students, 9/1 for international students. Applications are processed on a rolling basis. Application fee: $45. Electronic applications accepted. *Expenses:* Tuition, state resident: full-time $7956; part-time $442 per credit. Tuition, nonresident: full-time $11,934; part-time $663 per credit. *Required fees:* $2134.20; $106.24 per credit. Tuition and fees vary according to campus/location and program. *Financial support:* Unspecified assistantships available. Support available to part-time students. Financial award application deadline: 2/15; financial award applicants required to submit FAFSA. *Unit head:* Dr. Donna Wandry, Chair, 610-436-3431, Fax: 610-436-3102, E-mail: dwandry@wcupa.edu. *Application contact:* Dr. Vicki McGinley, Graduate Coordinator, 610-436-2867, E-mail: vmcginley@wcupa.edu.
Website: http://www.wcupa.edu/_academics/sch_sed.earlyspecialed/.

Western Connecticut State University, Division of Graduate Studies, School of Professional Studies, Department of Education and Educational Psychology, Special Education Option, Danbury, CT 06810-6885. Offers MS. Part-time programs available. *Degree requirements:* For master's, thesis or research project. *Entrance requirements:* For master's, minimum GPA of 2.8, teaching certificate. Additional exam requirements/recommendations for international students: Recommended—TOEFL (minimum score 550 paper-based; 79 iBT), IELTS (minimum score 6). *Faculty research:* Education and development of exceptional, gifted, talented, and disabled students in a regular (mainstream) classroom.

Western Governors University, Teachers College, Salt Lake City, UT 84107. Offers curriculum and instruction (MS); educational leadership (MS); educational studies (MA); educational studies (5-12) (MA), including mathematics; elementary education (K-8) (MAT, Postbaccalaureate Certificate); elementary education (PreK-8) (MAT); English language learning (K-12) (MA); instructional design (MAT); learning and technology (M Ed, MA); management and innovation (M Ed); mathematics (5-12) (MAT, Postbaccalaureate Certificate); mathematics (5-9) (MAT, Postbaccalaureate Certificate); mathematics education (5-12) (MA); mathematics education (5-9) (MA); mathematics education (K-6) (MA); measurement and evaluation (M Ed); science (5-12) (Postbaccalaureate Certificate); science (5-9) (MAT, Postbaccalaureate Certificate); science education (5-12) (MA), including biology, chemistry, geology, physics; science education (5-9) (MA); social science (5-12) (MAT, Postbaccalaureate Certificate); special education (MAT, MS). *Accreditation:* NCATE. Evening/weekend programs available. Postbaccalaureate distance learning degree programs offered (no on-campus study). *Degree requirements:* For master's, capstone project. *Entrance requirements:* For master's and Postbaccalaureate Certificate, Readiness Assessment, transcripts. Additional exam requirements/recommendations for international students: Required—TOEFL (minimum score 450 paper-based; 80 iBT). Electronic applications accepted. *Expenses:* Contact institution.

Western Illinois University, School of Graduate Studies, College of Education and Human Services, Department of Curriculum and Instruction, Program in Special Education, Macomb, IL 61455-1390. Offers MS Ed. *Accreditation:* NCATE. Part-time programs available. *Students:* 1 (woman) full-time, 27 part-time (25 women); includes 2 minority (1 American Indian or Alaska Native, non-Hispanic/Latino; 1 Hispanic/Latino). Average age 36. In 2013, 8 master's awarded. *Degree requirements:* For master's, comprehensive exam, thesis or alternative. *Entrance requirements:* For master's, teacher certification. Additional exam requirements/recommendations for international students: Required—TOEFL (minimum score 550 paper-based; 80 iBT). *Application deadline:* Applications are processed on a rolling basis. Application fee: $30. Electronic applications accepted. *Financial support:* Applicants required to submit FAFSA. *Unit head:* Dr. Anne Gregory, Chairperson, 309-298-1961. *Application contact:* Dr. Nancy Parsons, Associate Provost and Director of Graduate Studies, 309-298-1806, Fax: 309-298-2345, E-mail: grad-office@wiu.edu.
Website: http://www.wiu.edu/coehs/curriculum_and_instruction/prospective_students/spedgrad.php.

Western Kentucky University, Graduate Studies, College of Education and Behavioral Sciences, School of Teacher Education, Bowling Green, KY 42101. Offers elementary education (MAE, Ed S); exceptional education: learning and behavioral disorders (MAE); exceptional education: moderate and severe disabilities (MAE); instructional design (MS); interdisciplinary early childhood education (MAE); library media education (MS); literacy education (MAE); middle grades education (MAE); secondary education (MAE, Ed S). Part-time and evening/weekend programs available. Postbaccalaureate distance learning degree programs offered (minimal on-campus study). *Degree requirements:* For master's, comprehensive exam. *Entrance requirements:* For master's, GRE General Test. Additional exam requirements/recommendations for international students: Required—TOEFL (minimum score 555 paper-based; 79 iBT). *Faculty research:* Teacher preparation in moderate/severe disabilities.

Western Michigan University, Graduate College, College of Education and Human Development, Department of Special Education and Literacy Studies, Kalamazoo, MI 49008. Offers literacy studies (MA); special education (MA, Ed D); teaching children with visual impairments (MA).

Western New Mexico University, Graduate Division, School of Education, Silver City, NM 88062-0680. Offers bilingual education (MAT); counseling (MA); educational leadership (MA); elementary education (MAT); reading (MAT); school psychology (MA); secondary education (MAT); special education (MAT); TESOL (teaching English to speakers of other languages) (MAT). *Accreditation:* NCATE. *Degree requirements:* For master's, comprehensive exam. *Entrance requirements:* For master's, GRE General Test, GRE Subject Test, minimum GPA of 3.2 in last 64 hours of undergraduate study. Additional exam requirements/recommendations for international students: Required—TOEFL (minimum score 550 paper-based). Electronic applications accepted.

Western Oregon University, Graduate Programs, College of Education, Division of Special Education, Program in Deaf Education, Monmouth, OR 97361-1394. Offers MS Ed. *Accreditation:* NCATE. Part-time and evening/weekend programs available. *Degree requirements:* For master's, thesis, portfolio. *Entrance requirements:* For master's, California Basic Educational Skills Test or PRAXIS, GRE General Test or MAT, interview, minimum GPA of 3.0, teaching license. Additional exam requirements/recommendations for international students: Required—TOEFL (minimum score 550 paper-based; 79 iBT), IELTS (minimum score 6.5). *Faculty research:* Effects of infant massage on the interactions between high-risk infants and their caregivers, work sample methodology.

Western Oregon University, Graduate Programs, College of Education, Division of Special Education, Special Education Program, Monmouth, OR 97361-1394. Offers MS Ed. Part-time and evening/weekend programs available. *Degree requirements:* For master's, comprehensive exam (for some programs), thesis optional, oral exam, portfolio, written exam. *Entrance requirements:* For master's, California Basic Educational Skills Test or PRAXIS, GRE General Test or MAT, interview, minimum GPA of 3.0, teaching license. Additional exam requirements/recommendations for international students: Required—TOEFL (minimum score 550 paper-based; 79 iBT), IELTS (minimum score 6.5). *Faculty research:* Interpreter teacher training, hearing disabilities, mental retardation.

Westfield State University, Division of Graduate and Continuing Education, Department of Education, Program in Special Education, Westfield, MA 01086. Offers M Ed. *Accreditation:* NCATE. Part-time and evening/weekend programs available. *Degree requirements:* For master's, comprehensive exam, practicum. *Entrance requirements:* For master's, GRE General Test or MAT, minimum undergraduate GPA of 2.7.

West Texas A&M University, College of Education and Social Sciences, Department of Education, Program in Special Education, Canyon, TX 79016-0001. Offers M Ed. *Degree requirements:* For master's, comprehensive exam, thesis optional. *Entrance requirements:* For master's, GRE, standard classroom teaching certificate. Additional exam requirements/recommendations for international students: Required—TOEFL.

West Virginia University, College of Human Resources and Education, Department of Curriculum and Instruction/Literacy Studies, Morgantown, WV 26506. Offers curriculum and instruction (Ed D); elementary education (MA); reading (MA); secondary education (MA), including higher education curriculum and teaching, secondary education; special education (Ed D), including special education. *Accreditation:* NCATE. Part-time and evening/weekend programs available. *Degree requirements:* For doctorate, comprehensive exam, thesis/dissertation. *Entrance requirements:* For master's, minimum GPA of 2.75; for doctorate, GRE General Test or MAT, 3 letters of recommendation, curriculum vitae. Additional exam requirements/recommendations for international students: Required—TOEFL. *Faculty research:* Teacher education, curriculum development, educational technology, curriculum assessment.

West Virginia University, College of Human Resources and Education, Department of Special Education, Morgantown, WV 26506. Offers autism spectrum disorder (5-adult) (MA); autism spectrum disorder (K-6) (MA); early intervention/early childhood special education (MA); gifted education (1-12) (MA); low vision (PreK-adult) (MA); multicategorical special education (5-adult) (MA); multicategorical special education (K-6) (MA); severe/multiple disabilities (K-adult) (MA); special education (MA, Ed D); vision impairments (PreK-adult) (MA). *Accreditation:* NCATE. Part-time and evening/weekend programs available. Postbaccalaureate distance learning degree programs offered (no on-campus study). *Degree requirements:* For master's, thesis optional; for doctorate, comprehensive exam, thesis/dissertation. *Entrance requirements:* For master's, minimum GPA of 2.75 passing scores on PRAXIS PPST; for doctorate, GRE General Test or MAT. Additional exam requirements/recommendations for international students: Required—TOEFL.

Wheelock College, Graduate Programs, Division of Education, Boston, MA 02215-4176. Offers early childhood education (MS); education leadership (MS); elementary education (MS); language, literacy, and reading (MS); teaching students with moderate disabilities (MS). *Accreditation:* NCATE. Postbaccalaureate distance learning degree programs offered (minimal on-campus study). *Degree requirements:* For master's, comprehensive exam. *Entrance requirements:* Additional exam requirements/recommendations for international students: Required—TOEFL. Electronic applications accepted. *Faculty research:* Symbolic learning, emergent literacy, diversity inclusion, beginning reading language and culture, math education.

Whitworth University, School of Education, Graduate Studies in Education, Program in Special Education, Spokane, WA 99251-0001. Offers MAT. *Accreditation:* NCATE. Part-time and evening/weekend programs available. *Degree requirements:* For master's, comprehensive exam, internship, practicum, research project, or thesis. *Entrance requirements:* For master's, GRE General Test, MAT. Additional exam requirements/recommendations for international students: Required—TOEFL.

Wichita State University, Graduate School, College of Education, Department of Curriculum and Instruction, Wichita, KS 67260. Offers curriculum and instruction (M Ed); special education (M Ed), including adaptive, early childhood unified (M Ed, MAT), functional, gifted; teaching (MAT), including curriculum and instruction, early childhood unified (M Ed, MAT). *Accreditation:* NCATE. Part-time and evening/weekend programs available. *Entrance requirements:* For master's, MAT, minimum GPA of 2.75. *Unit head:* Dr. Janice Ewing, Chairperson, 316-978-3322, E-mail: janice.ewing@wichita.edu. *Application contact:* Jordan Oleson, Admission Coordinator, 316-978-3095, Fax: 316-978-3253, E-mail: jordan.oleson@wichita.edu.

Widener University, School of Human Service Professions, Center for Education, Chester, PA 19013-5792. Offers adult education (M Ed); counseling in higher education (M Ed); counselor education (M Ed); early childhood education (M Ed); educational foundations (M Ed); educational leadership (M Ed); educational psychology (M Ed); elementary education (M Ed); English and language arts (M Ed); health education (M Ed); higher education leadership (Ed D); home and school visitor (M Ed); human sexuality (M Ed, PhD); mathematics education (M Ed); middle school education (M Ed);

principalship (M Ed); reading and language arts (Ed D); reading education (M Ed); school administration (Ed D); science education (M Ed); social studies education (M Ed); special education (M Ed); technology education (M Ed). *Accreditation:* NCATE. Part-time and evening/weekend programs available. *Faculty:* 34 full-time (22 women), 37 part-time/adjunct (14 women). *Students:* 64 full-time (44 women), 209 part-time (146 women); includes 49 minority (39 Black or African American, non-Hispanic/Latino; 1 American Indian or Alaska Native, non-Hispanic/Latino; 4 Asian, non-Hispanic/Latino; 4 Hispanic/Latino; 1 Two or more races, non-Hispanic/Latino), 8 international. Average age 39. 139 applicants, 88% accepted. In 2013, 168 master's, 31 doctorates awarded. Terminal master's awarded for partial completion of doctoral program. *Degree requirements:* For doctorate, thesis/dissertation. *Entrance requirements:* For master's, minimum GPA of 2.5; for doctorate, GRE or MAT, minimum GPA of 2.0 (undergraduate), 3.5 (graduate). *Application deadline:* Applications are processed on a rolling basis. Application fee: $25 ($300 for international students). Electronic applications accepted. *Expenses:* Contact institution. *Financial support:* Career-related internships or fieldwork, tuition waivers (full and partial), and unspecified assistantships available. Support available to part-time students. Financial award application deadline: 5/1. *Faculty research:* Reading and cognition, adult education, technology education, educational leadership, special education. *Unit head:* Dr. Michael W. LeDoux, Associate Dean, 610-499-4294, Fax: 610-499-4623, E-mail: mwledoux@widener.edu. *Application contact:* Dr. Roberta Nolan, Director of Graduate Admissions, 610-499-4125, E-mail: rdnolan@widener.edu.

Wilkes University, College of Graduate and Professional Studies, School of Education, Wilkes-Barre, PA 18766-0002. Offers art and science of teaching (MS Ed); classroom technology (MS Ed); early childhood literacy (MS Ed); educational development and strategies (MS Ed); educational leadership (MS Ed); educational technology (Ed D); higher education administration (Ed D); instructional media (MS Ed); instructional technology (MS Ed); international school leadership (MS Ed); K-12 administration (Ed D); middle level education (MS Ed); online teaching (MS Ed); reading (MS Ed); school business leadership (MS Ed); secondary education (MS Ed), including biology, chemistry, English, history, mathematics; special education (MS Ed); teaching English as a second language (MS Ed); twenty-first century teaching and learning (MS Ed). Part-time and evening/weekend programs available. Postbaccalaureate distance learning degree programs offered (minimal on-campus study). *Students:* 46 full-time (37 women), 1,410 part-time (1,039 women); includes 67 minority (12 Black or African American, non-Hispanic/Latino; 2 American Indian or Alaska Native, non-Hispanic/Latino; 11 Asian, non-Hispanic/Latino; 28 Hispanic/Latino; 1 Native Hawaiian or other Pacific Islander, non-Hispanic/Latino; 13 Two or more races, non-Hispanic/Latino), 6 international. Average age 34. In 2013, 852 master's, 10 doctorates awarded. *Entrance requirements:* Additional exam requirements/recommendations for international students: Required—TOEFL (minimum score 550 paper-based; 79 iBT). *Application deadline:* Applications are processed on a rolling basis. Application fee: $45. Electronic applications accepted. *Expenses:* Contact institution. *Financial support:* Federal Work-Study and unspecified assistantships available. Financial award application deadline: 3/1; financial award applicants required to submit FAFSA. *Unit head:* Dr. Rhonda Waskiewicz, Interim Dean, Education, 570-408-4332, Fax: 570-408-7872, E-mail: rhonda.waskiewicz@wilkes.edu. *Application contact:* Joanne Thomas, Interim Director of Graduate Education, 570-408-4234, Fax: 570-408-7846, E-mail: joanne.thomas1@wilkes.edu.
Website: http://www.wilkes.edu/pages/383.asp.

Willamette University, Graduate School of Education, Salem, OR 97301-3931. Offers environmental literacy (M Ed); reading (M Ed); special education (M Ed); teaching (MAT). *Accreditation:* NCATE. Evening/weekend programs available. *Degree requirements:* For master's, leadership project (action research). *Entrance requirements:* For master's, California Basic Educational Skills Test, Multiple Subject Assessment for Teachers, PRAXIS, minimum GPA of 3.0, classroom experience, 2 letters of reference. Additional exam requirements/recommendations for international students: Recommended—TOEFL. Electronic applications accepted. *Expenses:* Contact institution. *Faculty research:* Educational leadership, multicultural education, middle school education, clinical supervision, educational technology.

William Carey University, School of Education, Hattiesburg, MS 39401-5499. Offers art education (M Ed); art of teaching (M Ed); elementary education (M Ed, Ed S); English education (M Ed); gifted education (M Ed); history and social science (M Ed); mild/moderate disabilities (M Ed); secondary education (M Ed). *Accreditation:* NCATE. Part-time programs available. *Degree requirements:* For master's, comprehensive exam. *Entrance requirements:* For master's, GRE, MAT, minimum GPA of 2.5, Class A teacher's license. Additional exam requirements/recommendations for international students: Required—TOEFL (minimum score 550 paper-based).

William Paterson University of New Jersey, College of Education, Wayne, NJ 07470-8420. Offers curriculum and learning (M Ed); educational leadership (M Ed); reading (M Ed); special education and counseling services (M Ed), including counseling services, special education; teaching (MAT). *Accreditation:* NCATE. Part-time and evening/weekend programs available. Postbaccalaureate distance learning degree programs offered. *Faculty:* 33 full-time (8 women), 32 part-time/adjunct (9 women). *Students:* 118 full-time (92 women), 519 part-time (431 women); includes 134 minority (35 Black or African American, non-Hispanic/Latino; 1 American Indian or Alaska Native, non-Hispanic/Latino; 6 Asian, non-Hispanic/Latino; 86 Hispanic/Latino; 6 Two or more races, non-Hispanic/Latino). Average age 34. 439 applicants, 74% accepted, 240 enrolled. In 2013, 144 master's awarded. *Degree requirements:* For master's, comprehensive exam, thesis (for some programs), exit interview (for some programs), practicum/internship. *Entrance requirements:* For master's, GRE/MAT, minimum GPA of 2.75, teaching certificate. Additional exam requirements/recommendations for international students: Required—TOEFL (minimum score 550 paper-based; 79 iBT), IELTS (minimum score 6). *Application deadline:* For fall admission, 6/1 for domestic students, 5/1 for international students; for spring admission, 11/1 for domestic students, 10/1 for international students. Applications are processed on a rolling basis. Application fee: $50. Electronic applications accepted. *Financial support:* Research assistantships with full tuition reimbursements, career-related internships or fieldwork, Federal Work-Study, and unspecified assistantships available. Support available to part-time students. Financial award application deadline: 4/1; financial award applicants required to submit FAFSA. *Faculty research:* IPads in the classroom, characteristics of effective elementary teachers in language arts and mathematics, gender issues in science, after-school programs, middle class parents' roles and gentrifying school districts. *Unit head:* Dr. Candace Burns, Dean, 973-720-2137, Fax: 973-720-2955, E-mail: burnsc@wpunj.edu. *Application contact:* Liana Fornarotto, Assistant Director, Graduate Admissions, 973-720-3578, Fax: 973-720-2035, E-mail: fornarottol@wpunj.edu.
Website: http://www.wpunj.edu/coe.

Wilmington College, Department of Education, Wilmington, OH 45177. Offers reading (M Ed); special education (M Ed). Part-time programs available. *Degree requirements:* For master's, comprehensive exam. *Entrance requirements:* For master's, GRE or MAT, minimum GPA of 3.0, 2 letters of recommendation. Additional exam requirements/recommendations for international students: Required—TOEFL. *Faculty research:* Reading instruction, special education practices, conflict resolution in the schools, models of higher education for teachers.

Wilmington University, College of Education, New Castle, DE 19720-6491. Offers applied technology in education (M Ed); career and technical education (M Ed); educational leadership (Ed D); elementary and secondary school counseling (M Ed); elementary studies (M Ed); ESOL literacy (M Ed); higher education leadership (Ed D); instruction: gifted and talented (M Ed); instruction: teacher of reading (M Ed); instruction: teaching and learning (M Ed); organizational leadership (Ed D); school leadership (M Ed); secondary education (MAT); special education (M Ed). *Accreditation:* NCATE. Part-time and evening/weekend programs available. *Entrance requirements:* For master's, 2 letters of recommendation, interview. Additional exam requirements/recommendations for international students: Required—TOEFL (minimum score 500 paper-based). Electronic applications accepted.

Winona State University, College of Education, Department of Special Education, Winona, MN 55987. Offers special education (MS), including developmental disabilities, learning disabilities. Part-time and evening/weekend programs available. *Degree requirements:* For master's, comprehensive exam, thesis.

Winthrop University, College of Education, Program in Special Education, Rock Hill, SC 29733. Offers M Ed. *Accreditation:* NCATE. Part-time programs available. *Entrance requirements:* For master's, PRAXIS, South Carolina Class III Teaching Certificate, sample of written work. Electronic applications accepted.

Worcester State University, Graduate Studies, Department of Education, Program in Moderate Special Needs, Worcester, MA 01602-2597. Offers M Ed, Postbaccalaureate Certificate. Part-time and evening/weekend programs available. *Faculty:* 14 full-time (11 women), 22 part-time/adjunct (10 women). *Students:* 25 part-time (18 women); includes 1 minority (Black or African American, non-Hispanic/Latino). Average age 32. 40 applicants, 53% accepted, 6 enrolled. In 2013, 4 master's, 13 other advanced degrees awarded. *Degree requirements:* For master's, comprehensive exam (for some programs), thesis optional. *Entrance requirements:* For master's, GRE General Test or MAT, teaching certificate. Additional exam requirements/recommendations for international students: Required—TOEFL (minimum score 500 paper-based; 61 iBT). *Application deadline:* For fall admission, 6/15 for domestic and international students; for spring admission, 4/1 for domestic and international students. Applications are processed on a rolling basis. Application fee: $40. Electronic applications accepted. *Expenses: Tuition, area resident:* Part-time $150 per credit. Tuition, state resident: part-time $150 per credit. Tuition, nonresident: part-time $150 per credit. *Required fees:* $114.50 per credit. *Financial support:* Career-related internships or fieldwork, scholarships/grants, and unspecified assistantships available. Financial award application deadline: 3/1; financial award applicants required to submit FAFSA. *Unit head:* Dr. Sue Fan Foo, Coordinator, 508-929-8071, Fax: 508-929-8164, E-mail: sfoo@worcester.edu. *Application contact:* Sara Grady, Assistant Dean of Graduate and Continuing Education, 508-929-8787, Fax: 508-929-8100, E-mail: sara.grady@worcester.edu.

Wright State University, School of Graduate Studies, College of Education and Human Services, Department of Teacher Education, Programs in Intervention Specialist, Dayton, OH 45435. Offers gifted educational needs (M Ed, MA); mild to moderate educational needs (M Ed, MA); moderate to intensive educational needs (M Ed, MA). *Accreditation:* NCATE. *Degree requirements:* For master's, thesis (for some programs). *Entrance requirements:* For master's, GRE General Test, MAT. Additional exam requirements/recommendations for international students: Required—TOEFL.

Xavier University, College of Social Sciences, Health and Education, School of Education, Department of Secondary and Special Education, Program in Special Education, Cincinnati, OH 45207. Offers M Ed. Part-time programs available. *Faculty:* 4 full-time (all women), 16 part-time/adjunct (13 women). *Students:* 23 full-time (15 women), 56 part-time (41 women); includes 10 minority (8 Black or African American, non-Hispanic/Latino; 1 Hispanic/Latino; 1 Two or more races, non-Hispanic/Latino), 1 international. Average age 34. 7 applicants, 100% accepted, 7 enrolled. In 2013, 45 master's awarded. *Degree requirements:* For master's, comprehensive exam, presentation of research. *Entrance requirements:* For master's, MAT, GRE. Application fee: $35. *Expenses: Tuition:* Part-time $594 per credit hour. *Required fees:* $3 per semester. *Financial support:* In 2013–14, 69 students received support. Applicants required to submit FAFSA. *Faculty research:* Autism, collaboration of general education and special education, mental health/special education, training criminal justice personnel in special education, technology and learning. *Unit head:* Dr. Michael Flick, Chair, 513-745-3225, Fax: 513-745-3410, E-mail: flick@xavier.edu. *Application contact:* Dr. Sharon Merrill, Director, 513-745-1078, Fax: 513-745-3410, E-mail: merrill@xavier.edu.
Website: http://www.xavier.edu/education/secondary-special-education/.

Youngstown State University, Graduate School, Beeghly College of Education, Department of Teacher Education, Program in Special Education, Youngstown, OH 44555-0001. Offers gifted and talented education (MS Ed); special education (MS Ed). *Accreditation:* NCATE. Part-time and evening/weekend programs available. *Degree requirements:* For master's, comprehensive exam. *Entrance requirements:* For master's, GRE, MAT, or teaching certificate; interview; minimum GPA of 2.7. Additional exam requirements/recommendations for international students: Required—TOEFL. *Faculty research:* Learning disabilities, learning styles, developing self-esteem and social skills of severe behaviorally handicapped students, inclusion.

Urban Education

Alvernia University, Graduate Studies, Program in Education, Reading, PA 19607-1799. Offers urban education (M Ed). Part-time and evening/weekend programs available. *Degree requirements:* For master's, thesis optional. *Entrance requirements:* For master's, GRE or MAT (alumni excluded). Electronic applications accepted.

Urban Education

Bakke Graduate University, Programs in Pastoral Ministry and Business, Seattle, WA 98104. Offers business administration (MBA); church and ministry multiplication (D Min); global urban leadership (MA); leadership (D Min); ministry in complex contexts (D Min); social and civic entrepreneurship (MA); theology of work (D Min); theology reflection (D Min); transformational leadership (DTL); urban youth ministry (D Min). Part-time programs available. Postbaccalaureate distance learning degree programs offered (minimal on-campus study). *Faculty:* 5 full-time (3 women), 19 part-time/adjunct (7 women). *Students:* 72 full-time (36 women), 129 part-time (51 women). *Degree requirements:* For master's, thesis; for doctorate, thesis/dissertation. *Entrance requirements:* For master's, 2 years of ministry experience, BA in Biblical studies or theology; for doctorate, 3 years of ministry experience, M Div. Additional exam requirements/recommendations for international students: Required—TOEFL. *Application deadline:* For fall admission, 7/1 priority date for domestic students; for winter admission, 12/1 for domestic students; for spring admission, 3/15 for domestic students. Applications are processed on a rolling basis. Application fee: $75. Electronic applications accepted. *Financial support:* Scholarships/grants and tuition waivers (partial) available. Financial award applicants required to submit FAFSA. *Faculty research:* Theological systems, church management, worship. *Unit head:* Dr. Gwen Dewey, Academic Dean, 206-264-9119, Fax: 206-264-8828, E-mail: gwend@bgu.edu. *Application contact:* Dr. Judith A. Melton, Registrar, 206-246-9114, Fax: 206-264-8828. Website: http://www.bgu.edu/.

Bloomsburg University of Pennsylvania, School of Graduate Studies, College of Education, Department of Early Childhood and Adolescent Education, Bloomsburg, PA 17815-1301. Offers early childhood education (M Ed); middle level education grades 4-8 (M Ed), including language arts, math, science, social studies; reading (M Ed). *Faculty:* 7 full-time (4 women). *Students:* 22 full-time (20 women), 8 part-time (all women). Average age 28. 28 applicants, 82% accepted, 8 enrolled. In 2013, 34 master's awarded. *Degree requirements:* For master's, thesis optional. *Entrance requirements:* For master's, MAT or PRAXIS, minimum QPA of 3.0. Additional exam requirements/recommendations for international students: Required—TOEFL (minimum score 550 paper-based). *Application deadline:* Applications are processed on a rolling basis. Application fee: $35 ($60 for international students). Electronic applications accepted. *Expenses:* Tuition, state resident: full-time $7956; part-time $442 per credit. Tuition, nonresident: full-time $11,934; part-time $663 per credit. *Required fees:* $95.50 per credit. $55 per semester. Tuition and fees vary according to course load. *Financial support:* Unspecified assistantships available. *Unit head:* Dr. Tegan Kotarski, College of Education Graduate Coordinator, 570-389-3883, Fax: 570-389-5049, E-mail: tkotarsk@bloomu.edu. *Application contact:* Jennifer Richard, Administrative Assistant, 570-389-4015, Fax: 570-389-3054, E-mail: jrichard@bloomu.edu. Website: http://www.bloomu.edu/early_childhood_adolescent.

Brown University, Graduate School, Department of Education, Program in Urban Education Policy, Providence, RI 02912. Offers AM. *Entrance requirements:* For master's, GRE General Test, official transcripts, 3 letters of recommendation, personal statement. Additional exam requirements/recommendations for international students: Required—TOEFL. Electronic applications accepted. *Faculty research:* Mayoral control of school systems.

California State University, East Bay, Office of Academic Programs and Graduate Studies, College of Education and Allied Studies, Department of Educational Leadership, Hayward, CA 94542-3000. Offers educational leadership (MS, Ed D); urban teaching leadership (MS). *Accreditation:* NCATE. Part-time and evening/weekend programs available. Postbaccalaureate distance learning degree programs offered. *Degree requirements:* For master's, comprehensive exam, project or thesis; for doctorate, thesis/dissertation. *Entrance requirements:* For master's, CBEST, teaching or services credential and experience; minimum GPA of 3.0; for doctorate, GRE, MA with minimum GPA of 3.0; PK-12 leadership position; portfolio of work samples; employer/district support agreement. Additional exam requirements/recommendations for international students: Required—TOEFL (minimum score 550 paper-based). Electronic applications accepted.

Cardinal Stritch University, College of Education, Department of Education, Milwaukee, WI 53217-3985. Offers education (ME); educational leadership (MS); leadership for the advancement of learning and service (Ed D, PhD); teaching (MAT); urban education (MA). *Accreditation:* NCATE. Evening/weekend programs available. *Degree requirements:* For master's, comprehensive exam, thesis (for some programs), research project, faculty recommendation; for doctorate, thesis/dissertation, practica, field experience. *Entrance requirements:* For master's, letters of recommendation (3), minimum GPA of 3.0; for doctorate, minimum GPA of 3.5 in master's coursework, letters of recommendation (3).

Cheyney University of Pennsylvania, Graduate Programs, Program in Urban Education, Cheyney, PA 19319. Offers M Ed. Part-time and evening/weekend programs available. *Degree requirements:* For master's, thesis or alternative. Electronic applications accepted.

Claremont Graduate University, Graduate Programs, School of Educational Studies, Claremont, CA 91711-6160. Offers Africana education (Certificate); education and policy (MA, PhD); higher education/student affairs (MA, PhD); human development (MA, PhD); public school administration (MA, PhD); quantitative evaluation (MA, PhD); special education (MA, PhD); teacher education (MA); teaching and learning (MA, PhD); urban leadership (PhD); MBA/PhD. PhD program offered jointly with San Diego State University. Part-time programs available. *Faculty:* 16 full-time (9 women), 1 part-time/adjunct (0 women). *Students:* 224 full-time (158 women), 221 part-time (151 women); includes 229 minority (52 Black or African American, non-Hispanic/Latino; 3 American Indian or Alaska Native, non-Hispanic/Latino; 43 Asian, non-Hispanic/Latino; 113 Hispanic/Latino; 1 Native Hawaiian or other Pacific Islander, non-Hispanic/Latino; 17 Two or more races, non-Hispanic/Latino), 15 international. Average age 39. In 2013, 51 master's, 33 doctorates, 5 other advanced degrees awarded. Terminal master's awarded for partial completion of doctoral program. *Entrance requirements:* For master's and doctorate, GRE General Test. Additional exam requirements/recommendations for international students: Required—TOEFL (minimum score 550 paper-based; 80 iBT). *Application deadline:* For fall admission, 4/1 priority date for domestic and international students. Applications are processed on a rolling basis. Application fee: $80. Electronic applications accepted. *Expenses: Tuition:* Full-time $40,560; part-time $1690 per credit. *Required fees:* $275 per semester. Tuition and fees vary according to program. *Financial support:* Fellowships, research assistantships, Federal Work-Study, institutionally sponsored loans, and scholarships/grants available. Support available to part-time students. Financial award application deadline: 2/15; financial award applicants required to submit FAFSA. *Faculty research:* Education administration, K-12 and higher education, multicultural education, education policy, diversity in higher education, faculty issues. *Unit head:* Scott Thomas, Dean, 909-621-8075, Fax: 909-621-8734, E-mail: scott.thomas@cgu.edu. *Application contact:* Julia Wendt, Director of Central Recruitment, 909-607-3689, Fax: 909-607-7285, E-mail: admiss@cgu.edu. Website: http://www.cgu.edu/pages/267.asp.

Cleveland State University, College of Graduate Studies, College of Education and Human Services, Program in Urban Education, Cleveland, OH 44115. Offers adult, continuing, and higher education (PhD); counseling psychology (PhD); counselor education (PhD); learning and development (PhD); nursing education (PhD); policy studies (PhD); school administration (PhD). Part-time programs available. *Faculty:* 16 full-time (8 women), 15 part-time/adjunct (12 women). *Students:* 24 full-time (18 women), 88 part-time (61 women); includes 32 minority (26 Black or African American, non-Hispanic/Latino; 3 Asian, non-Hispanic/Latino; 3 Hispanic/Latino), 9 international. Average age 40. 62 applicants, 58% accepted, 6 enrolled. In 2013, 8 doctorates awarded. *Degree requirements:* For doctorate, one foreign language, comprehensive exam, thesis/dissertation. *Entrance requirements:* For doctorate, GRE General Test, minimum graduate GPA of 3.25. Additional exam requirements/recommendations for international students: Required—TOEFL (minimum score 525 paper-based), IELTS (minimum score 6). *Application deadline:* For fall admission, 2/5 for domestic students. Application fee: $30. *Expenses:* Tuition, state resident: full-time $8335; part-time $521 per credit hour. Tuition, nonresident: full-time $15,670; part-time $979 per credit hour. *Required fees:* $50; $25 per semester. *Financial support:* In 2013–14, 24 students received support, including 21 research assistantships with full and partial tuition reimbursements available (averaging $7,700 per year), 3 teaching assistantships with full and partial tuition reimbursements available (averaging $18,682 per year); tuition waivers (full and partial) and unspecified assistantships also available. Financial award applicants required to submit FAFSA. *Faculty research:* Equity issues (race, ethnicity, and gender), education development consequences for special needs of urban populations, urban education programming, counseling the violent or aggressive adolescent. *Total annual research expenditures:* $5,662. *Unit head:* Dr. Graham Stead, Director, 216-875-9869, Fax: 216-875-9697, E-mail: g.b.stead@csuohio.edu. *Application contact:* Wanda Pruett-Butler, Administrative Coordinator, 216-687-4697, Fax: 216-875-9697, E-mail: w.pruett-butler@csuohio.edu. Website: http://www.csuohio.edu/cehs/departments/DOC/doc_dept.html.

Cleveland State University, College of Graduate Studies, School of Nursing, Cleveland, OH 44115. Offers clinical nurse leader (MSN); forensic nursing (MSN); nursing education (MSN); specialized population (MSN); urban education (PhD), including nursing education; MSN/MBA. *Accreditation:* AACN. Part-time programs available. Postbaccalaureate distance learning degree programs offered (no on-campus study). *Faculty:* 6 full-time (all women), 1 (woman) part-time/adjunct. *Students:* 20 full-time (all women), 28 part-time (26 women); includes 12 minority (8 Black or African American, non-Hispanic/Latino; 3 Hispanic/Latino; 1 Two or more races, non-Hispanic/Latino), 1 international. Average age 38. 65 applicants, 62% accepted, 20 enrolled. In 2013, 6 master's awarded. *Degree requirements:* For master's, thesis optional, portfolio, capstone practicum project; for doctorate, comprehensive exam, thesis/dissertation. *Entrance requirements:* For master's, RN license, BSN with minimum cumulative GPA of 3.0, recent (5 years) course work in statistics; for doctorate, GRE, MSN with minimum cumulative GPA of 3.25. Additional exam requirements/recommendations for international students: Required—TOEFL (minimum score 525 paper-based; 65 iBT), IELTS (minimum score 6). *Application deadline:* For fall admission, 3/1 priority date for domestic and international students. Application fee: $55. Electronic applications accepted. *Expenses:* Tuition, state resident: full-time $8335; part-time $521 per credit hour. Tuition, nonresident: full-time $15,670; part-time $979 per credit hour. *Required fees:* $50; $25 per semester. *Financial support:* In 2013–14, 4 students received support. Tuition waivers (full) and unspecified assistantships available. Financial award application deadline: 3/1; financial award applicants required to submit FAFSA. *Faculty research:* Diabetes management, African-American elders medication compliance, risk in home visiting, suffering, COPD and stress, nursing education, disaster health preparedness. *Total annual research expenditures:* $330,000. *Unit head:* Dr. Vida Lock, Dean, 216-523-7237, Fax: 216-687-3556, E-mail: v.lock@csuohio.edu. *Application contact:* Maureen Mitchell, Assistant Professor and Graduate Program Director, 216-523-7128, Fax: 216-687-3556, E-mail: m.m.mitchell1@csuohio.edu. Website: http://www.csuohio.edu/nursing/.

College of Mount Saint Vincent, School of Professional and Continuing Studies, Department of Teacher Education, Riverdale, NY 10471-1093. Offers instructional technology and global perspectives (Certificate); middle level education (Certificate); multicultural studies (Certificate); urban and multicultural education (MS Ed). *Accreditation:* Teacher Education Accreditation Council. Part-time programs available. *Degree requirements:* For master's, comprehensive exam. *Entrance requirements:* For master's, interview, New York teaching certificate. Additional exam requirements/recommendations for international students: Required—TOEFL.

Florida International University, College of Education, Department of Leadership and Professional Studies, Miami, FL 33199. Offers adult education and human resource development (MS, Ed D); counseling (MS), including rehabilitation counseling, school counseling; counselor education (MS), including clinical mental health counseling; educational administration and supervision (Ed D); educational leadership (MS, Certificate, Ed S); higher education (Ed D); higher education administration (MS); recreation and sport management (MS), including recreation and sport management, recreational therapy; school psychology (Ed S); urban education (MS), including instruction in urban settings, learning technologies, multicultural/bilingual, multicultural/TESOL, urban education. Part-time and evening/weekend programs available. *Degree requirements:* For doctorate, thesis/dissertation. *Entrance requirements:* For master's, minimum GPA of 3.0; for doctorate and other advanced degree, GRE General Test. Additional exam requirements/recommendations for international students: Required—TOEFL (minimum score 550 paper-based; 80 iBT), IELTS (minimum score 6.3). Electronic applications accepted.

Georgia State University, College of Education, Department of Early Childhood Education, Atlanta, GA 30302-3083. Offers early childhood and elementary education (PhD); early childhood education (M Ed, Ed S); mathematics education (M Ed); urban education (M Ed). *Accreditation:* NCATE. Part-time and evening/weekend programs available. *Faculty:* 20 full-time (16 women). *Students:* 104 full-time (93 women), 37 part-time (36 women); includes 70 minority (54 Black or African American, non-Hispanic/Latino; 7 Asian, non-Hispanic/Latino; 6 Hispanic/Latino; 3 Two or more races, non-Hispanic/Latino), 2 international. Average age 29. 51 applicants, 55% accepted, 27 enrolled. In 2013, 73 master's, 1 doctorate, 17 other advanced degrees awarded. *Degree requirements:* For master's, comprehensive exam (for some programs), thesis (for some programs); for doctorate, comprehensive exam, thesis/dissertation (for some programs); for Ed S, comprehensive exam (for some programs). *Entrance requirements:* For master's, GRE, undergraduate diploma; for doctorate and Ed S, GRE, master's degree. Additional exam requirements/recommendations for international students: Required—TOEFL (minimum score 550 paper-based; 79 iBT) or IELTS (minimum score 6.5). *Application deadline:* Applications are processed on a rolling basis. Application fee: $50. Electronic applications accepted. *Expenses: Tuition, area resident:* Full-time $4176; part-time $348 per credit hour. Tuition, state resident: full-time $14,544; part-time $1212 per credit hour. Tuition, nonresident: full-time $14,544; part-time $1212 per credit hour. Tuition and fees vary according to course load and program. *Financial support:* In 2013–14, fellowships with full tuition reimbursements (averaging $24,000 per year), research assistantships with full and partial tuition reimbursements (averaging $4,000 per year), teaching assistantships with full tuition reimbursements (averaging $2,000 per year) were awarded; career-related internships or fieldwork, Federal Work-Study, institutionally sponsored loans, scholarships/grants, traineeships, health care

benefits, tuition waivers (partial), and unspecified assistantships also available. Support available to part-time students. Financial award applicants required to submit FAFSA. *Faculty research:* Teacher development; language arts/literacy education; mathematics education; intersection of science, urban, and multicultural education; diversity in education. *Unit head:* Dr. Barbara Meyers, Department Chair, 404-413-8021, Fax: 404-413-8023, E-mail: barbara@gsu.edu. *Application contact:* Elaine King Jones, Administrative Curriculum Specialist, 404-413-8234, Fax: 404-413-8023, E-mail: ekjones@gsu.edu.
Website: http://education.gsu.edu/ece/index.htm.

Georgia State University, College of Education, Department of Educational Policy Studies, Program in Educational Leadership, Atlanta, GA 30302-3083. Offers educational leadership (M Ed, Ed D, Ed S); urban teacher leadership (M Ed). *Accreditation:* NCATE. Part-time programs available. *Students:* Average age 0. *Degree requirements:* For master's, comprehensive exam, thesis or alternative, 36 semester hours; for doctorate, comprehensive exam, thesis/dissertation, 54 semester hours (for EdD); 69 semester hours (for PhD); for Ed S, thesis, 30 semester hours of coursework. *Entrance requirements:* For master's, GRE; for doctorate and Ed S, GRE, MAT. Additional exam requirements/recommendations for international students: Required—TOEFL (minimum score 550 paper-based; 79 iBT) or IELTS (minimum score 6.5). *Application deadline:* For fall admission, 5/1 for domestic and international students; for winter admission, 2/1 for domestic students; for spring admission, 10/1 for domestic and international students. Applications are processed on a rolling basis. Application fee: $50. Electronic applications accepted. *Expenses: Tuition, area resident:* Full-time $4176; part-time $348 per credit hour. Tuition, state resident: full-time $14,544; part-time $1212 per credit hour. Tuition, nonresident: full-time $14,544; part-time $1212 per credit hour. Tuition and fees vary according to course load and program. *Financial support:* In 2013–14, research assistantships with full tuition reimbursements (averaging $6,000 per year) were awarded; fellowships, teaching assistantships with full tuition reimbursements, career-related internships or fieldwork, scholarships/grants, health care benefits, tuition waivers, and unspecified assistantships also available. Support available to part-time students. Financial award application deadline: 3/15. *Faculty research:* Practices with diverse populations, leadership and success, the cohort model of instruction, technology in the schools, instructional supervision and academic coaching. *Unit head:* Dr. Jami Berry, Clinical Assistant Professor, 404-413-8030, Fax: 404-413-8003, E-mail: jberry2@gsu.edu. *Application contact:* Aishah Cowan, Administrative Academic Specialist, 404-413-8273, Fax: 404-413-8033, E-mail: acowan@gsu.edu.
Website: http://education.gsu.edu/eps/4580.html.

The Graduate Center, City University of New York, Graduate Studies, Program in Urban Education, New York, NY 10016-4039. Offers PhD. *Entrance requirements:* For doctorate, GRE General Test. Additional exam requirements/recommendations for international students: Required—TOEFL. Electronic applications accepted.

Holy Names University, Graduate Division, Department of Education, Oakland, CA 94619-1699. Offers educational therapy (Certificate); mild/moderate disabilities (Ed S); multiple subject teaching (Credential); single subject teaching (Credential); teaching English as a second language (TESL) (M Ed); urban education: educational therapy (M Ed); urban education: K-12 education (M Ed); urban education: special education (M Ed). Part-time programs available. *Faculty:* 4 full-time, 14 part-time/adjunct. *Students:* 25 full-time (19 women), 127 part-time (93 women); includes 74 minority (37 Black or African American, non-Hispanic/Latino; 7 Asian, non-Hispanic/Latino; 28 Hispanic/Latino; 1 Native Hawaiian or other Pacific Islander, non-Hispanic/Latino; 1 Two or more races, non-Hispanic/Latino), 2 international. Average age 35. 72 applicants, 75% accepted, 37 enrolled. In 2013, 15 master's, 22 Certificates awarded. *Degree requirements:* For master's, comprehensive exam, research paper, thesis or project. *Entrance requirements:* For master's, minimum undergraduate GPA of 2.6 overall, 3.0 in major, personal statement, two recommendations, interview. Additional exam requirements/recommendations for international students: Required—TOEFL (minimum score 550 paper-based; 79 iBT). *Application deadline:* For fall admission, 8/1 priority date for domestic students, 7/15 for international students; for spring admission, 12/1 priority date for domestic students, 12/1 for international students; for summer admission, 5/1 priority date for domestic students, 5/1 for international students. Applications are processed on a rolling basis. Application fee: $65. Electronic applications accepted. Application fee is waived when completed online. *Expenses: Tuition:* Part-time $866 per unit. *Financial support:* Career-related internships or fieldwork, Federal Work-Study, scholarships/grants, and unspecified assistantships available. Support available to part-time students. Financial award application deadline: 3/2; financial award applicants required to submit FAFSA. *Faculty research:* Cognitive development, language development, learning handicaps. *Unit head:* Dr. Kimberly Mayfiel, 510-436-1396, Fax: 510-436-1325, E-mail: mayfield@hnu.edu. *Application contact:* Graduate Admission, 800-430-1321, Fax: 510-436-1325, E-mail: graduateadmissions@hnu.edu.
Website: http://www.hnu.edu/academics/graduatePrograms/education.html.

Johns Hopkins University, School of Education, Certificate Programs in Education, Baltimore, MD 21218-2699. Offers advanced methods for differentiated instruction and inclusive education (Certificate); applied behavior analysis (Certificate); counseling (CAGS); data-based decision making and organizational improvement (Certificate); early intervention/preschool special education specialist (Certificate); education leadership for independent schools (Certificate); education of students with autism and other pervasive developmental disorders (Certificate); evidence-based teaching in the health professions (Certificate); gifted education (Certificate); K-8 mathematics lead-teacher (Certificate); K-8 STEM education lead-teacher (Certificate); leadership for school, family, and community collaboration (Certificate); leadership in technology integration (Certificate); mental health counseling (Certificate); mind, brain, and teaching (Certificate); school administration and supervision (Certificate); urban education (Certificate). Part-time and evening/weekend programs available. Postbaccalaureate distance learning degree programs offered (no on-campus study). *Students:* 7 full-time (4 women), 216 part-time (169 women); includes 66 minority (35 Black or African American, non-Hispanic/Latino; 17 Asian, non-Hispanic/Latino; 6 Hispanic/Latino; 8 Two or more races, non-Hispanic/Latino), 6 international. Average age 35. 257 applicants, 81% accepted, 62 enrolled. In 2013, 202 CAGSs awarded. *Entrance requirements:* For degree, bachelor's degree from regionally- or nationally-accredited institution (master's for some programs), minimum GPA of 3.0 in all previous programs of study, official transcripts from all post-secondary institutions attended, essay, curriculum vitae/resume, minimum of two letters of recommendation. Additional exam requirements/recommendations for international students: Required—TOEFL (minimum score 600 paper-based; 100 iBT) or IELTS (minimum score 7). *Application deadline:* For fall admission, 4/1 for domestic students; for spring admission, 10/1 for domestic students; for summer admission, 2/1 for domestic students. Application fee: $80. Electronic applications accepted. *Financial support:* Application deadline: 6/1; applicants required to submit FAFSA. *Unit head:* Dr. David A. Andrews, Dean, 410-516-7820, Fax: 410-516-6697, E-mail: davidandrews@jhu.edu. *Application contact:* Catherine Wilson, Associate Director of Admissions, 410-516-9797, Fax: 410-516-9799, E-mail: soe.info@jhu.edu.

Langston University, School of Education and Behavioral Sciences, Langston, OK 73050. Offers bilingual/multicultural (M Ed); elementary education (M Ed); English as a second language (M Ed); rehabilitation counseling (M Sc); urban education (M Ed). *Accreditation:* CORE; NCATE (one or more programs are accredited). Part-time programs available. *Degree requirements:* For master's, comprehensive exam, thesis optional. *Entrance requirements:* For master's, GRE, writing skills test, minimum GPA of 2.5, 3 letters of recommendation. Additional exam requirements/recommendations for international students: Required—TOEFL, TWE. *Faculty research:* Bilingual/multicultural education, financing post-secondary education.

Loyola Marymount University, School of Education, Department of Specialized Programs in Urban Education, Program in Urban Education, Los Angeles, CA 90045. Offers MA. *Faculty:* 11 full-time (6 women), 39 part-time/adjunct (30 women). *Students:* 119 full-time (74 women), 5 part-time (3 women); includes 64 minority (7 Black or African American, non-Hispanic/Latino; 16 Asian, non-Hispanic/Latino; 36 Hispanic/Latino; 5 Two or more races, non-Hispanic/Latino). Average age 24. 14 applicants, 100% accepted, 10 enrolled. In 2013, 43 master's awarded. *Entrance requirements:* For master's, CBEST, CSET, letters of recommendation, statement of intent, interview, verification of employment as full-time teacher. Additional exam requirements/recommendations for international students: Required—TOEFL (minimum score 600 paper-based; 100 iBT). *Application deadline:* For fall admission, 6/15 for domestic students; for spring admission, 11/15 for domestic students. Application fee: $50. Electronic applications accepted. *Financial support:* In 2013–14, 121 students received support. Scholarships/grants and unspecified assistantships available. Support available to part-time students. Financial award application deadline: 6/30; financial award applicants required to submit FAFSA. Total annual research expenditures: $260,672. *Unit head:* Dr. Mary McCullough, Chair, 310-338-7312, E-mail: mmccullo@lmu.edu. *Application contact:* Chake H. Kouyoumjian, Director, Graduate Admissions, 310-338-2721, E-mail: ckouyoum@lmu.edu.
Website: http://soe.lmu.edu/admissions/programs/.

Marygrove College, Graduate Division, Griot Program, Detroit, MI 48221-2599. Offers M Ed.

Morgan State University, School of Graduate Studies, School of Education and Urban Studies, Department of Advanced Studies, Leadership and Policy, Program in Educational Administration and Supervision, Baltimore, MD 21251. Offers urban educational leadership (Ed D). *Accreditation:* NCATE. Part-time and evening/weekend programs available. *Faculty research:* Multicultural education, cooperative learning, psychology of cognition.

New Jersey City University, Graduate Studies and Continuing Education, Debra Cannon Partridge Wolfe College of Education, Department of Educational Leadership, Jersey City, NJ 07305-1597. Offers basics and urban studies (MA); bilingual/bicultural education and English as a second language (MA); educational administration and supervision (MA). Part-time and evening/weekend programs available. *Faculty:* 9 full-time (7 women), 7 part-time/adjunct (4 women). *Students:* 25 full-time (17 women), 206 part-time (155 women); includes 121 minority (17 Black or African American, non-Hispanic/Latino; 7 Asian, non-Hispanic/Latino; 97 Hispanic/Latino), 2 international. Average age 37. In 2013, 71 master's awarded. *Entrance requirements:* Additional exam requirements/recommendations for international students: Required—TOEFL (minimum score 61 iBT). *Application deadline:* For fall admission, 8/1 priority date for domestic students; for spring admission, 12/1 for domestic students. Applications are processed on a rolling basis. Application fee: $0. *Expenses: Tuition, area resident:* Part-time $527.90 per credit. Tuition, nonresident: part-time $947.75 per credit. *Financial support:* Fellowships, teaching assistantships, career-related internships or fieldwork, and unspecified assistantships available. *Unit head:* Dr. Catherine Rogers, Chairperson, 201-200-3012, E-mail: cshevey@njcu.edu. *Application contact:* Dr. William Bajor, Dean of Graduate Studies, 201-200-3409, Fax: 201-200-3411, E-mail: wbajor@njcu.edu.

Norfolk State University, School of Graduate Studies, School of Education, Department of Secondary Education and School Leadership, Program in Urban Education/Administration, Norfolk, VA 23504. Offers teaching (MA). *Accreditation:* NCATE. Part-time programs available. *Students:* 64 full-time (48 women), 98 part-time (78 women); includes 140 minority (135 Black or African American, non-Hispanic/Latino; 3 Hispanic/Latino; 2 Two or more races, non-Hispanic/Latino). In 2013, 94 master's awarded. *Entrance requirements:* For master's, GRE General Test, PRAXIS I, minimum GPA of 3.0 in major, 2.5 overall. *Application deadline:* For fall admission, 3/1 for domestic students; for spring admission, 10/1 for domestic students. Application fee: $30. *Financial support:* Fellowships and career-related internships or fieldwork available. *Unit head:* Dr. Margaret Knight, Acting Head, 757-823-8715, Fax: 757-823-8757, E-mail: mknight@nsu.edu. *Application contact:* Karen Fauntleroy, Education Specialist, 757-823-8178, Fax: 757-823-8757, E-mail: kfauntleroy@nsu.edu.

Northeastern Illinois University, College of Graduate Studies and Research, College of Education, Program in Inner City Studies, Chicago, IL 60625-4699. Offers MA. Part-time and evening/weekend programs available. *Degree requirements:* For master's, comprehensive exam, thesis or alternative. *Entrance requirements:* For master's, minimum GPA of 2.75. Additional exam requirements/recommendations for international students: Required—TOEFL (minimum score 550 paper-based; 79 iBT). Electronic applications accepted.

Providence College, Program in Urban Teaching, Providence, RI 02918. Offers M Ed. Part-time and evening/weekend programs available. *Faculty:* 4 full-time (2 women), 1 (woman) part-time/adjunct. *Students:* 5 full-time (4 women), 4 part-time (all women), 1 international. Average age 24. 3 applicants, 100% accepted, 3 enrolled. In 2013, 2 master's awarded. *Degree requirements:* For master's, symposium at which research results are presented. *Entrance requirements:* Additional exam requirements/recommendations for international students: Required—TOEFL (minimum score 550 paper-based; 80 iBT). *Application deadline:* For fall admission, 8/1 for domestic and international students; for spring admission, 12/1 for domestic and international students. Applications are processed on a rolling basis. Application fee: $55. *Expenses: Tuition:* Part-time $432 per credit. *Required fees:* $432 per credit. *Financial support:* Career-related internships or fieldwork, institutionally sponsored loans, and unspecified assistantships available. Support available to part-time students. Financial award application deadline: 8/1; financial award applicants required to submit FAFSA. *Unit head:* Dr. Brian M. McCadden, Director, 401-865-2503, E-mail: bmccadde@providence.edu. *Application contact:* Rev. Mark D. Nowel, Dean of Undergraduate and Graduate Studies, 401-865-2649, Fax: 401-865-1496, E-mail: mnowel@providence.edu.
Website: http://www.providence.edu/professional-studies/graduate-degrees/Pages/master-education-urban-teaching.aspx.

Sojourner-Douglass College, Graduate Program, Baltimore, MD 21205-1814. Offers human services (MASS); public administration (MASS); urban education (reading) (MASS). Part-time and evening/weekend programs available. *Degree requirements:* For master's, comprehensive exam, written proposal oral defense. *Entrance requirements:* For master's, Graduate Examination.

Urban Education

Temple University, College of Education, Department of Curriculum, Instruction, and Technology in Education, Program in Urban Education, Philadelphia, PA 19122-6096. Offers Ed M, PhD.

University of Central Florida, College of Education and Human Performance, School of Teaching, Learning, and Leadership, Applied Learning and Instruction Program, Orlando, FL 32816. Offers applied learning and instruction (MA); community college education (Certificate); gifted education (Certificate); global and comparative education (Certificate); initial teacher professional preparation (Certificate); urban education (Certificate). *Accreditation:* NCATE. Part-time and evening/weekend programs available. *Students:* 11 full-time (9 women), 80 part-time (62 women); includes 27 minority (10 Black or African American, non-Hispanic/Latino; 2 Asian, non-Hispanic/Latino; 13 Hispanic/Latino; 2 Two or more races, non-Hispanic/Latino). Average age 33. 61 applicants, 70% accepted, 29 enrolled. In 2013, 19 master's, 26 other advanced degrees awarded. *Degree requirements:* For Certificate, thesis or alternative, final exam. *Entrance requirements:* For degree, GRE General Test, minimum GPA of 3.0, resume. Additional exam requirements/recommendations for international students: Required—TOEFL. *Application deadline:* For fall admission, 2/20 for domestic students; for spring admission, 9/20 for domestic students. Application fee: $30. Electronic applications accepted. *Financial support:* In 2013–14, 3 students received support, including 1 research assistantship with partial tuition reimbursement available (averaging $8,100 per year), 2 teaching assistantships with partial tuition reimbursements available (averaging $6,900 per year); fellowships, career-related internships or fieldwork, Federal Work-Study, institutionally sponsored loans, and unspecified assistantships also available. Financial award application deadline: 3/1; financial award applicants required to submit FAFSA. *Unit head:* Dr. Bobby Hoffman, Program Coordinator, 407-823-1770, E-mail: bobby.hoffman@ucf.edu. *Application contact:* Barbara Rodriguez Lamas, Director, Admissions and Student Services, 407-823-2766, Fax: 407-823-6442, E-mail: gradadmissions@ucf.edu.
Website: http://education.ucf.edu/departments.cfm.

University of Chicago, Graham School of Continuing Liberal and Professional Studies, Urban Teacher Education Program, Chicago, IL 60637-1513. Offers MAT.

University of Houston–Downtown, College of Public Service, Department of Urban Education, Houston, TX 77002. Offers curriculum and instruction (MAT); elementary (EC-6) generalist certification (MAT); elementary/middle school (4-8) generalist certification (MAT); secondary education certification (MAT). Part-time and evening/weekend programs available. Postbaccalaureate distance learning degree programs offered. *Faculty:* 7 full-time (3 women). *Students:* 4 full-time (3 women), 28 part-time (19 women); includes 22 minority (14 Black or African American, non-Hispanic/Latino; 1 Asian, non-Hispanic/Latino; 6 Hispanic/Latino; 1 Two or more races, non-Hispanic/Latino). Average age 36. 31 applicants, 87% accepted, 27 enrolled. In 2013, 10 master's awarded. *Degree requirements:* For master's, capstone course with completed project, position paper, grant proposal, empirical study, curriculum development/revision, or advanced technology project presented at annual Graduate Project Exhibition. *Entrance requirements:* For master's, GRE, personal statement, 3 recommendation forms. Additional exam requirements/recommendations for international students: Required—TOEFL (minimum score 550 paper-based; 80 iBT). *Application deadline:* For fall admission, 7/15 for domestic and international students; for spring admission, 11/15 for domestic and international students. Application fee: $35 ($60 for international students). Electronic applications accepted. *Expenses:* Tuition, state resident: full-time $4212; part-time $234 per credit hour. Tuition, nonresident: full-time $9684; part-time $538 per credit hour. *Required fees:* $1074. Tuition and fees vary according to program. *Financial support:* Scholarships/grants available. Financial award applicants required to submit FAFSA. *Unit head:* Dr. Viola Garcia, Department Chair, 713-221-8165, Fax: 713-226-5294, E-mail: garciav@uhd.edu. *Application contact:* Ceshia Love, Assistant Director of Graduate Admissions, 713-221-8093, Fax: 713-223-7408, E-mail: gradadmissions@uhd.edu.
Website: http://www.uhd.edu/academic/colleges/publicservice/urbaned/.

University of Illinois at Chicago, Graduate College, College of Education, Department of Educational Policy Studies, Chicago, IL 60607-7128. Offers policy studies (M Ed); policy studies in urban education (PhD); urban education leadership (Ed D). *Faculty:* 12 full-time (6 women). *Students:* 45 full-time (33 women), 103 part-time (69 women); includes 78 minority (38 Black or African American, non-Hispanic/Latino; 4 Asian, non-Hispanic/Latino; 31 Hispanic/Latino; 5 Two or more races, non-Hispanic/Latino), 2 international. Average age 36. 71 applicants, 44% accepted, 22 enrolled. In 2013, 14 master's, 16 doctorates awarded. *Expenses:* Tuition, state resident: full-time $11,066; part-time $3689 per term. Tuition, nonresident: full-time $23,064; part-time $7688 per term. *Required fees:* $3004; $1190 per term. Tuition and fees vary according to course level and program. *Total annual research expenditures:* $290,000. *Unit head:* Prof. David Mayrowetz, Chair, 312-996-3326, E-mail: dmayro@uic.edu. *Application contact:* Receptionist, 312-413-2550, E-mail: gradcoll@uic.edu.
Website: http://education.uic.edu.

University of Massachusetts Boston, Office of Graduate Studies, Graduate College of Education, School Organization, Curriculum and Instruction Department, Boston, MA 02125-3393. Offers education (M Ed, Ed D), including elementary and secondary education/certification (M Ed), higher education administration (Ed D), teacher certification (M Ed), urban school leadership (Ed D); educational administration (M Ed, CAGS); special education (M Ed). *Degree requirements:* For master's and CAGS, comprehensive exam; for doctorate, comprehensive exam, thesis/dissertation. *Entrance requirements:* For master's, GRE General Test or MAT; for doctorate, GRE General Test or MAT, minimum GPA of 2.75; for CAGS, minimum GPA of 2.75.

University of Massachusetts Boston, Office of Graduate Studies, Graduate College of Education, School Organization, Curriculum and Instruction Department, Program in Education, Track in Urban School Leadership, Boston, MA 02125-3393. Offers Ed D. Part-time and evening/weekend programs available. *Degree requirements:* For doctorate, comprehensive exam, thesis/dissertation. *Entrance requirements:* For doctorate, GRE General Test or MAT, minimum GPA of 2.75. *Faculty research:* School reform, race and culture in schools, race and higher education, language, literacy and writing.

University of Michigan–Dearborn, College of Education, Health, and Human Services, Doctoral Program in Education, Dearborn, MI 48126. Offers curriculum and practice (Ed D); educational leadership (Ed D); metropolitan education (Ed D). Part-time and evening/weekend programs available. *Faculty:* 7 full-time (5 women), 2 part-time/adjunct (0 women). *Students:* 4 full-time (all women), 35 part-time (27 women); includes 15 minority (11 Black or African American, non-Hispanic/Latino; 1 Asian, non-Hispanic/Latino; 3 Hispanic/Latino). Average age 40. 26 applicants, 42% accepted, 7 enrolled. *Degree requirements:* For doctorate, comprehensive exam, thesis/dissertation. *Entrance requirements:* For doctorate, GRE (taken within the last 5 years), master's degree with minimum GPA of 3.3, 3 letters of recommendation (1 from faculty), 3 years' professional and/or teaching experience. Additional exam requirements/recommendations for international students: Required—TOEFL (minimum score 560 paper-based; 84 iBT). *Application deadline:* For fall admission, 3/1 for domestic and international students. Application fee: $60. Electronic applications accepted. *Expenses:* Tuition, state resident: full-time $11,838; part-time $686 per credit hour. Tuition, nonresident: full-time $20,926; part-time $1206 per credit hour. *Required fees:* $760; $286 per semester. Tuition and fees vary according to course load and program. *Financial support:* Scholarships/grants available. Financial award application deadline: 2/1; financial award applicants required to submit FAFSA. *Faculty research:* Educational leadership, metropolitan education, curriculum and practice, educational psychology, special education, assessment. *Unit head:* Dr. Bonnie M. Beyer, Coordinator, 313-593-5583, E-mail: beyer@umd.umich.edu. *Application contact:* Elizabeth Morden, Program Assistant, 313-583-6333, Fax: 313-593-4748, E-mail: emorden@umich.edu.
Website: http://cehhs.umd.umich.edu/cehhs_edd/.

University of Nebraska at Omaha, Graduate Studies, College of Education, Department of Teacher Education, Omaha, NE 68182. Offers elementary education (MS); instruction in urban schools (Certificate); reading education (MS); secondary education (MA, MS). Part-time and evening/weekend programs available. *Faculty:* 24 full-time (18 women). *Students:* 19 full-time (12 women), 324 part-time (278 women); includes 39 minority (7 Black or African American, non-Hispanic/Latino; 5 Asian, non-Hispanic/Latino; 19 Hispanic/Latino; 8 Two or more races, non-Hispanic/Latino), 2 international. Average age 34. 42 applicants, 76% accepted, 23 enrolled. In 2013, 73 master's awarded. *Degree requirements:* For master's, comprehensive exam (for some programs), thesis (for some programs). *Entrance requirements:* Additional exam requirements/recommendations for international students: Required—TOEFL, IELTS, PTE. *Application deadline:* For fall admission, 8/1 priority date for domestic students; for spring admission, 12/1 priority date for domestic students; for summer admission, 6/1 for domestic students. Applications are processed on a rolling basis. Application fee: $45. Electronic applications accepted. *Financial support:* In 2013–14, 6 students received support, including 5 research assistantships with tuition reimbursements available, 1 teaching assistantship with tuition reimbursement available; fellowships, Federal Work-Study, institutionally sponsored loans, scholarships/grants, tuition waivers (partial), and unspecified assistantships also available. Support available to part-time students. Financial award application deadline: 3/1; financial award applicants required to submit FAFSA. *Unit head:* Dr. Sarah Edwards, Chairperson, 402-554-3512. *Application contact:* Dr. Wilma Kuhlman, Graduate Program Chair, 402-554-3926, E-mail: graduate@unomaha.edu.

University of Pennsylvania, Graduate School of Education, Teach for America Program, Philadelphia, PA 19104. Offers MS Ed. Program designed for Teach For America corps members teaching in Philadelphia public and charter schools. *Students:* 168 full-time (112 women), 8 part-time (all women); includes 66 minority (27 Black or African American, non-Hispanic/Latino; 16 Asian, non-Hispanic/Latino; 17 Hispanic/Latino; 6 Two or more races, non-Hispanic/Latino), 2 international. 116 applicants, 92% accepted, 95 enrolled. In 2013, 96 master's awarded. *Unit head:* Dr. Andrew Porter, Dean, 215-898-7014. *Application contact:* 215-898-6415, Fax: 215-746-6884, E-mail: admissions@gse.upenn.edu.
Website: http://tfa.gse.upenn.edu/.

University of Southern California, Graduate School, Rossier School of Education, Doctor of Education Programs, Los Angeles, CA 90089. Offers educational psychology (Ed D); higher education administration (Ed D); K-12 leadership in urban school settings (Ed D); teacher education in multicultural societies (Ed D). Part-time and evening/weekend programs available. *Degree requirements:* For doctorate, thesis/dissertation. *Entrance requirements:* For doctorate, GRE. Additional exam requirements/recommendations for international students: Required—TOEFL (minimum score 100 iBT). Electronic applications accepted. *Faculty research:* Data-driven decision-making in K-12 schools and districts; examination of college and university leadership and management in U. S. and Asia; studies in facilitating student learning; organizational change and the role of leaders; leadership, diversity, learning and accountability.

University of Wisconsin–Milwaukee, Graduate School, School of Education, Department of Curriculum and Instruction, Milwaukee, WI 53201-0413. Offers curriculum planning and instruction improvement (MS); early childhood education (MS); elementary education (MS); junior high/middle school education (MS); reading education (MS); secondary education (MS); teaching in an urban setting (MS). Part-time programs available. *Faculty:* 18 full-time (13 women). *Students:* 17 full-time (10 women), 46 part-time (42 women); includes 15 minority (7 Black or African American, non-Hispanic/Latino; 1 Asian, non-Hispanic/Latino; 7 Two or more races, non-Hispanic/Latino), 1 international. Average age 32. 35 applicants, 69% accepted, 11 enrolled. In 2013, 31 master's awarded. *Degree requirements:* For master's, thesis or alternative. *Entrance requirements:* Additional exam requirements/recommendations for international students: Required—TOEFL (minimum score 550 paper-based; 79 iBT), IELTS (minimum score 6.5). *Application deadline:* For fall admission, 1/1 priority date for domestic students; for spring admission, 9/1 for domestic students. Applications are processed on a rolling basis. Application fee: $56 ($96 for international students). Electronic applications accepted. *Financial support:* In 2013–14, 1 fellowship was awarded; research assistantships, teaching assistantships, career-related internships or fieldwork, health care benefits, unspecified assistantships, and project assistantships also available. Support available to part-time students. Financial award application deadline: 4/15; financial award applicants required to submit FAFSA. *Unit head:* Raquel Oxford, Department Chair, 414-229-4884, Fax: 414-229-5571, E-mail: roxford@uwm.edu. *Application contact:* General Information Contact, 414-229-4982, Fax: 414-229-6967, E-mail: gradschool@uwm.edu.
Website: http://www.uwm.edu/SOE/.

University of Wisconsin–Milwaukee, Graduate School, School of Education, Urban Education Doctoral Program, Milwaukee, WI 53201-0413. Offers adult, continuing and higher education leadership (PhD); curriculum and instruction (PhD); educational administration (PhD); exceptional education (PhD); multicultural studies (PhD); social foundations of education (PhD). *Students:* 51 full-time (37 women), 40 part-time (25 women); includes 32 minority (16 Black or African American, non-Hispanic/Latino; 1 American Indian or Alaska Native, non-Hispanic/Latino; 3 Asian, non-Hispanic/Latino; 5 Hispanic/Latino; 7 Two or more races, non-Hispanic/Latino), 3 international. Average age 41. 25 applicants, 44% accepted, 4 enrolled. In 2013, 11 doctorates awarded. *Degree requirements:* For doctorate, comprehensive exam, thesis/dissertation. *Entrance requirements:* For doctorate, GRE General Test, minimum undergraduate GPA of 2.85, graduate 3.5. Additional exam requirements/recommendations for international students: Required—TOEFL (minimum score 550 paper-based; 79 iBT), IELTS (minimum score 6.5). *Application deadline:* For fall admission, 1/1 priority date for domestic students; for spring admission, 9/1 for domestic students. Applications are processed on a rolling basis. Application fee: $56 ($96 for international students). Electronic applications accepted. *Financial support:* In 2013–14, 11 fellowships, 1 teaching assistantship were awarded; research assistantships, career-related internships or fieldwork, health care benefits, unspecified assistantships, and project assistantships also available. Support available to part-time students. Financial award application deadline: 4/15; financial award applicants required to submit FAFSA. *Unit head:* Raji Swaminathan, Representative, 414-229-6740, Fax: 414-229-2920, E-mail: swaminar@uwm.edu. *Application contact:* General Information Contact, 414-229-4982, Fax: 414-229-6967, E-mail: gradschool@uwm.edu.
Website: http://www4.uwm.edu/soe/academics/urban_ed/.

Vanderbilt University, Peabody College, Department of Teaching and Learning, Nashville, TN 37240-1001. Offers elementary education (M Ed); English language learners (M Ed); learning and instruction (M Ed); learning, diversity, and urban studies (M Ed); reading education (M Ed); secondary education (M Ed). *Accreditation:* NCATE. *Faculty:* 35 full-time (25 women), 20 part-time/adjunct (14 women). *Students:* 103 full-time (74 women), 44 part-time (39 women); includes 22 minority (8 Black or African American, non-Hispanic/Latino; 5 Asian, non-Hispanic/Latino; 5 Hispanic/Latino; 1 Native Hawaiian or other Pacific Islander, non-Hispanic/Latino; 3 Two or more races, non-Hispanic/Latino), 21 international. Average age 25. 264 applicants, 73% accepted, 57 enrolled. In 2013, 95 master's awarded. *Degree requirements:* For master's, comprehensive exam, thesis optional. *Entrance requirements:* For master's, GRE General Test, MAT. Additional exam requirements/recommendations for international students: Required—TOEFL (minimum score 550 paper-based; 80 iBT). *Application deadline:* For fall admission, 12/31 priority date for domestic and international students; for spring admission, 11/1 priority date for domestic and international students. Applications are processed on a rolling basis. Application fee: $0. Electronic applications accepted. *Financial support:* Fellowships with full and partial tuition reimbursements, research assistantships with full and partial tuition reimbursements, teaching assistantships with full and partial tuition reimbursements, Federal Work-Study, institutionally sponsored loans, scholarships/grants, tuition waivers (partial), and unspecified assistantships available. Support available to part-time students. Financial award application deadline: 1/15; financial award applicants required to submit FAFSA. *Faculty research:* Learning environments for mathematics of space and motion, visual programming tools for children's learning of basic science concepts, pathways for elementary and middle school children's learning about measurement and statistics, early reading intervention, professional development for ambitious mathematics teaching. *Unit head:* Dr. Rogers Hall, Chair, 615-322-8100, Fax: 615-322-8999, E-mail: rogers.hall@vanderbilt.edu. *Application contact:* Angela Saylor, Educational Coordinator, 615-322-8092, Fax: 615-322-8999, E-mail: angela.saylor@vanderbilt.edu.

Virginia Commonwealth University, Graduate School, School of Education, Doctoral Program in Education, Urban Services Leadership Track, Richmond, VA 23284-9005. Offers PhD. *Entrance requirements:* For doctorate, GRE. Additional exam requirements/recommendations for international students: Required—TOEFL (minimum score 600 paper-based; 100 iBT). Electronic applications accepted.

Wayne State University, School of Library and Information Science, Detroit, MI 48202. Offers academic libraries (MLIS); archival administration (MLIS, Certificate); general librarianship (MLIS); health sciences librarianship (MLIS); information management for librarians (Certificate); information science (MLIS); law librarianship (MLIS); library and information science (Spec); organization of information (MLIS); public libraries (MLIS); public library services to children and young adults (MLIS, Certificate); records management (MLIS); references services (MLIS); school library media specialist endorsement (MLIS); special libraries (MLIS); urban libraries (MLIS); MLIS/MA. *Accreditation:* ALA (one or more programs are accredited). Part-time and evening/weekend programs available. Postbaccalaureate distance learning degree programs offered (no on-campus study). *Faculty:* 13 full-time (9 women), 17 part-time/adjunct (13 women). *Students:* 112 full-time (80 women), 372 part-time (296 women); includes 65 minority (26 Black or African American, non-Hispanic/Latino; 11 Asian, non-Hispanic/Latino; 18 Hispanic/Latino; 10 Two or more races, non-Hispanic/Latino), 2 international. Average age 33. 275 applicants, 61% accepted, 109 enrolled. In 2013, 179 master's, 42 other advanced degrees awarded. *Entrance requirements:* For master's and other advanced degree, GRE or MAT (if undergraduate GPA is between 2.5 and 2.99), minimum undergraduate GPA of 3.0 or graduate degree, personal statement, resume or curriculum vitae. Additional exam requirements/recommendations for international students: Required—TOEFL (minimum score 550 paper-based; 79 iBT); Recommended—IELTS (minimum score 6.5), TWE (minimum score 5.5). *Application deadline:* For fall admission, 7/1 for domestic students, 5/1 priority date for international students; for winter admission, 10/1 for domestic students, 9/1 priority date for international students; for spring admission, 3/15 for domestic students, 1/1 priority date for international students. Applications are processed on a rolling basis. Application fee: $0. Electronic applications accepted. *Expenses:* Contact institution. *Financial support:* In 2013–14, 65 students received support. Fellowships with tuition reimbursements available, research assistantships with tuition reimbursements available, institutionally sponsored loans, scholarships/grants, and unspecified assistantships available. Support available to part-time students. Financial award application deadline: 3/31; financial award applicants required to submit FAFSA. *Faculty research:* Library services, information management issues, digital content management, library/community engagement, archives and preservation. *Unit head:* Dr. Stephen Bajjaly, Associate Dean and Professor, 313-577-0350, Fax: 313-577-7563, E-mail: bajjaly@wayne.edu. *Application contact:* Matthew Fredericks, Academic Services Officer I, 313-577-2446, Fax: 313-577-7563, E-mail: mfredericks@wayne.edu. Website: http://slis.wayne.edu/.

Section 26
Subject Areas

This section contains a directory of institutions offering graduate work in subject areas of education. Additional information about programs listed in the directory may be obtained by writing directly to the dean of a graduate school or chair of a department at the address given in the directory.

For programs offering related work, see also in this book *Administration, Instruction, and Theory; Business Administration and Management; Education; Instructional Levels; Leisure Studies and Recreation; Physical Education and Kinesiology;* and *Special Focus*. In the other guides in this series:

Graduate Programs in the Humanities, Arts & Social Sciences

See *Art and Art History; Family and Consumer Sciences; Language and Literature; Performing Arts; Psychology and Counseling (School Psychology); Public, Regional, and Industrial Affairs (Urban Studies); Religious Studies;* and *Social Sciences*

Graduate Programs in the Biological/Biomedical Sciences & Health-Related Medical Professions

See *Health-Related Professions*

Graduate Programs in the Physical Sciences, Mathematics, Agricultural Sciences, the Environment & Natural Resources

See *Mathematical Sciences*

Graduate Programs in Engineering & Applied Sciences

See *Computer Science and Information Technology*

CONTENTS

Program Directories

Agricultural Education	1248
Art Education	1252
Business Education	1266
Computer Education	1270
Counselor Education	1273
Developmental Education	1319
English Education	1320
Environmental Education	1340
Foreign Languages Education	1343
Health Education	1358
Home Economics Education	1378
Mathematics Education	1380
Museum Education	1410
Music Education	1411
Reading Education	1433
Religious Education	1477
Science Education	1483
Social Sciences Education	1512
Vocational and Technical Education	1530

Agricultural Education

Alcorn State University, School of Graduate Studies, School of Psychology and Education, Alcorn State, MS 39096-7500. Offers agricultural education (MS Ed); elementary education (MS Ed, Ed S); guidance and counseling (MS Ed); industrial education (MS Ed); secondary education (MS Ed), including health and physical education; special education (MS Ed). *Accreditation:* NCATE. *Degree requirements:* For master's, thesis optional.

Arkansas State University, Graduate School, College of Agriculture and Technology, Jonesboro, AR 72467. Offers agricultural education (SCCT); agriculture (MSA); vocational-technical administration (SCCT). Part-time programs available. *Faculty:* 15 full-time (3 women). *Students:* 9 full-time (4 women), 16 part-time (8 women); includes 6 minority (all Black or African American, non-Hispanic/Latino), 2 international. Average age 32. 21 applicants, 81% accepted, 13 enrolled. In 2013, 11 master's, 1 SCCT awarded. *Degree requirements:* For master's, comprehensive exam, thesis or alternative; for SCCT, comprehensive exam. *Entrance requirements:* For master's, GRE General Test or MAT, appropriate bachelor's degree, official transcripts, immunization records; for SCCT, GRE General Test or MAT, interview, master's degree, official transcript, immunization records. Additional exam requirements/recommendations for international students: Required—TOEFL (minimum score 550 paper-based; 79 iBT), IELTS (minimum score 6), PTE (minimum score 56). *Application deadline:* For fall admission, 7/1 for domestic and international students; for spring admission, 11/15 for domestic students, 11/14 for international students. Applications are processed on a rolling basis. Application fee: $30 ($40 for international students). Electronic applications accepted. *Expenses:* Tuition, state resident: full-time $4284; part-time $238 per credit hour. Tuition, nonresident: full-time $8568; part-time $476 per credit hour. *International tuition:* $9268 full-time. *Required fees:* $1098; $61 per credit hour. $25 per term. Tuition and fees vary according to course load and program. *Financial support:* In 2013–14, 5 students received support. Teaching assistantships, career-related internships or fieldwork, scholarships/grants, and unspecified assistantships available. Financial award application deadline: 7/1; financial award applicants required to submit FAFSA. *Unit head:* Dr. Timothy Burcham, Dean, 870-972-2085, Fax: 870-972-3885, E-mail: tburcham@astate.edu. *Application contact:* Vickey Ring, Graduate Admissions Coordinator, 870-972-3029, Fax: 870-972-3857, E-mail: vickeyring@astate.edu.
Website: http://www.astate.edu/college/agriculture-and-technology/index.dot.

California Polytechnic State University, San Luis Obispo, College of Agriculture, Food and Environmental Sciences, Department of Agricultural Education and Communication, San Luis Obispo, CA 93407. Offers MAE. Part-time programs available. *Faculty:* 7 full-time (1 woman). *Students:* 23 full-time (18 women), 1 (woman) part-time; includes 4 minority (all Hispanic/Latino). Average age 25. 16 applicants, 94% accepted, 10 enrolled. In 2013, 10 master's awarded. *Degree requirements:* For master's, comprehensive exam. *Entrance requirements:* For master's, minimum GPA of 2.75 in last 90 quarter units of course work. Additional exam requirements/recommendations for international students: Required—TOEFL (minimum score 550 paper-based) or IELTS (minimum score 6). *Application deadline:* For fall admission, 4/1 for domestic students, 11/30 for international students; for winter admission, 10/1 for domestic students, 6/30 for international students; for spring admission, 10/1 for domestic students. Applications are processed on a rolling basis. Application fee: $55. Electronic applications accepted. *Financial support:* Application deadline: 3/2; applicants required to submit FAFSA. *Faculty research:* Agricultural education with emphasis on public school teaching. *Unit head:* Dr. William C. Kellogg, Graduate Coordinator, 805-756-2973, Fax: 805-756-2799, E-mail: bkellogg@calpoly.edu. *Application contact:* Dr. Mark Shelton, Associate Dean/Graduate Coordinator, 805-756-2161, Fax: 805-756-6577, E-mail: mshelton@calpoly.edu.
Website: http://aged.calpoly.edu/.

Clemson University, Graduate School, College of Agriculture, Forestry and Life Sciences, Program in Agricultural Education, Clemson, SC 29634. Offers M Ag Ed. *Accreditation:* NCATE. Part-time programs available. *Students:* 9 full-time (8 women), 5 part-time (all women); includes 1 minority (Black or African American, non-Hispanic/Latino), 1 international. Average age 27. 8 applicants, 100% accepted, 8 enrolled. In 2013, 4 master's awarded. *Entrance requirements:* For master's, GRE General Test. Additional exam requirements/recommendations for international students: Required—TOEFL. *Application deadline:* For fall admission, 3/15 for domestic students; for spring admission, 11/1 for domestic students. Application fee: $70 ($80 for international students). Electronic applications accepted. *Financial support:* In 2013–14, 4 students received support, including 2 research assistantships with partial tuition reimbursements available (averaging $10,373 per year), 3 teaching assistantships with partial tuition reimbursements available (averaging $10,985 per year); career-related internships or fieldwork, institutionally sponsored loans, scholarships/grants, health care benefits, and unspecified assistantships also available. Support available to part-time students. Financial award application deadline: 4/1; financial award applicants required to submit FAFSA. *Faculty research:* Adaptation and change, curriculum assessment and innovation, career development, adult and extension education, technology transfer. *Unit head:* Dr. Young Jo Han, Chair, 864-656-3250, Fax: 864-656-0338, E-mail: yhan@clemson.edu. *Application contact:* Dr. Tom Dobbins, Coordinator, 864-656-3834, Fax: 864-656-5675, E-mail: tdbbns@clemson.edu.
Website: http://www.clemson.edu/cafls/departments/agbioeng/aged/.

Cornell University, Graduate School, Graduate Fields of Agriculture and Life Sciences, Field of Education, Ithaca, NY 14853-0001. Offers adult and extension education (MPS, MS, PhD); learning, teaching, and social policy (MPS, MS, PhD); mathematics 7-12 (MS). *Faculty:* 21 full-time (8 women). *Students:* 14 full-time (9 women); includes 2 minority (1 Asian, non-Hispanic/Latino; 1 Hispanic/Latino), 1 international. Average age 32. 20 applicants, 20% accepted, 2 enrolled. In 2013, 17 master's, 4 doctorates awarded. Terminal master's awarded for partial completion of doctoral program. *Degree requirements:* For master's, thesis (MS); for doctorate, comprehensive exam, thesis/dissertation. *Entrance requirements:* For master's and doctorate, GRE General Test, sample of written work (recommended), 2 letters of recommendation. Additional exam requirements/recommendations for international students: Required—TOEFL (minimum score 550 paper-based; 77 iBT). *Application deadline:* For fall admission, 2/15 for domestic students. Application fee: $95. Electronic applications accepted. *Financial support:* In 2013–14, 4 students received support, including 3 fellowships with full tuition reimbursements available, 1 research assistantship with full tuition reimbursement available; teaching assistantships with full tuition reimbursements available, institutionally sponsored loans, scholarships/grants, health care benefits, tuition waivers (full and partial), and unspecified assistantships also available. Financial award applicants required to submit FAFSA. *Faculty research:* Moral development and professional ethics, public issues education and community development, socio/political issues in public education, teacher education and curriculum in agricultural science and mathematics, extension research. *Unit head:* Director of Graduate Studies, 607-255-4278, Fax: 607-255-7905. *Application contact:* Graduate Field Assistant, 607-255-4278, Fax: 607-255-7905, E-mail: rh22@cornell.edu.
Website: http://www.gradschool.cornell.edu/fields.php?id-80&a-2.

Eastern Kentucky University, The Graduate School, College of Education, Department of Curriculum and Instruction, Program in Secondary and Higher Education, Richmond, KY 40475-3102. Offers secondary education (MA Ed), including agricultural education, art education, biological sciences education, business education, English education, geography education, history education, home economics education, industrial education, mathematical sciences education, physical education, school health education. *Accreditation:* NCATE. Part-time programs available. *Entrance requirements:* For master's, GRE General Test, minimum GPA of 2.5.

Iowa State University of Science and Technology, Department of Agricultural Education and Studies, Ames, IA 50011. Offers MS, PhD. *Entrance requirements:* For master's and doctorate, resume. Additional exam requirements/recommendations for international students: Required—TOEFL (minimum score 550 paper-based; 79 iBT), IELTS (minimum score 6.5). Electronic applications accepted. *Faculty research:* Agricultural extension education, teaching, learning processes, distance education, international education, adult education.

Kansas State University, Graduate School, College of Agriculture, Department of Communications and Agricultural Education, Manhattan, KS 66506. Offers agricultural education and communication (MS). Part-time programs available. Postbaccalaureate distance learning degree programs offered (no on-campus study). *Faculty:* 5 full-time (2 women). *Students:* 7 full-time (5 women), 6 part-time (4 women). Average age 25. 10 applicants, 80% accepted, 8 enrolled. *Degree requirements:* For master's, comprehensive exam, thesis or alternative. *Entrance requirements:* For master's, GRE if GPA on last 60 undergraduate credits is less than 3.0. *Application deadline:* For fall admission, 5/1 for domestic students, 1/1 for international students; for spring admission, 10/1 for domestic students, 8/1 for international students; for summer admission, 3/1 for domestic students, 12/1 for international students. Application fee: $50 ($75 for international students). Electronic applications accepted. *Faculty research:* Curriculum development, instructional design, strategic communications, risk and crisis communications. *Total annual research expenditures:* $31,491. *Unit head:* Dr. Kristina M. Boone, Head, 785-532-5804, Fax: 785-532-5633, E-mail: kboone@ksu.edu. *Application contact:* Dr. Jason D. Ellis, Associate Professor, 785-532-5804, Fax: 785-532-5633, E-mail: jdellis@ksu.edu.
Website: http://www.communications.k-state.edu/.

Louisiana State University and Agricultural & Mechanical College, Graduate School, College of Human Sciences and Education, School of Human Resource Education and Workforce Development, Baton Rouge, LA 70803. Offers agriculture and extension education and youth development (MS, PhD); career and technical education (MS, PhD); comprehensive vocational education (MS, PhD); extension and international education (MS, PhD); human resource and leadership development (MS, PhD); industrial education (MS); vocational agriculture education (MS, PhD); vocational business education (MS); vocational home economics education (MS). *Accreditation:* NCATE. Part-time programs available. *Faculty:* 10 full-time (5 women). *Students:* 46 full-time (28 women), 138 part-time (96 women); includes 65 minority (52 Black or African American, non-Hispanic/Latino; 2 American Indian or Alaska Native, non-Hispanic/Latino; 2 Asian, non-Hispanic/Latino; 6 Hispanic/Latino; 3 Two or more races, non-Hispanic/Latino), 6 international. Average age 35. 120 applicants, 62% accepted, 49 enrolled. In 2013, 23 master's, 14 doctorates awarded. Terminal master's awarded for partial completion of doctoral program. *Degree requirements:* For master's, thesis (for some programs); for doctorate, thesis/dissertation. *Entrance requirements:* For master's and doctorate, GRE General Test, minimum GPA of 3.0. Additional exam requirements/recommendations for international students: Required—TOEFL (minimum score 550 paper-based; 79 IBT), IELTS (minimum score 6.5), or PTE (minimum score 59). *Application deadline:* For fall admission, 1/25 priority date for domestic students, 5/15 for international students; for spring admission, 10/15 for international students. Applications are processed on a rolling basis. Application fee: $50 ($70 for international students). Electronic applications accepted. *Financial support:* In 2013–14, 85 students received support, including 4 fellowships with full and partial tuition reimbursements available (averaging $31,175 per year), 9 research assistantships with full and partial tuition reimbursements available (averaging $15,422 per year), 14 teaching assistantships with partial tuition reimbursements available (averaging $14,289 per year); career-related internships or fieldwork, Federal Work-Study, institutionally sponsored loans, health care benefits, tuition waivers (full and partial), and unspecified assistantships also available. Financial award application deadline: 3/1; financial award applicants required to submit FAFSA. *Faculty research:* Adult education, history and philosophy of vocational education, curriculum and instruction, career decision-making. *Total annual research expenditures:* $4,454. *Unit head:* Dr. Ed Holton, Director, 225-578-5748, Fax: 225-578-5755, E-mail: eholton@lsu.edu.
Website: http://www.lsu.edu/hrleader/.

Mississippi State University, College of Agriculture and Life Sciences, School of Human Sciences, Mississippi State, MS 39762. Offers agricultural sciences (PhD), including agriculture and extension education; agriculture and extension education (MS); human development and family studies (MS, PhD). *Accreditation:* NCATE (one or more programs are accredited). Part-time programs available. *Faculty:* 9 full-time (3 women). *Students:* 23 full-time (15 women), 72 part-time (44 women); includes 19 minority (18 Black or African American, non-Hispanic/Latino; 1 Two or more races, non-Hispanic/Latino), 3 international. Average age 36. 74 applicants, 42% accepted, 28 enrolled. In 2013, 10 master's, 2 doctorates awarded. *Degree requirements:* For master's, thesis optional, comprehensive oral or written exam. *Entrance requirements:* For master's, GRE, minimum GPA of 2.75 in last 4 semesters of course work; for doctorate, minimum GPA of 3.0 on prior graduate work. Additional exam requirements/recommendations for international students: Required—TOEFL (minimum score 477 paper-based; 53 iBT); Recommended—IELTS (minimum score 4.5). *Application deadline:* For fall admission, 7/1 for domestic students, 5/1 for international students; for spring admission, 11/1 for domestic students, 9/1 for international students. Applications are processed on a rolling basis. Application fee: $60. Electronic applications accepted. *Financial support:* In 2013–14, 12 research assistantships (averaging $12,190 per year), 2 teaching assistantships with full tuition reimbursements (averaging $13,088 per year) were awarded; Federal Work-Study, institutionally sponsored loans, and unspecified assistantships also available. Financial award application deadline: 4/1; financial award applicants required to submit FAFSA. *Faculty research:* Animal welfare, agroscience, information technology, learning styles, problem solving. *Unit head:* Dr. Michael Newman, Director and Professor, 662-325-2950, E-mail: mnewman@

humansci.msstate.edu. *Application contact:* Dr. Tommy Phillips, Graduate Coordinator, 662-325-0655, E-mail: tphillips@humansci.msstate.edu.
Website: http://www.humansci.msstate.edu.

Montana State University, College of Graduate Studies, College of Agriculture, Division of Agricultural Education, Bozeman, MT 59717. Offers MS. Part-time programs available. Postbaccalaureate distance learning degree programs offered (no on-campus study). *Degree requirements:* For master's, comprehensive exam. *Entrance requirements:* For master's, GRE General Test. Additional exam requirements/recommendations for international students: Required—TOEFL (minimum score 550 paper-based). Electronic applications accepted. *Faculty research:* Extension systems, youth leadership, agricultural, adult and youth education in agriculture, international agricultural education, enzymology of vitamins, coenzymes and metal ions, steroid metabolism, protein structure, impact of wolves on big game hunting demand, prescription drug price dispersion in heterogeneous markets, divorce risk and the labor force participation of women with and without children, the economics of terraces in the Peruvian Andes.

Murray State University, School of Agriculture, Murray, KY 42071. Offers agriculture (MS); agriculture education (MS). Evening/weekend programs available. Postbaccalaureate distance learning degree programs offered (minimal on-campus study). *Degree requirements:* For master's, comprehensive exam, thesis (for some programs). *Entrance requirements:* Additional exam requirements/recommendations for international students: Required—TOEFL. *Faculty research:* Ultrasound in beef, corn and soybean research, tobacco research.

New Mexico State University, Graduate School, College of Agricultural, Consumer and Environmental Sciences, Department of Agricultural and Extension Education, Las Cruces, NM 88003. Offers MA. *Accreditation:* NCATE. Part-time and evening/weekend programs available. Postbaccalaureate distance learning degree programs offered (minimal on-campus study). *Faculty:* 5 full-time (2 women). *Students:* 13 full-time (10 women), 13 part-time (9 women); includes 11 minority (1 American Indian or Alaska Native, non-Hispanic/Latino; 10 Hispanic/Latino). Average age 31. 11 applicants, 91% accepted, 7 enrolled. In 2013, 12 master's awarded. *Degree requirements:* For master's, comprehensive exam, thesis or creative component. *Entrance requirements:* For master's, 3 letters of recommendation. Additional exam requirements/recommendations for international students: Required—TOEFL (minimum score 550 paper-based; 79 iBT), IELTS (minimum score 6.5). *Application deadline:* For fall admission, 7/1 priority date for domestic and international students; for spring admission, 11/1 priority date for domestic and international students. Applications are processed on a rolling basis. Application fee: $40 ($50 for international students). Electronic applications accepted. *Expenses:* Tuition, state resident: full-time $5398; part-time $224.90 per credit. Tuition, nonresident: full-time $18,821; part-time $784.20 per credit. *Required fees:* $1310; $54.60 per credit. *Financial support:* In 2013–14, 8 students received support, including 6 teaching assistantships (averaging $7,151 per year); career-related internships or fieldwork, institutionally sponsored loans, scholarships/grants, health care benefits, and unspecified assistantships also available. Financial award application deadline: 3/1. *Faculty research:* Secondary agricultural education programs, teaching and learning, agricultural technology and safety, volunteer programs, youth leadership development, agricultural development, youth development. *Total annual research expenditures:* $486,951. *Unit head:* Dr. Frank E. Hodnett, Interim Head, 575-646-4511, Fax: 575-646-4082, E-mail: fhodnett@nmsu.edu. *Application contact:* Dr. Brenda S. Seevers, Professor, 575-646-4511, Fax: 575-646-4082, E-mail: bseevers@nmsu.edu.
Website: http://aces.nmsu.edu/academics/axed.

North Carolina Agricultural and Technical State University, School of Graduate Studies, School of Agriculture and Environmental Sciences, Department of Agribusiness, Applied Economics, and Agriscience Education, Greensboro, NC 27411. Offers agricultural economics (MS); agricultural education (MS). *Accreditation:* NCATE. Part-time and evening/weekend programs available. *Degree requirements:* For master's, comprehensive exam, thesis or alternative, qualifying exam. *Entrance requirements:* For master's, GRE General Test, minimum GPA of 3.0. *Faculty research:* Aid for small farmers, agricultural technology resources, labor force mobility, agrology.

North Carolina State University, Graduate School, College of Agriculture and Life Sciences, Department of Agricultural and Extension Education, Program in Agricultural Education, Raleigh, NC 27695. Offers MAE, MS, Certificate. Postbaccalaureate distance learning degree programs offered. *Degree requirements:* For master's, thesis optional. *Entrance requirements:* For master's, GRE or MAT. Electronic applications accepted. *Faculty research:* Instructional methodology, distance education, leadership development, foundations, curriculum development.

North Dakota State University, College of Graduate and Interdisciplinary Studies, College of Human Development and Education, School of Education, Program in Agricultural Education, Fargo, ND 58108. Offers agricultural education (M Ed, MS); agricultural extension education (MS). *Accreditation:* NCATE. Part-time programs available. *Students:* 2 part-time (1 woman). Average age 36. In 2013, 1 master's awarded. *Degree requirements:* For master's, comprehensive exam, thesis or alternative. *Entrance requirements:* Additional exam requirements/recommendations for international students: Required—TOEFL (minimum score 525 paper-based; 71 iBT). *Application deadline:* Applications are processed on a rolling basis. Application fee: $45 ($60 for international students). *Financial support:* Research assistantships, career-related internships or fieldwork, Federal Work-Study, institutionally sponsored loans, and tuition waivers (full) available. Financial award application deadline: 4/15. *Faculty research:* Vocational and cooperative extension education, rural leadership, rural education, international extension. *Unit head:* Dr. William Martin, Chair, 701-231-7202, Fax: 701-231-7416, E-mail: william.martin@ndsu.edu. *Application contact:* Dr. Brent Young, Assistant Professor, 701-231-7439, Fax: 701-231-9685, E-mail: brent.young@ndsu.edu.

Northwest Missouri State University, Graduate School, Melvin and Valorie Booth College of Business and Professional Studies, Department of Agricultural Sciences, Maryville, MO 64468-6001. Offers agricultural economics (MBA); agriculture (MS); teaching agriculture (MS Ed). Part-time programs available. *Degree requirements:* For master's, comprehensive exam, thesis (for some programs). *Entrance requirements:* For master's, GRE General Test, minimum undergraduate GPA of 2.5, writing sample. Additional exam requirements/recommendations for international students: Required—TOEFL (minimum score 550 paper-based).

The Ohio State University, Graduate School, College of Food, Agricultural, and Environmental Sciences, Department of Agricultural Communication, Education and Leadership, Columbus, OH 43210. Offers agricultural and extension education (M Ed, MS, PhD). Postbaccalaureate distance learning degree programs offered (minimal on-campus study). *Faculty:* 8. *Students:* 25 full-time (12 women), 14 part-time (13 women); includes 2 minority (both Black or African American, non-Hispanic/Latino), 3 international. Average age 36. In 2013, 9 master's, 2 doctorates awarded. *Degree requirements:* For master's, thesis optional; for doctorate, thesis/dissertation. *Entrance requirements:* For master's, GRE General Test; for doctorate, GRE General Test. Additional exam requirements/recommendations for international students: Required—TOEFL (minimum score 550 paper-based; 79 iBT), Michigan English Language Assessment Battery (minimum score 82); Recommended—IELTS (minimum score 7). *Application deadline:* For fall admission, 12/13 priority date for domestic students, 11/30 priority date for international students; for spring admission, 12/6 for domestic students, 11/11 for international students. Applications are processed on a rolling basis. Application fee: $60 ($70 for international students). Electronic applications accepted. *Financial support:* Fellowships with tuition reimbursements, research assistantships with tuition reimbursements, teaching assistantships with tuition reimbursements, Federal Work-Study, institutionally sponsored loans, and unspecified assistantships available. Support available to part-time students. *Unit head:* Gary Straquadine, Chair, 614-292-6909, E-mail: straquadine.5@osu.edu. *Application contact:* Graduate Admissions, 614-292-6031, Fax: 614-292-3656, E-mail: gradadmissions@osu.edu.
Website: http://acel.osu.edu/.

Oklahoma State University, College of Agricultural Science and Natural Resources, Department of Agricultural Education, Communications and Leadership, Stillwater, OK 74078. Offers M Ag, MS, PhD. Postbaccalaureate distance learning degree programs offered. *Faculty:* 10 full-time (4 women), 2 part-time/adjunct (0 women). *Students:* 30 full-time (22 women), 50 part-time (37 women); includes 10 minority (2 Black or African American, non-Hispanic/Latino; 3 American Indian or Alaska Native, non-Hispanic/Latino; 2 Hispanic/Latino; 3 Two or more races, non-Hispanic/Latino), 5 international. Average age 29. 52 applicants, 62% accepted, 23 enrolled. In 2013, 23 master's, 4 doctorates awarded. *Degree requirements:* For master's, thesis (for some programs), thesis or report; for doctorate, comprehensive exam, thesis/dissertation. *Entrance requirements:* For master's and doctorate, GRE or GMAT. Additional exam requirements/recommendations for international students: Required—TOEFL (minimum score 550 paper-based; 79 iBT). *Application deadline:* For fall admission, 3/1 priority date for international students; for spring admission, 8/1 priority date for international students. Applications are processed on a rolling basis. Application fee: $40 ($75 for international students). Electronic applications accepted. *Expenses:* Tuition, state resident: full-time $4272; part-time $178 per credit hour. Tuition, nonresident: full-time $17,472; part-time $709 per credit hour. *Required fees:* $2413.20; $100.55 per credit hour. One-time fee: $50 full-time. Part-time tuition and fees vary according to course load and campus/location. *Financial support:* In 2013–14, 2 research assistantships (averaging $12,000 per year), 21 teaching assistantships (averaging $12,285 per year) were awarded; career-related internships or fieldwork, Federal Work-Study, scholarships/grants, health care benefits, tuition waivers (partial), and unspecified assistantships also available. Support available to part-time students. Financial award application deadline: 3/1; financial award applicants required to submit FAFSA. *Faculty research:* Teaching in and learning about agriculture, agriculture teacher evaluation, evaluation of information dissemination delivery methods, agricultural literacy curriculum model development, distance education delivery methods. *Unit head:* Dr. Robert Terry, Department Head, 405-744-8036, Fax: 405-744-5176, E-mail: rob.terry@okstate.edu.
Website: http://aged.okstate.edu/.

Oregon State University, College of Agricultural Sciences, Program in Agricultural Education, Corvallis, OR 97331. Offers M Ag, MS. Part-time programs available. *Faculty:* 5 full-time (1 woman). *Students:* 8 full-time (6 women), 1 part-time (0 women). Average age 25. 11 applicants, 91% accepted, 7 enrolled. In 2013, 5 master's awarded. *Entrance requirements:* Additional exam requirements/recommendations for international students: Required—TOEFL (minimum score 80 iBT), IELTS (minimum score 6.5). *Application deadline:* For fall admission, 6/1 for domestic students, 4/1 for international students; for winter admission, 9/1 for domestic students, 7/1 for international students; for spring admission, 12/1 for domestic students, 10/1 for international students; for summer admission, 3/1 for domestic students, 1/1 for international students. Application fee: $60. *Expenses:* Tuition, state resident: full-time $11,664; part-time $432 per credit hour. Tuition, nonresident: full-time $19,197; part-time $711 per credit hour. *Required fees:* $1446; $443 per quarter. One-time fee: $300. Tuition and fees vary according to course load and program. *Unit head:* Dr. Greg Thompson, Head, 541-737-1337, Fax: 541-737-3178, E-mail: greg.thompson@oregonstate.edu.
Website: http://oregonstate.edu/ag-ed/programs/agricultural-education.

Penn State University Park, Graduate School, College of Agricultural Sciences, Department of Agricultural Economics, Sociology, and Education, State College, PA 16802. Offers agricultural and extension education (M Ed, MS, PhD, Certificate); agricultural, environmental and regional economics (MS, PhD); applied youth, family and community education (M Ed); community and economic development (MPS); rural sociology (MS, PhD). *Unit head:* Dr. Barbara J. Christ, Interim Dean, 814-865-2541, Fax: 814-865-3103, E-mail: ebf@psu.edu. *Application contact:* Cynthia E. Nicosia, Director of Graduate Enrollment Services, 814-865-1834, Fax: 814-863-4627, E-mail: cey1@psu.edu.
Website: http://aese.psu.edu/.

Purdue University, Graduate School, College of Agriculture, Department of Youth Development and Agricultural Education, West Lafayette, IN 47907. Offers MA, PhD. *Faculty:* 11 full-time (5 women), 1 (woman) part-time/adjunct. *Students:* 9 full-time (7 women), 11 part-time (9 women); includes 2 minority (1 Black or African American, non-Hispanic/Latino; 1 Hispanic/Latino), 5 international. Average age 29. 12 applicants, 42% accepted, 3 enrolled. In 2013, 7 master's, 1 doctorate awarded. *Degree requirements:* For doctorate, comprehensive exam. *Entrance requirements:* For master's and doctorate, GRE General Test (minimum combined score of 1000), minimum undergraduate GPA of 3.0 or equivalent. Additional exam requirements/recommendations for international students: Required—TOEFL (minimum score 550 paper-based; 77 iBT), TWE with minimum score of 5 (recommended for MA, required for PhD). *Application deadline:* For fall admission, 3/15 priority date for domestic students, 3/1 for international students; for spring admission, 10/15 priority date for domestic students, 8/1 for international students; for summer admission, 3/15 for domestic students, 1/1 for international students. Applications are processed on a rolling basis. Application fee: $60 ($75 for international students). Electronic applications accepted. *Unit head:* Roger L. Tormoehlen, Head, 765-494-8422, E-mail: torm@purdue.edu. *Application contact:* Neil A. Knobloch, Chair of the Graduate Committee, 765-494-8439, E-mail: nknobloc@purdue.edu.
Website: https://ag.purdue.edu/ydae.

Purdue University, Graduate School, College of Education, Department of Curriculum and Instruction, West Lafayette, IN 47907. Offers agricultural and extension education (PhD, Ed S); agriculture and extension education (MS, MS Ed); art education (PhD); curriculum studies (MS Ed, PhD, Ed S); educational technology (MS Ed, PhD, Ed S); elementary education (MS Ed); family and consumer sciences education (MS Ed, PhD, Ed S); foreign language education (MS Ed, PhD, Ed S); industrial technology (PhD, Ed S); language arts (MS Ed, PhD, Ed S); literacy (MS Ed, PhD, Ed S); mathematics/science education (MS, MS Ed, PhD, Ed S); social studies (MS Ed, PhD); social studies education (Ed S); vocational/industrial education (MS Ed, PhD, Ed S); vocational/technical education (MS Ed, PhD, Ed S). *Accreditation:* NCATE. Part-time and evening/weekend programs available. *Faculty:* 29 full-time (19 women), 33 part-time/adjunct (29 women). *Students:* 85 full-time (53 women), 271 part-time (195 women); includes 62 minority (19 Black or African American, non-Hispanic/Latino; 3 American Indian or Alaska Native, non-Hispanic/Latino; 13 Asian, non-Hispanic/Latino; 22 Hispanic/Latino;

1 Native Hawaiian or other Pacific Islander, non-Hispanic/Latino; 4 Two or more races, non-Hispanic/Latino), 41 international. Average age 36. 155 applicants, 71% accepted, 71 enrolled. In 2013, 60 master's, 20 doctorates awarded. *Degree requirements:* For master's, thesis optional; for doctorate, thesis/dissertation, oral and written exams; for Ed S, oral presentation, project. *Entrance requirements:* For master's, GRE General Test (if undergraduate GPA is below 3.0), minimum undergraduate GPA of 3.0 or equivalent; for doctorate, GRE General Test (minimum combined verbal and quantitative score of 1000, 300 for new scoring), minimum undergraduate GPA of 3.0 or equivalent; master's degree with minimum GPA of 3.0 or equivalent; for Ed S, GRE General Test (minimum combined verbal and quantitative score of 1000, 300 for new scoring), minimum undergraduate GPA of 3.0 or equivalent; master's degree. Additional exam requirements/recommendations for international students: Required—TOEFL (minimum score 550 paper-based; 77 iBT). *Application deadline:* For fall admission, 12/15 for domestic students, 3/1 for international students; for spring admission, 9/15 for domestic students, 8/1 for international students. Application fee: $60 ($75 for international students). Electronic applications accepted. *Financial support:* Fellowships with full tuition reimbursements, research assistantships with full tuition reimbursements, teaching assistantships with full tuition reimbursements, career-related internships or fieldwork, and tuition waivers (full) available. Support available to part-time students. Financial award application deadline: 3/1; financial award applicants required to submit FAFSA. *Faculty research:* Literacy acquisition and development, teacher beliefs and knowledge, recruitment and retention of underrepresented students, economic education, literacy discourse. *Unit head:* Dr. Phillip J. VanFossen, Head, 765-494-7935, Fax: 765-496-1622, E-mail: vanfoss@purdue.edu. *Application contact:* Cindy Blankenship, Graduate Contact, 765-494-2345, Fax: 765-494-5832, E-mail: prater0@purdue.edu.
Website: http://www.edci.purdue.edu/.

State University of New York at Oswego, Graduate Studies, School of Education, Department of Vocational Teacher Preparation, Oswego, NY 13126. Offers agriculture (MS Ed); business and marketing (MS Ed); family and consumer sciences (MS Ed); health careers (MS Ed); technical education (MS Ed); trade education (MS Ed). *Accreditation:* NCATE. Part-time and evening/weekend programs available. *Degree requirements:* For master's, comprehensive exam, thesis or alternative. *Entrance requirements:* Additional exam requirements/recommendations for international students: Required—TOEFL (minimum score 560 paper-based).

Stephen F. Austin State University, Graduate School, College of Forestry and Agriculture, Department of Agriculture, Nacogdoches, TX 75962. Offers MS. *Accreditation:* NCATE. *Degree requirements:* For master's, comprehensive exam, thesis (for some programs). *Entrance requirements:* For master's, GRE General Test, minimum GPA of 2.8 in last half of major, 2.5 overall. Additional exam requirements/recommendations for international students: Required—TOEFL (minimum score 550 paper-based). *Faculty research:* Asian vegetables, soil fertility, animal breeding, animal nutrition.

Tarleton State University, College of Graduate Studies, College of Agricultural and Environmental Sciences, Department of Agricultural and Consumer Sciences, Stephenville, TX 76402. Offers agriculture education (MS). Part-time and evening/weekend programs available. Postbaccalaureate distance learning degree programs offered (minimal on-campus study). *Faculty:* 6 full-time (3 women), 4 part-time/adjunct (1 woman). *Students:* 28 full-time (17 women), 27 part-time (17 women); includes 4 minority (2 Hispanic/Latino; 2 Two or more races, non-Hispanic/Latino), 1 international. Average age 27. 27 applicants, 81% accepted, 19 enrolled. In 2013, 22 master's awarded. *Degree requirements:* For master's, comprehensive exam. *Entrance requirements:* For master's, GRE General Test, minimum GPA of 3.0. Additional exam requirements/recommendations for international students: Required—TOEFL (minimum score 550 paper-based; 80 iBT). *Application deadline:* For fall admission, 8/5 priority date for domestic students; for spring admission, 12/1 for domestic students. Applications are processed on a rolling basis. Application fee: $30 ($130 for international students). Electronic applications accepted. *Expenses:* Tuition, state resident: full-time $3312; part-time $184 per credit hour. Tuition, nonresident: full-time $9144; part-time $508 per credit hour. *Required fees:* $1916. Tuition and fees vary according to course load and campus/location. *Financial support:* Research assistantships, Federal Work-Study, institutionally sponsored loans, scholarships/grants, and unspecified assistantships available. Financial award application deadline: 5/1; financial award applicants required to submit FAFSA. *Unit head:* Dr. Rudy Tarpley, Head, 254-968-9201, Fax: 254-968-9199, E-mail: tarpley@tarleton.edu. *Application contact:* Information Contact, 254-968-9104, Fax: 254-968-9670, E-mail: gradoffice@tarleton.edu.
Website: http://www.tarleton.edu/COAHSWEB/agservices/.

Tennessee State University, The School of Graduate Studies and Research, College of Agriculture, Human and Natural Sciences, Nashville, TN 37209-1561. Offers agricultural sciences (MS), including agribusiness, agricultural and extension education, animal science, plant and soil science; biological sciences (MS, PhD); biotechnology (PhD); chemistry (MS). Part-time and evening/weekend programs available. *Students:* 112 full-time (65 women), 58 part-time (37 women); includes 80 minority (64 Black or African American, non-Hispanic/Latino; 1 American Indian or Alaska Native, non-Hispanic/Latino; 14 Asian, non-Hispanic/Latino; 1 Hispanic/Latino), 68 international. Average age 30. *Degree requirements:* For master's, thesis. *Entrance requirements:* For master's, GRE General Test, GRE Subject Test, MAT. *Application deadline:* For fall admission, 4/1 priority date for domestic students. Application fee: $25. *Financial support:* Research assistantships, teaching assistantships, Federal Work-Study, and unspecified assistantships available. *Faculty research:* Small farm economics, ornamental horticulture, beef cattle production, rural elderly. *Unit head:* Dr. Chandra Reddy, Dean, 615-963-5438, Fax: 615-963-5888. *Application contact:* Deborah Chisom, Director of Graduate Admissions, 615-963-5962, Fax: 615-963-5963, E-mail: dchiscom@tnstate.edu.
Website: http://www.tnstate.edu/agriculture/.

Texas A&M University, College of Agriculture and Life Sciences, Department of Agricultural Leadership, Education and Communications, College Station, TX 77843. Offers agricultural development (M Agr); agricultural education (Ed D); agricultural leadership, education and communication (M Ed, MS, Ed D, PhD). Part-time programs available. Postbaccalaureate distance learning degree programs offered (no on-campus study). *Faculty:* 23. *Students:* 70 full-time (45 women), 78 part-time (44 women); includes 29 minority (9 Black or African American, non-Hispanic/Latino; 3 Asian, non-Hispanic/Latino; 15 Hispanic/Latino; 2 Two or more races, non-Hispanic/Latino), 4 international. Average age 31. 49 applicants, 92% accepted, 36 enrolled. In 2013, 44 master's, 15 doctorates awarded. Terminal master's awarded for partial completion of doctoral program. *Degree requirements:* For master's, comprehensive exam, thesis (for some programs); for doctorate, comprehensive exam, thesis/dissertation. *Entrance requirements:* For master's, GRE General Test, letters of reference, curriculum vitae; for doctorate, GRE General Test, 3 years of professional experience, letters of reference, curriculum vitae. Additional exam requirements/recommendations for international students: Required—TOEFL. *Application deadline:* For fall admission, 3/15 priority date for domestic students; for spring admission, 10/15 for domestic students. Application fee: $50 ($75 for international students). Electronic applications accepted. *Expenses:* Tuition, state resident: full-time $4078; part-time $226.55 per credit hour. Tuition, nonresident: full-time $10,450; part-time $580.55 per credit hour. *Required fees:* $2328; $278.50 per credit hour. $642.45 per semester. *Financial support:* In 2013–14, fellowships with partial tuition reimbursements (averaging $12,000 per year), research assistantships with partial tuition reimbursements (averaging $12,000 per year), teaching assistantships with partial tuition reimbursements (averaging $12,000 per year) were awarded; career-related internships or fieldwork, institutionally sponsored loans, scholarships/grants, tuition waivers (partial), and unspecified assistantships also available. Financial award application deadline: 3/15; financial award applicants required to submit FAFSA. *Faculty research:* Planning and needs assessment, instructional design, delivery strategies, evaluation and accountability, distance education. *Unit head:* Dr. Jack Elliot, Department Head, 979-862-3003, E-mail: jelliot@tamu.edu. *Application contact:* Clarice Fulton, Graduate Program Coordinator, 979-862-7180, E-mail: cfulton@tamu.edu.
Website: http://alec.tamu.edu/.

Texas A&M University–Commerce, Graduate School, College of Science, Engineering and Agriculture, Department of Agricultural Sciences, Commerce, TX 75429-3011. Offers agricultural education (M Ed, MS); agricultural sciences (M Ed, MS). Part-time programs available. *Degree requirements:* For master's, comprehensive exam, thesis (for some programs). *Entrance requirements:* For master's, GRE General Test. Electronic applications accepted. *Expenses:* Tuition, state resident: full-time $3630; part-time $2420 per year. Tuition, nonresident: full-time $9948; part-time $6632.16 per year. *Required fees:* $1006 per year. Tuition and fees vary according to course load. *Faculty research:* Soil conservation, retention.

Texas State University, Graduate School, College of Applied Arts, Program in Agricultural Education, San Marcos, TX 78666. Offers M Ed. Part-time and evening/weekend programs available. *Faculty:* 4 full-time (0 women). *Students:* 6 full-time (5 women), 11 part-time (5 women); includes 4 minority (all Hispanic/Latino). Average age 32. 11 applicants, 91% accepted, 8 enrolled. In 2013, 4 master's awarded. *Degree requirements:* For master's, comprehensive exam, thesis (for some programs). *Entrance requirements:* For master's, GRE (verbal and quantitative with minimum score of 950), minimum GPA of 2.5 in last 60 hours of course work, 3 letters of reference (2 from academia). Additional exam requirements/recommendations for international students: Required—TOEFL (minimum score 550 paper-based; 78 iBT). *Application deadline:* For fall admission, 6/15 priority date for domestic students, 6/1 for international students; for spring admission, 10/15 priority date for domestic students, 10/1 for international students. Applications are processed on a rolling basis. Application fee: $40 ($90 for international students). Electronic applications accepted. *Expenses:* Tuition, state resident: full-time $6663; part-time $278 per credit hour. Tuition, nonresident: full-time $15,159; part-time $632 per credit hour. *Required fees:* $1872; $54 per credit hour. $306 per term. Tuition and fees vary according to course load. *Financial support:* In 2013–14, 12 students received support, including 3 research assistantships (averaging $12,333 per year); teaching assistantships, career-related internships or fieldwork, Federal Work-Study, and institutionally sponsored loans also available. Support available to part-time students. Financial award application deadline: 4/1; financial award applicants required to submit FAFSA. *Faculty research:* Food safety and agroterrorism. *Total annual research expenditures:* $800,000. *Unit head:* Dr. Douglas Morrish, Graduate Advisor, 512-245-2130, Fax: 512-245-3320, E-mail: dm43@txstate.edu. *Application contact:* Dr. Douglas Morrish, Graduate Adviser, 512-245-2130, Fax: 512-245-3320, E-mail: dm43@txstate.edu.
Website: http://ag.txstate.edu/.

Texas Tech University, Graduate School, College of Agricultural Sciences and Natural Resources, Department of Agricultural Education and Communications, Lubbock, TX 79404-2131. Offers agricultural communications (MS); agricultural communications and education (PhD); agricultural education (MS, Ed D). Part-time and evening/weekend programs available. Postbaccalaureate distance learning degree programs offered (minimal on-campus study). *Faculty:* 11 full-time (3 women). *Students:* 34 full-time (28 women), 33 part-time (24 women); includes 9 minority (1 Black or African American, non-Hispanic/Latino; 7 Hispanic/Latino; 1 Two or more races, non-Hispanic/Latino), 6 international. Average age 28. 42 applicants, 67% accepted, 20 enrolled. In 2013, 16 master's, 8 doctorates awarded. Terminal master's awarded for partial completion of doctoral program. *Degree requirements:* For master's, variable foreign language requirement, comprehensive exam, thesis optional; for doctorate, variable foreign language requirement, comprehensive exam, thesis/dissertation, experience plan. *Entrance requirements:* For master's and doctorate, GRE. Additional exam requirements/recommendations for international students: Required—TOEFL (minimum score 550 paper-based; 79 iBT). *Application deadline:* For fall admission, 6/1 priority date for domestic students, 1/15 priority date for international students; for spring admission, 9/1 priority date for domestic students, 6/15 priority date for international students. Applications are processed on a rolling basis. Application fee: $60. Electronic applications accepted. *Expenses:* Tuition, state resident: full-time $6062; part-time $252.57 per credit hour. Tuition, nonresident: full-time $14,558; part-time $606.57 per credit hour. *Required fees:* $2655; $35 per credit hour. $907.50 per semester. Tuition and fees vary according to course load. *Financial support:* In 2013–14, 42 students received support, including 30 fellowships (averaging $2,634 per year), 23 research assistantships (averaging $4,007 per year), 1 teaching assistantship (averaging $5,066 per year); scholarships/grants also available. Financial award application deadline: 4/15; financial award applicants required to submit FAFSA. *Faculty research:* Sustainable agriculture, food safety, international development, use of technology in agriculture, improvement of teaching and pedagogy. *Total annual research expenditures:* $481,177. *Unit head:* Dr. Steve Dee Fraze, Department Chair/Professor, 806-742-2816, Fax: 806-742-2880, E-mail: steven.fraze@ttu.edu. *Application contact:* Dr. David L. Doerfert, Professor and Graduate Coordinator, 806-834-4477, Fax: 806-742-2880, E-mail: david.doerfert@ttu.edu.
Website: http://www.depts.ttu.edu/aged/.

The University of Arizona, College of Agriculture and Life Sciences, Department of Agricultural Education, Tucson, AZ 85721. Offers M Ag Ed, MS. *Faculty:* 2 full-time (0 women), 1 part-time/adjunct (0 women). *Students:* 8 full-time (5 women), 6 part-time (3 women); includes 4 minority (2 Hispanic/Latino; 2 Two or more races, non-Hispanic/Latino). Average age 32. 6 applicants, 83% accepted, 4 enrolled. In 2013, 5 master's awarded. *Degree requirements:* For master's, thesis. *Entrance requirements:* For master's, teaching/extension experience or equivalent, minimum GPA of 3.0, 2 letters of recommendation. Additional exam requirements/recommendations for international students: Required—TOEFL (minimum score 550 paper-based; 79 iBT). *Application deadline:* For fall admission, 6/1 for domestic students, 2/1 for international students. Applications are processed on a rolling basis. Application fee: $75. Electronic applications accepted. *Expenses:* Tuition, state resident: full-time $11,526. Tuition, nonresident: full-time $27,398. *Financial support:* In 2013–14, 5 students received support, including 1 teaching assistantship with full and partial tuition reimbursement available (averaging $19,776 per year); fellowships, research assistantships, career-related internships or fieldwork, scholarships/grants, health care benefits, tuition waivers (full), and unspecified assistantships also available. *Faculty research:* Career placement, learning styles, noise impact on learning, computer technology, vocational education. *Total annual research expenditures:* $1.6 million. *Unit head:* Dr. Robert

Torres, Head, 520-621-1523, Fax: 520-621-9889, E-mail: rtorres@cals.arizona.edu. *Application contact:* Roberta Pearson, Graduate Coordinator, 520-621-2239, Fax: 520-621-8662.
Website: http://ag.arizona.edu/aed/.

University of Arkansas, Graduate School, Dale Bumpers College of Agricultural, Food and Life Sciences, Department of Agricultural and Extension Education, Fayetteville, AR 72701-1201. Offers agricultural and extension education (MS). *Accreditation:* NCATE. Electronic applications accepted.

University of Connecticut, Graduate School, Neag School of Education, Department of Curriculum and Instruction, Storrs, CT 06269. Offers agriculture (MA), including agriculture education; agriculture education (PhD, Post-Master's Certificate); bilingual and bicultural education (MA, PhD, Post-Master's Certificate); elementary education (MA, PhD, Post-Master's Certificate); English education (MA, PhD, Post-Master's Certificate); history and social sciences education (MA, PhD, Post-Master's Certificate); mathematics education (MA, PhD, Post-Master's Certificate); reading education (MA, PhD, Post-Master's Certificate); science education (MA, PhD); secondary education (MA, PhD, Post-Master's Certificate); world languages education (MA, PhD, Post-Master's Certificate). *Accreditation:* NCATE. Terminal master's awarded for partial completion of doctoral program. *Degree requirements:* For master's, comprehensive exam, thesis or alternative; for doctorate, thesis/dissertation. *Entrance requirements:* For doctorate, GRE General Test. Additional exam requirements/recommendations for international students: Required—TOEFL (minimum score 550 paper-based). Electronic applications accepted.

University of Delaware, College of Agriculture and Natural Resources, Department of Food and Resource Economics, Agricultural Education Program, Newark, DE 19716. Offers MA.

University of Florida, Graduate School, College of Agricultural and Life Sciences, Department of Agricultural Education and Communication, Gainesville, FL 32611. Offers MS, PhD. Part-time and evening/weekend programs available. Postbaccalaureate distance learning degree programs offered. *Faculty:* 14 full-time (5 women), 5 part-time/adjunct (2 women). *Students:* 38 full-time (23 women), 35 part-time (25 women); includes 14 minority (9 Black or African American, non-Hispanic/Latino; 1 American Indian or Alaska Native, non-Hispanic/Latino; 4 Hispanic/Latino), 3 international. Average age 32. 20 applicants, 70% accepted, 9 enrolled. In 2013, 25 master's, 6 doctorates awarded. *Degree requirements:* For master's, comprehensive exam (for some programs), thesis (for some programs); for doctorate, comprehensive exam, thesis/dissertation. *Entrance requirements:* For master's, GRE General Test, minimum GPA of 3.0; for doctorate, GRE General Test, minimum GPA of 3.0. Additional exam requirements/recommendations for international students: Required—TOEFL (minimum score 550 paper-based; 80 iBT), IELTS (minimum score 6). *Application deadline:* For fall admission, 2/1 priority date for domestic students, 2/1 for international students; for spring admission, 9/1 for domestic and international students. Applications are processed on a rolling basis. Application fee: $30. Electronic applications accepted. *Expenses:* Tuition, state resident: full-time $12,640. Tuition, nonresident: full-time $30,000. *Financial support:* In 2013–14, 34 students received support, including 5 fellowships (averaging $16,245 per year), 8 research assistantships (averaging $18,765 per year), 33 teaching assistantships (averaging $15,985 per year); unspecified assistantships also available. Financial award application deadline: 1/1; financial award applicants required to submit FAFSA. *Faculty research:* Cooperative extension service, including home economics, agriculture, 4-H, foods, housing, and nutrition. *Unit head:* Edward W. Osborne, PhD, Professor and Department Chair, 352-273-2613, Fax: 352-392-9585, E-mail: ewo@ufl.edu. *Application contact:* Grady Roberts, PhD, Interim Graduate Coordinator, 352-273-2568 Ext. 236, Fax: 251-392-9585, E-mail: groberts@ufl.edu.
Website: http://aec.ifas.ufl.edu/.

University of Georgia, College of Agricultural and Environmental Sciences, Department of Agricultural Leadership, Education, and Communication, Athens, GA 30602. Offers MA Ext, MAL. *Degree requirements:* For master's, comprehensive exam, thesis optional. *Entrance requirements:* For master's, GRE General Test. Electronic applications accepted.

University of Idaho, College of Graduate Studies, College of Agricultural and Life Sciences, Department of Agricultural Education and 4-H Youth Development, Moscow, ID 83844-2040. Offers agricultural education (MS). *Accreditation:* NCATE. *Faculty:* 7 full-time. *Students:* 3 full-time, 4 part-time. Average age 29. In 2013, 9 master's awarded. *Entrance requirements:* For master's, minimum GPA of 2.8. Additional exam requirements/recommendations for international students: Required—TOEFL (minimum score 550 paper-based). *Application deadline:* For fall admission, 8/1 for domestic students; for spring admission, 12/15 for domestic students. Applications are processed on a rolling basis. Application fee: $60. Electronic applications accepted. *Expenses:* Tuition, state resident: full-time $5596; part-time $363 per credit hour. Tuition, nonresident: full-time $18,672; part-time $1089 per credit hour. *Financial support:* Applicants required to submit FAFSA. *Unit head:* Dr. James Joseph Connors, Department Head, 208-885-6358, Fax: 208-885-4039. *Application contact:* Erick Larson, Director of Graduate Admissions, 208-885-4723, E-mail: gadms@uidaho.edu.
Website: http://www.uidaho.edu/cals/ae4hyd.

University of Illinois at Urbana–Champaign, Graduate College, College of Agricultural, Consumer and Environmental Sciences, Agricultural Education Program, Champaign, IL 61820. Offers MS. Part-time programs available. Postbaccalaureate distance learning degree programs offered (no on-campus study). *Students:* 17 (12 women). Application fee: $75 ($90 for international students). *Unit head:* Richard W. Clark, Associate Professor, 217-244-6909, Fax: 217-244-2911, E-mail: clark6@illinois.edu. *Application contact:* Andrea L. Ray, Office Manager, 217-333-3165, E-mail: aray@illinois.edu.
Website: http://aged.illinois.edu/.

University of Minnesota, Twin Cities Campus, Graduate School, College of Education and Human Development, Department of Organizational Leadership, Policy and Development, Program in Agricultural, Food and Environmental Education, Minneapolis, MN 55455-0213. Offers M Ed, MA, Ed D, PhD. *Students:* 5 full-time (3 women), 7 part-time (4 women). Average age 34. 9 applicants, 89% accepted, 8 enrolled. In 2013, 10 master's awarded. Application fee: $75 ($95 for international students). *Unit head:* Dr. Rebecca Ropers-Huilman, Chair, 612-624-1006, Fax: 612-624-3377, E-mail: ropers@umn.edu. *Application contact:* Dr. Jennifer Engler, Assistant Dean, 612-626-2887, Fax: 612-626-7496, E-mail: engle009@umn.edu.
Website: http://www.cehd.umn.edu/WHRE//AFEE.

University of Missouri, Graduate School, College of Agriculture, Food and Natural Resources, Department of Agricultural Education, Columbia, MO 65211. Offers MS, PhD. *Faculty:* 3 full-time (1 woman). *Students:* 16 full-time (10 women), 15 part-time (12 women). Average age 28. 15 applicants, 73% accepted, 8 enrolled. In 2013, 5 master's, 2 doctorates awarded. *Degree requirements:* For doctorate, comprehensive exam, thesis/dissertation. *Entrance requirements:* For master's, minimum GPA of 3.0 for last 60 hours of undergraduate coursework; for doctorate, GRE (preferred minimum score of 1000), minimum GPA of 3.5 on prior graduate course work; minimum of 3 years of full-time appropriate teaching or other professional experience; correspondence with one department faculty member in proposed area of concentration. Additional exam requirements/recommendations for international students: Required—TOEFL (minimum score 550 paper-based; 80 iBT). *Application deadline:* For fall admission, 7/15 for domestic students. Applications are processed on a rolling basis. Application fee: $55 ($75 for international students). Electronic applications accepted. *Financial support:* Fellowships, research assistantships with tuition reimbursements, teaching assistantships with tuition reimbursements, Federal Work-Study, scholarships/grants, health care benefits, and unspecified assistantships available. *Faculty research:* Program and professional development, evaluation, teaching and learning theories and practices, educational methods, organization and administration, leadership and communication. *Unit head:* Dr. Anna Ball, Department Chair, 573-882-7451, E-mail: ballan@missouri.edu. *Application contact:* Dr. Tracy Kitchel, Director of Graduate Studies, 573-882-7451, E-mail: kitcheltj@missouri.edu.
Website: http://dass.missouri.edu/aged/grad/.

University of Missouri, Graduate School, College of Education, Department of Learning, Teaching and Curriculum, Columbia, MO 65211. Offers agricultural education (M Ed, PhD, Ed S); art education (M Ed, PhD, Ed S); business and office education (M Ed, PhD, Ed S); early childhood education (M Ed, PhD, Ed S); elementary education (M Ed, PhD, Ed S); English education (M Ed, PhD, Ed S); foreign language education (M Ed, PhD, Ed S); health education and promotion (M Ed, PhD); learning and instruction (M Ed); marketing education (M Ed, PhD, Ed S); mathematics education (M Ed, PhD, Ed S); music education (M Ed, PhD, Ed S); reading education (M Ed, PhD, Ed S); science education (M Ed, PhD, Ed S); social studies education (M Ed, PhD, Ed S); vocational education (M Ed, PhD, Ed S). Part-time programs available. *Faculty:* 26 full-time (16 women), 3 part-time/adjunct (2 women). *Students:* 186 full-time (143 women), 197 part-time (172 women); includes 19 minority (4 Black or African American, non-Hispanic/Latino; 4 Asian, non-Hispanic/Latino; 6 Hispanic/Latino; 5 Two or more races, non-Hispanic/Latino), 25 international. Average age 31. 288 applicants, 65% accepted, 160 enrolled. In 2013, 202 master's, 18 doctorates, 7 other advanced degrees awarded. Terminal master's awarded for partial completion of doctoral program. *Degree requirements:* For doctorate, thesis/dissertation. *Entrance requirements:* For master's and Ed S, GRE General Test or MAT, minimum GPA of 3.0; for doctorate, GRE General Test, minimum GPA of 3.0. Additional exam requirements/recommendations for international students: Required—TOEFL (minimum score 600 paper-based; 100 iBT). *Application deadline:* For fall admission, 12/1 priority date for domestic and international students. Applications are processed on a rolling basis. Application fee: $55 ($75 for international students). Electronic applications accepted. *Financial support:* Fellowships, research assistantships, teaching assistantships, institutionally sponsored loans, traineeships, health care benefits, and unspecified assistantships available. Support available to part-time students. *Faculty research:* Curriculum development and research, teacher education, art education, business and marketing, early childhood education, English education, literacy/reading education, mathematics education, music education, science education, social studies education. *Unit head:* Dr. James Tarr, Associate Division Director, 573-882-4034, E-mail: tarrj@missouri.edu. *Application contact:* Fran Colley, Academic Advisor, 573-882-6462, E-mail: colleyf@missouri.edu.
Website: http://education.missouri.edu/LTC/.

University of Nebraska–Lincoln, Graduate College, College of Agricultural Sciences and Natural Resources, Department of Agricultural Leadership, Education and Communication, Lincoln, NE 68588. Offers leadership development (MS); leadership education (MS); teaching and extension education (MS). *Accreditation:* Teacher Education Accreditation Council. *Degree requirements:* For master's, thesis optional. *Entrance requirements:* For master's, resume. Additional exam requirements/recommendations for international students: Required—TOEFL (minimum score 550 paper-based). Electronic applications accepted. *Faculty research:* Teaching and instruction, extension education, leadership and human resource development, international agricultural education.

University of Puerto Rico, Mayagüez Campus, Graduate Studies, College of Agricultural Sciences, Department of Agricultural Education, Mayagüez, PR 00681-9000. Offers agricultural education (MS); agricultural extension (MS). Part-time programs available. *Faculty:* 3 full-time (1 woman). *Students:* 11 full-time (5 women), 6 part-time (5 women). 6 applicants, 67% accepted, 3 enrolled. In 2013, 1 master's awarded. *Degree requirements:* For master's, comprehensive exam, thesis. *Entrance requirements:* For master's, BA in home economics; BS in agricultural education, agriculture, home economics, or equivalent. *Application deadline:* For fall admission, 2/15 for domestic and international students; for spring admission, 9/15 for domestic and international students. Applications are processed on a rolling basis. Application fee: $25. *Expenses: Tuition, area resident:* Full-time $2466; part-time $822 per year. *International tuition:* $6371 full-time. *Required fees:* $1095; $1095. Tuition and fees vary according to course level, course load and reciprocity agreements. *Financial support:* In 2013–14, 4 students received support, including 4 teaching assistantships with tuition reimbursements available (averaging $5,422 per year); fellowships with full tuition reimbursements available and unspecified assistantships also available. *Faculty research:* Curricular development and supervision, youth education, rural sociology. *Unit head:* Dr. David Padilla, Director, 787-832-4040 Ext. 3855, Fax: 787-265-3814, E-mail: david.padilla@upr.edu. *Application contact:* Nydia Sanchez, Secretary, 787-832-4040 Ext. 3120, Fax: 787-265-3814, E-mail: nsanchez@uprm.edu.
Website: http://www.uprm.edu/agricultura/edag.

The University of Tennessee, Graduate School, College of Agricultural Sciences and Natural Resources, Department of Agricultural Economics, Knoxville, TN 37996. Offers agricultural education (MS); agricultural extension education (MS). *Accreditation:* NCATE. Part-time programs available. Postbaccalaureate distance learning degree programs offered (minimal on-campus study). *Degree requirements:* For master's, thesis or alternative. *Entrance requirements:* For master's, minimum GPA of 2.7. Additional exam requirements/recommendations for international students: Required—TOEFL. Electronic applications accepted. *Expenses:* Tuition, state resident: full-time $9540; part-time $531 per credit hour. Tuition, nonresident: full-time $27,728; part-time $1542 per credit hour. *Required fees:* $1404; $67 per credit hour.

University of Wisconsin–River Falls, Outreach and Graduate Studies, College of Agriculture, Food, and Environmental Sciences, Department of Agricultural Education, River Falls, WI 54022. Offers MS. Part-time programs available. *Degree requirements:* For master's, comprehensive exam, thesis (for some programs). *Entrance requirements:* For master's, minimum GPA of 2.75. Additional exam requirements/recommendations for international students: Required—TOEFL (minimum score 500 paper-based; 65 iBT), IELTS (minimum score 5.5). Electronic applications accepted.

Utah State University, School of Graduate Studies, College of Agriculture, Department of Agricultural Systems Technology and Education, Logan, UT 84322. Offers agricultural systems technology (MS), including agricultural extension education, agricultural mechanization, international agricultural extension, secondary and postsecondary agricultural education; family and consumer sciences education (MS). Part-time programs available. Postbaccalaureate distance learning degree programs offered (minimal on-campus study). *Degree requirements:* For master's, comprehensive exam (for some programs), thesis (for some programs). *Entrance requirements:* For master's,

Agricultural Education

GRE General Test, MAT, BS in agricultural education, agricultural extension, or related agricultural or science discipline; minimum GPA of 3.0. Additional exam requirements/ recommendations for international students: Required—TOEFL. *Faculty research:* Extension and adult education; structures and environment; low-input agriculture; farm safety, systems, and mechanizations.

West Virginia University, Davis College of Agriculture, Forestry and Consumer Sciences, Division of Resource Management and Sustainable Development, Program in Agricultural and Extension Education, Morgantown, WV 26506. Offers agricultural and extension education (MS, PhD); teaching vocational-agriculture (MS). *Accreditation:* NCATE. Part-time programs available. *Degree requirements:* For master's, thesis. *Entrance requirements:* For master's, GRE General Test, minimum GPA of 2.75. Additional exam requirements/recommendations for international students: Required— TOEFL. *Faculty research:* Program development in vocational agriculture, agricultural extension, supervised experience programs, leadership development.

Art Education

Academy of Art University, Graduate Program, School of Art Education, San Francisco, CA 94105-3410. Offers MA. Part-time programs available. Postbaccalaureate distance learning degree programs offered (no on-campus study). *Faculty:* 15 part-time/adjunct (14 women). *Students:* 30 full-time (28 women), 17 part-time (12 women); includes 7 minority (2 Black or African American, non-Hispanic/Latino; 1 Asian, non-Hispanic/Latino; 4 Hispanic/Latino), 23 international. Average age 32. 25 applicants, 100% accepted, 12 enrolled. In 2013, 6 master's awarded. *Degree requirements:* For master's, final review. *Entrance requirements:* For master's, statement of intent; resume; portfolio/reel; official college transcripts. *Application deadline:* Applications are processed on a rolling basis. Application fee: $100. Electronic applications accepted. *Expenses: Tuition:* Part-time $885 per unit. *Financial support:* Career-related internships or fieldwork and Federal Work-Study available. Support available to part-time students. Financial award application deadline: 8/10; financial award applicants required to submit FAFSA. *Unit head:* 800-544-ARTS, E-mail: info@ academyart.edu. *Application contact:* 800-544-ARTS, Fax: 415-263-4130, E-mail: info@ academyart.edu.
Website: http://www.academyart.edu/art-education-school/index.html.

Adelphi University, Ruth S. Ammon School of Education, Program in Art Education, Garden City, NY 11530-0701. Offers MA. Part-time programs available. *Students:* 7 full-time (6 women), 6 part-time (5 women); includes 3 minority (1 Black or African American, non-Hispanic/Latino; 1 Asian, non-Hispanic/Latino; 1 Hispanic/Latino), 2 international. Average age 29. In 2013, 6 master's awarded. *Entrance requirements:* For master's, 2 letters of recommendation, visual arts portfolio, essay. Additional exam requirements/recommendations for international students: Required—TOEFL (minimum score 550 paper-based; 80 iBT). *Application deadline:* For fall admission, 4/1 for international students; for spring admission, 11/1 for international students. Application fee: $50. Electronic applications accepted. *Expenses: Tuition:* Full-time $32,530; part-time $1010 per credit. *Required fees:* $1150. Tuition and fees vary according to degree level and program. *Financial support:* Career-related internships or fieldwork, Federal Work-Study, institutionally sponsored loans, tuition waivers, and unspecified assistantships available. Support available to part-time students. Financial award application deadline: 2/15; financial award applicants required to submit FAFSA. *Unit head:* Courtney Lee Weida, Director, 516-877-4105, E-mail: cweida@adelphi.edu. *Application contact:* Christine Murphy, Director of Admissions, 516-877-3050, Fax: 516-877-3039, E-mail: graduateadmissions@adelphi.edu.

American University of Puerto Rico, Program in Education, Bayamón, PR 00960-2037. Offers art education (M Ed); elementary education 4-6 (M Ed); elementary education K-3 (M Ed); general science education (M Ed); physical education (M Ed); special education (M Ed). *Faculty:* 17 part-time/adjunct (7 women). *Students:* 55 full-time (42 women), 105 part-time (96 women); all minorities (all Hispanic/Latino). Average age 33. 120 applicants, 99% accepted, 81 enrolled. In 2013, 52 master's awarded. *Entrance requirements:* For master's, EXADEP, GRE, or MAT, 2 letters of recommendation, minimum GPA of 2.5. *Application deadline:* For fall admission, 8/1 for domestic students; for winter admission, 10/18 for domestic students; for spring admission, 3/15 for domestic students. Applications are processed on a rolling basis. Application fee: $25. *Expenses: Tuition:* Part-time $240 per credit. Tuition and fees vary according to course load. *Unit head:* Dr. Jose A. Ramirez-Figueroa, Education and Technology Department Director/Chancellor, 787-620-2040 Ext. 2010, Fax: 787-620-2958, E-mail: jramirez@aupr.edu. *Application contact:* Keren I. Llanos-Figueroa, Information Contact, 787-620-2040 Ext. 2021, Fax: 787-785-7377, E-mail: oficnaadmisiones@aupr.edu.

Anna Maria College, Graduate Division, Program in Visual Arts, Paxton, MA 01612. Offers art and visual art (MA); teacher of visual art (M Ed). Part-time and evening/ weekend programs available. *Degree requirements:* For master's, thesis. *Entrance requirements:* For master's, minimum GPA of 2.7, undergraduate major in art, portfolio. Additional exam requirements/recommendations for international students: Required— TOEFL (minimum score 500 paper-based). Electronic applications accepted.

Arcadia University, Graduate Studies, School of Education, Glenside, PA 19038-3295. Offers art education (M Ed); computer education (CAS); curriculum (CAS); curriculum studies (M Ed); early childhood education (M Ed, CAS), including individualized (M Ed); master teacher (M Ed), research in child development (M Ed); educational leadership (M Ed, Ed D, CAS); elementary education (M Ed, CAS); English education (MA Ed); environmental education (MA Ed, CAS); history education (MA Ed); instructional technology (M Ed); language arts (M Ed, CAS); library science (M Ed); mathematics education (M Ed, MA Ed, CAS); music education (MA Ed); psychology (MA Ed); reading (M Ed, CAS); science education (M Ed, CAS); secondary education (M Ed, CAS); special education (M Ed, Ed D, CAS); theater arts (MA Ed); written communication (MA Ed). *Accreditation:* NASAD. Part-time and evening/weekend programs available. Postbaccalaureate distance learning degree programs offered (minimal on-campus study). Electronic applications accepted. *Expenses:* Contact institution.

Arizona State University at the Tempe campus, Herberger Institute for Design and the Arts, School of Art, Tempe, AZ 85287-1505. Offers art (art education) (MA); art (art history) (MA); art (ceramics) (MFA); art (digital technology) (MFA); art (drawing) (MFA); art (fibers) (MFA); art (intermedia) (MFA); art (metals) (MFA); art (painting) (MFA); art (printmaking) (MFA); art (sculpture) (MFA); art (wood) (MFA); design, environment and the arts (history, theory and criticism) (PhD). Terminal master's awarded for partial completion of doctoral program. *Degree requirements:* For master's, thesis/exhibition (MFA, MA in art education); interactive Program of Study (iPOS) submitted before completing 50 percent of required credit hours; for doctorate, comprehensive exam, thesis/dissertation, interactive Program of Study (iPOS) submitted before completing 50 percent of required credit hours. *Entrance requirements:* For master's, GRE or MAT, minimum GPA of 3.0 or equivalent in last 2 years of work leading to bachelor's degree; for doctorate, GRE, master's degree in architecture, graphic design, industrial design, interior design, landscape architecture, or art history or equivalent standing; statement of purpose; 3 letters of recommendation; indication of potential faculty mentor; sample of written work. Additional exam requirements/recommendations for international students: Required—TOEFL, IELTS, or PTE. Electronic applications accepted.

Art Academy of Cincinnati, Program in Art Education, Cincinnati, OH 45202. Offers MAAE. Offered during summer only. *Accreditation:* NASAD. Part-time programs available. *Degree requirements:* For master's, thesis, portfolio/exhibit. *Entrance requirements:* For master's, 2 letters of recommendation, portfolio, state teaching license. Additional exam requirements/recommendations for international students: Required—TOEFL (minimum score 550 paper-based; 80 iBT). Electronic applications accepted.

Auburn University at Montgomery, School of Education, Department of Foundations, Technology, and Secondary Education, Montgomery, AL 36124-4023. Offers instructional technology (M Ed); secondary education (M Ed, Ed S), including art education (M Ed), biology (M Ed), English language arts (M Ed), general science (M Ed), history (M Ed), mathematics (M Ed), social science (M Ed). *Accreditation:* NCATE. Part-time and evening/weekend programs available. *Faculty:* 6 full-time (2 women), 1 (woman) part-time/adjunct. *Students:* 47 full-time (22 women), 77 part-time (48 women); includes 30 minority (29 Black or African American, non-Hispanic/Latino; 1 Asian, non-Hispanic/Latino), 1 international. Average age 30. In 2013, 86 master's awarded. *Degree requirements:* For master's and Ed S, comprehensive exam, thesis optional. *Entrance requirements:* For master's, GRE General Test or MAT, certification, BS in teaching; for Ed S, GRE General Test or MAT, certification. *Application deadline:* Applications are processed on a rolling basis. Electronic applications accepted. *Expenses:* Tuition, state resident: full-time $5994; part-time $333 per credit hour. Tuition, nonresident: full-time $17,982; part-time $999 per credit hour. *Financial support:* Teaching assistantships, career-related internships or fieldwork, and scholarships/ grants available. Support available to part-time students. Financial award application deadline: 3/1; financial award applicants required to submit FAFSA. *Unit head:* Dr. Sheila Austin, Dean, 334-244-3425, Fax: 334-244-3102, E-mail: saustin1@aum.edu. *Application contact:* Dr. Rhonda Morton, Associate Dean/Graduate Coordinator, 334-244-3287, Fax: 334-244-3978, E-mail: rmorton@aum.edu.
Website: http://www.education.aum.edu/departments/foundations-technology-and-secondary-education.

Averett University, Master in Education Program, Danville, VA 24541-3692. Offers administration and supervision (M Ed); art (M Ed); biology (M Ed); chemistry (M Ed); curriculum and instruction (M Ed); early childhood (M Ed); English (M Ed); mathematics (M Ed); middle grades (M Ed); physical science (M Ed); reading specialist (M Ed); science (M Ed); special education (M Ed); special education learning disability (M Ed). Program offered on Danville Campus only. Part-time and evening/weekend programs available. *Faculty:* 4 full-time (3 women), 13 part-time/adjunct (8 women). *Students:* 43 full-time (35 women), 44 part-time (35 women); includes 7 minority (all Black or African American, non-Hispanic/Latino). *Degree requirements:* For master's, 30-credit core curriculum, minimum GPA of 3.0 throughout program, completion of degree requirements within six years from start of program. *Entrance requirements:* For master's, PRAXIS I, GRE, or MAT; writing proficiency test, minimum cumulative GPA of 3.0 over the last 60 hours of undergraduate study toward a baccalaureate degree, three letters of recommendation, Virginia teaching license (or eligibility). Additional exam requirements/recommendations for international students: Required—TOEFL (minimum score 600 paper-based; 100 iBT). *Application deadline:* Applications are processed on a rolling basis. Application fee: $100. *Expenses:* Contact institution. *Financial support:* Career-related internships or fieldwork, Federal Work-Study, and scholarships/grants available. Financial award application deadline: 4/1; financial award applicants required to submit FAFSA. *Unit head:* Wilfred Lawrence, Department Chair of Education, 434-791-5752, E-mail: priedel@averett.edu. *Application contact:* Christy Pack, Executive Director of Enrollment, 804-887-8612, E-mail: dpack@averett.edu.
Website: http://www.averett.edu/adultprograms/degrees/MEDtrad.php.

Boise State University, College of Arts and Sciences, Department of Art, Boise, ID 83725-0399. Offers art education (MA); visual arts (MFA). *Degree requirements:* For master's, thesis optional. *Entrance requirements:* For master's, minimum GPA of 3.0, portfolio. Electronic applications accepted.

Boston University, College of Fine Arts, School of Visual Arts, Boston, MA 02215. Offers art education (MA); graphic design (MFA); painting (MFA); sculpture (MFA); studio teaching (MA). *Faculty:* 17 full-time, 4 part-time/adjunct. *Students:* 205 full-time (170 women), 19 part-time (16 women); includes 24 minority (5 Black or African American, non-Hispanic/Latino; 5 Asian, non-Hispanic/Latino; 9 Hispanic/Latino; 5 Two or more races, non-Hispanic/Latino), 34 international. Average age 33. 257 applicants, 27% accepted, 21 enrolled. In 2013, 15 master's awarded. *Entrance requirements:* For master's, portfolio. Additional exam requirements/recommendations for international students: Required—TOEFL, IELTS. *Application deadline:* For fall admission, 2/2 for domestic and international students. Applications are processed on a rolling basis. Application fee: $80. *Expenses: Tuition:* Full-time $43,970; part-time $1374 per credit hour. *Required fees:* $60 per semester. Tuition and fees vary according to class time, course level and program. *Financial support:* Fellowships and teaching assistantships available. Financial award application deadline: 2/15. *Unit head:* Lynne Allen, Director, 617-353-3371. *Application contact:* Mark Krone, Manager, Graduate Admissions, 617-353-3350, E-mail: arts@bu.edu.

Bowling Green State University, Graduate College, College of Arts and Sciences, School of Art, Bowling Green, OH 43403. Offers 2-D studio art (MA, MFA); 3-D studio art (MA, MFA); art education (MA); art history (MA); computer art (MA); design (MFA); digital arts (MFA); graphics (MFA). *Accreditation:* NASAD. Part-time programs available. *Degree requirements:* For master's, thesis or alternative, final exhibit (MFA). *Entrance requirements:* For master's, GRE General Test (MA), slide portfolio (15-20 slides). Additional exam requirements/recommendations for international students: Required— TOEFL. Electronic applications accepted. *Faculty research:* Computer animation and virtual reality, Spanish still-life painting from 1600 to 1800, art and psychotherapy, Japanese wood-firing techniques in ceramics, non-toxic printmaking technologies.

Bridgewater State University, School of Graduate Studies, School of Arts and Sciences, Department of Art, Bridgewater, MA 02325-0001. Offers MAT. Part-time and evening/weekend programs available. *Degree requirements:* For master's, comprehensive exam. *Entrance requirements:* For master's, GRE General Test.

Brigham Young University, Graduate Studies, College of Fine Arts and Communications, Department of Visual Arts, Provo, UT 84602-6414. Offers art education (MA); art history (MA); studio art (MFA). Art education applications accepted biennially. *Accreditation:* NASAD. *Faculty:* 16 full-time (4 women), 1 (woman) part-time/ adjunct. *Students:* 29 full-time (21 women). Average age 26. 21 applicants, 33% accepted, 6 enrolled. In 2013, 20 master's awarded. *Degree requirements:* For master's, one foreign language, comprehensive exam, thesis (art history), selected project (MFA), curriculum project (art education). *Entrance requirements:* For master's, GRE (art history and art education), minimum GPA of 3.0 (MFA, MA in art education), 3.5 (MA in art history), portfolio in CD format (MFA), writing samples (MA in art education, art history). Additional exam requirements/recommendations for international students: Required—TOEFL (minimum score 580 paper-based; 85 iBT). *Application deadline:* For fall admission, 2/1 for domestic and international students. Application fee: $50. Electronic applications accepted. *Expenses: Tuition:* Full-time $6130; part-time $340 per credit hour. Tuition and fees vary according to program and student's religious affiliation. *Financial support:* In 2013–14, 28 students received support. Research assistantships, teaching assistantships with partial tuition reimbursements available, scholarships/ grants, and tuition waivers (partial) available. Financial award application deadline: 2/1. *Faculty research:* Methodology-standards-assessment, medieval architecture, classical/ Islamic eighteenth and nineteenth century art, Netherlandish art, contemporary art, modern art, history of photography, exploration of art making processes, new genre. *Unit head:* Prof. Linda A. Reynolds, Chair, 801-422-4429, Fax: 801-422-0695, E-mail: lindareynolds@byu.edu. *Application contact:* Sharon Lyn Heelis, Secretary, 801-422-4429, Fax: 801-422-0695, E-mail: sharon_heelis@byu.edu.
Website: http://visualarts.byu.edu.

Brooklyn College of the City University of New York, Division of Graduate Studies, School of Education, Program in Adolescence Education and Special Subjects, Brooklyn, NY 11210-2889. Offers adolescence science education (MAT); art teacher (MA); biology teacher (MA); chemistry teacher (MA); earth science teacher (MAT); English teacher (MA); French teacher (MA); health and nutrition sciences: health teacher (MS Ed); mathematics teacher (MA); music education (CAS); music teacher (MA); physical education teacher (MS Ed); physics teacher (MA); social studies teacher (MA); Spanish teacher (MA). Part-time and evening/weekend programs available. *Degree requirements:* For master's, comprehensive exam (for some programs), thesis (for some programs). *Entrance requirements:* For master's, LAST, previous course work in education, resume, 2 letters of recommendation, essay. Additional exam requirements/recommendations for international students: Required—TOEFL (minimum score 500 paper-based; 61 iBT). Electronic applications accepted. *Faculty research:* Interdisciplinary education, semiotics, discourse analysis, autobiography, teacher identity.

Buffalo State College, State University of New York, The Graduate School, Faculty of Arts and Humanities, Department of Art Education, Buffalo, NY 14222-1095. Offers MS Ed. *Accreditation:* NASAD; NCATE. Part-time and evening/weekend programs available. *Degree requirements:* For master's, thesis or alternative, project. *Entrance requirements:* For master's, New York teaching certificate, interview, minimum GPA of 3.0. Additional exam requirements/recommendations for international students: Required—TOEFL (minimum score 550 paper-based).

California State University, Long Beach, Graduate Studies, College of the Arts, Department of Art, Long Beach, CA 90840. Offers art education (MA); art history (MA); studio art (MA, MFA). *Accreditation:* NASAD. Part-time programs available. *Degree requirements:* For master's, thesis (for some programs). *Entrance requirements:* For master's, minimum GPA of 3.0 in last 60 hours. Electronic applications accepted.

California State University, Los Angeles, Graduate Studies, College of Arts and Letters, Department of Art, Los Angeles, CA 90032-8530. Offers art (MA), including art education, art history, art therapy, ceramics, metals, and textiles, design (MA, MFA), painting, sculpture, and graphic arts, photography; fine arts (MFA), including crafts, design (MA, MFA), studio arts. *Accreditation:* NASAD (one or more programs are accredited). Part-time and evening/weekend programs available. *Faculty:* 8 full-time (3 women), 3 part-time/adjunct (1 woman). *Students:* 27 full-time (21 women), 22 part-time (16 women); includes 26 minority (6 Black or African American, non-Hispanic/Latino; 4 Asian, non-Hispanic/Latino; 16 Hispanic/Latino), 4 international. Average age 37. 62 applicants, 26% accepted, 11 enrolled. In 2013, 29 master's awarded. *Degree requirements:* For master's, comprehensive exam, project or thesis. *Entrance requirements:* For master's, portfolio. Additional exam requirements/recommendations for international students: Required—TOEFL (minimum score 500 paper-based). *Application deadline:* For fall admission, 5/1 for domestic and international students. Applications are processed on a rolling basis. Application fee: $55. Electronic applications accepted. *Financial support:* Federal Work-Study available. Support available to part-time students. Financial award application deadline: 3/1. *Faculty research:* The artist and the book, conceptual art, ceramic processes, computer graphics, architectural graphics. *Unit head:* Dr. Abbas Daneshvari, Chair, 323-343-4010, Fax: 323-343-4045, E-mail: adanesh@calstatela.edu. *Application contact:* Dr. Larry Fritz, Dean of Graduate Studies, 323-343-3820, Fax: 323-343-5653, E-mail: lfritz@calstatela.edu.
Website: http://www.calstatela.edu/academic/art/.

California State University, Northridge, Graduate Studies, College of Arts, Media, and Communication, Department of Art, Northridge, CA 91330. Offers art education (MA); art history (MA); studio art (MA, MFA); visual communications (MA, MFA). *Accreditation:* NASAD.

Carlow University, School of Education, Program in Art Education, Pittsburgh, PA 15213-3165. Offers M Ed. Part-time and evening/weekend programs available. *Students:* 3 full-time (1 woman), 1 (woman) part-time; includes 1 minority (Hispanic/Latino). Average age 31. 2 applicants, 100% accepted, 1 enrolled. In 2013, 7 master's awarded. *Degree requirements:* For master's, thesis or alternative. *Entrance requirements:* Additional exam requirements/recommendations for international students: Required—TOEFL (minimum score 550 paper-based). *Application deadline:* For fall admission, 6/15 priority date for domestic and international students; for spring admission, 11/15 priority date for domestic and international students. Applications are processed on a rolling basis. Application fee: $20. Electronic applications accepted. Application fee is waived when completed online. *Expenses: Tuition:* Full-time $9523; part-time $744 per credit. Tuition and fees vary according to course load, degree level and program. *Financial support:* Application deadline: 4/1; applicants required to submit FAFSA. *Unit head:* Dr. Marilyn Llewellyn, Dean, 412-578-6011, Fax: 412-578-0816, E-mail: llewellynmj@carlow.edu. *Application contact:* Jo Danhires, Administrative Assistant, Admissions, 412-578-6059, Fax: 412-578-6321, E-mail: gradstudies@carlow.edu.
Website: http://www.carlow.edu/.

Carlow University, School of Education, Program in Education, Pittsburgh, PA 15213-3165. Offers art education (M Ed); early childhood education (M Ed); secondary education (M Ed); special education (M Ed). Part-time and evening/weekend programs available. *Students:* 42 full-time (37 women), 36 part-time (34 women); includes 9 minority (6 Black or African American, non-Hispanic/Latino; 1 Asian, non-Hispanic/Latino; 2 Two or more races, non-Hispanic/Latino). Average age 31. 27 applicants, 100% accepted, 19 enrolled. In 2013, 17 master's awarded. *Entrance requirements:* For master's, resume, 3 letters of recommendation, minimum GPA of 3.0, interview. Additional exam requirements/recommendations for international students: Required—TOEFL. *Application deadline:* For fall admission, 6/15 priority date for domestic and international students; for spring admission, 11/15 priority date for domestic and international students. Applications are processed on a rolling basis. Application fee: $20. Electronic applications accepted. Application fee is waived when completed online. *Expenses: Tuition:* Full-time $9523; part-time $744 per credit. Tuition and fees vary according to course load, degree level and program. *Financial support:* Applicants required to submit FAFSA. *Unit head:* Dr. Marilyn Llewellyn, Dean, 412-578-6011, Fax: 412-578-0816, E-mail: llewellynmj@carlow.edu. *Application contact:* Jo Danhires, Administrative Assistant, Admissions, 412-578-6089, Fax: 412-578-6321, E-mail: gradstudies@carlow.edu.
Website: http://www.carlow.edu.

Carthage College, Division of Teacher Education, Kenosha, WI 53140. Offers classroom guidance and counseling (M Ed); creative arts (M Ed); gifted and talented children (M Ed); language arts (M Ed); modern language (M Ed); natural sciences (M Ed); reading (M Ed, Certificate); social sciences (M Ed); teacher leadership (M Ed). Part-time and evening/weekend programs available. *Degree requirements:* For master's, thesis optional. *Entrance requirements:* For master's, MAT, minimum B average, letters of reference.

Case Western Reserve University, School of Graduate Studies, Department of Art History and Art, Program in Art Education, Cleveland, OH 44106. Offers MA. Program offered jointly with The Cleveland Institute of Art. *Accreditation:* Teacher Education Accreditation Council. Part-time programs available. *Faculty:* 10 part-time/adjunct (6 women). *Students:* 6 full-time (5 women), 2 part-time (1 woman), 1 international. Average age 29. 10 applicants, 40% accepted, 4 enrolled. In 2013, 3 master's awarded. *Degree requirements:* For master's, thesis, art exhibit. *Entrance requirements:* For master's, NTE, interview, portfolio. Additional exam requirements/recommendations for international students: Required—TOEFL (minimum score 577 paper-based; 90 iBT); Recommended—IELTS (minimum score 7). *Application deadline:* For fall admission, 3/1 for domestic students; for spring admission, 11/1 for domestic students. Applications are processed on a rolling basis. Application fee: $50. Electronic applications accepted. *Faculty research:* Visual and aesthetic education, ethnographic arts, multiculturalism. *Unit head:* Tim Shuckerow, Director, 216-368-2714, Fax: 216-368-2715, E-mail: txs10@po.cwru.edu. *Application contact:* Debby Tenenbaum, Assistant, 216-368-4118, Fax: 216-368-4681, E-mail: deborah.tenenbaum@case.edu.
Website: http://www.case.edu/artsci/artedu/.

Central Connecticut State University, School of Graduate Studies, School of Arts and Sciences, Department of Art, New Britain, CT 06050-4010. Offers art education (MS, Certificate). Part-time and evening/weekend programs available. *Faculty:* 3 full-time (1 woman). *Students:* 12 full-time (11 women), 10 part-time (8 women). Average age 32. 15 applicants, 80% accepted, 7 enrolled. In 2013, 2 master's, 4 other advanced degrees awarded. *Degree requirements:* For master's, thesis or alternative, exhibit or special project; for Certificate, qualifying exam. *Entrance requirements:* For master's, portfolio, essay. Additional exam requirements/recommendations for international students: Required—TOEFL (minimum score 550 paper-based; 79 iBT). *Application deadline:* For fall admission, 6/1 for domestic students, 5/1 for international students; for spring admission, 11/1 for domestic and international students. Applications are processed on a rolling basis. Application fee: $50. Electronic applications accepted. Part-time tuition and fees vary according to degree level. *Financial support:* In 2013–14, 3 research assistantships were awarded; career-related internships or fieldwork, Federal Work-Study, scholarships/grants, and unspecified assistantships also available. Support available to part-time students. Financial award application deadline: 3/1; financial award applicants required to submit FAFSA. *Faculty research:* Visual arts. *Unit head:* Prof. Rachel Siporin, Chair, 860-832-2620, E-mail: siporinr@ccsu.edu. *Application contact:* Patricia Gardner, Associate Director of Graduate Studies, 860-832-2350, Fax: 860-832-2362, E-mail: graduateadmissions@ccsu.edu.
Website: http://www.art.ccsu.edu/.

Chatham University, Program in Education, Pittsburgh, PA 15232-2826. Offers early childhood education (MAT); elementary education (MAT); environmental education (K-12) (MAT); secondary art (MAT); secondary biology education (MAT); secondary chemistry education (MAT); secondary English education (MAT); secondary math education (MAT); secondary physics education (MAT); secondary social studies education (MAT); special education (MAT). *Faculty:* 1 (woman) full-time, 5 part-time/ adjunct (4 women). *Students:* 19 full-time (15 women), 4 part-time (all women); includes 2 minority (1 Black or African American, non-Hispanic/Latino; 1 Asian, non-Hispanic/Latino), 2 international. Average age 28. 22 applicants, 73% accepted, 6 enrolled. In 2013, 20 master's awarded. *Degree requirements:* For master's, thesis, teaching experience. *Entrance requirements:* For master's, minimum GPA of 3.0, sample of written work, recommendation letters. Additional exam requirements/recommendations for international students: Required—TOEFL (minimum score 600 paper-based; 100 iBT), IELTS (minimum score 7), TWE. *Application deadline:* For fall admission, 4/1 priority date for domestic and international students; for spring admission, 11/1 priority date for domestic students, 10/1 priority date for international students. Applications are processed on a rolling basis. Application fee: $45. Electronic applications accepted. Application fee is waived when completed online. *Expenses: Tuition:* Full-time $14,886; part-time $827 per credit hour. One-time fee: $396 full-time. *Financial support:* Career-related internships or fieldwork available. Financial award applicants required to submit FAFSA. *Faculty research:* Gifted education, environmental education, technology in education, writing as learning, class size and achievement. *Unit head:* Dr. Edward Donovan, Director of Education Programs, 412-365-2773, E-mail: edonovan@chatham.edu. *Application contact:* Katie Noel, Assistant Director of Graduate Admission, 412-365-2758, Fax: 412-365-1609, E-mail: gradadmissions@chatham.edu.
Website: http://www.chatham.edu/mat.

Christopher Newport University, Graduate Studies, Department of Teacher Preparation, Newport News, VA 23606-3072. Offers art (PK-12) (MAT); biology (6-12) (MAT); chemistry (6-12) (MAT); computer science (6-12) (MAT); elementary (PK-6) (MAT); English (6-12) (MAT); English as second language (PK-12) (MAT); French (PK-12) (MAT); history and social science (6-12) (MAT); mathematics (6-12) (MAT); music (PK-12) (MAT), including choral, instrumental; physics (6-12) (MAT); Spanish (PK-12) (MAT). Part-time programs available. *Faculty:* 15 full-time (7 women), 14 part-time/ adjunct (13 women). *Students:* 74 full-time (64 women), 2 part-time (both women); includes 6 minority (4 Hispanic/Latino; 2 Two or more races, non-Hispanic/Latino). Average age 23. 90 applicants, 100% accepted, 67 enrolled. In 2013, 96 master's awarded. *Degree requirements:* For master's, comprehensive exam, thesis or alternative. *Entrance requirements:* For master's, PRAXIS I, minimum GPA of 3.0.

Additional exam requirements/recommendations for international students: Required—TOEFL (minimum score 580 paper-based; 92 iBT). *Application deadline:* For fall admission, 4/1 for international students; for spring admission, 10/15 for domestic students, 10/1 for international students; for summer admission, 1/15 for domestic students, 3/1 for international students. Applications are processed on a rolling basis. Application fee: $50. Electronic applications accepted. *Expenses: Tuition, area resident:* Part-time $498 per credit hour. Tuition, state resident: part-time $498 per credit hour. Tuition, nonresident: part-time $899 per credit hour. *Financial support:* In 2013–14, 3 students received support, including 3 research assistantships with full tuition reimbursements available (averaging $2,000 per year); career-related internships or fieldwork, Federal Work-Study, and unspecified assistantships also available. Financial award application deadline: 3/1; financial award applicants required to submit FAFSA. *Faculty research:* Early literacy development, instructional innovations, professional teaching standards, multicultural issues, aesthetic education. *Total annual research expenditures:* $24,000. *Unit head:* Dr. Marsha Sprague, Director, 757-594-7388, Fax: 757-594-7803, E-mail: msprague@cnu.edu. *Application contact:* Lyn Sawyer, Associate Director, Graduate Admissions, 757-594-7544, Fax: 757-594-7649, E-mail: gradstdy@cnu.edu.

Cleveland State University, College of Graduate Studies, College of Education and Human Services, Department of Teacher Education, Cleveland, OH 44115. Offers art education (M Ed); early childhood education (M Ed); foreign language education (M Ed); mathematics and science education (M Ed); middle childhood education (M Ed); special education (M Ed), including mild/moderate disabilities, moderate/intensive disabilities; teaching English to speakers of other languages (M Ed). Part-time and evening/weekend programs available. *Faculty:* 20 full-time (12 women), 26 part-time/adjunct (20 women). *Students:* 108 full-time (78 women), 311 part-time (252 women); includes 103 minority (80 Black or African American, non-Hispanic/Latino; 2 Asian, non-Hispanic/Latino; 10 Hispanic/Latino; 1 Native Hawaiian or other Pacific Islander, non-Hispanic/Latino; 10 Two or more races, non-Hispanic/Latino), 52 international. Average age 32. 177 applicants, 55% accepted, 68 enrolled. In 2013, 192 master's awarded. *Degree requirements:* For master's, comprehensive exam (for some programs), thesis or alternative. *Entrance requirements:* For master's, GRE General Test or MAT, minimum GPA of 2.75. Additional exam requirements/recommendations for international students: Required—TOEFL (minimum score 525 paper-based), IELTS (minimum score 6). *Application deadline:* For fall admission, 7/15 priority date for domestic students. Applications are processed on a rolling basis. Application fee: $30. *Expenses:* Tuition, state resident: full-time $8335; part-time $521 per credit hour. Tuition, nonresident: full-time $15,670; part-time $979 per credit hour. *Required fees:* $50; $25 per semester. *Financial support:* In 2013–14, 12 research assistantships with full tuition reimbursements (averaging $3,480 per year) were awarded; tuition waivers (partial) and unspecified assistantships also available. *Faculty research:* Early literacy, professional development in reading, reading recovery, dual language, induction programs. *Total annual research expenditures:* $6.2 million. *Unit head:* Dr. Clifford T. Bennett, Chairperson, 216-523-7105, Fax: 216-687-5379, E-mail: c.t.bennett@csuohio.edu. *Application contact:* Deborah L. Brown, Interim Assistant Director, Graduate Admissions, 216-523-7572, E-mail: d.l.brown@csuohio.edu.
Website: http://www.csuohio.edu/cehs/departments/TE/te_dept.html.

Cleveland State University, College of Graduate Studies, College of Liberal Arts and Social Sciences, Department of Art, Cleveland, OH 44115. Offers art education (M Ed); art history (MA). *Faculty:* 3 full-time (2 women). *Students:* 1 (woman) full-time, 1 (woman) part-time. Average age 37. 6 applicants, 83% accepted. *Expenses:* Tuition, state resident: full-time $8335; part-time $521 per credit hour. Tuition, nonresident: full-time $15,670; part-time $979 per credit hour. *Required fees:* $50; $25 per semester. *Unit head:* Jennifer Visocky-O-Grady, Chair/Associate Professor, 216-523-7546, E-mail: j.visoky@csuohio.edu. *Application contact:* Jan Milic, Administrative Coordinator, 216-687-2065, Fax: 216-687-5400, E-mail: j.milic@csuohio.edu.
Website: https://www.csuohio.edu/class/art/art.

The College of New Rochelle, Graduate School, Division of Art and Communication Studies, Program in Art Education, New Rochelle, NY 10805-2308. Offers MA. Part-time and evening/weekend programs available. *Degree requirements:* For master's, thesis. *Entrance requirements:* For master's, interview, minimum GPA of 3.0 in field, 2.7 overall, portfolio, 36 credits of course work in studio art. *Expenses: Tuition:* Part-time $894 per credit. *Required fees:* $300 per semester. One-time fee: $200. Tuition and fees vary according to course load. *Faculty research:* Developmental stages in art, assessment and evaluation, curriculum development, multicultural education, art museum education.

The College of Saint Rose, Graduate Studies, School of Arts and Humanities, Center for Art and Design, Albany, NY 12203-1419. Offers art education (MS Ed, Certificate). *Accreditation:* NASAD; NCATE. Part-time and evening/weekend programs available. *Degree requirements:* For master's, final project. *Entrance requirements:* For master's, minimum undergraduate GPA of 3.0, art portfolio, undergraduate art degree; for Certificate, minimum undergraduate GPA of 3.0, slide portfolio. Additional exam requirements/recommendations for international students: Required—TOEFL (minimum score 550 paper-based). Electronic applications accepted.

The Colorado College, Education Department, Program in Secondary Education, Colorado Springs, CO 80903-3294. Offers art teaching (K-12) (MAT); English teaching (MAT); foreign language teaching (MAT); mathematics teaching (MAT); music teaching (MAT); science teaching (MAT); social studies teaching (MAT). *Degree requirements:* For master's, thesis, internship. Electronic applications accepted.

Colorado State University–Pueblo, College of Education, Engineering and Professional Studies, Education Program, Pueblo, CO 81001-4901. Offers art education (M Ed); foreign language education (M Ed); health and physical education (M Ed); instructional technology (M Ed); linguistically diverse education (M Ed); music education (M Ed); special education (M Ed). *Accreditation:* Teacher Education Accreditation Council. Part-time programs available. *Degree requirements:* For master's, portfolio. *Entrance requirements:* For master's, 3 recommendations, teaching license. Additional exam requirements/recommendations for international students: Required—TOEFL (minimum score 500 paper-based). Electronic applications accepted. *Faculty research:* Portfolio assessment, math education, science education.

Columbus State University, Graduate Studies, College of the Arts, Department of Art, Columbus, GA 31907-5645. Offers M Ed, MAT. *Accreditation:* NASAD; NCATE. Part-time and evening/weekend programs available. *Faculty:* 2 full-time (0 women). *Students:* 3 full-time (2 women), 7 part-time (6 women); includes 4 minority (3 Black or African American, non-Hispanic/Latino; 1 Two or more races, non-Hispanic/Latino). Average age 40. 2 applicants, 100% accepted, 1 enrolled. In 2013, 5 master's awarded. *Degree requirements:* For master's, exhibit. *Entrance requirements:* For master's, portfolio, interview. Additional exam requirements/recommendations for international students: Required—TOEFL (minimum score 550 paper-based; 79 iBT). *Application deadline:* For fall admission, 6/30 for domestic students, 5/1 for international students; for spring admission, 11/1 for domestic and international students; for summer admission, 3/1 for domestic and international students. Applications are processed on a rolling basis. Application fee: $40. Electronic applications accepted. *Expenses:* Tuition, state resident: full-time $4572; part-time $382 per credit hour. Tuition, nonresident: full-time $18,292; part-time $1526 per credit hour. *Required fees:* $1800; $196 per credit hour. Tuition and fees vary according to campus/location and program. *Financial support:* In 2013–14, 7 students received support, including 1 research assistantship; career-related internships or fieldwork, Federal Work-Study, institutionally sponsored loans, scholarships/grants, tuition waivers (partial), and unspecified assistantships also available. Support available to part-time students. Financial award application deadline: 5/1; financial award applicants required to submit FAFSA. *Unit head:* Prof. Joe Sanders, Acting Chair, 706-507-8302, E-mail: sanders_joe@columbusstate.edu. *Application contact:* Kristin Williams, Director of International and Graduate Recruitment, 706-507-8848, Fax: 706-568-5091, E-mail: williams_kristin@columbusstate.edu.
Website: http://art.columbusstate.edu/.

Concordia University, School of Graduate Studies, Faculty of Fine Arts, Department of Art Education, Montréal, QC H3G 1M8, Canada. Offers art education (MA, PhD), including art in education (MA). *Degree requirements:* For master's, thesis (for some programs), practicum; for doctorate, comprehensive exam, thesis/dissertation. *Entrance requirements:* For master's, teaching experience; for doctorate, teaching or related professional experience. *Faculty research:* Vernacular culture, museum education, psychotic art, adults and families.

Concordia University Wisconsin, Graduate Programs, Department of Education, Mequon, WI 53097-2402. Offers art education (MS Ed); curriculum and instruction (MS Ed); early childhood (MS Ed); educational administration (MS Ed); environmental education (MS Ed); family studies (MS Ed); reading (MS Ed); school counseling (MS Ed); special education (MS Ed). Part-time and evening/weekend programs available. Postbaccalaureate distance learning degree programs offered (minimal on-campus study). *Degree requirements:* For master's, comprehensive exam, thesis or alternative. *Entrance requirements:* For master's, minimum GPA of 3.0, teaching license. Additional exam requirements/recommendations for international students: Required—TOEFL. *Faculty research:* Motivation, developmental learning, learning styles.

Converse College, School of Education and Graduate Studies, Program in Art Education, Spartanburg, SC 29302-0006. Offers M Ed, MAT.

Delaware State University, Graduate Programs, College of Education, Health and Public Policy, Program in Art Education, Dover, DE 19901-2277. Offers MA. *Entrance requirements:* Additional exam requirements/recommendations for international students: Required—TOEFL (minimum score 550 paper-based). Electronic applications accepted.

East Carolina University, Graduate School, College of Fine Arts and Communication, School of Art and Design, Greenville, NC 27858-4353. Offers art education (MA Ed); ceramics (MFA); graphic design (MFA); illustration (MFA); metal design (MFA); painting and drawing (MFA); photography (MFA); printmaking (MFA); sculpture (MFA); textile design (MFA); wood design (MFA). *Accreditation:* NASAD (one or more programs are accredited). Part-time and evening/weekend programs available. *Degree requirements:* For master's, comprehensive exam, thesis (for some programs). *Entrance requirements:* For master's, GRE General Test or MAT, portfolio. Additional exam requirements/recommendations for international students: Required—TOEFL. *Expenses:* Tuition, state resident: full-time $4223. Tuition, nonresident: full-time $16,540. *Required fees:* $2184.

Eastern Illinois University, Graduate School, College of Arts and Humanities, Department of Art, Charleston, IL 61920-3099. Offers art (MA); art education (MA); community arts (MA). *Accreditation:* NASAD. Part-time and evening/weekend programs available. Postbaccalaureate distance learning degree programs offered (minimal on-campus study). In 2013, 7 master's awarded. *Degree requirements:* For master's, thesis or alternative, portfolio. *Application deadline:* For fall admission, 3/31 priority date for domestic students. Applications are processed on a rolling basis. Application fee: $30. *Expenses: Tuition, area resident:* Part-time $283 per credit hour. Tuition, state resident: part-time $283 per credit hour. Tuition, nonresident: part-time $679 per credit hour. *Financial support:* In 2013–14, research assistantships with tuition reimbursements (averaging $7,650 per year), 6 teaching assistantships with tuition reimbursements (averaging $7,650 per year) were awarded. *Unit head:* David Griffin, Chairperson, 217-581-3410. *Application contact:* Chris Kahler, Coordinator, 217-581-6259, E-mail: cbkahler@eiu.edu.

Eastern Kentucky University, The Graduate School, College of Education, Department of Curriculum and Instruction, Program in Secondary and Higher Education, Richmond, KY 40475-3102. Offers secondary education (MA Ed), including agricultural education, art education, biological sciences education, business education, English education, geography education, history education, home economics education, industrial education, mathematical sciences education, physical education, school health education. *Accreditation:* NCATE. Part-time programs available. *Entrance requirements:* For master's, GRE General Test, minimum GPA of 2.5.

Eastern Michigan University, Graduate School, College of Arts and Sciences, Department of Art, Program in Art Education, Ypsilanti, MI 48197. Offers MA. Part-time and evening/weekend programs available. Postbaccalaureate distance learning degree programs offered (minimal on-campus study). *Students:* 3 part-time (1 woman). Average age 40. 1 applicant, 100% accepted. *Entrance requirements:* Additional exam requirements/recommendations for international students: Required—TOEFL. *Application deadline:* Applications are processed on a rolling basis. *Expenses:* Tuition, state resident: full-time $12,300; part-time $466 per credit hour. Tuition, nonresident: full-time $23,159; part-time $918 per credit hour. *Required fees:* $71 per credit hour. $46 per semester. One-time fee: $100. Tuition and fees vary according to course level and degree level. *Financial support:* Fellowships with tuition reimbursements, research assistantships with full tuition reimbursements, teaching assistantships with full tuition reimbursements, career-related internships or fieldwork, Federal Work-Study, institutionally sponsored loans, scholarships/grants, and unspecified assistantships available. Support available to part-time students. Financial award applicants required to submit FAFSA. *Unit head:* Dr. Colin Blakely, Department Head, 734-487-1268, Fax: 734-487-2324, E-mail: cblakely@emich.edu. *Application contact:* Michael Reedy, Graduate Coordinator, 734-487-1268, Fax: 734-487-2324, E-mail: mreedy@emich.edu.

Endicott College, Van Loan School of Graduate and Professional Studies, Program in Arts and Learning, Beverly, MA 01915-2096. Offers M Ed. Part-time and evening/weekend programs available. Postbaccalaureate distance learning degree programs offered (minimal on-campus study). *Students:* 9 part-time (8 women). Average age 49. 11 applicants, 64% accepted. In 2013, 11 master's awarded. *Degree requirements:* For master's, portfolio, written integrative paper, major presentation. *Entrance requirements:* For master's, MAT or GRE, documentation of artistic involvement/skill, two letters of recommendation. Additional exam requirements/recommendations for international students: Required—TOEFL. *Application deadline:* Applications are processed on a rolling basis. Application fee: $50. Electronic applications accepted. *Expenses:* Contact institution. *Financial support:* Available to part-time students. Applicants required to submit FAFSA. *Faculty research:* Linkage of creative processes to effective teaching and learning. *Unit head:* Dr. Enid E. Larsen, Assistant Dean of Academic Programs, 978-232-2198, Fax: 978-232-3000, E-mail: elarsen@endicott.edu. *Application contact:* Dr. Mary Huegel, Vice President and Dean of the School of Graduate and Professional Studies, 978-232-2084, Fax: 978-232-3000, E-mail: mhuegel@endicott.edu.

Fitchburg State University, Division of Graduate and Continuing Education, Program in Arts Education, Fitchburg, MA 01420-2697. Offers arts education (M Ed); fine arts director (Certificate). *Accreditation:* NCATE. Part-time and evening/weekend programs available. *Entrance requirements:* Additional exam requirements/recommendations for international students: Required—TOEFL (minimum score 550 paper-based; 79 iBT). Electronic applications accepted.

Florida Atlantic University, College of Education, Department of Teaching and Learning, Boca Raton, FL 33431-0991. Offers curriculum and instruction (M Ed), including art, biology, chemistry, English, French, German, mathematics, music, physics, Pre-K and primary education, reading, social sciences, Spanish; elementary education (M Ed); environmental education (M Ed); reading education (M Ed); social foundations of education (M Ed), including educational psychology, educational technology, multilingual education. *Accreditation:* NCATE. Part-time and evening/weekend programs available. *Faculty:* 16 full-time (12 women), 1 (woman) part-time/adjunct. *Students:* 56 full-time (46 women), 96 part-time (78 women); includes 39 minority (10 Black or African American, non-Hispanic/Latino; 6 Asian, non-Hispanic/Latino; 20 Hispanic/Latino; 3 Two or more races, non-Hispanic/Latino), 4 international. Average age 32. 101 applicants, 54% accepted, 42 enrolled. In 2013, 64 master's awarded. *Entrance requirements:* For master's, GRE General Test, minimum GPA of 3.0 in last 2 years of undergraduate course work. Additional exam requirements/recommendations for international students: Required—TOEFL (minimum score 500 paper-based; 61 iBT), IELTS (minimum score 6). *Application deadline:* For fall admission, 7/1 for domestic students, 2/15 for international students; for spring admission, 11/1 for domestic students, 7/15 for international students. Applications are processed on a rolling basis. Application fee: $30. *Expenses:* Tuition, state resident: full-time $6660; part-time $370 per credit hour. Tuition, nonresident: full-time $18,450; part-time $1025 per credit hour. Tuition and fees vary according to course load. *Financial support:* Fellowships with partial tuition reimbursements, research assistantships with partial tuition reimbursements, teaching assistantships with partial tuition reimbursements, career-related internships or fieldwork, scholarships/grants, and unspecified assistantships available. *Faculty research:* Technology, teaching English to speakers of other languages, math teaching, electronic portfolio assessment, global perspectives through social studies. *Unit head:* Dr. Barbara Ridener, Chairperson, 561-297-3588. *Application contact:* Dr. Eliah Watlington, Associate Dean, 561-296-8520, Fax: 261-297-2991, E-mail: ewatling@fau.edu.
Website: http://www.coe.fau.edu/academicdepartments/tl/.

Florida International University, College of Education, Department of Teaching and Learning, Miami, FL 33199. Offers art education (MA, MS); curriculum and instruction (MS, Ed D, PhD, Ed S), including curriculum development (MS), elementary education (MS), English education (MS), learning technologies (MS), mathematics education (MS), modern language education (MS), physical education (MS), science education (MS), social studies education (MS), special education (MS); early childhood education (MS); exceptional student education (Ed D); foreign language education (MS), including foreign language education, teaching English to speakers of other languages (TESOL); international/intercultural education (MS); language, literacy and culture (PhD); mathematics, science, and learning technologies (PhD); physical education (MS), including sport and fitness; reading education (MS). Part-time and evening/weekend programs available. *Degree requirements:* For doctorate, comprehensive exam, thesis/dissertation. *Entrance requirements:* For master's, GRE General Test, Florida General Knowledge Test or Florida College Level Academic Skills Test; for doctorate and Ed S, GRE General Test. Additional exam requirements/recommendations for international students: Required—TOEFL (minimum score 550 paper-based; 80 iBT), IELTS (minimum score 6.3). Electronic applications accepted.

Florida State University, The Graduate School, College of Visual Arts, Theatre and Dance, Department of Art Education, Tallahassee, FL 32306. Offers MA, MS, Ed D, PhD, Ed S. *Accreditation:* NASAD (one or more programs are accredited). Part-time programs available. *Faculty:* 8 full-time (4 women). *Students:* 66 full-time (60 women), 14 part-time (10 women); includes 27 minority (6 Black or African American, non-Hispanic/Latino; 14 Asian, non-Hispanic/Latino; 7 Hispanic/Latino). Average age 33. 105 applicants, 50% accepted, 31 enrolled. In 2013, 21 master's, 3 doctorates awarded. *Degree requirements:* For master's, thesis (for some programs); for doctorate, thesis/dissertation. *Entrance requirements:* For master's, GRE, minimum GPA of 3.0 in last 2 years; for doctorate, GRE. Additional exam requirements/recommendations for international students: Required—TOEFL (minimum score 550 paper-based; 80 iBT). *Application deadline:* For fall admission, 1/15 priority date for domestic and international students; for spring admission, 10/15 priority date for domestic and international students. Applications are processed on a rolling basis. Application fee: $30. Electronic applications accepted. *Expenses:* Tuition, state resident: part-time $403.51 per credit hour. Tuition, nonresident: part-time $1004.85 per credit hour. *Required fees:* $75.81 per credit hour. One-time fee: $20 part-time. Tuition and fees vary according to course load, campus/location and student level. *Financial support:* In 2013–14, 27 students received support, including 20 research assistantships with full tuition reimbursements available (averaging $3,800 per year), 7 teaching assistantships with full tuition reimbursements available (averaging $8,500 per year); fellowships, career-related internships or fieldwork, Federal Work-Study, and scholarships/grants also available. Financial award applicants required to submit FAFSA. *Faculty research:* Teaching and learning in art, museum education, art therapy, arts administration, discipline-based art education. *Total annual research expenditures:* $110,000. *Unit head:* Dr. David E. Gussak, Chairman, 850-665-5663, Fax: 850-644-5067, E-mail: dgussak@fsu.edu. *Application contact:* Susan Messersmith, Academic Support Assistant, 850-644-5473, Fax: 850-644-6067, E-mail: smessersmith@fsu.edu.
Website: http://www.fsu.edu/~are/.

George Mason University, College of Visual and Performing Arts, Program in Art Education, Fairfax, VA 22030. Offers MAT. *Faculty:* 3 full-time (all women), 1 (woman) part-time/adjunct. *Students:* 2 full-time (both women), 31 part-time (27 women); includes 5 minority (1 American Indian or Alaska Native, non-Hispanic/Latino; 2 Asian, non-Hispanic/Latino; 1 Hispanic/Latino; 1 Two or more races, non-Hispanic/Latino). Average age 30. 21 applicants, 62% accepted, 10 enrolled. In 2013, 8 master's awarded. *Entrance requirements:* For master's, PRAXIS I or SAT equivalent, college transcript, expanded goals statement, 3 letters of recommendation, resume, portfolio, BFA or approved equivalent. Additional exam requirements/recommendations for international students: Required—TOEFL (minimum score 570 paper-based; 88 iBT), PTE. *Application deadline:* For fall admission, 4/1 for domestic students; for spring admission, 11/1 for domestic students. Application fee: $65 ($80 for international students). *Expenses:* Tuition, state resident: full-time $9350; part-time $390 per credit. Tuition, nonresident: full-time $25,754; part-time $1073 per credit. *Required fees:* $2688; $112 per credit. *Financial support:* Application deadline: 3/1; applicants required to submit FAFSA. *Unit head:* Renee Sandell, Professor, School of Art, 703-993-8564, Fax: 703-993-8798, E-mail: rsandell@gmu.edu. *Application contact:* Victoria N. Salmon, Graduate Studies Associate Dean, 703-993-4541, Fax: 703-993-9037, E-mail: vsalmon@gmu.edu.
Website: http://arteducation.gmu.edu/.

The George Washington University, Columbian College of Arts and Sciences, Corcoran College of Art and Design, Washington, DC 20007. Offers art and the book (MA); art education (MA, MAT); exhibition design (MA); interior design (MA); new media photojournalism (MA). *Accreditation:* NASAD. Part-time programs available. *Entrance requirements:* Additional exam requirements/recommendations for international students: Required—TOEFL (minimum score 95 iBT).

Georgia State University, College of Arts and Sciences, Ernest G. Welch School of Art and Design, Program in Art Education, Atlanta, GA 30302-3083. Offers MA Ed. *Accreditation:* NASAD. Part-time programs available. *Students:* Average age 0. *Degree requirements:* For master's, thesis. *Entrance requirements:* For master's, GRE. Additional exam requirements/recommendations for international students: Required—TOEFL. *Application deadline:* For fall admission, 4/15 for domestic and international students; for spring admission, 9/15 for domestic and international students. Application fee: $50. Electronic applications accepted. *Expenses: Tuition, area resident:* Full-time $4176; part-time $348 per credit hour. Tuition, state resident: full-time $14,544; part-time $1212 per credit hour. Tuition, nonresident: full-time $14,544; part-time $1212 per credit hour. Tuition and fees vary according to course load and program. *Financial support:* Tuition waivers (full) and unspecified assistantships available. Financial award application deadline: 4/15. *Faculty research:* Critical theories, museum education, instructional technology, multi-culture and interdisciplinary art education, Chinese art history. *Unit head:* Michael White, Director, Welch School of Art and Design, 404-413-5221, Fax: 404-413-5261, E-mail: mwhite@gsu.edu. *Application contact:* Hubert Stanley Anderson, Director of Graduate Studies, 404-413-5229, Fax: 404-413-5261, E-mail: artgrad@gsu.edu.
Website: http://www2.gsu.edu/~wwwart/8206.html.

Harding University, Cannon-Clary College of Education, Searcy, AR 72149-0001. Offers advanced studies in teaching and learning (M Ed); art (MSE); behavioral science (MSE); counseling (MS, Ed S); early childhood special education (M Ed, MSE); education (MSE); educational leadership (M Ed, Ed S); elementary education (M Ed); English (MSE); French (MSE); history/social science (MSE); kinesiology (MSE); math (MSE); reading (M Ed); secondary education (M Ed); Spanish (MSE); teaching (MAT); teaching English as a second language (MSE). *Accreditation:* NCATE. Part-time and evening/weekend programs available. *Faculty:* 13 full-time (5 women), 42 part-time/adjunct (24 women). *Students:* 154 full-time (119 women), 393 part-time (270 women); includes 108 minority (81 Black or African American, non-Hispanic/Latino; 5 American Indian or Alaska Native, non-Hispanic/Latino; 5 Asian, non-Hispanic/Latino; 9 Hispanic/Latino; 8 Two or more races, non-Hispanic/Latino), 15 international. Average age 36. 187 applicants, 79% accepted, 135 enrolled. In 2013, 138 master's, 17 other advanced degrees awarded. *Degree requirements:* For master's, comprehensive exam (for some programs), thesis optional, portfolio(s); for Ed S, comprehensive exam, portfolio, project. *Entrance requirements:* For master's, GRE, MAT, PRAXIS; for Ed S, MAT or GRE. Additional exam requirements/recommendations for international students: Required—TOEFL (minimum score 550 paper-based; 79 iBT). *Application deadline:* For fall admission, 8/1 for domestic and international students; for spring admission, 1/1 for domestic and international students. Applications are processed on a rolling basis. Application fee: $35. *Expenses: Tuition:* Full-time $11,574; part-time $643 per credit hour. *Required fees:* $432; $24 per credit hour. Tuition and fees vary according to course load, degree level and program. *Financial support:* In 2013–14, 36 students received support. Unspecified assistantships available. *Faculty research:* Reading, comprehension, school violence, educational technology, behavior, college choice, differentiated instruction, brain-based teaching. *Unit head:* Dr. Clara Carroll, Chair, 501-279-4501, Fax: 501-279-4083, E-mail: ccarroll@harding.edu. *Application contact:* Information Contact, 501-279-4315, E-mail: gradstudiesedu@harding.edu.
Website: http://www.harding.edu/education.

Harvard University, Harvard Graduate School of Education, Master's Programs in Education, Cambridge, MA 02138. Offers arts in education (Ed M); education policy and management (Ed M); higher education (Ed M); human development and psychology (Ed M); international education policy (Ed M); language and literacy (Ed M); learning and teaching (Ed M); mind, brain, and education (Ed M); prevention science and practice (Ed M); school leadership (Ed M); special studies (Ed M); teacher education (Ed M); technology, innovation, and education (Ed M). Part-time programs available. *Faculty:* 68 full-time (34 women), 77 part-time/adjunct (41 women). *Students:* 557 full-time (410 women), 69 part-time (50 women); includes 179 minority (34 Black or African American, non-Hispanic/Latino; 1 American Indian or Alaska Native, non-Hispanic/Latino; 62 Asian, non-Hispanic/Latino; 52 Hispanic/Latino; 2 Native Hawaiian or other Pacific Islander, non-Hispanic/Latino; 28 Two or more races, non-Hispanic/Latino), 100 international. Average age 28. 1,756 applicants, 47% accepted, 589 enrolled. In 2013, 673 master's awarded. *Entrance requirements:* For master's, GRE General Test, statement of purpose, 3 letters of recommendation, resume, official transcripts. Additional exam requirements/recommendations for international students: Required—TOEFL (minimum score 613 paper-based; 104 iBT), TWE (minimum score 5). *Application deadline:* For fall admission, 1/3 for domestic and international students. Application fee: $85. Electronic applications accepted. *Expenses:* Contact institution. *Financial support:* In 2013–14, 375 students received support, including 12 fellowships with full and partial tuition reimbursements available (averaging $13,925 per year), 2 research assistantships (averaging $2,174 per year); career-related internships or fieldwork, Federal Work-Study, institutionally sponsored loans, scholarships/grants, health care benefits, tuition waivers (full and partial), and unspecified assistantships also available. Support available to part-time students. Financial award application deadline: 2/1; financial award applicants required to submit FAFSA. *Faculty research:* Learning and development, educational leadership and organizations, education policy analysis. *Total annual research expenditures:* $34.3 million. *Unit head:* Jennifer L. Petrallia, Assistant Dean, 617-495-8445. *Application contact:* Information Contact, 617-495-3414, Fax: 617-496-3577, E-mail: gseadmissions@harvard.edu.
Website: http://www.gse.harvard.edu/.

Hofstra University, School of Education, Programs in Teaching - K-12, Hempstead, NY 11549. Offers bilingual education (MA, Advanced Certificate); family and consumer sciences (MS Ed); fine arts and music education (Advanced Certificate); fine arts education (MA, MS Ed); middle childhood extensions (Advanced Certificate), including grades 5-6 or 7-9; music education (MA, MS Ed); teaching languages other than English and TESOL (MS Ed); TESOL (MS Ed, Advanced Certificate); wind conducting (MA).

Indiana University Bloomington, School of Education, Department of Curriculum and Instruction, Bloomington, IN 47405-7000. Offers art education (MS, Ed D, PhD); curriculum studies (Ed D, PhD); elementary education (MS, Ed D, PhD, Ed S); mathematics education (MS, Ed D, PhD); science education (MS, Ed D, PhD); secondary education (MS, Ed D, PhD); social studies education (MS, PhD); special education (PhD, Ed S). *Accreditation:* NCATE. Part-time and evening/weekend programs available. Terminal master's awarded for partial completion of doctoral program. *Degree requirements:* For doctorate, thesis/dissertation; for Ed S, comprehensive exam or project. *Entrance requirements:* For master's, doctorate, and Ed S, GRE General Test. Electronic applications accepted.

Indiana University–Purdue University Indianapolis, Herron School of Art and Design, Indianapolis, IN 46202-2896. Offers art education (MAE); furniture design (MFA);

printmaking (MFA); sculpture (MFA); visual communication (MFA). *Accreditation:* NASAD. Part-time and evening/weekend programs available. *Faculty:* 2 full-time (both women). *Students:* 56 full-time (38 women), 6 part-time (2 women); includes 6 minority (1 Black or African American, non-Hispanic/Latino; 1 Asian, non-Hispanic/Latino; 1 Hispanic/Latino; 3 Two or more races, non-Hispanic/Latino), 4 international. Average age 30. 113 applicants, 54% accepted, 27 enrolled. In 2013, 13 master's awarded. *Entrance requirements:* For master's, portfolio, 44 hours of course work in art history and studio art. *Application deadline:* For fall admission, 5/1 priority date for domestic students, 3/15 priority date for international students; for spring admission, 11/1 priority date for domestic students, 10/15 priority date for international students. Applications are processed on a rolling basis. Application fee: $55 ($65 for international students). Electronic applications accepted. *Financial support:* Career-related internships or fieldwork, Federal Work-Study, institutionally sponsored loans, scholarships/grants, and tuition waivers (partial) available. Support available to part-time students. *Total annual research expenditures:* $6,097. *Unit head:* Valerie Eickmeier, Dean, 317-278-9470, Fax: 317-278-9471, E-mail: herron@iupui.edu. *Application contact:* Herron Student Services Office, 317-378-9400, E-mail: herrart@iupui.edu.
Website: http://www.herron.iupui.edu/.

Indiana University South Bend, Raclin School of the Arts, South Bend, IN 46634-7111. Offers music (MM); studio teaching (MM). Part-time programs available. *Faculty:* 1 full-time (0 women). *Students:* 13 full-time (7 women), 3 part-time (2 women); includes 2 minority (1 Black or African American, non-Hispanic/Latino; 1 Hispanic/Latino), 6 international. Average age 29. 15 applicants, 47% accepted, 5 enrolled. In 2013, 2 master's awarded. *Entrance requirements:* For master's, performance audition. *Application deadline:* For fall admission, 7/1 priority date for domestic students; for spring admission, 11/1 for domestic students. Applications are processed on a rolling basis. *Financial support:* Fellowships, teaching assistantships, and Federal Work-Study available. Support available to part-time students. Financial award application deadline: 3/1; financial award applicants required to submit FAFSA. *Faculty research:* Orchestral conducting. *Unit head:* Dr. Marvin V. Curtis, Dean, 574-520-4170, E-mail: mvcurtis@iusb.edu. *Application contact:* Admissions Counselor, 574-520-4839, Fax: 574-520-4834, E-mail: graduate@iusb.edu.
Website: https://www.iusb.edu/arts/index.php.

James Madison University, The Graduate School, College of Visual and Performing Arts, School of Art and Art History, Harrisonburg, VA 22807. Offers art education (MA); art history (MA); ceramics (MFA); drawing/painting (MFA); metal/jewelry (MFA); photography (MFA); printmaking (MFA); sculpture (MFA); studio art (MA); weaving/fibers (MFA). *Accreditation:* NASAD. Part-time programs available. *Faculty:* 13 full-time (10 women), 1 (woman) part-time/adjunct. *Students:* 10 full-time (7 women), 5 part-time (all women); includes 4 minority (1 Black or African American, non-Hispanic/Latino; 1 Asian, non-Hispanic/Latino; 2 Two or more races, non-Hispanic/Latino). Average age 27. In 2013, 4 master's awarded. *Degree requirements:* For master's, thesis (for some programs). *Entrance requirements:* For master's, GRE General Test, language exam in French or German, portfolio, 3 letters of recommendation, research paper. Additional exam requirements/recommendations for international students: Required—TOEFL. *Application deadline:* For fall admission, 2/15 priority date for domestic students, 2/15 for international students; for spring admission, 10/15 priority date for domestic students, 10/15 for international students. Applications are processed on a rolling basis. Application fee: $55. Electronic applications accepted. *Financial support:* In 2013–14, 10 students received support, including 2 teaching assistantships with full tuition reimbursements available (averaging $8,837 per year); Federal Work-Study and 8 graduate assistantships (averaging $7530) also available. Financial award application deadline: 3/1; financial award applicants required to submit FAFSA. *Unit head:* Dr. William Wightman, Director, 540-568-6216, E-mail: art-arthistory@jmu.edu. *Application contact:* Lynette M. Bible, Director of Graduate Admissions, 540-568-6395, Fax: 540-568-7860, E-mail: biblelm@jmu.edu.

Kean University, College of Visual and Performing Arts, Program in Fine Arts Education, Union, NJ 07083. Offers initial teaching certification (MA); studio (MA); supervision (MA). *Accreditation:* NASAD. Part-time programs available. *Faculty:* 10 full-time (4 women). *Students:* 7 full-time (6 women), 23 part-time (15 women); includes 7 minority (1 Black or African American, non-Hispanic/Latino; 1 Asian, non-Hispanic/Latino; 5 Hispanic/Latino), 3 international. Average age 36. 12 applicants, 100% accepted, 9 enrolled. In 2013, 14 master's awarded. *Degree requirements:* For master's, thesis (for some programs), exhibition, 3 years of teaching experience (supervision), PRAXIS and fieldwork (certification). *Entrance requirements:* For master's, studio portfolio, proficiencies in academic writing, dialogic skills, minimum GPA of 3.0, interview, 2 letters of recommendation, official transcripts from all institutions attended. Additional exam requirements/recommendations for international students: Required—TOEFL (minimum score 79 iBT). *Application deadline:* For fall admission, 6/1 for domestic and international students; for spring admission, 12/1 for domestic and international students. Applications are processed on a rolling basis. Application fee: $75 ($150 for international students). Electronic applications accepted. *Expenses:* Tuition, state resident: full-time $12,099; part-time $589 per credit. Tuition, nonresident: full-time $16,399; part-time $722 per credit. *Required fees:* $3050; $139 per credit. Part-time tuition and fees vary according to course level, course load, degree level and program. *Financial support:* In 2013–14, 4 research assistantships with full tuition reimbursements (averaging $3,713 per year) were awarded; unspecified assistantships also available. Financial award applicants required to submit FAFSA. *Unit head:* Dr. Joseph Amorino, Program Coordinator, 908-737-4403, E-mail: jamorino@kean.edu. *Application contact:* Steven Koch, Admissions Counselor, 908-737-5924, Fax: 908-737-5925, E-mail: skoch@kean.edu.
Website: http://grad.kean.edu/masters-programs/initial-teaching-certification.

Kennesaw State University, Leland and Clarice C. Bagwell College of Education, Program in Teaching, Kennesaw, GA 30144-5591. Offers art education (MAT); biology (MAT); chemistry (MAT); foreign language education (Chinese and Spanish) (MAT); physics (MAT); secondary English (MAT); secondary mathematics (MAT); special education (MAT); teaching English to speakers of other languages (MAT). Part-time and evening/weekend programs available. *Students:* 82 full-time (59 women), 16 part-time (12 women); includes 28 minority (14 Black or African American, non-Hispanic/Latino; 4 Asian, non-Hispanic/Latino; 7 Hispanic/Latino; 1 Native Hawaiian or other Pacific Islander, non-Hispanic/Latino; 2 Two or more races, non-Hispanic/Latino), 3 international. Average age 35. 28 applicants, 68% accepted, 15 enrolled. In 2013, 54 master's awarded. *Entrance requirements:* For master's, GRE, GACE I (state certificate exam), minimum GPA of 2.75, 2 recommendations, resume. Additional exam requirements/recommendations for international students: Required—TOEFL (minimum score 550 paper-based; 80 iBT), IELTS (minimum score 6). *Application deadline:* For fall admission, 6/1 for domestic and international students; for spring admission, 3/1 for domestic and international students; for summer admission, 4/15 for domestic and international students. Applications are processed on a rolling basis. Application fee: $60. Electronic applications accepted. *Expenses:* Tuition, state resident: full-time $4806; part-time $267 per semester hour. Tuition, nonresident: full-time $17,298; part-time $961 per semester hour. *Required fees:* $1834; $784.50 per semester. *Financial support:* In 2013–14, 2 research assistantships with tuition reimbursements (averaging $8,000 per year) were awarded; unspecified assistantships also available. Financial award application deadline: 4/1; financial award applicants required to submit FAFSA. *Unit head:* Dr. Jillian Ford, Director, 770-499-3093, E-mail: graded@kennesaw.edu. *Application contact:* Melinda Ross, Admissions Counselor, 770-423-6122, Fax: 770-423-6885, E-mail: ksugrad@kennesaw.edu.
Website: http://www.kennesaw.edu.

Kent State University, College of the Arts, School of Art, Kent, OH 44242-0001. Offers art education (MA); art history (MA); crafts (MA, MFA), including ceramics (MA), glass, jewelry/metals, textiles/art; fine art (MA, MFA), including drawing/painting, printmaking, sculpture. *Accreditation:* NASAD (one or more programs are accredited). *Degree requirements:* For master's, one foreign language, thesis. *Entrance requirements:* For master's, undergraduate degree in proposed area of study (for fine arts and crafts programs); minimum overall GPA of 2.75 (3.0 for art major); 3 letters of recommendation; portfolio (15-20 slides for MA, 20-25 for MFA). Additional exam requirements/recommendations for international students: Required—TOEFL. Electronic applications accepted.

Kutztown University of Pennsylvania, College of Visual and Performing Arts, Program in Art Education, Kutztown, PA 19530-0730. Offers M Ed. *Accreditation:* NASAD; NCATE. Part-time programs available. *Faculty:* 10 full-time (5 women). *Students:* 12 full-time (8 women), 29 part-time (26 women). Average age 31. 20 applicants, 80% accepted, 11 enrolled. In 2013, 12 master's awarded. *Degree requirements:* For master's, comprehensive exam, thesis optional. *Entrance requirements:* For master's, GRE, teacher certification. Additional exam requirements/recommendations for international students: Required—TOEFL (minimum score 550 paper-based; 79 iBT). *Application deadline:* For fall admission, 8/1 priority date for domestic and international students; for spring admission, 12/1 priority date for domestic and international students. Applications are processed on a rolling basis. Application fee: $35. Electronic applications accepted. *Expenses: Tuition, area resident:* Part-time $442 per credit. Tuition, state resident: part-time $442 per credit. Tuition, nonresident: part-time $663 per credit. *Required fees:* $80 per credit. *Financial support:* Career-related internships or fieldwork, Federal Work-Study, scholarships/grants, and unspecified assistantships available. Financial award application deadline: 3/1; financial award applicants required to submit FAFSA. *Faculty research:* Teaching of art history, child development in art, aesthetics and criticism curriculum, multicultural education, assessment in art. *Unit head:* Dr. John White, Chairperson, 610-683-4520, Fax: 610-683-4502, E-mail: white@kutztown.edu. *Application contact:* Kelly Hish, Admissions Clerk, 610-683-4200, Fax: 610-683-1393, E-mail: graduate@kutztown.edu.

Lake Forest College, Master of Arts in Teaching Program, Lake Forest, IL 60045. Offers elementary education (MAT); K-12 French (MAT); K-12 music (MAT); K-12 Spanish (MAT); K-12 visual art (MAT); secondary biology (MAT); secondary chemistry (MAT); secondary English (MAT); secondary history (MAT); secondary mathematics (MAT). *Degree requirements:* For master's, comprehensive exam, portfolio. *Entrance requirements:* For master's, GRE.

Lesley University, School of Education, Cambridge, MA 02138-2790. Offers arts, community, and education (M Ed); autism studies (Certificate); curriculum and instruction (M Ed, CAGS); early childhood education (M Ed); ecological teaching and learning (MS); educational studies (PhD), including adult learning, educational leadership, individually designed; elementary education (M Ed); emergent technologies for educators (Certificate); ESLArts: language learning through the arts (M Ed); high school education (M Ed); individually designed (M Ed); integrated teaching through the arts (M Ed); literacy for K-8 classroom teachers (M Ed); mathematics education (M Ed); middle school education (M Ed); moderate disabilities (M Ed); online learning (Certificate); reading (CAGS); science in education (M Ed); severe disabilities (M Ed); special needs (CAGS); specialist teacher of reading (M Ed); teacher of visual art (M Ed); technology in education (M Ed, CAGS). *Accreditation:* Teacher Education Accreditation Council. Part-time and evening/weekend programs available. Postbaccalaureate distance learning degree programs offered (no on-campus study). *Faculty:* 40 full-time (30 women), 104 part-time/adjunct (77 women). *Students:* 453 full-time (381 women), 1,672 part-time (1,435 women); includes 284 minority (139 Black or African American, non-Hispanic/Latino; 11 American Indian or Alaska Native, non-Hispanic/Latino; 38 Asian, non-Hispanic/Latino; 58 Hispanic/Latino; 5 Native Hawaiian or other Pacific Islander, non-Hispanic/Latino; 33 Two or more races, non-Hispanic/Latino), 22 international. Average age 35. In 2013, 1,137 master's, 18 doctorates, 51 other advanced degrees awarded. *Degree requirements:* For master's, practicum; for doctorate, thesis/dissertation. *Entrance requirements:* For master's, Massachusetts Tests for Educator Licensure (MTEL), transcripts, statement of purpose, recommendations; interview (for special education); for doctorate, GRE General Test, transcripts, statement of purpose, recommendations, interview, master's degree, resume; for other advanced degree, interview, master's degree. Additional exam requirements/recommendations for international students: Required—TOEFL (minimum score 550 paper-based; 80 iBT). *Application deadline:* Applications are processed on a rolling basis. Application fee: $50. Electronic applications accepted. *Expenses: Tuition:* Part-time $900 per credit. *Financial support:* In 2013–14, 15 fellowships (averaging $3,600 per year) were awarded; career-related internships or fieldwork, Federal Work-Study, scholarships/grants, tuition waivers, and unspecified assistantships also available. Financial award application deadline: 4/15; financial award applicants required to submit FAFSA. *Faculty research:* Assessment in literacy, mathematics and science; autism spectrum disorders; instructional technology and online learning; multicultural education and English language learners. *Unit head:* Dr. Jack Gillette, Dean, 617-349-8401, Fax: 617-349-8607, E-mail: jgillett@lesley.edu. *Application contact:* Martha Sheehan, Director of Admissions, 888-LESLEYU, Fax: 617-349-8313, E-mail: info@lesley.edu.
Website: http://www.lesley.edu/soe.html.

Long Island University–LIU Post, School of Education, Department of Curriculum and Instruction, Brookville, NY 11548-1300. Offers adolescence education (MS); adolescence education: biology (MS); adolescence education: earth science (MS); adolescence education: English (MS); adolescence education: mathematics (MS); adolescence education: social studies (MS); adolescence education: Spanish (MS); art education (MS); bilingual education (MS); childhood education (MS); early childhood education (MS); middle childhood education (MS); music education (MS); teaching English to speakers of other languages (MS). Part-time and evening/weekend programs available. *Degree requirements:* For master's, comprehensive exam or thesis, student teaching. *Entrance requirements:* For master's, minimum GPA of 2.75 in major, 2.5 overall. Electronic applications accepted. *Faculty research:* Ethics and education, teaching strategies.

Long Island University–LIU Post, School of Visual and Performing Arts, Department of Art, Brookville, NY 11548-1300. Offers art (MA); art education (MS); clinical art therapy (MA); fine art and design (MFA). Part-time and evening/weekend programs available. *Degree requirements:* For master's, thesis. Electronic applications accepted. *Faculty research:* Painting, sculpture, installation, computers, video.

Manhattanville College, School of Education, Program in Visual Arts Education, Purchase, NY 10577-2132. Offers MAT. Part-time and evening/weekend programs available. *Degree requirements:* For master's, comprehensive examination or final

project. *Entrance requirements:* Additional exam requirements/recommendations for international students: Required—TOEFL. Electronic applications accepted.

Mansfield University of Pennsylvania, Graduate Studies, Department of Art, Mansfield, PA 16933. Offers art education (M Ed). Part-time programs available. *Degree requirements:* For master's, thesis optional. *Entrance requirements:* For master's, minimum GPA of 3.0, portfolio. Additional exam requirements/recommendations for international students: Required—TOEFL (minimum score 550 paper-based). Electronic applications accepted.

Maryland Institute College of Art, Graduate Studies, Program in Art Education, Baltimore, MD 21217. Offers MA, MAT. MA program offered in summer only. *Accreditation:* NASAD. Part-time programs available. *Degree requirements:* For master's, thesis, seminar. *Entrance requirements:* For master's, portfolio, 40 studio credits, 6 credits in art history. Additional exam requirements/recommendations for international students: Required—TOEFL (minimum score 550 paper-based; 80 iBT).

Maryville University of Saint Louis, School of Education, St. Louis, MO 63141-7299. Offers art education (MA Ed); early childhood education (MA Ed); educational leadership (Ed D); educational leadership: principal certification (MA Ed); elementary education (MA Ed); gifted education (MA Ed); higher education leadership (Ed D); literacy specialist (MA Ed); middle grades education (MA Ed); secondary teaching and inquiry (MA Ed); teacher as leader (MA Ed); teacher leadership (Ed D). *Accreditation:* NCATE. Part-time and evening/weekend programs available. *Faculty:* 10 full-time (6 women), 17 part-time/adjunct (13 women). *Students:* 21 full-time (17 women), 238 part-time (167 women); includes 64 minority (54 Black or African American, non-Hispanic/Latino; 2 Asian, non-Hispanic/Latino; 4 Hispanic/Latino; 4 Two or more races, non-Hispanic/Latino), 2 international. Average age 39. In 2013, 61 master's, 40 doctorates awarded. *Degree requirements:* For master's, thesis, project. *Entrance requirements:* For master's, minimum cumulative GPA of 3.0, 3 professional recommendations, essays, interview with program faculty; for doctorate, minimum GPA of 3.0, 3 professional recommendations, essay, interview, on-site writing sample. Additional exam requirements/recommendations for international students: Required—TOEFL (minimum score 550 paper-based). *Application deadline:* Applications are processed on a rolling basis. Application fee: $40 ($60 for international students). Electronic applications accepted. Application fee is waived when completed online. *Expenses: Tuition:* Full-time $23,812; part-time $728 per credit hour. *Required fees:* $395 per year. Tuition and fees vary according to course load, degree level and program. *Financial support:* Career-related internships or fieldwork, Federal Work-Study, tuition waivers (partial), and professional educator discounts available. Financial award application deadline: 3/1; financial award applicants required to submit FAFSA. *Faculty research:* Collaboration with public schools, pre-service program development, mathematics, diversity, literacy. *Unit head:* Dr. Cathy Bear, Dean, 314-529-9692, Fax: 314-529-9921, E-mail: cbear@maryville.edu. *Application contact:* Holly Stanwich, Graduate Admissions Coordinator, 314-529-9542, Fax: 314-529-9921. E-mail: teachered@maryville.edu. Website: http://www.maryville.edu/ed/graduate-programs/.

Marywood University, Academic Affairs, Insalaco College of Creative and Performing Arts, Art Department, Program in Art Education, Scranton, PA 18509-1598. Offers MA. *Accreditation:* NASAD; NCATE. *Entrance requirements:* Additional exam requirements/recommendations for international students: Required—TOEFL (minimum score 550 paper-based; 79 iBT). *Application deadline:* For fall admission, 4/1 priority date for domestic students, 3/31 priority date for international students; for spring admission, 11/1 priority date for domestic students, 8/31 priority date for international students. Applications are processed on a rolling basis. Application fee: $35. Electronic applications accepted. *Expenses: Tuition:* Part-time $775 per credit. Tuition and fees vary according to degree level. *Financial support:* Career-related internships or fieldwork, scholarships/grants, and unspecified assistantships available. Support available to part-time students. Financial award application deadline: 6/30; financial award applicants required to submit FAFSA. *Faculty research:* Current trends in art education, color theories, research in Mariology. *Unit head:* Matthew Povse, Chair, 570-348-6211 Ext. 2476, E-mail: povse@marywood.edu. *Application contact:* Tammy Manka, Assistant Director of Graduate Admissions, 570-348-6211 Ext. 2322, E-mail: tmanka@marywood.edu.
Website: http://www.marywood.edu/art/graduate-programs/master-art-education.html.

Massachusetts College of Art and Design, Graduate Programs, Program in Art Education, Boston, MA 02115-5882. Offers MAT, Postbaccalaureate Certificate. *Accreditation:* NASAD. *Faculty:* 5 full-time (4 women), 11 part-time/adjunct (7 women). *Students:* 16 full-time (12 women), 2 part-time (1 woman); includes 2 minority (1 Black or African American, non-Hispanic/Latino; 1 Two or more races, non-Hispanic/Latino). 37 applicants, 46% accepted, 10 enrolled. In 2013, 22 master's, 3 other advanced degrees awarded. *Entrance requirements:* For master's and Postbaccalaureate Certificate, portfolio, college transcripts, resume, statement of purpose, letters of reference, interview. Additional exam requirements/recommendations for international students: Required—TOEFL (minimum score 563 paper-based; 85 iBT); Recommended—IELTS (minimum score 6.5). *Application deadline:* For fall admission, 1/6 priority date for domestic and international students. Application fee: $75. Electronic applications accepted. *Expenses:* Contact institution. *Financial support:* In 2013–14, 3 students received support, including 2 teaching assistantships (averaging $2,160 per year); career-related internships or fieldwork, scholarships/grants, unspecified assistantships, and 3 technical/work assistantships (averaging $2160 per year) also available. Support available to part-time students. Financial award application deadline: 3/1. *Unit head:* Ken Strickland, Provost/Senior Vice President for Academic Affairs, 617-879-7365, E-mail: ken.strickland@massart.edu. *Application contact:* Isaac Goldstein, Graduate Admissions Counselor, 617-879-7203, Fax: 617-879-7250, E-mail: igoldstein@massart.edu.
Website: http://www.massart.edu/Admissions/Graduate_Programs.html.

Memphis College of Art, Graduate Programs, Program in Art Education, Memphis, TN 38104-2764. Offers MA, MAT. Part-time and evening/weekend programs available. *Faculty:* 23 full-time (14 women), 13 part-time/adjunct (8 women). *Students:* 27 part-time (10 women); includes 10 minority (9 Black or African American, non-Hispanic/Latino; 1 Asian, non-Hispanic/Latino), 1 international. Average age 28. 28 applicants, 75% accepted, 13 enrolled. In 2013, 15 master's awarded. *Degree requirements:* For master's, thesis. *Entrance requirements:* For master's, portfolio, resume, interview. Additional exam requirements/recommendations for international students: Required—TOEFL (minimum score 525 paper-based). *Application deadline:* For fall admission, 3/1 for domestic and international students; for spring admission, 11/1 for domestic and international students. Applications are processed on a rolling basis. Application fee: $50. Electronic applications accepted. *Expenses: Tuition:* Full-time $28,100; part-time $1170 per credit hour. *Required fees:* $650; $3510 per credit hour. $325 per semester. Full-time tuition and fees vary according to course load, degree level and program. *Financial support:* Application deadline: 8/1; applicants required to submit FAFSA. *Unit head:* Dr. Shannon Elliott, Director of Graduate Education, 901-272-5100, Fax: 901-272-5158, E-mail: selliott@mca.edu. *Application contact:* Annette Moore, Dean of Admissions, 901-272-5153, Fax: 901-272-5158, E-mail: amoore@mca.edu.

Miami University, College of Creative Arts, Department of Art, Oxford, OH 45056. Offers art education (MA); studio art (MFA). *Accreditation:* NASAD (one or more

programs are accredited). *Students:* 15 full-time (5 women). Average age 32. In 2013, 4 master's awarded. *Entrance requirements:* For master's, portfolio, resume, statement of intent, letters of recommendation. Additional exam requirements/recommendations for international students: Recommended—TOEFL (minimum score 80 iBT), IELTS (minimum score 6.5), TSE (minimum score 54). *Application deadline:* For fall admission, 2/1 for domestic and international students. Application fee: $50. Electronic applications accepted. *Expenses:* Tuition, state resident: full-time $12,634; part-time $526 per credit hour. Tuition, nonresident: full-time $27,892; part-time $1162 per credit hour. Part-time tuition and fees vary according to course load, campus/location and program. *Financial support:* Research assistantships with full and partial tuition reimbursements, teaching assistantships with full and partial tuition reimbursements, Federal Work-Study, health care benefits, and unspecified assistantships available. Financial award application deadline: 2/15; financial award applicants required to submit FAFSA. *Unit head:* Dr. Peg Faimon, Chair/Professor, 513-529-2900, E-mail: peg.faimon@miamioh.edu. *Application contact:* 513-529-2900, E-mail: art@miamioh.edu.
Website: http://www.MiamiOH.edu/art.

Millersville University of Pennsylvania, College of Graduate and Professional Studies, School of Humanities and Social Sciences, Department of Art, Millersville, PA 17551-0302. Offers M Ed. *Accreditation:* NASAD; NCATE. Part-time programs available. *Faculty:* 14 full-time (9 women). *Students:* 2 full-time (both women), 4 part-time (3 women); includes 1 minority (Asian, non-Hispanic/Latino). Average age 29. 4 applicants, 75% accepted, 3 enrolled. In 2013, 2 master's awarded. *Degree requirements:* For master's, comprehensive exam, thesis optional. *Entrance requirements:* For master's, GRE or MAT, 3 letters of recommendation, portfolio, goal statement, official transcripts. Additional exam requirements/recommendations for international students: Required—TOEFL (minimum score 550 paper-based, 79 iBT) or IELTS (minimum score 6). *Application deadline:* For fall admission, 1/15 priority date for domestic and international students; for winter admission, 10/1 priority date for domestic and international students; for spring admission, 10/1 priority date for domestic and international students. Applications are processed on a rolling basis. Application fee: $40. Electronic applications accepted. *Expenses:* Tuition, state resident: full-time $7956; part-time $442 per credit. Tuition, nonresident: full-time $11,934; part-time $663 per credit. *Required fees:* $2196; $122 per credit. Tuition and fees vary according to course load. *Financial support:* Research assistantships with full tuition reimbursements, institutionally sponsored loans, and unspecified assistantships available. Support available to part-time students. Financial award application deadline: 3/15; financial award applicants required to submit FAFSA. *Faculty research:* Art education curriculum, democratic education, assessment in arts education, collaborative action research. *Total annual research expenditures:* $10,000. *Unit head:* Brant D. Schuller, Chair, 717-872-3304, Fax: 717-871-2004, E-mail: brant.schuller@millersville.edu. *Application contact:* Dr. Victor S. DeSantis, Dean of College of Graduate and Professional Studies/Associate Provost for Civic and Community Engagement, 717-872-3099, Fax: 717-872-3453, E-mail: victor.desantis@millersville.edu.
Website: http://www.millersville.edu/art/.

Mills College, Graduate Studies, School of Education, Oakland, CA 94613-1000. Offers child life in hospitals (MA); early childhood education (MA); education (MA), including art education, curriculum and instruction, elementary education, English education, foreign language education, mathematics education, science education, secondary education, social studies education, teaching; educational leadership (MA, Ed D). Part-time and evening/weekend programs available. *Faculty:* 10 full-time (7 women), 13 part-time/adjunct (10 women). *Students:* 154 full-time (136 women), 54 part-time (47 women); includes 96 minority (32 Black or African American, non-Hispanic/Latino; 1 American Indian or Alaska Native, non-Hispanic/Latino; 23 Asian, non-Hispanic/Latino; 27 Hispanic/Latino; 1 Native Hawaiian or other Pacific Islander, non-Hispanic/Latino; 12 Two or more races, non-Hispanic/Latino), 2 international. Average age 25. 222 applicants, 89% accepted, 110 enrolled. In 2013, 96 master's, 38 doctorates awarded. Terminal master's awarded for partial completion of doctoral program. *Degree requirements:* For master's, comprehensive exam, thesis (for some programs); for doctorate, thesis/dissertation. *Entrance requirements:* For master's, statement of purpose, official transcript, 3 recommendations. Additional exam requirements/recommendations for international students: Required—TOEFL (minimum score 550 paper-based; 80 iBT) or IELTS (minimum score 6). *Application deadline:* For fall admission, 12/31 priority date for domestic students, 12/15 for international students; for spring admission, 11/1 priority date for domestic students, 10/1 for international students. Applications are processed on a rolling basis. Application fee: $50. Electronic applications accepted. *Expenses: Tuition:* Full-time $29,860. *Required fees:* $1134. Part-time tuition and fees vary according to course load, degree level and program. *Financial support:* In 2013–14, 130 students received support, including 130 fellowships with full and partial tuition reimbursements available (averaging $7,565 per year); career-related internships or fieldwork and scholarships/grants also available. Support available to part-time students. Financial award application deadline: 2/1; financial award applicants required to submit FAFSA. *Faculty research:* Early childhood education, teacher preparation, educational leadership. *Total annual research expenditures:* $3.5 million. *Unit head:* Dr. Katherine Schultz, Department Head, 510-430-3384, Fax: 510-430-2159, E-mail: kschultz@mills.edu. *Application contact:* Shrim Bathey, Director of Graduate Admission, 510-430-3309, Fax: 510-430-2159, E-mail: grad-admission@mills.edu.
Website: http://www.mills.edu/education.

Minnesota State University Mankato, College of Graduate Studies, College of Arts and Humanities, Department of Art, Mankato, MN 56001. Offers studio art (MA); teaching art (MAT). *Accreditation:* NASAD (one or more programs are accredited). Part-time programs available. *Students:* 15 full-time (6 women), 11 part-time (4 women). *Degree requirements:* For master's, one foreign language, comprehensive exam, thesis or alternative. *Entrance requirements:* For master's, minimum GPA of 3.0 during previous 2 years, portfolio (MA). Additional exam requirements/recommendations for international students: Required—TOEFL. *Application deadline:* For fall admission, 7/1 priority date for domestic students, 5/1 for international students; for spring admission, 11/1 for domestic students, 10/1 for international students. Applications are processed on a rolling basis. Application fee: $40. Electronic applications accepted. *Financial support:* Research assistantships, teaching assistantships with full tuition reimbursements, and unspecified assistantships available. Financial award application deadline: 3/15; financial award applicants required to submit FAFSA. *Faculty research:* Photographic documentation. *Unit head:* Brian Frink, Graduate Coordinator, 507-389-6412. *Application contact:* 507-389-2321, E-mail: grad@mnsu.edu.
Website: http://www.mnsu.edu/artdept/.

Mississippi College, Graduate School, School of Education, Department of Teacher Education and Leadership, Clinton, MS 39058. Offers art (M Ed); biological science (M Ed); business education (M Ed); computer science (M Ed); dyslexia therapy (M Ed); educational leadership (M Ed, Ed D, Ed S); elementary education (M Ed, Ed S); English (M Ed); higher education administration (MS); mathematics (M Ed); secondary education (M Ed); social studies (history) (M Ed); teaching arts (M Ed). Part-time programs available. Postbaccalaureate distance learning degree programs offered (no on-campus study). *Degree requirements:* For master's, comprehensive exam, thesis optional. *Entrance requirements:* For master's, NTE. Additional exam requirements/

recommendations for international students: Recommended—TOEFL, IELTS. Electronic applications accepted.

Montclair State University, The Graduate School, College of Education and Human Services, Department of Secondary and Special Education, Program in Teaching in Subject Area, Montclair, NJ 07043-1624. Offers art (MAT); biology (MAT); chemistry (MAT); earth science (MAT); English (MAT); French (MAT); health and physical education (MAT); health education (MAT); mathematics (MAT); music (MAT); physical education (MAT); physical science (MAT); social studies (MAT); Spanish (MAT); teacher of English as a second language (MAT). *Degree requirements:* For master's, comprehensive exam, thesis or alternative. *Entrance requirements:* For master's, GRE General Test, interview, 2 letters of recommendation. Additional exam requirements/recommendations for international students: Required—TOEFL (minimum score 83 iBT), IELTS (minimum score 6.5). Electronic applications accepted.

Montclair State University, The Graduate School, College of the Arts, Department of Art and Design, Program in Art, Montclair, NJ 07043-1624. Offers MAT. Part-time and evening/weekend programs available. *Entrance requirements:* For master's, GRE General Test, 2 letters of recommendation, essay. Additional exam requirements/recommendations for international students: Required—TOEFL (minimum score 83 iBT), IELTS (minimum score 6.5). Electronic applications accepted.

Moore College of Art & Design, Program in Art Education, Philadelphia, PA 19103. Offers MA. Part-time programs available. *Degree requirements:* For master's, thesis, field practicum. *Entrance requirements:* For master's, minimum GPA of 3.0, on-site interview, portfolio, 3 letters of recommendation, resume.

Morehead State University, Graduate Programs, Caudill College of Arts, Humanities and Social Sciences, Department of Art and Design, Morehead, KY 40351. Offers art education (MA); graphic design (MA); studio art (MA). Part-time and evening/weekend programs available. *Degree requirements:* For master's, comprehensive exam, thesis (for some programs), oral exam during exhibition. *Entrance requirements:* For master's, GRE General Test, minimum undergraduate GPA of 3.0 in major, 2.5 overall; portfolio; bachelor's degree in art. Additional exam requirements/recommendations for international students: Required—TOEFL (minimum score 500 paper-based). Electronic applications accepted. *Faculty research:* Computer art, painting, drawing, ceramics, photography.

Nazareth College of Rochester, Graduate Studies, Department of Art, Program in Art Education, Rochester, NY 14618-3790. Offers MS Ed. *Accreditation:* Teacher Education Accreditation Council. Part-time and evening/weekend programs available. *Entrance requirements:* For master's, minimum GPA of 3.0, portfolio review.

New Hampshire Institute of Art, Graduate Programs, Manchester, NH 03104. Offers art education (MA); creative writing (MFA); photography (MFA); visual arts (MFA); writing for stage and screen (MFA).

New Jersey City University, Graduate Studies and Continuing Education, William J. Maxwell College of Arts and Sciences, Department of Art, Jersey City, NJ 07305-1597. Offers art (MFA); art education (MA); studio art (MFA). *Accreditation:* NASAD. Part-time and evening/weekend programs available. *Faculty:* 11 full-time (4 women), 3 part-time/adjunct (2 women). *Students:* 4 full-time (3 women), 10 part-time (4 women); includes 8 minority (3 Black or African American, non-Hispanic/Latino; 1 Asian, non-Hispanic/Latino; 4 Hispanic/Latino), 1 international. Average age 42. In 2013, 3 master's awarded. *Degree requirements:* For master's, thesis or alternative, exhibit. *Entrance requirements:* For master's, portfolio. Additional exam requirements/recommendations for international students: Required—TOEFL (minimum score 61 iBT). *Application deadline:* For fall admission, 8/1 priority date for domestic students; for spring admission, 12/1 for domestic students. Applications are processed on a rolling basis. Application fee: $0. *Expenses: Tuition, area resident:* Part-time $527.90 per credit. Tuition, nonresident: part-time $947.75 per credit. *Financial support:* Unspecified assistantships available. *Unit head:* Dr. Herbert Rosenberg, Chairperson, 201-200-2367. *Application contact:* Dr. William Bajor, Dean of Graduate Studies, 201-200-3409, Fax: 201-200-3411, E-mail: wbajor@njcu.edu.

New York University, Steinhardt School of Culture, Education, and Human Development, Department of Art and Art Professions, Program in Art Education, New York, NY 10003-5799. Offers art, education, and community practice (MA); teaching art and social studies (MA); teaching art, all grades (MA). *Accreditation:* Teacher Education Accreditation Council. Part-time programs available. *Faculty:* 2 full-time (1 woman). *Students:* 10 full-time (9 women), 12 part-time (9 women); includes 10 minority (1 Black or African American, non-Hispanic/Latino; 4 American Indian or Alaska Native, non-Hispanic/Latino; 3 Asian, non-Hispanic/Latino; 2 Hispanic/Latino), 4 international. Average age 35. 34 applicants, 94% accepted, 12 enrolled. In 2013, 14 master's awarded. *Degree requirements:* For master's, thesis (for some programs). *Entrance requirements:* For master's, portfolio. Additional exam requirements/recommendations for international students: Required—TOEFL (minimum score 100 iBT). *Application deadline:* For fall admission, 11/16 priority date for domestic and international students. Applications are processed on a rolling basis. Application fee: $75. Electronic applications accepted. *Expenses: Tuition:* Full-time $35,856; part-time $1494 per unit. *Required fees:* $1408; $64 per unit. $473 per term. Tuition and fees vary according to course load and program. *Financial support:* Career-related internships or fieldwork, Federal Work-Study, and tuition waivers (partial) available. Support available to part-time students. Financial award application deadline: 2/1; financial award applicants required to submit FAFSA. *Faculty research:* Multicultural aesthetic inquiry, urban art education, feminism, equity and social justice. *Unit head:* Prof. Dipti Desai, Director, 212-998-9022, Fax: 212-995-4320, E-mail: dd25@nyu.edu. *Application contact:* 212-998-5030, Fax: 212-995-4328, E-mail: steinhardt.gradadmissions@nyu.edu.
Website: http://steinhardt.nyu.edu/art/education.

New York University, Steinhardt School of Culture, Education, and Human Development, Department of Teaching and Learning, Program in Social Studies Education, New York, NY 10003. Offers history, social studies, and global education (PhD); teaching art and social studies 7-12 (MA); teaching social studies 7-12 (MA). *Accreditation:* Teacher Education Accreditation Council. Part-time and evening/weekend programs available. *Faculty:* 3 full-time (2 women). *Students:* 5 full-time (3 women), 5 part-time (2 women); includes 4 minority (all Hispanic/Latino). Average age 27. 48 applicants, 88% accepted, 6 enrolled. In 2013, 23 master's awarded. *Degree requirements:* For master's, thesis (for some programs). *Entrance requirements:* Additional exam requirements/recommendations for international students: Required—TOEFL (minimum score 100 iBT). *Application deadline:* For fall admission, 2/1 priority date for domestic and international students; for spring admission, 10/1 for domestic and international students. Applications are processed on a rolling basis. Application fee: $75. Electronic applications accepted. *Expenses: Tuition:* Full-time $35,856; part-time $1494 per unit. *Required fees:* $1408; $64 per unit. $473 per term. Tuition and fees vary according to course load and program. *Financial support:* Career-related internships or fieldwork, Federal Work-Study, institutionally sponsored loans, scholarships/grants, and tuition waivers (partial) available. Support available to part-time students. Financial award application deadline: 2/1; financial award applicants required to submit FAFSA. *Faculty research:* Social studies education reform, ethnography and oral history, civic education, labor history and social studies curriculum, material culture. *Unit head:* 212-998-5460, Fax: 212-995-4049. *Application contact:* 212-998-5030, Fax: 212-995-4328, E-mail: steinhardt.gradadmissions@nyu.edu.
Website: http://steinhardt.nyu.edu/teachlearn/social_studies.

The Ohio State University, Graduate School, College of Arts and Sciences, Division of Arts and Humanities, Department of Arts Administration, Education and Policy, Columbus, OH 43210. Offers art education (MA); art education online (MA); arts administration, education and policy (PhD); arts policy and administration (MA). *Accreditation:* NASAD; NCATE. Postbaccalaureate distance learning degree programs offered. *Faculty:* 14. *Students:* 50 full-time (39 women), 16 part-time (14 women); includes 9 minority (5 Black or African American, non-Hispanic/Latino; 1 Asian, non-Hispanic/Latino; 2 Hispanic/Latino; 1 Two or more races, non-Hispanic/Latino), 21 international. Average age 34. In 2013, 11 master's, 3 doctorates awarded. Terminal master's awarded for partial completion of doctoral program. *Degree requirements:* For master's, thesis; for doctorate, thesis/dissertation. *Entrance requirements:* For master's, GRE; for doctorate, GRE General Test. Additional exam requirements/recommendations for international students: Recommended—TOEFL (minimum score 550 paper-based; 100 iBT). *Application deadline:* For fall admission, 11/30 priority date for domestic and international students; for winter admission, 12/1 for domestic students, 11/1 for international students; for spring admission, 11/30 priority date for domestic and international students. Applications are processed on a rolling basis. Application fee: $60 ($70 for international students). Electronic applications accepted. *Financial support:* Fellowships with tuition reimbursements, research assistantships with tuition reimbursements, teaching assistantships with tuition reimbursements, career-related internships or fieldwork, Federal Work-Study, institutionally sponsored loans, and unspecified assistantships available. Support available to part-time students. Financial award applicants required to submit FAFSA. *Unit head:* Deborah L. Smith-Shank, Chair, 614-688-4346, E-mail: smith-shank.1@osu.edu. *Application contact:* Graduate Admissions, 614-292-9444, Fax: 614-292-3895, E-mail: gradadmissions@osu.edu.
Website: http://aaep.osu.edu/.

Penn State University Park, Graduate School, College of Arts and Architecture, School of Visual Arts, State College, PA 16802. Offers art (MFA); art education (MPS, MS, PhD, Certificate). *Accreditation:* NASAD. *Unit head:* Dr. Barbara O. Korner, Dean, 814-865-2592, Fax: 814-865-2018, E-mail: bok2@psu.edu. *Application contact:* Cynthia E. Nicosia, Director, Graduate Enrollment Services, 814-865-1834, Fax: 814-863-4627, E-mail: cey1@psu.edu.
Website: http://sova.psu.edu/.

Piedmont College, School of Education, Demorest, GA 30535-0010. Offers art education (MAT); early childhood education (MA, MAT); instructional technology (MAT); middle grades education (MA, MAT); music education (MAT); secondary education (MA, MAT); special education (MA, MAT); teacher leadership (Ed S). Part-time and evening/weekend programs available. *Students:* 312 full-time (242 women), 694 part-time (563 women); includes 153 minority (103 Black or African American, non-Hispanic/Latino; 3 American Indian or Alaska Native, non-Hispanic/Latino; 17 Asian, non-Hispanic/Latino; 19 Hispanic/Latino; 11 Two or more races, non-Hispanic/Latino), 1 international. Average age 37. 165 applicants, 72% accepted, 118 enrolled. In 2013, 333 master's, 15 doctorates, 457 other advanced degrees awarded. *Degree requirements:* For master's, thesis, field experience in the classroom teaching; for doctorate, thesis/dissertation. *Entrance requirements:* For master's, GRE General Test, MAT, minimum undergraduate GPA of 2.5; for Ed S, minimum graduate GPA of 3.5, valid teaching certificate. Additional exam requirements/recommendations for international students: Required—TOEFL (minimum score 550 paper-based). *Application deadline:* For fall admission, 7/15 for domestic students; for spring admission, 12/1 for domestic students. Applications are processed on a rolling basis. Electronic applications accepted. *Expenses: Tuition:* Full-time $7992; part-time $444 per credit hour. *Financial support:* Career-related internships or fieldwork, Federal Work-Study, and unspecified assistantships available. Support available to part-time students. Financial award applicants required to submit FAFSA. *Unit head:* Dr. Don Gnecco, Dean, 706-778-3000 Ext. 1201, Fax: 706-776-9608, E-mail: dgnecco@piedmont.edu. *Application contact:* Kathleen Anderson, Director of Graduate Enrollment Management, 706-778-8500 Ext. 1181, Fax: 706-778-0150, E-mail: kanderson@piedmont.edu.

Pittsburg State University, Graduate School, College of Arts and Sciences, Department of Art, Pittsburg, KS 66762. Offers art education (MA); studio art (MA). *Degree requirements:* For master's, thesis or alternative.

Plymouth State University, College of Graduate Studies, Graduate Studies in Education, Program in Teaching, Plymouth, NH 03264-1595. Offers art education (MAT); science education (MAT). Evening/weekend programs available. *Degree requirements:* For master's, internship or teaching experience.

Pratt Institute, School of Art, Program in Art and Design Education, Brooklyn, NY 11205-3899. Offers MS, Adv C. *Accreditation:* NASAD. Part-time programs available. *Faculty:* 4 full-time (all women), 3 part-time/adjunct (all women). *Students:* 13 full-time (11 women), 2 part-time (both women); includes 2 minority (1 Black or African American, non-Hispanic/Latino; 1 Hispanic/Latino), 2 international. Average age 35. 26 applicants, 85% accepted, 5 enrolled. In 2013, 12 master's awarded. *Degree requirements:* For master's, thesis. *Entrance requirements:* Additional exam requirements/recommendations for international students: Required—TOEFL (minimum score 600 paper-based; 100 iBT). *Application deadline:* For fall admission, 1/5 for domestic and international students; for spring admission, 10/1 for domestic and international students. Application fee: $50 ($90 for international students). *Expenses: Tuition:* Full-time $26,478; part-time $1471 per credit. *Required fees:* $1830; $1050 per year. *Financial support:* Career-related internships or fieldwork, Federal Work-Study, institutionally sponsored loans, scholarships/grants, health care benefits, and unspecified assistantships available. Support available to part-time students. Financial award application deadline: 2/1; financial award applicants required to submit FAFSA. *Unit head:* Aileen Wilson, Acting Chairperson, 718-636-3654, E-mail: awilson2@pratt.edu. *Application contact:* Young Hah, Director of Graduate Admissions, 718-636-3683, Fax: 718-399-4242, E-mail: yhah@pratt.edu.
Website: https://www.pratt.edu/academics/art-design/art-grad/art-and-design-education-grad/.

Purdue University, Graduate School, College of Education, Department of Curriculum and Instruction, West Lafayette, IN 47907. Offers agricultural and extension education (PhD, Ed S); agriculture and extension education (MS, MS Ed); art education (PhD); curriculum studies (MS Ed, PhD, Ed S); educational technology (MS Ed, PhD, Ed S); elementary education (MS Ed); family and consumer sciences education (MS Ed, PhD, Ed S); foreign language education (MS Ed, PhD, Ed S); industrial technology (PhD, Ed S); language arts (MS Ed, PhD, Ed S); literacy (MS Ed, PhD, Ed S); mathematics/science education (MS, MS Ed, PhD, Ed S); social studies (MS Ed, PhD); social studies education (Ed S); vocational/industrial education (MS Ed, PhD, Ed S); vocational/technical education (MS Ed, PhD, Ed S). *Accreditation:* NCATE. Part-time and evening/weekend programs available. *Faculty:* 29 full-time (19 women), 33 part-time/adjunct (29 women). *Students:* 85 full-time (53 women), 271 part-time (195 women); includes 62 minority (19 Black or African American, non-Hispanic/Latino; 3 American Indian or Alaska Native, non-Hispanic/Latino; 13 Asian, non-Hispanic/Latino; 22 Hispanic/Latino;

1 Native Hawaiian or other Pacific Islander, non-Hispanic/Latino; 4 Two or more races, non-Hispanic/Latino), 41 international. Average age 36. 155 applicants, 71% accepted, 71 enrolled. In 2013, 60 master's, 20 doctorates awarded. *Degree requirements:* For master's, thesis optional; for doctorate, thesis/dissertation, oral and written exams; for Ed S, oral presentation, project. *Entrance requirements:* For master's, GRE General Test (if undergraduate GPA is below 3.0), minimum undergraduate GPA of 3.0 or equivalent; for doctorate, GRE General Test (minimum combined verbal and quantitative score of 1000, 300 for new scoring), minimum undergraduate GPA of 3.0 or equivalent; master's degree with minimum GPA of 3.0 or equivalent; for Ed S, GRE General Test (minimum combined verbal and quantitative score of 1000, 300 for new scoring), minimum undergraduate GPA of 3.0 or equivalent; master's degree. Additional exam requirements/recommendations for international students: Required—TOEFL (minimum score 550 paper-based; 77 iBT). *Application deadline:* For fall admission, 12/15 for domestic students, 3/1 for international students; for spring admission, 9/15 for domestic students, 8/1 for international students. Application fee: $60 ($75 for international students). Electronic applications accepted. *Financial support:* Fellowships with full tuition reimbursements, research assistantships with full tuition reimbursements, teaching assistantships with full tuition reimbursements, career-related internships or fieldwork, and tuition waivers (full) available. Support available to part-time students. Financial award application deadline: 3/1; financial award applicants required to submit FAFSA. *Faculty research:* Literacy acquisition and development, teacher beliefs and knowledge, recruitment and retention of underrepresented students, economic education, literacy discourse. *Unit head:* Dr. Phillip J. VanFossen, Head, 765-494-7935, Fax: 765-496-1622, E-mail: vanfoss@purdue.edu. *Application contact:* Cindy Blankenship, Graduate Contact, 765-494-2345, Fax: 765-494-5832, E-mail: prater0@purdue.edu.
Website: http://www.edci.purdue.edu/.

Queens College of the City University of New York, Division of Graduate Studies, Division of Education, Department of Secondary Education, Flushing, NY 11367-1597. Offers art (MS Ed); biology (MS Ed, AC); chemistry (MS Ed, AC); earth sciences (MS Ed, AC); English (MS Ed, AC); French (MS Ed, AC); Italian (MS Ed, AC); mathematics (MS Ed, AC); music (MS Ed, AC); physics (MS Ed, AC); social studies (MS Ed, AC); Spanish (MS Ed, AC). Part-time and evening/weekend programs available. *Degree requirements:* For master's, research project; for AC, thesis optional. *Entrance requirements:* For master's, minimum GPA of 3.0. Additional exam requirements/recommendations for international students: Required—TOEFL.

Rhode Island College, School of Graduate Studies, Faculty of Arts and Sciences, Department of Art, Providence, RI 02908-1991. Offers art education (MA, MAT); media studies (MA). *Accreditation:* NASAD (one or more programs are accredited). Part-time and evening/weekend programs available. *Faculty:* 7 full-time (4 women), 4 part-time/adjunct (3 women). *Students:* 8 full-time (4 women), 12 part-time (9 women), 1 international. Average age 32. In 2013, 4 master's awarded. *Degree requirements:* For master's, thesis. *Entrance requirements:* For master's, GRE General Test, portfolio (MA), 3 letters of recommendation, interview. Additional exam requirements/recommendations for international students: Recommended—TOEFL (minimum score 550 paper-based; 79 iBT). *Application deadline:* For fall admission, 3/1 for domestic students. Applications are processed on a rolling basis. Application fee: $50. *Expenses:* Tuition, state resident: full-time $8928; part-time $372 per credit hour. Tuition, nonresident: full-time $17,376; part-time $724 per credit hour. *Required fees:* $602; $22 per credit. $72 per term. *Financial support:* In 2013–14, 2 teaching assistantships with full tuition reimbursements (averaging $1,500 per year) were awarded; career-related internships or fieldwork, Federal Work-Study, scholarships/grants, health care benefits, and unspecified assistantships also available. Support available to part-time students. Financial award application deadline: 5/15; financial award applicants required to submit FAFSA. *Unit head:* Prof. William Martin, Chair, 401-456-8054. *Application contact:* Graduate Studies, 401-456-8700.
Website: http://www.ric.edu/art/index.php.

Rhode Island School of Design, Graduate Studies, Program in Art Education, Providence, RI 02903-2784. Offers MA, MAT. *Accreditation:* NASAD. *Faculty:* 3 full-time (1 woman), 2 part-time/adjunct (both women). *Students:* 18 full-time (16 women); includes 6 minority (2 Asian, non-Hispanic/Latino; 3 Hispanic/Latino; 1 Two or more races, non-Hispanic/Latino), 3 international. Average age 29. In 2013, 9 master's awarded. *Degree requirements:* For master's, thesis, exhibit. *Entrance requirements:* For master's, portfolio, statement of purpose, letters of recommendation. Additional exam requirements/recommendations for international students: Required—TOEFL (minimum score 580 paper-based; 93 iBT). *Application deadline:* For fall admission, 2/1 for domestic and international students. Application fee: $60. *Expenses:* Tuition: Full-time $42,622. *Required fees:* $310. *Financial support:* Fellowships, teaching assistantships, career-related internships or fieldwork, Federal Work-Study, and institutionally sponsored loans available. Financial award application deadline: 2/15; financial award applicants required to submit FAFSA. *Unit head:* Paul Sproll, Head, 401-454-6695, Fax: 401-454-6694, E-mail: psproll@risd.edu. *Application contact:* Edward Newhall, Director of Admissions, 401-454-6307, E-mail: enewhall@risd.edu.

Rochester Institute of Technology, Graduate Enrollment Services, College of Imaging Arts and Sciences, School of Art, Program in Art Education, Rochester, NY 14623-5603. Offers MST. *Accreditation:* NASAD; Teacher Education Accreditation Council. *Students:* 10 full-time (9 women), 1 international. Average age 26. 19 applicants, 63% accepted, 10 enrolled. In 2013, 7 master's awarded. *Entrance requirements:* For master's, portfolio, minimum GPA of 3.0. Additional exam requirements/recommendations for international students: Required—TOEFL (minimum score 550 paper-based; 79 iBT) or IELTS (minimum score 6.5). *Application deadline:* For fall admission, 2/15 priority date for domestic and international students. Applications are processed on a rolling basis. Application fee: $60. Electronic applications accepted. *Expenses:* Tuition: Full-time $37,236; part-time $1552 per credit hour. *Required fees:* $250. *Financial support:* Career-related internships or fieldwork, institutionally sponsored loans, and scholarships/grants available. Financial award application deadline: 8/30; financial award applicants required to submit FAFSA. *Unit head:* Carol Woodlock, Graduate Program Director, 585-475-7556, E-mail: cmwfaa@rit.edu. *Application contact:* Diane Ellison, Assistant Vice President, Graduate Enrollment Services, 585-475-2229, Fax: 585-475-7164, E-mail: gradinfo@rit.edu.
Website: http://cias.rit.edu.

Rocky Mountain College of Art + Design, Program in Education, Leadership + Emerging Technologies, Lakewood, CO 80214. Offers MA. Postbaccalaureate distance learning degree programs offered (no on-campus study).

Sage Graduate School, Esteves School of Education, Program in Teaching, Troy, NY 12180-4115. Offers art education (MAT); English (MAT); mathematics (MAT); social studies (MAT). *Accreditation:* NASAD. Part-time and evening/weekend programs available. *Faculty:* 10 full-time (6 women), 6 part-time/adjunct (4 women). *Students:* 1 (woman) full-time, 12 part-time (10 women); includes 2 minority (1 Hispanic/Latino; 1 Two or more races, non-Hispanic/Latino). Average age 26. 13 applicants, 31% accepted, 1 enrolled. In 2013, 18 master's awarded. *Entrance requirements:* For master's, assessment of writing skills, minimum undergraduate GPA of 2.75 overall, 3.0 in content area; current resume; 2 letters of recommendation. Additional exam

requirements/recommendations for international students: Required—TOEFL (minimum score 550 paper-based). *Application deadline:* For fall admission, 8/1 for domestic students. Applications are processed on a rolling basis. Application fee: $40. *Expenses:* Tuition: Full-time $11,880; part-time $660 per credit hour. *Financial support:* Fellowships, research assistantships, Federal Work-Study, scholarships/grants, and unspecified assistantships available. Support available to part-time students. Financial award application deadline: 3/1; financial award applicants required to submit FAFSA. *Unit head:* Dr. Lori Quigley, Dean, Esteves School of Education, 518-244-2326, Fax: 518-244-4571, E-mail: l.quigley@sage.edu. *Application contact:* Kelly Jones, Director, 518-244-2433, Fax: 518-244-6880, E-mail: jonesk4@sage.edu.

Saint Michael's College, Graduate Programs, Program in Education, Colchester, VT 05439. Offers administration (M Ed, CAGS); arts in education (CAGS); curriculum and instruction (M Ed, CAGS); information technology (CAGS); reading (M Ed); special education (M Ed, CAGS); technology (M Ed). Part-time and evening/weekend programs available. *Degree requirements:* For master's, thesis. *Entrance requirements:* For master's, minimum GPA of 3.0. Electronic applications accepted. *Faculty research:* Integrative curriculum, moral and spiritual dimensions of education, learning styles, multiple intelligences, integrating technology into the curriculum.

Salem College, Department of Education, Winston-Salem, NC 27101. Offers art education (MAT); elementary education (M Ed, MAT); language and literacy (M Ed); middle school education (MAT); school counseling (M Ed); second language studies (MAT); secondary education (MAT); special education (M Ed, MAT). *Accreditation:* NCATE. Part-time and evening/weekend programs available. Postbaccalaureate distance learning degree programs offered (minimal on-campus study). *Degree requirements:* For master's, practicum (MAT), project (M Ed); oral and written comprehensive exams. *Entrance requirements:* For master's, minimum GPA of 2.5. *Faculty research:* Content area reading strategies, literacy development, brain compatible instruction.

Salem State University, School of Graduate Studies, Program in Art, Salem, MA 01970-5353. Offers MAT. *Accreditation:* NASAD. Part-time and evening/weekend programs available. *Students:* 17 part-time (16 women); includes 1 minority (Asian, non-Hispanic/Latino). 2 applicants, 50% accepted, 1 enrolled. In 2013, 15 master's awarded. *Entrance requirements:* For master's, GRE or MAT. Additional exam requirements/recommendations for international students: Required—TOEFL (minimum score 550 paper-based; 80 iBT) or IELTS (minimum score 5.5). *Application deadline:* For fall admission, 5/1 for domestic and international students; for spring admission, 10/1 for domestic and international students. Application fee: $50. *Financial support:* Career-related internships or fieldwork, Federal Work-Study, scholarships/grants, and unspecified assistantships available. Support available to part-time students. Financial award application deadline: 5/1; financial award applicants required to submit FAFSA. *Unit head:* Airisenne Angle, Program Coordinator, 978-542-6323, E-mail: aangle@salemstate.edu. *Application contact:* Dr. Lee A. Brossoit, Assistant Dean of Graduate Admissions, 978-542-6673, Fax: 978-542-7215, E-mail: lbrossoit@salemstate.edu.
Website: http://www.salemstate.edu/academics/schools/12113.php.

School of the Art Institute of Chicago, Graduate Division, Program in Art Education and Art Teaching, Chicago, IL 60603-3103. Offers MAAE, MAT. *Accreditation:* NASAD. *Entrance requirements:* Additional exam requirements/recommendations for international students: Required—TOEFL (minimum score 600 paper-based; 100 iBT), IELTS (minimum score 7).

School of the Museum of Fine Arts, Boston, Graduate Programs, Boston, MA 02115. Offers art education (MAT); studio art (MFA, Postbaccalaureate Certificate). *Accreditation:* NASAD (one or more programs are accredited). Postbaccalaureate distance learning degree programs offered. Terminal master's awarded for partial completion of doctoral program. *Degree requirements:* For master's, thesis (for some programs), exhibition thesis. *Entrance requirements:* For master's, BFA, bachelor's degree or equivalent in related area, portfolio; for Postbaccalaureate Certificate, portfolio, BFA or equivalent. Additional exam requirements/recommendations for international students: Required—TOEFL (minimum score 550 paper-based). Electronic applications accepted. *Faculty research:* Public art commissions, National Endowment for the Arts grant recipients, international exhibitions.

School of Visual Arts, Graduate Programs, Art Criticism and Writing Department, New York, NY 10010. Offers MFA. *Degree requirements:* For master's, thesis, 60 credits, including all required courses; residency of two academic years. *Entrance requirements:* For master's, typed writing sample between 2,500 and 3,000 words in length; personal interviews. Additional exam requirements/recommendations for international students: Required—TOEFL (minimum score 550 paper-based; 79 iBT). Electronic applications accepted. *Faculty research:* Art, writing, criticism, editing, art history, philosophy.

School of Visual Arts, Graduate Programs, Art Education Department, New York, NY 10010-3994. Offers MAT. Part-time programs available. *Degree requirements:* For master's, one foreign language, thesis, 60 credits, including all required courses; minimum cumulative GPA of 3.0; residency of two academic years. *Entrance requirements:* For master's, Liberal Arts and Sciences Test (strongly recommended), CD with 15 to 20 images (jpeg or tiff formats, and at least 600x500 pixels); 30 credits each in studio art and liberal arts and sciences; 12 credits in art history; coursework in language other than English; personal interview. Additional exam requirements/recommendations for international students: Required—TOEFL (minimum score 550 paper-based; 79 iBT). Electronic applications accepted. *Faculty research:* Teaching art to children in pre-kindergarten through grade 12.

Simon Fraser University, Office of Graduate Studies, Faculty of Education, Program in Arts Education, Burnaby, BC V5A 1S6, Canada. Offers M Ed, MA, Ed D, PhD. Part-time and evening/weekend programs available. *Faculty:* 8 full-time (5 women). *Degree requirements:* For master's, comprehensive exam (for some programs), thesis (for some programs); for doctorate, comprehensive exam (for some programs), thesis/dissertation (for some programs). *Entrance requirements:* For master's, minimum GPA of 3.0 (on scale of 4.33), or 3.33 based on last 60 credits of undergraduate courses; for doctorate, minimum GPA of 3.5 (on scale of 4.33). Additional exam requirements/recommendations for international students: Recommended—TOEFL (minimum score 580 paper-based; 93 iBT), IELTS (minimum score 7), TWE (minimum score 5). *Application deadline:* For fall admission, 1/31 for domestic and international students. Application fee: $90 ($125 for international students). *Expenses: Tuition, area resident:* Full-time $5084 Canadian dollars. *Required fees:* $840 Canadian dollars. *Financial support:* In 2013–14, fellowships (averaging $6,250 per year) were awarded; research assistantships, teaching assistantships, and scholarships/grants also available. *Faculty research:* Drama education, poetic and performative inquiry, the integration of the arts in education, art therapy, arts-based narrative and arts-informed research methodologies. *Unit head:* Dr. John Nesbit, Associate Dean, Graduate Studies in Education, 778-782-7123, Fax: 778-782-4320, E-mail: mesbit@sfu.ca. *Application contact:* Graduate Secretary, 778-782-3984, Fax: 778-782-4320, E-mail: educmast@sfu.ca.

Southern Connecticut State University, School of Graduate Studies, School of Arts and Sciences, Department of Art, New Haven, CT 06515-1355. Offers art education (MS). Part-time and evening/weekend programs available. *Degree requirements:* For

master's, thesis or alternative. *Entrance requirements:* For master's, interview. Electronic applications accepted.

Southwestern Oklahoma State University, College of Arts and Sciences, Department of Art, Weatherford, OK 73096-3098. Offers art education (M Ed). Part-time programs available. *Degree requirements:* For master's, exam. *Entrance requirements:* For master's, GRE General Test or minimum undergraduate GPA of 3.0. Additional exam requirements/recommendations for international students: Required—TOEFL.

Spalding University, Graduate Studies, College of Education, Programs in Education, Louisville, KY 40203-2188. Offers art teacher education (MAT); business teacher education (MAT); elementary school education (MAT); foreign language (MAT); general education (MA Ed); high school education (MAT); middle school education (MAT); school administration (MA Ed); secondary education (MAT); special education (learning and behavioral disorders) (MAT); student guidance counselor (MA); teacher education and professional development (MAT). *Accreditation:* NCATE. Part-time and evening/weekend programs available. *Faculty:* 12 full-time (11 women), 6 part-time/adjunct (4 women). *Students:* 92 full-time (63 women), 36 part-time (29 women); includes 43 minority (41 Black or African American, non-Hispanic/Latino; 2 Two or more races, non-Hispanic/Latino). Average age 35. 77 applicants, 48% accepted, 30 enrolled. In 2013, 81 master's awarded. *Degree requirements:* For master's, portfolio, final project, clinical experience. *Entrance requirements:* For master's, GRE General Test or MAT, interview, letters of recommendation, resume. Additional exam requirements/recommendations for international students: Required—TOEFL (minimum score 535 paper-based). *Application deadline:* Applications are processed on a rolling basis. Application fee: $30. Electronic applications accepted. *Expenses: Tuition:* Full-time $21,450. *Required fees:* $810. Tuition and fees vary according to course load, degree level, program and student level. *Financial support:* Scholarships/grants, traineeships, and unspecified assistantships available. Financial award application deadline: 3/30; financial award applicants required to submit FAFSA. *Faculty research:* Instructional technology, achievement gap, classroom management, assessment. *Unit head:* Dr. Beverly Keepers, Dean, 502-588-7121, Fax: 502-585-7123, E-mail: bkeepers@spalding.edu. *Application contact:* Bonnie Caughron, Administrative Assistant, College of Education, 502-873-4262, E-mail: bcaughron@spalding.edu.

State University of New York at New Paltz, Graduate School, School of Fine and Performing Arts, Department of Art Education, New Paltz, NY 12561. Offers visual arts education (MS Ed). *Accreditation:* NASAD. Part-time and evening/weekend programs available. *Faculty:* 2 full-time (1 woman). *Students:* 15 part-time (all women); includes 2 minority (both Hispanic/Latino). Average age 33. 10 applicants, 90% accepted, 9 enrolled. In 2013, 14 master's awarded. *Degree requirements:* For master's, thesis, portfolio. *Entrance requirements:* For master's, New York state art education teaching certificate, minimum GPA of 3.0, portfolio. Additional exam requirements/recommendations for international students: Required—TOEFL (minimum score 550 paper-based; 80 iBT), IELTS (minimum score 6.5). *Application deadline:* For fall admission, 4/15 for domestic and international students. Application fee: $50. Electronic applications accepted. *Expenses:* Tuition, state resident: full-time $9870; part-time $411 per credit. Tuition, nonresident: full-time $18,350; part-time $765 per credit. *Required fees:* $1213. Tuition and fees vary according to program. *Financial support:* In 2013–14, 1 research assistantship with partial tuition reimbursement (averaging $5,000 per year) was awarded. *Unit head:* Prof. Beth Thomas, Interim Director, 845-257-3850, E-mail: thomasb@newpaltz.edu. *Application contact:* Prof. Aaron Knochel, Graduate Coordinator, 845-257-3837, E-mail: knochela@newpaltz.edu.

State University of New York at Oswego, Graduate Studies, School of Education, Department of Curriculum and Instruction, Oswego, NY 13126. Offers adolescence education (MST); art education (MAT); childhood education (MST); elementary education (MS Ed); literacy education (MS Ed); secondary education (MS Ed); special education (MS Ed). Part-time and evening/weekend programs available. *Degree requirements:* For master's, comprehensive exam (for some programs), thesis optional. *Entrance requirements:* For master's, GRE General Test, minimum GPA of 2.7, provisional teaching certificate. Additional exam requirements/recommendations for international students: Required—TOEFL (minimum score 560 paper-based). *Faculty research:* Classroom applications for microcomputers; classroom questioning, wait-time, and achievement; values clarification and academic achievement.

Sul Ross State University, School of Arts and Sciences, Department of Fine Arts and Communication, Alpine, TX 79832. Offers art history (MA); studio art (MA), including art education, ceramics, painting, sculpture. Part-time programs available. *Degree requirements:* For master's, oral or written exam. *Entrance requirements:* For master's, GRE General Test, minimum GPA of 2.5 in last 60 hours of undergraduate work. *Faculty research:* Ceramic sculpture, watercolor, wood sculpture, rock art.

Syracuse University, School of Education, Program in Art Education, Syracuse, NY 13244. Offers preparation (MS); professional certification (MS). Part-time and evening/weekend programs available. *Students:* 2 full-time (1 woman), 3 part-time (2 women). Average age 29. 3 applicants, 100% accepted. In 2013, 9 master's awarded. *Degree requirements:* For master's, thesis or alternative. *Entrance requirements:* For master's, interview. Additional exam requirements/recommendations for international students: Required—TOEFL (minimum score 100 iBT). *Application deadline:* For fall admission, 1/15 priority date for domestic and international students; for spring admission, 10/15 priority date for domestic and international students. Applications are processed on a rolling basis. Application fee: $75. Electronic applications accepted. *Financial support:* Fellowships with full tuition reimbursements and teaching assistantships with full and partial tuition reimbursements available. *Unit head:* Dr. James Haywood Rolling, Jr., Director, 315-443-2355, E-mail: jrolling@syr.edu. *Application contact:* Laurie Deyo, Graduate Recruiter, School of Education, 315-443-2505, E-mail: e-gradrcrt@syr.edu.
Website: http://soeweb.syr.edu/future/degree_programs/masters_degrees.aspx.

Teachers College, Columbia University, Graduate Faculty of Education, Department of Arts and Humanities, Program in Art and Art Education, New York, NY 10027. Offers Ed M, MA, Ed D, Ed DCT. *Accreditation:* NCATE. Part-time and evening/weekend programs available. *Faculty:* 5 full-time, 8 part-time/adjunct. *Students:* 29 full-time (26 women), 87 part-time (78 women); includes 39 minority (8 Black or African American, non-Hispanic/Latino; 14 Asian, non-Hispanic/Latino; 10 Hispanic/Latino; 7 Two or more races, non-Hispanic/Latino), 15 international. Average age 34. 65 applicants, 72% accepted, 25 enrolled. In 2013, 35 master's, 5 doctorates awarded. *Degree requirements:* For doctorate, variable foreign language requirement, thesis/dissertation. *Entrance requirements:* For master's, portfolio; for doctorate, portfolio, five years of professional experience in arts/museum/studio education. Additional exam requirements/recommendations for international students: Required—TOEFL (minimum score 600 paper-based; 100 iBT). *Application deadline:* For fall admission, 1/2 priority date for domestic students; for spring admission, 11/1 for domestic students. Applications are processed on a rolling basis. Application fee: $65. Electronic applications accepted. *Financial support:* Research assistantships, teaching assistantships, career-related internships or fieldwork, Federal Work-Study, institutionally sponsored loans, and tuition waivers (full and partial) available. Support available to part-time students. Financial award application deadline: 2/1. *Faculty research:* Learning and transfer of learning in the arts, instructional methods in the arts, role of artists in the education of children, cultural experiences in arts education, twentieth-century and contemporary arts practice. *Unit head:* Prof. Judith M. Burton, Program Coordinator, 212-678-3336, E-mail: burton@exchange.tc.columbia.edu. *Application contact:* Thomas P. Rock, Director of Admissions, 212-678-3083, Fax: 212-678-4171, E-mail: rock@tc.edu.
Website: http://www.tc.edu/a%26h/ArtEd/.

Temple University, Center for the Arts, Tyler School of Art, Department of Art Education and Community Arts Practices, Philadelphia, PA 19122-6096. Offers art education (Ed M). Part-time and evening/weekend programs available. *Faculty:* 3 full-time (1 woman). *Students:* 8 full-time (6 women), 8 part-time (7 women); includes 3 minority (2 Black or African American, non-Hispanic/Latino; 1 Hispanic/Latino). 14 applicants, 50% accepted, 5 enrolled. In 2013, 7 master's awarded. *Degree requirements:* For master's, paper, portfolio review. *Entrance requirements:* For master's, GRE or MAT, minimum GPA of 3.0, slide portfolio, 40 credits in studio art, 9 credits in art history, letters of recommendation, resume/curriculum vitae. Additional exam requirements/recommendations for international students: Required—TOEFL (minimum score 550 paper-based; 79 iBT), IELTS (minimum score 6.5). *Application deadline:* For fall admission, 1/15 for domestic and international students; for spring admission, 11/1 for domestic and international students. Applications are processed on a rolling basis. Application fee: $60. Electronic applications accepted. *Expenses:* Contact institution. *Financial support:* Research assistantships with full tuition reimbursements, teaching assistantships, and Federal Work-Study available. Support available to part-time students. Financial award application deadline: 1/15; financial award applicants required to submit FAFSA. *Unit head:* Dr. Lisa Kay, Chair, 215-777-9763, E-mail: lisakay@temple.edu. *Application contact:* Nicole Hall, Director of Admissions, 215-777-9090, E-mail: tylerart@temple.edu.
Website: http://www.temple.edu/tyler/arted/.

Texas Tech University, Graduate School, College of Visual and Performing Arts, School of Art, Lubbock, TX 79409-2081. Offers art (MFA); art education (MAE); art history (MA). *Accreditation:* NASAD (one or more programs are accredited). Part-time programs available. Postbaccalaureate distance learning degree programs offered (minimal on-campus study). *Faculty:* 29 full-time (15 women). *Students:* 32 full-time (17 women), 20 part-time (17 women); includes 12 minority (11 Hispanic/Latino; 1 Two or more races, non-Hispanic/Latino), 6 international. Average age 32. 41 applicants, 59% accepted, 13 enrolled. In 2013, 25 master's awarded. *Degree requirements:* For master's, variable foreign language requirement, comprehensive exam, thesis (for some programs), exhibition (for MFA). *Entrance requirements:* For master's, GRE (for MA). Additional exam requirements/recommendations for international students: Required—TOEFL (minimum score 550 paper-based; 79 iBT), IELTS (minimum score 6.5). *Application deadline:* For fall admission, 6/1 priority date for domestic students, 1/15 priority date for international students; for spring admission, 9/1 priority date for domestic students, 6/15 priority date for international students. Applications are processed on a rolling basis. Application fee: $60. Electronic applications accepted. *Expenses:* Tuition, state resident: full-time $6062; part-time $252.57 per credit hour. Tuition, nonresident: full-time $14,558; part-time $606.57 per credit hour. *Required fees:* $2655; $35 per credit hour. $907.50 per semester. Tuition and fees vary according to course load. *Financial support:* In 2013–14, 44 students received support, including 32 fellowships (averaging $1,311 per year), 1 research assistantship (averaging $4,960 per year), 30 teaching assistantships (averaging $4,967 per year); Federal Work-Study, scholarships/grants, and unspecified assistantships also available. Financial award application deadline: 2/15; financial award applicants required to submit FAFSA. *Faculty research:* Modern and contemporary art; contemporary Chicano/a art; transformation of multidisciplinary approach to printmaking; figurative painting and an intense interest in space as metaphor for community; working-class, sexuality and race issues; letter press posters; creating and crafting of metalsmithing. *Unit head:* Prof. Lydia Thompson, Director and Professor, 806-742-3825 Ext. 255, E-mail: lydia.thompson@ttu.edu. *Application contact:* Ryan Scheckel, Academic Advisor, 806-742-3825 Ext. 222, E-mail: ryan.scheckel@ttu.edu.
Website: http://www.art.ttu.edu.

Towson University, Arts Integration Institute, Towson, MD 21252-0001. Offers Postbaccalaureate Certificate. Program offered jointly with The Johns Hopkins University, University of Maryland, College Park and University of Maryland, Baltimore County. *Students:* 24 part-time (all women). *Entrance requirements:* For degree, bachelor's degree, minimum GPA of 3.0 (based upon last 60 credits of study); teaching experience (preferred). *Application deadline:* Applications are processed on a rolling basis. Application fee: $45. Electronic applications accepted. *Unit head:* Prof. Susan Rotkovitz, Program Director, 410-704-3658, E-mail: srotkovitz@towson.edu. *Application contact:* Alicia Arkell-Kleis, Information Contact, 410-704-6004, E-mail: grads@towson.edu.
Website: http://grad.towson.edu/program/certificate/arin-pbc/.

Towson University, Program in Art Education, Towson, MD 21252-0001. Offers M Ed. *Accreditation:* NCATE. Part-time and evening/weekend programs available. *Students:* 1 (woman) full-time, 39 part-time (31 women); includes 1 minority (Black or African American, non-Hispanic/Latino), 1 international. *Degree requirements:* For master's, thesis optional. *Entrance requirements:* For master's, bachelor's degree and/or certification in art education, minimum GPA of 3.0, resume. *Application deadline:* Applications are processed on a rolling basis. Application fee: $45. Electronic applications accepted. *Financial support:* Application deadline: 4/1. *Unit head:* Dr. Ray Martens, Graduate Program Director, 410-704-3819, E-mail: rmartens@towson.edu. *Application contact:* Alicia Arkell-Kleis, Information Contact, 410-704-6004, E-mail: grads@towson.edu.
Website: http://grad.towson.edu/program/master/ared-med/.

Troy University, Graduate School, College of Education, Program in Teacher Education-Multiple Levels, Troy, AL 36082. Offers art education (MS); gifted education (MS); instrumental (MS); physical education (MS); reading specialist (MS); vocal/choral (MS). Part-time and evening/weekend programs available. *Faculty:* 8 full-time (4 women). *Students:* 2 full-time (both women), 17 part-time (15 women); includes 3 minority (all Black or African American, non-Hispanic/Latino). Average age 30. 9 applicants, 89% accepted, 4 enrolled. In 2013, 19 master's awarded. *Degree requirements:* For master's, comprehensive exam, thesis. *Entrance requirements:* For master's, GRE (minimum score of 850 on old exam or 290 on new exam), GMAT (minimum score of 380), or MAT (minimum score of 385), bachelor's degree; minimum undergraduate GPA of 2.5 or 3.0 on last 30 semester hours, letter of recommendation. Additional exam requirements/recommendations for international students: Required—TOEFL (minimum score 523 paper-based; 70 iBT), IELTS (minimum score 6). *Application deadline:* Applications are processed on a rolling basis. Application fee: $50. Electronic applications accepted. *Expenses:* Tuition, state resident: full-time $6084; part-time $338 per credit hour. Tuition, nonresident: full-time $12,168; part-time $676 per credit hour. *Required fees:* $630; $35 per credit hour. $50 per semester. *Financial support:* Available to part-time students. Applicants required to submit FAFSA. *Unit head:* Dr. Charlotte S. Minnick, Director, Teacher Education, 334-670-3544, Fax: 334-670-3548, E-mail: csminnick@troy.edu. *Application contact:* Brenda K. Campbell, Director of Graduate Admissions, 334-670-3178, Fax: 334-670-3733, E-mail: bcamp@troy.edu.

Tufts University, Graduate School of Arts and Sciences, Department of Education, Medford, MA 02155. Offers art education (MAT); education (MA, MAT, MS, PhD), including educational studies (MA), elementary education (MAT), middle and secondary education (MA, MAT), museum education (MA), secondary education (MA), STEM education (MS, PhD); school psychology (MA, Ed S). *Faculty:* 13 full-time, 9 part-time/adjunct. *Students:* 140 full-time (119 women); includes 33 minority (5 Black or African American, non-Hispanic/Latino; 1 American Indian or Alaska Native, non-Hispanic/Latino; 8 Asian, non-Hispanic/Latino; 11 Hispanic/Latino; 8 Two or more races, non-Hispanic/Latino), 5 international. Average age 27. 227 applicants, 60% accepted, 66 enrolled. In 2013, 121 master's, 11 other advanced degrees awarded. *Degree requirements:* For doctorate, thesis/dissertation. *Entrance requirements:* For master's and doctorate, GRE General Test. Additional exam requirements/recommendations for international students: Required—TOEFL (minimum score 550 paper-based; 80 iBT), IELTS (minimum score 6.5). *Application deadline:* For fall admission, 1/2 for domestic and international students; for spring admission, 10/15 for domestic students, 9/15 for international students. Applications are processed on a rolling basis. Application fee: $75. Electronic applications accepted. *Financial support:* Teaching assistantships with full and partial tuition reimbursements, Federal Work-Study, scholarships/grants, and tuition waivers (partial) available. Support available to part-time students. Financial award application deadline: 1/2. *Unit head:* David Hammer, Chair, 617-627-3244. *Application contact:* Patricia Romeo, Department Administrator, 617-627-3244.
Website: http://www.ase.tufts.edu/education/.

The University of Alabama at Birmingham, School of Education, Program in Arts Education, Birmingham, AL 35294. Offers MA Ed. *Accreditation:* NCATE. *Degree requirements:* For master's, thesis optional. *Entrance requirements:* For master's, GRE General Test, MAT, or NTE, minimum GPA of 3.0. Electronic applications accepted.

The University of Arizona, College of Fine Arts, School of Art, Program in Art Education, Tucson, AZ 85721. Offers MA. *Accreditation:* NASAD. *Faculty:* 29 full-time (16 women), 7 part-time/adjunct (4 women). *Students:* 9 full-time (7 women), 5 part-time (4 women); includes 3 minority (1 Asian, non-Hispanic/Latino; 1 Hispanic/Latino; 1 Two or more races, non-Hispanic/Latino). Average age 34. 8 applicants, 38% accepted, 1 enrolled. In 2013, 6 master's awarded. *Degree requirements:* For master's, thesis. *Entrance requirements:* For master's, portfolio, resume, autobiography, 3 letters of reference, writing sample. Additional exam requirements/recommendations for international students: Required—TOEFL (minimum score 550 paper-based; 79 iBT). *Application deadline:* For fall admission, 2/1 for domestic students, 12/1 for international students; for spring admission, 10/1 for domestic students, 9/1 for international students. Applications are processed on a rolling basis. Application fee: $75. Electronic applications accepted. *Expenses:* Tuition, state resident: full-time $11,526. Tuition, nonresident: full-time $27,398. *Financial support:* In 2013–14, 36 teaching assistantships with full tuition reimbursements (averaging $8,544 per year) were awarded; research assistantships with partial tuition reimbursements, career-related internships or fieldwork, Federal Work-Study, institutionally sponsored loans, scholarships/grants, tuition waivers (full and partial), and unspecified assistantships also available. Support available to part-time students. Financial award application deadline: 4/1; financial award applicants required to submit FAFSA. *Faculty research:* Artistic styles, visual perception, integration of arts into elementary curricula, aesthetics of the vanishing roadsides of America. *Unit head:* Dennis L. Jones, Chair, 520-621-7000, E-mail: dennisj@email.arizona.edu. *Application contact:* Megan Bartel, Graduate Coordinator, 520-621-8518, E-mail: mbartel@email.arizona.edu.
Website: http://www.arts.arizona.edu/arted/grad.html.

The University of Arizona, College of Fine Arts, School of Art, Program in Art History and Education, Tucson, AZ 85721. Offers PhD. *Faculty:* 29 full-time (16 women), 7 part-time/adjunct (4 women). *Students:* 25 full-time (19 women), 4 part-time (3 women); includes 2 minority (1 Asian, non-Hispanic/Latino; 1 Two or more races, non-Hispanic/Latino), 7 international. Average age 37. 18 applicants, 50% accepted, 6 enrolled. In 2013, 2 doctorates awarded. *Degree requirements:* For doctorate, thesis/dissertation. *Entrance requirements:* Additional exam requirements/recommendations for international students: Required—TOEFL (minimum score 550 paper-based; 79 iBT). *Application deadline:* For fall admission, 2/1 for domestic and international students. Application fee: $75. Electronic applications accepted. *Expenses:* Tuition, state resident: full-time $11,526. Tuition, nonresident: full-time $27,398. *Financial support:* In 2013–14, 36 teaching assistantships with full and partial tuition reimbursements (averaging $8,544 per year) were awarded; research assistantships with full and partial tuition reimbursements also available. *Unit head:* Dennis L. Jones, Director, 520-621-7000, Fax: 520-621-2955, E-mail: dennisj@email.arizona.edu. *Application contact:* Megan Bartel, Graduate Program Coordinator, 520-621-8518, Fax: 520-621-2955, E-mail: mbartel@email.arizona.edu.
Website: http://art.arizona.edu/students/programs-of-study/doctor-of-philosophy-in-art-history-and-education.

University of Arkansas at Little Rock, Graduate School, College of Arts, Humanities, and Social Science, Department of Art, Little Rock, AR 72204-1099. Offers art education (MA); art history (MA); studio art (MA). *Accreditation:* NASAD. Part-time programs available. *Degree requirements:* For master's, 4 foreign languages, oral exam, oral defense of thesis or exhibit. *Entrance requirements:* For master's, portfolio review or term paper evaluation, minimum GPA of 2.7. *Expenses:* Tuition, state resident: full-time $5690; part-time $284.50 per credit hour. Tuition, nonresident: full-time $13,030; part-time $651.50 per credit hour. *Required fees:* $1121; $672 per term. One-time fee: $40 full-time.

The University of British Columbia, Faculty of Education, Department of Curriculum and Pedagogy, Vancouver, BC V6T 1Z4, Canada. Offers art education (M Ed, MA); business education (MA); curriculum studies (M Ed, MA, PhD); home economics education (M Ed, MA); math education (M Ed, MA); music education (M Ed, MA); physical education (M Ed, MA); science education (M Ed, MA); social studies education (M Ed, MA); technology studies education (M Ed, MA). Part-time programs available. Postbaccalaureate distance learning degree programs offered (no on-campus study). *Faculty:* 32 full-time (14 women), 1 (woman) part-time/adjunct. *Students:* 163 full-time, 134 part-time, 42 international. Average age 40. 160 applicants, 75% accepted, 97 enrolled. In 2013, 68 master's, 7 doctorates awarded. *Degree requirements:* For master's, thesis (MA); for doctorate, comprehensive exam, thesis/dissertation. *Entrance requirements:* Additional exam requirements/recommendations for international students: Required—TOEFL (minimum score 580 paper-based; 92 iBT), IELTS (minimum score 6.5). *Application deadline:* For fall admission, 12/1 for domestic and international students; for spring admission, 10/1 for domestic students, 9/1 for international students. Application fee: $90 Canadian dollars ($150 Canadian dollars for international students). Electronic applications accepted. *Expenses:* Contact institution. *Financial support:* In 2013–14, 10 fellowships with partial tuition reimbursements (averaging $16,000 per year), 11 research assistantships with partial tuition reimbursements (averaging $14,000 per year), 27 teaching assistantships with partial tuition reimbursements (averaging $14,000 per year) were awarded; tuition waivers (partial) also available. *Faculty research:* School subjects, teaching and learning. *Unit head:* Dr. Peter Grimmett, Head, 604-822-5422, Fax: 604-822-4714, E-mail: anna.ip@ubc.ca. *Application contact:* Basia Zurek, Graduate Programs Assistant, 604-822-5367, Fax: 604-822-4714, E-mail: edcp.grad@ubc.ca.
Website: http://www.edcp.educ.ubc.ca/.

University of Central Florida, College of Education and Human Performance, School of Teaching, Learning, and Leadership, Orlando, FL 32816. Offers applied learning and instruction (MA, Certificate), including applied learning and instruction (MA), community college education (Certificate), gifted education (Certificate), global and comparative education (Certificate), initial teacher professional preparation (Certificate), urban education (Certificate); art education (M Ed, MAT), including teacher education (MAT), teacher leadership (M Ed); educational and instructional technology (MA, Certificate), including e-learning (Certificate), educational technology (Certificate), instructional design and technology (MA), instructional/educational technology (Certificate); educational leadership (Ed S); elementary education (M Ed, MA); English language arts education (M Ed, MAT), including teacher education (MAT), teacher leadership (M Ed); K-8 mathematics and science education (M Ed, Certificate); mathematics education (M Ed, MAT), including teacher education (MAT), teacher leadership (M Ed); reading education (M Ed, Certificate); science education (M Ed, MAT), including teacher education (MAT), teacher leadership (M Ed); social science education (M Ed, MAT), including teacher education (MAT), teacher leadership (M Ed); teacher leadership and educational leadership (M Ed, Ed S), including educational leadership (Ed S), teacher leadership (M Ed); teaching excellence (Certificate). Part-time and evening/weekend programs available. *Faculty:* 76 full-time (54 women), 75 part-time/adjunct (57 women). *Students:* 115 full-time (93 women), 476 part-time (364 women); includes 149 minority (49 Black or African American, non-Hispanic/Latino; 20 Asian, non-Hispanic/Latino; 69 Hispanic/Latino; 11 Two or more races, non-Hispanic/Latino), 8 international. Average age 31. 268 applicants, 79% accepted, 133 enrolled. In 2013, 212 master's, 48 other advanced degrees awarded. *Degree requirements:* For other advanced degree, thesis or alternative. *Entrance requirements:* For degree, GRE General Test, minimum GPA of 3.0. Additional exam requirements/recommendations for international students: Required—TOEFL. *Application deadline:* For fall admission, 7/15 for domestic students; for spring admission, 12/15 for domestic students. Application fee: $30. Electronic applications accepted. *Financial support:* In 2013–14, 8 students received support, including 5 research assistantships with partial tuition reimbursements available (averaging $7,300 per year), 3 teaching assistantships with partial tuition reimbursements available (averaging $7,000 per year); career-related internships or fieldwork, Federal Work-Study, institutionally sponsored loans, tuition waivers (partial), and unspecified assistantships also available. Financial award application deadline: 3/1; financial award applicants required to submit FAFSA. *Unit head:* Dr. Michael C. Hynes, Co-Director, 407-823-6076, E-mail: michael.hynes@ucf.edu. *Application contact:* Barbara Rodriguez Lamas, Director, Admissions and Student Services, 407-823-2766, Fax: 407-823-6442, E-mail: gradadmissions@ucf.edu.
Website: http://education.ucf.edu/departments.cfm.

University of Cincinnati, Graduate School, College of Design, Architecture, Art, and Planning, School of Art, Program in Art Education, Cincinnati, OH 45221. Offers MA. *Accreditation:* NASAD; NCATE. *Entrance requirements:* For master's, MAT. Electronic applications accepted.

University of Florida, Graduate School, College of Fine Arts, School of Art and Art History, Gainesville, FL 32611. Offers art (MA), including digital arts and sciences; art education (MA); art history (MA, PhD); museology (MA). *Accreditation:* NASAD. Postbaccalaureate distance learning degree programs offered (minimal on-campus study). *Faculty:* 32 full-time (14 women), 5 part-time/adjunct (3 women). *Students:* 82 full-time (67 women), 107 part-time (89 women); includes 42 minority (9 Black or African American, non-Hispanic/Latino; 3 American Indian or Alaska Native, non-Hispanic/Latino; 4 Asian, non-Hispanic/Latino; 26 Hispanic/Latino), 10 international. Average age 33. 178 applicants, 42% accepted, 56 enrolled. In 2013, 69 master's awarded. *Degree requirements:* For master's, project or thesis (MFA); 1 foreign language (MA in art history); for doctorate, 2 foreign languages, comprehensive exam, thesis/dissertation. *Entrance requirements:* For master's, GRE General Test, portfolio (MFA), writing sample (MA), minimum GPA 3.0; for doctorate, GRE General Test, minimum GPA of 3.0. Additional exam requirements/recommendations for international students: Required—TOEFL (minimum score 550 paper-based; 80 iBT), IELTS (minimum score 6). *Application deadline:* For fall admission, 1/1 priority date for domestic students, 1/1 for international students; for spring admission, 11/1 for domestic and international students. Applications are processed on a rolling basis. Application fee: $30. Electronic applications accepted. *Expenses:* Tuition, state resident: full-time $12,640. Tuition, nonresident: full-time $30,000. *Financial support:* In 2013–14, 80 students received support, including 10 fellowships (averaging $3,820 per year), 1 research assistantship with tuition reimbursement available (averaging $7,362 per year), 86 teaching assistantships with tuition reimbursements available (averaging $7,340 per year); Federal Work-Study, institutionally sponsored loans, and unspecified assistantships also available. Financial award applicants required to submit FAFSA. *Faculty research:* Studio production, art historical studies of style context. *Unit head:* Richard Heipp, Professor and Interim Director, 352-273-3021, Fax: 352-392-8453, E-mail: heipp@ufl.edu. *Application contact:* Maya Stanfield-Mazzi, PhD, Assistant Professor/Director of Graduate Studies for Art History, 352-273-3070, Fax: 352-392-8453, E-mail: mstanfield@ufl.edu.
Website: http://www.arts.ufl.edu/art.

University of Georgia, College of Education, Program in Art Education, Athens, GA 30602. Offers MA Ed, Ed D, PhD, Ed S. *Accreditation:* NASAD; NCATE. *Degree requirements:* For doctorate, thesis/dissertation. *Entrance requirements:* For master's, GRE General Test, MAT; for doctorate, GRE General Test; for Ed S, GRE General Test or MAT. Electronic applications accepted.

University of Idaho, College of Graduate Studies, College of Art and Architecture, Moscow, ID 83844-2461. Offers architecture (M Arch); art (MFA); integrated architecture and design (MS); landscape architecture (MLA); teaching art (MAT). *Accreditation:* NASAD. *Faculty:* 16 full-time, 2 part-time/adjunct. *Students:* 89 full-time, 16 part-time. Average age 29. In 2013, 57 master's awarded. *Entrance requirements:* Additional exam requirements/recommendations for international students: Required—TOEFL (minimum score 550 paper-based). *Application deadline:* For fall admission, 8/1 for domestic students; for spring admission, 12/15 for domestic students. Applications are processed on a rolling basis. Application fee: $60. Electronic applications accepted. *Expenses:* Tuition, state resident: full-time $5596; part-time $363 per credit hour. Tuition, nonresident: full-time $18,672; part-time $1089 per credit hour. *Financial support:* Applicants required to submit FAFSA. *Faculty research:* Sustainability in communities, urban research, virtual technology, bioregional planning, environment and behavior interaction. *Unit head:* Dr. Mark Hoversten, Dean, 208-885-5423, E-mail: caa@uidaho.edu. *Application contact:* Stephanie Thomas, Graduate Recruitment Coordinator, 208-885-4001, Fax: 208-885-4406, E-mail: gadms@uidaho.edu.
Website: http://www.uidaho.edu/caa.

University of Illinois at Urbana–Champaign, Graduate College, College of Fine and Applied Arts, School of Art and Design, Program in Art Education, Champaign, IL 61820. Offers Ed M, MA, PhD. *Accreditation:* NASAD. *Students:* 18 (11 women). Application fee: $75 ($90 for international students). *Unit head:* Joseph Squier, Chair, 217-333-

0855, Fax: 217-244-7688, E-mail: squier@illinois.edu. *Application contact:* Ellen de Waard, Coordinator of Graduate Academic Affairs, 217-333-0642, Fax: 217-244-7688, E-mail: edewaard@illinois.edu.
Website: http://www.art.illinois.edu.

University of Indianapolis, Graduate Programs, School of Education, Indianapolis, IN 46227-3697. Offers art education (MAT); biology (MAT); chemistry (MAT); curriculum and instruction (MA); earth sciences (MAT); education (MA, MAT); educational leadership (MA); elementary education (MA); English (MAT); French (MAT); math (MAT); physical education (MAT); physics (MAT); secondary education (MA), including art education, education, English education, social studies education; social studies (MAT); Spanish (MAT). *Accreditation:* NCATE. Part-time and evening/weekend programs available. *Faculty:* 5 full-time (4 women), 2 part-time/adjunct (1 woman). *Students:* 19 full-time (9 women), 54 part-time (27 women); includes 13 minority (5 Black or African American, non-Hispanic/Latino; 1 Asian, non-Hispanic/Latino; 5 Hispanic/Latino; 2 Two or more races, non-Hispanic/Latino), 1 international. Average age 32. In 2013, 52 master's awarded. *Entrance requirements:* For master's, GRE Subject Test, PRAXIS I, minimum GPA of 2.5, 3 letters of recommendation, interview. Additional exam requirements/recommendations for international students: Required—TOEFL (minimum score 550 paper-based). *Application deadline:* Applications are processed on a rolling basis. Application fee: $50. *Expenses: Tuition:* Full-time $5436; part-time $810 per credit hour. *Financial support:* Federal Work-Study available. Financial award application deadline: 5/1; financial award applicants required to submit FAFSA. *Faculty research:* Assessment of teacher education, perceptions of prospective teachers by parents. *Unit head:* Dr. Kathy Moran, Dean, 317-788-3285, Fax: 317-788-3300, E-mail: kmoran@uindy.edu. *Application contact:* Jeni Kirby, Administrative Assistant, Teacher Education, 317-788-2113, E-mail: kirbyj@uindy.edu.
Website: http://education.uindy.edu/.

The University of Iowa, Graduate College, College of Education, Department of Teaching and Learning, Program in Education, Iowa City, IA 52242-1316. Offers art education (MA); developmental reading (MA); elementary education (MA); English education (MA, MAT); foreign and second language education (MAT); foreign language education (MA); foreign language/ESL education (PhD); language, literacy and culture (PhD); mathematics education (MA, MAT, PhD); music education (MM, PhD); science education (MA); secondary education (MA); social studies (MA, PhD). *Degree requirements:* For master's, thesis optional, exam; for doctorate, comprehensive exam, thesis/dissertation. *Entrance requirements:* For master's and doctorate, GRE General Test, minimum GPA of 3.0. Additional exam requirements/recommendations for international students: Required—TOEFL (minimum score 550 paper-based; 81 iBT). Electronic applications accepted.

The University of Kansas, Graduate Studies, College of Liberal Arts and Sciences, Department of Visual Art, Program in Visual Art Education, Lawrence, KS 66045. Offers MA. Part-time programs available. *Faculty:* 3 full-time (2 women). *Students:* 9 full-time (8 women), 7 part-time (all women); includes 1 minority (Two or more races, non-Hispanic/Latino). Average age 27. 7 applicants, 86% accepted, 6 enrolled. In 2013, 2 master's awarded. *Degree requirements:* For master's, thesis or alternative. *Entrance requirements:* For master's, portfolio, 3 letters of recommendation, minimum GPA of 3.0. Additional exam requirements/recommendations for international students: Required—TOEFL (minimum score 570 paper-based) or IELTS (minimum score 6.5). *Application deadline:* For fall admission, 5/1 for domestic and international students; for spring admission, 10/15 for domestic and international students. Application fee: $55 ($65 for international students). Electronic applications accepted. *Financial support:* Teaching assistantships with full tuition reimbursements, Federal Work-Study, scholarships/grants, and unspecified assistantships available. Financial award application deadline: 5/1. *Faculty research:* Museum education, art educator education. *Unit head:* Mary Anne Jordan, Chairperson, 785-864-4042, Fax: 785-864-4404, E-mail: majordan@ku.edu. *Application contact:* Norman R. Akers, Director, 785-864-4042, Fax: 785-864-4404, E-mail: normanakers2@ku.edu.
Website: http://art.ku.edu/programs/visual_art_education/.

University of Kentucky, Graduate School, College of Fine Arts, Program in Art Education, Lexington, KY 40506-0032. Offers MA. *Degree requirements:* For master's, comprehensive exam, thesis optional. *Entrance requirements:* For master's, GRE General Test, minimum undergraduate GPA of 2.75. Additional exam requirements/recommendations for international students: Required—TOEFL (minimum score 550 paper-based). Electronic applications accepted. *Faculty research:* Multicultural art education, women's issues in art education, lifelong learning in the arts, the artist-teacher, art teaching as a form of art, place and art, children's home art and creativity as a basis for school art instruction.

University of Louisiana at Monroe, Graduate School, College of Arts, Education, and Sciences, School of Education, Program in Curriculum and Instruction, Monroe, LA 71209-0001. Offers art education (M Ed); biology education (M Ed); chemistry education (M Ed); curriculum and instruction (Ed D); early childhood education (M Ed); earth science education (M Ed); educational leadership (M Ed); elementary education (1-5) (M Ed); English as a second language (M Ed); English education (M Ed); family and consumer education (M Ed); French education (M Ed); history education (M Ed); math education (M Ed); middle school education (M Ed); music education (M Ed); reading education (K-12) (M Ed); Spanish education (M Ed); special education - academically gifted (M Ed); special education - early intervention (M Ed); special education - educational diagnostician (M Ed); special education - mild/moderate disabilities (M Ed); speech education (M Ed). *Accreditation:* NCATE. *Degree requirements:* For master's, comprehensive exam (for some programs), thesis; for doctorate, thesis/dissertation, internships. *Entrance requirements:* For master's, GRE General Test; for doctorate, GRE General Test, minimum undergraduate GPA of 2.75, graduate 3.25. Additional exam requirements/recommendations for international students: Required—TOEFL (minimum score 500 paper-based; 61 iBT). *Application deadline:* For fall admission, 8/24 priority date for domestic students, 7/1 for international students; for winter admission, 12/14 priority date for domestic students; for spring admission, 1/19 for domestic students, 11/1 for international students. Applications are processed on a rolling basis. Application fee: $20 ($30 for international students). Electronic applications accepted. *Expenses:* Tuition, state resident: full-time $6607. Tuition, nonresident: full-time $17,179. Full-time tuition and fees vary according to program. *Financial support:* Research assistantships, career-related internships or fieldwork, Federal Work-Study, and unspecified assistantships available. Financial award application deadline: 4/1; financial award applicants required to submit FAFSA. *Unit head:* Dr. Dorothy Schween, Director, 318-342-1268, Fax: 318-342-3131, E-mail: schween@ulm.edu. *Application contact:* Dr. Dorothy Schween, Director, 318-342-1268, Fax: 318-342-3131, E-mail: schween@ulm.edu.

University of Louisville, Graduate School, College of Education and Human Development, Department of Teaching and Learning, Louisville, KY 40292-0001. Offers art education (MAT); curriculum and instruction (PhD); early elementary education (MAT); instructional technology (M Ed); interdisciplinary early childhood education (MAT); middle school education (MAT); music education (MAT); secondary education (MAT); special education (MAT); teacher leadership (M Ed). Part-time and evening/weekend programs available. *Students:* 137 full-time (93 women), 208 part-time (131 women); includes 44 minority (25 Black or African American, non-Hispanic/Latino; 1 American Indian or Alaska Native, non-Hispanic/Latino; 3 Asian, non-Hispanic/Latino; 12 Hispanic/Latino; 3 Two or more races, non-Hispanic/Latino), 2 international. Average age 32. 150 applicants, 51% accepted, 54 enrolled. In 2013, 127 master's, 5 doctorates awarded. *Degree requirements:* For doctorate, comprehensive exam, thesis/dissertation. *Entrance requirements:* For master's, GRE General Test, PRAXIS II (for some programs); for doctorate, GRE General Test. Additional exam requirements/recommendations for international students: Required—TOEFL (minimum score 560 paper-based; 83 iBT). *Application deadline:* For fall admission, 5/1 priority date for international students; for spring admission, 11/1 priority date for international students; for summer admission, 4/1 priority date for international students. Application fee: $60. Electronic applications accepted. *Expenses:* Tuition, state resident: full-time $10,788; part-time $599 per credit hour. Tuition, nonresident: full-time $22,446; part-time $1247 per credit hour. *Required fees:* $196. Tuition and fees vary according to program and reciprocity agreements. *Financial support:* Fellowships, research assistantships, teaching assistantships, career-related internships or fieldwork, Federal Work-Study, scholarships/grants, and unspecified assistantships available. Financial award application deadline: 6/1; financial award applicants required to submit FAFSA. *Faculty research:* Mathematics teacher education and ongoing professional development in pedagogy and content knowledge; development of literacy, including early literacy in science and mathematics and literacy development for English language learners; immersive visualizations for promoting STEM education from nanoscience to cosmic scales; evidence-based practices for students with disabilities; urban education, including teacher response to intervention systems in schools and cross-cultural competence. *Unit head:* Dr. Ann E. Larson, Acting Chair, 502-852-6431, Fax: 502-852-1497, E-mail: ann@louisville.edu. *Application contact:* Libby Leggett, Director, Graduate Admissions, 502-852-3101, Fax: 502-852-6536, E-mail: gradadm@louisville.edu.
Website: http://louisville.edu/delphi.

University of Maryland, Baltimore County, Graduate School, College of Arts, Humanities and Social Sciences, Department of Education, Program in Teaching, Baltimore, MD 21250. Offers early childhood education (MAT); elementary education (MAT); secondary education (MAT), including art, biology, chemistry, dance, earth/space science, English, foreign language, mathematics, music, physics, social studies, theatre. Part-time and evening/weekend programs available. *Faculty:* 24 full-time (18 women), 25 part-time/adjunct (19 women). *Students:* 49 full-time (34 women), 35 part-time (23 women); includes 19 minority (9 Black or African American, non-Hispanic/Latino; 3 Asian, non-Hispanic/Latino; 6 Hispanic/Latino; 1 Two or more races, non-Hispanic/Latino). Average age 30. 40 applicants, 95% accepted, 35 enrolled. In 2013, 106 master's awarded. *Degree requirements:* For master's, comprehensive exam (for some programs), thesis (for some programs). *Entrance requirements:* For master's, PRAXIS I or SAT (minimum score of 1000), minimum GPA of 3.0. Additional exam requirements/recommendations for international students: Required—TOEFL. *Application deadline:* For fall admission, 6/1 for domestic students; for spring admission, 11/1 for domestic students. Applications are processed on a rolling basis. Application fee: $50. Electronic applications accepted. One-time fee: $200 full-time. *Financial support:* In 2013–14, 6 students received support, including teaching assistantships with full and partial tuition reimbursements available (averaging $12,000 per year); career-related internships or fieldwork, Federal Work-Study, scholarships/grants, tuition waivers, and unspecified assistantships also available. Financial award application deadline: 3/1. *Faculty research:* STEM teacher education, culturally sensitive pedagogy, ESOL/bilingual education, early childhood education, language, literacy and culture. *Unit head:* Dr. Susan M. Blunck, Graduate Program Director, 410-455-2869, Fax: 410-455-3986, E-mail: blunck@umbc.edu. *Application contact:* Dr. Susan M. Blunck, Graduate Program Director, 410-455-2869, Fax: 410-455-3986, E-mail: blunck@umbc.edu.
Website: http://www.umbc.edu/education/.

University of Massachusetts Amherst, Graduate School, College of Humanities and Fine Arts, Department of Art, Programs in Art, Amherst, MA 01003. Offers art education (MA); studio art (MFA). Part-time programs available. *Students:* 15 full-time (8 women), 6 part-time (3 women); includes 2 minority (1 Asian, non-Hispanic/Latino; 1 Hispanic/Latino), 1 international. Average age 33. 40 applicants, 30% accepted, 10 enrolled. In 2013, 10 master's awarded. *Degree requirements:* For master's, comprehensive exam (for some programs), thesis (for some programs). *Entrance requirements:* For master's, portfolio. Additional exam requirements/recommendations for international students: Required—TOEFL (minimum score 530 paper-based; 80 iBT), IELTS (minimum score 6.5). *Application deadline:* For fall admission, 2/1 for domestic and international students. Applications are processed on a rolling basis. Application fee: $75. Electronic applications accepted. *Financial support:* Fellowships with full and partial tuition reimbursements, research assistantships with full and partial tuition reimbursements, teaching assistantships with full and partial tuition reimbursements, career-related internships or fieldwork, Federal Work-Study, scholarships/grants, traineeships, health care benefits, tuition waivers (full and partial), and unspecified assistantships available. Support available to part-time students. Financial award application deadline: 2/1. *Unit head:* Dr. Shona Macdonald, Graduate Program Director, 413-545-1903, Fax: 413-545-3929. *Application contact:* Lindsay DeSantis, Supervisor of Admissions, 413-545-0722, Fax: 413-577-0100, E-mail: gradadm@grad.umass.edu.
Website: http://www.umass.edu/art/studio_arts.html.

University of Massachusetts Dartmouth, Graduate School, College of Visual and Performing Arts, Department of Art Education, North Dartmouth, MA 02747-2300. Offers MAE. *Accreditation:* NASAD. Part-time programs available. *Faculty:* 3 full-time (all women), 3 part-time/adjunct (2 women). *Students:* 4 full-time (2 women), 19 part-time (14 women); includes 2 minority (1 Asian, non-Hispanic/Latino; 1 Hispanic/Latino). Average age 31. 7 applicants, 100% accepted, 5 enrolled. In 2013, 9 master's awarded. *Degree requirements:* For master's, thesis. *Entrance requirements:* For master's, MTEL, statement of purpose (minimum of 300 words), resume, 3 letters of recommendation, official transcripts, portfolio (20 images representing applicant's art work). Additional exam requirements/recommendations for international students: Required—TOEFL (minimum score 533 paper-based; 72 iBT). *Application deadline:* For fall admission, 8/1 priority date for domestic students, 7/1 priority date for international students; for spring admission, 10/15 priority date for domestic students, 9/15 priority date for international students. Applications are processed on a rolling basis. Application fee: $60. Electronic applications accepted. *Expenses:* Tuition, state resident: full-time $2071; part-time $86.29 per credit. Tuition, nonresident: full-time $8099; part-time $337.46 per credit. Tuition and fees vary according to course load and reciprocity agreements. *Financial support:* In 2013–14, 4 teaching assistantships with partial tuition reimbursements (averaging $3,500 per year) were awarded; Federal Work-Study and unspecified assistantships also available. Support available to part-time students. Financial award application deadline: 3/1; financial award applicants required to submit FAFSA. *Faculty research:* Creative art, in-service and pre-service teachers, museum partnership in education, authentic visual arts integration. *Unit head:* Cathy Smilan, Graduate Program Director, 508-910-6594, Fax: 508-999-8901, E-mail: csmilan@umassd.edu. *Application contact:* Steven Briggs, Director of Marketing and Recruitment for Graduate Studies, 508-999-8604, Fax: 508-999-8183, E-mail: graduate@umassd.edu.
Website: http://www.umassd.edu/cvpa/graduate/arteducation.

University of Minnesota, Twin Cities Campus, Graduate School, College of Education and Human Development, Department of Curriculum and Instruction, Minneapolis, MN 55455-0213. Offers art education (M Ed, MA, PhD); children's literature (M Ed, MA, PhD); curriculum and instruction (MA, PhD); early childhood education (M Ed, PhD); elementary education (M Ed, MA, PhD); English education (MA, PhD); environmental education (M Ed); family education (M Ed, MA, Ed D, PhD); instructional systems and technology (M Ed, MA, PhD); language arts (MA, PhD); language immersion education (Certificate); literacy education (MA); mathematics education (MA, PhD); reading education (MA, PhD); science education (MA, PhD); second languages and cultures education (MA, PhD); social studies education (MA, PhD); teaching (M Ed), including Chinese, earth science, elementary special education, English, English as a second language, French, German, Hebrew, Japanese, life sciences, mathematics, middle school science, science, second languages and cultures, social studies, Spanish; technology enhanced learning (Certificate); writing education (M Ed, MA, PhD). *Faculty:* 29 full-time (16 women). *Students:* 425 full-time (301 women), 220 part-time (153 women); includes 85 minority (21 Black or African American, non-Hispanic/Latino; 6 American Indian or Alaska Native, non-Hispanic/Latino; 42 Asian, non-Hispanic/Latino; 16 Hispanic/Latino), 50 international. Average age 32. 551 applicants, 68% accepted, 340 enrolled. In 2013, 618 master's, 33 doctorates, 6 other advanced degrees awarded. Application fee: $75 ($95 for international students). *Financial support:* In 2013–14, 25 fellowships (averaging $28,500 per year), 23 research assistantships with full tuition reimbursements (averaging $8,082 per year), 81 teaching assistantships with full tuition reimbursements (averaging $9,974 per year) were awarded. *Faculty research:* Teaching and learning; quality of education; influence of cultural, linguistic, social, political, technological and economic factors on teaching, learning and educational research; relationship between educational practice and a democratic and just society. *Total annual research expenditures:* $272,048. *Unit head:* Dr. Nina Asher, Chair, 612-624-4772, Fax: 612-624-1357, E-mail: nasher@umn.edu. *Application contact:* Dr. Jennifer Engler, Assistant Dean, 612-626-2887, Fax: 612-626-7496, E-mail: engle009@umn.edu.
Website: http://www.cehd.umn.edu/ci.

University of Mississippi, Graduate School, College of Liberal Arts, Department of Art, Oxford, MS 38677. Offers art education (MA); art history (MA); fine arts (MFA). *Accreditation:* NASAD (one or more programs are accredited). Part-time programs available. *Faculty:* 18 full-time (11 women), 11 part-time/adjunct (7 women). *Students:* 11 full-time (2 women); includes 3 minority (1 Black or African American, non-Hispanic/Latino; 1 Hispanic/Latino; 1 Two or more races, non-Hispanic/Latino). In 2013, 7 master's awarded. *Degree requirements:* For master's, thesis (for some programs). *Entrance requirements:* For master's, GRE General Test, minimum GPA of 3.0. Additional exam requirements/recommendations for international students: Required—TOEFL. *Application deadline:* For fall admission, 3/1 for domestic students; for spring admission, 10/1 for domestic students. Applications are processed on a rolling basis. Application fee: $40. Electronic applications accepted. *Financial support:* Fellowships, scholarships/grants, and unspecified assistantships available. Financial award application deadline: 3/1; financial award applicants required to submit FAFSA. *Unit head:* Virginia R. Chavis, Interim Chair, 662-915-5015, Fax: 662-915-5013, E-mail: art@olemiss.edu. *Application contact:* Dr. Christy M. Wyandt, Associate Dean, 662-915-7474, Fax: 662-915-7577, E-mail: cwyandt@olemiss.edu.

University of Missouri, Graduate School, College of Education, Department of Learning, Teaching and Curriculum, Columbia, MO 65211. Offers agricultural education (M Ed, PhD, Ed S); art education (M Ed, PhD, Ed S); business and office education (M Ed, PhD, Ed S); early childhood education (M Ed, PhD, Ed S); elementary education (M Ed, PhD, Ed S); English education (M Ed, PhD, Ed S); foreign language education (M Ed, PhD, Ed S); health education and promotion (M Ed, PhD); learning and instruction (M Ed); marketing education (M Ed, PhD, Ed S); mathematics education (M Ed, PhD, Ed S); music education (M Ed, PhD, Ed S); reading education (M Ed, PhD, Ed S); science education (M Ed, PhD, Ed S); social studies education (M Ed, PhD, Ed S); vocational education (M Ed, PhD, Ed S). Part-time programs available. *Faculty:* 26 full-time (16 women), 3 part-time/adjunct (2 women). *Students:* 186 full-time (143 women), 197 part-time (172 women); includes 19 minority (4 Black or African American, non-Hispanic/Latino; 4 Asian, non-Hispanic/Latino; 6 Hispanic/Latino; 5 Two or more races, non-Hispanic/Latino), 25 international. Average age 31. 288 applicants, 65% accepted, 160 enrolled. In 2013, 202 master's, 18 doctorates, 7 other advanced degrees awarded. Terminal master's awarded for partial completion of doctoral program. *Degree requirements:* For doctorate, thesis/dissertation. *Entrance requirements:* For master's and Ed S, GRE General Test or MAT, minimum GPA of 3.0; for doctorate, GRE General Test, minimum GPA of 3.0. Additional exam requirements/recommendations for international students: Required—TOEFL (minimum score 600 paper-based; 100 iBT). *Application deadline:* For fall admission, 12/1 priority date for domestic and international students. Applications are processed on a rolling basis. Application fee: $55 ($75 for international students). Electronic applications accepted. *Financial support:* Fellowships, research assistantships, teaching assistantships, institutionally sponsored loans, traineeships, health care benefits, and unspecified assistantships available. Support available to part-time students. *Faculty research:* Curriculum development and research, teacher education, art education, business and marketing, early childhood education, English education, literacy/reading education, mathematics education, music education, science education, social studies education. *Unit head:* Dr. James Tarr, Associate Division Director, 573-882-4034, E-mail: tarrj@missouri.edu. *Application contact:* Fran Colley, Academic Advisor, 573-882-6462, E-mail: colleyf@missouri.edu. Website: http://education.missouri.edu/LTC/.

University of Nebraska at Kearney, Graduate Programs, College of Fine Arts and Humanities, Department of Art, Kearney, NE 68849-0001. Offers art education (MA Ed). *Accreditation:* NCATE. Part-time and evening/weekend programs available. Postbaccalaureate distance learning degree programs offered (no on-campus study). *Degree requirements:* For master's, thesis optional. *Entrance requirements:* For master's, slide portfolio (campus program only); two letters of recommendation, resume, statement of purpose, 24 undergraduate hours of art/art history/art education. Additional exam requirements/recommendations for international students: Required—TOEFL (minimum score 550 paper-based; 79 iBT). Electronic applications accepted. *Faculty research:* Fibers, art education, kiln design construction and low-fire glaze.

University of New Mexico, Graduate School, College of Education, Department of Educational Specialties, Program in Art Education, Albuquerque, NM 87131-2039. Offers MA. *Accreditation:* NCATE. Part-time and evening/weekend programs available. *Faculty:* 8 full-time (7 women), 6 part-time/adjunct (4 women). *Students:* 18 full-time (12 women), 14 part-time (10 women); includes 13 minority (1 Black or African American, non-Hispanic/Latino; 2 American Indian or Alaska Native, non-Hispanic/Latino; 1 Asian, non-Hispanic/Latino; 8 Hispanic/Latino; 1 Two or more races, non-Hispanic/Latino), 2 international. Average age 37. 6 applicants, 67% accepted, 3 enrolled. In 2013, 18 master's awarded. *Degree requirements:* For master's, comprehensive exam, thesis optional, participation in art exhibit. *Entrance requirements:* For master's, letter of intent, resume, 3 letters of recommendation, portfolio of 10 samples of art work. Additional exam requirements/recommendations for international students: Required—TOEFL. *Application deadline:* For fall admission, 3/30 for domestic and international students; for spring admission, 10/30 for domestic and international students. Application fee: $50.

Electronic applications accepted. *Financial support:* In 2013–14, 20 students received support, including 1 fellowship (averaging $3,600 per year), 2 research assistantships with full tuition reimbursements available (averaging $12,139 per year); teaching assistantships, Federal Work-Study, institutionally sponsored loans, scholarships/grants, and unspecified assistantships also available. Financial award application deadline: 3/1; financial award applicants required to submit FAFSA. *Faculty research:* Studio in art education, visual culture, curricular issues regarding gender and sexual identity, archetypal thought in art education, teacher preparation. *Unit head:* Prof. Ruth Luckasson, Chair, 505-277-6510, Fax: 505-277-6929, E-mail: ruthl@unm.edu. *Application contact:* Katherine Vazquez, Information Contact, 505-277-4112, Fax: 505-277-0576, E-mail: arted@unm.edu.
Website: http://www.unm.edu/~arted.

The University of North Carolina at Charlotte, The Graduate School, College of Education, Interdisciplinary Education Programs, Charlotte, NC 28223-0001. Offers art education (MAT); dance education (MAT); elementary education (MAT); English as a second language (MAT); foreign language education (MAT); middle grades education (MAT); music education (MAT); secondary education (MAT); special education (MAT); teacher certification (Graduate Certificate); teaching (Graduate Certificate); theater education (MAT). Part-time programs available. *Students:* 206 full-time (165 women), 791 part-time (628 women); includes 342 minority (247 Black or African American, non-Hispanic/Latino; 16 Asian, non-Hispanic/Latino; 62 Hispanic/Latino; 17 Two or more races, non-Hispanic/Latino), 14 international. Average age 32. 564 applicants, 91% accepted, 414 enrolled. In 2013, 145 master's, 271 other advanced degrees awarded. Terminal master's awarded for partial completion of doctoral program. *Degree requirements:* For master's, thesis. *Entrance requirements:* For master's, GRE or MAT. Additional exam requirements/recommendations for international students: Required—TOEFL (minimum score 550 paper-based; 83 iBT). *Application deadline:* For fall admission, 5/1 priority date for domestic and international students; for spring admission, 10/1 priority date for domestic and international students. Applications are processed on a rolling basis. Application fee: $75. Electronic applications accepted. *Expenses:* Tuition, state resident: full-time $3522. Tuition, nonresident: full-time $16,051. *Required fees:* $2585. Tuition and fees vary according to course load and program. *Total annual research expenditures:* $43,031. *Unit head:* Dr. Warren DiBiase, Chair, 704-687-8881, Fax: 704-687-4705, E-mail: wjdibias@uncc.edu. *Application contact:* Kathy B. Giddings, Director of Graduate Admissions, 704-687-5503, Fax: 704-687-1668, E-mail: gradadm@uncc.edu.
Website: http://education.uncc.edu/academic-programs.

The University of North Carolina at Pembroke, Graduate Studies, Department of Art, Pembroke, NC 28372-1510. Offers art education (MA, MAT). Part-time and evening/weekend programs available. *Degree requirements:* For master's, comprehensive exam, capstone show. *Entrance requirements:* For master's, GRE or MAT, minimum GPA of 3.0 in major or 2.5 overall. Additional exam requirements/recommendations for international students: Required—TOEFL. *Expenses:* Contact institution.

University of Northern Iowa, Graduate College, College of Humanities, Arts and Sciences, Department of Art, Cedar Falls, IA 50614. Offers art education (MA). *Accreditation:* NASAD. Part-time and evening/weekend programs available. *Degree requirements:* For master's, comprehensive exam (for some programs), thesis or alternative. *Entrance requirements:* For master's, minimum GPA of 3.0, portfolio. Additional exam requirements/recommendations for international students: Required—TOEFL (minimum score 500 paper-based; 61 iBT). *Application deadline:* For fall admission, 8/1 priority date for domestic students. Applications are processed on a rolling basis. Application fee: $50 ($70 for international students). Electronic applications accepted. *Financial support:* Career-related internships or fieldwork, Federal Work-Study, scholarships/grants, and tuition waivers (full and partial) available. Support available to part-time students. Financial award application deadline: 2/1. *Unit head:* Dr. Jeffery Byrd, Department Head/Professor, 319-273-2077, Fax: 319-273-7333, E-mail: jeffery.byrd@uni.edu. *Application contact:* Laurie S. Russell, Record Analyst, 319-273-2623, Fax: 319-273-2885, E-mail: laurie.russell@uni.edu.
Website: http://www.uni.edu/artdept/.

University of North Georgia, School of Education, Dahlonega, GA 30597. Offers art education (MAT); early childhood education (M Ed); English education (MAT); history education (MAT); math education (MAT); middle grades education (M Ed, MAT); physical education (MS); school leadership (Ed S); secondary education (M Ed), including English education, history education, mathematics education, physical education; teacher education (MAT). *Accreditation:* NCATE. Part-time and evening/weekend programs available. Postbaccalaureate distance learning degree programs offered (no on-campus study). *Degree requirements:* For master's, comprehensive exam, thesis optional. *Entrance requirements:* For master's, GRE or MAT, GACE, minimum GPA of 2.75; for Ed S, GRE General Test or MAT, 3 years of teaching experience, master's degree, minimum graduate GPA of 3.25, leadership position in the school. Additional exam requirements/recommendations for international students: Required—TOEFL (minimum score 550 paper-based; 79 iBT), IELTS (minimum score 6.5). Electronic applications accepted. *Faculty research:* Identification of professional development school structures supporting P-12 student achievement, impact of diverse field placement settings in teacher belief development among preservice teachers, use of inquiry methodology in social studies teaching with English language learners, use of instructional differentiation in the middle grades classroom, effects of international school placements on preservice teacher beliefs and attitudes.

University of North Texas, Robert B. Toulouse School of Graduate Studies, Denton, TN 76203-5017. Offers accounting (MS, PhD); applied anthropology (MA, MS); applied behavior analysis (Certificate); applied technology and performance improvement (M Ed, MS, PhD); art education (MA, PhD); art history (MA); art museum education (Certificate); arts leadership (Certificate); audiology (Au D); behavior analysis (MS); biochemistry and molecular biology (MS, PhD); biology (MA, MS, PhD); business (PhD); business computer information systems (PhD); chemistry (MS, PhD); clinical psychology (PhD); communication studies (MA, MS); computer engineering (MS); computer science (MS); computer science and engineering (PhD); counseling (M Ed, MS, PhD), including clinical mental health counseling (MS), college and university counseling (M Ed, MS), elementary school counseling (M Ed, MS), secondary school counseling (M Ed, MS); counseling psychology (PhD); creative writing (MA); criminal justice (MS); curriculum and instruction (M Ed, PhD), including curriculum studies (PhD), early childhood studies (PhD), language and literacy studies (PhD); decision sciences (MBA); design (MA, MFA), including fashion design (MFA), innovation studies, interior design (MFA); early childhood studies (MS); economics (MS); educational leadership (M Ed, Ed D, PhD); educational psychology (MS), including family studies, gifted and talented (MS, PhD); human development, learning and cognition, research, measurement and evaluation; educational research (PhD), including gifted and talented (MS, PhD), human development and family studies, psychological aspects of sports and exercise, research, measurement and statistics; electrical engineering (MS); emergency management (MPA); engineering systems (MS); English (MA, PhD); environmental science (MS, PhD); experimental psychology (PhD); finance (MBA, MS, PhD); financial management (MPA); French (MA); health psychology and behavioral medicine (PhD); health services management (MBA); higher education (M Ed, Ed D, PhD); history (MA, MS, PhD),

including European history (PhD), military history (PhD), United States history (PhD); hospitality management (MS); human resources management (MPA); information science (MS, PhD); information technologies (MBA); information technology and decision sciences (MS); interdisciplinary studies (MA, MS); international sustainable tourism (MS); jazz studies (MM); journalism (MA, MJ, Graduate Certificate), including interactive and virtual digital communication (Graduate Certificate), narrative journalism (Graduate Certificate), public relations (Graduate Certificate); kinesiology (MS); learning technologies (MS, PhD); library science (MS); local government management (MPA); logistics and supply chain management (MBA, PhD); long-term care, senior housing, and aging services (MA, MS); management science (PhD); marketing (MBA, PhD); materials science and engineering (MS, PhD); mathematics (MA, PhD); merchandising (MS); music (MA, MM Ed, PhD), including ethnomusicology (MA), music education (MM Ed, PhD), music theory (MA, PhD), musicology (MA, PhD), performance (MA); nonprofit management (MPA); operations and supply chain management (MBA); performance (MM, DMA); philosophy (MA, PhD); physics (MS, PhD); political science (MA, MS, PhD); public administration and management (PhD), including emergency management, nonprofit management, public financial management, urban management; radio, television and film (MA, MFA); recreation, event and sport management (MS); rehabilitation counseling (MS, Certificate); sociology (MA, MS, PhD); Spanish (MA); special education (M Ed, PhD), including autism intervention (PhD), emotional/behavioral disorders (PhD), mild/moderate disabilities (PhD); speech-language pathology (MA, MS); strategic management (MBA); studio art (MFA); taxation (MS); teaching (M Ed); MBA/MS; MS/MPH; MSES/MBA. Part-time and evening/weekend programs available. Postbaccalaureate distance learning degree programs offered. *Faculty:* 661 full-time (213 women), 240 part-time/adjunct (144 women). *Students:* 3,106 full-time (1,620 women), 3,543 part-time (2,221 women); includes 1,740 minority (533 Black or African American, non-Hispanic/Latino; 15 American Indian or Alaska Native, non-Hispanic/Latino; 286 Asian, non-Hispanic/Latino; 746 Hispanic/Latino; 3 Native Hawaiian or other Pacific Islander, non-Hispanic/Latino; 157 Two or more races, non-Hispanic/Latino), 1,145 international. Average age 32. 6,289 applicants, 43% accepted, 1751 enrolled. In 2013, 1,778 master's, 239 doctorates, 10 other advanced degrees awarded. Terminal master's awarded for partial completion of doctoral program. *Degree requirements:* For master's, variable foreign language requirement, comprehensive exam (for some programs), thesis (for some programs); for doctorate, variable foreign language requirement, comprehensive exam (for some programs), thesis/dissertation; for other advanced degree, variable foreign language requirement, comprehensive exam (for some programs). *Entrance requirements:* For master's and doctorate, GRE, GMAT. Additional exam requirements/recommendations for international students: Required—TOEFL (minimum score 550 paper-based; 79 iBT). *Application deadline:* For fall admission, 7/15 for domestic students, 3/15 for international students; for spring admission, 11/15 for domestic students, 9/15 for international students; for summer admission, 5/1 for domestic students. Applications are processed on a rolling basis. Application fee: $60. Electronic applications accepted. *Financial support:* Fellowships with partial tuition reimbursements, research assistantships with partial tuition reimbursements, teaching assistantships, career-related internships or fieldwork, Federal Work-Study, institutionally sponsored loans, scholarships/grants, health care benefits, and library assistantships available. Support available to part-time students. Financial award applicants required to submit FAFSA. *Unit head:* Mark Wardell, Dean, 940-565-2383, E-mail: mark.wardell@unt.edu. *Application contact:* Toulouse School of Graduate Studies, 940-565-2383, Fax: 940-565-2141, E-mail: gradsch@unt.edu.
Website: http://tsgs.unt.edu/.

University of Rio Grande, Graduate School, Rio Grande, OH 45674. Offers classroom teaching (M Ed), including fine arts, learning disabilities, mathematics, reading education. *Accreditation:* NCATE. Part-time and evening/weekend programs available. *Degree requirements:* For master's, final research project, portfolio. *Entrance requirements:* For master's, minimum GPA of 2.7 in major, 2.5 overall. Additional exam requirements/recommendations for international students: Required—TOEFL. *Faculty research:* Interagency collaboration, reading and mathematics, learning styles, college access, literacy.

University of St. Francis, College of Education, Joliet, IL 60435-6169. Offers educational leadership (MS, Ed D); elementary education (M Ed); higher education (MS); reading (MS); secondary education (M Ed), including English education, math education, science education, social studies education, visual arts education; special education (M Ed); teaching and learning (MS). *Accreditation:* NCATE. Part-time and evening/weekend programs available. Postbaccalaureate distance learning degree programs offered (no on-campus study). *Faculty:* 10 full-time (8 women), 34 part-time/adjunct (25 women). *Students:* 14 full-time (13 women), 250 part-time (183 women); includes 34 minority (20 Black or African American, non-Hispanic/Latino; 1 American Indian or Alaska Native, non-Hispanic/Latino; 13 Hispanic/Latino), 1 international. Average age 36. 133 applicants, 62% accepted, 71 enrolled. In 2013, 147 master's awarded. *Degree requirements:* For doctorate, thesis/dissertation. *Entrance requirements:* For doctorate, master's degree, IL Type 75 or Principal's endorsement, interview, minimum undergraduate GPA of 3.0, professional portfolio, letter of recommendation. Additional exam requirements/recommendations for international students: Required—TOEFL (minimum score 550 paper-based; 79 iBT), IELTS (minimum score 6.5). *Application deadline:* Applications are processed on a rolling basis. Application fee: $30. Electronic applications accepted. Application fee is waived when completed online. *Expenses:* Contact institution. *Financial support:* In 2013–14, 10 students received support. Scholarships/grants, tuition waivers (partial), and unspecified assistantships available. Support available to part-time students. Financial award applicants required to submit FAFSA. *Unit head:* Dr. John Gambro, Dean, 815-740-3829, Fax: 815-740-2264, E-mail: jgambro@stfrancis.edu. *Application contact:* Sandra Sloka, Director of Admissions for Graduate and Degree Completion Programs, 800-735-7500, Fax: 815-740-3431, E-mail: ssloka@stfrancis.edu.
Website: http://www.stfrancis.edu/academics/college-of-education/.

University of South Carolina, The Graduate School, College of Arts and Sciences, Department of Art, Program in Art Education, Columbia, SC 29208. Offers IMA, MA, MAT. IMA and MAT offered in cooperation with the College of Education. *Accreditation:* NCATE. *Degree requirements:* For master's, comprehensive exam, thesis (for some programs). *Entrance requirements:* For master's, GRE General Test or MAT, portfolio. Additional exam requirements/recommendations for international students: Required—TOEFL. Electronic applications accepted. *Faculty research:* Teaching art at the primary and secondary levels of education.

University of South Carolina, The Graduate School, College of Education, Department of Instruction and Teacher Education, Program in Secondary Education, Columbia, SC 29208. Offers art education (IMA, MAT); business education (IMA, MAT); English (MAT); foreign language (MAT); health education (MAT); mathematics (MAT); science (IMA, MAT); secondary (Ed D); secondary education (MT, PhD); social studies (MAT); theatre and speech (MAT). IMA and MT offered jointly with the subject areas. *Accreditation:* NCATE. *Degree requirements:* For master's, comprehensive exam, thesis (for some programs), foreign language (MA); for doctorate, one foreign language, comprehensive exam, thesis/dissertation. *Entrance requirements:* For master's, GRE General Test or MAT, teaching certificate (IMA, M Ed), interview; for doctorate, GRE General Test or MAT, interview. *Faculty research:* Middle school programs, professional development, school collaboration.

The University of Tennessee, Graduate School, College of Education, Health and Human Sciences, Program in Education, Knoxville, TN 37996. Offers art education (MS); counseling education (PhD); cultural studies in education (PhD); curriculum (MS, Ed S); curriculum, educational research and evaluation (Ed D, PhD); early childhood education (PhD); early childhood special education (MS); education of deaf and hard of hearing (MS); educational administration and policy studies (Ed D, PhD); educational administration and supervision (Ed S); educational psychology (Ed D, PhD); elementary education (MS, Ed S); elementary teaching (MS); English education (MS, Ed S); exercise science (PhD); foreign language/ESL education (MS, Ed S); instructional technology (MS, Ed D, PhD, Ed S); literacy, language and ESL education (PhD); literacy, language education, and ESL education (Ed D); mathematics education (MS, Ed S); modified and comprehensive special education (MS); reading education (MS, Ed S); school counseling (Ed S); school psychology (PhD, Ed S); science education (MS, Ed S); secondary teaching (MS); social foundations (MS); social science education (MS, Ed S); socio-cultural foundations of sports and education (PhD); special education (Ed S); teacher education (Ed D, PhD). *Accreditation:* NCATE. Part-time and evening/weekend programs available. *Degree requirements:* For master's and Ed S, thesis optional; for doctorate, variable foreign language requirement, thesis/dissertation. *Entrance requirements:* For master's, minimum GPA of 2.7; for doctorate and Ed S, GRE General Test, minimum GPA of 2.7. Additional exam requirements/recommendations for international students: Required—TOEFL. Electronic applications accepted. *Expenses:* Tuition, state resident: full-time $9540; part-time $531 per credit hour. Tuition, nonresident: full-time $27,728; part-time $1542 per credit hour. *Required fees:* $1404; $67 per credit hour.

The University of Texas at Austin, Graduate School, College of Fine Arts, Department of Art and Art History, Program in Art Education, Austin, TX 78712-1111. Offers MA. *Accreditation:* NASAD. Part-time programs available. *Degree requirements:* For master's, thesis, oral and written exam. *Entrance requirements:* For master's, GRE General Test, 2 samples of written work, 10 slides of art work. Electronic applications accepted. *Faculty research:* Museum education; community-based, environmental, and multicultural art education; interdisciplinary art education, elementary and secondary art education.

The University of Texas at El Paso, Graduate School, College of Liberal Arts, Department of Art, El Paso, TX 79968-0001. Offers art education (MA); studio art (MA). Part-time and evening/weekend programs available. *Degree requirements:* For master's, thesis optional. *Entrance requirements:* For master's, minimum GPA of 3.0, digital portfolio, letters of recommendation. Additional exam requirements/recommendations for international students: Required—TOEFL; Recommended—IELTS. Electronic applications accepted.

The University of the Arts, College of Art, Media and Design, Department of Art Education, Philadelphia, PA 19102-4944. Offers art education (MA); visual arts (MAT). *Accreditation:* NASAD (one or more programs are accredited). Part-time programs available. *Degree requirements:* For master's, student teaching (MAT); thesis (MA). *Entrance requirements:* For master's, portfolio, official transcripts from each undergraduate or graduate school attended, three letters of recommendation, one- to two-page statement of professional plans and goals, personal interview, writing sample. Additional exam requirements/recommendations for international students: Required—TOEFL (minimum score 580 paper-based, 92 iBT) or IELTS (minimum score 6.5). *Faculty research:* Using technology and visual arts concepts to develop critical and creative thinking skills.

The University of Toledo, College of Graduate Studies, Judith Herb College of Education, Department of Curriculum and Instruction, Toledo, OH 43606-3390. Offers art education (ME); career and technical education (ME); career-technical education (Ed S); curriculum and instruction (ME, PhD, Ed S); early childhood education (PhD, Ed S); education and biology (MES); education and chemistry (MES); education and economics (MAE); education and English (MAE); education and French (MAE); education and geography (MAE); education and geology (MES); education and German (MAE); education and history (MAE); education and mathematics (MAE, MES); education and physics (MES); education and political science (MAE); education and sociology (MAE); education and Spanish (MAE); educational media (PhD); educational technology (ME); educational technology: virtual educator (Certificate); elementary education (PhD); English as a second language (MAE); gifted and talented (PhD); middle childhood education licensure (ME); music education (MME); secondary education (PhD); secondary education licensure (ME); special education (PhD, Ed S). *Accreditation:* NCATE. Part-time and evening/weekend programs available. *Faculty:* 41. *Students:* 53 full-time (30 women), 154 part-time (111 women); includes 21 minority (16 Black or African American, non-Hispanic/Latino; 4 Hispanic/Latino; 1 Two or more races, non-Hispanic/Latino), 21 international. Average age 34. 82 applicants, 79% accepted, 47 enrolled. In 2013, 80 master's, 5 doctorates awarded. *Degree requirements:* For master's, comprehensive exam, thesis or alternative; for doctorate, comprehensive exam, thesis/dissertation; for other advanced degree, thesis optional. *Entrance requirements:* For master's, doctorate, and other advanced degree, minimum cumulative GPA of 2.7 for all previous academic work, letters of recommendation. Additional exam requirements/recommendations for international students: Required—TOEFL (minimum score 550 paper-based; 80 iBT). *Application deadline:* For fall admission, 1/15 priority date for domestic and international students. Applications are processed on a rolling basis. Application fee: $45 ($75 for international students). Electronic applications accepted. *Financial support:* In 2013–14, 5 research assistantships with full and partial tuition reimbursements (averaging $13,200 per year), 11 teaching assistantships with full and partial tuition reimbursements (averaging $8,809 per year) were awarded; career-related internships or fieldwork, Federal Work-Study, institutionally sponsored loans, scholarships/grants, tuition waivers (full and partial), unspecified assistantships, and administrative assistantships also available. Support available to part-time students. *Unit head:* Dr. Joan Kaderavek, Chair, 419-530-5373, E-mail: eigh.chiarelott@utoledo.edu. *Application contact:* Graduate School Office, 419-530-4723, Fax: 419-530-4724, E-mail: grdsch@utnet.utoledo.edu.
Website: http://www.utoledo.edu/eduhshs/.

University of Utah, Graduate School, College of Fine Arts, Department of Art and Art History, Salt Lake City, UT 84112-0380. Offers art history (MA); ceramics (MFA); community-based art education (MFA); drawing (MFA); graphic design (MFA); painting (MFA); photography/digital imaging (MFA); printmaking (MFA); sculpture/intermedia (MFA). *Faculty:* 20 full-time (10 women), 27 part-time/adjunct (13 women). *Students:* 20 full-time (13 women), 2 part-time (both women); includes 3 minority (all Hispanic/Latino), 1 international. Average age 29. 40 applicants, 23% accepted, 7 enrolled. In 2013, 5 master's awarded. *Degree requirements:* For master's, variable foreign language requirement, comprehensive exam (for some programs), thesis or alternative, exhibit and final project paper (for MFA). *Entrance requirements:* For master's, CD portfolio (MFA), writing sample (MA), curriculum vitae, letters of recommendation, letter of intent. Additional exam requirements/recommendations for international students: Required—TOEFL (minimum score 575 paper-based; 75 iBT). *Application deadline:* For fall admission, 1/2 priority date for domestic and international students. Application fee: $55

($65 for international students). Electronic applications accepted. *Expenses:* Tuition, state resident: full-time $5259. Tuition, nonresident: full-time $18,569. *Required fees:* $841. Tuition and fees vary according to course load. *Financial support:* In 2013–14, 2 fellowships, 6 research assistantships with partial tuition reimbursements, 34 teaching assistantships with partial tuition reimbursements were awarded; Federal Work-Study, institutionally sponsored loans, scholarships/grants, tuition waivers (partial), unspecified assistantships, and stipends also available. Financial award application deadline: 1/2; financial award applicants required to submit FAFSA. *Faculty research:* Studio art, European art history, Asian art history, Latin American art history, twentieth century/contemporary art history. *Total annual research expenditures:* $54,906. *Unit head:* Prof. Brian Snapp, Chair, 801-581-8677, Fax: 801-585-6171, E-mail: b.snapp@utah.edu. *Application contact:* Prof. Kim Martinez, Director of Graduate Studies, 801-581-8677, Fax: 801-585-6171, E-mail: kim.martinez@art.utah.edu.
Website: http://www.art.utah.edu/.

University of Victoria, Faculty of Graduate Studies, Faculty of Education, Department of Curriculum and Instruction, Victoria, BC V8W 2Y2, Canada. Offers art education (M Ed, PhD); curriculum studies (M Ed, MA, PhD); early childhood education (M Ed, PhD); educational studies (PhD); language and literacy (M Ed, MA, PhD); mathematics (M Ed, MA, PhD); music education (M Ed, MA, PhD); science (M Ed, MA, PhD); social studies (M Ed, MA); social, cultural and foundational studies (MA, PhD); technology and environmental education (PhD). Part-time programs available. *Degree requirements:* For master's, thesis, project (M Ed); for doctorate, comprehensive exam, thesis/dissertation. *Entrance requirements:* For master's, minimum B average. Additional exam requirements/recommendations for international students: Required—TOEFL (minimum score 575 paper-based), IELTS (minimum score 7). Electronic applications accepted. *Faculty research:* Elementary and secondary English, language arts, curriculum theory and practice, educational media and technology, educational administration and leadership, history and philosophy of education.

University of Wisconsin–Madison, Graduate School, School of Education, Department of Art and Department of Curriculum and Instruction, Program in Art Education, Madison, WI 53706-1380. Offers MA. *Accreditation:* NASAD. *Application deadline:* For fall admission, 1/10 for domestic students; for spring admission, 11/15 for domestic students. Application fee: $56. *Expenses:* Tuition, state resident: full-time $10,728; part-time $790 per credit. Tuition, nonresident: full-time $24,054; part-time $1623 per credit. *Required fees:* $1130; $119 per credit. *Financial support:* Fellowships with full tuition reimbursements, research assistantships with full tuition reimbursements, teaching assistantships with full tuition reimbursements, and project assistantships available. *Unit head:* Dr. Paul Sacaridiz, Chair, 608-262-1662, E-mail: tloeser@facstaff.wisc.edu. *Application contact:* 608-262-2433, Fax: 608-262-5134, E-mail: gradadmiss@mail.bascom.wisc.edu.
Website: http://www.education.wisc.edu/art.

University of Wisconsin–Madison, Graduate School, School of Education, Department of Curriculum and Instruction, Madison, WI 53706-1380. Offers art education (MA); curriculum and instruction (MS, PhD); education and mathematics (MA); French education (MA); German education (MA); music education (MS); science education (MS); Spanish education (MA). *Accreditation:* NASM (one or more programs are accredited). *Degree requirements:* For doctorate, thesis/dissertation. Application fee: $56. *Expenses:* Tuition, state resident: full-time $10,728; part-time $790 per credit. Tuition, nonresident: full-time $24,054; part-time $1623 per credit. *Required fees:* $1130; $119 per credit. *Financial support:* Project assistantships available. *Unit head:* Dr. Beth Graue, Chair, 608-263-4600, E-mail: graue@education.wisc.edu. *Application contact:* 608-262-2433, Fax: 608-262-5134, E-mail: gradadmiss@mail.bascom.wisc.edu.
Website: http://www.education.wisc.edu/ci.

University of Wisconsin–Milwaukee, Graduate School, Peck School of the Arts, Department of Art, Milwaukee, WI 53201-0413. Offers art education (MS); studio art (MA, MFA). Part-time programs available. *Faculty:* 20 full-time (15 women). *Students:* 20 full-time (6 women), 1 (woman) part-time; includes 2 minority (1 Black or African American, non-Hispanic/Latino; 1 Asian, non-Hispanic/Latino), 2 international. Average age 33. 49 applicants, 35% accepted, 12 enrolled. In 2013, 12 master's awarded. *Degree requirements:* For master's, comprehensive exam, thesis or alternative. *Entrance requirements:* For master's, portfolio. Additional exam requirements/recommendations for international students: Required—TOEFL (minimum score 550 paper-based; 79 iBT), IELTS (minimum score 6.5). *Application deadline:* For fall admission, 1/1 priority date for domestic students; for spring admission, 9/1 for domestic students. Applications are processed on a rolling basis. Application fee: $56 ($96 for international students). Electronic applications accepted. *Financial support:* In 2013–14, 10 teaching assistantships were awarded; career-related internships or fieldwork, health care benefits, unspecified assistantships, and project assistantships also available. Support available to part-time students. Financial award application deadline: 4/15. *Unit head:* Yevgeniya Kaganovich, Chair, 414-229-6216, E-mail: yk@uwm.edu. *Application contact:* General Information Contact, 414-229-4982, Fax: 414-229-6967, E-mail: gradschool@uwm.edu.
Website: http://www4.uwm.edu/psoa/artdesign/.

University of Wisconsin–Superior, Graduate Division, Department of Visual Arts, Superior, WI 54880-4500. Offers art education (MA); art history (MA); art therapy (MA); studio arts (MA). Part-time programs available. *Faculty:* 7 full-time (1 woman), 1 (woman) part-time/adjunct. *Students:* 3 full-time (1 woman), 9 part-time (all women); includes 2 minority (1 American Indian or Alaska Native, non-Hispanic/Latino; 1 Hispanic/Latino), 1 international. Average age 35. 10 applicants, 60% accepted, 4 enrolled. In 2013, 12 master's awarded. *Degree requirements:* For master's, comprehensive exam, exhibit. *Entrance requirements:* For master's, minimum GPA of 2.75, portfolio. *Application deadline:* For fall admission, 4/1 priority date for domestic and international students; for spring admission, 10/15 priority date for domestic and international students. Applications are processed on a rolling basis. Application fee: $45. Electronic applications accepted. *Expenses:* Tuition, state resident: full-time $4526; part-time $649.24 per credit. Tuition, nonresident: full-time $9091; part-time $1156.51 per credit. *Financial support:* Career-related internships or fieldwork, Federal Work-Study, scholarships/grants, and tuition waivers (partial) available. Support available to part-time students. Financial award application deadline: 4/15; financial award applicants required to submit FAFSA. *Unit head:* Tim Cleary, Coordinator, 715-394-8398, E-mail: tcleary@uwsuper.edu. *Application contact:* Suzie Finckler, Student Status Examiner, 715-394-8295, Fax: 715-394-8371, E-mail: gradstudy@uwsuper.edu.
Website: http://www.uwsuper.edu/.

Ursuline College, School of Graduate Studies, Program in Education, Pepper Pike, OH 44124-4398. Offers art education (MA); early childhood education (MA); language arts education (MA); life science education (MA); math education (MA); middle school education (MA); social studies education (MA); special education (MA). *Accreditation:* NCATE. *Faculty:* 4 full-time (all women), 7 part-time/adjunct (5 women). *Students:* 18 full-time (16 women), 7 part-time (all women); includes 8 minority (4 Black or African American, non-Hispanic/Latino; 2 Asian, non-Hispanic/Latino; 2 Hispanic/Latino). Average age 34. 1 applicant, 100% accepted, 1 enrolled. In 2013, 25 master's awarded. *Degree requirements:* For master's, comprehensive exam. *Entrance requirements:* For

master's, minimum undergraduate GPA of 3.0. Additional exam requirements/recommendations for international students: Required—TOEFL (minimum score 500 paper-based). *Application deadline:* For fall admission, 8/1 priority date for domestic students. Applications are processed on a rolling basis. Application fee: $25. *Expenses:* Contact institution. *Financial support:* In 2013–14, 1 student received support. Federal Work-Study available. Financial award application deadline: 3/1. *Unit head:* Dr. Edna West, Director, Master's Apprentice Program, 440-646-6134, Fax: 440-646-8328, E-mail: ewest@ursuline.edu. *Application contact:* Stephanie Pratt, Graduate Admission Coordinator, 440-646-8119, Fax: 440-684-6138, E-mail: graduateadmissions@ursuline.edu.

Virginia Commonwealth University, Graduate School, School of the Arts, Department of Art Education, Richmond, VA 23284-9005. Offers MAE. *Accreditation:* NASAD. *Degree requirements:* For master's, thesis optional. *Entrance requirements:* For master's, GRE if GPA is below 3.0, portfolio. Additional exam requirements/recommendations for international students: Required—TOEFL (minimum score 600 paper-based; 100 iBT). Electronic applications accepted. *Faculty research:* Teaching methods.

Wayne State University, College of Education, Division of Teacher Education, Detroit, MI 48202. Offers art education (M Ed), including art therapy; autism spectrum disorders (Certificate); bilingual/bicultural education (M Ed, Certificate); career and technical education (M Ed, Certificate); cognitive impairment (Certificate); curriculum and instruction (Ed D, PhD, Ed S), including art education (PhD), bilingual education (Ed D, Ed S), bilingual-bicultural education (PhD), career and technical education (MAT, Ed D, PhD, Ed S), early childhood education (MAT, Ed D, PhD, Ed S), elementary education, English as a second language (MAT, Ed D, Ed S), English education (MAT, Ed D, PhD, Ed S), foreign language education (MAT, PhD), K-12 curriculum, mathematics education (MAT, Ed D, PhD, Ed S), science education (MAT, Ed D, PhD, Ed S), secondary education, social studies education (MAT, Ed S), social studies education: secondary (Ed D, PhD); early childhood education (M Ed, Certificate); elementary education (M Ed, MAT), including children's literature (MAT), early childhood education (MAT, Ed D, PhD, Ed S), general elementary education (MAT); elementary or secondary education (MAT), including bilingual/bicultural education, English as a second language (MAT, Ed D, Ed S), mathematics education (MAT, Ed D, PhD, Ed S), science education (MAT, Ed D, PhD, Ed S), social studies education (MAT, Ed S); emotionally impaired (Certificate); English as a second language (Certificate); English education (M Ed), including secondary; foreign language education (M Ed); K-12 reading specialist (Certificate); learning disabilities (Certificate); mathematics education (M Ed), including secondary; reading (M Ed, Ed S); reading, language and literature (Ed D); science education (M Ed), including secondary; secondary education (MAT), including art education (K-12); career and technical education (MAT, Ed D, PhD, Ed S), English education (MAT, Ed D, PhD, Ed S), foreign language education (MAT, PhD), kinesiology; social studies education (M Ed), including secondary; special education (M Ed, MAT, Ed D, PhD, Ed S); visual arts education (Certificate). Part-time programs available. *Faculty:* 36 full-time (25 women), 55 part-time/adjunct (43 women). *Students:* 218 full-time (163 women), 448 part-time (344 women); includes 218 minority (177 Black or African American, non-Hispanic/Latino; 2 American Indian or Alaska Native, non-Hispanic/Latino; 11 Asian, non-Hispanic/Latino; 19 Hispanic/Latino; 1 Native Hawaiian or other Pacific Islander, non-Hispanic/Latino; 8 Two or more races, non-Hispanic/Latino), 10 international. Average age 37. 258 applicants, 30% accepted, 52 enrolled. In 2013, 183 master's, 10 doctorates, 35 other advanced degrees awarded. *Degree requirements:* For master's, thesis, essay or project (for some M Ed programs), professional field experience (for MAT programs); for doctorate, thesis/dissertation. *Entrance requirements:* For master's, Michigan Basic Skills Test (MA in teaching), admission to the graduate school, verification of participation in group work with children and Michigan State Police Criminal Background check; for doctorate, minimum undergraduate GPA of 3.0, graduate 3.5; interview, curriculum vitae; references. Additional exam requirements/recommendations for international students: Required—TOEFL (minimum score 550 paper-based; 79 iBT), TWE (minimum score 5.5), Michigan English Language Assessment Battery (minimum score 85); Recommended—IELTS (minimum score 6.5). *Application deadline:* For fall admission, 6/1 priority date for domestic students, 5/1 priority date for international students; for winter admission, 10/1 priority date for domestic students, 9/1 priority date for international students; for spring admission, 2/1 priority date for domestic students, 1/1 priority date for international students. Applications are processed on a rolling basis. Application fee: $0. Electronic applications accepted. *Expenses:* Tuition, state resident: part-time $554.15 per credit. Tuition, nonresident: part-time $1200.35 per credit. *Required fees:* $42.15 per credit. $268.30 per semester. Tuition and fees vary according to course load and program. *Financial support:* In 2013–14, 83 students received support, including 1 fellowship (averaging $16,842 per year), 1 research assistantship with tuition reimbursement available (averaging $21,229 per year); career-related internships or fieldwork, Federal Work-Study, scholarships/grants, health care benefits, and unspecified assistantships also available. Support available to part-time students. Financial award application deadline: 3/31; financial award applicants required to submit FAFSA. *Faculty research:* Improving students' skill achievement in mathematics; improving elementary children's understanding of informational text; teachers' use of their pedagogical and mathematical knowledge in the interactive work of teaching; the intersection of identity construction in teaching and learning; identifying effective methods of literacy instruction and assessments for bilingual students in elementary language arts classrooms. *Total annual research expenditures:* $368,105. *Unit head:* Dr. Kathleen Crawford-McKinney, Assistant Dean, 313-577-0122. *Application contact:* Janice Green, Assistant Dean, 313-577-1605, E-mail: jwgreen@wayne.edu.
Website: http://coe.wayne.edu/ted/index.php.

Western Kentucky University, Graduate Studies, Potter College of Arts and Letters, Department of Art, Bowling Green, KY 42101. Offers art education (MA Ed). *Accreditation:* NASAD; NCATE. Part-time and evening/weekend programs available. *Degree requirements:* For master's, comprehensive exam, final exam. *Entrance requirements:* For master's, GRE General Test, minimum GPA of 2.75. Additional exam requirements/recommendations for international students: Required—TOEFL (minimum score 555 paper-based; 79 iBT). *Faculty research:* Nineteenth century Kentucky women artists.

Western Michigan University, Graduate College, College of Fine Arts, Gwen Frostic School of Art, Kalamazoo, MI 49008. Offers art education (MA); studio art (MFA). *Accreditation:* NASAD (one or more programs are accredited). *Degree requirements:* For master's, thesis or alternative.

West Virginia University, College of Creative Arts, Division of Art and Design, Morgantown, WV 26506. Offers art education (MA); art history (MA); ceramics (MFA); graphic design (MFA); painting (MFA); printmaking (MFA); sculpture (MFA); studio art (MA). *Accreditation:* NASAD. *Degree requirements:* For master's, thesis, exhibit. *Entrance requirements:* For master's, minimum GPA of 2.75, portfolio. Additional exam requirements/recommendations for international students: Required—TOEFL. *Expenses:* Contact institution. *Faculty research:* Medieval art history.

William Carey University, School of Education, Hattiesburg, MS 39401-5499. Offers art education (M Ed); art of teaching (M Ed); elementary education (M Ed, Ed S);

English education (M Ed); gifted education (M Ed); history and social science (M Ed); mild/moderate disabilities (M Ed); secondary education (M Ed). *Accreditation:* NCATE. Part-time programs available. *Degree requirements:* For master's, comprehensive exam. *Entrance requirements:* For master's, GRE, MAT, minimum GPA of 2.5, Class A teacher's license. Additional exam requirements/recommendations for international students: Required—TOEFL (minimum score 550 paper-based).

Winthrop University, College of Visual and Performing Arts, Department of Art, Rock Hill, SC 29733. Offers art (MFA); art administration (MA); art education (MA). *Accreditation:* NASAD. Part-time programs available. *Degree requirements:* For master's, thesis, documented exhibit, oral exam. *Entrance requirements:* For master's, GRE General Test or MAT, PRAXIS (MA), minimum GPA of 3.0, resume, slide portfolio, teaching certificate (MA). Electronic applications accepted.

Business Education

Arkansas State University, Graduate School, College of Business, Department of Computer and Information Technology, Jonesboro, AR 72467. Offers business administration education (SCCT); business education (SCCT); business technology education (MSE, SCCT). Part-time programs available. *Faculty:* 9 full-time (1 woman). *Students:* 6 part-time (4 women); includes 4 minority (all Black or African American, non-Hispanic/Latino). Average age 36. 6 applicants, 83% accepted, 4 enrolled. In 2013, 8 master's awarded. *Degree requirements:* For master's, comprehensive exam, thesis or alternative. *Entrance requirements:* For master's, GRE General Test or MAT, appropriate bachelor's degree, official transcript, immunization records. Additional exam requirements/recommendations for international students: Required—TOEFL (minimum score 550 paper-based; 79 iBT), IELTS (minimum score 6), PTE (minimum score 56). *Application deadline:* For fall admission, 7/1 for domestic and international students; for spring admission, 11/15 for domestic students, 11/14 for international students. Applications are processed on a rolling basis. Application fee: $30 ($40 for international students). Electronic applications accepted. *Expenses:* Contact institution. *Financial support:* Career-related internships or fieldwork, scholarships/grants, and unspecified assistantships available. Financial award application deadline: 7/1; financial award applicants required to submit FAFSA. *Unit head:* Dr. John Robertson, Chair, 870-972-3416, Fax: 870-972-3868, E-mail: jfrobert@astate.edu. *Application contact:* Vickey Ring, Graduate Admissions Coordinator, 870-972-3029, Fax: 870-972-3857, E-mail: vickeyring@astate.edu.
Website: http://www.astate.edu/college/business/faculty-staff/computer-information-technology/.

Auburn University, Graduate School, College of Education, Department of Curriculum and Teaching, Auburn University, AL 36849. Offers business education (M Ed, MS, PhD); early childhood education (M Ed, MS, PhD, Ed S); elementary education (M Ed, MS, PhD, Ed S); foreign languages (M Ed, MS); music education (M Ed, MS, PhD, Ed S); postsecondary education (PhD); reading education (PhD, Ed S); secondary education (M Ed, MS, PhD, Ed S), including English language arts, mathematics, science, social studies. *Accreditation:* NASM (one or more programs are accredited); NCATE. Part-time programs available. *Faculty:* 29 full-time (21 women), 4 part-time/adjunct (all women). *Students:* 61 full-time (40 women), 153 part-time (108 women); includes 37 minority (32 Black or African American, non-Hispanic/Latino; 2 Asian, non-Hispanic/Latino; 3 Hispanic/Latino), 1 international. Average age 34. 150 applicants, 59% accepted, 74 enrolled. In 2013, 70 master's, 6 doctorates, 26 other advanced degrees awarded. *Degree requirements:* For master's, thesis (for some programs); for doctorate, thesis/dissertation; for Ed S, field project. *Entrance requirements:* For master's, doctorate, and Ed S, GRE General Test. *Application deadline:* For fall admission, 7/7 for domestic students; for spring admission, 11/24 for domestic students. Applications are processed on a rolling basis. Application fee: $50 ($60 for international students). Electronic applications accepted. *Expenses:* Tuition, state resident: full-time $8262; part-time $459 per credit hour. Tuition, nonresident: full-time $24,786; part-time $1377 per credit hour. Tuition and fees vary according to degree level and program. *Financial support:* Fellowships, teaching assistantships, career-related internships or fieldwork, and Federal Work-Study available. Support available to part-time students. Financial award application deadline: 3/15; financial award applicants required to submit FAFSA. *Faculty research:* Emerging literacy, reading attitudes, music for at-risk youth, portfolio assessment. *Unit head:* Dr. Kimberly Walls, Head, 334-844-4434. *Application contact:* Dr. George Flowers, Dean of the Graduate School, 334-844-2125.
Website: http://education.auburn.edu/academic_departments/curr/.

Ball State University, Graduate School, Miller College of Business, Department of Information Systems and Operations Management, Muncie, IN 47306-1099. Offers business education (MAE). *Accreditation:* NCATE. *Faculty:* 3 full-time (0 women). *Students:* 12 part-time (7 women). 1 applicant, 100% accepted, 1 enrolled. In 2013, 11 master's awarded. *Entrance requirements:* For master's, GMAT. Application fee: $50. *Financial support:* In 2013–14, 1 student received support, including 5 teaching assistantships with full tuition reimbursements available (averaging $9,762 per year). Financial award application deadline: 3/1. *Unit head:* Dr. Sushil Sharma, Chair, 765-285-5315, Fax: 765-285-8024, E-mail: ssharma@bsu.edu. *Application contact:* Jennifer Bott, Graduate Coordinator, 765-285-5323, Fax: 765-285-8818, E-mail: jpbott@bsu.edu.
Website: http://www.bsu.edu/business/beoa/.

Bloomsburg University of Pennsylvania, School of Graduate Studies, College of Business, Program in Business Education, Bloomsburg, PA 17815-1301. Offers M Ed. *Faculty:* 2 full-time (1 woman). *Students:* 4 part-time (0 women). Average age 31. 5 applicants, 60% accepted, 2 enrolled. In 2013, 4 master's awarded. *Degree requirements:* For master's, thesis optional, student teaching, minimum QPA of 3.0. *Entrance requirements:* For master's, PRAXIS, minimum QPA of 3.0, 2 letters of recommendation, personal statement, resume. Additional exam requirements/recommendations for international students: Required—TOEFL. *Application deadline:* Applications are processed on a rolling basis. Application fee: $35 ($60 for international students). Electronic applications accepted. *Expenses:* Tuition, state resident: full-time $7956; part-time $442 per credit. Tuition, nonresident: full-time $11,934; part-time $663 per credit. *Required fees:* $95.50 per credit. $55 per semester. Tuition and fees vary according to course load. *Financial support:* Unspecified assistantships available. *Unit head:* Dr. Margaret O'Connor, Chair, 570-389-4771, Fax: 570-389-3892, E-mail: moconno1@bloomu.edu. *Application contact:* Jennifer Richard, Administrative Assistant, 570-389-4015, Fax: 570-389-3054, E-mail: jrichard@bloomu.edu.
Website: http://www.bloomu.edu/gradschool/business-education.

Bowling Green State University, Graduate College, College of Education and Human Development, School of Education and Intervention Services, Teaching and Learning Division, Department of Business Education, Bowling Green, OH 43403. Offers M Ed. *Accreditation:* NCATE. Part-time programs available. *Degree requirements:* For master's, thesis or alternative. *Entrance requirements:* For master's, GRE General Test. Additional exam requirements/recommendations for international students: Required—TOEFL. Electronic applications accepted. *Faculty research:* School to work, workforce education, marketing education, contextual teaching and learning.

Buffalo State College, State University of New York, The Graduate School, Faculty of Applied Science and Education, Department of Business Studies, Buffalo, NY 14222-1095. Offers business and marketing education (MS Ed). Part-time and evening/weekend programs available. *Degree requirements:* For master's, thesis or alternative, project. *Entrance requirements:* For master's, minimum GPA of 2.5, New York teaching certificate.

Canisius College, Graduate Division, School of Education and Human Services, Department of Graduate Education and Leadership, Buffalo, NY 14208-1098. Offers business and marketing education (MS Ed); college student personnel (MS Ed); deaf education (MS Ed); deaf/adolescent education, grades 7-12 (MS Ed); deaf/childhood education, grades 1-6 (MS Ed); differentiated instruction (MS Ed); education administration (MS); educational administration (MS Ed); educational technologies (Certificate); gifted education extension (Certificate); literacy (MS Ed); reading (Certificate); school building leadership (MS Ed, Certificate); school district leadership (Certificate); teacher leader (Certificate); TESOL (MS Ed). *Accreditation:* NCATE. Part-time and evening/weekend programs available. Postbaccalaureate distance learning degree programs offered (minimal on-campus study). *Faculty:* 6 full-time (5 women), 33 part-time/adjunct (20 women). *Students:* 134 full-time (106 women), 267 part-time (213 women); includes 36 minority (22 Black or African American, non-Hispanic/Latino; 1 American Indian or Alaska Native, non-Hispanic/Latino; 3 Asian, non-Hispanic/Latino; 8 Hispanic/Latino; 2 Two or more races, non-Hispanic/Latino), 2 international. Average age 30. 282 applicants, 80% accepted, 120 enrolled. In 2013, 178 master's awarded. *Entrance requirements:* For master's, GRE if cumulative GPA less than 2.7, transcripts, two letters of recommendation. Additional exam requirements/recommendations for international students: Required—TOEFL (minimum score 550 paper-based, 80 iBT), IELTS (minimum score 6.5), or CAEL (minimum score 70). *Application deadline:* Applications are processed on a rolling basis. Application fee: $25. Electronic applications accepted. Application fee is waived when completed online. *Expenses: Tuition:* Part-time $750 per credit hour. *Financial support:* Career-related internships or fieldwork, Federal Work-Study, scholarships/grants, tuition waivers (partial), and unspecified assistantships available. Support available to part-time students. Financial award application deadline: 4/30; financial award applicants required to submit FAFSA. *Faculty research:* Asperger's disease, autism, private higher education, reading strategies. *Unit head:* Dr. Rosemary K. Murray, Chair/Associate Professor of Graduate Education and Leadership, 716-888-3723, E-mail: murray1@canisius.edu. *Application contact:* Julie A. Zulewski, Director of Graduate Admissions, 716-888-2548, Fax: 716-888-3195, E-mail: zulewskj@canisius.edu.
Website: http://www.canisius.edu/graduate/.

Capella University, School of Business and Technology, Doctoral Programs in Business, Minneapolis, MN 55402. Offers accounting (DBA, PhD); business intelligence (DBA); finance (DBA, PhD); general business management (PhD); human resource management (DBA, PhD); leadership (DBA, PhD); management education (PhD); marketing (DBA, PhD); project management (DBA, PhD); strategy and innovation (DBA, PhD).

Chadron State College, School of Professional and Graduate Studies, Department of Education, Chadron, NE 69337. Offers business (MA Ed); community counseling (MA Ed); educational administration (MS Ed, Sp Ed); elementary education (MS Ed); history (MA Ed); language and literature (MA Ed); secondary administration (MS Ed); secondary education (MS Ed). *Accreditation:* NCATE. Part-time and evening/weekend programs available. Postbaccalaureate distance learning degree programs offered. *Degree requirements:* For master's, thesis optional. *Entrance requirements:* For master's, GRE General Test, GRE Writing Test, minimum GPA of 2.75 or 12 graduate hours at CSC with minimum GPA of 3.25. Additional exam requirements/recommendations for international students: Required—TOEFL. Electronic applications accepted. *Faculty research:* Rural education, technology, mental health.

Colorado Christian University, Program in Curriculum and Instruction, Lakewood, CO 80226. Offers corporate education (MACI); early childhood educator (MACI); elementary educator (MACI); instructional technology (MACI); master educator (MACI); online course developer (MACI); online teaching and learning (MACI); special education generalist (MACI). Part-time and evening/weekend programs available. *Degree requirements:* For master's, thesis optional, practicum. *Entrance requirements:* For master's, interviews, letters of recommendation. Additional exam requirements/recommendations for international students: Required—TOEFL. Electronic applications accepted. *Expenses:* Contact institution.

East Carolina University, Graduate School, College of Education, Department of Business and Information Technologies Education, Greenville, NC 27858-4353. Offers business education (MA Ed); elementary education (MAT); English education (MAT); family and consumer science (MAT); health education (MAT); Hispanic studies (MAT); history education (MAT); marketing education (MA Ed); middle grades education (MAT); music education (MAT); physical education (MAT); science education (MAT); special education (MAT), including general curriculum; vocation education (MS). *Accreditation:* NCATE. Part-time and evening/weekend programs available. Postbaccalaureate distance learning degree programs offered (no on-campus study). *Degree requirements:* For master's, comprehensive exam, thesis optional. *Entrance requirements:* For master's, GRE or MAT, minimum GPA of 2.5, bachelor's degree in related field, teaching license (MA Ed). Additional exam requirements/recommendations for international students: Required—TOEFL. *Expenses:* Tuition, state resident: full-time $4223. Tuition, nonresident: full-time $16,540. *Required fees:* $2184.

Eastern Kentucky University, The Graduate School, College of Education, Department of Curriculum and Instruction, Program in Secondary and Higher Education, Richmond, KY 40475-3102. Offers secondary education (MA Ed), including agricultural education, art education, biological sciences education, business education, English education, geography education, history education, home economics education, industrial education, mathematical sciences education, physical education, school health education. *Accreditation:* NCATE. Part-time programs available. *Entrance requirements:* For master's, GRE General Test, minimum GPA of 2.5.

Emporia State University, Program in Business Education, Emporia, KS 66801-5415. Offers MS. Part-time and evening/weekend programs available. Postbaccalaureate distance learning degree programs offered (no on-campus study). *Students:* 4 full-time (2 women), 13 part-time (7 women); includes 1 minority (Hispanic/Latino). 4 applicants, 100% accepted, 1 enrolled. In 2013, 4 master's awarded. *Entrance requirements:* For master's, GRE, 15 undergraduate credits in business; minimum undergraduate GPA of 2.7 over last 60 hours. Additional exam requirements/recommendations for international students: Required—TOEFL (minimum score 520 paper-based; 68 iBT). *Application deadline:* For fall admission, 8/15 priority date for domestic students. Applications are processed on a rolling basis. Application fee: $30 ($75 for international students). Electronic applications accepted. *Expenses: Tuition, area resident:* Part-time $220 per credit hour. Tuition, state resident: part-time $220 per credit hour. Tuition, nonresident: part-time $685 per credit hour. *Required fees:* $73 per credit hour. *Financial support:* Career-related internships or fieldwork, institutionally sponsored loans, health care benefits, and unspecified assistantships available. Financial award application deadline: 3/15; financial award applicants required to submit FAFSA. *Unit head:* Dr. Jack Sterrett, Chair, 620-341-5345, Fax: 620-341-6345, E-mail: jsterret@emporia.edu. *Application contact:* Dr. Nancy Hite, Information Contact, 620-341-5345, Fax: 620-341-6345, E-mail: nhite@emporia.edu.

Florida Agricultural and Mechanical University, Division of Graduate Studies, Research, and Continuing Education, College of Education, Department of Vocational Education, Tallahassee, FL 32307-3200. Offers business education (MBE); industrial education (M Ed, MS Ed). *Accreditation:* NCATE. *Degree requirements:* For master's, thesis (for some programs). *Entrance requirements:* For master's, GRE General Test, minimum GPA of 3.0. Additional exam requirements/recommendations for international students: Required—TOEFL.

Georgia Southern University, Jack N. Averitt College of Graduate Studies, College of Education, Department of Teaching and Learning, Program in Business Education, Statesboro, GA 30460. Offers MAT. *Accreditation:* NCATE. Part-time and evening/weekend programs available. *Students:* 1 (woman) full-time; minority (Black or African American, non-Hispanic/Latino). Average age 43. 1 applicant. *Degree requirements:* For master's, transition point assessments. *Entrance requirements:* For master's, GRE General Test or MAT, GACE Basic Skills and Content Assessments, minimum cumulative GPA of 2.5. Additional exam requirements/recommendations for international students: Required—TOEFL (minimum score 550 paper-based; 80 iBT), IELTS (minimum score 6). *Application deadline:* For fall admission, 3/1 priority date for domestic and international students; for spring admission, 10/1 priority date for domestic students, 10/1 for international students. Applications are processed on a rolling basis. Application fee: $50. Electronic applications accepted. *Expenses:* Tuition, state resident: full-time $7068; part-time $270 per semester hour. Tuition, nonresident: full-time $26,446; part-time $1077 per semester hour. *Required fees:* $2092. *Financial support:* In 2013–14, research assistantships with partial tuition reimbursements (averaging $7,200 per year), teaching assistantships with partial tuition reimbursements (averaging $7,200 per year) were awarded; Federal Work-Study, scholarships/grants, tuition waivers (partial), and unspecified assistantships also available. Support available to part-time students. Financial award application deadline: 4/15; financial award applicants required to submit FAFSA. *Faculty research:* Technology applications. *Unit head:* Dr. Greg Chamblee, Program Coordinator, 912-478-5783, Fax: 912-478-0026, E-mail: gchamblee@georgiasouthern.edu. *Application contact:* Amanda Gilliland, Coordinator for Graduate Student Recruitment, 912-478-5384, Fax: 912-478-0740, E-mail: gradadmissions@georgiasouthern.edu.
Website: http://coe.georgiasouthern.edu/ger/.

Hofstra University, School of Education, Programs in Teaching - Secondary Education, Hempstead, NY 11549. Offers business education (MS Ed); education technology (Advanced Certificate); English education (MA, MS Ed); foreign language and TESOL (MS Ed); foreign language education (MA, MS Ed), including French, German, Russian, Spanish; mathematics education (MA, MS Ed); science education (MA, MS Ed), including biology, chemistry, earth science, geology, physics; secondary education (Advanced Certificate); social studies education (MA, MS Ed); technology for learning (MA).

Indiana University of Pennsylvania, School of Graduate Studies and Research, Eberly College of Business and Information Technology, Department of Technology Support and Training, Program in Business/Business Specialist, Indiana, PA 15705-1087. Offers M Ed. Part-time programs available. *Faculty:* 2 full-time (both women). *Students:* 1 part-time (0 women). Average age 45. 5 applicants. In 2013, 5 master's awarded. *Degree requirements:* For master's, thesis optional. *Entrance requirements:* For master's, GMAT or GRE. Additional exam requirements/recommendations for international students: Required—TOEFL (minimum score 540 paper-based). *Application deadline:* Applications are processed on a rolling basis. Application fee: $50. Electronic applications accepted. *Expenses:* Tuition, state resident: full-time $3978; part-time $442 per credit. Tuition, nonresident: full-time $5967; part-time $663 per credit. *Required fees:* $2080; $115.55 per credit. $93 per semester. Tuition and fees vary according to degree level and program. *Financial support:* Career-related internships or fieldwork, Federal Work-Study, scholarships/grants, and unspecified assistantships available. Financial award application deadline: 4/15; financial award applicants required to submit FAFSA. *Unit head:* Dr. Lucinda Willis, Graduate Coordinator, 724-357-2061, E-mail: willisl@iup.edu.
Website: http://www.iup.edu/upper.aspx?id-89005.

Inter American University of Puerto Rico, Metropolitan Campus, Graduate Programs, Program in Commerical Education, San Juan, PR 00919-1293. Offers MA.

Inter American University of Puerto Rico, San Germán Campus, Graduate Studies Center, Program in Business Education, San Germán, PR 00683-5008. Offers MA. Part-time and evening/weekend programs available. *Faculty:* 16 full-time (8 women), 17 part-time/adjunct (10 women). *Students:* 18 full-time (all women), 3 part-time (all women); all minorities (all Hispanic/Latino). Average age 33. 6 applicants, 83% accepted, 5 enrolled. In 2013, 6 master's awarded. *Degree requirements:* For master's, comprehensive exam. *Entrance requirements:* For master's, GRE General Test or EXADEP, minimum GPA of 3.0. *Application deadline:* For fall admission, 4/30 priority date for domestic students; for spring admission, 11/15 for domestic students. Applications are processed on a rolling basis. Application fee: $31. *Expenses: Tuition:* Full-time $2424; part-time $202 per credit hour. *Required fees:* $260 per semester. Tuition and fees vary according to course level, course load, degree level and program. *Financial support:* Teaching assistantships, Federal Work-Study, and unspecified assistantships available. *Unit head:* Dr. Elba T. Irizarry, Director of Graduate Studies Center, 787-264-1912 Ext. 7357, Fax: 787-892-6350, E-mail: elbat@sg.inter.edu. *Application contact:* Dr. Ailin Padilla, Coordinator, 787-264-1912 Ext. 7355, E-mail: ailin_padilla@intersg.edu.

International College of the Cayman Islands, Graduate Program in Management, Newlands, Cayman Islands. Offers business administration (MBA); management (MS), including education, human resources. Part-time and evening/weekend programs available. *Degree requirements:* For master's, comprehensive exam. *Entrance requirements:* Additional exam requirements/recommendations for international students: Recommended—TOEFL. *Faculty research:* International human resources administration.

Johnson & Wales University, MAT Program in Teacher Education, Providence, RI 02903-3703. Offers business education and secondary special education (MAT); elementary education and elementary special education (MAT); elementary education and elementary/secondary special education (MAT); elementary education and secondary special education (MAT); food service education (MAT). Part-time and evening/weekend programs available. *Entrance requirements:* For master's, MAT, minimum GPA of 2.75. Additional exam requirements/recommendations for international students: Required—TOEFL (minimum score 550 paper-based) or IELTS (recommended). *Faculty research:* Secondary education, student teaching, educational reform, evaluation procedures.

Lehman College of the City University of New York, Division of Education, Department of Middle and High School Education, Program in Business Education, Bronx, NY 10468-1589. Offers MS Ed. *Accreditation:* NCATE. Part-time and evening/weekend programs available. *Degree requirements:* For master's, thesis. *Entrance requirements:* For master's, minimum GPA of 2.7.

Louisiana State University and Agricultural & Mechanical College, Graduate School, College of Human Sciences and Education, School of Human Resource Education and Workforce Development, Baton Rouge, LA 70803. Offers agriculture and extension education and youth development (MS, PhD); career and technical education (MS, PhD); comprehensive vocational education (MS, PhD); extension and international education (MS, PhD); human resource and leadership development (MS, PhD); industrial education (MS); vocational agriculture education (MS, PhD); vocational business education (MS); vocational home economics education (MS). *Accreditation:* NCATE. Part-time programs available. *Faculty:* 10 full-time (5 women). *Students:* 46 full-time (28 women), 138 part-time (96 women); includes 65 minority (52 Black or African American, non-Hispanic/Latino; 2 American Indian or Alaska Native, non-Hispanic/Latino; 2 Asian, non-Hispanic/Latino; 6 Hispanic/Latino; 3 Two or more races, non-Hispanic/Latino), 6 international. Average age 35. 120 applicants, 62% accepted, 49 enrolled. In 2013, 23 master's, 14 doctorates awarded. Terminal master's awarded for partial completion of doctoral program. *Degree requirements:* For master's, thesis (for some programs); for doctorate, thesis/dissertation. *Entrance requirements:* For master's and doctorate, GRE General Test, minimum GPA of 3.0. Additional exam requirements/recommendations for international students: Required—TOEFL (minimum score 550 paper-based; 79 IBT), IELTS (minimum score 6.5), or PTE (minimum score 59). *Application deadline:* For fall admission, 1/25 priority date for domestic students, 5/15 for international students; for spring admission, 10/15 for international students. Applications are processed on a rolling basis. Application fee: $50 ($70 for international students). Electronic applications accepted. *Financial support:* In 2013–14, 85 students received support, including 4 fellowships with full and partial tuition reimbursements available (averaging $31,175 per year), 9 research assistantships with full and partial tuition reimbursements available (averaging $15,422 per year), 14 teaching assistantships with partial tuition reimbursements available (averaging $14,289 per year); career-related internships or fieldwork, Federal Work-Study, institutionally sponsored loans, health care benefits, tuition waivers (full and partial), and unspecified assistantships also available. Financial award application deadline: 3/1; financial award applicants required to submit FAFSA. *Faculty research:* Adult education, history and philosophy of vocational education, curriculum and instruction, career decision-making. *Total annual research expenditures:* $4,454. *Unit head:* Dr. Ed Holton, Director, 225-578-5748, Fax: 225-578-5755, E-mail: eholton@lsu.edu.
Website: http://www.lsu.edu/hrleader/.

Middle Tennessee State University, College of Graduate Studies, Jennings A. Jones College of Business, Department of Business Communication and Entrepreneurship, Murfreesboro, TN 37132. Offers business education (MBE). Part-time and evening/weekend programs available. Postbaccalaureate distance learning degree programs offered. *Faculty:* 8 full-time (5 women). *Students:* 9 full-time (5 women), 13 part-time (8 women); includes 4 minority (2 Black or African American, non-Hispanic/Latino; 1 Asian, non-Hispanic/Latino; 1 Hispanic/Latino). 11 applicants, 73% accepted. In 2013, 15 master's awarded. *Degree requirements:* For master's, comprehensive exam. *Entrance requirements:* For master's, GRE or MAT. Additional exam requirements/recommendations for international students: Required—TOEFL (minimum score 525 paper-based; 71 iBT) or IELTS (minimum score 6). *Application deadline:* For fall admission, 6/1 for domestic and international students. Applications are processed on a rolling basis. Application fee: $25 ($30 for international students). Electronic applications accepted. *Financial support:* In 2013–14, 10 students received support. Tuition waivers available. Support available to part-time students. Financial award application deadline: 5/1. *Unit head:* Dr. Stephen D. Lewis, Chair, 615-898-2902, Fax: 615-898-5438, E-mail: steve.lewis@mtsu.edu. *Application contact:* Dr. Michael D. Allen, Vice Provost for Research and Dean, 615-898-2840, Fax: 615-904-8020, E-mail: michael.allen@mtsu.edu.

Mississippi College, Graduate School, School of Business, Clinton, MS 39058. Offers accounting (Certificate); business administration (MBA), including accounting; business education (M Ed); finance (MBA, Certificate); JD/MBA. Part-time and evening/weekend programs available. *Degree requirements:* For master's, comprehensive exam, thesis optional. *Entrance requirements:* For master's, GMAT, minimum GPA of 2.5, 24 hours of undergraduate course work in business. Additional exam requirements/recommendations for international students: Recommended—TOEFL, IELTS. Electronic applications accepted.

Mississippi College, Graduate School, School of Education, Department of Teacher Education and Leadership, Clinton, MS 39058. Offers art (M Ed); biological science (M Ed); business education (M Ed); computer science (M Ed); dyslexia therapy (M Ed); educational leadership (M Ed, Ed D, Ed S); elementary education (M Ed, Ed S); English (M Ed); higher education administration (MS); mathematics (M Ed); secondary education (M Ed); social studies (history) (M Ed); teaching arts (M Ed). Part-time programs available. Postbaccalaureate distance learning degree programs offered (no on-campus study). *Degree requirements:* For master's, comprehensive exam, thesis optional. *Entrance requirements:* For master's, NTE. Additional exam requirements/recommendations for international students: Recommended—TOEFL, IELTS. Electronic applications accepted.

Mississippi State University, College of Education, Department of Leadership and Foundations, Mississippi State, MS 39762. Offers community college education (MAT); community college leadership (PhD); education (Ed S), including school administration; elementary, middle and secondary education administration (PhD); school administration (MS); workforce education leadership (MS). MS in workforce educational leadership held jointly with Alcorn State University. *Faculty:* 9 full-time (3 women). *Students:* 50 full-time (26 women), 156 part-time (100 women); includes 104 minority (99 Black or African American, non-Hispanic/Latino; 1 American Indian or Alaska Native, non-Hispanic/Latino; 1 Asian, non-Hispanic/Latino; 1 Hispanic/Latino; 1 Native Hawaiian or other Pacific Islander, non-Hispanic/Latino; 1 Two or more races, non-Hispanic/Latino). Average age 39. 121 applicants, 32% accepted, 33 enrolled. In 2013, 47 master's, 15 doctorates, 7 other advanced degrees awarded. *Degree requirements:* For master's and Ed S, comprehensive exam, thesis; for doctorate, comprehensive exam, thesis/dissertation. *Entrance requirements:* For master's, GRE, minimum GPA of 2.75 in junior and senior courses; for doctorate, GRE, minimum GPA of 3.4 on previous

graduate work; for Ed S, GRE, minimum GPA of 3.2, master's degree. Additional exam requirements/recommendations for international students: Required—TOEFL (minimum score 550 paper-based; 79 iBT); Recommended—IELTS (minimum score 6.5). *Application deadline:* For fall admission, 7/1 for domestic students, 5/1 for international students; for spring admission, 11/1 for domestic students, 9/1 for international students. Application fee: $60. *Financial support:* In 2013–14, 3 research assistantships with full tuition reimbursements (averaging $12,400 per year), 1 teaching assistantship with full tuition reimbursement (averaging $10,194 per year) were awarded; Federal Work-Study, institutionally sponsored loans, and unspecified assistantships also available. Financial award application deadline: 4/1; financial award applicants required to submit FAFSA. *Unit head:* Dr. David Morse, Interim Department Head and Professor, 662-325-0969, Fax: 662-325-0975, E-mail: dmorse@colled.msstate.edu.
Website: http://www.leadershipandfoundations.msstate.edu/.

Morehead State University, Graduate Programs, College of Education, Department of Foundational and Graduate Studies in Education, Morehead, KY 40351. Offers adult and higher education (MA, Ed S); certified professional counselor (Ed S); counseling P-12 (MA); curriculum and instruction (Ed S); educational technology (MA Ed); instructional leadership (Ed S); school administration (MA); school counseling (Ed S); teacher leader business and marketing content (MA Ed); teacher leader business and marketing technology (MA Ed); teacher leader educational technology (MA Ed); teacher leader English (MA Ed); teacher leader gifted education (MA Ed); teacher leader IECE certification (MA Ed); teacher leader interdisciplinary education P-5 (MA Ed); teacher leader middle grades (MA Ed); teacher leader non IECE certification (MA Ed); teacher leader reading/writing - non-certification (MA Ed); teacher leader reading/writing certification (MA Ed); teacher leader school communication - certification (MA Ed); teacher leader school communication - non-certification (MA Ed); teacher leader social studies (MA Ed); teacher leader special education (MA Ed). *Accreditation:* NCATE. Part-time and evening/weekend programs available. *Degree requirements:* For master's, thesis optional, oral and/or written comprehensive exams; for Ed S, thesis, oral exam. *Entrance requirements:* For master's, GRE General Test, minimum overall undergraduate GPA of 2.5; for Ed S, GRE General Test, interview, master's degree, minimum GPA of 3.5, work experience. Additional exam requirements/recommendations for international students: Required—TOEFL (minimum score 500 paper-based). Electronic applications accepted. *Faculty research:* Character education, school accountability, computer applications for school administrators.

Morehead State University, Graduate Programs, College of Education, Department of Middle Grades and Secondary Education, Morehead, KY 40351. Offers business and marketing education (MAT); English/language arts 5-9 (MAT); French (MAT); health P-12 (MAT); mathematics 5-9 (MAT); physical education P-12 (MAT); science 5-9 (MAT); secondary biology (MAT); secondary chemistry (MAT); secondary earth science (MAT); secondary English (MAT); secondary math (MAT); secondary physics (MAT); secondary social studies (MAT); social studies 5-9 (MAT); Spanish (MAT). Part-time and evening/weekend programs available. *Degree requirements:* For master's, portfolio. *Entrance requirements:* For master's, GRE or PRAXIS II content exam, minimum overall undergraduate GPA of 2.5. Additional exam requirements/recommendations for international students: Required—TOEFL (minimum score 500 paper-based). Electronic applications accepted.

Nazareth College of Rochester, Graduate Studies, Department of Business, Program in Business Education, Rochester, NY 14618-3790. Offers MS Ed. Part-time and evening/weekend programs available. *Entrance requirements:* For master's, minimum GPA of 3.0.

New York University, Steinhardt School of Culture, Education, and Human Development, Department of Administration, Leadership, and Technology, Program in Business Education, New York, NY 10003. Offers business and workplace education (MA, Advanced Certificate); workplace learning (Advanced Certificate). *Accreditation:* Teacher Education Accreditation Council. Part-time programs available. *Faculty:* 1 (woman) full-time. *Students:* 5 full-time (3 women), 13 part-time (11 women); includes 4 minority (3 Black or African American, non-Hispanic/Latino; 1 Asian, non-Hispanic/Latino), 4 international. Average age 31. 20 applicants, 75% accepted, 7 enrolled. In 2013, 6 master's awarded. *Degree requirements:* For master's, thesis (for some programs). *Entrance requirements:* For degree, master's degree. Additional exam requirements/recommendations for international students: Required—TOEFL (minimum score 100 iBT). *Application deadline:* For fall admission, 12/1 priority date for domestic and international students; for spring admission, 10/1 for domestic and international students. Applications are processed on a rolling basis. Application fee: $75. Electronic applications accepted. *Expenses: Tuition:* Full-time $35,856; part-time $1494 per unit. *Required fees:* $1408; $64 per unit. $473 per term. Tuition and fees vary according to course load and program. *Financial support:* Career-related internships or fieldwork, Federal Work-Study, institutionally sponsored loans, scholarships/grants, tuition waivers (partial), and unspecified assistantships available. Support available to part-time students. Financial award application deadline: 2/1; financial award applicants required to submit FAFSA. *Faculty research:* Applications of technology to instruction, workplace and corporate education, adult learning. *Unit head:* Dr. Bridget N. O'Connor, Director, 212-998-5488, Fax: 212-995-4041, E-mail: bridget.oconnor@nyu.edu. *Application contact:* 212-998-5030, Fax: 212-995-4328, E-mail: steinhardt.gradadmissions@nyu.edu.
Website: http://steinhardt.nyu.edu/alt/businessed.

North Carolina Agricultural and Technical State University, School of Graduate Studies, School of Business and Economics, Greensboro, NC 27411. Offers accounting (MSM); business education (MAT); human resources management (MSM); supply chain systems (MSM).

North Carolina State University, Graduate School, College of Education, Department of Curriculum and Instruction, Program in Business and Marketing Education, Raleigh, NC 27695. Offers M Ed, MS. *Entrance requirements:* For master's, MAT or GRE, minimum GPA of 3.0, teaching license, 3 letters of reference.

Old Dominion University, Darden College of Education, Programs in Occupational and Technical Studies, Norfolk, VA 23529. Offers business and industry training (MS); career and technical education (MS, PhD); community college teaching (MS); human resources training (PhD); STEM education (MS); technology education (PhD). *Accreditation:* NCATE (one or more programs are accredited). Part-time and evening/weekend programs available. Postbaccalaureate distance learning degree programs offered (minimal on-campus study). *Faculty:* 6 full-time (2 women), 2 part-time/adjunct (both women). *Students:* 8 full-time (3 women), 41 part-time (21 women); includes 19 minority (13 Black or African American, non-Hispanic/Latino; 1 American Indian or Alaska Native, non-Hispanic/Latino; 1 Asian, non-Hispanic/Latino; 3 Hispanic/Latino; 1 Two or more races, non-Hispanic/Latino), 2 international. Average age 43. 12 applicants, 83% accepted, 10 enrolled. In 2013, 16 master's, 8 doctorates awarded. *Degree requirements:* For master's, comprehensive exam, thesis optional, writing exam, candidacy exam; for doctorate, comprehensive exam, thesis/dissertation, writing exam, candidacy exam. *Entrance requirements:* For master's, GRE General Test or MAT, minimum GPA of 2.8, 2 letters of reference; for doctorate, GRE, minimum GPA of 3.0, 3 letters of reference. Additional exam requirements/recommendations for international students: Required—TOEFL. *Application deadline:* For fall admission, 6/1 priority date for domestic students, 6/1 for international students; for winter admission, 11/1 priority date for domestic students, 11/1 for international students; for spring admission, 3/1 priority date for domestic students, 3/1 for international students. Applications are processed on a rolling basis. Application fee: $50. Electronic applications accepted. *Expenses:* Tuition, state resident: full-time $9888; part-time $412 per credit. Tuition, nonresident: full-time $25,152; part-time $1048 per credit. *Required fees:* $59 per semester. One-time fee: $50. *Financial support:* In 2013–14, 19 students received support, including fellowships with full tuition reimbursements available (averaging $15,000 per year), research assistantships with partial tuition reimbursements available (averaging $9,000 per year), 2 teaching assistantships with partial tuition reimbursements available (averaging $15,000 per year); career-related internships or fieldwork, scholarships/grants, tuition waivers (partial), and unspecified assistantships also available. Support available to part-time students. Financial award application deadline: 2/15; financial award applicants required to submit FAFSA. *Faculty research:* Training and development, marketing, technology, special populations, STEM education. *Total annual research expenditures:* $799,773. *Unit head:* Dr. Cynthia L. Tomovic, Graduate Program Director, 757-683-5228, Fax: 757-683-5228, E-mail: ctomovic@odu.edu. *Application contact:* William Heffelfinger, Director of Graduate Admissions, 757-683-5554, Fax: 757-683-3255, E-mail: gradadmit@odu.edu.
Website: http://education.odu.edu/ots/.

Pontifical Catholic University of Puerto Rico, College of Education, Doctoral Program in Business Teacher Education, Ponce, PR 00717-0777. Offers PhD. *Degree requirements:* For doctorate, thesis/dissertation. *Entrance requirements:* For doctorate, EXADEP, GRE General Test or MAT, 3 letters of recommendation.

Pontifical Catholic University of Puerto Rico, College of Education, Master's Program in Business Teacher Education, Ponce, PR 00717-0777. Offers M Ed. *Degree requirements:* For master's, comprehensive exam, thesis (for some programs). *Entrance requirements:* For master's, GRE, 2 letters of recommendation, interview, minimum GPA of 2.75.

Rider University, Department of Graduate Education, Leadership and Counseling, Teacher Certification Program, Lawrenceville, NJ 08648-3001. Offers business education (Certificate); elementary education (Certificate); English as a second language (Certificate); English education (Certificate); mathematics education (Certificate); preschool to grade 3 (Certificate); science education (Certificate); social studies education (Certificate); world languages (Certificate), including French, German, Spanish. Part-time programs available. *Degree requirements:* For Certificate, internship, professional portfolio. *Entrance requirements:* For degree, PRAXIS, resume. Additional exam requirements/recommendations for international students: Required—TOEFL (minimum score 550 paper-based). Electronic applications accepted. *Faculty research:* Conceptual foundations for optimal development of creativity; creative theory, cognitive processes in mathematics learning, teacher collaboration.

Robert Morris University, Graduate Studies, School of Education and Social Sciences, Moon Township, PA 15108-1189. Offers business education (MS); education (Postbaccalaureate Certificate); instructional leadership (MS), including education, sport management; instructional management and leadership (PhD). *Accreditation:* Teacher Education Accreditation Council. Part-time and evening/weekend programs available. Postbaccalaureate distance learning degree programs offered (no on-campus study). *Faculty:* 20 full-time (9 women), 6 part-time/adjunct (3 women). *Students:* 203 part-time (127 women); includes 20 minority (11 Black or African American, non-Hispanic/Latino; 3 Asian, non-Hispanic/Latino; 2 Hispanic/Latino; 4 Two or more races, non-Hispanic/Latino), 4 international. Average age 26. 126 applicants, 44% accepted, 43 enrolled. In 2013, 102 master's, 6 doctorates awarded. *Degree requirements:* For doctorate, thesis/dissertation. *Entrance requirements:* Additional exam requirements/recommendations for international students: Required—TOEFL (minimum score 550 paper-based; 79 iBT). *Application deadline:* For fall admission, 7/1 priority date for domestic and international students; for spring admission, 11/1 priority date for domestic and international students. Applications are processed on a rolling basis. Application fee: $35. Electronic applications accepted. *Expenses:* Contact institution. *Unit head:* Dr. Mary Ann Rafoth, Dean, 412-397-3488, Fax: 412-397-2524, E-mail: rafoth@rmu.edu. *Application contact:* Assistant Dean, Graduate Admissions, 412-397-5200, Fax: 412-397-5915, E-mail: graduateadmissions@rmu.edu.
Website: http://www.rmu.edu/web/cms/schools/sess/.

South Carolina State University, School of Graduate and Professional Studies, Department of Education, Orangeburg, SC 29117-0001. Offers early childhood and special education (M Ed); early childhood education (MAT); elementary education (M Ed, MAT); general science (MAT); mathematics (MAT); secondary education (M Ed), including biology education, business education, counselor education, English education, home economics education, industrial education, mathematics education, science education, social studies education; special education (M Ed), including emotionally handicapped, learning disabilities, mentally handicapped. *Accreditation:* NCATE. Part-time and evening/weekend programs available. *Faculty:* 9 full-time (3 women), 4 part-time/adjunct (3 women). *Students:* 32 full-time (26 women), 33 part-time (26 women); includes 63 minority (61 Black or African American, non-Hispanic/Latino; 2 Asian, non-Hispanic/Latino). Average age 31. 21 applicants, 100% accepted, 21 enrolled. In 2013, 15 master's awarded. *Degree requirements:* For master's, thesis optional, departmental qualifying exam. *Entrance requirements:* For master's, GRE General Test, NTE, interview, teaching certificate. *Application deadline:* For fall admission, 6/15 priority date for domestic students, 6/15 for international students; for spring admission, 11/1 for domestic and international students. Applications are processed on a rolling basis. Application fee: $25. Electronic applications accepted. *Expenses:* Tuition, state resident: full-time $8906; part-time $543 per credit hour. Tuition, nonresident: full-time $18,040; part-time $1051 per credit hour. *Financial support:* Fellowships, career-related internships or fieldwork, Federal Work-Study, and institutionally sponsored loans available. Financial award application deadline: 6/1. *Faculty research:* Critical thinking, child abuse, stress, test-taking skills, conflict resolution, mainstreaming. *Unit head:* Dr. Margaret Evelyn Fields, Interim Chair, 803-536-7098, Fax: 803-516-4568, E-mail: efields@scsu.edu. *Application contact:* Curtis Foskey, Coordinator of Graduate Studies, 803-536-8419, Fax: 803-536-8812, E-mail: cfoskey@scsu.edu.

Southern New Hampshire University, School of Education, Manchester, NH 03106-1045. Offers business education (M Ed); child development (M Ed); curriculum and instruction (M Ed), including education leadership, reading, special education, technology integration; education (M Ed); educational leadership (M Ed, Ed D); educational studies (M Ed); elementary education (M Ed); English (MAT); English for speakers of other languages (M Ed); reading and writing specialist (M Ed); school business administration (Certificate); secondary education (M Ed); special education (M Ed); technology integration specialist (M Ed). Part-time and evening/weekend programs available. Postbaccalaureate distance learning degree programs offered (no on-campus study). *Degree requirements:* For master's, comprehensive exam (for some programs), thesis or alternative. *Entrance requirements:* For master's, PRAXIS I, minimum GPA of 2.75. Additional exam requirements/recommendations for international students: Required—TOEFL (minimum score 550 paper-based). Electronic applications accepted. *Expenses:* Contact institution.

Spalding University, Graduate Studies, College of Education, Programs in Education, Louisville, KY 40203-2188. Offers art teacher education (MAT); business teacher education (MAT); elementary school education (MAT); foreign language (MAT); general education (MA Ed); high school education (MAT); middle school education (MAT); school administration (MA Ed); secondary education (MAT); special education (learning and behavioral disorders) (MAT); student guidance counselor (MA); teacher education and professional development (MAT). *Accreditation:* NCATE. Part-time and evening/weekend programs available. *Faculty:* 12 full-time (11 women), 6 part-time/adjunct (4 women). *Students:* 92 full-time (63 women), 36 part-time (29 women); includes 43 minority (41 Black or African American, non-Hispanic/Latino; 2 Two or more races, non-Hispanic/Latino). Average age 35. 77 applicants, 48% accepted, 30 enrolled. In 2013, 81 master's awarded. *Degree requirements:* For master's, portfolio, final project, clinical experience. *Entrance requirements:* For master's, GRE General Test or MAT, interview, letters of recommendation, resume. Additional exam requirements/recommendations for international students: Required—TOEFL (minimum score 535 paper-based). *Application deadline:* Applications are processed on a rolling basis. Application fee: $30. Electronic applications accepted. *Expenses: Tuition:* Full-time $21,450. *Required fees:* $810. Tuition and fees vary according to course load, degree level, program and student level. *Financial support:* Scholarships/grants, traineeships, and unspecified assistantships available. Financial award application deadline: 3/30; financial award applicants required to submit FAFSA. *Faculty research:* Instructional technology, achievement gap, classroom management, assessment. *Unit head:* Dr. Beverly Keepers, Dean, 502-588-7121, Fax: 502-585-7123, E-mail: bkeepers@spalding.edu. *Application contact:* Bonnie Caughron, Administrative Assistant, College of Education, 502-873-4262, E-mail: bcaughron@spalding.edu.

State University of New York at Oswego, Graduate Studies, School of Education, Department of Vocational Teacher Preparation, Oswego, NY 13126. Offers agriculture (MS Ed); business and marketing (MS Ed); family and consumer sciences (MS Ed); health careers (MS Ed); technical education (MS Ed); trade education (MS Ed). *Accreditation:* NCATE. Part-time and evening/weekend programs available. *Degree requirements:* For master's, comprehensive exam, thesis or alternative. *Entrance requirements:* Additional exam requirements/recommendations for international students: Required—TOEFL (minimum score 560 paper-based).

Temple University, College of Education, Department of Curriculum, Instruction, and Technology in Education, Philadelphia, PA 19122-6096. Offers career and technical education (Ed M), including business, computing, and information technology, industrial education, marketing education; middle grades education (Ed M), including math and language arts, math and science, science and language arts; secondary education (Ed M), including English, math, social studies; teaching English to speakers of other languages (MS Ed); urban education (Ed M). Part-time and evening/weekend programs available. *Students:* 66 full-time (48 women), 120 part-time (67 women); includes 50 minority (35 Black or African American, non-Hispanic/Latino; 1 American Indian or Alaska Native, non-Hispanic/Latino; 2 Asian, non-Hispanic/Latino; 7 Hispanic/Latino; 5 Two or more races, non-Hispanic/Latino), 1 international. 229 applicants, 41% accepted, 60 enrolled. In 2013, 41 master's awarded. Terminal master's awarded for partial completion of doctoral program. *Degree requirements:* For master's, thesis or alternative. *Entrance requirements:* Additional exam requirements/recommendations for international students: Required—TOEFL (minimum score 550 paper-based; 79 iBT). *Application deadline:* For fall admission, 4/1 for domestic students, 12/15 for international students; for spring admission, 10/1 for domestic students, 8/1 for international students. Application fee: $60. Electronic applications accepted. *Financial support:* Fellowships, research assistantships, and teaching assistantships available. Financial award application deadline: 1/15; financial award applicants required to submit FAFSA. *Faculty research:* Workforce development, vocational education, technical education, industrial education, professional development, literacy, classroom management, school communities, curriculum development, instruction, applied linguistics, crosslinguistic influence, bilingual education, oral proficiency, multilingualism. *Application contact:* Felicia Neuber, Enrollment Management, 215-204-8011, E-mail: educate@temple.edu.
Website: http://www.temple.edu/education/tl/.

Thomas College, Graduate School, Programs in Business, Waterville, ME 04901-5097. Offers business (MBA); computer technology education (MS); education (MS); human resource management (MBA). Part-time and evening/weekend programs available. *Entrance requirements:* For master's, GMAT, GRE, MAT or minimum GPA of 3.3 in first 3 graduate-level courses. Additional exam requirements/recommendations for international students: Recommended—TOEFL.

The University of British Columbia, Faculty of Education, Department of Curriculum and Pedagogy, Vancouver, BC V6T 1Z4, Canada. Offers art education (M Ed, MA); business education (MA); curriculum studies (M Ed, MA, PhD); home economics education (M Ed, MA); math education (M Ed, MA); music education (M Ed, MA); physical education (M Ed, MA); science education (M Ed, MA); social studies education (M Ed, MA); technology studies education (M Ed, MA). Part-time programs available. Postbaccalaureate distance learning degree programs offered (no on-campus study). *Faculty:* 32 full-time (14 women), 1 (woman) part-time/adjunct. *Students:* 163 full-time, 134 part-time, 42 international. Average age 40. 160 applicants, 75% accepted, 97 enrolled. In 2013, 68 master's, 7 doctorates awarded. *Degree requirements:* For master's, thesis (MA); for doctorate, comprehensive exam, thesis/dissertation. *Entrance requirements:* Additional exam requirements/recommendations for international students: Required—TOEFL (minimum score 580 paper-based; 92 iBT), IELTS (minimum score 6.5). *Application deadline:* For fall admission, 12/1 for domestic and international students; for spring admission, 10/1 for domestic students, 9/1 for international students. Application fee: $90 Canadian dollars ($150 Canadian dollars for international students). Electronic applications accepted. *Expenses:* Contact institution. *Financial support:* In 2013–14, 10 fellowships with partial tuition reimbursements (averaging $16,000 per year), 11 research assistantships with partial tuition reimbursements (averaging $14,000 per year), 27 teaching assistantships with partial tuition reimbursements (averaging $14,000 per year) were awarded; tuition waivers (partial) also available. *Faculty research:* School subjects, teaching and learning. *Unit head:* Dr. Peter Grimmett, Head, 604-822-5422, Fax: 604-822-4714, E-mail: anna.ip@ubc.ca. *Application contact:* Basia Zurek, Graduate Programs Assistant, 604-822-5367, Fax: 604-822-4714, E-mail: edcp.grad@ubc.ca.
Website: http://www.edcp.educ.ubc.ca/.

University of Delaware, Alfred Lerner College of Business and Economics, Department of Economics, Newark, DE 19716. Offers economic education (PhD); economics (MA, MS, PhD); economics for entrepreneurship and educators (MA); MA/MBA. Part-time programs available. *Degree requirements:* For master's, comprehensive exam, thesis (for some programs), mathematics review exam, research project; for doctorate, comprehensive exam, thesis/dissertation, field exam. *Entrance requirements:* For master's, GMAT or GRE General Test, minimum GPA of 2.5; for doctorate, GRE General Test, minimum GPA of 3.5 in graduate economics course work. Additional exam requirements/recommendations for international students: Required—TOEFL (minimum score 550 paper-based). Electronic applications accepted. *Faculty research:* Applied quantitative economics, industrial organization, resource economics, monetary economics, labor economics.

University of Georgia, College of Education, Department of Career and Information Studies, Athens, GA 30602. Offers learning, design, and technology (M Ed, PhD, Ed S), including instructional design and development (M Ed, Ed S), instructional technology (M Ed), learning, design, and technology (M Ed), school library media (M Ed, Ed S); workforce education (M Ed, MAT, Ed D, PhD, Ed S), including business education (MAT), family and consumer sciences education (MAT), health science and technology education (MAT), marketing education (MAT), technology education (MAT), trade and industry education (MAT). *Accreditation:* NCATE. *Entrance requirements:* For master's, GRE General Test, MAT; for doctorate, GRE General Test; for Ed S, GRE General Test or MAT. Electronic applications accepted.

University of Minnesota, Twin Cities Campus, Graduate School, College of Education and Human Development, Department of Organizational Leadership, Policy and Development, Program in Business and Industry Education, Minneapolis, MN 55455-0213. Offers M Ed, MA, Ed D, PhD. *Students:* 1 (woman). In 2013, 1 master's awarded. Application fee: $75 ($95 for international students). *Unit head:* Dr. Rebecca Ropers-Huilman, Chair, 612-624-1006, E-mail: ropers@umn.edu. *Application contact:* Dr. Jennifer Engler, Assistant Dean, 612-626-2887, Fax: 612-626-7496, E-mail: engle009@umn.edu.
Website: http://www.cehd.umn.edu/WHRE//BIE.

University of Missouri, Graduate School, College of Education, Department of Learning, Teaching and Curriculum, Columbia, MO 65211. Offers agricultural education (M Ed, PhD, Ed S); art education (M Ed, PhD, Ed S); business and office education (M Ed, PhD, Ed S); early childhood education (M Ed, PhD, Ed S); elementary education (M Ed, PhD, Ed S); English education (M Ed, PhD, Ed S); foreign language education (M Ed, PhD, Ed S); health education and promotion (M Ed, PhD); learning and instruction (M Ed); marketing education (M Ed, PhD, Ed S); mathematics education (M Ed, PhD, Ed S); music education (M Ed, PhD, Ed S); reading education (M Ed, PhD, Ed S); science education (M Ed, PhD, Ed S); social studies education (M Ed, PhD, Ed S); vocational education (M Ed, PhD, Ed S). Part-time programs available. *Faculty:* 26 full-time (16 women), 3 part-time/adjunct (2 women). *Students:* 186 full-time (143 women), 197 part-time (172 women); includes 19 minority (4 Black or African American, non-Hispanic/Latino; 4 Asian, non-Hispanic/Latino; 6 Hispanic/Latino; 5 Two or more races, non-Hispanic/Latino), 25 international. Average age 31. 288 applicants, 65% accepted, 160 enrolled. In 2013, 202 master's, 18 doctorates, 7 other advanced degrees awarded. Terminal master's awarded for partial completion of doctoral program. *Degree requirements:* For doctorate, thesis/dissertation. *Entrance requirements:* For master's and Ed S, GRE General Test or MAT, minimum GPA of 3.0; for doctorate, GRE General Test, minimum GPA of 3.0. Additional exam requirements/recommendations for international students: Required—TOEFL (minimum score 600 paper-based; 100 iBT). *Application deadline:* For fall admission, 12/1 priority date for domestic and international students. Applications are processed on a rolling basis. Application fee: $55 ($75 for international students). Electronic applications accepted. *Financial support:* Fellowships, research assistantships, teaching assistantships, institutionally sponsored loans, traineeships, health care benefits, and unspecified assistantships available. Support available to part-time students. *Faculty research:* Curriculum development and research, teacher education, art education, business and marketing, early childhood education, English education, literacy/reading education, mathematics education, music education, science education, social studies education. *Unit head:* Dr. James Tarr, Associate Division Director, 573-882-4034, E-mail: tarrj@missouri.edu. *Application contact:* Fran Colley, Academic Advisor, 573-882-6462, E-mail: colleyf@missouri.edu.
Website: http://education.missouri.edu/LTC/.

University of St. Francis, College of Business and Health Administration, School of Professional Studies, Joliet, IL 60435-6169. Offers management of training and development (Certificate); training and development (MS); training specialist (Certificate). *Accreditation:* ACBSP. Part-time and evening/weekend programs available. Postbaccalaureate distance learning degree programs offered (no on-campus study). *Faculty:* 1 full-time (0 women), 1 part-time/adjunct (0 women). *Students:* 9 full-time (7 women), 33 part-time (27 women); includes 14 minority (13 Black or African American, non-Hispanic/Latino; 1 Hispanic/Latino). Average age 40. 58 applicants, 62% accepted, 30 enrolled. In 2013, 9 master's awarded. *Entrance requirements:* For master's, minimum GPA of 2.75, 2 letters recommendation, personal essay, computer proficiency. Additional exam requirements/recommendations for international students: Required—TOEFL (minimum score 550 paper-based; 79 iBT), IELTS (minimum score 6.5). *Application deadline:* Applications are processed on a rolling basis. Application fee: $30. Electronic applications accepted. Application fee is waived when completed online. *Expenses: Tuition:* Part-time $710 per credit hour. *Required fees:* $125 per semester. Part-time tuition and fees vary according to degree level and program. *Financial support:* In 2013–14, 9 students received support. Federal Work-Study, tuition waivers (partial), and unspecified assistantships available. Support available to part-time students. Financial award applicants required to submit FAFSA. *Unit head:* Dr. Christopher Clott, Dean, 815-740-3395, Fax: 815-740-3537, E-mail: cclott@stfrancis.edu. *Application contact:* Sandra Sloka, Director of Admissions for Graduate and Degree Completion Programs, 800-735-7500, Fax: 815-740-3431, E-mail: ssloka@stfrancis.edu.
Website: http://www.stfrancis.edu/academics/college-of-business-health-administration/school-of-professional-studies/.

University of South Carolina, The Graduate School, College of Education, Department of Instruction and Teacher Education, Program in Secondary Education, Columbia, SC 29208. Offers art education (IMA, MAT); business education (IMA, MAT); English (MAT); foreign language (MAT); health education (MAT); mathematics (MAT); science (IMA, MAT); secondary (Ed D); secondary education (MT, PhD); social studies (MAT); theatre and speech (MAT). IMA and MT offered jointly with the subject areas. *Accreditation:* NCATE. *Degree requirements:* For master's, comprehensive exam, thesis (for some programs), foreign language (MA); for doctorate, one foreign language, comprehensive exam, thesis/dissertation. *Entrance requirements:* For master's, GRE General Test or MAT, teaching certificate (IMA, M Ed), interview; for doctorate, GRE General Test or MAT, interview. *Faculty research:* Middle school programs, professional development, school collaboration.

University of the Cumberlands, Graduate Programs in Education, Williamsburg, KY 40769-1372. Offers all grades (P-12) (M Ed); business and marketing (MA Ed, MAT); counselor education and supervision (Ed D); director of pupil personnel (Certificate); director of special education (Certificate); educational administration and supervision (Ed S); educational leadership (Ed D); elementary education (MA Ed, MAT); instructional leadership - principalship (MA Ed); instructional leadership - school principal (Certificate); middle school education (MA Ed, MAT); reading and writing (MA Ed); school counseling (MA Ed); school superintendent (Certificate); secondary education (MA Ed, MAT); special education (MAT); supervisor of instruction (Certificate); teacher leader (MA Ed). Part-time and evening/weekend programs available. Postbaccalaureate distance learning degree programs offered. *Degree requirements:* For master's, comprehensive exam. Electronic applications accepted.

The University of Toledo, College of Graduate Studies, Judith Herb College of Education, Department of Curriculum and Instruction, Toledo, OH 43606-3390. Offers

art education (ME); career and technical education (ME); career-technical education (Ed S); curriculum and instruction (ME, PhD, Ed S); early childhood education (PhD, Ed S); education and biology (MES); education and chemistry (MES); education and economics (MAE); education and English (MAE); education and French (MAE); education and geography (MAE); education and geology (MES); education and German (MAE); education and history (MAE); education and mathematics (MAE, MES); education and physics (MES); education and political science (MAE); education and sociology (MAE); education and Spanish (MAE); educational media (PhD); educational technology (ME); educational technology: virtual educator (Certificate); elementary education (PhD); English as a second language (MAE); gifted and talented (PhD); middle childhood education licensure (ME); music education (MME); secondary education (PhD); secondary education licensure (ME); special education (PhD, Ed S). *Accreditation:* NCATE. Part-time and evening/weekend programs available. *Faculty:* 41. *Students:* 53 full-time (30 women), 154 part-time (111 women); includes 21 minority (16 Black or African American, non-Hispanic/Latino; 4 Hispanic/Latino; 1 Two or more races, non-Hispanic/Latino), 21 international. Average age 34. 82 applicants, 79% accepted, 47 enrolled. In 2013, 80 master's, 5 doctorates awarded. *Degree requirements:* For master's, comprehensive exam, thesis or alternative; for doctorate, comprehensive exam, thesis/dissertation; for other advanced degree, thesis optional. *Entrance requirements:* For master's, doctorate, and other advanced degree, minimum cumulative GPA of 2.7 for all previous academic work, letters of recommendation. Additional exam requirements/recommendations for international students: Required—TOEFL (minimum score 550 paper-based; 80 iBT). *Application deadline:* For fall admission, 1/15 priority date for domestic and international students. Applications are processed on a rolling basis. Application fee: $45 ($75 for international students). Electronic applications accepted. *Financial support:* In 2013–14, 5 research assistantships with full and partial tuition reimbursements (averaging $13,200 per year), 11 teaching assistantships with full and partial tuition reimbursements (averaging $8,809 per year) were awarded; career-related internships or fieldwork, Federal Work-Study, institutionally sponsored loans, scholarships/grants, tuition waivers (full and partial), unspecified assistantships, and administrative assistantships also available. Support available to part-time students. *Unit head:* Dr. Joan Kaderavek, Chair, 419-530-5373, E-mail: eigh.chiarelott@utoledo.edu. *Application contact:* Graduate School Office, 419-530-4723, Fax: 419-530-4724, E-mail: grdsch@utnet.utoledo.edu.
Website: http://www.utoledo.edu/eduhshs/.

University of Washington, Graduate School, Michael G. Foster School of Business, Seattle, WA 98195-3200. Offers auditing and assurance (MP Acc); business administration (MBA, PhD); executive business administration (MBA); global executive business administration (MBA); taxation (MP Acc); technology management (MBA); JD/MBA; MBA/MAIS; MBA/MHA. *Accreditation:* AACSB. Part-time and evening/weekend programs available. *Faculty:* 100 full-time (28 women), 55 part-time/adjunct (22 women). *Students:* 407 full-time (130 women), 369 part-time (110 women); includes 199 minority (16 Black or African American, non-Hispanic/Latino; 5 American Indian or Alaska Native, non-Hispanic/Latino; 139 Asian, non-Hispanic/Latino; 25 Hispanic/Latino; 7 Native Hawaiian or other Pacific Islander, non-Hispanic/Latino; 7 Two or more races, non-Hispanic/Latino), 178 international. Average age 32. 2,474 applicants, 40% accepted, 776 enrolled. In 2013, 468 master's, 8 doctorates awarded. Terminal master's awarded for partial completion of doctoral program. *Degree requirements:* For doctorate, comprehensive exam, thesis/dissertation. *Entrance requirements:* For master's, GMAT; for doctorate, GMAT, GRE. Additional exam requirements/recommendations for international students: Required—TOEFL (minimum score 600 paper-based; 100 iBT). *Application deadline:* For fall admission, 3/15 for domestic students, 1/20 for international students. Application fee: $85. Electronic applications accepted. *Expenses:* Contact institution. *Financial support:* Fellowships with partial tuition reimbursements, research assistantships with partial tuition reimbursements, teaching assistantships with partial tuition reimbursements, Federal Work-Study, institutionally sponsored loans, and scholarships/grants available. Financial award application deadline: 2/28; financial award applicants required to submit FAFSA. *Faculty research:* Finance, marketing, organizational behavior, information technology, strategy. *Unit head:* Dr. James Jiambalvo, Dean, 206-543-4750. *Application contact:* Erin Town, Director of Admissions, 206-543-4661, Fax: 206-616-7351, E-mail: mba@uw.edu.
Website: http://www.foster.washington.edu/.

University of Wisconsin–Whitewater, School of Graduate Studies, College of Business and Economics, Program in Business and Marketing Education, Whitewater, WI 53190-1790. Offers MS. *Accreditation:* NCATE. Part-time and evening/weekend programs available. Postbaccalaureate distance learning degree programs offered (no on-campus study). *Degree requirements:* For master's, thesis or alternative. *Entrance requirements:* For master's, interview, teaching license. Additional exam requirements/recommendations for international students: Required—TOEFL (minimum score 550 paper-based; 80 iBT), IELTS (minimum score 6). Electronic applications accepted. *Faculty research:* Active learning and performance strategies, technology-enhanced formative assessment, computer-supported cooperative work, privacy surveillance.

Utah State University, School of Graduate Studies, College of Business, Department of Business Information Systems, Logan, UT 84322. Offers business education (MS); business information systems (MS); business information systems and education (Ed D); education (PhD). Part-time programs available. Terminal master's awarded for partial completion of doctoral program. *Degree requirements:* For master's, thesis optional; for doctorate, thesis/dissertation. *Entrance requirements:* For master's, GMAT, minimum GPA of 3.2; for doctorate, GRE General Test, minimum GPA of 3.0. Additional exam requirements/recommendations for international students: Required—TOEFL. *Faculty research:* Oral and written communication, methods of teaching, CASE tools, object-oriented programming, decision support systems.

Utah State University, School of Graduate Studies, Emma Eccles Jones College of Education and Human Services, Doctoral Program in Education, Logan, UT 84322. Offers business information systems (Ed D, PhD); curriculum and instruction (Ed D, PhD); research and evaluation (PhD). *Degree requirements:* For doctorate, comprehensive exam, thesis/dissertation. *Entrance requirements:* For doctorate, GRE General Test, minimum GPA of 3.0, master's degree. Additional exam requirements/recommendations for international students: Required—TOEFL. Electronic applications accepted. *Faculty research:* Language and literacy development, math and science education, instructional technology, hearing problems/deafness, domestic violence and animal abuse.

Washington State University, Graduate School, College of Education, Department of Educational Leadership and Counseling Psychology, Pullman, WA 99164. Offers community counseling (MA); counseling psychology (PhD); educational leadership (Ed M, MA, Ed D, PhD); educational psychology (Ed M, MA, PhD); sport management (MA). *Degree requirements:* For master's, comprehensive exam (for some programs), thesis (for some programs), oral or written exam; for doctorate, comprehensive exam, thesis/dissertation, oral and written exam, internship. *Entrance requirements:* For master's and doctorate, GRE General Test, minimum GPA of 3.0, 3 letters of recommendation, transcripts showing all college or university course work, statement of professional objectives, current curriculum vitae/resume. Additional exam requirements/recommendations for international students: Required—TOEFL (minimum score 550 paper-based; 80 iBT). Electronic applications accepted.

Wayne State College, School of Education and Counseling, Department of Educational Foundations and Leadership, Program in Curriculum and Instruction, Wayne, NE 68787. Offers alternative education (MSE); business and information technology education (MSE); communication arts education (MSE); early childhood education (MSE); elementary education (MSE); English as a second language (MSE); English education (MSE); family and consumer sciences education (MSE); industrial technology and vocational education (MSE); learning communities (MSE); mathematics education (MSE); music education (MSE); science education (MSE); social science education (MSE). *Accreditation:* NCATE. Part-time and evening/weekend programs available. *Degree requirements:* For master's, comprehensive exam, thesis optional. *Entrance requirements:* For master's, GRE General Test. Additional exam requirements/recommendations for international students: Required—TOEFL (minimum score 550 paper-based).

Wright State University, School of Graduate Studies, College of Education and Human Services, Department of Teacher Education, Programs in Workforce Education, Dayton, OH 45435. Offers career, technology and vocational education (M Ed, MA); computer/technology education (M Ed, MA); library/media (M Ed, MA); vocational education (M Ed, MA). *Accreditation:* NCATE. *Degree requirements:* For master's, thesis (for some programs). *Entrance requirements:* For master's, GRE General Test, MAT. Additional exam requirements/recommendations for international students: Required—TOEFL.

Computer Education

Arcadia University, Graduate Studies, School of Education, Glenside, PA 19038-3295. Offers art education (M Ed); computer education (CAS); curriculum (CAS); curriculum studies (M Ed); early childhood education (M Ed, CAS), including individualized (M Ed), master teacher (M Ed), research in child development (M Ed); educational leadership (M Ed, Ed D, CAS); elementary education (M Ed, CAS); English education (MA Ed); environmental education (MA Ed, CAS); history education (MA Ed); instructional technology (M Ed); language arts (M Ed, CAS); library science (M Ed); mathematics education (M Ed, MA Ed, CAS); music education (MA Ed); psychology (MA Ed); reading (M Ed, CAS); science education (M Ed, CAS); secondary education (M Ed, CAS); special education (M Ed, Ed D, CAS); theater arts (MA Ed); written communication (MA Ed). *Accreditation:* NASAD. Part-time and evening/weekend programs available. Postbaccalaureate distance learning degree programs offered (minimal on-campus study). Electronic applications accepted. *Expenses:* Contact institution.

California State University, Dominguez Hills, College of Education, Division of Graduate Education, Program in Technology-Based Education, Carson, CA 90747-0001. Offers MA, Certificate. Part-time and evening/weekend programs available. *Faculty:* 1 (woman) full-time. *Students:* 11 full-time (10 women), 17 part-time (10 women); includes 11 minority (5 Black or African American, non-Hispanic/Latino; 5 Hispanic/Latino; 1 Two or more races, non-Hispanic/Latino), 7 international. Average age 37. 17 applicants, 100% accepted, 13 enrolled. In 2013, 14 master's awarded. *Degree requirements:* For master's, comprehensive exam, thesis or alternative. *Entrance requirements:* For master's, minimum GPA of 2.75. *Application deadline:* For fall admission, 6/1 for domestic students. Application fee: $55. *Expenses:* Tuition, state resident: full-time $6738. Tuition, nonresident: full-time $13,434. *Required fees:* $622. *Faculty research:* Media literacy, assistive technology. *Unit head:* Dr. Peter Desberg, Unit Head, 310-243-3908, E-mail: pdesberg@csudh.edu. *Application contact:* Admissions Office, 310-243-3530.
Website: http://www4.csudh.edu/coe/programs/grad-prgs/technology-based-edu/index.

Cardinal Stritch University, College of Education, Department of Educational Computing, Milwaukee, WI 53217-3985. Offers instructional technology (ME, MS). Part-time and evening/weekend programs available. *Degree requirements:* For master's, comprehensive exam, thesis, faculty recommendation. *Entrance requirements:* For master's, letters of recommendation (2), minimum GPA of 2.75.

Christopher Newport University, Graduate Studies, Department of Teacher Preparation, Newport News, VA 23606-3072. Offers art (PK-12) (MAT); biology (6-12) (MAT); chemistry (6-12) (MAT); computer science (6-12) (MAT); elementary (PK-6) (MAT); English (6-12) (MAT); English as second language (PK-12) (MAT); French (PK-12) (MAT); history and social science (6-12) (MAT); mathematics (6-12) (MAT); music (PK-12) (MAT), including choral, instrumental; physics (6-12) (MAT); Spanish (PK-12) (MAT). Part-time programs available. *Faculty:* 15 full-time (7 women), 14 part-time/adjunct (13 women). *Students:* 74 full-time (64 women), 2 part-time (both women); includes 6 minority (4 Hispanic/Latino; 2 Two or more races, non-Hispanic/Latino). Average age 23. 90 applicants, 100% accepted, 67 enrolled. In 2013, 96 master's awarded. *Degree requirements:* For master's, comprehensive exam, thesis or alternative. *Entrance requirements:* For master's, PRAXIS I, minimum GPA of 3.0. Additional exam requirements/recommendations for international students: Required—TOEFL (minimum score 580 paper-based; 92 iBT). *Application deadline:* For fall admission, 4/1 for international students; for spring admission, 10/15 for domestic students, 10/1 for international students; for summer admission, 1/15 for domestic students, 3/1 for international students. Applications are processed on a rolling basis. Application fee: $50. Electronic applications accepted. *Expenses: Tuition, area resident:* Part-time $498 per credit hour. Tuition, state resident: part-time $498 per credit hour. Tuition, nonresident: part-time $899 per credit hour. *Financial support:* In 2013–14, 3 students received support, including 3 research assistantships with full tuition reimbursements available (averaging $2,000 per year); career-related internships or fieldwork, Federal Work-Study, and unspecified assistantships also available. Financial award application deadline: 3/1; financial award applicants required to submit FAFSA. *Faculty research:* Early literacy development, instructional innovations, professional teaching standards, multicultural issues, aesthetic education. *Total annual research expenditures:* $24,000. *Unit head:* Dr. Marsha Sprague, Director, 757-594-7388, Fax: 757-594-7803, E-mail: msprague@cnu.edu. *Application contact:* Lyn Sawyer, Associate

Director, Graduate Admissions, 757-594-7544, Fax: 757-594-7649, E-mail: gradstdy@cnu.edu.

East Carolina University, Graduate School, College of Education, Department of Mathematics, Science, and Instructional Technology Education, Greenville, NC 27858-4353. Offers computer-based instruction (Certificate); distance learning and administration (Certificate); instructional technology (MA Ed, MS); mathematics (MA Ed); performance improvement (Certificate); science education (MA, MA Ed); special endorsement in computer education (Certificate). Part-time and evening/weekend programs available. *Degree requirements:* For master's, comprehensive exam, thesis optional. *Entrance requirements:* For master's, GRE General Test or MAT, interview, minimum GPA of 2.5, bachelor's degree in related field, teaching license (MA Ed). Additional exam requirements/recommendations for international students: Required—TOEFL. *Expenses:* Tuition, state resident: full-time $4223. Tuition, nonresident: full-time $16,540. *Required fees:* $2184.

Eastern Washington University, Graduate Studies, College of Science, Health and Engineering, Department of Computer Science, Cheney, WA 99004-2431. Offers computer and technology-supported education (M Ed); computer science (MS). Part-time programs available. *Faculty:* 13 full-time (1 woman). *Students:* 23 full-time (3 women), 7 part-time (0 women). Average age 31. 22 applicants, 36% accepted, 7 enrolled. In 2013, 4 master's awarded. *Degree requirements:* For master's, comprehensive exam, thesis or alternative. *Entrance requirements:* For master's, minimum GPA of 3.0. *Application deadline:* For fall admission, 4/1 priority date for domestic students; for spring admission, 1/15 for domestic students. Applications are processed on a rolling basis. Application fee: $50. *Financial support:* In 2013–14, 17 teaching assistantships with partial tuition reimbursements (averaging $12,000 per year) were awarded; career-related internships or fieldwork, Federal Work-Study, institutionally sponsored loans, scholarships/grants, health care benefits, tuition waivers (partial), and unspecified assistantships also available. Support available to part-time students. Financial award application deadline: 2/1. *Unit head:* Dr. Ray Hamel, Chair, 509-359-4758, Fax: 509-358-2061. *Application contact:* Dr. Timothy Rolfe, Adviser, 509-359-4276, Fax: 509-359-2215.
Website: http://www.ewu.edu/cshe/programs/computer-science.xml.

Florida Institute of Technology, Graduate Programs, College of Science, Department of Education and Interdisciplinary Studies, Melbourne, FL 32901-6975. Offers computer education (MS); elementary science education (M Ed); environmental education (MS); interdisciplinary science (MS); mathematics education (MS, PhD, Ed S); science education (MS, PhD, Ed S), including informal science education (MS); teaching (MAT). Part-time and evening/weekend programs available. *Faculty:* 4 full-time (1 woman), 5 part-time/adjunct (2 women). *Students:* 47 full-time (29 women), 40 part-time (25 women); includes 10 minority (4 Black or African American, non-Hispanic/Latino; 4 Asian, non-Hispanic/Latino; 2 Hispanic/Latino), 48 international. Average age 32. 90 applicants, 63% accepted, 23 enrolled. In 2013, 16 master's awarded. Terminal master's awarded for partial completion of doctoral program. *Degree requirements:* For master's, comprehensive exam (for some programs), thesis optional; for doctorate, comprehensive exam, thesis/dissertation; for Ed S, comprehensive exam. *Entrance requirements:* For master's, minimum GPA of 3.0, resume, 3 letters of recommendation (elementary science education), statement of objectives; for doctorate, minimum GPA of 3.2, resume, 3 letters of recommendation, statement of objectives, 3 years of teaching experience (recommended); for Ed S, minimum GPA of 3.0, resume, 3 letters of recommendation, statement of objectives. Additional exam requirements/recommendations for international students: Required—TOEFL (minimum score 550 paper-based; 79 iBT). *Application deadline:* For fall admission, 4/1 for international students; for spring admission, 9/30 for international students. Applications are processed on a rolling basis. Electronic applications accepted. *Expenses: Tuition:* Full-time $20,214; part-time $1123 per credit. Tuition and fees vary according to campus/location. *Financial support:* In 2013–14, 2 teaching assistantships with full and partial tuition reimbursements (averaging $12,623 per year) were awarded; research assistantships with full and partial tuition reimbursements, career-related internships or fieldwork, institutionally sponsored loans, tuition waivers (partial), unspecified assistantships, and tuition remissions also available. Support available to part-time students. Financial award application deadline: 3/1; financial award applicants required to submit FAFSA. *Faculty research:* Measurement and evaluation, computers in education, educational technology. *Total annual research expenditures:* $644,517. *Unit head:* Dr. Kastro Hamed, Department Head, 321-674-8126, Fax: 321-674-7598, E-mail: khamed@fit.edu. *Application contact:* Cheryl A. Brown, Associate Director of Graduate Admissions, 321-674-7581, Fax: 321-723-9468, E-mail: cbrown@fit.edu.
Website: http://cos.fit.edu/education/.

Fontbonne University, Graduate Programs, Department of Mathematics and Computer Science, St. Louis, MO 63105-3098. Offers computer education (MS). Part-time and evening/weekend programs available. Postbaccalaureate distance learning degree programs offered (no on-campus study). *Degree requirements:* For master's, thesis optional. *Entrance requirements:* For master's, minimum GPA of 3.0. *Expenses: Tuition:* Full-time $11,646; part-time $647 per credit hour. *Required fees:* $324; $18 per credit hour. Tuition and fees vary according to course load and program.

Illinois Institute of Technology, Graduate College, College of Science and Letters, Department of Computer Science, Chicago, IL 60616. Offers business (MCS); computational intelligence (MCS); computer networking and telecommunications (MCS); computer science (MCS, MS, PhD); cyber-physical systems (MCS); data analytics (MCS); distributed and cloud computing (MCS); education (MCS); finance (MCS); information security and assurance (MCS); information systems (MCS); software engineering (MCS); teaching (MST). Part-time and evening/weekend programs available. Postbaccalaureate distance learning degree programs offered (no on-campus study). Terminal master's awarded for partial completion of doctoral program. *Degree requirements:* For master's, thesis optional; for doctorate, comprehensive exam, thesis/dissertation. *Entrance requirements:* For master's, GRE General Test (minimum scores: 1000 Quantitative and Verbal, 3.0 Analytical Writing), minimum undergraduate GPA of 3.0; for doctorate, GRE General Test (minimum scores: 1100 Quantitative and Verbal, 3.5 Analytical Writing), minimum undergraduate GPA of 3.0. Additional exam requirements/recommendations for international students: Required—TOEFL (minimum score 523 paper-based; 70 iBT). Electronic applications accepted. *Faculty research:* Algorithms, data structures, artificial intelligence, computer architecture, computer graphics, computer networking and telecommunications, computer vision, database systems, distributed and parallel processing, I/O systems, image processing, information retrieval, natural language processing, software engineering and system software, machine learning, cloud computing.

Indiana University–Purdue University Indianapolis, School of Education, Indianapolis, IN 46202-2896. Offers computer education (Certificate); curriculum and instruction (MS); early childhood (MS); educational leadership (MS, Certificate); English as a second language (Certificate); higher education and student affairs (MS); kindergarten (Certificate); language education (MS); reading (Certificate); school counseling (MS); special education (MS, Certificate). Part-time and evening/weekend programs available. *Faculty:* 41 full-time, 80 part-time/adjunct. *Students:* 113 full-time (78 women), 263 part-time (200 women); includes 88 minority (51 Black or African

American, non-Hispanic/Latino; 1 American Indian or Alaska Native, non-Hispanic/Latino; 10 Asian, non-Hispanic/Latino; 19 Hispanic/Latino; 7 Two or more races, non-Hispanic/Latino), 5 international. Average age 33. 93 applicants, 54% accepted, 40 enrolled. In 2013, 179 master's awarded. *Degree requirements:* For master's, thesis optional. *Entrance requirements:* For master's, GRE General Test, minimum GPA of 3.0. Additional exam requirements/recommendations for international students: Required—TOEFL. *Application deadline:* For fall admission, 5/1 priority date for domestic students; for spring admission, 11/1 for domestic students. Application fee: $55 ($65 for international students). *Financial support:* Fellowships, research assistantships with partial tuition reimbursements, teaching assistantships, Federal Work-Study, institutionally sponsored loans, scholarships/grants, and tuition waivers (partial) available. Support available to part-time students. *Faculty research:* Teachers in the process of change, learning cycles, children's concepts of science. *Total annual research expenditures:* $614,458. *Unit head:* Dr. Pat Rogan, Executive Associate Dean, 317-274-6862, E-mail: progan@iupui.edu. *Application contact:* Donnella Dillon, Graduate Admissions Coordinator, 317-274-0645, E-mail: dmdillon@iupui.edu.
Website: http://education.iupui.edu/.

Kent State University, Graduate School of Education, Health, and Human Services, School of Lifespan Development and Educational Sciences, Program in Instructional Technology, Kent, OH 44242-0001. Offers computer technology (M Ed); general instructional technology (M Ed). *Accreditation:* NCATE. *Faculty:* 5 full-time (1 woman). *Students:* 6 full-time (3 women), 52 part-time (37 women); includes 4 minority (2 Black or African American, non-Hispanic/Latino; 2 Native Hawaiian or other Pacific Islander, non-Hispanic/Latino), 1 international. 28 applicants, 61% accepted. In 2013, 25 master's awarded. *Degree requirements:* For master's, thesis (for some programs). *Entrance requirements:* For master's, 2 letters of reference, goals statement, minimum GPA of 2.75. Additional exam requirements/recommendations for international students: Required—TOEFL (minimum score 550 paper-based; 80 iBT). *Application deadline:* Applications are processed on a rolling basis. Application fee: $30 ($60 for international students). *Financial support:* Research assistantships with full tuition reimbursements, teaching assistantships with full tuition reimbursements, Federal Work-Study, scholarships/grants, and unspecified assistantships available. Financial award application deadline: 4/1; financial award applicants required to submit FAFSA. *Faculty research:* Cooperative learning, aesthetics, computers in schools. *Unit head:* Dr. Drew Tiene, Coordinator, 330-672-0607, E-mail: dtiene@kent.edu. *Application contact:* Nancy Miller, Academic Program Director, Office of Graduate Student Services, 330-672-2576, Fax: 330-672-9162, E-mail: ogs@kent.edu.
Website: http://www.kent.edu/ehhs/itec/.

Lesley University, School of Education, Cambridge, MA 02138-2790. Offers arts, community, and education (M Ed); autism studies (Certificate); curriculum and instruction (M Ed, CAGS); early childhood education (M Ed); ecological teaching and learning (MS); educational studies (PhD), including adult learning, educational leadership, individually designed; elementary education (M Ed); emergent technologies for educators (Certificate); ESLArts: language learning through the arts (M Ed); high school education (M Ed); individually designed (M Ed); integrated teaching through the arts (M Ed); literacy for K-8 classroom teachers (M Ed); mathematics education (M Ed); middle school education (M Ed); moderate disabilities (M Ed); online learning (Certificate); reading (CAGS); science in education (M Ed); severe disabilities (M Ed); special needs (CAGS); specialist teacher of reading (M Ed); teacher of visual art (M Ed); technology in education (M Ed, CAGS). *Accreditation:* Teacher Education Accreditation Council. Part-time and evening/weekend programs available. Postbaccalaureate distance learning degree programs offered (no on-campus study). *Faculty:* 40 full-time (30 women), 104 part-time/adjunct (77 women). *Students:* 453 full-time (381 women), 1,672 part-time (1,435 women); includes 284 minority (139 Black or African American, non-Hispanic/Latino; 11 American Indian or Alaska Native, non-Hispanic/Latino; 38 Asian, non-Hispanic/Latino; 58 Hispanic/Latino; 5 Native Hawaiian or other Pacific Islander, non-Hispanic/Latino; 33 Two or more races, non-Hispanic/Latino), 22 international. Average age 35. In 2013, 1,137 master's, 18 doctorates, 51 other advanced degrees awarded. *Degree requirements:* For master's, practicum; for doctorate, thesis/dissertation. *Entrance requirements:* For master's, Massachusetts Tests for Educator Licensure (MTEL), transcripts, statement of purpose, recommendations; interview (for special education); for doctorate, GRE General Test, transcripts, statement of purpose, recommendations, interview, master's degree, resume; for other advanced degree, interview, master's degree. Additional exam requirements/recommendations for international students: Required—TOEFL (minimum score 550 paper-based; 80 iBT). *Application deadline:* Applications are processed on a rolling basis. Application fee: $50. Electronic applications accepted. *Expenses: Tuition:* Part-time $900 per credit. *Financial support:* In 2013–14, 15 fellowships (averaging $3,600 per year) were awarded; career-related internships or fieldwork, Federal Work-Study, scholarships/grants, tuition waivers, and unspecified assistantships also available. Financial award application deadline: 4/15; financial award applicants required to submit FAFSA. *Faculty research:* Assessment in literacy, mathematics and science; autism spectrum disorders; instructional technology and online learning; multicultural education and English language learners. *Unit head:* Dr. Jack Gillette, Dean, 617-349-8401, Fax: 617-349-8607, E-mail: jgillett@lesley.edu. *Application contact:* Martha Sheehan, Director of Admissions, 888-LESLEYU, Fax: 617-349-8313, E-mail: info@lesley.edu.
Website: http://www.lesley.edu/soe.html.

Long Island University–LIU Post, College of Information and Computer Science, Department of Computer Science/Management Engineering, Brookville, NY 11548-1300. Offers information systems (MS); information technology education (MS); management engineering (MS). Part-time and evening/weekend programs available. *Degree requirements:* For master's, comprehensive exam, thesis or alternative. *Entrance requirements:* For master's, bachelor's degree in science, mathematics, or engineering; minimum GPA of 2.5. Additional exam requirements/recommendations for international students: Required—TOEFL (minimum score 500 paper-based). Electronic applications accepted. *Faculty research:* Inductive music learning, re-engineering business process, technology and ethics.

Marlboro College, Graduate and Professional Studies, Program in Teaching with Technology, Brattleboro, VT 05301. Offers MAT, Certificate. Part-time and evening/weekend programs available. Postbaccalaureate distance learning degree programs offered (minimal on-campus study). *Faculty:* 1 full-time (0 women), 10 part-time/adjunct (7 women). *Students:* 2 full-time (1 woman), 19 part-time (13 women). Average age 44. 6 applicants, 67% accepted, 2 enrolled. In 2013, 11 master's awarded. *Degree requirements:* For master's, 30 credits including capstone project. *Entrance requirements:* For master's, letter of intent, 2 letters of recommendation, transcripts. *Application deadline:* For fall admission, 7/1 priority date for domestic students; for winter admission, 11/1 priority date for domestic students; for spring admission, 3/1 priority date for domestic students. Applications are processed on a rolling basis. Application fee: $0. Electronic applications accepted. *Expenses: Tuition:* Part-time $685 per credit. Tuition and fees vary according to course load and program. *Financial support:* Applicants required to submit FAFSA. *Unit head:* Caleb Clark, Degree Chair, 802-258-9207, Fax: 802-258-9201, E-mail: cclark@marlboro.edu. *Application contact:*

Matthew Livingston, Director of Graduate Admissions, 802-258-9209, Fax: 802-258-9201, E-mail: mlivingston@marlboro.edu.
Website: https://www.marlboro.edu/academics/graduate/mat.

Mississippi College, Graduate School, School of Education, Department of Teacher Education and Leadership, Clinton, MS 39058. Offers art (M Ed); biological science (M Ed); business education (M Ed); computer science (M Ed); dyslexia therapy (M Ed); educational leadership (M Ed, Ed D, Ed S); elementary education (M Ed, Ed S); English (M Ed); higher education administration (MS); mathematics (M Ed); secondary education (M Ed); social studies (history) (M Ed); teaching arts (M Ed). Part-time programs available. Postbaccalaureate distance learning degree programs offered (no on-campus study). *Degree requirements:* For master's, comprehensive exam, thesis optional. *Entrance requirements:* For master's, NTE. Additional exam requirements/recommendations for international students: Recommended—TOEFL, IELTS. Electronic applications accepted.

Ohio University, Graduate College, Gladys W. and David H. Patton College of Education and Human Services, Department of Educational Studies, Athens, OH 45701-2979. Offers computer education and technology (M Ed); cultural studies (M Ed); educational administration (M Ed, Ed D); educational research and evaluation (M Ed, PhD); instructional technology (PhD). Part-time and evening/weekend programs available. Postbaccalaureate distance learning degree programs offered (minimal on-campus study). *Degree requirements:* For master's, thesis or alternative; for doctorate, comprehensive exam, thesis/dissertation. *Entrance requirements:* For master's, GRE General Test (if GPA less than 2.9); for doctorate, GRE General Test, GRE Subject Test, minimum GPA of 2.9, work experience, 3 letters of reference, autobiography. Additional exam requirements/recommendations for international students: Required—TOEFL (minimum score 550 paper-based; 80 iBT) or IELTS (minimum score 6.5). Electronic applications accepted. *Faculty research:* Race, class and gender; computer programs; development and organization theory; evaluation/development of instruments, leadership.

Stony Brook University, State University of New York, Graduate School, College of Engineering and Applied Sciences, Department of Technology and Society, Program in Educational Technology, Stony Brook, NY 11794. Offers MS. *Accreditation:* NCATE. *Application deadline:* For fall admission, 1/15 for domestic students; for spring admission, 10/1 for domestic students. Electronic applications accepted. *Expenses:* Tuition, state resident: full-time $9870; part-time $411 per credit. Tuition, nonresident: full-time $18,350; part-time $765 per credit. *Financial support:* Research assistantships and teaching assistantships available. *Unit head:* Dr. David Ferguson, Chair, 631-632-8770, E-mail: david.ferguson@stonybrook.edu. *Application contact:* Dr. Sheldon Reaven, Graduate Program Director, 631-632-8770, E-mail: sheldon.raven@sunysb.edu.
Website: http://www.stonybrook.edu/est/graduate/msedtech.shtml.

Teachers College, Columbia University, Graduate Faculty of Education, Department of Math, Science and Technology, Program in Computing in Education, New York, NY 10027-6696. Offers MA. *Accreditation:* NCATE. Part-time and evening/weekend programs available. Postbaccalaureate distance learning degree programs offered (no on-campus study). *Faculty:* 8 full-time, 6 part-time/adjunct. *Students:* 3 full-time (2 women), 42 part-time (27 women); includes 17 minority (8 Black or African American, non-Hispanic/Latino; 6 Asian, non-Hispanic/Latino; 2 Hispanic/Latino; 1 Two or more races, non-Hispanic/Latino), 4 international. Average age 34. 20 applicants, 70% accepted, 5 enrolled. In 2013, 28 master's awarded. *Degree requirements:* For master's, integrative project. *Application deadline:* For fall admission, 1/15 priority date for domestic students; for spring admission, 11/1 for domestic students. Applications are processed on a rolling basis. Application fee: $65. Electronic applications accepted. *Financial support:* Career-related internships or fieldwork, Federal Work-Study, institutionally sponsored loans, and tuition waivers (full and partial) available. Support available to part-time students. Financial award application deadline: 2/1; financial award applicants required to submit FAFSA. *Faculty research:* Visual and interactive learning, global curriculum, cognition and learning. *Unit head:* Prof. Lalitha Vasudevan, Program Coordinator, 212-678-6660, E-mail: lmv2102@columbia.edu. *Application contact:* Deanna Ghozati, Assistant Director of Admission, 212-678-3710, Fax: 212-678-4171, E-mail: tcinfo@tc.edu.

Thomas College, Graduate School, Programs in Business, Waterville, ME 04901-5097. Offers business (MBA); computer technology education (MS); education (MS); human resource management (MBA). Part-time and evening/weekend programs available. *Entrance requirements:* For master's, GMAT, GRE, MAT or minimum GPA of 3.3 in first 3 graduate-level courses. Additional exam requirements/recommendations for international students: Recommended—TOEFL.

Troy University, Graduate School, College of Education, Program in Secondary Education, Troy, AL 36082. Offers 5th year biology (MS); 5th year computer science (MS); 5th year history (MS); 5th year language arts (MS); 5th year mathematics (MS); 5th year social science (MS); traditional biology (MS); traditional computer science (MS); traditional history (MS); traditional language arts (MS); traditional mathematics (MS); traditional social science (MS). *Accreditation:* NCATE. Part-time and evening/weekend programs available. *Faculty:* 2 full-time (1 woman). *Students:* 10 full-time (9 women), 21 part-time (14 women); includes 8 minority (6 Black or African American, non-Hispanic/Latino; 2 Hispanic/Latino). Average age 29. 15 applicants, 87% accepted, 6 enrolled. In 2013, 12 master's awarded. *Degree requirements:* For master's, comprehensive exam, thesis. *Entrance requirements:* For master's, GRE (minimum score of 850 on old exam or 290 on new exam), GMAT (minimum score of 380), or MAT (minimum score of 385), bachelor's degree; minimum undergraduate GPA of 2.5 or 3.0 on last 30 semester hours, letter of recommendation. Additional exam requirements/recommendations for international students: Required—TOEFL (minimum score 523 paper-based; 70 iBT), IELTS (minimum score 6). *Application deadline:* Applications are processed on a rolling basis. Application fee: $50. Electronic applications accepted. *Expenses:* Tuition, state resident: full-time $6084; part-time $338 per credit hour. Tuition, nonresident: full-time $12,168; part-time $676 per credit hour. *Required fees:* $630; $35 per credit hour. $50 per semester. *Financial support:* Career-related internships or fieldwork available. Support available to part-time students. Financial award applicants required to submit FAFSA. *Unit head:* Dr. Jan Oliver, Associate Professor, 334-670-3444, Fax: 334-670-3548, E-mail: oliver@troy.edu. *Application contact:* Brenda K. Campbell, Director of Graduate Admissions, 334-670-3178, Fax: 334-670-3733, E-mail: bcamp@troy.edu.

Union Graduate College, School of Education, Schenectady, NY 12308-3107. Offers biology (MAT); chemistry (MAT); Chinese (MAT); earth science (MAT); English (MA, MAT); English and history (MA); French (MAT); general science (MAT); German (MAT); history (MA); Latin (MAT); life sciences (MS); mathematics (MAT); mathematics and computer technology (MS); mentoring and teacher leadership (AC); middle childhood extension (AC); national board certification and teacher leadership (AC); physical sciences (MS); physics (MAT); social studies (MAT); Spanish (MAT); technology (MAT). *Accreditation:* Teacher Education Accreditation Council. *Faculty:* 3 full-time (1 woman), 56 part-time/adjunct (34 women). *Students:* 32 full-time (16 women), 27 part-time (22 women); includes 15 minority (1 Black or African American, non-Hispanic/Latino; 4 Asian, non-Hispanic/Latino; 6 Hispanic/Latino; 4 Two or more races, non-Hispanic/Latino), 1 international. Average age 32. In 2013, 25 master's, 11 other advanced degrees awarded. *Degree requirements:* For master's, thesis or project. *Entrance requirements:* For master's, minimum GPA of 3.0, letters of recommendation. Additional exam requirements/recommendations for international students: Required—TOEFL (minimum score 550 paper-based). *Application deadline:* Applications are processed on a rolling basis. Application fee: $60. Electronic applications accepted. *Expenses:* Contact institution. *Financial support:* Career-related internships or fieldwork, Federal Work-Study, scholarships/grants, health care benefits, and tuition waivers (partial) available. Support available to part-time students. Financial award applicants required to submit FAFSA. *Faculty research:* Transformative learning, science education, National Board Certification, teacher leadership, teacher quality. *Unit head:* Dr. Lynn Gelzheiser, Dean, 518-631-9870, Fax: 518-631-9901. *Application contact:* Nicki Foley, Assistant, 518-631-9871, Fax: 518-631-9903, E-mail: foleyn@uniongraduatecollege.edu.

University of Bridgeport, School of Education, Department of Education, Bridgeport, CT 06604. Offers education (MS); educational management (Ed D, Diploma), including intermediate administrator or supervisor (Diploma), leadership (Ed D); elementary education (MS, Diploma), including early childhood education, elementary education; middle school education (MS); music education (MS); remedial reading and language arts (Diploma); secondary education (MS, Diploma), including computer specialist (Diploma), international education (Diploma), reading specialist, secondary education. Part-time and evening/weekend programs available. *Faculty:* 12 full-time (5 women), 108 part-time/adjunct (60 women). *Students:* 155 full-time (108 women), 139 part-time (98 women); includes 48 minority (22 Black or African American, non-Hispanic/Latino; 9 Asian, non-Hispanic/Latino; 15 Hispanic/Latino; 2 Two or more races, non-Hispanic/Latino), 2 international. Average age 30. 306 applicants, 55% accepted, 107 enrolled. In 2013, 153 master's, 16 other advanced degrees awarded. *Degree requirements:* For master's, final exam, final project, or thesis; for doctorate, comprehensive exam, thesis/dissertation; for Diploma, thesis or alternative, final project. *Entrance requirements:* For master's, minimum undergraduate QPA of 2.67; for doctorate, GRE, MAT; for Diploma, GRE General Test or MAT, minimum graduate QPA of 3.0. Additional exam requirements/recommendations for international students: Recommended—TOEFL (minimum score 550 paper-based; 80 iBT), IELTS (minimum score 6.5). *Application deadline:* For fall admission, 8/1 priority date for domestic and international students; for spring admission, 12/1 priority date for domestic and international students. Applications are processed on a rolling basis. Application fee: $50. Electronic applications accepted. *Expenses:* Contact institution. *Financial support:* In 2013–14, 120 students received support. Fellowships, research assistantships, teaching assistantships, career-related internships or fieldwork, Federal Work-Study, and institutionally sponsored loans available. Support available to part-time students. Financial award application deadline: 6/1; financial award applicants required to submit FAFSA. *Faculty research:* Self-concept, internship assessment, stress and situational development, follow-up of graduation, trend analysis. *Unit head:* Dr. Allen P. Cook, Dean, 203-576-4192, Fax: 203-576-4200, E-mail: acook@bridgeport.edu. *Application contact:* Leanne Proctor, Director of Graduate Admissions, 203-576-4552, Fax: 203-576-4941, E-mail: admit@bridgeport.edu.

University of Detroit Mercy, College of Engineering and Science, Department of Mathematics and Computer Science, Detroit, MI 48221. Offers computer science (MSCS), including computer systems applications, software engineering; computer science education (MATM); mathematics education (MATM). Evening/weekend programs available. *Entrance requirements:* For master's, minimum GPA of 3.0.

University of Illinois at Chicago, Graduate College, Program in Learning Sciences, Chicago, IL 60607-7128. Offers PhD. *Expenses:* Tuition, state resident: full-time $11,066; part-time $3689 per term. Tuition, nonresident: full-time $23,064; part-time $7688 per term. *Required fees:* $3004; $1190 per term. Tuition and fees vary according to course level and program. *Unit head:* Dr. Clark Hulse, Dean, 312-413-2550. *Application contact:* Receptionist, 312-413-2550, E-mail: gradcoll@uic.edu.

University of Mary Hardin-Baylor, Graduate Studies in Information Systems, Belton, TX 76513. Offers computer technology (MS); systems management (MS). Part-time and evening/weekend programs available. *Faculty:* 3 full-time (1 woman), 1 part-time/adjunct (0 women). *Students:* 24 full-time (18 women), 69 part-time (53 women); includes 3 minority (1 Asian, non-Hispanic/Latino; 2 Two or more races, non-Hispanic/Latino), 82 international. Average age 24. 251 applicants, 85% accepted, 69 enrolled. In 2013, 18 master's awarded. *Degree requirements:* For master's, comprehensive exam. *Entrance requirements:* For master's, minimum GPA of 3.0, interview. Additional exam requirements/recommendations for international students: Required—TOEFL (minimum score 550 paper-based; 80 iBT), IELTS (minimum score 6). *Application deadline:* For fall admission, 6/1 for domestic students, 6/15 priority date for international students; for spring admission, 11/1 for domestic students, 10/15 priority date for international students. Applications are processed on a rolling basis. Application fee: $35 ($135 for international students). Electronic applications accepted. *Expenses: Tuition:* Full-time $14,130; part-time $785 per credit hour. *Required fees:* $1350; $75 per credit hour. $50 per term. *Financial support:* Federal Work-Study, unspecified assistantships, and scholarships (for some active duty military personnel only) available. Support available to part-time students. Financial award applicants required to submit FAFSA. *Unit head:* Dr. Nancy Bonner, Assistant Professor/Program Director, Master of Science in Information Systems, 254-295-5405, E-mail: nbonner@umhb.edu. *Application contact:* Melissa Ford, Director of Graduate Admissions, 254-295-4020, Fax: 254-295-5038, E-mail: mford@umhb.edu.
Website: http://www.graduate.umhb.edu/msis.

University of Phoenix–Central Valley Campus, College of Education, Fresno, CA 93720-1562. Offers curriculum and instruction (MA Ed); curriculum and instruction-computer education (MA Ed); elementary teacher education (MA Ed); secondary teacher education (MA Ed).

University of Phoenix–North Florida Campus, College of Education, Jacksonville, FL 32216-0959. Offers administration and supervision (MA Ed); curriculum and instruction (MA Ed), including computer education, mathematics education; early childhood education (MA Ed); elementary teacher education (MA Ed); secondary teacher education (MA Ed). Evening/weekend programs available. *Degree requirements:* For master's, thesis (for some programs). *Entrance requirements:* For master's, 3 years of work experience, minimum undergraduate GPA of 2.5. Additional exam requirements/recommendations for international students: Required—TOEFL (minimum score 550 paper-based; 49 iBT). Electronic applications accepted.

University of Phoenix–Omaha Campus, College of Education, Omaha, NE 68154-5240. Offers administration and supervision (MA Ed); curriculum and instruction (MA Ed), including adult education, computer education, curriculum and instruction, English and language arts education, English as a second language, mathematics education; elementary teacher education (MA Ed); secondary teacher education (MA Ed); special education (MA Ed).

University of Phoenix–Online Campus, College of Education, Phoenix, AZ 85034-7209. Offers administration and supervision (MAEd, Certificate); adult education and training (MAEd); curriculum and instruction (MAEd), including computer education, curriculum and instruction, English as a second language, language arts, mathematics, reading; early childhood education (MAEd); educational studies (MAEd); elementary

teacher education (MAEd), including early childhood, elementary teacher education, high school middle level, middle level; principal licensure (Certificate); secondary teacher education (MAEd); special education (MAEd, Certificate); teacher education (MAEd), including middle level generalist; teacher education middle level mathematics (MAEd), including middle level mathematics; teacher education middle level science (MAEd), including middle level science; teacher education secondary mathematics (MAEd); teacher education secondary science (MAEd); teacher leadership (MAEd); teachers of English learners (Certificate); transition to teaching (Certificate), including elementary education, secondary education. *Accreditation:* Teacher Education Accreditation Council. Evening/weekend programs available. Postbaccalaureate distance learning degree programs offered. *Entrance requirements:* Additional exam requirements/recommendations for international students: Required—TOEFL, TOEIC (Test of English as an International Communication), Berlitz Online English Proficiency Exam, PTE, or IELTS. Electronic applications accepted. *Expenses:* Contact institution.

University of Phoenix–San Diego Campus, College of Education, San Diego, CA 92123. Offers curriculum and instruction (MA Ed), including computer education, curriculum and instruction, English as a second language; elementary teacher education (MA Ed); secondary teacher education (MA Ed). Evening/weekend programs available. *Degree requirements:* For master's, thesis (for some programs). *Entrance requirements:* For master's, 3 years of work experience, minimum undergraduate GPA of 3.0. Additional exam requirements/recommendations for international students: Required—TOEFL (minimum score 550 paper-based; 79 iBT). Electronic applications accepted.

University of Phoenix–South Florida Campus, College of Education, Miramar, FL 33030. Offers administration and supervision (MA Ed); curriculum and instruction (MA Ed), including computer education, curriculum and instruction, mathematics education; early childhood education (MA Ed); elementary teacher education (MA Ed); secondary teacher education (MA Ed). Evening/weekend programs available. *Degree requirements:* For master's, thesis (for some programs). *Entrance requirements:* For master's, 3 years of work experience, minimum undergraduate GPA of 2.5. Additional exam requirements/recommendations for international students: Required—TOEFL (minimum score 550 paper-based; 79 iBT). Electronic applications accepted.

University of Phoenix–Springfield Campus, College of Education, Springfield, MO 65804-7211. Offers administration and supervision (MA Ed); curriculum and instruction (MA Ed), including computer education, curriculum and instruction, English and language arts education, English as a second language, mathematics education; English and language arts education (MA Ed).

University of Phoenix–Washington D.C. Campus, College of Education, Washington, DC 20001. Offers administration and supervision (MA Ed); adult education and training (MA Ed); computer education (MA Ed); curriculum and instruction (MA Ed, Ed D); early childhood education (MA Ed); education (Ed S); educational leadership (Ed D); educational technology (Ed D); elementary teacher education (MA Ed); English and language arts education (MA Ed); English as a second language (MA Ed); higher education administration (PhD); mathematics education (MA Ed); secondary teacher education (MA Ed); special education (MA Ed); teacher leadership (MA Ed).

University of Phoenix–West Florida Campus, College of Education, Temple Terrace, FL 33637. Offers administration and supervision (MA Ed); curriculum and instruction (MA Ed), including computer education, curriculum and instruction, mathematics education; curriculum and technology (MA Ed); early childhood education (MA Ed); elementary teacher education (MA Ed); secondary teacher education (MA Ed). Evening/weekend programs available. *Degree requirements:* For master's, thesis (for some programs). *Entrance requirements:* For master's, 3 years of work experience, minimum undergraduate GPA of 2.5. Additional exam requirements/recommendations for international students: Required—TOEFL (minimum score 550 paper-based; 79 iBT).

Wright State University, School of Graduate Studies, College of Education and Human Services, Department of Teacher Education, Programs in Workforce Education, Dayton, OH 45435. Offers career, technology and vocational education (M Ed, MA); computer/technology education (M Ed, MA); library/media (M Ed, MA); vocational education (M Ed, MA). *Accreditation:* NCATE. *Degree requirements:* For master's, thesis (for some programs). *Entrance requirements:* For master's, GRE General Test, MAT. Additional exam requirements/recommendations for international students: Required—TOEFL.

Counselor Education

Acadia University, Faculty of Professional Studies, School of Education, Program in Counseling, Wolfville, NS B4P 2R6, Canada. Offers M Ed. Part-time programs available. *Degree requirements:* For master's, thesis optional. *Entrance requirements:* For master's, B Ed, minimum B average in undergraduate course work, 2 years of teaching or related experience. Additional exam requirements/recommendations for international students: Required—TOEFL (minimum score 580 paper-based; 93 iBT), IELTS (minimum score 6.5). *Faculty research:* Computer-assisted supervision, rural/remote school counseling, non-custodial fathers, spirituality, counseling relationships.

Adams State University, The Graduate School, Department of Counselor Education, Alamosa, CO 81101. Offers counseling (MA). *Accreditation:* ACA. Part-time programs available. *Degree requirements:* For master's, internship, qualifying exam. *Entrance requirements:* For master's, GRE General Test or MAT, minimum undergraduate GPA of 2.75.

Adler Graduate School, Program in Adlerian Counseling and Psychotherapy, Richfield, MN 55423. Offers art therapy (MA); career development (MA); clinical counseling (MA); co-occurring disorders (MA); marriage and family therapy (MA); non-licensing Adlerian studies (MA); online Adlerian studies (MA); school counseling (MA). Part-time and evening/weekend programs available. *Faculty:* 10 full-time (5 women), 47 part-time/adjunct (33 women). *Students:* 380 part-time (300 women); includes 61 minority (35 Black or African American, non-Hispanic/Latino; 4 American Indian or Alaska Native, non-Hispanic/Latino; 14 Asian, non-Hispanic/Latino; 8 Hispanic/Latino). Average age 40. In 2013, 90 master's awarded. *Degree requirements:* For master's, thesis or alternative, 500-700 hour internship (depending on license choice). *Entrance requirements:* For master's, personal goal statement, three letters of reference, resume or work history, official transcripts. *Application deadline:* Applications are processed on a rolling basis. Application fee: $50. Electronic applications accepted. *Financial support:* Career-related internships or fieldwork and tuition waivers available. Support available to part-time students. Financial award applicants required to submit FAFSA. *Unit head:* Dr. Dan Haugen, President, 612-767-7048, Fax: 612-861-7559, E-mail: haugen@alfredadler.edu. *Application contact:* Evelyn B. Haas, Director of Student Services and Admissions, 612-767-7044, Fax: 612-861-7559, E-mail: ev@alfredadler.edu. Website: http://www.alfredadler.edu/academics/index.htm.

Alabama Agricultural and Mechanical University, School of Graduate Studies, School of Education, Department of Counseling and Special Education, Huntsville, AL 35811. Offers communicative disorders (M Ed, MS); psychology and counseling (MS, Ed S), including clinical psychology (MS), counseling and guidance, counseling psychology (MS), personnel management (MS), psychometry (MS), school psychology (MS); special education (M Ed, MS). *Accreditation:* CORE; NCATE. Part-time and evening/weekend programs available. *Degree requirements:* For master's, comprehensive exam. *Entrance requirements:* For master's, GRE General Test. Additional exam requirements/recommendations for international students: Required—TOEFL (minimum score 500 paper-based; 61 iBT). *Faculty research:* Increasing numbers of minorities in special education and speech-language pathology.

Alabama State University, College of Education, Department of Instructional Support Programs, Montgomery, AL 36101-0271. Offers counselor education (M Ed, MS, Ed S), including general counseling (MS, Ed S), school counseling (M Ed, Ed S); educational administration (M Ed, Ed D, Ed S), including educational administration (Ed S); educational leadership, policy and law (Ed D); instructional leadership (M Ed); library education media (M Ed, Ed S). Part-time programs available. *Faculty:* 8 full-time (4 women), 14 part-time/adjunct (8 women). *Students:* 57 full-time (41 women), 175 part-time (126 women); includes 209 minority (203 Black or African American, non-Hispanic/Latino; 2 Asian, non-Hispanic/Latino; 4 Hispanic/Latino). Average age 39. 86 applicants, 48% accepted, 34 enrolled. In 2013, 28 master's, 14 doctorates, 7 other advanced degrees awarded. *Degree requirements:* For master's, comprehensive exam; for Ed S, comprehensive exam, thesis. *Entrance requirements:* For master's and Ed S, GRE General Test, MAT, writing competency test. Additional exam requirements/recommendations for international students: Required—TOEFL (minimum score 500 paper-based). *Application deadline:* For fall admission, 7/15 for domestic students; for spring admission, 12/15 for domestic students. Applications are processed on a rolling basis. Application fee: $10. *Expenses:* Tuition, state resident: full-time $7958; part-time $343 per credit hour. Tuition, nonresident: full-time $14,132; part-time $686 per credit hour. *Required fees:* $446 per term. One-time fee: $1784 full-time; $892 part-time.

Tuition and fees vary according to course load. *Financial support:* In 2013–14, research assistantships (averaging $9,450 per year) were awarded. *Unit head:* Dr. Necoal Driver, Chair, 334-229-6882, Fax: 334-229-6904, E-mail: ndriver@alasu.edu. *Application contact:* Dr. Doris Screws, Dean of Graduate Studies, 334-229-4274, Fax: 334-229-4928, E-mail: dscrews@alasu.edu.
Website: http://www.alasu.edu/academics/colleges—departments/college-of-education/instructional-support-programs/index.aspx.

Albany State University, College of Education, Albany, GA 31705-2717. Offers early childhood education (M Ed); education specialist (Ed S); educational leadership and administration (M Ed); health, physical education and recreation (M Ed); middle grades education (M Ed); school counseling (M Ed); special education (M Ed). *Accreditation:* NCATE. Part-time and evening/weekend programs available. Postbaccalaureate distance learning degree programs offered (minimal on-campus study). *Degree requirements:* For master's, comprehensive exam, internship, GACE Content Exam. *Entrance requirements:* For master's, GRE or MAT. Electronic applications accepted. *Faculty research:* GACE preparation, STEM (science, technology, engineering, and mathematics), technology education, special education, professional teacher development, health implications liberation philosophy, NET-Q, learning community, disabled or at-risk students.

Alcorn State University, School of Graduate Studies, School of Psychology and Education, Alcorn State, MS 39096-7500. Offers agricultural education (MS Ed); elementary education (MS Ed, Ed S); guidance and counseling (MS Ed); industrial education (MS Ed); secondary education (MS Ed), including health and physical education; special education (MS Ed). *Accreditation:* NCATE. *Degree requirements:* For master's, thesis optional.

Alfred University, Graduate School, Counseling and School Psychology Program, Alfred, NY 14802-1205. Offers mental health counseling (MS Ed); school counseling (MS Ed, CAS); school psychology (MA, Psy D, CAS). *Accreditation:* APA. *Faculty:* 11 full-time (6 women), 4 part-time/adjunct (2 women). *Students:* 60 full-time (48 women), 33 part-time (26 women). Average age 25. 53 applicants, 79% accepted, 28 enrolled. In 2013, 20 master's, 4 doctorates, 13 other advanced degrees awarded. *Degree requirements:* For master's, internship; for doctorate, thesis/dissertation, internship. *Entrance requirements:* For master's and doctorate, GRE General Test. Additional exam requirements/recommendations for international students: Required—TOEFL (minimum score 590 paper-based; 90 iBT), IELTS (minimum score 6.5). *Application deadline:* For fall admission, 1/15 priority date for domestic and international students. Application fee: $60. Electronic applications accepted. *Expenses:* Tuition: Full-time $38,020; part-time $810 per credit hour. *Required fees:* $950; $160 per semester. Part-time tuition and fees vary according to campus/location and program. *Financial support:* In 2013–14, 26 research assistantships with partial tuition reimbursements (averaging $19,010 per year) were awarded; career-related internships or fieldwork and unspecified assistantships also available. Financial award application deadline: 8/1; financial award applicants required to submit FAFSA. *Faculty research:* Family processes, alternative assessment approaches, behavior disorders in children, parent involvement, school psychology training issues. *Unit head:* Dr. Nancy Evangelista, Chair, 607-871-2212, E-mail: fevangel@alfred.edu. *Application contact:* Sara Love, Coordinator of Graduate Admissions, 607-871-2115, Fax: 607-871-2198, E-mail: gradinquiry@alfred.edu.

Alliant International University–San Francisco, California School of Professional Psychology, Program in Clinical Counseling, San Francisco, CA 94133-1221. Offers MA. *Faculty:* 2 full-time (both women), 1 part-time/adjunct (0 women). *Students:* 14 full-time (8 women), 6 part-time (5 women); includes 8 minority (2 Black or African American, non-Hispanic/Latino; 1 American Indian or Alaska Native, non-Hispanic/Latino; 4 Hispanic/Latino; 1 Two or more races, non-Hispanic/Latino), 3 international. Average age 29. 25 applicants, 68% accepted, 6 enrolled. In 2013, 4 master's awarded. *Degree requirements:* For master's, comprehensive exam, project. *Entrance requirements:* For master's, minimum GPA of 3.0, recommendations, essay, interview. Additional exam requirements/recommendations for international students: Required—TOEFL (minimum score 550 paper-based; 80 iBT), TWE (minimum score 5). *Application deadline:* For fall admission, 4/1 priority date for domestic and international students; for spring admission, 11/1 priority date for domestic and international students. Applications are processed on a rolling basis. Application fee: $55. Electronic applications accepted. *Financial support:* Teaching assistantships, Federal Work-Study, and scholarships/

grants available. Financial award application deadline: 2/15; financial award applicants required to submit FAFSA. *Faculty research:* Systems of privilege and oppression, multicultural and social justice advocacy competence, rural issues, LGBTQ affirmative therapy and identity development, college student mental health. *Unit head:* Dr. Janie Pinterits, Program Director, 415-955-2026, E-mail: admissions@alliant.edu. *Application contact:* Alliant International University Central Contact Center, 866-U-ALLIANT, Fax: 858-635-4555, E-mail: admissions@alliant.edu.
Website: http://www.alliant.edu/cspp/programs-degrees/clinical-counseling/clin-couns-ma-sf.php.

American International College, School of Graduate and Adult Education, Department of Education, Springfield, MA 01109-3189. Offers early childhood education (M Ed, CAGS); educational leadership and supervision (Ed D); elementary education (M Ed, CAGS); middle/secondary education (M Ed, CAGS); moderate disabilities (M Ed, CAGS); reading (M Ed, CAGS); school adjustment counseling (MA, CAGS); school guidance counseling (MA, CAGS); school leadership preparation (M Ed, CAGS); teaching and learning (Ed D). Evening/weekend programs available. *Faculty:* 11 full-time (9 women), 235 part-time/adjunct. *Students:* 1,530 full-time (1,219 women), 184 part-time (143 women); includes 100 minority (58 Black or African American, non-Hispanic/Latino; 3 American Indian or Alaska Native, non-Hispanic/Latino; 14 Asian, non-Hispanic/Latino; 6 Hispanic/Latino; 19 Two or more races, non-Hispanic/Latino). Average age 36. 695 applicants, 82% accepted, 508 enrolled. In 2013, 449 master's, 17 doctorates, 135 other advanced degrees awarded. Terminal master's awarded for partial completion of doctoral program. *Degree requirements:* For master's, comprehensive exam (for some programs), thesis (for some programs), practicum/culminating experience; for doctorate, comprehensive exam (for some programs), thesis/dissertation; for CAGS, practicum/culminating experience. *Entrance requirements:* For master's, graduate of accredited four-year college with minimum B-average in undergraduate course work; for doctorate, master's degree, minimum GPA of 3.0; for CAGS, M Ed or master's degree in field related to licensure from accredited institution. Additional exam requirements/recommendations for international students: Required—TOEFL or IELTS. *Application deadline:* For fall admission, 7/1 for domestic and international students; for spring admission, 12/1 for domestic and international students. Applications are processed on a rolling basis. Application fee: $50. Electronic applications accepted. *Expenses: Tuition:* Full-time $14,040; part-time $780 per credit. Tuition and fees vary according to course load, degree level and program. *Financial support:* Career-related internships or fieldwork available. Financial award applicants required to submit FAFSA. *Unit head:* Esta Sobey, Associate Dean, 413-205-3453, Fax: 413-205-3943, E-mail: esta.sobey@aic.edu. *Application contact:* Kaitlyn Rickard, Director of XCP Admissions, 413-205-3090, Fax: 413-205-3911, E-mail: kaitlyn.rickard@aic.edu.
Website: http://www.aic.edu/academics.

American Public University System, AMU/APU Graduate Programs, Charles Town, WV 25414. Offers accounting (MBA, MS); criminal justice (MA), including business administration, emergency and disaster management, general (MA, MS); educational leadership (M Ed); emergency and disaster management (MA); entrepreneurship (MBA); environmental policy and management (MS), including environmental planning, environmental sustainability, fish and wildlife management, general (MA, MS), global environmental management; finance (MBA); general (MBA); global business management (MBA); history (MA), including American history, ancient and classical history, European history, global history, public history; homeland security (MA), including business administration, counter-terrorism studies, criminal justice, cyber, emergency management and public health, intelligence studies, transportation security; homeland security resource allocation (MBA); humanities (MA); information technology (MS), including digital forensics, enterprise software development, information assurance and security, IT project management; information technology management (MBA); intelligence studies (MA), including criminal intelligence, cyber, general (MA, MS), homeland security, intelligence analysis, intelligence collection, intelligence management, intelligence operations, terrorism studies; international relations and conflict resolution (MA), including comparative and security issues, conflict resolution, international and transnational security issues, peacekeeping; legal studies (MA); management (MA), including defense management, general (MA, MS), human resource management, organizational leadership, public administration; marketing (MBA); military history (MA), including American military history, American Revolution, civil war, war since 1945, World War II; military studies (MA), including joint warfare, strategic leadership; national security studies (MA), including general (MA, MS), homeland security, regional security studies, security and intelligence analysis, terrorism studies; nonprofit management (MBA); political science (MA), including American politics and government, comparative government and development, general (MA, MS), international relations, public policy; psychology (MA), including general (MA, MS), maritime engineering management, reverse logistics management; public administration (MPA), including disaster management, environmental policy, health policy, human resources, national security, organizational management, security management; public health (MPH); reverse logistics management (MA); school counseling (M Ed); security management (MA); space studies (MS), including aerospace science, general (MA, MS), planetary science; sports and health sciences (MS); teaching (M Ed), including curriculum and instruction for elementary teachers, elementary reading, English language learners, instructional leadership, online learning, special education; transportation and logistics management (MA), including general (MA, MS), maritime engineering management, reverse logistics management. Programs offered via distance learning only. Part-time and evening/weekend programs available. Postbaccalaureate distance learning degree programs offered (no on-campus study). *Faculty:* 432 full-time (242 women), 1,722 part-time/adjunct (829 women). *Students:* 511 full-time (241 women), 10,947 part-time (4,294 women); includes 3,760 minority (2,058 Black or African American, non-Hispanic/Latino; 88 American Indian or Alaska Native, non-Hispanic/Latino; 293 Asian, non-Hispanic/Latino; 876 Hispanic/Latino; 91 Native Hawaiian or other Pacific Islander, non-Hispanic/Latino; 354 Two or more races, non-Hispanic/Latino), 134 international. Average age 36. In 2013, 3,323 master's awarded. *Degree requirements:* For master's, comprehensive exam or practicum. *Entrance requirements:* For master's, official transcript showing earned bachelor's degree from institution accredited by recognized accrediting body. Additional exam requirements/recommendations for international students: Required—TOEFL (minimum score 550 paper-based), IELTS (minimum score 6.5). *Application deadline:* Applications are processed on a rolling basis. Application fee: $0. Electronic applications accepted. *Expenses: Tuition:* Part-time $325 per semester hour. *Financial support:* Applicants required to submit FAFSA. *Faculty research:* Military history, criminal justice, management performance, national security. *Unit head:* Dr. Karan Powell, Executive Vice President and Provost, 877-468-6268, Fax: 304-724-3780. *Application contact:* Terry Grant, Vice President of Enrollment Management, 877-468-6268, Fax: 304-724-3780, E-mail: info@apus.edu.
Website: http://www.apus.edu.

Amridge University, Graduate and Professional Programs, Montgomery, AL 36117. Offers behavioral leadership and management (MA); Biblical studies (MA, PhD); family therapy (D Min); leadership and management (MS); marriage and family therapy (M Div, MA, PhD); ministerial leadership (M Div, MS); pastoral counseling (M Div, MS); practical ministry (MA); professional counseling (M Div, MA, PhD); theology (M Div, D Min). Part-time and evening/weekend programs available. Postbaccalaureate distance learning degree programs offered (no on-campus study). *Faculty:* 48 full-time (9 women), 27 part-time/adjunct (12 women). *Students:* 124 full-time (62 women), 189 part-time (112 women); includes 196 minority (189 Black or African American, non-Hispanic/Latino; 3 Asian, non-Hispanic/Latino; 4 Hispanic/Latino). Average age 35. *Degree requirements:* For master's, one foreign language, comprehensive exam (for some programs), thesis (for some programs); for doctorate, comprehensive exam (for some programs), thesis/dissertation. *Entrance requirements:* For master's and doctorate, GRE General Test or MAT. Additional exam requirements/recommendations for international students: Required—TOEFL. *Application deadline:* For fall admission, 9/1 priority date for domestic students; for spring admission, 1/1 priority date for domestic students. Applications are processed on a rolling basis. Application fee: $50. Electronic applications accepted. *Financial support:* Federal Work-Study and scholarships/grants available. Support available to part-time students. Financial award applicants required to submit FAFSA. *Faculty research:* Homiletics, hermeneutics, ancient Near Eastern history. *Unit head:* Carl Byrd, Student Affairs Coordinator, 800-351-4040 Ext. 7569, Fax: 334-387-3878. *Application contact:* Ora Davis, Admissions Officer, 334-387-3877 Ext. 7524, Fax: 334-387-3878, E-mail: admissions@amridgeuniversity.edu.

Angelo State University, College of Graduate Studies, College of Education, Department of Curriculum and Instruction, Program in Guidance and Counseling, San Angelo, TX 76909. Offers M Ed. Part-time and evening/weekend programs available. *Degree requirements:* For master's, comprehensive exam. *Entrance requirements:* Additional exam requirements/recommendations for international students: Required—TOEFL or IELTS. Electronic applications accepted.

Antioch University Seattle, Graduate Programs, Program in Psychology, Seattle, WA 98121-1814. Offers counseling (MA); psychology (MA, Psy D). Part-time and evening/weekend programs available. *Degree requirements:* For master's, internship; for doctorate, thesis/dissertation. Electronic applications accepted. *Faculty research:* Trauma and post-traumatic stress disorders, workplace harassment and violence, multicultural issues and diversity.

Appalachian State University, Cratis D. Williams Graduate School, Department of Human Development and Psychological Counseling, Boone, NC 28608. Offers clinical mental health counseling (MA); college student development (MA); marriage and family therapy (MA); school counseling (MA). *Accreditation:* AAMFT/COAMFTE; ACA; NCATE. Part-time programs available. *Degree requirements:* For master's, comprehensive exam (for some programs), thesis optional, internships. *Entrance requirements:* For master's, GRE General Test, 3 letters of recommendation. Additional exam requirements/recommendations for international students: Required—TOEFL (minimum score 570 paper-based; 79 iBT), IELTS (minimum score 6.5). Electronic applications accepted. *Faculty research:* Multicultural counseling, addictions counseling, play therapy, expressive arts, child and adolescent therapy, sexual abuse counseling.

Argosy University, Atlanta, College of Psychology and Behavioral Sciences, Atlanta, GA 30328. Offers clinical psychology (MA, Psy D, Postdoctoral Respecialization Certificate), including child and family psychology (Psy D), general adult clinical (Psy D), health psychology (Psy D), neuropsychology/geropsychology (Psy D); community counseling (MA), including marriage and family therapy; counselor education and supervision (Ed D); forensic psychology (MA); industrial organizational psychology (MA); marriage and family therapy (Certificate); sport-exercise psychology (MA). *Accreditation:* APA.

Argosy University, Chicago, College of Psychology and Behavioral Sciences, Program in Counseling Psychology, Chicago, IL 60601. Offers counselor education and supervision (Ed D). *Accreditation:* ACA. Postbaccalaureate distance learning degree programs offered (minimal on-campus study).

Argosy University, Dallas, College of Psychology and Behavioral Sciences, Program in Counselor Education and Supervision, Farmers Branch, TX 75244. Offers Ed D.

Argosy University, Denver, College of Psychology and Behavioral Sciences, Denver, CO 80231. Offers clinical mental health counseling (MA); clinical psychology (MA, Psy D); counseling psychology (Ed D); counselor education and supervision (Ed D); forensic psychology (MA); industrial organizational psychology (MA); marriage and family therapy (MA, DMFT).

Argosy University, Nashville, College of Psychology and Behavioral Sciences, Program in Counselor Education and Supervision, Nashville, TN 37214. Offers Ed D.

Argosy University, Salt Lake City, College of Psychology and Behavioral Sciences, Draper, UT 84020. Offers counseling psychology (Ed D); counselor education and supervision (Ed D); forensic psychology (MA); marriage and family therapy (MA, DMFT); mental health counseling (MA).

Argosy University, Sarasota, College of Education, Sarasota, FL 34235. Offers community college executive leadership (Ed D); educational leadership (MA Ed, Ed D, Ed S), including higher education administration (Ed D), K-12 education (Ed D); school counseling (MA, Ed S); school psychology (MA); teaching and learning (MA Ed, Ed D, Ed S), including education technology (Ed D), higher education (Ed D), K-12 education (Ed D).

Argosy University, Sarasota, College of Psychology and Behavioral Sciences, Sarasota, FL 34235. Offers community counseling (MA); counseling psychology (Ed D); counselor education and supervision (Ed D); forensic psychology (MA); marriage and family therapy (MA); mental health counseling (MA); pastoral community counseling (Ed D).

Argosy University, Schaumburg, College of Psychology and Behavioral Sciences, Schaumburg, IL 60173-5403. Offers clinical health psychology (Post-Graduate Certificate); clinical psychology (MA, Psy D), including child and family psychology (Psy D), clinical health psychology (Psy D), diversity and multicultural psychology (Psy D), forensic psychology (Psy D), neuropsychology (Psy D); community counseling (MA); counseling psychology (Ed D), including counselor education and supervision; counselor education and supervision (Ed D); forensic psychology (Post-Graduate Certificate); industrial organizational psychology (MA). *Accreditation:* ACA; APA.

Argosy University, Tampa, College of Education, Tampa, FL 33607. Offers community college executive leadership (Ed D); educational leadership (MA Ed, Ed D, Ed S), including higher education administration (Ed D), K-12 education (Ed D); school counseling (MA); teaching and learning (MA Ed, Ed D, Ed S), including higher education (Ed D), K-12 education (Ed D).

Argosy University, Tampa, College of Psychology and Behavioral Sciences, Tampa, FL 33607. Offers clinical psychology (MA, Psy D), including clinical psychology; counselor education and supervision (Ed D); industrial organizational psychology (MA); marriage and family therapy (MA); mental health counseling (MA).

Argosy University, Washington DC, College of Psychology and Behavioral Sciences, Arlington, VA 22209. Offers clinical psychology (MA, Psy D), including child and family psychology (Psy D), diversity and multicultural psychology (Psy D), forensic psychology (Psy D), health and neuropsychology (Psy D); community counseling (MA); counseling

psychology (Ed D), including counselor education and supervision; counselor education and supervision (Ed D); forensic psychology (MA). *Accreditation:* APA.

Arizona State University at the Tempe campus, School of Letters and Sciences, Program in Counseling, Tempe, AZ 85287-0811. Offers MC. *Accreditation:* ACA. *Degree requirements:* For master's, comprehensive exam (for some programs), thesis (for some programs), interactive Program of Study (iPOS) submitted before completing 50 percent of required credit hours. *Entrance requirements:* For master's, GRE, minimum GPA of 3.0 or equivalent in last 2 years of work leading to bachelor's degree; 3 letters of recommendation; 3-5 page personal statement with information on significant life experiences, professional experiences and goals. Additional exam requirements/recommendations for international students: Required—TOEFL (minimum score 80 iBT), TOEFL, IELTS, or PTE. Electronic applications accepted.

Arkansas State University, Graduate School, College of Education and Behavioral Science, Department of Psychology and Counseling, Jonesboro, AR 72467. Offers college student personnel services (MS); mental health counseling (Certificate); psychology and counseling (Ed S); rehabilitation counseling (MRC); school counseling (MSE); student affairs (Certificate). *Accreditation:* ACA (one or more programs are accredited); CORE (one or more programs are accredited); NCATE. Part-time programs available. *Faculty:* 15 full-time (9 women). *Students:* 50 full-time (33 women), 73 part-time (56 women); includes 33 minority (31 Black or African American, non-Hispanic/Latino; 1 American Indian or Alaska Native, non-Hispanic/Latino; 1 Two or more races, non-Hispanic/Latino), 1 international. Average age 32. 87 applicants, 53% accepted, 42 enrolled. In 2013, 17 master's, 11 other advanced degrees awarded. *Degree requirements:* For master's and other advanced degree, comprehensive exam, thesis or alternative. *Entrance requirements:* For master's, GRE General Test or MAT (for MSE), appropriate bachelor's degree, interview, letters of reference, official transcripts, immunization records, written statement, 2-3 page autobiography; for other advanced degree, GRE General Test, interview, master's degree, letters of reference, official transcript, personal statement, immunization records. Additional exam requirements/recommendations for international students: Required—TOEFL (minimum score 550 paper-based; 79 iBT), IELTS (minimum score 6), PTE (minimum score 56). *Application deadline:* Applications are processed on a rolling basis. Application fee: $30 ($40 for international students). Electronic applications accepted. *Expenses:* Tuition, state resident: full-time $4284; part-time $238 per credit hour. Tuition, nonresident: full-time $8568; part-time $476 per credit hour. *International tuition:* $9268 full-time. *Required fees:* $1098; $61 per credit hour. $25 per term. Tuition and fees vary according to course load and program. *Financial support:* In 2013–14, 17 students received support. Teaching assistantships, career-related internships or fieldwork, scholarships/grants, and unspecified assistantships available. Financial award application deadline: 7/1; financial award applicants required to submit FAFSA. *Unit head:* Dr. Loretta McGregor, Chair, 870-972-3064, Fax: 870-972-3962, E-mail: lmcgregor@astate.edu. *Application contact:* Vickey Ring, Graduate Admissions Coordinator, 870-972-3029, Fax: 870-972-3857, E-mail: vickeyring@astate.edu.
Website: http://www.astate.edu/college/education/departments/psychology-and-counseling/index.dot.

Arkansas Tech University, Center for Leadership and Learning, Russellville, AR 72801. Offers educational leadership (M Ed, Ed S); school counseling and leadership (M Ed); teaching, learning and leadership (M Ed). Part-time and evening/weekend programs available. *Students:* 144 part-time (117 women); includes 17 minority (8 Black or African American, non-Hispanic/Latino; 1 Asian, non-Hispanic/Latino; 4 Hispanic/Latino; 4 Two or more races, non-Hispanic/Latino). Average age 35. In 2013, 20 master's, 5 Ed Ss awarded. *Degree requirements:* For master's, comprehensive exam (for some programs), thesis (for some programs), project, internship, portfolio. *Entrance requirements:* For master's, PRAXIS; for Ed S, teaching and administrative licenses. Additional exam requirements/recommendations for international students: Required—TOEFL (minimum score 550 paper-based; 79 iBT), IELTS (minimum score 6.5). *Application deadline:* For fall admission, 3/1 priority date for domestic students, 5/1 priority date for international students; for spring admission, 10/1 priority date for domestic and international students. Applications are processed on a rolling basis. Application fee: $25 ($75 for international students). Electronic applications accepted. *Expenses:* Tuition, state resident: full-time $5976; part-time $249 per credit hour. Tuition, nonresident: full-time $11,952; part-time $498 per credit hour. *Required fees:* $411 per semester. Tuition and fees vary according to course load. *Financial support:* In 2013–14, research assistantships with full tuition reimbursements (averaging $4,800 per year), teaching assistantships with full tuition reimbursements (averaging $4,800 per year) were awarded; career-related internships or fieldwork, Federal Work-Study, scholarships/grants, health care benefits, and unspecified assistantships also available. Support available to part-time students. Financial award application deadline: 4/15; financial award applicants required to submit FAFSA. *Unit head:* Dr. Mona Chadwick, Head, Center for Leadership and Learning, 479-498-6022, Fax: 479-498-6075, E-mail: cll@atu.edu. *Application contact:* Dr. Mary B. Gunter, Dean of Graduate College, 479-968-0398, Fax: 479-964-0542, E-mail: gradcollege@atu.edu.
Website: http://www.atu.edu/cll/.

Ashland Theological Seminary, Graduate Programs, Ashland, OH 44805. Offers biblical and theological studies (MAR); Biblical, historical and theological studies (MA), including Anabaptism and Pietism, Christian theology, church history, New Testament, Old Testament; Christian ministry (MAPT), including Black church studies (M Div, MAPT, D Min), chaplaincy (M Div, MAPT), Christian formation (M Div, MAPT), evangelism/church renewal and missions (M Div, MAPT), general ministry (M Div, MAPT), pastoral counseling and care (M Div, MAPT), specialized ministry, spiritual formation (M Div, MAPT, D Min); Christian studies (Diploma); clinical counseling (MACC); counseling (MAC); ministry (D Min), including Black church studies (M Div, MAPT, D Min), Canadian church studies, formational counseling, independent design, spiritual formation (M Div, MAPT, D Min), transformational leadership, Wesleyan practices; pastoral ministry (M Div), including Biblical studies - Old or New Testament, Black church studies (M Div, MAPT, D Min), chaplaincy (M Div, MAPT), Christian formation (M Div, MAPT), evangelism/church renewal and missions (M Div, MAPT), general Biblical studies, general ministry (M Div, MAPT), pastoral counseling and care (M Div, MAPT), spiritual formation (M Div, MAPT, D Min), theology or history. MAC program offered in Detroit, MI. *Accreditation:* ATS. Part-time programs available. *Degree requirements:* For master's, 2 foreign languages, comprehensive exam (for some programs), thesis (for some programs); for doctorate, thesis/dissertation. *Entrance requirements:* For master's, bachelor's degree from accredited institution with a minimum undergraduate GPA of 2.75; for doctorate, M Div, minimum undergraduate GPA of 3.0. Additional exam requirements/recommendations for international students: Required—TOEFL (minimum score 500 paper-based; 65 iBT). Electronic applications accepted. *Faculty research:* Semitic languages and linguistics, rhetorical and social-scientific criticism, Anabaptist studies, inner spiritual healing, African-American clergy in film and literature.

Athabasca University, Graduate Centre for Applied Psychology, Athabasca, AB T9S 3A3, Canada. Offers art therapy (MC); career counseling (MC); counseling (Advanced Certificate); counseling psychology (MC); school counseling (MC).

Auburn University at Montgomery, School of Education, Department of Counselor, Leadership, and Special Education, Montgomery, AL 36124-4023. Offers counseling education (M Ed, Ed S), including counseling and development (Ed S); school counseling (Ed S); early childhood special education (M Ed); instructional leadership (Ed S); special education (Ed S); special education/collaborative teacher (M Ed). *Accreditation:* ACA; NCATE. Part-time and evening/weekend programs available. *Faculty:* 6 full-time (5 women), 2 part-time/adjunct (1 woman). *Students:* 15 full-time (11 women), 55 part-time (42 women); includes 32 minority (31 Black or African American, non-Hispanic/Latino; 1 Hispanic/Latino). Average age 33. In 2013, 22 master's awarded. *Degree requirements:* For master's and Ed S, comprehensive exam. *Entrance requirements:* For master's, GRE General Test or MAT, certification, BS in teaching; for Ed S, GRE General Test or MAT, certification. *Application deadline:* Applications are processed on a rolling basis. Electronic applications accepted. *Expenses:* Tuition, state resident: full-time $5994; part-time $333 per credit hour. Tuition, nonresident: full-time $17,982; part-time $999 per credit hour. *Financial support:* Career-related internships or fieldwork and scholarships/grants available. Support available to part-time students. Financial award application deadline: 3/1; financial award applicants required to submit FAFSA. *Unit head:* Dr. Sheila Austin, Dean, 334-244-3425, Fax: 334-244-3102, E-mail: saustin1@aum.edu. *Application contact:* Dr. Rhonda Morton, Associate Dean/Graduate Coordinator, 334-244-3287, Fax: 334-244-3978, E-mail: rmorton@aum.edu.
Website: http://www.aum.edu/Education.

Austin Peay State University, College of Graduate Studies, College of Behavioral and Health Sciences, Department of Psychology, Clarksville, TN 37044. Offers counseling (MS); industrial-organizational psychology (MA). Part-time programs available. Postbaccalaureate distance learning degree programs offered (no on-campus study). *Faculty:* 11 full-time (7 women), 1 (woman) part-time/adjunct. *Students:* 53 full-time (44 women), 22 part-time (16 women); includes 17 minority (8 Black or African American, non-Hispanic/Latino; 1 Asian, non-Hispanic/Latino; 6 Hispanic/Latino; 2 Two or more races, non-Hispanic/Latino). Average age 30. 46 applicants, 78% accepted, 24 enrolled. In 2013, 33 master's awarded. *Degree requirements:* For master's, comprehensive exam, thesis (for some programs). *Entrance requirements:* For master's, GRE General Test, minimum undergraduate GPA of 2.5, 3 letters of recommendation, bachelor's degree. Additional exam requirements/recommendations for international students: Required—TOEFL (minimum score 500 paper-based). *Application deadline:* For fall admission, 8/5 priority date for domestic students. Applications are processed on a rolling basis. Application fee: $25. Electronic applications accepted. *Expenses:* Tuition, state resident: full-time $7500; part-time $375 per credit hour. Tuition, nonresident: full-time $20,800; part-time $1040 per credit hour. *Required fees:* $1284; $64.20 per credit hour. *Financial support:* In 2013–14, research assistantships with full tuition reimbursements (averaging $6,500 per year) were awarded; career-related internships or fieldwork, Federal Work-Study, institutionally sponsored loans, scholarships/grants, and unspecified assistantships also available. Support available to part-time students. Financial award application deadline: 3/1; financial award applicants required to submit FAFSA. *Unit head:* Dr. Kevin Harris, Chair, 931-221-7232, Fax: 931-221-6267, E-mail: harrisk@apsu.edu. *Application contact:* June D. Lee, Graduate Coordinator, 800-859-4723, Fax: 931-221-7641, E-mail: gradadmissions@apsu.edu.
Website: http://www.apsu.edu/psychology.

Azusa Pacific University, School of Education, Department of School Counseling and School Psychology, Program in Educational Counseling, Azusa, CA 91702-7000. Offers MA.

Baptist Bible College of Pennsylvania, Graduate Studies, Clarks Summit, PA 18411-1297. Offers Bible (MA); counseling (MA, MS); curriculum and instruction (M Ed); educational administration (M Ed); intercultural studies (MA); literature (MA); missions (MA); organizational leadership (MA); reading specialist (M Ed); secondary English/communications (M Ed); social entrepreneurship (MA); worldview studies (MA). MA in missions program available only for Association of Baptists for World Evangelism missionary personnel. Part-time and evening/weekend programs available. Postbaccalaureate distance learning degree programs offered (no on-campus study). *Entrance requirements:* Additional exam requirements/recommendations for international students: Required—TOEFL (minimum score 500 paper-based).

Barry University, School of Education, Program in Counseling, Miami Shores, FL 33161-6695. Offers MS, PhD, Ed S. *Accreditation:* ACA. Part-time and evening/weekend programs available. *Degree requirements:* For master's, comprehensive exam. *Entrance requirements:* For master's, GRE General Test or MAT, minimum GPA of 3.0; for doctorate, GRE, minimum GPA of 3.25; for Ed S, GRE General Test, minimum GPA of 3.0.

Barry University, School of Education, Program in Mental Health Counseling, Miami Shores, FL 33161-6695. Offers MS, Ed S. *Accreditation:* ACA. Part-time and evening/weekend programs available. *Degree requirements:* For master's, comprehensive exam, scholarly paper; for Ed S, comprehensive exam. *Entrance requirements:* For master's, GRE General Test or MAT, minimum GPA of 3.0; for Ed S, GRE General Test, minimum GPA of 3.0. Electronic applications accepted.

Barry University, School of Education, Program in School Counseling, Miami Shores, FL 33161-6695. Offers MS, Ed S. *Accreditation:* ACA (one or more programs are accredited). Part-time and evening/weekend programs available. *Degree requirements:* For master's, comprehensive exam, scholarly paper; for Ed S, comprehensive exam. *Entrance requirements:* For master's, GRE General Test or MAT, minimum GPA of 3.0; for Ed S, GRE General Test, minimum GPA of 3.0. Electronic applications accepted.

Bayamón Central University, Graduate Programs, Program in Education, Bayamón, PR 00960-1725. Offers administration and supervision (MA Ed); commercial education (MA Ed); elementary education (K–3) (MA Ed); family counseling (Graduate Certificate); guidance and counseling (MA Ed); pre-elementary teacher (MA Ed); rehabilitation counseling (MA Ed); special education (MA Ed), including attention deficit disorder, education of the autistic, learning disabilities. Part-time and evening/weekend programs available. *Degree requirements:* For master's, comprehensive exam. *Entrance requirements:* For master's, EXADEP, bachelor's degree in education or related field.

Bellevue University, Graduate School, College of Arts and Sciences, Bellevue, NE 68005-3098. Offers clinical counseling (MS); healthcare administration (MHA); human services (MA); international security and intelligence studies (MS); managerial communication (MA). Postbaccalaureate distance learning degree programs offered.

Bloomsburg University of Pennsylvania, School of Graduate Studies, College of Education, Department of Educational Studies and Secondary Education, Program in School Counseling and Student Affairs, Bloomsburg, PA 17815-1301. Offers college student affairs (M Ed); elementary school (M Ed); secondary school (M Ed). *Faculty:* 5 full-time (3 women), 5 part-time/adjunct (2 women). *Students:* 8 full-time (6 women), 59 part-time (40 women); includes 16 minority (10 Black or African American, non-Hispanic/Latino; 4 Hispanic/Latino; 2 Two or more races, non-Hispanic/Latino), 1 international. Average age 25. 48 applicants, 79% accepted, 30 enrolled. *Degree requirements:* For master's, practicum. *Entrance requirements:* For master's, 3 letters of recommendation, resume, minimum QPA of 3.0, personal statement, interview. Additional exam requirements/recommendations for international students: Required—TOEFL. Application fee: $35 ($60 for international students). Electronic applications accepted.

Expenses: Tuition, state resident: full-time $7956; part-time $442 per credit. Tuition, nonresident: full-time $11,934; part-time $663 per credit. *Required fees:* $95.50 per credit. $55 per semester. Tuition and fees vary according to course load. *Unit head:* Dr. Tegan Kotarski, College of Education Graduate Coordinator, 570-389-3883, Fax: 570-389-5049, E-mail: tkotarsk@bloomu.edu. *Application contact:* Jennifer Richard, Administrative Assistant, 570-389-4015, Fax: 570-389-3054, E-mail: jrichard@bloomu.edu.
Website: http://www.bloomu.edu/gradschool/counseling-student-affairs.

Bob Jones University, Graduate Programs, Greenville, SC 29614. Offers accountancy (MS); Bible (MA); Bible translation (MA); Biblical studies (Certificate); broadcast management (MS); business administration (MBA); church history (MA, PhD); church ministries (MA); church music (MM); cinema and video production (MA); counseling (MS); curriculum and instruction (Ed D); divinity (M Div); dramatic production (MA); educational leadership (MS, Ed D, Ed S); elementary education (M Ed, MAT); English (M Ed, MA, MAT); fine arts (MA); graphic design (MA); history (M Ed, MA); illustration (MA); interpretative speech (MA); mathematics (M Ed, MAT); medical missions (Certificate); ministry (MM, D Min); multi-categorical special education (M Ed, MAT); music (M Ed); New Testament interpretation (PhD); Old Testament interpretation (PhD); orchestral instrument performance (MM); organ performance (MM); pastoral studies (MA); personnel services (MS, Ed S); piano pedagogy (MM); piano performance (MM); platform arts (MA); radio and television broadcasting (MS); rhetoric and public address (MA); secondary education (M Ed); studio art (MA); teaching Bible (MA); theology (MA, PhD); voice performance (MM); youth ministries (MA); M Div/MM.

Boston College, Lynch Graduate School of Education, Program in Counseling, Chestnut Hill, MA 02467-3800. Offers counseling psychology (PhD); mental health counseling (MA); school counseling (MA); MA/MA. *Accreditation:* APA (one or more programs are accredited). *Students:* 57 full-time (44 women), 4 part-time (3 women). 454 applicants, 41% accepted, 61 enrolled. In 2013, 81 master's, 4 doctorates awarded. Terminal master's awarded for partial completion of doctoral program. *Degree requirements:* For master's, comprehensive exam; for doctorate, comprehensive exam, thesis/dissertation. *Entrance requirements:* For master's and doctorate, GRE General Test. Additional exam requirements/recommendations for international students: Required—TOEFL (minimum score 550 paper-based; 100 iBT). *Application deadline:* For fall admission, 12/1 priority date for domestic and international students; for spring admission, 11/1 for domestic and international students. Application fee: $65. Electronic applications accepted. *Financial support:* Fellowships with full and partial tuition reimbursements, research assistantships with full and partial tuition reimbursements, teaching assistantships with full and partial tuition reimbursements, career-related internships or fieldwork, Federal Work-Study, scholarships/grants, traineeships, health care benefits, tuition waivers (full and partial), and unspecified assistantships available. Support available to part-time students. Financial award applicants required to submit FAFSA. *Faculty research:* Reducing non-academic barriers to learning; race, gender, culture and social class issues in mental health; domestic violence; career development; community intervention and prevention. *Unit head:* Dr. M. Brinton Lykes, Chairperson, 617-552-4214, Fax: 617-552-0812. *Application contact:* Domenic Lomanno, Director, Graduate Admission and Financial Aid, 617-552-4214, Fax: 617-552-0398, E-mail: lomanno@bc.edu.

Bowie State University, Graduate Programs, Program in Guidance and Counseling, Bowie, MD 20715-9465. Offers M Ed. Part-time and evening/weekend programs available. *Degree requirements:* For master's, comprehensive exam, thesis optional, research paper. *Entrance requirements:* For master's, teaching experience, minimum GPA of 2.5, 3 recommendations. Electronic applications accepted. *Expenses:* Tuition, state resident: full-time $8665. Tuition, nonresident: full-time $16,007. *Required fees:* $1927.

Bowling Green State University, Graduate College, College of Education and Human Development, School of Education and Intervention Services, Intervention Services Division, Program in Counseling, Bowling Green, OH 43403. Offers mental health counseling (MA); school counseling (M Ed). *Accreditation:* ACA; NCATE. Part-time programs available. *Degree requirements:* For master's, thesis or alternative. *Entrance requirements:* For master's, GRE General Test. Additional exam requirements/recommendations for international students: Required—TOEFL. Electronic applications accepted. *Faculty research:* Perfectionism, multicultural counseling, suicide, ethics and legal issues related to counseling, play therapy.

Bradley University, Graduate School, College of Education and Health Sciences, Department of Educational Leadership and Human Development, Peoria, IL 61625-0002. Offers human development counseling (MA), including community and agency counseling, school counseling; leadership in educational administration (MA); leadership in human service administration (MA). *Accreditation:* ACA; NCATE. Part-time and evening/weekend programs available. *Degree requirements:* For master's, comprehensive exam, thesis optional. *Entrance requirements:* For master's, GRE General Test or MAT, interview, 3 letters of recommendation. Additional exam requirements/recommendations for international students: Required—TOEFL (minimum score 550 paper-based; 79 iBT). *Expenses: Tuition:* Full-time $14,580; part-time $810 per credit hour. Tuition and fees vary according to course load and program.

Brandman University, School of Education, Irvine, CA 92618. Offers education (MA); educational leadership (MA); school counseling (MA); special education (MA); teaching (MA).

Brandon University, Faculty of Education, Brandon, MB R7A 6A9, Canada. Offers curriculum and instruction (M Ed, Diploma); educational administration (M Ed, Diploma); guidance and counseling (M Ed, Diploma); special education (M Ed, Diploma). *Degree requirements:* For master's, thesis. *Entrance requirements:* For master's, minimum GPA of 3.0, teaching certificate or equivalent. Additional exam requirements/recommendations for international students: Required—TOEFL. *Faculty research:* Comparative education, environmental studies, parent/school council.

Bridgewater State University, School of Graduate Studies, School of Education and Allied Studies, Department of Secondary Education and Professional Programs, Program in Counseling, Bridgewater, MA 02325-0001. Offers M Ed, CAGS. *Accreditation:* ACA; NCATE. Part-time and evening/weekend programs available. *Entrance requirements:* For master's, GRE General Test.

Brooklyn College of the City University of New York, Division of Graduate Studies, School of Education, Program in School Counseling, Brooklyn, NY 11210-2889. Offers MS Ed, CAS. *Accreditation:* ACA. Part-time programs available. *Degree requirements:* For master's, comprehensive exam, internship. *Entrance requirements:* For master's, interview, 2 letters of recommendation, resume, essay, supplemental application; for CAS, master's degree. Additional exam requirements/recommendations for international students: Required—TOEFL (minimum score 500 paper-based; 61 iBT). Electronic applications accepted. *Faculty research:* Urban school counseling, parent involvement, multicultural competence and counselor training.

Buena Vista University, School of Education, Storm Lake, IA 50588. Offers curriculum and instruction (M Ed), including effective teaching, TESL; school guidance and counseling (MS Ed). Program offered in summer only. Part-time and evening/weekend programs available. Postbaccalaureate distance learning degree programs offered (minimal on-campus study). *Degree requirements:* For master's, thesis, fieldwork/practicum, capstone portfolio. *Entrance requirements:* For master's, Analytical Writing Assessment (in-house), minimum undergraduate GPA of 2.75. Electronic applications accepted. *Faculty research:* Reading, curriculum, educational psychology, special education.

Butler University, College of Education, Indianapolis, IN 46208-3485. Offers educational administration (MS); effective teaching and leadership (MS); school counseling (MS). *Accreditation:* ACA; NCATE. Part-time and evening/weekend programs available. *Faculty:* 6 full-time (4 women), 19 part-time/adjunct (14 women). *Students:* 14 full-time (12 women), 96 part-time (71 women); includes 19 minority (13 Black or African American, non-Hispanic/Latino; 3 Asian, non-Hispanic/Latino; 2 Hispanic/Latino; 1 Two or more races, non-Hispanic/Latino), 3 international. Average age 31. 58 applicants, 79% accepted, 15 enrolled. In 2013, 51 master's awarded. *Entrance requirements:* For master's, GRE General Test, MAT, interview. *Application deadline:* For fall admission, 8/15 priority date for domestic students. Applications are processed on a rolling basis. Application fee: $35. Electronic applications accepted. *Financial support:* Institutionally sponsored loans available. Support available to part-time students. Financial award application deadline: 7/15; financial award applicants required to submit FAFSA. *Unit head:* Dr. Ena Shelley, Dean, 317-940-9752, Fax: 317-940-6481. *Application contact:* Diane Dubord, Graduate Student Services Specialist, 317-940-8100, Fax: 317-940-8250, E-mail: ddubord@butler.edu.
Website: http://www.butler.edu/academics/graduate-coe/.

Caldwell University, Graduate Studies, Department of Psychology, Caldwell, NJ 07006-6195. Offers art therapy (MA); counseling (MA), including art therapy, mental health, school counseling; director of school counseling (Post-Master's Certificate); professional counselor (Post-Master's Certificate); school counselor (Post-Master's Certificate). *Accreditation:* ACA. Part-time and evening/weekend programs available. *Faculty:* 7 full-time (4 women), 10 part-time/adjunct (6 women). *Students:* 58 full-time (51 women), 63 part-time (55 women); includes 30 minority (16 Black or African American, non-Hispanic/Latino; 3 Asian, non-Hispanic/Latino; 10 Hispanic/Latino; 1 Two or more races, non-Hispanic/Latino). Average age 34. 126 applicants, 32% accepted, 33 enrolled. In 2013, 40 master's awarded. *Degree requirements:* For master's, comprehensive exam. *Entrance requirements:* For master's, GRE or MAT, interview. *Application deadline:* For fall admission, 7/1 for domestic and international students; for spring admission, 12/1 for domestic and international students. Applications are processed on a rolling basis. Application fee: $40. Electronic applications accepted. *Financial support:* Career-related internships or fieldwork available. Financial award applicants required to submit FAFSA. *Faculty research:* Counseling, school counseling, art therapy. *Unit head:* Dr. Stacey Solomon, Program Coordinator, 973-618-3387, E-mail: ssolomon@caldwell.edu. *Application contact:* Vilma Mueller, Director of Graduate Studies, 973-618-3544, E-mail: graduate@caldwell.edu.

California Baptist University, Program in Education, Riverside, CA 92504-3206. Offers educational leadership for faith-based institutions (MS); educational leadership for public institutions (MS); educational technology (MS); instructional computer applications (MS); international education (MS); leadership and adult learning (MS); leadership and organizational studies (MS); reading (MS); school counseling (MS); school psychology (MS); science education (MS); special education in mild/moderate disabilities (MS); special education in moderate/severe disabilities (MS); teaching (MS); teaching and learning (MS); TESOL (teachers of English to speakers of other languages) (MS). Part-time and evening/weekend programs available. Postbaccalaureate distance learning degree programs offered (minimal on-campus study). *Faculty:* 18 full-time (9 women), 8 part-time/adjunct (5 women). *Students:* 158 full-time (127 women), 228 part-time (179 women); includes 159 minority (27 Black or African American, non-Hispanic/Latino; 4 American Indian or Alaska Native, non-Hispanic/Latino; 13 Asian, non-Hispanic/Latino; 107 Hispanic/Latino; 1 Native Hawaiian or other Pacific Islander, non-Hispanic/Latino; 7 Two or more races, non-Hispanic/Latino), 2 international. Average age 33. 298 applicants, 74% accepted, 113 enrolled. In 2013, 70 master's awarded. *Degree requirements:* For master's, comprehensive exam, project, or thesis. *Entrance requirements:* For master's, minimum undergraduate GPA of 3.0; 18 semester units of prerequisite course work in education; three recommendations; 500-word essay; interview. Additional exam requirements/recommendations for international students: Required—TOEFL (minimum score 80 iBT). *Application deadline:* For fall admission, 8/1 priority date for domestic students, 7/1 for international students; for spring admission, 12/1 priority date for domestic students, 11/1 for international students. Applications are processed on a rolling basis. Application fee: $45. Electronic applications accepted. *Expenses:* Contact institution. *Financial support:* Institutionally sponsored loans available. Financial award applicants required to submit CSS PROFILE or FAFSA. *Faculty research:* Leadership development, complexity theory, faith and learning, special education, social and philosophical contexts of education. *Unit head:* Dr. John Shoup, Dean, School of Education, 951-343-4205, Fax: 951-343-4516, E-mail: jshoup@calbaptist.edu. *Application contact:* Dr. Kathryn Norwood, Director, Master of Science Program in Education, 951-343-4760, E-mail: knorwood@calbaptist.edu.
Website: http://www.calbaptist.edu/mastersined/.

California Lutheran University, Graduate Studies, Graduate School of Education, Thousand Oaks, CA 91360-2787. Offers counseling and guidance (MS), including college student personnel, counseling and guidance; educational leadership (MA, Ed D), including educational leadership (K-12) (Ed D), higher education leadership (Ed D); special education (MS); teacher leadership (M Ed); teaching (M Ed). *Accreditation:* NCATE. Part-time and evening/weekend programs available. *Faculty:* 18 full-time (14 women), 28 part-time/adjunct (20 women). *Students:* 327 full-time (260 women), 96 part-time (77 women); includes 150 minority (7 Black or African American, non-Hispanic/Latino; 20 Asian, non-Hispanic/Latino; 112 Hispanic/Latino; 11 Two or more races, non-Hispanic/Latino), 1 international. Average age 33. 123 applicants, 85% accepted, 80 enrolled. In 2013, 117 master's, 9 doctorates awarded. *Entrance requirements:* For master's, GRE General Test, interview, minimum GPA of 3.0. *Application deadline:* For fall admission, 7/1 priority date for domestic students; for spring admission, 11/1 priority date for domestic students; for summer admission, 4/1 priority date for domestic students. Applications are processed on a rolling basis. Application fee: $50. *Unit head:* Dr. Robert Fraisse, Dean, 805-493-3421. *Application contact:* 805-493-3325, Fax: 805-493-3861, E-mail: clugrad@callutheran.edu.

California State University, Bakersfield, Division of Graduate Studies, School of Social Sciences and Education, Program in Counseling, Bakersfield, CA 93311. Offers school counseling (MS); student affairs (MS). *Accreditation:* NCATE. *Degree requirements:* For master's, thesis or alternative, culminating projects. *Entrance requirements:* For master's, CBEST (school counseling). *Application deadline:* Applications are processed on a rolling basis. Application fee: $55. *Unit head:* Julia Bavier, Evaluator, Advanced Educational Studies, 661-654-3193, Fax: 661-665-6916, E-mail: jbavier@csub.edu. *Application contact:* Debbie Blowers, Assistant Director of Admissions, 661-664-3381, E-mail: dblowers@csub.edu.
Website: http://www.csub.edu/sse/departments/advancededucationalstudies/educational_counseling/index.html.

California State University, Dominguez Hills, College of Education, Division of Graduate Education, Program in Counseling, Carson, CA 90747-0001. Offers MA. Part-

time and evening/weekend programs available. *Faculty:* 4 full-time (all women), 3 part-time/adjunct (all women). *Students:* 43 full-time (36 women), 14 part-time (11 women); includes 47 minority (7 Black or African American, non-Hispanic/Latino; 4 Asian, non-Hispanic/Latino; 35 Hispanic/Latino; 1 Two or more races, non-Hispanic/Latino). Average age 31. 41 applicants, 49% accepted, 18 enrolled. In 2013, 43 master's awarded. *Degree requirements:* For master's, comprehensive exam. *Entrance requirements:* For master's, minimum GPA of 3.0. *Application deadline:* For fall admission, 4/1 for domestic students; for spring admission, 10/1 for domestic students. Applications are processed on a rolling basis. Application fee: $55. *Expenses:* Tuition, state resident: full-time $6738. Tuition, nonresident: full-time $13,434. *Required fees:* $622. *Faculty research:* Social development. *Unit head:* Dr. Adriean Mancillas, Associate Professor, 310-243-2680, E-mail: amancillas@csudh.edu. *Application contact:* Admissions Office, 310-243-3530.
Website: http://www4.csudh.edu/coe/programs/grad-prgs/pupil-personnel/index.

California State University, East Bay, Office of Academic Programs and Graduate Studies, College of Education and Allied Studies, Department of Educational Psychology, Counseling Program, Hayward, CA 94542-3000. Offers clinical child/school psychology (MS); marriage and family therapy (MS); school counseling (MS). *Accreditation:* NCATE. *Degree requirements:* For master's, comprehensive exam, project or thesis. *Entrance requirements:* For master's, GRE or MAT, interview, minimum GPA of 2.5 during previous 2 years of course work. Additional exam requirements/recommendations for international students: Required—TOEFL (minimum score 550 paper-based). Electronic applications accepted.

California State University, Fresno, Division of Graduate Studies, School of Education and Human Development, Department of Counseling and Special Education, Program in Counseling and Student Services, Fresno, CA 93740-8027. Offers MS. *Accreditation:* NCATE. Part-time and evening/weekend programs available. *Degree requirements:* For master's, thesis or alternative. *Entrance requirements:* For master's, GRE General Test, MAT, minimum GPA of 3.0. Additional exam requirements/recommendations for international students: Required—TOEFL. Electronic applications accepted.

California State University, Fullerton, Graduate Studies, College of Health and Human Development, Department of Counseling, Fullerton, CA 92834-9480. Offers MS. *Accreditation:* ACA; NCATE. Part-time programs available. *Students:* 121 full-time (100 women), 75 part-time (62 women); includes 90 minority (4 Black or African American, non-Hispanic/Latino; 1 American Indian or Alaska Native, non-Hispanic/Latino; 29 Asian, non-Hispanic/Latino; 51 Hispanic/Latino; 5 Two or more races, non-Hispanic/Latino), 2 international. Average age 30. 240 applicants, 26% accepted, 58 enrolled. In 2013, 80 master's awarded. *Degree requirements:* For master's, comprehensive exam, project or thesis. *Entrance requirements:* For master's, minimum GPA of 3.0 in behavioral science and for undergraduate degree. Application fee: $55. *Financial support:* Career-related internships or fieldwork, Federal Work-Study, institutionally sponsored loans, and scholarships/grants available. Support available to part-time students. Financial award application deadline: 3/1; financial award applicants required to submit FAFSA. *Unit head:* Dr. Leah Brew, Chair, 657-278-2708. *Application contact:* Admissions/Applications, 657-278-2371.

California State University, Long Beach, Graduate Studies, College of Education, Department of Advanced Studies in Education and Counseling, Master of Science in Counseling Program, Long Beach, CA 90840. Offers marriage and family therapy (MS); school counseling (MS); student development in higher education (MS). *Accreditation:* NCATE. *Degree requirements:* For master's, comprehensive exam or thesis. Electronic applications accepted.

California State University, Los Angeles, Graduate Studies, Charter College of Education, Division of Special Education and Counseling, Los Angeles, CA 90032-8530. Offers counseling (MS), including applied behavior analysis, community college counseling, rehabilitation counseling, school counseling, school psychology; special education (MA, PhD). *Accreditation:* ACA. Part-time and evening/weekend programs available. *Faculty:* 18 full-time (11 women), 18 part-time/adjunct (12 women). *Students:* 299 full-time (237 women), 278 part-time (211 women); includes 389 minority (32 Black or African American, non-Hispanic/Latino; 1 American Indian or Alaska Native, non-Hispanic/Latino; 53 Asian, non-Hispanic/Latino; 280 Hispanic/Latino; 8 Native Hawaiian or other Pacific Islander, non-Hispanic/Latino; 15 Two or more races, non-Hispanic/Latino), 26 international. Average age 33. 274 applicants, 42% accepted, 100 enrolled. In 2013, 154 master's awarded. *Entrance requirements:* For master's, minimum GPA of 2.75 in last 90 units of course work, teaching certificate. Additional exam requirements/recommendations for international students: Required—TOEFL (minimum score 500 paper-based). *Application deadline:* For fall admission, 5/1 for domestic and international students. Applications are processed on a rolling basis. Application fee: $55. Electronic applications accepted. *Financial support:* Career-related internships or fieldwork and Federal Work-Study available. Support available to part-time students. Financial award application deadline: 3/1. *Unit head:* Dr. Andrea Zetlin, Acting Chair, 323-343-4400, Fax: 323-343-5605, E-mail: azetlin@calstatela.edu. *Application contact:* Dr. Larry Fritz, Dean of Graduate Studies, 323-343-3820, Fax: 323-343-5653, E-mail: lfritz@calstatela.edu.
Website: http://www.calstatela.edu/academic/ccoe/index_edsp.htm.

California State University, Northridge, Graduate Studies, College of Education, Department of Educational Psychology and Counseling, Northridge, CA 91330. Offers counseling (MS), including career counseling, college counseling and student services, marriage and family therapy, school counseling, school psychology; educational psychology (MA Ed), including development, learning, and instruction, early childhood education. *Accreditation:* ACA (one or more programs are accredited); NCATE. Part-time and evening/weekend programs available. *Entrance requirements:* For master's, GRE General Test or minimum GPA of 3.0. Additional exam requirements/recommendations for international students: Required—TOEFL.

California State University, Sacramento, Office of Graduate Studies, College of Education, Department of Counseling, Sacramento, CA 95819. Offers career (MS); marriage, family and child (MS); school counseling (MS); vocational rehabilitation (MS). *Accreditation:* ACA. *Degree requirements:* For master's, thesis or project; writing proficiency exam. *Entrance requirements:* For master's, minimum GPA of 2.5. Additional exam requirements/recommendations for international students: Required—TOEFL. *Application deadline:* For fall admission, 1/14 for domestic students, 3/1 for international students; for spring admission, 9/30 for international students. Applications are processed on a rolling basis. Application fee: $55. Electronic applications accepted. *Financial support:* Career-related internships or fieldwork and Federal Work-Study available. Support available to part-time students. Financial award application deadline: 3/1; financial award applicants required to submit FAFSA. *Unit head:* Rose Borunda, Chair, 916-278-6310, E-mail: rborunda@csus.edu. *Application contact:* Jose Martinez, Graduate Admissions Supervisor, 916-278-7871, E-mail: martinj@skymail.csus.edu.
Website: http://www.edweb.csus.edu/edc.

California State University, San Bernardino, Graduate Studies, College of Education, Program in Educational Psychology and Counseling, San Bernardino, CA 92407-2397. Offers correctional and alternative education (MA); counseling and guidance (MS); rehabilitation counseling (MA). *Accreditation:* NCATE. Part-time and evening/weekend programs available. *Students:* 82 full-time (72 women), 30 part-time (23 women); includes 79 minority (5 Black or African American, non-Hispanic/Latino; 3 Asian, non-Hispanic/Latino; 70 Hispanic/Latino; 1 Native Hawaiian or other Pacific Islander, non-Hispanic/Latino). Average age 28. 55 applicants, 69% accepted, 37 enrolled. In 2013, 25 master's awarded. *Degree requirements:* For master's, comprehensive exam, thesis or alternative, counselor preparation comprehensive examination. *Entrance requirements:* For master's, minimum GPA of 3.0 in education. *Application deadline:* For fall admission, 8/31 priority date for domestic students. Application fee: $55. *Financial support:* Career-related internships or fieldwork and Federal Work-Study available. Support available to part-time students. *Unit head:* Dr. Todd Jennings, Chair, 909-537-5655, Fax: 909-537-7040, E-mail: tjennin@csusb.edu. *Application contact:* Dr. Jeffrey Thompson, Dean of Graduate Studies, 909-537-5058, E-mail: jthompso@csusb.edu.

California State University, Stanislaus, College of Education, Program in Education (MA), Turlock, CA 95382. Offers curriculum and instruction (MA), including education technology, elementary education, multilingual education, physical education, reading, secondary education, special education; school administration (MA); school counseling (MA). Part-time and evening/weekend programs available. *Degree requirements:* For master's, comprehensive exam (for some programs), thesis (for some programs). *Entrance requirements:* For master's, MAT, GRE, or CBEST (varies by concentration), 3 letters of recommendation, personal statement. Additional exam requirements/recommendations for international students: Required—TOEFL (minimum score 550 paper-based). Electronic applications accepted. *Faculty research:* Children's perspectives on historical events, method elementary schools dual language education, K-12 reading programs.

California University of Pennsylvania, School of Graduate Studies and Research, College of Education and Human Services, Department of Counselor Education, California, PA 15419-1394. Offers community and agency counseling (MS); school counseling (M Ed). *Accreditation:* ACA; NCATE. Part-time and evening/weekend programs available. *Degree requirements:* For master's, comprehensive exam, thesis optional. *Entrance requirements:* For master's, MAT, minimum GPA of 3.0, resume, letters of reference. Additional exam requirements/recommendations for international students: Required—TOEFL (minimum score 550 paper-based; 80 iBT). Electronic applications accepted. *Faculty research:* Mind-body theories and practice, grief issues, career development, supervision, sports counseling.

Cambridge College, School of Education, Cambridge, MA 02138-5304. Offers autism specialist (M Ed); autism/behavior analyst (M Ed); behavior analyst (Post-Master's Certificate); behavioral management (M Ed); early childhood teacher (M Ed); education specialist in curriculum and instruction (CAGS); educational leadership (Ed D); elementary teacher (M Ed); English as a second language (M Ed, Certificate); general science (M Ed); health education (Post-Master's Certificate); health/family and consumer sciences (M Ed); history (M Ed); individualized (M Ed); information technology literacy (M Ed); instructional technology (M Ed); interdisciplinary studies (M Ed); library teacher (M Ed); literacy education (M Ed); mathematics (M Ed); mathematics specialist (Certificate); middle school mathematics and science (M Ed); school administration (M Ed, CAGS); school guidance counselor (M Ed); school nurse education (M Ed); school social worker/school adjustment counselor (M Ed); special education administrator (CAGS); special education/moderate disabilities (M Ed); teaching skills and methodologies (M Ed). Part-time and evening/weekend programs available. Postbaccalaureate distance learning degree programs offered (minimal on-campus study). *Degree requirements:* For master's, thesis, internship/practicum (licensure program only); for doctorate, thesis/dissertation; for other advanced degree, thesis. *Entrance requirements:* For master's, interview, resume, documentation of licensure, 2 professional references; for doctorate, official transcripts, interview, resume, documentation of licensure (if any), written personal statement/essay, portfolio of scholarly and professional work, qualifying assessment, 2 professional references, health insurance, immunizations form; for other advanced degree, official transcripts, interview, resume, documentation of licensure (if any), written personal statement/essay, 2 professional references, health insurance, immunizations form. Additional exam requirements/recommendations for international students: Required—TOEFL (minimum score 550 paper-based; 79 iBT), Michigan English Language Assessment Battery (minimum score 85); Recommended—IELTS (minimum score 6). Electronic applications accepted. *Expenses:* Contact institution. *Faculty research:* Adult education, accelerated learning, mathematics education, brain compatible learning, special education and law.

Cambridge College, School of Psychology and Counseling, Cambridge, MA 02138-5304. Offers addiction counseling (M Ed); alcohol and drug counseling (Certificate); counseling psychology (M Ed, CAGS); counseling psychology: forensic counseling (M Ed); marriage and family therapy (M Ed); mental health and addiction counseling (M Ed); mental health counseling (M Ed); mental health counseling for school guidance counselors (Post Master's Certificate); psychological studies (M Ed); school adjustment and mental health counseling (M Ed); school adjustment, mental health and addiction counseling (M Ed); school guidance counselor (M Ed); trauma studies (Certificate). Part-time and evening/weekend programs available. *Degree requirements:* For master's and other advanced degree, thesis, practicum/internship. *Entrance requirements:* For master's, resume, 2 professional references; for other advanced degree, official transcripts, documents for transfer credit evaluation, resume, written personal statement/essay, 2 professional references, health insurance, immunizations form. Additional exam requirements/recommendations for international students: Required—TOEFL (minimum score 550 paper-based; 79 iBT), Michigan English Language Assessment Battery (minimum score 85); Recommended—IELTS (minimum score 6). Electronic applications accepted. *Expenses:* Contact institution. *Faculty research:* Trauma, drug and alcohol counseling, cross-cultural issues, school counseling, trauma in schools.

Campbellsville University, Carver School of Social Work, Campbellsville, KY 42718-2799. Offers counseling (MA); social work (MA). *Accreditation:* CSWE. Part-time and evening/weekend programs available. Postbaccalaureate distance learning degree programs offered (minimal on-campus study). *Entrance requirements:* For master's, GRE. Electronic applications accepted.

Campbell University, Graduate and Professional Programs, School of Education, Buies Creek, NC 27506. Offers administration (MSA); community counseling (MA); elementary education (M Ed); English education (M Ed); interdisciplinary studies (M Ed); mathematics education (M Ed); middle grades education (M Ed); physical education (M Ed); school counseling (M Ed); secondary education (M Ed); social science education (M Ed). *Accreditation:* NCATE. Part-time and evening/weekend programs available. *Degree requirements:* For master's, comprehensive exam. *Entrance requirements:* For master's, GRE General Test, minimum GPA of 2.7. *Faculty research:* Spiritual values and wellness issues in counseling, stress and professional burnout among counselors, thinking strategies, leadership, adaptive technology.

Canisius College, Graduate Division, School of Education and Human Services, Programs in Counseling and Human Services, Buffalo, NY 14208-1098. Offers community mental health counseling (MS); counseling and human services (MS); school agency counseling (MS). *Accreditation:* ACA. Part-time and evening/weekend programs available. *Faculty:* 7 full-time (4 women), 10 part-time/adjunct (8 women). *Students:* 89

full-time (76 women), 60 part-time (48 women); includes 26 minority (16 Black or African American, non-Hispanic/Latino; 4 Asian, non-Hispanic/Latino; 6 Hispanic/Latino). Average age 28. 102 applicants, 80% accepted, 42 enrolled. In 2013, 51 master's awarded. *Degree requirements:* For master's, thesis, research project. *Entrance requirements:* For master's, GRE if cumulative GPA less than 2.7, transcripts, two letters of recommendation, interview, BA. Additional exam requirements/recommendations for international students: Required—TOEFL (minimum score 550 paper-based, 80 iBT), IELTS (minimum score 6.5), or CAEL (minimum score 70). *Application deadline:* Applications are processed on a rolling basis. Application fee: $25. Electronic applications accepted. Application fee is waived when completed online. *Expenses: Tuition:* Part-time $750 per credit hour. *Financial support:* Research assistantships, career-related internships or fieldwork, Federal Work-Study, scholarships/grants, tuition waivers (partial), and unspecified assistantships available. Support available to part-time students. Financial award application deadline: 4/30; financial award applicants required to submit FAFSA. *Faculty research:* Impact of trauma on adults, long term psych-social impact on police officers. *Unit head:* Dr. Christine Moll, Chair, 716-888-3287, E-mail: moll@canisius.edu. *Application contact:* Julie A. Zulewski, Director of Graduate Admissions, 716-888-2548, Fax: 716-888-3195, E-mail: zulewskj@canisius.edu. Website: http://www.canisius.edu/masters-counseling/.

Capella University, Harold Abel School of Social and Behavioral Science, Doctoral Programs in Counseling, Minneapolis, MN 55402. Offers general counselor education and supervision (PhD); general social work (DSW).

Capella University, Harold Abel School of Social and Behavioral Science, Master's Programs in Counseling, Minneapolis, MN 55402. Offers child and adolescent development (MS); general addiction counseling (MS); general marriage and family counseling/therapy (MS); general mental health counseling (MS); general school counseling (MS).

Carlow University, School for Social Change, Program in Professional Counseling, Pittsburgh, PA 15213-3165. Offers drug and alcohol counseling (MS); professional counseling (MS); school counseling (MS); school counselor (Certificate). Part-time and evening/weekend programs available. *Students:* 193 full-time (163 women), 23 part-time (21 women); includes 39 minority (28 Black or African American, non-Hispanic/Latino; 2 Asian, non-Hispanic/Latino; 3 Hispanic/Latino; 6 Two or more races, non-Hispanic/Latino). Average age 31. 104 applicants, 95% accepted, 45 enrolled. In 2013, 63 master's awarded. *Entrance requirements:* For master's, personal essay; resume or curriculum vitae; three recommendations; official transcripts; interview; minimum undergraduate GPA of 3.0; undergraduate courses in statistics, abnormal psychology, and personality theory; undergraduate work or work experience in the helping professions. Additional exam requirements/recommendations for international students: Required—TOEFL (minimum score 550 paper-based). Application fee: $20. Application fee is waived when completed online. *Expenses: Tuition:* Full-time $9523; part-time $744 per credit. Tuition and fees vary according to course load, degree level and program. *Unit head:* Dr. Joseph Roberts, Director, Master in Professional Counseling Program, 412-575-6331, E-mail: jmroberts@carlow.edu. *Application contact:* Dr. Kathleen A. Chrisman, Associate Director, Graduate Admissions, 412-578-8812, Fax: 412-578-6321, E-mail: kachrisman@carlow.edu. Website: http://www.carlow.edu/Master_of_Science_in_Professional_Counseling.aspx.

Carson-Newman University, Graduate Program in Education, Jefferson City, TN 37760. Offers curriculum and instruction (M Ed); educational leadership (M Ed); elementary education (MAT); school counseling (MS); secondary education (MAT); teaching English as a second language (MATESL). *Accreditation:* NCATE. Part-time and evening/weekend programs available. *Faculty:* 5 full-time (2 women), 10 part-time/adjunct (3 women). *Students:* 25 full-time (12 women), 100 part-time (70 women); includes 8 minority (4 Black or African American, non-Hispanic/Latino; 1 Asian, non-Hispanic/Latino; 1 Hispanic/Latino; 2 Two or more races, non-Hispanic/Latino), 1 international. Average age 32. In 2013, 34 master's awarded. *Degree requirements:* For master's, thesis or alternative. *Entrance requirements:* For master's, NTE, minimum GPA of 3.0 in major, 2.5 overall. *Application deadline:* For fall admission, 7/15 priority date for domestic students. Applications are processed on a rolling basis. Application fee: $25 ($50 for international students). *Expenses: Tuition:* Part-time $390 per credit hour. *Financial support:* Federal Work-Study and unspecified assistantships available. Financial award application deadline: 4/1; financial award applicants required to submit FAFSA. *Unit head:* Dr. Sharon Teets, Chair, 865-471-3461. *Application contact:* Graduate Admissions and Services Adviser, 865-471-3460, Fax: 865-471-3875.

Carson-Newman University, Program in School Counseling, Jefferson City, TN 37760. Offers MSC. *Expenses: Tuition:* Part-time $390 per credit hour.

Carthage College, Division of Teacher Education, Kenosha, WI 53140. Offers classroom guidance and counseling (M Ed); creative arts (M Ed); gifted and talented children (M Ed); language arts (M Ed); modern language (M Ed); natural sciences (M Ed); reading (M Ed, Certificate); social sciences (M Ed); teacher leadership (M Ed). Part-time and evening/weekend programs available. *Degree requirements:* For master's, thesis optional. *Entrance requirements:* For master's, MAT, minimum B average, letters of reference.

Central Connecticut State University, School of Graduate Studies, School of Education and Professional Studies, Department of Counseling and Family Therapy, New Britain, CT 06050-4010. Offers marriage and family therapy (MS); professional counseling (MS, AC, Certificate); school counseling (MS); student development in higher education (MS). *Accreditation:* AAMFT/COAMFTE; ACA. Part-time and evening/weekend programs available. *Faculty:* 8 full-time (5 women), 24 part-time/adjunct (20 women). *Students:* 154 full-time (124 women), 213 part-time (168 women); includes 105 minority (58 Black or African American, non-Hispanic/Latino; 5 Asian, non-Hispanic/Latino; 36 Hispanic/Latino; 6 Two or more races, non-Hispanic/Latino), 2 international. Average age 35. 238 applicants, 49% accepted, 94 enrolled. In 2013, 91 master's, 6 other advanced degrees awarded. *Degree requirements:* For master's, comprehensive exam, thesis or alternative; for other advanced degree, qualifying exam. *Entrance requirements:* For master's, minimum undergraduate GPA of 2.7, essay, interview, letters of recommendation. Additional exam requirements/recommendations for international students: Required—TOEFL (minimum score 550 paper-based; 79 iBT). *Application deadline:* For fall admission, 4/1 for domestic and international students; for spring admission, 11/1 for domestic and international students. Applications are processed on a rolling basis. Application fee: $50. Electronic applications accepted. Part-time tuition and fees vary according to degree level. *Financial support:* In 2013–14, 38 students received support, including 14 research assistantships; career-related internships or fieldwork, Federal Work-Study, scholarships/grants, and unspecified assistantships also available. Support available to part-time students. Financial award application deadline: 3/1; financial award applicants required to submit FAFSA. *Faculty research:* Elementary/secondary school counseling, marriage/family therapy, rehabilitation counseling, counseling in higher educational settings. *Unit head:* Dr. Connie Tait, Chair, 860-832-2154, E-mail: taitc@ccsu.edu. *Application contact:* Patricia Gardner, Associate Director of Graduate Studies, 860-832-2350, Fax: 860-832-2362, E-mail: graduateadmissions@ccsu.edu. Website: http://www.ccsu.edu/page.cfm?p=1354.

Central Methodist University, College of Graduate and Extended Studies, Fayette, MO 65248-1198. Offers clinical counseling (MS); clinical nurse leader (MSN); education (M Ed); music education (MME); nurse educator (MSN). Part-time and evening/weekend programs available. Postbaccalaureate distance learning degree programs offered (no on-campus study). *Degree requirements:* For master's, thesis. *Entrance requirements:* For master's, GRE General Test, minimum GPA of 2.75. *Application deadline:* Applications are processed on a rolling basis. Application fee: $25. Electronic applications accepted. *Expenses: Tuition:* Part-time $360 per credit hour. Part-time tuition and fees vary according to campus/location and program. *Financial support:* Tuition waivers available. Support available to part-time students. Financial award application deadline: 6/5; financial award applicants required to submit FAFSA. *Unit head:* Dr. Rita Gulstad, Provost, 660-248-6212, Fax: 660-248-6392, E-mail: rgulstad@centralmethodist.edu. *Application contact:* Aimee Sage, Director of Graduate Admissions, 660-248-6651, Fax: 660-248-6392, E-mail: asage@centralmethodist.edu. Website: http://www.centralmethodist.edu/graduate/.

Central Michigan University, Central Michigan University Global Campus, Program in Counseling, Mount Pleasant, MI 48859. Offers professional counseling (MA); school counseling (MA). *Accreditation:* Teacher Education Accreditation Council. Part-time and evening/weekend programs available. *Entrance requirements:* For master's, MAT, minimum GPA of 2.7. Additional exam requirements/recommendations for international students: Required—TOEFL. Electronic applications accepted. *Financial support:* Scholarships/grants available. Support available to part-time students. *Unit head:* Dr. Twinet Parmer, Chair, 989-774-3776, E-mail: parme1t@cmich.edu. *Application contact:* 877-268-4636, E-mail: cmuglobal@cmich.edu.

Central Michigan University, College of Graduate Studies, College of Education and Human Services, Department of Counseling and Special Education, Program in Counseling, Mount Pleasant, MI 48859. Offers counseling (MA), including professional counseling, school counseling. *Accreditation:* Teacher Education Accreditation Council. Part-time programs available. *Degree requirements:* For master's, comprehensive exam, thesis or alternative. *Entrance requirements:* For master's, MAT, eligible for Michigan Teacher Certification (for school counseling). Electronic applications accepted. *Faculty research:* School counseling, professional counseling.

Central Washington University, Graduate Studies and Research, College of the Sciences, Department of Psychology, Program in School Counseling, Ellensburg, WA 98926. Offers M Ed. *Degree requirements:* For master's, thesis or alternative, internship. *Entrance requirements:* For master's, GRE General Test, minimum GPA of 3.0. Additional exam requirements/recommendations for international students: Required—TOEFL (minimum score 550 paper-based; 79 iBT). Electronic applications accepted.

Chadron State College, School of Professional and Graduate Studies, Department of Education, Chadron, NE 69337. Offers business (MA Ed); community counseling (MA Ed); educational administration (MS Ed, Sp Ed); elementary education (MS Ed); history (MA Ed); language and literature (MA Ed); secondary administration (MS Ed); secondary education (MS Ed). *Accreditation:* NCATE. Part-time and evening/weekend programs available. Postbaccalaureate distance learning degree programs offered. *Degree requirements:* For master's, thesis optional. *Entrance requirements:* For master's, GRE General Test, GRE Writing Test, minimum GPA of 2.75 or 12 graduate hours at CSC with minimum GPA of 3.25. Additional exam requirements/recommendations for international students: Required—TOEFL. Electronic applications accepted. *Faculty research:* Rural education, technology, mental health.

Chapman University, College of Educational Studies, Orange, CA 92866. Offers communication sciences and disorders (MS); counseling (MA), including school counseling (MA, Credential); education (PhD), including cultural and curricular studies, disability studies, leadership studies, school psychology (PhD, Credential); educational psychology (MA); leadership development (MA); pupil personnel services (Credential), including school counseling (MA, Credential), school psychology (PhD, Credential); school psychology (Ed S); single subject (Credential); special education (MA, Credential), including mild/moderate (Credential), moderate/severe (Credential); speech language pathology (Credential); teaching (MA), including elementary education, secondary education. *Accreditation:* Teacher Education Accreditation Council. Part-time and evening/weekend programs available. *Faculty:* 29 full-time (18 women), 56 part-time/adjunct (38 women). *Students:* 251 full-time (208 women), 194 part-time (150 women); includes 185 minority (13 Black or African American, non-Hispanic/Latino; 61 Asian, non-Hispanic/Latino; 97 Hispanic/Latino; 1 Native Hawaiian or other Pacific Islander, non-Hispanic/Latino; 13 Two or more races, non-Hispanic/Latino), 7 international. Average age 29. 580 applicants, 42% accepted, 166 enrolled. In 2013, 140 master's, 10 doctorates awarded. *Entrance requirements:* Additional exam requirements/recommendations for international students: Required—TOEFL (minimum score 550 paper-based; 80 iBT). *Application deadline:* Applications are processed on a rolling basis. Application fee: $60. Electronic applications accepted. Tuition and fees vary according to program. *Financial support:* Fellowships and scholarships/grants available. Financial award application deadline: 6/30; financial award applicants required to submit FAFSA. *Unit head:* Dr. Don Cardinal, Dean, 714-997-6781, E-mail: cardinal@chapman.edu. *Application contact:* Admissions Coordinator, 714-997-6714. Website: http://www.chapman.edu/CES/.

Chicago State University, School of Graduate and Professional Studies, College of Arts and Sciences, Department of Psychology, Chicago, IL 60628. Offers counseling (MA). *Accreditation:* ACA; NCATE. *Degree requirements:* For master's, comprehensive exam, thesis optional. *Entrance requirements:* For master's, minimum GPA of 3.0 for last 60 semester hours of course work or essay; interview.

The Citadel, The Military College of South Carolina, Citadel Graduate College, Department of Psychology, Charleston, SC 29409. Offers psychology (MA), including clinical counseling; school psychology (Ed S), including school psychology. Part-time and evening/weekend programs available. *Faculty:* 11 full-time (3 women), 3 part-time/adjunct (2 women). *Students:* 61 full-time (54 women), 60 part-time (55 women); includes 15 minority (9 Black or African American, non-Hispanic/Latino; 3 Asian, non-Hispanic/Latino; 3 Hispanic/Latino). Average age 28. In 2013, 14 master's, 11 other advanced degrees awarded. *Degree requirements:* For master's, comprehensive exam, thesis optional; for Ed S, comprehensive exam, thesis, internship. *Entrance requirements:* For master's, GRE (minimum score of 297, 150 on the verbal reasoning and 141 on the quantitative reasoning section) or MAT (minimum score of 410), minimum undergraduate GPA of 3.0; 2 letters of reference; for Ed S, GRE (minimum score of 297, 150 on the verbal reasoning and 141 on the quantitative reasoning section) or MAT (minimum score of 410), minimum undergraduate or graduate GPA of 3.0; 2 letters of reference. Additional exam requirements/recommendations for international students: Required—TOEFL (minimum score 550 paper-based). *Application deadline:* For fall admission, 3/15 for domestic students. Application fee: $30. Electronic applications accepted. *Expenses: Tuition, area resident:* Part-time $525 per credit hour. Tuition, state resident: part-time $525 per credit hour. Tuition, nonresident: part-time $865 per credit hour. *Financial support:* Research assistantships, career-related internships or fieldwork, health care benefits, and unspecified assistantships available. Support available to part-time students. Financial award application deadline: 7/1; financial award applicants required to submit FAFSA. *Faculty*

research: Ostracism and social exclusion, bullying, social concerns of special-needs children, childhood obesity, phantom limb pain, validation of psychological tests, perfectionism, school-based interventions with at-risk children. *Unit head:* Dr. Steve A. Nida, Department Head, 843-953-6702, Fax: 843-953-6797, E-mail: steve.nida@citadel.edu. *Application contact:* Dr. William G. Johnson, Program Director, 843-953-6827, Fax: 843-953-6769, E-mail: will.johnson@citadel.edu.
Website: http://www.citadel.edu/root/psychology-graduateprograms.

The Citadel, The Military College of South Carolina, Citadel Graduate College, School of Education, Program in Guidance and Counseling, Charleston, SC 29409. Offers elementary/secondary school counseling (M Ed); student affairs and college counseling (M Ed). *Accreditation:* ACA; NCATE. Part-time and evening/weekend programs available. *Faculty:* 10 full-time (6 women), 8 part-time/adjunct (3 women). *Students:* 15 full-time (14 women), 40 part-time (35 women); includes 13 minority (12 Black or African American, non-Hispanic/Latino; 1 Two or more races, non-Hispanic/Latino). Average age 30. In 2013, 27 master's awarded. *Degree requirements:* For master's, comprehensive exam, practicum or internship. *Entrance requirements:* For master's, GRE (minimum score 290; 900 on old scoring system) or MAT (minimum score 396), minimum undergraduate GPA of 3.0, 3 letters of reference, group interview. Additional exam requirements/recommendations for international students: Required—TOEFL (minimum score 550 paper-based; 79 iBT). *Application deadline:* For fall admission, 6/1 for domestic students; for spring admission, 10/1 for domestic students. Application fee: $30. Electronic applications accepted. *Expenses: Tuition, area resident:* Part-time $525 per credit hour. Tuition, state resident: part-time $525 per credit hour. Tuition, nonresident: part-time $865 per credit hour. *Financial support:* Career-related internships or fieldwork, health care benefits, and unspecified assistantships available. Support available to part-time students. Financial award application deadline: 7/1; financial award applicants required to submit FAFSA. *Unit head:* Dr. George T. Williams, Director, 843-953-2205, Fax: 843-953-7258, E-mail: williamsg@citadel.edu. *Application contact:* Dr. Robert H. McNamara, Associate Provost, The Citadel Graduate College, 843-953-5089, Fax: 843-953-7630, E-mail: cgc@citadel.edu.
Website: http://www.citadel.edu/education/counselor.html.

Clark Atlanta University, School of Education, Department of Counseling and Psychological Studies, Atlanta, GA 30314. Offers MA. *Accreditation:* ACA. Part-time programs available. *Faculty:* 4 full-time (1 woman), 4 part-time/adjunct (2 women). *Students:* 33 full-time (28 women), 5 part-time (all women); includes 36 minority (all Black or African American, non-Hispanic/Latino). Average age 26. 23 applicants, 96% accepted, 17 enrolled. In 2013, 10 master's awarded. *Degree requirements:* For master's, comprehensive exam. *Entrance requirements:* For master's, GRE General Test, minimum undergraduate GPA of 2.6. Additional exam requirements/recommendations for international students: Required—TOEFL (minimum score 500 paper-based; 61 iBT). *Application deadline:* For fall admission, 4/1 for domestic and international students; for spring admission, 11/1 for domestic and international students. Applications are processed on a rolling basis. Application fee: $40 ($55 for international students). Electronic applications accepted. *Expenses: Tuition:* Full-time $14,616; part-time $812 per credit hour. *Required fees:* $706; $353 per semester. *Financial support:* Career-related internships or fieldwork, Federal Work-Study, scholarships/grants, and unspecified assistantships available. Support available to part-time students. Financial award application deadline: 4/30; financial award applicants required to submit FAFSA. *Unit head:* Dr. Noran Moffett, Interim Chairperson, 404-880-6330, E-mail: nmoffett@cau.edu. *Application contact:* Michelle Clark-Davis, Graduate Program Admissions, 404-880-6605, E-mail: cauadmissions@cau.edu.

Clemson University, Graduate School, College of Health, Education, and Human Development, Eugene T. Moore School of Education, Program in Counselor Education, Clemson, SC 29634. Offers clinical mental health counseling (M Ed); community mental health (M Ed); school counseling (K-12) (M Ed); student affairs (higher education) (M Ed). *Accreditation:* ACA; NCATE. Part-time and evening/weekend programs available. *Students:* 135 full-time (109 women), 14 part-time (10 women); includes 29 minority (17 Black or African American, non-Hispanic/Latino; 3 Asian, non-Hispanic/Latino; 6 Hispanic/Latino; 1 Native Hawaiian or other Pacific Islander, non-Hispanic/Latino; 2 Two or more races, non-Hispanic/Latino), 1 international. Average age 24. 271 applicants, 43% accepted, 63 enrolled. In 2013, 47 master's awarded. *Degree requirements:* For master's, comprehensive exam. *Entrance requirements:* For master's, GRE General Test. Additional exam requirements/recommendations for international students: Required—TOEFL; Recommended—IELTS. *Application deadline:* For fall admission, 2/1 priority date for domestic students; for spring admission, 10/1 for domestic students. Applications are processed on a rolling basis. Application fee: $70 ($80 for international students). Electronic applications accepted. *Expenses:* Contact institution. *Financial support:* In 2013–14, 84 students received support, including 9 research assistantships with partial tuition reimbursements available (averaging $7,586 per year), 3 teaching assistantships with partial tuition reimbursements available (averaging $22,987 per year); institutionally sponsored loans, health care benefits, and unspecified assistantships also available. Financial award application deadline: 6/1; financial award applicants required to submit FAFSA. *Faculty research:* At-risk youth, ethnic identity development across the life span, postsecondary transitions and college readiness, distance and distributed learning environments, the student veteran experience in college, student development theory. *Unit head:* Dr. Michael J. Padilla, Director/Associate Dean, 864-656-4444, Fax: 864-656-0311, E-mail: padilla@clemson.edu. *Application contact:* Dr. David Fleming, Graduate Coordinator, 864-656-1881, Fax: 864-656-0311, E-mail: dflemin@clemson.edu.

Cleveland State University, College of Graduate Studies, College of Education and Human Services, Department of Counseling, Administration, Supervision and Adult Learning (CASAL), Cleveland, OH 44115. Offers adult learning and development (M Ed); chemical dependency counseling (Certificate); clinical mental health counseling (M Ed); early childhood mental health counseling (Certificate); educational administration and supervision (M Ed); organizational leadership (M Ed); school administration (Ed S); school counseling (M Ed). *Accreditation:* ACA (one or more programs are accredited). Part-time and evening/weekend programs available. *Faculty:* 15 full-time (8 women), 19 part-time/adjunct (10 women). *Students:* 79 full-time (61 women), 237 part-time (188 women); includes 101 minority (86 Black or African American, non-Hispanic/Latino; 3 Asian, non-Hispanic/Latino; 11 Hispanic/Latino; 1 Two or more races, non-Hispanic/Latino), 8 international. Average age 36. 131 applicants, 69% accepted, 49 enrolled. In 2013, 99 master's, 7 Certificates awarded. *Degree requirements:* For master's, comprehensive exam (for some programs), thesis optional, internship. *Entrance requirements:* For master's, GRE General Test or MAT, letter of recommendation and minimum GPA of 2.75 (for counseling); 2 letters of recommendation and interviews (for organizational leadership). Additional exam requirements/recommendations for international students: Required—TOEFL (minimum score 525 paper-based), IELTS (minimum score 6). *Application deadline:* For fall admission, 6/21 for domestic students, 5/15 for international students; for spring admission, 8/31 for domestic students, 11/1 for international students. Application fee: $30. Electronic applications accepted. *Expenses:* Tuition, state resident: full-time $8335; part-time $521 per credit hour. Tuition, nonresident: full-time $15,670; part-time $979 per credit hour. *Required fees:* $50; $25 per semester. *Financial support:* In 2013–14, 19 students received support, including 10 research assistantships with full and partial tuition reimbursements available (averaging $11,882 per year), 5 teaching assistantships with full and partial tuition reimbursements available (averaging $11,882 per year); scholarships/grants and unspecified assistantships also available. Support available to part-time students. *Faculty research:* Education law, career development, bullying, psychopharmacology, counseling and spirituality. *Total annual research expenditures:* $225,821. *Unit head:* Dr. Ann L. Bauer, Chairperson, 216-687-4582, Fax: 216-687-5378, E-mail: a.l.bauer@csuohio.edu. *Application contact:* Deborah L. Brown, Interim Assistant Director, Graduate Admissions, 216-523-7572, Fax: 216-687-5400, E-mail: d.l.brown@csuohio.edu.
Website: http://www.csuohio.edu/cehs/departments/CASAL/casal_dept.html.

Cleveland State University, College of Graduate Studies, College of Education and Human Services, Program in Urban Education, Specialization in Counselor Education, Cleveland, OH 44115. Offers PhD. Part-time programs available. *Faculty:* 8 full-time (5 women). *Students:* 7 full-time (5 women), 14 part-time (11 women); includes 3 minority (2 Black or African American, non-Hispanic/Latino; 1 Two or more races, non-Hispanic/Latino), 2 international. Average age 37. 36 applicants, 28% accepted, 3 enrolled. *Degree requirements:* For doctorate, one foreign language, comprehensive exam, thesis/dissertation. *Entrance requirements:* For doctorate, General GRE Test (minimum score of 297 for combined Verbal and Quantitative exams, 4.0 preferred for Analytical Writing), minimum graduate GPA of 3.25 in counseling, psychology, or social work, curriculum vitae or resume, personal statement, 2 letters of recommendation. Additional exam requirements/recommendations for international students: Required—TOEFL (minimum score 525 paper-based), IELTS (minimum score 6). *Expenses:* Tuition, state resident: full-time $8335; part-time $521 per credit hour. Tuition, nonresident: full-time $15,670; part-time $979 per credit hour. *Required fees:* $50; $25 per semester. *Financial support:* Application deadline: 4/1; applicants required to submit FAFSA. *Faculty research:* Theory and practice of counseling within a multicultural, diverse urban society. *Unit head:* Dr. Graham Stead, Director, Doctoral Studies, 216-875-9869, E-mail: g.b.stead@csuohio.edu. *Application contact:* Rita M. Grabowski, Administrative Coordinator, 216-687-4697, Fax: 216-875-9697, E-mail: r.grabowski@csuohio.edu.
Website: http://www.csuohio.edu/cehs/departments/DOC/ce_doc.html.

The College at Brockport, State University of New York, School of Education and Human Services, Department of Counselor Education, Brockport, NY 14420-2997. Offers college counseling (MS Ed, CAS); mental health counseling (MS, CAS); school counseling (MS Ed, CAS); school counselor supervision (CAS). *Accreditation:* ACA (one or more programs are accredited). Part-time programs available. *Faculty:* 6 full-time (4 women), 5 part-time/adjunct (4 women). *Students:* 26 full-time (22 women), 62 part-time (48 women); includes 19 minority (11 Black or African American, non-Hispanic/Latino; 1 American Indian or Alaska Native, non-Hispanic/Latino; 1 Asian, non-Hispanic/Latino; 4 Hispanic/Latino; 2 Two or more races, non-Hispanic/Latino). 73 applicants, 30% accepted, 15 enrolled. In 2013, 20 master's, 7 other advanced degrees awarded. *Degree requirements:* For master's, thesis, internship. *Entrance requirements:* For master's, group interview, letters of recommendation, written objectives; for CAS, master's degree, New York state school counselor certificate. Additional exam requirements/recommendations for international students: Required—TOEFL (minimum score 550 paper-based; 79 iBT), IELTS (minimum score 6.5). *Application deadline:* For fall admission, 2/1 priority date for domestic and international students; for spring admission, 9/1 priority date for domestic and international students; for summer admission, 2/1 priority date for domestic and international students. Application fee: $80. Electronic applications accepted. *Expenses:* Tuition, state resident: full-time $9870. Tuition, nonresident: full-time $18,350. *Required fees:* $1848. *Financial support:* In 2013–14, 1 fellowship with full tuition reimbursement (averaging $7,500 per year), 1 teaching assistantship with full tuition reimbursement (averaging $6,000 per year) were awarded; Federal Work-Study, scholarships/grants, and unspecified assistantships also available. Support available to part-time students. Financial award application deadline: 3/15; financial award applicants required to submit FAFSA. *Faculty research:* Gender and diversity issues; counseling outcomes; spirituality; school, college and mental health counseling; obesity. *Unit head:* Dr. Thomas Hernandez, Chair, 585-395-2258, Fax: 585-395-2366, E-mail: thernandez@brockport.edu. *Application contact:* Danielle A. Welch, Graduate Admissions Counselor, 585-395-5465, Fax: 585-395-2515.
Website: http://www.brockport.edu/edc/.

The College of New Jersey, Graduate Studies, School of Education, Department of Counselor Education, Program in Community Counseling: Human Services Specialization, Ewing, NJ 08628. Offers MA. *Accreditation:* ACA. Part-time programs available. *Degree requirements:* For master's, comprehensive exam. *Entrance requirements:* For master's, GRE General Test, minimum GPA of 3.0 in field or 2.75 overall, interview. Additional exam requirements/recommendations for international students: Required—TOEFL. Electronic applications accepted.

The College of New Jersey, Graduate Studies, School of Education, Department of Counselor Education, Program in School Counseling, Ewing, NJ 08628. Offers MA. *Accreditation:* ACA; NCATE. Part-time programs available. *Degree requirements:* For master's, comprehensive exam. *Entrance requirements:* For master's, GRE General Test, minimum GPA of 3.0 in field or 2.75 overall, interview. Additional exam requirements/recommendations for international students: Required—TOEFL. Electronic applications accepted.

College of St. Joseph, Graduate Programs, Division of Psychology and Human Services, Rutland, VT 05701-3899. Offers alcohol and substance abuse counseling (MS); clinical mental health counseling (MS); clinical psychology (MS); community counseling (MS); school guidance counseling (MS). Part-time and evening/weekend programs available. *Degree requirements:* For master's, comprehensive exam, thesis optional. *Entrance requirements:* For master's, official college transcripts; 2 letters of reference. Additional exam requirements/recommendations for international students: Required—TOEFL (minimum score 550 paper-based). Electronic applications accepted.

The College of Saint Rose, Graduate Studies, School of Education, Program in Counseling, Albany, NY 12203-1419. Offers counseling (MS Ed), including mental health counseling, school counseling; mental health counseling (Certificate); school counseling (Certificate). Part-time and evening/weekend programs available. *Entrance requirements:* For master's, minimum undergraduate GPA of 3.0. Additional exam requirements/recommendations for international students: Required—TOEFL (minimum score 550 paper-based). Electronic applications accepted.

The College of William and Mary, School of Education, Program in Counselor Education, Williamsburg, VA 23187-8795. Offers community and addictions counseling (M Ed); community counseling (M Ed); counselor education (PhD); family counseling (M Ed); school counseling (M Ed). *Accreditation:* ACA; NCATE. Part-time and evening/weekend programs available. *Faculty:* 7 full-time (3 women), 8 part-time/adjunct (4 women). *Students:* 73 full-time (55 women), 11 part-time (9 women); includes 13 minority (6 Black or African American, non-Hispanic/Latino; 1 American Indian or Alaska Native, non-Hispanic/Latino; 2 Asian, non-Hispanic/Latino; 2 Hispanic/Latino; 2 Two or more races, non-Hispanic/Latino), 2 international. Average age 29. 173 applicants, 42% accepted, 36 enrolled. In 2013, 22 master's, 5 doctorates awarded. *Degree requirements:* For doctorate, comprehensive exam, thesis/dissertation. *Entrance requirements:* For master's, GRE, minimum GPA of 3.0; for doctorate, GRE, minimum GPA of 3.5. Additional exam requirements/recommendations for international students:

Required—TOEFL, IELTS. *Application deadline:* For fall admission, 1/15 for domestic and international students. Application fee: $50. Electronic applications accepted. *Expenses:* Tuition, state resident: full-time $7120; part-time $405 per credit hour. Tuition, nonresident: full-time $21,639; part-time $1050 per credit hour. *Required fees:* $4764. *Financial support:* In 2013–14, 31 students received support, including 28 research assistantships with full tuition reimbursements available (averaging $15,000 per year); career-related internships or fieldwork, Federal Work-Study, institutionally sponsored loans, scholarships/grants, and unspecified assistantships also available. Financial award application deadline: 1/15; financial award applicants required to submit FAFSA. *Faculty research:* Sexuality, multicultural education, substance abuse, transpersonal psychology. *Unit head:* Dr. Charles F. Gressard, Area Coordinator, 757-221-2352, E-mail: cfgres@wm.edu. *Application contact:* Dorothy Smith Osborne, Assistant Dean for Academic Programs and Student Services, 757-221-2317, Fax: 757-221-2293, E-mail: dsosbo@wm.edu.
Website: http://education.wm.edu.

Colorado State University, Graduate School, College of Health and Human Sciences, School of Education, Fort Collins, CO 80523-1588. Offers adult education and training (M Ed); community college leadership (PhD); counseling and career development (M Ed); education and human resource studies (M Ed, PhD); educational leadership (M Ed, PhD); interdisciplinary studies (PhD); organizational performance and change (M Ed, PhD); student affairs in higher education (MS). *Accreditation:* ACA; Teacher Education Accreditation Council. Part-time and evening/weekend programs available. *Faculty:* 19 full-time (10 women). *Students:* 84 full-time (60 women), 545 part-time (356 women); includes 115 minority (26 Black or African American, non-Hispanic/Latino; 5 American Indian or Alaska Native, non-Hispanic/Latino; 13 Asian, non-Hispanic/Latino; 56 Hispanic/Latino; 15 Two or more races, non-Hispanic/Latino), 22 international. Average age 37. 475 applicants, 38% accepted, 147 enrolled. In 2013, 1,157 master's, 43 doctorates awarded. *Degree requirements:* For master's, comprehensive exam, thesis optional; for doctorate, comprehensive exam, thesis/dissertation, minimum of 60 credits. *Entrance requirements:* For master's and doctorate, GRE, minimum GPA of 3.0. Additional exam requirements/recommendations for international students: Required—TOEFL (minimum score 550 paper-based; 80 iBT), IELTS. *Application deadline:* For fall admission, 3/1 priority date for domestic and international students; for spring admission, 9/1 for domestic and international students. Applications are processed on a rolling basis. Application fee: $50. Electronic applications accepted. *Expenses:* Tuition, state resident: full-time $9075.40; part-time $504 per credit. Tuition, nonresident: full-time $22,248; part-time $1236 per credit. *Required fees:* $1819; $60 per credit. *Financial support:* In 2013–14, 7 students received support, including 1 research assistantship with partial tuition reimbursement available (averaging $16,135 per year), 6 teaching assistantships with partial tuition reimbursements available (averaging $10,106 per year); career-related internships or fieldwork, scholarships/grants, and unspecified assistantships also available. Financial award application deadline: 3/1; financial award applicants required to submit FAFSA. *Faculty research:* Issues in STEM education, diversity and multiculturalism, teacher education leadership, distance learning and teaching. *Total annual research expenditures:* $498,539. *Unit head:* Dr. Daniel H. Robinson, Director, 970-491-6316, Fax: 970-491-1317, E-mail: dan.robinson@colostate.edu. *Application contact:* Kelli M. Clark, Academic Coordinator, 970-491-2093, Fax: 970-491-1317, E-mail: kelli.clark@colostate.edu.
Website: http://www.soe.chhs.colostate.edu/.

Columbia International University, Columbia Graduate School, Columbia, SC 29230-3122. Offers Bible teaching (MABT); Christian higher education leadership (Ed D); Christian school educational leadership (Ed D); counseling (MACN); curriculum and instruction (M Ed), including Christian school guidance, English as a second language, learning disabilities, school technology; early childhood and elementary education (MAT); educational administration (M Ed); teaching English as a foreign language (Certificate); teaching English as a foreign language and intercultural studies (MATF). Part-time and evening/weekend programs available. *Degree requirements:* For master's, internships, professional project. *Entrance requirements:* For master's, Minnesota Multiphasic Personality Inventory, MAT, minimum GPA of 2.7. Additional exam requirements/recommendations for international students: Required—TOEFL. Electronic applications accepted.

Columbus State University, Graduate Studies, College of Education and Health Professions, Department of Counseling, Foundations, and Leadership, Columbus, GA 31907-5645. Offers community counseling (MS); curriculum and leadership (Ed D); educational leadership (M Ed, Ed S); higher education (M Ed); school counseling (M Ed, Ed S). *Accreditation:* ACA; NCATE. Part-time and evening/weekend programs available. Postbaccalaureate distance learning degree programs offered (minimal on-campus study). *Faculty:* 13 full-time (5 women), 11 part-time/adjunct (7 women). *Students:* 94 full-time (64 women), 120 part-time (96 women); includes 95 minority (78 Black or African American, non-Hispanic/Latino; 1 American Indian or Alaska Native, non-Hispanic/Latino; 2 Asian, non-Hispanic/Latino; 9 Hispanic/Latino; 5 Two or more races, non-Hispanic/Latino). Average age 35. 139 applicants, 58% accepted, 49 enrolled. In 2013, 44 master's, 4 doctorates, 14 other advanced degrees awarded. *Degree requirements:* For master's, thesis, exit exam; for doctorate, comprehensive exam, thesis/dissertation; for Ed S, thesis or alternative. *Entrance requirements:* For master's, GRE General Test, minimum undergraduate GPA of 2.75; for doctorate, GRE General Test, minimum graduate GPA of 3.5, four years of professional service; for Ed S, GRE General Test, minimum undergraduate GPA of 2.75, graduate 3.0. Additional exam requirements/recommendations for international students: Required—TOEFL (minimum score 550 paper-based; 79 iBT). *Application deadline:* For fall admission, 6/30 for domestic and international students; for spring admission, 11/1 for domestic and international students; for summer admission, 3/1 for domestic and international students. Applications are processed on a rolling basis. Application fee: $40. Electronic applications accepted. *Expenses:* Tuition, state resident: full-time $4572; part-time $382 per credit hour. Tuition, nonresident: full-time $18,292; part-time $1526 per credit hour. *Required fees:* $1800; $196 per credit hour. Tuition and fees vary according to campus/location and program. *Financial support:* In 2013–14, 143 students received support, including 9 research assistantships with partial tuition reimbursements available (averaging $3,000 per year); career-related internships or fieldwork, Federal Work-Study, institutionally sponsored loans, scholarships/grants, tuition waivers (partial), and unspecified assistantships also available. Support available to part-time students. Financial award application deadline: 5/1; financial award applicants required to submit FAFSA. *Unit head:* Dr. Michael L. Baltimore, Department Chair, 706-569-3013, Fax: 706-569-3134, E-mail: baltimore_michael@columbusstate.edu. *Application contact:* Kristin Williams, Director of International and Graduate Recruitment, 706-507-8848, Fax: 706-568-5091, E-mail: williams_kristin@columbusstate.edu.
Website: http://cfl.columbusstate.edu/.

Concordia University, School of Education, Irvine, CA 92612-3299. Offers curriculum and instruction (MA); education and preliminary teaching credential (M Ed); educational administration and preliminary administrative services credential (MA); educational technology (MA); school counseling with pupil personnel services credential (MA). Part-time and evening/weekend programs available. Postbaccalaureate distance learning degree programs offered (no on-campus study). *Faculty:* 15 full-time (12 women), 96 part-time/adjunct (59 women). *Students:* 885 full-time (690 women), 96 part-time (74 women); includes 282 minority (39 Black or African American, non-Hispanic/Latino; 42 Asian, non-Hispanic/Latino; 182 Hispanic/Latino; 3 Native Hawaiian or other Pacific Islander, non-Hispanic/Latino; 16 Two or more races, non-Hispanic/Latino), 1 international. Average age 39. 402 applicants, 79% accepted, 311 enrolled. In 2013, 469 master's awarded. *Degree requirements:* For master's, action research project. *Entrance requirements:* For master's, California Basic Educational Skills Test, California Subject Examinations for Teachers (M Ed and MA in educational administration and preliminary administrative services credential), official college transcript(s), signed statement of intent, two references, copy of credential. Additional exam requirements/recommendations for international students: Required—TOEFL. *Application deadline:* For fall admission, 7/15 priority date for domestic students, 6/1 for international students; for spring admission, 11/30 priority date for domestic students, 10/1 for international students. Applications are processed on a rolling basis. Application fee: $50 ($125 for international students). Electronic applications accepted. *Expenses:* Contact institution. *Financial support:* In 2013–14, 23 students received support. Scholarships/grants and unspecified assistantships available. Financial award applicants required to submit FAFSA. *Unit head:* Dr. Janice Nelson, Dean, 949-214-3334, E-mail: janice.nelson@cui.edu. *Application contact:* Patty Hunt, Admissions Coordinator, 949-214-3362, Fax: 949-214-3362, E-mail: patricia.hunt@cui.edu.

Concordia University Chicago, College of Graduate and Innovative Programs, Program in School Counseling, River Forest, IL 60305-1499. Offers MA, CAS. *Accreditation:* ACA (one or more programs are accredited); NCATE. Part-time and evening/weekend programs available. *Degree requirements:* For master's, comprehensive exam, thesis optional; for CAS, thesis, final project. *Entrance requirements:* For master's, minimum GPA of 2.9; for CAS, master's degree. Additional exam requirements/recommendations for international students: Required—TOEFL (minimum score 550 paper-based). Electronic applications accepted. *Faculty research:* Development of comprehensive school counseling education, training of school counselors for parochial schools.

Concordia University Wisconsin, Graduate Programs, Department of Education, Mequon, WI 53097-2402. Offers art education (MS Ed); curriculum and instruction (MS Ed); early childhood (MS Ed); educational administration (MS Ed); environmental education (MS Ed); family studies (MS Ed); reading (MS Ed); school counseling (MS Ed); special education (MS Ed). Part-time and evening/weekend programs available. Postbaccalaureate distance learning degree programs offered (minimal on-campus study). *Degree requirements:* For master's, comprehensive exam, thesis or alternative. *Entrance requirements:* For master's, minimum GPA of 3.0, teaching license. Additional exam requirements/recommendations for international students: Required—TOEFL. *Faculty research:* Motivation, developmental learning, learning styles.

Creighton University, Graduate School, College of Arts and Sciences, Department of Education, Program in Counselor Education, Omaha, NE 68178-0001. Offers college student affairs (MS); community counseling (MS); elementary school guidance (MS); secondary school guidance (MS). Part-time and evening/weekend programs available. Postbaccalaureate distance learning degree programs offered (minimal on-campus study). *Faculty:* 4 full-time (2 women). *Students:* 24 part-time (20 women), 1 international. Average age 36. 8 applicants, 63% accepted, 4 enrolled. In 2013, 8 master's awarded. *Degree requirements:* For master's, comprehensive exam. *Entrance requirements:* For master's, GRE General Test, resume, 3 letters of recommendation, personal statement, background check. Additional exam requirements/recommendations for international students: Required—TOEFL (minimum score 550 paper-based; 80 iBT). *Application deadline:* For fall admission, 7/1 for domestic students, 3/1 for international students; for winter admission, 10/1 for domestic students, 7/1 for international students; for spring admission, 3/1 for domestic students, 9/1 for international students; for summer admission, 3/1 for domestic and international students. Applications are processed on a rolling basis. Application fee: $50. Electronic applications accepted. *Expenses: Tuition:* Full-time $13,608; part-time $756 per credit hour. *Required fees:* $149 per semester. Tuition and fees vary according to course load, campus/location, program, reciprocity agreements and student's religious affiliation. *Financial support:* Scholarships/grants available. Support available to part-time students. Financial award applicants required to submit FAFSA. *Unit head:* Dr. Jeffrey Smith, Associate Professor of Education, 402-280-2413, E-mail: jefsmith@creighton.edu. *Application contact:* Valerie Mattix, Senior Program Coordinator, 402-280-2425, Fax: 402-280-2423, E-mail: valeriemattix@creighton.edu.

Dallas Baptist University, Dorothy M. Bush College of Education, Program in School Counseling, Dallas, TX 75211-9299. Offers M Ed, Advanced Certificate. Part-time and evening/weekend programs available. *Entrance requirements:* For master's, GRE General Test, minimum GPA of 3.0. Additional exam requirements/recommendations for international students: Required—TOEFL, IELTS. *Application deadline:* Applications are processed on a rolling basis. Application fee: $25. Electronic applications accepted. *Expenses: Tuition:* Full-time $13,410; part-time $745 per credit hour. *Required fees:* $300; $150 per semester. Tuition and fees vary according to degree level. *Financial support:* Federal Work-Study, institutionally sponsored loans, scholarships/grants, and tuition waivers (full and partial) available. Support available to part-time students. Financial award applicants required to submit FAFSA. *Unit head:* Dr. Bonnie B. Bond, Director, 214-333-5413, Fax: 214-333-5551, E-mail: graduate@dbu.edu. *Application contact:* Kit P. Montgomery, Director of Graduate Programs, 214-333-5242, Fax: 214-333-5579, E-mail: graduate@dbu.edu.
Website: http://www3.dbu.edu/graduate/education_counseling.asp.

Delta State University, Graduate Programs, College of Education, Division of Counselor Education and Psychology, Cleveland, MS 38733-0001. Offers counseling (M Ed). *Accreditation:* ACA; NCATE. Part-time and evening/weekend programs available. *Faculty:* 7 full-time (5 women), 1 part-time/adjunct (0 women). *Students:* 48 full-time (43 women), 44 part-time (42 women); includes 71 minority (68 Black or African American, non-Hispanic/Latino; 3 Hispanic/Latino), 1 international. Average age 33. 49 applicants, 98% accepted, 33 enrolled. In 2013, 12 master's awarded. *Degree requirements:* For master's, thesis optional, practicum. *Application deadline:* For fall admission, 8/1 priority date for domestic students; for spring admission, 12/1 priority date for domestic students. Applications are processed on a rolling basis. Application fee: $0. Electronic applications accepted. *Expenses:* Tuition, state resident: full-time $3006; part-time $334 per credit hour. Tuition, nonresident: full-time $3006; part-time $334 per credit hour. *Financial support:* In 2013–14, research assistantships (averaging $4,000 per year) were awarded; career-related internships or fieldwork, Federal Work-Study, and institutionally sponsored loans also available. Support available to part-time students. Financial award application deadline: 6/1. *Unit head:* Dr. Matthew Buckley, Chair, 662-846-4355, Fax: 662-846-4402. *Application contact:* Dr. Albert Nylander, Dean of Graduate Studies, 662-846-4875, Fax: 662-846-4313, E-mail: grad-info@deltastate.edu.
Website: http://www.deltastate.edu/pages/567.asp.

Delta State University, Graduate Programs, College of Education, Thad Cochran Center for Rural School Leadership and Research, Program in Professional Studies, Cleveland, MS 38733-0001. Offers counselor education (Ed D); educational leadership (Ed D); elementary education (Ed D); higher education (Ed D). Part-time and evening/

weekend programs available. *Students:* 3 full-time (all women), 90 part-time (58 women); includes 31 minority (all Black or African American, non-Hispanic/Latino), 1 international. Average age 38. 44 applicants, 95% accepted, 28 enrolled. In 2013, 2 doctorates awarded. *Degree requirements:* For doctorate, thesis/dissertation. *Entrance requirements:* For doctorate, GRE General Test. *Application deadline:* For fall admission, 8/1 priority date for domestic students; for spring admission, 12/1 priority date for domestic students. Applications are processed on a rolling basis. Application fee: $0. *Expenses:* Tuition, state resident: full-time $3006; part-time $334 per credit hour. Tuition, nonresident: full-time $3006; part-time $334 per credit hour. *Financial support:* Research assistantships, career-related internships or fieldwork, Federal Work-Study, and institutionally sponsored loans available. Support available to part-time students. Financial award application deadline: 6/1. *Unit head:* Dr. Dan McFall, Interim Chair, 662-846-4395, Fax: 662-846-4402. *Application contact:* Dr. Albert Nylander, Dean of Graduate Studies, 662-846-4875, Fax: 662-846-4313, E-mail: grad-info@deltastate.edu.

DePaul University, College of Education, Chicago, IL 60614. Offers bilingual bicultural education (M Ed, MA); counseling (M Ed, MA), including clinical mental health counseling, college student development, school counseling; curriculum studies (M Ed, MA, Ed D); early childhood education (M Ed, MA, Ed D); educating adults (MA); educational leadership (M Ed, MA, Ed D), including administration and supervision (M Ed, MA), principal preparation (M Ed, MA); elementary education (MA); mathematics education (MA); mathematics for teaching (MS); middle school mathematics education (MS); reading specialist (M Ed, MA); secondary education (M Ed); social and cultural foundations in education (MA); special education (M Ed, MA); world languages education (M Ed, MA). Part-time and evening/weekend programs available. Postbaccalaureate distance learning degree programs offered (no on-campus study). *Faculty:* 61 full-time (35 women), 59 part-time/adjunct (43 women). *Students:* 628 full-time (486 women), 324 part-time (243 women); includes 304 minority (144 Black or African American, non-Hispanic/Latino; 1 American Indian or Alaska Native, non-Hispanic/Latino; 38 Asian, non-Hispanic/Latino; 98 Hispanic/Latino; 23 Two or more races, non-Hispanic/Latino), 24 international. Average age 30. In 2013, 465 master's, 4 doctorates awarded. *Degree requirements:* For doctorate, thesis/dissertation. *Application deadline:* For fall admission, 8/15 for domestic students; for winter admission, 12/1 for domestic students; for spring admission, 3/1 for domestic students. Applications are processed on a rolling basis. Application fee: $40. Electronic applications accepted. Tuition and fees vary according to course level, course load and degree level. *Financial support:* Application deadline: 12/31; applicants required to submit FAFSA. *Unit head:* Dr. Paul Zionts, Dean, 773-325-7581, Fax: 773-325-7713, E-mail: pzionts@depaul.edu. *Application contact:* Farrah Dalal, Assistant Director, 773-325-2465, Fax: 773-325-2270, E-mail: fdalal@depaul.edu.
Website: http://education.depaul.edu.

Doane College, Program in Counseling, Crete, NE 68333-2430. Offers MAC. Evening/weekend programs available. *Faculty:* 2 full-time (1 woman), 14 part-time/adjunct (9 women). *Students:* 111 full-time (92 women), 26 part-time (18 women); includes 17 minority (3 Black or African American, non-Hispanic/Latino; 10 Hispanic/Latino; 4 Two or more races, non-Hispanic/Latino). Average age 33. In 2013, 51 master's awarded. *Degree requirements:* For master's, thesis. *Entrance requirements:* For master's, minimum GPA of 3.0. Additional exam requirements/recommendations for international students: Required—TOEFL. *Application deadline:* Applications are processed on a rolling basis. Application fee: $25. *Expenses:* Contact institution. *Financial support:* Unspecified assistantships available. Financial award application deadline: 6/1; financial award applicants required to submit FAFSA. *Unit head:* Thomas Gilligan, Dean, 402-466-4774, Fax: 402-466-4228, E-mail: tom.gilligan@doane.edu. *Application contact:* Wilma Daddario, Assistant Dean, 402-466-4774, Fax: 404-466-4228, E-mail: wilma.daddario@doane.edu.
Website: http://www.doane.edu/master-of-arts-in-counseling-0.

Duquesne University, School of Education, Department of Counseling, Psychology, and Special Education, Program in Counselor Education, Pittsburgh, PA 15282-0001. Offers clinical mental health counseling (MS Ed, Post-Master's Certificate); counselor education and supervision (Ed D); counselor licensure (Post-Master's Certificate); marriage and family counseling (MS Ed); school counseling (MS Ed). *Accreditation:* ACA (one or more programs are accredited). Part-time and evening/weekend programs available. *Faculty:* 10 full-time (5 women). *Students:* 162 full-time (119 women), 26 part-time (18 women); includes 39 minority (26 Black or African American, non-Hispanic/Latino; 1 American Indian or Alaska Native, non-Hispanic/Latino; 2 Asian, non-Hispanic/Latino; 6 Hispanic/Latino; 4 Two or more races, non-Hispanic/Latino), 5 international. Average age 31. 184 applicants, 46% accepted, 53 enrolled. In 2013, 57 master's, 8 doctorates awarded. *Degree requirements:* For master's, thesis optional; for doctorate, thesis/dissertation. *Entrance requirements:* For master's, letters of recommendation, essay, interview, bachelor's degree; for doctorate, GRE, letters of recommendation, essay, interview, master's degree; for Post-Master's Certificate, GRE, letters of recommendation, essay, interview, bachelor's/master's degree. Additional exam requirements/recommendations for international students: Required—TOEFL (minimum score 550 paper-based), IELTS (minimum score 7). *Application deadline:* For fall admission, 3/1 for domestic students; for spring admission, 9/1 for domestic students. Applications are processed on a rolling basis. Application fee: $0. Electronic applications accepted. Application fee is waived when completed online. *Expenses: Tuition:* Full-time $18,162; part-time $1009 per credit. *Required fees:* $1728; $96 per credit. Tuition and fees vary according to program. *Financial support:* Research assistantships, teaching assistantships, and Federal Work-Study available. Support available to part-time students. *Unit head:* Dr. Jered Kolbert, Professor/Director, 412-396-4471, Fax: 412-396-1340, E-mail: kolbertj@duq.edu. *Application contact:* Michael Dolinger, Director of Student and Academic Services, 412-396-6647, Fax: 412-396-5585, E-mail: dolingerm@duq.edu.
Website: http://www.duq.edu/academics/schools/education/graduate-programs-education/ms-ed-counselor-education.

East Carolina University, Graduate School, College of Education, Department of Higher, Adult, and Counselor Education, Greenville, NC 27858-4353. Offers adult education (MA Ed); counselor education (MS); higher education administration (Ed D). *Accreditation:* NCATE. Part-time and evening/weekend programs available. *Degree requirements:* For master's, comprehensive exam, thesis optional. *Entrance requirements:* For master's, GRE General Test or MAT, interview, minimum GPA of 2.5, bachelor's degree in related field, teaching license (MA Ed). Additional exam requirements/recommendations for international students: Required—TOEFL. *Expenses:* Tuition, state resident: full-time $4223. Tuition, nonresident: full-time $16,540. *Required fees:* $2184.

East Central University, School of Graduate Studies, Department of Human Resources, Ada, OK 74820-6899. Offers administration (MSHR); counseling (MSHR); criminal justice (MSHR); human services (MSHR); rehabilitation counseling (MSHR). *Accreditation:* CORE. Part-time and evening/weekend programs available. *Degree requirements:* For master's, thesis optional. *Entrance requirements:* For master's, GRE General Test, MAT, minimum GPA of 2.5. Electronic applications accepted.

Eastern Illinois University, Graduate School, College of Education and Professional Studies, Department of Counseling and Student Development, Charleston, IL 61920-3099. Offers clinical counseling (MS); college student affairs (MS); school counseling (MS). *Accreditation:* ACA; NCATE. Part-time and evening/weekend programs available. *Degree requirements:* For master's, comprehensive exam. *Entrance requirements:* For master's, GRE General Test or MAT. *Expenses: Tuition, area resident:* Part-time $283 per credit hour. Tuition, state resident: part-time $283 per credit hour. Tuition, nonresident: part-time $679 per credit hour.

Eastern Kentucky University, The Graduate School, College of Education, Department of Counseling and Educational Leadership, Richmond, KY 40475-3102. Offers human services (MA); instructional leadership (MA Ed); mental health counseling (MA); school counseling (MA Ed). *Accreditation:* ACA (one or more programs are accredited); NCATE. Part-time programs available. Postbaccalaureate distance learning degree programs offered. *Entrance requirements:* For master's, GRE General Test, minimum GPA of 2.5.

Eastern Mennonite University, Master of Arts in Counseling Program, Harrisonburg, VA 22802-2462. Offers MA, M Div/MA. *Accreditation:* ACA (one or more programs are accredited); ACIPE. Part-time programs available. *Degree requirements:* For master's, practicum, internship. *Entrance requirements:* For master's, minimum GPA of 3.0. Additional exam requirements/recommendations for international students: Required—TOEFL (minimum score 550 paper-based). Electronic applications accepted. *Expenses:* Contact institution. *Faculty research:* Career and gender, empathy and consciousness, emotion theory, education models.

Eastern Michigan University, Graduate School, College of Education, Department of Leadership and Counseling, Programs in Counseling, Ypsilanti, MI 48197. Offers clinical mental health counseling (MA); college counseling (MA); helping interventions in a multicultural society (Graduate Certificate); school counseling (MA); school counselor licensure (Post Master's Certificate). Part-time and evening/weekend programs available. *Students:* 22 full-time (17 women), 91 part-time (73 women); includes 31 minority (24 Black or African American, non-Hispanic/Latino; 5 Asian, non-Hispanic/Latino; 2 Two or more races, non-Hispanic/Latino), 4 international. Average age 32. 84 applicants, 43% accepted, 15 enrolled. In 2013, 24 master's, 13 other advanced degrees awarded. *Degree requirements:* For master's, comprehensive exam, internship. *Entrance requirements:* Additional exam requirements/recommendations for international students: Required—TOEFL. *Application deadline:* For fall admission, 5/1 for domestic and international students; for winter admission, 9/15 for domestic and international students; for spring admission, 2/10 for domestic and international students. Applications are processed on a rolling basis. Application fee: $35. *Expenses:* Tuition, state resident: full-time $12,300; part-time $466 per credit hour. Tuition, nonresident: full-time $23,159; part-time $918 per credit hour. *Required fees:* $71 per credit hour. $46 per semester. One-time fee: $100. Tuition and fees vary according to course level and degree level. *Financial support:* Fellowships, research assistantships with full tuition reimbursements, teaching assistantships with full tuition reimbursements, career-related internships or fieldwork, Federal Work-Study, institutionally sponsored loans, scholarships/grants, tuition waivers (partial), and unspecified assistantships available. Support available to part-time students. Financial award applicants required to submit FAFSA. *Unit head:* Department Head. *Application contact:* Dr. Dibya Choudhuri, Coordinator of Advising for Programs in Counseling, 734-487-0255, Fax: 734-487-4608, E-mail: dchoudhur@emich.edu.

Eastern New Mexico University, Graduate School, College of Education and Technology, Department of Educational Studies, Program in Counseling, Portales, NM 88130. Offers MA. Part-time programs available. *Degree requirements:* For master's, comprehensive exam, thesis optional, 48-hour course work including a 600-hour internship in field placement. *Entrance requirements:* For master's, minimum GPA of 3.0, 3 letters of recommendation, interview. Additional exam requirements/recommendations for international students: Required—TOEFL (minimum score 550 paper-based; 79 iBT), IELTS (minimum score 6). Electronic applications accepted.

Eastern New Mexico University, Graduate School, College of Education and Technology, Department of Educational Studies, Program in School Counseling, Portales, NM 88130. Offers M Ed. Part-time programs available. *Degree requirements:* For master's, comprehensive exam, thesis optional, 48-hour curriculum, 600-hour internship in field placement. *Entrance requirements:* For master's, minimum GPA of 3.0, three letters of recommendation, interview. Additional exam requirements/recommendations for international students: Required—TOEFL (minimum score 550 paper-based; 79 iBT), IELTS (minimum score 6). Electronic applications accepted.

Eastern University, Department of Counseling Psychology, St. Davids, PA 19087-3696. Offers applied behavior analysis (MA); counseling (MA); school counseling (MA, Certificate); school psychology (MS, Certificate). Part-time programs available. *Faculty:* 6 full-time (3 women), 8 part-time/adjunct (6 women). *Students:* 68 full-time (55 women), 118 part-time (100 women); includes 62 minority (54 Black or African American, non-Hispanic/Latino; 3 Asian, non-Hispanic/Latino; 4 Hispanic/Latino; 1 Two or more races, non-Hispanic/Latino), 1 international. Average age 30. 101 applicants, 80% accepted, 45 enrolled. In 2013, 56 master's awarded. *Degree requirements:* For master's, internship. *Entrance requirements:* For master's, minimum GPA of 2.8 (3.0 for school psychology). Additional exam requirements/recommendations for international students: Required—TOEFL (minimum score 550 paper-based; 79 iBT). *Application deadline:* For fall admission, 6/15 for domestic students, 5/30 for international students. Applications are processed on a rolling basis. Application fee: $35. Electronic applications accepted. Application fee is waived when completed online. *Expenses: Tuition:* Full-time $15,600; part-time $650 per credit. *Required fees:* $27.50 per semester. One-time fee: $50. Tuition and fees vary according to course load, degree level and program. *Financial support:* In 2013–14, 21 students received support, including 6 research assistantships with partial tuition reimbursements available (averaging $8,115 per year); scholarships/grants and unspecified assistantships also available. Financial award application deadline: 3/15. *Unit head:* Dr. Susan Edgar-Smith, Co-Chair, 610-341-4379. *Application contact:* Katelyn Ambrose, Enrollment Counselor, 610-225-5564, Fax: 610-341-1585, E-mail: kambrose@eastern.edu.
Website: http://www.eastern.edu/academics/programs/counseling-psychology-department.

Eastern Washington University, Graduate Studies, College of Social and Behavioral Sciences and Social Work, Program in School Counseling, Cheney, WA 99004-2431. Offers applied psychology (MS); school counseling (MS). *Accreditation:* ACA. *Students:* 14 full-time (12 women); includes 1 minority (Hispanic/Latino). Average age 28. 17 applicants, 24% accepted, 4 enrolled. In 2013, 12 master's awarded. *Degree requirements:* For master's, comprehensive exam, thesis or alternative. *Entrance requirements:* For master's, GRE General Test, minimum GPA of 3.0. *Application deadline:* For fall admission, 2/1 for domestic students. Applications are processed on a rolling basis. Application fee: $50. *Financial support:* In 2013–14, teaching assistantships with partial tuition reimbursements (averaging $7,000 per year) were awarded; career-related internships or fieldwork, Federal Work-Study, institutionally sponsored loans, scholarships/grants, health care benefits, tuition waivers (partial), and unspecified assistantships also available. Support available to part-time students. Financial award application deadline: 2/1; financial award applicants required to submit

FAFSA. *Unit head:* Dr. Marty Slyter, Director, 509-359-6499, E-mail: mslyter@ewu.edu. *Application contact:* Julie Marr, Advisor/Recruiter for Graduate Studies, 509-359-6656, E-mail: gradprograms@ewu.edu.
Website: http://www.ewu.edu/grad/programs/applied-psychology—school-counseling.xml.

Edinboro University of Pennsylvania, School of Education, Department of Professional Studies, Edinboro, PA 16444. Offers counseling (MA); educational leadership (M Ed); educational psychology (M Ed); reading (M Ed); school psychology (MS, Ed S). Part-time and evening/weekend programs available. *Degree requirements:* For master's, thesis or alternative, competency exam; for Ed S, thesis or alternative. *Entrance requirements:* For master's and Ed S, GRE or MAT, minimum QPA of 2.5. Electronic applications accepted.

Emporia State University, Program in School Counseling, Emporia, KS 66801-5415. Offers MS. *Accreditation:* ACA; NCATE. Part-time programs available. *Students:* 27 full-time (22 women), 54 part-time (47 women); includes 10 minority (4 Black or African American, non-Hispanic/Latino; 4 Hispanic/Latino; 2 Two or more races, non-Hispanic/Latino). 29 applicants, 83% accepted, 16 enrolled. In 2013, 22 master's awarded. *Degree requirements:* For master's, comprehensive exam or thesis, practicum. *Entrance requirements:* For master's, GRE or MAT, essay exam, appropriate bachelor's degree, interview, letters of recommendation. *Application deadline:* For fall admission, 8/15 priority date for domestic students. Applications are processed on a rolling basis. Application fee: $30 ($75 for international students). Electronic applications accepted. *Expenses: Tuition, area resident:* Part-time $220 per credit hour. Tuition, state resident: part-time $220 per credit hour. Tuition, nonresident: part-time $685 per credit hour. *Required fees:* $73 per credit hour. *Financial support:* Career-related internships or fieldwork, Federal Work-Study, institutionally sponsored loans, health care benefits, and unspecified assistantships available. Financial award application deadline: 3/15; financial award applicants required to submit FAFSA. *Unit head:* Dr. James Costello, Chair, 620-341-5791, E-mail: jcostell@emporia.edu. *Application contact:* Mary Sewell, Admissions Coordinator, 800-950-GRAD, Fax: 620-341-5909, E-mail: msewell@emporia.edu.

Evangel University, School Counseling Program, Springfield, MO 65802. Offers MS. Part-time programs available. *Faculty:* 1 (woman) full-time, 6 part-time/adjunct (4 women). *Students:* 6 full-time (5 women), 43 part-time (36 women); includes 4 minority (1 Black or African American, non-Hispanic/Latino; 2 American Indian or Alaska Native, non-Hispanic/Latino; 1 Two or more races, non-Hispanic/Latino). Average age 32. 31 applicants, 45% accepted, 14 enrolled. In 2013, 27 master's awarded. *Degree requirements:* For master's, comprehensive exam (for some programs), thesis or alternative. *Entrance requirements:* For master's, MAT (preferred) or GRE, teaching certificate. Additional exam requirements/recommendations for international students: Required—TOEFL (minimum score 550 paper-based). *Application deadline:* For fall admission, 7/15 priority date for domestic students, 7/1 for international students; for spring admission, 11/15 priority date for domestic students, 12/1 for international students. Applications are processed on a rolling basis. Application fee: $25. Electronic applications accepted. *Financial support:* In 2013–14, 15 students received support. Career-related internships or fieldwork, scholarships/grants, and unspecified assistantships available. Support available to part-time students. Financial award application deadline: 3/1; financial award applicants required to submit FAFSA. *Unit head:* Debbie Bicket, Program Coordinator, 417-865-2815 Ext. 8567, Fax: 417-575-5484, E-mail: bicketd@evangel.edu. *Application contact:* Karen Benitez, Admissions Representative, Graduate Studies, 417-865-2815 Ext. 7227, Fax: 417-575-5484, E-mail: benitezk@evangel.edu.
Website: http://www.evangel.edu/academics/graduate-studies/graduate-programs.

Fairfield University, Graduate School of Education and Allied Professions, Fairfield, CT 06824-5195. Offers applied behavior analysis (ATC); applied psychology (MA); clinical mental health counseling (MA, CAS); early childhood studies (ATC); educational technology (MA); elementary education (MA, CAS); family studies (MA); integration of spirituality and religion in counseling (ATC); marriage and family therapy (MA); school counseling (MA, CAS); school psychology (MA, CAS); school-based marriage and family therapy (ATC); secondary education (MA); special education (MA, CAS); substance abuse counseling (ATC); teaching (Certificate); teaching and foundations (MA, CAS); TESOL, world languages, and bilingual education (MA, CAS). *Accreditation:* NCATE. Part-time and evening/weekend programs available. *Faculty:* 24 full-time (21 women), 39 part-time/adjunct (27 women). *Students:* 154 full-time (130 women), 307 part-time (248 women); includes 75 minority (14 Black or African American, non-Hispanic/Latino; 1 American Indian or Alaska Native, non-Hispanic/Latino; 10 Asian, non-Hispanic/Latino; 44 Hispanic/Latino; 6 Two or more races, non-Hispanic/Latino), 13 international. Average age 34. 263 applicants, 41% accepted, 91 enrolled. In 2013, 149 master's, 21 other advanced degrees awarded. *Degree requirements:* For master's, comprehensive exam. *Entrance requirements:* For master's, PRAXIS I (for certification programs), minimum GPA of 3.0, 2 recommendations, resume. Additional exam requirements/recommendations for international students: Required—TOEFL (minimum score 550 paper-based; 84 iBT) or IELTS (minimum score 7.5). *Application deadline:* For fall admission, 2/15 for international students; for spring admission, 10/1 for international students. Application fee: $60. Electronic applications accepted. *Expenses: Tuition:* Part-time $675 per credit hour. Tuition and fees vary according to program. *Financial support:* In 2013–14, 55 students received support. Career-related internships or fieldwork and unspecified assistantships available. Financial award applicants required to submit FAFSA. *Faculty research:* Literacy, adolescent psychology, special education, teaching development, mentoring for professional development, multicultural education. *Total annual research expenditures:* $325,000. *Unit head:* Dr. Robert D. Hannafin, Dean, 203-254-4250, Fax: 203-254-4241, E-mail: rhannafin@fairfield.edu. *Application contact:* Marianne Gumpper, Director of Graduate and Continuing Studies Admission, 203-254-4184, Fax: 203-254-4073, E-mail: gradadmis@fairfield.edu.
Website: http://www.fairfield.edu/academics/schoolscollegescenters/graduateschoolofeducationalliedprofessions/graduateprograms/.

Faulkner University, Alabama Christian College of Arts and Sciences, Department of Social and Behavioral Sciences, Montgomery, AL 36109-3398. Offers counseling (MS). Postbaccalaureate distance learning degree programs offered (no on-campus study).

Fitchburg State University, Division of Graduate and Continuing Education, Programs in Counseling, Fitchburg, MA 01420-2697. Offers elementary school guidance counseling (MS); mental health counseling (MS); secondary school guidance counseling (MS). *Accreditation:* NCATE. Part-time and evening/weekend programs available. *Entrance requirements:* Additional exam requirements/recommendations for international students: Required—TOEFL (minimum score 550 paper-based; 79 iBT). Electronic applications accepted.

Florida Agricultural and Mechanical University, Division of Graduate Studies, Research, and Continuing Education, College of Education, Department of Educational Leadership and Human Services, Tallahassee, FL 32307-3200. Offers administration and supervision (M Ed, MS Ed, PhD); adult education (M Ed, MS Ed); educational leadership (PhD); guidance and counseling (M Ed, MS Ed). *Accreditation:* NCATE. *Degree requirements:* For master's, thesis (for some programs); for doctorate, thesis/dissertation. *Entrance requirements:* For master's, GRE General Test, minimum GPA of 3.0. Additional exam requirements/recommendations for international students: Required—TOEFL.

Florida Atlantic University, College of Education, Department of Counselor Education, Boca Raton, FL 33431-0991. Offers counselor education (M Ed, PhD, Ed S); marriage and family therapy (Ed S); mental health counseling (M Ed, Ed S); rehabilitation counseling (M Ed); school counseling (M Ed, Ed S). *Accreditation:* ACA; NCATE. Part-time and evening/weekend programs available. *Faculty:* 8 full-time (3 women), 4 part-time/adjunct (all women). *Students:* 60 full-time (49 women), 85 part-time (68 women); includes 45 minority (25 Black or African American, non-Hispanic/Latino; 3 Asian, non-Hispanic/Latino; 15 Hispanic/Latino; 2 Two or more races, non-Hispanic/Latino), 3 international. Average age 31. 126 applicants, 31% accepted, 34 enrolled. In 2013, 42 master's, 6 doctorates, 4 other advanced degrees awarded. *Degree requirements:* For Ed S, departmental qualifying exam. *Entrance requirements:* For master's, GRE General Test, minimum GPA of 3.0 during previous 2 years; for Ed S, GRE General Test, minimum graduate GPA of 3.25. Additional exam requirements/recommendations for international students: Required—TOEFL (minimum score 500 paper-based; 61 iBT), IELTS (minimum score 6). *Application deadline:* For fall admission, 3/1 for domestic students, 2/1 for international students; for spring admission, 9/15 for domestic students, 7/1 for international students. Applications are processed on a rolling basis. Application fee: $30. *Expenses:* Tuition, state resident: full-time $6660; part-time $370 per credit hour. Tuition, nonresident: full-time $18,450; part-time $1025 per credit hour. Tuition and fees vary according to course load. *Financial support:* Research assistantships with partial tuition reimbursements, teaching assistantships, career-related internships or fieldwork, scholarships/grants, and unspecified assistantships available. *Faculty research:* Brief therapy, psychological type, marriage and family counseling, international programs, integrated services. *Unit head:* Dr. Paul Peluso, Interim Chair, 561-297-3625, Fax: 561-297-2309, E-mail: ppeluso@fau.edu. *Application contact:* Darlene Epperson, Office Assistant, 561-297-3601, Fax: 561-297-2309, E-mail: frederic@fau.edu.
Website: http://www.coe.fau.edu/academicdepartments/ce/.

Florida Gulf Coast University, College of Education, Program in Counseling, Fort Myers, FL 33965-6565. Offers MA. *Accreditation:* ACA. Part-time and evening/weekend programs available. *Degree requirements:* For master's, thesis or alternative. *Entrance requirements:* For master's, GRE General Test, MAT, minimum GPA of 3.0. Additional exam requirements/recommendations for international students: Required—TOEFL (minimum score 550 paper-based). Electronic applications accepted. *Faculty research:* Sexuality, confidentiality, school counselor roles, distance learning, exceptional students.

Florida International University, College of Education, Department of Leadership and Professional Studies, Miami, FL 33199. Offers adult education and human resource development (MS, Ed D); counseling (MS), including rehabilitation counseling, school counseling; counselor education (MS), including clinical mental health counseling; educational administration and supervision (Ed D); educational leadership (MS, Certificate, Ed S); higher education (Ed D); higher education administration (MS); recreation and sport management (MS), including recreation and sport management, recreational therapy; school psychology (Ed S); urban education (MS), including instruction in urban settings, learning technologies, multicultural/bilingual, multicultural/TESOL, urban education. Part-time and evening/weekend programs available. *Degree requirements:* For doctorate, thesis/dissertation. *Entrance requirements:* For master's, minimum GPA of 3.0; for doctorate and other advanced degree, GRE General Test. Additional exam requirements/recommendations for international students: Required—TOEFL (minimum score 550 paper-based; 80 iBT), IELTS (minimum score 6.3). Electronic applications accepted.

Fordham University, Graduate School of Education, Division of Psychological and Educational Services, New York, NY 10023. Offers counseling and personnel services (MSE, Adv C); counseling psychology (PhD); educational psychology (MSE, PhD); school psychology (PhD); urban and urban bilingual school psychology (Adv C). *Accreditation:* APA (one or more programs are accredited); NCATE. *Degree requirements:* For doctorate, thesis/dissertation. *Entrance requirements:* For doctorate, GRE General Test.

Fort Hays State University, Graduate School, College of Education and Technology, Department of Educational Administration and Counseling, Program in Counseling, Hays, KS 67601-4099. Offers MS. *Accreditation:* NCATE. Part-time programs available. *Degree requirements:* For master's, comprehensive exam, thesis or alternative. *Entrance requirements:* For master's, GRE General Test or MAT, minimum undergraduate GPA of 3.0 in last 60 hours. Additional exam requirements/recommendations for international students: Required—TOEFL (minimum score 550 paper-based). Electronic applications accepted. *Faculty research:* Career education, evaluation and plans, counseling the disabled, marriage and family parenting, underemployment and work in the family.

Fort Valley State University, College of Graduate Studies and Extended Education, Department of Counseling Psychology, Fort Valley, GA 31030. Offers guidance and counseling (Ed S); mental health counseling (MS); rehabilitation counseling (MS). Part-time programs available. *Degree requirements:* For master's, comprehensive exam (for some programs), thesis optional. *Entrance requirements:* For master's and Ed S, GRE General Test or MAT.

Freed-Hardeman University, Program in Counseling, Henderson, TN 38340-2399. Offers MS. Part-time and evening/weekend programs available. *Degree requirements:* For master's, comprehensive exam, practicum. *Entrance requirements:* For master's, GRE General Test or MAT. Additional exam requirements/recommendations for international students: Required—TOEFL (minimum score 500 paper-based).

Freed-Hardeman University, Program in Education, Henderson, TN 38340-2399. Offers curriculum and instruction (M Ed); school counseling (M Ed), including administration and supervision, special education; school leadership (Ed S). *Accreditation:* NCATE. Part-time and evening/weekend programs available. *Degree requirements:* For master's, comprehensive exam, thesis optional; for Ed S, thesis. *Entrance requirements:* For master's, GRE General Test or NTE; for Ed S, 3 years of teaching experience. Additional exam requirements/recommendations for international students: Required—TOEFL (minimum score 500 paper-based).

Fresno Pacific University, Graduate Programs, School of Education, Division of Pupil Personnel Services, Program in School Counseling, Fresno, CA 93702-4709. Offers MA. Part-time and evening/weekend programs available. *Students:* 46 full-time (42 women), 2 part-time (1 woman); includes 37 minority (1 Black or African American, non-Hispanic/Latino; 1 American Indian or Alaska Native, non-Hispanic/Latino; 4 Asian, non-Hispanic/Latino; 29 Hispanic/Latino; 2 Native Hawaiian or other Pacific Islander, non-Hispanic/Latino). Average age 30. In 2013, 19 master's awarded. *Degree requirements:* For master's, thesis or alternative. *Entrance requirements:* Additional exam requirements/recommendations for international students: Required—TOEFL (minimum score 550 paper-based). *Application deadline:* For fall admission, 7/15 for domestic and international students; for spring admission, 11/15 for domestic and international students. Applications are processed on a rolling basis. Application fee: $90. *Expenses: Tuition:* Full-time $8910; part-time $495 per unit. *Required fees:* $270. Tuition and fees

vary according to course load and program. *Financial support:* Scholarships/grants and tuition waivers (full and partial) available. Support available to part-time students. Financial award applicants required to submit FAFSA. *Unit head:* Dr. Diane Talbot, Program Director, 559-453-2024, Fax: 559-453-7168, E-mail: diane.talbot@fresno.edu. *Application contact:* Amanda Krum-Stovall, Director of Graduate Admissions, 559-453-2016, E-mail: amanda.krum-stovall@fresno.edu.
Website: http://grad.fresno.edu/programs/master-arts-school-counseling.

Frostburg State University, Graduate School, College of Education, Department of Educational Professions, Program in School Counseling, Frostburg, MD 21532-1099. Offers M Ed. *Accreditation:* NCATE. Part-time and evening/weekend programs available. *Degree requirements:* For master's, comprehensive exam, thesis or alternative. *Entrance requirements:* For master's, GRE General Test or MAT, interview. Additional exam requirements/recommendations for international students: Required—TOEFL. Electronic applications accepted. *Expenses: Tuition, area resident:* Part-time $340 per credit hour. Tuition, state resident: part-time $340 per credit hour. Tuition, nonresident: part-time $437 per credit hour.

Gallaudet University, The Graduate School, Washington, DC 20002-3625. Offers ASL/English bilingual early childhood education: birth to 5 (Certificate); audiology (Au D); clinical psychology (PhD); critical studies in the education of deaf learners (PhD); deaf and hard of hearing infants, toddlers, and their families (Certificate); deaf education (Ed S); deaf education: advanced studies (MA); deaf education: special programs (MA); deaf history (Certificate); deaf studies (MA, Certificate); educating deaf students with disabilities (Certificate); education: teacher preparation (MA), including deaf education, early childhood education and deaf education, elementary education and deaf education, secondary education and deaf education; educational neuroscience (PhD); hearing, speech and language sciences (MS, PhD); international development (MA); interpretation (MA, PhD), including combined interpreting practice and research (MA), interpreting research (MA); linguistics (MA, PhD); mental health counseling (MA); peer mentoring (Certificate); public administration (MPA); school counseling (MA); school psychology (Psy S); sign language teaching (MA); social work (MSW); speech-language pathology (MS). Part-time programs available. *Faculty:* 55 full-time (37 women). *Students:* 361 full-time (279 women), 108 part-time (73 women); includes 98 minority (39 Black or African American, non-Hispanic/Latino; 1 American Indian or Alaska Native, non-Hispanic/Latino; 12 Asian, non-Hispanic/Latino; 36 Hispanic/Latino; 1 Native Hawaiian or other Pacific Islander, non-Hispanic/Latino; 9 Two or more races, non-Hispanic/Latino), 31 international. Average age 30. 602 applicants, 49% accepted, 177 enrolled. In 2013, 140 master's, 32 doctorates, 11 other advanced degrees awarded. Terminal master's awarded for partial completion of doctoral program. *Degree requirements:* For master's, comprehensive exam (for some programs), thesis optional; for doctorate, comprehensive exam, thesis/dissertation. *Entrance requirements:* For master's and doctorate, GRE General Test or MAT, letters of recommendation, interviews, goals statement, ASL proficiency interview, written English competency. Additional exam requirements/recommendations for international students: Required—TOEFL. *Application deadline:* For fall admission, 2/15 for domestic students. Applications are processed on a rolling basis. Application fee: $75. Electronic applications accepted. *Expenses: Tuition:* Full-time $14,774; part-time $821 per credit. *Required fees:* $198 per semester. *Financial support:* In 2013–14, 325 students received support. Fellowships, research assistantships, teaching assistantships, career-related internships or fieldwork, Federal Work-Study, scholarships/grants, tuition waivers (partial), and unspecified assistantships available. Support available to part-time students. Financial award applicants required to submit FAFSA. *Faculty research:* Bimodal bilingualism development, cochlear implants, telecommunications access, cancer genetics, linguistics, visual language and visual learning, advancement of avatar and robotics translation, algal productivity and physiology in the Anacostia River. *Unit head:* Dr. Carol J. Erting, Dean, Research, Graduate School, Continuing Studies, and International Programs, 202-651-5520, Fax: 202-651-5027, E-mail: carol.erting@gallaudet.edu. *Application contact:* Wednesday Luria, Coordinator of Prospective Graduate Student Services, 202-651-5400, Fax: 202-651-5295, E-mail: graduate.school@gallaudet.edu.
Website: http://www.gallaudet.edu/x26696.xml.

Geneva College, Master of Arts in Counseling Program, Beaver Falls, PA 15010-3599. Offers clinical mental health counseling (MA); marriage and family counseling (MA); school counseling (MA). *Accreditation:* ACA. Part-time and evening/weekend programs available. *Faculty:* 6 full-time (3 women), 5 part-time/adjunct (3 women). *Students:* 57 full-time (47 women), 41 part-time (28 women); includes 5 minority (all Black or African American, non-Hispanic/Latino). Average age 32. 43 applicants, 100% accepted, 33 enrolled. In 2013, 11 master's awarded. *Degree requirements:* For master's, 50-60 credits (depending on program), practicum, internship. *Entrance requirements:* For master's, minimum GPA of 3.0 (preferred), 3 letters of recommendation, essay on career goals, resume of educational and professional experiences. Additional exam requirements/recommendations for international students: Required—TOEFL. *Application deadline:* For fall admission, 9/1 for domestic students; for spring admission, 1/10 for domestic students. Applications are processed on a rolling basis. Electronic applications accepted. *Expenses:* Contact institution. *Financial support:* In 2013–14, 24 students received support, including 6 research assistantships (averaging $300 per year), 11 teaching assistantships (averaging $800 per year); career-related internships or fieldwork and unspecified assistantships also available. Financial award application deadline: 8/1; financial award applicants required to submit FAFSA. *Unit head:* Dr. Shannon Shiderly, Program Director, 724-847-6649, Fax: 724-847-6101, E-mail: slshider@geneva.edu. *Application contact:* Marina Frazier, Graduate Program Manager, 724-847-6697, E-mail: counseling@geneva.edu.
Website: http://www.geneva.edu/page/grad_counseling.

George Fox University, College of Education, Graduate Department of Counseling, Newberg, OR 97132-2697. Offers clinical mental health counseling (MA); marriage, couple and family counseling (MA, Certificate); mental health trauma (Certificate); school counseling (MA, Certificate); school psychology (Certificate, Ed S). Part-time programs available. *Faculty:* 9 full-time (3 women), 12 part-time/adjunct (7 women). *Students:* 89 full-time (71 women), 159 part-time (135 women); includes 20 minority (4 Black or African American, non-Hispanic/Latino; 3 American Indian or Alaska Native, non-Hispanic/Latino; 5 Asian, non-Hispanic/Latino; 6 Hispanic/Latino; 1 Native Hawaiian or other Pacific Islander, non-Hispanic/Latino; 1 Two or more races, non-Hispanic/Latino), 2 international. Average age 36. 107 applicants, 70% accepted, 50 enrolled. In 2013, 58 master's, 4 other advanced degrees awarded. *Degree requirements:* For master's, clinical project. *Entrance requirements:* For master's, MAT or GRE, bachelor's degree from regionally-accredited college or university, minimum cumulative GPA of 3.0, 1 professional and 1 academic reference, resume, on-campus interview, official transcripts. Additional exam requirements/recommendations for international students: Required—TOEFL (minimum score 577 paper-based; 90 iBT), IELTS (minimum score 7). *Application deadline:* For fall admission, 5/30 for domestic and international students; for winter admission, 11/1 for domestic and international students; for spring admission, 2/28 for domestic and international students. Applications are processed on a rolling basis. Application fee: $40. Electronic applications accepted. *Expenses:* Contact institution. *Financial support:* Career-related internships or fieldwork available. Financial award applicants required to submit FAFSA. *Unit head:* Dr. Richard Shaw, Associate Professor of Marriage and Family Therapy/Chair, 503-554-6142, E-mail: rshaw@georgefox.edu. *Application contact:* Joel Moore, Graduate Admissions Counselor, 800-493-4937, Fax: 503-554-6111, E-mail: counseling@georgefox.edu.
Website: http://counseling.georgefox.edu/.

George Mason University, College of Education and Human Development, Program in Counseling and Development, Fairfax, VA 22030. Offers M Ed. *Accreditation:* NCATE. *Faculty:* 7 full-time (4 women), 9 part-time/adjunct (8 women). *Students:* 35 full-time (31 women), 92 part-time (76 women); includes 53 minority (20 Black or African American, non-Hispanic/Latino; 11 Asian, non-Hispanic/Latino; 20 Hispanic/Latino; 2 Two or more races, non-Hispanic/Latino), 4 international. Average age 31. 137 applicants, 31% accepted, 22 enrolled. In 2013, 56 master's awarded. *Degree requirements:* For master's, thesis (for some programs). *Entrance requirements:* For master's, bachelor's degree from regionally-accredited institution with minimum GPA of 3.0 overall or in last 60 credit hours; 2 copies of official transcripts; expanded goals statement; 3 letters of recommendation with recommendation form; 12 credits of undergraduate behavioral sciences; 1,000 hours of counseling or related experience. Additional exam requirements/recommendations for international students: Required—TOEFL (minimum score 575 paper-based; 88 iBT), IELTS (minimum score 6.5), PTE. *Application deadline:* For fall admission, 2/1 for domestic students; for spring admission, 10/1 for domestic students. Application fee: $65 ($80 for international students). Electronic applications accepted. *Expenses:* Tuition, state resident: full-time $9350; part-time $390 per credit. Tuition, nonresident: full-time $25,754; part-time $1073 per credit. *Required fees:* $2688; $112 per credit. *Financial support:* In 2013–14, 2 students received support, including 2 research assistantships with full and partial tuition reimbursements available (averaging $6,796 per year); career-related internships or fieldwork, Federal Work-Study, scholarships/grants, unspecified assistantships, and health care benefits (for full-time research or teaching assistantship recipients) also available. Support available to part-time students. Financial award application deadline: 3/1; financial award applicants required to submit FAFSA. *Faculty research:* Leadership, multiculturalism, social justice, and advocacy; global well-being; social psychological, physical, and spiritual health of individuals, families, communities, and organizations. *Unit head:* Fred Bemak, Academic Program Coordinator, 703-993-3941, Fax: 703-993-5577, E-mail: fbemak@gmu.edu. *Application contact:* Stephanie O'Neill, Office Manager, 703-993-2087, Fax: 703-993-5577, E-mail: soneill@gmu.edu.
Website: http://gse.gmu.edu/programs/counseling/.

The George Washington University, Graduate School of Education and Human Development, Department of Counseling and Human Development, Program in Counseling, Washington, DC 20052. Offers PhD, Ed S. *Accreditation:* ACA (one or more programs are accredited); NCATE. Part-time and evening/weekend programs available. *Students:* 1 (woman) full-time, 4 part-time (all women); includes 1 minority (Black or African American, non-Hispanic/Latino), 1 international. Average age 40. 11 applicants, 100% accepted. In 2013, 1 other advanced degree awarded. *Degree requirements:* For doctorate, comprehensive exam, thesis/dissertation; for Ed S, comprehensive exam. *Entrance requirements:* For doctorate, GRE General Test, interview, minimum GPA of 3.3; for Ed S, GRE General Test or MAT, minimum GPA of 3.3. *Application deadline:* For fall admission, 1/15 priority date for domestic students; for spring admission, 10/1 for domestic students. Applications are processed on a rolling basis. Application fee: $75. *Financial support:* Fellowships, research assistantships, teaching assistantships, career-related internships or fieldwork, Federal Work-Study, and tuition waivers (partial) available. Financial award application deadline: 1/15; financial award applicants required to submit FAFSA. *Faculty research:* Values in counseling, religion and counseling. *Unit head:* Dr. Pat Schwallie-Giddis, Director, 202-994-6856, E-mail: drpat@gwu.edu. *Application contact:* Sarah Lang, Director of Graduate Admissions, 202-994-1447, Fax: 202-994-7207, E-mail: slang@gwu.edu.

The George Washington University, Graduate School of Education and Human Development, Department of Counseling and Human Development, Program in School Counseling, Washington, DC 20052. Offers MA Ed, Graduate Certificate. *Students:* 55 full-time (49 women), 12 part-time (9 women); includes 23 minority (13 Black or African American, non-Hispanic/Latino; 6 Asian, non-Hispanic/Latino; 4 Hispanic/Latino), 3 international. Average age 31. 79 applicants, 92% accepted, 31 enrolled. In 2013, 32 master's awarded. *Unit head:* Dr. Pat Schwallie-Giddis, Chair, 202-994-6856, E-mail: drpat@gwu.edu. *Application contact:* Sarah Lang, Director of Graduate Admissions, 202-994-1447, Fax: 202-994-7207, E-mail: slang@gwu.edu.

Georgian Court University, School of Arts and Sciences, Lakewood, NJ 08701-2697. Offers applied behavior analysis (MA); Catholic school leadership (Certificate); clinical mental health counseling (MA); holistic health studies (MA, Certificate); homeland security (MS); parish administration (Certificate); pastoral ministry (Certificate); professional counseling (Certificate); religious education (Certificate); school psychology (MA, Certificate); theology (MA, Certificate). Part-time and evening/weekend programs available. *Faculty:* 20 full-time (9 women), 9 part-time/adjunct (6 women). *Students:* 94 full-time (82 women), 134 part-time (117 women); includes 43 minority (13 Black or African American, non-Hispanic/Latino; 2 Asian, non-Hispanic/Latino; 25 Hispanic/Latino; 3 Two or more races, non-Hispanic/Latino), 1 international. In 2013, 60 master's awarded. *Degree requirements:* For master's, comprehensive exam (for some programs), thesis (for some programs). *Entrance requirements:* For master's, GRE, MAT, or NTE/PRAXIS, 3 letters of recommendation. Additional exam requirements/recommendations for international students: Required—TOEFL (minimum score 550 paper-based). *Application deadline:* For fall admission, 8/1 priority date for domestic students, 4/1 for international students; for spring admission, 1/1 priority date for domestic students, 7/1 for international students. Applications are processed on a rolling basis. Application fee: $40. Electronic applications accepted. *Expenses: Tuition:* Full-time $18,912; part-time $788 per credit. *Required fees:* $906. *Financial support:* Scholarships/grants, health care benefits, and unspecified assistantships available. Financial award application deadline: 4/15; financial award applicants required to submit FAFSA. *Unit head:* Dr. Rita Kipp, Dean, 732-987-2493, Fax: 732-987-2007. *Application contact:* Patrick Givens, Director of Graduate Admissions, 732-987-2736, Fax: 732-987-2084, E-mail: graduateadmissions@georgian.edu.
Website: http://www.georgian.edu/arts_sciences/index.htm.

Georgia Regents University, The Graduate School, College of Education, Program in Counseling/Guidance, Augusta, GA 30912. Offers M Ed. *Accreditation:* ACA; NCATE. Part-time and evening/weekend programs available. *Faculty:* 3 full-time (2 women), 3 part-time/adjunct (2 women). *Students:* 30 full-time (26 women), 38 part-time (33 women); includes 14 minority (10 Black or African American, non-Hispanic/Latino; 1 Asian, non-Hispanic/Latino; 1 Hispanic/Latino; 2 Two or more races, non-Hispanic/Latino), 1 international. Average age 37. 33 applicants, 73% accepted, 24 enrolled. In 2013, 26 master's awarded. *Degree requirements:* For master's, comprehensive exam, portfolio. *Entrance requirements:* For master's, GRE, MAT, minimum GPA of 2.5. *Application deadline:* For fall admission, 8/1 priority date for domestic students. Applications are processed on a rolling basis. Application fee: $20. *Financial support:* Federal Work-Study, institutionally sponsored loans, and unspecified assistantships available. Support available to part-time students. Financial award application deadline: 4/15; financial award applicants required to submit FAFSA. *Faculty research:* Counseling for AIDS patients, counseling for drug and alcohol abuse. *Unit head:* Dr.

Counselor Education

Charles Jackson, Chair, 706-737-1497, Fax: 706-667-4706, E-mail: cjackson@aug.edu. *Application contact:* Andrea M. Scott, Secretary to the Dean, 706-737-1499, Fax: 706-667-4706, E-mail: ascott1@aug.edu.

Georgia Southern University, Jack N. Averitt College of Graduate Studies, College of Education, Department of Leadership, Technology, and Human Development, Program in Counselor Education, Statesboro, GA 30460. Offers M Ed, Ed S. *Accreditation:* ACA; NCATE. Part-time and evening/weekend programs available. *Students:* 67 full-time (57 women), 22 part-time (all women); includes 39 minority (all Black or African American, non-Hispanic/Latino), 1 international. Average age 28. 18 applicants, 61% accepted, 8 enrolled. In 2013, 27 master's, 8 Ed Ss awarded. *Degree requirements:* For master's, comprehensive exam, transition point assessments; for Ed S, comprehensive exam. *Entrance requirements:* For master's, GRE General Test or MAT, minimum GPA of 2.5, letters of recommendation, interview; for Ed S, GRE General Test or MAT, minimum graduate GPA of 3.25, letters of recommendation. Additional exam requirements/recommendations for international students: Required—TOEFL (minimum score 550 paper-based; 80 iBT), IELTS (minimum score 6). *Application deadline:* For fall admission, 3/15 for domestic and international students; for spring admission, 10/15 for domestic students, 10/1 for international students. Applications are processed on a rolling basis. Application fee: $50. Electronic applications accepted. *Expenses:* Tuition, state resident: full-time $7068; part-time $270 per semester hour. Tuition, nonresident: full-time $26,446; part-time $1077 per semester hour. *Required fees:* $2092. *Financial support:* In 2013–14, 24 students received support, including research assistantships with partial tuition reimbursements available (averaging $7,200 per year); teaching assistantships with partial tuition reimbursements available (averaging $7,200 per year); career-related internships or fieldwork, Federal Work-Study, scholarships/grants, tuition waivers (partial), and unspecified assistantships also available. Support available to part-time students. Financial award application deadline: 4/15; financial award applicants required to submit FAFSA. *Faculty research:* School counseling, test development, gender equity, career counseling, mental health counseling. *Unit head:* Dr. James Bergin, Program Coordinator, 912-478-0873, Fax: 912-478-7104, E-mail: jim_bergin@georgiasouthern.edu. *Application contact:* Amanda Gilliland, Coordinator for Graduate Student Recruitment, 912-478-5384, Fax: 912-478-0740, E-mail: gradadmissions@georgiasouthern.edu.
Website: http://coe.georgiasouthern.edu/coun/.

Georgia State University, College of Education, Department of Counseling and Psychological Services, Program in School Counseling, Atlanta, GA 30302-3083. Offers M Ed, Ed S. *Accreditation:* ACA (one or more programs are accredited); NCATE. *Students:* Average age 0. *Degree requirements:* For master's, comprehensive exam. *Entrance requirements:* For master's, GRE, goal statement, resume, 3 letters of recommendation, transcripts. Additional exam requirements/recommendations for international students: Required—TOEFL. *Application deadline:* For fall admission, 12/1 for domestic and international students. Application fee: $50. Electronic applications accepted. *Expenses: Tuition, area resident:* Full-time $4176; part-time $348 per credit hour. Tuition, state resident: full-time $14,544; part-time $1212 per credit hour. Tuition, nonresident: full-time $14,544; part-time $1212 per credit hour. Tuition and fees vary according to course load and program. *Financial support:* Research assistantships with full and partial tuition reimbursements, teaching assistantships with full and partial tuition reimbursements, career-related internships or fieldwork, institutionally sponsored loans, scholarships/grants, health care benefits, and unspecified assistantships available. Financial award application deadline: 4/1. *Faculty research:* Mattering, adolescent counseling, school counselor identity, group leadership of school counselors, play therapy. *Unit head:* Dr. Brian Dew, Chairperson, 404-413-8168, Fax: 404-413-8013, E-mail: bdew@gsu.edu. *Application contact:* CPS Admissions Office, 404-413-8200, E-mail: nkeita@gsu.edu.
Website: http://education.gsu.edu/CPS/4512.html.

Grambling State University, School of Graduate Studies and Research, College of Education, Department of Educational Leadership, Grambling, LA 71245. Offers developmental education (MS, Ed D, PMC), including curriculum and instructional design (Ed D), English (MS), guidance and counseling (MS), higher education administration and management (Ed D), mathematics (MS), reading (MS), science (MS), student development and personnel services (Ed D); educational leadership (M Ed). Part-time and evening/weekend programs available. *Faculty:* 10 full-time (7 women). *Students:* 19 full-time (13 women), 89 part-time (70 women); includes 83 minority (82 Black or African American, non-Hispanic/Latino; 1 Hispanic/Latino), 6 international. Average age 40. In 2013, 13 master's, 6 doctorates, 1 other advanced degree awarded. *Degree requirements:* For master's, comprehensive exam, thesis (for some programs); for doctorate, comprehensive exam, thesis/dissertation. *Entrance requirements:* For master's, GRE, minimum GPA of 2.5 on last degree; for doctorate, GRE (minimum score 1000, 500 on Verbal), master's degree, minimum GPA of 3.0 on last degree. Additional exam requirements/recommendations for international students: Required—TOEFL (minimum score 500 paper-based; 62 iBT). *Application deadline:* For fall admission, 7/1 for domestic and international students; for spring admission, 12/1 for domestic and international students; for summer admission, 5/1 for domestic and international students. Applications are processed on a rolling basis. Application fee: $20 ($30 for international students). Electronic applications accepted. *Financial support:* Research assistantships, health care benefits, tuition waivers (full), and unspecified assistantships available. Financial award application deadline: 5/31; financial award applicants required to submit FAFSA. *Unit head:* Dr. Olatunde Ogunyemi, Department Head, 318-274-2549, Fax: 318-274-6249, E-mail: ogunyemio@gram.edu. *Application contact:* Brenda Cooper, Administrative Assistant III, 318-274-2238, Fax: 318-274-6249, E-mail: cooper@gram.edu.
Website: http://www.gram.edu/academics/majors/education/departments/leadership/.

Gwynedd Mercy University, School of Education, Gwynedd Valley, PA 19437-0901. Offers educational administration (MS); master teacher (MS); reading (MS); school counseling (MS); special education (MS). Part-time and evening/weekend programs available. *Degree requirements:* For master's, thesis, internship, practicum. *Entrance requirements:* For master's, GRE or MAT; PRAXIS I, minimum GPA of 3.0. *Faculty research:* Learning and the brain, reading literacy, ethics and moral judgment, leadership, teaching and multicultural education.

Hampton University, Graduate College, College of Education and Continuing Studies, Program in Counseling, Hampton, VA 23668. Offers college student development (MA); community agency counseling (MA); pastoral counseling (MA); school counseling (MA). *Accreditation:* NCATE. Part-time and evening/weekend programs available. *Entrance requirements:* For master's, GRE General Test.

Harding University, Cannon-Clary College of Education, Searcy, AR 72149-0001. Offers advanced studies in teaching and learning (M Ed); art (MSE); behavioral science (MSE); counseling (MS, Ed S); early childhood special education (M Ed, MSE); education (MSE); educational leadership (M Ed, Ed S); elementary education (M Ed); English (MSE); French (MSE); history/social science (MSE); kinesiology (MSE); math (MSE); reading (M Ed); secondary education (M Ed); Spanish (MSE); teaching (MAT); teaching English as a second language (MSE). *Accreditation:* NCATE. Part-time and evening/weekend programs available. *Faculty:* 13 full-time (5 women), 42 part-time/adjunct (24 women). *Students:* 154 full-time (119 women), 393 part-time (270 women);

includes 108 minority (81 Black or African American, non-Hispanic/Latino; 5 American Indian or Alaska Native, non-Hispanic/Latino; 5 Asian, non-Hispanic/Latino; 9 Hispanic/Latino; 8 Two or more races, non-Hispanic/Latino), 15 international. Average age 36. 187 applicants, 79% accepted, 135 enrolled. In 2013, 138 master's, 17 other advanced degrees awarded. *Degree requirements:* For master's, comprehensive exam (for some programs), thesis optional, portfolio(s); for Ed S, comprehensive exam, portfolio, project. *Entrance requirements:* For master's, GRE, MAT, PRAXIS; for Ed S, MAT or GRE. Additional exam requirements/recommendations for international students: Required—TOEFL (minimum score 550 paper-based; 79 iBT). *Application deadline:* For fall admission, 8/1 for domestic and international students; for spring admission, 1/1 for domestic and international students. Applications are processed on a rolling basis. Application fee: $35. *Expenses: Tuition:* Full-time $11,574; part-time $643 per credit hour. *Required fees:* $432; $24 per credit hour. Tuition and fees vary according to course load, degree level and program. *Financial support:* In 2013–14, 36 students received support. Unspecified assistantships available. *Faculty research:* Reading, comprehension, school violence, educational technology, behavior, college choice, differentiated instruction, brain-based teaching. *Unit head:* Dr. Clara Carroll, Chair, 501-279-4501, Fax: 501-279-4083, E-mail: ccarroll@harding.edu. *Application contact:* Information Contact, 501-279-4315, E-mail: gradstudiesedu@harding.edu.
Website: http://www.harding.edu/education.

Hardin-Simmons University, Graduate School, Irvin School of Education, Department of Counseling and Human Development, Abilene, TX 79698-0001. Offers M Ed. Part-time programs available. *Faculty:* 3 full-time (2 women), 3 part-time/adjunct (2 women). *Students:* 31 full-time (20 women), 7 part-time (2 women); includes 12 minority (3 Black or African American, non-Hispanic/Latino; 9 Hispanic/Latino). Average age 30. 16 applicants, 94% accepted, 13 enrolled. In 2013, 21 master's awarded. *Degree requirements:* For master's, comprehensive exam, practicum. *Entrance requirements:* For master's, minimum undergraduate GPA of 3.0 in major, 2.7 overall; interview; 3 letters of recommendation; resume. Additional exam requirements/recommendations for international students: Required—TOEFL (minimum score 550 paper-based; 75 iBT). *Application deadline:* For fall admission, 8/15 priority date for domestic students, 4/1 for international students; for spring admission, 1/5 priority date for domestic students, 9/1 for international students. Applications are processed on a rolling basis. Application fee: $50. *Expenses: Tuition:* Full-time $13,410; part-time $745 per credit hour. *Required fees:* $325; $110 per semester. Tuition and fees vary according to program. *Financial support:* In 2013–14, 20 students received support, including 3 fellowships (averaging $2,400 per year); career-related internships or fieldwork and scholarships/grants also available. Support available to part-time students. Financial award application deadline: 6/30; financial award applicants required to submit FAFSA. *Unit head:* Dr. Robert Barnes, Head, 325-670-1451, Fax: 325-670-5859, E-mail: rbarnes@hsutx.edu. *Application contact:* Dr. Nancy Kucinski, Dean of Graduate Studies, 325-670-1298, Fax: 325-670-1564, E-mail: gradoff@hsutx.edu.
Website: http://www.hsutx.edu/academics/irvin/graduate/counseling.

Henderson State University, Graduate Studies, Teachers College, Department of Counselor Education, Arkadelphia, AR 71999-0001. Offers clinical mental health counseling (MS); developmental therapy (MS, Graduate Certificate); elementary school counseling (MSE); secondary school counseling (MSE). *Accreditation:* ACA; NCATE. Part-time programs available. *Faculty:* 5 full-time (3 women). *Students:* 37 full-time (26 women), 54 part-time (42 women); includes 29 minority (24 Black or African American, non-Hispanic/Latino; 2 Hispanic/Latino; 3 Two or more races, non-Hispanic/Latino). Average age 34. 16 applicants, 100% accepted, 16 enrolled. In 2013, 20 master's awarded. *Entrance requirements:* For master's, GRE General Test or MAT, letters of recommendation, minimum GPA of 2.7, teacher certification. Additional exam requirements/recommendations for international students: Required—TOEFL (minimum score 600 paper-based); Recommended—IELTS (minimum score 6.5). *Application deadline:* For fall admission, 8/1 priority date for domestic students, 6/30 priority date for international students; for spring admission, 1/1 priority date for domestic students, 11/30 priority date for international students. Applications are processed on a rolling basis. Application fee: $25 ($75 for international students). *Expenses:* Tuition, state resident: full-time $4284; part-time $238 per credit hour. Tuition, nonresident: full-time $8802; part-time $489 per credit hour. Tuition and fees vary according to course load and campus/location. *Financial support:* In 2013–14, 1 teaching assistantship with partial tuition reimbursement (averaging $4,000 per year) was awarded; scholarships/grants and unspecified assistantships also available. *Unit head:* Dr. Mike Kelly, Interim Chairperson, 870-230-5216, Fax: 870-230-5459, E-mail: kellym@hsu.edu. *Application contact:* Dr. Ken Taylor, Graduate Dean, 870-230-5126, Fax: 870-230-5479, E-mail: taylorke@hsu.edu.
Website: http://www.hsu.edu/counselor-education/.

Heritage University, Graduate Programs in Education, Program in Counseling, Toppenish, WA 98948-9599. Offers M Ed. Part-time programs available. *Degree requirements:* For master's, comprehensive exam. *Entrance requirements:* For master's, interview, letters of recommendation, at least 9 semester-credits of behavioral sciences.

Hofstra University, School of Health Sciences and Human Services, Programs in Counseling, Hempstead, NY 11549. Offers counseling (MS Ed, PD); creative arts therapy (MA); interdisciplinary transition specialist (Advanced Certificate); marriage and family therapy (MA); mental health counseling (MA); rehabilitation counseling (MS Ed, Advanced Certificate, PD); rehabilitation counseling in mental health (MS Ed, Advanced Certificate); school counselor-bilingual extension (Advanced Certificate).

Houston Baptist University, College of Education and Behavioral Sciences, Programs in Education, Houston, TX 77074-3298. Offers bilingual education (M Ed); counselor education (M Ed); curriculum and instruction (M Ed); educational administration (M Ed); educational diagnostician (M Ed); reading education (M Ed). Part-time programs available. Postbaccalaureate distance learning degree programs offered (no on-campus study). *Entrance requirements:* For master's, GRE General Test or MAT. Additional exam requirements/recommendations for international students: Required—TOEFL (minimum score 550 paper-based).

Howard University, School of Education, Department of Human Development and Psychoeducational Studies, Program in School Psychology and Counseling Services, Washington, DC 20059-0002. Offers M Ed. *Accreditation:* NCATE. Part-time programs available. *Faculty:* 2 full-time (1 woman), 2 part-time/adjunct (both women). *Students:* 6 full-time (all women), 3 part-time (2 women); includes 8 minority (all Black or African American, non-Hispanic/Latino), 1 international. Average age 31. 10 applicants, 50% accepted, 1 enrolled. In 2013, 14 master's awarded. *Degree requirements:* For master's, comprehensive exam, expository writing exam, practicum. *Entrance requirements:* Additional exam requirements/recommendations for international students: Required—TOEFL (minimum score 550 paper-based; 79 iBT). *Application deadline:* For fall admission, 2/15 priority date for domestic students; for spring admission, 11/1 for domestic students. Applications are processed on a rolling basis. Application fee: $45. Electronic applications accepted. *Financial support:* Fellowships with full and partial tuition reimbursements, career-related internships or fieldwork, Federal Work-Study, institutionally sponsored loans, scholarships/grants, and unspecified assistantships available. Financial award application deadline: 3/15; financial award applicants required

to submit FAFSA. *Faculty research:* Law and forensic evaluation, juvenile justice, ethics, clinical assessment, personality disorders, substance abuse. *Unit head:* Dr. Mercedes Ebanks, Assistant Professor/Coordinator, 202-806-5780, Fax: 202-806-5205, E-mail: mebanks@howard.edu. *Application contact:* Georgina Jarrett, Administration Assistant, Department of Human Development and Psychoeducational Studies, 202-806-7351, Fax: 202-806-5205, E-mail: gjarrett@howard.edu.

Hunter College of the City University of New York, Graduate School, School of Education, Department of Educational Foundations and Counseling Programs, Programs in School Counselor, New York, NY 10065-5085. Offers school counseling (MS Ed); school counseling with bilingual extension (MS Ed). *Accreditation:* ACA; NCATE. *Faculty:* 7 full-time (4 women), 17 part-time/adjunct (9 women). *Students:* 42 full-time (33 women), 81 part-time (74 women); includes 52 minority (14 Black or African American, non-Hispanic/Latino; 10 Asian, non-Hispanic/Latino; 28 Hispanic/Latino), 2 international. Average age 29. 227 applicants, 23% accepted, 16 enrolled. In 2013, 33 master's awarded. *Degree requirements:* For master's, thesis, internship, practicum, research seminar. *Entrance requirements:* For master's, interview, minimum GPA of 2.7. Additional exam requirements/recommendations for international students: Required—TOEFL, TWE. *Application deadline:* For fall admission, 4/1 for domestic students, 2/1 for international students; for spring admission, 11/1 for domestic students, 9/1 for international students. Applications are processed on a rolling basis. Application fee: $125. *Financial support:* Federal Work-Study and tuition waivers (partial) available. Support available to part-time students. *Unit head:* Dr. Tamara Buckley, Coordinator, 212-772-4758, E-mail: tamara.buckley@hunter.cuny.edu. *Application contact:* Milena Solo, Director for Graduate Admissions, 212-772-4480, E-mail: admissions@hunter.cuny.edu.
Website: http://www.hunter.cuny.edu/school-of-education/programs/graduate/counseling.

Husson University, Graduate Programs in Counseling and Human Relations, Bangor, ME 04401-2999. Offers clinical mental health counseling (MS); human relations (MS); pastoral counseling (MS); school counseling (MS). Part-time and evening/weekend programs available. *Faculty:* 3 full-time (2 women), 1 (woman) part-time/adjunct. *Students:* 36 full-time (30 women), 27 part-time (21 women); includes 3 minority (1 Black or African American, non-Hispanic/Latino; 1 Asian, non-Hispanic/Latino; 1 Two or more races, non-Hispanic/Latino), 1 international. 49 applicants, 71% accepted, 32 enrolled. In 2013, 17 master's awarded. *Degree requirements:* For master's, comprehensive exam (for some programs), thesis optional. *Entrance requirements:* For master's, GRE, BS with minimum GPA of 3.0. Additional exam requirements/recommendations for international students: Required—TOEFL (minimum score 550 paper-based). *Application deadline:* For fall admission, 2/1 for domestic students. Applications are processed on a rolling basis. Application fee: $40. *Expenses: Tuition:* Full-time $5556; part-time $463 per credit. One-time fee: $100. Tuition and fees vary according to course load, degree level and program. *Financial support:* In 2013–14, 2 students received support, including 3 research assistantships; Federal Work-Study, scholarships/grants, and unspecified assistantships also available. Financial award application deadline: 4/15; financial award applicants required to submit FAFSA. *Faculty research:* Challenges and rewards of counseling practice in rural, small town and "neighborhood" settings. *Unit head:* Dr. Deborah Drew, Director, Graduate Counseling Programs, 207-992-4912, Fax: 207-992-4952, E-mail: drewd@husson.edu. *Application contact:* Kristen Card, Director of Graduate Admissions, 207-404-5660, Fax: 207-941-7935, E-mail: cardk@husson.edu.
Website: http://www.husson.edu/human-relations.

Idaho State University, Office of Graduate Studies, Kasiska College of Health Professions, Department of Counseling, Pocatello, ID 83209-8120. Offers counseling (M Coun, Ed S), including marriage and family counseling (M Coun), mental health counseling (M Coun), school counseling (M Coun), student affairs and college counseling (M Coun); counselor education and counseling (PhD). *Accreditation:* ACA (one or more programs are accredited). Part-time programs available. *Degree requirements:* For master's, comprehensive exam, thesis, 4 semesters resident graduate study, practicum/internship; for doctorate, comprehensive exam, thesis/dissertation, 3 semesters internship, 4 consecutive semesters doctoral-level study on campus; for Ed S, comprehensive exam, thesis, case studies, oral exam. *Entrance requirements:* For master's, GRE General Test, MAT, minimum GPA of 3.0, bachelors degree, interview, 3 letters of recommendation; for doctorate, GRE General Test, MAT, minimum graduate GPA of 3.0, resume, interview, counseling license, master's degree; for Ed S, GRE General Test, minimum graduate GPA of 3.0, master's degree in counseling, 3 letters of recommendation, 2 years work experience. Additional exam requirements/recommendations for international students: Required—TOEFL (minimum score 600 paper-based; 80 iBT). Electronic applications accepted. *Faculty research:* Group counseling, multicultural counseling, family counseling, child therapy, supervision.

Immaculata University, College of Graduate Studies, Department of Psychology, Immaculata, PA 19345. Offers clinical psychology (Psy D); counseling psychology (MA, Certificate), including school guidance counselor (Certificate), school psychologist (Certificate). *Accreditation:* APA. Part-time and evening/weekend programs available. Terminal master's awarded for partial completion of doctoral program. *Degree requirements:* For master's, comprehensive exam, thesis optional; for doctorate, comprehensive exam, thesis/dissertation. *Entrance requirements:* For master's, GRE General Test or MAT, minimum GPA of 3.0; for doctorate, GRE General Test or MAT, minimum GPA of 3.5. Additional exam requirements/recommendations for international students: Required—TOEFL, IELTS. Electronic applications accepted. *Faculty research:* Supervision ethics, psychology of teaching, gender.

Indiana State University, College of Graduate and Professional Studies, College of Education, Department of Communication Disorders, Counseling and School and Educational Psychology, Terre Haute, IN 47809. Offers counseling psychology (MS, PhD); counselor education (PhD); mental health counseling (MS); school counseling (M Ed); school psychology (PhD, Ed S); MA/MS. *Accreditation:* ACA; NCATE. Part-time and evening/weekend programs available. *Degree requirements:* For master's, thesis optional; for doctorate, thesis/dissertation, research tools proficiency tests. *Entrance requirements:* For master's, GRE General Test or MAT, minimum undergraduate GPA of 2.75; for doctorate, GRE General Test, master's degree, minimum undergraduate GPA of 3.5. Electronic applications accepted. *Faculty research:* Vocational development supervision.

Indiana University Bloomington, School of Education, Department of Counseling and Educational Psychology, Bloomington, IN 47405-1006. Offers counseling (MS, PhD, Ed S); counselor education (MS, Ed S); educational psychology (MS, PhD); inquiry methodology (PhD); learning and developmental sciences (MS, PhD); school psychology (PhD, Ed S). *Accreditation:* ACA (one or more programs are accredited); APA (one or more programs are accredited); NCATE. Terminal master's awarded for partial completion of doctoral program. *Degree requirements:* For master's, thesis optional; for doctorate, thesis/dissertation; for Ed S, comprehensive exam or project. *Entrance requirements:* For master's, doctorate, and Ed S, GRE General Test. Additional exam requirements/recommendations for international students: Required—TOEFL. Electronic applications accepted. *Faculty research:* Counseling psychology, inquiry methodology, school psychology, learning sciences, human development, educational psychology.

Indiana University of Pennsylvania, School of Graduate Studies and Research, College of Education and Educational Technology, Department of Counseling, Program in School Counseling, Indiana, PA 15705-1087. Offers M Ed. Part-time programs available. *Faculty:* 12 full-time (9 women), 5 part-time/adjunct (all women). *Students:* 25 full-time (18 women), 35 part-time (25 women); includes 3 minority (2 Black or African American, non-Hispanic/Latino; 1 Hispanic/Latino). Average age 28. 55 applicants, 65% accepted, 29 enrolled. In 2013, 32 master's awarded. *Entrance requirements:* Additional exam requirements/recommendations for international students: Required—TOEFL (minimum score 540 paper-based). *Application deadline:* Applications are processed on a rolling basis. Application fee: $50. Electronic applications accepted. *Expenses:* Tuition, state resident: full-time $3978; part-time $442 per credit. Tuition, nonresident: full-time $5967; part-time $663 per credit. *Required fees:* $2080; $115.55 per credit. $93 per semester. Tuition and fees vary according to degree level and program. *Financial support:* In 2013–14, 1 fellowship with full tuition reimbursement (averaging $625 per year), 11 research assistantships with full and partial tuition reimbursements (averaging $2,062 per year) were awarded; career-related internships or fieldwork, Federal Work-Study, scholarships/grants, and unspecified assistantships also available. Financial award application deadline: 4/15; financial award applicants required to submit FAFSA. *Unit head:* Dr. Claire Dandeneau, Chairperson/Graduate Coordinator, 724-357-2306, E-mail: candean@iup.edu. *Application contact:* Dr. Edward Nardi, Associate Dean, 724-357-2480, Fax: 724-357-5595, E-mail: ewnardi@iup.edu. Website: http://www.iup.edu/grad/schoolcounseling/default.aspx.

Indiana University–Purdue University Fort Wayne, College of Education and Public Policy, Department of Professional Studies, Fort Wayne, IN 46805-1499. Offers counselor education (MS Ed); couple and family counseling (MS Ed); educational leadership (MS Ed); school counseling (MS Ed); special education (MS Ed, Certificate). Part-time programs available. *Faculty:* 7 full-time (6 women). *Students:* 5 full-time (2 women), 100 part-time (80 women); includes 11 minority (8 Black or African American, non-Hispanic/Latino; 1 Asian, non-Hispanic/Latino; 2 Hispanic/Latino), 1 international. Average age 32. 14 applicants, 100% accepted, 9 enrolled. In 2013, 57 master's awarded. *Degree requirements:* For master's, comprehensive exam, practicum, internship, portfolio. *Entrance requirements:* For master's, minimum GPA of 2.5, three professional letters of recommendation. Additional exam requirements/recommendations for international students: Required—TOEFL (minimum score 550 paper-based; 79 iBT). *Application deadline:* For fall admission, 4/1 priority date for domestic and international students. Applications are processed on a rolling basis. Application fee: $55. *Financial support:* In 2013–14, 1 research assistantship with partial tuition reimbursement (averaging $13,322 per year), 1 teaching assistantship with partial tuition reimbursement (averaging $13,322 per year) were awarded; scholarships/grants also available. Support available to part-time students. Financial award application deadline: 3/1; financial award applicants required to submit FAFSA. *Faculty research:* Perceptions of children and early adolescents at-risk. *Unit head:* Dr. Jane Leatherman, Acting Chair, 260-481-5742, Fax: 260-481-5408, E-mail: leatherj@ipfw.edu. *Application contact:* Vicky L. Schmidt, Graduate Recorder, 260-481-6450, Fax: 260-481-5408, E-mail: schmidt@ipfw.edu.
Website: http://new.ipfw.edu/education.

Indiana University–Purdue University Indianapolis, School of Education, Indianapolis, IN 46202-2896. Offers computer education (Certificate); curriculum and instruction (MS); early childhood (MS); educational leadership (MS, Certificate); English as a second language (Certificate); higher education and student affairs (MS); kindergarten (Certificate); language education (MS); reading (Certificate); school counseling (MS); special education (MS, Certificate). Part-time and evening/weekend programs available. *Faculty:* 41 full-time, 80 part-time/adjunct. *Students:* 113 full-time (78 women), 263 part-time (200 women); includes 88 minority (51 Black or African American, non-Hispanic/Latino; 1 American Indian or Alaska Native, non-Hispanic/Latino; 10 Asian, non-Hispanic/Latino; 19 Hispanic/Latino; 7 Two or more races, non-Hispanic/Latino), 5 international. Average age 33. 93 applicants, 54% accepted, 40 enrolled. In 2013, 179 master's awarded. *Degree requirements:* For master's, thesis optional. *Entrance requirements:* For master's, GRE General Test, minimum GPA of 3.0. Additional exam requirements/recommendations for international students: Required—TOEFL. *Application deadline:* For fall admission, 5/1 priority date for domestic students; for spring admission, 11/1 for domestic students. Application fee: $55 ($65 for international students). *Financial support:* Fellowships, research assistantships with partial tuition reimbursements, teaching assistantships, Federal Work-Study, institutionally sponsored loans, scholarships/grants, and tuition waivers (partial) available. Support available to part-time students. *Faculty research:* Teachers in the process of change, learning cycles, children's concepts of science. *Total annual research expenditures:* $614,458. *Unit head:* Dr. Pat Rogan, Executive Associate Dean, 317-274-6862, E-mail: progan@iupui.edu. *Application contact:* Donnella Dillon, Graduate Admissions Coordinator, 317-274-0645, E-mail: dmdillon@iupui.edu.
Website: http://education.iupui.edu/.

Indiana University South Bend, School of Education, South Bend, IN 46634-7111. Offers counseling and human services (MS Ed); elementary and secondary education leadership (MS Ed); elementary education (MS Ed); secondary education (MS Ed); special education (MAT, MS Ed). *Accreditation:* NCATE. Part-time and evening/weekend programs available. *Faculty:* 21 full-time (11 women), 9 part-time/adjunct (3 women). *Students:* 12 full-time (8 women), 103 part-time (85 women); includes 18 minority (8 Black or African American, non-Hispanic/Latino; 1 Asian, non-Hispanic/Latino; 5 Hispanic/Latino; 4 Two or more races, non-Hispanic/Latino), 3 international. Average age 36. 24 applicants, 63% accepted, 9 enrolled. In 2013, 41 master's awarded. *Degree requirements:* For master's, thesis or alternative, exit project. *Entrance requirements:* For master's, letters of recommendation, GRE or minimum GPA of 3.0. Additional exam requirements/recommendations for international students: Required—TOEFL. *Application deadline:* For fall admission, 7/1 for domestic students; for spring admission, 11/1 for domestic students. Applications are processed on a rolling basis. Electronic applications accepted. *Financial support:* Career-related internships or fieldwork available. Support available to part-time students. Financial award application deadline: 3/1; financial award applicants required to submit FAFSA. *Faculty research:* Professional dispositions, early childhood literacy, online learning, program assessments, problem-based learning. *Unit head:* Dr. Marvin Lynn, Dean, 574-520-4339. *Application contact:* Yvonne Walker, Student Services Representative, 574-520-4185, E-mail: ydwalker@iusb.edu.
Website: http://www.iusb.edu/~edud/.

Indiana University Southeast, School of Education, New Albany, IN 47150-6405. Offers counselor education (MS Ed); elementary education (MS Ed); secondary education (MS Ed). *Accreditation:* NCATE. Part-time and evening/weekend programs available. *Students:* 23 full-time (21 women), 324 part-time (248 women); includes 44 minority (34 Black or African American, non-Hispanic/Latino; 1 American Indian or Alaska Native, non-Hispanic/Latino; 1 Asian, non-Hispanic/Latino; 5 Hispanic/Latino; 3 Two or more races, non-Hispanic/Latino). Average age 33. 36 applicants, 81% accepted, 25 enrolled. In 2013, 147 master's awarded. *Entrance requirements:* For

master's, minimum undergraduate GPA of 2.5, graduate 3.0. *Application deadline:* Applications are processed on a rolling basis. *Financial support:* Career-related internships or fieldwork, Federal Work-Study, and institutionally sponsored loans available. Support available to part-time students. Financial award applicants required to submit FAFSA. *Faculty research:* Learning styles, technology, constructivism, group process, innovative math strategies. *Unit head:* Dr. Gloria Murray, Dean, 812-941-2169, Fax: 812-941-2667, E-mail: soeinfo@ius.edu. *Application contact:* Admissions Counselor, 812-941-2212, Fax: 812-941-2595, E-mail: admissions@ius.edu. Website: http://www.ius.edu/education/.

Indiana Wesleyan University, Graduate School, College of Arts and Sciences, Marion, IN 46953. Offers addictions counseling (MS); clinical mental health counseling (MS); community counseling (MS); marriage and family therapy (MS); school counseling (MS); student development counseling and administration (MS). *Accreditation:* ACA. Part-time programs available. *Degree requirements:* For master's, thesis or alternative. *Entrance requirements:* For master's, GRE General Test. Additional exam requirements/ recommendations for international students: Required—TOEFL. Electronic applications accepted. *Expenses:* Contact institution. *Faculty research:* Community counseling, multicultural counseling, addictions.

Inter American University of Puerto Rico, Arecibo Campus, Programs in Education, Arecibo, PR 00614-4050. Offers administration and educational supervision (MA Ed); counseling and guidance (MA Ed); curriculum and teaching (MA Ed), including biology education, English as a second language, history education, math education, Spanish; elementary education (MA Ed). *Degree requirements:* For master's, comprehensive exam, thesis optional. *Entrance requirements:* For master's, GRE, EXADEP, bachelor's degree in education or teaching license (administration and supervision) or courses in education and psychology (counseling and guidance), minimum GPA of 2.5 in last 60 credits.

Inter American University of Puerto Rico, Metropolitan Campus, Graduate Programs, Program in Education, San Juan, PR 00919-1293. Offers curriculum and instruction (Ed D); educational administration (Ed D); guidance and counseling (MA, Ed D); special education administration (Ed D). *Degree requirements:* For doctorate, comprehensive exam, thesis/dissertation. *Entrance requirements:* For doctorate, GRE, MAT, or EXADEP. Electronic applications accepted.

Inter American University of Puerto Rico, San Germán Campus, Graduate Studies Center, Program in Counseling and Guidance, San Germán, PR 00683-5008. Offers education: counseling (MA, PhD). Part-time and evening/weekend programs available. *Faculty:* 8 full-time (6 women), 13 part-time/adjunct (7 women). *Students:* 29 full-time (23 women), 8 part-time (7 women); all minorities (all Hispanic/Latino). Average age 31. 11 applicants, 73% accepted, 8 enrolled. In 2013, 5 master's awarded. *Degree requirements:* For master's, comprehensive exam. *Entrance requirements:* For master's, GRE General Test or EXADEP, minimum GPA of 3.0. *Application deadline:* For fall admission, 4/30 priority date for domestic students; for spring admission, 11/15 for domestic students. Applications are processed on a rolling basis. Application fee: $31. *Expenses; Tuition:* Full-time $2424; part-time $202 per credit hour. *Required fees:* $260 per semester. Tuition and fees vary according to course level, course load, degree level and program. *Financial support:* Teaching assistantships, Federal Work-Study, and unspecified assistantships available. *Unit head:* Dr. Elba T. Irizarry, Director of Graduate Studies Center, 787-264-1912 Ext. 7357, Fax: 787-892-6350, E-mail: elbat@sg.inter.edu. *Application contact:* Dr. Evelyn Acevedo, Coordinator, 787-264-7912 Ext. 7358, E-mail: eacevedo@intersg.edu.

Iowa State University of Science and Technology, Department of Educational Leadership and Policy Studies, Ames, IA 50011. Offers counselor education (M Ed, MS); educational administration (M Ed, MS); educational leadership (PhD); higher education (M Ed, MS); organizational learning and human resource development (M Ed, MS); research and evaluation (MS); student affairs (MS). *Degree requirements:* For master's, thesis or alternative; for doctorate, thesis/dissertation. *Entrance requirements:* For master's and doctorate, GRE General Test. Additional exam requirements/ recommendations for international students: Required—TOEFL (minimum score 560 paper-based; 83 iBT), IELTS (minimum score 6.5). Electronic applications accepted.

Jackson State University, Graduate School, College of Education and Human Development, Department of School, Community and Rehabilitation Counseling, Jackson, MS 39217. Offers community and agency counseling (MS); guidance and counseling (MS, MS Ed); rehabilitation counseling (MS Ed). *Accreditation:* ACA; CORE (one or more programs are accredited); NCATE. Part-time and evening/weekend programs available. *Degree requirements:* For master's, comprehensive exam, thesis. *Entrance requirements:* For master's, GRE General Test. Additional exam requirements/ recommendations for international students: Required—TOEFL (minimum score 520 paper-based; 67 iBT).

Jacksonville State University, College of Graduate Studies and Continuing Education, College of Education and Professional Studies, Program in Guidance and Counseling, Jacksonville, AL 36265-1602. Offers MS. *Accreditation:* ACA; NCATE. Part-time and evening/weekend programs available. *Degree requirements:* For master's, comprehensive exam, thesis (for some programs). *Entrance requirements:* For master's, GRE General Test or MAT. Additional exam requirements/recommendations for international students: Required—TOEFL (minimum score 61 iBT). Electronic applications accepted.

John Brown University, Graduate Counseling Programs, Siloam Springs, AR 72761-2121. Offers clinical mental health counseling (MS); marriage and family therapy (MS); school counseling (MS). *Accreditation:* NCATE. Part-time and evening/weekend programs available. *Faculty:* 5 full-time (0 women), 19 part-time/adjunct (6 women). *Students:* 104 full-time (82 women), 100 part-time (75 women); includes 46 minority (15 Black or African American, non-Hispanic/Latino; 4 American Indian or Alaska Native, non-Hispanic/Latino; 3 Asian, non-Hispanic/Latino; 19 Hispanic/Latino; 5 Two or more races, non-Hispanic/Latino). Average age 33. 102 applicants, 84% accepted, 71 enrolled. *Degree requirements:* For master's, practica or internships. *Entrance requirements:* For master's, GRE (minimum score of 300), recommendation forms from three people, 200-word essay describing professional plans and reason for seeking acceptance. Additional exam requirements/recommendations for international students: Required—TOEFL (minimum score 550 paper-based; 70 iBT). *Application deadline:* Applications are processed on a rolling basis. Application fee: $35 ($100 for international students). Electronic applications accepted. *Expenses: Tuition:* Part-time $515 per credit hour. *Financial support:* Fellowships, institutionally sponsored loans, scholarships/ grants, and unspecified assistantships available. Financial award applicants required to submit FAFSA. *Unit head:* Dr. John V. Carmack, Program Director, 479-524-8630, E-mail: jcarmack@jbu.edu. *Application contact:* Nikki Rader, Graduate Counseling Representative, 479-549-5478, E-mail: nrader@jbu.edu. Website: http://www.jbu.edu/.

John Carroll University, Graduate School, Department of Education and Allied Studies, Program in School Counseling, University Heights, OH 44118-4581. Offers M Ed, MA. *Accreditation:* ACA; NCATE. Part-time and evening/weekend programs available. *Degree requirements:* For master's, comprehensive exam, research essay or thesis (MA only). *Entrance requirements:* For master's, GRE General Test or MAT,

minimum GPA of 2.75, interview. Additional exam requirements/recommendations for international students: Required—TOEFL. Electronic applications accepted.

John Carroll University, Graduate School, Program in Community Counseling, University Heights, OH 44118-4581. Offers clinical counseling (Certificate); community counseling (MA). *Accreditation:* ACA. Part-time and evening/weekend programs available. *Degree requirements:* For master's, comprehensive exam, internship, practicum. *Entrance requirements:* For master's, MAT or GRE, minimum GPA of 2.75, statement of volunteer experience, interview, 12-18 hours social science course work, survey. Additional exam requirements/recommendations for international students: Required—TOEFL. Electronic applications accepted. *Faculty research:* Child and adolescent development, HIV, hypnosis, wellness, women's issues.

Johns Hopkins University, School of Education, Certificate Programs in Education, Baltimore, MD 21218-2699. Offers advanced methods for differentiated instruction and inclusive education (Certificate); applied behavior analysis (Certificate); counseling (CAGS); data-based decision making and organizational improvement (Certificate); early intervention/preschool special education specialist (Certificate); education leadership for independent schools (Certificate); education of students with autism and other pervasive developmental disorders (Certificate); evidence-based teaching in the health professions (Certificate); gifted education (Certificate); K-8 mathematics lead-teacher (Certificate); K-8 STEM education lead-teacher (Certificate); leadership for school, family, and community collaboration (Certificate); leadership in technology integration (Certificate); mental health counseling (Certificate); mind, brain, and teaching (Certificate); school administration and supervision (Certificate); urban education (Certificate). Part-time and evening/weekend programs available. Postbaccalaureate distance learning degree programs offered (no on-campus study). *Students:* 7 full-time (4 women), 216 part-time (169 women); includes 66 minority (35 Black or African American, non-Hispanic/Latino; 17 Asian, non-Hispanic/Latino; 6 Hispanic/Latino; 8 Two or more races, non-Hispanic/Latino), 6 international. Average age 35. 257 applicants, 81% accepted, 62 enrolled. In 2013, 202 CAGSs awarded. *Entrance requirements:* For degree, bachelor's degree from regionally- or nationally-accredited institution (master's for some programs), minimum GPA of 3.0 in all previous programs of study, official transcripts from all post-secondary institutions attended, essay, curriculum vitae/ resume, minimum of two letters of recommendation. Additional exam requirements/ recommendations for international students: Required—TOEFL (minimum score 600 paper-based; 100 iBT) or IELTS (minimum score 7). *Application deadline:* For fall admission, 4/1 for domestic students; for spring admission, 10/1 for domestic students; for summer admission, 2/1 for domestic students. Application fee: $80. Electronic applications accepted. *Financial support:* Application deadline: 6/1; applicants required to submit FAFSA. *Unit head:* Dr. David A. Andrews, Dean, 410-516-7820, Fax: 410-516-6697, E-mail: davidandrews@jhu.edu. *Application contact:* Catherine Wilson, Associate Director of Admissions, 410-516-9797, Fax: 410-516-9799, E-mail: soe.info@jhu.edu.

Johns Hopkins University, School of Education, Master's Programs in Education, Baltimore, MD 21218-2699. Offers counseling (MS), including mental health counseling, school counseling; education (MS), including educational studies, gifted education, reading, school administration and supervision, technology for educators; elementary education (MAT); health professions (M Ed); intelligence analysis (MS); management (MS); secondary education (MAT); special education (MS), including early childhood special education, general special education studies, mild to moderate disabilities, severe disabilities. Part-time and evening/weekend programs available. Postbaccalaureate distance learning degree programs offered (no on-campus study). *Students:* 183 full-time (123 women), 1,001 part-time (757 women); includes 380 minority (160 Black or African American, non-Hispanic/Latino; 4 American Indian or Alaska Native, non-Hispanic/Latino; 91 Asian, non-Hispanic/Latino; 78 Hispanic/Latino; 4 Native Hawaiian or other Pacific Islander, non-Hispanic/Latino; 43 Two or more races, non-Hispanic/Latino), 28 international. Average age 28. 508 applicants, 90% accepted, 337 enrolled. In 2013, 565 degrees awarded. *Degree requirements:* For master's, comprehensive exam (for some programs), portfolio, capstone project and/or internship; PRAXIS II (for teacher preparation programs that lead to licensure). *Entrance requirements:* For master's, GRE (for full-time programs only); PRAXIS I or equivalent (for teacher preparation programs that lead to licensure), bachelor's degree from regionally- or nationally-accredited institution, minimum GPA of 3.0 in all previous programs of study, official transcripts from all post-secondary institutions attended, essay, curriculum vitae/resume, minimum of two letters of recommendation. Additional exam requirements/recommendations for international students: Required—TOEFL (minimum score 600 paper-based; 100 iBT) or IELTS (minimum score 7). *Application deadline:* For fall admission, 4/1 for domestic and international students; for spring admission, 10/1 for domestic and international students; for summer admission, 2/1 for domestic and international students. Application fee: $80. Electronic applications accepted. *Financial support:* Application deadline: 6/1; applicants required to submit FAFSA. *Unit head:* Dr. David A. Andrews, Dean, 410-516-7820, Fax: 410-516-6697, E-mail: davidandrews@jhu.edu. *Application contact:* Catherine Wilson, Associate Director of Admissions, 410-516-9797, Fax: 410-516-9799, E-mail: soe.info@jhu.edu.

Johnson State College, Program in Counseling, Johnson, VT 05656. Offers college counseling (MA); school guidance counseling (MA); substance abuse and mental health counseling (MA). Part-time programs available. *Faculty:* 3 full-time (1 woman), 6 part-time/adjunct (3 women). *Students:* 28 full-time (18 women), 66 part-time (59 women). Average age 32. In 2013, 25 master's awarded. *Degree requirements:* For master's, comprehensive exam. *Entrance requirements:* For master's, interview. Additional exam requirements/recommendations for international students: Required—TOEFL. *Application deadline:* For fall admission, 3/15 priority date for domestic students, 2/15 priority date for international students; for spring admission, 10/1 priority date for domestic students, 7/15 priority date for international students. Applications are processed on a rolling basis. *Expenses:* Tuition, state resident: full-time $11,448; part-time $477 per credit. Tuition, nonresident: full-time $24,720; part-time $1030 per credit. Tuition and fees vary according to reciprocity agreements. *Financial support:* Career-related internships or fieldwork and unspecified assistantships available. Support available to part-time students. Financial award application deadline: 3/1; financial award applicants required to submit FAFSA. *Application contact:* Catherine H. Higley, Administrative Assistant, 800-635-2356 Ext. 1244, Fax: 802-635-1248, E-mail: catherine.higley@jsc.edu.

Johnson University, Graduate and Professional Programs, Knoxville, TN 37998-1001. Offers educational technology (MA); intercultural studies (MA); leadership studies (PhD); marriage and family therapy/professional counseling (MA); New Testament (MA); school counseling (MA); teacher education (MA). *Degree requirements:* For master's, variable foreign language requirement, comprehensive exam, thesis (for some programs), internship (500 client contact hours). *Entrance requirements:* For master's, interview, minimum GPA of 3.0, 20 credits of course work in psychology, 15 credits of course work in Bible. Additional exam requirements/recommendations for international students: Required—TOEFL.

Kansas State University, Graduate School, College of Education, Department of Special Education, Counseling and Student Affairs, Manhattan, KS 66506. Offers academic advising (MS); counseling and student development (MS, Ed D, PhD), including college student development (MS), counselor education and supervision

(PhD), school counseling (MS), student affairs in higher education (PhD); special education (MS, Ed D). *Accreditation:* ACA; NCATE. Part-time programs available. *Faculty:* 18 full-time (8 women), 15 part-time/adjunct (5 women). *Students:* 117 full-time (80 women), 327 part-time (257 women); includes 83 minority (42 Black or African American, non-Hispanic/Latino; 2 American Indian or Alaska Native, non-Hispanic/Latino; 9 Asian, non-Hispanic/Latino; 23 Hispanic/Latino; 1 Native Hawaiian or other Pacific Islander, non-Hispanic/Latino; 6 Two or more races, non-Hispanic/Latino), 9 international. Average age 33. 247 applicants, 69% accepted, 117 enrolled. In 2013, 117 master's, 7 doctorates awarded. *Degree requirements:* For master's, comprehensive exam; for doctorate, comprehensive exam, thesis/dissertation. *Entrance requirements:* For master's, minimum undergraduate GPA of 3.0; for doctorate, GRE General Test, minimum GPA of 3.0 in last 60 hours. Additional exam requirements/recommendations for international students: Required—TOEFL. *Application deadline:* For fall admission, 2/1 priority date for domestic and international students; for spring admission, 8/1 priority date for domestic and international students. Applications are processed on a rolling basis. Application fee: $50 ($75 for international students). Electronic applications accepted. *Financial support:* In 2013–14, 3 teaching assistantships (averaging $18,090 per year) were awarded; career-related internships or fieldwork, institutionally sponsored loans, and scholarships/grants also available. Financial award application deadline: 3/1; financial award applicants required to submit FAFSA. *Faculty research:* Counseling supervision, academic advising, career development, student development, universal design for learning, autism, learning disabilities. *Unit head:* Kenneth Hughey, Head, 785-532-6445, Fax: 785-532-7304, E-mail: khughey@ksu.edu. *Application contact:* Dona Deam, Application Contact, 785-532-5595, Fax: 785-532-7304, E-mail: ddeam@ksu.edu.
Website: http://www.coe.k-state.edu/departments/secsa/.

Kean University, Nathan Weiss Graduate College, Program in Counselor Education, Union, NJ 07083. Offers alcohol and drug abuse counseling (MA); clinical mental health counseling (MA); school counseling (MA). *Accreditation:* ACA; NCATE. Part-time programs available. *Faculty:* 7 full-time (5 women). *Students:* 103 full-time (75 women), 153 part-time (125 women); includes 99 minority (46 Black or African American, non-Hispanic/Latino; 6 Asian, non-Hispanic/Latino; 45 Hispanic/Latino; 2 Two or more races, non-Hispanic/Latino), 1 international. Average age 32. 168 applicants, 54% accepted, 58 enrolled. In 2013, 64 master's awarded. *Degree requirements:* For master's, practicum, internship, portfolio. *Entrance requirements:* For master's, GRE General Test or MAT, minimum GPA of 3.0, 2 letters of recommendation, interview, personal statement. Additional exam requirements/recommendations for international students: Required—TOEFL (minimum score 550 paper-based; 79 iBT). *Application deadline:* For fall admission, 5/1 for domestic students, 6/1 for international students; for spring admission, 12/1 for domestic and international students. Applications are processed on a rolling basis. Application fee: $75 ($150 for international students). Electronic applications accepted. *Expenses:* Tuition, state resident: full-time $12,099; part-time $589 per credit. Tuition, nonresident: full-time $16,399; part-time $722 per credit. *Required fees:* $3050; $139 per credit. Part-time tuition and fees vary according to course level, course load, degree level and program. *Financial support:* In 2013–14, 8 research assistantships with full tuition reimbursements (averaging $3,713 per year) were awarded; unspecified assistantships also available. Financial award applicants required to submit FAFSA. *Unit head:* Dr. J. Barry Mascari, Program Coordinator, 908-737-3863, E-mail: jmascari@kean.edu. *Application contact:* Steven Koch, Admissions Counselor, 908-737-5924, Fax: 908-737-5925, E-mail: skoch@kean.edu.
Website: http://grad.kean.edu/counseling.

Keene State College, School of Professional and Graduate Studies, Keene, NH 03435. Offers curriculum and instruction (M Ed); education leadership (PMC); educational leadership (M Ed); safety and occupational health applied science (MS); school counselor (M Ed, PMC); special education (M Ed); teacher certification (Postbaccalaureate Certificate). *Accreditation:* NCATE. Part-time and evening/weekend programs available. *Faculty:* 8 full-time (5 women), 12 part-time/adjunct (6 women). *Students:* 39 full-time (33 women), 46 part-time (32 women); includes 8 minority (1 American Indian or Alaska Native, non-Hispanic/Latino; 2 Asian, non-Hispanic/Latino; 5 Hispanic/Latino). Average age 30. 46 applicants, 61% accepted, 13 enrolled. In 2013, 26 master's, 1 other advanced degree awarded. *Entrance requirements:* For master's, PRAXIS I, 3 references; official transcripts; minimum GPA of 2.5; interview. Additional exam requirements/recommendations for international students: Required—TOEFL (minimum score 550 paper-based; 61 iBT). *Application deadline:* For fall admission, 4/1 for domestic students; for spring admission, 12/1 for domestic students. Applications are processed on a rolling basis. Application fee: $50. Electronic applications accepted. *Expenses:* Tuition, state resident: full-time $10,410; part-time $480 per credit. Tuition, nonresident: full-time $17,795; part-time $530 per credit. *Required fees:* $2366; $94 per credit. Full-time tuition and fees vary according to course load. *Financial support:* Career-related internships or fieldwork, Federal Work-Study, institutionally sponsored loans, scholarships/grants, and unspecified assistantships available. Support available to part-time students. Financial award application deadline: 3/1; financial award applicants required to submit FAFSA. *Unit head:* Dr. Wayne Hartz, Interim Dean of Professional and Graduate Studies, 603-358-2220, E-mail: whartz@keene.edu. *Application contact:* Peggy Richmond, Director of Admissions, 603-358-2276, Fax: 603-358-2767, E-mail: admissions@keene.edu.
Website: http://www.keene.edu/gradstudies/.

Kent State University, Graduate School of Education, Health, and Human Services, School of Lifespan Development and Educational Sciences, Program in Counseling, Kent, OH 44242-0001. Offers Ed S. *Accreditation:* ACA. *Faculty:* 10 full-time (5 women), 9 part-time/adjunct (7 women). *Students:* 11 part-time (8 women); includes 2 minority (1 Black or African American, non-Hispanic/Latino; 1 Native Hawaiian or other Pacific Islander, non-Hispanic/Latino). 3 applicants, 33% accepted. In 2013, 4 Ed Ss awarded. *Entrance requirements:* For degree, 2 letters of reference, goals statement, interview. Additional exam requirements/recommendations for international students: Required—TOEFL (minimum score 550 paper-based; 80 iBT). *Application deadline:* Applications are processed on a rolling basis. Application fee: $30 ($60 for international students). Electronic applications accepted. *Financial support:* Research assistantships, teaching assistantships, Federal Work-Study, scholarships/grants, and unspecified assistantships available. *Unit head:* Dr. Jason McGlothlin, Coordinator, 330-672-0716, E-mail: jmcgloth@kent.edu. *Application contact:* Nancy Miller, Academic Program Director, Office of Graduate Student Services, 330-672-2576, Fax: 330-672-9162, E-mail: ogs@kent.edu.

Kent State University, Graduate School of Education, Health, and Human Services, School of Lifespan Development and Educational Sciences, Program in Counseling and Human Development Services, Kent, OH 44242-0001. Offers PhD. *Accreditation:* ACA; NCATE. *Faculty:* 10 full-time (5 women), 9 part-time/adjunct (7 women). *Students:* 54 full-time (35 women), 12 part-time (9 women); includes 10 minority (7 Black or African American, non-Hispanic/Latino; 3 Asian, non-Hispanic/Latino), 3 international. 29 applicants, 38% accepted. In 2013, 3 doctorates awarded. *Degree requirements:* For doctorate, comprehensive exam, thesis/dissertation. *Entrance requirements:* For doctorate, GRE General Test, preliminary written exam, 2 letters of reference, resume, interview. Additional exam requirements/recommendations for international students: Required—TOEFL (minimum score 550 paper-based; 80 iBT). *Application deadline:* For fall admission, 2/1 for domestic students. Application fee: $30 ($60 for international students). Electronic applications accepted. *Financial support:* In 2013–14, 6 research assistantships with full tuition reimbursements (averaging $12,000 per year), 6 teaching assistantships with full tuition reimbursements (averaging $12,000 per year) were awarded; career-related internships or fieldwork, Federal Work-Study, institutionally sponsored loans, scholarships/grants, health care benefits, unspecified assistantships, and 1 administrative assistantship (averaging $12,000 per year) also available. Support available to part-time students. Financial award application deadline: 4/1; financial award applicants required to submit FAFSA. *Faculty research:* Family/child therapy, clinical supervision, group work, experiential training methods. *Unit head:* Dr. Jane Cox, Coordinator, 330-672-0698, Fax: 330-672-5396, E-mail: jcox8@kent.edu. *Application contact:* Nancy Miller, Academic Program Director, Office of Graduate Student Services, 330-672-2576, Fax: 330-672-9162, E-mail: ogs@kent.edu.
Website: http://www.kent.edu/ehhs/chds/.

Kent State University, Graduate School of Education, Health, and Human Services, School of Lifespan Development and Educational Sciences, Program in School Counseling, Kent, OH 44242-0001. Offers M Ed. *Accreditation:* ACA; NCATE. *Faculty:* 10 full-time (5 women), 9 part-time/adjunct (7 women). *Students:* 26 full-time (22 women), 39 part-time (35 women); includes 5 minority (4 Black or African American, non-Hispanic/Latino; 1 Hispanic/Latino), 4 international. 34 applicants, 38% accepted. In 2013, 34 master's awarded. *Entrance requirements:* For master's, minimum undergraduate GPA of 2.75, 2 letters of reference, goals statement, moral character statement, interview. Additional exam requirements/recommendations for international students: Required—TOEFL (minimum score 550 paper-based; 80 iBT). *Application deadline:* For fall admission, 6/1 for domestic students; for spring admission, 10/1 for domestic students. Application fee: $30 ($60 for international students). Electronic applications accepted. *Financial support:* In 2013–14, 1 research assistantship with full tuition reimbursement (averaging $8,500 per year) was awarded; Federal Work-Study, scholarships/grants, and unspecified assistantships also available. Financial award application deadline: 4/1; financial award applicants required to submit FAFSA. *Faculty research:* Appraisal, diagnosis, group work. *Unit head:* Dr. Jason McGlothlin, Coordinator, 330-672-0716, E-mail: jmcgloth@kent.edu. *Application contact:* Nancy Miller, Academic Program Director, Office of Graduate Student Services, 330-672-2576, Fax: 330-672-9162, E-mail: ogs@kent.edu.

Kutztown University of Pennsylvania, College of Education, Program in Guidance and Counseling, Kutztown, PA 19530-0730. Offers counselor education (M Ed), including elementary counseling, secondary counseling. *Accreditation:* NCATE. Part-time and evening/weekend programs available. *Faculty:* 1 (woman) full-time. *Students:* 27 full-time (21 women), 44 part-time (36 women); includes 7 minority (2 Black or African American, non-Hispanic/Latino; 5 Hispanic/Latino). Average age 31. 33 applicants, 58% accepted, 13 enrolled. In 2013, 27 master's awarded. *Degree requirements:* For master's, comprehensive exam, thesis optional. *Entrance requirements:* For master's, GRE General Test, interview. Additional exam requirements/recommendations for international students: Required—TOEFL (minimum score 550 paper-based; 79 iBT). *Application deadline:* For fall admission, 3/1 for domestic and international students; for spring admission, 10/1 for domestic and international students. Application fee: $35. Electronic applications accepted. *Expenses: Tuition, area resident:* Part-time $442 per credit. Tuition, state resident: part-time $442 per credit. Tuition, nonresident: part-time $663 per credit. *Required fees:* $80 per credit. *Financial support:* Career-related internships or fieldwork, Federal Work-Study, scholarships/grants, and unspecified assistantships available. Financial award application deadline: 3/1; financial award applicants required to submit FAFSA. *Faculty research:* Family addictions, family roles. *Unit head:* Dr. Margaret Herrick, Chairperson, 610-683-4225, Fax: 610-683-1585, E-mail: herrick@kutztown.edu. *Application contact:* Kelly Hish, Admissions Clerk, 610-683-4200, Fax: 610-683-1393, E-mail: graduate@kutztown.edu.

Lakeland College, Graduate Studies Division, Program in Counseling, Sheboygan, WI 53082-0359. Offers MA.

Lamar University, College of Graduate Studies, College of Education and Human Development, Department of Counseling and Special Populations, Beaumont, TX 77710. Offers counseling and development (M Ed); school counseling (M Ed); special education (M Ed); student affairs (Certificate).

Lamar University, College of Graduate Studies, College of Education and Human Development, Department of Educational Leadership, Beaumont, TX 77710. Offers counseling and development (M Ed, Certificate); education administration (M Ed); educational leadership (DE); principal (Certificate); school superintendent (Certificate); supervision (M Ed); technology application (Certificate). Part-time and evening/weekend programs available. Terminal master's awarded for partial completion of doctoral program. *Degree requirements:* For master's, comprehensive exam, thesis optional; for doctorate, thesis/dissertation. *Entrance requirements:* For master's, GRE General Test, minimum GPA of 2.5; for doctorate, GRE. Additional exam requirements/recommendations for international students: Required—TOEFL. *Faculty research:* School dropouts, suicide prevention in public school students, school climate and gifted performance, teacher evaluation.

Lancaster Bible College, Graduate School, Lancaster, PA 17601-5036. Offers adult ministries (MA); Bible (MA); children and family ministry (MA); church planting (MA); consulting resource teacher (M Ed); elementary school counseling (M Ed); leadership (PhD); leadership studies (MA); marriage and family counseling (MA); mental health counseling (MA); pastoral studies (MA); secondary school counseling (M Ed); sports ministry (MA); student ministry (MA); town and country ministry (MA). Part-time and evening/weekend programs available. *Degree requirements:* For master's, comprehensive exam (for some programs), thesis (for some programs). *Entrance requirements:* For master's, bachelor's degree with a minimum of 30 credits of course work in Bible, minimum undergraduate GPA of 3.0, interview. Additional exam requirements/recommendations for international students: Required—TOEFL.

La Sierra University, School of Education, Department of School Psychology and Counseling, Riverside, CA 92515. Offers counseling (MA); educational psychology (Ed S); school psychology (Ed S). Part-time and evening/weekend programs available. *Degree requirements:* For master's, thesis optional; for Ed S, practicum (educational psychology). *Entrance requirements:* For master's, California Basic Educational Skills Test, NTE, minimum GPA of 3.0; for Ed S, minimum GPA of 3.3. *Faculty research:* Equivalent score scales, self perception.

Lee University, Graduate Studies in Counseling, Cleveland, TN 37320-3450. Offers college student development (MS); holistic child development (MS); marriage and family therapy (MS); mental health counseling (MS); school counseling (MS). Part-time programs available. *Faculty:* 9 full-time (3 women), 4 part-time/adjunct (0 women). *Students:* 65 full-time (52 women), 37 part-time (32 women); includes 16 minority (7 Black or African American, non-Hispanic/Latino; 1 Asian, non-Hispanic/Latino; 7 Hispanic/Latino; 1 Native Hawaiian or other Pacific Islander, non-Hispanic/Latino). Average age 27. 52 applicants, 75% accepted, 28 enrolled. In 2013, 42 master's awarded. *Degree requirements:* For master's, variable foreign language requirement, comprehensive exam, thesis, internship. *Entrance requirements:* For master's, GRE General Test or MAT, minimum undergraduate GPA of 3.0, 3 letters of recommendation,

interview, official transcripts, essay. Additional exam requirements/recommendations for international students: Required—TOEFL (minimum score 450 paper-based). *Application deadline:* For fall admission, 4/1 priority date for domestic and international students; for spring admission, 10/1 priority date for domestic and international students. Applications are processed on a rolling basis. Application fee: $25. *Expenses: Tuition:* Full-time $9900; part-time $550 per credit hour. *Required fees:* $35 per term. One-time fee: $25. *Financial support:* In 2013–14, 52 students received support, including 1 teaching assistantship (averaging $250 per year); career-related internships or fieldwork, Federal Work-Study, institutionally sponsored loans, scholarships/grants, and unspecified assistantships also available. Financial award application deadline: 3/1; financial award applicants required to submit FAFSA. *Unit head:* Dr. Trevor Milliron, Director, 423-614-8126, Fax: 423-614-8129, E-mail: tmilliron@leeuniversity.edu. *Application contact:* Vicki Glasscock, Graduate Admissions Director, 423-614-8059, E-mail: vglasscock@leeuniversity.edu.
Website: http://www.leeuniversity.edu/academics/graduate/counseling/.

Lehigh University, College of Education, Program in Comparative and International Education, Bethlehem, PA 18015. Offers comparative and international education (MA, PhD); globalization and educational change (M Ed); international counseling (Certificate); international development in education (Certificate); special education (Certificate); technology use in schools (Certificate); TESOL (Certificate). Part-time and evening/weekend programs available. Postbaccalaureate distance learning degree programs offered (minimal on-campus study). *Faculty:* 4 full-time (2 women). *Students:* 20 full-time (18 women), 26 part-time (17 women); includes 3 minority (2 Asian, non-Hispanic/Latino; 1 Hispanic/Latino), 14 international. Average age 33. 59 applicants, 63% accepted, 10 enrolled. In 2013, 17 master's awarded. Terminal master's awarded for partial completion of doctoral program. *Degree requirements:* For master's, thesis (MA); for doctorate, comprehensive exam, thesis/dissertation. *Entrance requirements:* For master's, 2 letters of recommendation; for doctorate, GRE, transcripts, 2 letters of recommendation, essay, and TOEFL if International applicant. Additional exam requirements/recommendations for international students: Required—TOEFL (minimum score 600 paper-based; 93 iBT). *Application deadline:* For fall and spring admission, 2/1 for domestic and international students. Application fee: $65. Electronic applications accepted. *Financial support:* Application deadline: 3/15. *Faculty research:* Comparative education, rural education, gender equity in education, post-socialist education transformation, educational borrowing, comparing education systems, education policy and globalization, family-school relationships, China, international testing, social inequities. *Unit head:* Dr. Iveta Silova, Program Director and Associate Professor, 610-758-5750, Fax: 610-758-6223, E-mail: ism207@lehigh.edu. *Application contact:* Sharon Y. Warden, Coordinator, 610-758-3256, Fax: 610-758-6223, E-mail: sy00@lehigh.edu.
Website: http://www.lehigh.edu/education/cie.

Lehigh University, College of Education, Program in Counseling Psychology, Bethlehem, PA 18015. Offers counseling and human services (M Ed); counseling psychology (PhD); elementary counseling with certification (M Ed); international counseling (M Ed, Certificate); secondary school counseling with certification (M Ed). *Accreditation:* APA (one or more programs are accredited). Part-time programs available. Postbaccalaureate distance learning degree programs offered (minimal on-campus study). *Faculty:* 6 full-time (4 women), 4 part-time/adjunct (3 women). *Students:* 50 full-time (43 women), 45 part-time (37 women); includes 14 minority (6 Black or African American, non-Hispanic/Latino; 2 Asian, non-Hispanic/Latino; 5 Hispanic/Latino; 1 Two or more races, non-Hispanic/Latino), 17 international. Average age 30. 177 applicants, 34% accepted, 25 enrolled. In 2013, 43 master's, 5 doctorates awarded. *Degree requirements:* For doctorate, comprehensive exam, thesis/dissertation. *Entrance requirements:* For master's, minimum GPA of 3.0, 2 letters of recommendation, essay, transcript; for doctorate, GRE General Test, 2 letters of recommendation, transcript, essay; for Certificate, minimum GPA of 3.0. Additional exam requirements/recommendations for international students: Required—TOEFL (minimum score 600 paper-based; 93 iBT). *Application deadline:* For fall admission, 2/15 for domestic students, 11/15 for international students; for winter admission, 2/1 for international students. Application fee: $65. Electronic applications accepted. Application fee is waived when completed online. *Financial support:* In 2013–14, 21 students received support, including 2 fellowships with full and partial tuition reimbursements available (averaging $16,000 per year), 6 research assistantships with partial tuition reimbursements available (averaging $9,000 per year); career-related internships or fieldwork, Federal Work-Study, institutionally sponsored loans, scholarships/grants, tuition waivers (full and partial), and unspecified assistantships also available. Financial award application deadline: 2/15; financial award applicants required to submit FAFSA. *Faculty research:* Maternal/infant attachment, multicultural training and counseling, career development and health interventions, intersection of identities. *Unit head:* Dr. Arnold R. Spokane, Director, 610-758-3257, Fax: 610-758-3227, E-mail: ars1@lehigh.edu. *Application contact:* Donna M. Johnson, Manager, Graduate Programs Admissions, 610-758-3231, Fax: 610-758-6223, E-mail: dmj4@lehigh.edu.
Website: http://coe.lehigh.edu/academics/disciplines/cp.

Lehman College of the City University of New York, Division of Education, Department of Specialized Services in Education, Program in Guidance and Counseling, Bronx, NY 10468-1589. Offers MS Ed. *Accreditation:* ACA; NCATE. Part-time and evening/weekend programs available. *Degree requirements:* For master's, thesis. *Entrance requirements:* For master's, minimum GPA of 2.7. *Faculty research:* Crisis intervention, domestic violence, alcohol abuse, gender issues.

Lenoir-Rhyne University, Graduate Programs, School of Counseling and Human Services, Program in School Counseling, Hickory, NC 28601. Offers MA. Part-time and evening/weekend programs available. *Degree requirements:* For master's, comprehensive exam, thesis optional. *Entrance requirements:* For master's, GRE General Test, minimum undergraduate GPA of 2.7, graduate 3.0; writing sample. Additional exam requirements/recommendations for international students: Required—TOEFL (minimum score 600 paper-based). Electronic applications accepted.

Lenoir-Rhyne University, Graduate Programs, School of Counseling and Human Services, Programs in Counseling, Hickory, NC 28601. Offers agency counseling (MA); community counseling (MA). Part-time and evening/weekend programs available. *Degree requirements:* For master's, comprehensive exam, thesis optional. *Entrance requirements:* For master's, GRE General Test, writing sample, minimum undergraduate GPA of 2.7, minimum graduate GPA of 3.0. Additional exam requirements/recommendations for international students: Required—TOEFL (minimum score 600 paper-based). Electronic applications accepted.

Lewis University, College of Arts and Sciences, Program in School Counseling, Romeoville, IL 60446. Offers MA. Part-time and evening/weekend programs available. *Students:* 39 full-time (33 women), 86 part-time (70 women); includes 23 minority (15 Black or African American, non-Hispanic/Latino; 1 American Indian or Alaska Native, non-Hispanic/Latino; 7 Hispanic/Latino). Average age 30. *Degree requirements:* For master's, comprehensive exam. *Entrance requirements:* For master's, letters of recommendation, interview, minimum GPA of 2.75. Additional exam requirements/recommendations for international students: Required—TOEFL (minimum score 550 paper-based; 80 iBT). *Application deadline:* For fall admission, 5/1 priority date for international students; for spring admission, 11/15 priority date for international students. Applications are processed on a rolling basis. Application fee: $40. Electronic applications accepted. *Financial support:* Federal Work-Study, scholarships/grants, tuition waivers (full and partial), and unspecified assistantships available. Financial award application deadline: 5/1; financial award applicants required to submit FAFSA. *Unit head:* Dr. Judith Zito, Director, 815-838-0500 Ext. 5971, E-mail: zitoju@lewisu.edu. *Application contact:* Assistant Director, Graduate and Adult Admission, 815-836-5610, Fax: 815-836-5578, E-mail: grad@lewisu.edu.

Liberty University, School of Education, Lynchburg, VA 24515. Offers administration and supervision (M Ed); curriculum and instruction (Ed D, Ed S); early childhood education (M Ed); educational leadership (Ed D, Ed S); educational technology and online instruction (M Ed); elementary education (M Ed, MAT); English (M Ed); gifted education (M Ed); history (M Ed); leadership (M Ed); math specialist (M Ed); middle grades (M Ed, MAT); outdoor adventure sport (MS); reading specialist (M Ed); school counseling (M Ed); secondary education (MAT); special education (M Ed, MAT); sport management (MS), including administration, outdoor recreation, sport management, tourism; sports administration (MS); student service (M Ed); teaching and learning (M Ed); tourism (MS). *Accreditation:* NCATE. Part-time programs available. Postbaccalaureate distance learning degree programs offered (minimal on-campus study). *Students:* 2,241 full-time (1,639 women), 4,413 part-time (3,240 women); includes 2,052 minority (1,588 Black or African American, non-Hispanic/Latino; 37 American Indian or Alaska Native, non-Hispanic/Latino; 67 Asian, non-Hispanic/Latino; 173 Hispanic/Latino; 37 Native Hawaiian or other Pacific Islander, non-Hispanic/Latino; 150 Two or more races, non-Hispanic/Latino), 15 international. Average age 37. 6,185 applicants, 43% accepted, 1603 enrolled. In 2013, 1,256 master's, 117 doctorates, 470 other advanced degrees awarded. *Degree requirements:* For doctorate, comprehensive exam, thesis/dissertation. *Entrance requirements:* For master's, GRE General Test or MAT (if taken in or before 1999), 2 letters of recommendation, minimum undergraduate GPA of 3.0, curriculum vitae; for doctorate and Ed S, GRE General Test or MAT (if taken before 1999), minimum master's GPA of 3.0, 3 years of teaching experience. Additional exam requirements/recommendations for international students: Required—TOEFL (minimum score 600 paper-based; 100 iBT). *Application deadline:* For fall admission, 6/1 for domestic students; for spring admission, 11/1 for domestic students. Applications are processed on a rolling basis. Application fee: $50. Electronic applications accepted. *Expenses:* Contact institution. *Financial support:* Federal Work-Study and tuition waivers (partial) available. *Faculty research:* Self-determination, character education, bibliotherapy, learning styles, distance education. *Unit head:* Dr. Karen L. Parker, Dean, 434-582-2195, Fax: 434-582-2468, E-mail: kparker@liberty.edu. *Application contact:* Jay Bridge, Director of Graduate Admissions, 800-424-9595, Fax: 800-628-7977, E-mail: gradadmissions@liberty.edu.
Website: http://www.liberty.edu/academics/education/graduate/.

Lincoln Memorial University, Carter and Moyers School of Education, Harrogate, TN 37752-1901. Offers administration and supervision (M Ed, Ed S); counseling and guidance (M Ed); curriculum and instruction (M Ed, Ed D, Ed S); English (M Ed); executive leadership (Ed D); higher education administration (Ed D); human resource development (Ed D); leadership and administration (Ed D). Part-time and evening/weekend programs available. Postbaccalaureate distance learning degree programs offered. *Degree requirements:* For master's, comprehensive exam, thesis optional; for Ed S, comprehensive exam. *Entrance requirements:* For master's, PRAXIS, NTE, GRE, MAT, letters of recommendation; for Ed S, graduate transcripts. Additional exam requirements/recommendations for international students: Recommended—TOEFL. *Faculty research:* Brain compatible teaching and learning; poverty in Appalachia; leadership for change; ethics, moral responsibility and social justice; human and organizational learning.

Lincoln University, Graduate Studies, Jefferson City, MO 65101. Offers business administration (MBA), including accounting, entrepreneurship, management, public administration and policy; educational leadership (Ed S), including elementary leadership, secondary leadership, superintendency; guidance and counseling (M Ed), including community/agency counseling, elementary school, secondary school; history (MA); school administration and supervision (M Ed), including elementary school administration, secondary school administration, special education administration; school teaching (M Ed), including elementary school teaching, secondary school teaching; sociology (MA); sociology/criminal justice (MA). Part-time and evening/weekend programs available. Postbaccalaureate distance learning degree programs offered (minimal on-campus study). *Students:* 42 full-time (29 women), 109 part-time (66 women); includes 51 minority (37 Black or African American, non-Hispanic/Latino; 10 American Indian or Alaska Native, non-Hispanic/Latino; 1 Asian, non-Hispanic/Latino; 2 Hispanic/Latino; 1 Two or more races, non-Hispanic/Latino), 10 international. Average age 33. 84 applicants, 76% accepted, 51 enrolled. In 2013, 73 master's, 6 other advanced degrees awarded. *Degree requirements:* For master's and Ed S, comprehensive exam, thesis optional. *Entrance requirements:* For master's and Ed S, GRE, MAT or GMAT, minimum GPA of 2.75 in major, 2.5 overall; 3 letters of recommendation; minimum C average in English composition; personal statement of purpose. Additional exam requirements/recommendations for international students: Required—TOEFL (minimum score 500 paper-based; 61 iBT). *Application deadline:* For fall admission, 8/1 priority date for domestic and international students; for spring admission, 12/1 priority date for domestic and international students; for summer admission, 5/1 priority date for domestic and international students. Applications are processed on a rolling basis. Application fee: $30. *Expenses:* Tuition, state resident: full-time $6840; part-time $285 per credit hour. Tuition, nonresident: full-time $12,720; part-time $530 per credit hour. *Required fees:* $587; $587 per year. Tuition and fees vary according to course load. *Financial support:* Federal Work-Study and scholarships/grants available. Support available to part-time students. Financial award application deadline: 3/1; financial award applicants required to submit FAFSA. *Unit head:* Dr. Linda S. Bickel, Dean, 573-681-5247, Fax: 573-681-5106, E-mail: gradschool@lincolnu.edu. *Application contact:* Irasema Steck, Administrative Assistant, 573-681-5247, Fax: 573-681-5106, E-mail: gradschool@lincolnu.edu.
Website: http://www.lincolnu.edu/web/graduate-studies/graduate-studies.

Lindenwood University–Belleville, Graduate Programs, Belleville, IL 62226. Offers business administration (MBA); communications (MA), including digital and multimedia, media management, promotions, training and development; counseling (MA); criminal justice administration (MS); education (MA); healthcare administration (MS); human resource management (MS); school administration (MA); teaching (MAT).

Loma Linda University, School of Science and Technology, Department of Counseling and Family Science, Loma Linda, CA 92350. Offers MA, MS, DMFT, PhD, Certificate, MA/Certificate. *Degree requirements:* For master's, comprehensive exam, thesis optional; for doctorate, comprehensive exam, thesis/dissertation (for some programs). *Entrance requirements:* For master's, minimum GPA of 3.0; for doctorate, GRE. Additional exam requirements/recommendations for international students: Required—TOEFL (minimum score 550 paper-based), MTELP. Electronic applications accepted.

Long Island University–Brentwood Campus, School of Education, Brentwood, NY 11717. Offers childhood education (MS); early childhood education (MS); literacy (MS); mental health counseling (MS); school counseling (MS); special education (MS). Part-time and evening/weekend programs available.

Long Island University–Hudson at Rockland, Graduate School, Program in Counseling and Development, Orangeburg, NY 10962. Offers mental health counseling (MS); school counselor (MS Ed). Part-time and evening/weekend programs available. *Entrance requirements:* For master's, transcripts, letters of recommendation, personal statement, interview. Additional exam requirements/recommendations for international students: Required—TOEFL (minimum score 79 iBT).

Long Island University–Hudson at Westchester, Programs in Education-School Counselor and School Psychology, Purchase, NY 10577. Offers school counselor (MS Ed); school psychologist (MS Ed). Part-time and evening/weekend programs available.

Long Island University–LIU Brooklyn, School of Education, Department of Human Development and Leadership, Program in Counseling and Development, Brooklyn, NY 11201-8423. Offers MS, MS Ed, Certificate. *Degree requirements:* For master's, thesis optional. *Entrance requirements:* For master's, 2 letters of recommendation. Additional exam requirements/recommendations for international students: Required—TOEFL (minimum score 500 paper-based).

Long Island University–LIU Post, School of Education, Department of Counseling and Development, Brookville, NY 11548-1300. Offers mental health counseling (MS); school counseling (MS). *Accreditation:* ACA. Part-time and evening/weekend programs available. *Degree requirements:* For master's, comprehensive exam or thesis, internship. *Entrance requirements:* For master's, interview, minimum GPA of 3.0. Electronic applications accepted. *Faculty research:* Community prevention programs, youth gang violence, community mental health counseling.

Longwood University, College of Graduate and Professional Studies, College of Education and Human Services, Farmville, VA 23909. Offers education (MS), including algebra and middle school math, counselor education, elementary and middle school math, elementary education, elementary education initial licensure, health and physical education, school librarianship, special education general curriculum, special education initial licensure; social work and communication sciences and disorders (MS). *Accreditation:* NCATE. Part-time and evening/weekend programs available. *Faculty:* 28 full-time (15 women), 9 part-time/adjunct (7 women). *Students:* 86 full-time (80 women), 187 part-time (173 women); includes 38 minority (26 Black or African American, non-Hispanic/Latino; 1 Asian, non-Hispanic/Latino; 5 Hispanic/Latino; 1 Native Hawaiian or other Pacific Islander, non-Hispanic/Latino; 5 Two or more races, non-Hispanic/Latino). 98 applicants, 89% accepted, 85 enrolled. In 2013, 132 master's awarded. *Degree requirements:* For master's, comprehensive exam (for some programs), thesis optional, professional portfolio, internship, clinical experience, or practicum. *Entrance requirements:* For master's, bachelor's degree from regionally-accredited institution, 2 recommendations, 500-word personal essay, official transcripts, minimum GPA of 2.75, valid teaching license (for some programs), passing Praxis I scores for initial teaching licensure programs. Additional exam requirements/recommendations for international students: Required—TOEFL (minimum score 570 paper-based), IELTS (minimum score 6.5). *Application deadline:* For fall admission, 5/1 priority date for domestic students; for spring admission, 10/1 priority date for domestic students; for summer admission, 2/1 priority date for domestic students. Applications are processed on a rolling basis. Application fee: $50. Electronic applications accepted. *Expenses:* Tuition, state resident: full-time $7506; part-time $327 per credit hour. Tuition, nonresident: full-time $17,100; part-time $837 per credit hour. Tuition and fees vary according to course load and campus/location. *Financial support:* Career-related internships or fieldwork and Federal Work-Study available. Financial award applicants required to submit FAFSA. *Unit head:* Dr. Peggy L. Tarpley, Chair of the Department of Education and Special Education, 434-395-2337, E-mail: tarpleypl@longwood.edu. *Application contact:* College of Graduate and Professional Studies, 434-395-2380, Fax: 434-395-2750, E-mail: graduate@longwood.edu.
Website: http://www.longwood.edu/cehs/.

Louisiana State University and Agricultural & Mechanical College, Graduate School, College of Human Sciences and Education, Department of Educational Theory, Policy and Practice, Baton Rouge, LA 70803. Offers counseling (M Ed, MA, Ed S); educational administration (M Ed, MA, PhD, Ed S); educational technology (MA); elementary education (M Ed, MAT); higher education (PhD); research methodology (PhD); secondary education (M Ed, MAT). PhD programs offered jointly with Louisiana State University in Shreveport. *Accreditation:* ACA (one or more programs are accredited); NCATE. Part-time and evening/weekend programs available. *Faculty:* 39 full-time (22 women). *Students:* 185 full-time (136 women), 177 part-time (140 women); includes 110 minority (90 Black or African American, non-Hispanic/Latino; 1 American Indian or Alaska Native, non-Hispanic/Latino; 5 Asian, non-Hispanic/Latino; 9 Hispanic/Latino; 5 Two or more races, non-Hispanic/Latino), 5 international. Average age 31. 167 applicants, 66% accepted, 76 enrolled. In 2013, 134 master's, 23 doctorates, 17 other advanced degrees awarded. Terminal master's awarded for partial completion of doctoral program. *Degree requirements:* For doctorate, thesis/dissertation; for Ed S, thesis optional. *Entrance requirements:* For master's and doctorate, GRE General Test, minimum GPA of 3.0. Additional exam requirements/recommendations for international students: Required—TOEFL (minimum score 550 paper-based; 79 IBT), IELTS (minimum score 6.5), or PTE (minimum score 59). *Application deadline:* For fall admission, 1/25 priority date for domestic students, 5/15 for international students; for spring admission, 10/15 for international students. Applications are processed on a rolling basis. Application fee: $50 ($70 for international students). Electronic applications accepted. *Financial support:* In 2013–14, 253 students received support, including 5 fellowships (averaging $32,204 per year), 27 research assistantships with full and partial tuition reimbursements available (averaging $10,199 per year), 68 teaching assistantships with full and partial tuition reimbursements available (averaging $12,316 per year); career-related internships or fieldwork, Federal Work-Study, institutionally sponsored loans, health care benefits, and unspecified assistantships also available. Support available to part-time students. Financial award applicants required to submit FAFSA. *Faculty research:* Literary, curriculum studies, science education, K-12 leadership, higher education. *Total annual research expenditures:* $735,835. *Unit head:* Dr. Earl Cheek, Jr., Chair, 225-578-1258, Fax: 225-578-2267, E-mail: echeek@lsu.edu. *Application contact:* Dr. Kristin Gansle, Graduate Coordinator, 225-578-6780, Fax: 225-578-2267, E-mail: kgansle@lsu.edu.

Louisiana State University in Shreveport, College of Business, Education, and Human Development, Program in Education, Shreveport, LA 71115-2399. Offers curriculum and instruction (M Ed); educational leadership (M Ed); school counseling (M Ed). *Accreditation:* NCATE. Part-time programs available. *Students:* 1 (woman) full-time, 99 part-time (80 women); includes 26 minority (20 Black or African American, non-Hispanic/Latino; 4 Hispanic/Latino; 2 Two or more races, non-Hispanic/Latino), 1 international. Average age 37. 111 applicants, 97% accepted, 42 enrolled. In 2013, 24 master's awarded. *Degree requirements:* For master's, orally-presented project, 200-hour internship (educational leadership). *Entrance requirements:* For master's, GRE, minimum GPA of 2.5; teacher certification; recommendations and interview (for educational leadership). Additional exam requirements/recommendations for international students: Required—TOEFL (minimum score 550 paper-based; 80 iBT). *Application deadline:* For fall admission, 6/30 for domestic and international students; for spring admission, 11/30 for domestic and international students. Applications are

processed on a rolling basis. Application fee: $10 ($20 for international students). *Expenses: Tuition, area resident:* Part-time $182 per credit hour. *Required fees:* $51. *Financial support:* In 2013–14, 5 research assistantships (averaging $2,150 per year) were awarded. *Unit head:* Dr. Pat Doerr, Coordinator, 318-797-5033, Fax: 318-798-4144, E-mail: pat.doerr@lsus.edu. *Application contact:* Christianne Wojcik, Director of Academic Services, 318-797-5247, Fax: 318-798-4120, E-mail: christianne.wojcik@lsus.edu.

Louisiana Tech University, Graduate School, College of Education, Department of Psychology and Behavioral Sciences, Ruston, LA 71272. Offers counseling and guidance (MA); counseling psychology (PhD); industrial and organizational psychology (MA, PhD). *Accreditation:* APA (one or more programs are accredited). Part-time programs available. *Degree requirements:* For master's, thesis or alternative; for doctorate, thesis/dissertation. *Entrance requirements:* For master's and doctorate, GRE General Test. *Application deadline:* For fall admission, 7/29 for domestic students; for spring admission, 2/3 for domestic students. Application fee: $20 ($30 for international students). *Financial support:* Fellowships, research assistantships, teaching assistantships, and career-related internships or fieldwork available. Financial award application deadline: 2/1. *Unit head:* Dr. Donna Thomas, Head, 318-257-5066, Fax: 318-257-2379. *Application contact:* Dr. Cathy Stockton, Associate Dean of Graduate Studies, 318-257-3229, Fax: 318-257-2379, E-mail: cstock@latech.edu.
Website: http://www.latech.edu/education/psychology/.

Loyola Marymount University, School of Education, Department of Educational Support Services, Program in Guidance and Counseling, Los Angeles, CA 90045. Offers MA. Part-time programs available. *Faculty:* 12 full-time (6 women), 35 part-time/adjunct (26 women). *Students:* 30 full-time (25 women), 13 part-time (8 women); includes 32 minority (4 Black or African American, non-Hispanic/Latino; 4 Asian, non-Hispanic/Latino; 23 Hispanic/Latino; 1 Two or more races, non-Hispanic/Latino), 1 international. Average age 29. 16 applicants, 81% accepted, 14 enrolled. In 2013, 15 master's awarded. *Degree requirements:* For master's, comprehensive exam. *Entrance requirements:* For master's, CBEST, 2 letters of recommendation, letter of intent. Additional exam requirements/recommendations for international students: Required—TOEFL (minimum score 600 paper-based; 100 iBT). *Application deadline:* For fall admission, 6/15 for domestic students; for spring admission, 11/15 for domestic students. Application fee: $50. Electronic applications accepted. *Financial support:* In 2013–14, 14 students received support. Scholarships/grants and unspecified assistantships available. Support available to part-time students. Financial award application deadline: 6/30; financial award applicants required to submit FAFSA. *Total annual research expenditures:* $132,233. *Unit head:* Dr. Nicholas Ladany, Program Director, 310-258-5591, E-mail: nladany@lmu.edu. *Application contact:* Chake H. Kouyoumjian, Associate Dean of Graduate Studies, 310-338-2721, E-mail: ckouyoum@lmu.edu.
Website: http://soe.lmu.edu/admissions/programs/counseling/.

Loyola Marymount University, School of Education, Department of Educational Support Services, Program in School Counseling, Los Angeles, CA 90045. Offers MA. Part-time programs available. *Faculty:* 12 full-time (6 women), 35 part-time/adjunct (26 women). *Students:* 60 full-time (50 women), 22 part-time (20 women); includes 64 minority (17 Black or African American, non-Hispanic/Latino; 7 Asian, non-Hispanic/Latino; 36 Hispanic/Latino; 4 Two or more races, non-Hispanic/Latino). Average age 30. 22 applicants, 86% accepted, 11 enrolled. In 2013, 58 master's awarded. *Degree requirements:* For master's, comprehensive exam. *Entrance requirements:* For master's, CBEST, 2 letters of recommendation, letter of intent. Additional exam requirements/recommendations for international students: Required—TOEFL (minimum score 600 paper-based; 100 iBT). *Application deadline:* For fall admission, 6/15 for domestic students; for spring admission, 11/15 for domestic students. Application fee: $50. Electronic applications accepted. *Financial support:* In 2013–14, 19 students received support, including 1 research assistantship (averaging $720 per year); scholarships/grants and unspecified assistantships also available. Support available to part-time students. Financial award application deadline: 6/30; financial award applicants required to submit FAFSA. *Total annual research expenditures:* $132,233. *Unit head:* Dr. Nicholas Ladany, Director, 310-258-5591, E-mail: nladany@lmu.edu. *Application contact:* Chake H. Kouyoumjian, Associate Dean of Graduate Studies, 310-338-2721, E-mail: ckouyoum@lmu.edu.
Website: http://soe.lmu.edu/admissions/programs/counseling/.

Loyola University Chicago, School of Education, Program in School Counseling, Chicago, IL 60660. Offers M Ed, Certificate. *Accreditation:* NCATE. *Faculty:* 5 full-time (3 women), 14 part-time/adjunct (8 women). *Students:* 22. Average age 25. 38 applicants, 74% accepted, 10 enrolled. In 2013, 9 master's awarded. *Degree requirements:* For master's, comprehensive exam. *Entrance requirements:* For master's, GRE General Test, minimum GPA of 3.0, letters of recommendation, resume. Additional exam requirements/recommendations for international students: Required—TOEFL (minimum score 550 paper-based; 79 iBT). *Application deadline:* For fall admission, 1/1 for domestic and international students. Application fee: $50. Electronic applications accepted. Application fee is waived when completed online. *Expenses: Tuition:* Full-time $16,740; part-time $930 per credit. *Required fees:* $135 per semester. *Financial support:* Career-related internships or fieldwork, institutionally sponsored loans, scholarships/grants, and tuition waivers (partial) available. Support available to part-time students. Financial award application deadline: 2/15; financial award applicants required to submit FAFSA. *Faculty research:* Career development, group counseling, family therapy, child and adolescent development, multicultural counseling. *Unit head:* Dr. Steven Brown, Director, 312-915-6311, E-mail: sbrown@luc.edu. *Application contact:* Marie Rosin-Dittmar, Information Contact, 312-915-6800, E-mail: schleduc@luc.edu.

Loyola University Maryland, Graduate Programs, School of Education, Program in School Counseling, Baltimore, MD 21210-2699. Offers M Ed, MA, CAS. *Accreditation:* ACA; NCATE. Part-time programs available. *Degree requirements:* For master's, thesis. *Entrance requirements:* For master's, essay, transcript, 2 letters of recommendation. Additional exam requirements/recommendations for international students: Required—TOEFL (minimum score 550 paper-based). Electronic applications accepted.

Loyola University New Orleans, College of Social Sciences, Department of Counseling, Program in Counseling, New Orleans, LA 70118-6195. Offers MS. *Accreditation:* ACA. Part-time and evening/weekend programs available. *Faculty:* 5 full-time (2 women), 2 part-time/adjunct (both women). *Students:* 23 full-time (22 women), 47 part-time (40 women); includes 11 minority (6 Black or African American, non-Hispanic/Latino; 2 Asian, non-Hispanic/Latino; 3 Hispanic/Latino), 1 international. Average age 28. 61 applicants, 41% accepted, 16 enrolled. In 2013, 17 master's awarded. *Degree requirements:* For master's, comprehensive exam. *Entrance requirements:* For master's, GRE, resume, transcripts, interview, letters of recommendation, writing sample, work experience. Additional exam requirements/recommendations for international students: Required—TOEFL (minimum score 550 paper-based). *Application deadline:* For fall admission, 2/15 priority date for domestic and international students; for spring admission, 9/15 priority date for domestic and international students. Applications are processed on a rolling basis. Application fee: $20. Electronic applications accepted. *Expenses:* Contact institution. *Financial support:*

Research assistantships, career-related internships or fieldwork, and Federal Work-Study available. Support available to part-time students. Financial award application deadline: 5/1; financial award applicants required to submit FAFSA. *Faculty research:* Counseling theory, spirituality issues, group counseling, multicultural applications. *Unit head:* Dr. Christine H. Ebrahim, Chair, 504-864-7840, Fax: 504-864-7844, E-mail: counselingdept@loyno.edu. *Application contact:* Dianna Whitfield, Department Assistant, 504-864-7840, Fax: 504-865-7844, E-mail: counselingdept@loyno.edu. Website: http://css.loyno.edu/counseling.

Lynchburg College, Graduate Studies, School of Education and Human Development, M Ed Program in School Counseling, Lynchburg, VA 24501-3199. Offers M Ed. *Accreditation:* ACA. Part-time and evening/weekend programs available. *Faculty:* 5 full-time (3 women). *Students:* 11 full-time (9 women), 12 part-time (11 women); includes 5 minority (3 Black or African American, non-Hispanic/Latino; 1 Asian, non-Hispanic/Latino; 1 Hispanic/Latino). Average age 31. In 2013, 5 master's awarded. *Degree requirements:* For master's, counseling internship. *Entrance requirements:* For master's, GRE, minimum GPA of 3.0 (preferred), official transcripts (bachelor's, others as relevant), three letters of recommendation, career goals statement. Additional exam requirements/recommendations for international students: Required—TOEFL (minimum score 550 paper-based; 79 iBT), IELTS (minimum score 6.5). *Application deadline:* For fall admission, 7/31 for domestic students, 6/1 for international students; for spring admission, 11/30 for domestic students, 10/15 for international students. Applications are processed on a rolling basis. Application fee: $30. Electronic applications accepted. Application fee is waived when completed online. *Financial support:* Fellowships, research assistantships, Federal Work-Study, scholarships/grants, health care benefits, and unspecified assistantships available. Support available to part-time students. Financial award application deadline: 7/31; financial award applicants required to submit FAFSA. *Unit head:* Dr. Jeanne Booth, Associate Professor/Coordinator of M Ed in School Counseling, 434-544-8551, Fax: 434-544-8483, E-mail: booth@lynchburg.edu. *Application contact:* Anne Pingstock, Executive Assistant, Graduate Studies, 434-544-8383, Fax: 434-544-8483, E-mail: gradstudies@lynchburg.edu.
Website: http://www.lynchburg.edu/master-education-counselor-education/school-counseling-program.

Lyndon State College, Graduate Programs in Education, Department of Education, Lyndonville, VT 05851-0919. Offers curriculum and instruction (M Ed); reading specialist (M Ed); special education (M Ed); teaching and counseling (M Ed). Part-time and evening/weekend programs available. *Degree requirements:* For master's, exam or major field project. *Entrance requirements:* Additional exam requirements/recommendations for international students: Recommended—TOEFL (minimum score 500 paper-based).

Malone University, Graduate Program in Counseling and Human Development, Canton, OH 44709. Offers clinical counseling (MA); school counseling (MA). *Accreditation:* ACA. Part-time and evening/weekend programs available. *Faculty:* 4 full-time (all women), 7 part-time/adjunct (5 women). *Students:* 29 full-time (21 women), 84 part-time (66 women); includes 16 minority (8 Black or African American, non-Hispanic/Latino; 1 American Indian or Alaska Native, non-Hispanic/Latino; 1 Asian, non-Hispanic/Latino; 4 Hispanic/Latino; 2 Two or more races, non-Hispanic/Latino). Average age 33. In 2013, 35 master's awarded. *Entrance requirements:* For master's, minimum undergraduate GPA of 3.0. Additional exam requirements/recommendations for international students: Required—TOEFL (minimum score 550 paper-based; 79 iBT). *Application deadline:* Applications are processed on a rolling basis. *Financial support:* Tuition waivers (partial) available. Support available to part-time students. Financial award application deadline: 6/30. *Faculty research:* Spirituality and clinical counseling supervision, ethical and legal issues in counseling regarding supervision, resilience in adolescent offenders, protective factors for suicidal clients. *Unit head:* Dr. Susan L. Steiner, Director, 330-471-8510, Fax: 330-471-8343, E-mail: ssteiner@malone.edu. *Application contact:* Dan DePasquale, Senior Recruiter, 330-471-8381, Fax: 330-471-8343, E-mail: depasquale@malone.edu.
Website: http://www.malone.edu/admissions/graduate/counseling/.

Manhattan College, Graduate Programs, School of Education and Health, Program in Counseling, Riverdale, NY 10471. Offers bilingual pupil personnel services (Professional Diploma); mental health counseling (MS, Professional Diploma); school counseling (MA, Professional Diploma). Part-time and evening/weekend programs available. *Faculty:* 2 full-time (1 woman), 16 part-time/adjunct (9 women). *Students:* 64 full-time (51 women), 55 part-time (45 women); includes 64 minority (25 Black or African American, non-Hispanic/Latino; 11 Asian, non-Hispanic/Latino; 28 Hispanic/Latino). 123 applicants, 89% accepted, 58 enrolled. In 2013, 42 master's, 4 other advanced degrees awarded. *Degree requirements:* For master's, thesis, internship. *Entrance requirements:* For master's, minimum GPA of 3.0. Additional exam requirements/recommendations for international students: Recommended—TOEFL. *Application deadline:* For fall admission, 7/1 priority date for domestic students; for spring admission, 12/20 priority date for domestic students. Applications are processed on a rolling basis. Application fee: $60. *Expenses: Tuition:* Part-time $890 per credit. Part-time tuition and fees vary according to program. *Financial support:* In 2013–14, 1 research assistantship with partial tuition reimbursement (averaging $18,000 per year) was awarded; Federal Work-Study, scholarships/grants, health care benefits, and unspecified assistantships also available. Financial award application deadline: 2/1; financial award applicants required to submit FAFSA. *Faculty research:* College advising, cognition, family counseling, group dynamics, cultural attitudes, bullying. *Unit head:* Dr. Corine Fitzpatrick, Director, 718-862-7497, Fax: 718-862-7472, E-mail: corine.fitzpatrick@manhattan.edu. *Application contact:* William Bisset, Vice President for Enrollment, 718-862-7199, Fax: 718-862-8019, E-mail: william.bisset@manhattan.edu.

Marquette University, Graduate School, College of Education, Department of Counselor Education and Counseling Psychology, Milwaukee, WI 53201-1881. Offers clinical mental health counseling (MS); community counseling (MA); counseling psychology (PhD); school counseling (MA). Part-time programs available. *Faculty:* 8 full-time (4 women). *Students:* 66 full-time (52 women), 11 part-time (7 women); includes 9 minority (3 Black or African American, non-Hispanic/Latino; 1 Asian, non-Hispanic/Latino; 2 Hispanic/Latino; 3 Two or more races, non-Hispanic/Latino), 3 international. Average age 26. 152 applicants, 40% accepted, 32 enrolled. In 2013, 38 master's, 4 doctorates awarded. Terminal master's awarded for partial completion of doctoral program. *Degree requirements:* For master's, comprehensive exam, thesis (for some programs); for doctorate, thesis/dissertation, qualifying exam, supporting minor. *Entrance requirements:* For master's, GRE General Test or MAT, official transcripts from all current and previous colleges/universities except Marquette, three letters of recommendation, statement of purpose; for doctorate, GRE General Test, MAT, sample of written work, official transcripts from all current and previous colleges/universities except Marquette, three letters of recommendation, statement of purpose, resume/curriculum vitae. Additional exam requirements/recommendations for international students: Required—TOEFL (minimum score 530 paper-based). *Application deadline:* For fall admission, 1/15 for domestic and international students. Application fee: $50. *Financial support:* In 2013–14, 25 students received support, including 1 fellowship with partial tuition reimbursement available (averaging $17,500 per year), 6 research assistantships with partial tuition reimbursements available (averaging $13,404 per year); scholarships/grants, health care benefits, tuition waivers (partial), and unspecified assistantships also available. Support available to part-time students. Financial award application deadline: 2/15. *Faculty research:* Ethical and legal issues in education, anxiety disorders, multicultural counseling, child psychopathology, group counseling and dynamics. *Total annual research expenditures:* $4,398. *Unit head:* Dr. Alan Burkard, Chair, 414-288-3434, E-mail: alan.burkard@marquette.edu. *Application contact:* Dr. Alan Burkard, Chair, 414-288-3434, E-mail: alan.burkard@marquette.edu.

Marshall University, Academic Affairs Division, College of Education and Professional Development, Program in Counseling, Huntington, WV 25755. Offers MA, Ed S. *Accreditation:* NCATE. Part-time and evening/weekend programs available. *Students:* 106 full-time (91 women), 61 part-time (52 women); includes 15 minority (7 Black or African American, non-Hispanic/Latino; 1 American Indian or Alaska Native, non-Hispanic/Latino; 1 Asian, non-Hispanic/Latino; 1 Hispanic/Latino; 5 Two or more races, non-Hispanic/Latino), 4 international. Average age 32. In 2013, 49 master's awarded. *Degree requirements:* For master's, thesis optional, comprehensive or oral assessment. *Entrance requirements:* For master's, GRE General Test, MAT. Application fee: $40. *Financial support:* Career-related internships or fieldwork, Federal Work-Study, tuition waivers (full), and unspecified assistantships available. Support available to part-time students. Financial award applicants required to submit FAFSA. *Unit head:* Dr. Bob Rubenstein, Director, 304-746-1953, E-mail: brubenstein@marshall.edu. *Application contact:* Information Contact, 304-746-1900, Fax: 304-746-1902, E-mail: services@marshall.edu.

Marymount University, School of Education and Human Services, Program in Counseling, Arlington, VA 22207-4299. Offers clinical mental health counseling (MA); counseling (Certificate); pastoral and spiritual care (MA); pastoral counseling (MA); school counseling (MA). *Accreditation:* ACA (one or more programs are accredited). Part-time and evening/weekend programs available. *Faculty:* 9 full-time (5 women), 7 part-time/adjunct (all women). *Students:* 90 full-time (80 women), 51 part-time (43 women); includes 42 minority (15 Black or African American, non-Hispanic/Latino; 1 American Indian or Alaska Native, non-Hispanic/Latino; 8 Asian, non-Hispanic/Latino; 17 Hispanic/Latino; 1 Two or more races, non-Hispanic/Latino), 5 international. Average age 30. 84 applicants, 76% accepted, 31 enrolled. In 2013, 45 master's awarded. *Entrance requirements:* For master's, GRE, 2 letters of recommendation, interview, resume, personal statement; for Certificate, master's degree in counseling. Additional exam requirements/recommendations for international students: Required—TOEFL (minimum score 600 paper-based; 96 iBT), IELTS (minimum score 6.5). *Application deadline:* For fall admission, 2/3 priority date for domestic students, 7/1 for international students; for spring admission, 10/5 for domestic students. Application fee: $40. Electronic applications accepted. *Expenses: Tuition:* Part-time $850 per credit. *Required fees:* $10 per credit. One-time fee: $200 part-time. Tuition and fees vary according to program. *Financial support:* In 2013–14, 9 students received support, including 2 research assistantships with full and partial tuition reimbursements available, 1 teaching assistantship with full and partial tuition reimbursement available; career-related internships or fieldwork, Federal Work-Study, scholarships/grants, and unspecified assistantships also available. Support available to part-time students. Financial award applicants required to submit FAFSA. *Unit head:* Dr. Lisa Jackson-Cherry, Director, 703-284-1633, Fax: 703-284-5708, E-mail: lisa.jackson-cherry@marymount.edu. *Application contact:* Francesca Reed, Director, Graduate Admissions, 703-284-5901, Fax: 703-527-3815, E-mail: grad.admissions@marymount.edu.

Marymount University, School of Education and Human Services, Program in Education, Arlington, VA 22207-4299. Offers counselor education and supervision (Ed D); elementary education (M Ed); English as a second language (M Ed); professional studies (M Ed); secondary education (M Ed); special education: general curriculum (M Ed). *Accreditation:* NCATE. Part-time and evening/weekend programs available. *Faculty:* 8 full-time (6 women), 13 part-time/adjunct (9 women). *Students:* 76 full-time (67 women), 83 part-time (70 women); includes 30 minority (12 Black or African American, non-Hispanic/Latino; 2 American Indian or Alaska Native, non-Hispanic/Latino; 9 Asian, non-Hispanic/Latino; 6 Hispanic/Latino; 1 Two or more races, non-Hispanic/Latino), 12 international. Average age 31. 63 applicants, 95% accepted, 44 enrolled. In 2013, 88 master's awarded. *Degree requirements:* For master's, thesis or alternative; for doctorate, thesis/dissertation. *Entrance requirements:* For master's, GRE or MAT and PRAXIS I or SAT/ACT and VCLA, 2 letters of recommendation, resume, interview. Additional exam requirements/recommendations for international students: Required—TOEFL (minimum score 600 paper-based; 96 iBT), IELTS (minimum score 6.5). *Application deadline:* For fall admission, 7/1 for international students. Applications are processed on a rolling basis. Application fee: $40. Electronic applications accepted. *Expenses: Tuition:* Part-time $850 per credit. *Required fees:* $10 per credit. One-time fee: $200 part-time. Tuition and fees vary according to program. *Financial support:* In 2013–14, 41 students received support, including 4 research assistantships with full and partial tuition reimbursements available, 1 teaching assistantship with full and partial tuition reimbursement available; career-related internships or fieldwork, Federal Work-Study, scholarships/grants, and unspecified assistantships also available. Support available to part-time students. Financial award applicants required to submit FAFSA. *Unit head:* Dr. Lisa Turissini, Chair, 703-526-1668, Fax: 703-284-1631, E-mail: lisa.turissini@marymount.edu. *Application contact:* Francesca Reed, Director, Graduate Admissions, 703-284-5901, Fax: 703-527-3815, E-mail: grad.admissions@marymount.edu.
Website: http://www.marymount.edu/academics/schools/sehs/grad.aspx.

Marywood University, Academic Affairs, Reap College of Education and Human Development, Department of Psychology and Counseling, Program in Counselor Education, Scranton, PA 18509-1598. Offers MS. *Entrance requirements:* Additional exam requirements/recommendations for international students: Required—TOEFL (minimum score 550 paper-based; 79 iBT). *Application deadline:* For fall admission, 4/1 priority date for domestic students, 3/31 priority date for international students; for spring admission, 11/1 priority date for domestic students, 8/31 priority date for international students. Applications are processed on a rolling basis. Application fee: $35. Electronic applications accepted. *Expenses: Tuition:* Part-time $775 per credit. Tuition and fees vary according to degree level. *Financial support:* Career-related internships or fieldwork, scholarships/grants, and unspecified assistantships available. Support available to part-time students. Financial award application deadline: 6/30; financial award applicants required to submit FAFSA. *Unit head:* Dr. Jennifer Barna, Coordinator, 570-348-6211 Ext. 2328, E-mail: jbarna@marywood.edu. *Application contact:* Tammy Manka, Associate Director of Graduate Admissions, 570-348-6211 Ext. 2322, E-mail: tmanka@marywood.edu.
Website: http://www.marywood.edu/psych-couns/graduate/counselor-education/.

McDaniel College, Graduate and Professional Studies, Program in Counselor Education, Westminster, MD 21157-4390. Offers MS. Part-time and evening/weekend programs available. *Degree requirements:* For master's, comprehensive exam, thesis optional, internship. *Entrance requirements:* For master's, GRE General Test, MAT, or NTE/PRAXIS I, 3 letters of reference. Additional exam requirements/recommendations for international students: Required—TOEFL.

McNeese State University, Doré School of Graduate Studies, Burton College of Education, Office of Graduate Education Programs, Program in School Counseling,

Lake Charles, LA 70609. Offers M Ed. *Accreditation:* NCATE. Evening/weekend programs available. *Entrance requirements:* For master's, GRE, 18 hours in professional education.

McNeese State University, Doré School of Graduate Studies, Burton College of Education, Office of Student Teaching and Professional Education Services, Program in Counseling, Grades K-12, Lake Charles, LA 70609. Offers Graduate Certificate. *Entrance requirements:* For degree, bachelor's degree, teaching certificate.

Mercer University, Graduate Studies, Cecil B. Day Campus, Penfield College, Macon, GA 31207-0003. Offers clinical mental health (MS); counselor education and supervision (PhD); organizational leadership (MS); public safety leadership (MS); school counseling (MS). *Faculty:* 19 full-time (10 women), 16 part-time/adjunct (12 women). *Students:* 130 full-time (105 women), 233 part-time (188 women); includes 184 minority (159 Black or African American, non-Hispanic/Latino; 11 Asian, non-Hispanic/Latino; 11 Hispanic/Latino; 2 Native Hawaiian or other Pacific Islander, non-Hispanic/Latino; 1 Two or more races, non-Hispanic/Latino), 3 international. Average age 33. In 2013, 80 master's awarded. *Unit head:* Dr. Priscilla R. Danheiser, Dean, 678-547-6028, E-mail: danheiser_p@mercer.edu. *Application contact:* Tracey M. Wofford, Associate Director of Admissions, 678-547-6422, E-mail: wofford_tm@mercer.edu.
Website: http://ccps.mercer.edu/graduate/.

Mercy College, School of Social and Behavioral Sciences, Dobbs Ferry, NY 10522-1189. Offers counseling (MS, Certificate), including counseling (MS), family counseling (Certificate); health services management (MPA, MS); marriage and family therapy (MS); mental health counseling (MS); psychology (MS); school counseling (Certificate); school psychology (MS). Part-time and evening/weekend programs available. Postbaccalaureate distance learning degree programs offered (minimal on-campus study). *Students:* 248 full-time (212 women), 315 part-time (274 women); includes 394 minority (194 Black or African American, non-Hispanic/Latino; 2 American Indian or Alaska Native, non-Hispanic/Latino; 10 Asian, non-Hispanic/Latino; 171 Hispanic/Latino; 4 Native Hawaiian or other Pacific Islander, non-Hispanic/Latino; 13 Two or more races, non-Hispanic/Latino), 5 international. Average age 34. 542 applicants, 39% accepted, 146 enrolled. In 2013, 172 master's, 7 other advanced degrees awarded. *Degree requirements:* For master's, comprehensive exam (for some programs), thesis (for some programs). *Entrance requirements:* For master's, essay, 2 letters of recommendation, interview, resume, undergraduate transcript. Additional exam requirements/recommendations for international students: Required—TOEFL (minimum score 600 paper-based; 100 iBT), IELTS (minimum score 8). *Application deadline:* For fall admission, 8/1 for international students. Applications are processed on a rolling basis. Application fee: $40. Electronic applications accepted. *Expenses: Tuition:* Full-time $19,344; part-time $806 per credit. *Required fees:* $580; $806 per credit. $145 per term. Tuition and fees vary according to course load, degree level and program. *Financial support:* Career-related internships or fieldwork, Federal Work-Study, scholarships/grants, and unspecified assistantships available. Support available to part-time students. Financial award applicants required to submit FAFSA. *Unit head:* Dr. Mary Knopp Kelly, Interim Dean, School of Social and Behavioral Sciences, 914-674-7809, E-mail: mkkelly@mercy.edu. *Application contact:* Allison Gurdineer, Senior Director of Admissions, 877-637-2946, Fax: 914-674-7382, E-mail: admissions@mercy.edu.
Website: https://www.mercy.edu/academics/school-of-social-and-behavioral-sciences/.

Messiah College, Program in Counseling, Mechanicsburg, PA 17055. Offers clinical mental health counseling (MAC); counseling (CAGS); marriage, couple, and family counseling (MAC); school counseling (MAC). *Accreditation:* ACA. Part-time programs available. Postbaccalaureate distance learning degree programs offered (no on-campus study). *Entrance requirements:* For master's, minimum undergraduate cumulative GPA of 3.0, 2 recommendations, resume or curriculum vitae, interview; for CAGS, bachelor's degree, minimum undergraduate cumulative GPA of 3.0, essay, two recommendations, resume or curriculum vitae, interview. Electronic applications accepted. *Expenses: Tuition:* Part-time $595 per credit hour. *Required fees:* $30 per course.

Michigan State University, The Graduate School, College of Education, Department of Counseling, Educational Psychology and Special Education, East Lansing, MI 48824. Offers counseling (MA); educational psychology and educational technology (PhD); educational technology (MA); measurement and quantitative methods (PhD); rehabilitation counseling (MA); rehabilitation counselor education (PhD); school psychology (MA, PhD, Ed S); special education (MA, PhD). *Accreditation:* APA (one or more programs are accredited); CORE (one or more programs are accredited). Part-time programs available. *Entrance requirements:* Additional exam requirements/recommendations for international students: Required—TOEFL. Electronic applications accepted.

Middle Tennessee State University, College of Graduate Studies, College of Education, Department of Educational Leadership, Program in Professional Counseling, Murfreesboro, TN 37132. Offers mental health counseling (M Ed); school counseling (M Ed). *Accreditation:* ACA; NCATE. Part-time and evening/weekend programs available. Postbaccalaureate distance learning degree programs offered. *Students:* 20 full-time (19 women), 53 part-time (47 women); includes 5 minority (4 Black or African American, non-Hispanic/Latino; 1 Hispanic/Latino). 63 applicants, 81% accepted. In 2013, 16 master's awarded. *Degree requirements:* For master's, comprehensive exam. *Entrance requirements:* For master's, GRE or MAT. Additional exam requirements/recommendations for international students: Required—TOEFL (minimum score 525 paper-based; 71 iBT) or IELTS (minimum score 6). *Application deadline:* For fall admission, 6/1 for domestic and international students. Applications are processed on a rolling basis. Application fee: $25 ($30 for international students). Electronic applications accepted. *Financial support:* Application deadline: 5/1. *Unit head:* Dr. James O. Huffman, Chair, 615-898-2855, Fax: 615-898-2859, E-mail: jim.huffman@mtsu.edu. *Application contact:* Dr. Michael D. Allen, Vice Provost for Research and Dean, 615-898-2840, Fax: 615-904-8020, E-mail: michael.allen@mtsu.edu.

Midwestern State University, Graduate School, West College of Education, Program in Counseling, Wichita Falls, TX 76308. Offers counseling (MA); human resource development (MA); school counseling (M Ed); training and development (MA). Part-time and evening/weekend programs available. *Degree requirements:* For master's, comprehensive exam, thesis (for some programs). *Entrance requirements:* For master's, GRE General Test, MAT, or GMAT, valid teaching certificate (M Ed). Additional exam requirements/recommendations for international students: Required—TOEFL (minimum score 550 paper-based). *Application deadline:* For fall admission, 7/1 priority date for domestic students, 4/1 for international students; for spring admission, 11/1 priority date for domestic students, 8/1 for international students. Applications are processed on a rolling basis. Application fee: $35 ($50 for international students). Electronic applications accepted. *Expenses:* Tuition, state resident: full-time $3627; part-time $201.50 per credit hour. Tuition, nonresident: full-time $10,899; part-time $605.50 per credit hour. *Required fees:* $1357. *Financial support:* Teaching assistantships with partial tuition reimbursements, career-related internships or fieldwork, Federal Work-Study, institutionally sponsored loans, scholarships/grants, tuition waivers (partial), and unspecified assistantships available. Support available to part-time students. Financial award application deadline: 3/1; financial award applicants required to submit FAFSA. *Faculty research:* Social development of students with disabilities, autism, criminal justice counseling, conflict resolution issues, leadership. *Unit head:* Dr. Michaelle Kitchen, Chair, 940-397-4141, Fax: 940-397-4694, E-mail: michaelle.kitchen@mwsu.edu.
Website: http://www.mwsu.edu/academics/education/.

Minnesota State University Mankato, College of Graduate Studies, College of Education, Department of Counseling and Student Personnel, Mankato, MN 56001. Offers college student affairs (MS); counselor education and supervision (Ed D); marriage and family counseling (Certificate); mental health counseling (MS); professional school counseling (MS). *Accreditation:* ACA (one or more programs are accredited); NCATE. *Students:* 69 full-time (59 women), 45 part-time (33 women). *Degree requirements:* For master's, comprehensive exam, thesis or alternative. *Entrance requirements:* For master's, GRE General Test or MAT (if GPA less than 3.0 for last 2 years), minimum GPA of 3.0 during previous 2 years, 3 letters of reference. Additional exam requirements/recommendations for international students: Required—TOEFL. *Application deadline:* For fall admission, 1/15 priority date for domestic students. Applications are processed on a rolling basis. Application fee: $40. Electronic applications accepted. *Financial support:* Research assistantships with full tuition reimbursements, teaching assistantships with full tuition reimbursements, career-related internships or fieldwork, Federal Work-Study, institutionally sponsored loans, and unspecified assistantships available. Support available to part-time students. Financial award application deadline: 3/15; financial award applicants required to submit FAFSA. *Unit head:* Dr. Richard Auger, Chairperson, 507-389-5658. *Application contact:* 507-389-2321, E-mail: grad@mnsu.edu.

Minnesota State University Moorhead, Graduate Studies, College of Education and Human Services, Program in Counseling and Student Affairs, Moorhead, MN 56563-0002. Offers MS. *Accreditation:* ACA; NCATE. Part-time and evening/weekend programs available. *Degree requirements:* For master's, comprehensive exam, final oral exam, internship, project or thesis. *Entrance requirements:* For master's, GRE or MAT, interview, 3 letters of recommendation, minimum GPA of 3.0. Additional exam requirements/recommendations for international students: Required—TOEFL (minimum score 550 paper-based). Electronic applications accepted.

Mississippi College, Graduate School, School of Education, Department of Psychology and Counseling, Clinton, MS 39058. Offers counseling (Ed S); marriage and family counseling (MS); mental health counseling (MS); school counseling (M Ed). Part-time programs available. *Degree requirements:* For master's and Ed S, comprehensive exam, thesis optional. *Entrance requirements:* For master's, GRE or NTE. Additional exam requirements/recommendations for international students: Recommended—TOEFL, IELTS. Electronic applications accepted.

Mississippi State University, College of Education, Department of Counseling and Educational Psychology, Mississippi State, MS 39762. Offers college/postsecondary student counseling and personnel services (PhD); counselor education (MS), including clinical mental health, college counseling, rehabilitation, school counseling, student affairs in higher education; counselor education/student counseling and guidance services (PhD); education (Ed S), including counselor education, school psychology (PhD, Ed S); educational psychology (MS, PhD), including general education psychology (MS), general educational psychology (PhD), psychometry (MS), school psychology (PhD, Ed S). *Accreditation:* ACA (one or more programs are accredited); APA; CORE (one or more programs are accredited); NCATE. Part-time programs available. Postbaccalaureate distance learning degree programs offered (minimal on-campus study). *Faculty:* 17 full-time (13 women). *Students:* 137 full-time (104 women), 81 part-time (73 women); includes 57 minority (47 Black or African American, non-Hispanic/Latino; 4 American Indian or Alaska Native, non-Hispanic/Latino; 3 Asian, non-Hispanic/Latino; 1 Hispanic/Latino; 2 Two or more races, non-Hispanic/Latino), 5 international. Average age 32. 287 applicants, 36% accepted, 72 enrolled. In 2013, 70 master's, 3 doctorates, 4 other advanced degrees awarded. Terminal master's awarded for partial completion of doctoral program. *Degree requirements:* For master's, comprehensive exam, thesis optional; for doctorate, thesis/dissertation, comprehensive oral and written exam. *Entrance requirements:* For master's, GRE (taken within the last five years), BS with minimum GPA of 2.75 on last 60 hours; for doctorate, GRE, MS from CACREP- or CORE-accredited program in counseling; for Ed S, GRE, MS in counseling or related field, minimum GPA of 3.3 on all graduate work. Additional exam requirements/recommendations for international students: Required—TOEFL (minimum score 550 paper-based; 79 iBT); Recommended—IELTS (minimum score 6.5). *Application deadline:* For fall admission, 2/1 priority date for domestic and international students. Applications are processed on a rolling basis. Application fee: $60. Electronic applications accepted. *Financial support:* In 2013–14, 1 research assistantship (averaging $10,800 per year), 11 teaching assistantships with full tuition reimbursements (averaging $8,401 per year) were awarded; career-related internships or fieldwork, Federal Work-Study, institutionally sponsored loans, and unspecified assistantships also available. Financial award application deadline: 2/1; financial award applicants required to submit FAFSA. *Faculty research:* HIV/AIDS in college population, substance abuse in youth and college students, ADHD and conduct disorders in youth, assessment and identification of early childhood disabilities, assessment and vocational transition of the disabled. *Unit head:* Dr. Daniel Wong, Professor/Head, 662-325-7928, Fax: 662-325-3263, E-mail: dwong@colled.msstate.edu. *Application contact:* Dr. Charles Palmer, Graduate Coordinator, Counselor Education, 662-325-7917, Fax: 662-325-3263, E-mail: cpalmer@colled.msstate.edu.
Website: http://www.cep.msstate.edu/.

Missouri Baptist University, Graduate Programs, St. Louis, MO 63141-8660. Offers business administration (MBA); Christian ministries (MACM); counseling (MAC); education (MSE); education administration (MEA); educational leadership (MSE, Ed S); teaching (MAT).

Missouri State University, Graduate College, College of Education, Department of Counseling, Leadership, and Special Education, Program in Counseling, Springfield, MO 65897. Offers counseling and assessment (Ed S); elementary school counseling (MS); mental health counseling (MS); secondary school counseling (MS). Part-time and evening/weekend programs available. *Students:* 51 full-time (44 women), 66 part-time (54 women); includes 11 minority (2 Black or African American, non-Hispanic/Latino; 1 American Indian or Alaska Native, non-Hispanic/Latino; 1 Asian, non-Hispanic/Latino; 4 Hispanic/Latino; 3 Two or more races, non-Hispanic/Latino), 4 international. Average age 33. 59 applicants, 51% accepted, 16 enrolled. In 2013, 39 master's awarded. *Degree requirements:* For master's, comprehensive exam, thesis or alternative. *Entrance requirements:* For master's, GRE or MAT, minimum GPA of 2.75. Additional exam requirements/recommendations for international students: Required—TOEFL (minimum score 550 paper-based; 79 iBT). *Application deadline:* For fall admission, 2/1 priority date for domestic students, 1/1 priority date for international students; for spring admission, 10/1 priority date for domestic students, 9/1 priority date for international students. Application fee: $35 ($50 for international students). Electronic applications accepted. *Expenses:* Tuition, state resident: full-time $4500; part-time $250 per credit hour. Tuition, nonresident: full-time $9018; part-time $501 per credit hour. *Required fees:* $361 per semester. Tuition and fees vary according to course level, course load and program. *Financial support:* Federal Work-Study, institutionally sponsored loans, scholarships/grants, and unspecified assistantships available. Financial award application deadline: 3/31; financial award applicants required to submit FAFSA. *Unit*

head: Dr. Jeffrey Cornelius-White, Program Coordinator, 417-836-6517, Fax: 417-836-4918, E-mail: jcornelius-white@missouristate.edu. *Application contact:* Misty Stewart, Coordinator of Admissions and Recruitment, 417-836-6079, Fax: 417-836-6200, E-mail: mistystewart@missouristate.edu.
Website: http://education.missouristate.edu/clse/.

Montana State University Billings, College of Education, Department of Educational Theory and Practice, Billings, MT 59101-0298. Offers educational technology (M Ed); general curriculum (M Ed); interdisciplinary studies (M Ed); reading (M Ed); school counseling (M Ed); special education (MS Sp Ed), including special education generalist; special education (MS Sp Ed), including advanced studies; teaching (Certificate). Part-time programs available. Postbaccalaureate distance learning degree programs offered (minimal on-campus study). *Degree requirements:* For master's, thesis optional. *Entrance requirements:* For master's, GRE General Test or MAT, minimum GPA of 3.0 (undergraduate), 3.25 (graduate). *Application deadline:* For fall admission, 7/15 for international students; for spring admission, 12/1 for international students. Applications are processed on a rolling basis. Application fee: $40. *Expenses:* Tuition, state resident: full-time $2653.75; part-time $1718 per semester. Tuition, nonresident: full-time $7015; part-time $4640 per semester. *Required fees:* $2445; $444 per credit. *Financial support:* Teaching assistantships with partial tuition reimbursements, career-related internships or fieldwork, Federal Work-Study, institutionally sponsored loans, scholarships/grants, tuition waivers (partial), and unspecified assistantships available. Support available to part-time students. Financial award application deadline: 5/1; financial award applicants required to submit FAFSA. *Unit head:* Dr. Ken Miller, Chair, 406-657-2034, E-mail: kmiller@msubillings.edu. *Application contact:* David M. Sullivan, Graduate Studies Counselor, 406-657-2053, Fax: 406-657-2299, E-mail: dsullivan@msubillings.edu.

Montana State University Billings, College of Education, Department of Special Education, Counseling, Reading and Early Childhood, Option in School Counseling, Billings, MT 59101-0298. Offers M Ed. *Accreditation:* NCATE. Part-time programs available. *Degree requirements:* For master's, thesis or professional paper and/or field experience. *Entrance requirements:* For master's, GRE General Test or MAT, minimum GPA of 3.0 (undergraduate), 3.25 (graduate). *Application deadline:* Applications are processed on a rolling basis. Application fee: $40. *Expenses:* Tuition, state resident: full-time $2653.75; part-time $1718 per semester. Tuition, nonresident: full-time $7015; part-time $4640 per semester. *Required fees:* $2445; $444 per credit. *Financial support:* Teaching assistantships, career-related internships or fieldwork, Federal Work-Study, institutionally sponsored loans, scholarships/grants, tuition waivers (partial), and unspecified assistantships available. Support available to part-time students. Financial award application deadline: 5/1; financial award applicants required to submit FAFSA. *Unit head:* Dr. Ken Miller, Chair, 406-657-2034, E-mail: kmiller@msubillings.edu. *Application contact:* David M. Sullivan, Graduate Studies Counselor, 406-657-2053, Fax: 406-657-2299, E-mail: dsullivan@msubillings.edu.

Montana State University–Northern, Graduate Programs, Option in Counselor Education, Havre, MT 59501-7751. Offers M Ed. Part-time and evening/weekend programs available. *Degree requirements:* For master's, comprehensive exam, thesis optional, oral exams. *Entrance requirements:* For master's, GRE General Test or MAT, minimum GPA of 3.0. Electronic applications accepted.

Montclair State University, The Graduate School, College of Education and Human Services, Department of Counseling and Educational Leadership, Advanced Counseling Certificate Program, Montclair, NJ 07043-1624. Offers Post-Master's Certificate. *Accreditation:* ACA. Part-time and evening/weekend programs available. *Entrance requirements:* Additional exam requirements/recommendations for international students: Required—TOEFL (minimum score 83 iBT), IELTS (minimum score 6.5). Electronic applications accepted.

Montclair State University, The Graduate School, College of Education and Human Services, Department of Counseling and Educational Leadership, Doctoral Program in Counselor Education, Montclair, NJ 07043-1624. Offers PhD. *Accreditation:* ACA. Part-time and evening/weekend programs available. *Degree requirements:* For doctorate, comprehensive exam, thesis/dissertation. *Entrance requirements:* For doctorate, GRE General Test, interview, 3 letters of recommendation. Additional exam requirements/recommendations for international students: Required—TOEFL (minimum score 83 iBT), IELTS (minimum score 6.5). Electronic applications accepted.

Montclair State University, The Graduate School, College of Education and Human Services, Department of Counseling and Educational Leadership, Program in Counseling, Montclair, NJ 07043-1624. Offers MA. *Accreditation:* ACA. Part-time and evening/weekend programs available. *Degree requirements:* For master's, comprehensive exam, thesis or alternative. *Entrance requirements:* For master's, GRE General Test, interview, 2 letters of recommendation. Additional exam requirements/recommendations for international students: Required—TOEFL (minimum score 83 iBT), IELTS (minimum score 6.5). Electronic applications accepted.

Morehead State University, Graduate Programs, College of Education, Department of Foundational and Graduate Studies in Education, Morehead, KY 40351. Offers adult and higher education (MA, Ed S); certified professional counselor (Ed S); counseling P-12 (MA); curriculum and instruction (Ed S); educational technology (MA Ed); instructional leadership (Ed S); school administration (MA); school counseling (Ed S); teacher leader business and marketing content (MA Ed); teacher leader business and marketing technology (MA Ed); teacher leader educational technology (MA Ed); teacher leader English (MA Ed); teacher leader gifted education (MA Ed); teacher leader IECE certification (MA Ed); teacher leader interdisciplinary education P-5 (MA Ed); teacher leader middle grades (MA Ed); teacher leader non IECE certification (MA Ed); teacher leader reading/writing - non-certification (MA Ed); teacher leader reading/writing certification (MA Ed); teacher leader school communication - certification (MA Ed); teacher leader school communication - non-certification (MA Ed); teacher leader social studies (MA Ed); teacher leader special education (MA Ed). *Accreditation:* NCATE. Part-time and evening/weekend programs available. *Degree requirements:* For master's, thesis optional, oral and/or written comprehensive exams; for Ed S, thesis, oral exam. *Entrance requirements:* For master's, GRE General Test, minimum overall undergraduate GPA of 2.5; for Ed S, GRE General Test, interview, master's degree, minimum GPA of 3.5, work experience. Additional exam requirements/recommendations for international students: Required—TOEFL (minimum score 500 paper-based). Electronic applications accepted. *Faculty research:* Character education, school accountability, computer applications for school administrators.

Mount Mary University, Graduate Division, Program in Counseling, Milwaukee, WI 53222-4597. Offers clinical mental health counseling (MS, Certificate); school counseling (MS, Certificate). Part-time and evening/weekend programs available. *Faculty:* 6 full-time (all women), 15 part-time/adjunct (12 women). *Students:* 125 full-time (115 women), 38 part-time (35 women); includes 59 minority (38 Black or African American, non-Hispanic/Latino; 1 American Indian or Alaska Native, non-Hispanic/Latino; 12 Hispanic/Latino; 1 Native Hawaiian or other Pacific Islander, non-Hispanic/Latino; 7 Two or more races, non-Hispanic/Latino), 2 international. Average age 33. 46 applicants, 91% accepted, 29 enrolled. In 2013, 39 master's, 4 other advanced degrees awarded. *Degree requirements:* For master's, comprehensive exam, thesis or alternative. *Entrance requirements:* For master's, minimum GPA of 3.0. Additional exam requirements/recommendations for international students: Required—TOEFL (minimum score 80 iBT) or IELTS (minimum score 6.5). *Application deadline:* For fall admission, 7/15 for domestic and international students; for spring admission, 11/15 for domestic and international students. Applications are processed on a rolling basis. Application fee: $45 ($100 for international students). Electronic applications accepted. *Expenses:* Contact institution. *Financial support:* Career-related internships or fieldwork, Federal Work-Study, and unspecified assistantships available. Support available to part-time students. Financial award application deadline: 5/1; financial award applicants required to submit FAFSA. *Faculty research:* Cognitive behavioral interventions for depression, eating disorders and compliance. *Unit head:* Dr. Carrie King, Graduate Program Director, 414-258-4810 Ext. 318, E-mail: kingc@mtmary.edu. *Application contact:* Dr. Douglas J. Mickelson, Dean for Graduate Education, 414-256-1252, Fax: 414-256-0167, E-mail: mickelsd@mtmary.edu.
Website: http://www.mtmary.edu/majors-programs/graduate/counseling/index.html.

Multnomah University, Multnomah Bible College Graduate Degree Programs, Portland, OR 97220-5898. Offers counseling (MA); global development and justice (MA); teaching (MA); TESOL (MA). *Faculty:* 6 full-time (4 women), 23 part-time/adjunct (11 women). *Students:* 124 full-time (84 women), 21 part-time (12 women); includes 16 minority (4 Black or African American, non-Hispanic/Latino; 1 Asian, non-Hispanic/Latino; 7 Hispanic/Latino; 4 Two or more races, non-Hispanic/Latino), 1 international. Average age 30. 103 applicants, 94% accepted, 53 enrolled. In 2013, 49 master's awarded. *Degree requirements:* For master's, variable foreign language requirement, comprehensive exam (for some programs), thesis (for some programs). *Entrance requirements:* For master's, CBEST or WEST-B (for MAT), interview; references (4 for teaching); writing sample (for counseling). Additional exam requirements/recommendations for international students: Required—TOEFL (minimum score 550 paper-based). *Application deadline:* For fall admission, 8/1 for domestic students, 12/1 for international students; for spring admission, 12/1 for domestic and international students. Application fee: $40. *Expenses: Tuition:* Full-time $7360; part-time $460 per credit hour. *Financial support:* Career-related internships or fieldwork and scholarships/grants available. Support available to part-time students. Financial award application deadline: 7/1; financial award applicants required to submit FAFSA. *Unit head:* Dr. Rex Koivisto, Academic Dean, 503-251-6401. *Application contact:* Stephanie Pollard, Admissions Counselor, 503-251-5166, Fax: 503-254-1268, E-mail: admiss@multnomah.edu.

Murray State University, College of Education, Department of Educational Studies, Leadership and Counseling, Program in Community and Agency Counseling, Murray, KY 42071. Offers Ed S. *Accreditation:* NCATE. Part-time programs available. *Degree requirements:* For Ed S, comprehensive exam, thesis. *Entrance requirements:* For degree, GRE General Test. Additional exam requirements/recommendations for international students: Required—TOEFL.

Murray State University, College of Education, Department of Educational Studies, Leadership and Counseling, Programs in School Guidance and Counseling, Murray, KY 42071. Offers MA Ed, Ed S. *Accreditation:* NCATE. Part-time programs available. *Degree requirements:* For master's, comprehensive exam, thesis (for some programs), portfolio; for Ed S, comprehensive exam, portfolio. *Entrance requirements:* For master's, GRE General Test or MAT. Additional exam requirements/recommendations for international students: Required—TOEFL.

Naropa University, Graduate Programs, Program in Transpersonal Counseling Psychology, Concentration in Counseling Psychology, Boulder, CO 80302-6697. Offers MA. *Faculty:* 7 full-time (5 women), 20 part-time/adjunct (13 women). *Students:* 99 full-time (74 women), 50 part-time (35 women); includes 23 minority (3 Black or African American, non-Hispanic/Latino; 1 American Indian or Alaska Native, non-Hispanic/Latino; 4 Asian, non-Hispanic/Latino; 8 Hispanic/Latino; 7 Two or more races, non-Hispanic/Latino), 6 international. Average age 33. 88 applicants, 81% accepted, 52 enrolled. In 2013, 46 master's awarded. *Degree requirements:* For master's, internships, counseling practicum. *Entrance requirements:* For master's, in-person interview; course work in psychology, resume, 2 letters of recommendation, transcripts, minimum 100 hours of paid or volunteer work in a helping profession (mental health, teaching, healthcare, etc.). Additional exam requirements/recommendations for international students: Required—TOEFL (minimum score 600 paper-based; 80 iBT). *Application deadline:* For fall admission, 1/13 priority date for domestic students, 1/15 priority date for international students. Applications are processed on a rolling basis. Application fee: $60. Electronic applications accepted. *Expenses: Tuition:* Full-time $16,848; part-time $936 per credit. *Required fees:* $335 per semester. *Financial support:* In 2013–14, 31 students received support, including 9 research assistantships with partial tuition reimbursements available (averaging $6,028 per year); career-related internships or fieldwork, Federal Work-Study, scholarships/grants, health care benefits, tuition waivers (partial), and unspecified assistantships also available. Financial award application deadline: 3/1; financial award applicants required to submit FAFSA. *Unit head:* Dr. MacAndrew Jack, Director, Graduate School of Psychology, 303-245-4752, E-mail: mjack@naropa.edu. *Application contact:* Office of Admissions, 303-546-3572, Fax: 303-546-3583, E-mail: admissions@naropa.edu.
Website: http://www.naropa.edu/academics/gsp/grad/somatic-counseling-psychology-ma/index.php.

National Louis University, College of Arts and Sciences, Chicago, IL 60603. Offers adult education (Ed D); counseling and human services (MS); language and academic development (M Ed, Certificate); psychology (MA, PhD, Certificate); public policy (MA); written communication (MS, Certificate). Part-time and evening/weekend programs available. Postbaccalaureate distance learning degree programs offered (minimal on-campus study). *Degree requirements:* For master's and Certificate, comprehensive exam (for some programs), thesis (for some programs); for doctorate, thesis/dissertation. *Entrance requirements:* For master's, MAT or GRE, 3 professional or academic references, interview, minimum GPA of 3.0; for doctorate, GRE General Test, MAT, or Watson-Glaser Critical Thinking Appraisal, three professional or academic references, statement of academic and professional goals, 3 years of experience in field, interview, master's degree, resume, writing sample; for Certificate, GRE, MAT, or Watson-Glaser Critical Thinking Appraisal, three professional or academic references, statement of academic and professional goals, interview, minimum GPA of 3.0. Additional exam requirements/recommendations for international students: Required—Department of Language Studies Assessment or TOEFL (minimum score 550 paper-based; 79 iBT). Electronic applications accepted.

National University, Academic Affairs, School of Education, La Jolla, CA 92037-1011. Offers applied behavior analysis (Certificate); applied school leadership (MS); autism (Certificate); best practices (Certificate); e-teaching and learning (Certificate); early childhood education (Certificate); education (MA), including best practices (M Ed, MA), e-teaching and learning (M Ed, MA), education technology, teacher leadership (M Ed, MA), teaching and learning in a global society (M Ed, MA), teaching mathematics (M Ed, MA); education with preliminary multiple or single subject (M Ed), including best practices (M Ed, MA), e-teaching and learning (M Ed, MA), educational technology (M Ed, MA), teacher leadership (M Ed, MA), teaching and learning in a global society (M Ed, MA), teaching mathematics (M Ed, MA); educational administration (MS);

educational and instructional technology (MS); educational counseling (MS); educational technology (Certificate); higher education administration (MS); innovative school leadership (MS); instructional leadership (MS); juvenile justice special education (MS); reading (Certificate); school psychology (MS); special education (MS), including deaf and hard-of-hearing, mild/moderate disabilities, moderate/severe disabilities; teacher leadership (Certificate); teaching (MA), including applied behavioral analysis, autism, best practices (M Ed, MA), e-teaching and learning (M Ed, MA), early childhood education, educational technology (M Ed, MA), reading, special education, teacher leadership (M Ed, MA), teaching and learning in a global society (M Ed, MA), teaching mathematics (M Ed, MA); teaching mathematics (Certificate). Part-time and evening/weekend programs available. Postbaccalaureate distance learning degree programs offered (no on-campus study). *Faculty:* 72 full-time (43 women), 287 part-time/adjunct (170 women). *Students:* 2,433 full-time (1,744 women), 2,017 part-time (1,371 women); includes 1,834 minority (358 Black or African American, non-Hispanic/Latino; 15 American Indian or Alaska Native, non-Hispanic/Latino; 250 Asian, non-Hispanic/Latino; 1,056 Hispanic/Latino; 29 Native Hawaiian or other Pacific Islander, non-Hispanic/Latino; 126 Two or more races, non-Hispanic/Latino), 1 international. Average age 34. 1,339 applicants, 100% accepted, 1035 enrolled. In 2013, 1,662 master's awarded. *Degree requirements:* For master's, thesis (for some programs). *Entrance requirements:* For master's, interview, minimum GPA of 2.5. Additional exam requirements/recommendations for international students: Required—TOEFL (minimum score 550 paper-based; 79 iBT), IELTS (minimum score 6). *Application deadline:* Applications are processed on a rolling basis. Application fee: $60 ($65 for international students). Electronic applications accepted. *Expenses: Tuition:* Full-time $13,824; part-time $1728 per course. One-time fee: $160. *Financial support:* Career-related internships or fieldwork, institutionally sponsored loans, scholarships/grants, and tuition waivers (partial) available. Support available to part-time students. Financial award application deadline: 6/30. *Faculty research:* Teacher education, special education, educational effectiveness, teaching abroad, school counseling. *Unit head:* School of Education, 800-628-8648, E-mail: soe@nu.edu. *Application contact:* Louis Cruz, Interim Vice President for Enrollment Services, 800-628-8648, E-mail: advisor@nu.edu.
Website: http://www.nu.edu/OurPrograms/SchoolOfEducation.html.

New Jersey City University, Graduate Studies and Continuing Education, Debra Cannon Partridge Wolfe College of Education, Program in Counseling, Jersey City, NJ 07305-1597. Offers MA. Part-time and evening/weekend programs available. *Faculty:* 8 full-time (7 women), 5 part-time/adjunct (2 women). *Students:* 68 full-time (54 women), 117 part-time (95 women); includes 116 minority (53 Black or African American, non-Hispanic/Latino; 12 Asian, non-Hispanic/Latino; 51 Hispanic/Latino), 2 international. Average age 34. In 2013, 43 master's awarded. *Entrance requirements:* Additional exam requirements/recommendations for international students: Required—TOEFL (minimum score 61 iBT). *Expenses: Tuition, area resident:* Part-time $527.90 per credit. Tuition, nonresident: part-time $947.75 per credit. *Unit head:* Dr. Jane Webber, Coordinator, 201-200-3124, E-mail: jwebber@njcu.edu. *Application contact:* Dr. William Bajor, Dean of Graduate Studies, 201-200-3409, Fax: 201-200-3411, E-mail: wbajor@njcu.edu.

New Mexico Highlands University, Graduate Studies, School of Education, Las Vegas, NM 87701. Offers curriculum and instruction (MA); educational leadership (MA); professional counseling (MA); special education (MA), including). Part-time programs available. *Faculty:* 25 full-time (12 women), 26 part-time/adjunct (22 women). *Students:* 139 full-time (106 women), 245 part-time (180 women); includes 207 minority (10 Black or African American, non-Hispanic/Latino; 20 American Indian or Alaska Native, non-Hispanic/Latino; 3 Asian, non-Hispanic/Latino; 172 Hispanic/Latino; 1 Native Hawaiian or other Pacific Islander, non-Hispanic/Latino; 1 Two or more races, non-Hispanic/Latino), 17 international. Average age 39. 137 applicants, 99% accepted, 102 enrolled. In 2013, 112 master's awarded. *Degree requirements:* For master's, comprehensive exam, thesis or alternative. *Entrance requirements:* For master's, minimum undergraduate GPA of 3.0. Additional exam requirements/recommendations for international students: Required—TOEFL (minimum score 540 paper-based). *Application deadline:* For fall admission, 8/1 priority date for domestic students. Applications are processed on a rolling basis. Application fee: $15. *Expenses:* Tuition, state resident: full-time $4278; part-time $178 per credit hour. Tuition, nonresident: full-time $6716; part-time $281 per credit hour. One-time fee: $15. *Financial support:* Career-related internships or fieldwork, Federal Work-Study, institutionally sponsored loans, scholarships/grants, traineeships, tuition waivers (partial), and unspecified assistantships available. Support available to part-time students. Financial award application deadline: 3/1; financial award applicants required to submit FAFSA. *Faculty research:* Middle school curriculum, integrated computer applications for pre-service classroom teachers, adolescent literacy, narrative cognitive modes in New Mexico multicultural setting, math and math education. *Unit head:* Dr. Belinda Laumbach, Interim Dean, 505-454-3146, Fax: 505-454-8884, E-mail: laumbach_b@nmhu.edu. *Application contact:* Diane Trujillo, Administrative Assistant for Graduate Studies, 505-454-3266, Fax: 505-426-2117, E-mail: dtrujillo@nmhu.edu.

New Mexico State University, Graduate School, College of Education, Department of Counseling and Educational Psychology, Las Cruces, NM 88003-8001. Offers counseling and guidance (MA), including counseling and guidance, educational diagnostics; counseling psychology (PhD); school psychology (Ed S). *Accreditation:* ACA; APA (one or more programs are accredited); NCATE. Part-time programs available. *Faculty:* 14 full-time (12 women). *Students:* 72 full-time (53 women), 23 part-time (17 women); includes 55 minority (3 Black or African American, non-Hispanic/Latino; 3 American Indian or Alaska Native, non-Hispanic/Latino; 4 Asian, non-Hispanic/Latino; 43 Hispanic/Latino; 2 Two or more races, non-Hispanic/Latino). Average age 31. 68 applicants, 35% accepted, 22 enrolled. In 2013, 16 master's, 5 doctorates, 9 other advanced degrees awarded. *Degree requirements:* For master's, comprehensive exam, thesis optional, internship; for doctorate, comprehensive exam, thesis/dissertation, internship; for Ed S, comprehensive exam, thesis or alternative, internship. *Entrance requirements:* For master's, doctorate, and Ed S, GRE General Test, minimum GPA of 3.0. Additional exam requirements/recommendations for international students: Required—IELTS (minimum score 6.5); Recommended—TOEFL (minimum score 550 paper-based; 79 iBT). *Application deadline:* For fall admission, 12/15 for domestic and international students; for winter admission, 1/15 for domestic and international students; for spring admission, 2/1 priority date for domestic students, 2/1 for international students. Application fee: $40 ($50 for international students). Electronic applications accepted. *Expenses:* Tuition, state resident: full-time $5398; part-time $224.90 per credit. Tuition, nonresident: full-time $18,821; part-time $784.20 per credit. *Required fees:* $1310; $54.60 per credit. *Financial support:* In 2013–14, 57 students received support, including 6 fellowships (averaging $4,050 per year), 6 research assistantships (averaging $10,227 per year), 16 teaching assistantships (averaging $9,456 per year); career-related internships or fieldwork, Federal Work-Study, institutionally sponsored loans, scholarships/grants, traineeships, health care benefits, and unspecified assistantships also available. Support available to part-time students. Financial award application deadline: 4/1; financial award applicants required to submit FAFSA. *Faculty research:* Multicultural counseling and training, integrative health psychology, social justice, academic success, mental health disparities. *Total annual research expenditures:* $99,768. *Unit head:* Dr. Elsa Corina Arroyos, Interim Head, 575-

646-2121, Fax: 575-646-8035, E-mail: earroyos@nmsu.edu. *Application contact:* Jeanette Jones, Program Coordinator, 575-646-5485, Fax: 575-646-8035, E-mail: jjjones@nmsu.edu.
Website: http://cep.education.nmsu.edu.

New York Institute of Technology, School of Education, Department of Counseling, Old Westbury, NY 11568-8000. Offers MS. Part-time and evening/weekend programs available. *Faculty:* 3 full-time (all women), 14 part-time/adjunct (10 women). *Students:* 2 full-time (both women), 63 part-time (48 women); includes 31 minority (13 Black or African American, non-Hispanic/Latino; 1 American Indian or Alaska Native, non-Hispanic/Latino; 2 Asian, non-Hispanic/Latino; 13 Hispanic/Latino; 1 Native Hawaiian or other Pacific Islander, non-Hispanic/Latino; 1 Two or more races, non-Hispanic/Latino), 1 international. Average age 32. 59 applicants, 49% accepted, 21 enrolled. In 2013, 16 master's awarded. *Degree requirements:* For master's, internship. *Entrance requirements:* For master's, minimum GPA of 3.0, interview, 3 letters of reference. Additional exam requirements/recommendations for international students: Required—TOEFL (minimum score 550 paper-based; 79 iBT), IELTS (minimum score 6). *Application deadline:* For fall admission, 7/1 priority date for domestic students, 6/1 for international students; for spring admission, 12/1 priority date for domestic students, 12/1 for international students. Applications are processed on a rolling basis. Application fee: $50. Electronic applications accepted. *Expenses: Tuition:* Full-time $18,900; part-time $1050 per credit. *Financial support:* Research assistantships, career-related internships or fieldwork, scholarships/grants, health care benefits, tuition waivers (partial), and unspecified assistantships available. Support available to part-time students. *Faculty research:* School counselor accountability, school counselor evaluation (Race to the Top), comprehensive school counseling programs' design and evaluation, cultural competence, college and career readiness. *Unit head:* Dr. Carol Dahir, Department Chair, 516-686-7616, Fax: 516-686-7655, E-mail: cdahir@nyit.edu. *Application contact:* Alice Dolitsky, Director, Graduate Admissions, 516-686-7520, Fax: 516-686-1116, E-mail: nyitgrad@nyit.edu.
Website: http://www.nyit.edu/education/counseling.

New York University, Steinhardt School of Culture, Education, and Human Development, Department of Applied Psychology, Program in Counseling, New York, NY 10003. Offers counseling and guidance (MA), including bilingual school counseling K-12, counseling and guidance; counseling and guidance: K-12 (Advanced Certificate); counseling for mental health and wellness (MA); counseling psychology (PhD); LGBT health, education, and social services (Advanced Certificate). *Accreditation:* APA (one or more programs are accredited). Part-time programs available. *Faculty:* 12 full-time (9 women). *Students:* 140 full-time (118 women), 48 part-time (39 women); includes 75 minority (22 Black or African American, non-Hispanic/Latino; 19 Asian, non-Hispanic/Latino; 30 Hispanic/Latino; 1 Native Hawaiian or other Pacific Islander, non-Hispanic/Latino; 3 Two or more races, non-Hispanic/Latino), 18 international. Average age 29. 715 applicants, 32% accepted, 64 enrolled. In 2013, 80 master's, 1 doctorate awarded. *Degree requirements:* For master's, thesis (for some programs); for doctorate, thesis/dissertation. *Entrance requirements:* For doctorate, GRE General Test, interview. Additional exam requirements/recommendations for international students: Required—TOEFL (minimum score 100 iBT). *Application deadline:* For fall admission, 12/1 priority date for domestic and international students. Applications are processed on a rolling basis. Application fee: $75. Electronic applications accepted. *Expenses: Tuition:* Full-time $35,856; part-time $1494 per unit. *Required fees:* $1408; $64 per unit. $473 per term. Tuition and fees vary according to course load and program. *Financial support:* Fellowships with full and partial tuition reimbursements, research assistantships, teaching assistantships with partial tuition reimbursements, career-related internships or fieldwork, Federal Work-Study, institutionally sponsored loans, scholarships/grants, tuition waivers (partial), and unspecified assistantships available. Support available to part-time students. Financial award application deadline: 2/1; financial award applicants required to submit FAFSA. *Faculty research:* Sexual and gender identities, group dynamics, psychopathy and personality, multicultural assessment, working people's lives. *Unit head:* 212-998-5555, Fax: 212-995-4358. *Application contact:* 212-998-5030, Fax: 212-995-4328, E-mail: steinhardt.gradadmissions@nyu.edu.
Website: http://steinhardt.nyu.edu/appsych/counseling.

Niagara University, Graduate Division of Education, Concentration in Mental Health Counseling, Niagara Falls, NY 14109. Offers MS, Certificate. Part-time programs available. *Students:* 47 full-time (40 women), 6 part-time (all women); includes 6 minority (3 Black or African American, non-Hispanic/Latino; 1 Asian, non-Hispanic/Latino; 2 Hispanic/Latino), 8 international. Average age 26. In 2013, 10 master's awarded. *Entrance requirements:* For master's, GRE General Test or MAT. Additional exam requirements/recommendations for international students: Required—TOEFL (minimum score 550 paper-based, 79 iBT) or IELTS (minimum score 6). *Application deadline:* For fall admission, 8/1 for domestic students. Applications are processed on a rolling basis. Application fee: $30. *Expenses:* Contact institution. *Financial support:* Research assistantships with full and partial tuition reimbursements, teaching assistantships with full and partial tuition reimbursements, career-related internships or fieldwork, Federal Work-Study, scholarships/grants, and unspecified assistantships available. Financial award application deadline: 4/15; financial award applicants required to submit FAFSA. *Unit head:* Dr. Shannon Hodges, Chair, 716-286-8328. *Application contact:* Dr. Debra A. Colley, Dean of Education, 716-286-8560, Fax: 716-286-8561, E-mail: dcolley@niagara.edu.
Website: http://www.niagara.edu/mental-health-counseling.

Niagara University, Graduate Division of Education, Concentration in School Counseling, Niagara Falls, NY 14109. Offers MS Ed, Certificate. *Accreditation:* NCATE. Part-time and evening/weekend programs available. *Students:* 9 full-time (8 women), 7 part-time (5 women); includes 2 minority (both Black or African American, non-Hispanic/Latino). Average age 33. In 2013, 12 master's, 10 Certificates awarded. *Entrance requirements:* For master's, GRE General Test or MAT; for Certificate, GRE General Test, GRE Subject Test or MAT. Additional exam requirements/recommendations for international students: Required—TOEFL (minimum score 550 paper-based, 79 iBT) or IELTS (minimum score 6). *Application deadline:* For fall admission, 8/1 for domestic students. Applications are processed on a rolling basis. Application fee: $30. *Expenses:* Contact institution. *Financial support:* Research assistantships with full and partial tuition reimbursements, teaching assistantships with full and partial tuition reimbursements, career-related internships or fieldwork, Federal Work-Study, scholarships/grants, and unspecified assistantships available. Financial award application deadline: 4/15. *Unit head:* Dr. Kristine Augustyniak, Chair, 716-286-8548, E-mail: kma@niagara.edu. *Application contact:* Dr. Debra A. Colley, Dean of Education, 716-286-8560, Fax: 716-286-8561, E-mail: dcolley@niagara.edu.
Website: http://www.niagara.edu/school-counseling.

Nicholls State University, Graduate Studies, College of Education, Department of Teacher Education, Thibodaux, LA 70310. Offers administration and supervision (M Ed); counselor education (M Ed); curriculum and instruction (M Ed). *Accreditation:* NCATE. Part-time and evening/weekend programs available. *Degree requirements:* For master's, comprehensive exam, portfolio. *Entrance requirements:* For master's, GRE General Test, teaching license. Electronic applications accepted.

Counselor Education

North Carolina Agricultural and Technical State University, School of Graduate Studies, School of Education, Department of Human Development and Services, Greensboro, NC 27411. Offers adult education (MS); counseling (MS); school administration (MS). *Accreditation:* ACA. Part-time and evening/weekend programs available. *Degree requirements:* For master's, comprehensive exam, thesis, qualifying exam. *Entrance requirements:* For master's, GRE General Test, minimum GPA of 3.0.

North Carolina Central University, School of Education, Department of Counselor Education, Durham, NC 27707-3129. Offers career counseling (MA); community agency counseling (MA); school counseling (MA). *Accreditation:* ACA; NCATE. Part-time and evening/weekend programs available. *Degree requirements:* For master's, comprehensive exam, thesis or alternative. *Entrance requirements:* For master's, GRE, minimum GPA of 3.0 in major, 2.5 overall. Additional exam requirements/recommendations for international students: Required—TOEFL. *Faculty research:* Becoming a leader, skill building in academia.

North Carolina State University, Graduate School, College of Education, Department of Curriculum and Instruction, Program in Counselor Education, Raleigh, NC 27695. Offers M Ed, MS, PhD. *Accreditation:* ACA. *Degree requirements:* For master's, thesis (for some programs). *Entrance requirements:* For master's, GRE or MAT. Electronic applications accepted. *Faculty research:* Career development, retention of at-risk students in higher education, psycho-social development, multicultural issues, cognitive-developmental interventions.

North Dakota State University, College of Graduate and Interdisciplinary Studies, College of Human Development and Education, School of Education, Program in Counseling, Fargo, ND 58108. Offers M Ed, MS, PhD. *Accreditation:* ACA; NCATE. Part-time programs available. Postbaccalaureate distance learning degree programs offered (minimal on-campus study). *Students:* 47 full-time (39 women), 18 part-time (16 women); includes 5 minority (1 Black or African American, non-Hispanic/Latino; 1 American Indian or Alaska Native, non-Hispanic/Latino; 3 Two or more races, non-Hispanic/Latino), 1 international. Average age 29. 2 applicants, 100% accepted, 2 enrolled. In 2013, 15 master's, 1 doctorate awarded. *Degree requirements:* For master's, comprehensive exam, thesis or alternative; for doctorate, comprehensive exam, thesis/dissertation. *Entrance requirements:* For master's, GRE, MAT, interview. Additional exam requirements/recommendations for international students: Required—TOEFL. *Application deadline:* For fall admission, 2/15 for domestic students. Applications are processed on a rolling basis. Application fee: $35. *Financial support:* Teaching assistantships, career-related internships or fieldwork, Federal Work-Study, institutionally sponsored loans, and tuition waivers (full) available. Financial award application deadline: 4/15. *Faculty research:* Supervision, program assessment, multicultural issues. *Unit head:* Dr. Jill R. Nelson, Coordinator, 701-231-7921, Fax: 701-231-7416, E-mail: jill.r.nelson@ndsu.edu. *Application contact:* Sonya Goergen, Marketing, Recruitment, and Public Relations Coordinator, 701-231-7033; Fax: 701-231-6524.

Northeastern Illinois University, College of Graduate Studies and Research, College of Education, Program in School Counseling, Chicago, IL 60625-4699. Offers MA. *Accreditation:* ACA.

Northeastern State University, College of Education, Department of Psychology and Counseling, Program in School Counseling, Tahlequah, OK 74464-2399. Offers M Ed. Part-time and evening/weekend programs available. *Faculty:* 32 full-time (19 women), 17 part-time/adjunct (8 women). *Students:* 11 full-time (9 women), 18 part-time (all women); includes 2 minority (both American Indian or Alaska Native, non-Hispanic/Latino). Average age 34. In 2013, 18 master's awarded. *Degree requirements:* For master's, thesis or alternative, innovative project or research paper, written and oral exams. *Entrance requirements:* For master's, MAT or GRE, minimum GPA of 2.5. Additional exam requirements/recommendations for international students: Required—TOEFL. *Application deadline:* For fall admission, 6/1 priority date for domestic students. Applications are processed on a rolling basis. Application fee: $0 ($25 for international students). Electronic applications accepted. *Expenses:* Tuition, state resident: full-time $3029; part-time $168.25 per credit hour. Tuition, nonresident: full-time $7709; part-time $428.25 per credit hour. *Required fees:* $35.90 per credit hour. *Financial support:* Teaching assistantships and Federal Work-Study available. Financial award application deadline: 3/1. *Unit head:* Dr. Elizabeth Keller-Dupree, School Counseling Chair, 918-444-3847, E-mail: kellere@nsuok.edu. *Application contact:* Margie Railey, Administrative Assistant, 918-456-5511 Ext. 2093, Fax: 918-458-2061, E-mail: railey@nsouk.edu.
Website: http://academics.nsuok.edu/education/DegreePrograms/GraduatePrograms/SchoolCounseling.aspx.

Northeastern University, Bouvé College of Health Sciences, Boston, MA 02115-5096. Offers audiology (Au D); biotechnology (MS); counseling psychology (MS, PhD, CAGS); counseling/school psychology (PhD); exercise physiology (MS), including exercise physiology, public health; health informatics (MS); nursing (MS, PhD, CAGS), including acute care (MS), administration (MS), anesthesia (MS), primary care (MS), psychiatric mental health (MS); pharmaceutical sciences (PhD); pharmaceutics and drug delivery systems (MS); pharmacology (MS); physical therapy (DPT); physician assistant (MS); school psychology (PhD, CAGS); school/counseling psychology (PhD); speech language pathology (MS); urban public health (MPH); MS/MBA. *Accreditation:* ACPE (one or more programs are accredited). Part-time and evening/weekend programs available. *Degree requirements:* For doctorate, thesis/dissertation (for some programs); for CAGS, comprehensive exam.

Northern Arizona University, Graduate College, College of Education, Department of Educational Psychology, Flagstaff, AZ 86011. Offers counseling (MA); educational psychology (PhD), including counseling psychology, school psychology; human relations (M Ed); school counseling (M Ed); school psychology (Ed S); student affairs (M Ed). Part-time programs available. Postbaccalaureate distance learning degree programs offered. *Faculty:* 22 full-time (9 women), 3 part-time/adjunct (1 woman). *Students:* 232 full-time (175 women), 237 part-time (187 women); includes 155 minority (21 Black or African American, non-Hispanic/Latino; 27 American Indian or Alaska Native, non-Hispanic/Latino; 3 Asian, non-Hispanic/Latino; 91 Hispanic/Latino; 1 Native Hawaiian or other Pacific Islander, non-Hispanic/Latino; 12 Two or more races, non-Hispanic/Latino), 4 international. Average age 34. 234 applicants, 71% accepted, 101 enrolled. In 2013, 232 master's, 6 doctorates awarded. Terminal master's awarded for partial completion of doctoral program. *Degree requirements:* For master's, internship (for some programs); for doctorate, comprehensive exam, thesis/dissertation, internship. *Entrance requirements:* Additional exam requirements/recommendations for international students: Required—TOEFL (minimum score 550 paper-based; 80 iBT), IELTS (minimum score 7). *Application deadline:* For fall admission, 9/15 for domestic students; for spring admission, 1/15 for domestic students. Applications are processed on a rolling basis. Application fee: $65. Electronic applications accepted. *Financial support:* In 2013–14, 20 students received support, including 11 teaching assistantships with full tuition reimbursements available (averaging $9,660 per year); research assistantships, career-related internships or fieldwork, Federal Work-Study, scholarships/grants, health care benefits, tuition waivers (full and partial), and unspecified assistantships also available. Financial award applicants required to submit FAFSA. *Unit head:* Dr. Robert Horn, Chair, 928-523-0362, Fax: 928-523-9284, E-mail: robert.horn@nau.edu. *Application contact:* Hope DeMello, Administrative Assistant, 928-523-7103, Fax: 928-523-9284, E-mail: eps@nau.edu.
Website: http://nau.edu/coe/ed-psych/.

Northern Illinois University, Graduate School, College of Education, Department of Counseling, Adult and Higher Education, De Kalb, IL 60115-2854. Offers adult and higher education (MS Ed, Ed D); counseling (MS Ed, Ed D). *Accreditation:* ACA. Part-time and evening/weekend programs available. *Faculty:* 19 full-time (11 women), 2 part-time/adjunct (1 woman). *Students:* 121 full-time (94 women), 252 part-time (182 women); includes 149 minority (102 Black or African American, non-Hispanic/Latino; 1 American Indian or Alaska Native, non-Hispanic/Latino; 11 Asian, non-Hispanic/Latino; 28 Hispanic/Latino; 7 Two or more races, non-Hispanic/Latino), 9 international. Average age 36. 115 applicants, 48% accepted, 37 enrolled. In 2013, 73 master's, 19 doctorates awarded. Terminal master's awarded for partial completion of doctoral program. *Degree requirements:* For master's, comprehensive exam, thesis optional; for doctorate, thesis/dissertation, candidacy exam, dissertation defense. *Entrance requirements:* For master's, GRE General Test or MAT, minimum undergraduate GPA of 2.75, interview (for counseling); for doctorate, GRE General Test, minimum undergraduate GPA of 2.75, 3.2 graduate, interview (for counseling). Additional exam requirements/recommendations for international students: Required—TOEFL (minimum score 550 paper-based). *Application deadline:* For fall admission, 6/1 for domestic students, 5/1 for international students; for spring admission, 11/1 for domestic students, 10/1 for international students. Applications are processed on a rolling basis. Application fee: $40. Electronic applications accepted. *Financial support:* In 2013–14, 13 research assistantships with full tuition reimbursements, 2 teaching assistantships with full tuition reimbursements were awarded; fellowships with full tuition reimbursements, career-related internships or fieldwork, Federal Work-Study, scholarships/grants, tuition waivers (full), and staff assistantships also available. Support available to part-time students. Financial award applicants required to submit FAFSA. *Unit head:* Dr. Suzanne Degges-White, Interim Chair, 815-753-1448, E-mail: cahe@niu.edu. *Application contact:* Graduate School Office, 815-753-0395, E-mail: gradsch@niu.edu.
Website: http://www.cedu.niu.edu/cahe/index.html.

Northern Kentucky University, Office of Graduate Programs, College of Education and Human Services, Program in School Counseling, Highland Heights, KY 41099. Offers MA. *Accreditation:* ACA. Part-time and evening/weekend programs available. *Faculty:* 8 full-time (4 women), 1 (woman) part-time/adjunct. *Students:* 22 full-time (20 women), 22 part-time (18 women); includes 5 minority (3 Black or African American, non-Hispanic/Latino; 2 Native Hawaiian or other Pacific Islander, non-Hispanic/Latino). Average age 27. 31 applicants, 61% accepted, 17 enrolled. In 2013, 15 master's awarded. *Degree requirements:* For master's, portfolio, practicum, internship. *Entrance requirements:* For master's, GRE or MAT or PLT, interview, 3 letters of recommendation, minimum GPA of 2.75, criminal background check (state and federal), essay, interview. Additional exam requirements/recommendations for international students: Required—TOEFL (minimum score 550 paper-based; 79 iBT); Recommended—IELTS (minimum score 6.5). *Application deadline:* For fall admission, 2/1 priority date for domestic students, 6/1 priority date for international students; for spring admission, 11/1 for domestic students, 10/1 priority date for international students; for summer admission, 2/1 priority date for domestic students. Applications are processed on a rolling basis. Application fee: $40. Electronic applications accepted. *Expenses:* Tuition, state resident: full-time $4446; part-time $494 per credit hour. Tuition, nonresident: full-time $6885; part-time $765 per credit hour. *Required fees:* $72 per semester. One-time fee: $125.50. Part-time tuition and fees vary according to course load, degree level, program and reciprocity agreements. *Financial support:* In 2013–14, 11 students received support. Unspecified assistantships available. Financial award applicants required to submit FAFSA. *Faculty research:* Impact of school counseling on achievement, counselor supervision, equity and social justice issues, instrument development and assessment. *Unit head:* Brett Zyromski, Program Director, 859-572-5943, Fax: 859-572-6592, E-mail: zyromskib1@nku.edu. *Application contact:* Dr. Christian Gamm, Director of Graduate Programs, 859-572-6364, Fax: 859-572-6670, E-mail: gammc1@nku.edu.
Website: http://coehs.nku.edu/gradprograms/counseling.html.

Northern Michigan University, College of Graduate Studies, College of Health Sciences and Professional Studies, School of Education, Leadership and Public Service, Program in School Guidance Counseling, Marquette, MI 49855-5301. Offers MAE. *Expenses:* Tuition, state resident: part-time $427 per credit. Tuition, nonresident: part-time $614.50 per credit. *Required fees:* $325 per semester. Tuition and fees vary according to course load and program. *Unit head:* Rodney Clarken, Associate Dean, 906-227-1880, E-mail: rclarken@nmu.edu. *Application contact:* Dr. Cynthia A. Prosen, Dean of Graduate Studies and Research, 906-227-2300, Fax: 906-227-2315, E-mail: cprosen@nmu.edu.

Northern State University, MS Ed Program in Counseling, Aberdeen, SD 57401-7198. Offers clinical mental health counseling (MS Ed); school counseling (MS Ed). *Accreditation:* NCATE. Part-time programs available. Postbaccalaureate distance learning degree programs offered (minimal on-campus study). *Faculty:* 3 full-time (1 woman), 2 part-time/adjunct (0 women). *Students:* 30 full-time (21 women), 22 part-time (18 women); includes 2 minority (1 Black or African American, non-Hispanic/Latino; 1 American Indian or Alaska Native, non-Hispanic/Latino). Average age 25. 22 applicants, 64% accepted, 12 enrolled. In 2013, 16 master's awarded. *Degree requirements:* For master's, comprehensive exam, thesis optional. *Entrance requirements:* For master's, minimum GPA of 2.75. Additional exam requirements/recommendations for international students: Required—TOEFL (minimum score 550 paper-based; 78 iBT), IELTS (minimum score 6). *Application deadline:* For fall admission, 8/15 for domestic and international students; for spring admission, 12/15 for domestic and international students. Applications are processed on a rolling basis. Application fee: $35. Electronic applications accepted. *Expenses:* Tuition, state resident: full-time $3634. Tuition, nonresident: full-time $7690. One-time fee: $35 full-time. Part-time tuition and fees vary according to course load, degree level, campus/location and reciprocity agreements. *Financial support:* In 2013–14, 6 students received support, including 5 teaching assistantships with partial tuition reimbursements available (averaging $6,478 per year); career-related internships or fieldwork, Federal Work-Study, institutionally sponsored loans, scholarships/grants, and unspecified assistantships also available. Support available to part-time students. Financial award application deadline: 3/1; financial award applicants required to submit FAFSA. *Unit head:* Dr. Constance Geier, Dean of Education, 605-626-2558, Fax: 605-626-7190, E-mail: connie.geier@northern.edu. *Application contact:* Tammy K. Griffith, Program Assistant, 605-626-2558, Fax: 605-626-7190, E-mail: tammy.griffith@northern.edu.

Northwest Christian University, School of Education and Counseling, Eugene, OR 97401-3745. Offers clinical mental health counseling (MA); curriculum and instructional technology (M Ed); education (M Ed); school counseling (MA). Part-time and evening/weekend programs available. *Entrance requirements:* For master's, MAT, interview, minimum GPA of 3.0. Electronic applications accepted.

Northwestern Oklahoma State University, School of Professional Studies, Program in School Counseling, Alva, OK 73717-2799. Offers M Ed. *Accreditation:* NCATE. Part-time programs available. *Degree requirements:* For master's, thesis optional, portfolio.

Entrance requirements: For master's, GRE General Test or MAT, minimum GPA of 2.75.

Northwestern State University of Louisiana, Graduate Studies and Research, College of Education and Human Development, Program in School Counseling, Natchitoches, LA 71497. Offers MA. *Degree requirements:* For master's, comprehensive exam, thesis (for some programs). *Entrance requirements:* For master's, GRE General Test. Additional exam requirements/recommendations for international students: Required—TOEFL. Electronic applications accepted.

Northwestern State University of Louisiana, Graduate Studies and Research, College of Education and Human Development, Programs in Educational Leadership and Instruction, Natchitoches, LA 71497. Offers counseling (Ed S); educational leadership (M Ed, Ed S); educational technology (Ed S); elementary teaching (Ed S); reading (Ed S); secondary teaching (Ed S); special education (Ed S). *Accreditation:* NASAD. *Degree requirements:* For master's, comprehensive exam, thesis (for some programs). *Entrance requirements:* For master's and Ed S, GRE General Test. Additional exam requirements/recommendations for international students: Required—TOEFL. Electronic applications accepted.

Northwest Missouri State University, Graduate School, College of Education and Human Services, Department of Behavioral Sciences, Program in Guidance and Counseling, Maryville, MO 64468-6001. Offers MS Ed. *Accreditation:* NCATE. *Degree requirements:* For master's, comprehensive exam, thesis. *Entrance requirements:* For master's, GRE General Test, teaching certificate; 2 years of experience; minimum undergraduate GPA of 2.5, 3.0 in major; writing sample. Additional exam requirements/recommendations for international students: Required—TOEFL (minimum score 550 paper-based).

Northwest Nazarene University, Graduate Studies, Program in Counselor Education, Nampa, ID 83686-5897. Offers clinical counseling (MS); marriage and family counseling (MS); school counseling (MS). Part-time programs available. *Faculty:* 6 full-time (4 women), 10 part-time/adjunct (6 women). *Students:* 94 full-time (67 women), 29 part-time (22 women); includes 10 minority (2 Black or African American, non-Hispanic/Latino; 6 Hispanic/Latino; 2 Two or more races, non-Hispanic/Latino), 1 international. Average age 35. 47 applicants, 66% accepted, 25 enrolled. *Degree requirements:* For master's, comprehensive exam. *Entrance requirements:* For master's, minimum GPA of 3.0, BA. Additional exam requirements/recommendations for international students: Required—TOEFL. *Application deadline:* For fall admission, 2/15 for domestic and international students; for spring admission, 9/15 for domestic and international students. Application fee: $50. Electronic applications accepted. *Expenses: Tuition:* Part-time $565 per credit. *Unit head:* Dr. Michael Pitts, Chair, 208-467-8040, Fax: 208-467-8339. *Application contact:* Marilyn Holly, Graduate Admissions Counselor, 208-467-8688, E-mail: mholly@nnu.edu.

Nova Southeastern University, Center for Psychological Studies, Fort Lauderdale, FL 33314-7796. Offers clinical psychology (PhD, Psy D); clinical psychopharmacology (MS); counseling (MS); forensic psychology (MS); general psychology (MS); mental health counseling (MS); school counseling (MS); school psychology (Psy D, Psy S). *Accreditation:* APA (one or more programs are accredited). Postbaccalaureate distance learning degree programs offered. *Faculty:* 41 full-time (15 women), 134 part-time/adjunct (80 women). *Students:* 1,820 (1,568 women); includes 832 minority (289 Black or African American, non-Hispanic/Latino; 4 American Indian or Alaska Native, non-Hispanic/Latino; 46 Asian, non-Hispanic/Latino; 464 Hispanic/Latino; 29 Two or more races, non-Hispanic/Latino), 38 international. Average age 31. 1,185 applicants, 52% accepted, 403 enrolled. In 2013, 462 master's, 73 doctorates, 16 other advanced degrees awarded. Terminal master's awarded for partial completion of doctoral program. *Degree requirements:* For master's, comprehensive exam, 3 practica; for doctorate, thesis/dissertation, clinical internship, competency exam; for Psy S, comprehensive exam, internship. *Entrance requirements:* For doctorate, GRE General Test, GRE Subject Test (recommended), minimum undergraduate GPA of 3.0; for Psy S, GRE General Test. Additional exam requirements/recommendations for international students: Required—TOEFL (minimum score 550 paper-based). *Application deadline:* Applications are processed on a rolling basis. Application fee: $50. Electronic applications accepted. *Expenses:* Contact institution. *Financial support:* In 2013–14, 5 research assistantships, 34 teaching assistantships (averaging $1,000 per year) were awarded; career-related internships or fieldwork, Federal Work-Study, institutionally sponsored loans, scholarships/grants, and unspecified assistantships also available. Support available to part-time students. Financial award application deadline: 4/1. *Faculty research:* Clinical and child clinical psychology, geriatrics, interpersonal violence. *Unit head:* Karen Grosby, EdD, Dean, 954-262-5701, Fax: 954-262-3859, E-mail: grosby@nova.edu. *Application contact:* Carlos Perez, Enrollment Management, 954-262-5790, Fax: 954-262-3893, E-mail: cpsinfo@cps.nova.edu.
Website: http://www.cps.nova.edu/.

Nyack College, Alliance Graduate School of Counseling, Nyack, NY 10960-3698. Offers marriage and family therapy (MA); mental health counseling (MA). Part-time and evening/weekend programs available. *Students:* 114 full-time (93 women), 176 part-time (147 women); includes 217 minority (115 Black or African American, non-Hispanic/Latino; 36 Asian, non-Hispanic/Latino; 63 Hispanic/Latino; 3 Two or more races, non-Hispanic/Latino), 8 international. Average age 38. In 2013, 58 master's awarded. *Degree requirements:* For master's, comprehensive exam, counselor-in-training therapy, internship, CPCE exam. *Entrance requirements:* For master's, Millon Clinical Multiaxial Inventory-3, Minnesota Multiphasic Personality Inventory-2, transcripts, statement of Christian life and experience, statement of support systems. Additional exam requirements/recommendations for international students: Required—TOEFL (minimum score 83 iBT). *Application deadline:* For fall admission, 8/1 for domestic students, 2/15 for international students; for spring admission, 7/15 for international students. Applications are processed on a rolling basis. Application fee: $35. Electronic applications accepted. *Expenses:* Contact institution. *Financial support:* Career-related internships or fieldwork and scholarships/grants available. Financial award applicants required to submit FAFSA. *Unit head:* Dr. Carol Robles, Director, 845-770-5730, Fax: 845-348-3923. *Application contact:* Traci Piescki, Director of Admissions, 800-541-6891, Fax: 845-348-3912, E-mail: admissions.grad@nyack.edu.
Website: http://www.nyack.edu/agsc.

Ohio University, Graduate College, Gladys W. and David H. Patton College of Education and Human Services, Department of Counseling and Higher Education, Athens, OH 45701-2979. Offers college student personnel (M Ed); community/agency counseling (M Ed); counselor education (PhD); higher education (PhD); rehabilitation counseling (M Ed); school counseling (M Ed). *Accreditation:* ACA; CORE. Part-time and evening/weekend programs available. *Degree requirements:* For master's, comprehensive exam (for some programs), thesis or alternative; for doctorate, comprehensive exam, thesis/dissertation. *Entrance requirements:* For master's, GRE General Test or MAT (if GPA less than 2.9), 3 letters of reference; for doctorate, GRE General Test, work experience, minimum GPA of 3.4. Additional exam requirements/recommendations for international students: Required—TOEFL (minimum score 550 paper-based; 80 iBT) or IELTS (minimum score 6.5). Electronic applications accepted. *Faculty research:* Youth violence, gender studies, student affairs, chemical dependency, disabilities issues.

Old Dominion University, Darden College of Education, Counseling Program, Norfolk, VA 23529. Offers clinical mental health counseling (MS Ed); college counseling (MS Ed); counseling (PhD, Ed S); school counseling (MS Ed). *Accreditation:* ACA. Part-time and evening/weekend programs available. Postbaccalaureate distance learning degree programs offered (minimal on-campus study). *Faculty:* 13 full-time (6 women), 8 part-time/adjunct (7 women). *Students:* 136 full-time (110 women), 67 part-time (53 women); includes 64 minority (44 Black or African American, non-Hispanic/Latino; 2 Asian, non-Hispanic/Latino; 12 Hispanic/Latino; 1 Native Hawaiian or other Pacific Islander, non-Hispanic/Latino; 5 Two or more races, non-Hispanic/Latino), 3 international. Average age 31. 128 applicants, 56% accepted, 63 enrolled. In 2013, 67 master's, 12 doctorates, 3 other advanced degrees awarded. *Degree requirements:* For master's and Ed S, comprehensive exam; for doctorate, comprehensive exam, thesis/dissertation. *Entrance requirements:* For master's and Ed S, GRE General Test, resume, essay, transcripts; for doctorate, GRE General Test, resume, interview, essay, transcripts. Additional exam requirements/recommendations for international students: Required—TOEFL. *Application deadline:* For fall admission, 3/1 for domestic and international students; for winter admission, 1/10 for domestic students; for spring admission, 11/1 for domestic students, 10/1 for international students; for summer admission, 3/1 for domestic students, 2/1 for international students. Application fee: $50. Electronic applications accepted. *Expenses:* Tuition, state resident: full-time $9888; part-time $412 per credit. Tuition, nonresident: full-time $25,152; part-time $1048 per credit. *Required fees:* $59 per semester. One-time fee: $50. *Financial support:* In 2013–14, 125 students received support, including 2 fellowships with full tuition reimbursements available (averaging $15,000 per year), 20 research assistantships with partial tuition reimbursements available (averaging $10,000 per year), 14 teaching assistantships with full tuition reimbursements available (averaging $15,000 per year); career-related internships or fieldwork, Federal Work-Study, institutionally sponsored loans, scholarships/grants, traineeships, tuition waivers (partial), and unspecified assistantships also available. Support available to part-time students. Financial award applicants required to submit FAFSA. *Faculty research:* Group counseling, counselor education, career counseling, spirituality and counseling, school counseling, GLBT counseling, legal and ethical issues. *Total annual research expenditures:* $75,000. *Unit head:* Dr. Tim Grothaus, Graduate Program Director, 757-683-3326, Fax: 757-683-5756, E-mail: tgrothau@odu.edu. *Application contact:* Kelly Olds, Graduate Assistant, 757-683-3326, Fax: 757-683-5756, E-mail: kolds@odu.edu.
Website: http://www.education.odu.edu/chs/academics/counseling.

Oregon State University, College of Education, Program in Counseling, Corvallis, OR 97331. Offers M Coun, MS, PhD. *Accreditation:* ACA (one or more programs are accredited); NCATE. Part-time programs available. *Faculty:* 8 full-time (3 women), 12 part-time/adjunct (9 women). *Students:* 6 full-time (4 women), 65 part-time (48 women); includes 23 minority (5 Black or African American, non-Hispanic/Latino; 1 American Indian or Alaska Native, non-Hispanic/Latino; 5 Asian, non-Hispanic/Latino; 9 Hispanic/Latino; 3 Two or more races, non-Hispanic/Latino), 1 international. Average age 39. 160 applicants, 40% accepted, 22 enrolled. In 2013, 27 master's, 11 doctorates awarded. *Degree requirements:* For master's, thesis or alternative; for doctorate, one foreign language, thesis/dissertation. *Entrance requirements:* For master's, minimum GPA of 3.0 in last 90 hours; for doctorate, GRE or MAT, master's degree, minimum GPA of 3.0 in last 90 hours of course work, 2 years of teaching experience. Additional exam requirements/recommendations for international students: Required—TOEFL (minimum score 575 paper-based). *Application deadline:* For fall admission, 1/31 for domestic students. Applications are processed on a rolling basis. Application fee: $60. *Expenses:* Tuition, state resident: full-time $11,664; part-time $432 per credit hour. Tuition, nonresident: full-time $19,197; part-time $711 per credit hour. *Required fees:* $1446; $443 per quarter. One-time fee: $300. Tuition and fees vary according to course load and program. *Financial support:* Teaching assistantships, career-related internships or fieldwork, Federal Work-Study, and institutionally sponsored loans available. Support available to part-time students. Financial award application deadline: 2/1. *Faculty research:* Counseling and guidance improvement in social services agencies, elementary and secondary schools. *Unit head:* Dr. Larry Flick, Dean, 541-737-3664, E-mail: larry.flick@oregonstate.edu. *Application contact:* Laurie Brendle-Sleipness, Program Assistant, 541-737-4317, E-mail: laurie.brendle@oregonstate.edu.
Website: http://education.oregonstate.edu/counseling.

Ottawa University, Graduate Studies-Arizona, Program in Education, Ottawa, KS 66067-3399. Offers community college counseling (MA); curriculum and instruction (MA); early childhood (MA); education intervention (MA); education leadership (MA); education technology (MA); Montessori early childhood education (MA); Montessori elementary education (MA); professional development (MA); school guidance counseling (MA); special education - cross categorical (MA). Programs offered in Mesa, Phoenix, Tempe and West Valley, AZ. *Accreditation:* NCATE. Part-time programs available. *Degree requirements:* For master's, thesis or alternative. *Entrance requirements:* For master's, minimum undergraduate GPA of 3.0, copy of current state certification or teaching license. Additional exam requirements/recommendations for international students: Required—TOEFL (minimum score 550 paper-based). Electronic applications accepted. *Expenses:* Contact institution.

Our Lady of Holy Cross College, Program in Education and Counseling, New Orleans, LA 70131-7399. Offers administration and supervision (M Ed); curriculum and instruction (M Ed); marriage and family counseling (MA); school counseling (M Ed, MA). *Accreditation:* ACA; NCATE. Part-time and evening/weekend programs available. *Degree requirements:* For master's, thesis. *Entrance requirements:* For master's, GRE General Test, minimum GPA of 2.7.

Our Lady of the Lake University of San Antonio, School of Professional Studies, Program in School Counseling, San Antonio, TX 78207-4689. Offers M Ed. Part-time and evening/weekend programs available. *Faculty:* 6 full-time (4 women), 3 part-time/adjunct (all women). *Students:* 16 full-time (14 women), 3 part-time (all women); includes 16 minority (1 Black or African American, non-Hispanic/Latino; 15 Hispanic/Latino). Average age 38. 21 applicants, 62% accepted, 7 enrolled. In 2013, 4 master's awarded. *Degree requirements:* For master's, comprehensive exam, thesis optional, practicum. *Entrance requirements:* For master's, GRE General Test or MAT. Additional exam requirements/recommendations for international students: Required—TOEFL. *Application deadline:* For fall admission, 4/1 priority date for domestic and international students; for spring admission, 11/1 priority date for domestic and international students; for summer admission, 2/1 priority date for international students. Applications are processed on a rolling basis. Application fee: $25 ($50 for international students). Electronic applications accepted. *Expenses: Tuition:* Full-time $9120; part-time $760 per credit. *Required fees:* $698; $334 per trimester. Tuition and fees vary according to course load, degree level, campus/location and program. *Financial support:* Research assistantships, teaching assistantships, career-related internships or fieldwork, Federal Work-Study, institutionally sponsored loans, scholarships/grants, and tuition waivers (partial) available. Support available to part-time students. Financial award application deadline: 4/15. *Faculty research:* Professional educator to understand and meet the comprehensive needs of a diverse student population, life-long learners, innovative practices. *Unit head:* Dr. Jerrie Jackson, Chair, 210-434-6711 Ext. 2698, E-mail:

jjackson@lake.ollusa.edu. *Application contact:* Graduate Admission, 210-431-3961 Ext. 2314, Fax: 210-431-4013, E-mail: gradadm@lake.ollusa.edu.
Website: http://www.ollusa.edu/s/1190/ollu-3-column-noads.aspx?sid=1190&gid=1&pgid=3855.

Palm Beach Atlantic University, School of Education and Behavioral Studies, West Palm Beach, FL 33416-4708. Offers counseling psychology (MS), including addictions/mental health, general counseling, marriage and family therapy, mental health counseling, school guidance counseling. Part-time and evening/weekend programs available. *Faculty:* 9 full-time (3 women), 12 part-time/adjunct (4 women). *Students:* 272 full-time (225 women), 65 part-time (57 women); includes 152 minority (81 Black or African American, non-Hispanic/Latino; 3 Asian, non-Hispanic/Latino; 55 Hispanic/Latino; 1 Native Hawaiian or other Pacific Islander, non-Hispanic/Latino; 12 Two or more races, non-Hispanic/Latino), 10 international. Average age 35. 110 applicants, 87% accepted, 87 enrolled. In 2013, 112 master's awarded. *Entrance requirements:* For master's, GRE or MAT and MMPI-2, minimum GPA of 3.0. Additional exam requirements/recommendations for international students: Required—TOEFL (minimum score 550 paper-based; 79 iBT). *Application deadline:* For fall admission, 7/15 priority date for domestic students; for spring admission, 11/15 priority date for domestic students. Applications are processed on a rolling basis. Application fee: $45. Electronic applications accepted. *Expenses: Tuition:* Part-time $495 per credit hour. *Required fees:* $495 per credit hour. Part-time tuition and fees vary according to course load and program. *Financial support:* Application deadline: 5/1; applicants required to submit FAFSA. *Unit head:* Dr. Gene Sale, Program Director, 561-803-2352. *Application contact:* Graduate Admissions, 888-468-6722, E-mail: grad@pba.edu.
Website: http://www.pba.edu/graduate-counseling-program.

Penn State University Park, Graduate School, College of Education, Department of Educational Psychology, Counseling and Special Education, State College, PA 16802. Offers counselor education (M Ed, D Ed, PhD, Certificate); educational psychology (MS, PhD, Certificate); school psychology (M Ed, MS, PhD, Certificate); special education (M Ed, MS, PhD, Certificate). *Unit head:* Dr. David H. Monk, Dean, 814-865-2523, Fax: 814-865-0555, E-mail: dhm6@psu.edu. *Application contact:* Cynthia E. Nicosia, Director, Graduate Enrollment Services, 814-865-1834, Fax: 814-863-4627, E-mail: cey1@psu.edu.
Website: http://www.ed.psu.edu/educ/epcse.

Phillips Graduate Institute, Programs in Marriage and Family Therapy and School Counseling, Encino, CA 91316-1509. Offers art therapy (MA); marriage and family therapy (MA); school counseling (MA). Evening/weekend programs available. *Degree requirements:* For master's, comprehensive exam, thesis. *Entrance requirements:* For master's, minimum GPA of 2.5. Electronic applications accepted. *Faculty research:* Integration of interpersonal psychological theory, systems approach, firsthand experiential learning.

Pittsburg State University, Graduate School, College of Education, Department of Psychology and Counseling, Program in Counselor Education, Pittsburg, KS 66762. Offers community counseling (MS); school counseling (MS). *Accreditation:* ACA; NCATE. *Degree requirements:* For master's, thesis or alternative. *Entrance requirements:* For master's, GRE General Test, minimum GPA of 2.8.

Plymouth State University, College of Graduate Studies, Graduate Studies in Education, Programs in Counseling, Plymouth, NH 03264-1595. Offers human relations (M Ed); school counseling (M Ed); school psychology (M Ed). *Accreditation:* ACA; NCATE. Part-time and evening/weekend programs available. *Degree requirements:* For master's, PRAXIS I. *Entrance requirements:* For master's, MAT, minimum GPA of 3.0.

Point Loma Nazarene University, School of Education, Program in Education, San Diego, CA 92106-2899. Offers counseling and guidance (MA); educational leadership (MA); teaching and learning (MA). Part-time and evening/weekend programs available. *Students:* 26 full-time (24 women), 126 part-time (92 women); includes 68 minority (11 Black or African American, non-Hispanic/Latino; 2 American Indian or Alaska Native, non-Hispanic/Latino; 8 Asian, non-Hispanic/Latino; 42 Hispanic/Latino; 4 Native Hawaiian or other Pacific Islander, non-Hispanic/Latino; 1 Two or more races, non-Hispanic/Latino). Average age 50. 65 applicants, 71% accepted, 41 enrolled. In 2013, 103 master's awarded. *Entrance requirements:* For master's, interview, letters of recommendation, essay. Additional exam requirements/recommendations for international students: Required—TOEFL. *Application deadline:* For fall admission, 8/4 priority date for domestic students; for spring admission, 12/8 priority date for domestic students; for summer admission, 4/12 priority date for domestic students. Applications are processed on a rolling basis. Application fee: $50. Electronic applications accepted. *Expenses: Tuition:* Full-time $6900; part-time $567 per credit hour. *Financial support:* Applicants required to submit FAFSA. *Unit head:* Dr. Deborah Erickson, Dean of the School of Education, 619-849-2332, Fax: 619-849-2579, E-mail: deberickson@pointloma.edu. *Application contact:* Laura Leinweber, Director of Graduate Admission, 866-693-4723, E-mail: lauraleinweber@pointloma.edu.
Website: http://www.pointloma.edu/discover/graduate-school-san-diego/san-diego-graduate-programs-masters-degree-san-diego/education/master-arts-education.

Pontifical Catholic University of Puerto Rico, College of Education, Program in Counselor Education, Ponce, PR 00717-0777. Offers M Ed. *Degree requirements:* For master's, comprehensive exam, thesis (for some programs). *Entrance requirements:* For master's, GRE, 2 letters of recommendation, interview, minimum GPA of 2.75.

Portland State University, Graduate Studies, School of Education, Department of Special Education and Counselor Education, Portland, OR 97207-0751. Offers counselor education (MA, MS); special and counselor education (Ed D); special education (MA, MS). *Accreditation:* ACA (one or more programs are accredited). Part-time and evening/weekend programs available. *Faculty:* 23 full-time (13 women), 79 part-time/adjunct (56 women). *Students:* 191 full-time (159 women), 128 part-time (91 women); includes 52 minority (3 Black or African American, non-Hispanic/Latino; 2 American Indian or Alaska Native, non-Hispanic/Latino; 12 Asian, non-Hispanic/Latino; 24 Hispanic/Latino; 1 Native Hawaiian or other Pacific Islander, non-Hispanic/Latino; 10 Two or more races, non-Hispanic/Latino), 6 international. Average age 35. 390 applicants, 34% accepted, 119 enrolled. In 2013, 149 master's awarded. *Degree requirements:* For master's, thesis or alternative. *Entrance requirements:* For master's, California Basic Educational Skills Test, minimum GPA of 3.0 in upper-division course work or 2.75 overall. Additional exam requirements/recommendations for international students: Required—TOEFL (minimum score 550 paper-based). *Application deadline:* For fall admission, 2/1 for domestic and international students. Application fee: $50. *Expenses:* Tuition, state resident: full-time $9207; part-time $341 per credit. Tuition, nonresident: full-time $14,391; part-time $533 per credit. *Required fees:* $1263; $22 per credit. $98 per quarter. One-time fee: $150. Tuition and fees vary according to program. *Financial support:* In 2013–14, 1 research assistantship with full tuition reimbursement (averaging $6,372 per year) was awarded; career-related internships or fieldwork, Federal Work-Study, and institutionally sponsored loans also available. Support available to part-time students. Financial award application deadline: 3/1; financial award applicants required to submit FAFSA. *Faculty research:* Transition of students with disabilities, functional curriculum, supported/inclusive education, leisure/recreation, autism. *Total annual research expenditures:* $1.2 million. *Unit head:* Rick Johnson, Chair, 503-725-9764, Fax: 503-725-5599, E-mail: johnsonp@pdx.edu. *Application contact:* Kris Smith, Admission Specialist, 503-725-4654, Fax: 503-725-5599, E-mail: kmsmith@pdx.edu.

Prairie View A&M University, College of Education, Department of Educational Leadership and Counseling, Prairie View, TX 77446-0519. Offers counseling (MA, MS Ed); educational administration (M Ed, MS Ed); educational leadership (PhD). *Accreditation:* NCATE. Part-time and evening/weekend programs available. *Faculty:* 28 full-time (10 women), 13 part-time/adjunct (9 women). *Students:* 193 full-time (144 women), 450 part-time (359 women); includes 607 minority (571 Black or African American, non-Hispanic/Latino; 6 Asian, non-Hispanic/Latino; 26 Hispanic/Latino; 4 Two or more races, non-Hispanic/Latino), 5 international. Average age 34. 337 applicants, 55% accepted, 125 enrolled. In 2013, 197 master's, 5 doctorates awarded. *Degree requirements:* For master's, thesis optional; for doctorate, comprehensive exam, thesis/dissertation. *Entrance requirements:* For master's, GRE General Test, 3 letters of reference, minimum undergraduate GPA of 2.5; for doctorate, GRE General Test, 3 letters of reference. Additional exam requirements/recommendations for international students: Required—TOEFL (minimum score 550 paper-based). *Application deadline:* For fall admission, 7/1 priority date for domestic students, 7/1 for international students; for spring admission, 11/1 priority date for domestic students, 11/1 for international students. Applications are processed on a rolling basis. Application fee: $50. Electronic applications accepted. *Expenses:* Tuition, state resident: full-time $3776; part-time $209.77 per credit hour. Tuition, nonresident: full-time $10,183; part-time $565.77 per credit hour. *Required fees:* $2037; $446.50 per credit hour. *Financial support:* In 2013–14, 600 students received support. Career-related internships or fieldwork available. Support available to part-time students. Financial award application deadline: 4/1; financial award applicants required to submit FAFSA. *Faculty research:* Mentoring, personality assessment, holistic/humanistic education. *Unit head:* Dr. Pamela Barber-Freeman, Interim Head, 936-261-3530, Fax: 936-261-3617, E-mail: ptfreeman@pvamu.edu. *Application contact:* Head.

Prescott College, Graduate Programs, Program in Education, Prescott, AZ 86301. Offers early childhood education (MA); early childhood special education (MA); education (MA); elementary education (MA); environmental education leadership and administration (MA); equine-assisted learning (MA); school guidance counseling (MA); secondary education (MA); special education: learning disabilities (MA); special education: mental retardation (MA); special education: serious emotional disabilities (MA); student-directed independent study (MA); sustainability education (PhD). Part-time programs available. Postbaccalaureate distance learning degree programs offered (minimal on-campus study). *Degree requirements:* For master's, thesis, fieldwork or internship, practicum; for doctorate, thesis/dissertation. *Entrance requirements:* For master's, 2 letters of recommendation, resume; for doctorate, 3 letters of recommendation, resume, official transcripts, personal statement, program proposal. Additional exam requirements/recommendations for international students: Required—TOEFL (minimum score 500 paper-based). Electronic applications accepted.

Providence College, Program in Counseling, Providence, RI 02918. Offers M Ed. Part-time and evening/weekend programs available. *Faculty:* 2 full-time (both women), 16 part-time/adjunct (7 women). *Students:* 41 full-time (33 women), 52 part-time (36 women); includes 16 minority (8 Black or African American, non-Hispanic/Latino; 1 American Indian or Alaska Native, non-Hispanic/Latino; 2 Asian, non-Hispanic/Latino; 4 Hispanic/Latino; 1 Two or more races, non-Hispanic/Latino), 1 international. Average age 30. 31 applicants, 100% accepted, 27 enrolled. In 2013, 33 master's awarded. *Degree requirements:* For master's, comprehensive exam, portfolio. *Entrance requirements:* For master's, GRE General Test. Additional exam requirements/recommendations for international students: Required—TOEFL (minimum score 550 paper-based; 80 iBT). *Application deadline:* For fall admission, 8/1 priority date for domestic and international students; for spring admission, 12/1 priority date for domestic and international students. Applications are processed on a rolling basis. Application fee: $55. *Expenses: Tuition:* Part-time $432 per credit. *Required fees:* $432 per credit. *Financial support:* Career-related internships or fieldwork, institutionally sponsored loans, and unspecified assistantships available. Support available to part-time students. Financial award application deadline: 8/1; financial award applicants required to submit FAFSA. *Unit head:* John T. Hogan, Director, 401-865-2922, Fax: 401-865-1147, E-mail: jhogan@providence.edu. *Application contact:* Rev. Mark D. Nowel, Dean of Undergraduate and Graduate Studies, 401-865-2649, Fax: 401-865-1496, E-mail: mnowel@providence.edu.
Website: http://www.providence.edu/professional-studies/graduate-degrees/Pages/master-education-counseling.aspx.

Purdue University, Graduate School, College of Education, Department of Educational Studies, West Lafayette, IN 47907. Offers administration (MS Ed, PhD, Ed S); counseling and development (MS Ed, PhD); education of the gifted (MS Ed); educational psychology (MS Ed, PhD); foundations of education (MS Ed, PhD); higher education administration (MS Ed, PhD); special education (MS Ed, PhD). *Accreditation:* ACA (one or more programs are accredited); NCATE (one or more programs are accredited). Part-time and evening/weekend programs available. *Faculty:* 21 full-time (17 women), 7 part-time/adjunct (4 women). *Students:* 102 full-time (73 women), 45 part-time (27 women); includes 23 minority (10 Black or African American, non-Hispanic/Latino; 5 Asian, non-Hispanic/Latino; 5 Hispanic/Latino; 3 Two or more races, non-Hispanic/Latino), 32 international. Average age 35. 165 applicants, 40% accepted, 33 enrolled. In 2013, 26 master's, 21 doctorates awarded. *Degree requirements:* For master's, thesis optional; for doctorate, thesis/dissertation, oral and written exams; for Ed S, oral presentation, project. *Entrance requirements:* For master's, GRE General Test (except for special education if undergraduate GPA is higher than a 3.0), minimum undergraduate GPA of 3.0; for doctorate and Ed S, GRE General Test (minimum combined score of 1000, 300 for new scoring), minimum undergraduate GPA of 3.0. Additional exam requirements/recommendations for international students: Required—TOEFL (minimum score 550 paper-based; 77 iBT), TWE (minimum score 5). *Application deadline:* Applications are processed on a rolling basis. Application fee: $60 ($75 for international students). Electronic applications accepted. *Financial support:* Fellowships with full tuition reimbursements, research assistantships with full tuition reimbursements, teaching assistantships with full tuition reimbursements, career-related internships or fieldwork, and tuition waivers (full) available. Support available to part-time students. Financial award application deadline: 3/1; financial award applicants required to submit FAFSA. *Faculty research:* Motivation, learning disabilities, school learning, group processes, cognitive development. *Unit head:* Dr. Ala Samrapungavan, Head, 765-494-9170, Fax: 765-496-1228, E-mail: ala@purdue.edu. *Application contact:* Cindy Blankenship, Graduate Contact, 765-494-2345, Fax: 765-494-5832, E-mail: prater0@purdue.edu.
Website: http://www.edst.purdue.edu/.

Purdue University Calumet, Graduate Studies Office, School of Education, Program in Counseling, Hammond, IN 46323-2094. Offers human services (MS Ed); mental health counseling (MS Ed); school counseling (MS Ed). *Entrance requirements:* Additional exam requirements/recommendations for international students: Required—TOEFL.

Queens College of the City University of New York, Division of Graduate Studies, Division of Education, Department of Educational and Community Programs, Program in

Counselor Education, Flushing, NY 11367-1597. Offers MS Ed. Part-time programs available. *Degree requirements:* For master's, research project. *Entrance requirements:* For master's, minimum GPA of 3.0. Additional exam requirements/recommendations for international students: Required—TOEFL.

Quincy University, Program in Counseling, Quincy, IL 62301-2699. Offers education (MS Ed), including clinical mental health counseling, school counseling. Part-time and evening/weekend programs available. *Faculty:* 2 full-time (1 woman). *Students:* 11 full-time (10 women), 25 part-time (21 women); includes 3 minority (1 American Indian or Alaska Native, non-Hispanic/Latino; 1 Asian, non-Hispanic/Latino; 1 Hispanic/Latino). In 2013, 2 master's awarded. *Degree requirements:* For master's, comprehensive exam, practicum, internship. *Entrance requirements:* For master's, MAT or GRE. Additional exam requirements/recommendations for international students: Required—TOEFL (minimum score 550 paper-based; 79 iBT). *Application deadline:* Applications are processed on a rolling basis. Application fee: $25. Electronic applications accepted. *Expenses: Tuition:* Full-time $9600; part-time $400 per semester hour. *Required fees:* $720; $30 per semester hour. Tuition and fees vary according to course load and program. *Financial support:* Applicants required to submit FAFSA. *Unit head:* Dr. Kenneth Oliver, Director, 217-228-5432 Ext. 3113, E-mail: oliveke@quincy.edu. *Application contact:* Office of Admissions, 217-228-5210, Fax: 217-228-5479, E-mail: admissions@quincy.edu.
Website: http://www.quincy.edu/academics/graduate-programs/counseling.

Radford University, College of Graduate and Professional Studies, College of Education and Human Development, Department of Counselor Education, Radford, VA 24142. Offers clinical mental health counseling (MS); school counseling (MS). *Accreditation:* ACA; NCATE. Part-time and evening/weekend programs available. *Faculty:* 6 full-time (3 women), 5 part-time/adjunct (all women). *Students:* 60 full-time (47 women), 27 part-time (23 women); includes 14 minority (8 Black or African American, non-Hispanic/Latino; 1 Asian, non-Hispanic/Latino; 2 Hispanic/Latino; 3 Two or more races, non-Hispanic/Latino), 2 international. Average age 28. 50 applicants, 84% accepted, 31 enrolled. In 2013, 29 master's awarded. *Degree requirements:* For master's, comprehensive exam, thesis optional. *Entrance requirements:* For master's, GRE or MAT, minimum GPA of 2.75, 3 letters of reference, personal essay, resume, official transcripts. Additional exam requirements/recommendations for international students: Required—TOEFL (minimum score 550 paper-based; 79 iBT). *Application deadline:* For fall admission, 2/15 priority date for domestic students, 12/1 for international students; for spring admission, 7/1 for international students. Applications are processed on a rolling basis. Application fee: $50. Electronic applications accepted. *Expenses:* Tuition, state resident: full-time $6800; part-time $283 per credit hour. Tuition, nonresident: full-time $15,610; part-time $627 per credit hour. *Required fees:* $2944; $123 per credit hour. Tuition and fees vary according to program. *Financial support:* In 2013–14, 17 students received support, including 14 research assistantships (averaging $8,036 per year), 3 teaching assistantships with partial tuition reimbursements available (averaging $11,000 per year); career-related internships or fieldwork, Federal Work-Study, institutionally sponsored loans, scholarships/grants, and unspecified assistantships also available. Financial award application deadline: 3/1; financial award applicants required to submit FAFSA. *Unit head:* Dr. Alan Forrest, Chair, 540-831-5214, Fax: 540-831-6755, E-mail: cquesnb@radford.edu. *Application contact:* Rebecca Conner, Director, Graduate Enrollment, 540-831-6296, Fax: 540-831-6061, E-mail: gradcollege@radford.edu.
Website: http://www.radford.edu/content/cehd/home/departments/counselor-education.html.

Regent University, Graduate School, School of Psychology and Counseling, Virginia Beach, VA 23464-9800. Offers clinical psychology (Psy D); counseling (MA), including clinical mental health counseling, marriage, couple, and family counseling, school counseling; counseling studies (CAGS); counselor education and supervision (PhD); human services counseling (MA); M Div/MA; M Ed/MA; MBA/MA. PhD program offered online only. *Accreditation:* ACA; APA (one or more programs are accredited). Part-time and evening/weekend programs available. Postbaccalaureate distance learning degree programs offered (minimal on-campus study). *Faculty:* 28 full-time (13 women), 39 part-time/adjunct (26 women). *Students:* 236 full-time (191 women), 245 part-time (193 women); includes 124 minority (98 Black or African American, non-Hispanic/Latino; 2 American Indian or Alaska Native, non-Hispanic/Latino; 9 Asian, non-Hispanic/Latino; 15 Hispanic/Latino), 26 international. Average age 34. 599 applicants, 39% accepted, 144 enrolled. In 2013, 129 master's, 43 doctorates awarded. *Median time to degree:* Of those who began their doctoral program in fall 2005, 87% received their degree in 8 years or less. *Degree requirements:* For master's, thesis or alternative, internship, practicum, written competency exam; for doctorate, thesis/dissertation or alternative. *Entrance requirements:* For master's, GRE General Test (including writing exam), minimum undergraduate GPA of 2.75, 3 recommendations, resume, transcripts, writing sample; for doctorate, GRE General Test (including writing exam), GRE Subject Test, minimum undergraduate GPA of 3.0, 3.5 (PhD), 10-15 minute VHS tape demonstrating counseling skills, writing sample, 3 recommendations, resume. Additional exam requirements/recommendations for international students: Required—TOEFL (minimum score 577 paper-based). *Application deadline:* For fall admission, 4/1 priority date for domestic students; for spring admission, 11/1 priority date for domestic students. Applications are processed on a rolling basis. Application fee: $50. Electronic applications accepted. *Expenses:* Contact institution. *Financial support:* Research assistantships with full and partial tuition reimbursements, teaching assistantships with full and partial tuition reimbursements, career-related internships or fieldwork, scholarships/grants, and tuition waivers (full and partial) available. Support available to part-time students. Financial award application deadline: 9/1; financial award applicants required to submit FAFSA. *Faculty research:* Marriage enrichment, AIDS counseling, troubled youth, faith and learning, trauma. *Unit head:* Dr. William Hathaway, Dean, 757-352-4294, Fax: 757-352-4282, E-mail: willhat@regent.edu. *Application contact:* Matthew Chadwick, Director of Enrollment Support Services, 800-373-5504, Fax: 757-352-4381, E-mail: admissions@regent.edu.
Website: http://www.regent.edu/psychology/.

Rhode Island College, School of Graduate Studies, Feinstein School of Education and Human Development, Department of Counseling, Educational Leadership, and School Psychology, Providence, RI 02908-1991. Offers advanced counseling (CGS); agency counseling (MA); co-occurring disorders (MA, CGS); educational leadership (M Ed); mental health counseling (CAGS); school counseling (MA); school psychology (CAGS); teacher leadership (CGS). *Accreditation:* NCATE. Part-time and evening/weekend programs available. *Faculty:* 10 full-time (6 women), 8 part-time/adjunct (7 women). *Students:* 38 full-time (32 women), 133 part-time (99 women); includes 18 minority (7 Black or African American, non-Hispanic/Latino; 2 Asian, non-Hispanic/Latino; 8 Hispanic/Latino; 1 Two or more races, non-Hispanic/Latino), 1 international. Average age 34. In 2013, 50 master's, 23 other advanced degrees awarded. *Degree requirements:* For master's and other advanced degree, comprehensive exam (for some programs), thesis (for some programs). *Entrance requirements:* For master's, GRE General Test or MAT, undergraduate transcripts; minimum undergraduate GPA of 3.0; for other advanced degree, GRE or MAT (for most programs), undergraduate transcripts; minimum undergraduate GPA of 3.0; 3 letters of recommendation; current resume. Additional exam requirements/recommendations for international students:

Recommended—TOEFL (minimum score 550 paper-based; 79 iBT). *Application deadline:* For fall admission, 3/1 for domestic students; for spring admission, 11/1 for domestic students. Applications are processed on a rolling basis. Application fee: $50. *Expenses:* Tuition, state resident: full-time $8928; part-time $372 per credit hour. Tuition, nonresident: full-time $17,376; part-time $724 per credit hour. *Required fees:* $602; $22 per credit. $72 per term. *Financial support:* In 2013–14, 4 teaching assistantships with full tuition reimbursements (averaging $2,250 per year) were awarded; career-related internships or fieldwork, Federal Work-Study, scholarships/grants, health care benefits, and unspecified assistantships also available. Support available to part-time students. Financial award application deadline: 5/15; financial award applicants required to submit FAFSA. *Unit head:* Dr. Kalina Brabeck, Chair, 401-456-8023. *Application contact:* Graduate Studies, 401-456-8700.
Website: http://www.ric.edu/counselingEducationalLeadershipSchoolPsychology/index.php.

Richmont Graduate University, School of Counseling, Atlanta, GA 30327. Offers marriage and family therapy (MA); professional counseling (MA).

Rider University, Department of Graduate Education, Leadership and Counseling, Program in Counseling Services, Lawrenceville, NJ 08648-3001. Offers counseling services (MA, Ed S); director of school counseling (Certificate); school counseling services (Certificate). *Accreditation:* ACA; NCATE. Part-time and evening/weekend programs available. *Degree requirements:* For master's, comprehensive exam, research project; for other advanced degree, specialty seminar. *Entrance requirements:* For master's, GRE or MAT, interview, resume, 2 letters of recommendation; for other advanced degree, GRE or MAT, interview, professional experience, 2 letters of recommendation. Additional exam requirements/recommendations for international students: Required—TOEFL (minimum score 550 paper-based). Electronic applications accepted. *Faculty research:* Diversity in counseling.

Rivier University, School of Graduate Studies, Department of Education, Nashua, NH 03060. Offers curriculum and instruction (M Ed); early childhood education (M Ed); educational administration (M Ed); educational studies (M Ed); elementary education (M Ed); elementary education and general special education (M Ed); emotional and behavioral disorders (M Ed); general social education (M Ed); leadership and learning (Ed D, CAGS); learning disabilities (M Ed); learning disabilities and reading (M Ed); mental health counseling (MA); reading (M Ed); school counseling (M Ed). Part-time and evening/weekend programs available. *Degree requirements:* For master's, comprehensive exam (for some programs), internships. *Entrance requirements:* For master's, GRE General Test or MAT.

Roberts Wesleyan College, Department of Psychology, Rochester, NY 14624-1997. Offers school counseling (MS); school psychology (MS). Part-time and evening/weekend programs available. *Faculty:* 8 full-time (6 women), 4 part-time/adjunct (3 women). *Students:* 34 full-time (30 women), 6 part-time (5 women); includes 5 minority (3 Black or African American, non-Hispanic/Latino; 2 Asian, non-Hispanic/Latino). Average age 28. 34 applicants, 82% accepted, 19 enrolled. In 2013, 17 master's awarded. *Degree requirements:* For master's, comprehensive exam, Praxis II for school psychology. *Entrance requirements:* For master's, GRE. *Application deadline:* For fall admission, 2/15 for domestic students. Applications are processed on a rolling basis. Electronic applications accepted. Application fee is waived when completed online. *Expenses: Tuition:* Full-time $12,816; part-time $712 per credit hour. One-time fee: $300. Tuition and fees vary according to course load and program. *Financial support:* In 2013–14, 8 students received support. Career-related internships or fieldwork, scholarships/grants, and unspecified assistantships available. Financial award application deadline: 4/15; financial award applicants required to submit FAFSA. *Faculty research:* Counselor supervision, forgiveness, community health psychology, applied research in group process. *Unit head:* Dr. Julia Grimm, Department Chair, 585-594-6133, Fax: 585-594-6124, E-mail: grimmj@roberts.edu. *Application contact:* Darlene Heitz, Graduate Admissions Office, 585-594-6011, Fax: 585-594-6124, E-mail: gradpsychadmissions@roberts.edu.
Website: https://www.roberts.edu/department-of-psychology.aspx.

Rollins College, Hamilton Holt School, Master of Arts in Counseling Program, Winter Park, FL 32789. Offers mental health counseling (MA). *Accreditation:* ACA. Part-time and evening/weekend programs available. *Faculty:* 5 full-time (3 women), 7 part-time/adjunct (5 women). *Students:* 35 full-time (30 women), 49 part-time (43 women); includes 20 minority (8 Black or African American, non-Hispanic/Latino; 1 American Indian or Alaska Native, non-Hispanic/Latino; 2 Asian, non-Hispanic/Latino; 8 Hispanic/Latino; 1 Two or more races, non-Hispanic/Latino), 1 international. Average age 32. 41 applicants, 100% accepted, 23 enrolled. In 2013, 22 master's awarded. *Degree requirements:* For master's, satisfactory completion of pre-practicum, practicum, and internship (1,000 hours total). *Entrance requirements:* For master's, GRE General Test or MAT, official transcripts, minimum GPA of 3.0, three letters of recommendation, essay, current resume. Additional exam requirements/recommendations for international students: Required—TOEFL (minimum score 550 paper-based; 80 iBT). *Application deadline:* For fall admission, 3/15 for domestic students. Application fee: $50. *Expenses:* Contact institution. *Financial support:* In 2013–14, 23 students received support. Federal Work-Study, scholarships/grants, and unspecified assistantships available. Support available to part-time students. Financial award applicants required to submit FAFSA. *Unit head:* Dr. Kathryn Norsworthy, Faculty Director, 407-646-2132, E-mail: knorsworthy@rollins.edu. *Application contact:* 407-646-1568, Fax: 407-975-6430, E-mail: graduateeducation@rollins.edu.
Website: http://www.rollins.edu/holt/graduate/mac.html.

Roosevelt University, Graduate Division, College of Education, Program in Counseling and Human Services, Chicago, IL 60605. Offers MA. *Accreditation:* ACA.

Rosemont College, Schools of Graduate and Professional Studies, Counseling Psychology Program, Rosemont, PA 19010-1699. Offers human services (MA); school counseling (MA). Part-time and evening/weekend programs available. *Degree requirements:* For master's, thesis or alternative, practicum. *Entrance requirements:* For master's, minimum undergraduate GPA of 3.0, 3 letters of recommendation. Additional exam requirements/recommendations for international students: Required—TOEFL. Electronic applications accepted. Application fee is waived when completed online. *Expenses:* Contact institution. *Faculty research:* Addictions counseling.

Rowan University, Graduate School, College of Education, Department of Special Educational Services/Instruction, Program in Counseling in Educational Settings, Glassboro, NJ 08028-1701. Offers MA. *Accreditation:* ACA. Part-time and evening/weekend programs available. *Faculty:* 7 full-time (3 women), 3 part-time/adjunct (all women). *Students:* 51 full-time (44 women), 30 part-time (27 women); includes 15 minority (10 Black or African American, non-Hispanic/Latino; 1 Asian, non-Hispanic/Latino; 3 Hispanic/Latino; 1 Two or more races, non-Hispanic/Latino), 1 international. Average age 27. 57 applicants, 91% accepted, 39 enrolled. In 2013, 42 master's awarded. *Degree requirements:* For master's, thesis. *Entrance requirements:* For master's, GRE General Test, minimum GPA of 2.8, 1 year of teaching experience. Additional exam requirements/recommendations for international students: Required—TOEFL. *Application deadline:* For fall admission, 7/1 priority date for domestic students; for spring admission, 11/15 priority date for domestic students. Applications are

processed on a rolling basis. Application fee: $65. Electronic applications accepted. *Expenses: Tuition, area resident:* Part-time $638 per credit. Tuition, state resident: full-time $5742. *Required fees:* $142 per credit. Tuition and fees vary according to course level and program. *Financial support:* Career-related internships or fieldwork, scholarships/grants, health care benefits, and unspecified assistantships available. Support available to part-time students. *Unit head:* Dr. Horacio Sosa, Dean, College of Graduate and Continuing Education, 856-256-4747, Fax: 856-256-5638, E-mail: sosa@rowan.edu. *Application contact:* Admissions and Enrollment Services, 856-256-5435, Fax: 856-256-5637, E-mail: cgceadmissions@rowan.edu.

Rutgers, The State University of New Jersey, New Brunswick, Graduate School of Education, Department of Educational Psychology, Programs in School Counseling and Counseling Psychology, Piscataway, NJ 08854-8097. Offers Ed M. Part-time and evening/weekend programs available. *Entrance requirements:* For master's, GRE General Test, 3 letters of recommendation. Additional exam requirements/recommendations for international students: Required—TOEFL (minimum score 550 paper-based; 83 iBT). Electronic applications accepted. *Faculty research:* Children and family in cross-cultural context, attachment theory, multicultural counseling, therapy relationship.

Sage Graduate School, Esteves School of Education, Program in Guidance and Counseling, Troy, NY 12180-4115. Offers MS, Post Master's Certificate. *Accreditation:* NCATE. Part-time and evening/weekend programs available. *Faculty:* 10 full-time (5 women), 2 part-time/adjunct (1 woman). *Students:* 29 full-time (27 women), 12 part-time (10 women); includes 2 minority (1 Black or African American, non-Hispanic/Latino; 1 Asian, non-Hispanic/Latino). Average age 26. 38 applicants, 53% accepted, 11 enrolled. In 2013, 27 master's, 7 other advanced degrees awarded. *Entrance requirements:* For master's, minimum GPA of 2.75, current resume, essay, official transcripts, 2 letters of recommendation. Additional exam requirements/recommendations for international students: Required—TOEFL (minimum score 550 paper-based). *Application deadline:* Applications are processed on a rolling basis. Application fee: $40. *Expenses: Tuition:* Full-time $11,880; part-time $660 per credit hour. *Financial support:* Fellowships, research assistantships, Federal Work-Study, scholarships/grants, and unspecified assistantships available. Support available to part-time students. Financial award application deadline: 3/1; financial award applicants required to submit FAFSA. *Faculty research:* Roles and responsibilities of guidance personnel, projections of need for guidance counselors. *Unit head:* Dr. Lori Quigley, Dean, Esteves School of Education, 518-244-2326, Fax: 518-244-4571, E-mail: l.quigley@sage.edu. *Application contact:* Dr. Michael Stahl, Director, 518-244-2499, Fax: 518-244-4571, E-mail: stahlm@sage.edu.

St. Bonaventure University, School of Graduate Studies, School of Education, Program in Counselor Education, St. Bonaventure, NY 14778-2284. Offers community mental health counseling (MS Ed); rehabilitation counseling (MS Ed); school counseling (MS Ed); school counselor (Adv C). Program offered in Olean and Buffalo Center (Hamburg, NY). *Accreditation:* ACA. Part-time and evening/weekend programs available. *Faculty:* 6 full-time (2 women), 6 part-time/adjunct (4 women). *Students:* 61 full-time (51 women), 20 part-time (13 women); includes 4 minority (1 Black or African American, non-Hispanic/Latino; 1 American Indian or Alaska Native, non-Hispanic/Latino; 1 Hispanic/Latino; 1 Two or more races, non-Hispanic/Latino), 1 international. Average age 33. 53 applicants, 87% accepted, 27 enrolled. In 2013, 68 master's, 3 Adv Cs awarded. *Degree requirements:* For master's, comprehensive exam, thesis optional, internship, portfolio; for Adv C, internship. *Entrance requirements:* For master's, interview, writing sample, minimum undergraduate GPA of 3.0, two letters of recommendation, bachelor's degree; for Adv C, interview, writing sample, minimum undergraduate GPA of 3.0, two letters of recommendation, master's degree, transcripts. Additional exam requirements/recommendations for international students: Required—TOEFL (minimum score 550 paper-based; 79 iBT). *Application deadline:* For fall admission, 8/15 priority date for domestic students, 2/1 priority date for international students; for spring admission, 11/15 priority date for domestic students, 7/1 priority date for international students. Applications are processed on a rolling basis. Application fee: $0. Electronic applications accepted. *Financial support:* In 2013–14, 5 research assistantships with full and partial tuition reimbursements were awarded; career-related internships or fieldwork, Federal Work-Study, scholarships/grants, health care benefits, tuition waivers (partial), and unspecified assistantships also available. Support available to part-time students. Financial award application deadline: 4/15; financial award applicants required to submit FAFSA. *Unit head:* Dr. Alan Silliker, Director, 716-375-2368, Fax: 716-375-2360, E-mail: silliker@sbu.edu. *Application contact:* Bruce Campbell, Director of Graduate Admissions, 716-375-2429, Fax: 716-375-4015, E-mail: gradsch@sbu.edu.
Website: http://www.sbu.edu/academics/schools/education.

St. Cloud State University, School of Graduate Studies, School of Education, Department of Educational Leadership and Higher Education, Program in College Counseling and Student Development, St. Cloud, MN 56301-4498. Offers MS. *Degree requirements:* For master's, comprehensive exam, thesis or alternative. *Entrance requirements:* For master's, GRE General Test, minimum GPA of 2.75. Additional exam requirements/recommendations for international students: Required—Michigan English Language Assessment Battery; Recommended—TOEFL (minimum score 550 paper-based), IELTS (minimum score 6.5). Electronic applications accepted.

St. Cloud State University, School of Graduate Studies, School of Education, Department of Educational Leadership and Higher Education, Program in School Counseling, St. Cloud, MN 56301-4498. Offers MS. *Accreditation:* ACA; NCATE. *Degree requirements:* For master's, comprehensive exam (for some programs), thesis or alternative. *Entrance requirements:* For master's, GRE General Test, minimum GPA of 2.75. Additional exam requirements/recommendations for international students: Required—Michigan English Language Assessment Battery; Recommended—TOEFL (minimum score 550 paper-based), IELTS. Electronic applications accepted.

St. John's University, The School of Education, Department of Human Services and Counseling, Program in Mental Health Counseling, Queens, NY 11439. Offers MS Ed, Adv C. Part-time and evening/weekend programs available. *Students:* 30 full-time (24 women), 37 part-time (31 women); includes 34 minority (12 Black or African American, non-Hispanic/Latino; 5 Asian, non-Hispanic/Latino; 16 Hispanic/Latino; 1 Two or more races, non-Hispanic/Latino), 2 international. Average age 28. 57 applicants, 84% accepted, 14 enrolled. In 2013, 22 master's awarded. *Degree requirements:* For master's, internship, state examination. *Entrance requirements:* For master's, bachelor's degree from an accredited college or university, minimum GPA of 3.0, 2 letters of recommendation, interview, 18 credits in behavioral and social science. Additional exam requirements/recommendations for international students: Required—TOEFL (minimum score 600 paper-based; 100 iBT), IELTS (minimum score 5.5). *Application deadline:* For fall admission, 4/1 for domestic students, 4/1 priority date for international students; for spring admission, 11/1 for domestic students, 11/1 priority date for international students. Applications are processed on a rolling basis. Application fee: $70. Electronic applications accepted. *Expenses: Tuition:* Full-time $19,800; part-time $1100 per credit. *Required fees:* $170 per semester. *Financial support:* Research assistantships and career-related internships or fieldwork available. Support available to part-time students. Financial award application deadline: 3/1; financial award applicants required to submit FAFSA. *Unit head:* Dr. E. Francine Guastello, Chair, 718-990-1475, E-mail: guastelf@stjohns.edu. *Application contact:* Dr. Kelly K. Ronayne, Associate Dean for Graduate Admissions, 718-990-2304, Fax: 718-990-2343, E-mail: graded@stjohns.edu.

St. John's University, The School of Education, Department of Human Services and Counseling, Program in School Counseling, Queens, NY 11439. Offers MS Ed, Adv C. *Accreditation:* ACA (one or more programs are accredited). Part-time and evening/weekend programs available. *Students:* 29 full-time (26 women), 16 part-time (12 women); includes 20 minority (7 Black or African American, non-Hispanic/Latino; 6 Asian, non-Hispanic/Latino; 6 Hispanic/Latino; 1 Two or more races, non-Hispanic/Latino). Average age 26. 45 applicants, 87% accepted, 15 enrolled. In 2013, 24 master's awarded. *Degree requirements:* For master's, comprehensive exam. *Entrance requirements:* For master's, bachelor's degree from accredited college or university, minimum GPA of 3.0, 2 letters of recommendation, interview, minimum of 18 credits in behavioral or social science; for Adv C, master's degree in counseling or related field, essay, official transcript showing minimum GPA of 3.0, 2 letters of recommendation, interview. Additional exam requirements/recommendations for international students: Required—TOEFL (minimum score 600 paper-based; 100 iBT), IELTS (minimum score 5.5). *Application deadline:* For fall admission, 4/1 for domestic students, 4/1 priority date for international students; for spring admission, 11/1 for domestic students, 11/1 priority date for international students. Applications are processed on a rolling basis. Application fee: $70. Electronic applications accepted. *Expenses: Tuition:* Full-time $19,800; part-time $1100 per credit. *Required fees:* $170 per semester. *Financial support:* Research assistantships and career-related internships or fieldwork available. Support available to part-time students. Financial award application deadline: 3/1; financial award applicants required to submit FAFSA. *Faculty research:* Counseling/client engagement; counseling accountability; pipe-line mentoring from grade 4 to college; stress, coping and resilience for children and adults; helping parents deal with aggressive children; effects of bullying and cyber bullying with adolescents; creative connections through the arts. *Unit head:* Dr. E. Francine Guastello, Chair, 718-990-1475, E-mail: guastelf@stjohns.edu. *Application contact:* Dr. Kelly K. Ronayne, Associate Dean for Graduate Admissions, 718-990-2304, Fax: 718-990-2343, E-mail: graded@stjohns.edu.

St. John's University, The School of Education, Department of Human Services and Counseling, Program in School Counseling with Bilingual Extension, Queens, NY 11439. Offers MS Ed. Part-time and evening/weekend programs available. *Students:* 3 full-time (2 women), 1 (woman) part-time; includes 3 minority (1 Asian, non-Hispanic/Latino; 2 Hispanic/Latino). Average age 30. 4 applicants, 100% accepted, 1 enrolled. In 2013, 14 master's awarded. *Degree requirements:* For master's, comprehensive exam. *Entrance requirements:* For master's, GRE, New York State Bilingual Assessment (BEA), bachelor's degree from an accredited college or university, minimum GPA of 3.0, 2 letters of recommendation, interview, minimum of 18 credits in behavioral or social science. Additional exam requirements/recommendations for international students: Required—TOEFL (minimum score 600 paper-based; 100 iBT), IELTS (minimum score 5.5). *Application deadline:* For fall admission, 4/1 for domestic students, 4/1 priority date for international students; for spring admission, 11/1 for domestic students, 11/1 priority date for international students. Applications are processed on a rolling basis. Application fee: $70. Electronic applications accepted. *Expenses: Tuition:* Full-time $19,800; part-time $1100 per credit. *Required fees:* $170 per semester. *Financial support:* Research assistantships, career-related internships or fieldwork, and scholarships/grants available. Support available to part-time students. Financial award application deadline: 3/1; financial award applicants required to submit FAFSA. *Faculty research:* Cross-cultural comparisons of predictors of active coping. *Unit head:* Dr. E. Francine Guastello, Chair, 718-990-1475, E-mail: guastelf@stjohns.edu. *Application contact:* Dr. Kelly K. Ronayne, Associate Dean for Graduate Admissions, 718-990-2304, Fax: 718-990-2343, E-mail: graded@stjohns.edu.

St. Lawrence University, Department of Education, Program in Counseling and Human Development, Canton, NY 13617-1455. Offers mental health counseling (MS); school counseling (M Ed, CAS). Part-time and evening/weekend programs available. *Entrance requirements:* For master's, GRE General Test. *Faculty research:* Defense mechanisms and mediation.

Saint Louis University, Graduate Education, College of Education and Public Service and Graduate Education, Department of Counseling and Family Therapy, St. Louis, MO 63103-2097. Offers counseling and family therapy (PhD); human development counseling (MA); marriage and family therapy (Certificate); school counseling (MA, MA-R). *Accreditation:* AAMFT/COAMFTE; NCATE. Part-time programs available. *Degree requirements:* For master's, comprehensive exam, thesis (for some programs); for doctorate, comprehensive exam, thesis/dissertation, preliminary oral and written exams. *Entrance requirements:* For master's, GRE General Test, letters of recommendation, resume; for doctorate, GRE General Test, letters of recommendation, resumé, transcripts, goal statement. Additional exam requirements/recommendations for international students: Required—TOEFL (minimum score 550 paper-based). Electronic applications accepted. *Faculty research:* Medical family therapy/collaborative health care multicultural counseling, mental health needs of diverse, minority, or Immigrant/refugee populations, divorce, aging families.

Saint Martin's University, Office of Graduate Studies, College of Education, Lacey, WA 98503. Offers administration (M Ed); English as a second language (M Ed); guidance and counseling (M Ed); reading (M Ed); special education (M Ed); teaching (MIT). *Accreditation:* Teacher Education Accreditation Council. Part-time and evening/weekend programs available. *Faculty:* 10 full-time (6 women), 15 part-time/adjunct (12 women). *Students:* 57 full-time (35 women), 52 part-time (38 women); includes 20 minority (7 Black or African American, non-Hispanic/Latino; 1 American Indian or Alaska Native, non-Hispanic/Latino; 2 Asian, non-Hispanic/Latino; 6 Hispanic/Latino; 1 Native Hawaiian or other Pacific Islander, non-Hispanic/Latino; 3 Two or more races, non-Hispanic/Latino). Average age 35. 63 applicants, 25% accepted, 13 enrolled. In 2013, 12 master's awarded. *Degree requirements:* For master's, comprehensive exam (for some programs), thesis or alternative, project or comprehensives. *Entrance requirements:* For master's, GRE General Test or MAT, three letters of recommendations; curriculum vitae. Additional exam requirements/recommendations for international students: Required—TOEFL (minimum score 550 paper-based; 79 iBT); Recommended—IELTS (minimum score 6.5). *Application deadline:* For fall admission, 4/1 priority date for domestic and international students; for spring admission, 11/1 priority date for domestic and international students. Applications are processed on a rolling basis. Application fee: $50. Electronic applications accepted. *Expenses: Tuition:* Part-time $990 per credit hour. Tuition and fees vary according to course level and program. *Financial support:* Career-related internships or fieldwork, Federal Work-Study, institutionally sponsored loans, and unspecified assistantships available. Support available to part-time students. Financial award application deadline: 3/1; financial award applicants required to submit FAFSA. *Faculty research:* Reader's theatre and reader/writer workshops, curriculum and assessment integration, gender and equity, classroom evaluations, organizational leadership. *Unit head:* Dr. Joyce Westgard, Dean, College of Education and Professional Psychology, 360-438-4509, Fax: 360-438-4486, E-mail: westgard@stmartin.edu. *Application contact:* Marie C. Boisvert, Administrative Assistant, 360-412-6145, E-mail: gradstudies@stmartin.edu.
Website: http://www.stmartin.edu/gradstudies.

Saint Mary's College of California, Kalmanovitz School of Education, Program in Counseling, Moraga, CA 94575. Offers general counseling (MA); marital and family therapy (MA); school counseling (MA). Part-time and evening/weekend programs available. *Degree requirements:* For master's, thesis or alternative. *Entrance requirements:* For master's, interview, minimum GPA of 3.0. *Faculty research:* Counselor training effectiveness, multicultural development, empathy, the interface of spirituality and psychotherapy, gender issues.

St. Mary's University, Graduate School, Department of Counseling and Human Services, Program in Counseling Education and Supervision, San Antonio, TX 78228-8507. Offers PhD. *Accreditation:* ACA. Part-time programs available. *Degree requirements:* For doctorate, comprehensive exam, thesis/dissertation. *Entrance requirements:* For doctorate, GRE, master's degree, work experience, letters of recommendation. Additional exam requirements/recommendations for international students: Required—TOEFL (minimum score 550 paper-based; 80 iBT). Electronic applications accepted.

Saint Peter's University, Graduate Programs in Education, Program in School Counseling, Jersey City, NJ 07306-5997. Offers MA, Certificate.

St. Thomas University, Biscayne College, Department of Social Sciences and Counseling, Program in Guidance and Counseling, Miami Gardens, FL 33054-6459. Offers MS, Post-Master's Certificate. Part-time and evening/weekend programs available. *Degree requirements:* For master's, comprehensive exam. *Entrance requirements:* For master's, interview, minimum GPA of 3.0 or GRE. Additional exam requirements/recommendations for international students: Required—TOEFL (minimum score 550 paper-based; 79 iBT). Electronic applications accepted.

Saint Xavier University, Graduate Studies, School of Education, Program in Counseling, Chicago, IL 60655-3105. Offers MA. *Degree requirements:* For master's, practicum, internship. *Entrance requirements:* For master's, 3 letters of recommendation, interview. Additional exam requirements/recommendations for international students: Required—TOEFL. Electronic applications accepted.

Salem College, Department of Education, Winston-Salem, NC 27101. Offers art education (MAT); elementary education (M Ed, MAT); language and literacy (M Ed); middle school education (MAT); school counseling (M Ed); second language studies (MAT); secondary education (MAT); special education (M Ed, MAT). *Accreditation:* NCATE. Part-time and evening/weekend programs available. Postbaccalaureate distance learning degree programs offered (minimal on-campus study). *Degree requirements:* For master's, practicum (MAT), project (M Ed), oral and written comprehensive exams. *Entrance requirements:* For master's, minimum GPA of 2.5. *Faculty research:* Content area reading strategies, literacy development, brain compatible instruction.

Salem State University, School of Graduate Studies, Program in School Counseling, Salem, MA 01970-5353. Offers M Ed. *Accreditation:* NCATE. Part-time and evening/weekend programs available. *Students:* 7 full-time (5 women), 37 part-time (31 women); includes 2 minority (both Hispanic/Latino). 16 applicants, 94% accepted, 11 enrolled. In 2013, 20 master's awarded. *Entrance requirements:* For master's, GRE or MAT. Additional exam requirements/recommendations for international students: Required—TOEFL (minimum score 550 paper-based; 80 iBT) or IELTS (minimum score 5.5). *Application deadline:* For fall admission, 5/1 for domestic students; for spring admission, 10/1 for domestic students. Applications are processed on a rolling basis. Application fee: $50. *Financial support:* Career-related internships or fieldwork, Federal Work-Study, scholarships/grants, and unspecified assistantships available. Support available to part-time students. Financial award application deadline: 5/1; financial award applicants required to submit FAFSA. *Application contact:* Dr. Lee A. Brossoit, Assistant Dean of Graduate Admissions, 978-542-6675, Fax: 978-542-7215, E-mail: lbrossoit@salemstate.edu.
Website: http://www.salemstate.edu/academics/schools/12643.php.

Sam Houston State University, College of Education and Applied Science, Department of Educational Leadership and Counseling, Huntsville, TX 77341. Offers administration (M Ed); clinical mental health counseling (MA); counselor education (PhD); developmental education administration (Ed D); educational leadership (Ed D); higher education administration (MA); instructional leadership (M Ed, MA); school counseling (M Ed). Part-time and evening/weekend programs available. Postbaccalaureate distance learning degree programs offered (no on-campus study). *Faculty:* 29 full-time (16 women). *Students:* 220 full-time (178 women), 463 part-time (374 women); includes 265 minority (128 Black or African American, non-Hispanic/Latino; 3 American Indian or Alaska Native, non-Hispanic/Latino; 6 Asian, non-Hispanic/Latino; 115 Hispanic/Latino; 13 Two or more races, non-Hispanic/Latino), 24 international. Average age 35. 294 applicants, 96% accepted, 130 enrolled. In 2013, 166 master's, 32 doctorates awarded. *Degree requirements:* For master's, comprehensive exam, thesis (for some programs); for doctorate, comprehensive exam, thesis/dissertation. *Entrance requirements:* For master's, GRE General Test. Additional exam requirements/recommendations for international students: Required—TOEFL (minimum score 550 paper-based; 79 iBT). *Application deadline:* For fall admission, 8/1 for domestic students, 6/25 for international students; for spring admission, 12/1 for domestic students, 11/12 for international students. Applications are processed on a rolling basis. Application fee: $45 ($75 for international students). Electronic applications accepted. *Financial support:* In 2013–14, 7 research assistantships (averaging $9,335 per year), 3 teaching assistantships (averaging $6,183 per year) were awarded; career-related internships or fieldwork, Federal Work-Study, institutionally sponsored loans, scholarships/grants, tuition waivers (partial), and unspecified assistantships also available. Support available to part-time students. Financial award application deadline: 5/31; financial award applicants required to submit FAFSA. *Unit head:* Dr. Stacey Edmonson, Chair, 936-294-1752, Fax: 936-294-3886, E-mail: edu_sle01@shsu.edu. *Application contact:* Dr. Barbara Polnick, Advisor, 936-294-3859, E-mail: bpolnick@shsu.edu.
Website: http://www.shsu.edu/~edu_elc/.

San Diego State University, Graduate and Research Affairs, College of Education, Department of Counseling and School Psychology, San Diego, CA 92182. Offers MS. *Accreditation:* NCATE. Evening/weekend programs available. *Degree requirements:* For master's, comprehensive exam (for some programs), thesis (for some programs). *Entrance requirements:* For master's, GRE General Test, interview, letters of reference. Additional exam requirements/recommendations for international students: Required—TOEFL. Electronic applications accepted. *Faculty research:* Multicultural and cross-cultural counseling and training, AIDS counseling.

San Francisco State University, Division of Graduate Studies, College of Health and Social Sciences, Department of Counseling, San Francisco, CA 94132-1722. Offers counseling (MS); marriage, family, and child counseling (MSC); rehabilitation counseling (MS); school counseling (Credential). *Accreditation:* ACA (one or more programs are accredited). Part-time programs available. *Application deadline:* Applications are processed on a rolling basis. *Unit head:* Dr. Robert A. Williams, Chair, 415-338-2005, E-mail: counsel@sfsu.edu. *Application contact:* Prof. Graciela Orozco, Graduate Coordinator, 415-338-2394, E-mail: orozco@sfsu.edu.
Website: http://counseling.sfsu.edu.

San Jose State University, Graduate Studies and Research, Connie L. Lurie College of Education, Department of Counselor Education, San Jose, CA 95192-0001. Offers MA. *Accreditation:* NCATE. Evening/weekend programs available. *Degree requirements:* For master's, thesis or alternative. Electronic applications accepted.

Santa Clara University, School of Education and Counseling Psychology, Santa Clara, CA 95053. Offers alternative and correctional education (Certificate); counseling (MA); counseling psychology (MA); educational administration (MA); interdisciplinary education (MA); teaching (MA). Part-time and evening/weekend programs available. *Faculty:* 56 full-time (21 women), 41 part-time/adjunct (23 women). *Students:* 232 full-time (192 women), 329 part-time (262 women); includes 162 minority (14 Black or African American, non-Hispanic/Latino; 1 American Indian or Alaska Native, non-Hispanic/Latino; 59 Asian, non-Hispanic/Latino; 75 Hispanic/Latino; 2 Native Hawaiian or other Pacific Islander, non-Hispanic/Latino; 11 Two or more races, non-Hispanic/Latino), 21 international. Average age 31. 322 applicants, 77% accepted, 178 enrolled. In 2013, 176 master's, 36 other advanced degrees awarded. *Degree requirements:* For master's, comprehensive exam (for some programs), thesis (for some programs); for Certificate, comprehensive exam. *Entrance requirements:* For master's, GRE or MAT, transcript, letters of recommendation, essay. Additional exam requirements/recommendations for international students: Required—TOEFL. *Application deadline:* For fall admission, 6/15 for domestic and international students; for winter admission, 10/15 for domestic and international students; for spring admission, 1/31 for domestic and international students. Applications are processed on a rolling basis. Application fee: $50. Electronic applications accepted. *Expenses:* Contact institution. *Financial support:* In 2013–14, 281 students received support. Fellowships, research assistantships, Federal Work-Study, institutionally sponsored loans, and scholarships/grants available. Support available to part-time students. Financial award application deadline: 5/15; financial award applicants required to submit FAFSA. *Faculty research:* Cognitive behavioral therapies and positive psychology, multicultural counseling and Latino mental health. *Unit head:* Nicholas Ladany, Dean, 408-554-4455, Fax: 408-554-5038, E-mail: nladany@scu.edu. *Application contact:* Kelly Pjesky, Admissions Director, 408-554-7884, Fax: 408-554-4367, E-mail: kpjesky@scu.edu.
Website: http://www.scu.edu/ecppm/.

Seattle Pacific University, Master of Education in School Counseling Program, Seattle, WA 98119-1997. Offers counselor education (PhD); school counseling (M Ed, Certificate). *Accreditation:* NCATE. Part-time programs available. *Students:* 27 full-time (25 women), 17 part-time (13 women); includes 7 minority (4 Asian, non-Hispanic/Latino; 1 Native Hawaiian or other Pacific Islander, non-Hispanic/Latino; 2 Two or more races, non-Hispanic/Latino), 1 international. Average age 28. 38 applicants, 32% accepted, 12 enrolled. In 2013, 10 master's awarded. *Degree requirements:* For master's, year-long internship. *Entrance requirements:* For master's, GRE General Test or MAT, copy of teaching certificate; official transcript(s) from each college/university attended; resume; personal statement, including long-term professional goals (maximum of 500 words); 2 letters of recommendation. *Application deadline:* For fall admission, 4/1 priority date for domestic students. Application fee: $50. Electronic applications accepted. *Expenses:* Contact institution. *Financial support:* Scholarships/grants available. Financial award applicants required to submit FAFSA. *Unit head:* Dr. Cher Edwards, Chair, 206-281-2286, Fax: 206-281-2756, E-mail: edwards@spu.edu. *Application contact:* 206-281-2091.
Website: http://spu.edu/academics/school-of-education/graduate-programs/masters-programs/school-counseling-med.

Seattle Pacific University, PhD in Counselor Education Program, Seattle, WA 98119-1997. Offers PhD. *Students:* 3 full-time (1 woman), 2 part-time (both women); includes 3 minority (1 Black or African American, non-Hispanic/Latino; 1 Asian, non-Hispanic/Latino; 1 Two or more races, non-Hispanic/Latino). Average age 30. 3 applicants, 33% accepted, 1 enrolled. *Entrance requirements:* For doctorate, GRE (minimum revised score of 153 Verbal Reasoning, 152 Quantitative Reasoning, taken within five years of application; minimum combined score of 1200 on old test), official transcripts, personal statement, four recent letters of recommendation, writing sample, resume. *Application deadline:* For fall admission, 8/15 for domestic students; for winter admission, 11/15 for domestic students; for spring admission, 2/15 for domestic students; for summer admission, 5/15 for domestic students. Application fee: $50. *Unit head:* Dr. Andrew Lumpe, Director, 206-281-2369, E-mail: lumpea@spu.edu. *Application contact:* John Glancy, Director, Graduate Admissions and Marketing, 206-281-2325, Fax: 206-281-2877, E-mail: jglancy@spu.edu.
Website: http://spu.edu/academics/school-of-education/graduate-programs/doctoral-programs/doctor-of-philosophy-counselor-education-phd.

Seattle University, College of Education, Program in Counseling and School Psychology, Seattle, WA 98122-1090. Offers MA, Certificate, Ed S. *Accreditation:* ACA; NCATE. Part-time and evening/weekend programs available. *Faculty:* 11 full-time (6 women), 3 part-time/adjunct (all women). *Students:* 52 full-time (43 women), 125 part-time (99 women); includes 64 minority (5 Black or African American, non-Hispanic/Latino; 1 American Indian or Alaska Native, non-Hispanic/Latino; 16 Asian, non-Hispanic/Latino; 23 Hispanic/Latino; 19 Two or more races, non-Hispanic/Latino), 1 international. Average age 29. 167 applicants, 34% accepted, 44 enrolled. In 2013, 23 master's, 12 other advanced degrees awarded. *Degree requirements:* For master's, comprehensive exam. *Entrance requirements:* For master's, interview; GRE, MAT, or minimum GPA of 3.0; related work experience. Additional exam requirements/recommendations for international students: Required—TOEFL. *Application deadline:* For fall admission, 7/1 for domestic students; for winter admission, 10/20 for domestic students; for spring admission, 1/20 for domestic students. Application fee: $55. *Unit head:* Hutch Haney, Director, 206-296-5750, E-mail: schpsy@seattleu.edu. *Application contact:* Janet Shandley, Associate Dean of Graduate Admissions, 206-296-5900, Fax: 206-298-5656, E-mail: grad_admissions@seattleu.edu.

Shippensburg University of Pennsylvania, School of Graduate Studies, College of Education and Human Services, Department of Counseling, Shippensburg, PA 17257-2299. Offers clinical mental health counseling (MS); college counseling (MS); college student personnel (MS); couple and family counseling (Certificate); school counseling (M Ed). *Accreditation:* ACA (one or more programs are accredited); NCATE. Part-time and evening/weekend programs available. *Faculty:* 8 full-time (3 women), 3 part-time/adjunct (2 women). *Students:* 87 full-time (70 women), 53 part-time (42 women); includes 23 minority (15 Black or African American, non-Hispanic/Latino; 1 American Indian or Alaska Native, non-Hispanic/Latino; 2 Asian, non-Hispanic/Latino; 1 Hispanic/Latino; 4 Two or more races, non-Hispanic/Latino). Average age 28. 101 applicants, 54% accepted, 38 enrolled. In 2013, 47 master's awarded. *Degree requirements:* For master's, fieldwork, research project, internship, candidacy. *Entrance requirements:* For master's, GRE or MAT (for clinical mental health, student personnel, and college counseling applicants if GPA is less than 2.75), minimum GPA of 2.75 (3.0 for M Ed), resume, 3 letters of recommendation, one year of relevant work experience, on-campus interview, autobiographical statement. Additional exam requirements/recommendations for international students: Required—TOEFL (minimum score 580 paper-based); Recommended—IELTS (minimum score 6). *Application deadline:* For fall admission, 4/30 for international students; for spring admission, 9/30 for international students. Applications are processed on a rolling basis. Application fee: $45. Electronic

applications accepted. *Expenses: Tuition, area resident:* Part-time $442 per credit. Tuition, state resident: part-time $442 per credit. Tuition, nonresident: part-time $663 per credit. *Required fees:* $127 per credit. *Financial support:* In 2013–14, 60 research assistantships with full tuition reimbursements (averaging $5,000 per year) were awarded; career-related internships or fieldwork, scholarships/grants, unspecified assistantships, and resident hall director and student payroll positions also available. Support available to part-time students. Financial award application deadline: 3/1; financial award applicants required to submit FAFSA. *Unit head:* Dr. Kurt L. Kraus, Chairperson, 717-477-1603, Fax: 717-477-4016, E-mail: klkrau@ship.edu. *Application contact:* Jeremy R. Goshorn, Assistant Dean of Graduate Admissions, 717-477-1231, Fax: 717-477-4016, E-mail: jrgoshorn@ship.edu.
Website: http://www.ship.edu/counsel/.

Simon Fraser University, Office of Graduate Studies, Faculty of Education, Program in Counseling Psychology, Burnaby, BC V5A 1S6, Canada. Offers M Ed, MA. Part-time and evening/weekend programs available. *Faculty:* 6 full-time (3 women). *Students:* 11 full-time (9 women). 74 applicants, 26% accepted, 9 enrolled. *Degree requirements:* For master's, comprehensive exam (for some programs), thesis (for some programs), practicum. *Entrance requirements:* For master's, minimum GPA of 3.0 (on scale of 4.33), or 3.33 based on last 60 credits of undergraduate courses. Additional exam requirements/recommendations for international students: Recommended—TOEFL (minimum score 580 paper-based; 93 iBT), IELTS (minimum score 7), TWE (minimum score 5). *Application deadline:* For fall admission, 1/15 for domestic and international students. Application fee: $90 ($125 for international students). Electronic applications accepted. *Expenses: Tuition, area resident:* Full-time $5084 Canadian dollars. *Required fees:* $840 Canadian dollars. *Financial support:* In 2013–14, fellowships (averaging $6,250 per year) were awarded; research assistantships, teaching assistantships, career-related internships or fieldwork, and scholarships/grants also available. *Faculty research:* Cultural and personal dimensions in psychological development, "psychology of working" and career development, social justice and multicultural competence issues, traumatic stress studies, counselor education. *Unit head:* Dr. John Nesbit, Associate Dean, Graduate Studies in Education, 778-782-7123, Fax: 778-782-4320, E-mail: mesbit@sfu.ca. *Application contact:* Bridget Fox, Graduate Secretary, 778-782-4215, E-mail: educmast@sfu.ca.

Slippery Rock University of Pennsylvania, Graduate Studies (Recruitment), College of Education, Department of Counseling and Development, Slippery Rock, PA 16057-1383. Offers community counseling (MA), including addiction, adult, child/adolescent, older adult, youth; school counseling (M Ed); student affairs (MA), including higher education; student affairs in higher education (MA), including college counseling. *Accreditation:* ACA (one or more programs are accredited); NCATE. Part-time and evening/weekend programs available. *Faculty:* 9 full-time (5 women). *Students:* 85 full-time (69 women), 26 part-time (21 women); includes 9 minority (7 Black or African American, non-Hispanic/Latino; 1 American Indian or Alaska Native, non-Hispanic/Latino; 1 Hispanic/Latino). Average age 28. 137 applicants, 49% accepted, 51 enrolled. In 2013, 45 master's awarded. *Degree requirements:* For master's, comprehensive exam, thesis (for some programs). *Entrance requirements:* For master's, GRE General Test, MAT, minimum GPA of 2.75 or 3.0 (depending on program), personal statement, three letters of recommendation, interview. Additional exam requirements/recommendations for international students: Required—TOEFL (minimum score 550 paper-based; 80 iBT). *Application deadline:* For fall admission, 1/15 priority date for domestic and international students. Application fee: $25 ($30 for international students). Electronic applications accepted. *Expenses:* Tuition, state resident: full-time $7956; part-time $442 per credit. Tuition, nonresident: full-time $11,934; part-time $663 per credit. *Required fees:* $2896; $148 per credit. Tuition and fees vary according to degree level and program. *Financial support:* Career-related internships or fieldwork, Federal Work-Study, institutionally sponsored loans, scholarships/grants, tuition waivers (partial), and unspecified assistantships available. Support available to part-time students. Financial award application deadline: 5/1; financial award applicants required to submit FAFSA. *Unit head:* Dr. Donald Strano, Graduate Coordinator, 724-738-2035, Fax: 724-738-4859, E-mail: donald.strano@sru.edu. *Application contact:* Brandi Weber-Mortimer, Director of Graduate Admissions, 724-738-2051, Fax: 724-738-2146, E-mail: graduate.admissions@sru.edu.

Sonoma State University, School of Social Sciences, Department of Counseling, Rohnert Park, CA 94928. Offers counseling (MA); licensed professional clinical counseling (MA); marriage, family, and child counseling (MA); pupil personnel services (MA). *Accreditation:* ACA. Part-time programs available. *Faculty:* 3 full-time (2 women), 4 part-time/adjunct (2 women). *Students:* 67 full-time (57 women), 11 part-time (10 women); includes 19 minority (1 Black or African American, non-Hispanic/Latino; 1 American Indian or Alaska Native, non-Hispanic/Latino; 2 Asian, non-Hispanic/Latino; 9 Hispanic/Latino; 1 Native Hawaiian or other Pacific Islander, non-Hispanic/Latino; 5 Two or more races, non-Hispanic/Latino). Average age 33. 113 applicants, 42% accepted, 22 enrolled. In 2013, 33 master's awarded. *Degree requirements:* For master's, internship. *Entrance requirements:* For master's, minimum GPA of 3.0. Additional exam requirements/recommendations for international students: Required—TOEFL (minimum score 500 paper-based). *Application deadline:* For fall admission, 11/30 for domestic students. Application fee: $55. *Expenses:* Tuition, state resident: full-time $8500. Tuition, nonresident: full-time $12,964. *Required fees:* $1762. *Financial support:* In 2013–14, 9 fellowships (averaging $1,520 per year) were awarded; career-related internships or fieldwork also available. Financial award application deadline: 3/2; financial award applicants required to submit FAFSA. *Unit head:* Dr. Adam Hill, Department Chair, 707-664-2340, E-mail: adam.hill@sonoma.edu. *Application contact:* Dr. Adam Zagelbaum, Program Coordinator, 707-664-2266, Fax: 707-664-2266, E-mail: zagelbau@sonoma.edu.
Website: http://www.sonoma.edu/counseling.

South Carolina State University, School of Graduate and Professional Studies, Department of Education, Orangeburg, SC 29117-0001. Offers early childhood and special education (M Ed); early childhood education (MAT); elementary education (M Ed, MAT); general science (MAT); mathematics (MAT); secondary education (M Ed), including biology education, business education, counselor education, English education, home economics education, industrial education, mathematics education, science education, social studies education; special education (M Ed), including emotionally handicapped, learning disabilities, mentally handicapped. *Accreditation:* NCATE. Part-time and evening/weekend programs available. *Faculty:* 9 full-time (3 women), 4 part-time/adjunct (3 women). *Students:* 32 full-time (26 women), 33 part-time (26 women); includes 63 minority (61 Black or African American, non-Hispanic/Latino; 2 Asian, non-Hispanic/Latino). Average age 31. 21 applicants, 100% accepted, 21 enrolled. In 2013, 15 master's awarded. *Degree requirements:* For master's, thesis optional, departmental qualifying exam. *Entrance requirements:* For master's, GRE General Test, NTE, interview, teaching certificate. *Application deadline:* For fall admission, 6/15 priority date for domestic students, 6/15 for international students; for spring admission, 11/1 for domestic and international students. Applications are processed on a rolling basis. Application fee: $25. Electronic applications accepted. *Expenses:* Tuition, state resident: full-time $8906; part-time $543 per credit hour. Tuition, nonresident: full-time $18,040; part-time $1051 per credit hour. *Financial support:* Fellowships, career-related internships or fieldwork, Federal Work-Study, and institutionally sponsored loans available. Financial award application deadline: 6/1. *Faculty research:* Critical thinking, child abuse, stress, test-taking skills, conflict resolution, mainstreaming. *Unit head:* Dr. Margaret Evelyn Fields, Interim Chair, 803-536-7098, Fax: 803-516-4568, E-mail: efields@scsu.edu. *Application contact:* Curtis Foskey, Coordinator of Graduate Studies, 803-536-8419, Fax: 803-536-8812, E-mail: cfoskey@scsu.edu.

South Carolina State University, School of Graduate and Professional Studies, Department of Human Services, Orangeburg, SC 29117-0001. Offers counselor education (M Ed); rehabilitation counseling (MA). *Accreditation:* CORE. Part-time and evening/weekend programs available. *Faculty:* 9 full-time (6 women), 8 part-time/adjunct (5 women). *Students:* 107 full-time (74 women), 35 part-time (27 women); includes 135 minority (all Black or African American, non-Hispanic/Latino). Average age 31. 54 applicants, 93% accepted, 50 enrolled. In 2013, 54 master's awarded. *Degree requirements:* For master's, comprehensive exam (for some programs), departmental qualifying exam, internship. *Entrance requirements:* For master's, GRE, MAT, minimum GPA of 2.7. *Application deadline:* For fall admission, 6/15 priority date for domestic students, 6/15 for international students; for spring admission, 11/1 for domestic and international students. Applications are processed on a rolling basis. Application fee: $25. Electronic applications accepted. *Expenses:* Tuition, state resident: full-time $8906; part-time $543 per credit hour. Tuition, nonresident: full-time $18,040; part-time $1051 per credit hour. *Financial support:* In 2013–14, 35 students received support. Fellowships, career-related internships or fieldwork, institutionally sponsored loans, and unspecified assistantships available. Financial award application deadline: 6/1. *Faculty research:* Handicap, disability, rehabilitation evaluation, vocation. *Unit head:* Dr. Cassandra Sligh Conway, Chair, 803-536-7075, Fax: 803-533-3636, E-mail: csligh-dewalt@scsu.edu. *Application contact:* Curtis Foskey, Coordinator of Graduate Admissions, 803-536-8419, Fax: 803-536-8812, E-mail: cfoskey@scsu.edu.

South Dakota State University, Graduate School, College of Education and Human Sciences, Department of Counseling and Human Resource Development, Brookings, SD 57007. Offers MS. *Accreditation:* ACA; NCATE. Part-time and evening/weekend programs available. *Degree requirements:* For master's, comprehensive exam, thesis (for some programs), oral exams. *Entrance requirements:* For master's, minimum GPA of 2.75. Additional exam requirements/recommendations for international students: Required—TOEFL (minimum score 525 paper-based; 71 iBT). *Faculty research:* Rural mental health, family issues, character education, student affairs, solution focused therapy.

Southeastern Louisiana University, College of Nursing and Health Sciences, Department of Health and Human Sciences, Hammond, LA 70402. Offers communication sciences and disorders (MS); counselor education (M Ed). *Accreditation:* ASHA; NCATE. *Faculty:* 15 full-time (all women), 1 (woman) part-time/adjunct. *Students:* 87 full-time (83 women), 70 part-time (60 women); includes 35 minority (24 Black or African American, non-Hispanic/Latino; 7 Hispanic/Latino; 4 Two or more races, non-Hispanic/Latino). Average age 26. 221 applicants, 64% accepted, 26 enrolled. In 2013, 33 master's awarded. *Degree requirements:* For master's, comprehensive exam, thesis optional, 25 clock hours of clinical observation. *Entrance requirements:* For master's, GRE (verbal and quantitative), minimum GPA of 2.75; undergraduate degree; three letters of reference; favorable criminal background check. Additional exam requirements/recommendations for international students: Required—TOEFL (minimum score 500 paper-based; 61 iBT). *Application deadline:* For fall admission, 3/1 priority date for domestic students, 6/1 priority date for international students; for spring admission, 10/1 priority date for domestic and international students. Applications are processed on a rolling basis. Application fee: $20 ($30 for international students). Electronic applications accepted. *Expenses:* Tuition, state resident: full-time $5047. Tuition, nonresident: full-time $17,066. *Required fees:* $1213. Tuition and fees vary according to degree level. *Financial support:* In 2013–14, 1 research assistantship (averaging $9,000 per year) was awarded; career-related internships or fieldwork, Federal Work-Study, institutionally sponsored loans, scholarships/grants, and unspecified assistantships also available. Support available to part-time students. Financial award application deadline: 5/1; financial award applicants required to submit FAFSA. *Faculty research:* Aphasia, autism spectrum disorders, child language and literacy, language and dementia, clinical supervision. *Unit head:* Dr. Jacqueline Guendouzi, Interim Department Head, 985-549-2309, Fax: 985-549-5030, E-mail: jguendouzi@selu.edu. *Application contact:* Sandra Meyers, Graduate Admissions Analyst, 985-549-5620, Fax: 985-549-5632, E-mail: admissions@selu.edu.
Website: http://www.southeastern.edu/acad_research/depts/hhs/.

Southeastern Oklahoma State University, School of Behavioral Sciences, Durant, OK 74701-0609. Offers clinical mental health counseling (MS). Part-time and evening/weekend programs available. *Degree requirements:* For master's, comprehensive exam, thesis optional. *Entrance requirements:* For master's, GRE General Test, minimum GPA of 3.0 in last 60 hours or 2.75 overall. Additional exam requirements/recommendations for international students: Required—TOEFL (minimum score 550 paper-based; 79 iBT). Electronic applications accepted.

Southeastern Oklahoma State University, School of Education, Durant, OK 74701-0609. Offers math specialist (M Ed); reading specialist (M Ed); school administration (M Ed); school counseling (M Ed). *Accreditation:* NCATE. Part-time and evening/weekend programs available. *Degree requirements:* For master's, comprehensive exam, thesis optional, portfolio (M Ed). *Entrance requirements:* For master's, GRE General Test (for school counseling), minimum GPA of 3.0 in last 60 hours or 2.75 overall. Additional exam requirements/recommendations for international students: Required—TOEFL (minimum score 550 paper-based; 79 iBT). Electronic applications accepted.

Southeastern University, Department of Behavioral and Social Sciences, Lakeland, FL 33801-6099. Offers human services (MA); professional counseling (MS); school counseling (MS). Evening/weekend programs available.

Southeast Missouri State University, School of Graduate Studies, Department of Educational Leadership and Counseling, Counseling Program, Cape Girardeau, MO 63701-4799. Offers career counseling (MA); counseling education (Ed S); mental health counseling (MA); school counseling (MA). *Accreditation:* ACA; NCATE. Part-time and evening/weekend programs available. *Faculty:* 4 full-time (3 women), 2 part-time/adjunct (both women). *Students:* 32 full-time (28 women), 44 part-time (40 women); includes 9 minority (7 Black or African American, non-Hispanic/Latino; 1 Hispanic/Latino; 1 Native Hawaiian or other Pacific Islander, non-Hispanic/Latino), 1 international. Average age 33. 39 applicants, 90% accepted, 26 enrolled. In 2013, 22 master's, 8 other advanced degrees awarded. *Degree requirements:* For master's and Ed S, comprehensive exam, thesis. *Entrance requirements:* For master's, GRE General Test or MAT, minimum undergraduate GPA of 3.5; 3 letters of recommendation; 18 undergraduate hours in social science including statistics (for mental health counseling and career counseling); for Ed S, GRE General Test or MAT, minimum graduate GPA of 3.7; master's degree in counseling, education or related field; 4 letters of recommendation. Additional exam requirements/recommendations for international students: Required—TOEFL (minimum score 550 paper-based; 79 iBT), IELTS (minimum score 6), PTE (minimum score 53). *Application deadline:* For fall admission, 3/1 for domestic and international students; for spring admission, 11/21 for domestic students, 10/1 for international students; for

summer admission, 3/1 for domestic students. Applications are processed on a rolling basis. Application fee: $30 ($40 for international students). Electronic applications accepted. *Expenses:* Tuition, state resident: full-time $5139; part-time $285.50 per credit hour. Tuition, nonresident: full-time $9099; part-time $505.50 per credit hour. *Financial support:* In 2013–14, 8 students received support. Career-related internships or fieldwork, Federal Work-Study, scholarships/grants, traineeships, tuition waivers (full), and unspecified assistantships available. Financial award application deadline: 6/30; financial award applicants required to submit FAFSA. *Faculty research:* School counseling, mental health, career and family. *Unit head:* Dr. Jan Ward, Graduate Program Coordinator, 573-651-2415, E-mail: jward@semo.edu. *Application contact:* Alisa Aleen McFerron, Assistant Director of Admissions for Operations, 573-651-5937, E-mail: amcferron@semo.edu.
Website: http://www4.semo.edu/counsel/.

Southern Adventist University, School of Education and Psychology, Collegedale, TN 37315-0370. Offers clinical mental health counseling (MS); inclusive education (MS Ed); instructional leadership (MS Ed); literacy education (MS Ed); outdoor teacher education (MS Ed); school counseling (MS). *Accreditation:* NCATE. Part-time and evening/weekend programs available. *Degree requirements:* For master's, comprehensive exam (for some programs), thesis optional, position paper (MS), portfolio (MS Ed in outdoor teacher education). *Entrance requirements:* For master's, interview (MS); 9 semester hours of upper-division course work in psychology or related field, including 1 course in psychology research or statistics; 9 semester hours of education (MS Ed). Additional exam requirements/recommendations for international students: Required—TOEFL (minimum score 600 paper-based; 100 iBT). Electronic applications accepted.

Southern Arkansas University–Magnolia, Graduate Programs, Magnolia, AR 71753. Offers agriculture (MS); business administration (MBA); computer and information sciences (MS); education (M Ed), including counseling and development, curriculum and instruction, educational administration and supervision, elementary education, reading, secondary education, TESOL; kinesiology (M Ed); library media and information specialist (M Ed); mental health and clinical counseling (MS); public administration (MPA); school counseling (M Ed); teaching (MAT). *Accreditation:* NCATE. Part-time and evening/weekend programs available. Postbaccalaureate distance learning degree programs offered. *Faculty:* 34 full-time (15 women), 8 part-time/adjunct (5 women). *Students:* 48 full-time (22 women), 269 part-time (167 women); includes 85 minority (78 Black or African American, non-Hispanic/Latino; 2 Asian, non-Hispanic/Latino; 2 Hispanic/Latino; 1 Native Hawaiian or other Pacific Islander, non-Hispanic/Latino; 2 Two or more races, non-Hispanic/Latino), 5 international. Average age 33. 149 applicants, 73% accepted, 109 enrolled. In 2013, 149 master's awarded. *Degree requirements:* For master's, comprehensive exam (for some programs), thesis optional. *Entrance requirements:* For master's, GRE, MAT or GMAT, minimum GPA of 2.5. Additional exam requirements/recommendations for international students: Required—TOEFL, IELTS. *Application deadline:* For fall admission, 7/10 for domestic and international students; for winter admission, 12/1 for domestic and international students; for spring admission, 12/1 for domestic and international students; for summer admission, 4/1 for domestic students. Applications are processed on a rolling basis. Application fee: $25 ($50 for international students). Electronic applications accepted. *Expenses:* Tuition, state resident: part-time $254 per credit hour. Tuition, nonresident: part-time $370 per credit hour. *Required fees:* $136 per credit hour. $259 per semester. Tuition and fees vary according to course load and program. *Financial support:* Career-related internships or fieldwork, Federal Work-Study, scholarships/grants, tuition waivers (full), and unspecified assistantships available. Financial award applicants required to submit FAFSA. *Faculty research:* Alternative certification for teachers, supervision of instruction, instructional leadership, counseling. *Unit head:* Dr. Kim Bloss, Dean, School of Graduate Studies, 870-235-4150, Fax: 870-235-5227, E-mail: kkbloss@saumag.edu. *Application contact:* Shrijana Malaka, Admissions Specialist, 870-235-4150, Fax: 870-235-5227, E-mail: smalakar@saumag.edu.
Website: http://www.saumag.edu/graduate.

Southern Connecticut State University, School of Graduate Studies, School of Education, Department of Counseling and School Psychology, New Haven, CT 06515-1355. Offers community counseling (MS); counseling (Diploma); school counseling (MS); school psychology (MS, Diploma). *Accreditation:* ACA (one or more programs are accredited); NCATE. *Degree requirements:* For master's, comprehensive exam. *Entrance requirements:* For master's, interview, previous course work in behavioral sciences, minimum QPA of 2.7. Electronic applications accepted.

Southern Illinois University Carbondale, Graduate School, College of Education and Human Services, Department of Educational Psychology and Special Education, Program in Educational Psychology, Carbondale, IL 62901-4701. Offers counselor education (MS Ed, PhD); educational psychology (PhD); human learning and development (MS Ed); measurement and statistics (PhD). *Accreditation:* NCATE. *Faculty:* 19 full-time (9 women), 7 part-time/adjunct (2 women). *Students:* 40 full-time (30 women), 28 part-time (16 women); includes 13 minority (11 Black or African American, non-Hispanic/Latino; 1 Asian, non-Hispanic/Latino; 1 Hispanic/Latino), 11 international. Average age 36. 22 applicants, 50% accepted, 8 enrolled. In 2013, 6 master's, 1 doctorate awarded. *Degree requirements:* For master's, thesis; for doctorate, thesis/dissertation. *Entrance requirements:* For master's, GRE General Test, minimum GPA of 2.7; for doctorate, minimum GPA of 3.25. Additional exam requirements/recommendations for international students: Required—TOEFL. *Application deadline:* For fall admission, 6/15 priority date for domestic students. Applications are processed on a rolling basis. Application fee: $50. *Financial support:* In 2013–14, 36 students received support, including 2 fellowships with full tuition reimbursements available, 4 research assistantships with full tuition reimbursements available; teaching assistantships with full tuition reimbursements available, career-related internships or fieldwork, Federal Work-Study, institutionally sponsored loans, and tuition waivers (full) also available. Support available to part-time students. Financial award application deadline: 5/1. *Faculty research:* Career development, problem-solving, learning and instruction, cognitive development, family assessment. *Total annual research expenditures:* $10,000. *Unit head:* Dr. Lyle White, Chairperson, 618-536-7763, E-mail: lwhite@siu.edu. *Application contact:* Brenda Prell, Administrative Clerk, 618-453-6932, E-mail: bprell@siu.edu.

Southern Methodist University, Annette Caldwell Simmons School of Education and Human Development, Department of Dispute Resolution and Counseling, Dallas, TX 75275. Offers counseling (MS); dispute resolution (MA). Part-time programs available. *Degree requirements:* For master's, practica experience, 2 internships (counseling). *Entrance requirements:* For master's, minimum undergraduate GPA of 2.75 (for dispute resolution), 3.0 (for counseling); 3 letters of recommendation. Additional exam requirements/recommendations for international students: Required—TOEFL. Electronic applications accepted.

Southern University and Agricultural and Mechanical College, Graduate School, College of Education, Department of Behavioral Studies and Educational Leadership, Baton Rouge, LA 70813. Offers administration and supervision (M Ed); counselor education (MA); educational leadership (M Ed); mental health counseling (MA). *Accreditation:* ACA; NCATE. *Degree requirements:* For master's, comprehensive exam, thesis optional. *Entrance requirements:* For master's, GRE General Test. Additional

exam requirements/recommendations for international students: Required—TOEFL (minimum score 525 paper-based). *Faculty research:* Mental health, computer assisted programs, families relations, head start improvements, careers.

Southwestern Oklahoma State University, College of Professional and Graduate Studies, School of Behavioral Sciences and Education, Specialization in Community Counseling, Weatherford, OK 73096-3098. Offers M Ed. M Ed distance learning degree program offered to Oklahoma residents only. *Accreditation:* NCATE. Part-time and evening/weekend programs available. Postbaccalaureate distance learning degree programs offered (minimal on-campus study). *Degree requirements:* For master's, exam. *Entrance requirements:* For master's, GRE General Test or minimum undergraduate GPA of 3.0. Additional exam requirements/recommendations for international students: Required—TOEFL.

Southwestern Oklahoma State University, College of Professional and Graduate Studies, School of Behavioral Sciences and Education, Specialization in School Counseling, Weatherford, OK 73096-3098. Offers M Ed. M Ed distance learning degree program offered to Oklahoma residents only. *Accreditation:* NCATE. Part-time and evening/weekend programs available. Postbaccalaureate distance learning degree programs offered (minimal on-campus study). *Degree requirements:* For master's, exam. *Entrance requirements:* For master's, GRE General Test or minimum undergraduate GPA of 3.0, portfolio. Additional exam requirements/recommendations for international students: Required—TOEFL.

Spalding University, Graduate Studies, College of Education, Programs in Education, Louisville, KY 40203-2188. Offers art teacher education (MAT); business teacher education (MAT); elementary school education (MAT); foreign language (MAT); general education (MA Ed); high school education (MAT); middle school education (MAT); school administration (MA Ed); secondary education (MAT); special education (learning and behavioral disorders) (MAT); student guidance counselor (MA); teacher education and professional development (MAT). *Accreditation:* NCATE. Part-time and evening/weekend programs available. *Faculty:* 12 full-time (11 women), 6 part-time/adjunct (4 women). *Students:* 92 full-time (63 women), 36 part-time (29 women); includes 43 minority (41 Black or African American, non-Hispanic/Latino; 2 Two or more races, non-Hispanic/Latino). Average age 35. 77 applicants, 48% accepted, 30 enrolled. In 2013, 81 master's awarded. *Degree requirements:* For master's, portfolio, final project, clinical experience. *Entrance requirements:* For master's, GRE General Test or MAT, interview, letters of recommendation, resume. Additional exam requirements/recommendations for international students: Required—TOEFL (minimum score 535 paper-based). *Application deadline:* Applications are processed on a rolling basis. Application fee: $30. Electronic applications accepted. *Expenses:* Tuition: Full-time $21,450. *Required fees:* $810. Tuition and fees vary according to course load, degree level, program and student level. *Financial support:* Scholarships/grants, traineeships, and unspecified assistantships available. Financial award application deadline: 3/30; financial award applicants required to submit FAFSA. *Faculty research:* Instructional technology, achievement gap, classroom management, assessment. *Unit head:* Dr. Beverly Keepers, Dean, 502-588-7121, Fax: 502-585-7123, E-mail: bkeepers@spalding.edu. *Application contact:* Bonnie Caughron, Administrative Assistant, College of Education, 502-873-4262, E-mail: bcaughron@spalding.edu.

Springfield College, Graduate Programs, Program in Education, Springfield, MA 01109-3797. Offers counseling and secondary education (M Ed, MS); early childhood education (M Ed, MS); education (M Ed, MS); educational administration (M Ed, MS); educational studies (M Ed, MS); elementary education (M Ed, MS); secondary education (M Ed, MS); special education (M Ed, MS). Part-time and evening/weekend programs available. *Faculty:* 6 full-time. *Students:* 47 full-time. 45 applicants, 87% accepted, 35 enrolled. In 2013, 15 master's awarded. *Entrance requirements:* Additional exam requirements/recommendations for international students: Required—TOEFL (minimum score 550 paper-based); Recommended—IELTS (minimum score 6). *Application deadline:* For fall admission, 1/15 for domestic and international students; for winter admission, 11/1 for domestic and international students; for spring admission, 11/1 for domestic and international students. Applications are processed on a rolling basis. Application fee: $50. Electronic applications accepted. *Expenses: Tuition:* Full-time $13,620; part-time $908 per credit. *Financial support:* Fellowships with partial tuition reimbursements, teaching assistantships with partial tuition reimbursements, career-related internships or fieldwork, Federal Work-Study, institutionally sponsored loans, and unspecified assistantships available. Financial award application deadline: 3/1; financial award applicants required to submit FAFSA. *Unit head:* Jennifer Johnston, Program Coordinator, 413-748-3348, E-mail: jjohnston@springfieldcollege.edu. *Application contact:* Evelyn Cohen, Associate Director of Graduate Admissions, 413-748-3479, Fax: 413-748-3694, E-mail: ecohen@springfieldcollege.edu.

Springfield College, Graduate Programs, Programs in Psychology and Counseling, Springfield, MA 01109-3797. Offers athletic counseling (M Ed, MS, Psy D, CAGS); clinical mental health counseling (Psy D); couples and family therapy (Psy D); industrial/organizational psychology (M Ed, MS, CAGS); marriage and family therapy (M Ed, MS, CAGS); mental health counseling (M Ed, MS, CAGS); school guidance and counseling (M Ed, MS, CAGS); student personnel in higher education (M Ed, MS, CAGS). Part-time programs available. *Faculty:* 13 full-time (6 women), 12 part-time/adjunct (3 women). *Students:* 151 full-time, 52 part-time. Average age 30. 198 applicants, 73% accepted, 74 enrolled. In 2013, 84 master's, 4 other advanced degrees awarded. *Degree requirements:* For master's, research project, portfolio; for doctorate, dissertation project, 1500 hours of counseling psychology practicum, full-year internship. *Entrance requirements:* Additional exam requirements/recommendations for international students: Required—TOEFL (minimum score 550 paper-based). *Application deadline:* For fall admission, 1/15 priority date for domestic students, 1/15 for international students; for winter admission, 11/1 for domestic and international students; for spring admission, 11/1 for domestic and international students. Applications are processed on a rolling basis. Application fee: $50. Electronic applications accepted. *Expenses: Tuition:* Full-time $13,620; part-time $908 per credit. *Financial support:* Fellowships with partial tuition reimbursements, teaching assistantships with partial tuition reimbursements, career-related internships or fieldwork, Federal Work-Study, institutionally sponsored loans, and unspecified assistantships available. Financial award application deadline: 3/1; financial award applicants required to submit FAFSA. *Unit head:* Dr. Allison Cumming-McCann, Graduate Program Director, 413-748-3075, Fax: 413-748-3854, E-mail: acumming@springfieldcollege.edu. *Application contact:* Evelyn Cohen, Director of Graduate Admissions, 413-748-3225, E-mail: ecohen@springfieldcollege.edu.
Website: http://www.springfieldcollege.edu/academic-programs/psychology-department/graduate-programs-in-psychology/index#.U1F-dKJWiSo.

State University of New York at New Paltz, Graduate School, School of Liberal Arts and Sciences, Department of Psychology, New Paltz, NY 12561. Offers mental health counseling (MS, AC); psychology (MA); school counseling (MS). Part-time and evening/weekend programs available. *Faculty:* 23 full-time (12 women), 6 part-time/adjunct (all women). *Students:* 50 full-time (40 women), 19 part-time (17 women); includes 12 minority (3 Black or African American, non-Hispanic/Latino; 3 Asian, non-Hispanic/Latino; 4 Hispanic/Latino; 2 Two or more races, non-Hispanic/Latino). Average age 28. 71 applicants, 70% accepted, 28 enrolled. In 2013, 22 master's awarded. *Degree requirements:* For master's, comprehensive exam, thesis. *Entrance requirements:* For

master's, GRE General Test, minimum GPA of 3.0. Additional exam requirements/ recommendations for international students: Required—TOEFL (minimum score 550 paper-based; 80 iBT), IELTS (minimum score 6.5). *Application deadline:* For fall admission, 1/20 priority date for domestic and international students; for spring admission, 11/15 for domestic and international students. Application fee: $50. Electronic applications accepted. *Expenses:* Tuition, state resident: full-time $9870; part-time $411 per credit. Tuition, nonresident: full-time $18,350; part-time $765 per credit. *Required fees:* $1213. Tuition and fees vary according to program. *Financial support:* In 2013–14, 6 teaching assistantships with partial tuition reimbursements (averaging $5,000 per year) were awarded. Financial award application deadline: 8/1. *Faculty research:* Disaster mental health, women's objectification, mate selection, cultural psychology, achievement motivation. *Unit head:* Dr. Glenn Geher, Chair, 845-257-3091, E-mail: geherg@newpaltz.edu. *Application contact:* Dr. Melanie Hill, Coordinator, 845-257-3475, E-mail: hillm@newpaltz.edu.
Website: http://www.newpaltz.edu/psychology/.

State University of New York at Plattsburgh, Division of Education, Health, and Human Services, Department of Counselor Education, Plattsburgh, NY 12901-2681. Offers clinical mental health counseling (MS, Advanced Certificate); school counselor (MS Ed, CAS); student affairs counseling (MS). *Accreditation:* ACA (one or more programs are accredited); Teacher Education Accreditation Council. Part-time programs available. *Students:* 50 full-time (36 women), 14 part-time (10 women); includes 9 minority (4 Black or African American, non-Hispanic/Latino; 5 Hispanic/Latino), 3 international. Average age 27. *Entrance requirements:* For master's, GRE General Test or MAT, minimum GPA of 2.8. Additional exam requirements/recommendations for international students: Required—TOEFL. *Application deadline:* For fall admission, 2/15 priority date for domestic students; for spring admission, 10/15 priority date for domestic students. Applications are processed on a rolling basis. Application fee: $75. *Financial support:* Research assistantships, teaching assistantships, career-related internships or fieldwork, Federal Work-Study, and administrative assistantships, editorial assistantships available. Support available to part-time students. Financial award application deadline: 4/15; financial award applicants required to submit FAFSA. *Faculty research:* Campus violence, program accreditation, substance abuse, vocational assessment, group counseling, divorce. *Unit head:* Dr. Julia Davis, Coordinator, 518-564-4179, E-mail: jdavi004@plattsburgh.edu. *Application contact:* Betsy Kane, Director, Graduate Admissions, 518-564-4723, Fax: 518-564-4722, E-mail: bkane002@plattsburgh.edu.

State University of New York College at Oneonta, Graduate Education, Division of Education, Department of Educational Psychology and Counseling, Oneonta, NY 13820-4015. Offers school counselor K-12 (MS Ed, CAS). *Accreditation:* NCATE. Part-time and evening/weekend programs available. *Degree requirements:* For master's, comprehensive exam. *Entrance requirements:* For master's, GRE General Test.

Stephen F. Austin State University, Graduate School, College of Education, Department of Human Services, Nacogdoches, TX 75962. Offers counseling (MA); school psychology (MA); special education (M Ed); speech pathology (MS). *Accreditation:* ACA (one or more programs are accredited); ASHA (one or more programs are accredited); CORE; NCATE. *Degree requirements:* For master's, comprehensive exam, thesis (for some programs). *Entrance requirements:* For master's, GRE General Test, minimum GPA of 2.8. Additional exam requirements/ recommendations for international students: Required—TOEFL.

Stephens College, Division of Graduate and Continuing Studies, Programs in Counseling, Columbia, MO 65215-0002. Offers counseling (M Ed, PGC), including marriage and family therapy (M Ed), professional counseling (M Ed), school counseling (M Ed). Part-time and evening/weekend programs available. *Degree requirements:* For master's, thesis. *Entrance requirements:* For master's, minimum GPA of 3.0 in last 60 hours. Additional exam requirements/recommendations for international students: Required—TOEFL. Electronic applications accepted.

Stetson University, College of Arts and Sciences, Division of Education, Department of Counselor Education, DeLand, FL 32723. Offers clinical mental health counseling (MS); marriage couple family counseling (MS); school counseling (MS). *Accreditation:* ACA. Evening/weekend programs available. *Faculty:* 5 full-time (all women), 4 part-time/ adjunct (3 women). *Students:* 82 full-time (74 women), 12 part-time (11 women); includes 22 minority (4 Black or African American, non-Hispanic/Latino; 1 American Indian or Alaska Native, non-Hispanic/Latino; 17 Hispanic/Latino), 1 international. Average age 29. 44 applicants, 75% accepted, 30 enrolled. In 2013, 29 master's awarded. *Entrance requirements:* For master's, GRE or MAT. Additional exam requirements/recommendations for international students: Required—TOEFL (minimum score 90 iBT), IELTS (minimum score 7). *Application deadline:* For fall admission, 8/1 priority date for domestic students; for spring admission, 1/1 priority date for domestic students; for summer admission, 5/1 priority date for domestic students. Applications are processed on a rolling basis. Application fee: $50. Electronic applications accepted. *Unit head:* Dr. Brigid Noonan-Klima, Chair, 386-822-8992. *Application contact:* Jamie Vanderlip, Assistant Director of Graduate Admissions, 386-822-7100, Fax: 386-822-7112, E-mail: jlszarol@stetson.edu.

Suffolk University, College of Arts and Sciences, Department of Psychology, Boston, MA 02108-2770. Offers clinical psychology (PhD); college admission counseling (Certificate); mental health counseling (MS, CAGS); school counseling (MS, CAGS). *Accreditation:* APA. *Faculty:* 14 full-time (6 women), 4 part-time/adjunct (2 women). *Students:* 70 full-time (58 women), 43 part-time (40 women); includes 24 minority (6 Black or African American, non-Hispanic/Latino; 9 Asian, non-Hispanic/Latino; 8 Hispanic/Latino; 1 Two or more races, non-Hispanic/Latino), 4 international. Average age 27. 385 applicants, 25% accepted, 45 enrolled. In 2013, 22 master's, 11 doctorates, 8 other advanced degrees awarded. *Degree requirements:* For doctorate, thesis/ dissertation, practicum. *Entrance requirements:* For doctorate, GRE General Test or MAT, 2 letters of recommendation, resume. Additional exam requirements/ recommendations for international students: Required—TOEFL (minimum score 550 paper-based; 80 iBT). *Application deadline:* For fall admission, 12/15 for domestic and international students. Applications are processed on a rolling basis. Application fee: $50. Electronic applications accepted. *Expenses:* Contact institution. *Financial support:* In 2013–14, 71 students received support, including 68 fellowships (averaging $15,506 per year); career-related internships or fieldwork, Federal Work-Study, and institutionally sponsored loans also available. Support available to part-time students. Financial award application deadline: 4/1; financial award applicants required to submit FAFSA. *Faculty research:* Assessing exposure in the context of a family-based cognitive behavioral treatment for pediatric OCD, a mindfulness approach to designing and testing the efficacy of a new sexual revictimization prevention program for college women, olfaction and decision-making in substance-dependent individuals, the role of experiential avoidance in Generalized Anxiety Disorder, ego development as a predictor of dogmatism and intolerance in the political right and left. *Unit head:* Dr. Gary Fireman, Chairperson, 617-305-6368, Fax: 617-367-2924, E-mail: gfireman@suffolk.edu. *Application contact:* Cory Meyers, Director of Graduate Admissions, 617-573-8302, Fax: 617-305-1733, E-mail: grad.admission@suffolk.edu.
Website: http://www.suffolk.edu/college/departments/9912.php.

Sul Ross State University, Rio Grande College of Sul Ross State University, Alpine, TX 79832. Offers business administration (MBA); teacher education (M Ed), including bilingual education, counseling, educational diagnostics, elementary education, general education, reading, school administration, secondary education. Part-time and evening/ weekend programs available. Postbaccalaureate distance learning degree programs offered (no on-campus study). *Degree requirements:* For master's, comprehensive exam, thesis optional, minimum GPA of 3.0. *Entrance requirements:* For master's, GMAT or GRE General Test, minimum GPA of 2.5 in last 60 hours of undergraduate work. Additional exam requirements/recommendations for international students: Required—TOEFL.

Sul Ross State University, School of Professional Studies, Department of Teacher Education, Program in Counseling, Alpine, TX 79832. Offers M Ed. Part-time and evening/weekend programs available. *Degree requirements:* For master's, thesis optional. *Entrance requirements:* For master's, GMAT or GRE General Test, minimum GPA of 2.5 in last 60 hours of undergraduate work.

Syracuse University, School of Education, Program in Counseling and Counselor Education, Syracuse, NY 13244. Offers PhD. *Accreditation:* ACA. Part-time programs available. *Students:* 11 full-time (8 women), 5 part-time (2 women); includes 6 minority (4 Black or African American, non-Hispanic/Latino; 2 Hispanic/Latino), 2 international. Average age 35. 23 applicants, 22% accepted, 4 enrolled. In 2013, 1 doctorate awarded. *Degree requirements:* For doctorate, comprehensive exam, thesis/dissertation. *Entrance requirements:* For doctorate, GRE, video of counseling interview, master's degree, interview. Additional exam requirements/recommendations for international students: Required—TOEFL (minimum score 100 iBT). *Application deadline:* For fall admission, 12/1 priority date for domestic and international students; for spring admission, 10/15 priority date for domestic and international students. Applications are processed on a rolling basis. Application fee: $75. Electronic applications accepted. *Financial support:* Fellowships with full tuition reimbursements and teaching assistantships with full tuition reimbursements available. Financial award application deadline: 1/1; financial award applicants required to submit FAFSA. *Unit head:* Dr. Nicole Hill, Chair, 315-443-2266, Fax: 315-443-5732, E-mail: nrhill@syr.edu. *Application contact:* Laurie Deyo, Graduate Recruiter, School of Education, 315-443-2505, E-mail: e-gradrcrt@syr.edu.
Website: http://soeweb.syr.edu/.

Syracuse University, School of Education, Program in Student Affairs Counseling, Syracuse, NY 13244. Offers MS. Part-time programs available. *Students:* 3 full-time (all women), 5 part-time (all women); includes 3 minority (1 Black or African American, non-Hispanic/Latino; 1 Asian, non-Hispanic/Latino; 1 Hispanic/Latino). Average age 28. 11 applicants, 36% accepted, 1 enrolled. In 2013, 2 master's awarded. *Entrance requirements:* For master's, GRE General Test or MAT, interview. Additional exam requirements/recommendations for international students: Required—TOEFL (minimum score 100 iBT). *Application deadline:* For fall admission, 1/15 priority date for domestic and international students; for spring admission, 10/15 priority date for domestic and international students. Applications are processed on a rolling basis. Application fee: $75. Electronic applications accepted. *Financial support:* Fellowships with full tuition reimbursements and teaching assistantships with full and partial tuition reimbursements available. Financial award application deadline: 1/1. *Unit head:* Dr. Derek Seward, 315-443-2266, E-mail: bernard@syr.edu. *Application contact:* Laurie Deyo, Graduate Recruiter, School of Education, 315-443-2505, E-mail: dxseward@syr.ed.
Website: http://soeweb.syr.edu/.

Tarleton State University, College of Graduate Studies, College of Education, Department of Psychology and Counseling, Stephenville, TX 76402. Offers counseling and psychology (M Ed), including counseling, counseling psychology, educational psychology; educational administration (M Ed); secondary education (Certificate); special education (Certificate). Part-time and evening/weekend programs available. Postbaccalaureate distance learning degree programs offered (minimal on-campus study). *Faculty:* 8 full-time (6 women), 14 part-time/adjunct (7 women). *Students:* 60 full-time (48 women), 183 part-time (157 women); includes 63 minority (21 Black or African American, non-Hispanic/Latino; 3 Asian, non-Hispanic/Latino; 30 Hispanic/Latino; 9 Two or more races, non-Hispanic/Latino). Average age 34. 78 applicants, 81% accepted, 47 enrolled. In 2013, 76 master's awarded. *Degree requirements:* For master's, comprehensive exam, thesis optional. *Entrance requirements:* For master's, GRE General Test, minimum GPA of 3.0. Additional exam requirements/recommendations for international students: Required—TOEFL (minimum score 550 paper-based; 80 iBT). *Application deadline:* For fall admission, 8/15 priority date for domestic students; for spring admission, 1/7 for domestic students. Applications are processed on a rolling basis. Application fee: $30 ($130 for international students). Electronic applications accepted. *Expenses:* Tuition, state resident: full-time $3312; part-time $184 per credit hour. Tuition, nonresident: full-time $9144; part-time $508 per credit hour. *Required fees:* $1916. Tuition and fees vary according to course load and campus/location. *Financial support:* Research assistantships, teaching assistantships, career-related internships or fieldwork, Federal Work-Study, institutionally sponsored loans, and tuition waivers (partial) available. Support available to part-time students. Financial award application deadline: 5/1; financial award applicants required to submit FAFSA. *Unit head:* Dr. Bob Newby, Department Head, 254-968-9813, Fax: 254-968-1991, E-mail: newby@tarleton.edu. *Application contact:* Information Contact, 254-968-9104, Fax: 254-968-9670, E-mail: gradoffice@tarleton.edu.
Website: http://www.tarleton.edu/COEWEB/pc/.

Tennessee State University, The School of Graduate Studies and Research, College of Education, Department of Psychology, Nashville, TN 37209-1561. Offers counseling psychology (MS, PhD); professional school counseling (MS); psychology (MS, PhD); school psychology (MS, PhD). *Accreditation:* APA. *Degree requirements:* For doctorate, thesis/dissertation (for some programs). *Entrance requirements:* For master's, GRE General Test or MAT; for doctorate, GRE General Test or MAT, minimum GPA of 3.25, work experience. Electronic applications accepted.

Texas A&M International University, Office of Graduate Studies and Research, College of Education, Department of Professional Programs, Laredo, TX 78041-1900. Offers educational administration (MS Ed); generic special education (MS Ed); school counseling (MS). *Faculty:* 7 full-time (4 women), 4 part-time/adjunct (2 women). *Students:* 19 full-time (18 women), 137 part-time (104 women); includes 150 minority (2 Black or African American, non-Hispanic/Latino; 148 Hispanic/Latino), 1 international. Average age 33. 61 applicants, 75% accepted, 42 enrolled. In 2013, 87 master's awarded. *Entrance requirements:* Additional exam requirements/recommendations for international students: Required—TOEFL (minimum score 550 paper-based; 79 iBT). *Application deadline:* For fall admission, 4/30 priority date for domestic students, 4/30 for international students; for spring admission, 11/30 priority date for domestic students, 10/1 for international students. Application fee: $35 ($50 for international students). *Expenses:* Tuition, state resident: full-time $5184. *International tuition:* $11,556 full-time. *Financial support:* In 2013–14, 5 students received support, including 1 teaching assistantship; fellowships, research assistantships, Federal Work-Study, scholarships/ grants, and unspecified assistantships also available. Financial award application deadline: 4/1. *Unit head:* Dr. Randel Brown, Chair, 956-326-2679, E-mail: brown@

tamiu.edu. *Application contact:* Suzanne H. Alford, Director of Admissions, 956-326-3023, E-mail: graduateschool@tamiu.edu.
Website: http://www.tamiu.edu/coedu/DOPPPrograms.shtml.

Texas A&M University–Commerce, Graduate School, College of Education and Human Services, Department of Counseling, Commerce, TX 75429-3011. Offers M Ed, MS, PhD. *Accreditation:* ACA (one or more programs are accredited). Part-time programs available. Terminal master's awarded for partial completion of doctoral program. *Degree requirements:* For master's, comprehensive exam, thesis (for some programs); for doctorate, thesis/dissertation, departmental qualifying exam. *Entrance requirements:* For master's and doctorate, GRE General Test. *Expenses:* Tuition, state resident: full-time $3630; part-time $2420 per year. Tuition, nonresident: full-time $9948; part-time $6632.16 per year. *Required fees:* $1006 per year. Tuition and fees vary according to course load. *Faculty research:* Emergency responders, efficacy and effect of web-based instruction, family violence, play therapy.

Texas A&M University–Corpus Christi, Graduate Studies and Research, College of Education, Programs in Counseling, Corpus Christi, TX 78412-5503. Offers counseling (MS); counselor education (PhD). *Accreditation:* ACA. Part-time and evening/weekend programs available. *Degree requirements:* For master's, comprehensive exam, thesis (for some programs). *Entrance requirements:* For master's, GRE General Test. Additional exam requirements/recommendations for international students: Required—TOEFL. Electronic applications accepted.

Texas A&M University–Kingsville, College of Graduate Studies, College of Education, Department of Education, Program in Guidance and Counseling, Kingsville, TX 78363. Offers MA, MS. MS offered jointly with University of North Texas. Part-time and evening/weekend programs available. *Faculty:* 10 full-time (8 women), 9 part-time/adjunct (5 women). *Students:* 38 full-time (29 women), 59 part-time (48 women); includes 86 minority (3 Black or African American, non-Hispanic/Latino; 82 Hispanic/Latino; 1 Native Hawaiian or other Pacific Islander, non-Hispanic/Latino), 2 international. Average age 31. 41 applicants, 98% accepted, 26 enrolled. In 2013, 36 master's awarded. *Degree requirements:* For master's, comprehensive exam, mini-thesis. *Entrance requirements:* For master's, GRE General Test, MAT, minimum GPA of 3.0. *Application deadline:* For fall admission, 6/1 for domestic students; for spring admission, 11/15 for domestic students. Applications are processed on a rolling basis. Application fee: $35 ($50 for international students). *Financial support:* Application deadline: 5/15. *Faculty research:* Diagnostician requirements for certification, teaching methods for adult learner. *Unit head:* Prof. Gary R. Low, Assistant Dean and Interim Chair, 361-593-2980, Fax: 361-593-2136, E-mail: gary.low@tamuk.edu. *Application contact:* Dr. Alberto M. Olivares, Dean, College of Graduate Studies, 361-593-2808, Fax: 361-593-3412, E-mail: a-olivares@tamuk.edu.

Texas A&M University–San Antonio, Department of Leadership and Counseling, San Antonio, TX 78224. Offers counseling and guidance (MA); educational leadership (MA). Part-time and evening/weekend programs available. *Degree requirements:* For master's, comprehensive exam, thesis or alternative. *Entrance requirements:* For master's, MAT. Additional exam requirements/recommendations for international students: Required—TOEFL (minimum score 550 paper-based; 80 iBT), IELTS (minimum score 6). Electronic applications accepted.

Texas Christian University, College of Education, Program in Counseling, Fort Worth, TX 76129-0002. Offers counseling (M Ed); counseling and counselor education (PhD); school counseling (Certificate). Part-time and evening/weekend programs available. *Students:* 18 full-time (15 women), 35 part-time (32 women); includes 14 minority (4 Black or African American, non-Hispanic/Latino; 2 Asian, non-Hispanic/Latino; 7 Hispanic/Latino; 1 Two or more races, non-Hispanic/Latino). Average age 30. 30 applicants, 47% accepted, 8 enrolled. In 2013, 14 master's awarded. *Degree requirements:* For master's, oral exam; for doctorate, comprehensive exam, thesis/dissertation. *Entrance requirements:* For master's and doctorate, GRE, interview. Additional exam requirements/recommendations for international students: Required—TOEFL (minimum score 550 paper-based; 80 iBT). *Application deadline:* For fall admission, 11/16 for domestic and international students; for winter admission, 2/1 for domestic and international students; for spring admission, 3/1 for domestic and international students. Application fee: $60. Electronic applications accepted. *Expenses: Tuition:* Part-time $1270 per credit hour. Tuition and fees vary according to course load and program. *Financial support:* Teaching assistantships with full tuition reimbursements, career-related internships or fieldwork, scholarships/grants, and unspecified assistantships available. Financial award application deadline: 2/1; financial award applicants required to submit FAFSA. *Unit head:* Dr. Jan Lacina, Associate Dean, 817-257-6786, E-mail: j.lacina@tcu.edu. *Application contact:* Lori Kimball, Administrative Program Specialist, 817-257-7661, E-mail: l.kimball@tcu.edu.
Website: http://www.coe.tcu.edu/graduate-students-graduate-programs.asp.

Texas Southern University, College of Education, Department of Counselor Education, Houston, TX 77004-4584. Offers counseling (M Ed); counselor education (Ed D). Part-time and evening/weekend programs available. *Faculty:* 5 full-time (4 women), 6 part-time/adjunct (5 women). *Students:* 51 full-time (43 women), 92 part-time (79 women); includes 135 minority (130 Black or African American, non-Hispanic/Latino; 1 Asian, non-Hispanic/Latino; 4 Hispanic/Latino), 1 international. Average age 35. 72 applicants, 47% accepted, 30 enrolled. In 2013, 19 master's, 3 doctorates awarded. *Degree requirements:* For master's, one foreign language, comprehensive exam; for doctorate, comprehensive exam, thesis/dissertation. *Entrance requirements:* For master's, GRE General Test, minimum GPA of 2.5; for doctorate, GRE General Test or MAT, master's degree, minimum B+ average. Additional exam requirements/recommendations for international students: Required—TOEFL. *Application deadline:* For fall admission, 7/1 priority date for domestic students, 7/1 for international students; for spring admission, 11/1 priority date for domestic students, 11/1 for international students. Applications are processed on a rolling basis. Application fee: $50 ($75 for international students). Electronic applications accepted. *Financial support:* Fellowships, research assistantships, teaching assistantships, scholarships/grants, and unspecified assistantships available. Support available to part-time students. Financial award application deadline: 5/1. *Faculty research:* Clinical and urban psychology. *Unit head:* Dr. Candy Ratliff, Interim Chair, 713-313-6721, Fax: 713-313-7481, E-mail: ratliff_ch@tsu.edu. *Application contact:* Dr. Gregory Maddox, Dean of the Graduate School, 713-313-7011 Ext. 4410, Fax: 713-639-1876, E-mail: maddox_gh@tsu.edu.
Website: http://www.tsu.edu/academics/colleges__schools/College_of_Education/Departments/default.php.

Texas State University, Graduate School, College of Education, Department of Counseling, Leadership, Adult Education, and School Psychology, Program in Professional Counseling, San Marcos, TX 78666. Offers MA. *Accreditation:* ACA. Part-time programs available. *Faculty:* 12 full-time (9 women), 5 part-time/adjunct (4 women). *Students:* 89 full-time (76 women), 117 part-time (94 women); includes 48 minority (7 Black or African American, non-Hispanic/Latino; 7 Asian, non-Hispanic/Latino; 25 Hispanic/Latino; 9 Two or more races, non-Hispanic/Latino). Average age 32. 141 applicants, 43% accepted, 27 enrolled. In 2013, 33 master's awarded. *Degree requirements:* For master's, comprehensive exam, internship. *Entrance requirements:* For master's, GRE General Test, minimum GPA of 3.0 in last 60 hours. Additional exam requirements/recommendations for international students: Required—TOEFL (minimum score 550 paper-based; 78 iBT). *Application deadline:* For fall admission, 2/15 for domestic and international students; for spring admission, 10/1 for domestic and international students. Applications are processed on a rolling basis. Application fee: $40 ($90 for international students). Electronic applications accepted. *Expenses:* Tuition, state resident: full-time $6663; part-time $278 per credit hour. Tuition, nonresident: full-time $15,159; part-time $632 per credit hour. *Required fees:* $1872; $54 per credit hour. $306 per term. Tuition and fees vary according to course load. *Financial support:* In 2013–14, 113 students received support, including 9 research assistantships (averaging $12,668 per year), 7 teaching assistantships (averaging $7,251 per year); Federal Work-Study and institutionally sponsored loans also available. Support available to part-time students. Financial award application deadline: 4/1; financial award applicants required to submit FAFSA. *Unit head:* Dr. Kevin Fall, Graduate Advisor, 512-245-2575, Fax: 512-245-8872, E-mail: profcounadm@txstate.edu. *Application contact:* Dr. Andrea Golato, Dean of Graduate School, 512-245-2581, Fax: 512-245-8365, E-mail: gradcollege@txstate.edu.
Website: http://www.txstate.edu/clas/Professional-Counseling/Program-Information.html.

Texas Tech University, Graduate School, College of Education, Department of Educational Psychology and Leadership, Lubbock, TX 79409-1071. Offers counselor education (M Ed, PhD); educational leadership (M Ed, Ed D); educational psychology (M Ed, PhD); higher education (M Ed, Ed D); higher education research (PhD); instructional technology (M Ed, Ed D); special education (M Ed, Ed D, PhD). *Accreditation:* ACA; NCATE. Part-time and evening/weekend programs available. Postbaccalaureate distance learning degree programs offered (minimal on-campus study). *Faculty:* 42 full-time (20 women). *Students:* 220 full-time (171 women), 549 part-time (404 women); includes 219 minority (73 Black or African American, non-Hispanic/Latino; 5 American Indian or Alaska Native, non-Hispanic/Latino; 6 Asian, non-Hispanic/Latino; 122 Hispanic/Latino; 13 Two or more races, non-Hispanic/Latino), 48 international. Average age 36. 437 applicants, 72% accepted, 215 enrolled. In 2013, 137 master's, 38 doctorates awarded. Terminal master's awarded for partial completion of doctoral program. *Degree requirements:* For master's, comprehensive exam, thesis optional; for doctorate, comprehensive exam, thesis/dissertation. *Entrance requirements:* For master's, GRE (for some programs); for doctorate, GRE. Additional exam requirements/recommendations for international students: Required—TOEFL (minimum score 550 paper-based; 79 iBT). *Application deadline:* For fall admission, 6/1 priority date for domestic students, 1/15 priority date for international students; for spring admission, 9/1 priority date for domestic students, 6/15 priority date for international students. Applications are processed on a rolling basis. Application fee: $60. Electronic applications accepted. *Expenses:* Tuition, state resident: full-time $6062; part-time $252.57 per credit hour. Tuition, nonresident: full-time $14,558; part-time $606.57 per credit hour. *Required fees:* $2655; $35 per credit hour. $907.50 per semester. Tuition and fees vary according to course load. *Financial support:* In 2013–14, 188 students received support, including 179 fellowships (averaging $2,580 per year), 39 research assistantships (averaging $4,550 per year), 8 teaching assistantships (averaging $4,647 per year); scholarships/grants and unspecified assistantships also available. Support available to part-time students. Financial award application deadline: 1/3; financial award applicants required to submit FAFSA. *Faculty research:* Cognitive, motivational, and developmental processes in learning; counseling education; instructional technology; generic special education and sensory impairment; community college administration; K-12 school administration. *Total annual research expenditures:* $708,063. *Unit head:* Dr. Fred Hartmeister, Chair, 806-834-0248, Fax: 806-742-2179, E-mail: fred.hartmeister@ttu.edu. *Application contact:* Pam Smith, Admissions Advisor, 806-834-2969, Fax: 806-742-2179, E-mail: pam.smith@ttu.edu.
Website: http://www.educ.ttu.edu/.

Texas Wesleyan University, Graduate Programs, Programs in Education, Fort Worth, TX 76105-1536. Offers education (M Ed, Ed D); marriage and family therapy (MSMFT); professional counseling (MA); school counseling (MS). Part-time and evening/weekend programs available. Postbaccalaureate distance learning degree programs offered (no on-campus study). *Entrance requirements:* For master's, GRE General Test, minimum GPA of 3.0 in final 60 hours of undergraduate course work, interview. *Faculty research:* Teacher effectiveness, bilingual education, analytic teaching.

Texas Woman's University, Graduate School, College of Professional Education, Department of Family Sciences, Denton, TX 76201. Offers child development (MS); counseling and development (MS); early childhood development and education (PhD); early childhood education (M Ed, MA, MS); family studies (MS, PhD); family therapy (MS, PhD). *Accreditation:* ACA (one or more programs are accredited). Part-time and evening/weekend programs available. *Faculty:* 23 full-time (18 women), 11 part-time/adjunct (9 women). *Students:* 138 full-time (130 women), 296 part-time (272 women); includes 198 minority (117 Black or African American, non-Hispanic/Latino; 5 American Indian or Alaska Native, non-Hispanic/Latino; 15 Asian, non-Hispanic/Latino; 61 Hispanic/Latino), 18 international. Average age 35. 187 applicants, 41% accepted, 56 enrolled. In 2013, 88 master's, 12 doctorates awarded. Terminal master's awarded for partial completion of doctoral program. *Degree requirements:* For master's, comprehensive exam (for some programs), thesis (for some programs); for doctorate, comprehensive exam, thesis/dissertation. *Entrance requirements:* Additional exam requirements/recommendations for international students: Required—TOEFL (minimum score 550 paper-based; 79 iBT). *Application deadline:* For fall admission, 7/1 priority date for domestic students, 2/15 for international students; for spring admission, 9/15 priority date for domestic students, 7/1 for international students. Applications are processed on a rolling basis. Application fee: $50 ($75 for international students). Electronic applications accepted. *Expenses:* Tuition, state resident: full-time $4182; part-time $233.32 per credit hour. Tuition, nonresident: full-time $10,716; part-time $595.32 per credit hour. *Financial support:* In 2013–14, 137 students received support, including 15 research assistantships (averaging $5,637 per year), 8 teaching assistantships (averaging $5,637 per year); career-related internships or fieldwork, Federal Work-Study, institutionally sponsored loans, scholarships/grants, traineeships, health care benefits, and unspecified assistantships also available. Support available to part-time students. Financial award application deadline: 3/1; financial award applicants required to submit FAFSA. *Faculty research:* Parenting/parent education, military families, play therapy, family sexuality, diversity, healthy relationships/healthy marriages, childhood obesity, male communication. *Unit head:* Dr. Karen Petty, Chair, 940-898-2685, Fax: 940-898-2676, E-mail: famsci@twu.edu. *Application contact:* Dr. Samuel Wheeler, Assistant Director of Admissions, 940-898-3188, Fax: 940-898-3081, E-mail: wheelersr@twu.edu.
Website: http://www.twu.edu/family-sciences/.

Touro College, Graduate School of Psychology, New York, NY 10010. Offers general psychology (MS); industrial/organizational psychology (MS); mental health counseling (MS); school counseling (MS); school psychology (MS). *Students:* 44 full-time (35 women), 169 part-time (151 women); includes 96 minority (52 Black or African American, non-Hispanic/Latino; 1 American Indian or Alaska Native, non-Hispanic/Latino; 8 Asian, non-Hispanic/Latino; 32 Hispanic/Latino; 3 Two or more races, non-Hispanic/Latino). *Unit head:* Dr. Richard Waxman, Dean, 212-242-4668 Ext. 6077, E-mail: richard.waxman@touro.edu.
Website: http://www.touro.edu/dgsp/Programs.asp.

Counselor Education

Trevecca Nazarene University, Graduate Counseling Program, Nashville, TN 37210-2877. Offers clinical counseling (PhD); counseling (MA); marriage and family therapy (MMFT). Part-time and evening/weekend programs available. *Faculty:* 8 full-time (1 woman), 13 part-time/adjunct (8 women). *Students:* 165 full-time (122 women), 47 part-time (35 women); includes 45 minority (31 Black or African American, non-Hispanic/Latino; 2 American Indian or Alaska Native, non-Hispanic/Latino; 1 Asian, non-Hispanic/Latino; 5 Hispanic/Latino; 1 Native Hawaiian or other Pacific Islander, non-Hispanic/Latino; 5 Two or more races, non-Hispanic/Latino). Average age 34. In 2013, 89 master's, 5 doctorates awarded. *Degree requirements:* For master's, comprehensive exam; for doctorate, comprehensive exam, thesis/dissertation. *Entrance requirements:* For master's, MAT minimum score of 380 or GRE minimum score of 290 (combined verbal and quantitative), minimum GPA of 2.7, official transcript from regionally accredited institution, 2 reference assessment forms; for doctorate, GRE (minimum scores: 300 combined verbal and quantitative, 3.5 analytical writing), minimum GPA of 3.25, official transcript of master's degree from regionally-accredited institution, 3 recommendation forms, 400-word letter of intent, professional vitae, interview. Additional exam requirements/recommendations for international students: Required—TOEFL (minimum score 600 paper-based). *Application deadline:* Applications are processed on a rolling basis. Application fee: $25. *Expenses:* Contact institution. *Financial support:* Applicants required to submit FAFSA. *Unit head:* Dr. Peter Wilson, Director, 615-248-1384, Fax: 615-248-1662, E-mail: admissions_gradcouns@trevecca.edu. *Application contact:* 615-248-1384, Fax: 615-248-1662, E-mail: admissions_gradcouns@trevecca.edu.
Website: http://www.trevecca.edu/gradcounseling.

Trinity Washington University, School of Education, Washington, DC 20017-1094. Offers clinical mental health counseling (MA); early childhood education (MAT); educating for change (M Ed); educational administration (MSA); elementary education (MAT); reading (M Ed); school counseling (MA); secondary education (MAT), including English, social studies; special education (MAT). *Accreditation:* NCATE. Part-time and evening/weekend programs available. *Degree requirements:* For master's, thesis (for some programs), capstone project(s). *Entrance requirements:* For master's, PRAXIS I, minimum GPA of 2.8. Additional exam requirements/recommendations for international students: Required—TOEFL (minimum score 550 paper-based). *Application deadline:* For fall admission, 4/1 priority date for domestic students; for winter admission, 11/1 priority date for domestic students; for spring admission, 11/1 priority date for domestic students. Applications are processed on a rolling basis. Application fee: $40. *Expenses: Tuition:* Part-time $715 per credit. *Financial support:* Career-related internships or fieldwork, health care benefits, and unspecified assistantships available. Support available to part-time students. Financial award application deadline: 4/1; financial award applicants required to submit FAFSA. *Faculty research:* Technology, literacy, special education, organizations, inclusion models. *Unit head:* Dr. Janet Stocks, Dean, 202-884-9380, Fax: 202-884-9506, E-mail: stocksj@trinitydc.edu. *Application contact:* Erika Davis, Director of Admissions for School of Education, 202-884-9400, Fax: 202-884-9229, E-mail: daviser@trinitydc.edu.
Website: http://www.trinitydc.edu/education/.

Troy University, Graduate School, College of Education, Program in Counseling and Psychology, Troy, AL 36082. Offers agency counseling (Ed S); clinical mental health (MS); community counseling (MS, Ed S); corrections counseling (MS); rehabilitation counseling (MS); school psychology (MS, Ed S); school psychometry (MS); social service counseling (MS); student affairs counseling (MS); substance abuse counseling (MS). *Accreditation:* ACA; CORE; NCATE. Part-time and evening/weekend programs available. *Faculty:* 63 full-time (34 women), 4 part-time/adjunct (2 women). *Students:* 344 full-time (284 women), 616 part-time (502 women); includes 615 minority (520 Black or African American, non-Hispanic/Latino; 3 American Indian or Alaska Native, non-Hispanic/Latino; 5 Asian, non-Hispanic/Latino; 68 Hispanic/Latino; 19 Two or more races, non-Hispanic/Latino). Average age 34. 293 applicants, 88% accepted, 156 enrolled. In 2013, 253 master's awarded. *Degree requirements:* For master's, comprehensive exam, thesis. *Entrance requirements:* For master's, GRE (minimum score of 850 on old exam or 290 on new exam), GMAT (minimum score of 380), or MAT (minimum score of 385), bachelor's degree; minimum undergraduate GPA of 2.5 or 3.0 on last 30 semester hours, letter of recommendation. Additional exam requirements/recommendations for international students: Required—TOEFL (minimum score 523 paper-based; 70 iBT), IELTS (minimum score 6). *Application deadline:* Applications are processed on a rolling basis. Application fee: $50. Electronic applications accepted. *Expenses:* Tuition, state resident: full-time $6084; part-time $338 per credit hour. Tuition, nonresident: full-time $12,168; part-time $676 per credit hour. *Required fees:* $630; $35 per credit hour. $50 per semester. *Unit head:* Dr. Andrew Creamer, Chair, 334-670-3350, Fax: 334-670-3291, E-mail: drcreamer@troy.edu. *Application contact:* Brenda K. Campbell, Director of Graduate Admissions, 334-670-3178, Fax: 334-670-3733, E-mail: bcamp@troy.edu.

Troy University, Graduate School, College of Education, Program in School Counseling, Troy, AL 36082. Offers school counseling (MS, Ed S). *Accreditation:* ACA; CORE; NCATE. Part-time and evening/weekend programs available. *Faculty:* 6 full-time (4 women), 3 part-time/adjunct (2 women). *Students:* 27 full-time (24 women), 71 part-time (64 women); includes 71 minority (68 Black or African American, non-Hispanic/Latino; 1 American Indian or Alaska Native, non-Hispanic/Latino; 2 Two or more races, non-Hispanic/Latino). Average age 35. 29 applicants, 86% accepted, 11 enrolled. In 2013, 15 master's, 5 other advanced degrees awarded. *Degree requirements:* For master's, comprehensive exam, thesis. *Entrance requirements:* For master's, GRE (minimum score of 850 on old exam or 290 on new exam), GMAT (minimum score of 380), or MAT (minimum score of 385), bachelor's degree; minimum undergraduate GPA of 2.5 or 3.0 on last 30 semester hours, letter of recommendation; teaching certification, 2 years of teaching experience. Additional exam requirements/recommendations for international students: Required—TOEFL (minimum score 523 paper-based; 70 iBT), IELTS (minimum score 6). *Application deadline:* Applications are processed on a rolling basis. Application fee: $50. Electronic applications accepted. *Expenses:* Tuition, state resident: full-time $6084; part-time $338 per credit hour. Tuition, nonresident: full-time $12,168; part-time $676 per credit hour. *Required fees:* $630; $35 per credit hour. $50 per semester. *Unit head:* Dr. Andrew Creamer, Chair, 334-670-3350, Fax: 334-670-3291, E-mail: drcreamer@troy.edu. *Application contact:* Brenda K. Campbell, Director of Graduate Admissions, 334-670-3178, Fax: 334-670-3733, E-mail: bcamp@troy.edu.

Universidad del Turabo, Graduate Programs, Programs in Education, Program in Guidance Counseling, Gurabo, PR 00778-3030. Offers M Ed.

Université de Moncton, Faculty of Education, Graduate Studies in Education, Moncton, NB E1A 3E9, Canada. Offers educational psychology (M Ed, MA Ed); guidance (M Ed, MA Ed); school administration (M Ed, MA Ed); teaching (M Ed, MA Ed). Part-time programs available. *Degree requirements:* For master's, proficiency in English and French. *Entrance requirements:* For master's, minimum GPA of 3.0. *Faculty research:* Guidance, ethnolinguistic vitality, children's rights, ecological education, entrepreneurship.

Université Laval, Faculty of Education, Department of Foundations and Interventions in Education, Programs in Orientation Sciences, Québec, QC G1K 7P4, Canada. Offers MA, PhD. Terminal master's awarded for partial completion of doctoral program. *Degree requirements:* For master's, thesis (for some programs); for doctorate, comprehensive exam, thesis/dissertation. *Entrance requirements:* For master's, English test (comprehension of written English), knowledge of French; for doctorate, oral exam (subject of thesis), knowledge of French and English. Electronic applications accepted. *Faculty research:* Counseling psychology, psychological education, vocational guidance, growth and development.

University at Albany, State University of New York, School of Education, Department of Educational and Counseling Psychology, Albany, NY 12222-0001. Offers counseling psychology (MS, PhD, CAS); educational psychology (Ed D); educational psychology and statistics (MS); measurements and evaluation (Ed D); rehabilitation counseling (MS), including counseling psychology; school counselor (CAS); school psychology (Psy D, CAS); special education (MS); statistics and research design (Ed D). *Accreditation:* APA (one or more programs are accredited). Evening/weekend programs available. *Degree requirements:* For doctorate, thesis/dissertation. *Entrance requirements:* For doctorate, GRE General Test. Additional exam requirements/recommendations for international students: Required—TOEFL (minimum score 550 paper-based). Electronic applications accepted.

University at Buffalo, the State University of New York, Graduate School, Graduate School of Education, Department of Counseling, School, and Educational Psychology, Buffalo, NY 14260. Offers counseling/school psychology (PhD); counselor education (PhD); education studies (Ed M); educational psychology (MA, PhD); mental health counseling (MS, Certificate); rehabilitation counseling (MS, Advanced Certificate); school counseling (Ed M, Certificate). *Accreditation:* CORE (one or more programs are accredited). Part-time programs available. Postbaccalaureate distance learning degree programs offered (no on-campus study). *Faculty:* 20 full-time (12 women), 36 part-time/adjunct (29 women). *Students:* 167 full-time (134 women), 131 part-time (109 women); includes 44 minority (24 Black or African American, non-Hispanic/Latino; 5 American Indian or Alaska Native, non-Hispanic/Latino; 6 Asian, non-Hispanic/Latino; 9 Hispanic/Latino), 18 international. Average age 31. 333 applicants, 54% accepted, 120 enrolled. In 2013, 64 master's, 15 doctorates, 19 other advanced degrees awarded. *Degree requirements:* For master's, comprehensive exam (for some programs), thesis (for some programs); for doctorate, comprehensive exam, thesis/dissertation. *Entrance requirements:* For master's, GRE General Test, interview, letters of reference; for doctorate, GRE General Test, interview, letters of reference, writing sample. Additional exam requirements/recommendations for international students: Required—TOEFL (minimum score 79 iBT). *Application deadline:* For fall admission, 2/1 priority date for domestic and international students. Application fee: $50. Electronic applications accepted. *Financial support:* In 2013–14, 21 fellowships (averaging $13,105 per year), 23 research assistantships with tuition reimbursements (averaging $9,652 per year) were awarded; teaching assistantships, career-related internships or fieldwork, Federal Work-Study, institutionally sponsored loans, scholarships/grants, tuition waivers, and unspecified assistantships also available. Financial award application deadline: 2/1; financial award applicants required to submit FAFSA. *Faculty research:* Multicultural counseling, class size effects, good work in counseling, eating disorders, outcome assessment, change agents and therapeutic factors in group counseling. *Total annual research expenditures:* $1.9 million. *Unit head:* Dr. Timothy Janikowski, Chair, 716-645-2484, Fax: 716-645-6616, E-mail: tjanikow@buffalo.edu. *Application contact:* Joanne Laska, Admissions Assistant, 716-645-2110, Fax: 716-645-7937, E-mail: jlaska@buffalo.edu.
Website: http://gse.buffalo.edu/csep.

The University of Akron, Graduate School, College of Education, Department of Counseling, Program in Counselor Education and Supervision, Akron, OH 44325. Offers PhD. *Accreditation:* ACA. *Students:* 11 full-time (7 women), 8 part-time (all women); includes 3 minority (2 Black or African American, non-Hispanic/Latino; 1 Native Hawaiian or other Pacific Islander, non-Hispanic/Latino), 1 international. Average age 33. 17 applicants, 35% accepted, 4 enrolled. In 2013, 2 doctorates awarded. *Degree requirements:* For doctorate, comprehensive exam, thesis/dissertation, written and oral exams. *Entrance requirements:* For doctorate, GRE, minimum GPA of 3.25, three letters of recommendation, professional resume, interview. Additional exam requirements/recommendations for international students: Required—TOEFL (minimum score 550 paper-based; 79 iBT). *Application deadline:* For fall admission, 1/15 for domestic and international students. Application fee: $40 ($60 for international students). Electronic applications accepted. *Expenses:* Tuition, state resident: full-time $7430; part-time $412.80 per credit hour. Tuition, nonresident: full-time $12,722; part-time $706.80 per credit hour. *Required fees:* $53 per credit hour. $12 per semester. Tuition and fees vary according to course load and program. *Unit head:* Dr. Karin Jordan, Department Chair, 330-972-5155, E-mail: kj25@uakron.edu. *Application contact:* Dr. Varunee Faii Sangganjanavanich, Program Coordinator, 330-972-6851, E-mail: vs45@uakron.edu.

The University of Alabama, Graduate School, College of Education, Department of Educational Studies in Psychology, Research Methodology and Counseling, Tuscaloosa, AL 35487. Offers MA, Ed D, PhD, Ed S. *Accreditation:* ACA (one or more programs are accredited); CORE; NCATE. Part-time programs available. *Faculty:* 19 full-time (8 women), 1 (woman) part-time/adjunct. *Students:* 84 full-time (64 women), 96 part-time (77 women); includes 55 minority (41 Black or African American, non-Hispanic/Latino; 1 American Indian or Alaska Native, non-Hispanic/Latino; 3 Asian, non-Hispanic/Latino; 6 Hispanic/Latino; 4 Two or more races, non-Hispanic/Latino), 8 international. Average age 33. 149 applicants, 56% accepted, 40 enrolled. In 2013, 36 master's, 5 doctorates, 12 other advanced degrees awarded. *Degree requirements:* For master's, comprehensive exam, thesis optional; for doctorate, comprehensive exam, thesis/dissertation; for Ed S, comprehensive exam. *Entrance requirements:* For master's and doctorate, GRE General Test, MAT, or NTE, minimum GPA of 3.0; for Ed S, minimum GPA of 3.0 during previous 2 years. Additional exam requirements/recommendations for international students: Required—TOEFL (minimum score 550 paper-based), IELTS (minimum score 6.5). *Application deadline:* For fall admission, 7/1 for domestic students; for spring admission, 11/1 for domestic students. Applications are processed on a rolling basis. Application fee: $50 ($60 for international students). Electronic applications accepted. *Expenses:* Tuition, state resident: full-time $9450. Tuition, nonresident: full-time $23,950. *Financial support:* Research assistantships with tuition reimbursements, teaching assistantships with tuition reimbursements, and career-related internships or fieldwork available. Financial award application deadline: 7/14; financial award applicants required to submit FAFSA. *Faculty research:* Moral development, positive psychology, children's fears, digital storytelling. *Total annual research expenditures:* $23,833. *Unit head:* Dr. Rick House, Department Head, 205-348-0283. *Application contact:* Marie S. Marshall, Office Associate II, 205-348-8362, Fax: 205-348-0683, E-mail: mmarshal@bamaed.ua.edu.
Website: http://education.ua.edu/departments/esprmc/.

The University of Alabama at Birmingham, School of Education, Program in Counseling, Birmingham, AL 35294. Offers MA. *Accreditation:* ACA; CORE; NCATE. *Degree requirements:* For master's, thesis optional. *Entrance requirements:* For master's, GRE General Test or MAT, minimum GPA of 3.0, interview. Electronic applications accepted.

University of Alaska Anchorage, College of Education, Program in Counseling and Guidance, Anchorage, AK 99508. Offers M Ed. Part-time programs available. *Entrance*

requirements: For master's, GRE or MAT, interview, resume. Additional exam requirements/recommendations for international students: Required—TOEFL (minimum score 550 paper-based).

University of Alaska Fairbanks, School of Education, Program in Counseling, Fairbanks, AK 99775-7520. Offers counseling (M Ed), including community counseling, school counseling. *Students:* 22 full-time (19 women), 38 part-time (31 women); includes 9 minority (2 Black or African American, non-Hispanic/Latino; 4 American Indian or Alaska Native, non-Hispanic/Latino; 1 Hispanic/Latino; 1 Native Hawaiian or other Pacific Islander, non-Hispanic/Latino; 1 Two or more races, non-Hispanic/Latino). Average age 37. 40 applicants, 58% accepted, 21 enrolled. In 2013, 17 master's awarded. *Degree requirements:* For master's, comprehensive exam, thesis, oral defense. *Entrance requirements:* For master's, 1 year of teaching or administrative experience. *Application deadline:* For fall admission, 6/1 for domestic students, 3/1 for international students; for spring admission, 10/15 for domestic students, 9/1 for international students. Applications are processed on a rolling basis. Application fee: $60. Electronic applications accepted. *Expenses:* Tuition, state resident: full-time $7254; part-time $403 per credit. Tuition, nonresident: full-time $14,814; part-time $823 per credit. Tuition and fees vary according to course level, course load and reciprocity agreements. *Financial support:* In 2013–14, 3 teaching assistantships with tuition reimbursements (averaging $10,906 per year) were awarded; fellowships with tuition reimbursements, career-related internships or fieldwork, Federal Work-Study, scholarships/grants, health care benefits, and unspecified assistantships also available. Support available to part-time students. Financial award application deadline: 7/1; financial award applicants required to submit FAFSA. *Unit head:* Allan Morotti, Interim Dean, 907-474-7341, Fax: 907-474-5451, E-mail: uaf-soe-school@alaska.edu. *Application contact:* Libby Eddy, Registrar and Director of Admissions, 907-474-7500, Fax: 907-474-7097, E-mail: admissions@uaf.edu.
Website: https://sites.google.com/a/alaska.edu/soe-graduate/.

University of Alberta, Faculty of Graduate Studies and Research, Department of Educational Psychology, Edmonton, AB T6G 2E1, Canada. Offers counseling psychology (M Ed, PhD); educational psychology (M Ed, PhD); instructional technology (M Ed); school counseling (M Ed); school psychology (M Ed, PhD); special education (M Ed, PhD); special education-deafness studies (M Ed); teaching English as a second language (M Ed). Part-time programs available. *Degree requirements:* For master's, thesis optional; for doctorate, comprehensive exam, thesis/dissertation. *Entrance requirements:* For master's and doctorate, minimum GPA of 3.0. Additional exam requirements/recommendations for international students: Required—TOEFL. *Faculty research:* Human learning, development and assessment.

The University of Arizona, College of Education, Department of Disability and Psychoeducational Studies, Program in School Counseling, Tucson, AZ 85721. Offers M Ed. Part-time programs available. *Faculty:* 15 full-time (8 women), 1 (woman) part-time/adjunct. *Students:* 4 full-time (all women), 4 part-time (2 women); includes 2 minority (both Hispanic/Latino), 2 international. Average age 40. In 2013, 10 master's awarded. *Degree requirements:* For master's, presentation or thesis. *Entrance requirements:* Additional exam requirements/recommendations for international students: Required—TOEFL (minimum score 550 paper-based; 79 iBT). *Application deadline:* For fall admission, 3/1 for domestic students, 12/1 for international students. Application fee: $75. Electronic applications accepted. *Expenses:* Tuition, state resident: full-time $11,526. Tuition, nonresident: full-time $27,398. *Unit head:* Dr. Linda R. Shaw, Department Head, 520-621-7822, Fax: 520-621-3821, E-mail: lshaw@email.arizona.edu. *Application contact:* Cecilia Carlon, Coordinator, 520-621-7822, Fax: 520-621-3821, E-mail: ccarlon@email.arizona.edu.
Website: https://www.coe.arizona.edu/counseling.

University of Arkansas, Graduate School, College of Education and Health Professions, Department of Rehabilitation, Human Resources and Communication Disorders, Program in Counseling, Fayetteville, AR 72701-1201. Offers MS, PhD, Ed S. *Accreditation:* ACA; NCATE. Part-time and evening/weekend programs available. *Degree requirements:* For master's, thesis optional; for doctorate, thesis/dissertation. *Entrance requirements:* For master's, GRE General Test or MAT; for doctorate, GRE General Test. Electronic applications accepted.

University of Arkansas at Little Rock, Graduate School, College of Education, Department of Counseling, Adult and Rehabilitation Education, Program in Counselor Education, Little Rock, AR 72204-1099. Offers school counseling (M Ed). Part-time and evening/weekend programs available. *Degree requirements:* For master's, comprehensive exam, portfolio or thesis. *Entrance requirements:* For master's, GRE General Test, minimum GPA of 2.75, teaching certificate. *Expenses:* Tuition, state resident: full-time $5690; part-time $284.50 per credit hour. Tuition, nonresident: full-time $13,030; part-time $651.50 per credit hour. *Required fees:* $1121; $672 per term. One-time fee: $40 full-time.

University of Central Arkansas, Graduate School, College of Education, Department of Leadership Studies, Program in School Counseling, Conway, AR 72035-0001. Offers MS. *Accreditation:* NCATE. Part-time and evening/weekend programs available. Postbaccalaureate distance learning degree programs offered (minimal on-campus study). *Degree requirements:* For master's, comprehensive exam, thesis optional. *Entrance requirements:* For master's, GRE General Test, minimum GPA of 2.7. Additional exam requirements/recommendations for international students: Required—TOEFL (minimum score 550 paper-based). Electronic applications accepted.

University of Central Florida, College of Education and Human Performance, Department of Educational and Human Sciences, Program in Counselor Education, Orlando, FL 32816. Offers mental health counseling (MA); school counseling (M Ed, MA, Ed S). *Accreditation:* ACA. Part-time and evening/weekend programs available. *Students:* 137 full-time (117 women), 47 part-time (38 women); includes 55 minority (19 Black or African American, non-Hispanic/Latino; 12 Asian, non-Hispanic/Latino; 21 Hispanic/Latino; 3 Two or more races, non-Hispanic/Latino), 3 international. Average age 27. 184 applicants, 42% accepted, 51 enrolled. In 2013, 63 master's, 19 other advanced degrees awarded. *Degree requirements:* For master's, comprehensive exam, thesis or alternative. *Entrance requirements:* For master's, GRE General Test, interview, minimum GPA of 3.0. Additional exam requirements/recommendations for international students: Required—TOEFL. *Application deadline:* For fall admission, 2/1 for domestic students; for spring admission, 9/1 for domestic students. Application fee: $30. Electronic applications accepted. *Financial support:* In 2013–14, 23 students received support, including 13 fellowships with partial tuition reimbursements available (averaging $2,100 per year), 13 research assistantships with partial tuition reimbursements available (averaging $6,700 per year), 1 teaching assistantship with partial tuition reimbursement available (averaging $7,100 per year); career-related internships or fieldwork, Federal Work-Study, institutionally sponsored loans, tuition waivers (partial), and unspecified assistantships also available. Financial award application deadline: 3/1; financial award applicants required to submit FAFSA. *Unit head:* Dr. W. Bryce Hagedorn, Program Coordinator, 407-823-2999, E-mail: bryce.hagedorn@ucf.edu. *Application contact:* Barbara Rodriguez Lamas, Director, Admissions and Student Services, 407-823-2766, Fax: 407-823-6442, E-mail: gradadmissions@ucf.edu.

University of Central Florida, College of Education and Human Performance, Education Doctoral Programs, Orlando, FL 32816. Offers communication sciences and disorders (PhD); counselor education (PhD); early childhood education (PhD); education (Ed D); elementary education (PhD); exceptional education (PhD); exercise physiology (PhD); higher education (PhD); hospitality education (PhD); instructional technology (PhD); mathematics education (PhD); reading education (PhD); science education (PhD); social science education (PhD); TESOL (PhD). *Students:* 137 full-time (94 women), 86 part-time (64 women); includes 45 minority (24 Black or African American, non-Hispanic/Latino; 5 Asian, non-Hispanic/Latino; 13 Hispanic/Latino; 3 Two or more races, non-Hispanic/Latino), 22 international. Average age 39. 132 applicants, 54% accepted, 54 enrolled. In 2013, 38 doctorates awarded. Application fee: $30. Electronic applications accepted. *Financial support:* In 2013–14, 84 students received support, including 38 fellowships with partial tuition reimbursements available (averaging $6,600 per year), 41 research assistantships with partial tuition reimbursements available (averaging $7,800 per year), 53 teaching assistantships with partial tuition reimbursements available (averaging $7,700 per year). *Unit head:* Dr. Edward Robinson, Director of Doctoral Programs, 407-823-6106, E-mail: edward.robinson@ucf.edu. *Application contact:* Barbara Rodriguez Lamas, Associate Director, Admissions and Student Services, 407-823-2766, Fax: 407-823-6442, E-mail: gradadmissions@ucf.edu.
Website: http://education.ucf.edu/departments.cfm.

University of Central Missouri, The Graduate School, Warrensburg, MO 6409. Offers accountancy (MA); accounting (MBA); applied mathematics (MS); aviation safety (MA); biology (MS); business administration (MBA); career and technical education leadership (MS); college student personnel administration (MS); communication (MA); computer science (MS); counseling (MS); criminal justice (MS); educational leadership (Ed D); educational technology (MS); elementary and early childhood education (MSE); English (MA); environmental studies (MA); finance (MBA); history (MA); human services/educational technology (Ed S); human services/learning resources (Ed S); human services/professional counseling (Ed S); industrial hygiene (MS); industrial management (MS); information systems (MBA); information technology (MS); kinesiology (MS); library science and information services (MS); literacy education (MSE); marketing (MBA); mathematics (MS); music (MA); occupational safety management (MS); psychology (MS); rural family nursing (MS); school administration (MSE); social gerontology (MS); sociology (MA); special education (MSE); speech language pathology (MS); superintendency (Ed S); teaching (MAT); teaching English as a second language (MA); technology (MS); technology management (PhD); theatre (MA). Part-time programs available. *Faculty:* 233. *Students:* 890 full-time (396 women), 1,486 part-time (1,001 women); includes 192 minority (97 Black or African American, non-Hispanic/Latino; 9 American Indian or Alaska Native, non-Hispanic/Latino; 32 Asian, non-Hispanic/Latino; 40 Hispanic/Latino; 3 Native Hawaiian or other Pacific Islander, non-Hispanic/Latino; 11 Two or more races, non-Hispanic/Latino), 539 international. Average age 31. 1,953 applicants, 75% accepted. In 2013, 719 master's, 58 other advanced degrees awarded. *Degree requirements:* For master's and Ed S, comprehensive exam (for some programs), thesis (for some programs). *Entrance requirements:* Additional exam requirements/recommendations for international students: Required—TOEFL (minimum score 550 paper-based; 79 iBT). *Application deadline:* For fall admission, 6/1 for domestic students; for spring admission, 10/1 for domestic and international students. Applications are processed on a rolling basis. Application fee: $30 ($75 for international students). Electronic applications accepted. *Expenses:* Tuition, state resident: full-time $7326; part-time $276.25 per credit hour. Tuition, nonresident: full-time $13,956; part-time $552.50 per credit hour. *Required fees:* $29 per credit hour. *Financial support:* In 2013–14, 118 students received support, including 271 research assistantships with full and partial tuition reimbursements available (averaging $7,500 per year), 109 teaching assistantships with full and partial tuition reimbursements available (averaging $7,500 per year); career-related internships or fieldwork, Federal Work-Study, scholarships/grants, and administrative and laboratory assistantships also available. Support available to part-time students. Financial award application deadline: 3/1; financial award applicants required to submit FAFSA. *Unit head:* Dr. Joseph Vaughn, Assistant Provost for Research/Dean, 660-543-4092, Fax: 660-543-4778, E-mail: vaughn@ucmo.edu. *Application contact:* Brittany Lawrence, Graduate Student Services Coordinator, 660-543-4621, Fax: 660-543-4778, E-mail: gradinfo@ucmo.edu.
Website: http://www.ucmo.edu/graduate/.

University of Central Oklahoma, The Jackson College of Graduate Studies, College of Education and Professional Studies, Department of Advanced Professional and Special Services, Edmond, OK 73034-5209. Offers educational leadership (M Ed); library media education (M Ed); reading (M Ed); school counseling (M Ed); special education (M Ed), including mild/moderate disabilities, severe-profound/multiple disabilities, special education; speech-language pathology (MS). Part-time programs available. *Faculty:* 14 full-time (9 women), 16 part-time/adjunct (8 women). *Students:* 87 full-time (80 women), 298 part-time (251 women); includes 77 minority (32 Black or African American, non-Hispanic/Latino; 10 American Indian or Alaska Native, non-Hispanic/Latino; 2 Asian, non-Hispanic/Latino; 15 Hispanic/Latino; 18 Two or more races, non-Hispanic/Latino), 9 international. Average age 34. 147 applicants, 94% accepted, 89 enrolled. In 2013, 163 master's awarded. *Degree requirements:* For master's, comprehensive exam (for some programs), thesis (for some programs). *Entrance requirements:* For master's, GRE. Additional exam requirements/recommendations for international students: Required—TOEFL (minimum score 550 paper-based; 79 iBT), IELTS (minimum score 6.5). *Application deadline:* For fall admission, 7/1 for international students; for spring admission, 7/1 for international students. Applications are processed on a rolling basis. Application fee: $50. Electronic applications accepted. *Expenses:* Tuition, state resident: full-time $4137; part-time $206.85 per credit hour. Tuition, nonresident: full-time $10,359; part-time $517.95 per credit hour. *Required fees:* $481. Tuition and fees vary according to course load and program. *Financial support:* In 2013–14, 93 students received support, including 4 research assistantships with partial tuition reimbursements available (averaging $8,133 per year); teaching assistantships with partial tuition reimbursements available, career-related internships or fieldwork, scholarships/grants, tuition waivers (partial), and unspecified assistantships also available. Financial award application deadline: 3/31; financial award applicants required to submit FAFSA. *Faculty research:* Intellectual freedom, fair use copyright, technology integration, young adult literature, distance learning. *Unit head:* Dr. Patsy Couts, Chair, 405-974-3888, Fax: 405-974-3857, E-mail: pcouts@uco.edu. *Application contact:* Dr. Richard Bernard, Dean, Graduate College, 405-974-3493, Fax: 405-974-3852, E-mail: gradcoll@uco.edu.
Website: http://www.uco.edu/ceps/dept/apss/.

University of Cincinnati, Graduate School, College of Education, Criminal Justice, and Human Services, Division of Human Services, Program in Counseling, Cincinnati, OH 45221. Offers counseling (Ed D); counselor education (CAGS); mental health (MA); school counseling (M Ed). *Accreditation:* ACA (one or more programs are accredited); NCATE. Part-time programs available. Terminal master's awarded for partial completion of doctoral program. *Degree requirements:* For master's, comprehensive exam; for doctorate, comprehensive exam, thesis/dissertation. *Entrance requirements:* For master's, GRE General Test, interview; for doctorate, GRE General Test, GRE Subject Test, interview. Additional exam requirements/recommendations for international students: Required—TOEFL (minimum score 620 paper-based), OEPT. Electronic

applications accepted. *Faculty research:* Group work, career development, ecology, prevention, multicultural.

University of Colorado Colorado Springs, College of Education, Colorado Springs, CO 80933-7150. Offers counseling and human services (MA); curriculum and instruction (MA); educational administration (MA); educational leadership (MA, PhD); special education (MA). *Accreditation:* ACA; NCATE. Part-time and evening/weekend programs available. Postbaccalaureate distance learning degree programs offered (minimal on-campus study). *Faculty:* 25 full-time (17 women), 39 part-time/adjunct (29 women). *Students:* 220 full-time (146 women), 237 part-time (163 women); includes 86 minority (18 Black or African American, non-Hispanic/Latino; 3 American Indian or Alaska Native, non-Hispanic/Latino; 11 Asian, non-Hispanic/Latino; 46 Hispanic/Latino; 8 Two or more races, non-Hispanic/Latino), 16 international. Average age 35. 182 applicants, 88% accepted, 118 enrolled. In 2013, 140 master's, 8 doctorates awarded. *Degree requirements:* For master's, comprehensive exam, thesis or alternative, microcomputer proficiency; for doctorate, comprehensive exam, thesis/dissertation, research lab. *Entrance requirements:* For master's, GRE General Test. Additional exam requirements/recommendations for international students: Recommended—TOEFL. *Application deadline:* For fall admission, 2/28 priority date for domestic students, 2/28 for international students; for spring admission, 10/15 for domestic and international students. Applications are processed on a rolling basis. Application fee: $60 ($75 for international students). *Expenses:* Tuition, state resident: full-time $8882; part-time $1622 per course. Tuition, nonresident: full-time $17,435; part-time $3048 per course. One-time fee: $100. Tuition and fees vary according to course load, degree level, campus/location and program. *Financial support:* In 2013–14, 23 students received support, including 23 fellowships (averaging $1,577 per year); career-related internships or fieldwork, Federal Work-Study, and scholarships/grants also available. Support available to part-time students. Financial award application deadline: 3/1; financial award applicants required to submit FAFSA. *Faculty research:* Linguistically diverse education (LDE), educational policy, evidence-based reading and writing instruction, relational and social aggression, positive behavior supports (PBS), inclusive schooling, K-12 education policy. *Total annual research expenditures:* $136,574. *Unit head:* Dr. Mary Snyder, Dean, 719-255-3701, Fax: 719-262-4133, E-mail: msnyder3@uccs.edu. *Application contact:* Juliane Field, Director, 719-255-4526, Fax: 719-255-4110, E-mail: jfield@uccs.edu.
Website: http://www.uccs.edu/coe.

University of Colorado Denver, School of Education and Human Development, Program in Counseling Psychology and Counselor Education, Denver, CO 80217-3364. Offers counseling (MA), including clinical mental health counseling, couple and family counseling, multicultural counseling, school counseling; school counseling (MA). *Accreditation:* ACA; NCATE. Part-time and evening/weekend programs available. *Students:* 171 full-time (138 women), 46 part-time (44 women); includes 32 minority (6 Black or African American, non-Hispanic/Latino; 5 Asian, non-Hispanic/Latino; 19 Hispanic/Latino; 2 Two or more races, non-Hispanic/Latino). Average age 31. 139 applicants, 35% accepted, 24 enrolled. In 2013, 59 master's awarded. *Degree requirements:* For master's, thesis or alternative, 63-66 hours. *Entrance requirements:* For master's, GRE or MAT (unless applicant already holds a graduate degree), letters of recommendation, interview, resume. Additional exam requirements/recommendations for international students: Required—TOEFL (minimum score 525 paper-based; 71 iBT); Recommended—IELTS (minimum score 6.3). *Application deadline:* For fall admission, 1/15 for domestic students, 1/1 for international students; for spring admission, 9/15 for domestic students, 9/1 for international students. Application fee: $50 ($75 for international students). Electronic applications accepted. *Expenses:* Contact institution. *Financial support:* In 2013–14, 12 students received support. Research assistantships, Federal Work-Study, institutionally sponsored loans, scholarships/grants, and traineeships available. Financial award application deadline: 4/1; financial award applicants required to submit FAFSA. *Faculty research:* Spiritual issues in counseling, multicultural and diversity issues in counseling, adolescent suicide, career development. *Unit head:* Farah Ibrahim, Counseling Professor, 303-315-6329, E-mail: farah.ibrahim@ucdenver.edu. *Application contact:* Student Services Coordinator, 303-315-6300, Fax: 303-315-6311, E-mail: education@ucdenver.edu.
Website: http://www.ucdenver.edu/academics/colleges/SchoolOfEducation/Academics/MASTERS/counseling/Pages/default.aspx.

University of Connecticut, Graduate School, Neag School of Education, Department of Educational Psychology, Program in Counseling Psychology, Storrs, CT 06269. Offers counseling psychology (PhD); school counseling (MA, Post-Master's Certificate). *Accreditation:* ACA. Terminal master's awarded for partial completion of doctoral program. *Degree requirements:* For master's, comprehensive exam, thesis or alternative; for doctorate, thesis/dissertation. *Entrance requirements:* For doctorate, GRE General Test. Additional exam requirements/recommendations for international students: Required—TOEFL (minimum score 550 paper-based). Electronic applications accepted.

University of Dayton, Department of Counselor Education and Human Services, Dayton, OH 45469-1300. Offers clinical mental health counseling (MS Ed); college student personnel (MS Ed); higher education administration (MS Ed); human services (MS Ed); school counseling (MS Ed); school psychology (MS Ed, Ed S). *Accreditation:* ACA; NCATE. Part-time and evening/weekend programs available. *Faculty:* 11 full-time (7 women), 46 part-time/adjunct (31 women). *Students:* 212 full-time (170 women), 151 part-time (118 women); includes 73 minority (61 Black or African American, non-Hispanic/Latino; 1 Asian, non-Hispanic/Latino; 8 Hispanic/Latino; 3 Two or more races, non-Hispanic/Latino), 4 international. Average age 32. 295 applicants, 47% accepted, 103 enrolled. In 2013, 147 master's, 5 Ed Ss awarded. *Degree requirements:* For master's, comprehensive exam (for some programs), thesis (for some programs), exit exam. *Entrance requirements:* For master's, MAT or GRE (if GPA less than 2.75), interview, writing sample. Additional exam requirements/recommendations for international students: Required—TOEFL (minimum score 550 paper-based; 80 iBT). *Application deadline:* For fall admission, 4/10 for domestic students, 4/10 priority date for international students; for winter admission, 9/10 for domestic students, 7/1 for international students; for spring admission, 9/10 for domestic students, 9/10 priority date for international students. Application fee: $0 ($50 for international students). Electronic applications accepted. *Expenses:* Tuition: Full-time $10,296; part-time $858 per credit hour. *Required fees:* $50; $25. *Financial support:* In 2013–14, 10 research assistantships with full tuition reimbursements (averaging $8,720 per year) were awarded; career-related internships or fieldwork, institutionally sponsored loans, health care benefits, and unspecified assistantships also available. Financial award application deadline: 3/1; financial award applicants required to submit FAFSA. *Faculty research:* Mindfulness, forgiveness in relationships, positive psychology in couples counseling, traumatic brain injury responses, college student development. *Unit head:* Dr. Molly Schaller, Chairperson, 937-229-3644, Fax: 937-229-1055, E-mail: mschaller1@udayton.edu. *Application contact:* Kathleen Brown, Administrative Assistant, 937-229-3644, Fax: 937-229-1055, E-mail: kbrown1@udayton.edu.
Website: http://www.udayton.edu/education/edc/index.php.

University of Detroit Mercy, College of Liberal Arts and Education, Department of Counseling and Addiction Studies, Program in Counseling, Detroit, MI 48221. Offers

addiction counseling (MA); community counseling (MA); school counseling (MA). *Accreditation:* ACA. Part-time and evening/weekend programs available. *Degree requirements:* For master's, thesis or alternative. *Entrance requirements:* For master's, minimum GPA of 2.75.

University of Florida, Graduate School, College of Education, School of Human Development and Organizational Studies in Education, Gainesville, FL 32611. Offers counseling and counselor education (Ed D, PhD), including counseling and counselor education, marriage and family counseling, mental health counseling, school counseling and guidance; educational leadership (M Ed, MAE, Ed D, PhD, Ed S), including educational leadership (Ed D, PhD), educational policy (Ed D, PhD); higher education administration (Ed D, PhD, Ed S), including education policy (Ed D), educational policy (Ed D, PhD), higher education administration (Ed D, PhD); marriage and family counseling (M Ed, MAE, Ed S); mental health counseling (M Ed, MAE, Ed S); research and evaluation methodology (M Ed, MAE, Ed D, PhD, Ed S); school counseling and guidance (M Ed, MAE, Ed S); student personnel in higher education (M Ed, MAE, Ed S). *Accreditation:* ACA (one or more programs are accredited); NCATE. Part-time programs available. Postbaccalaureate distance learning degree programs offered. *Faculty:* 20 full-time (11 women), 4 part-time/adjunct (1 woman). *Students:* 291 full-time (232 women), 212 part-time (157 women); includes 145 minority (71 Black or African American, non-Hispanic/Latino; 3 American Indian or Alaska Native, non-Hispanic/Latino; 11 Asian, non-Hispanic/Latino; 60 Hispanic/Latino), 38 international. Average age 31. 271 applicants, 42% accepted, 75 enrolled. In 2013, 71 master's, 31 doctorates, 62 other advanced degrees awarded. Terminal master's awarded for partial completion of doctoral program. *Degree requirements:* For master's, thesis optional; for doctorate, comprehensive exam, thesis/dissertation. *Entrance requirements:* For master's and doctorate, GRE General Test, minimum GPA of 3.0 (undergraduate), 3.5 (graduate); for Ed S, GRE General Test. Additional exam requirements/recommendations for international students: Required—TOEFL (minimum score 550 paper-based; 80 iBT), IELTS (minimum score 6). *Application deadline:* Applications are processed on a rolling basis. Application fee: $30. Electronic applications accepted. *Expenses:* Tuition, state resident: full-time $12,640. Tuition, nonresident: full-time $30,000. *Financial support:* In 2013–14, 85 students received support, including 6 fellowships (averaging $12,190 per year), 48 research assistantships (averaging $15,155 per year), 50 teaching assistantships (averaging $9,080 per year); career-related internships or fieldwork and unspecified assistantships also available. Financial award applicants required to submit FAFSA. *Unit head:* Glenn E. Good, PhD, Dean and Professor, 352-273-4135, Fax: 352-846-2697, E-mail: ggood@ufl.edu. *Application contact:* Thomasenia L. Adams, PhD, Professor and Associate Dean, 352-273-4119, Fax: 352-846-2697, E-mail: tla@coe.ufl.edu.
Website: http://education.ufl.edu/hdose/.

University of Georgia, College of Education, Department of Counseling and Human Development Services, Athens, GA 30602. Offers college student affairs administration (M Ed, PhD); counseling and student personnel (PhD); counseling psychology (PhD); professional counseling (M Ed); professional school counseling (Ed S); recreation and leisure studies (M Ed, MA, PhD). *Accreditation:* ACA (one or more programs are accredited); APA (one or more programs are accredited); NCATE. *Degree requirements:* For master's, thesis (MA); for doctorate, variable foreign language requirement, thesis/dissertation. *Entrance requirements:* For master's, GRE General Test or MAT; for doctorate, GRE General Test. Electronic applications accepted.

University of Guam, Office of Graduate Studies, School of Education, Program in Counseling, Mangilao, GU 96923. Offers MA. *Degree requirements:* For master's, comprehensive oral and written exams, special project or thesis. *Entrance requirements:* For master's, GRE General Test. Additional exam requirements/recommendations for international students: Required—TOEFL. *Faculty research:* Drugs in the local schools, standardized teaching procedures in the elementary school, how to address the dropout problems.

University of Hartford, College of Education, Nursing, and Health Professions, Program in Counseling, West Hartford, CT 06117-1599. Offers M Ed, MS, Sixth Year Certificate. *Accreditation:* NCATE. Part-time and evening/weekend programs available. *Degree requirements:* For master's and Sixth Year Certificate, comprehensive exam. *Entrance requirements:* For master's, GRE General Test or MAT, PRAXIS I or waiver, interview, 2 letters of recommendation; for Sixth Year Certificate, GRE General Test or MAT, PRAXIS I or waiver, interview. Additional exam requirements/recommendations for international students: Required—TOEFL (minimum score 550 paper-based). Electronic applications accepted.

University of Houston–Clear Lake, School of Education, Program in Foundations and Professional Studies, Houston, TX 77058-1002. Offers counseling (MS); instructional technology (MS); multicultural studies (MS). Part-time and evening/weekend programs available. *Degree requirements:* For master's, thesis optional. *Entrance requirements:* For master's, GRE or minimum GPA of 3.0 in last 60 hours. Additional exam requirements/recommendations for international students: Required—TOEFL (minimum score 550 paper-based). Electronic applications accepted.

University of Houston–Victoria, School of Education and Human Development, Victoria, TX 77901-4450. Offers administration and supervision (M Ed); adult and higher education (M Ed); counseling (M Ed); curriculum and instruction (M Ed); special education (M Ed). Part-time and evening/weekend programs available. Postbaccalaureate distance learning degree programs offered (minimal on-campus study). *Faculty:* 22 full-time (19 women). *Students:* 56 full-time (52 women), 325 part-time (274 women); includes 211 minority (113 Black or African American, non-Hispanic/Latino; 2 American Indian or Alaska Native, non-Hispanic/Latino; 16 Asian, non-Hispanic/Latino; 68 Hispanic/Latino; 12 Two or more races, non-Hispanic/Latino), 3 international. *Degree requirements:* For master's, comprehensive exam, project or thesis. *Entrance requirements:* For master's, GRE General Test. Additional exam requirements/recommendations for international students: Required—TOEFL. *Application deadline:* For fall admission, 6/1 for international students; for spring admission, 10/1 for international students. Applications are processed on a rolling basis. Application fee: $0. Electronic applications accepted. *Expenses:* Tuition, state resident: full-time $4534; part-time $251 per credit hour. Tuition, nonresident: full-time $10,906; part-time $606 per contact hour. *Required fees:* $68 per semester hour. Tuition and fees vary according to course load. *Financial support:* In 2013–14, research assistantships with partial tuition reimbursements (averaging $2,000 per year), teaching assistantships with partial tuition reimbursements (averaging $2,000 per year) were awarded; Federal Work-Study, scholarships/grants, and unspecified assistantships also available. Support available to part-time students. Financial award application deadline: 4/15; financial award applicants required to submit FAFSA. *Faculty research:* Reading and language arts education, evaluation and diagnosis of special children's abilities. *Unit head:* Freddie W. Litton, Dean, 361-570-4260, Fax: 361-580-5580. *Application contact:* Sandy Hybner, Senior Recruitment Coordinator, 361-570-4252, Fax: 361-580-5580, E-mail: hybners@uhv.edu.
Website: http://www.uhv.edu/edu/.

University of Idaho, College of Graduate Studies, College of Education, Department of Leadership and Counseling, Boise, ID 83844-2282. Offers adult/organizational learning and leadership (MS, Ed S); educational leadership (M Ed, Ed S); rehabilitation

counseling and human services (M Ed, MS); school counseling (M Ed, MS); special education (M Ed). *Faculty:* 13 full-time, 11 part-time/adjunct. *Students:* 58 full-time (39 women), 200 part-time (121 women). Average age 39. In 2013, 83 master's, 38 other advanced degrees awarded. *Entrance requirements:* Additional exam requirements/recommendations for international students: Required—TOEFL (minimum score 550 paper-based). *Application deadline:* Applications are processed on a rolling basis. Application fee: $60. Electronic applications accepted. *Expenses:* Tuition, state resident: full-time $5596; part-time $363 per credit hour. Tuition, nonresident: full-time $18,672; part-time $1089 per credit hour. *Financial support:* Applicants required to submit FAFSA. *Unit head:* Dr. Jeffrey Brooks, Chair, 208-364-4047, E-mail: mweitz@uidaho.edu. *Application contact:* Stephanie Thomas, Graduate Recruitment Coordinator, 208-885-4001, Fax: 208-885-4406, E-mail: gadms@uidaho.edu.
Website: http://www.uidaho.edu/ed/leadershipcounseling.

University of Illinois at Urbana–Champaign, Graduate College, College of Education, Department of Educational Psychology, Champaign, IL 61820. Offers Ed M, MA, MS, PhD, CAS. *Accreditation:* APA (one or more programs are accredited). Part-time programs available. Postbaccalaureate distance learning degree programs offered (no on-campus study). *Students:* 84 (60 women). Application fee: $75 ($90 for international students). *Unit head:* Jose Mestre, Chair, 217-333-0098, Fax: 217-244-7620, E-mail: mestre@illinois.edu. *Application contact:* Myranda Lyons, Office Support Specialist, 217-244-3391, Fax: 217-244-7620, E-mail: mjlyons@illinois.edu.
Website: http://education.illinois.edu/EDPSY/.

The University of Iowa, Graduate College, College of Education, Department of Rehabilitation and Counselor Education, Iowa City, IA 52242-1316. Offers counselor education and supervision (PhD); couple and family therapy (PhD); rehabilitation and mental health counseling (MA); rehabilitation counselor education (PhD); school counseling (MA). *Accreditation:* ACA (one or more programs are accredited); CORE (one or more programs are accredited). *Degree requirements:* For master's, thesis optional, exam; for doctorate, comprehensive exam, thesis/dissertation. *Entrance requirements:* For master's and doctorate, GRE General Test, minimum GPA of 3.0. Additional exam requirements/recommendations for international students: Required—TOEFL (minimum score 550 paper-based; 81 iBT). Electronic applications accepted.

University of La Verne, College of Education and Organizational Leadership, Program in Educational Counseling, La Verne, CA 91750-4443. Offers educational counseling (MS); pupil personnel services (Credential); school psychology (MS). Part-time programs available. *Faculty:* 3 full-time (2 women), 3 part-time/adjunct (all women). *Students:* 14 full-time (13 women), 52 part-time (39 women); includes 51 minority (8 Black or African American, non-Hispanic/Latino; 2 Asian, non-Hispanic/Latino; 39 Hispanic/Latino; 2 Two or more races, non-Hispanic/Latino), 1 international. Average age 31. In 2013, 90 master's awarded. *Degree requirements:* For master's, thesis optional. *Entrance requirements:* For master's, California Basic Educational Skills Test, minimum undergraduate GPA of 2.75, graduate 3.0; interview; 1 year's experience working with children; 3 letters of reference. Additional exam requirements/recommendations for international students: Required—TOEFL (minimum score 550 paper-based). *Application deadline:* Applications are processed on a rolling basis. Application fee: $50. *Expenses:* Contact institution. *Financial support:* Institutionally sponsored loans and unspecified assistantships available. Financial award application deadline: 3/2; financial award applicants required to submit FAFSA. *Unit head:* Lynn Stanton-Riggs, Chairperson, 909-448-4625, E-mail: lstanton-riggs@laverne.edu. *Application contact:* Christy Ranells, Admissions Information Specialist, 909-448-4644, Fax: 909-392-2744, E-mail: cranells@laverne.edu.
Website: http://www.laverne.edu/education/.

University of La Verne, Regional and Online Campuses, Graduate Credential Program in Education, California Statewide Campus, La Verne, CA 91750-4443. Offers administration services (preliminary) (Credential); education specialist: mild/moderate (Credential); multiple subject teaching (Credential); pupil personnel services: school counseling (Credential); single subject teaching (Credential). *Accreditation:* NCATE. Part-time programs available. *Faculty:* 10 full-time (7 women), 1 (woman) part-time/adjunct. *Students:* 128 full-time (92 women), 49 part-time (43 women); includes 58 minority (6 Black or African American, non-Hispanic/Latino; 1 American Indian or Alaska Native, non-Hispanic/Latino; 3 Asian, non-Hispanic/Latino; 44 Hispanic/Latino; 4 Two or more races, non-Hispanic/Latino). Average age 32. In 2013, 24 Credentials awarded. *Entrance requirements:* For degree, California Basic Educational Skills Test, minimum undergraduate GPA of 2.75, 3 letters of recommendation, interview. *Application deadline:* Applications are processed on a rolling basis. Application fee: $50. *Expenses:* Contact institution. *Financial support:* Institutionally sponsored loans available. Financial award application deadline: 3/2; financial award applicants required to submit FAFSA. *Unit head:* Pam Bergovoy, Assistant Dean, Regional and Online Campuses/Director, Center for Educators, 909-448-4953, E-mail: pbergovoy@laverne.edu.
Website: http://www.laverne.edu/locations.

University of La Verne, Regional and Online Campuses, Graduate Programs, Central Coast/Vandenberg Air Force Base Campuses, La Verne, CA 91750-4443. Offers business administration for experienced professionals (MBA), including health services management, information technology; education (special emphasis) (M Ed); educational counseling (MS); educational leadership (M Ed); multiple subject (elementary) (Credential); preliminary administrative services (Credential); pupil personnel services (Credential); single subject (secondary) (Credential). Part-time programs available. *Faculty:* 11 part-time/adjunct (2 women). *Students:* 17 full-time (7 women), 34 part-time (22 women); includes 15 minority (1 Black or African American, non-Hispanic/Latino; 1 American Indian or Alaska Native, non-Hispanic/Latino; 1 Asian, non-Hispanic/Latino; 10 Hispanic/Latino; 2 Two or more races, non-Hispanic/Latino). Average age 38. In 2013, 25 master's awarded. *Application deadline:* Applications are processed on a rolling basis. Application fee: $50. *Expenses:* Contact institution. *Financial support:* Institutionally sponsored loans available. Financial award application deadline: 3/2; financial award applicants required to submit FAFSA. *Unit head:* Kitt Vincent, Director, Central Coast Campus, 805-788-6202, Fax: 805-788-6201, E-mail: kvincent@laverne.edu. *Application contact:* Gene Teal, Admissions, 805-788-6205, Fax: 805-788-6201, E-mail: eteal@laverne.edu.
Website: http://www.laverne.edu/locations.

University of La Verne, Regional and Online Campuses, Graduate Programs, High Desert Campus, Victorville, CA 92392. Offers business administration for experienced professionals (MBA); educational counseling (MS); educational leadership (M Ed); multiple subject (elementary) (Credential); preliminary administrative services (Credential); pupil personnel services (Credential); single subject (secondary) (Credential). *Faculty:* 3 part-time/adjunct (0 women). *Students:* 10 full-time (6 women), 17 part-time (12 women); includes 14 minority (3 Black or African American, non-Hispanic/Latino; 3 Asian, non-Hispanic/Latino; 6 Hispanic/Latino; 1 Native Hawaiian or other Pacific Islander, non-Hispanic/Latino; 1 Two or more races, non-Hispanic/Latino). Average age 38. In 2013, 6 master's awarded. *Application deadline:* Applications are processed on a rolling basis. Application fee: $50. *Expenses:* Contact institution. *Financial support:* Application deadline: 3/2; applicants required to submit FAFSA. *Unit head:* Juli Roberts, Regional Campus Director, 760-955-6448, Fax: 760-843-9505, E-mail: jroberts@laverne.edu. *Application contact:* Donald Parker, Associate Director of Admissions, 760-955-6477, E-mail: dparker@laverne.edu.
Website: http://www.laverne.edu/locations/victorville/.

University of La Verne, Regional and Online Campuses, Graduate Programs, Kern County Campus, Bakersfield, CA 93301. Offers business administration for experienced professionals (MBA-EP); education (special emphasis) (M Ed); educational counseling (MS); educational leadership (M Ed); health administration (MHA); leadership and management (MS); mild/moderate education specialist preliminary (Credential); multiple subject (elementary) (Credential); organizational leadership (Ed D); preliminary administrative services (Credential); single subject (secondary) (Credential); special education studies (MS). Part-time and evening/weekend programs available. *Faculty:* 2 part-time/adjunct (1 woman). *Students:* 1 (woman) full-time, 5 part-time (3 women); includes 4 minority (3 Hispanic/Latino; 1 Two or more races, non-Hispanic/Latino). Average age 36. In 2013, 4 master's awarded. *Application deadline:* Applications are processed on a rolling basis. Application fee: $50. *Expenses:* Contact institution. *Financial support:* Institutionally sponsored loans available. Financial award application deadline: 3/2; financial award applicants required to submit FAFSA. *Unit head:* Nora Dominguez, Regional Campus Director, 661-861-6802, E-mail: ndominguez@laverne.edu. *Application contact:* Regina Benavides, Associate Director of Admissions, 661-861-6807, E-mail: rbenavides@laverne.edu.
Website: http://laverne.edu/locations/bakersfield/.

University of La Verne, Regional and Online Campuses, Graduate Programs, Orange County Campus, Irvine, CA 92606. Offers business administration for experienced professionals (MBA); educational counseling (MS); educational leadership (M Ed); health administration (MHA); leadership and management (MS); preliminary administrative services (Credential); pupil personnel services (Credential). Part-time programs available. *Faculty:* 3 full-time (all women), 12 part-time/adjunct (3 women). *Students:* 38 full-time (21 women), 78 part-time (36 women); includes 69 minority (7 Black or African American, non-Hispanic/Latino; 1 American Indian or Alaska Native, non-Hispanic/Latino; 19 Asian, non-Hispanic/Latino; 40 Hispanic/Latino; 1 Native Hawaiian or other Pacific Islander, non-Hispanic/Latino; 1 Two or more races, non-Hispanic/Latino). Average age 37. In 2013, 30 master's awarded. *Application deadline:* Applications are processed on a rolling basis. Application fee: $50. *Expenses:* Contact institution. *Financial support:* Institutionally sponsored loans available. Financial award application deadline: 3/2; financial award applicants required to submit FAFSA. *Unit head:* Pam Bergovoy, Director, Center for Educators, 909-448-4953, E-mail: pbergovoy@laverne.edu. *Application contact:* Alison Rodriguez-Balles, Associate Director of Admissions, 714-505-6943, E-mail: arodriguez2@laverne.edu.
Website: http://laverne.edu/locations/irvine/.

University of La Verne, Regional and Online Campuses, Graduate Programs, San Fernando Valley Campus, Burbank, CA 91505. Offers business administration for experienced professionals (MBA-EP); educational counseling (MS); educational leadership (M Ed); leadership and management (MS); preliminary administrative services (Credential); pupil personnel services (Credential). Part-time and evening/weekend programs available. *Faculty:* 2 full-time (1 woman), 12 part-time/adjunct (5 women). *Students:* 46 full-time (20 women), 128 part-time (76 women); includes 121 minority (29 Black or African American, non-Hispanic/Latino; 19 Asian, non-Hispanic/Latino; 66 Hispanic/Latino; 1 Native Hawaiian or other Pacific Islander, non-Hispanic/Latino; 6 Two or more races, non-Hispanic/Latino). Average age 38. In 2013, 79 master's awarded. *Application deadline:* Applications are processed on a rolling basis. Application fee: $50. *Expenses:* Contact institution. *Financial support:* Institutionally sponsored loans available. Financial award application deadline: 3/2; financial award applicants required to submit FAFSA. *Unit head:* Dr. Nelly Kazman, Senior Executive Director, 818-295-6502, E-mail: nkazman@laverne.edu. *Application contact:* Debi Hrboka, Associate Director of Admissions, 818-295-6508, E-mail: dhrboka@laverne.edu.
Website: http://laverne.edu/locations/burbank/.

University of La Verne, Regional and Online Campuses, Graduate Programs, Ventura County/Point Mugu Naval Air Station Campuses, Oxnard, CA 93036. Offers business administration for experienced professionals (MS); educational counseling (MS); educational leadership (M Ed); leadership and management (MS); multiple subject (elementary) (Credential); pupil personnel services (Credential); single subject (secondary) (Credential). Part-time and evening/weekend programs available. *Faculty:* 12 part-time/adjunct (2 women). *Students:* 34 full-time (13 women), 37 part-time (20 women); includes 39 minority (3 Black or African American, non-Hispanic/Latino; 2 American Indian or Alaska Native, non-Hispanic/Latino; 3 Asian, non-Hispanic/Latino; 29 Hispanic/Latino; 2 Two or more races, non-Hispanic/Latino). Average age 38. In 2013, 31 master's awarded. Application fee: $50. *Expenses:* Contact institution. *Financial support:* Institutionally sponsored loans available. Financial award application deadline: 3/2; financial award applicants required to submit FAFSA. *Unit head:* Jamie Dempsey, Director, Point Mugu, 661-986-6902, E-mail: jdempsey@laverne.edu. *Application contact:* Kevin Laack, Regional Campus Director, Ventura, 805-981-6022, E-mail: klaack@laverne.edu.
Website: http://laverne.edu/locations/oxnard/.

University of La Verne, Regional and Online Campuses, Master's Programs in Education, California Statewide Campus, La Verne, CA 91750-4443. Offers administration services (preliminary) (Credential); education specialist: mild/moderate (Credential); educational counseling (MS); educational leadership (M Ed); multiple subject teaching (Credential); pupil personnel services: school counseling (Credential); single subject teaching (Credential); special education studies (MS); special emphasis (M Ed). *Accreditation:* NCATE. *Faculty:* 6 full-time (2 women), 23 part-time/adjunct (16 women). *Students:* 109 full-time (88 women), 63 part-time (53 women); includes 94 minority (8 Black or African American, non-Hispanic/Latino; 6 Asian, non-Hispanic/Latino; 76 Hispanic/Latino; 4 Two or more races, non-Hispanic/Latino). Average age 33. In 2013, 76 master's awarded. *Entrance requirements:* For master's, California Basic Educational Skills Test, 3 letters of recommendation, teaching credential. *Application deadline:* Applications are processed on a rolling basis. Application fee: $50. *Expenses:* Contact institution. *Financial support:* Fellowships and institutionally sponsored loans available. Financial award application deadline: 3/2; financial award applicants required to submit FAFSA. *Unit head:* Pam Bergovoy, Assistant Dean, Regional and Online Campuses/Director, Center for Educators, 909-448-4953, E-mail: pbergovoy@laverne.edu.
Website: http://www.laverne.edu/locations.

University of Lethbridge, School of Graduate Studies, Lethbridge, AB T1K 3M4, Canada. Offers accounting (MScM); addictions counseling (M Sc); agricultural biotechnology (M Sc); agricultural studies (M Sc, MA); anthropology (MA); archaeology (M Sc, MA); art (MA, MFA); biochemistry (M Sc); biological sciences (M Sc); biomolecular science (PhD); biosystems and biodiversity (PhD); Canadian studies (MA); chemistry (M Sc); computer science (M Sc); computer science and geographical information science (M Sc); counseling (MC); counseling psychology (M Ed); dramatic arts (MA); earth, space, and physical science (PhD); economics (MA); education (MA); educational leadership (M Ed); English (MA); environmental science (M Sc); evolution and behavior (PhD); exercise science (M Sc); finance (MScM); French (MA); French/

German (MA); French/Spanish (MA); general education (M Ed); general management (MScM); geography (M Sc, MA); German (MA); health sciences (M Sc); human resource management and labour relations (MScM); individualized multidisciplinary (M Sc, MA); information systems (MScM); international management (MScM); kinesiology (M Sc, MA); marketing (MScM); mathematics (M Sc); modern languages (MA); music (M Mus, MA); Native American studies (MA); neuroscience (M Sc, PhD); new media (MA, MFA); nursing (M Sc); philosophy (MA); physics (M Sc); policy and strategy (MScM); political science (MA); psychology (M Sc, MA); religious studies (MA); sociology (MA); theatre and dramatic arts (MFA); theoretical and computational science (PhD); urban and regional studies (MA); women and gender studies (MA). Part-time and evening/weekend programs available. *Degree requirements:* For doctorate, comprehensive exam, thesis/dissertation. *Entrance requirements:* For master's, GMAT (for M Sc in management), bachelor's degree in related field, minimum GPA of 3.0 during previous 20 graded semester courses, 2 years teaching or related experience (M Ed); for doctorate, master's degree, minimum graduate GPA of 3.5. Additional exam requirements/recommendations for international students: Required—TOEFL. Application fee: $60 Canadian dollars. *Financial support:* Fellowships, research assistantships, teaching assistantships, scholarships/grants, health care benefits, and unspecified assistantships available. *Faculty research:* Movement and brain plasticity, gibberellin physiology, photosynthesis, carbon cycling, molecular properties of main-group ring components. *Application contact:* School of Graduate Studies, 403-329-2793, Fax: 403-332-5239, E-mail: sgsinquiries@uleth.ca.
Website: http://www.uleth.ca/graduatestudies/.

University of Louisiana at Lafayette, Department of Counselor Education, Lafayette, LA 70504. Offers MS. *Entrance requirements:* For master's, GRE General Test, minimum GPA of 2.75. Additional exam requirements/recommendations for international students: Required—TOEFL (minimum score 550 paper-based). Electronic applications accepted.

University of Louisiana at Monroe, Graduate School, College of Health and Pharmaceutical Sciences, Programs in Counseling, Monroe, LA 71209-0001. Offers clinical mental health counseling (MS); school counseling (MS). *Accreditation:* ACA; NCATE. Part-time and evening/weekend programs available. Postbaccalaureate distance learning degree programs offered (minimal on-campus study). *Degree requirements:* For master's, comprehensive exam, thesis. *Entrance requirements:* For master's, GRE General Test, minimum GPA of 2.8 in last 60 hours. Additional exam requirements/recommendations for international students: Required—TOEFL (minimum score 500 paper-based; 61 iBT). *Application deadline:* For fall admission, 8/24 priority date for domestic students, 7/1 for international students; for winter admission, 12/14 priority date for domestic students; for spring admission, 1/19 for domestic students, 11/1 for international students. Applications are processed on a rolling basis. Application fee: $20 ($30 for international students). Electronic applications accepted. *Expenses:* Tuition, state resident: full-time $6607. Tuition, nonresident: full-time $17,179. Full-time tuition and fees vary according to program. *Financial support:* Career-related internships or fieldwork, Federal Work-Study, and unspecified assistantships available. Financial award application deadline: 4/1; financial award applicants required to submit FAFSA. *Unit head:* Dr. John-Nelson Pope, Director, 318-342-1246, E-mail: pope@ulm.edu. *Application contact:* Dr. John-Nelson Pope, Director, 318-342-1246, E-mail: pope@ulm.edu.
Website: http://www.ulm.edu/counseling/.

University of Louisville, Graduate School, College of Education and Human Development, Department of Educational and Counseling Psychology, Louisville, KY 40292-0001. Offers counseling and personnel services (M Ed, PhD). *Accreditation:* APA; NCATE. Part-time and evening/weekend programs available. *Faculty:* 15 full-time (8 women), 4 part-time/adjunct (2 women). *Students:* 192 full-time (158 women), 72 part-time (55 women); includes 59 minority (38 Black or African American, non-Hispanic/Latino; 1 American Indian or Alaska Native, non-Hispanic/Latino; 5 Asian, non-Hispanic/Latino; 9 Hispanic/Latino; 6 Two or more races, non-Hispanic/Latino), 7 international. Average age 29. 222 applicants, 50% accepted, 77 enrolled. In 2013, 46 master's, 2 doctorates awarded. *Degree requirements:* For doctorate, comprehensive exam, thesis/dissertation. *Entrance requirements:* For master's and doctorate, GRE General Test. Additional exam requirements/recommendations for international students: Required—TOEFL (minimum score 560 paper-based; 83 iBT). *Application deadline:* For fall admission, 5/1 priority date for international students; for winter admission, 11/1 for international students; for summer admission, 4/1 priority date for international students. Application fee: $60. Electronic applications accepted. *Expenses:* Tuition, state resident: full-time $10,788; part-time $599 per credit hour. Tuition, nonresident: full-time $22,446; part-time $1247 per credit hour. *Required fees:* $196. Tuition and fees vary according to program and reciprocity agreements. *Financial support:* Fellowships, research assistantships, teaching assistantships, career-related internships or fieldwork, Federal Work-Study, scholarships/grants, health care benefits, and unspecified assistantships available. Financial award application deadline: 6/1; financial award applicants required to submit FAFSA. *Faculty research:* Classroom processes, school outcomes, adolescent and adult development issues/prevention and treatment, multicultural counseling, spirituality, therapeutic outcomes, college student success, college student affairs administration, career development. *Unit head:* Dr. Michael Cuyjet, Acting Chair, 502-852-0628, Fax: 502-852-0629, E-mail: cuyjet@louisville.edu. *Application contact:* Libby Leggett, Director, Graduate Admissions, 502-852-3101, Fax: 502-852-6536, E-mail: gradadm@louisville.edu.
Website: http://www.louisville.edu/education/departments/ecpy.

University of Maine, Graduate School, College of Education and Human Development, Department of Teacher and Counselor Education, Orono, ME 04469. Offers counselor education (M Ed, MA, MS, CAS); early childhood teacher (CGS); education (PhD), including counselor education, literacy education, prevention and intervention studies; elementary education (M Ed, CAS); individualized education (M Ed); literacy education (M Ed, MS, CAS); response to intervention for behavior (CGS); secondary education (M Ed, MAT, CAS); social studies education (M Ed); special education (M Ed, CAS); teacher consultant in writing (CGS). Part-time programs available. *Students:* 147 full-time (118 women), 15 part-time (2 women); includes 8 minority (4 Black or African American, non-Hispanic/Latino; 2 American Indian or Alaska Native, non-Hispanic/Latino; 1 Hispanic/Latino; 1 Two or more races, non-Hispanic/Latino), 3 international. Average age 37. 100 applicants, 58% accepted, 50 enrolled. In 2013, 83 master's, 5 doctorates, 17 other advanced degrees awarded. *Degree requirements:* For master's, thesis (for some programs); for doctorate, comprehensive exam, thesis/dissertation. *Entrance requirements:* For master's, GRE General Test, MAT. Additional exam requirements/recommendations for international students: Required—TOEFL. *Application deadline:* For fall admission, 2/1 priority date for domestic students. Applications are processed on a rolling basis. Application fee: $65. Electronic applications accepted. *Expenses:* Tuition, state resident: full-time $7524. Tuition, nonresident: full-time $23,112. *Required fees:* $1970. *Financial support:* In 2013–14, 46 students received support, including 1 research assistantship (averaging $14,600 per year), 11 teaching assistantships (averaging $14,600 per year). Financial award application deadline: 3/1. *Unit head:* Dr. Janet Spector, Coordinator, 207-581-2459.

Application contact: Scott G. Delcourt, Associate Dean of the Graduate School, 207-581-3291, Fax: 207-581-3232, E-mail: graduate@maine.edu.
Website: http://umaine.edu/edhd/.

University of Manitoba, Faculty of Graduate Studies, Faculty of Education, Department of Educational Administration, Foundations and Psychology, Winnipeg, MB R3T 2N2, Canada. Offers adult and post-secondary education (M Ed); educational administration (M Ed); guidance and counseling (M Ed); inclusive special education (M Ed); social foundations of education (M Ed). *Degree requirements:* For master's, thesis or alternative.

University of Mary Hardin-Baylor, Graduate Studies in Counseling, Belton, TX 76513. Offers Christian marriage and family counseling (MA); clinical and mental health counseling (MA); marriage, family and child counseling (MA); non-clinical professional studies (MA). Part-time and evening/weekend programs available. *Faculty:* 5 full-time (3 women), 3 part-time/adjunct (2 women). *Students:* 55 full-time (46 women), 19 part-time (14 women); includes 26 minority (7 Black or African American, non-Hispanic/Latino; 2 American Indian or Alaska Native, non-Hispanic/Latino; 7 Asian, non-Hispanic/Latino; 10 Hispanic/Latino), 5 international. Average age 29. 36 applicants, 81% accepted, 23 enrolled. In 2013, 21 master's awarded. *Degree requirements:* For master's, comprehensive exam. *Entrance requirements:* For master's, GRE General Test (waived if GPA greater than 3.0), minimum GPA of 3.0 cumulative or last 60 hours, three letters of recommendation, interview. Additional exam requirements/recommendations for international students: Required—TOEFL (minimum score 550 paper-based; 80 iBT), IELTS (minimum score 6). *Application deadline:* For fall admission, 6/1 for domestic students, 6/15 priority date for international students; for spring admission, 11/1 for domestic students, 10/15 priority date for international students. Applications are processed on a rolling basis. Application fee: $35 ($135 for international students). Electronic applications accepted. *Expenses:* Tuition: Full-time $14,130; part-time $785 per credit hour. *Required fees:* $1350; $75 per credit hour. $50 per term. *Financial support:* Federal Work-Study, unspecified assistantships, and scholarships (for some active duty military personnel only) available. Support available to part-time students. Financial award applicants required to submit FAFSA. *Unit head:* Dr. Marta Garrett, Associate Professor/Director, Graduate Counseling, 254-295-5018, E-mail: mgarrett@umhb.edu. *Application contact:* Melissa Ford, Director of Graduate Admissions, 254-295-4020, Fax: 254-295-5038, E-mail: mford@umhb.edu.
Website: http://graduate.umhb.edu/counseling/.

University of Maryland, College Park, Academic Affairs, College of Education, Department of Counseling, Higher Education and Special Education, College Park, MD 20742. Offers college student personnel (M Ed, MA); college student personnel administration (PhD); community counseling (CAGS); community/career counseling (M Ed, MA); counseling and personnel services (M Ed, MA, PhD), including art therapy (M Ed), college student personnel (M Ed), counseling and personnel services (PhD), counseling psychology (M Ed), mental health counseling (M Ed), school counseling (M Ed); counseling psychology (PhD); counselor education (PhD); rehabilitation counseling (M Ed, MA, AGSC); school counseling (M Ed, MA); school psychology (M Ed, MA, PhD). *Accreditation:* ACA (one or more programs are accredited); APA (one or more programs are accredited); NCATE. Part-time and evening/weekend programs available. Postbaccalaureate distance learning degree programs offered (no on-campus study). *Faculty:* 63 full-time (43 women), 9 part-time/adjunct (8 women). *Students:* 244 full-time (189 women), 76 part-time (54 women); includes 96 minority (40 Black or African American, non-Hispanic/Latino; 1 American Indian or Alaska Native, non-Hispanic/Latino; 23 Asian, non-Hispanic/Latino; 26 Hispanic/Latino; 6 Two or more races, non-Hispanic/Latino), 34 international. 623 applicants, 21% accepted, 83 enrolled. In 2013, 64 master's, 41 doctorates awarded. *Degree requirements:* For master's, thesis (for some programs); for doctorate, thesis/dissertation. *Entrance requirements:* For master's, GRE General Test or MAT, minimum GPA of 3.0, 3 letters of recommendation; for doctorate, GRE General Test or MAT, minimum GPA of 3.5, 3 letters of recommendation. Additional exam requirements/recommendations for international students: Required—TOEFL. *Application deadline:* For fall admission, 12/1 for domestic students, 12/15 for international students; for spring admission, 12/1 for domestic students, 6/1 for international students. Applications are processed on a rolling basis. Application fee: $75. Electronic applications accepted. *Expenses:* Tuition, state resident: full-time $10,314; part-time $573 per credit hour. Tuition, nonresident: full-time $22,248; part-time $1236 per credit. *Required fees:* $1446; $403.15 per semester. Tuition and fees vary according to program. *Financial support:* In 2013–14, 31 fellowships with full and partial tuition reimbursements (averaging $21,772 per year), 7 research assistantships with tuition reimbursements (averaging $17,202 per year), 100 teaching assistantships with tuition reimbursements (averaging $16,637 per year) were awarded; career-related internships or fieldwork, Federal Work-Study, and scholarships/grants also available. Support available to part-time students. Financial award applicants required to submit FAFSA. *Faculty research:* Educational psychology, counseling, health. *Total annual research expenditures:* $3.2 million. *Unit head:* Dennis Kivlighan, Chair, 301-405-2858, E-mail: dennisk@umd.edu. *Application contact:* Dr. Charles A. Caramello, Dean of Graduate School, 301-405-0358, Fax: 301-314-9305, E-mail: ccaramel@umd.edu.

University of Maryland Eastern Shore, Graduate Programs, Department of Education, Program in Guidance and Counseling, Princess Anne, MD 21853-1299. Offers M Ed. Evening/weekend programs available. *Degree requirements:* For master's, comprehensive exam, practicum, seminar paper. *Entrance requirements:* For master's, interview, minimum GPA of 3.0. Additional exam requirements/recommendations for international students: Required—TOEFL (minimum score 80 iBT). Electronic applications accepted.

University of Massachusetts Amherst, Graduate School, College of Education, Program in Education, Amherst, MA 01003. Offers bilingual/English as a second language/multicultural education (M Ed, Ed S); child study and early education (M Ed); children, families and schools (Ed D, Ed S); early childhood and elementary teacher education (M Ed); educational leadership (M Ed); educational policy and leadership (Ed D); higher education (M Ed); international education (M Ed); language, literacy and culture (Ed D); learning, media and technology (M Ed, Ed S); mathematics, science, and learning technologies (Ed D); psychometric methods, educational statistics and research methods (Ed D); reading and writing (M Ed); school counselor education (M Ed, Ed S); school psychology (Ed S); science education (Ed S); secondary teacher education (M Ed); social justice education (M Ed, Ed D, Ed S); special education (M Ed, Ed D, Ed S); teacher education and school improvement (Ed D, Ed S). *Accreditation:* NCATE. Part-time programs available. Postbaccalaureate distance learning degree programs offered (minimal on-campus study). *Faculty:* 95 full-time (55 women). *Students:* 357 full-time (240 women), 264 part-time (194 women); includes 114 minority (41 Black or African American, non-Hispanic/Latino; 4 American Indian or Alaska Native, non-Hispanic/Latino; 10 Asian, non-Hispanic/Latino; 47 Hispanic/Latino; 12 Two or more races, non-Hispanic/Latino), 100 international. Average age 34. 761 applicants, 51% accepted, 200 enrolled. In 2013, 186 master's, 31 doctorates, 22 other advanced degrees awarded. Terminal master's awarded for partial completion of doctoral program. *Degree requirements:* For doctorate, comprehensive exam, thesis/dissertation. *Entrance requirements:* Additional exam requirements/recommendations

for international students: Required—TOEFL (minimum score 550 paper-based; 80 iBT), IELTS (minimum score 6.5). *Application deadline:* For fall admission, 1/15 for domestic and international students. Applications are processed on a rolling basis. Application fee: $75. Electronic applications accepted. *Financial support:* Fellowships with full and partial tuition reimbursements, research assistantships with full and partial tuition reimbursements, teaching assistantships with full and partial tuition reimbursements, career-related internships or fieldwork, Federal Work-Study, scholarships/grants, traineeships, health care benefits, tuition waivers (full and partial), and unspecified assistantships available. Support available to part-time students. Financial award application deadline: 1/15; financial award applicants required to submit FAFSA. *Unit head:* Dr. Linda L. Griffin, Graduate Program Director, 413-545-6984, Fax: 413-545-1523. *Application contact:* Lindsay DeSantis, Supervisor of Admissions, 413-545-0722, Fax: 413-577-0010, E-mail: gradadm@grad.umass.edu.
Website: http://www.umass.edu/education/.

University of Massachusetts Boston, Office of Graduate Studies, Graduate College of Education, Counseling and School Psychology Department, Program in School Guidance Counseling, Boston, MA 02125-3393. Offers M Ed, CAGS.

University of Memphis, Graduate School, College of Education, Department of Counseling, Educational Psychology and Research, Memphis, TN 38152. Offers counseling (MS, Ed D), including community counseling (MS), rehabilitation counseling (MS), school counseling (MS); counseling psychology (PhD); educational psychology and research (MS, PhD), including educational psychology, educational research. *Accreditation:* ACA (one or more programs are accredited); APA (one or more programs are accredited); CORE (one or more programs are accredited); NCATE. *Faculty:* 27 full-time (13 women), 12 part-time/adjunct (9 women). *Students:* 137 full-time (105 women), 97 part-time (74 women); includes 60 minority (44 Black or African American, non-Hispanic/Latino; 1 American Indian or Alaska Native, non-Hispanic/Latino; 7 Hispanic/Latino; 8 Two or more races, non-Hispanic/Latino), 9 international. Average age 32. 129 applicants, 50% accepted, 30 enrolled. In 2013, 46 master's, 14 doctorates awarded. *Degree requirements:* For master's, comprehensive exam, thesis or alternative; for doctorate, comprehensive exam, thesis/dissertation. *Entrance requirements:* For master's, GRE General Test or MAT, minimum GPA of 2.5; for doctorate, GRE General Test. *Application deadline:* For fall admission, 10/1 for domestic students; for spring admission, 4/1 for domestic students. Application fee: $35 ($60 for international students). *Financial support:* In 2013–14, 130 students received support. Fellowships with full tuition reimbursements available, research assistantships with full tuition reimbursements available, teaching assistantships with full tuition reimbursements available, career-related internships or fieldwork, Federal Work-Study, scholarships/grants, and unspecified assistantships available. Financial award application deadline: 2/15; financial award applicants required to submit FAFSA. *Faculty research:* Anger management, aging and disability, supervision, multicultural counseling. *Unit head:* Dr. Douglas C. Strohmer, Chair, 901-678-2841, Fax: 901-678-5114. *Application contact:* Dr. Ernest A. Rakow, Associate Dean of Administration and Graduate Programs, 901-678-2399, Fax: 901-678-4778.
Website: http://coe.memphis.edu/cepr/.

University of Miami, Graduate School, School of Education and Human Development, Department of Educational and Psychological Studies, Program in Counseling, Coral Gables, FL 33124. Offers counseling and research (MS Ed); Latino mental health (Certificate); marriage and family therapy (MS Ed); mental health counseling (MS Ed). Part-time and evening/weekend programs available. *Faculty:* 6 full-time (2 women). *Students:* 37 full-time (35 women), 4 part-time (all women); includes 21 minority (4 Black or African American, non-Hispanic/Latino; 2 Asian, non-Hispanic/Latino; 14 Hispanic/Latino; 1 Native Hawaiian or other Pacific Islander, non-Hispanic/Latino), 2 international. Average age 26. 91 applicants, 18% accepted, 16 enrolled. In 2013, 19 master's awarded. *Degree requirements:* For master's, comprehensive exam, personal growth experience. *Entrance requirements:* For master's, GRE General Test. Additional exam requirements/recommendations for international students: Required—TOEFL (minimum score 550 paper-based; 80 iBT); Recommended—IELTS (minimum score 6.5). *Application deadline:* For fall admission, 2/1 for domestic students. Application fee: $65. Electronic applications accepted. *Financial support:* In 2013–14, 10 students received support. Career-related internships or fieldwork and institutionally sponsored loans available. Support available to part-time students. Financial award application deadline: 3/1; financial award applicants required to submit FAFSA. *Faculty research:* Cocaine recidivism, HIV, non-traditional families, health psychology, diversity. *Unit head:* Dr. Anabel Bejarano, Clinical Assistant Professor and Program Director, 305-284-4829, Fax: 305-284-3003, E-mail: bejarano@miami.edu. *Application contact:* Lois Heffernan, Graduate Admissions Coordinator, 305-284-2167, Fax: 305-284-9395, E-mail: lheffernan@miami.edu.
Website: http://www.education.miami.edu/career/graduate.asp.

University of Minnesota, Twin Cities Campus, Graduate School, College of Education and Human Development, Department of Educational Psychology, Program in Counseling and Student Personnel Psychology, Minneapolis, MN 55455-0213. Offers MA, PhD, Ed S. *Students:* 90 full-time (72 women), 13 part-time (9 women); includes 20 minority (5 Black or African American, non-Hispanic/Latino; 2 American Indian or Alaska Native, non-Hispanic/Latino; 6 Asian, non-Hispanic/Latino; 7 Hispanic/Latino), 15 international. Average age 28. 134 applicants, 56% accepted, 37 enrolled. In 2013, 31 master's, 6 doctorates awarded. Application fee: $75 ($95 for international students). *Unit head:* Geoff Maruyama, Chair, 612-624-1003, Fax: 612-625-5861, E-mail: geoff@umn.edu. *Application contact:* Dr. Jennifer Engler, Assistant Dean, 612-626-2887, Fax: 612-626-7496, E-mail: engle009@umn.edu.
Website: http://www.cehd.umn.edu/EdPsych/CSPP.

University of Mississippi, Graduate School, School of Education, Department of Leadership and Counselor Education, Oxford, MS 38677. Offers counselor education (M Ed, PhD); educational leadership (M Ed, PhD, Ed S); higher education/student personnel (MA, PhD); play therapy (Ed S). *Accreditation:* ACA; NCATE. *Faculty:* 13 full-time (6 women), 9 part-time/adjunct (6 women). *Students:* 155 full-time (123 women), 181 part-time (127 women); includes 136 minority (116 Black or African American, non-Hispanic/Latino; 3 American Indian or Alaska Native, non-Hispanic/Latino; 8 Hispanic/Latino; 9 Two or more races, non-Hispanic/Latino), 6 international. In 2013, 104 master's, 9 doctorates awarded. *Degree requirements:* For doctorate, thesis/dissertation. *Entrance requirements:* For master's, GRE General Test, minimum GPA of 3.0; for doctorate, GRE General Test. Additional exam requirements/recommendations for international students: Required—TOEFL. *Application deadline:* For fall admission, 4/1 for domestic students; for spring admission, 10/1 for domestic students. Applications are processed on a rolling basis. Application fee: $40. Electronic applications accepted. *Financial support:* Scholarships/grants available. Financial award application deadline: 3/1; financial award applicants required to submit FAFSA. *Unit head:* Dr. Timothy Letzring, Chair, 662-915-7069, Fax: 662-915-7230. *Application contact:* Dr. Christy M. Wyandt, Associate Dean, 662-915-7474, Fax: 662-915-7577, E-mail: cwyandt@olemiss.edu.
Website: http://education.olemiss.edu/dco/leadership_counselor_education.html.

University of Missouri–Kansas City, School of Education, Kansas City, MO 64110-2499. Offers administration (Ed D); counseling and guidance (MA, Ed S), including mental health counseling (Ed S), school counseling (Ed S); counseling psychology (PhD); curriculum and instruction (MA, Ed S), including language and literacy (Ed S); education (PhD), including higher education administration, PK-12 education administration; educational administration (MA, Ed S), including advanced principal (Ed S), beginning principal (Ed S), district-level administration (Ed S); reading education (MA, Ed S); special education (MA). PhD in education offered through the School of Graduate Studies. *Accreditation:* NCATE. Part-time and evening/weekend programs available. *Faculty:* 44 full-time (34 women), 60 part-time/adjunct (45 women). *Students:* 206 full-time (145 women), 394 part-time (291 women); includes 154 minority (99 Black or African American, non-Hispanic/Latino; 13 Asian, non-Hispanic/Latino; 30 Hispanic/Latino; 1 Native Hawaiian or other Pacific Islander, non-Hispanic/Latino; 11 Two or more races, non-Hispanic/Latino), 16 international. Average age 32. 401 applicants, 48% accepted, 188 enrolled. In 2013, 156 master's, 9 doctorates, 24 other advanced degrees awarded. *Degree requirements:* For doctorate, thesis/dissertation, internship, practicum. *Entrance requirements:* For master's, GRE, minimum GPA of 2.75, 2 letters of reference, written statement of purpose; for doctorate, GRE, minimum GPA of 3.0; for Ed S, minimum GPA of 3.0. Additional exam requirements/recommendations for international students: Required—TOEFL (minimum score 550 paper-based; 80 iBT). *Application deadline:* For fall admission, 4/1 priority date for domestic and international students; for spring admission, 11/1 priority date for domestic and international students. Applications are processed on a rolling basis. Application fee: $45 ($50 for international students). *Expenses:* Tuition, state resident: full-time $6073; part-time $337.40 per credit hour. Tuition, nonresident: full-time $15,680; part-time $871.10 per credit hour. *Required fees:* $97.59 per credit hour. Full-time tuition and fees vary according to program. *Financial support:* In 2013–14, 12 research assistantships with partial tuition reimbursements (averaging $11,140 per year) were awarded; career-related internships or fieldwork, Federal Work-Study, institutionally sponsored loans, and tuition waivers (full and partial) also available. Support available to part-time students. Financial award application deadline: 3/1; financial award applicants required to submit FAFSA. *Faculty research:* Urban education, inquiry-based field study, theories of counseling and psychotherapy, school literacy, educational technology. *Unit head:* Dr. Wanda Blanchett, Dean, 816-235-2234, Fax: 816-235-5270, E-mail: education@umkc.edu. *Application contact:* Erica Hernandez-Scott, Student Recruiter, 816-235-1295, Fax: 816-235-5270, E-mail: hernandeze@umkc.edu.
Website: http://education.umkc.edu.

University of Missouri–St. Louis, College of Education, Division of Counseling, St. Louis, MO 63121. Offers clinical mental health counseling (M Ed); elementary school counseling (M Ed); secondary school counseling (M Ed). *Accreditation:* ACA; NCATE. Part-time and evening/weekend programs available. *Faculty:* 6 full-time (3 women), 19 part-time/adjunct (13 women). *Students:* 65 full-time (53 women), 131 part-time (108 women); includes 46 minority (32 Black or African American, non-Hispanic/Latino; 1 American Indian or Alaska Native, non-Hispanic/Latino; 3 Asian, non-Hispanic/Latino; 6 Hispanic/Latino; 4 Two or more races, non-Hispanic/Latino), 2 international. Average age 32. 73 applicants, 73% accepted, 37 enrolled. In 2013, 54 master's awarded. *Degree requirements:* For master's, comprehensive exam. *Entrance requirements:* For master's, 3 letters of recommendation. Additional exam requirements/recommendations for international students: Recommended—TOEFL (minimum score 550 paper-based; 79 iBT), IELTS (minimum score 6.5). *Application deadline:* For fall admission, 6/1 for domestic and international students; for spring admission, 10/1 for domestic and international students. Application fee: $50 ($40 for international students). Electronic applications accepted. *Expenses:* Tuition, state resident: full-time $7364; part-time $409.10 per credit hour. Tuition, nonresident: full-time $19,162; part-time $1008.50 per credit hour. *Financial support:* In 2013–14, 1 research assistantship with full and partial tuition reimbursement (averaging $12,500 per year), 2 teaching assistantships with full and partial tuition reimbursements (averaging $8,470 per year) were awarded. Financial award application deadline: 4/1; financial award applicants required to submit FAFSA. *Faculty research:* Vocational interests, self-concept, decision-making factors, developmental differences. *Unit head:* Dr. Mark Pope, Chair, 314-516-5782. *Application contact:* 314-516-5458, Fax: 314-516-6996, E-mail: gradadm@umsl.edu.

University of Missouri–St. Louis, College of Education, Interdisciplinary Doctoral Programs, St. Louis, MO 63121. Offers adult and higher education (Ed D); counseling (PhD); counselor education (Ed D); educational administration (Ed D); educational leadership and policy studies (PhD); educational psychology (PhD); teaching-learning processes (Ed D, PhD). *Faculty:* 72 full-time (33 women). *Students:* 58 full-time (46 women), 240 part-time (154 women); includes 106 minority (86 Black or African American, non-Hispanic/Latino; 4 American Indian or Alaska Native, non-Hispanic/Latino; 6 Asian, non-Hispanic/Latino; 8 Hispanic/Latino; 2 Two or more races, non-Hispanic/Latino), 9 international. Average age 42. 67 applicants, 58% accepted, 24 enrolled. In 2013, 24 doctorates awarded. *Degree requirements:* For doctorate, thesis/dissertation. *Entrance requirements:* For doctorate, GRE General Test, 3 letters of recommendation; personal interview. Additional exam requirements/recommendations for international students: Recommended—TOEFL (minimum score 550 paper-based; 79 iBT), IELTS (minimum score 6.5). *Application deadline:* For fall admission, 3/1 for domestic and international students; for spring admission, 10/1 for domestic and international students. Application fee: $50 ($40 for international students). Electronic applications accepted. *Expenses:* Tuition, state resident: full-time $7364; part-time $409.10 per credit hour. Tuition, nonresident: full-time $19,162; part-time $1008.50 per credit hour. *Financial support:* In 2013–14, 13 research assistantships (averaging $12,240 per year), 9 teaching assistantships (averaging $12,240 per year) were awarded. Financial award application deadline: 4/1; financial award applicants required to submit FAFSA. *Faculty research:* Higher education law and policy, gender and higher education, student retention, lifelong learning orientation, school counselor's role in violence prevention. *Unit head:* Dr. Kathleen Haywood, Director of Graduate Studies, 314-516-5483, Fax: 314-516-5227, E-mail: kathleen_haywood@umsl.edu. *Application contact:* 314-516-5458, Fax: 314-516-6996, E-mail: gradadm@umsl.edu.

The University of Montana, Graduate School, Phyllis J. Washington College of Education and Human Sciences, Department of Educational Leadership and Counseling, Program in Counselor Education, Missoula, MT 59812-0002. Offers counselor education (Ed S); counselor education and supervision (Ed D); mental health counseling (MA); school counseling (MA). *Accreditation:* ACA. *Degree requirements:* For doctorate, thesis/dissertation. *Entrance requirements:* For master's, doctorate, and Ed S, GRE General Test. Additional exam requirements/recommendations for international students: Required—TOEFL.

University of Montevallo, College of Education, Program in Counseling, Montevallo, AL 35115. Offers community counseling (M Ed); couple, marriage and family (M Ed); school counseling (M Ed). *Accreditation:* ACA; NCATE. Part-time and evening/weekend programs available. *Students:* 41 full-time (34 women), 42 part-time (37 women); includes 20 minority (16 Black or African American, non-Hispanic/Latino; 2 Hispanic/Latino; 2 Two or more races, non-Hispanic/Latino). In 2013, 11 master's awarded. *Entrance requirements:* For master's, GRE General Test or MAT, minimum undergraduate GPA of 2.75 in last 60 hours or 2.5 overall, interview. Additional exam requirements/recommendations for international students: Required—TOEFL (minimum score 550 paper-based). *Application deadline:* For fall admission, 7/15 for domestic students; for spring admission, 11/15 for domestic students. Application fee: $25.

Financial support: Federal Work-Study, scholarships/grants, and unspecified assistantships available. *Unit head:* Dr. Charlotte Daughhetee, Chair, 205-665-6358, E-mail: daughc@montevallo.edu. *Application contact:* Kevin Thornthwaite, Director, Graduate Admissions and Records, 205-665-6350, E-mail: graduate@montevallo.edu.
Website: http://www.montevallo.edu/education/college-of-education/traditional-masters-degrees/counseling/.

University of Nebraska at Kearney, Graduate Programs, College of Education, Department of Counseling and School Psychology, Kearney, NE 68849-0001. Offers clinical mental health counseling (MS Ed); school counseling (MS Ed), including elementary, secondary, student affairs; school psychology (Ed S). *Accreditation:* ACA; NCATE. Part-time and evening/weekend programs available. *Degree requirements:* For master's, thesis optional; for Ed S, thesis. *Entrance requirements:* For master's and Ed S, personal statement, recommendations, resume, interview. Additional exam requirements/recommendations for international students: Required—TOEFL (minimum score: 550 paper-based, 79 iBT) or IELTS (6.5). Electronic applications accepted. *Faculty research:* Multicultural counseling and diversity issues, team decision-making, adult development, women's issues, brief therapy.

University of Nebraska at Omaha, Graduate Studies, College of Education, Department of Counseling, Omaha, NE 68182. Offers MA, MS. *Accreditation:* ACA (one or more programs are accredited); NCATE. Part-time and evening/weekend programs available. *Faculty:* 5 full-time (2 women). *Students:* 50 full-time (30 women), 104 part-time (84 women); includes 16 minority (6 Black or African American, non-Hispanic/Latino; 1 American Indian or Alaska Native, non-Hispanic/Latino; 1 Asian, non-Hispanic/Latino; 4 Hispanic/Latino; 4 Two or more races, non-Hispanic/Latino), 2 international. Average age 31. 59 applicants, 31% accepted, 16 enrolled. In 2013, 52 master's awarded. *Degree requirements:* For master's, comprehensive exam, thesis (for some programs). *Entrance requirements:* For master's, GRE General Test, MAT, interview, minimum GPA of 3.0, 3 letters of recommendation, transcripts. Additional exam requirements/recommendations for international students: Required—TOEFL, IELTS, PTE. *Application deadline:* For fall admission, 3/1 for domestic students; for spring admission, 10/1 for domestic students; for summer admission, 3/1 for domestic students. Applications are processed on a rolling basis. Application fee: $45. Electronic applications accepted. *Financial support:* In 2013–14, 10 students received support, including 6 research assistantships with tuition reimbursements available, 4 teaching assistantships with tuition reimbursements available; fellowships, Federal Work-Study, institutionally sponsored loans, scholarships/grants, tuition waivers (partial), and unspecified assistantships also available. Support available to part-time students. Financial award application deadline: 3/1; financial award applicants required to submit FAFSA. *Unit head:* Dr. Paul Barnes, Chairperson and Graduate Program Chair, 402-554-2306, E-mail: graduate@unomaha.edu.

University of Nevada, Las Vegas, Graduate College, College of Education, Department of Educational and Clinical Studies, Las Vegas, NV 89154-3066. Offers addiction studies (Advanced Certificate); counselor education (Ed D, Ed S), including clinical mental health (Ed D), school counseling (Ed S); mental health counseling (Advanced Certificate); rehabilitation counseling (Advanced Certificate); special education (MS, Ed D, PhD, Ed S), including early childhood education (Ed D), special education (Ed D). Part-time and evening/weekend programs available. *Faculty:* 16 full-time (7 women), 17 part-time/adjunct (16 women). *Students:* 161 full-time (136 women), 184 part-time (148 women); includes 153 minority (31 Black or African American, non-Hispanic/Latino; 13 Asian, non-Hispanic/Latino; 53 Hispanic/Latino; 3 Native Hawaiian or other Pacific Islander, non-Hispanic/Latino; 53 Two or more races, non-Hispanic/Latino), 14 international. Average age 33. 140 applicants, 84% accepted, 100 enrolled. In 2013, 133 master's, 11 doctorates, 2 other advanced degrees awarded. *Degree requirements:* For master's, comprehensive exam (for some programs), thesis (for some programs); for other advanced degree, thesis (for some programs). *Entrance requirements:* Additional exam requirements/recommendations for international students: Required—TOEFL (minimum score 550 paper-based; 80 iBT), IELTS (minimum score 7). *Application deadline:* For fall admission, 2/1 for domestic students, 5/1 for international students; for spring admission, 10/1 for domestic and international students. Application fee: $60 ($95 for international students). Electronic applications accepted. *Expenses:* Tuition, state resident: full-time $4752; part-time $264 per credit. Tuition, nonresident: full-time $18,662; part-time $554.50 per credit. *International tuition:* $18,952 full-time. *Required fees:* $532; $12 per credit. $266 per semester. One-time fee: $35. Tuition and fees vary according to course load and program. *Financial support:* In 2013–14, 35 students received support, including 27 research assistantships with partial tuition reimbursements available (averaging $9,213 per year), 8 teaching assistantships with partial tuition reimbursements available (averaging $11,438 per year); institutionally sponsored loans, scholarships/grants, health care benefits, and unspecified assistantships also available. Financial award application deadline: 3/1. *Faculty research:* Multicultural issues in counseling, academic interventions for students with disabilities, rough and tumble play in early childhood, inclusive strategies for students with disabilities, addictions. *Total annual research expenditures:* $343,782. *Unit head:* Dr. Thomas Pierce, Interim Chair/Associate Professor, 702-895-1104, Fax: 702-895-5550, E-mail: tom.pierce@unlv.edu. *Application contact:* Graduate College Admissions Evaluator, 702-895-3320, Fax: 702-895-4180, E-mail: gradcollege@unlv.edu.
Website: http://education.unlv.edu/ecs/.

University of Nevada, Reno, Graduate School, College of Education, Department of Counseling and Educational Psychology, Reno, NV 89557. Offers M Ed, MA, MS, Ed D, PhD, Ed S. *Accreditation:* ACA (one or more programs are accredited); NCATE. Terminal master's awarded for partial completion of doctoral program. *Degree requirements:* For master's, comprehensive exam, thesis optional; for doctorate, comprehensive exam, thesis/dissertation, qualifying exam. *Entrance requirements:* For master's, GRE, minimum GPA of 2.75; for doctorate, GRE, minimum GPA of 3.0. Additional exam requirements/recommendations for international students: Required—TOEFL (minimum score 500 paper-based; 61 iBT), IELTS (minimum score 6). Electronic applications accepted. *Faculty research:* Marriage and family counseling, substance abuse attitudes of teachers, current supply of counseling educators, HIV-positive services for patients, family counseling for youth at risk.

University of New Hampshire, Graduate School, College of Liberal Arts, Department of Education, Program in Counseling, Durham, NH 03824. Offers M Ed. Part-time programs available. *Faculty:* 32 full-time. *Students:* 16 full-time (14 women), 15 part-time (13 women); includes 2 minority (both Asian, non-Hispanic/Latino). Average age 32. 28 applicants, 79% accepted, 10 enrolled. In 2013, 16 master's awarded. *Degree requirements:* For master's, thesis (for some programs). *Entrance requirements:* For master's, GRE General Test. Additional exam requirements/recommendations for international students: Required—TOEFL (minimum score 550 paper-based; 80 iBT). *Application deadline:* For fall admission, 2/1 priority date for domestic students, 2/1 for international students; for spring admission, 12/1 for domestic students. Applications are processed on a rolling basis. Application fee: $65. Electronic applications accepted. *Expenses:* Tuition, state resident: full-time $13,500; part-time $750 per credit hour. Tuition, nonresident: full-time $26,200; part-time $1100 per credit hour. *Required fees:* $1741; $435.25 per term. Tuition and fees vary according to course level, course load, campus/location and program. *Financial support:* In 2013–14, 5 students received support, including 2 teaching assistantships; fellowships, research assistantships, career-related internships or fieldwork, Federal Work-Study, scholarships/grants, and tuition waivers (full and partial) also available. Support available to part-time students. Financial award application deadline: 2/15. *Faculty research:* Generic approach to counseling. *Unit head:* Dr. Mike Middleton, Chair, 603-862-7054, E-mail: education.department@unh.edu. *Application contact:* Lisa Wilder, Administrative Assistant, 603-862-2381, E-mail: education.department@unh.edu.
Website: http://www.unh.edu/education.

University of New Hampshire, Graduate School Manchester Campus, Manchester, NH 03101. Offers business administration (MBA); counseling (M Ed); education (M Ed, MAT); educational administration and supervision (M Ed, Ed S); information technology (MS); management of technology (MS); public administration (MPA); public health (MPH, Certificate); social work (MSW); software systems engineering (Certificate). Part-time and evening/weekend programs available. *Students:* 2 full-time (0 women), 5 part-time (0 women), 2 international. Average age 38. 6 applicants, 17% accepted, 1 enrolled. In 2013, 1 master's awarded. *Degree requirements:* For master's, thesis or alternative. *Entrance requirements:* Additional exam requirements/recommendations for international students: Required—TOEFL (minimum score 550 paper-based; 80 iBT). *Application deadline:* For fall admission, 6/1 for domestic students, 4/1 for international students; for spring admission, 12/1 for domestic students. Applications are processed on a rolling basis. Application fee: $65. Electronic applications accepted. *Expenses:* Tuition, state resident: full-time $13,500; part-time $750 per credit hour. Tuition, nonresident: full-time $26,200; part-time $1100 per credit hour. *Required fees:* $1741; $435.25 per term. Tuition and fees vary according to course level, course load, campus/location and program. *Financial support:* Fellowships, research assistantships, teaching assistantships, Federal Work-Study, scholarships/grants, health care benefits, and unspecified assistantships available. Support available to part-time students. Financial award application deadline: 3/1; financial award applicants required to submit FAFSA. *Unit head:* Candice Brown, Director, 603-641-4313, E-mail: unhm.gradcenter@unh.edu. *Application contact:* Graduate Admissions Office, 603-862-3000, Fax: 603-862-0275, E-mail: grad.school@unh.edu.
Website: http://www.gradschool.unh.edu/manchester/.

University of New Mexico, Graduate School, College of Education, Department of Individual, Family and Community Education, Program in Counselor Education, Albuquerque, NM 87131. Offers counseling (MA); counselor education (PhD). *Accreditation:* ACA (one or more programs are accredited); NCATE. Part-time programs available. *Faculty:* 5 full-time (2 women), 2 part-time/adjunct (0 women). *Students:* 63 full-time (49 women), 39 part-time (28 women); includes 48 minority (4 Black or African American, non-Hispanic/Latino; 3 American Indian or Alaska Native, non-Hispanic/Latino; 2 Asian, non-Hispanic/Latino; 39 Hispanic/Latino), 2 international. Average age 34. 103 applicants, 35% accepted, 33 enrolled. In 2013, 24 master's, 1 doctorate awarded. *Degree requirements:* For master's, comprehensive exam; for doctorate, comprehensive exam, thesis/dissertation. *Entrance requirements:* For master's, 3 letters of recommendation, personal statement; for doctorate, GRE General Test, 3 letters of recommendation, writing sample, personal statement. Additional exam requirements/recommendations for international students: Required—TOEFL. *Application deadline:* For fall admission, 11/1 for domestic and international students; for spring admission, 9/15 for domestic and international students. Application fee: $50. Electronic applications accepted. *Financial support:* In 2013–14, 73 students received support. Unspecified assistantships available. Financial award application deadline: 3/1; financial award applicants required to submit FAFSA. *Faculty research:* Counselor education and supervision, school counseling, LGBTQQI, crisis and trauma, multiculturalism. *Unit head:* Dr. Jean Keim, Program Coordinator, 505-277-4535, Fax: 505-277-8361, E-mail: divbse@unm.edu. *Application contact:* Cynthia Salas, Department Administrator, 505-277-4535, Fax: 505-277-8361, E-mail: divbse@unm.edu.
Website: http://coe.unm.edu/departments/ifce/counselor-education.html.

University of New Orleans, Graduate School, College of Education and Human Development, Department of Educational Leadership, Counseling, and Foundations, Program in Counselor Education, New Orleans, LA 70148. Offers M Ed, PhD. *Accreditation:* ACA (one or more programs are accredited); NCATE. Evening/weekend programs available. Terminal master's awarded for partial completion of doctoral program. *Degree requirements:* For master's, thesis (for some programs); for doctorate, variable foreign language requirement, thesis/dissertation. *Entrance requirements:* For master's and doctorate, GRE General Test. Additional exam requirements/recommendations for international students: Required—TOEFL (minimum score 550 paper-based; 79 iBT). Electronic applications accepted.

University of North Alabama, College of Education, Department of Counselor Education, Florence, AL 35632-0001. Offers community counseling (MA); school counseling P-12 (MA Ed). *Accreditation:* ACA; NCATE. Part-time and evening/weekend programs available. *Faculty:* 4 full-time (3 women). *Students:* 19 full-time (16 women), 36 part-time (30 women); includes 5 minority (3 Black or African American, non-Hispanic/Latino; 1 American Indian or Alaska Native, non-Hispanic/Latino; 1 Two or more races, non-Hispanic/Latino), 2 international. Average age 34. 28 applicants, 61% accepted, 13 enrolled. In 2013, 27 master's awarded. *Degree requirements:* For master's, comprehensive exam. *Entrance requirements:* For master's, GRE, MAT, or NTE, minimum GPA of 2.5, Alabama Class B Certificate or equivalent, teaching experience. Additional exam requirements/recommendations for international students: Required—TOEFL (minimum score 550 paper-based; 79 iBT), IELTS (minimum score 6). *Application deadline:* For fall admission, 7/1 priority date for domestic students, 7/1 for international students; for spring admission, 12/1 for domestic and international students. Applications are processed on a rolling basis. Application fee: $25 ($50 for international students). Electronic applications accepted. *Expenses:* Tuition, state resident: full-time $4968; part-time $3312 per year. Tuition, nonresident: full-time $9936; part-time $6624 per year. *Required fees:* $970; $60.33 per credit. $362 per semester. *Financial support:* Federal Work-Study available. Support available to part-time students. Financial award application deadline: 4/1; financial award applicants required to submit FAFSA. *Unit head:* Dr. Paul Baird, Chair, 256-765-4763, Fax: 256-765-4159, E-mail: jpbaird@una.edu. *Application contact:* Russ Darracott, Graduate Admissions Counselor, 256-765-4447, E-mail: erdarracott@una.edu.
Website: http://www.una.edu/education/departments/counselor-education.html.

The University of North Carolina at Chapel Hill, Graduate School, School of Education, Program in School Counseling, Chapel Hill, NC 27599. Offers M Ed. *Accreditation:* ACA; NCATE. *Degree requirements:* For master's, comprehensive exam. *Entrance requirements:* For master's, GRE General Test, minimum GPA of 3.0 during last 2 years of undergraduate course work. Additional exam requirements/recommendations for international students: Required—TOEFL (minimum score 550 paper-based). Electronic applications accepted. *Faculty research:* Career counseling, development and assessment, multicultural counseling, measurement.

The University of North Carolina at Charlotte, The Graduate School, College of Education, Department of Counseling, Charlotte, NC 28223-0001. Offers counseling (MA, PhD, Graduate Certificate); play therapy (Postbaccalaureate Certificate); school counseling (MA); substance abuse counseling (Postbaccalaureate Certificate). *Accreditation:* ACA. Part-time and evening/weekend programs available.

Postbaccalaureate distance learning degree programs offered (no on-campus study). *Faculty:* 11 full-time (7 women), 4 part-time/adjunct (all women). *Students:* 114 full-time (98 women), 102 part-time (90 women); includes 55 minority (43 Black or African American, non-Hispanic/Latino; 2 American Indian or Alaska Native, non-Hispanic/Latino; 2 Asian, non-Hispanic/Latino; 6 Hispanic/Latino; 2 Two or more races, non-Hispanic/Latino), 1 international. Average age 31. 131 applicants, 82% accepted, 97 enrolled. In 2013, 60 master's, 7 doctorates, 24 other advanced degrees awarded. Terminal master's awarded for partial completion of doctoral program. *Degree requirements:* For master's, thesis; for doctorate, thesis/dissertation. *Entrance requirements:* For master's, GRE or MAT; for doctorate, GRE. Additional exam requirements/recommendations for international students: Required—TOEFL (minimum score 557 paper-based; 83 iBT). *Application deadline:* For fall admission, 12/1 for domestic and international students; for spring admission, 11/1 for domestic students, 10/1 for international students. Applications are processed on a rolling basis. Application fee: $75. Electronic applications accepted. *Expenses:* Tuition, state resident: full-time $3522. Tuition, nonresident: full-time $16,051. *Required fees:* $2585. Tuition and fees vary according to course load and program. *Financial support:* In 2013–14, 12 students received support, including 2 research assistantships (averaging $15,855 per year), 10 teaching assistantships (averaging $5,650 per year); career-related internships or fieldwork, institutionally sponsored loans, scholarships/grants, unspecified assistantships, and administrative assistantships also available. Support available to part-time students. Financial award application deadline: 4/1; financial award applicants required to submit FAFSA. *Unit head:* Dr. Henry Harris, Chair, 704-687-8971, Fax: 704-687-1636, E-mail: srfurr@uncc.edu. *Application contact:* Kathy B. Giddings, Director of Graduate Admissions, 704-687-5503, Fax: 704-687-1668, E-mail: gradadm@uncc.edu. Website: http://education.uncc.edu/counseling/.

The University of North Carolina at Greensboro, Graduate School, School of Education, Department of Counseling and Educational Development, Greensboro, NC 27412-5001. Offers advanced school counseling (PMC); counseling and counselor education (PhD); counseling and educational development (MS); couple and family counseling (PMC); school counseling (PMC); MS/Ed S. *Accreditation:* ACA (one or more programs are accredited); NCATE. *Degree requirements:* For master's, comprehensive exam, practicum, internship; for doctorate, comprehensive exam, thesis/dissertation. *Entrance requirements:* For master's, doctorate, and PMC, GRE General Test. Additional exam requirements/recommendations for international students: Required—TOEFL. Electronic applications accepted. *Faculty research:* Gerontology, invitational theory, career development, marriage and family therapy, drug and alcohol abuse prevention.

The University of North Carolina at Pembroke, Graduate Studies, School of Education, Programs in Counseling, Pembroke, NC 28372-1510. Offers clinical mental health counseling (MA Ed); professional school counseling (MA Ed). *Accreditation:* NCATE. Part-time and evening/weekend programs available. *Degree requirements:* For master's, comprehensive exam, thesis optional. *Entrance requirements:* For master's, GRE General Test or MAT, minimum GPA of 3.0 in major, 2.5 overall. Additional exam requirements/recommendations for international students: Required—TOEFL.

University of Northern Colorado, Graduate School, College of Education and Behavioral Sciences, Department of Counselor Education and Supervision, Greeley, CO 80639. Offers PhD. *Accreditation:* ACA. Part-time and evening/weekend programs available. *Degree requirements:* For doctorate, comprehensive exam, thesis/dissertation. *Entrance requirements:* For doctorate, GRE General Test. Electronic applications accepted.

University of Northern Colorado, Graduate School, College of Education and Behavioral Sciences, Program in Clinical Counseling, Greeley, CO 80639. Offers MA. Part-time programs available. Electronic applications accepted.

University of Northern Colorado, Graduate School, College of Education and Behavioral Sciences, Program in School Counseling, Greeley, CO 80639. Offers MA. *Accreditation:* ACA. Part-time programs available. Electronic applications accepted.

University of Northern Iowa, Graduate College, College of Social and Behavioral Sciences, School of Applied Human Sciences, MA Program in Counseling, Cedar Falls, IA 50614. Offers mental health counseling (MA); school counseling (MAE). *Accreditation:* ACA (one or more programs are accredited). Part-time and evening/weekend programs available. *Students:* 52 full-time (44 women), 31 part-time (22 women); includes 8 minority (5 Black or African American, non-Hispanic/Latino; 1 Asian, non-Hispanic/Latino; 2 Hispanic/Latino), 1 international. 72 applicants, 35% accepted, 23 enrolled. In 2013, 20 master's awarded. *Degree requirements:* For master's, comprehensive exam, thesis or alternative. *Entrance requirements:* For master's, minimum GPA of 3.0. Additional exam requirements/recommendations for international students: Required—TOEFL (minimum score 500 paper-based; 61 iBT). *Application deadline:* For fall admission, 8/1 priority date for domestic students. Applications are processed on a rolling basis. Application fee: $50 ($70 for international students). Electronic applications accepted. *Financial support:* Career-related internships or fieldwork, Federal Work-Study, and tuition waivers (full and partial) available. Support available to part-time students. Financial award application deadline: 2/1. *Unit head:* Dr. Robert Swazo, Coordinator, 319-273-2675, Fax: 319-273-5175, E-mail: roberto.swazo@uni.edu. *Application contact:* Laurie S. Russell, Record Analyst, 319-273-2623, Fax: 319-273-2885, E-mail: laurie.russell@uni.edu. Website: http://www.uni.edu/csbs/sahs/counseling.

University of North Florida, College of Education and Human Services, Department of Leadership, School Counseling and Sport Management, Jacksonville, FL 32224. Offers counselor education (M Ed), including school counseling; educational leadership (M Ed, Ed D), including athletic administration (M Ed), educational leadership, educational technology (M Ed), instructional leadership (M Ed). Part-time and evening/weekend programs available. *Faculty:* 16 full-time (8 women), 1 (woman) part-time/adjunct. *Students:* 76 full-time (59 women), 212 part-time (153 women); includes 91 minority (65 Black or African American, non-Hispanic/Latino; 1 American Indian or Alaska Native, non-Hispanic/Latino; 3 Asian, non-Hispanic/Latino; 13 Hispanic/Latino; 1 Native Hawaiian or other Pacific Islander, non-Hispanic/Latino; 8 Two or more races, non-Hispanic/Latino), 6 international. Average age 35. 151 applicants, 60% accepted, 71 enrolled. In 2013, 59 master's, 12 doctorates awarded. *Degree requirements:* For doctorate, thesis/dissertation. *Entrance requirements:* For master's, GRE General Test, minimum GPA of 3.0 in last 60 hours, interview, 3 letters of recommendation; for doctorate, GRE General Test, master's degree, interview, 3 letters of recommendation, writing sample. Additional exam requirements/recommendations for international students: Required—TOEFL (minimum score 500 paper-based). *Application deadline:* For fall admission, 7/1 priority date for domestic students, 5/1 for international students; for spring admission, 11/1 priority date for domestic students, 10/1 for international students. Application fee: $30. Electronic applications accepted. *Expenses:* Tuition, state resident: full-time $9794; part-time $408.10 per credit hour. Tuition, nonresident: full-time $22,383; part-time $932.61 per credit hour. *Required fees:* $2020; $84.20 per credit hour. Tuition and fees vary according to course load and program. *Financial support:* In 2013–14, 49 students received support, including 8 research assistantships (averaging $2,573 per year); teaching assistantships, career-related internships or fieldwork, Federal Work-Study, scholarships/grants, tuition waivers (partial), and

unspecified assistantships also available. Support available to part-time students. Financial award application deadline: 4/1; financial award applicants required to submit FAFSA. *Faculty research:* Counseling: ethics; lesbian, bisexual and transgender issues; educational leadership: school culture and climate; educational assessment and accountability; school safety and student discipline. *Total annual research expenditures:* $128,099. *Unit head:* Dr. Jennifer Kane, Chair, 904-620-2465, E-mail: jkane@unf.edu. *Application contact:* Dr. Amanda Pascale, Director, The Graduate School, 904-620-1360, Fax: 904-620-1362, E-mail: graduateschool@unf.edu. Website: http://www.unf.edu/coehs/lscsm/.

University of North Texas, Robert B. Toulouse School of Graduate Studies, Denton, TN 76203-5017. Offers accounting (MS, PhD); applied anthropology (MA, MS); applied behavior analysis (Certificate); applied technology and performance improvement (M Ed, MS, PhD); art education (MA, PhD); art history (MA); art museum education (Certificate); arts leadership (Certificate); audiology (Au D); behavior analysis (MS); biochemistry and molecular biology (MS, PhD); biology (MA, MS, PhD); business (PhD); business computer information systems (PhD); chemistry (MS, PhD); clinical psychology (PhD); communication studies (MA, MS); computer engineering (MS); computer science (MS); computer science and engineering (PhD); counseling (M Ed, MS, PhD), including clinical mental health counseling (MS), college and university counseling (M Ed, MS), elementary school counseling (M Ed, MS), secondary school counseling (M Ed, MS); counseling psychology (PhD); creative writing (MA); criminal justice (MS); curriculum and instruction (M Ed, PhD), including curriculum studies (PhD), early childhood studies (PhD), language and literacy studies (PhD); decision sciences (MBA); design (MA, MFA), including fashion design (MFA), innovation studies, interior design (MFA); early childhood studies (MS); economics (MS); educational leadership (M Ed, Ed D, PhD); educational psychology (MS), including family studies, gifted and talented (MS, PhD), human development, learning and cognition, research, measurement and evaluation; educational research (PhD), including gifted and talented (MS, PhD), human development and family studies, psychological aspects of sports and exercise, research, measurement and statistics; electrical engineering (MS); emergency management (MPA); engineering systems (MS); English (MA, PhD); environmental science (MS, PhD); experimental psychology (PhD); finance (MBA, MS, PhD); financial management (MPA); French (MA); health psychology and behavioral medicine (PhD); health services management (MBA); higher education (M Ed, Ed D, PhD); history (MA, MS, PhD), including European history (PhD), military history (PhD), United States history (PhD); hospitality management (MS); human resources management (MPA); information science (MS, PhD); information technologies (MBA); information technology and decision sciences (MS); interdisciplinary studies (MA, MS); international sustainable tourism (MS); jazz studies (MM); journalism (MA, MJ, Graduate Certificate), including interactive and virtual digital communication (Graduate Certificate), narrative journalism (Graduate Certificate), public relations (Graduate Certificate); kinesiology (MS); learning technologies (MS, PhD); library science (MS); local government management (MPA); logistics and supply chain management (MBA, PhD); long-term care, senior housing, and aging services (MA, MS); management science (PhD); marketing (MBA, PhD); materials science and engineering (MS, PhD); mathematics (MA, PhD); merchandising (MS); music (MA, MM Ed, PhD), including ethnomusicology (MA), music education (MM Ed, PhD), music theory (MA, PhD), musicology (MA, PhD), performance (MA); nonprofit management (MPA); operations and supply chain management (MBA); performance (MM, DMA); philosophy (MA, PhD); physics (MS, PhD); political science (MA, MS, PhD); public administration and management (PhD), including emergency management, nonprofit management, public financial management, urban management; radio, television and film (MA, MFA); recreation, event and sport management (MS); rehabilitation counseling (MS, Certificate); sociology (MA, MS, PhD); Spanish (MA); special education (M Ed, PhD), including autism intervention (PhD), emotional/behavioral disorders (PhD), mild/moderate disabilities (PhD); speech-language pathology (MA, MS); strategic management (MBA); studio art (MFA); taxation (MS); teaching (M Ed); MBA/MS; MS/MPH; MSES/MBA. Part-time and evening/weekend programs available. Postbaccalaureate distance learning degree programs offered. *Faculty:* 661 full-time (213 women), 240 part-time/adjunct (144 women). *Students:* 3,106 full-time (1,620 women), 3,543 part-time (2,221 women); includes 1,740 minority (533 Black or African American, non-Hispanic/Latino; 15 American Indian or Alaska Native, non-Hispanic/Latino; 286 Asian, non-Hispanic/Latino; 746 Hispanic/Latino; 3 Native Hawaiian or other Pacific Islander, non-Hispanic/Latino; 157 Two or more races, non-Hispanic/Latino), 1,145 international. Average age 32. 6,289 applicants, 43% accepted, 1751 enrolled. In 2013, 1,778 master's, 239 doctorates, 10 other advanced degrees awarded. Terminal master's awarded for partial completion of doctoral program. *Degree requirements:* For master's, variable foreign language requirement, comprehensive exam (for some programs), thesis (for some programs); for doctorate, variable foreign language requirement, comprehensive exam (for some programs), thesis/dissertation; for other advanced degree, variable foreign language requirement, comprehensive exam (for some programs). *Entrance requirements:* For master's and doctorate, GRE, GMAT. Additional exam requirements/recommendations for international students: Required—TOEFL (minimum score 550 paper-based; 79 iBT). *Application deadline:* For fall admission, 7/15 for domestic students, 3/15 for international students; for spring admission, 11/15 for domestic students, 9/15 for international students; for summer admission, 5/1 for domestic students. Applications are processed on a rolling basis. Application fee: $60. Electronic applications accepted. *Financial support:* Fellowships with partial tuition reimbursements, research assistantships with partial tuition reimbursements, teaching assistantships, career-related internships or fieldwork, Federal Work-Study, institutionally sponsored loans, scholarships/grants, health care benefits, and library assistantships available. Support available to part-time students. Financial award applicants required to submit FAFSA. *Unit head:* Mark Wardell, Dean, 940-565-2383, E-mail: mark.wardell@unt.edu. *Application contact:* Toulouse School of Graduate Studies, 940-565-2383, Fax: 940-565-2141, E-mail: gradsch@unt.edu. Website: http://tsgs.unt.edu/.

University of Phoenix–Las Vegas Campus, College of Human Services, Las Vegas, NV 89135. Offers marriage, family, and child therapy (MSC); mental health counseling (MSC); school counseling (MSC). Postbaccalaureate distance learning degree programs offered. *Entrance requirements:* For master's, minimum undergraduate GPA of 2.5, 3 years of work experience. Additional exam requirements/recommendations for international students: Required—TOEFL (minimum score 550 paper-based; 79 iBT). Electronic applications accepted.

University of Phoenix–New Mexico Campus, College of Education, Albuquerque, NM 87113-1570. Offers administration and supervision (MAEd); curriculum and instruction (MAEd); elementary teacher education (MAEd); school counseling (MSC); secondary teacher education (MAEd). Evening/weekend programs available. *Degree requirements:* For master's, thesis (for some programs). *Entrance requirements:* For master's, minimum undergraduate GPA of 2.5, 3 years of work experience. Additional exam requirements/recommendations for international students: Required—TOEFL (minimum score 550 paper-based; 79 iBT). Electronic applications accepted.

University of Phoenix–Phoenix Campus, College of Social Sciences, Tempe, AZ 85282-2371. Offers counseling (MS), including clinical mental health counseling, community counseling, counseling, marriage, family and child therapy; psychology (MS).

Evening/weekend programs available. Postbaccalaureate distance learning degree programs offered. *Entrance requirements:* Additional exam requirements/recommendations for international students: Required—TOEFL, TOEIC (Test of English as an International Communication), Berlitz Online English Proficiency Exam, PTE, or IELTS. Electronic applications accepted. *Expenses:* Contact institution.

University of Phoenix–Southern Arizona Campus, College of Education, Tucson, AZ 85711. Offers administration and supervision (MA Ed); adult education and training (MA Ed); curriculum instruction (MA Ed); educational counseling (MA Ed); elementary teacher education (MA Ed); school counseling (MSC); secondary teacher education (MA Ed); special education (MA Ed, Certificate). Evening/weekend programs available. *Degree requirements:* For master's, thesis (for some programs). *Entrance requirements:* For master's, minimum undergraduate GPA of 2.5, 3 years of work experience. Additional exam requirements/recommendations for international students: Required—TOEFL (minimum score 550 paper-based; 79 iBT). Electronic applications accepted.

University of Phoenix–Southern California Campus, College of Social Sciences, Costa Mesa, CA 92626. Offers counseling (MS), including counseling, marriage, family and child therapy; psychology (MS), including behavioral health. Evening/weekend programs available. Postbaccalaureate distance learning degree programs offered. *Entrance requirements:* Additional exam requirements/recommendations for international students: Required—TOEFL, TOEIC (Test of English as an International Communication), Berlitz Online English Proficiency Exam, PTE, or IELTS. Electronic applications accepted. *Expenses:* Contact institution.

University of Puerto Rico, Río Piedras Campus, College of Education, Program in Guidance and Counseling, San Juan, PR 00931-3300. Offers M Ed, Ed D. Part-time programs available. *Degree requirements:* For master's, thesis; for doctorate, thesis/dissertation, internship. *Entrance requirements:* For master's, PAEG or GRE, interview, minimum GPA of 3.0, letter of recommendation; for doctorate, GRE or PAEG, master's degree, minimum GPA of 3.0, letter of recommendation (2), interview.

University of Puget Sound, Graduate Studies, School of Education, Program in Counseling, Tacoma, WA 98416. Offers learning, teaching, and leadership (M Ed); mental health counseling (M Ed); school counseling (M Ed). Part-time programs available. *Degree requirements:* For master's, capstone course. *Entrance requirements:* For master's, GRE General Test, minimum baccalaureate GPA of 3.0. Additional exam requirements/recommendations for international students: Required—TOEFL (minimum score 550 paper-based; 90 iBT). Electronic applications accepted. *Expenses:* Contact institution. *Faculty research:* Cross-role professional preparation, suicide prevention.

University of Rochester, Margaret Warner Graduate School of Education and Human Development, Doctoral Programs in Education, Rochester, NY 14627. Offers counseling (Ed D); educational administration (Ed D); educational policy and theory (PhD); higher education (PhD); human development in educational context (PhD); teaching, curriculum, and change (PhD). *Expenses: Tuition:* Full-time $44,580; part-time $1394 per credit hour. *Required fees:* $492.

University of Rochester, Margaret Warner Graduate School of Education and Human Development, Master's Program in Counseling, Rochester, NY 14627. Offers school and community counseling (MS); school counseling (MS). *Expenses: Tuition:* Full-time $44,580; part-time $1394 per credit hour. *Required fees:* $492.

University of Saint Francis, Graduate School, Department of Psychology and Counseling, Fort Wayne, IN 46808-3994. Offers clinical mental health counseling (MS, Post Master's Certificate); pastoral counseling (MS, Post Master's Certificate); psychology (MS); rehabilitation counseling (MS, Post Master's Certificate); school counseling (MS Ed). Part-time and evening/weekend programs available. *Faculty:* 4. *Students:* 38 full-time (32 women), 23 part-time (18 women); includes 14 minority (10 Black or African American, non-Hispanic/Latino; 3 Hispanic/Latino; 1 Two or more races, non-Hispanic/Latino), 1 international. Average age 34. 20 applicants, 100% accepted, 20 enrolled. In 2013, 20 master's, 1 other advanced degree awarded. *Application deadline:* For fall admission, 7/1 priority date for domestic students; for spring admission, 11/1 priority date for domestic students. Applications are processed on a rolling basis. Application fee: $20. Application fee is waived when completed online. *Financial support:* Federal Work-Study, scholarships/grants, and unspecified assistantships available. Support available to part-time students. Financial award application deadline: 3/10. *Unit head:* Dr. John Brinkman, Associate Professor/Chair in the Department of Psychology and Counseling, 260-399-7700 Ext. 8425, Fax: 260-399-8170, E-mail: jbrinkman@sf.edu. *Application contact:* James Cashdollar, Admissions Counselor, 260-399-7700 Ext. 6302, Fax: 260-399-8152, E-mail: jcashdollar@sf.edu.
Website: http://www.sf.edu/sf/psychology.

University of Saint Joseph, Department of Counselor Education, West Hartford, CT 06117-2700. Offers clinical mental health counseling (MA); school counseling (MA). Part-time and evening/weekend programs available. *Degree requirements:* For master's, comprehensive exam, thesis optional. *Entrance requirements:* For master's, 2 letters of recommendation. Electronic applications accepted. Application fee is waived when completed online.

University of St. Thomas, School of Education, Houston, TX 77006-4696. Offers all level education (M Ed); bilingual/dual language (M Ed); Catholic school teaching (M Ed); Catholic/private school leadership (M Ed); counselor education (M Ed); curriculum and instruction (M Ed); educational leadership (M Ed); elementary teaching (M Ed); English as a second language (M Ed); exceptionality/educational diagnostician (M Ed); exceptionality/special education (M Ed); generalist (M Ed); reading (M Ed); secondary teaching (M Ed). *Accreditation:* Teacher Education Accreditation Council. Part-time and evening/weekend programs available. Postbaccalaureate distance learning degree programs offered (no on-campus study). *Faculty:* 40 full-time (26 women), 43 part-time/adjunct (31 women). *Students:* 27 full-time (20 women), 1,091 part-time (981 women); includes 691 minority (247 Black or African American, non-Hispanic/Latino; 1 American Indian or Alaska Native, non-Hispanic/Latino; 44 Asian, non-Hispanic/Latino; 379 Hispanic/Latino; 2 Native Hawaiian or other Pacific Islander, non-Hispanic/Latino; 18 Two or more races, non-Hispanic/Latino), 28 international. Average age 36. 858 applicants, 83% accepted, 458 enrolled. In 2013, 454 master's awarded. *Degree requirements:* For master's, thesis, field experience. *Entrance requirements:* For master's, GRE or MAT if GPA is below 3.0, bachelor's degree; minimum GPA of 2.75 in bachelor's degree or last 60 credit hours; official transcripts from all institutions; goal statement of 250-300 words; 1 reference. Additional exam requirements/recommendations for international students: Required—TOEFL. *Application deadline:* Applications are processed on a rolling basis. Application fee: $35. Electronic applications accepted. *Expenses:* Contact institution. *Financial support:* In 2013–14, 41 students received support. Federal Work-Study, scholarships/grants, and state work-study, institutional employment available. Support available to part-time students. Financial award application deadline: 4/15; financial award applicants required to submit FAFSA. *Faculty research:* Leadership, diversity, personality traits, second language acquisition. *Unit head:* Dr. Robert LeBlanc, Dean, 713-525-3540, Fax: 713-525-3871, E-mail: education@stthom.edu. *Application contact:* Rita Paredes, Administrative Assistant, 713-525-3442, Fax: 713-525-3871, E-mail: rparede@stthom.edu.
Website: http://www.stthom.edu/Academics/School_of_Education/Index.aqf.

University of San Diego, School of Leadership and Education Sciences, School, Family, and Mental Health Professions Programs, San Diego, CA 92110-2492. Offers clinical mental health counseling (MA); marital and family therapy (MA); school counseling (MA). *Accreditation:* ACA. Part-time and evening/weekend programs available. *Faculty:* 11 full-time (6 women), 25 part-time/adjunct (17 women). *Students:* 162 full-time (142 women), 24 part-time (23 women); includes 115 minority (17 Black or African American, non-Hispanic/Latino; 34 Asian, non-Hispanic/Latino; 56 Hispanic/Latino; 8 Two or more races, non-Hispanic/Latino), 14 international. Average age 26. 346 applicants, 51% accepted, 85 enrolled. In 2013, 63 master's awarded. *Degree requirements:* For master's, comprehensive exam, international experience. *Entrance requirements:* For master's, minimum GPA of 3.0, interview with faculty member. Additional exam requirements/recommendations for international students: Required—TOEFL (minimum score 580 paper-based; 83 iBT), TWE. *Application deadline:* For fall admission, 2/21 for domestic students, 2/22 for international students. Applications are processed on a rolling basis. Application fee: $45. Electronic applications accepted. *Expenses: Tuition:* Full-time $23,580; part-time $1310 per credit. *Required fees:* $350. *Financial support:* In 2013–14, 152 students received support. Career-related internships or fieldwork, Federal Work-Study, institutionally sponsored loans, unspecified assistantships, and stipends available. Support available to part-time students. Financial award application deadline: 4/1; financial award applicants required to submit FAFSA. *Faculty research:* Action research, collaboration between family therapists and medical professionals, family therapy training and supervision, multicultural counseling, school counseling. *Unit head:* Dr. Ann Garland, Director, 619-260-7879, E-mail: agarland@sandiego.edu. *Application contact:* Monica Mahon, Director of Admissions and Enrollment, 619-260-4524, Fax: 619-260-4158, E-mail: grads@sandiego.edu.
Website: http://www.sandiego.edu/soles/departments/school-family-mental-health-professions/.

University of San Francisco, School of Education, Department of Counseling Psychology, San Francisco, CA 94117-1080. Offers counseling (MA), including educational counseling, life transitions counseling, marital and family therapy. *Faculty:* 5 full-time (2 women), 37 part-time/adjunct (26 women). *Students:* 251 full-time (209 women), 15 part-time (13 women); includes 120 minority (20 Black or African American, non-Hispanic/Latino; 24 Asian, non-Hispanic/Latino; 65 Hispanic/Latino; 1 Native Hawaiian or other Pacific Islander, non-Hispanic/Latino; 10 Two or more races, non-Hispanic/Latino), 2 international. Average age 29. 275 applicants, 83% accepted, 122 enrolled. In 2013, 179 master's awarded. *Application deadline:* For fall admission, 3/1 priority date for domestic students, 3/1 for international students; for spring admission, 10/15 priority date for domestic students, 10/15 for international students. Applications are processed on a rolling basis. Application fee: $55 ($65 for international students). Electronic applications accepted. *Expenses: Tuition:* Full-time $21,150; part-time $1175 per unit. Tuition and fees vary according to course load, campus/location and program. *Financial support:* In 2013–14, 19 students received support. Fellowships, research assistantships, and teaching assistantships available. Financial award application deadline: 3/2; financial award applicants required to submit FAFSA. *Unit head:* Dr. Brian Gerrard, Chair, 415-422-6868. *Application contact:* Amy Fogliani, Associate Director of Graduate Outreach, 415-422-5467, E-mail: schoolofeducation@usfca.edu.

The University of Scranton, College of Graduate and Continuing Education, Department of Counseling and Human Services, Program in School Counseling, Scranton, PA 18510. Offers MS. *Accreditation:* ACA; NCATE. Part-time and evening/weekend programs available. *Students:* 48 full-time (40 women), 5 part-time (all women); includes 1 minority (Hispanic/Latino). Average age 26. 23 applicants, 87% accepted. In 2013, 16 master's awarded. *Degree requirements:* For master's, comprehensive exam, capstone experience. *Entrance requirements:* For master's, minimum GPA of 3.0. Additional exam requirements/recommendations for international students: Required—TOEFL (minimum score 500 paper-based), IELTS (minimum score 6). *Application deadline:* For fall admission, 3/1 for domestic students. Application fee: $0. *Financial support:* Teaching assistantships, career-related internships or fieldwork, and Federal Work-Study available. Support available to part-time students. Financial award application deadline: 3/1. *Unit head:* Dr. Lee Ann M. Eschbach, Co-Director, 570-941-6299, Fax: 570-941-4201, E-mail: eschbach@scranton.edu. *Application contact:* Joseph M. Roback, Director of Admissions, 570-941-4385, Fax: 570-941-5928, E-mail: robackj2@scranton.edu.

University of South Africa, College of Human Sciences, Pretoria, South Africa. Offers adult education (M Ed); African languages (MA, PhD); African politics (MA, PhD); Afrikaans (MA, PhD); ancient history (MA, PhD); ancient Near Eastern studies (MA, PhD); anthropology (MA, PhD); applied linguistics (MA); Arabic (MA, PhD); archaeology (MA); art history (MA); Biblical archaeology (MA); Biblical studies (M Th, D Th, PhD); Christian spirituality (M Th, D Th); church history (M Th, D Th); classical studies (MA, PhD); clinical psychology (MA); communication (MA, PhD); comparative education (M Ed, Ed D); consulting psychology (D Admin, D Com, PhD); curriculum studies (M Ed, Ed D); development studies (M Admin, MA, D Admin, PhD); didactics (M Ed, Ed D); education (M Tech); education management (M Ed, Ed D); educational psychology (M Ed); English (MA); environmental education (M Ed); French (MA, PhD); German (MA, PhD); Greek (MA); guidance and counseling (M Ed); health studies (MA, PhD), including health sciences education (MA), health services management (MA), medical and surgical nursing science (critical care general) (MA), midwifery and neonatal nursing science (MA), trauma and emergency care (MA); history (MA, PhD); history of education (Ed D); inclusive education (M Ed, Ed D); information and communications technology policy and regulation (MA); information science (MA, MIS, PhD); international politics (MA, PhD); Islamic studies (MA, PhD); Italian (MA, PhD); Judaica (MA, PhD); linguistics (MA, PhD); mathematical education (M Ed); mathematics education (MA); missiology (M Th, D Th); modern Hebrew (MA, PhD); musicology (MA, MMus, D Mus, PhD); natural science education (M Ed); New Testament (M Th, D Th); Old Testament (D Th); pastoral therapy (M Th, D Th); philosophy (MA); philosophy of education (M Ed, Ed D); politics (MA, PhD); Portuguese (MA, PhD); practical theology (M Th, D Th); psychology (MA, MS, PhD); psychology of education (M Ed, Ed D); public health (MA); religious studies (MA, D Th, PhD); Romance languages (MA); Russian (MA, PhD); Semitic languages (MA, PhD); social behavior studies in HIV/AIDS (MA); social science (mental health) (MA); social science in development studies (MA); social science in psychology (MA); social science in social work (MA); social science in sociology (MA); social work (MSW, DSW, PhD); socio-education (M Ed, Ed D); sociolinguistics (MA); sociology (MA, PhD); Spanish (MA, PhD); systematic theology (M Th, D Th); TESOL (teaching English to speakers of other languages) (MA); theological ethics (M Th, D Th); theory of literature (MA, PhD); urban ministries (D Th); urban ministry (M Th).

University of South Carolina, The Graduate School, College of Education, Department of Educational Studies, Program in Counseling Education, Columbia, SC 29208. Offers PhD, Ed S. *Accreditation:* ACA (one or more programs are accredited); NCATE. Part-time programs available. *Degree requirements:* For doctorate, one foreign language, comprehensive exam, thesis/dissertation; for Ed S, comprehensive exam. *Entrance requirements:* For doctorate, GRE General Test or MAT, interview, resume, references; for Ed S, GRE General Test or MAT, interview, resum&e, transcripts, letter of intent, references. Electronic applications accepted. *Faculty research:* Multicultural counseling, children's fears, career development, family counseling.

The University of South Dakota, Graduate School, School of Education, Division of Counseling and Psychology in Education, Vermillion, SD 57069-2390. Offers counseling (MA, PhD, Ed S); human development and educational psychology (MA, PhD, Ed S); school psychology (PhD, Ed S). *Accreditation:* ACA (one or more programs are accredited); NCATE. Part-time programs available. *Degree requirements:* For master's and Ed S, comprehensive exam, thesis or alternative; for doctorate, comprehensive exam, thesis/dissertation. *Entrance requirements:* For master's and doctorate, GRE General Test, minimum GPA of 3.0. Additional exam requirements/recommendations for international students: Required—TOEFL (minimum score 550 paper-based; 79 iBT). Electronic applications accepted.

University of Southern California, Graduate School, Rossier School of Education, Master's Programs in Education, Los Angeles, CA 90089-4038. Offers educational counseling (ME); marriage, family and child counseling (MMFT); postsecondary administration and student affairs [PASA] (ME); school counseling (ME); teaching (online) (MAT); teaching and teaching credential (MAT); teaching English to speakers of other languages (MAT). Part-time and evening/weekend programs available. Postbaccalaureate distance learning degree programs offered (no on-campus study). *Degree requirements:* For master's, thesis optional. *Entrance requirements:* For master's, GRE (for all programs except MAT). Additional exam requirements/recommendations for international students: Required—TOEFL (minimum score 100 iBT). Electronic applications accepted. *Faculty research:* College access and equity, preparing teachers for culturally diverse populations, sociocultural basis of learning as mediated by instruction with focus on reading and literacy in English learners, social and political aspects of teaching and learning English, school counselor development and training.

University of Southern Maine, College of Management and Human Service, School of Education and Human Development, Program in Counselor Education, Portland, ME 04104-9300. Offers clinical mental health counseling (MS); counseling (CAS); culturally responsive practices in education and human development (CGS); mental health rehabilitation technician/community (Certificate); rehabilitation counseling (MS); school counseling (MS); substance abuse counseling (CGS). *Accreditation:* ACA (one or more programs are accredited); CORE; Teacher Education Accreditation Council. Part-time and evening/weekend programs available. *Faculty:* 6 full-time (4 women), 3 part-time/adjunct (2 women). *Students:* 57 full-time (42 women), 71 part-time (53 women); includes 5 minority (1 Black or African American, non-Hispanic/Latino; 2 American Indian or Alaska Native, non-Hispanic/Latino; 1 Asian, non-Hispanic/Latino; 1 Hispanic/Latino. Average age 36. 89 applicants, 72% accepted, 44 enrolled. In 2013, 37 master's, 7 other advanced degrees awarded. *Degree requirements:* For master's, comprehensive exam, thesis or alternative; for other advanced degree, thesis or alternative. *Entrance requirements:* For master's, GRE General Test or MAT, interview; for other advanced degree, master's degree. Additional exam requirements/recommendations for international students: Required—TOEFL (minimum score 550 paper-based; 79 iBT). *Application deadline:* For fall admission, 11/15 for domestic students. Application fee: $65. Electronic applications accepted. *Expenses:* Tuition, state resident: part-time $380 per credit. Tuition, nonresident: part-time $1026 per credit. Part-time tuition and fees vary according to program. *Financial support:* Research assistantships, career-related internships or fieldwork, Federal Work-Study, institutionally sponsored loans, scholarships/grants, and unspecified assistantships available. Support available to part-time students. Financial award application deadline: 3/1; financial award applicants required to submit FAFSA. *Faculty research:* Counselor licensure, group dynamics, counseling theories, healthy adaptation, counselor educator well-being. *Unit head:* Adele Baruch, Program Coordinator, 207-780-5317, E-mail: abaruch@usm.maine.edu. *Application contact:* Mary Sloan, Assistant Dean of Graduate Studies and Director of Graduate Admissions, 207-780-4386, E-mail: gradstudies@usm.maine.edu.
Website: http://usm.maine.edu/counselor-education.

University of Southern Mississippi, Graduate School, College of Education and Psychology, Department of Educational Leadership and School Counseling, Hattiesburg, MS 39401. Offers education (Ed D, PhD, Ed S), including educational leadership and school counseling (Ed D, PhD); educational administration (M Ed). Part-time programs available. *Faculty:* 9 full-time (5 women), 3 part-time/adjunct (1 woman). *Students:* 42 full-time (27 women), 158 part-time (110 women); includes 63 minority (53 Black or African American, non-Hispanic/Latino; 3 Asian, non-Hispanic/Latino; 2 Hispanic/Latino; 5 Two or more races, non-Hispanic/Latino). Average age 39. 35 applicants, 86% accepted, 19 enrolled. In 2013, 43 master's, 30 doctorates, 5 other advanced degrees awarded. *Degree requirements:* For master's, comprehensive exam, thesis optional, internship; for doctorate, comprehensive exam, thesis/dissertation; for Ed S, comprehensive exam, thesis optional. *Entrance requirements:* For master's, GRE General Test, minimum GPA of 2.75; for doctorate, GRE General Test, minimum GPA of 3.5; for Ed S, GRE General Test, minimum GPA of 3.25. Additional exam requirements/recommendations for international students: Required—TOEFL, IELTS. *Application deadline:* For fall admission, 3/1 priority date for domestic and international students; for spring admission, 1/10 for domestic and international students. Application fee: $50. *Financial support:* In 2013–14, research assistantships (averaging $9,000 per year), teaching assistantships (averaging $9,000 per year) were awarded; career-related internships or fieldwork, Federal Work-Study, institutionally sponsored loans, scholarships/grants, health care benefits, and unspecified assistantships also available. Financial award application deadline: 3/15; financial award applicants required to submit FAFSA. *Unit head:* Dr. Thelma Roberson, Interim Chair, 601-266-4556, Fax: 601-266-4233, E-mail: thelma.roberson@usm.edu. *Application contact:* Shonna Breland, Manager of Graduate Admissions, 601-266-6563, Fax: 601-266-5138.
Website: http://www.usm.edu/graduateschool/table.php.

University of Southern Mississippi, Graduate School, College of Education and Psychology, Department of Educational Studies and Research, Hattiesburg, MS 39406-0001. Offers adult education (Graduate Certificate); community college leadership (Graduate Certificate); counseling and personnel services (college) (M Ed); education (PhD, Ed S), including adult education, research, evaluation and statistics (PhD); education (Ed D), including educational administration, educational research; education: educational leadership and research (Ed S), including higher education administration; educational administration and supervision (M Ed); higher education administration (Ed D, PhD); institutional research (Graduate Certificate). *Faculty:* 7 full-time (1 woman), 5 part-time/adjunct (1 woman). *Students:* 32 full-time (21 women), 103 part-time (70 women); includes 44 minority (39 Black or African American, non-Hispanic/Latino; 2 Hispanic/Latino; 3 Two or more races, non-Hispanic/Latino; 4 international). Average age 36. 36 applicants, 72% accepted, 15 enrolled. In 2013, 18 master's, 9 doctorates, 7 other advanced degrees awarded. *Degree requirements:* For master's and other advanced degree, comprehensive exam, thesis (for some programs); for doctorate, comprehensive exam, thesis/dissertation. *Entrance requirements:* For master's, doctorate, and other advanced degree, GRE General Test, minimum GPA of 2.75. Additional exam requirements/recommendations for international students: Required—TOEFL. *Application deadline:* For fall admission, 2/1 for domestic students, 3/1 for international students. Applications are processed on a rolling basis. Application fee: $35. *Financial support:* Career-related internships or fieldwork, Federal Work-Study, and institutionally sponsored loans available. Financial award application deadline: 3/15;

financial award applicants required to submit FAFSA. *Total annual research expenditures:* $88,500. *Unit head:* Dr. Thomas V. O'Brien, Chair, 601-266-6093, E-mail: thomas.obrien@usm.edu. *Application contact:* Shonna Breland, Manager of Graduate Admissions, 601-266-6563, Fax: 601-266-5138.
Website: http://www.usm.edu/cep/esr/.

University of South Florida, College of Education, Department of Psychological and Social Foundations, Tampa, FL 33620-9951. Offers college student affairs (M Ed); counselor education (MA, PhD, Ed S); interdisciplinary (PhD, Ed S); school psychology (PhD, Ed S). Part-time and evening/weekend programs available. *Degree requirements:* For master's, comprehensive exam, thesis (for some programs); for doctorate, comprehensive exam, thesis/dissertation, multiple research methods; philosophies of inquiry (for some programs). *Entrance requirements:* For master's, GRE General Test, minimum GPA of 3.5 in last 60 hours of course work; for doctorate, GRE General Test, MAT, minimum GPA of 3.5 in last 60 hours of course work; for Ed S, GRE General Test. Additional exam requirements/recommendations for international students: Required—TOEFL (minimum score 550 paper-based; 79 iBT). Electronic applications accepted. *Faculty research:* College student affairs, counselor education, educational psychology, school psychology, social foundations.

University of South Florida, University College/Distance Education, Tampa, FL 33620-9951. *Unit head:* Kathy Barnes, Interdisciplinary Programs Coordinator, 813-974-8031, Fax: 813-974-7061, E-mail: barnesk@usf.edu. *Application contact:* Karen Tylinski, Metro Initiatives, 813-974-9943, Fax: 813-974-7061, E-mail: ktylinsk@usf.edu.
Website: http://uc.usf.edu/.

The University of Tennessee, Graduate School, College of Education, Health and Human Sciences, Department of Educational Psychology and Counseling, Knoxville, TN 37996. Offers adult education (MS); applied educational psychology (MS); collaborative learning (Ed D); college student personnel (MS); mental health counseling (MS); rehabilitation counseling (MS); school counseling (MS). *Accreditation:* ACA (one or more programs are accredited); CORE (one or more programs are accredited); NCATE. Part-time and evening/weekend programs available. *Degree requirements:* For master's, thesis optional. *Entrance requirements:* For master's, GRE General Test, minimum GPA of 2.7. Additional exam requirements/recommendations for international students: Required—TOEFL. Electronic applications accepted. *Expenses:* Tuition, state resident: full-time $9540; part-time $531 per credit hour. Tuition, nonresident: full-time $27,728; part-time $1542 per credit hour. *Required fees:* $1404; $67 per credit hour.

The University of Tennessee, Graduate School, College of Education, Health and Human Sciences, Program in Education, Knoxville, TN 37996. Offers art education (MS); counseling education (PhD); cultural studies in education (PhD); curriculum (MS, Ed S); curriculum, educational research and evaluation (Ed D, PhD); early childhood education (PhD); early childhood special education (MS); education of deaf and hard of hearing (MS); educational administration and policy studies (Ed D, PhD); educational administration and supervision (Ed S); educational psychology (Ed D, PhD); elementary education (MS, Ed S); elementary teaching (MS); English education (MS, Ed S); exercise science (PhD); foreign language/ESL education (MS, Ed S); instructional technology (MS, Ed D, PhD, Ed S); literacy, language and ESL education (PhD); literacy, language education, and ESL education (Ed D); mathematics education (MS, Ed S); modified and comprehensive special education (MS); reading education (MS, Ed S); school counseling (Ed S); school psychology (PhD, Ed S); science education (MS, Ed S); secondary teaching (MS); social foundations (MS); social science education (MS, Ed S); socio-cultural foundations of sports and education (PhD); special education (Ed S); teacher education (Ed D, PhD). *Accreditation:* NCATE. Part-time and evening/weekend programs available. *Degree requirements:* For master's and Ed S, thesis optional; for doctorate, variable foreign language requirement, thesis/dissertation. *Entrance requirements:* For master's, minimum GPA of 2.7; for doctorate and Ed S, GRE General Test, minimum GPA of 2.7. Additional exam requirements/recommendations for international students: Required—TOEFL. Electronic applications accepted. *Expenses:* Tuition, state resident: full-time $9540; part-time $531 per credit hour. Tuition, nonresident: full-time $27,728; part-time $1542 per credit hour. *Required fees:* $1404; $67 per credit hour.

The University of Tennessee at Chattanooga, Graduate School, College of Health, Education and Professional Studies, School of Education, Chattanooga, TN 37403. Offers counseling (M Ed), including community counseling, school counseling; education (M Ed, Post-Master's Certificate), including elementary education (M Ed), school leadership, secondary education (M Ed), special education (M Ed); educational specialist (Ed S), including educational technology, school psychology; learning and leadership (Ed D), including educational leadership. *Accreditation:* ACA; NCATE. Part-time and evening/weekend programs available. Postbaccalaureate distance learning degree programs offered (no on-campus study). *Faculty:* 24 full-time (17 women), 6 part-time/adjunct (4 women). *Students:* 107 full-time (86 women), 263 part-time (192 women); includes 71 minority (46 Black or African American, non-Hispanic/Latino; 2 American Indian or Alaska Native, non-Hispanic/Latino; 5 Asian, non-Hispanic/Latino; 11 Hispanic/Latino; 7 Two or more races, non-Hispanic/Latino), 2 international. Average age 34. 121 applicants, 83% accepted, 67 enrolled. In 2013, 125 master's, 10 doctorates, 3 other advanced degrees awarded. *Degree requirements:* For master's, comprehensive exam, thesis optional, culminating experience; for doctorate, comprehensive exam, thesis/dissertation; for other advanced degree, internship. *Entrance requirements:* For master's, GRE General Test, PPST 1, teaching certificate; for doctorate, GRE General Test, master's degree, two years of practical work experience in organizational environment; for other advanced degree, GRE General Test, letters of reference. Additional exam requirements/recommendations for international students: Required—TOEFL (minimum score 550 paper-based; 79 iBT), IELTS (minimum score 6). *Application deadline:* For fall admission, 6/13 for domestic students, 6/1 for international students; for spring admission, 10/15 for domestic students, 10/1 for international students. Applications are processed on a rolling basis. Application fee: $30 ($35 for international students). Electronic applications accepted. *Financial support:* In 2013–14, 20 research assistantships with tuition reimbursements (averaging $6,340 per year), 4 teaching assistantships with tuition reimbursements (averaging $7,234 per year) were awarded; career-related internships or fieldwork, institutionally sponsored loans, scholarships/grants, and unspecified assistantships also available. Support available to part-time students. Financial award applicants required to submit FAFSA. *Faculty research:* School counseling, community counseling, elementary and secondary education, school leadership and administration. *Total annual research expenditures:* $967,880. *Unit head:* Dr. Linda Johnston, Director, 423-425-4122, Fax: 423-425-5380, E-mail: linda-johnston@utc.edu. *Application contact:* Dr. J. Randy Walker, Interim Dean of Graduate Studies, 423-425-4478, Fax: 423-425-5223, E-mail: randy-walker@utc.edu.
Website: http://www.utc.edu/school-education/abouttheschool/gradprograms.php.

The University of Tennessee at Martin, Graduate Programs, College of Education, Health and Behavioral Sciences, Program in Counseling, Martin, TN 38238. Offers community counseling (MS Ed); school counseling (MS Ed). *Accreditation:* NCATE. Part-time programs available. *Students:* 18 full-time (17 women), 58 part-time (50 women); includes 12 minority (11 Black or African American, non-Hispanic/Latino; 1 Two or more races, non-Hispanic/Latino). 28 applicants, 57% accepted, 15 enrolled. In 2013,

15 master's awarded. *Degree requirements:* For master's, comprehensive exam. *Entrance requirements:* For master's, GRE General Test, minimum GPA of 2.5, resume, letters of reference. Additional exam requirements/recommendations for international students: Required—TOEFL (minimum score 525 paper-based; 71 iBT). *Application deadline:* For fall admission, 7/29 priority date for domestic and international students; for spring admission, 12/12 priority date for domestic and international students. Applications are processed on a rolling basis. Application fee: $30 ($130 for international students). Electronic applications accepted. *Financial support:* Scholarships/grants and unspecified assistantships available. Support available to part-time students. Financial award application deadline: 2/15; financial award applicants required to submit FAFSA. *Unit head:* Dr. Gail Stephens, Interim Dean, 731-881-7127, Fax: 731-881-7975, E-mail: gstephe6@utm.edu. *Application contact:* Jolene L. Cunningham, Student Services Specialist, 731-881-7012, Fax: 731-881-7499, E-mail: jcunningham@utm.edu.

The University of Texas at Austin, Graduate School, College of Education, Department of Educational Psychology, Austin, TX 78712-1111. Offers academic educational psychology (M Ed, MA); counseling psychology (PhD); counselor education (M Ed); human development, culture and learning sciences (PhD); program evaluation (MA); quantitative methods (M Ed, MA, PhD); school psychology (MA, PhD). *Accreditation:* APA (one or more programs are accredited). *Degree requirements:* For master's, thesis optional; for doctorate, thesis/dissertation. *Entrance requirements:* For master's and doctorate, GRE General Test, 3 letters of recommendation. Additional exam requirements/recommendations for international students: Required—TOEFL.

The University of Texas at Brownsville, Graduate Studies, College of Education, Brownsville, TX 78520-4991. Offers bilingual education (M Ed); counseling and guidance (M Ed); curriculum and instruction (M Ed); early childhood education (M Ed); educational leadership (M Ed); educational technology (M Ed); exercise science (MS); special education (M Ed). Part-time and evening/weekend programs available. Postbaccalaureate distance learning degree programs offered (no on-campus study). *Faculty:* 51 full-time (28 women). *Students:* 60 full-time (43 women), 496 part-time (363 women); includes 467 minority (4 Black or African American, non-Hispanic/Latino; 1 American Indian or Alaska Native, non-Hispanic/Latino; 10 Asian, non-Hispanic/Latino; 451 Hispanic/Latino; 1 Native Hawaiian or other Pacific Islander, non-Hispanic/Latino), 12 international. 161 applicants, 67% accepted, 81 enrolled. In 2013, 142 master's awarded. *Degree requirements:* For master's, comprehensive exam (for some programs), thesis optional, electronic portfolio. *Entrance requirements:* For master's, GRE General Test, curriculum vitae or resume, teaching certificate. Additional exam requirements/recommendations for international students: Required—TOEFL (minimum score 550 paper-based; 77 iBT). *Application deadline:* For fall admission, 7/1 priority date for domestic students, 7/1 for international students; for spring admission, 12/1 priority date for domestic students, 12/1 for international students. Applications are processed on a rolling basis. Application fee: $30. Electronic applications accepted. *Expenses:* Tuition, state resident: full-time $3444; part-time $1148 per semester. Tuition, nonresident: full-time $9816. *Required fees:* $1018; $221 per credit hour. $401 per semester. *Financial support:* In 2013–14, 136 students received support, including 6 research assistantships (averaging $10,000 per year); career-related internships or fieldwork, Federal Work-Study, scholarships/grants, tuition waivers (partial), and unspecified assistantships also available. Support available to part-time students. Financial award application deadline: 3/1; financial award applicants required to submit FAFSA. *Unit head:* Dr. Miguel Angel Escotet, Dean, 956-882-7220, Fax: 956-882-7431, E-mail: miguel.escotet@utb.edu. *Application contact:* Mari E. Stevens, Graduate Studies Specialist, 956-882-6587, Fax: 956-882-7279, E-mail: mari.stevens@utb.edu. Website: http://www.utb.edu/vpaa/coe/Pages/default.aspx.

The University of Texas at El Paso, Graduate School, College of Education, Department of Educational Psychology and Special Services, El Paso, TX 79968-0001. Offers educational diagnostics (M Ed); guidance and counseling (M Ed); special education (M Ed). Part-time and evening/weekend programs available. *Degree requirements:* For master's, thesis optional. *Entrance requirements:* For master's, minimum GPA of 3.0. Additional exam requirements/recommendations for international students: Required—TOEFL. Electronic applications accepted.

The University of Texas at San Antonio, College of Education and Human Development, Department of Counseling, San Antonio, TX 78249-0617. Offers counseling (MA); counselor education and supervision (PhD). *Accreditation:* ACA. Part-time and evening/weekend programs available. *Faculty:* 20 full-time (10 women), 6 part-time/adjunct (5 women). *Students:* 181 full-time (147 women), 272 part-time (221 women); includes 272 minority (42 Black or African American, non-Hispanic/Latino; 14 Asian, non-Hispanic/Latino; 203 Hispanic/Latino; 13 Two or more races, non-Hispanic/Latino), 7 international. Average age 31. 163 applicants, 83% accepted, 102 enrolled. In 2013, 161 master's, 6 doctorates awarded. *Degree requirements:* For master's, comprehensive exam, thesis optional; for doctorate, comprehensive exam, thesis/dissertation. *Entrance requirements:* For master's, GRE if GPA is below 3.0 on the last 60 hours, minimum of 48 semester credit hours, bachelor's degree with 18 credit hours in field of study or in another appropriate field of study; for doctorate, GRE, minimum GPA of 3.0 in master's-level courses in counseling or in related mental health field; resume; three letters of recommendation; statement of purpose; Counseling Experience Form. Additional exam requirements/recommendations for international students: Required—TOEFL (minimum score 550 paper-based; 79 iBT), IELTS (minimum score 6.5). *Application deadline:* For fall admission, 7/1 for domestic students, 4/1 for international students; for spring admission, 10/1 for domestic students, 9/1 for international students. Applications are processed on a rolling basis. Application fee: $45 ($80 for international students). Electronic applications accepted. *Expenses:* Tuition, state resident: full-time $4671. Tuition, nonresident: full-time $8708. *International tuition:* $17,415 full-time. *Required fees:* $1924.60. Tuition and fees vary according to course load and degree level. *Financial support:* Scholarships/grants and unspecified assistantships available. *Faculty research:* Life-threatening behaviors, self-injurious behavior, youth mentoring, relationships/relational competencies and development, addiction counseling. *Unit head:* Dr. Thelma Duffey, Department Chair, 210-458-2600, Fax: 210-458-2605, E-mail: thelma.duffey@utsa.edu. *Application contact:* Dr. Heather Trepal, Graduate Assistant of Record, 210-458-2928, Fax: 210-458-2605, E-mail: heather.trepal@utsa.edu. Website: http://coehd.utsa.edu/counseling.

The University of Texas of the Permian Basin, Office of Graduate Studies, School of Education, Program in Counseling, Odessa, TX 79762-0001. Offers MA. *Degree requirements:* For master's, comprehensive exam (for some programs), thesis (for some programs). *Entrance requirements:* For master's, GRE General Test. Additional exam requirements/recommendations for international students: Required—TOEFL (minimum score 550 paper-based).

The University of Texas–Pan American, College of Education, Department of Educational Psychology, Edinburg, TX 78539. Offers educational diagnostician (M Ed); gifted education (M Ed); guidance and counseling (M Ed); school psychology (MA); special education (M Ed). Part-time and evening/weekend programs available. *Degree requirements:* For master's, comprehensive exam (for some programs), thesis (for some programs). *Entrance requirements:* For master's, GRE General Test, interview. *Expenses:* Tuition, state resident: full-time $5986; part-time $333 per credit hour.

Tuition, nonresident: full-time $12,358; part-time $687 per credit hour. *Required fees:* $782. Tuition and fees vary according to program. *Faculty research:* Reading instruction, assessment practice, behavior interventions consultation, mental retardation.

University of the Cumberlands, Graduate Programs in Education, Williamsburg, KY 40769-1372. Offers all grades (P-12) (M Ed); business and marketing (MA Ed, MAT); counselor education and supervision (Ed D); director of pupil personnel (Certificate); director of special education (Certificate); educational administration and supervision (Ed S); educational leadership (Ed D); elementary education (MA Ed, MAT); instructional leadership - principalship (MA Ed); instructional leadership - school principal (Certificate); middle school education (MA Ed, MAT); reading and writing (MA Ed); school counseling (MA Ed); school superintendent (Certificate); secondary education (MA Ed, MAT); special education (MAT); supervisor of instruction (Certificate); teacher leader (MA Ed). Part-time and evening/weekend programs available. Postbaccalaureate distance learning degree programs offered. *Degree requirements:* For master's, comprehensive exam. Electronic applications accepted.

University of the District of Columbia, College of Arts and Sciences, Department of Psychology and Counseling, Washington, DC 20008-1175. Offers clinical psychology (MS); counseling (MS). *Accreditation:* ACA. *Degree requirements:* For master's, comprehensive exam, thesis optional, seminar paper. *Entrance requirements:* For master's, GRE General Test, writing proficiency exam. *Expenses: Tuition, area resident:* Full-time $7883.28; part-time $437.96 per credit hour. Tuition, state resident: full-time $8923.14. Tuition, nonresident: full-time $15,163; part-time $842.40 per credit hour. *Required fees:* $620; $30 per credit hour.

University of the Southwest, Graduate Programs, Hobbs, NM 88240-9129. Offers business administration (MBA); curriculum and instruction (MSE); curriculum and instruction: bilingual (MSE); curriculum and instruction: TESOL (MSE); early childhood education (MSE); educational administration (MSE); mental health counseling (MSE); school counseling (MSE); special education (MSE); sports management (MBA). Part-time and evening/weekend programs available. Postbaccalaureate distance learning degree programs offered (no on-campus study). *Degree requirements:* For master's, comprehensive exam, thesis (for some programs). *Entrance requirements:* Additional exam requirements/recommendations for international students: Recommended—TOEFL. Electronic applications accepted.

The University of Toledo, College of Graduate Studies, College of Social Justice and Human Service, Department of School Psychology, Higher Education and Counselor Education, Toledo, OH 43606-3390. Offers counselor education (MA, PhD); higher education (ME, PhD, Certificate); school psychology (MA, Ed S). Part-time programs available. *Faculty:* 63. *Students:* 49 full-time (42 women), 174 part-time (111 women); includes 52 minority (35 Black or African American, non-Hispanic/Latino; 7 Asian, non-Hispanic/Latino; 10 Hispanic/Latino), 6 international. Average age 37. 103 applicants, 59% accepted, 42 enrolled. In 2013, 60 master's, 20 doctorates awarded. *Degree requirements:* For master's, comprehensive exam, thesis or alternative; for doctorate, comprehensive exam, thesis/dissertation; for other advanced degree, thesis optional. *Entrance requirements:* For master's, doctorate, and other advanced degree, minimum cumulative GPA of 2.7 for all previous academic work, letters of recommendation. Additional exam requirements/recommendations for international students: Required—TOEFL (minimum score 550 paper-based; 80 iBT). *Application deadline:* For fall admission, 1/15 priority date for domestic and international students. Applications are processed on a rolling basis. Application fee: $45 ($75 for international students). Electronic applications accepted. *Financial support:* In 2013–14, 1 research assistantship with full and partial tuition reimbursement (averaging $12,000 per year), 19 teaching assistantships with full and partial tuition reimbursements (averaging $9,841 per year) were awarded; career-related internships or fieldwork, Federal Work-Study, institutionally sponsored loans, scholarships/grants, tuition waivers (full and partial), unspecified assistantships, and administrative assistantships also available. *Unit head:* Dr. John Laux, Chair, 419-530-4705, E-mail: martin.laux@utoledo.edu. *Application contact:* Graduate School Office, 419-530-4723, Fax: 419-530-4724, E-mail: grdsch@utnet.utoledo.edu. Website: http://www.utoledo.edu/csjhs/depts/sphece/index.html.

University of Utah, Graduate School, College of Education, Department of Educational Psychology, Salt Lake City, UT 84112. Offers clinical mental health counseling (M Ed); counseling psychology (PhD); educational psychology (M Ed, MA, MS); elementary education (M Ed); instructional design and educational technology (M Ed); instructional design and technology (MS); learning and cognition (MS, PhD); reading and literacy (M Ed, MS, PhD); school counseling (M Ed); school psychology (M Ed, PhD); statistics (M Stat). *Accreditation:* APA (one or more programs are accredited). *Faculty:* 18 full-time (8 women), 20 part-time/adjunct (17 women). *Students:* 109 full-time (88 women), 108 part-time (68 women); includes 29 minority (2 Black or African American, non-Hispanic/Latino; 1 American Indian or Alaska Native, non-Hispanic/Latino; 7 Asian, non-Hispanic/Latino; 14 Hispanic/Latino; 1 Native Hawaiian or other Pacific Islander, non-Hispanic/Latino; 4 Two or more races, non-Hispanic/Latino), 7 international. Average age 32. 222 applicants, 35% accepted, 61 enrolled. In 2013, 51 master's, 10 doctorates awarded. *Degree requirements:* For master's, variable foreign language requirement, comprehensive exam (for some programs), thesis (for some programs), projects; for doctorate, variable foreign language requirement, comprehensive exam, thesis/dissertation, oral exam. *Entrance requirements:* For master's and doctorate, GRE General Test, minimum GPA of 3.0. Additional exam requirements/recommendations for international students: Required—TOEFL (minimum score 80 iBT). *Application deadline:* For fall admission, 4/1 for domestic and international students; for winter admission, 11/1 for domestic and international students; for spring admission, 3/15 for domestic and international students. Application fee: $55 ($65 for international students). Electronic applications accepted. *Expenses:* Contact institution. *Financial support:* In 2013–14, 81 students received support, including 29 fellowships with full and partial tuition reimbursements available (averaging $11,200 per year), 11 research assistantships with full and partial tuition reimbursements available (averaging $9,100 per year), 38 teaching assistantships with full and partial tuition reimbursements available (averaging $10,400 per year); career-related internships or fieldwork, Federal Work-Study, institutionally sponsored loans, scholarships/grants, health care benefits, and unspecified assistantships also available. Financial award application deadline: 4/1; financial award applicants required to submit FAFSA. *Faculty research:* Autism, computer technology and instruction, cognitive behavior, aging, group counseling. *Total annual research expenditures:* $441,375. *Unit head:* Dr. Anne E. Cook, Chair, 801-581-7148, Fax: 801-581-5566, E-mail: anne.cook@utah.edu. *Application contact:* JoLynn N. Yates, Academic Program Specialist, 801-581-7148, Fax: 801-581-5566, E-mail: jo.yates@utah.edu. Website: http://www.ed.utah.edu/edps/.

University of Vermont, Graduate College, College of Education and Social Services, Department of Leadership and Developmental Sciences, Counseling Program, Burlington, VT 05405. Offers MS. *Accreditation:* ACA; NCATE. *Faculty:* 3 full-time (2 women), 6 part-time/adjunct (2 women). *Students:* 37 (28 women); includes 2 minority (1 Black or African American, non-Hispanic/Latino; 1 Hispanic/Latino). 56 applicants, 73% accepted, 16 enrolled. In 2013, 21 master's awarded. *Entrance requirements:* For master's, GRE General Test, resume. Additional exam requirements/recommendations

for international students: Required—TOEFL (minimum score 550 paper-based; 80 iBT). *Application deadline:* For fall admission, 2/1 priority date for domestic students, 2/1 for international students. Applications are processed on a rolling basis. Application fee: $65. Electronic applications accepted. *Financial support:* Fellowships, research assistantships, and teaching assistantships available. Financial award application deadline: 2/1. *Faculty research:* Women and tenure, counseling children and adolescents. *Unit head:* Jane Okech, Director, 802-656-3888, Fax: 802-656-3173.
Website: http://www.uvm.edu/~cslgprog/.

University of Victoria, Faculty of Graduate Studies, Faculty of Education, Department of Educational Psychology and Leadership Studies, Victoria, BC V8W 2Y2, Canada. Offers aboriginal communities counseling (M Ed); counseling (M Ed, MA); educational psychology (M Ed, MA, PhD), including counseling psychology (M Ed, MA), leadership studies (PhD), learning and development (MA, PhD), measurement and evaluation, special education (M Ed, MA); leadership studies (M Ed, MA). Part-time programs available. *Degree requirements:* For master's, thesis (for some programs), comprehensive exam (M Ed); for doctorate, comprehensive exam, thesis/dissertation, candidacy exam. *Entrance requirements:* For master's, 2 years of work experience in a relevant field; for doctorate, GRE, 2 years of work experience in a relevant field, minimum B average. Additional exam requirements/recommendations for international students: Required—TOEFL (minimum score 575 paper-based), IELTS (minimum score 7). *Faculty research:* Learning and development (child, adolescent and adult), special education and exceptional children.

University of Virginia, Curry School of Education, Department of Human Services, Program in Counselor Education, Charlottesville, VA 22903. Offers M Ed, Ed S. *Accreditation:* ACA (one or more programs are accredited). *Students:* 13 full-time (12 women); includes 3 minority (1 Black or African American, non-Hispanic/Latino; 1 Hispanic/Latino; 1 Two or more races, non-Hispanic/Latino). Average age 24. 33 applicants, 58% accepted, 7 enrolled. In 2013, 9 master's awarded. *Entrance requirements:* For master's, GRE General Test, 2 letters of recommendation; for Ed S, GRE General Test. Additional exam requirements/recommendations for international students: Required—TOEFL (minimum score 600 paper-based; 90 iBT), IELTS. *Application deadline:* For fall admission, 1/5 for domestic and international students. Applications are processed on a rolling basis. Application fee: $60. Electronic applications accepted. *Expenses:* Tuition, state resident: part-time $334 per credit hour. Tuition, nonresident: part-time $1224 per credit hour. *Financial support:* Applicants required to submit FAFSA. *Unit head:* Antoinette Thomas, Program Coordinator, 434-924-6958, E-mail: art8u@virginia.edu. *Application contact:* Lynn Renfroe, Information Contact, 434-924-6254, E-mail: ldr9t@virginia.edu.
Website: http://curry.edschool.virginia.edu/counselor-ed-home-counslered-347?task-view.

University of Virginia, Curry School of Education, Program in Education, Charlottesville, VA 22903. Offers administration and supervision (PhD); applied developmental science (PhD); counselor education (PhD); curriculum and instruction (PhD); early childhood special education (MT); education evaluation (PhD); educational psychology (PhD); educational research (PhD); elementary education (MT); English education (MT, PhD); foreign language education (MT); higher education (PhD); instructional technology (PhD); kinesiology (MT, PhD); math education (PhD); reading education (PhD); research, statistics and evaluation (PhD); school psychology (PhD); science education (PhD); social studies education (MT, PhD); special education (PhD); world languages education (MT). *Students:* 474 full-time (379 women), 35 part-time (19 women); includes 89 minority (30 Black or African American, non-Hispanic/Latino; 1 American Indian or Alaska Native, non-Hispanic/Latino; 26 Asian, non-Hispanic/Latino; 19 Hispanic/Latino; 13 Two or more races, non-Hispanic/Latino), 21 international. Average age 26. 312 applicants, 49% accepted, 80 enrolled. In 2013, 137 master's, 38 doctorates awarded. *Degree requirements:* For master's, comprehensive exam (for some programs), field project; for doctorate, comprehensive exam, thesis/dissertation. *Entrance requirements:* For doctorate, GRE General Test. Additional exam requirements/recommendations for international students: Required—TOEFL (minimum score 600 paper-based; 90 iBT), IELTS (minimum score 7). *Application deadline:* Applications are processed on a rolling basis. Application fee: $60. Electronic applications accepted. *Expenses:* Tuition, state resident: part-time $334 per credit hour. Tuition, nonresident: part-time $1224 per credit hour. *Financial support:* Fellowships, research assistantships, and teaching assistantships available. Financial award application deadline: 1/5; financial award applicants required to submit FAFSA. *Unit head:* Robert C. Pianta, Dean, 434-924-3334, E-mail: pianta@virginia.edu. *Application contact:* Office of Admissions and Student Services, 434-924-0742, E-mail: curry-admissions@virginia.edu.
Website: http://curry.virginia.edu/teacher-education.

The University of West Alabama, School of Graduate Studies, College of Education, Departments of Instructional Leadership and Support/Curriculum and Instruction, Program in Continuing Education, Livingston, AL 35470. Offers college student development (MSCE); continuing education (MSCE); counseling and psychology (MSCE); family counseling (MSCE); guidance and counseling (MSCE). *Accreditation:* NCATE. Part-time and evening/weekend programs available. Postbaccalaureate distance learning degree programs offered (no on-campus study). *Faculty:* 16 full-time (10 women), 38 part-time/adjunct (28 women). *Students:* 757 (662 women); includes 581 minority (572 Black or African American, non-Hispanic/Latino; 3 American Indian or Alaska Native, non-Hispanic/Latino; 1 Asian, non-Hispanic/Latino; 3 Hispanic/Latino; 2 Two or more races, non-Hispanic/Latino). 212 applicants, 100% accepted, 173 enrolled. In 2013, 152 master's awarded. *Degree requirements:* For master's, comprehensive exam, thesis optional. *Entrance requirements:* For master's, GRE General Test, MAT, minimum GPA of 2.75. Additional exam requirements/recommendations for international students: Required—TOEFL (minimum score 500 paper-based; 61 iBT). *Application deadline:* For fall admission, 8/12 priority date for domestic students; for spring admission, 3/24 for domestic students. Applications are processed on a rolling basis. Application fee: $25 ($50 for international students). Electronic applications accepted. Tuition and fees vary according to course load. *Financial support:* Teaching assistantships, career-related internships or fieldwork, Federal Work-Study, scholarships/grants, and unspecified assistantships available. Support available to part-time students. Financial award applicants required to submit FAFSA. *Unit head:* Dr. Reenay Rogers, Chair of Instructional Leadership and Support, 205-652-5423, Fax: 205-652-3706, E-mail: rrogers@uwa.edu. *Application contact:* Dr. Kathy Chandler, Dean of Graduate Studies, 205-652-3421, Fax: 205-652-3670, E-mail: kchandler@uwa.edu.

The University of West Alabama, School of Graduate Studies, College of Education, Departments of Instructional Leadership and Support/Curriculum and Instruction, Program in School Counseling, Livingston, AL 35470. Offers counseling (Ed S); school counseling (M Ed, Ed S). *Accreditation:* NCATE. Part-time and evening/weekend programs available. Postbaccalaureate distance learning degree programs offered (no on-campus study). *Faculty:* 8 full-time (4 women), 20 part-time/adjunct (14 women). *Students:* 498 (447 women); includes 257 minority (240 Black or African American, non-Hispanic/Latino; 5 American Indian or Alaska Native, non-Hispanic/Latino; 1 Asian, non-Hispanic/Latino; 5 Hispanic/Latino; 6 Two or more races, non-Hispanic/Latino). 157 applicants, 96% accepted, 107 enrolled. In 2013, 187 master's, 54 Ed Ss awarded. *Degree requirements:* For master's, comprehensive exam, thesis optional. *Entrance requirements:* For master's, GRE General Test, MAT, minimum GPA of 2.75. Additional exam requirements/recommendations for international students: Required—TOEFL (minimum score 500 paper-based; 61 iBT). *Application deadline:* For fall admission, 8/12 priority date for domestic students; for spring admission, 3/21 for domestic students. Applications are processed on a rolling basis. Application fee: $25 ($50 for international students). Electronic applications accepted. Tuition and fees vary according to course load. *Financial support:* Teaching assistantships, career-related internships or fieldwork, Federal Work-Study, scholarships/grants, and unspecified assistantships available. Support available to part-time students. Financial award application deadline: 3/1; financial award applicants required to submit FAFSA. *Unit head:* Dr. Reenay Rogers, Chair of Instructional Leadership and Support, 205-652-5423, Fax: 205-652-3706, E-mail: rrogers@uwa.edu. *Application contact:* Dr. Kathy Chandler, Dean of Graduate Studies, 205-652-3421, Fax: 205-652-3706, E-mail: kchandler@uwa.edu.
Website: http://www.uwa.edu/medschoolcounseling.aspx.

University of West Florida, College of Professional Studies, Department of Research and Advanced Studies, Program in College Student Personnel Administration, Pensacola, FL 32514-5750. Offers college personnel administration (M Ed); guidance and counseling (M Ed). Part-time and evening/weekend programs available. *Degree requirements:* For master's, internship. *Entrance requirements:* For master's, GRE General Test, minimum GPA of 3.0. Additional exam requirements/recommendations for international students: Required—TOEFL (minimum score 550 paper-based).

University of West Georgia, College of Education, Department of Clinical and Professional Studies, Carrollton, GA 30118. Offers professional counseling (M Ed, Ed S); professional counseling and supervision (Ed D); speech pathology (M Ed). Part-time and evening/weekend programs available. *Faculty:* 10 full-time (6 women), 1 (woman) part-time/adjunct. *Students:* 212 full-time (177 women), 89 part-time (83 women); includes 106 minority (84 Black or African American, non-Hispanic/Latino; 6 Asian, non-Hispanic/Latino; 7 Hispanic/Latino; 9 Two or more races, non-Hispanic/Latino), 3 international. Average age 29. 167 applicants, 89% accepted, 92 enrolled. In 2013, 82 master's, 6 doctorates, 10 other advanced degrees awarded. *Degree requirements:* For master's, comprehensive exam; for Ed S, research project. *Entrance requirements:* For master's, minimum GPA of 2.7, GRE, GACE basic skills (school counseling); for Ed S, GRE, master's degree, minimum graduate GPA of 2.7. Additional exam requirements/recommendations for international students: Required—TOEFL (minimum score 523 paper-based; 69 iBT); Recommended—IELTS (minimum score 6). *Application deadline:* For fall admission, 6/3 for domestic students, 6/1 for international students; for spring admission, 10/7 for domestic students, 10/15 for international students. Applications are processed on a rolling basis. Application fee: $40. Electronic applications accepted. *Expenses:* Tuition, state resident: full-time $4600; part-time $192 per semester hour. Tuition, nonresident: full-time $17,880; part-time $745 per semester hour. *Required fees:* $1858; $46.34 per semester hour. $512 per semester. Tuition and fees vary according to course load, degree level, campus/location and program. *Financial support:* In 2013–14, 15 students received support, including 5 research assistantships with full tuition reimbursements available (averaging $3,000 per year); career-related internships or fieldwork and scholarships/grants also available. Support available to part-time students. Financial award application deadline: 4/1; financial award applicants required to submit FAFSA. *Total annual research expenditures:* $134,000. *Unit head:* Dr. Mark S. Parrish, Chair, 678-839-6117, Fax: 678-839-6162, E-mail: mparrish@westga.edu. *Application contact:* Deanna Richards, Coordinator, Graduate Studies, 678-839-5946, E-mail: drichard@westga.edu.
Website: http://www.westga.edu/coecps/.

University of Wisconsin–Madison, Graduate School, School of Education, Department of Counseling Psychology, Program in Counseling, Madison, WI 53706-1380. Offers MS. *Entrance requirements:* For master's, GRE General Test. *Application deadline:* For fall admission, 12/15 for domestic and international students. Application fee: $56. Electronic applications accepted. *Expenses:* Tuition, state resident: full-time $10,728; part-time $790 per credit. Tuition, nonresident: full-time $24,054; part-time $1623 per credit. *Required fees:* $1130; $119 per credit. *Financial support:* Fellowships with full tuition reimbursements, research assistantships with full tuition reimbursements, teaching assistantships with full tuition reimbursements, and project assistantships available. *Unit head:* Dr. Alberta Gloria, Chair, 608-263-9503, E-mail: agloria@education.wisc.edu. *Application contact:* 608-262-2433, Fax: 608-262-5134, E-mail: gradadmiss@mail.bascom.wisc.edu.
Website: http://www.education.wisc.edu/cp.

University of Wisconsin–Milwaukee, Graduate School, School of Education, Department of Educational Psychology, Milwaukee, WI 53201-0413. Offers counseling psychology (PhD); educational statistics and measurement (MS, PhD); learning and development (MS, PhD); school and community counseling (MS); school psychology (PhD). *Accreditation:* APA. Part-time programs available. *Faculty:* 15 full-time (9 women), 1 (woman) part-time/adjunct. *Students:* 149 full-time (112 women), 41 part-time (27 women); includes 38 minority (12 Black or African American, non-Hispanic/Latino; 6 Asian, non-Hispanic/Latino; 5 Hispanic/Latino; 15 Two or more races, non-Hispanic/Latino), 9 international. Average age 31. 243 applicants, 52% accepted, 47 enrolled. In 2013, 61 master's, 5 doctorates awarded. *Degree requirements:* For master's, comprehensive exam, thesis; for doctorate, thesis/dissertation. *Entrance requirements:* For master's, minimum GPA of 3.0; for doctorate, GRE General Test, minimum GPA of 3.0. Additional exam requirements/recommendations for international students: Required—TOEFL (minimum score 550 paper-based; 79 iBT), IELTS (minimum score 6.5). *Application deadline:* For fall admission, 1/1 priority date for domestic students; for spring admission, 9/1 for domestic students. Applications are processed on a rolling basis. Application fee: $56 ($96 for international students). Electronic applications accepted. *Financial support:* In 2013–14, 14 fellowships, 1 research assistantship, 8 teaching assistantships were awarded; career-related internships or fieldwork, health care benefits, unspecified assistantships, and project assistantships also available. Support available to part-time students. Financial award application deadline: 4/15; financial award applicants required to submit FAFSA. *Unit head:* Nadya Fouad, Department Chair, 414-229-6830, Fax: 414-229-4939, E-mail: nadya@uwm.edu. *Application contact:* General Information Contact, 414-229-4982, Fax: 414-229-6967, E-mail: gradschool@uwm.edu.
Website: http://www4.uwm.edu/soe/academics/ed_psych/.

University of Wisconsin–Oshkosh, Graduate Studies, College of Education and Human Services, Department of Professional Counseling, Oshkosh, WI 54901. Offers counseling (MSE). *Accreditation:* ACA. Part-time and evening/weekend programs available. *Degree requirements:* For master's, thesis optional, practicum. *Entrance requirements:* For master's, MAT, interview, minimum GPA of 3.0, letters of recommendation. Additional exam requirements/recommendations for international students: Required—TOEFL (minimum score 550 paper-based; 79 iBT). Electronic applications accepted. *Faculty research:* Gender issues, grief and loss, addictions, career development, close relationships.

University of Wisconsin–Platteville, School of Graduate Studies, College of Liberal Arts and Education, Counselor Education Program, Platteville, WI 53818-3099. Offers

MSE. *Accreditation:* NCATE. Part-time programs available. *Faculty:* 5 full-time (2 women). *Students:* 38 full-time (30 women), 2 part-time (both women); includes 5 minority (3 Black or African American, non-Hispanic/Latino; 1 American Indian or Alaska Native, non-Hispanic/Latino; 1 Asian, non-Hispanic/Latino). 15 applicants, 93% accepted, 12 enrolled. In 2013, 20 master's awarded. *Degree requirements:* For master's, comprehensive exam, thesis or alternative. *Entrance requirements:* Additional exam requirements/recommendations for international students: Required—TOEFL (minimum score 500 paper-based; 61 iBT), IELTS (minimum score 6). *Application deadline:* For fall admission, 7/1 priority date for domestic students; for spring admission, 11/1 for domestic students. Applications are processed on a rolling basis. Application fee: $56. Electronic applications accepted. *Financial support:* Research assistantships with partial tuition reimbursements, career-related internships or fieldwork, Federal Work-Study, institutionally sponsored loans, scholarships/grants, and unspecified assistantships available. Support available to part-time students. Financial award applicants required to submit FAFSA. *Unit head:* Dr. Kimberly Tuescher, Coordinator, 608-342-1252, E-mail: tueschek@uwplatt.edu. *Application contact:* Dee Dunbar, School of Graduate Studies, 608-342-1322, Fax: 608-342-1389, E-mail: dunbard@uwplatt.edu.

University of Wisconsin–River Falls, Outreach and Graduate Studies, College of Education and Professional Studies, Department of Counseling and School Psychology, River Falls, WI 54022. Offers counseling (MSE); school psychology (MSE, Ed S). Part-time programs available. *Entrance requirements:* For master's, minimum GPA of 2.75, resume, 3 letters of reference, vita. Additional exam requirements/recommendations for international students: Required—TOEFL (minimum score 500 paper-based; 65 iBT), IELTS (minimum score 5.5). Electronic applications accepted.

University of Wisconsin–Stevens Point, College of Professional Studies, School of Education, Program in Guidance and Counseling, Stevens Point, WI 54481-3897. Offers MSE. Program offered jointly with University of Wisconsin–Oshkosh. *Degree requirements:* For master's, comprehensive exam, thesis or alternative.

University of Wisconsin–Superior, Graduate Division, Department of Counseling and Psychological Professions, Superior, WI 54880-4500. Offers community counseling (MSE); human relations (MSE); school counseling (MSE). Part-time and evening/weekend programs available. *Faculty:* 3 full-time (1 woman), 4 part-time/adjunct (all women). *Students:* 18 full-time (15 women), 31 part-time (26 women); includes 4 minority (1 American Indian or Alaska Native, non-Hispanic/Latino; 1 Asian, non-Hispanic/Latino; 2 Two or more races, non-Hispanic/Latino). Average age 33. 25 applicants, 56% accepted, 10 enrolled. In 2013, 17 master's awarded. *Degree requirements:* For master's, position paper, practicum. *Entrance requirements:* For master's, GRE and/or MAT, minimum GPA of 2.75. *Application deadline:* For fall admission, 4/1 priority date for domestic students; for spring admission, 10/15 priority date for domestic students. Applications are processed on a rolling basis. Application fee: $56. Electronic applications accepted. *Expenses:* Tuition, state resident: full-time $4526; part-time $649.24 per credit. Tuition, nonresident: full-time $9091; part-time $1156.51 per credit. *Financial support:* Career-related internships or fieldwork, Federal Work-Study, institutionally sponsored loans, scholarships/grants, traineeships, and tuition waivers (partial) available. Support available to part-time students. Financial award application deadline: 4/15; financial award applicants required to submit FAFSA. *Faculty research:* Women and power, intrafamily dynamics. *Unit head:* Terri Kronzer, Chairperson, 715-394-8506. *Application contact:* Suzie Finckler, Student Status Examiner, 715-394-8295, Fax: 715-394-8371, E-mail: gradstudy@uwsuper.edu.

University of Wisconsin–Whitewater, School of Graduate Studies, College of Education and Professional Studies, Department of Counselor Education, Whitewater, WI 53190-1790. Offers community counseling (MS Ed); higher education (MS Ed); school counseling (MS Ed). *Accreditation:* ACA; NCATE. Part-time and evening/weekend programs available. *Degree requirements:* For master's, thesis or alternative. *Entrance requirements:* For master's, resume, 2 letters of reference, goal statement, autobiography. Additional exam requirements/recommendations for international students: Required—TOEFL (minimum score 550 paper-based; 80 iBT), IELTS (minimum score 6). Electronic applications accepted. *Faculty research:* Alcohol and other drugs, counseling effectiveness, teacher mentoring.

University of Wyoming, College of Education, Programs in Counselor Education, Laramie, WY 82071. Offers community mental health (MS); counselor education and supervision (PhD); school counseling (MS); student affairs (MS). *Accreditation:* ACA (one or more programs are accredited). *Degree requirements:* For master's, comprehensive exam (for some programs), thesis optional; for doctorate, thesis/dissertation, video demonstration. *Entrance requirements:* For master's, interview, background check; for doctorate, video tape session, interview, writing sample, master's degree, background check. Additional exam requirements/recommendations for international students: Required—TOEFL. *Faculty research:* Wyoming SAGE photovoice project; accountable school counseling programs; GLBT issues; addictions; play therapy-early childhood mental health.

Utah State University, School of Graduate Studies, Emma Eccles Jones College of Education and Human Services, Department of Psychology, Logan, UT 84322. Offers clinical/counseling/school psychology (PhD); research and evaluation methodology (PhD); school counseling (MS); school psychology (MS). *Accreditation:* APA (one or more programs are accredited). Part-time and evening/weekend programs available. Postbaccalaureate distance learning degree programs offered (no on-campus study). Terminal master's awarded for partial completion of doctoral program. *Degree requirements:* For master's, thesis (for some programs); for doctorate, thesis/dissertation. *Entrance requirements:* For master's, GRE General Test (school psychology), MAT (school counseling), minimum GPA of 3.5; for doctorate, GRE General Test, minimum GPA of 3.5. Additional exam requirements/recommendations for international students: Required—TOEFL. *Faculty research:* Hearing loss detection in infancy, ADHD, eating disorders, domestic violence, neuropsychology, bilingual/Spanish speaking students/parents.

Valdosta State University, Department of Psychology and Counseling, Valdosta, GA 31698. Offers clinical/counseling psychology (MS); industrial/organizational psychology (MS); school counseling (M Ed, Ed S). Part-time and evening/weekend programs available. *Faculty:* 18 full-time (6 women). *Students:* 61 full-time (42 women), 23 part-time (21 women); includes 21 minority (15 Black or African American, non-Hispanic/Latino; 1 Asian, non-Hispanic/Latino; 3 Hispanic/Latino; 2 Two or more races, non-Hispanic/Latino), 3 international. Average age 23. 43 applicants, 72% accepted, 29 enrolled. In 2013, 19 master's awarded. *Degree requirements:* For master's, thesis or alternative, comprehensive written and/or oral exams; for Ed S, thesis. *Entrance requirements:* For master's and Ed S, GRE General Test or MAT. Additional exam requirements/recommendations for international students: Required—TOEFL (minimum score 523 paper-based). *Application deadline:* For fall admission, 7/1 for domestic and international students; for spring admission, 11/15 for domestic and international students. Applications are processed on a rolling basis. Application fee: $35. Electronic applications accepted. *Expenses:* Tuition, state resident: full-time $4140; part-time $230 per credit hour. Tuition, nonresident: full-time $14,904; part-time $828 per credit hour. *Required fees:* $995 per semester. Tuition and fees vary according to course load. *Financial support:* In 2013–14, 5 students received support, including 2 research

assistantships with full tuition reimbursements available (averaging $3,652 per year); institutionally sponsored loans and unspecified assistantships also available. Support available to part-time students. Financial award application deadline: 7/1; financial award applicants required to submit FAFSA. *Unit head:* Dr. Jackson Rainer, Chair, 229-333-5930, Fax: 229-259-5576, E-mail: jprainer@valdosta.edu. *Application contact:* Jessica Powers, Coordinator of Graduate Admissions, 229-333-5694, Fax: 229-245-3853, E-mail: jldevane@valdosta.edu.
Website: http://www.valdosta.edu/colleges/education/psychology-and-counseling/welcome.php.

Valparaiso University, Graduate School, Department of Education, Program in School Counseling, Valparaiso, IN 46383. Offers M Ed/Ed S. *Accreditation:* ACA. Part-time and evening/weekend programs available. *Students:* 10 full-time (9 women), 1 (woman) part-time; includes 2 minority (1 Asian, non-Hispanic/Latino; 1 Hispanic/Latino), 1 international. Average age 26. *Entrance requirements:* Additional exam requirements/recommendations for international students: Required—TOEFL (minimum score 550 paper-based; 80 iBT), IELTS (minimum score 6). *Application deadline:* For fall admission, 3/1 priority date for domestic students. Applications are processed on a rolling basis. Application fee: $30 ($50 for international students). Electronic applications accepted. *Expenses:* Tuition: Full-time $10,350; part-time $575 per credit hour. *Required fees:* $378; $101 per term. Tuition and fees vary according to course load and program. *Financial support:* Available to part-time students. Applicants required to submit FAFSA. *Unit head:* Dr. Jon Kilpinen, Acting Chair, Department of Education, 219-464-5314, Fax: 219-464-6720. *Application contact:* Jessica Choquette, Graduate Admissions Specialist, 219-464-5313, Fax: 219-464-5381, E-mail: jessica.choquette@valpo.edu.
Website: http://www.valpo.edu/education/programs/schoolcounseling/mededsschoolcounseling.php.

Vanderbilt University, Peabody College, Department of Human and Organizational Development, Nashville, TN 37240-1001. Offers community development and action (M Ed); human development counseling (M Ed). *Accreditation:* ACA; NCATE. Part-time programs available. *Faculty:* 26 full-time (15 women), 23 part-time/adjunct (13 women). *Students:* 111 full-time (92 women), 13 part-time (11 women); includes 19 minority (12 Black or African American, non-Hispanic/Latino; 4 Asian, non-Hispanic/Latino; 1 Hispanic/Latino; 2 Two or more races, non-Hispanic/Latino). Average age 26. 182 applicants, 66% accepted, 68 enrolled. In 2013, 32 master's awarded. *Degree requirements:* For master's, comprehensive exam, thesis optional. *Entrance requirements:* For master's, GRE General Test, MAT. Additional exam requirements/recommendations for international students: Required—TOEFL (minimum score 550 paper-based; 80 iBT). *Application deadline:* For fall admission, 12/31 priority date for domestic and international students; for spring admission, 11/1 priority date for domestic and international students. Applications are processed on a rolling basis. Application fee: $0. Electronic applications accepted. *Financial support:* Fellowships with full and partial tuition reimbursements, research assistantships with full and partial tuition reimbursements, teaching assistantships with full and partial tuition reimbursements, Federal Work-Study, institutionally sponsored loans, scholarships/grants, tuition waivers (partial), and unspecified assistantships available. Support available to part-time students. Financial award application deadline: 1/15; financial award applicants required to submit FAFSA. *Faculty research:* Community psychology and community development; counseling and mental health services, prevention and positive youth development; organizational and community change; youth physical and behavioral health in schools and communities. *Unit head:* Dr. Marybeth Shinn, Chair, 615-322-6881, Fax: 615-322-1141, E-mail: marybeth.shinn@vanderbilt.edu. *Application contact:* Sherrie Lane, Educational Coordinator, 615-322-8484, Fax: 615-322-1141, E-mail: sherrie.a.lane@vanderbilt.edu.

Villanova University, Graduate School of Liberal Arts and Sciences, Department of Education and Counseling, Program in Clinical Mental Health Counseling, Villanova, PA 19085-1699. Offers counseling and human relations (MS). Part-time and evening/weekend programs available. *Students:* 32 full-time (24 women), 7 part-time (6 women); includes 5 minority (3 Black or African American, non-Hispanic/Latino; 2 Hispanic/Latino), 2 international. Average age 28. In 2013, 12 master's awarded. *Degree requirements:* For master's, comprehensive exam. *Entrance requirements:* For master's, GRE or MAT, minimum GPA of 3.0, statement of goals, 3 letters of recommendation. Additional exam requirements/recommendations for international students: Required—TOEFL. *Application deadline:* For fall admission, 5/1 priority date for international students; for spring admission, 11/15 for international students. Applications are processed on a rolling basis. Application fee: $50. Electronic applications accepted. *Financial support:* Applicants required to submit FAFSA. *Unit head:* Dr. Edward Fierros, Director, 610-519-4625. *Application contact:* Dean, Graduate School of Liberal Arts and Sciences.

Villanova University, Graduate School of Liberal Arts and Sciences, Department of Education and Counseling, Program in Elementary School Counseling, Villanova, PA 19085-1699. Offers counseling and human relations (MS). Part-time and evening/weekend programs available. *Students:* 4 full-time (all women), 1 (woman) part-time. Average age 23. In 2013, 4 master's awarded. *Degree requirements:* For master's, comprehensive exam. *Entrance requirements:* For master's, GRE or MAT, minimum GPA of 3.0, statement of goals, 3 letters of recommendation. Additional exam requirements/recommendations for international students: Required—TOEFL. *Application deadline:* For fall admission, 5/1 for international students; for spring admission, 10/15 for international students. Applications are processed on a rolling basis. Application fee: $50. Electronic applications accepted. *Financial support:* Career-related internships or fieldwork and Federal Work-Study available. Financial award applicants required to submit FAFSA. *Unit head:* Dr. Edward Fierros, Chair, 610-519-4625. *Application contact:* Dean, Graduate School of Liberal Arts and Sciences.

Villanova University, Graduate School of Liberal Arts and Sciences, Department of Education and Counseling, Program in Secondary School Counseling, Villanova, PA 19085-1699. Offers counseling and human relations (MS). *Students:* 10 full-time (all women), 5 part-time (2 women); includes 3 minority (1 Black or African American, non-Hispanic/Latino; 1 Hispanic/Latino; 1 Two or more races, non-Hispanic/Latino). Average age 27. In 2013, 13 master's awarded. *Degree requirements:* For master's, comprehensive exam. *Entrance requirements:* For master's, GRE or MAT, minimum GPA of 3.0, statement of goals, 3 letters of recommendation. *Application deadline:* Applications are processed on a rolling basis. Application fee: $50. Electronic applications accepted. *Financial support:* Applicants required to submit FAFSA. *Unit head:* Dr. Krista Malott, Director, 610-519-4642. *Application contact:* Dean, Graduate School of Liberal Arts and Sciences.

Virginia Commonwealth University, Graduate School, School of Education, Program in Counselor Education, Richmond, VA 23284-9005. Offers college student development and counseling (M Ed); school counseling (M Ed). *Accreditation:* ACA; NCATE. *Entrance requirements:* For master's, GRE General Test or MAT. Additional exam requirements/recommendations for international students: Required—TOEFL (minimum score 600 paper-based; 100 iBT). Electronic applications accepted.

Virginia Polytechnic Institute and State University, Graduate School, College of Liberal Arts and Human Sciences, Blacksburg, VA 24061. Offers career and technical

education (MS Ed, Ed D, PhD, Ed S); communication (MA); counselor education (MA Ed, Ed D, PhD, Ed S); creative writing (MFA); curriculum and instruction (MA Ed, Ed D, PhD, Ed S); educational leadership and policy studies (MA Ed, Ed D, PhD, Ed S); educational research and evaluation (PhD); English (MA); foreign languages, cultures, and literatures (MA); higher education and student affairs (MA Ed); history (MA); human development (MS, PhD); material culture and public humanities (MA); philosophy (MA); political science (MA); rhetoric and writing (PhD); science and technology studies (MS, PhD); social, political, ethical, and cultural thought (PhD); sociology (MS, PhD); theater arts (MFA). *Faculty:* 410 full-time (211 women), 6 part-time/adjunct (5 women). *Students:* 688 full-time (464 women), 576 part-time (372 women); includes 243 minority (144 Black or African American, non-Hispanic/Latino; 3 American Indian or Alaska Native, non-Hispanic/Latino; 29 Asian, non-Hispanic/Latino; 48 Hispanic/Latino; 1 Native Hawaiian or other Pacific Islander, non-Hispanic/Latino; 18 Two or more races, non-Hispanic/Latino), 84 international. Average age 34. 1,054 applicants, 48% accepted, 374 enrolled. In 2013, 314 master's, 74 doctorates, 14 other advanced degrees awarded. *Degree requirements:* For master's, comprehensive exam (for some programs), thesis (for some programs); for doctorate, comprehensive exam (for some programs), thesis/dissertation (for some programs). *Entrance requirements:* For master's and doctorate, GRE/GMAT (may vary by department). Additional exam requirements/recommendations for international students: Required—TOEFL (minimum score 550 paper-based). *Application deadline:* For fall admission, 8/1 for domestic students, 4/1 for international students; for spring admission, 1/1 for domestic students, 9/1 for international students. Applications are processed on a rolling basis. Application fee: $75. Electronic applications accepted. *Expenses:* Tuition, state resident: full-time $11,185; part-time $621.50 per credit hour. Tuition, nonresident: full-time $22,146; part-time $1230.25 per credit hour. *Required fees:* $2442; $449.25 per semester. Tuition and fees vary according to course load, campus/location and program. *Financial support:* In 2013–14, 19 research assistantships with full tuition reimbursements (averaging $17,115 per year), 205 teaching assistantships with full tuition reimbursements (averaging $14,433 per year) were awarded. Financial award application deadline: 3/1; financial award applicants required to submit FAFSA. *Total annual research expenditures:* $6.8 million. *Unit head:* Joan Hirt, Interim Dean, 540-231-6779, Fax: 540-231-7157, E-mail: jbhirt@vt.edu. *Application contact:* Melissa Elliott, Executive Assistant, 540-231-6779, Fax: 540-231-7157, E-mail: elliott1@vt.edu. Website: http://www.clahs.vt.edu/.

Wake Forest University, Graduate School of Arts and Sciences, Counseling Program, Winston-Salem, NC 27109. Offers MA, M Div/MA. *Accreditation:* ACA. *Entrance requirements:* For master's, GRE General Test. Additional exam requirements/recommendations for international students: Required—TOEFL (minimum score 79 iBT). Electronic applications accepted.

Walden University, Graduate Programs, School of Counseling, Minneapolis, MN 55401. Offers addiction counseling (MS), including addictions and public health, child and adolescent counseling, family studies and interventions, forensic counseling, general program (MS, PhD), trauma and crisis counseling; counselor education and supervision (PhD), including consultation, counseling and social change, forensic mental health counseling, general program (MS, PhD), nonprofit management and leadership, trauma and crisis; marriage, couple, and family counseling (MS), including forensic counseling, general program (MS, PhD), trauma and crisis counseling; mental health counseling (MS), including forensic counseling, general program (MS, PhD), trauma and crisis counseling; school counseling (MS), including addictions counseling, crisis and trauma, general program (MS, PhD), military. Part-time and evening/weekend programs available. Postbaccalaureate distance learning degree programs offered (minimal on-campus study). *Faculty:* 50 full-time (38 women), 238 part-time/adjunct (172 women). *Students:* 2,019 full-time (1,709 women), 1,566 part-time (1,345 women); includes 1,622 minority (1,223 Black or African American, non-Hispanic/Latino; 21 American Indian or Alaska Native, non-Hispanic/Latino; 36 Asian, non-Hispanic/Latino; 231 Hispanic/Latino; 8 Native Hawaiian or other Pacific Islander, non-Hispanic/Latino; 103 Two or more races, non-Hispanic/Latino), 19 international. Average age 38. 789 applicants, 90% accepted, 623 enrolled. In 2013, 410 master's awarded. *Degree requirements:* For master's, residency, field experience, professional development plan, licensure plan; for doctorate, thesis/dissertation, residency, practicum, internship. *Entrance requirements:* For master's, bachelor's degree or higher; minimum GPA of 2.5; official transcripts; goal statement (for some programs); access to computer and Internet; for doctorate, master's degree or higher; three years of related professional or academic experience (preferred); minimum GPA of 3.0; goal statement and current resume (select programs); official transcripts; access to computer and Internet. Additional exam requirements/recommendations for international students: Required—TOEFL (minimum score 550 paper-based; 79 iBT), IELTS (minimum score 6.5), Michigan English Language Assessment Battery (minimum score 82), or PTE. *Application deadline:* Applications are processed on a rolling basis. Application fee: $0. Electronic applications accepted. *Expenses: Tuition:* Full-time $11,813.55; part-time $500 per credit. *Required fees:* $618.76. *Financial support:* Federal Work-Study, scholarships/grants, unspecified assistantships, and family tuition reduction, active duty/veteran tuition reduction, group tuition reduction, interest-free payment plans, employee tuition reduction available. Support available to part-time students. Financial award applicants required to submit FAFSA. *Unit head:* Dr. Savitri Dixon-Saxon, Associate Dean, 800-925-3368. *Application contact:* Jennifer Hall, Vice President of Enrollment Management, 866-4-WALDEN, E-mail: info@waldenu.edu.

Walsh University, Graduate Studies, Program in Counseling and Human Development, North Canton, OH 44720-3396. Offers clinical mental health counseling (MA); school counseling (MA); student affairs in higher education (MA). *Accreditation:* ACA. Part-time and evening/weekend programs available. *Faculty:* 5 full-time (all women), 6 part-time/adjunct (2 women). *Students:* 38 full-time (27 women), 47 part-time (41 women); includes 3 minority (2 Black or African American, non-Hispanic/Latino; 1 Hispanic/Latino), 2 international. Average age 28. 94 applicants, 37% accepted, 26 enrolled. In 2013, 21 master's awarded. *Degree requirements:* For master's, comprehensive exam, internship, practicum. *Entrance requirements:* For master's, GRE (minimum score of 145 verbal and 146 quantitative) or MAT (minimum score of 397), interview, minimum GPA of 3.0, writing sample, reference forms, notarized affidavit of good moral conduct. Additional exam requirements/recommendations for international students: Required—TOEFL (minimum score 500 paper-based; 61 iBT). *Application deadline:* For fall admission, 7/15 priority date for domestic students. Applications are processed on a rolling basis. Application fee: $25. Electronic applications accepted. *Expenses: Tuition:* Full-time $10,890; part-time $605 per credit hour. *Required fees:* $100; $100. *Financial support:* In 2013–14, 73 students received support, including 3 research assistantships with partial tuition reimbursements available (averaging $8,065 per year), 11 teaching assistantships with partial tuition reimbursements available (averaging $5,610 per year); scholarships/grants, tuition waivers (full and partial), and unspecified assistantships also available. Support available to part-time students. Financial award application deadline: 12/31. *Faculty research:* Clinical training and supervision of clinical mental health counselors, supervision of school counselors, cross-cultural training in counselor education, outcomes in adventure-based therapies with children, counseling for intimate partner violence and relational issues, refugee mental health and trauma, career counseling for refugees using ecological and social learning models, integration of neuroscience and culture in clinical mental health counseling. *Unit head:* Dr. Linda Barclay, Program Director, 330-490-7264, Fax: 330-490-7323, E-mail: lbarclay@walsh.edu. *Application contact:* Audra Dice, Graduate and Transfer Admissions Counselor, 330-490-7181, Fax: 330-244-4925, E-mail: adice@walsh.edu. Website: http://www.walsh.edu/counseling-graduate-program.

Washington State University, Graduate School, College of Education, Department of Educational Leadership and Counseling Psychology, Program in Community Counseling, Pullman, WA 99164. Offers MA. *Degree requirements:* For master's, comprehensive exam (for some programs), thesis (for some programs), oral and written exam. *Entrance requirements:* For master's, GRE General Test, minimum GPA of 3.0, 3 letters of recommendation, transcripts showing all college or university course work, statement of professional objectives, current curriculum vitae/resume. Additional exam requirements/recommendations for international students: Required—TOEFL (minimum score 550 paper-based; 80 iBT). Electronic applications accepted. *Faculty research:* Hypnosis supervision, multicultural counseling, American Indian mental health, eating disorders.

Wayne State College, School of Education and Counseling, Department of Counseling and Special Education, Program in Guidance and Counseling, Wayne, NE 68787. Offers counseling (MSE); counselor education (MSE); school counseling (MSE). *Accreditation:* NCATE. Part-time and evening/weekend programs available. *Degree requirements:* For master's, comprehensive exam, thesis optional. *Entrance requirements:* For master's, GRE General Test, minimum GPA of 3.0. Additional exam requirements/recommendations for international students: Required—TOEFL (minimum score 550 paper-based). Electronic applications accepted.

Wayne State University, College of Education, Division of Theoretical and Behavioral Foundations, Detroit, MI 48202. Offers counseling (M Ed, MA, Ed D, PhD, Ed S); education evaluation and research (M Ed, Ed D, PhD); educational psychology (M Ed, PhD), including learning and instruction sciences (PhD), school psychology (PhD); educational sociology (M Ed); history and philosophy of education (M Ed); rehabilitation counseling and community inclusion (MA); school and community psychology (MA); school psychology (Certificate). *Accreditation:* ACA (one or more programs are accredited); CORE (one or more programs are accredited). Evening/weekend programs available. *Students:* 239 full-time (199 women), 214 part-time (190 women); includes 181 minority (141 Black or African American, non-Hispanic/Latino; 2 American Indian or Alaska Native, non-Hispanic/Latino; 14 Asian, non-Hispanic/Latino; 10 Hispanic/Latino; 1 Native Hawaiian or other Pacific Islander, non-Hispanic/Latino; 13 Two or more races, non-Hispanic/Latino), 21 international. Average age 33. 271 applicants, 35% accepted, 62 enrolled. In 2013, 55 master's, 19 doctorates, 8 other advanced degrees awarded. *Degree requirements:* For master's, thesis (for some programs); for doctorate, thesis/dissertation. *Entrance requirements:* For master's, GRE; for doctorate, GRE, interview, minimum GPA of 3.0, curriculum vitae, references. Additional exam requirements/recommendations for international students: Required—TOEFL (minimum score 550 paper-based; 79 iBT), Michigan English Language Assessment Battery (minimum score 85); Recommended—IELTS (minimum score 6.5), TWE (minimum score 5.5). *Application deadline:* For fall admission, 6/1 priority date for domestic students, 5/1 priority date for international students; for winter admission, 10/1 priority date for domestic students, 9/1 priority date for international students; for spring admission, 2/1 priority date for domestic students, 1/1 priority date for international students. Applications are processed on a rolling basis. Application fee: $0. Electronic applications accepted. *Expenses:* Tuition, state resident: part-time $554.15 per credit. Tuition, nonresident: part-time $1200.35 per credit. *Required fees:* $42.15 per credit. $268.30 per semester. Tuition and fees vary according to course load and program. *Financial support:* In 2013–14, 83 students received support, including 2 research assistantships with tuition reimbursements available (averaging $16,508 per year); fellowships with tuition reimbursements available, teaching assistantships with tuition reimbursements available, scholarships/grants, health care benefits, and unspecified assistantships also available. Financial award application deadline: 3/31; financial award applicants required to submit FAFSA. *Faculty research:* Adolescents at risk, supervision of counseling. *Unit head:* Dr. Joanne Holbert, Interim Assistant Dean, 313-577-1691, E-mail: jholbert@wayne.edu. *Application contact:* Janice Green, Assistant Dean, 313-577-1605, E-mail: jwgreen@wayne.edu.
Website: http://coe.wayne.edu/tbf/index.php.

West Chester University of Pennsylvania, College of Education, Department of Counselor Education, West Chester, PA 19383. Offers counseling (Teaching Certificate); elementary school counseling (M Ed); higher education counseling (MS); higher education counseling/student affairs (Certificate); secondary school counseling (M Ed). *Accreditation:* ACA; NCATE. Part-time and evening/weekend programs available. *Faculty:* 10 full-time (6 women), 7 part-time/adjunct (5 women). *Students:* 116 full-time (100 women), 110 part-time (93 women); includes 36 minority (19 Black or African American, non-Hispanic/Latino; 2 American Indian or Alaska Native, non-Hispanic/Latino; 2 Asian, non-Hispanic/Latino; 7 Hispanic/Latino; 6 Two or more races, non-Hispanic/Latino). Average age 28. 145 applicants, 76% accepted, 59 enrolled. In 2013, 83 master's awarded. *Degree requirements:* For master's, comprehensive exam. *Entrance requirements:* For master's, minimum GPA of 3.0, three letters of reference. Additional exam requirements/recommendations for international students: Required—TOEFL (minimum score 550 paper-based; 80 iBT). *Application deadline:* For fall admission, 4/15 priority date for domestic students, 3/15 for international students; for spring admission, 10/15 priority date for domestic students, 9/1 for international students. Applications are processed on a rolling basis. Application fee: $45. Electronic applications accepted. *Expenses:* Tuition, state resident: full-time $7956; part-time $442 per credit. Tuition, nonresident: full-time $11,934; part-time $663 per credit. *Required fees:* $2134.20; $106.24 per credit. Tuition and fees vary according to campus/location and program. *Financial support:* Unspecified assistantships available. Support available to part-time students. Financial award application deadline: 2/15; financial award applicants required to submit FAFSA. *Faculty research:* Teacher and student cognition, adolescent cognitive development, college counseling, motivational interviewing. *Unit head:* Dr. Kathryn (Tina) Alessandria, Chair, 610-436-2559, Fax: 610-425-7432, E-mail: kalessandria@wcupa.edu. *Application contact:* Dr. Eric W. Owens, Graduate Coordinator, 610-436-2559, Fax: 610-425-7432, E-mail: eowens@wcupa.edu. Website: http://www.wcupa.edu/_academics/sch_sed.counseling&edpsych/.

Western Carolina University, Graduate School, College of Education and Allied Professions, Department of Human Services, Cullowhee, NC 28723. Offers counseling (M Ed, MA Ed, MS), including community counseling (M Ed, MS), school counseling (MA Ed); human resources (MS). *Accreditation:* ACA (one or more programs are accredited). Part-time and evening/weekend programs available. Postbaccalaureate distance learning degree programs offered. *Degree requirements:* For master's, comprehensive exam, thesis or alternative. *Entrance requirements:* For master's, GRE General Test, appropriate undergraduate degree with minimum GPA of 3.0, 3 recommendations, writing sample, resume. Additional exam requirements/recommendations for international students: Required—TOEFL (minimum score 550 paper-based; 79 iBT). *Faculty research:* Marital and family development, spirituality in counseling, home school law, sexuality education, employee recruitment/retention.

Counselor Education

Western Connecticut State University, Division of Graduate Studies, School of Professional Studies, Department of Education and Educational Psychology, Program in School Counseling, Danbury, CT 06810-6885. Offers MS. *Accreditation:* ACA. Part-time programs available. *Degree requirements:* For master's, practicum, internship, completion of program in 6 years. *Entrance requirements:* For master's, PRAXIS I, minimum GPA of 2.8, 3 letters of reference, essay, 6 hours of psychology. Additional exam requirements/recommendations for international students: Recommended—TOEFL (minimum score 550 paper-based; 79 iBT), IELTS (minimum score 6). *Faculty research:* The effect of affective factors on cognition and learning, statistics and research methods, interviewing, individual and multicultural counseling.

Western Illinois University, School of Graduate Studies, College of Education and Human Services, Department of Counselor Education, Macomb, IL 61455-1390. Offers counseling (MS Ed). *Accreditation:* ACA. Part-time programs available. *Students:* 32 full-time (29 women), 40 part-time (33 women); includes 6 minority (2 Black or African American, non-Hispanic/Latino; 4 Hispanic/Latino). Average age 30. In 2013, 26 master's awarded. *Degree requirements:* For master's, thesis or alternative. *Entrance requirements:* For master's, GRE, interview. Additional exam requirements/recommendations for international students: Required—TOEFL (minimum score 550 paper-based; 80 iBT). *Application deadline:* Applications are processed on a rolling basis. Application fee: $30. Electronic applications accepted. *Financial support:* In 2013–14, 5 students received support, including 5 research assistantships with full tuition reimbursements available (averaging $7,544 per year). Financial award applicants required to submit FAFSA. *Unit head:* Dr. Rebecca Newgent, Chairperson, 309-762-1876. *Application contact:* Dr. Nancy Parsons, Assistant Director of Graduate Studies, 309-298-1806, Fax: 309-298-2345, E-mail: grad-office@wiu.edu.
Website: http://wiu.edu/counselored.

Western Kentucky University, Graduate Studies, College of Education and Behavioral Sciences, Department of Counseling and Student Affairs, Bowling Green, KY 42101. Offers counseling (MA Ed), including marriage and family therapy, mental health counseling; school counseling (P-12) (MA Ed); student affairs in higher education (MA Ed). *Accreditation:* ACA; NCATE. Part-time and evening/weekend programs available. *Degree requirements:* For master's, comprehensive exam, thesis optional. *Entrance requirements:* For master's, GRE General Test. Additional exam requirements/recommendations for international students: Required—TOEFL (minimum score 555 paper-based; 79 iBT). *Faculty research:* Counselor education, research for residential workers.

Western Michigan University, Graduate College, College of Education and Human Development, Department of Counselor Education and Counseling Psychology, Kalamazoo, MI 49008. Offers counseling psychology (MA, PhD); counselor education (MA, PhD); human resources development (MA). *Accreditation:* ACA (one or more programs are accredited); APA (one or more programs are accredited); CORE; NCATE. *Degree requirements:* For doctorate, thesis/dissertation, oral exams. *Entrance requirements:* For doctorate, GRE General Test.

Western New Mexico University, Graduate Division, School of Education, Silver City, NM 88062-0680. Offers bilingual education (MAT); counseling (MA); educational leadership (MA); elementary education (MAT); reading (MAT); school psychology (MA); secondary education (MAT); special education (MAT); TESOL (teaching English to speakers of other languages) (MAT). *Accreditation:* NCATE. *Degree requirements:* For master's, comprehensive exam. *Entrance requirements:* For master's, GRE General Test, GRE Subject Test, minimum GPA of 3.2 in last 64 hours of undergraduate study. Additional exam requirements/recommendations for international students: Required—TOEFL (minimum score 550 paper-based). Electronic applications accepted.

Western Washington University, Graduate School, College of Humanities and Social Sciences, Department of Psychology, Program in School Counseling, Bellingham, WA 98225-5996. Offers M Ed. *Accreditation:* ACA. *Degree requirements:* For master's, comprehensive exam. *Entrance requirements:* For master's, GRE General Test, minimum GPA of 3.0 in last 60 semester hours or last 90 quarter hours. Additional exam requirements/recommendations for international students: Required—TOEFL (minimum score 567 paper-based). Electronic applications accepted.

Westfield State University, Division of Graduate and Continuing Education, Department of Psychology, Westfield, MA 01086. Offers applied behavior analysis (MA); mental health counseling (MA); school guidance (MA). Part-time and evening/weekend programs available. *Degree requirements:* For master's, comprehensive exam. *Entrance requirements:* For master's, GRE General Test, MAT, minimum undergraduate GPA of 2.7.

Westminster College, Programs in Education, Program in School Counseling, New Wilmington, PA 16172-0001. Offers M Ed, Certificate. Part-time and evening/weekend programs available. *Degree requirements:* For master's, comprehensive exam. *Entrance requirements:* For master's, minimum GPA of 3.0.

West Texas A&M University, College of Education and Social Sciences, Department of Education, Program in Clinical Mental Health, Canyon, TX 79016-0001. Offers MA. Part-time programs available. *Degree requirements:* For master's, comprehensive exam. *Entrance requirements:* For master's, GRE General Test, interview, 12 semester hours in education and/or psychology, approval from the Counselor Admissions Committee. Additional exam requirements/recommendations for international students: Required—TOEFL (minimum score 550 paper-based). Electronic applications accepted.

West Texas A&M University, College of Education and Social Sciences, Department of Education, Program in School Counseling, Canyon, TX 79016-0001. Offers M Ed. Part-time and evening/weekend programs available. *Degree requirements:* For master's, comprehensive exam, thesis or alternative. *Entrance requirements:* For master's, GRE General Test, interview. Additional exam requirements/recommendations for international students: Required—TOEFL (minimum score 550 paper-based). Electronic applications accepted. *Faculty research:* Reducing the somatoform patient's reliance on primary care through cognitive-relational group therapy, determining effects of premarital sex.

West Virginia University, College of Human Resources and Education, Department of Counseling, Rehabilitation Counseling, and Counseling Psychology, Program in Counseling, Morgantown, WV 26506. Offers MA. *Accreditation:* ACA; APA. *Degree requirements:* For master's, content exams. *Entrance requirements:* For master's, GRE General Test, minimum GPA of 2.8, interview 2.8. Additional exam requirements/recommendations for international students: Required—TOEFL (minimum score 550 paper-based; 65 iBT). Electronic applications accepted. *Faculty research:* Career development and placement, family therapy, conflict resolution, interviewing technique, multicultural counseling.

Whitworth University, School of Education, Graduate Studies in Education, Program in Counseling, Spokane, WA 99251-0001. Offers school counselors (M Ed); social agency/church setting (M Ed). *Accreditation:* NCATE. Part-time and evening/weekend programs available. *Degree requirements:* For master's, comprehensive exam, internship, practicum, research project, or thesis. *Entrance requirements:* For master's, GRE General Test, MAT. *Faculty research:* Church counseling service support.

Wichita State University, Graduate School, College of Education, Department of Counseling, Educational Leadership, Educational and School Psychology, Wichita, KS 67260. Offers counseling (M Ed); educational leadership (M Ed, Ed D); educational psychology (M Ed); school psychology (Ed S). *Accreditation:* NCATE. Part-time and evening/weekend programs available. *Unit head:* Dr. Jean Patterson, Chairperson, 316-978-3325, Fax: 316-978-3102, E-mail: jean.patterson@wichita.edu. *Application contact:* Jordan Oleson, Admissions Coordinator, 316-978-3095, Fax: 316-978-3253, E-mail: jordan.oleson@wichita.edu.
Website: http://www.wichita.edu/.

Widener University, School of Human Service Professions, Center for Education, Chester, PA 19013-5792. Offers adult education (M Ed); counseling in higher education (M Ed); counselor education (M Ed); early childhood education (M Ed); educational foundations (M Ed); educational leadership (M Ed); educational psychology (M Ed); elementary education (M Ed); English and language arts (M Ed); health education (M Ed); higher education leadership (Ed D); home and school visitor (M Ed); human sexuality (M Ed, PhD); mathematics education (M Ed); middle school education (M Ed); principalship (M Ed); reading and language arts (Ed D); reading education (M Ed); school administration (Ed D); science education (M Ed); social studies education (M Ed); special education (M Ed); technology education (M Ed). *Accreditation:* NCATE. Part-time and evening/weekend programs available. *Faculty:* 34 full-time (22 women), 37 part-time/adjunct (14 women). *Students:* 64 full-time (44 women), 209 part-time (146 women); includes 49 minority (39 Black or African American, non-Hispanic/Latino; 1 American Indian or Alaska Native, non-Hispanic/Latino; 4 Asian, non-Hispanic/Latino; 4 Hispanic/Latino; 1 Two or more races, non-Hispanic/Latino), 8 international. Average age 39. 139 applicants, 88% accepted. In 2013, 168 master's, 31 doctorates awarded. Terminal master's awarded for partial completion of doctoral program. *Degree requirements:* For doctorate, thesis/dissertation. *Entrance requirements:* For master's, minimum GPA of 2.5; for doctorate, GRE or MAT, minimum GPA of 2.0 (undergraduate), 3.5 (graduate). *Application deadline:* Applications are processed on a rolling basis. Application fee: $25 ($300 for international students). Electronic applications accepted. *Expenses:* Contact institution. *Financial support:* Career-related internships or fieldwork, tuition waivers (full and partial), and unspecified assistantships available. Support available to part-time students. Financial award application deadline: 5/1. *Faculty research:* Reading and cognition, adult education, technology education, educational leadership, special education. *Unit head:* Dr. Michael W. LeDoux, Associate Dean, 610-499-4294, Fax: 610-499-4623, E-mail: mwledoux@widener.edu. *Application contact:* Dr. Roberta Nolan, Director of Graduate Admissions, 610-499-4125, E-mail: rdnolan@widener.edu.

William Paterson University of New Jersey, College of Education, Wayne, NJ 07470-8420. Offers curriculum and learning (M Ed); educational leadership (M Ed); reading (M Ed); special education and counseling services (M Ed), including counseling services, special education; teaching (MAT). *Accreditation:* NCATE. Part-time and evening/weekend programs available. Postbaccalaureate distance learning degree programs offered. *Faculty:* 33 full-time (8 women), 32 part-time/adjunct (9 women). *Students:* 118 full-time (92 women), 519 part-time (431 women); includes 134 minority (35 Black or African American, non-Hispanic/Latino; 1 American Indian or Alaska Native, non-Hispanic/Latino; 6 Asian, non-Hispanic/Latino; 86 Hispanic/Latino; 6 Two or more races, non-Hispanic/Latino). Average age 34. 439 applicants, 74% accepted, 240 enrolled. In 2013, 144 master's awarded. *Degree requirements:* For master's, comprehensive exam, thesis (for some programs), exit interview (for some programs), practicum/internship. *Entrance requirements:* For master's, GRE/MAT, minimum GPA of 2.75, teaching certificate. Additional exam requirements/recommendations for international students: Required—TOEFL (minimum score 550 paper-based; 79 iBT), IELTS (minimum score 6). *Application deadline:* For fall admission, 6/1 for domestic students, 5/1 for international students; for spring admission, 11/1 for domestic students, 10/1 for international students. Applications are processed on a rolling basis. Application fee: $50. Electronic applications accepted. *Financial support:* Research assistantships with full tuition reimbursements, career-related internships or fieldwork, Federal Work-Study, and unspecified assistantships available. Support available to part-time students. Financial award application deadline: 4/1; financial award applicants required to submit FAFSA. *Faculty research:* IPads in the classroom, characteristics of effective elementary teachers in language arts and mathematics, gender issues in science, after-school programs, middle class parents' roles and gentrifying school districts. *Unit head:* Dr. Candace Burns, Dean, 973-720-2137, Fax: 973-720-2955, E-mail: burnsc@wpunj.edu. *Application contact:* Liana Fornarotto, Assistant Director, Graduate Admissions, 973-720-3578, Fax: 973-720-2035, E-mail: fornarottol@wpunj.edu.
Website: http://www.wpunj.edu/coe.

Wilmington University, College of Education, New Castle, DE 19720-6491. Offers applied technology in education (M Ed); career and technical education (M Ed); educational leadership (Ed D); elementary and secondary school counseling (M Ed); elementary studies (M Ed); ESOL literacy (M Ed); higher education leadership (Ed D); instruction: gifted and talented (M Ed); instruction: teacher of reading (M Ed); instruction: teaching and learning (M Ed); organizational leadership (Ed D); school leadership (M Ed); secondary education (MAT); special education (M Ed). *Accreditation:* NCATE. Part-time and evening/weekend programs available. *Entrance requirements:* For master's, 2 letters of recommendation, interview. Additional exam requirements/recommendations for international students: Required—TOEFL (minimum score 500 paper-based). Electronic applications accepted.

Winona State University, College of Education, Counselor Education Department, Winona, MN 55987. Offers community counseling (MS); professional development (MS); school counseling (MS). *Accreditation:* ACA; NCATE. Part-time and evening/weekend programs available. *Degree requirements:* For master's, thesis or alternative. *Entrance requirements:* For master's, letters of reference, interview, group activity, on-site writing. Electronic applications accepted.

Winthrop University, College of Education, Program in Counseling and Development, Rock Hill, SC 29733. Offers agency counseling (M Ed); school counseling (M Ed). *Accreditation:* ACA; NCATE. Part-time programs available. *Degree requirements:* For master's, comprehensive exam. *Entrance requirements:* For master's, GRE General Test or MAT, interview. Electronic applications accepted.

Wright State University, School of Graduate Studies, College of Education and Human Services, Department of Human Services, Programs in Counseling, Dayton, OH 45435. Offers counseling (MA, MS), including business and industrial management, community counseling, exceptional children, marriage and family, mental health counseling; pupil personnel services (M Ed, MA), including school counseling. *Accreditation:* ACA (one or more programs are accredited); NCATE. *Degree requirements:* For master's, comprehensive exam, thesis (for some programs). *Entrance requirements:* For master's, GRE General Test, MAT, interview. Additional exam requirements/recommendations for international students: Required—TOEFL.

Xavier University, College of Social Sciences, Health and Education, School of Education, Department of Counseling, Master of Arts in School Counseling Program, Cincinnati, OH 45207. Offers MA. *Accreditation:* ACA. Part-time and evening/weekend programs available. *Faculty:* 2 full-time (0 women), 4 part-time/adjunct (2 women). *Students:* 9 full-time (6 women), 45 part-time (36 women); includes 9 minority (6 Black or

African American, non-Hispanic/Latino; 2 Hispanic/Latino; 1 Native Hawaiian or other Pacific Islander, non-Hispanic/Latino). Average age 31. 6 applicants, 67% accepted, 5 enrolled. In 2013, 16 master's awarded. *Degree requirements:* For master's, internship. *Entrance requirements:* For master's, MAT or GRE, minimum GPA of 3.0, letters of recommendation, resume. Additional exam requirements/recommendations for international students: Required—TOEFL (minimum score 550 paper-based; 79 iBT). *Application deadline:* For fall admission, 3/1 priority date for domestic and international students; for winter admission, 4/1 for domestic and international students; for spring admission, 10/1 priority date for domestic and international students; for summer admission, 3/1 priority date for domestic and international students. Application fee: $35. Electronic applications accepted. *Expenses: Tuition:* Part-time $594 per credit hour. *Required fees:* $3 per semester. *Financial support:* In 2013–14, 30 students received support. Tuition waivers (partial) and unspecified assistantships available. Financial award applicants required to submit FAFSA. *Faculty research:* Supervision, ethics, consultation, self-injury, bullying. *Unit head:* Dr. Brent Richardson, Chair, 513-745-4294, Fax: 513-745-2920, E-mail: richardb@xavier.edu. *Application contact:* Roger Bosse,

Graduate Services Director, 513-745-3357, Fax: 513-745-1048, E-mail: bosse@xavier.edu.
Website: http://www.xavier.edu/school-counseling/.

Xavier University of Louisiana, Graduate School, Programs in Education, New Orleans, LA 70125-1098. Offers curriculum and instruction (MA); education administration and supervision (MA); guidance and counseling (MA). *Accreditation:* NCATE. Part-time and evening/weekend programs available. *Degree requirements:* For master's, comprehensive exam, thesis or alternative. *Entrance requirements:* For master's, GRE General Test, MAT, minimum GPA of 2.5. Additional exam requirements/recommendations for international students: Required—TOEFL.

Youngstown State University, Graduate School, Beeghly College of Education, Department of Counseling, Youngstown, OH 44555-0001. Offers community counseling (MS Ed); school counseling (MS Ed). *Accreditation:* ACA; NCATE. Part-time and evening/weekend programs available. *Degree requirements:* For master's, comprehensive exam. *Entrance requirements:* For master's, MAT, interview, minimum GPA of 2.7. Additional exam requirements/recommendations for international students: Required—TOEFL. *Faculty research:* Suicide, euthanasia, ethical issues, marriage and family.

Developmental Education

Eastern Michigan University, Graduate School, College of Education, Department of Teacher Education, Programs in Educational Psychology and Assessment, Ypsilanti, MI 48197. Offers educational assessment (Graduate Certificate); educational psychology (MA), including development/personality, research and assessment, research and evaluation, the developing learner. *Accreditation:* NCATE. Part-time and evening/weekend programs available. Postbaccalaureate distance learning degree programs offered (minimal on-campus study). *Students:* 14 part-time (12 women); includes 2 minority (1 Black or African American, non-Hispanic/Latino; 1 Hispanic/Latino), 1 international. Average age 40. 6 applicants, 100% accepted, 4 enrolled. In 2013, 17 master's, 3 other advanced degrees awarded. *Degree requirements:* For master's, thesis or alternative. *Entrance requirements:* For master's, GRE. Additional exam requirements/recommendations for international students: Required—TOEFL. *Application deadline:* Applications are processed on a rolling basis. Application fee: $35. *Expenses:* Tuition, state resident: full-time $12,300; part-time $466 per credit hour. Tuition, nonresident: full-time $23,159; part-time $918 per credit hour. *Required fees:* $71 per credit hour. $46 per semester. One-time fee: $100. Tuition and fees vary according to course level and degree level. *Financial support:* Fellowships, research assistantships with full tuition reimbursements, teaching assistantships with full tuition reimbursements, career-related internships or fieldwork, Federal Work-Study, institutionally sponsored loans, scholarships/grants, tuition waivers (partial), and unspecified assistantships available. Support available to part-time students. Financial award applicants required to submit FAFSA. *Unit head:* Dr. Martha Kinney-Sedgwick, Interim Department Head, 734-487-3260, Fax: 734-487-2101, E-mail: mkinneys@emich.edu. *Application contact:* Dr. Patricia Pokay, Coordinator, 734-487-3260, Fax: 734-487-2101, E-mail: ppokay@emich.edu.

Ferris State University, College of Education and Human Services, School of Education, Big Rapids, MI 49307. Offers curriculum and instruction (M Ed), including reading, special education, subject area; educational leadership (MS); instructor (MSCTE); post-secondary administration (MSCTE); training and development (MSCTE). Part-time and evening/weekend programs available. Postbaccalaureate distance learning degree programs offered (minimal on-campus study). *Faculty:* 7 full-time (5 women), 9 part-time/adjunct (6 women). *Students:* 17 full-time (14 women), 88 part-time (53 women); includes 8 minority (3 Black or African American, non-Hispanic/Latino; 1 American Indian or Alaska Native, non-Hispanic/Latino; 1 Asian, non-Hispanic/Latino; 3 Two or more races, non-Hispanic/Latino), 12 international. Average age 35. 16 applicants, 63% accepted, 6 enrolled. In 2013, 31 master's awarded. *Degree requirements:* For master's, thesis, research paper or project. *Entrance requirements:* For master's, minimum undergraduate degree GPA of 3.0. Additional exam requirements/recommendations for international students: Required—TOEFL (minimum score 500 paper-based; 61 iBT), IELTS. *Application deadline:* For fall admission, 7/1 priority date for domestic and international students; for spring admission, 11/1 priority date for domestic and international students; for summer admission, 3/1 priority date for domestic and international students. Applications are processed on a rolling basis. Application fee: $30. Electronic applications accepted. Application fee is waived when completed online. *Financial support:* Career-related internships or fieldwork and scholarships/grants available. Support available to part-time students. Financial award applicants required to submit FAFSA. *Faculty research:* Suicide prevention, reading, women in education, special needs, administration. *Unit head:* Dr. James Powell, Director, 231-591-3512, Fax: 231-591-2043, E-mail: powelj20@ferris.edu. *Application contact:* Kimisue Worrall, Secretary, 231-591-5361, Fax: 231-591-2043.
Website: http://www.ferris.edu/education/education/.

Grambling State University, School of Graduate Studies and Research, College of Education, Department of Educational Leadership, Grambling, LA 71245. Offers developmental education (MS, Ed D, PMC), including curriculum and instructional design (Ed D), English (MS), guidance and counseling (MS), higher education administration and management (Ed D), mathematics (MS), reading (MS), science (MS), student development and personnel services (Ed D); educational leadership (M Ed). Part-time and evening/weekend programs available. *Faculty:* 10 full-time (7 women). *Students:* 19 full-time (13 women), 89 part-time (70 women); includes 83 minority (82 Black or African American, non-Hispanic/Latino; 1 Hispanic/Latino), 6 international. Average age 40. In 2013, 13 master's, 6 doctorates, 1 other advanced degree awarded. *Degree requirements:* For master's, comprehensive exam, thesis (for some programs); for doctorate, comprehensive exam, thesis/dissertation. *Entrance requirements:* For master's, GRE, minimum GPA of 2.5 on last degree; for doctorate, GRE (minimum score 1000, 500 on Verbal), master's degree, minimum GPA of 3.0 on last degree. Additional exam requirements/recommendations for international students: Required—TOEFL (minimum score 500 paper-based; 62 iBT). *Application deadline:* For fall admission, 7/1 for domestic and international students; for spring admission, 12/1 for domestic and international students; for summer admission, 5/1 for domestic and international students. Applications are processed on a rolling basis. Application fee: $20 ($30 for international students). Electronic applications accepted. *Financial support:* Research assistantships, health care benefits, tuition waivers (full), and unspecified assistantships available. Financial award application deadline: 5/31; financial award applicants required to submit FAFSA. *Unit head:* Dr. Olatunde Ogunyemi, Department Head, 318-274-2549, Fax: 318-274-6249, E-mail: ogunyemio@gram.edu. *Application*

contact: Brenda Cooper, Administrative Assistant III, 318-274-2238, Fax: 318-274-6249, E-mail: cooper@gram.edu.
Website: http://www.gram.edu/academics/majors/education/departments/leadership/.

Instituto Tecnológico y de Estudios Superiores de Monterrey, Campus Ciudad Obregón, Programs in Education, Program in Cognitive Development, Ciudad Obregón, Mexico. Offers ME.

National Louis University, College of Arts and Sciences, Chicago, IL 60603. Offers adult education (Ed D); counseling and human services (MS); language and academic development (M Ed, Certificate); psychology (MA, PhD, Certificate); public policy (MA); written communication (MS, Certificate). Part-time and evening/weekend programs available. Postbaccalaureate distance learning degree programs offered (minimal on-campus study). *Degree requirements:* For master's and Certificate, comprehensive exam (for some programs), thesis (for some programs); for doctorate, thesis/dissertation. *Entrance requirements:* For master's, MAT or GRE, 3 professional or academic references, interview, minimum GPA of 3.0; for doctorate, GRE General Test, MAT, or Watson-Glaser Critical Thinking Appraisal, three professional or academic references, statement of academic and professional goals, 3 years of experience in field, interview, master's degree, resume, writing sample; for Certificate, GRE, MAT, or Watson-Glaser Critical Thinking Appraisal, three professional or academic references, statement of academic and professional goals, interview, minimum GPA of 3.0. Additional exam requirements/recommendations for international students: Required—Department of Language Studies Assessment or TOEFL (minimum score 550 paper-based; 79 iBT). Electronic applications accepted.

North Carolina State University, Graduate School, College of Education, Department of Adult and Higher Education, Program in Training and Development, Raleigh, NC 27695. Offers M Ed, Ed D, Certificate. Postbaccalaureate distance learning degree programs offered. *Degree requirements:* For master's, thesis optional. *Entrance requirements:* For master's, GRE General Test or MAT, minimum GPA of 3.0 in major. Electronic applications accepted.

Penn State Harrisburg, Graduate School, School of Behavioral Sciences and Education, Middletown, PA 17057-4898. Offers applied behavior analysis (MA); applied clinical psychology (MA); applied psychological research (MA); community psychology and social change (MA); health education (M Ed); literacy education (M Ed); teaching and curriculum (M Ed, Certificate); training and development (M Ed). Part-time and evening/weekend programs available. *Financial support:* Career-related internships or fieldwork available. *Unit head:* Dr. Mukund S. Kulkarni, Chancellor, 717-948-6105, Fax: 717-948-6452, E-mail: msk5@psu.edu. *Application contact:* Robert W. Coffman, Jr., Director of Enrollment Management, Admissions, 717-948-6250, Fax: 717-948-6325, E-mail: ric1@psu.edu.
Website: http://harrisburg.psu.edu/behavioral-sciences-and-education/.

Rutgers, The State University of New Jersey, New Brunswick, Graduate School of Education, Department of Educational Psychology, Program in Learning, Cognition and Development, Piscataway, NJ 08854-8097. Offers Ed M. Part-time and evening/weekend programs available. *Entrance requirements:* For master's, GRE General Test, 3 letters of recommendation. Additional exam requirements/recommendations for international students: Required—TOEFL (minimum score 550 paper-based; 83 iBT). Electronic applications accepted. *Faculty research:* Cognitive development, gender roles, cognition and instruction, peer learning, infancy and early childhood.

Sam Houston State University, College of Education and Applied Science, Department of Educational Leadership and Counseling, Huntsville, TX 77341. Offers administration (M Ed); clinical mental health counseling (MA); counselor education (PhD); developmental education administration (Ed D); educational leadership (Ed D); higher education administration (MA); instructional leadership (M Ed, MA); school counseling (M Ed). Part-time and evening/weekend programs available. Postbaccalaureate distance learning degree programs offered (no on-campus study). *Faculty:* 29 full-time (16 women). *Students:* 220 full-time (178 women), 463 part-time (374 women); includes 265 minority (128 Black or African American, non-Hispanic/Latino; 3 American Indian or Alaska Native, non-Hispanic/Latino; 6 Asian, non-Hispanic/Latino; 115 Hispanic/Latino; 13 Two or more races, non-Hispanic/Latino), 24 international. Average age 35. 294 applicants, 96% accepted, 130 enrolled. In 2013, 166 master's, 32 doctorates awarded. *Degree requirements:* For master's, comprehensive exam, thesis (for some programs); for doctorate, comprehensive exam, thesis/dissertation. *Entrance requirements:* For master's, GRE General Test. Additional exam requirements/recommendations for international students: Required—TOEFL (minimum score 550 paper-based; 79 iBT). *Application deadline:* For fall admission, 8/1 for domestic students, 6/25 for international students; for spring admission, 12/1 for domestic students, 11/12 for international students. Applications are processed on a rolling basis. Application fee: $45 ($75 for international students). Electronic applications accepted. *Financial support:* In 2013–14, 7 research assistantships (averaging $9,335 per year), 3 teaching assistantships (averaging $6,183 per year) were awarded; career-related internships or fieldwork, Federal Work-Study, institutionally sponsored loans, scholarships/grants, tuition waivers (partial), and unspecified assistantships also available. Support available to part-time students. Financial award application deadline: 5/31; financial award applicants required to submit FAFSA. *Unit head:* Dr. Stacey

Edmonson, Chair, 936-294-1752, Fax: 936-294-3886, E-mail: edu_sle01@shsu.edu. *Application contact:* Dr. Barbara Polnick, Advisor, 936-294-3859, E-mail: bpolnick@shsu.edu.
Website: http://www.shsu.edu/~edu_elc/.

Texas State University, Graduate School, College of Education, Department of Curriculum and Instruction, San Marcos, TX 78666. Offers developmental education (MA, Ed D, PhD); educational technology (M Ed); elementary education (M Ed, MA); elementary education-bilingual/bicultural (M Ed, MA); reading education (M Ed); secondary education (M Ed, MA); special education (M Ed). Part-time and evening/weekend programs available. *Faculty:* 3 full-time (1 woman). *Students:* 26 full-time (21 women), 5 part-time (4 women); includes 13 minority (5 Black or African American, non-Hispanic/Latino; 1 Asian, non-Hispanic/Latino; 7 Hispanic/Latino), 1 international. Average age 38. 26 applicants, 65% accepted, 13 enrolled. In 2013, 3 master's awarded. *Degree requirements:* For master's, comprehensive exam, thesis (for some programs). *Entrance requirements:* For master's, GRE General Test (preferred), minimum GPA of 2.75 in last 60 hours of course work, teaching experience; for doctorate, GRE (minimum preferred score of 299 with no less than 150 verbal and 149 quantitative), master's Degree with relevant developmental education course work and minimum GPA of 3.0. Additional exam requirements/recommendations for international students: Required—TOEFL (minimum score 550 paper-based; 78 iBT). *Application deadline:* For fall admission, 6/15 priority date for domestic students, 6/1 for international students; for spring admission, 10/15 priority date for domestic students, 10/1 for international students. Applications are processed on a rolling basis. Application fee: $40 ($90 for international students). Electronic applications accepted. *Expenses:* Tuition, state resident: full-time $6663; part-time $278 per credit hour. Tuition, nonresident: full-time $15,159; part-time $632 per credit hour. *Required fees:* $1872; $54 per credit hour. $306 per term. Tuition and fees vary according to course load. *Financial support:* In 2013–14, 21 students received support, including 2 research assistantships (averaging $28,889 per year), 13 teaching assistantships (averaging $27,534 per year); fellowships, career-related internships or fieldwork, Federal Work-Study, and institutionally sponsored loans also available. Support available to part-time students. Financial award application deadline: 4/1; financial award applicants required to submit FAFSA. *Unit head:* Dr. Eric Paulson, Doctoral Program Director, 512-245-2048, Fax: 512-245-7911, E-mail: ep27@txstate.edu. *Application contact:* Dr. Andrea Golato, Dean of Graduate School, 512-245-2581, Fax: 512-245-8365, E-mail: gradcollege@txstate.edu.
Website: http://www.txstate.edu/ci.

The University of Iowa, Graduate College, College of Education, Department of Teaching and Learning, Program in Education, Iowa City, IA 52242-1316. Offers art education (MA); developmental reading (MA); elementary education (MA); English education (MA, MAT); foreign and second language education (MAT); foreign language education (MA); foreign language/ESL education (PhD); language, literacy and culture (PhD); mathematics education (MA, MAT, PhD); music education (MM, PhD); science education (MA); secondary education (MA); social studies (MA, PhD). *Degree requirements:* For master's, thesis optional, exam; for doctorate, comprehensive exam, thesis/dissertation. *Entrance requirements:* For master's and doctorate, GRE General Test, minimum GPA of 3.0. Additional exam requirements/recommendations for international students: Required—TOEFL (minimum score 550 paper-based; 81 iBT). Electronic applications accepted.

Walden University, Graduate Programs, Richard W. Riley College of Education and Leadership, Minneapolis, MN 55401. *Accreditation:* NCATE. Part-time and evening/weekend programs available. Postbaccalaureate distance learning degree programs offered (minimal on-campus study). *Faculty:* 23 full-time (15 women), 830 part-time/adjunct (569 women). *Students:* 8,671 full-time (7,197 women), 2,122 part-time (1,735 women); includes 4,734 minority (3,802 Black or African American, non-Hispanic/Latino; 50 American Indian or Alaska Native, non-Hispanic/Latino; 136 Asian, non-Hispanic/Latino; 539 Hispanic/Latino; 35 Native Hawaiian or other Pacific Islander, non-Hispanic/Latino; 172 Two or more races, non-Hispanic/Latino), 73 international. Average age 40. 2,646 applicants, 96% accepted, 2074 enrolled. In 2013, 2,214 master's, 354 doctorates, 479 other advanced degrees awarded. *Degree requirements:* For doctorate, thesis/dissertation (for some programs), residency; for other advanced degree, residency (for some programs). *Entrance requirements:* For master's, bachelor's degree or higher; minimum GPA of 2.5; official transcripts; goal statement (for some programs); access to computer and Internet; for doctorate, master's degree or higher; three years of related professional or academic experience (preferred); minimum GPA of 3.0; goal statement and current resume (select programs); official transcripts; access to computer and Internet; for other advanced degree, relevant work experience; access to computer and Internet. Additional exam requirements/recommendations for international students: Required—TOEFL (minimum score 550 paper-based; 79 iBT), IELTS (minimum score 6.5), Michigan English Language Assessment Battery (minimum score 82), or PTE. *Application deadline:* Applications are processed on a rolling basis. Application fee: $0. Electronic applications accepted. *Expenses:* *Tuition:* Full-time $11,813.55; part-time $500 per credit. *Required fees:* $618.76. *Financial support:* In 2013–14, 1 fellowship was awarded; Federal Work-Study, scholarships/grants, unspecified assistantships, and family tuition reduction, active duty/veteran tuition reduction, group tuition reduction, interest-free payment plans, employee tuition reduction also available. Support available to part-time students. Financial award applicants required to submit FAFSA. *Unit head:* Dr. Kate Steffens, Dean, 800-925-3368. *Application contact:* Jennifer Hall, Vice President of Enrollment Management, 866-4-WALDEN, E-mail: info@waldenu.edu.
Website: http://www.waldenu.edu/colleges-schools/riley-college-of-education/.

English Education

Alabama State University, College of Education, Department of Curriculum and Instruction, Montgomery, AL 36101-0271. Offers early childhood education (M Ed, Ed S); elementary education (M Ed, Ed S); secondary education (M Ed, Ed S), including biology education, English language arts education (M Ed), history education, math education, music education (M Ed), reading education (M Ed), social science education; special education (M Ed). Part-time programs available. *Faculty:* 11 full-time (8 women), 13 part-time/adjunct (10 women). *Students:* 32 full-time (19 women), 162 part-time (136 women); includes 189 minority (187 Black or African American, non-Hispanic/Latino; 1 Hispanic/Latino; 1 Two or more races, non-Hispanic/Latino). Average age 33. 99 applicants, 45% accepted, 34 enrolled. In 2013, 74 master's, 20 Ed Ss awarded. *Degree requirements:* For master's, comprehensive exam, thesis optional; for Ed S, comprehensive exam, thesis. *Entrance requirements:* For master's, GRE General Test, MAT, writing competency test; for Ed S, writing competency test, GRE, MAT. Additional exam requirements/recommendations for international students: Required—TOEFL (minimum score 500 paper-based). *Application deadline:* For fall admission, 7/15 for domestic students; for spring admission, 12/15 for domestic students. Applications are processed on a rolling basis. Application fee: $25. *Expenses:* Tuition, state resident: full-time $7958; part-time $343 per credit hour. Tuition, nonresident: full-time $14,132; part-time $686 per credit hour. *Required fees:* $446 per term. One-time fee: $1784 full-time; $892 part-time. Tuition and fees vary according to course load. *Financial support:* In 2013–14, research assistantships (averaging $9,450 per year) were awarded. *Unit head:* Dr. Joyce Johnson, Acting Chairperson, 334-229-4485, Fax: 334-229-5603, E-mail: jjohnson@alasu.edu. *Application contact:* Dr. William Person, Dean of Graduate Studies, 334-229-4274, Fax: 334-229-4928, E-mail: wperson@alasu.edu.
Website: http://www.alasu.edu/academics/colleges—departments/college-of-education/curriculum—instruction/index.aspx.

Albany State University, College of Arts and Humanities, Albany, GA 31705-2717. Offers English education (M Ed); public administration (MPA), including community and economic development administration, criminal justice administration, general administration, health administration and policy, human resources management, public policy, water resources management; social work (MSW). Part-time programs available. *Degree requirements:* For master's, comprehensive exam, professional portfolio (for MPA), internship, capstone report. *Entrance requirements:* For master's, GRE, MAT, minimum GPA of 3.0, official transcript, pre-medical record/certificate of immunization, letters of reference. Electronic applications accepted. *Faculty research:* HIV prevention for minority students.

Andrews University, School of Graduate Studies, College of Arts and Sciences, Department of English, Berrien Springs, MI 49104. Offers MA, MAT. Part-time programs available. *Faculty:* 9 full-time (4 women), 1 (woman) part-time/adjunct. *Students:* 4 full-time (all women), 12 part-time (7 women); includes 4 minority (1 Asian, non-Hispanic/Latino; 2 Hispanic/Latino; 1 Two or more races, non-Hispanic/Latino), 2 international. Average age 35. 10 applicants, 40% accepted, 2 enrolled. In 2013, 5 master's awarded. *Degree requirements:* For master's, one foreign language, thesis optional. *Entrance requirements:* For master's, GRE Subject Test. Additional exam requirements/recommendations for international students: Required—TOEFL (minimum score 550 paper-based). *Application deadline:* For fall admission, 8/15 for domestic students. Applications are processed on a rolling basis. Application fee: $40. *Financial support:* Fellowships, research assistantships, teaching assistantships, career-related internships or fieldwork, and Federal Work-Study available. *Faculty research:* Christianity and literature, Victorian literature, social linguistics, rhetoric, American literature. *Unit head:* Dr. Douglas Jones, Chairperson, 269-471-3298. *Application contact:* Monica Wringer, Supervisor of Graduate Admission, 800-253-2874, Fax: 269-471-6321, E-mail: graduate@andrews.edu.

Andrews University, School of Graduate Studies, School of Education, Department of Teaching, Learning, and Curriculum, Berrien Springs, MI 49104. Offers curriculum and instruction (MA, Ed D, PhD, Ed S); elementary education (MAT); secondary education (MAT), including biology, education, English, English as a second language, French, history, physics; teacher education (MAT). *Faculty:* 7 full-time (4 women). *Students:* 16 full-time (11 women), 26 part-time (22 women); includes 14 minority (11 Black or African American, non-Hispanic/Latino; 1 Asian, non-Hispanic/Latino; 1 Hispanic/Latino; 1 Two or more races, non-Hispanic/Latino), 13 international. Average age 40. 33 applicants, 42% accepted, 3 enrolled. In 2013, 7 master's, 1 doctorate, 1 other advanced degree awarded. *Entrance requirements:* For master's, GRE Subject Test. Additional exam requirements/recommendations for international students: Required—TOEFL (minimum score 550 paper-based). *Application deadline:* For fall admission, 8/15 for domestic students. Applications are processed on a rolling basis. Application fee: $40. *Unit head:* Dr. Lee C. Davidson, Chair, 269-471-6364. *Application contact:* Monica Wringer, Supervisor of Graduate Admission, 800-253-2874, Fax: 269-471-6321, E-mail: graduate@andrews.edu.

Anna Maria College, Graduate Division, Program in Education, Paxton, MA 01612. Offers early childhood education (M Ed); education (CAGS); elementary education (M Ed); English language arts (M Ed); visual arts (M Ed). Part-time and evening/weekend programs available. *Entrance requirements:* For master's, bachelor's degree in liberal arts or sciences, minimum GPA of 3.0. Additional exam requirements/recommendations for international students: Required—TOEFL (minimum score 500 paper-based). Electronic applications accepted.

Appalachian State University, Cratis D. Williams Graduate School, Department of Curriculum and Instruction, Boone, NC 28608. Offers curriculum specialist (MA); educational media (MA); elementary education (MA); middle grades education (MA), including language arts, mathematics, science, social studies. *Accreditation:* NCATE. Part-time and evening/weekend programs available. Postbaccalaureate distance learning degree programs offered (no on-campus study). *Degree requirements:* For master's, comprehensive exam, thesis or alternative. *Entrance requirements:* For master's, GRE General Test or MAT, 3 letters of recommendation. Additional exam requirements/recommendations for international students: Required—TOEFL (minimum score 570 paper-based; 79 iBT), IELTS (minimum score 6.5). Electronic applications accepted. *Faculty research:* Media literacy, elementary teaching, curriculum development, online learning environments.

Appalachian State University, Cratis D. Williams Graduate School, Department of English, Boone, NC 28608. Offers English (MA); English education (MA). Part-time programs available. Postbaccalaureate distance learning degree programs offered (no on-campus study). *Degree requirements:* For master's, one foreign language, comprehensive exam, thesis (for some programs). *Entrance requirements:* For master's, GRE General Test, 3 letters of recommendation. Additional exam requirements/recommendations for international students: Required—TOEFL (minimum score 570 paper-based; 79 iBT), IELTS (minimum score 6.5). Electronic applications accepted. *Faculty research:* Contemporary Irish literature, Romantic psychology, cultural practices of everyday life, Gullah linguistics, Renaissance women's writing.

Arcadia University, Graduate Studies, School of Education, Glenside, PA 19038-3295. Offers art education (M Ed); computer education (CAS); curriculum (CAS); curriculum studies (M Ed); early childhood education (M Ed, CAS), including individualized (M Ed), master teacher (M Ed), research in child development (M Ed); educational leadership (M Ed, Ed D, CAS); elementary education (M Ed, CAS); English education (MA Ed); environmental education (MA Ed, CAS); history education (MA Ed); instructional technology (M Ed); language arts (M Ed, CAS); library science (M Ed); mathematics education (M Ed, MA Ed, CAS); music education (MA Ed); psychology (MA Ed); reading

(M Ed, CAS); science education (M Ed, CAS); secondary education (M Ed, CAS); special education (M Ed, Ed D, CAS); theater arts (MA Ed); written communication (MA Ed). *Accreditation:* NASAD. Part-time and evening/weekend programs available. Postbaccalaureate distance learning degree programs offered (minimal on-campus study). Electronic applications accepted. *Expenses:* Contact institution.

Arkansas State University, Graduate School, College of Humanities and Social Sciences, Department of English and Philosophy, Jonesboro, AR 72467. Offers English (MA); English education (MSE, SCCT). Part-time programs available. *Faculty:* 19 full-time (6 women). *Students:* 11 full-time (7 women), 16 part-time (9 women); includes 3 minority (2 Black or African American, non-Hispanic/Latino; 1 Two or more races, non-Hispanic/Latino). Average age 30. 28 applicants, 68% accepted, 13 enrolled. In 2013, 6 master's, 1 other advanced degree awarded. *Degree requirements:* For master's, variable foreign language requirement, comprehensive exam, thesis or alternative, preliminary exam; for SCCT, comprehensive exam. *Entrance requirements:* For master's, GRE General Test or MAT, appropriate bachelor's degree, official transcript, valid teaching certificate (for MSE), immunization records; for SCCT, GRE General Test or MAT, interview, master's degree, official transcript, immunization records. Additional exam requirements/recommendations for international students: Required—TOEFL (minimum score 550 paper-based; 79 iBT), IELTS (minimum score 6), PTE (minimum score 56). *Application deadline:* For fall admission, 7/1 for domestic and international students; for spring admission, 11/15 for domestic students, 11/14 for international students. Applications are processed on a rolling basis. Application fee: $30 ($40 for international students). Electronic applications accepted. *Expenses:* Tuition, state resident: full-time $4284; part-time $238 per credit hour. Tuition, nonresident: full-time $8568; part-time $476 per credit hour. *International tuition:* $9268 full-time. *Required fees:* $1098; $61 per credit hour. $25 per term. Tuition and fees vary according to course load and program. *Financial support:* In 2013–14, 9 students received support. Teaching assistantships, career-related internships or fieldwork, scholarships/grants, and unspecified assistantships available. Financial award application deadline: 7/1; financial award applicants required to submit FAFSA. *Unit head:* Dr. Janelle Collins, Chair, 870-972-3043, Fax: 870-972-3045, E-mail: jcollins@astate.edu. *Application contact:* Vickey Ring, Graduate Admissions Coordinator, 870-972-3029, Fax: 870-972-3857, E-mail: vickeyring@astate.edu.
Website: http://www.astate.edu/college/humanities-and-social-sciences/departments/english-and-philosophy.

Arkansas Tech University, College of Arts and Humanities, Russellville, AR 72801. Offers English (M Ed, MA); history (MA); liberal arts (MLA); multi-media journalism (MA); psychology (MS); Spanish (MA); teaching English as a second language (MA). Part-time programs available. *Students:* 64 full-time (45 women), 81 part-time (62 women); includes 22 minority (3 Black or African American, non-Hispanic/Latino; 2 American Indian or Alaska Native, non-Hispanic/Latino; 2 Asian, non-Hispanic/Latino; 12 Hispanic/Latino; 3 Two or more races, non-Hispanic/Latino), 36 international. Average age 29. In 2013, 67 master's awarded. *Degree requirements:* For master's, comprehensive exam (for some programs), thesis (for some programs), project. *Entrance requirements:* For master's, GRE General Test or GMAT. Additional exam requirements/recommendations for international students: Required—TOEFL (minimum score 550 paper-based; 79 iBT), IELTS (minimum score 6). *Application deadline:* For fall admission, 3/1 priority date for domestic students, 5/1 priority date for international students; for spring admission, 10/1 priority date for domestic and international students. Applications are processed on a rolling basis. Application fee: $25 ($75 for international students). Electronic applications accepted. *Expenses:* Tuition, state resident: full-time $5976; part-time $249 per credit hour. Tuition, nonresident: full-time $11,952; part-time $498 per credit hour. *Required fees:* $411 per semester. Tuition and fees vary according to course load. *Financial support:* In 2013–14, research assistantships with full tuition reimbursements (averaging $4,800 per year), teaching assistantships with full tuition reimbursements (averaging $4,800 per year) were awarded; career-related internships or fieldwork, Federal Work-Study, scholarships/grants, health care benefits, and unspecified assistantships also available. Support available to part-time students. Financial award application deadline: 4/15; financial award applicants required to submit FAFSA. *Unit head:* Dr. Jeffrey Woods, Dean, 479-968-0274, Fax: 479-964-0812, E-mail: jwoods@atu.edu. *Application contact:* Dr. Mary B. Gunter, Dean of Graduate College, 479-968-0398, Fax: 479-964-0542, E-mail: gradcollege@atu.edu.
Website: http://www.atu.edu/humanities/.

Auburn University, Graduate School, College of Education, Department of Curriculum and Teaching, Auburn University, AL 36849. Offers business education (M Ed, MS, PhD); early childhood education (M Ed, MS, PhD, Ed S); elementary education (M Ed, MS, PhD, Ed S); foreign languages (M Ed, MS); music education (M Ed, MS, PhD, Ed S); postsecondary education (PhD); reading education (PhD, Ed S); secondary education (M Ed, MS, PhD, Ed S), including English language arts, mathematics, science, social studies. *Accreditation:* NASM (one or more programs are accredited); NCATE. Part-time programs available. *Faculty:* 29 full-time (21 women), 4 part-time/adjunct (all women). *Students:* 61 full-time (40 women), 153 part-time (108 women); includes 37 minority (32 Black or African American, non-Hispanic/Latino; 2 Asian, non-Hispanic/Latino; 3 Hispanic/Latino), 1 international. Average age 34. 150 applicants, 59% accepted, 74 enrolled. In 2013, 70 master's, 6 doctorates, 26 other advanced degrees awarded. *Degree requirements:* For master's, thesis (for some programs); for doctorate, thesis/dissertation; for Ed S, field project. *Entrance requirements:* For master's, doctorate, and Ed S, GRE General Test. *Application deadline:* For fall admission, 7/7 for domestic students; for spring admission, 11/24 for domestic students. Applications are processed on a rolling basis. Application fee: $50 ($60 for international students). Electronic applications accepted. *Expenses:* Tuition, state resident: full-time $8262; part-time $459 per credit hour. Tuition, nonresident: full-time $24,786; part-time $1377 per credit hour. Tuition and fees vary according to degree level and program. *Financial support:* Fellowships, teaching assistantships, career-related internships or fieldwork, and Federal Work-Study available. Support available to part-time students. Financial award application deadline: 3/15; financial award applicants required to submit FAFSA. *Faculty research:* Emerging literacy, reading attitudes, music for at-risk youth, portfolio assessment. *Unit head:* Dr. Kimberly Walls, Head, 334-844-4434. *Application contact:* Dr. George Flowers, Dean of the Graduate School, 334-844-2125.
Website: http://education.auburn.edu/academic_departments/curr/.

Auburn University at Montgomery, School of Education, Department of Foundations, Technology, and Secondary Education, Montgomery, AL 36124-4023. Offers instructional technology (M Ed); secondary education (M Ed, Ed S), including art education (M Ed), biology (M Ed), English language arts (M Ed), general science (M Ed), history (M Ed), mathematics (M Ed), social science (M Ed). *Accreditation:* NCATE. Part-time and evening/weekend programs available. *Faculty:* 6 full-time (2 women), 1 (woman) part-time/adjunct. *Students:* 47 full-time (22 women), 77 part-time (48 women); includes 30 minority (29 Black or African American, non-Hispanic/Latino; 1 Asian, non-Hispanic/Latino), 1 international. Average age 30. In 2013, 86 master's awarded. *Degree requirements:* For master's and Ed S, comprehensive exam, thesis optional. *Entrance requirements:* For master's, GRE General Test or MAT, certification, BS in teaching; for Ed S, GRE General Test or MAT, certification. *Application deadline:* Applications are processed on a rolling basis. Electronic applications accepted. *Expenses:* Tuition, state resident: full-time $5994; part-time $333 per credit hour. Tuition, nonresident: full-time $17,982; part-time $999 per credit hour. *Financial support:* Teaching assistantships, career-related internships or fieldwork, and scholarships/grants available. Support available to part-time students. Financial award application deadline: 3/1; financial award applicants required to submit FAFSA. *Unit head:* Dr. Sheila Austin, Dean, 334-244-3425, Fax: 334-244-3102, E-mail: saustin1@aum.edu. *Application contact:* Dr. Rhonda Morton, Associate Dean/Graduate Coordinator, 334-244-3287, Fax: 334-244-3978, E-mail: rmorton@aum.edu.
Website: http://www.education.aum.edu/departments/foundations-technology-and-secondary-education.

Averett University, Master in Education Program, Danville, VA 24541-3692. Offers administration and supervision (M Ed); art (M Ed); biology (M Ed); chemistry (M Ed); curriculum and instruction (M Ed); early childhood (M Ed); English (M Ed); mathematics (M Ed); middle grades (M Ed); physical science (M Ed); reading specialist (M Ed); science (M Ed); special education (M Ed); special education learning disability (M Ed). Program offered on Danville Campus only. Part-time and evening/weekend programs available. *Faculty:* 4 full-time (3 women), 13 part-time/adjunct (8 women). *Students:* 43 full-time (35 women), 44 part-time (35 women); includes 7 minority (all Black or African American, non-Hispanic/Latino). *Degree requirements:* For master's, 30-credit core curriculum, minimum GPA of 3.0 throughout program, completion of degree requirements within six years from start of program. *Entrance requirements:* For master's, PRAXIS I, GRE, or MAT; writing proficiency test, minimum cumulative GPA of 3.0 over the last 60 hours of undergraduate study toward a baccalaureate degree, three letters of recommendation, Virginia teaching license (or eligibility). Additional exam requirements/recommendations for international students: Required—TOEFL (minimum score 600 paper-based; 100 iBT). *Application deadline:* Applications are processed on a rolling basis. Application fee: $100. *Expenses:* Contact institution. *Financial support:* Career-related internships or fieldwork, Federal Work-Study, and scholarships/grants available. Financial award application deadline: 4/1; financial award applicants required to submit FAFSA. *Unit head:* Wilfred Lawrence, Department Chair of Education, 434-791-5752, E-mail: priedel@averett.edu. *Application contact:* Christy Pack, Executive Director of Enrollment, 804-887-8612, E-mail: dpack@averett.edu.
Website: http://www.averett.edu/adultprograms/degrees/MEDtrad.php.

Binghamton University, State University of New York, Graduate School, School of Education, Program in Adolescence Education, Vestal, NY 13850. Offers biology education (MAT, MS Ed); chemistry education (MAT, MS Ed); earth science education (MAT, MS Ed); English education (MAT, MS Ed); French education (MAT, MS Ed); literacy education (MS Ed); mathematical sciences education (MAT, MS Ed); physics (MAT, MS Ed); social studies (MAT, MS Ed); Spanish education (MAT, MS Ed). *Accreditation:* Teacher Education Accreditation Council. Part-time and evening/weekend programs available. *Students:* 48 full-time (29 women), 5 part-time (3 women); includes 7 minority (2 Black or African American, non-Hispanic/Latino; 3 Asian, non-Hispanic/Latino; 2 Hispanic/Latino), 1 international. Average age 26. 37 applicants, 86% accepted, 21 enrolled. In 2013, 34 master's awarded. *Entrance requirements:* For master's, GRE General Test. Additional exam requirements/recommendations for international students: Required—TOEFL (minimum score 550 paper-based; 80 iBT). *Application deadline:* For fall admission, 2/1 priority date for domestic and international students; for spring admission, 10/15 priority date for domestic and international students. Applications are processed on a rolling basis. Application fee: $75. Electronic applications accepted. *Financial support:* In 2013–14, 7 students received support, including 1 fellowship with partial tuition reimbursement available (averaging $4,500 per year); career-related internships or fieldwork, Federal Work-Study, institutionally sponsored loans, scholarships/grants, health care benefits, tuition waivers (full), and unspecified assistantships also available. Financial award application deadline: 2/15; financial award applicants required to submit FAFSA. *Unit head:* Dr. S. G. Grant, Dean of School of Education, 607-777-7329, E-mail: sggrant@binghamton.edu. *Application contact:* Kishan Zuber, Recruiting and Admissions Coordinator, 607-777-2151, Fax: 607-777-2501, E-mail: kzuber@binghamton.edu.

Bloomsburg University of Pennsylvania, School of Graduate Studies, College of Education, Department of Early Childhood and Adolescent Education, Program in Middle Level Education Grades 4-8, Bloomsburg, PA 17815-1301. Offers language arts (M Ed); math (M Ed); science (M Ed); social studies (M Ed). *Accreditation:* NCATE. *Faculty:* 14 full-time (6 women), 3 part-time/adjunct (2 women). In 2013, 2 master's awarded. *Degree requirements:* For master's, thesis optional, student teaching. *Entrance requirements:* For master's, MAT, GRE, or PRAXIS, minimum QPA of 3.0, teaching certificate, U.S. citizenship, related undergraduate coursework, professional liability insurance, recent TB test. Additional exam requirements/recommendations for international students: Required—TOEFL (minimum score 550 paper-based). *Application deadline:* Applications are processed on a rolling basis. Application fee: $35 ($60 for international students). Electronic applications accepted. *Expenses:* Tuition, state resident: full-time $7956; part-time $442 per credit. Tuition, nonresident: full-time $11,934; part-time $663 per credit. *Required fees:* $95.50 per credit. $55 per semester. Tuition and fees vary according to course load. *Financial support:* Unspecified assistantships available. *Unit head:* Dr. Tegan Kotarski, College of Education Graduate Coordinator, 570-389-3883, Fax: 570-389-5049, E-mail: tkotarsk@bloomu.edu. *Application contact:* Jennifer Richard, Administrative Assistant, 570-389-4015, Fax: 570-389-3054, E-mail: jrichard@bloomu.edu.
Website: http://www.bloomu.edu/gradschool/middle-level-education.

Bob Jones University, Graduate Programs, Greenville, SC 29614. Offers accountancy (MS); Bible (MA); Bible translation (MA); Biblical studies (Certificate); broadcast management (MS); business administration (MBA); church history (MA, PhD); church ministries (MA); church music (MM); cinema and video production (MA); counseling (MS); curriculum and instruction (Ed D); divinity (M Div); dramatic production (MA); educational leadership (MS, Ed D, Ed S); elementary education (M Ed, MAT); English (M Ed, MA, MAT); fine arts (MA); graphic design (MA); history (M Ed, MA); illustration (MA); interpretative speech (MA); mathematics (M Ed, MAT); medical missions (Certificate); ministry (MM, D Min); multi-categorical special education (M Ed, MAT); music (M Ed); New Testament interpretation (PhD); Old Testament interpretation (PhD); orchestral instrument performance (MM); organ performance (MM); pastoral studies (MA); personnel services (MS, Ed S); piano pedagogy (MM); piano performance (MM); platform arts (MA); radio and television broadcasting (MS); rhetoric and public address (MA); secondary education (M Ed); studio art (MA); teaching Bible (MA); theology (MA, PhD); voice performance (MM); youth ministries (MA); M Div/MM.

Brooklyn College of the City University of New York, Division of Graduate Studies, School of Education, Program in Adolescence Education and Special Subjects, Brooklyn, NY 11210-2889. Offers adolescence science education (MAT); art teacher (MA); biology teacher (MA); chemistry teacher (MA); earth science teacher (MAT); English teacher (MA); French teacher (MA); health and nutrition sciences: health teacher (MS Ed); mathematics teacher (MA); music education (CAS); music teacher (MA); physical education teacher (MS Ed); physics teacher (MA); social studies teacher (MA); Spanish teacher (MA). Part-time and evening/weekend programs available. *Degree requirements:* For master's, comprehensive exam (for some programs), thesis (for some programs). *Entrance requirements:* For master's, LAST, previous course work in education, resume, 2 letters of recommendation, essay. Additional exam

requirements/recommendations for international students: Required—TOEFL (minimum score 500 paper-based; 61 iBT). Electronic applications accepted. *Faculty research:* Interdisciplinary education, semiotics, discourse analysis, autobiography, teacher identity.

Brown University, Graduate School, Department of Education, Program in Teaching, Providence, RI 02912. Offers elementary education (MAT); English (MAT); history/social studies (MAT); science (MAT); secondary education (MAT). *Degree requirements:* For master's, student teaching, portfolio. *Entrance requirements:* For master's, GRE General Test, transcript, personal statement, 3 letters of recommendation, interview, writing sample (English applicants only). Additional exam requirements/recommendations for international students: Required—TOEFL (minimum score 577 paper-based). Electronic applications accepted. *Faculty research:* Literacy, English language learners, diversity, special education, biodiversity.

Buffalo State College, State University of New York, The Graduate School, Faculty of Arts and Humanities, Department of English, Buffalo, NY 14222-1095. Offers English (MA); secondary education (MS Ed), including English. Part-time and evening/weekend programs available. *Degree requirements:* For master's, thesis or project, 1 foreign language (MS Ed). *Entrance requirements:* For master's, minimum GPA of 2.75, 36 hours in English, New York teaching certificate (MS Ed). Additional exam requirements/recommendations for international students: Required—TOEFL (minimum score 550 paper-based).

California Baptist University, Program in English, Riverside, CA 92504-3206. Offers English pedagogy (MA); literature (MA); teaching English to speakers of other languages (TESOL) (MA). Part-time and evening/weekend programs available. *Faculty:* 8 full-time (5 women), 1 (woman) part-time/adjunct. *Students:* 1 (woman) full-time, 21 part-time (17 women); includes 5 minority (1 Black or African American, non-Hispanic/Latino; 1 Asian, non-Hispanic/Latino; 3 Hispanic/Latino), 1 international. Average age 31. 8 applicants, 75% accepted, 3 enrolled. In 2013, 7 master's awarded. *Degree requirements:* For master's, comprehensive exam, research thesis, or project. *Entrance requirements:* For master's, minimum undergraduate GPA of 3.0; 18 semester hours of course work in English beyond freshman level; three recommendations; essay; demonstration of writing; interview. Additional exam requirements/recommendations for international students: Required—TOEFL (minimum score 80 iBT). *Application deadline:* For fall admission, 8/1 priority date for domestic students, 7/1 for international students; for spring admission, 12/1 priority date for domestic students, 11/1 for international students. Applications are processed on a rolling basis. Application fee: $45. Electronic applications accepted. *Expenses:* Contact institution. *Financial support:* Institutionally sponsored loans available. Financial award applicants required to submit CSS PROFILE or FAFSA. *Faculty research:* Classical mythology and folklore, multicultural literature, genre studies, science fiction and fantasy literature, intercultural rhetoric. *Unit head:* Dr. Gayne Anacker, Dean, College of Arts and Sciences, 951-343-4682, E-mail: ganacker@calbaptist.edu. *Application contact:* Dr. Jennifer Newton, Director, Master of Arts Program in English, 951-343-4276, Fax: 951-343-4661, E-mail: jnewton@calbaptist.edu.
Website: http://www.calbaptist.edu/maenglish/.

California State University, Northridge, Graduate Studies, College of Education, Department of Secondary Education, Northridge, CA 91330. Offers educational technology (MA); English education (MA); mathematics education (MA); secondary science education (MA); teaching and learning (MA). *Accreditation:* NCATE. Part-time programs available. *Degree requirements:* For master's, thesis optional. *Entrance requirements:* For master's, GRE General Test or minimum GPA of 3.0. Additional exam requirements/recommendations for international students: Required—TOEFL.

California State University, San Bernardino, Graduate Studies, College of Education, San Bernardino, CA 92407-2397. Offers bilingual/cross-cultural education (MA); curriculum and instruction (MA); educational administration (MA); educational leadership and curriculum (Ed D); educational psychology and counseling (MA, MS), including correctional and alternative education (MA), counseling and guidance (MS), rehabilitation counseling (MA); English as a second language (MA); general education (MA); history and English for secondary teachers (MA); instructional technology (MA); reading (MA); secondary education (MA); special education and rehabilitation counseling (MA), including rehabilitation counseling, special education; teaching of science (MA); vocational and career education (MA). *Accreditation:* NCATE. Part-time and evening/weekend programs available. *Students:* 217 full-time (172 women), 353 part-time (263 women); includes 283 minority (41 Black or African American, non-Hispanic/Latino; 1 American Indian or Alaska Native, non-Hispanic/Latino; 21 Asian, non-Hispanic/Latino; 204 Hispanic/Latino; 1 Native Hawaiian or other Pacific Islander, non-Hispanic/Latino; 15 Two or more races, non-Hispanic/Latino), 35 international. Average age 34. 349 applicants, 76% accepted, 207 enrolled. In 2013, 215 master's awarded. *Degree requirements:* For master's, comprehensive exam (for some programs), thesis (for some programs), advancement to candidacy. *Entrance requirements:* For master's, minimum GPA of 3.0 in education. *Application deadline:* For fall admission, 8/31 priority date for domestic students. Application fee: $55. *Financial support:* Career-related internships or fieldwork and Federal Work-Study available. Support available to part-time students. *Faculty research:* Multicultural education, brain-based learning, science education, social studies/global education. *Unit head:* Dr. Jay Fiene, Dean, 909-537-5600, Fax: 909-537-7011, E-mail: jfiene@csusb.edu. *Application contact:* Dr. Jeffrey Thompson, Dean of Graduate Studies, 909-537-5808, E-mail: jthompso@csusb.edu.

Campbell University, Graduate and Professional Programs, School of Education, Buies Creek, NC 27506. Offers administration (MSA); community counseling (MA); elementary education (M Ed); English education (M Ed); interdisciplinary studies (M Ed); mathematics education (M Ed); middle grades education (M Ed); physical education (M Ed); school counseling (M Ed); secondary education (M Ed); social science education (M Ed). *Accreditation:* NCATE. Part-time and evening/weekend programs available. *Degree requirements:* For master's, comprehensive exam. *Entrance requirements:* For master's, GRE General Test, minimum GPA of 2.7. *Faculty research:* Spiritual values and wellness issues in counseling, stress and professional burnout among counselors, thinking strategies, leadership, adaptive technology.

Caribbean University, Graduate School, Bayamón, PR 00960-0493. Offers administration and supervision (MA Ed); criminal justice (MA); curriculum and instruction (MA Ed, PhD), including elementary education (MA Ed), English education (MA Ed), history education (MA Ed), mathematics education (MA Ed), primary education (MA Ed), science education (MA Ed), Spanish education (MA Ed); educational technology in instructional systems (MA Ed); gerontology (MSN); human resources (MBA); museology, archiving and art history (MA Ed); neonatal pediatrics (MSN); physical education (MA Ed); special education (MA Ed). *Entrance requirements:* For master's, interview, minimum GPA of 2.5.

Carthage College, Division of Teacher Education, Kenosha, WI 53140. Offers classroom guidance and counseling (M Ed); creative arts (M Ed); gifted and talented children (M Ed); language arts (M Ed); modern language (M Ed); natural sciences (M Ed); reading (M Ed, Certificate); social sciences (M Ed); teacher leadership (M Ed). Part-time and evening/weekend programs available. *Degree requirements:* For master's, thesis optional. *Entrance requirements:* For master's, MAT, minimum B average, letters of reference.

Chadron State College, School of Professional and Graduate Studies, Department of Education, Chadron, NE 69337. Offers business (MA Ed); community counseling (MA Ed); educational administration (MS Ed, Sp Ed); elementary education (MS Ed); history (MA Ed); language and literature (MA Ed); secondary administration (MS Ed); secondary education (MS Ed). *Accreditation:* NCATE. Part-time and evening/weekend programs available. Postbaccalaureate distance learning degree programs offered. *Degree requirements:* For master's, thesis optional. *Entrance requirements:* For master's, GRE General Test, GRE Writing Test, minimum GPA of 2.75 or 12 graduate hours at CSC with minimum GPA of 3.25. Additional exam requirements/recommendations for international students: Required—TOEFL. Electronic applications accepted. *Faculty research:* Rural education, technology, mental health.

Chaminade University of Honolulu, Graduate Services, Program in Education, Honolulu, HI 96816-1578. Offers child development (M Ed); early childhood education (M Ed); educational leadership (M Ed); elementary education (MAT); instructional leadership (M Ed); Montessori education (M Ed); secondary education (MAT), including English, math, science, social studies; special education (MAT). Part-time and evening/weekend programs available. Postbaccalaureate distance learning degree programs offered (minimal on-campus study). *Degree requirements:* For master's, thesis or alternative. *Entrance requirements:* For master's, PRAXIS (for MAT only), minimum GPA of 2.75, 3 letters of recommendation. Additional exam requirements/recommendations for international students: Required—TOEFL (minimum score 550 paper-based). Electronic applications accepted. *Faculty research:* Peace and curriculum education.

Chatham University, Program in Education, Pittsburgh, PA 15232-2826. Offers early childhood education (MAT); elementary education (MAT); environmental education (K-12) (MAT); secondary art (MAT); secondary biology education (MAT); secondary chemistry education (MAT); secondary English education (MAT); secondary math education (MAT); secondary physics education (MAT); secondary social studies education (MAT); special education (MAT). *Faculty:* 1 (woman) full-time, 5 part-time/adjunct (4 women). *Students:* 19 full-time (15 women), 4 part-time (all women); includes 2 minority (1 Black or African American, non-Hispanic/Latino; 1 Asian, non-Hispanic/Latino), 2 international. Average age 28. 22 applicants, 73% accepted, 6 enrolled. In 2013, 20 master's awarded. *Degree requirements:* For master's, thesis, teaching experience. *Entrance requirements:* For master's, minimum GPA of 3.0, sample of written work, recommendation letters. Additional exam requirements/recommendations for international students: Required—TOEFL (minimum score 600 paper-based; 100 iBT), IELTS (minimum score 7), TWE. *Application deadline:* For fall admission, 4/1 priority date for domestic and international students; for spring admission, 11/1 priority date for domestic students, 10/1 priority date for international students. Applications are processed on a rolling basis. Application fee: $45. Electronic applications accepted. Application fee is waived when completed online. *Expenses: Tuition:* Full-time $14,886; part-time $827 per credit hour. One-time fee: $396 full-time. *Financial support:* Career-related internships or fieldwork available. Financial award applicants required to submit FAFSA. *Faculty research:* Gifted education, environmental education, technology in education, writing as learning, class size and achievement. *Unit head:* Dr. Edward Donovan, Director of Education Programs, 412-365-2773, E-mail: edonovan@chatham.edu. *Application contact:* Katie Noel, Assistant Director of Graduate Admission, 412-365-2758, Fax: 412-365-1609, E-mail: gradadmissions@chatham.edu.
Website: http://www.chatham.edu/mat.

Christopher Newport University, Graduate Studies, Department of Teacher Preparation, Newport News, VA 23606-3072. Offers art (PK-12) (MAT); biology (6-12) (MAT); chemistry (6-12) (MAT); computer science (6-12) (MAT); elementary (PK-6) (MAT); English (6-12) (MAT); English as second language (PK-12) (MAT); French (PK-12) (MAT); history and social science (6-12) (MAT); mathematics (6-12) (MAT); music (PK-12) (MAT), including choral, instrumental; physics (6-12) (MAT); Spanish (PK-12) (MAT). Part-time programs available. *Faculty:* 15 full-time (7 women), 14 part-time/adjunct (13 women). *Students:* 74 full-time (64 women), 2 part-time (both women); includes 6 minority (4 Hispanic/Latino; 2 Two or more races, non-Hispanic/Latino). Average age 23. 90 applicants, 100% accepted, 67 enrolled. In 2013, 96 master's awarded. *Degree requirements:* For master's, comprehensive exam, thesis or alternative. *Entrance requirements:* For master's, PRAXIS I, minimum GPA of 3.0. Additional exam requirements/recommendations for international students: Required—TOEFL (minimum score 580 paper-based; 92 iBT). *Application deadline:* For fall admission, 4/1 for international students; for spring admission, 10/15 for domestic students, 10/1 for international students; for summer admission, 1/15 for domestic students, 3/1 for international students. Applications are processed on a rolling basis. Application fee: $50. Electronic applications accepted. *Expenses: Tuition, area resident:* Part-time $498 per credit hour. Tuition, state resident: part-time $498 per credit hour. Tuition, nonresident: part-time $899 per credit hour. *Financial support:* In 2013–14, 3 students received support, including 3 research assistantships with full tuition reimbursements available (averaging $2,000 per year); career-related internships or fieldwork, Federal Work-Study, and unspecified assistantships also available. Financial award application deadline: 3/1; financial award applicants required to submit FAFSA. *Faculty research:* Early literacy development, instructional innovations, professional teaching standards, multicultural issues, aesthetic education. *Total annual research expenditures:* $24,000. *Unit head:* Dr. Marsha Sprague, Director, 757-594-7388, Fax: 757-594-7803, E-mail: msprague@cnu.edu. *Application contact:* Lyn Sawyer, Associate Director, Graduate Admissions, 757-594-7544, Fax: 757-594-7649, E-mail: gradstdy@cnu.edu.

The Citadel, The Military College of South Carolina, Citadel Graduate College, School of Education, Program in Secondary Education, Charleston, SC 29409. Offers biology (MAT); English language arts (MAT); mathematics (MAT); mathematics education (MAE); physical education (MAT); social studies (MAT). *Accreditation:* NCATE. Part-time and evening/weekend programs available. *Faculty:* 10 full-time (6 women), 8 part-time/adjunct (3 women). *Students:* 14 full-time (9 women), 56 part-time (31 women); includes 9 minority (8 Black or African American, non-Hispanic/Latino; 1 Hispanic/Latino). Average age 30. In 2013, 24 master's awarded. *Degree requirements:* For master's, comprehensive exam, internship. *Entrance requirements:* For master's, GRE (minimum score 290; 900 on old scoring system) or MAT (minimum score 396), minimum undergraduate GPA of 2.5. Additional exam requirements/recommendations for international students: Required—TOEFL (minimum score 550 paper-based). *Application deadline:* Applications are processed on a rolling basis. Application fee: $30. Electronic applications accepted. *Expenses: Tuition, area resident:* Part-time $525 per credit hour. Tuition, state resident: part-time $525 per credit hour. Tuition, nonresident: part-time $865 per credit hour. *Financial support:* Career-related internships or fieldwork, health care benefits, and unspecified assistantships available. Support available to part-time students. Financial award application deadline: 7/1; financial award applicants required to submit FAFSA. *Unit head:* Dr. Kathryn A. Richardson-Jones, Coordinator, 843-953-3163, Fax: 843-953-7258, E-mail: kathryn.jones@

citadel.edu. *Application contact:* Dr. Robert H. McNamara, Associate Provost, The Citadel Graduate College, 843-953-5089, Fax: 843-953-7630, E-mail: cgc@citadel.edu. Website: http://www.citadel.edu/education/teacher-education/mat-master-of-arts-in-teaching.html.

City College of the City University of New York, Graduate School, School of Education, Department of Secondary Education, New York, NY 10031-9198. Offers adolescent mathematics education (MA, AC); English education (MA); middle school mathematics education (MS); science education (MA); social studies education (AC). *Accreditation:* NCATE. *Entrance requirements:* For master's, Liberal Arts and Sciences Test (LAST), Content Specialty Test (CST). Additional exam requirements/recommendations for international students: Required—TOEFL.

Clayton State University, School of Graduate Studies, College of Arts and Sciences, Program in Education, Morrow, GA 30260-0285. Offers English (MAT); mathematics (MAT). *Accreditation:* NCATE. *Entrance requirements:* For master's, GRE, GACE, 2 official copies of transcripts, 3 recommendation letters, statement of purpose. Additional exam requirements/recommendations for international students: Required—TOEFL (minimum score 550 paper-based). Electronic applications accepted.

Clemson University, Graduate School, College of Health, Education, and Human Development, Eugene T. Moore School of Education, Program in Teaching and Learning, Clemson, SC 29634. Offers elementary education (M Ed); English education (M Ed); mathematics education (M Ed); science education (M Ed); social studies education (M Ed). *Students:* 6 full-time (5 women), 8 part-time (7 women), 3 international. Average age 28. 6 applicants, 100% accepted, 4 enrolled. In 2013, 9 master's awarded. *Entrance requirements:* For master's, GRE, baccalaureate degree from regionally-accredited institution, official transcripts, copy of valid teaching certificate, two letters of recommendation. *Financial support:* In 2013–14, 1 teaching assistantship (averaging $6,812 per year) was awarded. *Unit head:* Dr. Michael J. Padilla, Director/Associate Dean, 864-656-4444, Fax: 864-656-0311, E-mail: padilla@clemson.edu. *Application contact:* Dr. David Fleming, Graduate Programs Coordinator, 864-656-1881, Fax: 864-656-0311, E-mail: dflemin@clemson.edu.
Website: http://www.grad.clemson.edu/programs/Teaching-Learning/.

The College at Brockport, State University of New York, School of Education and Human Services, Department of Education and Human Development, Program in Adolescence Education, Brockport, NY 14420-2997. Offers adolescence biology education (MS Ed); adolescence chemistry education (MS Ed); adolescence earth science education (MS Ed); adolescence English education (MS Ed); adolescence mathematics education (MS Ed); adolescence physics education (MS Ed); adolescence social studies education (MS Ed). *Accreditation:* NCATE. Part-time programs available. *Students:* 13 full-time (7 women), 47 part-time (28 women); includes 3 minority (1 Black or African American, non-Hispanic/Latino; 1 American Indian or Alaska Native, non-Hispanic/Latino; 1 Asian, non-Hispanic/Latino). 26 applicants, 88% accepted, 14 enrolled. In 2013, 27 master's awarded. *Degree requirements:* For master's, thesis or alternative. *Entrance requirements:* For master's, minimum GPA of 3.0, letters of recommendation; statement of objectives, current resume. Additional exam requirements/recommendations for international students: Required—TOEFL (minimum score 550 paper-based; 79 iBT), IELTS (minimum score 6.5). *Application deadline:* For fall admission, 3/15 priority date for domestic and international students; for spring admission, 10/15 priority date for domestic and international students; for summer admission, 3/15 priority date for domestic students, 3/13 priority date for international students. Application fee: $80. Electronic applications accepted. *Expenses:* Tuition, state resident: full-time $9870. Tuition, nonresident: full-time $18,350. *Required fees:* $1848. *Financial support:* Federal Work-Study, scholarships/grants, and unspecified assistantships available. Support available to part-time students. Financial award application deadline: 3/15; financial award applicants required to submit FAFSA. *Unit head:* Dr. Don Halquist, Chairperson, 585-395-5550, Fax: 585-395-2172, E-mail: dhalquis@brockport.edu. *Application contact:* Michael Harrison, Coordinator of Certification and Graduate Advisement, 585-395-2326, Fax: 585-395-2172, E-mail: mharriso@brockport.edu.
Website: http://www.brockport.edu/ehd/.

The College at Brockport, State University of New York, School of Education and Human Services, Department of Education and Human Development, Program in Adolescence Inclusive Generalist Education, Brockport, NY 14420-2997. Offers English (MS Ed); mathematics (MS Ed); science (MS Ed); social studies (MS Ed). *Students:* 30 full-time (18 women), 24 part-time (17 women); includes 6 minority (3 Black or African American, non-Hispanic/Latino; 2 Hispanic/Latino; 1 Two or more races, non-Hispanic/Latino). 16 applicants, 75% accepted, 8 enrolled. In 2013, 15 master's awarded. *Degree requirements:* For master's, thesis or alternative. *Entrance requirements:* For master's, minimum GPA of 3.0, letters of recommendation, statement of objectives, academic major (or equivalent) in program discipline; current resume. Additional exam requirements/recommendations for international students: Required—TOEFL (minimum score 550 paper-based; 79 iBT), IELTS (minimum score 6.5). *Application deadline:* For fall admission, 3/15 priority date for domestic and international students; for spring admission, 10/15 priority date for domestic and international students; for summer admission, 3/15 for domestic and international students. Application fee: $80. Electronic applications accepted. *Expenses:* Tuition, state resident: full-time $9870. Tuition, nonresident: full-time $18,350. *Required fees:* $1848. *Financial support:* Federal Work-Study, scholarships/grants, and unspecified assistantships available. Support available to part-time students. Financial award application deadline: 3/15; financial award applicants required to submit FAFSA. *Unit head:* Dr. Don Halquist, Chairperson, 585-395-2205, Fax: 585-395-2171, E-mail: dhalquis@brockport.edu. *Application contact:* Michael Harrison, Coordinator of Certification and Graduate Advisement, 585-395-2326, Fax: 585-395-2172, E-mail: mharriso@brockport.edu.
Website: http://www.brockport.edu/ehd/.

College of St. Joseph, Graduate Programs, Division of Education, Program in Secondary Education, Rutland, VT 05701-3899. Offers English (M Ed); social studies (M Ed). Part-time and evening/weekend programs available. *Degree requirements:* For master's, comprehensive exam. *Entrance requirements:* For master's, PRAXIS I, official college transcripts; 2 letters of reference; minimum GPA of 3.0 (initial licensure) or 2.7 (nonlicensure); interview. Additional exam requirements/recommendations for international students: Required—TOEFL (minimum score 550 paper-based). Electronic applications accepted.

The College of William and Mary, School of Education, Program in Curriculum and Instruction, Williamsburg, VA 23187-8795. Offers elementary education (MA Ed); gifted education (MA Ed); literacy leadership (MA Ed); math specialist (MA Ed); secondary education (MA Ed), including English education, mathematics education, modern foreign languages education, science education, social studies education; special education (MA Ed), including collaborating master educator, general curriculum. *Accreditation:* NCATE. Part-time programs available. *Faculty:* 15 full-time (10 women), 44 part-time/adjunct (38 women). *Students:* 66 full-time (55 women), 27 part-time (26 women); includes 17 minority (4 Black or African American, non-Hispanic/Latino; 1 American Indian or Alaska Native, non-Hispanic/Latino; 3 Asian, non-Hispanic/Latino; 5 Hispanic/Latino; 4 Two or more races, non-Hispanic/Latino). Average age 28. 179 applicants, 72% accepted, 92 enrolled. In 2013, 76 master's awarded. *Degree requirements:* For master's, project. *Entrance requirements:* For master's, GRE or MAT, minimum GPA of 2.5. Additional exam requirements/recommendations for international students: Required—TOEFL, IELTS. *Application deadline:* For fall admission, 1/15 for domestic and international students; for spring admission, 10/1 for domestic and international students. Application fee: $50. Electronic applications accepted. *Expenses:* Tuition, state resident: full-time $7120; part-time $405 per credit hour. Tuition, nonresident: full-time $21,639; part-time $1050 per credit hour. *Required fees:* $4764. *Financial support:* In 2013–14, 49 students received support, including 6 research assistantships with full and partial tuition reimbursements available (averaging $8,269 per year); career-related internships or fieldwork, Federal Work-Study, institutionally sponsored loans, scholarships/grants, and unspecified assistantships also available. Financial award application deadline: 1/15; financial award applicants required to submit FAFSA. *Faculty research:* National Council of Teachers of Mathematics standards, counseling, self-concept and self-esteem, special education, curriculum development. *Unit head:* Dr. Mark Hofer, Area Coordinator, 757-221-1713, E-mail: mjhofe@wm.edu. *Application contact:* Dorothy Smith Osborne, Assistant Dean for Academic Programs and Student Services, 757-221-2317, Fax: 757-221-2293, E-mail: dsosbo@wm.edu.
Website: http://education.wm.edu.

The Colorado College, Education Department, Program in Secondary Education, Colorado Springs, CO 80903-3294. Offers art teaching (K-12) (MAT); English teaching (MAT); foreign language teaching (MAT); mathematics teaching (MAT); music teaching (MAT); science teaching (MAT); social studies teaching (MAT). *Degree requirements:* For master's, thesis, internship. Electronic applications accepted.

Columbus State University, Graduate Studies, College of Education and Health Professions, Department of Teacher Education, Columbus, GA 31907-5645. Offers accomplished teaching (M Ed); early childhood education (M Ed, MAT, Ed S); middle grades education (M Ed, MAT, Ed S); school library media (M Ed, MAT); secondary education (M Ed, MAT, Ed S), including English/language arts (M Ed, Ed S), general science (M Ed), mathematics (M Ed, Ed S), science (Ed S), social science (M Ed, Ed S); special education (M Ed, MAT, Ed S), including general curriculum (M Ed, MAT); teacher leadership (M Ed). *Accreditation:* NCATE. Part-time and evening/weekend programs available. Postbaccalaureate distance learning degree programs offered (minimal on-campus study). *Faculty:* 17 full-time (12 women), 31 part-time/adjunct (28 women). *Students:* 59 full-time (48 women), 190 part-time (150 women); includes 85 minority (68 Black or African American, non-Hispanic/Latino; 1 American Indian or Alaska Native, non-Hispanic/Latino; 6 Asian, non-Hispanic/Latino; 4 Hispanic/Latino; 6 Two or more races, non-Hispanic/Latino), 2 international. Average age 34. 132 applicants, 58% accepted, 50 enrolled. In 2013, 86 master's, 26 other advanced degrees awarded. *Degree requirements:* For master's, thesis, exit exam; for Ed S, thesis or alternative. *Entrance requirements:* For master's, GRE General Test, minimum undergraduate GPA of 2.75; for Ed S, GRE General Test, minimum undergraduate GPA of 2.75, graduate 3.0. Additional exam requirements/recommendations for international students: Required—TOEFL (minimum score 550 paper-based; 79 iBT). *Application deadline:* For fall admission, 6/30 for domestic students, 5/1 for international students; for spring admission, 11/1 for domestic and international students; for summer admission, 3/1 for domestic and international students. Applications are processed on a rolling basis. Application fee: $40. Electronic applications accepted. *Expenses:* Tuition, state resident: full-time $4572; part-time $382 per credit hour. Tuition, nonresident: full-time $18,292; part-time $1526 per credit hour. *Required fees:* $1800; $196 per credit hour. Tuition and fees vary according to campus/location and program. *Financial support:* In 2013–14, 173 students received support, including 12 research assistantships with partial tuition reimbursements available (averaging $3,000 per year); career-related internships or fieldwork, Federal Work-Study, institutionally sponsored loans, scholarships/grants, tuition waivers (partial), and unspecified assistantships also available. Support available to part-time students. Financial award application deadline: 5/1; financial award applicants required to submit FAFSA. *Unit head:* Dr. Deirdre Greer, Department Chair, 706-507-8034, Fax: 706-568-3134, E-mail: greer_deirdre@columbusstate.edu. *Application contact:* Kristin Williams, Director of International and Graduate Recruitment, 706-507-8848, Fax: 706-568-5091, E-mail: williams_kristin@columbusstate.edu.
Website: http://te.columbusstate.edu/.

Converse College, School of Education and Graduate Studies, Program in Secondary Education, Spartanburg, SC 29302-0006. Offers biology (MAT); chemistry (MAT); English (M Ed, MAT); mathematics (M Ed, MAT); natural sciences (M Ed); social sciences (M Ed, MAT). Part-time programs available. *Degree requirements:* For master's, capstone paper. *Entrance requirements:* For master's, NTE or PRAXIS II (M Ed), minimum GPA of 2.75, 2 recommendations. Electronic applications accepted.

Delta State University, Graduate Programs, College of Arts and Sciences, Division of Languages and Literature, Cleveland, MS 38733-0001. Offers secondary education (M Ed), including English. Part-time programs available. *Faculty:* 8 full-time (2 women). *Students:* 10 full-time (7 women), 11 part-time (7 women); includes 3 minority (all Black or African American, non-Hispanic/Latino). Average age 30. 15 applicants, 100% accepted, 9 enrolled. *Degree requirements:* For master's, thesis or alternative. *Application deadline:* For fall admission, 8/1 priority date for domestic students; for spring admission, 12/1 priority date for domestic students. Applications are processed on a rolling basis. Application fee: $0. *Expenses:* Tuition, state resident: full-time $3006; part-time $334 per credit hour. Tuition, nonresident: full-time $3006; part-time $334 per credit hour. *Financial support:* In 2013–14, research assistantships (averaging $4,000 per year) were awarded; career-related internships or fieldwork, Federal Work-Study, and institutionally sponsored loans also available. Support available to part-time students. Financial award application deadline: 6/1. *Unit head:* Dr. Bill Hays, Chair, 662-846-4060, Fax: 662-846-4016. *Application contact:* Dr. Beverly Moon, Dean of Graduate Studies, 662-846-4873, Fax: 662-846-4313, E-mail: grad-info@deltastate.edu.
Website: http://www.deltastate.edu/pages/2000.asp.

Duquesne University, School of Education, Department of Instruction and Leadership, Program in Secondary Education, Pittsburgh, PA 15282-0001. Offers biology (MS Ed); chemistry (MS Ed); English (MS Ed); K-12 education (MS Ed), including Latin; mathematics (MS Ed); physics (MS Ed); social studies (MS Ed). Part-time and evening/weekend programs available. *Faculty:* 4 full-time (2 women). *Students:* 44 full-time (23 women), 3 part-time (2 women); includes 7 minority (6 Black or African American, non-Hispanic/Latino; 1 Two or more races, non-Hispanic/Latino), 1 international. Average age 27. 43 applicants, 35% accepted, 15 enrolled. In 2013, 28 master's awarded. *Degree requirements:* For master's, thesis optional. *Entrance requirements:* For master's, letters of recommendation, letter of intent, interview, bachelor's degree. Additional exam requirements/recommendations for international students: Required—TOEFL (minimum score 550 paper-based), IELTS (minimum score 7). *Application deadline:* For fall admission, 9/1 for domestic students; for spring admission, 1/1 for domestic students. Applications are processed on a rolling basis. Application fee: $0. Electronic applications accepted. Application fee is waived when completed online. *Expenses: Tuition:* Full-time $18,162; part-time $1009 per credit. *Required fees:* $1728; $96 per credit. Tuition and fees vary according to program. *Financial support:* Research assistantships and Federal Work-Study available. Support available to part-time students. *Unit head:* Dr. Melissa Boston, Associate Professor and Director, 412-396-

6109, E-mail: bostonm@duq.edu. *Application contact:* Michael Dolinger, Director of Student and Academic Services, 412-396-6647, Fax: 412-396-5585, E-mail: dolingerm@duq.edu.
Website: http://www.duq.edu/academics/schools/education/graduate-programs-education/ms-ed-secondary-education.

East Carolina University, Graduate School, College of Education, Department of Business and Information Technologies Education, Greenville, NC 27858-4353. Offers business education (MA Ed); elementary education (MAT); English education (MAT); family and consumer science (MAT); health education (MAT); Hispanic studies (MAT); history education (MAT); marketing education (MA Ed); middle grades education (MAT); music education (MAT); physical education (MAT); science education (MAT); special education (MAT), including general curriculum; vocation education (MS). *Accreditation:* NCATE. Part-time and evening/weekend programs available. Postbaccalaureate distance learning degree programs offered (no on-campus study). *Degree requirements:* For master's, comprehensive exam, thesis optional. *Entrance requirements:* For master's, GRE or MAT, minimum GPA of 2.5, bachelor's degree in related field, teaching license (MA Ed). Additional exam requirements/recommendations for international students: Required—TOEFL. *Expenses:* Tuition, state resident: full-time $4223. Tuition, nonresident: full-time $16,540. *Required fees:* $2184.

East Carolina University, Graduate School, College of Education, Department of Curriculum and Instruction, Greenville, NC 27858-4353. Offers assistive technology (Certificate); autism (Certificate); deaf/blindness (Certificate); elementary education (MA Ed); English education (MA Ed); history (MA Ed); middle grade education (MA Ed); reading education (MA Ed); special education (MA Ed); teaching (MAT). Part-time programs available. Postbaccalaureate distance learning degree programs offered. *Degree requirements:* For master's, comprehensive exam, thesis optional. *Entrance requirements:* For master's, GRE General Test or MAT, interview, bachelor's degree in related field, minimum GPA of 2.5, teaching license. Additional exam requirements/recommendations for international students: Required—TOEFL. *Expenses:* Tuition, state resident: full-time $4223. Tuition, nonresident: full-time $16,540. *Required fees:* $2184.

Eastern Kentucky University, The Graduate School, College of Education, Department of Curriculum and Instruction, Program in Secondary and Higher Education, Richmond, KY 40475-3102. Offers secondary education (MA Ed), including agricultural education, art education, biological sciences education, business education, English education, geography education, history education, home economics education, industrial education, mathematical sciences education, physical education, school health education. *Accreditation:* NCATE. Part-time programs available. *Entrance requirements:* For master's, GRE General Test, minimum GPA of 2.5.

Eastern Michigan University, Graduate School, College of Arts and Sciences, Department of English Language and Literature, Program in English Studies for Teachers, Ypsilanti, MI 48197. Offers MA. Part-time and evening/weekend programs available. *Students:* 7 part-time (5 women); includes 1 minority (Black or African American, non-Hispanic/Latino). Average age 32. 3 applicants, 67% accepted. In 2013, 2 master's awarded. *Entrance requirements:* Additional exam requirements/recommendations for international students: Required—TOEFL. *Expenses:* Tuition, state resident: full-time $12,300; part-time $466 per credit hour. Tuition, nonresident: full-time $23,159; part-time $918 per credit hour. *Required fees:* $71 per credit hour. $46 per semester. One-time fee: $100. Tuition and fees vary according to course level and degree level. *Financial support:* Research assistantships with full tuition reimbursements, teaching assistantships with full tuition reimbursements, career-related internships or fieldwork, Federal Work-Study, institutionally sponsored loans, scholarships/grants, and unspecified assistantships available. Support available to part-time students. *Unit head:* Dr. Mary Ramsey, Department Head, 734-487-4220, Fax: 734-483-9744, E-mail: mramsey6@emich.edu. *Application contact:* Dr. Douglas Baker, Program Advisor, 734-487-2296, Fax: 734-487-9744, E-mail: douglas.baker@emich.edu.

Eastern Michigan University, Graduate School, College of Arts and Sciences, Department of English Language and Literature, Program in Teaching of Writing, Ypsilanti, MI 48197. Offers Graduate Certificate. Application fee: $35. *Expenses:* Tuition, state resident: full-time $12,300; part-time $466 per credit hour. Tuition, nonresident: full-time $23,159; part-time $918 per credit hour. *Required fees:* $71 per credit hour. $46 per semester. One-time fee: $100. Tuition and fees vary according to course level and degree level. *Unit head:* Dr. Joseph Csicsila, Interim Department Head, 734-487-4220, Fax: 734-483-9744, E-mail: jcsicsila@emich.edu. *Application contact:* Dr. Steven Krause, Program Advisor, 734-487-3172, Fax: 734-483-9744, E-mail: skrause@emich.edu.

Eastern University, Graduate Education Programs, St. Davids, PA 19087-3696. Offers ESL program specialist (K-12) (Certificate); general supervisor (PreK-12) (Certificate); health and physical education (K-12) (Certificate); middle level (4-8) (Certificate); multicultural education (M Ed); pre K-4 (Certificate); pre K-4 with special education (Certificate); reading (M Ed); reading specialist (K-12) (Certificate); reading supervisor (K-12) (Certificate); school health services (M Ed); school health supervisor (Certificate); school nurse (Certificate); school principalship (K-12) (Certificate); secondary biology education (7-12) (Certificate); secondary chemistry education (7-12) (Certificate); secondary communication education (7-12) (Certificate); secondary education (7-12) (Certificate); secondary English education (7-12) (Certificate); secondary math education (7-12) (Certificate); secondary social studies education (7-12) (Certificate); special education (M Ed); special education (7-12) (Certificate); special education (Pre K-8) (Certificate); special education supervisor (N-12) (Certificate); TESOL (M Ed); world language (Certificate), including French, Mandarin Chinese, Spanish. Part-time and evening/weekend programs available. Postbaccalaureate distance learning degree programs offered (no on-campus study). *Faculty:* 22 full-time (11 women), 26 part-time/adjunct (18 women). *Students:* 77 full-time (58 women), 223 part-time (149 women); includes 112 minority (81 Black or African American, non-Hispanic/Latino; 1 American Indian or Alaska Native, non-Hispanic/Latino; 9 Asian, non-Hispanic/Latino; 18 Hispanic/Latino; 1 Native Hawaiian or other Pacific Islander, non-Hispanic/Latino; 2 Two or more races, non-Hispanic/Latino), 7 international. Average age 34. 94 applicants, 100% accepted, 81 enrolled. In 2013, 120 master's awarded. *Entrance requirements:* For master's, minimum GPA of 2.5 (for M Ed); for Certificate, minimum GPA of 3.0 for certifications. Additional exam requirements/recommendations for international students: Required—TOEFL. *Application deadline:* For fall admission, 8/14 for domestic students; for spring admission, 12/20 for domestic students. Applications are processed on a rolling basis. Application fee: $35. Application fee is waived when completed online. *Expenses: Tuition:* Full-time $15,600; part-time $650 per credit. *Required fees:* $27.50 per semester. One-time fee: $50. Tuition and fees vary according to course load, degree level and program. *Financial support:* In 2013–14, 84 students received support, including 6 research assistantships with partial tuition reimbursements available (averaging $7,710 per year); scholarships/grants and unspecified assistantships also available. Financial award application deadline: 3/15; financial award applicants required to submit FAFSA. *Unit head:* Harry Gutelius, Associate Dean, 610-341-1729. *Application contact:* Michael Perpiglia, Associate Director of Enrollment, 610-341-5947, Fax: 484-581-1276, E-mail: mperpigl@eastern.edu.
Website: http://www.eastern.edu/academics/programs/loeb-school-education-0/graduateprograms.

Elms College, Division of Education, Chicopee, MA 01013-2839. Offers early childhood education (MAT); education (M Ed, CAGS); elementary education (MAT); English as a second language (MAT); reading (MAT); secondary education (MAT), including biology education, English education, Spanish education; special education (MAT). Part-time and evening/weekend programs available. *Degree requirements:* For master's, thesis (for some programs). *Entrance requirements:* For master's, Massachusetts Educators Certification Test, minimum GPA of 3.0; for CAGS, master's degree in education. Additional exam requirements/recommendations for international students: Required—TOEFL.

Fitchburg State University, Division of Graduate and Continuing Education, Programs in English and Teaching English (Secondary Level), Fitchburg, MA 01420-2697. Offers MA, MAT, Certificate. *Accreditation:* NCATE. Part-time and evening/weekend programs available. *Entrance requirements:* Additional exam requirements/recommendations for international students: Required—TOEFL (minimum score 550 paper-based; 79 iBT). Electronic applications accepted.

Florida Agricultural and Mechanical University, Division of Graduate Studies, Research, and Continuing Education, College of Education, Program in Secondary Education and Foundation, Tallahassee, FL 32307-3200. Offers biology (M Ed); chemistry (MS Ed); English (MS Ed); history (MS Ed); math (MS Ed); physics (MS Ed). *Accreditation:* NCATE. *Degree requirements:* For master's, thesis (for some programs). *Entrance requirements:* For master's, GRE General Test, minimum GPA of 3.0. Additional exam requirements/recommendations for international students: Required—TOEFL.

Florida Atlantic University, College of Education, Department of Teaching and Learning, Boca Raton, FL 33431-0991. Offers curriculum and instruction (M Ed), including art, biology, chemistry, English, French, German, mathematics, music, physics, Pre-K and primary education, reading, social sciences, Spanish; elementary education (M Ed); environmental education (M Ed); reading education (M Ed); social foundations of education (M Ed), including educational psychology, educational technology, multilingual education. *Accreditation:* NCATE. Part-time and evening/weekend programs available. *Faculty:* 16 full-time (12 women), 1 (woman) part-time/adjunct. *Students:* 56 full-time (46 women), 96 part-time (78 women); includes 39 minority (10 Black or African American, non-Hispanic/Latino; 6 Asian, non-Hispanic/Latino; 20 Hispanic/Latino; 3 Two or more races, non-Hispanic/Latino), 4 international. Average age 32. 101 applicants, 54% accepted, 42 enrolled. In 2013, 64 master's awarded. *Entrance requirements:* For master's, GRE General Test, minimum GPA of 3.0 in last 2 years of undergraduate course work. Additional exam requirements/recommendations for international students: Required—TOEFL (minimum score 500 paper-based; 61 iBT), IELTS (minimum score 6). *Application deadline:* For fall admission, 7/1 for domestic students, 2/15 for international students; for spring admission, 11/1 for domestic students, 7/15 for international students. Applications are processed on a rolling basis. Application fee: $30. *Expenses:* Tuition, state resident: full-time $6660; part-time $370 per credit hour. Tuition, nonresident: full-time $18,450; part-time $1025 per credit hour. Tuition and fees vary according to course load. *Financial support:* Fellowships with partial tuition reimbursements, research assistantships with partial tuition reimbursements, teaching assistantships with partial tuition reimbursements, career-related internships or fieldwork, scholarships/grants, and unspecified assistantships available. *Faculty research:* Technology, teaching English to speakers of other languages, math teaching, electronic portfolio assessment, global perspectives through social studies. *Unit head:* Dr. Barbara Ridener, Chairperson, 561-297-3588. *Application contact:* Dr. Eliah Watlington, Associate Dean, 561-296-8520, Fax: 261-297-2991, E-mail: ewatling@fau.edu.
Website: http://www.coe.fau.edu/academicdepartments/tl/.

Florida Atlantic University, Dorothy F. Schmidt College of Arts and Letters, Department of English, Boca Raton, FL 33431-0991. Offers American literature (MA); British literature (MA); creative nonfiction (MFA); creative writing (MA); English (MAT); fiction (MFA); multicultural and world literacies (MA); poetry (MFA); rhetoric and composition (MA); science fiction and fantasy (MA). Part-time programs available. *Faculty:* 25 full-time (10 women). *Students:* 35 full-time (23 women), 33 part-time (21 women); includes 20 minority (7 Black or African American, non-Hispanic/Latino; 2 Asian, non-Hispanic/Latino; 9 Hispanic/Latino; 2 Two or more races, non-Hispanic/Latino). Average age 30. 82 applicants, 43% accepted, 11 enrolled. In 2013, 33 master's awarded. *Degree requirements:* For master's, one foreign language, thesis. *Entrance requirements:* For master's, GRE General Test, minimum GPA of 3.0, writing samples, 2 letters of recommendation. Additional exam requirements/recommendations for international students: Required—TOEFL (minimum score 500 paper-based; 61 iBT), IELTS (minimum score 6). *Application deadline:* For fall admission, 3/1 for domestic students, 2/15 for international students; for spring admission, 11/1 for domestic students, 7/15 for international students. Applications are processed on a rolling basis. Application fee: $30. Electronic applications accepted. *Expenses:* Tuition, state resident: full-time $6660; part-time $370 per credit hour. Tuition, nonresident: full-time $18,450; part-time $1025 per credit hour. Tuition and fees vary according to course load. *Financial support:* Fellowships, teaching assistantships with partial tuition reimbursements, Federal Work-Study, and tuition waivers available. Support available to part-time students. Financial award application deadline: 3/1. *Faculty research:* African-American writers, critical theory, British-American, Asian-American. *Unit head:* Dr. Andy Furman, Chair, 561-297-2065, Fax: 561-297-3807, E-mail: afurman@fau.edu. *Application contact:* Dr. Mark Scroggins, Director of Graduate Studies, 561-297-3561, Fax: 561-297-3807, E-mail: mscroggi@fau.edu.
Website: http://www.fau.edu/english/.

Florida Gulf Coast University, College of Education, Program in Curriculum and Instruction, Fort Myers, FL 33965-6565. Offers curriculum and instruction (Ed D, Ed S); educational technology (M Ed, MA); English education (M Ed). Part-time and evening/weekend programs available. Postbaccalaureate distance learning degree programs offered (minimal on-campus study). *Degree requirements:* For master's, final project or portfolio. *Entrance requirements:* For master's, GRE General Test, MAT, minimum undergraduate GPA of 3.0 in last 2 years. Additional exam requirements/recommendations for international students: Required—TOEFL (minimum score 550 paper-based). Electronic applications accepted. *Faculty research:* Internet in schools, technology in pre-service and in-service teacher training.

Florida International University, College of Education, Department of Teaching and Learning, Miami, FL 33199. Offers art education (MA, MS); curriculum and instruction (MS, Ed D, PhD, Ed S), including curriculum development (MS), elementary education (MS), English education (MS), learning technologies (MS), mathematics education (MS), modern language education (MS), physical education (MS), science education (MS), social studies education (MS), special education (MS); early childhood education (MS); exceptional student education (Ed D); foreign language education (MS), including foreign language education, teaching English to speakers of other languages (TESOL); international/intercultural education (MS); language, literacy and culture (PhD);

mathematics, science, and learning technologies (PhD); physical education (MS), including sport and fitness; reading education (MS). Part-time and evening/weekend programs available. *Degree requirements:* For doctorate, comprehensive exam, thesis/dissertation. *Entrance requirements:* For master's, GRE General Test, Florida General Knowledge Test or Florida College Level Academic Skills Test; for doctorate and Ed S, GRE General Test. Additional exam requirements/recommendations for international students: Required—TOEFL (minimum score 550 paper-based; 80 iBT), IELTS (minimum score 6.3). Electronic applications accepted.

Florida State University, The Graduate School, College of Education, School of Teacher Education, Tallahassee, FL 32306. Offers curriculum and instruction (MS, MST, PhD, Ed S), including early childhood education (MS, PhD, Ed S), elementary education (MS, PhD, Ed S), English education (MS, PhD, Ed S), English teaching (MST), exceptional student education (MST), foreign and second language education (MS, PhD, Ed S), foreign and second language teaching (MST), math education (MS, PhD, Ed S), math teaching (MST), reading education and language arts (MS, PhD, Ed S), science education (MS, PhD, Ed S), social science education (MS, PhD, Ed S), social science teaching (MST), special education (MS, PhD, Ed S), special education studies (MST), visual disabilities (MS, Ed S). Part-time programs available. *Faculty:* 30 full-time (20 women), 22 part-time/adjunct (18 women). *Students:* 183 full-time (151 women), 92 part-time (80 women); includes 47 minority (20 Black or African American, non-Hispanic/Latino; 3 American Indian or Alaska Native, non-Hispanic/Latino; 1 Asian, non-Hispanic/Latino; 20 Hispanic/Latino; 3 Two or more races, non-Hispanic/Latino), 61 international. Average age 30. 199 applicants, 79% accepted, 86 enrolled. In 2013, 119 master's, 9 doctorates, 4 other advanced degrees awarded. *Degree requirements:* For master's and Ed S, comprehensive exam, thesis optional; for doctorate, comprehensive exam, thesis/dissertation, preliminary exam, prospectus defense. *Entrance requirements:* For master's, doctorate, and Ed S, GRE General Test, minimum GPA of 3.0. Additional exam requirements/recommendations for international students: Required—TOEFL (minimum score 550 paper-based; 80 iBT). *Application deadline:* For fall admission, 7/1 for domestic and international students; for winter admission, 10/1 for domestic students, 11/1 for international students; for spring admission, 3/1 for domestic and international students. Applications are processed on a rolling basis. Application fee: $30. Electronic applications accepted. *Expenses:* Tuition, state resident: part-time $403.51 per credit hour. Tuition, nonresident: part-time $1004.85 per credit hour. *Required fees:* $75.81 per credit hour. One-time fee: $20 part-time. Tuition and fees vary according to course load, campus/location and student level. *Financial support:* In 2013–14, 113 students received support, including 55 research assistantships with full and partial tuition reimbursements available, 18 teaching assistantships with full and partial tuition reimbursements available; fellowships with full and partial tuition reimbursements available, career-related internships or fieldwork, scholarships/grants, health care benefits, and unspecified assistantships also available. Financial award application deadline: 1/15; financial award applicants required to submit FAFSA. *Faculty research:* Effective intervention and assessment strategies to improve reading skills; literacy teaching and learning through technology; understanding of student sense-making through instructions, especially STEM learning for all students; international education and consequences of globalization; support professional teacher development and adoption of effective/transformative practices. *Total annual research expenditures:* $1.3 million. *Unit head:* Dr. Sherry Southerland, Chair, 850-644-4880, Fax: 850-644-7736, E-mail: ssoutherland@admin.fsu.edu. *Application contact:* Dawn Matthews, Academic Support Assistant, 850-644-2122, Fax: 850-644-7736, E-mail: dmatthews@fsu.edu.
Website: http://www.coe.fsu.edu/STE.

Framingham State University, Continuing Education, Program in English, Framingham, MA 01701-9101. Offers M Ed.

Gardner-Webb University, Graduate School, Department of English, Boiling Springs, NC 28017. Offers English (MA); English education (MA). Part-time and evening/weekend programs available. *Students:* 7 part-time (5 women). Average age 25. 8 applicants, 25% accepted, 2 enrolled. In 2013, 1 master's awarded. *Degree requirements:* For master's, comprehensive exam. *Entrance requirements:* For master's, GRE General Test, MAT, or NTE; PRAXIS, minimum GPA of 2.5. *Application deadline:* For fall admission, 8/1 priority date for domestic students. Applications are processed on a rolling basis. Application fee: $40. Electronic applications accepted. *Expenses: Tuition:* Full-time $7200; part-time $400 per credit hour. Tuition and fees vary according to course load and program. *Financial support:* Unspecified assistantships available. *Unit head:* Dr. June Hobbs, Chair, 704-406-4412, Fax: 704-406-3921, E-mail: jhobbs@gardner-webb.edu. *Application contact:* Office of Graduate Admissions, 877-498-4723, Fax: 704-406-3895, E-mail: gradinfo@gardner-webb.edu.

Georgia Southern University, Jack N. Averitt College of Graduate Studies, College of Education, Department of Teaching and Learning, Program in English Education, Statesboro, GA 30460. Offers MAT. *Accreditation:* NCATE. Part-time and evening/weekend programs available. *Students:* 4 full-time (all women), 1 (woman) part-time. Average age 24. 4 applicants, 100% accepted, 3 enrolled. In 2013, 4 master's awarded. *Degree requirements:* For master's, portfolio, transition point assessments, exit assessment. *Entrance requirements:* For master's, GRE General Test or MAT; GACE Basic Skills and Content Assessments (for MAT), minimum cumulative GPA of 2.5. Additional exam requirements/recommendations for international students: Required—TOEFL (minimum score 550 paper-based; 80 iBT), IELTS (minimum score 6). *Application deadline:* For fall admission, 3/1 priority date for domestic and international students; for spring admission, 10/1 priority date for domestic students, 10/1 for international students. Applications are processed on a rolling basis. Application fee: $50. Electronic applications accepted. *Expenses:* Tuition, state resident: full-time $7068; part-time $270 per semester hour. Tuition, nonresident: full-time $26,446; part-time $1077 per semester hour. *Required fees:* $2092. *Financial support:* In 2013–14, research assistantships with partial tuition reimbursements (averaging $7,200 per year), teaching assistantships with partial tuition reimbursements (averaging $7,200 per year) were awarded; Federal Work-Study, scholarships/grants, tuition waivers (partial), and unspecified assistantships also available. Support available to part-time students. Financial award application deadline: 4/15; financial award applicants required to submit FAFSA. *Faculty research:* Literacy for at-risk students. *Unit head:* Dr. Greg Chamblee, Coordinator, 912-478-5783, Fax: 912-478-0026, E-mail: gchamblee@georgiasouthern.edu. *Application contact:* Amanda Gilliland, Coordinator for Graduate Student Recruitment, 912-478-5384, Fax: 912-478-0740, E-mail: gradadmissions@georgiasouthern.edu.
Website: http://coe.georgiasouthern.edu/ger/.

Georgia State University, College of Education, Department of Middle-Secondary Education and Instructional Technology, Atlanta, GA 30302-3083. Offers English education (M Ed, MAT); English speakers of other languages (MAT); instructional design and technology (MS); instructional technology (PhD), including alternative instructional delivery systems, consulting, instructional design, management, research; mathematics education (M Ed, MAT); middle level education (MAT); reading, language and literacy education (M Ed), including reading instruction; science education (MAT), including biology, broad field science, chemistry, earth science, physics; social studies education (M Ed, MAT), including economics (MAT), geography (MAT), history (MAT), political science (MAT); teaching and learning (PhD), including language and literacy, mathematics education, music education, science education, social studies, teaching and teacher education. *Accreditation:* NCATE. Part-time and evening/weekend programs available. Postbaccalaureate distance learning degree programs offered (minimal on-campus study). *Faculty:* 27 full-time (19 women). *Students:* 181 full-time (113 women), 203 part-time (145 women); includes 161 minority (127 Black or African American, non-Hispanic/Latino; 1 American Indian or Alaska Native, non-Hispanic/Latino; 10 Asian, non-Hispanic/Latino; 11 Hispanic/Latino; 1 Native Hawaiian or other Pacific Islander, non-Hispanic/Latino; 11 Two or more races, non-Hispanic/Latino), 9 international. Average age 36. 2 applicants, 50% accepted, 1 enrolled. In 2013, 213 master's, 17 doctorates awarded. *Degree requirements:* For master's, comprehensive exam (for some programs), thesis or alternative, exit portfolio; for doctorate, comprehensive exam, thesis/dissertation. *Entrance requirements:* For master's, GRE; GACE I (for initial teacher preparation degree programs), baccalaureate degree or equivalent, resume, goals statement, two letters of recommendation, minimum undergraduate GPA of 2.5; proof of initial teacher certification in the content area (for M Ed); for doctorate, GRE, resume, goals statement, writing sample, two letters of recommendation, minimum graduate GPA of 3.3, interview. Additional exam requirements/recommendations for international students: Required—TOEFL (minimum score 550 paper-based; 79 iBT) or IELTS (minimum score 6.5). *Application deadline:* For fall admission, 1/15 priority date for domestic and international students; for spring admission, 10/1 for domestic and international students. Application fee: $50. Electronic applications accepted. *Expenses: Tuition, area resident:* Full-time $4176; part-time $348 per credit hour. Tuition, state resident: full-time $14,544; part-time $1212 per credit hour. Tuition, nonresident: full-time $14,544; part-time $1212 per credit hour. Tuition and fees vary according to course load and program. *Financial support:* In 2013–14, fellowships with full tuition reimbursements (averaging $19,667 per year), research assistantships with full tuition reimbursements (averaging $5,436 per year), teaching assistantships with full tuition reimbursements (averaging $2,779 per year) were awarded; career-related internships or fieldwork, Federal Work-Study, scholarships/grants, health care benefits, tuition waivers (full and partial), and unspecified assistantships also available. Financial award application deadline: 3/15. *Faculty research:* Teacher education in language and literacy, mathematics, science, and social studies in urban middle and secondary school settings; learning technologies in school, community, and corporate settings; multicultural education and education for social justice; urban education; international education. *Unit head:* Dr. Dana L. Fox, Chair, 404-413-8060, Fax: 404-413-8063, E-mail: dfox@gsu.edu. *Application contact:* Bobbie Turner, Administrative Coordinator I, 404-413-8405, Fax: 404-413-8063, E-mail: bnturner@gsu.edu.
Website: http://msit.gsu.edu/msit_programs.htm.

Grand Valley State University, College of Education, Program in Reading and Language Arts, Allendale, MI 49401-9403. Offers M Ed. *Accreditation:* NCATE. Part-time and evening/weekend programs available. *Degree requirements:* For master's, thesis. *Entrance requirements:* For master's, GRE General Test or minimum GPA of 3.0. Additional exam requirements/recommendations for international students: Required—TOEFL. Electronic applications accepted. *Faculty research:* Culture of literacy, literacy acquisition, assessment, content area literacy, writing pedagogy.

Harding University, Cannon-Clary College of Education, Searcy, AR 72149-0001. Offers advanced studies in teaching and learning (M Ed); art (MSE); behavioral science (MSE); counseling (MS, Ed S); early childhood special education (M Ed, MSE); education (MSE); educational leadership (M Ed, Ed S); elementary education (M Ed); English (MSE); French (MSE); history/social science (MSE); kinesiology (MSE); math (MSE); reading (M Ed); secondary education (M Ed); Spanish (MSE); teaching (MAT); teaching English as a second language (MSE). *Accreditation:* NCATE. Part-time and evening/weekend programs available. *Faculty:* 13 full-time (5 women), 42 part-time/adjunct (24 women). *Students:* 154 full-time (119 women), 393 part-time (270 women); includes 108 minority (81 Black or African American, non-Hispanic/Latino; 5 American Indian or Alaska Native, non-Hispanic/Latino; 5 Asian, non-Hispanic/Latino; 9 Hispanic/Latino; 8 Two or more races, non-Hispanic/Latino), 15 international. Average age 36. 187 applicants, 79% accepted, 135 enrolled. In 2013, 138 master's, 17 other advanced degrees awarded. *Degree requirements:* For master's, comprehensive exam (for some programs), thesis optional, portfolio(s); for Ed S, comprehensive exam, portfolio, project. *Entrance requirements:* For master's, GRE, MAT, PRAXIS; for Ed S, MAT or GRE. Additional exam requirements/recommendations for international students: Required—TOEFL (minimum score 550 paper-based; 79 iBT). *Application deadline:* For fall admission, 8/1 for domestic and international students; for spring admission, 1/1 for domestic and international students. Applications are processed on a rolling basis. Application fee: $35. *Expenses: Tuition:* Full-time $11,574; part-time $643 per credit hour. *Required fees:* $432; $24 per credit hour. Tuition and fees vary according to course load, degree level and program. *Financial support:* In 2013–14, 36 students received support. Unspecified assistantships available. *Faculty research:* Reading, comprehension, school violence, educational technology, behavior, college choice, differentiated instruction, brain-based teaching. *Unit head:* Dr. Clara Carroll, Chair, 501-279-4501, Fax: 501-279-4083, E-mail: ccarroll@harding.edu. *Application contact:* Information Contact, 501-279-4315, E-mail: gradstudiesedu@harding.edu.
Website: http://www.harding.edu/education.

Hofstra University, School of Education, Programs in Teaching - Secondary Education, Hempstead, NY 11549. Offers business education (MS Ed); education technology (Advanced Certificate); English education (MA, MS Ed); foreign language and TESOL (MS Ed); foreign language education (MA, MS Ed), including French, German, Russian, Spanish; mathematics education (MA, MS Ed); science education (MA, MS Ed), including biology, chemistry, earth science, geology, physics; secondary education (Advanced Certificate); social studies education (MA, MS Ed); technology for learning (MA).

Hunter College of the City University of New York, Graduate School, School of Arts and Sciences, Department of English, New York, NY 10065-5085. Offers British and American literature (MA); creative writing (MFA), including creative writing, fiction, nonfiction, poetry; English education (MA). Part-time and evening/weekend programs available. *Faculty:* 24 full-time (11 women). *Students:* 1 full-time (0 women), 85 part-time (54 women); includes 12 minority (4 Black or African American, non-Hispanic/Latino; 4 Asian, non-Hispanic/Latino; 4 Hispanic/Latino), 1 international. Average age 31. 670 applicants, 5% accepted, 26 enrolled. In 2013, 38 master's awarded. *Entrance requirements:* Additional exam requirements/recommendations for international students: Required—TOEFL. *Application deadline:* For fall admission, 4/1 for domestic students, 2/1 for international students; for spring admission, 11/1 for domestic students, 9/1 for international students. Application fee: $125. *Financial support:* Fellowships, Federal Work-Study, and tuition waivers (partial) available. Support available to part-time students. *Faculty research:* Medieval, early modern, late century, Asian-American, and post-colonial literatures. *Unit head:* Dr. Christina Alfar, Chair, 212-772-5070, Fax: 212-772-5411, E-mail: calfar@hunter.cuny.edu. *Application contact:* Sarah Chinn, Adviser, 212-772-5187, E-mail: gradenghish@hunter.cuny.edu.
Website: http://www.hunter.cuny.edu/.

English Education

Hunter College of the City University of New York, Graduate School, School of Education, Programs in Secondary Education, Concentration in English Education, New York, NY 10065-5085. Offers MA. *Accreditation:* NCATE. *Faculty:* 3 full-time (1 woman), 20 part-time/adjunct (9 women). *Students:* 7 full-time (3 women), 49 part-time (30 women); includes 20 minority (5 Black or African American, non-Hispanic/Latino; 6 Asian, non-Hispanic/Latino; 9 Hispanic/Latino), 1 international. Average age 30. 17 applicants, 100% accepted, 17 enrolled. In 2013, 37 master's awarded. *Degree requirements:* For master's, thesis, professional teaching portfolio, New York State Teacher Certification Exam, research project. *Entrance requirements:* For master's, minimum GPA of 2.8, 2 letters of reference, minimum of 21 credits in English. Additional exam requirements/recommendations for international students: Required—TOEFL, TWE. *Application deadline:* For fall admission, 4/1 for domestic students, 2/1 for international students; for spring admission, 11/1 for domestic students, 9/1 for international students. Applications are processed on a rolling basis. Application fee: $125. *Financial support:* Federal Work-Study and tuition waivers (partial) available. Support available to part-time students. *Unit head:* Melissa Schieble, Education Program Coordinator, 212-772-4773, E-mail: mschiebl@hunter.cuny.edu. *Application contact:* Candice Jenkins, English Department Program Coordinator, 212-772-5172, E-mail: candice.jenkins@hunter.cuny.edu.
Website: http://www.hunter.cuny.edu/school-of-education/programs/graduate/adolescent/english.

Indiana State University, College of Graduate and Professional Studies, College of Arts and Sciences, Department of English, Terre Haute, IN 47809. Offers English teaching (MA); history (MA); literature (MA). Part-time and evening/weekend programs available. *Faculty:* 16 full-time (4 women), 7 part-time/adjunct (2 women). *Students:* 12 full-time (10 women), 16 part-time (11 women); includes 1 minority (Black or African American, non-Hispanic/Latino). Average age 32. 11 applicants, 100% accepted, 6 enrolled. In 2013, 14 master's awarded. *Degree requirements:* For master's, one foreign language, thesis optional. *Entrance requirements:* For master's, minimum GPA of 2.75 in all English courses above freshman level. Additional exam requirements/recommendations for international students: Required—TOEFL (minimum score 550 paper-based). *Application deadline:* For fall admission, 7/1 priority date for domestic students; for spring admission, 11/1 priority date for domestic students. Applications are processed on a rolling basis. Application fee: $35. Electronic applications accepted. *Financial support:* In 2013–14, 11 teaching assistantships with partial tuition reimbursements (averaging $3,000 per year) were awarded; career-related internships or fieldwork, Federal Work-Study, and tuition waivers (partial) also available. Support available to part-time students. Financial award application deadline: 3/1; financial award applicants required to submit FAFSA. *Unit head:* Dr. Robert Perrin, Interim Chairperson, 812-237-3160. *Application contact:* Dr. Jay Gatrell, Dean, 800-444-GRAD, Fax: 812-237-8060, E-mail: jay.gatrell@indstate.edu.

Indiana University of Pennsylvania, School of Graduate Studies and Research, College of Humanities and Social Sciences, Department of English, Program in Composition and Teaching English to Speakers of Other Languages, Indiana, PA 15705-1087. Offers PhD. Part-time programs available. *Faculty:* 30 full-time (15 women). *Students:* 23 full-time (17 women), 104 part-time (73 women); includes 10 minority (5 Black or African American, non-Hispanic/Latino; 3 Asian, non-Hispanic/Latino; 1 Hispanic/Latino; 1 Two or more races, non-Hispanic/Latino), 33 international. Average age 39. 190 applicants, 18% accepted, 17 enrolled. In 2013, 25 doctorates awarded. *Degree requirements:* For doctorate, one foreign language, comprehensive exam, thesis/dissertation. *Entrance requirements:* For doctorate, 2 letters of recommendation. Additional exam requirements/recommendations for international students: Required—TOEFL (minimum score 600 paper-based). *Application deadline:* For fall admission, 2/1 priority date for domestic students; for summer admission, 11/1 priority date for domestic students. Applications are processed on a rolling basis. Application fee: $50. Electronic applications accepted. *Expenses:* Tuition, state resident: full-time $3978; part-time $442 per credit. Tuition, nonresident: full-time $5967; part-time $663 per credit. *Required fees:* $2080; $115.55 per credit. $93 per semester. Tuition and fees vary according to degree level and program. *Financial support:* In 2013–14, 15 fellowships with full tuition reimbursements (averaging $392 per year), 15 research assistantships with full and partial tuition reimbursements (averaging $6,710 per year), 6 teaching assistantships with partial tuition reimbursements (averaging $22,848 per year) were awarded; career-related internships or fieldwork, Federal Work-Study, scholarships/grants, and unspecified assistantships also available. Support available to part-time students. Financial award application deadline: 4/15; financial award applicants required to submit FAFSA. *Unit head:* Dr. Sharon Deckert, Graduate Coordinator, 724-357-2261, E-mail: sharon.deckert@iup.edu. *Application contact:* Paula Stossel, Assistant Dean for Administration, 724-357-4511, Fax: 724-357-4862, E-mail: graduate-admissions@iup.edu.
Website: http://www.iup.edu/upper.aspx?id-49407.

Indiana University of Pennsylvania, School of Graduate Studies and Research, College of Humanities and Social Sciences, Department of English, Program in Teaching English, Indiana, PA 15705-1087. Offers MA. Part-time programs available. *Faculty:* 30 full-time (15 women). *Students:* 6 full-time (4 women), 7 part-time (5 women); includes 1 minority (Black or African American, non-Hispanic/Latino). Average age 28. 8 applicants, 75% accepted, 4 enrolled. In 2013, 8 master's awarded. *Degree requirements:* For master's, thesis optional. *Entrance requirements:* For master's, two letters of recommendation. Additional exam requirements/recommendations for international students: Required—TOEFL (minimum score 540 paper-based). *Application deadline:* Applications are processed on a rolling basis. Application fee: $50. Electronic applications accepted. *Expenses:* Tuition, state resident: full-time $3978; part-time $442 per credit. Tuition, nonresident: full-time $5967; part-time $663 per credit. *Required fees:* $2080; $115.55 per credit. $93 per semester. Tuition and fees vary according to degree level and program. *Financial support:* In 2013–14, 1 research assistantship with full and partial tuition reimbursement (averaging $1,000 per year) was awarded; career-related internships or fieldwork, Federal Work-Study, scholarships/grants, and unspecified assistantships also available. Financial award application deadline: 4/16; financial award applicants required to submit FAFSA. *Unit head:* Dr. Linda Norris, Coordinator, 724-357-2263, E-mail: lnorris@iup.edu. *Application contact:* Paula Stossel, Assistant Dean, 724-357-2222, Fax: 724-357-4862, E-mail: graduate-admissions@iup.edu.
Website: http://www.iup.edu/upper.aspx?id-92695.

Indiana University–Purdue University Fort Wayne, College of Arts and Sciences, Department of English and Linguistics, Fort Wayne, IN 46805-1499. Offers English (MA, MAT); TENL (teaching English as a new language) (Certificate). Part-time programs available. *Faculty:* 22 full-time (9 women), 1 (woman) part-time/adjunct. *Students:* 8 full-time (7 women), 18 part-time (13 women); includes 2 minority (both Two or more races, non-Hispanic/Latino), 1 international. Average age 30. 5 applicants, 100% accepted, 3 enrolled. In 2013, 16 master's awarded. *Degree requirements:* For master's, one foreign language, thesis (for some programs), teaching certificate (MAT). *Entrance requirements:* For master's, GRE General Test, minimum GPA of 3.0, major or minor in English, 3 letters of recommendation; for Certificate, bachelor's degree with minimum GPA of 2.5. Additional exam requirements/recommendations for international students: Required—TOEFL (minimum score 600 paper-based; 79 iBT). *Application deadline:* For

fall admission, 8/1 for domestic students; for spring admission, 10/15 for domestic students. Applications are processed on a rolling basis. Application fee: $50. *Financial support:* In 2013–14, 9 teaching assistantships with partial tuition reimbursements (averaging $13,322 per year) were awarded; career-related internships or fieldwork, scholarships/grants, and unspecified assistantships also available. Support available to part-time students. Financial award application deadline: 3/1; financial award applicants required to submit FAFSA. *Faculty research:* Feminism to post-feminism, Shanghai telephone service, customer-employee interaction. *Total annual research expenditures:* $97,110. *Unit head:* Dr. Hardin Aasand, Chair/Professor, 260-481-6750, Fax: 260-481-6985, E-mail: aasandh@ipfw.edu. *Application contact:* Dr. Lewis Roberts, Graduate Program Director, 260-481-6754, Fax: 260-481-6985, E-mail: robertlc@ipfw.edu.
Website: http://www.ipfw.edu/english.

Iona College, School of Arts and Science, Department of Education, New Rochelle, NY 10801-1890. Offers adolescence education: biology (MS Ed, MST); adolescence education: English (MS Ed, MST); adolescence education: Italian (MS Ed, MST); adolescence education: mathematics (MS Ed, MST); adolescence education: social studies (MS Ed, MST); adolescence education: Spanish (MS Ed, MST); adolescence special education 5-12 (MST); adolescence special education and literacy (MS Ed); childhood and special education (MST); childhood education (MST); early childhood and childhood (MST); educational leadership (MS Ed); literacy education: birth-grade 6 (MS Ed). *Accreditation:* NCATE. Part-time and evening/weekend programs available. *Faculty:* 11 full-time (9 women), 7 part-time/adjunct (6 women). *Students:* 34 full-time (25 women), 61 part-time (47 women); includes 5 minority (2 Asian, non-Hispanic/Latino; 3 Hispanic/Latino), 1 international. Average age 25. 27 applicants, 93% accepted, 16 enrolled. In 2013, 54 master's awarded. *Degree requirements:* For master's, thesis or alternative. *Entrance requirements:* For master's, minimum GPA of 3.0, NY State teaching certificate (for all MS Ed programs). Additional exam requirements/recommendations for international students: Required—TOEFL (minimum score 550 paper-based; 80 iBT), IELTS (minimum score 6.5). *Application deadline:* For fall admission, 8/1 priority date for domestic students, 5/1 priority date for international students; for spring admission, 1/1 priority date for domestic students, 9/1 priority date for international students. Applications are processed on a rolling basis. Application fee: $50. Electronic applications accepted. *Expenses: Tuition:* Part-time $948 per credit. *Required fees:* $235 per term. *Financial support:* In 2013–14, 84 students received support. Unspecified assistantships available. Support available to part-time students. Financial award application deadline: 4/15; financial award applicants required to submit FAFSA. *Faculty research:* Reading/writing, educational technology, administration, early literacy assessment, literacy development. *Unit head:* Margaret Smith, PhD, Chair, 914-633-2210, Fax: 914-633-2608, E-mail: msmith@iona.edu. *Application contact:* Veronica Jarek-Prinz, Director, Graduate Admissions, 914-633-2420, Fax: 914-633-2277, E-mail: vjarekprinz@iona.edu.
Website: http://www.iona.edu/Academics/School-of-Arts-Science/Departments/Education/Graduate-Programs.aspx.

Ithaca College, School of Humanities and Sciences, Program in Adolescence Education, Ithaca, NY 14850. Offers biology 7-12 (MAT); chemistry 7-12 (MAT); English 7-12 (MAT); French 7-12 (MAT); math 7-12 (MAT); physics 7-12 (MAT); social studies 7-12 (MAT); Spanish (MAT). Part-time programs available. *Faculty:* 31 full-time (11 women). *Students:* 12 full-time (4 women); includes 1 minority (Hispanic/Latino). Average age 24. 27 applicants, 81% accepted, 12 enrolled. In 2013, 7 master's awarded. *Degree requirements:* For master's, thesis or alternative, student teaching. *Entrance requirements:* For master's, minimum GPA of 3.0. Additional exam requirements/recommendations for international students: Required—TOEFL (minimum score 550 paper-based; 80 iBT). *Application deadline:* For fall admission, 2/15 priority date for domestic and international students; for spring admission, 12/1 for domestic and international students. Applications are processed on a rolling basis. Application fee: $40. Electronic applications accepted. *Expenses:* Contact institution. *Financial support:* In 2013–14, 7 students received support, including 7 teaching assistantships (averaging $9,781 per year); career-related internships or fieldwork, Federal Work-Study, scholarships/grants, and unspecified assistantships also available. Support available to part-time students. Financial award application deadline: 2/15; financial award applicants required to submit CSS PROFILE or FAFSA. *Faculty research:* Teacher preparation (elementary and secondary education), equity and social justice in education, language and literacy, multicultural education/sociocultural studies, reflective practice and teacher research. *Unit head:* Dr. Linda Hanrahan, Chair, 607-274-3143, Fax: 607-274-1263, E-mail: gps@ithaca.edu. *Application contact:* Gerard Turbide, Director, Office of Admission, 607-274-3143, Fax: 607-274-1263, E-mail: gps@ithaca.edu.
Website: http://www.ithaca.edu/gradprograms/education/programs/aded.

Jackson State University, Graduate School, College of Liberal Arts, Department of English and Modern Foreign Languages, Jackson, MS 39217. Offers English (MA); teaching English (MAT). Part-time and evening/weekend programs available. *Degree requirements:* For master's, comprehensive exam, thesis or alternative. *Entrance requirements:* For master's, GRE General Test. Additional exam requirements/recommendations for international students: Required—TOEFL (minimum score 520 paper-based; 67 iBT).

Kansas State University, Graduate School, College of Education, Department of Curriculum and Instruction, Manhattan, KS 66506. Offers career and technical education (Ed D, PhD); curriculum studies (Ed D, PhD); digital teaching and learning (MS); educational computing, design and online learning (MS); educational technology (Ed D, PhD); elementary/middle level curriculum and instruction (MS); English as a second language (MS); language/diversity education (Ed D, PhD); literacy education (Ed D, PhD); mathematics education (Ed D, PhD); middle level/secondary curriculum and instruction (MS); reading and language arts (MS); reading specialist endorsement (MS); science education (Ed D, PhD); social science education (Ed D, PhD); teacher education (Ed D, PhD); teacher leader/school improvement (MS, Ed D). *Accreditation:* NCATE. Part-time programs available. Postbaccalaureate distance learning degree programs offered (minimal on-campus study). *Faculty:* 18 full-time (13 women), 7 part-time/adjunct (4 women). *Students:* 39 full-time (23 women), 122 part-time (94 women); includes 19 minority (3 Black or African American, non-Hispanic/Latino; 2 Asian, non-Hispanic/Latino; 12 Hispanic/Latino; 2 Two or more races, non-Hispanic/Latino), 12 international. Average age 36. 80 applicants, 50% accepted, 34 enrolled. In 2013, 40 master's, 13 doctorates awarded. *Degree requirements:* For master's, comprehensive exam, portfolio, project, report or thesis; for doctorate, comprehensive exam, thesis/dissertation, preliminary exam. *Entrance requirements:* For master's, minimum GPA of 3.0, letters of recommendation; for doctorate, GRE, minimum GPA of 3.0, letters of recommendation, evidence of scholarly writing. Additional exam requirements/recommendations for international students: Required—TOEFL (minimum score 550 paper-based; 80 iBT). *Application deadline:* For fall admission, 3/1 priority date for domestic students, 2/1 priority date for international students; for spring admission, 10/1 priority date for domestic students, 8/1 priority date for international students. Applications are processed on a rolling basis. Application fee: $50 ($75 for international students). Electronic applications accepted. *Financial support:* In 2013–14, 1 research assistantship (averaging $16,900 per year), 8 teaching assistantships (averaging $12,466 per year) were awarded; career-related internships or fieldwork, institutionally

sponsored loans, and scholarships/grants also available. Support available to part-time students. Financial award application deadline: 3/1; financial award applicants required to submit FAFSA. *Faculty research:* Literacy and technology, critical race theory and diversity, achievement gaps, school improvement, teacher education. *Total annual research expenditures:* $543,677. *Unit head:* Dr. Todd Goodson, Chair, 785-532-5904, Fax: 785-532-7304, E-mail: tgoodson@ksu.edu. *Application contact:* Dona Deam, Application Contact, 785-532-5595, Fax: 785-532-7304, E-mail: ddeam@ksu.edu.
Website: http://www.coe.k-state.edu/departments/edci/.

Kennesaw State University, Leland and Clarice C. Bagwell College of Education, Program in Teaching, Kennesaw, GA 30144-5591. Offers art education (MAT); biology (MAT); chemistry (MAT); foreign language education (Chinese and Spanish) (MAT); physics (MAT); secondary English (MAT); secondary mathematics (MAT); special education (MAT); teaching English to speakers of other languages (MAT). Part-time and evening/weekend programs available. *Students:* 82 full-time (59 women), 16 part-time (12 women); includes 28 minority (14 Black or African American, non-Hispanic/Latino; 4 Asian, non-Hispanic/Latino; 7 Hispanic/Latino; 1 Native Hawaiian or other Pacific Islander, non-Hispanic/Latino; 2 Two or more races, non-Hispanic/Latino), 3 international. Average age 35. 28 applicants, 68% accepted, 15 enrolled. In 2013, 54 master's awarded. *Entrance requirements:* For master's, GRE, GACE I (state certificate exam), minimum GPA of 2.75, 2 recommendations, resume. Additional exam requirements/recommendations for international students: Required—TOEFL (minimum score 550 paper-based; 80 iBT), IELTS (minimum score 6). *Application deadline:* For fall admission, 6/1 for domestic and international students; for spring admission, 3/1 for domestic and international students; for summer admission, 4/15 for domestic and international students. Applications are processed on a rolling basis. Application fee: $60. Electronic applications accepted. *Expenses:* Tuition, state resident: full-time $4806; part-time $267 per semester hour. Tuition, nonresident: full-time $17,298; part-time $961 per semester hour. *Required fees:* $1834; $784.50 per semester. *Financial support:* In 2013–14, 2 research assistantships with tuition reimbursements (averaging $8,000 per year) were awarded; unspecified assistantships also available. Financial award application deadline: 4/1; financial award applicants required to submit FAFSA. *Unit head:* Dr. Jillian Ford, Director, 770-499-3093, E-mail: graded@kennesaw.edu. *Application contact:* Melinda Ross, Admissions Counselor, 770-423-6122, Fax: 770-423-6885, E-mail: ksugrad@kennesaw.edu.
Website: http://www.kennesaw.edu.

Kent State University, College of Arts and Sciences, Department of English, Kent, OH 44242-0001. Offers comparative literature (MA); creative writing (MFA); English (PhD); English for teachers (MA); literature and writing (MA); rhetoric and composition (PhD); teaching English as a second language (MA). MFA program offered jointly with Cleveland State University, The University of Akron, and Youngstown State University. Part-time programs available. Terminal master's awarded for partial completion of doctoral program. *Degree requirements:* For master's, one foreign language, thesis optional; for doctorate, one foreign language, thesis/dissertation, qualifying exams. *Entrance requirements:* For master's and doctorate, GRE General Test, writing sample, letters of recommendation. Additional exam requirements/recommendations for international students: Required—TOEFL (minimum score 600 paper-based). Electronic applications accepted. *Faculty research:* British and American literature, textual editing, rhetoric and composition, cultural studies, linguistic and critical theories.

Kutztown University of Pennsylvania, College of Education, Program in Secondary Education, Kutztown, PA 19530-0730. Offers biology (M Ed); curriculum and instruction (M Ed); English (M Ed); mathematics (M Ed); social studies (M Ed). *Accreditation:* NCATE. Part-time and evening/weekend programs available. *Faculty:* 6 full-time (2 women). *Students:* 34 full-time (17 women), 46 part-time (34 women); includes 4 minority (1 Asian, non-Hispanic/Latino; 3 Hispanic/Latino). Average age 31. 50 applicants, 70% accepted, 26 enrolled. In 2013, 31 master's awarded. *Degree requirements:* For master's, comprehensive exam, thesis optional. *Entrance requirements:* For master's, GRE General Test. Additional exam requirements/recommendations for international students: Required—TOEFL (minimum score 550 paper-based; 79 iBT). *Application deadline:* For fall admission, 8/1 priority date for domestic and international students; for spring admission, 12/1 priority date for domestic and international students. Applications are processed on a rolling basis. Application fee: $35. Electronic applications accepted. *Expenses: Tuition, area resident:* Part-time $442 per credit. Tuition, state resident: part-time $442 per credit. Tuition, nonresident: part-time $663 per credit. *Required fees:* $80 per credit. *Financial support:* Career-related internships or fieldwork, Federal Work-Study, scholarships/grants, and unspecified assistantships available. Financial award application deadline: 3/1; financial award applicants required to submit FAFSA. *Unit head:* Dr. Theresa Stahler, Chairperson, 610-683-4259, Fax: 610-683-1338, E-mail: stahler@kutztown.edu. *Application contact:* Kelly Hish, Admissions Clerk, 610-683-4200, Fax: 610-683-1393, E-mail: graduate@kutztown.edu.

Lake Forest College, Master of Arts in Teaching Program, Lake Forest, IL 60045. Offers elementary education (MAT); K-12 French (MAT); K-12 music (MAT); K-12 Spanish (MAT); K-12 visual art (MAT); secondary biology (MAT); secondary chemistry (MAT); secondary English (MAT); secondary history (MAT); secondary mathematics (MAT). *Degree requirements:* For master's, comprehensive exam, portfolio. *Entrance requirements:* For master's, GRE.

La Salle University, School of Arts and Sciences, Program in English, Philadelphia, PA 19141-1199. Offers American studies (Certificate); English for educators (MA); English in literary and cultural studies (MA); global literature (Certificate); media studies and the performing and visual arts (Certificate); Philadelphia and regional studies (Certificate). Part-time and evening/weekend programs available. *Faculty:* 4 full-time (2 women). *Students:* 17 part-time (11 women). Average age 33. 2 applicants, 100% accepted, 1 enrolled. In 2013, 1 master's awarded. *Degree requirements:* For master's, critical-pedagogical project (for English for educators), thesis or comprehensive examination (for English in literary and cultural studies). *Entrance requirements:* For master's, GRE General Test or MAT, 18 hours of undergraduate course work in English or a related discipline with minimum GPA of 3.0; three letters of recommendation; brief personal statement; writing sample; for Certificate, undergraduate degree in English or a related discipline with minimum GPA of 3.0; 3 letters of recommendation. Additional exam requirements/recommendations for international students: Required—TOEFL. *Application deadline:* For fall admission, 8/15 priority date for domestic students, 7/15 for international students; for spring admission, 12/15 priority date for domestic students, 11/15 for international students; for summer admission, 4/15 priority date for domestic students, 3/15 for international students. Applications are processed on a rolling basis. Application fee: $35. Electronic applications accepted. Application fee is waived when completed online. *Expenses: Tuition:* Full-time $20,750; part-time $695 per credit hour. *Required fees:* $300; $200 per year. Tuition and fees vary according to program. *Financial support:* In 2013–14, 7 students received support. Federal Work-Study and scholarships/grants available. Support available to part-time students. Financial award application deadline: 8/31; financial award applicants required to submit FAFSA. *Unit head:* Dr. Stephen Smith, Director, 215-951-1145, E-mail: smiths@lasalle.edu. *Application contact:* Paul J. Reilly, Assistant Vice President, Enrollment Services, 215-951-1946, Fax: 215-951-1462, E-mail: reilly@lasalle.edu.
Website: http://www.lasalle.edu/grad/index.php?section-english&page-index.

Lehman College of the City University of New York, Division of Education, Department of Middle and High School Education, Program in English Education, Bronx, NY 10468-1589. Offers MS Ed. *Accreditation:* NCATE. *Entrance requirements:* For master's, minimum GPA of 3.0 in English, 2.8 overall; teaching certificate.

Le Moyne College, Department of Education, Syracuse, NY 13214. Offers adolescent education (MS Ed, MST); adolescent education/special education (MS Ed, MST); adolescent English (MST), including grades 7-12 (MS Ed, MST); adolescent English/special education (MST), including grades 7-12 (MS Ed, MST); adolescent foreign language (MST), including grades 7-12 (MS Ed, MST); adolescent history (MST), including grades 7-12 (MS Ed, MST); childhood education (MS Ed); childhood education/special education (MS Ed); elementary education (MS Ed); general education (MS Ed); inclusive childhood education (MST); literacy education (MS Ed), including birth to grade 6, grades 5-12; school building leader (MS Ed); school building leadership (CAS); school district business leader (MS Ed, CAS); school district leader (MS Ed); school district leadership (CAS); secondary education (MS Ed); special education (MS Ed); students with disabilities-generalist (MS Ed), including grades 7-12 (MS Ed, MST); teaching English to speakers of other languages (MS Ed); urban studies (MS Ed). *Accreditation:* Teacher Education Accreditation Council. Part-time and evening/weekend programs available. *Faculty:* 8 full-time (5 women), 61 part-time/adjunct (38 women). *Students:* 24 full-time (20 women), 178 part-time (133 women); includes 22 minority (12 Black or African American, non-Hispanic/Latino; 1 American Indian or Alaska Native, non-Hispanic/Latino; 3 Asian, non-Hispanic/Latino; 6 Hispanic/Latino), 1 international. Average age 31. 248 applicants, 90% accepted, 86 enrolled. In 2013, 158 master's, 37 CASs awarded. *Degree requirements:* For master's, thesis. *Entrance requirements:* For master's, GRE General Test, bachelor's degree, 2 letters of recommendation, written statement, transcripts. Additional exam requirements/recommendations for international students: Required—TOEFL (minimum score 550 paper-based; 79 iBT). *Application deadline:* For fall admission, 4/1 priority date for domestic and international students; for spring admission, 10/1 priority date for domestic and international students; for summer admission, 3/1 priority date for domestic and international students. Applications are processed on a rolling basis. Application fee: $50. *Expenses:* Contact institution. *Financial support:* In 2013–14, 26 students received support. Career-related internships or fieldwork and health care benefits available. Support available to part-time students. Financial award applicants required to submit FAFSA. *Faculty research:* Minority teachers, special education, multiculturalism, literacy, technology, media literacy learning, autism, school district organization, service-learning, higher level problem solving, teacher leadership. *Unit head:* Dr. Suzanne L. Gilmour, Chair, Department of Education/Director of Graduate Education Programs, 315-445-4376, Fax: 315-445-4744, E-mail: gilmous@lemoyne.edu. *Application contact:* Kristen P. Trapasso, Senior Director of Enrollment Management, 315-445-4265, Fax: 315-445-6092, E-mail: trapaskp@lemoyne.edu.
Website: http://www.lemoyne.edu/education.

Lincoln Memorial University, Carter and Moyers School of Education, Harrogate, TN 37752-1901. Offers administration and supervision (M Ed, Ed S); counseling and guidance (M Ed); curriculum and instruction (M Ed, Ed D, Ed S); English (M Ed); executive leadership (Ed D); higher education administration (Ed D); human resource development (Ed D); leadership and administration (Ed D). Part-time and evening/weekend programs available. Postbaccalaureate distance learning degree programs offered. *Degree requirements:* For master's, comprehensive exam, thesis optional; for Ed S, comprehensive exam. *Entrance requirements:* For master's, PRAXIS, NTE, GRE, MAT, letters of recommendation; for Ed S, graduate transcripts. Additional exam requirements/recommendations for international students: Recommended—TOEFL. *Faculty research:* Brain compatible teaching and learning; poverty in Appalachia; leadership for change; ethics, moral responsibility and social justice; human and organizational learning.

Lipscomb University, Program in Education, Nashville, TN 37204-3951. Offers applied behavior analysis (Certificate); collaborative professional learning (M Ed, Ed S); educational leadership (M Ed, Ed S); English language learning (M Ed, Ed S); instructional coaching (Certificate); instructional practice (M Ed); learning organizations and strategic change (Ed D); math specialty (M Ed); reading specialty (M Ed, Ed S); special education (M Ed); teaching, learning, and leading (M Ed); technology integration (M Ed); technology integration specialist (Certificate). *Accreditation:* NCATE. Part-time and evening/weekend programs available. Postbaccalaureate distance learning degree programs offered (no on-campus study). *Faculty:* 19 full-time (13 women), 28 part-time/adjunct (22 women). *Students:* 171 full-time (123 women), 509 part-time (429 women); includes 118 minority (91 Black or African American, non-Hispanic/Latino; 1 American Indian or Alaska Native, non-Hispanic/Latino; 4 Asian, non-Hispanic/Latino; 15 Hispanic/Latino; 1 Native Hawaiian or other Pacific Islander, non-Hispanic/Latino; 6 Two or more races, non-Hispanic/Latino). Average age 32. 237 applicants, 65% accepted, 150 enrolled. In 2013, 212 master's awarded. *Degree requirements:* For master's, comprehensive exam, portfolio, research project and presentation; for doctorate, practical capstone project in experiential setting. *Entrance requirements:* For master's, MAT (minimum 31) or GRE General Test (minimum 294), 2 reference letters, goals statement, writing sample, interview; for doctorate, MAT or GRE General Test, 3 reference letters, artifact of demonstrated academic excellence, written personal statements, interview. Additional exam requirements/recommendations for international students: Required—TOEFL (minimum score 570 paper-based). *Application deadline:* For fall admission, 8/29 priority date for domestic students; for spring admission, 1/15 priority date for domestic students. Applications are processed on a rolling basis. Application fee: $50 ($75 for international students). *Expenses: Tuition:* Full-time $15,570; part-time $865 per credit hour. Tuition and fees vary according to degree level and program. *Financial support:* Scholarships/grants and unspecified assistantships available. Financial award applicants required to submit FAFSA. *Faculty research:* Facilitative learning styles, leadership, student assessment, interactive multimedia inclusion, learning organizations and strategic change. *Unit head:* Dr. Deborah Boyd, Director of Graduate Studies, 615-966-6263, E-mail: deborah.boyd@lipscomb.edu. *Application contact:* Kristin Baese, Director of Enrollment and Outreach, 615-966-7628 Ext. 6081, Fax: 615-966-5173, E-mail: kristin.baese@lipscomb.edu.
Website: http://www.lipscomb.edu/education/graduate-programs.

Long Island University–LIU Brooklyn, Richard L. Conolly College of Liberal Arts and Sciences, Department of English, Brooklyn, NY 11201-8423. Offers creative writing (MFA); literature (MA); professional writing (MA); writing and rhetoric (MA). Part-time and evening/weekend programs available. *Degree requirements:* For master's, thesis or alternative. *Entrance requirements:* For master's, 2 letters of recommendation (at least 1 from a former professor or teacher). Additional exam requirements/recommendations for international students: Required—TOEFL (minimum score 550 paper-based). Electronic applications accepted.

Long Island University–LIU Post, School of Education, Department of Curriculum and Instruction, Brookville, NY 11548-1300. Offers adolescence education (MS); adolescence education: biology (MS); adolescence education: earth science (MS);

adolescence education: English (MS); adolescence education: mathematics (MS); adolescence education: social studies (MS); adolescence education: Spanish (MS); art education (MS); bilingual education (MS); childhood education (MS); early childhood education (MS); middle childhood education (MS); music education (MS); teaching English to speakers of other languages (MS). Part-time and evening/weekend programs available. *Degree requirements:* For master's, comprehensive exam or thesis, student teaching. *Entrance requirements:* For master's, minimum GPA of 2.75 in major, 2.5 overall. Electronic applications accepted. *Faculty research:* Ethics and education, teaching strategies.

Longwood University, College of Graduate and Professional Studies, Department of English and Modern Languages, Farmville, VA 23909. Offers 6-12 initial teaching licensure (MA); creative writing (MA); English education and writing (MA); literature (MA). Part-time programs available. *Faculty:* 24 full-time (9 women). *Students:* 9 full-time (6 women), 8 part-time (5 women); includes 4 minority (1 Black or African American, non-Hispanic/Latino; 1 Hispanic/Latino; 2 Two or more races, non-Hispanic/Latino). 11 applicants, 64% accepted, 4 enrolled. In 2013, 11 master's awarded. *Degree requirements:* For master's, comprehensive exam (for some programs), thesis (for some programs). *Entrance requirements:* For master's, minimum GPA of 2.75 (for creative writing), 3.0 (for all others); bachelor's degree from regionally-accredited institution; 2 recommendations; 500-word personal essay; official transcripts. Additional exam requirements/recommendations for international students: Required—TOEFL (minimum score 570 paper-based), IELTS (minimum score 6.5). *Application deadline:* For fall admission, 5/1 priority date for domestic students; for spring admission, 10/1 priority date for domestic students; for summer admission, 2/1 priority date for domestic students. Applications are processed on a rolling basis. Application fee: $50. Electronic applications accepted. *Expenses:* Tuition, state resident: full-time $7506; part-time $327 per credit hour. Tuition, nonresident: full-time $17,100; part-time $837 per credit hour. Tuition and fees vary according to course load and campus/location. *Financial support:* Career-related internships or fieldwork and Federal Work-Study available. Support available to part-time students. Financial award applicants required to submit FAFSA. *Unit head:* Dr. Wade A. Edwards, Chair of the Department of English and Modern Languages, 434-395-2181, E-mail: edwardswa@longwood.edu. *Application contact:* College of Graduate and Professional Studies, 434-395-2380, Fax: 434-395-2750, E-mail: graduate@longwood.edu.
Website: http://www.longwood.edu/english/.

Louisiana Tech University, Graduate School, College of Education, Department of Curriculum, Instruction and Leadership, Ruston, LA 71272. Offers curriculum and instruction (M Ed, Ed D), including adult education (M Ed), early childhood (M Ed), English education (M Ed), mathematics education (M Ed), science education (M Ed), social studies education (M Ed), special education (M Ed); educational leadership (M Ed, Ed D). *Accreditation:* NCATE. Part-time programs available. *Degree requirements:* For doctorate, thesis/dissertation. *Entrance requirements:* For master's and doctorate, GRE General Test. *Application deadline:* For fall admission, 7/29 for domestic students; for spring admission, 2/3 for domestic students. Application fee: $20 ($30 for international students). *Financial support:* Fellowships, research assistantships, and teaching assistantships available. Financial award application deadline: 2/1. *Unit head:* Dr. Pauline Leonard, Head, 318-257-4609, Fax: 318-257-2379. *Application contact:* Dr. John Harrison, Associate Dean of Graduate Studies, 318-257-3229, Fax: 318-257-2379, E-mail: johnharrison@latech.edu.
Website: http://www.latech.edu/education/cil/.

Loyola University Maryland, Graduate Programs, School of Education, Master of Arts in Teaching Program, Baltimore, MD 21210-2699. Offers elementary/middle education (MAT); secondary education (MAT); secondary education: biology (MAT); secondary education: chemistries (MAT); secondary education: earth science (MAT); secondary education: English (MAT); secondary education: mathematics (MAT); secondary education: physics (MAT). Part-time programs available. *Entrance requirements:* For master's, essay, 2 letters of recommendation, resume, transcipt. Additional exam requirements/recommendations for international students: Required—TOEFL (minimum score 550 paper-based).

Manhattanville College, School of Education, Program in Middle Childhood/ Adolescence Education (Grades 5-12), Purchase, NY 10577-2132. Offers biology (MAT); biology and special education (MPS); chemistry (MAT); chemistry and special education (MPS); English (MAT); English and special education (MPS); literacy and special education (MPS); literacy specialist (MPS); math and special education (MPS); mathematics (MAT); physics (MAT); social studies (MAT); social studies and special education (MPS); special education (MPS); teaching languages other than English (MAT), including French, Italian, Latin, Spanish. Part-time and evening/weekend programs available. *Degree requirements:* For master's, comprehensive exam or research project, field experience. *Entrance requirements:* For master's, minimum undergraduate GPA of 3.0, 2 letters of recommendation. Additional exam requirements/ recommendations for international students: Required—TOEFL. Electronic applications accepted.

Mills College, Graduate Studies, School of Education, Oakland, CA 94613-1000. Offers child life in hospitals (MA); early childhood education (MA); education (MA), including art education, curriculum and instruction, elementary education, English education, foreign language education, mathematics education, science education, secondary education, social studies education, teaching; educational leadership (MA, Ed D). Part-time and evening/weekend programs available. *Faculty:* 10 full-time (7 women), 13 part-time/ adjunct (10 women). *Students:* 154 full-time (136 women), 54 part-time (47 women); includes 96 minority (32 Black or African American, non-Hispanic/Latino; 1 American Indian or Alaska Native, non-Hispanic/Latino; 23 Asian, non-Hispanic/Latino; 27 Hispanic/Latino; 1 Native Hawaiian or other Pacific Islander, non-Hispanic/Latino; 12 Two or more races, non-Hispanic/Latino), 2 international. Average age 25. 222 applicants, 89% accepted, 110 enrolled. In 2013, 96 master's, 38 doctorates awarded. Terminal master's awarded for partial completion of doctoral program. *Degree requirements:* For master's, comprehensive exam, thesis (for some programs); for doctorate, thesis/dissertation. *Entrance requirements:* For master's, statement of purpose, official transcript, 3 recommendations. Additional exam requirements/ recommendations for international students: Required—TOEFL (minimum score 550 paper-based; 80 iBT) or IELTS (minimum score 6). *Application deadline:* For fall admission, 12/31 priority date for domestic students, 12/15 for international students; for spring admission, 11/1 priority date for domestic students, 10/1 for international students. Applications are processed on a rolling basis. Application fee: $50. Electronic applications accepted. *Expenses: Tuition:* Full-time $29,860. *Required fees:* $1134. Part-time tuition and fees vary according to course load, degree level and program. *Financial support:* In 2013–14, 130 students received support, including 130 fellowships with full and partial tuition reimbursements available (averaging $7,565 per year); career-related internships or fieldwork and scholarships/grants also available. Support available to part-time students. Financial award application deadline: 2/1; financial award applicants required to submit FAFSA. *Faculty research:* Early childhood education, teacher preparation, educational leadership. *Total annual research expenditures:* $3.5 million. *Unit head:* Dr. Katherine Schultz, Department Head, 510-430-3384, Fax: 510-430-2159, E-mail: kschultz@mills.edu. *Application contact:* Shrim

Bathey, Director of Graduate Admission, 510-430-3309, Fax: 510-430-2159, E-mail: grad-admission@mills.edu.
Website: http://www.mills.edu/education.

Minnesota State University Mankato, College of Graduate Studies, College of Arts and Humanities, Department of English, Mankato, MN 56001. Offers creative writing (MFA); English (MAT); English studies (MA); teaching English as a second language (MA, Certificate); technical communication (MA, Certificate). Part-time programs available. *Students:* 46 full-time (29 women), 136 part-time (87 women). *Degree requirements:* For master's, one foreign language, comprehensive exam, thesis or alternative. *Entrance requirements:* For master's, minimum GPA of 3.0 during previous 2 years, writing sample (MFA). Additional exam requirements/recommendations for international students: Required—TOEFL (minimum score 500 paper-based; 61 iBT). *Application deadline:* For fall admission, 7/1 for domestic students, 5/1 for international students. Applications are processed on a rolling basis. Application fee: $40. Electronic applications accepted. *Financial support:* Research assistantships with full tuition reimbursements, teaching assistantships with full tuition reimbursements, career-related internships or fieldwork, Federal Work-Study, and unspecified assistantships available. Financial award application deadline: 3/15; financial award applicants required to submit FAFSA. *Faculty research:* Keats and Christianity. *Unit head:* Dr. John Banschbach, Chairperson, 507-389-2117. *Application contact:* 507-389-2321, E-mail: grad@mnsu.edu.
Website: http://english.mnsu.edu/.

Mississippi College, Graduate School, School of Education, Department of Teacher Education and Leadership, Clinton, MS 39058. Offers art (M Ed); biological science (M Ed); business education (M Ed); computer science (M Ed); dyslexia therapy (M Ed); educational leadership (M Ed, Ed D, Ed S); elementary education (M Ed, Ed S); English (M Ed); higher education administration (MS); mathematics (M Ed); secondary education (M Ed); social studies (history) (M Ed); teaching arts (M Ed). Part-time programs available. Postbaccalaureate distance learning degree programs offered (no on-campus study). *Degree requirements:* For master's, comprehensive exam, thesis optional. *Entrance requirements:* For master's, NTE. Additional exam requirements/ recommendations for international students: Recommended—TOEFL, IELTS. Electronic applications accepted.

Montclair State University, The Graduate School, College of Education and Human Services, Department of Secondary and Special Education, Program in Teaching in Subject Area, Montclair, NJ 07043-1624. Offers art (MAT); biology (MAT); chemistry (MAT); earth science (MAT); English (MAT); French (MAT); health and physical education (MAT); health education (MAT); mathematics (MAT); music (MAT); physical education (MAT); physical science (MAT); social studies (MAT); Spanish (MAT); teacher of English as a second language (MAT). *Degree requirements:* For master's, comprehensive exam, thesis or alternative. *Entrance requirements:* For master's, GRE General Test, interview, 2 letters of recommendation. Additional exam requirements/ recommendations for international students: Required—TOEFL (minimum score 83 iBT), IELTS (minimum score 6.5). Electronic applications accepted.

Montclair State University, The Graduate School, College of Humanities and Social Sciences, Department of English, Teaching Writing Certificate Program, Montclair, NJ 07043-1624. Offers Certificate. Part-time and evening/weekend programs available. *Entrance requirements:* For degree, 2 letters of recommendation, essay. Additional exam requirements/recommendations for international students: Required—TOEFL (minimum score 83 iBT), IELTS (minimum score 6.5). Electronic applications accepted. *Faculty research:* Pedagogy in writing.

Morehead State University, Graduate Programs, College of Education, Department of Foundational and Graduate Studies in Education, Morehead, KY 40351. Offers adult and higher education (MA, Ed S); certified professional counselor (Ed S); counseling P-12 (MA); curriculum and instruction (Ed S); educational technology (MA Ed); instructional leadership (Ed S); school administration (MA); school counseling (Ed S); teacher leader business and marketing content (MA Ed); teacher leader business and marketing technology (MA Ed); teacher leader educational technology (MA Ed); teacher leader English (MA Ed); teacher leader gifted education (MA Ed); teacher leader IECE certification (MA Ed); teacher leader interdisciplinary education P-5 (MA Ed); teacher leader middle grades (MA Ed); teacher leader non IECE certification (MA Ed); teacher leader reading/writing - non-certification (MA Ed); teacher leader reading/writing certification (MA Ed); teacher leader school communication - certification (MA Ed); teacher leader school communication - non-certification (MA Ed); teacher leader social studies (MA Ed); teacher leader special education (MA Ed). *Accreditation:* NCATE. Part-time and evening/weekend programs available. *Degree requirements:* For master's, thesis optional, oral and/or written comprehensive exams; for Ed S, thesis, oral exam. *Entrance requirements:* For master's, GRE General Test, minimum overall undergraduate GPA of 2.5; for Ed S, GRE General Test, interview, master's degree, minimum GPA of 3.5, work experience. Additional exam requirements/ recommendations for international students: Required—TOEFL (minimum score 500 paper-based). Electronic applications accepted. *Faculty research:* Character education, school accountability, computer applications for school administrators.

Morehead State University, Graduate Programs, College of Education, Department of Middle Grades and Secondary Education, Morehead, KY 40351. Offers business and marketing education (MAT); English/language arts 5-9 (MAT); French (MAT); health P-12 (MAT); mathematics 5-9 (MAT); physical education P-12 (MAT); science 5-9 (MAT); secondary biology (MAT); secondary chemistry (MAT); secondary earth science (MAT); secondary English (MAT); secondary math (MAT); secondary physics (MAT); secondary social studies (MAT); social studies 5-9 (MAT); Spanish (MAT). Part-time and evening/ weekend programs available. *Degree requirements:* For master's, portfolio. *Entrance requirements:* For master's, GRE or PRAXIS II content exam, minimum overall undergraduate GPA of 2.5. Additional exam requirements/recommendations for international students: Required—TOEFL (minimum score 500 paper-based). Electronic applications accepted.

National Louis University, National College of Education, Chicago, IL 60603. Offers administration and supervision (M Ed, Ed D, CAS, Ed S); curriculum and instruction (M Ed, MS Ed, CAS); early childhood administration (M Ed, CAS); early childhood education (M Ed, MAT, MS Ed, CAS); education (Ed D); educational psychology/human learning and development (M Ed, MS Ed, CAS, Ed S); elementary education (MAT); interdisciplinary curriculum and instruction (M Ed); mathematics education (M Ed, MS Ed, CAS); reading and language (M Ed, MS Ed, CAS); school psychology (M Ed, Ed S); science education (M Ed, MS Ed, CAS); secondary education (MAT); special education (M Ed, MAT, CAS); technology in education (M Ed, CAS). *Accreditation:* NCATE. Part-time and evening/weekend programs available. *Degree requirements:* For doctorate, comprehensive exam, thesis/dissertation. *Entrance requirements:* For master's, MAT or GRE, minimum GPA of 3.0; for doctorate, GRE General Test, minimum GPA of 3.25, interview, resume, writing sample, 4 recommendations. Additional exam requirements/recommendations for international students: Required—TOEFL (minimum score 550 paper-based; 79 iBT).

New York University, Steinhardt School of Culture, Education, and Human Development, Department of Music and Performing Arts Professions, Program in

Educational Theatre, New York, NY 10012. Offers educational theatre (Ed D, Advanced Certificate); educational theatre and English 7-12: dual certificate (MA); educational theatre and social studies 7-12: dual certificate (MA); educational theatre in colleges and communities (MA, PhD); educational theatre, all grades (MA). Part-time programs available. *Faculty:* 5 full-time (2 women). *Students:* 51 full-time (34 women), 36 part-time (24 women); includes 20 minority (10 Black or African American, non-Hispanic/Latino; 1 Asian, non-Hispanic/Latino; 7 Hispanic/Latino; 2 Two or more races, non-Hispanic/Latino), 5 international. Average age 28. 66 applicants, 80% accepted, 25 enrolled. In 2013, 51 master's, 1 doctorate awarded. *Degree requirements:* For master's, thesis (for some programs); for doctorate, thesis/dissertation. *Entrance requirements:* For master's, audition; for doctorate, GRE General Test, interview; for Advanced Certificate, master's degree. Additional exam requirements/recommendations for international students: Required—TOEFL (minimum score 100 iBT). *Application deadline:* For fall admission, 12/1 priority date for domestic and international students; for spring admission, 10/1 for domestic and international students. Applications are processed on a rolling basis. Application fee: $75. Electronic applications accepted. *Expenses: Tuition:* Full-time $35,856; part-time $1494 per unit. *Required fees:* $1408; $64 per unit. $473 per term. Tuition and fees vary according to course load and program. *Financial support:* Teaching assistantships with partial tuition reimbursements, career-related internships or fieldwork, Federal Work-Study, institutionally sponsored loans, and scholarships/grants available. Support available to part-time students. Financial award application deadline: 2/1; financial award applicants required to submit FAFSA. *Faculty research:* Theatre for young audiences, drama in education, applied theatre, arts education assessment, reflective praxis. *Unit head:* Prof. David Montgomery, Director, 212-998-5869, Fax: 212-995-4043, E-mail: dm635@nyu.edu. *Application contact:* 212-998-5030, Fax: 212-995-4328, E-mail: steinhardt.gradadmissions@nyu.edu.
Website: http://steinhardt.nyu.edu/music/edtheatre.

New York University, Steinhardt School of Culture, Education, and Human Development, Department of Teaching and Learning, Program in English Education, New York, NY 10012-1019. Offers clinically-based English education, grades 7-12 (MA, Postbaccalaureate Certificate); English education (Advanced Certificate); English education, grades 7-12 (MA); literature, reading, and media education (PhD), including applied linguistics, comparative education. *Accreditation:* Teacher Education Accreditation Council. Part-time programs available. *Faculty:* 6 full-time (4 women). *Students:* 21 full-time (15 women), 34 part-time (24 women); includes 24 minority (9 Black or African American, non-Hispanic/Latino; 5 Asian, non-Hispanic/Latino; 9 Hispanic/Latino; 1 Two or more races, non-Hispanic/Latino), 1 international. Average age 31. 104 applicants, 75% accepted, 28 enrolled. In 2013, 26 master's, 2 doctorates awarded. *Degree requirements:* For master's, thesis (for some programs); for doctorate, thesis/dissertation. *Entrance requirements:* For doctorate, GRE General Test, interview; for other advanced degree, master's degree. Additional exam requirements/recommendations for international students: Required—TOEFL (minimum score 100 iBT). *Application deadline:* For fall admission, 12/1 priority date for domestic and international students; for spring admission, 10/1 for domestic and international students. Applications are processed on a rolling basis. Application fee: $75. Electronic applications accepted. *Expenses: Tuition:* Full-time $35,856; part-time $1494 per unit. *Required fees:* $1408; $64 per unit. $473 per term. Tuition and fees vary according to course load and program. *Financial support:* Fellowships with full and partial tuition reimbursements, teaching assistantships with full and partial tuition reimbursements, career-related internships or fieldwork, Federal Work-Study, institutionally sponsored loans, scholarships/grants, tuition waivers (partial), and unspecified assistantships available. Support available to part-time students. Financial award application deadline: 2/1; financial award applicants required to submit FAFSA. *Faculty research:* Making meaning of literature, teaching of literature, urban adolescent literacy and equity, literacy development and globalization, digital media and literacy. *Unit head:* Prof. Sarah W. Beck, Chairperson, 212-998-5473, Fax: 212-995-4049, E-mail: sarah.beck@nyu.edu. *Application contact:* 212-998-5030, Fax: 212-995-4328, E-mail: steinhardt.gradadmissions@nyu.edu.
Website: http://steinhardt.nyu.edu/teachlearn/english.

North Carolina Agricultural and Technical State University, School of Graduate Studies, College of Arts and Sciences, Department of English, Greensboro, NC 27411. Offers English (MA); English and African-American literature (MA); English education (MAT, MS). Part-time and evening/weekend programs available. *Degree requirements:* For master's, comprehensive exam, qualifying exam. *Entrance requirements:* For master's, GRE General Test, minimum GPA of 3.0.

North Carolina State University, Graduate School, College of Education, Department of Curriculum and Instruction, Program in Secondary English Education, Raleigh, NC 27695. Offers M Ed, MS Ed. *Degree requirements:* For master's, thesis optional.

Northern Arizona University, Graduate College, College of Arts and Letters, Department of English, Flagstaff, AZ 86011. Offers applied linguistics (PhD); English (MA, MFA), including creative writing (MFA), general English studies (MA), literature (MA), rhetoric and the teaching of writing (MA), secondary English education (MA); professional writing (Certificate); teaching English as a second language (MA, Certificate). Part-time programs available. *Faculty:* 62 full-time (43 women), 15 part-time/adjunct (9 women). *Students:* 168 full-time (120 women), 133 part-time (100 women); includes 52 minority (12 Black or African American, non-Hispanic/Latino; 4 American Indian or Alaska Native, non-Hispanic/Latino; 5 Asian, non-Hispanic/Latino; 22 Hispanic/Latino; 9 Two or more races, non-Hispanic/Latino), 37 international. Average age 33. 230 applicants, 69% accepted, 92 enrolled. In 2013, 117 master's, 3 doctorates, 16 other advanced degrees awarded. *Degree requirements:* For master's, comprehensive exam (for some programs), thesis (for some programs), departmental qualifying exam; for doctorate, comprehensive exam, thesis/dissertation, departmental qualifying exam. *Entrance requirements:* For master's, minimum GPA of 3.0 or GRE; for doctorate, GRE General Test. Additional exam requirements/recommendations for international students: Required—TOEFL (minimum score 550 paper-based; 80 iBT), IELTS (minimum score 7), TOEFL (minimum score 600 paper-based; 100 iBT) for PhD; TOEFL (minimum score 570 paper-based; 89 iBT) for MA. *Application deadline:* For fall admission, 4/15 priority date for domestic students, 2/15 priority date for international students; for spring admission, 11/15 priority date for domestic and international students. Applications are processed on a rolling basis. Application fee: $65. Electronic applications accepted. *Financial support:* In 2013–14, 73 teaching assistantships with full tuition reimbursements (averaging $13,500 per year) were awarded; Federal Work-Study, scholarships/grants, health care benefits, tuition waivers (full and partial), and unspecified assistantships also available. Financial award applicants required to submit FAFSA. *Unit head:* Dr. John Rothfork, Chair, 928-523-0559, Fax: 928-523-4911, E-mail: john.rothfork@nau.edu. *Application contact:* Yvette Loeffler-Schmelzle, Secretary, 928-523-6842, Fax: 928-523-4911, E-mail: yvette.schmelzle@nau.edu.
Website: http://nau.edu/cal/english/.

Northwest Missouri State University, Graduate School, College of Arts and Sciences, Department of English and Modern Languages, Maryville, MO 64468-6001. Offers English (MA, MS Ed); English with English pedagogy emphasis (MA). Part-time programs available. *Degree requirements:* For master's, comprehensive exam, thesis optional. *Entrance requirements:* For master's, GRE General Test (verbal and analytical writing portions), minimum undergraduate GPA of 3.0, writing sample. Additional exam requirements/recommendations for international students: Required—TOEFL (minimum score 550 paper-based).

Occidental College, Graduate Studies, Department of Education, Los Angeles, CA 90041-3314. Offers elementary education (MAT), including liberal studies; secondary education (MAT), including English and comparative literary studies, history, life science, mathematics, physical science, social science, Spanish. Part-time programs available. *Degree requirements:* For master's, comprehensive exam, synthesis paper. *Entrance requirements:* For master's, GRE General Test, minimum GPA of 3.0. Additional exam requirements/recommendations for international students: Required—TOEFL (minimum score 625 paper-based). *Expenses:* Contact institution. *Faculty research:* Preparing teacher-leaders, curriculum development.

Our Lady of the Lake University of San Antonio, College of Arts and Sciences, Program in English, San Antonio, TX 78207-4689. Offers English and communication arts (MA); English education (MA); English language and literature (MA); writing (MA); MA/MFA. Program offered jointly with University of the Incarnate Word and St. Mary's University. Part-time and evening/weekend programs available. *Faculty:* 6 full-time (3 women). *Students:* 13 full-time (9 women), 5 part-time (2 women); includes 13 minority (2 Black or African American, non-Hispanic/Latino; 11 Hispanic/Latino). Average age 35. 7 applicants, 86% accepted, 3 enrolled. In 2013, 8 master's awarded. *Degree requirements:* For master's, comprehensive exam, thesis optional. *Entrance requirements:* For master's, GRE General Test or MAT, minimum GPA of 3.0 in last 60 hours, 2.5 overall. Additional exam requirements/recommendations for international students: Required—TOEFL. *Application deadline:* For fall admission, 4/1 priority date for domestic and international students; for spring admission, 11/1 priority date for domestic and international students; for summer admission, 2/1 priority date for domestic and international students. Applications are processed on a rolling basis. Application fee: $25 ($50 for international students). Electronic applications accepted. *Expenses: Tuition:* Full-time $9120; part-time $760 per credit. *Required fees:* $698; $334 per trimester. Tuition and fees vary according to course load, degree level, campus/location and program. *Financial support:* Research assistantships, teaching assistantships, career-related internships or fieldwork, Federal Work-Study, institutionally sponsored loans, scholarships/grants, and tuition waivers (partial) available. Financial award application deadline: 4/15. *Faculty research:* Writing theory and research, contemporary Southern literature, popular culture, poetry, literature of the Southwest. *Unit head:* David Sanor, Chair of Mass Communication and Drama Department, 210-434-6711 Ext. 2243, E-mail: dsanor@lake.ollusa.edu. *Application contact:* Graduate Admission, 210-431-3961, Fax: 210-431-4036, E-mail: gradadm@lake.ollusa.edu.
Website: http://www.ollusa.edu/s/1190/ollu-3-column-noads.aspx?sid=1190&gid=1&pgid=1426.

Plymouth State University, College of Graduate Studies, Graduate Studies in Education, Program in English Education, Plymouth, NH 03264-1595. Offers M Ed. Part-time and evening/weekend programs available. *Degree requirements:* For master's, capstone, research, or thesis. *Entrance requirements:* For master's, MAT.

Purdue University, Graduate School, College of Education, Department of Curriculum and Instruction, West Lafayette, IN 47907. Offers agricultural and extension education (PhD, Ed S); agriculture and extension education (MS, MS Ed); art education (PhD); curriculum studies (MS Ed, PhD, Ed S); educational technology (MS Ed, PhD, Ed S); elementary education (MS Ed); family and consumer sciences education (MS Ed, PhD, Ed S); foreign language education (MS Ed, PhD, Ed S); industrial technology (PhD, Ed S); language arts (MS Ed, PhD, Ed S); literacy (MS Ed, PhD, Ed S); mathematics/science education (MS, MS Ed, PhD, Ed S); social studies (MS Ed, PhD); social studies education (Ed S); vocational/industrial education (MS Ed, PhD, Ed S); vocational/technical education (MS Ed, PhD, Ed S). *Accreditation:* NCATE. Part-time and evening/weekend programs available. *Faculty:* 29 full-time (19 women), 33 part-time/adjunct (29 women). *Students:* 85 full-time (53 women), 271 part-time (195 women); includes 62 minority (19 Black or African American, non-Hispanic/Latino; 3 American Indian or Alaska Native, non-Hispanic/Latino; 13 Asian, non-Hispanic/Latino; 22 Hispanic/Latino; 1 Native Hawaiian or other Pacific Islander, non-Hispanic/Latino; 4 Two or more races, non-Hispanic/Latino), 41 international. Average age 36. 155 applicants, 71% accepted, 71 enrolled. In 2013, 60 master's, 20 doctorates awarded. *Degree requirements:* For master's, thesis optional; for doctorate, thesis/dissertation, oral and written exams; for Ed S, oral presentation, project. *Entrance requirements:* For master's, GRE General Test (if undergraduate GPA is below 3.0), minimum undergraduate GPA of 3.0 or equivalent; for doctorate, GRE General Test (minimum combined verbal and quantitative score of 1000, 300 for new scoring), minimum undergraduate GPA of 3.0 or equivalent; master's degree with minimum GPA of 3.0 or equivalent; for Ed S, GRE General Test (minimum combined verbal and quantitative score of 1000, 300 for new scoring), minimum undergraduate GPA of 3.0 or equivalent; master's degree. Additional exam requirements/recommendations for international students: Required—TOEFL (minimum score 550 paper-based; 77 iBT). *Application deadline:* For fall admission, 12/15 for domestic students, 3/1 for international students; for spring admission, 9/15 for domestic students, 8/1 for international students. Application fee: $60 ($75 for international students). Electronic applications accepted. *Financial support:* Fellowships with full tuition reimbursements, research assistantships with full tuition reimbursements, teaching assistantships with full tuition reimbursements, career-related internships or fieldwork, and tuition waivers (full) available. Support available to part-time students. Financial award application deadline: 3/1; financial award applicants required to submit FAFSA. *Faculty research:* Literacy acquisition and development, teacher beliefs and knowledge, recruitment and retention of underrepresented students, economic education, literacy discourse. *Unit head:* Dr. Phillip J. VanFossen, Head, 765-494-7935, Fax: 765-496-1622, E-mail: vanfoss@purdue.edu. *Application contact:* Cindy Blankenship, Graduate Contact, 765-494-2345, Fax: 765-494-5832, E-mail: prater0@purdue.edu.
Website: http://www.edci.purdue.edu/.

Queens College of the City University of New York, Division of Graduate Studies, Division of Education, Department of Secondary Education, Flushing, NY 11367-1597. Offers art (MS Ed); biology (MS Ed, AC); chemistry (MS Ed, AC); earth sciences (MS Ed, AC); English (MS Ed, AC); French (MS Ed, AC); Italian (MS Ed, AC); mathematics (MS Ed, AC); music (MS Ed, AC); physics (MS Ed, AC); social studies (MS Ed, AC); Spanish (MS Ed, AC). Part-time and evening/weekend programs available. *Degree requirements:* For master's, research project; for AC, thesis optional. *Entrance requirements:* For master's, minimum GPA of 3.0. Additional exam requirements/recommendations for international students: Required—TOEFL.

Quinnipiac University, School of Education, Program in Secondary Education, Hamden, CT 06518-1940. Offers biology (MAT); English (MAT); history/social studies (MAT); mathematics (MAT); Spanish (MAT). *Accreditation:* NCATE. *Faculty:* 14 full-time (7 women), 46 part-time/adjunct (27 women). *Students:* 44 full-time (37 women), 1 (woman) part-time; includes 2 minority (both Hispanic/Latino). 45 applicants, 93% accepted, 32 enrolled. In 2013, 32 master's awarded. *Entrance requirements:* For master's, PRAXIS I, minimum GPA of 2.67, interview. *Application deadline:* For fall admission, 4/1 priority date for domestic students. Applications are processed on a

rolling basis. Application fee: $45. Electronic applications accepted. *Expenses: Tuition:* Part-time $920 per credit. *Required fees:* $37 per credit. *Financial support:* Career-related internships or fieldwork, tuition waivers (full and partial), and unspecified assistantships available. Support available to part-time students. Financial award application deadline: 6/1; financial award applicants required to submit FAFSA. *Faculty research:* Multicultural and urban education/leadership, challenges of teaching diverse learners, scholarship of teaching and learning, technology and teaching, humor and education. *Unit head:* Mordechai Gordon, Program Director, E-mail: mordechai.gordon@quinnipiac.edu. *Application contact:* Office of Graduate Admissions, 800-462-1944, Fax: 203-582-3443, E-mail: graduate@quinnipiac.edu.
Website: http://www.quinnipiac.edu/gradeducation.

Rhode Island College, School of Graduate Studies, Feinstein School of Education and Human Development, Department of Educational Studies, Providence, RI 02908-1991. Offers advanced studies in teaching and learning (M Ed); English (MAT); French (MAT); history (MAT); math (MAT); secondary education (MAT); Spanish (MAT); teaching English as a second language (M Ed). *Accreditation:* NCATE. Part-time and evening/weekend programs available. *Faculty:* 10 full-time (6 women), 7 part-time/adjunct (all women). *Students:* 4 full-time (3 women), 61 part-time (54 women); includes 2 minority (both Hispanic/Latino). Average age 37. In 2013, 27 master's awarded. *Degree requirements:* For master's, capstone or comprehensive assessment. *Entrance requirements:* For master's, GRE or MAT (for most programs), minimum undergraduate GPA of 3.0; baccalaureate degree in English, French, history, math or Spanish; evaluation of content area knowledge; 3 letters of recommendation; interview. Additional exam requirements/recommendations for international students: Recommended—TOEFL (minimum score 550 paper-based; 79 iBT). *Application deadline:* For fall admission, 3/1 for domestic students; for spring admission, 11/1 for domestic students. Applications are processed on a rolling basis. Application fee: $50. *Expenses:* Tuition, state resident: full-time $8928; part-time $372 per credit hour. Tuition, nonresident: full-time $17,376; part-time $724 per credit hour. *Required fees:* $602; $22 per credit. $72 per term. *Financial support:* In 2013–14, 2 teaching assistantships with full tuition reimbursements (averaging $2,250 per year) were awarded; career-related internships or fieldwork, Federal Work-Study, scholarships/grants, health care benefits, and unspecified assistantships also available. Support available to part-time students. Financial award application deadline: 5/15; financial award applicants required to submit FAFSA. *Faculty research:* School administration, school/college articulation. *Unit head:* Dr. Paul Tiskus, Chair, 401-456-8170. *Application contact:* Graduate Studies, 401-456-8700.
Website: http://www.ric.edu/educationalStudies/.

Rider University, Department of Graduate Education, Leadership and Counseling, Teacher Certification Program, Lawrenceville, NJ 08648-3001. Offers business education (Certificate); elementary education (Certificate); English as a second language (Certificate); English education (Certificate); mathematics education (Certificate); preschool to grade 3 (Certificate); science education (Certificate); social studies education (Certificate); world languages (Certificate), including French, German, Spanish. Part-time programs available. *Degree requirements:* For Certificate, internship, professional portfolio. *Entrance requirements:* For degree, PRAXIS, resume. Additional exam requirements/recommendations for international students: Required—TOEFL (minimum score 550 paper-based). Electronic applications accepted. *Faculty research:* Conceptual foundations for optimal development of creativity; creative theory, cognitive processes in mathematics learning, teacher collaboration.

Rowan University, Graduate School, College of Communication and Creative Arts, Writing, Composition, and Rhetoric Certificate of Graduate Study Program, Glassboro, NJ 08028-1701. Offers CGS. *Faculty:* 1 full-time (0 women). *Students:* 2 part-time (both women). Average age 31. 1 applicant, 100% accepted, 1 enrolled. *Expenses: Tuition, area resident:* Part-time $638 per credit. Tuition, state resident: full-time $5742. *Required fees:* $142 per credit. Tuition and fees vary according to course level and program. *Unit head:* Dr. Horacio Sosa, Dean, College of Graduate and Continuing Education, 856-256-4747, Fax: 856-256-5638, E-mail: sosa@rowan.edu. *Application contact:* Admissions and Enrollment Services, 856-256-5435, Fax: 856-256-5637, E-mail: cgceadmissions@rowan.edu.

Rutgers, The State University of New Jersey, New Brunswick, Graduate School of Education, Department of Learning and Teaching, Program in English Education, Piscataway, NJ 08854-8097. Offers Ed M. Part-time programs available. *Degree requirements:* For master's, comprehensive exam or paper. *Entrance requirements:* For master's, GRE General Test, minimum GPA of 3.0. Additional exam requirements/recommendations for international students: Required—TOEFL. Electronic applications accepted.

Sage Graduate School, Esteves School of Education, Program in Teaching, Troy, NY 12180-4115. Offers art education (MAT); English (MAT); mathematics (MAT); social studies (MAT). *Accreditation:* NASAD. Part-time and evening/weekend programs available. *Faculty:* 10 full-time (6 women), 6 part-time/adjunct (4 women). *Students:* 1 (woman) full-time, 12 part-time (10 women); includes 2 minority (1 Hispanic/Latino; 1 Two or more races, non-Hispanic/Latino). Average age 26. 13 applicants, 31% accepted, 1 enrolled. In 2013, 18 master's awarded. *Entrance requirements:* For master's, assessment of writing skills, minimum undergraduate GPA of 2.75 overall, 3.0 in content area; current resume; 2 letters of recommendation. Additional exam requirements/recommendations for international students: Required—TOEFL (minimum score 550 paper-based). *Application deadline:* For fall admission, 8/1 for domestic students. Applications are processed on a rolling basis. Application fee: $40. *Expenses: Tuition:* Full-time $11,880; part-time $660 per credit hour. *Financial support:* Fellowships, research assistantships, Federal Work-Study, scholarships/grants, and unspecified assistantships available. Support available to part-time students. Financial award application deadline: 3/1; financial award applicants required to submit FAFSA. *Unit head:* Dr. Lori Quigley, Dean, Esteves School of Education, 518-244-2326, Fax: 518-244-4571, E-mail: l.quigley@sage.edu. *Application contact:* Kelly Jones, Director, 518-244-2433, Fax: 518-244-6880, E-mail: jonesk4@sage.edu.

St. John Fisher College, Ralph C. Wilson Jr. School of Education, Program in Adolescence Education and Special Education, Rochester, NY 14618-3597. Offers adolescence education: English with special education (MS Ed); adolescence education: French with special education (MS Ed); adolescence education: social studies with special education (MS Ed); adolescence education: Spanish with special education (MS Ed). Part-time and evening/weekend programs available. *Faculty:* 4 full-time (2 women), 4 part-time/adjunct (all women). *Students:* 20 full-time (10 women), 27 part-time (21 women); includes 4 minority (1 Black or African American, non-Hispanic/Latino; 1 Asian, non-Hispanic/Latino; 1 Hispanic/Latino; 1 Two or more races, non-Hispanic/Latino). Average age 27. 45 applicants, 89% accepted, 28 enrolled. In 2013, 28 master's awarded. *Degree requirements:* For master's, field experiences, student teaching, LAST. *Entrance requirements:* For master's, 2 letters of recommendation, personal statement, current resume. Additional exam requirements/recommendations for international students: Required—TOEFL (minimum score 575 paper-based; 80 iBT). *Application deadline:* Applications are processed on a rolling basis. Application fee: $30. Electronic applications accepted. *Expenses: Tuition:* Part-time $795 per credit hour. *Required fees:* $10 per credit hour. Tuition and fees vary according to course load,

degree level and program. *Financial support:* In 2013–14, 11 students received support. Scholarships/grants available. Financial award applicants required to submit FAFSA. *Faculty research:* Arts and humanities, urban schools, constructivist learning, at-risk students, mentoring. *Unit head:* Dr. Susan Schultz, Program Director, 585-385-7296, E-mail: sschultz@sjfc.edu. *Application contact:* Jose Perales, Director of Graduate Admissions, 585-385-8067, E-mail: jperales@sjfc.edu.
Website: http://www.sjfc.edu/academics/education/departments/ms-special-ed/options/initial-adolescence.dot.

San Francisco State University, Division of Graduate Studies, College of Education, Department of Elementary Education, Program in Language and Literacy Education, San Francisco, CA 94132-1722. Offers language and literacy education (MA); reading (Certificate); reading and language arts (Credential). *Unit head:* Dr. Debra Luna, Chair, 415-338-1562, E-mail: dluna@sfsu.edu. *Application contact:* Dr. Ali Borjian, MA Program Coordinator, 415-338-1838, E-mail: borjian@sfsu.edu.
Website: http://coe.sfsu.edu/eed/language-and-literacy-education.

San Francisco State University, Division of Graduate Studies, College of Liberal and Creative Arts, Department of English Language and Literature, San Francisco, CA 94132-1722. Offers composition (MA); immigrant literacies (Certificate); linguistics (MA); literature (MA); teaching English to speakers of other languages (MA); teaching of composition (Certificate); teaching post-secondary reading (Certificate). Part-time programs available. *Application deadline:* Applications are processed on a rolling basis. *Unit head:* Dr. Sugie Goen-Salter, Chair, 415-338-2264, E-mail: english@sfsu.edu. *Application contact:* Cynthia Losinsky, Administrative Support, Graduate Programs, 415-338-2660, E-mail: english@sfsu.edu.
Website: http://english.sfsu.edu/.

Simon Fraser University, Office of Graduate Studies, Faculty of Arts and Social Sciences, Department of English, Burnaby, BC V5A 1S6, Canada. Offers English (MA, PhD); teachers of English (MA). Part-time programs available. *Faculty:* 34 full-time (14 women). *Students:* 46 full-time (26 women). 63 applicants, 38% accepted, 12 enrolled. In 2013, 34 master's, 5 doctorates awarded. *Degree requirements:* For master's, one foreign language, thesis or alternative; for doctorate, one foreign language, thesis/dissertation, field exams. *Entrance requirements:* For master's, minimum GPA of 3.0 (on scale of 4.33), or 3.33 based on last 60 credits of undergraduate courses; for doctorate, minimum GPA of 3.5 (on scale of 4.33). Additional exam requirements/recommendations for international students: Recommended—TOEFL (minimum score 580 paper-based; 93 iBT), IELTS (minimum score 7), TWE (minimum score 5). *Application deadline:* For fall admission, 1/25 for domestic and international students; for spring admission, 2/1 for domestic students. Application fee: $90 ($125 for international students). Electronic applications accepted. *Expenses: Tuition, area resident:* Full-time $5084 Canadian dollars. *Required fees:* $840 Canadian dollars. *Financial support:* In 2013–14, 24 students received support, including 25 fellowships (averaging $6,250 per year), teaching assistantships (averaging $5,608 per year); research assistantships and scholarships/grants also available. *Faculty research:* Literary criticism, literature and psychoanalysis, Renaissance drama and poetry, Shakespeare, Canadian and American literature. *Unit head:* Dr. Jeff Derkson, Graduate Chair, 778-782-5431, E-mail: engl-grad-chair@sfu.ca. *Application contact:* Christa Gruninger, Graduate Secretary, 778-782-4614, Fax: 778-782-3136, E-mail: englgrad@sfu.ca.
Website: http://www.english.sfu.ca/.

Slippery Rock University of Pennsylvania, Graduate Studies (Recruitment), College of Education, Department of Secondary Education/Foundations of Education, Slippery Rock, PA 16057-1383. Offers educational leadership (M Ed); secondary education (M Ed), including English, math/science, social studies/history. *Accreditation:* NCATE. Part-time and evening/weekend programs available. *Faculty:* 12 full-time (5 women). *Students:* 48 full-time (24 women), 10 part-time (6 women). Average age 27. 50 applicants, 84% accepted, 29 enrolled. In 2013, 28 master's awarded. *Degree requirements:* For master's, comprehensive exam, thesis (for some programs). *Entrance requirements:* For master's, GRE General Test, MAT, minimum GPA of 2.8 or 3.0 (depending on program); copy of teaching certification and two letters of recommendation (for some programs). Additional exam requirements/recommendations for international students: Required—TOEFL (minimum score 550 paper-based; 80 iBT). *Application deadline:* For fall admission, 3/1 priority date for domestic students, 5/1 priority date for international students; for spring admission, 10/1 priority date for domestic students, 9/1 priority date for international students. Applications are processed on a rolling basis. Application fee: $25 ($30 for international students). Electronic applications accepted. *Expenses:* Tuition, state resident: full-time $7956; part-time $442 per credit. Tuition, nonresident: full-time $11,934; part-time $663 per credit. *Required fees:* $2896; $148 per credit. Tuition and fees vary according to degree level and program. *Financial support:* Career-related internships or fieldwork, Federal Work-Study, institutionally sponsored loans, scholarships/grants, tuition waivers (partial), and unspecified assistantships available. Support available to part-time students. Financial award application deadline: 5/1; financial award applicants required to submit FAFSA. *Unit head:* Dr. Jeffrey Lehman, Graduate Coordinator, 724-738-2311, Fax: 724-738-4987, E-mail: jeffrey.lehman@sru.edu. *Application contact:* Brandi Weber-Mortimer, Interim Director of Graduate Studies, 724-738-2051, Fax: 724-738-2146, E-mail: graduate.admissions@sru.edu.

Smith College, Graduate and Special Programs, Department of Education and Child Study, Program in Secondary Education, Northampton, MA 01063. Offers biological sciences education (MAT); chemistry education (MAT); English education (MAT); French education (MAT); geology education (MAT); government education (MAT); history education (MAT); mathematics education (MAT); physics education (MAT); Spanish education (MAT). Part-time programs available. *Faculty:* 6 full-time (4 women), 3 part-time/adjunct (2 women). *Students:* 4 full-time (3 women), 1 (woman) part-time, 2 international. Average age 33. 12 applicants, 92% accepted, 4 enrolled. In 2013, 6 master's awarded. *Entrance requirements:* Additional exam requirements/recommendations for international students: Required—TOEFL (minimum score 595 paper-based; 97 iBT). *Application deadline:* For fall admission, 4/1 for domestic students, 1/15 priority date for international students; for spring admission, 12/1 for domestic students. Application fee: $60. *Expenses: Tuition:* Full-time $32,160; part-time $1340 per credit. *Financial support:* In 2013–14, 5 students received support, including 2 fellowships with full tuition reimbursements available; career-related internships or fieldwork, institutionally sponsored loans, and scholarships/grants also available. Support available to part-time students. Financial award application deadline: 1/15; financial award applicants required to submit CSS PROFILE or FAFSA. *Unit head:* Rosetta Cohen, Graduate Student Advisor, 413-585-3266, E-mail: rcohen@smith.edu. *Application contact:* Ruth Morgan, Administrative Assistant, 413-585-3050, Fax: 413-585-3054, E-mail: gradstdy@smith.edu.
Website: http://www.smith.edu/educ/.

Smith College, Graduate and Special Programs, Department of English Language and Literature, Northampton, MA 01063. Offers MAT. Part-time programs available. *Faculty:* 20 full-time (8 women). *Students:* 1 (woman) full-time, all international. Average age 25. 4 applicants, 75% accepted, 1 enrolled. In 2013, 4 master's awarded. *Entrance requirements:* Additional exam requirements/recommendations for international students: Required—TOEFL (minimum score 595 paper-based; 97 iBT). *Application*

deadline: For fall admission, 4/1 for domestic students, 1/15 for international students; for spring admission, 12/1 for domestic students. Application fee: $60. *Expenses: Tuition:* Full-time $32,160; part-time $1340 per credit. *Financial support:* In 2013–14, 1 student received support. Career-related internships or fieldwork, institutionally sponsored loans, and scholarships/grants available. Support available to part-time students. Financial award application deadline: 1/15; financial award applicants required to submit CSS PROFILE or FAFSA. *Unit head:* Robert Hosmer, Graduate Adviser, 413-585-3315, E-mail: rhosmer@smith.edu. *Application contact:* Ruth Morgan, Administrative Assistant, 413-585-3050, Fax: 413-585-3054, E-mail: gradstdy@smith.edu.
Website: http://www.smith.edu/english/.

South Carolina State University, School of Graduate and Professional Studies, Department of Education, Orangeburg, SC 29117-0001. Offers early childhood and special education (M Ed); early childhood education (MAT); elementary education (M Ed, MAT); general science (MAT); mathematics (MAT); secondary education (M Ed), including biology education, business education, counselor education, English education, home economics education, industrial education, mathematics education, science education, social studies education; special education (M Ed), including emotionally handicapped, learning disabilities, mentally handicapped. *Accreditation:* NCATE. Part-time and evening/weekend programs available. *Faculty:* 9 full-time (3 women), 4 part-time/adjunct (3 women). *Students:* 32 full-time (26 women), 33 part-time (26 women); includes 63 minority (61 Black or African American, non-Hispanic/Latino; 2 Asian, non-Hispanic/Latino). Average age 31. 21 applicants, 100% accepted, 21 enrolled. In 2013, 15 master's awarded. *Degree requirements:* For master's, thesis optional, departmental qualifying exam. *Entrance requirements:* For master's, GRE General Test, NTE, interview, teaching certificate. *Application deadline:* For fall admission, 6/15 priority date for domestic students, 6/15 for international students; for spring admission, 11/1 for domestic and international students. Applications are processed on a rolling basis. Application fee: $25. Electronic applications accepted. *Expenses:* Tuition, state resident: full-time $8906; part-time $543 per credit hour. Tuition, nonresident: full-time $18,040; part-time $1051 per credit hour. *Financial support:* Fellowships, career-related internships or fieldwork, Federal Work-Study, and institutionally sponsored loans available. Financial award application deadline: 6/1. *Faculty research:* Critical thinking, child abuse, stress, test-taking skills, conflict resolution, mainstreaming. *Unit head:* Dr. Margaret Evelyn Fields, Interim Chair, 803-536-7098, Fax: 803-516-4568, E-mail: efields@scsu.edu. *Application contact:* Curtis Foskey, Coordinator of Graduate Studies, 803-536-8419, Fax: 803-536-8812, E-mail: cfoskey@scsu.edu.

Southeastern Louisiana University, College of Arts, Humanities and Social Sciences, Department of English, Hammond, LA 70402. Offers creative writing (MA); language and theory (MA); professional writing (MA). Part-time programs available. *Faculty:* 19 full-time (8 women), 1 part-time/adjunct (0 women). *Students:* 13 full-time (7 women), 21 part-time (17 women); includes 4 minority (1 Asian, non-Hispanic/Latino; 3 Hispanic/Latino), 1 international. Average age 29. 13 applicants, 54% accepted, 5 enrolled. In 2013, 15 master's awarded. *Degree requirements:* For master's, comprehensive exam, thesis optional. *Entrance requirements:* For master's, GRE General Test (minimum score of 850), bachelor's degree; minimum undergraduate GPA of 2.5; 24 hours of undergraduate English courses. Additional exam requirements/recommendations for international students: Required—TOEFL (minimum score 500 paper-based; 61 iBT), IELTS (minimum score 5.5). *Application deadline:* For fall admission, 7/15 priority date for domestic students, 6/1 priority date for international students; for spring admission, 12/1 priority date for domestic students, 10/1 priority date for international students. Applications are processed on a rolling basis. Application fee: $20 ($30 for international students). Electronic applications accepted. *Expenses:* Tuition, state resident: full-time $5047. Tuition, nonresident: full-time $17,066. *Required fees:* $1213. Tuition and fees vary according to degree level. *Financial support:* In 2013–14, 1 fellowship (averaging $10,800 per year), 7 research assistantships (averaging $6,900 per year), 1 teaching assistantship (averaging $9,000 per year) were awarded; career-related internships or fieldwork, Federal Work-Study, institutionally sponsored loans, scholarships/grants, and traineeships also available. Support available to part-time students. Financial award application deadline: 5/1; financial award applicants required to submit FAFSA. *Faculty research:* Creole studies, modernism, digital humanities, library studies, John Donne. *Total annual research expenditures:* $47,697. *Unit head:* Dr. David Hanson, Department Head, 985-549-2100, Fax: 985-549-5021, E-mail: dhanson@selu.edu. *Application contact:* Sandra Meyers, Graduate Admissions Analyst, 985-549-5620, Fax: 985-549-5632, E-mail: admissions@selu.edu.
Website: http://www.selu.edu/acad_research/depts/engl.

Southern Illinois University Edwardsville, Graduate School, College of Arts and Sciences, Department of English Language and Literature, Program in Teaching of Writing, Edwardsville, IL 62026-0001. Offers MA, Postbaccalaureate Certificate. Part-time and evening/weekend programs available. *Students:* 2 full-time (1 woman), 12 part-time (10 women); includes 2 minority (both Black or African American, non-Hispanic/Latino). 4 applicants, 100% accepted. In 2013, 5 master's, 1 other advanced degree awarded. *Degree requirements:* For master's, thesis or alternative, final exam. *Entrance requirements:* Additional exam requirements/recommendations for international students: Required—TOEFL (minimum score 550 paper-based, 79 iBT), IELTS (minimum score 6.5), Michigan Test of English Language Proficiency or PTE. *Application deadline:* For fall admission, 7/15 for domestic students, 6/1 for international students; for spring admission, 12/15 for domestic students, 10/1 for international students; for summer admission, 4/24 for domestic students, 3/1 for international students. Applications are processed on a rolling basis. Application fee: $30. Electronic applications accepted. *Expenses:* Tuition, state resident: full-time $3551. Tuition, nonresident: full-time $8378. *Financial support:* Fellowships with full tuition reimbursements, research assistantships with full tuition reimbursements, teaching assistantships with full tuition reimbursements, scholarships/grants, and unspecified assistantships available. Financial award application deadline: 3/1; financial award applicants required to submit FAFSA. *Unit head:* Dr. Jessica DeSpain, Program Director, 618-650-2051, E-mail: jdespai@siue.edu. *Application contact:* Melissa K. Mace, Assistant Director of Graduate and International Recruitment, 618-650-2756, Fax: 618-650-3618, E-mail: mmace@siue.edu.
Website: http://www.siue.edu/ENGLISH/TOW/.

Southern New Hampshire University, School of Education, Manchester, NH 03106-1045. Offers business education (M Ed); child development (M Ed); curriculum and instruction (M Ed), including education leadership, reading, special education, technology integration; education (M Ed); educational leadership (M Ed, Ed D); educational studies (M Ed); elementary education (M Ed); English (MAT); English for speakers of other languages (M Ed); reading and writing specialist (M Ed); school business administration (Certificate); secondary education (M Ed); special education (M Ed); technology integration specialist (M Ed). Part-time and evening/weekend programs available. Postbaccalaureate distance learning degree programs offered (no on-campus study). *Degree requirements:* For master's, comprehensive exam (for some programs), thesis or alternative. *Entrance requirements:* For master's, PRAXIS I, minimum GPA of 2.75. Additional exam requirements/recommendations for international students: Required—TOEFL (minimum score 550 paper-based). Electronic applications accepted. *Expenses:* Contact institution.

Southwestern Oklahoma State University, College of Arts and Sciences, Specialization in English, Weatherford, OK 73096-3098. Offers M Ed. M Ed distance learning degree program offered to Oklahoma residents only. *Accreditation:* NCATE. Part-time programs available. *Degree requirements:* For master's, exam. *Entrance requirements:* For master's, GRE General Test or minimum undergraduate GPA of 3.0. Additional exam requirements/recommendations for international students: Required—TOEFL.

State University of New York at New Paltz, Graduate School, School of Education, Department of Secondary Education, New Paltz, NY 12561. Offers adolescence education: biology (MAT, MS Ed); adolescence education: chemistry (MAT, MS Ed); adolescence education: earth science (MAT, MS Ed); adolescence education: English (MAT, MS Ed); adolescence education: French (MAT, MS Ed); adolescence education: social studies (MAT, MS Ed); adolescence education: Spanish (MAT, MS Ed); second language education (MS Ed, AC), including second language education (MS Ed), teaching English language learners (AC). *Accreditation:* NCATE. Part-time and evening/weekend programs available. *Faculty:* 10 full-time (8 women), 15 part-time/adjunct (10 women). *Students:* 73 full-time (47 women), 52 part-time (39 women); includes 27 minority (2 Black or African American, non-Hispanic/Latino; 6 Asian, non-Hispanic/Latino; 16 Hispanic/Latino; 3 Two or more races, non-Hispanic/Latino), 1 international. Average age 29. 81 applicants, 84% accepted, 51 enrolled. In 2013, 85 master's awarded. *Degree requirements:* For master's, comprehensive exam (for some programs), portfolio. *Entrance requirements:* For master's, minimum GPA of 3.0, New York state teaching certificate (MS Ed). Additional exam requirements/recommendations for international students: Required—TOEFL (minimum score 550 paper-based; 80 iBT), IELTS (minimum score 6.5). *Application deadline:* For fall admission, 3/1 priority date for domestic students, 3/1 for international students; for spring admission, 10/1 priority date for domestic students, 10/1 for international students. Application fee: $50. Electronic applications accepted. *Expenses:* Tuition, state resident: full-time $9870; part-time $411 per credit. Tuition, nonresident: full-time $18,350; part-time $765 per credit. *Required fees:* $1213. Tuition and fees vary according to program. *Financial support:* Application deadline: 8/1. *Unit head:* Dr. Laura Dull, Chair, 845-257-2850, E-mail: dulll@newpaltz.edu. *Application contact:* Caroline Murphy, Graduate Admissions Advisor, 845-257-3285, Fax: 845-257-3284, E-mail: gradschool@newpaltz.edu.
Website: http://www.newpaltz.edu/secondaryed/.

State University of New York at Plattsburgh, Division of Education, Health, and Human Services, Program in Teacher Education: Adolescence, Plattsburgh, NY 12901-2681. Offers adolescence education (MST); biology 7-12 (MST); chemistry 7-12 (MST); earth science 7-12 (MST); English 7-12 (MST); French 7-12 (MST); mathematics 7-12 (MST); physics 7-12 (MST); social studies 7-12 (MST); Spanish 7-12 (MST). *Accreditation:* Teacher Education Accreditation Council. Part-time and evening/weekend programs available. *Students:* 75 full-time (47 women), 5 part-time (3 women); includes 10 minority (1 Black or African American, non-Hispanic/Latino; 4 Asian, non-Hispanic/Latino; 5 Hispanic/Latino), 1 international. Average age 25. *Entrance requirements:* For master's, minimum GPA of 2.75. Additional exam requirements/recommendations for international students: Required—TOEFL. *Application deadline:* For fall admission, 2/15 priority date for domestic students. Applications are processed on a rolling basis. Application fee: $75. *Financial support:* Application deadline: 4/15; applicants required to submit FAFSA. *Unit head:* Dr. Robert Ackland, Coordinator, 518-564-5131, E-mail: acklanrt@plattsburgh.edu. *Application contact:* Betsy Kane, Director, Graduate Admissions, 518-564-4723, Fax: 518-564-4722, E-mail: bkane002@plattsburgh.edu.

State University of New York College at Cortland, Graduate Studies, School of Arts and Sciences, Programs in Adolescence Education, Cortland, NY 13045. Offers biology (MAT, MS Ed); chemistry (MAT, MS Ed); earth science (MAT, MS Ed); English (MAT, MS Ed); mathematics (MAT, MS Ed); physics (MAT, MS Ed); physics and mathematics (MS Ed); social studies (MS Ed), including geography, history. *Accreditation:* NCATE. Part-time and evening/weekend programs available. *Degree requirements:* For master's, one foreign language, comprehensive exam (for some programs), thesis (for some programs). *Entrance requirements:* For master's, GRE General Test. *Expenses:* Tuition, state resident: full-time $9870; part-time $411 per credit hour. Tuition, nonresident: full-time $18,350; part-time $765 per credit hour. *Required fees:* $1458; $65 per credit hour.

State University of New York College at Old Westbury, Program in Adolescent Education, Old Westbury, NY 11568-0210. Offers biology (MAT, MS); chemistry (MAT, MS); English language arts (MAT, MS); math (MAT, MS); social studies (MAT, MS); Spanish (MAT, MS). Part-time and evening/weekend programs available. *Faculty:* 19 full-time (11 women), 6 part-time/adjunct (1 woman). *Students:* 33 full-time (20 women), 33 part-time (19 women); includes 16 minority (2 Black or African American, non-Hispanic/Latino; 4 Asian, non-Hispanic/Latino; 9 Hispanic/Latino; 1 Two or more races, non-Hispanic/Latino). 25 applicants, 84% accepted, 19 enrolled. In 2013, 29 master's awarded. *Entrance requirements:* For master's, Liberal Arts and Sciences Test, undergraduate degree with at least 30 semester hours of appropriate coursework as defined by the respective discipline; minimum cumulative undergraduate GPA of 3.0; two letters of recommendation (one from an academic source); essay. Additional exam requirements/recommendations for international students: Required—TOEFL (minimum score 550 paper-based); Recommended—IELTS. *Expenses:* Tuition, state resident: full-time $9370; part-time $390 per credit. Tuition, nonresident: full-time $16,680; part-time $695 per credit. *Required fees:* $45.85 per credit. $47 per term. *Application contact:* Philip D'Angelo, Graduate Admissions Office, 516-876-3073, E-mail: enroll@oldwestbury.edu.

State University of New York College at Potsdam, School of Education and Professional Studies, Program in Secondary Education, Potsdam, NY 13676. Offers English education (MST); mathematics education (MST); science education (MST), including biology, chemistry, earth science, physics; social studies education (MST). *Accreditation:* NCATE. *Degree requirements:* For master's, culminating experience. *Entrance requirements:* For master's, minimum GPA of 2.75 in last 60 hours of course work (3.0 for English program). Additional exam requirements/recommendations for international students: Required—TOEFL (minimum score 550 paper-based; 80 iBT), IELTS (minimum score 6). Electronic applications accepted.

Stony Brook University, State University of New York, Graduate School, College of Arts and Sciences, Department of English, Stony Brook, NY 11794. Offers English (MA, PhD); English education (MAT). MAT offered through the School of Professional Development. Evening/weekend programs available. *Faculty:* 21 full-time (7 women), 3 part-time/adjunct (2 women). *Students:* 77 full-time (48 women), 24 part-time (19 women); includes 17 minority (2 Black or African American, non-Hispanic/Latino; 7 Asian, non-Hispanic/Latino; 6 Hispanic/Latino; 2 Two or more races, non-Hispanic/Latino), 5 international. Average age 32. 104 applicants, 23% accepted, 10 enrolled. In 2013, 22 master's, 10 doctorates awarded. Terminal master's awarded for partial completion of doctoral program. *Degree requirements:* For doctorate, thesis/dissertation. *Entrance requirements:* For master's and doctorate, GRE General Test. Additional exam requirements/recommendations for international students: Required—

TOEFL. *Application deadline:* For fall admission, 1/15 for domestic students; for spring admission, 10/1 for domestic students. Application fee: $100. *Expenses:* Tuition, state resident: full-time $9870; part-time $411 per credit. Tuition, nonresident: full-time $18,350; part-time $765 per credit. *Financial support:* In 2013–14, 23 teaching assistantships were awarded; fellowships and research assistantships also available. *Faculty research:* American literature, British literature, literary critical theory, rhetoric and composition theory, women's studies. *Unit head:* Dr. Eugene Hammond, Chair, 631-632-9277, Fax: 631-632-7568, E-mail: eugene.hammond@stonybrook.edu. *Application contact:* Dorothy Mason, Director, 631-632-7373, Fax: 631-632-7568, E-mail: dorothy.mason@stonybrook.edu.
Website: http://www.stonybrook.edu/english/.

Stony Brook University, State University of New York, School of Professional Development, Stony Brook, NY 11794. Offers biology (MAT); chemistry (MAT); coaching (Graduate Certificate); earth science (MAT); educational computing (Graduate Certificate); educational leadership (Advanced Certificate); English (MAT); environmental management (Graduate Certificate); French (MAT); German (MAT); higher education administration (MA, Certificate); human resource management (MS, Graduate Certificate); industrial management (Graduate Certificate); information systems management (Graduate Certificate); Italian (MAT); liberal studies (MA); mathematics (MAT); operations research (Graduate Certificate); physics (MAT); school district business leadership (Advanced Certificate); social science and the professions (MPS), including environmental management, human resource management; social studies (MAT); Spanish (MAT). Part-time and evening/weekend programs available. Postbaccalaureate distance learning degree programs offered. *Faculty:* 2 full-time (1 woman), 70 part-time/adjunct (30 women). *Students:* 241 full-time (135 women), 954 part-time (673 women); includes 209 minority (65 Black or African American, non-Hispanic/Latino; 2 American Indian or Alaska Native, non-Hispanic/Latino; 32 Asian, non-Hispanic/Latino; 104 Hispanic/Latino; 6 Two or more races, non-Hispanic/Latino), 7 international. Average age 28. 353 applicants, 92% accepted, 248 enrolled. In 2013, 312 master's, 131 other advanced degrees awarded. *Degree requirements:* For master's, one foreign language, thesis or alternative. *Application deadline:* For fall admission, 1/15 for domestic students; for spring admission, 10/1 for domestic students. Applications are processed on a rolling basis. Application fee: $100. *Expenses:* Tuition, state resident: full-time $9870; part-time $411 per credit. Tuition, nonresident: full-time $18,350; part-time $765 per credit. *Financial support:* Fellowships, research assistantships, teaching assistantships, and career-related internships or fieldwork available. Support available to part-time students. *Unit head:* Dr. Thomas Sexton, Interim Dean, 631-632-7181, Fax: 631-632-9046, E-mail: thomas.sexton@stonybrook.edu. *Application contact:* 631-632-7050 Ext. 1, E-mail: spd@stonybrook.edu.
Website: http://www.stonybrook.edu/spd/.

Syracuse University, School of Education, Program in English Education: Preparation 7-12, Syracuse, NY 13244. Offers MS. Part-time programs available. *Students:* 4 full-time (3 women), 1 part-time (0 women); includes 1 minority (Asian, non-Hispanic/Latino). Average age 27. 12 applicants, 92% accepted, 4 enrolled. In 2013, 3 master's awarded. *Degree requirements:* For master's, thesis or alternative. *Entrance requirements:* For master's, GRE. Additional exam requirements/recommendations for international students: Required—TOEFL (minimum score 100 iBT). *Application deadline:* For fall admission, 1/15 priority date for domestic and international students; for spring admission, 10/15 priority date for domestic and international students. Applications are processed on a rolling basis. Application fee: $75. Electronic applications accepted. *Financial support:* Fellowships with full tuition reimbursements and teaching assistantships with full and partial tuition reimbursements available. Financial award application deadline: 1/1. *Unit head:* Dr. Marcelle Haddix, Program Director, 315-443-4755, E-mail: mhaddix@syr.edu. *Application contact:* Laurie Deyo, Graduate Recruiter, School of Education, 315-443-2505, E-mail: e-gradrcrt@syr.edu.
Website: http://soeweb.syr.edu/.

Teachers College, Columbia University, Graduate Faculty of Education, Department of Arts and Humanities, Program in Teaching of English and English Education, New York, NY 10027. Offers Ed M, MA, Ed D, PhD. *Accreditation:* NCATE. Part-time and evening/weekend programs available. *Faculty:* 9 full-time, 6 part-time/adjunct. *Students:* 49 full-time (34 women), 145 part-time (113 women); includes 43 minority (15 Black or African American, non-Hispanic/Latino; 7 Asian, non-Hispanic/Latino; 15 Hispanic/Latino; 6 Two or more races, non-Hispanic/Latino), 11 international. Average age 30. 118 applicants, 87% accepted, 53 enrolled. In 2013, 111 master's, 7 doctorates awarded. Terminal master's awarded for partial completion of doctoral program. *Degree requirements:* For master's, project; for doctorate, comprehensive exam, thesis/dissertation. *Entrance requirements:* For master's, at least 24 undergraduate and/or graduate credits in English or their equivalent; writing sample and master's degree (for Ed M applicants); for doctorate, at least five years of classroom teaching experience; MA in English, English education or closely-related field; writing sample. *Application deadline:* For fall admission, 1/2 priority date for domestic students; for spring admission, 11/1 for domestic students. Application fee: $65. *Financial support:* Fellowships, research assistantships, teaching assistantships, career-related internships or fieldwork, Federal Work-Study, institutionally sponsored loans, and tuition waivers (full and partial) available. Support available to part-time students. Financial award application deadline: 2/1. *Faculty research:* Teaching of writing and reading, language and curriculum, literacy and health, narrative and action research. *Unit head:* Prof. Sheridan Blau, Program Coordinator, 212-678-7430, E-mail: sb2908@columbia.edu. *Application contact:* Thomas P. Rock, Director of Admissions, 212-678-3083, Fax: 212-678-4171, E-mail: rock@tc.edu.
Website: http://www.tc.edu/a%26h/EnglishEd/.

Temple University, College of Education, Department of Curriculum, Instruction, and Technology in Education, Philadelphia, PA 19122-6096. Offers career and technical education (Ed M), including business, computing, and information technology, industrial education, marketing education; middle grades education (Ed M), including math and language arts, math and science, science and language arts; secondary education (Ed M), including English, math, social studies; teaching English to speakers of other languages (MS Ed); urban education (Ed M). Part-time and evening/weekend programs available. *Students:* 66 full-time (48 women), 120 part-time (67 women); includes 50 minority (35 Black or African American, non-Hispanic/Latino; 1 American Indian or Alaska Native, non-Hispanic/Latino; 2 Asian, non-Hispanic/Latino; 7 Hispanic/Latino; 5 Two or more races, non-Hispanic/Latino), 1 international. 229 applicants, 41% accepted, 60 enrolled. In 2013, 41 master's awarded. Terminal master's awarded for partial completion of doctoral program. *Degree requirements:* For master's, thesis or alternative. *Entrance requirements:* Additional exam requirements/recommendations for international students: Required—TOEFL (minimum score 550 paper-based; 79 iBT). *Application deadline:* For fall admission, 4/1 for domestic students, 12/15 for international students; for spring admission, 10/1 for domestic students, 8/1 for international students. Application fee: $60. Electronic applications accepted. *Financial support:* Fellowships, research assistantships, and teaching assistantships available. Financial award application deadline: 1/15; financial award applicants required to submit FAFSA. *Faculty research:* Workforce development, vocational education, technical education, industrial education, professional development, literacy, classroom management, school communities, curriculum development, instruction, applied linguistics, crosslinguistic influence, bilingual education, oral proficiency, multilingualism. *Application contact:* Felicia Neuber, Enrollment Management, 215-204-8011, E-mail: educate@temple.edu.
Website: http://www.temple.edu/education/tl/.

Texas A&M University–Commerce, Graduate School, College of Humanities, Social Sciences and Arts, Department of Literature and Languages, Commerce, TX 75429-3011. Offers college teaching of English (PhD); English (MA, MS); Spanish (MA). Part-time programs available. Terminal master's awarded for partial completion of doctoral program. *Degree requirements:* For master's, comprehensive exam, thesis (for some programs); for doctorate, one foreign language, thesis/dissertation, departmental qualifying exam. *Entrance requirements:* For master's and doctorate, GRE General Test. Electronic applications accepted. *Expenses:* Tuition, state resident: full-time $3630; part-time $2420 per year. Tuition, nonresident: full-time $9948; part-time $6632.16 per year. *Required fees:* $1006 per year. Tuition and fees vary according to course load. *Faculty research:* Latino literature, American film studies, ethnographic research, Willa Carter.

Trinity Washington University, School of Education, Washington, DC 20017-1094. Offers clinical mental health counseling (MA); early childhood education (MAT); educating for change (M Ed); educational administration (MSA); elementary education (MAT); reading (M Ed); school counseling (MA); secondary education (MAT), including English, social studies; special education (MAT). *Accreditation:* NCATE. Part-time and evening/weekend programs available. *Degree requirements:* For master's, thesis (for some programs), capstone project(s). *Entrance requirements:* For master's, PRAXIS I, minimum GPA of 2.8. Additional exam requirements/recommendations for international students: Required—TOEFL (minimum score 550 paper-based). *Application deadline:* For fall admission, 4/1 priority date for domestic students; for winter admission, 11/1 priority date for domestic students; for spring admission, 11/1 priority date for domestic students. Applications are processed on a rolling basis. Application fee: $40. *Expenses: Tuition:* Part-time $715 per credit. *Financial support:* Career-related internships or fieldwork, health care benefits, and unspecified assistantships available. Support available to part-time students. Financial award application deadline: 4/1; financial award applicants required to submit FAFSA. *Faculty research:* Technology, literacy, special education, organizations, inclusion models. *Unit head:* Dr. Janet Stocks, Dean, 202-884-9380, Fax: 202-884-9506, E-mail: stocksj@trinitydc.edu. *Application contact:* Erika Davis, Director of Admissions for School of Education, 202-884-9400, Fax: 202-884-9229, E-mail: daviser@trinitydc.edu.
Website: http://www.trinitydc.edu/education/.

Troy University, Graduate School, College of Education, Program in Postsecondary Education, Troy, AL 36082. Offers adult education (M Ed); biology (M Ed); criminal justice (M Ed); English (M Ed); foundations of education (M Ed); general science (M Ed); higher education administration (M Ed); history (M Ed); instructional technology (M Ed); mathematics (M Ed); music industry (M Ed); physical fitness (M Ed); political science (M Ed); public administration (M Ed); social science (M Ed); teaching English (M Ed). *Accreditation:* NCATE. Part-time and evening/weekend programs available. *Faculty:* 30 full-time (11 women), 8 part-time/adjunct (1 woman). *Students:* 17 full-time (13 women), 106 part-time (84 women); includes 55 minority (45 Black or African American, non-Hispanic/Latino; 3 Asian, non-Hispanic/Latino; 2 Hispanic/Latino; 5 Two or more races, non-Hispanic/Latino). Average age 34. 109 applicants, 83% accepted, 5 enrolled. In 2013, 130 master's awarded. *Degree requirements:* For master's, comprehensive exam (for some programs), thesis (for some programs), thesis or comprehensive exam. *Entrance requirements:* For master's, GRE (minimum score of 850 on old exam or 290 on new exam), GMAT (minimum score of 380), or MAT (minimum score of 385), bachelor's degree; minimum undergraduate GPA of 2.5 or 3.0 on last 30 semester hours, letter of recommendation. Additional exam requirements/recommendations for international students: Required—TOEFL (minimum score 523 paper-based; 70 iBT), IELTS (minimum score 6). *Application deadline:* Applications are processed on a rolling basis. Application fee: $50. Electronic applications accepted. *Expenses:* Tuition, state resident: full-time $6084; part-time $338 per credit hour. Tuition, nonresident: full-time $12,168; part-time $676 per credit hour. *Required fees:* $630; $35 per credit hour. $50 per semester. *Financial support:* Available to part-time students. Applicants required to submit FAFSA. *Unit head:* Dr. Jan Oliver, Associate Professor, 334-670-3444, Fax: 334-670-3474, E-mail: oliver@troy.edu. *Application contact:* Brenda K. Campbell, Director of Graduate Admissions, 334-670-3178, Fax: 334-670-3733, E-mail: bcamp@troy.edu.

Union Graduate College, School of Education, Schenectady, NY 12308-3107. Offers biology (MAT); chemistry (MAT); Chinese (MAT); earth science (MAT); English (MA, MAT); English and history (MA); French (MAT); general science (MAT); German (MAT); history (MA); Latin (MAT); life sciences (MS); mathematics (MAT); mathematics and computer technology (MS); mentoring and teacher leadership (AC); middle childhood extension (AC); national board certification and teacher leadership (AC); physical sciences (MS); physics (MAT); social studies (MAT); Spanish (MAT); technology (MAT). *Accreditation:* Teacher Education Accreditation Council. *Faculty:* 3 full-time (1 woman), 56 part-time/adjunct (34 women). *Students:* 32 full-time (16 women), 27 part-time (22 women); includes 15 minority (1 Black or African American, non-Hispanic/Latino; 4 Asian, non-Hispanic/Latino; 6 Hispanic/Latino; 4 Two or more races, non-Hispanic/Latino), 1 international. Average age 32. In 2013, 25 master's, 11 other advanced degrees awarded. *Degree requirements:* For master's, thesis or project. *Entrance requirements:* For master's, minimum GPA of 3.0, letters of recommendation. Additional exam requirements/recommendations for international students: Required—TOEFL (minimum score 550 paper-based). *Application deadline:* Applications are processed on a rolling basis. Application fee: $60. Electronic applications accepted. *Expenses:* Contact institution. *Financial support:* Career-related internships or fieldwork, Federal Work-Study, scholarships/grants, health care benefits, and tuition waivers (partial) available. Support available to part-time students. Financial award applicants required to submit FAFSA. *Faculty research:* Transformative learning, science education, National Board Certification, teacher leadership, teacher quality. *Unit head:* Dr. Lynn Gelzheiser, Dean, 518-631-9870, Fax: 518-631-9901. *Application contact:* Nicki Foley, Assistant, 518-631-9871, Fax: 518-631-9903, E-mail: foleyn@uniongraduatecollege.edu.

University at Buffalo, the State University of New York, Graduate School, Graduate School of Education, Department of Learning and Instruction, Buffalo, NY 14260. Offers biology education (Ed M, Certificate); chemistry education (Ed M, Certificate); childhood education (Ed M); childhood education with bilingual extension (Ed M); curriculum, instruction and the science of learning (PhD); early childhood education (Ed M); early childhood education with bilingual extension (birth-grade 2) (Ed M); earth science education (Ed M, Certificate); education studies (Ed M); educational technology and new literacies (Certificate); elementary education (Ed D); English education (Ed M, Certificate); English for speakers of other languages (Ed M); foreign and second language education (PhD); French education (Ed M, Certificate); German education (Ed M, Certificate); gifted education (Certificate); Latin education (Ed M, Certificate); literacy specialist (Ed M); literacy teaching and learning (Certificate); mathematics education (Ed M, Certificate); music education (Ed M, Certificate); physics education (Ed M, Certificate); science and the public (Ed M); social studies education (Ed M, Certificate); Spanish education (Ed M, Certificate); special education (PhD); teaching English to speakers of other languages (Ed M). Part-time and evening/weekend

programs available. Postbaccalaureate distance learning degree programs offered (no on-campus study). *Faculty:* 31 full-time (23 women), 64 part-time/adjunct (53 women). *Students:* 275 full-time (215 women), 293 part-time (205 women); includes 35 minority (16 Black or African American, non-Hispanic/Latino; 5 American Indian or Alaska Native, non-Hispanic/Latino; 11 Asian, non-Hispanic/Latino; 3 Hispanic/Latino), 97 international. Average age 30. 544 applicants, 81% accepted, 246 enrolled. In 2013, 222 master's, 17 doctorates, 35 other advanced degrees awarded. *Degree requirements:* For master's, comprehensive exam; for doctorate, thesis/dissertation, research analysis exam, research experience component. *Entrance requirements:* For master's, content test in science and math, letters of reference; for doctorate, GRE General Test or MAT, interview, writing sample, letters of recommendation. Additional exam requirements/ recommendations for international students: Required—TOEFL (minimum score 600 paper-based; 96 iBT). *Application deadline:* For fall admission, 2/1 priority date for domestic and international students; for spring admission, 11/15 priority date for domestic students, 10/1 for international students. Applications are processed on a rolling basis. Application fee: $50. Electronic applications accepted. *Financial support:* In 2013–14, 50 fellowships (averaging $8,589 per year), 31 research assistantships with tuition reimbursements (averaging $11,406 per year) were awarded; teaching assistantships, career-related internships or fieldwork, Federal Work-Study, institutionally sponsored loans, scholarships/grants, tuition waivers, and unspecified assistantships also available. Financial award application deadline: 2/28; financial award applicants required to submit FAFSA. *Faculty research:* Science assessment, foreign language teaching and learning, early learning, new literacies, gender and education. *Total annual research expenditures:* $1.7 million. *Unit head:* Dr. Suzanne Miller, Chair, 716-645-2455, Fax: 716-645-3161, E-mail: smiller@buffalo.edu. *Application contact:* Cathy Dimino, Admissions Assistant, 716-645-2110, Fax: 716-645-7937, E-mail: cadimino@buffalo.edu.
Website: http://gse.buffalo.edu/lai.

The University of Alabama in Huntsville, School of Graduate Studies, College of Liberal Arts, Department of English, Huntsville, AL 35899. Offers education (MA); English (MA); language arts (MA); reading specialist (MA); technical communications (Certificate). Part-time and evening/weekend programs available. *Faculty:* 16 full-time (8 women). *Students:* 15 full-time (12 women), 26 part-time (18 women); includes 7 minority (all Black or African American, non-Hispanic/Latino). Average age 32. 27 applicants, 56% accepted, 10 enrolled. In 2013, 20 master's, 3 other advanced degrees awarded. *Degree requirements:* For master's, one foreign language, comprehensive exam, thesis or alternative, oral and written exams. *Entrance requirements:* For master's and Certificate, GRE General Test, minimum GPA of 3.0. Additional exam requirements/ recommendations for international students: Required—TOEFL (minimum score 500 paper-based; 80 iBT), IELTS (minimum score 6.5). *Application deadline:* For fall admission, 7/15 priority date for domestic students, 4/1 priority date for international students; for spring admission, 11/30 priority date for domestic students, 9/1 priority date for international students. Applications are processed on a rolling basis. Application fee: $50. Electronic applications accepted. *Expenses:* Tuition, state resident: full-time $8912; part-time $540 per credit hour. Tuition, nonresident: full-time $20,774; part-time $1252 per credit hour. *Required fees:* $148 per semester. One-time fee: $150. *Financial support:* In 2013–14, 10 students received support, including 7 teaching assistantships with full tuition reimbursements available (averaging $8,460 per year); career-related internships or fieldwork, Federal Work-Study, institutionally sponsored loans, scholarships/grants, health care benefits, tuition waivers (full and partial), and unspecified assistantships also available. Support available to part-time students. Financial award application deadline: 4/1; financial award applicants required to submit FAFSA. *Faculty research:* Fiction and identity, Shakespeare, science fiction, eighteenth-century literature, technical writing. *Total annual research expenditures:* $3,356. *Unit head:* Dr. Dan Schenker, Chair, 256-824-6320, Fax: 256-824-6949, E-mail: schenkd@uah.edu. *Application contact:* Kim Gray, Graduate Studies Admissions Coordinator, 256-824-6002, Fax: 256-824-6405, E-mail: deangrad@uah.edu.
Website: http://www.uah.edu/colleges/liberal/english/index.php.

University of Alaska Fairbanks, School of Education, Program in Education, Fairbanks, AK 99775. Offers curriculum and instruction (M Ed); education (M Ed, Graduate Certificate); elementary education (M Ed); language and literacy (M Ed); reading (M Ed); secondary education (M Ed); special education (M Ed). *Faculty:* 23 full-time (14 women), 1 part-time/adjunct (0 women). *Students:* 37 full-time (26 women), 78 part-time (54 women); includes 15 minority (6 American Indian or Alaska Native, non-Hispanic/Latino; 6 Hispanic/Latino; 3 Two or more races, non-Hispanic/Latino), 2 international. Average age 34. 37 applicants, 68% accepted, 19 enrolled. In 2013, 39 master's, 28 other advanced degrees awarded. *Degree requirements:* For master's, comprehensive exam, thesis, oral defense. *Entrance requirements:* Additional exam requirements/recommendations for international students: Required—TOEFL (minimum score 550 paper-based; 80 iBT). *Application deadline:* For fall admission, 5/1 for domestic students, 3/1 for international students; for spring admission, 10/15 for domestic students, 8/1 for international students. Applications are processed on a rolling basis. Application fee: $60. Electronic applications accepted. *Expenses:* Tuition, state resident: full-time $7254; part-time $403 per credit. Tuition, nonresident: full-time $14,814; part-time $823 per credit. Tuition and fees vary according to course level, course load and reciprocity agreements. *Financial support:* In 2013–14, 1 teaching assistantship with tuition reimbursement (averaging $11,011 per year) was awarded; fellowships with tuition reimbursements, research assistantships with tuition reimbursements, career-related internships or fieldwork, Federal Work-Study, scholarships/grants, health care benefits, and unspecified assistantships also available. Support available to part-time students. Financial award application deadline: 6/1; financial award applicants required to submit FAFSA. *Unit head:* Allan Morotti, Interim Dean, 907-474-7341, Fax: 907-474-5451, E-mail: uaf-soe-school@alaska.edu. *Application contact:* Libby Eddy, Director of Admissions, 907-474-7500, Fax: 907-474-7097, E-mail: admissions@uaf.edu.
Website: https://sites.google.com/a/alaska.edu/soe-graduate/.

The University of Arizona, College of Humanities, Department of English, Rhetoric, Composition and the Teaching of English Program, Tucson, AZ 85721. Offers MA, PhD. *Faculty:* 45 full-time (17 women), 3 part-time/adjunct (1 woman). *Students:* 41 full-time (26 women), 2 part-time (both women); includes 11 minority (1 Black or African American, non-Hispanic/Latino; 4 Asian, non-Hispanic/Latino; 3 Hispanic/Latino; 3 Two or more races, non-Hispanic/Latino), 1 international. Average age 32. 50 applicants, 14% accepted, 4 enrolled. In 2013, 11 doctorates awarded. *Degree requirements:* For master's, one foreign language, comprehensive exam; for doctorate, one foreign language, comprehensive exam, thesis/dissertation. *Entrance requirements:* For doctorate, GRE General Test, 3 letters of recommendation, writing sample. Additional exam requirements/recommendations for international students: Required—TOEFL (minimum score 550 paper-based; 79 iBT). *Application deadline:* Applications are processed on a rolling basis. Application fee: $75. Electronic applications accepted. *Expenses:* Tuition, state resident: full-time $11,526. Tuition, nonresident: full-time $27,398. *Financial support:* In 2013–14, 1 research assistantship with full tuition reimbursement (averaging $11,258 per year), 128 teaching assistantships with full tuition reimbursements (averaging $20,796 per year) were awarded. *Total annual research expenditures:* $420,173. *Unit head:* Dr. Lawrence J. Evers, Director, 520-621-

3287, Fax: 520-621-7397, E-mail: levers@email.arizona.edu. *Application contact:* Sharon Meyerson, Administrative Assistant, 520-621-7216, Fax: 520-621-7397, E-mail: sharonne@email.arizona.edu.
Website: http://grad.arizona.edu/live/programs/description/139.

University of Arkansas at Pine Bluff, School of Education, Pine Bluff, AR 71601-2799. Offers early childhood education (M Ed); secondary education (M Ed), including English education, mathematics education, physical education, science education, social studies education; teaching (MAT). *Accreditation:* NCATE. Part-time and evening/ weekend programs available. *Degree requirements:* For master's, comprehensive exam. *Entrance requirements:* For master's, GRE, minimum GPA of 2.75, NTE or Standard Arkansas Teaching Certificate. *Faculty research:* Teacher certification, accreditation, assessment, standards, portfolio development, rehabilitation, technology.

University of Central Florida, College of Education and Human Performance, School of Teaching, Learning, and Leadership, Orlando, FL 32816. Offers applied learning and instruction (MA, Certificate), including applied learning and instruction (MA), community college education (Certificate), gifted education (Certificate), global and comparative education (Certificate), initial teacher professional preparation (Certificate), urban education (Certificate); art education (M Ed, MAT), including teacher education (MAT), teacher leadership (M Ed); educational and instructional technology (MA, Certificate), including e-learning (Certificate), educational technology (Certificate), instructional design and technology (MA), instructional/educational technology (Certificate); educational leadership (Ed S); elementary education (M Ed, MA); English language arts education (M Ed, MAT), including teacher education (MAT), teacher leadership (M Ed); K-8 mathematics and science education (M Ed, Certificate); mathematics education (M Ed, MAT), including teacher education (MAT), teacher leadership (M Ed); reading education (M Ed, Certificate); science education (M Ed, MAT), including teacher education (MAT), teacher leadership (M Ed); social science education (M Ed, MAT), including teacher education (MAT), teacher leadership (M Ed); teacher leadership and educational leadership (M Ed, Ed S), including educational leadership (Ed S), teacher leadership (M Ed); teaching excellence (Certificate). Part-time and evening/weekend programs available. *Faculty:* 76 full-time (54 women), 75 part-time/adjunct (57 women). *Students:* 115 full-time (93 women), 476 part-time (364 women); includes 149 minority (49 Black or African American, non-Hispanic/Latino; 20 Asian, non-Hispanic/Latino; 69 Hispanic/Latino; 11 Two or more races, non-Hispanic/Latino), 8 international. Average age 31. 268 applicants, 79% accepted, 133 enrolled. In 2013, 212 master's, 48 other advanced degrees awarded. *Degree requirements:* For other advanced degree, thesis or alternative. *Entrance requirements:* For degree, GRE General Test, minimum GPA of 3.0. Additional exam requirements/recommendations for international students: Required—TOEFL. *Application deadline:* For fall admission, 7/15 for domestic students; for spring admission, 12/15 for domestic students. Application fee: $30. Electronic applications accepted. *Financial support:* In 2013–14, 8 students received support, including 5 research assistantships with partial tuition reimbursements available (averaging $7,300 per year), 3 teaching assistantships with partial tuition reimbursements available (averaging $7,000 per year); career-related internships or fieldwork, Federal Work-Study, institutionally sponsored loans, tuition waivers (partial), and unspecified assistantships also available. Financial award application deadline: 3/1; financial award applicants required to submit FAFSA. *Unit head:* Dr. Michael C. Hynes, Co-Director, 407-823-6076, E-mail: michael.hynes@ucf.edu. *Application contact:* Barbara Rodriguez Lamas, Director, Admissions and Student Services, 407-823-2766, Fax: 407-823-6442, E-mail: gradadmissions@ucf.edu.
Website: http://education.ucf.edu/departments.cfm.

University of Colorado Denver, College of Liberal Arts and Sciences, Department of English, Denver, CO 80217. Offers applied linguistics (MA); literature (MA); rhetoric and teaching of writing (MA). Part-time and evening/weekend programs available. *Faculty:* 20 full-time (12 women). *Students:* 24 full-time (18 women), 21 part-time (10 women); includes 4 minority (1 Black or African American, non-Hispanic/Latino; 3 Hispanic/ Latino), 3 international. Average age 29. 30 applicants, 60% accepted, 14 enrolled. In 2013, 21 master's awarded. *Degree requirements:* For master's, variable foreign language requirement, comprehensive exam (for some programs), thesis (for some programs), minimum of 33 credit hours for literature, 30 for rhetoric and teaching of writing and applied linguistics. *Entrance requirements:* For master's, GRE General Test, minimum GPA of 3.0, critical writing sample, letters of recommendation, completion of 24 semester hours in English courses (at least 16 at the upper-division level), statement of purpose. Additional exam requirements/recommendations for international students: Required—TOEFL (minimum score 537 paper-based; 75 iBT); Recommended—IELTS (minimum score 6.5). *Application deadline:* For fall admission, 4/1 for domestic and international students; for spring admission, 10/1 for domestic and international students. Application fee: $50 ($75 for international students). Electronic applications accepted. *Financial support:* In 2013–14, 10 students received support. Fellowships, research assistantships, teaching assistantships, Federal Work-Study, institutionally sponsored loans, scholarships/grants, traineeships, and unspecified assistantships available. Financial award application deadline: 4/1; financial award applicants required to submit FAFSA. *Faculty research:* Literature, rhetoric, teaching of writing, applied linguistics. *Unit head:* Prof. Nancy Ciccone, Chair, 303-556-8395, Fax: 303-556-2959, E-mail: nancy.ciccone@ucdenver.edu. *Application contact:* English Department, 303-556-2584, Fax: 303-556-2959.
Website: http://www.ucdenver.edu/academics/colleges/CLAS/Departments/english/Programs/Masters/Pages/Overview.aspx.

University of Colorado Denver, School of Education and Human Development, Teacher Education Programs, Denver, CO 80217. Offers elementary linguistically diverse education (MA); elementary math and science education (MA); elementary math education (MA); elementary reading and writing (MA); elementary science education (MA); secondary English education (MA); secondary linguistically diverse education (MA); secondary math education (MA); secondary reading and writing (MA); secondary science education (MA); special education (MA). *Accreditation:* NCATE. Part-time and evening/weekend programs available. *Students:* 269 full-time (208 women), 141 part-time (111 women); includes 55 minority (4 Black or African American, non-Hispanic/ Latino; 1 American Indian or Alaska Native, non-Hispanic/Latino; 10 Asian, non-Hispanic/Latino; 39 Hispanic/Latino; 1 Two or more races, non-Hispanic/Latino), 7 international. Average age 31. 97 applicants, 81% accepted, 62 enrolled. In 2013, 180 master's awarded. *Degree requirements:* For master's, comprehensive exam. *Entrance requirements:* For master's, GRE or MAT (for those with GPA below 2.75), transcripts, resume, letters of recommendation. Additional exam requirements/recommendations for international students: Required—TOEFL (minimum score 537 paper-based; 75 iBT); Recommended—IELTS (minimum score 6.5). *Application deadline:* For fall admission, 4/15 priority date for domestic students, 4/1 for international students; for spring admission, 9/15 priority date for domestic students, 9/1 for international students. Applications are processed on a rolling basis. Application fee: $50 ($75 for international students). Electronic applications accepted. *Expenses:* Contact institution. *Financial support:* In 2013–14, 42 students received support. Fellowships, research assistantships, teaching assistantships, Federal Work-Study, institutionally sponsored loans, scholarships/grants, and traineeships available. Financial award application deadline: 4/1; financial award applicants required to submit FAFSA. *Faculty research:* Linguistically diverse education/ESL, elementary reading and writing, elementary

teacher education, secondary teacher education, special education. *Unit head:* Cindy Gutierrez, Director, 303-315-4982, E-mail: cindy.gutierrez@ucdenver.edu. *Application contact:* Lori Sisneros, Student Services Center, 303-315-4979, E-mail: education@ucdenver.edu.
Website: http://www.ucdenver.edu/academics/colleges/SchoolOfEducation/Academics/MASTERS/Pages/default.aspx.

University of Connecticut, Graduate School, Neag School of Education, Department of Curriculum and Instruction, Program in English Education, Storrs, CT 06269. Offers MA, PhD, Post-Master's Certificate. *Accreditation:* NCATE. Terminal master's awarded for partial completion of doctoral program. *Degree requirements:* For master's, comprehensive exam, thesis or alternative; for doctorate, thesis/dissertation. *Entrance requirements:* For doctorate, GRE General Test. Additional exam requirements/recommendations for international students: Required—TOEFL (minimum score 550 paper-based). Electronic applications accepted.

University of Florida, Graduate School, College of Education, School of Teaching and Learning, Gainesville, FL 32611. Offers curriculum and instruction (M Ed, MAE, Ed D, PhD, Ed S), including bilingual/ESOL specialization; elementary education (M Ed, MAE); English education (M Ed, MAE); mathematics education (M Ed, MAE); reading education (M Ed, MAE); science education (M Ed, MAE); social studies education (M Ed, MAE). *Accreditation:* NCATE. Part-time and evening/weekend programs available. Postbaccalaureate distance learning degree programs offered (no on-campus study). *Faculty:* 24 full-time (17 women), 12 part-time/adjunct (7 women). *Students:* 201 full-time (162 women), 325 part-time (255 women); includes 124 minority (36 Black or African American, non-Hispanic/Latino; 4 American Indian or Alaska Native, non-Hispanic/Latino; 10 Asian, non-Hispanic/Latino; 74 Hispanic/Latino), 47 international. Average age 34. 220 applicants, 55% accepted, 64 enrolled. In 2013, 215 master's, 15 doctorates, 14 other advanced degrees awarded. Terminal master's awarded for partial completion of doctoral program. *Degree requirements:* For master's, comprehensive exam (for some programs), thesis (for some programs); for doctorate, comprehensive exam (for some programs), thesis/dissertation (for some programs). *Entrance requirements:* For master's and doctorate, GRE General Test, minimum GPA of 3.0; for Ed S, GRE General Test. Additional exam requirements/recommendations for international students: Required—TOEFL (minimum score 550 paper-based; 80 iBT), IELTS (minimum score 6). *Application deadline:* For fall admission, 2/15 for domestic students, 12/1 for international students; for spring admission, 9/15 for domestic students, 3/1 for international students. Applications are processed on a rolling basis. Application fee: $30. Electronic applications accepted. *Expenses:* Tuition, state resident: full-time $12,640. Tuition, nonresident: full-time $30,000. *Financial support:* In 2013–14, 52 students received support, including 3 fellowships (averaging $2,365 per year), 20 research assistantships (averaging $11,715 per year), 58 teaching assistantships (averaging $8,410 per year); career-related internships or fieldwork and unspecified assistantships also available. Financial award applicants required to submit FAFSA. *Faculty research:* Early childhood, child and adolescents, diverse learners, race/ethnicity issues, teacher education, professional development, language and literacy development, policy development. *Unit head:* Elizabeth Bondy, PhD, Interim Director and Professor, 352-273-4242, Fax: 352-392-9193, E-mail: bondy@coe.ufl.edu. *Application contact:* Sevan Terzian, Graduate Coordinator, 352-273-4216, Fax: 352-392-9193, E-mail: sterzian@coe.ufl.edu.
Website: http://education.ufl.edu/school-teaching-learning/.

University of Georgia, College of Education, Department of Language and Literacy Education, Athens, GA 30602. Offers English education (M Ed, Ed S); language and literacy education (PhD); reading education (M Ed, Ed D, Ed S); teaching additional languages (M Ed, Ed S). *Accreditation:* NCATE. *Degree requirements:* For doctorate, variable foreign language requirement. *Entrance requirements:* For master's and Ed S, GRE General Test or MAT; for doctorate, GRE General Test. Additional exam requirements/recommendations for international students: Required—TOEFL (minimum score 550 paper-based). Electronic applications accepted. *Faculty research:* Comprehension, critical literacy, literacy and technology, vocabulary instruction, content area reading.

University of Illinois at Chicago, Graduate College, College of Liberal Arts and Sciences, Department of English, Chicago, IL 60607-7128. Offers English (MA, PhD), including creative writing (PhD), English education (MA), English studies, writing (MA). Part-time and evening/weekend programs available. *Faculty:* 27 full-time (11 women), 10 part-time/adjunct (7 women). *Students:* 92 full-time (49 women), 16 part-time (8 women); includes 16 minority (6 Black or African American, non-Hispanic/Latino; 3 Asian, non-Hispanic/Latino; 3 Hispanic/Latino; 4 Two or more races, non-Hispanic/Latino), 6 international. Average age 32. 308 applicants, 24% accepted, 20 enrolled. In 2013, 13 master's, 10 doctorates awarded. *Degree requirements:* For doctorate, variable foreign language requirement, thesis/dissertation, written and oral exams. *Entrance requirements:* For master's, GRE General Test, GRE Subject Test; for doctorate, GRE General Test, GRE Subject Test, minimum GPA of 2.0. Additional exam requirements/recommendations for international students: Required—TOEFL. *Application deadline:* For fall admission, 1/1 for domestic and international students. Applications are processed on a rolling basis. Application fee: $40 ($50 for international students). Electronic applications accepted. *Expenses:* Tuition, state resident: full-time $11,066; part-time $3689 per term. Tuition, nonresident: full-time $23,064; part-time $7688 per term. *Required fees:* $3004; $1190 per term. Tuition and fees vary according to course level and program. *Financial support:* In 2013–14, 3 fellowships with full tuition reimbursements were awarded; research assistantships with full tuition reimbursements, teaching assistantships with full tuition reimbursements, career-related internships or fieldwork, Federal Work-Study, institutionally sponsored loans, scholarships/grants, traineeships, tuition waivers (full), and unspecified assistantships also available. Financial award application deadline: 3/1; financial award applicants required to submit FAFSA. *Faculty research:* Literary history and theory. *Unit head:* Prof. John Huntington, Head, 312-413-2203, Fax: 312-413-1005, E-mail: juntingj@uic.edu. *Application contact:* Madhu Dubey, Director of Graduate Studies, 312-413-2239, E-mail: madhud@uic.edu.
Website: http://www.uic.edu/depts/engl/.

University of Illinois at Springfield, Graduate Programs, College of Liberal Arts and Sciences, Program in English, Springfield, IL 62703-5407. Offers English (MA); teaching English (Graduate Certificate). Part-time and evening/weekend programs available. *Faculty:* 8 full-time (7 women). *Students:* 14 part-time (9 women); includes 3 minority (2 Asian, non-Hispanic/Latino; 1 Hispanic/Latino). Average age 32. 2 applicants. In 2013, 3 master's awarded. *Degree requirements:* For master's, comprehensive exam, thesis, or project. *Entrance requirements:* For master's, GRE General Test, analytical writing sample, two letters of recommendation. Additional exam requirements/recommendations for international students: Required—TOEFL (minimum score 500 paper-based; 61 iBT). *Application deadline:* Applications are processed on a rolling basis. Application fee: $60 ($75 for international students). Electronic applications accepted. *Expenses:* Tuition, state resident: full-time $7440. Tuition, nonresident: full-time $15,744. *Required fees:* $2985.60. *Financial support:* In 2013–14, fellowships with full tuition reimbursements (averaging $9,900 per year), research assistantships with full tuition reimbursements (averaging $9,550 per year), teaching assistantships with full tuition reimbursements (averaging $9,700 per year) were awarded; career-related internships or fieldwork, Federal Work-Study, scholarships/grants, health care benefits, and unspecified assistantships also available. Support available to part-time students. Financial award application deadline: 11/15; financial award applicants required to submit FAFSA. *Unit head:* Dr. Tena Helton, Program Administrator, 217-206-7441, Fax: 217-206-6217, E-mail: thelt2@uis.edu. *Application contact:* Dr. Lynn Pardie, Office of Graduate Studies, 800-252-8533, Fax: 217-206-7623, E-mail: lpard1@uis.edu.

University of Indianapolis, Graduate Programs, School of Education, Indianapolis, IN 46227-3697. Offers art education (MAT); biology (MAT); chemistry (MAT); curriculum and instruction (MA); earth sciences (MAT); education (MA, MAT); educational leadership (MA); elementary education (MA); English (MAT); French (MAT); math (MAT); physical education (MAT); physics (MAT); secondary education (MA), including art education, education, English education, social studies education; social studies (MAT); Spanish (MAT). *Accreditation:* NCATE. Part-time and evening/weekend programs available. *Faculty:* 5 full-time (4 women), 2 part-time/adjunct (1 woman). *Students:* 19 full-time (9 women), 54 part-time (27 women); includes 13 minority (5 Black or African American, non-Hispanic/Latino; 1 Asian, non-Hispanic/Latino; 5 Hispanic/Latino; 2 Two or more races, non-Hispanic/Latino), 1 international. Average age 32. In 2013, 52 master's awarded. *Entrance requirements:* For master's, GRE Subject Test, PRAXIS I, minimum GPA of 2.5, 3 letters of recommendation, interview. Additional exam requirements/recommendations for international students: Required—TOEFL (minimum score 550 paper-based). *Application deadline:* Applications are processed on a rolling basis. Application fee: $50. *Expenses:* *Tuition:* Full-time $5436; part-time $810 per credit hour. *Financial support:* Federal Work-Study available. Financial award application deadline: 5/1; financial award applicants required to submit FAFSA. *Faculty research:* Assessment of teacher education, perceptions of prospective teachers by parents. *Unit head:* Dr. Kathy Moran, Dean, 317-788-3285, Fax: 317-788-3300, E-mail: kmoran@uindy.edu. *Application contact:* Jeni Kirby, Administrative Assistant, Teacher Education, 317-788-2113, E-mail: kirbyj@uindy.edu.
Website: http://education.uindy.edu/.

The University of Iowa, Graduate College, College of Education, Department of Teaching and Learning, Program in Education, Iowa City, IA 52242-1316. Offers art education (MA); developmental reading (MA); elementary education (MA); English education (MA, MAT); foreign and second language education (MAT); foreign language education (MA); foreign language/ESL education (PhD); language, literacy and culture (PhD); mathematics education (MA, MAT, PhD); music education (MM, PhD); science education (MA); secondary education (MA); social studies (MA, PhD). *Degree requirements:* For master's, thesis optional, exam; for doctorate, comprehensive exam, thesis/dissertation. *Entrance requirements:* For master's and doctorate, GRE General Test, minimum GPA of 3.0. Additional exam requirements/recommendations for international students: Required—TOEFL (minimum score 550 paper-based; 81 iBT). Electronic applications accepted.

University of Louisiana at Monroe, Graduate School, College of Arts, Education, and Sciences, School of Education, Program in Curriculum and Instruction, Monroe, LA 71209-0001. Offers art education (M Ed); biology education (M Ed); chemistry education (M Ed); curriculum and instruction (Ed D); early childhood education (M Ed); earth science education (M Ed); educational leadership (M Ed); elementary education (1-5) (M Ed); English as a second language (M Ed); English education (M Ed); family and consumer education (M Ed); French education (M Ed); history education (M Ed); math education (M Ed); middle school education (M Ed); music education (M Ed); reading education (K-12) (M Ed); Spanish education (M Ed); special education - academically gifted (M Ed); special education - early intervention (M Ed); special education - educational diagnostician (M Ed); special education - mild/moderate disabilities (M Ed); speech education (M Ed). *Accreditation:* NCATE. *Degree requirements:* For master's, comprehensive exam (for some programs), thesis; for doctorate, thesis/dissertation, internships. *Entrance requirements:* For master's, GRE General Test; for doctorate, GRE General Test, minimum undergraduate GPA of 2.75, graduate 3.25. Additional exam requirements/recommendations for international students: Required—TOEFL (minimum score 500 paper-based; 61 iBT). *Application deadline:* For fall admission, 8/24 priority date for domestic students, 7/1 for international students; for winter admission, 12/14 priority date for domestic students; for spring admission, 1/19 for domestic students, 11/1 for international students. Applications are processed on a rolling basis. Application fee: $20 ($30 for international students). Electronic applications accepted. *Expenses:* Tuition, state resident: full-time $6607. Tuition, nonresident: full-time $17,179. Full-time tuition and fees vary according to program. *Financial support:* Research assistantships, career-related internships or fieldwork, Federal Work-Study, and unspecified assistantships available. Financial award application deadline: 4/1; financial award applicants required to submit FAFSA. *Unit head:* Dr. Dorothy Schween, Director, 318-342-1268, Fax: 318-342-3131, E-mail: schween@ulm.edu. *Application contact:* Dr. Dorothy Schween, Director, 318-342-1268, Fax: 318-342-3131, E-mail: schween@ulm.edu.

University of Maine, Graduate School, College of Liberal Arts and Sciences, Department of English, Orono, ME 04469. Offers composition and pedagogy (MA); creative writing (MA); gender and literature (MA); poetry and poetics (MA); women's studies (MA). Part-time and evening/weekend programs available. *Faculty:* 20 full-time (10 women). *Students:* 24 full-time (12 women), 2 part-time (1 woman), 2 international. Average age 26. 31 applicants, 65% accepted, 12 enrolled. In 2013, 11 master's awarded. *Degree requirements:* For master's, one foreign language, thesis optional. *Entrance requirements:* For master's, GRE General Test, minimum GPA of 3.0. Additional exam requirements/recommendations for international students: Required—TOEFL. *Application deadline:* For fall admission, 1/15 priority date for domestic students. Applications are processed on a rolling basis. Application fee: $65. Electronic applications accepted. *Expenses:* Tuition, state resident: full-time $7524. Tuition, nonresident: full-time $23,112. *Required fees:* $1970. *Financial support:* In 2013–14, 24 students received support, including 1 fellowship (averaging $15,000 per year), 1 research assistantship (averaging $14,600 per year), 20 teaching assistantships with full tuition reimbursements available (averaging $14,600 per year); Federal Work-Study and tuition waivers (full and partial) also available. Financial award application deadline: 3/1. *Faculty research:* Utopia and utopianism, women's literature, restoration, writing pedagogy, British Romantic period. *Unit head:* Dr. Richard Brucher, Chair, 207-581-3823, Fax: 207-581-1604. *Application contact:* Scott G. Delcourt, Associate Dean of the Graduate School, 207-581-3291, Fax: 207-581-3232, E-mail: graduate@maine.edu.
Website: http://english.umaine.edu/.

University of Manitoba, Faculty of Graduate Studies, Faculty of Education, Department of Curriculum, Teaching and Learning, Winnipeg, MB R3T 2N2, Canada. Offers language and literacy (M Ed); second language education (M Ed); studies in curriculum, teaching and learning (M Ed). *Degree requirements:* For master's, thesis or alternative.

University of Maryland, Baltimore County, Graduate School, College of Arts, Humanities and Social Sciences, Department of Education, Program in Teaching, Baltimore, MD 21250. Offers early childhood education (MAT); elementary education (MAT); secondary education (MAT), including art, biology, chemistry, dance, earth/space science, English, foreign language, mathematics, music, physics, social studies, theatre. Part-time and evening/weekend programs available. *Faculty:* 24 full-time (18

women), 25 part-time/adjunct (19 women). *Students:* 49 full-time (34 women), 35 part-time (23 women); includes 19 minority (9 Black or African American, non-Hispanic/Latino; 3 Asian, non-Hispanic/Latino; 6 Hispanic/Latino; 1 Two or more races, non-Hispanic/Latino). Average age 30. 40 applicants, 95% accepted, 35 enrolled. In 2013, 106 master's awarded. *Degree requirements:* For master's, comprehensive exam (for some programs), thesis (for some programs). *Entrance requirements:* For master's, PRAXIS I or SAT (minimum score of 1000), minimum GPA of 3.0. Additional exam requirements/recommendations for international students: Required—TOEFL. *Application deadline:* For fall admission, 6/1 for domestic students; for spring admission, 11/1 for domestic students. Applications are processed on a rolling basis. Application fee: $50. Electronic applications accepted. One-time fee: $200 full-time. *Financial support:* In 2013–14, 6 students received support, including teaching assistantships with full and partial tuition reimbursements available (averaging $12,000 per year); career-related internships or fieldwork, Federal Work-Study, scholarships/grants, tuition waivers, and unspecified assistantships also available. Financial award application deadline: 3/1. *Faculty research:* STEM teacher education, culturally sensitive pedagogy, ESOL/bilingual education, early childhood education, language, literacy and culture. *Unit head:* Dr. Susan M. Blunck, Graduate Program Director, 410-455-2869, Fax: 410-455-3986, E-mail: blunck@umbc.edu. *Application contact:* Dr. Susan M. Blunck, Graduate Program Director, 410-455-2869, Fax: 410-455-3986, E-mail: blunck@umbc.edu.
Website: http://www.umbc.edu/education/.

University of Michigan, Horace H. Rackham School of Graduate Studies, Joint PhD Program in English and Education, Ann Arbor, MI 48109. Offers PhD. *Accreditation:* Teacher Education Accreditation Council. *Faculty:* 34 full-time (20 women). *Students:* 29 full-time (23 women); includes 2 minority (1 Black or African American, non-Hispanic/Latino; 1 Hispanic/Latino). 43 applicants, 14% accepted, 5 enrolled. In 2013, 1 doctorate awarded. *Degree requirements:* For doctorate, one foreign language, comprehensive exam, thesis/dissertation, 3 preliminary exams, oral defense of dissertation. *Entrance requirements:* For doctorate, GRE General Test, master's degree, teaching experience. Additional exam requirements/recommendations for international students: Required—TOEFL. *Application deadline:* For fall admission, 1/5 for domestic and international students. Application fee: $75 ($90 for international students). Electronic applications accepted. Tuition and fees vary according to course level, course load, degree level, program and student level. *Financial support:* In 2013–14, 29 students received support, including 8 fellowships with full tuition reimbursements available, 5 research assistantships with full tuition reimbursements available, 25 teaching assistantships with full tuition reimbursements available; health care benefits and unspecified assistantships also available. *Faculty research:* Literacy, teacher education, discourse analysis, rhetoric and composition studies. *Unit head:* Dr. Anne Ruggles Gere, Co-Chair, 734-763-6643, Fax: 734-615-6524, E-mail: argere@umich.edu. *Application contact:* Jeanie Mahoney Laubenthal, Graduate Coordinator, 734-763-6643, Fax: 734-615-6524, E-mail: laubenth@umich.edu.
Website: http://www.soe.umich.edu/academics/doctoral_programs/ee/.

University of Minnesota, Twin Cities Campus, Graduate School, College of Education and Human Development, Department of Curriculum and Instruction, Program in Teaching, Minneapolis, MN 55455-0213. Offers Chinese (M Ed); earth science (M Ed); elementary special education (M Ed); English (M Ed); English as a second language (M Ed); French (M Ed); German (M Ed); Hebrew (M Ed); Japanese (M Ed); life sciences (M Ed); mathematics (M Ed); middle school science (M Ed); science (M Ed); second languages and cultures (M Ed); social studies (M Ed); Spanish (M Ed). *Students:* 220 full-time (154 women), 83 part-time (60 women); includes 43 minority (10 Black or African American, non-Hispanic/Latino; 26 Asian, non-Hispanic/Latino; 7 Hispanic/Latino), 4 international. Average age 27. 261 applicants, 87% accepted, 222 enrolled. In 2013, 561 master's awarded. Application fee: $75 ($95 for international students). *Unit head:* Dr. Nina Asher, Chair, 612-624-1357, Fax: 612-624-8277, E-mail: nasher@umn.edu. *Application contact:* Dr. Jennifer Engler, Assistant Dean, 612-626-2887, Fax: 612-626-7496, E-mail: engle009@umn.edu.
Website: http://www.cehd.umn.edu/ci/.

University of Missouri, Graduate School, College of Education, Department of Learning, Teaching and Curriculum, Columbia, MO 65211. Offers agricultural education (M Ed, PhD, Ed S); art education (M Ed, PhD, Ed S); business and office education (M Ed, PhD, Ed S); early childhood education (M Ed, PhD, Ed S); elementary education (M Ed, PhD, Ed S); English education (M Ed, PhD, Ed S); foreign language education (M Ed, PhD, Ed S); health education and promotion (M Ed, PhD); learning and instruction (M Ed); marketing education (M Ed, PhD, Ed S); mathematics education (M Ed, PhD, Ed S); music education (M Ed, PhD, Ed S); reading education (M Ed, PhD, Ed S); science education (M Ed, PhD, Ed S); social studies education (M Ed, PhD, Ed S); vocational education (M Ed, PhD, Ed S). Part-time programs available. *Faculty:* 26 full-time (16 women), 3 part-time/adjunct (2 women). *Students:* 186 full-time (143 women), 197 part-time (172 women); includes 19 minority (4 Black or African American, non-Hispanic/Latino; 4 Asian, non-Hispanic/Latino; 6 Hispanic/Latino; 5 Two or more races, non-Hispanic/Latino), 25 international. Average age 31. 288 applicants, 65% accepted, 160 enrolled. In 2013, 202 master's, 18 doctorates, 7 other advanced degrees awarded. Terminal master's awarded for partial completion of doctoral program. *Degree requirements:* For doctorate, thesis/dissertation. *Entrance requirements:* For master's and Ed S, GRE General Test or MAT, minimum GPA of 3.0; for doctorate, GRE General Test, minimum GPA of 3.0. Additional exam requirements/recommendations for international students: Required—TOEFL (minimum score 600 paper-based; 100 iBT). *Application deadline:* For fall admission, 12/1 priority date for domestic and international students. Applications are processed on a rolling basis. Application fee: $55 ($75 for international students). Electronic applications accepted. *Financial support:* Fellowships, research assistantships, teaching assistantships, institutionally sponsored loans, traineeships, health care benefits, and unspecified assistantships available. Support available to part-time students. *Faculty research:* Curriculum development and research, teacher education, art education, business and marketing, early childhood education, English education, literacy/reading education, mathematics education, music education, science education, social studies education. *Unit head:* Dr. James Tarr, Associate Division Director, 573-882-4034, E-mail: tarrj@missouri.edu. *Application contact:* Fran Colley, Academic Advisor, 573-882-6462, E-mail: colleyf@missouri.edu.
Website: http://education.missouri.edu/LTC/.

The University of Montana, Graduate School, College of Arts and Sciences, Department of English, Program in Teaching, Missoula, MT 59812-0002. Offers MA. *Entrance requirements:* For master's, GRE General Test, sample of written work.

University of New Hampshire, Graduate School, College of Liberal Arts, Department of English, Durham, NH 03824. Offers English (MA, PhD); English education (MST); language and linguistics (MA); literature (MA); writing (MFA). Part-time programs available. *Faculty:* 36 full-time (19 women). *Students:* 62 full-time (43 women), 36 part-time (21 women); includes 4 minority (2 Black or African American, non-Hispanic/Latino; 2 Hispanic/Latino), 8 international. Average age 30. 196 applicants, 49% accepted, 31 enrolled. In 2013, 34 master's, 3 doctorates awarded. *Degree requirements:* For master's, one foreign language; for doctorate, 2 foreign languages, thesis/dissertation. *Entrance requirements:* For master's, GRE General Test, sample of written work; for doctorate, GRE General Test, GRE Subject Test, sample of written work. Additional exam requirements/recommendations for international students: Required—TOEFL (minimum score 550 paper-based; 80 iBT). *Application deadline:* For fall admission, 6/1 priority date for domestic students, 2/15 for international students; for spring admission, 12/1 for domestic students. Applications are processed on a rolling basis. Application fee: $65. Electronic applications accepted. *Expenses:* Tuition, state resident: full-time $13,500; part-time $750 per credit hour. Tuition, nonresident: full-time $26,200; part-time $1100 per credit hour. *Required fees:* $1741; $435.25 per term. Tuition and fees vary according to course level, course load, campus/location and program. *Financial support:* In 2013–14, 57 students received support, including 1 fellowship, 44 teaching assistantships; research assistantships, career-related internships or fieldwork, Federal Work-Study, scholarships/grants, and tuition waivers (full and partial) also available. Support available to part-time students. Financial award application deadline: 2/15. *Unit head:* Dr. Andrew Merton, Chairperson, 603-862-3967. *Application contact:* Janine Wilks, Administrative Assistant, 603-862-3963, E-mail: engl.grad@unh.edu.
Website: http://www.unh.edu/english/.

University of New Mexico, Graduate School, College of Education, Department of Language, Literacy and Sociocultural Studies, Program in Language, Literacy and Sociocultural Studies, Albuquerque, NM 87131. Offers American Indian education (MA); bilingual education (MA, PhD); educational linguistics (PhD); educational thought and sociocultural studies (MA, PhD); literacy/language arts (MA, PhD); social studies (MA); TESOL (MA, PhD). *Faculty:* 10 full-time (6 women), 3 part-time/adjunct (1 woman). *Students:* 63 full-time (48 women), 117 part-time (105 women); includes 96 minority (8 Black or African American, non-Hispanic/Latino; 16 American Indian or Alaska Native, non-Hispanic/Latino; 6 Asian, non-Hispanic/Latino; 62 Hispanic/Latino; 4 Two or more races, non-Hispanic/Latino), 20 international. Average age 39. 67 applicants, 63% accepted, 30 enrolled. In 2013, 30 master's, 8 doctorates awarded. *Degree requirements:* For master's, comprehensive exam, thesis optional; for doctorate, comprehensive exam, thesis/dissertation, research skills. *Entrance requirements:* For master's, letter of intent, 3 letters of recommendation, resume, BA/BS, department demographic form, transcripts; for doctorate, writing sample, letter of intent, 3 letters of recommendation, resume, BA/BS, MA, department demographic form, transcripts. Additional exam requirements/recommendations for international students: Required—TOEFL. *Application deadline:* For fall admission, 12/1 for domestic and international students; for spring admission, 9/15 for domestic and international students. Application fee: $50. Electronic applications accepted. *Financial support:* In 2013–14, 7 students received support, including 7 fellowships (averaging $3,170 per year), 1,318 teaching assistantships with tuition reimbursements available (averaging $3,789 per year); research assistantships, career-related internships or fieldwork, institutionally sponsored loans, scholarships/grants, and unspecified assistantships also available. Support available to part-time students. Financial award application deadline: 3/1; financial award applicants required to submit FAFSA. *Faculty research:* School reform, professional development, history of education, Native American education, politics of education, feminism and issues of sexual identity, critical race theory, bilingualism, literacy reading, adolescent literature, second language acquisition, critical theory and schooling, indigenous languages. *Unit head:* Dr. Lois M. Meyer, Chair, 505-277-7244, Fax: 505-277-8362, E-mail: lsmeyer@unm.edu. *Application contact:* Debra Schaffer, Administrative Assistant, 505-277-0437, Fax: 505-277-8362, E-mail: schaffer@unm.edu.
Website: http://coe.unm.edu/departments/department-of-language-literacy-and-sociocultural-studies/llss-program.html.

The University of North Carolina at Chapel Hill, Graduate School, School of Education, Program in Secondary Education, Chapel Hill, NC 27599. Offers English (Grades 9-12) (MAT); English as a second language (MAT); French (Grades K-12) (MAT); German (Grades K-12) (MAT); Japanese (Grades K-12) (MAT); Latin (Grades 9-12) (MAT); mathematics (Grades 9-12) (MAT); music (Grades K-12) (MAT); science (Grades 9-12) (MAT); social studies (Grades 9-12) (MAT); Spanish (Grades K-12) (MAT). *Accreditation:* NCATE. *Degree requirements:* For master's, comprehensive exam. *Entrance requirements:* For master's, GRE General Test, minimum GPA of 3.0 during last 2 years of undergraduate course work. Additional exam requirements/recommendations for international students: Required—TOEFL (minimum score 550 paper-based). Electronic applications accepted.

The University of North Carolina at Charlotte, The Graduate School, College of Liberal Arts and Sciences, Department of English, Charlotte, NC 28223-0001. Offers English (MA); English education (MA); technical communication (Graduate Certificate). Part-time and evening/weekend programs available. *Faculty:* 32 full-time (17 women). *Students:* 24 full-time (16 women), 56 part-time (41 women); includes 16 minority (9 Black or African American, non-Hispanic/Latino; 1 American Indian or Alaska Native, non-Hispanic/Latino; 1 Asian, non-Hispanic/Latino; 4 Hispanic/Latino; 1 Native Hawaiian or other Pacific Islander, non-Hispanic/Latino), 1 international. Average age 32. 51 applicants, 94% accepted, 29 enrolled. In 2013, 45 master's, 2 other advanced degrees awarded. *Degree requirements:* For master's, comprehensive exam, thesis optional. *Entrance requirements:* For master's, GRE General Test, minimum undergraduate GPA of 3.0 in major, 2.75 overall. Additional exam requirements/recommendations for international students: Required—TOEFL (minimum score 557 paper-based; 83 iBT). *Application deadline:* For fall admission, 5/1 priority date for domestic students, 5/1 for international students; for spring admission, 10/1 priority date for domestic students, 10/1 for international students. Applications are processed on a rolling basis. Application fee: $75. Electronic applications accepted. *Expenses:* Tuition, state resident: full-time $3522. Tuition, nonresident: full-time $16,051. *Required fees:* $2585. Tuition and fees vary according to course load and program. *Financial support:* In 2013–14, 15 students received support, including 1 research assistantship (averaging $8,000 per year), 14 teaching assistantships (averaging $7,794 per year); career-related internships or fieldwork, institutionally sponsored loans, scholarships/grants, and unspecified assistantships also available. Support available to part-time students. Financial award application deadline: 4/1; financial award applicants required to submit FAFSA. *Faculty research:* Narrative, pragmatics and stance in: medical discourse and Alzheimer's speech; online discourse and digital corpora of speech. *Total annual research expenditures:* $114,250. *Unit head:* Dr. Mark West, Interim Chair, 704-687-0618, Fax: 704-687-1401, E-mail: miwest@uncc.edu. *Application contact:* Kathy B. Giddings, Director of Graduate Admissions, 704-687-5503, Fax: 704-687-1668, E-mail: gradadm@uncc.edu.
Website: http://english.uncc.edu/MA-English/graduate-programs.html.

The University of North Carolina at Greensboro, Graduate School, College of Arts and Sciences, Department of English, Program in English, Greensboro, NC 27412-5001. Offers American literature (PhD); English (M Ed, MA); English literature (PhD); rhetoric and composition (PhD). *Degree requirements:* For master's, comprehensive exam, thesis or alternative; for doctorate, variable foreign language requirement, thesis/dissertation, preliminary exam. *Entrance requirements:* For master's, GRE General Test, GRE Subject Test, minimum GPA of 3.0; for doctorate, GRE General Test, GRE Subject Test, critical writing sample, minimum GPA of 3.0. Additional exam requirements/recommendations for international students: Required—TOEFL. Electronic applications accepted.

English Education

The University of North Carolina at Pembroke, Graduate Studies, Department of English, Theatre and Foreign Languages, Program in English Education, Pembroke, NC 28372-1510. Offers MA, MAT. *Accreditation:* NCATE. Part-time and evening/weekend programs available. *Degree requirements:* For master's, comprehensive exam, thesis optional. *Entrance requirements:* For master's, GRE, MAT, or NTE, minimum GPA of 3.0 in major or 2.5 overall. Additional exam requirements/recommendations for international students: Required—TOEFL.

University of Northern Iowa, Graduate College, College of Humanities, Arts and Sciences, Department of Languages and Literatures, Program in Teaching English in Secondary Schools, Cedar Falls, IA 50614. Offers MA. *Students:* 15 part-time (13 women); includes 1 minority (Asian, non-Hispanic/Latino). Application fee: $50 ($70 for international students). *Unit head:* Dr. Anne Myles, Coordinator, 319-273-6911, Fax: 319-273-5807, E-mail: anne.myles@uni.edu. *Application contact:* Laurie S. Russell, Record Analyst, 319-273-2623, Fax: 319-273-2885, E-mail: laurie.russell@uni.edu.

University of North Georgia, School of Education, Dahlonega, GA 30597. Offers art education (MAT); early childhood education (M Ed); English education (MAT); history education (MAT); math education (MAT); middle grades education (M Ed, MAT); physical education (MS); school leadership (Ed S); secondary education (M Ed), including English education, history education, mathematics education, physical education; teacher education (MAT). *Accreditation:* NCATE. Part-time and evening/weekend programs available. Postbaccalaureate distance learning degree programs offered (no on-campus study). *Degree requirements:* For master's, comprehensive exam, thesis optional. *Entrance requirements:* For master's, GRE or MAT, GACE, minimum GPA of 2.75; for Ed S, GRE General Test or MAT, 3 years of teaching experience, master's degree, minimum graduate GPA of 3.25, leadership position in the school. Additional exam requirements/recommendations for international students: Required—TOEFL (minimum score 550 paper-based; 79 iBT), IELTS (minimum score 6.5). Electronic applications accepted. *Faculty research:* Identification of professional development school structures supporting P-12 student achievement, impact of diverse field placement settings in teacher belief development among preservice teachers, use of inquiry methodology in social studies teaching with English language learners, use of instructional differentiation in the middle grades classroom, effects of international school placements on preservice teacher beliefs and attitudes.

University of Oklahoma, Jeannine Rainbolt College of Education, Department of Instructional Leadership and Academic Curriculum, Norman, OK 73072. Offers communication, culture and pedagogy for Hispanic populations in educational settings (Graduate Certificate); instructional leadership and academic curriculum (M Ed, PhD), including bilingual education (PhD), early childhood education, elementary education, English education, instructional leadership, mathematics education, reading education, science education, science, technology, engineering and mathematics education (M Ed), secondary education, social studies education, teacher education (M Ed), world language education (M Ed). *Accreditation:* NCATE. Part-time and evening/weekend programs available. Postbaccalaureate distance learning degree programs offered (no on-campus study). *Faculty:* 22 full-time (15 women), 1 (woman) part-time/adjunct. *Students:* 64 full-time (49 women), 103 part-time (81 women); includes 33 minority (8 Black or African American, non-Hispanic/Latino; 9 American Indian or Alaska Native, non-Hispanic/Latino; 5 Asian, non-Hispanic/Latino; 4 Hispanic/Latino; 1 Native Hawaiian or other Pacific Islander, non-Hispanic/Latino; 6 Two or more races, non-Hispanic/Latino), 10 international. Average age 34. 50 applicants, 84% accepted, 36 enrolled. In 2013, 26 master's, 11 doctorates awarded. Terminal master's awarded for partial completion of doctoral program. *Degree requirements:* For master's, comprehensive exam (for some programs), thesis (for some programs); for doctorate, comprehensive exam, thesis/dissertation. *Entrance requirements:* For master's, essay; for doctorate, GRE, 3 recommendation letters; autobiography, statement of objectives; essay on chosen major; transcripts; writing sample. Additional exam requirements/recommendations for international students: Required—TOEFL (minimum score 79 iBT). *Application deadline:* For fall admission, 4/30 for domestic and international students; for spring admission, 10/31 for domestic and international students; for summer admission, 3/15 for domestic and international students. Applications are processed on a rolling basis. Application fee: $50 ($100 for international students). Electronic applications accepted. *Expenses:* Tuition, state resident: full-time $4205; part-time $175.20 per credit hour. Tuition, nonresident: full-time $16,205; part-time $675.20 per credit hour. *Required fees:* $2745; $103.85 per credit hour. $126.50 per semester. *Financial support:* In 2013–14, 98 students received support, including 10 research assistantships with partial tuition reimbursements available (averaging $10,671 per year), 7 teaching assistantships with partial tuition reimbursements available (averaging $10,753 per year); Federal Work-Study, institutionally sponsored loans, scholarships/grants, and unspecified assistantships also available. Support available to part-time students. Financial award application deadline: 6/1; financial award applicants required to submit FAFSA. *Total annual research expenditures:* $1 million. *Unit head:* Dr. Stacy Reeder, Chair/Graduate Liaison, 405-325-1498, Fax: 405-325-4061, E-mail: reeder@ou.edu. *Application contact:* Lynn Crussel, Graduate Programs Officer, 405-325-1498, Fax: 405-325-4061, E-mail: lcrussel@ou.edu.
Website: http://education.ou.edu/departments/ilac.

University of Pennsylvania, Graduate School of Education, Division of Reading, Writing, and Literacy, Program in Reading/Writing/Literacy, Philadelphia, PA 19104. Offers MS Ed, Ed D, PhD. *Students:* 71 full-time (53 women), 30 part-time (26 women); includes 25 minority (9 Black or African American, non-Hispanic/Latino; 7 Asian, non-Hispanic/Latino; 5 Hispanic/Latino; 4 Two or more races, non-Hispanic/Latino), 4 international. 118 applicants, 53% accepted, 37 enrolled. In 2013, 36 master's, 11 doctorates awarded. *Degree requirements:* For master's and doctorate, internship. *Unit head:* Dr. Andrew Porter, Dean, 215-898-7014. *Application contact:* 215-898-6415, Fax: 215-746-6884, E-mail: admissions@gse.upenn.edu.
Website: http://www.gse.upenn.edu/rwl.

University of Phoenix–Omaha Campus, College of Education, Omaha, NE 68154-5240. Offers administration and supervision (MA Ed); curriculum and instruction (MA Ed), including adult education, computer education, curriculum and instruction, English and language arts education, English as a second language, mathematics education; elementary teacher education (MA Ed); secondary teacher education (MA Ed); special education (MA Ed).

University of Phoenix–Online Campus, College of Education, Phoenix, AZ 85034-7209. Offers administration and supervision (MAEd, Certificate); adult education and training (MAEd); curriculum and instruction (MAEd), including computer education, curriculum and instruction, English as a second language, language arts, mathematics, reading; early childhood education (MAEd); educational studies (MAEd); elementary teacher education (MAEd), including early childhood, elementary teacher education, high school middle level, middle level; principal licensure (Certificate); secondary teacher education (MAEd); special education (MAEd, Certificate); teacher education (MAEd), including middle level generalist; teacher education middle level mathematics (MAEd), including middle level mathematics; teacher education middle level science (MAEd), including middle level science; teacher education secondary mathematics (MAEd); teacher education secondary science (MAEd); teacher leadership (MAEd); teachers of English learners (Certificate); transition to teaching (Certificate), including elementary education, secondary education. *Accreditation:* Teacher Education Accreditation Council. Evening/weekend programs available. Postbaccalaureate distance learning degree programs offered. *Entrance requirements:* Additional exam requirements/recommendations for international students: Required—TOEFL, TOEIC (Test of English as an International Communication), Berlitz Online English Proficiency Exam, PTE, or IELTS. Electronic applications accepted. *Expenses:* Contact institution.

University of Phoenix–Springfield Campus, College of Education, Springfield, MO 65804-7211. Offers administration and supervision (MA Ed); curriculum and instruction (MA Ed), including computer education, curriculum and instruction, English and language arts education, English as a second language, mathematics education; English and language arts education (MA Ed).

University of Phoenix–Washington D.C. Campus, College of Education, Washington, DC 20001. Offers administration and supervision (MA Ed); adult education and training (MA Ed); computer education (MA Ed); curriculum and instruction (MA Ed, Ed D); early childhood education (MA Ed); education (Ed S); educational leadership (Ed D); educational technology (Ed D); elementary teacher education (MA Ed); English and language arts education (MA Ed); English as a second language (MA Ed); higher education administration (PhD); mathematics education (MA Ed); secondary teacher education (MA Ed); special education (MA Ed); teacher leadership (MA Ed).

University of Pittsburgh, School of Education, Department of Instruction and Learning, Program in Secondary Education, Pittsburgh, PA 15260. Offers English/communications education (M Ed, MAT); foreign languages education (M Ed, MAT); mathematics education (M Ed, MAT, Ed D); science education (M Ed, MAT, Ed D); secondary education (PhD); social studies education (M Ed, MAT). Part-time and evening/weekend programs available. *Students:* 116 full-time (78 women), 47 part-time (36 women); includes 16 minority (4 Black or African American, non-Hispanic/Latino; 3 Asian, non-Hispanic/Latino; 5 Hispanic/Latino; 4 Two or more races, non-Hispanic/Latino), 29 international. Average age 30. 279 applicants, 66% accepted, 91 enrolled. In 2013, 113 master's, 8 doctorates awarded. *Degree requirements:* For master's, thesis; for doctorate, thesis/dissertation. *Entrance requirements:* For master's, PRAXIS I; for doctorate, GRE General Test. Additional exam requirements/recommendations for international students: Required—TOEFL. *Application deadline:* For fall admission, 2/1 priority date for domestic students; for spring admission, 11/15 priority date for domestic students. Applications are processed on a rolling basis. Application fee: $50. Electronic applications accepted. *Expenses:* Tuition, state resident: full-time $19,964; part-time $807 per credit. Tuition, nonresident: full-time $32,686; part-time $1337 per credit. *Required fees:* $740; $200. Tuition and fees vary according to program. *Financial support:* Fellowships, teaching assistantships, career-related internships or fieldwork, Federal Work-Study, tuition waivers (partial), and unspecified assistantships available. Support available to part-time students. Financial award application deadline: 3/15; financial award applicants required to submit FAFSA. *Unit head:* Dr. Richard Donato, Chairman, 412-624-7248, Fax: 412-648-7081, E-mail: donato@pitt.edu. *Application contact:* Marianne L. Budziszewski, Director of Admissions and Enrollment Services, 412-648-2230, Fax: 412-648-1899, E-mail: soeinfo@pitt.edu.
Website: http://www.education.pitt.edu/.

University of Puerto Rico, Mayagüez Campus, Graduate Studies, College of Arts and Sciences, Department of English, Mayagüez, PR 00681-9000. Offers English education (MA). Part-time programs available. *Faculty:* 34 full-time (24 women), 1 (woman) part-time/adjunct. *Students:* 40 full-time (29 women), 9 part-time (4 women). 24 applicants, 63% accepted, 11 enrolled. In 2013, 9 master's awarded. *Degree requirements:* For master's, comprehensive exam, thesis optional. *Entrance requirements:* For master's, course work in linguistics or language, American literature, British literature, and structure/grammar or syntax. Additional exam requirements/recommendations for international students: Required—TOEFL (minimum score 550 paper-based). *Application deadline:* For fall admission, 2/15 for domestic and international students; for spring admission, 9/15 for domestic and international students. Applications are processed on a rolling basis. Application fee: $25. *Expenses: Tuition, area resident:* Full-time $2466; part-time $822 per year. *International tuition:* $6371 full-time. *Required fees:* $1095; $1095. Tuition and fees vary according to course level, course load and reciprocity agreements. *Financial support:* In 2013–14, 31 students received support, including 3 research assistantships (averaging $5,533 per year), 28 teaching assistantships (averaging $6,245 per year); fellowships with full tuition reimbursements available, Federal Work-Study, institutionally sponsored loans, and unspecified assistantships also available. *Faculty research:* Teaching English as a second language, linguistics, American literature, British literature. *Unit head:* Dr. Rosita Rivera, Director, 787-265-3847, Fax: 787-265-3847, E-mail: rosita.rivera1@upr.edu. *Application contact:* Dr. Ricia Chansky, Graduate Coordinator, 787-265-3847, E-mail: ricia.chansky@upr.edu.
Website: http://www.uprm.edu./english/.

University of St. Francis, College of Education, Joliet, IL 60435-6169. Offers educational leadership (MS, Ed D); elementary education (M Ed); higher education (MS); reading (MS); secondary education (M Ed), including English education, math education, science education, social studies education, visual arts education; special education (M Ed); teaching and learning (MS). *Accreditation:* NCATE. Part-time and evening/weekend programs available. Postbaccalaureate distance learning degree programs offered (no on-campus study). *Faculty:* 10 full-time (8 women), 34 part-time/adjunct (25 women). *Students:* 14 full-time (13 women), 250 part-time (183 women); includes 34 minority (20 Black or African American, non-Hispanic/Latino; 1 American Indian or Alaska Native, non-Hispanic/Latino; 13 Hispanic/Latino), 1 international. Average age 36. 133 applicants, 62% accepted, 71 enrolled. In 2013, 147 master's awarded. *Degree requirements:* For doctorate, thesis/dissertation. *Entrance requirements:* For doctorate, master's degree, IL Type 75 or Principal's endorsement, interview, minimum undergraduate GPA of 3.0, professional portfolio, letter of recommendation. Additional exam requirements/recommendations for international students: Required—TOEFL (minimum score 550 paper-based; 79 iBT), IELTS (minimum score 6.5). *Application deadline:* Applications are processed on a rolling basis. Application fee: $30. Electronic applications accepted. Application fee is waived when completed online. *Expenses:* Contact institution. *Financial support:* In 2013–14, 10 students received support. Scholarships/grants, tuition waivers (partial), and unspecified assistantships available. Support available to part-time students. Financial award applicants required to submit FAFSA. *Unit head:* Dr. John Gambro, Dean, 815-740-3829, Fax: 815-740-2264, E-mail: jgambro@stfrancis.edu. *Application contact:* Sandra Sloka, Director of Admissions for Graduate and Degree Completion Programs, 800-735-7500, Fax: 815-740-3431, E-mail: ssloka@stfrancis.edu.
Website: http://www.stfrancis.edu/academics/college-of-education/.

University of South Carolina, The Graduate School, College of Arts and Sciences, Department of English Language and Literature, Columbia, SC 29208. Offers creative writing (MFA); English (MA, PhD); English education (MAT); MLIS/MA. MAT offered in cooperation with the College of Education. Part-time programs available. *Degree requirements:* For master's, one foreign language, comprehensive exam, thesis; for doctorate, 2 foreign languages, comprehensive exam, thesis/dissertation. *Entrance requirements:* For master's, GRE General Test (MFA), GRE Subject Test (MA, MAT), sample of written work; for doctorate, GRE General Test, GRE Subject Test, sample of

written work. Additional exam requirements/recommendations for international students: Required—TOEFL. Electronic applications accepted. *Faculty research:* American literature, British literature, composition and rhetoric, linguistics, speech communication.

University of South Carolina, The Graduate School, College of Education, Department of Instruction and Teacher Education, Program in Secondary Education, Columbia, SC 29208. Offers art education (IMA, MAT); business education (IMA, MAT); English (MAT); foreign language (MAT); health education (MAT); mathematics (MAT); science (IMA, MAT); secondary (Ed D); secondary education (MT, PhD); social studies (MAT); theatre and speech (MAT). IMA and MT offered jointly with the subject areas. *Accreditation:* NCATE. *Degree requirements:* For master's, comprehensive exam, thesis (for some programs), foreign language (MA); for doctorate, one foreign language, comprehensive exam, thesis/dissertation. *Entrance requirements:* For master's, GRE General Test or MAT, teaching certificate (IMA, M Ed), interview; for doctorate, GRE General Test or MAT, interview. *Faculty research:* Middle school programs, professional development, school collaboration.

University of South Florida, College of Education, Department of Secondary Education, Tampa, FL 33620-9951. Offers English education (M Ed, MA, MAT, PhD); foreign language education/ESOL (M Ed, MA, MAT); instructional technology (M Ed, PhD, Ed S); mathematics education (M Ed, MA, MAT, PhD, Ed S); science education (M Ed, MA, MAT, PhD); second language acquisition/instructional technology (PhD); secondary education (M Ed, PhD); secondary education/TESOL (M Ed); social science education (M Ed, MA, MAT); teaching and learning in the content area (PhD). *Accreditation:* NCATE. Part-time and evening/weekend programs available. *Degree requirements:* For master's, variable foreign language requirement, comprehensive exam, project (for some programs); for doctorate, variable foreign language requirement, comprehensive exam, thesis/dissertation, philosophies of inquiry; multiple research methods. *Entrance requirements:* For master's, GRE General Test or General Knowledge Test, minimum GPA of 3.0; for doctorate, GRE General Test, minimum GPA of 3.5; for Ed S, GRE General Test. Additional exam requirements/recommendations for international students: Required—TOEFL (minimum score 550 paper-based; 79 iBT). Electronic applications accepted. *Faculty research:* English language learners/multicultural, social science education, mathematics education, science education, instructional technology.

University of South Florida–St. Petersburg Campus, College of Education, St. Petersburg, FL 33701. Offers educational leadership development (M Ed); elementary education (MA), including math/science; English education (MA); middle grades STEM education (MS); reading education (MA). Part-time programs available. *Degree requirements:* For master's, comprehensive exam, practicum, internship, comprehensive portfolio. *Entrance requirements:* For master's, State of Florida General Knowledge Test (GKT), Florida Teaching Certificate (for non-initial certification programs), letters of recommendation. Additional exam requirements/recommendations for international students: Required—TOEFL (minimum score 550 paper-based; 79 iBT); Recommended—IELTS. Electronic applications accepted.

University of South Florida Sarasota-Manatee, College of Education, Sarasota, FL 34243. Offers education (MA); educational leadership (M Ed), including curriculum leadership, K-12, non-public/charter school leadership; English education (MA); teaching K-6 with ESOL endorsement (MAT). Part-time and evening/weekend programs available. *Faculty:* 7 full-time (all women), 5 part-time/adjunct (3 women). *Students:* 11 full-time (9 women), 43 part-time (33 women); includes 6 minority (2 Black or African American, non-Hispanic/Latino; 2 Hispanic/Latino; 1 Native Hawaiian or other Pacific Islander, non-Hispanic/Latino; 1 Two or more races, non-Hispanic/Latino). Average age 33. 46 applicants, 39% accepted, 15 enrolled. In 2013, 33 master's awarded. *Degree requirements:* For master's, comprehensive exam (for some programs). *Entrance requirements:* For master's, GRE (within last 5 years) or minimum GPA of 3.0, letters of recommendation. Additional exam requirements/recommendations for international students: Required—TOEFL (minimum score 550 paper-based; 79 iBT), IELTS (minimum score 6.5). *Application deadline:* For fall admission, 3/1 priority date for domestic students, 3/1 for international students; for spring admission, 10/1 priority date for domestic students, 10/1 for international students. Applications are processed on a rolling basis. Application fee: $30. Electronic applications accepted. *Expenses:* Tuition, state resident: full-time $10,029; part-time $418 per credit. Tuition, nonresident: full-time $20,727; part-time $863 per credit. *Required fees:* $10; $5. Tuition and fees vary according to program. *Financial support:* In 2013–14, 10 students received support. Career-related internships or fieldwork, institutionally sponsored loans, scholarships/grants, health care benefits, and unspecified assistantships available. Support available to part-time students. Financial award application deadline: 3/1; financial award applicants required to submit FAFSA. *Faculty research:* Child development, student achievement, inter-generational studies, equitable implementation of educational policy, linguistics and its applications. *Unit head:* Dr. Terry A. Osborn, Dean, 941-359-4531, Fax: 941-359-4778, E-mail: terryosborn@sar.usf.edu. *Application contact:* Andy Telatovich, Director, Admissions, 941-359-4330, Fax: 941-359-4585, E-mail: atelatovich@sar.usf.edu.
Website: http://usfsm.edu/college-of-education/.

The University of Tennessee, Graduate School, College of Education, Health and Human Sciences, Program in Education, Knoxville, TN 37996. Offers art education (MS); counseling education (PhD); cultural studies in education (PhD); curriculum (MS, Ed S); curriculum, educational research and evaluation (Ed D, PhD); early childhood education (PhD); early childhood special education (MS); education of deaf and hard of hearing (MS); educational administration and policy studies (Ed D, PhD); educational administration and supervision (Ed S); educational psychology (Ed D, PhD); elementary education (MS, Ed S); elementary teaching (MS); English education (MS, Ed S); exercise science (PhD); foreign language/ESL education (MS, Ed S); instructional technology (MS, Ed D, PhD, Ed S); literacy, language and ESL education (PhD); literacy, language education, and ESL education (Ed D); mathematics education (MS, Ed S); modified and comprehensive special education (MS); reading education (MS, Ed S); school counseling (Ed S); school psychology (PhD, Ed S); science education (MS, Ed S); secondary teaching (MS); social foundations (MS); social science education (MS, Ed S); socio-cultural foundations of sports and education (PhD); special education (Ed S); teacher education (Ed D, PhD). *Accreditation:* NCATE. Part-time and evening/weekend programs available. *Degree requirements:* For master's and Ed S, thesis optional; for doctorate, variable foreign language requirement, thesis/dissertation. *Entrance requirements:* For master's, minimum GPA of 2.7; for doctorate and Ed S, GRE General Test, minimum GPA of 2.7. Additional exam requirements/recommendations for international students: Required—TOEFL. Electronic applications accepted. *Expenses:* Tuition, state resident: full-time $9540; part-time $531 per credit hour. Tuition, nonresident: full-time $27,728; part-time $1542 per credit hour. *Required fees:* $1404; $67 per credit hour.

The University of Texas at El Paso, Graduate School, College of Liberal Arts, Department of English, El Paso, TX 79968-0001. Offers bilingual professional writing (Certificate); English and American literature (MA); rhetoric and composition (PhD); rhetoric and writing studies (MA); teaching English (MAT). Part-time and evening/weekend programs available. *Degree requirements:* For master's, thesis optional. *Entrance requirements:* For master's, GRE General Test, minimum GPA of 3.0.

Additional exam requirements/recommendations for international students: Required—TOEFL. Electronic applications accepted. *Faculty research:* Literature, creative writing, literary theory.

University of the Sacred Heart, Graduate Programs, Department of Education, San Juan, PR 00914-0383. Offers early childhood education (M Ed); information technology and multimedia (Certificate); instruction systems and education technology (M Ed), including English, information technology and multimedia, instructional design, mathematics, Spanish. Part-time and evening/weekend programs available. *Degree requirements:* For master's, thesis. *Entrance requirements:* For master's, EXADEP, minimum undergraduate GPA of 2.75, interview.

The University of Toledo, College of Graduate Studies, Judith Herb College of Education, Department of Curriculum and Instruction, Toledo, OH 43606-3390. Offers art education (ME); career and technical education (ME); career-technical education (Ed S); curriculum and instruction (ME, PhD, Ed S); early childhood education (PhD, Ed S); education and biology (MES); education and chemistry (MES); education and economics (MAE); education and English (MAE); education and French (MAE); education and geography (MAE); education and geology (MES); education and German (MAE); education and history (MAE); education and mathematics (MAE, MES); education and physics (MES); education and political science (MAE); education and sociology (MAE); education and Spanish (MAE); educational media (PhD); educational technology (ME); educational technology: virtual educator (Certificate); elementary education (PhD); English as a second language (MAE); gifted and talented (PhD); middle childhood education licensure (ME); music education (MME); secondary education (PhD); secondary education licensure (ME); special education (PhD, Ed S). *Accreditation:* NCATE. Part-time and evening/weekend programs available. *Faculty:* 41. *Students:* 53 full-time (30 women), 154 part-time (111 women); includes 21 minority (16 Black or African American, non-Hispanic/Latino; 4 Hispanic/Latino; 1 Two or more races, non-Hispanic/Latino), 21 international. Average age 34. 82 applicants, 79% accepted, 47 enrolled. In 2013, 80 master's, 5 doctorates awarded. *Degree requirements:* For master's, comprehensive exam, thesis or alternative; for doctorate, comprehensive exam, thesis/dissertation; for other advanced degree, thesis optional. *Entrance requirements:* For master's, doctorate, and other advanced degree, minimum cumulative GPA of 2.7 for all previous academic work, letters of recommendation. Additional exam requirements/recommendations for international students: Required—TOEFL (minimum score 550 paper-based; 80 iBT). *Application deadline:* For fall admission, 1/15 priority date for domestic and international students. Applications are processed on a rolling basis. Application fee: $45 ($75 for international students). Electronic applications accepted. *Financial support:* In 2013–14, 5 research assistantships with full and partial tuition reimbursements (averaging $13,200 per year), 11 teaching assistantships with full and partial tuition reimbursements (averaging $8,809 per year) were awarded; career-related internships or fieldwork, Federal Work-Study, institutionally sponsored loans, scholarships/grants, tuition waivers (full and partial), unspecified assistantships, and administrative assistantships also available. Support available to part-time students. *Unit head:* Dr. Joan Kaderavek, Chair, 419-530-5373, E-mail: eigh.chiarelott@utoledo.edu. *Application contact:* Graduate School Office, 419-530-4723, Fax: 419-530-4724, E-mail: grdsch@utnet.utoledo.edu.
Website: http://www.utoledo.edu/eduhshs/.

The University of Tulsa, Graduate School, College of Arts and Sciences, School of Urban Education, Program in Teaching Arts, Tulsa, OK 74104-3189. Offers art (MTA); biology (MTA); English (MTA); history (MTA); mathematics (MTA). Part-time programs available. *Students:* 1 full-time (0 women), 1 part-time (0 women); includes 1 minority (Black or African American, non-Hispanic/Latino). Average age 30. 2 applicants, 100% accepted, 2 enrolled. *Entrance requirements:* For master's, GRE General Test. Additional exam requirements/recommendations for international students: Required—TOEFL (minimum score 577 paper-based), IELTS (minimum score 6.5). *Application deadline:* Applications are processed on a rolling basis. Application fee: $40. Electronic applications accepted. *Expenses:* Tuition: Full-time $19,566; part-time $1087 per credit hour. *Required fees:* $1690; $5 per credit hour. $160 per semester. Tuition and fees vary according to course load. *Financial support:* In 2013–14, 1 student received support, including 1 research assistantship with full and partial tuition reimbursement available (averaging $12,766 per year); fellowships with full and partial tuition reimbursements available, teaching assistantships with full and partial tuition reimbursements available, career-related internships or fieldwork, Federal Work-Study, scholarships/grants, health care benefits, tuition waivers (full and partial), and unspecified assistantships also available. Support available to part-time students. Financial award application deadline: 2/1; financial award applicants required to submit FAFSA. *Unit head:* Dr. Kara Gae Neal, Chair, 918-631-2238, Fax: 918-631-3721, E-mail: karagae-neal@utulsa.edu. *Application contact:* Dr. David Brown, Advisor, 918-631-2719, Fax: 918-631-2133, E-mail: david-brown@utulsa.edu.

University of Victoria, Faculty of Graduate Studies, Faculty of Education, Department of Curriculum and Instruction, Victoria, BC V8W 2Y2, Canada. Offers art education (M Ed, PhD); curriculum studies (M Ed, MA, PhD); early childhood education (M Ed, PhD); educational studies (PhD); language and literacy (M Ed, MA, PhD); mathematics (M Ed, MA, PhD); music education (M Ed, MA, PhD); science (M Ed, MA, PhD); social studies (M Ed, MA); social, cultural and foundational studies (MA, PhD); technology and environmental education (PhD). Part-time programs available. *Degree requirements:* For master's, thesis, project (M Ed); for doctorate, comprehensive exam, thesis/dissertation. *Entrance requirements:* For master's, minimum B average. Additional exam requirements/recommendations for international students: Required—TOEFL (minimum score 575 paper-based), IELTS (minimum score 7). Electronic applications accepted. *Faculty research:* Elementary and secondary English, language arts, curriculum theory and practice, educational media and technology, educational administration and leadership, history and philosophy of education.

University of Virginia, Curry School of Education, Department of Curriculum, Instruction, and Special Education, Program in Curriculum and Instruction, Charlottesville, VA 22903. Offers curriculum and instruction (M Ed, Ed S); elementary education (M Ed, Ed D); English (M Ed, Ed D); foreign language (M Ed); mathematics (M Ed, Ed D); reading (M Ed, Ed D, Ed S); science (Ed D); social studies (M Ed). *Students:* 42 full-time (30 women), 37 part-time (32 women); includes 4 minority (1 Black or African American, non-Hispanic/Latino; 2 Hispanic/Latino; 1 Two or more races, non-Hispanic/Latino), 1 international. Average age 31. 76 applicants, 74% accepted, 39 enrolled. In 2013, 84 master's, 3 doctorates, 23 other advanced degrees awarded. *Degree requirements:* For master's, comprehensive exam (for some programs); for doctorate, comprehensive exam, thesis/dissertation; for Ed S, comprehensive exam. *Entrance requirements:* For master's, doctorate, and Ed S, GRE General Test, 2 letters of recommendation. Additional exam requirements/recommendations for international students: Required—TOEFL (minimum score 600 paper-based; 90 iBT), IELTS (minimum score 7). *Application deadline:* Applications are processed on a rolling basis. Application fee: $60. Electronic applications accepted. *Expenses:* Tuition, state resident: part-time $334 per credit hour. Tuition, nonresident: part-time $1224 per credit hour. *Financial support:* Fellowships with tuition reimbursements, research assistantships with tuition reimbursements, and teaching assistantships with tuition reimbursements available. Financial award application deadline: 1/5; financial award

applicants required to submit FAFSA. *Unit head:* Stephanie van Hover, Chair, 434-924-0841, E-mail: sdv2w@virginia.edu. *Application contact:* Karen Dwier, Information Contact, 434-924-0831, E-mail: kgd9g@virginia.edu.
Website: http://curry.virginia.edu/academics/areas-of-study/curriculum-teaching-learning.

University of Virginia, Curry School of Education, Program in Education, Charlottesville, VA 22903. Offers administration and supervision (PhD); applied developmental science (PhD); counselor education (PhD); curriculum and instruction (PhD); early childhood special education (MT); education evaluation (PhD); educational psychology (PhD); educational research (PhD); elementary education (MT); English education (MT, PhD); foreign language education (MT); higher education (PhD); instructional technology (PhD); kinesiology (MT, PhD); math education (PhD); reading education (PhD); research, statistics and evaluation (PhD); school psychology (PhD); science education (PhD); social studies education (MT, PhD); special education (PhD); world languages education (MT). *Students:* 474 full-time (379 women), 35 part-time (19 women); includes 89 minority (30 Black or African American, non-Hispanic/Latino; 1 American Indian or Alaska Native, non-Hispanic/Latino; 26 Asian, non-Hispanic/Latino; 19 Hispanic/Latino; 13 Two or more races, non-Hispanic/Latino), 21 international. Average age 26. 312 applicants, 49% accepted, 80 enrolled. In 2013, 137 master's, 38 doctorates awarded. *Degree requirements:* For master's, comprehensive exam (for some programs), field project; for doctorate, comprehensive exam, thesis/dissertation. *Entrance requirements:* For doctorate, GRE General Test. Additional exam requirements/recommendations for international students: Required—TOEFL (minimum score 600 paper-based; 90 iBT), IELTS (minimum score 7). *Application deadline:* Applications are processed on a rolling basis. Application fee: $60. Electronic applications accepted. *Expenses:* Tuition, state resident: part-time $334 per credit hour. Tuition, nonresident: part-time $1224 per credit hour. *Financial support:* Fellowships, research assistantships, and teaching assistantships available. Financial award application deadline: 1/5; financial award applicants required to submit FAFSA. *Unit head:* Robert C. Pianta, Dean, 434-924-3334, E-mail: pianta@virginia.edu. *Application contact:* Office of Admissions and Student Services, 434-924-0742, E-mail: curry-admissions@virginia.edu.
Website: http://curry.virginia.edu/teacher-education.

University of Washington, Graduate School, College of Arts and Sciences, Department of English, Seattle, WA 98195. Offers creative writing (MFA); English as a second language (MAT); English literature and language (MA, MAT, PhD). Part-time programs available. Terminal master's awarded for partial completion of doctoral program. *Degree requirements:* For master's, one foreign language, thesis (for some programs); for doctorate, one foreign language, thesis/dissertation. *Entrance requirements:* For master's, GRE General Test, GRE Subject Test (MA and MAT in English), minimum GPA of 3.0; for doctorate, GRE General Test, GRE Subject Test. Additional exam requirements/recommendations for international students: Required—TOEFL. Electronic applications accepted. *Faculty research:* English and American literature, critical theory, creative writing, language theory.

University of Washington, Graduate School, College of Education, Seattle, WA 98195. Offers curriculum and instruction (M Ed, Ed D, PhD), including educational technology, general curriculum (Ed D, PhD), language, literacy, and culture, mathematics education, multicultural education, reading and language arts education (Ed D), science education, social studies education, teaching and curriculum (M Ed); educational leadership and policy studies (M Ed, Ed D, PhD), including administration (Ed D), educational policy, organization, and leadership (M Ed, PhD), higher education, leadership for learning (Ed D), social and cultural foundations of education (M Ed, PhD); educational psychology (M Ed, PhD), including educational psychology (PhD), human development and cognition (M Ed), learning sciences, measurement, statistics and research design (M Ed), school psychology (M Ed); instructional leadership (M Ed); intercollegiate athletic leadership (M Ed); special education (M Ed, Ed D, PhD), including early childhood special education (M Ed), emotional and behavioral disabilities (M Ed), learning disabilities (M Ed), low-incidence disabilities (M Ed), severe disabilities (M Ed), special education (Ed D, PhD); teacher education (MIT). *Accreditation:* APA. Part-time and evening/weekend programs available. *Degree requirements:* For master's, thesis optional; for doctorate, thesis/dissertation. *Entrance requirements:* For master's and doctorate, GRE General Test, minimum GPA of 3.0. Additional exam requirements/recommendations for international students: Required—TOEFL. Electronic applications accepted. *Faculty research:* School restructuring/effective schools, special education interventions, literacy and writing, technology, school partnerships, teacher preparation.

The University of West Alabama, School of Graduate Studies, College of Education, Departments of Instructional Leadership and Support/Curriculum and Instruction, Program in Secondary Education, Livingston, AL 35470. Offers biology (MAT); English language arts (MAT); history (MAT); mathematics (MAT); physical education (MAT); science (MAT); secondary education (M Ed); social science (MAT). Part-time and evening/weekend programs available. Postbaccalaureate distance learning degree programs offered (no on-campus study). *Faculty:* 20 full-time (4 women), 5 part-time/adjunct (2 women). *Students:* 210 (139 women); includes 86 minority (80 Black or African American, non-Hispanic/Latino; 2 Asian, non-Hispanic/Latino; 2 Hispanic/Latino; 2 Two or more races, non-Hispanic/Latino). 115 applicants, 86% accepted, 72 enrolled. In 2013, 61 master's awarded. *Degree requirements:* For master's, comprehensive exam, thesis optional. *Entrance requirements:* For master's, GRE General Test, MAT, minimum GPA of 2.75. Additional exam requirements/recommendations for international students: Required—TOEFL (minimum score 500 paper-based; 61 iBT). *Application deadline:* For fall admission, 8/12 priority date for domestic students; for spring admission, 3/24 for domestic students. Applications are processed on a rolling basis. Application fee: $25 ($50 for international students). Electronic applications accepted. Tuition and fees vary according to course load. *Financial support:* Teaching assistantships, career-related internships or fieldwork, Federal Work-Study, scholarships/grants, and unspecified assistantships available. Support available to part-time students. Financial award application deadline: 3/1; financial award applicants required to submit FAFSA. *Faculty research:* Integrated arts in the curriculum, moral development of children. *Unit head:* Dr. Esther Howard, Chair of Curriculum and Instruction, 205-652-3428, Fax: 205-652-3706, E-mail: ehoward@uwa.edu. *Application contact:* Dr. Kathy Chandler, Dean of Graduate Studies, 205-652-3421, Fax: 205-652-3706, E-mail: kchandler@uwa.edu.
Website: http://www.uwa.edu/highschool612.aspx.

University of Wisconsin–Platteville, School of Graduate Studies, College of Liberal Arts and Education, School of Education, Platteville, WI 53818-3099. Offers adult education (MSE); elementary education (MSE); English education (MSE); middle school education (MSE); secondary education (MSE). *Accreditation:* NCATE. Part-time programs available. *Faculty:* 5 full-time (3 women), 13 part-time/adjunct (7 women). *Students:* 90 full-time (70 women), 30 part-time (16 women); includes 25 minority (21 Black or African American, non-Hispanic/Latino; 1 American Indian or Alaska Native, non-Hispanic/Latino; 2 Asian, non-Hispanic/Latino; 1 Hispanic/Latino), 3 international. 45 applicants, 96% accepted, 38 enrolled. In 2013, 82 master's awarded. *Degree requirements:* For master's, comprehensive exam, thesis or alternative. *Entrance requirements:* Additional exam requirements/recommendations for international students: Required—TOEFL (minimum score 500 paper-based; 61 iBT), IELTS (minimum score 6). *Application deadline:* For fall admission, 7/1 priority date for domestic students; for spring admission, 11/1 for domestic students. Applications are processed on a rolling basis. Application fee: $56. Electronic applications accepted. *Financial support:* Research assistantships with partial tuition reimbursements, career-related internships or fieldwork, Federal Work-Study, institutionally sponsored loans, scholarships/grants, and unspecified assistantships available. Support available to part-time students. Financial award applicants required to submit FAFSA. *Unit head:* Dr. Karen Stinson, Director, 608-342-1131, Fax: 608-342-1133, E-mail: stinsonk@uwplatt.edu. *Application contact:* Dee Dunbar, School of Graduate Studies, 608-342-1322, Fax: 608-342-1389, E-mail: dunbard@uwplatt.edu.
Website: http://www.uwplatt.edu/.

Valdosta State University, Department of English, Valdosta, GA 31698. Offers literature (MA); rhetoric and composition (MA); studies for language arts teachers (MA). Part-time programs available. *Faculty:* 12 full-time (9 women). *Students:* 5 full-time (3 women), 14 part-time (8 women); includes 1 minority (Black or African American, non-Hispanic/Latino). Average age 23. 4 applicants, 100% accepted, 3 enrolled. In 2013, 4 master's awarded. *Degree requirements:* For master's, one foreign language, thesis, comprehensive written and/or oral exams. *Entrance requirements:* For master's, GRE General Test, minimum GPA of 3.0. Additional exam requirements/recommendations for international students: Required—TOEFL (minimum score 523 paper-based). *Application deadline:* For fall admission, 7/1 for domestic and international students; for spring admission, 11/1 for domestic and international students. Applications are processed on a rolling basis. Application fee: $35. Electronic applications accepted. *Expenses:* Tuition, state resident: full-time $4140; part-time $230 per credit hour. Tuition, nonresident: full-time $14,904; part-time $828 per credit hour. *Required fees:* $995 per semester. Tuition and fees vary according to course load. *Financial support:* In 2013–14, 11 students received support, including 6 research assistantships with full tuition reimbursements available (averaging $4,000 per year), 7 teaching assistantships with full tuition reimbursements available (averaging $8,000 per year); institutionally sponsored loans, scholarships/grants, and unspecified assistantships also available. Support available to part-time students. Financial award application deadline: 7/1; financial award applicants required to submit FAFSA. *Faculty research:* American literature, creative writing. *Unit head:* Dr. Mark Smith, Head, 229-333-5946, E-mail: marksmit@valdosta.edu. *Application contact:* Jessica DeVane, Admissions Specialist, 229-333-5694, Fax: 229-245-3853, E-mail: jldevane@valdosta.edu.

Valley City State University, Online Master of Education Program, Valley City, ND 58072. Offers elementary education (M Ed); English education (M Ed); library and information technologies (M Ed); teaching and technology (M Ed); teaching English language learners (ELL) (M Ed); technology education (M Ed). *Accreditation:* NCATE. Part-time and evening/weekend programs available. Postbaccalaureate distance learning degree programs offered (no on-campus study). *Faculty:* 21 full-time (14 women), 7 part-time/adjunct (all women). *Students:* 2 full-time (both women), 151 part-time (102 women); includes 10 minority (1 Black or African American, non-Hispanic/Latino; 3 Asian, non-Hispanic/Latino; 2 Hispanic/Latino; 4 Two or more races, non-Hispanic/Latino), 1 international. Average age 34. 27 applicants, 93% accepted, 21 enrolled. In 2013, 45 master's awarded. *Degree requirements:* For master's, action research report, comprehensive portfolio. *Entrance requirements:* For master's, GRE, MAT, PRAXIS II or National Teaching Board for Professional Standards (if GPA is less than 3.0). Additional exam requirements/recommendations for international students: Required—TOEFL (minimum score 525 paper-based; 71 iBT); Recommended—IELTS (minimum score 5.5). *Application deadline:* For fall admission, 7/19 priority date for domestic and international students; for spring admission, 12/13 priority date for domestic and international students; for summer admission, 5/9 priority date for domestic and international students. Applications are processed on a rolling basis. Application fee: $35. Electronic applications accepted. *Expenses:* Contact institution. *Financial support:* In 2013–14, 24 students received support. Scholarships/grants and tuition waivers (full and partial) available. Financial award application deadline: 5/15; financial award applicants required to submit FAFSA. *Faculty research:* Academically at-risk students in higher education, communication pedagogy and technology, gender communication, computer-mediated communication, creativity in music, STEM education in K-12. *Total annual research expenditures:* $26,000. *Unit head:* Dr. Gary Thompson, Dean, 701-845-7197, E-mail: gary.thompson@vcsu.edu. *Application contact:* Misty Lindgren, Graduate Studies, 701-845-7303, Fax: 701-845-7190, E-mail: misty.lindgren@vcsu.edu.
Website: http://www.vcsu.edu/graduate.

Vanderbilt University, Peabody College, Department of Teaching and Learning, Nashville, TN 37240-1001. Offers elementary education (M Ed); English language learners (M Ed); learning and instruction (M Ed); learning, diversity, and urban studies (M Ed); reading education (M Ed); secondary education (M Ed). *Accreditation:* NCATE. *Faculty:* 35 full-time (25 women), 20 part-time/adjunct (14 women). *Students:* 103 full-time (74 women), 44 part-time (39 women); includes 22 minority (8 Black or African American, non-Hispanic/Latino; 5 Asian, non-Hispanic/Latino; 5 Hispanic/Latino; 1 Native Hawaiian or other Pacific Islander, non-Hispanic/Latino; 3 Two or more races, non-Hispanic/Latino), 21 international. Average age 25. 264 applicants, 73% accepted, 57 enrolled. In 2013, 95 master's awarded. *Degree requirements:* For master's, comprehensive exam, thesis optional. *Entrance requirements:* For master's, GRE General Test, MAT. Additional exam requirements/recommendations for international students: Required—TOEFL (minimum score 550 paper-based; 80 iBT). *Application deadline:* For fall admission, 12/31 priority date for domestic and international students; for spring admission, 11/1 priority date for domestic and international students. Applications are processed on a rolling basis. Application fee: $0. Electronic applications accepted. *Financial support:* Fellowships with full and partial tuition reimbursements, research assistantships with full and partial tuition reimbursements, teaching assistantships with full and partial tuition reimbursements, Federal Work-Study, institutionally sponsored loans, scholarships/grants, tuition waivers (partial), and unspecified assistantships available. Support available to part-time students. Financial award application deadline: 1/15; financial award applicants required to submit FAFSA. *Faculty research:* Learning environments for mathematics of space and motion, visual programming tools for children's learning of basic science concepts, pathways for elementary and middle school children's learning about measurement and statistics, early reading intervention, professional development for ambitious mathematics teaching. *Unit head:* Dr. Rogers Hall, Chair, 615-322-8100, Fax: 615-322-8999, E-mail: rogers.hall@vanderbilt.edu. *Application contact:* Angela Saylor, Educational Coordinator, 615-322-8092, Fax: 615-322-8999, E-mail: angela.saylor@vanderbilt.edu.

Wagner College, Division of Graduate Studies, Department of Education, Program in Secondary Education/Special Education, Staten Island, NY 10301-4495. Offers language arts (MS Ed); languages other than English (MS Ed); mathematics and technology (MS Ed); science and technology (MS Ed); social studies (MS Ed). Part-time and evening/weekend programs available. *Degree requirements:* For master's, thesis (for some programs). *Entrance requirements:* For master's, minimum GPA of 3.0, interview, recommendations. Electronic applications accepted. *Expenses: Tuition:* Full-time $17,496; part-time $972 per credit. Tuition and fees vary according to course load.

Washington State University, Graduate School, College of Arts and Sciences, Department of English, Pullman, WA 99164. Offers composition (MA); English (MA, PhD); teaching of English (MA). *Degree requirements:* For master's, one foreign language, comprehensive exam (for some programs), thesis (for some programs), oral exam; for doctorate, 2 foreign languages, comprehensive exam, thesis/dissertation, oral exam, written exam. *Entrance requirements:* For master's and doctorate, GRE General Test, GRE Subject Test, official transcripts; writing sample (approximately 10 pages); three letters of recommendation; statement of purpose (approximately 500 words); undergraduate major in English or other appropriate discipline. Additional exam requirements/recommendations for international students: Required—TOEFL, IELTS. Electronic applications accepted. *Faculty research:* Nationalism and gender in the American West, slavery and exploitation in nineteenth century Britain, photography and the color line, D.H. Lawrence and Mexico, social movement cultures and the arts.

Wayland Baptist University, Graduate Programs, Program in Education, Plainview, TX 79072-6998. Offers education administration (M Ed); education diagnostics (M Ed); education literacy (M Ed); elementary certification (M Ed); English (M Ed); English as a second language (M Ed); higher education administration (M Ed); human resources (M Ed); instructional leadership (M Ed); instructional technology (M Ed); science education (M Ed); secondary certification (M Ed); social studies (M Ed); special education (M Ed). Part-time and evening/weekend programs available. Postbaccalaureate distance learning degree programs offered (no on-campus study). *Faculty:* 33 full-time (17 women), 28 part-time/adjunct (17 women). *Students:* 22 full-time (15 women), 316 part-time (189 women); includes 130 minority (48 Black or African American, non-Hispanic/Latino; 3 American Indian or Alaska Native, non-Hispanic/Latino; 71 Hispanic/Latino; 1 Native Hawaiian or other Pacific Islander, non-Hispanic/Latino; 7 Two or more races, non-Hispanic/Latino). Average age 39. 80 applicants, 96% accepted, 44 enrolled. In 2013, 170 master's awarded. *Degree requirements:* For master's, comprehensive exam, capstone course. *Entrance requirements:* For master's, GRE, GMAT or MAT. Additional exam requirements/recommendations for international students: Required—TOEFL (minimum score 500 paper-based; 61 iBT). *Application deadline:* Applications are processed on a rolling basis. Application fee: $50. Electronic applications accepted. *Expenses: Tuition:* Full-time $8190; part-time $455 per credit hour. *Required fees:* $970; $455 per credit hour. $485 per semester. *Financial support:* Federal Work-Study, institutionally sponsored loans, and scholarships/grants available. Support available to part-time students. Financial award application deadline: 5/1; financial award applicants required to submit FAFSA. *Unit head:* Dr. Jim Todd, Chairman, 806-291-1045, Fax: 806-291-1951. *Application contact:* Amanda Stanton, Coordinator of Graduate Studies, 806-291-3423, Fax: 806-291-1950, E-mail: stanton@wbu.edu.

Wayne State College, School of Education and Counseling, Department of Educational Foundations and Leadership, Program in Curriculum and Instruction, Wayne, NE 68787. Offers alternative education (MSE); business and information technology education (MSE); communication arts education (MSE); early childhood education (MSE); elementary education (MSE); English as a second language (MSE); English education (MSE); family and consumer sciences education (MSE); industrial technology and vocational education (MSE); learning communities (MSE); mathematics education (MSE); music education (MSE); science education (MSE); social science education (MSE). *Accreditation:* NCATE. Part-time and evening/weekend programs available. *Degree requirements:* For master's, comprehensive exam, thesis optional. *Entrance requirements:* For master's, GRE General Test. Additional exam requirements/recommendations for international students: Required—TOEFL (minimum score 550 paper-based).

Wayne State University, College of Education, Division of Teacher Education, Detroit, MI 48202. Offers art education (M Ed), including art therapy; autism spectrum disorders (Certificate); bilingual/bicultural education (M Ed, Certificate); career and technical education (M Ed, Certificate); cognitive impairment (Certificate); curriculum and instruction (Ed D, PhD, Ed S), including art education (PhD), bilingual education (Ed D, Ed S), bilingual-bicultural education (PhD), career and technical education (MAT, Ed D, PhD, Ed S), early childhood education (MAT, Ed D, PhD, Ed S), elementary education, English as a second language (MAT, Ed D, Ed S), English education (MAT, Ed D, PhD, Ed S), foreign language education (MAT, PhD), K-12 curriculum, mathematics education (MAT, Ed D, PhD, Ed S), science education (MAT, Ed D, PhD, Ed S), secondary education, social studies education (MAT, Ed S), social studies education: secondary (Ed D, PhD); early childhood education (M Ed, Certificate); elementary education (M Ed, MAT), including children's literature (MAT), early childhood education (MAT, Ed D, PhD, Ed S), general elementary education (MAT); elementary or secondary education (MAT), including bilingual/bicultural education, English as a second language (MAT, Ed D, Ed S), mathematics education (MAT, Ed D, PhD, Ed S), science education (MAT, Ed D, PhD, Ed S), social studies education (MAT, Ed S); emotionally impaired (Certificate); English as a second language (Certificate); English education (M Ed), including secondary; foreign language education (M Ed); K-12 reading specialist (Certificate); learning disabilities (Certificate); mathematics education (M Ed), including secondary; reading (M Ed, Ed S); reading, language and literature (Ed D); science education (M Ed), including secondary; secondary education (MAT), including art education (K-12), career and technical education (MAT, Ed D, PhD, Ed S), English education (MAT, Ed D, PhD, Ed S), foreign language education (MAT, PhD), kinesiology; social studies education (M Ed), including secondary; special education (M Ed, MAT, Ed D, PhD, Ed S); visual arts education (Certificate). Part-time programs available. *Faculty:* 36 full-time (25 women), 55 part-time/adjunct (43 women). *Students:* 218 full-time (163 women), 448 part-time (344 women); includes 218 minority (177 Black or African American, non-Hispanic/Latino; 2 American Indian or Alaska Native, non-Hispanic/Latino; 11 Asian, non-Hispanic/Latino; 19 Hispanic/Latino; 1 Native Hawaiian or other Pacific Islander, non-Hispanic/Latino; 8 Two or more races, non-Hispanic/Latino), 10 international. Average age 37. 258 applicants, 30% accepted, 52 enrolled. In 2013, 183 master's, 10 doctorates, 35 other advanced degrees awarded. *Degree requirements:* For master's, thesis, essay or project (for some M Ed programs), professional field experience (for MAT programs); for doctorate, thesis/dissertation. *Entrance requirements:* For master's, Michigan Basic Skills Test (MA in teaching), admission to the graduate school, verification of participation in group work with children and Michigan State Police Criminal Background check; for doctorate, minimum undergraduate GPA of 3.0, graduate 3.5; interview, curriculum vitae; references. Additional exam requirements/recommendations for international students: Required—TOEFL (minimum score 550 paper-based; 79 iBT), TWE (minimum score 5.5), Michigan English Language Assessment Battery (minimum score 85); Recommended—IELTS (minimum score 6.5). *Application deadline:* For fall admission, 6/1 priority date for domestic students, 5/1 priority date for international students; for winter admission, 10/1 priority date for domestic students, 9/1 priority date for international students; for spring admission, 2/1 priority date for domestic students, 1/1 priority date for international students. Applications are processed on a rolling basis. Application fee: $0. Electronic applications accepted. *Expenses:* Tuition, state resident: part-time $554.15 per credit. Tuition, nonresident: part-time $1200.35 per credit. *Required fees:* $42.15 per credit. $268.30 per semester. Tuition and fees vary according to course load and program. *Financial support:* In 2013–14, 83 students received support, including 1 fellowship (averaging $16,842 per year), 1 research assistantship with tuition reimbursement available (averaging $21,229 per year); career-related internships or fieldwork, Federal Work-Study, scholarships/grants, health care benefits, and unspecified assistantships also available. Support available to part-time students. Financial award application deadline: 3/31; financial award applicants required to submit FAFSA. *Faculty research:* Improving students' skill achievement in mathematics; improving elementary children's understanding of informational text; teachers' use of their pedagogical and mathematical knowledge in the interactive work of teaching; the intersection of identity construction in teaching and learning; identifying effective methods of literacy instruction and assessments for bilingual students in elementary language arts classrooms. *Total annual research expenditures:* $368,105. *Unit head:* Dr. Kathleen Crawford-McKinney, Assistant Dean, 313-577-0122. *Application contact:* Janice Green, Assistant Dean, 313-577-1605, E-mail: jwgreen@wayne.edu.
Website: http://coe.wayne.edu/ted/index.php.

Western Connecticut State University, Division of Graduate Studies, School of Professional Studies, Department of Education and Educational Psychology, English Education Option, Danbury, CT 06810-6885. Offers MS. Part-time programs available. *Degree requirements:* For master's, comprehensive exam (for some programs), thesis or comprehensive exam, completion of program in 6 years. *Entrance requirements:* For master's, minimum GPA of 2.8, teaching certificate. Additional exam requirements/recommendations for international students: Recommended—TOEFL (minimum score 550 paper-based; 79 iBT), IELTS (minimum score 6).

Western Governors University, Teachers College, Salt Lake City, UT 84107. Offers curriculum and instruction (MS); educational leadership (MS); educational studies (MA); educational studies (5-12) (MA), including mathematics; elementary education (K-8) (MAT, Postbaccalaureate Certificate); elementary education (PreK-8) (MAT); English language learning (K-12) (MA); instructional design (MAT); learning and technology (M Ed, MA); management and innovation (M Ed); mathematics (5-12) (MAT, Postbaccalaureate Certificate); mathematics (5-9) (MAT, Postbaccalaureate Certificate); mathematics education (5-12) (MA); mathematics education (5-9) (MA); mathematics education (K-6) (MA); measurement and evaluation (M Ed); science (5-12) (Postbaccalaureate Certificate); science (5-9) (MAT, Postbaccalaureate Certificate); science education (5-12) (MA), including biology, chemistry, geology, physics; science education (5-9) (MA); social science (5-12) (MAT, Postbaccalaureate Certificate); special education (MAT, MS). *Accreditation:* NCATE. Evening/weekend programs available. Postbaccalaureate distance learning degree programs offered (no on-campus study). *Degree requirements:* For master's, capstone project. *Entrance requirements:* For master's and Postbaccalaureate Certificate, Readiness Assessment, transcripts. Additional exam requirements/recommendations for international students: Required—TOEFL (minimum score 450 paper-based; 80 iBT). Electronic applications accepted. *Expenses:* Contact institution.

Western Kentucky University, Graduate Studies, Potter College of Arts and Letters, Department of English, Bowling Green, KY 42101. Offers education (MA); English (MA Ed); literature (MA), including American literature, British literature, literary theory, women writers, world literature; teaching English as a second language (MA); writing (MA). Part-time and evening/weekend programs available. *Degree requirements:* For master's, comprehensive exam, thesis optional, final exam. *Entrance requirements:* For master's, GRE General Test, minimum GPA of 2.75. Additional exam requirements/recommendations for international students: Required—TOEFL (minimum score 555 paper-based; 79 iBT). *Faculty research:* Improving writing, linking teacher knowledge and performance, Victorian women writers, Kentucky women writers, Kentucky poets.

Western Michigan University, Graduate College, College of Arts and Sciences, Department of English, Kalamazoo, MI 49008. Offers creative writing (MFA, PhD); English (MA, PhD); English education (MA, PhD). *Degree requirements:* For master's, oral exams; for doctorate, one foreign language, thesis/dissertation, oral exam, written exams. *Entrance requirements:* For master's and doctorate, GRE General Test, GRE Subject Test.

Western New England University, College of Arts and Sciences, Program in English for Teachers, Springfield, MA 01119. Offers MAET. Part-time and evening/weekend programs available. *Faculty:* 3 full-time (2 women). *Students:* 14 part-time (8 women); includes 1 minority (Asian, non-Hispanic/Latino). Average age 32. 39 applicants. In 2013, 14 master's awarded. *Entrance requirements:* For master's, two letters of recommendation, official transcript, personal statement, resume. Additional exam requirements/recommendations for international students: Required—TOEFL. *Application deadline:* Applications are processed on a rolling basis. Application fee: $30. Electronic applications accepted. Tuition and fees vary according to program. *Financial support:* Application deadline: 4/15; applicants required to submit FAFSA. *Unit head:* Dr. Saeed Ghahramani, Dean, 413-782-1218, Fax: 413-796-2118, E-mail: sghahram@wne.edu. *Application contact:* Matthew Fox, Director of Recruiting and Marketing for Adult Learners, 413-782-1517, Fax: 413-782-1779, E-mail: study@wne.edu.
Website: http://www1.wne.edu/artsandsciences/index.cfm?selection-doc.859.

Widener University, School of Human Service Professions, Center for Education, Chester, PA 19013-5792. Offers adult education (M Ed); counseling in higher education (M Ed); counselor education (M Ed); early childhood education (M Ed); educational foundations (M Ed); educational leadership (M Ed); educational psychology (M Ed); elementary education (M Ed); English and language arts (M Ed); health education (M Ed); higher education leadership (Ed D); home and school visitor (M Ed); human sexuality (M Ed, PhD); mathematics education (M Ed); middle school education (M Ed); principalship (M Ed); reading and language arts (Ed D); reading education (M Ed); school administration (Ed D); science education (M Ed); social studies education (M Ed); special education (M Ed); technology education (M Ed). *Accreditation:* NCATE. Part-time and evening/weekend programs available. *Faculty:* 34 full-time (22 women), 37 part-time/adjunct (14 women). *Students:* 64 full-time (44 women), 209 part-time (146 women); includes 49 minority (39 Black or African American, non-Hispanic/Latino; 1 American Indian or Alaska Native, non-Hispanic/Latino; 4 Asian, non-Hispanic/Latino; 4 Hispanic/Latino; 1 Two or more races, non-Hispanic/Latino), 8 international. Average age 39. 139 applicants, 88% accepted. In 2013, 168 master's, 31 doctorates awarded. Terminal master's awarded for partial completion of doctoral program. *Degree requirements:* For doctorate, thesis/dissertation. *Entrance requirements:* For master's, minimum GPA of 2.5; for doctorate, GRE or MAT, minimum GPA of 2.0 (undergraduate), 3.5 (graduate). *Application deadline:* Applications are processed on a rolling basis. Application fee: $25 ($300 for international students). Electronic applications accepted. *Expenses:* Contact institution. *Financial support:* Career-related internships or fieldwork, tuition waivers (full and partial), and unspecified assistantships available. Support available to part-time students. Financial award application deadline: 5/1. *Faculty research:* Reading and cognition, adult education, technology education, educational leadership, special education. *Unit head:* Dr. Michael W. LeDoux, Associate Dean, 610-499-4294, Fax: 610-499-4623, E-mail: mwledoux@widener.edu. *Application contact:* Dr. Roberta Nolan, Director of Graduate Admissions, 610-499-4125, E-mail: rdnolan@widener.edu.

Wilkes University, College of Graduate and Professional Studies, School of Education, Wilkes-Barre, PA 18766-0002. Offers art and science of teaching (MS Ed); classroom technology (MS Ed); early childhood literacy (MS Ed); educational development and strategies (MS Ed); educational leadership (MS Ed); educational technology (Ed D);

higher education administration (Ed D); instructional media (MS Ed); instructional technology (MS Ed); international school leadership (MS Ed); K-12 administration (Ed D); middle level education (MS Ed); online teaching (MS Ed); reading (MS Ed); school business leadership (MS Ed); secondary education (MS Ed), including biology, chemistry, English, history, mathematics; special education (MS Ed); teaching English as a second language (MS Ed); twenty-first century teaching and learning (MS Ed). Part-time and evening/weekend programs available. Postbaccalaureate distance learning degree programs offered (minimal on-campus study). *Students:* 46 full-time (37 women), 1,410 part-time (1,039 women); includes 67 minority (12 Black or African American, non-Hispanic/Latino; 2 American Indian or Alaska Native, non-Hispanic/Latino; 11 Asian, non-Hispanic/Latino; 28 Hispanic/Latino; 1 Native Hawaiian or other Pacific Islander, non-Hispanic/Latino; 13 Two or more races, non-Hispanic/Latino), 6 international. Average age 34. In 2013, 852 master's, 10 doctorates awarded. *Entrance requirements:* Additional exam requirements/recommendations for international students: Required—TOEFL (minimum score 550 paper-based; 79 iBT). *Application deadline:* Applications are processed on a rolling basis. Application fee: $45. Electronic applications accepted. *Expenses:* Contact institution. *Financial support:* Federal Work-Study and unspecified assistantships available. Financial award application deadline: 3/1; financial award applicants required to submit FAFSA. *Unit head:* Dr. Rhonda Waskiewicz, Interim Dean, Education, 570-408-4332, Fax: 570-408-7872, E-mail: rhonda.waskiewicz@wilkes.edu. *Application contact:* Joanne Thomas, Interim Director of Graduate Education, 570-408-4234, Fax: 570-408-7846, E-mail: joanne.thomas1@wilkes.edu.
Website: http://www.wilkes.edu/pages/383.asp.

William Carey University, School of Education, Hattiesburg, MS 39401-5499. Offers art education (M Ed); art of teaching (M Ed); elementary education (M Ed, Ed S); English education (M Ed); gifted education (M Ed); history and social science (M Ed); mild/moderate disabilities (M Ed); secondary education (M Ed). *Accreditation:* NCATE. Part-time programs available. *Degree requirements:* For master's, comprehensive exam. *Entrance requirements:* For master's, GRE, MAT, minimum GPA of 2.5, Class A teacher's license. Additional exam requirements/recommendations for international students: Required—TOEFL (minimum score 550 paper-based).

Worcester State University, Graduate Studies, Program in English, Worcester, MA 01602-2597. Offers MA. Part-time programs available. *Faculty:* 5 full-time (3 women). *Students:* 1 full-time (0 women), 14 part-time (8 women). Average age 39. 7 applicants, 71% accepted. In 2013, 7 master's awarded. *Degree requirements:* For master's, comprehensive exam (for some programs), thesis optional. *Entrance requirements:* For master's, GRE General Test or MAT, 18 undergraduate credits in English, excluding composition. Additional exam requirements/recommendations for international students: Required—TOEFL (minimum score 500 paper-based; 61 iBT). *Application deadline:* For fall admission, 6/15 for domestic and international students; for spring admission, 4/1 for domestic and international students. Applications are processed on a rolling basis. Application fee: $40. Electronic applications accepted. *Expenses: Tuition, area resident:* Part-time $150 per credit. Tuition, state resident: part-time $150 per credit. Tuition, nonresident: part-time $150 per credit. *Required fees:* $114.50 per credit. *Financial support:* In 2013–14, 1 student received support, including 1 research assistantship (averaging $4,800 per year); career-related internships or fieldwork, scholarships/grants, and unspecified assistantships also available. Financial award application deadline: 3/1; financial award applicants required to submit FAFSA. *Unit head:* Dr. Ruth Haber, Coordinator, 508-929-8706, Fax: 508-929-8174, E-mail: rhaber@worcester.edu. *Application contact:* Sara Grady, Assistant Dean of Graduate and Continuing Education, 508-929-8787, Fax: 508-929-8100, E-mail: sara.grady@worcester.edu.

Environmental Education

Alaska Pacific University, Graduate Programs, Environmental Science Department, Program in Outdoor and Environmental Education, Anchorage, AK 99508-4672. Offers MSOEE. Part-time programs available. *Degree requirements:* For master's, thesis. *Entrance requirements:* For master's, MAT or GRE, minimum GPA of 3.0. Additional exam requirements/recommendations for international students: Required—TOEFL (minimum score 550 paper-based).

Antioch University New England, Graduate School, Department of Environmental Studies, Program in Environmental Education, Keene, NH 03431-3552. Offers MS. *Degree requirements:* For master's, practicum. *Entrance requirements:* For master's, previous undergraduate course work in biology, chemistry, and mathematics; resume; 3 letters of recommendation. Additional exam requirements/recommendations for international students: Required—TOEFL (minimum score 550 paper-based). Electronic applications accepted. *Expenses:* Contact institution. *Faculty research:* Sustainability, natural resources inventory.

Arcadia University, Graduate Studies, School of Education, Glenside, PA 19038-3295. Offers art education (M Ed); computer education (CAS); curriculum (CAS); curriculum studies (M Ed); early childhood education (M Ed, CAS), including individualized (M Ed), master teacher (M Ed), research in child development (M Ed); educational leadership (M Ed, Ed D, CAS); elementary education (M Ed, CAS); English education (MA Ed); environmental education (MA Ed, CAS); history education (MA Ed); instructional technology (M Ed); language arts (M Ed, CAS); library science (M Ed); mathematics education (M Ed, MA Ed, CAS); music education (MA Ed); psychology (MA Ed); reading (M Ed, CAS); science education (M Ed, CAS); secondary education (M Ed, CAS); special education (M Ed, Ed D, CAS); theater arts (MA Ed); written communication (MA Ed). *Accreditation:* NASAD. Part-time and evening/weekend programs available. Postbaccalaureate distance learning degree programs offered (minimal on-campus study). Electronic applications accepted. *Expenses:* Contact institution.

Brooklyn College of the City University of New York, Division of Graduate Studies, School of Education, Program in Childhood Education, Brooklyn, NY 11210-2889. Offers bilingual education (MS Ed); liberal arts (MS Ed); mathematics (MS Ed); science/environmental education (MS Ed). Part-time and evening/weekend programs available. *Entrance requirements:* For master's, LAST, interview, previous course work in education, writing sample, resume, 2 letters of recommendation. Additional exam requirements/recommendations for international students: Required—TOEFL (minimum score 500 paper-based; 61 iBT). Electronic applications accepted. *Faculty research:* Emotional intelligence, multiculturalism, arts immersion, the Holocaust.

Chatham University, Program in Education, Pittsburgh, PA 15232-2826. Offers early childhood education (MAT); elementary education (MAT); environmental education (K-12) (MAT); secondary art (MAT); secondary biology education (MAT); secondary chemistry education (MAT); secondary English education (MAT); secondary math education (MAT); secondary physics education (MAT); secondary social studies education (MAT); special education (MAT). *Faculty:* 1 (woman) full-time, 5 part-time/adjunct (4 women). *Students:* 19 full-time (15 women), 4 part-time (all women); includes 2 minority (1 Black or African American, non-Hispanic/Latino; 1 Asian, non-Hispanic/Latino), 2 international. Average age 28. 22 applicants, 73% accepted, 6 enrolled. In 2013, 20 master's awarded. *Degree requirements:* For master's, thesis, teaching experience. *Entrance requirements:* For master's, minimum GPA of 3.0, sample of written work, recommendation letters. Additional exam requirements/recommendations for international students: Required—TOEFL (minimum score 600 paper-based; 100 iBT), IELTS (minimum score 7), TWE. *Application deadline:* For fall admission, 4/1 priority date for domestic and international students; for spring admission, 11/1 priority date for domestic students, 10/1 priority date for international students. Applications are processed on a rolling basis. Application fee: $45. Electronic applications accepted. Application fee is waived when completed online. *Expenses: Tuition:* Full-time $14,886; part-time $827 per credit hour. One-time fee: $396 full-time. *Financial support:* Career-related internships or fieldwork available. Financial award applicants required to submit FAFSA. *Faculty research:* Gifted education, environmental education, technology in education, writing as learning, class size and achievement. *Unit head:* Dr. Edward Donovan, Director of Education Programs, 412-365-2773, E-mail: edonovan@chatham.edu. *Application contact:* Katie Noel, Assistant Director of Graduate Admission, 412-365-2758, Fax: 412-365-1609, E-mail: gradadmissions@chatham.edu.
Website: http://www.chatham.edu/mat.

Concordia University, College of Education, Portland, OR 97211-6099. Offers career and technical education (M Ed); curriculum and instruction (M Ed), including adolescent literacy, career and technical education, e-learning/technology education, early childhood education, English for speakers of other languages, English language development, environmental education, mathematics, methods and curriculum, reading, science, teacher leadership, the inclusive classroom; early childhood (MAT); education leadership (Ed D); educational administration (M Ed); elementary education (MAT); secondary education (MAT); special education (M Ed); teacher leadership (Ed D). Part-time programs available. Postbaccalaureate distance learning degree programs offered (no on-campus study). *Degree requirements:* For master's, comprehensive exam, work samples/portfolio. *Entrance requirements:* For master's, California Basic Educational Skills Test or PRAXIS I, minimum undergraduate GPA of 2.8, graduate 3.0; 2 letters of recommendation. Additional exam requirements/recommendations for international students: Required—TOEFL (minimum score 525 paper-based). Electronic applications accepted. *Faculty research:* Learner-centered classroom, brain-based learning, future of online learning.

Concordia University Wisconsin, Graduate Programs, Department of Education, Mequon, WI 53097-2402. Offers art education (MS Ed); curriculum and instruction (MS Ed); early childhood (MS Ed); educational administration (MS Ed); environmental education (MS Ed); family studies (MS Ed); reading (MS Ed); school counseling (MS Ed); special education (MS Ed). Part-time and evening/weekend programs available. Postbaccalaureate distance learning degree programs offered (minimal on-campus study). *Degree requirements:* For master's, comprehensive exam, thesis or alternative. *Entrance requirements:* For master's, minimum GPA of 3.0, teaching license. Additional exam requirements/recommendations for international students: Required—TOEFL. *Faculty research:* Motivation, developmental learning, learning styles.

Florida Atlantic University, College of Education, Department of Teaching and Learning, Boca Raton, FL 33431-0991. Offers curriculum and instruction (M Ed), including art, biology, chemistry, English, French, German, mathematics, music, physics, Pre-K and primary education, reading, social sciences, Spanish; elementary education (M Ed); environmental education (M Ed); reading education (M Ed); social foundations of education (M Ed), including educational psychology, educational technology, multilingual education. *Accreditation:* NCATE. Part-time and evening/weekend programs available. *Faculty:* 16 full-time (12 women), 1 (woman) part-time/adjunct. *Students:* 56 full-time (46 women), 96 part-time (78 women); includes 39 minority (10 Black or African American, non-Hispanic/Latino; 6 Asian, non-Hispanic/Latino; 20 Hispanic/Latino; 3 Two or more races, non-Hispanic/Latino), 4 international. Average age 32. 101 applicants, 54% accepted, 42 enrolled. In 2013, 64 master's awarded. *Entrance requirements:* For master's, GRE General Test, minimum GPA of 3.0 in last 2 years of undergraduate course work. Additional exam requirements/recommendations for international students: Required—TOEFL (minimum score 500 paper-based; 61 iBT), IELTS (minimum score 6). *Application deadline:* For fall admission, 7/1 for domestic students, 2/15 for international students; for spring admission, 11/1 for domestic students, 7/15 for international students. Applications are processed on a rolling basis. Application fee: $30. *Expenses:* Tuition, state resident: full-time $6660; part-time $370 per credit hour. Tuition, nonresident: full-time $18,450; part-time $1025 per credit hour. Tuition and fees vary according to course load. *Financial support:* Fellowships with partial tuition reimbursements, research assistantships with partial tuition reimbursements, teaching assistantships with partial tuition reimbursements, career-related internships or fieldwork, scholarships/grants, and unspecified assistantships available. *Faculty research:* Technology, teaching English to speakers of other languages, math teaching, electronic portfolio assessment, global perspectives through social studies. *Unit head:* Dr. Barbara Ridener, Chairperson, 561-297-3588. *Application contact:* Dr. Eliah Watlington, Associate Dean, 561-296-8520, Fax: 261-297-2991, E-mail: ewatling@fau.edu.
Website: http://www.coe.fau.edu/academicdepartments/tl/.

Florida Institute of Technology, Graduate Programs, College of Science, Department of Education and Interdisciplinary Studies, Melbourne, FL 32901-6975. Offers computer education (MS); elementary science education (M Ed); environmental education (MS); interdisciplinary science (MS); mathematics education (MS, PhD, Ed S); science education (MS, PhD, Ed S), including informal science education (MS); teaching (MAT). Part-time and evening/weekend programs available. *Faculty:* 4 full-time (1 woman), 5 part-time/adjunct (2 women). *Students:* 47 full-time (29 women), 40 part-time (25 women); includes 10 minority (4 Black or African American, non-Hispanic/Latino; 4 Asian, non-Hispanic/Latino; 2 Hispanic/Latino), 48 international. Average age 32. 90 applicants, 63% accepted, 23 enrolled. In 2013, 16 master's awarded. Terminal master's awarded for partial completion of doctoral program. *Degree requirements:* For master's, comprehensive exam (for some programs), thesis optional; for doctorate, comprehensive exam, thesis/dissertation; for Ed S, comprehensive exam. *Entrance requirements:* For master's, minimum GPA of 3.0, resume, 3 letters of recommendation (elementary science education), statement of objectives; for doctorate, minimum GPA of 3.2, resume, 3 letters of recommendation, statement of objectives, 3 years of teaching experience (recommended); for Ed S, minimum GPA of 3.0, resume, 3 letters of

recommendation, statement of objectives. Additional exam requirements/recommendations for international students: Required—TOEFL (minimum score 550 paper-based; 79 iBT). *Application deadline:* For fall admission, 4/1 for international students; for spring admission, 9/30 for international students. Applications are processed on a rolling basis. Electronic applications accepted. *Expenses: Tuition:* Full-time $20,214; part-time $1123 per credit. Tuition and fees vary according to campus/location. *Financial support:* In 2013–14, 2 teaching assistantships with full and partial tuition reimbursements (averaging $12,623 per year) were awarded; research assistantships with full and partial tuition reimbursements, career-related internships or fieldwork, institutionally sponsored loans, tuition waivers (partial), unspecified assistantships, and tuition remissions also available. Support available to part-time students. Financial award application deadline: 3/1; financial award applicants required to submit FAFSA. *Faculty research:* Measurement and evaluation, computers in education, educational technology. *Total annual research expenditures:* $644,517. *Unit head:* Dr. Kastro Hamed, Department Head, 321-674-8126, Fax: 321-674-7598, E-mail: khamed@fit.edu. *Application contact:* Cheryl A. Brown, Associate Director of Graduate Admissions, 321-674-7581, Fax: 321-723-9468, E-mail: cbrown@fit.edu. Website: http://cos.fit.edu/education/.

Goshen College, Merry Lea Environmental Learning Center, Goshen, IN 46526-4794. Offers MA. *Accreditation:* NCATE. *Faculty:* 7 full-time (0 women), 1 (woman) part-time/adjunct. *Students:* 15 full-time (6 women), 2 part-time (0 women); includes 2 minority (both Black or African American, non-Hispanic/Latino), 2 international. *Entrance requirements:* For master's, resume, official transcripts, three letters of reference, personal written statement. Additional exam requirements/recommendations for international students: Required—TOEFL. *Application deadline:* For fall admission, 3/1 for domestic students. Application fee: $50. Electronic applications accepted. *Expenses: Tuition:* Full-time $28,800. Tuition and fees vary according to course load and program. *Financial support:* Application deadline: 9/10; applicants required to submit FAFSA. *Unit head:* Dr. Luke Gascho, Executive Director, 260-799-5869, E-mail: lukeag@goshen.edu. *Application contact:* Dr. David Ostergren, Director of the Graduate Program, 260-799-5869, E-mail: daveo@goshen.edu. Website: http://merrylea.goshen.edu/.

Hamline University, School of Education, St. Paul, MN 55104-1284. Offers education (MA Ed, Ed D); English as a second language (MA); literacy education (MA); natural science and environmental education (MA Ed); teaching (MAT). *Accreditation:* NCATE (one or more programs are accredited). Part-time and evening/weekend programs available. Postbaccalaureate distance learning degree programs offered (no on-campus study). *Faculty:* 19 full-time (14 women), 44 part-time/adjunct (38 women). *Students:* 107 full-time (75 women), 997 part-time (744 women); includes 71 minority (23 Black or African American, non-Hispanic/Latino; 4 American Indian or Alaska Native, non-Hispanic/Latino; 17 Asian, non-Hispanic/Latino; 21 Hispanic/Latino; 6 Two or more races, non-Hispanic/Latino), 10 international. Average age 33. 395 applicants, 74% accepted, 224 enrolled. In 2013, 221 master's, 13 doctorates awarded. *Degree requirements:* For master's, foreign language (for MA in English as a second language only); thesis or capstone project; for doctorate, comprehensive exam, thesis/dissertation. *Entrance requirements:* For master's, written essay, official transcripts, 2 letters of recommendation, minimum GPA of 3.0 from bachelor's work; for doctorate, personal statement, master's degree with minimum GPA of 3.0, 3 letters of recommendation, writing sample, interview. Additional exam requirements/recommendations for international students: Required—TOEFL (minimum score 550 paper-based; 80 iBT), TOEFL (625 paper-based, 107 iBT) or IELTS (minimum 7.5) for MA in ESL. *Application deadline:* Applications are processed on a rolling basis. Application fee: $0 ($100 for international students). Electronic applications accepted. *Financial support:* Career-related internships or fieldwork, Federal Work-Study, and scholarships/grants available. Support available to part-time students. Financial award applicants required to submit FAFSA. *Faculty research:* Adult basic education, service-learning, teacher dispositions, diversity, technology. *Unit head:* Dr. Nancy Sorenson, Dean, 651-523-2600, Fax: 651-523-2489, E-mail: nsorenson01@hamline.edu. *Application contact:* Shawn Skoog, Director of Graduate Recruitment and Admission, 651-523-2900, Fax: 651-523-3058, E-mail: sskoog03@hamline.edu. Website: http://www.hamline.edu/education.

Instituto Tecnologico de Santo Domingo, Graduate School, Area of Basic And Environmental Sciences, Santo Domingo, Dominican Republic. Offers environmental science (M En S), including environmental education, environmental management, marine resources, natural resources management; mathematics (MS, PhD); renewable energy technology (MS, Certificate).

Montclair State University, The Graduate School, College of Science and Mathematics, Department of Earth and Environmental Studies, Program in Environmental Studies, Montclair, NJ 07043-1624. Offers environmental education (MA); environmental management (MA); environmental science (MA). Part-time and evening/weekend programs available. *Degree requirements:* For master's, thesis. *Entrance requirements:* For master's, GRE General Test, 2 letters of recommendation, essay. Additional exam requirements/recommendations for international students: Required—TOEFL (minimum score 83 iBT), IELTS (minimum score 6.5). Electronic applications accepted. *Faculty research:* Environmental geochemistry/remediation/forensics, environmental law and policy, regional climate modeling, remote sensing, Cenozoic marine sediment records from polar regions, sustainability science.

Montreat College, School of Professional and Adult Studies, Montreat, NC 28757-1267. Offers business administration (MBA); clinical mental health counseling (MA); environmental education (MS); management and leadership (MS). Evening/weekend programs available. Postbaccalaureate distance learning degree programs offered (minimal on-campus study). *Faculty:* 12 full-time (3 women), 14 part-time/adjunct (3 women). *Students:* 108 full-time (65 women), 179 part-time (111 women); includes 130 minority (116 Black or African American, non-Hispanic/Latino; 5 American Indian or Alaska Native, non-Hispanic/Latino; 2 Asian, non-Hispanic/Latino; 6 Hispanic/Latino; 1 Two or more races, non-Hispanic/Latino). Average age 34. 145 applicants, 41% accepted, 57 enrolled. In 2013, 142 master's awarded. *Degree requirements:* For master's, business consulting project (for MBA). *Entrance requirements:* For master's, GMAT. Additional exam requirements/recommendations for international students: Required—TOEFL (minimum score 550 paper-based; 80 iBT). *Application deadline:* Applications are processed on a rolling basis. *Financial support:* Available to part-time students. Application deadline: 7/1; applicants required to submit FAFSA. *Unit head:* Joseph Kirkland, Interim President, 828-669-8012, Fax: 828-669-0500, E-mail: jkirkland@montreat.edu. *Application contact:* Julia Pacilli, Director of Enrollment, 828-669-8012 Ext. 2756, Fax: 828-669-0500, E-mail: jpacilli@montreat.edu. Website: http://www.montreat.edu/.

New York University, Steinhardt School of Culture, Education, and Human Development, Department of Teaching and Learning, Program in Environmental Conservation Education, New York, NY 10003. Offers MA. *Accreditation:* Teacher Education Accreditation Council. Part-time programs available. *Faculty:* 2 full-time (1 woman). *Students:* 17 full-time (all women), 23 part-time (22 women); includes 8 minority (1 Black or African American, non-Hispanic/Latino; 7 Hispanic/Latino), 6 international. Average age 28. 32 applicants, 78% accepted, 12 enrolled. In 2013, 17 master's awarded. *Degree requirements:* For master's, thesis (for some programs). *Entrance requirements:* Additional exam requirements/recommendations for international students: Required—TOEFL (minimum score 100 iBT). *Application deadline:* For fall admission, 2/1 priority date for domestic and international students; for spring admission, 10/1 for domestic and international students. Applications are processed on a rolling basis. Application fee: $75. Electronic applications accepted. *Expenses: Tuition:* Full-time $35,856; part-time $1494 per unit. *Required fees:* $1408; $64 per unit. $473 per term. Tuition and fees vary according to course load and program. *Financial support:* Career-related internships or fieldwork, Federal Work-Study, institutionally sponsored loans, and tuition waivers (partial) available. Support available to part-time students. Financial award application deadline: 2/1; financial award applicants required to submit FAFSA. *Faculty research:* Environmental ethics, values and policy, philosophy and geography. *Unit head:* Dr. Mary Leou, Acting Director, 212-998-5474, Fax: 212-995-4832, E-mail: mary.leou@nyu.edu. *Application contact:* 212-998-5030, Fax: 212-995-4328, E-mail: steinhardt.gradadmissions@nyu.edu. Website: http://steinhardt.nyu.edu/teachlearn/environmental.

Prescott College, Graduate Programs, Program in Education, Prescott, AZ 86301. Offers early childhood education (MA); early childhood special education (MA); education (MA); elementary education (MA); environmental education leadership and administration (MA); equine-assisted learning (MA); school guidance counseling (MA); secondary education (MA); special education: learning disabilities (MA); special education: mental retardation (MA); special education: serious emotional disabilities (MA); student-directed independent study (MA); sustainability education (PhD). Part-time programs available. Postbaccalaureate distance learning degree programs offered (minimal on-campus study). *Degree requirements:* For master's, thesis, fieldwork or internship, practicum; for doctorate, thesis/dissertation. *Entrance requirements:* For master's, 2 letters of recommendation, resume; for doctorate, 3 letters of recommendation, resume, official transcripts, personal statement, program proposal. Additional exam requirements/recommendations for international students: Required—TOEFL (minimum score 500 paper-based). Electronic applications accepted.

Royal Roads University, Graduate Studies, Environment and Sustainability Program, Victoria, BC V9B 5Y2, Canada. Offers environment and management (M Sc, MA); environmental education and communication (MA, G Dip, Graduate Certificate); MA/MS. Postbaccalaureate distance learning degree programs offered (minimal on-campus study). *Degree requirements:* For master's, thesis. *Entrance requirements:* For master's, 5-7 years of related work experience. Electronic applications accepted. *Faculty research:* Sustainable development, atmospheric processes, sustainable communities, chemical fate and transport of persistent organic pollutants, educational technology.

Saint Vincent College, Program in Education, Latrobe, PA 15650-2690. Offers curriculum and instruction (MS); educational media and technology (MS); environmental education (MS); school administration and supervision (MS); special education (MS). Part-time and evening/weekend programs available. *Degree requirements:* For master's, comprehensive exam. *Entrance requirements:* For master's, GRE (if undergraduate GPA less than 3.0). Additional exam requirements/recommendations for international students: Required—TOEFL (minimum score 550 paper-based). *Faculty research:* Assessment and instructional technology.

Slippery Rock University of Pennsylvania, Graduate Studies (Recruitment), College of Health, Environment, and Science, Department of Parks, Recreation, and Environmental Education, Slippery Rock, PA 16057-1383. Offers environmental education (M Ed); parks and resource management (MS). Part-time and evening/weekend programs available. Postbaccalaureate distance learning degree programs offered (no on-campus study). *Faculty:* 2 full-time (0 women), 3 part-time/adjunct (2 women). *Students:* 19 full-time (11 women), 79 part-time (44 women); includes 5 minority (1 Black or African American, non-Hispanic/Latino; 2 Hispanic/Latino; 2 Two or more races, non-Hispanic/Latino), 2 international. Average age 31. 70 applicants, 90% accepted, 38 enrolled. In 2013, 45 master's awarded. *Degree requirements:* For master's, comprehensive exam (for some programs), thesis (for some programs). *Entrance requirements:* For master's, GRE General Test, MAT, minimum GPA of 2.75. Additional exam requirements/recommendations for international students: Required—TOEFL (minimum score 550 paper-based; 80 iBT). *Application deadline:* For fall admission, 3/1 priority date for domestic students, 5/1 priority date for international students; for spring admission, 10/1 priority date for domestic students, 9/1 priority date for international students. Applications are processed on a rolling basis. Application fee: $25 ($30 for international students). Electronic applications accepted. *Expenses:* Tuition, state resident: full-time $7956; part-time $442 per credit. Tuition, nonresident: full-time $11,934; part-time $663 per credit. *Required fees:* $2896; $148 per credit. Tuition and fees vary according to degree level and program. *Financial support:* Career-related internships or fieldwork, Federal Work-Study, institutionally sponsored loans, scholarships/grants, and tuition waivers (partial) available. Support available to part-time students. Financial award application deadline: 5/1; financial award applicants required to submit FAFSA. *Unit head:* Dr. Daniel Dziubek, Graduate Coordinator, 724-738-2958, Fax: 724-738-2938, E-mail: daniel.dziubek@sru.edu. *Application contact:* Brandi Weber-Mortimer, Director of Graduate Admissions, 724-738-2051, Fax: 724-738-2146, E-mail: graduate.admissions@sru.edu.

Southern Connecticut State University, School of Graduate Studies, School of Arts and Sciences, Department of Science Education and Environmental Studies, New Haven, CT 06515-1355. Offers environmental education (MS); science education (MS, Diploma). *Accreditation:* NCATE. Part-time and evening/weekend programs available. *Degree requirements:* For master's, thesis or alternative. *Entrance requirements:* For master's, interview; for Diploma, master's degree. Electronic applications accepted.

Southern Oregon University, Graduate Studies, Program in Environmental Education, Ashland, OR 97520. Offers MS. Part-time programs available. Postbaccalaureate distance learning degree programs offered (minimal on-campus study). *Faculty:* 12 full-time (4 women), 1 (woman) part-time/adjunct. *Students:* 15 full-time (12 women), 5 part-time (all women); includes 3 minority (2 Asian, non-Hispanic/Latino; 1 Two or more races, non-Hispanic/Latino). Average age 35. 13 applicants, 23% accepted, 2 enrolled. In 2013, 13 master's awarded. *Degree requirements:* For master's, thesis (for some programs), comprehensive exam (MA). *Entrance requirements:* For master's, GRE General Test, minimum cumulative GPA of 3.0 in the last 90 quarter credits (60 semester credits) of undergraduate coursework. Additional exam requirements/recommendations for international students: Required—TOEFL (minimum score 540 paper-based; 76 iBT), IELTS (minimum score 6), ELPT (minimum score 964) or ELS (minimum score 112). *Application deadline:* For fall admission, 7/31 priority date for domestic and international students; for winter admission, 11/15 priority date for domestic and international students; for spring admission, 1/7 priority date for domestic and international students. Applications are processed on a rolling basis. Application fee: $50. Electronic applications accepted. *Expenses:* Tuition, state resident: full-time $13,635; part-time $378.72 per credit hour. Tuition, nonresident: full-time $17,042; part-time $473.40 per credit hour. *Required fees:* $408 per quarter. *Financial support:* In 2013–14, 4 students received support, including 4 research assistantships with partial tuition reimbursements available; career-related internships or fieldwork, institutionally sponsored loans, scholarships/grants, and unspecified assistantships also available. *Unit head:* Dr. Stuart Janes, Graduate Program Coordinator, 541-552-6797, E-mail:

janes@sou.edu. *Application contact:* Kelly Moutsatson, Director of Admissions, 541-552-6411, Fax: 541-552-8403, E-mail: admissions@sou.edu.
Website: http://www.sou.edu/ee/.

Université du Québec à Montréal, Graduate Programs, Program in Education, Montréal, QC H3C 3P8, Canada. Offers education (M Ed, MA, PhD); education of the environmental sciences (Diploma). PhD offered jointly with Université du Québec à Chicoutimi, Université du Québec à Rimouski, Université du Québec à Trois-Rivières, Université du Québec en Outaouais, and Université du Québec en Abitibi-Témiscamingue. Part-time programs available. *Degree requirements:* For master's, thesis (for some programs); for doctorate, thesis/dissertation. *Entrance requirements:* For master's and Diploma, appropriate bachelor's degree or equivalent, proficiency in French; for doctorate, appropriate master's degree or equivalent, proficiency in French.

University of Colorado Denver, College of Liberal Arts and Sciences, Department of Geography and Environmental Sciences, Denver, CO 80217. Offers environmental sciences (MS), including air quality, ecosystems, environmental health, environmental science education, geo-spatial analysis, hazardous waste, water quality. Part-time and evening/weekend programs available. *Faculty:* 12 full-time (4 women), 6 part-time/adjunct (1 woman). *Students:* 35 full-time (26 women), 3 part-time (2 women); includes 7 minority (1 Asian, non-Hispanic/Latino; 5 Hispanic/Latino; 1 Two or more races, non-Hispanic/Latino), 7 international. Average age 29. 34 applicants, 74% accepted, 15 enrolled. In 2013, 16 master's awarded. *Degree requirements:* For master's, thesis or alternative, 30 credits including 21 of core requirements and 9 of environmental science electives. *Entrance requirements:* For master's, GRE General Test, BA in one of the natural/physical sciences or engineering (or equivalent background); prerequisite coursework in calculus and physics (one semester each), general chemistry with lab and general biology with lab (two semesters each), three letters of recommendation. Additional exam requirements/recommendations for international students: Required—TOEFL (minimum score 537 paper-based; 75 iBT); Recommended—IELTS (minimum score 6.5). *Application deadline:* For fall admission, 4/1 for domestic and international students; for spring admission, 10/1 for domestic and international students. Application fee: $50 ($75 for international students). Electronic applications accepted. *Financial support:* In 2013–14, 7 students received support. Fellowships, research assistantships, teaching assistantships, Federal Work-Study, institutionally sponsored loans, scholarships/grants, and traineeships available. Financial award application deadline: 4/1; financial award applicants required to submit FAFSA. *Faculty research:* Air quality, environmental health, ecosystems, hazardous waste, water quality, geo-spatial analysis and environmental science education. *Unit head:* Dr. Frederick Chambers, Director of MS in Environmental Sciences Program, 303-556-2619, Fax: 303-556-6197, E-mail: frederick.chambers@ucdenver.edu. *Application contact:* Sue Eddleman, Program Assistant, 303-556-2276, E-mail: sue.eddleman@ucdenver.edu.
Website: http://www.ucdenver.edu/academics/colleges/CLAS/Departments/ges/Programs/MasterofScience/Pages/MasterofScience.aspx.

University of Florida, Graduate School, College of Agricultural and Life Sciences, Department of Wildlife Ecology and Conservation, Gainesville, FL 32611. Offers environmental education and communications (Certificate); wildlife ecology and conservation (MS, PhD). *Faculty:* 21 full-time (6 women), 4 part-time/adjunct (2 women). *Students:* 43 full-time (26 women), 10 part-time (3 women); includes 6 minority (4 Black or African American, non-Hispanic/Latino; 2 Hispanic/Latino), 17 international. Average age 31. 47 applicants, 13% accepted, 6 enrolled. In 2013, 7 master's, 6 doctorates awarded. *Degree requirements:* For master's, comprehensive exam, thesis optional; for doctorate, comprehensive exam, thesis/dissertation. *Entrance requirements:* For master's and doctorate, GRE General Test, minimum GPA of 3.3. Additional exam requirements/recommendations for international students: Required—TOEFL (minimum score 550 paper-based; 80 iBT), IELTS (minimum score 6). *Application deadline:* For fall admission, 6/1 priority date for domestic students; for spring admission, 12/1 for domestic students. Applications are processed on a rolling basis. Application fee: $30. Electronic applications accepted. *Expenses:* Tuition, state resident: full-time $12,640. Tuition, nonresident: full-time $30,000. *Financial support:* In 2013–14, 36 students received support, including 4 fellowships (averaging $11,235 per year), 27 research assistantships (averaging $21,960 per year), 8 teaching assistantships (averaging $16,465 per year); institutionally sponsored loans also available. Financial award applicants required to submit FAFSA. *Faculty research:* Wildlife biology and management, tropical ecology and conservation, conservation biology, landscape ecology and restoration, conservation education. *Unit head:* Eric C. Hellgren, PhD, Professor and Department Chair, 352-846-0552, E-mail: hellgren@ufl.edu. *Application contact:* Katie Sieving, PhD, Professor and Graduate Coordinator, 352-846-0569, Fax: 352-846-0841, E-mail: chucao@ufl.edu.
Website: http://www.wec.ufl.edu/.

University of Minnesota, Twin Cities Campus, Graduate School, College of Education and Human Development, Department of Curriculum and Instruction, Minneapolis, MN 55455-0213. Offers art education (M Ed, MA, PhD); children's literature (M Ed, MA, PhD); curriculum and instruction (MA, PhD); early childhood education (M Ed, PhD); elementary education (M Ed, MA, PhD); English education (MA, PhD); environmental education (M Ed); family education (M Ed, MA, Ed D, PhD); instructional systems and technology (M Ed, MA, PhD); language arts (MA, PhD); language immersion education (Certificate); literacy education (MA); mathematics education (MA, PhD); reading education (MA, PhD); science education (MA, PhD); second languages and cultures education (MA, PhD); social studies education (MA, PhD); teaching (M Ed), including Chinese, earth science, elementary special education, English, English as a second language, French, German, Hebrew, Japanese, life sciences, mathematics, middle school science, science, second languages and cultures, social studies, Spanish; technology enhanced learning (Certificate); writing education (M Ed, MA, PhD). *Faculty:* 29 full-time (16 women). *Students:* 425 full-time (301 women), 220 part-time (153 women); includes 85 minority (21 Black or African American, non-Hispanic/Latino; 6 American Indian or Alaska Native, non-Hispanic/Latino; 42 Asian, non-Hispanic/Latino; 16 Hispanic/Latino), 50 international. Average age 32. 551 applicants, 68% accepted, 340 enrolled. In 2013, 618 master's, 33 doctorates, 6 other advanced degrees awarded. Application fee: $75 ($95 for international students). *Financial support:* In 2013–14, 25 fellowships (averaging $28,500 per year), 23 research assistantships with full tuition reimbursements (averaging $8,082 per year), 81 teaching assistantships with full tuition reimbursements (averaging $9,974 per year) were awarded. *Faculty research:* Teaching and learning; quality of education; influence of cultural, linguistic, social, political, technological and economic factors on teaching, learning and educational research; relationship between educational practice and a democratic and just society. *Total annual research expenditures:* $272,048. *Unit head:* Dr. Nina Asher, Chair, 612-624-4772, Fax: 612-624-1357, E-mail: nasher@umn.edu. *Application contact:* Dr. Jennifer Engler, Assistant Dean, 612-626-2887, Fax: 612-626-7496, E-mail: engle009@umn.edu.
Website: http://www.cehd.umn.edu/ci.

University of New Hampshire, Graduate School, Interdisciplinary Programs, Program in Environmental Education, Durham, NH 03824. Offers MA. Program offered in summer only. Part-time programs available. *Students:* 2 full-time (both women), 2 part-time (1 woman); includes 1 minority (Two or more races, non-Hispanic/Latino). Average age 29. 2 applicants, 50% accepted. In 2013, 6 master's awarded. *Entrance requirements:* Additional exam requirements/recommendations for international students: Required—TOEFL (minimum score 550 paper-based; 80 iBT). *Application deadline:* For fall admission, 6/1 for domestic students, 4/1 for international students; for spring admission, 12/1 for domestic students. Applications are processed on a rolling basis. Application fee: $65. Electronic applications accepted. *Expenses:* Tuition, state resident: full-time $13,500; part-time $750 per credit hour. Tuition, nonresident: full-time $26,200; part-time $1100 per credit hour. *Required fees:* $1741; $435.25 per term. Tuition and fees vary according to course level, course load, campus/location and program. *Financial support:* Fellowships, research assistantships, and teaching assistantships available. Financial award application deadline: 2/15. *Unit head:* Dr. Eleanor Abrams, Chairperson, 603-862-2990, E-mail: education.department@unh.edu. *Application contact:* Lisa Canfield, Administrative Assistant, 603-862-2310, E-mail: education.department@unh.edu.

The University of North Carolina Wilmington, College of Arts and Sciences, Department of Environmental Studies, Wilmington, NC 28403-3297. Offers coastal management (MA); environmental education and interpretation (MA); environmental management (MA); individualized study (MA). Part-time programs available. *Faculty:* 6 full-time (0 women), 1 part-time/adjunct (0 women). *Students:* 26 full-time (20 women), 14 part-time (9 women); includes 4 minority (1 Asian, non-Hispanic/Latino; 2 Hispanic/Latino; 1 Two or more races, non-Hispanic/Latino). Average age 29. 52 applicants, 87% accepted, 38 enrolled. In 2013, 6 master's awarded. *Degree requirements:* For master's, comprehensive exam, thesis or alternative, final project, practicum. *Entrance requirements:* For master's, GRE, 3 letters of recommendation. Additional exam requirements/recommendations for international students: Required—TOEFL (minimum score 550 paper-based; 79 iBT), IELTS (minimum score 6.5). *Application deadline:* For fall admission, 4/15 for domestic and international students; for spring admission, 10/15 for domestic and international students. Application fee: $60. Electronic applications accepted. *Expenses:* Tuition, state resident: full-time $4163. Tuition, nonresident: full-time $16,098. *Financial support:* In 2013–14, 5 fellowships with full tuition reimbursements (averaging $1,000 per year), 5 teaching assistantships with full and partial tuition reimbursements (averaging $10,000 per year) were awarded; research assistantships, career-related internships or fieldwork, scholarships/grants, and unspecified assistantships also available. *Faculty research:* Coastal management, environmental management, environmental education, environmental law, natural resource management. *Unit head:* Dr. Jack Hall, Chair, 910-962-3488, Fax: 910-962-7634, E-mail: hallj@uncw.edu. *Application contact:* Dr. Jeffery Hill, Graduate Program Coordinator, 910-962-3264, Fax: 910-962-7634, E-mail: hillj@uncw.edu.
Website: http://www.uncw.edu/evs/.

University of South Africa, College of Human Sciences, Pretoria, South Africa. Offers adult education (M Ed); African languages (MA, PhD); African politics (MA, PhD); Afrikaans (MA, PhD); ancient history (MA, PhD); ancient Near Eastern studies (MA, PhD); anthropology (MA, PhD); applied linguistics (MA); Arabic (MA, PhD); archaeology (MA); art history (MA); Biblical archaeology (MA); Biblical studies (M Th, D Th, PhD); Christian spirituality (M Th, D Th); church history (M Th, D Th); classical studies (MA, PhD); clinical psychology (MA); communication (MA, PhD); comparative education (M Ed, Ed D); consulting psychology (D Admin, D Com, PhD); curriculum studies (M Ed, Ed D); development studies (M Admin, MA, D Admin, PhD); didactics (M Ed, Ed D); education (M Tech); education management (M Ed, Ed D); educational psychology (M Ed); English (MA); environmental education (M Ed); French (MA, PhD); German (MA, PhD); Greek (MA); guidance and counseling (M Ed); health studies (MA, PhD), including health sciences education (MA), health services management (MA), medical and surgical nursing science (critical care general) (MA), midwifery and neonatal nursing science (MA), trauma and emergency care (MA); history (MA, PhD); history of education (Ed D); inclusive education (M Ed, Ed D); information and communications technology policy and regulation (MA); information science (MA, MIS, PhD); international politics (MA, PhD); Islamic studies (MA, PhD); Italian (MA, PhD); Judaica (MA, PhD); linguistics (MA, PhD); mathematical education (M Ed); mathematics education (MA); missiology (M Th, D Th); modern Hebrew (MA, PhD); musicology (MA, MMus, D Mus, PhD); natural science education (M Ed); New Testament (M Th, D Th); Old Testament (D Th); pastoral therapy (M Th, D Th); philosophy (MA); philosophy of education (M Ed, Ed D); politics (MA, PhD); Portuguese (MA, PhD); practical theology (M Th, D Th); psychology (MA, MS, PhD); psychology of education (M Ed, Ed D); public health (MA); religious studies (MA, D Th, PhD); Romance languages (MA); Russian (MA, PhD); Semitic languages (MA, PhD); social behavior studies in HIV/AIDS (MA); social science (mental health) (MA); social science in development studies (MA); social science in psychology (MA); social science in social work (MA); social science in sociology (MA); social work (MSW, DSW, PhD); socio-education (M Ed, Ed D); sociolinguistics (MA); sociology (MA, PhD); Spanish (MA, PhD); systematic theology (M Th, D Th); TESOL (teaching English to speakers of other languages) (MA); theological ethics (M Th, D Th); theory of literature (MA, PhD); urban ministries (D Th); urban ministry (M Th).

University of Victoria, Faculty of Graduate Studies, Faculty of Education, Department of Curriculum and Instruction, Victoria, BC V8W 2Y2, Canada. Offers art education (M Ed, PhD); curriculum studies (M Ed, MA, PhD); early childhood education (M Ed, PhD); educational studies (PhD); language and literacy (M Ed, MA, PhD); mathematics (M Ed, MA, PhD); music education (M Ed, MA, PhD); science (M Ed, MA, PhD); social studies (M Ed, MA); social, cultural and foundational studies (MA, PhD); technology and environmental education (PhD). Part-time programs available. *Degree requirements:* For master's, thesis, project (M Ed); for doctorate, comprehensive exam, thesis/dissertation. *Entrance requirements:* For master's, minimum B average. Additional exam requirements/recommendations for international students: Required—TOEFL (minimum score 575 paper-based), IELTS (minimum score 7). Electronic applications accepted. *Faculty research:* Elementary and secondary English, language arts, curriculum theory and practice, educational media and technology, educational administration and leadership, history and philosophy of education.

Western Washington University, Graduate School, Huxley College of the Environment, Department of Environmental Studies, Program in Environmental Education, Bellingham, WA 98225-5996. Offers M Ed. Part-time programs available. *Degree requirements:* For master's, comprehensive exam, thesis optional. *Entrance requirements:* For master's, GRE or MAT, minimum GPA of 3.0 in last 60 semester hours. Additional exam requirements/recommendations for international students: Required—TOEFL (minimum score 567 paper-based). Electronic applications accepted. *Faculty research:* Role of wilderness in national park history; history of the conservation movement and sense of place in environmental education; environmental care and responsibility; conservation psychology and environmental education.

West Virginia University, Davis College of Agriculture, Forestry and Consumer Sciences, Division of Resource Management and Sustainable Development, Program in Agricultural and Extension Education, Morgantown, WV 26506. Offers agricultural and extension education (MS, PhD); teaching vocational-agriculture (MS). *Accreditation:* NCATE. Part-time programs available. *Degree requirements:* For master's, thesis. *Entrance requirements:* For master's, GRE General Test, minimum GPA of 2.75. Additional exam requirements/recommendations for international students: Required—TOEFL. *Faculty research:* Program development in vocational agriculture, agricultural extension, supervised experience programs, leadership development.

Foreign Languages Education

The American University in Cairo, School of Humanities and Social Sciences, Arabic Language Institute, Cairo, Egypt. Offers teaching Arabic as a foreign language (MA). *Entrance requirements:* Additional exam requirements/recommendations for international students: Required—English entrance exam and/or TOEFL. Tuition and fees vary according to course level, course load and program.

Andrews University, School of Graduate Studies, School of Education, Department of Teaching, Learning, and Curriculum, Berrien Springs, MI 49104. Offers curriculum and instruction (MA, Ed D, PhD, Ed S); elementary education (MAT); secondary education (MAT), including biology, education, English, English as a second language, French, history, physics; teacher education (MAT). *Faculty:* 7 full-time (4 women). *Students:* 16 full-time (11 women), 26 part-time (22 women); includes 14 minority (11 Black or African American, non-Hispanic/Latino; 1 Asian, non-Hispanic/Latino; 1 Hispanic/Latino; 1 Two or more races, non-Hispanic/Latino), 13 international. Average age 40. 33 applicants, 42% accepted, 3 enrolled. In 2013, 7 master's, 1 doctorate, 1 other advanced degree awarded. *Entrance requirements:* For master's, GRE Subject Test. Additional exam requirements/recommendations for international students: Required—TOEFL (minimum score 550 paper-based). *Application deadline:* For fall admission, 8/15 for domestic students. Applications are processed on a rolling basis. Application fee: $40. *Unit head:* Dr. Lee C. Davidson, Chair, 269-471-6364. *Application contact:* Monica Wringer, Supervisor of Graduate Admission, 800-253-2874, Fax: 269-471-6321, E-mail: graduate@andrews.edu.

Appalachian State University, Cratis D. Williams Graduate School, Department of Foreign Languages and Literatures, Boone, NC 28608. Offers romance languages (MA), including Spanish or French teaching. Part-time programs available. Postbaccalaureate distance learning degree programs offered (no on-campus study). *Degree requirements:* For master's, one foreign language, comprehensive exam, thesis optional. *Entrance requirements:* For master's, GRE General Test, 3 letters of recommendation. Additional exam requirements/recommendations for international students: Required—TOEFL (minimum score 570 paper-based; 79 iBT) or IELTS (minimum score 6.5). Electronic applications accepted. *Faculty research:* French and Spanish literature, Latin American culture, teaching foreign languages.

Arizona State University at the Tempe campus, College of Liberal Arts and Sciences, School of International Letters and Cultures, Program in Spanish, Tempe, AZ 85287-0202. Offers Spanish (cultural studies) (PhD); Spanish (linguistics) (MA), including second language acquisition/applied linguistics; sociolinguistics; Spanish (literature and culture) (MA); Spanish (literature) (PhD). Part-time programs available. Terminal master's awarded for partial completion of doctoral program. *Degree requirements:* For master's, thesis, oral defense; written comprehensive exam (literature and culture); portfolio review (linguistics); interactive Program of Study (iPOS) submitted before completing 50 percent of required credit hours; for doctorate, comprehensive exam, thesis/dissertation, interactive Program of Study (iPOS) submitted before completing 50 percent of required credit hours. *Entrance requirements:* For master's, GRE (recommended), BA in Spanish or close equivalent from accredited institution with minimum GPA of 3.5, 3 letters of recommendation, personal statement, academic writing sample; for doctorate, GRE (recommended), MA in Spanish or equivalent from accredited institution with minimum GPA of 3.75, 3 letters of recommendation, personal statement, academic writing sample. Additional exam requirements/recommendations for international students: Required—TOEFL (minimum score 550 paper-based; 83 iBT), IELTS (minimum score 6.5). Electronic applications accepted.

Auburn University, Graduate School, College of Education, Department of Curriculum and Teaching, Auburn University, AL 36849. Offers business education (M Ed, MS, PhD); early childhood education (M Ed, MS, PhD, Ed S); elementary education (M Ed, MS, PhD, Ed S); foreign languages (M Ed, MS); music education (M Ed, MS, PhD, Ed S); postsecondary education (PhD); reading education (PhD, Ed S); secondary education (M Ed, MS, PhD, Ed S), including English language arts, mathematics, science, social studies. *Accreditation:* NASM (one or more programs are accredited); NCATE. Part-time programs available. *Faculty:* 29 full-time (21 women), 4 part-time/adjunct (all women). *Students:* 61 full-time (40 women), 153 part-time (108 women); includes 37 minority (32 Black or African American, non-Hispanic/Latino; 2 Asian, non-Hispanic/Latino; 3 Hispanic/Latino), 1 international. Average age 34. 150 applicants, 59% accepted, 74 enrolled. In 2013, 70 master's, 6 doctorates, 26 other advanced degrees awarded. *Degree requirements:* For master's, thesis (for some programs); for doctorate, thesis/dissertation; for Ed S, field project. *Entrance requirements:* For master's, doctorate, and Ed S, GRE General Test. *Application deadline:* For fall admission, 7/7 for domestic students; for spring admission, 11/24 for domestic students. Applications are processed on a rolling basis. Application fee: $50 ($60 for international students). Electronic applications accepted. *Expenses:* Tuition, state resident: full-time $8262; part-time $459 per credit hour. Tuition, nonresident: full-time $24,786; part-time $1377 per credit hour. Tuition and fees vary according to degree level and program. *Financial support:* Fellowships, teaching assistantships, career-related internships or fieldwork, and Federal Work-Study available. Support available to part-time students. Financial award application deadline: 3/15; financial award applicants required to submit FAFSA. *Faculty research:* Emerging literacy, reading attitudes, music for at-risk youth, portfolio assessment. *Unit head:* Dr. Kimberly Walls, Head, 334-844-4434. *Application contact:* Dr. George Flowers, Dean of the Graduate School, 334-844-2125. Website: http://education.auburn.edu/academic_departments/curr/.

Bennington College, Graduate Programs, MA in Teaching a Second Language Program, Bennington, VT 05201. Offers education (MATSL); foreign language education (MATSL); French (MATSL); Spanish (MATSL). Part-time programs available. *Degree requirements:* For master's, one foreign language, 2 major projects and presentations. *Entrance requirements:* For master's, Oral Proficiency Interview (OPI). Additional exam requirements/recommendations for international students: Required—TOEFL (minimum score 577 paper-based; 91 iBT). *Expenses:* Contact institution. *Faculty research:* Acquisition, evaluation, assessment, conceptual teaching and learning, content-driven communication, applied linguistics.

Binghamton University, State University of New York, Graduate School, School of Education, Program in Adolescence Education, Vestal, NY 13850. Offers biology education (MAT, MS Ed); chemistry education (MAT, MS Ed); earth science education (MAT, MS Ed); English education (MAT, MS Ed); French education (MAT, MS Ed); literacy education (MS Ed); mathematical sciences education (MAT, MS Ed); physics (MAT, MS Ed); social studies (MAT, MS Ed); Spanish education (MAT, MS Ed). *Accreditation:* Teacher Education Accreditation Council. Part-time and evening/weekend programs available. *Students:* 48 full-time (29 women), 5 part-time (3 women); includes 7 minority (2 Black or African American, non-Hispanic/Latino; 3 Asian, non-Hispanic/Latino; 2 Hispanic/Latino), 1 international. Average age 26. 37 applicants, 86% accepted, 21 enrolled. In 2013, 34 master's awarded. *Entrance requirements:* For

master's, GRE General Test. Additional exam requirements/recommendations for international students: Required—TOEFL (minimum score 550 paper-based; 80 iBT). *Application deadline:* For fall admission, 2/1 priority date for domestic and international students; for spring admission, 10/15 priority date for domestic and international students. Applications are processed on a rolling basis. Application fee: $75. Electronic applications accepted. *Financial support:* In 2013–14, 7 students received support, including 1 fellowship with partial tuition reimbursement available (averaging $4,500 per year); career-related internships or fieldwork, Federal Work-Study, institutionally sponsored loans, scholarships/grants, health care benefits, tuition waivers (full), and unspecified assistantships also available. Financial award application deadline: 2/15; financial award applicants required to submit FAFSA. *Unit head:* Dr. S. G. Grant, Dean of School of Education, 607-777-7329, E-mail: sggrant@binghamton.edu. *Application contact:* Kishan Zuber, Recruiting and Admissions Coordinator, 607-777-2151, Fax: 607-777-2501, E-mail: kzuber@binghamton.edu.

Bowling Green State University, Graduate College, College of Arts and Sciences, Department of German, Russian, and East Asian Languages, Bowling Green, OH 43403. Offers German (MA, MAT); MA/MA. Part-time programs available. *Degree requirements:* For master's, one foreign language, thesis or alternative. *Entrance requirements:* For master's, GRE General Test. Additional exam requirements/recommendations for international students: Required—TOEFL. Electronic applications accepted.

Bowling Green State University, Graduate College, College of Arts and Sciences, Department of Romance and Classical Studies, Program in French, Bowling Green, OH 43403. Offers French (MA); French education (MAT). Part-time programs available. *Degree requirements:* For master's, one foreign language, thesis or alternative. *Entrance requirements:* For master's, GRE General Test. Additional exam requirements/recommendations for international students: Required—TOEFL. Electronic applications accepted. *Faculty research:* Francophone literature, French cinema, business French, nineteenth- and twentieth-century literature.

Bowling Green State University, Graduate College, College of Arts and Sciences, Department of Romance and Classical Studies, Program in Spanish, Bowling Green, OH 43403. Offers Spanish (MA); Spanish education (MAT). Part-time programs available. *Degree requirements:* For master's, one foreign language, thesis or alternative. *Entrance requirements:* For master's, GRE General Test. Additional exam requirements/recommendations for international students: Required—TOEFL. Electronic applications accepted. *Faculty research:* U.S. Latino literature and culture, Latin American film and popular culture, applied linguistics, Spanish popular culture.

Brigham Young University, Graduate Studies, College of Humanities, Center for Language Studies, Provo, UT 84602-1001. Offers second language teaching (MA). *Faculty:* 26 full-time (7 women). *Students:* 5 full-time (4 women), 12 part-time (9 women); includes 5 minority (4 Asian, non-Hispanic/Latino; 1 Hispanic/Latino). Average age 31. 8 applicants, 63% accepted, 5 enrolled. In 2013, 5 master's awarded. *Degree requirements:* For master's, one foreign language, comprehensive exam, thesis. *Entrance requirements:* For master's, GRE General Test (minimum score in 50th percentile on the verbal section and a rating of 4 on the analytical/writing section), demonstrated proficiency in ACTFL OPI rating in the language of specialization, English writing sample, minimum GPA of 3.0, three letters of recommendation, letter of intent, completion of teaching method class. Additional exam requirements/recommendations for international students: Required—TOEFL (minimum score 85 iBT). *Application deadline:* For fall admission, 2/1 for domestic and international students. Application fee: $50. Electronic applications accepted. *Expenses: Tuition:* Full-time $6130; part-time $340 per credit hour. Tuition and fees vary according to program and student's religious affiliation. *Financial support:* In 2013–14, 11 students received support, including 21 fellowships with partial tuition reimbursements available (averaging $1,955 per year); career-related internships or fieldwork, scholarships/grants, traineeships, tuition waivers (partial), and unspecified assistantships also available. Support available to part-time students. Financial award application deadline: 2/1. *Faculty research:* Second language vocabulary, applied linguistics, computer-assisted learning and instructing, language comprehension, testing sociolinguists. *Total annual research expenditures:* $875,000. *Unit head:* Dr. Ray T. Clifford, Director, 801-422-3263, Fax: 801-422-9741, E-mail: rayc@byu.edu. *Application contact:* Agnes Y. Welch, Program Manager/Graduate Secretary, 801-422-5199, Fax: 801-422-9741, E-mail: agnes_welch@byu.edu. Website: http://slat.byu.edu.

Brigham Young University, Graduate Studies, College of Humanities, Department of Spanish and Portuguese, Provo, UT 84602. Offers Portuguese (MA), including Luso-Brazilian literature, Portuguese linguistics, Portuguese pedagogy; Spanish (MA), including Hispanic linguistics, Hispanic literatures, Spanish pedagogy. *Faculty:* 28 full-time (5 women). *Students:* 21 full-time (10 women), 25 part-time (17 women); includes 19 minority (all Hispanic/Latino). Average age 32. 22 applicants, 68% accepted, 14 enrolled. In 2013, 10 master's awarded. *Degree requirements:* For master's, one foreign language, comprehensive exam, thesis, 1 semester of teaching. *Entrance requirements:* For master's, GRE, minimum GPA of 3.5 in Spanish or Portuguese, 3.3 overall. Additional exam requirements/recommendations for international students: Required—TOEFL (minimum score 580 paper-based; 85 iBT). *Application deadline:* For fall admission, 2/1 for domestic and international students. Application fee: $50. Electronic applications accepted. *Expenses: Tuition:* Full-time $6130; part-time $340 per credit hour. Tuition and fees vary according to program and student's religious affiliation. *Financial support:* In 2013–14, 30 students received support, including 71 teaching assistantships with partial tuition reimbursements available (averaging $3,500 per year); institutionally sponsored loans, scholarships/grants, tuition waivers (partial), and unspecified assistantships also available. Support available to part-time students. Financial award application deadline: 7/1. *Faculty research:* Mexican prose; Latin American theater, literature, phonetics and phonology; pedagogy; classical Portuguese literature; Peninsular prose and theater. *Unit head:* Dr. David P. Laraway, Chair, 801-422-3807, Fax: 801-422-0628, E-mail: david_laraway@byu.edu. *Application contact:* Jasmine S. Talbot, Graduate Secretary, 801-422-2196, Fax: 801-422-0628, E-mail: jasmine_talbot@byu.edu. Website: http://spanport.byu.edu/.

Brooklyn College of the City University of New York, Division of Graduate Studies, School of Education, Program in Adolescence Education and Special Subjects, Brooklyn, NY 11210-2889. Offers adolescence science education (MAT); art teacher (MA); biology teacher (MA); chemistry teacher (MA); earth science teacher (MAT); English teacher (MA); French teacher (MA); health and nutrition sciences: health teacher (MS Ed); mathematics teacher (MA); music education (CAS); music teacher (MA); physical education teacher (MS Ed); physics teacher (MA); social studies teacher (MA); Spanish teacher (MA). Part-time and evening/weekend programs available.

Degree requirements: For master's, comprehensive exam (for some programs), thesis (for some programs). *Entrance requirements:* For master's, LAST, previous course work in education, resume, 2 letters of recommendation, essay. Additional exam requirements/recommendations for international students: Required—TOEFL (minimum score 500 paper-based; 61 iBT). Electronic applications accepted. *Faculty research:* Interdisciplinary education, semiotics, discourse analysis, autobiography, teacher identity.

California State University, Chico, Office of Graduate Studies, College of Communication and Education, School of Education, Program in Teaching International Languages, Chico, CA 95929-0722. Offers MA. Part-time programs available. *Degree requirements:* For master's, comprehensive exam (for some programs), thesis or project. *Entrance requirements:* For master's, GRE, faculty mentor, statement of purpose. Additional exam requirements/recommendations for international students: Required—TOEFL (minimum score 550 paper-based; 80 iBT), IELTS (minimum score 6.5), PTE (minimum score 59). Electronic applications accepted.

California State University, Sacramento, Office of Graduate Studies, College of Arts and Letters, Department of Foreign Languages, Sacrament, CA 95819. Offers MA. Part-time programs available. *Entrance requirements:* For master's, interview, minimum GPA of 2.5 during previous 2 years of course work. Additional exam requirements/recommendations for international students: Required—TOEFL. *Application deadline:* For fall admission, 3/1 for domestic and international students; for spring admission, 9/30 for international students. Applications are processed on a rolling basis. Application fee: $55. Electronic applications accepted. *Financial support:* Teaching assistantships, career-related internships or fieldwork, and Federal Work-Study available. Support available to part-time students. Financial award application deadline: 3/1; financial award applicants required to submit FAFSA. *Unit head:* Bernice Bass de Martinez, Chair, 916-278-6333, Fax: 916-278-5502, E-mail: bbdem@csus.edu. *Application contact:* Jose Martinez, Graduate Admissions Supervisor, 916-278-7871, E-mail: martinj@skymail.csus.edu.
Website: http://www.csus.edu/fl.

Caribbean University, Graduate School, Bayamón, PR 00960-0493. Offers administration and supervision (MA Ed); criminal justice (MA); curriculum and instruction (MA Ed, PhD), including elementary education (MA Ed), English education (MA Ed), history education (MA Ed), mathematics education (MA Ed), primary education (MA Ed), science education (MA Ed), Spanish education (MA Ed); educational technology in instructional systems (MA Ed); gerontology (MSN); human resources (MBA); museology, archiving and art history (MA Ed); neonatal pediatrics (MSN); physical education (MA Ed); special education (MA Ed). *Entrance requirements:* For master's, interview, minimum GPA of 2.5.

Central Connecticut State University, School of Graduate Studies, School of Arts and Sciences, Department of Modern Languages, New Britain, CT 06050-4010. Offers modern language (MA, Certificate), including French, German (Certificate), Italian (Certificate), modern language (MA), Spanish language and Hispanic culture (MA); Spanish (MS, Certificate). Part-time and evening/weekend programs available. *Faculty:* 5 full-time (4 women). *Students:* 5 full-time (3 women), 28 part-time (23 women); includes 18 minority (2 Black or African American, non-Hispanic/Latino; 16 Hispanic/Latino). Average age 37. 20 applicants, 85% accepted, 14 enrolled. In 2013, 11 master's awarded. *Degree requirements:* For master's, one foreign language, comprehensive exam, thesis or alternative; for Certificate, qualifying exam. *Entrance requirements:* For master's, minimum undergraduate GPA of 2.7, 24 credits of undergraduate courses in either Italian or Spanish. Additional exam requirements/recommendations for international students: Required—TOEFL (minimum score 550 paper-based; 79 iBT). *Application deadline:* For fall admission, 6/1 for domestic students, 5/1 for international students; for spring admission, 11/1 for domestic and international students. Applications are processed on a rolling basis. Application fee: $50. Electronic applications accepted. Part-time tuition and fees vary according to degree level. *Financial support:* In 2013–14, 2 students received support, including 2 research assistantships; career-related internships or fieldwork, Federal Work-Study, scholarships/grants, and unspecified assistantships also available. Support available to part-time students. Financial award application deadline: 3/1; financial award applicants required to submit FAFSA. *Faculty research:* Quebecois literature, Caribbean literature, modern French/Spanish drama, Puerto Rican novel and drama. *Unit head:* Dr. Lilian Uribe, Chair, 860-832-2875, E-mail: uribe@ccsu.edu. *Application contact:* Patricia Gardner, Associate Director of Graduate Studies, 860-832-2350, Fax: 860-832-2362, E-mail: graduateadmissions@ccsu.edu.
Website: http://www.modlang.ccsu.edu/.

Christopher Newport University, Graduate Studies, Department of Teacher Preparation, Newport News, VA 23606-3072. Offers art (PK-12) (MAT); biology (6-12) (MAT); chemistry (6-12) (MAT); computer science (6-12) (MAT); elementary (PK-6) (MAT); English (6-12) (MAT); English as second language (PK-12) (MAT); French (PK-12) (MAT); history and social science (6-12) (MAT); mathematics (6-12) (MAT); music (PK-12) (MAT), including choral, instrumental; physics (6-12) (MAT); Spanish (PK-12) (MAT). Part-time programs available. *Faculty:* 15 full-time (7 women), 14 part-time/adjunct (13 women). *Students:* 74 full-time (64 women), 2 part-time (both women); includes 6 minority (4 Hispanic/Latino; 2 Two or more races, non-Hispanic/Latino). Average age 23. 90 applicants, 100% accepted, 67 enrolled. In 2013, 96 master's awarded. *Degree requirements:* For master's, comprehensive exam, thesis or alternative. *Entrance requirements:* For master's, PRAXIS I, minimum GPA of 3.0. Additional exam requirements/recommendations for international students: Required—TOEFL (minimum score 580 paper-based; 92 iBT). *Application deadline:* For fall admission, 4/1 for international students; for spring admission, 10/15 for domestic students, 10/1 for international students; for summer admission, 1/15 for domestic students, 3/1 for international students. Applications are processed on a rolling basis. Application fee: $50. Electronic applications accepted. *Expenses: Tuition, area resident:* Part-time $498 per credit hour. Tuition, state resident: part-time $498 per credit hour. Tuition, nonresident: part-time $899 per credit hour. *Financial support:* In 2013–14, 3 students received support, including 3 research assistantships with full tuition reimbursements available (averaging $2,000 per year); career-related internships or fieldwork, Federal Work-Study, and unspecified assistantships also available. Financial award application deadline: 3/1; financial award applicants required to submit FAFSA. *Faculty research:* Early literacy development, instructional innovations, professional teaching standards, multicultural issues, aesthetic education. *Total annual research expenditures:* $24,000. *Unit head:* Dr. Marsha Sprague, Director, 757-594-7388, Fax: 757-594-7803, E-mail: msprague@cnu.edu. *Application contact:* Lyn Sawyer, Associate Director, Graduate Admissions, 757-594-7544, Fax: 757-594-7649, E-mail: gradstdy@cnu.edu.

Cleveland State University, College of Graduate Studies, College of Education and Human Services, Department of Teacher Education, Cleveland, OH 44115. Offers art education (M Ed); early childhood education (M Ed); foreign language education (M Ed); mathematics and science education (M Ed); middle childhood education (M Ed); special education (M Ed), including mild/moderate disabilities, moderate/intensive disabilities; teaching English to speakers of other languages (M Ed). Part-time and evening/weekend programs available. *Faculty:* 20 full-time (12 women), 26 part-time/adjunct (20 women). *Students:* 108 full-time (78 women), 311 part-time (252 women); includes 103 minority (80 Black or African American, non-Hispanic/Latino; 2 Asian, non-Hispanic/Latino; 10 Hispanic/Latino; 1 Native Hawaiian or other Pacific Islander, non-Hispanic/Latino; 10 Two or more races, non-Hispanic/Latino), 52 international. Average age 32. 177 applicants, 55% accepted, 68 enrolled. In 2013, 192 master's awarded. *Degree requirements:* For master's, comprehensive exam (for some programs), thesis or alternative. *Entrance requirements:* For master's, GRE General Test or MAT, minimum GPA of 2.75. Additional exam requirements/recommendations for international students: Required—TOEFL (minimum score 525 paper-based), IELTS (minimum score 6). *Application deadline:* For fall admission, 7/15 priority date for domestic students. Applications are processed on a rolling basis. Application fee: $30. *Expenses:* Tuition, state resident: full-time $8335; part-time $521 per credit hour. Tuition, nonresident: full-time $15,670; part-time $979 per credit hour. *Required fees:* $50; $25 per semester. *Financial support:* In 2013–14, 12 research assistantships with full tuition reimbursements (averaging $3,480 per year) were awarded; tuition waivers (partial) and unspecified assistantships also available. *Faculty research:* Early literacy, professional development in reading, reading recovery, dual language, induction programs. *Total annual research expenditures:* $6.2 million. *Unit head:* Dr. Clifford T. Bennett, Chairperson, 216-523-7105, Fax: 216-687-5379, E-mail: c.t.bennett@csuohio.edu. *Application contact:* Deborah L. Brown, Interim Assistant Director, Graduate Admissions, 216-523-7572, E-mail: d.l.brown@csuohio.edu.
Website: http://www.csuohio.edu/cehs/departments/TE/te_dept.html.

The College at Brockport, State University of New York, School of Education and Human Services, Department of Education and Human Development, Brockport, NY 14420-2997. Offers adolescence education (MS Ed), including adolescence biology education, adolescence chemistry education, adolescence earth science education, adolescence English education, adolescence mathematics education, adolescence physics education, adolescence social studies education; adolescence inclusive generalist education (MS Ed), including English, mathematics, science, social studies; bilingual education (MS Ed, AGC), including bilingual education, Spanish (AGC); childhood curriculum specialist (MS Ed); childhood literacy (MS Ed). *Accreditation:* NCATE. *Faculty:* 14 full-time (10 women), 11 part-time/adjunct (7 women). *Students:* 52 full-time (34 women), 177 part-time (138 women); includes 19 minority (5 Black or African American, non-Hispanic/Latino; 1 American Indian or Alaska Native, non-Hispanic/Latino; 2 Asian, non-Hispanic/Latino; 9 Hispanic/Latino; 2 Two or more races, non-Hispanic/Latino). 81 applicants, 81% accepted, 44 enrolled. In 2013, 71 master's, 3 AGCs awarded. *Degree requirements:* For master's, thesis or alternative. *Entrance requirements:* For master's, minimum GPA of 3.0, letters of recommendation, interview (for some programs); statement of objectives, current resume. Additional exam requirements/recommendations for international students: Required—TOEFL (minimum score 550 paper-based; 79 iBT), IELTS (minimum score 6.5). *Application deadline:* For fall admission, 3/15 priority date for domestic and international students; for spring admission, 10/15 priority date for domestic and international students; for summer admission, 3/15 priority date for domestic and international students. Application fee: $80. Electronic applications accepted. *Expenses:* Tuition, state resident: full-time $9870. Tuition, nonresident: full-time $18,350. *Required fees:* $1848. *Financial support:* In 2013–14, 1 fellowship with full tuition reimbursement (averaging $7,500 per year), 1 teaching assistantship with full tuition reimbursement (averaging $6,000 per year) were awarded; Federal Work-Study, scholarships/grants, and unspecified assistantships also available. Support available to part-time students. Financial award application deadline: 3/15; financial award applicants required to submit FAFSA. *Faculty research:* Educational assessment, literacy education, inclusive education, teacher preparation, qualitative methodology. *Unit head:* Dr. Don Halquist, Chairperson, 585-395-5550, Fax: 585-395-2172, E-mail: snovinge@brockport.edu. *Application contact:* Michael Harrison, Coordinator of Certification and Graduate Advisement, 585-395-2326, Fax: 585-395-2172, E-mail: mharriso@brockport.edu.
Website: http://www.brockport.edu/ehd/.

College of Charleston, Graduate School, School of Education, Health, and Human Performance, Program in Languages, Charleston, SC 29424-0001. Offers M Ed. Part-time and evening/weekend programs available. *Degree requirements:* For master's, comprehensive exam or portfolio. *Entrance requirements:* For master's, minimum GPA of 2.5. Additional exam requirements/recommendations for international students: Required—TOEFL (minimum score 81 iBT). Electronic applications accepted.

The College of William and Mary, School of Education, Program in Curriculum and Instruction, Williamsburg, VA 23187-8795. Offers elementary education (MA Ed); gifted education (MA Ed); literacy leadership (MA Ed); math specialist (MA Ed); secondary education (MA Ed), including English education, mathematics education, modern foreign languages education, science education, social studies education; special education (MA Ed), including collaborating master educator, general curriculum. *Accreditation:* NCATE. Part-time programs available. *Faculty:* 15 full-time (10 women), 44 part-time/adjunct (38 women). *Students:* 66 full-time (55 women), 27 part-time (26 women); includes 17 minority (4 Black or African American, non-Hispanic/Latino; 1 American Indian or Alaska Native, non-Hispanic/Latino; 3 Asian, non-Hispanic/Latino; 5 Hispanic/Latino; 4 Two or more races, non-Hispanic/Latino). Average age 28. 179 applicants, 72% accepted, 92 enrolled. In 2013, 76 master's awarded. *Degree requirements:* For master's, project. *Entrance requirements:* For master's, GRE or MAT, minimum GPA of 2.5. Additional exam requirements/recommendations for international students: Required—TOEFL, IELTS. *Application deadline:* For fall admission, 1/15 for domestic and international students; for spring admission, 10/1 for domestic and international students. Application fee: $50. Electronic applications accepted. *Expenses:* Tuition, state resident: full-time $7120; part-time $405 per credit hour. Tuition, nonresident: full-time $21,639; part-time $1050 per credit hour. *Required fees:* $4764. *Financial support:* In 2013–14, 49 students received support, including 6 research assistantships with full and partial tuition reimbursements available (averaging $8,269 per year); career-related internships or fieldwork, Federal Work-Study, institutionally sponsored loans, scholarships/grants, and unspecified assistantships also available. Financial award application deadline: 1/15; financial award applicants required to submit FAFSA. *Faculty research:* National Council of Teachers of Mathematics standards, counseling, self-concept and self-esteem, special education, curriculum development. *Unit head:* Dr. Mark Hofer, Area Coordinator, 757-221-1713, E-mail: mjhofe@wm.edu. *Application contact:* Dorothy Smith Osborne, Assistant Dean for Academic Programs and Student Services, 757-221-2317, Fax: 757-221-2293, E-mail: dsosbo@wm.edu.
Website: http://education.wm.edu.

The Colorado College, Education Department, Program in Secondary Education, Colorado Springs, CO 80903-3294. Offers art teaching (K-12) (MAT); English teaching (MAT); foreign language teaching (MAT); mathematics teaching (MAT); music teaching (MAT); science teaching (MAT); social studies teaching (MAT). *Degree requirements:* For master's, thesis, internship. Electronic applications accepted.

Colorado State University, Graduate School, College of Liberal Arts, Department of Foreign Languages and Literatures, Fort Collins, CO 80523-1774. Offers MA. Part-time programs available. *Faculty:* 14 full-time (6 women). *Students:* 14 full-time (10 women), 3 part-time (2 women); includes 1 minority (Hispanic/Latino), 4 international. Average age 27. 23 applicants, 57% accepted, 8 enrolled. In 2013, 8 master's awarded. *Degree*

requirements: For master's, one foreign language, comprehensive exam (for some programs), thesis or paper, competitive exams. *Entrance requirements:* For master's, minimum GPA of 3.0; undergraduate major/proficiency in foreign languages, BA/BS in related field, statement of purpose, biographical statement, 3 letters of recommendation, resume, transcripts, writing sample. Additional exam requirements/recommendations for international students: Required—TOEFL (minimum score 550 paper-based; 80 iBT). *Application deadline:* For fall admission, 2/15 priority date for domestic students; for spring admission, 7/15 priority date for domestic students. Applications are processed on a rolling basis. Application fee: $50. Electronic applications accepted. *Expenses:* Tuition, state resident: full-time $9075.40; part-time $504 per credit. Tuition, nonresident: full-time $22,248; part-time $1236 per credit. *Required fees:* $1819; $60 per credit. *Financial support:* In 2013–14, 11 students received support, including 11 teaching assistantships with full tuition reimbursements available (averaging $12,888 per year); career-related internships or fieldwork, scholarships/grants, and unspecified assistantships also available. Financial award application deadline: 3/1; financial award applicants required to submit FAFSA. *Faculty research:* French, German, and Hispanic literatures and cultures; video-assisted language learning; computer-assisted language learners; foreign language teaching methodologies; linguistics. *Total annual research expenditures:* $388. *Unit head:* Dr. Paola Malpezzi-Price, Chair, 970-491-3838, Fax: 970-491-2822, E-mail: paola.malpezzi_price@colostate.edu. *Application contact:* Dr. Frederique Grim, Graduate Coordinator, 970-491-3867, Fax: 970-491-2822, E-mail: frederique.grim@colostate.edu.
Website: http://languages.colostate.edu/.

Colorado State University–Pueblo, College of Education, Engineering and Professional Studies, Education Program, Pueblo, CO 81001-4901. Offers art education (M Ed); foreign language education (M Ed); health and physical education (M Ed); instructional technology (M Ed); linguistically diverse education (M Ed); music education (M Ed); special education (M Ed). *Accreditation:* Teacher Education Accreditation Council. Part-time programs available. *Degree requirements:* For master's, portfolio. *Entrance requirements:* For master's, 3 recommendations, teaching license. Additional exam requirements/recommendations for international students: Required—TOEFL (minimum score 500 paper-based). Electronic applications accepted. *Faculty research:* Portfolio assessment, math education, science education.

Columbia University, Graduate School of Arts and Sciences, New York, NY 10027. Offers African-American studies (MA); American studies (MA); anthropology (MA, PhD); art history and archaeology (MA, PhD); astronomy (PhD); biological sciences (PhD); biotechnology (MA); chemical physics (PhD); chemistry (PhD); classical studies (MA, PhD); classics (MA, PhD); climate and society (MA); earth and environmental sciences (PhD); East Asia: regional studies (MA); East Asian languages and cultures (MA, PhD); ecology, evolution and environmental biology (MA), including conservation biology; ecology, evolution, and environmental biology (PhD), including ecology and evolutionary biology, evolutionary primatology; economics (PhD); English and comparative literature (MA, PhD); French and Romance philology (MA, PhD); Germanic languages (MA, PhD); global French studies (MA); Hispanic cultural studies (MA); history (PhD); history and literature (MA); human rights studies (MA); Islamic studies (MA); Italian (MA, PhD); Japanese pedagogy (MA); Jewish studies (MA); Latin America and the Caribbean: regional studies (MA); Latin American and Iberian cultures (PhD); mathematics (MA, PhD), including finance (MA); medieval and Renaissance studies (MA); Middle Eastern, South Asian, and African studies (MA, PhD); modern art: critical and curatorial studies (MA); modern European studies (MA); museum anthropology (MA); music (DMA, PhD); oral history (MA); philosophical foundations of physics (MA); philosophy (MA, PhD); physics (PhD); political science (MA, PhD); psychology (PhD); quantitative methods in the social sciences (MA); religion (MA, PhD); Russia, Eurasia and East Europe: regional studies (MA); Russian translation (MA); Slavic cultures (MA); Slavic languages (MA, PhD); sociology (MA, PhD); South Asian studies (MA); statistics (MA, PhD); theatre (PhD); JD/PhD; MA/MS; MD/PhD; MPA/MA. Dual-degree programs require admission to both Graduate School of Arts and Sciences and another Columbia school. Part-time and evening/weekend programs available. *Faculty:* 808 full-time (310 women). *Students:* 2,755 full-time, 354 part-time; includes 493 minority (80 Black or African American, non-Hispanic/Latino; 6 American Indian or Alaska Native, non-Hispanic/Latino; 215 Asian, non-Hispanic/Latino; 135 Hispanic/Latino; 3 Native Hawaiian or other Pacific Islander, non-Hispanic/Latino; 54 Two or more races, non-Hispanic/Latino), 1,433 international. 12,949 applicants, 19% accepted, 998 enrolled. In 2013, 969 master's, 461 doctorates awarded. Terminal master's awarded for partial completion of doctoral program. *Degree requirements:* For master's, thesis (for some programs); for doctorate, comprehensive exam, thesis/dissertation. *Entrance requirements:* For master's and doctorate, GRE General Test, GRE Subject Test (for some programs). Application fee: $105. Electronic applications accepted. *Financial support:* Application deadline: 12/15. *Faculty research:* Humanities, natural sciences, social sciences. *Unit head:* Carlos J. Alonso, Dean of the Graduate School of Arts and Sciences, 212-854-5177. *Application contact:* GSAS Office of Admissions, 212-854-8903, E-mail: gsas-admissions@columbia.edu.
Website: http://gsas.columbia.edu/.

Concordia College, Program in Education, Moorhead, MN 56562. Offers world language instruction (M Ed). *Degree requirements:* For master's, thesis/seminar. *Entrance requirements:* For master's, 2 professional references, 1 personal reference.

Cornell University, Graduate School, Graduate Fields of Arts and Sciences, Field of Linguistics, Ithaca, NY 14853-0001. Offers applied linguistics (MA, PhD); East Asian linguistics (MA, PhD); English linguistics (MA, PhD); general linguistics (MA, PhD); Germanic linguistics (MA, PhD); Indo-European linguistics (MA, PhD); phonetics (MA, PhD); phonological theory (MA, PhD); Romance linguistics (MA, PhD); second language acquisition (MA, PhD); semantics (MA, PhD); Slavic linguistics (MA, PhD); sociolinguistics (MA, PhD); South Asian linguistics (MA, PhD); Southeast Asian linguistics (MA, PhD); syntactic theory (MA, PhD). *Faculty:* 18 full-time (7 women). *Students:* 29 full-time (17 women); includes 5 minority (1 Asian, non-Hispanic/Latino; 2 Hispanic/Latino; 2 Two or more races, non-Hispanic/Latino), 13 international. Average age 28. 98 applicants, 16% accepted, 11 enrolled. In 2013, 9 master's, 2 doctorates awarded. Terminal master's awarded for partial completion of doctoral program. *Degree requirements:* For master's, one foreign language, thesis; for doctorate, one foreign language, comprehensive exam, thesis/dissertation. *Entrance requirements:* For master's and doctorate, GRE General Test, 2 letters of recommendation. Additional exam requirements/recommendations for international students: Required—TOEFL (minimum score 600 paper-based; 77 iBT). *Application deadline:* For fall admission, 1/15 for domestic students. Application fee: $95. Electronic applications accepted. *Financial support:* In 2013–14, 26 students received support, including 13 fellowships with full tuition reimbursements available, 13 teaching assistantships with full tuition reimbursements available; research assistantships with full tuition reimbursements available, institutionally sponsored loans, scholarships/grants, health care benefits, tuition waivers (full and partial), and unspecified assistantships also available. Financial award applicants required to submit FAFSA. *Faculty research:* Phonology and phonetics, syntax and semantics, historical linguistics, philosophy of language, language acquisition. *Unit head:* Director of Graduate Studies, 607-255-1105. *Application contact:* Graduate Field Assistant, 607-255-1105, E-mail: lingfield@cornell.edu.
Website: http://www.gradschool.cornell.edu/fields.php?id-90&a-2.

Delaware State University, Graduate Programs, Department of English and Foreign Languages, Dover, DE 19901-2277. Offers French (MA); Spanish (MA). *Entrance requirements:* Additional exam requirements/recommendations for international students: Required—TOEFL (minimum score 550 paper-based). Electronic applications accepted.

DePaul University, College of Education, Chicago, IL 60614. Offers bilingual bicultural education (M Ed, MA); counseling (M Ed, MA), including clinical mental health counseling, college student development, school counseling; curriculum studies (M Ed, MA, Ed D); early childhood education (M Ed, MA, Ed D); educating adults (MA); educational leadership (M Ed, MA, Ed D), including administration and supervision (M Ed, MA), principal preparation (M Ed, MA); elementary education (MA); mathematics education (MA); mathematics for teaching (MS); middle school mathematics education (MS); reading specialist (M Ed, MA); secondary education (M Ed); social and cultural foundations in education (MA); special education (M Ed, MA); world languages education (M Ed, MA). Part-time and evening/weekend programs available. Postbaccalaureate distance learning degree programs offered (no on-campus study). *Faculty:* 61 full-time (35 women), 59 part-time/adjunct (43 women). *Students:* 628 full-time (486 women), 324 part-time (243 women); includes 304 minority (144 Black or African American, non-Hispanic/Latino; 1 American Indian or Alaska Native, non-Hispanic/Latino; 38 Asian, non-Hispanic/Latino; 98 Hispanic/Latino; 23 Two or more races, non-Hispanic/Latino), 24 international. Average age 30. In 2013, 465 master's, 4 doctorates awarded. *Degree requirements:* For doctorate, thesis/dissertation. *Application deadline:* For fall admission, 8/15 for domestic students; for winter admission, 12/1 for domestic students; for spring admission, 3/1 for domestic students. Applications are processed on a rolling basis. Application fee: $40. Electronic applications accepted. Tuition and fees vary according to course level, course load and degree level. *Financial support:* Application deadline: 12/31; applicants required to submit FAFSA. *Unit head:* Dr. Paul Zionts, Dean, 773-325-7581, Fax: 773-325-7713, E-mail: pzionts@depaul.edu. *Application contact:* Farrah Dalal, Assistant Director, 773-325-2465, Fax: 773-325-2270, E-mail: fdalal@depaul.edu.
Website: http://education.depaul.edu.

Drew University, Caspersen School of Graduate Studies, Program in Education, Madison, NJ 07940-1493. Offers biology (MAT); chemistry (MAT); English (MAT); French (MAT); Italian (MAT); math (MAT); physics (MAT); social studies (MAT); Spanish (MAT); theatre arts (MAT). Part-time programs available. *Degree requirements:* For master's, student teaching internship and seminar. *Entrance requirements:* For master's, transcripts, statement of purpose, three letters of recommendation. Additional exam requirements/recommendations for international students: Required—TOEFL. *Expenses:* Contact institution.

Duquesne University, School of Education, Department of Instruction and Leadership, Program in Secondary Education, Pittsburgh, PA 15282-0001. Offers biology (MS Ed); chemistry (MS Ed); English (MS Ed); K-12 education (MS Ed), including Latin; mathematics (MS Ed); physics (MS Ed); social studies (MS Ed). Part-time and evening/weekend programs available. *Faculty:* 4 full-time (2 women). *Students:* 44 full-time (23 women), 3 part-time (2 women); includes 7 minority (6 Black or African American, non-Hispanic/Latino; 1 Two or more races, non-Hispanic/Latino), 1 international. Average age 27. 43 applicants, 35% accepted, 15 enrolled. In 2013, 28 master's awarded. *Degree requirements:* For master's, thesis optional. *Entrance requirements:* For master's, letters of recommendation, letter of intent, interview, bachelor's degree. Additional exam requirements/recommendations for international students: Required—TOEFL (minimum score 550 paper-based), IELTS (minimum score 7). *Application deadline:* For fall admission, 9/1 for domestic students; for spring admission, 1/1 for domestic students. Applications are processed on a rolling basis. Application fee: $0. Electronic applications accepted. Application fee is waived when completed online. *Expenses: Tuition:* Full-time $18,162; part-time $1009 per credit. *Required fees:* $1728; $96 per credit. Tuition and fees vary according to program. *Financial support:* Research assistantships and Federal Work-Study available. Support available to part-time students. *Unit head:* Dr. Melissa Boston, Associate Professor and Director, 412-396-6109, E-mail: bostonm@duq.edu. *Application contact:* Michael Dolinger, Director of Student and Academic Services, 412-396-6647, Fax: 412-396-5585, E-mail: dolingerm@duq.edu.
Website: http://www.duq.edu/academics/schools/education/graduate-programs-education/ms-ed-secondary-education.

Eastern University, Graduate Education Programs, St. Davids, PA 19087-3696. Offers ESL program specialist (K-12) (Certificate); general supervisor (PreK-12) (Certificate); health and physical education (K-12) (Certificate); middle level (4-8) (Certificate); multicultural education (M Ed); pre K-4 (Certificate); pre K-4 with special education (Certificate); reading (M Ed); reading specialist (K-12) (Certificate); reading supervisor (K-12) (Certificate); school health services (M Ed); school health supervisor (Certificate); school nurse (Certificate); school principalship (K-12) (Certificate); secondary biology education (7-12) (Certificate); secondary chemistry education (7-12) (Certificate); secondary communication education (7-12) (Certificate); secondary education (7-12) (Certificate); secondary English education (7-12) (Certificate); secondary math education (7-12) (Certificate); secondary social studies education (7-12) (Certificate); special education (M Ed); special education (7-12) (Certificate); special education (Pre K-8) (Certificate); special education supervisor (N-12) (Certificate); TESOL (M Ed); world language (Certificate), including French, Mandarin Chinese, Spanish. Part-time and evening/weekend programs available. Postbaccalaureate distance learning degree programs offered (no on-campus study). *Faculty:* 22 full-time (11 women), 26 part-time/adjunct (18 women). *Students:* 77 full-time (58 women), 223 part-time (149 women); includes 112 minority (81 Black or African American, non-Hispanic/Latino; 1 American Indian or Alaska Native, non-Hispanic/Latino; 9 Asian, non-Hispanic/Latino; 18 Hispanic/Latino; 1 Native Hawaiian or other Pacific Islander, non-Hispanic/Latino; 2 Two or more races, non-Hispanic/Latino), 7 international. Average age 34. 94 applicants, 100% accepted, 81 enrolled. In 2013, 120 master's awarded. *Entrance requirements:* For master's, minimum GPA of 2.5 (for M Ed); for Certificate, minimum GPA of 3.0 for certifications. Additional exam requirements/recommendations for international students: Required—TOEFL. *Application deadline:* For fall admission, 8/14 for domestic students; for spring admission, 12/20 for domestic students. Applications are processed on a rolling basis. Application fee: $35. Application fee is waived when completed online. *Expenses: Tuition:* Full-time $15,600; part-time $650 per credit. *Required fees:* $27.50 per semester. One-time fee: $50. Tuition and fees vary according to course load, degree level and program. *Financial support:* In 2013–14, 84 students received support, including 6 research assistantships with partial tuition reimbursements available (averaging $7,710 per year); scholarships/grants and unspecified assistantships also available. Financial award application deadline: 3/15; financial award applicants required to submit FAFSA. *Unit head:* Harry Gutelius, Associate Dean, 610-341-1729. *Application contact:* Michael Perpiglia, Associate Director of Enrollment, 610-341-5947, Fax: 484-581-1276, E-mail: mperpigl@eastern.edu.
Website: http://www.eastern.edu/academics/programs/loeb-school-education-0/graduateprograms.

Elms College, Division of Education, Chicopee, MA 01013-2839. Offers early childhood education (MAT); education (M Ed, CAGS); elementary education (MAT); English as a

second language (MAT); reading (MAT); secondary education (MAT), including biology education, English education, Spanish education; special education (MAT). Part-time and evening/weekend programs available. *Degree requirements:* For master's, thesis (for some programs). *Entrance requirements:* For master's, Massachusetts Educators Certification Test, minimum GPA of 3.0; for CAGS, master's degree in education. Additional exam requirements/recommendations for international students: Required—TOEFL.

Florida International University, College of Education, Department of Teaching and Learning, Miami, FL 33199. Offers art education (MA, MS); curriculum and instruction (MS, Ed D, PhD, Ed S), including curriculum development (MS), elementary education (MS), English education (MS), learning technologies (MS), mathematics education (MS), modern language education (MS), physical education (MS), science education (MS), social studies education (MS), special education (MS); early childhood education (MS); exceptional student education (Ed D); foreign language education (MS), including foreign language education, teaching English to speakers of other languages (TESOL); international/intercultural education (MS); language, literacy and culture (PhD); mathematics, science, and learning technologies (PhD); physical education (MS), including sport and fitness; reading education (MS). Part-time and evening/weekend programs available. *Degree requirements:* For doctorate, comprehensive exam, thesis/dissertation. *Entrance requirements:* For master's, GRE General Test, Florida General Knowledge Test or Florida College Level Academic Skills Test; for doctorate and Ed S, GRE General Test. Additional exam requirements/recommendations for international students: Required—TOEFL (minimum score 550 paper-based; 80 iBT), IELTS (minimum score 6.3). Electronic applications accepted.

Florida State University, The Graduate School, College of Education, School of Teacher Education, Tallahassee, FL 32306. Offers curriculum and instruction (MS, MST, PhD, Ed S), including early childhood education (MS, PhD, Ed S), elementary education (MS, PhD, Ed S), English education (MS, PhD, Ed S), English teaching (MST), exceptional student education (MST), foreign and second language education (MS, PhD, Ed S), foreign and second language teaching (MST), math education (MS, PhD, Ed S), math teaching (MST), reading education and language arts (MS, PhD, Ed S), science education (MS, PhD, Ed S), social science education (MS, PhD, Ed S), social science teaching (MST), special education (MS, PhD, Ed S), special education studies (MST), visual disabilities (MS, Ed S). Part-time programs available. *Faculty:* 30 full-time (20 women), 22 part-time/adjunct (18 women). *Students:* 183 full-time (151 women), 92 part-time (80 women); includes 47 minority (20 Black or African American, non-Hispanic/Latino; 3 American Indian or Alaska Native, non-Hispanic/Latino; 1 Asian, non-Hispanic/Latino; 20 Hispanic/Latino; 3 Two or more races, non-Hispanic/Latino), 61 international. Average age 30. 199 applicants, 79% accepted, 86 enrolled. In 2013, 119 master's, 9 doctorates, 4 other advanced degrees awarded. *Degree requirements:* For master's and Ed S, comprehensive exam, thesis optional; for doctorate, comprehensive exam, thesis/dissertation, preliminary exam, prospectus defense. *Entrance requirements:* For master's, doctorate, and Ed S, GRE General Test, minimum GPA of 3.0. Additional exam requirements/recommendations for international students: Required—TOEFL (minimum score 550 paper-based; 80 iBT). *Application deadline:* For fall admission, 7/1 for domestic and international students; for winter admission, 10/1 for domestic students, 11/1 for international students; for spring admission, 3/1 for domestic and international students. Applications are processed on a rolling basis. Application fee: $30. Electronic applications accepted. *Expenses:* Tuition, state resident: part-time $403.51 per credit hour. Tuition, nonresident: part-time $1004.85 per credit hour. *Required fees:* $75.81 per credit hour. One-time fee: $20 part-time. Tuition and fees vary according to course load, campus/location and student level. *Financial support:* In 2013–14, 113 students received support, including 55 research assistantships with full and partial tuition reimbursements available, 18 teaching assistantships with full and partial tuition reimbursements available; fellowships with full and partial tuition reimbursements available, career-related internships or fieldwork, scholarships/grants, health care benefits, and unspecified assistantships also available. Financial award application deadline: 1/15; financial award applicants required to submit FAFSA. *Faculty research:* Effective intervention and assessment strategies to improve reading skills; literacy teaching and learning through technology; understanding of student sense-making through instructions, especially STEM learning for all students; international education and consequences of globalization; support professional teacher development and adoption of effective/transformative practices. *Total annual research expenditures:* $1.3 million. *Unit head:* Dr. Sherry Southerland, Chair, 850-644-4880, Fax: 850-644-7736, E-mail: ssoutherland@admin.fsu.edu. *Application contact:* Dawn Matthews, Academic Support Assistant, 850-644-2122, Fax: 850-644-7736, E-mail: dmatthews@fsu.edu.
Website: http://www.coe.fsu.edu/STE.

Framingham State University, Continuing Education, Program in Spanish, Framingham, MA 01701-9101. Offers M Ed.

George Mason University, College of Humanities and Social Sciences, Department of Modern and Classical Languages, Fairfax, VA 22030. Offers foreign languages (MA). *Faculty:* 32 full-time (25 women), 39 part-time/adjunct (32 women). *Students:* 8 full-time (6 women), 20 part-time (18 women); includes 13 minority (4 Black or African American, non-Hispanic/Latino; 1 Asian, non-Hispanic/Latino; 6 Hispanic/Latino; 2 Two or more races, non-Hispanic/Latino), 1 international. Average age 35. 22 applicants, 77% accepted, 9 enrolled. In 2013, 12 master's awarded. *Degree requirements:* For master's, comprehensive exam, thesis optional. *Entrance requirements:* For master's, 3 letters of recommendation; official transcripts; goals statement; baccalaureate degree in French or Spanish with minimum GPA of 3.0 (recommended). Additional exam requirements/recommendations for international students: Required—TOEFL (minimum score 570 paper-based; 88 iBT), IELTS (minimum score 6.5), PTE. *Application deadline:* For fall admission, 5/15 priority date for domestic students; for spring admission, 11/1 priority date for domestic students. Application fee: $65 ($80 for international students). Electronic applications accepted. *Expenses:* Tuition, state resident: full-time $9350; part-time $390 per credit. Tuition, nonresident: full-time $25,754; part-time $1073 per credit. *Required fees:* $2688; $112 per credit. *Financial support:* In 2013–14, 2 students received support, including 2 teaching assistantships with full and partial tuition reimbursements available (averaging $11,572 per year); career-related internships or fieldwork, Federal Work-Study, scholarships/grants, unspecified assistantships, and health care benefits (for full-time research or teaching assistantship recipients) also available. Support available to part-time students. Financial award application deadline: 3/1; financial award applicants required to submit FAFSA. *Faculty research:* French Renaissance studies, early Modern (sixteenth-eighteenth centuries) literary and cultural studies, history, literature and philosophy, women's studies. *Unit head:* Julie Christensen, Chair, 703-993-1228, Fax: 703-993-1245, E-mail: jchriste@gmu.edu. *Application contact:* Jen Barnard, Information Contact, 703-993-1230, Fax: 703-993-1245, E-mail: jbarnard@gmu.edu.
Website: http://mcl.gmu.edu/.

Georgia Southern University, Jack N. Averitt College of Graduate Studies, College of Liberal Arts and Social Sciences, Department of Foreign Languages, Statesboro, GA 30460. Offers Spanish (MA). Part-time and evening/weekend programs available. *Students:* 13 full-time (8 women); includes 6 minority (2 Black or African American, non-Hispanic/Latino; 1 Asian, non-Hispanic/Latino; 3 Hispanic/Latino). Average age 26. 14 applicants, 71% accepted, 7 enrolled. In 2013, 11 master's awarded. *Degree requirements:* For master's, one foreign language, thesis optional. *Entrance requirements:* For master's, GRE, minimum GPA of 3.0, letters of reference. Additional exam requirements/recommendations for international students: Required—TOEFL (minimum score 550 paper-based; 80 iBT), IELTS (minimum score 6). *Application deadline:* For fall admission, 3/1 priority date for domestic and international students; for spring admission, 10/1 priority date for domestic students, 10/1 for international students. Applications are processed on a rolling basis. Application fee: $50. Electronic applications accepted. *Expenses:* Tuition, state resident: full-time $7068; part-time $270 per semester hour. Tuition, nonresident: full-time $26,446; part-time $1077 per semester hour. *Required fees:* $2092. *Financial support:* In 2013–14, 3 students received support, including research assistantships with partial tuition reimbursements available (averaging $7,200 per year), teaching assistantships with partial tuition reimbursements available (averaging $7,200 per year); career-related internships or fieldwork, Federal Work-Study, scholarships/grants, tuition waivers (partial), and unspecified assistantships also available. Support available to part-time students. Financial award application deadline: 4/15; financial award applicants required to submit FAFSA. *Faculty research:* Lettrism, twentieth-century France, Spanish medieval studies, Spanish Renaissance studies, Spanish-American colonial period, Mexican studies, Spanish linguistics, foreign language acquisition and education, drama and cinema of Spain and Latin America. *Unit head:* Dr. Eric Kartchner, Department Chair, 912-478-1381, Fax: 912-478-0652, E-mail: ekartchner@georgiasouthern.edu. *Application contact:* Amanda Gilliland, Coordinator for Graduate Student Recruitment, 912-478-5384, Fax: 912-478-0740, E-mail: gradadmissions@georgiasouthern.edu.
Website: http://class.georgiasouthern.edu/fl.

Georgia State University, College of Arts and Sciences, Department of Modern and Classical Languages, Program in French, Atlanta, GA 30302-3083. Offers applied linguistics and pedagogy (MA); French studies (MA); literature and culture (MA). Part-time programs available. *Students:* Average age 0. *Degree requirements:* For master's, one foreign language, comprehensive exam, thesis or alternative, Graduate Foreign Language Reading Exam. *Entrance requirements:* For master's, GRE, statement of purpose, writing sample in the target language, 2 letters of recommendation, official transcripts. Additional exam requirements/recommendations for international students: Required—TOEFL (minimum score 79 iBT). *Application deadline:* For fall admission, 3/15 priority date for domestic and international students; for spring admission, 11/15 priority date for domestic and international students. Application fee: $50. Electronic applications accepted. *Expenses: Tuition, area resident:* Full-time $4176; part-time $348 per credit hour. Tuition, state resident: full-time $14,544; part-time $1212 per credit hour. Tuition, nonresident: full-time $14,544; part-time $1212 per credit hour. Tuition and fees vary according to course load and program. *Financial support:* Institutionally sponsored loans available. Financial award applicants required to submit FAFSA. *Faculty research:* The nineteenth century novel, narratology, genetic criticism, poetics, semiotics, and intertextuality; Francophone and transnational studies; early modern travel literature; post/colonial and Diaspora studies; film studies; social and gender studies; eighteenth century French literature and history of ideas; history of civilization; Enlightenment, encyclopedism. *Unit head:* Dr. Fernando Reati, Department Chair, 404-413-5984, Fax: 404-413-5982, E-mail: freati@gsu.edu. *Application contact:* Lita Malveaux, Administrative Academic Specialist, 404-413-5046, Fax: 404-413-5036, E-mail: lmalveaux@gsu.edu.
Website: http://www.gsu.edu/~wwwmcl/.

Harding University, Cannon-Clary College of Education, Searcy, AR 72149-0001. Offers advanced studies in teaching and learning (M Ed); art (MSE); behavioral science (MSE); counseling (MS, Ed S); early childhood special education (M Ed, MSE); education (MSE); educational leadership (M Ed, Ed S); elementary education (M Ed); English (MSE); French (MSE); history/social science (MSE); kinesiology (MSE); math (MSE); reading (M Ed); secondary education (M Ed); Spanish (MSE); teaching (MAT); teaching English as a second language (MSE). *Accreditation:* NCATE. Part-time and evening/weekend programs available. *Faculty:* 13 full-time (5 women), 42 part-time/adjunct (24 women). *Students:* 154 full-time (119 women), 393 part-time (270 women); includes 108 minority (81 Black or African American, non-Hispanic/Latino; 5 American Indian or Alaska Native, non-Hispanic/Latino; 5 Asian, non-Hispanic/Latino; 9 Hispanic/Latino; 8 Two or more races, non-Hispanic/Latino), 15 international. Average age 36. 187 applicants, 79% accepted, 135 enrolled. In 2013, 138 master's, 17 other advanced degrees awarded. *Degree requirements:* For master's, comprehensive exam (for some programs), thesis optional, portfolio(s); for Ed S, comprehensive exam, portfolio, project. *Entrance requirements:* For master's, GRE, MAT, PRAXIS; for Ed S, MAT or GRE. Additional exam requirements/recommendations for international students: Required—TOEFL (minimum score 550 paper-based; 79 iBT). *Application deadline:* For fall admission, 8/1 for domestic and international students; for spring admission, 1/1 for domestic and international students. Applications are processed on a rolling basis. Application fee: $35. *Expenses: Tuition:* Full-time $11,574; part-time $643 per credit hour. *Required fees:* $432; $24 per credit hour. Tuition and fees vary according to course load, degree level and program. *Financial support:* In 2013–14, 36 students received support. Unspecified assistantships available. *Faculty research:* Reading, comprehension, school violence, educational technology, behavior, college choice, differentiated instruction, brain-based teaching. *Unit head:* Dr. Clara Carroll, Chair, 501-279-4501, Fax: 501-279-4083, E-mail: ccarroll@harding.edu. *Application contact:* Information Contact, 501-279-4315, E-mail: gradstudiesedu@harding.edu.
Website: http://www.harding.edu/education.

Hofstra University, School of Education, Programs in Teaching - K-12, Hempstead, NY 11549. Offers bilingual education (MA, Advanced Certificate); family and consumer sciences (MS Ed); fine arts and music education (Advanced Certificate); fine arts education (MA, MS Ed); middle childhood extensions (Advanced Certificate), including grades 5-6 or 7-9; music education (MA, MS Ed); teaching languages other than English and TESOL (MS Ed); TESOL (MS Ed, Advanced Certificate); wind conducting (MA).

Hofstra University, School of Education, Programs in Teaching - Secondary Education, Hempstead, NY 11549. Offers business education (MS Ed); education technology (Advanced Certificate); English education (MA, MS Ed); foreign language and TESOL (MS Ed); foreign language education (MA, MS Ed), including French, German, Russian, Spanish; mathematics education (MA, MS Ed); science education (MA, MS Ed), including biology, chemistry, earth science, geology, physics; secondary education (Advanced Certificate); social studies education (MA, MS Ed); technology for learning (MA).

Hunter College of the City University of New York, Graduate School, School of Arts and Sciences, Department of Romance Languages, Program in French, New York, NY 10065-5085. Offers French (MA); French education (MA). Part-time and evening/weekend programs available. *Faculty:* 4 full-time (all women). *Students:* 1 full-time (0 women), 9 part-time (8 women); includes 2 minority (1 Black or African American, non-Hispanic/Latino; 1 Hispanic/Latino). Average age 44. 3 applicants, 67% accepted, 1 enrolled. In 2013, 1 master's awarded. *Degree requirements:* For master's, 2 foreign languages, comprehensive exam, thesis optional. *Entrance requirements:* For master's, GRE General Test, GRE Subject Test, ability to read, speak, and write French;

interview. Additional exam requirements/recommendations for international students: Required—TOEFL. *Application deadline:* For fall admission, 4/1 for domestic students, 2/1 for international students; for spring admission, 11/1 for domestic students, 9/1 for international students. Application fee: $125. *Financial support:* Fellowships, Federal Work-Study, scholarships/grants, and tuition waivers (partial) available. Support available to part-time students. Financial award application deadline: 4/15. *Faculty research:* Contemporary French theater, Villiers de l 'Isle-Adam, Voltaire, medieval folklore, fin-de-sicle. *Unit head:* Prof. Marlene Barsoum, Graduate Advisor, 212-650-3511, E-mail: mbarsoum@hunter.cuny.edu. *Application contact:* Milena Solo, Director for Graduate Admissions, 212-772-4480, E-mail: milena.solo@hunter.cuny.edu.
Website: http://www.hunter.cuny.edu/romancelanguages/graduate/ma-requirements.

Hunter College of the City University of New York, Graduate School, School of Arts and Sciences, Department of Romance Languages, Program in Italian, New York, NY 10065-5085. Offers Italian (MA); Italian education (MA). *Faculty:* 2 full-time (1 woman), 1 (woman) part-time/adjunct. *Students:* 5 part-time (3 women); includes 1 minority (Hispanic/Latino), 1 international. Average age 32. 3 applicants, 67% accepted, 1 enrolled. In 2013, 2 master's awarded. *Degree requirements:* For master's, 2 foreign languages, comprehensive exam, thesis optional. *Entrance requirements:* For master's, GRE General Test, GRE Subject Test, ability to read, speak, and write Italian; interview. Additional exam requirements/recommendations for international students: Required—TOEFL. *Application deadline:* For fall admission, 4/1 for domestic students, 2/1 for international students; for spring admission, 11/1 for domestic students, 9/1 for international students. Application fee: $125. *Financial support:* Federal Work-Study, scholarships/grants, and tuition waivers (partial) available. Support available to part-time students. Financial award application deadline: 4/15. *Faculty research:* Dante, Middle Ages, Renaissance, contemporary Italian novel and poetry, late Renaissance and Baroque. *Unit head:* Dr. Paolo Fasoli, Chairperson and Associate Professor, 212-772-5129, Fax: 212-772-5094, E-mail: pfasoli@hunter.cuny.edu. *Application contact:* Milena Solo, Director for Graduate Admissions, 212-772-4480, E-mail: milena.solo@hunter.cuny.edu.
Website: http://www.hunter.cuny.edu/romancelanguages/graduate/ma-requirements.

Hunter College of the City University of New York, Graduate School, School of Arts and Sciences, Department of Romance Languages, Program in Spanish, New York, NY 10065-5085. Offers Spanish (MA); Spanish education (MA). Part-time and evening/weekend programs available. *Faculty:* 3 full-time (all women), 1 part-time/adjunct (0 women). *Students:* 2 full-time (both women), 16 part-time (9 women); includes 10 minority (all Hispanic/Latino), 4 international. Average age 37. 3 applicants, 67% accepted, 1 enrolled. In 2013, 8 master's awarded. *Degree requirements:* For master's, 2 foreign languages, comprehensive exam, thesis optional. *Entrance requirements:* For master's, GRE General Test, GRE Subject Test, ability to read, speak, and write Spanish; interview. Additional exam requirements/recommendations for international students: Required—TOEFL. *Application deadline:* For fall admission, 4/1 for domestic students, 2/1 for international students; for spring admission, 11/1 for domestic students, 9/1 for international students. Application fee: $125. *Financial support:* Federal Work-Study and tuition waivers (partial) available. Support available to part-time students. Financial award application deadline: 4/15. *Faculty research:* Galician studies, contemporary Spanish poetry, Lope de Vega, comparative Hispanic literatures, contemporary Hispanic poetry. *Unit head:* Dr. Alicia O. Ramos, Associate Professor and Coordinator, 212-772-5130, E-mail: rosramos@hunter.cuny.edu. *Application contact:* Milena Solo, Director for Graduate Admissions, 212-772-4480, E-mail: admissions@hunter.cuny.edu.
Website: http://www.hunter.cuny.edu/romancelanguages/graduate/ma-requirements.

Hunter College of the City University of New York, Graduate School, School of Education, Programs in Secondary Education, Concentration in French Education, New York, NY 10065-5085. Offers MA. *Accreditation:* NCATE. *Faculty:* 3 full-time (1 woman), 20 part-time/adjunct (9 women). *Students:* 1 full-time (0 women), 6 part-time (5 women); includes 2 minority (1 Black or African American, non-Hispanic/Latino; 1 Hispanic/Latino). Average age 31. 1 applicant, 100% accepted, 1 enrolled. *Degree requirements:* For master's, thesis, professional teaching portfolio, New York State Teacher Certification Exam. *Entrance requirements:* For master's, 24 credits in French; minimum GPA of 3.0 in French, 2.8 overall; 2 letters of reference; interview. Additional exam requirements/recommendations for international students: Required—TOEFL, TWE. *Application deadline:* For fall admission, 4/1 for domestic students, 2/1 for international students; for spring admission, 11/1 for domestic students, 9/1 for international students. Applications are processed on a rolling basis. Application fee: $125. *Financial support:* Federal Work-Study and tuition waivers (partial) available. Support available to part-time students. *Unit head:* Dr. Jenny M. Castillo, Graduate Advisor, 212-772-4614, E-mail: jmcastil@hunter.cuny.edu. *Application contact:* Milena Solo, Director for Graduate Admissions, 212-772-4480, E-mail: admissions@hunter.cuny.edu.
Website: http://www.hunter.cuny.edu/school-of-education/programs/graduate/adolescent/foreign-languages/french.

Hunter College of the City University of New York, Graduate School, School of Education, Programs in Secondary Education, Concentration in Italian Education, New York, NY 10065-5085. Offers MA. *Accreditation:* NCATE. *Students:* 3 part-time (1 woman). Average age 43. 1 applicant, 100% accepted, 1 enrolled. In 2013, 7 master's awarded. *Degree requirements:* For master's, thesis, professional teaching portfolio, New York State Teacher Certification Exam, research project. *Entrance requirements:* For master's, minimum GPA of 3.0 in Italian, 2.8 overall; 24 credits of course work in Italian; 2 letters of reference; interview. Additional exam requirements/recommendations for international students: Required—TOEFL, TWE. *Application deadline:* For fall admission, 4/1 for domestic students, 2/1 for international students; for spring admission, 11/1 for domestic students, 9/1 for international students. Applications are processed on a rolling basis. Application fee: $125. *Financial support:* Federal Work-Study and tuition waivers (partial) available. Support available to part-time students. *Unit head:* Prof. Jenny Castillo, Education Program Coordinator, 212-772-4614, Fax: 212-772-5094, E-mail: jmcasti@hunter.cuny.edu. *Application contact:* Milena Solo, Director for Graduate Admissions, 212-772-4482, E-mail: admissions@hunter.cuny.edu.
Website: http://www.hunter.cuny.edu/school-of-education/programs/graduate/adolescent/foreign-languages/italian.

Hunter College of the City University of New York, Graduate School, School of Education, Programs in Secondary Education, Concentration in Spanish Education, New York, NY 10065-5085. Offers MA. *Accreditation:* NCATE. *Students:* 2 full-time (both women), 8 part-time (4 women); includes 5 minority (all Hispanic/Latino), 2 international. Average age 32. 4 applicants, 25% accepted, 1 enrolled. In 2013, 8 master's awarded. *Degree requirements:* For master's, thesis, professional teaching portfolio, New York State Teacher Certification Exam. *Entrance requirements:* For master's, minimum GPA of 3.0 in Spanish, 2.8 overall; 24 credits of course work in Spanish; 2 letters of reference; interview. Additional exam requirements/recommendations for international students: Required—TOEFL, TWE. *Application deadline:* For fall admission, 4/1 for domestic students, 2/1 for international students; for spring admission, 11/1 for domestic students, 9/1 for international students. Applications are processed on a rolling basis. Application fee: $125. *Financial support:* Federal Work-Study and tuition waivers (partial) available. Support available to part-time students. *Unit head:* Dr. Magdalena Perkowska, Romance Language Advisor (Spanish), 212-772-5132, E-mail: mperkowsk@hunter.cuny.edu. *Application contact:* Milena Solo, Director for Graduate Admissions, 212-772-4482, E-mail: admissions@hunter.cuny.edu.
Website: http://www.hunter.cuny.edu/school-of-education/programs/graduate/bilingual.

Indiana University Bloomington, University Graduate School, College of Arts and Sciences, Department of East Asian Languages and Cultures, Bloomington, IN 47408. Offers Chinese (MA, PhD); Chinese language pedagogy (MA); East Asian studies (MA); Japanese (MA, PhD); Japanese language pedagogy (MA). Part-time programs available. *Faculty:* 17 full-time (7 women), 17 part-time/adjunct (8 women). *Students:* 16 full-time (7 women), 18 part-time (13 women); includes 2 minority (1 Black or African American, non-Hispanic/Latino; 1 Hispanic/Latino), 16 international. 93 applicants, 40% accepted, 18 enrolled. In 2013, 9 master's, 2 doctorates awarded. *Degree requirements:* For master's, one foreign language, thesis; for doctorate, 2 foreign languages, comprehensive exam, thesis/dissertation. *Entrance requirements:* Additional exam requirements/recommendations for international students: Required—TOEFL (minimum score 93 iBT). *Application deadline:* For fall admission, 1/15 for domestic students, 12/1 for international students. Application fee: $55 ($65 for international students). Electronic applications accepted. *Financial support:* In 2013–14, fellowships with full tuition reimbursements (averaging $15,000 per year), teaching assistantships with full tuition reimbursements (averaging $15,750 per year) were awarded. Financial award application deadline: 2/15. *Faculty research:* Modern East Asian history; politics and society; traditional Chinese thought and society; medieval and premodern Japanese history, literature and society; modern Chinese and Japanese film and literature; Chinese, Japanese, Korean language and linguistics. *Unit head:* Prof. Natsuko Tsujimura, Chair, 812-855-0856, Fax: 812-855-6402, E-mail: tsujimur@indiana.edu. *Application contact:* Rachel Gray, Graduate Secretary, 812-856-4959, E-mail: rtgray@indiana.edu.
Website: http://www.indiana.edu/~ealc/index.shtml.

Indiana University Bloomington, University Graduate School, College of Arts and Sciences, Department of French and Italian, Bloomington, IN 47405-7000. Offers French (MA, PhD), including French instruction (MA), French linguistics, French literature; Italian (MA, PhD). Part-time programs available. *Faculty:* 23 full-time. *Students:* 66 full-time (42 women), 2 part-time (both women); includes 3 minority (1 Black or African American, non-Hispanic/Latino; 2 Hispanic/Latino), 19 international. Average age 30. 43 applicants, 60% accepted, 10 enrolled. In 2013, 7 master's, 8 doctorates awarded. Terminal master's awarded for partial completion of doctoral program. *Degree requirements:* For master's, one foreign language, comprehensive exam, thesis optional; for doctorate, 2 foreign languages, comprehensive exam, thesis/dissertation. *Entrance requirements:* For master's and doctorate, GRE General Test. Additional exam requirements/recommendations for international students: Required—TOEFL (minimum score 550 paper-based; 79 iBT). *Application deadline:* For fall admission, 1/15 priority date for domestic students, 12/1 priority date for international students; for spring admission, 9/1 priority date for domestic and international students. Application fee: $55 ($65 for international students). Electronic applications accepted. *Financial support:* In 2013–14, 7 fellowships with partial tuition reimbursements (averaging $18,000 per year), 6 research assistantships with partial tuition reimbursements (averaging $15,750 per year), 38 teaching assistantships with partial tuition reimbursements (averaging $15,750 per year) were awarded. Financial award application deadline: 1/15. *Faculty research:* French and Italian literature, French linguistics, including the novel and political theory, literature and fine arts, literary theory, postcolonialism, French-Creole studies, French literature of Africa and its Diaspora, humanism, medieval folklore and mythology, humor in medieval and Renaissance literature, cinema Old Occitan and Old French, emigration, second language acquisition, syntax, sociolinguistics, phonology, lexicography. *Unit head:* Prof. Andrea Ciccarelli, Chair, 812-855-5458, Fax: 812-855-8877, E-mail: fritchr@indiana.edu. *Application contact:* Casey Green, Graduate Secretary, 812-855-1088, Fax: 812-855-8877, E-mail: fritgs@indiana.edu.
Website: http://www.indiana.edu/~frithome/.

Indiana University Bloomington, University Graduate School, College of Arts and Sciences, Department of Germanic Studies, Bloomington, IN 47405-7000. Offers German philology and linguistics (PhD); German studies (MA, PhD), including German (MA), German literature and culture (MA), German literature and linguistics (MA); medieval German studies (PhD); teaching German (MAT). *Faculty:* 13 full-time (4 women), 6 part-time/adjunct (2 women). *Students:* 30 full-time (17 women); includes 1 minority (Asian, non-Hispanic/Latino), 7 international. Average age 31. 24 applicants, 42% accepted, 5 enrolled. In 2013, 1 doctorate awarded. Terminal master's awarded for partial completion of doctoral program. *Degree requirements:* For master's, one foreign language, project; for doctorate, one foreign language, comprehensive exam, thesis/dissertation. *Entrance requirements:* For master's, GRE General Test, BA in German or equivalent; for doctorate, GRE General Test, MA in German or equivalent. Additional exam requirements/recommendations for international students: Required—TOEFL. *Application deadline:* For fall admission, 1/15 priority date for domestic students, 12/1 for international students; for spring admission, 9/1 priority date for domestic students, 9/1 for international students. Applications are processed on a rolling basis. Application fee: $55 ($65 for international students). Electronic applications accepted. *Financial support:* In 2013–14, 8 fellowships with full and partial tuition reimbursements (averaging $17,000 per year), 19 teaching assistantships with full tuition reimbursements (averaging $15,750 per year) were awarded; research assistantships, Federal Work-Study, institutionally sponsored loans, scholarships/grants, and unspecified assistantships also available. Support available to part-time students. Financial award application deadline: 1/15; financial award applicants required to submit FAFSA. *Faculty research:* German and other European literature: medieval to modern/postmodern, German and culture studies, Germanic philology, literary theory, literature and the other arts. *Unit head:* Fritz Breithaupt, Department Chairman, 812-855-7947, Fax: 812-855-8292, E-mail: fbreitha@indiana.edu. *Application contact:* Michelle Dunbar, Graduate Secretary, 812-855-7947, E-mail: midunbar@indiana.edu.
Website: http://www.indiana.edu/~germanic/.

Indiana University of Pennsylvania, School of Graduate Studies and Research, College of Humanities and Social Sciences, Department of Foreign Languages, Program in Spanish/Applied Linguistics and Teaching Methodology, Indiana, PA 15705-1087. Offers MA. *Faculty:* 5 full-time (3 women). *Students:* 3 full-time (1 woman), 1 part-time (0 women); includes 1 minority (Hispanic/Latino), 1 international. Average age 30. 2 applicants, 100% accepted, 1 enrolled. Application fee: $50. *Expenses:* Tuition, state resident: full-time $3978; part-time $442 per credit. Tuition, nonresident: full-time $5967; part-time $663 per credit. *Required fees:* $2080; $115.55 per credit. $93 per semester. Tuition and fees vary according to degree level and program. *Financial support:* In 2013–14, 1 fellowship with full tuition reimbursement (averaging $500 per year), 3 research assistantships with full and partial tuition reimbursements (averaging $4,435 per year) were awarded. *Unit head:* Dr. Sean McDaniel, Chairperson, 724-357-7532, E-mail: mcdaniel@iup.edu.

Indiana University–Purdue University Indianapolis, School of Education, Indianapolis, IN 46202-2896. Offers computer education (Certificate); curriculum and

instruction (MS); early childhood (MS); educational leadership (MS, Certificate); English as a second language (Certificate); higher education and student affairs (MS); kindergarten (Certificate); language education (MS); reading (Certificate); school counseling (MS); special education (MS, Certificate). Part-time and evening/weekend programs available. *Faculty:* 41 full-time, 80 part-time/adjunct. *Students:* 113 full-time (78 women), 263 part-time (200 women); includes 88 minority (51 Black or African American, non-Hispanic/Latino; 1 American Indian or Alaska Native, non-Hispanic/Latino; 10 Asian, non-Hispanic/Latino; 19 Hispanic/Latino; 7 Two or more races, non-Hispanic/Latino), 5 international. Average age 33. 93 applicants, 54% accepted, 40 enrolled. In 2013, 179 master's awarded. *Degree requirements:* For master's, thesis optional. *Entrance requirements:* For master's, GRE General Test, minimum GPA of 3.0. Additional exam requirements/recommendations for international students: Required—TOEFL. *Application deadline:* For fall admission, 5/1 priority date for domestic students; for spring admission, 11/1 for domestic students. Application fee: $55 ($65 for international students). *Financial support:* Fellowships, research assistantships with partial tuition reimbursements, teaching assistantships, Federal Work-Study, institutionally sponsored loans, scholarships/grants, and tuition waivers (partial) available. Support available to part-time students. *Faculty research:* Teachers in the process of change, learning cycles, children's concepts of science. *Total annual research expenditures:* $614,458. *Unit head:* Dr. Pat Rogan, Executive Associate Dean, 317-274-6862, E-mail: progan@iupui.edu. *Application contact:* Donnella Dillon, Graduate Admissions Coordinator, 317-274-0645, E-mail: dmdillon@iupui.edu.
Website: http://education.iupui.edu/.

Inter American University of Puerto Rico, Arecibo Campus, Programs in Education, Arecibo, PR 00614-4050. Offers administration and educational supervision (MA Ed); counseling and guidance (MA Ed); curriculum and teaching (MA Ed), including biology education, English as a second language, history education, math education, Spanish; elementary education (MA Ed). *Degree requirements:* For master's, comprehensive exam, thesis optional. *Entrance requirements:* For master's, GRE, EXADEP, bachelor's degree in education or teaching license (administration and supervision) or courses in education and psychology (counseling and guidance), minimum GPA of 2.5 in last 60 credits.

Inter American University of Puerto Rico, Barranquitas Campus, Program in Education, Barranquitas, PR 00794. Offers curriculum and teaching (M Ed), including biology education, English as a second language, history education, mathematics education, Spanish; educational leadership and management (MA); elementary education (M Ed); information and library service technology (M Ed); special education (MA). *Degree requirements:* For master's, comprehensive exam, thesis optional. *Entrance requirements:* For master's, EXADEP, letter of recommendation. Electronic applications accepted.

Inter American University of Puerto Rico, Metropolitan Campus, Graduate Programs, Program in Spanish Education, San Juan, PR 00919-1293. Offers MA.

Iona College, School of Arts and Science, Department of Education, New Rochelle, NY 10801-1890. Offers adolescence education: biology (MS Ed, MST); adolescence education: English (MS Ed, MST); adolescence education: Italian (MS Ed, MST); adolescence education: mathematics (MS Ed, MST); adolescence education: social studies (MS Ed, MST); adolescence education: Spanish (MS Ed, MST); adolescence special education 5-12 (MST); adolescence special education and literacy (MS Ed); childhood and special education (MST); childhood education (MST); early childhood and childhood (MST); educational leadership (MS Ed); literacy education: birth-grade 6 (MS Ed). *Accreditation:* NCATE. Part-time and evening/weekend programs available. *Faculty:* 11 full-time (9 women), 7 part-time/adjunct (6 women). *Students:* 34 full-time (25 women), 61 part-time (47 women); includes 5 minority (2 Asian, non-Hispanic/Latino; 3 Hispanic/Latino), 1 international. Average age 25. 27 applicants, 93% accepted, 16 enrolled. In 2013, 54 master's awarded. *Degree requirements:* For master's, thesis or alternative. *Entrance requirements:* For master's, minimum GPA of 3.0, NY State teaching certificate (for all MS Ed programs). Additional exam requirements/recommendations for international students: Required—TOEFL (minimum score 550 paper-based; 80 iBT), IELTS (minimum score 6.5). *Application deadline:* For fall admission, 8/1 priority date for domestic students, 5/1 priority date for international students; for spring admission, 1/1 priority date for domestic students, 9/1 priority date for international students. Applications are processed on a rolling basis. Application fee: $50. Electronic applications accepted. *Expenses: Tuition:* Part-time $948 per credit. *Required fees:* $235 per term. *Financial support:* In 2013–14, 84 students received support. Unspecified assistantships available. Support available to part-time students. Financial award application deadline: 4/15; financial award applicants required to submit FAFSA. *Faculty research:* Reading/writing, educational technology, administration, early literacy assessment, literacy development. *Unit head:* Margaret Smith, PhD, Chair, 914-633-2210, Fax: 914-633-2608, E-mail: msmith@iona.edu. *Application contact:* Veronica Jarek-Prinz, Director, Graduate Admissions, 914-633-2420, Fax: 914-633-2277, E-mail: vjarekprinz@iona.edu.
Website: http://www.iona.edu/Academics/School-of-Arts-Science/Departments/Education/Graduate-Programs.aspx.

Iona College, School of Arts and Science, Department of Modern Language, New Rochelle, NY 10801-1890. Offers Spanish (MA). Part-time and evening/weekend programs available. *Faculty:* 4 full-time (2 women). *Students:* 1 (woman) full-time, 6 part-time (5 women); includes 2 minority (1 Black or African American, non-Hispanic/Latino; 1 Hispanic/Latino). Average age 36. 1 applicant, 100% accepted. In 2013, 4 master's awarded. *Degree requirements:* For master's, comprehensive exam (for some programs), thesis optional. *Entrance requirements:* For master's, minimum GPA of 3.0. Additional exam requirements/recommendations for international students: Required—TOEFL (minimum score 550 paper-based; 80 iBT), IELTS (minimum score 6.5). *Application deadline:* For fall admission, 8/1 priority date for domestic students, 5/1 priority date for international students; for spring admission, 1/1 priority date for domestic students, 9/1 priority date for international students. Applications are processed on a rolling basis. Application fee: $50. Electronic applications accepted. *Expenses: Tuition:* Part-time $948 per credit. *Required fees:* $235 per term. *Financial support:* In 2013–14, 3 students received support. Unspecified assistantships available. Support available to part-time students. Financial award application deadline: 4/15; financial award applicants required to submit FAFSA. *Faculty research:* Colonial literature, contemporary Peninsular literature, African diaspora, travel literature, pedagogy. *Unit head:* Dr. Victoria L. Katz, Chair, 914-633-2425, E-mail: vketz@iona.edu. *Application contact:* Veronica Jarek-Prinz, Director, Graduate Admissions, 914-633-2420, Fax: 914-633-2277, E-mail: vjarekprinz@iona.edu.
Website: http://www.iona.edu/Academics/School-of-Arts-Science/Departments/Foreign-Languages/Graduate-Programs/Spanish.aspx.

Ithaca College, School of Humanities and Sciences, Program in Adolescence Education, Ithaca, NY 14850. Offers biology 7-12 (MAT); chemistry 7-12 (MAT); English 7-12 (MAT); French 7-12 (MAT); math 7-12 (MAT); physics 7-12 (MAT); social studies 7-12 (MAT); Spanish (MAT). Part-time programs available. *Faculty:* 31 full-time (11 women). *Students:* 12 full-time (4 women); includes 1 minority (Hispanic/Latino). Average age 24. 27 applicants, 81% accepted, 12 enrolled. In 2013, 7 master's awarded. *Degree requirements:* For master's, thesis or alternative, student teaching. *Entrance requirements:* For master's, minimum GPA of 3.0. Additional exam requirements/recommendations for international students: Required—TOEFL (minimum score 550 paper-based; 80 iBT). *Application deadline:* For fall admission, 2/15 priority date for domestic and international students; for spring admission, 12/1 for domestic and international students. Applications are processed on a rolling basis. Application fee: $40. Electronic applications accepted. *Expenses:* Contact institution. *Financial support:* In 2013–14, 7 students received support, including 7 teaching assistantships (averaging $9,781 per year); career-related internships or fieldwork, Federal Work-Study, scholarships/grants, and unspecified assistantships also available. Support available to part-time students. Financial award application deadline: 2/15; financial award applicants required to submit CSS PROFILE or FAFSA. *Faculty research:* Teacher preparation (elementary and secondary education), equity and social justice in education, language and literacy, multicultural education/sociocultural studies, reflective practice and teacher research. *Unit head:* Dr. Linda Hanrahan, Chair, 607-274-3143, Fax: 607-274-1263, E-mail: gps@ithaca.edu. *Application contact:* Gerard Turbide, Director, Office of Admission, 607-274-3143, Fax: 607-274-1263, E-mail: gps@ithaca.edu.
Website: http://www.ithaca.edu/gradprograms/education/programs/aded.

Kean University, College of Education, Program in Instruction and Curriculum, Union, NJ 07083. Offers bilingual/bicultural education (MA); classroom instruction (MA); earth science (MA); mathematics/science/computer education (MA); teaching (MA); teaching English as a second language (MA); world languages (Spanish) (MA). *Accreditation:* NCATE. Part-time programs available. *Faculty:* 22 full-time (12 women). *Students:* 16 full-time (10 women), 100 part-time (72 women); includes 57 minority (8 Black or African American, non-Hispanic/Latino; 3 Asian, non-Hispanic/Latino; 45 Hispanic/Latino; 1 Two or more races, non-Hispanic/Latino). Average age 35. 56 applicants, 100% accepted, 38 enrolled. In 2013, 42 master's awarded. *Degree requirements:* For master's, comprehensive exam, thesis (for some programs), two-semester advanced seminar. *Entrance requirements:* For master's, GRE General Test or MAT, PRAXIS, minimum GPA of 3.0, personal statement, professional resume/curriculum vitae, commitment to working with children, certification (for some programs). Additional exam requirements/recommendations for international students: Required—TOEFL (minimum score 550 paper-based; 79 iBT). *Application deadline:* For fall admission, 6/1 for domestic and international students; for spring admission, 12/1 for domestic and international students. Applications are processed on a rolling basis. Application fee: $75 ($150 for international students). Electronic applications accepted. *Expenses:* Tuition, state resident: full-time $12,099; part-time $589 per credit. Tuition, nonresident: full-time $16,399; part-time $722 per credit. *Required fees:* $3050; $139 per credit. Part-time tuition and fees vary according to course level, course load, degree level and program. *Financial support:* In 2013–14, 6 research assistantships with full tuition reimbursements (averaging $3,713 per year) were awarded; unspecified assistantships also available. Financial award applicants required to submit FAFSA. *Unit head:* Dr. Gail Verdi, Program Coordinator, 908-737-3908, E-mail: gverdi@kean.edu. *Application contact:* Ann-Marie Kay, Assistant Director for Graduate Admissions, 908-737-5922, Fax: 908-737-5925, E-mail: akay@kean.edu.
Website: http://grad.kean.edu/masters-programs/bilingualbicultural-education-instruction-and-curriculum.

Kennesaw State University, Leland and Clarice C. Bagwell College of Education, Program in Teaching, Kennesaw, GA 30144-5591. Offers art education (MAT); biology (MAT); chemistry (MAT); foreign language education (Chinese and Spanish) (MAT); physics (MAT); secondary English (MAT); secondary mathematics (MAT); special education (MAT); teaching English to speakers of other languages (MAT). Part-time and evening/weekend programs available. *Students:* 82 full-time (59 women), 16 part-time (12 women); includes 28 minority (14 Black or African American, non-Hispanic/Latino; 4 Asian, non-Hispanic/Latino; 7 Hispanic/Latino; 1 Native Hawaiian or other Pacific Islander, non-Hispanic/Latino; 2 Two or more races, non-Hispanic/Latino), 3 international. Average age 35. 28 applicants, 68% accepted, 15 enrolled. In 2013, 54 master's awarded. *Entrance requirements:* For master's, GRE, GACE I (state certificate exam), minimum GPA of 2.75, 2 recommendations, resume. Additional exam requirements/recommendations for international students: Required—TOEFL (minimum score 550 paper-based; 80 iBT), IELTS (minimum score 6). *Application deadline:* For fall admission, 6/1 for domestic and international students; for spring admission, 3/1 for domestic and international students; for summer admission, 4/15 for domestic and international students. Applications are processed on a rolling basis. Application fee: $60. Electronic applications accepted. *Expenses:* Tuition, state resident: full-time $4806; part-time $267 per semester hour. Tuition, nonresident: full-time $17,298; part-time $961 per semester hour. *Required fees:* $1834; $784.50 per semester. *Financial support:* In 2013–14, 2 research assistantships with tuition reimbursements (averaging $8,000 per year) were awarded; unspecified assistantships also available. Financial award application deadline: 4/1; financial award applicants required to submit FAFSA. *Unit head:* Dr. Jillian Ford, Director, 770-499-3093, E-mail: graded@kennesaw.edu. *Application contact:* Melinda Ross, Admissions Counselor, 770-423-6122, Fax: 770-423-6885, E-mail: ksugrad@kennesaw.edu.
Website: http://www.kennesaw.edu.

Kent State University, College of Arts and Sciences, Department of Modern and Classical Language Studies, Kent, OH 44242-0001. Offers French literature (MA); French, Spanish, German and Latin pedagogy (MA); German literature (MA); Spanish literature (MA); translation (MA), including French, German, Japanese, Russian, Spanish; translation studies (PhD). Part-time and evening/weekend programs available. *Degree requirements:* For master's, one foreign language, comprehensive exam (for some programs), thesis (for some programs); for doctorate, comprehensive exam, thesis/dissertation (for some programs). *Entrance requirements:* For master's, minimum GPA of 3.0, writing sample, audio tape or CD; for doctorate, 3 recommendations. Additional exam requirements/recommendations for international students: Required—TOEFL. Electronic applications accepted. *Faculty research:* Literature, pedagogy, applied linguistics, translation studies.

Le Moyne College, Department of Education, Syracuse, NY 13214. Offers adolescent education (MS Ed, MST); adolescent education/special education (MS Ed, MST); adolescent English (MST), including grades 7-12 (MS Ed, MST); adolescent English/special education (MST), including grades 7-12 (MS Ed, MST); adolescent foreign language (MST), including grades 7-12 (MS Ed, MST); adolescent history (MST), including grades 7-12 (MS Ed, MST); childhood education (MS Ed); childhood education/special education (MS Ed); elementary education (MS Ed); general education (MS Ed); inclusive childhood education (MST); literacy education (MS Ed), including birth to grade 6, grades 5-12; school building leader (MS Ed); school building leadership (CAS); school district business leader (MS Ed, CAS); school district leader (MS Ed); school district leadership (CAS); secondary education (MS Ed); special education (MS Ed); students with disabilities-generalist (MS Ed), including grades 7-12 (MS Ed, MST); teaching English to speakers of other languages (MS Ed); urban studies (MS Ed). *Accreditation:* Teacher Education Accreditation Council. Part-time and evening/weekend programs available. *Faculty:* 8 full-time (5 women), 61 part-time/adjunct (38 women). *Students:* 24 full-time (20 women), 178 part-time (133 women); includes 22 minority (12 Black or African American, non-Hispanic/Latino; 1 American Indian or Alaska Native, non-Hispanic/Latino; 3 Asian, non-Hispanic/Latino; 6 Hispanic/Latino), 1 international.

Average age 31. 248 applicants, 90% accepted, 86 enrolled. In 2013, 158 master's, 37 CASs awarded. *Degree requirements:* For master's, thesis. *Entrance requirements:* For master's, GRE General Test, bachelor's degree, 2 letters of recommendation, written statement, transcripts. Additional exam requirements/recommendations for international students: Required—TOEFL (minimum score 550 paper-based; 79 iBT). *Application deadline:* For fall admission, 4/1 priority date for domestic and international students; for spring admission, 10/1 priority date for domestic and international students; for summer admission, 3/1 priority date for domestic and international students. Applications are processed on a rolling basis. Application fee: $50. *Expenses:* Contact institution. *Financial support:* In 2013–14, 26 students received support. Career-related internships or fieldwork and health care benefits available. Support available to part-time students. Financial award applicants required to submit FAFSA. *Faculty research:* Minority teachers, special education, multiculturalism, literacy, technology, media literacy learning, autism, school district organization, service-learning, higher level problem solving, teacher leadership. *Unit head:* Dr. Suzanne L. Gilmour, Chair, Department of Education/Director of Graduate Education Programs, 315-445-4376, Fax: 315-445-4744, E-mail: gilmous@lemoyne.edu. *Application contact:* Kristen P. Trapasso, Senior Director of Enrollment Management, 315-445-4265, Fax: 315-445-6092, E-mail: trapaskp@lemoyne.edu.
Website: http://www.lemoyne.edu/education.

Long Island University–LIU Post, College of Liberal Arts and Sciences, Department of Foreign Languages, Brookville, NY 11548-1300. Offers Spanish (MA); Spanish education (MS). Part-time programs available. *Degree requirements:* For master's, 2 foreign languages, comprehensive exam, thesis or alternative. *Entrance requirements:* For master's, 24 credits of undergraduate course work in Spanish. Electronic applications accepted. *Faculty research:* Making of a superhero, dialogue in the 19th century novel, nicknames, Menendez Pidal and Spanish School of Philology, women writers of Latin America.

Long Island University–LIU Post, School of Education, Department of Curriculum and Instruction, Brookville, NY 11548-1300. Offers adolescence education (MS); adolescence education: biology (MS); adolescence education: earth science (MS); adolescence education: English (MS); adolescence education: mathematics (MS); adolescence education: social studies (MS); adolescence education: Spanish (MS); art education (MS); bilingual education (MS); childhood education (MS); early childhood education (MS); middle childhood education (MS); music education (MS); teaching English to speakers of other languages (MS). Part-time and evening/weekend programs available. *Degree requirements:* For master's, comprehensive exam or thesis, student teaching. *Entrance requirements:* For master's, minimum GPA of 2.75 in major, 2.5 overall. Electronic applications accepted. *Faculty research:* Ethics and education, teaching strategies.

Manhattanville College, School of Education, Program in Middle Childhood/Adolescence Education (Grades 5-12), Purchase, NY 10577-2132. Offers biology (MAT); biology and special education (MPS); chemistry (MAT); chemistry and special education (MPS); English (MAT); English and special education (MPS); literacy and special education (MPS); literacy specialist (MPS); math and special education (MPS); mathematics (MAT); physics (MAT); social studies (MAT); social studies and special education (MPS); special education (MPS); teaching languages other than English (MAT), including French, Italian, Latin, Spanish. Part-time and evening/weekend programs available. *Degree requirements:* For master's, comprehensive exam or research project, field experience. *Entrance requirements:* For master's, minimum undergraduate GPA of 3.0, 2 letters of recommendation. Additional exam requirements/recommendations for international students: Required—TOEFL. Electronic applications accepted.

Marquette University, Graduate School, College of Arts and Sciences, Department of Foreign Languages and Literatures, Milwaukee, WI 53201-1881. Offers Spanish (MA). Part-time and evening/weekend programs available. *Faculty:* 32 full-time (21 women), 5 part-time/adjunct (3 women). *Students:* 8 full-time (4 women), 2 part-time (1 woman); includes 3 minority (all Hispanic/Latino), 1 international. Average age 29. 10 applicants, 70% accepted, 2 enrolled. In 2013, 6 master's awarded. *Degree requirements:* For master's, one foreign language, comprehensive exam. *Entrance requirements:* For master's, official transcripts from all current and previous colleges/universities except Marquette, three letters of recommendation, tape recording of foreign speaking voice. Additional exam requirements/recommendations for international students: Required—TOEFL (minimum score 530 paper-based). *Application deadline:* For fall admission, 12/15 for domestic and international students. Application fee: $50. Electronic applications accepted. *Financial support:* In 2013–14, 11 students received support, including 8 teaching assistantships with full tuition reimbursements available (averaging $13,285 per year); fellowships, institutionally sponsored loans, scholarships/grants, health care benefits, tuition waivers (full and partial), and unspecified assistantships also available. Support available to part-time students. Financial award application deadline: 2/15. *Faculty research:* Latin American literature, Afro-Hispanic literature, descriptive Spanish linguistics, inter-American studies, foreign language education. *Total annual research expenditures:* $44,719. *Unit head:* Dr. Anne Pasero, Chair and Professor, 414-288-7063. *Application contact:* Dr. Armando Gonzales-Percz, Director of Graduate Studies, 414-288-7268, Fax: 414-288-1578.
Website: http://www.marquette.edu/fola/grad_director_intro.shtml.

McGill University, Faculty of Graduate and Postdoctoral Studies, Faculty of Education, Department of Integrated Studies in Education, Montréal, QC H3A 2T5, Canada. Offers culture and values in education (MA, PhD); curriculum studies (MA); educational leadership (MA, Certificate); educational studies (PhD); integrated studies in education (M Ed); second language education (MA, PhD).

Michigan State University, The Graduate School, College of Arts and Letters, Program in Second Language Studies, East Lansing, MI 48824. Offers PhD. *Accreditation:* Teacher Education Accreditation Council. *Entrance requirements:* Additional exam requirements/recommendations for international students: Required—TOEFL, Michigan State University ELT (minimum score 85), Michigan English Language Assessment Battery (minimum score 83). Electronic applications accepted.

Middle Tennessee State University, College of Graduate Studies, College of Liberal Arts, Department of Foreign Languages and Literatures, Murfreesboro, TN 37132. Offers foreign language (MAT). Part-time and evening/weekend programs available. Postbaccalaureate distance learning degree programs offered. *Faculty:* 16 full-time (12 women). *Students:* 13 full-time (8 women), 8 part-time (4 women); includes 8 minority (2 Black or African American, non-Hispanic/Latino; 1 Asian, non-Hispanic/Latino; 4 Hispanic/Latino; 1 Two or more races, non-Hispanic/Latino). 15 applicants, 73% accepted. In 2013, 8 master's awarded. *Degree requirements:* For master's, one foreign language, comprehensive exam, thesis optional. *Entrance requirements:* For master's, GRE. Additional exam requirements/recommendations for international students: Required—TOEFL (minimum score 525 paper-based; 71 iBT) or IELTS (minimum score 6). *Application deadline:* For fall admission, 6/1 for domestic and international students. Applications are processed on a rolling basis. Application fee: $25 ($30 for international students). Electronic applications accepted. *Financial support:* In 2013–14, 15 students received support. Tuition waivers available. Support available to part-time students. Financial award application deadline: 5/1; financial award applicants required to submit FAFSA. *Faculty research:* Linguistics, holocaust studies, foreign language pedagogy. *Unit head:* Dr. Joan McRae, Chair, 615-898-2981, Fax: 615-898-5735, E-mail: joan.mcrae@mtsu.edu. *Application contact:* Dr. Michael D. Allen, Vice Provost for Research and Dean, 615-898-2840, Fax: 615-904-8020, E-mail: michael.allen@mtsu.edu.

Mills College, Graduate Studies, School of Education, Oakland, CA 94613-1000. Offers child life in hospitals (MA); early childhood education (MA); education (MA), including art education, curriculum and instruction, elementary education, English education, foreign language education, mathematics education, science education, secondary education, social studies education, teaching; educational leadership (MA, Ed D). Part-time and evening/weekend programs available. *Faculty:* 10 full-time (7 women), 13 part-time/adjunct (10 women). *Students:* 154 full-time (136 women), 54 part-time (47 women); includes 96 minority (32 Black or African American, non-Hispanic/Latino; 1 American Indian or Alaska Native, non-Hispanic/Latino; 23 Asian, non-Hispanic/Latino; 27 Hispanic/Latino; 1 Native Hawaiian or other Pacific Islander, non-Hispanic/Latino; 12 Two or more races, non-Hispanic/Latino), 2 international. Average age 25. 222 applicants, 89% accepted, 110 enrolled. In 2013, 96 master's, 38 doctorates awarded. Terminal master's awarded for partial completion of doctoral program. *Degree requirements:* For master's, comprehensive exam, thesis (for some programs); for doctorate, thesis/dissertation. *Entrance requirements:* For master's, statement of purpose, official transcript, 3 recommendations. Additional exam requirements/recommendations for international students: Required—TOEFL (minimum score 550 paper-based; 80 iBT) or IELTS (minimum score 6). *Application deadline:* For fall admission, 12/31 priority date for domestic students, 12/15 for international students; for spring admission, 11/1 priority date for domestic students, 10/1 for international students. Applications are processed on a rolling basis. Application fee: $50. Electronic applications accepted. *Expenses: Tuition:* Full-time $29,860. *Required fees:* $1134. Part-time tuition and fees vary according to course load, degree level and program. *Financial support:* In 2013–14, 130 students received support, including 130 fellowships with full and partial tuition reimbursements available (averaging $7,565 per year); career-related internships or fieldwork and scholarships/grants also available. Support available to part-time students. Financial award application deadline: 2/1; financial award applicants required to submit FAFSA. *Faculty research:* Early childhood education, teacher preparation, educational leadership. *Total annual research expenditures:* $3.5 million. *Unit head:* Dr. Katherine Schultz, Department Head, 510-430-3384, Fax: 510-430-2159, E-mail: kschultz@mills.edu. *Application contact:* Shrim Bathey, Director of Graduate Admission, 510-430-3309, Fax: 510-430-2159, E-mail: grad-admission@mills.edu.
Website: http://www.mills.edu/education.

Mississippi State University, College of Arts and Sciences, Department of Classical and Modern Languages and Literatures, Mississippi State, MS 39762. Offers French (MA); German (MA); Spanish (MA). Part-time programs available. *Faculty:* 5 full-time (1 woman). *Students:* 14 full-time (9 women), 2 part-time (0 women); includes 5 minority (1 Black or African American, non-Hispanic/Latino; 3 Hispanic/Latino; 1 Two or more races, non-Hispanic/Latino), 1 international. Average age 30. 11 applicants, 36% accepted, 3 enrolled. In 2013, 4 master's awarded. *Degree requirements:* For master's, one foreign language, thesis optional, comprehensive oral or written exam. *Entrance requirements:* For master's, minimum GPA of 2.75 on last two years of undergraduate courses. Additional exam requirements/recommendations for international students: Required—TOEFL (minimum score 525 paper-based; 70 iBT); Recommended—IELTS (minimum score 6). *Application deadline:* For fall admission, 7/1 for domestic students, 5/1 for international students; for spring admission, 11/1 for domestic students, 9/1 for international students. Applications are processed on a rolling basis. Application fee: $60. Electronic applications accepted. *Financial support:* In 2013–14, 12 teaching assistantships with full tuition reimbursements (averaging $8,766 per year) were awarded; Federal Work-Study, institutionally sponsored loans, and unspecified assistantships also available. Financial award application deadline: 4/1; financial award applicants required to submit FAFSA. *Faculty research:* French, German, Spanish literature from medieval era to present; gender and cultural studies in French; Spanish-American literature; foreign language methodology; linguistics. *Unit head:* Dr. Jack Jordan, Professor/Head, 662-325-3480, Fax: 662-325-8209, E-mail: jordan@ra.msstate.edu. *Application contact:* Dr. Edward T. Potter, Assistant Professor/Graduate Coordinator, 662-325-2399, Fax: 662-325-8209, E-mail: ep75@.msstate.edu.
Website: http://www.cmll.msstate.edu/.

Montclair State University, The Graduate School, College of Humanities and Social Sciences, Department of Spanish and Italian, Program in Teaching Spanish, Montclair, NJ 07043-1624. Offers MAT. *Degree requirements:* For master's, comprehensive exam. *Entrance requirements:* For master's, GRE General Test, 2 letters of recommendation, essay, interview. Additional exam requirements/recommendations for international students: Required—TOEFL (minimum score 83 iBT), IELTS (minimum score 6.5). Electronic applications accepted. *Faculty research:* Second language acquisition, theory and practice.

Monterey Institute of International Studies, Graduate School of Translation, Interpretation and Language Education, Program in Teaching Foreign Language, Monterey, CA 93940-2691. Offers MATFL. *Degree requirements:* For master's, one foreign language, portfolio, oral defense. *Entrance requirements:* For master's, minimum GPA of 3.0, proficiency in foreign language. Additional exam requirements/recommendations for international students: Required—TOEFL (minimum score 600 paper-based; 100 iBT). Electronic applications accepted. *Expenses: Tuition:* Full-time $34,970; part-time $1665 per credit. *Required fees:* $28 per semester.

Morehead State University, Graduate Programs, College of Education, Department of Middle Grades and Secondary Education, Morehead, KY 40351. Offers business and marketing education (MAT); English/language arts 5-9 (MAT); French (MAT); health P-12 (MAT); mathematics 5-9 (MAT); physical education P-12 (MAT); science 5-9 (MAT); secondary biology (MAT); secondary chemistry (MAT); secondary earth science (MAT); secondary English (MAT); secondary math (MAT); secondary physics (MAT); secondary social studies (MAT); social studies 5-9 (MAT); Spanish (MAT). Part-time and evening/weekend programs available. *Degree requirements:* For master's, portfolio. *Entrance requirements:* For master's, GRE or PRAXIS II content exam, minimum overall undergraduate GPA of 2.5. Additional exam requirements/recommendations for international students: Required—TOEFL (minimum score 500 paper-based). Electronic applications accepted.

New York University, Steinhardt School of Culture, Education, and Human Development, Department of Teaching and Learning, Program in Multilingual/Multicultural Studies, New York, NY 10003. Offers bilingual education (MA, PhD, Advanced Certificate); foreign language education (MA, Advanced Certificate); foreign language education (7-12) and TESOL (K-12) (MA); teaching English to speakers of other languages (MA, PhD, Advanced Certificate); teaching foreign languages, 7-12 (MA), including Chinese, French, Italian, Japanese, Spanish; teaching foreign languages, college and adult (MA); teaching French as a foreign language and TESOL (MA); teaching Spanish as a foreign language and TESOL (MA). *Accreditation:* Teacher Education Accreditation Council. Part-time and evening/weekend programs available. *Faculty:* 5 full-time (4 women). *Students:* 134 full-time (112 women), 77 part-time (68

women); includes 43 minority (6 Black or African American, non-Hispanic/Latino; 18 Asian, non-Hispanic/Latino; 15 Hispanic/Latino; 4 Two or more races, non-Hispanic/ Latino), 113 international. Average age 31. 501 applicants, 39% accepted, 68 enrolled. In 2013, 91 master's, 3 doctorates, 7 other advanced degrees awarded. *Degree requirements:* For master's, thesis (for some programs); for doctorate, thesis/ dissertation. *Entrance requirements:* For doctorate, GRE General Test, interview; for Advanced Certificate, master's degree. Additional exam requirements/recommendations for international students: Required—TOEFL (minimum score 100 iBT). *Application deadline:* For fall admission, 12/1 priority date for domestic and international students; for spring admission, 10/1 for domestic and international students. Applications are processed on a rolling basis. Application fee: $75. Electronic applications accepted. *Expenses: Tuition:* Full-time $35,856; part-time $1494 per unit. *Required fees:* $1408; $64 per unit. $473 per term. Tuition and fees vary according to course load and program. *Financial support:* Fellowships with full and partial tuition reimbursements, career-related internships or fieldwork, Federal Work-Study, institutionally sponsored loans, scholarships/grants, and tuition waivers (partial) available. Support available to part-time students. Financial award application deadline: 2/1; financial award applicants required to submit FAFSA. *Faculty research:* Second language acquisition, cross-cultural communication, technology-enhanced language learning, language variation, action learning. *Unit head:* Prof. Shondel Nero, Director, 212-998-5757, E-mail: shondel.nero@nyu.edu. *Application contact:* 212-998-5030, Fax: 212-995-4328, E-mail: steinhardt.gradadmissions@nyu.edu.
Website: http://steinhardt.nyu.edu/teachlearn/mms.

Northern Arizona University, Graduate College, College of Arts and Letters, Department of Global Languages and Cultures, Flagstaff, AZ 86011. Offers Spanish teaching (MAT); Spanish teaching/Spanish education (MAT). Part-time programs available. *Faculty:* 27 full-time (18 women), 5 part-time/adjunct (all women). *Students:* 15 full-time (11 women), 2 part-time (both women); includes 7 minority (all Hispanic/ Latino), 2 international. Average age 28. 10 applicants, 70% accepted, 5 enrolled. In 2013, 8 master's awarded. *Degree requirements:* For master's, comprehensive exam, thesis optional. *Entrance requirements:* For master's, bachelor's degree in Spanish (coupled with preparation in general or foreign language education courses) or Spanish secondary education, or degree/experience in related field (e.g., bilingual education); minimum GPA of 3.0 or equivalent. Additional exam requirements/recommendations for international students: Required—TOEFL (minimum score 550 paper-based; 80 iBT), IELTS (minimum score 7). *Application deadline:* For fall admission, 4/21 priority date for domestic and international students; for spring admission, 10/21 priority date for domestic students. Applications are processed on a rolling basis. Application fee: $65. Electronic applications accepted. *Financial support:* In 2013–14, 17 teaching assistantships with full tuition reimbursements (averaging $13,500 per year) were awarded; Federal Work-Study, scholarships/grants, health care benefits, tuition waivers (full and partial), and unspecified assistantships also available. Financial award applicants required to submit FAFSA. *Application contact:* Alexandria McConocha, Administrative Associate, 928-523-2361, Fax: 928-523-0963, E-mail: alexandria.mcconocha@nau.edu.
Website: http://www.nau.edu/cal/modern-languages/.

Occidental College, Graduate Studies, Department of Education, Los Angeles, CA 90041-3314. Offers elementary education (MAT), including liberal studies; secondary education (MAT), including English and comparative literary studies, history, life science, mathematics, physical science, social science, Spanish. Part-time programs available. *Degree requirements:* For master's, comprehensive exam, synthesis paper. *Entrance requirements:* For master's, GRE General Test, minimum GPA of 3.0. Additional exam requirements/recommendations for international students: Required—TOEFL (minimum score 625 paper-based). *Expenses:* Contact institution. *Faculty research:* Preparing teacher-leaders, curriculum development.

Plymouth State University, College of Graduate Studies, Graduate Studies in Education, Program in Secondary Education, Plymouth, NH 03264-1595. Offers curriculum and instruction (M Ed); language education (M Ed); library media (M Ed); physical education (M Ed); social studies education (M Ed); special education (M Ed). Part-time and evening/weekend programs available. *Entrance requirements:* For master's, MAT.

Portland State University, Graduate Studies, College of Liberal Arts and Sciences, Department of World Languages and Literature, Portland, OR 97207-0751. Offers foreign literature and language (MA); French (MA); German (MA); Japanese (MA); Spanish (MA). Part-time programs available. *Faculty:* 47 full-time (29 women), 32 part-time/adjunct (24 women). *Students:* 20 full-time (15 women), 4 part-time (2 women); includes 1 minority (Hispanic/Latino), 8 international. Average age 30. 31 applicants, 48% accepted, 9 enrolled. In 2013, 13 master's awarded. *Degree requirements:* For master's, one foreign language, thesis (for some programs). *Entrance requirements:* Additional exam requirements/recommendations for international students: Required—TOEFL (minimum score 550 paper-based). *Application deadline:* For fall admission, 4/1 for domestic students, 3/1 for international students; for winter admission, 9/1 for domestic students, 7/1 for international students; for spring admission, 11/1 for domestic and international students. Applications are processed on a rolling basis. Application fee: $50. *Expenses:* Tuition, state resident: full-time $9207; part-time $341 per credit. Tuition, nonresident: full-time $14,391; part-time $533 per credit. *Required fees:* $1263; $22 per credit. $98 per quarter. One-time fee: $150. Tuition and fees vary according to program. *Financial support:* In 2013–14, 1 research assistantship with full tuition reimbursement (averaging $9,438 per year), 21 teaching assistantships with full and partial tuition reimbursements (averaging $9,254 per year) were awarded; Federal Work-Study, scholarships/grants, and unspecified assistantships also available. Support available to part-time students. Financial award application deadline: 3/1; financial award applicants required to submit FAFSA. *Faculty research:* Foreign language pedagogy, applied and social linguistics, literary history and criticism. *Total annual research expenditures:* $460,377. *Unit head:* Dr. Jennifer Perlmutter, Chair, 503-725-8783, Fax: 503-725-5276, E-mail: jrp@pdx.edu. *Application contact:* Amanda Dodds, Graduate Admissions Coordinator, 503-725-3243, E-mail: adodds@pdx.edu.
Website: http://www.pdx.edu/wll/.

Purdue University, Graduate School, College of Education, Department of Curriculum and Instruction, West Lafayette, IN 47907. Offers agricultural and extension education (PhD, Ed S); agriculture and extension education (MS, MS Ed); art education (PhD); curriculum studies (MS Ed, PhD, Ed S); educational technology (MS Ed, PhD, Ed S); elementary education (MS Ed); family and consumer sciences education (MS Ed, PhD, Ed S); foreign language education (MS Ed, PhD, Ed S); industrial technology (PhD, Ed S); language arts (MS Ed, PhD, Ed S); literacy (MS Ed, PhD, Ed S); mathematics/ science education (MS, MS Ed, PhD, Ed S); social studies (MS Ed, PhD); social studies education (Ed S); vocational/industrial education (MS Ed, PhD, Ed S); vocational/ technical education (MS Ed, PhD, Ed S). *Accreditation:* NCATE. Part-time and evening/ weekend programs available. *Faculty:* 29 full-time (19 women), 33 part-time/adjunct (29 women). *Students:* 85 full-time (53 women), 271 part-time (195 women); includes 62 minority (19 Black or African American, non-Hispanic/Latino; 3 American Indian or Alaska Native, non-Hispanic/Latino; 13 Asian, non-Hispanic/Latino; 22 Hispanic/Latino; 1 Native Hawaiian or other Pacific Islander, non-Hispanic/Latino; 4 Two or more races, non-Hispanic/Latino), 41 international. Average age 36. 155 applicants, 71% accepted, 71 enrolled. In 2013, 60 master's, 20 doctorates awarded. *Degree requirements:* For master's, thesis optional; for doctorate, thesis/dissertation, oral and written exams; for Ed S, oral presentation, project. *Entrance requirements:* For master's, GRE General Test (if undergraduate GPA is below 3.0), minimum undergraduate GPA of 3.0 or equivalent; for doctorate, GRE General Test (minimum combined verbal and quantitative score of 1000, 300 for new scoring), minimum undergraduate GPA of 3.0 or equivalent; master's degree with minimum GPA of 3.0 or equivalent; for Ed S, GRE General Test (minimum combined verbal and quantitative score of 1000, 300 for new scoring), minimum undergraduate GPA of 3.0 or equivalent; master's degree. Additional exam requirements/recommendations for international students: Required—TOEFL (minimum score 550 paper-based; 77 iBT). *Application deadline:* For fall admission, 12/ 15 for domestic students, 3/1 for international students; for spring admission, 9/15 for domestic students, 8/1 for international students. Application fee: $60 ($75 for international students). Electronic applications accepted. *Financial support:* Fellowships with full tuition reimbursements, research assistantships with full tuition reimbursements, teaching assistantships with full tuition reimbursements, career-related internships or fieldwork, and tuition waivers (full) available. Support available to part-time students. Financial award application deadline: 3/1; financial award applicants required to submit FAFSA. *Faculty research:* Literacy acquisition and development, teacher beliefs and knowledge, recruitment and retention of underrepresented students, economic education, literacy discourse. *Unit head:* Dr. Phillip J. VanFossen, Head, 765-494-7935, Fax: 765-496-1622, E-mail: vanfoss@purdue.edu. *Application contact:* Cindy Blankenship, Graduate Contact, 765-494-2345, Fax: 765-494-5832, E-mail: prater0@ purdue.edu.
Website: http://www.edci.purdue.edu/.

Purdue University, Graduate School, College of Liberal Arts, School of Languages and Cultures, West Lafayette, IN 47907. Offers French (MA, MAT, PhD), including French (MA, PhD), French education (MAT); German (MA, MAT, PhD), including German (MA, PhD), German education (MAT); Japanese pedagogy (MA); Spanish (MA, MAT, PhD), including Spanish (MA, PhD), Spanish education (MAT). *Faculty:* 52 full-time (30 women), 21 part-time/adjunct (16 women). *Students:* 58 full-time (42 women), 39 part-time (23 women); includes 8 minority (1 Asian, non-Hispanic/Latino; 7 Hispanic/Latino), 67 international. Average age 32. 76 applicants, 64% accepted, 18 enrolled. In 2013, 12 master's, 5 doctorates awarded. Terminal master's awarded for partial completion of doctoral program. *Degree requirements:* For master's, one foreign language; for doctorate, 2 foreign languages, thesis/dissertation. *Entrance requirements:* For master's, GRE General Test (minimum score 600, 160 for new scoring), two writing samples, one in English, one in language (French, German, Japanese, or Spanish); sample recording of English and language of study; for doctorate, GRE General Test (minimum score 600, 160 for new scoring), master's degree with minimum GPA of 3.5 or equivalent; two writing samples, one in English, one in language (French, German, Japanese, or Spanish); sample recording of English and language of study. Additional exam requirements/recommendations for international students: Required—TOEFL (minimum score 550 paper-based; 77 iBT); Recommended—TWE. *Application deadline:* For fall admission, 12/12 for domestic and international students; for spring admission, 10/1 for domestic and international students. Applications are processed on a rolling basis. Application fee: $60 ($75 for international students). Electronic applications accepted. *Financial support:* In 2013–14, fellowships with tuition reimbursements (averaging $15,750 per year), teaching assistantships with tuition reimbursements (averaging $13,463 per year) were awarded. Support available to part-time students. Financial award applicants required to submit FAFSA. *Faculty research:* Linguistics, semiotics, literary criticism, pedagogy. *Unit head:* Dr. Madeleine M. Henry, Interim Head, 765-494-3867, E-mail: henry48@purdue.edu. *Application contact:* Joni L. Hipsher, Graduate Contact, 765-494-3842, E-mail: jlhipshe@purdue.edu.
Website: http://www.cla.purdue.edu/slc/main/.

Queens College of the City University of New York, Division of Graduate Studies, Division of Education, Department of Secondary Education, Flushing, NY 11367-1597. Offers art (MS Ed); biology (MS Ed, AC); chemistry (MS Ed, AC); earth sciences (MS Ed, AC); English (MS Ed, AC); French (MS Ed, AC); Italian (MS Ed, AC); mathematics (MS Ed, AC); music (MS Ed, AC); physics (MS Ed, AC); social studies (MS Ed, AC); Spanish (MS Ed, AC). Part-time and evening/weekend programs available. *Degree requirements:* For master's, research project; for AC, thesis optional. *Entrance requirements:* For master's, minimum GPA of 3.0. Additional exam requirements/recommendations for international students: Required—TOEFL.

Quinnipiac University, School of Education, Program in Secondary Education, Hamden, CT 06518-1940. Offers biology (MAT); English (MAT); history/social studies (MAT); mathematics (MAT); Spanish (MAT). *Accreditation:* NCATE. *Faculty:* 14 full-time (7 women), 46 part-time/adjunct (27 women). *Students:* 44 full-time (37 women), 1 (woman) part-time; includes 2 minority (both Hispanic/Latino). 45 applicants, 93% accepted, 32 enrolled. In 2013, 32 master's awarded. *Entrance requirements:* For master's, PRAXIS I, minimum GPA of 2.67, interview. *Application deadline:* For fall admission, 4/1 priority date for domestic students. Applications are processed on a rolling basis. Application fee: $45. Electronic applications accepted. *Expenses: Tuition:* Part-time $920 per credit. *Required fees:* $37 per credit. *Financial support:* Career-related internships or fieldwork, tuition waivers (full and partial), and unspecified assistantships available. Support available to part-time students. Financial award application deadline: 6/1; financial award applicants required to submit FAFSA. *Faculty research:* Multicultural and urban education/leadership, challenges of teaching diverse learners, scholarship of teaching and learning, technology and teaching, humor and education. *Unit head:* Mordechai Gordon, Program Director, E-mail: mordechai.gordon@quinnipiac.edu. *Application contact:* Office of Graduate Admissions, 800-462-1944, Fax: 203-582-3443, E-mail: graduate@quinnipiac.edu.
Website: http://www.quinnipiac.edu/gradeducation.

Rhode Island College, School of Graduate Studies, Feinstein School of Education and Human Development, Department of Educational Studies, Providence, RI 02908-1991. Offers advanced studies in teaching and learning (M Ed); English (MAT); French (MAT); history (MAT); math (MAT); secondary education (MAT); Spanish (MAT); teaching English as a second language (M Ed). *Accreditation:* NCATE. Part-time and evening/ weekend programs available. *Faculty:* 10 full-time (6 women), 7 part-time/adjunct (all women). *Students:* 4 full-time (3 women), 61 part-time (54 women); includes 2 minority (both Hispanic/Latino). Average age 37. In 2013, 27 master's awarded. *Degree requirements:* For master's, capstone or comprehensive assessment. *Entrance requirements:* For master's, GRE or MAT (for most programs), minimum undergraduate GPA of 3.0; baccalaureate degree in English, French, history, math or Spanish; evaluation of content area knowledge; 3 letters of recommendation; interview. Additional exam requirements/recommendations for international students: Recommended—TOEFL (minimum score 550 paper-based; 79 iBT). *Application deadline:* For fall admission, 3/1 for domestic students; for spring admission, 11/1 for domestic students. Applications are processed on a rolling basis. Application fee: $50. *Expenses:* Tuition, state resident: full-time $8928; part-time $372 per credit hour. Tuition, nonresident: full-time $17,376; part-time $724 per credit hour. *Required fees:* $602; $22 per credit. $72 per term. *Financial support:* In 2013–14, 2 teaching assistantships with full tuition reimbursements (averaging $2,250 per year) were awarded; career-related internships

or fieldwork, Federal Work-Study, scholarships/grants, health care benefits, and unspecified assistantships also available. Support available to part-time students. Financial award application deadline: 5/15; financial award applicants required to submit FAFSA. *Faculty research:* School administration, school/college articulation. *Unit head:* Dr. Paul Tiskus, Chair, 401-456-8170. *Application contact:* Graduate Studies, 401-456-8700.

Website: http://www.ric.edu/educationalStudies/.

Rider University, Department of Graduate Education, Leadership and Counseling, Teacher Certification Program, Lawrenceville, NJ 08648-3001. Offers business education (Certificate); elementary education (Certificate); English as a second language (Certificate); English education (Certificate); mathematics education (Certificate); preschool to grade 3 (Certificate); science education (Certificate); social studies education (Certificate); world languages (Certificate), including French, German, Spanish. Part-time programs available. *Degree requirements:* For Certificate, internship, professional portfolio. *Entrance requirements:* For degree, PRAXIS, resume. Additional exam requirements/recommendations for international students: Required—TOEFL (minimum score 550 paper-based). Electronic applications accepted. *Faculty research:* Conceptual foundations for optimal development of creativity; creative theory, cognitive processes in mathematics learning, teacher collaboration.

Rivier University, School of Graduate Studies, Department of Modern Languages, Nashua, NH 03060. Offers Spanish (MAT). Part-time and evening/weekend programs available.

Rowan University, Graduate School, College of Education, Department of Teacher Education, Glassboro, NJ 08028-1701. Offers bilingual/bicultural education (CGS); collaborative teaching (MST); educational technology (CGS); elementary education (MST); elementary school teaching (MA); ESL education (CGS); foreign language education (MST); music education (MA); science teaching (MST); secondary education (MST); subject matter teaching (MA); teacher leadership (M Ed); teaching and learning (CGS); theatre education (MST). *Accreditation:* NCATE. Part-time and evening/weekend programs available. *Faculty:* 7 full-time (5 women), 1 (woman) part-time/adjunct. *Students:* 35 full-time (22 women), 78 part-time (66 women); includes 23 minority (4 Black or African American, non-Hispanic/Latino; 3 Asian, non-Hispanic/Latino; 16 Hispanic/Latino). Average age 28. 58 applicants, 100% accepted, 37 enrolled. In 2013, 12 master's awarded. *Degree requirements:* For master's, comprehensive exam, thesis. *Entrance requirements:* For master's, GRE General Test, PRAXIS I, PRAXIS II, interview, minimum GPA of 2.8. Additional exam requirements/recommendations for international students: Required—TOEFL. *Application deadline:* For spring admission, 2/15 priority date for domestic students. Applications are processed on a rolling basis. Application fee: $65. Electronic applications accepted. *Expenses: Tuition, area resident:* Part-time $638 per credit. Tuition, state resident: full-time $5742. *Required fees:* $142 per credit. Tuition and fees vary according to course level and program. *Financial support:* Career-related internships or fieldwork, scholarships/grants, health care benefits, and unspecified assistantships available. Support available to part-time students. *Unit head:* Dr. Horacio Sosa, Dean, College of Graduate and Continuing Education, 856-256-4747, Fax: 856-256-5638, E-mail: sosa@rowan.edu. *Application contact:* Karen Haynes, Graduate Coordinator, 856-256-4052, Fax: 856-256-4436, E-mail: haynes@rowan.edu.

Rutgers, The State University of New Jersey, New Brunswick, Graduate School-New Brunswick, Program in French, Piscataway, NJ 08854-8097. Offers French (MA, PhD); French studies (MAT). Part-time and evening/weekend programs available. Terminal master's awarded for partial completion of doctoral program. *Degree requirements:* For master's, one foreign language, written and oral exams (MA); for doctorate, 3 foreign languages, thesis/dissertation, qualifying exam. *Entrance requirements:* For master's and doctorate, GRE General Test. *Faculty research:* Literatures in French, literary history and theory, rhetoric and poetics.

Rutgers, The State University of New Jersey, New Brunswick, Graduate School-New Brunswick, Program in Italian, Piscataway, NJ 08854-8097. Offers Italian (MA, PhD); Italian literature and literary criticism (MA); language, literature and culture (MAT). Part-time and evening/weekend programs available. Terminal master's awarded for partial completion of doctoral program. *Degree requirements:* For master's, one foreign language, comprehensive exam (for some programs), thesis optional; for doctorate, 2 foreign languages, thesis/dissertation, qualifying exam. *Entrance requirements:* For master's and doctorate, GRE General Test. Additional exam requirements/recommendations for international students: Required—TOEFL. *Faculty research:* Literature.

Rutgers, The State University of New Jersey, New Brunswick, Graduate School-New Brunswick, Program in Spanish, Piscataway, NJ 08854-8097. Offers bilingualism and second language acquisition (MA, PhD); Spanish (MA, MAT, PhD); Spanish literature (MA, PhD); translation (MA). Part-time programs available. *Degree requirements:* For master's, comprehensive exam (for some programs), thesis (for some programs); for doctorate, 2 foreign languages, comprehensive exam, thesis/dissertation. *Entrance requirements:* For master's and doctorate, GRE General Test. Additional exam requirements/recommendations for international students: Required—TOEFL. Electronic applications accepted. *Faculty research:* Hispanic literature, Luso-Brazilian literature, Spanish linguistics, Spanish translation.

Rutgers, The State University of New Jersey, New Brunswick, Graduate School of Education, Department of Learning and Teaching, Program in Language Education, Piscataway, NJ 08854-8097. Offers English as a second language education (Ed M); language education (Ed M, Ed D). Part-time programs available. Terminal master's awarded for partial completion of doctoral program. *Degree requirements:* For master's, comprehensive exam; for doctorate, thesis/dissertation, concept paper, qualifying exam. *Entrance requirements:* For master's, GRE General Test, minimum GPA of 3.0; for doctorate, GRE General Test, minimum GPA of 3.5. Additional exam requirements/recommendations for international students: Required—TOEFL. Electronic applications accepted. *Faculty research:* Linguistics, sociolinguistics, cross-cultural/international communication.

St. John Fisher College, Ralph C. Wilson Jr. School of Education, Program in Adolescence Education and Special Education, Rochester, NY 14618-3597. Offers adolescence education: English with special education (MS Ed); adolescence education: French with special education (MS Ed); adolescence education: social studies with special education (MS Ed); adolescence education: Spanish with special education (MS Ed). Part-time and evening/weekend programs available. *Faculty:* 4 full-time (2 women), 4 part-time/adjunct (all women). *Students:* 20 full-time (10 women), 27 part-time (21 women); includes 4 minority (1 Black or African American, non-Hispanic/Latino; 1 Asian, non-Hispanic/Latino; 1 Hispanic/Latino; 1 Two or more races, non-Hispanic/Latino). Average age 27. 45 applicants, 89% accepted, 28 enrolled. In 2013, 28 master's awarded. *Degree requirements:* For master's, field experiences, student teaching, LAST. *Entrance requirements:* For master's, 2 letters of recommendation, personal statement, current resume. Additional exam requirements/recommendations for international students: Required—TOEFL (minimum score 575 paper-based; 80 iBT). *Application deadline:* Applications are processed on a rolling basis. Application fee: $30. Electronic applications accepted. *Expenses: Tuition:* Part-time $795 per credit hour.

Required fees: $10 per credit hour. Tuition and fees vary according to course load, degree level and program. *Financial support:* In 2013–14, 11 students received support. Scholarships/grants available. Financial award applicants required to submit FAFSA. *Faculty research:* Arts and humanities, urban schools, constructivist learning, at-risk students, mentoring. *Unit head:* Dr. Susan Schultz, Program Director, 585-385-7296, E-mail: sschultz@sjfc.edu. *Application contact:* Jose Perales, Director of Graduate Admissions, 585-385-8067, E-mail: jperales@sjfc.edu.

Website: http://www.sjfc.edu/academics/education/departments/ms-special-ed/options/initial-adolescence.dot.

Saint Xavier University, Graduate Studies, School of Education, Chicago, IL 60655-3105. Offers counseling (MA); curriculum and instruction (MA); early childhood education (MA); educational administration (MA); elementary education (MA); individualized studies (MA), including educational technology, English as a second language (ESL), ISTEM (integrative science, technology, engineering, and math), science education; music education (MA); reading (MA); secondary education (MA); Spanish education (MA); special education (MA); teaching and leadership (MA). *Accreditation:* NCATE. Part-time and evening/weekend programs available. *Degree requirements:* For master's, thesis or project. *Entrance requirements:* For master's, minimum GPA of 3.0. *Expenses:* Contact institution.

Shippensburg University of Pennsylvania, School of Graduate Studies, College of Education and Human Services, Department of Teacher Education, Shippensburg, PA 17257-2299. Offers curriculum and instruction (M Ed), including biology, early childhood education, elementary education, geography/earth science, history, mathematics, middle level education, modern languages; reading (M Ed). *Accreditation:* NCATE. Part-time and evening/weekend programs available. *Faculty:* 13 full-time (9 women), 2 part-time/adjunct (both women). *Students:* 6 full-time (all women), 72 part-time (61 women); includes 5 minority (1 Black or African American, non-Hispanic/Latino; 1 Asian, non-Hispanic/Latino; 2 Hispanic/Latino; 1 Two or more races, non-Hispanic/Latino), 1 international. Average age 30. 55 applicants, 60% accepted, 24 enrolled. In 2013, 63 master's awarded. *Degree requirements:* For master's, comprehensive exam (for some programs), thesis optional, practicum or internship; capstone seminar (for some programs). *Entrance requirements:* For master's, MAT or GRE (if GPA less than 2.75), interview, 3 letters of reference, questionnaire of teaching background and future goals. Additional exam requirements/recommendations for international students: Required—TOEFL (minimum score 580 paper-based); Recommended—IELTS (minimum score 6). *Application deadline:* For fall admission, 4/1 priority date for domestic students, 4/30 for international students; for spring admission, 9/1 priority date for domestic students, 9/30 for international students. Applications are processed on a rolling basis. Application fee: $45. Electronic applications accepted. *Expenses: Tuition, area resident:* Part-time $442 per credit. Tuition, state resident: part-time $442 per credit. Tuition, nonresident: part-time $663 per credit. *Required fees:* $127 per credit. *Financial support:* In 2013–14, 4 research assistantships with full tuition reimbursements (averaging $5,000 per year) were awarded; career-related internships or fieldwork, scholarships/grants, unspecified assistantships, and resident hall director and student payroll positions also available. Support available to part-time students. Financial award application deadline: 3/1; financial award applicants required to submit FAFSA. *Unit head:* Dr. Christine A. Royce, Chairperson, 717-477-1688, Fax: 717-477-4046, E-mail: caroyc@ship.edu. *Application contact:* Jeremy R. Goshorn, Assistant Dean of Graduate Admissions, 717-477-1231, Fax: 717-477-4016, E-mail: jrgoshorn@ship.edu.

Website: http://www.ship.edu/teacher/.

SIT Graduate Institute, Graduate Programs, Programs in Language Teacher Education, Brattleboro, VT 05302-0676. Offers TESOL (MAT). *Degree requirements:* For master's, one foreign language, thesis, teaching practice. *Entrance requirements:* For master's, 4 letters of reference. Additional exam requirements/recommendations for international students: Required—TOEFL. *Faculty research:* Teaching English to speakers of other languages (TESOL).

Smith College, Graduate and Special Programs, Department of Education and Child Study, Program in Secondary Education, Northampton, MA 01063. Offers biological sciences education (MAT); chemistry education (MAT); English education (MAT); French education (MAT); geology education (MAT); government education (MAT); history education (MAT); mathematics education (MAT); physics education (MAT); Spanish education (MAT). Part-time programs available. *Faculty:* 6 full-time (4 women), 3 part-time/adjunct (2 women). *Students:* 4 full-time (3 women), 1 (woman) part-time, 2 international. Average age 33. 12 applicants, 92% accepted, 4 enrolled. In 2013, 6 master's awarded. *Entrance requirements:* Additional exam requirements/recommendations for international students: Required—TOEFL (minimum score 595 paper-based; 97 iBT). *Application deadline:* For fall admission, 4/1 for domestic students, 1/15 priority date for international students; for spring admission, 12/1 for domestic students. Application fee: $60. *Expenses: Tuition:* Full-time $32,160; part-time $1340 per credit. *Financial support:* In 2013–14, 5 students received support, including 2 fellowships with full tuition reimbursements available; career-related internships or fieldwork, institutionally sponsored loans, and scholarships/grants also available. Support available to part-time students. Financial award application deadline: 1/15; financial award applicants required to submit CSS PROFILE or FAFSA. *Unit head:* Rosetta Cohen, Graduate Student Advisor, 413-585-3266, E-mail: rcohen@smith.edu. *Application contact:* Ruth Morgan, Administrative Assistant, 413-585-3050, Fax: 413-585-3054, E-mail: gradstdy@smith.edu.

Website: http://www.smith.edu/educ/.

Smith College, Graduate and Special Programs, Department of Spanish and Portuguese, Northampton, MA 01063. Offers Spanish (MAT). Part-time programs available. *Faculty:* 9 full-time (6 women). *Degree requirements:* For master's, one foreign language. *Entrance requirements:* Additional exam requirements/recommendations for international students: Required—TOEFL (minimum score 595 paper-based; 97 iBT). *Application deadline:* For fall admission, 4/1 for domestic students, 1/15 for international students; for spring admission, 12/1 for domestic students. Application fee: $60. *Expenses: Tuition:* Full-time $32,160; part-time $1340 per credit. *Financial support:* Career-related internships or fieldwork, institutionally sponsored loans, and scholarships/grants available. Support available to part-time students. Financial award application deadline: 1/15; financial award applicants required to submit CSS PROFILE or FAFSA. *Unit head:* Marguerite Harrison, Chair, 413-585-3450, E-mail: mharriso@smith.edu. *Application contact:* Ruth Morgan, Administrative Assistant, 413-585-3050, Fax: 413-585-3054, E-mail: gradstdy@smith.edu.

Website: http://www.smith.edu/spp/.

Soka University of America, Graduate School, Aliso Viejo, CA 92656. Offers teaching Japanese as a foreign language (Certificate). Evening/weekend programs available. *Entrance requirements:* For degree, bachelor's degree with minimum GPA of 3.0, proficiency in Japanese. Additional exam requirements/recommendations for international students: Required—TOEFL (minimum score 600 paper-based; 100 iBT).

Southern Connecticut State University, School of Graduate Studies, School of Arts and Sciences, Department of World Languages and Literatures, New Haven, CT 06515-1355. Offers multicultural-bilingual education/teaching English to speakers of other languages (MS); romance languages (MA). Part-time and evening/weekend programs available. *Degree requirements:* For master's, one foreign language, thesis or

alternative. *Entrance requirements:* For master's, interview, minimum undergraduate GPA of 2.7. Electronic applications accepted.

Southern Oregon University, Graduate Studies, College of Arts and Sciences, Department of Foreign Languages and Literatures, Ashland, OR 97520. Offers French language teaching (MA); Spanish language teaching (MA). Part-time programs available. Postbaccalaureate distance learning degree programs offered (minimal on-campus study). *Faculty:* 11 full-time (6 women), 1 (woman) part-time/adjunct. *Students:* 55 full-time (48 women), 5 part-time (2 women); includes 15 minority (2 Asian, non-Hispanic/Latino; 12 Hispanic/Latino; 1 Two or more races, non-Hispanic/Latino). Average age 36. In 2013, 4 master's awarded. *Degree requirements:* For master's, thesis (for some programs). *Entrance requirements:* For master's, GRE General Test, minimum cumulative GPA of 3.0 in the last 90 quarter credits (60 semester credits) of undergraduate coursework. Additional exam requirements/recommendations for international students: Required—TOEFL (minimum score 540 paper-based; 76 iBT), IELTS (minimum score 6), ELPT (minimum score 964) or ELS (minimum score 112). *Application deadline:* For fall admission, 7/31 priority date for domestic and international students; for winter admission, 11/15 priority date for domestic and international students; for spring admission, 1/7 priority date for domestic and international students. Applications are processed on a rolling basis. Application fee: $50. Electronic applications accepted. *Expenses:* Tuition, state resident: full-time $13,635; part-time $378.72 per credit hour. Tuition, nonresident: full-time $17,042; part-time $473.40 per credit hour. *Required fees:* $408 per quarter. *Financial support:* Research assistantships with partial tuition reimbursements, career-related internships or fieldwork, institutionally sponsored loans, scholarships/grants, and unspecified assistantships available. *Unit head:* Dr. Dan Morris, French Language Graduate Program Coordinator, 541-552-6740, E-mail: morris@sou.edu. *Application contact:* Dr. Anne Connor, Graduate Spanish Language Program Coordinator, 541-552-6743, E-mail: connora@sou.edu.
Website: http://www.sou.edu/language/.

Spalding University, Graduate Studies, College of Education, Programs in Education, Louisville, KY 40203-2188. Offers art teacher education (MAT); business teacher education (MAT); elementary school education (MAT); foreign language (MAT); general education (MA Ed); high school education (MAT); middle school education (MAT); school administration (MA Ed); secondary education (MAT); special education (learning and behavioral disorders) (MAT); student guidance counselor (MA); teacher education and professional development (MAT). *Accreditation:* NCATE. Part-time and evening/weekend programs available. *Faculty:* 12 full-time (11 women), 6 part-time/adjunct (4 women). *Students:* 92 full-time (63 women), 36 part-time (29 women); includes 43 minority (41 Black or African American, non-Hispanic/Latino; 2 Two or more races, non-Hispanic/Latino). Average age 35. 77 applicants, 48% accepted, 30 enrolled. In 2013, 81 master's awarded. *Degree requirements:* For master's, portfolio, final project, clinical experience. *Entrance requirements:* For master's, GRE General Test or MAT, interview, letters of recommendation, resume. Additional exam requirements/recommendations for international students: Required—TOEFL (minimum score 535 paper-based). *Application deadline:* Applications are processed on a rolling basis. Application fee: $30. Electronic applications accepted. *Expenses: Tuition:* Full-time $21,450. *Required fees:* $810. Tuition and fees vary according to course load, degree level, program and student level. *Financial support:* Scholarships/grants, traineeships, and unspecified assistantships available. Financial award application deadline: 3/30; financial award applicants required to submit FAFSA. *Faculty research:* Instructional technology, achievement gap, classroom management, assessment. *Unit head:* Dr. Beverly Keepers, Dean, 502-588-7121, Fax: 502-585-7123, E-mail: bkeepers@spalding.edu. *Application contact:* Bonnie Caughron, Administrative Assistant, College of Education, 502-873-4262, E-mail: bcaughron@spalding.edu.

State University of New York at Plattsburgh, Division of Education, Health, and Human Services, Program in Teacher Education: Adolescence, Plattsburgh, NY 12901-2681. Offers adolescence education (MST); biology 7-12 (MST); chemistry 7-12 (MST); earth science 7-12 (MST); English 7-12 (MST); French 7-12 (MST); mathematics 7-12 (MST); physics 7-12 (MST); social studies 7-12 (MST); Spanish 7-12 (MST). *Accreditation:* Teacher Education Accreditation Council. Part-time and evening/weekend programs available. *Students:* 75 full-time (47 women), 5 part-time (3 women); includes 10 minority (1 Black or African American, non-Hispanic/Latino; 4 Asian, non-Hispanic/Latino; 5 Hispanic/Latino), 1 international. Average age 25. *Entrance requirements:* For master's, minimum GPA of 2.75. Additional exam requirements/recommendations for international students: Required—TOEFL. *Application deadline:* For fall admission, 2/15 priority date for domestic students. Applications are processed on a rolling basis. Application fee: $75. *Financial support:* Application deadline: 4/15; applicants required to submit FAFSA. *Unit head:* Dr. Robert Ackland, Coordinator, 518-564-5131, E-mail: acklanrt@plattsburgh.edu. *Application contact:* Betsy Kane, Director, Graduate Admissions, 518-564-4723, Fax: 518-564-4722, E-mail: bkane002@plattsburgh.edu.

State University of New York College at Cortland, Graduate Studies, School of Arts and Sciences, Department of Second Language Education, Cortland, NY 13045. Offers ESL (MS Ed); French (MS Ed); Spanish (MS Ed). *Accreditation:* NCATE. *Expenses:* Tuition, state resident: full-time $9870; part-time $411 per credit hour. Tuition, nonresident: full-time $18,350; part-time $765 per credit hour. *Required fees:* $1458; $65 per credit hour.

State University of New York College at Old Westbury, Program in Adolescent Education, Old Westbury, NY 11568-0210. Offers biology (MAT, MS); chemistry (MAT, MS); English language arts (MAT, MS); math (MAT, MS); social studies (MAT, MS); Spanish (MAT, MS). Part-time and evening/weekend programs available. *Faculty:* 19 full-time (11 women), 6 part-time/adjunct (1 woman). *Students:* 33 full-time (20 women), 33 part-time (19 women); includes 16 minority (2 Black or African American, non-Hispanic/Latino; 4 Asian, non-Hispanic/Latino; 9 Hispanic/Latino; 1 Two or more races, non-Hispanic/Latino). 25 applicants, 84% accepted, 19 enrolled. In 2013, 29 master's awarded. *Entrance requirements:* For master's, Liberal Arts and Sciences Test, undergraduate degree with at least 30 semester hours of appropriate coursework as defined by the respective discipline; minimum cumulative undergraduate GPA of 3.0; two letters of recommendation (one from an academic source); essay. Additional exam requirements/recommendations for international students: Required—TOEFL (minimum score 550 paper-based); Recommended—IELTS. *Expenses:* Tuition, state resident: full-time $9370; part-time $390 per credit. Tuition, nonresident: full-time $16,680; part-time $695 per credit. *Required fees:* $45.85 per credit. $47 per term. *Application contact:* Philip D'Angelo, Graduate Admissions Office, 516-876-3073, E-mail: enroll@oldwestbury.edu.

Stony Brook University, State University of New York, School of Professional Development, Stony Brook, NY 11794. Offers biology (MAT); chemistry (MAT); coaching (Graduate Certificate); earth science (MAT); educational computing (Graduate Certificate); educational leadership (Advanced Certificate); English (MAT); environmental management (Graduate Certificate); French (MAT); German (MAT); higher education administration (MA, Certificate); human resource management (MS, Graduate Certificate); industrial management (Graduate Certificate); information systems management (Graduate Certificate); Italian (MAT); liberal studies (MA); mathematics (MAT); operations research (Graduate Certificate); physics (MAT); school district business leadership (Advanced Certificate); social science and the professions (MPS), including environmental management, human resource management; social studies (MAT); Spanish (MAT). Part-time and evening/weekend programs available. Postbaccalaureate distance learning degree programs offered. *Faculty:* 2 full-time (1 woman), 70 part-time/adjunct (30 women). *Students:* 241 full-time (135 women), 954 part-time (673 women); includes 209 minority (65 Black or African American, non-Hispanic/Latino; 2 American Indian or Alaska Native, non-Hispanic/Latino; 32 Asian, non-Hispanic/Latino; 104 Hispanic/Latino; 6 Two or more races, non-Hispanic/Latino), 7 international. Average age 28. 353 applicants, 92% accepted, 248 enrolled. In 2013, 312 master's, 131 other advanced degrees awarded. *Degree requirements:* For master's, one foreign language, thesis or alternative. *Application deadline:* For fall admission, 1/15 for domestic students; for spring admission, 10/1 for domestic students. Applications are processed on a rolling basis. Application fee: $100. *Expenses:* Tuition, state resident: full-time $9870; part-time $411 per credit. Tuition, nonresident: full-time $18,350; part-time $765 per credit. *Financial support:* Fellowships, research assistantships, teaching assistantships, and career-related internships or fieldwork available. Support available to part-time students. *Unit head:* Dr. Thomas Sexton, Interim Dean, 631-632-7181, Fax: 631-632-9046, E-mail: thomas.sexton@stonybrook.edu. *Application contact:* 631-632-7050 Ext. 1, E-mail: spd@stonybrook.edu.
Website: http://www.stonybrook.edu/spd/.

Texas A&M International University, Office of Graduate Studies and Research, College of Arts and Sciences, Department of Humanities, Laredo, TX 78041-1900. Offers English (MA); Hispanic studies (PhD); history and political thought (MA); language, literature and translation (MA). *Faculty:* 10 full-time (3 women), 2 part-time/adjunct (0 women). *Students:* 10 full-time (6 women), 43 part-time (27 women); includes 48 minority (all Hispanic/Latino), 1 international. Average age 36. 37 applicants, 81% accepted, 27 enrolled. In 2013, 15 master's awarded. *Degree requirements:* For master's, comprehensive exam (for some programs), thesis (for some programs). *Entrance requirements:* For master's, GRE General Test. Additional exam requirements/recommendations for international students: Required—TOEFL (minimum score 550 paper-based; 79 iBT). *Application deadline:* For fall admission, 4/30 priority date for domestic students, 4/30 for international students; for spring admission, 11/30 for domestic students, 10/1 for international students. Applications are processed on a rolling basis. Application fee: $35 ($50 for international students). *Expenses:* Tuition, state resident: full-time $5184. *International tuition:* $11,556 full-time. *Financial support:* In 2013–14, 2 fellowships, 9 research assistantships, 3 teaching assistantships were awarded. Financial award application deadline: 4/1. *Unit head:* Dr. Stephen Duffy, Chair, 956-326-2543, E-mail: sduffy@tamiu.edu. *Application contact:* Suzanne Hansen-Alford, Director of Graduate Recruiting, 956-326-3023, Fax: 956-326-3021, E-mail: enroll@tamiu.edu.
Website: http://www.tamiu.edu/coas/lla/.

Texas A&M University–Kingsville, College of Graduate Studies, College of Arts and Sciences, Department of Language and Literature, Kingsville, TX 78363. Offers English (MA, MS); Hispanic culture (PhD); Spanish (MA). Part-time and evening/weekend programs available. *Faculty:* 8 full-time (5 women), 1 (woman) part-time/adjunct. *Students:* 1 (woman) full-time, 9 part-time (6 women); includes 9 minority (all Hispanic/Latino). Average age 40. In 2013, 5 master's awarded. *Degree requirements:* For master's, comprehensive exam, thesis or alternative. *Entrance requirements:* For master's, GRE General Test, minimum GPA of 3.0. Additional exam requirements/recommendations for international students: Required—TOEFL. *Application deadline:* For fall admission, 6/1 for domestic students; for spring admission, 11/15 for domestic students. Applications are processed on a rolling basis. Application fee: $35 ($50 for international students). *Financial support:* Teaching assistantships, Federal Work-Study, and institutionally sponsored loans available. Financial award application deadline: 5/15. *Faculty research:* Linguistics, culture, Spanish American literature, Spanish peninsular literature, American literature. *Unit head:* Dr. David Sabrio, Chair, 361-593-4960, E-mail: d-sabrio@tamuk.edu. *Application contact:* Dr. D. Wayne Gunnz, Graduate Coordinator, 361-593-2597.

Union Graduate College, School of Education, Schenectady, NY 12308-3107. Offers biology (MAT); chemistry (MAT); Chinese (MAT); earth science (MAT); English (MA, MAT); English and history (MA); French (MAT); general science (MAT); German (MAT); history (MA); Latin (MAT); life sciences (MS); mathematics (MAT); mathematics and computer technology (MS); mentoring and teacher leadership (AC); middle childhood extension (AC); national board certification and teacher leadership (AC); physical sciences (MS); physics (MAT); social studies (MAT); Spanish (MAT); technology (MAT). *Accreditation:* Teacher Education Accreditation Council. *Faculty:* 3 full-time (1 woman), 56 part-time/adjunct (34 women). *Students:* 32 full-time (16 women), 27 part-time (22 women); includes 15 minority (1 Black or African American, non-Hispanic/Latino; 4 Asian, non-Hispanic/Latino; 6 Hispanic/Latino; 4 Two or more races, non-Hispanic/Latino), 1 international. Average age 32. In 2013, 25 master's, 11 other advanced degrees awarded. *Degree requirements:* For master's, thesis or project. *Entrance requirements:* For master's, minimum GPA of 3.0, letters of recommendation. Additional exam requirements/recommendations for international students: Required—TOEFL (minimum score 550 paper-based). *Application deadline:* Applications are processed on a rolling basis. Application fee: $60. Electronic applications accepted. *Expenses:* Contact institution. *Financial support:* Career-related internships or fieldwork, Federal Work-Study, scholarships/grants, health care benefits, and tuition waivers (partial) available. Support available to part-time students. Financial award applicants required to submit FAFSA. *Faculty research:* Transformative learning, science education, National Board Certification, teacher leadership, teacher quality. *Unit head:* Dr. Lynn Gelzheiser, Dean, 518-631-9870, Fax: 518-631-9901. *Application contact:* Nicki Foley, Assistant, 518-631-9871, Fax: 518-631-9903, E-mail: foleyn@uniongraduatecollege.edu.

United States University, School of Education, Cypress, CA 90630. Offers administration (MA Ed); early childhood education (MA Ed); general (MA Ed); higher education administration (MA Ed); Spanish language education (MA Ed); special education (MA Ed). *Degree requirements:* For master's, portfolio. *Entrance requirements:* For master's, minimum undergraduate GPA of 2.5. Additional exam requirements/recommendations for international students: Required—TOEFL (minimum score 500 paper-based; 61 iBT).

Universidad del Este, Graduate School, Carolina, PR 00984. Offers accounting (MBA); adult education (M Ed); agribusiness (MBA); criminal justice and criminology (MA); curriculum and instruction - early education (M Ed); curriculum and instruction - elementary (M Ed); curriculum and instruction - English (M Ed); curriculum and instruction - Spanish (M Ed); human resources (MBA); information security management (MBA); information technology and Web business development (MBA); management (MBA); public policy (MPA); social work (MA), including clinical social work; special education (M Ed); strategic leadership (MBA). *Students:* 464 full-time (322 women), 669 part-time (499 women); all minorities (all Hispanic/Latino). Average age 35. 693 applicants, 61% accepted, 332 enrolled. In 2013, 228 master's awarded. *Unit head:* Jose R. Clintron, Dean, 787-257-7373 Ext. 3007, E-mail: ue_jcintron@suagm.edu. *Application contact:* Clotilde Santiago, Director of Admissions, 787-257-7373 Ext. 3400, E-mail: ue_csantiago@suagm.edu.

Université du Québec en Outaouais, Graduate Programs, Department of Language Studies, Gatineau, QC J8X 3X7, Canada. Offers second and foreign language teaching (Diploma).

University at Buffalo, the State University of New York, Graduate School, Graduate School of Education, Department of Learning and Instruction, Buffalo, NY 14260. Offers biology education (Ed M, Certificate); chemistry education (Ed M, Certificate); childhood education (Ed M); childhood education with bilingual extension (Ed M); curriculum, instruction and the science of learning (PhD); early childhood education (Ed M); early childhood education with bilingual extension (birth-grade 2) (Ed M); earth science education (Ed M, Certificate); education studies (Ed M); educational technology and new literacies (Certificate); elementary education (Ed D); English education (Ed M, Certificate); English for speakers of other languages (Ed M); foreign and second language education (PhD); French education (Ed M, Certificate); German education (Ed M, Certificate); gifted education (Certificate); Latin education (Ed M, Certificate); literacy specialist (Ed M); literacy teaching and learning (Certificate); mathematics education (Ed M, Certificate); music education (Ed M, Certificate); physics education (Ed M, Certificate); science and the public (Ed M); social studies education (Ed M, Certificate); Spanish education (Ed M, Certificate); special education (PhD); teaching English to speakers of other languages (Ed M). Part-time and evening/weekend programs available. Postbaccalaureate distance learning degree programs offered (no on-campus study). *Faculty:* 31 full-time (23 women), 64 part-time/adjunct (53 women). *Students:* 275 full-time (215 women), 293 part-time (205 women); includes 35 minority (16 Black or African American, non-Hispanic/Latino; 5 American Indian or Alaska Native, non-Hispanic/Latino; 11 Asian, non-Hispanic/Latino; 3 Hispanic/Latino), 97 international. Average age 30. 544 applicants, 81% accepted, 246 enrolled. In 2013, 222 master's, 17 doctorates, 35 other advanced degrees awarded. *Degree requirements:* For master's, comprehensive exam; for doctorate, thesis/dissertation, research analysis exam, research experience component. *Entrance requirements:* For master's, content test in science and math, letters of reference; for doctorate, GRE General Test or MAT, interview, writing sample, letters of recommendation. Additional exam requirements/recommendations for international students: Required—TOEFL (minimum score 600 paper-based; 96 iBT). *Application deadline:* For fall admission, 2/1 priority date for domestic and international students; for spring admission, 11/15 priority date for domestic students, 10/1 for international students. Applications are processed on a rolling basis. Application fee: $50. Electronic applications accepted. *Financial support:* In 2013–14, 50 fellowships (averaging $8,589 per year), 31 research assistantships with tuition reimbursements (averaging $11,406 per year) were awarded; teaching assistantships, career-related internships or fieldwork, Federal Work-Study, institutionally sponsored loans, scholarships/grants, tuition waivers, and unspecified assistantships also available. Financial award application deadline: 2/28; financial award applicants required to submit FAFSA. *Faculty research:* Science assessment, foreign language teaching and learning, early learning, new literacies, gender and education. *Total annual research expenditures:* $1.7 million. *Unit head:* Dr. Suzanne Miller, Chair, 716-645-2455, Fax: 716-645-3161, E-mail: smiller@buffalo.edu. *Application contact:* Cathy Dimino, Admissions Assistant, 716-645-2110, Fax: 716-645-7937, E-mail: cadimino@buffalo.edu.
Website: http://gse.buffalo.edu/lai.

University of Arkansas at Little Rock, Graduate School, College of Arts, Humanities, and Social Science, Department of International and Second Language Studies, Little Rock, AR 72204-1099. Offers second languages (MA). *Expenses:* Tuition, state resident: full-time $5690; part-time $284.50 per credit hour. Tuition, nonresident: full-time $13,030; part-time $651.50 per credit hour. *Required fees:* $1121; $672 per term. One-time fee: $40 full-time.

University of California, Irvine, School of Humanities, Department of Spanish and Portuguese, Irvine, CA 92697. Offers Spanish (MA, MAT, PhD). *Students:* 32 full-time (15 women), 5 part-time (3 women); includes 27 minority (all Hispanic/Latino). Average age 36. 31 applicants, 32% accepted, 5 enrolled. In 2013, 2 master's, 3 doctorates awarded. *Degree requirements:* For doctorate, thesis/dissertation. *Entrance requirements:* For master's and doctorate, GRE General Test, minimum GPA of 3.0. Additional exam requirements/recommendations for international students: Required—TOEFL (minimum score 550 paper-based). *Application deadline:* For fall admission, 1/2 priority date for domestic students, 1/2 for international students. Applications are processed on a rolling basis. Application fee: $80 ($100 for international students). Electronic applications accepted. *Financial support:* Fellowships, teaching assistantships, institutionally sponsored loans, traineeships, health care benefits, and unspecified assistantships available. Financial award application deadline: 3/1; financial award applicants required to submit FAFSA. *Faculty research:* Latin American literature, Spanish literature, Spanish linguistics in Creole studies, Hispanic literature in the U.S., Luso-Brazilian literature. *Unit head:* Horacio Legras, Department Chair, 949-824-7265, Fax: 949-824-2803, E-mail: hlegras@uci.edu. *Application contact:* Linda Le, Department Manager, 949-824-7726, Fax: 949-824-2803, E-mail: ttle@uci.edu.
Website: http://www.hnet.uci.edu/spanishandportuguese/.

University of Central Arkansas, Graduate School, College of Liberal Arts, Department of Foreign Languages, Conway, AR 72035-0001. Offers MA. Part-time programs available. *Degree requirements:* For master's, one foreign language, comprehensive exam, thesis optional. *Entrance requirements:* For master's, GRE General Test, minimum GPA of 2.7. Additional exam requirements/recommendations for international students: Required—TOEFL (minimum score 550 paper-based). Electronic applications accepted.

University of Connecticut, Graduate School, Neag School of Education, Department of Curriculum and Instruction, Program in World Languages Education, Storrs, CT 06269. Offers MA, PhD, Post-Master's Certificate. *Accreditation:* NCATE. Terminal master's awarded for partial completion of doctoral program. *Degree requirements:* For master's, comprehensive exam, thesis or alternative; for doctorate, thesis/dissertation. *Entrance requirements:* For doctorate, GRE General Test. Additional exam requirements/recommendations for international students: Required—TOEFL (minimum score 550 paper-based). Electronic applications accepted.

University of Delaware, College of Arts and Sciences, Department of Foreign Languages and Literatures, Newark, DE 19716. Offers foreign languages and literatures (MA), including French, German, Spanish; foreign languages pedagogy (MA), including French, German, Spanish; technical Chinese translation (MA). *Degree requirements:* For master's, one foreign language, comprehensive exam, thesis optional. *Entrance requirements:* For master's, GRE General Test, letters of recommendation, writing sample. Additional exam requirements/recommendations for international students: Required—TOEFL. Electronic applications accepted. *Faculty research:* Medieval to Modern French and Spanish literature, twentieth-century German, French, Spanish literature by women, computer-assisted instruction.

University of Georgia, College of Education, Department of Language and Literacy Education, Athens, GA 30602. Offers English education (M Ed, Ed S); language and literacy education (PhD); reading education (M Ed, Ed D, Ed S); teaching additional languages (M Ed, Ed S). *Accreditation:* NCATE. *Degree requirements:* For doctorate, variable foreign language requirement. *Entrance requirements:* For master's and Ed S, GRE General Test or MAT; for doctorate, GRE General Test. Additional exam requirements/recommendations for international students: Required—TOEFL (minimum score 550 paper-based). Electronic applications accepted. *Faculty research:* Comprehension, critical literacy, literacy and technology, vocabulary instruction, content area reading.

University of Hawaii at Hilo, Program in Hawaiian and Indigenous Language and Culture Revitalization, Hilo, HI 96720-4091. Offers PhD. *Faculty:* 6 full-time (2 women). *Students:* 1 full-time (0 women), 4 part-time (2 women); all minorities (all Two or more races, non-Hispanic/Latino). Average age 40. 6 applicants, 67% accepted, 4 enrolled. In 2013, 1 doctorate awarded. *Entrance requirements:* Additional exam requirements/recommendations for international students: Required—TOEFL, IELTS. *Application deadline:* For fall admission, 2/1 priority date for domestic students. Application fee: $50. Electronic applications accepted. *Expenses:* Tuition, state resident: full-time $4668. Tuition, nonresident: full-time $10,704. Tuition and fees vary according to course load and program. *Financial support:* Application deadline: 3/1; applicants required to submit FAFSA. *Unit head:* Scott Saft, Program Coordinator, 808-932-7221, Fax: 808-932-7218, E-mail: saft@hawaii.edu. *Application contact:* UH Hilo Admissions Office, 808-932-7446, Fax: 808-932-7459, E-mail: uhhadm@hawaii.edu.
Website: http://hilo.hawaii.edu/studentaffairs/admissions/phdh.php.

University of Hawaii at Hilo, Program in Hawaiian Language and Literature, Hilo, HI 96720-4091. Offers MA. *Faculty:* 3 full-time (0 women). *Students:* 12 part-time (8 women); includes 11 minority (5 Native Hawaiian or other Pacific Islander, non-Hispanic/Latino; 6 Two or more races, non-Hispanic/Latino). Average age 34. 8 applicants, 75% accepted, 4 enrolled. *Entrance requirements:* Additional exam requirements/recommendations for international students: Required—TOEFL, IELTS. *Application deadline:* For fall admission, 2/1 priority date for domestic students. Application fee: $50. Electronic applications accepted. *Expenses:* Tuition, state resident: full-time $4668. Tuition, nonresident: full-time $10,704. Tuition and fees vary according to course load and program. *Financial support:* Application deadline: 3/1; applicants required to submit FAFSA. *Unit head:* Hiapo Perreira, 808-932-7432, E-mail: hiapokei@hawaii.edu. *Application contact:* UH Hilo Admissions Office, 808-932-7446, Fax: 808-932-7459, E-mail: uhhadm@hawaii.edu.
Website: http://hilo.hawaii.edu/studentaffairs/admissions/mahll_000.php.

University of Hawaii at Hilo, Program in Indigenous Language and Culture Education, Hilo, HI 96720-4091. Offers MA. *Faculty:* 4 full-time (all women). *Students:* 6 part-time (4 women); all minorities (all Native Hawaiian or other Pacific Islander, non-Hispanic/Latino). Average age 35. In 2013, 4 master's awarded. *Entrance requirements:* Additional exam requirements/recommendations for international students: Required—TOEFL, IELTS. *Application deadline:* For fall admission, 2/1 for domestic students. Application fee: $50. Electronic applications accepted. *Expenses:* Tuition, state resident: full-time $4668. Tuition, nonresident: full-time $10,704. Tuition and fees vary according to course load and program. *Financial support:* Application deadline: 3/1; applicants required to submit FAFSA. *Unit head:* Makalapua Alencastre, Coordinator, 808-932-7411, E-mail: kaawa@hawaii.edu. *Application contact:* UH Hilo Admissions Office, 808-932-7446, Fax: 808-932-7459, E-mail: uhhadm@hawaii.edu.
Website: http://www.olelo.hawaii.edu/khuok/ma_hoonaauao.php.

University of Hawaii at Manoa, Graduate Division, College of Languages, Linguistics and Literature, Department of Second Language Studies, Honolulu, HI 96822. Offers English as a second language (MA, Graduate Certificate); second language acquisition (PhD). Part-time programs available. *Degree requirements:* For master's, 2 foreign languages, thesis optional; for doctorate, 2 foreign languages, comprehensive exam, thesis/dissertation. *Entrance requirements:* For master's, GRE General Test, minimum GPA of 3.0; for doctorate, GRE General Test, MA, scholarly publications. Additional exam requirements/recommendations for international students: Required—TOEFL (minimum score 600 paper-based; 100 iBT), IELTS (minimum score 7). *Faculty research:* Second language use, second language analysis, second language pedagogy and testing, second language learning, qualitative and quantitative research methods for second languages.

University of Hawaii at Manoa, Graduate Division, Hawai'inuaka School of Hawaiian Knowledge, Program in Hawaiian, Honolulu, HI 96822. Offers MA. Part-time programs available. *Degree requirements:* For master's, thesis optional. *Entrance requirements:* Additional exam requirements/recommendations for international students: Required—TOEFL (minimum score 500 paper-based; 61 iBT), IELTS (minimum score 5).

University of Hawaii at Manoa, Graduate Division, Hawai'inuaka School of Hawaiian Knowledge, Program in Hawaiian Studies, Honolulu, HI 96822. Offers MA. Part-time programs available. *Degree requirements:* For master's, thesis optional. *Entrance requirements:* Additional exam requirements/recommendations for international students: Required—TOEFL (minimum score 500 paper-based; 61 iBT), IELTS (minimum score 5).

University of Illinois at Chicago, Graduate College, College of Liberal Arts and Sciences, School of Literatures, Cultural Studies and Linguistics, Department of Hispanic and Italian Studies, Chicago, IL 60607-7128. Offers Hispanic linguistics (MA, PhD); Hispanic literary and cultural studies (MA, PhD); teaching of Spanish (MAT). Part-time programs available. *Faculty:* 10 full-time (6 women), 2 part-time/adjunct (1 woman). *Students:* 47 full-time (31 women), 17 part-time (10 women); includes 23 minority (22 Hispanic/Latino; 1 Two or more races, non-Hispanic/Latino), 22 international. Average age 30. 63 applicants, 52% accepted, 19 enrolled. In 2013, 10 master's, 3 doctorates awarded. Terminal master's awarded for partial completion of doctoral program. *Degree requirements:* For master's, one foreign language, departmental qualifying exam. *Entrance requirements:* For master's, GRE General Test, minimum GPA of 2.75, undergraduate major in Spanish. Additional exam requirements/recommendations for international students: Required—TOEFL. *Application deadline:* For fall admission, 2/1 for domestic and international students. Applications are processed on a rolling basis. Application fee: $40 ($50 for international students). Electronic applications accepted. *Expenses:* Tuition, state resident: full-time $11,066; part-time $3689 per term. Tuition, nonresident: full-time $23,064; part-time $7688 per term. *Required fees:* $3004; $1190 per term. Tuition and fees vary according to course level and program. *Financial support:* In 2013–14, 2 fellowships with full tuition reimbursements were awarded; research assistantships with full tuition reimbursements, teaching assistantships with full tuition reimbursements, Federal Work-Study, scholarships/grants, traineeships, tuition waivers (full), and unspecified assistantships also available. Financial award application deadline: 3/1; financial award applicants required to submit FAFSA. *Faculty research:* Linguistic competence of bilingual speakers as a window to understanding the human faculty of language, neurocognitive processing of language among different speakers and learners, how languages are used within their social contexts. *Unit head:* Prof. Luis Lopez, Professor and Head of the Department of Hispanic and Italian Studies, 312-413-2646, E-mail: luislope@uic.edu. *Application contact:* Prof. Steven Marsh, Associate Professor and Director of Graduate Studies, 312-996-5845, E-mail: marshsw@uic.edu.
Website: http://lcsl.uic.edu/hispanic-italian.

University of Illinois at Urbana–Champaign, Graduate College, College of Liberal Arts and Sciences, School of Literatures, Cultures and Linguistics, Department of Spanish, Italian and Portuguese, Champaign, IL 61820. Offers Italian (MA, PhD); Portuguese (MA, PhD); Spanish (MA, PhD). *Students:* 49 (35 women). Application fee:

Foreign Languages Education

$75 ($90 for international students). *Financial support:* Tuition waivers available. *Unit head:* Jose Ignacio Hualde, Head, 217-333-3390, Fax: 217-244-8430, E-mail: jihualde@illinois.edu. *Application contact:* Lynn Stanke, Office Support Specialist, 217-333-6269, Fax: 217-244-3050, E-mail: stanke@illinois.edu. Website: http://www.sip.illinois.edu/.

University of Illinois at Urbana–Champaign, Graduate College, College of Liberal Arts and Sciences, School of Literatures, Cultures and Linguistics, Department of the Classics, Champaign, IL 61820. Offers classical philology (PhD); classics (MA); teaching of Latin (MA). *Students:* 17 (6 women). Application fee: $75 ($90 for international students). *Unit head:* Ariana Traill, Head, 217-333-1008, Fax: 217-244-8430, E-mail: traill@illinois.edu. *Application contact:* Lynn Stanke, Office Support Specialist, 217-333-6269, Fax: 217-244-3050, E-mail: stanke@illinois.edu. Website: http://www.classics.illinois.edu/.

University of Indianapolis, Graduate Programs, School of Education, Indianapolis, IN 46227-3697. Offers art education (MAT); biology (MAT); chemistry (MAT); curriculum and instruction (MA); earth sciences (MAT); education (MA, MAT); educational leadership (MA); elementary education (MA); English (MAT); French (MAT); math (MAT); physical education (MAT); physics (MAT); secondary education (MA), including art education, education, English education, social studies education; social studies (MAT); Spanish (MAT). *Accreditation:* NCATE. Part-time and evening/weekend programs available. *Faculty:* 5 full-time (4 women), 2 part-time/adjunct (1 woman). *Students:* 19 full-time (9 women), 54 part-time (27 women); includes 13 minority (5 Black or African American, non-Hispanic/Latino; 1 Asian, non-Hispanic/Latino; 5 Hispanic/Latino; 2 Two or more races, non-Hispanic/Latino), 1 international. Average age 32. In 2013, 52 master's awarded. *Entrance requirements:* For master's, GRE Subject Test, PRAXIS I, minimum GPA of 2.5, 3 letters of recommendation, interview. Additional exam requirements/recommendations for international students: Required—TOEFL (minimum score 550 paper-based). *Application deadline:* Applications are processed on a rolling basis. Application fee: $50. *Expenses: Tuition:* Full-time $5436; part-time $810 per credit hour. *Financial support:* Federal Work-Study available. Financial award application deadline: 5/1; financial award applicants required to submit FAFSA. *Faculty research:* Assessment of teacher education, perceptions of prospective teachers by parents. *Unit head:* Dr. Kathy Moran, Dean, 317-788-3285, Fax: 317-788-3300, E-mail: kmoran@uindy.edu. *Application contact:* Jeni Kirby, Administrative Assistant, Teacher Education, 317-788-2113, E-mail: kirbyj@uindy.edu. Website: http://education.uindy.edu/.

The University of Iowa, Graduate College, College of Education, Department of Teaching and Learning, Program in Education, Iowa City, IA 52242-1316. Offers art education (MA); developmental reading (MA); elementary education (MA); English education (MA, MAT); foreign and second language education (MAT); foreign language education (MA); foreign language/ESL education (PhD); language, literacy and culture (PhD); mathematics education (MA, MAT, PhD); music education (MM, PhD); science education (MA); secondary education (MA); social studies (MA, PhD). *Degree requirements:* For master's, thesis optional, exam; for doctorate, comprehensive exam, thesis/dissertation. *Entrance requirements:* For master's and doctorate, GRE General Test, minimum GPA of 3.0. Additional exam requirements/recommendations for international students: Required—TOEFL (minimum score 550 paper-based; 81 iBT). Electronic applications accepted.

The University of Iowa, Graduate College, College of Liberal Arts and Sciences, Program in Second Language Acquisition, Iowa City, IA 52242-1316. Offers PhD. *Degree requirements:* For doctorate, comprehensive exam, thesis/dissertation. *Entrance requirements:* For doctorate, GRE General Test, minimum GPA of 3.0. Additional exam requirements/recommendations for international students: Required—TOEFL (minimum score 600 paper-based; 100 iBT). Electronic applications accepted.

University of Kentucky, Graduate School, College of Arts and Sciences and College of Education, Program in Teaching World Languages, Lexington, KY 40506-0032. Offers MA. *Entrance requirements:* For master's, GRE General Test, minimum undergraduate GPA of 2.75. Additional exam requirements/recommendations for international students: Required—TOEFL (minimum score 550 paper-based). Electronic applications accepted.

University of Lethbridge, School of Graduate Studies, Lethbridge, AB T1K 3M4, Canada. Offers accounting (MScM); addictions counseling (M Sc); agricultural biotechnology (M Sc); agricultural studies (M Sc, MA); anthropology (MA); archaeology (M Sc, MA); art (MA, MFA); biochemistry (M Sc); biological sciences (M Sc); biomolecular science (PhD); biosystems and biodiversity (PhD); Canadian studies (MA); chemistry (M Sc); computer science (M Sc); computer science and geographical information science (M Sc); counseling (MC); counseling psychology (M Ed); dramatic arts (MA); earth, space, and physical science (PhD); economics (MA); education (MA); educational leadership (M Ed); English (MA); environmental science (M Sc); evolution and behavior (PhD); exercise science (M Sc); finance (MScM); French (MA); French/German (MA); French/Spanish (MA); general education (M Ed); general management (MScM); geography (M Sc, MA); German (MA); health sciences (M Sc); human resource management and labour relations (MScM); individualized multidisciplinary (M Sc, MA); information systems (MScM); international management (MScM); kinesiology (M Sc, MA); marketing (MScM); mathematics (M Sc); modern languages (MA); music (M Mus, MA); Native American studies (MA); neuroscience (M Sc, PhD); new media (MA, MFA); nursing (M Sc); philosophy (MA); physics (M Sc); policy and strategy (MScM); political science (MA); psychology (M Sc, MA); religious studies (MA); sociology (MA); theatre and dramatic arts (MFA); theoretical and computational science (PhD); urban and regional studies (MA); women and gender studies (MA). Part-time and evening/weekend programs available. *Degree requirements:* For doctorate, comprehensive exam, thesis/dissertation. *Entrance requirements:* For master's, GMAT (for M Sc in management), bachelor's degree in related field, minimum GPA of 3.0 during previous 20 graded semester courses, 2 years teaching or related experience (M Ed); for doctorate, master's degree, minimum graduate GPA of 3.5. Additional exam requirements/recommendations for international students: Required—TOEFL. Application fee: $60 Canadian dollars. *Financial support:* Fellowships, research assistantships, teaching assistantships, scholarships/grants, health care benefits, and unspecified assistantships available. *Faculty research:* Movement and brain plasticity, gibberellin physiology, photosynthesis, carbon cycling, molecular properties of main-group ring components. *Application contact:* School of Graduate Studies, 403-329-2793, Fax: 403-332-5239, E-mail: sgsinquiries@uleth.ca. Website: http://www.uleth.ca/graduatestudies/.

University of Louisiana at Monroe, Graduate School, College of Arts, Education, and Sciences, School of Education, Program in Curriculum and Instruction, Monroe, LA 71209-0001. Offers art education (M Ed); biology education (M Ed); chemistry education (M Ed); curriculum and instruction (Ed D); early childhood education (M Ed); earth science education (M Ed); educational leadership (M Ed); elementary education (1-5) (M Ed); English as a second language (M Ed); English education (M Ed); family and consumer education (M Ed); French education (M Ed); history education (M Ed); math education (M Ed); middle school education (M Ed); music education (M Ed); reading education (K-12) (M Ed); Spanish education (M Ed); special education - academically gifted (M Ed); special education - early intervention (M Ed); special education - educational diagnostician (M Ed); special education - mild/moderate disabilities (M Ed);

speech education (M Ed). *Accreditation:* NCATE. *Degree requirements:* For master's, comprehensive exam (for some programs), thesis; for doctorate, thesis/dissertation, internships. *Entrance requirements:* For master's, GRE General Test; for doctorate, GRE General Test, minimum undergraduate GPA of 2.75, graduate 3.25. Additional exam requirements/recommendations for international students: Required—TOEFL (minimum score 500 paper-based; 61 iBT). *Application deadline:* For fall admission, 8/24 priority date for domestic students, 7/1 for international students; for winter admission, 12/14 priority date for domestic students; for spring admission, 1/19 for domestic students, 11/1 for international students. Applications are processed on a rolling basis. Application fee: $20 ($30 for international students). Electronic applications accepted. *Expenses:* Tuition, state resident: full-time $6607. Tuition, nonresident: full-time $17,179. Full-time tuition and fees vary according to program. *Financial support:* Research assistantships, career-related internships or fieldwork, Federal Work-Study, and unspecified assistantships available. Financial award application deadline: 4/1; financial award applicants required to submit FAFSA. *Unit head:* Dr. Dorothy Schween, Director, 318-342-1268, Fax: 318-342-3131, E-mail: schween@ulm.edu. *Application contact:* Dr. Dorothy Schween, Director, 318-342-1268, Fax: 318-342-3131, E-mail: schween@ulm.edu.

University of Maine, Graduate School, College of Liberal Arts and Sciences, Department of Modern Languages and Classics, Orono, ME 04469. Offers French (MAT); French literature (MA); North American French (MA); Spanish (MAT). Part-time programs available. *Faculty:* 10 full-time (7 women), 2 part-time/adjunct (1 woman). *Students:* 5 full-time (4 women), 3 part-time (all women), 1 international. Average age 34. 4 applicants, 75% accepted, 2 enrolled. In 2013, 4 master's awarded. *Degree requirements:* For master's, one foreign language, thesis (for some programs). *Entrance requirements:* For master's, GRE General Test. Additional exam requirements/recommendations for international students: Required—TOEFL. *Application deadline:* For fall admission, 2/1 priority date for domestic students. Applications are processed on a rolling basis. Application fee: $65. Electronic applications accepted. *Expenses:* Tuition, state resident: full-time $7524. Tuition, nonresident: full-time $23,112. *Required fees:* $1970. *Financial support:* In 2013–14, 2 students received support, including 2 teaching assistantships with tuition reimbursements available (averaging $14,600 per year); Federal Work-Study and tuition waivers (full and partial) also available. Financial award application deadline: 3/1. *Faculty research:* Narratology, poetics, Quebec literature, theater, women's studies. *Unit head:* Dr. Jane Smith, Chair, 207-581-2075, Fax: 207-581-1832. *Application contact:* Scott G. Delcourt, Associate Dean of the Graduate School, 207-581-3291, Fax: 207-581-3232, E-mail: graduate@maine.edu. Website: http://umaine.edu/mlandc/.

University of Maryland, Baltimore County, Graduate School, College of Arts, Humanities and Social Sciences, Department of Education, Program in Teaching, Baltimore, MD 21250. Offers early childhood education (MAT); elementary education (MAT); secondary education (MAT), including art, biology, chemistry, dance, earth/space science, English, foreign language, mathematics, music, physics, social studies, theatre. Part-time and evening/weekend programs available. *Faculty:* 24 full-time (18 women), 25 part-time/adjunct (19 women). *Students:* 49 full-time (34 women), 35 part-time (23 women); includes 19 minority (9 Black or African American, non-Hispanic/Latino; 3 Asian, non-Hispanic/Latino; 6 Hispanic/Latino; 1 Two or more races, non-Hispanic/Latino). Average age 30. 40 applicants, 95% accepted, 35 enrolled. In 2013, 106 master's awarded. *Degree requirements:* For master's, comprehensive exam (for some programs), thesis (for some programs). *Entrance requirements:* For master's, PRAXIS I or SAT (minimum score of 1000), minimum GPA of 3.0. Additional exam requirements/recommendations for international students: Required—TOEFL. *Application deadline:* For fall admission, 6/1 for domestic students; for spring admission, 11/1 for domestic students. Applications are processed on a rolling basis. Application fee: $50. Electronic applications accepted. One-time fee: $200 full-time. *Financial support:* In 2013–14, 6 students received support, including teaching assistantships with full and partial tuition reimbursements available (averaging $12,000 per year); career-related internships or fieldwork, Federal Work-Study, scholarships/grants, tuition waivers, and unspecified assistantships also available. Financial award application deadline: 3/1. *Faculty research:* STEM teacher education, culturally sensitive pedagogy, ESOL/bilingual education, early childhood education, language, literacy and culture. *Unit head:* Dr. Susan M. Blunck, Graduate Program Director, 410-455-2869, Fax: 410-455-3986, E-mail: blunck@umbc.edu. *Application contact:* Dr. Susan M. Blunck, Graduate Program Director, 410-455-2869, Fax: 410-455-3986, E-mail: blunck@umbc.edu. Website: http://www.umbc.edu/education/.

University of Maryland, College Park, Academic Affairs, College of Arts and Humanities, School of Languages, Literatures, and Cultures, Program in Second Language Acquisition and Application, College Park, MD 20742. Offers second language instruction (PhD); second language learning (PhD); second language measurement and assessment (PhD); second language use (PhD). *Students:* 23 full-time (15 women), 4 part-time (3 women); includes 3 minority (all Asian, non-Hispanic/Latino), 13 international. 100 applicants, 14% accepted, 5 enrolled. In 2013, 4 doctorates awarded. *Application deadline:* For fall admission, 1/15 for domestic students, 2/1 for international students; for spring admission, 10/15 for domestic students, 6/1 for international students. Applications are processed on a rolling basis. Application fee: $75. Electronic applications accepted. *Expenses:* Tuition, state resident: full-time $10,314; part-time $573 per credit hour. Tuition, nonresident: full-time $22,248; part-time $1236 per credit. *Required fees:* $1446; $403.15 per semester. Tuition and fees vary according to program. *Financial support:* In 2013–14, 3 fellowships with full and partial tuition reimbursements (averaging $18,117 per year), 4 research assistantships (averaging $20,032 per year), 8 teaching assistantships (averaging $20,107 per year) were awarded. *Faculty research:* Second language acquisition, pedagogical perspectives, technological applications, language use in professional contexts. *Unit head:* Steven J. Ross, Director, 301-405-4246, E-mail: krudolf@umd.edu. *Application contact:* Dr. Charles A. Caramello, Dean of Graduate School, 301-405-0358, Fax: 301-314-9305, E-mail: ccaramel@umd.edu.

University of Massachusetts Amherst, Graduate School, College of Humanities and Fine Arts, Department of Languages, Literatures, and Cultures, Program in French and Francophone Studies, Amherst, MA 01003. Offers French (MA, MAT). Part-time programs available. *Faculty:* 8 full-time (4 women). *Students:* 8 full-time (6 women), 2 part-time (1 woman); includes 1 minority (Hispanic/Latino), 2 international. Average age 27. 5 applicants, 80% accepted, 3 enrolled. In 2013, 3 master's awarded. *Degree requirements:* For master's, thesis or alternative. *Entrance requirements:* For master's, GRE General Test. Additional exam requirements/recommendations for international students: Required—TOEFL (minimum score 550 paper-based; 80 iBT), IELTS (minimum score 6.5). *Application deadline:* For fall admission, 2/1 for domestic and international students; for spring admission, 10/1 for domestic and international students. Applications are processed on a rolling basis. Application fee: $75. Electronic applications accepted. *Financial support:* Fellowships with full and partial tuition reimbursements, research assistantships with full and partial tuition reimbursements, teaching assistantships with full and partial tuition reimbursements, career-related internships or fieldwork, Federal Work-Study, scholarships/grants, traineeships, health care benefits, tuition waivers (full and partial), and unspecified assistantships available. Support available to part-time students. Financial award application deadline: 2/1. *Unit*

head: Dr. Luke P. Bouvier, Graduate Program Director, 413-545-2314, Fax: 412-545-4778. *Application contact:* Lindsay DeSantis, Supervisor of Admissions, 413-545-0722, Fax: 413-577-0100, E-mail: gradadm@grad.umass.edu. Website: http://www.umass.edu/french/.

University of Massachusetts Boston, Office of Graduate Studies, College of Liberal Arts, Program in Applied Linguistics, Boston, MA 02125-3393. Offers bilingual education (MA); English as a second language (MA); foreign language pedagogy (MA). Part-time and evening/weekend programs available. *Degree requirements:* For master's, one foreign language, comprehensive exam. *Entrance requirements:* For master's, minimum GPA of 2.75. *Faculty research:* Multicultural theory and curriculum development, foreign language pedagogy, language and culture, applied psycholinguistics, bilingual education.

University of Michigan, Horace H. Rackham School of Graduate Studies, College of Literature, Science, and the Arts, Department of Classical Studies, Ann Arbor, MI 48109. Offers classical studies (PhD); teaching Latin (MAT). *Faculty:* 18 full-time (9 women), 9 part-time/adjunct (3 women). *Students:* 26 full-time (11 women); includes 2 minority (both Hispanic/Latino), 3 international. Average age 27. 74 applicants, 15% accepted, 3 enrolled. In 2013, 7 master's, 1 doctorate awarded. Terminal master's awarded for partial completion of doctoral program. *Degree requirements:* For master's, one foreign language, comprehensive exam; for doctorate, 4 foreign languages, comprehensive exam, thesis/dissertation, oral defense of dissertation, preliminary exams, qualifying exams. *Entrance requirements:* For master's, GRE General Test, 2-3 years of Latin (for the Latin MAT); for doctorate, GRE General Test, strict minimum of 3 years of college-level Latin and 2 years of college-level Greek. Additional exam requirements/recommendations for international students: Required—TOEFL (minimum score 560 paper-based). *Application deadline:* For fall admission, 12/15 for domestic students, 1/5 for international students. Application fee: $75 ($90 for international students). Electronic applications accepted. Tuition and fees vary according to course level, course load, degree level, program and student level. *Financial support:* In 2013–14, 25 students received support, including 6 fellowships with full tuition reimbursements available (averaging $19,000 per year), 1 research assistantship with full tuition reimbursement available (averaging $18,600 per year), 18 teaching assistantships with full tuition reimbursements available (averaging $18,600 per year); career-related internships or fieldwork, Federal Work-Study, institutionally sponsored loans, scholarships/grants, traineeships, tuition waivers (full), unspecified assistantships, and summer stipends, year-round health care also available. Financial award application deadline: 3/15. *Faculty research:* Greek and Latin literature, ancient history, papyrology, archaeology. *Unit head:* Prof. Sara Forsdyke, Chair and Professor, 734-764-0360, Fax: 734-763-4959, E-mail: classics@umich.edu. *Application contact:* Michelle M. Biggs, Graduate Program Coordinator, 734-647-2330, Fax: 734-763-4959, E-mail: mbiggs@umich.edu. Website: http://www.lsa.umich.edu/classics.

University of Minnesota, Twin Cities Campus, Graduate School, College of Education and Human Development, Department of Curriculum and Instruction, Program in Teaching, Minneapolis, MN 55455-0213. Offers Chinese (M Ed); earth science (M Ed); elementary special education (M Ed); English (M Ed); English as a second language (M Ed); French (M Ed); German (M Ed); Hebrew (M Ed); Japanese (M Ed); life sciences (M Ed); mathematics (M Ed); middle school science (M Ed); science (M Ed); second languages and cultures (M Ed); social studies (M Ed); Spanish (M Ed). *Students:* 220 full-time (154 women), 83 part-time (60 women); includes 43 minority (10 Black or African American, non-Hispanic/Latino; 26 Asian, non-Hispanic/Latino; 7 Hispanic/Latino), 4 international. Average age 27. 261 applicants, 87% accepted, 222 enrolled. In 2013, 561 master's awarded. Application fee: $75 ($95 for international students). *Unit head:* Dr. Nina Asher, Chair, 612-624-1357, Fax: 612-624-8277, E-mail: nasher@umn.edu. *Application contact:* Dr. Jennifer Engler, Assistant Dean, 612-626-2887, Fax: 612-626-7496, E-mail: engle009@umn.edu. Website: http://www.cehd.umn.edu/ci/.

University of Missouri, Graduate School, College of Arts and Science, Department of Romance Languages and Literature, Columbia, MO 65211. Offers French (MA, PhD); literature (MA); Spanish (MA, PhD); teaching (MA). *Faculty:* 25 full-time (12 women), 1 (woman) part-time/adjunct. *Students:* 26 full-time (16 women), 15 part-time (10 women); includes 8 minority (4 Black or African American, non-Hispanic/Latino; 3 Hispanic/Latino; 1 Two or more races, non-Hispanic/Latino), 18 international. Average age 33. 16 applicants, 69% accepted, 7 enrolled. In 2013, 3 master's, 1 doctorate awarded. Terminal master's awarded for partial completion of doctoral program. *Degree requirements:* For master's, one foreign language; for doctorate, 4 foreign languages, comprehensive exam, thesis/dissertation. *Entrance requirements:* For master's, GRE General Test, minimum GPA of 3.0 in field of major; bachelor's degree; for doctorate, GRE General Test, minimum GPA of 3.0 in field of major; master's degree. Additional exam requirements/recommendations for international students: Required—TOEFL (minimum score 500 paper-based; 61 iBT). *Application deadline:* For fall admission, 2/15 priority date for domestic students; for winter admission, 10/15 for domestic students. Applications are processed on a rolling basis. Application fee: $55 ($75 for international students). Electronic applications accepted. *Financial support:* Research assistantships, teaching assistantships with full tuition reimbursements, institutionally sponsored loans, health care benefits, and unspecified assistantships available. *Faculty research:* Afro-Romance studies. *Unit head:* Dr. Flore Zephir, Department Chair, 573-882-5048, E-mail: zephirf@missouri.edu. *Application contact:* Mary Harris, Administrative Assistant, 573-882-5039, E-mail: harrisma@missouri.edu. Website: http://romancelanguages.missouri.edu/grad.shtml.

University of Missouri, Graduate School, College of Education, Department of Learning, Teaching and Curriculum, Columbia, MO 65211. Offers agricultural education (M Ed, PhD, Ed S); art education (M Ed, PhD, Ed S); business and office education (M Ed, PhD, Ed S); early childhood education (M Ed, PhD, Ed S); elementary education (M Ed, PhD, Ed S); English education (M Ed, PhD, Ed S); foreign language education (M Ed, PhD, Ed S); health education and promotion (M Ed, PhD); learning and instruction (M Ed); marketing education (M Ed, PhD, Ed S); mathematics education (M Ed, PhD, Ed S); music education (M Ed, PhD, Ed S); reading education (M Ed, PhD, Ed S); science education (M Ed, PhD, Ed S); social studies education (M Ed, PhD, Ed S); vocational education (M Ed, PhD, Ed S). Part-time programs available. *Faculty:* 26 full-time (16 women), 3 part-time/adjunct (2 women). *Students:* 186 full-time (143 women), 197 part-time (172 women); includes 19 minority (4 Black or African American, non-Hispanic/Latino; 4 Asian, non-Hispanic/Latino; 6 Hispanic/Latino; 5 Two or more races, non-Hispanic/Latino), 25 international. Average age 31. 288 applicants, 65% accepted, 160 enrolled. In 2013, 202 master's, 18 doctorates, 7 other advanced degrees awarded. Terminal master's awarded for partial completion of doctoral program. *Degree requirements:* For doctorate, thesis/dissertation. *Entrance requirements:* For master's and Ed S, GRE General Test or MAT, minimum GPA of 3.0; for doctorate, GRE General Test, minimum GPA of 3.0. Additional exam requirements/recommendations for international students: Required—TOEFL (minimum score 600 paper-based; 100 iBT). *Application deadline:* For fall admission, 12/1 priority date for domestic and international students. Applications are processed on a rolling basis. Application fee: $55 ($75 for international students). Electronic applications accepted. *Financial support:* Fellowships, research assistantships, teaching assistantships, institutionally sponsored

loans, traineeships, health care benefits, and unspecified assistantships available. Support available to part-time students. *Faculty research:* Curriculum development and research, teacher education, art education, business and marketing, early childhood education, English education, literacy/reading education, mathematics education, music education, science education, social studies education. *Unit head:* Dr. James Tarr, Associate Division Director, 573-882-4034, E-mail: tarrj@missouri.edu. *Application contact:* Fran Colley, Academic Advisor, 573-882-6462, E-mail: colleyf@missouri.edu. Website: http://education.missouri.edu/LTC/.

University of Nebraska at Kearney, Graduate Programs, College of Fine Arts and Humanities, Department of Modern Languages, Kearney, NE 68849-0001. Offers Spanish education (MA Ed). *Accreditation:* NCATE. Part-time and evening/weekend programs available. *Degree requirements:* For master's, thesis optional. *Entrance requirements:* For master's, 21 semester hours of upper-level Spanish; two-page Spanish essay; one-page English essay; two letters of recommendation. Additional exam requirements/recommendations for international students: Required—TOEFL (minimum score 550 paper-based; 79 iBT). Electronic applications accepted. *Faculty research:* Translation theory, Spanish linguistics; Heidegger, Rilke and Nietzsche; symotolistic poetry.

University of Nebraska at Omaha, Graduate Studies, College of Arts and Sciences, Program in Language Teaching, Omaha, NE 68182. Offers MA. Part-time and evening/weekend programs available. *Faculty:* 12 full-time (6 women). *Students:* 6 full-time (all women), 14 part-time (12 women), 1 international. Average age 32. 7 applicants, 43% accepted, 2 enrolled. In 2013, 11 master's awarded. *Degree requirements:* For master's, comprehensive exam, thesis (for some programs). *Entrance requirements:* For master's, minimum GPA of 3.0, official transcripts, 2 letters of recommendation, oral language sample, writing sample. Additional exam requirements/recommendations for international students: Required—TOEFL, IELTS, PTE. *Application deadline:* For fall admission, 4/15 priority date for domestic students; for spring admission, 11/15 priority date for domestic students; for summer admission, 4/15 for domestic students. Applications are processed on a rolling basis. Application fee: $45. Electronic applications accepted. *Financial support:* In 2013–14, 2 students received support, including 2 research assistantships with tuition reimbursements available; teaching assistantships with tuition reimbursements available and tuition waivers (partial) also available. Financial award application deadline: 3/1; financial award applicants required to submit FAFSA. *Unit head:* Dr. Melanie Bloom, Chairperson, 402-554-4841. *Application contact:* Dr. Carolyn Gascoigne, Graduate Program Chair, 402-554-2862, E-mail: graduate@unomaha.edu.

University of Nevada, Reno, Graduate School, College of Liberal Arts, Department of Foreign Languages and Literatures, Reno, NV 89557. Offers French (MA); German (MA); Spanish (MA). *Degree requirements:* For master's, one foreign language, thesis optional. *Entrance requirements:* For master's, GRE General Test, minimum GPA of 2.75. Additional exam requirements/recommendations for international students: Required—TOEFL (minimum score 500 paper-based; 61 iBT), IELTS (minimum score 6). *Faculty research:* Thirteenth century mysticism, contemporary Spanish and Latin American poetry and theater, French interrelation between narration and photography, exile literature and Holocaust.

The University of North Carolina at Chapel Hill, Graduate School, School of Education, Program in Secondary Education, Chapel Hill, NC 27599. Offers English (Grades 9-12) (MAT); English as a second language (MAT); French (Grades K-12) (MAT); German (Grades K-12) (MAT); Japanese (Grades K-12) (MAT); Latin (Grades 9-12) (MAT); mathematics (Grades 9-12) (MAT); music (Grades K-12) (MAT); science (Grades 9-12) (MAT); social studies (Grades 9-12) (MAT); Spanish (Grades K-12) (MAT). *Accreditation:* NCATE. *Degree requirements:* For master's, comprehensive exam. *Entrance requirements:* For master's, GRE General Test, minimum GPA of 3.0 during last 2 years of undergraduate course work. Additional exam requirements/recommendations for international students: Required—TOEFL (minimum score 550 paper-based). Electronic applications accepted.

The University of North Carolina at Charlotte, The Graduate School, College of Education, Interdisciplinary Education Programs, Charlotte, NC 28223-0001. Offers art education (MAT); dance education (MAT); elementary education (MAT); English as a second language (MAT); foreign language education (MAT); middle grades education (MAT); music education (MAT); secondary education (MAT); special education (MAT); teacher certification (Graduate Certificate); teaching (Graduate Certificate); theater education (MAT). Part-time programs available. *Students:* 206 full-time (165 women), 791 part-time (628 women); includes 342 minority (247 Black or African American, non-Hispanic/Latino; 16 Asian, non-Hispanic/Latino; 62 Hispanic/Latino; 17 Two or more races, non-Hispanic/Latino), 14 international. Average age 32. 564 applicants, 91% accepted, 414 enrolled. In 2013, 145 master's, 271 other advanced degrees awarded. Terminal master's awarded for partial completion of doctoral program. *Degree requirements:* For master's, thesis. *Entrance requirements:* For master's, GRE or MAT. Additional exam requirements/recommendations for international students: Required—TOEFL (minimum score 550 paper-based; 83 iBT). *Application deadline:* For fall admission, 5/1 priority date for domestic and international students; for spring admission, 10/1 priority date for domestic and international students. Applications are processed on a rolling basis. Application fee: $75. Electronic applications accepted. *Expenses:* Tuition, state resident: full-time $3522. Tuition, nonresident: full-time $16,051. *Required fees:* $2585. Tuition and fees vary according to course load and program. *Total annual research expenditures:* $43,031. *Unit head:* Dr. Warren DiBiase, Chair, 704-687-8881, Fax: 704-687-4705, E-mail: wjdibias@uncc.edu. *Application contact:* Kathy B. Giddings, Director of Graduate Admissions, 704-687-5503, Fax: 704-687-1668, E-mail: gradadm@uncc.edu. Website: http://education.uncc.edu/academic-programs.

The University of North Carolina at Greensboro, Graduate School, School of Education, Department of Curriculum and Instruction, Greensboro, NC 27412-5001. Offers college teaching and adult learning (Certificate); curriculum and instruction (M Ed), including chemistry education, elementary education, English as a second language, French education, instructional technology, mathematics education, middle grades education, reading education, science education, social studies education, Spanish education; curriculum and teaching (PhD), including higher education, teacher education and development; English as a second language (Certificate); higher education (M Ed); supervision (M Ed). *Accreditation:* NCATE. Part-time programs available. *Degree requirements:* For doctorate, thesis/dissertation. *Entrance requirements:* For master's and doctorate, GRE General Test. Additional exam requirements/recommendations for international students: Required—TOEFL. Electronic applications accepted. *Faculty research:* Community college literacy program, middle school mathematics/computer mathematics.

University of Northern Colorado, Graduate School, College of Humanities and Social Sciences, School of Modern Languages and Cultural Studies, Program in Foreign Languages, Greeley, CO 80639. Offers Spanish/teaching (MA). Part-time programs available. *Degree requirements:* For master's, comprehensive exam, thesis or alternative. *Entrance requirements:* For master's, minimum undergraduate GPA of 3.0, BA in Spanish, 1 year of secondary teaching. Electronic applications accepted.

Foreign Languages Education

University of Northern Iowa, Graduate College, College of Humanities, Arts and Sciences, Department of Languages and Literatures, MA Program in Spanish, Cedar Falls, IA 50614. Offers Spanish (MA); Spanish teaching (MA). Part-time and evening/weekend programs available. *Students:* 4 full-time (3 women), 1 (woman) part-time; includes 1 minority (Hispanic/Latino), 1 international. 5 applicants, 40% accepted, 2 enrolled. In 2013, 21 master's awarded. *Degree requirements:* For master's, one foreign language, comprehensive exam, thesis or alternative. *Entrance requirements:* For master's, minimum GPA of 3.0, valid teaching license, documentation of successful teaching experience. Additional exam requirements/recommendations for international students: Required—TOEFL (minimum score 600 paper-based; 100 iBT). *Application deadline:* For fall admission, 8/1 priority date for domestic students. Applications are processed on a rolling basis. Application fee: $50 ($70 for international students). Electronic applications accepted. *Financial support:* Career-related internships or fieldwork, Federal Work-Study, and tuition waivers (full and partial) available. Support available to part-time students. Financial award application deadline: 2/1. *Unit head:* Dr. Gabriela Olivares-Cuhat, Coordinator, 319-273-6102, Fax: 319-273-5807, E-mail: gabriela.olivares@uni.edu. *Application contact:* Laurie S. Russell, Record Analyst, 319-273-2623, Fax: 319-273-2885, E-mail: laurie.russell@uni.edu.
Website: http://www.uni.edu/langlit/.

University of Northern Iowa, Graduate College, College of Humanities, Arts and Sciences, Department of Languages and Literatures, Program in TESOL/Spanish, Cedar Falls, IA 50614. Offers MA. *Students:* 3 full-time (all women), 1 part-time (0 women), 2 international. 2 applicants, 50% accepted. In 2013, 2 master's awarded. Application fee: $50 ($70 for international students). *Unit head:* Dr. Joyce Milambiling, Coordinator, 319-273-6099, Fax: 319-273-5807, E-mail: joyce.milambiling@uni.edu. *Application contact:* Laurie S. Russell, Record Analyst, 319-273-2623, Fax: 319-273-2885, E-mail: laurie.russell@uni.edu.

University of Pittsburgh, School of Education, Department of Instruction and Learning, Program in Secondary Education, Pittsburgh, PA 15260. Offers English/communications education (M Ed, MAT); foreign languages education (M Ed, MAT); mathematics education (M Ed, MAT, Ed D); science education (M Ed, MAT, Ed D); secondary education (PhD); social studies education (M Ed, MAT). Part-time and evening/weekend programs available. *Students:* 116 full-time (78 women), 47 part-time (36 women); includes 16 minority (4 Black or African American, non-Hispanic/Latino; 3 Asian, non-Hispanic/Latino; 5 Hispanic/Latino; 4 Two or more races, non-Hispanic/Latino), 29 international. Average age 30. 279 applicants, 66% accepted, 91 enrolled. In 2013, 113 master's, 8 doctorates awarded. *Degree requirements:* For master's, thesis; for doctorate, thesis/dissertation. *Entrance requirements:* For master's, PRAXIS I; for doctorate, GRE General Test. Additional exam requirements/recommendations for international students: Required—TOEFL. *Application deadline:* For fall admission, 2/1 priority date for domestic students; for spring admission, 11/15 priority date for domestic students. Applications are processed on a rolling basis. Application fee: $50. Electronic applications accepted. *Expenses:* Tuition, state resident: full-time $19,964; part-time $807 per credit. Tuition, nonresident: full-time $32,686; part-time $1337 per credit. *Required fees:* $740; $200. Tuition and fees vary according to program. *Financial support:* Fellowships, teaching assistantships, career-related internships or fieldwork, Federal Work-Study, tuition waivers (partial), and unspecified assistantships available. Support available to part-time students. Financial award application deadline: 3/15; financial award applicants required to submit FAFSA. *Unit head:* Dr. Richard Donato, Chairman, 412-624-7248, Fax: 412-648-7081, E-mail: donato@pitt.edu. *Application contact:* Marianne L. Budziszewski, Director of Admissions and Enrollment Services, 412-648-2230, Fax: 412-648-1899, E-mail: soeinfo@pitt.edu.
Website: http://www.education.pitt.edu/.

University of Puerto Rico, Río Piedras Campus, College of Education, Program in Curriculum and Teaching, San Juan, PR 00931-3300. Offers biology education (M Ed); chemistry education (M Ed); curriculum and teaching (Ed D); history education (M Ed); mathematics education (M Ed); physics education (M Ed); Spanish education (M Ed). Part-time programs available. *Degree requirements:* For master's, thesis; for doctorate, thesis/dissertation, internship. *Entrance requirements:* For master's, PAEG or GRE, minimum GPA of 3.0, letter of recommendation; for doctorate, GRE or PAEG, master's degree, minimum GPA of 3.0, letter of recommendation (2), interview. *Faculty research:* Curriculum, math teaching.

University of South Carolina, The Graduate School, College of Arts and Sciences, Department of Languages, Literatures, and Cultures, Columbia, SC 29208. Offers comparative literature (MA, PhD); foreign languages (MAT), including French, German, Spanish; French (MA); German (MA); Spanish (MA). MAT offered in cooperation with the College of Education. Part-time programs available. *Degree requirements:* For master's, one foreign language, comprehensive exam, thesis optional; for doctorate, 2 foreign languages, comprehensive exam, thesis/dissertation. *Entrance requirements:* For master's and doctorate, GRE General Test, writing sample. Additional exam requirements/recommendations for international students: Required—TOEFL (minimum score 75 iBT). Electronic applications accepted. *Faculty research:* Modern literature, linguistics, literature and culture, medieval literature, literary theory.

University of South Carolina, The Graduate School, College of Education, Department of Instruction and Teacher Education, Program in Secondary Education, Columbia, SC 29208. Offers art education (IMA, MAT); business education (IMA, MAT); English (MAT); foreign language (MAT); health education (MAT); mathematics (MAT); science (IMA, MAT); secondary (Ed D); secondary education (MT, PhD); social studies (MAT); theatre and speech (MAT). IMA and MT offered jointly with the subject areas. *Accreditation:* NCATE. *Degree requirements:* For master's, comprehensive exam, thesis (for some programs), foreign language (MA); for doctorate, one foreign language, comprehensive exam, thesis/dissertation. *Entrance requirements:* For master's, GRE General Test or MAT, teaching certificate (IMA, M Ed), interview; for doctorate, GRE General Test or MAT, interview. *Faculty research:* Middle school programs, professional development, school collaboration.

University of Southern Mississippi, Graduate School, College of Arts and Letters, Department of Foreign Languages and Literatures, Hattiesburg, MS 39406-0001. Offers French (MATL); Spanish (MATL); teaching English to speakers of other languages (TESOL) (MATL). *Faculty:* 9 full-time (5 women). *Students:* 13 full-time (8 women), 61 part-time (47 women); includes 11 minority (4 Black or African American, non-Hispanic/Latino; 6 Hispanic/Latino; 1 Two or more races, non-Hispanic/Latino), 4 international. Average age 36. 19 applicants, 74% accepted, 10 enrolled. In 2013, 20 master's awarded. *Degree requirements:* For master's, comprehensive exam. *Entrance requirements:* For master's, GRE General Test, minimum GPA of 3.0 in field of study, 2.75 in last 2 years. Additional exam requirements/recommendations for international students: Required—TOEFL, IELTS. *Application deadline:* For fall admission, 3/1 for domestic and international students. Applications are processed on a rolling basis. Application fee: $50. *Financial support:* In 2013–14, 8 teaching assistantships with full tuition reimbursements (averaging $8,350 per year) were awarded; Federal Work-Study, institutionally sponsored loans, scholarships/grants, health care benefits, and unspecified assistantships also available. Financial award application deadline: 3/15; financial award applicants required to submit FAFSA. *Unit head:* Dr. Leah Fonder-Solano, Chair, 601-266-4964, Fax: 601-266-4853. *Application contact:* Dr. Joanne Burnett, Director, Graduate Studies, 601-266-4964, E-mail: graduateschool@usm.edu.
Website: http://www.usm.edu/graduateschool/table.php.

University of South Florida, College of Education, Department of Secondary Education, Tampa, FL 33620-9951. Offers English education (M Ed, MA, MAT, PhD); foreign language education/ESOL (M Ed, MA, MAT); instructional technology (M Ed, PhD, Ed S); mathematics education (M Ed, MA, MAT, PhD, Ed S); science education (M Ed, MA, MAT, PhD); second language acquisition/instructional technology (PhD); secondary education (M Ed, PhD); secondary education/TESOL (M Ed); social science education (M Ed, MA, MAT); teaching and learning in the content area (PhD). *Accreditation:* NCATE. Part-time and evening/weekend programs available. *Degree requirements:* For master's, variable foreign language requirement, comprehensive exam, project (for some programs); for doctorate, variable foreign language requirement, comprehensive exam, thesis/dissertation, philosophies of inquiry; multiple research methods. *Entrance requirements:* For master's, GRE General Test or General Knowledge Test, minimum GPA of 3.0; for doctorate, GRE General Test, minimum GPA of 3.5; for Ed S, GRE General Test. Additional exam requirements/recommendations for international students: Required—TOEFL (minimum score 550 paper-based; 79 iBT). Electronic applications accepted. *Faculty research:* English language learners/multicultural, social science education, mathematics education, science education, instructional technology.

University of South Florida, University College/Distance Education, Tampa, FL 33620-9951. *Unit head:* Kathy Barnes, Interdisciplinary Programs Coordinator, 813-974-8031, Fax: 813-974-7061, E-mail: barnesk@usf.edu. *Application contact:* Karen Tylinski, Metro Initiatives, 813-974-9943, Fax: 813-974-7061, E-mail: ktylinsk@usf.edu.
Website: http://uc.usf.edu/.

The University of Tennessee, Graduate School, College of Education, Health and Human Sciences, Program in Education, Knoxville, TN 37996. Offers art education (MS); counseling education (PhD); cultural studies in education (PhD); curriculum (MS, Ed S); curriculum, educational research and evaluation (Ed D, PhD); early childhood education (PhD); early childhood special education (MS); education of deaf and hard of hearing (MS); educational administration and policy studies (Ed D, PhD); educational administration and supervision (Ed S); educational psychology (Ed D, PhD); elementary education (MS, Ed S); elementary teaching (MS); English education (MS, Ed S); exercise science (PhD); foreign language/ESL education (MS, Ed S); instructional technology (MS, Ed D, PhD, Ed S); literacy, language and ESL education (PhD); literacy, language education, and ESL education (Ed D); mathematics education (MS, Ed S); modified and comprehensive special education (MS); reading education (MS, Ed S); school counseling (Ed S); school psychology (PhD, Ed S); science education (MS, Ed S); secondary teaching (MS); social foundations (MS); social science education (MS, Ed S); socio-cultural foundations of sports and education (PhD); special education (Ed S); teacher education (Ed D, PhD). *Accreditation:* NCATE. Part-time and evening/weekend programs available. *Degree requirements:* For master's and Ed S, thesis optional; for doctorate, variable foreign language requirement, thesis/dissertation. *Entrance requirements:* For master's, minimum GPA of 2.7; for doctorate and Ed S, GRE General Test, minimum GPA of 2.7. Additional exam requirements/recommendations for international students: Required—TOEFL. Electronic applications accepted. *Expenses:* Tuition, state resident: full-time $9540; part-time $531 per credit hour. Tuition, nonresident: full-time $27,728; part-time $1542 per credit hour. *Required fees:* $1404; $67 per credit hour.

University of the Sacred Heart, Graduate Programs, Department of Education, San Juan, PR 00914-0383. Offers early childhood education (M Ed); information technology and multimedia (Certificate); instruction systems and education technology (M Ed), including English, information technology and multimedia, instructional design, mathematics, Spanish. Part-time and evening/weekend programs available. *Degree requirements:* For master's, thesis. *Entrance requirements:* For master's, EXADEP, minimum undergraduate GPA of 2.75, interview.

The University of Toledo, College of Graduate Studies, Judith Herb College of Education, Department of Curriculum and Instruction, Toledo, OH 43606-3390. Offers art education (ME); career and technical education (ME); career-technical education (Ed S); curriculum and instruction (ME, PhD, Ed S); early childhood education (PhD, Ed S); education and biology (MES); education and chemistry (MES); education and economics (MAE); education and English (MAE); education and French (MAE); education and geography (MAE); education and geology (MES); education and German (MAE); education and history (MAE); education and mathematics (MAE, MES); education and physics (MES); education and political science (MAE); education and sociology (MAE); education and Spanish (MAE); educational media (PhD); educational technology (ME); educational technology: virtual educator (Certificate); elementary education (PhD); English as a second language (MAE); gifted and talented (PhD); middle childhood education licensure (ME); music education (MME); secondary education (PhD); secondary education licensure (ME); special education (PhD, Ed S). *Accreditation:* NCATE. Part-time and evening/weekend programs available. *Faculty:* 41. *Students:* 53 full-time (30 women), 154 part-time (111 women); includes 21 minority (16 Black or African American, non-Hispanic/Latino; 4 Hispanic/Latino; 1 Two or more races, non-Hispanic/Latino), 21 international. Average age 34. 82 applicants, 79% accepted, 47 enrolled. In 2013, 80 master's, 5 doctorates awarded. *Degree requirements:* For master's, comprehensive exam, thesis or alternative; for doctorate, comprehensive exam, thesis/dissertation; for other advanced degree, thesis optional. *Entrance requirements:* For master's, doctorate, and other advanced degree, minimum cumulative GPA of 2.7 for all previous academic work, letters of recommendation. Additional exam requirements/recommendations for international students: Required—TOEFL (minimum score 550 paper-based; 80 iBT). *Application deadline:* For fall admission, 1/15 priority date for domestic and international students. Applications are processed on a rolling basis. Application fee: $45 ($75 for international students). Electronic applications accepted. *Financial support:* In 2013–14, 5 research assistantships with full and partial tuition reimbursements (averaging $13,200 per year), 11 teaching assistantships with full and partial tuition reimbursements (averaging $8,809 per year) were awarded; career-related internships or fieldwork, Federal Work-Study, institutionally sponsored loans, scholarships/grants, tuition waivers (full and partial), unspecified assistantships, and administrative assistantships also available. Support available to part-time students. *Unit head:* Dr. Joan Kaderavek, Chair, 419-530-5373, E-mail: eigh.chiarelott@utoledo.edu. *Application contact:* Graduate School Office, 419-530-4723, Fax: 419-530-4724, E-mail: grdsch@utnet.utoledo.edu.
Website: http://www.utoledo.edu/eduhshs/.

University of Utah, Graduate School, College of Humanities, Department of Languages and Literature, Salt Lake City, UT 84112. Offers comparative literary and cultural studies (MA, PhD); French (MA); Spanish (MA, MALP, PhD); world languages (MA). Part-time programs available. *Faculty:* 33 full-time (20 women), 15 part-time/adjunct (10 women). *Students:* 44 full-time (30 women), 7 part-time (4 women); includes 11 minority (1 Black or African American, non-Hispanic/Latino; 1 American Indian or Alaska Native, non-Hispanic/Latino; 1 Asian, non-Hispanic/Latino; 8 Hispanic/Latino), 14 international. Average age 32. 35 applicants, 60% accepted, 19 enrolled. In 2013, 21 master's awarded. Terminal master's awarded for partial completion of doctoral program. *Degree*

requirements: For master's, comprehensive exam (for some programs), thesis (for some programs), standard proficiency in 2 languages other than English; for doctorate, comprehensive exam, thesis/dissertation, standard proficiency in 2 languages other than English and language of study, advanced proficiency in 1 language other than English and language of study. *Entrance requirements:* For master's, GRE (except for French), bachelor's degree or strong undergraduate record in target languages, minimum GPA of 3.0; for doctorate, GRE, MA, advanced proficiency in a target language. Additional exam requirements/recommendations for international students: Required—TOEFL (minimum score 550 paper-based; 80 iBT). *Application deadline:* For fall admission, 1/15 priority date for domestic students, 12/15 priority date for international students. Application fee: $55 ($65 for international students). Electronic applications accepted. *Expenses:* Tuition, state resident: full-time $5259. Tuition, nonresident: full-time $18,569. *Required fees:* $841. Tuition and fees vary according to course load. *Financial support:* In 2013–14, 22 teaching assistantships with full and partial tuition reimbursements (averaging $11,424 per year) were awarded; health care benefits and unspecified assistantships also available. Financial award application deadline: 1/15; financial award applicants required to submit FAFSA. *Faculty research:* Literary study, literary theory, linguistics, cultural studies, comparative studies. *Unit head:* Dr. Margaret Toscano, Director of Graduate Studies, 801-581-4768, Fax: 801-581-4768, E-mail: margaret.toscano@utah.edu. *Application contact:* Marcie Leek, Academic Coordinator, 801-581-5401, Fax: 801-581-5401, E-mail: marcie.leek@utah.edu.
Website: http://languages.utah.edu/.

University of Vermont, Graduate College, College of Arts and Sciences, Department of Classics, Burlington, VT 05405. Offers Greek (MA); Greek and Latin (MAT); Latin (MA). *Students:* 5 (3 women); includes 3 minority (1 Black or African American, non-Hispanic/Latino; 1 Asian, non-Hispanic/Latino; 1 Hispanic/Latino), 1 international. 15 applicants, 53% accepted, 2 enrolled. In 2013, 1 master's awarded. *Degree requirements:* For master's, one foreign language, thesis. *Entrance requirements:* For master's, GRE General Test. Additional exam requirements/recommendations for international students: Required—TOEFL (minimum score 550 paper-based; 80 iBT). *Application deadline:* For fall admission, 3/1 priority date for domestic students, 3/1 for international students. Applications are processed on a rolling basis. Application fee: $65. Electronic applications accepted. *Financial support:* Fellowships and teaching assistantships available. Financial award application deadline: 3/1. *Faculty research:* Early Greek literature. *Unit head:* Dr. Mark Usher, Chair, 802-656-3210. *Application contact:* Prof. Jacques Bailly, Coordinator, 802-656-3210.

University of Victoria, Faculty of Graduate Studies, Faculty of Humanities, Department of French, Victoria, BC V8W 2Y2, Canada. Offers literature (MA); teaching emphasis (MA). Part-time and evening/weekend programs available. *Degree requirements:* For master's, 2 foreign languages, thesis optional. *Entrance requirements:* For master's, BA in French. Additional exam requirements/recommendations for international students: Required—TOEFL (minimum score 575 paper-based), IELTS (minimum score 7). Electronic applications accepted. *Faculty research:* French-Canadian literature, stylistics, comparative literature, Francophone literature.

University of Virginia, Curry School of Education, Department of Curriculum, Instruction, and Special Education, Program in Curriculum and Instruction, Charlottesville, VA 22903. Offers curriculum and instruction (M Ed, Ed S); elementary education (M Ed, Ed D); English (M Ed, Ed D); foreign language (M Ed); mathematics (M Ed, Ed D); reading (M Ed, Ed D, Ed S); science (Ed D); social studies (M Ed). *Students:* 42 full-time (30 women), 37 part-time (32 women); includes 4 minority (1 Black or African American, non-Hispanic/Latino; 2 Hispanic/Latino; 1 Two or more races, non-Hispanic/Latino), 1 international. Average age 31. 76 applicants, 74% accepted, 39 enrolled. In 2013, 84 master's, 3 doctorates, 23 other advanced degrees awarded. *Degree requirements:* For master's, comprehensive exam (for some programs); for doctorate, comprehensive exam, thesis/dissertation; for Ed S, comprehensive exam. *Entrance requirements:* For master's, doctorate, and Ed S, GRE General Test, 2 letters of recommendation. Additional exam requirements/recommendations for international students: Required—TOEFL (minimum score 600 paper-based; 90 iBT), IELTS (minimum score 7). *Application deadline:* Applications are processed on a rolling basis. Application fee: $60. Electronic applications accepted. *Expenses:* Tuition, state resident: part-time $334 per credit hour. Tuition, nonresident: part-time $1224 per credit hour. *Financial support:* Fellowships with tuition reimbursements, research assistantships with tuition reimbursements, and teaching assistantships with tuition reimbursements available. Financial award application deadline: 1/5; financial award applicants required to submit FAFSA. *Unit head:* Stephanie van Hover, Chair, 434-924-0841, E-mail: sdv2w@virginia.edu. *Application contact:* Karen Dwier, Information Contact, 434-924-0831, E-mail: kgd9g@virginia.edu.
Website: http://curry.virginia.edu/academics/areas-of-study/curriculum-teaching-learning.

University of Virginia, Curry School of Education, Program in Education, Charlottesville, VA 22903. Offers administration and supervision (PhD); applied developmental science (PhD); counselor education (PhD); curriculum and instruction (PhD); early childhood special education (MT); education evaluation (PhD); educational psychology (PhD); educational research (PhD); elementary education (MT); English education (MT, PhD); foreign language education (MT); higher education (PhD); instructional technology (PhD); kinesiology (MT, PhD); math education (PhD); reading education (PhD); research, statistics and evaluation (PhD); school psychology (PhD); science education (PhD); social studies education (MT, PhD); special education (PhD); world languages education (MT). *Students:* 474 full-time (379 women), 35 part-time (19 women); includes 89 minority (30 Black or African American, non-Hispanic/Latino; 1 American Indian or Alaska Native, non-Hispanic/Latino; 26 Asian, non-Hispanic/Latino; 19 Hispanic/Latino; 13 Two or more races, non-Hispanic/Latino), 21 international. Average age 26. 312 applicants, 49% accepted, 80 enrolled. In 2013, 137 master's, 38 doctorates awarded. *Degree requirements:* For master's, comprehensive exam (for some programs), field project; for doctorate, comprehensive exam, thesis/dissertation. *Entrance requirements:* For doctorate, GRE General Test. Additional exam requirements/recommendations for international students: Required—TOEFL (minimum score 600 paper-based; 90 iBT), IELTS (minimum score 7). *Application deadline:* Applications are processed on a rolling basis. Application fee: $60. Electronic applications accepted. *Expenses:* Tuition, state resident: part-time $334 per credit hour. Tuition, nonresident: part-time $1224 per credit hour. *Financial support:* Fellowships, research assistantships, and teaching assistantships available. Financial award application deadline: 1/5; financial award applicants required to submit FAFSA. *Unit head:* Robert C. Pianta, Dean, 434-924-3334, E-mail: pianta@virginia.edu. *Application contact:* Office of Admissions and Student Services, 434-924-0742, E-mail: curry-admissions@virginia.edu.
Website: http://curry.virginia.edu/teacher-education.

University of Wisconsin–Madison, Graduate School, School of Education, Department of Curriculum and Instruction, Madison, WI 53706-1380. Offers art education (MA); curriculum and instruction (MS, PhD); education and mathematics (MA); French education (MA); German education (MA); music education (MS); science education (MS); Spanish education (MA). *Accreditation:* NASM (one or more programs

are accredited). *Degree requirements:* For doctorate, thesis/dissertation. Application fee: $56. *Expenses:* Tuition, state resident: full-time $10,728; part-time $790 per credit. Tuition, nonresident: full-time $24,054; part-time $1623 per credit. *Required fees:* $1130; $119 per credit. *Financial support:* Project assistantships available. *Unit head:* Dr. Beth Graue, Chair, 608-263-4600, E-mail: graue@education.wisc.edu. *Application contact:* 608-262-2433, Fax: 608-262-5134, E-mail: gradadmiss@mail.bascom.wisc.edu.
Website: http://www.education.wisc.edu/ci.

Vanderbilt University, Graduate School, Department of French and Italian, Nashville, TN 37240-1001. Offers French (MA, MAT, PhD). *Faculty:* 11 full-time (5 women). *Students:* 9 full-time (7 women), 3 international. Average age 28. 28 applicants. In 2013, 1 master's, 4 doctorates awarded. Terminal master's awarded for partial completion of doctoral program. *Degree requirements:* For master's, one foreign language, comprehensive exam; for doctorate, 2 foreign languages, comprehensive exam, thesis/dissertation, final and qualifying exams. *Entrance requirements:* For master's and doctorate, GRE General Test. Additional exam requirements/recommendations for international students: Required—TOEFL (minimum score 570 paper-based; 88 iBT). *Application deadline:* For fall admission, 1/15 for domestic and international students. Electronic applications accepted. *Financial support:* Fellowships with full and partial tuition reimbursements, teaching assistantships with full and partial tuition reimbursements, career-related internships or fieldwork, Federal Work-Study, institutionally sponsored loans, scholarships/grants, and health care benefits available. Financial award application deadline: 1/15; financial award applicants required to submit CSS PROFILE or FAFSA. *Faculty research:* Baudelaire, Rabelais, voyage literature, postcolonial literature, medieval epic. *Unit head:* Paul Miller, Director of Graduate Studies, 615-322-6906, Fax: 615-343-6909, E-mail: paul.b.miller@vanderbilt.edu. *Application contact:* Tamra Hicks, Department Administrator, 615-343-6900, Fax: 615-343-6909, E-mail: tamra.m.hicks@vanderbilt.edu.
Website: http://as.vanderbilt.edu/french-italian/.

Vanderbilt University, Graduate School, Department of Germanic and Slavic Languages, Nashville, TN 37240-1001. Offers German (MA, MAT, PhD). *Faculty:* 6 full-time (3 women). *Students:* 20 full-time (16 women); includes 4 minority (1 Asian, non-Hispanic/Latino; 2 Hispanic/Latino; 1 Two or more races, non-Hispanic/Latino), 8 international. Average age 32. 15 applicants, 33% accepted, 1 enrolled. In 2013, 2 master's, 4 doctorates awarded. Terminal master's awarded for partial completion of doctoral program. *Degree requirements:* For master's, one foreign language, comprehensive exam; for doctorate, 2 foreign languages, comprehensive exam, thesis/dissertation, qualifying and final exams. *Entrance requirements:* For master's and doctorate, GRE General Test, sample of written work. Additional exam requirements/recommendations for international students: Required—TOEFL (minimum score 570 paper-based; 88 iBT). *Application deadline:* For fall admission, 1/15 for domestic and international students. Electronic applications accepted. *Financial support:* Fellowships with full and partial tuition reimbursements, teaching assistantships with full and partial tuition reimbursements, career-related internships or fieldwork, Federal Work-Study, institutionally sponsored loans, scholarships/grants, and health care benefits available. Financial award application deadline: 1/15; financial award applicants required to submit CSS PROFILE or FAFSA. *Faculty research:* 1750 to present, Middle Ages, Baroque, language pedagogy, linguistics. *Unit head:* Dr. Meike Werner, Director of Graduate Studies, 615-343-0404, Fax: 615-343-7258, E-mail: meike.werner@vanderbilt.edu. *Application contact:* Rose M. Dudney, Administrative Assistant, 615-322-2611, Fax: 615-343-7258, E-mail: rose.m.dudney@vanderbilt.edu.
Website: http://www.vanderbilt.edu/german/graduate/.

Vanderbilt University, Graduate School, Department of Spanish and Portuguese, Nashville, TN 37240-1001. Offers Portuguese (MA); Spanish (MA, MAT, PhD); Spanish and Portuguese (PhD). *Faculty:* 13 full-time (6 women). *Students:* 22 full-time (10 women); includes 3 minority (1 Black or African American, non-Hispanic/Latino; 2 Hispanic/Latino), 8 international. Average age 32. 62 applicants, 8% accepted, 2 enrolled. In 2013, 2 doctorates awarded. *Degree requirements:* For master's, one foreign language, thesis; for doctorate, 2 foreign languages, thesis/dissertation, final and qualifying exams. *Entrance requirements:* For master's, GRE General Test; for doctorate, GRE General Test, writing sample in Spanish. Additional exam requirements/recommendations for international students: Required—TOEFL (minimum score 570 paper-based; 88 iBT). *Application deadline:* For fall admission, 1/15 for domestic and international students. Electronic applications accepted. *Financial support:* Fellowships with full and partial tuition reimbursements, teaching assistantships with full tuition reimbursements, Federal Work-Study, institutionally sponsored loans, and health care benefits available. Financial award application deadline: 1/15; financial award applicants required to submit CSS PROFILE or FAFSA. *Faculty research:* Spanish, Portuguese, and Latin American literatures; foreign language pedagogy; Renaissance and Baroque poetry; nineteenth-century Spanish novel. *Unit head:* Dr. Andres Zamora, Director of Graduate Studies, 615-322-6858, Fax: 615-343-7260, E-mail: andres.zamora@vanderbilt.edu. *Application contact:* Cindy Martinez, Administrative Assistant, 615-322-6930, Fax: 615-343-7260, E-mail: cindy.m.martinez@vanderbilt.edu.
Website: http://as.vanderbilt.edu/spanish-portuguese/graduate/index.php.

Virginia Polytechnic Institute and State University, Graduate School, College of Liberal Arts and Human Sciences, Blacksburg, VA 24061. Offers career and technical education (MS Ed, Ed D, PhD, Ed S); communication (MA); counselor education (MA Ed, Ed D, PhD, Ed S); creative writing (MFA); curriculum and instruction (MA Ed, Ed D, PhD, Ed S); educational leadership and policy studies (MA Ed, Ed D, PhD, Ed S); educational research and evaluation (PhD); English (MA); foreign languages, cultures, and literatures (MA); higher education and student affairs (MA Ed); history (MA); human development (MS, PhD); material culture and public humanities (MA); philosophy (MA); political science (MA); rhetoric and writing (PhD); science and technology studies (MS, PhD); social, political, ethical, and cultural thought (PhD); sociology (MS, PhD); theater arts (MFA). *Faculty:* 410 full-time (211 women), 6 part-time/adjunct (5 women). *Students:* 688 full-time (464 women), 576 part-time (372 women); includes 243 minority (144 Black or African American, non-Hispanic/Latino; 3 American Indian or Alaska Native, non-Hispanic/Latino; 29 Asian, non-Hispanic/Latino; 48 Hispanic/Latino; 1 Native Hawaiian or other Pacific Islander, non-Hispanic/Latino; 18 Two or more races, non-Hispanic/Latino), 84 international. Average age 34. 1,054 applicants, 48% accepted, 374 enrolled. In 2013, 314 master's, 74 doctorates, 14 other advanced degrees awarded. *Degree requirements:* For master's, comprehensive exam (for some programs), thesis (for some programs); for doctorate, comprehensive exam (for some programs), thesis/dissertation (for some programs). *Entrance requirements:* For master's and doctorate, GRE/GMAT (may vary by department). Additional exam requirements/recommendations for international students: Required—TOEFL (minimum score 550 paper-based). *Application deadline:* For fall admission, 8/1 for domestic students, 4/1 for international students; for spring admission, 1/1 for domestic students, 9/1 for international students. Applications are processed on a rolling basis. Application fee: $75. Electronic applications accepted. *Expenses:* Tuition, state resident: full-time $11,185; part-time $621.50 per credit hour. Tuition, nonresident: full-time $22,146; part-time $1230.25 per credit hour. *Required fees:* $2442; $449.25 per semester. Tuition and fees vary according to course load, campus/location and program. *Financial support:* In 2013–14, 19 research assistantships with full tuition reimbursements (averaging

$17,115 per year), 205 teaching assistantships with full tuition reimbursements (averaging $14,433 per year) were awarded. Financial award application deadline: 3/1; financial award applicants required to submit FAFSA. *Total annual research expenditures:* $6.8 million. *Unit head:* Joan Hirt, Interim Dean, 540-231-6779, Fax: 540-231-7157, E-mail: jbhirt@vt.edu. *Application contact:* Melissa Elliott, Executive Assistant, 540-231-6779, Fax: 540-231-7157, E-mail: elliott1@vt.edu.
Website: http://www.clahs.vt.edu/.

Wagner College, Division of Graduate Studies, Department of Education, Program in Secondary Education/Special Education, Staten Island, NY 10301-4495. Offers language arts (MS Ed); languages other than English (MS Ed); mathematics and technology (MS Ed); science and technology (MS Ed); social studies (MS Ed). Part-time and evening/weekend programs available. *Degree requirements:* For master's, thesis (for some programs). *Entrance requirements:* For master's, minimum GPA of 3.0, interview, recommendations. Electronic applications accepted. *Expenses: Tuition:* Full-time $17,496; part-time $972 per credit. Tuition and fees vary according to course load.

Washington State University, Graduate School, College of Arts and Sciences, Department of Foreign Languages and Cultures, Pullman, WA 99164. Offers foreign languages with emphasis in Spanish (MA). *Degree requirements:* For master's, comprehensive exam (for some programs), thesis (for some programs), 4 written exams, oral exam, paper. *Entrance requirements:* For master's, three current letters of recommendation; all original transcripts including an official English translation; two writing samples; letter of application stating qualifications and personal goals; brief (3-5 minute) tape recordings of two informal dialogues between applicant and native speaker. Additional exam requirements/recommendations for international students: Required—TOEFL (minimum score 550 paper-based). Electronic applications accepted. *Faculty research:* Spanish and Latin American literature, film, and culture; pedagogy; computer-aided instruction.

Wayne State University, College of Education, Division of Teacher Education, Detroit, MI 48202. Offers art education (M Ed), including art therapy; autism spectrum disorders (Certificate); bilingual/bicultural education (M Ed, Certificate); career and technical education (M Ed, Certificate); cognitive impairment (Certificate); curriculum and instruction (Ed D, PhD, Ed S), including art education (PhD), bilingual education (Ed D, Ed S), bilingual-bicultural education (PhD), career and technical education (MAT, Ed D, PhD, Ed S), early childhood education (MAT, Ed D, PhD, Ed S), elementary education, English as a second language (MAT, Ed D, Ed S), English education (MAT, Ed D, PhD, Ed S), foreign language education (MAT, PhD), K-12 curriculum, mathematics education (MAT, Ed D, PhD, Ed S), science education (MAT, Ed D, PhD, Ed S), secondary education, social studies education (MAT, Ed S), social studies education: secondary (Ed D, PhD); early childhood education (M Ed, Certificate); elementary education (M Ed, MAT), including children's literature (MAT), early childhood education (MAT, Ed D, PhD, Ed S), general elementary education (MAT); elementary or secondary education (MAT), including bilingual/bicultural education, English as a second language (MAT, Ed D, Ed S), mathematics education (MAT, Ed D, PhD, Ed S), science education (MAT, Ed D, PhD, Ed S), social studies education (MAT, Ed S); emotionally impaired (Certificate); English as a second language (Certificate); English education (M Ed), including secondary; foreign language education (M Ed); K-12 reading specialist (Certificate); learning disabilities (Certificate); mathematics education (M Ed), including secondary; reading (M Ed, Ed S); reading, language and literature (Ed D); science education (M Ed), including secondary; secondary education (MAT), including art education (K-12), career and technical education (MAT, Ed D, PhD, Ed S), English education (MAT, Ed D, PhD, Ed S), foreign language education (MAT, PhD), kinesiology; social studies education (M Ed), including secondary; special education (M Ed, MAT, Ed D, PhD, Ed S); visual arts education (Certificate). Part-time programs available. *Faculty:* 36 full-time (25 women), 55 part-time/adjunct (43 women). *Students:* 218 full-time (163 women), 448 part-time (344 women); includes 218 minority (177 Black or African American, non-Hispanic/Latino; 2 American Indian or Alaska Native, non-Hispanic/Latino; 11 Asian, non-Hispanic/Latino; 19 Hispanic/Latino; 1 Native Hawaiian or other Pacific Islander, non-Hispanic/Latino; 8 Two or more races, non-Hispanic/Latino), 10 international. Average age 37. 258 applicants, 30% accepted, 52 enrolled. In 2013, 183 master's, 10 doctorates, 35 other advanced degrees awarded. *Degree requirements:* For master's, thesis, essay or project (for some M Ed programs), professional field experience (for MAT programs); for doctorate, thesis/dissertation. *Entrance requirements:* For master's, Michigan Basic Skills Test (MA in teaching), admission to the graduate school, verification of participation in group work with children and Michigan State Police Criminal Background check; for doctorate, minimum undergraduate GPA of 3.0, graduate 3.5; interview, curriculum vitae; references. Additional exam requirements/recommendations for international students: Required—TOEFL (minimum score 550 paper-based; 79 iBT), TWE (minimum score 5.5), Michigan English Language Assessment Battery (minimum score 85); Recommended—IELTS (minimum score 6.5). *Application deadline:* For fall admission, 6/1 priority date for domestic students, 5/1 priority date for international students; for winter admission, 10/1 priority date for domestic students, 9/1 priority date for international students; for spring admission, 2/1 priority date for domestic students, 1/1 priority date for international students. Applications are processed on a rolling basis. Application fee: $0. Electronic applications accepted. *Expenses:* Tuition, state resident: part-time $554.15 per credit. Tuition, nonresident: part-time $1200.35 per credit. *Required fees:* $42.15 per credit. $268.30 per semester. Tuition and fees vary according to course load and program. *Financial support:* In 2013–14, 83 students received support, including 1 fellowship (averaging $16,842 per year), 1 research assistantship with tuition reimbursement available (averaging $21,229 per year); career-related internships or fieldwork, Federal Work-Study, scholarships/grants, health care benefits, and unspecified assistantships also available. Support available to part-time students. Financial award application deadline: 3/31; financial award applicants required to submit FAFSA. *Faculty research:* Improving students' skill achievement in mathematics; improving elementary children's understanding of informational text; teachers' use of their pedagogical and mathematical knowledge in the interactive work of teaching; the intersection of identity construction in teaching and learning; identifying effective methods of literacy instruction and assessments for bilingual students in elementary language arts classrooms. *Total annual research expenditures:* $368,105. *Unit head:* Dr. Kathleen Crawford-McKinney, Assistant Dean, 313-577-0122. *Application contact:* Janice Green, Assistant Dean, 313-577-1605, E-mail: jwgreen@wayne.edu.
Website: http://coe.wayne.edu/ted/index.php.

Wayne State University, College of Liberal Arts and Sciences, Department of Classical and Modern Languages, Literatures, and Cultures, Program in Language Learning, Detroit, MI 48202. Offers Arabic (MALL); classics (MALL); French (MALL); German (MALL); Italian (MALL); Spanish (MALL). *Students:* 8 part-time (6 women); includes 2 minority (1 Black or African American, non-Hispanic/Latino; 1 Hispanic/Latino). Average age 30. 7 applicants, 71% accepted. In 2013, 2 master's awarded. *Degree requirements:* For master's, one foreign language, three-credit essay. *Entrance requirements:* For master's, GRE (recommended), target language proficiency, statement of purpose, three letters of recommendation, minimum GPA of 2.6 from accredited institution or 3.2 from non-accredited institution. Additional exam requirements/recommendations for international students: Required—TOEFL (minimum score 550 paper-based; 79 iBT), TWE (minimum score 5.5), Michigan English Language Assessment Battery (minimum score 85); Recommended—IELTS (minimum score 6.5). *Application deadline:* For fall admission, 6/1 priority date for domestic students, 5/1 for international students; for winter admission, 10/1 priority date for domestic students, 9/1 priority date for international students; for spring admission, 2/1 priority date for domestic students, 1/1 priority date for international students. Applications are processed on a rolling basis. Application fee: $0. Electronic applications accepted. *Expenses:* Tuition, state resident: part-time $554.15 per credit. Tuition, nonresident: part-time $1200.35 per credit. *Required fees:* $42.15 per credit. $268.30 per semester. Tuition and fees vary according to course load and program. *Financial support:* Scholarships/grants and unspecified assistantships available. Financial award application deadline: 3/31; financial award applicants required to submit FAFSA. *Unit head:* Dr. Donald Spinelli, Department Chair, 313-577-3002, E-mail: aa1471@wayne.edu. *Application contact:* Dr. Catherine Barrette, Associate Professor/Graduate Advisor, 313-577-6243, E-mail: c.barrette@wayne.edu.
Website: http://clasweb.clas.wayne.edu/MALL.

West Chester University of Pennsylvania, College of Arts and Sciences, Department of Languages and Cultures, West Chester, PA 19383. Offers French (M Ed, MA, Teaching Certificate); Spanish (M Ed, MA, Teaching Certificate). Part-time and evening/weekend programs available. *Faculty:* 12 full-time (7 women), 1 (woman) part-time/adjunct. *Students:* 4 full-time (2 women), 19 part-time (16 women); includes 7 minority (3 Black or African American, non-Hispanic/Latino; 4 Hispanic/Latino), 1 international. Average age 35. 6 applicants, 100% accepted, 7 enrolled. In 2013, 8 master's awarded. *Degree requirements:* For master's, 2 foreign languages, exit exam capstone project; thesis (for MA); for Teaching Certificate, 2 foreign languages, PA K-12 Certification completion. *Entrance requirements:* For master's, placement test. Additional exam requirements/recommendations for international students: Required—TOEFL (minimum score 550 paper-based; 80 iBT). *Application deadline:* For fall admission, 4/15 priority date for domestic students, 3/15 for international students; for spring admission, 10/15 priority date for domestic students, 9/1 for international students. Applications are processed on a rolling basis. Application fee: $45. Electronic applications accepted. *Expenses:* Tuition, state resident: full-time $7956; part-time $442 per credit. Tuition, nonresident: full-time $11,934; part-time $663 per credit. *Required fees:* $2134.20; $106.24 per credit. Tuition and fees vary according to campus/location and program. *Financial support:* Unspecified assistantships available. Support available to part-time students. Financial award application deadline: 2/15; financial award applicants required to submit FAFSA. *Faculty research:* Language structure, literature, film, culture, pedagogy, technology. *Unit head:* Dr. Jerome Williams, Chair, 610-436-2700, Fax: 610-436-3048, E-mail: jwilliams2@wcupa.edu. *Application contact:* Dr. Rebecca Pauly, Graduate Coordinator, 610-436-2382, Fax: 610-436-3048, E-mail: rpauly@wcupa.edu.
Website: http://www.wcupa.edu/_academics/sch_cas.flg/.

Western Kentucky University, Graduate Studies, Potter College of Arts and Letters, Department of Modern Languages, Bowling Green, KY 42101. Offers French (MA Ed); German (MA Ed); Spanish (MA Ed).

Worcester State University, Graduate Studies, Program in Spanish, Worcester, MA 01602-2597. Offers MA. Part-time programs available. *Faculty:* 3 full-time (2 women). *Students:* 17 part-time (16 women); includes 5 minority (all Hispanic/Latino). Average age 35. 12 applicants, 92% accepted, 4 enrolled. In 2013, 8 master's awarded. *Degree requirements:* For master's, comprehensive exam (for some programs), thesis optional. *Entrance requirements:* For master's, GRE, MAT, BA in Spanish or related field and/or interview with faculty member. Additional exam requirements/recommendations for international students: Required—TOEFL (minimum score 500 paper-based; 61 iBT). *Application deadline:* For fall admission, 6/15 for domestic and international students; for spring admission, 4/1 for domestic and international students. Applications are processed on a rolling basis. Application fee: $40. Electronic applications accepted. *Expenses: Tuition, area resident:* Part-time $150 per credit. Tuition, state resident: part-time $150 per credit. Tuition, nonresident: part-time $150 per credit. *Required fees:* $114.50 per credit. *Financial support:* Career-related internships or fieldwork, scholarships/grants, and unspecified assistantships available. Financial award application deadline: 3/1; financial award applicants required to submit FAFSA. *Unit head:* Dr. Juan Orbe, Head, 508-929-8704, Fax: 508-929-8174, E-mail: jorbe@worcester.edu. *Application contact:* Sara Grady, Assistant Dean of Graduate and Continuing Education, 508-929-8787, Fax: 508-929-8100, E-mail: sara.grady@worcester.edu.

Health Education

Adelphi University, Ruth S. Ammon School of Education, Program in Health Studies, Garden City, NY 11530-0701. Offers community health education (MA, Certificate); school health education (MA). Part-time and evening/weekend programs available. *Students:* 12 full-time (7 women), 34 part-time (18 women); includes 5 minority (2 Black or African American, non-Hispanic/Latino; 3 Hispanic/Latino), 1 international. Average age 26. In 2013, 13 master's awarded. *Degree requirements:* For master's, internship. *Entrance requirements:* For master's, 3 letters of recommendation, resume, minimum cumulative GPA of 2.75. Additional exam requirements/recommendations for international students: Required—TOEFL (minimum score 550 paper-based; 80 iBT). *Application deadline:* For fall admission, 4/1 for international students; for spring admission, 11/1 for international students. Applications are processed on a rolling basis. Application fee: $50. Electronic applications accepted. *Expenses: Tuition:* Full-time $32,530; part-time $1010 per credit. *Required fees:* $1150. Tuition and fees vary according to degree level and program. *Financial support:* Fellowships, research assistantships with partial tuition reimbursements, teaching assistantships, career-related internships or fieldwork, Federal Work-Study, institutionally sponsored loans, and tuition waivers (full) available. Support available to part-time students. Financial award application deadline: 2/15; financial award applicants required to submit FAFSA. *Faculty research:* Alcohol abuse, tobacco cessation, drug abuse, healthy family lives, healthy personal living. *Unit head:* Dr. Ronald Feingold, Director, 516-877-4764, E-mail:

feingold@adelphi.edu. *Application contact:* Christine Murphy, Director of Admissions, 516-877-3050, Fax: 516-877-3039, E-mail: graduateadmissions@adelphi.edu.

Alabama State University, College of Education, Department of Health, Physical Education, and Recreation, Montgomery, AL 36101-0271. Offers health education (M Ed); physical education (M Ed). Part-time programs available. *Faculty:* 4 full-time (all women), 1 part-time/adjunct (0 women). *Students:* 5 full-time (2 women), 8 part-time (3 women); includes 12 minority (all Black or African American, non-Hispanic/Latino). Average age 27. 20 applicants, 55% accepted, 9 enrolled. In 2013, 6 master's awarded. *Degree requirements:* For master's, comprehensive exam. *Entrance requirements:* For master's, GRE General Test, MAT, writing competency test. Additional exam requirements/recommendations for international students: Required—TOEFL (minimum score 500 paper-based). *Application deadline:* For fall admission, 7/15 for domestic students; for spring admission, 12/15 for domestic students. Applications are processed on a rolling basis. Application fee: $10. *Expenses:* Tuition, state resident: full-time $7958; part-time $343 per credit hour. Tuition, nonresident: full-time $14,132; part-time $686 per credit hour. *Required fees:* $446 per term. One-time fee: $1784 full-time; $892 part-time. Tuition and fees vary according to course load. *Financial support:* In 2013–14, research assistantships (averaging $9,450 per year) were awarded. *Faculty research:* Risk factors for heart disease in the college-age population, cardiovascular reactivity for the Cold Pressor Test. *Unit head:* Dr. Doris Screws, Chair, 334-229-4504, Fax: 334-229-4928, E-mail: dscrews@alasu.edu. *Application contact:* Dr. William Person, Dean of Graduate Studies, 334-229-4274, Fax: 334-229-4928, E-mail: wperson@alasu.edu.
Website: http://www.alasu.edu/academics/colleges—departments/college-of-education/health-physical-education—recreation/index.aspx.

Albany State University, College of Education, Albany, GA 31705-2717. Offers early childhood education (M Ed); education specialist (Ed S); educational leadership and administration (M Ed); health, physical education and recreation (M Ed); middle grades education (M Ed); school counseling (M Ed); special education (M Ed). *Accreditation:* NCATE. Part-time and evening/weekend programs available. Postbaccalaureate distance learning degree programs offered (minimal on-campus study). *Degree requirements:* For master's, comprehensive exam, internship, GACE Content Exam. *Entrance requirements:* For master's, GRE or MAT. Electronic applications accepted. *Faculty research:* GACE preparation, STEM (science, technology, engineering, and mathematics), technology education, special education, professional teacher development, health implications liberation philosophy, NET-Q, learning community, disabled or at-risk students.

Alcorn State University, School of Graduate Studies, School of Psychology and Education, Alcorn State, MS 39096-7500. Offers agricultural education (MS Ed); elementary education (MS Ed, Ed S); guidance and counseling (MS Ed); industrial education (MS Ed); secondary education (MS Ed), including health and physical education; special education (MS Ed). *Accreditation:* NCATE. *Degree requirements:* For master's, thesis optional.

Allen College, Program in Nursing, Waterloo, IA 50703. Offers acute care nurse practitioner (MSN, Post-Master's Certificate); adult nurse practitioner (MSN, Post-Master's Certificate); adult psychiatric-mental health nurse practitioner (MSN, Post-Master's Certificate); community public health (MSN, Post-Master's Certificate); family nurse practitioner (MSN, Post-Master's Certificate); gerontological nurse practitioner (MSN, Post-Master's Certificate); health education (MSN); leadership in health care delivery (MSN, Post-Master's Certificate); nursing (DNP). Part-time programs available. Postbaccalaureate distance learning degree programs offered (minimal on-campus study). *Faculty:* 3 full-time (all women), 21 part-time/adjunct (20 women). *Students:* 21 full-time (19 women), 162 part-time (150 women); includes 5 minority (1 Black or African American, non-Hispanic/Latino; 2 Asian, non-Hispanic/Latino; 1 Hispanic/Latino; 1 Two or more races, non-Hispanic/Latino). Average age 34. 213 applicants, 57% accepted, 94 enrolled. In 2013, 41 master's, 4 other advanced degrees awarded. *Degree requirements:* For master's, thesis optional. *Entrance requirements:* For master's, minimum GPA of 3.0 in the last 60 hours of undergraduate coursework; for doctorate, minimum GPA of 3.25 in graduate coursework. Additional exam requirements/recommendations for international students: Recommended—TOEFL (minimum score 580 paper-based; 92 iBT), IELTS (minimum score 6). *Application deadline:* For fall admission, 2/1 priority date for domestic students; for spring admission, 9/1 priority date for domestic students. Applications are processed on a rolling basis. Application fee: $50. Electronic applications accepted. *Expenses: Tuition:* Full-time $14,534; part-time $755 per credit hour. *Required fees:* $935; $75 per credit hour. One-time fee: $275 part-time. Tuition and fees vary according to course load. *Financial support:* In 2013–14, 60 students received support. Institutionally sponsored loans, scholarships/grants, and traineeships available. Support available to part-time students. Financial award application deadline: 8/15; financial award applicants required to submit FAFSA. *Unit head:* Kendra Williams-Perez, Dean, School of Nursing, 319-226-2044, Fax: 319-226-2070, E-mail: kendra.williams-perez@allencollege.edu. *Application contact:* Molly Quinn, Admissions Counselor, 319-226-2001, Fax: 319-226-2010, E-mail: molly.quinn@allencollege.edu.
Website: http://www.allencollege.edu/.

American University, College of Arts and Sciences, Washington, DC 20016-8012. Offers addiction and addictive behavior (Certificate); anthropology (PhD); applied microeconomics (Certificate); applied statistics (Certificate); art history (MA); arts management (MA, Certificate); Asian studies (Certificate); audio production (Certificate); audio technology (MA); behavior, cognition, and neuroscience (PhD); bilingual education (MA, Certificate); biology (MA, MS); chemistry (MS); clinical psychology (PhD); computer science (MS, Certificate); creative writing (MFA); curriculum and instruction (M Ed, Certificate); economics (MA, PhD); environmental assessment (Certificate); environmental science (MS); ethics, peace, and global affairs (MA); gender analysis in economics (Certificate); health promotion management (MS); history (MA, PhD); international arts management (Certificate); international economic relations (Certificate); international economics (MA); international training and education (MA); literature (MA); mathematics (MA); North American studies (Certificate); nutrition education (MS, Certificate); philosophy (MA); professional science: biotechnology (MS); professional science: environmental assessment (MS); professional science: quantitative analysis (MS); psychobiology of healing (Certificate); psychology (MA); psychology: general (PhD); public anthropology (MA, Certificate); public sociology (Certificate); social research (Certificate); sociology (MA); Spanish: Latin American studies (MA); special education: learning disabilities (MA); statistics (MS); studio art (MFA); teaching (MAT); teaching English as a foreign language (MA); teaching: early childhood (Certificate); teaching: elementary (Certificate); teaching: ESOL (Certificate); teaching: secondary (Certificate); technology in arts management (Certificate); TESOL (MA); translation: French (Certificate); translation: Russian (Certificate); translation: Spanish (Certificate); women's, gender, and sexuality studies (Certificate). Part-time and evening/weekend programs available. Postbaccalaureate distance learning degree programs offered (no on-campus study). *Faculty:* 358 full-time (187 women), 254 part-time/adjunct (127 women). *Students:* 627 full-time (411 women), 416 part-time (300 women); includes 206 minority (91 Black or African American, non-Hispanic/Latino; 5 American Indian or Alaska Native, non-Hispanic/Latino; 32 Asian, non-Hispanic/Latino;

64 Hispanic/Latino; 1 Native Hawaiian or other Pacific Islander, non-Hispanic/Latino; 13 Two or more races, non-Hispanic/Latino), 124 international. Average age 29. 1,672 applicants, 52% accepted, 361 enrolled. In 2013, 382 master's, 38 doctorates, 33 other advanced degrees awarded. Terminal master's awarded for partial completion of doctoral program. *Degree requirements:* For master's, comprehensive exam (for some programs), thesis (for some programs); for doctorate, comprehensive exam (for some programs), thesis/dissertation. *Entrance requirements:* For master's, GRE, minimum GPA of 3.0 in last 60 credit hours, letter of recommendation, statement of purpose, resume, unofficial transcript; for doctorate, GRE, minimum GPA of 3.0 for all graduate work, letter of recommendation, statement of purpose, resume, unofficial transcript. Additional exam requirements/recommendations for international students: Required—TOEFL (minimum score 600 paper-based; 100 iBT), IELTS (minimum score 7). *Application deadline:* For fall admission, 2/1 for domestic students; for spring admission, 10/1 for domestic students. Applications are processed on a rolling basis. Application fee: $55. Electronic applications accepted. *Expenses: Tuition:* Full-time $25,920; part-time $1482 per credit hour. *Required fees:* $430. Tuition and fees vary according to course load and program. *Financial support:* Fellowships, research assistantships with full and partial tuition reimbursements, teaching assistantships with full and partial tuition reimbursements, career-related internships or fieldwork, Federal Work-Study, institutionally sponsored loans, scholarships/grants, traineeships, tuition waivers (full and partial), and unspecified assistantships available. Support available to part-time students. Financial award applicants required to submit FAFSA. *Unit head:* Dr. Peter Starr, Dean, 202-885-2446, Fax: 202-885-2429, E-mail: pstarr@american.edu. *Application contact:* Kathleen Clowery, Associate Director, Graduate Enrollment Management, 202-885-3621, Fax: 202-885-1505, E-mail: clowery@american.edu.
Website: http://www.american.edu/cas/.

Arcadia University, Graduate Studies, Department of Medical Science and Community Health, Program in Health Education, Glenside, PA 19038-3295. Offers MA, MSHE. Part-time and evening/weekend programs available. *Entrance requirements:* For master's, GMAT or GRE (MHA).

Arizona State University at the Tempe campus, School of Letters and Sciences, Program in Behavioral Health, Phoenix, AZ 85004-2135. Offers DBH. Part-time and evening/weekend programs available. Postbaccalaureate distance learning degree programs offered (minimal on-campus study). *Degree requirements:* For doctorate, thesis/dissertation or alternative, 16 hours/week practicum (400 hours total), applied research paper focused on design, implementation and evaluation of a clinical intervention in primary care or related setting, interactive Program of Study (iPOS) submitted before completing 50 percent of required credit hours. *Entrance requirements:* For doctorate, minimum GPA of 3.0 or equivalent in last 2 years of work leading to bachelor's degree; 3 professional reference letters; copy of current clinical license(s) to practice behavioral health; interview. Additional exam requirements/recommendations for international students: Required—TOEFL (minimum score 80 iBT), TOEFL, IELTS, or PTE. Electronic applications accepted. *Expenses:* Contact institution.

Arkansas State University, Graduate School, College of Nursing and Health Professions, School of Nursing, Jonesboro, AR 72467. Offers aging studies (Certificate); health care management (Certificate); health communications (Certificate); health sciences (MS); health sciences education (Certificate); nurse anesthesia (MSN); nursing (MSN); nursing practice (DNP). *Accreditation:* AANA/CANAEP (one or more programs are accredited). Part-time programs available. *Faculty:* 16 full-time (14 women). *Students:* 96 full-time (34 women), 120 part-time (108 women); includes 38 minority (26 Black or African American, non-Hispanic/Latino; 3 American Indian or Alaska Native, non-Hispanic/Latino; 2 Asian, non-Hispanic/Latino; 4 Hispanic/Latino; 3 Two or more races, non-Hispanic/Latino). Average age 33. 153 applicants, 32% accepted, 44 enrolled. In 2013, 103 master's awarded. *Degree requirements:* For master's, comprehensive exam, thesis or alternative; for doctorate, comprehensive exam, thesis/dissertation. *Entrance requirements:* For master's, GRE General Test or MAT, appropriate bachelor's degree, current Arkansas nursing license, CPR certification, physical examination, professional liability insurance, critical care experience, ACLS Certification, PALS Certification, interview, immunization records, personal goal statement, health assessment; for doctorate, GRE or MAT, appropriate master's degree, current Arkansas nursing license, CPR certification, physical examination, professional liability insurance, critical care experience, ACLS Certification, PALS Certification, interview, immunization records, personal goal statement, health assessment, TB skin test, NCLEX-RN Exam, background check. Additional exam requirements/recommendations for international students: Required—TOEFL (minimum score 550 paper-based; 79 iBT), IELTS (minimum score 6), PTE (minimum score 56). *Application deadline:* Applications are processed on a rolling basis. Electronic applications accepted. *Expenses:* Contact institution. *Financial support:* In 2013–14, 9 students received support. Fellowships, career-related internships or fieldwork, scholarships/grants, and unspecified assistantships available. Financial award application deadline: 7/1; financial award applicants required to submit FAFSA. *Unit head:* Dr. Marilyn Duran, Chair, 870-972-3074, Fax: 870-972-2954, E-mail: mduran@astate.edu. *Application contact:* Vickey Ring, Graduate Admissions Coordinator, 870-972-3029, Fax: 870-972-3857, E-mail: vickeyring@astate.edu.
Website: http://www.astate.edu/college/conhp/departments/nursing/.

A.T. Still University, School of Health Management, Kirksville, MO 63501. Offers dental public health (MPH); health administration (MHA, DHA); health education (DH Ed); public health (MPH). Part-time and evening/weekend programs available. Postbaccalaureate distance learning degree programs offered (no on-campus study). *Faculty:* 20 full-time (10 women), 49 part-time/adjunct (27 women). *Students:* 164 full-time (123 women), 256 part-time (144 women); includes 143 minority (61 Black or African American, non-Hispanic/Latino; 4 American Indian or Alaska Native, non-Hispanic/Latino; 46 Asian, non-Hispanic/Latino; 25 Hispanic/Latino; 3 Native Hawaiian or other Pacific Islander, non-Hispanic/Latino; 4 Two or more races, non-Hispanic/Latino), 12 international. Average age 34. 154 applicants, 93% accepted, 114 enrolled. In 2013, 132 master's, 13 doctorates awarded. *Degree requirements:* For master's, thesis, integrated terminal project, practicum; for doctorate, thesis/dissertation. *Entrance requirements:* For master's, minimum GPA of 3.0, bachelor's degree or equivalent, background check, essay, three references; for doctorate, minimum GPA of 3.0, master's or terminal degree, background check, essay, three references. Additional exam requirements/recommendations for international students: Required—TOEFL (minimum score 550 paper-based; 80 iBT). *Application deadline:* For fall admission, 5/31 for domestic and international students; for winter admission, 8/2 for domestic and international students; for spring admission, 11/8 for domestic and international students; for summer admission, 1/24 for domestic and international students. Application fee: $70. Electronic applications accepted. *Expenses:* Contact institution. *Financial support:* Scholarships/grants available. Financial award application deadline: 5/1; financial award applicants required to submit FAFSA. *Faculty research:* Public health: influence of availability of comprehensive wellness resources online, student wellness, oral health care needs assessment of community, oral health knowledge and behaviors of Medicaid-eligible pregnant women and mothers of young children in relations to early childhood caries and tooth decay, alcohol use and alcohol related problems among college students. *Unit head:* Dr. Donald Altman, Interim Dean, 660-626-2820, Fax: 660-626-2826, E-mail: daltman@atsu.edu. *Application contact:* Sarah

Spencer, Associate Director, Admissions, 660-626-2820 Ext. 2669, Fax: 660-626-2826, E-mail: sspencer@atsu.edu. Website: http://www.atsu.edu/shm.

Auburn University, Graduate School, College of Education, Department of Kinesiology, Auburn University, AL 36849. Offers exercise science (M Ed, MS, PhD); health promotion (M Ed, MS); kinesiology (PhD); physical education/teacher education (M Ed, MS, Ed D, Ed S). *Accreditation:* NCATE. Part-time programs available. *Faculty:* 19 full-time (9 women). *Students:* 89 full-time (43 women), 21 part-time (9 women); includes 17 minority (15 Black or African American, non-Hispanic/Latino; 1 Asian, non-Hispanic/Latino; 1 Hispanic/Latino), 5 international. Average age 26. 136 applicants, 71% accepted, 60 enrolled. In 2013, 38 master's, 10 doctorates awarded. *Degree requirements:* For master's, thesis (for some programs); for doctorate, thesis/dissertation; for Ed S, exam, field project. *Entrance requirements:* For master's, GRE General Test; for doctorate and Ed S, GRE General Test, interview, master's degree. *Application deadline:* For fall admission, 7/7 for domestic students; for spring admission, 11/24 for domestic students. Applications are processed on a rolling basis. Application fee: $50 ($60 for international students). Electronic applications accepted. *Expenses:* Tuition, state resident: full-time $8262; part-time $459 per credit hour. Tuition, nonresident: full-time $24,786; part-time $1377 per credit hour. Tuition and fees vary according to degree level and program. *Financial support:* Research assistantships, teaching assistantships, and Federal Work-Study available. Support available to part-time students. Financial award application deadline: 3/15; financial award applicants required to submit FAFSA. *Faculty research:* Biomechanics, exercise physiology, motor skill learning, school health, curriculum development. *Unit head:* Dr. Mary E. Rudisill, Head, 334-844-1458. *Application contact:* Dr. George Flowers, Dean of the Graduate School, 334-844-2125.

Austin Peay State University, College of Graduate Studies, College of Behavioral and Health Sciences, Department of Health and Human Performance, Clarksville, TN 37044. Offers health leadership (MS). Part-time and evening/weekend programs available. Postbaccalaureate distance learning degree programs offered (no on-campus study). *Faculty:* 6 full-time (3 women). *Students:* 15 full-time (6 women), 30 part-time (21 women); includes 14 minority (13 Black or African American, non-Hispanic/Latino; 1 Hispanic/Latino). Average age 27. 41 applicants, 90% accepted, 32 enrolled. In 2013, 32 master's awarded. *Degree requirements:* For master's, comprehensive exam, thesis optional. *Entrance requirements:* For master's, GRE General Test, 3 letters of recommendation, minimum undergraduate GPA of 2.5. Additional exam requirements/recommendations for international students: Required—TOEFL (minimum score 500 paper-based). *Application deadline:* For fall admission, 8/5 priority date for domestic students. Applications are processed on a rolling basis. Application fee: $25. Electronic applications accepted. *Expenses:* Tuition, state resident: full-time $7500; part-time $375 per credit hour. Tuition, nonresident: full-time $20,800; part-time $1040 per credit hour. *Required fees:* $1284; $64.20 per credit hour. *Financial support:* In 2013–14, research assistantships with full tuition reimbursements (averaging $6,500 per year) were awarded; career-related internships or fieldwork, Federal Work-Study, institutionally sponsored loans, scholarships/grants, and unspecified assistantships also available. Support available to part-time students. Financial award application deadline: 3/1; financial award applicants required to submit FAFSA. *Unit head:* Dr. Marcy Maurer, Chair, 931-221-6105, Fax: 931-221-7040, E-mail: maurerm@apsu.edu. *Application contact:* June D. Lee, Graduate Coordinator, 800-859-4723, Fax: 931-221-7641, E-mail: gradadmissions@apsu.edu.
Website: http://www.apsu.edu/hhp/.

Baylor University, Graduate School, School of Education, Department of Health, Human Performance and Recreation, Waco, TX 76798. Offers community health education (MPH); exercise physiology (MS Ed); kinesiology, exercise nutrition and health promotion (PhD); sport management (MS Ed); sport pedagogy (MS Ed). *Accreditation:* NCATE. Part-time programs available. *Faculty:* 13 full-time (5 women), 3 part-time/adjunct (1 woman). *Students:* 79 full-time (40 women), 28 part-time (14 women); includes 26 minority (9 Black or African American, non-Hispanic/Latino; 1 American Indian or Alaska Native, non-Hispanic/Latino; 3 Asian, non-Hispanic/Latino; 8 Hispanic/Latino; 5 Two or more races, non-Hispanic/Latino), 9 international. 30 applicants, 87% accepted. In 2013, 48 master's awarded. *Degree requirements:* For master's, comprehensive exam, thesis optional; for doctorate, comprehensive exam, thesis/dissertation. *Entrance requirements:* For master's and doctorate, GRE General Test. Additional exam requirements/recommendations for international students: Required—TOEFL. *Application deadline:* For fall admission, 2/1 priority date for domestic students, 2/1 for international students; for spring admission, 10/1 for domestic and international students. Applications are processed on a rolling basis. Application fee: $25. Electronic applications accepted. *Expenses:* Tuition: Full-time $25,866; part-time $1437 per credit hour. *Required fees:* $2736; $152 per credit hour. Tuition and fees vary according to course load and program. *Financial support:* In 2013–14, 35 students received support, including 1 research assistantship with tuition reimbursement available, 33 teaching assistantships with tuition reimbursements available; career-related internships or fieldwork, Federal Work-Study, institutionally sponsored loans, tuition waivers (partial), and unspecified assistantships also available. Financial award application deadline: 2/1. *Faculty research:* Behavior change theory, nutrition and enzyme therapy, exercise testing, health planning, sport management. *Unit head:* Dr. Jeffrey Petersen, Graduate Program Director, 254-710-4007, Fax: 254-710-3527, E-mail: jeffrey_petersen@baylor.edu. *Application contact:* Kathy Mirick, Administrative Assistant, 254-710-3526, Fax: 254-710-3527, E-mail: kathy_mirick@baylor.edu.
Website: http://www.baylor.edu/HHPR/.

Benedictine University, Graduate Programs, Program in Public Health, Lisle, IL 60532-0900. Offers administration of health care institutions (MPH); dietetics (MPH); disaster management (MPH); health education (MPH); health information systems (MPH); MBA/MPH; MPH/MS. Part-time and evening/weekend programs available. Postbaccalaureate distance learning degree programs offered. *Students:* 78 full-time (62 women), 340 part-time (254 women); includes 159 minority (97 Black or African American, non-Hispanic/Latino; 3 American Indian or Alaska Native, non-Hispanic/Latino; 47 Asian, non-Hispanic/Latino; 11 Hispanic/Latino; 1 Native Hawaiian or other Pacific Islander, non-Hispanic/Latino), 14 international. Average age 33. 195 applicants, 86% accepted, 143 enrolled. In 2013, 207 master's awarded. *Entrance requirements:* For master's, MAT, GRE, or GMAT. Additional exam requirements/recommendations for international students: Required—TOEFL (minimum score 550 paper-based). *Application deadline:* For fall admission, 9/1 for domestic students; for winter admission, 12/1 for domestic students; for spring admission, 2/15 for domestic students. Application fee: $40. *Expenses:* Tuition: Part-time $590 per credit hour. *Financial support:* Career-related internships or fieldwork and health care benefits available. Support available to part-time students. *Unit head:* Dr. Georgeen Polyak, Director, 630-829-6217, E-mail: gpolyak@ben.edu. *Application contact:* Kari Gibbons, Associate Vice President, Enrollment Center, 630-829-6200, Fax: 630-829-6584, E-mail: kgibbons@ben.edu.

Brandeis University, The Heller School for Social Policy and Management, Program in Social Policy, Waltham, MA 02454-9110. Offers assets and inequalities (PhD); children, youth and families (PhD); global health and development (PhD); health and behavioral health (PhD). *Degree requirements:* For doctorate, comprehensive exam, thesis/

dissertation, qualifying paper, 2-year residency. *Entrance requirements:* For doctorate, GRE General Test, 3 letters of recommendation, statement of purpose, writing sample, at least 3-5 years of professional experience. Additional exam requirements/recommendations for international students: Required—TOEFL (minimum score 600 paper-based; 100 iBT). Electronic applications accepted. *Faculty research:* Health; mental health; substance abuse; children, youth, and families; aging; international and community development; disabilities; work and inequality; hunger and poverty.

Brigham Young University, Graduate Studies, College of Life Sciences, Department of Health Science, Provo, UT 84602. Offers MPH. *Faculty:* 21 full-time (4 women). *Students:* 30 full-time (24 women); includes 5 minority (1 American Indian or Alaska Native, non-Hispanic/Latino; 1 Hispanic/Latino; 1 Native Hawaiian or other Pacific Islander, non-Hispanic/Latino; 2 Two or more races, non-Hispanic/Latino), 4 international. Average age 25. 47 applicants, 38% accepted, 15 enrolled. In 2013, 9 master's awarded. *Degree requirements:* For master's, thesis, oral defense. *Entrance requirements:* For master's, GRE General Test (minimum score of 300), minimum GPA of 3.2 in last 60 hours. Additional exam requirements/recommendations for international students: Required—TOEFL (minimum score 580 paper-based; 85 iBT), IELTS (minimum score 7). *Application deadline:* For fall admission, 2/1 for domestic and international students. Application fee: $50. Electronic applications accepted. *Expenses:* Tuition: Full-time $6130; part-time $340 per credit hour. Tuition and fees vary according to program and student's religious affiliation. *Financial support:* In 2013–14, 31 students received support, including 30 fellowships with partial tuition reimbursements available (averaging $2,500 per year), 17 research assistantships (averaging $1,405 per year), 2 teaching assistantships (averaging $546 per year); career-related internships or fieldwork, scholarships/grants, and tuition waivers (partial) also available. Financial award application deadline: 3/1. *Faculty research:* Social marketing, health communication, cancer, epidemiology, tobacco prevention and control, maternal and child health. *Total annual research expenditures:* $60,938. *Unit head:* Dr. Michael Dean Barnes, Chair, 801-422-3327, Fax: 801-422-0273, E-mail: michael_barnes@byu.edu. *Application contact:* Dr. Carl Lee Hanson, Graduate Coordinator, 801-422-9103, Fax: 801-422-0273, E-mail: carl_hanson@byu.edu.
Website: http://healthscience.byu.edu/.

Brooklyn College of the City University of New York, Division of Graduate Studies, School of Education, Program in Adolescence Education and Special Subjects, Brooklyn, NY 11210-2889. Offers adolescence science education (MAT); art teacher (MA); biology teacher (MA); chemistry teacher (MA); earth science teacher (MAT); English teacher (MA); French teacher (MA); health and nutrition sciences: health teacher (MS Ed); mathematics teacher (MA); music education (CAS); music teacher (MA); physical education teacher (MS Ed); physics teacher (MA); social studies teacher (MA); Spanish teacher (MA). Part-time and evening/weekend programs available. *Degree requirements:* For master's, comprehensive exam (for some programs), thesis (for some programs). *Entrance requirements:* For master's, LAST, previous course work in education, resume, 2 letters of recommendation, essay. Additional exam requirements/recommendations for international students: Required—TOEFL (minimum score 500 paper-based; 61 iBT). Electronic applications accepted. *Faculty research:* Interdisciplinary education, semiotics, discourse analysis, autobiography, teacher identity.

California State University, Long Beach, Graduate Studies, College of Health and Human Services, Department of Health Science, Long Beach, CA 90840. Offers MPH, MS, MSN/MPH. *Accreditation:* CEPH; NCATE. Part-time programs available. *Degree requirements:* For master's, thesis optional. *Entrance requirements:* For master's, GRE, minimum GPA of 3.0 in last 60 units. Electronic applications accepted.

California State University, Los Angeles, Graduate Studies, College of Health and Human Services, School of Nursing, Los Angeles, CA 90032-8530. Offers health science (MA); nursing (MS). *Accreditation:* AACN. Part-time and evening/weekend programs available. *Faculty:* 21 full-time (18 women), 1 (woman) part-time/adjunct. *Students:* 130 full-time (111 women), 61 part-time (52 women); includes 107 minority (11 Black or African American, non-Hispanic/Latino; 65 Asian, non-Hispanic/Latino; 19 Hispanic/Latino; 2 Native Hawaiian or other Pacific Islander, non-Hispanic/Latino; 10 Two or more races, non-Hispanic/Latino), 18 international. Average age 33. 239 applicants, 25% accepted, 50 enrolled. In 2013, 63 master's awarded. *Degree requirements:* For master's, comprehensive exam, project or thesis. *Entrance requirements:* For master's, minimum GPA of 3.0 in nursing, course work in nursing and statistics. Additional exam requirements/recommendations for international students: Required—TOEFL (minimum score 500 paper-based). *Application deadline:* For fall admission, 5/1 for domestic and international students. Applications are processed on a rolling basis. Application fee: $55. *Financial support:* Federal Work-Study available. Support available to part-time students. Financial award application deadline: 3/1. *Faculty research:* Family stress, geripsychiatric nursing, self-care counseling, holistic nursing, adult health. *Unit head:* Dr. Cynthia Hughes, Director, 323-343-4700, Fax: 323-343-6454, E-mail: chughes2@calstatela.edu. *Application contact:* Dr. Larry Fritz, Dean of Graduate Studies, 323-343-3820, Fax: 323-343-5653, E-mail: lfritz@calstatela.edu.
Website: http://web.calstatela.edu/academic/hhs/nursing/.

California State University, Northridge, Graduate Studies, The Tseng College of Extended Learning, Northridge, CA 91330. Offers business administration (Graduate Certificate); health administration (MPA); health education (MPH); knowledge management (MKM); music industry administration (MA); nonprofit-sector management (Graduate Certificate); public administration (MPA); public sector management and leadership (MPA); social work (MSW); taxation (MS); tourism, hospitality and recreation management (MS). *Entrance requirements:* For master's, GRE (if cumulative undergraduate GPA less than 3.0).

California State University, San Bernardino, Graduate Studies, College of Natural Sciences, Program in Health Science, San Bernardino, CA 92407-2397. Offers health science (MS); public health (MPH). *Students:* 8 full-time (7 women), 12 part-time (9 women); includes 12 minority (1 Black or African American, non-Hispanic/Latino; 3 Asian, non-Hispanic/Latino; 6 Hispanic/Latino; 2 Two or more races, non-Hispanic/Latino), 2 international. Average age 28. 3 applicants. In 2013, 18 master's awarded. *Unit head:* Dr. Marsha Greer, Chair, 909-537-5339, Fax: 909-537-7037, E-mail: mgreer@csusb.edu. *Application contact:* Dr. Jeffrey Thompson, Dean of Graduate Studies, 909-537-5058, E-mail: jthompso@csusb.edu.

Cambridge College, School of Education, Cambridge, MA 02138-5304. Offers autism specialist (M Ed); autism/behavior analyst (M Ed); behavior analyst (Post-Master's Certificate); behavioral management (M Ed); early childhood teacher (M Ed); education specialist in curriculum and instruction (CAGS); educational leadership (Ed D); elementary teacher (M Ed); English as a second language (M Ed, Certificate); general science (M Ed); health education (Post-Master's Certificate); health/family and consumer sciences (M Ed); history (M Ed); individualized (M Ed); information technology literacy (M Ed); instructional technology (M Ed); interdisciplinary studies (M Ed); library teacher (M Ed); literacy education (M Ed); mathematics (M Ed); mathematics specialist (Certificate); middle school mathematics and science (M Ed); school administration (M Ed, CAGS); school guidance counselor (M Ed); school nurse education (M Ed); school social worker/school adjustment counselor (M Ed); special education administrator (CAGS); special education/moderate disabilities (M Ed);

teaching skills and methodologies (M Ed). Part-time and evening/weekend programs available. Postbaccalaureate distance learning degree programs offered (minimal on-campus study). *Degree requirements:* For master's, thesis, internship/practicum (licensure program only); for doctorate, thesis/dissertation; for other advanced degree, thesis. *Entrance requirements:* For master's, interview, resume, documentation of licensure, 2 professional references; for doctorate, official transcripts, interview, resume, documentation of licensure (if any), written personal statement/essay, portfolio of scholarly and professional work, qualifying assessment, 2 professional references, health insurance, immunizations form; for other advanced degree, official transcripts, interview, resume, documentation of licensure (if any), written personal statement/essay, 2 professional references, health insurance, immunizations form. Additional exam requirements/recommendations for international students: Required—TOEFL (minimum score 550 paper-based; 79 iBT), Michigan English Language Assessment Battery (minimum score 85); Recommended—IELTS (minimum score 6). Electronic applications accepted. *Expenses:* Contact institution. *Faculty research:* Adult education, accelerated learning, mathematics education, brain compatible learning, special education and law.

Central Washington University, Graduate Studies and Research, College of Education and Professional Studies, Department of Physical Education, School and Public Health, Ellensburg, WA 98926. Offers athletic administration (MS); health and physical education (MS). Part-time programs available. *Degree requirements:* For master's, comprehensive exam, thesis or alternative. *Entrance requirements:* For master's, minimum GPA of 3.0. Additional exam requirements/recommendations for international students: Required—TOEFL (minimum score 550 paper-based; 79 iBT), IELTS. Electronic applications accepted.

The Citadel, The Military College of South Carolina, Citadel Graduate College, Department of Health, Exercise, and Sport Science, Charleston, SC 29409. Offers health, exercise, and sport science (MS); physical education (MAT). *Accreditation:* NCATE. Part-time and evening/weekend programs available. *Faculty:* 10 full-time (4 women). *Students:* 9 full-time (5 women), 29 part-time (16 women); includes 7 minority (all Black or African American, non-Hispanic/Latino), 2 international. Average age 26. In 2013, 25 master's awarded. *Degree requirements:* For master's, comprehensive exam, thesis optional. *Entrance requirements:* For master's, GRE (minimum score 900) or MAT (minimum score 396), minimum undergraduate GPA of 2.5, 3 letters of recommendation, resume detailing previous work experience (for MS only). Additional exam requirements/recommendations for international students: Required—TOEFL (minimum score 550 paper-based; 79 iBT). *Application deadline:* Applications are processed on a rolling basis. Application fee: $30. Electronic applications accepted. *Expenses: Tuition, area resident:* Part-time $525 per credit hour. Tuition, state resident: part-time $525 per credit hour. Tuition, nonresident: part-time $865 per credit hour. *Financial support:* Career-related internships or fieldwork, health care benefits, and unspecified assistantships available. Support available to part-time students. Financial award application deadline: 7/1; financial award applicants required to submit FAFSA. *Faculty research:* Risk management in sport and physical activity programs, school-wide physical activity programs, exercise intervention among HIV-infected individuals, factors influencing motor skill in SC physical education programs, effect of mouthpiece use on human performance. *Unit head:* Dr. Harry D. Davakos, Department Head, 843-953-5060, Fax: 843-953-6798, E-mail: harry.davakos@citadel.edu. *Application contact:* Dr. Robert H. McNamara, Associate Provost, The Citadel Graduate College, 843-953-5089, Fax: 843-953-7630, E-mail: cgc@citadel.edu.
Website: http://www.citadel.edu/hess/index.htm.

Cleveland State University, College of Graduate Studies, College of Education and Human Services, Department of Health, Physical Education, Recreation and Dance, Cleveland, OH 44115. Offers community health education (M Ed); exercise science (M Ed); human performance (M Ed); physical education pedagogy (M Ed); public health (MPH); school health education (M Ed); sport and exercise psychology (M Ed); sports management (M Ed). Part-time programs available. *Faculty:* 7 full-time (4 women), 3 part-time/adjunct (2 women). *Students:* 49 full-time (31 women), 79 part-time (46 women); includes 32 minority (25 Black or African American, non-Hispanic/Latino; 2 Asian, non-Hispanic/Latino; 5 Hispanic/Latino), 7 international. Average age 35. 103 applicants, 72% accepted, 35 enrolled. In 2013, 40 master's awarded. *Degree requirements:* For master's, comprehensive exam, thesis optional. *Entrance requirements:* For master's, GRE General Test or MAT (if undergraduate GPA less than 2.75), minimum undergraduate GPA of 2.75. Additional exam requirements/recommendations for international students: Required—TOEFL (minimum score 525 paper-based), IELTS (minimum score 6). *Application deadline:* For fall admission, 7/15 priority date for domestic students; for spring admission, 12/15 priority date for domestic students. Applications are processed on a rolling basis. Application fee: $30. Electronic applications accepted. *Expenses:* Tuition, state resident: full-time $8335; part-time $521 per credit hour. Tuition, nonresident: full-time $15,670; part-time $979 per credit hour. *Required fees:* $50; $25 per semester. *Financial support:* In 2013–14, 6 research assistantships with full and partial tuition reimbursements (averaging $3,480 per year), 1 teaching assistantship with full and partial tuition reimbursement (averaging $3,480 per year) were awarded; career-related internships or fieldwork, tuition waivers (full), and unspecified assistantships also available. Financial award application deadline: 3/15. *Faculty research:* Bone density, marketing fitness centers, motor development of disabled, online learning and survey research. *Unit head:* Dr. Sheila M. Patterson, Chairperson, 216-687-4870, Fax: 216-687-5410, E-mail: s.m.patterson@csuohio.edu. *Application contact:* Deborah L. Brown, Interim Assistant Director, Graduate Admissions, 216-523-7572, Fax: 216-687-5400, E-mail: d.l.brown@csuohio.edu.
Website: http://www.csuohio.edu/cehs/departments/HPERD/hperd_dept.html.

The College at Brockport, State University of New York, School of Health and Human Performance, Department of Health Science, Brockport, NY 14420-2997. Offers health education (MS Ed), including community health education, health education K-12. *Faculty:* 4 full-time (1 woman), 5 part-time/adjunct (1 woman). *Students:* 9 full-time (4 women), 8 part-time (5 women); includes 1 minority (Hispanic/Latino). 13 applicants, 85% accepted, 8 enrolled. In 2013, 13 master's awarded. *Degree requirements:* For master's, thesis or alternative. *Entrance requirements:* For master's, minimum GPA of 3.0, letters of recommendation. Additional exam requirements/recommendations for international students: Required—TOEFL (minimum score 550 paper-based; 79 iBT), IELTS (minimum score 6.5). *Application deadline:* For fall admission, 3/1 priority date for domestic and international students; for spring admission, 10/1 priority date for domestic and international students; for summer admission, 3/1 priority date for domestic and international students. Application fee: $80. Electronic applications accepted. *Expenses:* Tuition, state resident: full-time $9870. Tuition, nonresident: full-time $18,350. *Required fees:* $1848. *Financial support:* In 2013–14, 1 teaching assistantship with full tuition reimbursement (averaging $6,000 per year) was awarded; Federal Work-Study, scholarships/grants, and unspecified assistantships also available. Support available to part-time students. Financial award application deadline: 3/15; financial award applicants required to submit FAFSA. *Faculty research:* Nutrition, substance use, HIV/AIDS, bioethics, worksite health. *Unit head:* Dr. Patti Follansbee, Chairperson, 585-395-5483, Fax: 585-395-5246, E-mail: pfollans@brockport.edu. *Application contact:* Danielle A. Welch, Graduate Admissions Counselor, 585-395-5465, Fax: 585-395-2515.
Website: http://www.brockport.edu/healthsci/graduate/.

The College of New Jersey, Graduate Studies, School of Nursing, Health and Exercise Science, Department of Health and Exercise Science, Program in Health Education, Ewing, NJ 08628. Offers health (MAT); physical education (M Ed). *Accreditation:* NCATE. Part-time programs available. *Degree requirements:* For master's, comprehensive exam. *Entrance requirements:* For master's, GRE, minimum GPA of 3.0 in field or 2.75 overall. Additional exam requirements/recommendations for international students: Required—TOEFL. Electronic applications accepted.

College of Saint Mary, Program in Health Professions Education, Omaha, NE 68106. Offers Ed D. Part-time programs available.

Colorado State University–Pueblo, College of Education, Engineering and Professional Studies, Education Program, Pueblo, CO 81001-4901. Offers art education (M Ed); foreign language education (M Ed); health and physical education (M Ed); instructional technology (M Ed); linguistically diverse education (M Ed); music education (M Ed); special education (M Ed). *Accreditation:* Teacher Education Accreditation Council. Part-time programs available. *Degree requirements:* For master's, portfolio. *Entrance requirements:* For master's, 3 recommendations, teaching license. Additional exam requirements/recommendations for international students: Required—TOEFL (minimum score 500 paper-based). Electronic applications accepted. *Faculty research:* Portfolio assessment, math education, science education.

Columbus State University, Graduate Studies, College of Education and Health Professions, Department of Health, Physical Education and Exercise Science, Columbus, GA 31907-5645. Offers exercise science (MS); health and physical education (M Ed). Part-time and evening/weekend programs available. *Faculty:* 6 full-time (3 women). *Students:* 25 full-time (10 women), 14 part-time (9 women); includes 17 minority (15 Black or African American, non-Hispanic/Latino; 2 Hispanic/Latino), 1 international. Average age 28. 23 applicants, 70% accepted, 12 enrolled. In 2013, 20 master's awarded. *Degree requirements:* For master's, thesis optional. *Entrance requirements:* For master's, GRE, minimum undergraduate GPA of 2.75. Additional exam requirements/recommendations for international students: Required—TOEFL (minimum score 550 paper-based; 79 iBT). *Application deadline:* For fall admission, 5/1 for domestic students, 4/1 for international students; for spring admission, 11/1 for domestic and international students; for summer admission, 2/1 for domestic students, 3/1 for international students. Application fee: $40. *Expenses:* Tuition, state resident: full-time $4572; part-time $382 per credit hour. Tuition, nonresident: full-time $18,292; part-time $1526 per credit hour. *Required fees:* $1800; $196 per credit hour. Tuition and fees vary according to campus/location and program. *Financial support:* In 2013–14, 30 students received support, including 18 research assistantships (averaging $3,000 per year). *Unit head:* Dr. Tara Underwood, Chair, 706-568-2485, E-mail: underwood_tara@columbusstate.edu. *Application contact:* Kristin Williams, Director of International and Graduate Admissions, 706-507-8848, Fax: 706-568-5091, E-mail: williams_kristin@columbusstate.edu.
Website: http://hpex.columbusstate.edu/.

Dalhousie University, Faculty of Health Professions, School of Health and Human Performance, Program in Health Promotion, Halifax, NS B3H 3J5, Canada. Offers MA. Part-time programs available. *Degree requirements:* For master's, thesis. *Entrance requirements:* Additional exam requirements/recommendations for international students: Required—TOEFL, IELTS, CANTEST, CAEL, or Michigan English Language Assessment Battery. Electronic applications accepted. *Faculty research:* AIDS research, health knowledge of adolescents, evaluating health promotion, program evaluation.

Delta State University, Graduate Programs, College of Education, Division of Health, Physical Education, and Recreation, Cleveland, MS 38733-0001. Offers health, physical education, and recreation (M Ed); sport and human performance (MS). Part-time and evening/weekend programs available. *Faculty:* 5 full-time (1 woman), 1 part-time/adjunct (0 women). *Students:* 37 full-time (12 women), 13 part-time (4 women); includes 15 minority (11 Black or African American, non-Hispanic/Latino; 1 Hispanic/Latino; 3 Two or more races, non-Hispanic/Latino), 4 international. Average age 27. 35 applicants, 91% accepted, 29 enrolled. In 2013, 11 master's awarded. *Degree requirements:* For master's, thesis optional. *Entrance requirements:* For master's, GRE General Test or MAT, Class A teaching certificate. *Application deadline:* For fall admission, 8/1 priority date for domestic students; for spring admission, 12/1 priority date for domestic students. Applications are processed on a rolling basis. Application fee: $0. *Expenses:* Tuition, state resident: full-time $3006; part-time $334 per credit hour. Tuition, nonresident: full-time $3006; part-time $334 per credit hour. *Financial support:* In 2013–14, research assistantships (averaging $4,000 per year) were awarded; career-related internships or fieldwork, Federal Work-Study, and institutionally sponsored loans also available. Support available to part-time students. Financial award application deadline: 6/1. *Faculty research:* Blood pressure, body fat, power and reaction time, learning disorders for athletes, effects of walking. *Unit head:* Tim Colbert, Chair, 662-846-4555, Fax: 662-846-4571. *Application contact:* Dr. Albert Nylander, Dean of Graduate Studies, 662-846-4875, Fax: 662-846-4313, E-mail: grad-info@deltastate.edu.
Website: http://www.deltastate.edu/pages/2963.asp.

D'Youville College, Department of Health Services Administration, Buffalo, NY 14201-1084. Offers clinical research associate (Certificate); health administration (Ed D); health policy and health education (Ed D); health services administration (MS, Certificate); long term care administration (Certificate). Part-time and evening/weekend programs available. *Students:* 38 full-time (25 women), 80 part-time (60 women); includes 28 minority (24 Black or African American, non-Hispanic/Latino; 2 American Indian or Alaska Native, non-Hispanic/Latino; 1 Hispanic/Latino; 1 Two or more races, non-Hispanic/Latino), 20 international. Average age 38. 81 applicants, 54% accepted, 25 enrolled. In 2013, 5 master's, 2 doctorates, 2 other advanced degrees awarded. *Degree requirements:* For master's, project or thesis. *Entrance requirements:* For master's, minimum GPA of 3.0 in major. Additional exam requirements/recommendations for international students: Required—TOEFL (minimum score 500 paper-based). *Application deadline:* For fall admission, 5/1 priority date for international students; for spring admission, 9/1 priority date for international students. Applications are processed on a rolling basis. Application fee: $25. Electronic applications accepted. *Financial support:* Career-related internships or fieldwork, Federal Work-Study, and scholarships/grants available. Support available to part-time students. Financial award application deadline: 3/1; financial award applicants required to submit FAFSA. *Faculty research:* Outcomes research in rehabilitation medicine, cost/benefit analysis of prospective payment systems. *Unit head:* Dr. Lisa Rafalson, Chair, 716-829-8489, Fax: 716-829-8184. *Application contact:* Linda Fisher, Graduate Admissions Director, 716-829-8400, Fax: 716-829-7900, E-mail: graduateadmissions@dyc.edu.

East Carolina University, Graduate School, College of Education, Department of Business and Information Technologies Education, Greenville, NC 27858-4353. Offers business education (MA Ed); elementary education (MAT); English education (MAT); family and consumer science (MAT); health education (MAT); Hispanic studies (MAT); history education (MAT); marketing education (MA Ed); middle grades education (MAT); music education (MAT); physical education (MAT); science education (MAT); special education (MAT), including general curriculum; vocation education (MS). *Accreditation:* NCATE. Part-time and evening/weekend programs available. Postbaccalaureate distance learning degree programs offered (no on-campus study). *Degree requirements:* For master's, comprehensive exam, thesis optional. *Entrance requirements:* For

master's, GRE or MAT, minimum GPA of 2.5, bachelor's degree in related field, teaching license (MA Ed). Additional exam requirements/recommendations for international students: Required—TOEFL. *Expenses:* Tuition, state resident: full-time $4223. Tuition, nonresident: full-time $16,540. *Required fees:* $2184.

East Carolina University, Graduate School, College of Health and Human Performance, Department of Health Education and Promotion, Greenville, NC 27858-4353. Offers athletic training (MS); environmental health (MS); health education (MA, MA Ed). *Accreditation:* NCATE. *Degree requirements:* For master's, comprehensive exam, thesis optional. *Entrance requirements:* For master's, GRE General Test or MAT. Additional exam requirements/recommendations for international students: Required—TOEFL. *Expenses:* Tuition, state resident: full-time $4223. Tuition, nonresident: full-time $16,540. *Required fees:* $2184. *Faculty research:* Community health education, worksite health promotion, school health education, environmental health.

Eastern Kentucky University, The Graduate School, College of Education, Department of Curriculum and Instruction, Program in Secondary and Higher Education, Richmond, KY 40475-3102. Offers secondary education (MA Ed), including agricultural education, art education, biological sciences education, business education, English education, geography education, history education, home economics education, industrial education, mathematical sciences education, physical education, school health education. *Accreditation:* NCATE. Part-time programs available. *Entrance requirements:* For master's, GRE General Test, minimum GPA of 2.5.

Eastern Michigan University, Graduate School, College of Health and Human Services, School of Health Promotion and Human Performance, Program in Health Education, Ypsilanti, MI 48197. Offers MS. Part-time and evening/weekend programs available. *Students:* 2 full-time (both women), 20 part-time (18 women); includes 8 minority (all Black or African American, non-Hispanic/Latino), 1 international. Average age 32. 16 applicants, 75% accepted, 6 enrolled. In 2013, 1 master's awarded. *Degree requirements:* For master's, thesis or project. *Entrance requirements:* For master's, teaching credential. Additional exam requirements/recommendations for international students: Required—TOEFL. *Application deadline:* For fall admission, 8/1 for domestic students, 5/1 for international students; for winter admission, 12/1 for domestic students, 10/1 for international students; for spring admission, 4/15 for domestic students, 3/1 for international students. Application fee: $35. *Expenses:* Tuition, state resident: full-time $12,300; part-time $466 per credit hour. Tuition, nonresident: full-time $23,159; part-time $918 per credit hour. *Required fees:* $71 per credit hour. $46 per semester. One-time fee: $100. Tuition and fees vary according to course level and degree level. *Unit head:* Dr. Christopher Herman, Director, 734-487-2185, Fax: 734-487-2024, E-mail: cherman2@emich.edu. *Application contact:* Dr. Donna (Kay) Woodiel, Program Coordinator, 734-487-2832, Fax: 734-487-2024, E-mail: dwoodiel@emich.edu.

Eastern University, Graduate Education Programs, St. Davids, PA 19087-3696. Offers ESL program specialist (K-12) (Certificate); general supervisor (PreK-12) (Certificate); health and physical education (K-12) (Certificate); middle level (4-8) (Certificate); multicultural education (M Ed); pre K-4 (Certificate); pre K-4 with special education (Certificate); reading (M Ed); reading specialist (K-12) (Certificate); reading supervisor (K-12) (Certificate); school health services (M Ed); school health supervisor (Certificate); school nurse (Certificate); school principalship (K-12) (Certificate); secondary biology education (7-12) (Certificate); secondary chemistry education (7-12) (Certificate); secondary communication education (7-12) (Certificate); secondary education (7-12) (Certificate); secondary English education (7-12) (Certificate); secondary math education (7-12) (Certificate); secondary social studies education (7-12) (Certificate); special education (M Ed); special education (7-12) (Certificate); special education (Pre K-8) (Certificate); special education supervisor (N-12) (Certificate); TESOL (M Ed); world language (Certificate), including French, Mandarin Chinese, Spanish. Part-time and evening/weekend programs available. Postbaccalaureate distance learning degree programs offered (no on-campus study). *Faculty:* 22 full-time (11 women), 26 part-time/adjunct (18 women). *Students:* 77 full-time (58 women), 223 part-time (149 women); includes 112 minority (81 Black or African American, non-Hispanic/Latino; 1 American Indian or Alaska Native, non-Hispanic/Latino; 9 Asian, non-Hispanic/Latino; 18 Hispanic/Latino; 1 Native Hawaiian or other Pacific Islander, non-Hispanic/Latino; 2 Two or more races, non-Hispanic/Latino), 7 international. Average age 34. 94 applicants, 100% accepted, 81 enrolled. In 2013, 120 master's awarded. *Entrance requirements:* For master's, minimum GPA of 2.5 (for M Ed); for Certificate, minimum GPA of 3.0 for certifications. Additional exam requirements/recommendations for international students: Required—TOEFL. *Application deadline:* For fall admission, 8/14 for domestic students; for spring admission, 12/20 for domestic students. Applications are processed on a rolling basis. Application fee: $35. Application fee is waived when completed online. *Expenses: Tuition:* Full-time $15,600; part-time $650 per credit. *Required fees:* $27.50 per semester. One-time fee: $50. Tuition and fees vary according to course load, degree level and program. *Financial support:* In 2013–14, 84 students received support, including 6 research assistantships with partial tuition reimbursements available (averaging $7,710 per year); scholarships/grants and unspecified assistantships also available. Financial award application deadline: 3/15; financial award applicants required to submit FAFSA. *Unit head:* Harry Gutelius, Associate Dean, 610-341-1729. *Application contact:* Michael Perpiglia, Associate Director of Enrollment, 610-341-5947, Fax: 484-581-1276, E-mail: mperpigl@eastern.edu.
Website: http://www.eastern.edu/academics/programs/loeb-school-education-0/graduateprograms.

East Stroudsburg University of Pennsylvania, Graduate College, College of Health Sciences, Department of Exercise Science, East Stroudsburg, PA 18301-2999. Offers cardiac rehabilitation and exercise science (MS). Part-time and evening/weekend programs available. Postbaccalaureate distance learning degree programs offered. *Faculty:* 7 full-time (2 women). *Students:* 48 full-time (28 women), 2 part-time (1 woman); includes 11 minority (6 Black or African American, non-Hispanic/Latino; 3 Hispanic/Latino; 2 Two or more races, non-Hispanic/Latino), 1 international. Average age 23. 114 applicants, 75% accepted, 54 enrolled. In 2013, 38 master's awarded. *Degree requirements:* For master's, comprehensive exam, thesis or alternative, computer literacy. *Entrance requirements:* Additional exam requirements/recommendations for international students: Required—TOEFL (minimum score 560 paper-based; 83 iBT) or IELTS. *Application deadline:* For fall admission, 3/1 priority date for domestic and international students; for spring admission, 11/30 for domestic students, 10/31 for international students. Applications are processed on a rolling basis. Application fee: $50. Electronic applications accepted. *Expenses:* Tuition, state resident: full-time $7956; part-time $442 per credit. Tuition, nonresident: full-time $11,934; part-time $663 per credit. *Required fees:* $2129; $118 per credit. *Financial support:* Research assistantships with full and partial tuition reimbursements, Federal Work-Study, and institutionally sponsored loans available. Financial award application deadline: 3/1. *Unit head:* Dr. Shala Davis, Graduate Coordinator, 570-422-3302, Fax: 570-422-3616, E-mail: sdavis@po-box.esu.edu. *Application contact:* Kevin Quintero, Graduate Admissions Coordinator, 570-422-3536, Fax: 570-422-2711, E-mail: kquintero@esu.edu.

East Stroudsburg University of Pennsylvania, Graduate College, College of Health Sciences, Department of Health, East Stroudsburg, PA 18301-2999. Offers community health education (MPH); health education (MS). *Accreditation:* CEPH (one or more programs are accredited). Part-time and evening/weekend programs available. Postbaccalaureate distance learning degree programs offered. *Faculty:* 6 full-time (3 women), 2 part-time/adjunct (both women). *Students:* 20 full-time (14 women), 24 part-time (21 women); includes 16 minority (8 Black or African American, non-Hispanic/Latino; 1 Asian, non-Hispanic/Latino; 6 Hispanic/Latino; 1 Two or more races, non-Hispanic/Latino), 2 international. Average age 34. 47 applicants, 68% accepted, 20 enrolled. In 2013, 6 master's awarded. *Degree requirements:* For master's, oral comprehensive exam. *Entrance requirements:* For master's, GRE General Test, minimum GPA of 3.0 in major, 2.8 overall; undergraduate prerequisites in anatomy and physiology; 3 verifiable letters of recommendation; professional resume. Additional exam requirements/recommendations for international students: Required—TOEFL (minimum score 560 paper-based; 83 iBT) or IELTS. *Application deadline:* For fall admission, 7/31 priority date for domestic students, 6/30 priority date for international students; for spring admission, 11/30 for domestic students, 10/31 for international students. Applications are processed on a rolling basis. Application fee: $50. Electronic applications accepted. *Expenses:* Tuition, state resident: full-time $7956; part-time $442 per credit. Tuition, nonresident: full-time $11,934; part-time $663 per credit. *Required fees:* $2129; $118 per credit. *Financial support:* Research assistantships with full and partial tuition reimbursements, Federal Work-Study, and institutionally sponsored loans available. Financial award application deadline: 3/1; financial award applicants required to submit FAFSA. *Faculty research:* HIV prevention, wellness, international health issues. *Unit head:* Dr. Kathleen Hillman, Graduate Coordinator, 570-422-3727, Fax: 570-422-3848, E-mail: khillman@po-box.esu.edu. *Application contact:* Kevin Quintero, Graduate Admissions Coordinator, 570-422-3536, Fax: 570-422-2711, E-mail: kquintero@esu.edu.

Emory University, Rollins School of Public Health, Department of Behavioral Sciences and Health Education, Atlanta, GA 30322-1100. Offers MPH, PhD. *Accreditation:* CEPH. Part-time programs available. *Degree requirements:* For master's, comprehensive exam (for some programs), thesis, practicum. *Entrance requirements:* For master's, GRE General Test. Additional exam requirements/recommendations for international students: Required—TOEFL (minimum score 550 paper-based; 80 iBT). Electronic applications accepted.

Excelsior College, School of Health Sciences, Albany, NY 12203-5159. Offers health care informatics (Certificate); health professions education (MSHS); public health (MSHS). Part-time and evening/weekend programs available. Postbaccalaureate distance learning degree programs offered (no on-campus study). *Faculty:* 12 part-time/adjunct (9 women). *Students:* 35 part-time (24 women); includes 14 minority (9 Black or African American, non-Hispanic/Latino; 2 American Indian or Alaska Native, non-Hispanic/Latino; 1 Hispanic/Latino; 1 Native Hawaiian or other Pacific Islander, non-Hispanic/Latino; 1 Two or more races, non-Hispanic/Latino). Average age 46. *Entrance requirements:* For degree, bachelor's degree in applicable field. *Application deadline:* Applications are processed on a rolling basis. Application fee: $50. Electronic applications accepted. *Expenses: Tuition:* Part-time $565 per credit. *Financial support:* In 2013–14, 1 student received support. Scholarships/grants available. Support available to part-time students. *Faculty research:* Use of technology in online learning. *Unit head:* Dr. Deborah Sopczyk, Dean, 518-464-8500, Fax: 518-464-8777, E-mail: informatics@excelsior.edu. *Application contact:* Laura Goff, Director of Advisement and Evaluation, 518-464-8500, Fax: 518-464-8777, E-mail: lgoff@excelsior.edu.

Florida Agricultural and Mechanical University, Division of Graduate Studies, Research, and Continuing Education, College of Education, Department of Health, Physical Education, and Recreation, Tallahassee, FL 32307-3200. Offers M Ed, MS Ed. *Accreditation:* NCATE. Part-time and evening/weekend programs available. *Degree requirements:* For master's, thesis optional. *Entrance requirements:* For master's, GRE General Test, minimum GPA of 3.0. Additional exam requirements/recommendations for international students: Required—TOEFL. *Faculty research:* Administration/curriculum, work behavior, psychology.

Florida State University, The Graduate School, College of Human Sciences, Department of Nutrition, Food and Exercise Sciences, Tallahassee, FL 32306-1493. Offers exercise physiology (MS, PhD); nutrition and food science (MS, PhD), including clinical nutrition (MS), food science, human nutrition (PhD), nutrition education and health promotion (MS), nutrition science (MS); sports nutrition (MS); sports sciences (MS). Part-time programs available. *Faculty:* 19 full-time (12 women). *Students:* 102 full-time (55 women), 17 part-time (13 women); includes 21 minority (7 Black or African American, non-Hispanic/Latino; 3 Asian, non-Hispanic/Latino; 2 Hispanic/Latino; 9 Two or more races, non-Hispanic/Latino), 24 international. Average age 26. 168 applicants, 51% accepted, 43 enrolled. In 2013, 29 master's, 3 doctorates awarded. *Degree requirements:* For master's, comprehensive exam (for some programs), thesis optional; for doctorate, thesis/dissertation. *Entrance requirements:* For master's, GRE General Test, minimum upper-division GPA of 3.0; for doctorate, GRE General Test, minimum upper-division GPA of 3.0, MS. Additional exam requirements/recommendations for international students: Required—TOEFL (minimum score 550 paper-based; 80 iBT). *Application deadline:* For fall admission, 7/1 for domestic and international students; for spring admission, 11/1 for domestic and international students. Applications are processed on a rolling basis. Application fee: $30. Electronic applications accepted. *Expenses:* Tuition, state resident: part-time $403.51 per credit hour. Tuition, nonresident: part-time $1004.85 per credit hour. *Required fees:* $75.81 per credit hour. One-time fee: $20 part-time. Tuition and fees vary according to course load, campus/location and student level. *Financial support:* In 2013–14, 54 students received support, including 3 fellowships with partial tuition reimbursements available (averaging $2,362 per year), 21 research assistantships with full tuition reimbursements available (averaging $3,902 per year), 42 teaching assistantships with full tuition reimbursements available (averaging $10,993 per year); career-related internships or fieldwork, Federal Work-Study, institutionally sponsored loans, scholarships/grants, and unspecified assistantships also available. Financial award application deadline: 2/1; financial award applicants required to submit FAFSA. *Faculty research:* Body composition, functional food, chronic disease and aging response; food safety, food allergy, and safety/quality detection methods; sports nutrition, energy and human performance; strength training, functional performance, cardiovascular physiology, sarcopenia. *Total annual research expenditures:* $497,515. *Unit head:* Dr. Bahram H. Arjmandi, Professor/Chair, 850-645-1517, Fax: 850-645-5000, E-mail: barjmandi@fsu.edu. *Application contact:* Ann R. Smith, Office Administrator, 850-644-1828, Fax: 850-645-5000, E-mail: asmith@fsu.edu.
Website: http://www.chs.fsu.edu/Departments/Nutrition-Food-Exercise-Sciences.

Fort Hays State University, Graduate School, College of Health and Life Sciences, Department of Health and Human Performance, Hays, KS 67601-4099. Offers MS. Part-time programs available. *Degree requirements:* For master's, comprehensive exam, thesis optional. *Entrance requirements:* For master's, GRE General Test or MAT. Additional exam requirements/recommendations for international students: Required—TOEFL (minimum score 550 paper-based). Electronic applications accepted. *Faculty research:* Isoproterenol hydrochloride and exercise, dehydrogenase and high-density lipoprotein levels in athletics, venous blood parameters to adipose fat.

Framingham State University, Continuing Education, Programs in Food and Nutrition, Program in Human Nutrition: Education and Media Technologies, Framingham, MA 01701-9101. Offers MS.

Georgia College & State University, Graduate School, College of Health Sciences, Department of Kinesiology, Milledgeville, GA 31061. Offers health promotion (M Ed); human performance (M Ed); outdoor education (M Ed); physical education (MAT). *Accreditation:* NCATE (one or more programs are accredited). Part-time and evening/weekend programs available. *Students:* 31 full-time (14 women), 13 part-time (12 women); includes 11 minority (all Black or African American, non-Hispanic/Latino), 1 international. Average age 26. In 2013, 25 master's awarded. *Degree requirements:* For master's, comprehensive exam, thesis optional. *Entrance requirements:* For master's, GRE General Test or MAT, minimum GPA of 2.75 in upper-level undergraduate courses, 2 letters of reference. Additional exam requirements/recommendations for international students: Recommended—TOEFL (minimum score 550 paper-based; 79 iBT). *Application deadline:* For fall admission, 7/1 priority date for domestic students, 4/1 priority date for international students; for spring admission, 11/15 priority date for domestic students, 9/1 priority date for international students. Applications are processed on a rolling basis. Application fee: $40. Electronic applications accepted. *Financial support:* In 2013–14, 26 research assistantships with full tuition reimbursements were awarded; career-related internships or fieldwork and unspecified assistantships also available. Support available to part-time students. Financial award applicants required to submit FAFSA. *Unit head:* Dr. Lisa Griffin, Chair, 478-445-4072, Fax: 478-445-4074, E-mail: lisa.griffin@gcsu.edu. *Application contact:* 800-342-0471, E-mail: grad-admit@gcsu.edu.

Georgia Regents University, The Graduate School, College of Education, Program in Health and Physical Education, Augusta, GA 30912. Offers M Ed. *Entrance requirements:* For master's, GRE, MAT, minimum GPA of 2.5.

Georgia Southern University, Jack N. Averitt College of Graduate Studies, Jiann-Ping Hsu College of Public Health, Program in Public Health, Statesboro, GA 30460. Offers biostatistics (MPH, Dr PH); community health behavior and education (Dr PH); community health education (MPH); environmental health sciences (MPH); epidemiology (MPH); health policy and management (MPH, Dr PH). *Accreditation:* CEPH. Part-time programs available. *Students:* 130 full-time (96 women), 50 part-time (39 women); includes 95 minority (80 Black or African American, non-Hispanic/Latino; 5 Asian, non-Hispanic/Latino; 4 Hispanic/Latino; 1 Native Hawaiian or other Pacific Islander, non-Hispanic/Latino; 5 Two or more races, non-Hispanic/Latino), 32 international. Average age 30. 213 applicants, 68% accepted, 61 enrolled. In 2013, 29 master's, 9 doctorates awarded. *Degree requirements:* For master's, thesis optional, practicum; for doctorate, comprehensive exam, thesis/dissertation, practicum. *Entrance requirements:* For master's, GRE General Test, minimum GPA of 2.75, resume, 3 letters of reference; for doctorate, GRE, GMAT, MCAT, LSAT, 3 letters of reference, statement of purpose, resume or curriculum vitae. Additional exam requirements/recommendations for international students: Required—TOEFL (minimum score 550 paper-based; 80 iBT), IELTS (minimum score 6). *Application deadline:* For fall admission, 3/1 priority date for domestic and international students; for spring admission, 10/1 priority date for domestic students, 10/1 for international students. Applications are processed on a rolling basis. Application fee: $50. Electronic applications accepted. *Expenses:* Contact institution. *Financial support:* In 2013–14, 54 students received support, including research assistantships with partial tuition reimbursements available (averaging $7,200 per year), teaching assistantships with partial tuition reimbursements available (averaging $7,200 per year); career-related internships or fieldwork, Federal Work-Study, scholarships/grants, tuition waivers (partial), and unspecified assistantships also available. Support available to part-time students. Financial award application deadline: 4/15; financial award applicants required to submit FAFSA. *Faculty research:* Rural public health best practices, health disparity elimination, community initiatives to enhance public health, cost effectiveness analysis, epidemiology of rural public health, environmental health issues, health care system assessment, rural health care, health policy and healthcare financing, survival analysis, nonparametric statistics and resampling methods, micro-arrays and genomics, data imputation techniques and clinical trial methodology. *Total annual research expenditures:* $281,707. *Unit head:* Sarah Peterson, Student Services Coordinator, 912-478-2413, Fax: 912-478-5811, E-mail: speterson@georgiasouthern.edu. *Application contact:* Amanda Gilliland, Coordinator for Graduate Student Recruitment, 912-478-5384, Fax: 912-478-0740, E-mail: gradadmissions@georgiasouthern.edu.
Website: http://chhs.georgiasouthern.edu/health/.

Georgia Southwestern State University, Graduate Studies, School of Education, Americus, GA 31709-4693. Offers early childhood education (M Ed, Ed S); health and physical education (M Ed); middle grades education (M Ed, Ed S); reading (M Ed); secondary education (M Ed); special education (M Ed). *Accreditation:* NCATE. *Degree requirements:* For master's, comprehensive exam. *Entrance requirements:* For master's, GRE General Test or MAT, minimum GPA of 2.5; for Ed S, GRE General Test or MAT, minimum graduate GPA of 3.25, M Ed from accredited college or university, 3 years teaching experience. Electronic applications accepted.

Georgia State University, College of Education, Department of Kinesiology and Health, Program in Health and Physical Education, Atlanta, GA 30302-3083. Offers M Ed. Part-time and evening/weekend programs available. *Degree requirements:* For master's, comprehensive exam. *Entrance requirements:* For master's, GRE General Test, minimum GPA of 2.5. *Application deadline:* For fall admission, 5/1 for domestic students; for spring admission, 10/1 for domestic students. Application fee: $50. *Expenses: Tuition, area resident:* Full-time $4176; part-time $348 per credit hour. Tuition, state resident: full-time $14,544; part-time $1212 per credit hour. Tuition, nonresident: full-time $14,544; part-time $1212 per credit hour. Tuition and fees vary according to course load and program. *Financial support:* Teaching assistantships and career-related internships or fieldwork available. *Faculty research:* Exercise science, teacher behavior. *Unit head:* Dr. Jacalyn Lea Lund, Chair, 404-413-8051, E-mail: jlund@gsu.edu. *Application contact:* Dr. Rachel Gurvitch, Program Coordinator, 404-413-8374, E-mail: rgurvitch@gsu.edu.
Website: http://education.gsu.edu/KIN/kh_programs.htm.

Grand Canyon University, College of Doctoral Studies, Phoenix, AZ 85017-1097. Offers business administration (DBA); general psychology (PhD), including cognition and instruction, industrial and organizational psychology; organizational leadership (Ed D, PhD), including behavioral health (PhD), education and effective schools (PhD), higher education (PhD), instructional leadership (PhD), organizational development (Ed D). *Degree requirements:* For doctorate, comprehensive exam, thesis/dissertation. *Entrance requirements:* For doctorate, minimum GPA of 3.4 on earned advanced degree from regionally-accredited institution; transcripts; goals statement.

Harding University, Cannon-Clary College of Education, Searcy, AR 72149-0001. Offers advanced studies in teaching and learning (M Ed); art (MSE); behavioral science (MSE); counseling (MS, Ed S); early childhood special education (M Ed, MSE); education (MSE); educational leadership (M Ed, Ed S); elementary education (M Ed); English (MSE); French (MSE); history/social science (MSE); kinesiology (MSE); math (MSE); reading (M Ed); secondary education (M Ed); Spanish (MSE); teaching (MAT); teaching English as a second language (MSE). *Accreditation:* NCATE. Part-time and evening/weekend programs available. *Faculty:* 13 full-time (5 women), 42 part-time/adjunct (24 women). *Students:* 154 full-time (119 women), 393 part-time (270 women); includes 108 minority (81 Black or African American, non-Hispanic/Latino; 5 American Indian or Alaska Native, non-Hispanic/Latino; 5 Asian, non-Hispanic/Latino; 9 Hispanic/Latino; 8 Two or more races, non-Hispanic/Latino), 15 international. Average age 36. 187 applicants, 79% accepted, 135 enrolled. In 2013, 138 master's, 17 other advanced degrees awarded. *Degree requirements:* For master's, comprehensive exam (for some programs), thesis optional, portfolio(s); for Ed S, comprehensive exam, portfolio, project. *Entrance requirements:* For master's, GRE, MAT, PRAXIS; for Ed S, MAT or GRE. Additional exam requirements/recommendations for international students: Required—TOEFL (minimum score 550 paper-based; 79 iBT). *Application deadline:* For fall admission, 8/1 for domestic and international students; for spring admission, 1/1 for domestic and international students. Applications are processed on a rolling basis. Application fee: $35. *Expenses: Tuition:* Full-time $11,574; part-time $643 per credit hour. *Required fees:* $432; $24 per credit hour. Tuition and fees vary according to course load, degree level and program. *Financial support:* In 2013–14, 36 students received support. Unspecified assistantships available. *Faculty research:* Reading, comprehension, school violence, educational technology, behavior, college choice, differentiated instruction, brain-based teaching. *Unit head:* Dr. Clara Carroll, Chair, 501-279-4501, Fax: 501-279-4083, E-mail: ccarroll@harding.edu. *Application contact:* Information Contact, 501-279-4315, E-mail: gradstudiesedu@harding.edu.
Website: http://www.harding.edu/education.

Hofstra University, School of Education, Programs in Physical and Health Education, Hempstead, NY 11549. Offers adventure education (Advanced Certificate); health education (MS), including PK-12 teaching certification; physical education (MA, MS), including adventure education, curriculum (MA), strength and conditioning; sport science (MS), including adventure education (MA, MS), strength and conditioning (MA, MS).

Howard University, Graduate School, Department of Health, Human Performance and Leisure Studies, Washington, DC 20059-0002. Offers exercise physiology (MS); health education (MS); sports studies (MS), including sociology of sports, sports management; urban recreation (MS), including leisure studies. Part-time and evening/weekend programs available. *Degree requirements:* For master's, comprehensive exam, thesis. *Entrance requirements:* For master's, BS in human performance or related field. Additional exam requirements/recommendations for international students: Recommended—TOEFL. Electronic applications accepted. *Faculty research:* Health promotion, cardiovascular hypertension, physical activity, sport and human rights issues.

Idaho State University, Office of Graduate Studies, Kasiska College of Health Professions, Department of Health and Nutrition Sciences, Program in Health Education, Pocatello, ID 83209-8109. Offers MHE. Part-time programs available. *Degree requirements:* For master's, comprehensive exam, thesis or project. *Entrance requirements:* For master's, GRE General Test, previous coursework in statistics, natural sciences, tests and measurements. Additional exam requirements/recommendations for international students: Required—TOEFL (minimum score 600 paper-based). Electronic applications accepted. *Faculty research:* Health and wellness.

Illinois State University, Graduate School, College of Applied Science and Technology, School of Kinesiology and Recreation, Normal, IL 61790-2200. Offers health education (MS); physical education (MS). *Degree requirements:* For master's, thesis or alternative. *Entrance requirements:* For master's, GRE General Test, minimum GPA of 2.6 in last 60 hours of course work. *Faculty research:* Influences on positive youth development through sport, country-wide health fitness project, graduate practicum in athletic training, perceived exertion and self-selected intensity during resistance exercise in younger and older.

Indiana State University, College of Graduate and Professional Studies, College of Nursing, Health and Human Services, Department of Health, Safety, and Environmental Health Sciences, Terre Haute, IN 47809. Offers community health promotion (MA, MS); health and safety education (MA, MS); occupational safety management (MA, MS). *Accreditation:* NCATE (one or more programs are accredited). *Degree requirements:* For master's, thesis or alternative. *Entrance requirements:* For master's, GRE General Test. Electronic applications accepted.

Indiana University Bloomington, School of Public Health, Department of Applied Health Science, Bloomington, IN 47405. Offers behavioral, social, and community health (MPH); family health (MPH); health behavior (PhD); nutrition science (MS); professional health education (MPH); public health administration (MPH); safety management (MS); school and college health education (MS). *Accreditation:* CEPH (one or more programs are accredited). *Faculty:* 30 full-time (19 women). *Students:* 144 full-time (104 women), 26 part-time (16 women); includes 46 minority (23 Black or African American, non-Hispanic/Latino; 1 American Indian or Alaska Native, non-Hispanic/Latino; 8 Asian, non-Hispanic/Latino; 10 Hispanic/Latino; 4 Two or more races, non-Hispanic/Latino), 32 international. Average age 30. 129 applicants, 71% accepted, 58 enrolled. In 2013, 53 master's, 6 doctorates awarded. *Degree requirements:* For master's, thesis optional; for doctorate, comprehensive exam, thesis/dissertation. *Entrance requirements:* For master's, GRE (for MS in nutrition science), 3 recommendations; for doctorate, GRE, 3 recommendations. Additional exam requirements/recommendations for international students: Required—TOEFL (minimum score 550 paper-based; 80 iBT). *Application deadline:* For fall admission, 2/1 priority date for domestic students, 12/1 priority date for international students; for spring admission, 11/15 priority date for domestic students, 9/1 priority date for international students. Application fee: $55 ($65 for international students). Electronic applications accepted. *Financial support:* Fellowships, research assistantships with full and partial tuition reimbursements, teaching assistantships with full and partial tuition reimbursements, career-related internships or fieldwork, Federal Work-Study, institutionally sponsored loans, scholarships/grants, health care benefits, tuition waivers (partial), unspecified assistantships, and fee remissions available. Financial award application deadline: 3/1; financial award applicants required to submit FAFSA. *Faculty research:* Cancer education, HIV/AIDS and drug education, public health, parent-child interactions, safety education, obesity, public health policy, public health administration, school health, health education, human development, nutrition, human sexuality, chronic disease, early childhood health. *Total annual research expenditures:* $1.4 million. *Unit head:* Dr. David K. Lohrmann, Chair, 812-856-5101, Fax: 812-855-3936, E-mail: dlohrman@indiana.edu. *Application contact:* Dr. Susan Middlestadt, Associate Professor and Graduate Coordinator, 812-856-5768, Fax: 812-855-3936, E-mail: semiddle@indiana.edu.
Website: http://www.publichealth.indiana.edu/departments/applied-health-science/index.shtml.

Indiana University of Pennsylvania, School of Graduate Studies and Research, College of Health and Human Services, Department of Health and Physical Education, Program in Health and Physical Education, Indiana, PA 15705-1087. Offers M Ed. Part-time programs available. *Faculty:* 8 full-time (4 women). *Students:* 12 full-time (9 women), 3 part-time (1 woman); includes 2 minority (both Black or African American, non-Hispanic/Latino). Average age 26. 8 applicants, 75% accepted, 4 enrolled. In 2013, 20 master's awarded. *Entrance requirements:* Additional exam requirements/recommendations for international students: Required—TOEFL (minimum score 540 paper-based). *Application deadline:* Applications are processed on a rolling basis.

Application fee: $50. Electronic applications accepted. *Expenses:* Tuition, state resident: full-time $3978; part-time $442 per credit. Tuition, nonresident: full-time $5967; part-time $663 per credit. *Required fees:* $2080; $115.55 per credit. $93 per semester. Tuition and fees vary according to degree level and program. *Financial support:* In 2013–14, 6 research assistantships with full and partial tuition reimbursements (averaging $5,440 per year) were awarded; career-related internships or fieldwork, Federal Work-Study, scholarships/grants, and unspecified assistantships also available. Support available to part-time students. Financial award application deadline: 4/15; financial award applicants required to submit FAFSA. *Unit head:* Dr. Keri Kulik, Coordinator, 724-357-5656, E-mail: kskulik@iup.edu.
Website: http://www.iup.edu/grad/healthphysed/default.aspx.

Indiana University–Purdue University Indianapolis, School of Health and Rehabilitation Sciences, Indianapolis, IN 46202. Offers health and rehabilitation sciences (PhD); health sciences (MS); nutrition and dietetics (MS); occupational therapy (MS); physical therapy (DPT); physician assistant (MPAS). Part-time and evening/weekend programs available. *Faculty:* 4 full-time (3 women). *Students:* 266 full-time (201 women), 13 part-time (12 women); includes 21 minority (6 Black or African American, non-Hispanic/Latino; 7 Asian, non-Hispanic/Latino; 4 Hispanic/Latino; 1 Native Hawaiian or other Pacific Islander, non-Hispanic/Latino; 3 Two or more races, non-Hispanic/Latino), 11 international. Average age 26. 381 applicants, 23% accepted, 77 enrolled. In 2013, 33 master's, 39 doctorates awarded. *Degree requirements:* For master's, thesis (for some programs). *Entrance requirements:* For master's, GRE General Test, minimum GPA of 3.0 (for MS in health sciences, nutrition and dietetics), 3.2 (for MS in occupational therapy), 3.0 cumulative and prerequisite math/science (for MPAS); for doctorate, GRE, minimum cumulative and prerequisite math/science GPA of 3.2. Additional exam requirements/recommendations for international students: Required—TOEFL (minimum score 550 paper-based; 79 iBT), IELTS (minimum score 6.5), PTE (minimum score 54). *Application deadline:* For fall admission, 10/1 for domestic students; for spring admission, 10/15 for domestic students. Electronic applications accepted. *Expenses:* Contact institution. *Financial support:* Fellowships, research assistantships, Federal Work-Study, institutionally sponsored loans, and scholarships/grants available. Support available to part-time students. Financial award applicants required to submit FAFSA. *Faculty research:* Function and mobility across the lifespan, pediatric nutrition, driving and mobility rehabilitation, neurorehabilitation and biomechanics, rehabilitation and integrative therapy. *Total annual research expenditures:* $1.1 million. *Unit head:* Dr. Augustine Agho, Dean, 317-274-4704, E-mail: aagho@iu.edu. *Application contact:* Kim Crockett, Student Data Coordinator, 317-278-6744, E-mail: kimecroc@iu.edu.
Website: http://shrs.iupui.edu/.

Inter American University of Puerto Rico, Metropolitan Campus, Graduate Programs, Program in Physical Education, San Juan, PR 00919-1293. Offers teaching of physical education (MA); training and sport performance (MA). *Degree requirements:* For master's, comprehensive exam. *Entrance requirements:* For master's, GRE or EXADEP, interview. Electronic applications accepted.

Inter American University of Puerto Rico, San Germán Campus, Graduate Studies Center, Program in Health and Physical Education, San Germán, PR 00683-5008. Offers MA. Part-time and evening/weekend programs available. *Faculty:* 12 full-time (7 women), 27 part-time/adjunct (17 women). *Students:* 20 full-time (9 women), 2 part-time (1 woman); all minorities (all Hispanic/Latino). Average age 29. 7 applicants, 86% accepted, 5 enrolled. In 2013, 8 master's awarded. *Degree requirements:* For master's, comprehensive exam. *Entrance requirements:* For master's, GRE General Test or EXADEP, minimum GPA of 3.0. *Application deadline:* For fall admission, 4/30 priority date for domestic students; for spring admission, 11/15 for domestic students. Applications are processed on a rolling basis. Application fee: $31. *Expenses: Tuition:* Full-time $2424; part-time $202 per credit hour. *Required fees:* $260 per semester. Tuition and fees vary according to course level, course load, degree level and program. *Financial support:* Teaching assistantships available. *Unit head:* Dr. Elba T. Irizarry, Director of Graduate Studies Center, 787-264-1912 Ext. 7357, Fax: 787-892-6350, E-mail: elbat@sg.inter.edu. *Application contact:* Dr. Elba T. Irizarry, Director of Graduate Studies Center, 787-264-1912 Ext. 7357, Fax: 787-892-6350, E-mail: elbat@sg.inter.edu.

Ithaca College, School of Health Sciences and Human Performance, Program in Health Education, Ithaca, NY 14850. Offers MS. Part-time programs available. *Faculty:* 7 full-time (5 women). *Students:* 10 full-time (9 women), 3 international. Average age 24. 19 applicants, 84% accepted, 10 enrolled. In 2013, 14 master's awarded. *Degree requirements:* For master's, thesis optional. *Entrance requirements:* For master's, minimum GPA of 3.0. Additional exam requirements/recommendations for international students: Required—TOEFL (minimum score 550 paper-based; 80 iBT). *Application deadline:* For fall admission, 3/1 priority date for domestic and international students; for spring admission, 12/1 for domestic and international students. Applications are processed on a rolling basis. Application fee: $40. Electronic applications accepted. *Expenses:* Contact institution. *Financial support:* In 2013–14, 10 students received support, including 10 teaching assistantships (averaging $8,170 per year); career-related internships or fieldwork, Federal Work-Study, scholarships/grants, and unspecified assistantships also available. Support available to part-time students. Financial award application deadline: 3/1; financial award applicants required to submit CSS PROFILE or FAFSA. *Faculty research:* Needs assessment evaluation of health education programs, minority health (includes diversity), employee health assessment and program planning, youth at risk/families, multicultural/international health, program planning/health behaviors, sexuality education in the family and school setting, parent-teacher and student-teacher relationships, attitude/interest/motivation, teaching effectiveness, student learning/achievement. *Unit head:* Dr. Srijana Bajracharya, Chairperson, 607-274-3143, Fax: 607-274-1263, E-mail: gps@ithaca.edu. *Application contact:* Gerard Turbide, Director, Office of Admission, 607-274-3143, Fax: 607-274-1263, E-mail: gps@ithaca.edu.
Website: http://www.ithaca.edu/gps/gradprograms/hppe/programs/healthed.

Jackson State University, Graduate School, College of Education and Human Development, Department of Health, Physical Education and Recreation, Jackson, MS 39217. Offers MS Ed. *Accreditation:* NCATE. Part-time and evening/weekend programs available. *Degree requirements:* For master's, comprehensive exam, thesis or alternative. *Entrance requirements:* For master's, GRE General Test. Additional exam requirements/recommendations for international students: Required—TOEFL (minimum score 520 paper-based; 67 iBT).

James Madison University, The Graduate School, College of Health and Behavioral Studies, Department of Health Sciences, Program in Health Education, Harrisonburg, VA 22807. Offers MS, MS Ed. Part-time programs available. *Students:* 8 full-time (7 women), 6 part-time (all women); includes 4 minority (1 Black or African American, non-Hispanic/Latino; 3 Hispanic/Latino). Average age 27. In 2013, 4 master's awarded. *Entrance requirements:* For master's, GRE General Test. Additional exam requirements/recommendations for international students: Required—TOEFL. *Application deadline:* For fall admission, 5/1 priority date for domestic students; for spring admission, 9/1 priority date for domestic students. Application fee: $55. *Financial support:* In 2013–14, 4 students received support. 4 graduate assistantships (averaging $7530) available. Financial award application deadline: 3/1. *Unit head:* Dr. Maria T. Wessel, Director, 540-568-3955, E-mail: wesselmt@jmu.edu. *Application contact:* Lynette M. Bible, Director of Graduate Admissions, 540-568-6395, Fax: 540-568-7860, E-mail: biblelm@jmu.edu.

John F. Kennedy University, Graduate School of Holistic Studies, Department of Integral Studies, Program in Holistic Health Education, Pleasant Hill, CA 94523-4817. Offers MA. Part-time and evening/weekend programs available. *Degree requirements:* For master's, thesis or alternative. *Entrance requirements:* For master's, interview. Additional exam requirements/recommendations for international students: Required—TOEFL.

Johns Hopkins University, Bloomberg School of Public Health, Department of Health, Behavior and Society, Baltimore, MD 21218-2699. Offers genetic counseling (Sc M); health education and health communication (MHS); social and behavioral sciences (Dr PH, PhD, Sc D); social factors in health (MHS). *Faculty:* 43 full-time (30 women), 59 part-time/adjunct (40 women). *Students:* 107 full-time (97 women), 10 part-time (8 women); includes 33 minority (11 Black or African American, non-Hispanic/Latino; 11 Asian, non-Hispanic/Latino; 7 Hispanic/Latino; 4 Two or more races, non-Hispanic/Latino), 14 international. Average age 29. 241 applicants, 33% accepted, 35 enrolled. In 2013, 27 master's, 18 doctorates awarded. *Degree requirements:* For master's, comprehensive exam (for some programs), thesis (for some programs); for doctorate, comprehensive exam, thesis/dissertation. *Entrance requirements:* For master's, GRE, curriculum vitae, 3 letters of recommendation; for doctorate, GRE, transcripts, curriculum vitae, 3 recommendation letters. Additional exam requirements/recommendations for international students: Required—TOEFL (minimum score 600 paper-based; 100 iBT). *Application deadline:* For fall admission, 12/1 for domestic and international students. Applications are processed on a rolling basis. Application fee: $45. Electronic applications accepted. *Financial support:* Fellowships with tuition reimbursements, research assistantships, teaching assistantships, career-related internships or fieldwork, Federal Work-Study, scholarships/grants, traineeships, health care benefits, unspecified assistantships, and stipends available. Financial award application deadline: 3/15. *Faculty research:* Social determinants of health and structural and community-level inventions to improve health, communication and health education, behavioral and social aspects of genetic counseling. *Total annual research expenditures:* $6.3 million. *Unit head:* David R. Holtgrave, Department Chair, 410-502-4076, Fax: 410-502-4080, E-mail: dholtgra@jhsph.edu. *Application contact:* Barbara W. Diehl, Senior Academic Program Coordinator, 410-502-4415, Fax: 410-502-4333, E-mail: bdiehl@jhsph.edu.
Website: http://jhsph.edu/dept/hbs.

Johns Hopkins University, School of Education, Certificate Programs in Education, Baltimore, MD 21218-2699. Offers advanced methods for differentiated instruction and inclusive education (Certificate); applied behavior analysis (Certificate); counseling (CAGS); data-based decision making and organizational improvement (Certificate); early intervention/preschool special education specialist (Certificate); education leadership for independent schools (Certificate); education of students with autism and other pervasive developmental disorders (Certificate); evidence-based teaching in the health professions (Certificate); gifted education (Certificate); K-8 mathematics lead-teacher (Certificate); K-8 STEM education lead-teacher (Certificate); leadership for school, family, and community collaboration (Certificate); leadership in technology integration (Certificate); mental health counseling (Certificate); mind, brain, and teaching (Certificate); school administration and supervision (Certificate); urban education (Certificate). Part-time and evening/weekend programs available. Postbaccalaureate distance learning degree programs offered (no on-campus study). *Students:* 7 full-time (4 women), 216 part-time (169 women); includes 66 minority (35 Black or African American, non-Hispanic/Latino; 17 Asian, non-Hispanic/Latino; 6 Hispanic/Latino; 8 Two or more races, non-Hispanic/Latino), 6 international. Average age 35. 257 applicants, 81% accepted, 62 enrolled. In 2013, 202 CAGSs awarded. *Entrance requirements:* For degree, bachelor's degree from regionally- or nationally-accredited institution (master's for some programs), minimum GPA of 3.0 in all previous programs of study, official transcripts from all post-secondary institutions attended, essay, curriculum vitae/resume, minimum of two letters of recommendation. Additional exam requirements/recommendations for international students: Required—TOEFL (minimum score 600 paper-based; 100 iBT) or IELTS (minimum score 7). *Application deadline:* For fall admission, 4/1 for domestic students; for spring admission, 10/1 for domestic students; for summer admission, 2/1 for domestic students. Application fee: $80. Electronic applications accepted. *Financial support:* Application deadline: 6/1; applicants required to submit FAFSA. *Unit head:* Dr. David A. Andrews, Dean, 410-516-7820, Fax: 410-516-6697, E-mail: davidandrews@jhu.edu. *Application contact:* Catherine Wilson, Associate Director of Admissions, 410-516-9797, Fax: 410-516-9799, E-mail: soe.info@jhu.edu.

Johns Hopkins University, School of Education, Master's Programs in Education, Baltimore, MD 21218-2699. Offers counseling (MS), including mental health counseling, school counseling; education (MS), including educational studies, gifted education, reading, school administration and supervision, technology for educators; elementary education (MAT); health professions (M Ed); intelligence analysis (MS); management (MS); secondary education (MAT); special education (MS), including early childhood special education, general special education studies, mild to moderate disabilities, severe disabilities. Part-time and evening/weekend programs available. Postbaccalaureate distance learning degree programs offered (no on-campus study). *Students:* 183 full-time (123 women), 1,001 part-time (757 women); includes 380 minority (160 Black or African American, non-Hispanic/Latino; 4 American Indian or Alaska Native, non-Hispanic/Latino; 91 Asian, non-Hispanic/Latino; 78 Hispanic/Latino; 4 Native Hawaiian or other Pacific Islander, non-Hispanic/Latino; 43 Two or more races, non-Hispanic/Latino), 28 international. Average age 28. 508 applicants, 90% accepted, 337 enrolled. In 2013, 565 degrees awarded. *Degree requirements:* For master's, comprehensive exam (for some programs), portfolio, capstone project and/or internship; PRAXIS II (for teacher preparation programs that lead to licensure). *Entrance requirements:* For master's, GRE (for full-time programs only); PRAXIS I or equivalent (for teacher preparation programs that lead to licensure), bachelor's degree from regionally- or nationally-accredited institution, minimum GPA of 3.0 in all previous programs of study, official transcripts from all post-secondary institutions attended, essay, curriculum vitae/resume, minimum of two letters of recommendation. Additional exam requirements/recommendations for international students: Required—TOEFL (minimum score 600 paper-based; 100 iBT) or IELTS (minimum score 7). *Application deadline:* For fall admission, 4/1 for domestic and international students; for spring admission, 10/1 for domestic and international students; for summer admission, 2/1 for domestic and international students. Application fee: $80. Electronic applications accepted. *Financial support:* Application deadline: 6/1; applicants required to submit FAFSA. *Unit head:* Dr. David A. Andrews, Dean, 410-516-7820, Fax: 410-516-6697, E-mail: davidandrews@jhu.edu. *Application contact:* Catherine Wilson, Associate Director of Admissions, 410-516-9797, Fax: 410-516-9799, E-mail: soe.info@jhu.edu.

Keiser University, Master of Science in Education Program, Ft. Lauderdale, FL 33309. Offers allied health teaching and leadership (MS Ed); career college administration (MS Ed); leadership (MS Ed); online teaching and learning (MS Ed); teaching and learning (MS Ed). Part-time programs available. Postbaccalaureate distance learning degree programs offered (no on-campus study).

Kent State University, Graduate School of Education, Health, and Human Services, School of Health Sciences, Program in Health Education and Promotion, Kent, OH 44242-0001. Offers M Ed, PhD. *Accreditation:* NCATE. *Faculty:* 7 full-time (6 women), 1 (woman) part-time/adjunct. *Students:* 17 full-time (14 women), 12 part-time (9 women); includes 7 minority (6 Black or African American, non-Hispanic/Latino; 1 Hispanic/Latino), 1 international. 34 applicants, 38% accepted. In 2013, 13 master's, 1 doctorate awarded. *Degree requirements:* For doctorate, comprehensive exam, thesis/dissertation. *Entrance requirements:* For master's, 2 letters of reference, goals statement; for doctorate, GRE General Test, goals statement, resume, interview. Additional exam requirements/recommendations for international students: Required—TOEFL (minimum score 550 paper-based; 80 iBT). *Application deadline:* Applications are processed on a rolling basis. Application fee: $30 ($60 for international students). Electronic applications accepted. *Financial support:* In 2013–14, 1 research assistantship with full tuition reimbursement (averaging $8,500 per year), 5 teaching assistantships with full tuition reimbursements (averaging $12,000 per year) were awarded; Federal Work-Study, scholarships/grants, and unspecified assistantships also available. Financial award application deadline: 4/1; financial award applicants required to submit FAFSA. *Faculty research:* Substance use/abuse, sexuality, community health assessment, epidemiology, HIV/AIDS. *Unit head:* Dr. Kele Ding, Coordinator, 330-672-0688, E-mail: kding@kent.edu. *Application contact:* Nancy Miller, Academic Program Director, Office of Graduate Student Services, 330-672-2586, Fax: 330-672-9162, E-mail: ogs@kent.edu.
Website: http://www.kent.edu/ehhs/Schools/hs/programs/hedp/.

Lake Erie College of Osteopathic Medicine, Professional Programs, Erie, PA 16509-1025. Offers biomedical sciences (Postbaccalaureate Certificate); medical education (MS); osteopathic medicine (DO); pharmacy (Pharm D). *Accreditation:* ACPE; AOsA. *Degree requirements:* For doctorate, comprehensive exam, National Osteopathic Medical Licensing Exam, Levels 1 and 2; for Postbaccalaureate Certificate, comprehensive exam, North American Pharmacist Licensure Examination (NAPLEX). *Entrance requirements:* For doctorate, MCAT, minimum GPA of 3.2, letters of recommendation; for Postbaccalaureate Certificate, PCAT, letters of recommendation, minimum GPA of 3.5. Electronic applications accepted. *Faculty research:* Cardiac smooth and skeletal muscle mechanics, chemotherapeutics and vitamins, osteopathic manipulation.

Lehman College of the City University of New York, School of Natural and Social Sciences, Department of Health Sciences, Program in Health Education and Promotion, Bronx, NY 10468-1589. Offers MA. *Accreditation:* CEPH; NCATE. Part-time and evening/weekend programs available. *Degree requirements:* For master's, thesis or alternative. *Entrance requirements:* For master's, minimum GPA of 2.7.

Lehman College of the City University of New York, School of Natural and Social Sciences, Department of Health Sciences, Program in Health N–12 Teacher, Bronx, NY 10468-1589. Offers MS Ed. *Accreditation:* NCATE. *Degree requirements:* For master's, thesis or alternative.

Loma Linda University, School of Public Health, Programs in Health Promotion and Education, Loma Linda, CA 92350. Offers MPH, Dr PH. *Accreditation:* CEPH (one or more programs are accredited). *Degree requirements:* For doctorate, thesis/dissertation. *Entrance requirements:* For doctorate, GRE General Test. Additional exam requirements/recommendations for international students: Required—Michigan English Language Assessment Battery or TOEFL.

Long Island University–LIU Brooklyn, School of Health Professions, Division of Sports Sciences, Brooklyn, NY 11201-8423. Offers adapted physical education (MS); athletic training and sports sciences (MS); exercise physiology (MS); health sciences (MS). Part-time and evening/weekend programs available. *Entrance requirements:* For master's, 2 letters of recommendation. Additional exam requirements/recommendations for international students: Required—TOEFL (minimum score 500 paper-based). Electronic applications accepted.

Longwood University, College of Graduate and Professional Studies, College of Education and Human Services, Farmville, VA 23909. Offers education (MS), including algebra and middle school math, counselor education, elementary and middle school math, elementary education, elementary education initial licensure, health and physical education, school librarianship, special education general curriculum, special education initial licensure; social work and communication sciences and disorders (MS). *Accreditation:* NCATE. Part-time and evening/weekend programs available. *Faculty:* 28 full-time (15 women), 9 part-time/adjunct (7 women). *Students:* 86 full-time (80 women), 187 part-time (173 women); includes 38 minority (26 Black or African American, non-Hispanic/Latino; 1 Asian, non-Hispanic/Latino; 5 Hispanic/Latino; 1 Native Hawaiian or other Pacific Islander, non-Hispanic/Latino; 5 Two or more races, non-Hispanic/Latino). 98 applicants, 89% accepted, 85 enrolled. In 2013, 132 master's awarded. *Degree requirements:* For master's, comprehensive exam (for some programs), thesis optional, professional portfolio, internship, clinical experience, or practicum. *Entrance requirements:* For master's, bachelor's degree from regionally-accredited institution, 2 recommendations, 500-word personal essay, official transcripts, minimum GPA of 2.75, valid teaching license (for some programs), passing Praxis I scores for initial teaching licensure programs. Additional exam requirements/recommendations for international students: Required—TOEFL (minimum score 570 paper-based), IELTS (minimum score 6.5). *Application deadline:* For fall admission, 5/1 priority date for domestic students; for spring admission, 10/1 priority date for domestic students; for summer admission, 2/1 priority date for domestic students. Applications are processed on a rolling basis. Application fee: $50. Electronic applications accepted. *Expenses:* Tuition, state resident: full-time $7506; part-time $327 per credit hour. Tuition, nonresident: full-time $17,100; part-time $837 per credit hour. Tuition and fees vary according to course load and campus/location. *Financial support:* Career-related internships or fieldwork and Federal Work-Study available. Financial award applicants required to submit FAFSA. *Unit head:* Dr. Peggy L. Tarpley, Chair of the Department of Education and Special Education, 434-395-2337, E-mail: tarpleypl@longwood.edu. *Application contact:* College of Graduate and Professional Studies, 434-395-2380, Fax: 434-395-2750, E-mail: graduate@longwood.edu.
Website: http://www.longwood.edu/cehs/.

Marshall University, Academic Affairs Division, College of Information Technology and Engineering, Division of Applied Science and Technology, Program in Safety, Huntington, WV 25755. Offers MS. *Accreditation:* NCATE. *Students:* 6 full-time (1 woman), 10 part-time (1 woman). Average age 36. In 2013, 10 master's awarded. *Degree requirements:* For master's, thesis optional, comprehensive assessment. Application fee: $40. *Unit head:* Dr. D. Allen Stern, Division Chair, 304-696-3069, E-mail: stern@marshall.edu. *Application contact:* Information Contact, 304-746-1900, Fax: 304-746-1902, E-mail: services@marshall.edu.
Website: http://muwww-new.marshall.edu/cite/dast/safety-technology-graduate-degree-program/.

Marymount University, School of Health Professions, Program in Health Education Management, Arlington, VA 22207-4299. Offers MS. Part-time and evening/weekend programs available. *Faculty:* 3 full-time (2 women). *Students:* 6 full-time (5 women), 13 part-time (11 women); includes 7 minority (5 Black or African American, non-Hispanic/Latino; 2 Asian, non-Hispanic/Latino), 2 international. Average age 32. 16 applicants, 100% accepted, 11 enrolled. In 2013, 22 master's awarded. *Entrance requirements:* For master's, GRE or MAT, 2 letters of recommendation, interview, resume. Additional exam requirements/recommendations for international students: Required—TOEFL (minimum score 600 paper-based; 96 iBT), IELTS (minimum score 6.5). *Application deadline:* For fall admission, 7/1 for international students. Applications are processed on a rolling basis. Application fee: $40. Electronic applications accepted. *Expenses: Tuition:* Part-time $850 per credit. *Required fees:* $10 per credit. One-time fee: $200 part-time. Tuition and fees vary according to program. *Financial support:* In 2013–14, 2 students received support, including 1 research assistantship with full and partial tuition reimbursement available; career-related internships or fieldwork, Federal Work-Study, scholarships/grants, and unspecified assistantships also available. Support available to part-time students. Financial award applicants required to submit FAFSA. *Unit head:* Dr. Michelle Walters-Edwards, Chair, 703-526-1597, Fax: 703-284-3819, E-mail: michelle.walters-edwards@marymount.edu. *Application contact:* Francesca Reed, Director, Graduate Admissions, 703-284-5901, Fax: 703-527-3815, E-mail: grad.admissions@marymount.edu.
Website: http://www.marymount.edu/academics/programs/healthPromo.

Marywood University, Academic Affairs, Reap College of Education and Human Development, Doctoral Program in Human Development, Emphasis in Health Promotion, Scranton, PA 18509-1598. Offers PhD. *Entrance requirements:* Additional exam requirements/recommendations for international students: Required—TOEFL (minimum score 550 paper-based; 79 iBT). *Application deadline:* For fall admission, 1/30 for domestic and international students. Application fee: $35. Electronic applications accepted. *Expenses:* Contact institution. *Financial support:* Career-related internships or fieldwork, scholarships/grants, and unspecified assistantships available. Support available to part-time students. Financial award application deadline: 6/30; financial award applicants required to submit FAFSA. *Unit head:* Dr. Alice McDonnell, Coordinator, 570-348-6279, E-mail: mcdonnell@marywood.edu. *Application contact:* Tammy Manka, Assistant Director of Graduate Admissions, 570-348-6211 Ext. 2322, E-mail: tmanka@marywood.edu.
Website: http://www.marywood.edu/phd/specializations.html.

Massachusetts College of Liberal Arts, Graduate Programs, North Adams, MA 01247-4100. Offers business (MBA); educational administration (M Ed); educational leadership (CAGS); instruction and curriculum (M Ed); instructional technology (M Ed); physical education and health (M Ed); reading (M Ed); special education (M Ed). Part-time and evening/weekend programs available. *Degree requirements:* For master's, thesis. *Entrance requirements:* For master's, writing sample.

Middle Tennessee State University, College of Graduate Studies, College of Behavioral and Health Sciences, Department of Health and Human Performance, Program in Health, Physical Education and Recreation, Murfreesboro, TN 37132. Offers health and human performance (MS); leisure and sport management (MS). Part-time and evening/weekend programs available. Postbaccalaureate distance learning degree programs offered. *Faculty:* 24 full-time (9 women), 5 part-time/adjunct (3 women). *Students:* 26 full-time (15 women), 40 part-time (23 women); includes 20 minority (15 Black or African American, non-Hispanic/Latino; 1 Asian, non-Hispanic/Latino; 3 Hispanic/Latino; 1 Two or more races, non-Hispanic/Latino). 87 applicants, 61% accepted. In 2013, 31 master's awarded. *Degree requirements:* For master's, comprehensive exam, thesis optional. *Entrance requirements:* For master's, GRE. Additional exam requirements/recommendations for international students: Required—TOEFL (minimum score 525 paper-based; 71 iBT) or IELTS (minimum score 6). *Application deadline:* For fall admission, 6/1 for domestic and international students. Applications are processed on a rolling basis. Application fee: $25 ($30 for international students). *Financial support:* In 2013–14, 14 students received support. Tuition waivers available. Support available to part-time students. Financial award application deadline: 5/1. *Faculty research:* Kinesiometrics, leisure behavior, health, lifestyles. *Unit head:* Dr. Harold D. Whiteside, Interim Dean, 615-898-2900, Fax: 615-494-7704, E-mail: harold.whiteside@mtsu.edu. *Application contact:* Dr. Michael D. Allen, Vice Provost for Research and Dean, 615-898-2840, Fax: 615-904-8020, E-mail: michael.allen@mtsu.edu.

Mills College, Graduate Studies, School of Education, Oakland, CA 94613-1000. Offers child life in hospitals (MA); early childhood education (MA); education (MA), including art education, curriculum and instruction, elementary education, English education, foreign language education, mathematics education, science education, secondary education, social studies education, teaching; educational leadership (MA, Ed D). Part-time and evening/weekend programs available. *Faculty:* 10 full-time (7 women), 13 part-time/adjunct (10 women). *Students:* 154 full-time (136 women), 54 part-time (47 women); includes 96 minority (32 Black or African American, non-Hispanic/Latino; 1 American Indian or Alaska Native, non-Hispanic/Latino; 23 Asian, non-Hispanic/Latino; 27 Hispanic/Latino; 1 Native Hawaiian or other Pacific Islander, non-Hispanic/Latino; 12 Two or more races, non-Hispanic/Latino), 2 international. Average age 25. 222 applicants, 89% accepted, 110 enrolled. In 2013, 96 master's, 38 doctorates awarded. Terminal master's awarded for partial completion of doctoral program. *Degree requirements:* For master's, comprehensive exam, thesis (for some programs); for doctorate, thesis/dissertation. *Entrance requirements:* For master's, statement of purpose, official transcript, 3 recommendations. Additional exam requirements/recommendations for international students: Required—TOEFL (minimum score 550 paper-based; 80 iBT) or IELTS (minimum score 6). *Application deadline:* For fall admission, 12/31 priority date for domestic students, 12/15 for international students; for spring admission, 11/1 priority date for domestic students, 10/1 for international students. Applications are processed on a rolling basis. Application fee: $50. Electronic applications accepted. *Expenses: Tuition:* Full-time $29,860. *Required fees:* $1134. Part-time tuition and fees vary according to course load, degree level and program. *Financial support:* In 2013–14, 130 students received support, including 130 fellowships with full and partial tuition reimbursements available (averaging $7,565 per year); career-related internships or fieldwork and scholarships/grants also available. Support available to part-time students. Financial award application deadline: 2/1; financial award applicants required to submit FAFSA. *Faculty research:* Early childhood education, teacher preparation, educational leadership. *Total annual research expenditures:* $3.5 million. *Unit head:* Dr. Katherine Schultz, Department Head, 510-430-3384, Fax: 510-430-2159, E-mail: kschultz@mills.edu. *Application contact:* Shrim Bathey, Director of Graduate Admission, 510-430-3309, Fax: 510-430-2159, E-mail: grad-admission@mills.edu.
Website: http://www.mills.edu/education.

Minnesota State University Mankato, College of Graduate Studies, College of Allied Health and Nursing, Department of Health Science, Mankato, MN 56001. Offers community health education (MS); school health education (MS, Postbaccalaureate Certificate). Part-time programs available. *Students:* 5 full-time (all women), 25 part-time (18 women). *Degree requirements:* For master's, comprehensive exam, thesis or alternative. *Entrance requirements:* For master's, minimum GPA of 3.0 during previous 2 years; for Postbaccalaureate Certificate, teaching license. Additional exam requirements/recommendations for international students: Required—TOEFL (minimum score 500 paper-based; 61 iBT). *Application deadline:* For fall admission, 7/1 for

domestic students, 5/1 for international students; for spring admission, 11/1 for domestic students, 10/1 for international students. Applications are processed on a rolling basis. Application fee: $40. Electronic applications accepted. *Financial support:* Research assistantships with full tuition reimbursements, teaching assistantships with full tuition reimbursements, career-related internships or fieldwork, and Federal Work-Study available. Support available to part-time students. Financial award application deadline: 3/15; financial award applicants required to submit FAFSA. *Faculty research:* Teaching methods, stress prophylaxis and management, effects of alcohol. *Unit head:* Dr. Dawn Larsen, Graduate Coordinator, 507-389-2113. *Application contact:* 507-389-2321, E-mail: grad@mnsu.edu.
Website: http://ahn.mnsu.edu/health/.

Mississippi University for Women, Graduate School, Department of Health and Kinesiology, Columbus, MS 39701-9998. Offers health education (MS). *Degree requirements:* For master's, comprehensive exam.

Montana State University, College of Graduate Studies, College of Education, Health, and Human Development, Department of Health and Human Development, Bozeman, MT 59717. Offers family and consumer sciences (MS). *Accreditation:* ACA. Part-time programs available. Postbaccalaureate distance learning degree programs offered (no on-campus study). *Degree requirements:* For master's, comprehensive exam. *Entrance requirements:* For master's, GRE (minimum scores: verbal 480; quantitative 480). Additional exam requirements/recommendations for international students: Required—TOEFL (minimum score 550 paper-based). Electronic applications accepted. *Faculty research:* Community food systems, ethic of care for teachers and coaches, influence of public policy on families and communities, cost effectiveness of early childhood education, exercise metabolism, winter sport performance enhancement, assessment of physical activity.

Montclair State University, The Graduate School, College of Education and Human Services, Department of Secondary and Special Education, Program in Teaching in Subject Area, Montclair, NJ 07043-1624. Offers art (MAT); biology (MAT); chemistry (MAT); earth science (MAT); English (MAT); French (MAT); health and physical education (MAT); health education (MAT); mathematics (MAT); music (MAT); physical education (MAT); physical science (MAT); social studies (MAT); Spanish (MAT); teacher of English as a second language (MAT). *Degree requirements:* For master's, comprehensive exam, thesis or alternative. *Entrance requirements:* For master's, GRE General Test, interview, 2 letters of recommendation. Additional exam requirements/recommendations for international students: Required—TOEFL (minimum score 83 iBT), IELTS (minimum score 6.5). Electronic applications accepted.

Morehead State University, Graduate Programs, College of Education, Department of Middle Grades and Secondary Education, Morehead, KY 40351. Offers business and marketing education (MAT); English/language arts 5-9 (MAT); French (MAT); health P-12 (MAT); mathematics 5-9 (MAT); physical education P-12 (MAT); science 5-9 (MAT); secondary biology (MAT); secondary chemistry (MAT); secondary earth science (MAT); secondary English (MAT); secondary math (MAT); secondary physics (MAT); secondary social studies (MAT); social studies 5-9 (MAT); Spanish (MAT). Part-time and evening/weekend programs available. *Degree requirements:* For master's, portfolio. *Entrance requirements:* For master's, GRE or PRAXIS II content exam, minimum overall undergraduate GPA of 2.5. Additional exam requirements/recommendations for international students: Required—TOEFL (minimum score 500 paper-based). Electronic applications accepted.

Morehead State University, Graduate Programs, College of Science and Technology, Department of Health, Wellness and Human Performance, Morehead, KY 40351. Offers health/physical education (MA). *Accreditation:* NCATE. Part-time and evening/weekend programs available. *Degree requirements:* For master's, comprehensive exam, thesis, oral exam, written core exam. *Entrance requirements:* For master's, GRE General Test or MAT, minimum GPA of 2.5; undergraduate major/minor in health, physical education, or recreation. Additional exam requirements/recommendations for international students: Required—TOEFL (minimum score 500 paper-based). Electronic applications accepted. *Faculty research:* Child growth and performance, instructional strategies, outdoor leadership qualities, exercise science, athletic training.

Morehouse School of Medicine, Master of Public Health Program, Atlanta, GA 30310-1495. Offers epidemiology (MPH); health administration, management and policy (MPH); health education/health promotion (MPH); international health (MPH). *Accreditation:* CEPH. Part-time programs available. *Students:* 37 full-time (27 women), 5 part-time (3 women); includes 33 minority (32 Black or African American, non-Hispanic/Latino; 1 American Indian or Alaska Native, non-Hispanic/Latino). Average age 28. In 2013, 13 master's awarded. *Degree requirements:* For master's, thesis, practicum, public health leadership seminar. *Entrance requirements:* For master's, GRE General Test, writing test, public health or human service experience. Additional exam requirements/recommendations for international students: Required—TOEFL (minimum score 550 paper-based). *Application deadline:* For fall admission, 3/1 for domestic and international students. Application fee: $50. Electronic applications accepted. *Expenses:* Contact institution. *Financial support:* Fellowships, research assistantships with partial tuition reimbursements, teaching assistantships, career-related internships or fieldwork, Federal Work-Study, institutionally sponsored loans, scholarships/grants, and unspecified assistantships available. Support available to part-time students. Financial award application deadline: 5/1; financial award applicants required to submit FAFSA. *Faculty research:* Women's and adolescent health, violence prevention, cancer epidemiology/disparities, substance abuse prevention. *Unit head:* Dr. Stephanie Miles-Richardson, Interim Director, 404-752-1944, Fax: 404-752-1051, E-mail: smiles-richardson@msm.edu. *Application contact:* Brandon Hunter, Director of Admissions, 404-752-1650, Fax: 404-752-1512, E-mail: mphadmissions@msm.edu.
Website: http://www.msm.edu/educationTraining/degreePrograms/mph.aspx.

Mount Mary University, Graduate Division, Program in Dietetics, Milwaukee, WI 53222-4597. Offers administrative dietetics (MS); clinical dietetics (MS); nutrition education (MS). Part-time and evening/weekend programs available. *Faculty:* 3 full-time (all women), 1 part-time/adjunct (0 women). *Students:* 13 full-time (all women), 20 part-time (all women); includes 1 minority (Hispanic/Latino), 1 international. Average age 29. 91 applicants, 18% accepted, 13 enrolled. In 2013, 10 master's awarded. *Degree requirements:* For master's, thesis or alternative. *Entrance requirements:* For master's, minimum GPA of 2.75, completion of ADA and DPD requirements. Additional exam requirements/recommendations for international students: Required—TOEFL (minimum score 80 iBT) or IELTS (minimum score 6.5). *Application deadline:* For fall admission, 8/1 for domestic and international students; for spring admission, 12/1 for domestic and international students. Applications are processed on a rolling basis. Application fee: $45 ($100 for international students). Electronic applications accepted. *Expenses:* Contact institution. *Financial support:* Career-related internships or fieldwork and Federal Work-Study available. Support available to part-time students. Financial award application deadline: 5/1; financial award applicants required to submit FAFSA. *Unit head:* Lisa Stark, Director, 414-258-4810 Ext. 398, E-mail: starkl@mtmary.edu. *Application contact:* Dr. Douglas J. Mickelson, Dean for Graduate Education, 414-256-1252, Fax: 414-256-0167, E-mail: mickelsd@mtmary.edu.
Website: http://www.mtmary.edu/majors-programs/graduate/dietetics/index.html.

New Jersey City University, Graduate Studies and Continuing Education, College of Professional Studies, Department of Health Sciences, Jersey City, NJ 07305-1597. Offers community health education (MS); health administration (MS); school health education (MS). Part-time and evening/weekend programs available. *Faculty:* 5 full-time (all women), 7 part-time/adjunct (2 women). *Students:* 10 full-time (7 women), 58 part-time (50 women); includes 32 minority (15 Black or African American, non-Hispanic/Latino; 7 Asian, non-Hispanic/Latino; 10 Hispanic/Latino), 2 international. Average age 40. In 2013, 18 master's awarded. *Degree requirements:* For master's, thesis or alternative, internship. *Entrance requirements:* Additional exam requirements/recommendations for international students: Required—TOEFL (minimum score 61 iBT). *Application deadline:* For fall admission, 8/1 priority date for domestic students; for spring admission, 12/1 for domestic students. Applications are processed on a rolling basis. Application fee: $0. *Expenses: Tuition, area resident:* Part-time $527.90 per credit. Tuition, nonresident: part-time $947.75 per credit. *Financial support:* Career-related internships or fieldwork and unspecified assistantships available. *Unit head:* Dr. Lilliam Rosado, Chairperson, 201-200-3431, E-mail: lrosado@njcu.edu. *Application contact:* Dr. William Bajor, Dean of Graduate Studies, 201-200-3409, Fax: 201-200-3411, E-mail: wbajor@njcu.edu.

New Mexico Highlands University, Graduate Studies, College of Arts and Sciences, Department of Exercise and Sport Sciences, Las Vegas, NM 87701. Offers human performance and sport (MA), including human performance and sport sciences, sports administration, teacher education. Part-time programs available. *Faculty:* 5 full-time (2 women). *Students:* 22 full-time (10 women), 28 part-time (8 women); includes 35 minority (13 Black or African American, non-Hispanic/Latino; 1 American Indian or Alaska Native, non-Hispanic/Latino; 1 Asian, non-Hispanic/Latino; 19 Hispanic/Latino; 1 Two or more races, non-Hispanic/Latino), 3 international. Average age 31. 18 applicants, 83% accepted, 13 enrolled. In 2013, 22 master's awarded. *Degree requirements:* For master's, comprehensive exam, thesis or alternative. *Entrance requirements:* For master's, minimum undergraduate GPA of 3.0. Additional exam requirements/recommendations for international students: Required—TOEFL (minimum score 540 paper-based). *Application deadline:* For fall admission, 8/1 priority date for domestic students. Applications are processed on a rolling basis. Application fee: $15. *Expenses:* Tuition, state resident: full-time $4278; part-time $178 per credit hour. Tuition, nonresident: full-time $6716; part-time $281 per credit hour. One-time fee: $15. *Financial support:* Career-related internships or fieldwork, Federal Work-Study, institutionally sponsored loans, scholarships/grants, tuition waivers (partial), and unspecified assistantships available. Support available to part-time students. Financial award application deadline: 3/1; financial award applicants required to submit FAFSA. *Faculty research:* Child obesity and physical inactivity, body composition and fitness assessment, motor development, sport marketing, sport finance. *Unit head:* Dr. Yongseek Kim, Department Head, 505-454-3490, E-mail: ykim@nmhu.edu. *Application contact:* Diane Trujillo, Administrative Assistant, Graduate Studies, 505-454-3266, Fax: 505-426-2117, E-mail: dtrujillo@nmhu.edu.

New Mexico State University, Graduate School, College of Health and Social Services, Department of Public Health Sciences, Las Cruces, NM 88003-8001. Offers community health education (MPH); health management, administration and policy (MPH). Part-time programs available. Postbaccalaureate distance learning degree programs offered (minimal on-campus study). *Faculty:* 11 full-time (6 women), 2 part-time/adjunct (1 woman). *Students:* 32 full-time (30 women), 28 part-time (21 women); includes 24 minority (3 Black or African American, non-Hispanic/Latino; 4 American Indian or Alaska Native, non-Hispanic/Latino; 2 Asian, non-Hispanic/Latino; 14 Hispanic/Latino; 1 Two or more races, non-Hispanic/Latino), 1 international. Average age 34. 37 applicants, 68% accepted, 18 enrolled. In 2013, 25 master's awarded. *Degree requirements:* For master's, thesis optional. *Entrance requirements:* For master's, GRE. Additional exam requirements/recommendations for international students: Required—TOEFL (minimum score 550 paper-based; 79 iBT), IELTS (minimum score 6.5). *Application deadline:* For fall admission, 2/15 for domestic and international students. Application fee: $40 ($50 for international students). Electronic applications accepted. *Expenses:* Tuition, state resident: full-time $5398; part-time $224.90 per credit. Tuition, nonresident: full-time $18,821; part-time $784.20 per credit. *Required fees:* $1310; $54.60 per credit. *Financial support:* In 2013–14, 19 students received support, including 8 teaching assistantships (averaging $8,131 per year); career-related internships or fieldwork, Federal Work-Study, health care benefits, and unspecified assistantships also available. Financial award application deadline: 4/1. *Faculty research:* Community health education, health issues of U.S.-Mexico border, health policy and management, victims of violence, environmental and occupational health issues. *Total annual research expenditures:* $79,183. *Unit head:* Dr. Mark J. Kittleson, Head, 575-646-4300, Fax: 575-646-4343, E-mail: kittle@nmsu.edu. *Application contact:* Dr. James Robinson, III, Graduate Coordinator, 575-646-7431, E-mail: jrobin3@nmsu.edu.
Website: http://publichealth.nmsu.edu.

New York Medical College, School of Health Sciences and Practice, Department of Epidemiology and Community Health, Graduate Certificate Program in Health Education, Valhalla, NY 10595-1691. Offers Graduate Certificate. Part-time and evening/weekend programs available. Postbaccalaureate distance learning degree programs offered (no on-campus study). *Students:* Average age 32. 9 applicants. *Entrance requirements:* Additional exam requirements/recommendations for international students: Required—TOEFL (minimum score 637 paper-based; 110 iBT), IELTS (minimum score 7). *Application deadline:* For fall admission, 8/1 for domestic students; for spring admission, 12/1 for domestic students. Applications are processed on a rolling basis. Application fee: $50 ($100 for international students). Electronic applications accepted. *Expenses: Tuition:* Full-time $49,170; part-time $910 per credit. Tuition and fees vary according to program. *Unit head:* Dr. Chia-Ching Chen, Director, 914-594-3379, E-mail: chiaching_chen@nymc.edu. *Application contact:* Pamela Suett, Director of Recruitment, 914-594-4510, Fax: 914-594-4292, E-mail: shsp_admissions@nymc.edu.
Website: http://www.nymc.edu/Academics/SchoolOfHealthSciencesAndPractice/Programs/GraduateCertificateInHealthEducation/index.html.

North Carolina Agricultural and Technical State University, School of Graduate Studies, School of Education, Department of Human Performance and Leisure Studies, Greensboro, NC 27411. Offers physical education (MAT, MS). *Accreditation:* NCATE. Part-time and evening/weekend programs available. *Degree requirements:* For master's, comprehensive exam, thesis or alternative, qualifying exam. *Entrance requirements:* For master's, GRE General Test or MAT.

Northeastern State University, College of Education, Department of Health and Kinesiology, Tahlequah, OK 74464-2399. Offers MS. Part-time and evening/weekend programs available. *Faculty:* 17 full-time (12 women), 7 part-time/adjunct (2 women). *Students:* 11 full-time (4 women), 22 part-time (7 women); includes 13 minority (9 American Indian or Alaska Native, non-Hispanic/Latino; 1 Hispanic/Latino; 3 Two or more races, non-Hispanic/Latino), 4 international. Average age 27. In 2013, 15 master's awarded. *Entrance requirements:* For master's, MAT or GRE, minimum GPA of 2.5. Additional exam requirements/recommendations for international students: Required—TOEFL. *Application deadline:* For fall admission, 6/1 for domestic and international

students; for winter admission, 11/1 for domestic and international students; for spring admission, 3/1 for domestic students, 2/1 for international students. Applications are processed on a rolling basis. Application fee: $25. Electronic applications accepted. *Expenses:* Tuition, state resident: full-time $3029; part-time $168.25 per credit hour. Tuition, nonresident: full-time $7709; part-time $428.25 per credit hour. *Required fees:* $35.90 per credit hour. *Unit head:* Dr. Mark Giese, Chair, 918-456-5511 Ext. 3950. *Application contact:* Margie Railey, Administrative Assistant, 918-456-5511 Ext. 2093, Fax: 918-458-2061, E-mail: railey@nsouk.edu.
Website: http://academics.nsuok.edu/education/DegreePrograms/GraduatePrograms/HealthandKinesiology.aspx.

Northwestern State University of Louisiana, Graduate Studies and Research, Department of Health and Human Performance, Natchitoches, LA 71497. Offers MS. *Degree requirements:* For master's, comprehensive exam, thesis or alternative. *Entrance requirements:* For master's, GRE General Test, minimum undergraduate GPA of 2.5. Additional exam requirements/recommendations for international students: Required—TOEFL. Electronic applications accepted.

Northwest Missouri State University, Graduate School, College of Education and Human Services, Department of Health and Human Services, Maryville, MO 64468-6001. Offers applied health science (MS); health and physical education (MS Ed); recreation (MS). *Accreditation:* NCATE. Part-time programs available. *Degree requirements:* For master's, comprehensive exam. *Entrance requirements:* For master's, GRE General Test, minimum undergraduate GPA of 2.75, teaching certificate, writing sample. Additional exam requirements/recommendations for international students: Required—TOEFL (minimum score 550 paper-based).

Oklahoma State University, College of Education, School of Applied Health and Educational Psychology, Stillwater, OK 74078. Offers applied behavioral studies (Ed D); applied health and educational psychology (MS, PhD, Ed S). *Accreditation:* APA (one or more programs are accredited). Part-time programs available. *Faculty:* 40 full-time (21 women), 17 part-time/adjunct (10 women). *Students:* 172 full-time (121 women), 187 part-time (123 women); includes 88 minority (19 Black or African American, non-Hispanic/Latino; 13 American Indian or Alaska Native, non-Hispanic/Latino; 6 Asian, non-Hispanic/Latino; 25 Hispanic/Latino; 25 Two or more races, non-Hispanic/Latino), 10 international. Average age 32. 303 applicants, 31% accepted, 75 enrolled. In 2013, 56 master's, 31 doctorates awarded. *Degree requirements:* For master's, thesis (for some programs); for doctorate, comprehensive exam, thesis/dissertation. *Entrance requirements:* For master's and doctorate, GRE or GMAT. Additional exam requirements/recommendations for international students: Required—TOEFL (minimum score 550 paper-based; 79 iBT). *Application deadline:* For fall admission, 3/1 priority date for international students; for spring admission, 8/1 priority date for international students. Applications are processed on a rolling basis. Application fee: $40 ($75 for international students). Electronic applications accepted. *Expenses:* Tuition, state resident: full-time $4272; part-time $178 per credit hour. Tuition, nonresident: full-time $17,472; part-time $709 per credit hour. *Required fees:* $2413.20; $100.55 per credit hour. One-time fee: $50 full-time. Part-time tuition and fees vary according to course load and campus/location. *Financial support:* In 2013–14, 26 research assistantships (averaging $9,164 per year), 58 teaching assistantships (averaging $8,917 per year) were awarded; career-related internships or fieldwork, Federal Work-Study, scholarships/grants, health care benefits, tuition waivers (partial), and unspecified assistantships also available. Support available to part-time students. Financial award application deadline: 3/1; financial award applicants required to submit FAFSA. *Unit head:* Dr. John Romans, Interim Head, 405-744-6040, Fax: 405-744-6779, E-mail: steve.harrist@okstate.edu.
Website: http://education.okstate.edu/sahep.

Penn State Harrisburg, Graduate School, School of Behavioral Sciences and Education, Middletown, PA 17057-4898. Offers applied behavior analysis (MA); applied clinical psychology (MA); applied psychological research (MA); community psychology and social change (MA); health education (M Ed); literacy education (M Ed); teaching and curriculum (M Ed, Certificate); training and development (M Ed). Part-time and evening/weekend programs available. *Financial support:* Career-related internships or fieldwork available. *Unit head:* Dr. Mukund S. Kulkarni, Chancellor, 717-948-6105, Fax: 717-948-6452, E-mail: msk5@psu.edu. *Application contact:* Robert W. Coffman, Jr., Director of Enrollment Management, Admissions, 717-948-6250, Fax: 717-948-6325, E-mail: ric1@psu.edu.
Website: http://harrisburg.psu.edu/behavioral-sciences-and-education/.

Plymouth State University, College of Graduate Studies, Graduate Studies in Education, Program in Health Education, Plymouth, NH 03264-1595. Offers M Ed. Part-time and evening/weekend programs available. *Degree requirements:* For master's, PRAXIS. *Entrance requirements:* For master's, MAT, minimum GPA of 3.0.

Portland State University, Graduate Studies, College of Urban and Public Affairs, School of Community Health, Portland, OR 97207-0751. Offers aging (Certificate); health education (MA, MS); health education and health promotion (MPH); health studies (MPA, MPH), including health administration. MPH offered jointly with Oregon Health & Science University. *Accreditation:* CEPH. Part-time programs available. *Faculty:* 21 full-time (16 women), 28 part-time/adjunct (13 women). *Students:* 39 full-time (33 women), 28 part-time (27 women); includes 13 minority (2 Black or African American, non-Hispanic/Latino; 1 American Indian or Alaska Native, non-Hispanic/Latino; 2 Asian, non-Hispanic/Latino; 4 Hispanic/Latino; 4 Two or more races, non-Hispanic/Latino), 3 international. Average age 30. 127 applicants, 40% accepted, 45 enrolled. In 2013, 45 master's awarded. *Degree requirements:* For master's, oral and written exams. *Entrance requirements:* For master's, GRE General Test, 3 letters of recommendation, minimum GPA of 3.0. Additional exam requirements/recommendations for international students: Required—TOEFL (minimum score 550 paper-based). *Application deadline:* For fall admission, 2/1 for domestic and international students. Application fee: $50. *Expenses:* Tuition, state resident: full-time $9207; part-time $341 per credit. Tuition, nonresident: full-time $14,391; part-time $533 per credit. *Required fees:* $1263; $22 per credit. $98 per quarter. One-time fee: $150. Tuition and fees vary according to program. *Financial support:* In 2013–14, 7 research assistantships with full and partial tuition reimbursements (averaging $5,695 per year), 1 teaching assistantship with full tuition reimbursement (averaging $3,186 per year) were awarded; career-related internships or fieldwork, Federal Work-Study, scholarships/grants, and unspecified assistantships also available. Support available to part-time students. Financial award application deadline: 3/1; financial award applicants required to submit FAFSA. *Total annual research expenditures:* $1.2 million. *Unit head:* Dr. Carlos J. Crespo, Director, 503-725-5120, Fax: 503-725-5100. *Application contact:* Elizabeth Bull, Assistant to the Director, 503-725-4592, Fax: 503-725-5100, E-mail: bulle@pdx.edu.
Website: http://www.healthed.pdx.edu/.

Prairie View A&M University, College of Education, Department of Health and Human Performance, Prairie View, TX 77446-0519. Offers health education (M Ed, MS); physical education (M Ed, MS). *Accreditation:* NCATE. Part-time and evening/weekend programs available. *Faculty:* 1 (woman) full-time, 2 part-time/adjunct (0 women). *Students:* 18 full-time (10 women), 14 part-time (7 women); includes 27 minority (24 Black or African American, non-Hispanic/Latino; 3 Hispanic/Latino), 1 international.

Average age 31. 36 applicants, 100% accepted. In 2013, 12 master's awarded. *Entrance requirements:* For master's, GRE General Test. Additional exam requirements/recommendations for international students: Required—TOEFL. *Application deadline:* For fall admission, 7/1 priority date for domestic students, 7/1 for international students; for spring admission, 11/1 for domestic and international students. Applications are processed on a rolling basis. Application fee: $50. *Expenses:* Tuition, state resident: full-time $3776; part-time $209.77 per credit hour. Tuition, nonresident: full-time $10,183; part-time $565.77 per credit hour. *Required fees:* $2037; $446.50 per credit hour. *Financial support:* In 2013–14, 8 fellowships with tuition reimbursements (averaging $1,200 per year), 10 research assistantships with tuition reimbursements (averaging $15,000 per year) were awarded; teaching assistantships with tuition reimbursements, career-related internships or fieldwork, Federal Work-Study, and institutionally sponsored loans also available. Support available to part-time students. Financial award application deadline: 4/1. *Unit head:* Dr. Patricia Hoffman-Miller, Interim Department Head, 936-261-3530, Fax: 936-261-3617, E-mail: phmiller@pvamu.edu. *Application contact:* Dr. William H. Parker, Dean of Graduate School, 936-261-3500, Fax: 936-261-3529, E-mail: whparker@pvamu.edu.

Purdue University, Graduate School, College of Health and Human Sciences, Department of Health and Kinesiology, West Lafayette, IN 47907. Offers athletic training education administration (MS, PhD); biomechanics (MS, PhD); exercise physiology (MS, PhD); health education (MS, PhD); history/philosophy of sport (MS, PhD); motor control and development (MS, PhD); physical education pedagogy (PhD); physical education teacher education (MS); recreation and sport management (MS, PhD); sport and exercise psychology (MS, PhD). Part-time programs available. *Faculty:* 16 full-time (8 women), 20 part-time/adjunct (3 women). *Students:* 43 full-time (29 women), 21 part-time (11 women); includes 6 minority (2 Black or African American, non-Hispanic/Latino; 1 American Indian or Alaska Native, non-Hispanic/Latino; 1 Asian, non-Hispanic/Latino; 2 Two or more races, non-Hispanic/Latino), 12 international. Average age 28. 103 applicants, 32% accepted, 16 enrolled. In 2013, 15 master's, 8 doctorates awarded. *Degree requirements:* For master's, thesis optional; for doctorate, comprehensive exam, thesis/dissertation, qualifying examination, preliminary examination. *Entrance requirements:* For master's, GRE General Test (minimum score 1000 combined verbal and quantitative), minimum undergraduate GPA of 3.0 or equivalent; for doctorate, GRE General Test (minimum score 1100 combined verbal and quantitative), minimum undergraduate GPA of 3.0 or equivalent; master's degree with minimum GPA of 3.25 (recommended). Additional exam requirements/recommendations for international students: Required—TOEFL (minimum score 77 iBT); Recommended—TWE. *Application deadline:* For fall admission, 4/30 for domestic and international students; for spring admission, 10/15 for domestic and international students. Applications are processed on a rolling basis. Application fee: $60 ($75 for international students). Electronic applications accepted. *Financial support:* Fellowships with partial tuition reimbursements, research assistantships with partial tuition reimbursements, teaching assistantships with partial tuition reimbursements, and Federal Work-Study available. Support available to part-time students. Financial award applicants required to submit FAFSA. *Faculty research:* Wellness, motivation, teaching effectiveness, learning and development. *Unit head:* Dr. Timothy P. Gavin, Head of the Graduate Program, 765-494-3178, Fax: 765-494-1239, E-mail: gavin1@purdue.edu. *Application contact:* Lisa Duncan, Graduate Contact, 765-494-3162, E-mail: llduncan@purdue.edu.
Website: http://www.purdue.edu/hhs/hk/.

Purdue University, Graduate School, College of Health and Human Sciences, Department of Nutrition Science, West Lafayette, IN 47907. Offers animal health (MS, PhD); biochemical and molecular nutrition (MS, PhD); growth and development (MS, PhD); human and clinical nutrition (MS, PhD); public health and education (MS, PhD). *Faculty:* 22 full-time (14 women), 10 part-time/adjunct (all women). *Students:* 44 full-time (37 women), 2 part-time (both women); includes 5 minority (2 Black or African American, non-Hispanic/Latino; 1 Asian, non-Hispanic/Latino; 1 Hispanic/Latino; 1 Two or more races, non-Hispanic/Latino), 20 international. Average age 27. 78 applicants, 21% accepted, 10 enrolled. In 2013, 2 master's, 4 doctorates awarded. *Degree requirements:* For master's, thesis; for doctorate, thesis/dissertation. *Entrance requirements:* For master's and doctorate, GRE General Test (minimum scores in verbal and quantitative areas of 1000 or 300 on new scoring), minimum undergraduate GPA of 3.0 or equivalent. Additional exam requirements/recommendations for international students: Required—TOEFL (minimum score 600 paper-based; 77 iBT). *Application deadline:* For fall admission, 1/10 for domestic and international students. Applications are processed on a rolling basis. Application fee: $60 ($75 for international students). Electronic applications accepted. *Financial support:* Fellowships, research assistantships, and teaching assistantships available. Support available to part-time students. Financial award applicants required to submit FAFSA. *Faculty research:* Nutrient requirements, nutrient metabolism, nutrition and disease prevention. *Unit head:* Dr. Connie M. Weaver, Head, 765-494-8237, Fax: 765-494-0674, E-mail: weavercm@purdue.edu. *Application contact:* James C. Smith, Chair of the Graduate Committee, 765-494-0302, E-mail: fleet@purdue.edu.
Website: http://www.cfs.purdue.edu/fn/.

Rhode Island College, School of Graduate Studies, Feinstein School of Education and Human Development, Department of Health and Physical Education, Providence, RI 02908-1991. Offers health education (M Ed); physical education (CGS). *Accreditation:* NCATE. Part-time and evening/weekend programs available. *Faculty:* 2 full-time (1 woman), 1 part-time/adjunct (0 women). *Students:* 9 part-time (all women); includes 1 minority (Native Hawaiian or other Pacific Islander, non-Hispanic/Latino). Average age 42. In 2013, 2 master's awarded. *Degree requirements:* For master's, comprehensive assessment. *Entrance requirements:* For master's, GRE General Test or MAT, undergraduate transcripts; minimum undergraduate GPA of 3.0; 3 letters of recommendation; for CGS, GRE or MAT (for most programs), undergraduate transcripts; minimum undergraduate GPA of 3.0; 3 letters of recommendation. Additional exam requirements/recommendations for international students: Recommended—TOEFL (minimum score 550 paper-based; 79 iBT). *Application deadline:* For fall admission, 3/1 for domestic students; for spring admission, 11/1 for domestic students. Applications are processed on a rolling basis. Application fee: $50. *Expenses:* Tuition, state resident: full-time $8928; part-time $372 per credit hour. Tuition, nonresident: full-time $17,376; part-time $724 per credit hour. *Required fees:* $602; $22 per credit. $72 per term. *Financial support:* Teaching assistantships with full tuition reimbursements, Federal Work-Study, scholarships/grants, health care benefits, and unspecified assistantships available. Support available to part-time students. Financial award application deadline: 5/15; financial award applicants required to submit FAFSA. *Unit head:* Dr. Robin Auld, Chair, 401-456-8046. *Application contact:* Graduate Studies, 401-456-8700.
Website: http://www.ric.edu/healthPhysicalEducation/.

Rosalind Franklin University of Medicine and Science, College of Health Professions, Department of Nutrition, North Chicago, IL 60064-3095. Offers clinical nutrition (MS); nutrition education (MS). Part-time and evening/weekend programs available. Postbaccalaureate distance learning degree programs offered (no on-campus study). *Degree requirements:* For master's, thesis optional, portfolio. *Entrance requirements:* For master's, minimum GPA of 2.75, registered dietitian (RD), professional certificate or license. Additional exam requirements/recommendations for

international students: Required—TOEFL. *Expenses:* Contact institution. *Faculty research:* Nutrition education, distance learning, computer-based graduate education, childhood obesity, nutrition medical education.

Rutgers, The State University of New Jersey, Newark, School of Health Related Professions, Department of Interdisciplinary Studies, Program in Health Sciences, Newark, NJ 07102. Offers health sciences (MS, PhD). Part-time and evening/weekend programs available. Postbaccalaureate distance learning degree programs offered (no on-campus study). *Degree requirements:* For doctorate, thesis/dissertation. *Entrance requirements:* For master's, BS, 2 reference letters, statement of career goals, curriculum vitae; for doctorate, GRE, interview, writing sample, 3 reference letters, curriculum vitae. Additional exam requirements/recommendations for international students: Required—TOEFL. Electronic applications accepted.

Rutgers, The State University of New Jersey, New Brunswick, School of Public Health, Piscataway, NJ 08854. Offers biostatistics (MPH, MS, Dr PH, PhD); clinical epidemiology (Certificate); environmental and occupational health (MPH, Dr PH, PhD, Certificate); epidemiology (MPH, Dr PH, PhD); general public health (Certificate); health education and behavioral science (MPH, Dr PH, PhD); health systems and policy (MPH, PhD); public health preparedness (Certificate); DO/MPH; JD/MPH; MD/MPH; MPH/MBA; MPH/MSPA; MS/MPH; Psy D/MPH. *Accreditation:* CEPH. Part-time and evening/weekend programs available. *Degree requirements:* For master's, thesis, internship; for doctorate, comprehensive exam, thesis/dissertation. *Entrance requirements:* For master's, GRE General Test; for doctorate, GRE General Test, MPH (Dr PH); MA, MPH, or MS (PhD). Additional exam requirements/recommendations for international students: Required—TOEFL. Electronic applications accepted.

Sage Graduate School, Esteves School of Education, Program in Community Health Education, Troy, NY 12180-4115. Offers MS. Part-time and evening/weekend programs available. *Faculty:* 10 full-time (6 women), 2 part-time/adjunct (both women). *Students:* 1 (woman) full-time, 4 part-time (all women); includes 2 minority (1 Black or African American, non-Hispanic/Latino; 1 Two or more races, non-Hispanic/Latino). Average age 32. 2 applicants. In 2013, 9 master's awarded. *Degree requirements:* For master's, thesis optional. *Entrance requirements:* For master's, minimum GPA of 2.75, resume, 2 letters of recommendation, interview, assessment of writing skills. Additional exam requirements/recommendations for international students: Required—TOEFL (minimum score 550 paper-based). *Application deadline:* Applications are processed on a rolling basis. Application fee: $40. *Expenses: Tuition:* Full-time $11,880; part-time $660 per credit hour. *Financial support:* Federal Work-Study, scholarships/grants, tuition waivers (partial), and unspecified assistantships available. Support available to part-time students. Financial award application deadline: 3/1; financial award applicants required to submit FAFSA. *Unit head:* Dr. Lori Quigley, Dean, Esteves School of Education, 518-244-2326, Fax: 518-244-4571, E-mail: l.quigley@sage.edu. *Application contact:* Dr. Nancy DeKorp, Director, 518-244-2496, Fax: 518-244-4571, E-mail: dekorn@sage.edu.

Sage Graduate School, Esteves School of Education, Program in School Health Education, Troy, NY 12180-4115. Offers MS. *Accreditation:* NCATE. Part-time and evening/weekend programs available. *Faculty:* 10 full-time (5 women), 2 part-time/adjunct (1 woman). *Students:* 4 full-time (1 woman), 17 part-time (6 women); includes 1 minority (Asian, non-Hispanic/Latino). Average age 27. 9 applicants, 44% accepted, 4 enrolled. In 2013, 21 master's awarded. *Degree requirements:* For master's, thesis optional. *Entrance requirements:* For master's, minimum GPA of 2.75, resume, 2 letters of recommendation, interview, assessment of writing skills. Additional exam requirements/recommendations for international students: Required—TOEFL (minimum score 550 paper-based). *Application deadline:* Applications are processed on a rolling basis. Application fee: $40. *Expenses: Tuition:* Full-time $11,880; part-time $660 per credit hour. *Financial support:* Fellowships, research assistantships, Federal Work-Study, scholarships/grants, and unspecified assistantships available. Support available to part-time students. Financial award application deadline: 3/1; financial award applicants required to submit FAFSA. *Faculty research:* Policy development in health education and health care. *Unit head:* Dr. Lori Quigley, Dean, Esteves School of Education, 518-244-2326, Fax: 518-244-4571, E-mail: l.quigley@sage.edu. *Application contact:* Dr. John J. Pelizza, Director, 518-244-2051, Fax: 518-244-2334, E-mail: pelizj@sage.edu.

Saint Francis University, Department of Physician Assistant Sciences, Health Science Program, Loretto, PA 15940-0600. Offers MHS. Part-time and evening/weekend programs available. Postbaccalaureate distance learning degree programs offered (no on-campus study). *Faculty:* 2 full-time (both women), 8 part-time/adjunct (5 women). *Students:* 106 part-time (79 women); includes 40 minority (20 Black or African American, non-Hispanic/Latino; 1 American Indian or Alaska Native, non-Hispanic/Latino; 3 Asian, non-Hispanic/Latino; 13 Hispanic/Latino; 3 Two or more races, non-Hispanic/Latino). Average age 38. 39 applicants, 64% accepted, 25 enrolled. In 2013, 42 master's awarded. *Degree requirements:* For master's, minimum GPA of 2.8. *Entrance requirements:* For master's, undergraduate transcript, letters of reference, minimum QPA of 2.5, resume. Additional exam requirements/recommendations for international students: Recommended—TOEFL (minimum score 80 iBT). *Application deadline:* For fall admission, 7/19 for domestic and international students; for spring admission, 11/15 for domestic and international students; for summer admission, 3/22 for domestic and international students. Applications are processed on a rolling basis. Application fee: $50. Electronic applications accepted. *Expenses:* Contact institution. *Financial support:* Available to part-time students. Applicants required to submit FAFSA. *Faculty research:* Distance education, health sciences, medical sciences, communication, adult education. *Unit head:* Deborah E. Budash, Director, 814-472-3919, Fax: 814-472-3066, E-mail: dbudash@francis.edu. *Application contact:* Jean A. Kline, Administrative Assistant, 814-472-3357, Fax: 814-472-3066, E-mail: jkline@francis.edu.
Website: http://onlinemhsc.francis.edu.

Saint Joseph's College of Maine, Master of Science in Education Program, Standish, ME 04084. Offers adult education and training (MS Ed); Catholic school leadership (MS Ed); health care educator (MS Ed); school educator (MS Ed). Program available by correspondence. Part-time programs available. Postbaccalaureate distance learning degree programs offered (minimal on-campus study). Electronic applications accepted.

Saint Joseph's University, College of Arts and Sciences, Department of Health Services, Philadelphia, PA 19131-1395. Offers health administration (MS, Post-Master's Certificate); health care ethics (Post-Master's Certificate); health education (MS, Post-Master's Certificate); health informatics (Post-Master's Certificate); healthcare ethics (MS); long-term care administration (MS); nurse anesthesia (MS); school nurse certification (MS). Part-time and evening/weekend programs available. *Faculty:* 5 full-time (1 woman), 16 part-time/adjunct (6 women). *Students:* 46 full-time (25 women), 431 part-time (315 women); includes 168 minority (120 Black or African American, non-Hispanic/Latino; 29 Asian, non-Hispanic/Latino; 15 Hispanic/Latino; 2 Native Hawaiian or other Pacific Islander, non-Hispanic/Latino; 2 Two or more races, non-Hispanic/Latino), 14 international. Average age 34. 234 applicants, 74% accepted, 135 enrolled. In 2013, 83 master's awarded. *Entrance requirements:* For master's, GRE (if GPA less than 3.0), 2 letters of recommendation, resume, personal statement, official transcripts. Additional exam requirements/recommendations for international students: Required—TOEFL (minimum score 550 paper-based; 80 iBT), IELTS (minimum score 6.5). *Application deadline:* For fall admission, 7/15 priority date for domestic students, 4/15 for international students; for winter admission, 1/15 for international students; for spring admission, 11/15 priority date for domestic students, 10/15 for international students. Applications are processed on a rolling basis. Application fee: $35. Electronic applications accepted. *Expenses: Tuition:* Part-time $786 per credit hour. Tuition and fees vary according to degree level and program. *Financial support:* Career-related internships or fieldwork and unspecified assistantships available. Financial award applicants required to submit FAFSA. *Unit head:* Nakia Henderson, Director, 610-660-3131, E-mail: gradstudies@sju.edu. *Application contact:* Elisabeth Woodward, Director of Marketing and Admissions, Graduate Arts and Sciences, 610-660-3131, Fax: 610-660-3230, E-mail: gradstudies@sju.edu.
Website: http://sju.edu/majors-programs/graduate-arts-sciences/masters/health-administration-ms.

San Francisco State University, Division of Graduate Studies, College of Health and Social Sciences, Human Sexuality Studies Program, San Francisco, CA 94132-1722. Offers MA. *Unit head:* Dr. Ed McCaughan, Chair, 415-405-3570, E-mail: sxsdept@sfsu.edu. *Application contact:* Dr. Jessica Fields, Graduate Coordinator, 415-405-0589, E-mail: jfields@sfsu.edu.
Website: http://sxs.sfsu.edu/.

San Jose State University, Graduate Studies and Research, College of Applied Sciences and Arts, Department of Health Science, San Jose, CA 95192-0001. Offers applied social gerontology (Certificate); community health education (MPH). *Accreditation:* CEPH (one or more programs are accredited). Postbaccalaureate distance learning degree programs offered. *Entrance requirements:* For master's, GRE General Test. Electronic applications accepted. *Faculty research:* Behavioral science in occupational and health care settings, epidemiology in health care settings.

Simmons College, School of Nursing and Health Sciences, Boston, MA 02115. Offers didactic dietetics (Certificate); dietetic internship (Certificate); health professions education (CAGS); nursing (MS); nursing practice (DNP); nutrition and health promotion (MS); physical therapy (DPT); sports nutrition (Certificate). Part-time programs available. Postbaccalaureate distance learning degree programs offered (minimal on-campus study). *Students:* 143 full-time (129 women), 347 part-time (329 women); includes 72 minority (31 Black or African American, non-Hispanic/Latino; 17 Asian, non-Hispanic/Latino; 15 Hispanic/Latino; 9 Two or more races, non-Hispanic/Latino), 4 international. 196 applicants, 56% accepted, 88 enrolled. In 2013, 70 master's, 45 doctorates awarded. *Entrance requirements:* For doctorate, GRE. Additional exam requirements/recommendations for international students: Required—TOEFL (minimum score 570 paper-based; 88 iBT). *Application deadline:* For fall admission, 6/1 for international students. Application fee: $50. Electronic applications accepted. *Financial support:* In 2013–14, 33 students received support, including 24 teaching assistantships (averaging $6,000 per year); scholarships/grants and unspecified assistantships also available. *Unit head:* Dr. Judy Beal, Dean, 617-521-2139. *Application contact:* Carmen Fortin, Assistant Dean/Director of Admission, 617-521-2651, Fax: 617-521-3137, E-mail: gshsadm@simmons.edu.
Website: http://www.simmons.edu/snhs/.

South Dakota State University, Graduate School, College of Education and Human Sciences, Department of Health, Physical Education and Recreation, Brookings, SD 57007. Offers MS. Part-time programs available. *Degree requirements:* For master's, thesis, oral and written exams. *Entrance requirements:* Additional exam requirements/recommendations for international students: Required—TOEFL (minimum score 550 paper-based; 71 iBT). *Faculty research:* Effective teaching behaviors in physical education, sports nutrition, muscle/bone interaction, hormonal response to exercise.

Southeastern Louisiana University, College of Nursing and Health Sciences, Department of Kinesiology and Health Studies, Hammond, LA 70402. Offers health and kinesiology (MA), including exercise science, health promotion and exercise science, health studies, kinesiology. *Accreditation:* NCATE. Part-time programs available. *Faculty:* 10 full-time (4 women). *Students:* 26 full-time (13 women), 17 part-time (9 women); includes 10 minority (7 Black or African American, non-Hispanic/Latino; 2 Asian, non-Hispanic/Latino; 1 Hispanic/Latino), 1 international. Average age 28. 38 applicants, 66% accepted, 12 enrolled. In 2013, 21 master's awarded. *Degree requirements:* For master's, comprehensive exam (for some programs), thesis (for some programs). *Entrance requirements:* For master's, GRE General Test (minimum score 800), undergraduate human anatomy and physiology course. Additional exam requirements/recommendations for international students: Required—TOEFL (minimum score 500 paper-based; 61 iBT). *Application deadline:* For fall admission, 7/15 priority date for domestic students, 6/1 priority date for international students; for spring admission, 12/1 priority date for domestic students, 10/1 priority date for international students. Applications are processed on a rolling basis. Application fee: $20 ($30 for international students). Electronic applications accepted. *Expenses:* Tuition, state resident: full-time $5047. Tuition, nonresident: full-time $17,066. *Required fees:* $1213. Tuition and fees vary according to degree level. *Financial support:* In 2013–14, 3 fellowships (averaging $10,800 per year), 4 research assistantships (averaging $8,425 per year), 5 teaching assistantships (averaging $8,540 per year) were awarded; career-related internships or fieldwork, Federal Work-Study, institutionally sponsored loans, scholarships/grants, and unspecified assistantships also available. Support available to part-time students. Financial award application deadline: 5/1; financial award applicants required to submit FAFSA. *Faculty research:* Exercise endocrinology, perceptions of exercise intensity and pain, spirituality and health, alternative health practices, use of podcasting and other technology to promote healthy behaviors. *Unit head:* Dr. Edward Hebert, Department Head, 985-549-2129, Fax: 985-549-5119, E-mail: ehebert@selu.edu. *Application contact:* Sandra Meyers, Graduate Admissions Analyst, 985-549-5620, Fax: 985-549-5632, E-mail: admissions@selu.edu.
Website: http://www.selu.edu/acad_research/depts/kin_hs.

Southern Connecticut State University, School of Graduate Studies, School of Education, Department of Exercise Science, Program in School Health Education, New Haven, CT 06515-1355. Offers MS. *Accreditation:* NCATE. Part-time and evening/weekend programs available. *Entrance requirements:* For master's, interview. Electronic applications accepted.

Southern Illinois University Carbondale, Graduate School, College of Education and Human Services, Department of Health Education and Recreation, Program in Community Health Education, Carbondale, IL 62901-4701. Offers MPH. *Accreditation:* CEPH. *Faculty:* 7 full-time (4 women). *Students:* 38 full-time (28 women), 7 part-time (5 women); includes 17 minority (14 Black or African American, non-Hispanic/Latino; 2 Asian, non-Hispanic/Latino; 1 Hispanic/Latino), 3 international. 42 applicants, 50% accepted, 15 enrolled. In 2013, 13 master's awarded. *Entrance requirements:* Additional exam requirements/recommendations for international students: Required—TOEFL. Application fee: $50. *Unit head:* Dr. Stephen L. Brown, Chair, 618-453-2777, Fax: 618-453-1829, E-mail: slbrown@siu.edu. *Application contact:* Carol Reynolds, Administrative Assistant, 618-453-2415, Fax: 618-453-1829, E-mail: creynolds@siu.edu.

Southern Illinois University Carbondale, Graduate School, College of Education and Human Services, Department of Health Education and Recreation, Program in Health Education, Carbondale, IL 62901-4701. Offers MS Ed, PhD. *Accreditation:* NCATE.

Part-time programs available. *Faculty:* 9 full-time (6 women). *Students:* 14 full-time (11 women), 23 part-time (16 women); includes 9 minority (8 Black or African American, non-Hispanic/Latino; 1 American Indian or Alaska Native, non-Hispanic/Latino), 5 international. Average age 30. 16 applicants, 19% accepted, 2 enrolled. In 2013, 1 master's, 13 doctorates awarded. *Degree requirements:* For master's, thesis; for doctorate, thesis/dissertation. *Entrance requirements:* For master's, MAT, minimum GPA of 2.7; for doctorate, MAT, minimum GPA of 3.25. Additional exam requirements/recommendations for international students: Required—TOEFL. *Application deadline:* For fall admission, 2/15 for domestic students; for spring admission, 9/15 for domestic students. Application fee: $50. *Financial support:* In 2013–14, 33 students received support, including 1 fellowship with full tuition reimbursement available, 10 teaching assistantships with full tuition reimbursements available; research assistantships with full tuition reimbursements available, career-related internships or fieldwork, Federal Work-Study, institutionally sponsored loans, and tuition waivers (full) also available. Support available to part-time students. *Faculty research:* Sexuality education, research design, injury control, program evaluation. *Unit head:* Dr. Stephen Brown, Director of Graduate Studies, 618-453-2777, Fax: 618-453-1829, E-mail: slbrown@siu.edu. *Application contact:* Pam Battaglia, Administrative Assistant, 618-453-2415, Fax: 618-453-1829, E-mail: pbatta@siu.edu.
Website: http://ehs.siu.edu/her/graduate/index.php.

Southern Illinois University Edwardsville, Graduate School, School of Education, Department of Kinesiology and Health Education, Edwardsville, IL 62026. Offers exercise physiology (MS); physical education and sport pedagogy (MS Ed); sport and exercise behavior (MS). *Accreditation:* NCATE. Part-time and evening/weekend programs available. *Faculty:* 12 full-time (7 women). *Students:* 39 full-time (17 women), 60 part-time (30 women); includes 26 minority (16 Black or African American, non-Hispanic/Latino; 1 American Indian or Alaska Native, non-Hispanic/Latino; 3 Asian, non-Hispanic/Latino; 3 Hispanic/Latino; 3 Two or more races, non-Hispanic/Latino), 5 international. 78 applicants, 77% accepted. In 2013, 53 master's awarded. *Degree requirements:* For master's, comprehensive exam (for some programs), thesis (for some programs). *Entrance requirements:* Additional exam requirements/recommendations for international students: Required—TOEFL (minimum score 550 paper-based, 79 iBT), IELTS (minimum score 6.5), Michigan Test of English Language Proficiency or PTE. *Application deadline:* For fall admission, 7/18 for domestic students, 6/1 for international students; for spring admission, 12/12 for domestic students, 10/1 for international students; for summer admission, 4/24 for domestic students, 3/1 for international students. Applications are processed on a rolling basis. Application fee: $30. Electronic applications accepted. *Expenses:* Tuition, state resident: full-time $3551. Tuition, nonresident: full-time $8378. *Financial support:* In 2013–14, 6 research assistantships with full tuition reimbursements (averaging $9,585 per year), 16 teaching assistantships with full tuition reimbursements (averaging $9,585 per year) were awarded; fellowships, institutionally sponsored loans, scholarships/grants, and unspecified assistantships also available. Financial award application deadline: 3/1; financial award applicants required to submit FAFSA. *Unit head:* Dr. Curt Lox, Chair, 618-650-2938, E-mail: clox@siue.edu. *Application contact:* Dr. Erik Kirk, Program Director, 618-650-2718, E-mail: ekirk@siue.edu.
Website: http://www.siue.edu/education/khe.

Springfield College, Graduate Programs, Programs in Physical Education, Springfield, MA 01109-3797. Offers adapted physical education (M Ed, MPE, MS); advanced level coaching (M Ed, MPE, MS); athletic administration (M Ed, MPE, MS); general physical education (PhD, CAGS); health education licensure (MPE, MS); health education licensure program (M Ed); physical education licensure (MPE, MS); physical education licensure program (M Ed); teaching and administration (MS). Part-time programs available. *Faculty:* 33 full-time, 5 part-time/adjunct. *Students:* 52 full-time. 44 applicants, 86% accepted, 26 enrolled. In 2013, 22 master's, 4 doctorates awarded. *Degree requirements:* For master's, comprehensive exam, thesis (for some programs). *Entrance requirements:* For master's and doctorate, GRE General Test. Additional exam requirements/recommendations for international students: Required—TOEFL (minimum score 550 paper-based); Recommended—IELTS (minimum score 6). *Application deadline:* For fall admission, 1/15 priority date for domestic students, 1/15 for international students; for winter admission, 11/1 for domestic and international students; for spring admission, 11/1 for domestic and international students. Applications are processed on a rolling basis. Application fee: $50. Electronic applications accepted. *Expenses:* Tuition: Full-time $13,620; part-time $908 per credit. *Financial support:* Fellowships with partial tuition reimbursements, teaching assistantships with partial tuition reimbursements, career-related internships or fieldwork, Federal Work-Study, institutionally sponsored loans, and unspecified assistantships available. Financial award application deadline: 3/1; financial award applicants required to submit FAFSA. *Unit head:* Dr. Michelle Moosbrugger, Director, 413-748-3486, E-mail: mmoosbrugger@springfieldcollege.edu. *Application contact:* Evelyn Cohen, Associate Director of Graduate Admissions, 413-748-3479, Fax: 413-748-3694, E-mail: ecohen@springfieldcollege.edu.

State University of New York College at Cortland, Graduate Studies, School of Professional Studies, Department of Health Education, Cortland, NY 13045. Offers MS, MS Ed, MST. *Accreditation:* NCATE. Part-time and evening/weekend programs available. *Entrance requirements:* Additional exam requirements/recommendations for international students: Required—TOEFL. *Expenses:* Tuition, state resident: full-time $9870; part-time $411 per credit hour. Tuition, nonresident: full-time $18,350; part-time $765 per credit hour. *Required fees:* $1458; $65 per credit hour.

Teachers College, Columbia University, Graduate Faculty of Education, Department of Health and Behavioral Studies, Program in Health Education, New York, NY 10027-6696. Offers MA, MS, Ed D. *Accreditation:* NCATE. Part-time and evening/weekend programs available. *Faculty:* 8 full-time, 5 part-time/adjunct. *Students:* 20 full-time (19 women), 72 part-time (59 women); includes 49 minority (21 Black or African American, non-Hispanic/Latino; 8 Asian, non-Hispanic/Latino; 15 Hispanic/Latino; 1 Native Hawaiian or other Pacific Islander, non-Hispanic/Latino; 4 Two or more races, non-Hispanic/Latino), 5 international. Average age 37. 34 applicants, 85% accepted, 15 enrolled. In 2013, 15 master's, 16 doctorates awarded. Terminal master's awarded for partial completion of doctoral program. *Degree requirements:* For master's, thesis optional, integrative project; for doctorate, comprehensive exam, thesis/dissertation. *Entrance requirements:* For doctorate, GRE or MAT. *Application deadline:* For fall admission, 1/2 for domestic students; for spring admission, 11/1 for domestic students. Applications are processed on a rolling basis. Application fee: $65. Electronic applications accepted. *Financial support:* Fellowships and research assistantships available. Financial award application deadline: 2/1; financial award applicants required to submit FAFSA. *Faculty research:* Health behavior, disease self-management, and health outcomes in chronic disease; health education in schools and patient-care settings; behavioral epidemiology. *Unit head:* Prof. Barbara Wallace, Program Coordinator, 212-678-3966, E-mail: wallace@tc.columbia.edu. *Application contact:* Elizabeth Puleio, Assistant Director of Admission, 212-678-3730, E-mail: eap2136@tc.columbia.edu.

Temple University, College of Health Professions and Social Work, Department of Public Health, Philadelphia, PA 19122. Offers clinical research and translational medicine (MS); environmental health (MPH); epidemiology (MS); epidemiology and biostatistics (MPH); health policy (PhD); health policy and management (MPH); school health education (Ed M); social and behavioral sciences (MPH, PhD). *Accreditation:* CEPH (one or more programs are accredited). Part-time and evening/weekend programs available. *Faculty:* 27 full-time (18 women). *Students:* 47 full-time (30 women), 45 part-time (37 women); includes 27 minority (9 Black or African American, non-Hispanic/Latino; 10 Asian, non-Hispanic/Latino; 7 Hispanic/Latino; 1 Two or more races, non-Hispanic/Latino), 9 international. 188 applicants, 45% accepted, 29 enrolled. In 2013, 29 master's, 3 doctorates awarded. Terminal master's awarded for partial completion of doctoral program. *Degree requirements:* For master's, thesis (for some programs), capstone project; for doctorate, comprehensive exam, thesis/dissertation. *Entrance requirements:* For master's, GRE General Test (for MS only); DAT, GMAT, MCAT, OAT, PCAT (alternates for MPH, Ed M), minimum undergraduate GPA of 3.0, letters of reference, statement of goals, writing sample, resume, interview (only for MS); for doctorate, GRE General Test, minimum undergraduate GPA of 3.0, 3 letters of reference, statement of goals, writing sample, resume. Additional exam requirements/recommendations for international students: Required—TOEFL (minimum score 550 paper-based; 79 iBT). *Application deadline:* For fall admission, 3/1 for domestic students, 2/1 for international students; for spring admission, 10/15 for domestic students, 8/1 for international students. Applications are processed on a rolling basis. Application fee: $60. Electronic applications accepted. *Financial support:* In 2013–14, 1 fellowship with tuition reimbursement, 4 research assistantships with tuition reimbursements, 8 teaching assistantships with tuition reimbursements were awarded; career-related internships or fieldwork, Federal Work-Study, scholarships/grants, tuition waivers (partial), and unspecified assistantships also available. Financial award application deadline: 1/15. *Faculty research:* Smoking cessation, obesity prevention, tobacco policy, community engagement, health communication. *Total annual research expenditures:* $3.9 million. *Unit head:* Dr. Alice J. Hausman, Chair, 215-204-5112, Fax: 215-204-1854, E-mail: hausman@temple.edu. *Application contact:* Joyce Hankins, 215-204-7213, E-mail: joyce.hankins@temple.edu.
Website: http://chpsw.temple.edu/publichealth/home.

Tennessee Technological University, College of Graduate Studies, College of Education, Department of Exercise Science, Physical Education and Wellness, Cookeville, TN 38505. Offers adapted physical education (MA); elementary/middle school physical education (MA); lifetime wellness (MA); sport management (MA). *Accreditation:* NCATE. Part-time programs available. Postbaccalaureate distance learning degree programs offered (no on-campus study). *Faculty:* 7 full-time (0 women). *Students:* 10 full-time (0 women), 38 part-time (11 women); includes 5 minority (all Black or African American, non-Hispanic/Latino). Average age 27. 38 applicants, 58% accepted, 20 enrolled. In 2013, 23 master's awarded. *Degree requirements:* For master's, comprehensive exam, thesis or alternative. *Entrance requirements:* For master's, MAT or GRE. Additional exam requirements/recommendations for international students: Required—TOEFL (minimum score 527 paper-based; 71 iBT), IELTS (minimum score 5.5), PTE (minimum score 48), or TOEIC (Test of English as an International Communication). *Application deadline:* For fall admission, 8/1 for domestic students, 5/1 for international students; for spring admission, 12/1 for domestic students, 10/1 for international students. Applications are processed on a rolling basis. Application fee: $35 ($40 for international students). Electronic applications accepted. *Expenses:* Tuition, state resident: full-time $9347; part-time $465 per credit hour. Tuition, nonresident: full-time $23,635; part-time $1152 per credit hour. *Financial support:* In 2013–14, fellowships (averaging $8,000 per year), 3 research assistantships (averaging $4,000 per year), 4 teaching assistantships (averaging $4,000 per year) were awarded; career-related internships or fieldwork also available. Financial award application deadline: 4/1. *Unit head:* Dr. John Steven Smith, Interim Chairperson, 931-372-3467, Fax: 931-372-6319, E-mail: jssmith@tntech.edu. *Application contact:* Shelia K. Kendrick, Coordinator of Graduate Studies, 931-372-3808, Fax: 931-372-3497, E-mail: skendrick@tntech.edu.

Texas A&M Health Science Center, Baylor College of Dentistry, Department of Endodontics, Program in Health Professions Education, College Station, TX 77840. Offers MS. Part-time programs available. *Degree requirements:* For master's, thesis. *Entrance requirements:* For master's, GRE General Test, DDS or DMD. Additional exam requirements/recommendations for international students: Required—TOEFL. *Faculty research:* Craniofacial biology, dermatoglyphics, alternative curricula, admissions criteria, competency-based program assessment.

Texas A&M University, College of Education and Human Development, Department of Health and Kinesiology, College Station, TX 77843. Offers athletic training (MS); health education (M Ed, MS, Ed D, PhD); kinesiology (MS, PhD); sport management (MS). Part-time programs available. *Faculty:* 38. *Students:* 206 full-time (113 women), 71 part-time (38 women); includes 81 minority (35 Black or African American, non-Hispanic/Latino; 8 Asian, non-Hispanic/Latino; 33 Hispanic/Latino; 5 Two or more races, non-Hispanic/Latino), 43 international. Average age 29. 167 applicants, 71% accepted, 79 enrolled. In 2013, 68 master's, 16 doctorates awarded. *Degree requirements:* For master's, thesis (for some programs); for doctorate, comprehensive exam, thesis/dissertation. *Entrance requirements:* For master's and doctorate, GRE General Test. Additional exam requirements/recommendations for international students: Required—TOEFL. *Application deadline:* Applications are processed on a rolling basis. Application fee: $50 ($75 for international students). Electronic applications accepted. *Expenses:* Tuition, state resident: full-time $4078; part-time $226.55 per credit hour. Tuition, nonresident: full-time $10,450; part-time $580.55 per credit hour. *Required fees:* $2328; $278.50 per credit hour. $642.45 per semester. *Financial support:* Fellowships with partial tuition reimbursements, research assistantships, teaching assistantships, career-related internships or fieldwork, and institutionally sponsored loans available. Financial award application deadline: 2/15; financial award applicants required to submit FAFSA. *Unit head:* Dr. Richard Kreider, Head, 979-845-1333, Fax: 979-847-8987, E-mail: rkreider@hlkn.tamu.edu. *Application contact:* Christina Escamilla, Senior Academic Advisor I, 979-845-4530, E-mail: cescamil@tamu.edu.
Website: http://hlknweb.tamu.edu/.

Texas A&M University–Commerce, Graduate School, College of Education and Human Services, Department of Health and Human Performance, Commerce, TX 75429-3011. Offers exercise physiology (MS); health and human performance (M Ed); health promotion (MS); health, kinesiology and sports studies (Ed D); motor performance (MS); sport studies (MS). Part-time programs available. *Degree requirements:* For master's, comprehensive exam, thesis (for some programs). *Entrance requirements:* For master's, GRE General Test. Electronic applications accepted. *Expenses:* Tuition, state resident: full-time $3630; part-time $2420 per year. Tuition, nonresident: full-time $9948; part-time $6632.16 per year. *Required fees:* $1006 per year. Tuition and fees vary according to course load. *Faculty research:* Teaching, physical fitness.

Texas A&M University–Kingsville, College of Graduate Studies, College of Education, Department of Health and Kinesiology, Kingsville, TX 78363. Offers MA, MS. Part-time programs available. *Faculty:* 4 full-time (0 women). *Students:* 16 full-time (7 women), 15 part-time (11 women); includes 15 minority (1 Black or African American, non-Hispanic/Latino; 12 Hispanic/Latino; 2 Two or more races, non-Hispanic/Latino), 4 international.

Average age 26. 16 applicants, 94% accepted, 11 enrolled. In 2013, 7 master's awarded. *Degree requirements:* For master's, comprehensive exam, thesis or alternative. *Entrance requirements:* For master's, GRE General Test, minimum GPA of 3.0. *Application deadline:* For fall admission, 6/1 for domestic students; for spring admission, 11/15 for domestic students. Applications are processed on a rolling basis. Application fee: $35 ($50 for international students). *Financial support:* Teaching assistantships, Federal Work-Study, institutionally sponsored loans, and tuition waivers (partial) available. Financial award application deadline: 5/15. *Faculty research:* Body composition, electromyography. *Unit head:* Dr. Mike Daniel, Head, 361-593-2301, E-mail: m-daniel@tamuk.edu. *Application contact:* Dr. Alberto M. Olivares, Dean, College of Graduate Studies, 361-593-2808, Fax: 361-593-3412, E-mail: a-olivares@tamuk.edu.

Texas Southern University, College of Education, Department of Health and Kinesiology, Houston, TX 77004-4584. Offers health education (MS); human performance (MS). Part-time and evening/weekend programs available. *Faculty:* 3 full-time (0 women), 2 part-time/adjunct (1 woman). *Students:* 32 full-time (15 women), 19 part-time (12 women); includes 49 minority (45 Black or African American, non-Hispanic/Latino; 4 Hispanic/Latino), 1 international. Average age 30. 31 applicants, 55% accepted, 12 enrolled. In 2013, 22 master's awarded. *Degree requirements:* For master's, comprehensive exam, thesis optional. *Entrance requirements:* For master's, GRE General Test, minimum GPA of 2.5. Additional exam requirements/recommendations for international students: Required—TOEFL. *Application deadline:* For fall admission, 7/1 for domestic and international students; for spring admission, 11/1 for domestic and international students. Applications are processed on a rolling basis. Application fee: $50 ($75 for international students). Electronic applications accepted. *Financial support:* Teaching assistantships, scholarships/grants, and unspecified assistantships available. Support available to part-time students. Financial award application deadline: 5/1. *Unit head:* Dr. Dwalah Fisher, Interim Chair, 713-313-7272, E-mail: fisher_dl@tsu.edu. *Application contact:* Dr. Gregory Maddox, Interim Dean of the Graduate School, 713-313-7011 Ext. 4410, Fax: 713-639-1876, E-mail: maddox_gh@tsu.edu.
Website: http://www.tsu.edu/academics/colleges__schools/College_of_Education/Departments/default.php.

Texas State University, Graduate School, College of Education, Department of Health and Human Performance, Program in Health Education, San Marcos, TX 78666. Offers M Ed. Part-time and evening/weekend programs available. *Faculty:* 3 full-time (1 woman). *Students:* 19 full-time (17 women), 8 part-time (6 women); includes 13 minority (8 Black or African American, non-Hispanic/Latino; 5 Hispanic/Latino), 2 international. Average age 28. 28 applicants, 71% accepted, 13 enrolled. In 2013, 11 master's awarded. *Degree requirements:* For master's, comprehensive exam, thesis optional. *Entrance requirements:* For master's, GRE General Test, minimum GPA of 2.75 in last 60 hours of course work, 18 hours of health education background courses. Additional exam requirements/recommendations for international students: Required—TOEFL (minimum score 550 paper-based; 78 iBT). *Application deadline:* For fall admission, 6/15 priority date for domestic students, 6/1 for international students; for spring admission, 10/15 priority date for domestic students, 10/1 for international students. Applications are processed on a rolling basis. Application fee: $40 ($90 for international students). Electronic applications accepted. *Expenses:* Tuition, state resident: full-time $6663; part-time $278 per credit hour. Tuition, nonresident: full-time $15,159; part-time $632 per credit hour. *Required fees:* $1872; $54 per credit hour. $306 per term. Tuition and fees vary according to course load. *Financial support:* In 2013–14, 18 students received support, including 5 research assistantships (averaging $11,430 per year), 4 teaching assistantships (averaging $9,870 per year); career-related internships or fieldwork, Federal Work-Study, and institutionally sponsored loans also available. Support available to part-time students. Financial award application deadline: 4/1; financial award applicants required to submit FAFSA. *Faculty research:* AIDS education, employee wellness, isometric strength evaluation. *Unit head:* Dr. David C. Wiley, Graduate Advisor, 512-245-2946, E-mail: dw13@txstate.edu. *Application contact:* Dr. Andrea Golato, Dean of the Graduate College, 512-245-2581, Fax: 512-245-8365, E-mail: gradcollege@txstate.edu.
Website: http://www.hhp.txstate.edu/Degree-Plans/Graduate.html.

Texas Woman's University, Graduate School, College of Health Sciences, Department of Health Studies, Denton, TX 76201. Offers MS, Ed D, PhD. Part-time and evening/weekend programs available. *Faculty:* 9 full-time (7 women), 3 part-time/adjunct (1 woman). *Students:* 7 full-time (all women), 58 part-time (53 women); includes 35 minority (19 Black or African American, non-Hispanic/Latino; 2 American Indian or Alaska Native, non-Hispanic/Latino; 2 Asian, non-Hispanic/Latino; 12 Hispanic/Latino), 3 international. Average age 38. 28 applicants, 57% accepted, 12 enrolled. In 2013, 9 master's awarded. *Degree requirements:* For master's, comprehensive exam, thesis or alternative; for doctorate, comprehensive exam, thesis/dissertation, qualifying exam. *Entrance requirements:* For master's, GRE General Test (preferred minimum scores 150 [450 old version] Verbal, 140 [400 old version] Quantitative), 2 letters of recommendation, curriculum vitae, essay; for doctorate, GRE General Test (preferred minimum scores 152 [480 old version] Verbal, 140 [400 old version] Quantitative), minimum GPA of 3.5 on all master's course work, 2 letters of recommendation, curriculum vitae, essay, writing sample. Additional exam requirements/recommendations for international students: Required—TOEFL (minimum score 575 paper-based; 90 iBT). *Application deadline:* For fall admission, 4/1 for domestic students, 3/1 for international students; for spring admission, 10/1 for domestic students, 7/1 for international students. Applications are processed on a rolling basis. Application fee: $50 ($75 for international students). Electronic applications accepted. *Expenses:* Tuition, state resident: full-time $4182; part-time $233.32 per credit hour. Tuition, nonresident: full-time $10,716; part-time $595.32 per credit hour. *Financial support:* In 2013–14, 7 students received support, including 4 research assistantships (averaging $7,798 per year), 1 teaching assistantship (averaging $7,798 per year); career-related internships or fieldwork, Federal Work-Study, institutionally sponsored loans, scholarships/grants, traineeships, health care benefits, tuition waivers (partial), and unspecified assistantships also available. Support available to part-time students. Financial award application deadline: 3/1; financial award applicants required to submit FAFSA. *Faculty research:* Body image and eating disorder prevention, health communication/health literacy, violence prevention, chronic diseases, HIV/AIDS prevention. *Unit head:* Dr. Kimberly A. Parker, Graduate Program Coordinator and Assistant Professor, 940-898-2860, Fax: 940-898-2859, E-mail: kparker6@twu.edu. *Application contact:* Dr. Samuel Wheeler, Assistant Director of Admissions, 940-898-3188, Fax: 940-898-3081, E-mail: wheelersr@twu.edu.
Website: http://www.twu.edu/health-studies/.

Thomas Jefferson University, Jefferson School of Health Professions, Professional and Continuing Studies Program, Philadelphia, PA 19107. Offers healthcare education (Certificate). *Application deadline:* For fall admission, 8/1 for domestic students. Applications are processed on a rolling basis. Electronic applications accepted. *Financial support:* Application deadline: 4/1; applicants required to submit FAFSA. *Unit head:* Debra S. Zelnick, Interim Chair, Department of Professional and Continuing Studies, 215-503-8707, E-mail: debra.zelnick@jefferson.edu. *Application contact:* Lee

E. Bryant, Director, Undergraduate and Pre-College Programs, 215-503-1868, E-mail: lee.bryant@jefferson.edu.
Website: http://www.jefferson.edu/university/health_professions/departments/professional_studies.html.

Thomas Jefferson University, Jefferson School of Population Health, Philadelphia, PA 19107. Offers applied health economics and outcomes research (MS, PhD, Certificate); behavioral health science (PhD); health policy (MS, Certificate); healthcare quality and safety (MS, PhD); healthcare quality and safety management (MS); population health (Certificate); public health (MPH, Certificate). Part-time and evening/weekend programs available. Postbaccalaureate distance learning degree programs offered (no on-campus study). Terminal master's awarded for partial completion of doctoral program. *Degree requirements:* For master's, thesis; for doctorate, comprehensive exam, thesis/dissertation. *Entrance requirements:* For master's, GRE or other graduate entrance exam (MCAT, LSAT, DAT, etc.), two letters of recommendation, curriculum vitae, transcripts from all undergraduate and graduate institutions; for doctorate, GRE (taken within the last 5 years), three letters of recommendation, curriculum vitae, transcripts from all undergraduate and graduate institutions. Additional exam requirements/recommendations for international students: Required—TOEFL. Electronic applications accepted. *Faculty research:* Applied health economics and outcomes research, behavioral and health sciences, chronic disease management, health policy, healthcare quality and patient safety, wellness and prevention.

Trident University International, College of Health Sciences, Program in Health Sciences, Cypress, CA 90630. Offers clinical research administration (MS, Certificate); emergency and disaster management (MS, Certificate); environmental health science (Certificate); health care administration (PhD); health care management (MS), including health informatics; health education (MS, Certificate); health informatics (Certificate); health sciences (PhD); international health (MS); international health: educator or researcher option (PhD); international health: practitioner option (PhD); law and expert witness studies (MS, Certificate); public health (MS); quality assurance (Certificate). Part-time and evening/weekend programs available. Postbaccalaureate distance learning degree programs offered (no on-campus study). *Degree requirements:* For doctorate, comprehensive exam, thesis/dissertation, defense of dissertation. *Entrance requirements:* For master's, minimum GPA of 2.5 (students with GPA 3.0 or greater may transfer up to 30% of graduate level credits); for doctorate, minimum GPA of 3.4, curriculum vitae, course work in research methods or statistics. Additional exam requirements/recommendations for international students: Required—TOEFL. Electronic applications accepted.

Tulane University, School of Public Health and Tropical Medicine, Department of Community Health Sciences, Program in Health Education and Communication, New Orleans, LA 70118-5669. Offers MPH. *Accreditation:* CEPH; Teacher Education Accreditation Council. *Degree requirements:* For master's, comprehensive exam. *Entrance requirements:* For master's, GRE General Test. Additional exam requirements/recommendations for international students: Required—TOEFL.

Union College, Graduate Programs, Department of Education, Barbourville, KY 40906-1499. Offers elementary education (MA); health and physical education (MA); middle grades (MA); music education (MA); principalship (MA); reading specialist (MA); secondary education (MA); special education (MA). *Degree requirements:* For master's, thesis optional. *Entrance requirements:* For master's, GRE General Test, NTE.

Union College, Graduate Programs, Department of Health and Physical Education, Barbourville, KY 40906-1499. Offers health (MA Ed). *Degree requirements:* For master's, thesis optional. *Entrance requirements:* For master's, GRE General Test, NTE.

United States University, School of Health Science, Cypress, CA 90630. Offers health education (MSHS). *Entrance requirements:* For master's, undergraduate degree from accredited institution, minimum cumulative GPA of 2.5, official transcripts.

Universidad Adventista de las Antillas, EGECED Department, Mayagüez, PR 00681-0118. Offers curriculum and instruction (M Ed); health education (M Ed); medical surgical nursing (MN); school administration and supervision (M Ed). *Degree requirements:* For master's, comprehensive exam (for some programs), thesis (for some programs). *Entrance requirements:* For master's, EXADEP or GRE General Test, recommendations. Application fee: $175. Electronic applications accepted. *Expenses:* Tuition: Full-time $2400; part-time $200 per credit. *Required fees:* $235 per semester. One-time fee: $30. Tuition and fees vary according to course load. *Financial support:* Fellowships and Federal Work-Study available. *Unit head:* Director, 787-834-9595 Ext. 2282, Fax: 787-834-9595. *Application contact:* Prof. Yolanda Ferrer, Director of Admission, 787-834-9595 Ext. 2261, Fax: 787-834-9597, E-mail: admissions@uaa.edu.
Website: http://www.uaa.edu.

The University of Alabama, Graduate School, College of Human Environmental Sciences, Department of Health Science, Tuscaloosa, AL 35487-0311. Offers health education and promotion (PhD); health studies (MA). Part-time programs available. Postbaccalaureate distance learning degree programs offered (no on-campus study). *Faculty:* 10 full-time (6 women). *Students:* 58 full-time (47 women), 156 part-time (129 women); includes 53 minority (43 Black or African American, non-Hispanic/Latino; 2 American Indian or Alaska Native, non-Hispanic/Latino; 1 Asian, non-Hispanic/Latino; 3 Hispanic/Latino; 4 Two or more races, non-Hispanic/Latino), 1 international. Average age 33. 113 applicants, 66% accepted, 54 enrolled. In 2013, 83 master's, 3 doctorates awarded. *Degree requirements:* For master's, comprehensive exam, thesis optional; for doctorate, one foreign language, comprehensive exam, thesis/dissertation. *Entrance requirements:* For master's, minimum GPA of 3.0; for doctorate, GRE General Test, minimum GPA of 3.0, prerequisites in health education. Additional exam requirements/recommendations for international students: Required—TOEFL. *Application deadline:* For fall admission, 3/15 priority date for domestic students, 3/15 for international students. Applications are processed on a rolling basis. Application fee: $50 ($60 for international students). Electronic applications accepted. *Expenses:* Tuition, state resident: full-time $9450. Tuition, nonresident: full-time $23,950. *Financial support:* In 2013–14, 2 research assistantships with full tuition reimbursements (averaging $10,500 per year), 6 teaching assistantships with full tuition reimbursements (averaging $10,500 per year) were awarded; career-related internships or fieldwork, Federal Work-Study, institutionally sponsored loans, health care benefits, and unspecified assistantships also available. Financial award application deadline: 4/14. *Faculty research:* Program planning, substance abuse prevention, obesity prevention, nutrition, physical activity, athletic training, osteoporosis, health behavior. Total annual research expenditures: $49,063. *Unit head:* Dr. Lori W. Turner, Department Head and Professor, 205-348-2956, Fax: 205-348-7568, E-mail: lwturner@ches.ua.edu. *Application contact:* Dr. Stuart Usdan, Associate Professor and Doctoral Program Coordinator, 205-348-8373, Fax: 205-348-7568, E-mail: susdan@ches.ua.edu.
Website: http://ches.ua.edu/.

The University of Alabama at Birmingham, School of Education, Program in Health Education, Birmingham, AL 35294. Offers MA Ed. *Accreditation:* NCATE. *Degree requirements:* For master's, comprehensive exam (for some programs), thesis optional. *Entrance requirements:* For master's, GRE General Test, MAT, or NTE, minimum GPA of 3.0. Electronic applications accepted.

The University of Alabama at Birmingham, School of Education, Program in Health Education and Promotion, Birmingham, AL 35294. Offers PhD. Program offered jointly with School of Public Health, School of Health Professions, and The University of Alabama (Tuscaloosa). *Accreditation:* NCATE. *Degree requirements:* For doctorate, thesis/dissertation. *Entrance requirements:* For doctorate, GRE General Test (preferred minimum scores of 156 or greater for each section), minimum GPA of 3.0, letters of recommendation. Electronic applications accepted.

The University of Alabama at Birmingham, School of Public Health, Program in Health Education and Promotion, Birmingham, AL 35294. Offers PhD. Program offered jointly with The University of Alabama (Tuscaloosa). *Entrance requirements:* For doctorate, GRE, letters of recommendation. Additional exam requirements/recommendations for international students: Recommended—TOEFL, IELTS.

University of Arkansas, Graduate School, College of Education and Health Professions, Department of Health, Human Performance and Recreation, Program in Health Science, Fayetteville, AR 72701-1201. Offers MS, PhD. *Accreditation:* NCATE. *Degree requirements:* For doctorate, thesis/dissertation. *Entrance requirements:* For doctorate, GRE General Test. Electronic applications accepted.

University of Arkansas for Medical Sciences, College of Public Health, Little Rock, AR 72205-7199. Offers biostatistics (MPH); environmental and occupational health (MPH, Certificate); epidemiology (MPH, PhD); health behavior and health education (MPH); health policy and management (MPH); health promotion and prevention research (PhD); health services administration (MHSA); health systems research (PhD); public health (Certificate); public health leadership (Dr PH). Part-time programs available. *Faculty:* 37 full-time (19 women), 9 part-time/adjunct (5 women). *Students:* 56 full-time (35 women), 85 part-time (58 women); includes 54 minority (38 Black or African American, non-Hispanic/Latino; 1 American Indian or Alaska Native, non-Hispanic/Latino; 8 Asian, non-Hispanic/Latino; 3 Hispanic/Latino; 1 Native Hawaiian or other Pacific Islander, non-Hispanic/Latino; 3 Two or more races, non-Hispanic/Latino), 5 international. Average age 30. 70 applicants, 91% accepted, 33 enrolled. In 2013, 2 master's, 1 doctorate, 2 other advanced degrees awarded. *Degree requirements:* For master's, preceptorship, culminating experience, internship; for doctorate, comprehensive exam, capstone. *Entrance requirements:* For master's, GRE, GMAT, LSAT, PCAT, MCAT, DAT; for doctorate, GRE. Additional exam requirements/recommendations for international students: Required—TOEFL (minimum score 80 iBT), IELTS. *Application deadline:* For fall admission, 3/1 for domestic students, 2/1 for international students; for spring admission, 8/1 for domestic and international students; for summer admission, 2/1 for domestic and international students. Application fee: $25 ($50 for international students). Electronic applications accepted. *Expenses:* Contact institution. *Financial support:* In 2013–14, 8 research assistantships with full tuition reimbursements (averaging $13,000 per year) were awarded; scholarships/grants and tuition waivers (full and partial) also available. *Faculty research:* Health systems, tobacco prevention control, obesity prevention, environmental and occupational exposure, cancer prevention. *Unit head:* Dr. James M. Raczynski, Dean, 501-526-6600, E-mail: raczynskijameson@uams.edu. *Application contact:* Angie Choi, Director of Admission, 501-526-4620, Fax: 501-526-6750, E-mail: anchoi@uams.edu.
Website: http://publichealth.uams.edu/.

University of Central Arkansas, Graduate School, College of Health and Behavioral Sciences, Department of Health Sciences, Conway, AR 72035-0001. Offers health education (MS). Part-time and evening/weekend programs available. Postbaccalaureate distance learning degree programs offered (minimal on-campus study). *Degree requirements:* For master's, comprehensive exam, thesis optional. *Entrance requirements:* For master's, GRE General Test, minimum GPA of 2.7. Additional exam requirements/recommendations for international students: Required—TOEFL (minimum score 550 paper-based). Electronic applications accepted.

University of Central Oklahoma, The Jackson College of Graduate Studies, College of Education and Professional Studies, Department of Adult Education and Safety Science, Edmond, OK 73034-5209. Offers adult and higher education (M Ed), including adult and higher education, interdisciplinary studies, student personnel, training. Part-time programs available. *Faculty:* 7 full-time (4 women), 12 part-time/adjunct (5 women). *Students:* 37 full-time (23 women), 91 part-time (57 women); includes 50 minority (24 Black or African American, non-Hispanic/Latino; 3 American Indian or Alaska Native, non-Hispanic/Latino; 5 Asian, non-Hispanic/Latino; 12 Hispanic/Latino; 6 Two or more races, non-Hispanic/Latino), 5 international. Average age 36. 59 applicants, 78% accepted, 28 enrolled. In 2013, 17 master's awarded. *Degree requirements:* For master's, comprehensive exam (for some programs), thesis (for some programs). *Entrance requirements:* For master's, GRE General Test. Additional exam requirements/recommendations for international students: Required—TOEFL (minimum score 550 paper-based; 79 iBT), IELTS (minimum score 6.5). *Application deadline:* For fall admission, 7/1 for international students; for spring admission, 11/1 for international students. Applications are processed on a rolling basis. Application fee: $50. Electronic applications accepted. *Expenses:* Tuition, state resident: full-time $4137; part-time $206.85 per credit hour. Tuition, nonresident: full-time $10,359; part-time $517.95 per credit hour. *Required fees:* $481. Tuition and fees vary according to course load and program. *Financial support:* In 2013–14, 31 students received support, including 2 research assistantships with partial tuition reimbursements available (averaging $2,958 per year), 1 teaching assistantship with partial tuition reimbursement available (averaging $15,382 per year); career-related internships or fieldwork, scholarships/grants, tuition waivers (partial), and unspecified assistantships also available. Financial award application deadline: 3/31; financial award applicants required to submit FAFSA. *Faculty research:* Violence in the workplace/schools, aging issues, trade and industrial education. *Unit head:* Dr. Candy Sebert, Chair, 405-974-5780, Fax: 405-974-3822. *Application contact:* Dr. Richard Bernard, Dean, Graduate College, 405-974-3493, Fax: 405-974-3852, E-mail: gradcoll@uco.edu.

University of Cincinnati, Graduate School, College of Education, Criminal Justice, and Human Services, Division of Human Services, Program in Health Promotion/Education, Cincinnati, OH 45221. Offers community health (MS); health education (MS, PhD); health promotion and education (M Ed). *Accreditation:* NCATE. Part-time and evening/weekend programs available. *Degree requirements:* For master's, thesis or alternative. *Entrance requirements:* For master's and doctorate, GRE General Test. Additional exam requirements/recommendations for international students: Required—TOEFL (minimum score 580 paper-based), OEPT. Electronic applications accepted.

University of Colorado Denver, College of Liberal Arts and Sciences, Program in Health and Behavioral Sciences, Denver, CO 80217. Offers PhD. Part-time and evening/weekend programs available. *Faculty:* 10 full-time (8 women), 1 (woman) part-time/adjunct. *Students:* 15 full-time (12 women), 7 part-time (6 women); includes 7 minority (2 Black or African American, non-Hispanic/Latino; 2 Asian, non-Hispanic/Latino; 3 Hispanic/Latino). Average age 35. 16 applicants, 38% accepted, 6 enrolled. In 2013, 8 doctorates awarded. *Degree requirements:* For doctorate, comprehensive exam, thesis/dissertation, minimum of 62 credit hours of course work. *Entrance requirements:* For doctorate, GRE, master's or equivalent graduate degree; prior coursework or experience in social or behavioral sciences (minimum 15 semester hours); human biology or physiology (minimum six semester hours); statistics and epidemiology (minimum three semester hours each); minimum undergraduate GPA of 3.25, graduate 3.5, three letters of recommendation, essay. Additional exam requirements/recommendations for international students: Required—TOEFL (minimum score 525 paper-based; 71 iBT). *Application deadline:* For fall admission, 2/15 for domestic students, 1/15 priority date for international students. Application fee: $50 ($75 for international students). Electronic applications accepted. *Financial support:* In 2013–14, 20 students received support. Fellowships with tuition reimbursements available, research assistantships with tuition reimbursements available, teaching assistantships, Federal Work-Study, institutionally sponsored loans, scholarships/grants, and traineeships available. Financial award application deadline: 4/1; financial award applicants required to submit FAFSA. *Faculty research:* HIV/AIDS prevention, tobacco control, globalization and primary health care, social inequality and health, maternal and child health. *Unit head:* Dr. David Tracer, Professor/Chair, 303-556-6792, E-mail: david.tracer@ucdenver.edu. *Application contact:* Abby Fitch, Program Assistant, 303-556-4300, Fax: 303-556-8501, E-mail: abby.fitch@ucdenver.edu.
Website: http://www.ucdenver.edu/academics/colleges/CLAS/Departments/hbsc/Pages/HealthBehavioralSciences.aspx.

University of Colorado Denver, Colorado School of Public Health, Program in Public Health, Aurora, CO 80045. Offers community and behavioral health (MPH, Dr PH); environmental and occupational health (MPH); epidemiology (MPH); health systems, management and policy (MPH). *Accreditation:* CEPH. Part-time and evening/weekend programs available. *Faculty:* 14 full-time (13 women). *Students:* 295 full-time (247 women), 49 part-time (39 women); includes 77 minority (17 Black or African American, non-Hispanic/Latino; 3 American Indian or Alaska Native, non-Hispanic/Latino; 16 Asian, non-Hispanic/Latino; 31 Hispanic/Latino; 10 Two or more races, non-Hispanic/Latino), 5 international. Average age 30. 657 applicants, 71% accepted, 132 enrolled. In 2013, 106 master's awarded. *Degree requirements:* For master's, thesis or alternative, 42 credit hours; for doctorate, comprehensive exam, thesis/dissertation, 67 credit hours. *Entrance requirements:* For master's, GRE, MCAT, DAT, LSAT, PCAT, GMAT or master's degree from accredited institution, baccalaureate degree or equivalent; minimum GPA of 3.0; transcripts; references; resume; essay; for doctorate, GRE, MCAT, DAT, LSAT, PCAT or GMAT, MPH or master's or higher degree in related field or equivalent; 2 years of previous work experience in public health; essay; resume. Additional exam requirements/recommendations for international students: Required—TOEFL (minimum score 550 paper-based; 80 iBT). *Application deadline:* For fall admission, 12/15 priority date for domestic students, 12/1 priority date for international students. Application fee: $65. Electronic applications accepted. *Expenses:* Contact institution. *Financial support:* In 2013–14, 125 students received support. Fellowships, research assistantships, teaching assistantships, Federal Work-Study, institutionally sponsored loans, scholarships/grants, traineeships, and unspecified assistantships available. Financial award application deadline: 3/15; financial award applicants required to submit FAFSA. *Faculty research:* Cancer prevention by nutrition, cancer survivorship outcomes, social and cultural factors related to health. *Unit head:* Dr. Lori Crane, Chair, 303-724-4385, E-mail: lori.crane@ucdenver.edu. *Application contact:* Carla Denerstein, Departmental Assistant, 303-724-4446, E-mail: carla.denerstein@ucdenver.edu.
Website: http://www.ucdenver.edu/academics/colleges/PublicHealth/departments/CommunityBehavioralHealth/Pages/CommunityBehavioralHealth.aspx.

University of Colorado Denver, School of Medicine, Physician Assistant Program, Aurora, CO 80045. Offers child health associate (MPAS), including global health, leadership, education, advocacy, development, and scholarship, rural health, urban/underserved populations. *Accreditation:* ARC-PA. *Students:* 132 full-time (107 women); includes 15 minority (1 American Indian or Alaska Native, non-Hispanic/Latino; 6 Asian, non-Hispanic/Latino; 8 Hispanic/Latino). Average age 27. 1,313 applicants, 3% accepted, 44 enrolled. In 2013, 43 master's awarded. *Degree requirements:* For master's, comprehensive exam, successful completion of all coursework and rotations. *Entrance requirements:* For master's, GRE General Test, minimum GPA of 2.8, 3 letters of recommendation, prerequisite courses in chemistry, biology, general genetics, psychology and statistics, interviews. Additional exam requirements/recommendations for international students: Required—TOEFL (minimum score 550 paper-based; 80 iBT). *Application deadline:* For fall admission, 9/1 for domestic students, 8/15 for international students. Application fee: $170. Electronic applications accepted. *Expenses:* Contact institution. *Financial support:* In 2013–14, 85 students received support. Fellowships, research assistantships, teaching assistantships, career-related internships or fieldwork, Federal Work-Study, institutionally sponsored loans, scholarships/grants, traineeships, and unspecified assistantships available. Financial award application deadline: 3/15; financial award applicants required to submit FAFSA. *Faculty research:* Clinical genetics and genetic counseling, evidence-based medicine, pediatric allergy and asthma, childhood diabetes, standardized patient assessment. *Unit head:* Jonathan Bowser, Program Director, 303-724-1349, E-mail: jonathan.bowser@ucdenver.edu. *Application contact:* Kay Denler, Director of Admissions, 303-724-7963, E-mail: kay.denler@ucdenver.edu.
Website: http://www.ucdenver.edu/academics/colleges/medicalschool/education/degree_programs/PAProgram/Pages/Home.aspx.

University of Florida, Graduate School, College of Health and Human Performance, Department of Health Education and Behavior, Gainesville, FL 32611. Offers health and human performance (PhD), including health behavior; health communication (Graduate Certificate); health education and behavior (MS). *Accreditation:* NCATE (one or more programs are accredited). Part-time programs available. *Faculty:* 10 full-time (3 women), 3 part-time/adjunct (2 women). *Students:* 31 full-time (24 women), 7 part-time (5 women); includes 12 minority (4 Black or African American, non-Hispanic/Latino; 5 Asian, non-Hispanic/Latino; 3 Hispanic/Latino), 1 international. Average age 29. 12 applicants, 58% accepted, 6 enrolled. In 2013, 28 master's, 4 doctorates awarded. Terminal master's awarded for partial completion of doctoral program. *Degree requirements:* For master's, comprehensive exam, thesis (for some programs); for doctorate, comprehensive exam, thesis/dissertation. *Entrance requirements:* For master's and doctorate, GRE General Test, minimum GPA of 3.0. Additional exam requirements/recommendations for international students: Required—TOEFL (minimum score 550 paper-based; 80 iBT), IELTS (minimum score 6). *Application deadline:* For fall admission, 6/1 priority date for domestic students; for spring admission, 10/1 for domestic and international students. Applications are processed on a rolling basis. Application fee: $30. Electronic applications accepted. *Expenses:* Tuition, state resident: full-time $12,640. Tuition, nonresident: full-time $30,000. *Financial support:* In 2013–14, 17 students received support, including 6 research assistantships (averaging $13,500 per year), 11 teaching assistantships (averaging $9,807 per year); career-related internships or fieldwork and institutionally sponsored loans also available. Financial award application deadline: 2/1; financial award applicants required to submit FAFSA. *Faculty research:* Information technology and digital health for health promotion and disease prevention; prevention of high risk drinking among college students; scale development and measurement of youth prescription drug use; evaluation of state, regional, and community-based health education interventions. *Unit head:* Thomas Clanton, PhD, Professor and Interim Department Chair, 352-294-1712 Ext. 1281, Fax: 352-392-1909, E-mail: tclanton@hhp.ufl.edu. *Application contact:* Robert M Weiler, PhD, Professor and Graduate Coordinator, 352-294-1808, Fax: 352-392-1909, E-mail: rweiler@hhp.ufl.edu.
Website: http://heb.hhp.ufl.edu/.

Health Education

University of Georgia, Biomedical and Health Sciences Institute, Athens, GA 30602. Offers neuroscience (PhD). *Entrance requirements:* For doctorate, GRE, official transcripts, 3 letters of recommendation, statement of interest. Additional exam requirements/recommendations for international students: Required—TOEFL.

University of Georgia, College of Education, Department of Career and Information Studies, Athens, GA 30602. Offers learning, design, and technology (M Ed, PhD, Ed S), including instructional design and development (M Ed, Ed S), instructional technology (M Ed), learning, design, and technology (M Ed), school library media (M Ed, Ed S); workforce education (M Ed, MAT, Ed D, PhD, Ed S), including business education (MAT), family and consumer sciences education (MAT), health science and technology education (MAT), marketing education (MAT), technology education (MAT), trade and industry education (MAT). *Accreditation:* NCATE. *Entrance requirements:* For master's, GRE General Test, MAT; for doctorate, GRE General Test; for Ed S, GRE General Test or MAT. Electronic applications accepted.

University of Georgia, College of Public Health, Department of Health Promotion and Behavior, Athens, GA 30602. Offers MPH, PhD. *Accreditation:* CEPH; NCATE (one or more programs are accredited). *Degree requirements:* For master's, thesis (MA); for doctorate, thesis/dissertation. *Entrance requirements:* For master's, GRE General Test or MAT; for doctorate, GRE General Test. Electronic applications accepted.

University of Houston, College of Liberal Arts and Social Sciences, Department of Health and Human Performance, Houston, TX 77204. Offers exercise science (MS); human nutrition (MS); human space exploration sciences (MS); kinesiology (PhD); physical education (M Ed). *Accreditation:* NCATE (one or more programs are accredited). Part-time and evening/weekend programs available. *Degree requirements:* For master's, comprehensive exam (for some programs), thesis (for some programs); for doctorate, comprehensive exam, thesis/dissertation, qualifying exam, candidacy paper. *Entrance requirements:* For master's, GRE (minimum 35th percentile on each section), minimum cumulative GPA of 3.0; for doctorate, GRE (minimum 35th percentile on each section), minimum cumulative GPA of 3.3. Additional exam requirements/ recommendations for international students: Required—TOEFL (minimum score 550 paper-based; 79 iBT). Electronic applications accepted. *Faculty research:* Biomechanics, exercise physiology, obesity, nutrition, space exploration science.

University of Illinois at Chicago, College of Medicine and Graduate College, Graduate Programs in Medicine, Department of Medical Education, Chicago, IL 60607-7128. Offers MHPE. Part-time programs available. *Faculty:* 13 full-time (7 women), 1 part-time/ adjunct (0 women). *Students:* 7 full-time (4 women), 35 part-time (20 women); includes 10 minority (1 Black or African American, non-Hispanic/Latino; 7 Asian, non-Hispanic/ Latino; 1 Hispanic/Latino; 1 Two or more races, non-Hispanic/Latino), 9 international. Average age 40. 58 applicants, 41% accepted, 19 enrolled. In 2013, 9 master's awarded. *Degree requirements:* For master's, thesis. *Entrance requirements:* For master's, GRE General Test. Additional exam requirements/recommendations for international students: Required—TOEFL. *Application deadline:* For fall admission, 3/15 for domestic students, 2/15 for international students; for spring admission, 7/15 for domestic students. Applications are processed on a rolling basis. Application fee: $40 ($50 for international students). Electronic applications accepted. *Expenses:* Tuition, state resident: full-time $11,066; part-time $3689 per term. Tuition, nonresident: full-time $23,064; part-time $7688 per term. *Required fees:* $3004; $1190 per term. Tuition and fees vary according to course level and program. *Financial support:* In 2013–14, 2 students received support. Fellowships with full tuition reimbursements available, research assistantships with full tuition reimbursements available, teaching assistantships with full tuition reimbursements available, Federal Work-Study, tuition waivers (full), and unspecified assistantships available. Financial award application deadline: 3/1; financial award applicants required to submit FAFSA. *Unit head:* Dr. Ilene Harris, Head, 312-355-0800, E-mail: ibharris@uic.edu. *Application contact:* Jackie Perry, Graduate College Receptionist, 312-413-2550, Fax: 312-413-0185, E-mail: gradcoll@uic.edu.
Website: http://chicago.medicine.uic.edu/departments___programs/departments/ meded/educational_programs/mhpe/.

The University of Kansas, Graduate Studies, School of Education, Department of Health, Sport, and Exercise Sciences, Lawrence, KS 66045. Offers health and physical education (MS Ed, Ed D, PhD). *Accreditation:* NCATE. Part-time and evening/weekend programs available. *Faculty:* 21. *Students:* 56 full-time (20 women), 25 part-time (12 women); includes 7 minority (3 Black or African American, non-Hispanic/Latino; 2 American Indian or Alaska Native, non-Hispanic/Latino; 1 Asian, non-Hispanic/Latino; 1 Hispanic/Latino), 3 international. Average age 28. 59 applicants, 53% accepted, 19 enrolled. In 2013, 20 master's, 3 doctorates awarded. *Degree requirements:* For master's, comprehensive exam (for some programs), thesis (for some programs); for doctorate, variable foreign language requirement, comprehensive exam, thesis/ dissertation. *Entrance requirements:* For master's, GRE General Test (minimum score 1000, 450 verbal, 450 quantitative, 4.0 analytical), minimum GPA of 3.0; for doctorate, GRE General Test (minimum score 1100, verbal 500, quantitative 500, analytical 4.5), minimum graduate GPA of 3.5, undergraduate 3.0. Additional exam requirements/ recommendations for international students: Required—TOEFL (minimum score 570 paper-based). *Application deadline:* For fall admission, 3/15 priority date for domestic students; for spring admission, 10/15 priority date for domestic students. Applications are processed on a rolling basis. Application fee: $55 ($65 for international students). Electronic applications accepted. *Financial support:* Research assistantships with full and partial tuition reimbursements and teaching assistantships with full and partial tuition reimbursements available. Financial award application deadline: 4/1. *Faculty research:* Exercise and sport psychology, obesity prevention, sexuality health, sport ethics, skeletal muscle cell signaling and performance. *Unit head:* Dr. Joseph Weir, Chair, 785-864-0784, Fax: 785-864-3343, E-mail: joseph.weir@ku.edu. *Application contact:* Linda Faust, Graduate Admissions Coordinator, 785-864-0783, Fax: 785-864-3343, E-mail: lfaust@ku.edu.
Website: http://hses.soe.ku.edu/.

The University of Kansas, University of Kansas Medical Center, School of Nursing, Kansas City, KS 66160. Offers adult/gerontological clinical nurse specialist (PMC); adult/gerontological nurse practitioner (PMC); clinical research management (PMC); health care informatics (PMC); health professions educator (PMC); nurse midwife (PMC); nursing (MS, DNP, PhD); organizational leadership (PMC); psychiatric/mental health nurse practitioner (PMC); public health nursing (PMC). *Accreditation:* AACN; ACNM/ACME. Part-time programs available. Postbaccalaureate distance learning degree programs offered (minimal on-campus study). *Faculty:* 59. *Students:* 55 full-time (53 women), 323 part-time (303 women); includes 57 minority (23 Black or African American, non-Hispanic/Latino; 14 Asian, non-Hispanic/Latino; 16 Hispanic/Latino; 1 Native Hawaiian or other Pacific Islander, non-Hispanic/Latino; 3 Two or more races, non-Hispanic/Latino), 1 international. Average age 38. 113 applicants, 59% accepted, 61 enrolled. In 2013, 77 master's, 18 doctorates, 11 other advanced degrees awarded. Terminal master's awarded for partial completion of doctoral program. *Degree requirements:* For master's, comprehensive exam, thesis (for some programs), general oral exam; for doctorate, variable foreign language requirement, thesis/dissertation, comprehensive oral exam (for DNP); comprehensive written and oral exam (for PhD). *Entrance requirements:* For master's, bachelor's degree in nursing, minimum GPA of 3.0, 1 year of clinical experience, RN license in KS and MO; for doctorate, GRE General Test, bachelor's degree in nursing, minimum GPA of 3.5, RN license in KS and MO. Additional exam requirements/recommendations for international students: Required—TOEFL. *Application deadline:* For fall admission, 4/1 for domestic and international students; for spring admission, 9/1 for domestic and international students. Application fee: $60. Electronic applications accepted. *Financial support:* Research assistantships with full and partial tuition reimbursements, teaching assistantships with full and partial tuition reimbursements, scholarships/grants, and traineeships available. Financial award application deadline: 3/1; financial award applicants required to submit FAFSA. *Faculty research:* Breastfeeding practices of teen mothers, national database of nursing quality indicators, caregiving of families of patients using technology in the home, simulation in nursing education, diaphragm fatigue. *Total annual research expenditures:* $6.4 million. *Unit head:* Dr. Karen L. Miller, Dean, 913-588-1601, Fax: 913-588-1660, E-mail: kmiller@kumc.edu. *Application contact:* Dr. Pamela K. Barnes, Associate Dean, Student Affairs, 913-588-1619, Fax: 913-588-1615, E-mail: pbarnes2@kumc.edu.
Website: http://nursing.kumc.edu.

University of Louisville, Graduate School, College of Education and Human Development, Department of Health and Sport Sciences, Louisville, KY 40292-0001. Offers community health education (M Ed); exercise physiology (MS); health and physical education (MAT); sport administration (MS). Part-time and evening/weekend programs available. *Students:* 54 full-time (22 women), 11 part-time (9 women); includes 12 minority (6 Black or African American, non-Hispanic/Latino; 1 American Indian or Alaska Native, non-Hispanic/Latino; 1 Asian, non-Hispanic/Latino; 3 Hispanic/Latino; 1 Two or more races, non-Hispanic/Latino), 3 international. Average age 27. 91 applicants, 70% accepted, 40 enrolled. In 2013, 16 master's awarded. *Entrance requirements:* For master's, GRE General Test. Additional exam requirements/ recommendations for international students: Required—TOEFL (minimum score 560 paper-based; 83 iBT). Application fee: $60. Electronic applications accepted. *Expenses:* Tuition, state resident: full-time $10,788; part-time $599 per credit hour. Tuition, nonresident: full-time $22,446; part-time $1247 per credit hour. *Required fees:* $196. Tuition and fees vary according to program and reciprocity agreements. *Financial support:* Fellowships, research assistantships, teaching assistantships, career-related internships or fieldwork, Federal Work-Study, scholarships/grants, health care benefits, and unspecified assistantships available. Financial award application deadline: 6/1; financial award applicants required to submit FAFSA. *Faculty research:* Impact of sports and sport marketing on society, factors associated with school and community health, cardiac and pulmonary rehabilitation, impact of participation in activities on student retention and graduation, strength and conditioning. *Unit head:* Dr. Anita Moorman, Chair, 502-852-0553, Fax: 502-852-4534, E-mail: amm@louisville.edu. *Application contact:* Libby Leggett, Director, Graduate Admissions, 502-852-3101, Fax: 502-852-6536, E-mail: gradadm@louisville.edu.
Website: http://www.louisville.edu/education/departments/hss.

University of Louisville, Graduate School, School of Nursing, Louisville, KY 40202. Offers adult nurse practitioner (MSN); family nurse practitioner (MSN); health professions education (MSN); neonatal nurse practitioner (MSN); nursing research (PhD); psychiatric mental health nurse practitioner (MSN). *Accreditation:* AACN. Part-time programs available. *Students:* 91 full-time (81 women), 47 part-time (42 women); includes 16 minority (8 Black or African American, non-Hispanic/Latino; 3 Asian, non-Hispanic/Latino; 3 Hispanic/Latino; 2 Two or more races, non-Hispanic/Latino), 6 international. Average age 36. 58 applicants, 74% accepted, 36 enrolled. In 2013, 33 master's, 3 doctorates awarded. Terminal master's awarded for partial completion of doctoral program. *Degree requirements:* For master's, thesis optional; for doctorate, comprehensive exam, thesis/dissertation. *Entrance requirements:* For master's, GRE General Test, bachelor's degree in nursing, minimum GPA of 3.0, RN license; for doctorate, GRE General Test, BSN or MSN with recommended minimum GPA of 3.0. Additional exam requirements/recommendations for international students: Required—TOEFL. *Application deadline:* For fall admission, 4/1 priority date for domestic students, 4/1 for international students. Applications are processed on a rolling basis. Application fee: $60. Electronic applications accepted. *Expenses:* Tuition, state resident: full-time $10,788; part-time $599 per credit hour. Tuition, nonresident: full-time $22,446; part-time $1247 per credit hour. *Required fees:* $196. Tuition and fees vary according to program and reciprocity agreements. *Financial support:* Fellowships with full tuition reimbursements, research assistantships with full tuition reimbursements, teaching assistantships with full tuition reimbursements, institutionally sponsored loans, scholarships/grants, traineeships, health care benefits, and unspecified assistantships available. Support available to part-time students. Financial award application deadline: 4/15; financial award applicants required to submit FAFSA. *Faculty research:* Maternal-child/family stress after pregnancy loss, postpartum depression, access to healthcare (underserved populations), quality of life issues, physical activity (impact on chronic/ acute conditions). *Total annual research expenditures:* $718,934. *Unit head:* Dr. Marcia J. Hern, Dean, 502-852-8300, Fax: 502-852-5044, E-mail: m.hern@gwise.louisville.edu. *Application contact:* Dr. Lee Ridner, Interim Associate Dean for Academic Affairs and Director of MSN Programs, 502-852-8518, Fax: 502-852-0704, E-mail: romain01@ louisville.edu.
Website: http://www.louisville.edu/nursing/.

University of Maryland, Baltimore County, Graduate School, College of Arts, Humanities and Social Sciences, Department of Emergency Health Services, Baltimore, MD 21250. Offers administration, planning, and policy (MS); education (MS); emergency health services (MS); emergency management (Postbaccalaureate Certificate); preventive medicine and epidemiology (MS). Part-time and evening/weekend programs available. Postbaccalaureate distance learning degree programs offered (no on-campus study). *Faculty:* 1 full-time (0 women), 9 part-time/adjunct (1 woman). *Students:* 20 full-time (8 women), 21 part-time (10 women); includes 2 minority (both Black or African American, non-Hispanic/Latino), 6 international. Average age 32. 13 applicants, 85% accepted, 10 enrolled. In 2013, 13 master's awarded. *Degree requirements:* For master's, comprehensive exam, thesis (for some programs), capstone project. *Entrance requirements:* For master's, GRE General Test, minimum GPA of 3.0. Additional exam requirements/recommendations for international students: Required—TOEFL (minimum score 85 iBT). *Application deadline:* For fall admission, 7/1 for domestic students, 4/1 for international students; for spring admission, 10/15 for domestic students, 9/1 for international students. Applications are processed on a rolling basis. Application fee: $50. Electronic applications accepted. One-time fee: $200 full-time. *Financial support:* In 2013–14, 2 students received support, including 1 fellowship with tuition reimbursement available (averaging $70,000 per year), 1 research assistantship with tuition reimbursement available (averaging $21,000 per year); career-related internships or fieldwork, Federal Work-Study, scholarships/grants, health care benefits, and unspecified assistantships also available. Financial award application deadline: 5/30; financial award applicants required to submit FAFSA. *Faculty research:* EMS management, disaster health services, emergency management. *Total annual research expenditures:* $50,000. *Unit head:* Dr. Bruce Walz, Chairman, 410-455-3223. *Application contact:* Dr. Rick Bissell, Program Director, 410-455-3776, Fax: 410-455-3045, E-mail: bissell@umbc.edu.
Website: http://ehs.umbc.edu/.

University of Maryland, College Park, Academic Affairs, School of Public Health, Department of Behavioral and Community Health, College Park, MD 20742. Offers community health education (MPH); public/community health (PhD). *Accreditation:* CEPH. Part-time and evening/weekend programs available. *Faculty:* 36 full-time (25 women), 6 part-time/adjunct (5 women). *Students:* 34 full-time (31 women), 14 part-time (all women); includes 22 minority (13 Black or African American, non-Hispanic/Latino; 1 American Indian or Alaska Native, non-Hispanic/Latino; 7 Asian, non-Hispanic/Latino; 1 Two or more races, non-Hispanic/Latino), 3 international. 147 applicants, 29% accepted, 9 enrolled. In 2013, 11 master's, 4 doctorates awarded. *Degree requirements:* For master's, thesis optional; for doctorate, comprehensive exam, thesis/dissertation. *Entrance requirements:* For master's, GRE General Test, minimum GPA of 3.0, 3 letters of recommendation; for doctorate, GRE General Test, minimum GPA of 3.5, 3 letters of recommendation. Additional exam requirements/recommendations for international students: Required—TOEFL. *Application deadline:* For fall admission, 1/15 for domestic and international students. Applications are processed on a rolling basis. Application fee: $75. Electronic applications accepted. *Expenses:* Tuition, state resident: full-time $10,314; part-time $573 per credit hour. Tuition, nonresident: full-time $22,248; part-time $1236 per credit. *Required fees:* $1446; $403.15 per semester. Tuition and fees vary according to program. *Financial support:* In 2013–14, 3 fellowships with partial tuition reimbursements (averaging $9,167 per year), 22 teaching assistantships (averaging $16,041 per year) were awarded; career-related internships or fieldwork, Federal Work-Study, and scholarships/grants also available. Support available to part-time students. Financial award applicants required to submit FAFSA. *Faculty research:* Controlling stress and tension, women's health, aging and public policy, adolescent health, long-term care. *Total annual research expenditures:* $3.9 million. *Unit head:* Dr. Elbert Glover, Chair, 301-405-2467, Fax: 301-314-9167, E-mail: eglover1@umd.edu. *Application contact:* Dr. Charles A. Caramello, Dean of Graduate School, 301-405-0358, Fax: 301-314-9305, E-mail: ccaramel@umd.edu.
Website: http://www.sph.umd.edu/bch/.

University of Massachusetts Amherst, Graduate School, School of Public Health and Health Sciences, Department of Public Health, Amherst, MA 01003. Offers biostatistics (MPH, MS, PhD); community health education (MPH, MS, PhD); environmental health sciences (MPH, MS, PhD); epidemiology (MPH, MS, PhD); health policy and management (MPH, MS, PhD); nutrition (MPH, PhD); public health practice (MPH); MPH/MPPA. *Accreditation:* CEPH (one or more programs are accredited). Part-time and evening/weekend programs available. Postbaccalaureate distance learning degree programs offered (no on-campus study). *Faculty:* 53 full-time (29 women). *Students:* 117 full-time (83 women), 271 part-time (213 women); includes 89 minority (34 Black or African American, non-Hispanic/Latino; 23 Asian, non-Hispanic/Latino; 25 Hispanic/Latino; 7 Two or more races, non-Hispanic/Latino), 45 international. Average age 36. 359 applicants, 69% accepted, 94 enrolled. In 2013, 120 master's, 1 doctorate awarded. Terminal master's awarded for partial completion of doctoral program. *Degree requirements:* For master's, thesis (for some programs); for doctorate, comprehensive exam, thesis/dissertation. *Entrance requirements:* For master's and doctorate, GRE General Test. Additional exam requirements/recommendations for international students: Required—TOEFL (minimum score 550 paper-based; 80 iBT), IELTS (minimum score 6.5). *Application deadline:* For fall admission, 2/1 for domestic and international students. Applications are processed on a rolling basis. Application fee: $75. Electronic applications accepted. *Financial support:* Fellowships with full and partial tuition reimbursements, research assistantships with full and partial tuition reimbursements, teaching assistantships with full and partial tuition reimbursements, career-related internships or fieldwork, Federal Work-Study, scholarships/grants, traineeships, health care benefits, tuition waivers (full and partial), and unspecified assistantships available. Support available to part-time students. Financial award application deadline: 2/1; financial award applicants required to submit FAFSA. *Unit head:* Dr. Paula Stamps, Graduate Program Director, 413-545-2861, Fax: 413-545-1645. *Application contact:* Lindsay DeSantis, Supervisor of Admissions, 413-545-0722, Fax: 413-577-0010, E-mail: gradadm@grad.umass.edu.
Website: http://www.umass.edu/sphhs/public_health/.

University of Michigan, School of Public Health, Department of Health Behavior and Health Education, Ann Arbor, MI 48109. Offers MPH, PhD, MPH/MSW. PhD offered through the Horace H. Rackham School of Graduate Studies. *Accreditation:* CEPH (one or more programs are accredited). Terminal master's awarded for partial completion of doctoral program. *Degree requirements:* For doctorate, oral defense of dissertation, preliminary exam. *Entrance requirements:* For master's, GRE General Test (preferred); MCAT; for doctorate, GRE General Test. Additional exam requirements/recommendations for international students: Required—TOEFL (minimum score 560 paper-based; 100 iBT). Electronic applications accepted. Tuition and fees vary according to course level, course load, degree level, program and student level. *Faculty research:* Empowerment theory; structure, culture, and health; health disparities; community-based participatory research; health and medical decision-making.

University of Michigan–Flint, School of Health Professions and Studies, Program in Health Education, Flint, MI 48502-1950. Offers MS. Part-time programs available. *Faculty:* 3 full-time (all women), 4 part-time/adjunct (all women). *Students:* 10 full-time (all women), 14 part-time (12 women); includes 11 minority (10 Black or African American, non-Hispanic/Latino; 1 Hispanic/Latino), 1 international. Average age 35. 20 applicants, 50% accepted, 6 enrolled. In 2013, 7 master's awarded. *Degree requirements:* For master's, thesis or alternative, internship or current employment as health educator. *Entrance requirements:* For master's, minimum GPA of 2.8; course work completion in anatomy, physiology, speech, and developmental psychology. Additional exam requirements/recommendations for international students: Required—TOEFL (minimum score 560 paper-based; 84 iBT), IELTS (minimum score 6.5). *Application deadline:* For fall admission, 8/1 for domestic students, 5/1 for international students; for winter admission, 11/15 for domestic students, 9/1 for international students; for spring admission, 3/15 for domestic students, 1/1 for international students. Applications are processed on a rolling basis. Application fee: $55. Electronic applications accepted. *Expenses:* Contact institution. *Financial support:* Career-related internships or fieldwork, Federal Work-Study, scholarships/grants, and unspecified assistantships available. Support available to part-time students. Financial award application deadline: 3/1; financial award applicants required to submit FAFSA. *Faculty research:* Minority health, health disparities, cultural competency, HIV/AIDS, women's health. *Unit head:* Dr. Shan Parker, Associate Director, 810-762-3172, Fax: 810-762-3003, E-mail: shanpark@umich.edu. *Application contact:* Bradley T. Maki, Director of Graduate Admissions, 810-762-3171, Fax: 810-766-6789, E-mail: bmaki@umflint.edu.
Website: http://www.umflint.edu/graduateprograms/health-education-ms.

University of Mississippi, Graduate School, School of Applied Sciences, Department of Health, Exercise Science, and Recreation Management, Oxford, MS 38677. Offers exercise science (MS); health and kinesiology (PhD); health promotion (MS); park and recreation management (MA). *Faculty:* 9 full-time (3 women), 3 part-time/adjunct (1 woman). *Students:* 45 full-time (23 women), 14 part-time (9 women); includes 11 minority (8 Black or African American, non-Hispanic/Latino; 1 Asian, non-Hispanic/Latino; 2 Hispanic/Latino), 5 international. In 2013, 19 master's, 1 doctorate awarded. *Degree requirements:* For master's, thesis (for some programs); for doctorate, thesis/dissertation. *Entrance requirements:* For master's, GRE General Test, minimum GPA of 3.0; for doctorate, GRE General Test. Additional exam requirements/recommendations for international students: Required—TOEFL. *Application deadline:* For fall admission, 4/1 for domestic students; for spring admission, 10/1 for domestic students. Applications are processed on a rolling basis. *Financial support:* Scholarships/grants available. Financial award application deadline: 3/1; financial award applicants required to submit FAFSA. *Unit head:* Dr. Scott G. Owens, Chair, 662-915-5844, Fax: 662-915-5525, E-mail: dbramlett@olemiss.edu. *Application contact:* Dr. Christy M. Wyandt, Associate Dean, 662-915-7474, Fax: 662-915-7577, E-mail: cwyandt@olemiss.edu.

University of Missouri, Graduate School, College of Education, Department of Learning, Teaching and Curriculum, Columbia, MO 65211. Offers agricultural education (M Ed, PhD, Ed S); art education (M Ed, PhD, Ed S); business and office education (M Ed, PhD, Ed S); early childhood education (M Ed, PhD, Ed S); elementary education (M Ed, PhD, Ed S); English education (M Ed, PhD, Ed S); foreign language education (M Ed, PhD, Ed S); health education and promotion (M Ed, PhD); learning and instruction (M Ed); marketing education (M Ed, PhD, Ed S); mathematics education (M Ed, PhD, Ed S); music education (M Ed, PhD, Ed S); reading education (M Ed, PhD, Ed S); science education (M Ed, PhD, Ed S); social studies education (M Ed, PhD, Ed S); vocational education (M Ed, PhD, Ed S). Part-time programs available. *Faculty:* 26 full-time (16 women), 3 part-time/adjunct (2 women). *Students:* 186 full-time (143 women), 197 part-time (172 women); includes 19 minority (4 Black or African American, non-Hispanic/Latino; 4 Asian, non-Hispanic/Latino; 6 Hispanic/Latino; 5 Two or more races, non-Hispanic/Latino), 25 international. Average age 31. 288 applicants, 65% accepted, 160 enrolled. In 2013, 202 master's, 18 doctorates, 7 other advanced degrees awarded. Terminal master's awarded for partial completion of doctoral program. *Degree requirements:* For doctorate, thesis/dissertation. *Entrance requirements:* For master's and Ed S, GRE General Test or MAT, minimum GPA of 3.0; for doctorate, GRE General Test, minimum GPA of 3.0. Additional exam requirements/recommendations for international students: Required—TOEFL (minimum score 600 paper-based; 100 iBT). *Application deadline:* For fall admission, 12/1 priority date for domestic and international students. Applications are processed on a rolling basis. Application fee: $55 ($75 for international students). Electronic applications accepted. *Financial support:* Fellowships, research assistantships, teaching assistantships, institutionally sponsored loans, traineeships, health care benefits, and unspecified assistantships available. Support available to part-time students. *Faculty research:* Curriculum development and research, teacher education, art education, business and marketing, early childhood education, English education, literacy/reading education, mathematics education, music education, science education, social studies education. *Unit head:* Dr. James Tarr, Associate Division Director, 573-882-4034, E-mail: tarrj@missouri.edu. *Application contact:* Fran Colley, Academic Advisor, 573-882-6462, E-mail: colleyf@missouri.edu.
Website: http://education.missouri.edu/LTC/.

University of Missouri–Kansas City, School of Medicine, Kansas City, MO 64110-2499. Offers anesthesia (MS); bioinformatics (MS); health professions education (MS); medicine (MD); physician assistant (MMS); MD/PhD. *Accreditation:* LCME/AMA. *Faculty:* 49 full-time (20 women), 13 part-time/adjunct (6 women). *Students:* 462 full-time (241 women), 16 part-time (8 women); includes 253 minority (33 Black or African American, non-Hispanic/Latino; 2 American Indian or Alaska Native, non-Hispanic/Latino; 196 Asian, non-Hispanic/Latino; 14 Hispanic/Latino; 1 Native Hawaiian or other Pacific Islander, non-Hispanic/Latino; 7 Two or more races, non-Hispanic/Latino), 3 international. Average age 24. 1,070 applicants, 11% accepted, 94 enrolled. In 2013, 12 master's, 88 doctorates awarded. *Degree requirements:* For doctorate, one foreign language, United States Medical Licensing Exam Step 1 and 2. *Entrance requirements:* For doctorate, interview. *Application deadline:* For fall admission, 11/15 for domestic and international students. Application fee: $50. *Expenses:* Contact institution. *Financial support:* In 2013–14, 4 fellowships (averaging $38,964 per year), 4 research assistantships (averaging $17,373 per year) were awarded; career-related internships or fieldwork, Federal Work-Study, institutionally sponsored loans, scholarships/grants, and tuition waivers (partial) also available. Financial award application deadline: 3/1; financial award applicants required to submit FAFSA. *Faculty research:* Cardiovascular disease, women's and children's health, trauma and infectious diseases, neurological, metabolic disease. *Unit head:* Dr. Betty Drees, Dean, 816-235-1808, E-mail: dreesb@umkc.edu. *Application contact:* Janine Kluckhohn, Admissions Coordinator, 816-235-1870, Fax: 816-235-6579, E-mail: kluckhohnj@umkc.edu.
Website: http://www.med.umkc.edu/.

The University of Montana, Graduate School, Phyllis J. Washington College of Education and Human Sciences, Department of Health and Human Performance, Missoula, MT 59812-0002. Offers exercise science (MS); health and human performance (MS); health promotion (MS). Part-time programs available. *Entrance requirements:* For master's, GRE General Test. Additional exam requirements/recommendations for international students: Required—TOEFL. *Faculty research:* Exercise physiology, performance psychology, nutrition, pre-employment physical screening, program evaluation.

University of Nebraska at Omaha, Graduate Studies, College of Education, School of Health, Physical Education, and Recreation, Omaha, NE 68182. Offers athletic training (MA); exercise science (PhD); health, physical education, and recreation (MA, MS). Part-time and evening/weekend programs available. *Faculty:* 15 full-time (7 women). *Students:* 54 full-time (24 women), 32 part-time (9 women); includes 8 minority (2 Asian, non-Hispanic/Latino; 3 Hispanic/Latino; 3 Two or more races, non-Hispanic/Latino), 4 international. Average age 28. 79 applicants, 51% accepted, 22 enrolled. In 2013, 27 master's awarded. *Degree requirements:* For master's, comprehensive exam, thesis (for some programs). *Entrance requirements:* For master's, GRE; entrance exam, minimum GPA of 3.0, official transcripts, statement of purpose, 2 letters of recommendation; for doctorate, GRE, minimum GPA of 3.2, official transcripts, statement of purpose, 3 letters of recommendation, resume, writing sample. Additional exam requirements/recommendations for international students: Required—TOEFL, IELTS, PTE. *Application deadline:* For fall admission, 7/1 priority date for domestic students; for spring admission, 11/1 priority date for domestic students; for summer admission, 2/1 for domestic students. Applications are processed on a rolling basis. Application fee: $45. Electronic applications accepted. *Financial support:* In 2013–14, 19 students received support, including 12 research assistantships with tuition reimbursements available, 7 teaching assistantships with tuition reimbursements available; fellowships, Federal Work-Study, institutionally sponsored loans, scholarships/grants, tuition waivers (full), and unspecified assistantships also available. Support available to part-time students. Financial award application deadline: 3/1; financial award applicants required to submit FAFSA. *Unit head:* Dr. Daniel Blanke, Director, 402-554-2670. *Application contact:* Dr. Kris Berg, Graduate Program Chair, 402-554-2670, E-mail: graduate@unomaha.edu.

University of New England, College of Osteopathic Medicine, Program in Medical Education Leadership, Biddeford, ME 04005-9526. Offers leadership development in academic medicine (Certificate); medical education leadership (MS); program development in academic medicine (Certificate). Part-time and evening/weekend programs available. Postbaccalaureate distance learning degree programs offered (no on-campus study). *Faculty:* 1 (woman) full-time, 4 part-time/adjunct (1 woman). *Students:* 40 full-time (21 women), 10 part-time (6 women); includes 6 minority (1 Black or African American, non-Hispanic/Latino; 5 Asian, non-Hispanic/Latino). Average age

40. 35 applicants, 83% accepted, 21 enrolled. In 2013, 18 master's, 2 other advanced degrees awarded. *Application deadline:* For fall admission, 8/1 for domestic students; for spring admission, 12/1 for domestic students. Applications are processed on a rolling basis. Application fee: $40. Electronic applications accepted. *Financial support:* Application deadline: 5/1; applicants required to submit FAFSA. *Unit head:* Dr. India L. Broyles, Director, Master of Medical Education Leadership Program/Associate Professor, 207-602-2694, Fax: 207-602-5977, E-mail: ibroyles@une.edu. *Application contact:* Dr. Cynthia Forrest, Vice President for Student Affairs, 207-221-4225, Fax: 207-523-1925, E-mail: gradadmissions@une.edu.
Website: http://www.une.edu/com/mmel/index.cfm.

University of New Mexico, Graduate School, College of Education, Department of Health, Exercise and Sports Sciences, Program in Health Education, Albuquerque, NM 87131-2039. Offers community health education (MS). *Accreditation:* NCATE. Part-time programs available. *Faculty:* 6 full-time (3 women). *Students:* 16 full-time (all women), 20 part-time (17 women); includes 21 minority (1 Black or African American, non-Hispanic/Latino; 6 American Indian or Alaska Native, non-Hispanic/Latino; 12 Hispanic/Latino; 1 Native Hawaiian or other Pacific Islander, non-Hispanic/Latino; 1 Two or more races, non-Hispanic/Latino), 4 international. Average age 30. 15 applicants, 60% accepted, 9 enrolled. In 2013, 14 master's awarded. *Degree requirements:* For master's, comprehensive exam, thesis optional. *Entrance requirements:* For master's, 3 letters of reference, resume, minimum cumulative GPA of 3.0 in last 2 years of bachelor's degree, letter of intent. Additional exam requirements/recommendations for international students: Required—TOEFL (minimum score 550 paper-based). *Application deadline:* For fall admission, 6/15 priority date for domestic students; for spring admission, 11/1 priority date for domestic students. Applications are processed on a rolling basis. Application fee: $50. Electronic applications accepted. *Financial support:* In 2013–14, 23 students received support, including 2 fellowships (averaging $2,290 per year), 3 teaching assistantships with full tuition reimbursements available (averaging $11,911 per year); career-related internships or fieldwork, institutionally sponsored loans, scholarships/grants, and health care benefits also available. Financial award application deadline: 3/1; financial award applicants required to submit FAFSA. *Faculty research:* Alcohol and families, health behaviors and sexuality, multicultural health behavior, health promotion policy, school/community-based prevention, health and aging. *Total annual research expenditures:* $91,910. *Unit head:* Dr. Elias Duryea, Coordinator, 505-277-5151, Fax: 505-277-6227, E-mail: duryea@unm.edu. *Application contact:* Carol Catania, Graduate Coordinator, 505-277-5151, Fax: 505-277-6227, E-mail: catania@unm.edu.
Website: http://coe.unm.edu/departments/hess/health-education/health-education-ms.html.

University of Northern Colorado, Graduate School, College of Natural and Health Sciences, School of Human Sciences, Program in Public Health, Greeley, CO 80639. Offers public health education (MPH). *Accreditation:* CEPH. *Degree requirements:* For master's, comprehensive exam, thesis or alternative. *Entrance requirements:* For master's, GRE General Test, 2 letters of recommendation. Electronic applications accepted.

University of Northern Iowa, Graduate College, College of Education, School of Health, Physical Education, and Leisure Services, MA Program in Health Promotion and Education, Cedar Falls, IA 50614. Offers health education (MA); health promotion/fitness (MA); school health education (MA). Part-time and evening/weekend programs available. *Students:* 10 full-time (6 women), 6 part-time (all women); includes 1 minority (Black or African American, non-Hispanic/Latino), 2 international. 14 applicants, 79% accepted, 5 enrolled. In 2013, 9 master's awarded. *Degree requirements:* For master's, comprehensive exam, thesis or alternative. *Entrance requirements:* For master's, minimum GPA of 3.0. Additional exam requirements/recommendations for international students: Required—TOEFL (minimum score 500 paper-based; 61 iBT). *Application deadline:* For fall admission, 8/1 priority date for domestic students. Applications are processed on a rolling basis. Application fee: $50 ($70 for international students). Electronic applications accepted. *Financial support:* Career-related internships or fieldwork, Federal Work-Study, and tuition waivers (full and partial) available. Support available to part-time students. Financial award application deadline: 2/1. *Unit head:* Dr. Susan Roberts-Dobie, Coordinator, 319-273-5930, Fax: 319-273-5958, E-mail: susan.dobie@uni.edu. *Application contact:* Laurie S. Russell, Record Analyst, 319-273-2623, Fax: 319-273-2885, E-mail: laurie.russell@uni.edu.
Website: http://www.uni.edu/coe/departments/school-health-physical-education-leisure-services/health-promotion-and-education.

University of Oklahoma Health Sciences Center, Graduate College, College of Allied Health, Department of Allied Health Sciences, Oklahoma City, OK 73190. Offers PhD. *Faculty:* 1 (woman) full-time, 1 part-time/adjunct (0 women). *Students:* 5 full-time (4 women), 5 part-time (3 women); includes 4 minority (1 American Indian or Alaska Native, non-Hispanic/Latino; 2 Asian, non-Hispanic/Latino; 1 Hispanic/Latino). Average age 31. 22 applicants, 23% accepted, 4 enrolled. *Degree requirements:* For doctorate, one foreign language, comprehensive exam, thesis/dissertation optional. *Entrance requirements:* For doctorate, GRE General Test, 3 letters of recommendation, master's degree. Additional exam requirements/recommendations for international students: Required—TOEFL (minimum score 550 paper-based). *Application deadline:* For fall admission, 7/1 for domestic students; for spring admission, 12/1 for domestic students. Application fee: $50. *Expenses:* Tuition, state resident: full-time $3504; part-time $175.20 per credit hour. Tuition, nonresident: full-time $13,504; part-time $675.20 per credit hour. *Required fees:* $1545; $52.70 per credit hour. $245.25 per semester. Tuition and fees vary according to course load. *Financial support:* In 2013–14, research assistantships (averaging $15,000 per year) were awarded. *Unit head:* Dr. Jan Womack, Associate Dean, Academic and Student Affairs, 405-271-6588, Fax: 405-271-3120, E-mail: jan-womack@ouhsc.edu. *Application contact:* Dr. Carole Sullivan, Dean, 405-271-2288, Fax: 405-271-1190, E-mail: carole-sullivan@ouhsc.edu.

University of Phoenix–Charlotte Campus, College of Nursing, Charlotte, NC 28273-3409. Offers education (MHA); gerontology (MHA); health administration (MHA); informatics (MHA, MSN); nursing (MSN); nursing/health care education (MSN). Evening/weekend programs available. *Degree requirements:* For master's, thesis (for some programs). *Entrance requirements:* For master's, minimum undergraduate GPA of 2.5, 3 years work experience. Additional exam requirements/recommendations for international students: Required—TOEFL (minimum score 550 paper-based; 79 iBT). Electronic applications accepted.

University of Phoenix–Des Moines Campus, College of Nursing, Des Moines, IA 50309. Offers education (MHA); gerontology (MHA); health administration (MHA, DHA); informatics (MHA, MSN); nursing (MSN, PhD); nursing/health care education (MSN).

University of Phoenix–Online Campus, College of Health Sciences and Nursing, Phoenix, AZ 85034-7209. Offers family nurse practitioner (Certificate); health care (Certificate); health care education (Certificate); health care informatics (Certificate); informatics (MSN); nursing (MSN); nursing and health care education (MSN); MSN/MBA; MSN/MHA. *Accreditation:* AACN. Evening/weekend programs available. Postbaccalaureate distance learning degree programs offered. *Entrance requirements:* Additional exam requirements/recommendations for international students: Required—TOEFL, TOEIC (Test of English as an International Communication), Berlitz Online English Proficiency Exam, PTE, or IELTS. Electronic applications accepted. *Expenses:* Contact institution.

University of Phoenix–Southern Colorado Campus, College of Nursing, Colorado Springs, CO 80903. Offers education (MHA); gerontology (MHA); health administration (MHA); nursing (MSN); MSN/MBA. Evening/weekend programs available. *Degree requirements:* For master's, thesis (for some programs). *Entrance requirements:* For master's, minimum undergraduate GPA of 2.5, 3 years of work experience, RN license. Additional exam requirements/recommendations for international students: Required—TOEFL (minimum score 550 paper-based; 79 iBT). Electronic applications accepted.

University of Phoenix–Washington D.C. Campus, College of Nursing, Washington, DC 20001. Offers education (MHA); gerontology (MHA); health administration (MHA, DHA); informatics (MHA, MSN); nursing (MSN, PhD); nursing/health care education (MSN); MSN/MBA; MSN/MHA.

University of Pittsburgh, Graduate School of Public Health, Department of Infectious Diseases and Microbiology, Pittsburgh, PA 15260. Offers infectious disease management, intervention, and community practice (MPH); infectious disease pathogenesis, eradication, and laboratory practice (MPH); infectious diseases and microbiology (MS, PhD). Part-time programs available. *Faculty:* 19 full-time (6 women), 4 part-time/adjunct (1 woman). *Students:* 50 full-time (42 women), 15 part-time (10 women); includes 8 minority (2 Black or African American, non-Hispanic/Latino; 4 Asian, non-Hispanic/Latino; 1 Hispanic/Latino; 1 Two or more races, non-Hispanic/Latino), 11 international. Average age 27. 155 applicants, 63% accepted, 15 enrolled. In 2013, 25 master's, 4 doctorates awarded. Terminal master's awarded for partial completion of doctoral program. *Degree requirements:* For master's, one foreign language, comprehensive exam (for some programs), thesis; for doctorate, one foreign language, comprehensive exam, thesis/dissertation. *Entrance requirements:* For master's and doctorate, GRE General Test, MCAT, or DAT. Additional exam requirements/recommendations for international students: Required—TOEFL (minimum score 550 paper-based; 80 iBT) or IELTS (minimum score 6.5). *Application deadline:* For fall admission, 1/15 for domestic and international students; for spring admission, 10/15 for domestic students, 8/1 for international students; for summer admission, 12/1 for international students. Applications are processed on a rolling basis. Application fee: $120. Electronic applications accepted. *Expenses:* Tuition, state resident: full-time $19,964; part-time $807 per credit. Tuition, nonresident: full-time $32,686; part-time $1337 per credit. *Required fees:* $740; $200. Tuition and fees vary according to program. *Financial support:* In 2013–14, 12 research assistantships with full and partial tuition reimbursements (averaging $8,754 per year) were awarded. Financial award applicants required to submit FAFSA. *Faculty research:* HIV, Epstein-Barr virus, virology, immunology, malaria. *Total annual research expenditures:* $14.8 million. *Unit head:* Dr. Charles R. Rinaldo, Jr., Chairman, 412-624-3928, Fax: 412-624-4953, E-mail: rinaldo@pitt.edu. *Application contact:* Dr. Jeremy Martinson, Assistant Professor, 412-624-5646, Fax: 412-383-8926, E-mail: jmartins@pitt.edu.
Website: http://www.idm.pitt.edu/.

University of Pittsburgh, School of Medicine, Medical Education Graduate Programs, Pittsburgh, PA 15260. Offers medical education (MS, Certificate). Part-time programs available. *Faculty:* 44 full-time (26 women). *Students:* 25 part-time (19 women); includes 7 minority (3 Black or African American, non-Hispanic/Latino; 3 Asian, non-Hispanic/Latino; 1 Two or more races, non-Hispanic/Latino). Average age 35. 11 applicants, 45% accepted, 5 enrolled. In 2013, 10 master's awarded. *Degree requirements:* For master's, thesis. *Entrance requirements:* For master's, MCAT, GRE, or GMAT. Additional exam requirements/recommendations for international students: Required—TOEFL (minimum score 600 paper-based; 100 iBT). *Application deadline:* For fall admission, 10/31 priority date for domestic and international students; for spring admission, 4/15 priority date for domestic and international students. Applications are processed on a rolling basis. Application fee: $0. Electronic applications accepted. *Expenses:* Tuition, state resident: full-time $19,964; part-time $807 per credit. Tuition, nonresident: full-time $32,686; part-time $1337 per credit. *Required fees:* $740; $200. Tuition and fees vary according to program. *Financial support:* Tuition waivers (partial) available. *Faculty research:* Medical education. *Unit head:* Dr. Wishwa Kapoor, Program Director, 412-692-2686, Fax: 412-586-9672, E-mail: kapoorwn@upmc.edu. *Application contact:* Jennifer Holliman, Program Coordinator, 412-586-9673, Fax: 412-586-9672, E-mail: hollimanjm@upmc.edu.
Website: http://www.icre.pitt.edu/degrees/degrees.html.

University of Puerto Rico, Medical Sciences Campus, Graduate School of Public Health, Department of Social Sciences, Program in Public Health Education, San Juan, PR 00936-5067. Offers MPHE. Part-time and evening/weekend programs available. *Degree requirements:* For master's, thesis. *Entrance requirements:* For master's, GRE, previous course work in education, social sciences, algebra, and natural sciences.

University of Rhode Island, Graduate School, College of Human Science and Services, Department of Kinesiology, Kingston, RI 02881. Offers cultural studies of sport and physical culture (MS); exercise science (MS); physical education pedagogy (MS); psychosocial/behavioral aspects of physical activity (MS). *Accreditation:* NCATE. Part-time programs available. *Faculty:* 17 full-time (11 women). *Students:* 13 full-time (8 women), 5 part-time (2 women); includes 4 minority (1 Black or African American, non-Hispanic/Latino; 1 American Indian or Alaska Native, non-Hispanic/Latino; 2 Hispanic/Latino). In 2013, 12 master's awarded. *Degree requirements:* For master's, thesis optional. *Entrance requirements:* For master's, GRE, 2 letters of recommendation. Additional exam requirements/recommendations for international students: Required—TOEFL (minimum score 550 paper-based). *Application deadline:* For fall admission, 7/15 for domestic students, 2/1 for international students; for spring admission, 11/15 for domestic students, 7/15 for international students. Application fee: $65. Electronic applications accepted. *Expenses:* Tuition, state resident: full-time $11,532; part-time $641 per credit. Tuition, nonresident: full-time $23,606; part-time $1311 per credit. *Required fees:* $1388; $36 per credit. $35 per semester. One-time fee: $130. *Financial support:* In 2013–14, 5 teaching assistantships with full and partial tuition reimbursements (averaging $9,903 per year) were awarded. Financial award application deadline: 7/15; financial award applicants required to submit FAFSA. *Faculty research:* Strength training and older adults, interventions to promote a healthy lifestyle as well as analysis of the psychosocial outcomes of those interventions, effects of exercise and nutrition on skeletal muscle of aging healthy adults with CVD and other metabolic related diseases, physical activity and fitness of deaf children and youth. *Total annual research expenditures:* $51,804. *Unit head:* Dr. Deborah Riebe, Chair, 401-874-5444, Fax: 401-874-4215, E-mail: debriebe@uri.edu. *Application contact:* Dr. Matthew Delmonico, Graduate Program Director, 401-874-5440, E-mail: delmonico@uri.edu.
Website: http://www.uri.edu/hss/.

University of St. Augustine for Health Sciences, Graduate Programs, Division of Advanced Studies, St. Augustine, FL 32086. Offers health science (DH Sc); health sciences education (Ed D). Part-time programs available. Postbaccalaureate distance learning degree programs offered (minimal on-campus study). *Faculty:* 22 part-time/adjunct (5 women). *Students:* 20 applicants, 100% accepted. In 2013, 3 doctorates awarded. *Entrance requirements:* For doctorate, GRE General Test, master's degree in related field. Additional exam requirements/recommendations for international students: Required—TOEFL. *Application deadline:* For fall admission, 12/15 for domestic

students; for spring admission, 6/15 for domestic students; for summer admission, 10/1 for domestic students. Application fee: $50. Tuition and fees vary according to course level, course load, campus/location and program. *Financial support:* In 2013–14, 1 teaching assistantship was awarded; career-related internships or fieldwork and tuition waivers (partial) also available. Support available to part-time students. *Unit head:* Dr. Richard Jensen, Director, 904-826-0084 Ext. 262, Fax: 904-826-0085, E-mail: rhjensen@usa.edu. *Application contact:* Dian Hartley, Director of Admissions, 904-826-0084 Ext. 207, Fax: 904-826-0085, E-mail: dhartley@usa.edu.

University of San Francisco, School of Nursing and Health Professions, Master's Programs, San Francisco, CA 94117-1080. Offers behavioral health (MSBH); clinical nurse leader (MS); public health (MPH). *Faculty:* 14 full-time (12 women), 30 part-time/adjunct (24 women). *Students:* 355 full-time (301 women), 108 part-time (97 women); includes 237 minority (26 Black or African American, non-Hispanic/Latino; 2 American Indian or Alaska Native, non-Hispanic/Latino; 122 Asian, non-Hispanic/Latino; 61 Hispanic/Latino; 5 Native Hawaiian or other Pacific Islander, non-Hispanic/Latino; 21 Two or more races, non-Hispanic/Latino), 4 international. Average age 33. 524 applicants, 52% accepted, 170 enrolled. In 2013, 106 master's awarded. *Application deadline:* For fall admission, 5/15 priority date for domestic students; for spring admission, 11/30 priority date for domestic students. *Expenses: Tuition:* Full-time $21,150; part-time $1175 per unit. Tuition and fees vary according to course load, campus/location and program. *Financial support:* In 2013–14, 50 students received support. *Unit head:* Dr. Michelle Montagno, Director, 415-422-4074, E-mail: mjmontagno@usfca.edu. *Application contact:* Ingrid McVanner, Information Contact, 415-422-2746, Fax: 415-422-2217.

University of South Africa, College of Human Sciences, Pretoria, South Africa. Offers adult education (M Ed); African languages (MA, PhD); African politics (MA, PhD); Afrikaans (MA, PhD); ancient history (MA, PhD); ancient Near Eastern studies (MA, PhD); anthropology (MA, PhD); applied linguistics (MA); Arabic (MA, PhD); archaeology (MA); art history (MA); Biblical archaeology (MA); Biblical studies (M Th, D Th, PhD); Christian spirituality (M Th, D Th); church history (M Th, D Th); classical studies (MA, PhD); clinical psychology (MA); communication (MA, PhD); comparative education (M Ed, Ed D); consulting psychology (D Admin, D Com, PhD); curriculum studies (M Ed, Ed D); development studies (M Admin, MA, D Admin, PhD); didactics (M Ed, Ed D); education (M Tech); education management (M Ed, Ed D); educational psychology (M Ed); English (MA); environmental education (M Ed); French (MA, PhD); German (MA, PhD); Greek (MA); guidance and counseling (M Ed); health studies (MA, PhD), including health sciences education (MA), health services management (MA), medical and surgical nursing science (critical care general) (MA), midwifery and neonatal nursing science (MA), trauma and emergency care (MA); history (MA, PhD); history of education (Ed D); inclusive education (M Ed, Ed D); information and communications technology policy and regulation (MA); information science (MA, MIS, PhD); international politics (MA, PhD); Islamic studies (MA, PhD); Italian (MA, PhD); Judaica (MA, PhD); linguistics (MA, PhD); mathematical education (M Ed); mathematics education (MA); missiology (M Th, D Th); modern Hebrew (MA, PhD); musicology (MA, MMus, D Mus, PhD); natural science education (M Ed); New Testament (M Th, D Th); Old Testament (D Th); pastoral therapy (M Th, D Th); philosophy (MA); philosophy of education (M Ed, Ed D); politics (MA, PhD); Portuguese (MA, PhD); practical theology (M Th, D Th); psychology (MA, MS, PhD); psychology of education (M Ed, Ed D); public health (MA); religious studies (MA, D Th, PhD); Romance languages (MA); Russian (MA, PhD); Semitic languages (MA, PhD); social behavior studies in HIV/AIDS (MA); social science (mental health) (MA); social science in development studies (MA); social science in psychology (MA); social science in social work (MA); social science in sociology (MA); social work (MSW, DSW, PhD); socio-education (M Ed, Ed D); sociolinguistics (MA); sociology (MA, PhD); Spanish (MA, PhD); systematic theology (M Th, D Th); TESOL (teaching English to speakers of other languages) (MA); theological ethics (M Th, D Th); theory of literature (MA, PhD); urban ministries (D Th); urban ministry (M Th).

University of South Alabama, Graduate School, College of Education, Department of Health, Physical Education and Leisure Services, Mobile, AL 36688-0002. Offers exercise science (MS); health education (M Ed); physical education (M Ed); therapeutic recreation (MS). *Accreditation:* NCATE (one or more programs are accredited). Part-time programs available. *Faculty:* 4 full-time (1 woman), 2 part-time/adjunct (0 women). *Students:* 34 full-time (16 women), 5 part-time (1 woman); includes 12 minority (9 Black or African American, non-Hispanic/Latino; 3 Two or more races, non-Hispanic/Latino), 4 international. 36 applicants, 61% accepted, 18 enrolled. In 2013, 16 master's awarded. *Degree requirements:* For master's, comprehensive exam. *Entrance requirements:* For master's, GRE General Test or MAT. *Application deadline:* For fall admission, 7/15 priority date for domestic students, 6/15 priority date for international students; for spring admission, 12/1 priority date for domestic students, 11/1 priority date for international students. Applications are processed on a rolling basis. Application fee: $35. *Expenses:* Tuition, state resident: full-time $8976; part-time $374 per credit hour. Tuition, nonresident: full-time $17,952; part-time $748 per credit hour. *Financial support:* In 2013–14, 10 teaching assistantships were awarded; career-related internships or fieldwork also available. Support available to part-time students. Financial award application deadline: 4/1. *Unit head:* Dr. Frederick M. Scaffidi, Chair, 251-460-7131. *Application contact:* Dr. Abigail Baxter, Director of Graduate Studies, 251-460-7131.

University of South Carolina, The Graduate School, Arnold School of Public Health, Department of Health Promotion, Education, and Behavior, Columbia, SC 29208. Offers health education (MAT); health promotion, education, and behavior (MPH, MS, MSPH, Dr PH, PhD); school health education (Certificate); MSW/MPH. MAT offered in cooperation with the College of Education. *Accreditation:* CEPH (one or more programs are accredited); NCATE (one or more programs are accredited). Part-time programs available. *Degree requirements:* For master's, comprehensive exam, thesis or alternative, practicum (MPH), project (MS); for doctorate, comprehensive exam, thesis/dissertation. *Entrance requirements:* For master's and doctorate, GRE General Test. Additional exam requirements/recommendations for international students: Required—TOEFL (minimum score 570 paper-based; 75 iBT). Electronic applications accepted. *Faculty research:* Health disparities and inequalities in communities, global health and nutrition, cancer and HIV/AIDS prevention, health communication, policy and program design.

University of South Carolina, The Graduate School, College of Education, Department of Instruction and Teacher Education, Program in Secondary Education, Columbia, SC 29208. Offers art education (IMA, MAT); business education (IMA, MAT); English (MAT); foreign language (MAT); health education (MAT); mathematics (MAT); science (IMA, MAT); secondary (Ed D); secondary education (MT, PhD); social studies (MAT); theatre and speech (MAT). IMA and MT offered jointly with the subject areas. *Accreditation:* NCATE. *Degree requirements:* For master's, comprehensive exam, thesis (for some programs), foreign language (MA); for doctorate, one foreign language, comprehensive exam, thesis/dissertation. *Entrance requirements:* For master's, GRE General Test or MAT, teaching certificate (IMA, M Ed), interview; for doctorate, GRE General Test or MAT, interview. *Faculty research:* Middle school programs, professional development, school collaboration.

University of Southern California, Keck School of Medicine and Graduate School, Graduate Programs in Medicine, Department of Preventive Medicine, Master of Public Health Program, Los Angeles, CA 90032. Offers biostatistics-epidemiology (MPH); child and family health (MPH); environmental health (MPH); global health leadership (MPH); health communication (MPH); health education and promotion (MPH); public health policy (MPH). *Accreditation:* CEPH. Part-time and evening/weekend programs available. *Faculty:* 22 full-time (12 women), 3 part-time/adjunct (0 women). *Students:* 179 full-time (136 women), 31 part-time (24 women); includes 120 minority (19 Black or African American, non-Hispanic/Latino; 64 Asian, non-Hispanic/Latino; 37 Hispanic/Latino), 36 international. Average age 24. 205 applicants, 70% accepted, 73 enrolled. In 2013, 90 master's awarded. *Degree requirements:* For master's, practicum, final report, oral presentation. *Entrance requirements:* For master's, GRE General Test, MCAT, GMAT, minimum GPA of 3.0. Additional exam requirements/recommendations for international students: Required—TOEFL (minimum score 600 paper-based; 90 iBT). *Application deadline:* For fall admission, 6/1 priority date for domestic and international students; for spring admission, 10/1 priority date for domestic and international students; for summer admission, 3/1 for domestic and international students. Applications are processed on a rolling basis. Application fee: $85. Electronic applications accepted. *Financial support:* Career-related internships or fieldwork, Federal Work-Study, institutionally sponsored loans, and scholarships/grants available. Support available to part-time students. Financial award application deadline: 5/4; financial award applicants required to submit CSS PROFILE or FAFSA. *Faculty research:* Substance abuse prevention, cancer and heart disease prevention, mass media and health communication research, health promotion, treatment compliance. *Unit head:* Dr. Louise A. Rohrbach, Director, 323-442-8237, Fax: 323-442-8297, E-mail: rohrbac@usc.edu. *Application contact:* Valerie Burris, Admissions Counselor, 323-442-7257, Fax: 323-442-8297, E-mail: valeriem@usc.edu. Website: http://mph.usc.edu/.

University of Southern Mississippi, Graduate School, College of Health, Department of Community Health Sciences, Hattiesburg, MS 39406-0001. Offers epidemiology and biostatistics (MPH); health education (MPH); health policy/administration (MPH); occupational/environmental health (MPH); public health nutrition (MPH). *Accreditation:* CEPH. Part-time and evening/weekend programs available. *Faculty:* 8 full-time (4 women), 1 part-time/adjunct (0 women). *Students:* 92 full-time (60 women), 9 part-time (4 women); includes 38 minority (29 Black or African American, non-Hispanic/Latino; 1 American Indian or Alaska Native, non-Hispanic/Latino; 2 Asian, non-Hispanic/Latino; 6 Two or more races, non-Hispanic/Latino), 13 international. Average age 34. 71 applicants, 93% accepted, 45 enrolled. *Degree requirements:* For master's, comprehensive exam, thesis (for some programs). *Entrance requirements:* For master's, GRE General Test, minimum GPA of 2.75 in last 60 hours. Additional exam requirements/recommendations for international students: Required—TOEFL, IELTS. *Application deadline:* For fall admission, 3/1 priority date for domestic and international students; for spring admission, 1/10 priority date for domestic and international students. Applications are processed on a rolling basis. Application fee: $50. Electronic applications accepted. *Financial support:* In 2013–14, 5 research assistantships with full tuition reimbursements (averaging $7,000 per year), 1 teaching assistantship with full tuition reimbursement (averaging $8,263 per year) were awarded; career-related internships or fieldwork, Federal Work-Study, institutionally sponsored loans, scholarships/grants, health care benefits, and unspecified assistantships also available. Financial award application deadline: 3/15; financial award applicants required to submit FAFSA. *Faculty research:* Rural health care delivery, school health, nutrition of pregnant teens, risk factor reduction, sexually transmitted diseases. *Unit head:* Dr. Ray Newman, Interim Chair, 601-266-5437, Fax: 601-266-5043. *Application contact:* Shonna Breland, Manager of Graduate Admissions, 601-266-6563, Fax: 601-266-5138. Website: http://www.usm.edu/chs.

The University of Tennessee, Graduate School, College of Education, Health and Human Sciences, Program in Health Promotion and Health Education, Knoxville, TN 37996. Offers MS. *Accreditation:* CEPH. Part-time programs available. *Degree requirements:* For master's, thesis optional. *Entrance requirements:* For master's, minimum GPA of 2.7. Additional exam requirements/recommendations for international students: Required—TOEFL. Electronic applications accepted. *Expenses:* Tuition, state resident: full-time $9540; part-time $531 per credit hour. Tuition, nonresident: full-time $27,728; part-time $1542 per credit hour. *Required fees:* $1404; $67 per credit hour.

The University of Tennessee, Graduate School, College of Education, Health and Human Sciences, Program in Safety, Knoxville, TN 37996. Offers MS. *Accreditation:* NCATE. Part-time programs available. *Degree requirements:* For master's, thesis optional. *Entrance requirements:* For master's, minimum GPA of 2.7. Additional exam requirements/recommendations for international students: Required—TOEFL. Electronic applications accepted. *Expenses:* Tuition, state resident: full-time $9540; part-time $531 per credit hour. Tuition, nonresident: full-time $27,728; part-time $1542 per credit hour. *Required fees:* $1404; $67 per credit hour.

The University of Texas at Austin, Graduate School, College of Education, Department of Kinesiology and Health Education, Austin, TX 78712-1111. Offers behavioral health (PhD); exercise and sport psychology (M Ed, MA); exercise science (M Ed, MS, PhD); health education (M Ed, MS, Ed D, PhD). Part-time programs available. Terminal master's awarded for partial completion of doctoral program. *Degree requirements:* For master's, thesis (for some programs); for doctorate, thesis/dissertation. *Entrance requirements:* For master's and doctorate, GRE General Test. Additional exam requirements/recommendations for international students: Required—TOEFL. Electronic applications accepted. *Faculty research:* Health promotion, human performance and exercise biochemistry, motor behavior and biomechanics, sport management, aging and pediatric development.

The University of Texas at San Antonio, College of Education and Human Development, Department of Kinesiology, Health, and Nutrition, San Antonio, TX 78249-0617. Offers dietetics studies (MSD); health and kinesiology (MS). Part-time and evening/weekend programs available. *Faculty:* 17 full-time (7 women), 1 part-time/adjunct (0 women). *Students:* 65 full-time (38 women), 66 part-time (29 women); includes 88 minority (12 Black or African American, non-Hispanic/Latino; 4 Asian, non-Hispanic/Latino; 71 Hispanic/Latino; 1 Two or more races, non-Hispanic/Latino), 9 international. Average age 28. 79 applicants, 95% accepted, 45 enrolled. In 2013, 48 master's awarded. *Degree requirements:* For master's, comprehensive exam, thesis optional. *Entrance requirements:* For master's, bachelor's degree with minimum GPA of 3.0 in last 60 hours of coursework; resume; statement of purpose; two letters of recommendation. Additional exam requirements/recommendations for international students: Required—TOEFL (minimum score 550 paper-based; 79 iBT), IELTS (minimum score 6.5). *Application deadline:* For fall admission, 7/1 for domestic students, 4/1 for international students; for spring admission, 11/1 for domestic students, 9/1 for international students; for summer admission, 4/1 for domestic students, 3/1 for international students. Applications are processed on a rolling basis. Application fee: $45 ($80 for international students). Electronic applications accepted. *Expenses:* Tuition, state resident: full-time $4671. Tuition, nonresident: full-time $8708. *International tuition:* $17,415 full-time. *Required fees:* $1924.60. Tuition and fees vary according to course load and degree level. *Faculty research:* Motor behavior, motor skills, exercise and nutrition, athlete efficacy, diabetes prevention. *Unit head:* Dr. Wan Xiang Yao, Chair, 210-458-6224, Fax: 210-452-5873, E-mail: wanxiang.yao@utsa.edu.

Application contact: Dr. Alberto Cordova, Graduate Advisor of Record, 210-458-6226, Fax: 210-458-5873, E-mail: alberto.cordova@utsa.edu.
Website: http://education.utsa.edu/health_and_kinesiology.

The University of Texas at Tyler, College of Nursing and Health Sciences, Department of Health and Kinesiology, Tyler, TX 75799-0001. Offers health and kinesiology (M Ed, MA); health sciences (MS); kinesiology (MS). *Accreditation:* Teacher Education Accreditation Council. Part-time programs available. Postbaccalaureate distance learning degree programs offered. *Degree requirements:* For master's, comprehensive exam (for some programs), thesis (for some programs). *Entrance requirements:* Additional exam requirements/recommendations for international students: Required—TOEFL. Electronic applications accepted. *Faculty research:* Osteoporosis, muscle soreness, economy of locomotion, adoption of rehabilitation programs, effect of inactivity and aging on muscle blood vessels, territoriality.

The University of Toledo, College of Graduate Studies, College of Health Sciences, Department of Health and Recreation Professions, Toledo, OH 43606-3390. Offers health education (PhD); recreation and leisure studies (MA). Part-time programs available. *Faculty:* 12. *Students:* 36 full-time (30 women), 38 part-time (20 women); includes 14 minority (10 Black or African American, non-Hispanic/Latino; 1 Asian, non-Hispanic/Latino; 2 Hispanic/Latino; 1 Two or more races, non-Hispanic/Latino), 2 international. Average age 28. 41 applicants, 80% accepted, 26 enrolled. In 2013, 10 master's, 3 doctorates awarded. *Degree requirements:* For master's, comprehensive exam, thesis; for doctorate, thesis/dissertation. *Entrance requirements:* For master's and doctorate, minimum cumulative GPA of 2.7 for all previous academic work, letters of recommendation. Additional exam requirements/recommendations for international students: Required—TOEFL (minimum score 550 paper-based; 80 iBT). *Application deadline:* For fall admission, 1/15 priority date for domestic and international students. Applications are processed on a rolling basis. Application fee: $45 ($75 for international students). Electronic applications accepted. *Financial support:* In 2013–14, 1 research assistantship with full and partial tuition reimbursement (averaging $9,000 per year), 17 teaching assistantships with full and partial tuition reimbursements (averaging $11,588 per year) were awarded; career-related internships or fieldwork, Federal Work-Study, institutionally sponsored loans, scholarships/grants, tuition waivers (full and partial), unspecified assistantships, and administrative assistantships also available. Support available to part-time students. Financial award applicants required to submit FAFSA. *Unit head:* Dr. Joseph Dake, Chair, 419-530-2767, E-mail: joseph.dake@utoledo.edu. *Application contact:* Graduate School Office, 419-530-4723, Fax: 419-530-4724, E-mail: grdsch@utnet.utoledo.edu.
Website: http://www.utoledo.edu/eduhshs/.

The University of Toledo, College of Graduate Studies, College of Medicine and Life Sciences, Department of Public Health and Preventative Medicine, Toledo, OH 43606-3390. Offers biostatistics and epidemiology (Certificate); contemporary gerontological practice (Certificate); environmental and occupational health and safety (MPH); epidemiology (Certificate); global public health (Certificate); health promotion and education (MPH); industrial hygiene (MSOH); medical and health science teaching and learning (Certificate); occupational health (Certificate); public health administration (MPH); public health and emergency response (Certificate); public health epidemiology (MPH); public health nutrition (MPH); MD/MPH. Part-time and evening/weekend programs available. *Faculty:* 9. *Students:* 69 full-time (50 women), 88 part-time (66 women); includes 50 minority (35 Black or African American, non-Hispanic/Latino; 10 Asian, non-Hispanic/Latino; 4 Hispanic/Latino; 1 Two or more races, non-Hispanic/Latino), 6 international. Average age 30. 92 applicants, 80% accepted, 52 enrolled. In 2013, 59 master's, 15 other advanced degrees awarded. *Degree requirements:* For master's, thesis or alternative. *Entrance requirements:* For master's, GRE, minimum undergraduate GPA of 3.0, three letters of recommendation, statement of purpose, transcripts from all prior institutions attended, resume; for Certificate, minimum undergraduate GPA of 3.0, three letters of recommendation, statement of purpose, transcripts from all prior institutions attended, resume. Additional exam requirements/recommendations for international students: Required—TOEFL (minimum score 550 paper-based; 80 iBT), IELTS (minimum score 6.5). *Application deadline:* For fall admission, 6/15 for domestic students, 3/15 priority date for international students; for spring admission, 10/15 for domestic students, 6/15 for international students; for summer admission, 3/15 for domestic students, 10/15 for international students. Applications are processed on a rolling basis. Application fee: $45 ($75 for international students). Electronic applications accepted. *Financial support:* In 2013–14, 4 research assistantships with full tuition reimbursements (averaging $10,000 per year) were awarded; Federal Work-Study, institutionally sponsored loans, scholarships/grants, tuition waivers (full and partial), and unspecified assistantships also available. *Unit head:* Dr. Sheryl A. Milz, Chair, 419-383-3976, Fax: 419-383-6140, E-mail: sheryl.milz@utoledo.edu. *Application contact:* Admissions Analyst, 419-383-4112, Fax: 419-383-6140.
Website: http://nocphmph.org/.

University of Utah, Graduate School, College of Health, Department of Health Promotion and Education, Salt Lake City, UT 84112. Offers M Phil, MS, Ed D, PhD. Part-time and evening/weekend programs available. *Faculty:* 5 full-time (3 women), 9 part-time/adjunct (4 women). *Students:* 28 full-time (20 women), 29 part-time (21 women); includes 11 minority (2 Black or African American, non-Hispanic/Latino; 3 Asian, non-Hispanic/Latino; 3 Hispanic/Latino; 1 Native Hawaiian or other Pacific Islander, non-Hispanic/Latino; 2 Two or more races, non-Hispanic/Latino), 6 international. Average age 32. 36 applicants, 58% accepted, 18 enrolled. In 2013, 8 master's, 3 doctorates awarded. Terminal master's awarded for partial completion of doctoral program. *Degree requirements:* For master's, comprehensive exam, thesis or alternative, field experience; for doctorate, comprehensive exam, thesis/dissertation, field experience. *Entrance requirements:* For master's, GRE (for thesis option), minimum GPA of 3.0; for doctorate, GRE General Test, minimum GPA of 3.2. Additional exam requirements/recommendations for international students: Required—TOEFL (minimum score 500 paper-based). *Application deadline:* For fall admission, 2/1 for domestic and international students; for spring admission, 2/15 for domestic and international students; for summer admission, 2/1 for domestic and international students. Applications are processed on a rolling basis. Application fee: $55 ($65 for international students). Electronic applications accepted. *Expenses:* Tuition, state resident: full-time $5259. Tuition, nonresident: full-time $18,569. *Required fees:* $841. Tuition and fees vary according to course load. *Financial support:* In 2013–14, 14 students received support, including 2 research assistantships with full and partial tuition reimbursements available (averaging $12,000 per year), 4 teaching assistantships with full tuition reimbursements available (averaging $12,000 per year); career-related internships or fieldwork, Federal Work-Study, institutionally sponsored loans, and scholarships/grants also available. Financial award application deadline: 2/15; financial award applicants required to submit FAFSA. *Faculty research:* Health behavior and counseling, health service administration, evaluation of health programs. *Unit head:* Leslie K. Chatelain, Department Chair, 801-581-4512, Fax: 801-585-3646, E-mail: les.chatelain@utah.edu. *Application contact:* Dr. Justine J. Reel, Director of Graduate Studies, 801-581-3481, Fax: 801-585-3646, E-mail: justine.reel@hsc.utah.edu.
Website: http://www.health.utah.edu/healthed/index.htm.

University of Virginia, Curry School of Education, Department of Human Services, Program in Health and Physical Education, Charlottesville, VA 22903. Offers M Ed, Ed D. *Students:* 42 full-time (25 women), 7 part-time (3 women); includes 1 minority (Asian, non-Hispanic/Latino), 1 international. Average age 26. 32 applicants, 53% accepted, 6 enrolled. In 2013, 39 master's, 1 doctorate awarded. *Entrance requirements:* For master's and doctorate, GRE General Test, 2 letters of recommendation. Additional exam requirements/recommendations for international students: Required—TOEFL (minimum score 600 paper-based; 90 iBT), IELTS (minimum score 7). *Application deadline:* Applications are processed on a rolling basis. Application fee: $60. Electronic applications accepted. *Expenses:* Tuition, state resident: part-time $334 per credit hour. Tuition, nonresident: part-time $1224 per credit hour. *Financial support:* Applicants required to submit FAFSA. *Unit head:* Arthur L. Weltman, Chair, Kinesiology, 434-924-6191, E-mail: alw2v@virginia.edu. *Application contact:* Lynn Renfroe, Information Contact, 434-924-6254, E-mail: ldr9t@virginia.edu.
Website: http://curry.virginia.edu/academics/degrees/bachelor-master-in-teaching/b-mt-in-health-physical-education.

University of Waterloo, Graduate Studies, Faculty of Applied Health Sciences, School of Public Health and Health Systems, Waterloo, ON N2L 3G1, Canada. Offers health studies and gerontology (M Sc, PhD); public health (MPH). Part-time programs available. *Degree requirements:* For master's, thesis; for doctorate, comprehensive exam, thesis/dissertation. *Entrance requirements:* For master's, honors degree, minimum B average, resume, writing sample; for doctorate, GRE (recommended), master's degree, minimum B average, resumé, writing sample. Additional exam requirements/recommendations for international students: Required—TOEFL, TWE. Electronic applications accepted. *Faculty research:* Population health, health promotion and disease prevention, healthy aging, health policy, planning and evaluation, health information management and health informatics, aging, health and well-being, work and health.

University of West Florida, College of Professional Studies, Department of Health, Leisure, and Exercise Science, Community Health Education Program, Pensacola, FL 32514-5750. Offers aging studies (MS); health promotion and worksite wellness (MS); psychosocial (MS). Part-time and evening/weekend programs available. *Degree requirements:* For master's, thesis or alternative. *Entrance requirements:* For master's, GRE or MAT, official transcripts; minimum GPA of 3.0; letter of intent; three personal references. Additional exam requirements/recommendations for international students: Required—TOEFL (minimum score 550 paper-based).

University of West Florida, College of Professional Studies, Department of Health, Leisure, and Exercise Science, Program in Health, Leisure, and Exercise Science, Pensacola, FL 32514-5750. Offers exercise science (MS); physical education (MS). Part-time and evening/weekend programs available. *Degree requirements:* For master's, thesis or alternative. *Entrance requirements:* For master's, GRE or MAT, official transcripts; minimum GPA of 3.0; letter of intent; two personal references; work experience. Additional exam requirements/recommendations for international students: Required—TOEFL (minimum score 550 paper-based). Electronic applications accepted.

University of Wisconsin–La Crosse, Graduate Studies, College of Science and Health, Department of Health Education and Health Promotion, Program in Community Health Education, La Crosse, WI 54601-3742. Offers MPH, MS. *Accreditation:* CEPH. *Faculty:* 7 full-time (4 women), 1 (woman) part-time/adjunct. *Students:* 15 full-time (13 women), 8 part-time (6 women); includes 2 minority (1 Black or African American, non-Hispanic/Latino; 1 Hispanic/Latino), 1 international. Average age 30. 18 applicants, 94% accepted, 10 enrolled. In 2013, 7 master's awarded. *Degree requirements:* For master's, thesis. *Entrance requirements:* For master's, GRE General Test, GRE Subject Test (MPH), 3 letters of recommendation. Additional exam requirements/recommendations for international students: Required—TOEFL (minimum score 550 paper-based; 79 iBT). Electronic applications accepted. *Financial support:* Research assistantships with partial tuition reimbursements, Federal Work-Study, scholarships/grants, health care benefits, and tuition waivers (partial) available. Support available to part-time students. Financial award applicants required to submit FAFSA. *Unit head:* Dr. Gary Gilmore, Director, 608-785-8163, E-mail: gilmore.gary@uwlax.edu. *Application contact:* Corey Sjoquist, Director of Admissions, 608-785-8939, E-mail: admissions@uwlax.edu.
Website: http://www.uwlax.edu/sah/hehp/.

University of Wisconsin–La Crosse, Graduate Studies, College of Science and Health, Department of Health Education and Health Promotion, Program in School Health Education, La Crosse, WI 54601-3742. Offers MS. *Students:* 1 applicant. *Entrance requirements:* For master's, GRE General Test, minimum GPA of 2.85. Additional exam requirements/recommendations for international students: Required—TOEFL (minimum score 550 paper-based; 79 iBT). *Application deadline:* Applications are processed on a rolling basis. Application fee: $0. Electronic applications accepted. *Financial support:* Federal Work-Study, scholarships/grants, and tuition waivers available. Support available to part-time students. Financial award applicants required to submit FAFSA. *Unit head:* Dr. Tracy Caravella, Director, 608-785-6788, E-mail: caravell.trac@uwlax.edu. *Application contact:* Corey Sjoquist, Director of Admissions, 608-785-8939, E-mail: admissions@uwlax.edu.
Website: http://www.uwlax.edu/sah/hehp/html/gr_she.htm.

University of Wisconsin–Milwaukee, Graduate School, College of Nursing, Milwaukee, WI 53201. Offers family nursing practitioner (Post Master's Certificate); health professional education (Certificate); nursing (MN, PhD); public health (Certificate). *Accreditation:* AACN. Part-time programs available. *Faculty:* 30 full-time (29 women), 2 part-time/adjunct (both women). *Students:* 157 full-time (142 women), 90 part-time (79 women); includes 32 minority (13 Black or African American, non-Hispanic/Latino; 10 Asian, non-Hispanic/Latino; 1 Hispanic/Latino; 8 Two or more races, non-Hispanic/Latino), 7 international. Average age 38. 160 applicants, 57% accepted, 51 enrolled. In 2013, 42 master's, 8 doctorates awarded. *Degree requirements:* For master's, thesis; for doctorate, thesis/dissertation. *Entrance requirements:* For master's, GRE General Test or MAT, autobiographical sketch; for doctorate, GRE, minimum GPA of 3.2. Additional exam requirements/recommendations for international students: Required—TOEFL (minimum score 550 paper-based; 79 iBT), IELTS (minimum score 6.5). *Application deadline:* For fall admission, 1/1 priority date for domestic students; for spring admission, 9/1 for domestic students. Applications are processed on a rolling basis. Application fee: $56 ($96 for international students). Electronic applications accepted. *Financial support:* In 2013–14, 3 fellowships, 1 research assistantship, 9 teaching assistantships were awarded; career-related internships or fieldwork, Federal Work-Study, health care benefits, unspecified assistantships, and project assistantships also available. Support available to part-time students. Financial award application deadline: 4/15; financial award applicants required to submit FAFSA. *Total annual research expenditures:* $3.2 million. *Unit head:* Dr. Sally Lundeen, Dean, 414-229-4189, E-mail: slundeen@uwm.edu. *Application contact:* Kim Litwack, Representative, 414-229-5098.
Website: http://www.uwm.edu/Dept/Nursing/.

University of Wyoming, College of Health Sciences, Division of Kinesiology and Health, Laramie, WY 82071. Offers MS. *Accreditation:* NCATE. Part-time programs available. Postbaccalaureate distance learning degree programs offered (no on-campus study). *Degree requirements:* For master's, comprehensive exam (for some programs),

thesis (for some programs). *Entrance requirements:* For master's, GRE General Test, minimum GPA of 3.0. Additional exam requirements/recommendations for international students: Required—TOEFL. Electronic applications accepted. *Faculty research:* Teacher effectiveness, effects of exercising on heart function, physiological responses of overtraining, psychological benefits of physical activity, health behavior.

Utah State University, School of Graduate Studies, Emma Eccles Jones College of Education and Human Services, Department of Health, Physical Education and Recreation, Logan, UT 84322. Offers M Ed, MS. Part-time and evening/weekend programs available. Postbaccalaureate distance learning degree programs offered (minimal on-campus study). *Degree requirements:* For master's, thesis (for some programs). *Entrance requirements:* For master's, GRE General Test or MAT, minimum GPA of 3.0. Additional exam requirements/recommendations for international students: Required—TOEFL. *Faculty research:* Sport psychology intervention, motor learning biomechanics, pedagogy, physiology.

Virginia Commonwealth University, Graduate School, School of Education, Program in Teaching and Learning, Richmond, VA 23284-9005. Offers early and elementary education (MT); health and physical education (MT); secondary 6-12 education (MT); secondary education (Certificate). *Accreditation:* NCATE. Part-time programs available. *Entrance requirements:* For master's, GRE General Test or MAT. Additional exam requirements/recommendations for international students: Required—TOEFL (minimum score 600 paper-based; 100 iBT). Electronic applications accepted.

Virginia State University, School of Graduate Studies, Research, and Outreach, School of Engineering, Science and Technology, Department of Psychology, Petersburg, VA 23806-0001. Offers behavioral and community health sciences (PhD); clinical health psychology (PhD); clinical psychology (MS); general psychology (MS). *Degree requirements:* For master's, one foreign language, thesis. *Entrance requirements:* For master's, GRE General Test.

Walden University, Graduate Programs, School of Health Sciences, Minneapolis, MN 55401. Offers clinical research administration (MS, Graduate Certificate); health education and promotion (MS); health informatics (MS); health services (PhD), including community health, healthcare administration, leadership, public health policy, self-designed; healthcare administration (MHA); public health (MPH, Dr PH, PhD), including community health and education (PhD), epidemiology (PhD). Part-time and evening/weekend programs available. Postbaccalaureate distance learning degree programs offered (minimal on-campus study). *Faculty:* 18 full-time (12 women), 236 part-time/adjunct (120 women). *Students:* 2,563 full-time (1,867 women), 1,775 part-time (1,233 women); includes 2,532 minority (1,963 Black or African American, non-Hispanic/Latino; 29 American Indian or Alaska Native, non-Hispanic/Latino; 212 Asian, non-Hispanic/Latino; 238 Hispanic/Latino; 15 Native Hawaiian or other Pacific Islander, non-Hispanic/Latino; 75 Two or more races, non-Hispanic/Latino), 97 international. Average age 39. 1,191 applicants, 94% accepted, 861 enrolled. In 2013, 723 master's, 121 doctorates, 17 other advanced degrees awarded. *Degree requirements:* For doctorate, thesis/dissertation, residency. *Entrance requirements:* For master's, bachelor's degree or higher; minimum GPA of 2.5; official transcripts; goal statement (for some programs); access to computer and Internet; for doctorate, master's degree or higher; three years of related professional or academic experience (preferred); minimum GPA of 3.0; goal statement and current resume (select programs); official transcripts; access to computer and Internet; for Graduate Certificate, relevant work experience; access to computer and Internet. Additional exam requirements/recommendations for international students: Required—TOEFL (minimum score 550 paper-based; 79 iBT), IELTS (minimum score 6.5), Michigan English Language Assessment Battery (minimum score 82), or PTE. *Application deadline:* Applications are processed on a rolling basis. Application fee: $0. Electronic applications accepted. *Expenses: Tuition:* Full-time $11,813.55; part-time $500 per credit. *Required fees:* $618.76. *Financial support:* Fellowships, Federal Work-Study, scholarships/grants, unspecified assistantships, and family tuition reduction, active duty/veteran tuition reduction, group tuition reduction, interest-free payment plans, employee tuition reduction available. Support available to part-time students. Financial award applicants required to submit FAFSA. *Unit head:* Dr. Jorg Westermann, Associate Dean, 800-925-3368. *Application contact:* Jennifer Hall, Vice President of Enrollment Management, 866-4-WALDEN, E-mail: info@waldenu.edu.
Website: http://www.waldenu.edu/colleges-schools/school-of-health-sciences.

Washburn University, School of Applied Studies, Department of Allied Health, Topeka, KS 66621. Offers health care education (MHS). Part-time programs available. *Students:* 14 part-time (12 women). Average age 35. *Degree requirements:* For master's, internship, practicum. *Entrance requirements:* For master's, bachelor's degree, two years of professional work experience in a health care environment, official transcripts, minimum cumulative GPA of 3.0 in last 60 hours, personal statement, resume, college algebra course with grade no lower than a C. Additional exam requirements/recommendations for international students: Required—TOEFL (minimum score 80 iBT). *Application deadline:* For fall admission, 3/15 priority date for domestic students. *Expenses:* Tuition, state resident: full-time $5850; part-time $325 per credit hour. Tuition, nonresident: full-time $11,916; part-time $662 per credit hour. *Required fees:* $86; $43 per semester. Tuition and fees vary according to program. *Unit head:* Dr. Pat Munzer, Dean, 785-670-2111, Fax: 785-670-1027, E-mail: nancy.tate@washburn.edu. *Application contact:* Kris Klima, Director of Admissions, 785-670-1030, Fax: 785-670-1113, E-mail: admissions@washburn.edu.
Website: http://www.washburn.edu/academics/college-schools/applied-studies/departments/allied-health/.

Washington University in St. Louis, School of Medicine, Program in Applied Health Behavior Research, Saint Louis, MO 63110. Offers health behavior planning and evaluation (Graduate Certificate); health behavior research (MS); health education, program planning and evaluation (MS). Part-time and evening/weekend programs available. *Faculty:* 15 part-time/adjunct (10 women). *Students:* 1 full-time (0 women), 17 part-time (12 women); includes 4 minority (1 Black or African American, non-Hispanic/Latino; 2 Asian, non-Hispanic/Latino; 1 Hispanic/Latino). Average age 40. In 2013, 1 master's, 1 other advanced degree awarded. *Entrance requirements:* For master's and Graduate Certificate, baccalaureate degree in psychology, biology, social work, public health, anthropology or other related field; experience working in the health care field, including health promotion research, social research, or community programs. Additional exam requirements/recommendations for international students: Required—TOEFL. *Application deadline:* Applications are processed on a rolling basis. Application fee: $35. *Financial support:* Applicants required to submit FAFSA. *Faculty research:* Health behavior, health disparities, health education, program management, program evaluation. *Unit head:* Dr. Anjali Deshpande, Program Director, 314-286-0148, E-mail: adeshpan@wustl.edu. *Application contact:* Debbie Pfeiffer, Program Manager, 314-454-8956, Fax: 314-454-8279, E-mail: dpfeiffer@wustl.edu.
Website: http://crtc.wustl.edu/degrees/ahbr.html.

Wayne State University, College of Education, Division of Kinesiology, Health and Sports Studies, Detroit, MI 48202. Offers adapted physical education (Certificate); coaching (Certificate); elementary physical education (Certificate); exercise and sport science (M Ed); health education (M Ed, Certificate); kinesiology (M Ed, PhD), including exercise and sport science (PhD), physical education pedagogy (PhD); physical education (M Ed); secondary physical education (Certificate); sports administration (MA); wellness clinician/research (M Ed). Part-time programs available. *Students:* 42 full-time (27 women), 78 part-time (38 women); includes 43 minority (35 Black or African American, non-Hispanic/Latino; 1 Asian, non-Hispanic/Latino; 5 Hispanic/Latino; 2 Two or more races, non-Hispanic/Latino), 5 international. Average age 30. 120 applicants, 48% accepted, 30 enrolled. In 2013, 32 master's awarded. *Degree requirements:* For master's, thesis (for some programs); for doctorate, thesis/dissertation. *Entrance requirements:* For master's and doctorate, minimum undergraduate GPA of 3.0, undergraduate degree directly relating to the field of specialization being applied for, or undergraduate degree accompanied by extensive educational background in a closely-related field. Additional exam requirements/recommendations for international students: Required—TOEFL (minimum score 79 iBT), TWE (minimum score 5.5), Michigan English Language Assessment Battery (minimum score 85); Recommended—IELTS (minimum score 6.5). *Application deadline:* For fall admission, 6/1 priority date for domestic students, 5/1 priority date for international students; for winter admission, 10/1 priority date for domestic students, 9/1 priority date for international students; for spring admission, 2/1 priority date for domestic students, 1/1 priority date for international students. Applications are processed on a rolling basis. Application fee: $0. Electronic applications accepted. *Expenses:* Tuition, state resident: part-time $554.15 per credit. Tuition, nonresident: part-time $1200.35 per credit. *Required fees:* $42.15 per credit. $268.30 per semester. Tuition and fees vary according to course load and program. *Financial support:* In 2013–14, 22 students received support, including 4 fellowships with tuition reimbursements available (averaging $13,050 per year), 5 research assistantships with tuition reimbursements available (averaging $16,508 per year); career-related internships or fieldwork, Federal Work-Study, scholarships/grants, health care benefits, and unspecified assistantships also available. Support available to part-time students. Financial award application deadline: 3/31; financial award applicants required to submit FAFSA. *Faculty research:* Exercise and sport science, nutrition and physical activity interventions, school and community health, obesity prevention. *Total annual research expenditures:* $1.3 million. *Unit head:* Dr. Nate McCaughtry, Assistant Dean, Division of Kinesiology, Health and Sport Studies/Director, Center for School Health, 313-577-0014, Fax: 313-577-5002, E-mail: aj4391@wayne.edu. *Application contact:* Janice Green, Assistant Dean, 313-577-1605, E-mail: jwgreen@wayne.edu.
Website: http://coe.wayne.edu/kinesiology/index.php.

Wayne State University, School of Medicine, Graduate Programs in Medicine, Medical Research Program, Detroit, MI 48202. Offers MS. Program open only to individuals actively participating in post-graduate professional training in Wayne State University affiliated programs. In 2013, 1 master's awarded. *Degree requirements:* For master's, thesis. *Entrance requirements:* For master's, GRE or MCAT, minimum GPA of 3.0, MD or equivalent professional degree in human health care. Additional exam requirements/recommendations for international students: Required—TOEFL, TWE (minimum score 6). *Application deadline:* For fall admission, 6/1 for domestic students, 4/1 for international students; for winter admission, 12/1 for domestic and international students. Application fee: $0. Electronic applications accepted. *Expenses:* Contact institution. *Financial support:* Scholarships/grants available. *Faculty research:* Clinical research (cardiovascular, pediatrics, infectious diseases), basic research (stem cell biology, electrophysiology, drugs/drug abuse). *Unit head:* Dr. Thomas Holland, Director/Graduate Program Officer, Master of Science in Medical Research, 313-577-1455, Fax: 313-577-1455.
Website: http://gradprograms.med.wayne.edu/program-spotlight.php?id=33.

West Chester University of Pennsylvania, College of Health Sciences, Department of Health, West Chester, PA 19383. Offers community health (MPH); emergency preparedness (Certificate); environmental health (MPH); health care management (MPH, Certificate); integrative health (MPH, Certificate); nutrition (MPH); school health (M Ed). *Accreditation:* CEPH. Part-time and evening/weekend programs available. *Faculty:* 17 full-time (13 women), 3 part-time/adjunct (all women). *Students:* 115 full-time (85 women), 95 part-time (73 women); includes 79 minority (66 Black or African American, non-Hispanic/Latino; 1 American Indian or Alaska Native, non-Hispanic/Latino; 5 Asian, non-Hispanic/Latino; 3 Hispanic/Latino; 4 Two or more races, non-Hispanic/Latino), 15 international. Average age 31. 156 applicants, 83% accepted, 76 enrolled. In 2013, 101 master's, 18 other advanced degrees awarded. *Degree requirements:* For master's, thesis or alternative, minimum GPA of 3.0; research report (for M Ed); major project and practicum (for MPH); for Certificate, minimum GPA of 3.0. *Entrance requirements:* For master's, goal statement, two letters of recommendation, undergraduate Introduction to Statistics course. Additional exam requirements/recommendations for international students: Required—TOEFL (minimum score 550 paper-based; 80 iBT). *Application deadline:* For fall admission, 4/15 priority date for domestic students, 3/15 for international students; for spring admission, 10/15 priority date for domestic students, 9/1 for international students. Applications are processed on a rolling basis. Application fee: $45. Electronic applications accepted. *Expenses:* Tuition, state resident: full-time $7956; part-time $442 per credit. Tuition, nonresident: full-time $11,934; part-time $663 per credit. *Required fees:* $2134.20; $106.24 per credit. Tuition and fees vary according to campus/location and program. *Financial support:* Unspecified assistantships available. Support available to part-time students. Financial award application deadline: 2/15; financial award applicants required to submit FAFSA. *Faculty research:* Healthy school communities, community health issues and evidence-based programs, environment and health, nutrition and health, integrative health. *Unit head:* Dr. Bethann Cinelli, Chair, 610-436-2267, E-mail: bcinelli@wcupa.edu. *Application contact:* Dr. Lynn Carson, Graduate Coordinator, 610-436-2138, E-mail: lcarson@wcupa.edu.
Website: http://www.wcupa.edu/_ACADEMICS/HealthSciences/health/.

Western Illinois University, School of Graduate Studies, College of Education and Human Services, Department of Health Sciences, Macomb, IL 61455-1390. Offers health education (MS); health services administration (Certificate). *Accreditation:* NCATE. Part-time programs available. *Students:* 24 full-time (18 women), 24 part-time (17 women); includes 10 minority (5 Black or African American, non-Hispanic/Latino; 3 Asian, non-Hispanic/Latino; 2 Hispanic/Latino), 7 international. Average age 29. In 2013, 15 master's, 8 other advanced degrees awarded. *Degree requirements:* For master's, comprehensive exam, thesis or alternative. *Entrance requirements:* Additional exam requirements/recommendations for international students: Required—TOEFL (minimum score 550 paper-based; 80 iBT). *Application deadline:* Applications are processed on a rolling basis. Application fee: $30. Electronic applications accepted. *Financial support:* In 2013–14, 11 students received support, including 9 research assistantships with full tuition reimbursements available (averaging $7,544 per year), 2 teaching assistantships with full tuition reimbursements available (averaging $8,688 per year). Financial award applicants required to submit FAFSA. *Unit head:* Dr. Lorette Oden, Interim Chairperson, 309-298-1076. *Application contact:* Dr. Nancy Parsons, Associate Provost and Director of Graduate Studies, 309-298-1806, Fax: 309-298-2345, E-mail: grad-office@wiu.edu.
Website: http://wiu.edu/health.

Western Michigan University, Graduate College, College of Health and Human Services, Interdisciplinary Health Sciences Program, Kalamazoo, MI 49008. Offers PhD.

Western Oregon University, Graduate Programs, College of Education, Division of Teacher Education, Program in Secondary Education, Monmouth, OR 97361-1394. Offers bilingual education (MS Ed); health (MS Ed); humanities (MAT, MS Ed); initial

licensure (MAT); mathematics (MAT, MS Ed); science (MAT, MS Ed); social science (MAT, MS Ed). *Accreditation:* NCATE. Part-time and evening/weekend programs available. *Degree requirements:* For master's, thesis optional, written exam. *Entrance requirements:* For master's, minimum GPA of 3.0, teaching license. Additional exam requirements/recommendations for international students: Required—TOEFL (minimum score 550 paper-based; 79 iBT), IELTS (minimum score 6.5). *Faculty research:* Literacy, science in primary grades, geography education, retention, teacher burnout.

Western University of Health Sciences, College of Allied Health Professions, Program in Health Sciences, Pomona, CA 91766-1854. Offers MS. Part-time and evening/weekend programs available. *Faculty:* 2 full-time (1 woman). *Students:* 16 full-time (15 women), 20 part-time (17 women); includes 22 minority (6 Black or African American, non-Hispanic/Latino; 10 Asian, non-Hispanic/Latino; 5 Hispanic/Latino; 1 Two or more races, non-Hispanic/Latino), 3 international. Average age 29. 16 applicants, 31% accepted, 3 enrolled. In 2013, 15 master's awarded. *Degree requirements:* For master's, thesis. *Entrance requirements:* For master's, GRE, minimum undergraduate GPA of 2.5, graduate 3.0; letters of recommendation; interview. Additional exam requirements/recommendations for international students: Required—TOEFL. *Application deadline:* For fall admission, 5/31 priority date for domestic students; for spring admission, 10/31 priority date for domestic students. Applications are processed on a rolling basis. Application fee: $35. Electronic applications accepted. *Expenses:* Contact institution. *Financial support:* Institutionally sponsored loans, scholarships/grants, and veterans educational benefits available. Financial award application deadline: 3/2; financial award applicants required to submit FAFSA. *Unit head:* Dr. Tina Meyer, Chair, 909-469-5397, Fax: 909-469-5407, E-mail: tmeyer@westernu.edu. *Application contact:* Susan Hanson, Director of Admissions for the College of Osteopathic Medicine of the Pacific and for Health Professions Education, 909-469-5335, Fax: 909-469-5570, E-mail: admissions@westernu.edu.
Website: http://prospective.westernu.edu/health-sciences/welcome-3/.

West Virginia University, School of Physical Education, Morgantown, WV 26506. Offers athletic coaching education (MS); athletic training (MS); physical education/teacher education (MS, PhD), including curriculum and instruction (PhD), motor behavior (PhD), physical education supervision (PhD); sport and exercise psychology (PhD); sport management (MS). *Degree requirements:* For doctorate, comprehensive exam, thesis/dissertation, oral exam. *Entrance requirements:* For master's, GRE or MAT, minimum GPA of 3.0; for doctorate, GRE General Test or MAT, minimum GPA of 3.5. Additional exam requirements/recommendations for international students: Required—TOEFL (minimum score 550 paper-based). Electronic applications accepted. *Faculty research:* Sport psychosociology, teacher education, exercise psychology, counseling.

Widener University, School of Human Service Professions, Center for Education, Chester, PA 19013-5792. Offers adult education (M Ed); counseling in higher education (M Ed); counselor education (M Ed); early childhood education (M Ed); educational foundations (M Ed); educational leadership (M Ed); educational psychology (M Ed); elementary education (M Ed); English and language arts (M Ed); health education (M Ed); higher education leadership (Ed D); home and school visitor (M Ed); human sexuality (M Ed, PhD); mathematics education (M Ed); middle school education (M Ed); principalship (M Ed); reading and language arts (Ed D); reading education (M Ed); school administration (Ed D); science education (M Ed); social studies education (M Ed); special education (M Ed); technology education (M Ed). *Accreditation:* NCATE. Part-time and evening/weekend programs available. *Faculty:* 34 full-time (22 women), 37 part-time/adjunct (14 women). *Students:* 64 full-time (44 women), 209 part-time (146 women); includes 49 minority (39 Black or African American, non-Hispanic/Latino; 1 American Indian or Alaska Native, non-Hispanic/Latino; 4 Asian, non-Hispanic/Latino; 4 Hispanic/Latino; 1 Two or more races, non-Hispanic/Latino), 8 international. Average age 39. 139 applicants, 88% accepted. In 2013, 168 master's, 31 doctorates awarded. Terminal master's awarded for partial completion of doctoral program. *Degree requirements:* For doctorate, thesis/dissertation. *Entrance requirements:* For master's, minimum GPA of 2.5; for doctorate, GRE or MAT, minimum GPA of 2.0 (undergraduate), 3.5 (graduate). *Application deadline:* Applications are processed on a rolling basis. Application fee: $25 ($300 for international students). Electronic applications accepted. *Expenses:* Contact institution. *Financial support:* Career-related internships or fieldwork, tuition waivers (full and partial), and unspecified assistantships available. Support available to part-time students. Financial award application deadline: 5/1. *Faculty research:* Reading and cognition, adult education, technology education, educational leadership, special education. *Unit head:* Dr. Michael W. LeDoux, Associate Dean, 610-499-4294, Fax: 610-499-4623, E-mail: mwledoux@widener.edu. *Application contact:* Dr. Roberta Nolan, Director of Graduate Admissions, 610-499-4125, E-mail: rdnolan@widener.edu.

Wingate University, Thayer School of Education, Wingate, NC 28174-0159. Offers community college leadership (Ed D); educational leadership (MA Ed, Ed D); elementary education (MA Ed, MAT); health and physical education (MA Ed); sport administration (MA Ed). *Accreditation:* NCATE. Part-time and evening/weekend programs available. *Degree requirements:* For master's, portfolio. *Entrance requirements:* For master's, GRE General Test or MAT, teaching certificate (MA Ed).

Worcester State University, Graduate Studies, Department of Education, Program in Health Education, Worcester, MA 01602-2597. Offers M Ed. Part-time programs available. *Faculty:* 14 full-time (11 women), 22 part-time/adjunct (10 women). *Students:* 7 part-time (6 women). Average age 40. 3 applicants, 100% accepted. In 2013, 8 master's awarded. *Degree requirements:* For master's, comprehensive exam (for some programs), thesis optional. *Entrance requirements:* For master's, GRE General Test or MAT. Additional exam requirements/recommendations for international students: Required—TOEFL (minimum score 500 paper-based; 61 iBT). *Application deadline:* For fall admission, 6/15 for domestic and international students; for spring admission, 4/1 for domestic and international students. Applications are processed on a rolling basis. Application fee: $40. Electronic applications accepted. *Expenses: Tuition, area resident:* Part-time $150 per credit. Tuition, state resident: part-time $150 per credit. Tuition, nonresident: part-time $150 per credit. *Required fees:* $114.50 per credit. *Financial support:* Career-related internships or fieldwork, scholarships/grants, and unspecified assistantships available. Financial award application deadline: 3/1; financial award applicants required to submit FAFSA. *Unit head:* Dr. Marianna Calle, Coordinator, 508-929-8739, Fax: 508-929-8164, E-mail: mcalle@worcester.edu. *Application contact:* Sara Grady, Assistant Dean of Graduate and Continuing Education, 508-929-8787, Fax: 508-929-8100, E-mail: sara.grady@worcester.edu.

Wright State University, School of Graduate Studies, College of Education and Human Services, Department of Health, Physical Education, and Recreation, Dayton, OH 45435. Offers M Ed, MA. *Accreditation:* NCATE. *Degree requirements:* For master's, comprehensive exam, thesis (for some programs). *Entrance requirements:* For master's, GRE General Test, MAT. Additional exam requirements/recommendations for international students: Required—TOEFL. *Faculty research:* Motor learning, motor development, exercise physiology, adapted physical education.

Wright State University, School of Medicine, Program in Public Health, Dayton, OH 45435. Offers health promotion and education (MPH); public health management (MPH); public health nursing (MPH). *Accreditation:* CEPH.

Home Economics Education

Cambridge College, School of Education, Cambridge, MA 02138-5304. Offers autism specialist (M Ed); autism/behavior analyst (M Ed); behavior analyst (Post-Master's Certificate); behavioral management (M Ed); early childhood teacher (M Ed); education specialist in curriculum and instruction (CAGS); educational leadership (Ed D); elementary teacher (M Ed); English as a second language (M Ed, Certificate); general science (M Ed); health education (Post-Master's Certificate); health/family and consumer sciences (M Ed); history (M Ed); individualized (M Ed); information technology literacy (M Ed); instructional technology (M Ed); interdisciplinary studies (M Ed); library teacher (M Ed); literacy education (M Ed); mathematics (M Ed); mathematics specialist (Certificate); middle school mathematics and science (M Ed); school administration (M Ed, CAGS); school guidance counselor (M Ed); school nurse education (M Ed); school social worker/school adjustment counselor (M Ed); special education administrator (CAGS); special education/moderate disabilities (M Ed); teaching skills and methodologies (M Ed). Part-time and evening/weekend programs available. Postbaccalaureate distance learning degree programs offered (minimal on-campus study). *Degree requirements:* For master's, thesis, internship/practicum (licensure program only); for doctorate, thesis/dissertation; for other advanced degree, thesis. *Entrance requirements:* For master's, interview, resume, documentation of licensure, 2 professional references; for doctorate, official transcripts, interview, resume, documentation of licensure (if any), written personal statement/essay, portfolio of scholarly and professional work, qualifying assessment, 2 professional references, health insurance, immunizations form; for other advanced degree, official transcripts, interview, resume, documentation of licensure (if any), written personal statement/essay, 2 professional references, health insurance, immunizations form. Additional exam requirements/recommendations for international students: Required—TOEFL (minimum score 550 paper-based; 79 iBT), Michigan English Language Assessment Battery (minimum score 85); Recommended—IELTS (minimum score 6). Electronic applications accepted. *Expenses:* Contact institution. *Faculty research:* Adult education, accelerated learning, mathematics education, brain compatible learning, special education and law.

Central Washington University, Graduate Studies and Research, College of Education and Professional Studies, Department of Family and Consumer Sciences, Ellensburg, WA 98926. Offers career and technical education (MS); family and consumer sciences education (MS); family studies (MS). Part-time programs available. *Degree requirements:* For master's, thesis or alternative. *Entrance requirements:* For master's, minimum GPA of 3.0. Additional exam requirements/recommendations for international students: Required—TOEFL (minimum score 550 paper-based; 79 iBT). Electronic applications accepted.

Eastern Kentucky University, The Graduate School, College of Education, Department of Curriculum and Instruction, Program in Secondary and Higher Education, Richmond, KY 40475-3102. Offers secondary education (MA Ed), including agricultural education, art education, biological sciences education, business education, English education, geography education, history education, home economics education, industrial education, mathematical sciences education, physical education, school health education. *Accreditation:* NCATE. Part-time programs available. *Entrance requirements:* For master's, GRE General Test, minimum GPA of 2.5.

Indiana State University, College of Graduate and Professional Studies, College of Arts and Sciences, Department of Family and Consumer Sciences, Terre Haute, IN 47809. Offers dietetics (MS); family and consumer sciences education (MS); inter-area option (MS). *Accreditation:* AND. Part-time programs available. *Faculty:* 5 full-time (4 women). *Students:* 12 full-time (all women), 7 part-time (6 women); includes 4 minority (3 Black or African American, non-Hispanic/Latino; 1 Asian, non-Hispanic/Latino), 2 international. Average age 33. 13 applicants, 100% accepted, 5 enrolled. In 2013, 9 master's awarded. *Degree requirements:* For master's, thesis optional. *Application deadline:* For fall admission, 7/1 priority date for domestic students; for spring admission, 11/1 priority date for domestic students. Applications are processed on a rolling basis. Application fee: $35. Electronic applications accepted. *Financial support:* In 2013–14, 2 research assistantships with partial tuition reimbursements (averaging $7,000 per year) were awarded; teaching assistantships and tuition waivers (partial) also available. Financial award application deadline: 3/1; financial award applicants required to submit FAFSA. *Unit head:* Dr. Frederica Kramer, Chairperson, 812-237-3297. *Application contact:* Dr. Jay Gatrell, Dean, 800-444-GRAD, Fax: 812-237-8060, E-mail: jay.gatrell@indstate.edu.

Iowa State University of Science and Technology, Department of Apparel, Education Studies, and Hospitality Management, Ames, IA 50011. Offers family and consumer sciences education and studies (M Ed, MS, PhD); foodservice and lodging management (MFCS, MS, PhD); textiles and clothing (MFCS, MS, PhD). *Degree requirements:* For doctorate, thesis/dissertation. *Entrance requirements:* For master's and doctorate, GRE General Test. Additional exam requirements/recommendations for international students: Required—TOEFL (minimum score 550 paper-based; 79 iBT), IELTS (minimum score 6.5). Electronic applications accepted.

Louisiana State University and Agricultural & Mechanical College, Graduate School, College of Human Sciences and Education, School of Human Resource Education and Workforce Development, Baton Rouge, LA 70803. Offers agriculture and extension education and youth development (MS, PhD); career and technical education (MS, PhD); comprehensive vocational education (MS, PhD); extension and international education (MS, PhD); human resource and leadership development (MS, PhD); industrial education (MS); vocational agriculture education (MS, PhD); vocational business education (MS); vocational home economics education (MS). *Accreditation:* NCATE. Part-time programs available. *Faculty:* 10 full-time (5 women). *Students:* 46 full-time (28 women), 138 part-time (96 women); includes 65 minority (52 Black or African American, non-Hispanic/Latino; 2 American Indian or Alaska Native, non-Hispanic/

Latino; 2 Asian, non-Hispanic/Latino; 6 Hispanic/Latino; 3 Two or more races, non-Hispanic/Latino), 6 international. Average age 35. 120 applicants, 62% accepted, 49 enrolled. In 2013, 23 master's, 14 doctorates awarded. Terminal master's awarded for partial completion of doctoral program. *Degree requirements:* For master's, thesis (for some programs); for doctorate, thesis/dissertation. *Entrance requirements:* For master's and doctorate, GRE General Test, minimum GPA of 3.0. Additional exam requirements/recommendations for international students: Required—TOEFL (minimum score 550 paper-based; 79 iBT), IELTS (minimum score 6.5), or PTE (minimum score 59). *Application deadline:* For fall admission, 1/25 priority date for domestic students, 5/15 for international students; for spring admission, 10/15 for international students. Applications are processed on a rolling basis. Application fee: $50 ($70 for international students). Electronic applications accepted. *Financial support:* In 2013–14, 85 students received support, including 4 fellowships with full and partial tuition reimbursements available (averaging $31,175 per year), 9 research assistantships with full and partial tuition reimbursements available (averaging $15,422 per year), 14 teaching assistantships with partial tuition reimbursements available (averaging $14,289 per year); career-related internships or fieldwork, Federal Work-Study, institutionally sponsored loans, health care benefits, tuition waivers (full and partial), and unspecified assistantships also available. Financial award application deadline: 3/1; financial award applicants required to submit FAFSA. *Faculty research:* Adult education, history and philosophy of vocational education, curriculum and instruction, career decision-making. *Total annual research expenditures:* $4,454. *Unit head:* Dr. Ed Holton, Director, 225-578-5748, Fax: 225-578-5755, E-mail: eholton@lsu.edu. Website: http://www.lsu.edu/hrleader/.

Montana State University, College of Graduate Studies, College of Education, Health, and Human Development, Department of Health and Human Development, Bozeman, MT 59717. Offers family and consumer sciences (MS). *Accreditation:* ACA. Part-time programs available. Postbaccalaureate distance learning degree programs offered (no on-campus study). *Degree requirements:* For master's, comprehensive exam. *Entrance requirements:* For master's, GRE (minimum scores: verbal 480; quantitative 480). Additional exam requirements/recommendations for international students: Required—TOEFL (minimum score 550 paper-based). Electronic applications accepted. *Faculty research:* Community food systems, ethic of care for teachers and coaches, influence of public policy on families and communities, cost effectiveness of early childhood education, exercise metabolism, winter sport performance enhancement, assessment of physical activity.

Purdue University, Graduate School, College of Education, Department of Curriculum and Instruction, West Lafayette, IN 47907. Offers agricultural and extension education (PhD, Ed S); agriculture and extension education (MS, MS Ed); art education (PhD); curriculum studies (MS Ed, PhD, Ed S); educational technology (MS Ed, PhD, Ed S); elementary education (MS Ed); family and consumer sciences education (MS Ed, PhD, Ed S); foreign language education (MS Ed, PhD, Ed S); industrial technology (PhD, Ed S); language arts (MS Ed, PhD, Ed S); literacy (MS Ed, PhD, Ed S); mathematics/science education (MS, MS Ed, PhD, Ed S); social studies (MS Ed, PhD); social studies education (Ed S); vocational/industrial education (MS Ed, PhD, Ed S); vocational/technical education (MS Ed, PhD, Ed S). *Accreditation:* NCATE. Part-time and evening/weekend programs available. *Faculty:* 29 full-time (19 women), 33 part-time/adjunct (29 women). *Students:* 85 full-time (53 women), 271 part-time (195 women); includes 62 minority (19 Black or African American, non-Hispanic/Latino; 3 American Indian or Alaska Native, non-Hispanic/Latino; 13 Asian, non-Hispanic/Latino; 22 Hispanic/Latino; 1 Native Hawaiian or other Pacific Islander, non-Hispanic/Latino; 4 Two or more races, non-Hispanic/Latino), 41 international. Average age 36. 155 applicants, 71% accepted, 71 enrolled. In 2013, 60 master's, 20 doctorates awarded. *Degree requirements:* For master's, thesis optional; for doctorate, thesis/dissertation, oral and written exams; for Ed S, oral presentation, project. *Entrance requirements:* For master's, GRE General Test (if undergraduate GPA is below 3.0), minimum undergraduate GPA of 3.0 or equivalent; for doctorate, GRE General Test (minimum combined verbal and quantitative score of 1000, 300 for new scoring), minimum undergraduate GPA of 3.0 or equivalent; master's degree with minimum GPA of 3.0 or equivalent; for Ed S, GRE General Test (minimum combined verbal and quantitative score of 1000, 300 for new scoring), minimum undergraduate GPA of 3.0 or equivalent; master's degree. Additional exam requirements/recommendations for international students: Required—TOEFL (minimum score 550 paper-based; 77 iBT). *Application deadline:* For fall admission, 12/15 for domestic students, 3/1 for international students; for spring admission, 9/15 for domestic students, 8/1 for international students. Application fee: $60 ($75 for international students). Electronic applications accepted. *Financial support:* Fellowships with full tuition reimbursements, research assistantships with full tuition reimbursements, teaching assistantships with full tuition reimbursements, career-related internships or fieldwork, and tuition waivers (full) available. Support available to part-time students. Financial award application deadline: 3/1; financial award applicants required to submit FAFSA. *Faculty research:* Literacy acquisition and development, teacher beliefs and knowledge, recruitment and retention of underrepresented students, economic education, literacy discourse. *Unit head:* Dr. Phillip J. VanFossen, Head, 765-494-7935, Fax: 765-496-1622, E-mail: vanfoss@purdue.edu. *Application contact:* Cindy Blankenship, Graduate Contact, 765-494-2345, Fax: 765-494-5832, E-mail: prater0@purdue.edu.
Website: http://www.edci.purdue.edu/.

Queens College of the City University of New York, Division of Graduate Studies, Mathematics and Natural Sciences Division, Department of Family, Nutrition and Exercise Sciences, Flushing, NY 11367-1597. Offers home economics (MS Ed); physical education and exercise sciences (MS Ed). Part-time and evening/weekend programs available. *Degree requirements:* For master's, research project. *Entrance requirements:* For master's, minimum GPA of 3.0. Additional exam requirements/recommendations for international students: Required—TOEFL.

South Carolina State University, School of Graduate and Professional Studies, Department of Education, Orangeburg, SC 29117-0001. Offers early childhood and special education (M Ed); early childhood education (MAT); elementary education (M Ed, MAT); general science (MAT); mathematics (MAT); secondary education (M Ed), including biology education, business education, counselor education, English education, home economics education, industrial education, mathematics education, science education, social studies education; special education (M Ed), including emotionally handicapped, learning disabilities, mentally handicapped. *Accreditation:* NCATE. Part-time and evening/weekend programs available. *Faculty:* 9 full-time (3 women), 4 part-time/adjunct (3 women). *Students:* 32 full-time (26 women), 33 part-time (26 women); includes 63 minority (61 Black or African American, non-Hispanic/Latino; 2 Asian, non-Hispanic/Latino). Average age 31. 21 applicants, 100% accepted, 21 enrolled. In 2013, 15 master's awarded. *Degree requirements:* For master's, thesis optional, departmental qualifying exam. *Entrance requirements:* For master's, GRE General Test, NTE, interview, teaching certificate. *Application deadline:* For fall admission, 6/15 priority date for domestic students, 6/15 for international students; for spring admission, 11/1 for domestic and international students. Applications are processed on a rolling basis. Application fee: $25. Electronic applications accepted.

Expenses: Tuition, state resident: full-time $8906; part-time $543 per credit hour. Tuition, nonresident: full-time $18,040; part-time $1051 per credit hour. *Financial support:* Fellowships, career-related internships or fieldwork, Federal Work-Study, and institutionally sponsored loans available. Financial award application deadline: 6/1. *Faculty research:* Critical thinking, child abuse, stress, test-taking skills, conflict resolution, mainstreaming. *Unit head:* Dr. Margaret Evelyn Fields, Interim Chair, 803-536-7098, Fax: 803-516-4568, E-mail: efields@scsu.edu. *Application contact:* Curtis Foskey, Coordinator of Graduate Studies, 803-536-8419, Fax: 803-536-8812, E-mail: cfoskey@scsu.edu.

Texas Tech University, Graduate School, College of Human Sciences, Program in Family and Consumer Sciences Education, Lubbock, TX 79409. Offers MS, PhD. Part-time and evening/weekend programs available. Postbaccalaureate distance learning degree programs offered (no on-campus study). Terminal master's awarded for partial completion of doctoral program. *Degree requirements:* For master's, thesis or alternative; for doctorate, comprehensive exam, thesis/dissertation. *Entrance requirements:* For master's and doctorate, GRE General Test. Additional exam requirements/recommendations for international students: Required—TOEFL (minimum score 500 paper-based; 79 iBT). *Application deadline:* For fall admission, 6/1 for domestic students, 1/15 for international students; for spring admission, 9/1 for domestic students, 6/15 for international students. Applications are processed on a rolling basis. Electronic applications accepted. *Expenses:* Tuition, state resident: full-time $6062; part-time $252.57 per credit hour. Tuition, nonresident: full-time $14,558; part-time $606.57 per credit hour. *Required fees:* $2655; $35 per credit hour. $907.50 per semester. Tuition and fees vary according to course load. *Financial support:* Application deadline: 4/15; applicants required to submit FAFSA.
Website: http://www.depts.ttu.edu/hs/fcse/.

The University of British Columbia, Faculty of Education, Department of Curriculum and Pedagogy, Vancouver, BC V6T 1Z4, Canada. Offers art education (M Ed, MA); business education (MA); curriculum studies (M Ed, MA, PhD); home economics education (M Ed, MA); math education (M Ed, MA); music education (M Ed, MA); physical education (M Ed, MA); science education (M Ed, MA); social studies education (M Ed, MA); technology studies education (M Ed, MA). Part-time programs available. Postbaccalaureate distance learning degree programs offered (no on-campus study). *Faculty:* 32 full-time (14 women), 1 (woman) part-time/adjunct. *Students:* 163 full-time, 134 part-time, 42 international. Average age 40. 160 applicants, 75% accepted, 97 enrolled. In 2013, 68 master's, 7 doctorates awarded. *Degree requirements:* For master's, thesis (MA); for doctorate, comprehensive exam, thesis/dissertation. *Entrance requirements:* Additional exam requirements/recommendations for international students: Required—TOEFL (minimum score 580 paper-based; 92 iBT), IELTS (minimum score 6.5). *Application deadline:* For fall admission, 12/1 for domestic and international students; for spring admission, 10/1 for domestic students, 9/1 for international students. Application fee: $90 Canadian dollars ($150 Canadian dollars for international students). Electronic applications accepted. *Expenses:* Contact institution. *Financial support:* In 2013–14, 10 fellowships with partial tuition reimbursements (averaging $16,000 per year), 11 research assistantships with partial tuition reimbursements (averaging $14,000 per year), 27 teaching assistantships with partial tuition reimbursements (averaging $14,000 per year) were awarded; tuition waivers (partial) also available. *Faculty research:* School subjects, teaching and learning. *Unit head:* Dr. Peter Grimmett, Head, 604-822-5422, Fax: 604-822-4714, E-mail: anna.ip@ubc.ca. *Application contact:* Basia Zurek, Graduate Programs Assistant, 604-822-5367, Fax: 604-822-4714, E-mail: edcp.grad@ubc.ca.
Website: http://www.edcp.educ.ubc.ca/.

University of Georgia, College of Education, Department of Career and Information Studies, Athens, GA 30602. Offers learning, design, and technology (M Ed, PhD, Ed S), including instructional design and development (M Ed, Ed S), instructional technology (M Ed), learning, design, and technology (M Ed); school library media (M Ed, Ed S); workforce education (M Ed, MAT, Ed D, PhD, Ed S), including business education (MAT), family and consumer sciences education (MAT), health science and technology education (MAT), marketing education (MAT), technology education (MAT), trade and industry education (MAT). *Accreditation:* NCATE. *Entrance requirements:* For master's, GRE General Test, MAT; for doctorate, GRE General Test; for Ed S, GRE General Test or MAT. Electronic applications accepted.

University of Nebraska–Lincoln, Graduate College, College of Education and Human Sciences, Department of Child, Youth and Family Studies, Lincoln, NE 68588. Offers child development/early childhood education (MS, PhD); child, youth and family studies (MS); family and consumer sciences education (MS, PhD); family financial planning (MS); family science (MS, PhD); gerontology (PhD); human sciences (PhD), including child, youth and family studies, gerontology, medical family therapy; marriage and family therapy (MS); medical family therapy (PhD); youth development (MS). *Accreditation:* AAMFT/COAMFTE (one or more programs are accredited). Postbaccalaureate distance learning degree programs offered. *Degree requirements:* For master's, thesis optional. *Entrance requirements:* For master's, GRE. Additional exam requirements/recommendations for international students: Required—TOEFL (minimum score 550 paper-based). Electronic applications accepted. *Faculty research:* Marriage and family therapy, child development/early childhood education, family financial management.

Utah State University, School of Graduate Studies, College of Agriculture, Department of Agricultural Systems Technology and Education, Logan, UT 84322. Offers agricultural systems technology (MS), including agricultural extension education, agricultural mechanization, international agricultural extension, secondary and postsecondary agricultural education; family and consumer sciences education (MS). Part-time programs available. Postbaccalaureate distance learning degree programs offered (minimal on-campus study). *Degree requirements:* For master's, comprehensive exam (for some programs), thesis (for some programs). *Entrance requirements:* For master's, GRE General Test, MAT, BS in agricultural education, agricultural extension, or related agricultural or science discipline; minimum GPA of 3.0. Additional exam requirements/recommendations for international students: Required—TOEFL. *Faculty research:* Extension and adult education; structures and environment; low-input agriculture; farm safety, systems, and mechanizations.

Wayne State College, School of Education and Counseling, Department of Educational Foundations and Leadership, Program in Curriculum and Instruction, Wayne, NE 68787. Offers alternative education (MSE); business and information technology education (MSE); communication arts education (MSE); early childhood education (MSE); elementary education (MSE); English as a second language (MSE); English education (MSE); family and consumer sciences education (MSE); industrial technology and vocational education (MSE); learning communities (MSE); mathematics education (MSE); music education (MSE); science education (MSE); social science education (MSE). *Accreditation:* NCATE. Part-time and evening/weekend programs available. *Degree requirements:* For master's, comprehensive exam, thesis optional. *Entrance requirements:* For master's, GRE General Test. Additional exam requirements/recommendations for international students: Required—TOEFL (minimum score 550 paper-based).

Mathematics Education

Acadia University, Faculty of Professional Studies, School of Education, Program in Curriculum Studies, Wolfville, NS B4P 2R6, Canada. Offers cultural and media studies (M Ed); learning and technology (M Ed); science, math and technology (M Ed). Part-time programs available. *Degree requirements:* For master's, thesis optional. *Entrance requirements:* For master's, B Ed or the equivalent, minimum B average in undergraduate course work, 2 years of teaching experience. Additional exam requirements/recommendations for international students: Required—TOEFL (minimum score 580 paper-based; 93 iBT), IELTS (minimum score 6.5). *Faculty research:* Literacy development, postmodern philosophy and curriculum theory, historiography, philosophy of education, learning and technology.

Alabama State University, College of Education, Department of Curriculum and Instruction, Montgomery, AL 36101-0271. Offers early childhood education (M Ed, Ed S); elementary education (M Ed, Ed S); secondary education (M Ed, Ed S), including biology education, English language arts education (M Ed), history education, math education, music education (M Ed), reading education (M Ed), social science education; special education (M Ed). Part-time programs available. *Faculty:* 11 full-time (8 women), 13 part-time/adjunct (10 women). *Students:* 32 full-time (19 women), 162 part-time (136 women); includes 189 minority (187 Black or African American, non-Hispanic/Latino; 1 Hispanic/Latino; 1 Two or more races, non-Hispanic/Latino). Average age 33. 99 applicants, 45% accepted, 34 enrolled. In 2013, 74 master's, 20 Ed Ss awarded. *Degree requirements:* For master's, comprehensive exam, thesis optional; for Ed S, comprehensive exam, thesis. *Entrance requirements:* For master's, GRE General Test, MAT, writing competency test; for Ed S, writing competency test, GRE, MAT. Additional exam requirements/recommendations for international students: Required—TOEFL (minimum score 500 paper-based). *Application deadline:* For fall admission, 7/15 for domestic students; for spring admission, 12/15 for domestic students. Applications are processed on a rolling basis. Application fee: $25. *Expenses:* Tuition, state resident: full-time $7958; part-time $343 per credit hour. Tuition, nonresident: full-time $14,132; part-time $686 per credit hour. *Required fees:* $446 per term. One-time fee: $1784 full-time; $892 part-time. Tuition and fees vary according to course load. *Financial support:* In 2013–14, research assistantships (averaging $9,450 per year) were awarded. *Unit head:* Dr. Joyce Johnson, Acting Chairperson, 334-229-4485, Fax: 334-229-5603, E-mail: jjohnson@alasu.edu. *Application contact:* Dr. William Person, Dean of Graduate Studies, 334-229-4274, Fax: 334-229-4928, E-mail: wperson@alasu.edu.
Website: http://www.alasu.edu/academics/colleges—departments/college-of-education/curriculum—instruction/index.aspx.

Albany State University, College of Sciences and Health Professions, Albany, GA 31705-2717. Offers criminal justice (MS), including corrections, forensic science, law enforcement, public administration; mathematics education (M Ed); nursing (MSN), including RN to MSN family nurse practitioner, RN to MSN nurse educator; science education (M Ed). Part-time and evening/weekend programs available. Postbaccalaureate distance learning degree programs offered. *Degree requirements:* For master's, comprehensive exam, thesis. *Entrance requirements:* For master's, GRE or MAT, official transcript, letters of recommendations, pre-medical/certificate of immunizations. Electronic applications accepted.

Appalachian State University, Cratis D. Williams Graduate School, Department of Curriculum and Instruction, Boone, NC 28608. Offers curriculum specialist (MA); educational media (MA); elementary education (MA); middle grades education (MA), including language arts, mathematics, science, social studies. *Accreditation:* NCATE. Part-time and evening/weekend programs available. Postbaccalaureate distance learning degree programs offered (no on-campus study). *Degree requirements:* For master's, comprehensive exam, thesis or alternative. *Entrance requirements:* For master's, GRE General Test or MAT, 3 letters of recommendation. Additional exam requirements/recommendations for international students: Required—TOEFL (minimum score 570 paper-based; 79 iBT), IELTS (minimum score 6.5). Electronic applications accepted. *Faculty research:* Media literacy, elementary teaching, curriculum development, online learning environments.

Appalachian State University, Cratis D. Williams Graduate School, Department of Mathematical Sciences, Boone, NC 28608. Offers mathematics (MA); mathematics education (MA). Part-time programs available. Postbaccalaureate distance learning degree programs offered (no on-campus study). *Degree requirements:* For master's, comprehensive exam, thesis optional. *Entrance requirements:* For master's, GRE General Test, 3 letters of recommendation. Additional exam requirements/recommendations for international students: Required—TOEFL (minimum score 570 paper-based; 79 iBT), IELTS (minimum score 6.5). Electronic applications accepted. *Faculty research:* Graph theory, differential equations, logic, geometry, complex analysis, topology, algebra, mathematics education.

Arcadia University, Graduate Studies, School of Education, Glenside, PA 19038-3295. Offers art education (M Ed); computer education (CAS); curriculum (CAS); curriculum studies (M Ed); early childhood education (M Ed, CAS), including individualized (M Ed), master teacher (M Ed), research in child development (M Ed); educational leadership (M Ed, Ed D, CAS); elementary education (M Ed, CAS); English education (MA Ed); environmental education (MA Ed, CAS); history education (MA Ed); instructional technology (M Ed); language arts (M Ed, CAS); library science (M Ed); mathematics education (M Ed, MA Ed, CAS); music education (MA Ed); psychology (MA Ed); reading (M Ed, CAS); science education (M Ed, CAS); secondary education (M Ed, CAS); special education (M Ed, Ed D, CAS); theater arts (MA Ed); written communication (MA Ed). *Accreditation:* NASAD. Part-time and evening/weekend programs available. Postbaccalaureate distance learning degree programs offered (minimal on-campus study). Electronic applications accepted. *Expenses:* Contact institution.

Arizona State University at the Tempe campus, College of Liberal Arts and Sciences, Department of Mathematics and Statistics, Tempe, AZ 85287-1804. Offers applied mathematics (PhD); computational biosciences (PhD); mathematics (MA, MNS, PhD); mathematics education (PhD); statistics (PhD). Part-time programs available. Terminal master's awarded for partial completion of doctoral program. *Degree requirements:* For master's, thesis or alternative, interactive Program of Study (iPOS) submitted before completing 50 percent of required credit hours; for doctorate, comprehensive exam, thesis/dissertation, interactive Program of Study (iPOS) submitted before completing 50 percent of required credit hours. *Entrance requirements:* For master's and doctorate, GRE General Test, minimum GPA of 3.0 or equivalent in last 2 years of work leading to bachelor's degree. Additional exam requirements/recommendations for international students: Required—TOEFL (minimum score 80 iBT), TOEFL, IELTS, or PTE. Electronic applications accepted. *Expenses:* Contact institution.

Arkansas State University, Graduate School, College of Sciences and Mathematics, Department of Mathematics and Statistics, Jonesboro, AR 72467. Offers mathematics (MS); mathematics education (MSE). Part-time programs available. *Faculty:* 11 full-time (5 women). *Students:* 10 full-time (7 women), 8 part-time (6 women); includes 3 minority (2 Black or African American, non-Hispanic/Latino; 1 Hispanic/Latino), 2 international. Average age 29. 12 applicants, 67% accepted, 6 enrolled. In 2013, 9 master's awarded. *Degree requirements:* For master's, comprehensive exam, thesis or alternative. *Entrance requirements:* For master's, GRE General Test or MAT, appropriate bachelor's degree, official transcripts, immunization records, valid teaching certificate (for MSE). Additional exam requirements/recommendations for international students: Required—TOEFL (minimum score 550 paper-based; 79 iBT), IELTS (minimum score 6), PTE (minimum score 56). *Application deadline:* For fall admission, 7/1 for domestic and international students; for spring admission, 11/15 for domestic students, 11/14 for international students. Applications are processed on a rolling basis. Application fee: $30 ($40 for international students). Electronic applications accepted. *Expenses:* Tuition, state resident: full-time $4284; part-time $238 per credit hour. Tuition, nonresident: full-time $8568; part-time $476 per credit hour. *International tuition:* $9268 full-time. *Required fees:* $1098; $61 per credit hour. $25 per term. Tuition and fees vary according to course load and program. *Financial support:* In 2013–14, 9 students received support. Teaching assistantships, career-related internships or fieldwork, scholarships/grants, and unspecified assistantships available. Financial award application deadline: 7/1; financial award applicants required to submit FAFSA. *Unit head:* Dr. Debra Ingram, Chair, 870-972-3090, Fax: 870-972-3950, E-mail: dingram@astate.edu. *Application contact:* Vickey Ring, Graduate Admissions Coordinator, 870-972-3029, Fax: 870-972-3857, E-mail: vickeyring@astate.edu.
Website: http://www.astate.edu/college/sciences-and-mathematics/departments/math-statistics/index.dot.

Asbury University, School of Graduate and Professional Studies, Wilmore, KY 40390-1198. Offers biology: alternative certificate (MA Ed); chemistry: alternative certificate (MA Ed); English (MA Ed); English as a second language (MA Ed); ESL (MA Ed); French (MA Ed); Latin: alternative certificate (MA Ed); mathematics: alternative certificate (MA Ed); reading/writing endorsement (MA Ed); social studies (MA Ed); social work (MSW), including child and family services; Spanish (MA Ed); special education (MA Ed); special education: alternative certificate (MA Ed); teacher as leader endorsement (MA Ed). *Accreditation:* NCATE. Part-time programs available. *Degree requirements:* For master's, action research project, portfolio. *Entrance requirements:* For master's, PRAXIS/NTE, minimum GPA of 2.75, letters of recommendation. Additional exam requirements/recommendations for international students: Required—TOEFL (minimum score 550 paper-based). Electronic applications accepted.

Auburn University, Graduate School, College of Education, Department of Curriculum and Teaching, Auburn University, AL 36849. Offers business education (M Ed, MS, PhD); early childhood education (M Ed, MS, PhD, Ed S); elementary education (M Ed, MS, PhD, Ed S); foreign languages (M Ed, MS); music education (M Ed, MS, PhD, Ed S); postsecondary education (PhD); reading education (PhD, Ed S); secondary education (M Ed, MS, PhD, Ed S), including English language arts, mathematics, science, social studies. *Accreditation:* NASM (one or more programs are accredited); NCATE. Part-time programs available. *Faculty:* 29 full-time (21 women), 4 part-time/adjunct (all women). *Students:* 61 full-time (40 women), 153 part-time (108 women); includes 37 minority (32 Black or African American, non-Hispanic/Latino; 2 Asian, non-Hispanic/Latino; 3 Hispanic/Latino), 1 international. Average age 34. 150 applicants, 59% accepted, 74 enrolled. In 2013, 70 master's, 6 doctorates, 26 other advanced degrees awarded. *Degree requirements:* For master's, thesis (for some programs); for doctorate, thesis/dissertation; for Ed S, field project. *Entrance requirements:* For master's, doctorate, and Ed S, GRE General Test. *Application deadline:* For fall admission, 7/7 for domestic students; for spring admission, 11/24 for domestic students. Applications are processed on a rolling basis. Application fee: $50 ($60 for international students). Electronic applications accepted. *Expenses:* Tuition, state resident: full-time $8262; part-time $459 per credit hour. Tuition, nonresident: full-time $24,786; part-time $1377 per credit hour. Tuition and fees vary according to degree level and program. *Financial support:* Fellowships, teaching assistantships, career-related internships or fieldwork, and Federal Work-Study available. Support available to part-time students. Financial award application deadline: 3/15; financial award applicants required to submit FAFSA. *Faculty research:* Emerging literacy, reading attitudes, music for at-risk youth, portfolio assessment. *Unit head:* Dr. Kimberly Walls, Head, 334-844-4434. *Application contact:* Dr. George Flowers, Dean of the Graduate School, 334-844-2125.
Website: http://education.auburn.edu/academic_departments/curr/.

Auburn University at Montgomery, School of Education, Department of Foundations, Technology, and Secondary Education, Montgomery, AL 36124-4023. Offers instructional technology (M Ed); secondary education (M Ed, Ed S), including art education (M Ed), biology (M Ed), English language arts (M Ed), general science (M Ed), history (M Ed), mathematics (M Ed), social science (M Ed). *Accreditation:* NCATE. Part-time and evening/weekend programs available. *Faculty:* 6 full-time (2 women), 1 (woman) part-time/adjunct. *Students:* 47 full-time (22 women), 77 part-time (48 women); includes 30 minority (29 Black or African American, non-Hispanic/Latino; 1 Asian, non-Hispanic/Latino), 1 international. Average age 30. In 2013, 86 master's awarded. *Degree requirements:* For master's and Ed S, comprehensive exam, thesis optional. *Entrance requirements:* For master's, GRE General Test or MAT, certification, BS in teaching; for Ed S, GRE General Test or MAT, certification. *Application deadline:* Applications are processed on a rolling basis. Electronic applications accepted. *Expenses:* Tuition, state resident: full-time $5994; part-time $333 per credit hour. Tuition, nonresident: full-time $17,982; part-time $999 per credit hour. *Financial support:* Teaching assistantships, career-related internships or fieldwork, and scholarships/grants available. Support available to part-time students. Financial award application deadline: 3/1; financial award applicants required to submit FAFSA. *Unit head:* Dr. Sheila Austin, Dean, 334-244-3425, Fax: 334-244-3102, E-mail: saustin1@aum.edu. *Application contact:* Dr. Rhonda Morton, Associate Dean/Graduate Coordinator, 334-244-3287, Fax: 334-244-3978, E-mail: rmorton@aum.edu.
Website: http://www.education.aum.edu/departments/foundations-technology-and-secondary-education.

Aurora University, College of Arts and Sciences, Aurora, IL 60506-4892. Offers elementary math and science (MATL); life science (MATL); mathematics (MATL, MS). Part-time and evening/weekend programs available. *Entrance requirements:* Additional exam requirements/recommendations for international students: Required—TOEFL (minimum score 550 paper-based). Electronic applications accepted. *Expenses:* Contact institution.

Averett University, Master in Education Program, Danville, VA 24541-3692. Offers administration and supervision (M Ed); art (M Ed); biology (M Ed); chemistry (M Ed); curriculum and instruction (M Ed); early childhood (M Ed); English (M Ed); mathematics (M Ed); middle grades (M Ed); physical science (M Ed); reading specialist (M Ed); science (M Ed); special education (M Ed); special education learning disability (M Ed).

Program offered on Danville Campus only. Part-time and evening/weekend programs available. *Faculty:* 4 full-time (3 women), 13 part-time/adjunct (8 women). *Students:* 43 full-time (35 women), 44 part-time (35 women); includes 7 minority (all Black or African American, non-Hispanic/Latino). *Degree requirements:* For master's, 30-credit core curriculum, minimum GPA of 3.0 throughout program, completion of degree requirements within six years from start of program. *Entrance requirements:* For master's, PRAXIS I, GRE, or MAT; writing proficiency test, minimum cumulative GPA of 3.0 over the last 60 hours of undergraduate study toward a baccalaureate degree, three letters of recommendation, Virginia teaching license (or eligibility). Additional exam requirements/recommendations for international students: Required—TOEFL (minimum score 600 paper-based; 100 iBT). *Application deadline:* Applications are processed on a rolling basis. Application fee: $100. *Expenses:* Contact institution. *Financial support:* Career-related internships or fieldwork, Federal Work-Study, and scholarships/grants available. Financial award application deadline: 4/1; financial award applicants required to submit FAFSA. *Unit head:* Wilfred Lawrence, Department Chair of Education, 434-791-5752, E-mail: priedel@averett.edu. *Application contact:* Christy Pack, Executive Director of Enrollment, 804-887-8612, E-mail: dpack@averett.edu.
Website: http://www.averett.edu/adultprograms/degrees/MEDtrad.php.

Ball State University, Graduate School, College of Sciences and Humanities, Department of Mathematical Sciences, Program in Mathematics, Muncie, IN 47306-1099. Offers mathematics (MA, MS); mathematics education (MA). *Students:* 11 full-time (2 women), 18 part-time (9 women); includes 1 minority (Black or African American, non-Hispanic/Latino), 6 international. Average age 39. 16 applicants, 50% accepted, 4 enrolled. In 2013, 10 master's awarded. Application fee: $50. *Financial support:* In 2013–14, 4 students received support. Application deadline: 3/1. *Unit head:* Dr. Sheryl Stump, Director, 765-285-8680, Fax: 765-285-1721, E-mail: sstump@bsu.edu. *Application contact:* Dr. Hanspeter Fischer, Director, 765-285-8640, Fax: 765-285-1721, E-mail: hfischer@bsu.edu.
Website: http://cms.bsu.edu/Academics/CollegesandDepartments/Math/AcademicsAdmissions/Programs/Masters/MAorMSinMath.aspx.

Bank Street College of Education, Graduate School, Programs in Educational Leadership, New York, NY 10025. Offers early childhood leadership (MS Ed); educational leadership (MS Ed); leadership for educational change (Ed M, MS Ed); leadership in community-based learning (MS Ed); leadership in mathematics education (MS Ed); leadership in museum education (MS Ed); leadership in the arts: creative writing (MS Ed); leadership in the arts: visual arts (MS Ed). *Degree requirements:* For master's, thesis. *Entrance requirements:* For master's, interview, essays, minimum of 2 years experience as a classroom teacher. Additional exam requirements/recommendations for international students: Required—TOEFL (minimum score 600 paper-based; 100 iBT), IELTS (minimum score 7). Electronic applications accepted. *Faculty research:* Leadership in urban schools, leadership in small schools, mathematics in elementary schools, professional development in early childhood, leadership in arts education, leadership in special education, museum leadership, community-based leadership.

Bemidji State University, School of Graduate Studies, Bemidji, MN 56601. Offers biology (MS); education (MS); English (MA, MS); environmental studies (MS); mathematics (MS); mathematics (elementary and middle level education) (MS); special education (M Sp Ed, MS). Part-time programs available. Postbaccalaureate distance learning degree programs offered (no on-campus study). *Faculty:* 117 full-time (53 women), 20 part-time/adjunct (15 women). *Students:* 30 full-time (17 women), 157 part-time (108 women); includes 16 minority (2 Black or African American, non-Hispanic/Latino; 4 American Indian or Alaska Native, non-Hispanic/Latino; 2 Asian, non-Hispanic/Latino; 1 Hispanic/Latino; 7 Two or more races, non-Hispanic/Latino), 1 international. Average age 35. 73 applicants, 93% accepted, 38 enrolled. In 2013, 49 master's awarded. *Degree requirements:* For master's, comprehensive exam, thesis (for some programs). *Entrance requirements:* For master's, GRE; GMAT, letters of recommendation, letters of interest. Additional exam requirements/recommendations for international students: Required—TOEFL (minimum score 550 paper-based; 80 iBT). *Application deadline:* Applications are processed on a rolling basis. Application fee: $20. Electronic applications accepted. *Expenses:* Tuition, state resident: full-time $6941; part-time $365 per credit. Tuition, nonresident: full-time $6941; part-time $365 per credit. *Required fees:* $16 per credit. Tuition and fees vary according to program and reciprocity agreements. *Financial support:* In 2013–14, 131 students received support, including 18 research assistantships with partial tuition reimbursements available (averaging $12,889 per year), 23 teaching assistantships with partial tuition reimbursements available (averaging $12,889 per year); scholarships/grants and unspecified assistantships also available. Financial award application deadline: 3/31; financial award applicants required to submit FAFSA. *Faculty research:* Human performance, sport, and health: physical education teacher education, continuum models, spiritual health, intellectual health, resiliency, health priorities; psychology: health psychology, college student drinking behavior, micro-aggressions, infant cognition, false memories, leadership assessment; biology: structure and dynamics of forest communities, aquatic and riverine ecology, interaction between animal populations and aquatic environments, cellular motility. *Unit head:* Dr. James Barta, Interim Dean of Health Sciences and Human Ecology, 218-755-3874, Fax: 218-755-2258, E-mail: jbarta@bemidjistate.edu. *Application contact:* Joan Miller, Director, School of Graduate Studies, 218-755-2027, Fax: 218-755-2258, E-mail: jmiller@bemidjistate.edu.
Website: http://www.bemidjistate.edu/academics/graduate_studies/.

Binghamton University, State University of New York, Graduate School, School of Education, Program in Adolescence Education, Vestal, NY 13850. Offers biology education (MAT, MS Ed); chemistry education (MAT, MS Ed); earth science education (MAT, MS Ed); English education (MAT, MS Ed); French education (MAT, MS Ed); literacy education (MS Ed); mathematical sciences education (MAT, MS Ed); physics (MAT, MS Ed); social studies (MAT, MS Ed); Spanish education (MAT, MS Ed). *Accreditation:* Teacher Education Accreditation Council. Part-time and evening/weekend programs available. *Students:* 48 full-time (29 women), 5 part-time (3 women); includes 7 minority (2 Black or African American, non-Hispanic/Latino; 3 Asian, non-Hispanic/Latino; 2 Hispanic/Latino), 1 international. Average age 26. 37 applicants, 86% accepted, 21 enrolled. In 2013, 34 master's awarded. *Entrance requirements:* For master's, GRE General Test. Additional exam requirements/recommendations for international students: Required—TOEFL (minimum score 550 paper-based; 80 iBT). *Application deadline:* For fall admission, 2/1 priority date for domestic and international students; for spring admission, 10/15 priority date for domestic and international students. Applications are processed on a rolling basis. Application fee: $75. Electronic applications accepted. *Financial support:* In 2013–14, 7 students received support, including 1 fellowship with partial tuition reimbursement available (averaging $4,500 per year); career-related internships or fieldwork, Federal Work-Study, institutionally sponsored loans, scholarships/grants, health care benefits, tuition waivers (full), and unspecified assistantships also available. Financial award application deadline: 2/15; financial award applicants required to submit FAFSA. *Unit head:* Dr. S. G. Grant, Dean of School of Education, 607-777-7329, E-mail: sggrant@binghamton.edu. *Application contact:* Kishan Zuber, Recruiting and Admissions Coordinator, 607-777-2151, Fax: 607-777-2501, E-mail: kzuber@binghamton.edu.

Bloomsburg University of Pennsylvania, School of Graduate Studies, College of Education, Department of Early Childhood and Adolescent Education, Program in Middle Level Education Grades 4-8, Bloomsburg, PA 17815-1301. Offers language arts (M Ed); math (M Ed); science (M Ed); social studies (M Ed). *Accreditation:* NCATE. *Faculty:* 14 full-time (6 women), 3 part-time/adjunct (2 women). In 2013, 2 master's awarded. *Degree requirements:* For master's, thesis optional, student teaching. *Entrance requirements:* For master's, MAT, GRE, or PRAXIS, minimum QPA of 3.0, teaching certificate, U.S. citizenship, related undergraduate coursework, professional liability insurance, recent TB test. Additional exam requirements/recommendations for international students: Required—TOEFL (minimum score 550 paper-based). *Application deadline:* Applications are processed on a rolling basis. Application fee: $35 ($60 for international students). Electronic applications accepted. *Expenses:* Tuition, state resident: full-time $7956; part-time $442 per credit. Tuition, nonresident: full-time $11,934; part-time $663 per credit. *Required fees:* $95.50 per credit. $55 per semester. Tuition and fees vary according to course load. *Financial support:* Unspecified assistantships available. *Unit head:* Dr. Tegan Kotarski, College of Education Graduate Coordinator, 570-389-3883, Fax: 570-389-5049, E-mail: tkotarsk@bloomu.edu. *Application contact:* Jennifer Richard, Administrative Assistant, 570-389-4015, Fax: 570-389-3054, E-mail: jrichard@bloomu.edu.
Website: http://www.bloomu.edu/gradschool/middle-level-education.

Bob Jones University, Graduate Programs, Greenville, SC 29614. Offers accountancy (MS); Bible (MA); Bible translation (MA); Biblical studies (Certificate); broadcast management (MS); business administration (MBA); church history (MA, PhD); church ministries (MA); church music (MM); cinema and video production (MA); counseling (MS); curriculum and instruction (Ed D); divinity (M Div); dramatic production (MA); educational leadership (MS, Ed D, Ed S); elementary education (M Ed, MAT); English (M Ed, MA, MAT); fine arts (MA); graphic design (MA); history (M Ed, MA); illustration (MA); interpretative speech (MA); mathematics (M Ed, MAT); medical missions (Certificate); ministry (MM, D Min); multi-categorical special education (M Ed, MAT); music (M Ed); New Testament interpretation (PhD); Old Testament interpretation (PhD); orchestral instrument performance (MM); organ performance (MM); pastoral studies (MA); personnel services (MS, Ed S); piano pedagogy (MM); piano performance (MM); platform arts (MA); radio and television broadcasting (MS); rhetoric and public address (MA); secondary education (M Ed); studio art (MA); teaching Bible (MA); theology (MA, PhD); voice performance (MM); youth ministries (MA); M Div/MM.

Boise State University, College of Arts and Sciences, Department of Mathematics, Boise, ID 83725-0399. Offers mathematics (MS); mathematics education (MS).

Bowling Green State University, Graduate College, College of Arts and Sciences, Department of Mathematics and Statistics, Bowling Green, OH 43403. Offers applied statistics (MS); mathematics (MA, MAT, PhD); statistics (PhD). Part-time programs available. *Degree requirements:* For master's, thesis or alternative; for doctorate, comprehensive exam, thesis/dissertation. *Entrance requirements:* For master's and doctorate, GRE General Test. Additional exam requirements/recommendations for international students: Required—TOEFL. Electronic applications accepted. *Faculty research:* Statistics and probability, algebra, analysis.

Bridgewater State University, School of Graduate Studies, School of Arts and Sciences, Department of Mathematics and Computer Science, Bridgewater, MA 02325-0001. Offers computer science (MS); mathematics (MAT). Part-time and evening/weekend programs available. *Entrance requirements:* For master's, GRE General Test.

Brigham Young University, Graduate Studies, College of Physical and Mathematical Sciences, Department of Mathematics Education, Provo, UT 84602-1001. Offers MA. Part-time programs available. *Faculty:* 7 full-time (2 women). *Students:* 11 full-time (7 women), 11 part-time (5 women); includes 2 minority (1 Hispanic/Latino; 1 Native Hawaiian or other Pacific Islander, non-Hispanic/Latino). Average age 30. 13 applicants, 54% accepted, 7 enrolled. In 2013, 7 master's awarded. *Degree requirements:* For master's, comprehensive exam, project or thesis. *Entrance requirements:* For master's, GRE General Test, teaching certificate, bachelor's degree in math education or equivalent. Additional exam requirements/recommendations for international students: Required—TOEFL. *Application deadline:* For fall admission, 3/1 priority date for domestic and international students; for spring admission, 3/1 for domestic and international students; for summer admission, 3/1 priority date for domestic and international students. Application fee: $50. Electronic applications accepted. *Expenses:* *Tuition:* Full-time $6130; part-time $340 per credit hour. Tuition and fees vary according to program and student's religious affiliation. *Financial support:* In 2013–14, 18 students received support, including 3 research assistantships with full tuition reimbursements available (averaging $6,500 per year), 12 teaching assistantships with full tuition reimbursements available (averaging $13,000 per year); institutionally sponsored loans and scholarships/grants also available. Financial award application deadline: 3/1. *Faculty research:* Understanding characteristics of high-quality mathematics instruction, understanding the complexities of teaching and learning to teach mathematics, process of learning to teach mathematics, discourse and literacy in mathematics classrooms, national policy and mathematics curriculum, advanced mathematical thinking. *Unit head:* Steven R. Williams, Chair, 801-422-2887, Fax: 801-422-0511, E-mail: williams@mathed.byu.edu. *Application contact:* Kathy Lee Garrett, Administrative Assistant, 801-422-1840, Fax: 801-422-0511, E-mail: kathylee@mathed.byu.edu.
Website: https://mathed.byu.edu/.

Brooklyn College of the City University of New York, Division of Graduate Studies, School of Education, Program in Adolescence Education and Special Subjects, Brooklyn, NY 11210-2889. Offers adolescence science education (MAT); art teacher (MA); biology teacher (MA); chemistry teacher (MA); earth science teacher (MAT); English teacher (MA); French teacher (MA); health and nutrition sciences: health teacher (MS Ed); mathematics teacher (MA); music education (CAS); music teacher (MA); physical education teacher (MS Ed); physics teacher (MA); social studies teacher (MA); Spanish teacher (MA). Part-time and evening/weekend programs available. *Degree requirements:* For master's, comprehensive exam (for some programs), thesis (for some programs). *Entrance requirements:* For master's, LAST, previous course work in education, resume, 2 letters of recommendation, essay. Additional exam requirements/recommendations for international students: Required—TOEFL (minimum score 500 paper-based; 61 iBT). Electronic applications accepted. *Faculty research:* Interdisciplinary education, semiotics, discourse analysis, autobiography, teacher identity.

Brooklyn College of the City University of New York, Division of Graduate Studies, School of Education, Program in Childhood Education, Brooklyn, NY 11210-2889. Offers bilingual education (MS Ed); liberal arts (MS Ed); mathematics (MS Ed); science/environmental education (MS Ed). Part-time and evening/weekend programs available. *Entrance requirements:* For master's, LAST, interview, previous course work in education, writing sample, resume, 2 letters of recommendation. Additional exam requirements/recommendations for international students: Required—TOEFL (minimum score 500 paper-based; 61 iBT). Electronic applications accepted. *Faculty research:* Emotional intelligence, multiculturalism, arts immersion, the Holocaust.

Brooklyn College of the City University of New York, Division of Graduate Studies, School of Education, Program in Middle Childhood Education (Math), Brooklyn, NY

11210-2889. Offers MS Ed. *Entrance requirements:* For master's, LAST, 2 letters of recommendation, essay, resume. Additional exam requirements/recommendations for international students: Required—TOEFL (minimum score 500 paper-based; 61 iBT). Electronic applications accepted.

Buffalo State College, State University of New York, The Graduate School, Faculty of Natural and Social Sciences, Department of Mathematics, Buffalo, NY 14222-1095. Offers mathematics education (MS Ed). *Accreditation:* NCATE. Part-time and evening/weekend programs available. *Degree requirements:* For master's, thesis or alternative. *Entrance requirements:* For master's, 18 undergraduate hours in upper-level mathematics, minimum GPA of 2.5 in undergraduate math courses. Additional exam requirements/recommendations for international students: Required—TOEFL (minimum score 550 paper-based).

California State University, Bakersfield, Division of Graduate Studies, School of Natural Sciences, Mathematics, and Engineering, Program in Teaching Mathematics, Bakersfield, CA 93311. Offers MA. *Entrance requirements:* For master's, minimum GPA of 2.5 for last 90 quarter units. *Unit head:* Dr. Joseph Fiedler, Head, 661-654-2058, Fax: 661-664-2039. *Application contact:* Debbie Blowers, Assistant Director of Admissions, 661-664-3381, E-mail: dblowers@csub.edu.

California State University, Chico, Office of Graduate Studies, College of Natural Sciences, Program in Math Education, Chico, CA 95929-0722. Offers math education (MS). Part-time programs available. *Degree requirements:* For master's, thesis or project. *Entrance requirements:* For master's, GRE, teaching credential in mathematics, statement of purpose. Additional exam requirements/recommendations for international students: Required—TOEFL (minimum score 550 paper-based; 80 iBT), IELTS (minimum score 6.5), PTE (minimum score 59). Electronic applications accepted.

California State University, Dominguez Hills, College of Natural and Behavioral Sciences, Program in Teaching of Mathematics, Carson, CA 90747-0001. Offers MA. Part-time and evening/weekend programs available. *Faculty:* 2 full-time (0 women). *Students:* 11 part-time (7 women); includes 9 minority (2 Black or African American, non-Hispanic/Latino; 6 Hispanic/Latino; 1 Native Hawaiian or other Pacific Islander, non-Hispanic/Latino). Average age 38. 6 applicants, 67% accepted, 3 enrolled. In 2013, 10 master's awarded. *Degree requirements:* For master's, comprehensive exam, thesis. *Entrance requirements:* For master's, 2 years of teaching experience. Additional exam requirements/recommendations for international students: Required—TOEFL. *Application deadline:* For fall admission, 6/1 priority date for domestic students; for spring admission, 11/1 priority date for domestic students. Applications are processed on a rolling basis. Application fee: $55. Electronic applications accepted. *Expenses:* Tuition, state resident: full-time $6738. Tuition, nonresident: full-time $13,434. *Required fees:* $622. *Unit head:* Dr. John Wilkins, Chair, 310-243-3380, E-mail: jwilkins@csudh.edu. *Application contact:* Dr. John Wilkins, Associate Professor, 310-243-3380, E-mail: jwilkins@csudh.edu.
Website: http://www.csudh.edu/math.

California State University, East Bay, Office of Academic Programs and Graduate Studies, College of Science, Department of Mathematics and Computer Science, Mathematics Program, Hayward, CA 94542-3000. Offers applied math (MS); mathematics (MS); mathematics teaching (MS). Part-time and evening/weekend programs available. *Degree requirements:* For master's, comprehensive exam or thesis. *Entrance requirements:* For master's, minimum GPA of 3.0 in field. Additional exam requirements/recommendations for international students: Required—TOEFL (minimum score 550 paper-based). Electronic applications accepted.

California State University, Fresno, Division of Graduate Studies, College of Science and Mathematics, Department of Mathematics, Fresno, CA 93740-8027. Offers mathematics (MA); teaching (MA). Part-time programs available. *Degree requirements:* For master's, thesis or alternative. *Entrance requirements:* For master's, GRE General Test. Additional exam requirements/recommendations for international students: Required—TOEFL. Electronic applications accepted. *Faculty research:* Diagnostic testing project.

California State University, Fullerton, Graduate Studies, College of Education, Department of Secondary Education, Fullerton, CA 92834-9480. Offers secondary education (MS); teaching foundational mathematics (MS). Part-time programs available. *Students:* 5 full-time (3 women), 42 part-time (26 women); includes 29 minority (2 Black or African American, non-Hispanic/Latino; 9 Asian, non-Hispanic/Latino; 18 Hispanic/Latino). Average age 32. 28 applicants, 71% accepted, 18 enrolled. In 2013, 20 master's awarded. Application fee: $55. *Financial support:* Career-related internships or fieldwork, Federal Work-Study, institutionally sponsored loans, and scholarships/grants available. Support available to part-time students. Financial award application deadline: 3/1; financial award applicants required to submit FAFSA. *Unit head:* Dr. Grace Cho, Chair, 657-278-3283, E-mail: gcho@fullerton.edu. *Application contact:* Admissions/Applications, 657-278-2371.

California State University, Fullerton, Graduate Studies, College of Natural Science and Mathematics, Department of Mathematics, Fullerton, CA 92834-9480. Offers applied mathematics (MA); mathematics (MA); teaching (MA). Part-time programs available. *Students:* 19 full-time (8 women), 69 part-time (34 women); includes 46 minority (3 Black or African American, non-Hispanic/Latino; 25 Asian, non-Hispanic/Latino; 17 Hispanic/Latino; 1 Two or more races, non-Hispanic/Latino), 11 international. Average age 31. 95 applicants, 68% accepted, 39 enrolled. In 2013, 23 degrees awarded. *Degree requirements:* For master's, comprehensive exam or project. *Entrance requirements:* For master's, minimum GPA of 2.5 in last 60 units of course work, major in mathematics or related field. Application fee: $55. *Financial support:* Research assistantships, teaching assistantships, career-related internships or fieldwork, Federal Work-Study, institutionally sponsored loans, and scholarships/grants available. Support available to part-time students. Financial award application deadline: 3/1; financial award applicants required to submit FAFSA. *Unit head:* Dr. Stephen W. Goode, Chair, 657-278-3631. *Application contact:* Admissions/Applications, 657-278-2371.

California State University, Long Beach, Graduate Studies, College of Natural Sciences and Mathematics, Department of Mathematics and Statistics, Long Beach, CA 90840. Offers mathematics (MS), including applied mathematics, applied statistics, mathematics education for secondary school teachers. Part-time programs available. *Degree requirements:* For master's, comprehensive exam or thesis. Electronic applications accepted. *Faculty research:* Algebra, functional analysis, partial differential equations, operator theory, numerical analysis.

California State University, Northridge, Graduate Studies, College of Education, Department of Secondary Education, Northridge, CA 91330. Offers educational technology (MA); English education (MA); mathematics education (MA); secondary science education (MA); teaching and learning (MA). *Accreditation:* NCATE. Part-time programs available. *Degree requirements:* For master's, thesis optional. *Entrance requirements:* For master's, GRE General Test or minimum GPA of 3.0. Additional exam requirements/recommendations for international students: Required—TOEFL.

California State University, Northridge, Graduate Studies, College of Science and Mathematics, Department of Mathematics, Northridge, CA 91330. Offers applied mathematics (MS); mathematics (MS); mathematics for educational careers (MS). Part-time and evening/weekend programs available. *Degree requirements:* For master's, thesis (for some programs). *Entrance requirements:* For master's, GRE (if cumulative undergraduate GPA less than 3.0). Additional exam requirements/recommendations for international students: Required—TOEFL.

California State University, San Bernardino, Graduate Studies, College of Natural Sciences, Department of Mathematics, San Bernardino, CA 92407-2397. Offers mathematics (MA); teaching mathematics (MAT). Part-time programs available. *Students:* 9 full-time (6 women), 55 part-time (30 women); includes 42 minority (2 Black or African American, non-Hispanic/Latino; 6 Asian, non-Hispanic/Latino; 31 Hispanic/Latino; 3 Two or more races, non-Hispanic/Latino), 3 international. Average age 31. 33 applicants, 67% accepted, 15 enrolled. In 2013, 15 master's awarded. *Degree requirements:* For master's, advancement to candidacy. *Entrance requirements:* For master's, writing exam, minimum GPA of 3.0 in math courses. Application fee: $55. *Financial support:* Teaching assistantships available. *Faculty research:* Mathematics education, technology in education, algebra, combinatorics, real analysis. *Unit head:* Dr. Peter D. Williams, Chair, 909-537-5361, Fax: 909-537-7119, E-mail: pwilliam@csusb.edu. *Application contact:* Dr. Jeffrey Thompson, Assistant Dean of Graduate Studies, 909-537-5058, E-mail: jthompso@csusb.edu.

Cambridge College, School of Education, Cambridge, MA 02138-5304. Offers autism specialist (M Ed); autism/behavior analyst (M Ed); behavior analyst (Post-Master's Certificate); behavioral management (M Ed); early childhood teacher (M Ed); education specialist in curriculum and instruction (CAGS); educational leadership (Ed D); elementary teacher (M Ed); English as a second language (M Ed, Certificate); general science (M Ed); health education (Post-Master's Certificate); health/family and consumer sciences (M Ed); history (M Ed); individualized (M Ed); information technology literacy (M Ed); instructional technology (M Ed); interdisciplinary studies (M Ed); library teacher (M Ed); literacy education (M Ed); mathematics (M Ed); mathematics specialist (Certificate); middle school mathematics and science (M Ed); school administration (M Ed, CAGS); school guidance counselor (M Ed); school nurse education (M Ed); school social worker/school adjustment counselor (M Ed); special education administrator (CAGS); special education/moderate disabilities (M Ed); teaching skills and methodologies (M Ed). Part-time and evening/weekend programs available. Postbaccalaureate distance learning degree programs offered (minimal on-campus study). *Degree requirements:* For master's, thesis, internship/practicum (licensure program only); for doctorate, thesis/dissertation; for other advanced degree, thesis. *Entrance requirements:* For master's, interview, resume, documentation of licensure, 2 professional references; for doctorate, official transcripts, interview, resume, documentation of licensure (if any), written personal statement/essay, portfolio of scholarly and professional work, qualifying assessment, 2 professional references, health insurance, immunizations form; for other advanced degree, official transcripts, interview, resume, documentation of licensure (if any), written personal statement/essay, 2 professional references, health insurance, immunizations form. Additional exam requirements/recommendations for international students: Required—TOEFL (minimum score 550 paper-based; 79 iBT), Michigan English Language Assessment Battery (minimum score 85); Recommended—IELTS (minimum score 6). Electronic applications accepted. *Expenses:* Contact institution. *Faculty research:* Adult education, accelerated learning, mathematics education, brain compatible learning, special education and law.

Campbell University, Graduate and Professional Programs, School of Education, Buies Creek, NC 27506. Offers administration (MSA); community counseling (MA); elementary education (M Ed); English education (M Ed); interdisciplinary studies (M Ed); mathematics education (M Ed); middle grades education (M Ed); physical education (M Ed); school counseling (M Ed); secondary education (M Ed); social science education (M Ed). *Accreditation:* NCATE. Part-time and evening/weekend programs available. *Degree requirements:* For master's, comprehensive exam. *Entrance requirements:* For master's, GRE General Test, minimum GPA of 2.7. *Faculty research:* Spiritual values and wellness issues in counseling, stress and professional burnout among counselors, thinking strategies, leadership, adaptive technology.

Caribbean University, Graduate School, Bayamón, PR 00960-0493. Offers administration and supervision (MA Ed); criminal justice (MA); curriculum and instruction (MA Ed, PhD), including elementary education (MA Ed), English education (MA Ed), history education (MA Ed), mathematics education (MA Ed), primary education (MA Ed), science education (MA Ed), Spanish education (MA Ed); educational technology in instructional systems (MA Ed); gerontology (MSN); human resources (MBA); museology, archiving and art history (MA Ed); neonatal pediatrics (MSN); physical education (MA Ed); special education (MA Ed). *Entrance requirements:* For master's, interview, minimum GPA of 2.5.

Central Michigan University, College of Graduate Studies, College of Science and Technology, Department of Mathematics, Mount Pleasant, MI 48859. Offers mathematics (MA, PhD), including teaching of college mathematics (PhD). Part-time programs available. *Degree requirements:* For master's, thesis or alternative; for doctorate, thesis/dissertation. *Entrance requirements:* For master's, minimum GPA of 2.7, 20 hours of course work in mathematics; for doctorate, GRE, minimum GPA of 3.0, 20 hours of course work in mathematics. Electronic applications accepted. *Faculty research:* Combinatorics, approximation theory, applied mathematics, statistics, functional analysis and operator theory.

Chaminade University of Honolulu, Graduate Services, Program in Education, Honolulu, HI 96816-1578. Offers child development (M Ed); early childhood education (M Ed); educational leadership (M Ed); elementary education (MAT); instructional leadership (M Ed); Montessori education (M Ed); secondary education (MAT), including English, math, science, social studies; special education (MAT). Part-time and evening/weekend programs available. Postbaccalaureate distance learning degree programs offered (minimal on-campus study). *Degree requirements:* For master's, thesis or alternative. *Entrance requirements:* For master's, PRAXIS (for MAT only), minimum GPA of 2.75, 3 letters of recommendation. Additional exam requirements/recommendations for international students: Required—TOEFL (minimum score 550 paper-based). Electronic applications accepted. *Faculty research:* Peace and curriculum education.

Chatham University, Program in Education, Pittsburgh, PA 15232-2826. Offers early childhood education (MAT); elementary education (MAT); environmental education (K-12) (MAT); secondary art (MAT); secondary biology education (MAT); secondary chemistry education (MAT); secondary English education (MAT); secondary math education (MAT); secondary physics education (MAT); secondary social studies education (MAT); special education (MAT). *Faculty:* 1 (woman) full-time, 5 part-time/adjunct (4 women). *Students:* 19 full-time (15 women), 4 part-time (all women); includes 2 minority (1 Black or African American, non-Hispanic/Latino; 1 Asian, non-Hispanic/Latino), 2 international. Average age 28. 22 applicants, 73% accepted, 6 enrolled. In 2013, 20 master's awarded. *Degree requirements:* For master's, thesis, teaching experience. *Entrance requirements:* For master's, minimum GPA of 3.0, sample of written work, recommendation letters. Additional exam requirements/recommendations for international students: Required—TOEFL (minimum score 600 paper-based; 100 iBT), IELTS (minimum score 7), TWE. *Application deadline:* For fall admission, 4/1 priority date for domestic and international students; for spring admission, 11/1 priority

date for domestic students, 10/1 priority date for international students. Applications are processed on a rolling basis. Application fee: $45. Electronic applications accepted. Application fee is waived when completed online. *Expenses: Tuition:* Full-time $14,886; part-time $827 per credit hour. One-time fee: $396 full-time. *Financial support:* Career-related internships or fieldwork available. Financial award applicants required to submit FAFSA. *Faculty research:* Gifted education, environmental education, technology in education, writing as learning, class size and achievement. *Unit head:* Dr. Edward Donovan, Director of Education Programs, 412-365-2773, E-mail: edonovan@chatham.edu. *Application contact:* Katie Noel, Assistant Director of Graduate Admission, 412-365-2758, Fax: 412-365-1609, E-mail: gradadmissions@chatham.edu.
Website: http://www.chatham.edu/mat.

Christopher Newport University, Graduate Studies, Department of Teacher Preparation, Newport News, VA 23606-3072. Offers art (PK-12) (MAT); biology (6-12) (MAT); chemistry (6-12) (MAT); computer science (6-12) (MAT); elementary (PK-6) (MAT); English (6-12) (MAT); English as second language (PK-12) (MAT); French (PK-12) (MAT); history and social science (6-12) (MAT); mathematics (6-12) (MAT); music (PK-12) (MAT), including choral, instrumental; physics (6-12) (MAT); Spanish (PK-12) (MAT). Part-time programs available. *Faculty:* 15 full-time (7 women), 14 part-time/adjunct (13 women). *Students:* 74 full-time (64 women), 2 part-time (both women); includes 6 minority (4 Hispanic/Latino; 2 Two or more races, non-Hispanic/Latino). Average age 23. 90 applicants, 100% accepted, 67 enrolled. In 2013, 96 master's awarded. *Degree requirements:* For master's, comprehensive exam, thesis or alternative. *Entrance requirements:* For master's, PRAXIS I, minimum GPA of 3.0. Additional exam requirements/recommendations for international students: Required—TOEFL (minimum score 580 paper-based; 92 iBT). *Application deadline:* For fall admission, 4/1 for international students; for spring admission, 10/15 for domestic students, 10/1 for international students; for summer admission, 1/15 for domestic students, 3/1 for international students. Applications are processed on a rolling basis. Application fee: $50. Electronic applications accepted. *Expenses: Tuition, area resident:* Part-time $498 per credit hour. Tuition, state resident: part-time $498 per credit hour. Tuition, nonresident: part-time $899 per credit hour. *Financial support:* In 2013–14, 3 students received support, including 3 research assistantships with full tuition reimbursements available (averaging $2,000 per year); career-related internships or fieldwork, Federal Work-Study, and unspecified assistantships also available. Financial award application deadline: 3/1; financial award applicants required to submit FAFSA. *Faculty research:* Early literacy development, instructional innovations, professional teaching standards, multicultural issues, aesthetic education. *Total annual research expenditures:* $24,000. *Unit head:* Dr. Marsha Sprague, Director, 757-594-7388, Fax: 757-594-7803, E-mail: msprague@cnu.edu. *Application contact:* Lyn Sawyer, Associate Director, Graduate Admissions, 757-594-7544, Fax: 757-594-7649, E-mail: gradstdy@cnu.edu.

The Citadel, The Military College of South Carolina, Citadel Graduate College, Department of Mathematics and Computer Science, Charleston, SC 29409. Offers computer and information science (MS); mathematics education (MAE). *Accreditation:* NCATE (one or more programs are accredited). Part-time and evening/weekend programs available. *Faculty:* 5 full-time (3 women). *Students:* 1 full-time (0 women), 3 part-time (0 women); includes 1 minority (Asian, non-Hispanic/Latino). Average age 33. In 2013, 3 master's awarded. *Degree requirements:* For master's, comprehensive exam (for some programs), thesis (for some programs). *Entrance requirements:* For master's, GRE General Test with minimum combined score of 300 on the verbal and quantitative sections [1000 under the old grading system], 4.0 on the writing assessment (for MS); MAT with minimum raw score of 396 (for MA Ed), minimum undergraduate GPA of 3.0 (MS) or 2.5 (MAT); competency, demonstrated through coursework, approved work experience, or a program-administrated competency exam, in the areas of basic computer architecture, object-oriented programming, discrete mathematics, and data structures (MS); successful completion of 7 courses (MAT). Additional exam requirements/recommendations for international students: Required—TOEFL (minimum score 550 paper-based; 79 iBT). *Application deadline:* Applications are processed on a rolling basis. Application fee: $30. Electronic applications accepted. *Expenses: Tuition, area resident:* Part-time $525 per credit hour. Tuition, state resident: part-time $525 per credit hour. Tuition, nonresident: part-time $865 per credit hour. *Financial support:* Health care benefits and unspecified assistantships available. Support available to part-time students. Financial award application deadline: 7/1; financial award applicants required to submit FAFSA. *Faculty research:* Mathematics: numerical linear algebra, inverse problems, operator algebras, geometric group theory, integral equations; computer science: computer networks, database systems, software engineering, computational systems biology, mobile systems. *Unit head:* Dr. John I. Moore, Jr., Department Head, 843-953-5048, Fax: 843-953-7391, E-mail: john.moore@citadel.edu. *Application contact:* Dr. Shankar M. Banik, Computer and Information Science Program Director, 843-953-5039, Fax: 843-953-7391, E-mail: shankar.banik@citadel.edu.
Website: http://www.mathcs.citadel.edu/.

The Citadel, The Military College of South Carolina, Citadel Graduate College, School of Education, Program in Secondary Education, Charleston, SC 29409. Offers biology (MAT); English language arts (MAT); mathematics (MAT); mathematics education (MAE); physical education (MAT); social studies (MAT). *Accreditation:* NCATE. Part-time and evening/weekend programs available. *Faculty:* 10 full-time (6 women), 8 part-time/adjunct (3 women). *Students:* 14 full-time (9 women), 56 part-time (31 women); includes 9 minority (8 Black or African American, non-Hispanic/Latino; 1 Hispanic/Latino). Average age 30. In 2013, 24 master's awarded. *Degree requirements:* For master's, comprehensive exam, internship. *Entrance requirements:* For master's, GRE (minimum score 290; 900 on old scoring system) or MAT (minimum score 396), minimum undergraduate GPA of 2.5. Additional exam requirements/recommendations for international students: Required—TOEFL (minimum score 550 paper-based). *Application deadline:* Applications are processed on a rolling basis. Application fee: $30. Electronic applications accepted. *Expenses: Tuition, area resident:* Part-time $525 per credit hour. Tuition, state resident: part-time $525 per credit hour. Tuition, nonresident: part-time $865 per credit hour. *Financial support:* Career-related internships or fieldwork, health care benefits, and unspecified assistantships available. Support available to part-time students. Financial award application deadline: 7/1; financial award applicants required to submit FAFSA. *Unit head:* Dr. Kathryn A. Richardson-Jones, Coordinator, 843-953-3163, Fax: 843-953-7258, E-mail: kathryn.jones@citadel.edu. *Application contact:* Dr. Robert H. McNamara, Associate Provost, The Citadel Graduate College, 843-953-5089, Fax: 843-953-7630, E-mail: cgc@citadel.edu.
Website: http://www.citadel.edu/education/teacher-education/mat-master-of-arts-in-teaching.html.

City College of the City University of New York, Graduate School, School of Education, Department of Secondary Education, New York, NY 10031-9198. Offers adolescent mathematics education (MA, AC); English education (MA); middle school mathematics education (MS); science education (MA); social studies education (AC). *Accreditation:* NCATE. *Entrance requirements:* For master's, Liberal Arts and Sciences Test (LAST), Content Specialty Test (CST). Additional exam requirements/recommendations for international students: Required—TOEFL.

Clarion University of Pennsylvania, Office of Transfer, Adult and Graduate Admissions, Master of Education Program, Clarion, PA 16214. Offers curriculum and instruction (M Ed); early childhood (M Ed); math education (M Ed); reading (M Ed); science education (M Ed); special education (M Ed); technology (M Ed). *Accreditation:* NCATE. Part-time programs available. Postbaccalaureate distance learning degree programs offered (no on-campus study). *Faculty:* 17 full-time (10 women). *Students:* 231 full-time (191 women), 535 part-time (448 women); includes 39 minority (12 Black or African American, non-Hispanic/Latino; 8 Asian, non-Hispanic/Latino; 11 Hispanic/Latino; 1 Native Hawaiian or other Pacific Islander, non-Hispanic/Latino; 7 Two or more races, non-Hispanic/Latino). Average age 31. 28 applicants, 75% accepted, 18 enrolled. In 2013, 99 master's awarded. *Degree requirements:* For master's, comprehensive exam, thesis, or portfolio. *Entrance requirements:* For master's, minimum QPA of 3.0. Additional exam requirements/recommendations for international students: Required—TOEFL (minimum score 550 paper-based; 80 iBT), IELTS (minimum score 7). *Application deadline:* For fall admission, 8/1 for domestic students, 4/15 for international students; for spring admission, 8/1 for domestic students, 9/15 for international students. Applications are processed on a rolling basis. Application fee: $40. Electronic applications accepted. *Expenses:* Tuition, state resident: part-time $442 per credit. Tuition, nonresident: part-time $451 per credit. *Required fees:* $142.40 per semester. One-time fee: $150 part-time. *Financial support:* In 2013–14, 8 research assistantships with full and partial tuition reimbursements (averaging $9,420 per year) were awarded; career-related internships or fieldwork also available. Support available to part-time students. Financial award application deadline: 3/1. *Unit head:* Ray Puller, Interim Dean, 814-393-2146, Fax: 514-393-2446, E-mail: rpuller@clarion.edu. *Application contact:* Susan Staub, Assistant Director, Graduate Programs, 814-393-2337, Fax: 814-393-2722, E-mail: gradstudies@clarion.edu.
Website: http://www.clarion.edu/25887/.

Clark Atlanta University, School of Education, Department of Curriculum, Atlanta, GA 30314. Offers special education general curriculum (MA); teaching math and science (MAT). Part-time programs available. *Faculty:* 2 full-time (1 woman), 1 (woman) part-time/adjunct. *Students:* 9 full-time (8 women), 3 part-time (1 woman); includes 11 minority (all Black or African American, non-Hispanic/Latino). Average age 28. 8 applicants, 88% accepted, 7 enrolled. In 2013, 4 master's awarded. *Degree requirements:* For master's, one foreign language, comprehensive exam. *Entrance requirements:* For master's, GRE General Test, minimum undergraduate GPA of 2.6. Additional exam requirements/recommendations for international students: Required—TOEFL (minimum score 500 paper-based; 61 iBT). *Application deadline:* For fall admission, 4/1 for domestic and international students; for spring admission, 11/1 for domestic and international students. Applications are processed on a rolling basis. Application fee: $40 ($55 for international students). *Expenses: Tuition:* Full-time $14,616; part-time $812 per credit hour. *Required fees:* $706; $353 per semester. *Financial support:* Career-related internships or fieldwork, Federal Work-Study, scholarships/grants, and unspecified assistantships available. Support available to part-time students. Financial award application deadline: 4/30; financial award applicants required to submit FAFSA. *Unit head:* Dr. Doris Terrell, Chairperson, 404-880-6336, E-mail: dterrell@cau.edu. *Application contact:* Michelle Clark-Davis, Graduate Program Admissions, 404-880-6605, E-mail: cauadmissions@cau.edu.
Website: http://www.cau.edu/School_of_Education_curriculum_dept.aspx.

Clayton State University, School of Graduate Studies, College of Arts and Sciences, Program in Education, Morrow, GA 30260-0285. Offers English (MAT); mathematics (MAT). *Accreditation:* NCATE. *Entrance requirements:* For master's, GRE, GACE, 2 official copies of transcripts, 3 recommendation letters, statement of purpose. Additional exam requirements/recommendations for international students: Required—TOEFL (minimum score 550 paper-based). Electronic applications accepted.

Clemson University, Graduate School, College of Health, Education, and Human Development, Eugene T. Moore School of Education, Program in Secondary Education: Math and Science, Clemson, SC 29634. Offers MAT. *Accreditation:* NCATE. *Students:* 18 full-time (13 women); includes 1 minority (Black or African American, non-Hispanic/Latino). Average age 27. 4 applicants, 50% accepted, 1 enrolled. In 2013, 11 master's awarded. *Degree requirements:* For master's, digital portfolio. *Entrance requirements:* For master's, PRAXIS II. Additional exam requirements/recommendations for international students: Required—TOEFL; Recommended—IELTS. *Application deadline:* For fall admission, 4/1 for domestic students. Applications are processed on a rolling basis. Application fee: $70 ($80 for international students). Electronic applications accepted. *Expenses:* Contact institution. *Financial support:* In 2013–14, 4 students received support, including 12 fellowships with partial tuition reimbursements available (averaging $3,599 per year); institutionally sponsored loans, scholarships/grants, health care benefits, and unspecified assistantships also available. Financial award application deadline: 6/1; financial award applicants required to submit FAFSA. *Faculty research:* Science education, math education. *Unit head:* Dr. Michael J. Padilla, Director/Associate Dean, 864-656-4444, Fax: 864-656-0311, E-mail: padilla@clemson.edu. *Application contact:* Dr. David Fleming, Graduate Coordinator, 864-656-1881, Fax: 864-656-0311, E-mail: dflemin@clemson.edu.
Website: http://www.clemson.edu/hehd/departments/education/academics/graduate/MAT/secondary.html.

Clemson University, Graduate School, College of Health, Education, and Human Development, Eugene T. Moore School of Education, Program in Teaching and Learning, Clemson, SC 29634. Offers elementary education (M Ed); English education (M Ed); mathematics education (M Ed); science education (M Ed); social studies education (M Ed). *Students:* 6 full-time (5 women), 8 part-time (7 women), 3 international. Average age 28. 6 applicants, 100% accepted, 4 enrolled. In 2013, 9 master's awarded. *Entrance requirements:* For master's, GRE, baccalaureate degree from regionally-accredited institution, official transcripts, copy of valid teaching certificate, two letters of recommendation. *Financial support:* In 2013–14, 1 teaching assistantship (averaging $6,812 per year) was awarded. *Unit head:* Dr. Michael J. Padilla, Director/Associate Dean, 864-656-4444, Fax: 864-656-0311, E-mail: padilla@clemson.edu. *Application contact:* Dr. David Fleming, Graduate Programs Coordinator, 864-656-1881, Fax: 864-656-0311, E-mail: dflemin@clemson.edu.
Website: http://www.grad.clemson.edu/programs/Teaching-Learning/.

Cleveland State University, College of Graduate Studies, College of Education and Human Services, Department of Teacher Education, Cleveland, OH 44115. Offers art education (M Ed); early childhood education (M Ed); foreign language education (M Ed); mathematics and science education (M Ed); middle childhood education (M Ed); special education (M Ed), including mild/moderate disabilities, moderate/intensive disabilities; teaching English to speakers of other languages (M Ed). Part-time and evening/weekend programs available. *Faculty:* 20 full-time (12 women), 26 part-time/adjunct (20 women). *Students:* 108 full-time (78 women), 311 part-time (252 women); includes 103 minority (80 Black or African American, non-Hispanic/Latino; 2 Asian, non-Hispanic/Latino; 10 Hispanic/Latino; 1 Native Hawaiian or other Pacific Islander, non-Hispanic/Latino; 10 Two or more races, non-Hispanic/Latino), 52 international. Average age 32. 177 applicants, 55% accepted, 68 enrolled. In 2013, 192 master's awarded. *Degree requirements:* For master's, comprehensive exam (for some programs), thesis or alternative. *Entrance requirements:* For master's, GRE General Test or MAT, minimum

GPA of 2.75. Additional exam requirements/recommendations for international students: Required—TOEFL (minimum score 525 paper-based), IELTS (minimum score 6). *Application deadline:* For fall admission, 7/15 priority date for domestic students. Applications are processed on a rolling basis. Application fee: $30. *Expenses:* Tuition, state resident: full-time $8335; part-time $521 per credit hour. Tuition, nonresident: full-time $15,670; part-time $979 per credit hour. *Required fees:* $50; $25 per semester. *Financial support:* In 2013–14, 12 research assistantships with full tuition reimbursements (averaging $3,480 per year) were awarded; tuition waivers (partial) and unspecified assistantships also available. *Faculty research:* Early literacy, professional development in reading, reading recovery, dual language, induction programs. *Total annual research expenditures:* $6.2 million. *Unit head:* Dr. Clifford T. Bennett, Chairperson, 216-523-7105, Fax: 216-687-5379, E-mail: c.t.bennett@csuohio.edu. *Application contact:* Deborah L. Brown, Interim Assistant Director, Graduate Admissions, 216-523-7572, E-mail: d.l.brown@csuohio.edu.
Website: http://www.csuohio.edu/cehs/departments/TE/te_dept.html.

The College at Brockport, State University of New York, School of Education and Human Services, Department of Education and Human Development, Program in Adolescence Education, Brockport, NY 14420-2997. Offers adolescence biology education (MS Ed); adolescence chemistry education (MS Ed); adolescence earth science education (MS Ed); adolescence English education (MS Ed); adolescence mathematics education (MS Ed); adolescence physics education (MS Ed); adolescence social studies education (MS Ed). *Accreditation:* NCATE. Part-time programs available. *Students:* 13 full-time (7 women), 47 part-time (28 women); includes 3 minority (1 Black or African American, non-Hispanic/Latino; 1 American Indian or Alaska Native, non-Hispanic/Latino; 1 Asian, non-Hispanic/Latino). 26 applicants, 88% accepted, 14 enrolled. In 2013, 27 master's awarded. *Degree requirements:* For master's, thesis or alternative. *Entrance requirements:* For master's, minimum GPA of 3.0, letters of recommendation; statement of objectives, current resume. Additional exam requirements/recommendations for international students: Required—TOEFL (minimum score 550 paper-based; 79 iBT), IELTS (minimum score 6.5). *Application deadline:* For fall admission, 3/15 priority date for domestic and international students; for spring admission, 10/15 priority date for domestic and international students; for summer admission, 3/15 priority date for domestic students, 3/13 priority date for international students. Application fee: $80. Electronic applications accepted. *Expenses:* Tuition, state resident: full-time $9870. Tuition, nonresident: full-time $18,350. *Required fees:* $1848. *Financial support:* Federal Work-Study, scholarships/grants, and unspecified assistantships available. Support available to part-time students. Financial award application deadline: 3/15; financial award applicants required to submit FAFSA. *Unit head:* Dr. Don Halquist, Chairperson, 585-395-5550, Fax: 585-395-2172, E-mail: dhalquis@brockport.edu. *Application contact:* Michael Harrison, Coordinator of Certification and Graduate Advisement, 585-395-2326, Fax: 585-395-2172, E-mail: mharriso@brockport.edu.
Website: http://www.brockport.edu/ehd/.

The College at Brockport, State University of New York, School of Education and Human Services, Department of Education and Human Development, Program in Adolescence Inclusive Generalist Education, Brockport, NY 14420-2997. Offers English (MS Ed); mathematics (MS Ed); science (MS Ed); social studies (MS Ed). *Students:* 30 full-time (18 women), 24 part-time (17 women); includes 6 minority (3 Black or African American, non-Hispanic/Latino; 2 Hispanic/Latino; 1 Two or more races, non-Hispanic/Latino). 16 applicants, 75% accepted, 8 enrolled. In 2013, 15 master's awarded. *Degree requirements:* For master's, thesis or alternative. *Entrance requirements:* For master's, minimum GPA of 3.0, letters of recommendation, statement of objectives, academic major (or equivalent) in program discipline; current resume. Additional exam requirements/recommendations for international students: Required—TOEFL (minimum score 550 paper-based; 79 iBT), IELTS (minimum score 6.5). *Application deadline:* For fall admission, 3/15 priority date for domestic and international students; for spring admission, 10/15 priority date for domestic and international students; for summer admission, 3/15 for domestic and international students. Application fee: $80. Electronic applications accepted. *Expenses:* Tuition, state resident: full-time $9870. Tuition, nonresident: full-time $18,350. *Required fees:* $1848. *Financial support:* Federal Work-Study, scholarships/grants, and unspecified assistantships available. Support available to part-time students. Financial award application deadline: 3/15; financial award applicants required to submit FAFSA. *Unit head:* Dr. Don Halquist, Chairperson, 585-395-2205, Fax: 585-395-2171, E-mail: dhalquis@brockport.edu. *Application contact:* Michael Harrison, Coordinator of Certification and Graduate Advisement, 585-395-2326, Fax: 585-395-2172, E-mail: mharriso@brockport.edu.
Website: http://www.brockport.edu/ehd/.

College of Charleston, Graduate School, School of Education, Health, and Human Performance, Program in Science and Mathematics for Teachers, Charleston, SC 29424-0001. Offers M Ed. *Accreditation:* NCATE. Part-time and evening/weekend programs available. *Degree requirements:* For master's, capstone project. *Entrance requirements:* For master's, GRE or PRAXIS, 2 letters of recommendation, copy of teaching certificate. Additional exam requirements/recommendations for international students: Required—TOEFL (minimum score 81 iBT). Electronic applications accepted.

The College of William and Mary, School of Education, Program in Curriculum and Instruction, Williamsburg, VA 23187-8795. Offers elementary education (MA Ed); gifted education (MA Ed); literacy leadership (MA Ed); math specialist (MA Ed); secondary education (MA Ed), including English education, mathematics education, modern foreign languages education, science education, social studies education; special education (MA Ed), including collaborating master educator, general curriculum. *Accreditation:* NCATE. Part-time programs available. *Faculty:* 15 full-time (10 women), 44 part-time/adjunct (38 women). *Students:* 66 full-time (55 women), 27 part-time (26 women); includes 17 minority (4 Black or African American, non-Hispanic/Latino; 1 American Indian or Alaska Native, non-Hispanic/Latino; 3 Asian, non-Hispanic/Latino; 5 Hispanic/Latino; 4 Two or more races, non-Hispanic/Latino). Average age 28. 179 applicants, 72% accepted, 92 enrolled. In 2013, 76 master's awarded. *Degree requirements:* For master's, project. *Entrance requirements:* For master's, GRE or MAT, minimum GPA of 2.5. Additional exam requirements/recommendations for international students: Required—TOEFL, IELTS. *Application deadline:* For fall admission, 1/15 for domestic and international students; for spring admission, 10/1 for domestic and international students. Application fee: $50. Electronic applications accepted. *Expenses:* Tuition, state resident: full-time $7120; part-time $405 per credit hour. Tuition, nonresident: full-time $21,639; part-time $1050 per credit hour. *Required fees:* $4764. *Financial support:* In 2013–14, 49 students received support, including 6 research assistantships with full and partial tuition reimbursements available (averaging $8,269 per year); career-related internships or fieldwork, Federal Work-Study, institutionally sponsored loans, scholarships/grants, and unspecified assistantships also available. Financial award application deadline: 1/15; financial award applicants required to submit FAFSA. *Faculty research:* National Council of Teachers of Mathematics standards, counseling, self-concept and self-esteem, special education, curriculum development. *Unit head:* Dr. Mark Hofer, Area Coordinator, 757-221-1713, E-mail: mjhofe@wm.edu. *Application contact:* Dorothy Smith Osborne, Assistant Dean for Academic Programs and Student Services, 757-221-2317, Fax: 757-221-2293, E-mail: dsosbo@wm.edu.
Website: http://education.wm.edu.

The Colorado College, Education Department, Program in Secondary Education, Colorado Springs, CO 80903-3294. Offers art teaching (K-12) (MAT); English teaching (MAT); foreign language teaching (MAT); mathematics teaching (MAT); music teaching (MAT); science teaching (MAT); social studies teaching (MAT). *Degree requirements:* For master's, thesis, internship. Electronic applications accepted.

Columbus State University, Graduate Studies, College of Education and Health Professions, Department of Teacher Education, Columbus, GA 31907-5645. Offers accomplished teaching (M Ed); early childhood education (M Ed, MAT, Ed S); middle grades education (M Ed, MAT, Ed S); school library media (M Ed, MAT); secondary education (M Ed, MAT, Ed S), including English/language arts (M Ed, Ed S), general science (M Ed), mathematics (M Ed, Ed S), science (Ed S), social science (M Ed, Ed S); special education (M Ed, MAT, Ed S), including general curriculum (M Ed, MAT); teacher leadership (M Ed). *Accreditation:* NCATE. Part-time and evening/weekend programs available. Postbaccalaureate distance learning degree programs offered (minimal on-campus study). *Faculty:* 17 full-time (12 women), 31 part-time/adjunct (28 women). *Students:* 59 full-time (48 women), 190 part-time (150 women); includes 85 minority (68 Black or African American, non-Hispanic/Latino; 1 American Indian or Alaska Native, non-Hispanic/Latino; 6 Asian, non-Hispanic/Latino; 4 Hispanic/Latino; 6 Two or more races, non-Hispanic/Latino), 2 international. Average age 34. 132 applicants, 58% accepted, 50 enrolled. In 2013, 86 master's, 26 other advanced degrees awarded. *Degree requirements:* For master's, thesis, exit exam; for Ed S, thesis or alternative. *Entrance requirements:* For master's, GRE General Test, minimum undergraduate GPA of 2.75; for Ed S, GRE General Test, minimum undergraduate GPA of 2.75, graduate 3.0. Additional exam requirements/recommendations for international students: Required—TOEFL (minimum score 550 paper-based; 79 iBT). *Application deadline:* For fall admission, 6/30 for domestic students, 5/1 for international students; for spring admission, 11/1 for domestic and international students; for summer admission, 3/1 for domestic and international students. Applications are processed on a rolling basis. Application fee: $40. Electronic applications accepted. *Expenses:* Tuition, state resident: full-time $4572; part-time $382 per credit hour. Tuition, nonresident: full-time $18,292; part-time $1526 per credit hour. *Required fees:* $1800; $196 per credit hour. Tuition and fees vary according to campus/location and program. *Financial support:* In 2013–14, 173 students received support, including 12 research assistantships with partial tuition reimbursements available (averaging $3,000 per year); career-related internships or fieldwork, Federal Work-Study, institutionally sponsored loans, scholarships/grants, tuition waivers (partial), and unspecified assistantships also available. Support available to part-time students. Financial award application deadline: 5/1; financial award applicants required to submit FAFSA. *Unit head:* Dr. Deirdre Greer, Department Chair, 706-507-8034, Fax: 706-568-3134, E-mail: greer_deirdre@columbusstate.edu. *Application contact:* Kristin Williams, Director of International and Graduate Recruitment, 706-507-8848, Fax: 706-568-5091, E-mail: williams_kristin@columbusstate.edu.
Website: http://te.columbusstate.edu/.

Concordia University, College of Education, Portland, OR 97211-6099. Offers career and technical education (M Ed); curriculum and instruction (M Ed), including adolescent literacy, career and technical education, e-learning/technology education, early childhood education, English for speakers of other languages, English language development, environmental education, mathematics, methods and curriculum, reading, science, teacher leadership, the inclusive classroom; early childhood (MAT); education leadership (Ed D); educational administration (M Ed); elementary education (MAT); secondary education (MAT); special education (M Ed); teacher leadership (Ed D). Part-time programs available. Postbaccalaureate distance learning degree programs offered (no on-campus study). *Degree requirements:* For master's, comprehensive exam, work samples/portfolio. *Entrance requirements:* For master's, California Basic Educational Skills Test or PRAXIS I, minimum undergraduate GPA of 2.8, graduate 3.0; 2 letters of recommendation. Additional exam requirements/recommendations for international students: Required—TOEFL (minimum score 525 paper-based). Electronic applications accepted. *Faculty research:* Learner-centered classroom, brain-based learning, future of online learning.

Concordia University, School of Graduate Studies, Faculty of Arts and Science, Department of Mathematics and Statistics, Montréal, QC H3G 1M8, Canada. Offers mathematics (M Sc, MA, PhD); teaching of mathematics (MTM). *Degree requirements:* For master's, thesis optional; for doctorate, comprehensive exam, thesis/dissertation. *Entrance requirements:* For master's, honors degree in mathematics or equivalent. *Faculty research:* Number theory, computational algebra, mathematical physics, differential geometry, dynamical systems and statistics.

Converse College, School of Education and Graduate Studies, Program in Middle Level Education, Spartanburg, SC 29302-0006. Offers language arts/English (MAT); mathematics (MAT); middle level education (M Ed); science (MAT); social studies (MAT).

Converse College, School of Education and Graduate Studies, Program in Secondary Education, Spartanburg, SC 29302-0006. Offers biology (MAT); chemistry (MAT); English (M Ed, MAT); mathematics (M Ed, MAT); natural sciences (M Ed); social sciences (M Ed, MAT). Part-time programs available. *Degree requirements:* For master's, capstone paper. *Entrance requirements:* For master's, NTE or PRAXIS II (M Ed), minimum GPA of 2.75, 2 recommendations. Electronic applications accepted.

Cornell University, Graduate School, Graduate Fields of Agriculture and Life Sciences, Field of Education, Ithaca, NY 14853-0001. Offers adult and extension education (MPS, MS, PhD); learning, teaching, and social policy (MPS, MS, PhD); mathematics 7-12 (MS). *Faculty:* 21 full-time (8 women). *Students:* 14 full-time (9 women); includes 2 minority (1 Asian, non-Hispanic/Latino; 1 Hispanic/Latino), 1 international. Average age 32. 20 applicants, 20% accepted, 2 enrolled. In 2013, 17 master's, 4 doctorates awarded. Terminal master's awarded for partial completion of doctoral program. *Degree requirements:* For master's, thesis (MS); for doctorate, comprehensive exam, thesis/dissertation. *Entrance requirements:* For master's and doctorate, GRE General Test, sample of written work (recommended), 2 letters of recommendation. Additional exam requirements/recommendations for international students: Required—TOEFL (minimum score 550 paper-based; 77 iBT). *Application deadline:* For fall admission, 2/15 for domestic students. Application fee: $95. Electronic applications accepted. *Financial support:* In 2013–14, 4 students received support, including 3 fellowships with full tuition reimbursements available, 1 research assistantship with full tuition reimbursement available; teaching assistantships with full tuition reimbursements available, institutionally sponsored loans, scholarships/grants, health care benefits, tuition waivers (full and partial), and unspecified assistantships also available. Financial award applicants required to submit FAFSA. *Faculty research:* Moral development and professional ethics, public issues education and community development, socio/political issues in public education, teacher education and curriculum in agricultural science and mathematics, extension research. *Unit head:* Director of Graduate Studies, 607-255-4278, Fax: 607-255-7905. *Application contact:* Graduate Field Assistant, 607-255-4278, Fax: 607-255-7905, E-mail: rh22@cornell.edu.
Website: http://www.gradschool.cornell.edu/fields.php?id-80&a-2.

Delaware State University, Graduate Programs, Department of Mathematics, Program in Mathematics Education, Dover, DE 19901-2277. Offers MS. *Entrance requirements:*

Additional exam requirements/recommendations for international students: Required—TOEFL (minimum score 550 paper-based). Electronic applications accepted.

DePaul University, College of Education, Chicago, IL 60614. Offers bilingual bicultural education (M Ed, MA); counseling (M Ed, MA), including clinical mental health counseling, college student development, school counseling; curriculum studies (M Ed, MA, Ed D); early childhood education (M Ed, MA, Ed D); educating adults (MA); educational leadership (M Ed, MA, Ed D), including administration and supervision (M Ed, MA), principal preparation (M Ed, MA); elementary education (MA); mathematics education (MA); mathematics for teaching (MS); middle school mathematics education (MS); reading specialist (M Ed, MA); secondary education (M Ed); social and cultural foundations in education (MA); special education (M Ed, MA); world languages education (M Ed, MA). Part-time and evening/weekend programs available. Postbaccalaureate distance learning degree programs offered (no on-campus study). *Faculty:* 61 full-time (35 women), 59 part-time/adjunct (43 women). *Students:* 628 full-time (486 women), 324 part-time (243 women); includes 304 minority (144 Black or African American, non-Hispanic/Latino; 1 American Indian or Alaska Native, non-Hispanic/Latino; 38 Asian, non-Hispanic/Latino; 98 Hispanic/Latino; 23 Two or more races, non-Hispanic/Latino), 24 international. Average age 30. In 2013, 465 master's, 4 doctorates awarded. *Degree requirements:* For doctorate, thesis/dissertation. *Application deadline:* For fall admission, 8/15 for domestic students; for winter admission, 12/1 for domestic students; for spring admission, 3/1 for domestic students. Applications are processed on a rolling basis. Application fee: $40. Electronic applications accepted. Tuition and fees vary according to course level, course load and degree level. *Financial support:* Application deadline: 12/31; applicants required to submit FAFSA. *Unit head:* Dr. Paul Zionts, Dean, 773-325-7581, Fax: 773-325-7713, E-mail: pzionts@depaul.edu. *Application contact:* Farrah Dalal, Assistant Director, 773-325-2465, Fax: 773-325-2270, E-mail: fdalal@depaul.edu.
Website: http://education.depaul.edu.

DePaul University, College of Science and Health, Chicago, IL 60614. Offers applied mathematics (MS); applied statistics (MS); biological sciences (MA, MS); chemistry (MS); mathematics education (MA); mathematics for teaching (MS); nursing (MS); nursing practice (DNP); physics (MS); psychology (MS); pure mathematics (MS); science education (MS); MA/PhD. *Faculty:* 66 full-time (40 women), 23 part-time/adjunct (21 women). *Students:* 485 full-time (338 women), 207 part-time (132 women); includes 198 minority (55 Black or African American, non-Hispanic/Latino; 1 American Indian or Alaska Native, non-Hispanic/Latino; 64 Asian, non-Hispanic/Latino; 53 Hispanic/Latino; 2 Native Hawaiian or other Pacific Islander, non-Hispanic/Latino; 23 Two or more races, non-Hispanic/Latino), 48 international. Average age 29. In 2013, 244 master's, 20 doctorates awarded. *Application deadline:* Applications are processed on a rolling basis. Application fee: $40. Electronic applications accepted. Tuition and fees vary according to course level, course load and degree level. *Financial support:* Applicants required to submit FAFSA. *Application contact:* Ann Spittle, Director of Graduate Admission, 773-325-7315, Fax: 312-476-3244, E-mail: graddepaul@depaul.edu.
Website: http://csh.depaul.edu/.

Drew University, Caspersen School of Graduate Studies, Program in Education, Madison, NJ 07940-1493. Offers biology (MAT); chemistry (MAT); English (MAT); French (MAT); Italian (MAT); math (MAT); physics (MAT); social studies (MAT); Spanish (MAT); theatre arts (MAT). Part-time programs available. *Degree requirements:* For master's, student teaching internship and seminar. *Entrance requirements:* For master's, transcripts, statement of purpose, three letters of recommendation. Additional exam requirements/recommendations for international students: Required—TOEFL. *Expenses:* Contact institution.

Drury University, Graduate Programs in Education, Springfield, MO 65802. Offers elementary education (M Ed); gifted education (M Ed); human services (M Ed); instructional mathematics K-8 (M Ed); instructional technology (M Ed); middle school teaching (M Ed); secondary education (M Ed); special education (M Ed); special reading (M Ed). *Accreditation:* NCATE. Part-time and evening/weekend programs available. *Degree requirements:* For master's, thesis. *Entrance requirements:* For master's, GRE or MAT, minimum GPA of 2.75. Additional exam requirements/recommendations for international students: Required—TOEFL. Electronic applications accepted. *Faculty research:* Cultural enrichment, research skills, parental involvement relating to reading skills, reading strategies for mainstreaming children.

Duquesne University, School of Education, Department of Instruction and Leadership, Program in Secondary Education, Pittsburgh, PA 15282-0001. Offers biology (MS Ed); chemistry (MS Ed); English (MS Ed); K-12 education (MS Ed), including Latin; mathematics (MS Ed); physics (MS Ed); social studies (MS Ed). Part-time and evening/weekend programs available. *Faculty:* 4 full-time (2 women). *Students:* 44 full-time (23 women), 3 part-time (2 women); includes 7 minority (6 Black or African American, non-Hispanic/Latino; 1 Two or more races, non-Hispanic/Latino), 1 international. Average age 27. 43 applicants, 35% accepted, 15 enrolled. In 2013, 28 master's awarded. *Degree requirements:* For master's, thesis optional. *Entrance requirements:* For master's, letters of recommendation, letter of intent, interview, bachelor's degree. Additional exam requirements/recommendations for international students: Required—TOEFL (minimum score 550 paper-based), IELTS (minimum score 7). *Application deadline:* For fall admission, 9/1 for domestic students; for spring admission, 1/1 for domestic students. Applications are processed on a rolling basis. Application fee: $0. Electronic applications accepted. Application fee is waived when completed online. *Expenses: Tuition:* Full-time $18,162; part-time $1009 per credit. *Required fees:* $1728; $96 per credit. Tuition and fees vary according to program. *Financial support:* Research assistantships and Federal Work-Study available. Support available to part-time students. *Unit head:* Dr. Melissa Boston, Associate Professor and Director, 412-396-6109, E-mail: bostonm@duq.edu. *Application contact:* Michael Dolinger, Director of Student and Academic Services, 412-396-6647, Fax: 412-396-5585, E-mail: dolingerm@duq.edu.
Website: http://www.duq.edu/academics/schools/education/graduate-programs-education/ms-ed-secondary-education.

East Carolina University, Graduate School, College of Education, Department of Mathematics, Science, and Instructional Technology Education, Greenville, NC 27858-4353. Offers computer-based instruction (Certificate); distance learning and administration (Certificate); instructional technology (MA Ed, MS); mathematics (MA Ed); performance improvement (Certificate); science education (MA, MA Ed); special endorsement in computer education (Certificate). Part-time and evening/weekend programs available. *Degree requirements:* For master's, comprehensive exam, thesis optional. *Entrance requirements:* For master's, GRE General Test or MAT, interview, minimum GPA of 2.5, bachelor's degree in related field, teaching license (MA Ed). Additional exam requirements/recommendations for international students: Required—TOEFL. *Expenses:* Tuition, state resident: full-time $4223. Tuition, nonresident: full-time $16,540. *Required fees:* $2184.

Eastern Illinois University, Graduate School, College of Sciences, Department of Mathematics and Computer Science, Charleston, IL 61920-3099. Offers mathematics (MA); mathematics education (MA). *Entrance requirements:* For master's, GRE General Test. *Expenses: Tuition, area resident:* Part-time $283 per credit hour. Tuition, state resident: part-time $283 per credit hour. Tuition, nonresident: part-time $679 per credit hour.

Eastern Kentucky University, The Graduate School, College of Education, Department of Curriculum and Instruction, Program in Secondary and Higher Education, Richmond, KY 40475-3102. Offers secondary education (MA Ed), including agricultural education, art education, biological sciences education, business education, English education, geography education, history education, home economics education, industrial education, mathematical sciences education, physical education, school health education. *Accreditation:* NCATE. Part-time programs available. *Entrance requirements:* For master's, GRE General Test, minimum GPA of 2.5.

Eastern Michigan University, Graduate School, College of Arts and Sciences, Department of Mathematics, Ypsilanti, MI 48197. Offers applied statistics (MA); computer science (MA); mathematics (MA); mathematics education (MA). Part-time and evening/weekend programs available. Postbaccalaureate distance learning degree programs offered (minimal on-campus study). *Faculty:* 22 full-time (9 women). *Students:* 9 full-time (2 women), 26 part-time (10 women); includes 6 minority (2 Black or African American, non-Hispanic/Latino; 3 Asian, non-Hispanic/Latino; 1 Hispanic/Latino), 4 international. Average age 30. 35 applicants, 71% accepted, 10 enrolled. In 2013, 13 master's awarded. *Degree requirements:* For master's, thesis optional. *Entrance requirements:* Additional exam requirements/recommendations for international students: Required—TOEFL. *Application deadline:* Applications are processed on a rolling basis. Application fee: $35. *Expenses:* Tuition, state resident: full-time $12,300; part-time $466 per credit hour. Tuition, nonresident: full-time $23,159; part-time $918 per credit hour. *Required fees:* $71 per credit hour. $46 per semester. One-time fee: $100. Tuition and fees vary according to course level and degree level. *Financial support:* Fellowships, research assistantships with full tuition reimbursements, teaching assistantships with full tuition reimbursements, career-related internships or fieldwork, Federal Work-Study, institutionally sponsored loans, scholarships/grants, tuition waivers (partial), and unspecified assistantships available. Support available to part-time students. Financial award applicants required to submit FAFSA. *Unit head:* Dr. Christopher Gardiner, Department Head, 734-487-1444, Fax: 734-487-2489, E-mail: cgardiner@emich.edu. *Application contact:* Dr. Bingwu Wang, Graduate Coordinator, 734-487-5044, Fax: 734-487-2489, E-mail: bwang@emich.edu.
Website: http://www.math.emich.edu.

Eastern University, Graduate Education Programs, St. Davids, PA 19087-3696. Offers ESL program specialist (K-12) (Certificate); general supervisor (PreK-12) (Certificate); health and physical education (K-12) (Certificate); middle level (4-8) (Certificate); multicultural education (M Ed); pre K-4 (Certificate); pre K-4 with special education (Certificate); reading (M Ed); reading specialist (K-12) (Certificate); reading supervisor (K-12) (Certificate); school health services (M Ed); school health supervisor (Certificate); school nurse (Certificate); school principalship (K-12) (Certificate); secondary biology education (7-12) (Certificate); secondary chemistry education (7-12) (Certificate); secondary communication education (7-12) (Certificate); secondary education (7-12) (Certificate); secondary English education (7-12) (Certificate); secondary math education (7-12) (Certificate); secondary social studies education (7-12) (Certificate); special education (M Ed); special education (7-12) (Certificate); special education (Pre K-8) (Certificate); special education supervisor (N-12) (Certificate); TESOL (M Ed); world language (Certificate), including French, Mandarin Chinese, Spanish. Part-time and evening/weekend programs available. Postbaccalaureate distance learning degree programs offered (no on-campus study). *Faculty:* 22 full-time (11 women), 26 part-time/adjunct (18 women). *Students:* 77 full-time (58 women), 223 part-time (149 women); includes 112 minority (81 Black or African American, non-Hispanic/Latino; 1 American Indian or Alaska Native, non-Hispanic/Latino; 9 Asian, non-Hispanic/Latino; 18 Hispanic/Latino; 1 Native Hawaiian or other Pacific Islander, non-Hispanic/Latino; 2 Two or more races, non-Hispanic/Latino), 7 international. Average age 34. 94 applicants, 100% accepted, 81 enrolled. In 2013, 120 master's awarded. *Entrance requirements:* For master's, minimum GPA of 2.5 (for M Ed); for Certificate, minimum GPA of 3.0 for certifications. Additional exam requirements/recommendations for international students: Required—TOEFL. *Application deadline:* For fall admission, 8/14 for domestic students; for spring admission, 12/20 for domestic students. Applications are processed on a rolling basis. Application fee: $35. Application fee is waived when completed online. *Expenses: Tuition:* Full-time $15,600; part-time $650 per credit. *Required fees:* $27.50 per semester. One-time fee: $50. Tuition and fees vary according to course load, degree level and program. *Financial support:* In 2013–14, 84 students received support, including 6 research assistantships with partial tuition reimbursements available (averaging $7,710 per year); scholarships/grants and unspecified assistantships also available. Financial award application deadline: 3/15; financial award applicants required to submit FAFSA. *Unit head:* Harry Gutelius, Associate Dean, 610-341-1729. *Application contact:* Michael Perpiglia, Associate Director of Enrollment, 610-341-5947, Fax: 484-581-1276, E-mail: mperpigl@eastern.edu.
Website: http://www.eastern.edu/academics/programs/loeb-school-education-0/graduateprograms.

Eastern Washington University, Graduate Studies, College of Science, Health and Engineering, Department of Mathematics, Cheney, WA 99004-2431. Offers mathematics (MS); teaching mathematics (MA). Part-time programs available. *Faculty:* 11 full-time (4 women). In 2013, 17 master's awarded. *Degree requirements:* For master's, comprehensive exam, thesis (for some programs). *Entrance requirements:* For master's, GRE General Test, departmental qualifying exam, minimum GPA of 3.0. *Application deadline:* For fall admission, 4/1 priority date for domestic students; for spring admission, 1/15 for domestic students. Applications are processed on a rolling basis. Application fee: $50. *Financial support:* In 2013–14, 12 teaching assistantships with partial tuition reimbursements (averaging $12,000 per year) were awarded; career-related internships or fieldwork, Federal Work-Study, institutionally sponsored loans, scholarships/grants, health care benefits, tuition waivers (partial), and unspecified assistantships also available. Support available to part-time students. Financial award application deadline: 2/1; financial award applicants required to submit FAFSA. *Unit head:* Dr. Christian Hansen, Chair, 509-359-6225, Fax: 509-359-4700. *Application contact:* Dr. Yves Nievergelt, Adviser, 509-359-2219.

Elizabeth City State University, School of Mathematics, Science and Technology, Master of Science in Mathematics Program, Elizabeth City, NC 27909-7806. Offers applied mathematics (MS); community college teaching (MS); mathematics education (MS); remote sensing (MS). Part-time and evening/weekend programs available. *Faculty:* 7 full-time (2 women). *Students:* 25 part-time (13 women); includes 19 minority (all Black or African American, non-Hispanic/Latino). Average age 25. 5 applicants, 80% accepted, 4 enrolled. In 2013, 18 degrees awarded. *Degree requirements:* For master's, thesis. *Entrance requirements:* For master's, MAT and/or GRE, minimum GPA of 3.0, 3 letters of recommendation, two official transcripts from all undergraduate/graduate schools attended, typewritten one-page request for entry into program that includes description of student's educational preparation. Additional exam requirements/recommendations for international students: Required—TOEFL (minimum score 550 paper-based, 80 iBT) or IELTS (minimum score 6.5). *Application deadline:* For fall admission, 7/15 priority date for domestic and international students; for spring admission, 11/15 priority date for domestic and international students; for summer

admission, 3/15 priority date for domestic and international students. Applications are processed on a rolling basis. Application fee: $30. Electronic applications accepted. *Expenses:* Tuition, state resident: full-time $2916; part-time $364.48 per credit. Tuition, nonresident: full-time $14,199; part-time $1774.83 per credit. *Required fees:* $2972.23; $206.58 per credit. $571.06 per semester. *Financial support:* In 2013–14, 22 students received support, including 3 research assistantships (averaging $19,000 per year), 2 teaching assistantships (averaging $18,000 per year); scholarships/grants and tuition waivers also available. Financial award application deadline: 6/30; financial award applicants required to submit FAFSA. *Faculty research:* Oceanic temperature effects, mathematics strategies in elementary schools, multimedia, Antarctic temperature mapping, computer networks, water quality, remote sensing, polar ice, satellite imagery. *Total annual research expenditures:* $25,000. *Unit head:* Dr. Farrah Jackson, Chair, 252-335-8549, Fax: 252-335-3487, E-mail: fmjackson@mail.ecsu.edu. *Application contact:* Dr. Paula S. Viltz, Interim Dean, School of Education and Psychology and Graduate Education, 252-335-3297, Fax: 252-335-3146, E-mail: psviltz@mail.ecsu.edu.
Website: http://www.ecsu.edu/academics/mathsciencetechnology/.

Florida Agricultural and Mechanical University, Division of Graduate Studies, Research, and Continuing Education, College of Education, Program in Secondary Education and Foundation, Tallahassee, FL 32307-3200. Offers biology (M Ed); chemistry (MS Ed); English (MS Ed); history (MS Ed); math (MS Ed); physics (MS Ed). *Accreditation:* NCATE. *Degree requirements:* For master's, thesis (for some programs). *Entrance requirements:* For master's, GRE General Test, minimum GPA of 3.0. Additional exam requirements/recommendations for international students: Required—TOEFL.

Florida Atlantic University, College of Education, Department of Teaching and Learning, Boca Raton, FL 33431-0991. Offers curriculum and instruction (M Ed), including art, biology, chemistry, English, French, German, mathematics, music, physics, Pre-K and primary education, reading, social sciences, Spanish; elementary education (M Ed); environmental education (M Ed); reading education (M Ed); social foundations of education (M Ed), including educational psychology, educational technology, multilingual education. *Accreditation:* NCATE. Part-time and evening/weekend programs available. *Faculty:* 16 full-time (12 women), 1 (woman) part-time/adjunct. *Students:* 56 full-time (46 women), 96 part-time (78 women); includes 39 minority (10 Black or African American, non-Hispanic/Latino; 6 Asian, non-Hispanic/Latino; 20 Hispanic/Latino; 3 Two or more races, non-Hispanic/Latino), 4 international. Average age 32. 101 applicants, 54% accepted, 42 enrolled. In 2013, 64 master's awarded. *Entrance requirements:* For master's, GRE General Test, minimum GPA of 3.0 in last 2 years of undergraduate course work. Additional exam requirements/recommendations for international students: Required—TOEFL (minimum score 500 paper-based; 61 iBT), IELTS (minimum score 6). *Application deadline:* For fall admission, 7/1 for domestic students, 2/15 for international students; for spring admission, 11/1 for domestic students, 7/15 for international students. Applications are processed on a rolling basis. Application fee: $30. *Expenses:* Tuition, state resident: full-time $6660; part-time $370 per credit hour. Tuition, nonresident: full-time $18,450; part-time $1025 per credit hour. Tuition and fees vary according to course load. *Financial support:* Fellowships with partial tuition reimbursements, research assistantships with partial tuition reimbursements, teaching assistantships with partial tuition reimbursements, career-related internships or fieldwork, scholarships/grants, and unspecified assistantships available. *Faculty research:* Technology, teaching English to speakers of other languages, math teaching, electronic portfolio assessment, global perspectives through social studies. *Unit head:* Dr. Barbara Ridener, Chairperson, 561-297-3588. *Application contact:* Dr. Eliah Watlington, Associate Dean, 561-296-8520, Fax: 261-297-2991, E-mail: ewatling@fau.edu.
Website: http://www.coe.fau.edu/academicdepartments/tl/.

Florida Institute of Technology, Graduate Programs, College of Science, Department of Education and Interdisciplinary Studies, Melbourne, FL 32901-6975. Offers computer education (MS); elementary science education (M Ed); environmental education (MS); interdisciplinary science (MS); mathematics education (MS, PhD, Ed S); science education (MS, PhD, Ed S), including informal science education (MS); teaching (MAT). Part-time and evening/weekend programs available. *Faculty:* 4 full-time (1 woman), 5 part-time/adjunct (2 women). *Students:* 47 full-time (29 women), 40 part-time (25 women); includes 10 minority (4 Black or African American, non-Hispanic/Latino; 4 Asian, non-Hispanic/Latino; 2 Hispanic/Latino), 48 international. Average age 32. 90 applicants, 63% accepted, 23 enrolled. In 2013, 16 master's awarded. Terminal master's awarded for partial completion of doctoral program. *Degree requirements:* For master's, comprehensive exam (for some programs), thesis optional; for doctorate, comprehensive exam, thesis/dissertation; for Ed S, comprehensive exam. *Entrance requirements:* For master's, minimum GPA of 3.0, resume, 3 letters of recommendation (elementary science education), statement of objectives; for doctorate, minimum GPA of 3.2, resume, 3 letters of recommendation, statement of objectives, 3 years of teaching experience (recommended); for Ed S, minimum GPA of 3.0, resume, 3 letters of recommendation, statement of objectives. Additional exam requirements/recommendations for international students: Required—TOEFL (minimum score 550 paper-based; 79 iBT). *Application deadline:* For fall admission, 4/1 for international students; for spring admission, 9/30 for international students. Applications are processed on a rolling basis. Electronic applications accepted. *Expenses: Tuition:* Full-time $20,214; part-time $1123 per credit. Tuition and fees vary according to campus/location. *Financial support:* In 2013–14, 2 teaching assistantships with full and partial tuition reimbursements (averaging $12,623 per year) were awarded; research assistantships with full and partial tuition reimbursements, career-related internships or fieldwork, institutionally sponsored loans, tuition waivers (partial), unspecified assistantships, and tuition remissions also available. Support available to part-time students. Financial award application deadline: 3/1; financial award applicants required to submit FAFSA. *Faculty research:* Measurement and evaluation, computers in education, educational technology. *Total annual research expenditures:* $644,517. *Unit head:* Dr. Kastro Hamed, Department Head, 321-674-8126, Fax: 321-674-7598, E-mail: khamed@fit.edu. *Application contact:* Cheryl A. Brown, Associate Director of Graduate Admissions, 321-674-7581, Fax: 321-723-9468, E-mail: cbrown@fit.edu.
Website: http://cos.fit.edu/education/.

Florida International University, College of Education, Department of Teaching and Learning, Miami, FL 33199. Offers art education (MA, MS); curriculum and instruction (MS, Ed D, PhD, Ed S), including curriculum development (MS), elementary education (MS), English education (MS), learning technologies (MS), mathematics education (MS), modern language education (MS), physical education (MS), science education (MS), social studies education (MS), special education (MS); early childhood education (MS); exceptional student education (Ed D); foreign language education (MS), including foreign language education, teaching English to speakers of other languages (TESOL); international/intercultural education (MS); language, literacy and culture (PhD); mathematics, science, and learning technologies (PhD); physical education (MS), including sport and fitness; reading education (MS). Part-time and evening/weekend programs available. *Degree requirements:* For doctorate, comprehensive exam, thesis/dissertation. *Entrance requirements:* For master's, GRE General Test, Florida General Knowledge Test or Florida College Level Academic Skills Test; for doctorate and Ed S, GRE General Test. Additional exam requirements/recommendations for international students: Required—TOEFL (minimum score 550 paper-based; 80 iBT), IELTS (minimum score 6.3). Electronic applications accepted.

Florida State University, The Graduate School, College of Education, School of Teacher Education, Tallahassee, FL 32306. Offers curriculum and instruction (MS, MST, PhD, Ed S), including early childhood education (MS, PhD, Ed S), elementary education (MS, PhD, Ed S), English education (MS, PhD, Ed S), English teaching (MST), exceptional student education (MST), foreign and second language education (MS, PhD, Ed S), foreign and second language teaching (MST), math education (MS, PhD, Ed S), math teaching (MST), reading education and language arts (MS, PhD, Ed S), science education (MS, PhD, Ed S), social science education (MS, PhD, Ed S), social science teaching (MST), special education (MS, PhD, Ed S), special education studies (MST), visual disabilities (MS, Ed S). Part-time programs available. *Faculty:* 30 full-time (20 women), 22 part-time/adjunct (18 women). *Students:* 183 full-time (151 women), 92 part-time (80 women); includes 47 minority (20 Black or African American, non-Hispanic/Latino; 3 American Indian or Alaska Native, non-Hispanic/Latino; 1 Asian, non-Hispanic/Latino; 20 Hispanic/Latino; 3 Two or more races, non-Hispanic/Latino), 61 international. Average age 30. 199 applicants, 79% accepted, 86 enrolled. In 2013, 119 master's, 9 doctorates, 4 other advanced degrees awarded. *Degree requirements:* For master's and Ed S, comprehensive exam, thesis optional; for doctorate, comprehensive exam, thesis/dissertation, preliminary exam, prospectus defense. *Entrance requirements:* For master's, doctorate, and Ed S, GRE General Test, minimum GPA of 3.0. Additional exam requirements/recommendations for international students: Required—TOEFL (minimum score 550 paper-based; 80 iBT). *Application deadline:* For fall admission, 7/1 for domestic and international students; for winter admission, 10/1 for domestic students, 11/1 for international students; for spring admission, 3/1 for domestic and international students. Applications are processed on a rolling basis. Application fee: $30. Electronic applications accepted. *Expenses:* Tuition, state resident: part-time $403.51 per credit hour. Tuition, nonresident: part-time $1004.85 per credit hour. *Required fees:* $75.81 per credit hour. One-time fee: $20 part-time. Tuition and fees vary according to course load, campus/location and student level. *Financial support:* In 2013–14, 113 students received support, including 55 research assistantships with full and partial tuition reimbursements available, 18 teaching assistantships with full and partial tuition reimbursements available; fellowships with full and partial tuition reimbursements available, career-related internships or fieldwork, scholarships/grants, health care benefits, and unspecified assistantships also available. Financial award application deadline: 1/15; financial award applicants required to submit FAFSA. *Faculty research:* Effective intervention and assessment strategies to improve reading skills; literacy teaching and learning through technology; understanding of student sense-making through instructions, especially STEM learning for all students; international education and consequences of globalization; support professional teacher development and adoption of effective/transformative practices. *Total annual research expenditures:* $1.3 million. *Unit head:* Dr. Sherry Southerland, Chair, 850-644-4880, Fax: 850-644-7736, E-mail: ssoutherland@admin.fsu.edu. *Application contact:* Dawn Matthews, Academic Support Assistant, 850-644-2122, Fax: 850-644-7736, E-mail: dmatthews@fsu.edu.
Website: http://www.coe.fsu.edu/STE.

Framingham State University, Continuing Education, Program in Mathematics, Framingham, MA 01701-9101. Offers M Ed. *Entrance requirements:* For master's, GRE General Test, minimum GPA of 3.0.

Fresno Pacific University, Graduate Programs, School of Education, Division of Mathematics/Science/Computer Education, Program in Integrated Mathematics/Science Education, Fresno, CA 93702-4709. Offers MA Ed. Part-time and evening/weekend programs available. *Students:* 9 part-time (5 women); includes 4 minority (all Hispanic/Latino). Average age 42. *Degree requirements:* For master's, thesis or alternative. *Entrance requirements:* Additional exam requirements/recommendations for international students: Required—TOEFL (minimum score 550 paper-based). *Application deadline:* For fall admission, 7/15 for domestic and international students; for spring admission, 11/15 for domestic and international students. Applications are processed on a rolling basis. Application fee: $90. *Expenses: Tuition:* Full-time $8910; part-time $495 per unit. *Required fees:* $270. Tuition and fees vary according to course load and program. *Financial support:* Scholarships/grants and tuition waivers (full and partial) available. Support available to part-time students. Financial award applicants required to submit FAFSA. *Unit head:* Dr. Dave Youngs, Program Director, 559-453-2244, Fax: 559-453-7106, E-mail: dyoungs@fresno.edu. *Application contact:* Amanda Krum-Stovall, Director of Graduate Admissions, 559-453-2016, E-mail: amanda.krum-stovall@fresno.edu.
Website: http://grad.fresno.edu/programs/master-arts-education-integrated-mathematicsscience-education-emphasis.

Georgia Southern University, Jack N. Averitt College of Graduate Studies, College of Education, Department of Teaching and Learning, Program in Mathematics Education, Statesboro, GA 30460. Offers MAT. *Accreditation:* NCATE. Part-time and evening/weekend programs available. *Students:* 1 full-time (0 women), 1 part-time (0 women); includes 1 minority (Hispanic/Latino). Average age 30. In 2013, 5 master's awarded. *Degree requirements:* For master's, portfolio, transition point assessments, exit assessment. *Entrance requirements:* For master's, GRE General Test or MAT; GACE Basic Skills and Content Assessments (for MAT), minimum cumulative GPA of 2.5. Additional exam requirements/recommendations for international students: Required—TOEFL (minimum score 550 paper-based; 80 iBT), IELTS (minimum score 6). *Application deadline:* For fall admission, 3/1 priority date for domestic and international students; for spring admission, 10/1 priority date for domestic students, 10/1 for international students. Applications are processed on a rolling basis. Application fee: $50. Electronic applications accepted. *Expenses:* Tuition, state resident: full-time $7068; part-time $270 per semester hour. Tuition, nonresident: full-time $26,446; part-time $1077 per semester hour. *Required fees:* $2092. *Financial support:* In 2013–14, 2 students received support, including research assistantships with partial tuition reimbursements available (averaging $7,200 per year), teaching assistantships with partial tuition reimbursements available (averaging $7,200 per year); Federal Work-Study, scholarships/grants, tuition waivers (partial), and unspecified assistantships also available. Support available to part-time students. Financial award application deadline: 4/15; financial award applicants required to submit FAFSA. *Faculty research:* Technology applications. *Unit head:* Dr. Greg Chamblee, Program Coordinator, 912-478-5783, Fax: 912-478-0026, E-mail: gchamblee@georgiasouthern.edu. *Application contact:* Amanda Gilliland, Coordinator for Graduate Student Recruitment, 912-478-5384, Fax: 912-478-0740, E-mail: gradadmissions@georgiasouthern.edu.
Website: http://coe.georgiasouthern.edu/ger/.

Georgia State University, College of Education, Department of Early Childhood Education, Atlanta, GA 30302-3083. Offers early childhood and elementary education (PhD); early childhood education (M Ed, Ed S); mathematics education (M Ed); urban education (M Ed). *Accreditation:* NCATE. Part-time and evening/weekend programs available. *Faculty:* 20 full-time (16 women). *Students:* 104 full-time (93 women), 37 part-time (36 women); includes 70 minority (54 Black or African American, non-Hispanic/Latino; 7 Asian, non-Hispanic/Latino; 6 Hispanic/Latino; 3 Two or more races, non-Hispanic/Latino), 2 international. Average age 29. 51 applicants, 55% accepted, 27

enrolled. In 2013, 73 master's, 1 doctorate, 17 other advanced degrees awarded. *Degree requirements:* For master's, comprehensive exam (for some programs), thesis (for some programs); for doctorate, comprehensive exam, thesis/dissertation (for some programs); for Ed S, comprehensive exam (for some programs). *Entrance requirements:* For master's, GRE, undergraduate diploma; for doctorate and Ed S, GRE, master's degree. Additional exam requirements/recommendations for international students: Required—TOEFL (minimum score 550 paper-based; 79 iBT) or IELTS (minimum score 6.5). *Application deadline:* Applications are processed on a rolling basis. Application fee: $50. Electronic applications accepted. *Expenses: Tuition, area resident:* Full-time $4176; part-time $348 per credit hour. Tuition, state resident: full-time $14,544; part-time $1212 per credit hour. Tuition, nonresident: full-time $14,544; part-time $1212 per credit hour. Tuition and fees vary according to course load and program. *Financial support:* In 2013–14, fellowships with full tuition reimbursements (averaging $24,000 per year), research assistantships with full and partial tuition reimbursements (averaging $4,000 per year), teaching assistantships with full tuition reimbursements (averaging $2,000 per year) were awarded; career-related internships or fieldwork, Federal Work-Study, institutionally sponsored loans, scholarships/grants, traineeships, health care benefits, tuition waivers (partial), and unspecified assistantships also available. Support available to part-time students. Financial award applicants required to submit FAFSA. *Faculty research:* Teacher development; language arts/literacy education; mathematics education; intersection of science, urban, and multicultural education; diversity in education. *Unit head:* Dr. Barbara Meyers, Department Chair, 404-413-8021, Fax: 404-413-8023, E-mail: barbara@gsu.edu. *Application contact:* Elaine King Jones, Administrative Curriculum Specialist, 404-413-8234, Fax: 404-413-8023, E-mail: ekjones@gsu.edu.
Website: http://education.gsu.edu/ece/index.htm.

Georgia State University, College of Education, Department of Middle-Secondary Education and Instructional Technology, Atlanta, GA 30302-3083. Offers English education (M Ed, MAT); English speakers of other languages (MAT); instructional design and technology (MS); instructional technology (PhD), including alternative instructional delivery systems, consulting, instructional design, management, research; mathematics education (M Ed, MAT); middle level education (MAT); reading, language and literacy education (M Ed), including reading instruction; science education (MAT), including biology, broad field science, chemistry, earth science, physics; social studies education (M Ed, MAT), including economics (MAT), geography (MAT), history (MAT), political science (MAT); teaching and learning (PhD), including language and literacy, mathematics education, music education, science education, social studies, teaching and teacher education. *Accreditation:* NCATE. Part-time and evening/weekend programs available. Postbaccalaureate distance learning degree programs offered (minimal on-campus study). *Faculty:* 27 full-time (19 women). *Students:* 181 full-time (113 women), 203 part-time (145 women); includes 161 minority (127 Black or African American, non-Hispanic/Latino; 1 American Indian or Alaska Native, non-Hispanic/Latino; 10 Asian, non-Hispanic/Latino; 11 Hispanic/Latino; 1 Native Hawaiian or other Pacific Islander, non-Hispanic/Latino; 11 Two or more races, non-Hispanic/Latino), 9 international. Average age 36. 2 applicants, 50% accepted, 1 enrolled. In 2013, 213 master's, 17 doctorates awarded. *Degree requirements:* For master's, comprehensive exam (for some programs), thesis or alternative, exit portfolio; for doctorate, comprehensive exam, thesis/dissertation. *Entrance requirements:* For master's, GRE, GACE I (for initial teacher preparation degree programs), baccalaureate degree or equivalent, resume, goals statement, two letters of recommendation, minimum undergraduate GPA of 2.5; proof of initial teacher certification in the content area (for M Ed); for doctorate, GRE, resume, goals statement, writing sample, two letters of recommendation, minimum graduate GPA of 3.3, interview. Additional exam requirements/recommendations for international students: Required—TOEFL (minimum score 550 paper-based; 79 iBT) or IELTS (minimum score 6.5). *Application deadline:* For fall admission, 1/15 priority date for domestic and international students; for spring admission, 10/1 for domestic and international students. Application fee: $50. Electronic applications accepted. *Expenses: Tuition, area resident:* Full-time $4176; part-time $348 per credit hour. Tuition, state resident: full-time $14,544; part-time $1212 per credit hour. Tuition, nonresident: full-time $14,544; part-time $1212 per credit hour. Tuition and fees vary according to course load and program. *Financial support:* In 2013–14, fellowships with full tuition reimbursements (averaging $19,667 per year), research assistantships with full tuition reimbursements (averaging $5,436 per year), teaching assistantships with full tuition reimbursements (averaging $2,779 per year) were awarded; career-related internships or fieldwork, Federal Work-Study, scholarships/grants, health care benefits, tuition waivers (full and partial), and unspecified assistantships also available. Financial award application deadline: 3/15. *Faculty research:* Teacher education in language and literacy, mathematics, science, and social studies in urban middle and secondary school settings; learning technologies in school, community, and corporate settings; multicultural education and education for social justice; urban education; international education. *Unit head:* Dr. Dana L. Fox, Chair, 404-413-8060, Fax: 404-413-8063, E-mail: dfox@gsu.edu. *Application contact:* Bobbie Turner, Administrative Coordinator I, 404-413-8405, Fax: 404-413-8063, E-mail: bnturner@gsu.edu.
Website: http://msit.gsu.edu/msit_programs.htm.

Gordon College, Graduate Education Program, Wenham, MA 01984-1899. Offers education (M Ed); educational leadership (Ed S); English as a second language (ESL) (Ed S); mathematics specialist (Ed S); reading (Ed S). Part-time and evening/weekend programs available. *Faculty:* 1 (woman) full-time, 45 part-time/adjunct (27 women). *Students:* 106 full-time (86 women), 281 part-time (230 women); includes 30 minority (4 Black or African American, non-Hispanic/Latino; 7 Asian, non-Hispanic/Latino; 17 Hispanic/Latino; 2 Two or more races, non-Hispanic/Latino), 5 international. In 2013, 52 master's awarded. *Degree requirements:* For master's and Ed S, action research or clinical experience (for some programs). *Entrance requirements:* For master's, GRE or MAT, references, minimum undergraduate GPA of 3.0; for Ed S, references, minimum undergraduate GPA of 3.0. Additional exam requirements/recommendations for international students: Required—TOEFL (minimum score 550 paper-based, 80 iBT) or IELTS (minimum score 6.5). *Application deadline:* Applications are processed on a rolling basis. Application fee: $50. *Expenses: Tuition:* Part-time $325 per credit. Required fees: $50 per term. One-time fee: $50. Tuition and fees vary according to program. *Financial support:* Applicants required to submit FAFSA. *Faculty research:* Reading, early childhood development, English language learners. *Unit head:* Dr. Janet Arndt, Director of Graduate Studies, 978-867-4355, Fax: 978-867-4663. *Application contact:* Julie Lenocker, Program Administrator, 978-867-4322, Fax: 978-867-4663, E-mail: graduate-education@gordon.edu.
Website: http://www.gordon.edu/graduate.

Grambling State University, School of Graduate Studies and Research, College of Education, Department of Educational Leadership, Grambling, LA 71245. Offers developmental education (MS, Ed D, PMC), including curriculum and instructional design (Ed D), English (MS), guidance and counseling (MS), higher education administration and management (Ed D), mathematics (MS), reading (MS), science (MS), student development and personnel services (Ed D); educational leadership (M Ed). Part-time and evening/weekend programs available. *Faculty:* 10 full-time (7 women). *Students:* 19 full-time (13 women), 89 part-time (70 women); includes 83

minority (82 Black or African American, non-Hispanic/Latino; 1 Hispanic/Latino), 6 international. Average age 40. In 2013, 13 master's, 6 doctorates, 1 other advanced degree awarded. *Degree requirements:* For master's, comprehensive exam, thesis (for some programs); for doctorate, comprehensive exam, thesis/dissertation. *Entrance requirements:* For master's, GRE, minimum GPA of 2.5 on last degree; for doctorate, GRE (minimum score 1000, 500 on Verbal), master's degree, minimum GPA of 3.0 on last degree. Additional exam requirements/recommendations for international students: Required—TOEFL (minimum score 500 paper-based; 62 iBT). *Application deadline:* For fall admission, 7/1 for domestic and international students; for spring admission, 12/1 for domestic and international students; for summer admission, 5/1 for domestic and international students. Applications are processed on a rolling basis. Application fee: $20 ($30 for international students). Electronic applications accepted. *Financial support:* Research assistantships, health care benefits, tuition waivers (full), and unspecified assistantships available. Financial award application deadline: 5/31; financial award applicants required to submit FAFSA. *Unit head:* Dr. Olatunde Ogunyemi, Department Head, 318-274-2549, Fax: 318-274-6249, E-mail: ogunyemio@gram.edu. *Application contact:* Brenda Cooper, Administrative Assistant III, 318-274-2238, Fax: 318-274-6249, E-mail: cooper@gram.edu.
Website: http://www.gram.edu/academics/majors/education/departments/leadership/.

Harding University, Cannon-Clary College of Education, Searcy, AR 72149-0001. Offers advanced studies in teaching and learning (M Ed); art (MSE); behavioral science (MSE); counseling (MS, Ed S); early childhood special education (M Ed, MSE); education (MSE); educational leadership (M Ed, Ed S); elementary education (M Ed); English (MSE); French (MSE); history/social science (MSE); kinesiology (MSE); math (MSE); reading (M Ed); secondary education (M Ed); Spanish (MSE); teaching (MAT); teaching English as a second language (MSE). *Accreditation:* NCATE. Part-time and evening/weekend programs available. *Faculty:* 13 full-time (5 women), 42 part-time/adjunct (24 women). *Students:* 154 full-time (119 women), 393 part-time (270 women); includes 108 minority (81 Black or African American, non-Hispanic/Latino; 5 American Indian or Alaska Native, non-Hispanic/Latino; 5 Asian, non-Hispanic/Latino; 9 Hispanic/Latino; 8 Two or more races, non-Hispanic/Latino), 15 international. Average age 36. 187 applicants, 79% accepted, 135 enrolled. In 2013, 138 master's, 17 other advanced degrees awarded. *Degree requirements:* For master's, comprehensive exam (for some programs), thesis optional, portfolio(s); for Ed S, comprehensive exam, portfolio, project. *Entrance requirements:* For master's, GRE, MAT, PRAXIS; for Ed S, MAT or GRE. Additional exam requirements/recommendations for international students: Required—TOEFL (minimum score 550 paper-based; 79 iBT). *Application deadline:* For fall admission, 8/1 for domestic and international students; for spring admission, 1/1 for domestic and international students. Applications are processed on a rolling basis. Application fee: $35. *Expenses: Tuition:* Full-time $11,574; part-time $643 per credit hour. Required fees: $432; $24 per credit hour. Tuition and fees vary according to course load, degree level and program. *Financial support:* In 2013–14, 36 students received support. Unspecified assistantships available. *Faculty research:* Reading, comprehension, school violence, educational technology, behavior, college choice, differentiated instruction, brain-based teaching. *Unit head:* Dr. Clara Carroll, Chair, 501-279-4501, Fax: 501-279-4083, E-mail: ccarroll@harding.edu. *Application contact:* Information Contact, 501-279-4315, E-mail: gradstudiesedu@harding.edu.
Website: http://www.harding.edu/education.

Harvard University, Extension School, Cambridge, MA 02138-3722. Offers applied sciences (CAS); biotechnology (ALM); educational technologies (ALM); educational technology (CET); English for graduate and professional studies (DGP); environmental management (ALM, CEM); information technology (ALM); journalism (ALM); liberal arts (ALM); management (ALM, CM); mathematics for teaching (ALM); museum studies (ALM); premedical studies (Diploma); publication and communication (CPC). Part-time and evening/weekend programs available. *Degree requirements:* For master's, thesis. *Entrance requirements:* For master's, 3 completed graduate courses with grade of B or higher. Additional exam requirements/recommendations for international students: Required—TOEFL (minimum score 600 paper-based), TWE (minimum score 5). *Expenses:* Contact institution.

High Point University, Norcross Graduate School, High Point, NC 27262-3598. Offers business administration (MBA); educational leadership (M Ed); elementary education (M Ed); history (MA); nonprofit management (MA); secondary math (M Ed); special education (M Ed); strategic communication (MA); teaching elementary education k-6 (MAT); teaching secondary mathematics 9-12 (MAT). *Accreditation:* NCATE. Part-time and evening/weekend programs available. *Degree requirements:* For master's, comprehensive exam (for some programs), thesis (for some programs). *Entrance requirements:* For master's, GMAT (MBA), GRE, MAT, minimum GPA of 3.0. Additional exam requirements/recommendations for international students: Required—TOEFL (minimum score 550 paper-based). Electronic applications accepted.

Hofstra University, School of Education, Programs in Teaching - Elementary and Early Childhood Education, Hempstead, NY 11549. Offers early childhood and childhood education (MS Ed); early childhood education (MA, MS Ed); educational technology (MA); elementary education (MS Ed); literacy (MA); math specialist (Advanced Certificate); math, science, technology (MA); multiculturalism (MA).

Hofstra University, School of Education, Programs in Teaching - Secondary Education, Hempstead, NY 11549. Offers business education (MS Ed); education technology (Advanced Certificate); English education (MA, MS Ed); foreign language and TESOL (MS Ed); foreign language education (MA, MS Ed), including French, German, Russian, Spanish; mathematics education (MA, MS Ed); science education (MA, MS Ed), including biology, chemistry, earth science, geology, physics; secondary education (Advanced Certificate); social studies education (MA, MS Ed); technology for learning (MA).

Hood College, Graduate School, Department of Education, Frederick, MD 21701-8575. Offers curriculum and instruction (MS), including early childhood education, elementary education, elementary school science and mathematics, secondary education, special education; educational leadership (MS, Certificate); reading specialization (MS); STEM (Certificate). *Accreditation:* NCATE. Part-time and evening/weekend programs available. *Faculty:* 4 full-time (3 women), 33 part-time/adjunct (25 women). *Students:* 1 (woman) full-time, 340 part-time (282 women); includes 59 minority (31 Black or African American, non-Hispanic/Latino; 1 American Indian or Alaska Native, non-Hispanic/Latino; 10 Asian, non-Hispanic/Latino; 13 Hispanic/Latino; 4 Two or more races, non-Hispanic/Latino). Average age 33. 97 applicants, 99% accepted, 86 enrolled. In 2013, 64 master's, 40 other advanced degrees awarded. *Degree requirements:* For master's, action research project, portfolio (reading). *Entrance requirements:* For master's, minimum GPA of 2.75, teaching certification. Additional exam requirements/recommendations for international students: Required—TOEFL (minimum score 575 paper-based; 89 iBT), IELTS (minimum score 6.5). *Application deadline:* For fall admission, 7/15 priority date for domestic students, 7/15 for international students; for spring admission, 12/1 priority date for domestic students, 12/1 for international students. Applications are processed on a rolling basis. Application fee: $35. Electronic applications accepted. Application fee is waived when completed online. *Expenses: Tuition:* Part-time $405 per credit. Required fees: $100 per semester. *Financial support:* In 2013–14, 1 student received support. Tuition waivers (partial) and unspecified

assistantships available. Financial award applicants required to submit FAFSA. *Faculty research:* Leadership, action research, brain research, learning styles. *Unit head:* Dr. Ellen Koitz, Chairperson, 301-696-3466, Fax: 301-696-3597, E-mail: koitz@hood.edu. *Application contact:* Dr. Maria Green Cowles, Dean of Graduate School, 301-696-3811, Fax: 301-696-3597, E-mail: gofurther@hood.edu.
Website: http://www.hood.edu/academics/education/index.html.

Hood College, Graduate School, Program in Secondary Mathematics Education, Frederick, MD 21701-8575. Offers mathematics education (MS), including high school, middle school; secondary mathematics education (Certificate). Part-time and evening/weekend programs available. *Faculty:* 2 full-time (1 woman), 1 part-time/adjunct (0 women). *Students:* 1 full-time (0 women), 45 part-time (35 women); includes 1 minority (Hispanic/Latino). Average age 33. 9 applicants, 100% accepted, 8 enrolled. In 2013, 14 master's, 1 other advanced degree awarded. *Degree requirements:* For master's, capstone/research project. *Entrance requirements:* For master's, minimum GPA of 2.75. Additional exam requirements/recommendations for international students: Required—TOEFL (minimum score 575 paper-based; 89 iBT), IELTS (minimum score 6.5). *Application deadline:* For fall admission, 7/15 priority date for domestic students, 7/15 for international students; for spring admission, 12/1 priority date for domestic students, 12/1 for international students. Applications are processed on a rolling basis. Application fee: $35. Electronic applications accepted. Application fee is waived when completed online. *Expenses: Tuition:* Part-time $405 per credit. *Required fees:* $100 per semester. *Financial support:* Tuition waivers (partial) and unspecified assistantships available. Financial award applicants required to submit FAFSA. *Unit head:* Dr. Betty Mayfield, Chairperson, 301-696-3763, E-mail: mayfield@hood.edu. *Application contact:* Dr. Maria Green Cowles, Dean of Graduate School, 301-696-3811, Fax: 301-696-3597, E-mail: gofurther@hood.edu.
Website: http://www.hood.edu/graduate.

Hunter College of the City University of New York, Graduate School, School of Arts and Sciences, Department of Mathematics and Statistics, New York, NY 10065-5085. Offers applied mathematics (MA); mathematics for secondary education (MA); pure mathematics (MA). Part-time and evening/weekend programs available. *Faculty:* 10 full-time (2 women), 2 part-time/adjunct (1 woman). *Students:* 6 full-time (all women), 70 part-time (37 women); includes 39 minority (4 Black or African American, non-Hispanic/Latino; 1 American Indian or Alaska Native, non-Hispanic/Latino; 26 Asian, non-Hispanic/Latino; 8 Hispanic/Latino), 3 international. Average age 31. 54 applicants, 41% accepted, 13 enrolled. In 2013, 28 master's awarded. *Degree requirements:* For master's, one foreign language, comprehensive exam, thesis (for some programs). *Entrance requirements:* For master's, GRE General Test, 24 credits in mathematics. Additional exam requirements/recommendations for international students: Required—TOEFL. *Application deadline:* For fall admission, 4/1 for domestic students, 2/1 for international students; for spring admission, 11/1 for domestic students, 9/1 for international students. Application fee: $125. *Financial support:* Federal Work-Study, institutionally sponsored loans, scholarships/grants, and tuition waivers (partial) available. Support available to part-time students. *Faculty research:* Data analysis, dynamical systems, computer graphics, topology, statistical decision theory. *Unit head:* Robert Thompson, Chair, 212-772-5300, Fax: 212-772-4858, E-mail: robert.thompson@hunter.cuny.edu. *Application contact:* Ada Peluso, Director for Graduate Admissions, 212-772-4632, Fax: 212-772-4858, E-mail: peluso@math.hunter.cuny.edu.
Website: http://math.hunter.cuny.edu/.

Hunter College of the City University of New York, Graduate School, School of Education, Programs in Secondary Education, Concentration in Mathematics Education, New York, NY 10065-5085. Offers MA. *Accreditation:* NCATE. *Faculty:* 3 full-time (1 woman), 20 part-time/adjunct (9 women). *Students:* 6 full-time (all women), 58 part-time (34 women); includes 31 minority (4 Black or African American, non-Hispanic/Latino; 1 American Indian or Alaska Native, non-Hispanic/Latino; 19 Asian, non-Hispanic/Latino; 7 Hispanic/Latino), 2 international. Average age 32. 41 applicants, 71% accepted, 20 enrolled. In 2013, 41 master's awarded. *Degree requirements:* For master's, thesis, professional teaching portfolio, New York State Teacher Certification Exam, research project. *Entrance requirements:* For master's, minimum GPA of 2.8 overall, 2.7 in mathematics courses; 24 credits of course work in mathematics. Additional exam requirements/recommendations for international students: Required—TOEFL, TWE. *Application deadline:* For fall admission, 4/1 for domestic students, 2/1 for international students; for spring admission, 11/1 for domestic students, 9/1 for international students. Applications are processed on a rolling basis. Application fee: $125. *Financial support:* Federal Work-Study and tuition waivers (partial) available. Support available to part-time students. *Unit head:* Dr. Patrick Burke, Program Coordinator, 212-396-6043, E-mail: patrick.burke@hunter.cuny.edu. *Application contact:* Milena Solo, Director for Graduate Admissions, 212-772-4480, E-mail: admissions@hunter.cuny.edu.
Website: http://www.hunter.cuny.edu/school-of-education/programs/graduate/adolescent/mathematics.

Idaho State University, Office of Graduate Studies, College of Science and Engineering, Department of Mathematics, Pocatello, ID 83209-8085. Offers mathematics (MS, DA); mathematics for secondary teachers (MA). Part-time programs available. *Degree requirements:* For master's, comprehensive exam, thesis (for some programs), oral and written exams; for doctorate, comprehensive exam, thesis/dissertation, teaching internships. *Entrance requirements:* For master's, GRE General Test, GRE Subject Test, course work in modern algebra, differential equations, advanced calculus, introductory analysis; for doctorate, GRE General Test, GRE Subject Test, minimum graduate GPA of 3.5, MS in mathematics, teaching experience, 3 letters of recommendation. Additional exam requirements/recommendations for international students: Required—TOEFL (minimum score 550 paper-based; 80 iBT). Electronic applications accepted. *Faculty research:* Algebra, analysis geometry, statistics, applied mathematics.

Illinois Institute of Technology, Graduate College, College of Science and Letters, Department of Mathematics and Science Education, Chicago, IL 60616. Offers collegiate mathematics education (PhD); mathematics education (MME, MS, PhD); science education (MS, MSE, PhD). *Degree requirements:* For master's, comprehensive exam (for some programs), thesis optional; for doctorate, comprehensive exam, thesis/dissertation. *Entrance requirements:* For master's, GRE General Test, minimum undergraduate GPA of 3.0; for doctorate, GRE General Test, minimum GPA of 3.0, 3 years of teaching experience. Additional exam requirements/recommendations for international students: Required—TOEFL (minimum score 523 paper-based; 70 iBT). Electronic applications accepted. *Faculty research:* Informal science/math education, curriculum development, integration of science/math disciplines and across disciplines, instructional methods, students' and teachers' conceptions of scientific/mathematical inquiry and the nature of science/math, instructional models, evaluation, and research design.

Illinois State University, Graduate School, College of Arts and Sciences, Department of Mathematics, Program in Mathematics Education, Normal, IL 61790-2200. Offers PhD. *Degree requirements:* For doctorate, variable foreign language requirement, comprehensive exam, thesis/dissertation, 2 terms of residency. *Entrance requirements:* For doctorate, GRE General Test.

Indiana State University, College of Graduate and Professional Studies, College of Arts and Sciences, Department of Mathematics and Computer Science, Terre Haute, IN 47809. Offers math teaching (MA, MS); mathematics and computer science (MA); mathematics and computer sciences (MS). Part-time programs available. *Faculty:* 10 full-time (1 woman), 3 part-time/adjunct (2 women). *Students:* 33 full-time (15 women), 4 part-time (0 women); includes 2 minority (both Asian, non-Hispanic/Latino), 32 international. Average age 25. 27 applicants, 78% accepted, 4 enrolled. In 2013, 21 master's awarded. *Degree requirements:* For master's, thesis or alternative. *Entrance requirements:* For master's, 24 semester hours of course work in undergraduate mathematics. *Application deadline:* For fall admission, 7/1 priority date for domestic students; for spring admission, 11/1 priority date for domestic students. Applications are processed on a rolling basis. Application fee: $35. Electronic applications accepted. *Financial support:* In 2013–14, 4 teaching assistantships with partial tuition reimbursements (averaging $7,000 per year) were awarded; research assistantships with partial tuition reimbursements and tuition waivers (partial) also available. Financial award application deadline: 3/1; financial award applicants required to submit FAFSA. *Unit head:* Dr. Bhaskara Rao Kopparty, Interim Chairperson, 812-237-2130. *Application contact:* Dr. Jay Gatrell, Dean, 800-444-GRAD, Fax: 812-237-8060, E-mail: jay.gatrell@indstate.edu.

Indiana University Bloomington, School of Education, Department of Curriculum and Instruction, Bloomington, IN 47405-7000. Offers art education (MS, Ed D, PhD); curriculum studies (Ed D, PhD); elementary education (MS, Ed D, PhD, Ed S); mathematics education (MS, Ed D, PhD); science education (MS, Ed D, PhD); secondary education (MS, Ed D, PhD); social studies education (MS, PhD); special education (PhD, Ed S). *Accreditation:* NCATE. Part-time and evening/weekend programs available. Terminal master's awarded for partial completion of doctoral program. *Degree requirements:* For doctorate, thesis/dissertation; for Ed S, comprehensive exam or project. *Entrance requirements:* For master's, doctorate, and Ed S, GRE General Test. Electronic applications accepted.

Indiana University Bloomington, University Graduate School, College of Arts and Sciences, Department of Mathematics, Bloomington, IN 47405-7000. Offers applied mathematics (MA); mathematical physics (PhD); mathematics education (MAT); pure mathematics (MA, PhD). *Faculty:* 49 full-time (3 women). *Students:* 115 full-time (20 women), 1 (woman) part-time; includes 8 minority (1 Black or African American, non-Hispanic/Latino; 6 Asian, non-Hispanic/Latino; 1 Hispanic/Latino), 74 international. Average age 27. 225 applicants, 28% accepted, 24 enrolled. In 2013, 14 master's, 17 doctorates awarded. Terminal master's awarded for partial completion of doctoral program. *Degree requirements:* For doctorate, one foreign language, thesis/dissertation. *Entrance requirements:* For master's and doctorate, GRE General Test, GRE Subject Test. Additional exam requirements/recommendations for international students: Required—TOEFL. *Application deadline:* For fall admission, 1/15 priority date for domestic and international students. Applications are processed on a rolling basis. Application fee: $55 ($65 for international students). Electronic applications accepted. *Financial support:* In 2013–14, 4 fellowships with full tuition reimbursements (averaging $21,750 per year), 21 research assistantships with full tuition reimbursements (averaging $9,000 per year), 90 teaching assistantships with full tuition reimbursements (averaging $16,890 per year) were awarded; scholarships/grants, health care benefits, and unspecified assistantships also available. Financial award application deadline: 1/15. *Faculty research:* Topology, geometry, algebra, applied, analysis. *Unit head:* Kevin Zumbrun, Chair, 812-855-2200. *Application contact:* Kate Forrest, Graduate Secretary, 812-855-2645, Fax: 812-855-0046, E-mail: gradmath@indiana.edu.
Website: http://www.math.indiana.edu/.

Indiana University of Pennsylvania, School of Graduate Studies and Research, College of Natural Sciences and Mathematics, Department of Mathematics, Program in Elementary and Middle School Mathematics Education, Indiana, PA 15705-1087. Offers M Ed. *Accreditation:* NCATE. Part-time programs available. *Faculty:* 6 full-time (3 women). *Students:* 3 full-time (2 women), 4 part-time (all women); includes 1 minority (Black or African American, non-Hispanic/Latino), 2 international. Average age 27. 5 applicants, 80% accepted, 3 enrolled. In 2013, 6 master's awarded. *Degree requirements:* For master's, comprehensive exam (for some programs), thesis optional. *Entrance requirements:* For master's, 2 letters of recommendation. Additional exam requirements/recommendations for international students: Required—TOEFL (minimum score 540 paper-based). *Application deadline:* Applications are processed on a rolling basis. Application fee: $50. Electronic applications accepted. *Expenses:* Tuition, state resident: full-time $3978; part-time $442 per credit. Tuition, nonresident: full-time $5967; part-time $663 per credit. *Required fees:* $2080; $115.55 per credit. $93 per semester. Tuition and fees vary according to degree level and program. *Financial support:* In 2013–14, 1 research assistantship with full and partial tuition reimbursement (averaging $6,360 per year) was awarded; career-related internships or fieldwork and Federal Work-Study also available. Support available to part-time students. Financial award application deadline: 4/15; financial award applicants required to submit FAFSA. *Unit head:* Dr. Edel M. Reilly, Graduate Coordinator, 724-357-7907, E-mail: ereilly@iup.edu. *Application contact:* Dr. Larry Feldman, Co-Coordinator, 724-357-4767, E-mail: larry.feldman@iup.edu.
Website: http://www.iup.edu/grad/mathed/default.aspx.

Indiana University–Purdue University Fort Wayne, College of Arts and Sciences, Department of Mathematical Sciences, Fort Wayne, IN 46805-1499. Offers applied mathematics (MS); applied statistics (Certificate); mathematics (MS); operations research (MS); teaching (MAT). Part-time and evening/weekend programs available. *Faculty:* 19 full-time (5 women). *Students:* 1 (woman) full-time, 10 part-time (3 women), 1 international. Average age 29. 5 applicants, 100% accepted, 4 enrolled. In 2013, 6 master's, 2 other advanced degrees awarded. *Entrance requirements:* For master's, minimum GPA of 3.0, major or minor in mathematics, three letters of recommendation. Additional exam requirements/recommendations for international students: Required—TOEFL (minimum score 550 paper-based; 79 iBT); Recommended—TWE. *Application deadline:* For fall admission, 8/1 priority date for domestic students, 7/1 priority date for international students; for spring admission, 12/1 for domestic students, 10/1 for international students. Applications are processed on a rolling basis. Application fee: $55 ($60 for international students). Electronic applications accepted. *Financial support:* In 2013–14, 5 teaching assistantships with partial tuition reimbursements (averaging $13,322 per year) were awarded; scholarships/grants and unspecified assistantships also available. Support available to part-time students. Financial award application deadline: 3/1; financial award applicants required to submit FAFSA. *Faculty research:* Equilibrium measures, harmonic densities. *Total annual research expenditures:* $10,338. *Unit head:* Dr. Peter Dragnev, Interim Chair/Professor, 260-481-6382, Fax: 260-481-0155, E-mail: dragnevp@ipfw.edu. *Application contact:* Dr. W. Douglas Weakley, Director of Graduate Studies, 260-481-6233, Fax: 260-481-0155, E-mail: weakley@ipfw.edu.
Website: http://www.ipfw.edu/math/.

Indiana University–Purdue University Indianapolis, School of Science, Department of Mathematical Sciences, Indianapolis, IN 46202-3216. Offers mathematics (MS, PhD), including applied mathematics, applied statistics (MS), mathematical statistics (PhD), mathematics, mathematics education (MS). *Faculty:* 30 full-time (2 women). *Students:*

26 full-time (10 women), 36 part-time (13 women); includes 10 minority (1 Black or African American, non-Hispanic/Latino; 7 Asian, non-Hispanic/Latino; 2 Hispanic/Latino), 24 international. Average age 33. 71 applicants, 61% accepted, 24 enrolled. In 2013, 22 master's awarded. Terminal master's awarded for partial completion of doctoral program. *Degree requirements:* For master's, thesis optional; for doctorate, one foreign language, thesis/dissertation. *Entrance requirements:* For doctorate, GRE General Test. Additional exam requirements/recommendations for international students: Required—TOEFL. *Application deadline:* For fall admission, 2/1 priority date for domestic students. Application fee: $55 ($65 for international students). *Financial support:* In 2013–14, 14 students received support, including 23 research assistantships with tuition reimbursements available (averaging $20,000 per year); fellowships with tuition reimbursements available, teaching assistantships with tuition reimbursements available, and tuition waivers (full and partial) also available. Financial award application deadline: 2/1. *Faculty research:* Mathematical physics, integrable systems, partial differential equations, noncommutative geometry, biomathematics, computational neurosciences. *Unit head:* Dr. Jyoti Sarker, Interim Chair, 317-274-8112, E-mail: jsarkar@math.iupui.edu. *Application contact:* Kelly Matthews, Graduate Programs Coordinator, E-mail: kahouser@iupui.edu.
Website: http://www.math.iupui.edu/.

Instituto Tecnológico y de Estudios Superiores de Monterrey, Campus Ciudad Obregón, Programs in Education, Program in Mathematics, Ciudad Obregón, Mexico. Offers ME.

Inter American University of Puerto Rico, Arecibo Campus, Programs in Education, Arecibo, PR 00614-4050. Offers administration and educational supervision (MA Ed); counseling and guidance (MA Ed); curriculum and teaching (MA Ed), including biology education, English as a second language, history education, math education, Spanish; elementary education (MA Ed). *Degree requirements:* For master's, comprehensive exam, thesis optional. *Entrance requirements:* For master's, GRE, EXADEP, bachelor's degree in education or teaching license (administration and supervision) or courses in education and psychology (counseling and guidance), minimum GPA of 2.5 in last 60 credits.

Inter American University of Puerto Rico, Barranquitas Campus, Program in Education, Barranquitas, PR 00794. Offers curriculum and teaching (M Ed), including biology education, English as a second language, history education, mathematics education, Spanish; educational leadership and management (MA); elementary education (M Ed); information and library service technology (M Ed); special education (MA). *Degree requirements:* For master's, comprehensive exam, thesis optional. *Entrance requirements:* For master's, EXADEP, letter of recommendation. Electronic applications accepted.

Inter American University of Puerto Rico, Metropolitan Campus, Graduate Programs, Program in Teaching of Math, San Juan, PR 00919-1293. Offers MA.

Inter American University of Puerto Rico, Ponce Campus, Graduate School, Mercedita, PR 00715-1602. Offers accounting (MBA); biology (M Ed); chemistry (M Ed); criminal justice (MA); elementary education (M Ed); English as a Second Language (M Ed); finance (MBA); history (M Ed); human resources (MBA); marketing (MBA); mathematics (M Ed); Spanish (M Ed). *Entrance requirements:* For master's, minimum GPA of 2.5.

Inter American University of Puerto Rico, San Germán Campus, Graduate Studies Center, Program in Mathematics Education, San Germán, PR 00683-5008. Offers applied mathematics (MA). Part-time and evening/weekend programs available. *Faculty:* 10 full-time (6 women). *Students:* 17 full-time (4 women), 5 part-time (1 woman); all minorities (all Hispanic/Latino). Average age 32. 8 applicants, 88% accepted, 7 enrolled. In 2013, 20 master's awarded. *Degree requirements:* For master's, comprehensive exam. *Entrance requirements:* For master's, EXADEP or GRE General Test, minimum GPA of 3.0. *Application deadline:* For fall admission, 4/30 priority date for domestic students; for spring admission, 11/15 for domestic students. Application fee: $31. *Expenses: Tuition:* Full-time $2424; part-time $202 per credit hour. *Required fees:* $260 per semester. Tuition and fees vary according to course level, course load, degree level and program. *Financial support:* Teaching assistantships, Federal Work-Study, and unspecified assistantships available. *Unit head:* Dr. Elba T. Irizarry, Director of Graduate Studies Center, 787-264-1912 Ext. 7357, Fax: 787-892-6350, E-mail: elbat@sg.inter.edu. *Application contact:* Dr. Alvaro Lecompte, Coordinator, 787-264-1912 Ext. 7547, E-mail: alvarolecompte@cs.com.

Iona College, School of Arts and Science, Department of Education, New Rochelle, NY 10801-1890. Offers adolescence education: biology (MS Ed, MST); adolescence education: English (MS Ed, MST); adolescence education: Italian (MS Ed, MST); adolescence education: mathematics (MS Ed, MST); adolescence education: social studies (MS Ed, MST); adolescence education: Spanish (MS Ed, MST); adolescence special education 5-12 (MST); adolescence special education and literacy (MS Ed); childhood and special education (MST); childhood education (MST); early childhood and childhood (MST); educational leadership (MS Ed); literacy education: birth-grade 6 (MS Ed). *Accreditation:* NCATE. Part-time and evening/weekend programs available. *Faculty:* 11 full-time (9 women), 7 part-time/adjunct (6 women). *Students:* 34 full-time (25 women), 61 part-time (47 women); includes 5 minority (2 Asian, non-Hispanic/Latino; 3 Hispanic/Latino), 1 international. Average age 25. 27 applicants, 93% accepted, 16 enrolled. In 2013, 54 master's awarded. *Degree requirements:* For master's, thesis or alternative. *Entrance requirements:* For master's, minimum GPA of 3.0, NY State teaching certificate (for all MS Ed programs). Additional exam requirements/recommendations for international students: Required—TOEFL (minimum score 550 paper-based; 80 iBT), IELTS (minimum score 6.5). *Application deadline:* For fall admission, 8/1 priority date for domestic students, 5/1 priority date for international students; for spring admission, 1/1 priority date for domestic students, 9/1 priority date for international students. Applications are processed on a rolling basis. Application fee: $50. Electronic applications accepted. *Expenses: Tuition:* Part-time $948 per credit. *Required fees:* $235 per term. *Financial support:* In 2013–14, 84 students received support. Unspecified assistantships available. Support available to part-time students. Financial award application deadline: 4/15; financial award applicants required to submit FAFSA. *Faculty research:* Reading/writing, educational technology, administration, early literacy assessment, literacy development. *Unit head:* Margaret Smith, PhD, Chair, 914-633-2210, Fax: 914-633-2608, E-mail: msmith@iona.edu. *Application contact:* Veronica Jarek-Prinz, Director, Graduate Admissions, 914-633-2420, Fax: 914-633-2277, E-mail: vjarekprinz@iona.edu.
Website: http://www.iona.edu/Academics/School-of-Arts-Science/Departments/Education/Graduate-Programs.aspx.

Iowa State University of Science and Technology, Department of Mathematics, Ames, IA 50011. Offers applied mathematics (MS, PhD); mathematics (MS, PhD); school mathematics (MSM). *Degree requirements:* For master's, thesis or alternative; for doctorate, thesis/dissertation. *Entrance requirements:* For master's and doctorate, GRE General Test. Additional exam requirements/recommendations for international students: Required—TOEFL (minimum score 550 paper-based; 79 iBT), IELTS (minimum score 6.5). Electronic applications accepted.

Iowa State University of Science and Technology, Program in School Mathematics, Ames, IA 50011. Offers MSM. *Entrance requirements:* For master's, official academic transcripts, resume, three letters of recommendation, statement of purpose. Additional exam requirements/recommendations for international students: Required—TOEFL (minimum score 550 paper-based; 79 iBT), IELTS (minimum score 6.5). Electronic applications accepted.

Ithaca College, School of Humanities and Sciences, Program in Adolescence Education, Ithaca, NY 14850. Offers biology 7-12 (MAT); chemistry 7-12 (MAT); English 7-12 (MAT); French 7-12 (MAT); math 7-12 (MAT); physics 7-12 (MAT); social studies 7-12 (MAT); Spanish (MAT). Part-time programs available. *Faculty:* 31 full-time (11 women). *Students:* 12 full-time (4 women); includes 1 minority (Hispanic/Latino). Average age 24. 27 applicants, 81% accepted, 12 enrolled. In 2013, 7 master's awarded. *Degree requirements:* For master's, thesis or alternative, student teaching. *Entrance requirements:* For master's, minimum GPA of 3.0. Additional exam requirements/recommendations for international students: Required—TOEFL (minimum score 550 paper-based; 80 iBT). *Application deadline:* For fall admission, 2/15 priority date for domestic and international students; for spring admission, 12/1 for domestic and international students. Applications are processed on a rolling basis. Application fee: $40. Electronic applications accepted. *Expenses:* Contact institution. *Financial support:* In 2013–14, 7 students received support, including 7 teaching assistantships (averaging $9,781 per year); career-related internships or fieldwork, Federal Work-Study, scholarships/grants, and unspecified assistantships also available. Support available to part-time students. Financial award application deadline: 2/15; financial award applicants required to submit CSS PROFILE or FAFSA. *Faculty research:* Teacher preparation (elementary and secondary education), equity and social justice in education, language and literacy, multicultural education/sociocultural studies, reflective practice and teacher research. *Unit head:* Dr. Linda Hanrahan, Chair, 607-274-3143, Fax: 607-274-1263, E-mail: gps@ithaca.edu. *Application contact:* Gerard Turbide, Director, Office of Admission, 607-274-3143, Fax: 607-274-1263, E-mail: gps@ithaca.edu.
Website: http://www.ithaca.edu/gradprograms/education/programs/aded.

Jackson State University, Graduate School, College of Science, Engineering and Technology, Department of Physics, Atmospheric Sciences, and General Science, Jackson, MS 39217. Offers science and mathematics teaching (MST). Part-time and evening/weekend programs available. *Degree requirements:* For master's, comprehensive exam. *Entrance requirements:* For master's, GRE General Test. Additional exam requirements/recommendations for international students: Required—TOEFL (minimum score 520 paper-based; 67 iBT).

Johns Hopkins University, School of Education, Certificate Programs in Education, Baltimore, MD 21218-2699. Offers advanced methods for differentiated instruction and inclusive education (Certificate); applied behavior analysis (Certificate); counseling (CAGS); data-based decision making and organizational improvement (Certificate); early intervention/preschool special education specialist (Certificate); education leadership for independent schools (Certificate); education of students with autism and other pervasive developmental disorders (Certificate); evidence-based teaching in the health professions (Certificate); gifted education (Certificate); K-8 mathematics lead-teacher (Certificate); K-8 STEM education lead-teacher (Certificate); leadership for school, family, and community collaboration (Certificate); leadership in technology integration (Certificate); mental health counseling (Certificate); mind, brain, and teaching (Certificate); school administration and supervision (Certificate); urban education (Certificate). Part-time and evening/weekend programs available. Postbaccalaureate distance learning degree programs offered (no on-campus study). *Students:* 7 full-time (4 women), 216 part-time (169 women); includes 66 minority (35 Black or African American, non-Hispanic/Latino; 17 Asian, non-Hispanic/Latino; 6 Hispanic/Latino; 8 Two or more races, non-Hispanic/Latino), 6 international. Average age 35. 257 applicants, 81% accepted, 62 enrolled. In 2013, 202 CAGSs awarded. *Entrance requirements:* For degree, bachelor's degree from regionally- or nationally-accredited institution (master's for some programs), minimum GPA of 3.0 in all previous programs of study, official transcripts from all post-secondary institutions attended, essay, curriculum vitae/resume, minimum of two letters of recommendation. Additional exam requirements/recommendations for international students: Required—TOEFL (minimum score 600 paper-based; 100 iBT) or IELTS (minimum score 7). *Application deadline:* For fall admission, 4/1 for domestic students; for spring admission, 10/1 for domestic students; for summer admission, 2/1 for domestic students. Application fee: $80. Electronic applications accepted. *Financial support:* Application deadline: 6/1; applicants required to submit FAFSA. *Unit head:* Dr. David A. Andrews, Dean, 410-516-7820, Fax: 410-516-6697, E-mail: davidandrews@jhu.edu. *Application contact:* Catherine Wilson, Associate Director of Admissions, 410-516-9797, Fax: 410-516-9799, E-mail: soe.info@jhu.edu.

Kansas State University, Graduate School, College of Education, Department of Curriculum and Instruction, Manhattan, KS 66506. Offers career and technical education (Ed D, PhD); curriculum studies (Ed D, PhD); digital teaching and learning (MS); educational computing, design and online learning (MS); educational technology (Ed D, PhD); elementary/middle level curriculum and instruction (MS); English as a second language (MS); language/diversity education (Ed D, PhD); literacy education (Ed D, PhD); mathematics education (Ed D, PhD); middle level/secondary curriculum and instruction (MS); reading and language arts (MS); reading specialist endorsement (MS); science education (Ed D, PhD); social science education (Ed D, PhD); teacher education (Ed D, PhD); teacher leader/school improvement (MS, Ed D). *Accreditation:* NCATE. Part-time programs available. Postbaccalaureate distance learning degree programs offered (minimal on-campus study). *Faculty:* 18 full-time (13 women), 7 part-time/adjunct (4 women). *Students:* 39 full-time (23 women), 122 part-time (94 women); includes 19 minority (3 Black or African American, non-Hispanic/Latino; 2 Asian, non-Hispanic/Latino; 12 Hispanic/Latino; 2 Two or more races, non-Hispanic/Latino), 12 international. Average age 36. 80 applicants, 50% accepted, 34 enrolled. In 2013, 40 master's, 13 doctorates awarded. *Degree requirements:* For master's, comprehensive exam, portfolio, project, report or thesis; for doctorate, comprehensive exam, thesis/dissertation, preliminary exam. *Entrance requirements:* For master's, minimum GPA of 3.0, letters of recommendation; for doctorate, GRE, minimum GPA of 3.0, letters of recommendation, evidence of scholarly writing. Additional exam requirements/recommendations for international students: Required—TOEFL (minimum score 550 paper-based; 80 iBT). *Application deadline:* For fall admission, 3/1 priority date for domestic students, 2/1 priority date for international students; for spring admission, 10/1 priority date for domestic students, 8/1 priority date for international students. Applications are processed on a rolling basis. Application fee: $50 ($75 for international students). Electronic applications accepted. *Financial support:* In 2013–14, 1 research assistantship (averaging $16,900 per year), 8 teaching assistantships (averaging $12,466 per year) were awarded; career-related internships or fieldwork, institutionally sponsored loans, and scholarships/grants also available. Support available to part-time students. Financial award application deadline: 3/1; financial award applicants required to submit FAFSA. *Faculty research:* Literacy and technology, critical race theory and diversity, achievement gaps, school improvement, teacher education. *Total annual research expenditures:* $543,677. *Unit head:* Dr. Todd Goodson, Chair, 785-532-5904,

Fax: 785-532-7304, E-mail: tgoodson@ksu.edu. *Application contact:* Dona Deam, Application Contact, 785-532-5595, Fax: 785-532-7304, E-mail: ddeam@ksu.edu.
Website: http://www.coe.k-state.edu/departments/edci/.

Kaplan University, Davenport Campus, School of Teacher Education, Davenport, IA 52807-2095. Offers education (M Ed); secondary education (M Ed); teaching and learning (MA); teaching literacy and language: grades 6-12 (MA); teaching literacy and language: grades K-6 (MA); teaching mathematics: grades 6-8 (MA); teaching mathematics: grades 9-12 (MA); teaching mathematics: grades K-5 (MA); teaching science: grades 6-12 (MA); teaching science: grades K-6 (MA); teaching students with special needs (MA); teaching with technology (MA). Part-time and evening/weekend programs available. Postbaccalaureate distance learning degree programs offered (no on-campus study). *Entrance requirements:* Additional exam requirements/recommendations for international students: Required—TOEFL (minimum score 550 paper-based; 80 iBT).

Kean University, College of Education, Program in Instruction and Curriculum, Union, NJ 07083. Offers bilingual/bicultural education (MA); classroom instruction (MA); earth science (MA); mathematics/science/computer education (MA); teaching (MA); teaching English as a second language (MA); world languages (Spanish) (MA). *Accreditation:* NCATE. Part-time programs available. *Faculty:* 22 full-time (12 women). *Students:* 16 full-time (10 women), 100 part-time (72 women); includes 57 minority (8 Black or African American, non-Hispanic/Latino; 3 Asian, non-Hispanic/Latino; 45 Hispanic/Latino; 1 Two or more races, non-Hispanic/Latino). Average age 35. 56 applicants, 100% accepted, 38 enrolled. In 2013, 42 master's awarded. *Degree requirements:* For master's, comprehensive exam, thesis (for some programs), two-semester advanced seminar. *Entrance requirements:* For master's, GRE General Test or MAT, PRAXIS, minimum GPA of 3.0, personal statement, professional resume/curriculum vitae, commitment to working with children, certification (for some programs). Additional exam requirements/recommendations for international students: Required—TOEFL (minimum score 550 paper-based; 79 iBT). *Application deadline:* For fall admission, 6/1 for domestic and international students; for spring admission, 12/1 for domestic and international students. Applications are processed on a rolling basis. Application fee: $75 ($150 for international students). Electronic applications accepted. *Expenses:* Tuition, state resident: full-time $12,099; part-time $589 per credit. Tuition, nonresident: full-time $16,399; part-time $722 per credit. *Required fees:* $3050; $139 per credit. Part-time tuition and fees vary according to course level, course load, degree level and program. *Financial support:* In 2013–14, 6 research assistantships with full tuition reimbursements (averaging $3,713 per year) were awarded; unspecified assistantships also available. Financial award applicants required to submit FAFSA. *Unit head:* Dr. Gail Verdi, Program Coordinator, 908-737-3908, E-mail: gverdi@kean.edu. *Application contact:* Ann-Marie Kay, Assistant Director for Graduate Admissions, 908-737-5922, Fax: 908-737-5925, E-mail: akay@kean.edu.
Website: http://grad.kean.edu/masters-programs/bilingualbicultural-education-instruction-and-curriculum.

Kean University, College of Natural, Applied and Health Sciences, Program in Mathematics Education, Union, NJ 07083. Offers supervision of math education (MA); teaching of math (MA). Part-time programs available. *Faculty:* 15 full-time (4 women). *Students:* 1 (woman) full-time, 14 part-time (8 women); includes 5 minority (2 Asian, non-Hispanic/Latino; 3 Hispanic/Latino). Average age 36. 1 applicant, 100% accepted, 1 enrolled. In 2013, 4 master's awarded. *Degree requirements:* For master's, thesis optional, research. *Entrance requirements:* For master's, GRE General Test, baccalaureate degree from accredited college or university with major or strong minor in a mathematical science; minimum cumulative GPA of 3.0; official transcripts from all institutions attended; two letters of recommendation; personal statement; resume. Additional exam requirements/recommendations for international students: Required—TOEFL (minimum score 550 paper-based; 79 iBT). *Application deadline:* For fall admission, 6/1 for domestic and international students; for spring admission, 12/1 for domestic and international students. Applications are processed on a rolling basis. Application fee: $75 ($150 for international students). Electronic applications accepted. *Expenses:* Tuition, state resident: full-time $12,099; part-time $589 per credit. Tuition, nonresident: full-time $16,399; part-time $722 per credit. *Required fees:* $3050; $139 per credit. Part-time tuition and fees vary according to course level, course load, degree level and program. *Financial support:* In 2013–14, research assistantships with full tuition reimbursements (averaging $3,713 per year) were awarded; unspecified assistantships also available. Financial award applicants required to submit FAFSA. *Unit head:* Dr. Revathi Narasimhan, Program Coordinator, 908-737-3716, E-mail: rnarasim@kean.edu. *Application contact:* Reenat Hasan, Admissions Counselor, 908-737-5923, Fax: 908-737-5925, E-mail: rhasan@exchange.kean.edu.

Kennesaw State University, Leland and Clarice C. Bagwell College of Education, Program in Teaching, Kennesaw, GA 30144-5591. Offers art education (MAT); biology (MAT); chemistry (MAT); foreign language education (Chinese and Spanish) (MAT); physics (MAT); secondary English (MAT); secondary mathematics (MAT); special education (MAT); teaching English to speakers of other languages (MAT). Part-time and evening/weekend programs available. *Students:* 82 full-time (59 women), 16 part-time (12 women); includes 28 minority (14 Black or African American, non-Hispanic/Latino; 4 Asian, non-Hispanic/Latino; 7 Hispanic/Latino; 1 Native Hawaiian or other Pacific Islander, non-Hispanic/Latino; 2 Two or more races, non-Hispanic/Latino), 3 international. Average age 35. 28 applicants, 68% accepted, 15 enrolled. In 2013, 54 master's awarded. *Entrance requirements:* For master's, GRE, GACE I (state certificate exam), minimum GPA of 2.75, 2 recommendations, resume. Additional exam requirements/recommendations for international students: Required—TOEFL (minimum score 550 paper-based; 80 iBT), IELTS (minimum score 6). *Application deadline:* For fall admission, 6/1 for domestic and international students; for spring admission, 3/1 for domestic and international students; for summer admission, 4/15 for domestic and international students. Applications are processed on a rolling basis. Application fee: $60. Electronic applications accepted. *Expenses:* Tuition, state resident: full-time $4806; part-time $267 per semester hour. Tuition, nonresident: full-time $17,298; part-time $961 per semester hour. *Required fees:* $1834; $784.50 per semester. *Financial support:* In 2013–14, 2 research assistantships with tuition reimbursements (averaging $8,000 per year) were awarded; unspecified assistantships also available. Financial award application deadline: 4/1; financial award applicants required to submit FAFSA. *Unit head:* Dr. Jillian Ford, Director, 770-499-3093, E-mail: graded@kennesaw.edu. *Application contact:* Melinda Ross, Admissions Counselor, 770-423-6122, Fax: 770-423-6885, E-mail: ksugrad@kennesaw.edu.
Website: http://www.kennesaw.edu.

Kutztown University of Pennsylvania, College of Education, Program in Secondary Education, Kutztown, PA 19530-0730. Offers biology (M Ed); curriculum and instruction (M Ed); English (M Ed); mathematics (M Ed); social studies (M Ed). *Accreditation:* NCATE. Part-time and evening/weekend programs available. *Faculty:* 6 full-time (2 women). *Students:* 34 full-time (17 women), 46 part-time (34 women); includes 4 minority (1 Asian, non-Hispanic/Latino; 3 Hispanic/Latino). Average age 31. 50 applicants, 70% accepted, 26 enrolled. In 2013, 31 master's awarded. *Degree requirements:* For master's, comprehensive exam, thesis optional. *Entrance requirements:* For master's, GRE General Test. Additional exam requirements/recommendations for international students: Required—TOEFL (minimum score 550 paper-based; 79 iBT). *Application deadline:* For fall admission, 8/1 priority date for domestic and international students; for spring admission, 12/1 priority date for domestic and international students. Applications are processed on a rolling basis. Application fee: $35. Electronic applications accepted. *Expenses: Tuition, area resident:* Part-time $442 per credit. Tuition, state resident: part-time $442 per credit. Tuition, nonresident: part-time $663 per credit. *Required fees:* $80 per credit. *Financial support:* Career-related internships or fieldwork, Federal Work-Study, scholarships/grants, and unspecified assistantships available. Financial award application deadline: 3/1; financial award applicants required to submit FAFSA. *Unit head:* Dr. Theresa Stahler, Chairperson, 610-683-4259, Fax: 610-683-1338, E-mail: stahler@kutztown.edu. *Application contact:* Kelly Hish, Admissions Clerk, 610-683-4200, Fax: 610-683-1393, E-mail: graduate@kutztown.edu.

Lake Forest College, Master of Arts in Teaching Program, Lake Forest, IL 60045. Offers elementary education (MAT); K-12 French (MAT); K-12 music (MAT); K-12 Spanish (MAT); K-12 visual art (MAT); secondary biology (MAT); secondary chemistry (MAT); secondary English (MAT); secondary history (MAT); secondary mathematics (MAT). *Degree requirements:* For master's, comprehensive exam, portfolio. *Entrance requirements:* For master's, GRE.

Lehman College of the City University of New York, Division of Education, Department of Middle and High School Education, Program in Mathematics 7–12, Bronx, NY 10468-1589. Offers MS Ed. *Accreditation:* NCATE. Part-time and evening/weekend programs available. *Degree requirements:* For master's, comprehensive exam or thesis. *Entrance requirements:* For master's, 18 credits in mathematics, 12 credits in education. *Faculty research:* Mathematical problem solving, Piagetian cognitive theory.

Lesley University, School of Education, Cambridge, MA 02138-2790. Offers arts, community, and education (M Ed); autism studies (Certificate); curriculum and instruction (M Ed, CAGS); early childhood education (M Ed); ecological teaching and learning (MS); educational studies (PhD), including adult learning, educational leadership, individually designed; elementary education (M Ed); emergent technologies for educators (Certificate); ESLArts: language learning through the arts (M Ed); high school education (M Ed); individually designed (M Ed); integrated teaching through the arts (M Ed); literacy for K-8 classroom teachers (M Ed); mathematics education (M Ed); middle school education (M Ed); moderate disabilities (M Ed); online learning (Certificate); reading (CAGS); science in education (M Ed); severe disabilities (M Ed); special needs (CAGS); specialist teacher of reading (M Ed); teacher of visual art (M Ed); technology in education (M Ed, CAGS). *Accreditation:* Teacher Education Accreditation Council. Part-time and evening/weekend programs available. Postbaccalaureate distance learning degree programs offered (no on-campus study). *Faculty:* 40 full-time (30 women), 104 part-time/adjunct (77 women). *Students:* 453 full-time (381 women), 1,672 part-time (1,435 women); includes 284 minority (139 Black or African American, non-Hispanic/Latino; 11 American Indian or Alaska Native, non-Hispanic/Latino; 38 Asian, non-Hispanic/Latino; 58 Hispanic/Latino; 5 Native Hawaiian or other Pacific Islander, non-Hispanic/Latino; 33 Two or more races, non-Hispanic/Latino), 22 international. Average age 35. In 2013, 1,137 master's, 18 doctorates, 51 other advanced degrees awarded. *Degree requirements:* For master's, practicum; for doctorate, thesis/dissertation. *Entrance requirements:* For master's, Massachusetts Tests for Educator Licensure (MTEL), transcripts, statement of purpose, recommendations; interview (for special education); for doctorate, GRE General Test, transcripts, statement of purpose, recommendations, interview, master's degree, resume; for other advanced degree, interview, master's degree. Additional exam requirements/recommendations for international students: Required—TOEFL (minimum score 550 paper-based; 80 iBT). *Application deadline:* Applications are processed on a rolling basis. Application fee: $50. Electronic applications accepted. *Expenses: Tuition:* Part-time $900 per credit. *Financial support:* In 2013–14, 15 fellowships (averaging $3,600 per year) were awarded; career-related internships or fieldwork, Federal Work-Study, scholarships/grants, tuition waivers, and unspecified assistantships also available. Financial award application deadline: 4/15; financial award applicants required to submit FAFSA. *Faculty research:* Assessment in literacy, mathematics and science; autism spectrum disorders; instructional technology and online learning; multicultural education and English language learners. *Unit head:* Dr. Jack Gillette, Dean, 617-349-8401, Fax: 617-349-8607, E-mail: jgillett@lesley.edu. *Application contact:* Martha Sheehan, Director of Admissions, 888-LESLEYU, Fax: 617-349-8313, E-mail: info@lesley.edu.
Website: http://www.lesley.edu/soe.html.

Lewis University, College of Education, Program in Secondary Education, Romeoville, IL 60446. Offers biology (MA); chemistry (MA); English (MA); history (MA); math (MA); physics (MA); psychology and social science (MA). Part-time programs available. *Students:* 15 full-time (6 women), 15 part-time (9 women); includes 6 minority (2 Black or African American, non-Hispanic/Latino; 1 Asian, non-Hispanic/Latino; 3 Hispanic/Latino). Average age 30. *Entrance requirements:* For master's, departmental qualifying exam, writing exam, minimum GPA of 2.75, 2 letters of recommendation, interview. Additional exam requirements/recommendations for international students: Required—TOEFL (minimum score 550 paper-based; 80 iBT). *Application deadline:* For fall admission, 5/1 priority date for international students; for spring admission, 11/15 priority date for international students. Applications are processed on a rolling basis. Application fee: $40. Electronic applications accepted. *Financial support:* Federal Work-Study, scholarships/grants, and unspecified assistantships available. Financial award application deadline: 5/1; financial award applicants required to submit FAFSA. *Unit head:* Dr. Dorene Huvaere, Program Director, 815-838-0500 Ext. 5885, E-mail: huvaersdo@lewisu.edu. *Application contact:* Fran Welsh, Secretary, 815-838-0500 Ext. 5880, E-mail: welshfr@lewisu.edu.

Liberty University, School of Education, Lynchburg, VA 24515. Offers administration and supervision (M Ed); curriculum and instruction (Ed D, Ed S); early childhood education (M Ed); educational leadership (Ed D, Ed S); educational technology and online instruction (M Ed); elementary education (M Ed, MAT); English (M Ed); gifted education (M Ed); history (M Ed); leadership (M Ed); math specialist (M Ed); middle grades (M Ed, MAT); outdoor adventure sport (MS); reading specialist (M Ed); school counseling (M Ed); secondary education (MAT); special education (M Ed, MAT); sport management (MS), including administration, outdoor recreation, sport management, tourism; sports administration (MS); student service (M Ed); teaching and learning (M Ed); tourism (MS). *Accreditation:* NCATE. Part-time programs available. Postbaccalaureate distance learning degree programs offered (minimal on-campus study). *Students:* 2,241 full-time (1,639 women), 4,413 part-time (3,240 women); includes 2,052 minority (1,588 Black or African American, non-Hispanic/Latino; 37 American Indian or Alaska Native, non-Hispanic/Latino; 67 Asian, non-Hispanic/Latino; 173 Hispanic/Latino; 37 Native Hawaiian or other Pacific Islander, non-Hispanic/Latino; 150 Two or more races, non-Hispanic/Latino), 15 international. Average age 37. 6,185 applicants, 43% accepted, 1603 enrolled. In 2013, 1,256 master's, 117 doctorates, 470 other advanced degrees awarded. *Degree requirements:* For doctorate, comprehensive exam, thesis/dissertation. *Entrance requirements:* For master's, GRE General Test or MAT (if taken in or before 1999), 2 letters of recommendation, minimum undergraduate GPA of 3.0, curriculum vitae; for doctorate and Ed S, GRE General Test or MAT (if taken

before 1999), minimum master's GPA of 3.0, 3 years of teaching experience. Additional exam requirements/recommendations for international students: Required—TOEFL (minimum score 600 paper-based; 100 iBT). *Application deadline:* For fall admission, 6/1 for domestic students; for spring admission, 11/1 for domestic students. Applications are processed on a rolling basis. Application fee: $50. Electronic applications accepted. *Expenses:* Contact institution. *Financial support:* Federal Work-Study and tuition waivers (partial) available. *Faculty research:* Self-determination, character education, bibliotherapy, learning styles, distance education. *Unit head:* Dr. Karen L. Parker, Dean, 434-582-2195, Fax: 434-582-2468, E-mail: kparker@liberty.edu. *Application contact:* Jay Bridge, Director of Graduate Admissions, 800-424-9595, Fax: 800-628-7977, E-mail: gradadmissions@liberty.edu.
Website: http://www.liberty.edu/academics/education/graduate/.

Lipscomb University, Program in Education, Nashville, TN 37204-3951. Offers applied behavior analysis (Certificate); collaborative professional learning (M Ed, Ed S); educational leadership (M Ed, Ed S); English language learning (M Ed, Ed S); instructional coaching (Certificate); instructional practice (M Ed); learning organizations and strategic change (Ed D); math specialty (M Ed); reading specialty (M Ed, Ed S); special education (M Ed); teaching, learning, and leading (M Ed); technology integration (M Ed); technology integration specialist (Certificate). *Accreditation:* NCATE. Part-time and evening/weekend programs available. Postbaccalaureate distance learning degree programs offered (no on-campus study). *Faculty:* 19 full-time (13 women), 28 part-time/adjunct (22 women). *Students:* 171 full-time (123 women), 509 part-time (429 women); includes 118 minority (91 Black or African American, non-Hispanic/Latino; 1 American Indian or Alaska Native, non-Hispanic/Latino; 4 Asian, non-Hispanic/Latino; 15 Hispanic/Latino; 1 Native Hawaiian or other Pacific Islander, non-Hispanic/Latino; 6 Two or more races, non-Hispanic/Latino). Average age 32. 237 applicants, 65% accepted, 150 enrolled. In 2013, 212 master's awarded. *Degree requirements:* For master's, comprehensive exam, portfolio, research project and presentation; for doctorate, practical capstone project in experiential setting. *Entrance requirements:* For master's, MAT (minimum 31) or GRE General Test (minimum 294), 2 reference letters, goals statement, writing sample, interview; for doctorate, MAT or GRE General Test, 3 reference letters, artifact of demonstrated academic excellence, written personal statements, interview. Additional exam requirements/recommendations for international students: Required—TOEFL (minimum score 570 paper-based). *Application deadline:* For fall admission, 8/29 priority date for domestic students; for spring admission, 1/15 priority date for domestic students. Applications are processed on a rolling basis. Application fee: $50 ($75 for international students). *Expenses: Tuition:* Full-time $15,570; part-time $865 per credit hour. Tuition and fees vary according to degree level and program. *Financial support:* Scholarships/grants and unspecified assistantships available. Financial award applicants required to submit FAFSA. *Faculty research:* Facilitative learning styles, leadership, student assessment, interactive multimedia inclusion, learning organizations and strategic change. *Unit head:* Dr. Deborah Boyd, Director of Graduate Studies, 615-966-6263, E-mail: deborah.boyd@lipscomb.edu. *Application contact:* Kristin Baese, Director of Enrollment and Outreach, 615-966-7628 Ext. 6081, Fax: 615-966-5173, E-mail: kristin.baese@lipscomb.edu.
Website: http://www.lipscomb.edu/education/graduate-programs.

Long Island University–LIU Brooklyn, School of Education, Department of Teaching and Learning, Program in Secondary Education, Brooklyn, NY 11201-8423. Offers mathematics education (MS Ed). Part-time and evening/weekend programs available. *Degree requirements:* For master's, thesis optional. *Entrance requirements:* For master's, 2 letters of recommendation. Additional exam requirements/recommendations for international students: Required—TOEFL (minimum score 500 paper-based). Electronic applications accepted.

Long Island University–LIU Post, College of Liberal Arts and Sciences, Department of Mathematics, Brookville, NY 11548-1300. Offers applied mathematics (MS); mathematics education (MS); mathematics for secondary school teachers (MS). Part-time and evening/weekend programs available. *Degree requirements:* For master's, thesis or alternative, oral presentation. *Entrance requirements:* Additional exam requirements/recommendations for international students: Required—TOEFL. Electronic applications accepted. *Faculty research:* Differential geometry, topological groups, general topology, number theory, analysis and statistics, numerical analysis.

Long Island University–LIU Post, School of Education, Department of Curriculum and Instruction, Brookville, NY 11548-1300. Offers adolescence education (MS); adolescence education: biology (MS); adolescence education: earth science (MS); adolescence education: English (MS); adolescence education: mathematics (MS); adolescence education: social studies (MS); adolescence education: Spanish (MS); art education (MS); bilingual education (MS); childhood education (MS); early childhood education (MS); middle childhood education (MS); music education (MS); teaching English to speakers of other languages (MS). Part-time and evening/weekend programs available. *Degree requirements:* For master's, comprehensive exam or thesis, student teaching. *Entrance requirements:* For master's, minimum GPA of 2.75 in major, 2.5 overall. Electronic applications accepted. *Faculty research:* Ethics and education, teaching strategies.

Longwood University, College of Graduate and Professional Studies, College of Education and Human Services, Farmville, VA 23909. Offers education (MS), including algebra and middle school math, counselor education, elementary and middle school math, elementary education, elementary education initial licensure, health and physical education, school librarianship, special education general curriculum, special education initial licensure; social work and communication sciences and disorders (MS). *Accreditation:* NCATE. Part-time and evening/weekend programs available. *Faculty:* 28 full-time (15 women), 9 part-time/adjunct (7 women). *Students:* 86 full-time (80 women), 187 part-time (173 women); includes 38 minority (26 Black or African American, non-Hispanic/Latino; 1 Asian, non-Hispanic/Latino; 5 Hispanic/Latino; 1 Native Hawaiian or other Pacific Islander, non-Hispanic/Latino; 5 Two or more races, non-Hispanic/Latino). 98 applicants, 89% accepted, 85 enrolled. In 2013, 132 master's awarded. *Degree requirements:* For master's, comprehensive exam (for some programs), thesis optional, professional portfolio, internship, clinical experience, or practicum. *Entrance requirements:* For master's, bachelor's degree from regionally-accredited institution, 2 recommendations, 500-word personal essay, official transcripts, minimum GPA of 2.75, valid teaching license (for some programs), passing Praxis I scores for initial teaching licensure programs. Additional exam requirements/recommendations for international students: Required—TOEFL (minimum score 570 paper-based), IELTS (minimum score 6.5). *Application deadline:* For fall admission, 5/1 priority date for domestic students; for spring admission, 10/1 priority date for domestic students; for summer admission, 2/1 priority date for domestic students. Applications are processed on a rolling basis. Application fee: $50. Electronic applications accepted. *Expenses:* Tuition, state resident: full-time $7506; part-time $327 per credit hour. Tuition, nonresident: full-time $17,100; part-time $837 per credit hour. Tuition and fees vary according to course load and campus/location. *Financial support:* Career-related internships or fieldwork and Federal Work-Study available. Financial award applicants required to submit FAFSA. *Unit head:* Dr. Peggy L. Tarpley, Chair of the Department of Education and Special Education, 434-395-2337, E-mail: tarpleypl@longwood.edu. *Application contact:* College of Graduate and Professional Studies, 434-395-2380, Fax: 434-395-2750, E-mail: graduate@longwood.edu.
Website: http://www.longwood.edu/cehs/.

Louisiana Tech University, Graduate School, College of Education, Department of Curriculum, Instruction and Leadership, Ruston, LA 71272. Offers curriculum and instruction (M Ed, Ed D), including adult education (M Ed), early childhood (M Ed), English education (M Ed), mathematics education (M Ed), science education (M Ed), social studies education (M Ed), special education (M Ed); educational leadership (M Ed, Ed D). *Accreditation:* NCATE. Part-time programs available. *Degree requirements:* For doctorate, thesis/dissertation. *Entrance requirements:* For master's and doctorate, GRE General Test. *Application deadline:* For fall admission, 7/29 for domestic students; for spring admission, 2/3 for domestic students. Application fee: $20 ($30 for international students). *Financial support:* Fellowships, research assistantships, and teaching assistantships available. Financial award application deadline: 2/1. *Unit head:* Dr. Pauline Leonard, Head, 318-257-4609, Fax: 318-257-2379. *Application contact:* Dr. John Harrison, Associate Dean of Graduate Studies, 318-257-3229, Fax: 318-257-2379, E-mail: johnharrison@latech.edu.
Website: http://www.latech.edu/education/cil/.

Loyola Marymount University, College of Science and Engineering, Department of Mathematics, Program in Teaching in Mathematics, Los Angeles, CA 90045. Offers MAT. Part-time programs available. *Faculty:* 19 full-time (9 women). *Students:* 2 full-time (both women), 1 (woman) part-time; includes 1 minority (Hispanic/Latino), 1 international. Average age 35. 6 applicants, 83% accepted, 3 enrolled. *Entrance requirements:* For master's, letter of recommendation, personal statement. Additional exam requirements/recommendations for international students: Required—TOEFL (minimum score 550 paper-based; 80 iBT). *Application deadline:* For fall admission, 6/15 for domestic students; for spring admission, 11/15 for domestic students. Application fee: $50. Electronic applications accepted. *Financial support:* In 2013–14, 2 students received support. Scholarships/grants and unspecified assistantships available. Financial award application deadline: 6/30; financial award applicants required to submit FAFSA. *Total annual research expenditures:* $293,255. *Unit head:* Dr. Anne E. Bargagliotti, Chair, 310-338-4582, E-mail: abargagl@lmu.edu. *Application contact:* Chake H. Kouyoumjian, Associate Dean of Graduate Admissions, 310-338-2721, E-mail: ckouyoum@lmu.edu.
Website: http://cse.lmu.edu/department/math/degreesoffered/mainteachingmathematics/.

Loyola University Chicago, School of Education, Program in Teaching and Learning, Chicago, IL 60660. Offers behavior intervention specialist (M Ed); elementary education (M Ed); English as a second language (Certificate); English language teaching and learning (M Ed); math education (M Ed); reading specialist (M Ed); reading teacher endorsement (Certificate); school technology (M Ed); science education (M Ed); secondary education (M Ed); special education (M Ed). *Accreditation:* NCATE. *Faculty:* 23 full-time (16 women), 49 part-time/adjunct (42 women). *Students:* 109. Average age 28. 104 applicants, 71% accepted, 44 enrolled. In 2013, 39 master's awarded. *Degree requirements:* For master's, comprehensive exam. *Entrance requirements:* For master's, Illinois Basic Skills Test, 3 letters of recommendation, minimum GPA of 3.0, resume. Additional exam requirements/recommendations for international students: Required—TOEFL (minimum score 550 paper-based; 79 iBT). *Application deadline:* For fall admission, 7/1 priority date for domestic and international students; for spring admission, 11/1 priority date for domestic and international students; for summer admission, 4/1 for domestic and international students. Applications are processed on a rolling basis. Application fee: $50. Electronic applications accepted. Application fee is waived when completed online. *Expenses: Tuition:* Full-time $16,740; part-time $930 per credit. *Required fees:* $135 per semester. *Financial support:* In 2013–14, 58 fellowships with partial tuition reimbursements were awarded; research assistantships, teaching assistantships, institutionally sponsored loans, scholarships/grants, and unspecified assistantships also available. Support available to part-time students. Financial award application deadline: 2/1; financial award applicants required to submit FAFSA. *Faculty research:* Positive behavior support, school reform, school improvement. *Unit head:* Dr. Ann Marie Ryan, Director, 312-915-7027, E-mail: aryan3@luc.edu. *Application contact:* Marie Rosin-Dittmar, Information Contact, 312-915-6800, E-mail: schleduc@luc.edu.

Loyola University Maryland, Graduate Programs, School of Education, Master of Arts in Teaching Program, Baltimore, MD 21210-2699. Offers elementary/middle education (MAT); secondary education (MAT); secondary education: biology (MAT); secondary education: chemistries (MAT); secondary education: earth science (MAT); secondary education: English (MAT); secondary education: mathematics (MAT); secondary education: physics (MAT). Part-time programs available. *Entrance requirements:* For master's, essay, 2 letters of recommendation, resume, transcipt. Additional exam requirements/recommendations for international students: Required—TOEFL (minimum score 550 paper-based).

Manhattanville College, School of Education, Program in Middle Childhood/Adolescence Education (Grades 5-12), Purchase, NY 10577-2132. Offers biology (MAT); biology and special education (MPS); chemistry (MAT); chemistry and special education (MPS); English (MAT); English and special education (MPS); literacy and special education (MPS); literacy specialist (MPS); math and special education (MPS); mathematics (MAT); physics (MAT); social studies (MAT); social studies and special education (MPS); special education (MPS); teaching languages other than English (MAT), including French, Italian, Latin, Spanish. Part-time and evening/weekend programs available. *Degree requirements:* For master's, comprehensive exam or research project, field experience. *Entrance requirements:* For master's, minimum undergraduate GPA of 3.0, 2 letters of recommendation. Additional exam requirements/recommendations for international students: Required—TOEFL. Electronic applications accepted.

Marquette University, Graduate School, College of Arts and Sciences, Department of Mathematics, Statistics, and Computer Science, Milwaukee, WI 53201-1881. Offers bioinformatics (MS); computational sciences (MS, PhD); computing (MS); mathematics education (MS). Part-time and evening/weekend programs available. Postbaccalaureate distance learning degree programs offered (minimal on-campus study). *Faculty:* 27 full-time (7 women), 10 part-time/adjunct (4 women). *Students:* 15 full-time (4 women), 21 part-time (7 women); includes 4 minority (2 Black or African American, non-Hispanic/Latino; 1 Asian, non-Hispanic/Latino; 1 Hispanic/Latino), 16 international. Average age 29. 39 applicants, 54% accepted, 10 enrolled. In 2013, 11 master's, 3 doctorates awarded. Terminal master's awarded for partial completion of doctoral program. *Degree requirements:* For master's, thesis (for some programs), essay with oral presentation; for doctorate, comprehensive exam, thesis/dissertation, qualifying examination. *Entrance requirements:* For master's, official transcripts from all current and previous colleges/universities except Marquette, three letters of recommendation; for doctorate, GRE General Test, official transcripts from all current and previous colleges/universities except Marquette, three letters of recommendation. Additional exam requirements/recommendations for international students: Required—TOEFL (minimum score 530 paper-based). *Application deadline:* For fall admission, 1/15 for domestic and international students. Applications are processed on a rolling basis. Application fee:

$50. Electronic applications accepted. *Financial support:* In 2013–14, 23 students received support, including 4 fellowships (averaging $1,375 per year), 5 research assistantships with full tuition reimbursements available (averaging $17,000 per year), 15 teaching assistantships with full tuition reimbursements available (averaging $17,000 per year); scholarships/grants, health care benefits, tuition waivers (full and partial), and unspecified assistantships also available. Support available to part-time students. Financial award application deadline: 2/15. *Faculty research:* Models of physiological systems, mathematical immunology, computational group theory, mathematical logic, computational science. *Total annual research expenditures:* $1.1 million. *Unit head:* Dr. Gary Krenz, Chair, 414-288-7573, Fax: 414-288-1578. *Application contact:* Dr. Stephen Merrill, Professor, 414-288-5237.
Website: http://www.marquette.edu/mscs/grad.shtml.

Miami University, College of Arts and Science, Department of Mathematics, Oxford, OH 45056. Offers MA, MAT, MS. *Students:* 27 full-time (11 women); includes 3 minority (1 Black or African American, non-Hispanic/Latino; 1 Asian, non-Hispanic/Latino; 1 Two or more races, non-Hispanic/Latino), 8 international. Average age 24. In 2013, 19 master's awarded. *Entrance requirements:* Additional exam requirements/recommendations for international students: Recommended—TOEFL (minimum score 550 paper-based; 80 iBT), IELTS (minimum score 6.5), TSE (minimum score 54). *Application deadline:* For fall admission, 2/1 for domestic and international students. Application fee: $50. Electronic applications accepted. *Expenses:* Tuition, state resident: full-time $12,634; part-time $526 per credit hour. Tuition, nonresident: full-time $27,892; part-time $1162 per credit hour. Part-time tuition and fees vary according to course load, campus/location and program. *Financial support:* Research assistantships, teaching assistantships, health care benefits, and unspecified assistantships available. Financial award application deadline: 2/1; financial award applicants required to submit FAFSA. *Unit head:* Dr. Patrick Dowling, Department Chair, 513-529-5818, E-mail: dowlinpn@miamioh.edu. *Application contact:* Dr. Doug Ward, Director of Graduate Studies, 513-529-3534, E-mail: wardde@miamioh.edu.
Website: http://www.MiamiOH.edu/mathematics.

Michigan State University, The Graduate School, College of Natural Science, Department of Mathematics, East Lansing, MI 48824. Offers applied mathematics (MS, PhD); industrial mathematics (MS); mathematics (MAT, MS, PhD). *Entrance requirements:* Additional exam requirements/recommendations for international students: Required—TOEFL. Electronic applications accepted.

Michigan State University, The Graduate School, College of Natural Science and College of Education, Division of Science and Mathematics Education, East Lansing, MI 48824. Offers biological, physical and general science for teachers (MAT, MS), including biological science (MS), general science (MAT), physical science (MS); mathematics education (MS, PhD).

Middle Tennessee State University, College of Graduate Studies, College of Basic and Applied Sciences, Department of Mathematical Sciences, Murfreesboro, TN 37132. Offers mathematics (MS, MST). Part-time and evening/weekend programs available. Postbaccalaureate distance learning degree programs offered. *Faculty:* 26 full-time (12 women). *Students:* 16 full-time (9 women), 9 part-time (8 women); includes 10 minority (1 Black or African American, non-Hispanic/Latino; 6 Asian, non-Hispanic/Latino; 1 Hispanic/Latino; 2 Two or more races, non-Hispanic/Latino). 49 applicants, 55% accepted. In 2013, 15 master's awarded. *Degree requirements:* For master's, comprehensive exam, thesis optional. *Entrance requirements:* For master's, GRE General Test or MAT. Additional exam requirements/recommendations for international students: Required—TOEFL (minimum score 525 paper-based; 71 iBT) or IELTS (minimum score 6). *Application deadline:* For fall admission, 6/1 for domestic and international students. Applications are processed on a rolling basis. Application fee: $25 ($30 for international students). Electronic applications accepted. *Financial support:* In 2013–14, 11 students received support. Tuition waivers available. Support available to part-time students. Financial award application deadline: 5/1; financial award applicants required to submit FAFSA. *Faculty research:* Graph theory, computational science. *Unit head:* Dr. Donald A. Nelson, Chair, 615-898-2669, Fax: 615-898-5422, E-mail: donald.nelson@mtsu.edu. *Application contact:* Dr. Michael D. Allen, Vice Provost for Research and Dean, 615-898-2840, Fax: 615-904-8020, E-mail: michael.allen@mtsu.edu.

Middle Tennessee State University, College of Graduate Studies, Interdisciplinary Program in Mathematics and Science Education, Murfreesboro, TN 37132. Offers PhD. *Students:* 10 full-time (7 women), 25 part-time (12 women); includes 6 minority (3 Black or African American, non-Hispanic/Latino; 2 Asian, non-Hispanic/Latino; 1 Hispanic/Latino). 22 applicants, 77% accepted. *Unit head:* Dr. Michael D. Allen, Vice Provost for Research and Dean, 615-898-2840, Fax: 615-904-8020, E-mail: michael.allen@mtsu.edu. *Application contact:* Dr. Michael D. Allen, Vice Provost for Research and Dean, 615-898-2840, Fax: 615-904-8020, E-mail: michael.allen@mtsu.edu.

Millersville University of Pennsylvania, College of Graduate and Professional Studies, School of Science and Mathematics, Department of Mathematics, Millersville, PA 17551-0302. Offers M Ed. *Accreditation:* NCATE. Part-time and evening/weekend programs available. *Faculty:* 20 full-time (7 women), 6 part-time/adjunct (3 women). *Students:* 5 full-time (4 women), 11 part-time (8 women); includes 2 minority (1 Asian, non-Hispanic/Latino; 1 Hispanic/Latino), 1 international. Average age 31. 3 applicants, 67% accepted, 1 enrolled. In 2013, 11 master's awarded. *Degree requirements:* For master's, thesis optional. *Entrance requirements:* For master's, 3 letters of recommendation, official transcripts, goal statement. Additional exam requirements/recommendations for international students: Required—TOEFL (minimum score 550 paper-based, 79 iBT) or IELTS (minimum score 6). *Application deadline:* For fall admission, 1/15 priority date for domestic and international students; for winter admission, 10/1 priority date for domestic and international students; for spring admission, 10/1 priority date for domestic and international students. Applications are processed on a rolling basis. Application fee: $40. Electronic applications accepted. *Expenses:* Tuition, state resident: full-time $7956; part-time $442 per credit. Tuition, nonresident: full-time $11,934; part-time $663 per credit. *Required fees:* $2196; $122 per credit. Tuition and fees vary according to course load. *Financial support:* In 2013–14, 3 students received support, including 3 research assistantships with full tuition reimbursements available (averaging $5,267 per year); institutionally sponsored loans and unspecified assistantships also available. Support available to part-time students. Financial award application deadline: 3/15; financial award applicants required to submit FAFSA. *Faculty research:* Training of secondary mathematic teachers, the use of technology in mathematics classes, equity in mathematics, middle school mathematics, questioning techniques of teacher educators. *Unit head:* Dr. Delray J. Schultz, Chair, 717-872-3535, Fax: 717-871-2320, E-mail: delray.schultz@millersville.edu. *Application contact:* Dr. Victor S. DeSantis, Dean of College of Graduate and Professional Studies/Associate Provost for Civic and Community Engagement, 717-872-3099, Fax: 717-872-3453, E-mail: victor.desantis@millersville.edu.
Website: http://www.millersville.edu/math/.

Mills College, Graduate Studies, School of Education, Oakland, CA 94613-1000. Offers child life in hospitals (MA); early childhood education (MA); education (MA), including art education, curriculum and instruction, elementary education, English education, foreign language education, mathematics education, science education, secondary education, social studies education, teaching; educational leadership (MA, Ed D). Part-time and evening/weekend programs available. *Faculty:* 10 full-time (7 women), 13 part-time/adjunct (10 women). *Students:* 154 full-time (136 women), 54 part-time (47 women); includes 96 minority (32 Black or African American, non-Hispanic/Latino; 1 American Indian or Alaska Native, non-Hispanic/Latino; 23 Asian, non-Hispanic/Latino; 27 Hispanic/Latino; 1 Native Hawaiian or other Pacific Islander, non-Hispanic/Latino; 12 Two or more races, non-Hispanic/Latino), 2 international. Average age 25. 222 applicants, 89% accepted, 110 enrolled. In 2013, 96 master's, 38 doctorates awarded. Terminal master's awarded for partial completion of doctoral program. *Degree requirements:* For master's, comprehensive exam, thesis (for some programs); for doctorate, thesis/dissertation. *Entrance requirements:* For master's, statement of purpose, official transcript, 3 recommendations. Additional exam requirements/recommendations for international students: Required—TOEFL (minimum score 550 paper-based; 80 iBT) or IELTS (minimum score 6). *Application deadline:* For fall admission, 12/31 priority date for domestic students, 12/15 for international students; for spring admission, 11/1 priority date for domestic students, 10/1 for international students. Applications are processed on a rolling basis. Application fee: $50. Electronic applications accepted. *Expenses: Tuition:* Full-time $29,860. *Required fees:* $1134. Part-time tuition and fees vary according to course load, degree level and program. *Financial support:* In 2013–14, 130 students received support, including 130 fellowships with full and partial tuition reimbursements available (averaging $7,565 per year); career-related internships or fieldwork and scholarships/grants also available. Support available to part-time students. Financial award application deadline: 2/1; financial award applicants required to submit FAFSA. *Faculty research:* Early childhood education, teacher preparation, educational leadership. *Total annual research expenditures:* $3.5 million. *Unit head:* Dr. Katherine Schultz, Department Head, 510-430-3384, Fax: 510-430-2159, E-mail: kschultz@mills.edu. *Application contact:* Shrim Bathey, Director of Graduate Admission, 510-430-3309, Fax: 510-430-2159, E-mail: grad-admission@mills.edu.
Website: http://www.mills.edu/education.

Minnesota State University Mankato, College of Graduate Studies, College of Science, Engineering and Technology, Department of Mathematics and Statistics, Mankato, MN 56001. Offers mathematics (MA, MAT, MS); mathematics education (MS); statistics (MS). *Students:* 20 full-time (6 women), 19 part-time (11 women). *Degree requirements:* For master's, one foreign language, comprehensive exam, thesis or alternative. *Entrance requirements:* For master's, GRE General Test (if GPA less than 2.75), minimum GPA of 2.75 during previous 2 years of course work. Additional exam requirements/recommendations for international students: Required—TOEFL. *Application deadline:* For fall admission, 7/1 priority date for domestic students; for spring admission, 11/1 for domestic students. Applications are processed on a rolling basis. Application fee: $40. Electronic applications accepted. *Financial support:* Fellowships with partial tuition reimbursements, research assistantships with full tuition reimbursements, teaching assistantships with full tuition reimbursements, Federal Work-Study, institutionally sponsored loans, and unspecified assistantships available. Support available to part-time students. Financial award application deadline: 3/15; financial award applicants required to submit FAFSA. *Unit head:* Dr. Han Wu, Chairperson, 507-389-1453. *Application contact:* 507-389-2321, E-mail: grad@mnsu.edu.
Website: http://cset.mnsu.edu/mathstat/.

Minot State University, Graduate School, Department of Mathematics and Computer Science, Minot, ND 58707-0002. Offers mathematics (MAT). *Degree requirements:* For master's, thesis or alternative. *Entrance requirements:* For master's, minimum GPA of 2.75, undergraduate major in mathematics, teaching certificate. Additional exam requirements/recommendations for international students: Required—TOEFL. *Faculty research:* Mathematics education.

Mississippi College, Graduate School, School of Education, Department of Teacher Education and Leadership, Clinton, MS 39058. Offers art (M Ed); biological science (M Ed); business education (M Ed); computer science (M Ed); dyslexia therapy (M Ed); educational leadership (M Ed, Ed D, Ed S); elementary education (M Ed, Ed S); English (M Ed); higher education administration (MS); mathematics (M Ed); secondary education (M Ed); social studies (history) (M Ed); teaching arts (M Ed). Part-time programs available. Postbaccalaureate distance learning degree programs offered (no on-campus study). *Degree requirements:* For master's, comprehensive exam, thesis optional. *Entrance requirements:* For master's, NTE. Additional exam requirements/recommendations for international students: Recommended—TOEFL, IELTS. Electronic applications accepted.

Missouri University of Science and Technology, Graduate School, Department of Mathematics and Statistics, Rolla, MO 65409. Offers applied mathematics (MS); mathematics (MST, PhD), including mathematics (PhD), mathematics education (MST), statistics (PhD). Terminal master's awarded for partial completion of doctoral program. *Degree requirements:* For master's, thesis or alternative; for doctorate, one foreign language, thesis/dissertation. *Entrance requirements:* For master's and doctorate, GRE General Test, GRE Subject Test. Electronic applications accepted. *Faculty research:* Analysis, differential equations, topology, statistics.

Montana State University, College of Graduate Studies, College of Letters and Science, Department of Mathematical Sciences, Bozeman, MT 59717. Offers mathematics (MS, PhD), including mathematics education option (MS); statistics (MS, PhD). Part-time programs available. Postbaccalaureate distance learning degree programs offered (minimal on-campus study). *Degree requirements:* For master's, comprehensive exam, thesis (for some programs); for doctorate, comprehensive exam, thesis/dissertation. *Entrance requirements:* For master's and doctorate, GRE General Test. Additional exam requirements/recommendations for international students: Required—TOEFL (minimum score 550 paper-based). Electronic applications accepted. *Faculty research:* Applied mathematics, dynamical systems, statistics, mathematics education, mathematical and computational biology.

Montclair State University, The Graduate School, College of Education and Human Services, Department of Secondary and Special Education, Program in Teaching in Subject Area, Montclair, NJ 07043-1624. Offers art (MAT); biology (MAT); chemistry (MAT); earth science (MAT); English (MAT); French (MAT); health and physical education (MAT); health education (MAT); mathematics (MAT); music (MAT); physical education (MAT); physical science (MAT); social studies (MAT); Spanish (MAT); teacher of English as a second language (MAT). *Degree requirements:* For master's, comprehensive exam, thesis or alternative. *Entrance requirements:* For master's, GRE General Test, interview, 2 letters of recommendation. Additional exam requirements/recommendations for international students: Required—TOEFL (minimum score 83 iBT), IELTS (minimum score 6.5). Electronic applications accepted.

Montclair State University, The Graduate School, College of Science and Mathematics, Department of Mathematical Sciences, Program in Mathematics, Montclair, NJ 07043-1624. Offers mathematics education (MS); pure and applied mathematics (MS). Part-time and evening/weekend programs available. *Degree requirements:* For master's, comprehensive exam. *Entrance requirements:* For master's, GRE General Test, 2 letters of recommendation, essay. Additional exam requirements/recommendations for international students: Required—TOEFL (minimum

score 83 iBT), IELTS (minimum score 6.5). Electronic applications accepted. *Faculty research:* Computation, applied analysis.

Montclair State University, The Graduate School, College of Science and Mathematics, Department of Mathematical Sciences, Program in Mathematics Education, Montclair, NJ 07043-1624. Offers Ed D. *Degree requirements:* For doctorate, thesis/dissertation. *Entrance requirements:* For doctorate, GRE General Test, 2 letters of recommendation, essay. Additional exam requirements/recommendations for international students: Required—TOEFL (minimum score 83 iBT), IELTS (minimum score 6.5). Electronic applications accepted. *Faculty research:* Teacher development, student thinking.

Montclair State University, The Graduate School, College of Science and Mathematics, Department of Mathematical Sciences, Program in Teaching Middle Grades Mathematics, Montclair, NJ 07043-1624. Offers MA. Part-time and evening/weekend programs available. *Degree requirements:* For master's, comprehensive exam, thesis or alternative. *Entrance requirements:* For master's, GRE General Test, 2 letters of recommendation, essay. Additional exam requirements/recommendations for international students: Required—TOEFL (minimum score 83 iBT), IELTS (minimum score 6.5). Electronic applications accepted. *Faculty research:* Teacher knowledge, curriculum.

Morehead State University, Graduate Programs, College of Education, Department of Middle Grades and Secondary Education, Morehead, KY 40351. Offers business and marketing education (MAT); English/language arts 5-9 (MAT); French (MAT); health P-12 (MAT); mathematics 5-9 (MAT); physical education P-12 (MAT); science 5-9 (MAT); secondary biology (MAT); secondary chemistry (MAT); secondary earth science (MAT); secondary English (MAT); secondary math (MAT); secondary physics (MAT); secondary social studies (MAT); social studies 5-9 (MAT); Spanish (MAT). Part-time and evening/weekend programs available. *Degree requirements:* For master's, portfolio. *Entrance requirements:* For master's, GRE or PRAXIS II content exam, minimum overall undergraduate GPA of 2.5. Additional exam requirements/recommendations for international students: Required—TOEFL (minimum score 500 paper-based). Electronic applications accepted.

Morgan State University, School of Graduate Studies, School of Education and Urban Studies, Department of Advanced Studies, Leadership and Policy, Program in Mathematics Education, Baltimore, MD 21251. Offers MS, Ed D. *Degree requirements:* For doctorate, comprehensive exam, thesis/dissertation. *Entrance requirements:* For doctorate, GRE General Test or MAT. Additional exam requirements/recommendations for international students: Required—TOEFL (minimum score 550 paper-based).

National Louis University, National College of Education, Chicago, IL 60603. Offers administration and supervision (M Ed, Ed D, CAS, Ed S); curriculum and instruction (M Ed, MS Ed, CAS); early childhood administration (M Ed, CAS); early childhood education (M Ed, MAT, MS Ed, CAS); education (Ed D); educational psychology/human learning and development (M Ed, MS Ed, CAS, Ed S); elementary education (MAT); interdisciplinary curriculum and instruction (M Ed); mathematics education (M Ed, MS Ed, CAS); reading and language (M Ed, MS Ed, CAS); school psychology (M Ed, Ed S); science education (M Ed, MS Ed, CAS); secondary education (MAT); special education (M Ed, MAT, CAS); technology in education (M Ed, CAS). *Accreditation:* NCATE. Part-time and evening/weekend programs available. *Degree requirements:* For doctorate, comprehensive exam, thesis/dissertation. *Entrance requirements:* For master's, MAT or GRE, minimum GPA of 3.0; for doctorate, GRE General Test, minimum GPA of 3.25, interview, resume, writing sample, 4 recommendations. Additional exam requirements/recommendations for international students: Required—TOEFL (minimum score 550 paper-based; 79 iBT).

National University, Academic Affairs, College of Letters and Sciences, La Jolla, CA 92037-1011. Offers applied linguistics (MA); biology (MS); counseling psychology (MA), including licensed professional clinical counseling, marriage and family therapy; creative writing (MFA); English (MA), including Gothic studies, rhetoric; film studies (MA); forensic and crime science (Certificate); forensic studies (MFS), including criminalistics, investigation; gerontology (MA); history (MA); human behavior (MA); mathematics for educators (MS); performance psychology (MA); strategic communications (MA). Part-time and evening/weekend programs available. Postbaccalaureate distance learning degree programs offered (no on-campus study). *Faculty:* 62 full-time (29 women), 95 part-time/adjunct (54 women). *Students:* 708 full-time (525 women), 409 part-time (269 women); includes 503 minority (151 Black or African American, non-Hispanic/Latino; 8 American Indian or Alaska Native, non-Hispanic/Latino; 64 Asian, non-Hispanic/Latino; 221 Hispanic/Latino; 4 Native Hawaiian or other Pacific Islander, non-Hispanic/Latino; 55 Two or more races, non-Hispanic/Latino), 6 international. Average age 35. 265 applicants, 100% accepted, 204 enrolled. In 2013, 594 master's awarded. *Degree requirements:* For master's, thesis (for some programs). *Entrance requirements:* For master's, interview, minimum GPA of 2.5. Additional exam requirements/recommendations for international students: Required—TOEFL (minimum score 550 paper-based; 79 iBT), IELTS (minimum score 6). *Application deadline:* Applications are processed on a rolling basis. Application fee: $60 ($65 for international students). Electronic applications accepted. *Expenses: Tuition:* Full-time $13,824; part-time $1728 per course. One-time fee: $160. *Financial support:* Career-related internships or fieldwork, institutionally sponsored loans, scholarships/grants, and tuition waivers (partial) available. Support available to part-time students. Financial award application deadline: 6/30; financial award applicants required to submit FAFSA. *Unit head:* College of Letters and Sciences, 800-628-8648, E-mail: cols@nu.edu. *Application contact:* Louis Cruz, Interim Vice President for Enrollment Services, 800-628-8648, E-mail: advisor@nu.edu.
Website: http://www.nu.edu/OurPrograms/CollegeOfLettersAndSciences.html.

National University, Academic Affairs, School of Education, La Jolla, CA 92037-1011. Offers applied behavior analysis (Certificate); applied school leadership (MS); autism (Certificate); best practices (Certificate); e-teaching and learning (Certificate); early childhood education (Certificate); education (MA), including best practices (M Ed, MA), e-teaching and learning (M Ed, MA), education technology, teacher leadership (M Ed, MA), teaching and learning in a global society (M Ed, MA), teaching mathematics (M Ed, MA); education with preliminary multiple or single subject (M Ed), including best practices (M Ed, MA), e-teaching and learning (M Ed, MA), educational technology (M Ed, MA), teacher leadership (M Ed, MA), teaching and learning in a global society (M Ed, MA), teaching mathematics (M Ed, MA); educational administration (MS); educational and instructional technology (MS); educational counseling (MS); educational technology (Certificate); higher education administration (MS); innovative school leadership (MS); instructional leadership (MS); juvenile justice special education (MS); reading (Certificate); school psychology (MS); special education (MS), including deaf and hard-of-hearing, mild/moderate disabilities, moderate/severe disabilities; teacher leadership (Certificate); teaching (MA), including applied behavioral analysis, autism, best practices (M Ed, MA), e-teaching and learning (M Ed, MA), early childhood education, educational technology (M Ed, MA), reading, special education, teacher leadership (M Ed, MA), teaching and learning in a global society (M Ed, MA), teaching mathematics (M Ed, MA); teaching mathematics (Certificate). Part-time and evening/weekend programs available. Postbaccalaureate distance learning degree programs offered (no on-campus study). *Faculty:* 72 full-time (43 women), 287 part-time/adjunct (170 women). *Students:* 2,433 full-time (1,744 women), 2,017 part-time (1,371 women); includes 1,834 minority (358 Black or African American, non-Hispanic/Latino; 15 American Indian or Alaska Native, non-Hispanic/Latino; 250 Asian, non-Hispanic/Latino; 1,056 Hispanic/Latino; 29 Native Hawaiian or other Pacific Islander, non-Hispanic/Latino; 126 Two or more races, non-Hispanic/Latino), 1 international. Average age 34. 1,339 applicants, 100% accepted, 1035 enrolled. In 2013, 1,662 master's awarded. *Degree requirements:* For master's, thesis (for some programs). *Entrance requirements:* For master's, interview, minimum GPA of 2.5. Additional exam requirements/recommendations for international students: Required—TOEFL (minimum score 550 paper-based; 79 iBT), IELTS (minimum score 6). *Application deadline:* Applications are processed on a rolling basis. Application fee: $60 ($65 for international students). Electronic applications accepted. *Expenses: Tuition:* Full-time $13,824; part-time $1728 per course. One-time fee: $160. *Financial support:* Career-related internships or fieldwork, institutionally sponsored loans, scholarships/grants, and tuition waivers (partial) available. Support available to part-time students. Financial award application deadline: 6/30. *Faculty research:* Teacher education, special education, educational effectiveness, teaching abroad, school counseling. *Unit head:* School of Education, 800-628-8648, E-mail: soe@nu.edu. *Application contact:* Louis Cruz, Interim Vice President for Enrollment Services, 800-628-8648, E-mail: advisor@nu.edu.
Website: http://www.nu.edu/OurPrograms/SchoolOfEducation.html.

New Jersey City University, Graduate Studies and Continuing Education, William J. Maxwell College of Arts and Sciences, Department of Mathematics, Jersey City, NJ 07305-1597. Offers mathematics education (MA). Part-time and evening/weekend programs available. *Faculty:* 4 full-time (3 women), 1 part-time/adjunct (0 women). *Students:* 5 full-time (3 women), 37 part-time (17 women); includes 27 minority (7 Black or African American, non-Hispanic/Latino; 8 Asian, non-Hispanic/Latino; 9 Hispanic/Latino; 3 Two or more races, non-Hispanic/Latino), 1 international. Average age 39. In 2013, 16 master's awarded. *Degree requirements:* For master's, comprehensive exam, thesis optional. *Entrance requirements:* Additional exam requirements/recommendations for international students: Required—TOEFL (minimum score 61 iBT). *Application deadline:* For fall admission, 8/1 priority date for domestic students; for spring admission, 12/1 for domestic students. Applications are processed on a rolling basis. Application fee: $0. *Expenses: Tuition, area resident:* Part-time $527.90 per credit. Tuition, nonresident: part-time $947.75 per credit. *Financial support:* Unspecified assistantships available. *Unit head:* Dr. Bimnet Teclezghi, Chairperson, 201-200-3202, E-mail: bteclezghi@njcu.edu. *Application contact:* Dr. William Bajor, Dean of Graduate Studies, 201-200-3409, Fax: 201-200-3411, E-mail: wbajor@njcu.edu.

New York Institute of Technology, School of Education, Department of Education, Old Westbury, NY 11568-8000. Offers adolescence education: mathematics (MS); adolescence education: science (MS); childhood education (MS); science, technology, engineering, and math education (Advanced Certificate); teaching 21st century skills (Advanced Certificate). Part-time and evening/weekend programs available. Postbaccalaureate distance learning degree programs offered (minimal on-campus study). *Faculty:* 1 (woman) full-time, 6 part-time/adjunct (3 women). *Students:* 13 full-time (11 women), 21 part-time (19 women); includes 7 minority (2 Black or African American, non-Hispanic/Latino; 3 Asian, non-Hispanic/Latino; 1 Hispanic/Latino; 1 Two or more races, non-Hispanic/Latino), 1 international. Average age 31. 32 applicants, 75% accepted, 13 enrolled. In 2013, 6 master's, 58 other advanced degrees awarded. *Entrance requirements:* Additional exam requirements/recommendations for international students: Required—TOEFL (minimum score 550 paper-based; 79 iBT), IELTS (minimum score 6). *Application deadline:* For fall admission, 7/1 priority date for domestic students, 6/1 for international students; for spring admission, 12/1 priority date for domestic students, 12/1 for international students. Applications are processed on a rolling basis. Application fee: $50. Electronic applications accepted. *Expenses: Tuition:* Full-time $18,900; part-time $1050 per credit. *Financial support:* Research assistantships with partial tuition reimbursements, career-related internships or fieldwork, scholarships/grants, health care benefits, tuition waivers (full and partial), and unspecified assistantships available. Support available to part-time students. Financial award applicants required to submit FAFSA. *Faculty research:* Evolving definition of new literacies and its impact on teaching and learning (twenty-first century skills), new literacies practices in teacher education, teachers' professional development, English language and literacy learning through mobile learning, teaching reading to culturally and linguistically diverse children. *Unit head:* Dr. Hui-Yin Hsu, Associate Professor, 516-686-1322, Fax: 516-686-7655, E-mail: hhsu02@nyit.edu. *Application contact:* Alice Dolitsky, Director, Graduate Admissions, 516-686-7520, Fax: 516-686-1116, E-mail: nyitgrad@nyit.edu.
Website: http://www.nyit.edu/education/departments.

New York University, Steinhardt School of Culture, Education, and Human Development, Department of Teaching and Learning, Program in Mathematics Education, New York, NY 10003. Offers MA, PhD. *Accreditation:* Teacher Education Accreditation Council. Part-time and evening/weekend programs available. *Faculty:* 6 full-time (5 women). *Students:* 6 full-time (5 women), 1 (woman) part-time; includes 5 minority (3 Asian, non-Hispanic/Latino; 2 Hispanic/Latino), 2 international. Average age 24. 31 applicants, 81% accepted, 1 enrolled. In 2013, 25 master's awarded. *Degree requirements:* For master's, thesis (for some programs). *Entrance requirements:* Additional exam requirements/recommendations for international students: Required—TOEFL (minimum score 100 iBT). *Application deadline:* For fall admission, 2/1 priority date for domestic and international students; for spring admission, 11/1 for domestic and international students. Applications are processed on a rolling basis. Application fee: $75. Electronic applications accepted. *Expenses: Tuition:* Full-time $35,856; part-time $1494 per unit. *Required fees:* $1408; $64 per unit. $473 per term. Tuition and fees vary according to course load and program. *Financial support:* Career-related internships or fieldwork, Federal Work-Study, institutionally sponsored loans, scholarships/grants, and tuition waivers (partial) available. Support available to part-time students. Financial award application deadline: 2/1; financial award applicants required to submit FAFSA. *Faculty research:* Race, gender and mathematics learning; developing mathematical concepts through activity; innovative secondary school mathematics materials. *Unit head:* Dr. Orit Zaslavsky, Director, 212-998-5460, Fax: 212-995-4049. *Application contact:* 212-998-5030, Fax: 212-995-4328, E-mail: steinhardt.gradadmissions@nyu.edu.
Website: http://steinhardt.nyu.edu/teachlearn/math.

Niagara University, Graduate Division of Education, Concentration in Foundations of Teaching, Niagara Falls, NY 14109. Offers MS Ed. *Accreditation:* NCATE. Part-time programs available. *Students:* 1 (woman) full-time, 5 part-time (2 women). Average age 30. In 2013, 5 master's awarded. *Degree requirements:* For master's, thesis. *Entrance requirements:* For master's, GRE General Test or MAT. Additional exam requirements/recommendations for international students: Required—TOEFL (minimum score 550 paper-based, 79 iBT) or IELTS (minimum score 6). *Application deadline:* For fall admission, 8/1 for domestic students. Applications are processed on a rolling basis. Application fee: $30. *Expenses:* Contact institution. *Financial support:* Research assistantships with full and partial tuition reimbursements, teaching assistantships with full and partial tuition reimbursements, career-related internships or fieldwork, Federal Work-Study, scholarships/grants, and unspecified assistantships available. Financial award application deadline: 4/15; financial award applicants required to submit FAFSA.

Mathematics Education

Unit head: Dr. Leticia Hahn, 716-286-8760, E-mail: lhahn@niagara.edu. *Application contact:* Dr. Debra A. Colley, Dean of Education, 716-286-8560, Fax: 716-286-8560, E-mail: dcolley@niagara.edu.
Website: http://www.niagara.edu/foundations-of-teaching-math-science-and-technology-education.

Nicholls State University, Graduate Studies, College of Arts and Sciences, Department of Mathematics and Computer Science, Thibodaux, LA 70310. Offers community/technical college mathematics (MS). Part-time and evening/weekend programs available. *Degree requirements:* For master's, comprehensive exam. *Entrance requirements:* For master's, GRE General Test. Electronic applications accepted. *Faculty research:* Operations research, statistics, numerical analysis, algebra, topology.

North Carolina Central University, College of Science and Technology, Department of Mathematics and Computer Science, Durham, NC 27707-3129. Offers applied mathematics (MS); mathematics education (MS); pure mathematics (MS). Part-time and evening/weekend programs available. *Degree requirements:* For master's, one foreign language, comprehensive exam, thesis. *Entrance requirements:* For master's, minimum GPA of 3.0 in major, 2.5 overall. Additional exam requirements/recommendations for international students: Required—TOEFL. *Faculty research:* Structure theorems for Lie algebra, Kleene monoids and semi-groups, theoretical computer science, mathematics education.

North Carolina State University, Graduate School, College of Education, Department of Mathematics, Science, and Technology Education, Program in Mathematics Education, Raleigh, NC 27695. Offers M Ed, MS, PhD. *Accreditation:* NCATE. Part-time programs available. *Degree requirements:* For master's, thesis (for some programs), oral exam; for doctorate, one foreign language, thesis/dissertation, oral and written exams. *Entrance requirements:* For master's, GRE General Test or MAT, minimum GPA of 3.0; for doctorate, GRE General Test, minimum GPA of 3.0, interview. Electronic applications accepted. *Faculty research:* Teacher education using technology, curriculum development, scientific visualization, problem solving.

North Dakota State University, College of Graduate and Interdisciplinary Studies, College of Human Development and Education, School of Education, Fargo, ND 58108. Offers agricultural education (M Ed, MS), including agricultural education, agricultural extension education (MS); counseling (M Ed, MS, PhD); curriculum and instruction (M Ed, MS); education (PhD); educational leadership (M Ed, MS, Ed S); family and consumer sciences education (M Ed, MS); history education (M Ed, MS); institutional analysis (Ed D); mathematics education (M Ed, MS); music education (M Ed, MS); occupational and adult education (Ed D); science education (M Ed, MS). *Accreditation:* NCATE. Part-time and evening/weekend programs available. Postbaccalaureate distance learning degree programs offered (minimal on-campus study). *Faculty:* 25 full-time (11 women), 1 (woman) part-time/adjunct. *Students:* 110 full-time (82 women), 123 part-time (85 women); includes 14 minority (4 Black or African American, non-Hispanic/Latino; 4 American Indian or Alaska Native, non-Hispanic/Latino; 1 Native Hawaiian or other Pacific Islander, non-Hispanic/Latino; 5 Two or more races, non-Hispanic/Latino), 10 international. Average age 28. 57 applicants, 81% accepted, 42 enrolled. In 2013, 38 master's, 9 doctorates awarded. *Degree requirements:* For master's, comprehensive exam; for doctorate, thesis/dissertation; for Ed S, thesis. *Entrance requirements:* For degree, GRE General Test, master's degree, minimum GPA of 3.25. Additional exam requirements/recommendations for international students: Required—TOEFL. *Application deadline:* Applications are processed on a rolling basis. Application fee: $45 ($60 for international students). *Financial support:* Research assistantships, teaching assistantships, career-related internships or fieldwork, Federal Work-Study, institutionally sponsored loans, and tuition waivers (full) available. Financial award application deadline: 4/15. *Unit head:* Dr. William Martin, Chair, 701-231-7202, Fax: 701-231-7416, E-mail: william.martin@ndsu.edu. *Application contact:* Sonya Goergen, Marketing, Recruitment, and Public Relations Coordinator, 701-231-7033, Fax: 701-231-6524.
Website: http://www.ndsu.nodak.edu/school_of_education/.

North Dakota State University, College of Graduate and Interdisciplinary Studies, Program in STEM Education, Fargo, ND 58108. Offers PhD. In 2013, 1 doctorate awarded. Application fee: $35. Electronic applications accepted. *Unit head:* Dr. Donald Schwert, Director, 701-231-7496, Fax: 701-231-5924, E-mail: donald.schwert@ndsu.edu. *Application contact:* Sonya Goergen, Marketing, Recruitment, and Public Relations Coordinator, 701-231-7033, Fax: 701-231-6524.

Northeastern Illinois University, College of Graduate Studies and Research, College of Arts and Sciences, Program in Pedagogical Content Knowledge for Teaching Elementary and Middle School Mathematics, Chicago, IL 60625-4699. Offers MA. *Degree requirements:* For master's, portfolio, exit exam. *Entrance requirements:* For master's, current Illinois teaching certificate for teaching elementary or middle school; 6 or more credit hours of college mathematics content courses; essay.

Northeastern Illinois University, College of Graduate Studies and Research, College of Arts and Sciences, Program in Secondary Education Mathematics, Chicago, IL 60625-4699. Offers MS.

Northeastern State University, College of Science and Health Professions, Program in Mathematics Education, Tahlequah, OK 74464-2399. Offers M Ed. *Faculty:* 6 full-time (3 women). *Students:* 2 full-time (both women), 20 part-time (16 women); includes 4 minority (1 Black or African American, non-Hispanic/Latino; 3 American Indian or Alaska Native, non-Hispanic/Latino). Average age 35. In 2013, 7 master's awarded. *Entrance requirements:* For master's, GRE or MAT, minimum GPA of 2.5. Additional exam requirements/recommendations for international students: Required—TOEFL. *Application deadline:* For fall admission, 8/19 for domestic students; for spring admission, 1/7 for domestic students. Applications are processed on a rolling basis. Application fee: $25. Electronic applications accepted. *Expenses:* Tuition, state resident: full-time $3029; part-time $168.25 per credit hour. Tuition, nonresident: full-time $7709; part-time $428.25 per credit hour. *Required fees:* $35.90 per credit hour. *Unit head:* Dr. Martha Parrott, Department Chair of Mathematics, 918-449-6536, E-mail: parrott@nsuok.edu. *Application contact:* Margie Railey, Administrative Assistant, 918-456-5511 Ext. 2093, Fax: 918-458-2061, E-mail: railey@nsouk.edu.
Website: http://academics.nsuok.edu/mathematics/DegreesMajors/Graduate/MEdMathematicsEducation.aspx.

Northern Arizona University, Graduate College, College of Engineering, Forestry and Natural Sciences, Center for Science Teaching and Learning, Flagstaff, AZ 86011. Offers mathematics or science teaching (Certificate); science teaching and learning (MAST); teaching science (MAT). Part-time programs available. Postbaccalaureate distance learning degree programs offered (minimal on-campus study). *Faculty:* 7 full-time (3 women), 2 part-time/adjunct (both women). *Students:* 16 full-time (12 women), 4 part-time (3 women). Average age 31. 23 applicants, 83% accepted, 13 enrolled. In 2013, 11 master's, 3 other advanced degrees awarded. *Entrance requirements:* Additional exam requirements/recommendations for international students: Required—TOEFL (minimum score 550 paper-based; 80 iBT), IELTS (minimum score 7). *Application deadline:* For fall admission, 3/1 for international students; for spring admission, 9/15 for international students. Application fee: $65. *Financial support:* In 2013–14, 2 research assistantships (averaging $9,200 per year) were awarded; career-related internships or fieldwork, Federal Work-Study, and scholarships/grants also available. Financial award applicants required to submit FAFSA. *Unit head:* Max Dass, Director, 928-523-2066, E-mail: pradep.dass@nau.edu. *Application contact:* Ann Archuleta, Administrative Associate, 928-523-1709, E-mail: ann.archuleta@nau.edu.
Website: http://nau.edu/cefns/cstl/.

Northern Arizona University, Graduate College, College of Engineering, Forestry and Natural Sciences, Department of Mathematics and Statistics, Flagstaff, AZ 86011. Offers applied statistics (Certificate); mathematics (MS); mathematics education (MS); statistics (MS). Part-time programs available. *Faculty:* 39 full-time (15 women), 5 part-time/adjunct (3 women). *Students:* 36 full-time (15 women), 12 part-time (8 women); includes 11 minority (1 American Indian or Alaska Native, non-Hispanic/Latino; 4 Asian, non-Hispanic/Latino; 5 Hispanic/Latino; 1 Two or more races, non-Hispanic/Latino), 4 international. Average age 28. 39 applicants, 85% accepted, 24 enrolled. In 2013, 18 master's, 4 other advanced degrees awarded. *Degree requirements:* For master's, comprehensive exam (for some programs), thesis (for some programs). *Entrance requirements:* For master's, minimum GPA of 3.0. Additional exam requirements/recommendations for international students: Required—TOEFL (minimum score 550 paper-based; 80 iBT), IELTS (minimum score 7). *Application deadline:* For fall admission, 3/15 priority date for domestic and international students; for spring admission, 10/15 priority date for domestic and international students. Applications are processed on a rolling basis. Application fee: $65. Electronic applications accepted. *Financial support:* In 2013–14, 34 teaching assistantships with full tuition reimbursements (averaging $14,213 per year) were awarded; Federal Work-Study, scholarships/grants, health care benefits, tuition waivers (full and partial), and unspecified assistantships also available. Financial award applicants required to submit FAFSA. *Faculty research:* Topology, statistics, groups, ring theory, number theory. *Unit head:* Dr. Terence Blows, Chair, 928-523-6863, Fax: 928-523-5847, E-mail: terence.blows@nau.edu. *Application contact:* Jenny Buckinghorse, Administrative Assistant, 928-523-6881, Fax: 928-523-5847, E-mail: math.grad@nau.edu.
Website: http://nau.edu/CEFNS/NatSci/Math/Degrees-Programs/.

Northwest Missouri State University, Graduate School, College of Arts and Sciences, Department of Mathematics, Computer Science and Information Systems, Maryville, MO 64468-6001. Offers applied computer science (MS); teaching instructional technology (MS Ed); teaching mathematics (MS Ed). Part-time programs available. *Degree requirements:* For master's, comprehensive exam. *Entrance requirements:* For master's, GRE General Test, minimum undergraduate GPA of 2.5, writing sample. Additional exam requirements/recommendations for international students: Required—TOEFL (minimum score 550 paper-based).

Oakland University, Graduate Study and Lifelong Learning, School of Education and Human Services, Department of Human Development and Child Studies, Program in Early Childhood Education, Rochester, MI 48309-4401. Offers early childhood education (M Ed, PhD, Certificate); early mathematics education (Certificate). *Accreditation:* Teacher Education Accreditation Council. *Students:* 15 full-time (all women), 73 part-time (70 women); includes 12 minority (10 Black or African American, non-Hispanic/Latino; 2 Asian, non-Hispanic/Latino), 1 international. Average age 36. 66 applicants, 94% accepted, 59 enrolled. In 2013, 49 master's, 2 doctorates awarded. *Degree requirements:* For doctorate, thesis/dissertation. *Entrance requirements:* For master's, minimum GPA of 3.0 for unconditional admission; for doctorate, GRE General Test, minimum GPA of 3.0 for unconditional admission. Additional exam requirements/recommendations for international students: Required—TOEFL (minimum score 550 paper-based). *Application deadline:* For fall admission, 5/1 for domestic students, 5/1 priority date for international students; for winter admission, 2/1 for domestic students, 9/1 priority date for international students. Application fee: $0. *Financial support:* Career-related internships or fieldwork, Federal Work-Study, institutionally sponsored loans, and tuition waivers (full) available. Financial award application deadline: 3/1; financial award applicants required to submit FAFSA. *Unit head:* Dr. Sherri Oden, Coordinator, 248-370-3027, E-mail: oden@oakland.edu. *Application contact:* Christina J. Grabowski, Associate Director of Graduate Study and Lifelong Learning, 248-370-3167, Fax: 248-370-4114, E-mail: grabowsk@oakland.edu.

Occidental College, Graduate Studies, Department of Education, Los Angeles, CA 90041-3314. Offers elementary education (MAT), including liberal studies; secondary education (MAT), including English and comparative literary studies, history, life science, mathematics, physical science, social science, Spanish. Part-time programs available. *Degree requirements:* For master's, comprehensive exam, synthesis paper. *Entrance requirements:* For master's, GRE General Test, minimum GPA of 3.0. Additional exam requirements/recommendations for international students: Required—TOEFL (minimum score 625 paper-based). *Expenses:* Contact institution. *Faculty research:* Preparing teacher-leaders, curriculum development.

The Ohio State University, Graduate School, College of Arts and Sciences, Division of Natural and Mathematical Sciences, Department of Mathematics, Columbus, OH 43210. Offers computational sciences (MMS); mathematical biosciences (MMS); mathematics (MS, PhD); mathematics for educators (MMS). *Faculty:* 61. *Students:* 126 full-time (32 women), 8 part-time (1 woman); includes 8 minority (3 Asian, non-Hispanic/Latino; 3 Hispanic/Latino; 2 Two or more races, non-Hispanic/Latino), 64 international. Average age 26. In 2013, 15 master's, 9 doctorates awarded. *Degree requirements:* For master's, thesis optional; for doctorate, one foreign language, thesis/dissertation. *Entrance requirements:* For master's, GRE General Test; for doctorate, GRE General Test (recommended), GRE Subject Test (mathematics). Additional exam requirements/recommendations for international students: Required—TOEFL (minimum score 550 paper-based; 79 iBT), Michigan English Language Assessment Battery (minimum score 82); Recommended—IELTS (minimum score 7). *Application deadline:* For fall admission, 12/15 priority date for domestic and international students; for winter admission, 12/1 for domestic students, 11/1 for international students; for spring admission, 3/1 for domestic students, 2/1 for international students. Applications are processed on a rolling basis. Application fee: $60 ($70 for international students). Electronic applications accepted. *Financial support:* Fellowships with tuition reimbursements, research assistantships with tuition reimbursements, teaching assistantships with tuition reimbursements, Federal Work-Study, institutionally sponsored loans, and unspecified assistantships available. Support available to part-time students. *Unit head:* Luis Casian, Chair, 614-292-7173, E-mail: casian@math.ohio-state.edu. *Application contact:* Roman Nitze, Graduate Studies Coordinator, 614-292-6274, Fax: 614-292-1479, E-mail: nitze.1@osu.edu.
Website: http://www.math.osu.edu/.

Ohio University, Graduate College, Gladys W. and David H. Patton College of Education and Human Services, Department of Teacher Education, Athens, OH 45701-2979. Offers adolescent to young adult education (M Ed); curriculum and instruction (M Ed, PhD); early childhood/special education (M Ed); intervention specialist/mild-moderate needs (M Ed); intervention specialist/moderate-intensive needs (M Ed); mathematics education (PhD); middle childhood education (M Ed); reading education (M Ed); social studies education (PhD). Part-time and evening/weekend programs available. *Degree requirements:* For master's, thesis or alternative; for doctorate, comprehensive exam, thesis/dissertation. *Entrance requirements:* For master's, GRE

General Test or MAT (if GPA is below 2.9); for doctorate, GRE General Test, minimum GPA of 3.4, work experience. Additional exam requirements/recommendations for international students: Required—TOEFL (minimum score 550 paper-based; 80 iBT) or IELTS (minimum score 6.5). Electronic applications accepted. *Faculty research:* Cognition literacy, character education, teacher's education reform, disabilities.

Oklahoma State University, College of Arts and Sciences, Department of Mathematics, Stillwater, OK 74078. Offers applied mathematics (MS, PhD); mathematics education (MS, PhD); pure mathematics (MS, PhD). *Faculty:* 45 full-time (11 women), 9 part-time/adjunct (5 women). *Students:* 9 full-time (3 women), 29 part-time (12 women); includes 2 minority (1 Asian, non-Hispanic/Latino; 1 Hispanic/Latino), 21 international. Average age 30. 69 applicants, 28% accepted, 12 enrolled. In 2013, 6 master's, 4 doctorates awarded. *Degree requirements:* For master's, thesis, creative component, or report; for doctorate, comprehensive exam, thesis/dissertation. *Entrance requirements:* For master's and doctorate, GRE (recommended). Additional exam requirements/recommendations for international students: Required—TOEFL (minimum score 550 paper-based; 79 iBT). *Application deadline:* For fall admission, 3/1 for domestic and international students; for spring admission, 10/15 for domestic students, 10/15 priority date for international students. Applications are processed on a rolling basis. Application fee: $40 ($75 for international students). Electronic applications accepted. *Expenses:* Tuition, state resident: full-time $4272; part-time $178 per credit hour. Tuition, nonresident: full-time $17,472; part-time $709 per credit hour. *Required fees:* $2413.20; $100.55 per credit hour. One-time fee: $50 full-time. Part-time tuition and fees vary according to course load and campus/location. *Financial support:* In 2013–14, 1 research assistantship (averaging $10,878 per year), 35 teaching assistantships (averaging $20,074 per year) were awarded; health care benefits and tuition waivers (partial) also available. Financial award application deadline: 3/1; financial award applicants required to submit FAFSA. *Unit head:* Dr. Willam Jaco, Department Head, 405-744-5688, Fax: 405-744-8275.
Website: http://www.math.okstate.edu/.

Oregon State University, College of Education, Program in Mathematics Education, Corvallis, OR 97331. Offers MS, PhD. *Accreditation:* NCATE. Part-time programs available. Postbaccalaureate distance learning degree programs offered (no on-campus study). *Faculty:* 11 full-time (7 women), 1 part-time/adjunct (0 women). *Students:* 8 full-time (4 women), 27 part-time (23 women); includes 3 minority (1 American Indian or Alaska Native, non-Hispanic/Latino; 1 Asian, non-Hispanic/Latino; 1 Hispanic/Latino), 2 international. Average age 35. 22 applicants, 50% accepted, 9 enrolled. In 2013, 12 master's, 1 doctorate awarded. *Degree requirements:* For master's, variable foreign language requirement; for doctorate, one foreign language, thesis/dissertation. *Entrance requirements:* For master's, minimum GPA of 3.0 in last 90 hours of course work; for doctorate, GRE or MAT, minimum GPA of 3.0 in last 90 hours of course work. Additional exam requirements/recommendations for international students: Required—TOEFL (minimum score 80 iBT), IELTS (minimum score 6.5). *Application deadline:* For fall admission, 6/1 for domestic students. Applications are processed on a rolling basis. Application fee: $60. *Expenses:* Tuition, state resident: full-time $11,664; part-time $432 per credit hour. Tuition, nonresident: full-time $19,197; part-time $711 per credit hour. *Required fees:* $1446; $443 per quarter. One-time fee: $300. Tuition and fees vary according to course load and program. *Financial support:* Teaching assistantships, Federal Work-Study, and institutionally sponsored loans available. Support available to part-time students. Financial award application deadline: 2/1. *Faculty research:* Teacher action when focused on standards, teacher belief, integration of technology. *Unit head:* Dr. Larry Flick, Dean, 541-737-3664, Fax: 541-737-8971, E-mail: larry.flick@oregonstate.edu. *Application contact:* Dr. Wendy Rose Aaron, Assistant Professor, 541-737-1277, E-mail: wendy.aaron@oregonstate.edu.
Website: http://education.oregonstate.edu/academics.

Oregon State University, College of Education, Program in Teaching: Advanced Mathematics Education, Corvallis, OR 97331. Offers MAT. Part-time programs available. *Faculty:* 3 full-time (2 women), 8 part-time/adjunct (6 women). *Students:* 1 (woman) part-time. 4 applicants, 25% accepted. *Entrance requirements:* For master's, CBEST. Additional exam requirements/recommendations for international students: Required—TOEFL (minimum score 575 paper-based). Application fee: $60. *Expenses:* Tuition, state resident: full-time $11,664; part-time $432 per credit hour. Tuition, nonresident: full-time $19,197; part-time $711 per credit hour. *Required fees:* $1446; $443 per quarter. One-time fee: $300. Tuition and fees vary according to course load and program. *Unit head:* Dr. Carolyn Platt, Teacher Education Program Lead, 541-322-3120, E-mail: carolyn.platt@osucascades.edu.
Website: http://www.osucascades.edu/academics/teaching/secondary.

Our Lady of the Lake University of San Antonio, School of Professional Studies, Program in Curriculum and Instruction, San Antonio, TX 78207-4689. Offers bilingual education (M Ed); early childhood education (M Ed); English as a second language (M Ed); integrated math teaching (M Ed); integrated science teaching (M Ed); reading specialist (M Ed). Part-time and evening/weekend programs available. *Faculty:* 6 full-time (4 women), 3 part-time/adjunct (all women). *Students:* 4 full-time (all women), 84 part-time (72 women); includes 52 minority (2 Black or African American, non-Hispanic/Latino; 2 Asian, non-Hispanic/Latino; 48 Hispanic/Latino). Average age 40. 9 applicants, 56% accepted, 1 enrolled. In 2013, 8 master's awarded. *Degree requirements:* For master's, comprehensive exam. *Entrance requirements:* For master's, GRE General Test or MAT. Additional exam requirements/recommendations for international students: Required—TOEFL. *Application deadline:* For fall admission, 4/1 priority date for domestic and international students; for spring admission, 11/1 priority date for domestic and international students; for summer admission, 2/1 priority date for domestic students, 4/1 priority date for international students. Applications are processed on a rolling basis. Application fee: $25 ($50 for international students). Electronic applications accepted. *Expenses: Tuition:* Full-time $9120; part-time $760 per credit. *Required fees:* $698; $334 per trimester. Tuition and fees vary according to course load, degree level, campus/location and program. *Financial support:* Research assistantships, teaching assistantships, career-related internships or fieldwork, Federal Work-Study, institutionally sponsored loans, scholarships/grants, and tuition waivers (partial) available. Support available to part-time students. Financial award application deadline: 4/1. *Faculty research:* Professional educator to understand and meet the comprehensive needs of a diverse student population, life-long learners, innovative practices. *Unit head:* Dr. Jerrie Jackson, 210-434-6711 Ext. 2698, E-mail: jjackson@lake.ollusa.edu. *Application contact:* Graduate Admission, 210-431-3961, Fax: 210-431-4013, E-mail: gradadm@lake.ollusa.edu.
Website: http://www.ollusa.edu/s/1190/ollu-3-column-noads.aspx?sid=1190&gid=1&pgid=4173.

Our Lady of the Lake University of San Antonio, School of Professional Studies, Program in Intermediate Education, San Antonio, TX 78207-4689. Offers math/science education (M Ed); professional studies (M Ed). Part-time and evening/weekend programs available. *Faculty:* 6 full-time (4 women), 3 part-time/adjunct (all women). *Students:* 1 (woman) full-time; minority (Black or African American, non-Hispanic/Latino). Average age 50. 1 applicant, 100% accepted. In 2013, 1 master's awarded. *Degree requirements:* For master's, comprehensive exam. *Entrance requirements:* For master's, GRE General Test or MAT. Additional exam requirements/recommendations for international students: Required—TOEFL. *Application deadline:* For fall admission, 4/1 priority date for domestic and international students; for spring admission, 11/1 priority date for domestic and international students; for summer admission, 2/1 priority date for domestic and international students. Applications are processed on a rolling basis. Application fee: $25 ($50 for international students). Electronic applications accepted. *Expenses: Tuition:* Full-time $9120; part-time $760 per credit. *Required fees:* $698; $334 per trimester. Tuition and fees vary according to course load, degree level, campus/location and program. *Financial support:* Research assistantships, teaching assistantships, career-related internships or fieldwork, Federal Work-Study, institutionally sponsored loans, scholarships/grants, and tuition waivers (partial) available. Support available to part-time students. Financial award application deadline: 4/15. *Faculty research:* Professional educator to understand and meet the comprehensive needs of a diverse student population, life-long learners, innovative practices. *Unit head:* Dr. Jerrie Jackson, 210-434-6711 Ext. 2698, E-mail: jjackson@lake.ollusa.edu. *Application contact:* Graduate Admission, 210-431-3961, Fax: 210-431-4013, E-mail: gradadm@lake.ollusa.edu.
Website: http://www.ollusa.edu/s/1190/ollu-3-column-noads.aspx?sid=1190&gid=1&pgid=3855.

Plymouth State University, College of Graduate Studies, Graduate Studies in Education, Program in Mathematics Education, Plymouth, NH 03264-1595. Offers M Ed. Part-time and evening/weekend programs available. *Degree requirements:* For master's, comprehensive exam, thesis optional, internship or practicum. *Entrance requirements:* For master's, MAT, minimum GPA of 3.0.

Portland State University, Graduate Studies, College of Liberal Arts and Sciences, Department of Mathematics and Statistics, Portland, OR 97207-0751. Offers mathematical sciences (PhD); mathematics education (PhD); statistics (MS); MA/MS. *Faculty:* 30 full-time (9 women), 13 part-time/adjunct (3 women). *Students:* 65 full-time (25 women), 41 part-time (14 women); includes 18 minority (1 Black or African American, non-Hispanic/Latino; 3 American Indian or Alaska Native, non-Hispanic/Latino; 7 Asian, non-Hispanic/Latino; 5 Hispanic/Latino; 2 Two or more races, non-Hispanic/Latino), 10 international. Average age 33. 107 applicants, 42% accepted, 28 enrolled. In 2013, 23 master's, 2 doctorates awarded. *Degree requirements:* For master's, thesis or alternative, exams; for doctorate, 2 foreign languages, thesis/dissertation, exams. *Entrance requirements:* For master's, GRE General Test, GRE Subject Test, minimum GPA of 3.0 in upper-division course work or 2.75 overall; for doctorate, GRE General Test. Additional exam requirements/recommendations for international students: Required—TOEFL (minimum score 550 paper-based). *Application deadline:* For fall admission, 4/1 for domestic students, 3/1 for international students; for winter admission, 9/1 for domestic students, 8/1 for international students; for spring admission, 11/1 for domestic and international students. Applications are processed on a rolling basis. Application fee: $50. *Expenses:* Tuition, state resident: full-time $9207; part-time $341 per credit. Tuition, nonresident: full-time $14,391; part-time $533 per credit. *Required fees:* $1263; $22 per credit. $98 per quarter. One-time fee: $150. Tuition and fees vary according to program. *Financial support:* In 2013–14, 3 research assistantships with full tuition reimbursements (averaging $12,609 per year), 33 teaching assistantships with full tuition reimbursements (averaging $12,197 per year) were awarded; Federal Work-Study, scholarships/grants, tuition waivers (partial), and unspecified assistantships also available. Support available to part-time students. Financial award application deadline: 3/1; financial award applicants required to submit FAFSA. *Faculty research:* Algebra, topology, statistical distribution theory, control theory, statistical robustness. *Total annual research expenditures:* $497,723. *Unit head:* Steven A. Bleiler, Chair, 503-725-2208, Fax: 503-725-3661, E-mail: bleilers@pdx.edu. *Application contact:* Katie Gettling, Administrative Assistant, 503-725-3604, Fax: 503-725-3661, E-mail: ekatie@pdx.edu.
Website: http://www.mth.pdx.edu/.

Providence College, Program in Teaching Mathematics, Providence, RI 02918. Offers MA. Part-time and evening/weekend programs available. *Faculty:* 3 full-time (2 women). *Students:* 1 full-time (0 women), 15 part-time (7 women); includes 1 minority (Two or more races, non-Hispanic/Latino), 1 international. Average age 31. 4 applicants, 100% accepted, 3 enrolled. In 2013, 11 master's awarded. *Entrance requirements:* Additional exam requirements/recommendations for international students: Required—TOEFL (minimum score 550 paper-based; 80 iBT). *Application deadline:* For fall admission, 8/1 priority date for domestic and international students; for spring admission, 12/1 priority date for domestic and international students. Applications are processed on a rolling basis. Application fee: $55. *Expenses: Tuition:* Part-time $432 per credit. *Required fees:* $432 per credit. *Financial support:* Institutionally sponsored loans and unspecified assistantships available. Support available to part-time students. Financial award application deadline: 8/1; financial award applicants required to submit FAFSA. *Unit head:* Dr. Wataru Ishizuka, Program Director, 401-865-2784, E-mail: wishizuk@providence.edu. *Application contact:* Rev. Mark D. Nowel, Dean of Undergraduate and Graduate Studies, 401-865-2649, Fax: 401-865-1496, E-mail: mnowel@providence.edu.
Website: http://www.providence.edu/academics/Pages/master-teaching-math.aspx.

Purdue University, Graduate School, College of Education, Department of Curriculum and Instruction, West Lafayette, IN 47907. Offers agricultural and extension education (PhD, Ed S); agriculture and extension education (MS, MS Ed); art education (PhD); curriculum studies (MS Ed, PhD, Ed S); educational technology (MS Ed, PhD, Ed S); elementary education (MS Ed); family and consumer sciences education (MS Ed, PhD, Ed S); foreign language education (MS Ed, PhD, Ed S); industrial technology (PhD, Ed S); language arts (MS Ed, PhD, Ed S); literacy (MS Ed, PhD, Ed S); mathematics/science education (MS, MS Ed, PhD, Ed S); social studies (MS Ed, PhD); social studies education (Ed S); vocational/industrial education (MS Ed, PhD, Ed S); vocational/technical education (MS Ed, PhD, Ed S). *Accreditation:* NCATE. Part-time and evening/weekend programs available. *Faculty:* 29 full-time (19 women), 33 part-time/adjunct (29 women). *Students:* 85 full-time (53 women), 271 part-time (195 women); includes 62 minority (19 Black or African American, non-Hispanic/Latino; 3 American Indian or Alaska Native, non-Hispanic/Latino; 13 Asian, non-Hispanic/Latino; 22 Hispanic/Latino; 1 Native Hawaiian or other Pacific Islander, non-Hispanic/Latino; 4 Two or more races, non-Hispanic/Latino), 41 international. Average age 36. 155 applicants, 71% accepted, 71 enrolled. In 2013, 60 master's, 20 doctorates awarded. *Degree requirements:* For master's, thesis optional; for doctorate, thesis/dissertation, oral and written exams; for Ed S, oral presentation, project. *Entrance requirements:* For master's, GRE General Test (if undergraduate GPA is below 3.0), minimum undergraduate GPA of 3.0 or equivalent; for doctorate, GRE General Test (minimum combined verbal and quantitative score of 1000, 300 for new scoring), minimum undergraduate GPA of 3.0 or equivalent; master's degree with minimum GPA of 3.0 or equivalent; for Ed S, GRE General Test (minimum combined verbal and quantitative score of 1000, 300 for new scoring), minimum undergraduate GPA of 3.0 or equivalent; master's degree. Additional exam requirements/recommendations for international students: Required—TOEFL (minimum score 550 paper-based; 77 iBT). *Application deadline:* For fall admission, 12/15 for domestic students, 3/1 for international students; for spring admission, 9/15 for domestic students, 8/1 for international students. Application fee: $60 ($75 for international students). Electronic applications accepted. *Financial support:* Fellowships with full tuition reimbursements, research assistantships with full tuition reimbursements,

Mathematics Education

teaching assistantships with full tuition reimbursements, career-related internships or fieldwork, and tuition waivers (full) available. Support available to part-time students. Financial award application deadline: 3/1; financial award applicants required to submit FAFSA. *Faculty research:* Literacy acquisition and development, teacher beliefs and knowledge, recruitment and retention of underrepresented students, economic education, literacy discourse. *Unit head:* Dr. Phillip J. VanFossen, Head, 765-494-7935, Fax: 765-496-1622, E-mail: vanfoss@purdue.edu. *Application contact:* Cindy Blankenship, Graduate Contact, 765-494-2345, Fax: 765-494-5832, E-mail: prater0@purdue.edu.
Website: http://www.edci.purdue.edu/.

Purdue University Calumet, Graduate Studies Office, School of Engineering, Mathematics, and Science, Department of Mathematics, Computer Science, and Statistics, Hammond, IN 46323-2094. Offers computer science (MS); mathematics (MAT, MS). Part-time programs available. *Entrance requirements:* Additional exam requirements/recommendations for international students: Required—TOEFL. *Faculty research:* Topology, analysis, algebra, mathematics education.

Queens College of the City University of New York, Division of Graduate Studies, Division of Education, Department of Secondary Education, Flushing, NY 11367-1597. Offers art (MS Ed); biology (MS Ed, AC); chemistry (MS Ed, AC); earth sciences (MS Ed, AC); English (MS Ed, AC); French (MS Ed, AC); Italian (MS Ed, AC); mathematics (MS Ed, AC); music (MS Ed, AC); physics (MS Ed, AC); social studies (MS Ed, AC); Spanish (MS Ed, AC). Part-time and evening/weekend programs available. *Degree requirements:* For master's, research project; for AC, thesis optional. *Entrance requirements:* For master's, minimum GPA of 3.0. Additional exam requirements/recommendations for international students: Required—TOEFL.

Quinnipiac University, School of Education, Program in Secondary Education, Hamden, CT 06518-1940. Offers biology (MAT); English (MAT); history/social studies (MAT); mathematics (MAT); Spanish (MAT). *Accreditation:* NCATE. *Faculty:* 14 full-time (7 women), 46 part-time/adjunct (27 women). *Students:* 44 full-time (37 women), 1 (woman) part-time; includes 2 minority (both Hispanic/Latino). 45 applicants, 93% accepted, 32 enrolled. In 2013, 32 master's awarded. *Entrance requirements:* For master's, PRAXIS I, minimum GPA of 2.67, interview. *Application deadline:* For fall admission, 4/1 priority date for domestic students. Applications are processed on a rolling basis. Application fee: $45. Electronic applications accepted. *Expenses: Tuition:* Part-time $920 per credit. *Required fees:* $37 per credit. *Financial support:* Career-related internships or fieldwork, tuition waivers (full and partial), and unspecified assistantships available. Support available to part-time students. Financial award application deadline: 6/1; financial award applicants required to submit FAFSA. *Faculty research:* Multicultural and urban education/leadership, challenges of teaching diverse learners, scholarship of teaching and learning, technology and teaching, humor and education. *Unit head:* Mordechai Gordon, Program Director, E-mail: mordechai.gordon@quinnipiac.edu. *Application contact:* Office of Graduate Admissions, 800-462-1944, Fax: 203-582-3443, E-mail: graduate@quinnipiac.edu.
Website: http://www.quinnipiac.edu/gradeducation.

Radford University, College of Graduate and Professional Studies, College of Education and Human Development, School of Teacher Education and Leadership, Program in Education, Radford, VA 24142. Offers curriculum and instruction (MS); early childhood education (MS); educational technology (MS); math education content area studies (MS). *Accreditation:* NCATE. Part-time and evening/weekend programs available. *Faculty:* 6 full-time (4 women), 2 part-time/adjunct (1 woman). *Students:* 68 full-time (53 women), 30 part-time (20 women); includes 6 minority (3 Black or African American, non-Hispanic/Latino; 1 Asian, non-Hispanic/Latino; 1 Hispanic/Latino; 1 Two or more races, non-Hispanic/Latino). Average age 28. 38 applicants, 100% accepted, 28 enrolled. In 2013, 42 master's awarded. *Degree requirements:* For master's, comprehensive exam. *Entrance requirements:* For master's, GRE, minimum GPA of 3.0, 2 letters of professional reference, personal statement, resume, official transcripts. Additional exam requirements/recommendations for international students: Required—TOEFL (minimum score 550 paper-based; 79 iBT). *Application deadline:* For fall admission, 2/15 priority date for domestic students, 12/1 for international students; for spring admission, 7/1 for international students. Applications are processed on a rolling basis. Application fee: $50. Electronic applications accepted. *Expenses: Tuition,* state resident: full-time $6800; part-time $283 per credit hour. Tuition, nonresident: full-time $15,610; part-time $627 per credit hour. *Required fees:* $2944; $123 per credit hour. Tuition and fees vary according to program. *Financial support:* In 2013–14, 24 students received support, including 19 research assistantships (averaging $7,105 per year); career-related internships or fieldwork, Federal Work-Study, institutionally sponsored loans, scholarships/grants, and unspecified assistantships also available. Financial award application deadline: 3/1; financial award applicants required to submit FAFSA. *Faculty research:* Pedagogy of mathematics education. *Unit head:* Dr. Kristan Morrison, Coordinator, 540-831-7120, Fax: 540-831-5059, E-mail: kmorrison12@radford.edu. *Application contact:* Rebecca Conner, Director, Graduate Enrollment, 540-831-6296, Fax: 540-831-6061, E-mail: gradcollege@radford.edu.
Website: http://www.radford.edu/content/cehd/home/departments/STEL/programs/education-master.html.

Regent University, Graduate School, School of Education, Virginia Beach, VA 23464-9800. Offers adult education (Ed D, PhD); advanced educational leadership (Ed D, PhD); career switcher with licensure (M Ed), including alternative licensure; character education (Ed D, PhD); Christian education leadership (Ed D); Christian school administration (M Ed); curriculum and instruction (M Ed); distance education (Ed D, PhD); educational leadership (M Ed); educational leadership - special education (Ed S); educational psychology (Ed D); elementary education (M Ed); higher education (Ed D, PhD); higher education leadership and management (Ed D); K-12 school leadership (Ed D, PhD); leadership in mathematics education (M Ed); reading specialist (M Ed); special education (M Ed, Ed D, PhD); student affairs (M Ed); TESOL (M Ed), including adult education, PreK-12. *Accreditation:* Teacher Education Accreditation Council. Part-time and evening/weekend programs available. Postbaccalaureate distance learning degree programs offered (minimal on-campus study). *Faculty:* 25 full-time (12 women), 50 part-time/adjunct (31 women). *Students:* 100 full-time (78 women), 754 part-time (614 women); includes 225 minority (191 Black or African American, non-Hispanic/Latino; 1 American Indian or Alaska Native, non-Hispanic/Latino; 7 Asian, non-Hispanic/Latino; 26 Hispanic/Latino), 16 international. Average age 39. 487 applicants, 63% accepted, 233 enrolled. In 2013, 202 master's, 19 doctorates awarded. *Degree requirements:* For master's, thesis or alternative; for doctorate, comprehensive exam, thesis/dissertation. *Entrance requirements:* For master's, MAT, minimum undergraduate GPA of 2.75, writing sample, resume, recommendations, interview; for doctorate, GRE, writing sample, 3 years of relevant professional experience, master's-level paper, copies of published work, resume, transcripts, interview, recommendations. Additional exam requirements/recommendations for international students: Required—TOEFL (minimum score 577 paper-based). *Application deadline:* For fall admission, 4/1 priority date for domestic students; for spring admission, 10/15 priority date for domestic students. Applications are processed on a rolling basis. Application fee: $50. Electronic applications accepted. Tuition and fees vary according to course load and degree level. *Financial support:* Fellowships, career-related internships or fieldwork, scholarships/

grants, tuition waivers (full and partial), and unspecified assistantships available. Support available to part-time students. Financial award application deadline: 4/1; financial award applicants required to submit FAFSA. *Faculty research:* Character development and discipline for children, education leadership development, diversity in schools, classroom management, technology in education settings. *Unit head:* Dr. Alan Arroyo, Dean, 757-352-4261, Fax: 757-352-4318, E-mail: alanarr@regent.edu. *Application contact:* Matthew Chadwick, Director of Enrollment Support Services, 800-373-5504, Fax: 757-352-4381, E-mail: admissions@regent.edu.
Website: http://www.regent.edu/education/.

Rhode Island College, School of Graduate Studies, Feinstein School of Education and Human Development, Department of Educational Studies, Providence, RI 02908-1991. Offers advanced studies in teaching and learning (M Ed); English (MAT); French (MAT); history (MAT); math (MAT); secondary education (MAT); Spanish (MAT); teaching English as a second language (M Ed). *Accreditation:* NCATE. Part-time and evening/weekend programs available. *Faculty:* 10 full-time (6 women), 7 part-time/adjunct (all women). *Students:* 4 full-time (3 women), 61 part-time (54 women); includes 2 minority (both Hispanic/Latino). Average age 37. In 2013, 27 master's awarded. *Degree requirements:* For master's, capstone or comprehensive assessment. *Entrance requirements:* For master's, GRE or MAT (for most programs), minimum undergraduate GPA of 3.0; baccalaureate degree in English, French, history, math or Spanish; evaluation of content area knowledge; 3 letters of recommendation; interview. Additional exam requirements/recommendations for international students: Recommended—TOEFL (minimum score 550 paper-based; 79 iBT). *Application deadline:* For fall admission, 3/1 for domestic students; for spring admission, 11/1 for domestic students. Applications are processed on a rolling basis. Application fee: $50. *Expenses:* Tuition, state resident: full-time $8928; part-time $372 per credit hour. Tuition, nonresident: full-time $17,376; part-time $724 per credit hour. *Required fees:* $602; $22 per credit. $72 per term. *Financial support:* In 2013–14, 2 teaching assistantships with full tuition reimbursements (averaging $2,250 per year) were awarded; career-related internships or fieldwork, Federal Work-Study, scholarships/grants, health care benefits, and unspecified assistantships also available. Support available to part-time students. Financial award application deadline: 5/15; financial award applicants required to submit FAFSA. *Faculty research:* School administration, school/college articulation. *Unit head:* Dr. Paul Tiskus, Chair, 401-456-8170. *Application contact:* Graduate Studies, 401-456-8700.
Website: http://www.ric.edu/educationalStudies/.

Rider University, Department of Graduate Education, Leadership and Counseling, Teacher Certification Program, Lawrenceville, NJ 08648-3001. Offers business education (Certificate); elementary education (Certificate); English as a second language (Certificate); English education (Certificate); mathematics education (Certificate); preschool to grade 3 (Certificate); science education (Certificate); social studies education (Certificate); world languages (Certificate), including French, German, Spanish. Part-time programs available. *Degree requirements:* For Certificate, internship, professional portfolio. *Entrance requirements:* For degree, PRAXIS, resume. Additional exam requirements/recommendations for international students: Required—TOEFL (minimum score 550 paper-based). Electronic applications accepted. *Faculty research:* Conceptual foundations for optimal development of creativity; creative theory, cognitive processes in mathematics learning, teacher collaboration.

Rowan University, Graduate School, College of Liberal Arts and Sciences, Department of Mathematics, Program in Middle Grades Math Education, Glassboro, NJ 08028-1701. Offers CGS. *Faculty:* 1 (woman) full-time. *Students:* 27 part-time (24 women); includes 6 minority (4 Black or African American, non-Hispanic/Latino; 1 Hispanic/Latino; 1 Two or more races, non-Hispanic/Latino). Average age 42. 3 applicants, 100% accepted, 3 enrolled. *Application deadline:* For fall admission, 8/1 for domestic and international students; for spring admission, 11/1 for domestic and international students; for summer admission, 4/1 for domestic and international students. Application fee: $65. *Expenses: Tuition, area resident:* Part-time $638 per credit. Tuition, state resident: full-time $5742. *Required fees:* $142 per credit. Tuition and fees vary according to course level and program. *Unit head:* Dr. Horacio Sosa, Dean, College of Graduate and Continuing Education, 856-256-4747, Fax: 856-256-5638, E-mail: sosa@rowan.edu. *Application contact:* Admissions and Enrollment Services, 856-256-5145, Fax: 856-256-5637, E-mail: cgceadmissions@rowan.edu.

Rutgers, The State University of New Jersey, Camden, Graduate School of Arts and Sciences, Program in Mathematical Sciences, Camden, NJ 08102. Offers industrial mathematics (MBS); industrial/applied mathematics (MS); mathematical computer science (MS); pure mathematics (MS); teaching in mathematical sciences (MS). Part-time and evening/weekend programs available. *Degree requirements:* For master's, comprehensive exam, thesis optional, survey paper, 30 credits. *Entrance requirements:* For master's, GRE, BS/BA in math or related subject, 2 letters of recommendation. Additional exam requirements/recommendations for international students: Required—TOEFL (minimum score 550 paper-based), IELTS. Electronic applications accepted. *Faculty research:* Differential geometry, dynamical systems, vertex operator algebra, automorphic forms, CR-structures.

Rutgers, The State University of New Jersey, New Brunswick, Graduate School of Education, Department of Learning and Teaching, Program in Mathematics Education, Piscataway, NJ 08854-8097. Offers Ed M, Ed D. Part-time programs available. Terminal master's awarded for partial completion of doctoral program. *Degree requirements:* For master's, comprehensive exam (for some programs); for doctorate, thesis/dissertation, qualifying exam. *Entrance requirements:* For master's, GRE General Test, minimum GPA of 3.0; for doctorate, GRE General Test, minimum GPA of 3.5. Additional exam requirements/recommendations for international students: Required—TOEFL. Electronic applications accepted.

Rutgers, The State University of New Jersey, New Brunswick, Graduate School of Education, Doctoral Program in Education, New Brunswick, NJ 08901. Offers educational policy (PhD); educational psychology (PhD); literacy education (PhD); mathematics education (PhD). Part-time programs available. *Degree requirements:* For doctorate, thesis/dissertation, qualifying exam. *Entrance requirements:* For doctorate, GRE General Test, GRE Subject Test (mathematics education). Additional exam requirements/recommendations for international students: Required—TOEFL (minimum score 575 paper-based; 83 iBT). Electronic applications accepted. *Faculty research:* Literacy education, math education, educational psychology, educational policy, learning sciences.

Sage Graduate School, Esteves School of Education, Program in Teaching, Troy, NY 12180-4115. Offers art education (MAT); English (MAT); mathematics (MAT); social studies (MAT). *Accreditation:* NASAD. Part-time and evening/weekend programs available. *Faculty:* 10 full-time (6 women), 6 part-time/adjunct (4 women). *Students:* 1 (woman) full-time, 12 part-time (10 women); includes 2 minority (1 Hispanic/Latino; 1 Two or more races, non-Hispanic/Latino). Average age 26. 13 applicants, 31% accepted, 1 enrolled. In 2013, 18 master's awarded. *Entrance requirements:* For master's, assessment of writing skills, minimum undergraduate GPA of 2.75 overall, 3.0 in content area; current resume; 2 letters of recommendation. Additional exam requirements/recommendations for international students: Required—TOEFL (minimum score 550 paper-based). *Application deadline:* For fall admission, 8/1 for domestic

students. Applications are processed on a rolling basis. Application fee: $40. *Expenses: Tuition:* Full-time $11,880; part-time $660 per credit hour. *Financial support:* Fellowships, research assistantships, Federal Work-Study, scholarships/grants, and unspecified assistantships available. Support available to part-time students. Financial award application deadline: 3/1; financial award applicants required to submit FAFSA. *Unit head:* Dr. Lori Quigley, Dean, Esteves School of Education, 518-244-2326, Fax: 518-244-4571, E-mail: l.quigley@sage.edu. *Application contact:* Kelly Jones, Director, 518-244-2433, Fax: 518-244-6880, E-mail: jonesk4@sage.edu.

St. John Fisher College, School of Arts and Sciences, Mathematics/Science/Technology Education Program, Rochester, NY 14618-3597. Offers MS. Part-time and evening/weekend programs available. *Faculty:* 3 full-time (0 women), 3 part-time/adjunct (1 woman). *Students:* 6 full-time (4 women), 21 part-time (14 women); includes 4 minority (1 American Indian or Alaska Native, non-Hispanic/Latino; 1 Asian, non-Hispanic/Latino; 1 Hispanic/Latino; 1 Two or more races, non-Hispanic/Latino). Average age 30. 10 applicants, 70% accepted, 6 enrolled. In 2013, 15 master's awarded. *Degree requirements:* For master's, thesis, capstone experience. *Entrance requirements:* For master's, 2 letters of recommendation, personal statement, current resume, interview, teaching certification. Additional exam requirements/recommendations for international students: Required—TOEFL (minimum score 575 paper-based; 80 iBT). *Application deadline:* Applications are processed on a rolling basis. Application fee: $30. Electronic applications accepted. *Expenses: Tuition:* Part-time $795 per credit hour. *Required fees:* $10 per credit hour. Tuition and fees vary according to course load, degree level and program. *Financial support:* In 2013–14, 2 students received support. Scholarships/grants available. Financial award applicants required to submit FAFSA. *Faculty research:* Mathematics education, science and technology education. *Unit head:* Dr. Bernard Ricca, Graduate Director, 585-899-3866, E-mail: bricca@sjfc.edu. *Application contact:* Jose Perales, Director of Graduate Admissions, 585-385-8067, E-mail: jperales@sjfc.edu.

Saint Peter's University, Graduate Programs in Education, Jersey City, NJ 07306-5997. Offers director of school counseling services (Certificate); educational leadership (MA Ed, Ed D); higher education (Ed D); middle school mathematics (Certificate); professional/associate counselor (Certificate); reading (MA Ed); school business administrator (Certificate); school counseling (MA, Certificate); special education (MA Ed, Certificate), including applied behavioral analysis (MA Ed), literacy (MA Ed), teacher of students with disabilities (Certificate); teaching (MA Ed, Certificate), including 6-8 middle school education, K-12 secondary education, K-5 elementary education. *Accreditation:* Teacher Education Accreditation Council. Part-time and evening/weekend programs available. *Degree requirements:* For master's, comprehensive exam; for doctorate, comprehensive exam, thesis/dissertation. *Entrance requirements:* For master's and doctorate, GRE or MAT. Additional exam requirements/recommendations for international students: Required—TOEFL. Electronic applications accepted.

Salem State University, School of Graduate Studies, Program in Middle School Education, Salem, MA 01970-5353. Offers humanities (M Ed); math/science (MAT). Part-time and evening/weekend programs available. *Students:* 1 (woman) full-time, 9 part-time (6 women). 1 applicant, 100% accepted, 1 enrolled. In 2013, 9 master's awarded. *Entrance requirements:* For master's, GRE or MAT. Additional exam requirements/recommendations for international students: Required—TOEFL (minimum score 550 paper-based; 80 iBT) or IELTS (minimum score 5.5). *Application deadline:* For fall admission, 5/1 for domestic students; for spring admission, 10/1 for domestic students. Applications are processed on a rolling basis. Application fee: $50. *Financial support:* Career-related internships or fieldwork, Federal Work-Study, scholarships/grants, and unspecified assistantships available. Support available to part-time students. Financial award application deadline: 5/1; financial award applicants required to submit FAFSA. *Application contact:* Dr. Lee A. Brossoit, Assistant Dean of Graduate Admissions, 978-542-6675, Fax: 978-542-7215, E-mail: lbrossoit@salemstate.edu. Website: http://www.salemstate.edu/academics/schools/12610.php.

Salem State University, School of Graduate Studies, Program in Middle School Math, Salem, MA 01970-5353. Offers MAT. Part-time and evening/weekend programs available. *Students:* 1 full-time (0 women), 31 part-time (20 women); includes 1 minority (Two or more races, non-Hispanic/Latino). 10 applicants, 100% accepted, 8 enrolled. In 2013, 11 master's awarded. *Entrance requirements:* For master's, GRE or MAT. Additional exam requirements/recommendations for international students: Required—TOEFL (minimum score 550 paper-based; 80 iBT) or IELTS (minimum score 5.5). *Application deadline:* For fall admission, 5/1 for domestic students; for spring admission, 10/1 for domestic students. Applications are processed on a rolling basis. Application fee: $50. *Financial support:* Career-related internships or fieldwork, Federal Work-Study, scholarships/grants, and unspecified assistantships available. Support available to part-time students. Financial award application deadline: 5/1; financial award applicants required to submit FAFSA. *Application contact:* Dr. Lee A. Brossoit, Assistant Dean of Graduate Admissions, 978-542-6675, Fax: 978-542-7215, E-mail: lbrossoit@salemstate.edu. Website: http://www.salemstate.edu/academics/schools/5616.php.

San Diego State University, Graduate and Research Affairs, College of Sciences, Department of Mathematics and Statistics, San Diego, CA 92182. Offers applied mathematics (MS); mathematics (MA); mathematics and science education (PhD); statistics (MS). PhD offered jointly wtih University of California, San Diego. Part-time programs available. *Degree requirements:* For doctorate, thesis/dissertation. *Entrance requirements:* For master's, GRE General Test; for doctorate, GRE, minimum GPA of 3.25 in last 30 undergraduate semester units, minimum graduate GPA of 3.5, MSE recommendation form, 3 letters of recommendation. Additional exam requirements/recommendations for international students: Required—TOEFL. Electronic applications accepted. *Faculty research:* Teacher education in mathematics.

San Francisco State University, Division of Graduate Studies, College of Education, Department of Elementary Education, Program in Mathematics Education, San Francisco, CA 94132-1722. Offers MA. *Accreditation:* NCATE. *Unit head:* Dr. Debra Luna, Chair, 415-338-1562, E-mail: dluna@sfsu.edu. *Application contact:* Dr. Maria Zavala, MA Program Coordinator, 415-405-0465, E-mail: mza@sfsu.edu. Website: http://coe.sfsu.edu/eed/masters-arts-mathematics.

San Jose State University, Graduate Studies and Research, College of Science, Department of Mathematics, San Jose, CA 95192-0001. Offers applied mathematics (MS); mathematics (MA, MS); mathematics education (MA); statistics (MA). Part-time and evening/weekend programs available. *Degree requirements:* For master's, comprehensive exam, thesis (for some programs). *Entrance requirements:* For master's, GRE Subject Test. Electronic applications accepted. *Faculty research:* Artificial intelligence, algorithms, numerical analysis, software database, number theory.

Shippensburg University of Pennsylvania, School of Graduate Studies, College of Education and Human Services, Department of Teacher Education, Shippensburg, PA 17257-2299. Offers curriculum and instruction (M Ed), including biology, early childhood education, elementary education, geography/earth science, history, mathematics, middle level education, modern languages; reading (M Ed). *Accreditation:* NCATE. Part-time and evening/weekend programs available. *Faculty:* 13 full-time (9 women), 2 part-time/adjunct (both women). *Students:* 6 full-time (all women), 72 part-time (61 women); includes 5 minority (1 Black or African American, non-Hispanic/Latino; 1 Asian, non-Hispanic/Latino; 2 Hispanic/Latino; 1 Two or more races, non-Hispanic/Latino), 1 international. Average age 30. 55 applicants, 60% accepted, 24 enrolled. In 2013, 63 master's awarded. *Degree requirements:* For master's, comprehensive exam (for some programs), thesis optional, practicum or internship; capstone seminar (for some programs). *Entrance requirements:* For master's, MAT or GRE (if GPA less than 2.75), interview, 3 letters of reference, questionnaire of teaching background and future goals. Additional exam requirements/recommendations for international students: Required—TOEFL (minimum score 580 paper-based); Recommended—IELTS (minimum score 6). *Application deadline:* For fall admission, 4/1 priority date for domestic students, 4/30 for international students; for spring admission, 9/1 priority date for domestic students, 9/30 for international students. Applications are processed on a rolling basis. Application fee: $45. Electronic applications accepted. *Expenses: Tuition, area resident:* Part-time $442 per credit. Tuition, state resident: part-time $442 per credit. Tuition, nonresident: part-time $663 per credit. *Required fees:* $127 per credit. *Financial support:* In 2013–14, 4 research assistantships with full tuition reimbursements (averaging $5,000 per year) were awarded; career-related internships or fieldwork, scholarships/grants, unspecified assistantships, and resident hall director and student payroll positions also available. Support available to part-time students. Financial award application deadline: 3/1; financial award applicants required to submit FAFSA. *Unit head:* Dr. Christine A. Royce, Chairperson, 717-477-1688, Fax: 717-477-4046, E-mail: caroyc@ship.edu. *Application contact:* Jeremy R. Goshorn, Assistant Dean of Graduate Admissions, 717-477-1231, Fax: 717-477-4016, E-mail: jrgoshorn@ship.edu. Website: http://www.ship.edu/teacher/.

Simon Fraser University, Office of Graduate Studies, Faculty of Education, Program in Mathematics Education, Burnaby, BC V5A 1S6, Canada. Offers mathematics education (PhD); secondary mathematics education (M Ed, M Sc). Part-time and evening/weekend programs available. *Degree requirements:* For master's, comprehensive exam (for some programs), thesis; for doctorate, comprehensive exam, thesis/dissertation. *Entrance requirements:* For master's, minimum GPA of 3.0 (on scale of 4.33), or 3.33 based on last 60 credits of undergraduate courses; for doctorate, minimum GPA of 3.5 (on scale of 4.33). Additional exam requirements/recommendations for international students: Recommended—TOEFL (minimum score 580 paper-based; 93 iBT), IELTS (minimum score 7), TWE (minimum score 5). Electronic applications accepted. *Expenses: Tuition, area resident:* Full-time $5084 Canadian dollars. *Required fees:* $840 Canadian dollars. *Faculty research:* Historical and psychological development of mathematical thinking, math anxiety and concept formation, mathematical problem solving, numeracy, instructional design, cognition in mathematics thinking and learning, undergraduate math education.

Slippery Rock University of Pennsylvania, Graduate Studies (Recruitment), College of Education, Department of Elementary Education and Early Childhood, Slippery Rock, PA 16057-1383. Offers elementary education (M Ed), including K-12 reading specialist, math/science K-8, reading, reading specialist-instructional coach; literacy. *Accreditation:* NCATE. Part-time and evening/weekend programs available. Postbaccalaureate distance learning degree programs offered (no on-campus study). *Faculty:* 2 full-time (both women). *Students:* 4 full-time (all women), 23 part-time (all women); includes 1 minority (Black or African American, non-Hispanic/Latino). Average age 28. 47 applicants, 79% accepted, 11 enrolled. In 2013, 36 master's awarded. *Entrance requirements:* For master's, GRE General Test, MAT, minimum GPA of 3.0, resume, teaching certification, letters of recommendation, transcripts (depending on program). Additional exam requirements/recommendations for international students: Required—TOEFL (minimum score 550 paper-based; 80 iBT). *Application deadline:* For fall admission, 3/1 priority date for domestic students, 5/1 priority date for international students; for spring admission, 10/1 priority date for domestic students, 9/1 priority date for international students. Applications are processed on a rolling basis. Application fee: $25 ($30 for international students). Electronic applications accepted. *Expenses:* Tuition, state resident: full-time $7956; part-time $442 per credit. Tuition, nonresident: full-time $11,934; part-time $663 per credit. *Required fees:* $2896; $148 per credit. Tuition and fees vary according to degree level and program. *Financial support:* Career-related internships or fieldwork, Federal Work-Study, institutionally sponsored loans, scholarships/grants, tuition waivers (partial), and unspecified assistantships available. Support available to part-time students. Financial award application deadline: 5/1; financial award applicants required to submit FAFSA. *Unit head:* Dr. Suzanne Rose, Graduate Coordinator, 724-738-2042, Fax: 724-738-2779, E-mail: suzanne.rose@sru.edu. *Application contact:* Brandi Weber-Mortimer, Director of Graduate Admissions, 724-738-2051, Fax: 724-738-2146, E-mail: graduate.admissions@sru.edu.

Slippery Rock University of Pennsylvania, Graduate Studies (Recruitment), College of Education, Department of Secondary Education/Foundations of Education, Slippery Rock, PA 16057-1383. Offers educational leadership (M Ed); secondary education (M Ed), including English, math/science, social studies/history. *Accreditation:* NCATE. Part-time and evening/weekend programs available. *Faculty:* 12 full-time (5 women). *Students:* 48 full-time (24 women), 10 part-time (6 women). Average age 27. 50 applicants, 84% accepted, 29 enrolled. In 2013, 28 master's awarded. *Degree requirements:* For master's, comprehensive exam, thesis (for some programs). *Entrance requirements:* For master's, GRE General Test, MAT, minimum GPA of 2.8 or 3.0 (depending on program); copy of teaching certification and two letters of recommendation (for some programs). Additional exam requirements/recommendations for international students: Required—TOEFL (minimum score 550 paper-based; 80 iBT). *Application deadline:* For fall admission, 3/1 priority date for domestic students, 5/1 priority date for international students; for spring admission, 10/1 priority date for domestic students, 9/1 priority date for international students. Applications are processed on a rolling basis. Application fee: $25 ($30 for international students). Electronic applications accepted. *Expenses:* Tuition, state resident: full-time $7956; part-time $442 per credit. Tuition, nonresident: full-time $11,934; part-time $663 per credit. *Required fees:* $2896; $148 per credit. Tuition and fees vary according to degree level and program. *Financial support:* Career-related internships or fieldwork, Federal Work-Study, institutionally sponsored loans, scholarships/grants, tuition waivers (partial), and unspecified assistantships available. Support available to part-time students. Financial award application deadline: 5/1; financial award applicants required to submit FAFSA. *Unit head:* Dr. Jeffrey Lehman, Graduate Coordinator, 724-738-2311, Fax: 724-738-4987, E-mail: jeffrey.lehman@sru.edu. *Application contact:* Brandi Weber-Mortimer, Interim Director of Graduate Studies, 724-738-2051, Fax: 724-738-2146, E-mail: graduate.admissions@sru.edu.

Smith College, Graduate and Special Programs, Department of Education and Child Study, Program in Secondary Education, Northampton, MA 01063. Offers biological sciences education (MAT); chemistry education (MAT); English education (MAT); French education (MAT); geology education (MAT); government education (MAT); history education (MAT); mathematics education (MAT); physics education (MAT); Spanish education (MAT). Part-time programs available. *Faculty:* 6 full-time (4 women), 3 part-time/adjunct (2 women). *Students:* 4 full-time (3 women), 1 (woman) part-time, 2 international. Average age 33. 12 applicants, 92% accepted, 4 enrolled. In 2013, 6 master's awarded. *Entrance requirements:* Additional exam requirements/recommendations for international students: Required—TOEFL (minimum score 595 paper-based; 97 iBT). *Application deadline:* For fall admission, 4/1 for domestic

students, 1/15 priority date for international students; for spring admission, 12/1 for domestic students. Application fee: $60. *Expenses: Tuition:* Full-time $32,160; part-time $1340 per credit. *Financial support:* In 2013–14, 5 students received support, including 2 fellowships with full tuition reimbursements available; career-related internships or fieldwork, institutionally sponsored loans, and scholarships/grants also available. Support available to part-time students. Financial award application deadline: 1/15; financial award applicants required to submit CSS PROFILE or FAFSA. *Unit head:* Rosetta Cohen, Graduate Student Advisor, 413-585-3266, E-mail: rcohen@smith.edu. *Application contact:* Ruth Morgan, Administrative Assistant, 413-585-3050, Fax: 413-585-3054, E-mail: gradstdy@smith.edu.
Website: http://www.smith.edu/educ/.

Smith College, Graduate and Special Programs, Department of Mathematics, Northampton, MA 01063. Offers MAT. Part-time programs available. *Faculty:* 12 full-time (5 women). *Students:* 1 (woman) full-time, 1 (woman) part-time. Average age 45. 2 applicants, 100% accepted, 1 enrolled. *Entrance requirements:* Additional exam requirements/recommendations for international students: Required—TOEFL (minimum score 595 paper-based; 97 iBT). *Application deadline:* For fall admission, 4/1 for domestic students, 1/15 for international students; for spring admission, 12/1 for domestic students. Application fee: $60. *Expenses: Tuition:* Full-time $32,160; part-time $1340 per credit. *Financial support:* In 2013–14, 2 students received support. Career-related internships or fieldwork, institutionally sponsored loans, and scholarships/grants available. Support available to part-time students. Financial award application deadline: 1/15. *Unit head:* Mary Murphy, Graduate Adviser, 413-585-3876, E-mail: memurphy@smith.edu. *Application contact:* Ruth Morgan, Administrative Assistant, 413-585-3050, Fax: 413-585-3054, E-mail: gradstdy@smith.edu.
Website: http://www.math.smith.edu/.

South Carolina State University, School of Graduate and Professional Studies, Department of Education, Orangeburg, SC 29117-0001. Offers early childhood and special education (M Ed); early childhood education (MAT); elementary education (M Ed, MAT); general science (MAT); mathematics (MAT); secondary education (M Ed), including biology education, business education, counselor education, English education, home economics education, industrial education, mathematics education, science education, social studies education; special education (M Ed), including emotionally handicapped, learning disabilities, mentally handicapped. *Accreditation:* NCATE. Part-time and evening/weekend programs available. *Faculty:* 9 full-time (3 women), 4 part-time/adjunct (3 women). *Students:* 32 full-time (26 women), 33 part-time (26 women); includes 63 minority (61 Black or African American, non-Hispanic/Latino; 2 Asian, non-Hispanic/Latino). Average age 31. 21 applicants, 100% accepted, 21 enrolled. In 2013, 15 master's awarded. *Degree requirements:* For master's, thesis optional, departmental qualifying exam. *Entrance requirements:* For master's, GRE General Test, NTE, interview, teaching certificate. *Application deadline:* For fall admission, 6/15 priority date for domestic students, 6/15 for international students; for spring admission, 11/1 for domestic and international students. Applications are processed on a rolling basis. Application fee: $25. Electronic applications accepted. *Expenses:* Tuition, state resident: full-time $8906; part-time $543 per credit hour. Tuition, nonresident: full-time $18,040; part-time $1051 per credit hour. *Financial support:* Fellowships, career-related internships or fieldwork, Federal Work-Study, and institutionally sponsored loans available. Financial award application deadline: 6/1. *Faculty research:* Critical thinking, child abuse, stress, test-taking skills, conflict resolution, mainstreaming. *Unit head:* Dr. Margaret Evelyn Fields, Interim Chair, 803-536-7098, Fax: 803-516-4568, E-mail: efields@scsu.edu. *Application contact:* Curtis Foskey, Coordinator of Graduate Studies, 803-536-8419, Fax: 803-536-8812, E-mail: cfoskey@scsu.edu.

Southeastern Oklahoma State University, School of Education, Durant, OK 74701-0609. Offers math specialist (M Ed); reading specialist (M Ed); school administration (M Ed); school counseling (M Ed). *Accreditation:* NCATE. Part-time and evening/weekend programs available. *Degree requirements:* For master's, comprehensive exam, thesis optional, portfolio (M Ed). *Entrance requirements:* For master's, GRE General Test (for school counseling), minimum GPA of 3.0 in last 60 hours or 2.75 overall. Additional exam requirements/recommendations for international students: Required—TOEFL (minimum score 550 paper-based; 79 iBT). Electronic applications accepted.

Southern Illinois University Edwardsville, Graduate School, College of Arts and Sciences, Department of Mathematics and Statistics, Program in Postsecondary Mathematics Education, Edwardsville, IL 62026. Offers MS. Part-time programs available. *Students:* 4 part-time (0 women). 2 applicants, 50% accepted. In 2013, 2 master's awarded. *Degree requirements:* For master's, thesis (for some programs), special project. *Entrance requirements:* Additional exam requirements/recommendations for international students: Required—TOEFL (minimum score 550 paper-based, 79 iBT), IELTS (minimum score 6.5), Michigan Test of English Language Proficiency or PTE. *Application deadline:* For fall admission, 7/18 for domestic students, 6/1 for international students; for spring admission, 12/12 for domestic students, 10/1 for international students; for summer admission, 4/24 for domestic students, 3/1 for international students. Applications are processed on a rolling basis. Application fee: $30. Electronic applications accepted. *Expenses:* Tuition, state resident: full-time $3551. Tuition, nonresident: full-time $8378. *Financial support:* Institutionally sponsored loans, scholarships/grants, and unspecified assistantships available. Financial award application deadline: 3/1; financial award applicants required to submit FAFSA. *Unit head:* Dr. Myung Sin Song, Program Director, 618-650-2580, E-mail: msong@siue.edu. *Application contact:* Melissa K. Mace, Assistant Director of Graduate and International Recruitment, 618-650-2756, Fax: 618-650-3618, E-mail: mmace@siue.edu.
Website: http://www.siue.edu/artsandsciences/math/.

Southern University and Agricultural and Mechanical College, Graduate School, Department of Science/Mathematics Education, Baton Rouge, LA 70813. Offers PhD. *Accreditation:* NCATE. *Degree requirements:* For doctorate, thesis/dissertation. *Entrance requirements:* For doctorate, GRE General Test. Additional exam requirements/recommendations for international students: Required—TOEFL (minimum score 525 paper-based). *Faculty research:* Performance assessment in science/mathematics education, equity in science/mathematics education, technology and distance learning, science/mathematics concept formation, cognitive themes, problem solving in science/mathematics education.

Southwestern Oklahoma State University, College of Arts and Sciences, Department of Mathematics, Weatherford, OK 73096-3098. Offers M Ed. Part-time programs available. *Degree requirements:* For master's, exam. *Entrance requirements:* For master's, GRE General Test or minimum undergraduate GPA of 3.0. Additional exam requirements/recommendations for international students: Required—TOEFL.

Southwest Minnesota State University, Department of Education, Marshall, MN 56258. Offers ESL (MS); math (MS); reading (MS); special education (MS), including developmental disabilities, early childhood education, emotional behavioral disorders, learning disabilities; teaching, learning and leadership (MS). Part-time and evening/weekend programs available. Postbaccalaureate distance learning degree programs offered (no on-campus study). *Entrance requirements:* Additional exam requirements/recommendations for international students: Required—TOEFL or IELTS; Recommended—TOEFL (minimum score 550 paper-based; 80 iBT), IELTS.

State University of New York at New Paltz, Graduate School, School of Education, Department of Elementary Education, New Paltz, NY 12561. Offers childhood education 1-6 (MS Ed, MST), including childhood education 1-6 (MST), early childhood B-2 (MS Ed), mathematics, science and technology (MS Ed), reading/literacy (MS Ed); literacy education 5-12 (MS Ed); literacy education and childhood special education (MS Ed); literacy education B-6 (MS Ed). *Accreditation:* NCATE. Part-time and evening/weekend programs available. *Faculty:* 11 full-time (10 women), 9 part-time/adjunct (8 women). *Students:* 51 full-time (47 women), 128 part-time (117 women); includes 13 minority (2 Black or African American, non-Hispanic/Latino; 11 Hispanic/Latino). Average age 27. 103 applicants, 89% accepted, 57 enrolled. In 2013, 96 master's awarded. *Degree requirements:* For master's, comprehensive exam (for some programs), portfolio. *Entrance requirements:* For master's, GRE or MAT (for MST), minimum GPA of 3.0 (3.2 for literacy and special education), New York state teaching certificate (for MS Ed). Additional exam requirements/recommendations for international students: Required—TOEFL (minimum score 550 paper-based; 80 iBT), IELTS (minimum score 6.5). *Application deadline:* For fall admission, 4/1 for domestic and international students; for spring admission, 11/15 for domestic and international students. Application fee: $50. Electronic applications accepted. *Expenses:* Tuition, state resident: full-time $9870; part-time $411 per credit. Tuition, nonresident: full-time $18,350; part-time $765 per credit. *Required fees:* $1213. Tuition and fees vary according to program. *Financial support:* Application deadline: 8/1. *Faculty research:* Multi-sensory teaching methods, volunteer tutoring programs for struggling readers, school readiness and transition, math/science/technology, university-school partnerships. *Unit head:* Dr. Andrea Noel, Chair, 845-257-2860, E-mail: noela@newpaltz.edu. *Application contact:* Caroline Murphy, Graduate Admissions Advisor, 845-257-3285, Fax: 845-257-3284, E-mail: gradschool@newpaltz.edu.
Website: http://www.newpaltz.edu/elementaryed/.

State University of New York at Plattsburgh, Division of Education, Health, and Human Services, Program in Teacher Education: Adolescence, Plattsburgh, NY 12901-2681. Offers adolescence education (MST); biology 7-12 (MST); chemistry 7-12 (MST); earth science 7-12 (MST); English 7-12 (MST); French 7-12 (MST); mathematics 7-12 (MST); physics 7-12 (MST); social studies 7-12 (MST); Spanish 7-12 (MST). *Accreditation:* Teacher Education Accreditation Council. Part-time and evening/weekend programs available. *Students:* 75 full-time (47 women), 5 part-time (3 women); includes 10 minority (1 Black or African American, non-Hispanic/Latino; 4 Asian, non-Hispanic/Latino; 5 Hispanic/Latino), 1 international. Average age 25. *Entrance requirements:* For master's, minimum GPA of 2.75. Additional exam requirements/recommendations for international students: Required—TOEFL. *Application deadline:* For fall admission, 2/15 priority date for domestic students. Applications are processed on a rolling basis. Application fee: $75. *Financial support:* Application deadline: 4/15; applicants required to submit FAFSA. *Unit head:* Dr. Robert Ackland, Coordinator, 518-564-5131, E-mail: acklanrt@plattsburgh.edu. *Application contact:* Betsy Kane, Director, Graduate Admissions, 518-564-4723, Fax: 518-564-4722, E-mail: bkane002@plattsburgh.edu.

State University of New York College at Cortland, Graduate Studies, School of Arts and Sciences, Programs in Adolescence Education, Cortland, NY 13045. Offers biology (MAT, MS Ed); chemistry (MAT, MS Ed); earth science (MAT, MS Ed); English (MAT, MS Ed); mathematics (MAT, MS Ed); physics (MAT, MS Ed); physics and mathematics (MS Ed); social studies (MS Ed), including geography, history. *Accreditation:* NCATE. Part-time and evening/weekend programs available. *Degree requirements:* For master's, one foreign language, comprehensive exam (for some programs), thesis (for some programs). *Entrance requirements:* For master's, GRE General Test. *Expenses:* Tuition, state resident: full-time $9870; part-time $411 per credit hour. Tuition, nonresident: full-time $18,350; part-time $765 per credit hour. *Required fees:* $1458; $65 per credit hour.

State University of New York College at Old Westbury, Program in Adolescent Education, Old Westbury, NY 11568-0210. Offers biology (MAT, MS); chemistry (MAT, MS); English language arts (MAT, MS); math (MAT, MS); social studies (MAT, MS); Spanish (MAT, MS). Part-time and evening/weekend programs available. *Faculty:* 19 full-time (11 women), 6 part-time/adjunct (1 woman). *Students:* 33 full-time (20 women), 33 part-time (19 women); includes 16 minority (2 Black or African American, non-Hispanic/Latino; 4 Asian, non-Hispanic/Latino; 9 Hispanic/Latino; 1 Two or more races, non-Hispanic/Latino). 25 applicants, 84% accepted, 19 enrolled. In 2013, 29 master's awarded. *Entrance requirements:* For master's, Liberal Arts and Sciences Test, undergraduate degree with at least 30 semester hours of appropriate coursework as defined by the respective discipline; minimum cumulative undergraduate GPA of 3.0; two letters of recommendation (one from an academic source); essay. Additional exam requirements/recommendations for international students: Required—TOEFL (minimum score 550 paper-based); Recommended—IELTS. *Expenses:* Tuition, state resident: full-time $9370; part-time $390 per credit. Tuition, nonresident: full-time $16,680; part-time $695 per credit. *Required fees:* $45.85 per credit. $47 per term. *Application contact:* Philip D'Angelo, Graduate Admissions Office, 516-876-3073, E-mail: enroll@oldwestbury.edu.

State University of New York College at Potsdam, School of Education and Professional Studies, Program in Secondary Education, Potsdam, NY 13676. Offers English education (MST); mathematics education (MST); science education (MST), including biology, chemistry, earth science, physics; social studies education (MST). *Accreditation:* NCATE. *Degree requirements:* For master's, culminating experience. *Entrance requirements:* For master's, minimum GPA of 2.75 in last 60 hours of course work (3.0 for English program). Additional exam requirements/recommendations for international students: Required—TOEFL (minimum score 550 paper-based; 80 iBT), IELTS (minimum score 6). Electronic applications accepted.

Stephen F. Austin State University, Graduate School, College of Sciences and Mathematics, Department of Mathematics and Statistics, Nacogdoches, TX 75962. Offers mathematics (MS); mathematics education (MS); statistics (MS). *Degree requirements:* For master's, comprehensive exam, thesis optional. *Entrance requirements:* For master's, GRE General Test, minimum GPA of 2.8 in last 60 hours, 2.5 overall. Additional exam requirements/recommendations for international students: Required—TOEFL. *Faculty research:* Kernel type estimators, fractal mappings, spline curve fitting, robust regression continua theory.

Stony Brook University, State University of New York, School of Professional Development, Stony Brook, NY 11794. Offers biology (MAT); chemistry (MAT); coaching (Graduate Certificate); earth science (MAT); educational computing (Graduate Certificate); educational leadership (Advanced Certificate); English (MAT); environmental management (Graduate Certificate); French (MAT); German (MAT); higher education administration (MA, Certificate); human resource management (MS, Graduate Certificate); industrial management (Graduate Certificate); information systems management (Graduate Certificate); Italian (MAT); liberal studies (MA); mathematics (MAT); operations research (Graduate Certificate); physics (MAT); school district business leadership (Advanced Certificate); social science and the professions (MPS), including environmental management, human resource management; social studies (MAT); Spanish (MAT). Part-time and evening/weekend programs available.

Postbaccalaureate distance learning degree programs offered. *Faculty:* 2 full-time (1 woman), 70 part-time/adjunct (30 women). *Students:* 241 full-time (135 women), 954 part-time (673 women); includes 209 minority (65 Black or African American, non-Hispanic/Latino; 2 American Indian or Alaska Native, non-Hispanic/Latino; 32 Asian, non-Hispanic/Latino; 104 Hispanic/Latino; 6 Two or more races, non-Hispanic/Latino), 7 international. Average age 28. 353 applicants, 92% accepted, 248 enrolled. In 2013, 312 master's, 131 other advanced degrees awarded. *Degree requirements:* For master's, one foreign language, thesis or alternative. *Application deadline:* For fall admission, 1/15 for domestic students; for spring admission, 10/1 for domestic students. Applications are processed on a rolling basis. Application fee: $100. *Expenses:* Tuition, state resident: full-time $9870; part-time $411 per credit. Tuition, nonresident: full-time $18,350; part-time $765 per credit. *Financial support:* Fellowships, research assistantships, teaching assistantships, and career-related internships or fieldwork available. Support available to part-time students. *Unit head:* Dr. Thomas Sexton, Interim Dean, 631-632-7181, Fax: 631-632-9046, E-mail: thomas.sexton@stonybrook.edu. *Application contact:* 631-632-7050 Ext. 1, E-mail: spd@stonybrook.edu.
Website: http://www.stonybrook.edu/spd/.

Syracuse University, School of Education, Program in Mathematics Education, Syracuse, NY 13244. Offers mathematics education (PhD); teacher preparation 7-12 (MS). Part-time programs available. *Students:* 9 full-time (5 women), 3 part-time (2 women); includes 3 minority (2 Black or African American, non-Hispanic/Latino; 1 Hispanic/Latino), 4 international. Average age 32. 12 applicants, 67% accepted, 4 enrolled. In 2013, 1 master's, 1 doctorate awarded. *Degree requirements:* For master's, thesis or alternative; for doctorate, comprehensive exam, thesis/dissertation. *Entrance requirements:* For master's, GRE (for assistantship applicants); for doctorate, GRE, MS. Additional exam requirements/recommendations for international students: Required—TOEFL (minimum score 100 iBT). *Application deadline:* For fall admission, 1/15 priority date for domestic and international students; for spring admission, 10/15 for domestic students, 10/15 priority date for international students. Applications are processed on a rolling basis. Application fee: $75. Electronic applications accepted. *Financial support:* Fellowships with full tuition reimbursements and teaching assistantships with full and partial tuition reimbursements available. Financial award application deadline: 1/1. *Unit head:* Dr. Joanna Masingila, Chair, 315-443-1483, E-mail: jomasing@syr.edu. *Application contact:* Laurie Deyo, Graduate Recruiter, School of Education, 315-443-2505, E-mail: e-gradrcrt@syr.edu.
Website: http://soe.syr.edu/.

Teachers College, Columbia University, Graduate Faculty of Education, Department of Math, Science and Technology, Program in Mathematics Education, New York, NY 10027. Offers Ed M, MA, MS, Ed D, Ed DCT, PhD. *Accreditation:* NCATE. *Faculty:* 5 full-time, 5 part-time/adjunct. *Students:* 59 full-time (32 women), 106 part-time (60 women); includes 43 minority (20 Black or African American, non-Hispanic/Latino; 3 Asian, non-Hispanic/Latino; 15 Hispanic/Latino; 5 Two or more races, non-Hispanic/Latino), 21 international. Average age 32. 85 applicants, 84% accepted, 36 enrolled. In 2013, 32 master's, 14 doctorates awarded. *Degree requirements:* For doctorate, thesis/dissertation. *Entrance requirements:* For master's, undergraduate major or minor in mathematics; for doctorate, MA in mathematics or mathematics education. *Application deadline:* For fall admission, 1/15 for domestic students. Applications are processed on a rolling basis. Application fee: $65. Electronic applications accepted. *Financial support:* Career-related internships or fieldwork, Federal Work-Study, institutionally sponsored loans, and tuition waivers (full and partial) available. Support available to part-time students. Financial award applicants required to submit FAFSA. *Faculty research:* Problem solving, curriculum development, international education, history of mathematics. *Unit head:* Prof. Bruce R. Vogeli, Program Coordinator, 212-678-3840, E-mail: brv2@columbia.edu. *Application contact:* Deanna Ghozati, Assistant Director of Admission, 212-678-4018, Fax: 212-678-4171, E-mail: ghozati@tc.edu.
Website: http://www.tc.edu/mst/mathed/.

Temple University, College of Education, Department of Curriculum, Instruction, and Technology in Education, Philadelphia, PA 19122-6096. Offers career and technical education (Ed M), including business, computing, and information technology, industrial education, marketing education; middle grades education (Ed M), including math and language arts, math and science, science and language arts; secondary education (Ed M), including English, math, social studies; teaching English to speakers of other languages (MS Ed); urban education (Ed M). Part-time and evening/weekend programs available. *Students:* 66 full-time (48 women), 120 part-time (67 women); includes 50 minority (35 Black or African American, non-Hispanic/Latino; 1 American Indian or Alaska Native, non-Hispanic/Latino; 2 Asian, non-Hispanic/Latino; 7 Hispanic/Latino; 5 Two or more races, non-Hispanic/Latino), 1 international. 229 applicants, 41% accepted, 60 enrolled. In 2013, 41 master's awarded. Terminal master's awarded for partial completion of doctoral program. *Degree requirements:* For master's, thesis or alternative. *Entrance requirements:* Additional exam requirements/recommendations for international students: Required—TOEFL (minimum score 550 paper-based; 79 iBT). *Application deadline:* For fall admission, 4/1 for domestic students, 12/15 for international students; for spring admission, 10/1 for domestic students, 8/1 for international students. Application fee: $60. Electronic applications accepted. *Financial support:* Fellowships, research assistantships, and teaching assistantships available. Financial award application deadline: 1/15; financial award applicants required to submit FAFSA. *Faculty research:* Workforce development, vocational education, technical education, industrial education, professional development, literacy, classroom management, school communities, curriculum development, instruction, applied linguistics, crosslinguistic influence, bilingual education, oral proficiency, multilingualism. *Application contact:* Felicia Neuber, Enrollment Management, 215-204-8011, E-mail: educate@temple.edu.
Website: http://www.temple.edu/education/tl/.

Texas A&M University–Corpus Christi, Graduate Studies and Research, College of Science and Technology, Program in Mathematics, Corpus Christi, TX 78412-5503. Offers applied and computational mathematics (MS); curriculum content (MS). Part-time programs available. *Degree requirements:* For master's, thesis (for some programs). *Entrance requirements:* For master's, 2 letters of recommendation.

Texas Christian University, College of Education, Program in Mathematics Education, Fort Worth, TX 76129-0002. Offers M Ed. Part-time and evening/weekend programs available. *Students:* 4 full-time (all women), 2 part-time (both women). 2 applicants, 100% accepted, 2 enrolled. *Entrance requirements:* For master's, GRE. Additional exam requirements/recommendations for international students: Required—TOEFL (minimum score 550 paper-based). *Application deadline:* For fall admission, 3/1 for domestic and international students; for spring admission, 11/16 for domestic and international students. Application fee: $60. *Expenses: Tuition:* Part-time $1270 per credit hour. Tuition and fees vary according to course load and program. *Financial support:* Teaching assistantships with full tuition reimbursements, career-related internships or fieldwork, scholarships/grants, and unspecified assistantships available. Financial award application deadline: 3/1; financial award applicants required to submit FAFSA. *Unit head:* Dr. Jan Lacina, Associate Dean, 817-257-6786, E-mail: j.lacina@tcu.edu. *Application contact:* Lori Kimball, Administrative Program Specialist, 817-257-7661, E-mail: l.kimball@tcu.edu.
Website: http://www.coe.tcu.edu/graduate-students-graduate-programs.asp.

Texas State University, Graduate School, College of Science and Engineering, Department of Mathematics, PhD Program in Mathematics Education, San Marcos, TX 78666. Offers PhD. *Faculty:* 21 full-time (15 women). *Students:* 23 full-time (17 women), 7 part-time (3 women); includes 6 minority (3 Black or African American, non-Hispanic/Latino; 2 Hispanic/Latino; 1 Two or more races, non-Hispanic/Latino), 4 international. Average age 32. 30 applicants, 63% accepted, 6 enrolled. In 2013, 6 doctorates awarded. *Degree requirements:* For doctorate, comprehensive exam, thesis/dissertation. *Entrance requirements:* For doctorate, GRE General Test; GRE Subject Test in mathematics (minimum score in 75th percentile), bachelor's degree or higher in mathematics, mathematics education, or related field; minimum GPA of 3.0 in last 60 hours of undergraduate work. Additional exam requirements/recommendations for international students: Required—TOEFL (minimum score 550 paper-based; 78 iBT). *Application deadline:* For fall admission, 6/15 priority date for domestic students, 6/1 priority date for international students; for spring admission, 10/15 priority date for domestic students, 9/1 priority date for international students. Application fee: $40 ($90 for international students). *Expenses:* Tuition, state resident: full-time $6663; part-time $278 per credit hour. Tuition, nonresident: full-time $15,159; part-time $632 per credit hour. *Required fees:* $1872; $54 per credit hour. $306 per term. Tuition and fees vary according to course load. *Financial support:* In 2013–14, 1 research assistantship (averaging $29,756 per year), 23 teaching assistantships (averaging $28,345 per year) were awarded; Federal Work-Study, institutionally sponsored loans, scholarships/grants, health care benefits, and unspecified assistantships also available. Support available to part-time students. *Unit head:* Dr. Nathaniel Dean, Chair, Department of Mathematics, 512-245-3555, E-mail: nd17@txstate.edu. *Application contact:* Dr. Andrea Golato, Dean of the Graduate College, 512-245-2581, E-mail: gradcollege@txstate.edu.
Website: http://www.math.txstate.edu/degrees-programs/phd.html.

Texas State University, Graduate School, College of Science and Engineering, Department of Mathematics, Program in Middle School Mathematics Teaching, San Marcos, TX 78666. Offers M Ed. Part-time programs available. *Faculty:* 3 full-time (2 women). *Students:* 1 (woman) full-time, 4 part-time (2 women); includes 2 minority (both Hispanic/Latino). Average age 37. 9 applicants, 78% accepted. *Degree requirements:* For master's, comprehensive exam. *Entrance requirements:* For master's, GRE, minimum GPA of 2.75 in last 60 hours of undergraduate course work. Additional exam requirements/recommendations for international students: Required—TOEFL (minimum score 550 paper-based; 78 iBT). *Application deadline:* For fall admission, 6/15 priority date for domestic students, 6/1 priority date for international students; for spring admission, 10/15 priority date for domestic students, 10/1 priority date for international students. Applications are processed on a rolling basis. Application fee: $40 ($90 for international students). Electronic applications accepted. *Expenses:* Tuition, state resident: full-time $6663; part-time $278 per credit hour. Tuition, nonresident: full-time $15,159; part-time $632 per credit hour. *Required fees:* $1872; $54 per credit hour. $306 per term. Tuition and fees vary according to course load. *Financial support:* In 2013–14, 1 student received support, including 2 teaching assistantships (averaging $13,900 per year); Federal Work-Study and institutionally sponsored loans also available. Support available to part-time students. Financial award application deadline: 4/1; financial award applicants required to submit FAFSA. *Unit head:* Dr. Gregory Passty, Graduate Advisor, 512-245-2551, Fax: 512-245-3425, E-mail: gp02@txstate.edu. *Application contact:* Dr. Andrea Golato, Dean of the Graduate College, 512-245-2581, E-mail: gradcollege@txstate.edu.
Website: http://www.math.txstate.edu/degrees-programs/masters/middle-school.html.

Texas State University, Graduate School, College of Science and Engineering, Interdisciplinary Studies Program in Elementary Mathematics, Science, and Technology, San Marcos, TX 78666. Offers MSIS. *Students:* 3 full-time (2 women); includes 1 minority (Hispanic/Latino), 1 international. Average age 24. 1 applicant, 100% accepted. In 2013, 2 master's awarded. *Degree requirements:* For master's, comprehensive exam, thesis optional. *Entrance requirements:* For master's, minimum GPA of 2.75 in the last 60 hours of undergraduate work. Additional exam requirements/recommendations for international students: Required—TOEFL (minimum score 550 paper-based; 78 iBT). *Application deadline:* For fall admission, 6/15 priority date for domestic students, 6/1 priority date for international students; for spring admission, 10/15 priority date for domestic students, 10/1 priority date for international students. Applications are processed on a rolling basis. Application fee: $40 ($90 for international students). Electronic applications accepted. *Expenses:* Tuition, state resident: full-time $6663; part-time $278 per credit hour. Tuition, nonresident: full-time $15,159; part-time $632 per credit hour. *Required fees:* $1872; $54 per credit hour. $306 per term. Tuition and fees vary according to course load. *Financial support:* In 2013–14, 1 student received support, including 1 teaching assistantship (averaging $11,568 per year); research assistantships, Federal Work-Study, institutionally sponsored loans, scholarships/grants, health care benefits, and unspecified assistantships also available. Support available to part-time students. Financial award application deadline: 4/1; financial award applicants required to submit FAFSA. *Unit head:* Dr. Sandra West Moody, Acting Dean, 512-245-3360, Fax: 512-245-8095, E-mail: sw04@txstate.edu. *Application contact:* Dr. Andrea Golato, Dean of Graduate School, 512-245-2581, Fax: 512-245-8365, E-mail: gradcollege@txstate.edu.

Texas Tech University, Graduate School, Rawls College of Business Administration, Programs in Business Administration, Lubbock, TX 79409. Offers business administration (IMBA); general business (MBA); health organization management (MBA); STEM (MBA); JD/MBA; MBA/M Arch; MBA/MD; MBA/MS; MBA/Pharm D. Part-time and evening/weekend programs available. *Faculty:* 56 full-time (9 women), 1 part-time/adjunct (0 women). *Students:* 97 full-time (63 women), 296 part-time (88 women); includes 73 minority (21 Black or African American, non-Hispanic/Latino; 3 American Indian or Alaska Native, non-Hispanic/Latino; 30 Asian, non-Hispanic/Latino; 19 Hispanic/Latino), 19 international. Average age 31. 155 applicants, 79% accepted, 116 enrolled. In 2013, 225 master's awarded. *Degree requirements:* For master's, capstone course. *Entrance requirements:* For master's, GMAT, holistic review of academic credentials. Additional exam requirements/recommendations for international students: Required—TOEFL (minimum score 550 paper-based; 79 iBT). *Application deadline:* For fall admission, 6/1 priority date for domestic students, 1/15 for international students; for spring admission, 11/1 priority date for domestic students, 6/15 for international students; for summer admission, 4/15 for domestic students. Applications are processed on a rolling basis. Application fee: $60. Electronic applications accepted. *Expenses:* Tuition, state resident: full-time $6062; part-time $252.57 per credit hour. Tuition, nonresident: full-time $14,558; part-time $606.57 per credit hour. *Required fees:* $2655; $35 per credit hour. $907.50 per semester. Tuition and fees vary according to course load. *Financial support:* Research assistantships, teaching assistantships, Federal Work-Study, scholarships/grants, and unspecified assistantships available. Support available to part-time students. Financial award applicants required to submit FAFSA. *Unit head:* Dr. William J. Pasewark, Associate Dean, 806-742-3184, Fax: 806-742-3958, E-mail: w.pasewark@ttu.edu. *Application contact:* Terri Boston, Application Manager, 806-742-3184, Fax: 806-742-3958, E-mail: rawlsgrad@ttu.edu.
Website: http://mba.ba.ttu.edu/.

Mathematics Education

Texas Woman's University, Graduate School, College of Arts and Sciences, Department of Mathematics and Computer Science, Denton, TX 76201. Offers mathematics (MA, MS); mathematics teaching (MS). Part-time and evening/weekend programs available. *Faculty:* 12 full-time (9 women), 1 part-time/adjunct (0 women). *Students:* 7 full-time (6 women), 40 part-time (31 women); includes 15 minority (5 Black or African American, non-Hispanic/Latino; 3 Asian, non-Hispanic/Latino; 7 Hispanic/Latino), 3 international. Average age 35. 12 applicants, 83% accepted, 6 enrolled. In 2013, 9 master's awarded. *Degree requirements:* For master's, comprehensive exam, thesis. *Entrance requirements:* For master's, 2 letters of reference. Additional exam requirements/recommendations for international students: Required—TOEFL (minimum score 550 paper-based; 79 iBT). *Application deadline:* For fall admission, 7/1 priority date for domestic students, 3/1 for international students; for spring admission, 12/1 priority date for domestic students, 7/1 for international students. Applications are processed on a rolling basis. Application fee: $50 ($75 for international students). Electronic applications accepted. *Expenses:* Tuition, state resident: full-time $4182; part-time $233.32 per credit hour. Tuition, nonresident: full-time $10,716; part-time $595.32 per credit hour. *Financial support:* In 2013–14, 13 students received support, including 4 research assistantships (averaging $13,248 per year), 7 teaching assistantships (averaging $13,248 per year); career-related internships or fieldwork, Federal Work-Study, institutionally sponsored loans, scholarships/grants, traineeships, health care benefits, and unspecified assistantships also available. Support available to part-time students. Financial award application deadline: 3/1; financial award applicants required to submit FAFSA. *Faculty research:* Biopharmaceutical statistics, dynamic systems and control theory, Bayesian inference, math and computer science curriculum innovation, computer modeling of physical phenomenon. *Unit head:* Dr. Don E. Edwards, Chair, 940-898-2166, Fax: 940-898-2179, E-mail: mathcs@twu.edu. *Application contact:* Dr. Samuel Wheeler, Assistant Director of Admissions, 940-898-3188, Fax: 940-898-3081, E-mail: wheelersr@twu.edu. Website: http://www.twu.edu/math-computer-science/.

Touro College, Graduate School of Education, New York, NY 10010. Offers education and special education (MS); education biology (MS); instructional technology (MS); mathematics education (MS); school leadership (MS); teaching English to speakers of other languages (MS); teaching literacy (MS). Part-time and evening/weekend programs available. Postbaccalaureate distance learning degree programs offered (no on-campus study). *Faculty:* 75 full-time, 131 part-time/adjunct. *Students:* 327 full-time (272 women), 2,454 part-time (2,103 women); includes 840 minority (333 Black or African American, non-Hispanic/Latino; 4 American Indian or Alaska Native, non-Hispanic/Latino; 139 Asian, non-Hispanic/Latino; 334 Hispanic/Latino; 8 Native Hawaiian or other Pacific Islander, non-Hispanic/Latino; 22 Two or more races, non-Hispanic/Latino), 4 international. 1,422 applicants, 50% accepted, 675 enrolled. In 2013, 6 master's awarded. *Entrance requirements:* Additional exam requirements/recommendations for international students: Required—TOEFL (minimum score 83 iBT), IELTS (minimum score 6.5). *Application deadline:* For fall admission, 8/26 for domestic students, 7/15 for international students; for spring admission, 12/31 for domestic students, 12/15 for international students. Applications are processed on a rolling basis. Application fee: $50. *Financial support:* Federal Work-Study available. Financial award applicants required to submit FAFSA. *Faculty research:* Equity assistance, language development, scholar communications, Latin American studies and cultural sensitivity, behavior management techniques and strategies in special education. *Unit head:* Dr. LaMar Miller, Dean, 212-463-0400 Ext. 5561, Fax: 212-462-4889, E-mail: lpmiller@touro.edu. *Application contact:* Natalie Arroyo, Admissions, 212-463-0400.

Towson University, Program in Mathematics Education, Towson, MD 21252-0001. Offers MS. *Accreditation:* NCATE. Part-time and evening/weekend programs available. *Students:* 5 full-time (2 women), 83 part-time (65 women); includes 13 minority (6 Black or African American, non-Hispanic/Latino; 2 Asian, non-Hispanic/Latino; 2 Hispanic/Latino; 3 Two or more races, non-Hispanic/Latino), 1 international. *Entrance requirements:* For master's, undergraduate degree in mathematics or elementary education, current certification for teaching secondary school or elementary school mathematics, minimum GPA of 3.0. *Application deadline:* Applications are processed on a rolling basis. Application fee: $45. Electronic applications accepted. *Financial support:* Application deadline: 4/1. *Unit head:* Dr. Maureen Yarnevich, Graduate Program Director, 410-704-2988, E-mail: myarnevich@towson.edu. *Application contact:* Alicia Arkell-Kleis, Information Contact, 410-704-6004, E-mail: grads@towson.edu. Website: http://grad.towson.edu/program/master/mted-ms/.

Troy University, Graduate School, College of Education, Program in Postsecondary Education, Troy, AL 36082. Offers adult education (M Ed); biology (M Ed); criminal justice (M Ed); English (M Ed); foundations of education (M Ed); general science (M Ed); higher education administration (M Ed); history (M Ed); instructional technology (M Ed); mathematics (M Ed); music industry (M Ed); physical fitness (M Ed); political science (M Ed); public administration (M Ed); social science (M Ed); teaching English (M Ed). *Accreditation:* NCATE. Part-time and evening/weekend programs available. *Faculty:* 30 full-time (11 women), 8 part-time/adjunct (1 woman). *Students:* 17 full-time (13 women), 106 part-time (84 women); includes 55 minority (45 Black or African American, non-Hispanic/Latino; 3 Asian, non-Hispanic/Latino; 2 Hispanic/Latino; 5 Two or more races, non-Hispanic/Latino). Average age 34. 109 applicants, 83% accepted, 5 enrolled. In 2013, 130 master's awarded. *Degree requirements:* For master's, comprehensive exam (for some programs), thesis (for some programs), thesis or comprehensive exam. *Entrance requirements:* For master's, GRE (minimum score of 850 on old exam or 290 on new exam), GMAT (minimum score of 380), or MAT (minimum score of 385), bachelor's degree; minimum undergraduate GPA of 2.5 or 3.0 on last 30 semester hours, letter of recommendation. Additional exam requirements/recommendations for international students: Required—TOEFL (minimum score 523 paper-based; 70 iBT), IELTS (minimum score 6). *Application deadline:* Applications are processed on a rolling basis. Application fee: $50. Electronic applications accepted. *Expenses:* Tuition, state resident: full-time $6084; part-time $338 per credit hour. Tuition, nonresident: full-time $12,168; part-time $676 per credit hour. *Required fees:* $630; $35 per credit hour. $50 per semester. *Financial support:* Available to part-time students. Applicants required to submit FAFSA. *Unit head:* Dr. Jan Oliver, Associate Professor, 334-670-3444, Fax: 334-670-3474, E-mail: oliver@troy.edu. *Application contact:* Brenda K. Campbell, Director of Graduate Admissions, 334-670-3178, Fax: 334-670-3733, E-mail: bcamp@troy.edu.

Troy University, Graduate School, College of Education, Program in Secondary Education, Troy, AL 36082. Offers 5th year biology (MS); 5th year computer science (MS); 5th year history (MS); 5th year language arts (MS); 5th year mathematics (MS); 5th year social science (MS); traditional biology (MS); traditional computer science (MS); traditional history (MS); traditional language arts (MS); traditional mathematics (MS); traditional social science (MS). *Accreditation:* NCATE. Part-time and evening/weekend programs available. *Faculty:* 2 full-time (1 woman). *Students:* 10 full-time (9 women), 21 part-time (14 women); includes 8 minority (6 Black or African American, non-Hispanic/Latino; 2 Hispanic/Latino). Average age 29. 15 applicants, 87% accepted, 6 enrolled. In 2013, 12 master's awarded. *Degree requirements:* For master's, comprehensive exam, thesis. *Entrance requirements:* For master's, GRE (minimum score of 850 on old exam or 290 on new exam), GMAT (minimum score of 380), or MAT (minimum score of 385), bachelor's degree; minimum undergraduate GPA of 2.5 or 3.0 on last 30 semester hours, letter of recommendation. Additional exam requirements/recommendations for

international students: Required—TOEFL (minimum score 523 paper-based; 70 iBT), IELTS (minimum score 6). *Application deadline:* Applications are processed on a rolling basis. Application fee: $50. Electronic applications accepted. *Expenses:* Tuition, state resident: full-time $6084; part-time $338 per credit hour. Tuition, nonresident: full-time $12,168; part-time $676 per credit hour. *Required fees:* $630; $35 per credit hour. $50 per semester. *Financial support:* Career-related internships or fieldwork available. Support available to part-time students. Financial award applicants required to submit FAFSA. *Unit head:* Dr. Jan Oliver, Associate Professor, 334-670-3444, Fax: 334-670-3548, E-mail: oliver@troy.edu. *Application contact:* Brenda K. Campbell, Director of Graduate Admissions, 334-670-3178, Fax: 334-670-3733, E-mail: bcamp@troy.edu.

Tufts University, Graduate School of Arts and Sciences, Department of Education, Program in Education, Medford, MA 02155. Offers educational studies (MA); elementary education (MAT); middle and secondary education (MA, MAT); museum education (MA); secondary education (MA); STEM education (MS, PhD). *Faculty:* 13 full-time, 9 part-time/adjunct. *Students:* 85 full-time (72 women); includes 19 minority (4 Black or African American, non-Hispanic/Latino; 1 American Indian or Alaska Native, non-Hispanic/Latino; 3 Asian, non-Hispanic/Latino; 7 Hispanic/Latino; 4 Two or more races, non-Hispanic/Latino), 5 international. Average age 27. 154 applicants, 69% accepted, 50 enrolled. In 2013, 84 master's awarded. *Degree requirements:* For master's, thesis optional; for doctorate, thesis/dissertation. *Entrance requirements:* For master's and doctorate, GRE General Test. Additional exam requirements/recommendations for international students: Required—TOEFL (minimum score 550 paper-based; 80 iBT), IELTS (minimum score 6.5). *Application deadline:* For fall admission, 1/2 for domestic and international students; for spring admission, 10/15 for domestic students, 9/15 for international students. Applications are processed on a rolling basis. Application fee: $75. Electronic applications accepted. *Financial support:* Teaching assistantships with full and partial tuition reimbursements, Federal Work-Study, scholarships/grants, and tuition waivers (full and partial) available. Support available to part-time students. Financial award application deadline: 1/2. *Unit head:* Hammer David, Chair, 617-627-3244, Fax: 617-627-3901. *Application contact:* Patricia Romeo, Information Contact, 617-627-3244.

Union Graduate College, School of Education, Schenectady, NY 12308-3107. Offers biology (MAT); chemistry (MAT); Chinese (MAT); earth science (MAT); English (MA, MAT); English and history (MA); French (MAT); general science (MAT); German (MAT); history (MA); Latin (MAT); life sciences (MS); mathematics (MAT); mathematics and computer technology (MS); mentoring and teacher leadership (AC); middle childhood extension (AC); national board certification and teacher leadership (AC); physical sciences (MS); physics (MAT); social studies (MAT); Spanish (MAT); technology (MAT). *Accreditation:* Teacher Education Accreditation Council. *Faculty:* 3 full-time (1 woman), 56 part-time/adjunct (34 women). *Students:* 32 full-time (16 women), 27 part-time (22 women); includes 15 minority (1 Black or African American, non-Hispanic/Latino; 4 Asian, non-Hispanic/Latino; 6 Hispanic/Latino; 4 Two or more races, non-Hispanic/Latino), 1 international. Average age 32. In 2013, 25 master's, 11 other advanced degrees awarded. *Degree requirements:* For master's, thesis or project. *Entrance requirements:* For master's, minimum GPA of 3.0, letters of recommendation. Additional exam requirements/recommendations for international students: Required—TOEFL (minimum score 550 paper-based). *Application deadline:* Applications are processed on a rolling basis. Application fee: $60. Electronic applications accepted. *Expenses:* Contact institution. *Financial support:* Career-related internships or fieldwork, Federal Work-Study, scholarships/grants, health care benefits, and tuition waivers (partial) available. Support available to part-time students. Financial award applicants required to submit FAFSA. *Faculty research:* Transformative learning, science education, National Board Certification, teacher leadership, teacher quality. *Unit head:* Dr. Lynn Gelzheiser, Dean, 518-631-9870, Fax: 518-631-9901. *Application contact:* Nicki Foley, Assistant, 518-631-9871, Fax: 518-631-9903, E-mail: foleyn@uniongraduatecollege.edu.

Universidad Autonoma de Guadalajara, Graduate Programs, Guadalajara, Mexico. Offers administrative law and justice (LL M); advertising and corporate communications (MA); architecture (M Arch); business (MBA); computational science (MCC); education (Ed M, Ed D); English-Spanish translation (MA); entrepreneurship and management (MBA); integrated management of digital animation (MA); international business (MIB); international corporate law (LL M); internet technologies (MS); manufacturing systems (MMS); occupational health (MS); philosophy (MA, PhD); power electronics (MS); quality systems (MQS); renewable energy (MS); social evaluation of projects (MBA); strategic market research (MBA); tax law (MA); teaching mathematics (MA).

University at Albany, State University of New York, College of Arts and Sciences, Department of Mathematics and Statistics, Albany, NY 12222-0001. Offers mathematics (PhD); secondary teaching (MA); statistics (MA). *Degree requirements:* For doctorate, one foreign language, thesis/dissertation. *Entrance requirements:* For doctorate, GRE General Test. Additional exam requirements/recommendations for international students: Required—TOEFL (minimum score 550 paper-based). Electronic applications accepted.

University at Buffalo, the State University of New York, Graduate School, Graduate School of Education, Department of Learning and Instruction, Buffalo, NY 14260. Offers biology education (Ed M, Certificate); chemistry education (Ed M, Certificate); childhood education (Ed M); childhood education with bilingual extension (Ed M); curriculum, instruction and the science of learning (PhD); early childhood education (Ed M); early childhood education with bilingual extension (birth-grade 2) (Ed M); earth science education (Ed M, Certificate); education studies (Ed M); educational technology and new literacies (Certificate); elementary education (Ed D); English education (Ed M, Certificate); English for speakers of other languages (Ed M); foreign and second language education (PhD); French education (Ed M, Certificate); German education (Ed M, Certificate); gifted education (Certificate); Latin education (Ed M, Certificate); literacy specialist (Ed M); literacy teaching and learning (Certificate); mathematics education (Ed M, Certificate); music education (Ed M, Certificate); physics education (Ed M, Certificate); science and the public (Ed M); social studies education (Ed M, Certificate); Spanish education (Ed M, Certificate); special education (PhD); teaching English to speakers of other languages (Ed M). Part-time and evening/weekend programs available. Postbaccalaureate distance learning degree programs offered (no on-campus study). *Faculty:* 31 full-time (23 women), 64 part-time/adjunct (53 women). *Students:* 275 full-time (215 women), 293 part-time (205 women); includes 35 minority (16 Black or African American, non-Hispanic/Latino; 5 American Indian or Alaska Native, non-Hispanic/Latino; 11 Asian, non-Hispanic/Latino; 3 Hispanic/Latino), 97 international. Average age 30. 544 applicants, 81% accepted, 246 enrolled. In 2013, 222 master's, 17 doctorates, 35 other advanced degrees awarded. *Degree requirements:* For master's, comprehensive exam; for doctorate, thesis/dissertation, research analysis exam, research experience component. *Entrance requirements:* For master's, content test in science and math, letters of reference; for doctorate, GRE General Test or MAT, interview, writing sample, letters of recommendation. Additional exam requirements/recommendations for international students: Required—TOEFL (minimum score 600 paper-based; 96 iBT). *Application deadline:* For fall admission, 2/1 priority date for domestic and international students; for spring admission, 11/15 priority date for domestic students, 10/1 for international students. Applications are processed on a rolling basis. Application fee: $50. Electronic applications accepted. *Financial support:*

In 2013–14, 50 fellowships (averaging $8,589 per year), 31 research assistantships with tuition reimbursements (averaging $11,406 per year) were awarded; teaching assistantships, career-related internships or fieldwork, Federal Work-Study, institutionally sponsored loans, scholarships/grants, tuition waivers, and unspecified assistantships also available. Financial award application deadline: 2/28; financial award applicants required to submit FAFSA. *Faculty research:* Science assessment, foreign language teaching and learning, early learning, new literacies, gender and education. *Total annual research expenditures:* $1.7 million. *Unit head:* Dr. Suzanne Miller, Chair, 716-645-2455, Fax: 716-645-3161, E-mail: smiller@buffalo.edu. *Application contact:* Cathy Dimino, Admissions Assistant, 716-645-2110, Fax: 716-645-7937, E-mail: cadimino@buffalo.edu.
Website: http://gse.buffalo.edu/lai.

The University of Alabama in Huntsville, School of Graduate Studies, College of Science, Department of Mathematical Sciences, Huntsville, AL 35899. Offers applied mathematics (PhD); education (MA, MS); mathematics (MA, MS). PhD offered jointly with The University of Alabama (Tuscaloosa) and The University of Alabama at Birmingham. Part-time and evening/weekend programs available. *Faculty:* 14 full-time (1 woman). *Students:* 18 full-time (11 women), 8 part-time (1 woman); includes 5 minority (1 Black or African American, non-Hispanic/Latino; 2 Asian, non-Hispanic/Latino; 1 Hispanic/Latino; 1 Two or more races, non-Hispanic/Latino), 3 international. Average age 28. 24 applicants, 75% accepted, 8 enrolled. In 2013, 8 master's, 2 doctorates awarded. *Degree requirements:* For master's, comprehensive exam, thesis or alternative, oral and written exams; for doctorate, comprehensive exam, thesis/dissertation, oral and written exams. *Entrance requirements:* For master's and doctorate, GRE General Test, minimum GPA of 3.0. Additional exam requirements/recommendations for international students: Required—TOEFL (minimum score 550 paper-based; 80 iBT), IELTS (minimum score 6.5). *Application deadline:* For fall admission, 7/15 priority date for domestic students, 4/1 priority date for international students; for spring admission, 11/30 priority date for domestic students, 9/1 priority date for international students. Applications are processed on a rolling basis. Application fee: $50. Electronic applications accepted. *Expenses:* Tuition, state resident: full-time $8912; part-time $540 per credit hour. Tuition, nonresident: full-time $20,774; part-time $1252 per credit hour. *Required fees:* $148 per semester. One-time fee: $150. *Financial support:* In 2013–14, 16 students received support, including 1 fellowship (averaging $10,450 per year), 14 teaching assistantships with full and partial tuition reimbursements available (averaging $10,078 per year); career-related internships or fieldwork, Federal Work-Study, institutionally sponsored loans, scholarships/grants, health care benefits, and unspecified assistantships also available. Support available to part-time students. Financial award application deadline: 4/1; financial award applicants required to submit FAFSA. *Faculty research:* Combinatorics and graph theory, computational mathematics, differential equations and applications, mathematical biology, probability and stochastic processes. *Total annual research expenditures:* $184,281. *Unit head:* Dr. Jia Li, Chair, 256-824-6470, Fax: 256-824-6173, E-mail: li@math.uah.edu. *Application contact:* Kim Gray, Graduate Studies Admissions Coordinator, 256-824-6002, Fax: 256-824-6405, E-mail: deangrad@uah.edu.
Website: http://www.math.uah.edu/.

The University of Arizona, College of Science, Department of Mathematics, Program in Middle School Mathematics Teaching Leadership, Tucson, AZ 85721. Offers MA. Part-time programs available. *Students:* 18 full-time (14 women), 8 part-time (all women); includes 13 minority (1 Asian, non-Hispanic/Latino; 8 Hispanic/Latino; 1 Native Hawaiian or other Pacific Islander, non-Hispanic/Latino; 3 Two or more races, non-Hispanic/Latino). Average age 44. In 2013, 12 master's awarded. *Degree requirements:* For master's, thesis, internships, colloquium, business courses. *Entrance requirements:* For master's, GRE, minimum GPA of 3.0, statement of purpose. Additional exam requirements/recommendations for international students: Required—TOEFL (minimum score 550 paper-based). Application fee: $75. *Expenses:* Tuition, state resident: full-time $11,526. Tuition, nonresident: full-time $27,398. *Financial support:* Research assistantships, teaching assistantships, career-related internships or fieldwork, Federal Work-Study, scholarships/grants, health care benefits, and unspecified assistantships available. *Faculty research:* Algebra, coding theory, graph theory, combinatorics, probability. *Unit head:* William McCallum, Head, 520-621-2068, E-mail: stovall@math.arizona.edu. *Application contact:* Teresa Stoval, 520-626-6145, E-mail: stovall@math.arizona.edu.
Website: http://math.arizona.edu/.

University of Arkansas, Graduate School, J. William Fulbright College of Arts and Sciences, Department of Mathematical Sciences, Program in Secondary Mathematics, Fayetteville, AR 72701-1201. Offers MA. *Accreditation:* NCATE. *Degree requirements:* For master's, written exam. Electronic applications accepted.

University of Arkansas at Pine Bluff, School of Education, Pine Bluff, AR 71601-2799. Offers early childhood education (M Ed); secondary education (M Ed), including English education, mathematics education, physical education, science education, social studies education; teaching (MAT). *Accreditation:* NCATE. Part-time and evening/weekend programs available. *Degree requirements:* For master's, comprehensive exam. *Entrance requirements:* For master's, GRE, minimum GPA of 2.75, NTE or Standard Arkansas Teaching Certificate. *Faculty research:* Teacher certification, accreditation, assessment, standards, portfolio development, rehabilitation, technology.

The University of British Columbia, Faculty of Education, Department of Curriculum and Pedagogy, Vancouver, BC V6T 1Z4, Canada. Offers art education (M Ed, MA); business education (MA); curriculum studies (M Ed, MA, PhD); home economics education (M Ed, MA); math education (M Ed, MA); music education (M Ed, MA); physical education (M Ed, MA); science education (M Ed, MA); social studies education (M Ed, MA); technology studies education (M Ed, MA). Part-time programs available. Postbaccalaureate distance learning degree programs offered (no on-campus study). *Faculty:* 32 full-time (14 women), 1 (woman) part-time/adjunct. *Students:* 163 full-time, 134 part-time, 42 international. Average age 40. 160 applicants, 75% accepted, 97 enrolled. In 2013, 68 master's, 7 doctorates awarded. *Degree requirements:* For master's, thesis (MA); for doctorate, comprehensive exam, thesis/dissertation. *Entrance requirements:* Additional exam requirements/recommendations for international students: Required—TOEFL (minimum score 580 paper-based; 92 iBT), IELTS (minimum score 6.5). *Application deadline:* For fall admission, 12/1 for domestic and international students; for spring admission, 10/1 for domestic students, 9/1 for international students. Application fee: $90 Canadian dollars ($150 Canadian dollars for international students). Electronic applications accepted. *Expenses:* Contact institution. *Financial support:* In 2013–14, 10 fellowships with partial tuition reimbursements (averaging $16,000 per year), 11 research assistantships with partial tuition reimbursements (averaging $14,000 per year), 27 teaching assistantships with partial tuition reimbursements (averaging $14,000 per year) were awarded; tuition waivers (partial) also available. *Faculty research:* School subjects, teaching and learning. *Unit head:* Dr. Peter Grimmett, Head, 604-822-5422, Fax: 604-822-4714, E-mail: anna.ip@ubc.ca. *Application contact:* Basia Zurek, Graduate Programs Assistant, 604-822-5367, Fax: 604-822-4714, E-mail: edcp.grad@ubc.ca.
Website: http://www.edcp.educ.ubc.ca/.

University of California, Berkeley, Graduate Division, School of Education, Group in Science and Mathematics Education, Berkeley, CA 94720-1500. Offers PhD, MA/Credential. Electronic applications accepted.

University of California, Berkeley, Graduate Division, School of Education, Programs in Education, Berkeley, CA 94720-1500. Offers development in mathematics and science (MA); education in mathematics, science, and technology (MA, PhD); human development and education (MA, PhD); special education (PhD); MA/Credential; PhD/Credential; PhD/MA. Terminal master's awarded for partial completion of doctoral program. *Degree requirements:* For master's, exam or thesis; for doctorate, thesis/dissertation, oral qualifying exam. *Entrance requirements:* For master's and doctorate, GRE General Test, minimum GPA of 3.0 during last 2 years of undergraduate course work. Electronic applications accepted. *Faculty research:* Human development, social and moral educational psychology, developmental teacher preparation.

University of California, San Diego, Office of Graduate Studies, Program in Mathematics and Science Education, La Jolla, CA 92093. Offers PhD. Program offered jointly with San Diego State University. *Students:* 13 (6 women). In 2013, 5 doctorates awarded. *Degree requirements:* For doctorate, thesis/dissertation, teaching practicum. *Entrance requirements:* For doctorate, GRE General Test. Additional exam requirements/recommendations for international students: Required—TOEFL, IELTS. *Application deadline:* For fall admission, 1/7 for domestic students. Electronic applications accepted. *Expenses:* Tuition, state resident: full-time $11,220; part-time $1870 per quarter. Tuition, nonresident: full-time $26,322; part-time $4387 per quarter. *Required fees:* $519.50 per quarter. Part-time tuition and fees vary according to course load and program. *Financial support:* Scholarships/grants and stipends available. Financial award applicants required to submit FAFSA. *Faculty research:* Effective teaching of rational numbers, teacher development, development of number sense and estimation. *Unit head:* Gabriele Wienhausen, Co-Director, 858-534-2904, E-mail: gwienhausen@ucsd.edu. *Application contact:* Sherry Seethaler, Application Contact, 858-534-4656, E-mail: sseethaler@ucsd.edu.
Website: http://sci.sdsu.edu/CRMSE/msed/.

University of Central Arkansas, Graduate School, College of Natural Sciences and Math, Department of Mathematics, Conway, AR 72035-0001. Offers applied mathematics (MS); math education (MA). Part-time programs available. *Degree requirements:* For master's, comprehensive exam, thesis optional. *Entrance requirements:* For master's, GRE General Test, minimum GPA of 2.7. Additional exam requirements/recommendations for international students: Required—TOEFL (minimum score 550 paper-based; 80 iBT). Electronic applications accepted.

University of Central Florida, College of Education and Human Performance, Education Doctoral Programs, Orlando, FL 32816. Offers communication sciences and disorders (PhD); counselor education (PhD); early childhood education (PhD); education (Ed D); elementary education (PhD); exceptional education (PhD); exercise physiology (PhD); higher education (PhD); hospitality education (PhD); instructional technology (PhD); mathematics education (PhD); reading education (PhD); science education (PhD); social science education (PhD); TESOL (PhD). *Students:* 137 full-time (94 women), 86 part-time (64 women); includes 45 minority (24 Black or African American, non-Hispanic/Latino; 5 Asian, non-Hispanic/Latino; 13 Hispanic/Latino; 3 Two or more races, non-Hispanic/Latino), 22 international. Average age 39. 132 applicants, 54% accepted, 54 enrolled. In 2013, 38 doctorates awarded. Application fee: $30. Electronic applications accepted. *Financial support:* In 2013–14, 84 students received support, including 38 fellowships with partial tuition reimbursements available (averaging $6,600 per year), 41 research assistantships with partial tuition reimbursements available (averaging $7,800 per year), 53 teaching assistantships with partial tuition reimbursements available (averaging $7,700 per year). *Unit head:* Dr. Edward Robinson, Director of Doctoral Programs, 407-823-6106, E-mail: edward.robinson@ucf.edu. *Application contact:* Barbara Rodriguez Lamas, Associate Director, Admissions and Student Services, 407-823-2766, Fax: 407-823-6442, E-mail: gradadmissions@ucf.edu.
Website: http://education.ucf.edu/departments.cfm.

University of Central Florida, College of Education and Human Performance, School of Teaching, Learning, and Leadership, Program in K-8 Mathematics and Science Education, Orlando, FL 32816. Offers M Ed, Certificate. *Accreditation:* NCATE. *Students:* 14 part-time (11 women); includes 6 minority (1 Black or African American, non-Hispanic/Latino; 2 Asian, non-Hispanic/Latino; 3 Hispanic/Latino). Average age 31. 14 applicants, 71% accepted, 7 enrolled. In 2013, 8 master's awarded. Application fee: $30. *Unit head:* Dr. Juli K. Dixon, Program Coordinator, 407-823-4140, E-mail: juli.dixon@ucf.edu. *Application contact:* Barbara Rodriguez Lamas, Director, Admissions and Student Services, 407-823-2766, Fax: 407-823-6442, E-mail: gradadmissions@ucf.edu.

University of Central Florida, College of Education and Human Performance, School of Teaching, Learning, and Leadership, Program in Mathematics Education, Orlando, FL 32816. Offers teacher education (MAT), including mathematics education, middle school mathematics; teacher leadership (M Ed). *Accreditation:* NCATE. Part-time and evening/weekend programs available. *Students:* 3 full-time (1 woman), 35 part-time (22 women); includes 12 minority (2 Black or African American, non-Hispanic/Latino; 3 Asian, non-Hispanic/Latino; 7 Hispanic/Latino). Average age 24. 11 applicants, 64% accepted, 3 enrolled. In 2013, 23 master's awarded. *Entrance requirements:* For master's, GRE General Test. Additional exam requirements/recommendations for international students: Required—TOEFL. *Application deadline:* For fall admission, 7/15 for domestic students; for spring admission, 12/1 for domestic students. Application fee: $30. Electronic applications accepted. *Financial support:* In 2013–14, 1 student received support. Fellowships, research assistantships, teaching assistantships, career-related internships or fieldwork, Federal Work-Study, institutionally sponsored loans, tuition waivers (partial), and unspecified assistantships available. Financial award application deadline: 3/1; financial award applicants required to submit FAFSA. *Unit head:* Dr. Erhan Seluk Haciomeroglu, Program Coordinator, 407-823-4336, E-mail: erhan.haciomeroglu@ucf.edu. *Application contact:* Barbara Rodriguez Lamas, Director, Admissions and Student Support, 407-823-2766, Fax: 407-823-6442, E-mail: gradadmissions@ucf.edu.

University of Cincinnati, Graduate School, McMicken College of Arts and Sciences, Department of Mathematical Sciences, Cincinnati, OH 45221. Offers applied mathematics (MS, PhD); mathematics education (MAT); pure mathematics (MS, PhD); statistics (MS, PhD). Part-time programs available. Terminal master's awarded for partial completion of doctoral program. *Degree requirements:* For master's, comprehensive exam, thesis or alternative; for doctorate, one foreign language, comprehensive exam, thesis/dissertation. *Entrance requirements:* For master's, GRE, teacher certification (MAT); for doctorate, GRE. Additional exam requirements/recommendations for international students: Required—TOEFL. Electronic applications accepted. *Faculty research:* Algebra, analysis, differential equations, numerical analysis, statistics.

University of Colorado Denver, College of Liberal Arts and Sciences, Department of Mathematical and Statistical Sciences, Denver, CO 80217. Offers applied mathematics (MS, PhD), including applied mathematics, applied probability (MS), applied statistics

(MS), computational biology, computational mathematics (PhD), discrete mathematics, finite geometry (PhD), mathematics education (PhD), mathematics of engineering and science (MS), numerical analysis, operations research (MS), optimization and operations research (PhD), probability (PhD), statistics (PhD). Part-time programs available. *Faculty:* 20 full-time (6 women), 6 part-time/adjunct (0 women). *Students:* 41 full-time (10 women), 8 part-time (2 women); includes 10 minority (1 Black or African American, non-Hispanic/Latino; 4 Asian, non-Hispanic/Latino; 4 Hispanic/Latino; 1 Two or more races, non-Hispanic/Latino), 13 international. Average age 30. 75 applicants, 56% accepted, 9 enrolled. In 2013, 6 master's, 5 doctorates awarded. *Degree requirements:* For master's, comprehensive exam, thesis optional, 30 hours of course work with minimum GPA of 3.0; for doctorate, comprehensive exam, thesis/dissertation, 42 hours of course work with minimum GPA of 3.25. *Entrance requirements:* For master's, GRE General Test; GRE Subject Test in math (recommended), 30 hours of course work in mathematics (24 of which must be upper-division mathematics), bachelor's degree with minimum GPA of 3.0; for doctorate, GRE General Test; GRE Subject Test in math (recommended), 30 hours of course work in mathematics (24 of which must be upper-division mathematics), master's degree with minimum GPA of 3.25. Additional exam requirements/recommendations for international students: Required—TOEFL (minimum score 537 paper-based; 75 iBT); Recommended—IELTS (minimum score 6.5). *Application deadline:* For fall admission, 2/1 for domestic students, 2/1 priority date for international students; for spring admission, 10/1 for domestic students, 10/1 priority date for international students. Application fee: $50 ($75 for international students). Electronic applications accepted. *Financial support:* In 2013–14, 28 students received support. Fellowships with partial tuition reimbursements available, research assistantships with full tuition reimbursements available, teaching assistantships with full tuition reimbursements available, Federal Work-Study, institutionally sponsored loans, scholarships/grants, and traineeships available. Financial award application deadline: 4/1; financial award applicants required to submit FAFSA. *Faculty research:* Computational mathematics, computational biology, discrete mathematics and geometry, probability and statistics, optimization. *Unit head:* Dr. Jan Mandel, Professor and Chair, 303-315-1703, E-mail: jan.mandel@ucdenver.edu. *Application contact:* Margie Bopp, Graduate Program Assistant, 303-556-2341, E-mail: margie.bopp@ucdenver.edu.
Website: http://www.ucdenver.edu/academics/colleges/CLAS/Departments/math/Pages/MathStats.aspx.

University of Colorado Denver, School of Education and Human Development, Program in Educational Leadership and Innovation, Denver, CO 80217-3364. Offers educational studies and research (PhD), including administrative leadership and policy, early childhood special education, math education, research, assessment and evaluation, science education, urban ecologies. Part-time and evening/weekend programs available. *Students:* 16 full-time (12 women), 12 part-time (9 women); includes 6 minority (2 Black or African American, non-Hispanic/Latino; 3 Asian, non-Hispanic/Latino; 1 Hispanic/Latino), 1 international. Average age 39. 16 applicants, 31% accepted, 4 enrolled. In 2013, 10 doctorates awarded. *Degree requirements:* For doctorate, comprehensive exam, thesis/dissertation, 75 credit hours (for PhD). *Entrance requirements:* For doctorate, GRE or equivalent, resume or curriculum vitae, letters of recommendation, master's degree or equivalent, completion of basic or advanced statistics course with minimum B grade. Additional exam requirements/recommendations for international students: Required—TOEFL (minimum score 537 paper-based; 75 iBT); Recommended—IELTS (minimum score 6.5). *Application deadline:* For fall admission, 5/1 priority date for domestic students, 4/15 priority date for international students. Applications are processed on a rolling basis. Application fee: $50 ($75 for international students). Electronic applications accepted. *Expenses:* Contact institution. *Financial support:* In 2013–14, 19 students received support. Fellowships, research assistantships, teaching assistantships, Federal Work-Study, institutionally sponsored loans, scholarships/grants, and traineeships available. Financial award application deadline: 4/1; financial award applicants required to submit FAFSA. *Faculty research:* Administrative leadership and policy studies, early childhood education, research in diversity, paraprofessionals in education, urban schools lab. *Unit head:* Dr. Deanna Sands, Associate Dean, Research and Professional Development, 303-315-4931, E-mail: deanna.sands@ucdenver.edu. *Application contact:* Student Services Center, 303-315-6300, Fax: 303-315-6311, E-mail: education@ucdenver.edu.
Website: http://www.ucdenver.edu/academics/colleges/SchoolOfEducation/Academics/Doctorate/Pages/PhD.aspx.

University of Colorado Denver, School of Education and Human Development, Program in Mathematics Education, Denver, CO 80217-3364. Offers MS Ed. *Unit head:* Rebecca Kantor, Dean, 303-315-6343, E-mail: rebecca.kantor@ucdenver.edu. *Application contact:* Student Services Center, 303-315-6300, Fax: 303-315-6311, E-mail: education@ucdenver.edu.

University of Colorado Denver, School of Education and Human Development, Teacher Education Programs, Denver, CO 80217. Offers elementary linguistically diverse education (MA); elementary math and science education (MA); elementary math education (MA); elementary reading and writing (MA); elementary science education (MA); secondary English education (MA); secondary linguistically diverse education (MA); secondary math education (MA); secondary reading and writing (MA); secondary science education (MA); special education (MA). *Accreditation:* NCATE. Part-time and evening/weekend programs available. *Students:* 269 full-time (208 women), 141 part-time (111 women); includes 55 minority (4 Black or African American, non-Hispanic/Latino; 1 American Indian or Alaska Native, non-Hispanic/Latino; 10 Asian, non-Hispanic/Latino; 39 Hispanic/Latino; 1 Two or more races, non-Hispanic/Latino), 7 international. Average age 31. 97 applicants, 81% accepted, 62 enrolled. In 2013, 180 master's awarded. *Degree requirements:* For master's, comprehensive exam. *Entrance requirements:* For master's, GRE or MAT (for those with GPA below 2.75), transcripts, resume, letters of recommendation. Additional exam requirements/recommendations for international students: Required—TOEFL (minimum score 537 paper-based; 75 iBT); Recommended—IELTS (minimum score 6.5). *Application deadline:* For fall admission, 4/15 priority date for domestic students, 4/1 for international students; for spring admission, 9/15 priority date for domestic students, 9/1 for international students. Applications are processed on a rolling basis. Application fee: $50 ($75 for international students). Electronic applications accepted. *Expenses:* Contact institution. *Financial support:* In 2013–14, 42 students received support. Fellowships, research assistantships, teaching assistantships, Federal Work-Study, institutionally sponsored loans, scholarships/grants, and traineeships available. Financial award application deadline: 4/1; financial award applicants required to submit FAFSA. *Faculty research:* Linguistically diverse education/ESL, elementary reading and writing, elementary teacher education, secondary teacher education, special education. *Unit head:* Cindy Gutierrez, Director, 303-315-4982, E-mail: cindy.gutierrez@ucdenver.edu. *Application contact:* Lori Sisneros, Student Services Center, 303-315-4979, E-mail: education@ucdenver.edu.
Website: http://www.ucdenver.edu/academics/colleges/SchoolOfEducation/Academics/MASTERS/Pages/default.aspx.

University of Connecticut, Graduate School, Neag School of Education, Department of Curriculum and Instruction, Program in Mathematics Education, Storrs, CT 06269. Offers MA, PhD, Post-Master's Certificate. *Accreditation:* NCATE. Terminal master's awarded for partial completion of doctoral program. *Degree requirements:* For master's, comprehensive exam; for doctorate, thesis/dissertation. *Entrance requirements:* For doctorate, GRE General Test. Additional exam requirements/recommendations for international students: Required—TOEFL (minimum score 550 paper-based). Electronic applications accepted.

University of Dayton, Department of Mathematics, Dayton, OH 45469-1300. Offers applied mathematics (MAS); financial mathematics (MFM); mathematics education (MME). Part-time and evening/weekend programs available. *Faculty:* 15 full-time (5 women). *Students:* 33 full-time (18 women), 5 part-time (3 women); includes 2 minority (both Black or African American, non-Hispanic/Latino), 30 international. Average age 27. 121 applicants, 29% accepted, 10 enrolled. In 2013, 33 master's awarded. *Entrance requirements:* For master's, minimum undergraduate GPA of 2.8 (MAS), 3.0 (MFM, MME). Additional exam requirements/recommendations for international students: Required—TOEFL (minimum score 550 paper-based; 80 iBT). *Application deadline:* For fall admission, 3/1 priority date for domestic students, 5/1 priority date for international students; for winter admission, 7/1 for international students; for spring admission, 10/1 priority date for international students. Applications are processed on a rolling basis. Application fee: $0 ($50 for international students). Electronic applications accepted. *Expenses: Tuition:* Full-time $10,296; part-time $858 per credit hour. *Required fees:* $50; $25. *Financial support:* In 2013–14, 6 teaching assistantships with full tuition reimbursements (averaging $14,466 per year) were awarded; institutionally sponsored loans, health care benefits, and unspecified assistantships also available. Financial award application deadline: 3/1; financial award applicants required to submit FAFSA. *Faculty research:* Differential equations, integral equations, general topology, measure theory, graph theory, financial math, math education, numerical analysis. *Unit head:* Dr. Joe D. Mashburn, Chair, 937-229-2511, Fax: 937-229-2566, E-mail: jmashburn1@udayton.edu. *Application contact:* Dr. Paul W. Eloe, Graduate Program Director and Professor, 937-229-2016, E-mail: peloe1@udayton.edu.

University of Detroit Mercy, College of Engineering and Science, Department of Mathematics and Computer Science, Detroit, MI 48221. Offers computer science (MSCS), including computer systems applications, software engineering; computer science education (MATM); mathematics education (MATM). Evening/weekend programs available. *Entrance requirements:* For master's, minimum GPA of 3.0.

University of Florida, Graduate School, College of Education, School of Teaching and Learning, Gainesville, FL 32611. Offers curriculum and instruction (M Ed, MAE, Ed D, PhD, Ed S), including bilingual/ESOL specialization; elementary education (M Ed, MAE); English education (M Ed, MAE); mathematics education (M Ed, MAE); reading education (M Ed, MAE); science education (M Ed, MAE); social studies education (M Ed, MAE). *Accreditation:* NCATE. Part-time and evening/weekend programs available. Postbaccalaureate distance learning degree programs offered (no on-campus study). *Faculty:* 24 full-time (17 women), 12 part-time/adjunct (7 women). *Students:* 201 full-time (162 women), 325 part-time (255 women); includes 124 minority (36 Black or African American, non-Hispanic/Latino; 4 American Indian or Alaska Native, non-Hispanic/Latino; 10 Asian, non-Hispanic/Latino; 74 Hispanic/Latino), 47 international. Average age 34. 220 applicants, 55% accepted, 64 enrolled. In 2013, 215 master's, 15 doctorates, 14 other advanced degrees awarded. Terminal master's awarded for partial completion of doctoral program. *Degree requirements:* For master's, comprehensive exam (for some programs), thesis (for some programs); for doctorate, comprehensive exam (for some programs), thesis/dissertation (for some programs). *Entrance requirements:* For master's and doctorate, GRE General Test, minimum GPA of 3.0; for Ed S, GRE General Test. Additional exam requirements/recommendations for international students: Required—TOEFL (minimum score 550 paper-based; 80 iBT), IELTS (minimum score 6). *Application deadline:* For fall admission, 2/15 for domestic students, 12/1 for international students; for spring admission, 9/15 for domestic students, 3/1 for international students. Applications are processed on a rolling basis. Application fee: $30. Electronic applications accepted. *Expenses:* Tuition, state resident: full-time $12,640. Tuition, nonresident: full-time $30,000. *Financial support:* In 2013–14, 52 students received support, including 3 fellowships (averaging $2,365 per year), 20 research assistantships (averaging $11,715 per year), 58 teaching assistantships (averaging $8,410 per year); career-related internships or fieldwork and unspecified assistantships also available. Financial award applicants required to submit FAFSA. *Faculty research:* Early childhood, child and adolescents, diverse learners, race/ethnicity issues, teacher education, professional development, language and literacy development, policy development. *Unit head:* Elizabeth Bondy, PhD, Interim Director and Professor, 352-273-4242, Fax: 352-392-9193, E-mail: bondy@coe.ufl.edu. *Application contact:* Sevan Terzian, Graduate Coordinator, 352-273-4216, Fax: 352-392-9193, E-mail: sterzian@coe.ufl.edu.
Website: http://education.ufl.edu/school-teaching-learning/.

University of Georgia, College of Education, Department of Mathematics and Science Education, Athens, GA 30602. Offers mathematics education (M Ed, Ed D, PhD, Ed S); science education (M Ed, Ed D, PhD, Ed S).

University of Illinois at Chicago, Graduate College, College of Liberal Arts and Sciences, Department of Mathematics, Statistics, and Computer Science, Program in Teaching of Mathematics, Chicago, IL 60607-7128. Offers elementary school mathematics (MST); secondary school mathematics (MST). Part-time programs available. *Students:* 5 full-time (2 women), 23 part-time (18 women); includes 5 minority (4 Hispanic/Latino; 1 Two or more races, non-Hispanic/Latino). Average age 34. 9 applicants, 78% accepted, 7 enrolled. In 2013, 4 master's awarded. *Degree requirements:* For master's, comprehensive exam. *Entrance requirements:* For master's, GRE General Test, minimum GPA of 2.75. Additional exam requirements/recommendations for international students: Required—TOEFL. *Application deadline:* For fall admission, 1/1 for domestic and international students; for spring admission, 10/1 for domestic students, 7/15 for international students. Applications are processed on a rolling basis. Application fee: $40 ($50 for international students). Electronic applications accepted. *Expenses:* Tuition, state resident: full-time $11,066; part-time $3689 per term. Tuition, nonresident: full-time $23,064; part-time $7688 per term. *Required fees:* $3004; $1190 per term. Tuition and fees vary according to course level and program. *Financial support:* In 2013–14, 9 students received support, including 4 fellowships with full tuition reimbursements available; research assistantships with full tuition reimbursements available, teaching assistantships with full tuition reimbursements available, Federal Work-Study, scholarships/grants, traineeships, tuition waivers (full), and unspecified assistantships also available. Financial award application deadline: 3/1; financial award applicants required to submit FAFSA. *Unit head:* Alison Castro-Superfine, Director, 312-413-3019, E-mail: amcastro@uic.edu.
Website: http://www.math.uic.edu/mathed/secondary/MST.

University of Illinois at Chicago, Graduate College, Program in Learning Sciences, Chicago, IL 60607-7128. Offers PhD. *Expenses:* Tuition, state resident: full-time $11,066; part-time $3689 per term. Tuition, nonresident: full-time $23,064; part-time $7688 per term. *Required fees:* $3004; $1190 per term. Tuition and fees vary according to course level and program. *Unit head:* Dr. Clark Hulse, Dean, 312-413-2550. *Application contact:* Receptionist, 312-413-2550, E-mail: gradcoll@uic.edu.

University of Illinois at Urbana–Champaign, Graduate College, College of Liberal Arts and Sciences, Department of Mathematics, Champaign, IL 61820. Offers applied

mathematics (MS); applied mathematics: actuarial science (MS); mathematics (MS, PhD); teaching of mathematics (MS). *Students:* 211 (78 women). Application fee: $75 ($90 for international students). *Unit head:* Matthew Ando, Chair, 217-244-2846, Fax: 217-333-9576, E-mail: mando@illinois.edu. *Application contact:* Marci Blocher, Office Support Specialist, 217-333-5749, Fax: 217-333-9576, E-mail: mblocher@illinois.edu. Website: http://math.illinois.edu/.

University of Indianapolis, Graduate Programs, School of Education, Indianapolis, IN 46227-3697. Offers art education (MAT); biology (MAT); chemistry (MAT); curriculum and instruction (MA); earth sciences (MAT); education (MA, MAT); educational leadership (MA); elementary education (MA); English (MAT); French (MAT); math (MAT); physical education (MAT); physics (MAT); secondary education (MA), including art education, education, English education, social studies education; social studies (MAT); Spanish (MAT). *Accreditation:* NCATE. Part-time and evening/weekend programs available. *Faculty:* 5 full-time (4 women), 2 part-time/adjunct (1 woman). *Students:* 19 full-time (9 women), 54 part-time (27 women); includes 13 minority (5 Black or African American, non-Hispanic/Latino; 1 Asian, non-Hispanic/Latino; 5 Hispanic/Latino; 2 Two or more races, non-Hispanic/Latino), 1 international. Average age 32. In 2013, 52 master's awarded. *Entrance requirements:* For master's, GRE Subject Test, PRAXIS I, minimum GPA of 2.5, 3 letters of recommendation, interview. Additional exam requirements/recommendations for international students: Required—TOEFL (minimum score 550 paper-based). *Application deadline:* Applications are processed on a rolling basis. Application fee: $50. *Expenses: Tuition:* Full-time $5436; part-time $810 per credit hour. *Financial support:* Federal Work-Study available. Financial award application deadline: 5/1; financial award applicants required to submit FAFSA. *Faculty research:* Assessment of teacher education, perceptions of prospective teachers by parents. *Unit head:* Dr. Kathy Moran, Dean, 317-788-3285, Fax: 317-788-3300, E-mail: kmoran@uindy.edu. *Application contact:* Jeni Kirby, Administrative Assistant, Teacher Education, 317-788-2113, E-mail: kirbyj@uindy.edu.
Website: http://education.uindy.edu/.

The University of Iowa, Graduate College, College of Education, Department of Teaching and Learning, Program in Education, Iowa City, IA 52242-1316. Offers art education (MA); developmental reading (MA); elementary education (MA); English education (MA, MAT); foreign and second language education (MAT); foreign language education (MA); foreign language/ESL education (PhD); language, literacy and culture (PhD); mathematics education (MA, MAT, PhD); music education (MM, PhD); science education (MA); secondary education (MA); social studies (MA, PhD). *Degree requirements:* For master's, thesis optional, exam; for doctorate, comprehensive exam, thesis/dissertation. *Entrance requirements:* For master's and doctorate, GRE General Test, minimum GPA of 3.0. Additional exam requirements/recommendations for international students: Required—TOEFL (minimum score 550 paper-based; 81 iBT). Electronic applications accepted.

University of Louisiana at Monroe, Graduate School, College of Arts, Education, and Sciences, School of Education, Program in Curriculum and Instruction, Monroe, LA 71209-0001. Offers art education (M Ed); biology education (M Ed); chemistry education (M Ed); curriculum and instruction (Ed D); early childhood education (M Ed); earth science education (M Ed); educational leadership (M Ed); elementary education (1-5) (M Ed); English as a second language (M Ed); English education (M Ed); family and consumer education (M Ed); French education (M Ed); history education (M Ed); math education (M Ed); middle school education (M Ed); music education (M Ed); reading education (K-12) (M Ed); Spanish education (M Ed); special education - academically gifted (M Ed); special education - early intervention (M Ed); special education - educational diagnostician (M Ed); special education - mild/moderate disabilities (M Ed); speech education (M Ed). *Accreditation:* NCATE. *Degree requirements:* For master's, comprehensive exam (for some programs), thesis; for doctorate, thesis/dissertation, internships. *Entrance requirements:* For master's, GRE General Test; for doctorate, GRE General Test, minimum undergraduate GPA of 2.75, graduate 3.25. Additional exam requirements/recommendations for international students: Required—TOEFL (minimum score 500 paper-based; 61 iBT). *Application deadline:* For fall admission, 8/24 priority date for domestic students, 7/1 for international students; for winter admission, 12/14 priority date for domestic students; for spring admission, 1/19 for domestic students, 11/1 for international students. Applications are processed on a rolling basis. Application fee: $20 ($30 for international students). Electronic applications accepted. *Expenses: Tuition,* state resident: full-time $6607. *Tuition,* nonresident: full-time $17,179. Full-time tuition and fees vary according to program. *Financial support:* Research assistantships, career-related internships or fieldwork, Federal Work-Study, and unspecified assistantships available. Financial award application deadline: 4/1; financial award applicants required to submit FAFSA. *Unit head:* Dr. Dorothy Schween, Director, 318-342-1268, Fax: 318-342-3131, E-mail: schween@ulm.edu. *Application contact:* Dr. Dorothy Schween, Director, 318-342-1268, Fax: 318-342-3131, E-mail: schween@ulm.edu.

University of Maine, Graduate School, College of Education and Human Development, Department of Exercise Science and STEM Education, Orono, ME 04469. Offers classroom technology integrationist (CGS); education data specialist (CGS); educational technology coordinator (CGS); kinesiology and physical education (M Ed, MS); science education (M Ed, MS); STEM education (PhD). Part-time and evening/weekend programs available. *Students:* 25 full-time (13 women), 28 part-time (16 women); includes 5 minority (2 Black or African American, non-Hispanic/Latino; 2 American Indian or Alaska Native, non-Hispanic/Latino; 1 Asian, non-Hispanic/Latino), 2 international. Average age 34. 19 applicants, 84% accepted, 12 enrolled. In 2013, 6 master's awarded. *Degree requirements:* For master's, thesis (for some programs); for doctorate, comprehensive exam, thesis/dissertation. *Entrance requirements:* For master's, GRE General Test, MAT; for doctorate, GRE General Test. Additional exam requirements/recommendations for international students: Required—TOEFL. *Application deadline:* For fall admission, 1/15 for domestic students. Applications are processed on a rolling basis. Application fee: $65. Electronic applications accepted. *Expenses: Tuition,* state resident: full-time $7524. *Tuition,* nonresident: full-time $23,112. *Required fees:* $1970. *Financial support:* In 2013–14, 13 students received support, including 2 teaching assistantships (averaging $14,600 per year). Financial award application deadline: 3/1. *Faculty research:* Integration of technology in K-12 classrooms, instructional theory and practice in science, inquiry-based teaching, professional development, exercise science, adaptive physical education, neuromuscular function/dysfunction. *Unit head:* Dr. Janet Spector, Dean, 207-581-2441, Fax: 207-581-2423. *Application contact:* Scott G. Delcourt, Associate Dean of the Graduate School, 207-581-3291, Fax: 207-581-3232, E-mail: graduate@maine.edu. Website: http://umaine.edu/edhd/.

University of Maryland, Baltimore County, Graduate School, College of Arts, Humanities and Social Sciences, Department of Education, Master of Arts in Education Program, Baltimore, MD 21250. Offers K-8 mathematics instructional leadership (MAE); K-8 science education (MAE); K-8 STEM education (MAE); secondary mathematics education (MAE); secondary science education (MAE); secondary STEM education (MAE). Part-time and evening/weekend programs available. Postbaccalaureate distance learning degree programs offered (no on-campus study). *Faculty:* 5 full-time (4 women), 5 part-time/adjunct (all women). *Students:* 1 (woman) full-time, 133 part-time (100

women); includes 15 minority (13 Black or African American, non-Hispanic/Latino; 2 Hispanic/Latino). Average age 32. 47 applicants, 96% accepted, 45 enrolled. In 2013, 41 master's awarded. *Degree requirements:* For master's, comprehensive exam (for some programs), thesis (for some programs). *Application deadline:* For fall admission, 6/1 for domestic students; for spring admission, 11/1 for domestic students. Electronic applications accepted. One-time fee: $200 full-time. *Financial support:* Application deadline: 3/1. *Unit head:* Dr. Eugene Schaffer, Director, 410-455-8423, Fax: 410-455-1880, E-mail: schaffer@umbc.edu.
Website: http://www.umbc.edu/education/mae.

University of Maryland, Baltimore County, Graduate School, College of Arts, Humanities and Social Sciences, Department of Education, Program in Teaching, Baltimore, MD 21250. Offers early childhood education (MAT); elementary education (MAT); secondary education (MAT), including art, biology, chemistry, dance, earth/space science, English, foreign language, mathematics, music, physics, social studies, theatre. Part-time and evening/weekend programs available. *Faculty:* 24 full-time (18 women), 25 part-time/adjunct (19 women). *Students:* 49 full-time (34 women), 35 part-time (23 women); includes 19 minority (9 Black or African American, non-Hispanic/Latino; 3 Asian, non-Hispanic/Latino; 6 Hispanic/Latino; 1 Two or more races, non-Hispanic/Latino). Average age 30. 40 applicants, 95% accepted, 35 enrolled. In 2013, 106 master's awarded. *Degree requirements:* For master's, comprehensive exam (for some programs), thesis (for some programs). *Entrance requirements:* For master's, PRAXIS I or SAT (minimum score of 1000), minimum GPA of 3.0. Additional exam requirements/recommendations for international students: Required—TOEFL. *Application deadline:* For fall admission, 6/1 for domestic students; for spring admission, 11/1 for domestic students. Applications are processed on a rolling basis. Application fee: $50. Electronic applications accepted. One-time fee: $200 full-time. *Financial support:* In 2013–14, 6 students received support, including teaching assistantships with full and partial tuition reimbursements available (averaging $12,000 per year); career-related internships or fieldwork, Federal Work-Study, scholarships/grants, tuition waivers, and unspecified assistantships also available. Financial award application deadline: 3/1. *Faculty research:* STEM teacher education, culturally sensitive pedagogy, ESOL/bilingual education, early childhood education, language, literacy and culture. *Unit head:* Dr. Susan M. Blunck, Graduate Program Director, 410-455-2869, Fax: 410-455-3986, E-mail: blunck@umbc.edu. *Application contact:* Dr. Susan M. Blunck, Graduate Program Director, 410-455-2869, Fax: 410-455-3986, E-mail: blunck@umbc.edu.
Website: http://www.umbc.edu/education/.

University of Massachusetts Dartmouth, Graduate School, College of Arts and Sciences, School of Education, Program in Mathematics Education, North Dartmouth, MA 02747-2300. Offers math education (PhD). Part-time programs available. *Faculty:* 4 full-time (2 women), 2 part-time/adjunct (both women). *Students:* 9 full-time (2 women), 5 part-time (4 women); includes 1 minority (Black or African American, non-Hispanic/Latino), 2 international. Average age 34. 9 applicants, 89% accepted, 5 enrolled. In 2013, 1 doctorate awarded. *Degree requirements:* For doctorate, comprehensive exam, thesis/dissertation. *Entrance requirements:* For doctorate, GRE, statement of purpose (minimum of 300 words), resume, 3 letters of recommendation, official transcripts. Additional exam requirements/recommendations for international students: Required—TOEFL (minimum score 533 paper-based; 72 iBT). *Application deadline:* For fall admission, 3/31 priority date for domestic students, 2/28 priority date for international students; for spring admission, 11/15 priority date for domestic students, 10/15 priority date for international students. Applications are processed on a rolling basis. Application fee: $60. Electronic applications accepted. *Expenses:* Tuition, state resident: full-time $2071; part-time $86.29 per credit. Tuition, nonresident: full-time $8099; part-time $337.46 per credit. Tuition and fees vary according to course load and reciprocity agreements. *Financial support:* In 2013–14, 1 fellowship with full tuition reimbursement (averaging $2,769 per year), 2 research assistantships with full tuition reimbursements (averaging $21,500 per year), 4 teaching assistantships with full tuition reimbursements (averaging $16,000 per year) were awarded; Federal Work-Study and unspecified assistantships also available. Support available to part-time students. Financial award application deadline: 3/1; financial award applicants required to submit FAFSA. *Faculty research:* Role of metacognition in advanced mathematical thinking, conceptual and historical development of mathematical concepts, semiotics specific to the coevolution of symbolic thinking and digital technologies, relationship between teachers' organizations of proportional reasoning and understanding the ways they teach proportions in their classrooms, development of teachers' specialized knowledge for teaching science. Total annual research expenditures: $655,000. *Unit head:* Chandra Orrill, Graduate Program Director, 774-929-3052, Fax: 508-999-9215, E-mail: corrill@umassd.edu. *Application contact:* Steven Briggs, Director of Marketing and Recruitment for Graduate Studies, 508-999-8604, Fax: 508-999-8183, E-mail: graduate@umassd.edu.
Website: http://www.umassd.edu/mathedphd/.

University of Massachusetts Lowell, Graduate School of Education, Lowell, MA 01854-2881. Offers administration, planning, and policy (CAGS); curriculum and instruction (M Ed, CAGS); educational administration (M Ed); language arts and literacy (Ed D); leadership in schooling (Ed D); math and science education (Ed D); reading and language (M Ed, CAGS). *Accreditation:* NCATE. Part-time and evening/weekend programs available. Postbaccalaureate distance learning degree programs offered (no on-campus study). Terminal master's awarded for partial completion of doctoral program. *Degree requirements:* For doctorate, thesis/dissertation. *Entrance requirements:* For master's, doctorate, and CAGS, GRE General Test. Additional exam requirements/recommendations for international students: Required—TOEFL. Electronic applications accepted.

University of Miami, Graduate School, School of Education and Human Development, Department of Teaching and Learning, Program in Teaching and Learning, Coral Gables, FL 33124. Offers language and literacy learning in multilingual settings (PhD); science, technology, engineering and mathematics (PhD); special education (PhD). *Faculty:* 14 full-time (10 women), 9 part-time/adjunct (all women). *Students:* 24 full-time (21 women); includes 11 minority (3 Black or African American, non-Hispanic/Latino; 7 Hispanic/Latino; 1 Two or more races, non-Hispanic/Latino), 5 international. Average age 32. 29 applicants, 21% accepted, 5 enrolled. In 2013, 2 doctorates awarded. *Degree requirements:* For doctorate, thesis/dissertation, qualifying exam, electronic portfolio. *Entrance requirements:* For doctorate, GRE General Test. Additional exam requirements/recommendations for international students: Required—TOEFL (minimum score 550 paper-based; 80 iBT); Recommended—IELTS (minimum score 6.5). *Application deadline:* For fall admission, 2/15 for domestic students, 10/1 for international students. Application fee: $65. Electronic applications accepted. *Financial support:* In 2013–14, 24 students received support, including 11 research assistantships with full and partial tuition reimbursements available (averaging $18,900 per year), 8 teaching assistantships with full and partial tuition reimbursements available (averaging $18,900 per year). Financial award application deadline: 3/1; financial award applicants required to submit FAFSA. *Faculty research:* Teacher education, multicultural education, special education, second language acquisition, math and science education. *Unit head:* Dr. Elizabeth Harry, Department Chairperson and Program Director, 305-284-4961, Fax: 305-284-6998, E-mail: bharry@miami.edu. *Application contact:* Lois

Heffernan, Graduate Admission Coordinator, 305-284-2167, Fax: 305-284-9395, E-mail: lheffernan@miami.edu.

University of Minnesota, Twin Cities Campus, Graduate School, College of Education and Human Development, Department of Curriculum and Instruction, Program in Teaching, Minneapolis, MN 55455-0213. Offers Chinese (M Ed); earth science (M Ed); elementary special education (M Ed); English (M Ed); English as a second language (M Ed); French (M Ed); German (M Ed); Hebrew (M Ed); Japanese (M Ed); life sciences (M Ed); mathematics (M Ed); middle school science (M Ed); science (M Ed); second languages and cultures (M Ed); social studies (M Ed); Spanish (M Ed). *Students:* 220 full-time (154 women), 83 part-time (60 women); includes 43 minority (10 Black or African American, non-Hispanic/Latino; 26 Asian, non-Hispanic/Latino; 7 Hispanic/Latino), 4 international. Average age 27. 261 applicants, 87% accepted, 222 enrolled. In 2013, 561 master's awarded. Application fee: $75 ($95 for international students). *Unit head:* Dr. Nina Asher, Chair, 612-624-1357, Fax: 612-624-8277, E-mail: nasher@umn.edu. *Application contact:* Dr. Jennifer Engler, Assistant Dean, 612-626-2887, Fax: 612-626-7496, E-mail: engle009@umn.edu. Website: http://www.cehd.umn.edu/ci/.

University of Missouri, Graduate School, College of Arts and Science, Department of Mathematics, Columbia, MO 65211. Offers applied mathematics (MS); mathematics (MA, MST, PhD). *Faculty:* 40 full-time (6 women), 1 (woman) part-time/adjunct. *Students:* 64 full-time (10 women), 5 part-time (0 women); includes 2 minority (1 Hispanic/Latino; 1 Two or more races, non-Hispanic/Latino), 23 international. Average age 27. 100 applicants, 33% accepted, 15 enrolled. In 2013, 12 master's, 6 doctorates awarded. *Degree requirements:* For doctorate, 2 foreign languages, comprehensive exam, thesis/dissertation. *Entrance requirements:* For master's and doctorate, GRE General Test, minimum GPA of 3.0; bachelor's degree from accredited institution. Additional exam requirements/recommendations for international students: Required—TOEFL (minimum score 500 paper-based; 61 iBT). *Application deadline:* For fall admission, 1/15 priority date for domestic and international students. Applications are processed on a rolling basis. Application fee: $55 ($75 for international students). Electronic applications accepted. *Financial support:* Fellowships with full tuition reimbursements, research assistantships with full tuition reimbursements, teaching assistantships with full tuition reimbursements, institutionally sponsored loans, health care benefits, and unspecified assistantships available. Financial award applicants required to submit FAFSA. *Faculty research:* Algebraic geometry, analysis (real, complex, functional and harmonic), analytic functions, applied mathematics, financial mathematics and mathematics of insurance, commutative rings, scattering theory, differential equations (ordinary and partial), differential geometry, dynamical systems, general relativity, mathematical physics, number theory, probabilistic analysis and topology. *Unit head:* Dr. Glen Himmelberg, Department Chair, 573-882-6222, E-mail: himmelbergg@missouri.edu. *Application contact:* Amy Crews, Administrative Assistant, 573-882-6222, E-mail: crewsae@missouri.edu. Website: http://www.math.missouri.edu/degrees/graduate/index.html.

University of Missouri, Graduate School, College of Education, Department of Learning, Teaching and Curriculum, Columbia, MO 65211. Offers agricultural education (M Ed, PhD, Ed S); art education (M Ed, PhD, Ed S); business and office education (M Ed, PhD, Ed S); early childhood education (M Ed, PhD, Ed S); elementary education (M Ed, PhD, Ed S); English education (M Ed, PhD, Ed S); foreign language education (M Ed, PhD, Ed S); health education and promotion (M Ed, PhD); learning and instruction (M Ed); marketing education (M Ed, PhD, Ed S); mathematics education (M Ed, PhD, Ed S); music education (M Ed, PhD, Ed S); reading education (M Ed, PhD, Ed S); science education (M Ed, PhD, Ed S); social studies education (M Ed, PhD, Ed S); vocational education (M Ed, PhD, Ed S). Part-time programs available. *Faculty:* 26 full-time (16 women), 3 part-time/adjunct (2 women). *Students:* 186 full-time (143 women), 197 part-time (172 women); includes 19 minority (4 Black or African American, non-Hispanic/Latino; 4 Asian, non-Hispanic/Latino; 6 Hispanic/Latino; 5 Two or more races, non-Hispanic/Latino), 25 international. Average age 31. 288 applicants, 65% accepted, 160 enrolled. In 2013, 202 master's, 18 doctorates, 7 other advanced degrees awarded. Terminal master's awarded for partial completion of doctoral program. *Degree requirements:* For doctorate, thesis/dissertation. *Entrance requirements:* For master's and Ed S, GRE General Test or MAT, minimum GPA of 3.0; for doctorate, GRE General Test, minimum GPA of 3.0. Additional exam requirements/recommendations for international students: Required—TOEFL (minimum score 600 paper-based; 100 iBT). *Application deadline:* For fall admission, 12/1 priority date for domestic and international students. Applications are processed on a rolling basis. Application fee: $55 ($75 for international students). Electronic applications accepted. *Financial support:* Fellowships, research assistantships, teaching assistantships, institutionally sponsored loans, traineeships, health care benefits, and unspecified assistantships available. Support available to part-time students. *Faculty research:* Curriculum development and research, teacher education, art education, business and marketing, early childhood education, English education, literacy/reading education, mathematics education, music education, science education, social studies education. *Unit head:* Dr. James Tarr, Associate Division Director, 573-882-4034, E-mail: tarrj@missouri.edu. *Application contact:* Fran Colley, Academic Advisor, 573-882-6462, E-mail: colleyf@missouri.edu. Website: http://education.missouri.edu/LTC/.

The University of Montana, Graduate School, College of Arts and Sciences, Department of Mathematical Sciences, Missoula, MT 59812-0002. Offers mathematics (MA, PhD), including college teaching (PhD), traditional mathematics research (PhD); mathematics education (MA). Part-time programs available. Terminal master's awarded for partial completion of doctoral program. *Degree requirements:* For doctorate, thesis/dissertation. *Entrance requirements:* For master's and doctorate, GRE General Test. Additional exam requirements/recommendations for international students: Required—TOEFL (minimum score 525 paper-based).

University of Nebraska at Kearney, Graduate Programs, College of Natural and Social Sciences, Department of Biology, Kearney, NE 68849. Offers biology (MS); science/math education (MA Ed). Part-time and evening/weekend programs available. Postbaccalaureate distance learning degree programs offered (no on-campus study). *Degree requirements:* For master's, thesis optional. *Entrance requirements:* For master's, GRE (for thesis option and for online program applicants if undergraduate GPA is below 2.75), letter of interest. Additional exam requirements/recommendations for international students: Required—TOEFL (minimum score 550 paper-based; 79 iBT). Electronic applications accepted. *Faculty research:* Pollution injury, molecular biology-viral gene expression, prairie range condition modeling, evolution of symbiotic nitrogen fixation.

University of Nevada, Reno, Graduate School, College of Science, Department of Mathematics and Statistics, Reno, NV 89557. Offers mathematics (MS); teaching mathematics (MATM). *Degree requirements:* For master's, thesis optional. *Entrance requirements:* For master's, GRE General Test, minimum GPA of 2.75. Additional exam requirements/recommendations for international students: Required—TOEFL (minimum score 500 paper-based; 61 iBT), IELTS (minimum score 6). Electronic applications accepted. *Faculty research:* Operator algebra, nonlinear systems, differential equations.

University of New Hampshire, Graduate School, College of Engineering and Physical Sciences, Department of Mathematics and Statistics, Durham, NH 03824. Offers applied mathematics (MS); industrial statistics (Postbaccalaureate Certificate); mathematics (MS, MST, PhD); mathematics education (PhD); statistics (MS). *Faculty:* 21 full-time (5 women). *Students:* 29 full-time (8 women), 37 part-time (14 women); includes 4 minority (1 American Indian or Alaska Native, non-Hispanic/Latino; 3 Asian, non-Hispanic/Latino), 24 international. Average age 29. 76 applicants, 53% accepted, 20 enrolled. In 2013, 9 master's, 2 doctorates, 1 other advanced degree awarded. Terminal master's awarded for partial completion of doctoral program. *Degree requirements:* For doctorate, 2 foreign languages, thesis/dissertation. *Entrance requirements:* Additional exam requirements/recommendations for international students: Required—TOEFL (minimum score 550 paper-based; 80 iBT). *Application deadline:* For fall admission, 4/1 priority date for domestic students, 4/1 for international students; for spring admission, 12/1 for domestic students. Applications are processed on a rolling basis. Application fee: $65. Electronic applications accepted. *Expenses:* Tuition, state resident: full-time $13,500; part-time $750 per credit hour. Tuition, nonresident: full-time $26,200; part-time $1100 per credit hour. *Required fees:* $1741; $435.25 per term. Tuition and fees vary according to course level, course load, campus/location and program. *Financial support:* In 2013–14, 46 students received support, including 3 fellowships, 2 research assistantships, 40 teaching assistantships; Federal Work-Study, scholarships/grants, and tuition waivers (full and partial) also available. Support available to part-time students. Financial award application deadline: 2/15. *Faculty research:* Operator theory, complex analysis, algebra, nonlinear dynamics, statistics. *Unit head:* Dr. Edward Hinson, Chairperson, 603-862-2688. *Application contact:* Jan Jankowski, Administrative Assistant, 603-862-2320, E-mail: jan.jankowski@unh.edu. Website: http://www.math.unh.edu/.

The University of North Carolina at Chapel Hill, Graduate School, School of Education, Program in Secondary Education, Chapel Hill, NC 27599. Offers English (Grades 9-12) (MAT); English as a second language (MAT); French (Grades K-12) (MAT); German (Grades K-12) (MAT); Japanese (Grades K-12) (MAT); Latin (Grades 9-12) (MAT); mathematics (Grades 9-12) (MAT); music (Grades K-12) (MAT); science (Grades 9-12) (MAT); social studies (Grades 9-12) (MAT); Spanish (Grades K-12) (MAT). *Accreditation:* NCATE. *Degree requirements:* For master's, comprehensive exam. *Entrance requirements:* For master's, GRE General Test, minimum GPA of 3.0 during last 2 years of undergraduate course work. Additional exam requirements/recommendations for international students: Required—TOEFL (minimum score 550 paper-based). Electronic applications accepted.

The University of North Carolina at Charlotte, The Graduate School, College of Liberal Arts and Sciences, Department of Mathematics and Statistics, Charlotte, NC 28223-0001. Offers applied mathematics (MS, PhD); applied statistics (MS); general mathematics (MS); mathematics education (MA). Part-time and evening/weekend programs available. *Faculty:* 40 full-time (6 women). *Students:* 49 full-time (21 women), 21 part-time (15 women); includes 6 minority (2 Black or African American, non-Hispanic/Latino; 3 Asian, non-Hispanic/Latino; 1 Hispanic/Latino), 34 international. Average age 29. 64 applicants, 75% accepted, 11 enrolled. In 2013, 8 master's, 9 doctorates awarded. Terminal master's awarded for partial completion of doctoral program. *Degree requirements:* For master's, comprehensive exam, thesis or alternative; for doctorate, thesis/dissertation. *Entrance requirements:* For master's, GRE General Test, minimum GPA of 3.0 in undergraduate major, 2.75 overall; for doctorate, GRE General Test, minimum overall GPA of 3.0. Additional exam requirements/recommendations for international students: Required—TOEFL (minimum score 557 paper-based; 83 iBT), Michigan English Language Assessment Battery (minimum score 78) or IELTS (minimum score 6.5). *Application deadline:* For fall admission, 5/1 for domestic and international students; for spring admission, 10/1 for domestic and international students. Applications are processed on a rolling basis. Application fee: $75. Electronic applications accepted. *Expenses:* Tuition, state resident: full-time $3522. Tuition, nonresident: full-time $16,051. *Required fees:* $2585. Tuition and fees vary according to course load and program. *Financial support:* In 2013–14, 38 students received support, including 2 fellowships (averaging $17,457 per year), 2 research assistantships (averaging $3,560 per year), 34 teaching assistantships (averaging $14,243 per year); career-related internships or fieldwork, Federal Work-Study, institutionally sponsored loans, scholarships/grants, and unspecified assistantships also available. Support available to part-time students. Financial award application deadline: 4/1; financial award applicants required to submit FAFSA. *Faculty research:* Numerical analysis and scientific computation, probability and stochastic processes, partial differential equations and mathematical physics, algebra and combinatorics, analysis, biostatistics, topology. *Total annual research expenditures:* $1.1 million. *Unit head:* Dr. Yuanan Diao, Chair, 704-687-0635, Fax: 704-687-1392, E-mail: ydiao@uncc.edu. *Application contact:* Kathy B. Giddings, Director of Graduate Admissions, 704-687-5503, Fax: 704-687-1668, E-mail: gradadm@uncc.edu. Website: http://www.math.uncc.edu/.

The University of North Carolina at Greensboro, Graduate School, School of Education, Department of Curriculum and Instruction, Greensboro, NC 27412-5001. Offers college teaching and adult learning (Certificate); curriculum and instruction (M Ed), including chemistry education, elementary education, English as a second language, French education, instructional technology, mathematics education, middle grades education, reading education, science education, social studies education, Spanish education; curriculum and teaching (PhD), including higher education, teacher education and development; English as a second language (Certificate); higher education (M Ed); supervision (M Ed). *Accreditation:* NCATE. Part-time programs available. *Degree requirements:* For doctorate, thesis/dissertation. *Entrance requirements:* For master's and doctorate, GRE General Test. Additional exam requirements/recommendations for international students: Required—TOEFL. Electronic applications accepted. *Faculty research:* Community college literacy program, middle school mathematics/computer mathematics.

The University of North Carolina at Pembroke, Graduate Studies, Department of Mathematics and Computer Science, Program in Mathematics Education, Pembroke, NC 28372-1510. Offers MA. *Accreditation:* NCATE. Part-time and evening/weekend programs available. *Degree requirements:* For master's, comprehensive exam, thesis optional. *Entrance requirements:* For master's, GRE General Test or MAT, bachelor's degree in mathematics or mathematics education; minimum GPA of 3.0 in major, 2.5 overall. Additional exam requirements/recommendations for international students: Required—TOEFL.

University of Northern Colorado, Graduate School, College of Natural and Health Sciences, School of Mathematical Sciences, Greeley, CO 80639. Offers mathematical teaching (MA); mathematics (MA, PhD); mathematics education (PhD); mathematics: liberal arts (MA). Part-time programs available. *Degree requirements:* For master's, comprehensive exam, thesis or alternative; for doctorate, comprehensive exam, thesis/dissertation. *Entrance requirements:* For master's, GRE General Test (liberal arts), 3 letters of recommendation; for doctorate, GRE General Test, 3 letters of recommendation. Electronic applications accepted.

University of Northern Iowa, Graduate College, College of Humanities, Arts and Sciences, Department of Mathematics, Program in Mathematics, Cedar Falls, IA 50614. Offers community college teaching (MA); mathematics (MA); secondary teaching (MA). *Students:* 5 full-time (1 woman), 23 part-time (13 women); includes 1 minority (Black or

African American, non-Hispanic/Latino). 8 applicants, 50% accepted, 2 enrolled. In 2013, 4 master's awarded. Application fee: $50 ($70 for international students). *Unit head:* Dr. Michael Prophet, Coordinator, 319-273-2104, Fax: 319-273-2546, E-mail: mike.prophet@uni.edu. *Application contact:* Laurie S. Russell, Record Analyst, 319-273-2623, Fax: 319-273-2885, E-mail: laurie.russell@uni.edu.

University of Northern Iowa, Graduate College, College of Humanities, Arts and Sciences, Department of Mathematics, Program in Mathematics for the Middle Grades, Cedar Falls, IA 50614. Offers MA. *Students:* 11 part-time (all women). 1 applicant, 100% accepted. In 2013, 1 master's awarded. Application fee: $50 ($70 for international students). *Unit head:* Dr. Brian Townsend, Coordinator, 319-273-2397, Fax: 319-273-2546, E-mail: brian.townsend@uni.edu. *Application contact:* Laurie S. Russell, Record Analyst, 319-273-2623, Fax: 319-273-2885, E-mail: laurie.russell@uni.edu.

University of North Georgia, School of Education, Dahlonega, GA 30597. Offers art education (MAT); early childhood education (M Ed); English education (MAT); history education (MAT); math education (MAT); middle grades education (M Ed, MAT); physical education (MS); school leadership (Ed S); secondary education (M Ed), including English education, history education, mathematics education, physical education; teacher education (MAT). *Accreditation:* NCATE. Part-time and evening/weekend programs available. Postbaccalaureate distance learning degree programs offered (no on-campus study). *Degree requirements:* For master's, comprehensive exam, thesis optional. *Entrance requirements:* For master's, GRE or MAT, GACE, minimum GPA of 2.75; for Ed S, GRE General Test or MAT, 3 years of teaching experience, master's degree, minimum graduate GPA of 3.25, leadership position in the school. Additional exam requirements/recommendations for international students: Required—TOEFL (minimum score 550 paper-based; 79 iBT), IELTS (minimum score 6.5). Electronic applications accepted. *Faculty research:* Identification of professional development school structures supporting P-12 student achievement, impact of diverse field placement settings in teacher belief development among preservice teachers, use of inquiry methodology in social studies teaching with English language learners, use of instructional differentiation in the middle grades classroom, effects of international school placements on preservice teacher beliefs and attitudes.

University of Oklahoma, Jeannine Rainbolt College of Education, Department of Instructional Leadership and Academic Curriculum, Norman, OK 73072. Offers communication, culture and pedagogy for Hispanic populations in educational settings (Graduate Certificate); instructional leadership and academic curriculum (M Ed, PhD), including bilingual education (PhD), early childhood education, elementary education, English education, instructional leadership, mathematics education, reading education, science education, science, technology, engineering and mathematics education (M Ed), secondary education, social studies education, teacher education (M Ed), world language education (M Ed). *Accreditation:* NCATE. Part-time and evening/weekend programs available. Postbaccalaureate distance learning degree programs offered (no on-campus study). *Faculty:* 22 full-time (15 women), 1 (woman) part-time/adjunct. *Students:* 64 full-time (49 women), 103 part-time (81 women); includes 33 minority (8 Black or African American, non-Hispanic/Latino; 9 American Indian or Alaska Native, non-Hispanic/Latino; 5 Asian, non-Hispanic/Latino; 4 Hispanic/Latino; 1 Native Hawaiian or other Pacific Islander, non-Hispanic/Latino; 6 Two or more races, non-Hispanic/Latino), 10 international. Average age 34. 50 applicants, 84% accepted, 36 enrolled. In 2013, 26 master's, 11 doctorates awarded. Terminal master's awarded for partial completion of doctoral program. *Degree requirements:* For master's, comprehensive exam (for some programs), thesis (for some programs); for doctorate, comprehensive exam, thesis/dissertation. *Entrance requirements:* For master's, essay; for doctorate, GRE, 3 recommendation letters; autobiography, statement of objectives; essay on chosen major; transcripts; writing sample. Additional exam requirements/recommendations for international students: Required—TOEFL (minimum score 79 iBT). *Application deadline:* For fall admission, 4/30 for domestic and international students; for spring admission, 10/31 for domestic and international students; for summer admission, 3/15 for domestic and international students. Applications are processed on a rolling basis. Application fee: $50 ($100 for international students). Electronic applications accepted. *Expenses:* Tuition, state resident: full-time $4205; part-time $175.20 per credit hour. Tuition, nonresident: full-time $16,205; part-time $675.20 per credit hour. *Required fees:* $2745; $103.85 per credit hour. $126.50 per semester. *Financial support:* In 2013–14, 98 students received support, including 10 research assistantships with partial tuition reimbursements available (averaging $10,671 per year), 7 teaching assistantships with partial tuition reimbursements available (averaging $10,753 per year); Federal Work-Study, institutionally sponsored loans, scholarships/grants, and unspecified assistantships also available. Support available to part-time students. Financial award application deadline: 6/1; financial award applicants required to submit FAFSA. *Total annual research expenditures:* $1 million. *Unit head:* Dr. Stacy Reeder, Chair/Graduate Liaison, 405-325-1498, Fax: 405-325-4061, E-mail: reeder@ou.edu. *Application contact:* Lynn Crussel, Graduate Programs Officer, 405-325-1498, Fax: 405-325-4061, E-mail: lcrussel@ou.edu.
Website: http://education.ou.edu/departments/ilac.

University of Phoenix–North Florida Campus, College of Education, Jacksonville, FL 32216-0959. Offers administration and supervision (MA Ed); curriculum and instruction (MA Ed), including computer education, mathematics education; early childhood education (MA Ed); elementary teacher education (MA Ed); secondary teacher education (MA Ed). Evening/weekend programs available. *Degree requirements:* For master's, thesis (for some programs). *Entrance requirements:* For master's, 3 years of work experience, minimum undergraduate GPA of 2.5. Additional exam requirements/recommendations for international students: Required—TOEFL (minimum score 550 paper-based; 49 iBT). Electronic applications accepted.

University of Phoenix–Omaha Campus, College of Education, Omaha, NE 68154-5240. Offers administration and supervision (MA Ed); curriculum and instruction (MA Ed), including adult education, computer education, curriculum and instruction, English and language arts education, English as a second language, mathematics education; elementary teacher education (MA Ed); secondary teacher education (MA Ed); special education (MA Ed).

University of Phoenix–Online Campus, College of Education, Phoenix, AZ 85034-7209. Offers administration and supervision (MAEd, Certificate); adult education and training (MAEd); curriculum and instruction (MAEd), including computer education, curriculum and instruction, English as a second language, language arts, mathematics, reading; early childhood education (MAEd); educational studies (MAEd); elementary teacher education (MAEd), including early childhood, elementary teacher education, high school middle level, middle level; principal licensure (Certificate); secondary teacher education (MAEd); special education (MAEd, Certificate); teacher education (MAEd), including middle level generalist; teacher education middle level mathematics (MAEd), including middle level mathematics; teacher education middle level science (MAEd), including middle level science; teacher education secondary mathematics (MAEd); teacher education secondary science (MAEd); teacher leadership (MAEd); teachers of English learners (Certificate); transition to teaching (Certificate), including elementary education, secondary education. *Accreditation:* Teacher Education Accreditation Council. Evening/weekend programs available. Postbaccalaureate

distance learning degree programs offered. *Entrance requirements:* Additional exam requirements/recommendations for international students: Required—TOEFL, TOEIC (Test of English as an International Communication), Berlitz Online English Proficiency Exam, PTE, or IELTS. Electronic applications accepted. *Expenses:* Contact institution.

University of Phoenix–South Florida Campus, College of Education, Miramar, FL 33030. Offers administration and supervision (MA Ed); curriculum and instruction (MA Ed), including computer education, curriculum and instruction, mathematics education; early childhood education (MA Ed); elementary teacher education (MA Ed); secondary teacher education (MA Ed). Evening/weekend programs available. *Degree requirements:* For master's, thesis (for some programs). *Entrance requirements:* For master's, 3 years of work experience, minimum undergraduate GPA of 2.5. Additional exam requirements/recommendations for international students: Required—TOEFL (minimum score 550 paper-based; 79 iBT). Electronic applications accepted.

University of Phoenix–Springfield Campus, College of Education, Springfield, MO 65804-7211. Offers administration and supervision (MA Ed); curriculum and instruction (MA Ed), including computer education, curriculum and instruction, English and language arts education, English as a second language, mathematics education; English and language arts education (MA Ed).

University of Phoenix–Washington D.C. Campus, College of Education, Washington, DC 20001. Offers administration and supervision (MA Ed); adult education and training (MA Ed); computer education (MA Ed); curriculum and instruction (MA Ed, Ed D); early childhood education (MA Ed); education (Ed S); educational leadership (Ed D); educational technology (Ed D); elementary teacher education (MA Ed); English and language arts education (MA Ed); English as a second language (MA Ed); higher education administration (PhD); mathematics education (MA Ed); secondary teacher education (MA Ed); special education (MA Ed); teacher leadership (MA Ed).

University of Phoenix–West Florida Campus, College of Education, Temple Terrace, FL 33637. Offers administration and supervision (MA Ed); curriculum and instruction (MA Ed), including computer education, curriculum and instruction, mathematics education; curriculum and technology (MA Ed); early childhood education (MA Ed); elementary teacher education (MA Ed); secondary teacher education (MA Ed). Evening/weekend programs available. *Degree requirements:* For master's, thesis (for some programs). *Entrance requirements:* For master's, 3 years of work experience, minimum undergraduate GPA of 2.5. Additional exam requirements/recommendations for international students: Required—TOEFL (minimum score 550 paper-based; 79 iBT).

University of Pittsburgh, School of Education, Department of Instruction and Learning, Program in Secondary Education, Pittsburgh, PA 15260. Offers English/communications education (M Ed, MAT); foreign languages education (M Ed, MAT); mathematics education (M Ed, MAT, Ed D); science education (M Ed, MAT, Ed D); secondary education (PhD); social studies education (M Ed, MAT). Part-time and evening/weekend programs available. *Students:* 116 full-time (78 women), 47 part-time (36 women); includes 16 minority (4 Black or African American, non-Hispanic/Latino; 3 Asian, non-Hispanic/Latino; 5 Hispanic/Latino; 4 Two or more races, non-Hispanic/Latino), 29 international. Average age 30. 279 applicants, 66% accepted, 91 enrolled. In 2013, 113 master's, 8 doctorates awarded. *Degree requirements:* For master's, thesis; for doctorate, thesis/dissertation. *Entrance requirements:* For master's, PRAXIS I; for doctorate, GRE General Test. Additional exam requirements/recommendations for international students: Required—TOEFL. *Application deadline:* For fall admission, 2/1 priority date for domestic students; for spring admission, 11/15 priority date for domestic students. Applications are processed on a rolling basis. Application fee: $50. Electronic applications accepted. *Expenses:* Tuition, state resident: full-time $19,964; part-time $807 per credit. Tuition, nonresident: full-time $32,686; part-time $1337 per credit. *Required fees:* $740; $200. Tuition and fees vary according to program. *Financial support:* Fellowships, teaching assistantships, career-related internships or fieldwork, Federal Work-Study, tuition waivers (partial), and unspecified assistantships available. Support available to part-time students. Financial award application deadline: 3/15; financial award applicants required to submit FAFSA. *Unit head:* Dr. Richard Donato, Chairman, 412-624-7248, Fax: 412-648-7081, E-mail: donato@pitt.edu. *Application contact:* Marianne L. Budziszewski, Director of Admissions and Enrollment Services, 412-648-2230, Fax: 412-648-1899, E-mail: soeinfo@pitt.edu.
Website: http://www.education.pitt.edu.

University of Puerto Rico, Río Piedras Campus, College of Education, Program in Curriculum and Teaching, San Juan, PR 00931-3300. Offers biology education (M Ed); chemistry education (M Ed); curriculum and teaching (Ed D); history education (M Ed); mathematics education (M Ed); physics education (M Ed); Spanish education (M Ed). Part-time programs available. *Degree requirements:* For master's, thesis; for doctorate, thesis/dissertation, internship. *Entrance requirements:* For master's, PAEG or GRE, minimum GPA of 3.0, letter of recommendation; for doctorate, GRE or PAEG, master's degree, minimum GPA of 3.0, letter of recommendation (2), interview. *Faculty research:* Curriculum, math teaching.

University of Rio Grande, Graduate School, Rio Grande, OH 45674. Offers classroom teaching (M Ed), including fine arts, learning disabilities, mathematics, reading education. *Accreditation:* NCATE. Part-time and evening/weekend programs available. *Degree requirements:* For master's, final research project, portfolio. *Entrance requirements:* For master's, minimum GPA of 2.7 in major, 2.5 overall. Additional exam requirements/recommendations for international students: Required—TOEFL. *Faculty research:* Interagency collaboration, reading and mathematics, learning styles, college access, literacy.

University of St. Francis, College of Education, Joliet, IL 60435-6169. Offers educational leadership (MS, Ed D); elementary education (M Ed); higher education (MS); reading (MS); secondary education (M Ed), including English education, math education, science education, social studies education, visual arts education; special education (M Ed); teaching and learning (MS). *Accreditation:* NCATE. Part-time and evening/weekend programs available. Postbaccalaureate distance learning degree programs offered (no on-campus study). *Faculty:* 10 full-time (8 women), 34 part-time/adjunct (25 women). *Students:* 14 full-time (13 women), 250 part-time (183 women); includes 34 minority (20 Black or African American, non-Hispanic/Latino; 1 American Indian or Alaska Native, non-Hispanic/Latino; 13 Hispanic/Latino), 1 international. Average age 36. 133 applicants, 62% accepted, 71 enrolled. In 2013, 147 master's awarded. *Degree requirements:* For doctorate, thesis/dissertation. *Entrance requirements:* For doctorate, master's degree, IL Type 75 or Principal's endorsement, interview, minimum undergraduate GPA of 3.0, professional portfolio, letter of recommendation. Additional exam requirements/recommendations for international students: Required—TOEFL (minimum score 550 paper-based; 79 iBT), IELTS (minimum score 6.5). *Application deadline:* Applications are processed on a rolling basis. Application fee: $30. Electronic applications accepted. Application fee is waived when completed online. *Expenses:* Contact institution. *Financial support:* In 2013–14, 10 students received support. Scholarships/grants, tuition waivers (partial), and unspecified assistantships available. Support available to part-time students. Financial award applicants required to submit FAFSA. *Unit head:* Dr. John Gambro, Dean, 815-740-3829, Fax: 815-740-2264, E-mail: jgambro@stfrancis.edu. *Application contact:*

Sandra Sloka, Director of Admissions for Graduate and Degree Completion Programs, 800-735-7500, Fax: 815-740-3431, E-mail: ssloka@stfrancis.edu.
Website: http://www.stfrancis.edu/academics/college-of-education/.

University of St. Thomas, Graduate Studies, School of Education, Department of Teacher Education, St. Paul, MN 55105-1096. Offers curriculum and instruction (MA), including elementary, individualized, K-12, secondary; elementary education (MA); English as a second language (MA); math education (Certificate); multicultural education (Certificate); reading (MA, Certificate), including elementary (MA), K-12 (MA). *Accreditation:* NCATE. Part-time and evening/weekend programs available. *Entrance requirements:* For master's, minimum GPA of 3.0 or MAT. Additional exam requirements/recommendations for international students: Required—TOEFL (minimum score 550 paper-based; 80 iBT). *Application deadline:* For fall admission, 6/1 for domestic students; for spring admission, 11/1 for domestic students. Applications are processed on a rolling basis. Application fee: $50. *Financial support:* Fellowships, research assistantships, institutionally sponsored loans, and scholarships/grants available. Support available to part-time students. Financial award applicants required to submit FAFSA. *Unit head:* Dr. Jan L. H. Frank, Chair, 651-962-4446, Fax: 651-962-4169, E-mail: jlhfrank@stthomas.edu. *Application contact:* Rosemary R. Barreto, Department Assistant, 651-962-4420, Fax: 651-962-4169, E-mail: barr7879@stthomas.edu.

University of South Africa, College of Human Sciences, Pretoria, South Africa. Offers adult education (M Ed); African languages (MA, PhD); African politics (MA, PhD); Afrikaans (MA, PhD); ancient history (MA, PhD); ancient Near Eastern studies (MA, PhD); anthropology (MA, PhD); applied linguistics (MA); Arabic (MA, PhD); archaeology (MA); art history (MA); Biblical archaeology (MA); Biblical studies (M Th, D Th, PhD); Christian spirituality (M Th, D Th); church history (M Th, D Th); classical studies (MA, PhD); clinical psychology (MA); communication (MA, PhD); comparative education (M Ed, Ed D); consulting psychology (D Admin, D Com, PhD); curriculum studies (M Ed, Ed D); development studies (M Admin, MA, D Admin, PhD); didactics (M Ed, Ed D); education (M Tech); education management (M Ed, Ed D); educational psychology (M Ed); English (MA); environmental education (M Ed); French (MA, PhD); German (MA, PhD); Greek (MA); guidance and counseling (M Ed); health studies (MA, PhD), including health sciences education (MA), health services management (MA), medical and surgical nursing science (critical care general) (MA), midwifery and neonatal nursing science (MA), trauma and emergency care (MA); history (MA, PhD); history of education (Ed D); inclusive education (M Ed, Ed D); information and communications technology policy and regulation (MA); information science (MA, MIS, PhD); international politics (MA, PhD); Islamic studies (MA, PhD); Italian (MA, PhD); Judaica (MA, PhD); linguistics (MA, PhD); mathematical education (M Ed); mathematics education (MA); missiology (M Th, D Th); modern Hebrew (MA, PhD); musicology (MA, MMus, D Mus, PhD); natural science education (M Ed); New Testament (M Th, D Th); Old Testament (D Th); pastoral therapy (M Th, D Th); philosophy (MA); philosophy of education (M Ed, Ed D); politics (MA, PhD); Portuguese (MA, PhD); practical theology (M Th, D Th); psychology (MA, MS, PhD); psychology of education (M Ed, Ed D); public health (MA); religious studies (MA, D Th, PhD); Romance languages (MA); Russian (MA, PhD); Semitic languages (MA, PhD); social behavior studies in HIV/AIDS (MA); social science (mental health) (MA); social science in development studies (MA); social science in psychology (MA); social science in social work (MA); social science in sociology (MA); social work (MSW, DSW, PhD); socio-education (M Ed, Ed D); sociolinguistics (MA); sociology (MA, PhD); Spanish (MA, PhD); systematic theology (M Th, D Th); TESOL (teaching English to speakers of other languages) (MA); theological ethics (M Th, D Th); theory of literature (MA, PhD); urban ministries (D Th); urban ministry (M Th).

University of South Africa, Institute for Science and Technology Education, Pretoria, South Africa. Offers mathematics, science and technology education (M Sc, PhD).

University of South Carolina, The Graduate School, College of Arts and Sciences, Department of Mathematics, Columbia, SC 29208. Offers mathematics (MA, MS, PhD); mathematics education (M Math, MAT). MAT offered in cooperation with the College of Education. Part-time programs available. Terminal master's awarded for partial completion of doctoral program. *Degree requirements:* For master's, comprehensive exam, thesis (for some programs); for doctorate, one foreign language, comprehensive exam, thesis/dissertation, admission to candidacy exam, residency. *Entrance requirements:* For master's and doctorate, GRE General Test. Additional exam requirements/recommendations for international students: Required—TOEFL (minimum score 600 paper-based; 100 iBT). Electronic applications accepted. *Faculty research:* Computational mathematics, analysis (classical/modern), discrete mathematics, algebra, number theory.

University of South Carolina, The Graduate School, College of Education, Department of Instruction and Teacher Education, Program in Secondary Education, Columbia, SC 29208. Offers art education (IMA, MAT); business education (IMA, MAT); English (MAT); foreign language (MAT); health education (MAT); mathematics (MAT); science (IMA, MAT); secondary (Ed D); secondary education (MT, PhD); social studies (MAT); theatre and speech (MAT). IMA and MT offered jointly with the subject areas. *Accreditation:* NCATE. *Degree requirements:* For master's, comprehensive exam, thesis (for some programs), foreign language (MA); for doctorate, one foreign language, comprehensive exam, thesis/dissertation. *Entrance requirements:* For master's, GRE General Test or MAT, teaching certificate (IMA, M Ed), interview; for doctorate, GRE General Test or MAT, interview. *Faculty research:* Middle school programs, professional development, school collaboration.

University of Southern Mississippi, Graduate School, College of Science and Technology, Center for Science and Mathematics Education, Hattiesburg, MS 39406-0001. Offers MS, PhD. Part-time programs available. *Faculty:* 1 full-time (0 women), 1 (woman) part-time/adjunct. *Students:* 12 full-time (7 women), 28 part-time (18 women); includes 12 minority (9 Black or African American, non-Hispanic/Latino; 1 Asian, non-Hispanic/Latino; 1 Hispanic/Latino; 1 Two or more races, non-Hispanic/Latino), 5 international. Average age 37. 7 applicants, 100% accepted, 5 enrolled. In 2013, 2 master's, 10 doctorates awarded. *Degree requirements:* For master's, comprehensive exam, thesis or alternative; for doctorate, comprehensive exam, thesis/dissertation. *Entrance requirements:* For master's, GRE General Test, minimum GPA of 2.75 in last 60 hours; for doctorate, GRE General Test, minimum GPA of 3.5. Additional exam requirements/recommendations for international students: Required—TOEFL, IELTS. *Application deadline:* For fall admission, 3/15 priority date for domestic students, 3/15 for international students; for spring admission, 1/10 priority date for domestic and international students. Applications are processed on a rolling basis. Application fee: $50. *Financial support:* In 2013–14, 1 fellowship with full tuition reimbursement (averaging $21,000 per year), 1 research assistantship with full tuition reimbursement (averaging $14,500 per year), 8 teaching assistantships with full tuition reimbursements (averaging $8,400 per year) were awarded; Federal Work-Study, scholarships/grants, health care benefits, and unspecified assistantships also available. Financial award application deadline: 3/15; financial award applicants required to submit FAFSA. *Unit head:* Dr. Sherry Herron, Director, 601-266-4739, Fax: 601-266-4741. *Application contact:* Shonna Breland, Manager of Graduate School Admissions, 601-266-6567, Fax: 601-266-5138.
Website: http://www.usm.edu/graduateschool/table.php.

University of South Florida, College of Education, Department of Secondary Education, Tampa, FL 33620-9951. Offers English education (M Ed, MA, MAT, PhD); foreign language education/ESOL (M Ed, MA, MAT); instructional technology (M Ed, PhD, Ed S); mathematics education (M Ed, MA, MAT, PhD, Ed S); science education (M Ed, MA, MAT, PhD); second language acquisition/instructional technology (PhD); secondary education (M Ed, PhD); secondary education/TESOL (M Ed); social science education (M Ed, MA, MAT); teaching and learning in the content area (PhD). *Accreditation:* NCATE. Part-time and evening/weekend programs available. *Degree requirements:* For master's, variable foreign language requirement, comprehensive exam, project (for some programs); for doctorate, variable foreign language requirement, comprehensive exam, thesis/dissertation, philosophies of inquiry; multiple research methods. *Entrance requirements:* For master's, GRE General Test or General Knowledge Test, minimum GPA of 3.0; for doctorate, GRE General Test, minimum GPA of 3.5; for Ed S, GRE General Test. Additional exam requirements/recommendations for international students: Required—TOEFL (minimum score 550 paper-based; 79 iBT). Electronic applications accepted. *Faculty research:* English language learners/multicultural, social science education, mathematics education, science education, instructional technology.

University of South Florida–St. Petersburg Campus, College of Education, St. Petersburg, FL 33701. Offers educational leadership development (M Ed); elementary education (MA), including math/science; English education (MA); middle grades STEM education (MS); reading education (MA). Part-time programs available. *Degree requirements:* For master's, comprehensive exam, practicum, internship, comprehensive portfolio. *Entrance requirements:* For master's, State of Florida General Knowledge Test (GKT), Florida Teaching Certificate (for non-initial certification programs), letters of recommendation. Additional exam requirements/recommendations for international students: Required—TOEFL (minimum score 550 paper-based; 79 iBT); Recommended—IELTS. Electronic applications accepted.

The University of Tennessee, Graduate School, College of Education, Health and Human Sciences, Program in Education, Knoxville, TN 37996. Offers art education (MS); counseling education (PhD); cultural studies in education (PhD); curriculum (MS, Ed S); curriculum, educational research and evaluation (Ed D, PhD); early childhood education (PhD); early childhood special education (MS); education of deaf and hard of hearing (MS); educational administration and policy studies (Ed D, PhD); educational administration and supervision (Ed S); educational psychology (Ed D, PhD); elementary education (MS, Ed S); elementary teaching (MS); English education (MS, Ed S); exercise science (PhD); foreign language/ESL education (MS, Ed S); instructional technology (MS, Ed D, PhD, Ed S); literacy, language and ESL education (PhD); literacy, language education, and ESL education (Ed D); mathematics education (MS, Ed S); modified and comprehensive special education (MS); reading education (MS, Ed S); school counseling (Ed S); school psychology (PhD, Ed S); science education (MS, Ed S); secondary teaching (MS); social foundations (MS); social science education (MS, Ed S); socio-cultural foundations of sports and education (PhD); special education (Ed S); teacher education (Ed D, PhD). *Accreditation:* NCATE. Part-time and evening/weekend programs available. *Degree requirements:* For master's and Ed S, thesis optional; for doctorate, variable foreign language requirement, thesis/dissertation. *Entrance requirements:* For master's, minimum GPA of 2.7; for doctorate and Ed S, GRE General Test, minimum GPA of 2.7. Additional exam requirements/recommendations for international students: Required—TOEFL. Electronic applications accepted. *Expenses:* Tuition, state resident: full-time $9540; part-time $531 per credit hour. Tuition, nonresident: full-time $27,728; part-time $1542 per credit hour. *Required fees:* $1404; $67 per credit hour.

The University of Tennessee at Chattanooga, Graduate School, College of Arts and Sciences, Program in Mathematics, Chattanooga, TN 37403-2598. Offers applied mathematics (MS); applied statistics (MS); mathematics (MS); mathematics education (MS). Part-time and evening/weekend programs available. Postbaccalaureate distance learning degree programs offered (no on-campus study). *Faculty:* 8 full-time (1 woman). *Students:* 11 full-time (3 women), 5 part-time (1 woman); includes 3 minority (all Asian, non-Hispanic/Latino). Average age 27. 9 applicants, 78% accepted, 5 enrolled. In 2013, 5 master's awarded. *Entrance requirements:* For master's, two letters of recommendation. *Application deadline:* For fall admission, 6/13 for domestic students, 6/1 for international students; for spring admission, 10/15 for domestic students, 10/1 for international students. Applications are processed on a rolling basis. Application fee: $30 ($35 for international students). Electronic applications accepted. *Financial support:* In 2013–14, 15 research assistantships with tuition reimbursements (averaging $4,587 per year) were awarded. Financial award applicants required to submit FAFSA. *Total annual research expenditures:* $290,000. *Unit head:* Dr. John Graef, Department Head, 423-425-4545, E-mail: john-graef@utc.edu. *Application contact:* Dr. J. Randy Walker, Interim Dean of Graduate Studies, 423-425-4478, Fax: 423-425-5223, E-mail: randy-walker@utc.edu.
Website: http://www.utc.edu/Academic/Mathematics/.

The University of Texas at Arlington, Graduate School, College of Science, Department of Mathematics, Arlington, TX 76019. Offers applied math (MS); mathematics (PhD); mathematics education (MA). Part-time and evening/weekend programs available. *Degree requirements:* For master's, comprehensive exam, thesis or alternative; for doctorate, comprehensive exam, thesis/dissertation, preliminary examinations. *Entrance requirements:* For master's, GRE General Test (minimum score 350 verbal, 650 quantitative); for doctorate, GRE General Test (minimum score 350 verbal, 700 quantitative), 30 hours of graduate course work in mathematics, minimum GPA of 3.0 in last 60 hours of course work. Additional exam requirements/recommendations for international students: Required—TOEFL (minimum score 550 paper-based; 79 iBT). Electronic applications accepted. *Faculty research:* Algebra, combinatorics and geometry, applied mathematics and mathematical biology, computational mathematics, mathematics education, probability and statistics.

The University of Texas at Dallas, School of Natural Sciences and Mathematics, Department of Science/Mathematics Education, Richardson, TX 75080. Offers mathematics education (MAT); science education (MAT). Part-time and evening/weekend programs available. Postbaccalaureate distance learning degree programs offered (minimal on-campus study). *Faculty:* 6 full-time (2 women). *Students:* 10 full-time (6 women), 27 part-time (19 women); includes 15 minority (3 Black or African American, non-Hispanic/Latino; 8 Asian, non-Hispanic/Latino; 3 Hispanic/Latino; 1 Two or more races, non-Hispanic/Latino). Average age 34. 27 applicants, 56% accepted, 11 enrolled. In 2013, 16 master's awarded. *Degree requirements:* For master's, thesis optional. *Entrance requirements:* For master's, GRE General Test, minimum GPA of 3.0 in upper-level coursework in field. Additional exam requirements/recommendations for international students: Required—TOEFL (minimum score 550 paper-based). *Application deadline:* For fall admission, 7/15 for domestic students, 5/1 priority date for international students; for spring admission, 11/15 for domestic students, 9/1 priority date for international students. Applications are processed on a rolling basis. Application fee: $50 ($100 for international students). Electronic applications accepted. *Expenses:* Tuition, state resident: full-time $11,940; part-time $663.33 per credit hour. Tuition, nonresident: full-time $21,606; part-time $1200.33 per credit hour. *Financial support:* In 2013–14, 27 students received support. Research assistantships with partial tuition

reimbursements available, teaching assistantships with partial tuition reimbursements available, career-related internships or fieldwork, Federal Work-Study, institutionally sponsored loans, scholarships/grants, and unspecified assistantships available. Support available to part-time students. Financial award application deadline: 4/30; financial award applicants required to submit FAFSA. *Faculty research:* Innovative science/math education programs. *Unit head:* Dr. Mary L. Urquhart, Department Head, 972-883-2499, Fax: 972-883-6796, E-mail: scimathed@utdallas.edu. *Application contact:* Barbara Curry, Advisor, 972-883-4008, Fax: 972-883-6796, E-mail: barbc@utdallas.edu. Website: http://www.utdallas.edu/scimathed/.

The University of Texas at El Paso, Graduate School, College of Science, Department of Mathematical Sciences, El Paso, TX 79968-0001. Offers mathematical sciences (MS); mathematics (teaching) (MAT); statistics (MS). Part-time and evening/weekend programs available. *Degree requirements:* For master's, thesis optional. *Entrance requirements:* For master's, minimum GPA of 3.0, letters of recommendation. Additional exam requirements/recommendations for international students: Required—TOEFL; Recommended—IELTS. Electronic applications accepted.

The University of Texas at San Antonio, College of Sciences, Department of Mathematics, San Antonio, TX 78249-0617. Offers applied mathematics (MS), including industrial mathematics; mathematics (MS); mathematics education (MS). Part-time and evening/weekend programs available. *Faculty:* 10 full-time (1 woman). *Students:* 23 full-time (11 women), 34 part-time (12 women); includes 26 minority (2 Black or African American, non-Hispanic/Latino; 4 Asian, non-Hispanic/Latino; 20 Hispanic/Latino), 13 international. Average age 30. 27 applicants, 85% accepted, 8 enrolled. In 2013, 21 master's awarded. *Degree requirements:* For master's, comprehensive exam (for some programs), thesis or alternative. *Entrance requirements:* For master's, GRE General Test, minimum GPA of 3.0 in last 60 hours. Additional exam requirements/ recommendations for international students: Required—TOEFL (minimum score 550 paper-based; 79 iBT), IELTS (minimum score 6.5). *Application deadline:* For fall admission, 7/1 for domestic students, 4/1 for international students; for spring admission, 11/1 for domestic students, 9/1 for international students. Applications are processed on a rolling basis. Application fee: $45 ($80 for international students). Electronic applications accepted. *Expenses:* Tuition, state resident: full-time $4671. Tuition, nonresident: full-time $8708. *International tuition:* $17,415 full-time. *Required fees:* $1924.60. Tuition and fees vary according to course load and degree level. *Financial support:* In 2013–14, 15 students received support, including 15 teaching assistantships (averaging $10,000 per year). Financial award applicants required to submit FAFSA. *Faculty research:* Differential equations, functional analysis, numerical analysis, number theory, logic. *Total annual research expenditures:* $5,707. *Unit head:* Dr. F. Alexander Norman, Department Chair, 210-458-7254, Fax: 210-458-4439, E-mail: sandy.norman@utsa.edu. *Application contact:* Monica Rodriguez, Director of Graduate Admissions, 210-458-4331, Fax: 210-458-4332, E-mail: graduatestudies@utsa.edu. Website: http://math.utsa.edu/.

The University of Texas–Pan American, College of Science and Mathematics, Department of Mathematics, Edinburg, TX 78539. Offers applied mathematics (MS); mathematical sciences (MS); mathematics teaching (MS). Part-time and evening/ weekend programs available. *Faculty:* 13 full-time (1 woman). *Students:* 20 full-time (3 women), 17 part-time (7 women); includes 31 minority (2 Asian, non-Hispanic/Latino; 29 Hispanic/Latino), 5 international. Average age 30. 19 applicants, 95% accepted, 8 enrolled. In 2013, 28 master's awarded. *Degree requirements:* For master's, comprehensive exam, thesis optional. *Entrance requirements:* For master's, GRE General Test (strongly recommended for teaching assistantship applicants), bachelor's degree with at least 18 hours of math courses completed or in a related area. Additional exam requirements/recommendations for international students: Required—TOEFL (minimum score 500 paper-based; 61 iBT); Recommended—IELTS (minimum score 5.5). *Application deadline:* For fall admission, 8/1 for domestic students, 6/1 for international students; for spring admission, 12/1 for domestic students, 10/1 for international students; for summer admission, 5/1 for domestic students, 3/1 for international students. Applications are processed on a rolling basis. Application fee: $50. Electronic applications accepted. *Expenses:* Tuition, state resident: full-time $5986; part-time $333 per credit hour. Tuition, nonresident: full-time $12,358; part-time $687 per credit hour. *Required fees:* $782. Tuition and fees vary according to program. *Financial support:* Teaching assistantships, institutionally sponsored loans, and unspecified assistantships available. Financial award application deadline: 6/1. *Faculty research:* Boundary value problems in differential equations, training of public school teachers in methods of presenting mathematics, harmonic analysis, inverse problems, algebra. *Unit head:* Dr. Andras Balogh, Department Chair, 956-665-3460, E-mail: abalogh@utpa.edu. *Application contact:* Dr. Zhijun Qiao, Graduate Program Coordinator, 956-665-3406, E-mail: qiao@utpa.edu.

University of the District of Columbia, College of Arts and Sciences, Department of Mathematics, Washington, DC 20008-1175. Offers applied statistics (MS); teaching mathematics (MST). Part-time and evening/weekend programs available. *Degree requirements:* For master's, comprehensive exam. *Entrance requirements:* For master's, GRE General Test, writing proficiency exam. *Expenses: Tuition, area resident:* Full-time $7883.28; part-time $437.96 per credit hour. Tuition, state resident: full-time $8923.14. Tuition, nonresident: full-time $15,163; part-time $842.40 per credit hour. *Required fees:* $620; $30 per credit hour.

University of the Incarnate Word, School of Graduate Studies and Research, School of Mathematics, Science, and Engineering, Program in Mathematics, San Antonio, TX 78209-6397. Offers research statistics (MS); teaching (MA). Part-time and evening/ weekend programs available. *Faculty:* 4 full-time (2 women), 1 (woman) part-time/ adjunct. *Students:* 6 full-time (4 women), 2 part-time (1 woman); includes 1 minority (Hispanic/Latino), 5 international. Average age 31. 27 applicants, 48% accepted, 5 enrolled. In 2013, 2 master's awarded. *Degree requirements:* For master's, capstone or prerequisite knowledge (for research statistics). *Entrance requirements:* For master's, GRE (minimum score 800 verbal and quantitative), 18 hours of undergraduate mathematics with minimum GPA of 3.0; letter of recommendation by a professional in the field, writing sample, teaching experience at the precollege level. Additional exam requirements/recommendations for international students: Required—TOEFL (minimum score 560 paper-based; 83 iBT). *Application deadline:* Applications are processed on a rolling basis. Application fee: $20. Electronic applications accepted. *Expenses: Tuition:* Part-time $815 per credit hour. *Required fees:* $86 per credit hour. One-time fee: $40 part-time. Tuition and fees vary according to degree level and program. *Financial support:* Federal Work-Study and scholarships/grants available. Financial award applicants required to submit FAFSA. *Faculty research:* Scholarship and career development for undergraduate mathematics majors. *Total annual research expenditures:* $140,844. *Unit head:* Dr. Zhanbo Yang, Mathematics Graduate Program Coordinator, 210-283-5008, Fax: 210-829-3153, E-mail: yang@uiwtx.edu. *Application contact:* Andrea Cyterski-Acosta, Dean of Enrollment, 210-829-6005, Fax: 210-829-3921, E-mail: admis@uiwtx.edu.
Website: http://www.uiw.edu/math/mathprogramsgrad.html.

University of the Sacred Heart, Graduate Programs, Department of Education, San Juan, PR 00914-0383. Offers early childhood education (M Ed); information technology and multimedia (Certificate); instruction systems and education technology (M Ed), including English, information technology and multimedia, instructional design, mathematics, Spanish. Part-time and evening/weekend programs available. *Degree requirements:* For master's, thesis. *Entrance requirements:* For master's, EXADEP, minimum undergraduate GPA of 2.75, interview.

University of the Virgin Islands, Graduate Programs, Division of Science and Mathematics, Program in Mathematics, Saint Thomas, VI 00802-9990. Offers mathematics for secondary teachers (MA). *Degree requirements:* For master's, action research paper. *Entrance requirements:* For master's, GRE, minimum GPA of 2.5, BA or BS. Additional exam requirements/recommendations for international students: Required—TOEFL (minimum score 550 paper-based).

The University of Toledo, College of Graduate Studies, Judith Herb College of Education, Department of Curriculum and Instruction, Toledo, OH 43606-3390. Offers art education (ME); career and technical education (ME); career-technical education (Ed S); curriculum and instruction (ME, PhD, Ed S); early childhood education (PhD, Ed S); education and biology (MES); education and chemistry (MES); education and economics (MAE); education and English (MAE); education and French (MAE); education and geography (MAE); education and geology (MES); education and German (MAE); education and history (MAE); education and mathematics (MAE, MES); education and physics (MES); education and political science (MAE); education and sociology (MAE); education and Spanish (MAE); educational media (PhD); educational technology (ME); educational technology: virtual educator (Certificate); elementary education (PhD); English as a second language (MAE); gifted and talented (PhD); middle childhood education licensure (ME); music education (MME); secondary education (PhD); secondary education licensure (ME); special education (PhD, Ed S). *Accreditation:* NCATE. Part-time and evening/weekend programs available. *Faculty:* 41. *Students:* 53 full-time (30 women), 154 part-time (111 women); includes 21 minority (16 Black or African American, non-Hispanic/Latino; 4 Hispanic/Latino; 1 Two or more races, non-Hispanic/Latino), 21 international. Average age 34. 82 applicants, 79% accepted, 47 enrolled. In 2013, 80 master's, 5 doctorates awarded. *Degree requirements:* For master's, comprehensive exam, thesis or alternative; for doctorate, comprehensive exam, thesis/dissertation; for other advanced degree, thesis optional. *Entrance requirements:* For master's, doctorate, and other advanced degree, minimum cumulative GPA of 2.7 for all previous academic work, letters of recommendation. Additional exam requirements/recommendations for international students: Required—TOEFL (minimum score 550 paper-based; 80 iBT). *Application deadline:* For fall admission, 1/15 priority date for domestic and international students. Applications are processed on a rolling basis. Application fee: $45 ($75 for international students). Electronic applications accepted. *Financial support:* In 2013–14, 5 research assistantships with full and partial tuition reimbursements (averaging $13,200 per year), 11 teaching assistantships with full and partial tuition reimbursements (averaging $8,809 per year) were awarded; career-related internships or fieldwork, Federal Work-Study, institutionally sponsored loans, scholarships/grants, tuition waivers (full and partial), unspecified assistantships, and administrative assistantships also available. Support available to part-time students. *Unit head:* Dr. Joan Kaderavek, Chair, 419-530-5373, E-mail: eigh.chiarelott@utoledo.edu. *Application contact:* Graduate School Office, 419-530-4723, Fax: 419-530-4724, E-mail: grdsch@utnet.utoledo.edu.
Website: http://www.utoledo.edu/eduhshs/.

The University of Tulsa, Graduate School, College of Arts and Sciences, School of Urban Education, Program in Mathematics and Science Education, Tulsa, OK 74104-3189. Offers MSMSE. Part-time programs available. *Students:* 2 full-time (1 woman), 6 part-time (4 women), 1 international. Average age 31. 4 applicants, 100% accepted, 3 enrolled. In 2013, 1 master's awarded. *Entrance requirements:* For master's, GRE General Test. Additional exam requirements/recommendations for international students: Required—TOEFL (minimum score 577 paper-based), IELTS (minimum score 6.5). *Application deadline:* Applications are processed on a rolling basis. Application fee: $40. Electronic applications accepted. *Expenses: Tuition:* Full-time $19,566; part-time $1087 per credit hour. *Required fees:* $1690; $5 per credit hour. $160 per semester. Tuition and fees vary according to course load. *Financial support:* In 2013–14, 4 students received support, including 4 teaching assistantships with full and partial tuition reimbursements available (averaging $8,776 per year); fellowships with full and partial tuition reimbursements available, research assistantships, career-related internships or fieldwork, Federal Work-Study, scholarships/grants, health care benefits, tuition waivers (full and partial), and unspecified assistantships also available. Support available to part-time students. Financial award application deadline: 2/1; financial award applicants required to submit FAFSA. *Unit head:* Dr. Kara Gae Neal, Chair, 918-631-2238, Fax: 918-631-3721, E-mail: karagae-neal@utulsa.edu. *Application contact:* Dr. David Brown, Advisor, 918-631-2719, Fax: 918-631-2133, E-mail: david-brown@utulsa.edu.

University of Vermont, Graduate College, College of Engineering and Mathematics, Department of Mathematics and Statistics, Program in Mathematics, Burlington, VT 05405. Offers mathematics (MS, PhD); mathematics education (MST). *Students:* 28 (10 women), 2 international. 67 applicants, 43% accepted, 7 enrolled. In 2013, 7 master's, 1 doctorate awarded. *Degree requirements:* For doctorate, thesis/dissertation. *Entrance requirements:* For master's and doctorate, GRE General Test. Additional exam requirements/recommendations for international students: Required—TOEFL (minimum score 550 paper-based; 80 iBT). *Application deadline:* For fall admission, 1/15 priority date for domestic students, 1/15 for international students. Applications are processed on a rolling basis. Application fee: $65. Electronic applications accepted. *Financial support:* Fellowships, research assistantships, and teaching assistantships available. Financial award application deadline: 3/1. *Unit head:* Dr. James Burgmeier, Chair, 802-656-2940. *Application contact:* Prof. Jonathan Sands, Coordinator, 802-656-2940.

University of Victoria, Faculty of Graduate Studies, Faculty of Education, Department of Curriculum and Instruction, Victoria, BC V8W 2Y2, Canada. Offers art education (M Ed, PhD); curriculum studies (M Ed, MA, PhD); early childhood education (M Ed, PhD); educational studies (PhD); language and literacy (M Ed, MA, PhD); mathematics (M Ed, MA, PhD); music education (M Ed, MA, PhD); science (M Ed, MA, PhD); social studies (M Ed, MA); social, cultural and foundational studies (MA, PhD); technology and environmental education (PhD). Part-time programs available. *Degree requirements:* For master's, thesis, project (M Ed); for doctorate, comprehensive exam, thesis/ dissertation. *Entrance requirements:* For master's, minimum B average. Additional exam requirements/recommendations for international students: Required—TOEFL (minimum score 575 paper-based), IELTS (minimum score 7). Electronic applications accepted. *Faculty research:* Elementary and secondary English, language arts, curriculum theory and practice, educational media and technology, educational administration and leadership, history and philosophy of education.

University of Virginia, Curry School of Education, Department of Curriculum, Instruction, and Special Education, Program in Curriculum and Instruction, Charlottesville, VA 22903. Offers curriculum and instruction (M Ed, Ed S); elementary education (M Ed, Ed D); English (M Ed, Ed D); foreign language (M Ed); mathematics (M Ed, Ed D); reading (M Ed, Ed D, Ed S); science (Ed D); social studies (M Ed). *Students:* 42 full-time (30 women), 37 part-time (32 women); includes 4 minority (1 Black or African American, non-Hispanic/Latino; 2 Hispanic/Latino; 1 Two or more races, non-Hispanic/Latino), 1 international. Average age 31. 76 applicants, 74% accepted, 39 enrolled. In 2013, 84 master's, 3 doctorates, 23 other advanced degrees awarded.

Degree requirements: For master's, comprehensive exam (for some programs); for doctorate, comprehensive exam, thesis/dissertation; for Ed S, comprehensive exam. *Entrance requirements:* For master's, doctorate, and Ed S, GRE General Test, 2 letters of recommendation. Additional exam requirements/recommendations for international students: Required—TOEFL (minimum score 600 paper-based; 90 iBT), IELTS (minimum score 7). *Application deadline:* Applications are processed on a rolling basis. Application fee: $60. Electronic applications accepted. *Expenses:* Tuition, state resident: part-time $334 per credit hour. Tuition, nonresident: part-time $1224 per credit hour. *Financial support:* Fellowships with tuition reimbursements, research assistantships with tuition reimbursements, and teaching assistantships with tuition reimbursements available. Financial award application deadline: 1/5; financial award applicants required to submit FAFSA. *Unit head:* Stephanie van Hover, Chair, 434-924-0841, E-mail: sdv2w@virginia.edu. *Application contact:* Karen Dwier, Information Contact, 434-924-0831, E-mail: kgd9g@virginia.edu.
Website: http://curry.virginia.edu/academics/areas-of-study/curriculum-teaching-learning.

University of Virginia, Curry School of Education, Program in Education, Charlottesville, VA 22903. Offers administration and supervision (PhD); applied developmental science (PhD); counselor education (PhD); curriculum and instruction (PhD); early childhood special education (MT); education evaluation (PhD); educational psychology (PhD); educational research (PhD); elementary education (MT); English education (MT, PhD); foreign language education (MT); higher education (PhD); instructional technology (PhD); kinesiology (MT, PhD); math education (PhD); reading education (PhD); research, statistics and evaluation (PhD); school psychology (PhD); science education (PhD); social studies education (MT, PhD); special education (PhD); world languages education (MT). *Students:* 474 full-time (379 women), 35 part-time (19 women); includes 89 minority (30 Black or African American, non-Hispanic/Latino; 1 American Indian or Alaska Native, non-Hispanic/Latino; 26 Asian, non-Hispanic/Latino; 19 Hispanic/Latino; 13 Two or more races, non-Hispanic/Latino), 21 international. Average age 26. 312 applicants, 49% accepted, 80 enrolled. In 2013, 137 master's, 38 doctorates awarded. *Degree requirements:* For master's, comprehensive exam (for some programs), field project; for doctorate, comprehensive exam, thesis/dissertation. *Entrance requirements:* For doctorate, GRE General Test. Additional exam requirements/recommendations for international students: Required—TOEFL (minimum score 600 paper-based; 90 iBT), IELTS (minimum score 7). *Application deadline:* Applications are processed on a rolling basis. Application fee: $60. Electronic applications accepted. *Expenses:* Tuition, state resident: part-time $334 per credit hour. Tuition, nonresident: part-time $1224 per credit hour. *Financial support:* Fellowships, research assistantships, and teaching assistantships available. Financial award application deadline: 1/5; financial award applicants required to submit FAFSA. *Unit head:* Robert C. Pianta, Dean, 434-924-3334, E-mail: pianta@virginia.edu. *Application contact:* Office of Admissions and Student Services, 434-924-0742, E-mail: curry-admissions@virginia.edu.
Website: http://curry.virginia.edu/teacher-education.

University of Washington, Graduate School, College of Education, Seattle, WA 98195. Offers curriculum and instruction (M Ed, Ed D, PhD), including educational technology, general curriculum (Ed D, PhD), language, literacy, and culture, mathematics education, multicultural education, reading and language arts education (Ed D), science education, social studies education, teaching and curriculum (M Ed); educational leadership and policy studies (M Ed, Ed D, PhD), including administration (Ed D), educational policy, organization, and leadership (M Ed, PhD), higher education, leadership for learning (Ed D), social and cultural foundations of education (M Ed, PhD); educational psychology (M Ed, PhD), including educational psychology (PhD), human development and cognition (M Ed), learning sciences, measurement, statistics and research design (M Ed), school psychology (M Ed); instructional leadership (M Ed); intercollegiate athletic leadership (M Ed); special education (M Ed, Ed D, PhD), including early childhood special education (M Ed), emotional and behavioral disabilities (M Ed), learning disabilities (M Ed), low-incidence disabilities (M Ed), severe disabilities (M Ed), special education (Ed D, PhD); teacher education (MIT). *Accreditation:* APA. Part-time and evening/weekend programs available. *Degree requirements:* For master's, thesis optional; for doctorate, thesis/dissertation. *Entrance requirements:* For master's and doctorate, GRE General Test, minimum GPA of 3.0. Additional exam requirements/recommendations for international students: Required—TOEFL. Electronic applications accepted. *Faculty research:* School restructuring/effective schools, special education interventions, literacy and writing, technology, school partnerships, teacher preparation.

University of Washington, Tacoma, Graduate Programs, Program in Education, Tacoma, WA 98402-3100. Offers education (M Ed); educational administration (principal or program administrator certification) (M Ed); elementary education teacher certification (M Ed); elementary education/special education teacher certification (M Ed); secondary science or math teacher certification (M Ed). Part-time and evening/weekend programs available. *Degree requirements:* For master's, culminating project. *Entrance requirements:* For master's, WEST-B, WEST-E (teacher certification programs only), official sealed transcript from every college/university attended, personal goal statement, letters of recommendation, copy of valid teaching certificate. Additional exam requirements/recommendations for international students: Required—TOEFL (minimum score 580 paper-based; 92 iBT). Electronic applications accepted. *Faculty research:* Global learning communities for English/Chinese languages, evaluation of mathematics and reading intervention programs, response to intervention, school-wide behavioral and emotional support, mathematics education and culturally responsive mathematics education.

The University of West Alabama, School of Graduate Studies, College of Education, Departments of Instructional Leadership and Support/Curriculum and Instruction, Program in Secondary Education, Livingston, AL 35470. Offers biology (MAT); English language arts (MAT); history (MAT); mathematics (MAT); physical education (MAT); science (MAT); secondary education (M Ed); social science (MAT). Part-time and evening/weekend programs available. Postbaccalaureate distance learning degree programs offered (no on-campus study). *Faculty:* 20 full-time (4 women), 5 part-time/adjunct (2 women). *Students:* 210 (139 women); includes 86 minority (80 Black or African American, non-Hispanic/Latino; 2 Asian, non-Hispanic/Latino; 2 Hispanic/Latino; 2 Two or more races, non-Hispanic/Latino). 115 applicants, 86% accepted, 72 enrolled. In 2013, 61 master's awarded. *Degree requirements:* For master's, comprehensive exam, thesis optional. *Entrance requirements:* For master's, GRE General Test, MAT, minimum GPA of 2.75. Additional exam requirements/recommendations for international students: Required—TOEFL (minimum score 500 paper-based; 61 iBT). *Application deadline:* For fall admission, 8/12 priority date for domestic students; for spring admission, 3/24 for domestic students. Applications are processed on a rolling basis. Application fee: $25 ($50 for international students). Electronic applications accepted. Tuition and fees vary according to course load. *Financial support:* Teaching assistantships, career-related internships or fieldwork, Federal Work-Study, scholarships/grants, and unspecified assistantships available. Support available to part-time students. Financial award application deadline: 3/1; financial award applicants required to submit FAFSA. *Faculty research:* Integrated arts in the curriculum, moral development of children. *Unit head:* Dr. Esther Howard, Chair of Curriculum and Instruction, 205-652-3428, Fax: 205-652-3706, E-mail: ehoward@uwa.edu. *Application contact:* Dr. Kathy Chandler, Dean of Graduate Studies, 205-652-3421, Fax: 205-652-3706, E-mail: kchandler@uwa.edu.
Website: http://www.uwa.edu/highschool612.aspx.

University of West Georgia, College of Science and Mathematics, Department of Mathematics, Carrollton, GA 30118. Offers teaching and applied mathematics (MS). Part-time and evening/weekend programs available. *Faculty:* 16 full-time (4 women). *Students:* 4 full-time (2 women), 6 part-time (1 woman); includes 4 minority (1 Black or African American, non-Hispanic/Latino; 3 Asian, non-Hispanic/Latino), 3 international. Average age 35. 7 applicants, 86% accepted, 4 enrolled. In 2013, 4 master's awarded. *Degree requirements:* For master's, comprehensive exam, thesis optional, 36 credit hours. *Entrance requirements:* For master's, GRE General Test. Additional exam requirements/recommendations for international students: Recommended—TOEFL (minimum score 523 paper-based; 69 iBT), IELTS (minimum score 6). *Application deadline:* For fall admission, 6/1 for domestic and international students; for spring admission, 11/15 for domestic students, 10/15 for international students. Applications are processed on a rolling basis. Application fee: $40. Electronic applications accepted. *Expenses:* Tuition, state resident: full-time $4600; part-time $192 per semester hour. Tuition, nonresident: full-time $17,880; part-time $745 per semester hour. *Required fees:* $1858; $46.34 per semester hour. $512 per semester. Tuition and fees vary according to course load, degree level, campus/location and program. *Financial support:* In 2013–14, 6 teaching assistantships (averaging $6,800 per year) were awarded; unspecified assistantships also available. Financial award application deadline: 4/1; financial award applicants required to submit FAFSA. *Faculty research:* Graph coloring problems, labeling and domination in graphs, high dimension regression, inverse problem, spectral theory of operators, math teacher education. *Unit head:* Dr. Bruce Landman, Chair, 678-839-6489, Fax: 678-839-6490, E-mail: landman@westga.edu. *Application contact:* Alice Wesley, Departmental Assistant, 678-839-5192, E-mail: awesley@westga.edu.
Website: http://www.westga.edu/math/.

University of Wisconsin–Madison, Graduate School, School of Education, Department of Curriculum and Instruction, Madison, WI 53706-1380. Offers art education (MA); curriculum and instruction (MS, PhD); education and mathematics (MA); French education (MA); German education (MA); music education (MS); science education (MS); Spanish education (MA). *Accreditation:* NASM (one or more programs are accredited). *Degree requirements:* For doctorate, thesis/dissertation. Application fee: $56. *Expenses:* Tuition, state resident: full-time $10,728; part-time $790 per credit. Tuition, nonresident: full-time $24,054; part-time $1623 per credit. *Required fees:* $1130; $119 per credit. *Financial support:* Project assistantships available. *Unit head:* Dr. Beth Graue, Chair, 608-263-4600, E-mail: graue@education.wisc.edu. *Application contact:* 608-262-2433, Fax: 608-262-5134, E-mail: gradadmiss@mail.bascom.wisc.edu.
Website: http://www.education.wisc.edu/ci.

University of Wisconsin–Oshkosh, Graduate Studies, College of Letters and Science, Department of Mathematics, Oshkosh, WI 54901. Offers mathematics education (MS). Part-time programs available. *Degree requirements:* For master's, comprehensive exam, thesis optional. *Entrance requirements:* For master's, 30 undergraduate credits in mathematics. Additional exam requirements/recommendations for international students: Required—TOEFL (minimum score 550 paper-based; 79 iBT). Electronic applications accepted. *Faculty research:* Problem solving, number theory, discrete mathematics, statistics.

University of Wisconsin–River Falls, Outreach and Graduate Studies, College of Arts and Science, Program in Mathematics, River Falls, WI 54022. Offers mathematics education (MSE). Part-time programs available. *Degree requirements:* For master's, thesis (for some programs). *Entrance requirements:* For master's, minimum GPA of 2.75. Additional exam requirements/recommendations for international students: Required—TOEFL (minimum score 500 paper-based; 65 iBT), IELTS (minimum score 5.5). Electronic applications accepted.

University of Wyoming, College of Arts and Sciences, Department of Mathematics, Laramie, WY 82071. Offers mathematics (MA, MAT, MS, MST, PhD); mathematics/computer science (PhD). Part-time programs available. Terminal master's awarded for partial completion of doctoral program. *Degree requirements:* For master's, comprehensive exam, thesis, qualifying exam; for doctorate, comprehensive exam, thesis/dissertation, preliminary exam. *Entrance requirements:* For master's and doctorate, GRE General Test, minimum GPA of 3.0. Additional exam requirements/recommendations for international students: Required—TOEFL (minimum score 540 paper-based; 76 iBT). *Faculty research:* Numerical analysis, classical analysis, mathematical modeling, algebraic combinations.

Ursuline College, School of Graduate Studies, Program in Education, Pepper Pike, OH 44124-4398. Offers art education (MA); early childhood education (MA); language arts education (MA); life science education (MA); math education (MA); middle school education (MA); social studies education (MA); special education (MA). *Accreditation:* NCATE. *Faculty:* 4 full-time (all women), 7 part-time/adjunct (5 women). *Students:* 18 full-time (16 women), 7 part-time (all women); includes 8 minority (4 Black or African American, non-Hispanic/Latino; 2 Asian, non-Hispanic/Latino; 2 Hispanic/Latino). Average age 34. 1 applicant, 100% accepted, 1 enrolled. In 2013, 25 master's awarded. *Degree requirements:* For master's, comprehensive exam. *Entrance requirements:* For master's, minimum undergraduate GPA of 3.0. Additional exam requirements/recommendations for international students: Required—TOEFL (minimum score 500 paper-based). *Application deadline:* For fall admission, 8/1 priority date for domestic students. Applications are processed on a rolling basis. Application fee: $25. *Expenses:* Contact institution. *Financial support:* In 2013–14, 1 student received support. Federal Work-Study available. Financial award application deadline: 3/1. *Unit head:* Dr. Edna West, Director, Master's Apprentice Program, 440-646-6134, Fax: 440-646-8328, E-mail: ewest@ursuline.edu. *Application contact:* Stephanie Pratt, Graduate Admission Coordinator, 440-646-8119, Fax: 440-684-6138, E-mail: graduateadmissions@ursuline.edu.

Utah Valley University, Program in Education, Orem, UT 84058-5999. Offers educational technology (M Ed); elementary mathematics (M Ed); English as a second language (M Ed); models of instruction (M Ed). *Accreditation:* Teacher Education Accreditation Council. Part-time programs available. *Faculty:* 4 full-time (2 women). *Students:* 107 part-time (76 women); includes 2 minority (1 Asian, non-Hispanic/Latino; 1 Hispanic/Latino). Average age 33. *Degree requirements:* For master's, project. *Entrance requirements:* For master's, GRE, 3 letters of recommendation, interview. Additional exam requirements/recommendations for international students: Required—TOEFL (minimum score 83 iBT). *Application deadline:* For fall admission, 3/31 for domestic and international students. Application fee: $45 ($100 for international students). Electronic applications accepted. *Expenses:* Tuition, state resident: full-time $8520; part-time $355 per credit. Tuition, nonresident: full-time $21,232; part-time $885 per credit. *Required fees:* $700; $350 per semester. Tuition and fees vary according to program. *Financial support:* Application deadline: 5/1; applicants required to submit FAFSA. *Unit head:* Parker Fewson, Dean, School of Education, 801-863-8006. *Application contact:* Mary Sowder, Coordinator of Graduate Studies, 801-863-6723.

Virginia Polytechnic Institute and State University, Graduate School, College of Engineering, Blacksburg, VA 24061. Offers aerospace engineering (ME, MS, PhD); biological systems engineering (ME, MS, PhD); biomedical engineering (MS, PhD); chemical engineering (ME, MS, PhD); civil engineering (ME, MS, PhD); computer engineering (ME, MS, PhD); computer science and application (MS, PhD); electrical engineering (ME, PhD); engineering education (PhD); engineering mechanics (ME, MS, PhD); environmental engineering (MS); environmental science and engineering (MS); industrial and systems engineering (ME, MS, PhD); materials science and engineering (ME, MS, PhD); mechanical engineering (ME, MS, PhD); mining and minerals engineering (PhD); mining engineering (ME, MS); nuclear engineering (MS, PhD); ocean engineering (MS); systems engineering (ME, MS). *Accreditation:* ABET (one or more programs are accredited). *Faculty:* 345 full-time (56 women), 2 part-time/adjunct (0 women). *Students:* 1,752 full-time (388 women), 328 part-time (66 women); includes 211 minority (42 Black or African American, non-Hispanic/Latino; 1 American Indian or Alaska Native, non-Hispanic/Latino; 84 Asian, non-Hispanic/Latino; 58 Hispanic/Latino; 1 Native Hawaiian or other Pacific Islander, non-Hispanic/Latino; 25 Two or more races, non-Hispanic/Latino), 1,019 international. Average age 27. 4,856 applicants, 20% accepted, 493 enrolled. In 2013, 456 master's, 213 doctorates awarded. *Degree requirements:* For master's, comprehensive exam (for some programs), thesis (for some programs); for doctorate, comprehensive exam (for some programs), thesis/dissertation (for some programs). *Entrance requirements:* For master's and doctorate, GRE/GMAT (may vary by department). Additional exam requirements/recommendations for international students: Required—TOEFL (minimum score 550 paper-based). *Application deadline:* For fall admission, 8/1 for domestic students, 4/1 for international students; for spring admission, 1/1 for domestic students, 9/1 for international students. Applications are processed on a rolling basis. Application fee: $75. Electronic applications accepted. *Expenses:* Tuition, state resident: full-time $11,185; part-time $621.50 per credit hour. Tuition, nonresident: full-time $22,146; part-time $1230.25 per credit hour. *Required fees:* $2442; $449.25 per semester. Tuition and fees vary according to course load, campus/location and program. *Financial support:* In 2013–14, 166 fellowships with full tuition reimbursements (averaging $5,942 per year), 893 research assistantships with full tuition reimbursements (averaging $21,642 per year), 299 teaching assistantships with full tuition reimbursements (averaging $17,624 per year) were awarded. Financial award application deadline: 3/1; financial award applicants required to submit FAFSA. *Total annual research expenditures:* $100 million. *Unit head:* Dr. Richard C. Benson, Dean, 540-231-9752, Fax: 540-231-3031, E-mail: deaneng@vt.edu. *Application contact:* Linda Perkins, Executive Assistant, 540-231-9752, Fax: 540-231-3031, E-mail: lperkins@vt.edu.
Website: http://www.eng.vt.edu/.

Virginia State University, School of Graduate Studies, Research, and Outreach, School of Engineering, Science and Technology, Department of Mathematics and Computer Science, Petersburg, VA 23806-0001. Offers computer science (MS); mathematics (MS); mathematics education (M Ed). *Degree requirements:* For master's, thesis (for some programs).

Wagner College, Division of Graduate Studies, Department of Education, Program in Secondary Education/Special Education, Staten Island, NY 10301-4495. Offers language arts (MS Ed); languages other than English (MS Ed); mathematics and technology (MS Ed); science and technology (MS Ed); social studies (MS Ed). Part-time and evening/weekend programs available. *Degree requirements:* For master's, thesis (for some programs). *Entrance requirements:* For master's, minimum GPA of 3.0, interview, recommendations. Electronic applications accepted. *Expenses: Tuition:* Full-time $17,496; part-time $972 per credit. Tuition and fees vary according to course load.

Walden University, Graduate Programs, Richard W. Riley College of Education and Leadership, Minneapolis, MN 55401. *Accreditation:* NCATE. Part-time and evening/weekend programs available. Postbaccalaureate distance learning degree programs offered (minimal on-campus study). *Faculty:* 23 full-time (15 women), 830 part-time/adjunct (569 women). *Students:* 8,671 full-time (7,197 women), 2,122 part-time (1,735 women); includes 4,734 minority (3,802 Black or African American, non-Hispanic/Latino; 50 American Indian or Alaska Native, non-Hispanic/Latino; 136 Asian, non-Hispanic/Latino; 539 Hispanic/Latino; 35 Native Hawaiian or other Pacific Islander, non-Hispanic/Latino; 172 Two or more races, non-Hispanic/Latino), 73 international. Average age 40. 2,646 applicants, 96% accepted, 2074 enrolled. In 2013, 2,214 master's, 354 doctorates, 479 other advanced degrees awarded. *Degree requirements:* For doctorate, thesis/dissertation (for some programs), residency; for other advanced degree, residency (for some programs). *Entrance requirements:* For master's, bachelor's degree or higher; minimum GPA of 2.5; official transcripts; goal statement (for some programs); access to computer and Internet; for doctorate, master's degree or higher; three years of related professional or academic experience (preferred); minimum GPA of 3.0; goal statement and current resume (select programs); official transcripts; access to computer and Internet; for other advanced degree, relevant work experience; access to computer and Internet. Additional exam requirements/recommendations for international students: Required—TOEFL (minimum score 550 paper-based; 79 iBT), IELTS (minimum score 6.5), Michigan English Language Assessment Battery (minimum score 82), or PTE. *Application deadline:* Applications are processed on a rolling basis. Application fee: $0. Electronic applications accepted. *Expenses: Tuition:* Full-time $11,813.55; part-time $500 per credit. *Required fees:* $618.76. *Financial support:* In 2013–14, 1 fellowship was awarded; Federal Work-Study, scholarships/grants, unspecified assistantships, and family tuition reduction, active duty/veteran tuition reduction, group tuition reduction, interest-free payment plans, employee tuition reduction also available. Support available to part-time students. Financial award applicants required to submit FAFSA. *Unit head:* Dr. Kate Steffens, Dean, 800-925-3368. *Application contact:* Jennifer Hall, Vice President of Enrollment Management, 866-4-WALDEN, E-mail: info@waldenu.edu.
Website: http://www.waldenu.edu/colleges-schools/riley-college-of-education/.

Washington State University, Graduate School, College of Arts and Sciences, Department of Mathematics, Pullman, WA 99164. Offers applied mathematics (MS, PhD); mathematics (MS, PhD); mathematics computational finance (MS); mathematics teaching (MS, PhD). Part-time programs available. Terminal master's awarded for partial completion of doctoral program. *Degree requirements:* For master's, comprehensive exam (for some programs), thesis or alternative, oral exam, project; for doctorate, 2 foreign languages, comprehensive exam, thesis/dissertation, oral exam, written exam. *Entrance requirements:* For master's and doctorate, minimum GPA of 3.0, 3 letters of recommendation. Additional exam requirements/recommendations for international students: Required—TOEFL (minimum score 600 paper-based; 100 iBT) or IELTS (minimum score 7). Electronic applications accepted. *Faculty research:* Computational mathematics, operations research, modeling in the natural sciences, applied statistics.

Washington State University, Graduate School, College of Education, Department of Teaching and Learning, Program in Mathematics and Science Education, Pullman, WA 99164. Offers PhD. *Degree requirements:* For doctorate, comprehensive exam, thesis/dissertation, written and oral exam. *Entrance requirements:* For doctorate, GRE General Test, minimum GPA of 3.0, transcript showing all academic coursework, statement of purpose, current resume/curriculum vitae, letters of recommendation. Additional exam requirements/recommendations for international students: Required—TOEFL (minimum score 550 paper-based; 80 iBT). Electronic applications accepted. *Faculty research:* Student learning processes and the long-term development of mathematical understandings, assessment and learning of low-performing students (English language learners and special needs) in mathematics, mathematics instructional practices and professional development.

Wayne State College, School of Education and Counseling, Department of Educational Foundations and Leadership, Program in Curriculum and Instruction, Wayne, NE 68787. Offers alternative education (MSE); business and information technology education (MSE); communication arts education (MSE); early childhood education (MSE); elementary education (MSE); English as a second language (MSE); English education (MSE); family and consumer sciences education (MSE); industrial technology and vocational education (MSE); learning communities (MSE); mathematics education (MSE); music education (MSE); science education (MSE); social science education (MSE). *Accreditation:* NCATE. Part-time and evening/weekend programs available. *Degree requirements:* For master's, comprehensive exam, thesis optional. *Entrance requirements:* For master's, GRE General Test. Additional exam requirements/recommendations for international students: Required—TOEFL (minimum score 550 paper-based).

Wayne State University, College of Education, Division of Teacher Education, Detroit, MI 48202. Offers art education (M Ed), including art therapy; autism spectrum disorders (Certificate); bilingual/bicultural education (M Ed, Certificate); career and technical education (M Ed, Certificate); cognitive impairment (Certificate); curriculum and instruction (Ed D, PhD, Ed S), including art education (PhD), bilingual education (Ed D, Ed S), bilingual-bicultural education (PhD), career and technical education (MAT, Ed D, PhD, Ed S), early childhood education (MAT, Ed D, PhD, Ed S), elementary education, English as a second language (MAT, Ed D, Ed S), English education (MAT, Ed D, PhD, Ed S), foreign language education (MAT, PhD), K-12 curriculum, mathematics education (MAT, Ed D, PhD, Ed S), science education (MAT, Ed D, PhD, Ed S), secondary education, social studies education (MAT, Ed S), social studies education: secondary (Ed D, PhD); early childhood education (M Ed, Certificate); elementary education (M Ed, MAT), including children's literature (MAT), early childhood education (MAT, Ed D, PhD, Ed S), general elementary education (MAT); elementary or secondary education (MAT), including bilingual/bicultural education, English as a second language (MAT, Ed D, Ed S), mathematics education (MAT, Ed D, PhD, Ed S), science education (MAT, Ed D, PhD, Ed S), social studies education (MAT, Ed S); emotionally impaired (Certificate); English as a second language (Certificate); English education (M Ed), including secondary; foreign language education (M Ed); K-12 reading specialist (Certificate); learning disabilities (Certificate); mathematics education (M Ed), including secondary; reading (M Ed, Ed S); reading, language and literature (Ed D); science education (M Ed), including secondary; secondary education (MAT), including art education (K-12), career and technical education (MAT, Ed D, PhD, Ed S), English education (MAT, Ed D, PhD, Ed S), foreign language education (MAT, PhD), kinesiology; social studies education (M Ed), including secondary; special education (M Ed, MAT, Ed D, PhD, Ed S); visual arts education (Certificate). Part-time programs available. *Faculty:* 36 full-time (25 women), 55 part-time/adjunct (43 women). *Students:* 218 full-time (163 women), 448 part-time (344 women); includes 218 minority (177 Black or African American, non-Hispanic/Latino; 2 American Indian or Alaska Native, non-Hispanic/Latino; 11 Asian, non-Hispanic/Latino; 19 Hispanic/Latino; 1 Native Hawaiian or other Pacific Islander, non-Hispanic/Latino; 8 Two or more races, non-Hispanic/Latino), 10 international. Average age 37. 258 applicants, 30% accepted, 52 enrolled. In 2013, 183 master's, 10 doctorates, 35 other advanced degrees awarded. *Degree requirements:* For master's, thesis, essay or project (for some M Ed programs), professional field experience (for MAT programs); for doctorate, thesis/dissertation. *Entrance requirements:* For master's, Michigan Basic Skills Test (MA in teaching), admission to the graduate school, verification of participation in group work with children and Michigan State Police Criminal Background check; for doctorate, minimum undergraduate GPA of 3.0, graduate 3.5; interview, curriculum vitae; references. Additional exam requirements/recommendations for international students: Required—TOEFL (minimum score 550 paper-based; 79 iBT), TWE (minimum score 5.5), Michigan English Language Assessment Battery (minimum score 85); Recommended—IELTS (minimum score 6.5). *Application deadline:* For fall admission, 6/1 priority date for domestic students, 5/1 priority date for international students; for winter admission, 10/1 priority date for domestic students, 9/1 priority date for international students; for spring admission, 2/1 priority date for domestic students, 1/1 priority date for international students. Applications are processed on a rolling basis. Application fee: $0. Electronic applications accepted. *Expenses:* Tuition, state resident: part-time $554.15 per credit. Tuition, nonresident: part-time $1200.35 per credit. *Required fees:* $42.15 per credit. $268.30 per semester. Tuition and fees vary according to course load and program. *Financial support:* In 2013–14, 83 students received support, including 1 fellowship (averaging $16,842 per year), 1 research assistantship with tuition reimbursement available (averaging $21,229 per year); career-related internships or fieldwork, Federal Work-Study, scholarships/grants, health care benefits, and unspecified assistantships also available. Support available to part-time students. Financial award application deadline: 3/31; financial award applicants required to submit FAFSA. *Faculty research:* Improving students' skill achievement in mathematics; improving elementary children's understanding of informational text; teachers' use of their pedagogical and mathematical knowledge in the interactive work of teaching; the intersection of identity construction in teaching and learning; identifying effective methods of literacy instruction and assessments for bilingual students in elementary language arts classrooms. *Total annual research expenditures:* $368,105. *Unit head:* Dr. Kathleen Crawford-McKinney, Assistant Dean, 313-577-0122. *Application contact:* Janice Green, Assistant Dean, 313-577-1605, E-mail: jwgreen@wayne.edu.
Website: http://coe.wayne.edu/ted/index.php.

Webster University, School of Education, Department of Multidisciplinary Studies, St. Louis, MO 63119-3194. Offers education leadership (Ed S); educational technology (MAT); educational technology leadership (Ed S); mathematics (MA); multidisciplinary studies (MAT); school psychology (Ed S); school systems, superintendency and leadership (Ed S); social science (MAT); special education (MA). Part-time programs available. *Entrance requirements:* For master's, minimum GPA of 2.5. Additional exam requirements/recommendations for international students: Required—TOEFL. *Expenses: Tuition:* Full-time $11,610; part-time $645 per credit hour. Tuition and fees vary according to campus/location and program.

Western Connecticut State University, Division of Graduate Studies, School of Professional Studies, Department of Education and Educational Psychology, Mathematics Education Option, Danbury, CT 06810-6885. Offers MS. Part-time programs available. *Degree requirements:* For master's, thesis or alternative, completion of program in 6 years. *Entrance requirements:* For master's, minimum GPA of 2.8, teaching certificate. Additional exam requirements/recommendations for international students: Recommended—TOEFL (minimum score 550 paper-based; 79 iBT), IELTS (minimum score 6). *Faculty research:* Eulerian mathematical principles.

Western Connecticut State University, Division of Graduate Studies, School of Professional Studies, Department of Education and Educational Psychology, Program in Secondary Education, Danbury, CT 06810-6885. Offers biology (MAT); mathematics

(MAT). Part-time programs available. *Entrance requirements:* For master's, PRAXIS I Pre-Professional Skills Tests, PRAXIS II subject assessment(s), minimum combined undergraduate GPA of 2.8 or MAT (minimum score in 35th percentile). Additional exam requirements/recommendations for international students: Recommended—TOEFL (minimum score 550 paper-based; 79 iBT), IELTS (minimum score 6). *Faculty research:* Differentiated instruction, the transition of teacher learning, teacher retention, relationship building through the evaluation process and leadership development, culture development, differentiated instruction, scheduling, transitioning teacher learning and curriculum.

Western Governors University, Teachers College, Salt Lake City, UT 84107. Offers curriculum and instruction (MS); educational leadership (MS); educational studies (MA); educational studies (5-12) (MA), including mathematics; elementary education (K-8) (MAT, Postbaccalaureate Certificate); elementary education (PreK-8) (MAT); English language learning (K-12) (MA); instructional design (MAT); learning and technology (M Ed, MA); management and innovation (M Ed); mathematics (5-12) (MAT, Postbaccalaureate Certificate); mathematics (5-9) (MAT, Postbaccalaureate Certificate); mathematics education (5-12) (MA); mathematics education (5-9) (MA); mathematics education (K-6) (MA); measurement and evaluation (M Ed); science (5-12) (Postbaccalaureate Certificate); science (5-9) (MAT, Postbaccalaureate Certificate); science education (5-12) (MA), including biology, chemistry, geology, physics; science education (5-9) (MA); social science (5-12) (MAT, Postbaccalaureate Certificate); special education (MAT, MS). *Accreditation:* NCATE. Evening/weekend programs available. Postbaccalaureate distance learning degree programs offered (no on-campus study). *Degree requirements:* For master's, capstone project. *Entrance requirements:* For master's and Postbaccalaureate Certificate, Readiness Assessment, transcripts. Additional exam requirements/recommendations for international students: Required—TOEFL (minimum score 450 paper-based; 80 iBT). Electronic applications accepted. *Expenses:* Contact institution.

Western Michigan University, Graduate College, College of Arts and Sciences, Department of Mathematics, Programs in Mathematics, Kalamazoo, MI 49008. Offers mathematics (MA, PhD); mathematics education (MA, PhD). *Degree requirements:* For master's, oral exams; for doctorate, one foreign language, thesis/dissertation, oral exams, 3 comprehensive exams, internship. *Entrance requirements:* For doctorate, GRE General Test.

Western New England University, College of Arts and Sciences, Program in Mathematics for Teachers, Springfield, MA 01119. Offers MAMT. Part-time and evening/weekend programs available. *Faculty:* 3 full-time (2 women). *Students:* 9 part-time (7 women); includes 2 minority (both Asian, non-Hispanic/Latino). Average age 31. 18 applicants. In 2013, 8 master's awarded. *Entrance requirements:* For master's, two letters of recommendation, official transcript, personal statement, resume. Additional exam requirements/recommendations for international students: Required—TOEFL. *Application deadline:* Applications are processed on a rolling basis. Application fee: $30. Electronic applications accepted. Tuition and fees vary according to program. *Financial support:* Application deadline: 4/15; applicants required to submit FAFSA. *Unit head:* Dr. Dennis Luciano, Chair, 413-782-1275, E-mail: dluciano@wne.edu. *Application contact:* Matthew Fox, Director of Recruiting and Marketing for Adult Learners, 413-782-1517, Fax: 413-782-1779, E-mail: study@wne.edu.
Website: http://www1.wne.edu/artsandsciences/index.cfm?selection-doc.858.

Western Oregon University, Graduate Programs, College of Education, Division of Teacher Education, Program in Secondary Education, Monmouth, OR 97361-1394. Offers bilingual education (MS Ed); health (MS Ed); humanities (MAT, MS Ed); initial licensure (MAT); mathematics (MAT, MS Ed); science (MAT, MS Ed); social science (MAT, MS Ed). *Accreditation:* NCATE. Part-time and evening/weekend programs available. *Degree requirements:* For master's, thesis optional, written exam. *Entrance requirements:* For master's, minimum GPA of 3.0, teaching license. Additional exam requirements/recommendations for international students: Required—TOEFL (minimum score 550 paper-based; 79 iBT), IELTS (minimum score 6.5). *Faculty research:* Literacy, science in primary grades, geography education, retention, teacher burnout.

West Virginia University, Eberly College of Arts and Sciences, Department of Mathematics, Morgantown, WV 26506. Offers applied mathematics (MS, PhD); discrete mathematics (PhD); interdisciplinary mathematics (MS); mathematics for secondary education (MS); pure mathematics (MS). Part-time programs available. Terminal master's awarded for partial completion of doctoral program. *Degree requirements:* For master's, comprehensive exam (for some programs), thesis optional; for doctorate, one foreign language, comprehensive exam, thesis/dissertation. *Entrance requirements:* For master's, GRE Subject Test (recommended), minimum GPA of 2.5; for doctorate, GRE Subject Test (recommended), master's degree in mathematics. Additional exam requirements/recommendations for international students: Required—TOEFL (paper-based 550) or IELTS (6). *Faculty research:* Combinatorics and graph theory, differential equations, applied and computational mathematics.

Widener University, School of Human Service Professions, Center for Education, Chester, PA 19013-5792. Offers adult education (M Ed); counseling in higher education (M Ed); counselor education (M Ed); early childhood education (M Ed); educational foundations (M Ed); educational leadership (M Ed); educational psychology (M Ed); elementary education (M Ed); English and language arts (M Ed); health education (M Ed); higher education leadership (Ed D); home and school visitor (M Ed); human sexuality (M Ed, PhD); mathematics education (M Ed); middle school education (M Ed); principalship (M Ed); reading and language arts (Ed D); reading education (M Ed); school administration (Ed D); science education (M Ed); social studies education (M Ed); special education (M Ed); technology education (M Ed). *Accreditation:* NCATE. Part-time and evening/weekend programs available. *Faculty:* 34 full-time (22 women), 37 part-time/adjunct (14 women). *Students:* 64 full-time (44 women), 209 part-time (146 women); includes 49 minority (39 Black or African American, non-Hispanic/Latino; 1 American Indian or Alaska Native, non-Hispanic/Latino; 4 Asian, non-Hispanic/Latino; 4 Hispanic/Latino; 1 Two or more races, non-Hispanic/Latino), 8 international. Average age 39. 139 applicants, 88% accepted. In 2013, 168 master's, 31 doctorates awarded. Terminal master's awarded for partial completion of doctoral program. *Degree requirements:* For doctorate, thesis/dissertation. *Entrance requirements:* For master's, minimum GPA of 2.5; for doctorate, GRE or MAT, minimum GPA of 2.0 (undergraduate), 3.5 (graduate). *Application deadline:* Applications are processed on a rolling basis. Application fee: $25 ($300 for international students). Electronic applications accepted. *Expenses:* Contact institution. *Financial support:* Career-related internships or fieldwork, tuition waivers (full and partial), and unspecified assistantships available. Support available to part-time students. Financial award application deadline: 5/1. *Faculty research:* Reading and cognition, adult education, technology education, educational leadership, special education. *Unit head:* Dr. Michael W. LeDoux, Associate Dean, 610-499-4294, Fax: 610-499-4623, E-mail: mwledoux@widener.edu. *Application contact:* Dr. Roberta Nolan, Director of Graduate Admissions, 610-499-4125, E-mail: rdnolan@widener.edu.

Wilkes University, College of Graduate and Professional Studies, College of Science and Engineering, Department of Mathematics and Computer Science, Wilkes-Barre, PA 18766-0002. Offers mathematics (MS, MS Ed). Part-time programs available. *Students:* 2 full-time (1 woman). Average age 28. In 2013, 1 master's awarded. *Degree requirements:* For master's, thesis or alternative. *Entrance requirements:* For master's, GRE General Test. Additional exam requirements/recommendations for international students: Required—TOEFL (minimum score 550 paper-based; 79 iBT). *Application deadline:* Applications are processed on a rolling basis. Application fee: $45 ($65 for international students). Electronic applications accepted. *Financial support:* Federal Work-Study and unspecified assistantships available. Financial award application deadline: 3/1; financial award applicants required to submit FAFSA. *Unit head:* Dr. Barbara Bracken, Chair, 570-408-4836, Fax: 570-408-7883, E-mail: barbara.bracken@wilkes.edu. *Application contact:* Joanne Thomas, Interim Director of Graduate Enrollment, 570-408-4234, Fax: 570-408-7846, E-mail: joanne.thomas1@wilkes.edu.
Website: http://www.wilkes.edu/pages/389.asp.

Wilkes University, College of Graduate and Professional Studies, School of Education, Wilkes-Barre, PA 18766-0002. Offers art and science of teaching (MS Ed); classroom technology (MS Ed); early childhood literacy (MS Ed); educational development and strategies (MS Ed); educational leadership (MS Ed); educational technology (Ed D); higher education administration (Ed D); instructional media (MS Ed); instructional technology (MS Ed); international school leadership (MS Ed); K-12 administration (Ed D); middle level education (MS Ed); online teaching (MS Ed); reading (MS Ed); school business leadership (MS Ed); secondary education (MS Ed), including biology, chemistry, English, history, mathematics; special education (MS Ed); teaching English as a second language (MS Ed); twenty-first century teaching and learning (MS Ed). Part-time and evening/weekend programs available. Postbaccalaureate distance learning degree programs offered (minimal on-campus study). *Students:* 46 full-time (37 women), 1,410 part-time (1,039 women); includes 67 minority (12 Black or African American, non-Hispanic/Latino; 2 American Indian or Alaska Native, non-Hispanic/Latino; 11 Asian, non-Hispanic/Latino; 28 Hispanic/Latino; 1 Native Hawaiian or other Pacific Islander, non-Hispanic/Latino; 13 Two or more races, non-Hispanic/Latino), 6 international. Average age 34. In 2013, 852 master's, 10 doctorates awarded. *Entrance requirements:* Additional exam requirements/recommendations for international students: Required—TOEFL (minimum score 550 paper-based; 79 iBT). *Application deadline:* Applications are processed on a rolling basis. Application fee: $45. Electronic applications accepted. *Expenses:* Contact institution. *Financial support:* Federal Work-Study and unspecified assistantships available. Financial award application deadline: 3/1; financial award applicants required to submit FAFSA. *Unit head:* Dr. Rhonda Waskiewicz, Interim Dean, Education, 570-408-4332, Fax: 570-408-7872, E-mail: rhonda.waskiewicz@wilkes.edu. *Application contact:* Joanne Thomas, Interim Director of Graduate Education, 570-408-4234, Fax: 570-408-7846, E-mail: joanne.thomas1@wilkes.edu.
Website: http://www.wilkes.edu/pages/383.asp.

Wright State University, School of Graduate Studies, College of Science and Mathematics, Interdisciplinary Program in Science and Mathematics, Dayton, OH 45435. Offers MST.

Youngstown State University, Graduate School, College of Science, Technology, Engineering and Mathematics, Department of Mathematics and Statistics, Youngstown, OH 44555-0001. Offers applied mathematics (MS); computer science (MS); secondary mathematics (MS); statistics (MS). Part-time programs available. *Degree requirements:* For master's, comprehensive exam, thesis optional. *Entrance requirements:* For master's, minimum GPA of 2.7 in computer science and mathematics. Additional exam requirements/recommendations for international students: Required—TOEFL. *Faculty research:* Regression analysis, numerical analysis, statistics, Markov chain, topology and fuzzy sets.

Museum Education

Bank Street College of Education, Graduate School, Program in Museum Education, New York, NY 10025. Offers museum education (MS Ed); museum education: elementary education certification (MS Ed). *Degree requirements:* For master's, thesis. *Entrance requirements:* For master's, interview, essays. Additional exam requirements/recommendations for international students: Required—TOEFL (minimum score 600 paper-based; 100 iBT), IELTS (minimum score 7). Electronic applications accepted. *Faculty research:* Equitable access and openness to diversity in museum settings, exhibition display and development, museum and school partnerships.

Bank Street College of Education, Graduate School, Programs in Educational Leadership, New York, NY 10025. Offers early childhood leadership (MS Ed); educational leadership (MS Ed); leadership for educational change (Ed M, MS Ed); leadership in community-based learning (MS Ed); leadership in mathematics education (MS Ed); leadership in museum education (MS Ed); leadership in the arts: creative writing (MS Ed); leadership in the arts: visual arts (MS Ed). *Degree requirements:* For master's, thesis. *Entrance requirements:* For master's, interview, essays, minimum of 2 years experience as a classroom teacher. Additional exam requirements/recommendations for international students: Required—TOEFL (minimum score 600 paper-based; 100 iBT), IELTS (minimum score 7). Electronic applications accepted. *Faculty research:* Leadership in urban schools, leadership in small schools, mathematics in elementary schools, professional development in early childhood, leadership in arts education, leadership in special education, museum leadership, community-based leadership.

Eastern Michigan University, Graduate School, College of Arts and Sciences, Department of Sociology, Anthropology and Criminology, Program in Cultural Museum Studies, Ypsilanti, MI 48197. Offers Graduate Certificate. Part-time and evening/weekend programs available. Postbaccalaureate distance learning degree programs offered (minimal on-campus study). *Entrance requirements:* Additional exam requirements/recommendations for international students: Required—TOEFL. *Application deadline:* Applications are processed on a rolling basis. Application fee: $35. *Expenses:* Tuition, state resident: full-time $12,300; part-time $466 per credit hour.

Tuition, nonresident: full-time $23,159; part-time $918 per credit hour. *Required fees:* $71 per credit hour. $46 per semester. One-time fee: $100. Tuition and fees vary according to course level and degree level. *Financial support:* Fellowships, research assistantships with full tuition reimbursements, teaching assistantships with full tuition reimbursements, career-related internships or fieldwork, Federal Work-Study, institutionally sponsored loans, scholarships/grants, tuition waivers (partial), and unspecified assistantships available. Support available to part-time students. Financial award applicants required to submit FAFSA. *Unit head:* Dr. Anders Linde-Laursen, Department Head, 734-487-0012, Fax: 734-487-9666, E-mail: alindela@emich.edu. *Application contact:* Dr. Liza Cerroni-Long, Advisor, 734-487-0012, Fax: 734-487-9666, E-mail: liza.cerroni-long@emich.edu.

The George Washington University, Graduate School of Education and Human Development, Department of Educational Leadership, Program in Museum Education, Washington, DC 20052. Offers MAT. *Students:* 13 full-time (all women); includes 4 minority (1 Asian, non-Hispanic/Latino; 3 Hispanic/Latino), 1 international. Average age 24. 30 applicants, 93% accepted, 13 enrolled. In 2013, 14 master's awarded. *Degree requirements:* For master's, comprehensive exam. *Entrance requirements:* For master's, GRE General Test or MAT, minimum GPA of 2.75. *Application deadline:* For fall admission, 1/15 priority date for domestic students; for spring admission, 10/1 for domestic students. Applications are processed on a rolling basis. Application fee: $75. *Financial support:* In 2013–14, 7 students received support. Fellowships, career-related internships or fieldwork, Federal Work-Study, and tuition waivers available. Financial award application deadline: 1/15; financial award applicants required to submit FAFSA. *Unit head:* Dr. Carol B. Stapp, Director, 202-994-4960, E-mail: cstapp@gwu.edu. *Application contact:* Sarah Lang, Director of Graduate Admissions, 202-994-1447, Fax: 202-994-7207, E-mail: slang@gwu.edu. Website: http://gsehd.gwu.edu/MEP.

Seton Hall University, College of Arts and Sciences, Department of Communication and the Arts, South Orange, NJ 07079-2697. Offers corporate and professional communication (MA); museum professions (MA), including exhibition development, museum education, museum management, museum registration; strategic communication (MA); strategic communication and leadership (MA). Part-time and evening/weekend programs available. Postbaccalaureate distance learning degree programs offered (minimal on-campus study). *Degree requirements:* For master's, thesis. *Entrance requirements:* Additional exam requirements/recommendations for international students: Required—TOEFL. Electronic applications accepted. *Faculty research:* Managerial communication, communication consulting, communication and development.

Tufts University, Graduate School of Arts and Sciences, Department of Education, Program in Education, Medford, MA 02155. Offers educational studies (MA); elementary education (MAT); middle and secondary education (MA, MAT); museum education (MA); secondary education (MA); STEM education (MS, PhD). *Faculty:* 13 full-time, 9 part-time/adjunct. *Students:* 85 full-time (72 women); includes 19 minority (4 Black or African American, non-Hispanic/Latino; 1 American Indian or Alaska Native, non-Hispanic/Latino; 3 Asian, non-Hispanic/Latino; 7 Hispanic/Latino; 4 Two or more races, non-Hispanic/Latino), 5 international. Average age 27. 154 applicants, 69% accepted, 50 enrolled. In 2013, 84 master's awarded. *Degree requirements:* For master's, thesis optional; for doctorate, thesis/dissertation. *Entrance requirements:* For master's and doctorate, GRE General Test. Additional exam requirements/recommendations for international students: Required—TOEFL (minimum score 550 paper-based; 80 iBT), IELTS (minimum score 6.5). *Application deadline:* For fall admission, 1/2 for domestic and international students; for spring admission, 10/15 for domestic students, 9/15 for international students. Applications are processed on a rolling basis. Application fee: $75. Electronic applications accepted. *Financial support:* Teaching assistantships with full and partial tuition reimbursements, Federal Work-Study, scholarships/grants, and tuition waivers (full and partial) available. Support available to part-time students. Financial award application deadline: 1/2. *Unit head:* Hammer David, Chair, 617-627-3244, Fax: 617-627-3901. *Application contact:* Patricia Romeo, Information Contact, 617-627-3244.

The University of the Arts, College of Art, Media and Design, Department of Museum Studies, Philadelphia, PA 19102-4944. Offers museum communication (MA); museum education (MA); museum exhibition planning and design (MFA). *Accreditation:* NASAD. *Degree requirements:* For master's, thesis, internship. *Entrance requirements:* For master's, official transcripts, three letters of recommendation, one- to two-page statement, personal interview; academic writing sample and examples of work (for museum communication); two examples of academic and professional writing (for museum education); portfolio and/or writing samples (for museum exhibition planning and design). Additional exam requirements/recommendations for international students: Required—TOEFL (minimum score 580 paper-based, 92 iBT) or IELTS (minimum score 6.5).

Music Education

Alabama Agricultural and Mechanical University, School of Graduate Studies, School of Education, Area in Music Education, Huntsville, AL 35811. Offers music (MS); music education (M Ed). *Accreditation:* NCATE. Part-time and evening/weekend programs available. *Degree requirements:* For master's, comprehensive exam. *Entrance requirements:* For master's, GRE General Test. Additional exam requirements/recommendations for international students: Required—TOEFL (minimum score 500 paper-based; 61 iBT). Electronic applications accepted. *Faculty research:* Jazz and black music, Alabama folk music.

Alabama State University, College of Education, Department of Curriculum and Instruction, Montgomery, AL 36101-0271. Offers early childhood education (M Ed, Ed S); elementary education (M Ed, Ed S); secondary education (M Ed, Ed S), including biology education, English language arts education (M Ed), history education, math education, music education (M Ed), reading education (M Ed), social science education; special education (M Ed). Part-time programs available. *Faculty:* 11 full-time (8 women), 13 part-time/adjunct (10 women). *Students:* 32 full-time (19 women), 162 part-time (136 women); includes 189 minority (187 Black or African American, non-Hispanic/Latino; 1 Hispanic/Latino; 1 Two or more races, non-Hispanic/Latino). Average age 33. 99 applicants, 45% accepted, 34 enrolled. In 2013, 74 master's, 20 Ed Ss awarded. *Degree requirements:* For master's, comprehensive exam, thesis optional; for Ed S, comprehensive exam, thesis. *Entrance requirements:* For master's, GRE General Test, MAT, writing competency test; for Ed S, writing competency test, GRE, MAT. Additional exam requirements/recommendations for international students: Required—TOEFL (minimum score 500 paper-based). *Application deadline:* For fall admission, 7/15 for domestic students; for spring admission, 12/15 for domestic students. Applications are processed on a rolling basis. Application fee: $25. *Expenses:* Tuition, state resident: full-time $7958; part-time $343 per credit hour. Tuition, nonresident: full-time $14,132; part-time $686 per credit hour. *Required fees:* $446 per term. One-time fee: $1784 full-time; $892 part-time. Tuition and fees vary according to course load. *Financial support:* In 2013–14, research assistantships (averaging $9,450 per year) were awarded. *Unit head:* Dr. Joyce Johnson, Acting Chairperson, 334-229-4485, Fax: 334-229-5603, E-mail: jjohnson@alasu.edu. *Application contact:* Dr. William Person, Dean of Graduate Studies, 334-229-4274, Fax: 334-229-4928, E-mail: wperson@alasu.edu. Website: http://www.alasu.edu/academics/colleges—departments/college-of-education/curriculum—instruction/index.aspx.

Appalachian State University, Cratis D. Williams Graduate School, School of Music, Boone, NC 28608. Offers music education (MM); music performance (MM); music therapy (MMT). *Accreditation:* NASM. Part-time programs available. *Degree requirements:* For master's, comprehensive exam, thesis or alternative. *Entrance requirements:* For master's, GRE General Test, 3 letters of reference, audition. Additional exam requirements/recommendations for international students: Required—TOEFL (minimum score 550 paper-based; 79 iBT), IELTS (minimum score 6.5). Electronic applications accepted. *Faculty research:* Music of the Holocaust, Celtic folk music, early nineteenth-century performance practice, hypermeter and phase rhythm, world music, music and psychoneuroimmunology.

Arcadia University, Graduate Studies, School of Education, Glenside, PA 19038-3295. Offers art education (M Ed); computer education (CAS); curriculum (CAS); curriculum studies (M Ed); early childhood education (M Ed, CAS), including individualized (M Ed), master teacher (M Ed), research in child development (M Ed); educational leadership (M Ed, Ed D, CAS); elementary education (M Ed, CAS); English education (MA Ed); environmental education (MA Ed, CAS); history education (MA Ed); instructional technology (M Ed); language arts (M Ed, CAS); library science (M Ed); mathematics education (M Ed, MA Ed, CAS); music education (MA Ed); psychology (MA Ed); reading (M Ed, CAS); science education (M Ed, CAS); secondary education (M Ed, CAS); special education (M Ed, Ed D, CAS); theater arts (MA Ed); written communication (MA Ed). *Accreditation:* NASAD. Part-time and evening/weekend programs available. Postbaccalaureate distance learning degree programs offered (minimal on-campus study). Electronic applications accepted. *Expenses:* Contact institution.

Arizona State University at the Tempe campus, Herberger Institute for Design and the Arts, School of Music, Tempe, AZ 85287-0405. Offers composition (MM); music (conducting) (DMA); music (ethnomusicology) (MA); music (interdisciplinary digital media/performance) (DMA); music (music history and literature) (MA); music (performance) (DMA); music education (MM, PhD); music therapy (MM); performance (MM). *Accreditation:* NASM. Terminal master's awarded for partial completion of doctoral program. *Degree requirements:* For master's, thesis (for some programs), interactive Program of Study (iPOS) submitted before completing 50 percent of required credit hours; for doctorate, comprehensive exam, thesis/dissertation, interactive Program of Study (iPOS) submitted before completing 50 percent of required credit hours. *Entrance requirements:* For master's, minimum GPA of 3.0 or equivalent in last 2 years of work leading to bachelor's degree, 3 letters of recommendation, resume; for doctorate, GRE or MAT, minimum GPA of 3.0 or equivalent in last 2 years of work leading to bachelor's degree, 3 letters of recommendation, curriculum vitae, statement of intent. Additional exam requirements/recommendations for international students: Required—TOEFL, IELTS, or PTE. Electronic applications accepted.

Arkansas State University, Graduate School, College of Fine Arts, Department of Music, Jonesboro, AR 72467. Offers music education (MME, SCCT); performance (MM). *Accreditation:* NASM (one or more programs are accredited). Part-time programs available. *Faculty:* 21 full-time (6 women). *Students:* 6 full-time (1 woman), 12 part-time (4 women); includes 1 minority (Black or African American, non-Hispanic/Latino), 3 international. Average age 29. 10 applicants, 60% accepted, 6 enrolled. In 2013, 6 master's awarded. *Degree requirements:* For master's, 2 foreign languages, comprehensive exam, thesis or alternative; for SCCT, comprehensive exam. *Entrance requirements:* For master's, GRE General Test or MAT, university entrance exam, appropriate bachelor's degree, audition, letters of recommendation, teaching experience, official transcripts, immunization records, valid teaching certificate; for SCCT, GRE General Test or MAT, interview, master's degree, official transcript, immunization records, letters of recommendation. Additional exam requirements/recommendations for international students: Required—TOEFL (minimum score 550 paper-based; 79 iBT), IELTS (minimum score 6), PTE (minimum score 56). *Application deadline:* For fall admission, 7/1 for domestic and international students; for spring admission, 11/15 for domestic students, 11/14 for international students. Applications are processed on a rolling basis. Application fee: $30 ($40 for international students). Electronic applications accepted. *Expenses:* Tuition, state resident: full-time $4284; part-time $238 per credit hour. Tuition, nonresident: full-time $8568; part-time $476 per credit hour. *International tuition:* $9268 full-time. *Required fees:* $1098; $61 per credit hour. $25 per term. Tuition and fees vary according to course load and program. *Financial support:* In 2013–14, 10 students received support. Teaching assistantships, career-related internships or fieldwork, scholarships/grants, and unspecified assistantships available. Financial award application deadline: 7/1; financial award applicants required to submit FAFSA. *Unit head:* Ken Hatch, Chair, 870-972-2094, Fax: 870-972-3932, E-mail: khatch@astate.edu. *Application contact:* Vickey Ring, Graduate Admissions Coordinator, 870-972-3029, Fax: 870-972-3857, E-mail: vickeyring@astate.edu. Website: http://www.astate.edu/college/fine-arts/music/.

Auburn University, Graduate School, College of Education, Department of Curriculum and Teaching, Auburn University, AL 36849. Offers business education (M Ed, MS, PhD); early childhood education (M Ed, MS, PhD, Ed S); elementary education (M Ed, MS, PhD, Ed S); foreign languages (M Ed, MS); music education (M Ed, MS, PhD, Ed S); postsecondary education (PhD); reading education (PhD, Ed S); secondary education (M Ed, MS, PhD, Ed S), including English language arts, mathematics, science, social studies. *Accreditation:* NASM (one or more programs are accredited); NCATE. Part-time programs available. *Faculty:* 29 full-time (21 women), 4 part-time/adjunct (all women). *Students:* 61 full-time (40 women), 153 part-time (108 women); includes 37 minority (32 Black or African American, non-Hispanic/Latino; 2 Asian, non-Hispanic/Latino; 3 Hispanic/Latino), 1 international. Average age 34. 150 applicants, 59% accepted, 74 enrolled. In 2013, 70 master's, 6 doctorates, 26 other advanced

degrees awarded. *Degree requirements:* For master's, thesis (for some programs); for doctorate, thesis/dissertation; for Ed S, field project. *Entrance requirements:* For master's, doctorate, and Ed S, GRE General Test. *Application deadline:* For fall admission, 7/7 for domestic students; for spring admission, 11/24 for domestic students. Applications are processed on a rolling basis. Application fee: $50 ($60 for international students). Electronic applications accepted. *Expenses:* Tuition, state resident: full-time $8262; part-time $459 per credit hour. Tuition, nonresident: full-time $24,786; part-time $1377 per credit hour. Tuition and fees vary according to degree level and program. *Financial support:* Fellowships, teaching assistantships, career-related internships or fieldwork, and Federal Work-Study available. Support available to part-time students. Financial award application deadline: 3/15; financial award applicants required to submit FAFSA. *Faculty research:* Emerging literacy, reading attitudes, music for at-risk youth, portfolio assessment. *Unit head:* Dr. Kimberly Walls, Head, 334-844-4434. *Application contact:* Dr. George Flowers, Dean of the Graduate School, 334-844-2125.
Website: http://education.auburn.edu/academic_departments/curr/.

Austin Peay State University, College of Graduate Studies, College of Arts and Letters, Department of Music, Clarksville, TN 37044. Offers music education (M Mu); music performance (M Mu). *Accreditation:* NASM. Part-time programs available. *Faculty:* 16 full-time (8 women), 2 part-time/adjunct (both women). *Students:* 17 full-time (8 women), 5 part-time (0 women); includes 8 minority (2 Black or African American, non-Hispanic/Latino; 1 Asian, non-Hispanic/Latino; 1 Hispanic/Latino; 1 Native Hawaiian or other Pacific Islander, non-Hispanic/Latino; 3 Two or more races, non-Hispanic/Latino). Average age 30. 8 applicants, 88% accepted, 6 enrolled. In 2013, 5 master's awarded. *Degree requirements:* For master's, comprehensive exam, thesis optional. *Entrance requirements:* For master's, GRE General Test, diagnostic exams, audition, bachelor's degree, 3 letters of recommendation. Additional exam requirements/recommendations for international students: Required—TOEFL (minimum score 500 paper-based). *Application deadline:* For fall admission, 8/5 priority date for domestic students. Applications are processed on a rolling basis. Application fee: $25. Electronic applications accepted. *Expenses:* Tuition, state resident: full-time $7500; part-time $375 per credit hour. Tuition, nonresident: full-time $20,800; part-time $1040 per credit hour. *Required fees:* $1284; $64.20 per credit hour. *Financial support:* In 2013–14, research assistantships with full tuition reimbursements (averaging $6,500 per year) were awarded; career-related internships or fieldwork, Federal Work-Study, institutionally sponsored loans, scholarships/grants, and unspecified assistantships also available. Support available to part-time students. Financial award application deadline: 3/1; financial award applicants required to submit FAFSA. *Unit head:* Dr. Douglas Rose, Chair, 931-221-7808, Fax: 931-221-7529, E-mail: rosed@apsu.edu. *Application contact:* June D. Lee, Graduate Coordinator, 800-859-4723, Fax: 931-221-7641, E-mail: gradadmissions@apsu.edu.
Website: http://www.apsu.edu/music/.

Azusa Pacific University, School of Music, Azusa, CA 91702-7000. Offers education (M Mus); performance (M Mus). *Accreditation:* NASM. Part-time and evening/weekend programs available. *Degree requirements:* For master's, recital. *Entrance requirements:* For master's, interview, audition. Additional exam requirements/recommendations for international students: Required—TOEFL (minimum score 550 paper-based).

Ball State University, Graduate School, College of Fine Arts, School of Music, Muncie, IN 47306-1099. Offers music education (MA, MM, DA). *Accreditation:* NASM; NCATE (one or more programs are accredited). *Faculty:* 41 full-time (15 women), 2 part-time/adjunct (1 woman). *Students:* 49 full-time (28 women), 40 part-time (21 women); includes 8 minority (1 Black or African American, non-Hispanic/Latino; 7 Hispanic/Latino), 18 international. Average age 25. 105 applicants, 59% accepted, 22 enrolled. In 2013, 14 master's, 6 doctorates awarded. *Degree requirements:* For doctorate, thesis/dissertation. *Entrance requirements:* For master's, audition; for doctorate, GRE General Test, audition, minimum graduate GPA of 3.2, writing sample. Application fee: $50. *Financial support:* In 2013–14, 59 students received support, including 53 teaching assistantships with full tuition reimbursements available (averaging $9,975 per year); research assistantships with full tuition reimbursements available also available. Financial award application deadline: 3/1. *Unit head:* Dr. John Scheib, Unit Head, 765-285-5402, Fax: 765-285-5401, E-mail: jwscheib@bsu.edu. *Application contact:* Dr. Linda Pohly, Coordinator, 765-285-5502, Fax: 765-285-5401, E-mail: lpohly@bsu.edu.
Website: http://www.bsu.edu/music/.

Belmont University, College of Visual and Performing Arts, School of Music, Nashville, TN 37212-3757. Offers church music (MM); commercial music (MM); composition (MM); music education (MM); pedagogy (MM); performance (MM). *Accreditation:* NASM. Part-time programs available. *Students:* 46 full-time (24 women), 10 part-time (6 women); includes 9 minority (5 Black or African American, non-Hispanic/Latino; 1 American Indian or Alaska Native, non-Hispanic/Latino; 1 Hispanic/Latino; 2 Two or more races, non-Hispanic/Latino). Average age 27. 75 applicants, 40% accepted, 24 enrolled. *Degree requirements:* For master's, comprehensive exam, thesis (for some programs). *Entrance requirements:* For master's, placement exam, GRE or MAT, audition, interview, minimum GPA of 2.75. Additional exam requirements/recommendations for international students: Required—TOEFL (minimum score 500 paper-based). *Application deadline:* For fall admission, 5/1 priority date for domestic students, 5/1 for international students; for spring admission, 11/1 priority date for domestic students, 11/1 for international students. Applications are processed on a rolling basis. Application fee: $50. Electronic applications accepted. *Financial support:* Fellowships, teaching assistantships, career-related internships or fieldwork, scholarships/grants, and unspecified assistantships available. Financial award application deadline: 3/1; financial award applicants required to submit FAFSA. *Unit head:* Dr. Robert Gregg, Director, 615-460-8111, Fax: 615-386-0239, E-mail: greggr@mail.belmont.edu. *Application contact:* Ben Craine, Graduate Secretary, 615-460-8117, Fax: 615-386-0239, E-mail: ben.craine@belmont.edu.

Bob Jones University, Graduate Programs, Greenville, SC 29614. Offers accountancy (MS); Bible (MA); Bible translation (MA); Biblical studies (Certificate); broadcast management (MS); business administration (MBA); church history (MA, PhD); church ministries (MA); church music (MM); cinema and video production (MA); counseling (MS); curriculum and instruction (Ed D); divinity (M Div); dramatic production (MA); educational leadership (MS, Ed D, Ed S); elementary education (M Ed, MAT); English (M Ed, MA, MAT); fine arts (MA); graphic design (MA); history (M Ed, MA); illustration (MA); interpretative speech (MA); mathematics (M Ed, MAT); medical missions (Certificate); ministry (MM, D Min); multi-categorical special education (M Ed, MAT); music (M Ed); New Testament interpretation (PhD); Old Testament interpretation (PhD); orchestral instrument performance (MM); organ performance (MM); pastoral studies (MA); personnel services (MS, Ed S); piano pedagogy (MM); piano performance (MM); platform arts (MA); radio and television broadcasting (MS); rhetoric and public address (MA); secondary education (M Ed); studio art (MA); teaching Bible (MA); theology (MA, PhD); voice performance (MM); youth ministries (MA); M Div/MM.

Boise State University, College of Arts and Sciences, Department of Music, Boise, ID 83725-0399. Offers music (MM); music education (MM); pedagogy (MM); performance (MM). *Accreditation:* NASM. Part-time programs available. *Degree requirements:* For master's, thesis optional. *Entrance requirements:* For master's, minimum GPA of 3.0, performance demonstration. Electronic applications accepted.

The Boston Conservatory, Graduate Division, Boston, MA 02215. Offers choral conducting (MM); composition (MM); music (MM, ADP, Certificate), including music, music education (MM); music performance (MM, ADP, Certificate); opera (MM, ADP, Certificate); theater (MM). *Accreditation:* NASM (one or more programs are accredited). Part-time programs available. *Degree requirements:* For master's, recital or performance; for other advanced degree, recital. *Entrance requirements:* For master's and other advanced degree, audition. Additional exam requirements/recommendations for international students: Required—TOEFL (minimum score 580 paper-based). Electronic applications accepted.

The Boston Conservatory, Graduate Division, Music Division, Department of Music Education, Boston, MA 02215. Offers MM. *Accreditation:* NASM. Part-time programs available. *Degree requirements:* For master's, comprehensive oral exam, thesis or recital. *Entrance requirements:* For master's, audition, interview. Additional exam requirements/recommendations for international students: Required—TOEFL (minimum score 580 paper-based). Electronic applications accepted.

Boston University, College of Fine Arts, School of Music, Program in Music Education, Boston, MA 02215. Offers MM, DMA. *Accreditation:* NASM. *Faculty:* 9 full-time (3 women). *Students:* 352 full-time (172 women), 65 part-time (30 women); includes 66 minority (29 Black or African American, non-Hispanic/Latino; 4 American Indian or Alaska Native, non-Hispanic/Latino; 11 Asian, non-Hispanic/Latino; 16 Hispanic/Latino; 1 Native Hawaiian or other Pacific Islander, non-Hispanic/Latino; 5 Two or more races, non-Hispanic/Latino), 21 international. Average age 39. 36 applicants, 56% accepted, 7 enrolled. In 2013, 146 master's, 6 doctorates awarded. *Degree requirements:* For master's, thesis; for doctorate, 2 foreign languages, thesis/dissertation. *Entrance requirements:* For doctorate, GRE or MAT. Additional exam requirements/recommendations for international students: Required—TOEFL (minimum score 100 iBT). *Application deadline:* For fall admission, 1/1 priority date for domestic and international students. Application fee: $70. Electronic applications accepted. *Expenses: Tuition:* Full-time $43,970; part-time $1374 per credit hour. *Required fees:* $60 per semester. Tuition and fees vary according to class time, course level and program. *Financial support:* Fellowships and teaching assistantships available. Financial award application deadline: 1/1. *Unit head:* Richard Cornell, Interim Director, 617-353-8789, Fax: 617-353-7455, E-mail: rdodson@bu.edu. *Application contact:* Shaun Ramsay, Assistant Director, School of Music Admissions and Student Affairs, 617-353-3341, E-mail: arts@bu.edu.

Boston University, Graduate School of Arts and Sciences, Department of Music, Boston, MA 02215. Offers composition (MA); music education (MA); music history/theory (PhD); musicology (MA, PhD). *Accreditation:* NASM. *Students:* 13 full-time (8 women), 3 part-time (0 women); includes 1 minority (Hispanic/Latino), 1 international. Average age 34. 50 applicants, 12% accepted, 4 enrolled. *Degree requirements:* For master's, 2 foreign languages, comprehensive exam, thesis; for doctorate, 2 foreign languages, comprehensive exam, thesis/dissertation. *Entrance requirements:* For master's and doctorate, GRE General Test, musical composition or research paper, 3 letters of recommendation. Additional exam requirements/recommendations for international students: Required—TOEFL (minimum score 550 paper-based; 84 iBT). *Application deadline:* For fall admission, 1/1 for domestic and international students. Application fee: $80. Electronic applications accepted. *Expenses: Tuition:* Full-time $43,970; part-time $1374 per credit hour. *Required fees:* $60 per semester. Tuition and fees vary according to class time, course level and program. *Financial support:* In 2013–14, 14 students received support, including 4 fellowships (averaging $20,000 per year); Federal Work-Study, scholarships/grants, and unspecified assistantships also available. Support available to part-time students. Financial award application deadline: 1/1. *Unit head:* Victor Coelho, Director, 617-358-0628, Fax: 617-353-7455, E-mail: blues@bu.edu. *Application contact:* Jillian Hogan, Administrative Coordinator, 617-353-6887, Fax: 617-353-7455, E-mail: jhogan2@bu.edu.
Website: http://www.bu.edu/musicology/.

Bowling Green State University, Graduate College, College of Musical Arts, Bowling Green, OH 43403. Offers composition (MM); contemporary music (DMA), including composition, performance; ethnomusicology (MM); music education (MM), including choral, comprehensive, instrumental; music history (MM); music theory (MM); performance (MM). *Accreditation:* NASM. Part-time programs available. *Degree requirements:* For master's, thesis or alternative, recitals; for doctorate, comprehensive exam, thesis/dissertation. *Entrance requirements:* For master's, GRE General Test, diagnostic placement exams in music history and theory, audition, interview. Additional exam requirements/recommendations for international students: Required—TOEFL. Electronic applications accepted. *Faculty research:* Ethnomusicology.

Brandon University, School of Music, Brandon, MB R7A 6A9, Canada. Offers composition (M Mus); music education (M Mus); performance and literature (M Mus), including clarinet, conducting, jazz, piano, strings, trumpet. Part-time programs available. *Degree requirements:* For master's, comprehensive exam (for some programs), thesis (for some programs), 2 recitals. *Entrance requirements:* For master's, B Mus. Additional exam requirements/recommendations for international students: Required—TOEFL (minimum score 580 paper-based), IELTS (minimum score 7). Electronic applications accepted. *Faculty research:* Composition, evaluation and assessment, performance anxiety, philosophy of music, teacher education.

Brigham Young University, Graduate Studies, College of Fine Arts and Communications, School of Music, Provo, UT 84602-1001. Offers composition (MM); conducting (MM); music education (MA, MM); musicology (MA); performance (MM). *Accreditation:* NASM. *Faculty:* 47 full-time (8 women). *Students:* 43 full-time (29 women), 14 part-time (8 women); includes 6 minority (3 Asian, non-Hispanic/Latino; 2 Hispanic/Latino; 1 Native Hawaiian or other Pacific Islander, non-Hispanic/Latino). Average age 29. 58 applicants, 52% accepted, 21 enrolled. In 2013, 18 master's awarded. *Degree requirements:* For master's, comprehensive exam (for some programs), thesis (for some programs), recital, project, or composition (required for some programs). *Entrance requirements:* For master's, minimum GPA of 3.0 in last 60 hours, BM. Additional exam requirements/recommendations for international students: Required—TOEFL (minimum score 580 paper-based; 85 iBT). *Application deadline:* For fall admission, 12/15 priority date for domestic and international students. Application fee: $50. Electronic applications accepted. *Expenses: Tuition:* Full-time $6130; part-time $340 per credit hour. Tuition and fees vary according to program and student's religious affiliation. *Financial support:* In 2013–14, 60 students received support, including 46 teaching assistantships (averaging $3,500 per year); research assistantships, career-related internships or fieldwork, institutionally sponsored loans, scholarships/grants, tuition waivers (partial), and unspecified assistantships also available. Support available to part-time students. Financial award application deadline: 12/15; financial award applicants required to submit FAFSA. *Faculty research:* Improvisation and composition, music and globalism, adult-learning, expressive performance instruction in the ensemble setting, theorizing about music literacy. *Unit head:* Prof. Kory L. Katseanes, Director, 801-422-6304, Fax: 801-422-0533, E-mail: kory_katseanes@byu.edu. *Application contact:* Dr. A. Claudine Bigelow, Graduate Coordinator, 801-422-1315, Fax: 801-422-0533, E-mail: claudine_bigelow@byu.edu.
Website: https://cfac.byu.edu/music/.

Brooklyn College of the City University of New York, Division of Graduate Studies, Conservatory of Music, Brooklyn, NY 11210-2889. Offers composition (MM); music (DMA, PhD); music education (MA); musicology (MA); performance (MM); performance practice (MA). Part-time programs available. *Degree requirements:* For master's, one foreign language, comprehensive exam, thesis. *Entrance requirements:* For master's, placement exam, 36 credits in music, audition, completed composition, writing sample. Additional exam requirements/recommendations for international students: Required—TOEFL (minimum score 550 paper-based; 79 iBT). Electronic applications accepted. *Faculty research:* American music, computer music.

Brooklyn College of the City University of New York, Division of Graduate Studies, School of Education, Program in Adolescence Education and Special Subjects, Brooklyn, NY 11210-2889. Offers adolescence science education (MAT); art teacher (MA); biology teacher (MA); chemistry teacher (MA); earth science teacher (MAT); English teacher (MA); French teacher (MA); health and nutrition sciences: health teacher (MS Ed); mathematics teacher (MA); music education (CAS); music teacher (MA); physical education teacher (MS Ed); physics teacher (MA); social studies teacher (MA); Spanish teacher (MA). Part-time and evening/weekend programs available. *Degree requirements:* For master's, comprehensive exam (for some programs), thesis (for some programs). *Entrance requirements:* For master's, LAST, previous course work in education, resume, 2 letters of recommendation, essay. Additional exam requirements/recommendations for international students: Required—TOEFL (minimum score 500 paper-based; 61 iBT). Electronic applications accepted. *Faculty research:* Interdisciplinary education, semiotics, discourse analysis, autobiography, teacher identity.

Butler University, Jordan College of Fine Arts, Department of Music, Indianapolis, IN 46208-3485. Offers composition (MM); conducting (MM); double major (MM); music education (MM); music history (MM); music theory (MM); performance (MM). *Accreditation:* NASM. Part-time and evening/weekend programs available. *Faculty:* 8 full-time (1 woman), 2 part-time/adjunct (1 woman). *Students:* 13 full-time (5 women), 17 part-time (6 women); includes 2 minority (1 Asian, non-Hispanic/Latino; 1 Hispanic/Latino), 1 international. Average age 30. 39 applicants, 62% accepted, 12 enrolled. In 2013, 11 master's awarded. *Degree requirements:* For master's, thesis (for some programs). *Entrance requirements:* For master's, GRE General Test, GRE Subject Test, audition, interview. *Application deadline:* For fall admission, 8/15 priority date for domestic students. Applications are processed on a rolling basis. Application fee: $35. Electronic applications accepted. *Financial support:* Fellowships, teaching assistantships with tuition reimbursements, career-related internships or fieldwork, institutionally sponsored loans, and scholarships/grants available. Support available to part-time students. Financial award application deadline: 7/15; financial award applicants required to submit FAFSA. *Unit head:* Dr. Daniel Bolin, Head, 317-940-9988, Fax: 317-940-9658, E-mail: dbolin@butler.edu. *Application contact:* Diane Dubord, Graduate Student Services Specialist, 317-940-8107, E-mail: ddubord@butler.edu.
Website: http://www.butler.edu/academics/graduate-jca/.

California Baptist University, Program in Music, Riverside, CA 92504-3206. Offers conducting (MM); music education (MM); performance (MM). *Accreditation:* NASM. Part-time and evening/weekend programs available. *Faculty:* 9 full-time (2 women), 1 (woman) part-time/adjunct. *Students:* 14 full-time (10 women), 3 part-time (all women); includes 2 minority (1 Hispanic/Latino; 1 Two or more races, non-Hispanic/Latino), 9 international. Average age 26. 2 applicants, 100% accepted, 2 enrolled. In 2013, 4 master's awarded. *Degree requirements:* For master's, comprehensive exam (for some programs), comprehensive exam or thesis. *Entrance requirements:* For master's, minimum undergraduate GPA of 3.0; bachelor's degree in music; three recommendations; comprehensive essay; interview/audition. Additional exam requirements/recommendations for international students: Required—TOEFL (minimum score 80 iBT). *Application deadline:* For fall admission, 8/1 priority date for domestic students, 7/1 for international students; for spring admission, 12/1 priority date for domestic students, 11/1 for international students. Applications are processed on a rolling basis. Application fee: $45. Electronic applications accepted. *Expenses:* Contact institution. *Financial support:* Institutionally sponsored loans and scholarships/grants available. Financial award applicants required to submit CSS PROFILE or FAFSA. *Faculty research:* Choral conducting, church music, choir building, hymnology, music technology. *Unit head:* Dr. Judd Bonner, Dean, School of Music, 951-343-4256, Fax: 951-343-4570, E-mail: jbonner@calbaptist.edu. *Application contact:* Dr. Judd Bonner, Dean, School of Music, 951-343-4256, Fax: 951-343-4570, E-mail: jbonner@calbaptist.edu.
Website: http://www.calbaptist.edu/masterofmusic/.

California State University, Fresno, Division of Graduate Studies, College of Arts and Humanities, Department of Music, Fresno, CA 93740-8027. Offers music (MA); music education (MA); performance (MA). *Accreditation:* NASM. Part-time programs available. *Degree requirements:* For master's, thesis or alternative. *Entrance requirements:* For master's, GRE General Test, BA in music, minimum GPA of 3.0. Additional exam requirements/recommendations for international students: Required—TOEFL. Electronic applications accepted. *Faculty research:* Technology transfer, folk art.

California State University, Fullerton, Graduate Studies, College of the Arts, Department of Music, Fullerton, CA 92834-9480. Offers music education (MA); music history and literature (MA); performance (MM); piano pedagogy (MA); theory-composition (MM). *Accreditation:* NASM. Part-time programs available. *Students:* 19 full-time (8 women), 43 part-time (19 women); includes 20 minority (10 Asian, non-Hispanic/Latino; 7 Hispanic/Latino; 3 Two or more races, non-Hispanic/Latino), 14 international. Average age 29. 88 applicants, 28% accepted, 20 enrolled. In 2013, 13 master's awarded. *Degree requirements:* For master's, comprehensive exam, project or thesis. *Entrance requirements:* For master's, audition, major in music or related field, minimum GPA of 2.5 in last 60 units of course work. Application fee: $55. *Financial support:* Career-related internships or fieldwork, Federal Work-Study, institutionally sponsored loans, and scholarships/grants available. Support available to part-time students. Financial award application deadline: 3/1; financial award applicants required to submit FAFSA. *Unit head:* Dr. Marc Dickey, Chair, 657-278-3511. *Application contact:* Admissions/Applications, 657-278-2371.

California State University, Los Angeles, Graduate Studies, College of Arts and Letters, Department of Music, Los Angeles, CA 90032-8530. Offers music composition (MM); music education (MA); musicology (MA); performance (MM). *Accreditation:* NASM. Part-time and evening/weekend programs available. *Faculty:* 7 full-time (3 women), 9 part-time/adjunct (4 women). *Students:* 20 full-time (10 women), 33 part-time (13 women); includes 24 minority (4 Black or African American, non-Hispanic/Latino; 7 Asian, non-Hispanic/Latino; 12 Hispanic/Latino; 1 Two or more races, non-Hispanic/Latino), 15 international. Average age 33. 50 applicants, 54% accepted, 14 enrolled. In 2013, 22 master's awarded. *Degree requirements:* For master's, comprehensive exam, project or thesis. *Entrance requirements:* For master's, audition. Additional exam requirements/recommendations for international students: Required—TOEFL (minimum score 500 paper-based). *Application deadline:* For fall admission, 5/1 for domestic and international students. Applications are processed on a rolling basis. Application fee: $55. Electronic applications accepted. *Financial support:* Career-related internships or fieldwork and Federal Work-Study available. Support available to part-time students. Financial award application deadline: 3/1. *Faculty research:* Gregorian semiology, Baroque opera. *Unit head:* Dr. John Kennedy, Chair, 323-343-4060, Fax: 323-343-4063, E-mail: jkenned@calstatela.edu. *Application contact:* Dr. Larry Fritz, Dean of Graduate Studies, 323-343-3820, Fax: 323-343-5653, E-mail: lfritz@calstatela.edu.
Website: http://www.calstatela.edu/academic/music/.

California State University, Northridge, Graduate Studies, College of Arts, Media, and Communication, Department of Music, Northridge, CA 91330. Offers composition (MM); conducting (MM); music education (MA); performance (MM). *Accreditation:* NASM. *Degree requirements:* For master's, thesis. *Entrance requirements:* For master's, audition, GRE General Test or minimum GPA of 3.0. Additional exam requirements/recommendations for international students: Required—TOEFL. *Faculty research:* Touring program.

Campbellsville University, School of Music, Campbellsville, KY 42718-2799. Offers church music (MM); music (MA); music education (MM); music performance (MMP). *Accreditation:* NASM. Part-time programs available. *Degree requirements:* For master's, thesis (for some programs), paper or recital. *Entrance requirements:* For master's, GRE General Test or PRAXIS, minimum GPA of 2.75. Additional exam requirements/recommendations for international students: Required—TOEFL (minimum score 550 paper-based). Electronic applications accepted.

Capital University, Conservatory of Music, Columbus, OH 43209-2394. Offers music education (MM), including instrumental emphasis, Kodály emphasis. Program offered only in summer. *Accreditation:* NASM. Part-time programs available. *Degree requirements:* For master's, comprehensive exam, thesis or alternative, chamber performance exam. *Entrance requirements:* For master's, music theory exam, minimum undergraduate GPA of 3.0. Additional exam requirements/recommendations for international students: Required—TOEFL (minimum score 550 paper-based; 80 iBT). Electronic applications accepted. *Expenses:* Contact institution. *Faculty research:* Folk song research, Kodály method, performance, composition.

Carnegie Mellon University, College of Fine Arts, School of Music, Pittsburgh, PA 15213-3891. Offers composition (MM); conducting (MM); instrumental performance (MM); music and technology (MS); music education (MM); vocal performance (MM). *Accreditation:* NASM. Part-time programs available. *Degree requirements:* For master's, comprehensive exam, recital. *Entrance requirements:* For master's, audition. *Faculty research:* Computer music, music history.

Case Western Reserve University, School of Graduate Studies, Department of Music, Program in Music Education, Cleveland, OH 44106. Offers MA, PhD. *Accreditation:* NASM; Teacher Education Accreditation Council. *Faculty:* 5 full-time (2 women). *Students:* 13 full-time (5 women), 5 part-time (0 women), 2 international. Average age 30. 12 applicants, 67% accepted, 5 enrolled. In 2013, 2 master's, 1 doctorate awarded. *Degree requirements:* For master's, thesis (for some programs); for doctorate, thesis/dissertation. *Entrance requirements:* For master's, GRE, audition/interview, writing sample, 1 year of teaching; for doctorate, GRE, audition/interview, writing sample, statement of purpose. Additional exam requirements/recommendations for international students: Required—TOEFL (minimum score 577 paper-based; 90 iBT); Recommended—IELTS (minimum score 7). *Application deadline:* For fall admission, 1/1 priority date for domestic students. Application fee: $50. Electronic applications accepted. *Financial support:* Fellowships, teaching assistantships, career-related internships or fieldwork, tuition waivers (full), and unspecified assistantships available. Financial award application deadline: 1/1; financial award applicants required to submit FAFSA. *Faculty research:* Psychology of music, creative thinking, computer applications, educational psychology. *Unit head:* David Ake, Chair, 216-368-2400, Fax: 216-368-6557, E-mail: info@music.case.edu. *Application contact:* Laura Stauffer, Admissions, 216-368-2400, Fax: 216-368-6557, E-mail: info@music.case.edu.
Website: http://music.case.edu/.

Central Connecticut State University, School of Graduate Studies, School of Arts and Sciences, Department of Music, New Britain, CT 06050-4010. Offers music education (MS, Certificate). *Accreditation:* NASM. Part-time and evening/weekend programs available. *Faculty:* 2 full-time (0 women), 2 part-time/adjunct (both women). *Students:* 7 full-time (3 women), 14 part-time (12 women); includes 1 minority (Hispanic/Latino), 1 international. Average age 30. 9 applicants, 44% accepted, 4 enrolled. In 2013, 4 master's, 2 other advanced degrees awarded. *Degree requirements:* For master's, comprehensive exam, thesis or alternative; for Certificate, qualifying exam. *Entrance requirements:* For master's, audition, minimum undergraduate GPA of 2.7, essay, portfolio, resume. Additional exam requirements/recommendations for international students: Required—TOEFL (minimum score 550 paper-based; 79 iBT). *Application deadline:* For fall admission, 6/1 for domestic students, 5/1 for international students; for spring admission, 11/1 for domestic and international students. Applications are processed on a rolling basis. Application fee: $50. Electronic applications accepted. Part-time tuition and fees vary according to degree level. *Financial support:* In 2013–14, 1 research assistantship was awarded; career-related internships or fieldwork, Federal Work-Study, scholarships/grants, and unspecified assistantships also available. Support available to part-time students. Financial award application deadline: 3/1; financial award applicants required to submit FAFSA. *Faculty research:* Applied music. *Unit head:* Dr. Charles Menoche, Chair, 860-832-2912, E-mail: menochec@ccsu.edu. *Application contact:* Patricia Gardner, Associate Director of Graduate Studies, 860-832-2350, Fax: 860-832-2362, E-mail: graduateadmissions@ccsu.edu.
Website: http://www.ccsu.edu/page.cfm?p=10712.

Central Methodist University, College of Graduate and Extended Studies, Fayette, MO 65248-1198. Offers clinical counseling (MS); clinical nurse leader (MSN); education (M Ed); music education (MME); nurse educator (MSN). Part-time and evening/weekend programs available. Postbaccalaureate distance learning degree programs offered (no on-campus study). *Degree requirements:* For master's, thesis. *Entrance requirements:* For master's, GRE General Test, minimum GPA of 2.75. *Application deadline:* Applications are processed on a rolling basis. Application fee: $25. Electronic applications accepted. *Expenses: Tuition:* Part-time $360 per credit hour. Part-time tuition and fees vary according to campus/location and program. *Financial support:* Tuition waivers available. Support available to part-time students. Financial award application deadline: 6/5; financial award applicants required to submit FAFSA. *Unit head:* Dr. Rita Gulstad, Provost, 660-248-6212, Fax: 660-248-6392, E-mail: rgulstad@centralmethodist.edu. *Application contact:* Aimee Sage, Director of Graduate Admissions, 660-248-6651, Fax: 660-248-6392, E-mail: asage@centralmethodist.edu.
Website: http://www.centralmethodist.edu/graduate/.

Central Michigan University, College of Graduate Studies, College of Communication and Fine Arts, School of Music, Mount Pleasant, MI 48859. Offers composition (MM); conducting (MM); music education (MM); performance (MM). *Accreditation:* NASM. Part-time programs available. *Degree requirements:* For master's, thesis or alternative. Electronic applications accepted. *Faculty research:* Music education, music composition, conducting, music performance.

Christopher Newport University, Graduate Studies, Department of Teacher Preparation, Newport News, VA 23606-3072. Offers art (PK-12) (MAT); biology (6-12) (MAT); chemistry (6-12) (MAT); computer science (6-12) (MAT); elementary (PK-6) (MAT); English (6-12) (MAT); English as second language (PK-12) (MAT); French (PK-

12) (MAT); history and social science (6-12) (MAT); mathematics (6-12) (MAT); music (PK-12) (MAT), including choral, instrumental; physics (6-12) (MAT); Spanish (PK-12) (MAT). Part-time programs available. *Faculty:* 15 full-time (7 women), 14 part-time/adjunct (13 women). *Students:* 74 full-time (64 women), 2 part-time (both women); includes 6 minority (4 Hispanic/Latino; 2 Two or more races, non-Hispanic/Latino). Average age 23. 90 applicants, 100% accepted, 67 enrolled. In 2013, 96 master's awarded. *Degree requirements:* For master's, comprehensive exam, thesis or alternative. *Entrance requirements:* For master's, PRAXIS I, minimum GPA of 3.0. Additional exam requirements/recommendations for international students: Required—TOEFL (minimum score 580 paper-based; 92 iBT). *Application deadline:* For fall admission, 4/1 for international students; for spring admission, 10/15 for domestic students, 10/1 for international students; for summer admission, 1/15 for domestic students, 3/1 for international students. Applications are processed on a rolling basis. Application fee: $50. Electronic applications accepted. *Expenses: Tuition, area resident:* Part-time $498 per credit hour. Tuition, state resident: part-time $498 per credit hour. Tuition, nonresident: part-time $899 per credit hour. *Financial support:* In 2013–14, 3 students received support, including 3 research assistantships with full tuition reimbursements available (averaging $2,000 per year); career-related internships or fieldwork, Federal Work-Study, and unspecified assistantships also available. Financial award application deadline: 3/1; financial award applicants required to submit FAFSA. *Faculty research:* Early literacy development, instructional innovations, professional teaching standards, multicultural issues, aesthetic education. *Total annual research expenditures:* $24,000. *Unit head:* Dr. Marsha Sprague, Director, 757-594-7388, Fax: 757-594-7803, E-mail: msprague@cnu.edu. *Application contact:* Lyn Sawyer, Associate Director, Graduate Admissions, 757-594-7544, Fax: 757-594-7649, E-mail: gradstdy@cnu.edu.

Cleveland State University, College of Graduate Studies, College of Liberal Arts and Social Sciences, Department of Music, Cleveland, OH 44115. Offers composition (MM); music education (MM); performance (MM). *Accreditation:* NASM. Part-time and evening/weekend programs available. *Faculty:* 9 full-time (2 women), 19 part-time/adjunct (6 women). *Students:* 25 part-time (11 women); includes 3 minority (2 Black or African American, non-Hispanic/Latino; 1 Two or more races, non-Hispanic/Latino), 2 international. Average age 28. 38 applicants, 47% accepted. In 2013, 9 master's awarded. *Degree requirements:* For master's, comprehensive exam, thesis or recital. *Entrance requirements:* For master's, departmental assessment in music history, minimum undergraduate GPA of 2.75. Additional exam requirements/recommendations for international students: Required—TOEFL (minimum score 525 paper-based). *Application deadline:* For fall admission, 7/15 priority date for domestic students. Applications are processed on a rolling basis. Application fee: $30. *Expenses:* Tuition, state resident: full-time $8335; part-time $521 per credit hour. Tuition, nonresident: full-time $15,670; part-time $979 per credit hour. *Required fees:* $50; $25 per semester. *Financial support:* In 2013–14, 14 students received support, including 14 research assistantships with full tuition reimbursements available (averaging $3,612 per year); tuition waivers (partial) and unspecified assistantships also available. Financial award application deadline: 3/1. *Faculty research:* Ethnomusicology, classical-Romantic music, new performance practices, electronic music, interdisciplinary studies. *Total annual research expenditures:* $162,000. *Unit head:* Dr. Birch P. Browning, Chairperson, 216-687-2301, Fax: 216-687-9279, E-mail: b.browning@csuohio.edu. *Application contact:* Dr. Victor Liva, Coordinator of Graduate Studies and Admission, 216-687-6931, Fax: 216-687-9279, E-mail: v.liva@csuohio.edu.
Website: http://www.csuohio.edu/music/.

College of Charleston, Graduate School, School of Education, Health, and Human Performance, Department of Foundations, Secondary, and Special Education, Program in Performing Arts Education, Charleston, SC 29424-0001. Offers MAT. *Accreditation:* NASM. Part-time and evening/weekend programs available. *Entrance requirements:* For master's, GRE, minimum GPA of 2.5 overall, 3.0 in last 60 hours of undergraduate coursework; 2 letters of recommendation; audition/interview. Additional exam requirements/recommendations for international students: Required—TOEFL (minimum score 81 iBT). Electronic applications accepted.

The College of Saint Rose, Graduate Studies, School of Arts and Humanities, Music Department, Program in Music Education, Albany, NY 12203-1419. Offers MS Ed, Certificate. *Accreditation:* NASM; NCATE. *Degree requirements:* For master's, thesis optional, final project. *Entrance requirements:* For master's, audition, minimum undergraduate GPA of 3.0; for Certificate, placement test if undergraduate degree is not in music, audition. Additional exam requirements/recommendations for international students: Required—TOEFL (minimum score 550 paper-based). Electronic applications accepted.

The Colorado College, Education Department, Program in Secondary Education, Colorado Springs, CO 80903-3294. Offers art teaching (K-12) (MAT); English teaching (MAT); foreign language teaching (MAT); mathematics teaching (MAT); music teaching (MAT); science teaching (MAT); social studies teaching (MAT). *Degree requirements:* For master's, thesis, internship. Electronic applications accepted.

Colorado State University–Pueblo, College of Education, Engineering and Professional Studies, Education Program, Pueblo, CO 81001-4901. Offers art education (M Ed); foreign language education (M Ed); health and physical education (M Ed); instructional technology (M Ed); linguistically diverse education (M Ed); music education (M Ed); special education (M Ed). *Accreditation:* Teacher Education Accreditation Council. Part-time programs available. *Degree requirements:* For master's, portfolio. *Entrance requirements:* For master's, 3 recommendations, teaching license. Additional exam requirements/recommendations for international students: Required—TOEFL (minimum score 500 paper-based). Electronic applications accepted. *Faculty research:* Portfolio assessment, math education, science education.

Columbus State University, Graduate Studies, College of the Arts, Schwob School of Music, Columbus, GA 31907-5645. Offers artist diploma (Postbaccalaureate Certificate); music education (MM); music performance (M Ed). *Accreditation:* NASM; NCATE (one or more programs are accredited). Part-time and evening/weekend programs available. *Faculty:* 24 full-time (9 women), 2 part-time/adjunct (1 woman). *Students:* 17 full-time (0 women), 19 part-time (2 women); includes 6 minority (2 Black or African American, non-Hispanic/Latino; 1 Asian, non-Hispanic/Latino; 3 Hispanic/Latino), 13 international. Average age 26. 47 applicants, 34% accepted, 15 enrolled. In 2013, 7 master's, 5 other advanced degrees awarded. *Degree requirements:* For master's, exit exam. *Entrance requirements:* For master's, GRE General Test, audition, letters of recommendation, minimum undergraduate GPA of 2.5. Additional exam requirements/recommendations for international students: Required—TOEFL (minimum score 550 paper-based; 79 iBT). *Application deadline:* For fall admission, 6/30 for domestic students, 5/1 for international students; for spring admission, 11/1 for domestic and international students; for summer admission, 3/1 for domestic and international students. Applications are processed on a rolling basis. Application fee: $40. Electronic applications accepted. *Expenses:* Tuition, state resident: full-time $4572; part-time $382 per credit hour. Tuition, nonresident: full-time $18,292; part-time $1526 per credit hour. *Required fees:* $1800; $196 per credit hour. Tuition and fees vary according to campus/location and program. *Financial support:* In 2013–14, 34 students received support, including 28 research assistantships with partial tuition reimbursements available (averaging $3,000 per year); career-related internships or fieldwork, Federal Work-Study, institutionally sponsored loans, scholarships/grants, tuition waivers (full), and unspecified assistantships also available. Support available to part-time students. Financial award application deadline: 5/1; financial award applicants required to submit FAFSA. *Unit head:* Dr. Edwin Scott Harris, Director, 706-507-8419, E-mail: harris_scott@columbusstate.edu. *Application contact:* Kristin Williams, Director of International and Graduate Recruitment, 706-507-8848, Fax: 706-568-5091, E-mail: williams_kristin@columbusstate.edu.
Website: http://music.columbusstate.edu/.

Conservatorio de Musica de Puerto Rico, Program in Music Education, San Juan, PR 00907. Offers MM Ed. *Accreditation:* NASM. *Entrance requirements:* For master's, EXADEP, 3 letters of recommendation, audition, bachelor's degree in music education, interview, minimum GPA of 2.5, performance video, teaching video. Additional exam requirements/recommendations for international students: Required—TOEFL.

Converse College, School of Education and Graduate Studies, Petrie School of Music, Spartanburg, SC 29302-0006. Offers music education (M Mus); performance (M Mus). *Accreditation:* NASM. Part-time and evening/weekend programs available. *Degree requirements:* For master's, variable foreign language requirement, comprehensive exam, thesis (for some programs), recitals. *Entrance requirements:* For master's, NTE (music education), audition, 3 letters of recommendation. Additional exam requirements/recommendations for international students: Required—TOEFL. Electronic applications accepted. *Faculty research:* Chamber music, opera, performance, composition, recording.

DePaul University, School of Music, Chicago, IL 60614. Offers composition (MM); jazz studies (MM); music education (MM); music performance (MM); performance (Certificate). *Accreditation:* NASM (one or more programs are accredited). Part-time and evening/weekend programs available. *Faculty:* 22 full-time (10 women), 43 part-time/adjunct (10 women). *Students:* 99 full-time (48 women), 19 part-time (15 women); includes 26 minority (7 Black or African American, non-Hispanic/Latino; 4 Asian, non-Hispanic/Latino; 10 Hispanic/Latino; 5 Two or more races, non-Hispanic/Latino), 13 international. Average age 25. In 2013, 61 master's, 5 Certificates awarded. *Degree requirements:* For master's, comprehensive exam. *Entrance requirements:* For master's, bachelor's degree in music or related field, minimum GPA of 3.0, auditions (performance), scores (composition); for Certificate, master's degree in performance or related field, auditions (for performance majors). Additional exam requirements/recommendations for international students: Required—TOEFL (minimum score 550 paper-based; 80 iBT). *Application deadline:* For fall admission, 12/1 priority date for domestic and international students. Applications are processed on a rolling basis. Application fee: $40. Electronic applications accepted. *Expenses:* Contact institution. *Financial support:* Application deadline: 12/1; applicants required to submit FAFSA. *Unit head:* Dr. Donald E. Casey, Dean, 773-325-7256, Fax: 773-325-7429, E-mail: dcasey@depaul.edu. *Application contact:* Ross Beacraft, Director of Admission, 773-325-7444, Fax: 773-325-7429, E-mail: musicadmissions@depaul.edu.
Website: http://music.depaul.edu.

Duquesne University, Mary Pappert School of Music, Pittsburgh, PA 15282-0001. Offers music composition (MM); music education (MM); music performance (MM, AD); music technology (MM), including digital pedagogy, electronic composition, electronic performance; music theory (MM); sacred music (MM). *Accreditation:* NASM. Part-time programs available. *Faculty:* 26 full-time (8 women), 75 part-time/adjunct (24 women). *Students:* 64 full-time (29 women), 12 part-time (2 women); includes 5 minority (1 Asian, non-Hispanic/Latino; 3 Hispanic/Latino; 1 Two or more races, non-Hispanic/Latino), 19 international. Average age 26. 114 applicants, 54% accepted, 29 enrolled. In 2013, 26 master's, 6 ADs awarded. *Degree requirements:* For master's, comprehensive exam, thesis (for some programs), recital (music performance); for AD, recital. *Entrance requirements:* For master's, audition, minimum undergraduate QPA of 3.0 in music, portfolio of original compositions, or music education experience; for AD, audition. Additional exam requirements/recommendations for international students: Required—TOEFL (minimum score 550 paper-based; 79 iBT). *Application deadline:* For fall admission, 7/1 priority date for domestic and international students; for spring admission, 12/1 priority date for domestic and international students; for summer admission, 6/1 priority date for domestic students, 5/1 priority date for international students. Applications are processed on a rolling basis. Application fee: $50. Electronic applications accepted. *Expenses:* Contact institution. *Financial support:* In 2013–14, 59 students received support, including 59 fellowships with full and partial tuition reimbursements available (averaging $15,086 per year); scholarships/grants, tuition waivers (full and partial), and unspecified assistantships also available. Financial award application deadline: 4/1. *Faculty research:* Performance; computer-assisted instruction in music at elementary and secondary levels; electronic music; contemporary music, theory, and analysis; development of online graduate music courses. *Total annual research expenditures:* $59,349. *Unit head:* Dr. Edward W. Kocher, Dean, 412-396-6082, Fax: 412-396-1524, E-mail: kocher@duq.edu. *Application contact:* Peggy Eiseman, Administrative Assistant of Admissions, 412-396-5064, Fax: 412-396-5719, E-mail: eiseman@duq.edu.
Website: http://www.duq.edu/academics/schools/music.

East Carolina University, Graduate School, College of Education, Department of Business and Information Technologies Education, Greenville, NC 27858-4353. Offers business education (MA Ed); elementary education (MAT); English education (MAT); family and consumer science (MAT); health education (MAT); Hispanic studies (MAT); history education (MAT); marketing education (MA Ed); middle grades education (MAT); music education (MAT); physical education (MAT); science education (MAT); special education (MAT), including general curriculum; vocation education (MS). *Accreditation:* NCATE. Part-time and evening/weekend programs available. Postbaccalaureate distance learning degree programs offered (no on-campus study). *Degree requirements:* For master's, comprehensive exam, thesis optional. *Entrance requirements:* For master's, GRE or MAT, minimum GPA of 2.5, bachelor's degree in related field, teaching license (MA Ed). Additional exam requirements/recommendations for international students: Required—TOEFL. *Expenses:* Tuition, state resident: full-time $4223. Tuition, nonresident: full-time $16,540. *Required fees:* $2184.

East Carolina University, Graduate School, College of Fine Arts and Communication, School of Music, Greenville, NC 27858-4353. Offers advanced performance studies (Certificate); music education (MM); music therapy (MM); performance (MM), including choral conducting, instrumental conducting, jazz, organ, percussion, piano, piano pedagogy, sacred music, sacred music, choral conducting, string (Suzuki) pedagogy, vocal pedagogy, voice, wind instrument, woodwind specialist; theory and composition (MM). *Accreditation:* NASM. Part-time programs available. *Degree requirements:* For master's, comprehensive exam, thesis optional. *Entrance requirements:* For master's, GRE General Test or MAT. Additional exam requirements/recommendations for international students: Required—TOEFL. *Expenses:* Tuition, state resident: full-time $4223. Tuition, nonresident: full-time $16,540. *Required fees:* $2184.

Eastern Illinois University, Graduate School, College of Arts and Humanities, Department of Music, Charleston, IL 61920-3099. Offers music education (MA). *Accreditation:* NASM. Part-time and evening/weekend programs available. Postbaccalaureate distance learning degree programs offered (minimal on-campus

study). *Degree requirements:* For master's, thesis or alternative, recital. *Application deadline:* For fall admission, 3/31 priority date for domestic students. Applications are processed on a rolling basis. Application fee: $30. *Expenses: Tuition, area resident:* Part-time $283 per credit hour. Tuition, state resident: part-time $283 per credit hour. Tuition, nonresident: part-time $679 per credit hour. *Financial support:* In 2013–14, research assistantships with full tuition reimbursements (averaging $8,100 per year), 8 teaching assistantships with full tuition reimbursements (averaging $8,100 per year) were awarded. *Unit head:* Dr. Jerry Daniels, Chairperson, 217-581-3010, Fax: 217-581-2722, E-mail: jldaniels@eiu.edu. *Application contact:* Dr. Marilyn Coles, Coordinator, 217-581-2723, E-mail: mjcoles@eiu.edu.

Eastern Kentucky University, The Graduate School, College of Education, Department of Curriculum and Instruction, Richmond, KY 40475-3102. Offers elementary education (MA Ed), including early elementary education, reading; library science (MA Ed); music education (MA Ed); secondary and higher education (MA Ed), including secondary education; teaching (MAT). *Accreditation:* NCATE. Part-time programs available. *Degree requirements:* For master's, portfolio is part of exam. *Entrance requirements:* For master's, GRE General Test, PRAXIS II (KY), minimum GPA of 2.5. *Faculty research:* Technology in education, reading instruction, e-portfolios, induction to teacher education, dispositions of teachers.

Eastern Michigan University, Graduate School, College of Arts and Sciences, Department of Music and Dance, Ypsilanti, MI 48197. Offers music composition (MM); music education (MM); music pedagogy (MM); music performance (MM). *Accreditation:* NASM. Part-time and evening/weekend programs available. Postbaccalaureate distance learning degree programs offered (minimal on-campus study). *Faculty:* 23 full-time (11 women). *Students:* 6 full-time (5 women), 18 part-time (7 women); includes 1 minority (Asian, non-Hispanic/Latino), 7 international. Average age 30. 12 applicants, 50% accepted, 3 enrolled. In 2013, 8 master's awarded. *Entrance requirements:* Additional exam requirements/recommendations for international students: Required—TOEFL. *Application deadline:* Applications are processed on a rolling basis. Application fee: $35. *Expenses:* Tuition, state resident: full-time $12,300; part-time $466 per credit hour. Tuition, nonresident: full-time $23,159; part-time $918 per credit hour. *Required fees:* $71 per credit hour. $46 per semester. One-time fee: $100. Tuition and fees vary according to course level and degree level. *Financial support:* Fellowships, research assistantships with full tuition reimbursements, teaching assistantships with full tuition reimbursements, career-related internships or fieldwork, Federal Work-Study, institutionally sponsored loans, scholarships/grants, tuition waivers (partial), and unspecified assistantships available. Support available to part-time students. Financial award applicants required to submit FAFSA. *Unit head:* Dr. Diane Winder, Department Head, 734-487-4380, Fax: 734-487-6939, E-mail: dwinder@emich.edu. *Application contact:* Dr. David Pierce, Coordinator of Music Advising, 734-487-4380, Fax: 734-487-6939, E-mail: david.pierce@emich.edu.
Website: http://www.emich.edu/musicdance.

Eastern Washington University, Graduate Studies, College of Arts, Letters and Education, Department of Music, Cheney, WA 99004-2431. Offers composition (MA); general (MA); instrumental/vocal performance (MA); jazz pedagogy (MA); music education (MA). *Accreditation:* NASM. Part-time programs available. *Faculty:* 17 full-time (9 women), 10 part-time/adjunct (6 women). *Students:* 7 full-time (2 women), 3 part-time (1 woman); includes 1 minority (Asian, non-Hispanic/Latino). Average age 33. 20 applicants, 40% accepted, 6 enrolled. In 2013, 7 master's awarded. *Degree requirements:* For master's, comprehensive exam, thesis or alternative. *Entrance requirements:* For master's, GRE General Test, minimum GPA of 3.0. *Application deadline:* For fall admission, 4/1 priority date for domestic students; for spring admission, 1/15 for domestic students. Applications are processed on a rolling basis. Application fee: $50. *Financial support:* In 2013–14, 7 teaching assistantships with partial tuition reimbursements (averaging $7,000 per year) were awarded; career-related internships or fieldwork, Federal Work-Study, institutionally sponsored loans, scholarships/grants, health care benefits, tuition waivers (partial), and unspecified assistantships also available. Support available to part-time students. Financial award application deadline: 2/1; financial award applicants required to submit FAFSA. *Unit head:* Dr. Patrick Winters, Chair, 509-359-6129, Fax: 509-359-7028. *Application contact:* Dr. Jane Ellsworth, Assistant Professor, 509-359-7076, E-mail: gradprograms@ewu.edu.
Website: http://www.ewu.edu/cale/programs/music.xml.

Emporia State University, Department of Music, Emporia, KS 66801-5415. Offers music education (MM), including instrumental, vocal; performance (MM). *Accreditation:* NASM. Part-time programs available. *Faculty:* 12 full-time (4 women), 3 part-time/adjunct (all women). *Students:* 11 full-time (7 women), 14 part-time (10 women), 11 international. 5 applicants, 80% accepted, 4 enrolled. In 2013, 7 master's awarded. *Degree requirements:* For master's, comprehensive exam or thesis. *Entrance requirements:* For master's, music qualifying exam, appropriate undergraduate degree. Additional exam requirements/recommendations for international students: Required—TOEFL (minimum score 520 paper-based; 68 iBT). *Application deadline:* For fall admission, 8/15 priority date for domestic students. Applications are processed on a rolling basis. Application fee: $30 ($75 for international students). Electronic applications accepted. *Expenses: Tuition, area resident:* Part-time $220 per credit hour. Tuition, state resident: part-time $220 per credit hour. Tuition, nonresident: part-time $685 per credit hour. *Required fees:* $73 per credit hour. *Financial support:* In 2013–14, 5 teaching assistantships with full tuition reimbursements (averaging $7,200 per year) were awarded; Federal Work-Study, institutionally sponsored loans, health care benefits, and unspecified assistantships also available. Financial award application deadline: 3/15; financial award applicants required to submit FAFSA. *Unit head:* Dr. Allan D. Comstock, Chair, 620-341-5431, E-mail: acomstoc@emporia.edu. *Application contact:* Dr. Andrew Houchins, Graduate Coordinator, 620-341-6089, E-mail: ahouchin@emporia.edu.
Website: http://www.emporia.edu/music/.

Evangel University, Department of Music, Springfield, MO 65802. Offers music education (MME); music performance (MM). Part-time programs available. *Faculty:* 2 full-time (0 women), 2 part-time/adjunct (1 woman). *Students:* 1 (woman) full-time, 3 part-time (all women). Average age 32. In 2013, 4 master's awarded. *Entrance requirements:* For master's, entrance/diagnostic exam, performance audition (MM), teaching certificate (MME). Additional exam requirements/recommendations for international students: Required—TOEFL (minimum score 550 paper-based). *Application deadline:* For fall admission, 7/15 priority date for domestic students, 8/1 for international students; for spring admission, 11/15 priority date for domestic students, 12/1 for international students. Applications are processed on a rolling basis. Application fee: $25. Electronic applications accepted. *Financial support:* In 2013–14, 2 students received support. Scholarships/grants and unspecified assistantships available. Support available to part-time students. Financial award application deadline: 3/1; financial award applicants required to submit FAFSA. *Unit head:* Dr. Greg Morris, Program Coordinator, 417-865-2811 Ext. 7326, Fax: 417-575-5484, E-mail: morrisg@evangel.edu. *Application contact:* Karen Benitez, Admissions Representative, Graduate Studies, 417-865-2811 Ext. 7227, Fax: 417-575-5484, E-mail: benitezk@evangel.edu.
Website: http://www.evangel.edu/academics/graduate-studies/graduate-programs.

Five Towns College, Department of Music, Dix Hills, NY 11746-6055. Offers childhood education (MS Ed); composition and arranging (DMA); jazz/commercial music (MM); music education (MM, DMA); music history and literature (DMA); music performance (DMA). Part-time programs available. *Faculty:* 6 full-time (2 women), 10 part-time/adjunct (0 women). *Students:* 14 full-time (3 women), 28 part-time (12 women); includes 6 minority (3 Black or African American, non-Hispanic/Latino; 1 Asian, non-Hispanic/Latino; 2 Hispanic/Latino), 7 international. Average age 27. 19 applicants, 58% accepted, 9 enrolled. In 2013, 17 master's, 3 doctorates awarded. *Degree requirements:* For master's, thesis, exams, major composition or capstone project, recital; for doctorate, comprehensive exam, thesis/dissertation, final oral exam. *Entrance requirements:* For master's, audition, bachelor's degree in music or music education, minimum GPA of 2.75, 36 hours of course work in performance; for doctorate, master's degree in music or music education, minimum GPA of 3.0, 3 letters of recommendation, audition. Additional exam requirements/recommendations for international students: Required—TOEFL (minimum score 520 paper-based; 85 iBT); Recommended—IELTS (minimum score 7). *Application deadline:* For fall admission, 9/1 for domestic and international students; for spring admission, 1/25 for domestic and international students. Applications are processed on a rolling basis. Application fee: $50. Electronic applications accepted. *Expenses: Tuition:* Full-time $14,400; part-time $600 per credit. *Required fees:* $60 per semester. One-time fee: $85. Tuition and fees vary according to degree level. *Financial support:* Fellowships with tuition reimbursements, teaching assistantships with tuition reimbursements, and tuition waivers (partial) available. Financial award applicants required to submit FAFSA. *Faculty research:* Teaching methods, teaching strategies and techniques, analysis of modern music, jazz. *Unit head:* Dr. Jill Miller-Thorn, Dean of Graduate Music Studies, 631-656-2142, Fax: 631-656-2172, E-mail: jill.millerthorn@ftc.edu. *Application contact:* Jerry Cohen, Dean of Enrollment, 631-656-2110, Fax: 631-656-2172, E-mail: jerry.cohen@ftc.edu.

Florida Atlantic University, College of Education, Department of Teaching and Learning, Boca Raton, FL 33431-0991. Offers curriculum and instruction (M Ed), including art, biology, chemistry, English, French, German, mathematics, music, physics, Pre-K and primary education, reading, social sciences, Spanish; elementary education (M Ed); environmental education (M Ed); reading education (M Ed); social foundations of education (M Ed), including educational psychology, educational technology, multilingual education. *Accreditation:* NCATE. Part-time and evening/weekend programs available. *Faculty:* 16 full-time (12 women), 1 (woman) part-time/adjunct. *Students:* 56 full-time (46 women), 96 part-time (78 women); includes 39 minority (10 Black or African American, non-Hispanic/Latino; 6 Asian, non-Hispanic/Latino; 20 Hispanic/Latino; 3 Two or more races, non-Hispanic/Latino), 4 international. Average age 32. 101 applicants, 54% accepted, 42 enrolled. In 2013, 64 master's awarded. *Entrance requirements:* For master's, GRE General Test, minimum GPA of 3.0 in last 2 years of undergraduate course work. Additional exam requirements/recommendations for international students: Required—TOEFL (minimum score 500 paper-based; 61 iBT), IELTS (minimum score 6). *Application deadline:* For fall admission, 7/1 for domestic students, 2/15 for international students; for spring admission, 11/1 for domestic students, 7/15 for international students. Applications are processed on a rolling basis. Application fee: $30. *Expenses:* Tuition, state resident: full-time $6660; part-time $370 per credit hour. Tuition, nonresident: full-time $18,450; part-time $1025 per credit hour. Tuition and fees vary according to course load. *Financial support:* Fellowships with partial tuition reimbursements, research assistantships with partial tuition reimbursements, teaching assistantships with partial tuition reimbursements, career-related internships or fieldwork, scholarships/grants, and unspecified assistantships available. *Faculty research:* Technology, teaching English to speakers of other languages, math teaching, electronic portfolio assessment, global perspectives through social studies. *Unit head:* Dr. Barbara Ridener, Chairperson, 561-297-3588. *Application contact:* Dr. Eliah Watlington, Associate Dean, 561-296-8520, Fax: 261-297-2991, E-mail: ewatling@fau.edu.
Website: http://www.coe.fau.edu/academicdepartments/tl/.

Florida International University, College of Architecture and the Arts, School of Music, Program in Music Education, Miami, FL 33199. Offers MS. *Accreditation:* NASM. Part-time and evening/weekend programs available. *Degree requirements:* For master's, thesis. *Entrance requirements:* For master's, GRE, 2 letters of recommendation; audition, interview and/or writing sample (for some areas). Additional exam requirements/recommendations for international students: Required—TOEFL (minimum score 550 paper-based; 80 iBT). Electronic applications accepted. *Faculty research:* Psychology of music teaching, classroom methodology, biofeedback.

Florida State University, The Graduate School, College of Music, Program in Music Education, Tallahassee, FL 32306-1180. Offers MM Ed, PhD. *Accreditation:* NASM. *Faculty:* 20 full-time. *Students:* 46 full-time (23 women); includes 10 minority (6 Black or African American, non-Hispanic/Latino; 3 Asian, non-Hispanic/Latino; 1 Hispanic/Latino). Average age 25. 79 applicants, 46% accepted, 18 enrolled. In 2013, 20 master's, 9 doctorates awarded. *Degree requirements:* For master's, comprehensive exam (for some programs), thesis optional, departmental qualifying exam; for doctorate, thesis/dissertation, departmental qualifying exam. *Entrance requirements:* For master's, valid teacher certification, minimum GPA of 3.0; for doctorate, master's degree, minimum GPA of 3.0. Additional exam requirements/recommendations for international students: Required—TOEFL (minimum score 590 paper-based; 97 iBT), IELTS (minimum score 7.5), Michigan English Language Assessment Battery (minimum score 90). *Application deadline:* For fall admission, 7/1 for domestic and international students; for spring admission, 11/1 for domestic and international students. Applications are processed on a rolling basis. Application fee: $30. Electronic applications accepted. *Expenses:* Tuition, state resident: part-time $403.51 per credit hour. Tuition, nonresident: part-time $1004.85 per credit hour. *Required fees:* $75.81 per credit hour. One-time fee: $20 part-time. Tuition and fees vary according to course load, campus/location and student level. *Financial support:* In 2013–14, 31 students received support, including 9 teaching assistantships (averaging $4,400 per year); career-related internships or fieldwork, Federal Work-Study, tuition waivers, and unspecified assistantships also available. Support available to part-time students. Financial award application deadline: 2/28; financial award applicants required to submit FAFSA. *Unit head:* Dr. Patricia Flowers, Dean, 850-644-4361, Fax: 850-644-2033, E-mail: pjflowers@fsu.edu. *Application contact:* Dr. Seth Beckman, Senior Associate Dean for Academic Affairs/Director of Graduate Studies in Music, 850-644-5848, Fax: 850-644-2033, E-mail: sbeckman@admin.fsu.edu.
Website: http://www.music.fsu.edu/.

George Mason University, College of Visual and Performing Arts, School of Music, Program in Music, Fairfax, VA 22030. Offers composition (MM); conducting (MM); jazz studies (MM); music education (MM); pedagogy (MM); performance (MM). *Faculty:* 20 full-time (8 women), 20 part-time/adjunct (10 women). *Students:* 24 full-time (11 women), 18 part-time (9 women); includes 9 minority (4 Black or African American, non-Hispanic/Latino; 1 Asian, non-Hispanic/Latino; 4 Hispanic/Latino), 3 international. Average age 31. 58 applicants, 48% accepted, 13 enrolled. In 2013, 21 master's awarded. *Degree requirements:* For master's, comprehensive exam, foreign language in vocal emphasis. *Entrance requirements:* For master's, expanded goals statement; 2 letters of recommendation; official transcript. Additional exam requirements/recommendations for international students: Required—TOEFL (minimum score 570

paper-based; 88 iBT), IELTS (minimum score 6.5), PTE. *Application deadline:* For fall admission, 3/1 for domestic students; for spring admission, 11/1 for domestic students. Application fee: $65 ($80 for international students). Electronic applications accepted. *Expenses:* Tuition, state resident: full-time $9350; part-time $390 per credit. Tuition, nonresident: full-time $25,754; part-time $1073 per credit. *Required fees:* $2688; $112 per credit. *Financial support:* Career-related internships or fieldwork, Federal Work-Study, scholarships/grants, and unspecified assistantships available. Financial award application deadline: 3/1; financial award applicants required to submit FAFSA. *Unit head:* Dr. Dennis Layendecker, Chair/Director, 703-993-5082, Fax: 703-993-1394, E-mail: dlayende@gmu.edu. *Application contact:* Dr. Rachel Bergman, Graduate Director, 703-993-1395, Fax: 703-993-1394, E-mail: rbergman@gmu.edu.
Website: http://catalog.gmu.edu/preview_program.php?catoid-19&poid-17939&returnto-4105.

Georgia College & State University, Graduate School, College of Arts and Sciences, Department of Music, Milledgeville, GA 31061. Offers MM Ed. *Accreditation:* NASM. *Students:* 1 (woman) full-time, 8 part-time (3 women); includes 5 minority (4 Black or African American, non-Hispanic/Latino; 1 American Indian or Alaska Native, non-Hispanic/Latino). Average age 36. In 2013, 7 master's awarded. *Degree requirements:* For master's, comprehensive exam, thesis optional. *Entrance requirements:* For master's, GACE II or GRE, bachelor's degree in music (education), 3 letters of recommendation, interview. Additional exam requirements/recommendations for international students: Recommended—TOEFL (minimum score 550 paper-based; 79 iBT). *Application deadline:* For fall admission, 7/1 priority date for domestic students; for spring admission, 11/15 priority date for domestic students. Application fee: $40. Electronic applications accepted. *Financial support:* In 2013–14, 1 research assistantship was awarded. Financial award applicants required to submit FAFSA. *Unit head:* Dr. Jennifer Flory, Graduate Coordinator for Music Education, 478-445-4839, Fax: 478-445-1633, E-mail: jennifer.flory@gcsu.edu. *Application contact:* Kate Marshall, Graduate Admissions Coordinator, 478-445-1184, Fax: 478-445-1336, E-mail: grad-admit@gcsu.edu.
Website: http://www.gcsu.edu/music/graduate.htm.

Georgia State University, College of Arts and Sciences, School of Music, Atlanta, GA 30303. Offers choral conducting (MM); jazz studies (MM); music (Certificate); music composition (MM); music education (PhD); orchestral conducting (MM); performance (MM), including keyboard instruments: piano, harpsichord, organ, orchestral instruments, voice; piano pedagogy (MM); wind band conducting (MM). *Accreditation:* NASM. Part-time and evening/weekend programs available. *Faculty:* 24 full-time (6 women). *Students:* 57 full-time (24 women), 18 part-time (7 women); includes 30 minority (22 Black or African American, non-Hispanic/Latino; 4 Asian, non-Hispanic/Latino; 2 Hispanic/Latino; 2 Two or more races, non-Hispanic/Latino), 11 international. Average age 30. 92 applicants, 71% accepted, 35 enrolled. In 2013, 42 master's awarded. *Degree requirements:* For master's, comprehensive exam, thesis (for some programs), recital; for doctorate, comprehensive exam, thesis/dissertation; for Certificate, recital. *Entrance requirements:* For master's, GRE (music education, composition only), BM; for doctorate, GRE, MM; for Certificate, MM. Additional exam requirements/recommendations for international students: Required—TOEFL (minimum score 550 paper-based; 80 iBT). *Application deadline:* For fall admission, 3/1 priority date for domestic and international students; for spring admission, 10/1 priority date for domestic and international students. Applications are processed on a rolling basis. Application fee: $50. Electronic applications accepted. *Expenses: Tuition, area resident:* Full-time $4176; part-time $348 per credit hour. Tuition, state resident: full-time $14,544; part-time $1212 per credit hour. Tuition, nonresident: full-time $14,544; part-time $1212 per credit hour. Tuition and fees vary according to course load and program. *Financial support:* In 2013–14, research assistantships with full tuition reimbursements (averaging $4,000 per year) were awarded; Federal Work-Study, scholarships/grants, health care benefits, tuition waivers (partial), and unspecified assistantships also available. Financial award application deadline: 3/1. *Faculty research:* Male changing voice, nineteenth century chamber music, improvisation and learning, Garibunda, African-American classical musicians. *Unit head:* William Dwight Coleman, Director, School of Music, 404-413-5953, Fax: 404-413-5910, E-mail: wcoleman@gsu.edu. *Application contact:* Dr. Steven Andrew Harper, Graduate Director, 404-413-5943, Fax: 404-413-5910, E-mail: sharper@gsu.edu.
Website: http://www.music.gsu.edu/.

Georgia State University, College of Education, Department of Middle-Secondary Education and Instructional Technology, Atlanta, GA 30302-3083. Offers English education (M Ed, MAT); English speakers of other languages (MAT); instructional design and technology (MS); instructional technology (PhD), including alternative instructional delivery systems, consulting, instructional design, management, research; mathematics education (M Ed, MAT); middle level education (MAT); reading, language and literacy education (M Ed), including reading instruction; science education (MAT), including biology, broad field science, chemistry, earth science, physics; social studies education (M Ed, MAT), including economics (MAT), geography (MAT), history (MAT), political science (MAT); teaching and learning (PhD), including language and literacy, mathematics education, music education, science education, social studies, teaching and teacher education. *Accreditation:* NCATE. Part-time and evening/weekend programs available. Postbaccalaureate distance learning degree programs offered (minimal on-campus study). *Faculty:* 27 full-time (19 women). *Students:* 181 full-time (113 women), 203 part-time (145 women); includes 161 minority (127 Black or African American, non-Hispanic/Latino; 1 American Indian or Alaska Native, non-Hispanic/Latino; 10 Asian, non-Hispanic/Latino; 11 Hispanic/Latino; 1 Native Hawaiian or other Pacific Islander, non-Hispanic/Latino; 11 Two or more races, non-Hispanic/Latino), 9 international. Average age 36. 2 applicants, 50% accepted, 1 enrolled. In 2013, 213 master's, 17 doctorates awarded. *Degree requirements:* For master's, comprehensive exam (for some programs), thesis or alternative, exit portfolio; for doctorate, comprehensive exam, thesis/dissertation. *Entrance requirements:* For master's, GRE; GACE I (for initial teacher preparation degree programs), baccalaureate degree or equivalent, resume, goals statement, two letters of recommendation, minimum undergraduate GPA of 2.5; proof of initial teacher certification in the content area (for M Ed); for doctorate, GRE, resume, goals statement, writing sample, two letters of recommendation, minimum graduate GPA of 3.3, interview. Additional exam requirements/recommendations for international students: Required—TOEFL (minimum score 550 paper-based; 79 iBT) or IELTS (minimum score 6.5). *Application deadline:* For fall admission, 1/15 priority date for domestic and international students; for spring admission, 10/1 for domestic and international students. Application fee: $50. Electronic applications accepted. *Expenses: Tuition, area resident:* Full-time $4176; part-time $348 per credit hour. Tuition, state resident: full-time $14,544; part-time $1212 per credit hour. Tuition, nonresident: full-time $14,544; part-time $1212 per credit hour. Tuition and fees vary according to course load and program. *Financial support:* In 2013–14, fellowships with full tuition reimbursements (averaging $19,667 per year), research assistantships with full tuition reimbursements (averaging $5,436 per year), teaching assistantships with full tuition reimbursements (averaging $2,779 per year) were awarded; career-related internships or fieldwork, Federal Work-Study, scholarships/grants, health care benefits, tuition waivers (full and partial), and unspecified assistantships also available. Financial award application deadline: 3/15. *Faculty research:* Teacher education in language and literacy, mathematics, science, and social studies in urban middle and secondary school settings; learning technologies in school, community, and corporate settings; multicultural education and education for social justice; urban education; international education. *Unit head:* Dr. Dana L. Fox, Chair, 404-413-8060, Fax: 404-413-8063, E-mail: dfox@gsu.edu. *Application contact:* Bobbie Turner, Administrative Coordinator I, 404-413-8405, Fax: 404-413-8063, E-mail: bnturner@gsu.edu.
Website: http://msit.gsu.edu/msit_programs.htm.

Gordon College, Graduate Music Education Program, Wenham, MA 01984-1899. Offers MM Ed. Part-time programs available. *Faculty:* 4 part-time/adjunct (3 women). *Students:* 15 part-time (12 women); includes 1 minority (Hispanic/Latino). In 2013, 7 master's awarded. *Degree requirements:* For master's, clinical experience (for some programs). *Entrance requirements:* For master's, 15-20 minute video teaching demonstration, undergraduate degree in music education with minimum GPA of 2.85, at least one year of teaching experience, initial license in music (for professional licensure), professional resume, 3-4 page essay, two letters of recommendation. Additional exam requirements/recommendations for international students: Required—TOEFL (minimum score 550 paper-based, 80 iBT) or IELTS (minimum score 6.5). *Application deadline:* Applications are processed on a rolling basis. Application fee: $50. *Expenses:* Contact institution. *Financial support:* Applicants required to submit FAFSA. *Unit head:* Dr. Sandra Doneski, Associate Professor, 978-867-4818, E-mail: sandra.doneski@gordon.edu. *Application contact:* Kristen Harrington, Program Administrator, 978-867-4429, Fax: 978-867-4663, E-mail: kristen.harrington@gordon.edu.
Website: http://www.gordon.edu/gradmusic.

Hampton University, Graduate College, College of Education and Continuing Studies, Program in Teaching, Hampton, VA 23668. Offers early childhood education (MT); middle school education (MT); music education (MT); secondary education (MT); special education (MT). *Entrance requirements:* For master's, GRE General Test.

Hardin-Simmons University, Graduate School, School of Music and Fine Arts, Abilene, TX 79698-0001. Offers church music (MM); music education (MM); music performance (MM); theory-composition (MM). *Accreditation:* NASM. Part-time programs available. *Faculty:* 12 full-time (5 women). *Students:* 5 full-time (3 women), 1 part-time (0 women), 1 international. Average age 30. In 2013, 4 master's awarded. *Degree requirements:* For master's, one foreign language, comprehensive exam, thesis (for some programs). *Entrance requirements:* For master's, minimum undergraduate GPA of 3.0 in major, 2.7 overall; performance; writing sample; demonstrated knowledge in chosen area. Additional exam requirements/recommendations for international students: Required—TOEFL (minimum score 550 paper-based; 75 iBT). *Application deadline:* For fall admission, 8/15 priority date for domestic students, 4/1 for international students; for spring admission, 1/5 priority date for domestic students, 9/1 for international students. Applications are processed on a rolling basis. Application fee: $50. *Expenses: Tuition:* Full-time $13,410; part-time $745 per credit hour. *Required fees:* $325; $110 per semester. Tuition and fees vary according to program. *Financial support:* In 2013–14, 4 students received support, including 4 fellowships (averaging $3,150 per year); career-related internships or fieldwork and scholarships/grants also available. Support available to part-time students. Financial award application deadline: 6/30; financial award applicants required to submit FAFSA. *Unit head:* Dr. Lynette Chambers, Program Director, 325-670-1430, Fax: 325-670-5873, E-mail: lchambers@hsutx.edu. *Application contact:* Dr. Nancy Kucinski, Dean of Graduate Studies, 325-670-1298, Fax: 325-670-1564, E-mail: gradoff@hsutx.edu.
Website: http://www.hsutx.edu/academics/somfa.

Hebrew College, Program in Jewish Studies, Newton Centre, MA 02459. Offers Jewish liturgical music (Certificate); Jewish music education (Certificate); Jewish studies (MA). Part-time and evening/weekend programs available. Postbaccalaureate distance learning degree programs offered (minimal on-campus study). *Degree requirements:* For master's, one foreign language. *Entrance requirements:* For master's, GRE, interview. Additional exam requirements/recommendations for international students: Required—TOEFL.

Heidelberg University, Program in Music Education, Tiffin, OH 44883-2462. Offers MME. Summer program only. *Accreditation:* NASM. Part-time programs available. *Entrance requirements:* For master's, bachelor's degree in music education, minimum cumulative GPA of 2.8, three letters of recommendation, copy of teaching license or certificate, interview. Additional exam requirements/recommendations for international students: Required—TOEFL (minimum score 550 paper-based; 79 iBT), IELTS (minimum score 6.5). Electronic applications accepted.

Hofstra University, School of Education, Programs in Teaching - K-12, Hempstead, NY 11549. Offers bilingual education (MA, Advanced Certificate); family and consumer sciences (MS Ed); fine arts and music education (Advanced Certificate); fine arts education (MA, MS Ed); middle childhood extensions (Advanced Certificate), including grades 5-6 or 7-9; music education (MA, MS Ed); teaching languages other than English and TESOL (MS Ed); TESOL (MS Ed, Advanced Certificate); wind conducting (MA).

Holy Names University, Graduate Division, Department of Music, Oakland, CA 94619-1699. Offers Kodaly (Certificate); music education with Kodaly emphasis (MM); piano pedagogy (MM); piano pedagogy with Suzuki emphasis (MM); vocal pedagogy (MM). *Faculty:* 3 full-time, 7 part-time/adjunct. *Students:* 5 full-time (2 women), 15 part-time (10 women); includes 4 minority (all Asian, non-Hispanic/Latino), 4 international. Average age 33. 12 applicants, 83% accepted, 9 enrolled. In 2013, 7 master's awarded. *Degree requirements:* For master's, comprehensive exam, recital. *Entrance requirements:* For master's, audition; minimum undergraduate GPA of 2.6 overall, 3.0 in major. Additional exam requirements/recommendations for international students: Required—TOEFL (minimum score 550 paper-based; 79 iBT). *Application deadline:* For fall admission, 8/1 priority date for domestic students, 7/15 for international students; for spring admission, 12/1 priority date for domestic students, 12/1 for international students; for summer admission, 5/1 priority date for domestic students, 5/1 for international students. Applications are processed on a rolling basis. Application fee: $65. Electronic applications accepted. *Expenses: Tuition:* Part-time $866 per unit. *Financial support:* Career-related internships or fieldwork, Federal Work-Study, scholarships/grants, and unspecified assistantships available. Support available to part-time students. Financial award application deadline: 3/2; financial award applicants required to submit FAFSA. *Faculty research:* Performance practice with special interest in Baroque, Romantic, and twentieth-century instrumental and vocal music; choral pedagogy; Hungarian music education. *Unit head:* Dr. Steven Hofer, Chair of Music Department, 510-436-1244, E-mail: hofer@hnu.edu. *Application contact:* 800-430-1321, Fax: 510-436-1325, E-mail: graduateadmissions@hnu.edu.

Howard University, Graduate School, Division of Fine Arts, Department of Music, Washington, DC 20059-0002. Offers applied music (MM); instrument (MM Ed); jazz studies (MM); organ (MM Ed); piano (MM Ed); voice (MM Ed). *Accreditation:* NASM. Part-time programs available. *Degree requirements:* For master's, comprehensive exam, thesis or alternative, departmental qualifying exam, recital. *Entrance requirements:* For master's, minimum GPA of 3.0, bachelor's degree in music or music education. Additional exam requirements/recommendations for international students: Required—TOEFL.

Hunter College of the City University of New York, Graduate School, School of Arts and Sciences, Department of Music, New York, NY 10065-5085. Offers music (MA); music education (MA). Part-time and evening/weekend programs available. *Faculty:* 14 full-time (3 women), 2 part-time/adjunct (1 woman). *Students:* 5 full-time (1 woman), 58 part-time (29 women); includes 8 minority (2 Black or African American, non-Hispanic/Latino; 3 Asian, non-Hispanic/Latino; 3 Hispanic/Latino), 8 international. Average age 34. 32 applicants, 59% accepted, 9 enrolled. In 2013, 12 master's awarded. *Degree requirements:* For master's, one foreign language, thesis, composition, essay, or recital; proficiency exam. *Entrance requirements:* For master's, undergraduate major in music (minimum 24 credits) or equivalent, sample of work, research paper. Additional exam requirements/recommendations for international students: Required—TOEFL. *Application deadline:* For fall admission, 4/1 for domestic students, 2/1 for international students; for spring admission, 11/1 for domestic students, 9/1 for international students. Applications are processed on a rolling basis. Application fee: $125. *Financial support:* In 2013–14, 4 fellowships (averaging $1,000 per year) were awarded; Federal Work-Study, tuition waivers (partial), and lesson stipends also available. Support available to part-time students. Financial award application deadline: 4/15. *Faculty research:* African and African-American music, Bach, Renaissance music, early romantic music, theory of tonal music. *Unit head:* Dr. Paul Mueller, Department Chair, 212-772-5020, Fax: 212-772-5022, E-mail: music@hunter.cuny.edu. *Application contact:* Pondie Burstein, Graduate Adviser, 212-772-5152, E-mail: huntermust@aol.com.
Website: http://www.hunter.cuny.edu/music/.

Hunter College of the City University of New York, Graduate School, School of Education, Program in Music Education, New York, NY 10065-5085. Offers MA. *Accreditation:* NCATE. *Faculty:* 8 full-time (2 women), 2 part-time/adjunct (1 woman). *Students:* 5 full-time (1 woman), 20 part-time (9 women); includes 5 minority (1 Black or African American, non-Hispanic/Latino; 3 Asian, non-Hispanic/Latino; 1 Hispanic/Latino), 1 international. Average age 30. 20 applicants, 45% accepted, 7 enrolled. In 2013, 7 master's awarded. *Degree requirements:* For master's, one foreign language, comprehensive exam, thesis, professional teaching portfolio, New York State Teacher Certification Exams. *Entrance requirements:* For master's, minimum GPA of 2.8, 2 letters of reference. Additional exam requirements/recommendations for international students: Required—TOEFL, TWE. *Application deadline:* For fall admission, 4/1 for domestic students, 2/1 for international students; for spring admission, 11/1 for domestic students, 9/1 for international students. Applications are processed on a rolling basis. Application fee: $125. *Financial support:* Federal Work-Study and tuition waivers (partial) available. Support available to part-time students. *Unit head:* Matthew Caballero, Education Program Coordinator, 212-772-4621, E-mail: mc1360@hunter.cuny.edu. *Application contact:* Victor Bobetsky, Music Department Program Coordinator, 212-650-3574, E-mail: victor.bobetsky@hunter.cuny.edu.
Website: http://www.hunter.cuny.edu/school-of-education/programs/graduate/music.

Indiana University of Pennsylvania, School of Graduate Studies and Research, College of Fine Arts, Department of Music, Program in Music, Indiana, PA 15705-1087. Offers music education (MA); performance (MA). *Accreditation:* NASM. Part-time programs available. *Faculty:* 10 full-time (2 women). *Students:* 8 full-time (4 women), 5 part-time (2 women); includes 2 minority (1 Black or African American, non-Hispanic/Latino; 1 Hispanic/Latino), 2 international. Average age 27. 12 applicants, 75% accepted, 6 enrolled. In 2013, 4 master's awarded. *Degree requirements:* For master's, thesis optional. *Entrance requirements:* For master's, 2 letters of recommendation, audition. Additional exam requirements/recommendations for international students: Required—TOEFL (minimum score 550 paper-based). *Application deadline:* Applications are processed on a rolling basis. Application fee: $50. Electronic applications accepted. *Expenses:* Tuition, state resident: full-time $3978; part-time $442 per credit. Tuition, nonresident: full-time $5967; part-time $663 per credit. *Required fees:* $2080; $115.55 per credit. $93 per semester. Tuition and fees vary according to degree level and program. *Financial support:* In 2013–14, 1 fellowship with full tuition reimbursement (averaging $1,000 per year), 6 research assistantships with full and partial tuition reimbursements (averaging $3,793 per year) were awarded; career-related internships or fieldwork, Federal Work-Study, scholarships/grants, and unspecified assistantships also available. Support available to part-time students. Financial award application deadline: 4/15; financial award applicants required to submit FAFSA. *Unit head:* Dr. Matthew Baumer, Coordinator, 724-357-5646, E-mail: matthew.baumer@iup.edu.
Website: http://www.iup.edu/upper.aspx?id-89383.

Inter American University of Puerto Rico, Metropolitan Campus, Graduate Programs, Program in Music Education, San Juan, PR 00919-1293. Offers MM.

Inter American University of Puerto Rico, San Germán Campus, Graduate Studies Center, Program in Music Education, San Germán, PR 00683-5008. Offers music (MA); music teacher education (MA). Part-time and evening/weekend programs available. *Faculty:* 12 full-time (7 women), 19 part-time/adjunct (8 women). *Students:* 28 full-time (17 women), 7 part-time (4 women); all minorities (all Hispanic/Latino). Average age 32. 6 applicants, 100% accepted, 6 enrolled. In 2013, 9 master's awarded. Application fee: $31. *Expenses: Tuition:* Full-time $2424; part-time $202 per credit hour. *Required fees:* $260 per semester. Tuition and fees vary according to course level, course load, degree level and program. *Financial support:* Federal Work-Study available. *Unit head:* Dr. Elba T. Irizarry, Director of Graduate Studies Center, 787-264-1912 Ext. 7357, Fax: 787-892-6350, E-mail: elbat@sg.inter.edu. *Application contact:* Dr. Raquel Montalvo, Coordinator, 787-264-1912 Ext. 7378, E-mail: raquel_montalvo_benet@intersg.edu.

Ithaca College, School of Music, Programs in Music and Music Education, Ithaca, NY 14850. Offers composition (MM); conducting (MM); music education (MM, MS); performance (MM); Suzuki pedagogy (MM). *Accreditation:* NASM. Part-time programs available. *Faculty:* 57 full-time (20 women), 4 part-time/adjunct (3 women). *Students:* 58 full-time (29 women), 6 part-time (3 women); includes 7 minority (3 Black or African American, non-Hispanic/Latino; 2 Asian, non-Hispanic/Latino; 2 Hispanic/Latino), 19 international. Average age 24. 246 applicants, 35% accepted, 37 enrolled. In 2013, 33 master's awarded. *Degree requirements:* For master's, comprehensive exam (for some programs), thesis (for some programs). *Entrance requirements:* For master's, audition, minimum GPA of 3.0. Additional exam requirements/recommendations for international students: Required—TOEFL (minimum score 550 paper-based; 80 iBT). *Application deadline:* For fall admission, 3/1 for domestic and international students; for spring admission, 12/1 for domestic and international students. Applications are processed on a rolling basis. Application fee: $40. Electronic applications accepted. *Expenses:* Contact institution. *Financial support:* In 2013–14, 44 students received support, including 44 teaching assistantships (averaging $9,108 per year); career-related internships or fieldwork, Federal Work-Study, scholarships/grants, and unspecified assistantships also available. Support available to part-time students. Financial award application deadline: 3/1; financial award applicants required to submit CSS PROFILE or FAFSA. *Faculty research:* Musical performance and performance studies, musical composition, music theory and analysis, music education, teaching and learning, musical direction and conducting. *Unit head:* Dr. Les Black, Chair, Graduate Studies in Music, 607-274-3143, Fax: 607-274-1263, E-mail: gps@ithaca.edu. *Application contact:*

Gerard Turbide, Director, Office of Admission, 607-274-3143, Fax: 607-274-1263, E-mail: gps@ithaca.edu.
Website: http://www.ithaca.edu/music/grad.

Jackson State University, Graduate School, College of Liberal Arts, Department of Music, Jackson, MS 39217. Offers music education (MM Ed). *Accreditation:* NASM. Part-time and evening/weekend programs available. *Degree requirements:* For master's, comprehensive exam, thesis or alternative. *Entrance requirements:* For master's, GRE General Test. Additional exam requirements/recommendations for international students: Required—TOEFL (minimum score 520 paper-based; 67 iBT).

James Madison University, The Graduate School, College of Visual and Performing Arts, School of Music, Harrisonburg, VA 22807. Offers conducting (MM); music education (MM); musical arts (DMA); performance (MM); theory-composition (MM). *Accreditation:* NASM. Part-time programs available. *Faculty:* 51 full-time (17 women), 7 part-time/adjunct (5 women). *Students:* 21 full-time (8 women), 4 part-time (2 women); includes 1 minority (Black or African American, non-Hispanic/Latino), 2 international. Average age 27. In 2013, 8 master's awarded. *Degree requirements:* For master's, comprehensive exam. *Entrance requirements:* For master's, GRE General Test, audition, undergraduate degree with major in music and minimum GPA of 3.0. Additional exam requirements/recommendations for international students: Required—TOEFL. *Application deadline:* For fall admission, 4/1 priority date for domestic students, 4/1 for international students; for spring admission, 4/1 priority date for domestic students, 4/1 for international students. Applications are processed on a rolling basis. Application fee: $55. Electronic applications accepted. *Financial support:* In 2013–14, 12 students received support, including 1 teaching assistantship with full tuition reimbursement available (averaging $8,837 per year); Federal Work-Study and 11 graduate assistantships (averaging $7530) also available. Financial award application deadline: 3/1; financial award applicants required to submit FAFSA. *Unit head:* Eric Ruple, Interim Academic Unit Head, 540-568-3614, E-mail: rupleek@jmu.edu. *Application contact:* Dr. Mary Jane Speare, Graduate Coordinator, 540-568-3687.

Kansas State University, Graduate School, College of Arts and Sciences, School of Music, Theatre and Dance, Manhattan, KS 66506. Offers music (MM), including composition, keyboard pedagogy, music education, music history, performance; theatre (MA), including acting, directing, drama therapy, playwriting, scenic design, technical theatre. *Accreditation:* NASM. Part-time programs available. Postbaccalaureate distance learning degree programs offered (minimal on-campus study). *Faculty:* 54 full-time (21 women), 6 part-time/adjunct (2 women). *Students:* 35 full-time (19 women), 20 part-time (13 women); includes 6 minority (2 Black or African American, non-Hispanic/Latino; 2 Asian, non-Hispanic/Latino; 1 Hispanic/Latino; 1 Two or more races, non-Hispanic/Latino), 4 international. Average age 30. 56 applicants, 80% accepted, 20 enrolled. In 2013, 30 master's awarded. *Degree requirements:* For master's, thesis optional. *Entrance requirements:* For master's, GRE, audition (in person or recording), interview (for music education). Additional exam requirements/recommendations for international students: Required—TOEFL (minimum score 600 paper-based). *Application deadline:* For fall admission, 2/1 priority date for domestic and international students; for spring admission, 8/1 priority date for domestic and international students. Applications are processed on a rolling basis. Application fee: $50 ($75 for international students). Electronic applications accepted. *Financial support:* In 2013–14, 5 fellowships (averaging $5,000 per year), 24 teaching assistantships with full tuition reimbursements (averaging $7,500 per year) were awarded; institutionally sponsored loans, scholarships/grants, and tuition waivers (full and partial) also available. Support available to part-time students. Financial award application deadline: 3/1; financial award applicants required to submit FAFSA. *Faculty research:* American music, opera, drama therapy, directing, costume and scenic design, music by women composers. *Total annual research expenditures:* $17,913. *Unit head:* Dr. Gary Mortenson, Head, 785-532-3802, Fax: 785-532-5740, E-mail: garym@ksu.edu. *Application contact:* Dr. Fred Burrack, Director of Graduate Music Programs, 785-532-3429, Fax: 785-532-5740, E-mail: fburrack@ksu.edu.
Website: http://www.k-state.edu/mtd/.

Kent State University, College of the Arts, Hugh A. Glauser School of Music, Kent, OH 44242-0001. Offers composition (MA); conducting (MM); ethnomusicology (MA); music education (MM, PhD); musicology (MA); musicology-ethnomusicology (PhD); performance (MM); theory (MA); theory and composition (PhD). *Accreditation:* NASM. *Degree requirements:* For master's, variable foreign language requirement, comprehensive exam, 2 recitals, essay and recital, or thesis; for doctorate, variable foreign language requirement, comprehensive exam, thesis/dissertation. *Entrance requirements:* For master's, diagnostic exams in music history and theory, audition, minimum GPA of 2.75; for doctorate, diagnostic exams in music history and theory, master's thesis or scholarly paper, minimum GPA of 3.0. Additional exam requirements/recommendations for international students: Required—TOEFL. Electronic applications accepted. *Faculty research:* Music composition, performance, teaching and history.

Lake Forest College, Master of Arts in Teaching Program, Lake Forest, IL 60045. Offers elementary education (MAT); K-12 French (MAT); K-12 music (MAT); K-12 Spanish (MAT); K-12 visual art (MAT); secondary biology (MAT); secondary chemistry (MAT); secondary English (MAT); secondary history (MAT); secondary mathematics (MAT). *Degree requirements:* For master's, comprehensive exam, portfolio. *Entrance requirements:* For master's, GRE.

Lamar University, College of Graduate Studies, College of Fine Arts and Communication, Mary Morgan Moore Department of Music, Beaumont, TX 77710. Offers music education (MM Ed); music performance (MM). *Accreditation:* NASM (one or more programs are accredited). *Degree requirements:* For master's, comprehensive exam, thesis optional. *Entrance requirements:* For master's, GRE General Test, theory placement exams, audition. Additional exam requirements/recommendations for international students: Required—TOEFL. *Faculty research:* Performance: ensembles and personal.

Lebanon Valley College, Program in Music Education, Annville, PA 17003-1400. Offers MME. *Accreditation:* NASM. Part-time programs available. In 2013, 3 master's awarded. *Degree requirements:* For master's, thesis. *Entrance requirements:* For master's, minimum GPA of 3.0, teaching certificate. *Application deadline:* Applications are processed on a rolling basis. Application fee: $30. Electronic applications accepted. *Financial support:* Application deadline: 5/1; applicants required to submit FAFSA. *Unit head:* Dr. Marian T. Dura, Director of the Master of Music Education Program, 717-867-6919, E-mail: dura@lvc.edu. *Application contact:* Susan Greenawalt, Graduate Studies and Continuing Education Assistant/Records Coordinator, 717-867-6213, Fax: 717-867-6018, E-mail: greenawa@lvc.edu.
Website: http://www.lvc.edu/mme/.

Lee University, Program in Music, Cleveland, TN 37320-3450. Offers church music (MCM); conducting (MM); music education (MM); music performance (MM). *Accreditation:* NASM. Part-time programs available. *Faculty:* 19 full-time (5 women), 8 part-time/adjunct (2 women). *Students:* 26 full-time (17 women), 18 part-time (8 women); includes 11 minority (1 Black or African American, non-Hispanic/Latino; 8 Asian, non-Hispanic/Latino; 2 Hispanic/Latino). Average age 28. 19 applicants, 100% accepted, 15 enrolled. In 2013, 11 master's awarded. *Degree requirements:* For master's, variable

Music Education

foreign language requirement, comprehensive exam, thesis, internship. *Entrance requirements:* For master's, placement exercises in music theory, music history, diction, and piano proficiency, audition, resume, interview, minimum GPA of 2.75, official transcripts, essay, 3 recommendations. Additional exam requirements/recommendations for international students: Required—TOEFL (minimum score 450 paper-based). *Application deadline:* For fall admission, 4/1 priority date for domestic and international students; for spring admission, 10/1 priority date for domestic and international students. Applications are processed on a rolling basis. Application fee: $25. *Expenses: Tuition:* Full-time $9900; part-time $550 per credit hour. *Required fees:* $35 per term. One-time fee: $25. *Financial support:* In 2013–14, 36 students received support, including 3 teaching assistantships (averaging $346 per year); career-related internships or fieldwork, Federal Work-Study, institutionally sponsored loans, and scholarships/grants also available. Financial award application deadline: 3/1; financial award applicants required to submit FAFSA. *Unit head:* Dr. Brad W. Moffett, Director, 423-614-8240, Fax: 423-614-8242, E-mail: gradmusic@leeuniversity.edu. *Application contact:* Vicki Glasscock, Graduate Admissions Director, 423-614-8059, E-mail: vglasscock@leeuniversity.edu.
Website: http://www.leeuniversity.edu/academics/graduate/music.

Lehman College of the City University of New York, Division of Arts and Humanities, Department of Music, Bronx, NY 10468-1589. Offers MAT. *Accreditation:* NCATE. Part-time and evening/weekend programs available. *Entrance requirements:* For master's, audition. *Faculty research:* Music and music education.

Lehman College of the City University of New York, Division of Education, Department of Middle and High School Education, Program in Music Education, Bronx, NY 10468-1589. Offers MS Ed. Part-time and evening/weekend programs available.

Liberty University, School of Music, Lynchburg, VA 24515. Offers ethnomusicology (MA); music and worship (MA); music education (MA). *Students:* 15 full-time (5 women), 36 part-time (14 women); includes 10 minority (8 Black or African American, non-Hispanic/Latino; 1 American Indian or Alaska Native, non-Hispanic/Latino; 1 Hispanic/Latino). Average age 35. 144 applicants, 30% accepted, 33 enrolled. In 2013, 7 master's awarded. *Entrance requirements:* For master's, minimum GPA of 3.0; interview; letter of recommendation; statement of purpose; bachelor's/master's degree in music, worship, or related field, or 5 years of experience. Additional exam requirements/recommendations for international students: Required—TOEFL (minimum score 600 paper-based; 100 iBT). *Application deadline:* Applications are processed on a rolling basis. Application fee: $50. Electronic applications accepted. *Expenses: Tuition:* Full-time $9630; part-time $535 per credit hour. *Required fees:* $175 per term. One-time fee: $50. Tuition and fees vary according to course load, degree level, campus/location and program. *Unit head:* Dr. Vernon Whaley, 434-592-3463, E-mail: vwhaley@liberty.edu. *Application contact:* Jay Bridge, Director of Admissions, 800-424-9595, Fax: 800-628-7977, E-mail: gradadmissions@liberty.edu.
Website: http://www.liberty.edu/academics/music/.

Long Island University–LIU Post, School of Education, Department of Curriculum and Instruction, Brookville, NY 11548-1300. Offers adolescence education (MS); adolescence education: biology (MS); adolescence education: earth science (MS); adolescence education: English (MS); adolescence education: mathematics (MS); adolescence education: social studies (MS); adolescence education: Spanish (MS); art education (MS); bilingual education (MS); childhood education (MS); early childhood education (MS); middle childhood education (MS); music education (MS); teaching English to speakers of other languages (MS). Part-time and evening/weekend programs available. *Degree requirements:* For master's, comprehensive exam or thesis, student teaching. *Entrance requirements:* For master's, minimum GPA of 2.75 in major, 2.5 overall. Electronic applications accepted. *Faculty research:* Ethics and education, teaching strategies.

Long Island University–LIU Post, School of Education, Department of Music, Brookville, NY 11548-1300. Offers music education (MS).

Long Island University–LIU Post, School of Visual and Performing Arts, Department of Music, Brookville, NY 11548-1300. Offers music (MA); music education (MS). Part-time programs available. *Degree requirements:* For master's, thesis. *Entrance requirements:* For master's, GRE General Test (MA), GRE Subject Test in music, minimum undergraduate GPA of 3.0, 2 professional and/or academic letters of recommendation, current resume. Electronic applications accepted. *Faculty research:* Performance, composing, musicology, conducting, computer-based music technology.

Louisiana State University and Agricultural & Mechanical College, Graduate School, College of Music and Dramatic Arts, School of Music, Baton Rouge, LA 70803. Offers music (MM, DMA, PhD); music education (PhD). *Accreditation:* NASM. Part-time programs available. *Faculty:* 50 full-time (16 women), 1 (woman) part-time/adjunct. *Students:* 165 full-time (64 women), 32 part-time (13 women); includes 34 minority (17 Black or African American, non-Hispanic/Latino; 1 American Indian or Alaska Native, non-Hispanic/Latino; 4 Asian, non-Hispanic/Latino; 11 Hispanic/Latino; 1 Two or more races, non-Hispanic/Latino), 47 international. Average age 28. 209 applicants, 52% accepted, 62 enrolled. In 2013, 38 master's, 28 doctorates awarded. Terminal master's awarded for partial completion of doctoral program. *Degree requirements:* For doctorate, thesis/dissertation (for some programs). *Entrance requirements:* For master's, minimum GPA of 3.0, audition/interview; for doctorate, GRE General Test, minimum GPA of 3.0, audition/interview. Additional exam requirements/recommendations for international students: Required—TOEFL (minimum score 550 paper-based; 79 iBT), IELTS (minimum score 6.5), or PTE (minimum score 59). *Application deadline:* For fall admission, 3/15 priority date for domestic students, 5/15 for international students; for spring admission, 10/15 for international students. Applications are processed on a rolling basis. Application fee: $50 ($70 for international students). Electronic applications accepted. *Financial support:* In 2013–14, 162 students received support, including 8 fellowships (averaging $27,798 per year), 1 research assistantship with full and partial tuition reimbursement available (averaging $21,000 per year), 96 teaching assistantships with full and partial tuition reimbursements available (averaging $8,962 per year); Federal Work-Study, institutionally sponsored loans, scholarships/grants, health care benefits, tuition waivers (full and partial), and unspecified assistantships also available. Support available to part-time students. Financial award applicants required to submit FAFSA. *Faculty research:* Music education, music literature, formal and harmonic analysis, pedagogy, performance. *Unit head:* Dr. Stephen David Beck, Dean, 225-578-3261, Fax: 225-578-2562, E-mail: sdbeck@lsu.edu.
Website: http://www.music.lsu.edu/.

Loyola University Maryland, Graduate Programs, School of Education, Program in Kodaly Music Education, Baltimore, MD 21210-2699. Offers M Ed. *Entrance requirements:* For master's, essay, letter of recommendation, resume, transcript. Additional exam requirements/recommendations for international students: Required—TOEFL. Electronic applications accepted.

Manhattanville College, School of Education, Program in Music Education, Purchase, NY 10577-2132. Offers MAT. Part-time and evening/weekend programs available. *Degree requirements:* For master's, comprehensive exam or research project, field experience. *Entrance requirements:* For master's, audition, minimum undergraduate GPA of 3.0, 2 letters of recommendation. Additional exam requirements/

recommendations for international students: Required—TOEFL. Electronic applications accepted.

Marywood University, Academic Affairs, Insalaco College of Creative and Performing Arts, Music, Theatre and Dance Department, Scranton, PA 18509-1598. Offers music education (MA). *Accreditation:* NASM. *Entrance requirements:* Additional exam requirements/recommendations for international students: Required—TOEFL (minimum score 550 paper-based; 79 iBT). *Application deadline:* For fall admission, 4/1 for domestic students, 3/31 priority date for international students; for spring admission, 11/1 priority date for domestic students, 8/31 priority date for international students. Applications are processed on a rolling basis. Application fee: $35. Electronic applications accepted. *Expenses: Tuition:* Part-time $775 per credit. Tuition and fees vary according to degree level. *Financial support:* Career-related internships or fieldwork, scholarships/grants, and unspecified assistantships available. Support available to part-time students. Financial award application deadline: 6/30; financial award applicants required to submit FAFSA. *Faculty research:* Renaissance and American musicology, history of Gregorian chant, liturgical music. *Unit head:* Sr. Joan McCusker, Chair, 570-348-6268 Ext. 2531, E-mail: mccusker@maryu.marywood.edu. *Application contact:* Tammy Manka, Assistant Director of Graduate Admissions, 570-348-6211 Ext. 2322, E-mail: tmanka@marywood.edu.
Website: http://www.marywood.edu/mtd/.

McGill University, Faculty of Graduate and Postdoctoral Studies, Schulich School of Music, Montréal, QC H3A 2T5, Canada. Offers composition (M Mus, D Mus, PhD); music education (MA, PhD); music technology (MA, PhD); musicology (MA, PhD); performance (M Mus); performance studies (D Mus); sound recording (M Mus, PhD); theory (MA, PhD).

McKendree University, Graduate Programs, Programs in Education, Lebanon, IL 62254-1299. Offers curriculum design and instruction (Ed D, Ed S); educational administration and leadership (MA Ed); educational studies (MA Ed); higher education administrative services (MA Ed); music education (MA Ed); reading (MA Ed); special education (MA Ed); teacher leadership (MA Ed); teaching certification (MA Ed). *Accreditation:* NCATE. Part-time and evening/weekend programs available. Postbaccalaureate distance learning degree programs offered (no on-campus study). *Entrance requirements:* For master's, official transcripts from all institutions previously attended, minimum GPA of 3.0, resume, references; for doctorate, GRE (within the past 5 years), master's degree in education and Ed S, or the equivalent, from regionally-accredited institution; official transcripts from all institutions previously attended; curriculum vitae/resume; essay/personal statement; two years of teaching/professional experience; for Ed S, GRE (within the past 5 years), master's degree in education from regionally-accredited institution of higher education; official transcripts from all institutions previously attended; curriculum vitae/resume; essay/personal statement; two years of teaching/professional experience. Additional exam requirements/recommendations for international students: Required—TOEFL. Electronic applications accepted.

McNeese State University, Doré School of Graduate Studies, College of Liberal Arts, Department of Performing Arts, Lake Charles, LA 70609. Offers music education (Postbaccalaureate Certificate), including Kodaly studies. Evening/weekend programs available. *Entrance requirements:* For degree, GRE.

Miami University, College of Creative Arts, Department of Music, Oxford, OH 45056. Offers music education (MM); music performance (MM). *Accreditation:* NASM. *Students:* 22 full-time (13 women), 1 (woman) part-time; includes 5 minority (2 Black or African American, non-Hispanic/Latino; 1 Asian, non-Hispanic/Latino; 1 Hispanic/Latino; 1 Two or more races, non-Hispanic/Latino), 4 international. Average age 26. In 2013, 15 master's awarded. *Entrance requirements:* For master's, audition, personal statement, letters of recommendation, video recording of recent rehearsal or music class (Master of Music Education applicants only). Additional exam requirements/recommendations for international students: Recommended—TOEFL (minimum score 80 iBT), IELTS (minimum score 6.5), TSE (minimum score 54). Application fee: $50. Electronic applications accepted. *Expenses:* Tuition, state resident: full-time $12,634; part-time $526 per credit hour. Tuition, nonresident: full-time $27,892; part-time $1162 per credit hour. Part-time tuition and fees vary according to course load, campus/location and program. *Financial support:* Research assistantships with full and partial tuition reimbursements, teaching assistantships with full and partial tuition reimbursements, Federal Work-Study, health care benefits, and unspecified assistantships available. Financial award application deadline: 2/15. *Unit head:* Dr. Bruce Murray, Chair and Professor, 513-529-3014, E-mail: music@miamioh.edu. *Application contact:* Dr. Brenda Mitchell, Associate Professor of Music/Director of Graduate Studies, 513-529-1228, E-mail: mitchebs@miamioh.edu.
Website: http://www.MiamiOH.edu/music.

Michigan State University, The Graduate School, College of Music, East Lansing, MI 48824. Offers collaborative piano (M Mus); jazz studies (M Mus); music (PhD); music composition (M Mus, DMA); music conducting (M Mus, DMA); music education (M Mus); music performance (M Mus, DMA); music theory (M Mus); music therapy (M Mus); musicology (MA); piano pedagogy (M Mus). *Accreditation:* NASM. *Entrance requirements:* Additional exam requirements/recommendations for international students: Required—TOEFL. Electronic applications accepted.

Minot State University, Graduate School, Division of Music, Minot, ND 58707-0002. Offers music education (MME). Program offered during summer only. *Degree requirements:* For master's, thesis or alternative. *Entrance requirements:* For master's, music exam, minimum GPA of 2.75. Additional exam requirements/recommendations for international students: Required—TOEFL. *Faculty research:* Music education.

Mississippi College, Graduate School, College of Arts and Sciences, School of Christian Studies and the Arts, Department of Music, Clinton, MS 39058. Offers applied music performance (MM); conducting (MM); music education (MM); music performance: organ (MM); vocal pedagogy (MM). *Accreditation:* NASM. Part-time and evening/weekend programs available. *Degree requirements:* For master's, comprehensive exam, recital. *Entrance requirements:* For master's, GRE, minimum GPA of 2.5. Additional exam requirements/recommendations for international students: Recommended—TOEFL, IELTS. Electronic applications accepted.

Missouri State University, Graduate College, College of Arts and Letters, Department of Music, Springfield, MO 65897. Offers music (MM), including conducting, music education, music pedagogy, music theory and composition, performance; secondary education (MS Ed), including music. *Accreditation:* NASM. Part-time programs available. *Faculty:* 28 full-time (10 women), 1 (woman) part-time/adjunct. *Students:* 21 full-time (10 women), 12 part-time (8 women); includes 3 minority (1 Black or African American, non-Hispanic/Latino; 2 Hispanic/Latino), 6 international. Average age 27. 30 applicants, 83% accepted, 13 enrolled. In 2013, 17 master's awarded. *Degree requirements:* For master's, comprehensive exam, thesis or alternative. *Entrance requirements:* For master's, GRE, interview/audition (MM), 9-12 teaching certification (MS Ed). Additional exam requirements/recommendations for international students: Required—TOEFL (minimum score 550 paper-based; 79 iBT). *Application deadline:* For fall admission, 7/20 for domestic students, 5/1 for international students; for spring admission, 12/20 for domestic students, 9/1 for international students. Applications are

processed on a rolling basis. Application fee: $35 ($50 for international students). Electronic applications accepted. *Expenses:* Tuition, state resident: full-time $4500; part-time $250 per credit hour. Tuition, nonresident: full-time $9018; part-time $501 per credit hour. *Required fees:* $361 per semester. Tuition and fees vary according to course level, course load and program. *Financial support:* In 2013–14, 5 teaching assistantships with full tuition reimbursements (averaging $8,324 per year) were awarded; Federal Work-Study, institutionally sponsored loans, scholarships/grants, tuition waivers (partial), and unspecified assistantships also available. Financial award application deadline: 3/31; financial award applicants required to submit FAFSA. *Faculty research:* Bulgarian violin literature, Ozarks fiddle music, carillon, nineteenth-century piano. *Unit head:* Dr. Julie Combs, Head, 417-836-5648, Fax: 417-836-7665, E-mail: music@missouristate.edu. *Application contact:* Misty Stewart, Coordinator of Graduate Recruitment, 417-836-6079, Fax: 417-836-6200, E-mail: mistystewart@missouristate.edu.
Website: http://www.missouristate.edu/music/.

Montclair State University, The Graduate School, College of Education and Human Services, Department of Secondary and Special Education, Program in Teaching in Subject Area, Montclair, NJ 07043-1624. Offers art (MAT); biology (MAT); chemistry (MAT); earth science (MAT); English (MAT); French (MAT); health and physical education (MAT); health education (MAT); mathematics (MAT); music (MAT); physical education (MAT); physical science (MAT); social studies (MAT); Spanish (MAT); teacher of English as a second language (MAT). *Degree requirements:* For master's, comprehensive exam, thesis or alternative. *Entrance requirements:* For master's, GRE General Test, interview, 2 letters of recommendation. Additional exam requirements/recommendations for international students: Required—TOEFL (minimum score 83 iBT), IELTS (minimum score 6.5). Electronic applications accepted.

Montclair State University, The Graduate School, College of the Arts, John J. Cali School of Music, Program in Music, Montclair, NJ 07043-1624. Offers music education (MA); music therapy (MA); performance (MA); theory/composition (MA). Part-time and evening/weekend programs available. *Degree requirements:* For master's, thesis. *Entrance requirements:* For master's, GRE General Test, 2 letters of recommendation, essay. Additional exam requirements/recommendations for international students: Required—TOEFL (minimum score 83 iBT), IELTS (minimum score 6.5). Electronic applications accepted.

Morehead State University, Graduate Programs, Caudill College of Arts, Humanities and Social Sciences, Department of Music, Theatre and Dance, Morehead, KY 40351. Offers music education (MM); music performance (MM). *Accreditation:* NASM. Part-time and evening/weekend programs available. *Degree requirements:* For master's, comprehensive exam, oral and written exams. *Entrance requirements:* For master's, music entrance exam, BA in music with minimum GPA of 3.0, 2.5 overall; audition. Additional exam requirements/recommendations for international students: Required—TOEFL (minimum score 550 paper-based). Electronic applications accepted. *Faculty research:* Musical instrument digital interface (MIDI) applications, tonal concepts of euphonium and baritone horn, digital synthesis, computer-assisted instruction in music, musical composition.

Murray State University, College of Humanities and Fine Arts, Program in Music, Murray, KY 42071. Offers music education (MME). *Accreditation:* NASM. Part-time programs available. *Entrance requirements:* For master's, GRE General Test or MAT. Additional exam requirements/recommendations for international students: Required—TOEFL.

Nazareth College of Rochester, Graduate Studies, Department of Music, Program in Music Education, Rochester, NY 14618-3790. Offers MS Ed. *Accreditation:* NASM; Teacher Education Accreditation Council. Part-time and evening/weekend programs available. *Entrance requirements:* For master's, audition, minimum GPA of 3.0.

New Jersey City University, Graduate Studies and Continuing Education, William J. Maxwell College of Arts and Sciences, Department of Music, Dance and Theatre, Jersey City, NJ 07305-1597. Offers music education (MA); performance (MM). *Accreditation:* NASM. Part-time and evening/weekend programs available. *Faculty:* 6 full-time (4 women), 1 part-time/adjunct (0 women). *Students:* 15 full-time (10 women), 14 part-time (5 women); includes 8 minority (all Hispanic/Latino), 4 international. Average age 31. In 2013, 7 master's awarded. *Degree requirements:* For master's, thesis optional, recital. *Entrance requirements:* Additional exam requirements/recommendations for international students: Required—TOEFL (minimum score 61 iBT). *Application deadline:* For fall admission, 8/1 priority date for domestic students; for spring admission, 12/1 for domestic students. Applications are processed on a rolling basis. Application fee: $0. *Expenses: Tuition,* area resident: Part-time $527.90 per credit. Tuition, nonresident: part-time $947.75 per credit. *Financial support:* Unspecified assistantships available. *Unit head:* Dr. Min Kim, Chairperson, 201-200-3157, E-mail: mkim@njcu.edu. *Application contact:* Dr. William Bajor, Dean of Graduate Studies, 201-200-3409, Fax: 201-200-3411, E-mail: wbajor@njcu.edu.

New Mexico State University, Graduate School, College of Arts and Sciences, Department of Music, Las Cruces, NM 88003-8001. Offers conducting (MM); music education (MM); performance (MM). *Accreditation:* NASM. Part-time programs available. *Faculty:* 15 full-time (5 women), 3 part-time/adjunct (1 woman). *Students:* 10 full-time (5 women), 8 part-time (1 woman); includes 7 minority (all Hispanic/Latino), 5 international. Average age 32. 7 applicants, 100% accepted, 6 enrolled. In 2013, 8 master's awarded. *Degree requirements:* For master's, comprehensive exam (for some programs), thesis (for some programs), recital. *Entrance requirements:* For master's, diagnostic exam, audition, bachelor's degree or equivalent from an accredited institution. Additional exam requirements/recommendations for international students: Required—TOEFL (minimum score 550 paper-based; 79 iBT), IELTS (minimum score 6.5). *Application deadline:* For fall admission, 7/1 priority date for domestic students; for spring admission, 11/1 for domestic students. Applications are processed on a rolling basis. Application fee: $40 ($50 for international students). Electronic applications accepted. *Expenses:* Contact institution. *Financial support:* In 2013–14, 8 students received support, including 7 teaching assistantships (averaging $12,888 per year); Federal Work-Study, health care benefits, and unspecified assistantships also available. Support available to part-time students. Financial award application deadline: 3/1. *Faculty research:* Music education, contemporary wind band literature, performance. *Total annual research expenditures:* $10,598. *Unit head:* Dr. Lon W. Chaffin, Head, 575-646-2421, Fax: 575-646-8199, E-mail: lchaffin@nmsu.edu. *Application contact:* Dr. James Shearer, Assistant Professor, 575-646-2601, Fax: 575-646-8199, E-mail: jshearer@nmsu.edu.
Website: http://music.nmsu.edu.

New York University, Steinhardt School of Culture, Education, and Human Development, Department of Music and Performing Arts Professions, Program in Music Education, New York, NY 10012. Offers teaching music, all grades (MA). *Accreditation:* Teacher Education Accreditation Council. Part-time programs available. *Faculty:* 4 full-time (1 woman). *Students:* 25 full-time (14 women), 40 part-time (26 women); includes 8 minority (3 Black or African American, non-Hispanic/Latino; 4 Asian, non-Hispanic/Latino; 1 Hispanic/Latino), 32 international. Average age 29. 64 applicants, 80% accepted, 23 enrolled. In 2013, 29 master's awarded. *Degree requirements:* For

master's, thesis (for some programs). *Entrance requirements:* For master's, audition. Additional exam requirements/recommendations for international students: Required—TOEFL (minimum score 100 iBT). *Application deadline:* For fall admission, 12/1 priority date for domestic and international students; for spring admission, 10/1 for domestic and international students. Applications are processed on a rolling basis. Application fee: $75. Electronic applications accepted. *Expenses: Tuition* Full-time $35,856; part-time $1494 per unit. *Required fees:* $1408; $64 per unit. $473 per term. Tuition and fees vary according to course load and program. *Financial support:* Fellowships with full and partial tuition reimbursements, career-related internships or fieldwork, Federal Work-Study, scholarships/grants, and tuition waivers (partial) available. Support available to part-time students. Financial award application deadline: 2/1; financial award applicants required to submit FAFSA. *Faculty research:* Music education philosophy; community music education; integrated curriculum; multiple intelligences; technology in arts education; cognition, emotion, and music. *Unit head:* Dr. David Elliott, Director, 212-998-5424, E-mail: david.elliott@nyu.edu. *Application contact:* 212-998-5030, Fax: 212-995-4328, E-mail: steinhardt.gradadmissions@nyu.edu.
Website: http://steinhardt.nyu.edu/music/education/.

New York University, Steinhardt School of Culture, Education, and Human Development, Department of Music and Performing Arts Professions, Program in Music Performance and Composition, New York, NY 10012. Offers instrumental performance (MM), including instrumental performance, jazz instrumental performance; music composition (PhD); music theory and composition (MM), including composition for music theater, computer music composition, music theory and composition, scoring for film and multimedia, songwriting; piano performance (MM), including collaborative piano, solo piano; vocal pedagogy (Advanced Certificate); vocal performance (MM), including classical voice, musical theatre performance; vocal performance/vocal pedagogy (MM), including classical voice, musical theatre performance. Part-time programs available. *Faculty:* 22 full-time (6 women). *Students:* 216 full-time (102 women), 78 part-time (41 women); includes 50 minority (10 Black or African American, non-Hispanic/Latino; 19 Asian, non-Hispanic/Latino; 11 Hispanic/Latino; 10 Two or more races, non-Hispanic/Latino), 114 international. Average age 25. 555 applicants, 47% accepted, 130 enrolled. In 2013, 111 master's, 6 doctorates, 9 other advanced degrees awarded. *Degree requirements:* For master's, thesis (for some programs); for doctorate, thesis/dissertation. *Entrance requirements:* For master's, audition; for doctorate, GRE General Test, audition, interview. Additional exam requirements/recommendations for international students: Required—TOEFL (minimum score 100 iBT). *Application deadline:* For fall admission, 12/1 priority date for domestic and international students; for spring admission, 10/1 for domestic and international students. Applications are processed on a rolling basis. Application fee: $75. Electronic applications accepted. *Expenses: Tuition:* Full-time $35,856; part-time $1494 per unit. *Required fees:* $1408; $64 per unit. $473 per term. Tuition and fees vary according to course load and program. *Financial support:* Fellowships with full and partial tuition reimbursements, Federal Work-Study, scholarships/grants, and tuition waivers (partial) available. Support available to part-time students. Financial award application deadline: 2/1; financial award applicants required to submit FAFSA. *Faculty research:* Aesthetics, performance analysis, twentieth-century music, music methodologies for arts criticism and analysis. *Unit head:* 212-998-5424, Fax: 212-995-4043. *Application contact:* 212-998-5030, Fax: 212-995-4328, E-mail: steinhardt.gradadmissions@nyu.edu.
Website: http://steinhardt.nyu.edu/music/composition/programs/graduate.

Norfolk State University, School of Graduate Studies, School of Liberal Arts, Department of Music, Norfolk, VA 23504. Offers music (MM); music education (MM); performance (MM); theory and composition (MM). *Accreditation:* NASM. Part-time programs available. *Students:* 16 full-time (4 women), 3 part-time (1 woman); includes 16 minority (15 Black or African American, non-Hispanic/Latino; 1 Two or more races, non-Hispanic/Latino), 1 international. Average age 31. In 2013, 4 master's awarded. *Degree requirements:* For master's, thesis or alternative. *Entrance requirements:* For master's, minimum GPA of 2.7, letters of recommendation. Additional exam requirements/recommendations for international students: Required—TOEFL. *Application deadline:* For fall admission, 3/1 for domestic students, 3/1 priority date for international students; for spring admission, 10/1 for domestic and international students. Application fee: $30. *Financial support:* Fellowships with partial tuition reimbursements, Federal Work-Study, and unspecified assistantships available. *Unit head:* O'Neill Sanford, Head, 757-823-8544, Fax: 757-823-2605, E-mail: dsanford@nsu.edu. *Application contact:* Dr. Ernest Brown, Information Contact, 757-823-8544.
Website: http://www.nsu.edu/.

North Dakota State University, College of Graduate and Interdisciplinary Studies, College of Human Development and Education, School of Education, Fargo, ND 58108. Offers agricultural education (M Ed, MS), including agricultural education, agricultural extension education (MS); counseling (M Ed, MS, PhD); curriculum and instruction (M Ed, MS); education (PhD); educational leadership (M Ed, MS, Ed S); family and consumer sciences education (M Ed, MS); history education (M Ed, MS); institutional analysis (Ed D); mathematics education (M Ed, MS); music education (M Ed, MS); occupational and adult education (Ed D); science education (M Ed, MS). *Accreditation:* NCATE. Part-time and evening/weekend programs available. Postbaccalaureate distance learning degree programs offered (minimal on-campus study). *Faculty:* 25 full-time (11 women), 1 (woman) part-time/adjunct. *Students:* 110 full-time (82 women), 123 part-time (85 women); includes 14 minority (4 Black or African American, non-Hispanic/Latino; 4 American Indian or Alaska Native, non-Hispanic/Latino; 1 Native Hawaiian or other Pacific Islander, non-Hispanic/Latino; 5 Two or more races, non-Hispanic/Latino), 10 international. Average age 28. 57 applicants, 81% accepted, 42 enrolled. In 2013, 38 master's, 9 doctorates awarded. *Degree requirements:* For master's, comprehensive exam; for doctorate, thesis/dissertation; for Ed S, thesis. *Entrance requirements:* For degree, GRE General Test, master's degree, minimum GPA of 3.25. Additional exam requirements/recommendations for international students: Required—TOEFL. *Application deadline:* Applications are processed on a rolling basis. Application fee: $45 ($60 for international students). *Financial support:* Research assistantships, teaching assistantships, career-related internships or fieldwork, Federal Work-Study, institutionally sponsored loans, and tuition waivers (full) available. Financial award application deadline: 4/15. *Unit head:* Dr. William Martin, Chair, 701-231-7202, Fax: 701-231-7416, E-mail: william.martin@ndsu.edu. *Application contact:* Sonya Goergen, Marketing, Recruitment, and Public Relations Coordinator, 701-231-7033, Fax: 701-231-6524.
Website: http://www.ndsu.nodak.edu/school_of_education/.

Northern State University, MME Program in Music Education, Aberdeen, SD 57401-7198. Offers MME. Part-time programs available. Postbaccalaureate distance learning degree programs offered (minimal on-campus study). *Faculty:* 13 full-time (4 women). *Students:* 17 part-time (13 women). Average age 25. 8 applicants, 38% accepted, 3 enrolled. *Entrance requirements:* For master's, minimum GPA of 2.75. Additional exam requirements/recommendations for international students: Required—TOEFL (minimum score 550 paper-based; 78 iBT), IELTS (minimum score 6). *Application deadline:* Applications are processed on a rolling basis. Application fee: $35. Electronic applications accepted. *Expenses:* Tuition, state resident: full-time $3634. Tuition, nonresident: full-time $7690. One-time fee: $35 full-time. Part-time tuition and fees vary according to course load, degree level, campus/location and reciprocity agreements.

Music Education

Financial support: In 2013–14, 6 students received support. Institutionally sponsored loans and scholarships/grants available. Support available to part-time students. Financial award application deadline: 3/1; financial award applicants required to submit FAFSA. *Unit head:* Dr. Alan LaFave, Dean of Fine Arts, 605-626-2500, E-mail: alan.lafave@northern.edu. *Application contact:* Dr. Timothy Woods, Program Director, 605-626-7758, E-mail: timothy.woods@northern.edu.
Website: http://www.northern.edu/sfa.

Northwestern University, Henry and Leigh Bienen School of Music, Department of Music Performance, Evanston, IL 60208. Offers brass performance (MM, DMA); conducting (MM, DMA); jazz studies (MM); percussion performance (MM, DMA); performance (MM); piano pedagogy (MME); piano performance (MM, DMA); piano performance and collaborative arts (MM, DMA); piano performance and pedagogy (MM, DMA); string performance (MM, DMA); voice and opera performance (MM, DMA); woodwind performance (MM, DMA). *Accreditation:* NASM. *Degree requirements:* For master's, recital; for doctorate, comprehensive exam, thesis/dissertation, 3 recitals. *Entrance requirements:* For master's, audition, preliminary tapes in voice, flute, percussion; for doctorate, written essay exam (theory and music history), audition, preliminary tapes. Additional exam requirements/recommendations for international students: Required—TOEFL (minimum score 600 paper-based; 100 iBT).

Northwestern University, Henry and Leigh Bienen School of Music, Department of Music Studies, Evanston, IL 60208. Offers composition (DMA); music education (MME, PhD); music theory and cognition (PhD); musicology (MM, PhD); theory (MM). PhD admissions and degree offered through The Graduate School. *Accreditation:* NASM. *Degree requirements:* For doctorate, comprehensive exam, thesis/dissertation. *Entrance requirements:* For master's, portfolio or research papers; for doctorate, GRE General Test (for PhD), portfolio, research papers. Additional exam requirements/recommendations for international students: Required—TOEFL (minimum score 600 paper-based; 100 iBT). *Faculty research:* Music cognition, cognitive learning, aesthetic education, computer music, technology in education.

Northwest Missouri State University, Graduate School, College of Arts and Sciences, Department of Fine and Performing Arts, Maryville, MO 64468-6001. Offers teaching music (MS Ed). Part-time programs available. *Degree requirements:* For master's, comprehensive exam. *Entrance requirements:* For master's, GRE General Test, minimum undergraduate GPA of 2.5, writing sample. Additional exam requirements/recommendations for international students: Required—TOEFL (minimum score 550 paper-based).

Oakland University, Graduate Study and Lifelong Learning, College of Arts and Sciences, Department of Music, Rochester, MI 48309-4401. Offers music (MM); music education (PhD). *Accreditation:* NASM. *Faculty:* 13 full-time (3 women), 3 part-time/adjunct (1 woman). *Students:* 12 full-time (7 women), 33 part-time (19 women); includes 7 minority (3 Black or African American, non-Hispanic/Latino; 3 Asian, non-Hispanic/Latino; 1 Hispanic/Latino), 1 international. Average age 37. 31 applicants, 42% accepted, 13 enrolled. In 2013, 18 master's, 1 doctorate awarded. *Entrance requirements:* For master's, minimum GPA of 3.0 for unconditional admission. Additional exam requirements/recommendations for international students: Required—TOEFL (minimum score 550 paper-based). *Application deadline:* For fall admission, 7/15 priority date for domestic students, 5/1 priority date for international students; for winter admission, 12/1 priority date for domestic students, 9/1 priority date for international students; for spring admission, 3/15 priority date for domestic students. Applications are processed on a rolling basis. Application fee: $0. Electronic applications accepted. *Expenses:* Contact institution. *Financial support:* Federal Work-Study, institutionally sponsored loans, and tuition waivers (full) available. Financial award application deadline: 3/1; financial award applicants required to submit FAFSA. *Unit head:* Dr. Jacqueline H. Wiggins, Chair/Professor of Music Education/Doctoral Coordinator, 248-370-2030, Fax: 248-370-2041, E-mail: jwiggins@oakland.edu. *Application contact:* Joseph Shively, Graduate Program Coordinator/Associate Professor of Music Education, 248-370-2287, Fax: 248-370-2041, E-mail: shively@oakland.edu.

Oberlin College, Conservatory of Music, Oberlin, OH 44074-1588. Offers contemporary chamber music (MM); historical performance (MM); music education (MMT); performance (AD). *Accreditation:* NASM. *Students:* 15 full-time (6 women). 77 applicants, 23% accepted, 14 enrolled. In 2013, 2 master's awarded. *Degree requirements:* For master's, 2 recitals. *Entrance requirements:* For master's and AD, audition. Additional exam requirements/recommendations for international students: Required—TOEFL (minimum score 100 iBT). *Application deadline:* For fall admission, 12/1 for domestic and international students. Application fee: $100. Electronic applications accepted. *Financial support:* Career-related internships or fieldwork, Federal Work-Study, and scholarships/grants available. Financial award application deadline: 2/15; financial award applicants required to submit CSS PROFILE or FAFSA. *Unit head:* Andrea Kalyn, Dean, 440-775-8200. *Application contact:* Michael Manderen, Director of Conservatory Admissions, 440-775-8413, Fax: 440-775-6972, E-mail: conservatory.admissions@oberlin.edu.
Website: http://new.oberlin.edu/conservatory/.

Ohio University, Graduate College, College of Fine Arts, School of Music, Athens, OH 45701-2979. Offers accompanying (MM); composition (MM); conducting (MM); history/literature (MM); music education (MM); music therapy (MM); performance (MM, Certificate); performance/pedagogy (MM); theory (MM). *Accreditation:* NASM. Part-time and evening/weekend programs available. Postbaccalaureate distance learning degree programs offered (minimal on-campus study). *Degree requirements:* For master's, comprehensive exam, thesis (for some programs), oral exam. *Entrance requirements:* For master's, audition, interview, portfolio, recordings (varies by program). Additional exam requirements/recommendations for international students: Required—TOEFL (minimum score 550 paper-based; 80 iBT) or IELTS (minimum score 6.5). Electronic applications accepted.

Oklahoma State University, College of Arts and Sciences, Department of Music, Stillwater, OK 74078. Offers pedagogy and performance (MM). *Accreditation:* NASM. *Faculty:* 29 full-time (12 women), 6 part-time/adjunct (3 women). *Students:* 7 full-time (3 women), 10 part-time (5 women); includes 4 minority (1 Black or African American, non-Hispanic/Latino; 1 Asian, non-Hispanic/Latino; 2 Two or more races, non-Hispanic/Latino), 2 international. Average age 26. 26 applicants, 58% accepted, 8 enrolled. In 2013, 6 master's awarded. *Degree requirements:* For master's, final project, oral exam. *Entrance requirements:* For master's, GRE, audition. Additional exam requirements/recommendations for international students: Required—TOEFL (minimum score 550 paper-based; 79 iBT). *Application deadline:* For fall admission, 3/1 priority date for international students; for spring admission, 8/1 priority date for international students. Applications are processed on a rolling basis. Application fee: $40 ($75 for international students). Electronic applications accepted. *Expenses:* Tuition, state resident: full-time $4272; part-time $178 per credit hour. Tuition, nonresident: full-time $17,472; part-time $709 per credit hour. *Required fees:* $2413.20; $100.55 per credit hour. One-time fee: $50 full-time. Part-time tuition and fees vary according to course load and campus/location. *Financial support:* In 2013–14, 11 teaching assistantships (averaging $11,288 per year) were awarded; career-related internships or fieldwork, Federal Work-Study, scholarships/grants, health care benefits, tuition waivers (partial), and unspecified assistantships also available. Support available to part-time students. Financial award application deadline: 3/1; financial award applicants required to submit FAFSA. *Faculty research:* Discovery and presentation of music literature of other countries, transportation of ancient music literature to modern notation. *Unit head:* Dr. Brant Adams, Department Head, 405-744-6133, Fax: 405-744-9324, E-mail: osumusic@okstate.edu.
Website: http://music.okstate.edu/.

Old Dominion University, College of Arts and Letters, Program in Music Education, Norfolk, VA 23529. Offers MME. *Accreditation:* NASM. Part-time and evening/weekend programs available. *Faculty:* 11 full-time (2 women), 4 part-time/adjunct (1 woman). *Students:* 8 full-time (5 women), 9 part-time (7 women); includes 4 minority (3 Black or African American, non-Hispanic/Latino; 1 Asian, non-Hispanic/Latino). Average age 32. 8 applicants, 88% accepted, 7 enrolled. In 2013, 13 master's awarded. *Degree requirements:* For master's, comprehensive exam, thesis (for some programs), recital. *Entrance requirements:* For master's, music theory exam, diagnostic examination, GRE, baccalaureate degree in music theory, history, education, or applied music; audition. *Application deadline:* Applications are processed on a rolling basis. Application fee: $50. Electronic applications accepted. *Expenses:* Tuition, state resident: full-time $9888; part-time $412 per credit. Tuition, nonresident: full-time $25,152; part-time $1048 per credit. *Required fees:* $59 per semester. One-time fee: $50. *Financial support:* In 2013–14, 3 students received support, including 3 teaching assistantships (averaging $10,000 per year); scholarships/grants and unspecified assistantships also available. Financial award applicants required to submit FAFSA. *Faculty research:* Performance, composition, conducting, music education research. *Unit head:* Dr. Nancy K. Klein, Graduate Program Director, 757-683-4061, E-mail: nklein@odu.edu. *Application contact:* Dr. Robert Wojtowicz, Associate Dean, 757-683-6077, Fax: 757-683-5746, E-mail: rwojtowi@odu.edu.
Website: http://al.odu.edu/music/academics/grad.shtml.

Oregon State University, College of Education, Program in Music Education, Corvallis, OR 97331. Offers MAT. Part-time programs available. *Faculty:* 6 full-time (2 women), 4 part-time/adjunct (0 women). *Students:* 6 full-time (5 women). Average age 23. 15 applicants, 47% accepted, 6 enrolled. In 2013, 8 degrees awarded. *Degree requirements:* For master's, thesis optional. *Entrance requirements:* For master's, CBEST. Additional exam requirements/recommendations for international students: Required—TOEFL (minimum score 575 paper-based). *Application deadline:* For fall admission, 3/1 for domestic students. Application fee: $60. *Expenses:* Tuition, state resident: full-time $11,664; part-time $432 per credit hour. Tuition, nonresident: full-time $19,197; part-time $711 per credit hour. *Required fees:* $1446; $443 per quarter. One-time fee: $300. Tuition and fees vary according to course load and program. *Financial support:* Teaching assistantships, career-related internships or fieldwork, Federal Work-Study, and institutionally sponsored loans available. Support available to part-time students. Financial award application deadline: 2/1. *Faculty research:* Teaching skills and methods, verbal and nonverbal classroom teaching techniques. *Unit head:* Dr. Tina Bull, Associate Professor/Director of Graduate Studies, Music Education, 541-737-5603, E-mail: tina.bull@oregonstate.edu.
Website: http://www.osucascades.edu/academics/teaching/.

Penn State University Park, Graduate School, College of Arts and Architecture, School of Music, State College, PA 16802. Offers composition theory (M Mus); conducting (M Mus); music (MA); music education (MME, PhD, Certificate); pedagogy and performance (M Mus); performance (M Mus); piano performance (DMA). *Accreditation:* NASM. *Unit head:* Dr. Barbara O. Korner, Dean, 814-865-2592, Fax: 814-865-2018, E-mail: bok2@psu.edu. *Application contact:* Cynthia E. Nicosia, Director, Graduate Enrollment Services, 814-865-1834, Fax: 814-863-4627, E-mail: cey1@psu.edu.
Website: http://music.psu.edu/.

Piedmont College, School of Education, Demorest, GA 30535-0010. Offers art education (MAT); early childhood education (MA, MAT); instructional technology (MAT); middle grades education (MA, MAT); music education (MAT); secondary education (MA, MAT); special education (MA, MAT); teacher leadership (Ed S). Part-time and evening/weekend programs available. *Students:* 312 full-time (242 women), 694 part-time (563 women); includes 153 minority (103 Black or African American, non-Hispanic/Latino; 3 American Indian or Alaska Native, non-Hispanic/Latino; 17 Asian, non-Hispanic/Latino; 19 Hispanic/Latino; 11 Two or more races, non-Hispanic/Latino), 1 international. Average age 37. 165 applicants, 72% accepted, 118 enrolled. In 2013, 333 master's, 15 doctorates, 457 other advanced degrees awarded. *Degree requirements:* For master's, thesis, field experience in the classroom teaching; for doctorate, thesis/dissertation. *Entrance requirements:* For master's, GRE General Test, MAT, minimum undergraduate GPA of 2.5; for Ed S, minimum graduate GPA of 3.5, valid teaching certificate. Additional exam requirements/recommendations for international students: Required—TOEFL (minimum score 550 paper-based). *Application deadline:* For fall admission, 7/15 for domestic students; for spring admission, 12/1 for domestic students. Applications are processed on a rolling basis. Electronic applications accepted. *Expenses: Tuition:* Full-time $7992; part-time $444 per credit hour. *Financial support:* Career-related internships or fieldwork, Federal Work-Study, and unspecified assistantships available. Support available to part-time students. Financial award applicants required to submit FAFSA. *Unit head:* Dr. Don Gnecco, Dean, 706-778-3000 Ext. 1201, Fax: 706-776-9608, E-mail: dgnecco@piedmont.edu. *Application contact:* Kathleen Anderson, Director of Graduate Enrollment Management, 706-778-8500 Ext. 1181, Fax: 706-778-0150, E-mail: kanderson@piedmont.edu.

Pittsburg State University, Graduate School, College of Arts and Sciences, Department of Music, Pittsburg, KS 66762. Offers instrumental music education (MM); music history/music literature (MM); performance (MM), including orchestral performance, organ, piano, voice; theory and composition (MM); vocal music education (MM). *Accreditation:* NASM. *Degree requirements:* For master's, thesis or alternative.

Plymouth State University, College of Graduate Studies, Graduate Studies in Education, Program in Music Education, Plymouth, NH 03264-1595. Offers M Ed. Evening/weekend programs available.

Portland State University, Graduate Studies, College of the Arts, School of Music, Portland, OR 97207-0751. Offers conducting (MMC); music education (MAT, MST); performance (MMP). *Accreditation:* NASM. Part-time programs available. *Faculty:* 24 full-time (9 women), 40 part-time/adjunct (14 women). *Students:* 27 full-time (11 women), 14 part-time (7 women); includes 10 minority (2 Asian, non-Hispanic/Latino; 6 Hispanic/Latino; 2 Two or more races, non-Hispanic/Latino), 3 international. Average age 31. 63 applicants, 35% accepted, 16 enrolled. In 2013, 15 master's awarded. *Degree requirements:* For master's, variable foreign language requirement, exit exam. *Entrance requirements:* For master's, GRE General Test, departmental exam, minimum GPA of 3.0 in upper-division course work or 2.75 overall. Additional exam requirements/recommendations for international students: Required—TOEFL (minimum score 550 paper-based). *Application deadline:* For fall admission, 8/1 priority date for domestic students, 8/1 for international students; for winter admission, 11/15 for domestic students, 10/1 for international students; for spring admission, 2/1 for domestic and international students. Applications are processed on a rolling basis. Application fee: $50. *Expenses:* Tuition, state resident: full-time $9207; part-time $341 per credit. Tuition, nonresident: full-time $14,391; part-time $533 per credit. *Required fees:* $1263; $22 per credit. $98 per quarter. One-time fee: $150. Tuition and fees vary according to

program. *Financial support:* In 2013–14, 11 teaching assistantships with partial tuition reimbursements (averaging $5,040 per year) were awarded; Federal Work-Study, scholarships/grants, and unspecified assistantships also available. Support available to part-time students. Financial award application deadline: 3/1; financial award applicants required to submit FAFSA. *Faculty research:* Composition, music analysis, music history, jazz. *Unit head:* Bryan Johanson, Chair, 503-725-3003, Fax: 503-725-8215, E-mail: johansonb@pdx.edu. *Application contact:* Evan Brown, Office Coordinator, 503-725-3011, Fax: 503-725-5525, E-mail: music@pdx.edu.
Website: http://www.pdx.edu/the-arts/music.

Queens College of the City University of New York, Division of Graduate Studies, Division of Education, Department of Secondary Education, Flushing, NY 11367-1597. Offers art (MS Ed); biology (MS Ed, AC); chemistry (MS Ed, AC); earth sciences (MS Ed, AC); English (MS Ed, AC); French (MS Ed, AC); Italian (MS Ed, AC); mathematics (MS Ed, AC); music (MS Ed, AC); physics (MS Ed, AC); social studies (MS Ed, AC); Spanish (MS Ed, AC). Part-time and evening/weekend programs available. *Degree requirements:* For master's, research project; for AC, thesis optional. *Entrance requirements:* For master's, minimum GPA of 3.0. Additional exam requirements/recommendations for international students: Required—TOEFL.

Radford University, College of Graduate and Professional Studies, College of Visual and Performing Arts, Department of Music, Radford, VA 24142. Offers music (MA); music education (MS); music therapy (MS). *Accreditation:* NASM. Part-time programs available. *Faculty:* 8 full-time (1 woman), 4 part-time/adjunct (0 women). *Students:* 15 full-time (11 women), 6 part-time (3 women); includes 2 minority (1 Black or African American, non-Hispanic/Latino; 1 Asian, non-Hispanic/Latino), 1 international. Average age 28. 9 applicants, 89% accepted, 5 enrolled. In 2013, 5 master's awarded. *Degree requirements:* For master's, comprehensive exam, thesis or alternative. *Entrance requirements:* For master's, GRE, major field test in music or PRAXIS II (content knowledge), written diagnostics exams in music, minimum GPA of 2.75; 3 letters of reference, resume, official transcripts. Additional exam requirements/recommendations for international students: Required—TOEFL (minimum score 550 paper-based; 79 iBT). *Application deadline:* For fall admission, 2/15 priority date for domestic students, 12/1 for international students; for spring admission, 7/1 for international students. Applications are processed on a rolling basis. Application fee: $50. Electronic applications accepted. *Expenses:* Tuition, state resident: full-time $6800; part-time $283 per credit hour. Tuition, nonresident: full-time $15,610; part-time $627 per credit hour. *Required fees:* $2944; $123 per credit hour. Tuition and fees vary according to program. *Financial support:* In 2013–14, 12 students received support, including 4 research assistantships (averaging $6,750 per year), 7 teaching assistantships with partial tuition reimbursements available (averaging $8,429 per year); career-related internships or fieldwork, Federal Work-Study, institutionally sponsored loans, scholarships/grants, and unspecified assistantships also available. Financial award application deadline: 3/1; financial award applicants required to submit FAFSA. *Unit head:* Dr. Allen F. Wojtera, Chair, 540-831-5177, Fax: 540-831-6133, E-mail: awojtera@radford.edu. *Application contact:* Rebecca Conner, Director, Graduate Enrollment, 540-831-6296, Fax: 540-831-6061, E-mail: gradcollege@radford.edu.
Website: http://www.radford.edu/content/cvpa/home/music.html.

Reinhardt University, Program in Music, Waleska, GA 30183-2981. Offers conducting (MM); music education (MM); piano pedagogy (MM). *Accreditation:* NASM. Part-time and evening/weekend programs available. Postbaccalaureate distance learning degree programs offered. *Entrance requirements:* For master's, GRE, audition (for piano pedagogy and conducting), 2 letters of reference. Additional exam requirements/recommendations for international students: Required—TOEFL.

Rhode Island College, School of Graduate Studies, Faculty of Arts and Sciences, Department of Music, Theatre, and Dance, Providence, RI 02908-1991. Offers music education (MAT, MM Ed). Part-time and evening/weekend programs available. *Faculty:* 9 full-time (4 women), 14 part-time/adjunct (5 women). *Students:* 7 part-time (5 women); includes 1 minority (Hispanic/Latino). Average age 40. In 2013, 6 master's awarded. *Degree requirements:* For master's, comprehensive exam, thesis, final project (MFA). *Entrance requirements:* For master's, GRE General Test or MAT; exams in music education, theory, history and literature, audition, 3 letters of recommendation, evidence of musicianship, interview. Additional exam requirements/recommendations for international students: Recommended—TOEFL (minimum score 550 paper-based; 79 iBT). *Application deadline:* For fall admission, 3/1 for domestic students; for spring admission, 11/1 for domestic students. Applications are processed on a rolling basis. Application fee: $50. *Expenses:* Tuition, state resident: full-time $8928; part-time $372 per credit hour. Tuition, nonresident: full-time $17,376; part-time $724 per credit hour. *Required fees:* $602; $22 per credit. $72 per term. *Financial support:* Teaching assistantships with full tuition reimbursements, Federal Work-Study, scholarships/grants, health care benefits, and unspecified assistantships available. Support available to part-time students. Financial award application deadline: 5/15; financial award applicants required to submit FAFSA. *Unit head:* Prof. Ian Greitzer, Chair, 401-456-4654. *Application contact:* Graduate Studies, 401-456-8700.
Website: http://www.ric.edu/mtd/index.php.

Rider University, Westminster Choir College, Program in Music Education, Lawrenceville, NJ 08648-3001. Offers MAT, MM, MME. *Accreditation:* NASM. *Entrance requirements:* For master's, audition, interview, repertoire list, 2 letters of reference, resume. Additional exam requirements/recommendations for international students: Required—TOEFL (minimum score 525 paper-based). Electronic applications accepted.

Rider University, Westminster Choir College, Programs in Music, Lawrenceville, NJ 08648-3001. Offers choral conducting (MM); composition (MM); organ performance (MM); piano accompanying and coaching (MM); piano pedagogy and performance (MM); piano performance (MM); sacred music (MM); vocal pedagogy and performance (MM); vocal training (MVP). Part-time programs available. *Degree requirements:* For master's, variable foreign language requirement, departmental qualifying exam. *Entrance requirements:* For master's, audition, interview, repertoire list, 2 letters of reference, resume. Additional exam requirements/recommendations for international students: Required—TOEFL (minimum score 525 paper-based). Electronic applications accepted.

Roosevelt University, Graduate Division, Chicago College of Performing Arts, The Music Conservatory, Chicago, IL 60605. Offers music (MM); piano pedagogy (Diploma). *Accreditation:* NASM. Part-time and evening/weekend programs available.

Rutgers, The State University of New Jersey, New Brunswick, Mason Gross School of the Arts, Music Department, New Brunswick, NJ 08901. Offers collaborative piano (MM, DMA); conducting: choral (MM, DMA); conducting: instrumental (MM, DMA); conducting: orchestral (MM, DMA); jazz studies (MM); music (DMA, AD); music education (MM, DMA); music performance (MM). *Accreditation:* NASM. *Degree requirements:* For doctorate, one foreign language. *Entrance requirements:* For master's and doctorate, audition. Additional exam requirements/recommendations for international students: Required—TOEFL (minimum score 550 paper-based), IELTS (minimum score 7). Electronic applications accepted. *Faculty research:* Performance, twentieth century music, jazz, music education.

St. Cloud State University, School of Graduate Studies, College of Liberal Arts, Department of Music, St. Cloud, MN 56301-4498. Offers conducting and literature (MM); music education (MM); piano pedagogy (MM). *Degree requirements:* For master's, comprehensive exam (for some programs), thesis or alternative. *Entrance requirements:* For master's, GRE General Test, minimum GPA of 2.75. Additional exam requirements/recommendations for international students: Required—TOEFL (minimum score 550 paper-based; 79 iBT), IELTS (minimum score 6.5), Michigan English Language Assessment Battery. Electronic applications accepted.

Saint Xavier University, Graduate Studies, School of Education, Chicago, IL 60655-3105. Offers counseling (MA); curriculum and instruction (MA); early childhood education (MA); educational administration (MA); elementary education (MA); individualized studies (MA), including educational technology, English as a second language (ESL), ISTEM (integrative science, technology, engineering, and math), science education; music education (MA); reading (MA); secondary education (MA); Spanish education (MA); special education (MA); teaching and leadership (MA). *Accreditation:* NCATE. Part-time and evening/weekend programs available. *Degree requirements:* For master's, thesis or project. *Entrance requirements:* For master's, minimum GPA of 3.0. *Expenses:* Contact institution.

Samford University, School of the Arts, Birmingham, AL 35229. Offers church music (MM); music education (MME); piano performance and pedagogy (MM). MME program offered in Traditional, Fifth Year Non-Traditional, and National Board Cohort formats. *Accreditation:* NASM. Part-time programs available. *Faculty:* 8 full-time (2 women), 5 part-time/adjunct (2 women). *Students:* 8 full-time (3 women), 7 part-time (3 women); includes 1 minority (Black or African American, non-Hispanic/Latino), 2 international. Average age 25. 27 applicants, 85% accepted, 15 enrolled. In 2013, 10 master's awarded. *Degree requirements:* For master's, comprehensive oral exam; juried public recital (for MM). *Entrance requirements:* For master's, GRE General Test; PRAXIS II (for MME), minimum GPA of 3.0, undergraduate degree in music. Additional exam requirements/recommendations for international students: Required—TOEFL (minimum score 90 iBT). *Application deadline:* For fall admission, 2/15 priority date for domestic students; for spring admission, 10/15 priority date for domestic students. Applications are processed on a rolling basis. Application fee: $35. *Expenses: Tuition:* Full-time $11,552; part-time $722 per credit. *Required fees:* $500; $250 per term. *Financial support:* In 2013–14, 14 students received support, including research assistantships with partial tuition reimbursements available (averaging $6,000 per year); Federal Work-Study, scholarships/grants, tuition waivers (partial), and unspecified assistantships also available. Financial award application deadline: 9/1; financial award applicants required to submit FAFSA. *Faculty research:* Hymnology, choral techniques, assessment of music learning at elementary and secondary levels, piano pedagogy, special education and inclusion, learning theories; church music administration, worship and the arts. *Unit head:* Dr. Kathryn Fouse, Associate Dean, 205-726-2489, E-mail: klfouse@samford.edu. *Application contact:* Dr. Demondrae Thurman, Director, Graduate Studies, 205-726-2389, Fax: 205-726-2165, E-mail: dthurman@samford.edu.
Website: http://www.samford.edu/arts.

San Diego State University, Graduate and Research Affairs, College of Professional Studies and Fine Arts, School of Music and Dance, San Diego, CA 92182. Offers composition (acoustic and electronic) (MM); conducting (MM); ethnomusicology (MA); jazz studies (MM); musicology (MA); performance (MM); piano pedagogy (MA); theory (MA). *Degree requirements:* For master's, comprehensive exam (for some programs), thesis (for some programs). *Entrance requirements:* For master's, GRE General Test, bachelor's degree in related field, 2 letters of reference. Additional exam requirements/recommendations for international students: Required—TOEFL. Electronic applications accepted.

San Francisco State University, Division of Graduate Studies, College of Liberal and Creative Arts, School of Music and Dance, San Francisco, CA 94132-1722. Offers chamber music (MM); classical performance (MM); composition (MA); conducting (MM); music education (MA); music history (MA). *Accreditation:* NASM. *Unit head:* Dr. Dianthe Spencer, Director, 415-338-1431, E-mail: smd@sfsu.edu. *Application contact:* Dr. Cyrus Ginwala, Graduate Coordinator, 415-338-1431, E-mail: cginwala@sfsu.edu.
Website: http://musicdance.sfsu.edu/.

Shenandoah University, Shenandoah Conservatory, Winchester, VA 22601-5195. Offers artist diploma (Certificate); church music (MM, Certificate); collaborative piano (MM); composition (MM); conducting (MM); music education (MME); music therapy (MMT, Certificate); pedagogy (MM, DMA); performance (MM, DMA); performing arts leadership and management (MS). *Accreditation:* NASM. *Faculty:* 41 full-time (12 women), 6 part-time/adjunct (4 women). *Students:* 46 full-time (27 women), 98 part-time (58 women); includes 18 minority (6 Black or African American, non-Hispanic/Latino; 6 Asian, non-Hispanic/Latino; 6 Hispanic/Latino), 19 international. Average age 33. 101 applicants, 77% accepted, 44 enrolled. In 2013, 26 master's, 13 doctorates, 6 other advanced degrees awarded. *Degree requirements:* For master's, variable foreign language requirement, comprehensive exam, thesis (for some programs), minimum GPA of 3.0, internship (MS), recital (MM), research teaching project or thesis (MME), project (MA); for doctorate, variable foreign language requirement, comprehensive exam, thesis/dissertation, minimum GPA of 3.0, dissertation or teaching project, recital; for Certificate, variable foreign language requirement, comprehensive exam, thesis, minimum GPA of 3.0, research project, recital. *Entrance requirements:* For master's, diagnostic examination in music theory, vocal diction assessment (for MM in voice and choral conducting), bachelor's degree with minimum of GPA of 2.5, performance audition, writing sample, resume, all academic transcripts; for doctorate, diagnostic examination in music theory and music literature, vocal diction assessment (for voice), master's degree with minimum GPA of 3.25, performance audition, 2 letters of recommendation, writing sample, resume, all academic transcripts; for Certificate, bachelor's or master's degree; minimum GPA of 2.5; performance audition (for Artist Diploma). Additional exam requirements/recommendations for international students: Required—TOEFL (minimum score 550 paper-based; 79 iBT), IELTS (minimum score 6.5), Sakae Institute of Study Abroad (SISA) test (minimum score 15). *Application deadline:* For fall admission, 1/15 for domestic and international students; for summer admission, 5/1 for domestic and international students. Applications are processed on a rolling basis. Application fee: $30. Electronic applications accepted. *Expenses: Tuition:* Full-time $19,176; part-time $799 per credit. *Required fees:* $365 per term. Tuition and fees vary according to course level, course load and program. *Financial support:* In 2013–14, 34 students received support, including 31 teaching assistantships with partial tuition reimbursements available (averaging $6,810 per year); career-related internships or fieldwork, scholarships/grants, and unspecified assistantships also available. Support available to part-time students. Financial award application deadline: 3/15; financial award applicants required to submit FAFSA. *Faculty research:* CD Recording and Release Project, creative clinical therapy. *Unit head:* Dr. Michael J. Stepniak, Dean of Conservatory, 540-665-4600, Fax: 540-665-5402, E-mail: mstepnia@su.edu. *Application contact:* Andrew Woodall, Executive Director of Recruitment and Advancement, 540-665.4581, Fax: 540-665-4627, E-mail: admit@su.edu.
Website: http://www.conservatory.su.edu.

Silver Lake College of the Holy Family, Division of Graduate Studies, Program in Music Education, Manitowoc, WI 54220-9319. Offers music education-Kodaly emphasis

(MM). *Accreditation:* NASM. Part-time programs available. Postbaccalaureate distance learning degree programs offered (minimal on-campus study). *Faculty:* 1 (woman) full-time, 5 part-time/adjunct (2 women). *Students:* 5 part-time (all women). Average age 44. In 2013, 3 master's awarded. *Degree requirements:* For master's, comprehensive exam, thesis. *Entrance requirements:* For master's, examinations of music theory, music history and literature, and applied music and conducting, interview, minimum undergraduate GPA of 3.0, three letters of recommendation, video of teaching. Additional exam requirements/recommendations for international students: Required—TOEFL. *Application deadline:* For fall admission, 8/1 for domestic students; for spring admission, 12/1 for domestic students. Applications are processed on a rolling basis. Application fee: $0. Electronic applications accepted. *Expenses: Tuition:* Part-time $500 per credit. *Financial support:* Career-related internships or fieldwork, Federal Work-Study, and scholarships/grants available. Support available to part-time students. Financial award application deadline: 6/30; financial award applicants required to submit FAFSA. *Faculty research:* Effects of prenatal music on bonding and stimulation, music and the brain, early childhood music, effective use of Smart Music for choral and general music areas. *Unit head:* Rachel Ware Carlton, Interim Director, 920-686-6272, Fax: 920-684-7082, E-mail: rachel.warecarlton@sl.edu. *Application contact:* Jamie Grant, Director of Admissions, 920-686-6206, Fax: 920-686-6322, E-mail: jamie.grant@sl.edu.
Website: https://www.sl.edu/adult-education/academics/graduate-program/master-of-music/.

Southern Illinois University Carbondale, Graduate School, College of Liberal Arts, School of Music, Carbondale, IL 62901-4701. Offers composition and theory (MM); history and literature (MM); music education (MM); opera/music theater (MM); performance (MM); piano pedagogy (MM). *Accreditation:* NASM. Part-time programs available. *Faculty:* 22 full-time (6 women). *Students:* 26 full-time (12 women), 18 part-time (9 women); includes 2 minority (1 Asian, non-Hispanic/Latino; 1 Hispanic/Latino), 4 international. Average age 24. 39 applicants, 64% accepted, 16 enrolled. In 2013, 12 master's awarded. *Degree requirements:* For master's, one foreign language, thesis or alternative. *Entrance requirements:* For master's, audition, minimum GPA of 2.7. Additional exam requirements/recommendations for international students: Required—TOEFL. *Application deadline:* Applications are processed on a rolling basis. Application fee: $50. *Financial support:* In 2013–14, 16 students received support, including 2 fellowships with full tuition reimbursements available, 12 teaching assistantships with full tuition reimbursements available; research assistantships with full tuition reimbursements available, Federal Work-Study, institutionally sponsored loans, and tuition waivers (full) also available. Support available to part-time students. Financial award application deadline: 4/1. *Faculty research:* Performance practices, historical research, operatic development. *Unit head:* Dr. Frank Stemper, Director of Graduate Studies, 618-453-2541, E-mail: fstemp@siu.edu.

Southern Illinois University Edwardsville, Graduate School, College of Arts and Sciences, Department of Music, Program in Music, Edwardsville, IL 62026-0001. Offers music education (MM); music performance (MM). Part-time programs available. *Faculty:* 17 full-time (5 women). *Students:* 8 full-time (5 women), 6 part-time (4 women); includes 1 minority (Hispanic/Latino), 1 international. 8 applicants, 75% accepted. In 2013, 12 master's awarded. *Degree requirements:* For master's, one foreign language, thesis (for some programs), recital. *Entrance requirements:* Additional exam requirements/recommendations for international students: Required—TOEFL (minimum score 550 paper-based, 79 iBT), IELTS (minimum score 6.5), Michigan Test of English Language Proficiency or PTE. *Application deadline:* For fall admission, 7/18 for domestic students, 6/1 for international students; for spring admission, 12/12 for domestic students, 10/1 for international students; for summer admission, 4/24 for domestic students, 3/1 for international students. Applications are processed on a rolling basis. Application fee: $30. Electronic applications accepted. *Expenses:* Tuition, state resident: full-time $3551. Tuition, nonresident: full-time $8378. *Financial support:* In 2013–14, teaching assistantships with full tuition reimbursements (averaging $9,585 per year) were awarded; institutionally sponsored loans, scholarships/grants, and unspecified assistantships also available. Financial award application deadline: 3/1; financial award applicants required to submit FAFSA. *Unit head:* Dr. Marc Schapman, Program Director, 618-650-2034, E-mail: maschap@siue.edu. *Application contact:* Melissa K. Mace, Assistant Director of Graduate and International Recruitment, 618-650-2756, Fax: 618-650-3618, E-mail: mmace@siue.edu.
Website: http://www.siue.edu/artsandsciences/music/.

Southern Illinois University Edwardsville, Graduate School, College of Arts and Sciences, Department of Music, Program in Piano Pedagogy, Edwardsville, IL 62026. Offers Postbaccalaureate Certificate. Part-time programs available. *Students:* 1 (woman) part-time, all international. In 2013, 1 Postbaccalaureate Certificate awarded. *Entrance requirements:* Additional exam requirements/recommendations for international students: Required—TOEFL (minimum score 550 paper-based, 79 iBT), IELTS (minimum score 6.5), Michigan Test of English Language Proficiency or PTE. *Application deadline:* For fall admission, 7/18 for domestic students, 6/1 for international students; for spring admission, 12/12 for domestic students, 10/1 for international students; for summer admission, 4/24 for domestic students, 3/1 for international students. Applications are processed on a rolling basis. Application fee: $30. Electronic applications accepted. *Expenses:* Tuition, state resident: full-time $3551. Tuition, nonresident: full-time $8378. *Financial support:* Fellowships, research assistantships, teaching assistantships, institutionally sponsored loans, scholarships/grants, and unspecified assistantships available. Financial award application deadline: 3/1; financial award applicants required to submit FAFSA. *Unit head:* Dr. Kris Pineda, Program Director, 618-650-3593, E-mail: kpineda@siue.edu. *Application contact:* Melissa K. Mace, Assistant Director of Graduate and International Recruitment, 618-650-2756, Fax: 618-650-3618, E-mail: mmace@siue.edu.
Website: http://www.siue.edu/artsandsciences/music/.

Southern Illinois University Edwardsville, Graduate School, College of Arts and Sciences, Department of Music, Program in Vocal Pedagogy, Edwardsville, IL 62026. Offers Postbaccalaureate Certificate. Part-time programs available. *Students:* 1 (woman) part-time. In 2013, 3 Postbaccalaureate Certificates awarded. *Entrance requirements:* Additional exam requirements/recommendations for international students: Required—TOEFL (minimum score 550 paper-based, 79 iBT), IELTS (minimum score 6.5), Michigan Test of English Language Proficiency or PTE. *Application deadline:* For fall admission, 7/18 for domestic students, 6/1 for international students; for spring admission, 12/12 for domestic students, 10/1 for international students; for summer admission, 4/24 for domestic students, 3/1 for international students. Applications are processed on a rolling basis. Application fee: $30. Electronic applications accepted. *Expenses:* Tuition, state resident: full-time $3551. Tuition, nonresident: full-time $8378. *Financial support:* Fellowships, research assistantships, teaching assistantships, institutionally sponsored loans, scholarships/grants, and unspecified assistantships available. Financial award application deadline: 3/1; financial award applicants required to submit FAFSA. *Unit head:* Dr. Emily Truckenbrod, Program Director, 618-650-5394, E-mail: etrucke@siue.edu. *Application contact:* Melissa K. Mace, Assistant Director of Graduate and International Recruitment, 618-650-2756, Fax: 618-650-3618, E-mail: mmace@siue.edu.
Website: http://www.siue.edu/artsandsciences/music.

Southern Methodist University, Meadows School of the Arts, Division of Music, Dallas, TX 75275. Offers composition (MM); conducting (MM), including choral, instrumental; music education (MM); music history and literature (MM); performance (MM), including harpsichord, orchestral instrument, organ, piano, voice; piano performance and pedagogy (MM); theory pedagogy (MM). *Accreditation:* NASM. Part-time programs available. *Degree requirements:* For master's, variable foreign language requirement, comprehensive exam, project, recital, or thesis. *Entrance requirements:* For master's, placement exams in music history and theory, audition; bachelor's degree in music or equivalent; minimum GPA of 3.0; research paper in history, theory, education. Additional exam requirements/recommendations for international students: Required—TOEFL (minimum score 550 paper-based; 80 iBT). Electronic applications accepted. *Faculty research:* Music perception and cognition, computer-based instruction, music medicine and therapy, theoretical and historical analysis-medieval to contemporary.

Southwestern Oklahoma State University, College of Arts and Sciences, Department of Music, Weatherford, OK 73096-3098. Offers music education (MM); performance (MM). *Accreditation:* NASM. Part-time programs available. *Degree requirements:* For master's, comprehensive exam, recital (music performance). *Entrance requirements:* For master's, minimum GPA of 2.5. Additional exam requirements/recommendations for international students: Required—TOEFL.

State University of New York at Fredonia, Graduate Studies, School of Music, Program in Music Education, Fredonia, NY 14063-1136. Offers MM. *Accreditation:* NASM. Part-time and evening/weekend programs available. *Degree requirements:* For master's, thesis optional. *Expenses:* Tuition, state resident: full-time $7398; part-time $411 per credit hour. Tuition, nonresident: full-time $13,770; part-time $765 per credit hour. *Required fees:* $1143.90; $63.55 per credit hour. Tuition and fees vary according to course load.

State University of New York College at Potsdam, Crane School of Music, Potsdam, NY 13676. Offers music education (MM); music performance (MM). *Accreditation:* NASM. Part-time programs available. *Degree requirements:* For master's, variable foreign language requirement, thesis (for some programs). *Entrance requirements:* For master's, audition, minimum GPA of 3.0. Additional exam requirements/recommendations for international students: Required—TOEFL (minimum score 550 paper-based; 80 iBT), IELTS (minimum score 6). Electronic applications accepted.

Syracuse University, School of Education, Programs in Music Education, Syracuse, NY 13244. Offers music education/professional certification (M Mus, MS); music education: teacher preparation (MS). *Accreditation:* NASM. Part-time programs available. *Students:* 9 full-time (7 women), 5 part-time (all women); includes 2 minority (1 Hispanic/Latino; 1 Two or more races, non-Hispanic/Latino). Average age 25. 15 applicants, 67% accepted, 2 enrolled. In 2013, 13 master's awarded. *Degree requirements:* For master's, thesis or alternative. *Entrance requirements:* For master's, New York state teacher certification or eligibility. Additional exam requirements/recommendations for international students: Required—TOEFL (minimum score 100 iBT). *Application deadline:* For fall admission, 1/15 priority date for domestic and international students; for spring admission, 10/15 for domestic and international students. Applications are processed on a rolling basis. Application fee: $75. Electronic applications accepted. *Financial support:* Fellowships with full tuition reimbursements and teaching assistantships with full and partial tuition reimbursements available. Financial award application deadline: 1/1. *Unit head:* Prof. Colleen Reynolds, 315-443-4309, E-mail: cmreyn01@syr.edu. *Application contact:* Laurie Deyo, Graduate Recruiter, School of Education, 315-443-2505, E-mail: e-gradrcrt@syr.edu.
Website: http://soe.syr.edu/.

Tarleton State University, College of Graduate Studies, College of Liberal and Fine Arts, Department of Fine Arts, Stephenville, TX 76402. Offers music education (MM). *Accreditation:* NASM. Part-time and evening/weekend programs available. *Students:* 8 part-time (2 women). Average age 42. 3 applicants, 100% accepted, 3 enrolled. *Degree requirements:* For master's, comprehensive exam, thesis optional. *Entrance requirements:* For master's, GRE, minimum GPA of 3.0. Additional exam requirements/recommendations for international students: Required—TOEFL (minimum score 550 paper-based; 80 iBT). *Application deadline:* For fall admission, 8/15 priority date for domestic students; for spring admission, 1/7 for domestic students. Applications are processed on a rolling basis. Application fee: $30 ($130 for international students). Electronic applications accepted. *Expenses:* Tuition, state resident: full-time $3312; part-time $184 per credit hour. Tuition, nonresident: full-time $9144; part-time $508 per credit hour. *Required fees:* $1916. Tuition and fees vary according to course load and campus/location. *Financial support:* In 2013–14, 2 research assistantships (averaging $12,019 per year) were awarded; institutionally sponsored loans and scholarships/grants also available. Financial award application deadline: 5/1; financial award applicants required to submit FAFSA. *Unit head:* Dr. Teresa Davidian, Head, 254-968-9245, Fax: 254-968-9239, E-mail: davidian@tarleton.edu. *Application contact:* Information Contact, 254-968-9104, Fax: 254-968-9670, E-mail: gradoffice@tarleton.edu.
Website: http://www.tarleton.edu/COLFAWEB/finearts.

Teachers College, Columbia University, Graduate Faculty of Education, Department of Arts and Humanities, Program in Music and Music Education, New York, NY 10027. Offers Ed M, MA, Ed D, Ed DCT. *Accreditation:* NCATE. Part-time programs available. *Faculty:* 5 full-time, 4 part-time/adjunct. *Students:* 17 full-time (11 women), 112 part-time (81 women); includes 40 minority (7 Black or African American, non-Hispanic/Latino; 24 Asian, non-Hispanic/Latino; 4 Hispanic/Latino; 5 Two or more races, non-Hispanic/Latino), 22 international. Average age 32. 71 applicants, 66% accepted, 23 enrolled. In 2013, 51 master's, 14 doctorates awarded. Terminal master's awarded for partial completion of doctoral program. *Degree requirements:* For master's, cumulative integrative project, portfolio; for doctorate, comprehensive exam (for some programs), thesis/dissertation. *Entrance requirements:* For master's, initial certification (for MA); master's degree in music (for Ed M); for doctorate, academic writing sample; audition or performance CD/DVD (for Ed DCT). *Application deadline:* For fall admission, 1/2 priority date for domestic students; for spring admission, 11/1 for domestic students. Applications are processed on a rolling basis. Application fee: $65. Electronic applications accepted. *Financial support:* Fellowships, research assistantships, teaching assistantships, career-related internships or fieldwork, Federal Work-Study, institutionally sponsored loans, and tuition waivers (full and partial) available. Support available to part-time students. Financial award application deadline: 2/1. *Faculty research:* Artistry, creativity, and proficiency in production and performance; educational theory and practice; piano pedagogy; research strategies in music pedagogy. *Unit head:* Prof. Lori Custodero, Program Coordinator, 212-678-3285, E-mail: custodero@tc.edu. *Application contact:* Thomas P. Rock, Director of Admissions, 212-678-3083, Fax: 212-678-4171, E-mail: rock@tc.edu.
Website: http://www.tc.edu/a%26h/MusicEd/.

Temple University, Center for the Arts, Esther Boyer College of Music and Dance, Department of Music, Philadelphia, PA 19122-6096. Offers choral conducting (MM); collaborative piano/chamber music (MM); collaborative piano/opera coaching (MM); composition (MM, PhD); instrumental conducting (MM); music education (MM, PhD); music history (MM); music performance (MM, DMA), including instrumental (MM),

keyboard, voice (DMA), voice/opera (MM); music studies (PhD); music theory (MM, PhD); music therapy (MMT, PhD); musicology (MM, PhD); opera (MM); piano pedagogy (MM); string pedagogy (MM). Part-time programs available. Postbaccalaureate distance learning degree programs offered. *Faculty:* 50 full-time (17 women). *Students:* 170 full-time (101 women), 37 part-time (17 women); includes 31 minority (4 Black or African American, non-Hispanic/Latino; 12 Asian, non-Hispanic/Latino; 9 Hispanic/Latino; 6 Two or more races, non-Hispanic/Latino), 52 international. 407 applicants, 46% accepted, 78 enrolled. In 2013, 52 master's, 16 doctorates awarded. Terminal master's awarded for partial completion of doctoral program. *Degree requirements:* For doctorate, thesis/dissertation. *Entrance requirements:* Additional exam requirements/recommendations for international students: Required—TOEFL. *Application deadline:* For fall admission, 11/15 for international students; for spring admission, 8/1 for international students. Applications are processed on a rolling basis. Application fee: $60. Electronic applications accepted. *Financial support:* Fellowships with full and partial tuition reimbursements, research assistantships with full and partial tuition reimbursements, teaching assistantships with full and partial tuition reimbursements, career-related internships or fieldwork, Federal Work-Study, scholarships/grants, health care benefits, and unspecified assistantships available. Financial award application deadline: 3/1; financial award applicants required to submit FAFSA. *Unit head:* Dr. Robert Stroker, Dean, 215-204-5527, Fax: 215-204-4957, E-mail: rstroker@temple.edu. *Application contact:* James Short, 215-204-8301, Fax: 215-204-4957, E-mail: james.short@temple.edu.
Website: http://www.temple.edu/boyer/academicprograms/.

Tennessee State University, The School of Graduate Studies and Research, College of Liberal Arts, Department of Music, Nashville, TN 37209-1561. Offers music education (M Ed). *Accreditation:* NASM. *Degree requirements:* For master's, thesis optional. *Entrance requirements:* For master's, GRE or MAT. *Faculty research:* Applications of technology in music education; classical guitar performance practice.

Tennessee Technological University, College of Graduate Studies, College of Education, Department of Curriculum and Instruction, Program in Music, Cookeville, TN 38505. Offers MA. Part-time and evening/weekend programs available. *Students:* 2 full-time (0 women). 4 applicants, 50% accepted, 2 enrolled. In 2013, 1 master's awarded. *Degree requirements:* For master's, comprehensive exam, thesis or alternative. *Entrance requirements:* For master's, MAT or GRE. Additional exam requirements/recommendations for international students: Required—TOEFL (minimum score 527 paper-based; 71 iBT), IELTS (minimum score 5.5), PTE (minimum score 48), or TOEIC (Test of English as an International Communication). *Application deadline:* For fall admission, 8/1 for domestic students, 5/1 for international students; for spring admission, 12/1 for domestic students, 10/1 for international students. Applications are processed on a rolling basis. Application fee: $35 ($40 for international students). Electronic applications accepted. *Expenses:* Tuition, state resident: full-time $9347; part-time $465 per credit hour. Tuition, nonresident: full-time $23,635; part-time $1152 per credit hour. *Financial support:* Career-related internships or fieldwork available. *Unit head:* Dr. Jeremy Wendt, Interim Chairperson, 931-372-3181, Fax: 931-372-6270, E-mail: jwendt@tntech.edu. *Application contact:* Shelia K. Kendrick, Coordinator of Graduate Studies, 931-372-3808, Fax: 931-372-3497, E-mail: skendrick@tntech.edu.

Texas A&M University–Commerce, Graduate School, College of Humanities, Social Sciences and Arts, Department of Music, Commerce, TX 75429-3011. Offers music (MA, MS); music composition (MA, MM); music education (MA, MM, MS); music literature (MA); music performance (MA, MM); music theory (MA, MM). *Accreditation:* NASM. Part-time programs available. *Degree requirements:* For master's, comprehensive exam, thesis (for some programs). *Entrance requirements:* For master's, GRE General Test. Electronic applications accepted. *Expenses:* Tuition, state resident: full-time $3630; part-time $2420 per year. Tuition, nonresident: full-time $9948; part-time $6632.16 per year. *Required fees:* $1006 per year. Tuition and fees vary according to course load.

Texas A&M University–Kingsville, College of Graduate Studies, College of Arts and Sciences, Department of Music, Kingsville, TX 78363. Offers music education (MM). *Accreditation:* NASM. *Students:* 1 (woman) part-time; minority (Hispanic/Latino). Average age 41. In 2013, 2 master's awarded. *Degree requirements:* For master's, comprehensive exam, thesis or alternative. *Entrance requirements:* For master's, GRE General Test, minimum GPA of 3.0. Additional exam requirements/recommendations for international students: Required—TOEFL. *Application deadline:* For fall admission, 6/1 for domestic students; for spring admission, 11/15 for domestic students. Applications are processed on a rolling basis. Application fee: $35 ($50 for international students). *Financial support:* Fellowships available. Financial award application deadline: 5/15. *Unit head:* Dr. Robert Scott, Graduate Coordinator, 361-593-2804. *Application contact:* Director of Admissions, 361-593-2315.

Texas Christian University, College of Fine Arts, School of Music, Fort Worth, TX 76129-0002. Offers composition (DMA); conducting (M Mus, DMA); music education (MM Ed); musicology (M Mus); organ performance (M Mus); pedagogy (DMA); percussion (Artist Diploma); performance (DMA); piano (Artist Diploma); piano pedagogy (M Mus); piano performance (M Mus); string performance (M Mus); strings (Artist Diploma); theory/composition (M Mus); vocal performance (M Mus); voice (Artist Diploma); voice pedagogy (M Mus); wind and percussion performance (M Mus); winds (Artist Diploma). *Accreditation:* NASM. *Faculty:* 34 full-time (4 women), 1 (woman) part-time/adjunct. *Students:* 28 full-time (15 women), 25 part-time (9 women); includes 10 minority (4 Asian, non-Hispanic/Latino; 5 Hispanic/Latino; 1 Two or more races, non-Hispanic/Latino), 12 international. Average age 29. 65 applicants, 51% accepted, 21 enrolled. In 2013, 10 master's awarded. *Degree requirements:* For master's, comprehensive exam, thesis (for some programs), thesis or recital; for doctorate, comprehensive exam, thesis/dissertation. *Entrance requirements:* For master's, GRE (for musicology, music education, and music theory/composition), audition or composition/theory, letters of recommendation; for doctorate, GRE, audition, interview. Additional exam requirements/recommendations for international students: Required—TOEFL (minimum score 600 paper-based; 100 iBT). *Application deadline:* For fall admission, 12/1 for domestic and international students; for spring admission, 9/1 for domestic and international students. Application fee: $60. Electronic applications accepted. *Expenses:* Tuition: Part-time $1270 per credit hour. Tuition and fees vary according to course load and program. *Financial support:* In 2013–14, 52 research assistantships with full tuition reimbursements (averaging $6,000 per year) were awarded; career-related internships or fieldwork, institutionally sponsored loans, scholarships/grants, tuition waivers, and unspecified assistantships also available. Financial award application deadline: 12/1; financial award applicants required to submit CSS PROFILE or FAFSA. *Unit head:* Dr. Richard Gipson, Director, 817-257-7602. *Application contact:* Dr. Joseph Butler, Associate Dean, College of Fine Arts, 817-257-6629, E-mail: j.butler@tcu.edu.
Website: http://www.music.tcu.edu/.

Texas State University, Graduate School, College of Fine Arts and Communication, School of Music, Program in Music Education, San Marcos, TX 78666. Offers MM. *Accreditation:* NASM. Part-time programs available. *Faculty:* 12 full-time (1 woman), 4 part-time/adjunct (1 woman). *Students:* 9 full-time (3 women), 7 part-time (2 women); includes 4 minority (1 Black or African American, non-Hispanic/Latino; 3 Hispanic/Latino). Average age 30. 11 applicants, 55% accepted, 5 enrolled. In 2013, 4 master's awarded. *Degree requirements:* For master's, comprehensive exam. *Entrance requirements:* For master's, minimum GPA of 2.75 in last 60 hours of course work. Additional exam requirements/recommendations for international students: Required—TOEFL (minimum score 550 paper-based; 78 iBT). *Application deadline:* For fall admission, 6/15 priority date for domestic students, 6/1 for international students; for spring admission, 10/15 priority date for domestic students, 10/1 for international students. Applications are processed on a rolling basis. Application fee: $40 ($90 for international students). Electronic applications accepted. *Expenses:* Tuition, state resident: full-time $6663; part-time $278 per credit hour. Tuition, nonresident: full-time $15,159; part-time $632 per credit hour. *Required fees:* $1872; $54 per credit hour. $306 per term. Tuition and fees vary according to course load. *Financial support:* In 2013–14, 16 students received support, including 7 teaching assistantships (averaging $6,624 per year); career-related internships or fieldwork, Federal Work-Study, institutionally sponsored loans, scholarships/grants, and unspecified assistantships also available. Support available to part-time students. Financial award application deadline: 4/1; financial award applicants required to submit FAFSA. *Unit head:* Dr. Amy Simmons, Graduate Advisor, 512-245-2651, Fax: 512-245-8181, E-mail: as61@txstate.edu. *Application contact:* Dr. Andrea Golato, Dean of Graduate School, 512-245-2581, Fax: 512-245-8365, E-mail: gradcollege@txstate.edu.
Website: http://www.finearts.txstate.edu/music/.

Texas Tech University, Graduate School, College of Visual and Performing Arts, School of Music, Lubbock, TX 79409-2033. Offers music (MM, DMA); music education (MM Ed). *Accreditation:* NASM. Part-time programs available. *Faculty:* 50 full-time (16 women). *Students:* 95 full-time (49 women), 23 part-time (9 women); includes 19 minority (3 Black or African American, non-Hispanic/Latino; 3 Asian, non-Hispanic/Latino; 10 Hispanic/Latino; 3 Two or more races, non-Hispanic/Latino), 30 international. Average age 30. 114 applicants, 64% accepted, 43 enrolled. In 2013, 26 master's, 15 doctorates awarded. *Degree requirements:* For master's, thesis or alternative; for doctorate, thesis/dissertation. *Entrance requirements:* For master's and doctorate, GRE General Test. Additional exam requirements/recommendations for international students: Required—TOEFL (minimum score 550 paper-based; 79 iBT). *Application deadline:* For fall admission, 6/1 priority date for domestic students, 1/15 priority date for international students; for spring admission, 9/1 priority date for domestic students, 6/15 priority date for international students. Applications are processed on a rolling basis. Application fee: $60. Electronic applications accepted. *Expenses:* Tuition, state resident: full-time $6062; part-time $252.57 per credit hour. Tuition, nonresident: full-time $14,558; part-time $606.57 per credit hour. *Required fees:* $2655; $35 per credit hour. $907.50 per semester. Tuition and fees vary according to course load. *Financial support:* In 2013–14, 94 students received support, including 57 fellowships (averaging $1,908 per year), 65 teaching assistantships (averaging $5,429 per year). Financial award application deadline: 4/15; financial award applicants required to submit FAFSA. *Faculty research:* Strategies for music pedagogy in grades K-12, performance practice of traditional music, role of the woman piano virtuoso, vernacular music center, voice health and culture. Total annual research expenditures: $6,300. *Unit head:* Prof. William Ballenger, Director, 806-742-2270, Fax: 806-742-2294, E-mail: william.ballenger@ttu.edu. *Application contact:* Carin Wanner, Admissions and Scholarship Coordinator, 806-742-2270 Ext. 225, Fax: 806-742-2294, E-mail: melissacarin.wanner@ttu.edu.
Website: http://www.depts.ttu.edu/music.

Towson University, Program in Music Education, Towson, MD 21252-0001. Offers MS, Postbaccalaureate Certificate. *Accreditation:* NASM; NCATE. Part-time and evening/weekend programs available. *Students:* 8 full-time (4 women), 18 part-time (6 women); includes 3 minority (1 Black or African American, non-Hispanic/Latino; 1 Asian, non-Hispanic/Latino; 1 Hispanic/Latino). *Degree requirements:* For master's, thesis optional. *Entrance requirements:* For master's, bachelor's degree in music education or certification as public school music teacher, minimum GPA of 3.0, Placement Examination in Music History and Music Theory; for Postbaccalaureate Certificate, bachelor's degree with certification as a public school music teacher or a degree in music. *Application deadline:* Applications are processed on a rolling basis. Application fee: $45. Electronic applications accepted. *Financial support:* Application deadline: 4/1. *Unit head:* Dr. Dana Rothlisberger, Graduate Program Director, 410-704-2765, E-mail: drothlisberger@towson.edu. *Application contact:* Alicia Arkell-Kleis, Information Contact, 410-704-6004, E-mail: grads@towson.edu.

Troy University, Graduate School, College of Education, Program in Postsecondary Education, Troy, AL 36082. Offers adult education (M Ed); biology (M Ed); criminal justice (M Ed); English (M Ed); foundations of education (M Ed); general science (M Ed); higher education administration (M Ed); history (M Ed); instructional technology (M Ed); mathematics (M Ed); music industry (M Ed); physical fitness (M Ed); political science (M Ed); public administration (M Ed); social science (M Ed); teaching English (M Ed). *Accreditation:* NCATE. Part-time and evening/weekend programs available. *Faculty:* 30 full-time (11 women), 8 part-time/adjunct (1 woman). *Students:* 17 full-time (13 women), 106 part-time (84 women); includes 55 minority (45 Black or African American, non-Hispanic/Latino; 3 Asian, non-Hispanic/Latino; 2 Hispanic/Latino; 5 Two or more races, non-Hispanic/Latino). Average age 34. 109 applicants, 83% accepted, 5 enrolled. In 2013, 130 master's awarded. *Degree requirements:* For master's, comprehensive exam (for some programs), thesis (for some programs), thesis or comprehensive exam. *Entrance requirements:* For master's, GRE (minimum score of 850 on old exam or 290 on new exam), GMAT (minimum score of 380), or MAT (minimum score of 385), bachelor's degree; minimum undergraduate GPA of 2.5 or 3.0 on last 30 semester hours, letter of recommendation. Additional exam requirements/recommendations for international students: Required—TOEFL (minimum score 523 paper-based; 70 iBT), IELTS (minimum score 6). *Application deadline:* Applications are processed on a rolling basis. Application fee: $50. Electronic applications accepted. *Expenses:* Tuition, state resident: full-time $6084; part-time $338 per credit hour. Tuition, nonresident: full-time $12,168; part-time $676 per credit hour. *Required fees:* $630; $35 per credit hour. $50 per semester. *Financial support:* Available to part-time students. Applicants required to submit FAFSA. *Unit head:* Dr. Jan Oliver, Associate Professor, 334-670-3444, Fax: 334-670-3474, E-mail: oliver@troy.edu. *Application contact:* Brenda K. Campbell, Director of Graduate Admissions, 334-670-3178, Fax: 334-670-3733, E-mail: bcamp@troy.edu.

Troy University, Graduate School, College of Education, Program in Teacher Education-Multiple Levels, Troy, AL 36082. Offers art education (MS); gifted education (MS); instrumental (MS); physical education (MS); reading specialist (MS); vocal/choral (MS). Part-time and evening/weekend programs available. *Faculty:* 8 full-time (4 women). *Students:* 2 full-time (both women), 17 part-time (15 women); includes 3 minority (all Black or African American, non-Hispanic/Latino). Average age 30. 9 applicants, 89% accepted, 4 enrolled. In 2013, 19 master's awarded. *Degree requirements:* For master's, comprehensive exam, thesis. *Entrance requirements:* For master's, GRE (minimum score of 850 on old exam or 290 on new exam), GMAT (minimum score of 380), or MAT (minimum score of 385), bachelor's degree; minimum undergraduate GPA of 2.5 or 3.0 on last 30 semester hours, letter of recommendation. Additional exam requirements/recommendations for international students: Required—TOEFL (minimum score 523 paper-based; 70 iBT), IELTS (minimum score 6). *Application deadline:* Applications are processed on a rolling basis. Application fee: $50. Electronic applications accepted. *Expenses:* Tuition, state resident: full-time $6084;

part-time $338 per credit hour. Tuition, nonresident: full-time $12,168; part-time $676 per credit hour. *Required fees:* $630; $35 per credit hour. $50 per semester. *Financial support:* Available to part-time students. Applicants required to submit FAFSA. *Unit head:* Dr. Charlotte S. Minnick, Director, Teacher Education, 334-670-3544, Fax: 334-670-3548, E-mail: csminnick@troy.edu. *Application contact:* Brenda K. Campbell, Director of Graduate Admissions, 334-670-3178, Fax: 334-670-3733, E-mail: bcamp@troy.edu.

Union College, Graduate Programs, Department of Education, Barbourville, KY 40906-1499. Offers elementary education (MA); health and physical education (MA); middle grades (MA); music education (MA); principalship (MA); reading specialist (MA); secondary education (MA); special education (MA). *Degree requirements:* For master's, thesis optional. *Entrance requirements:* For master's, GRE General Test, NTE.

Université Laval, Faculty of Music, Programs in Music, Québec, QC G1K 7P4, Canada. Offers composition (M Mus); instrumental didactics (M Mus); interpretation (M Mus); music education (M Mus, PhD); musicology (M Mus, PhD). Terminal master's awarded for partial completion of doctoral program. *Degree requirements:* For master's, thesis (for some programs); for doctorate, comprehensive exam, thesis/dissertation. *Entrance requirements:* For master's, English exam, audition, knowledge of French; for doctorate, English exam, knowledge of French, third language. Electronic applications accepted.

University at Buffalo, the State University of New York, Graduate School, Graduate School of Education, Department of Learning and Instruction, Buffalo, NY 14260. Offers biology education (Ed M, Certificate); chemistry education (Ed M, Certificate); childhood education (Ed M); childhood education with bilingual extension (Ed M); curriculum, instruction and the science of learning (PhD); early childhood education (Ed M); early childhood education with bilingual extension (birth-grade 2) (Ed M); earth science education (Ed M, Certificate); education studies (Ed M); educational technology and new literacies (Certificate); elementary education (Ed D); English education (Ed M, Certificate); English for speakers of other languages (Ed M); foreign and second language education (PhD); French education (Ed M, Certificate); German education (Ed M, Certificate); gifted education (Certificate); Latin education (Ed M, Certificate); literacy specialist (Ed M); literacy teaching and learning (Certificate); mathematics education (Ed M, Certificate); music education (Ed M, Certificate); physics education (Ed M, Certificate); science and the public (Ed M); social studies education (Ed M, Certificate); Spanish education (Ed M, Certificate); special education (PhD); teaching English to speakers of other languages (Ed M). Part-time and evening/weekend programs available. Postbaccalaureate distance learning degree programs offered (no on-campus study). *Faculty:* 31 full-time (23 women), 64 part-time/adjunct (53 women). *Students:* 275 full-time (215 women), 293 part-time (205 women); includes 35 minority (16 Black or African American, non-Hispanic/Latino; 5 American Indian or Alaska Native, non-Hispanic/Latino; 11 Asian, non-Hispanic/Latino; 3 Hispanic/Latino), 97 international. Average age 30. 544 applicants, 81% accepted, 246 enrolled. In 2013, 222 master's, 17 doctorates, 35 other advanced degrees awarded. *Degree requirements:* For master's, comprehensive exam; for doctorate, thesis/dissertation, research analysis exam, research experience component. *Entrance requirements:* For master's, content test in science and math, letters of reference; for doctorate, GRE General Test or MAT, interview, writing sample, letters of recommendation. Additional exam requirements/recommendations for international students: Required—TOEFL (minimum score 600 paper-based; 96 iBT). *Application deadline:* For fall admission, 2/1 priority date for domestic and international students; for spring admission, 11/15 priority date for domestic students, 10/1 for international students. Applications are processed on a rolling basis. Application fee: $50. Electronic applications accepted. *Financial support:* In 2013–14, 50 fellowships (averaging $8,589 per year), 31 research assistantships with tuition reimbursements (averaging $11,406 per year) were awarded; teaching assistantships, career-related internships or fieldwork, Federal Work-Study, institutionally sponsored loans, scholarships/grants, tuition waivers, and unspecified assistantships also available. Financial award application deadline: 2/28; financial award applicants required to submit FAFSA. *Faculty research:* Science assessment, foreign language teaching and learning, early learning, new literacies, gender and education. *Total annual research expenditures:* $1.7 million. *Unit head:* Dr. Suzanne Miller, Chair, 716-645-2455, Fax: 716-645-3161, E-mail: smiller@buffalo.edu. *Application contact:* Cathy Dimino, Admissions Assistant, 716-645-2110, Fax: 716-645-7937, E-mail: cadimino@buffalo.edu.
Website: http://gse.buffalo.edu/lai.

The University of Akron, Graduate School, Buchtel College of Arts and Sciences, School of Music, Akron, OH 44325. Offers accompanying (MM); composition (MM); music education (MM); music history and literature (MM); music technology (MM); performance (MM); theory (MM). *Accreditation:* NASM. Part-time and evening/weekend programs available. *Faculty:* 17 full-time (5 women), 38 part-time/adjunct (10 women). *Students:* 56 full-time (27 women), 9 part-time (5 women); includes 6 minority (2 Black or African American, non-Hispanic/Latino; 3 Hispanic/Latino; 1 Two or more races, non-Hispanic/Latino), 8 international. Average age 29. 44 applicants, 80% accepted, 18 enrolled. In 2013, 35 master's awarded. *Degree requirements:* For master's, thesis optional. *Entrance requirements:* For master's, minimum GPA of 2.75, interview, audition, letters of recommendation, sample of scholarly writing, portfolio. Additional exam requirements/recommendations for international students: Required—TOEFL (minimum score 550 paper-based; 79 iBT). *Application deadline:* Applications are processed on a rolling basis. Application fee: $40 ($60 for international students). Electronic applications accepted. *Expenses:* Tuition, state resident: full-time $7430; part-time $412.80 per credit hour. Tuition, nonresident: full-time $12,722; part-time $706.80 per credit hour. *Required fees:* $53 per credit hour. $12 per semester. Tuition and fees vary according to course load and program. *Financial support:* In 2013–14, 48 teaching assistantships with full and partial tuition reimbursements were awarded; institutionally sponsored loans and tuition waivers (full and partial) also available. *Faculty research:* Educational reform in the arts, women in music, performance practices, early American composers, Olympic music. *Total annual research expenditures:* $69,902. *Unit head:* Dr. Ann Usher, Interim Director, 330-972-6923, E-mail: ausher@uakron.edu. *Application contact:* Dr. Brooks Toliver, Graduate Director, 330-972-5207, E-mail: brooks2@uakron.edu.
Website: http://www.uakron.edu/music/.

The University of Alabama, Graduate School, College of Arts and Sciences, School of Music, Tuscaloosa, AL 35487. Offers arranging (MM); choral conducting (MM, DMA); church music (MM); composition (MM, DMA); music education (MA, PhD); musicology (MM); performance (MM, DMA); theory (MM); wind conducting (MM, DMA). *Accreditation:* NASM. *Faculty:* 35 full-time (13 women), 1 part-time/adjunct (0 women). *Students:* 49 full-time (19 women), 27 part-time (5 women); includes 11 minority (3 Black or African American, non-Hispanic/Latino; 3 Asian, non-Hispanic/Latino; 3 Hispanic/Latino; 2 Two or more races, non-Hispanic/Latino), 12 international. Average age 30. 80 applicants, 59% accepted, 18 enrolled. In 2013, 12 master's, 14 doctorates awarded. *Degree requirements:* For master's, variable foreign language requirement, comprehensive exam, thesis or alternative, oral and recital; for doctorate, variable foreign language requirement, comprehensive exam, thesis/dissertation, oral and written exams, recitals. *Entrance requirements:* For master's and doctorate, School of Music Audition Exam, audition. Additional exam requirements/recommendations for international students: Required—TOEFL or IELTS. *Application deadline:* For fall admission, 2/1 for domestic students, 5/1 for international students; for winter admission, 2/1 for domestic and international students; for spring admission, 2/1 for domestic students, 10/1 for international students. Applications are processed on a rolling basis. Application fee: $50 ($60 for international students). Electronic applications accepted. *Expenses:* Tuition, state resident: full-time $9450. Tuition, nonresident: full-time $23,950. *Financial support:* In 2013–14, 22 students received support, including 1 fellowship with full tuition reimbursement available (averaging $8,600 per year), 37 teaching assistantships with full and partial tuition reimbursements available (averaging $10,161 per year); institutionally sponsored loans, scholarships/grants, health care benefits, and unspecified assistantships also available. Financial award application deadline: 7/14. *Faculty research:* Performance practice, musicology, theory, composition. *Unit head:* Charles G. Snead, Director, 205-348-7110, Fax: 205-348-1473, E-mail: ssnead@music.ua.edu. *Application contact:* Dr. Linda Cummins, Director of Graduate Studies, 205-348-1465, Fax: 205-348-1473, E-mail: lcummins@ua.edu.
Website: http://www.music.ua.edu/.

The University of Alabama, Graduate School, College of Education, Department of Music Education, Tuscaloosa, AL 35487-0366. Offers choral music education (MA); instrumental music education (MA); music education (Ed D, PhD, Ed S). *Accreditation:* NASM. Part-time programs available. *Degree requirements:* For master's, comprehensive exam, thesis optional; for doctorate, comprehensive exam, thesis/dissertation, oral exam (PhD). *Entrance requirements:* For master's, GRE or MAT, video of teaching, letters of recommendation; for doctorate, GRE or MAT, interview, writing sample, video of teaching, letters of recommendation; for Ed S, GRE or MAT. Additional exam requirements/recommendations for international students: Required—TOEFL (minimum score 550 paper-based). *Application deadline:* For fall admission, 7/1 priority date for domestic students; for spring admission, 11/1 priority date for domestic students. Applications are processed on a rolling basis. Application fee: $50 ($60 for international students). Electronic applications accepted. *Expenses:* Tuition, state resident: full-time $9450. Tuition, nonresident: full-time $23,950. *Financial support:* Research assistantships with full and partial tuition reimbursements and teaching assistantships with full and partial tuition reimbursements available. Financial award application deadline: 3/1. *Faculty research:* Elementary music, music for students with special needs, choral music. *Unit head:* Dr. Carol A. Prickett, Department Head and Professor, 205-348-1432, Fax: 205-348-1675, E-mail: cpricket@bama.ua.edu. *Application contact:* Cathie M. Daniels, Senior Office Associate, 205-348-6054, Fax: 205-348-1675, E-mail: cdaniels@bama.ua.edu.
Website: http://www.musiceducation.ua.edu.

University of Alaska Fairbanks, College of Liberal Arts, Department of Music, Fairbanks, AK 99775-5660. Offers conducting (MA); music education (MA); music history (MA); music theory/composition (MA); performance (MA). *Accreditation:* NASM. Part-time programs available. *Faculty:* 13 full-time (5 women). *Students:* 5 full-time (2 women), 1 (woman) part-time, 1 international. Average age 27. 9 applicants, 67% accepted, 3 enrolled. In 2013, 3 master's awarded. *Degree requirements:* For master's, comprehensive exam, thesis or alternative, oral exam, oral defense. *Entrance requirements:* For master's, evaluative preliminary examination in music theory and history. Additional exam requirements/recommendations for international students: Required—TOEFL (minimum score 550 paper-based; 80 iBT). *Application deadline:* For fall admission, 6/1 for domestic students, 3/1 for international students; for spring admission, 10/15 for domestic students, 9/1 for international students. Applications are processed on a rolling basis. Application fee: $60. Electronic applications accepted. *Expenses:* Tuition, state resident: full-time $7254; part-time $403 per credit. Tuition, nonresident: full-time $14,814; part-time $823 per credit. Tuition and fees vary according to course level, course load and reciprocity agreements. *Financial support:* In 2013–14, 5 teaching assistantships with tuition reimbursements (averaging $12,162 per year) were awarded; fellowships with tuition reimbursements, Federal Work-Study, scholarships/grants, health care benefits, and unspecified assistantships also available. Support available to part-time students. Financial award application deadline: 7/1; financial award applicants required to submit FAFSA. *Unit head:* Dr. Eduard Zilberkant, Department Chair, 907-474-7555, Fax: 907-474-6420, E-mail: uaf.music@alaska.edu. *Application contact:* Libby Eddy, Registrar and Director of Admissions, 907-474-7500, Fax: 907-474-7097, E-mail: admissions@uaf.edu.
Website: http://www.uaf.edu/music/.

The University of Arizona, College of Fine Arts, School of Music, Program in Music, Tucson, AZ 85721. Offers composition (MM); ethnomusicology (MM); music education (MM, PhD); music theory (MM, PhD); musicology (MM); performance (MM), including conducting - choral, conducting - instrumental, instrumental, keyboard, piano accompanying, piano and dance accompanying, vocal. *Faculty:* 40 full-time (11 women), 1 (woman) part-time/adjunct. *Students:* 52 full-time (18 women), 22 part-time (11 women); includes 9 minority (1 Black or African American, non-Hispanic/Latino; 2 Asian, non-Hispanic/Latino; 5 Hispanic/Latino; 1 Two or more races, non-Hispanic/Latino), 15 international. Average age 32. 117 applicants, 32% accepted, 20 enrolled. In 2013, 30 master's, 3 doctorates awarded. *Entrance requirements:* Additional exam requirements/recommendations for international students: Required—TOEFL (minimum score 550 paper-based; 79 iBT). *Application deadline:* For fall admission, 6/1 for domestic students, 12/1 for international students; for spring admission, 10/1 for domestic students, 6/1 for international students. Application fee: $75. Electronic applications accepted. *Expenses:* Tuition, state resident: full-time $11,526. Tuition, nonresident: full-time $27,398. *Financial support:* In 2013–14, 1 research assistantship with full and partial tuition reimbursement (averaging $8,058 per year), 50 teaching assistantships with full and partial tuition reimbursements (averaging $8,899 per year) were awarded. *Faculty research:* Music in general education, psychology of music learning, innovation in string music education, Zarzuela, Franz Liszt's work. *Total annual research expenditures:* $3,300. *Unit head:* Dr. Rex Wood, Director, 520-621-7023, Fax: 520-621-1351, E-mail: rawoods@u.arizona.edu. *Application contact:* Lyneen Elmore, Administrative Associate, 520-621-5929, Fax: 520-621-8118, E-mail: lyneen@u.arizona.edu.

University of Bridgeport, School of Education, Department of Education, Bridgeport, CT 06604. Offers education (MS); educational management (Ed D, Diploma), including intermediate administrator or supervisor (Diploma), leadership (Ed D); elementary education (MS, Diploma), including early childhood education, elementary education; middle school education (MS); music education (MS); remedial reading and language arts (Diploma); secondary education (MS, Diploma), including computer specialist (Diploma), international education (Diploma), reading specialist, secondary education. Part-time and evening/weekend programs available. *Faculty:* 12 full-time (5 women), 108 part-time/adjunct (60 women). *Students:* 155 full-time (108 women), 139 part-time (98 women); includes 48 minority (22 Black or African American, non-Hispanic/Latino; 9 Asian, non-Hispanic/Latino; 15 Hispanic/Latino; 2 Two or more races, non-Hispanic/Latino), 2 international. Average age 30. 306 applicants, 55% accepted, 107 enrolled. In 2013, 153 master's, 16 other advanced degrees awarded. *Degree requirements:* For master's, final exam, final project, or thesis; for doctorate, comprehensive exam, thesis/dissertation; for Diploma, thesis or alternative, final project. *Entrance requirements:* For master's, minimum undergraduate QPA of 2.67; for doctorate, GRE, MAT; for Diploma, GRE General Test or MAT, minimum graduate QPA of 3.0. Additional exam

requirements/recommendations for international students: Recommended—TOEFL (minimum score 550 paper-based; 80 iBT), IELTS (minimum score 6.5). *Application deadline:* For fall admission, 8/1 priority date for domestic and international students; for spring admission, 12/1 priority date for domestic and international students. Applications are processed on a rolling basis. Application fee: $50. Electronic applications accepted. *Expenses:* Contact institution. *Financial support:* In 2013–14, 120 students received support. Fellowships, research assistantships, teaching assistantships, career-related internships or fieldwork, Federal Work-Study, and institutionally sponsored loans available. Support available to part-time students. Financial award application deadline: 6/1; financial award applicants required to submit FAFSA. *Faculty research:* Self-concept, internship assessment, stress and situational development, follow-up of graduation, trend analysis. *Unit head:* Dr. Allen P. Cook, Dean, 203-576-4192, Fax: 203-576-4200, E-mail: acook@bridgeport.edu. *Application contact:* Leanne Proctor, Director of Graduate Admissions, 203-576-4552, Fax: 203-576-4941, E-mail: admit@bridgeport.edu.

The University of British Columbia, Faculty of Education, Department of Curriculum and Pedagogy, Vancouver, BC V6T 1Z4, Canada. Offers art education (M Ed, MA); business education (MA); curriculum studies (M Ed, MA, PhD); home economics education (M Ed, MA); math education (M Ed, MA); music education (M Ed, MA); physical education (M Ed, MA); science education (M Ed, MA); social studies education (M Ed, MA); technology studies education (M Ed, MA). Part-time programs available. Postbaccalaureate distance learning degree programs offered (no on-campus study). *Faculty:* 32 full-time (14 women), 1 (woman) part-time/adjunct. *Students:* 163 full-time, 134 part-time, 42 international. Average age 40. 160 applicants, 75% accepted, 97 enrolled. In 2013, 68 master's, 7 doctorates awarded. *Degree requirements:* For master's, thesis (MA); for doctorate, comprehensive exam, thesis/dissertation. *Entrance requirements:* Additional exam requirements/recommendations for international students: Required—TOEFL (minimum score 580 paper-based; 92 iBT), IELTS (minimum score 6.5). *Application deadline:* For fall admission, 12/1 for domestic and international students; for spring admission, 10/1 for domestic students, 9/1 for international students. Application fee: $90 Canadian dollars ($150 Canadian dollars for international students). Electronic applications accepted. *Expenses:* Contact institution. *Financial support:* In 2013–14, 10 fellowships with partial tuition reimbursements (averaging $16,000 per year), 11 research assistantships with partial tuition reimbursements (averaging $14,000 per year), 27 teaching assistantships with partial tuition reimbursements (averaging $14,000 per year) were awarded; tuition waivers (partial) also available. *Faculty research:* School subjects, teaching and learning. *Unit head:* Dr. Peter Grimmett, Head, 604-822-5422, Fax: 604-822-4714, E-mail: anna.ip@ubc.ca. *Application contact:* Basia Zurek, Graduate Programs Assistant, 604-822-5367, Fax: 604-822-4714, E-mail: edcp.grad@ubc.ca.
Website: http://www.edcp.educ.ubc.ca/.

University of Central Arkansas, Graduate School, College of Fine Arts and Communication, Department of Music, Conway, AR 72035-0001. Offers choral conducting (MM); instrumental conducting (MM); music (PC); music education (MM); music theory (MM); performance (MM). *Accreditation:* NASM. Part-time programs available. *Degree requirements:* For master's, comprehensive exam, thesis optional. *Entrance requirements:* For master's, GRE General Test, minimum GPA of 2.7. Additional exam requirements/recommendations for international students: Required—TOEFL (minimum score 550 paper-based). Electronic applications accepted.

University of Cincinnati, Graduate School, College-Conservatory of Music, Division of Music Education, Cincinnati, OH 45221. Offers MM. *Accreditation:* NASM; NCATE. *Degree requirements:* For master's, comprehensive exam, paper or thesis. *Entrance requirements:* For master's, GRE General Test, interview. Additional exam requirements/recommendations for international students: Required—TOEFL (minimum score 520 paper-based). Electronic applications accepted. *Faculty research:* Choral, orchestral, and wind conducting; Kodaly; Orff-Schulwerk; jazz studies; string education.

University of Colorado Boulder, Graduate School, College of Music, Boulder, CO 80309. Offers composition (M Mus, D Mus A); conducting (M Mus); instrumental conducting and literature (D Mus A); literature and performance of choral music (D Mus A); music education (M Mus Ed, PhD); musicology (PhD); performance (M Mus, D Mus A); performance/pedagogy (M Mus, D Mus A); theory (M Mus). *Accreditation:* NASM. *Faculty:* 55 full-time (20 women). *Students:* 173 full-time (80 women), 53 part-time (25 women); includes 31 minority (2 Black or African American, non-Hispanic/Latino; 14 Asian, non-Hispanic/Latino; 11 Hispanic/Latino; 4 Two or more races, non-Hispanic/Latino), 17 international. Average age 29. 516 applicants, 35% accepted, 70 enrolled. In 2013, 45 master's, 40 doctorates awarded. Terminal master's awarded for partial completion of doctoral program. *Degree requirements:* For master's, variable foreign language requirement, comprehensive exam, thesis or alternative, recital; for doctorate, variable foreign language requirement, thesis/dissertation. *Entrance requirements:* For master's, GRE General Test, GRE Subject Test (music literature), minimum undergraduate GPA of 2.75; for doctorate, GRE General Test, GRE Subject Test, audition, sample of research. *Application deadline:* For fall admission, 12/1 for domestic and international students; for spring admission, 10/1 for domestic and international students. Applications are processed on a rolling basis. Application fee: $50 ($60 for international students). Electronic applications accepted. *Financial support:* In 2013–14, 381 students received support, including 111 fellowships (averaging $2,916 per year), 109 teaching assistantships with full and partial tuition reimbursements available (averaging $18,378 per year); institutionally sponsored loans, scholarships/grants, health care benefits, and unspecified assistantships also available. Financial award application deadline: 3/1; financial award applicants required to submit FAFSA. *Faculty research:* Music, instrumental music, performing arts, chamber music, musicology/music theory.
Website: http://music.colorado.edu/.

University of Connecticut, Graduate School, School of Fine Arts, Department of Music, Storrs, CT 06269. Offers conducting (M Mus, DMA); historical musicology (MA); music (Performer's Certificate); music education (M Mus, PhD); music theory (MA); music theory and history (PhD); performance (M Mus, DMA). *Accreditation:* NASM. Terminal master's awarded for partial completion of doctoral program. *Degree requirements:* For master's, comprehensive exam; for doctorate, thesis/dissertation. *Entrance requirements:* For master's, GRE General Test, GRE Subject Test, audition; for doctorate, GRE Subject Test, MAT, audition. Additional exam requirements/recommendations for international students: Required—TOEFL (minimum score 550 paper-based).

University of Dayton, Department of Teacher Education, Dayton, OH 45469-1300. Offers adolescence to young adult education (MS Ed); early childhood education (MS Ed); early childhood leadership and advocacy (MS Ed); interdisciplinary education studies (MS Ed); intervention specialist education, mild/moderate (MS Ed); literacy (MS Ed); middle childhood education (MS Ed); multi-age education (MS Ed); music education (MS Ed); teacher as leader (MS Ed); technology enhanced learning (MS Ed). Part-time and evening/weekend programs available. Postbaccalaureate distance learning degree programs offered (no on-campus study). *Faculty:* 19 full-time (13 women), 21 part-time/adjunct (18 women). *Students:* 69 full-time (57 women), 86 part-time (75 women); includes 16 minority (10 Black or African American, non-Hispanic/Latino; 2 Asian, non-Hispanic/Latino; 4 Hispanic/Latino), 10 international. Average age 31. 140 applicants, 54% accepted, 39 enrolled. In 2013, 93 master's awarded. *Degree requirements:* For master's, variable foreign language requirement, comprehensive exam (for some programs), thesis. *Entrance requirements:* For master's, GRE or MAT, minimum GPA of 2.75. Additional exam requirements/recommendations for international students: Required—TOEFL (minimum score 550 paper-based; 80 iBT), IELTS (minimum score 6.5). *Application deadline:* For fall admission, 3/1 for domestic students, 5/1 for international students; for winter admission, 7/1 for international students; for spring admission, 11/1 for international students. Applications are processed on a rolling basis. Application fee: $0 ($50 for international students). Electronic applications accepted. *Expenses:* Contact institution. *Financial support:* In 2013–14, 61 students received support, including 5 research assistantships with full tuition reimbursements available (averaging $8,720 per year), 3 teaching assistantships with full tuition reimbursements available (averaging $8,720 per year); career-related internships or fieldwork, institutionally sponsored loans, scholarships/grants, traineeships, health care benefits, and unspecified assistantships also available. Support available to part-time students. Financial award application deadline: 3/1; financial award applicants required to submit FAFSA. *Faculty research:* Diversity, literacy, art representation by young children, preservice teacher preparation. *Unit head:* Dr. Connie L. Bowman, Chair, 937-229-3305, E-mail: cbowman1@udayton.edu. *Application contact:* Gina Seiter, Graduate Program Advisor, 937-229-3103, E-mail: gseiter1@udayton.edu.

University of Delaware, College of Arts and Sciences, Department of Music, Newark, DE 19716. Offers composition (MM); music education (MM); performance (MM). *Accreditation:* NASM. Part-time programs available. *Entrance requirements:* For master's, audition. Additional exam requirements/recommendations for international students: Required—TOEFL. Electronic applications accepted. *Faculty research:* Teaching of music.

University of Denver, Division of Arts, Humanities and Social Sciences, Lamont School of Music, Denver, CO 80208. Offers choral conducting (MM); composition (MM); jazz and commercial music (Certificate); jazz studies (MM); music theory (MA); musicology (MA); orchestral conducting (MM); performance (MM); piano pedagogy (MM); Suzuki pedagogy (MM), including cello, violin; Suzuki teaching (Certificate); wind conducting (MM). *Accreditation:* NASM. Part-time programs available. *Faculty:* 27 full-time (9 women), 36 part-time/adjunct (14 women). *Students:* 28 full-time (17 women), 48 part-time (16 women); includes 12 minority (1 Asian, non-Hispanic/Latino; 9 Hispanic/Latino; 2 Two or more races, non-Hispanic/Latino), 18 international. Average age 26. 118 applicants, 78% accepted, 47 enrolled. In 2013, 26 master's, 1 other advanced degree awarded. *Degree requirements:* For master's, one foreign language, comprehensive exam, recital or project (for performance), thesis (for musicology, music theory, piano pedagogy). *Entrance requirements:* For master's, GRE General Test (for MA only), bachelor's degree, transcripts, personal statement, resume, three letters of recommendation, pre-screen audition (for performance), portfolio (for composition), essay or research paper (for MA only); for Certificate, bachelor's degree, transcripts, personal statement, resume, letters of recommendation, pre-screen video recording or music audition. Additional exam requirements/recommendations for international students: Required—TOEFL (minimum score 550 paper-based; 80 iBT). *Application deadline:* For fall admission, 1/15 priority date for domestic and international students. Applications are processed on a rolling basis. Application fee: $65. Electronic applications accepted. *Financial support:* In 2013–14, 62 students received support, including 35 teaching assistantships with full and partial tuition reimbursements available (averaging $15,456 per year); career-related internships or fieldwork, Federal Work-Study, institutionally sponsored loans, scholarships/grants, tuition waivers, and unspecified assistantships also available. Support available to part-time students. Financial award application deadline: 2/15; financial award applicants required to submit FAFSA. *Faculty research:* Performance, jazz studies and commercial music, musicology, music theory, composition, music pedagogy, music recording and production. *Unit head:* Nancy Cochran, School Director, 303-871-6986, Fax: 303-871-3118, E-mail: nancy.cochran@du.edu. *Application contact:* Colby Carson, Director of Admission, 303-871-6973, Fax: 303-871-3118, E-mail: colby.carson@du.edu.
Website: http://www.du.edu/ahss/schools/lamont/index.html.

University of Florida, Graduate School, College of Fine Arts, School of Music, Gainesville, FL 32611. Offers choral conducting (MM); composition (MM, PhD); electronic music (MM); ethnomusicology (MM); instrumental conducting (MM); music (MM, PhD); music education (MM, PhD), including choral conducting (MM), composition (MM), electronic music (MM), ethnomusicology (MM), instrumental conducting (MM), music education (MM), music history (MM), music theory (MM), performance (MM), piano pedagogy (MM); music history and literature (MM, PhD); music theory (MM); performance (MM); sacred music (MM). *Accreditation:* NASM. *Faculty:* 28 full-time (8 women), 3 part-time/adjunct (0 women). *Students:* 76 full-time (28 women), 70 part-time (33 women); includes 24 minority (12 Black or African American, non-Hispanic/Latino; 1 American Indian or Alaska Native, non-Hispanic/Latino; 2 Asian, non-Hispanic/Latino; 9 Hispanic/Latino), 12 international. Average age 32. 113 applicants, 58% accepted, 45 enrolled. In 2013, 26 master's, 7 doctorates awarded. *Degree requirements:* For master's, variable foreign language requirement, comprehensive exam, thesis, recital; for doctorate, thesis/dissertation. *Entrance requirements:* For master's and doctorate, GRE General Test, audition, minimum GPA of 3.0. Additional exam requirements/recommendations for international students: Required—TOEFL (minimum score 550 paper-based; 80 iBT), IELTS (minimum score 6). *Application deadline:* For fall admission, 1/1 priority date for domestic students, 1/1 for international students; for spring admission, 11/1 for domestic and international students. Applications are processed on a rolling basis. Application fee: $30. Electronic applications accepted. *Expenses:* Tuition, state resident: full-time $12,640. Tuition, nonresident: full-time $30,000. *Financial support:* In 2013–14, 69 students received support, including 2 research assistantships with tuition reimbursements available (averaging $8,352 per year), 83 teaching assistantships with tuition reimbursements available (averaging $8,320 per year); unspecified assistantships also available. Financial award applicants required to submit FAFSA. *Unit head:* John A. Duff, PhD, Program Director and Professor, 352-392-8506, Fax: 352-392-0461, E-mail: jduff@arts.ufl.edu. *Application contact:* Dr. Leslie S. Odom, Associate Professor and Graduate Advisor, 352-273-3172, Fax: 352-352-0461, E-mail: lodom@arts.ufl.edu.
Website: http://www.arts.ufl.edu/welcome/music/.

University of Georgia, College of Education, Program in Music Education, Athens, GA 30602. Offers MM Ed, Ed D, Ed S. *Accreditation:* NASM; NCATE. *Degree requirements:* For doctorate, thesis/dissertation. *Entrance requirements:* For master's, GRE General Test, MAT; for doctorate, GRE General Test; for Ed S, GRE General Test or MAT. Electronic applications accepted.

University of Hartford, The Hartt School, West Hartford, CT 06117-1599. Offers choral conducting (MM Ed); composition (MM, DMA, Artist Diploma, Diploma); conducting (MM, DMA, Artist Diploma, Diploma), including choral (MM, Diploma), instrumental (MM, Diploma); early childhood education (MM Ed); instrumental conducting (MM Ed); Kodály (MM Ed); music (CAGS); music education (DMA, PhD); music history (MM); music theory (MM); pedagogy (MM Ed); performance (MM, MM Ed, DMA, Artist Diploma, Diploma); research (MM Ed); technology (MM Ed). *Accreditation:* NASD. Part-time

programs available. *Degree requirements:* For master's, variable foreign language requirement, thesis (for some programs), recital; for doctorate, variable foreign language requirement, thesis/dissertation (for some programs), recital; for other advanced degree, recital. *Entrance requirements:* For master's, audition, letters of recommendation; for doctorate, proficiency exam, audition, interview, research paper; for other advanced degree, audition. Additional exam requirements/recommendations for international students: Required—TOEFL. Electronic applications accepted. *Expenses:* Contact institution.

University of Houston, College of Liberal Arts and Social Sciences, Moores School of Music, Houston, TX 77204. Offers accompanying and chamber music (MM); applied music (MM); composition (MM); music education (DMA); music theory (MM); performance (DMA). *Accreditation:* NASM. Part-time programs available. *Degree requirements:* For master's, one foreign language, comprehensive exam, recital; for doctorate, one foreign language, comprehensive exam, thesis/dissertation. *Entrance requirements:* For master's, audition, resume, 3 letters of recommendation; for doctorate, writing sample, audition, statement of purpose, resume. Additional exam requirements/recommendations for international students: Required—TOEFL (minimum score 550 paper-based; 79 iBT), IELTS (minimum score 6.5). Electronic applications accepted. *Faculty research:* Twentieth century music, Baroque music, history of music theory, music analysis.

University of Illinois at Urbana–Champaign, Graduate College, College of Fine and Applied Arts, School of Music, Champaign, IL 61820. Offers music (M Mus, AD, DMA); music education (MME, PhD); musicology (PhD). *Accreditation:* NASM. *Students:* 349 (177 women). Application fee: $75 ($90 for international students). *Unit head:* Jeffrey S. Magee, Interim Director, 217-244-2676, Fax: 217-244-4585, E-mail: jmag@illinois.edu. *Application contact:* J. Michael Holmes, Enrollment Management Director, 217-244-9879, Fax: 217-244-4585, E-mail: holmes2@illinois.edu.
Website: http://www.music.illinois.edu/.

The University of Iowa, Graduate College, College of Education, Department of Teaching and Learning, Program in Education, Iowa City, IA 52242-1316. Offers art education (MA); developmental reading (MA); elementary education (MA); English education (MA, MAT); foreign and second language education (MAT); foreign language education (MA); foreign language/ESL education (PhD); language, literacy and culture (PhD); mathematics education (MA, MAT, PhD); music education (MM, PhD); science education (MA); secondary education (MA); social studies (MA, PhD). *Degree requirements:* For master's, thesis optional, exam; for doctorate, comprehensive exam, thesis/dissertation. *Entrance requirements:* For master's and doctorate, GRE General Test, minimum GPA of 3.0. Additional exam requirements/recommendations for international students: Required—TOEFL (minimum score 550 paper-based; 81 iBT). Electronic applications accepted.

The University of Kansas, Graduate Studies, School of Music, Program in Music Education, Lawrence, KS 66045. Offers MME, PhD. *Accreditation:* NASM. *Faculty:* 64. *Students:* 16 full-time (12 women), 7 part-time (all women); includes 1 minority (Asian, non-Hispanic/Latino), 1 international. Average age 39. 19 applicants, 95% accepted, 14 enrolled. In 2013, 7 master's, 3 doctorates awarded. *Degree requirements:* For master's, comprehensive exam, thesis or alternative; for doctorate, comprehensive exam, thesis/dissertation. *Entrance requirements:* For master's, GRE General Test, minimum undergraduate GPA of 3.0, video, letters of reference, transcripts; for doctorate, GRE General Test, MEMT Diagnostic Exam, minimum graduate GPA of 3.5, video, reference letters, transcripts, writing sample, proof of professional experience. Additional exam requirements/recommendations for international students: Required—TOEFL (minimum score 570 paper-based; 92 iBT) or IELTS (minimum score 6). *Application deadline:* For fall admission, 2/15 priority date for domestic students, 2/15 for international students. Applications are processed on a rolling basis. Application fee: $55 ($65 for international students). Electronic applications accepted. *Financial support:* Fellowships with tuition reimbursements, research assistantships, teaching assistantships with full and partial tuition reimbursements, institutionally sponsored loans, scholarships/grants, and unspecified assistantships available. Financial award application deadline: 12/15; financial award applicants required to submit FAFSA. *Faculty research:* Philosophy of music and music education; choral/voice pedagogy, choir acoustics; classroom management, teacher stress; the child voice, children's choirs; string pedagogy, history of string education in American public school systems. *Unit head:* Dr. Robert Walzel, Dean, 785-864-3421, Fax: 785-864-5866, E-mail: music@ku.edu. *Application contact:* Lois Elmer, Administrative Professional, 785-864-4748, Fax: 785-864-9640, E-mail: elmer@ku.edu.
Website: http://music.ku.edu/memt.

University of Kentucky, Graduate School, College of Fine Arts, School of Music, Lexington, KY 40506-0032. Offers music education (MM, PhD); music theory (MA, PhD); music therapy (MM); musical arts (DMA); musicology (MA, PhD); performance (MM); sacred music (MM). *Accreditation:* NASM. Part-time and evening/weekend programs available. *Degree requirements:* For master's, variable foreign language requirement, comprehensive exam, thesis (for some programs); for doctorate, variable foreign language requirement, comprehensive exam, thesis/dissertation. *Entrance requirements:* For master's, GRE General Test, minimum undergraduate GPA of 2.75; for doctorate, GRE General Test, minimum undergraduate GPA of 2.75, graduate 3.0. Additional exam requirements/recommendations for international students: Required—TOEFL (minimum score 550 paper-based). Electronic applications accepted. *Faculty research:* Musicology, music theory, jazz, music education, performance and conducting.

University of Louisiana at Lafayette, College of the Arts, School of Music, Lafayette, LA 70504. Offers conducting (MM); pedagogy (MM); vocal and instrumental performance (MM). *Accreditation:* NASM. *Degree requirements:* For master's, thesis or alternative. *Entrance requirements:* For master's, GRE General Test, minimum GPA of 2.75. Additional exam requirements/recommendations for international students: Required—TOEFL (minimum score 550 paper-based). Electronic applications accepted. *Faculty research:* Nineteenth century American music, trumpet pedagogy, fifteenth century Renaissance polyphony, Charles Ives.

University of Louisiana at Monroe, Graduate School, College of Arts, Education, and Sciences, School of Education, Program in Curriculum and Instruction, Monroe, LA 71209-0001. Offers art education (M Ed); biology education (M Ed); chemistry education (M Ed); curriculum and instruction (Ed D); early childhood education (M Ed); earth science education (M Ed); educational leadership (M Ed); elementary education (1-5) (M Ed); English as a second language (M Ed); English education (M Ed); family and consumer education (M Ed); French education (M Ed); history education (M Ed); math education (M Ed); middle school education (M Ed); music education (M Ed); reading education (K-12) (M Ed); Spanish education (M Ed); special education - academically gifted (M Ed); special education - early intervention (M Ed); special education - educational diagnostician (M Ed); special education - mild/moderate disabilities (M Ed); speech education (M Ed). *Accreditation:* NCATE. *Degree requirements:* For master's, comprehensive exam (for some programs), thesis; for doctorate, thesis/dissertation, internships. *Entrance requirements:* For master's, GRE General Test; for doctorate, GRE General Test, minimum undergraduate GPA of 2.75, graduate 3.25. Additional exam requirements/recommendations for international students: Required—TOEFL (minimum score 500 paper-based; 61 iBT). *Application deadline:* For fall admission, 8/24 priority date for domestic students, 7/1 for international students; for winter admission, 12/14 priority date for domestic students; for spring admission, 1/19 for domestic students, 11/1 for international students. Applications are processed on a rolling basis. Application fee: $20 ($30 for international students). Electronic applications accepted. *Expenses:* Tuition, state resident: full-time $6607. Tuition, nonresident: full-time $17,179. Full-time tuition and fees vary according to program. *Financial support:* Research assistantships, career-related internships or fieldwork, Federal Work-Study, and unspecified assistantships available. Financial award application deadline: 4/1; financial award applicants required to submit FAFSA. *Unit head:* Dr. Dorothy Schween, Director, 318-342-1268, Fax: 318-342-3131, E-mail: schween@ulm.edu. *Application contact:* Dr. Dorothy Schween, Director, 318-342-1268, Fax: 318-342-3131, E-mail: schween@ulm.edu.

University of Louisville, Graduate School, College of Education and Human Development, Department of Teaching and Learning, Louisville, KY 40292-0001. Offers art education (MAT); curriculum and instruction (PhD); early elementary education (MAT); instructional technology (M Ed); interdisciplinary early childhood education (MAT); middle school education (MAT); music education (MAT); secondary education (MAT); special education (MAT); teacher leadership (M Ed). Part-time and evening/weekend programs available. *Students:* 137 full-time (93 women), 208 part-time (131 women); includes 44 minority (25 Black or African American, non-Hispanic/Latino; 1 American Indian or Alaska Native, non-Hispanic/Latino; 3 Asian, non-Hispanic/Latino; 12 Hispanic/Latino; 3 Two or more races, non-Hispanic/Latino), 2 international. Average age 32. 150 applicants, 51% accepted, 54 enrolled. In 2013, 127 master's, 5 doctorates awarded. *Degree requirements:* For doctorate, comprehensive exam, thesis/dissertation. *Entrance requirements:* For master's, GRE General Test, PRAXIS II (for some programs); for doctorate, GRE General Test. Additional exam requirements/recommendations for international students: Required—TOEFL (minimum score 560 paper-based; 83 iBT). *Application deadline:* For fall admission, 5/1 priority date for international students; for spring admission, 11/1 priority date for international students; for summer admission, 4/1 priority date for international students. Application fee: $60. Electronic applications accepted. *Expenses:* Tuition, state resident: full-time $10,788; part-time $599 per credit hour. Tuition, nonresident: full-time $22,446; part-time $1247 per credit hour. *Required fees:* $196. Tuition and fees vary according to program and reciprocity agreements. *Financial support:* Fellowships, research assistantships, teaching assistantships, career-related internships or fieldwork, Federal Work-Study, scholarships/grants, and unspecified assistantships available. Financial award application deadline: 6/1; financial award applicants required to submit FAFSA. *Faculty research:* Mathematics teacher education and ongoing professional development in pedagogy and content knowledge; development of literacy, including early literacy in science and mathematics and literacy development for English language learners; immersive visualizations for promoting STEM education from nanoscience to cosmic scales; evidence-based practices for students with disabilities; urban education, including teacher response to intervention systems in schools and cross-cultural competence. *Unit head:* Dr. Ann E. Larson, Acting Chair, 502-852-6431, Fax: 502-852-1497, E-mail: ann@louisville.edu. *Application contact:* Libby Leggett, Director, Graduate Admissions, 502-852-3101, Fax: 502-852-6536, E-mail: gradadm@louisville.edu.
Website: http://louisville.edu/delphi.

University of Louisville, Graduate School, School of Music, Louisville, KY 40292-0001. Offers music composition (MM); music education (MME); music history and literature (MM); music theory (MM); performance (MM). *Accreditation:* NASM. Part-time and evening/weekend programs available. *Students:* 59 full-time (17 women), 5 part-time (1 woman); includes 6 minority (1 Black or African American, non-Hispanic/Latino; 2 Hispanic/Latino; 3 Two or more races, non-Hispanic/Latino), 10 international. Average age 26. 78 applicants, 67% accepted, 29 enrolled. In 2013, 25 master's awarded. *Degree requirements:* For master's, one foreign language, recital (performance), paper or thesis (music education), major composition (composition). *Entrance requirements:* For master's, GRE General Test, music history and theory entrance exams, jazz entrance exam, audition, portfolio. Additional exam requirements/recommendations for international students: Required—TOEFL (minimum score 550 paper-based; 79 iBT). *Application deadline:* For fall admission, 3/15 priority date for domestic and international students; for spring admission, 11/15 priority date for domestic and international students. Applications are processed on a rolling basis. Application fee: $60. Electronic applications accepted. *Expenses:* Tuition, state resident: full-time $10,788; part-time $599 per credit hour. Tuition, nonresident: full-time $22,446; part-time $1247 per credit hour. *Required fees:* $196. Tuition and fees vary according to program and reciprocity agreements. *Financial support:* Fellowships with full tuition reimbursements, teaching assistantships with full tuition reimbursements, scholarships/grants, health care benefits, tuition waivers (full and partial), and unspecified assistantships available. Financial award application deadline: 3/1; financial award applicants required to submit FAFSA. *Faculty research:* Performance, composition, music education, music therapy, music history. *Total annual research expenditures:* $129,384. *Unit head:* Dr. Christopher Doane, Dean, 502-852-6907, Fax: 502-852-1874, E-mail: doane@louisville.edu. *Application contact:* Toni Robinson, Admissions Counselor, 502-852-1623, Fax: 502-852-0520, E-mail: toni.robinson@louisville.edu.
Website: http://www.louisville.edu/music/.

University of Maine, Graduate School, College of Liberal Arts and Sciences, School of Performing Arts, Orono, ME 04469. Offers music education (MM); music performance (MM). Part-time programs available. *Faculty:* 24 full-time (9 women), 2 part-time/adjunct (1 woman). *Students:* 7 full-time (5 women), 1 (woman) part-time, 3 international. Average age 28. 6 applicants, 50% accepted, 2 enrolled. In 2013, 4 master's awarded. *Entrance requirements:* Additional exam requirements/recommendations for international students: Required—TOEFL. *Application deadline:* For fall admission, 2/1 priority date for domestic students. Applications are processed on a rolling basis. Application fee: $65. Electronic applications accepted. *Expenses:* Tuition, state resident: full-time $7524. Tuition, nonresident: full-time $23,112. *Required fees:* $1970. *Financial support:* In 2013–14, 4 students received support, including 4 teaching assistantships with full tuition reimbursements available (averaging $7,300 per year); career-related internships or fieldwork, Federal Work-Study, institutionally sponsored loans, scholarships/grants, and tuition waivers (full and partial) also available. Support available to part-time students. Financial award application deadline: 3/1. *Unit head:* Dr. Tom Mikotwicz, Chair, 207-581-4702, Fax: 207-581-4701. *Application contact:* Scott G. Delcourt, Associate Dean of the Graduate School, 207-581-3291, Fax: 207-581-3232, E-mail: graduate@maine.edu.
Website: http://umaine.edu/spa/academics/music/.

University of Maryland, Baltimore County, Graduate School, College of Arts, Humanities and Social Sciences, Department of Education, Program in Teaching, Baltimore, MD 21250. Offers early childhood education (MAT); elementary education (MAT); secondary education (MAT), including art, biology, chemistry, dance, earth/space science, English, foreign language, mathematics, music, physics, social studies, theatre. Part-time and evening/weekend programs available. *Faculty:* 24 full-time (18 women), 25 part-time/adjunct (19 women). *Students:* 49 full-time (34 women), 35 part-time (23 women); includes 19 minority (9 Black or African American, non-Hispanic/Latino; 3 Asian, non-Hispanic/Latino; 6 Hispanic/Latino; 1 Two or more races, non-

Hispanic/Latino). Average age 30. 40 applicants, 95% accepted, 35 enrolled. In 2013, 106 master's awarded. *Degree requirements:* For master's, comprehensive exam (for some programs), thesis (for some programs). *Entrance requirements:* For master's, PRAXIS I or SAT (minimum score of 1000), minimum GPA of 3.0. Additional exam requirements/recommendations for international students: Required—TOEFL. *Application deadline:* For fall admission, 6/1 for domestic students; for spring admission, 11/1 for domestic students. Applications are processed on a rolling basis. Application fee: $50. Electronic applications accepted. One-time fee: $200 full-time. *Financial support:* In 2013–14, 6 students received support, including teaching assistantships with full and partial tuition reimbursements available (averaging $12,000 per year); career-related internships or fieldwork, Federal Work-Study, scholarships/grants, tuition waivers, and unspecified assistantships also available. Financial award application deadline: 3/1. *Faculty research:* STEM teacher education, culturally sensitive pedagogy, ESOL/bilingual education, early childhood education, language, literacy and culture. *Unit head:* Dr. Susan M. Blunck, Graduate Program Director, 410-455-2869, Fax: 410-455-3986, E-mail: blunck@umbc.edu. *Application contact:* Dr. Susan M. Blunck, Graduate Program Director, 410-455-2869, Fax: 410-455-3986, E-mail: blunck@umbc.edu. Website: http://www.umbc.edu/education/.

University of Maryland, College Park, Academic Affairs, College of Arts and Humanities, School of Music, Program in Music, College Park, MD 20742. Offers M Ed, MA, MM, DMA, Ed D, PhD. *Students:* 160 full-time (79 women), 50 part-time (25 women); includes 43 minority (13 Black or African American, non-Hispanic/Latino; 17 Asian, non-Hispanic/Latino; 8 Hispanic/Latino; 5 Two or more races, non-Hispanic/Latino), 19 international. 621 applicants, 30% accepted, 86 enrolled. In 2013, 41 master's, 20 doctorates awarded. *Entrance requirements:* For master's, GRE General Test (for ethnomusicology, historical musicology and music theory), 3 letters of recommendation, audition/interview. Additional exam requirements/recommendations for international students: Required—TOEFL. *Application deadline:* For fall admission, 12/1 for domestic and international students. Application fee: $75. *Expenses:* Tuition, state resident: full-time $10,314; part-time $573 per credit hour. Tuition, nonresident: full-time $22,248; part-time $1236 per credit. *Required fees:* $1446; $403.15 per semester. Tuition and fees vary according to program. *Financial support:* In 2013–14, 3 fellowships with full tuition reimbursements (averaging $28,126 per year), 107 teaching assistantships (averaging $16,123 per year) were awarded. *Unit head:* Dr. Robert Gibson, Director, 301-405-5554, E-mail: rgibson@umd.edu. *Application contact:* Dr. Charles A. Caramello, Dean of Graduate School, 301-405-0358, Fax: 301-314-9305, E-mail: ccaramel@umd.edu.

University of Massachusetts Amherst, Graduate School, College of Humanities and Fine Arts, Department of Music and Dance, Amherst, MA 01003. Offers collaborative piano (MM); composition (MM); conducting (MM); jazz composition/arranging (MM); music education (MM); music history (MM); music theory (PhD); performance (MM). *Accreditation:* NASM. Part-time programs available. *Faculty:* 20 full-time (5 women). *Students:* 65 full-time (28 women), 13 part-time (3 women); includes 5 minority (3 Asian, non-Hispanic/Latino; 2 Hispanic/Latino), 8 international. Average age 28. 80 applicants, 58% accepted, 27 enrolled. In 2013, 27 master's, 1 doctorate awarded. Terminal master's awarded for partial completion of doctoral program. *Degree requirements:* For master's, thesis or alternative; for doctorate, comprehensive exam, thesis/dissertation. *Entrance requirements:* For master's and doctorate, placement tests, original scores, research, audition or tape. Additional exam requirements/recommendations for international students: Required—TOEFL (minimum score 550 paper-based; 80 iBT), IELTS (minimum score 6.5). *Application deadline:* For fall admission, 1/15 for domestic and international students; for spring admission, 10/1 for domestic and international students. Applications are processed on a rolling basis. Application fee: $75. Electronic applications accepted. *Financial support:* Fellowships with full and partial tuition reimbursements, research assistantships with full and partial tuition reimbursements, teaching assistantships with full and partial tuition reimbursements, career-related internships or fieldwork, Federal Work-Study, scholarships/grants, traineeships, health care benefits, tuition waivers (full and partial), and unspecified assistantships available. Support available to part-time students. Financial award application deadline: 1/15. *Unit head:* Dr. Jeff Cox, Graduate Program Director, 413-545-0311, Fax: 413-545-2092. *Application contact:* Lindsay DeSantis, Supervisor of Admissions, 413-545-0722, Fax: 413-577-0010, E-mail: gradadm@grad.umass.edu. Website: http://www.umass.edu/music/.

University of Massachusetts Lowell, College of Fine Arts, Humanities and Social Sciences, Department of Music, Lowell, MA 01854-2881. Offers music education (MM); sound recording technology (MM). *Accreditation:* NASM. Part-time programs available. *Degree requirements:* For master's, one foreign language, thesis. *Entrance requirements:* For master's, MAT, audition. Electronic applications accepted.

University of Memphis, Graduate School, College of Communication and Fine Arts, Rudi E. Scheidt School of Music, Memphis, TN 38152. Offers applied music (M Mu, DMA); composition (M Mu, DMA); conducting (M Mu, DMA); historical musicology (PhD); jazz and studio performance (M Mu); music education (M Mu, DMA); musicology (M Mu). *Accreditation:* NASM. Part-time programs available. *Faculty:* 35 full-time (6 women), 6 part-time/adjunct (3 women). *Students:* 75 full-time (25 women), 52 part-time (25 women); includes 24 minority (12 Black or African American, non-Hispanic/Latino; 3 Asian, non-Hispanic/Latino; 5 Hispanic/Latino; 4 Two or more races, non-Hispanic/Latino), 20 international. Average age 32. 84 applicants, 71% accepted, 23 enrolled. In 2013, 13 master's, 10 doctorates awarded. Terminal master's awarded for partial completion of doctoral program. *Degree requirements:* For master's, comprehensive exam, thesis or alternative; for doctorate, one foreign language, comprehensive exam, thesis/dissertation, exam. *Entrance requirements:* For master's, GRE General Test or MAT, proficiency exam, audition; for doctorate, GRE General Test or MAT, proficiency exam, audition, master's degree. Additional exam requirements/recommendations for international students: Required—TOEFL. *Application deadline:* For fall admission, 8/1 for domestic students; for spring admission, 12/1 for domestic students. Applications are processed on a rolling basis. Application fee: $35 ($60 for international students). *Financial support:* In 2013–14, 73 students received support. Research assistantships with full and partial tuition reimbursements available, teaching assistantships with full and partial tuition reimbursements available, Federal Work-Study, scholarships/grants, and unspecified assistantships available. Financial award application deadline: 2/15; financial award applicants required to submit FAFSA. *Faculty research:* Spanish Renaissance, twentieth-century music, Project OPTIMUS, composition, musical performance, regional music, performance, performance practice, composition. *Unit head:* Dr. Patricia J. Hoy, Director, 901-678-2541, Fax: 901-678-3096, E-mail: phoy@memphis.edu. *Application contact:* Dr. John Baur, Assistant Director for Graduate Admissions, 901-678-3362, Fax: 901-678-3096, E-mail: jbaur@memphis.edu. Website: http://www.memphis.edu/music/.

University of Miami, Graduate School, Frost School of Music, Department of Music Education and Music Therapy, Coral Gables, FL 33124. Offers music education (MM, PhD, Spec M); music therapy (MM). *Accreditation:* NASM. *Degree requirements:* For master's, thesis; for doctorate, thesis/dissertation, 2 research tools; for Spec M, thesis, research project. *Entrance requirements:* For master's and doctorate, GRE General Test. Additional exam requirements/recommendations for international students:

Required—TOEFL (minimum score 550 paper-based; 59 iBT). Electronic applications accepted. *Faculty research:* Motivation, quantitative research, early childhood, instrumental music, elementary music.

University of Michigan, Horace H. Rackham School of Graduate Studies, School of Music, Theatre, and Dance, Program in Music Education, Ann Arbor, MI 48109-2085. Offers MM, PhD, Spec M. *Accreditation:* NASM; Teacher Education Accreditation Council. *Degree requirements:* For doctorate, thesis/dissertation, oral and preliminary exams. *Entrance requirements:* For doctorate, MAT, writing sample, portfolio. Additional exam requirements/recommendations for international students: Required—TOEFL. *Application deadline:* For fall admission, 12/1 for domestic and international students. Applications are processed on a rolling basis. Application fee: $75 ($90 for international students). Electronic applications accepted. Tuition and fees vary according to course level, course load, degree level, program and student level. *Financial support:* Teaching assistantships with full and partial tuition reimbursements available. Financial award application deadline: 2/1. *Unit head:* Steven M. Whiting, Associate Dean for Graduate Studies, 734-764-0590, Fax: 734-764-5097, E-mail: stevenmw@umich.edu. *Application contact:* Kelsey Sieverding, Administrative Assistant, 734-764-0590, Fax: 734-763-5097, E-mail: hoshi@umich.edu. Website: http://www.music.umich.edu/.

University of Minnesota, Duluth, Graduate School, School of Fine Arts, Department of Music, Duluth, MN 55812-2496. Offers music education (MM); performance (MM). *Accreditation:* NASM. Part-time programs available. *Degree requirements:* For master's, comprehensive exam, thesis (for some programs), recital (MM in performance). *Entrance requirements:* For master's, audition, minimum GPA of 3.0, sample of written work, interview, bachelor's degree in music, video of teaching. Additional exam requirements/recommendations for international students: Required—TOEFL (minimum score 550 paper-based). *Faculty research:* Band composition, music aesthetics, learning theory, value theory, music advocacy.

University of Missouri, Graduate School, College of Education, Department of Learning, Teaching and Curriculum, Columbia, MO 65211. Offers agricultural education (M Ed, PhD, Ed S); art education (M Ed, PhD, Ed S); business and office education (M Ed, PhD, Ed S); early childhood education (M Ed, PhD, Ed S); elementary education (M Ed, PhD, Ed S); English education (M Ed, PhD, Ed S); foreign language education (M Ed, PhD, Ed S); health education and promotion (M Ed, PhD); learning and instruction (M Ed); marketing education (M Ed, PhD, Ed S); mathematics education (M Ed, PhD, Ed S); music education (M Ed, PhD, Ed S); reading education (M Ed, PhD, Ed S); science education (M Ed, PhD, Ed S); social studies education (M Ed, PhD, Ed S); vocational education (M Ed, PhD, Ed S). Part-time programs available. *Faculty:* 26 full-time (16 women), 3 part-time/adjunct (2 women). *Students:* 186 full-time (143 women), 197 part-time (172 women); includes 19 minority (4 Black or African American, non-Hispanic/Latino; 4 Asian, non-Hispanic/Latino; 6 Hispanic/Latino; 5 Two or more races, non-Hispanic/Latino), 25 international. Average age 31. 288 applicants, 65% accepted, 160 enrolled. In 2013, 202 master's, 18 doctorates, 7 other advanced degrees awarded. Terminal master's awarded for partial completion of doctoral program. *Degree requirements:* For doctorate, thesis/dissertation. *Entrance requirements:* For master's and Ed S, GRE General Test or MAT, minimum GPA of 3.0; for doctorate, GRE General Test, minimum GPA of 3.0. Additional exam requirements/recommendations for international students: Required—TOEFL (minimum score 600 paper-based; 100 iBT). *Application deadline:* For fall admission, 12/1 priority date for domestic and international students. Applications are processed on a rolling basis. Application fee: $55 ($75 for international students). Electronic applications accepted. *Financial support:* Fellowships, research assistantships, teaching assistantships, institutionally sponsored loans, traineeships, health care benefits, and unspecified assistantships available. Support available to part-time students. *Faculty research:* Curriculum development and research, teacher education, art education, business and marketing, early childhood education, English education, literacy/reading education, mathematics education, music education, science education, social studies education. *Unit head:* Dr. James Tarr, Associate Division Director, 573-882-4034, E-mail: tarrj@missouri.edu. *Application contact:* Fran Colley, Academic Advisor, 573-882-6462, E-mail: colleyf@missouri.edu. Website: http://education.missouri.edu/LTC/.

University of Missouri–Kansas City, Conservatory of Music and Dance, Kansas City, MO 64110-2499. Offers composition (MM, DMA); conducting (MM, DMA); music (MA); music education (MME, PhD); music history and literature (MM); music theory (MM); music therapy (MA); musicology (MM); performance (MM, DMA). PhD (interdisciplinary) offered through the School of Graduate Studies. *Accreditation:* NASM. Part-time programs available. *Faculty:* 56 full-time (22 women), 32 part-time/adjunct (13 women). *Students:* 141 full-time (62 women), 67 part-time (31 women); includes 19 minority (7 Black or African American, non-Hispanic/Latino; 6 Asian, non-Hispanic/Latino; 5 Hispanic/Latino; 1 Two or more races, non-Hispanic/Latino), 40 international. Average age 29. 364 applicants, 43% accepted, 75 enrolled. In 2013, 42 master's, 21 doctorates awarded. *Degree requirements:* For master's, variable foreign language requirement, comprehensive exam, thesis (for some programs); for doctorate, variable foreign language requirement, comprehensive exam, thesis/dissertation or alternative. *Entrance requirements:* For master's, minimum GPA of 3.0 in major, auditions (for MM in performance); for doctorate, minimum graduate GPA of 3.5, auditions (for DMA in performance), portfolio of compositions. Additional exam requirements/recommendations for international students: Required—TOEFL (minimum score 550 paper-based; 80 iBT). *Application deadline:* For fall admission, 1/15 priority date for domestic students, 1/15 for international students. Application fee: $45 ($50 for international students). *Expenses:* Tuition, state resident: full-time $6073; part-time $337.40 per credit hour. Tuition, nonresident: full-time $15,680; part-time $871.10 per credit hour. *Required fees:* $97.59 per credit hour. Full-time tuition and fees vary according to program. *Financial support:* In 2013–14, 57 teaching assistantships with partial tuition reimbursements (averaging $8,437 per year) were awarded; career-related internships or fieldwork, Federal Work-Study, institutionally sponsored loans, scholarships/grants, tuition waivers (partial), and unspecified assistantships also available. Support available to part-time students. Financial award application deadline: 3/1; financial award applicants required to submit FAFSA. *Faculty research:* Electro-acoustic composition, affective music responses, American music theatre, Russian choral music, music therapy and Alzheimer's. *Unit head:* Peter Witte, Dean, 816-235-2731, Fax: 816-235-5265, E-mail: wittep@umkc.edu. *Application contact:* William Everett, Associate Dean for Graduate Studies, 816-235-2857, Fax: 816-235-5264, E-mail: everettw@umkc.edu. Website: http://conservatory.umkc.edu/.

University of Missouri–St. Louis, College of Fine Arts and Communication, Program in Music Education, St. Louis, MO 63121. Offers MME. *Accreditation:* NASM. Part-time and evening/weekend programs available. *Faculty:* 13 full-time (6 women), 3 part-time/adjunct (1 woman). *Students:* 3 full-time (0 women), 17 part-time (9 women). Average age 29. 10 applicants, 90% accepted, 8 enrolled. *Entrance requirements:* For master's, 3 letters of recommendation, BA in music education. Additional exam requirements/recommendations for international students: Recommended—TOEFL (minimum score 550 paper-based; 79 iBT), IELTS (minimum score 6.5). *Application deadline:* For fall admission, 7/1 priority date for domestic and international students; for spring

admission, 12/1 for domestic students, 12/1 priority date for international students. Applications are processed on a rolling basis. Application fee: $50 ($40 for international students). Electronic applications accepted. *Expenses:* Tuition, state resident: full-time $7364; part-time $409.10 per credit hour. Tuition, nonresident: full-time $19,162; part-time $1008.50 per credit hour. *Financial support:* Applicants required to submit FAFSA. *Faculty research:* Music technology, musicology, music education methods, history of music education, psychology of music. *Unit head:* Dr. Jennifer Mishra, Director of Graduate Studies, 314-516-5894, Fax: 314-516-6593, E-mail: mishraj@umsl.edu. *Application contact:* 314-516-5458, Fax: 314-516-6996, E-mail: gradadm@umsl.edu. Website: http://www.umsl.edu/~umslmusic/.

The University of Montana, Graduate School, College of Visual and Performing Arts, School of Music, Missoula, MT 59812-0002. Offers music (MM), including composition/technology, music education, musical theater, performance. *Accreditation:* NASM. *Entrance requirements:* For master's, GRE General Test, GRE Subject Test, portfolio.

University of Nebraska at Kearney, Graduate Programs, College of Fine Arts and Humanities, Department of Music, Kearney, NE 68849-0001. Offers music education (MA Ed). *Accreditation:* NCATE. Part-time and evening/weekend programs available. *Degree requirements:* For master's, thesis optional. *Entrance requirements:* For master's, undergraduate degree in music, resume, philosophy of teaching, three letters of recommendation. Additional exam requirements/recommendations for international students: Required—TOEFL (minimum score 550 paper-based; 79 iBT). *Faculty research:* Contemporary American music, musical theatre, opera, woodwind performance and pedagogy.

University of Nebraska–Lincoln, Graduate College, College of Fine and Performing Arts, School of Music, Lincoln, NE 68588. Offers composition (MM, DMA); conducting (MM, DMA); music education (MM, PhD); music history (MM); music theory (MM); performance (MM, DMA); piano pedagogy (MM); woodwind specialties (MM). *Accreditation:* NASM. *Degree requirements:* For master's, thesis optional; for doctorate, comprehensive exam, thesis/dissertation. *Entrance requirements:* For master's and doctorate, audition. Additional exam requirements/recommendations for international students: Required—TOEFL. Electronic applications accepted. *Faculty research:* Mozart, Tchaikovsky, Josquin des Prez, practice of J.S. Bach's organ works, instructional strategies in music education.

University of New Mexico, Graduate School, College of Fine Arts, Department of Music, Albuquerque, NM 87131-0001. Offers collaborative piano (M Mu); conducting (M Mu); music education (M Mu); music history and literature (M Mu); performance (M Mu); theory and composition (M Mu). *Accreditation:* NASM. Part-time programs available. *Faculty:* 32 full-time (8 women), 7 part-time/adjunct (4 women). *Students:* 56 full-time (32 women), 36 part-time (22 women); includes 16 minority (1 Black or African American, non-Hispanic/Latino; 2 Asian, non-Hispanic/Latino; 13 Hispanic/Latino), 6 international. Average age 28. 72 applicants, 60% accepted, 31 enrolled. In 2013, 25 master's awarded. *Degree requirements:* For master's, variable foreign language requirement, comprehensive exam, thesis (for some programs), recital (for some programs). *Entrance requirements:* For master's, placement exams in music history and theory. Additional exam requirements/recommendations for international students: Required—TOEFL (minimum score 550 paper-based). *Application deadline:* For fall admission, 7/1 for domestic students, 5/1 for international students; for spring admission, 11/1 for domestic students, 10/1 for international students. Applications are processed on a rolling basis. Application fee: $50. Electronic applications accepted. *Financial support:* In 2013–14, 74 students received support, including 2 research assistantships (averaging $4,062 per year), 10 teaching assistantships with full and partial tuition reimbursements available (averaging $4,761 per year); Federal Work-Study, scholarships/grants, and unspecified assistantships also available. Support available to part-time students. Financial award application deadline: 2/1; financial award applicants required to submit FAFSA. *Faculty research:* Opera, twentieth-century and contemporary music, performance, conducting. *Total annual research expenditures:* $16,650. *Unit head:* Dr. Steven Block, Chair, 505-277-2127, Fax: 505-277-4202, E-mail: sblock@unm.edu. *Application contact:* Colleen M. Sheinberg, Graduate Coordinator, 505-277-8401, Fax: 505-277-4202, E-mail: colleens@unm.edu. Website: http://music.unm.edu/.

The University of North Carolina at Chapel Hill, Graduate School, School of Education, Program in Secondary Education, Chapel Hill, NC 27599. Offers English (Grades 9-12) (MAT); English as a second language (MAT); French (Grades K-12) (MAT); German (Grades K-12) (MAT); Japanese (Grades K-12) (MAT); Latin (Grades 9-12) (MAT); mathematics (Grades 9-12) (MAT); music (Grades K-12) (MAT); science (Grades 9-12) (MAT); social studies (Grades 9-12) (MAT); Spanish (Grades K-12) (MAT). *Accreditation:* NCATE. *Degree requirements:* For master's, comprehensive exam. *Entrance requirements:* For master's, GRE General Test, minimum GPA of 3.0 during last 2 years of undergraduate course work. Additional exam requirements/recommendations for international students: Required—TOEFL (minimum score 550 paper-based). Electronic applications accepted.

The University of North Carolina at Charlotte, The Graduate School, College of Education, Interdisciplinary Education Programs, Charlotte, NC 28223-0001. Offers art education (MAT); dance education (MAT); elementary education (MAT); English as a second language (MAT); foreign language education (MAT); middle grades education (MAT); music education (MAT); secondary education (MAT); special education (MAT); teacher certification (Graduate Certificate); teaching (Graduate Certificate); theater education (MAT). Part-time programs available. *Students:* 206 full-time (165 women), 791 part-time (628 women); includes 342 minority (247 Black or African American, non-Hispanic/Latino; 16 Asian, non-Hispanic/Latino; 62 Hispanic/Latino; 17 Two or more races, non-Hispanic/Latino), 14 international. Average age 32. 564 applicants, 91% accepted, 414 enrolled. In 2013, 145 master's, 271 other advanced degrees awarded. Terminal master's awarded for partial completion of doctoral program. *Degree requirements:* For master's, thesis. *Entrance requirements:* For master's, GRE or MAT. Additional exam requirements/recommendations for international students: Required—TOEFL (minimum score 550 paper-based; 83 iBT). *Application deadline:* For fall admission, 5/1 priority date for domestic and international students; for spring admission, 10/1 priority date for domestic and international students. Applications are processed on a rolling basis. Application fee: $75. Electronic applications accepted. *Expenses:* Tuition, state resident: full-time $3522. Tuition, nonresident: full-time $16,051. *Required fees:* $2585. Tuition and fees vary according to course load and program. *Total annual research expenditures:* $43,031. *Unit head:* Dr. Warren DiBiase, Chair, 704-687-8881, Fax: 704-687-4705, E-mail: wjdibias@uncc.edu. *Application contact:* Kathy B. Giddings, Director of Graduate Admissions, 704-687-5503, Fax: 704-687-1668, E-mail: gradadm@uncc.edu. Website: http://education.uncc.edu/academic-programs.

The University of North Carolina at Greensboro, Graduate School, School of Music, Theatre and Dance, Greensboro, NC 27412-5001. Offers composition (MM); dance (MA, MFA); education (MM); music education (PhD); performance (MM, DMA); theatre (M Ed, MFA), including acting (MFA), design (MFA), directing (MFA), theatre education (M Ed), theatre for youth (MFA); theory (MM). *Accreditation:* NASM. *Degree requirements:* For master's, variable foreign language requirement, thesis (for some programs), recital; for doctorate, comprehensive exam, thesis/dissertation, diagnostic

exam, recital. *Entrance requirements:* For master's, GRE General Test, NTE, audition; for doctorate, GRE General Test, GRE Subject Test (music), audition. Additional exam requirements/recommendations for international students: Required—TOEFL. Electronic applications accepted.

The University of North Carolina at Pembroke, Graduate Studies, Department of Music, Pembroke, NC 28372-1510. Offers music (MAT); music education (MA). *Accreditation:* NASM. *Entrance requirements:* For master's, GRE or MAT, minimum GPA of 3.0 in major, 2.5 overall; audition. Additional exam requirements/recommendations for international students: Required—TOEFL.

University of North Dakota, Graduate School, College of Arts and Sciences, Department of Music, Grand Forks, ND 58202. Offers music (M Mus); music education (M Mus, DMEd). *Accreditation:* NASM. Part-time programs available. *Degree requirements:* For master's, comprehensive exam, thesis or alternative. *Entrance requirements:* For master's, minimum GPA of 3.0. Additional exam requirements/recommendations for international students: Required—TOEFL (minimum score 550 paper-based; 79 iBT), IELTS (minimum score 6.5). Electronic applications accepted.

University of Northern Colorado, Graduate School, College of Performing and Visual Arts, School of Music, Greeley, CO 80639. Offers collaborative keyboard (MM); conducting (MM); instrumental performance (MM); jazz studies (MM); music conducting (DA); music education (MM, DA); music history and literature (MM, DA); music performance (DA); music theory and composition (MM, DA); vocal performance (MM). *Accreditation:* NASM; NCATE (one or more programs are accredited). Part-time programs available. *Degree requirements:* For master's, comprehensive exam, thesis or alternative; for doctorate, comprehensive exam, thesis/dissertation. *Entrance requirements:* For master's, audition; for doctorate, GRE General Test, audition, 3 letters of recommendation. Electronic applications accepted.

University of Northern Iowa, Graduate College, College of Humanities, Arts and Sciences, School of Music, MA Program in Music Education, Cedar Falls, IA 50614. Offers MM. *Accreditation:* NASM. Part-time and evening/weekend programs available. *Students:* 8 part-time (5 women). 2 applicants, 50% accepted. *Degree requirements:* For master's, comprehensive exam, thesis or alternative. *Entrance requirements:* For master's, written diagnostic exam in theory, music history, expository writing skills, and in the area of claimed competency, portfolio, tape recordings of compositions, in-person auditions, minimum GPA of 3.0. Additional exam requirements/recommendations for international students: Required—TOEFL (minimum score 500 paper-based; 61 iBT). *Application deadline:* For fall admission, 8/1 priority date for domestic students. Applications are processed on a rolling basis. Application fee: $50 ($70 for international students). Electronic applications accepted. *Financial support:* Career-related internships or fieldwork, Federal Work-Study, and tuition waivers (full and partial) available. Support available to part-time students. Financial award application deadline: 2/1. *Unit head:* Dr. Julia Bullard, Coordinator, 319-273-3074, Fax: 319-273-7320, E-mail: julia.bullard@uni.edu. *Application contact:* Laurie S. Russell, Record Analyst, 319-273-2623, Fax: 319-273-2885, E-mail: laurie.russell@uni.edu. Website: http://www.uni.edu/music/.

University of Northern Iowa, Graduate College, College of Humanities, Arts and Sciences, School of Music, Program in Jazz Pedagogy, Cedar Falls, IA 50614. Offers MM. *Students:* 2 applicants. In 2013, 2 master's awarded. *Degree requirements:* For master's, comprehensive exam. *Entrance requirements:* For master's, audition, interview, essay. Application fee: $50 ($70 for international students). *Unit head:* Chris Merz, Coordinator, 319-273-3077, E-mail: chris.merz@uni.edu. *Application contact:* Laurie S. Russell, Record Analyst, 319-273-2623, Fax: 319-273-2885, E-mail: laurie.russell@uni.edu.

University of Northern Iowa, Graduate College, College of Humanities, Arts and Sciences, School of Music, Program in Piano Performance and Pedagogy, Cedar Falls, IA 50614. Offers MM. *Students:* 2 full-time (both women), 2 part-time (both women), 1 international. 6 applicants, 50% accepted, 2 enrolled. In 2013, 2 master's awarded. Application fee: $50 ($70 for international students). *Unit head:* Dr. John F. Vallentine, Director, 319-273-2024, Fax: 319-273-7320, E-mail: john.vallentine@uni.edu. *Application contact:* Laurie S. Russell, Record Analyst, 319-273-2623, Fax: 319-273-2885, E-mail: laurie.russell@uni.edu.

University of North Texas, Robert B. Toulouse School of Graduate Studies, Denton, TN 76203-5017. Offers accounting (MS, PhD); applied anthropology (MA, MS); applied behavior analysis (Certificate); applied technology and performance improvement (M Ed, MS, PhD); art education (MA, PhD); art history (MA); art museum education (Certificate); arts leadership (Certificate); audiology (Au D); behavior analysis (MS); biochemistry and molecular biology (MS, PhD); biology (MA, MS, PhD); business (PhD); business computer information systems (PhD); chemistry (MS, PhD); clinical psychology (PhD); communication studies (MA, MS); computer engineering (MS); computer science (MS); computer science and engineering (PhD); counseling (M Ed, MS, PhD), including clinical mental health counseling (MS), college and university counseling (M Ed, MS), elementary school counseling (M Ed, MS), secondary school counseling (M Ed, MS); counseling psychology (PhD); creative writing (MA); criminal justice (MS); curriculum and instruction (M Ed, PhD), including curriculum studies (PhD), early childhood studies (PhD), language and literacy studies (PhD); decision sciences (MBA); design (MA, MFA), including fashion design (MFA), innovation studies, interior design (MFA); early childhood studies (MS); economics (MS); educational leadership (M Ed, Ed D, PhD); educational psychology (MS), including family studies, gifted and talented (MS, PhD); human development, learning and cognition, research, measurement and evaluation; educational research (PhD), including gifted and talented (MS, PhD), human development and family studies, psychological aspects of sports and exercise, research, measurement and statistics; electrical engineering (MS); emergency management (MPA); engineering systems (MS); English (MA, PhD); environmental science (MS, PhD); experimental psychology (PhD); finance (MBA, MS, PhD); financial management (MPA); French (MA); health psychology and behavioral medicine (PhD); health services management (MBA); higher education (M Ed, Ed D, PhD); history (MA, MS, PhD), including European history (PhD), military history (PhD), United States history (PhD); hospitality management (MS); human resources management (MPA); information science (MS, PhD); information technologies (MBA); information technology and decision sciences (MS); interdisciplinary studies (MA, MS); international sustainable tourism (MS); jazz studies (MM); journalism (MA, MJ, Graduate Certificate), including interactive and virtual digital communication (Graduate Certificate), narrative journalism (Graduate Certificate), public relations (Graduate Certificate); kinesiology (MS); learning technologies (MS, PhD); library science (MS); local government management (MPA); logistics and supply chain management (MBA, PhD); long-term care, senior housing, and aging services (MA, MS); management science (PhD); marketing (MBA, PhD); materials science and engineering (MS, PhD); mathematics (MA, PhD); merchandising (MS); music (MA, MM Ed, PhD), including ethnomusicology (MA), music education (MM Ed, PhD), music theory (MA, PhD), musicology (MA, PhD), performance (MA); nonprofit management (MPA); operations and supply chain management (MBA); performance (MM, DMA); philosophy (MA, PhD); physics (MS, PhD); political science (MA, MS, PhD); public administration and management (PhD), including emergency management, nonprofit management, public financial management, urban management; radio, television and film (MA, MFA); recreation, event and sport

management (MS); rehabilitation counseling (MS, Certificate); sociology (MA, MS, PhD); Spanish (MA); special education (M Ed, PhD), including autism intervention (PhD), emotional/behavioral disorders (PhD), mild/moderate disabilities (PhD); speech-language pathology (MA, MS); strategic management (MBA); studio art (MFA); taxation (MS); teaching (M Ed); MBA/MS; MS/MPH; MSES/MBA. Part-time and evening/weekend programs available. Postbaccalaureate distance learning degree programs offered. *Faculty:* 661 full-time (213 women), 240 part-time/adjunct (144 women). *Students:* 3,106 full-time (1,620 women), 3,543 part-time (2,221 women); includes 1,740 minority (533 Black or African American, non-Hispanic/Latino; 15 American Indian or Alaska Native, non-Hispanic/Latino; 286 Asian, non-Hispanic/Latino; 746 Hispanic/Latino; 3 Native Hawaiian or other Pacific Islander, non-Hispanic/Latino; 157 Two or more races, non-Hispanic/Latino), 1,145 international. Average age 32. 6,289 applicants, 43% accepted, 1751 enrolled. In 2013, 1,778 master's, 239 doctorates, 10 other advanced degrees awarded. Terminal master's awarded for partial completion of doctoral program. *Degree requirements:* For master's, variable foreign language requirement, comprehensive exam (for some programs), thesis (for some programs); for doctorate, variable foreign language requirement, comprehensive exam (for some programs), thesis/dissertation; for other advanced degree, variable foreign language requirement, comprehensive exam (for some programs). *Entrance requirements:* For master's and doctorate, GRE, GMAT. Additional exam requirements/recommendations for international students: Required—TOEFL (minimum score 550 paper-based; 79 iBT). *Application deadline:* For fall admission, 7/15 for domestic students, 3/15 for international students; for spring admission, 11/15 for domestic students, 9/15 for international students; for summer admission, 5/1 for domestic students. Applications are processed on a rolling basis. Application fee: $60. Electronic applications accepted. *Financial support:* Fellowships with partial tuition reimbursements, research assistantships with partial tuition reimbursements, teaching assistantships, career-related internships or fieldwork, Federal Work-Study, institutionally sponsored loans, scholarships/grants, health care benefits, and library assistantships available. Support available to part-time students. Financial award applicants required to submit FAFSA. *Unit head:* Mark Wardell, Dean, 940-565-2383, E-mail: mark.wardell@unt.edu. *Application contact:* Toulouse School of Graduate Studies, 940-565-2383, Fax: 940-565-2141, E-mail: gradsch@unt.edu.
Website: http://tsgs.unt.edu/.

University of Oklahoma, Weitzenhoffer Family College of Fine Arts, School of Music, Norman, OK 73019. Offers choral conducting (M Mus, M Mus Ed); conducting (DMA); instrumental conducting (M Mus, M Mus Ed); music composition (M Mus, DMA); music education (M Mus Ed, PhD), including choral or wind instrument conducting (PhD), general (PhD), Kodaly concepts, piano pedagogy (PhD), primary instruments (M Mus Ed), secondary instruments (M Mus Ed), voice pedagogy (M Mus Ed); music theory (M Mus); musicology (M Mus); organ (M Mus, DMA), including performance; piano (M Mus, DMA), including performance, performance and pedagogy; piano pedagogy (M Mus Ed); vocal/general (M Mus Ed); voice (M Mus, DMA), including performance, performance and pedagogy; wind/percussion/string (M Mus, DMA), including performance. *Accreditation:* NASM. *Faculty:* 58 full-time (21 women), 2 part-time/adjunct (0 women). *Students:* 92 full-time (47 women), 64 part-time (29 women); includes 26 minority (3 Black or African American, non-Hispanic/Latino; 3 American Indian or Alaska Native, non-Hispanic/Latino; 7 Asian, non-Hispanic/Latino; 7 Hispanic/Latino; 6 Two or more races, non-Hispanic/Latino), 21 international. Average age 30. 148 applicants, 51% accepted, 48 enrolled. In 2013, 40 master's, 12 doctorates awarded. *Degree requirements:* For master's, variable foreign language requirement, comprehensive exam (for some programs), thesis (for some programs), major recital (for performance, conducting and composition); for doctorate, variable foreign language requirement, comprehensive exam, thesis/dissertation, 3 public performances (for performance and conducting); 2 public performances (for composition). *Entrance requirements:* For master's, satisfactory auditions/teaching demonstrations/composition portfolios, recommendations, minimum GPA of 3.0; scholarly writing sample (for music theory and musicology programs); for doctorate, satisfactory auditions/teaching demonstrations/composition portfolios, scholarly writing sample, recommendations, minimum GPA of 3.0; 2 years of full-time, professional teaching experience (for PhD in music education). Additional exam requirements/recommendations for international students: Required—TOEFL (minimum score 79 iBT). *Application deadline:* For fall admission, 12/1 for domestic and international students; for spring admission, 9/1 for domestic and international students. Application fee: $50 ($100 for international students). Electronic applications accepted. *Expenses:* Tuition, state resident: full-time $4205; part-time $175.20 per credit hour. Tuition, nonresident: full-time $16,205; part-time $675.20 per credit hour. *Required fees:* $2745; $103.85 per credit hour. $126.50 per semester. *Financial support:* In 2013–14, 109 students received support, including 4 fellowships with full tuition reimbursements available (averaging $5,000 per year), 17 research assistantships with partial tuition reimbursements available (averaging $10,168 per year), 71 teaching assistantships with partial tuition reimbursements available (averaging $10,450 per year); Federal Work-Study and unspecified assistantships also available. Financial award application deadline: 6/1; financial award applicants required to submit FAFSA. *Faculty research:* Piano pedagogy, performance practice, music education, early music, non-Western music. *Total annual research expenditures:* $1,500. *Unit head:* Dr. Lawrence Mallett, Director, 405-325-2081, Fax: 405-325-7574, E-mail: lmallett@ou.edu. *Application contact:* Jan Russell, Graduate Admissions and Recruiting Advisor, 405-325-5393, Fax: 405-325-7574, E-mail: jrussell@ou.edu.
Website: http://music.ou.edu.

University of Oregon, Graduate School, School of Music, Program in Music Education, Eugene, OR 97403. Offers M Mus, DMA, PhD. *Accreditation:* NASM. Part-time programs available. Terminal master's awarded for partial completion of doctoral program. *Degree requirements:* For master's, variable foreign language requirement, thesis (for some programs); for doctorate, one foreign language, comprehensive exam, thesis/dissertation. *Entrance requirements:* For master's, minimum GPA of 3.0, videotape or interview; for doctorate, GRE General Test, minimum GPA of 3.0, videotape or interview. Additional exam requirements/recommendations for international students: Required—TOEFL. *Faculty research:* Psalms of DeLasso, stress and muscular tension in stringed instrument performance, piano music of Stravinsky, learning aptitudes in elementary music.

University of Ottawa, Faculty of Graduate and Postdoctoral Studies, Faculty of Arts, Department of Music, Ottawa, ON K1N 6N5, Canada. Offers music (M Mus, MA); orchestral studies (Certificate); piano pedagogy research (Certificate). *Degree requirements:* For master's, thesis optional. *Entrance requirements:* For master's, honors degree or equivalent, minimum B+ average. Electronic applications accepted. *Faculty research:* Performance, theory, musicology.

University of Rhode Island, Graduate School, College of Arts and Sciences, Department of Music, Kingston, RI 02881. Offers music education (MM); music performance (MM). *Accreditation:* NASM. Part-time programs available. *Faculty:* 12 full-time (5 women). *Students:* 5 full-time (1 woman), 6 part-time (2 women); includes 1 minority (Asian, non-Hispanic/Latino). In 2013, 8 master's awarded. *Entrance requirements:* For master's, 2 letters of recommendation, audition. Additional exam requirements/recommendations for international students: Required—TOEFL (minimum score 550 paper-based). *Application deadline:* For fall admission, 7/15 for domestic students, 2/1 for international students; for spring admission, 11/15 for domestic students, 7/15 for international students. Application fee: $65. Electronic applications accepted. *Expenses:* Tuition, state resident: full-time $11,532; part-time $641 per credit. Tuition, nonresident: full-time $23,606; part-time $1311 per credit. *Required fees:* $1388; $36 per credit. $35 per semester. One-time fee: $130. *Financial support:* In 2013–14, 3 teaching assistantships with full and partial tuition reimbursements (averaging $15,844 per year) were awarded. Financial award application deadline: 3/15; financial award applicants required to submit FAFSA. *Unit head:* Dr. Joe Parillo, Chair, 401-874-2431, Fax: 401-874-2772, E-mail: jparillo@uri.edu. *Application contact:* Dr. Manabu Takasawa, Co-Director of Graduate Studies, 401-874-2790, Fax: 401-874-2772, E-mail: takasawa@uri.edu.
Website: http://www.uri.edu/artsci/mus/.

University of Rhode Island, Graduate School, College of Human Science and Services, School of Education, Kingston, RI 02881. Offers adult education (MA); education (PhD); elementary education (MA); music education (MM); reading education (MA); secondary education (MA); special education (MA); MS/PhD. *Accreditation:* NCATE. Part-time and evening/weekend programs available. *Faculty:* 16 full-time (9 women). *Students:* 64 full-time (48 women), 91 part-time (68 women); includes 17 minority (8 Black or African American, non-Hispanic/Latino; 2 American Indian or Alaska Native, non-Hispanic/Latino; 2 Asian, non-Hispanic/Latino; 3 Hispanic/Latino; 2 Two or more races, non-Hispanic/Latino), 6 international. In 2013, 47 master's, 11 doctorates awarded. *Degree requirements:* For master's, comprehensive exam (for some programs), thesis optional; for doctorate, comprehensive exam, thesis/dissertation. *Entrance requirements:* For master's, 2 letters of recommendation; interview (for special education applicants); for doctorate, GRE, 3 letters of recommendation, resume. Additional exam requirements/recommendations for international students: Required—TOEFL (minimum score 600 paper-based; 100 iBT). *Application deadline:* For fall admission, 1/31 for domestic and international students. Application fee: $65. Electronic applications accepted. *Expenses:* Tuition, state resident: full-time $11,532; part-time $641 per credit. Tuition, nonresident: full-time $23,606; part-time $1311 per credit. *Required fees:* $1388; $36 per credit. $35 per semester. One-time fee: $130. *Financial support:* In 2013–14, 2 research assistantships with full and partial tuition reimbursements (averaging $11,883 per year), 4 teaching assistantships with full and partial tuition reimbursements (averaging $8,488 per year) were awarded; career-related internships or fieldwork also available. Financial award application deadline: 1/31; financial award applicants required to submit FAFSA. *Total annual research expenditures:* $1.1 million. *Unit head:* Dr. David Byrd, Director, 401-874-5484, Fax: 401-874-5471, E-mail: dbyrd@uri.edu. *Application contact:* Graduate Admissions, 401-874-2872, E-mail: gradadm@etal.uri.edu.
Website: http://www.uri.edu/hss/education/.

University of Rochester, Eastman School of Music, Programs in Music Education, Rochester, NY 14627. Offers MA, MM, DMA, PhD. *Expenses: Tuition:* Full-time $44,580; part-time $1394 per credit hour. *Required fees:* $492.

University of St. Thomas, Graduate Studies, College of Arts and Sciences, Graduate Programs in Music Education, St. Paul, MN 55105-1096. Offers choral (MA); instrumental (MA); Kodaly (MA); Orff (MA); piano pedagogy (MA). *Accreditation:* NASM; NCATE. Part-time programs available. *Faculty:* 10 full-time (4 women), 27 part-time/adjunct (12 women). *Students:* 24 part-time (16 women). Average age 30. 4 applicants, 50% accepted, 2 enrolled. In 2013, 26 master's awarded. *Degree requirements:* For master's, comprehensive exam, thesis, music history theory and diagnostic exam, piano recital (for piano pedagogy students). *Entrance requirements:* For master's, performance assessment hearing, interview. Additional exam requirements/recommendations for international students: Required—TOEFL (minimum score 550 paper-based; 80 iBT). *Application deadline:* For fall admission, 7/1 priority date for domestic and international students; for winter admission, 12/1 priority date for domestic and international students; for spring admission, 4/1 priority date for domestic and international students. Applications are processed on a rolling basis. Application fee: $50. Electronic applications accepted. Application fee is waived when completed online. *Financial support:* In 2013–14, 23 students received support. Fellowships, research assistantships, teaching assistantships, Federal Work-Study, institutionally sponsored loans, scholarships/grants, and tuition waivers (partial) available. Financial award application deadline: 4/1; financial award applicants required to submit FAFSA. *Faculty research:* Kodaly, choral, piano pedagogy, Orff, instrumental. *Unit head:* Dr. Doug C. Orzolek, Director, 800-328-6819 Ext. 25878, Fax: 651-962-5886, E-mail: dcorzolek@stthomas.edu. *Application contact:* Bev Johnson, Program Coordinator, Graduate Programs in Music Education, 800-328-6819 Ext. 25870, Fax: 651-962-5886, E-mail: bhjohnson@stthomas.edu.
Website: http://www.stthomas.edu/music/graduate.

University of South Carolina, The Graduate School, School of Music, Columbia, SC 29208. Offers composition (MM, DMA); conducting (MM, DMA); jazz studies (MM); music education (MM Ed, PhD); music history (MM); music performance (Certificate); music theory (MM); opera theater (MM); performance (MM, DMA); piano pedagogy (MM, DMA). *Accreditation:* NASM (one or more programs are accredited). Part-time programs available. *Degree requirements:* For master's, 5 foreign languages, comprehensive exam, thesis (for some programs); for doctorate, one foreign language, comprehensive exam, thesis/dissertation; for Certificate, recitals. *Entrance requirements:* For master's and doctorate, GRE General Test or MAT, music diagnostic exam. Additional exam requirements/recommendations for international students: Required—TOEFL (minimum score 570 paper-based). Electronic applications accepted. *Expenses:* Contact institution. *Faculty research:* Music skills in pre-school children, evaluation of school performing ensembles.

The University of South Dakota, Graduate School, College of Fine Arts, Department of Music, Vermillion, SD 57069-2390. Offers history of musical instruments (MM); music education (MM); music history (MM); music performance (MM). *Accreditation:* NASM. *Degree requirements:* For master's, thesis or alternative. *Entrance requirements:* For master's, minimum GPA of 2.7, audition or performance tape. Additional exam requirements/recommendations for international students: Required—TOEFL (minimum score 550 paper-based; 79 iBT). Electronic applications accepted.

University of Southern California, Graduate School, Thornton School of Music, Los Angeles, CA 90089. Offers brass performance (MM, DMA, Graduate Certificate); choral and sacred music (MM, DMA); classical guitar (MM, DMA, Graduate Certificate); composition (MM, DMA); early music (MA, DMA); harp performance (MM, DMA, Graduate Certificate); historical musicology (PhD); jazz studies (MM, DMA, Graduate Certificate); keyboard collaborative arts (MM, DMA, Graduate Certificate); music education (MM, DMA); organ performance (MM, DMA, Graduate Certificate); percussion performance (MM, DMA, Graduate Certificate); piano performance (MM, DMA, Graduate Certificate); scoring for motion pictures and television (Graduate Certificate); strings performance (MM, DMA, Graduate Certificate); studio jazz guitar (MM, DMA, Graduate Certificate); teaching music (MA); vocal arts (classical voice/opera) (MM, DMA, Graduate Certificate); woodwind performance (MM, DMA, Graduate Certificate). *Accreditation:* NASM. Part-time and evening/weekend programs available. Terminal master's awarded for partial completion of doctoral program. *Degree requirements:* For master's, variable foreign language requirement, comprehensive exam (for some

programs), thesis (for some programs); for doctorate, variable foreign language requirement, comprehensive exam, thesis/dissertation (for some programs). *Entrance requirements:* For master's, GRE (for MA in early music and MM in music education); for doctorate, GRE (for DMA). Additional exam requirements/recommendations for international students: Required—TOEFL (minimum score 560 paper-based; 83 iBT). Electronic applications accepted. *Expenses:* Contact institution. *Faculty research:* Early Modern musical improvisation and composition, maternal sound stimulation of the premature infant, physiological characteristics of jazz guitarists, the musical experience of the very young child, electronic music.

University of Southern Maine, College of Arts, Humanities, and Social Sciences, School of Music, Portland, ME 04104-9300. Offers composition (MM); conducting (MM); jazz studies (MM); music education (MM); pedagogy (MM); performance (MM). *Accreditation:* NASM. *Faculty:* 6 full-time (1 woman), 6 part-time/adjunct (1 woman). *Students:* 4 full-time (2 women), 10 part-time (5 women). Average age 35. 11 applicants, 82% accepted, 4 enrolled. In 2013, 13 master's awarded. Application fee: $65. *Expenses:* Tuition, state resident: part-time $380 per credit. Tuition, nonresident: part-time $1026 per credit. Part-time tuition and fees vary according to program. *Unit head:* Alan Kaschub, Director, 207-780-5387, E-mail: kaschulb@maine.edu. *Application contact:* Mary Sloan, Assistant Dean of Graduate Studies and Director of Graduate Admissions, 207-780-4812, Fax: 207-780-4969, E-mail: gradstudies@usm.maine.edu.
Website: http://usm.maine.edu/music.

University of Southern Mississippi, Graduate School, College of Arts and Letters, School of Music, Hattiesburg, MS 39406-0001. Offers conducting (MM); history and literature (MM); music education (MME, PhD); performance (MM); performance and pedagogy (DMA); theory and composition (MM); woodwind performance (MM). *Accreditation:* NASM. *Faculty:* 33 full-time (10 women), 2 part-time/adjunct (0 women). *Students:* 86 full-time (29 women), 39 part-time (12 women); includes 12 minority (5 Black or African American, non-Hispanic/Latino; 1 Hispanic/Latino; 6 Two or more races, non-Hispanic/Latino), 28 international. Average age 31. 67 applicants, 81% accepted, 43 enrolled. In 2013, 41 master's, 10 doctorates awarded. Terminal master's awarded for partial completion of doctoral program. *Degree requirements:* For master's, comprehensive exam, thesis (for some programs); for doctorate, comprehensive exam, thesis/dissertation. *Entrance requirements:* For master's, GRE General Test, minimum GPA of 2.75 in last 60 hours; for doctorate, GRE General Test, minimum GPA of 3.5. Additional exam requirements/recommendations for international students: Required—TOEFL, IELTS. *Application deadline:* For fall admission, 3/1 priority date for domestic students; for spring admission, 12/13 for domestic students. Applications are processed on a rolling basis. Application fee: $50. *Financial support:* In 2013–14, 1 fellowship with full tuition reimbursement (averaging $12,000 per year), 51 teaching assistantships with full tuition reimbursements (averaging $6,000 per year) were awarded; research assistantships, Federal Work-Study, institutionally sponsored loans, scholarships/grants, health care benefits, tuition waivers (partial), and unspecified assistantships also available. Financial award application deadline: 3/15; financial award applicants required to submit FAFSA. *Faculty research:* Music theory, composition, music performance. *Unit head:* Dr. Michael Miles, Director, 601-266-5543, Fax: 601-266-6427, E-mail: michael.a.miles@usm.edu. *Application contact:* Dr. Jennifer Shank, Director, Graduate Studies, 601-266-5369, Fax: 601-266-6427.
Website: http://www.usm.edu/graduateschool/table.php.

University of South Florida, College of The Arts, School of Music, Tampa, FL 33620-9951. Offers chamber music (MM); choral conducting (MM); electro-acoustic music (MM); instrumental conducting (MM); jazz composition (MM); jazz performance (MM); music composition (MM); music education (MA, PhD); music performance (MM); music theory (MM); piano pedagogy (MM). *Accreditation:* NASM. Part-time and evening/weekend programs available. *Faculty:* 29 full-time (8 women), 9 part-time/adjunct (2 women). *Students:* 77 full-time (30 women), 27 part-time (12 women); includes 19 minority (3 Black or African American, non-Hispanic/Latino; 3 Asian, non-Hispanic/Latino; 9 Hispanic/Latino; 1 Native Hawaiian or other Pacific Islander, non-Hispanic/Latino; 3 Two or more races, non-Hispanic/Latino), 15 international. Average age 31. 93 applicants, 82% accepted, 45 enrolled. In 2013, 32 master's, 3 doctorates awarded. *Degree requirements:* For master's, comprehensive exam, thesis optional; for doctorate, comprehensive exam, thesis/dissertation. *Entrance requirements:* For master's, minimum GPA of 3.0 in upper-division courses and music courses for bachelor's degree; resume; three letters of recommendation; at least 2 years of K-12 music teaching experience (for MA in music education); audition or interview (for MM); for doctorate, GRE General Test, master's degree from accredited institution with minimum GPA of 3.5, 3.0 in upper-division undergraduate courses; at least 2 years of K-12 music teaching experience; interview with faculty; 3 letters of recommendation; academic writing sample; curriculum vitae; personal goals statement; 15-20 minute video of applicant teaching music. Additional exam requirements/recommendations for international students: Required—TOEFL (minimum score 550 paper-based; 79 iBT) or IELTS (minimum score 6.5). *Application deadline:* For fall admission, 2/15 priority date for domestic students, 3/15 for international students; for spring admission, 10/15 for domestic students, 6/1 for international students. Application fee: $30. *Financial support:* In 2013–14, 47 students received support, including 1 research assistantship with tuition reimbursement available (averaging $15,724 per year), 46 teaching assistantships with tuition reimbursements available (averaging $10,099 per year); unspecified assistantships also available. Financial award application deadline: 2/15. *Faculty research:* Music education: alternate methods, community collaboration, contemporary changes, early childhood, general music, international perspectives, multicultural issues, technology, teacher behaviors, philosophy, psychology, sociology; music: chamber music, composition, conducting, jazz studies, music performance, music theory, pedagogy, electronic music. *Total annual research expenditures:* $19,223. *Unit head:* Dr. Josef Knott, Interim Director, 813-974-2311, Fax: 813-974-8721, E-mail: jknott1@usf.edu. *Application contact:* Dr. William Hayden, Associate Professor/Academic Advisor/Graduate Admissions Coordinator, 813-974-1753, Fax: 813-974-8721, E-mail: wphayden@usf.edu.
Website: http://music.arts.usf.edu/.

The University of Tennessee, Graduate School, College of Arts and Sciences, School of Music, Knoxville, TN 37996. Offers accompanying (MM); choral conducting (MM); composition (MM); instrumental conducting (MM); jazz (MM); music education (MM); music theory (MM); musicology (MM); performance (MM); piano pedagogy and literature (MM). *Accreditation:* NASM. Part-time programs available. *Degree requirements:* For master's, thesis (for some programs). *Entrance requirements:* For master's, audition, minimum GPA of 2.7. Additional exam requirements/recommendations for international students: Required—TOEFL. Electronic applications accepted. *Expenses:* Tuition, state resident: full-time $9540; part-time $531 per credit hour. Tuition, nonresident: full-time $27,728; part-time $1542 per credit hour. *Required fees:* $1404; $67 per credit hour.

The University of Tennessee at Chattanooga, Graduate School, College of Arts and Sciences, Program in Music, Chattanooga, TN 37403. Offers music education (MM); performance (MM). *Accreditation:* NASM. Part-time programs available. *Faculty:* 9 full-time (2 women), 1 part-time/adjunct (0 women). *Students:* 7 full-time (4 women), 6 part-time (4 women); includes 2 minority (1 Black or African American, non-Hispanic/Latino; 1 Hispanic/Latino), 1 international. Average age 32. 4 applicants, 100% accepted, 3 enrolled. In 2013, 2 master's awarded. *Degree requirements:* For master's, comprehensive exam, thesis or alternative, recital. *Entrance requirements:* For master's, GRE General Test or MAT, bachelor's degree in music, audition for placement. Additional exam requirements/recommendations for international students: Required—TOEFL (minimum score 550 paper-based; 79 iBT), IELTS (minimum score 6). *Application deadline:* For fall admission, 6/13 priority date for domestic students, 6/1 for international students; for spring admission, 10/15 priority date for domestic students, 10/1 for international students. Applications are processed on a rolling basis. Application fee: $30 ($35 for international students). Electronic applications accepted. *Financial support:* In 2013–14, 4 research assistantships with tuition reimbursements (averaging $5,503 per year) were awarded; Federal Work-Study, scholarships/grants, and unspecified assistantships also available. Financial award applicants required to submit FAFSA. *Faculty research:* Music education, conducting, opera, vocal instruction, orchestras. *Unit head:* Dr. Lee Harris, Department Head, 423-425-4601, Fax: 423-425-4603, E-mail: lee-harris@utc.edu. *Application contact:* Dr. J. Randy Walker, Interim Dean of Graduate Studies, 423-425-4478, Fax: 423-425-5223, E-mail: randy-walker@utc.edu.
Website: http://www.utc.edu/Academic/Music/.

The University of Texas at Arlington, Graduate School, College of Liberal Arts, Department of Music, Arlington, TX 76019. Offers education (MM); performance (MM). *Accreditation:* NASM. Part-time and evening/weekend programs available. *Degree requirements:* For master's, comprehensive exam, thesis optional. *Entrance requirements:* For master's, GRE, 3 letters of recommendation, minimum GPA of 3.0 in last 60 hours of course work. Additional exam requirements/recommendations for international students: Required—TOEFL (minimum score 550 paper-based). Electronic applications accepted.

The University of Texas at Austin, Graduate School, College of Fine Arts, Sarah and Ernest Butler School of Music, Austin, TX 78712-1111. Offers band and wind conducting (M Music, DMA); brass/woodwind/percussion (MM, DMA); chamber music (MM); choral conducting (MM, DMA); collaborative piano (MM, DMA); composition (MM, DMA), including composition, jazz, jazz (DMA); ethnomusicology (MM, PhD); literature and pedagogy (MM); music and human learning (MM, PhD); music and human learning (DMA), including jazz (MM, DMA), piano pedagogy; musicology (MM, PhD); opera performance (MM, DMA); orchestral conducting (MM, DMA); organ (MM), including sacred music; organ performance (MM, DMA); performance (MM), including jazz (MM, DMA); performance (DMA), including jazz (MM, DMA); piano (DMA), including jazz (MM, DMA); piano literature and pedagogy (MM); piano performance (MM, DMA); string performance (MM, DMA); theory (MM, PhD); vocal performance (MM, DMA); voice (DMA), including opera; voice performance pedagogy (DMA); woodwind, brass, percussion performance (MM). *Accreditation:* NASM. Part-time programs available. *Degree requirements:* For master's, one foreign language, comprehensive exam, thesis (for some programs), recital (performance or composition majors); for doctorate, one foreign language, comprehensive exam, thesis/dissertation (for some programs), recital (for performance or composition majors). *Entrance requirements:* For master's and doctorate, GRE General Test (except for performance or composition majors), audition (performance majors). Electronic applications accepted.

The University of Texas at Brownsville, Graduate Studies, College of Liberal Arts, Department of Music, Brownsville, TX 78520-4991. Offers music education (MM). *Accreditation:* NASM. Part-time and evening/weekend programs available. *Faculty:* 14 full-time (5 women). *Students:* 4 part-time (2 women); all minorities (all Hispanic/Latino). 2 applicants, 50% accepted, 1 enrolled. In 2013, 3 master's awarded. *Degree requirements:* For master's, capstone project. *Entrance requirements:* For master's, GRE, Fine Arts Department Music Diagnostic Exam (minimum score of 80%), copy of valid teaching certificate. *Application deadline:* For fall admission, 7/1 priority date for domestic students, 7/1 for international students; for spring admission, 12/1 priority date for domestic students, 12/1 for international students. Applications are processed on a rolling basis. Application fee: $30. Electronic applications accepted. *Expenses:* Tuition, state resident: full-time $3444; part-time $1148 per semester. Tuition, nonresident: full-time $9816. *Required fees:* $1018; $221 per credit hour. $401 per semester. *Unit head:* Dr. Tom Nevill, Chair, 956-882-8247, Fax: 956-882-3808, E-mail: tom.nevill@utb.edu. *Application contact:* Mari Montelongo, Graduate Studies Specialist, 956-882-7787, Fax: 956-882-7279, E-mail: mari.montelongo@utb.edu.
Website: http://www.utb.edu/vpaa/cla/music/Pages/default.aspx.

The University of Texas at El Paso, Graduate School, College of Liberal Arts, Department of Music, El Paso, TX 79968-0001. Offers music education (MM); music performance (MM). *Accreditation:* NASM. Part-time and evening/weekend programs available. *Degree requirements:* For master's, thesis optional. *Entrance requirements:* For master's, audition, interview, letters of recommendation. Additional exam requirements/recommendations for international students: Required—TOEFL; Recommended—IELTS. Electronic applications accepted.

The University of Texas–Pan American, College of Arts and Humanities, Department of Music, Edinburg, TX 78539. Offers ethnomusicology (M Mus); interdisciplinary studies (MAIS); music education (M Mus); performance (M Mus). *Accreditation:* NASM. Part-time programs available. *Degree requirements:* For master's, comprehensive exam, thesis optional, recital (performance). *Entrance requirements:* For master's, audition for performance area, bachelor's degree in music. *Expenses:* Tuition, state resident: full-time $5986; part-time $333 per credit hour. Tuition, nonresident: full-time $12,358; part-time $687 per credit hour. *Required fees:* $782. Tuition and fees vary according to program. *Faculty research:* Music history, instrumental pedagogy, vocal pedagogy, music education, ethnomusicology.

The University of the Arts, College of Performing Arts, School of Music, Division of Music Education, Philadelphia, PA 19102-4944. Offers MAT, MM. MM program offered in conjunction with Villanova University's Summer Music Studies program with summer enrollment only and priority application date of January 1. *Accreditation:* NASM. *Degree requirements:* For master's, student teaching (for MAT); thesis/project (for MM). *Entrance requirements:* For master's, official transcripts, three letters of recommendation, one- to two-page statement, personal interview, undergraduate degree with minimum cumulative GPA of 3.0, DVD/CD or link to uploaded film on YouTube or related site (or VHS video tape for MM), live or taped performance audition (for MAT). Additional exam requirements/recommendations for international students: Required—TOEFL (minimum score 580 paper-based, 92 iBT) or IELTS (minimum score 6.5).

University of the Pacific, Conservatory of Music, Stockton, CA 95211-0197. Offers music education (MM); music therapy (MA). *Accreditation:* NASM. *Faculty:* 4 full-time (2 women), 3 part-time/adjunct (2 women). *Students:* 7 full-time (5 women), 13 part-time (11 women); includes 7 minority (1 Black or African American, non-Hispanic/Latino; 3 Asian, non-Hispanic/Latino; 2 Hispanic/Latino; 1 Two or more races, non-Hispanic/Latino), 2 international. Average age 31. 38 applicants, 39% accepted, 8 enrolled. In 2013, 6 master's awarded. *Entrance requirements:* For master's, GRE General Test. Additional exam requirements/recommendations for international students: Required—TOEFL (minimum score 475 paper-based). *Application deadline:* For fall admission, 3/1 priority date for domestic students; for spring admission, 10/1 priority date for domestic students. Applications are processed on a rolling basis. Application fee: $75. *Financial*

support: Teaching assistantships and institutionally sponsored loans available. Support available to part-time students. Financial award application deadline: 3/1; financial award applicants required to submit FAFSA. *Unit head:* Dr. Giulio Ongaro, Dean, 209-946-2417, E-mail: musicdean@pacific.edu. *Application contact:* Dr. Ruth Brittin, Chairperson, 209-946-2408, E-mail: rbrittin@pacific.edu.

The University of Toledo, College of Graduate Studies, College of Communication and the Arts, Toledo, OH 43606-3390. Offers ME, MME, MMP, Certificate. *Accreditation:* NASM. *Faculty:* 32. *Students:* 2 full-time (0 women), 11 part-time (6 women); includes 1 minority (Hispanic/Latino), 1 international. Average age 28. 12 applicants, 67% accepted, 7 enrolled. In 2013, 6 master's, 11 Certificates awarded. *Degree requirements:* For master's, comprehensive exam, diagnostic theory and history exam. *Entrance requirements:* For master's, GRE if GPA is less than 3.0, minimum cumulative point-hour ratio of 2.7 for all previous academic work, audition. Additional exam requirements/recommendations for international students: Required—TOEFL (minimum score 550 paper-based; 80 iBT). *Application deadline:* For fall admission, 1/15 priority date for domestic and international students. Applications are processed on a rolling basis. Application fee: $45 ($75 for international students). Electronic applications accepted. *Financial support:* In 2013–14, 9 teaching assistantships with full and partial tuition reimbursements (averaging $6,189 per year) were awarded. *Unit head:* Dr. Debra Davis, Dean, 419-530-2448. *Application contact:* Graduate School Office, 419-530-4723, Fax: 419-530-4724, E-mail: grdsch@utnet.utoledo.edu.
Website: http://www.utoledo.edu/cvpa/.

The University of Toledo, College of Graduate Studies, Judith Herb College of Education, Department of Curriculum and Instruction, Toledo, OH 43606-3390. Offers art education (ME); career and technical education (ME); career-technical education (Ed S); curriculum and instruction (ME, PhD, Ed S); early childhood education (PhD, Ed S); education and biology (MES); education and chemistry (MES); education and economics (MAE); education and English (MAE); education and French (MAE); education and geography (MAE); education and geology (MES); education and German (MAE); education and history (MAE); education and mathematics (MAE, MES); education and physics (MES); education and political science (MAE); education and sociology (MAE); education and Spanish (MAE); educational media (PhD); educational technology (ME); educational technology: virtual educator (Certificate); elementary education (PhD); English as a second language (MAE); gifted and talented (PhD); middle childhood education licensure (ME); music education (MME); secondary education (PhD); secondary education licensure (ME); special education (PhD, Ed S). *Accreditation:* NCATE. Part-time and evening/weekend programs available. *Faculty:* 41. *Students:* 53 full-time (30 women), 154 part-time (111 women); includes 21 minority (16 Black or African American, non-Hispanic/Latino; 4 Hispanic/Latino; 1 Two or more races, non-Hispanic/Latino), 21 international. Average age 34. 82 applicants, 79% accepted, 47 enrolled. In 2013, 80 master's, 5 doctorates awarded. *Degree requirements:* For master's, comprehensive exam, thesis or alternative; for doctorate, comprehensive exam, thesis/dissertation; for other advanced degree, thesis optional. *Entrance requirements:* For master's, doctorate, and other advanced degree, minimum cumulative GPA of 2.7 for all previous academic work, letters of recommendation. Additional exam requirements/recommendations for international students: Required—TOEFL (minimum score 550 paper-based; 80 iBT). *Application deadline:* For fall admission, 1/15 priority date for domestic and international students. Applications are processed on a rolling basis. Application fee: $45 ($75 for international students). Electronic applications accepted. *Financial support:* In 2013–14, 5 research assistantships with full and partial tuition reimbursements (averaging $13,200 per year), 11 teaching assistantships with full and partial tuition reimbursements (averaging $8,809 per year) were awarded; career-related internships or fieldwork, Federal Work-Study, institutionally sponsored loans, scholarships/grants, tuition waivers (full and partial), unspecified assistantships, and administrative assistantships also available. Support available to part-time students. *Unit head:* Dr. Joan Kaderavek, Chair, 419-530-5373, E-mail: eigh.chiarelott@utoledo.edu. *Application contact:* Graduate School Office, 419-530-4723, Fax: 419-530-4724, E-mail: grdsch@utnet.utoledo.edu.
Website: http://www.utoledo.edu/eduhshs/.

University of Toronto, School of Graduate Studies, Faculty of Music, Toronto, ON M5S 1A1, Canada. Offers composition (M Mus, DMA); music education (MA, PhD); musicology/theory (MA, PhD); performance (M Mus, DMA). Part-time programs available. *Degree requirements:* For master's, comprehensive exam (for some programs), oral examination (M Mus in composition), 1 foreign language (MA); for doctorate, recital of original works (DMA), thesis (PhD). *Entrance requirements:* For master's, BM in area of specialization with minimum B average in final 2 years, original compositions (M Mus in composition); for doctorate, master's degree in area of specialization, minimum B+ average, at least 2 extended compositions (DMA). Additional exam requirements/recommendations for international students: Required—TOEFL (minimum score 580 paper-based; 93 iBT), TWE (minimum score 5). Electronic applications accepted.

University of Utah, Graduate School, College of Fine Arts, School of Music, Salt Lake City, UT 84112. Offers choral conducting (M Mus, DMA); collaborative piano (M Mus); composition (M Mus, PhD); instrumental conducting (M Mus); instrumental performance (M Mus, DMA); jazz studies (M Mus); music education (M Mus, PhD); music history and literature (M Mus); musicology (MA); organ performance (M Mus); piano performance (M Mus, DMA); string performance and pedagogy (M Mus); theory (M Mus); vocal performance (DMA). *Accreditation:* NASM. *Faculty:* 26 full-time (10 women), 49 part-time/adjunct (17 women). *Students:* 83 full-time (46 women), 42 part-time (19 women); includes 14 minority (1 Black or African American, non-Hispanic/Latino; 5 Asian, non-Hispanic/Latino; 4 Hispanic/Latino; 1 Native Hawaiian or other Pacific Islander, non-Hispanic/Latino; 3 Two or more races, non-Hispanic/Latino), 22 international. Average age 33. 90 applicants, 70% accepted, 33 enrolled. In 2013, 21 master's, 8 doctorates awarded. *Degree requirements:* For master's, variable foreign language requirement, comprehensive exam (for some programs), thesis (for some programs), 1-2 recitals (MM), final oral exam; for doctorate, variable foreign language requirement, comprehensive exam, thesis/dissertation, 4 recitals (DMA), final oral exam. *Entrance requirements:* For master's, placement exams, minimum GPA of 3.0, audition, bachelor's degree in music; for doctorate, placement exams, minimum GPA of 3.0, audition, master's degree in music. Additional exam requirements/recommendations for international students: Required—TOEFL (minimum score 85 iBT). *Application deadline:* For fall admission, 2/15 for domestic students, 1/15 for international students; for spring admission, 10/1 for domestic students, 9/1 for international students; for summer admission, 3/15 for domestic students, 2/15 for international students. Applications are processed on a rolling basis. Application fee: $55 ($65 for international students). Electronic applications accepted. *Expenses:* Tuition, state resident: full-time $5259. Tuition, nonresident: full-time $18,569. *Required fees:* $841. Tuition and fees vary according to course load. *Financial support:* In 2013–14, 76 students received support, including 65 teaching assistantships with full and partial tuition reimbursements available (averaging $9,750 per year); fellowships with full and partial tuition reimbursements available, research assistantships with full and partial tuition reimbursements available, scholarships/grants, health care benefits, and unspecified assistantships also available. Financial award application deadline: 2/1. *Faculty research:* Music education, conducting, musicology, composition, performance. *Total annual research expenditures:* $29,000. *Unit head:* Dr. James Gardner, Director, 801-581-6762, Fax: 801-581-5683, E-mail: jas.gardner@utah.edu. *Application contact:* Heather Severson, Academic Coordinator, 801-585-6972, Fax: 801-581-5683, E-mail: heather.severson@utah.edu.
Website: http://www.music.utah.edu/.

University of Victoria, Faculty of Graduate Studies, Faculty of Education, Department of Curriculum and Instruction, Victoria, BC V8W 2Y2, Canada. Offers art education (M Ed, PhD); curriculum studies (M Ed, MA, PhD); early childhood education (M Ed, PhD); educational studies (PhD); language and literacy (M Ed, MA, PhD); mathematics (M Ed, MA, PhD); music education (M Ed, MA, PhD); science (M Ed, MA, PhD); social studies (M Ed, MA); social, cultural and foundational studies (MA, PhD); technology and environmental education (PhD). Part-time programs available. *Degree requirements:* For master's, thesis, project (M Ed); for doctorate, comprehensive exam, thesis/dissertation. *Entrance requirements:* For master's, minimum B average. Additional exam requirements/recommendations for international students: Required—TOEFL (minimum score 575 paper-based), IELTS (minimum score 7). Electronic applications accepted. *Faculty research:* Elementary and secondary English, language arts, curriculum theory and practice, educational media and technology, educational administration and leadership, history and philosophy of education.

University of Washington, Graduate School, College of Arts and Sciences, School of Music, Concentration in Music Education, Seattle, WA 98195. Offers MA, PhD. *Degree requirements:* For doctorate, thesis/dissertation. *Entrance requirements:* For master's, GRE General Test, GRE Subject Test, minimum GPA of 3.0; for doctorate, GRE General Test, GRE Subject Test, minimum GPA of 3.0, sample of scholarly writing, videotape of teaching, 1 year of teaching experience. Additional exam requirements/recommendations for international students: Required—TOEFL. Electronic applications accepted. *Faculty research:* Multiethnic issues in music instruction, affective responses to music.

University of West Georgia, College of Arts and Humanities, Department of Music, Carrollton, GA 30118. Offers music education (M Mus); performance (M Mus). *Accreditation:* NASM. Part-time programs available. Postbaccalaureate distance learning degree programs offered (no on-campus study). *Faculty:* 8 full-time (3 women), 2 part-time/adjunct (both women). *Students:* 5 full-time (1 woman), 17 part-time (9 women); includes 10 minority (9 Black or African American, non-Hispanic/Latino; 1 American Indian or Alaska Native, non-Hispanic/Latino). Average age 32. 10 applicants, 60% accepted, 4 enrolled. In 2013, 1 master's awarded. *Degree requirements:* For master's, comprehensive exam, thesis optional, recital (for MM in performance), qualifying exam. *Entrance requirements:* For master's, minimum GPA of 2.5, bachelor's degree in music education or teacher certification and essay (for music education); performance evaluation (for performance). Additional exam requirements/recommendations for international students: Required—TOEFL (minimum score 523 paper-based; 69 iBT); Recommended—IELTS (minimum score 6). *Application deadline:* For fall admission, 8/1 for domestic students, 6/1 for international students; for spring admission, 11/15 for domestic students, 10/15 for international students. Applications are processed on a rolling basis. Application fee: $40. Electronic applications accepted. *Expenses:* Tuition, state resident: full-time $4600; part-time $192 per semester hour. Tuition, nonresident: full-time $17,880; part-time $745 per semester hour. *Required fees:* $1858; $46.34 per semester hour. $512 per semester. Tuition and fees vary according to course load, degree level, campus/location and program. *Financial support:* In 2013–14, 1 research assistantship with full tuition reimbursement (averaging $6,000 per year) was awarded; unspecified assistantships also available. Financial award application deadline: 4/1; financial award applicants required to submit FAFSA. *Faculty research:* Musicology, instrumental music/music education, jazz performance, French music. *Unit head:* Dr. Kevin Hibbard, Chair, 678-839-6516, Fax: 678-839-6259, E-mail: khibbard@westga.edu. *Application contact:* Kristy Gamble, Graduate Studies Associate, 678-839-5453, E-mail: kgamble@westga.edu.
Website: http://www.westga.edu/music.

University of Wisconsin–Madison, Graduate School, College of Letters and Science, School of Music, Program in Music Education, Madison, WI 53706-1380. Offers curriculum and instruction (MS, PhD); music education (MM). *Accreditation:* NASM. *Degree requirements:* For doctorate, 2 foreign languages, thesis/dissertation. *Entrance requirements:* For doctorate, GRE General Test. *Expenses:* Tuition, state resident: full-time $10,728; part-time $790 per credit. Tuition, nonresident: full-time $24,054; part-time $1623 per credit. *Required fees:* $1130; $119 per credit.

University of Wisconsin–Madison, Graduate School, School of Education, Department of Curriculum and Instruction, Madison, WI 53706-1380. Offers art education (MA); curriculum and instruction (MS, PhD); education and mathematics (MA); French education (MA); German education (MA); music education (MS); science education (MS); Spanish education (MA). *Accreditation:* NASM (one or more programs are accredited). *Degree requirements:* For doctorate, thesis/dissertation. Application fee: $56. *Expenses:* Tuition, state resident: full-time $10,728; part-time $790 per credit. Tuition, nonresident: full-time $24,054; part-time $1623 per credit. *Required fees:* $1130; $119 per credit. *Financial support:* Project assistantships available. *Unit head:* Dr. Beth Graue, Chair, 608-263-4600, E-mail: graue@education.wisc.edu. *Application contact:* 608-262-2433, Fax: 608-262-5134, E-mail: gradadmiss@mail.bascom.wisc.edu.
Website: http://www.education.wisc.edu/ci.

University of Wisconsin–Milwaukee, Graduate School, Peck School of the Arts, Department of Music, Milwaukee, WI 53201-0413. Offers chamber music performance (Certificate); music composition (MM); music education (MM); music history and literature (MM); opera and vocal arts (Certificate); string pedagogy (MM); MLIS/MM. *Accreditation:* NASM. Part-time programs available. *Faculty:* 16 full-time (5 women). *Students:* 52 full-time (32 women), 13 part-time (10 women); includes 10 minority (1 Asian, non-Hispanic/Latino; 4 Hispanic/Latino; 5 Two or more races, non-Hispanic/Latino), 8 international. Average age 27. 55 applicants, 65% accepted, 26 enrolled. In 2013, 34 master's awarded. *Degree requirements:* For master's, variable foreign language requirement, comprehensive exam, thesis or alternative. *Entrance requirements:* For master's, GRE General Test, GRE Subject Test, audition, interview. Additional exam requirements/recommendations for international students: Required—TOEFL (minimum score 550 paper-based; 79 iBT), IELTS (minimum score 6.5). *Application deadline:* For fall admission, 1/1 priority date for domestic students; for spring admission, 9/1 for domestic students. Applications are processed on a rolling basis. Application fee: $56 ($96 for international students). Electronic applications accepted. *Expenses:* Contact institution. *Financial support:* In 2013–14, 14 teaching assistantships were awarded; fellowships, career-related internships or fieldwork, health care benefits, unspecified assistantships, and project assistantships also available. Support available to part-time students. Financial award application deadline: 4/15. *Unit head:* Jon Welstead, Department Chair, 414-229-4594, E-mail: jonw@uwm.edu. *Application contact:* General Information Contact, 414-229-4982, Fax: 414-229-6967, E-mail: gradschool@uwm.edu.
Website: http://www4.uwm.edu/psoa/music/.

University of Wisconsin–Stevens Point, College of Fine Arts and Communication, Department of Music, Stevens Point, WI 54481-3897. Offers elementary/secondary

(MM Ed); studio pedagogy (MM Ed); Suzuki talent education (MM Ed). *Accreditation:* NASM. Part-time programs available. *Degree requirements:* For master's, thesis or alternative. *Entrance requirements:* For master's, teaching certificate. *Faculty research:* Music education, music composition, music performance.

University of Wyoming, College of Arts and Sciences, Department of Music, Laramie, WY 82071. Offers music education (MME); performance (MM). *Accreditation:* NASM. *Degree requirements:* For master's, comprehensive exam, thesis or alternative. *Entrance requirements:* For master's, minimum GPA of 3.0. Additional exam requirements/recommendations for international students: Required—TOEFL (minimum score 540 paper-based). Electronic applications accepted.

VanderCook College of Music, Master of Music Education Program, Chicago, IL 60616-3731. Offers MM Ed. *Accreditation:* NASM. Part-time programs available. *Faculty:* 9 full-time (5 women), 24 part-time/adjunct (11 women). *Students:* 135 full-time (64 women), 46 part-time (23 women); includes 17 minority (10 Black or African American, non-Hispanic/Latino; 4 Asian, non-Hispanic/Latino; 2 Hispanic/Latino; 1 Two or more races, non-Hispanic/Latino). Average age 30. In 2013, 53 master's awarded. *Degree requirements:* For master's, thesis, written comprehensive exam or professional teaching portfolio. *Entrance requirements:* For master's, minimum of one year of teaching experience, or its equivalent, in music; official transcripts; 3 letters of recommendation; bachelor's degree in music education from accredited college or university or minimum of 60 credits in undergraduate music and music education coursework. Additional exam requirements/recommendations for international students: Required—TOEFL (minimum score 500 paper-based; 70 iBT). *Application deadline:* For fall admission, 4/1 for domestic and international students; for spring admission, 11/1 for domestic and international students. Applications are processed on a rolling basis. Application fee: $50. *Expenses: Tuition:* Full-time $5868. *Required fees:* $525. *Financial support:* Federal Work-Study, scholarships/grants, and unspecified assistantships available. Financial award application deadline: 5/1; financial award applicants required to submit FAFSA. *Unit head:* Ruth Rhodes, Dean of Graduate Studies, 312-788-1145, Fax: 312-225-5211, E-mail: rrhodes@vandercook.edu. *Application contact:* Amy Lenting, Director of Admissions and Retention, 312-788-1120, Fax: 312-225-5211, E-mail: admissions@vandercook.edu.
Website: http://www.vandercook.edu/prospective/graduate.asp.

Virginia Commonwealth University, Graduate School, School of the Arts, Department of Music, Richmond, VA 23284-9005. Offers education (MM). *Accreditation:* NASM. *Degree requirements:* For master's, departmental qualifying exam, recital. *Entrance requirements:* For master's, department examination, audition or tapes, portfolio. Additional exam requirements/recommendations for international students: Required—TOEFL (minimum score 600 paper-based; 100 iBT). Electronic applications accepted. *Faculty research:* Composition, conducting, education, performance.

Washington State University, Graduate School, College of Arts and Sciences, School of Music and Theatre Arts, Pullman, WA 99164-5300. Offers composition (MA); jazz (MA); music (MA); music education (MA); performance (MA). *Accreditation:* NASM. Part-time programs available. *Degree requirements:* For master's, comprehensive exam, thesis (for some programs), oral exam. *Entrance requirements:* For master's, audition, minimum GPA of 3.0, 3 letters of recommendation, composition portfolio and recording (for composition); writing sample and written philosophy (for music education); writing sample (for music history); in-depth audition (for performance). Additional exam requirements/recommendations for international students: Required—TOEFL, IELTS. Electronic applications accepted. *Faculty research:* Music performance, composition, conducting, recording, pedagogy.

Wayne State College, School of Education and Counseling, Department of Educational Foundations and Leadership, Program in Curriculum and Instruction, Wayne, NE 68787. Offers alternative education (MSE); business and information technology education (MSE); communication arts education (MSE); early childhood education (MSE); elementary education (MSE); English as a second language (MSE); English education (MSE); family and consumer sciences education (MSE); industrial technology and vocational education (MSE); learning communities (MSE); mathematics education (MSE); music education (MSE); science education (MSE); social science education (MSE). *Accreditation:* NCATE. Part-time and evening/weekend programs available. *Degree requirements:* For master's, comprehensive exam, thesis optional. *Entrance requirements:* For master's, GRE General Test. Additional exam requirements/recommendations for international students: Required—TOEFL (minimum score 550 paper-based).

Wayne State University, College of Fine, Performing and Communication Arts, Department of Music, Detroit, MI 48202. Offers composition/theory (MM); conducting (MM); jazz performance (MM); music (MA); music education (MM); orchestral studies (Certificate); performance (MM). *Accreditation:* NASM. *Students:* 13 full-time (5 women), 5 part-time (1 woman); includes 3 minority (2 Black or African American, non-Hispanic/Latino; 1 American Indian or Alaska Native, non-Hispanic/Latino), 2 international. Average age 30. 16 applicants, 44% accepted, 3 enrolled. In 2013, 7 master's awarded. *Degree requirements:* For master's, thesis (for some programs), oral examination (for some programs), recital with program notes (for some programs). *Entrance requirements:* For master's, undergraduate degree in same field as desired field of graduate study or equivalent in course work, private study, or experience, audition/interview, apply at least one month before audition date. See department website for audition dates. Applicants are required to pass departmental diagnostic exam in theory and history; for Certificate, undergraduate degree in same field as desired field of graduate study or equivalent in course work, private study, or experience, audition/interview. Additional exam requirements/recommendations for international students: Required—TOEFL (minimum score 550 paper-based; 79 iBT), Michigan English Language Assessment Battery (minimum score 85); Recommended—IELTS (minimum score 6.5), TWE (minimum score 5.5). *Application deadline:* For fall admission, 1/1 for domestic and international students. Applications are processed on a rolling basis. Application fee: $0. Electronic applications accepted. *Expenses:* Contact institution. *Financial support:* In 2013–14, 15 students received support. Career-related internships or fieldwork, institutionally sponsored loans, and scholarships/grants available. Support available to part-time students. Financial award application deadline: 3/31; financial award applicants required to submit FAFSA. *Faculty research:* Teacher training, pedagogy, musicology, composition/theory, conducting/performance practice. *Unit head:* Dr. Norah Duncan, Interim Chair, Department of Music, 313-577-1775, E-mail: norah.duncan@wayne.edu. *Application contact:* Danny DeRose, Academic Services Officer II, 313-577-1783, E-mail: danny.derose@wayne.edu.
Website: http://music.wayne.edu/.

Webster University, Leigh Gerdine College of Fine Arts, Department of Music, St. Louis, MO 63119-3194. Offers church music (MM); composition (MM); jazz studies (MM); music (MA); music education (MM); organ (MM); performance (MM); piano (MM); voice (MM). *Accreditation:* NASM. *Entrance requirements:* Additional exam requirements/recommendations for international students: Required—TOEFL. *Expenses: Tuition:* Full-time $11,610; part-time $645 per credit hour. Tuition and fees vary according to campus/location and program.

West Chester University of Pennsylvania, College of Visual and Performing Arts, Department of Applied Music, West Chester, PA 19383. Offers performance (MM); piano pedagogy (MM, Certificate). Part-time and evening/weekend programs available. *Faculty:* 18 full-time (6 women), 3 part-time/adjunct (2 women). *Students:* 17 full-time (8 women), 16 part-time (6 women); includes 3 minority (1 Black or African American, non-Hispanic/Latino; 1 Hispanic/Latino; 1 Native Hawaiian or other Pacific Islander, non-Hispanic/Latino), 11 international. Average age 31. 20 applicants, 85% accepted, 11 enrolled. In 2013, 8 master's awarded. *Degree requirements:* For master's, comprehensive exam, thesis optional, recital. *Entrance requirements:* For master's and Certificate, School of Music Graduate Admission Test (GAT), audition, interview. Additional exam requirements/recommendations for international students: Required—TOEFL (minimum score 550 paper-based; 80 iBT). *Application deadline:* For fall admission, 4/15 priority date for domestic students, 3/15 for international students; for spring admission, 10/15 priority date for domestic students, 9/1 for international students. Applications are processed on a rolling basis. Application fee: $45. Electronic applications accepted. *Expenses:* Tuition, state resident: full-time $7956; part-time $442 per credit. Tuition, nonresident: full-time $11,934; part-time $663 per credit. *Required fees:* $2134.20; $106.24 per credit. Tuition and fees vary according to campus/location and program. *Financial support:* Unspecified assistantships available. Support available to part-time students. Financial award application deadline: 2/15; financial award applicants required to submit FAFSA. *Unit head:* Dr. Chris Hanning, Chair, 610-436-4178, Fax: 610-436-2873, E-mail: channing@wcupa.edu. *Application contact:* Dr. M. Gregory Martin, Graduate Coordinator, 610-436-2070, Fax: 610-436-2873, E-mail: mmartin@wcupa.edu.
Website: http://www.wcupa.edu/cvpa/music/am/grad.asp.

West Chester University of Pennsylvania, College of Visual and Performing Arts, Department of Music Education, West Chester, PA 19383. Offers Kodaly methodology (Certificate); music education (Teaching Certificate); music technology (Certificate); Orff-Schulwerk (Certificate); performance (MM); research (MM); technology (MM). *Accreditation:* NASM; NCATE. Part-time programs available. *Faculty:* 3 full-time (1 woman). *Students:* 3 full-time (1 woman), 30 part-time (18 women); includes 2 minority (1 Asian, non-Hispanic/Latino; 1 Hispanic/Latino). Average age 29. 21 applicants, 81% accepted, 11 enrolled. In 2013, 17 master's, 3 Certificates awarded. *Degree requirements:* For master's, comprehensive exam, thesis optional, recital. *Entrance requirements:* For master's and other advanced degree, School of Music Graduate Admission Test (GAT), audition, interview. Additional exam requirements/recommendations for international students: Required—TOEFL (minimum score 550 paper-based; 80 iBT). *Application deadline:* For fall admission, 4/15 priority date for domestic students, 3/15 for international students; for spring admission, 10/15 priority date for domestic students, 9/1 for international students. Applications are processed on a rolling basis. Application fee: $45. Electronic applications accepted. *Expenses:* Tuition, state resident: full-time $7956; part-time $442 per credit. Tuition, nonresident: full-time $11,934; part-time $663 per credit. *Required fees:* $2134.20; $106.24 per credit. Tuition and fees vary according to campus/location and program. *Financial support:* Unspecified assistantships available. Support available to part-time students. Financial award application deadline: 2/15; financial award applicants required to submit FAFSA. *Faculty research:* Developing music listening skills. *Unit head:* Dr. J. Bryan Burton, Chair and Graduate Coordinator, 610-436-2222, Fax: 610-436-2873, E-mail: jburton@wcupa.edu. *Application contact:* Dr. M. Gregory Martin, Graduate Coordinator, 610-436-2070, E-mail: mmartin@wcupa.edu.
Website: http://www.wcupa.edu/cvpa/music/me/grad.asp.

Western Connecticut State University, Division of Graduate Studies, School of Visual and Performing Arts, Music Department, Danbury, CT 06810-6885. Offers music education (MS). *Accreditation:* NASM. Part-time programs available. *Degree requirements:* For master's, thesis or comprehensive exam, completion of program within 6 years. *Entrance requirements:* For master's, minimum GPA of 2.8, teaching certificate. Additional exam requirements/recommendations for international students: Recommended—TOEFL (minimum score 550 paper-based; 79 iBT), IELTS (minimum score 6). *Faculty research:* Ear training.

Western Kentucky University, Graduate Studies, Potter College of Arts and Letters, Department of Music, Bowling Green, KY 42101. Offers MA Ed. *Accreditation:* NASM; NCATE. Part-time and evening/weekend programs available. *Degree requirements:* For master's, comprehensive exam, written exam. *Entrance requirements:* For master's, GRE General Test, minimum GPA of 3.0. Additional exam requirements/recommendations for international students: Required—TOEFL (minimum score 555 paper-based; 79 iBT). *Faculty research:* Music education, music technology, performance.

Western Michigan University, Graduate College, College of Fine Arts, School of Music, Kalamazoo, MI 49008. Offers composition (MM); conducting (MM); music (MA); music education (MM); music therapy (MM); performance (MM). *Accreditation:* NASM.

West Virginia University, College of Creative Arts, Division of Music, Morgantown, WV 26506. Offers music composition (MM, DMA); music education (MM, PhD); music history (MM); music performance (MM, DMA); music theory (MM). *Accreditation:* NASM. *Degree requirements:* For master's, comprehensive exam, thesis (for some programs), recitals; for doctorate, variable foreign language requirement, comprehensive exam, thesis/dissertation, recitals (DMA). *Entrance requirements:* For master's, GRE General Test (music history), minimum GPA of 3.0, audition; for doctorate, GRE General Test (music education), minimum GPA of 3.0, audition. Additional exam requirements/recommendations for international students: Required—TOEFL. *Faculty research:* Jazz history, seventeenth century French court music, nineteenth century composition theory.

Wichita State University, Graduate School, College of Fine Arts, School of Music, Wichita, KS 67260. Offers music (MM); music education (MME). *Accreditation:* NASM. Part-time programs available. *Unit head:* Prof. Russ Widener, Director, 316-978-6435, Fax: 316-978-3625, E-mail: russ.widener@wichita.edu. *Application contact:* Jordan Oleson, Admissions Coordinator, 316-978-3095, Fax: 316-978-3253, E-mail: jordan.oleson@wichita.edu.
Website: http://www.wichita.edu/.

Winthrop University, College of Visual and Performing Arts, Department of Music, Rock Hill, SC 29733. Offers conducting (MM); music education (MME); performance (MM). *Accreditation:* NASM. Part-time programs available. *Degree requirements:* For master's, oral and written exams, recital (MM). *Entrance requirements:* For master's, GRE General Test, audition, minimum GPA of 3.0, 2 recitals. Electronic applications accepted.

Wright State University, School of Graduate Studies, College of Liberal Arts, Department of Music, Dayton, OH 45435. Offers music education (M Mus); performance (M Mus). *Accreditation:* NASM. Part-time programs available. *Degree requirements:* For master's, thesis or alternative, oral exam. *Entrance requirements:* For master's, theory placement test, BA in music. Additional exam requirements/recommendations for international students: Required—TOEFL. *Faculty research:* General music, current needs, role of teacher, expectations in music education.

Youngstown State University, Graduate School, College of Fine and Performing Arts, Dana School of Music, Youngstown, OH 44555-0001. Offers jazz studies (MM); music

education (MM); music history and literature (MM); music theory and composition (MM); performance (MM). *Accreditation:* NASM. Part-time and evening/weekend programs available. *Degree requirements:* For master's, one foreign language, thesis optional; final qualifying exam. *Entrance requirements:* For master's, audition; GRE General Test

or minimum GPA of 2.7. Additional exam requirements/recommendations for international students: Required—TOEFL. *Faculty research:* Teaching education, use of computers, conducting.

Reading Education

Adelphi University, Ruth S. Ammon School of Education, Program in Literacy, Garden City, NY 11530-0701. Offers birth-grade 12 (MS); birth-grade 6 (MS); grades 5-12 (MS). Part-time and evening/weekend programs available. *Students:* 8 full-time (all women), 20 part-time (all women); includes 7 minority (2 Asian, non-Hispanic/Latino; 4 Hispanic/Latino; 1 Two or more races, non-Hispanic/Latino). Average age 29. In 2013, 15 master's awarded. *Entrance requirements:* For master's, 2 letters of recommendation, resume, valid New York state teaching certification. Additional exam requirements/recommendations for international students: Required—TOEFL (minimum score 550 paper-based; 80 iBT). *Application deadline:* For fall admission, 4/1 priority date for domestic students, 4/1 for international students; for spring admission, 11/1 priority date for domestic students, 11/1 for international students. Applications are processed on a rolling basis. Application fee: $50. Electronic applications accepted. *Expenses: Tuition:* Full-time $32,530; part-time $1010 per credit. *Required fees:* $1150. Tuition and fees vary according to degree level and program. *Financial support:* Career-related internships or fieldwork, Federal Work-Study, institutionally sponsored loans, and tuition waivers (full) available. Support available to part-time students. Financial award application deadline: 2/15; financial award applicants required to submit FAFSA. *Faculty research:* Assessment and intervention, literacy education and development, higher and teacher education, human and adult development, achieving styles and human motivation. *Unit head:* Dr. Lori Wolf, Director, 516-877-4104, E-mail: wolf@adelphi.edu. *Application contact:* Christine Murphy, Director of Admissions, 516-877-3050, Fax: 516-877-3039, E-mail: graduateadmissions@adelphi.edu.

Alabama State University, College of Education, Department of Curriculum and Instruction, Montgomery, AL 36101-0271. Offers early childhood education (M Ed, Ed S); elementary education (M Ed, Ed S); secondary education (M Ed, Ed S), including biology education, English language arts education (M Ed), history education, math education, music education (M Ed), reading education (M Ed), social science education; special education (M Ed). Part-time programs available. *Faculty:* 11 full-time (8 women), 13 part-time/adjunct (10 women). *Students:* 32 full-time (19 women), 162 part-time (136 women); includes 189 minority (187 Black or African American, non-Hispanic/Latino; 1 Hispanic/Latino; 1 Two or more races, non-Hispanic/Latino). Average age 33. 99 applicants, 45% accepted, 34 enrolled. In 2013, 74 master's, 20 Ed Ss awarded. *Degree requirements:* For master's, comprehensive exam, thesis optional; for Ed S, comprehensive exam, thesis. *Entrance requirements:* For master's, GRE General Test, MAT, writing competency test; for Ed S, writing competency test, GRE, MAT. Additional exam requirements/recommendations for international students: Required—TOEFL (minimum score 500 paper-based). *Application deadline:* For fall admission, 7/15 for domestic students; for spring admission, 12/15 for domestic students. Applications are processed on a rolling basis. Application fee: $25. *Expenses:* Tuition, state resident: full-time $7958; part-time $343 per credit hour. Tuition, nonresident: full-time $14,132; part-time $686 per credit hour. *Required fees:* $446 per term. One-time fee: $1784 full-time; $892 part-time. Tuition and fees vary according to course load. *Financial support:* In 2013–14, research assistantships (averaging $9,450 per year) were awarded. *Unit head:* Dr. Joyce Johnson, Acting Chairperson, 334-229-4485, Fax: 334-229-5603, E-mail: jjohnson@alasu.edu. *Application contact:* Dr. William Person, Dean of Graduate Studies, 334-229-4274, Fax: 334-229-4928, E-mail: wperson@alasu.edu.
Website: http://www.alasu.edu/academics/colleges—departments/college-of-education/curriculum—instruction/index.aspx.

Alfred University, Graduate School, Division of Education, Alfred, NY 14802-1205. Offers literacy (MS Ed). *Accreditation:* Teacher Education Accreditation Council. Part-time programs available. *Faculty:* 2 full-time (both women). *Students:* 3 full-time (all women), 4 part-time (1 woman). Average age 24. 8 applicants, 75% accepted, 5 enrolled. In 2013, 5 master's awarded. *Entrance requirements:* For master's, Liberal Arts and Sciences Test (LAST), Assessment of Teaching Skills (written) (ATS-W), Content Specialty Test (CST). Additional exam requirements/recommendations for international students: Required—TOEFL (minimum score 590 paper-based; 90 iBT), IELTS (minimum score 6.5). *Application deadline:* For fall admission, 8/1 for domestic students, 3/15 for international students; for spring admission, 12/1 for domestic students, 10/1 for international students. Applications are processed on a rolling basis. Application fee: $60. Electronic applications accepted. *Expenses: Tuition:* Full-time $38,020; part-time $810 per credit hour. *Required fees:* $950; $160 per semester. Part-time tuition and fees vary according to campus/location and program. *Financial support:* In 2013–14, 9 students received support, including 3 research assistantships with partial tuition reimbursements available (averaging $19,010 per year); tuition waivers (partial) and unspecified assistantships also available. Financial award applicants required to submit FAFSA. *Faculty research:* Literacy. *Unit head:* Dr. Ann Monroe-Baillargeon, Chair, Division of Education, 607-871-2219, E-mail: monroe@alfred.edu. *Application contact:* Sara Love, Coordinator of Graduate Admissions, 607-871-2115, Fax: 607-871-2198, E-mail: gradinquiry@alfred.edu.
Website: http://www.alfred.edu/gradschool/education/.

Alverno College, School of Education, Milwaukee, WI 53234-3922. Offers adaptive education (MA); administrative leadership (MA); adult education and organizational development (MA); adult educational and instructional design (MA); adult educational and instructional technology (MA); global connections in the humanities (MA); instructional leadership (MA); instructional technology for K-12 settings (MA); professional development (MA); reading education (MA); reading education with adaptive education (MA); science education (MA); teaching in alternative schools (MA). *Accreditation:* NCATE. Part-time and evening/weekend programs available. *Faculty:* 7 full-time (all women), 26 part-time/adjunct (23 women). *Students:* 48 full-time (41 women), 89 part-time (83 women); includes 41 minority (24 Black or African American, non-Hispanic/Latino; 3 Asian, non-Hispanic/Latino; 11 Hispanic/Latino; 3 Two or more races, non-Hispanic/Latino), 4 international. Average age 36. 89 applicants, 97% accepted, 59 enrolled. In 2013, 53 master's awarded. *Degree requirements:* For master's, presentation/defense of proposal, conference presentation of inquiry projects. *Entrance requirements:* For master's, bachelor's degree in related field, communication samples from work setting, 3 letters of recommendation. Additional exam requirements/recommendations for international students: Required—TOEFL. *Application deadline:* For fall admission, 7/15 priority date for domestic and international students; for spring admission, 12/15 priority date for domestic and international students. Applications are processed on a rolling basis. Application fee: $0. Electronic applications accepted.

Application fee is waived when completed online. Tuition and fees vary according to program. *Financial support:* In 2013–14, 9 students received support. Federal Work-Study and scholarships/grants available. Support available to part-time students. Financial award application deadline: 4/15; financial award applicants required to submit FAFSA. *Faculty research:* Student self-assessment, self-reflection, integration of curriculum, identifying needs of students in strategic situations and designing appropriate classroom strategies. *Unit head:* Dr. Desiree Pointer-Mace, Associate Dean, Graduate Program, 414-382-6345, Fax: 414-382-6332, E-mail: desiree.pointer-mace@alverno.edu. *Application contact:* Mary Claire Jones, Senior Graduate Admissions Counselor, 414-382-6106, Fax: 414-382-6354, E-mail: maryclaire.jones@alverno.edu.

American International College, School of Graduate and Adult Education, Department of Education, Springfield, MA 01109-3189. Offers early childhood education (M Ed, CAGS); educational leadership and supervision (Ed D); elementary education (M Ed, CAGS); middle/secondary education (M Ed, CAGS); moderate disabilities (M Ed, CAGS); reading (M Ed, CAGS); school adjustment counseling (MA, CAGS); school guidance counseling (MA, CAGS); school leadership preparation (M Ed, CAGS); teaching and learning (Ed D). Evening/weekend programs available. *Faculty:* 11 full-time (9 women), 235 part-time/adjunct. *Students:* 1,530 full-time (1,219 women), 184 part-time (143 women); includes 100 minority (58 Black or African American, non-Hispanic/Latino; 3 American Indian or Alaska Native, non-Hispanic/Latino; 14 Asian, non-Hispanic/Latino; 6 Hispanic/Latino; 19 Two or more races, non-Hispanic/Latino). Average age 36. 695 applicants, 82% accepted, 508 enrolled. In 2013, 449 master's, 17 doctorates, 135 other advanced degrees awarded. Terminal master's awarded for partial completion of doctoral program. *Degree requirements:* For master's, comprehensive exam (for some programs), thesis (for some programs), practicum/culminating experience; for doctorate, comprehensive exam (for some programs), thesis/dissertation; for CAGS, practicum/culminating experience. *Entrance requirements:* For master's, graduate of accredited four-year college with minimum B-average in undergraduate course work; for doctorate, master's degree, minimum GPA of 3.0; for CAGS, M Ed or master's degree in field related to licensure from accredited institution. Additional exam requirements/recommendations for international students: Required—TOEFL or IELTS. *Application deadline:* For fall admission, 7/1 for domestic and international students; for spring admission, 12/1 for domestic and international students. Applications are processed on a rolling basis. Application fee: $50. Electronic applications accepted. *Expenses: Tuition:* Full-time $14,040; part-time $780 per credit. Tuition and fees vary according to course load, degree level and program. *Financial support:* Career-related internships or fieldwork available. Financial award applicants required to submit FAFSA. *Unit head:* Esta Sobey, Associate Dean, 413-205-3453, Fax: 413-205-3943, E-mail: esta.sobey@aic.edu. *Application contact:* Kaitlyn Rickard, Director of XCP Admissions, 413-205-3090, Fax: 413-205-3911, E-mail: kaitlyn.rickard@aic.edu.
Website: http://www.aic.edu/academics.

American Public University System, AMU/APU Graduate Programs, Charles Town, WV 25414. Offers accounting (MBA, MS); criminal justice (MA), including business administration, emergency and disaster management, general (MA, MS); educational leadership (M Ed); emergency and disaster management (MA); entrepreneurship (MBA); environmental policy and management (MS), including environmental planning, environmental sustainability, fish and wildlife management, general (MA, MS), global environmental management; finance (MBA); general (MBA); global business management (MBA); history (MA), including American history, ancient and classical history, European history, global history, public history; homeland security (MA), including business administration, counter-terrorism studies, criminal justice, cyber, emergency management and public health, intelligence studies, transportation security; homeland security resource allocation (MBA); humanities (MA); information technology (MS), including digital forensics, enterprise software development, information assurance and security, IT project management; information technology management (MBA); intelligence studies (MA), including criminal intelligence, cyber, general (MA, MS), homeland security, intelligence analysis, intelligence collection, intelligence management, intelligence operations, terrorism studies; international relations and conflict resolution (MA), including comparative and security issues, conflict resolution, international and transnational security issues, peacekeeping; legal studies (MA); management (MA), including defense management, general (MA, MS), human resource management, organizational leadership, public administration; marketing (MBA); military history (MA), including American military history, American Revolution, civil war, war since 1945, World War II; military studies (MA), including joint warfare, strategic leadership; national security studies (MA), including general (MA, MS), homeland security, regional security studies, security and intelligence analysis, terrorism studies; nonprofit management (MBA); political science (MA), including American politics and government, comparative government and development, general (MA, MS), international relations, public policy; psychology (MA), including general (MA, MS), maritime engineering management, reverse logistics management; public administration (MPA), including disaster management, environmental policy, health policy, human resources, national security, organizational management, security management; public health (MPH); reverse logistics management (MA); school counseling (M Ed); security management (MA); space studies (MS), including aerospace science, general (MA, MS), planetary science; sports and health sciences (MS); teaching (M Ed), including curriculum and instruction for elementary teachers, elementary reading, English language learners, instructional leadership, online learning, special education; transportation and logistics management (MA), including general (MA, MS), maritime engineering management, reverse logistics management. Programs offered via distance learning only. Part-time and evening/weekend programs available. Postbaccalaureate distance learning degree programs offered (no on-campus study). *Faculty:* 432 full-time (242 women), 1,722 part-time/adjunct (829 women). *Students:* 511 full-time (241 women), 10,947 part-time (4,294 women); includes 3,760 minority (2,058 Black or African American, non-Hispanic/Latino; 88 American Indian or Alaska Native, non-Hispanic/Latino; 293 Asian, non-Hispanic/Latino; 876 Hispanic/Latino; 91 Native Hawaiian or other Pacific Islander, non-Hispanic/Latino; 354 Two or more races, non-Hispanic/Latino; 134 international. Average age 36. In 2013, 3,323 master's awarded. *Degree requirements:* For master's, comprehensive exam or practicum. *Entrance requirements:* For master's, official transcript showing earned bachelor's degree from

institution accredited by recognized accrediting body. Additional exam requirements/recommendations for international students: Required—TOEFL (minimum score 550 paper-based), IELTS (minimum score 6.5). *Application deadline:* Applications are processed on a rolling basis. Application fee: $0. Electronic applications accepted. *Expenses: Tuition:* Part-time $325 per semester hour. *Financial support:* Applicants required to submit FAFSA. *Faculty research:* Military history, criminal justice, management performance, national security. *Unit head:* Dr. Karan Powell, Executive Vice President and Provost, 877-468-6268, Fax: 304-724-3780. *Application contact:* Terry Grant, Vice President of Enrollment Management, 877-468-6268, Fax: 304-724-3780, E-mail: info@apus.edu.
Website: http://www.apus.edu.

Appalachian State University, Cratis D. Williams Graduate School, Department of Reading Education and Special Education, Boone, NC 28608. Offers reading education (MA); special education (MA). *Accreditation:* ASHA. Part-time and evening/weekend programs available. Postbaccalaureate distance learning degree programs offered (no on-campus study). *Degree requirements:* For master's, comprehensive exam, thesis optional. *Entrance requirements:* For master's, GRE General Test or MAT, 3 letters of recommendation. Additional exam requirements/recommendations for international students: Required—TOEFL (minimum score 570 paper-based; 79 iBT), IELTS (minimum score 6.5). Electronic applications accepted. *Faculty research:* Special education, language arts, reading.

Arcadia University, Graduate Studies, School of Education, Glenside, PA 19038-3295. Offers art education (M Ed); computer education (CAS); curriculum (CAS); curriculum studies (M Ed); early childhood education (M Ed, CAS), including individualized (M Ed); master teacher (M Ed), research in child development (M Ed); educational leadership (M Ed, Ed D, CAS); elementary education (M Ed, CAS); English education (MA Ed); environmental education (MA Ed, CAS); history education (MA Ed); instructional technology (M Ed); language arts (M Ed, CAS); library science (M Ed); mathematics education (M Ed, MA Ed, CAS); music education (MA Ed); psychology (MA Ed); reading (M Ed, CAS); science education (M Ed, CAS); secondary education (M Ed, CAS); special education (M Ed, Ed D, CAS); theater arts (MA Ed); written communication (MA Ed). *Accreditation:* NASAD. Part-time and evening/weekend programs available. Postbaccalaureate distance learning degree programs offered (minimal on-campus study). Electronic applications accepted. *Expenses:* Contact institution.

Arkansas State University, Graduate School, College of Education and Behavioral Science, School of Teacher Education and Leadership, Jonesboro, AR 72467. Offers community college administration (SCCT); curriculum and instruction (MSE); early childhood education (MAT, MSE); early childhood services (MS); educational leadership (MSE, Ed D, PhD, Ed S); educational theory and practice (MSE); middle level education (MAT, MSE); reading (MSE, Ed S); special education - gifted, talented, and creative (MSE); special education - instructional specialist grades 4-12 (MSE); special education - instructional specialist grades P-4 (MSE). *Accreditation:* NCATE. Part-time programs available. Postbaccalaureate distance learning degree programs offered. *Faculty:* 28 full-time (16 women). *Students:* 77 full-time (68 women), 1,934 part-time (1,449 women); includes 361 minority (290 Black or African American, non-Hispanic/Latino; 11 American Indian or Alaska Native, non-Hispanic/Latino; 3 Asian, non-Hispanic/Latino; 26 Hispanic/Latino; 1 Native Hawaiian or other Pacific Islander, non-Hispanic/Latino; 30 Two or more races, non-Hispanic/Latino), 5 international. Average age 36. 1,627 applicants, 71% accepted, 770 enrolled. In 2013, 1,182 master's, 12 doctorates, 76 other advanced degrees awarded. *Degree requirements:* For master's, comprehensive exam, thesis or alternative; for doctorate, comprehensive exam, thesis/dissertation; for other advanced degree, comprehensive exam. *Entrance requirements:* For master's, GRE General Test or MAT, appropriate bachelor's degree, official transcripts, immunization records, letters of reference, interview; for doctorate, GRE General Test or MAT, interview, master's degree, letters of reference, official transcript, personal statement, writing sample, immunization records; for other advanced degree, GRE General Test or MAT, interview, master's degree, official transcript, immunization records, letters of reference, 3 years of teaching experience, teaching license. Additional exam requirements/recommendations for international students: Required—TOEFL (minimum score 550 paper-based; 79 iBT), IELTS (minimum score 6), PTE (minimum score 56). *Application deadline:* For fall admission, 7/1 for domestic and international students; for spring admission, 11/15 for domestic students, 11/14 for international students. Applications are processed on a rolling basis. Electronic applications accepted. *Expenses:* Tuition, state resident: full-time $4284; part-time $238 per credit hour. Tuition, nonresident: full-time $8568; part-time $476 per credit hour. *International tuition:* $9268 full-time. *Required fees:* $1098; $61 per credit hour. $25 per term. Tuition and fees vary according to course load and program. *Financial support:* In 2013–14, 20 students received support. Fellowships, teaching assistantships, career-related internships or fieldwork, scholarships/grants, and unspecified assistantships available. Financial award application deadline: 7/1; financial award applicants required to submit FAFSA. *Unit head:* Dr. Annette Hux, Interim Chair, 870-972-3059, Fax: 870-972-3344, E-mail: ahux@astate.edu. *Application contact:* Vickey Ring, Graduate Admissions Coordinator, 870-972-3029, Fax: 870-972-3857, E-mail: vickeyring@astate.edu.
Website: http://www.astate.edu/college/education/departments/school-of-teacher-education-and-leadership/index.dot.

Armstrong State University, School of Graduate Studies, Department of Childhood and Exceptional Student Education, Savannah, GA 31419-1997. Offers early childhood education (M Ed, MAT); reading endorsement (Certificate); special education (M Ed, MAT). *Accreditation:* NCATE. Part-time and evening/weekend programs available. Postbaccalaureate distance learning degree programs offered (minimal on-campus study). *Faculty:* 12 full-time (9 women), 4 part-time/adjunct (0 women). *Students:* 26 full-time (22 women), 208 part-time (186 women); includes 74 minority (66 Black or African American, non-Hispanic/Latino; 1 Asian, non-Hispanic/Latino; 5 Hispanic/Latino; 2 Two or more races, non-Hispanic/Latino), 1 international. Average age 33. 107 applicants, 70% accepted, 69 enrolled. In 2013, 122 master's, 64 other advanced degrees awarded. *Degree requirements:* For master's, comprehensive exam. *Entrance requirements:* For master's, GRE General Test or MAT. Additional exam requirements/recommendations for international students: Required—TOEFL (minimum score 523 paper-based). *Application deadline:* For fall admission, 6/30 priority date for domestic students, 5/1 priority date for international students; for spring admission, 11/15 priority date for domestic students, 9/15 priority date for international students; for summer admission, 4/15 priority date for domestic students, 9/15 for international students. Applications are processed on a rolling basis. Application fee: $30. Electronic applications accepted. *Expenses:* Tuition, state resident: part-time $201 per credit hour. Tuition, nonresident: part-time $745 per credit hour. *Required fees:* $310 per semester. Tuition and fees vary according to course load, campus/location and program. *Financial support:* In 2013–14, research assistantships with full tuition reimbursements (averaging $5,000 per year) were awarded; career-related internships or fieldwork, Federal Work-Study, scholarships/grants, and unspecified assistantships also available. Support available to part-time students. Financial award application deadline: 3/15; financial award applicants required to submit FAFSA. *Faculty research:* Literacy, instructional design, poetry, working with local schools. *Unit head:* Dr. John Hobe, Department Head, 912-344-2564, Fax: 912-344-3443, E-mail: john.hobe@armstrong.edu. *Application contact:*

Jill Bell, Director, Graduate Enrollment Services, 912-344-2798, Fax: 912-344-3488, E-mail: graduate@armstrong.edu.
Website: http://www.armstrong.edu/Education/childhood_exceptional_education2/ceed_welcome.

Asbury University, School of Graduate and Professional Studies, Wilmore, KY 40390-1198. Offers biology: alternative certificate (MA Ed); chemistry: alternative certificate (MA Ed); English (MA Ed); English as a second language (MA Ed); ESL (MA Ed); French (MA Ed); Latin: alternative certificate (MA Ed); mathematics: alternative certificate (MA Ed); reading/writing endorsement (MA Ed); social studies (MA Ed); social work (MSW), including child and family services; Spanish (MA Ed); special education (MA Ed); special education: alternative certificate (MA Ed); teacher as leader endorsement (MA Ed). *Accreditation:* NCATE. Part-time programs available. *Degree requirements:* For master's, action research project, portfolio. *Entrance requirements:* For master's, PRAXIS/NTE, minimum GPA of 2.75, letters of recommendation. Additional exam requirements/recommendations for international students: Required—TOEFL (minimum score 550 paper-based). Electronic applications accepted.

Ashland University, Dwight Schar College of Education, Department of Curriculum and Instruction, Ashland, OH 44805-3702. Offers classroom instruction (M Ed); literacy (M Ed); technology facilitator (M Ed). *Accreditation:* NCATE. Part-time and evening/weekend programs available. *Degree requirements:* For master's, thesis or alternative, internship, practicum, inquiry seminar. *Entrance requirements:* For master's, teaching certificate or license, bachelor's degree, minimum cumulative GPA of 2.75. Additional exam requirements/recommendations for international students: Required—TOEFL. Electronic applications accepted. *Faculty research:* Gender equity, postmodern children's and young adult literature, outdoor/experimental education, re-examining literature study in middle grades, morality and giftedness.

Auburn University, Graduate School, College of Education, Department of Curriculum and Teaching, Auburn University, AL 36849. Offers business education (M Ed, MS, PhD); early childhood education (M Ed, MS, PhD, Ed S); elementary education (M Ed, MS, PhD, Ed S); foreign languages (M Ed, MS); music education (M Ed, MS, PhD, Ed S); postsecondary education (PhD); reading education (PhD, Ed S); secondary education (M Ed, MS, PhD, Ed S), including English language arts, mathematics, science, social studies. *Accreditation:* NASM (one or more programs are accredited); NCATE. Part-time programs available. *Faculty:* 29 full-time (21 women), 4 part-time/adjunct (all women). *Students:* 61 full-time (40 women), 153 part-time (108 women); includes 37 minority (32 Black or African American, non-Hispanic/Latino; 2 Asian, non-Hispanic/Latino; 3 Hispanic/Latino), 1 international. Average age 34. 150 applicants, 59% accepted, 74 enrolled. In 2013, 70 master's, 6 doctorates, 26 other advanced degrees awarded. *Degree requirements:* For master's, thesis (for some programs); for doctorate, thesis/dissertation; for Ed S, field project. *Entrance requirements:* For master's, doctorate, and Ed S, GRE General Test. *Application deadline:* For fall admission, 7/7 for domestic students; for spring admission, 11/24 for domestic students. Applications are processed on a rolling basis. Application fee: $50 ($60 for international students). Electronic applications accepted. *Expenses:* Tuition, state resident: full-time $8262; part-time $459 per credit hour. Tuition, nonresident: full-time $24,786; part-time $1377 per credit hour. Tuition and fees vary according to degree level and program. *Financial support:* Fellowships, teaching assistantships, career-related internships or fieldwork, and Federal Work-Study available. Support available to part-time students. Financial award application deadline: 3/15; financial award applicants required to submit FAFSA. *Faculty research:* Emerging literacy, reading attitudes, music for at-risk youth, portfolio assessment. *Unit head:* Dr. Kimberly Walls, Head, 334-844-4434. *Application contact:* Dr. George Flowers, Dean of the Graduate School, 334-844-2125.
Website: http://education.auburn.edu/academic_departments/curr/.

Augustana College, MA in Education Program, Sioux Falls, SD 57197. Offers instructional strategies (MA); reading (MA); special populations (MA); technology (MA). *Accreditation:* NCATE. Part-time and evening/weekend programs available. Postbaccalaureate distance learning degree programs offered (no on-campus study). *Faculty:* 9 full-time (6 women). *Students:* 48 part-time (40 women). Average age 33. 55 applicants, 100% accepted, 49 enrolled. In 2013, 14 master's awarded. *Degree requirements:* For master's, thesis. *Entrance requirements:* For master's, appropriate bachelor's degree, minimum GPA of 3.0, teaching certificate. Additional exam requirements/recommendations for international students: Required—TOEFL (minimum score 550 paper-based). *Application deadline:* For spring admission, 4/1 priority date for domestic and international students. Applications are processed on a rolling basis. Application fee: $50. Electronic applications accepted. *Expenses:* Contact institution. *Financial support:* Application deadline: 3/1; applicants required to submit FAFSA. *Unit head:* Dr. Sheryl Feinstein, MA in Education Program Director, 605-274-5211, E-mail: sheryl.feinstein@augie.edu. *Application contact:* Nancy Wright, Graduate Coordinator, 605-274-4043, Fax: 605-274-4450, E-mail: graduate@augie.edu.
Website: http://www.augie.edu/academics/graduate-education/master-arts-education.

Aurora University, College of Education, Aurora, IL 60506-4892. Offers curriculum and instruction (MA, Ed D); early childhood and special education (MA); education (MAT), including elementary certification; education and administration (Ed D); educational leadership (MEL); educational technology (MATL); reading instruction (MA); special education (MA). *Accreditation:* NCATE. Part-time and evening/weekend programs available. *Degree requirements:* For doctorate, comprehensive exam, thesis/dissertation. *Entrance requirements:* For master's, 2 years of teaching experience, valid teaching certificate. Additional exam requirements/recommendations for international students: Required—TOEFL (minimum score 550 paper-based). Electronic applications accepted. *Expenses:* Contact institution.

Austin Peay State University, College of Graduate Studies, College of Education, Department of Teaching and Learning, Clarksville, TN 37044. Offers elementary education K-6 (MAT); reading (MA Ed); secondary education 7-12 (MAT); special education K-12 (MAT). Part-time and evening/weekend programs available. Postbaccalaureate distance learning degree programs offered. *Faculty:* 7 full-time (4 women), 5 part-time/adjunct (all women). *Students:* 70 full-time (59 women), 77 part-time (55 women); includes 23 minority (10 Black or African American, non-Hispanic/Latino; 2 Asian, non-Hispanic/Latino; 5 Hispanic/Latino; 6 Two or more races, non-Hispanic/Latino). Average age 33. 50 applicants, 90% accepted, 37 enrolled. In 2013, 60 master's awarded. *Degree requirements:* For master's, comprehensive exam, thesis optional. *Entrance requirements:* For master's, GRE General Test, 3 letters of recommendation, minimum undergraduate GPA of 2.75. Additional exam requirements/recommendations for international students: Required—TOEFL (minimum score 500 paper-based). *Application deadline:* For fall admission, 8/5 priority date for domestic students. Applications are processed on a rolling basis. Application fee: $25. Electronic applications accepted. *Expenses:* Tuition, state resident: full-time $7500; part-time $375 per credit hour. Tuition, nonresident: full-time $20,800; part-time $1040 per credit hour. *Required fees:* $1284; $64.20 per credit hour. *Financial support:* Career-related internships or fieldwork, Federal Work-Study, institutionally sponsored loans, scholarships/grants, and unspecified assistantships available. Support available to part-time students. Financial award application deadline: 3/1; financial award applicants required to submit FAFSA. *Unit head:* Dr. Rebecca McMahan, Chair, 931-221-7513, Fax: 931-221-1292, E-mail: mcmahanb@apsu.edu. *Application contact:* June D. Lee,

Graduate Coordinator, 800-859-4723, Fax: 931-221-7641, E-mail: gradadmissions@apsu.edu.

Averett University, Master in Education Program, Danville, VA 24541-3692. Offers administration and supervision (M Ed); art (M Ed); biology (M Ed); chemistry (M Ed); curriculum and instruction (M Ed); early childhood (M Ed); English (M Ed); mathematics (M Ed); middle grades (M Ed); physical science (M Ed); reading specialist (M Ed); science (M Ed); special education (M Ed); special education learning disability (M Ed). Program offered on Danville Campus only. Part-time and evening/weekend programs available. *Faculty:* 4 full-time (3 women), 13 part-time/adjunct (8 women). *Students:* 43 full-time (35 women), 44 part-time (35 women); includes 7 minority (all Black or African American, non-Hispanic/Latino). *Degree requirements:* For master's, 30-credit core curriculum, minimum GPA of 3.0 throughout program, completion of degree requirements within six years from start of program. *Entrance requirements:* For master's, PRAXIS I, GRE, or MAT; writing proficiency test, minimum cumulative GPA of 3.0 over the last 60 hours of undergraduate study toward a baccalaureate degree, three letters of recommendation, Virginia teaching license (or eligibility). Additional exam requirements/recommendations for international students: Required—TOEFL (minimum score 600 paper-based; 100 iBT). *Application deadline:* Applications are processed on a rolling basis. Application fee: $100. *Expenses:* Contact institution. *Financial support:* Career-related internships or fieldwork, Federal Work-Study, and scholarships/grants available. Financial award application deadline: 4/1; financial award applicants required to submit FAFSA. *Unit head:* Wilfred Lawrence, Department Chair of Education, 434-791-5752, E-mail: priedel@averett.edu. *Application contact:* Christy Pack, Executive Director of Enrollment, 804-887-8612, E-mail: dpack@averett.edu.
Website: http://www.averett.edu/adultprograms/degrees/MEDtrad.php.

Baldwin Wallace University, Graduate Programs, Division of Education, Specialization in Literacy, Berea, OH 44017-2088. Offers MA Ed. *Accreditation:* NCATE. Part-time and evening/weekend programs available. Postbaccalaureate distance learning degree programs offered (minimal on-campus study). *Faculty:* 2 full-time (both women), 3 part-time/adjunct (all women). *Students:* 11 full-time (10 women), 33 part-time (32 women); includes 3 minority (2 Black or African American, non-Hispanic/Latino; 1 Two or more races, non-Hispanic/Latino). Average age 30. 16 applicants, 94% accepted, 12 enrolled. In 2013, 12 master's awarded. *Degree requirements:* For master's, comprehensive exam, capstone practicum. *Entrance requirements:* For master's, bachelor's degree in field, MAT or minimum GPA of 2.75. Additional exam requirements/recommendations for international students: Required—TOEFL (minimum score 523 paper-based; 70 iBT). *Application deadline:* For fall admission, 8/15 priority date for domestic students; for spring admission, 12/15 priority date for domestic students. Applications are processed on a rolling basis. Application fee: $25. Electronic applications accepted. Application fee is waived when completed online. *Expenses:* Contact institution. *Financial support:* Career-related internships or fieldwork available. Support available to part-time students. Financial award application deadline: 5/1; financial award applicants required to submit FAFSA. *Faculty research:* Metacognition and the reading process, language acquisition, genres and the reader response theory, cultural responsiveness, content area literacy. *Unit head:* Dr. Karen Kaye, Chair, 440-826-2168, Fax: 440-826-3779, E-mail: kkaye@bw.edu. *Application contact:* Winifred W. Gerhardt, Director of Admission, Adult and Graduate Programs, 440-826-2222, Fax: 440-826-3830, E-mail: admission@bw.edu.
Website: http://www.bw.edu/academic/mae/reading/.

Bank Street College of Education, Graduate School, Program in Reading and Literacy, New York, NY 10025. Offers advanced literacy specialization (Ed M); reading and literacy (MS Ed); teaching literacy (MS Ed); teaching literacy and childhood general education (MS Ed). *Degree requirements:* For master's, thesis. *Entrance requirements:* For master's, interview, essays. Additional exam requirements/recommendations for international students: Required—TOEFL (minimum score 600 paper-based; 100 iBT), IELTS (minimum score 7). Electronic applications accepted. *Faculty research:* Language development, children's literature, whole language, the reading and writing processes, reading difficulties in multicultural classrooms.

Baptist Bible College of Pennsylvania, Graduate Studies, Clarks Summit, PA 18411-1297. Offers Bible (MA); counseling (MA, MS); curriculum and instruction (M Ed); educational administration (M Ed); intercultural studies (MA); literature (MA); missions (MA); organizational leadership (MA); reading specialist (M Ed); secondary English/communications (M Ed); social entrepreneurship (MA); worldview studies (MA). MA in missions program available only for Association of Baptists for World Evangelism missionary personnel. Part-time and evening/weekend programs available. Postbaccalaureate distance learning degree programs offered (no on-campus study). *Entrance requirements:* Additional exam requirements/recommendations for international students: Required—TOEFL (minimum score 500 paper-based).

Barry University, School of Education, Program in Curriculum and Instruction, Miami Shores, FL 33161-6695. Offers accomplished teacher (Ed S); culture, language and literacy (TESOL) (PhD); curriculum evaluation and research (PhD); early childhood (Ed S); early childhood education (PhD); elementary (Ed S); elementary education (PhD); ESOL (Ed S); gifted (Ed S); Montessori (Ed S); PKP/elementary (Ed S); reading (Ed S); reading, language and cognition (PhD). *Entrance requirements:* For doctorate, GRE, minimum GPA of 3.25.

Barry University, School of Education, Program in Reading, Miami Shores, FL 33161-6695. Offers MS, Ed S. Part-time and evening/weekend programs available. *Degree requirements:* For master's, comprehensive exam, practicum; for Ed S, practicum. *Entrance requirements:* For master's, GRE General Test or MAT, minimum GPA of 3.0, course work in children's literature; for Ed S, GRE General Test, minimum GPA of 3.0. Electronic applications accepted.

Belhaven University, School of Education, Jackson, MS 39202-1789. Offers educational technology (M Ed); elementary education (M Ed, MAT); reading literacy (M Ed); secondary education (M Ed, MAT). Part-time and evening/weekend programs available. Postbaccalaureate distance learning degree programs offered (no on-campus study). *Faculty:* 7 full-time (6 women), 15 part-time/adjunct (10 women). *Students:* 1 full-time (0 women), 406 part-time (311 women); includes 254 minority (250 Black or African American, non-Hispanic/Latino; 2 Hispanic/Latino; 2 Two or more races, non-Hispanic/Latino). Average age 36. 273 applicants, 67% accepted, 162 enrolled. In 2013, 24 master's awarded. *Degree requirements:* For master's, comprehensive exam, portfolio. *Entrance requirements:* For master's, PRAXIS I and II, minimum GPA of 2.8. *Application deadline:* Applications are processed on a rolling basis. Application fee: $25. Electronic applications accepted. *Financial support:* Federal Work-Study, scholarships/grants, tuition waivers (full), and unspecified assistantships available. Support available to part-time students. Financial award applicants required to submit FAFSA. *Unit head:* Dr. David Hand, Dean, 601-965-7020, E-mail: dhand@belhaven.edu. *Application contact:* Amanda Slaughter, Assistant Vice President for Adult and Graduate Enrollment and Student Services, 601-968-8727, Fax: 601-968-5953, E-mail: gradadmission@belhaven.edu.
Website: http://graduateed.belhaven.edu.

Bellarmine University, Annsley Frazier Thornton School of Education, Louisville, KY 40205-0671. Offers education and social change (PhD); elementary education (MA Ed, MAT); learning and behavior disorders (MA Ed, MAT); middle grades education (MA Ed, MAT); principalship (Ed S); reading and writing (MA Ed); secondary education (MAT); teacher leadership (MA Ed). *Accreditation:* NCATE. Part-time and evening/weekend programs available. *Faculty:* 13 full-time (7 women), 14 part-time/adjunct (9 women). *Students:* 60 full-time (47 women), 191 part-time (140 women); includes 35 minority (22 Black or African American, non-Hispanic/Latino; 1 American Indian or Alaska Native, non-Hispanic/Latino; 3 Asian, non-Hispanic/Latino; 5 Hispanic/Latino; 4 Two or more races, non-Hispanic/Latino). Average age 33. In 2013, 108 master's awarded. *Degree requirements:* For master's, comprehensive exam, thesis (for some programs); for doctorate, comprehensive exam, thesis/dissertation. *Entrance requirements:* For master's, GRE, baccalaureate degree from accredited institution; minimum overall GPA of 2.75, 3.0 in major; letters of recommendation; valid Kentucky provisional or professional certificate; for doctorate, GRE, minimum GPA of 3.5 in all graduate coursework; baccalaureate and master's degrees in education (MA, MS) or fields directly relevant to education; three letters of recommendation; two essays (no more than 1000 words each); interview. Additional exam requirements/recommendations for international students: Required—TOEFL (minimum score 550 paper-based; 80 iBT). *Application deadline:* Applications are processed on a rolling basis. Application fee: $25. *Expenses:* Contact institution. *Financial support:* Scholarships/grants available. Financial award applicants required to submit FAFSA. *Faculty research:* Literacy, service-learning, dispositions, educational technology, special education. *Unit head:* Dr. Robert Cooter, Dean, 502-272-8191, Fax: 502-272-8189, E-mail: rcooter@bellarmine.edu. *Application contact:* Theresa Klapheke, Administrative Director of Graduate Programs, 502-272-8271, Fax: 502-272-8002, E-mail: tklapheke@bellarmine.edu.
Website: http://www.bellarmine.edu/education/graduate.

Benedictine University, Graduate Programs, Program in Education, Lisle, IL 60532-0900. Offers curriculum and instruction and collaborative teaching (M Ed); elementary education (MA Ed); leadership and administration (M Ed); reading and literacy (M Ed); secondary education (MA Ed); special education (MA Ed). Part-time and evening/weekend programs available. *Students:* 6 full-time (all women), 124 part-time (106 women); includes 14 minority (8 Black or African American, non-Hispanic/Latino; 1 American Indian or Alaska Native, non-Hispanic/Latino; 2 Asian, non-Hispanic/Latino; 3 Hispanic/Latino). 21 applicants, 62% accepted, 8 enrolled. In 2013, 120 master's awarded. *Degree requirements:* For master's, comprehensive exam, thesis (for some programs). *Entrance requirements:* For master's, GRE or MAT. Additional exam requirements/recommendations for international students: Required—TOEFL (minimum score 550 paper-based). *Application deadline:* For fall admission, 9/1 for domestic students; for winter admission, 12/1 for domestic students; for spring admission, 2/15 for domestic students. Applications are processed on a rolling basis. Application fee: $40. Electronic applications accepted. *Expenses:* Contact institution. *Financial support:* Career-related internships or fieldwork and health care benefits available. Support available to part-time students. *Unit head:* MeShelda Jackson, Director, 630-829-6282, E-mail: mjackson@ben.edu. *Application contact:* Kari Gibbons, Associate Vice President, Enrollment Center, 630-829-6200, Fax: 630-829-6584, E-mail: kgibbons@ben.edu.

Benedictine University at Springfield, Program in Reading/Literacy, Springfield, IL 62702. Offers M Ed. *Entrance requirements:* For master's, official transcript, minimum cumulative GPA of 3.0, 3 letters of recommendation, statement of goals.

Berry College, Graduate Programs, Graduate Programs in Education, Program in Middle Grades Education and Reading, Mount Berry, GA 30149-0159. Offers middle grades education (M Ed, MAT); reading (M Ed). *Accreditation:* NCATE. Part-time programs available. *Faculty:* 10 part-time/adjunct (6 women). *Students:* 1 (woman) full-time, 6 part-time (5 women). Average age 30. In 2013, 6 master's awarded. *Degree requirements:* For master's, thesis, portfolio, oral exams. *Entrance requirements:* For master's, GRE General Test or MAT, minimum GPA of 2.5. Additional exam requirements/recommendations for international students: Required—TOEFL (minimum score 550 paper-based). *Application deadline:* For fall admission, 7/25 for domestic students, 5/1 for international students; for spring admission, 12/1 for domestic students, 10/1 for international students. Applications are processed on a rolling basis. Application fee: $25 ($30 for international students). Electronic applications accepted. *Expenses:* Contact institution. *Financial support:* In 2013–14, 4 students received support, including 2 research assistantships with full tuition reimbursements available (averaging $1,158 per year); scholarships/grants, tuition waivers (partial), and unspecified assistantships also available. Support available to part-time students. Financial award application deadline: 3/1; financial award applicants required to submit FAFSA. *Unit head:* Dr. Jacqueline McDowell, Dean, 706-236-1717, Fax: 706-238-5827, E-mail: jmcdowell@berry.edu. *Application contact:* Brett Kennedy, Assistant Vice President of Enrollment Management, 706-236-2215, Fax: 706-290-2178, E-mail: admissions@berry.edu.
Website: http://www.berry.edu/academics/education/graduate/.

Bethel University, Graduate School, St. Paul, MN 55112-6999. Offers autism spectrum disorders (Certificate); business administration (MBA); communication (MA); counseling psychology (MA); educational leadership (Ed D); gerontology (MA); international baccalaureate education (Certificate); K-12 education (MA); literacy education (MA, Certificate); nurse educator (Certificate); nurse leader (Certificate); nurse-midwifery (MS); nursing (MS); physician assistant (MS); postsecondary teaching (Certificate); special education (MA); strategic leadership (MA); teaching (MA). Part-time and evening/weekend programs available. Postbaccalaureate distance learning degree programs offered (no on-campus study). *Faculty:* 13 full-time (7 women), 89 part-time/adjunct (43 women). *Students:* 692 full-time (457 women), 573 part-time (371 women); includes 170 minority (86 Black or African American, non-Hispanic/Latino; 1 American Indian or Alaska Native, non-Hispanic/Latino; 49 Asian, non-Hispanic/Latino; 20 Hispanic/Latino; 1 Native Hawaiian or other Pacific Islander, non-Hispanic/Latino; 13 Two or more races, non-Hispanic/Latino), 21 international. Average age 37. In 2013, 166 master's, 9 doctorates, 11 other advanced degrees awarded. *Degree requirements:* For master's, comprehensive exam (for some programs), thesis (for some programs); for doctorate, comprehensive exam, thesis/dissertation. *Entrance requirements:* Additional exam requirements/recommendations for international students: Required—TOEFL (minimum score 550 paper-based; 80 iBT). *Application deadline:* Applications are processed on a rolling basis. Electronic applications accepted. Tuition and fees vary according to course load, degree level and program. *Financial support:* Teaching assistantships, career-related internships or fieldwork, and scholarships/grants available. Support available to part-time students. Financial award applicants required to submit FAFSA. *Unit head:* Dick Crombie, Vice-President/Dean, 651-635-8000, Fax: 651-635-8004, E-mail: gs@bethel.edu. *Application contact:* Director of Admissions, 651-635-8000, Fax: 651-635-8004, E-mail: gs@bethel.edu.
Website: http://gs.bethel.edu/.

Binghamton University, State University of New York, Graduate School, School of Education, Program in Adolescence Education, Vestal, NY 13850. Offers biology education (MAT, MS Ed); chemistry education (MAT, MS Ed); earth science education (MAT, MS Ed); English education (MAT, MS Ed); French education (MAT, MS Ed); literacy education (MS Ed); mathematical sciences education (MAT, MS Ed); physics

(MAT, MS Ed); social studies (MAT, MS Ed); Spanish education (MAT, MS Ed). *Accreditation:* Teacher Education Accreditation Council. Part-time and evening/weekend programs available. *Students:* 48 full-time (29 women), 5 part-time (3 women); includes 7 minority (2 Black or African American, non-Hispanic/Latino; 3 Asian, non-Hispanic/Latino; 2 Hispanic/Latino), 1 international. Average age 26. 37 applicants, 86% accepted, 21 enrolled. In 2013, 34 master's awarded. *Entrance requirements:* For master's, GRE General Test. Additional exam requirements/recommendations for international students: Required—TOEFL (minimum score 550 paper-based; 80 iBT). *Application deadline:* For fall admission, 2/1 priority date for domestic and international students; for spring admission, 10/15 priority date for domestic and international students. Applications are processed on a rolling basis. Application fee: $75. Electronic applications accepted. *Financial support:* In 2013–14, 7 students received support, including 1 fellowship with partial tuition reimbursement available (averaging $4,500 per year); career-related internships or fieldwork, Federal Work-Study, institutionally sponsored loans, scholarships/grants, health care benefits, tuition waivers (full), and unspecified assistantships also available. Financial award application deadline: 2/15; financial award applicants required to submit FAFSA. *Unit head:* Dr. S. G. Grant, Dean of School of Education, 607-777-7329, E-mail: sggrant@binghamton.edu. *Application contact:* Kishan Zuber, Recruiting and Admissions Coordinator, 607-777-2151, Fax: 607-777-2501, E-mail: kzuber@binghamton.edu.

Binghamton University, State University of New York, Graduate School, School of Education, Program in Literacy Education, Vestal, NY 13850. Offers MS Ed. *Accreditation:* Teacher Education Accreditation Council. Part-time and evening/weekend programs available. *Students:* 13 full-time (12 women), 23 part-time (21 women). Average age 25. 28 applicants, 96% accepted, 16 enrolled. In 2013, 25 master's awarded. *Entrance requirements:* For master's, GRE General Test. Additional exam requirements/recommendations for international students: Required—TOEFL (minimum score 550 paper-based; 80 iBT). *Application deadline:* For fall admission, 2/1 priority date for domestic and international students; for spring admission, 10/15 priority date for domestic and international students. Applications are processed on a rolling basis. Application fee: $75. Electronic applications accepted. *Financial support:* In 2013–14, 6 students received support. Career-related internships or fieldwork, Federal Work-Study, institutionally sponsored loans, scholarships/grants, health care benefits, tuition waivers, and unspecified assistantships available. Financial award application deadline: 2/15; financial award applicants required to submit FAFSA. *Unit head:* Dr. S. G. Grant, Dean of School of Education, 607-777-7329, E-mail: sggrant@binghamton.edu. *Application contact:* Zuber Kishan, Recruiting and Admissions Coordinator, 607-777-2151, Fax: 607-777-2501, E-mail: kzuber@binghamton.edu.

Bloomsburg University of Pennsylvania, School of Graduate Studies, College of Education, Department of Early Childhood and Adolescent Education, Program in Reading, Bloomsburg, PA 17815-1301. Offers M Ed. *Faculty:* 3 full-time (2 women). *Students:* 19 full-time (17 women), 3 part-time (all women). Average age 28. 19 applicants, 84% accepted, 6 enrolled. In 2013, 15 master's awarded. *Degree requirements:* For master's, thesis, PRAXIS II. *Entrance requirements:* For master's, baccalaureate degree, letter of intent, two letters of recommendation, teaching certificate. Additional exam requirements/recommendations for international students: Required—TOEFL. *Application deadline:* Applications are processed on a rolling basis. Application fee: $35 ($60 for international students). Electronic applications accepted. *Expenses:* Tuition, state resident: full-time $7956; part-time $442 per credit. Tuition, nonresident: full-time $11,934; part-time $663 per credit. *Required fees:* $95.50 per credit. $55 per semester. Tuition and fees vary according to course load. *Financial support:* Tuition waivers (partial) and unspecified assistantships available. *Unit head:* Dr. Tegan Kotarski, College of Education Graduate Coordinator, 570-389-3883, Fax: 570-389-5049, E-mail: tkotarsk@bloomu.edu. *Application contact:* Jennifer Richard, Administrative Assistant, 570-389-4015, Fax: 570-389-3054, E-mail: jrichard@bloomu.edu.
Website: http://www.bloomu.edu/gradschool/reading.

Blue Mountain College, Program in Literacy/Reading (K-12), Blue Mountain, MS 38610. Offers M Ed. Part-time and evening/weekend programs available. *Faculty:* 3 full-time (all women). *Students:* 2 full-time (both women), 2 part-time (both women). 1 applicant, 100% accepted, 1 enrolled. In 2013, 4 master's awarded. *Degree requirements:* For master's, comprehensive exam. *Entrance requirements:* For master's, PRAXIS, GRE or MAT, official transcripts, bachelor's degree in a field of education from an accredited university or college, permanent teaching license, three recommendations. Additional exam requirements/recommendations for international students: Required—TOEFL (minimum score 550 paper-based). *Application deadline:* For fall admission, 7/1 priority date for domestic students; for spring admission, 1/1 priority date for domestic students; for summer admission, 5/1 priority date for domestic students. Applications are processed on a rolling basis. Application fee: $25. Electronic applications accepted. *Expenses: Tuition:* Full-time $8550; part-time $285 per hour. *Required fees:* $1160; $335 per term. *Financial support:* Scholarships/grants available. Financial award application deadline: 6/30; financial award applicants required to submit FAFSA. *Unit head:* Dr. Jenetta R. Waddell, Dean of Graduate Studies, 662-685-4771 Ext. 118, Fax: 662-815-2919, E-mail: jwaddell@bmc.edu. *Application contact:* Jean Harrington, Administrative Assistant, 662-685-4771 Ext. 118, Fax: 662-815-2919, E-mail: jharrington@bmc.edu.

Boise State University, College of Education, Department of Literacy, Boise, ID 83725-0399. Offers MA. *Accreditation:* NCATE. Part-time programs available. *Degree requirements:* For master's, thesis optional. *Entrance requirements:* For master's, minimum GPA of 3.0. Electronic applications accepted.

Boston College, Lynch Graduate School of Education, Program in Reading and Literacy, Chestnut Hill, MA 02467-3800. Offers M Ed, MAT, CAES. *Accreditation:* Teacher Education Accreditation Council. Part-time and evening/weekend programs available. *Students:* 2 part-time (both women). 12 applicants, 75% accepted, 2 enrolled. In 2013, 5 master's awarded. *Degree requirements:* For master's and CAES, comprehensive exam. *Entrance requirements:* For master's, GRE General Test or MAT, general licensure, one year of teaching experience; for CAES, GRE General Test or MAT. Additional exam requirements/recommendations for international students: Required—TOEFL (minimum score 100 iBT). *Application deadline:* For fall admission, 12/1 priority date for domestic students, 12/1 for international students; for spring admission, 11/1 for domestic and international students. Application fee: $65. Electronic applications accepted. *Financial support:* Fellowships with full and partial tuition reimbursements, research assistantships with full and partial tuition reimbursements, teaching assistantships with full and partial tuition reimbursements, career-related internships or fieldwork, Federal Work-Study, scholarships/grants, traineeships, health care benefits, tuition waivers (full and partial), and unspecified assistantships available. Support available to part-time students. Financial award applicants required to submit FAFSA. *Faculty research:* Creating literacy learning environments, critical literacy and literacy development. *Unit head:* Dr. Alec Peck, Chairperson, 617-552-4214, Fax: 617-552-0398. *Application contact:* Domenic Lomanno, Director, Graduate Admission and Financial Aid, 617-552-4214, Fax: 617-552-0398, E-mail: lomanno@bc.edu.

Bowie State University, Graduate Programs, Program in Reading Education, Bowie, MD 20715-9465. Offers M Ed. *Accreditation:* NCATE. Part-time and evening/weekend programs available. *Degree requirements:* For master's, comprehensive exam, thesis optional, research paper. *Entrance requirements:* For master's, minimum GPA of 2.5, teaching certificate, teaching experience. *Expenses:* Tuition, state resident: full-time $8665. Tuition, nonresident: full-time $16,007. *Required fees:* $1927. *Faculty research:* Literacy education, multicultural education.

Bowling Green State University, Graduate College, College of Education and Human Development, School of Education and Intervention Services, Teaching and Learning Division, Program in Reading, Bowling Green, OH 43403. Offers M Ed, Ed S. *Accreditation:* NCATE. Part-time programs available. *Degree requirements:* For master's, thesis or alternative; for Ed S, practicum or field experience. *Entrance requirements:* For master's and Ed S, GRE General Test. Additional exam requirements/recommendations for international students: Required—TOEFL. Electronic applications accepted. *Faculty research:* Children's literature, attention deficit disorder (ADD)/reading correlation, content area reading, reading instruction, reading/writing connection.

Bridgewater State University, School of Graduate Studies, School of Education and Allied Studies, Department of Elementary and Early Childhood Education, Program in Reading, Bridgewater, MA 02325-0001. Offers M Ed, CAGS. *Accreditation:* NCATE. Part-time and evening/weekend programs available. *Entrance requirements:* For master's, GRE General Test, 1 year of teaching experience.

Brigham Young University, Graduate Studies, David O. McKay School of Education, Department of Teacher Education, Provo, UT 84602. Offers integrative science-technology-engineering-mathematics (STEM) (MA); literacy education (MA); physical education teacher education (MA); teacher education (MA). *Faculty:* 27 full-time (14 women). *Students:* 15 full-time (9 women). Average age 33. In 2013, 7 master's awarded. *Degree requirements:* For master's, thesis. *Entrance requirements:* For master's, GRE General Test, minimum 1 year of teaching experience (preferred), minimum GPA of 3.25 in last 60 hours of course work. Additional exam requirements/recommendations for international students: Recommended—TOEFL. *Application deadline:* For fall admission, 2/1 for domestic and international students; for winter admission, 2/1 for domestic and international students; for spring admission, 3/15 for domestic students; for summer admission, 2/1 priority date for domestic and international students. Application fee: $50. Electronic applications accepted. *Expenses: Tuition:* Full-time $6130; part-time $340 per credit hour. Tuition and fees vary according to program and student's religious affiliation. *Financial support:* In 2013–14, 13 students received support. Scholarships/grants and tuition waivers (full and partial) available. *Faculty research:* Literacy education, stem education, teacher development and education, physical education teacher education. *Unit head:* Dr. Michael O. Tunnell, Chair, 801-422-3497, Fax: 801-422-0652, E-mail: mike_tunnell@byu.edu. *Application contact:* Dr. Janet R. Young, Associate Chair/Graduate Coordinator, 801-422-4979, Fax: 801-422-0652, E-mail: janet_young@byu.edu.
Website: http://education.byu.edu/ted/.

Buffalo State College, State University of New York, The Graduate School, Faculty of Applied Science and Education, Department of Elementary Education and Reading, Programs in Literacy Specialist, Buffalo, NY 14222-1095. Offers literacy specialist (birth-grade 6) (MS Ed); literacy specialist (grades 5-12) (MPS). *Accreditation:* NCATE. Part-time and evening/weekend programs available. *Degree requirements:* For master's, project. *Entrance requirements:* For master's, minimum GPA of 3.0 in last 60 hours. Additional exam requirements/recommendations for international students: Required—TOEFL (minimum score 550 paper-based).

Caldwell University, Graduate Studies, Division of Education, Caldwell, NJ 07006-6195. Offers curriculum and instruction (MA); education (Postbaccalaureate Certificate); educational administration (MA); learning disabilities teacher-consultant (Post-Master's Certificate); literacy instruction (MA); principal (Post-Master's Certificate); reading specialist (Post-Master's Certificate); special education (MA), including special education, teaching of students with disabilities, teaching of students with disabilities and learning disabilities teacher-consultant; superintendent (Post-Master's Certificate); supervisor (Post-Master's Certificate). Part-time and evening/weekend programs available. *Faculty:* 11 full-time (7 women), 12 part-time/adjunct (6 women). *Students:* 42 full-time (31 women), 255 part-time (219 women); includes 40 minority (14 Black or African American, non-Hispanic/Latino; 5 Asian, non-Hispanic/Latino; 18 Hispanic/Latino; 1 Native Hawaiian or other Pacific Islander, non-Hispanic/Latino; 2 Two or more races, non-Hispanic/Latino). Average age 37. 140 applicants, 71% accepted, 83 enrolled. In 2013, 63 master's awarded. *Degree requirements:* For master's, comprehensive exam (for some programs). *Entrance requirements:* For master's, PRAXIS, 3 years of work experience, prior teaching certification. Additional exam requirements/recommendations for international students: Required—TOEFL (minimum score 580 paper-based). *Application deadline:* Applications are processed on a rolling basis. Application fee: $40. Electronic applications accepted. *Financial support:* Career-related internships or fieldwork available. Financial award applicants required to submit FAFSA. *Faculty research:* Curriculum and instruction, secondary education, special education, education and technology. *Unit head:* Dr. Janice Stewart, Division Associate Dean, 973-618-3626, E-mail: jstewart@caldwell.edu. *Application contact:* Vilma Mueller, Director of Graduate Studies, 973-618-3544, E-mail: graduate@caldwell.edu.

California Baptist University, Program in Education, Riverside, CA 92504-3206. Offers educational leadership for faith-based institutions (MS); educational leadership for public institutions (MS); educational technology (MS); instructional computer applications (MS); international education (MS); leadership and adult learning (MS); leadership and organizational studies (MS); reading (MS); school counseling (MS); school psychology (MS); science education (MS); special education in mild/moderate disabilities (MS); special education in moderate/severe disabilities (MS); teaching (MS); teaching and learning (MS); TESOL (teachers of English to speakers of other languages) (MS). Part-time and evening/weekend programs available. Postbaccalaureate distance learning degree programs offered (minimal on-campus study). *Faculty:* 18 full-time (9 women), 8 part-time/adjunct (5 women). *Students:* 158 full-time (127 women), 228 part-time (179 women); includes 159 minority (27 Black or African American, non-Hispanic/Latino; 4 American Indian or Alaska Native, non-Hispanic/Latino; 13 Asian, non-Hispanic/Latino; 107 Hispanic/Latino; 1 Native Hawaiian or other Pacific Islander, non-Hispanic/Latino; 7 Two or more races, non-Hispanic/Latino), 2 international. Average age 33. 298 applicants, 74% accepted, 113 enrolled. In 2013, 70 master's awarded. *Degree requirements:* For master's, comprehensive exam, project, or thesis. *Entrance requirements:* For master's, minimum undergraduate GPA of 3.0; 18 semester units of prerequisite course work in education; three recommendations; 500-word essay; interview. Additional exam requirements/recommendations for international students: Required—TOEFL (minimum score 80 iBT). *Application deadline:* For fall admission, 8/1 priority date for domestic students, 7/1 for international students; for spring admission, 12/1 priority date for domestic students, 11/1 for international students. Applications are processed on a rolling basis. Application fee: $45. Electronic applications accepted. *Expenses:* Contact institution. *Financial support:* Institutionally sponsored loans available. Financial award applicants required to submit CSS PROFILE or FAFSA. *Faculty research:* Leadership development, complexity theory, faith and learning, special education, social and philosophical contexts of education. *Unit head:* Dr. John Shoup, Dean, School of Education, 951-343-4205, Fax: 951-343-4516, E-mail:

jshoup@calbaptist.edu. *Application contact:* Dr. Kathryn Norwood, Director, Master of Science Program in Education, 951-343-4760, E-mail: knorwood@calbaptist.edu.
Website: http://www.calbaptist.edu/mastersined/.

California State University, East Bay, Office of Academic Programs and Graduate Studies, College of Education and Allied Studies, Department of Teacher Education, Hayward, CA 94542-3000. Offers education (MS), including curriculum, early childhood education, educational technology leadership, reading instruction. Postbaccalaureate distance learning degree programs offered. *Degree requirements:* For master's, project or thesis. *Entrance requirements:* For master's, minimum GPA of 3.0 in field, 2.5 overall; teaching experience; baccalaureate degree; 3 letters of recommendation. Additional exam requirements/recommendations for international students: Required—TOEFL (minimum score 550 paper-based), IELTS. Electronic applications accepted. *Faculty research:* Online, pedagogy, writing, learning, teaching.

California State University, Fresno, Division of Graduate Studies, School of Education and Human Development, Department of Literacy and Early Education, Fresno, CA 93740-8027. Offers education (MA), including early childhood education, reading/language arts. *Accreditation:* NCATE. Part-time and evening/weekend programs available. *Degree requirements:* For master's, thesis or alternative. *Entrance requirements:* For master's, GRE General Test, MAT, minimum GPA of 2.75. Additional exam requirements/recommendations for international students: Required—TOEFL. Electronic applications accepted. *Faculty research:* Reading recovery, monitoring/tutoring programs, character and academics, professional ethics, low-performing partnership schools.

California State University, Fullerton, Graduate Studies, College of Education, Department of Reading, Fullerton, CA 92834-9480. Offers MS. Part-time programs available. *Students:* 9 full-time (all women), 93 part-time (89 women); includes 45 minority (2 Black or African American, non-Hispanic/Latino; 7 Asian, non-Hispanic/Latino; 32 Hispanic/Latino; 4 Two or more races, non-Hispanic/Latino), 2 international. Average age 36. 52 applicants, 94% accepted, 37 enrolled. In 2013, 30 master's awarded. Application fee: $55. *Financial support:* Career-related internships or fieldwork, Federal Work-Study, institutionally sponsored loans, and scholarships/grants available. Support available to part-time students. Financial award application deadline: 3/1; financial award applicants required to submit FAFSA. *Unit head:* Dr. Ula Manzo, Chair, 657-278-3357. *Application contact:* Admissions/Applications, 657-278-2371.

California State University, Los Angeles, Graduate Studies, Charter College of Education, Division of Curriculum and Instruction, Los Angeles, CA 90032-8530. Offers elementary teaching (MA); reading (MA); secondary teaching (MA). Part-time and evening/weekend programs available. *Faculty:* 4 full-time (2 women), 12 part-time/adjunct (8 women). *Students:* 144 full-time (104 women), 119 part-time (91 women); includes 188 minority (13 Black or African American, non-Hispanic/Latino; 39 Asian, non-Hispanic/Latino; 130 Hispanic/Latino; 6 Two or more races, non-Hispanic/Latino), 12 international. Average age 33. 78 applicants, 73% accepted, 41 enrolled. In 2013, 87 master's awarded. *Entrance requirements:* For master's, minimum GPA of 2.75 in last 90 units of course work, teaching certificate. Additional exam requirements/recommendations for international students: Required—TOEFL (minimum score 500 paper-based). *Application deadline:* For fall admission, 5/1 for domestic and international students. Applications are processed on a rolling basis. Application fee: $55. Electronic applications accepted. *Financial support:* Federal Work-Study available. Support available to part-time students. Financial award application deadline: 3/1. *Faculty research:* Media, language arts, mathematics, computers, drug-free schools. *Unit head:* Dr. Gay Yuen, Acting Chair, 323-343-4350, Fax: 323-343-5458, E-mail: gyuen@calstatela.edu. *Application contact:* Dr. Larry Fritz, Dean of Graduate Studies, 323-343-3827, Fax: 323-343-5653, E-mail: lfritz@calstatela.edu.
Website: http://www.calstatela.edu/academic/ccoe/index_edci.htm.

California State University, Northridge, Graduate Studies, College of Education, Department of Elementary Education, Northridge, CA 91330. Offers curriculum and instruction (MA); language and literacy (MA); multilingual/multicultural education (MA); teaching and learning (MA). *Accreditation:* NCATE. Part-time and evening/weekend programs available. *Degree requirements:* For master's, comprehensive exam. *Entrance requirements:* For master's, GRE General Test or minimum GPA of 3.0. Additional exam requirements/recommendations for international students: Required—TOEFL.

California State University, Sacramento, Office of Graduate Studies, College of Education, Department of Teacher Education, Sacramento, CA 95819. Offers behavioral sciences (MA), including gender equity studies; curriculum and instruction (MA); educational technology (MA); language and literacy (MA). Part-time programs available. *Entrance requirements:* Additional exam requirements/recommendations for international students: Required—TOEFL. *Application deadline:* For fall admission, 3/1 for domestic and international students; for spring admission, 9/15 for domestic students, 9/30 for international students. Applications are processed on a rolling basis. Application fee: $55. Electronic applications accepted. *Financial support:* Teaching assistantships, career-related internships or fieldwork, and Federal Work-Study available. Support available to part-time students. Financial award application deadline: 3/1; financial award applicants required to submit FAFSA. *Faculty research:* Technology integration and psychological implications for teaching and learning; inquiry-based research and learning in science and technology; uncovering the process of everyday creativity in teachers and other leaders; universal design as a foundation for inclusion; bullying, cyber-bullying and impact on school success; diversity, social justice in adult/vocational education. *Unit head:* Dr. Rita Johnson, Chair, 916-278-4356, E-mail: rjohnson@csus.edu. *Application contact:* Jose Martinez, Graduate Admissions Supervisor, 916-278-7871, E-mail: martinj@skymail.csus.edu.
Website: http://www.edweb.csus.edu/edte.

California State University, San Bernardino, Graduate Studies, College of Education, Program in Reading, San Bernardino, CA 92407-2397. Offers MA. *Accreditation:* NCATE. Part-time and evening/weekend programs available. *Students:* 8 full-time (6 women), 17 part-time (14 women); includes 11 minority (1 Black or African American, non-Hispanic/Latino; 10 Hispanic/Latino). Average age 32. 8 applicants, 100% accepted, 6 enrolled. In 2013, 17 master's awarded. *Degree requirements:* For master's, comprehensive exam (for some programs), thesis or alternative. *Entrance requirements:* For master's, minimum GPA of 3.0 in education. *Application deadline:* For fall admission, 8/31 priority date for domestic students. Application fee: $55. *Financial support:* Career-related internships or fieldwork and Federal Work-Study available. Support available to part-time students. *Unit head:* Dr. Kathryn Howard, Chair, 909-537-7626, Fax: 909-537-5992, E-mail: khoward@csusb.edu. *Application contact:* Dr. Jeffrey Thompson, Dean of Graduate Studies, 909-537-5058, E-mail: jthompso@csusb.edu.

California State University, San Marcos, School of Education, San Marcos, CA 92096-0001. Offers educational administration (MA); educational leadership (Ed D); general education (MA); literacy education (MA); special education (MA). *Accreditation:* NCATE (one or more programs are accredited). Part-time and evening/weekend programs available. *Degree requirements:* For master's, thesis. *Entrance requirements:* For master's, minimum GPA of 3.0, teaching credentials, 1 year of teaching experience. Tuition and fees vary according to program. *Faculty research:* Multicultural literature, art as knowledge, poetry and second language acquisition, restructuring K–12 education and improving the training of K–8 science teachers.

California State University, Stanislaus, College of Education, Program in Education (MA), Turlock, CA 95382. Offers curriculum and instruction (MA), including education technology, elementary education, multilingual education, physical education, reading, secondary education, special education; school administration (MA); school counseling (MA). Part-time and evening/weekend programs available. *Degree requirements:* For master's, comprehensive exam (for some programs), thesis (for some programs). *Entrance requirements:* For master's, MAT, GRE, or CBEST (varies by concentration), 3 letters of recommendation, personal statement. Additional exam requirements/recommendations for international students: Required—TOEFL (minimum score 550 paper-based). Electronic applications accepted. *Faculty research:* Children's perspectives on historical events, method elementary schools dual language education, K-12 reading programs.

California University of Pennsylvania, School of Graduate Studies and Research, College of Education and Human Services, Department of Elementary Education, Program in Reading Specialist, California, PA 15419-1394. Offers M Ed. *Accreditation:* NCATE. Part-time and evening/weekend programs available. *Degree requirements:* For master's, comprehensive exam, thesis optional, practicum. *Entrance requirements:* For master's, MAT, PRAXIS, minimum GPA of 3.0, teaching certificate. Additional exam requirements/recommendations for international students: Required—TOEFL (minimum score 550 paper-based; 80 iBT). Electronic applications accepted. *Faculty research:* Online education in reading supervision, phonetics education, remedial reading, injury and reading remediation in brain patients.

Calvin College, Graduate Programs in Education, Grand Rapids, MI 49546-4388. Offers curriculum and instruction (M Ed); educational leadership (M Ed); learning disabilities (M Ed); literacy (M Ed). Part-time programs available. *Faculty:* 12 full-time (5 women). *Students:* 9 full-time (7 women), 133 part-time (87 women); includes 12 minority (3 Black or African American, non-Hispanic/Latino; 3 Asian, non-Hispanic/Latino; 3 Hispanic/Latino; 3 Two or more races, non-Hispanic/Latino), 20 international. Average age 29. 15 applicants, 87% accepted, 13 enrolled. In 2013, 27 master's awarded. *Degree requirements:* For master's, thesis or seminar. *Entrance requirements:* For master's, teaching certificate. Additional exam requirements/recommendations for international students: Required—TOEFL (minimum score 550 paper-based; 80 iBT). *Application deadline:* For fall admission, 8/1 priority date for domestic students, 5/1 priority date for international students; for spring admission, 1/1 priority date for domestic students, 12/1 priority date for international students; for summer admission, 5/18 for domestic students. Applications are processed on a rolling basis. Application fee: $0. Electronic applications accepted. *Financial support:* Federal Work-Study, scholarships/grants, and tuition waivers (full and partial) available. Financial award application deadline: 4/3; financial award applicants required to submit FAFSA. *Faculty research:* Literacy, racialized gender and gendered identity, teacher learning, learning disabilities identification, leadership. *Unit head:* Dr. David Smith, Graduate Program Director, 616-526-6158, Fax: 616-526-6505, E-mail: dsmith@calvin.edu. *Application contact:* Cindi Hoekstra, Program Coordinator, 616-526-6158, Fax: 616-526-6505, E-mail: choekstr@calvin.edu.
Website: http://www.calvin.edu/academic/graduate_studies.

Cambridge College, School of Education, Cambridge, MA 02138-5304. Offers autism specialist (M Ed); autism/behavior analyst (M Ed); behavior analyst (Post-Master's Certificate); behavioral management (M Ed); early childhood teacher (M Ed); education specialist in curriculum and instruction (CAGS); educational leadership (Ed D); elementary teacher (M Ed); English as a second language (M Ed, Certificate); general science (M Ed); health education (Post-Master's Certificate); health/family and consumer sciences (M Ed); history (M Ed); individualized (M Ed); information technology literacy (M Ed); instructional technology (M Ed); interdisciplinary studies (M Ed); library teacher (M Ed); literacy education (M Ed); mathematics (M Ed); mathematics specialist (Certificate); middle school mathematics and science (M Ed); school administration (M Ed, CAGS); school guidance counselor (M Ed); school nurse education (M Ed); school social worker/school adjustment counselor (M Ed); special education administrator (CAGS); special education/moderate disabilities (M Ed); teaching skills and methodologies (M Ed). Part-time and evening/weekend programs available. Postbaccalaureate distance learning degree programs offered (minimal on-campus study). *Degree requirements:* For master's, thesis, internship/practicum (licensure program only); for doctorate, thesis/dissertation; for other advanced degree, thesis. *Entrance requirements:* For master's, interview, resume, documentation of licensure, 2 professional references; for doctorate, official transcripts, interview, resume, documentation of licensure (if any), written personal statement/essay, portfolio of scholarly and professional work, qualifying assessment, 2 professional references, health insurance, immunizations form; for other advanced degree, official transcripts, interview, resume, documentation of licensure (if any), written personal statement/essay, 2 professional references, health insurance, immunizations form. Additional exam requirements/recommendations for international students: Required—TOEFL (minimum score 550 paper-based; 79 iBT), Michigan English Language Assessment Battery (minimum score 85); Recommended—IELTS (minimum score 6). Electronic applications accepted. *Expenses:* Contact institution. *Faculty research:* Adult education, accelerated learning, mathematics education, brain compatible learning, special education and law.

Canisius College, Graduate Division, School of Education and Human Services, Department of Graduate Education and Leadership, Buffalo, NY 14208-1098. Offers business and marketing education (MS Ed); college student personnel (MS Ed); deaf education (MS Ed); deaf/adolescent education, grades 7-12 (MS Ed); deaf/childhood education, grades 1-6 (MS Ed); differentiated instruction (MS Ed); education administration (MS); educational administration (MS Ed); educational technologies (Certificate); gifted education extension (Certificate); literacy (MS Ed); reading (Certificate); school building leadership (MS Ed, Certificate); school district leadership (Certificate); teacher leader (Certificate); TESOL (MS Ed). *Accreditation:* NCATE. Part-time and evening/weekend programs available. Postbaccalaureate distance learning degree programs offered (minimal on-campus study). *Faculty:* 6 full-time (5 women), 33 part-time/adjunct (20 women). *Students:* 134 full-time (106 women), 267 part-time (213 women); includes 36 minority (22 Black or African American, non-Hispanic/Latino; 1 American Indian or Alaska Native, non-Hispanic/Latino; 3 Asian, non-Hispanic/Latino; 8 Hispanic/Latino; 2 Two or more races, non-Hispanic/Latino), 2 international. Average age 30. 282 applicants, 80% accepted, 120 enrolled. In 2013, 178 master's awarded. *Entrance requirements:* For master's, GRE if cumulative GPA less than 2.7, transcripts, two letters of recommendation. Additional exam requirements/recommendations for international students: Required—TOEFL (minimum score 550 paper-based, 80 iBT), IELTS (minimum score 6.5), or CAEL (minimum score 70). *Application deadline:* Applications are processed on a rolling basis. Application fee: $25. Electronic applications accepted. Application fee is waived when completed online. *Expenses: Tuition:* Part-time $750 per credit hour. *Financial support:* Career-related internships or fieldwork, Federal Work-Study, scholarships/grants, tuition waivers (partial), and unspecified assistantships available. Support available to part-time students. Financial award application deadline: 4/30; financial award applicants required to submit FAFSA.

Faculty research: Asperger's disease, autism, private higher education, reading strategies. *Unit head:* Dr. Rosemary K. Murray, Chair/Associate Professor of Graduate Education and Leadership, 716-888-3723, E-mail: murray1@canisius.edu. *Application contact:* Julie A. Zulewski, Director of Graduate Admissions, 716-888-2548, Fax: 716-888-3195, E-mail: zulewskj@canisius.edu.
Website: http://www.canisius.edu/graduate/.

Capella University, School of Education, Doctoral Programs in Education, Minneapolis, MN 55402. Offers curriculum and instruction (PhD); educational leadership and management (Ed D); instructional design for online learning (PhD); K-12 studies in education (PhD); leadership for higher education (PhD); leadership in educational administration (PhD); postsecondary and adult education (PhD); professional studies in education (PhD); reading and literacy (Ed D); special education leadership (PhD); training and performance improvement (PhD).

Capella University, School of Education, Master's Programs in Education, Minneapolis, MN 55402. Offers adult education (MS); curriculum and instruction (MS); early childhood education (MS); enrollment management (MS); higher education leadership and management (MS); instructional design for online learning (MS); integrative studies (MS); K-12 studies in education (MS); leadership in educational administration (MS); reading and literacy (MS); special education teaching (MS).

Cardinal Stritch University, College of Education, Department of Literacy, Milwaukee, WI 53217-3985. Offers literacy/English as a second language (MA); reading/language arts (MA); reading/learning disability (MA). *Accreditation:* NCATE. Part-time and evening/weekend programs available. *Degree requirements:* For master's, comprehensive exam, thesis, faculty recommendation, research project. *Entrance requirements:* For master's, letters of recommendation (2), minimum GPA of 2.75.

Carthage College, Division of Teacher Education, Kenosha, WI 53140. Offers classroom guidance and counseling (M Ed); creative arts (M Ed); gifted and talented children (M Ed); language arts (M Ed); modern language (M Ed); natural sciences (M Ed); reading (M Ed, Certificate); social sciences (M Ed); teacher leadership (M Ed). Part-time and evening/weekend programs available. *Degree requirements:* For master's, thesis optional. *Entrance requirements:* For master's, MAT, minimum B average, letters of reference.

Castleton State College, Division of Graduate Studies, Department of Education, Program in Language Arts and Reading, Castleton, VT 05735. Offers MA Ed, CAGS. Part-time and evening/weekend programs available. *Degree requirements:* For master's, thesis or alternative; for CAGS, publishable paper, written exams. *Entrance requirements:* For master's, GRE General Test, MAT, interview, minimum undergraduate GPA of 3.0; for CAGS, educational research, master's degree, minimum undergraduate GPA of 3.0.

Central Connecticut State University, School of Graduate Studies, School of Education and Professional Studies, Department of Reading and Language Arts, New Britain, CT 06050-4010. Offers MS, AC, Sixth Year Certificate. Part-time and evening/weekend programs available. *Faculty:* 5 full-time (4 women), 2 part-time/adjunct (1 woman). *Students:* 1 (woman) full-time, 88 part-time (87 women); includes 5 minority (3 Black or African American, non-Hispanic/Latino; 1 Asian, non-Hispanic/Latino; 1 Hispanic/Latino). Average age 32. 31 applicants, 65% accepted, 17 enrolled. In 2013, 44 master's, 5 other advanced degrees awarded. *Degree requirements:* For master's, comprehensive exam, thesis or alternative; for other advanced degree, qualifying exam. *Entrance requirements:* For master's, minimum undergraduate GPA of 2.7, teacher certification, interview, essay, letters of recommendation; for other advanced degree, master's degree, essay, teacher certification, interview, letters of recommendation. Additional exam requirements/recommendations for international students: Required—TOEFL (minimum score 550 paper-based; 79 iBT). *Application deadline:* For fall admission, 5/1 for domestic and international students; for spring admission, 11/1 for domestic and international students. Applications are processed on a rolling basis. Application fee: $50. Electronic applications accepted. Part-time tuition and fees vary according to degree level. *Financial support:* In 2013–14, 2 students received support. Career-related internships or fieldwork, Federal Work-Study, scholarships/grants, and unspecified assistantships available. Support available to part-time students. Financial award application deadline: 3/1; financial award applicants required to submit FAFSA. *Faculty research:* Developmental, clinical, and administrative aspects of reading and language arts instruction. *Unit head:* Dr. Helen Abadiano, Chair, 860-832-2175, E-mail: abadiano@ccsu.edu. *Application contact:* Patricia Gardner, Associate Director of Graduate Studies, 860-832-2350, Fax: 860-832-2362, E-mail: graduateadmissions@ccsu.edu.
Website: http://www.reading.ccsu.edu/.

Central Michigan University, Central Michigan University Global Campus, Program in Education, Mount Pleasant, MI 48859. Offers college teaching (Graduate Certificate); community college (MA); curriculum and instruction (MA); educational technology (MA); guidance and development (MA); reading and literacy K-12 (MA); school principalship (MA), including charter school leadership; training and development (MA). *Accreditation:* Teacher Education Accreditation Council. Part-time and evening/weekend programs available. *Entrance requirements:* For master's, minimum GPA of 2.7 in major. Additional exam requirements/recommendations for international students: Required—TOEFL. *Application deadline:* Applications are processed on a rolling basis. Application fee: $50. Electronic applications accepted. *Financial support:* Scholarships/grants available. Support available to part-time students. *Unit head:* Kaleb Patrick, Director, 989-774-3144, E-mail: patri1kg@cmich.edu. *Application contact:* 877-268-4636, E-mail: cmuglobal@cmich.edu.

Central Michigan University, College of Graduate Studies, College of Education and Human Services, Department of Teacher Education and Professional Development, Mount Pleasant, MI 48859. Offers educational technology (MA, Graduate Certificate); elementary education (MA), including classroom teaching, early childhood; reading and literacy K-12 (MA); secondary education (MA). Part-time and evening/weekend programs available. *Degree requirements:* For master's, thesis or alternative. Electronic applications accepted. *Faculty research:* Integrating literacy across the curriculum, science teaching and aesthetic learning in science, diversity education, educational technology, educational psychology and child development.

Central Washington University, Graduate Studies and Research, College of Education and Professional Studies, Department of Language, Literacy and Special Education, Program in Reading Education, Ellensburg, WA 98926. Offers M Ed. Part-time programs available. *Degree requirements:* For master's, thesis or alternative. *Entrance requirements:* For master's, minimum GPA of 3.0. Additional exam requirements/recommendations for international students: Required—TOEFL (minimum score 550 paper-based; 79 iBT), IELTS (minimum score 6.5). Electronic applications accepted.

Chestnut Hill College, School of Graduate Studies, Department of Education, Program in Reading, Philadelphia, PA 19118-2693. Offers M Ed, CAS. Part-time and evening/weekend programs available. *Faculty:* 10 full-time (7 women), 48 part-time/adjunct (34 women). *Students:* 5 part-time (3 women). Average age 31. 6 applicants, 100% accepted. In 2013, 3 CASs awarded. *Degree requirements:* For master's, thesis optional. *Entrance requirements:* Additional exam requirements/recommendations for international students: Required—TOEFL (minimum score 500 paper-based) or IELTS (minimum score 6). *Application deadline:* For fall admission, 7/1 for domestic and international students; for spring admission, 11/1 for domestic and international students; for summer admission, 4/1 for domestic and international students. Applications are processed on a rolling basis. *Expenses:* Contact institution. *Financial support:* Unspecified assistantships available. *Faculty research:* Inclusive education, cultural issues in education. *Unit head:* Dr. Debra Chiaradonna, Chair, Department of Education, 215-248-7147, Fax: 215-248-7155, E-mail: chiaradonnad@chc.edu. *Application contact:* Jayne Mashett, Director of Admissions, School of Graduate Studies, 215-248-7020, Fax: 215-248-7161, E-mail: gradadmissions@chc.edu.

Chicago State University, School of Graduate and Professional Studies, College of Education, Department of Reading, Elementary Education, Library Information and Media Studies, Program in Reading, Chicago, IL 60628. Offers teaching of reading (MS Ed). *Accreditation:* NCATE. *Entrance requirements:* For master's, minimum GPA of 2.75.

The Citadel, The Military College of South Carolina, Citadel Graduate College, School of Education, Program in Reading, Charleston, SC 29409. Offers literacy education (M Ed). *Accreditation:* NCATE. Part-time and evening/weekend programs available. *Faculty:* 10 full-time (6 women), 8 part-time/adjunct (3 women). *Students:* 1 (woman) full-time, 39 part-time (36 women); includes 4 minority (all Black or African American, non-Hispanic/Latino). Average age 31. In 2013, 11 master's awarded. *Degree requirements:* For master's, comprehensive exam. *Entrance requirements:* For master's, GRE (minimum score 290; 900 on old scoring system) or MAT (minimum score 396), minimum undergraduate GPA of 2.5, valid teaching certificate. Additional exam requirements/recommendations for international students: Required—TOEFL (minimum score 550 paper-based; 79 iBT). *Application deadline:* Applications are processed on a rolling basis. Application fee: $30. Electronic applications accepted. *Expenses: Tuition, area resident:* Part-time $525 per credit hour. Tuition, state resident: part-time $525 per credit hour. Tuition, nonresident: part-time $865 per credit hour. *Financial support:* Career-related internships or fieldwork, health care benefits, and unspecified assistantships available. Support available to part-time students. Financial award application deadline: 7/1; financial award applicants required to submit FAFSA. *Unit head:* Dr. Dan T. Ouzts, Coordinator, 843-953-6309, Fax: 843-953-7258, E-mail: dan.ouzts@citadel.edu. *Application contact:* Dr. Robert H. McNamara, Associate Provost, The Citadel Graduate College, 843-953-5089, Fax: 843-953-7630, E-mail: cgc@citadel.edu.
Website: http://www.citadel.edu/education/literacy-education.html.

City College of the City University of New York, Graduate School, College of Liberal Arts and Science, Division of the Humanities and Arts, Department of English, Program in Language and Literacy, New York, NY 10031-9198. Offers MA. *Accreditation:* NCATE. *Entrance requirements:* For master's, 2 writing samples. Additional exam requirements/recommendations for international students: Required—TOEFL (minimum score 600 paper-based; 100 iBT). Electronic applications accepted.

City University of Seattle, Graduate Division, Albright School of Education, Bellevue, WA 98005. Offers administrator certification (Certificate); curriculum and instruction (M Ed); educational leadership (Ed D); elementary education (MIT); guidance and counseling (M Ed); higher education leadership (Ed D); leadership (M Ed); leadership and school counseling (M Ed); organizational leadership (Ed D); reading and literacy (M Ed); special education (MIT); superintendent certification (Certificate). Part-time and evening/weekend programs available. Postbaccalaureate distance learning degree programs offered (no on-campus study). *Degree requirements:* For master's, comprehensive exam (for some programs), thesis (for some programs); for doctorate, comprehensive exam, thesis/dissertation. *Entrance requirements:* Additional exam requirements/recommendations for international students: Required—TOEFL (minimum score 567 paper-based; 87 iBT); Recommended—IELTS. Electronic applications accepted. *Expenses:* Contact institution.

Clarion University of Pennsylvania, Office of Transfer, Adult and Graduate Admissions, Master of Education Program, Clarion, PA 16214. Offers curriculum and instruction (M Ed); early childhood (M Ed); math education (M Ed); reading (M Ed); science education (M Ed); special education (M Ed); technology (M Ed). *Accreditation:* NCATE. Part-time programs available. Postbaccalaureate distance learning degree programs offered (no on-campus study). *Faculty:* 17 full-time (10 women). *Students:* 231 full-time (191 women), 535 part-time (448 women); includes 39 minority (12 Black or African American, non-Hispanic/Latino; 8 Asian, non-Hispanic/Latino; 11 Hispanic/Latino; 1 Native Hawaiian or other Pacific Islander, non-Hispanic/Latino; 7 Two or more races, non-Hispanic/Latino). Average age 31. 28 applicants, 75% accepted, 18 enrolled. In 2013, 99 master's awarded. *Degree requirements:* For master's, comprehensive exam, thesis, or portfolio. *Entrance requirements:* For master's, minimum QPA of 3.0. Additional exam requirements/recommendations for international students: Required—TOEFL (minimum score 550 paper-based; 80 iBT), IELTS (minimum score 7). *Application deadline:* For fall admission, 8/1 for domestic students, 4/15 for international students; for spring admission, 8/1 for domestic students, 9/15 for international students. Applications are processed on a rolling basis. Application fee: $40. Electronic applications accepted. *Expenses:* Tuition, state resident: part-time $442 per credit. Tuition, nonresident: part-time $451 per credit. *Required fees:* $142.40 per semester. One-time fee: $150 part-time. *Financial support:* In 2013–14, 8 research assistantships with full and partial tuition reimbursements (averaging $9,420 per year) were awarded; career-related internships or fieldwork also available. Support available to part-time students. Financial award application deadline: 3/1. *Unit head:* Ray Puller, Interim Dean, 814-393-2146, Fax: 514-393-2446, E-mail: rpuller@clarion.edu. *Application contact:* Susan Staub, Assistant Director, Graduate Programs, 814-393-2337, Fax: 814-393-2722, E-mail: gradstudies@clarion.edu.
Website: http://www.clarion.edu/25887/.

Clarke University, Program in Education, Dubuque, IA 52001-3198. Offers early childhood/special education (MAE); educational administration: elementary and secondary (MAE); educational media: elementary and secondary (MAE); multi-categorical resource k-12 (MAE); multidisciplinary studies (MAE); reading: elementary (MAE); technology in education (MAE). Part-time and evening/weekend programs available. Postbaccalaureate distance learning degree programs offered (minimal on-campus study). *Faculty:* 10 full-time (9 women), 1 (woman) part-time/adjunct. *Students:* 5 full-time (3 women), 27 part-time (24 women); includes 2 minority (1 Black or African American, non-Hispanic/Latino; 1 American Indian or Alaska Native, non-Hispanic/Latino). In 2013, 11 master's awarded. *Degree requirements:* For master's, comprehensive exam, thesis optional. *Entrance requirements:* For master's, GRE General Test or MAT, minimum GPA of 2.75. *Application deadline:* Applications are processed on a rolling basis. Application fee: $25. Electronic applications accepted. *Expenses: Tuition:* Part-time $660 per credit. *Required fees:* $15 per credit. *Financial support:* Career-related internships or fieldwork available. Financial award applicants required to submit FAFSA. *Unit head:* Dr. Michele Slover, Chair, 319-588-6397, Fax: 319-584-8604. *Application contact:* Kara Shroeder, Information Contact, 563-588-6354, Fax: 563-588-6789, E-mail: graduate@clarke.edu.

Clemson University, Graduate School, College of Health, Education, and Human Development, Eugene T. Moore School of Education, Program in Literacy, Clemson, SC

29634. Offers M Ed. *Accreditation:* NCATE. Part-time and evening/weekend programs available. *Students:* 3 part-time (2 women). Average age 33. 3 applicants, 100% accepted, 1 enrolled. In 2013, 30 master's awarded. *Degree requirements:* For master's, electronic portfolio. *Entrance requirements:* For master's, GRE General Test, teaching certificate; minimum undergraduate GPA of 3.0. Additional exam requirements/recommendations for international students: Required—TOEFL; Recommended—IELTS. *Application deadline:* For fall admission, 3/1 for domestic and international students; for winter admission, 3/1 for domestic and international students; for spring admission, 10/1 for domestic and international students. Applications are processed on a rolling basis. Application fee: $70 ($80 for international students). Electronic applications accepted. *Expenses:* Contact institution. *Financial support:* Research assistantships with partial tuition reimbursements, institutionally sponsored loans, health care benefits, and unspecified assistantships available. Financial award application deadline: 6/1; financial award applicants required to submit FAFSA. *Faculty research:* Assessment and at-risk readers, use of technology in literacy coaching, strategic reading processes, reading comprehension instruction, African-American children's literature. *Unit head:* Dr. Michael J. Padilla, Director/Associate Dean, 864-656-4444, Fax: 864-656-0311, E-mail: padilla@clemson.edu. *Application contact:* Dr. David Fleming, Graduate Coordinator, 864-656-1881, Fax: 864-656-0311, E-mail: dflemin@clemson.edu.
Website: http://www.clemson.edu/hehd/departments/education/academics/graduate/MEd-RE.html.

The College at Brockport, State University of New York, School of Education and Human Services, Department of Education and Human Development, Program in Childhood Literacy, Brockport, NY 14420-2997. Offers MS Ed. *Accreditation:* NCATE. Part-time programs available. *Students:* 8 full-time (all women), 79 part-time (72 women); includes 2 minority (1 Black or African American, non-Hispanic/Latino; 1 Hispanic/Latino). 36 applicants, 83% accepted, 22 enrolled. In 2013, 18 master's awarded. *Degree requirements:* For master's, thesis or alternative. *Entrance requirements:* For master's, minimum GPA of 3.0, letters of recommendation, interview. Additional exam requirements/recommendations for international students: Required—TOEFL (minimum score 550 paper-based; 79 iBT), IELTS (minimum score 6.5). *Application deadline:* For fall admission, 6/1 priority date for domestic and international students. Application fee: $80. Electronic applications accepted. *Expenses:* Tuition, state resident: full-time $9870. Tuition, nonresident: full-time $18,350. *Required fees:* $1848. *Financial support:* Federal Work-Study and scholarships/grants available. Support available to part-time students. Financial award application deadline: 3/15; financial award applicants required to submit FAFSA. *Unit head:* Dr. Don Halquist, Chairperson, 585-395-5550, Fax: 585-395-2172, E-mail: dhalquis@brockport.edu. *Application contact:* Michael Harrison, Coordinator of Certification and Graduate Advisement, 585-395-2326, Fax: 585-395-2172, E-mail: mharriso@brockport.edu. Website: http://www.brockport.edu/ehd.

The College of New Jersey, Graduate Studies, School of Education, Department of Special Education, Language and Literacy, Program in Developmental Reading, Ewing, NJ 08628. Offers M Ed. *Accreditation:* NCATE. Part-time programs available. *Degree requirements:* For master's, comprehensive exam. *Entrance requirements:* For master's, GRE General Test, minimum GPA of 3.0 in field or 2.75 overall. Additional exam requirements/recommendations for international students: Required—TOEFL. Electronic applications accepted.

The College of New Jersey, Graduate Studies, School of Education, Department of Special Education, Language and Literacy, Program in Reading Certification, Ewing, NJ 08628. Offers Certificate. Part-time programs available. *Entrance requirements:* Additional exam requirements/recommendations for international students: Required—TOEFL. Electronic applications accepted.

The College of New Rochelle, Graduate School, Division of Education, Program in Literacy Education, New Rochelle, NY 10805-2308. Offers MS Ed. Part-time and evening/weekend programs available. *Degree requirements:* For master's, practicum. *Entrance requirements:* For master's, interview, minimum GPA of 3.0 in field, 2.7 overall, early elementary teacher certification. *Expenses: Tuition:* Part-time $894 per credit. *Required fees:* $300 per semester. One-time fee: $200. Tuition and fees vary according to course load.

College of St. Joseph, Graduate Programs, Division of Education, Program in Reading, Rutland, VT 05701-3899. Offers M Ed. Part-time and evening/weekend programs available. *Degree requirements:* For master's, comprehensive exam. *Entrance requirements:* For master's, PRAXIS I, official college transcripts; 2 letters of reference; minimum GPA of 3.0 (initial licensure) or 2.7 (nonlicensure); interview. Additional exam requirements/recommendations for international students: Required—TOEFL (minimum score 550 paper-based). Electronic applications accepted.

The College of Saint Rose, Graduate Studies, School of Education, Department of Literacy, Albany, NY 12203-1419. Offers literacy: birth-grade 6 (MS Ed); literacy: grades 5-12 (MS Ed). Part-time and evening/weekend programs available. *Degree requirements:* For master's, field and clinical experiences. *Entrance requirements:* For master's, minimum undergraduate GPA of 3.0, current classroom teaching certification, baccalaureate degree from accredited institution, official transcripts from all colleges/universities attended. Additional exam requirements/recommendations for international students: Required—TOEFL (minimum score 550 paper-based). Electronic applications accepted.

The College of William and Mary, School of Education, Program in Curriculum and Instruction, Williamsburg, VA 23187-8795. Offers elementary education (MA Ed); gifted education (MA Ed); literacy leadership (MA Ed); math specialist (MA Ed); secondary education (MA Ed), including English education, mathematics education, modern foreign languages education, science education, social studies education; special education (MA Ed), including collaborating master educator, general curriculum. *Accreditation:* NCATE. Part-time programs available. *Faculty:* 15 full-time (10 women), 44 part-time/adjunct (38 women). *Students:* 66 full-time (55 women), 27 part-time (26 women); includes 17 minority (4 Black or African American, non-Hispanic/Latino; 1 American Indian or Alaska Native, non-Hispanic/Latino; 3 Asian, non-Hispanic/Latino; 5 Hispanic/Latino; 4 Two or more races, non-Hispanic/Latino). Average age 28. 179 applicants, 72% accepted, 92 enrolled. In 2013, 76 master's awarded. *Degree requirements:* For master's, project. *Entrance requirements:* For master's, GRE or MAT, minimum GPA of 2.5. Additional exam requirements/recommendations for international students: Required—TOEFL, IELTS. *Application deadline:* For fall admission, 1/15 for domestic and international students; for spring admission, 10/1 for domestic and international students. Application fee: $50. Electronic applications accepted. *Expenses:* Tuition, state resident: full-time $7120; part-time $405 per credit hour. Tuition, nonresident: full-time $21,639; part-time $1050 per credit hour. *Required fees:* $4764. *Financial support:* In 2013–14, 49 students received support, including 6 research assistantships with full and partial tuition reimbursements available (averaging $8,269 per year); career-related internships or fieldwork, Federal Work-Study, institutionally sponsored loans, scholarships/grants, and unspecified assistantships also available. Financial award application deadline: 1/15; financial award applicants required to submit FAFSA. *Faculty research:* National Council of Teachers of Mathematics standards, counseling, self-concept and self-esteem, special education, curriculum development.

Unit head: Dr. Mark Hofer, Area Coordinator, 757-221-1713, E-mail: mjhofe@wm.edu. *Application contact:* Dorothy Smith Osborne, Assistant Dean for Academic Programs and Student Services, 757-221-2317, Fax: 757-221-2293, E-mail: dsosbo@wm.edu. Website: http://education.wm.edu.

Concordia University, College of Education, Portland, OR 97211-6099. Offers career and technical education (M Ed); curriculum and instruction (M Ed), including adolescent literacy, career and technical education, e-learning/technology education, early childhood education, English for speakers of other languages, English language development, environmental education, mathematics, methods and curriculum, reading, science, teacher leadership, the inclusive classroom; early childhood (MAT); education leadership (Ed D); educational administration (M Ed); elementary education (MAT); secondary education (MAT); special education (M Ed); teacher leadership (Ed D). Part-time programs available. Postbaccalaureate distance learning degree programs offered (no on-campus study). *Degree requirements:* For master's, comprehensive exam, work samples/portfolio. *Entrance requirements:* For master's, California Basic Educational Skills Test or PRAXIS I, minimum undergraduate GPA of 2.8, graduate 3.0; 2 letters of recommendation. Additional exam requirements/recommendations for international students: Required—TOEFL (minimum score 525 paper-based). Electronic applications accepted. *Faculty research:* Learner-centered classroom, brain-based learning, future of online learning.

Concordia University Chicago, College of Education, Program in Reading Education, River Forest, IL 60305-1499. Offers MA. Part-time and evening/weekend programs available. *Degree requirements:* For master's, comprehensive exam, thesis optional. *Entrance requirements:* For master's, minimum GPA of 2.9. Additional exam requirements/recommendations for international students: Required—TOEFL (minimum score 550 paper-based). Electronic applications accepted. *Faculty research:* Early literacy, classroom management and organization in reading, minority students and reading.

Concordia University, Nebraska, Graduate Programs in Education, Program in Reading Education, Seward, NE 68434-1556. Offers M Ed. *Accreditation:* NCATE. Part-time programs available. *Degree requirements:* For master's, thesis or alternative. *Entrance requirements:* For master's, GRE, MAT, or NTE, minimum GPA of 3.0, BS in education or equivalent.

Concordia University, St. Paul, College of Education and Science, St. Paul, MN 55104-5494. Offers curriculum and instruction (MA Ed), including K-12 reading; differentiated instruction (MA Ed); early childhood education (MA Ed); educational leadership (MA Ed); educational technology (MA Ed); exercise science (MA); family life education (MA); K-12 principal licensure (Ed S); K-12 reading (Certificate); special education (MA Ed, Certificate), including autism spectrum disorder (MA Ed), emotional and behavioral disorders (MA Ed), learning disabilities (MA Ed); sports management (MA); superintendent (Ed S). *Accreditation:* NCATE. Part-time and evening/weekend programs available. Postbaccalaureate distance learning degree programs offered (minimal on-campus study). *Faculty:* 12 full-time (7 women), 92 part-time/adjunct (49 women). *Students:* 915 full-time (659 women), 64 part-time (53 women); includes 99 minority (47 Black or African American, non-Hispanic/Latino; 5 American Indian or Alaska Native, non-Hispanic/Latino; 18 Asian, non-Hispanic/Latino; 15 Hispanic/Latino; 2 Native Hawaiian or other Pacific Islander, non-Hispanic/Latino; 12 Two or more races, non-Hispanic/Latino), 24 international. Average age 34. 664 applicants, 67% accepted, 411 enrolled. In 2013, 275 master's, 69 other advanced degrees awarded. *Degree requirements:* For master's, thesis (for some programs). *Entrance requirements:* For master's, official transcripts from regionally-accredited institution stating the conferral of a bachelor's degree with minimum cumulative GPA of 3.0; personal statement; professional resume; practitioner in field through work or volunteerism; resume. Additional exam requirements/recommendations for international students: Recommended—TOEFL (minimum score 547 paper-based; 78 iBT), IELTS (minimum score 6). *Application deadline:* For fall admission, 8/1 for domestic and international students; for spring admission, 12/1 for domestic and international students; for summer admission, 5/1 for domestic and international students. Applications are processed on a rolling basis. Application fee: $50. Electronic applications accepted. *Expenses: Tuition:* Full-time $6200; part-time $425 per credit. Tuition and fees vary according to degree level and program. *Financial support:* Applicants required to submit FAFSA. *Unit head:* Dr. Donald Helmstetter, Dean, 651-641-8227, Fax: 651-641-8807, E-mail: helmstetter@csp.edu. *Application contact:* Kimberly Craig, Director of Graduate and Cohort Admission, 651-603-6223, Fax: 651-603-6320, E-mail: craig@csp.edu.

Concordia University Wisconsin, Graduate Programs, Department of Education, Program in Reading, Mequon, WI 53097-2402. Offers MS Ed. Part-time and evening/weekend programs available. Postbaccalaureate distance learning degree programs offered (minimal on-campus study). *Degree requirements:* For master's, comprehensive exam, thesis or alternative. *Entrance requirements:* For master's, minimum GPA of 3.0. Additional exam requirements/recommendations for international students: Required—TOEFL.

Concord University, Graduate Studies, Athens, WV 24712-1000. Offers educational leadership and supervision (M Ed); geography (M Ed); health promotion (MA); reading specialist (M Ed); special education (M Ed); teaching (MAT). Part-time and evening/weekend programs available. Postbaccalaureate distance learning degree programs offered (no on-campus study). *Degree requirements:* For master's, thesis (for some programs). *Entrance requirements:* For master's, GRE or MAT, baccalaureate degree with minimum GPA of 2.5 from regionally-accredited institution; teaching license; 2 letters of recommendation; completed disposition assessment form. Electronic applications accepted.

Converse College, School of Education and Graduate Studies, Education Specialist Program, Spartanburg, SC 29302-0006. Offers administration and leadership (Ed S); administration and supervision (Ed S); literacy (Ed S). *Accreditation:* AAMFT/COAMFTE. Part-time programs available. *Entrance requirements:* For degree, GRE or MAT (marriage and family therapy), minimum GPA of 3.0. Electronic applications accepted.

Coppin State University, Division of Graduate Studies, Division of Education, Department of Curriculum and Instruction, Program in Reading Education, Baltimore, MD 21216-3698. Offers MS. Part-time programs available. *Degree requirements:* For master's, 3 hours of capstone experience in urban literacy. *Entrance requirements:* For master's, MAT or GRE, resume, references, teacher certification, 3 years of teaching experience.

Curry College, Graduate Studies, Program in Education, Milton, MA 02186-9984. Offers elementary education (M Ed); foundations (non-license) (M Ed); reading (M Ed, Certificate); special education (M Ed). Part-time and evening/weekend programs available. *Degree requirements:* For master's, project or thesis. *Entrance requirements:* For master's, interview, recommendations, resume, written statement. Additional exam requirements/recommendations for international students: Required—TOEFL (minimum score 550 paper-based; 80 iBT). *Expenses:* Contact institution. *Faculty research:* Classroom trauma, therapeutic writing, inclusionary practices.

Dallas Baptist University, Dorothy M. Bush College of Education, Program in Reading and English as a Second Language, Dallas, TX 75211-9299. Offers bilingual education

(M Ed); English as a second language (M Ed); master reading teacher (M Ed); reading specialist (M Ed). Part-time and evening/weekend programs available. *Entrance requirements:* For master's, GRE General Test, minimum GPA of 3.0. Additional exam requirements/recommendations for international students: Required—TOEFL, IELTS. Application fee: $25. *Expenses: Tuition:* Full-time $13,410; part-time $745 per credit hour. *Required fees:* $300; $150 per semester. Tuition and fees vary according to degree level. *Financial support:* Federal Work-Study, institutionally sponsored loans, scholarships/grants, and tuition waivers (full and partial) available. Support available to part-time students. Financial award applicants required to submit FAFSA. *Unit head:* Amie Sarker, Director, 214-333-5200, Fax: 214-333-5551, E-mail: graduate@dbu.edu. *Application contact:* Kit P. Montgomery, Director of Graduate Programs, 214-333-5242, Fax: 214-333-5579, E-mail: graduate@dbu.edu.
Website: http://www3.dbu.edu/graduate/english_reading.asp.

Delaware State University, Graduate Programs, College of Education, Health and Public Policy, Program in Adult Literacy and Basic Education, Dover, DE 19901-2277. Offers MA. *Entrance requirements:* Additional exam requirements/recommendations for international students: Required—TOEFL (minimum score 550 paper-based). Electronic applications accepted.

DePaul University, College of Education, Chicago, IL 60614. Offers bilingual bicultural education (M Ed, MA); counseling (M Ed, MA), including clinical mental health counseling, college student development, school counseling; curriculum studies (M Ed, MA, Ed D); early childhood education (M Ed, MA, Ed D); educating adults (MA); educational leadership (M Ed, MA, Ed D), including administration and supervision (M Ed, MA), principal preparation (M Ed, MA); elementary education (MA); mathematics education (MA); mathematics for teaching (MS); middle school mathematics education (MS); reading specialist (M Ed, MA); secondary education (M Ed); social and cultural foundations in education (MA); special education (M Ed, MA); world languages education (M Ed, MA). Part-time and evening/weekend programs available. Postbaccalaureate distance learning degree programs offered (no on-campus study). *Faculty:* 61 full-time (35 women), 59 part-time/adjunct (43 women). *Students:* 628 full-time (486 women), 324 part-time (243 women); includes 304 minority (144 Black or African American, non-Hispanic/Latino; 1 American Indian or Alaska Native, non-Hispanic/Latino; 38 Asian, non-Hispanic/Latino; 98 Hispanic/Latino; 23 Two or more races, non-Hispanic/Latino), 24 international. Average age 30. In 2013, 465 master's, 4 doctorates awarded. *Degree requirements:* For doctorate, thesis/dissertation. *Application deadline:* For fall admission, 8/15 for domestic students; for winter admission, 12/1 for domestic students; for spring admission, 3/1 for domestic students. Applications are processed on a rolling basis. Application fee: $40. Electronic applications accepted. Tuition and fees vary according to course level, course load and degree level. *Financial support:* Application deadline: 12/31; applicants required to submit FAFSA. *Unit head:* Dr. Paul Zionts, Dean, 773-325-7581, Fax: 773-325-7713, E-mail: pzionts@depaul.edu. *Application contact:* Farrah Dalal, Assistant Director, 773-325-2465, Fax: 773-325-2270, E-mail: fdalal@depaul.edu.
Website: http://education.depaul.edu.

Dominican University, School of Education, River Forest, IL 60305-1099. Offers curriculum and instruction (MA Ed); early childhood education (MS); education (MAT); educational administration (MA); elementary education (MA Ed); English as a second language (MA Ed); reading (MA Ed); special education (MS). Part-time and evening/weekend programs available. Postbaccalaureate distance learning degree programs offered (no on-campus study). *Faculty:* 19 full-time (14 women), 51 part-time/adjunct (42 women). *Students:* 18 full-time (13 women), 334 part-time (274 women); includes 76 minority (26 Black or African American, non-Hispanic/Latino; 9 Asian, non-Hispanic/Latino; 41 Hispanic/Latino). Average age 32. 119 applicants, 77% accepted, 70 enrolled. In 2013, 246 master's awarded. *Entrance requirements:* For master's, Illinois Test of Basic Skills. Additional exam requirements/recommendations for international students: Required—TOEFL (minimum score 550 paper-based; 79 iBT). *Application deadline:* Applications are processed on a rolling basis. Application fee: $25. *Expenses:* Contact institution. *Financial support:* In 2013–14, 97 students received support. Career-related internships or fieldwork, scholarships/grants, and tuition waivers (partial) available. Support available to part-time students. Financial award application deadline: 8/15; financial award applicants required to submit FAFSA. *Faculty research:* Governance of private education institutions, reading and language arts, inclusion, organizational planning, leadership and vision. *Unit head:* Dr. Colleen Reardon, Dean, 718-524-6643, Fax: 708-524-6665, E-mail: creardon@dom.edu. *Application contact:* Keven Hansen, Coordinator of Recruitment and Admissions, 708-524-6921, Fax: 708-524-6665, E-mail: educate@dom.edu.
Website: http://educate.dom.edu/.

Dowling College, Graduate Programs in Education, Oakdale, NY 11769-1999. Offers adolescence education with middle childhood extension (MS); childhood and early childhood education (MS); childhood and gifted education (MS); childhood education (1-6) (MS); computers in education (AC); early childhood education (B-2) (MS); educational administration (Ed D); educational technology leadership (MS); educational technology specialist (AC); gifted education (AC); literacy education (MS, AC), including 5-12 (MS), B-12 (MS); literacy education (MS), including B-6; school building leader (AC); school district business leader (MBA, AC); school district leader (AC); special education (MS), including autism, severe disabilities; sport management (MS). *Accreditation:* NCATE. Part-time and evening/weekend programs available. Postbaccalaureate distance learning degree programs offered (minimal on-campus study). *Faculty:* 44 full-time (24 women), 17 part-time/adjunct (8 women). *Students:* 183 full-time (124 women), 314 part-time (231 women); includes 51 minority (19 Black or African American, non-Hispanic/Latino; 1 American Indian or Alaska Native, non-Hispanic/Latino; 3 Asian, non-Hispanic/Latino; 26 Hispanic/Latino; 2 Native Hawaiian or other Pacific Islander, non-Hispanic/Latino). Average age 32. 174 applicants, 80% accepted, 82 enrolled. In 2013, 198 master's, 33 doctorates, 48 other advanced degrees awarded. *Degree requirements:* For master's and AC, comprehensive exam; for doctorate, thesis/dissertation. *Entrance requirements:* For master's, minimum GPA of 3.0; for doctorate, GRE, master's degree; for AC, teaching certificate. Additional exam requirements/recommendations for international students: Required—TOEFL (minimum score 550 paper-based). *Application deadline:* For fall admission, 9/1 priority date for domestic students; for winter admission, 1/1 priority date for domestic students; for spring admission, 2/1 priority date for domestic students. Applications are processed on a rolling basis. Application fee: $50. Electronic applications accepted. *Expenses: Tuition:* Full-time $22,731; part-time $1029 per credit. *Required fees:* $956; $956. *Financial support:* Career-related internships or fieldwork and Federal Work-Study available. Support available to part-time students. Financial award application deadline: 6/30; financial award applicants required to submit FAFSA. *Faculty research:* Natural readers, Korean styles and learning strategies, mothers of children with disabilities, computers in instruction, cultural background and organizational roadblocks to problem solving. *Unit head:* Dr. Robert Manley, Dean, 631-244-3447, E-mail: manleyr@dowling.edu. *Application contact:* Mary Boullianne, Director of Admissions, 631-244-3274, Fax: 631-244-1059, E-mail: boulliam@dowling.edu.

Drury University, Graduate Programs in Education, Springfield, MO 65802. Offers elementary education (M Ed); gifted education (M Ed); human services (M Ed); instructional mathematics K-8 (M Ed); instructional technology (M Ed); middle school teaching (M Ed); secondary education (M Ed); special education (M Ed); special reading (M Ed). *Accreditation:* NCATE. Part-time and evening/weekend programs available. *Degree requirements:* For master's, thesis. *Entrance requirements:* For master's, GRE or MAT, minimum GPA of 2.75. Additional exam requirements/recommendations for international students: Required—TOEFL. Electronic applications accepted. *Faculty research:* Cultural enrichment, research skills, parental involvement relating to reading skills, reading strategies for mainstreaming children.

Duquesne University, School of Education, Department of Instruction and Leadership, Program in Reading and Language Arts, Pittsburgh, PA 15282-0001. Offers MS Ed. Part-time and evening/weekend programs available. *Faculty:* 1 (woman) full-time. *Students:* 14 full-time (all women), 13 part-time (all women); includes 1 minority (Black or African American, non-Hispanic/Latino), 1 international. Average age 30. 16 applicants, 56% accepted, 6 enrolled. In 2013, 15 master's awarded. *Degree requirements:* For master's, thesis optional. *Entrance requirements:* For master's, bachelor's degree. Additional exam requirements/recommendations for international students: Required—TOEFL (minimum score 550 paper-based), IELTS (minimum score 7). *Application deadline:* For fall admission, 9/1 for domestic students; for spring admission, 1/1 for domestic students. Applications are processed on a rolling basis. Application fee: $0. Electronic applications accepted. Application fee is waived when completed online. *Expenses: Tuition:* Full-time $18,162; part-time $1009 per credit. *Required fees:* $1728; $96 per credit. Tuition and fees vary according to program. *Financial support:* Research assistantships and Federal Work-Study available. Support available to part-time students. *Unit head:* Dr. Rosemary T. Mautino, Assistant Professor and Director, 412-396-6089, Fax: 412-396-1759, E-mail: mautino@duq.edu. *Application contact:* Michael Dolinger, Director of Student and Academic Services, 412-396-6647, Fax: 412-396-5585, E-mail: dolingerm@duq.edu.
Website: http://www.duq.edu/academics/schools/education/graduate-programs-education/ms-reading-language-arts.

East Carolina University, Graduate School, College of Education, Department of Curriculum and Instruction, Greenville, NC 27858-4353. Offers assistive technology (Certificate); autism (Certificate); deaf/blindness (Certificate); elementary education (MA Ed); English education (MA Ed); history (MA Ed); middle grade education (MA Ed); reading education (MA Ed); special education (MA Ed); teaching (MAT). Part-time programs available. Postbaccalaureate distance learning degree programs offered. *Degree requirements:* For master's, comprehensive exam, thesis optional. *Entrance requirements:* For master's, GRE General Test or MAT, interview, bachelor's degree in related field, minimum GPA of 2.5, teaching license. Additional exam requirements/recommendations for international students: Required—TOEFL. *Expenses:* Tuition, state resident: full-time $4223. Tuition, nonresident: full-time $16,540. *Required fees:* $2184.

Eastern Connecticut State University, School of Education and Professional Studies/Graduate Division, Program in Reading and Language Arts, Willimantic, CT 06226-2295. Offers MS. *Accreditation:* NCATE. Part-time and evening/weekend programs available. *Degree requirements:* For master's, comprehensive exam or thesis. *Entrance requirements:* For master's, minimum GPA of 2.7, teaching certificate. Additional exam requirements/recommendations for international students: Required—TOEFL (minimum score 550 paper-based).

Eastern Michigan University, Graduate School, College of Education, Department of Teacher Education, Program in Reading, Ypsilanti, MI 48197. Offers MA. *Accreditation:* NCATE. Part-time and evening/weekend programs available. Postbaccalaureate distance learning degree programs offered (minimal on-campus study). *Students:* 1 full-time (0 women), 61 part-time (58 women); includes 8 minority (7 Black or African American, non-Hispanic/Latino; 1 Asian, non-Hispanic/Latino). Average age 33. 15 applicants, 93% accepted, 10 enrolled. In 2013, 19 master's awarded. *Entrance requirements:* For master's, GRE. Additional exam requirements/recommendations for international students: Required—TOEFL. *Application deadline:* Applications are processed on a rolling basis. Application fee: $35. *Expenses:* Tuition, state resident: full-time $12,300; part-time $466 per credit hour. Tuition, nonresident: full-time $23,159; part-time $918 per credit hour. *Required fees:* $71 per credit hour. $46 per semester. One-time fee: $100. Tuition and fees vary according to course level and degree level. *Financial support:* Fellowships, research assistantships with full tuition reimbursements, teaching assistantships with full tuition reimbursements, career-related internships or fieldwork, Federal Work-Study, institutionally sponsored loans, scholarships/grants, tuition waivers (partial), and unspecified assistantships available. Support available to part-time students. Financial award applicants required to submit FAFSA. *Unit head:* Dr. Martha Kinney-Sedgwick, Interim Department Head, 734-487-3260, Fax: 734-487-2101, E-mail: mkinneys@emich.edu. *Application contact:* Dr. Linda Williams, Coordinator, 734-487-3260, Fax: 734-487-2101, E-mail: lwilli55@emich.edu.

Eastern Nazarene College, Adult and Graduate Studies, Division of Teacher Education, Quincy, MA 02170. Offers administration (M Ed); early childhood education (M Ed, Certificate); elementary education (M Ed, Certificate); English as a second language (Certificate); instructional enrichment and development (Certificate); middle school education (M Ed, Certificate); moderate special needs education (Certificate); principal (Certificate); program development and supervision (Certificate); secondary education (M Ed, Certificate); special education administrator (Certificate); special needs (M Ed); supervisor (Certificate); teacher of reading (M Ed, Certificate). M Ed also available through weekend program for administration, special needs, and teacher of reading only. Part-time and evening/weekend programs available. *Entrance requirements:* Additional exam requirements/recommendations for international students: Required—TOEFL (minimum score 550 paper-based).

Eastern New Mexico University, Graduate School, College of Education and Technology, Department of Curriculum and Instruction, Portales, NM 88130. Offers bilingual education (M Ed); educational technology (M Ed); elementary education (M Ed); English as a second language (M Ed); pedagogy and learning (M Ed); professional technical education (M Ed); reading/literacy (M Ed). Part-time programs available. Postbaccalaureate distance learning degree programs offered (minimal on-campus study). *Degree requirements:* For master's, comprehensive exam, thesis optional. *Entrance requirements:* For master's, minimum GPA of 3.0, photocopy of teaching license, writing assessment, letter of recommendation. Additional exam requirements/recommendations for international students: Required—TOEFL (minimum score 550 paper-based; 79 iBT), IELTS (minimum score 6). Electronic applications accepted.

Eastern University, Graduate Education Programs, St. Davids, PA 19087-3696. Offers ESL program specialist (K-12) (Certificate); general supervisor (PreK-12) (Certificate); health and physical education (K-12) (Certificate); middle level (4-8) (Certificate); multicultural education (M Ed); pre K-4 (Certificate); pre K-4 with special education (Certificate); reading (M Ed); reading specialist (K-12) (Certificate); reading supervisor (K-12) (Certificate); school health services (M Ed); school health supervisor (Certificate); school nurse (Certificate); school principalship (K-12) (Certificate); secondary biology education (7-12) (Certificate); secondary chemistry education (7-12) (Certificate); secondary communication education (7-12) (Certificate); secondary education (7-12) (Certificate); secondary English education (7-12) (Certificate); secondary math

education (7-12) (Certificate); secondary social studies education (7-12) (Certificate); special education (M Ed); special education (7-12) (Certificate); special education (Pre K-8) (Certificate); special education supervisor (N-12) (Certificate); TESOL (M Ed); world language (Certificate), including French, Mandarin Chinese, Spanish. Part-time and evening/weekend programs available. Postbaccalaureate distance learning degree programs offered (no on-campus study). *Faculty:* 22 full-time (11 women), 26 part-time/adjunct (18 women). *Students:* 77 full-time (58 women), 223 part-time (149 women); includes 112 minority (81 Black or African American, non-Hispanic/Latino; 1 American Indian or Alaska Native, non-Hispanic/Latino; 9 Asian, non-Hispanic/Latino; 18 Hispanic/Latino; 1 Native Hawaiian or other Pacific Islander, non-Hispanic/Latino; 2 Two or more races, non-Hispanic/Latino), 7 international. Average age 34. 94 applicants, 100% accepted, 81 enrolled. In 2013, 120 master's awarded. *Entrance requirements:* For master's, minimum GPA of 2.5 (for M Ed); for Certificate, minimum GPA of 3.0 for certifications. Additional exam requirements/recommendations for international students: Required—TOEFL. *Application deadline:* For fall admission, 8/14 for domestic students; for spring admission, 12/20 for domestic students. Applications are processed on a rolling basis. Application fee: $35. Application fee is waived when completed online. *Expenses: Tuition:* Full-time $15,600; part-time $650 per credit. *Required fees:* $27.50 per semester. One-time fee: $50. Tuition and fees vary according to course load, degree level and program. *Financial support:* In 2013–14, 84 students received support, including 6 research assistantships with partial tuition reimbursements available (averaging $7,710 per year); scholarships/grants and unspecified assistantships also available. Financial award application deadline: 3/15; financial award applicants required to submit FAFSA. *Unit head:* Harry Gutelius, Associate Dean, 610-341-1729. *Application contact:* Michael Perpiglia, Associate Director of Enrollment, 610-341-5947, Fax: 484-581-1276, E-mail: mperpigl@eastern.edu.
Website: http://www.eastern.edu/academics/programs/loeb-school-education-0/graduateprograms.

Eastern Washington University, Graduate Studies, College of Arts, Letters and Education, Department of Education, Program in Literacy, Cheney, WA 99004-2431. Offers M Ed. *Students:* 2 part-time (both women). Average age 33. In 2013, 4 master's awarded. *Degree requirements:* For master's, comprehensive exam. *Entrance requirements:* For master's, minimum GPA of 3.0. *Application deadline:* For fall admission, 4/1 priority date for domestic students; for spring admission, 1/15 for domestic students. Applications are processed on a rolling basis. Application fee: $50. *Financial support:* In 2013–14, teaching assistantships with partial tuition reimbursements (averaging $7,000 per year) were awarded; career-related internships or fieldwork, Federal Work-Study, institutionally sponsored loans, scholarships/grants, health care benefits, tuition waivers (partial), and unspecified assistantships also available. Support available to part-time students. Financial award application deadline: 2/1; financial award applicants required to submit FAFSA. *Unit head:* Robin Showalter, Program Coordinator, 509-359-6492, E-mail: rshowalter@mail.ewu.edu. *Application contact:* Dr. Kevin Pyatt, Assistant Professor, Science and Technology, 509-359-6091, E-mail: kpyatt@ewu.edu.

East Stroudsburg University of Pennsylvania, Graduate College, College of Education, Department of Reading, East Stroudsburg, PA 18301-2999. Offers M Ed. Part-time and evening/weekend programs available. Postbaccalaureate distance learning degree programs offered. *Faculty:* 3 full-time (all women). *Students:* 8 full-time (all women), 28 part-time (26 women); includes 3 minority (1 Black or African American, non-Hispanic/Latino; 1 Hispanic/Latino; 1 Two or more races, non-Hispanic/Latino). Average age 34. 20 applicants, 80% accepted, 14 enrolled. In 2013, 41 master's awarded. *Degree requirements:* For master's, comprehensive exam, research paper, electronic program portfolio. *Entrance requirements:* For master's, PRAXIS/teacher certification, letter of recommendation, Pennsylvania Department of Education requirements. Additional exam requirements/recommendations for international students: Required—TOEFL (minimum score 560 paper-based; 83 iBT) or IELTS. *Application deadline:* For fall admission, 7/31 priority date for domestic students, 6/30 priority date for international students; for spring admission, 11/30 for domestic students, 10/31 for international students. Applications are processed on a rolling basis. Application fee: $50. Electronic applications accepted. *Expenses:* Tuition, state resident: full-time $7956; part-time $442 per credit. Tuition, nonresident: full-time $11,934; part-time $663 per credit. *Required fees:* $2129; $118 per credit. *Financial support:* Research assistantships with full and partial tuition reimbursements, Federal Work-Study, and institutionally sponsored loans available. Financial award application deadline: 3/1; financial award applicants required to submit FAFSA. *Faculty research:* Portfolio assessment, reading assessment. *Unit head:* Dr. Stephanie Romano, Graduate Coordinator, 570-422-3415, Fax: 570-422-3920, E-mail: sromano@po-box.esu.edu. *Application contact:* Kevin Quintero, Graduate Admissions Coordinator, 570-422-3536, Fax: 570-422-2711, E-mail: kquintero@esu.edu.

East Tennessee State University, School of Graduate Studies, College of Education, Department of Curriculum and Instruction, Johnson City, TN 37614. Offers educational media and educational technology (M Ed), including educational communications and technology, school library media; elementary education (M Ed); reading (MA), including reading education, storytelling; school library professional (Post-Master's Certificate); secondary education (M Ed), including classroom technology, secondary education (M Ed, MAT); storytelling (Postbaccalaureate Certificate); teacher education with multiple levels (MAT), including elementary education, middle grades education, secondary education (M Ed, MAT). *Accreditation:* NCATE. Part-time and evening/weekend programs available. Postbaccalaureate distance learning degree programs offered (no on-campus study). *Faculty:* 25 full-time (18 women), 12 part-time/adjunct (8 women). *Students:* 66 full-time (50 women), 97 part-time (85 women); includes 5 minority (3 Black or African American, non-Hispanic/Latino; 2 Two or more races, non-Hispanic/Latino), 2 international. Average age 31. 144 applicants, 57% accepted, 70 enrolled. In 2013, 83 master's, 5 other advanced degrees awarded. *Degree requirements:* For master's, comprehensive exam, thesis optional, student teaching, practicum; for other advanced degree, field work (school library); culminating experience (storytelling). *Entrance requirements:* For master's, GRE, SAT, ACT, PRAXIS, minimum GPA of 3.0; for other advanced degree, master's degree, TN teaching license (for school library professional Post-Master's Certificate); three letters of recommendation (for storytelling Postbaccalaureate Certificate). Additional exam requirements/recommendations for international students: Required—TOEFL (minimum score 550 paper-based; 79 iBT). *Application deadline:* For fall admission, 6/1 for domestic students, 4/30 for international students; for spring admission, 11/1 for domestic students, 4/30 for international students. Application fee: $35 ($45 for international students). Electronic applications accepted. *Expenses:* Tuition, state resident: full-time $7900; part-time $395 per credit hour. Tuition, nonresident: full-time $21,960; part-time $1098 per credit hour. *Required fees:* $1345; $84 per credit hour. *Financial support:* In 2013–14, 43 students received support, including 6 research assistantships with full tuition reimbursements available (averaging $6,000 per year), 10 teaching assistantships with full tuition reimbursements available (averaging $6,000 per year); career-related internships or fieldwork, institutionally sponsored loans, scholarships/grants, and unspecified assistantships also available. Financial award application deadline: 7/1; financial award applicants required to submit FAFSA. *Faculty research:* Critical thinking; curriculum development in reading, math, and science education;

cultural diversity; cognitive processes; effective teaching strategies. *Unit head:* Dr. Rhona Hurwitz, Chair, 423-439-7598, Fax: 423-439-8362, E-mail: hurwitz@etsu.edu. *Application contact:* Fiona Goodyear, Graduate Specialist, 423-439-6148, Fax: 423-439-5624, E-mail: goodyear@etsu.edu.
Website: http://www.etsu.edu/coe/cuai/.

Edgewood College, Program in Education, Madison, WI 53711-1997. Offers adult learning (MA Ed); bilingual teaching and learning (MA Ed); director of instruction (Certificate); director of special education and pupil services (Certificate); education (MA Ed); educational administration (MA Ed); educational leadership (Ed D); professional studies (MA Ed); program coordinator (Certificate); reading administration (MA Ed); school business administration (Certificate); school principalship K-12 (Certificate); special education (MA Ed); sustainability leadership (MA Ed); teaching and learning (MA Ed); teaching English to speakers of other languages (TESOL) (MA Ed). *Accreditation:* NCATE (one or more programs are accredited). Part-time and evening/weekend programs available. *Students:* 159 full-time (95 women), 164 part-time (121 women); includes 61 minority (19 Black or African American, non-Hispanic/Latino; 9 Asian, non-Hispanic/Latino; 25 Hispanic/Latino; 8 Two or more races, non-Hispanic/Latino), 27 international. Average age 36. In 2013, 51 master's, 22 doctorates awarded. *Degree requirements:* For master's, practicum, research project; for doctorate, comprehensive exam, thesis/dissertation. *Entrance requirements:* For master's, minimum GPA of 2.75, 2 letters of recommendation, personal statement; for doctorate, resume, letter of intent, 2 letters of recommendation, interview, writing sample. Additional exam requirements/recommendations for international students: Required—TOEFL (minimum score 525 paper-based; 72 iBT). *Application deadline:* For fall admission, 8/15 for domestic students, 5/1 for international students; for spring admission, 1/8 for domestic students, 11/1 for international students. Applications are processed on a rolling basis. Application fee: $30. Electronic applications accepted. *Unit head:* Dr. Timothy Slekar, Dean, E-mail: tslekar@edgewood.edu. *Application contact:* Joann Eastman, Admissions Counselor, 608-663-3250, Fax: 608-663-2214, E-mail: gps@edgewood.edu.
Website: http://www.edgewood.edu/Academics/School-of-Education.

Edinboro University of Pennsylvania, School of Education, Department of Professional Studies, Edinboro, PA 16444. Offers counseling (MA); educational leadership (M Ed); educational psychology (M Ed); reading (M Ed); school psychology (MS, Ed S). Part-time and evening/weekend programs available. *Degree requirements:* For master's, thesis or alternative, competency exam; for Ed S, thesis or alternative. *Entrance requirements:* For master's and Ed S, GRE or MAT, minimum QPA of 2.5. Electronic applications accepted.

Elms College, Division of Education, Chicopee, MA 01013-2839. Offers early childhood education (MAT); education (M Ed, CAGS); elementary education (MAT); English as a second language (MAT); reading (MAT); secondary education (MAT), including biology education, English education, Spanish education; special education (MAT). Part-time and evening/weekend programs available. *Degree requirements:* For master's, thesis (for some programs). *Entrance requirements:* For master's, Massachusetts Educators Certification Test, minimum GPA of 3.0; for CAGS, master's degree in education. Additional exam requirements/recommendations for international students: Required—TOEFL.

Emory & Henry College, Graduate Programs, Emory, VA 24327-0947. Offers American history (MA Ed); organizational leadership (MCOL); professional studies (M Ed); reading specialist (MA Ed). Part-time and evening/weekend programs available. *Faculty:* 7 full-time (3 women). *Students:* 11 full-time (8 women), 32 part-time (22 women); includes 1 minority (Black or African American, non-Hispanic/Latino). Average age 36. 34 applicants, 85% accepted, 28 enrolled. In 2013, 36 master's awarded. *Entrance requirements:* For master's, GRE or PRAXIS I, recommendations, writing sample. Additional exam requirements/recommendations for international students: Recommended—TOEFL. *Application deadline:* Applications are processed on a rolling basis. Application fee: $30. *Financial support:* Applicants required to submit FAFSA. *Unit head:* Dr. Jack Roper, Director of Graduate Studies, 276-944-6188, Fax: 276-944-5223, E-mail: jroper@ehc.edu. *Application contact:* Dr. Jack Roper, Director of Graduate Studies, 276-944-6188, Fax: 276-944-5223, E-mail: jroper@ehc.edu.

Emporia State University, Program in Master Teacher, Emporia, KS 66801-5415. Offers elementary subject matter (MS); reading (MS). *Accreditation:* NCATE. Part-time programs available. *Students:* 3 full-time (all women), 60 part-time (59 women); includes 3 minority (1 Black or African American, non-Hispanic/Latino; 1 Hispanic/Latino; 1 Two or more races, non-Hispanic/Latino). 19 applicants, 79% accepted, 13 enrolled. In 2013, 22 master's awarded. *Degree requirements:* For master's, comprehensive exam or thesis, practicum. *Entrance requirements:* For master's, GRE General Test or MAT, essay exam, appropriate bachelor's degree, letters of recommendation. Additional exam requirements/recommendations for international students: Required—TOEFL (minimum score 520 paper-based; 68 iBT). *Application deadline:* For fall admission, 8/15 priority date for domestic students. Applications are processed on a rolling basis. Application fee: $30 ($75 for international students). Electronic applications accepted. *Expenses: Tuition, area resident:* Part-time $220 per credit hour. Tuition, state resident: part-time $220 per credit hour. Tuition, nonresident: part-time $685 per credit hour. *Required fees:* $73 per credit hour. *Financial support:* Federal Work-Study, institutionally sponsored loans, health care benefits, and unspecified assistantships available. Financial award application deadline: 3/15; financial award applicants required to submit FAFSA. *Unit head:* Dr. Jean Morrow, Chair, 620-341-5766, E-mail: jmorrow@emporia.edu. *Application contact:* Mary Sewell, Admissions Coordinator, 800-950-GRAD, Fax: 620-341-5909, E-mail: msewell@emporia.edu.

Endicott College, Van Loan School of Graduate and Professional Studies, Program in Reading and Literacy, Beverly, MA 01915-2096. Offers M Ed. Part-time and evening/weekend programs available. *Degree requirements:* For master's, comprehensive exam, practicum, seminar. *Entrance requirements:* For master's, MAT or GRE, Massachusetts teaching certificate, letters of recommendation. Additional exam requirements/recommendations for international students: Required—TOEFL. *Application deadline:* Applications are processed on a rolling basis. Application fee: $50. Electronic applications accepted. *Expenses:* Contact institution. *Financial support:* Career-related internships or fieldwork, Federal Work-Study, and institutionally sponsored loans available. Financial award applicants required to submit FAFSA. *Unit head:* Dr. John D. MacLean, Jr., Director of Licensure Programs, 978-232-2408, E-mail: jmaclean@endicott.edu.

Evangel University, Department of Education, Springfield, MO 65802. Offers educational leadership (M Ed); reading education (M Ed); secondary teaching (M Ed); teaching (MA). *Accreditation:* NCATE. Part-time and evening/weekend programs available. *Faculty:* 7 full-time (4 women), 5 part-time/adjunct (4 women). *Students:* 5 full-time (3 women), 37 part-time (28 women); includes 4 minority (3 Hispanic/Latino; 1 Two or more races, non-Hispanic/Latino). Average age 32. 17 applicants, 65% accepted, 11 enrolled. In 2013, 22 master's awarded. *Degree requirements:* For master's, comprehensive exam, thesis optional. *Entrance requirements:* For master's, PRAXIS II (preferred) or GRE. Additional exam requirements/recommendations for international students: Required—TOEFL (minimum score 550 paper-based). *Application deadline:* For fall admission, 7/15 priority date for domestic students, 8/1 for international students;

for spring admission, 11/15 priority date for domestic students, 12/1 for international students. Applications are processed on a rolling basis. Application fee: $25. Electronic applications accepted. *Financial support:* In 2013–14, 13 students received support. Career-related internships or fieldwork and scholarships/grants available. Support available to part-time students. Financial award application deadline: 3/1; financial award applicants required to submit FAFSA. *Unit head:* Dr. Matt Stringer, Program Coordinator, 417-865-2815 Ext. 8563, E-mail: stringerm@evangel.edu. *Application contact:* Karen Benitez, Admissions Representative, Graduate Studies, 417-865-2811 Ext. 7227, Fax: 417-865-9599, E-mail: benitezk@evangel.edu.
Website: http://www.evangel.edu/academics/graduate-studies/graduate-programs.

Fairleigh Dickinson University, College at Florham, University College: Arts, Sciences, and Professional Studies, Peter Sammartino School of Education, Madison, NJ 07940-1099. Offers education for certified teachers (MA, Certificate); educational leadership (MA); instructional technology (Certificate); literacy/reading (Certificate); teaching (MAT).

Fairleigh Dickinson University, Metropolitan Campus, University College: Arts, Sciences, and Professional Studies, Peter Sammartino School of Education, Teaneck, NJ 07666-1914. Offers dyslexia specialist (Certificate); education for certified teachers (MA); educational leadership (MA); instructional technology (Certificate); learning disabilities (MA); literacy/reading (Certificate); multilingual education (MA); teacher of the handicapped (Certificate); teaching (MAT). *Accreditation:* Teacher Education Accreditation Council. Part-time programs available. *Degree requirements:* For master's, research project (MAT).

Fairmont State University, Programs in Education, Fairmont, WV 26554. Offers digital media, new literacies and learning (M Ed); education (MAT); exercise science, fitness and wellness (M Ed); online learning (M Ed); professional studies (M Ed); reading (M Ed); special education (M Ed). *Accreditation:* NCATE. Part-time and evening/weekend programs available. Postbaccalaureate distance learning degree programs offered. *Faculty:* 18 part-time/adjunct (11 women). *Students:* 75 full-time (55 women), 120 part-time (96 women); includes 11 minority (5 Black or African American, non-Hispanic/Latino; 2 American Indian or Alaska Native, non-Hispanic/Latino; 1 Asian, non-Hispanic/Latino; 1 Hispanic/Latino; 2 Two or more races, non-Hispanic/Latino), 1 international. Average age 32. 69 applicants, 86% accepted, 45 enrolled. In 2013, 82 master's awarded. *Entrance requirements:* For master's, GRE. Additional exam requirements/recommendations for international students: Required—TOEFL. *Application deadline:* For fall admission, 5/1 for domestic and international students. Applications are processed on a rolling basis. Application fee: $40. *Expenses:* Tuition, state resident: full-time $6404; part-time $349 per credit hour. Tuition, nonresident: full-time $13,694; part-time $754 per credit hour. Part-time tuition and fees vary according to course load. *Financial support:* In 2013–14, 30 students received support. *Unit head:* Dr. Carolyn Crislip-Tacy, Interim Dean, School of Education, 304-367-4143, Fax: 304-367-4599, E-mail: carolyn.crislip-tacy@fairmontstate.edu. *Application contact:* Jack Kirby, Director of Graduate Studies, 304-367-4101, E-mail: jack.kirby@fairmontstate.edu.
Website: http://www.fairmontstate.edu/graduatestudies/default.asp.

Fayetteville State University, Graduate School, Programs in Middle Grades, Secondary and Special Education and Elementary Education, Fayetteville, NC 28301-4298. Offers biology (MA Ed); elementary education (MA Ed); history (MA Ed); mathematics (MA Ed); middle grades (MA Ed); political science (MA Ed); reading (MA Ed); sociology (MA Ed); special education (MA Ed), including behavioral-emotional handicaps, mentally handicapped, specific training disability. *Accreditation:* NCATE. Part-time and evening/weekend programs available. *Faculty:* 12 full-time (8 women), 4 part-time/adjunct (3 women). *Students:* 25 full-time (22 women), 49 part-time (45 women); includes 51 minority (48 Black or African American, non-Hispanic/Latino; 1 American Indian or Alaska Native, non-Hispanic/Latino; 2 Hispanic/Latino). Average age 35. 5 applicants, 100% accepted, 5 enrolled. In 2013, 29 master's awarded. *Degree requirements:* For master's, comprehensive exam, internship. *Application deadline:* For fall admission, 4/15 for domestic students; for spring admission, 10/15 for domestic students. Applications are processed on a rolling basis. Application fee: $40. Electronic applications accepted. *Faculty research:* Students with disabilities and selected leadership behaviors, new vision for professional development, gifted and talented students, emotional and behavioral disabilities, professional development for high school biology teachers. *Unit head:* Dr. Kimberly Smith-Burton, Interim Chair, 910-672-1182, E-mail: cbarringerbrown@uncfsu.edu. *Application contact:* Katrina Hoffman, Graduate Admission Officer, 910-672-1374, Fax: 910-672-1470, E-mail: khoffma1@uncfsu.edu.

Ferris State University, College of Education and Human Services, School of Education, Big Rapids, MI 49307. Offers curriculum and instruction (M Ed), including reading, special education, subject area; educational leadership (MS); instructor (MSCTE); post-secondary administration (MSCTE); training and development (MSCTE). Part-time and evening/weekend programs available. Postbaccalaureate distance learning degree programs offered (minimal on-campus study). *Faculty:* 7 full-time (5 women), 9 part-time/adjunct (6 women). *Students:* 17 full-time (14 women), 88 part-time (53 women); includes 8 minority (3 Black or African American, non-Hispanic/Latino; 1 American Indian or Alaska Native, non-Hispanic/Latino; 1 Asian, non-Hispanic/Latino; 3 Two or more races, non-Hispanic/Latino), 12 international. Average age 35. 16 applicants, 63% accepted, 6 enrolled. In 2013, 31 master's awarded. *Degree requirements:* For master's, thesis, research paper or project. *Entrance requirements:* For master's, minimum undergraduate degree GPA of 3.0. Additional exam requirements/recommendations for international students: Required—TOEFL (minimum score 500 paper-based; 61 iBT), IELTS. *Application deadline:* For fall admission, 7/1 priority date for domestic and international students; for spring admission, 11/1 priority date for domestic and international students; for summer admission, 3/1 priority date for domestic and international students. Applications are processed on a rolling basis. Application fee: $30. Electronic applications accepted. Application fee is waived when completed online. *Financial support:* Career-related internships or fieldwork and scholarships/grants available. Support available to part-time students. Financial award applicants required to submit FAFSA. *Faculty research:* Suicide prevention, reading, women in education, special needs, administration. *Unit head:* Dr. James Powell, Director, 231-591-3512, Fax: 231-591-2043, E-mail: powelj20@ferris.edu. *Application contact:* Kimisue Worrall, Secretary, 231-591-5361, Fax: 231-591-2043.
Website: http://www.ferris.edu/education/education/.

Florida Atlantic University, College of Education, Department of Teaching and Learning, Boca Raton, FL 33431-0991. Offers curriculum and instruction (M Ed), including art, biology, chemistry, English, French, German, mathematics, music, physics, Pre-K and primary education, reading, social sciences, Spanish; elementary education (M Ed); environmental education (M Ed); reading education (M Ed); social foundations of education (M Ed), including educational psychology, educational technology, multilingual education. *Accreditation:* NCATE. Part-time and evening/weekend programs available. *Faculty:* 16 full-time (12 women), 1 (woman) part-time/adjunct. *Students:* 56 full-time (46 women), 96 part-time (78 women); includes 39 minority (10 Black or African American, non-Hispanic/Latino; 6 Asian, non-Hispanic/Latino; 20 Hispanic/Latino; 3 Two or more races, non-Hispanic/Latino), 4 international.

Average age 32. 101 applicants, 54% accepted, 42 enrolled. In 2013, 64 master's awarded. *Entrance requirements:* For master's, GRE General Test, minimum GPA of 3.0 in last 2 years of undergraduate course work. Additional exam requirements/recommendations for international students: Required—TOEFL (minimum score 500 paper-based; 61 iBT), IELTS (minimum score 6). *Application deadline:* For fall admission, 7/1 for domestic students, 2/15 for international students; for spring admission, 11/1 for domestic students, 7/15 for international students. Applications are processed on a rolling basis. Application fee: $30. *Expenses:* Tuition, state resident: full-time $6660; part-time $370 per credit hour. Tuition, nonresident: full-time $18,450; part-time $1025 per credit hour. Tuition and fees vary according to course load. *Financial support:* Fellowships with partial tuition reimbursements, research assistantships with partial tuition reimbursements, teaching assistantships with partial tuition reimbursements, career-related internships or fieldwork, scholarships/grants, and unspecified assistantships available. *Faculty research:* Technology, teaching English to speakers of other languages, math teaching, electronic portfolio assessment, global perspectives through social studies. *Unit head:* Dr. Barbara Ridener, Chairperson, 561-297-3588. *Application contact:* Dr. Eliah Watlington, Associate Dean, 561-296-8520, Fax: 261-297-2991, E-mail: ewatling@fau.edu.
Website: http://www.coe.fau.edu/academicdepartments/tl/.

Florida Gulf Coast University, College of Education, Program in Reading Education, Fort Myers, FL 33965-6565. Offers M Ed. Part-time and evening/weekend programs available. *Entrance requirements:* For master's, GRE General Test, MAT, minimum GPA of 3.0. Additional exam requirements/recommendations for international students: Required—TOEFL (minimum score 550 paper-based). Electronic applications accepted. *Faculty research:* Struggling readers, reading and writing connection, involving families in reading.

Florida International University, College of Education, Department of Teaching and Learning, Miami, FL 33199. Offers art education (MA, MS); curriculum and instruction (MS, Ed D, PhD, Ed S), including curriculum development (MS), elementary education (MS), English education (MS), learning technologies (MS), mathematics education (MS), modern language education (MS), physical education (MS), science education (MS), social studies education (MS), special education (MS), early childhood education (MS); exceptional student education (Ed D); foreign language education (MS), including foreign language education, teaching English to speakers of other languages (TESOL); international/intercultural education (MS); language, literacy and culture (PhD); mathematics, science, and learning technologies (PhD); physical education (MS), including sport and fitness; reading education (MS). Part-time and evening/weekend programs available. *Degree requirements:* For doctorate, comprehensive exam, thesis/dissertation. *Entrance requirements:* For master's, GRE General Test, Florida General Knowledge Test or Florida College Level Academic Skills Test; for doctorate and Ed S, GRE General Test. Additional exam requirements/recommendations for international students: Required—TOEFL (minimum score 550 paper-based; 80 iBT), IELTS (minimum score 6.3). Electronic applications accepted.

Florida Memorial University, School of Education, Miami-Dade, FL 33054. Offers elementary education (MS); exceptional student education (MS); reading (MS). *Degree requirements:* For master's, comprehensive exam or thesis, field and clinical experiences, exit exam. *Entrance requirements:* For master's, GRE, CLAST, PRAXIS I, baccalaureate or graduate degree with minimum GPA of 3.0 in last 60 hours, 3 recommendations. Additional exam requirements/recommendations for international students: Recommended—TOEFL.

Florida State University, The Graduate School, College of Education, School of Teacher Education, Tallahassee, FL 32306. Offers curriculum and instruction (MS, MST, PhD, Ed S), including early childhood education (MS, PhD, Ed S), elementary education (MS, PhD, Ed S), English education (MS, PhD, Ed S), English teaching (MST), exceptional student education (MST), foreign and second language education (MS, PhD, Ed S), foreign and second language teaching (MST), math education (MS, PhD, Ed S), math teaching (MST), reading education and language arts (MS, PhD, Ed S), science education (MS, PhD, Ed S), social science education (MS, PhD, Ed S), social science teaching (MST), special education (MS, PhD, Ed S), special education studies (MST), visual disabilities (MS, Ed S). Part-time programs available. *Faculty:* 30 full-time (20 women), 22 part-time/adjunct (18 women). *Students:* 183 full-time (151 women), 92 part-time (80 women); includes 47 minority (20 Black or African American, non-Hispanic/Latino; 3 American Indian or Alaska Native, non-Hispanic/Latino; 1 Asian, non-Hispanic/Latino; 20 Hispanic/Latino; 3 Two or more races, non-Hispanic/Latino), 61 international. Average age 30. 199 applicants, 79% accepted, 86 enrolled. In 2013, 119 master's, 9 doctorates, 4 other advanced degrees awarded. *Degree requirements:* For master's and Ed S, comprehensive exam, thesis optional; for doctorate, comprehensive exam, thesis/dissertation, preliminary exam, prospectus defense. *Entrance requirements:* For master's, doctorate, and Ed S, GRE General Test, minimum GPA of 3.0. Additional exam requirements/recommendations for international students: Required—TOEFL (minimum score 550 paper-based; 80 iBT). *Application deadline:* For fall admission, 7/1 for domestic and international students; for winter admission, 10/1 for domestic students, 11/1 for international students; for spring admission, 3/1 for domestic and international students. Applications are processed on a rolling basis. Application fee: $30. Electronic applications accepted. *Expenses:* Tuition, state resident: part-time $403.51 per credit hour. Tuition, nonresident: part-time $1004.85 per credit hour. *Required fees:* $75.81 per credit hour. One-time fee: $20 part-time. Tuition and fees vary according to course load, campus/location and student level. *Financial support:* In 2013–14, 113 students received support, including 55 research assistantships with full and partial tuition reimbursements available, 18 teaching assistantships with full and partial tuition reimbursements available; fellowships with full and partial tuition reimbursements available, career-related internships or fieldwork, scholarships/grants, health care benefits, and unspecified assistantships also available. Financial award application deadline: 1/15; financial award applicants required to submit FAFSA. *Faculty research:* Effective intervention and assessment strategies to improve reading skills; literacy teaching and learning through technology; understanding of student sense-making through instructions, especially STEM learning for all students; international education and consequences of globalization; support professional teacher development and adoption of effective/transformative practices. *Total annual research expenditures:* $1.3 million. *Unit head:* Dr. Sherry Southerland, Chair, 850-644-4880, Fax: 850-644-7736, E-mail: ssoutherland@admin.fsu.edu. *Application contact:* Dawn Matthews, Academic Support Assistant, 850-644-2122, Fax: 850-644-7736, E-mail: dmatthews@fsu.edu.
Website: http://www.coe.fsu.edu/STE.

Fordham University, Graduate School of Education, Division of Curriculum and Teaching, New York, NY 10023. Offers adult education (MS, MSE); bilingual teacher education (MSE); curriculum and teaching (MSE); early childhood education (MSE); elementary education (MST); language, literacy, and learning (PhD); reading education (MSE, Adv C); secondary education (MAT, MSE); special education (MSE, Adv C); teaching English as a second language (MSE). *Accreditation:* NCATE. *Degree requirements:* For doctorate, thesis/dissertation; for Adv C, thesis. *Entrance requirements:* For doctorate, MAT, GRE General Test.

Framingham State University, Continuing Education, Program in Literacy and Language, Framingham, MA 01701-9101. Offers M Ed. Part-time and evening/weekend programs available. *Entrance requirements:* For master's, MAT.

Fresno Pacific University, Graduate Programs, School of Education, Division of Language, Literacy, and Culture, Program in Reading, Fresno, CA 93702-4709. Offers reading (Certificate); reading/English as a second language (MA Ed); reading/language arts (MA Ed). Part-time and evening/weekend programs available. *Faculty:* 1 (woman) full-time. *Students:* 1 part-time. Average age 40. In 2013, 2 master's awarded. *Degree requirements:* For master's, thesis or alternative. *Entrance requirements:* Additional exam requirements/recommendations for international students: Required—TOEFL (minimum score 550 paper-based). *Application deadline:* For fall admission, 7/15 for domestic and international students; for spring admission, 11/15 for domestic and international students. Applications are processed on a rolling basis. Application fee: $90. Electronic applications accepted. *Expenses: Tuition:* Full-time $8910; part-time $495 per unit. *Required fees:* $270. Tuition and fees vary according to course load and program. *Financial support:* Scholarships/grants and tuition waivers (full and partial) available. Support available to part-time students. Financial award applicants required to submit FAFSA. *Unit head:* Jo Ellen Misakian, Program Director, 559-453-2291, Fax: 559-453-7168, E-mail: jmisakian@fresno.edu. *Application contact:* Jon Endicott, Director of Graduate Admissions, 559-453-2016.

Frostburg State University, Graduate School, College of Education, Department of Educational Professions, Program in Reading, Frostburg, MD 21532-1099. Offers M Ed. *Accreditation:* NCATE. *Degree requirements:* For master's, thesis or alternative, in-service. *Entrance requirements:* For master's, teaching certificate. Additional exam requirements/recommendations for international students: Required—TOEFL. Electronic applications accepted. *Expenses: Tuition, area resident:* Part-time $340 per credit hour. Tuition, state resident: part-time $340 per credit hour. Tuition, nonresident: part-time $437 per credit hour.

Furman University, Graduate Division, Department of Education, Greenville, SC 29613. Offers curriculum and instruction (MA); early childhood education (MA); educational leadership (Ed S); English as a second language (MA); literacy (MA); school leadership (MA); special education (MA). *Accreditation:* NCATE. Part-time programs available. Postbaccalaureate distance learning degree programs offered (minimal on-campus study). *Degree requirements:* For master's, comprehensive exam (for some programs), thesis or alternative. *Entrance requirements:* For master's, PRAXIS II. *Faculty research:* Literacy, pedagogy and practice, social justice, advanced leadership, achievement in high poverty schools.

Gannon University, School of Graduate Studies, College of Humanities, Education, and Social Sciences, School of Education, Program in Reading, Erie, PA 16541-0001. Offers M Ed. Part-time and evening/weekend programs available. Postbaccalaureate distance learning degree programs offered. *Students:* 1 (woman) full-time, 16 part-time (15 women). Average age 30. 12 applicants, 92% accepted, 8 enrolled. In 2013, 9 master's awarded. *Degree requirements:* For master's, comprehensive exam, thesis or alternative, portfolio project. *Entrance requirements:* For master's, GRE, minimum GPA of 3.0, teacher certification. Additional exam requirements/recommendations for international students: Required—TOEFL (minimum score 79 iBT). *Application deadline:* Applications are processed on a rolling basis. Application fee: $25. Electronic applications accepted. *Expenses:* Contact institution. *Financial support:* Scholarships/grants available. Financial award application deadline: 7/1; financial award applicants required to submit FAFSA. *Unit head:* Dr. Robin Quick, Director, 814-871-5399, E-mail: quick003@gannon.edu. *Application contact:* Kara Morgan, Director of Graduate Admissions, 814-871-5831, Fax: 814-871-5827, E-mail: graduate@gannon.edu.

Gannon University, School of Graduate Studies, College of Humanities, Education, and Social Sciences, School of Education, Program in Reading Specialist, Erie, PA 16541-0001. Offers Certificate. Part-time and evening/weekend programs available. *Students:* 2 full-time (both women), 7 part-time (all women); includes 1 minority (Asian, non-Hispanic/Latino). Average age 35. 13 applicants, 77% accepted, 6 enrolled. *Entrance requirements:* For degree, GRE, teaching certification, minimum GPA of 3.0. Application fee: $25. *Expenses: Tuition:* Full-time $15,930; part-time $885 per credit. *Required fees:* $430; $18 per credit. Tuition and fees vary according to course load, degree level and program. *Unit head:* Dr. Robin Quick, Director, 814-871-5399, E-mail: quick003@gannon.edu. *Application contact:* Kara Morgan, Director of Graduate Admissions, 814-871-5831, Fax: 814-871-5827, E-mail: graduate@gannon.edu.

Geneva College, Master of Education in Reading Program, Beaver Falls, PA 15010-3599. Offers M Ed. Part-time and evening/weekend programs available. *Faculty:* 4 full-time (all women). *Students:* 10 part-time (9 women). Average age 32. 2 applicants, 100% accepted, 1 enrolled. In 2013, 6 master's awarded. *Degree requirements:* For master's, 100 hours of field experience. *Entrance requirements:* For master's, 2 letters of recommendation, resume, transcript. Additional exam requirements/recommendations for international students: Required—TOEFL. *Application deadline:* Applications are processed on a rolling basis. Electronic applications accepted. *Expenses: Tuition:* Full-time $14,640; part-time $640 per credit hour. Tuition and fees vary according to program. *Financial support:* In 2013–14, 1 student received support. Scholarships/grants available. Financial award application deadline: 9/1; financial award applicants required to submit FAFSA. *Unit head:* Dr. Adel Aiken, Program Director, 724-847-5002, E-mail: reading@geneva.edu. *Application contact:* Marina Frazier, Director of Graduate Enrollment, 724-846-6697, E-mail: reading@geneva.edu.
Website: http://www.geneva.edu/page/reading.

George Fox University, College of Education, Educational Foundations and Leadership Program, Newberg, OR 97132-2697. Offers continuing administrator license (Certificate); curriculum and instruction (M Ed); educational leadership (M Ed, Ed D); ESOL (Certificate); higher education (M Ed); initial administrator license (Certificate); instructional leadership (Ed S); library media (M Ed, Certificate); literacy (M Ed); reading (M Ed); secondary education (M Ed). *Accreditation:* NCATE. Part-time and evening/weekend programs available. Postbaccalaureate distance learning degree programs offered (minimal on-campus study). *Faculty:* 7 full-time (3 women), 5 part-time/adjunct (4 women). *Students:* 194 part-time (128 women); includes 15 minority (1 Black or African American, non-Hispanic/Latino; 1 American Indian or Alaska Native, non-Hispanic/Latino; 3 Asian, non-Hispanic/Latino; 6 Hispanic/Latino; 1 Native Hawaiian or other Pacific Islander, non-Hispanic/Latino; 3 Two or more races, non-Hispanic/Latino), 2 international. Average age 42. 46 applicants, 85% accepted, 39 enrolled. In 2013, 15 master's, 16 doctorates, 106 Certificates awarded. *Degree requirements:* For master's, thesis (for some programs); for doctorate, comprehensive exam, thesis/dissertation, project. *Entrance requirements:* For master's, minimum undergraduate GPA of 3.0 during previous 2 years of course work, resume, 3 professional recommendations on university forms, official transcripts; for doctorate, GRE, master's degree with minimum GPA of 3.25, 3 years of relevant professional experience, interview, personal essay, scholarly work, 3 professional recommendations on university forms along with 3 written letters of recommendation, official transcripts. Additional exam requirements/recommendations for international students: Required—TOEFL (minimum score 577 paper-based; 90 iBT). *Application deadline:* For fall admission, 7/15 for domestic and international students; for winter admission, 11/1 for domestic and international students; for spring admission, 4/1 for domestic and international students. Applications are processed on a rolling basis. Application fee: $40. Electronic applications accepted. *Expenses:* Contact institution. *Financial support:* Career-related internships or fieldwork available. Financial award applicants required to submit FAFSA. *Unit head:* Dr. Scot Headley, Professor/Chair, 503-554-2836, E-mail: sheadley@georgefox.edu. *Application contact:* Kipp Wilfong, Graduate Admissions Counselor, 800-631-0921, Fax: 503-554-3110, E-mail: kwilfong@georgefox.edu.
Website: http://www.georgefox.edu/education/index.html.

George Fox University, College of Education, Master of Arts in Teaching Program, Newberg, OR 97132-2697. Offers teaching (MAT); teaching plus ESOL (MAT); teaching plus ESOL/bilingual (MAT); teaching plus reading (MAT); teaching plus special education (MAT). Program offered in Oregon and Idaho. Part-time and evening/weekend programs available. *Faculty:* 11 full-time (9 women), 24 part-time/adjunct (16 women). *Students:* 64 full-time (44 women), 20 part-time (14 women); includes 11 minority (1 Black or African American, non-Hispanic/Latino; 2 Asian, non-Hispanic/Latino; 1 Hispanic/Latino; 2 Native Hawaiian or other Pacific Islander, non-Hispanic/Latino; 5 Two or more races, non-Hispanic/Latino), 1 international. Average age 30. 28 applicants, 100% accepted, 18 enrolled. In 2013, 116 master's awarded. *Entrance requirements:* For master's, CBEST, PRAXIS PPST, or EAS, bachelor's degree with minimum GPA of 3.0 in last two years of course work from regionally-accredited college or university, official transcripts. Additional exam requirements/recommendations for international students: Required—TOEFL (minimum score 577 paper-based; 90 iBT), IELTS (minimum score 7). *Application deadline:* For fall admission, 6/1 for domestic and international students; for winter admission, 10/1 for domestic and international students; for spring admission, 2/1 for domestic and international students. Applications are processed on a rolling basis. Application fee: $40. Electronic applications accepted. *Expenses:* Contact institution. *Financial support:* In 2013–14, 20 students received support. Scholarships/grants available. Financial award application deadline: 2/1; financial award applicants required to submit FAFSA. *Application contact:* Kipp Wilfong, Graduate Admissions Counselor, 800-631-0921, Fax: 503-554-3110, E-mail: mat@georgefox.edu.
Website: http://www.georgefox.edu/soe/mat/.

Georgetown College, Department of Education, Georgetown, KY 40324-1696. Offers reading and writing (MA Ed); special education (MA Ed); teaching (MA Ed). *Accreditation:* NCATE. Part-time programs available. *Degree requirements:* For master's, portfolio. *Entrance requirements:* For master's, teaching certificate, minimum GPA of 2.7 or GRE General Test.

The George Washington University, Graduate School of Education and Human Development, Department of Curriculum and Pedagogy, Program in Reading and Literacy, Washington, DC 20052. Offers Graduate Certificate. *Students:* 1 (woman) part-time; minority (Hispanic/Latino). Average age 31. 3 applicants, 100% accepted, 1 enrolled. *Entrance requirements:* For degree, GRE or MAT, official transcripts, statement of purpose, two letters of reference, teacher certification. *Unit head:* Dr. Colin Green, Chair, 202-994-0997, E-mail: colgreen@gwu.edu. *Application contact:* Sarah Lang, Director of Graduate Admissions, 202-994-1447, Fax: 202-994-7207, E-mail: slang@gwu.edu.
Website: http://gsehd.gwu.edu/academics/programs/certificates/reading-and-literacy/overview.

Georgia College & State University, Graduate School, The John H. Lounsbury College of Education, Program in Reading, Literacy, and Language, Milledgeville, GA 31061. Offers M Ed. *Students:* 10 part-time (9 women); includes 5 minority (all Black or African American, non-Hispanic/Latino). Average age 31. *Degree requirements:* For master's, comprehensive exam, minimum GPA of 3.0 on all work, complete program within 6 years. *Entrance requirements:* For master's, on-site writing assessment, two professional recommendations, level 4 teaching certificate, official transcripts, verification of immunization. Additional exam requirements/recommendations for international students: Recommended—TOEFL (minimum score 550 paper-based; 79 iBT). *Application deadline:* For fall admission, 7/1 for domestic students; for spring admission, 11/15 for domestic students. Application fee: $40. *Financial support:* In 2013–14, 1 research assistantship was awarded. Financial award applicants required to submit FAFSA. *Application contact:* Shanda Brand, Graduate Admissions Advisor, 478-445-1383, Fax: 478-445-6582, E-mail: shanda.brand@gcsu.edu.

Georgia Southern University, Jack N. Averitt College of Graduate Studies, College of Education, Department of Curriculum, Foundations, and Reading, Program in Reading Education, Statesboro, GA 30460. Offers M Ed, Ed S. *Accreditation:* NCATE. Part-time and evening/weekend programs available. *Students:* 4 full-time (2 women), 16 part-time (all women); includes 2 minority (both Black or African American, non-Hispanic/Latino), 1 international. Average age 33. 10 applicants, 90% accepted, 8 enrolled. In 2013, 3 master's awarded. *Degree requirements:* For master's, comprehensive exam, transition point assessments. *Entrance requirements:* For master's, GRE General Test or MAT, minimum GPA of 2.5. Additional exam requirements/recommendations for international students: Required—TOEFL (minimum score 550 paper-based; 80 iBT), IELTS (minimum score 6). *Application deadline:* For fall admission, 3/1 priority date for domestic and international students; for spring admission, 10/1 priority date for domestic students, 10/1 for international students. Applications are processed on a rolling basis. Application fee: $50. Electronic applications accepted. *Expenses:* Tuition, state resident: full-time $7068; part-time $270 per semester hour. Tuition, nonresident: full-time $26,446; part-time $1077 per semester hour. *Required fees:* $2092. *Financial support:* In 2013–14, research assistantships with partial tuition reimbursements (averaging $7,200 per year), teaching assistantships with partial tuition reimbursements (averaging $7,200 per year) were awarded; career-related internships or fieldwork, Federal Work-Study, scholarships/grants, tuition waivers (partial), and unspecified assistantships also available. Support available to part-time students. Financial award application deadline: 4/15; financial award applicants required to submit FAFSA. *Faculty research:* Emerging literacy, content literacy, digital literacies, English language learners, literature groups, phonics/whole language, interpreting literacy policy. *Unit head:* Dr. Michael Moore, Coordinator, 912-478-0211, Fax: 912-478-5382, E-mail: mmoore@georgiasouthern.edu. *Application contact:* Amanda Gilliland, Coordinator for Graduate Student Recruitment, 912-478-5384, Fax: 912-478-0740, E-mail: gradadmissions@georgiasouthern.edu.
Website: http://coe.georgiasouthern.edu/reading.

Georgia Southwestern State University, Graduate Studies, School of Education, Americus, GA 31709-4693. Offers early childhood education (M Ed, Ed S); health and physical education (M Ed); middle grades education (M Ed, Ed S); reading (M Ed); secondary education (M Ed); special education (M Ed). *Accreditation:* NCATE. *Degree requirements:* For master's, comprehensive exam. *Entrance requirements:* For master's, GRE General Test or MAT, minimum GPA of 2.5; for Ed S, GRE General Test or MAT, minimum graduate GPA of 3.25, M Ed from accredited college or university, 3 years teaching experience. Electronic applications accepted.

Georgia State University, College of Education, Department of Middle-Secondary Education and Instructional Technology, Atlanta, GA 30302-3083. Offers English education (M Ed, MAT); English speakers of other languages (MAT); instructional design and technology (MS); instructional technology (PhD), including alternative instructional delivery systems, consulting, instructional design, management, research;

mathematics education (M Ed, MAT); middle level education (MAT); reading, language and literacy education (M Ed), including reading instruction; science education (MAT), including biology, broad field science, chemistry, earth science, physics; social studies education (M Ed, MAT), including economics (MAT), geography (MAT), history (MAT), political science (MAT); teaching and learning (PhD), including language and literacy, mathematics education, music education, science education, social studies, teaching and teacher education. *Accreditation:* NCATE. Part-time and evening/weekend programs available. Postbaccalaureate distance learning degree programs offered (minimal on-campus study). *Faculty:* 27 full-time (19 women). *Students:* 181 full-time (113 women), 203 part-time (145 women); includes 161 minority (127 Black or African American, non-Hispanic/Latino; 1 American Indian or Alaska Native, non-Hispanic/Latino; 10 Asian, non-Hispanic/Latino; 11 Hispanic/Latino; 1 Native Hawaiian or other Pacific Islander, non-Hispanic/Latino; 11 Two or more races, non-Hispanic/Latino), 9 international. Average age 36. 2 applicants, 50% accepted, 1 enrolled. In 2013, 213 master's, 17 doctorates awarded. *Degree requirements:* For master's, comprehensive exam (for some programs), thesis or alternative, exit portfolio; for doctorate, comprehensive exam, thesis/dissertation. *Entrance requirements:* For master's, GRE; GACE I (for initial teacher preparation degree programs), baccalaureate degree or equivalent, resume, goals statement, two letters of recommendation, minimum undergraduate GPA of 2.5; proof of initial teacher certification in the content area (for M Ed); for doctorate, GRE, resume, goals statement, writing sample, two letters of recommendation, minimum graduate GPA of 3.3, interview. Additional exam requirements/recommendations for international students: Required—TOEFL (minimum score 550 paper-based; 79 iBT) or IELTS (minimum score 6.5). *Application deadline:* For fall admission, 1/15 priority date for domestic and international students; for spring admission, 10/1 for domestic and international students. Application fee: $50. Electronic applications accepted. *Expenses: Tuition, area resident:* Full-time $4176; part-time $348 per credit hour. Tuition, state resident: full-time $14,544; part-time $1212 per credit hour. Tuition, nonresident: full-time $14,544; part-time $1212 per credit hour. Tuition and fees vary according to course load and program. *Financial support:* In 2013–14, fellowships with full tuition reimbursements (averaging $19,667 per year), research assistantships with full tuition reimbursements (averaging $5,436 per year), teaching assistantships with full tuition reimbursements (averaging $2,779 per year) were awarded; career-related internships or fieldwork, Federal Work-Study, scholarships/grants, health care benefits, tuition waivers (full and partial), and unspecified assistantships also available. Financial award application deadline: 3/15. *Faculty research:* Teacher education in language and literacy, mathematics, science, and social studies in urban middle and secondary school settings; learning technologies in school, community, and corporate settings; multicultural education and education for social justice; urban education; international education. *Unit head:* Dr. Dana L. Fox, Chair, 404-413-8060, Fax: 404-413-8063, E-mail: dfox@gsu.edu. *Application contact:* Bobbie Turner, Administrative Coordinator I, 404-413-8405, Fax: 404-413-8063, E-mail: bnturner@gsu.edu.
Website: http://msit.gsu.edu/msit_programs.htm.

Gordon College, Graduate Education Program, Wenham, MA 01984-1899. Offers education (M Ed); educational leadership (Ed S); English as a second language (ESL) (Ed S); mathematics specialist (Ed S); reading (Ed S). Part-time and evening/weekend programs available. *Faculty:* 1 (woman) full-time, 45 part-time/adjunct (27 women). *Students:* 106 full-time (86 women), 281 part-time (230 women); includes 30 minority (4 Black or African American, non-Hispanic/Latino; 7 Asian, non-Hispanic/Latino; 17 Hispanic/Latino; 2 Two or more races, non-Hispanic/Latino), 5 international. In 2013, 52 master's awarded. *Degree requirements:* For master's and Ed S, action research or clinical experience (for some programs). *Entrance requirements:* For master's, GRE or MAT, references, minimum undergraduate GPA of 3.0; for Ed S, references, minimum undergraduate GPA of 3.0. Additional exam requirements/recommendations for international students: Required—TOEFL (minimum score 550 paper-based, 80 iBT) or IELTS (minimum score 6.5). *Application deadline:* Applications are processed on a rolling basis. Application fee: $50. *Expenses: Tuition:* Part-time $325 per credit. *Required fees:* $50 per term. One-time fee: $50. Tuition and fees vary according to program. *Financial support:* Applicants required to submit FAFSA. *Faculty research:* Reading, early childhood development, English language learners. *Unit head:* Dr. Janet Arndt, Director of Graduate Studies, 978-867-4355, Fax: 978-867-4663. *Application contact:* Julie Lenocker, Program Administrator, 978-867-4322, Fax: 978-867-4663, E-mail: graduate-education@gordon.edu.
Website: http://www.gordon.edu/graduate.

Governors State University, College of Education, Program in Reading, University Park, IL 60484. Offers MA. *Accreditation:* NCATE.

Graceland University, Gleazer School of Education, Independence, MO 64050. Offers differentiated instruction (M Ed); literacy and instruction (M Ed); management in the inclusive classroom (M Ed); mild/moderate special education (M Ed); technology integration (M Ed). *Accreditation:* NCATE. Part-time and evening/weekend programs available. Postbaccalaureate distance learning degree programs offered (no on-campus study). *Faculty:* 12 full-time (11 women), 18 part-time/adjunct (14 women). *Students:* 139 full-time (119 women), 18 part-time (14 women); includes 8 minority (3 Black or African American, non-Hispanic/Latino; 1 Asian, non-Hispanic/Latino; 4 Hispanic/Latino). Average age 36. 36 applicants, 81% accepted, 24 enrolled. In 2013, 196 master's awarded. *Degree requirements:* For master's, action research project. *Entrance requirements:* For master's, minimum GPA of 3.0, teaching certificate, current teaching contract. *Application deadline:* For fall admission, 7/15 for domestic students; for winter admission, 10/15 for domestic students; for spring admission, 1/15 priority date for domestic students. Application fee: $50. Electronic applications accepted. *Expenses: Tuition:* Part-time $450 per semester hour. Tuition and fees vary according to course load, degree level, campus/location and program. *Financial support:* Institutionally sponsored loans and scholarships/grants available. Financial award application deadline: 12/15; financial award applicants required to submit FAFSA. *Unit head:* Dr. Scott Huddleston, Dean, 641-784-5000 Ext. 4744, E-mail: huddlest@graceland.edu. *Application contact:* Cathy Porter, Program Consultant, 816-423-4716, Fax: 816-833-2990, E-mail: cgporter@graceland.edu.
Website: http://www.graceland.edu/education.

Grambling State University, School of Graduate Studies and Research, College of Education, Department of Educational Leadership, Grambling, LA 71245. Offers developmental education (MS, Ed D, PMC), including curriculum and instructional design (Ed D), English (MS), guidance and counseling (MS), higher education administration and management (Ed D), mathematics (MS), reading (MS), science (MS), student development and personnel services (Ed D); educational leadership (M Ed). Part-time and evening/weekend programs available. *Faculty:* 10 full-time (7 women). *Students:* 19 full-time (13 women), 89 part-time (70 women); includes 83 minority (82 Black or African American, non-Hispanic/Latino; 1 Hispanic/Latino), 6 international. Average age 40. In 2013, 13 master's, 6 doctorates, 1 other advanced degree awarded. *Degree requirements:* For master's, comprehensive exam, thesis (for some programs); for doctorate, comprehensive exam, thesis/dissertation. *Entrance requirements:* For master's, GRE, minimum GPA of 2.5 on last degree; for doctorate, GRE (minimum score 1000, 500 on Verbal), master's degree, minimum GPA of 3.0 on last degree. Additional exam requirements/recommendations for international students: Required—TOEFL (minimum score 500 paper-based; 62 iBT). *Application deadline:* For fall admission, 7/1 for domestic and international students; for spring admission, 12/1 for domestic and international students; for summer admission, 5/1 for domestic and international students. Applications are processed on a rolling basis. Application fee: $20 ($30 for international students). Electronic applications accepted. *Financial support:* Research assistantships, health care benefits, tuition waivers (full), and unspecified assistantships available. Financial award application deadline: 5/31; financial award applicants required to submit FAFSA. *Unit head:* Dr. Olatunde Ogunyemi, Department Head, 318-274-2549, Fax: 318-274-6249, E-mail: ogunyemio@gram.edu. *Application contact:* Brenda Cooper, Administrative Assistant III, 318-274-2238, Fax: 318-274-6249, E-mail: cooper@gram.edu.
Website: http://www.gram.edu/academics/majors/education/departments/leadership/.

Grand Valley State University, College of Education, Program in Literacy Studies, Allendale, MI 49401-9403. Offers M Ed.

Grand Valley State University, College of Education, Program in Reading and Language Arts, Allendale, MI 49401-9403. Offers M Ed. *Accreditation:* NCATE. Part-time and evening/weekend programs available. *Degree requirements:* For master's, thesis. *Entrance requirements:* For master's, GRE General Test or minimum GPA of 3.0. Additional exam requirements/recommendations for international students: Required—TOEFL. Electronic applications accepted. *Faculty research:* Culture of literacy, literacy acquisition, assessment, content area literacy, writing pedagogy.

Gwynedd Mercy University, School of Education, Gwynedd Valley, PA 19437-0901. Offers educational administration (MS); master teacher (MS); reading (MS); school counseling (MS); special education (MS). Part-time and evening/weekend programs available. *Degree requirements:* For master's, thesis, internship, practicum. *Entrance requirements:* For master's, GRE or MAT; PRAXIS I, minimum GPA of 3.0. *Faculty research:* Learning and the brain, reading literacy, ethics and moral judgment, leadership, teaching and multicultural education.

Hamline University, School of Education, St. Paul, MN 55104-1284. Offers education (MA Ed, Ed D); English as a second language (MA); literacy education (MA); natural science and environmental education (MA Ed); teaching (MAT). *Accreditation:* NCATE (one or more programs are accredited). Part-time and evening/weekend programs available. Postbaccalaureate distance learning degree programs offered (no on-campus study). *Faculty:* 19 full-time (14 women), 44 part-time/adjunct (38 women). *Students:* 107 full-time (75 women), 997 part-time (744 women); includes 71 minority (23 Black or African American, non-Hispanic/Latino; 4 American Indian or Alaska Native, non-Hispanic/Latino; 17 Asian, non-Hispanic/Latino; 21 Hispanic/Latino; 6 Two or more races, non-Hispanic/Latino), 10 international. Average age 33. 395 applicants, 74% accepted, 224 enrolled. In 2013, 221 master's, 13 doctorates awarded. *Degree requirements:* For master's, foreign language (for MA in English as a second language only); thesis or capstone project; for doctorate, comprehensive exam, thesis/dissertation. *Entrance requirements:* For master's, written essay, official transcripts, 2 letters of recommendation, minimum GPA of 3.0 from bachelor's work; for doctorate, personal statement, master's degree with minimum GPA of 3.0, 3 letters of recommendation, writing sample, interview. Additional exam requirements/recommendations for international students: Required—TOEFL (minimum score 550 paper-based; 80 iBT), TOEFL (625 paper-based, 107 iBT) or IELTS (minimum 7.5) for MA in ESL. *Application deadline:* Applications are processed on a rolling basis. Application fee: $0 ($100 for international students). Electronic applications accepted. *Financial support:* Career-related internships or fieldwork, Federal Work-Study, and scholarships/grants available. Support available to part-time students. Financial award applicants required to submit FAFSA. *Faculty research:* Adult basic education, service-learning, teacher dispositions, diversity, technology. *Unit head:* Dr. Nancy Sorenson, Dean, 651-523-2600, Fax: 651-523-2489, E-mail: nsorenson01@hamline.edu. *Application contact:* Shawn Skoog, Director of Graduate Recruitment and Admission, 651-523-2900, Fax: 651-523-3058, E-mail: sskoog03@hamline.edu.
Website: http://www.hamline.edu/education.

Hannibal-LaGrange University, Program in Education, Hannibal, MO 63401-1999. Offers literacy (MS Ed); teaching and learning (MS Ed). Part-time and evening/weekend programs available. *Degree requirements:* For master's, thesis, portfolio, documenting of program outcomes, public sharing of research. *Entrance requirements:* For master's, copy of current teaching certificate; minimum GPA of 2.75. *Faculty research:* Reading assessment, reading remediation, handwriting instruction, early childhood intervention.

Harding University, Cannon-Clary College of Education, Searcy, AR 72149-0001. Offers advanced studies in teaching and learning (M Ed); art (MSE); behavioral science (MSE); counseling (MS, Ed S); early childhood special education (M Ed, MSE); education (MSE); educational leadership (M Ed, Ed S); elementary education (M Ed); English (MSE); French (MSE); history/social science (MSE); kinesiology (MSE); math (MSE); reading (M Ed); secondary education (M Ed); Spanish (MSE); teaching (MAT); teaching English as a second language (MSE). *Accreditation:* NCATE. Part-time and evening/weekend programs available. *Faculty:* 13 full-time (5 women), 42 part-time/adjunct (24 women). *Students:* 154 full-time (119 women), 393 part-time (270 women); includes 108 minority (81 Black or African American, non-Hispanic/Latino; 5 American Indian or Alaska Native, non-Hispanic/Latino; 5 Asian, non-Hispanic/Latino; 9 Hispanic/Latino; 8 Two or more races, non-Hispanic/Latino), 15 international. Average age 36. 187 applicants, 79% accepted, 135 enrolled. In 2013, 138 master's, 17 other advanced degrees awarded. *Degree requirements:* For master's, comprehensive exam (for some programs), thesis optional, portfolio(s); for Ed S, comprehensive exam, portfolio, project. *Entrance requirements:* For master's, GRE, MAT, PRAXIS; for Ed S, MAT or GRE. Additional exam requirements/recommendations for international students: Required—TOEFL (minimum score 550 paper-based; 79 iBT). *Application deadline:* For fall admission, 8/1 for domestic and international students; for spring admission, 1/1 for domestic and international students. Applications are processed on a rolling basis. Application fee: $35. *Expenses: Tuition:* Full-time $11,574; part-time $643 per credit hour. *Required fees:* $432; $24 per credit hour. Tuition and fees vary according to course load, degree level and program. *Financial support:* In 2013–14, 36 students received support. Unspecified assistantships available. *Faculty research:* Reading, comprehension, school violence, educational technology, behavior, college choice, differentiated instruction, brain-based teaching. *Unit head:* Dr. Clara Carroll, Chair, 501-279-4501, Fax: 501-279-4083, E-mail: ccarroll@harding.edu. *Application contact:* Information Contact, 501-279-4315, E-mail: gradstudiesedu@harding.edu.
Website: http://www.harding.edu/education.

Hardin-Simmons University, Graduate School, Irvin School of Education, Department of Educational Studies, Program in Reading Specialist Education, Abilene, TX 79698-0001. Offers M Ed. Part-time programs available. *Faculty:* 1 (woman) full-time, 2 part-time/adjunct (1 woman). *Students:* 1 (woman) full-time, 3 part-time (all women); includes 1 minority (Hispanic/Latino), 1 international. Average age 31. 1 applicant, 100% accepted, 1 enrolled. *Degree requirements:* For master's, comprehensive exam. *Entrance requirements:* For master's, minimum undergraduate GPA of 3.0 in major, 2.7 overall. Additional exam requirements/recommendations for international students: Required—TOEFL (minimum score 550 paper-based; 75 iBT). *Application deadline:* For fall admission, 8/15 priority date for domestic students, 4/1 for international students; for spring admission, 1/5 priority date for domestic students, 9/1 for international students.

Applications are processed on a rolling basis. Application fee: $50. *Expenses: Tuition:* Full-time $13,410; part-time $745 per credit hour. *Required fees:* $325; $110 per semester. Tuition and fees vary according to program. *Financial support:* In 2013–14, 5 students received support, including 2 fellowships (averaging $1,800 per year); scholarships/grants also available. Support available to part-time students. Financial award application deadline: 6/30; financial award applicants required to submit FAFSA. *Faculty research:* Social networking as a gatekeeper, reflective process of teachers, growth of reflective practice in pre-service teachers, multicultural children's literature. *Unit head:* Dr. Diana Higgins, Director, 325-670-1354, Fax: 325-670-5859, E-mail: dihigg@hsutx.edu. *Application contact:* Dr. Nancy Kucinski, Dean of Graduate Studies, 325-670-1298, Fax: 325-670-1564, E-mail: gradoff@hsutx.edu.
Website: http://www.hsutx.edu/academics/irvin/graduate/readinged.

Harvard University, Harvard Graduate School of Education, Master's Programs in Education, Cambridge, MA 02138. Offers arts in education (Ed M); education policy and management (Ed M); higher education (Ed M); human development and psychology (Ed M); international education policy (Ed M); language and literacy (Ed M); learning and teaching (Ed M); mind, brain, and education (Ed M); prevention science and practice (Ed M); school leadership (Ed M); special studies (Ed M); teacher education (Ed M); technology, innovation, and education (Ed M). Part-time programs available. *Faculty:* 68 full-time (34 women), 77 part-time/adjunct (41 women). *Students:* 557 full-time (410 women), 69 part-time (50 women); includes 179 minority (34 Black or African American, non-Hispanic/Latino; 1 American Indian or Alaska Native, non-Hispanic/Latino; 62 Asian, non-Hispanic/Latino; 52 Hispanic/Latino; 2 Native Hawaiian or other Pacific Islander, non-Hispanic/Latino; 28 Two or more races, non-Hispanic/Latino), 100 international. Average age 28. 1,756 applicants, 47% accepted, 589 enrolled. In 2013, 673 master's awarded. *Entrance requirements:* For master's, GRE General Test, statement of purpose, 3 letters of recommendation, resume, official transcripts. Additional exam requirements/recommendations for international students: Required—TOEFL (minimum score 613 paper-based; 104 iBT), TWE (minimum score 5). *Application deadline:* For fall admission, 1/3 for domestic and international students. Application fee: $85. Electronic applications accepted. *Expenses:* Contact institution. *Financial support:* In 2013–14, 375 students received support, including 12 fellowships with full and partial tuition reimbursements available (averaging $13,925 per year), 2 research assistantships (averaging $2,174 per year); career-related internships or fieldwork, Federal Work-Study, institutionally sponsored loans, scholarships/grants, health care benefits, tuition waivers (full and partial), and unspecified assistantships also available. Support available to part-time students. Financial award application deadline: 2/1; financial award applicants required to submit FAFSA. *Faculty research:* Learning and development, educational leadership and organizations, education policy analysis. *Total annual research expenditures:* $34.3 million. *Unit head:* Jennifer L. Petrallia, Assistant Dean, 617-495-8445. *Application contact:* Information Contact, 617-495-3414, Fax: 617-496-3577, E-mail: gseadmissions@harvard.edu.
Website: http://www.gse.harvard.edu/.

Henderson State University, Graduate Studies, Teachers College, Department of Advanced Instructional Studies, Arkadelphia, AR 71999-0001. Offers early childhood (P-4) (MSE); education (MAT); English as a second language (Graduate Certificate); instructional facilitator (Graduate Certificate); middle school (MSE); reading (MSE); special education (MSE). *Accreditation:* NCATE. Part-time programs available. *Faculty:* 7 full-time (3 women), 2 part-time/adjunct (both women). *Students:* 1 (woman) full-time, 99 part-time (88 women); includes 20 minority (13 Black or African American, non-Hispanic/Latino; 1 American Indian or Alaska Native, non-Hispanic/Latino; 5 Hispanic/Latino; 1 Two or more races, non-Hispanic/Latino), 1 international. Average age 36. 7 applicants, 100% accepted, 7 enrolled. In 2013, 45 master's awarded. *Entrance requirements:* For master's, GRE General Test or MAT, minimum GPA of 2.7, teacher certification. Additional exam requirements/recommendations for international students: Required—TOEFL (minimum score 600 paper-based); Recommended—IELTS (minimum score 6.5). *Application deadline:* For fall admission, 8/1 priority date for domestic students, 6/30 priority date for international students; for spring admission, 1/1 priority date for domestic students, 11/30 priority date for international students. Applications are processed on a rolling basis. Application fee: $25 ($75 for international students). *Expenses:* Tuition, state resident: full-time $4284; part-time $238 per credit hour. Tuition, nonresident: full-time $8802; part-time $489 per credit hour. Tuition and fees vary according to course load and campus/location. *Financial support:* In 2013–14, 1 teaching assistantship with partial tuition reimbursement (averaging $4,000 per year) was awarded; scholarships/grants and unspecified assistantships also available. *Unit head:* Dr. Gary Smithey, Chairperson, 870-230-5361, Fax: 870-230-5455, E-mail: smitheg@hsu.edu. *Application contact:* Dr. Ken Taylor, Graduate Dean, 870-230-5126, Fax: 870-230-5479, E-mail: taylorke@hsu.edu.

Heritage University, Graduate Programs in Education, Program in Professional Studies, Toppenish, WA 98948-9599. Offers bilingual education/ESL (M Ed); biology (M Ed); English and literature (M Ed); reading/literacy (M Ed); special education (M Ed). Part-time and evening/weekend programs available. *Degree requirements:* For master's, comprehensive exam (for some programs), thesis (for some programs).

Hofstra University, School of Education, Programs in Literacy, Hempstead, NY 11549. Offers advanced literacy studies (PD), including birth-grade 6 (MA, MS Ed, PD); advanced literary studies (PD), including grades 5-12 (MA, PD); birth-grade 6 (MS Ed, Advanced Certificate); grades 5-12 (Advanced Certificate); literacy studies (Ed D, PhD); special education (MS Ed), including birth-grade 2, birth-grade 6 (MA, MS Ed, PD); teaching of writing (MA), including birth-grade 6 (MA, MS Ed, PD), grades 5-12 (MA, PD).

Hofstra University, School of Education, Programs in Teaching - Elementary and Early Childhood Education, Hempstead, NY 11549. Offers early childhood and childhood education (MS Ed); early childhood education (MA, MS Ed); educational technology (MA); elementary education (MS Ed); literacy (MA); math specialist (Advanced Certificate); math, science, technology (MA); multiculturalism (MA).

Holy Family University, Graduate School, School of Education, Master of Education Programs, Philadelphia, PA 19114. Offers early elementary education (PreK-Grade 4) (M Ed); education leadership (M Ed); general education (M Ed); middle level education (Grades 4-8) (M Ed); reading specialist (M Ed); secondary education (Grades 7-12) (M Ed); special education (M Ed); TESOL and literacy (M Ed). *Expenses: Tuition:* Full-time $12,060. *Required fees:* $250. Tuition and fees vary according to degree level. *Unit head:* Dr. Leonard Soroka, Dean, 267-341-3565, Fax: 215-824-2438, E-mail: lsoroka@holyfamily.edu. *Application contact:* Gidget Marie Montelibano, Associate Director of Graduate Admissions, 267-341-3358, Fax: 215-637-1478, E-mail: gmontelibano@holyfamily.edu.

Hood College, Graduate School, Department of Education, Frederick, MD 21701-8575. Offers curriculum and instruction (MS), including early childhood education, elementary education, elementary school science and mathematics, secondary education, special education; educational leadership (MS, Certificate); reading specialization (MS); STEM (Certificate). *Accreditation:* NCATE. Part-time and evening/weekend programs available. *Faculty:* 4 full-time (3 women), 33 part-time/adjunct (25 women). *Students:* 1 (woman) full-time, 340 part-time (282 women); includes 59 minority (31 Black or African American, non-Hispanic/Latino; 1 American Indian or Alaska Native, non-Hispanic/Latino; 10 Asian, non-Hispanic/Latino; 13 Hispanic/Latino; 4 Two or more races, non-Hispanic/Latino). Average age 33. 97 applicants, 99% accepted, 86 enrolled. In 2013, 64 master's, 40 other advanced degrees awarded. *Degree requirements:* For master's, action research project, portfolio (reading). *Entrance requirements:* For master's, minimum GPA of 2.75, teaching certification. Additional exam requirements/recommendations for international students: Required—TOEFL (minimum score 575 paper-based; 89 iBT), IELTS (minimum score 6.5). *Application deadline:* For fall admission, 7/15 priority date for domestic students, 7/15 for international students; for spring admission, 12/1 priority date for domestic students, 12/1 for international students. Applications are processed on a rolling basis. Application fee: $35. Electronic applications accepted. Application fee is waived when completed online. *Expenses: Tuition:* Part-time $405 per credit. *Required fees:* $100 per semester. *Financial support:* In 2013–14, 1 student received support. Tuition waivers (partial) and unspecified assistantships available. Financial award applicants required to submit FAFSA. *Faculty research:* Leadership, action research, brain research, learning styles. *Unit head:* Dr. Ellen Koitz, Chairperson, 301-696-3466, Fax: 301-696-3597, E-mail: koitz@hood.edu. *Application contact:* Dr. Maria Green Cowles, Dean of Graduate School, 301-696-3811, Fax: 301-696-3597, E-mail: gofurther@hood.edu.
Website: http://www.hood.edu/academics/education/index.html.

Houston Baptist University, College of Education and Behavioral Sciences, Programs in Education, Houston, TX 77074-3298. Offers bilingual education (M Ed); counselor education (M Ed); curriculum and instruction (M Ed); educational administration (M Ed); educational diagnostician (M Ed); reading education (M Ed). Part-time programs available. Postbaccalaureate distance learning degree programs offered (no on-campus study). *Entrance requirements:* For master's, GRE General Test or MAT. Additional exam requirements/recommendations for international students: Required—TOEFL (minimum score 550 paper-based).

Hunter College of the City University of New York, Graduate School, School of Education, Department of Curriculum and Teaching, New York, NY 10065-5085. Offers bilingual education (MS); corrective reading (K-12) (MS Ed); early childhood education (MS); educational supervision and administration (AC); elementary education (MS); literacy education (MS); teaching English as a second language (MA). *Faculty:* 18 full-time (10 women), 38 part-time/adjunct (26 women). *Students:* 61 full-time (54 women), 665 part-time (542 women); includes 256 minority (53 Black or African American, non-Hispanic/Latino; 1 American Indian or Alaska Native, non-Hispanic/Latino; 76 Asian, non-Hispanic/Latino; 126 Hispanic/Latino), 19 international. Average age 30. 443 applicants, 61% accepted, 176 enrolled. In 2013, 279 master's, 28 other advanced degrees awarded. *Degree requirements:* For master's, thesis; for AC, portfolio review. *Entrance requirements:* For degree, minimum B average in graduate course work, teaching certificate, minimum 3 years of full-time teaching experience, interview, 2 letters of support. Additional exam requirements/recommendations for international students: Required—TOEFL, TWE. *Application deadline:* For fall admission, 4/1 for domestic students; for spring admission, 11/1 for domestic students. Applications are processed on a rolling basis. Application fee: $125. *Financial support:* Federal Work-Study, scholarships/grants, and tuition waivers (partial) available. Support available to part-time students. *Faculty research:* Teacher opportunity corps (mentor program for first-year teachers), adult literacy, student literacy corporation. *Unit head:* Dr. Jennifer Tuten, Head, 212-777-4686, E-mail: jtuten@hunter.cuny.edu. *Application contact:* Milena Solo, Director for Graduate Admissions, 212-772-4482, E-mail: milena.solo@hunter.cuny.edu.
Website: http://www.hunter.cuny.edu/school-of-education/departments/curriculum-teaching.

Idaho State University, Office of Graduate Studies, College of Education, Department of Educational Foundations, Pocatello, ID 83209-8059. Offers child and family studies (M Ed); curriculum leadership (M Ed); education (M Ed); educational administration (M Ed); educational foundations (5th Year Certificate); elementary education (M Ed), including K-12 education, literacy, secondary education. Part-time programs available. *Degree requirements:* For master's, comprehensive exam, thesis optional, oral exam, written exam; for 5th Year Certificate, comprehensive exam, thesis (for some programs), oral exam, written exam. *Entrance requirements:* For master's, GRE General Test or MAT, minimum undergraduate GPA of 3.0; for 5th Year Certificate, GRE General Test, minimum undergraduate GPA of 3.0, master's degree. Additional exam requirements/recommendations for international students: Required—TOEFL (minimum score 550 paper-based; 80 iBT). Electronic applications accepted. *Faculty research:* Child and families studies; business education; special education; math, science, and technology education.

Idaho State University, Office of Graduate Studies, College of Education, Department of School Psychology, Literacy, and Special Education, Pocatello, ID 83209-8059. Offers deaf education (M Ed); human exceptionality (M Ed); literacy (M Ed); school psychology (Ed S); special education (Ed S). Part-time programs available. *Degree requirements:* For master's, comprehensive exam, thesis (for some programs), oral thesis defense or written comprehensive exam and oral exam; for Ed S, comprehensive exam, thesis (for some programs), oral exam, specialist paper or portfolio. *Entrance requirements:* For master's, GRE or MAT, minimum undergraduate GPA of 3.0, bachelor's degree, professional experience in an educational context; for Ed S, GRE or MAT, master's degree in related field. Additional exam requirements/recommendations for international students: Required—TOEFL (minimum score 550 paper-based; 80 iBT). Electronic applications accepted. *Faculty research:* Literacy, school psychology, special education.

Illinois State University, Graduate School, College of Education, Department of Curriculum and Instruction, Program in Reading, Normal, IL 61790-2200. Offers MS Ed. *Accreditation:* NCATE. *Degree requirements:* For master's, practicum. *Entrance requirements:* For master's, GRE General Test, minimum GPA of 3.0 in last 60 hours of course work, course work in reading.

Indiana University Bloomington, School of Education, Department of Literacy, Culture, and Language Education, Bloomington, IN 47405-7000. Offers MS, Ed D, PhD, Ed S. *Accreditation:* NCATE. Part-time and evening/weekend programs available. Postbaccalaureate distance learning degree programs offered (no on-campus study). Terminal master's awarded for partial completion of doctoral program. *Degree requirements:* For doctorate, thesis/dissertation, internship; for Ed S, comprehensive exam or project. *Entrance requirements:* For master's, GRE General Test or minimum GPA of 3.0; for doctorate, GRE General Test, minimum graduate GPA of 3.5; for Ed S, GRE General Test. Additional exam requirements/recommendations for international students: Required—TOEFL. *Faculty research:* Discourse analysis, sociolinguistics, critical literacy, cultural studies.

Indiana University of Pennsylvania, School of Graduate Studies and Research, College of Education and Educational Technology, Department of Professional Studies in Education, Program in Literacy, Indiana, PA 15705-1087. Offers literacy (M Ed); reading (Certificate). *Accreditation:* NCATE. Part-time programs available. *Faculty:* 19 full-time (12 women), 1 part-time/adjunct (0 women). *Students:* 3 full-time (all women), 10 part-time (9 women). Average age 25. 10 applicants, 80% accepted, 6 enrolled. In 2013, 23 master's awarded. *Degree requirements:* For master's, thesis optional. *Entrance requirements:* For master's, 2 letters of recommendation. Additional exam

requirements/recommendations for international students: Required—TOEFL (minimum score 540 paper-based). *Application deadline:* For fall admission, 7/1 for domestic students; for spring admission, 11/1 for domestic students. Applications are processed on a rolling basis. Application fee: $50. Electronic applications accepted. *Expenses:* Tuition, state resident: full-time $3978; part-time $442 per credit. Tuition, nonresident: full-time $5967; part-time $663 per credit. *Required fees:* $2080; $115.55 per credit. $93 per semester. Tuition and fees vary according to degree level and program. *Financial support:* Fellowships, research assistantships with full and partial tuition reimbursements, career-related internships or fieldwork, Federal Work-Study, scholarships/grants, and unspecified assistantships available. Support available to part-time students. Financial award application deadline: 4/15; financial award applicants required to submit FAFSA. *Unit head:* Dr. Anne Creany, Graduate Coordinator, 724-357-2409. *Application contact:* Paula Stossel, Assistant Dean for Administration, 724-357-4511, E-mail: graduate-admissions@iup.edu.
Website: http://www.iup.edu/upper.aspx?id=91232.

Indiana University–Purdue University Indianapolis, School of Education, Indianapolis, IN 46202-2896. Offers computer education (Certificate); curriculum and instruction (MS); early childhood (MS); educational leadership (MS, Certificate); English as a second language (Certificate); higher education and student affairs (MS); kindergarten (Certificate); language education (MS); reading (Certificate); school counseling (MS); special education (MS, Certificate). Part-time and evening/weekend programs available. *Faculty:* 41 full-time, 80 part-time/adjunct. *Students:* 113 full-time (78 women), 263 part-time (200 women); includes 88 minority (51 Black or African American, non-Hispanic/Latino; 1 American Indian or Alaska Native, non-Hispanic/Latino; 10 Asian, non-Hispanic/Latino; 19 Hispanic/Latino; 7 Two or more races, non-Hispanic/Latino), 5 international. Average age 33. 93 applicants, 54% accepted, 40 enrolled. In 2013, 179 master's awarded. *Degree requirements:* For master's, thesis optional. *Entrance requirements:* For master's, GRE General Test, minimum GPA of 3.0. Additional exam requirements/recommendations for international students: Required—TOEFL. *Application deadline:* For fall admission, 5/1 priority date for domestic students; for spring admission, 11/1 for domestic students. Application fee: $55 ($65 for international students). *Financial support:* Fellowships, research assistantships with partial tuition reimbursements, teaching assistantships, Federal Work-Study, institutionally sponsored loans, scholarships/grants, and tuition waivers (partial) available. Support available to part-time students. *Faculty research:* Teachers in the process of change, learning cycles, children's concepts of science. *Total annual research expenditures:* $614,458. *Unit head:* Dr. Pat Rogan, Executive Associate Dean, 317-274-6862, E-mail: progan@iupui.edu. *Application contact:* Donnella Dillon, Graduate Admissions Coordinator, 317-274-0645, E-mail: dmdillon@iupui.edu.
Website: http://education.iupui.edu/.

Iona College, School of Arts and Science, Department of Education, New Rochelle, NY 10801-1890. Offers adolescence education: biology (MS Ed, MST); adolescence education: English (MS Ed, MST); adolescence education: Italian (MS Ed, MST); adolescence education: mathematics (MS Ed, MST); adolescence education: social studies (MS Ed, MST); adolescence education: Spanish (MS Ed, MST); adolescence special education 5-12 (MST); adolescence special education and literacy (MS Ed); childhood and special education (MST); childhood education (MST); early childhood and childhood (MST); educational leadership (MS Ed); literacy education: birth-grade 6 (MS Ed). *Accreditation:* NCATE. Part-time and evening/weekend programs available. *Faculty:* 11 full-time (9 women), 7 part-time/adjunct (6 women). *Students:* 34 full-time (25 women), 61 part-time (47 women); includes 5 minority (2 Asian, non-Hispanic/Latino; 3 Hispanic/Latino), 1 international. Average age 25. 27 applicants, 93% accepted, 16 enrolled. In 2013, 54 master's awarded. *Degree requirements:* For master's, thesis or alternative. *Entrance requirements:* For master's, minimum GPA of 3.0, NY State teaching certificate (for all MS Ed programs). Additional exam requirements/recommendations for international students: Required—TOEFL (minimum score 550 paper-based; 80 iBT), IELTS (minimum score 6.5). *Application deadline:* For fall admission, 8/1 priority date for domestic students, 5/1 priority date for international students; for spring admission, 1/1 priority date for domestic students, 9/1 priority date for international students. Applications are processed on a rolling basis. Application fee: $50. Electronic applications accepted. *Expenses: Tuition:* Part-time $948 per credit. *Required fees:* $235 per term. *Financial support:* In 2013–14, 84 students received support. Unspecified assistantships available. Support available to part-time students. Financial award application deadline: 4/15; financial award applicants required to submit FAFSA. *Faculty research:* Reading/writing, educational technology, administration, early literacy assessment, literacy development. *Unit head:* Margaret Smith, PhD, Chair, 914-633-2210, Fax: 914-633-2608, E-mail: msmith@iona.edu. *Application contact:* Veronica Jarek-Prinz, Director, Graduate Admissions, 914-633-2420, Fax: 914-633-2277, E-mail: vjarekprinz@iona.edu.
Website: http://www.iona.edu/Academics/School-of-Arts-Science/Departments/Education/Graduate-Programs.aspx.

Jacksonville State University, College of Graduate Studies and Continuing Education, College of Education and Professional Studies, Program in Reading Specialist, Jacksonville, AL 36265-1602. Offers MS Ed. Part-time and evening/weekend programs available. *Degree requirements:* For master's, comprehensive exam, thesis (for some programs). *Entrance requirements:* Additional exam requirements/recommendations for international students: Required—TOEFL (minimum score 61 iBT). Electronic applications accepted.

James Madison University, The Graduate School, College of Education, Early, Elementary, and Reading Education Department, Harrisonburg, VA 22807. Offers early childhood education (MAT); elementary education (MAT); reading education (M Ed). *Students:* Average age 27. *Entrance requirements:* Additional exam requirements/recommendations for international students: Required—TOEFL. *Application deadline:* For fall admission, 5/1 for domestic students; for spring admission, 9/1 for domestic students. Applications are processed on a rolling basis. Application fee: $55. Electronic applications accepted. *Financial support:* Application deadline: 3/1; applicants required to submit FAFSA. *Unit head:* Dr. Martha Ross, Academic Unit Head, 540-568-6255. *Application contact:* Lynette M. Bible, Director of Graduate Admissions, 540-568-6395, Fax: 540-568-7860, E-mail: biblelm@jmu.edu.

Johns Hopkins University, School of Education, Master's Programs in Education, Baltimore, MD 21218-2699. Offers counseling (MS), including mental health counseling, school counseling; education (MS), including educational studies, gifted education, reading, school administration and supervision, technology for educators; elementary education (MAT); health professions (M Ed); intelligence analysis (MS); management (MS); secondary education (MAT); special education (MS), including early childhood special education, general special education studies, mild to moderate disabilities, severe disabilities. Part-time and evening/weekend programs available. Postbaccalaureate distance learning degree programs offered (no on-campus study). *Students:* 183 full-time (123 women), 1,001 part-time (757 women); includes 380 minority (160 Black or African American, non-Hispanic/Latino; 4 American Indian or Alaska Native, non-Hispanic/Latino; 91 Asian, non-Hispanic/Latino; 78 Hispanic/Latino; 4 Native Hawaiian or other Pacific Islander, non-Hispanic/Latino; 43 Two or more races, non-Hispanic/Latino), 28 international. Average age 28. 508 applicants, 90% accepted, 337 enrolled. In 2013, 565 degrees awarded. *Degree requirements:* For master's, comprehensive exam (for some programs), portfolio, capstone project and/or internship; PRAXIS II (for teacher preparation programs that lead to licensure). *Entrance requirements:* For master's, GRE (for full-time programs only); PRAXIS I or equivalent (for teacher preparation programs that lead to licensure), bachelor's degree from regionally- or nationally-accredited institution, minimum GPA of 3.0 in all previous programs of study, official transcripts from all post-secondary institutions attended, essay, curriculum vitae/resume, minimum of two letters of recommendation. Additional exam requirements/recommendations for international students: Required—TOEFL (minimum score 600 paper-based; 100 iBT) or IELTS (minimum score 7). *Application deadline:* For fall admission, 4/1 for domestic and international students; for spring admission, 10/1 for domestic and international students; for summer admission, 2/1 for domestic and international students. Application fee: $80. Electronic applications accepted. *Financial support:* Application deadline: 6/1; applicants required to submit FAFSA. *Unit head:* Dr. David A. Andrews, Dean, 410-516-7820, Fax: 410-516-6697, E-mail: davidandrews@jhu.edu. *Application contact:* Catherine Wilson, Associate Director of Admissions, 410-516-9797, Fax: 410-516-9799, E-mail: soe.info@jhu.edu.

Johnson State College, Graduate Program in Education, Johnson, VT 05656. Offers applied behavior analysis (MA Ed), including applied behavior analysis; curriculum and instruction (MA Ed); literacy (MA Ed); secondary education (MA Ed); special education (MA Ed). Part-time programs available. *Faculty:* 3 full-time (1 woman), 6 part-time/adjunct (5 women). *Students:* 6 full-time (5 women), 69 part-time (52 women). Average age 28. In 2013, 44 master's awarded. *Degree requirements:* For master's, comprehensive exam, thesis or alternative. *Entrance requirements:* For master's, interview. Additional exam requirements/recommendations for international students: Required—TOEFL. *Application deadline:* For fall admission, 4/1 priority date for domestic students, 1/15 priority date for international students; for spring admission, 11/1 for domestic students, 8/15 priority date for international students. Applications are processed on a rolling basis. Electronic applications accepted. *Expenses:* Tuition, state resident: full-time $11,448; part-time $477 per credit. Tuition, nonresident: full-time $24,720; part-time $1030 per credit. Tuition and fees vary according to reciprocity agreements. *Financial support:* Unspecified assistantships available. Financial award application deadline: 3/1; financial award applicants required to submit FAFSA. *Application contact:* Catherine H. Higley, Administrative Assistant, 800-635-2356 Ext. 1244, Fax: 802-635-1248, E-mail: catherine.higley@jsc.edu.

Judson University, Graduate Programs, Program in Literacy, Elgin, IL 60123-1498. Offers M Ed, Ed D. *Degree requirements:* For master's, thesis. *Entrance requirements:* For master's, copy of official teaching certificate; bachelor's degree with minimum GPA of 3.0; letters of reference; essay. *Faculty research:* Affective domain in reading, vocabulary acquisition, children's and adolescent literature, cross-curricular writing, critical thinking, human memory and learning strategies.

Kansas State University, Graduate School, College of Education, Department of Curriculum and Instruction, Manhattan, KS 66506. Offers career and technical education (Ed D, PhD); curriculum studies (Ed D, PhD); digital teaching and learning (MS); educational computing, design and online learning (MS); educational technology (Ed D, PhD); elementary/middle level curriculum and instruction (MS); English as a second language (MS); language/diversity education (Ed D, PhD); literacy education (Ed D, PhD); mathematics education (Ed D, PhD); middle level/secondary curriculum and instruction (MS); reading and language arts (MS); reading specialist endorsement (MS); science education (Ed D, PhD); social science education (Ed D, PhD); teacher education (Ed D, PhD); teacher leader/school improvement (MS, Ed D). *Accreditation:* NCATE. Part-time programs available. Postbaccalaureate distance learning degree programs offered (minimal on-campus study). *Faculty:* 18 full-time (13 women), 7 part-time/adjunct (4 women). *Students:* 39 full-time (23 women), 122 part-time (94 women); includes 19 minority (3 Black or African American, non-Hispanic/Latino; 2 Asian, non-Hispanic/Latino; 12 Hispanic/Latino; 2 Two or more races, non-Hispanic/Latino), 12 international. Average age 36. 80 applicants, 50% accepted, 34 enrolled. In 2013, 40 master's, 13 doctorates awarded. *Degree requirements:* For master's, comprehensive exam, portfolio, project, report or thesis; for doctorate, comprehensive exam, thesis/dissertation, preliminary exam. *Entrance requirements:* For master's, minimum GPA of 3.0, letters of recommendation; for doctorate, GRE, minimum GPA of 3.0, letters of recommendation, evidence of scholarly writing. Additional exam requirements/recommendations for international students: Required—TOEFL (minimum score 550 paper-based; 80 iBT). *Application deadline:* For fall admission, 3/1 priority date for domestic students, 2/1 priority date for international students; for spring admission, 10/1 priority date for domestic students, 8/1 priority date for international students. Applications are processed on a rolling basis. Application fee: $50 ($75 for international students). Electronic applications accepted. *Financial support:* In 2013–14, 1 research assistantship (averaging $16,900 per year), 8 teaching assistantships (averaging $12,466 per year) were awarded; career-related internships or fieldwork, institutionally sponsored loans, and scholarships/grants also available. Support available to part-time students. Financial award application deadline: 3/1; financial award applicants required to submit FAFSA. *Faculty research:* Literacy and technology, critical race theory and diversity, achievement gaps, school improvement, teacher education. *Total annual research expenditures:* $543,677. *Unit head:* Dr. Todd Goodson, Chair, 785-532-5904, Fax: 785-532-7304, E-mail: tgoodson@ksu.edu. *Application contact:* Dona Deam, Application Contact, 785-532-5595, Fax: 785-532-7304, E-mail: ddeam@ksu.edu.
Website: http://www.coe.k-state.edu/departments/edci/.

Kaplan University, Davenport Campus, School of Teacher Education, Davenport, IA 52807-2095. Offers education (M Ed); secondary education (M Ed); teaching and learning (MA); teaching literacy and language: grades 6-12 (MA); teaching literacy and language: grades K-6 (MA); teaching mathematics: grades 6-8 (MA); teaching mathematics: grades 9-12 (MA); teaching mathematics: grades K-5 (MA); teaching science: grades 6-12 (MA); teaching science: grades K-6 (MA); teaching students with special needs (MA); teaching with technology (MA). Part-time and evening/weekend programs available. Postbaccalaureate distance learning degree programs offered (no on-campus study). *Entrance requirements:* Additional exam requirements/recommendations for international students: Required—TOEFL (minimum score 550 paper-based; 80 iBT).

Kennesaw State University, Leland and Clarice C. Bagwell College of Education, Program in Graduate Education, Kennesaw, GA 30144-5591. Offers educational leadership (M Ed); educational leadership technology (M Ed); elementary and early childhood education (M Ed); instructional technology (M Ed); middle grades education (M Ed); reading (M Ed); secondary education (M Ed); special education (M Ed); teaching English to speakers of other languages (M Ed). *Accreditation:* NCATE. Part-time programs available. *Students:* 65 full-time (60 women), 229 part-time (158 women); includes 66 minority (46 Black or African American, non-Hispanic/Latino; 6 Asian, non-Hispanic/Latino; 9 Hispanic/Latino; 5 Two or more races, non-Hispanic/Latino), 1 international. Average age 34. 56 applicants, 86% accepted, 43 enrolled. In 2013, 109 master's awarded. *Degree requirements:* For master's, thesis or alternative. *Entrance requirements:* For master's, GRE General Test, T-4 state certification, minimum GPA of 2.75. Additional exam requirements/recommendations for international students: Required—TOEFL (minimum score 550 paper-based; 80 iBT), IELTS (minimum score

6.5). *Application deadline:* For fall admission, 7/1 for domestic and international students; for spring admission, 10/1 for domestic and international students; for summer admission, 4/15 for domestic and international students. Applications are processed on a rolling basis. Application fee: $60. Electronic applications accepted. *Expenses:* Tuition, state resident: full-time $4806; part-time $267 per semester hour. Tuition, nonresident: full-time $17,298; part-time $961 per semester hour. *Required fees:* $1834; $784.50 per semester. *Financial support:* In 2013–14, 10 research assistantships with tuition reimbursements (averaging $8,000 per year) were awarded; Federal Work-Study and unspecified assistantships also available. Support available to part-time students. Financial award application deadline: 4/1; financial award applicants required to submit FAFSA. *Unit head:* Melinda Ross, Administrative Coordinator for Graduate Programs in Education, 770-423-6043, E-mail: graded@kennesaw.edu. *Application contact:* Melinda Ross, Admissions Counselor, 770-423-6043, Fax: 770-423-6885, E-mail: ksugrad@kennesaw.edu.
Website: http://www.kennesaw.edu/education/grad/.

Kent State University, Graduate School of Education, Health, and Human Services, School of Teaching, Learning and Curriculum Studies, Program in Reading Specialization, Kent, OH 44242-0001. Offers M Ed, MA. *Accreditation:* NCATE. Part-time and evening/weekend programs available. *Faculty:* 5 full-time (3 women), 1 (woman) part-time/adjunct. *Students:* 3 full-time (all women), 20 part-time (all women). 18 applicants, 56% accepted. In 2013, 8 master's awarded. *Degree requirements:* For master's, thesis (for some programs). *Entrance requirements:* For master's, 2 letters of reference, goals statement. Additional exam requirements/recommendations for international students: Required—TOEFL (minimum score 550 paper-based; 80 iBT). *Application deadline:* Applications are processed on a rolling basis. Application fee: $30 ($60 for international students). Electronic applications accepted. *Financial support:* Research assistantships with full tuition reimbursements, Federal Work-Study, scholarships/grants, and unspecified assistantships available. Financial award application deadline: 4/1; financial award applicants required to submit FAFSA. *Faculty research:* Adolescent literacy, adult and family literacy, school change in literacy education, struggling readers. *Unit head:* Dr. Denise Morgan, Coordinator, 330-672-0663, E-mail: dmorgan2@kent.edu. *Application contact:* Nancy Miller, Academic Program Director, Office of Graduate Student Services, 330-672-2576, Fax: 330-672-9162, E-mail: ogs@kent.edu.
Website: http://www.kent.edu/ehhs/le/.

King's College, Program in Reading, Wilkes-Barre, PA 18711-0801. Offers M Ed. *Accreditation:* NCATE. Part-time and evening/weekend programs available. *Degree requirements:* For master's, thesis. *Entrance requirements:* Additional exam requirements/recommendations for international students: Required—TOEFL (minimum score 600 paper-based).

Kutztown University of Pennsylvania, College of Education, Program in Reading, Kutztown, PA 19530-0730. Offers M Ed. *Accreditation:* NCATE. Part-time and evening/weekend programs available. *Students:* 61 part-time (56 women); includes 1 minority (Hispanic/Latino). Average age 32. 31 applicants, 68% accepted, 19 enrolled. In 2013, 41 master's awarded. *Degree requirements:* For master's, comprehensive project. *Entrance requirements:* For master's, GRE General Test. Additional exam requirements/recommendations for international students: Required—TOEFL (minimum score 550 paper-based; 79 iBT). *Application deadline:* For fall admission, 8/1 priority date for domestic and international students; for spring admission, 12/1 priority date for domestic and international students. Applications are processed on a rolling basis. Application fee: $35. Electronic applications accepted. *Expenses: Tuition, area resident:* Part-time $442 per credit. Tuition, state resident: part-time $442 per credit. Tuition, nonresident: part-time $663 per credit. *Required fees:* $80 per credit. *Financial support:* Career-related internships or fieldwork, Federal Work-Study, scholarships/grants, and unspecified assistantships available. Financial award application deadline: 3/1; financial award applicants required to submit FAFSA. *Unit head:* Dr. Jeanie Burnett, Chairperson, 610-683-4286, Fax: 610-683-1327, E-mail: burnett@kutztown.edu. *Application contact:* Kelly Hish, Admissions Clerk, 610-683-4200, Fax: 610-683-1393, E-mail: graduate@kutztown.edu.

Lake Erie College, School of Education and Professional Studies, Painesville, OH 44077-3389. Offers curriculum and instruction (MS Ed); education (MS Ed); educational leadership (MS Ed); reading (MS Ed). Part-time and evening/weekend programs available. *Faculty:* 2 full-time (1 woman). *Students:* 7 part-time (4 women). Average age 27. 6 applicants, 33% accepted, 1 enrolled. In 2013, 10 master's awarded. *Degree requirements:* For master's, comprehensive exam (for some programs), thesis optional, applied research project. *Entrance requirements:* For master's, GRE General Test (minimum score of 440 verbal or 500 quantitative) or minimum GPA of 2.75; bachelor's degree from accredited 4-year institution; references; essay. Additional exam requirements/recommendations for international students: Required—TOEFL (minimum score 550 paper-based). *Application deadline:* For fall admission, 8/1 priority date for domestic students, 6/1 for international students; for spring admission, 12/15 for domestic students, 10/1 for international students. Applications are processed on a rolling basis. Application fee: $30. Electronic applications accepted. Application fee is waived when completed online. *Expenses:* Contact institution. *Financial support:* Tuition waivers and unspecified assistantships available. Financial award applicants required to submit FAFSA. *Unit head:* Prof. Dale Sheptak, Dean of the School of Education and Professional Studies, 440-375-7131, E-mail: dsheptak@lec.edu. *Application contact:* Milena Velez, Senior Admissions Counselor, 800-916-0904, Fax: 440-375-7000, E-mail: admissions@lec.edu.
Website: http://www.lec.edu/med.

La Salle University, School of Arts and Sciences, Program in Education, Philadelphia, PA 19141-1199. Offers American studies (MA); autism spectrum disorders (MA, Certificate); bilingual/bicultural studies (MA); classroom management (MA, Certificate); dual early childhood and special education (MA); dual middle-level science and math and special education secondary education (MA); education (MA); English (MA); English as a second language (Certificate); instructional coach (Certificate); instructional leadership (MA); reading specialist (MA, Certificate); secondary education (MA); special education (MA, Certificate). Part-time and evening/weekend programs available. *Faculty:* 5 full-time (4 women), 16 part-time/adjunct (10 women). *Students:* 18 full-time (13 women), 137 part-time (112 women); includes 33 minority (24 Black or African American, non-Hispanic/Latino; 9 Hispanic/Latino), 4 international. Average age 32. 47 applicants, 96% accepted, 28 enrolled. In 2013, 58 master's, 20 other advanced degrees awarded. *Degree requirements:* For master's, comprehensive exam. *Entrance requirements:* For master's and Certificate, MAT or GRE, 2 letters of recommendation. Additional exam requirements/recommendations for international students: Required—TOEFL. *Application deadline:* For fall admission, 8/15 priority date for domestic students, 7/15 for international students; for spring admission, 12/15 priority date for domestic students, 11/15 for international students; for summer admission, 4/15 priority date for domestic students, 3/15 for international students. Applications are processed on a rolling basis. Application fee: $35. Electronic applications accepted. Application fee is waived when completed online. *Expenses:* Contact institution. *Financial support:* In 2013–14, 28 students received support. Career-related internships or fieldwork, Federal Work-Study, and scholarships/grants available. Support available to part-time students. Financial award application deadline: 8/31; financial award applicants required to submit FAFSA. *Unit head:* Dr. Greer Richardson, Interim Director, 215-951-1806, Fax: 215-951-1843, E-mail: graded@lasalle.edu. *Application contact:* Paul J. Reilly, Assistant Vice President, Enrollment Services, 215-951-1946, Fax: 215-951-1462, E-mail: reilly@lasalle.edu.
Website: http://www.lasalle.edu/grad/index.php?section-education&page-index.

Lehman College of the City University of New York, Division of Education, Department of Specialized Services in Education, Program in Reading Teacher, Bronx, NY 10468-1589. Offers MS Ed. *Accreditation:* NCATE. Evening/weekend programs available. *Entrance requirements:* For master's, interview, minimum GPA of 2.7. *Faculty research:* Emergent literacy, language-based classrooms, primary and secondary social contexts of language and literacy, innovative in-service education models, adult literacy.

Le Moyne College, Department of Education, Syracuse, NY 13214. Offers adolescent education (MS Ed, MST); adolescent education/special education (MS Ed, MST); adolescent English (MST), including grades 7-12 (MS Ed, MST); adolescent English/special education (MST), including grades 7-12 (MS Ed, MST); adolescent foreign language (MST), including grades 7-12 (MS Ed, MST); adolescent history (MST), including grades 7-12 (MS Ed, MST); childhood education (MS Ed); childhood education/special education (MS Ed); elementary education (MS Ed); general education (MS Ed); inclusive childhood education (MST); literacy education (MS Ed), including birth to grade 6, grades 5-12; school building leader (MS Ed); school building leadership (CAS); school district business leader (MS Ed, CAS); school district leader (MS Ed); school district leadership (CAS); secondary education (MS Ed); special education (MS Ed); students with disabilities-generalist (MS Ed), including grades 7-12 (MS Ed, MST); teaching English to speakers of other languages (MS Ed); urban studies (MS Ed). *Accreditation:* Teacher Education Accreditation Council. Part-time and evening/weekend programs available. *Faculty:* 8 full-time (5 women), 61 part-time/adjunct (38 women). *Students:* 24 full-time (20 women), 178 part-time (133 women); includes 22 minority (12 Black or African American, non-Hispanic/Latino; 1 American Indian or Alaska Native, non-Hispanic/Latino; 3 Asian, non-Hispanic/Latino; 6 Hispanic/Latino), 1 international. Average age 31. 248 applicants, 90% accepted, 86 enrolled. In 2013, 158 master's, 37 CASs awarded. *Degree requirements:* For master's, thesis. *Entrance requirements:* For master's, GRE General Test, bachelor's degree, 2 letters of recommendation, written statement, transcripts. Additional exam requirements/recommendations for international students: Required—TOEFL (minimum score 550 paper-based; 79 iBT). *Application deadline:* For fall admission, 4/1 priority date for domestic and international students; for spring admission, 10/1 priority date for domestic and international students; for summer admission, 3/1 priority date for domestic and international students. Applications are processed on a rolling basis. Application fee: $50. *Expenses:* Contact institution. *Financial support:* In 2013–14, 26 students received support. Career-related internships or fieldwork and health care benefits available. Support available to part-time students. Financial award applicants required to submit FAFSA. *Faculty research:* Minority teachers, special education, multiculturalism, literacy, technology, media literacy learning, autism, school district organization, service-learning, higher level problem solving, teacher leadership. *Unit head:* Dr. Suzanne L. Gilmour, Chair, Department of Education/Director of Graduate Education Programs, 315-445-4376, Fax: 315-445-4744, E-mail: gilmous@lemoyne.edu. *Application contact:* Kristen P. Trapasso, Senior Director of Enrollment Management, 315-445-4265, Fax: 315-445-6092, E-mail: trapaskp@lemoyne.edu.
Website: http://www.lemoyne.edu/education.

Lesley University, School of Education, Cambridge, MA 02138-2790. Offers arts, community, and education (M Ed); autism studies (Certificate); curriculum and instruction (M Ed, CAGS); early childhood education (M Ed); ecological teaching and learning (MS); educational studies (PhD), including adult learning, educational leadership, individually designed; elementary education (M Ed); emergent technologies for educators (Certificate); ESLArts: language learning through the arts (M Ed); high school education (M Ed); individually designed (M Ed); integrated teaching through the arts (M Ed); literacy for K-8 classroom teachers (M Ed); mathematics education (M Ed); middle school education (M Ed); moderate disabilities (M Ed); online learning (Certificate); reading (CAGS); science in education (M Ed); severe disabilities (M Ed); special needs (CAGS); specialist teacher of reading (M Ed); teacher of visual art (M Ed); technology in education (M Ed, CAGS). *Accreditation:* Teacher Education Accreditation Council. Part-time and evening/weekend programs available. Postbaccalaureate distance learning degree programs offered (no on-campus study). *Faculty:* 40 full-time (30 women), 104 part-time/adjunct (77 women). *Students:* 453 full-time (381 women), 1,672 part-time (1,435 women); includes 284 minority (139 Black or African American, non-Hispanic/Latino; 11 American Indian or Alaska Native, non-Hispanic/Latino; 38 Asian, non-Hispanic/Latino; 58 Hispanic/Latino; 5 Native Hawaiian or other Pacific Islander, non-Hispanic/Latino; 33 Two or more races, non-Hispanic/Latino), 22 international. Average age 35. In 2013, 1,137 master's, 18 doctorates, 51 other advanced degrees awarded. *Degree requirements:* For master's, practicum; for doctorate, thesis/dissertation. *Entrance requirements:* For master's, Massachusetts Tests for Educator Licensure (MTEL), transcripts, statement of purpose, recommendations; interview (for special education); for doctorate, GRE General Test, transcripts, statement of purpose, recommendations, interview, master's degree, resume; for other advanced degree, interview, master's degree. Additional exam requirements/recommendations for international students: Required—TOEFL (minimum score 550 paper-based; 80 iBT). *Application deadline:* Applications are processed on a rolling basis. Application fee: $50. Electronic applications accepted. *Expenses: Tuition:* Part-time $900 per credit. *Financial support:* In 2013–14, 15 fellowships (averaging $3,600 per year) were awarded; career-related internships or fieldwork, Federal Work-Study, scholarships/grants, tuition waivers, and unspecified assistantships also available. Financial award application deadline: 4/15; financial award applicants required to submit FAFSA. *Faculty research:* Assessment in literacy, mathematics and science; autism spectrum disorders; instructional technology and online learning; multicultural education and English language learners. *Unit head:* Dr. Jack Gillette, Dean, 617-349-8401, Fax: 617-349-8607, E-mail: jgillett@lesley.edu. *Application contact:* Martha Sheehan, Director of Admissions, 888-LESLEYU, Fax: 617-349-8313, E-mail: info@lesley.edu.
Website: http://www.lesley.edu/soe.html.

Lewis University, College of Education, Programs in Reading and Literacy, Romeoville, IL 60446. Offers M Ed, MA. Part-time and evening/weekend programs available. *Students:* 40 part-time (38 women); includes 5 minority (3 Black or African American, non-Hispanic/Latino; 1 Asian, non-Hispanic/Latino; 1 Hispanic/Latino), 1 international. Average age 30. *Entrance requirements:* For master's, departmental qualifying exam, writing exam, minimum GPA of 2.75, 2 letters of recommendation, interview. Additional exam requirements/recommendations for international students: Required—TOEFL (minimum score 550 paper-based; 80 iBT). *Application deadline:* For fall admission, 5/1 priority date for international students; for spring admission, 11/15 priority date for international students. Application fee: $40. *Financial support:* Scholarships/grants and unspecified assistantships available. Support available to part-time students. Financial award application deadline: 5/1; financial award applicants required to submit FAFSA. *Unit head:* Dr. Deborah Augsburger, Program Director, 815-838-0500 Ext. 5883, E-mail: augsbude@lewisu.edu. *Application contact:* Linda

Campbell, Graduate Admission Counselor, 815-836-5704, Fax: 815-836-5578, E-mail: campbeli@lewisu.edu.

Liberty University, School of Education, Lynchburg, VA 24515. Offers administration and supervision (M Ed); curriculum and instruction (Ed D, Ed S); early childhood education (M Ed); educational leadership (Ed D, Ed S); educational technology and online instruction (M Ed); elementary education (M Ed, MAT); English (M Ed); gifted education (M Ed); history (M Ed); leadership (M Ed); math specialist (M Ed); middle grades (M Ed, MAT); outdoor adventure sport (MS); reading specialist (M Ed); school counseling (M Ed); secondary education (MAT); special education (M Ed, MAT); sport management (MS), including administration, outdoor recreation, sport management, tourism; sports administration (MS); student service (M Ed); teaching and learning (M Ed); tourism (MS). *Accreditation:* NCATE. Part-time programs available. Postbaccalaureate distance learning degree programs offered (minimal on-campus study). *Students:* 2,241 full-time (1,639 women), 4,413 part-time (3,240 women); includes 2,052 minority (1,588 Black or African American, non-Hispanic/Latino; 37 American Indian or Alaska Native, non-Hispanic/Latino; 67 Asian, non-Hispanic/Latino; 173 Hispanic/Latino; 37 Native Hawaiian or other Pacific Islander, non-Hispanic/Latino; 150 Two or more races, non-Hispanic/Latino), 15 international. Average age 37. 6,185 applicants, 43% accepted, 1603 enrolled. In 2013, 1,256 master's, 117 doctorates, 470 other advanced degrees awarded. *Degree requirements:* For doctorate, comprehensive exam, thesis/dissertation. *Entrance requirements:* For master's, GRE General Test or MAT (if taken in or before 1999), 2 letters of recommendation, minimum undergraduate GPA of 3.0, curriculum vitae; for doctorate and Ed S, GRE General Test or MAT (if taken before 1999), minimum master's GPA of 3.0, 3 years of teaching experience. Additional exam requirements/recommendations for international students: Required—TOEFL (minimum score 600 paper-based; 100 iBT). *Application deadline:* For fall admission, 6/1 for domestic students; for spring admission, 11/1 for domestic students. Applications are processed on a rolling basis. Application fee: $50. Electronic applications accepted. *Expenses:* Contact institution. *Financial support:* Federal Work-Study and tuition waivers (partial) available. *Faculty research:* Self-determination, character education, bibliotherapy, learning styles, distance education. *Unit head:* Dr. Karen L. Parker, Dean, 434-582-2195, Fax: 434-582-2468, E-mail: kparker@liberty.edu. *Application contact:* Jay Bridge, Director of Graduate Admissions, 800-424-9595, Fax: 800-628-7977, E-mail: gradadmissions@liberty.edu.
Website: http://www.liberty.edu/academics/education/graduate/.

Lincoln University, Graduate Programs, Philadelphia, PA 19104. Offers early childhood education (M Ed); educational leadership (M Ed); human resources (MSA), including finance, human resources management; human services (MHS); reading (MSR). Evening/weekend programs available. *Faculty:* 10 full-time (4 women), 34 part-time/adjunct (19 women). *Students:* 224 full-time (145 women), 115 part-time (74 women); includes 328 minority (311 Black or African American, non-Hispanic/Latino; 17 Hispanic/Latino). Average age 40. 237 applicants, 65% accepted, 64 enrolled. In 2013, 155 master's awarded. *Degree requirements:* For master's, thesis. *Entrance requirements:* For master's, working as full-time, paid staff member in the human services field, at least one year of paid experience in this field, and undergraduate degree in human services or a related field from an accredited institution (for MHS). *Application deadline:* For fall admission, 6/1 priority date for domestic and international students. Applications are processed on a rolling basis. Application fee: $50. *Expenses:* Tuition, state resident: full-time $10,106; part-time $567 per hour. Tuition, nonresident: full-time $17,636; part-time $949 per hour. *Financial support:* Application deadline: 8/1. *Unit head:* Dr. Cheryl Gooch, Dean, School of Humanities and Graduate Studies, 484-365-7664, E-mail: cgooch@lincoln.edu. *Application contact:* Jernice Lea, Director of Graduate Admissions, 215-590-8233, Fax: 215-387-3859, E-mail: jlea@lincoln.edu.
Website: http://www.lincoln.edu/academicaffairs/uc.html.

Lipscomb University, Program in Education, Nashville, TN 37204-3951. Offers applied behavior analysis (Certificate); collaborative professional learning (M Ed, Ed S); educational leadership (M Ed, Ed S); English language learning (M Ed, Ed S); instructional coaching (Certificate); instructional practice (M Ed); learning organizations and strategic change (Ed D); math specialty (M Ed); reading specialty (M Ed, Ed S); special education (M Ed); teaching, learning, and leading (M Ed); technology integration (M Ed); technology integration specialist (Certificate). *Accreditation:* NCATE. Part-time and evening/weekend programs available. Postbaccalaureate distance learning degree programs offered (no on-campus study). *Faculty:* 19 full-time (13 women), 28 part-time/adjunct (22 women). *Students:* 171 full-time (123 women), 509 part-time (429 women); includes 118 minority (91 Black or African American, non-Hispanic/Latino; 1 American Indian or Alaska Native, non-Hispanic/Latino; 4 Asian, non-Hispanic/Latino; 15 Hispanic/Latino; 1 Native Hawaiian or other Pacific Islander, non-Hispanic/Latino; 6 Two or more races, non-Hispanic/Latino). Average age 32. 237 applicants, 65% accepted, 150 enrolled. In 2013, 212 master's awarded. *Degree requirements:* For master's, comprehensive exam, portfolio, research project and presentation; for doctorate, practical capstone project in experiential setting. *Entrance requirements:* For master's, MAT (minimum 31) or GRE General Test (minimum 294), 2 reference letters, goals statement, writing sample, interview; for doctorate, MAT or GRE General Test, 3 reference letters, artifact of demonstrated academic excellence, written personal statements, interview. Additional exam requirements/recommendations for international students: Required—TOEFL (minimum score 570 paper-based). *Application deadline:* For fall admission, 8/29 priority date for domestic students; for spring admission, 1/15 priority date for domestic students. Applications are processed on a rolling basis. Application fee: $50 ($75 for international students). *Expenses: Tuition:* Full-time $15,570; part-time $865 per credit hour. Tuition and fees vary according to degree level and program. *Financial support:* Scholarships/grants and unspecified assistantships available. Financial award applicants required to submit FAFSA. *Faculty research:* Facilitative learning styles, leadership, student assessment, interactive multimedia inclusion, learning organizations and strategic change. *Unit head:* Dr. Deborah Boyd, Director of Graduate Studies, 615-966-6263, E-mail: deborah.boyd@lipscomb.edu. *Application contact:* Kristin Baese, Director of Enrollment and Outreach, 615-966-7628 Ext. 6081, Fax: 615-966-5173, E-mail: kristin.baese@lipscomb.edu.
Website: http://www.lipscomb.edu/education/graduate-programs.

Long Island University–Brentwood Campus, School of Education, Brentwood, NY 11717. Offers childhood education (MS); early childhood education (MS); literacy (MS); mental health counseling (MS); school counseling (MS); special education (MS). Part-time and evening/weekend programs available.

Long Island University–Hudson at Rockland, Graduate School, Programs in Special Education and Literacy, Orangeburg, NY 10962. Offers autism (MS Ed); childhood/literacy (MS Ed); childhood/special education (MS Ed); literacy (MS Ed); special education (MS Ed). Part-time programs available. *Entrance requirements:* For master's, college transcripts, two letters of recommendation, personal statement, resume.

Long Island University–Hudson at Westchester, Programs in Education-Teaching, Program in Literacy Education, Purchase, NY 10577. Offers MS Ed, Advanced Certificate. Part-time and evening/weekend programs available.

Long Island University–LIU Brooklyn, School of Education, Department of Teaching and Learning, Program in Reading, Brooklyn, NY 11201-8423. Offers MS Ed. Part-time and evening/weekend programs available. *Degree requirements:* For master's, thesis optional. *Entrance requirements:* For master's, 2 letters of recommendation. Additional exam requirements/recommendations for international students: Required—TOEFL (minimum score 500 paper-based). Electronic applications accepted.

Long Island University–LIU Post, School of Education, Department of Special Education and Literacy, Brookville, NY 11548-1300. Offers childhood education/literacy (MS); childhood education/special education (MS); literacy (MS Ed); special education (MS Ed). *Accreditation:* Teacher Education Accreditation Council. Part-time and evening/weekend programs available. *Degree requirements:* For master's, research project, comprehensive exam or thesis. *Entrance requirements:* For master's, interview; minimum GPA of 2.75 in major, 2.5 overall. Electronic applications accepted. *Faculty research:* Autism, mainstreaming, robotics and microcomputers in special education, transition from school to work.

Long Island University–Riverhead, Education Division, Program in Literacy Education, Riverhead, NY 11901. Offers MS Ed. *Accreditation:* Teacher Education Accreditation Council. Part-time programs available. *Degree requirements:* For master's, comprehensive exam. *Entrance requirements:* For master's, minimum undergraduate GPA of 2.75, New York State Provisional or Initial Teacher Certification. Additional exam requirements/recommendations for international students: Required—TOEFL (minimum score 550 paper-based). Electronic applications accepted.

Longwood University, College of Graduate and Professional Studies, College of Education and Human Services, Farmville, VA 23909. Offers education (MS), including algebra and middle school math, counselor education, elementary and middle school math, elementary education, elementary education initial licensure, health and physical education, school librarianship, special education general curriculum, special education initial licensure; social work and communication sciences and disorders (MS). *Accreditation:* NCATE. Part-time and evening/weekend programs available. *Faculty:* 28 full-time (15 women), 9 part-time/adjunct (7 women). *Students:* 86 full-time (80 women), 187 part-time (173 women); includes 38 minority (26 Black or African American, non-Hispanic/Latino; 1 Asian, non-Hispanic/Latino; 5 Hispanic/Latino; 1 Native Hawaiian or other Pacific Islander, non-Hispanic/Latino; 5 Two or more races, non-Hispanic/Latino). 98 applicants, 89% accepted, 85 enrolled. In 2013, 132 master's awarded. *Degree requirements:* For master's, comprehensive exam (for some programs), thesis optional, professional portfolio, internship, clinical experience, or practicum. *Entrance requirements:* For master's, bachelor's degree from regionally-accredited institution, 2 recommendations, 500-word personal essay, official transcripts, minimum GPA of 2.75, valid teaching license (for some programs), passing Praxis I scores for initial teaching licensure programs. Additional exam requirements/recommendations for international students: Required—TOEFL (minimum score 570 paper-based), IELTS (minimum score 6.5). *Application deadline:* For fall admission, 5/1 priority date for domestic students; for spring admission, 10/1 priority date for domestic students; for summer admission, 2/1 priority date for domestic students. Applications are processed on a rolling basis. Application fee: $50. Electronic applications accepted. *Expenses:* Tuition, state resident: full-time $7506; part-time $327 per credit hour. Tuition, nonresident: full-time $17,100; part-time $837 per credit hour. Tuition and fees vary according to course load and campus/location. *Financial support:* Career-related internships or fieldwork and Federal Work-Study available. Financial award applicants required to submit FAFSA. *Unit head:* Dr. Peggy L. Tarpley, Chair of the Department of Education and Special Education, 434-395-2337, E-mail: tarpleypl@longwood.edu. *Application contact:* College of Graduate and Professional Studies, 434-395-2380, Fax: 434-395-2750, E-mail: graduate@longwood.edu.
Website: http://www.longwood.edu/cehs/.

Lourdes University, Graduate School, Sylvania, OH 43560-2898. Offers business (MBA); leadership (M Ed); nurse anesthesia (MSN); nurse educator (MSN); nurse leader (MSN); organizational leadership (MOL); reading (M Ed); teaching and curriculum (M Ed); theology (MA). Evening/weekend programs available. *Entrance requirements:* Additional exam requirements/recommendations for international students: Required—TOEFL. *Application deadline:* For fall admission, 6/15 priority date for domestic students; for spring admission, 11/1 priority date for domestic students. Application fee: $25. *Application contact:* Melissa Bergfeld, Administrative Assistant, 419-824-3517, Fax: 419-824-3510, E-mail: mbergfeld2@lourdes.edu.
Website: http://www.lourdes.edu/gradschool.aspx.

Loyola Marymount University, School of Education, Department of Elementary and Secondary Education, Program in Literacy Education, Los Angeles, CA 90045. Offers MA. Part-time and evening/weekend programs available. *Faculty:* 5 full-time (4 women), 19 part-time/adjunct (11 women). *Students:* 5 full-time (all women), 1 (woman) part-time; includes 3 minority (all Hispanic/Latino). Average age 30. 1 applicant, 100% accepted, 2 enrolled. In 2013, 3 master's awarded. *Degree requirements:* For master's, comprehensive exam. *Entrance requirements:* For master's, CBEST. Additional exam requirements/recommendations for international students: Required—TOEFL (minimum score 600 paper-based; 100 iBT). *Application deadline:* For fall admission, 6/15 for domestic students; for spring admission, 11/15 for domestic students. Application fee: $50. Electronic applications accepted. *Financial support:* In 2013–14, 3 students received support. Scholarships/grants and unspecified assistantships available. Support available to part-time students. Financial award application deadline: 6/30; financial award applicants required to submit FAFSA. *Total annual research expenditures:* $132,233. *Unit head:* Dr. Candace Poindexter, Program Director, 310-338-7314, E-mail: cpoindex@lmu.edu. *Application contact:* Chake H. Kouyoumjian, Director, Graduate Admissions, 310-338-2721, E-mail: ckouyoum@lmu.edu.
Website: http://soe.lmu.edu/admissions/programs/literacyeducation/.

Loyola Marymount University, School of Education, Department of Elementary and Secondary Education, Program in Literacy/Language Arts, Los Angeles, CA 90045. Offers MA. Part-time and evening/weekend programs available. *Faculty:* 5 full-time (4 women), 19 part-time/adjunct (11 women). *Students:* 12 full-time (10 women), 4 part-time (all women); includes 6 minority (1 Black or African American, non-Hispanic/Latino; 2 Hispanic/Latino; 3 Two or more races, non-Hispanic/Latino). Average age 31. 7 applicants, 71% accepted, 6 enrolled. In 2013, 17 master's awarded. *Degree requirements:* For master's, comprehensive exam. *Entrance requirements:* For master's, CBEST, CSET, 3 letters of recommendation. Additional exam requirements/recommendations for international students: Required—TOEFL (minimum score 600 paper-based; 100 iBT). *Application deadline:* For fall admission, 6/15 for domestic students; for spring admission, 11/15 for domestic students. Application fee: $50. Electronic applications accepted. *Financial support:* In 2013–14, 5 students received support. Scholarships/grants and unspecified assistantships available. Support available to part-time students. Financial award application deadline: 6/30; financial award applicants required to submit FAFSA. *Unit head:* Dr. Irene Oliver, Chair, 310-338-7302, E-mail: ioliver@lmu.edu. *Application contact:* Chake H. Kouyoumjian, Director, Graduate Admissions, 310-338-2721, E-mail: ckouyoum@lmu.edu.
Website: http://soe.lmu.edu/admissions/programs/tcp/.

Loyola Marymount University, School of Education, Department of Elementary and Secondary Education, Program in Reading Instruction, Los Angeles, CA 90045. Offers MA. *Faculty:* 5 full-time (4 women), 19 part-time/adjunct (11 women). *Students:* 31 full-time (27 women), 8 part-time (7 women); includes 13 minority (1 Black or African American, non-Hispanic/Latino; 2 Asian, non-Hispanic/Latino; 8 Hispanic/Latino; 2 Two

or more races, non-Hispanic/Latino). Average age 28. 22 applicants, 68% accepted, 9 enrolled. In 2013, 28 master's awarded. *Entrance requirements:* For master's, statement of intent, 2 letters of recommendation. Additional exam requirements/recommendations for international students: Required—TOEFL (minimum score 600 paper-based; 100 iBT). *Application deadline:* For fall admission, 6/15 for domestic students. Application fee: $50. *Financial support:* In 2013–14, 26 students received support. Application deadline: 6/30; applicants required to submit FAFSA. *Total annual research expenditures:* $132,233. *Unit head:* Dr. Candace Poindexter, Director, 310-338-7314, E-mail: cpoindex@lmu.edu. *Application contact:* Chake H. Kouyoumjian, Graduate Admissions Director, 310-338-2721, E-mail: ckouyoum@lmu.edu.
Website: http://soe.lmu.edu/admissions/programs/literacyeducation/mainreadinginstruction/.

Loyola University Chicago, School of Education, Program in Teaching and Learning, Chicago, IL 60660. Offers behavior intervention specialist (M Ed); elementary education (M Ed); English as a second language (Certificate); English language teaching and learning (M Ed); math education (M Ed); reading specialist (M Ed); reading teacher endorsement (Certificate); school technology (M Ed); science education (M Ed); secondary education (M Ed); special education (M Ed). *Accreditation:* NCATE. *Faculty:* 23 full-time (16 women), 49 part-time/adjunct (42 women). *Students:* 109. Average age 28. 104 applicants, 71% accepted, 44 enrolled. In 2013, 39 master's awarded. *Degree requirements:* For master's, comprehensive exam. *Entrance requirements:* For master's, Illinois Basic Skills Test, 3 letters of recommendation, minimum GPA of 3.0, resume. Additional exam requirements/recommendations for international students: Required—TOEFL (minimum score 550 paper-based; 79 iBT). *Application deadline:* For fall admission, 7/1 priority date for domestic and international students; for spring admission, 11/1 priority date for domestic and international students; for summer admission, 4/1 for domestic and international students. Applications are processed on a rolling basis. Application fee: $50. Electronic applications accepted. Application fee is waived when completed online. *Expenses: Tuition:* Full-time $16,740; part-time $930 per credit. *Required fees:* $135 per semester. *Financial support:* In 2013–14, 58 fellowships with partial tuition reimbursements were awarded; research assistantships, teaching assistantships, institutionally sponsored loans, scholarships/grants, and unspecified assistantships also available. Support available to part-time students. Financial award application deadline: 2/1; financial award applicants required to submit FAFSA. *Faculty research:* Positive behavior support, school reform, school improvement. *Unit head:* Dr. Ann Marie Ryan, Director, 312-915-7027, E-mail: aryan3@luc.edu. *Application contact:* Marie Rosin-Dittmar, Information Contact, 312-915-6800, E-mail: schleduc@luc.edu.

Loyola University Maryland, Graduate Programs, School of Education, Program in Literacy/Reading, Baltimore, MD 21210-2699. Offers literacy (CAS); literacy teacher (M Ed); reading specialist (M Ed). *Accreditation:* NCATE. Part-time programs available. *Entrance requirements:* For master's, essay, 2 letters of recommendation, resume, transcripts. Additional exam requirements/recommendations for international students: Required—TOEFL (minimum score 550 paper-based). Electronic applications accepted.

Lynchburg College, Graduate Studies, School of Education and Human Development, M Ed Program in Reading, Lynchburg, VA 24501-3199. Offers reading instruction (M Ed); reading specialist (M Ed). Part-time and evening/weekend programs available. *Faculty:* 2 full-time (both women). *Students:* 1 full-time (0 women), 10 part-time (all women). Average age 33. In 2013, 4 master's awarded. *Degree requirements:* For master's, practicum; portfolio or comprehensive exam. *Entrance requirements:* For master's, GRE, minimum GPA of 3.0 (preferred), three letters of recommendation, official transcripts (bachelor's, others as relevant), career goals statement. Additional exam requirements/recommendations for international students: Required—TOEFL (minimum score 550 paper-based; 79 iBT), IELTS (minimum score 6.5). *Application deadline:* For fall admission, 7/31 for domestic students, 6/1 for international students; for spring admission, 11/30 for domestic students, 10/15 for international students. Applications are processed on a rolling basis. Application fee: $30. Electronic applications accepted. Application fee is waived when completed online. *Financial support:* Fellowships, research assistantships, Federal Work-Study, scholarships/grants, health care benefits, and unspecified assistantships available. Support available to part-time students. Financial award application deadline: 7/31; financial award applicants required to submit FAFSA. *Unit head:* Dr. Susan Thompson, Associate Professor/Director of M Ed in Reading, 434-544-8510, Fax: 434-544-8483, E-mail: thompson.s@lynchburg.edu. *Application contact:* Anne Pingstock, Executive Assistant, Graduate Studies, 434-544-8383, Fax: 434-544-8483, E-mail: gradstudies@lynchburg.edu.
Website: http://www.lynchburg.edu/master-education-reading.

Lyndon State College, Graduate Programs in Education, Department of Education, Lyndonville, VT 05851-0919. Offers curriculum and instruction (M Ed); reading specialist (M Ed); special education (M Ed); teaching and counseling (M Ed). Part-time and evening/weekend programs available. *Degree requirements:* For master's, exam or major field project. *Entrance requirements:* Additional exam requirements/recommendations for international students: Recommended—TOEFL (minimum score 500 paper-based).

Madonna University, Programs in Education, Livonia, MI 48150-1173. Offers Catholic school leadership (MSA); educational leadership (MSA); learning disabilities (MAT); literacy education (MAT); teaching and learning (MAT). *Accreditation:* NCATE. Part-time and evening/weekend programs available. *Degree requirements:* For master's, thesis or alternative. Electronic applications accepted.

Manhattanville College, School of Education, Program in Middle Childhood/Adolescence Education (Grades 5-12), Purchase, NY 10577-2132. Offers biology (MAT); biology and special education (MPS); chemistry (MAT); chemistry and special education (MPS); English (MAT); English and special education (MPS); literacy and special education (MPS); literacy specialist (MPS); math and special education (MPS); mathematics (MAT); physics (MAT); social studies (MAT); social studies and special education (MPS); special education (MPS); teaching languages other than English (MAT), including French, Italian, Latin, Spanish. Part-time and evening/weekend programs available. *Degree requirements:* For master's, comprehensive exam or research project, field experience. *Entrance requirements:* For master's, minimum undergraduate GPA of 3.0, 2 letters of recommendation. Additional exam requirements/recommendations for international students: Required—TOEFL. Electronic applications accepted.

Marquette University, Graduate School, College of Education, Department of Educational Policy and Leadership, Milwaukee, WI 53201-1881. Offers college student personnel administration (M Ed); curriculum and instruction (MA); education (MA); educational administration (M Ed); educational policy and foundations (MA); elementary education (Certificate); literacy (MA); principal (Certificate); reading specialist (Certificate); reading teacher (Certificate); secondary education (Certificate); superintendent (Certificate). Part-time and evening/weekend programs available. *Faculty:* 15 full-time (10 women), 3 part-time/adjunct (2 women). *Students:* 39 full-time (31 women), 107 part-time (70 women); includes 19 minority (7 Black or African American, non-Hispanic/Latino; 2 American Indian or Alaska Native, non-Hispanic/Latino; 3 Asian, non-Hispanic/Latino; 6 Hispanic/Latino; 1 Two or more races, non-Hispanic/Latino), 2 international. Average age 30. 144 applicants, 74% accepted, 67 enrolled. In 2013, 48 master's, 4 doctorates, 12 other advanced degrees awarded. Terminal master's awarded for partial completion of doctoral program. *Degree requirements:* For master's, comprehensive exam, thesis (for some programs); for doctorate, thesis/dissertation, qualifying exam, supporting minor. *Entrance requirements:* For master's, GRE General Test or MAT, official transcripts from all current and previous colleges/universities except Marquette, three letters of recommendation, statement of purpose; for doctorate, GRE General Test, MAT, sample of written work, official transcripts from all current and previous colleges/universities except Marquette, three letters of recommendation, statement of purpose, resume/curriculum vitae; for Certificate, GRE General Test or MAT, master's degree. Additional exam requirements/recommendations for international students: Required—TOEFL (minimum score 530 paper-based). *Application deadline:* For fall admission, 1/15 for domestic and international students. Application fee: $50. *Expenses:* Contact institution. *Financial support:* In 2013–14, 130 students received support, including 1 fellowship with full tuition reimbursement available (averaging $18,780 per year), 5 research assistantships with full tuition reimbursements available (averaging $13,404 per year); health care benefits, tuition waivers (partial), and unspecified assistantships also available. Support available to part-time students. Financial award application deadline: 2/15. *Faculty research:* Leadership; social justice in education; development of lifelong learners; race, class, and schooling in historical perspective; urban teacher education. *Unit head:* Dr. Ellen Eckman, Chair, 414-288-1561, E-mail: ellen.eckman@marquette.edu. *Application contact:* Dr. Sharon Chubbuck, Associate Professor, 414-288-5895.

Marshall University, Academic Affairs Division, College of Education and Professional Development, Program in Literacy Education, Huntington, WV 25755. Offers MA, Ed S. *Accreditation:* NCATE. Part-time and evening/weekend programs available. *Students:* 12 full-time (all women), 84 part-time (82 women); includes 2 minority (1 Hispanic/Latino; 1 Two or more races, non-Hispanic/Latino). Average age 34. In 2013, 16 master's awarded. *Degree requirements:* For master's, thesis optional, comprehensive or oral assessment, final project; for Ed S, thesis optional, research project. *Entrance requirements:* For master's, GRE General Test or MAT; for Ed S, master's degree in reading, minimum GPA of 3.0. Application fee: $40. *Financial support:* Federal Work-Study, tuition waivers (full and partial), and unspecified assistantships available. Support available to part-time students. Financial award applicants required to submit FAFSA. *Unit head:* Dr. Barbara O'Byrne, Program Director, 304-746-1986, E-mail: bobyrne@marshall.edu. *Application contact:* Information Contact, 304-746-1900, Fax: 304-746-1902, E-mail: services@marshall.edu.

Marygrove College, Graduate Division, Program in Reading and Literacy, Detroit, MI 48221-2599. Offers M Ed. Part-time and evening/weekend programs available. *Degree requirements:* For master's, practicum, research project. *Entrance requirements:* For master's, MAT, interview, minimum undergraduate GPA of 3.0, teaching certificate.

Maryville University of Saint Louis, School of Education, St. Louis, MO 63141-7299. Offers art education (MA Ed); early childhood education (MA Ed); educational leadership (Ed D); educational leadership: principal certification (MA Ed); elementary education (MA Ed); gifted education (MA Ed); higher education leadership (Ed D); literacy specialist (MA Ed); middle grades education (MA Ed); secondary teaching and inquiry (MA Ed); teacher as leader (MA Ed); teacher leadership (Ed D). *Accreditation:* NCATE. Part-time and evening/weekend programs available. *Faculty:* 10 full-time (6 women), 17 part-time/adjunct (13 women). *Students:* 21 full-time (17 women), 238 part-time (167 women); includes 64 minority (54 Black or African American, non-Hispanic/Latino; 2 Asian, non-Hispanic/Latino; 4 Hispanic/Latino; 4 Two or more races, non-Hispanic/Latino), 2 international. Average age 39. In 2013, 61 master's, 40 doctorates awarded. *Degree requirements:* For master's, thesis, project. *Entrance requirements:* For master's, minimum cumulative GPA of 3.0, 3 professional recommendations, essays, interview with program faculty; for doctorate, minimum GPA of 3.0, 3 professional recommendations, essay, interview, on-site writing sample. Additional exam requirements/recommendations for international students: Required—TOEFL (minimum score 550 paper-based). *Application deadline:* Applications are processed on a rolling basis. Application fee: $40 ($60 for international students). Electronic applications accepted. Application fee is waived when completed online. *Expenses: Tuition:* Full-time $23,812; part-time $728 per credit hour. *Required fees:* $395 per year. Tuition and fees vary according to course load, degree level and program. *Financial support:* Career-related internships or fieldwork, Federal Work-Study, tuition waivers (partial), and professional educator discounts available. Financial award application deadline: 3/1; financial award applicants required to submit FAFSA. *Faculty research:* Collaboration with public schools, pre-service program development, mathematics, diversity, literacy. *Unit head:* Dr. Cathy Bear, Dean, 314-529-9692, Fax: 314-529-9921, E-mail: cbear@maryville.edu. *Application contact:* Holly Stanwich, Graduate Admissions Coordinator, 314-529-9542, Fax: 314-529-9921, E-mail: teachered@maryville.edu.
Website: http://www.maryville.edu/ed/graduate-programs/.

Marywood University, Academic Affairs, Reap College of Education and Human Development, Department of Education, Program in Reading Education, Scranton, PA 18509-1598. Offers MS. *Accreditation:* NCATE. *Entrance requirements:* Additional exam requirements/recommendations for international students: Required—TOEFL (minimum score 550 paper-based; 79 iBT). *Application deadline:* For fall admission, 4/1 priority date for domestic students, 3/31 priority date for international students; for spring admission, 11/1 priority date for domestic students, 8/31 priority date for international students. Applications are processed on a rolling basis. Application fee: $30. Electronic applications accepted. *Expenses: Tuition:* Part-time $775 per credit. Tuition and fees vary according to degree level. *Financial support:* Career-related internships or fieldwork, scholarships/grants, and unspecified assistantships available. Support available to part-time students. Financial award application deadline: 6/30; financial award applicants required to submit FAFSA. *Faculty research:* Design of school reading programs, whole language. *Unit head:* Dr. Patricia S. Arter, Chairperson, 570-348-6211 Ext. 2511, E-mail: psarter@marywood.edu. *Application contact:* Tammy Manka, Assistant Director of Graduate Admissions, 570-348-6211 Ext. 2322, E-mail: tmanka@marywood.edu.
Website: http://www.marywood.edu/education/graduate-programs/m.s.-in-reading-education-.html.

Massachusetts College of Liberal Arts, Graduate Programs, North Adams, MA 01247-4100. Offers business (MBA); educational administration (M Ed); educational leadership (CAGS); instruction and curriculum (M Ed); instructional technology (M Ed); physical education and health (M Ed); reading (M Ed); special education (M Ed). Part-time and evening/weekend programs available. *Degree requirements:* For master's, thesis. *Entrance requirements:* For master's, writing sample.

McDaniel College, Graduate and Professional Studies, Program for Reading Specialists: Literacy Leadership, Westminster, MD 21157-4390. Offers MS. *Accreditation:* NCATE. Part-time and evening/weekend programs available. *Degree requirements:* For master's, comprehensive exam, thesis optional. *Entrance requirements:* For master's, GRE General Test, MAT, or NTE/PRAXIS I, 3 letters of reference. Additional exam requirements/recommendations for international students: Required—TOEFL.

Reading Education

McKendree University, Graduate Programs, Programs in Education, Lebanon, IL 62254-1299. Offers curriculum design and instruction (Ed D, Ed S); educational administration and leadership (MA Ed); educational studies (MA Ed); higher education administrative services (MA Ed); music education (MA Ed); reading (MA Ed); special education (MA Ed); teacher leadership (MA Ed); teaching certification (MA Ed). *Accreditation:* NCATE. Part-time and evening/weekend programs available. Postbaccalaureate distance learning degree programs offered (no on-campus study). *Entrance requirements:* For master's, official transcripts from all institutions previously attended, minimum GPA of 3.0, resume, references; for doctorate, GRE (within the past 5 years), master's degree in education and Ed S, or the equivalent, from regionally-accredited institution; official transcripts from all institutions previously attended; curriculum vitae/resume; essay/personal statement; two years of teaching/professional experience; for Ed S, GRE (within the past 5 years), master's degree in education from regionally-accredited institution of higher education; official transcripts from all institutions previously attended; curriculum vitae/resume; essay/personal statement; two years of teaching/professional experience. Additional exam requirements/recommendations for international students: Required—TOEFL. Electronic applications accepted.

McNeese State University, Doré School of Graduate Studies, Burton College of Education, Office of Graduate Education Programs, Program in Curriculum and Instruction, Lake Charles, LA 70609. Offers early childhood education (M Ed); elementary education (M Ed); reading (M Ed); secondary education (M Ed). Evening/weekend programs available. *Entrance requirements:* For master's, GRE, teaching certificate.

McNeese State University, Doré School of Graduate Studies, Burton College of Education, Office of Student Teaching and Professional Education Services, Program in Reading Specialist, Lake Charles, LA 70609. Offers Graduate Certificate. *Entrance requirements:* For degree, bachelor's degree, teaching certificate.

Medaille College, Program in Education, Buffalo, NY 14214-2695. Offers adolescent education (MS Ed); curriculum and instruction (MS Ed); education preparation (MS Ed); literacy (MS Ed); special education (MS). *Accreditation:* Teacher Education Accreditation Council. Part-time and evening/weekend programs available. *Faculty:* 12 full-time (9 women), 28 part-time/adjunct (19 women). *Students:* 159 full-time (123 women), 25 part-time (22 women); includes 8 minority (5 Black or African American, non-Hispanic/Latino; 3 Hispanic/Latino), 88 international. Average age 29. 209 applicants, 96% accepted, 61 enrolled. In 2013, 253 master's awarded. *Degree requirements:* For master's, comprehensive exam (for some programs), thesis or alternative. *Entrance requirements:* For master's, minimum undergraduate GPA of 2.7. Additional exam requirements/recommendations for international students: Required—TOEFL (minimum score 550 paper-based). *Application deadline:* For fall admission, 8/15 priority date for domestic students; for spring admission, 1/15 priority date for domestic students. Applications are processed on a rolling basis. Application fee: $35. Electronic applications accepted. *Financial support:* Federal Work-Study available. Financial award applicants required to submit FAFSA. *Faculty research:* Curriculum planning, truancy, tracking minority students, curriculum design, mentoring students. *Unit head:* Dr. Illana Lane, Dean, School of Education, 716-880-2553, E-mail: ilane@medaille.edu. *Application contact:* E-mail: sageadmissions@medaille.edu.
Website: http://www.medaille.edu.

Mercer University, Graduate Studies, Cecil B. Day Campus, Tift College of Education (Atlanta), Macon, GA 31207-0003. Offers curriculum and instruction (PhD); early childhood education (M Ed, MAT, Ed S); educational leadership (PhD, Ed S); higher education leadership (M Ed); independent and charter school leadership (M Ed); middle grades education (M Ed, MAT); reading education (M Ed); school counseling (Ed S); secondary education (M Ed, MAT); teacher leadership (Ed S). *Accreditation:* NCATE. Part-time and evening/weekend programs available. *Faculty:* 40 full-time (20 women), 9 part-time/adjunct (4 women). *Students:* 240 full-time (197 women), 382 part-time (320 women); includes 343 minority (315 Black or African American, non-Hispanic/Latino; 4 American Indian or Alaska Native, non-Hispanic/Latino; 9 Asian, non-Hispanic/Latino; 9 Hispanic/Latino; 1 Native Hawaiian or other Pacific Islander, non-Hispanic/Latino; 5 Two or more races, non-Hispanic/Latino), 4 international. Average age 36. In 2013, 233 master's, 24 doctorates, 47 other advanced degrees awarded. *Degree requirements:* For master's and Ed S, research project; for doctorate, comprehensive exam, thesis/dissertation. *Entrance requirements:* For master's, GRE or MAT, minimum undergraduate GPA of 2.75; for doctorate, GRE; for Ed S, GRE or MAT, minimum GPA of 3.25; for EDS degrees in educational leadership and teacher leadership: 3 years of certified teaching experience. Additional exam requirements/recommendations for international students: Required—TOEFL. *Application deadline:* For fall admission, 8/1 for domestic and international students; for spring admission, 12/1 for domestic and international students; for summer admission, 5/1 for domestic and international students. Applications are processed on a rolling basis. Application fee: $25. *Expenses:* Contact institution. *Financial support:* Federal Work-Study available. Support available to part-time students. Financial award application deadline: 5/1. *Faculty research:* Educational technology, multicultural and minority issues in education, educational leadership (P-12 and higher education), school discipline and school bullying, standards-based mathematics education. *Unit head:* Dr. Paige L. Tompkins, Interim Dean, 478-301-5397, Fax: 478-301-2280, E-mail: tompkins_pl@mercer.edu. *Application contact:* Dr. Allison Gilmore, Associate Dean for Graduate Teacher Education, 678-547-6333, Fax: 678-547-6055, E-mail: gilmore_a@mercer.edu.
Website: http://www.mercer.edu/education/.

Mercy College, School of Education, Program in Teaching Literacy, Dobbs Ferry, NY 10522-1189. Offers MS, Advanced Certificate. Part-time and evening/weekend programs available. Postbaccalaureate distance learning degree programs offered (no on-campus study). *Students:* 38 full-time (35 women), 167 part-time (146 women); includes 89 minority (24 Black or African American, non-Hispanic/Latino; 1 Asian, non-Hispanic/Latino; 61 Hispanic/Latino; 3 Two or more races, non-Hispanic/Latino). Average age 32. 79 applicants, 82% accepted, 60 enrolled. In 2013, 39 master's, 10 other advanced degrees awarded. *Degree requirements:* For master's, comprehensive exam (for some programs), thesis (for some programs). *Entrance requirements:* For master's, resume, undergraduate transcript. Additional exam requirements/recommendations for international students: Required—TOEFL (minimum score 600 paper-based; 100 iBT), IELTS (minimum score 8). *Application deadline:* For fall admission, 8/1 for international students. Applications are processed on a rolling basis. Application fee: $40. Electronic applications accepted. *Expenses: Tuition:* Full-time $19,344; part-time $806 per credit. *Required fees:* $580; $806 per credit. $145 per term. Tuition and fees vary according to course load, degree level and program. *Financial support:* Career-related internships or fieldwork, Federal Work-Study, scholarships/grants, and unspecified assistantships available. Support available to part-time students. Financial award applicants required to submit FAFSA. *Unit head:* Dr. Alfred S. Posamentier, Dean for the School of Education, 914-674-7350, E-mail: aposamentier@mercy.edu. *Application contact:* Allison Gurdineer, Senior Director of Admissions, 877-637-2946, Fax: 914-674-7382, E-mail: admissions@mercy.edu.
Website: https://www.mercy.edu/academics/school-of-education/department-of-literacy-and-multilingual-studies/.

Mercy College, School of Education, Program in Teaching Literacy, Birth-6, Dobbs Ferry, NY 10522. Offers MS. Part-time and evening/weekend programs available. *Students:* 8 full-time (all women), 42 part-time (all women); includes 18 minority (6 Black or African American, non-Hispanic/Latino; 1 Asian, non-Hispanic/Latino; 11 Hispanic/Latino). Average age 33. 35 applicants, 71% accepted, 17 enrolled. In 2013, 88 master's awarded. *Degree requirements:* For master's, thesis or alternative, capstone. *Entrance requirements:* For master's, resume, interview by faculty advisor and/or program director. Additional exam requirements/recommendations for international students: Required—TOEFL (minimum score 600 paper-based; 100 iBT), IELTS (minimum score 8). *Application deadline:* For fall admission, 8/1 for international students. Applications are processed on a rolling basis. Application fee: $40. Electronic applications accepted. *Expenses: Tuition:* Full-time $19,344; part-time $806 per credit. *Required fees:* $580; $806 per credit. $145 per term. Tuition and fees vary according to course load, degree level and program. *Financial support:* In 2013–14, 2 students received support. Career-related internships or fieldwork, Federal Work-Study, scholarships/grants, and unspecified assistantships available. Support available to part-time students. Financial award applicants required to submit FAFSA. *Faculty research:* Linguistics, literacy. *Unit head:* Dr. Andrew Peiser, Chairperson, 914-674-7489, Fax: 914-674-7352, E-mail: apeiser@mercy.edu. *Application contact:* Mary Ellen Hoffman, Director, Graduate Education Programs, 914-674-7334, E-mail: mhoffman@mercy.edu.

Mercy College, School of Education, Program in Teaching Literacy/Grades 5-12, Dobbs Ferry, NY 10522-1189. Offers MS. Part-time and evening/weekend programs available. *Students:* 1 (woman) full-time, 19 part-time (14 women); includes 3 minority (1 American Indian or Alaska Native, non-Hispanic/Latino; 2 Hispanic/Latino). Average age 30. 9 applicants, 67% accepted, 4 enrolled. In 2013, 13 master's awarded. *Entrance requirements:* Additional exam requirements/recommendations for international students: Required—TOEFL (minimum score 600 paper-based; 100 iBT). *Application deadline:* For fall admission, 8/1 for international students. Applications are processed on a rolling basis. Application fee: $40. Electronic applications accepted. *Expenses: Tuition:* Full-time $19,344; part-time $806 per credit. *Required fees:* $580; $806 per credit. $145 per term. Tuition and fees vary according to course load, degree level and program. *Faculty research:* Linguistics, literacy. *Unit head:* Dr. Andrew Peiser, Chairperson, 914-674-7489, Fax: 914-674-7352, E-mail: apeiser@mercy.edu. *Application contact:* Mary Ellen Hoffman, Director, Graduate Education Programs, 914-674-7334, E-mail: mhoffman@mercy.edu.

Merrimack College, School of Education, North Andover, MA 01845-5800. Offers community engagement (M Ed), including community organizations, higher education, K-12 education; early childhood education (M Ed); elementary education (M Ed); English as a second language (PreK-6) (M Ed); English language learners (M Ed); general studies (M Ed); higher education (M Ed), including leadership and organizational development, student affairs; middle (M Ed); moderate disabilities (PreK-8) (M Ed); secondary (M Ed); teacher leadership (CAGS), including instructional leadership, reading specialist. Part-time and evening/weekend programs available. *Faculty:* 4 full-time (all women), 23 part-time/adjunct (15 women). *Students:* 127 full-time (104 women), 61 part-time (52 women); includes 3 minority (1 Asian, non-Hispanic/Latino; 2 Hispanic/Latino), 2 international. Average age 25. 403 applicants, 47% accepted, 138 enrolled. In 2013, 140 master's awarded. *Degree requirements:* For master's, practicum, portfolio, and state test (for licensure track); capstone (for higher education and community engagement tracks). *Entrance requirements:* For master's, MTEL (Massachusetts Tests for Educator Licensure), official transcripts from other colleges, resume, personal statement, 2 letters of recommendation, additional essay requirements for fellowships. Additional exam requirements/recommendations for international students: Required—TOEFL (minimum score 84 iBT), IELTS (minimum score 6.5). *Application deadline:* For fall admission, 8/15 for domestic and international students; for winter admission, 12/1 for domestic students, 11/15 for international students; for spring admission, 1/10 for domestic and international students; for summer admission, 5/10 for domestic and international students. Applications are processed on a rolling basis. Application fee: $0. Electronic applications accepted. Tuition and fees vary according to course load and program. *Financial support:* In 2013–14, 91 fellowships with full tuition reimbursements were awarded; career-related internships or fieldwork, scholarships/grants, and health care benefits also available. Support available to part-time students. Financial award applicants required to submit FAFSA. *Faculty research:* Expressive language, civic engagement, family life education, reading genres, the psychological process of aging. *Application contact:* Kristen English, Interim Director of Graduate Admission, 978-837-5073, E-mail: englishkr@merrimack.edu.
Website: http://www.merrimack.edu/academics/graduate/education/.

MGH Institute of Health Professions, School of Health and Rehabilitation Sciences, Department of Communication Sciences and Disorders, Boston, MA 02129. Offers reading (Certificate); speech-language pathology (MS). *Accreditation:* ASHA (one or more programs are accredited). Part-time programs available. *Faculty:* 12 full-time (9 women), 2 part-time/adjunct (1 woman). *Students:* 111 full-time (104 women), 10 part-time (9 women); includes 37 minority (9 Black or African American, non-Hispanic/Latino; 18 Asian, non-Hispanic/Latino; 10 Hispanic/Latino). Average age 28. 527 applicants, 35% accepted, 82 enrolled. In 2013, 55 master's, 26 other advanced degrees awarded. *Degree requirements:* For master's, thesis or alternative, research proposal. *Entrance requirements:* For master's, GRE General Test, bachelor's degree from regionally-accredited college or university. Additional exam requirements/recommendations for international students: Required—TOEFL (minimum score 550 paper-based; 80 iBT). *Application deadline:* For fall admission, 1/1 for domestic and international students. Applications are processed on a rolling basis. Electronic applications accepted. *Expenses: Tuition:* Part-time $1114 per credit. *Required fees:* $620 per term. One-time fee: $475 part-time. *Financial support:* In 2013–14, 45 students received support, including 8 research assistantships (averaging $1,200 per year), 4 teaching assistantships (averaging $1,200 per year); career-related internships or fieldwork, scholarships/grants, and unspecified assistantships also available. Support available to part-time students. Financial award application deadline: 4/1; financial award applicants required to submit FAFSA. *Faculty research:* Children's language disorders, reading, speech disorders, voice disorders, augmentative communication, autism. *Unit head:* Dr. Gregory L. Lof, Department Chair, 617-724-6313, E-mail: glot@mghihp.edu. *Application contact:* Catherine Hamilton, Assistant Director of Admission and Multicultural Recruitment, 617-726-3140, Fax: 617-726-8010, E-mail: admissions@mghihp.edu.
Website: http://www.mghihp.edu/academics/communication-sciences-and-disorders/.

Miami University, College of Education, Health and Society, Department of Teacher Education, Oxford, OH 45056. Offers adolescent education (M Ed); elementary education (M Ed, MAT); reading education (M Ed); secondary education (MAT). Part-time and evening/weekend programs available. *Students:* 31 full-time (21 women), 26 part-time (23 women); includes 8 minority (3 Black or African American, non-Hispanic/Latino; 1 Asian, non-Hispanic/Latino; 2 Hispanic/Latino; 2 Two or more races, non-Hispanic/Latino), 2 international. Average age 31. In 2013, 31 master's awarded. *Entrance requirements:* Additional exam requirements/recommendations for international students: Recommended—TOEFL (minimum score 80 iBT), IELTS (minimum score 6.5), TSE (minimum score 54). *Application deadline:* Applications are processed on a rolling basis. Application fee: $50. Electronic applications accepted. *Expenses:* Tuition, state resident: full-time $12,634; part-time $526 per credit hour.

Tuition, nonresident: full-time $27,892; part-time $1162 per credit hour. Part-time tuition and fees vary according to course load, campus/location and program. *Financial support:* Research assistantships with full tuition reimbursements, teaching assistantships with full tuition reimbursements, career-related internships or fieldwork, Federal Work-Study, scholarships/grants, health care benefits, tuition waivers, and unspecified assistantships available. Financial award application deadline: 2/15. *Unit head:* Dr. Paula Saine, Interim Co-Chair, 513-529-6443, Fax: 513-529-4931, E-mail: sainep@miamioh.edu. *Application contact:* Linda Dennett, Program Associate, 513-529-5708, E-mail: dennetlg@miamioh.edu. Website: http://www.MiamiOH.edu/edt.

Michigan State University, The Graduate School, College of Education, Program in Literacy Instruction, East Lansing, MI 48824. Offers MA. *Accreditation:* Teacher Education Accreditation Council. Part-time programs available. *Degree requirements:* For master's, comprehensive exam (for some programs), final exam or portfolio. *Entrance requirements:* Additional exam requirements/recommendations for international students: Required—TOEFL, Michigan State University ELT (minimum score 85), Michigan English Language Assessment Battery (minimum score 83). Electronic applications accepted.

Middle Tennessee State University, College of Graduate Studies, College of Education, Department of Elementary and Special Education, Major in Reading, Murfreesboro, TN 37132. Offers M Ed. *Accreditation:* NCATE. Part-time and evening/weekend programs available. Postbaccalaureate distance learning degree programs offered. *Faculty:* 14 full-time (9 women), 7 part-time/adjunct (all women). *Students:* 1 (woman) full-time, 13 part-time (all women); includes 4 minority (3 Black or African American, non-Hispanic/Latino; 1 Hispanic/Latino). In 2013, 8 master's awarded. *Degree requirements:* For master's, comprehensive exam. *Entrance requirements:* For master's, GRE, MAT or PRAXIS. Additional exam requirements/recommendations for international students: Required—TOEFL (minimum score 525 paper-based; 71 iBT) or IELTS (minimum score 6). *Application deadline:* For fall admission, 6/1 for domestic and international students. Applications are processed on a rolling basis. Application fee: $25 ($30 for international students). Electronic applications accepted. *Financial support:* Tuition waivers available. Support available to part-time students. Financial award application deadline: 5/1. *Unit head:* Dr. Kathleen Burriss, Interim Chair, 615-898-2680, Fax: 615-898-5309, E-mail: kathleen.burriss@mtsu.edu. *Application contact:* Dr. Michael D. Allen, Vice Provost for Research and Dean, 615-898-2840, Fax: 615-904-8020, E-mail: michael.allen@mtsu.edu.

Middle Tennessee State University, College of Graduate Studies, College of Education, PhD in Literacy Studies Program, Murfreesboro, TN 37132. Offers PhD. Part-time and evening/weekend programs available. Postbaccalaureate distance learning degree programs offered. *Faculty:* 14 full-time (9 women), 7 part-time/adjunct (all women). *Students:* 8 full-time (6 women), 26 part-time (22 women); includes 12 minority (3 Black or African American, non-Hispanic/Latino; 6 Asian, non-Hispanic/Latino; 3 Two or more races, non-Hispanic/Latino). In 2013, 3 doctorates awarded. *Degree requirements:* For doctorate, comprehensive exam, thesis/dissertation. *Entrance requirements:* For doctorate, GRE. Additional exam requirements/recommendations for international students: Required—TOEFL (minimum score 525 paper-based; 71 iBT) or IELTS (minimum score 6). *Application deadline:* For fall admission, 6/1 for domestic and international students. Applications are processed on a rolling basis. Application fee: $25 ($30 for international students). *Financial support:* Institutionally sponsored loans and tuition waivers available. Support available to part-time students. Financial award application deadline: 5/1. *Unit head:* Kim Jwa, Director, 615-898-8434, E-mail: kim.jwa@mtsu.edu. *Application contact:* Dr. Michael D. Allen, Vice Provost for Research and Dean, 615-898-2840, Fax: 615-904-8020, E-mail: michael.allen@mtsu.edu.

Midwestern State University, Graduate School, West College of Education, Program in Reading Education, Wichita Falls, TX 76308. Offers M Ed. Part-time and evening/weekend programs available. *Degree requirements:* For master's, comprehensive exam. *Entrance requirements:* For master's, GRE General Test, MAT or GMAT. Additional exam requirements/recommendations for international students: Required—TOEFL (minimum score 550 paper-based). *Application deadline:* For fall admission, 7/1 priority date for domestic students, 4/1 for international students; for spring admission, 11/1 priority date for domestic students, 8/1 for international students. Applications are processed on a rolling basis. Application fee: $35 ($50 for international students). Electronic applications accepted. *Expenses:* Tuition, state resident: full-time $3627; part-time $201.50 per credit hour. Tuition, nonresident: full-time $10,899; part-time $605.50 per credit hour. *Required fees:* $1357. *Financial support:* Career-related internships or fieldwork, Federal Work-Study, institutionally sponsored loans, scholarships/grants, tuition waivers (partial), and unspecified assistantships available. Support available to part-time students. Financial award application deadline: 3/1; financial award applicants required to submit FAFSA. *Faculty research:* Collective learning, school culture, early literacy development, family literacy, brain-based learning. *Unit head:* Dr. Pamela Whitehouse, Chair, 940-397-4139, Fax: 940-397-4672, E-mail: pamela.whitehouse@mwsu.edu. Website: http://www.mwsu.edu/academics/education/.

Millersville University of Pennsylvania, College of Graduate and Professional Studies, School of Education, Department of Elementary and Early Childhood Education, Program in Language and Literacy Education, Millersville, PA 17551-0302. Offers ESL (M Ed); language and literacy education (M Ed). *Accreditation:* NCATE. Part-time and evening/weekend programs available. *Faculty:* 17 full-time (11 women), 18 part-time/adjunct (15 women). *Students:* 1 (woman) full-time, 58 part-time (52 women); includes 2 minority (1 Black or African American, non-Hispanic/Latino; 1 Hispanic/Latino). Average age 29. 12 applicants, 100% accepted, 11 enrolled. In 2013, 41 master's awarded. *Degree requirements:* For master's, thesis optional. *Entrance requirements:* For master's, GRE or MAT, 3 letters of recommendation, copy of teaching certificate, goal statement, official transcripts. Additional exam requirements/recommendations for international students: Required—TOEFL (minimum score 550 paper-based, 79 iBT) or IELTS (minimum score 6). *Application deadline:* For fall admission, 1/15 priority date for domestic and international students; for winter admission, 10/1 priority date for domestic and international students; for spring admission, 10/1 priority date for domestic and international students. Applications are processed on a rolling basis. Application fee: $40. Electronic applications accepted. *Expenses:* Tuition, state resident: full-time $7956; part-time $442 per credit. Tuition, nonresident: full-time $11,934; part-time $663 per credit. *Required fees:* $2196; $122 per credit. Tuition and fees vary according to course load. *Financial support:* In 2013–14, 3 students received support, including 3 research assistantships with full tuition reimbursements available (averaging $4,367 per year); institutionally sponsored loans and unspecified assistantships also available. Support available to part-time students. Financial award application deadline: 3/15; financial award applicants required to submit FAFSA. *Faculty research:* Academic vocabulary, new literacies, literacy coaching, trends and issues in multicultural children's literature, graphic novels and emergent readers, transgender characters in young adult literature. *Unit head:* Dr. Judith K. Wenrich, Coordinator, 717-872-3395, Fax: 717-871-5462, E-mail: judith.wenrich@millersville.edu. *Application contact:* Dr. Victor S. DeSantis, Dean of College of Graduate

and Professional Studies/Associate Provost for Civic and Community Engagement, 717-872-3099, Fax: 717-872-3453, E-mail: victor.desantis@millersville.edu. Website: http://www.millersville.edu/academics/educ/eled/graduate.php.

Minnesota State University Moorhead, Graduate Studies, College of Education and Human Services, Program in Reading, Moorhead, MN 56563-0002. Offers MS. *Accreditation:* NCATE. Part-time and evening/weekend programs available. *Degree requirements:* For master's, comprehensive exam, final oral exam, project or thesis. *Entrance requirements:* For master's, MAT, minimum GPA of 2.75, 2 years of teaching experience. Additional exam requirements/recommendations for international students: Required—TOEFL (minimum score 550 paper-based). Electronic applications accepted.

Misericordia University, College of Professional Studies and Social Sciences, Program in Education, Dallas, PA 18612-1098. Offers instructional technology (MS); reading specialist (MS); special education (MS). Part-time and evening/weekend programs available. *Faculty:* 1 full-time (0 women), 12 part-time/adjunct (8 women). *Students:* 44 part-time (35 women); includes 1 minority (Hispanic/Latino). Average age 32. In 2013, 24 master's awarded. *Entrance requirements:* For master's, minimum undergraduate GPA of 3.0. Additional exam requirements/recommendations for international students: Required—TOEFL. *Application deadline:* Applications are processed on a rolling basis. Application fee: $35. Electronic applications accepted. *Expenses:* Tuition: Full-time $14,450; part-time $680 per credit. Tuition and fees vary according to degree level. *Financial support:* In 2013–14, 11 students received support. Scholarships/grants available. Support available to part-time students. Financial award application deadline: 6/30; financial award applicants required to submit FAFSA. *Unit head:* Dr. Steven Broskoske, Associate Professor, Education Department, 570-674-6761, E-mail: sbroskos@misericordia.edu. *Application contact:* David Pasquini, Assistant Director of Admissions, 570-674-8183, Fax: 570-674-6232, E-mail: dpasquin@misericordia.edu. Website: http://www.misericordia.edu/misericordia_pg.cfm?page_id=387&subcat_id=108.

Mississippi State University, College of Education, Department of Curriculum, Instruction and Special Education, Mississippi State, MS 39762. Offers curriculum and instruction (PhD), including early childhood education (MS, PhD), elementary education (PhD, Ed S), general curriculum and instruction, reading education, secondary education (PhD, Ed S), special education (PhD, Ed S); education (Ed S), including elementary education (PhD, Ed S), secondary education (PhD, Ed S), special education (PhD, Ed S); elementary education (MS), including early childhood education (MS, PhD), general elementary education, middle level education; middle level alternate route (MAT); secondary education (MS); secondary teacher alternate route (MAT); special education (MS). *Accreditation:* NCATE. Part-time and evening/weekend programs available. *Faculty:* 11 full-time (9 women). *Students:* 58 full-time (40 women), 143 part-time (100 women); includes 62 minority (56 Black or African American, non-Hispanic/Latino; 2 American Indian or Alaska Native, non-Hispanic/Latino; 3 Hispanic/Latino; 1 Two or more races, non-Hispanic/Latino). Average age 33. 181 applicants, 32% accepted, 52 enrolled. In 2013, 44 master's, 1 doctorate, 7 other advanced degrees awarded. *Degree requirements:* For master's, comprehensive exam; for doctorate, thesis/dissertation; for Ed S, comprehensive exam, thesis or alternative. *Entrance requirements:* For master's, GRE, minimum GPA of 2.75 in junior and senior year, eligibility for initial teacher certification; for doctorate, GRE, minimum GPA of 3.4 on previous graduate work; for Ed S, GRE, minimum GPA of 3.2 on master's degree. Additional exam requirements/recommendations for international students: Required—TOEFL (minimum score 550 paper-based; 79 iBT); Recommended—IELTS (minimum score 6.5). *Application deadline:* For fall admission, 3/1 priority date for domestic students, 5/1 for international students; for spring admission, 9/1 priority date for domestic students, 9/1 for international students. Applications are processed on a rolling basis. Application fee: $60. Electronic applications accepted. *Financial support:* In 2013–14, 7 research assistantships with full and partial tuition reimbursements (averaging $9,623 per year), 2 teaching assistantships (averaging $11,382 per year) were awarded; Federal Work-Study, institutionally sponsored loans, scholarships/grants, and unspecified assistantships also available. Financial award application deadline: 4/1; financial award applicants required to submit FAFSA. *Faculty research:* Early childhood education, reading, rural schools, multicultural education, use of technology in instruction. *Unit head:* Dr. Devon Brenner, Professor and Interim Head, 662-325-7119, Fax: 662-325-7857, E-mail: devon@ra.msstate.edu. *Application contact:* Dr. Dana Franz, Graduate Coordinator, 662-325-3703, Fax: 662-325-7857, E-mail: tstevonson@colled.msstate.edu. Website: http://www.cise.msstate.edu/.

Mississippi University for Women, Graduate School, College of Education and Human Sciences, Columbus, MS 39701-9998. Offers differentiated instruction (M Ed); educational leadership (M Ed); gifted studies (M Ed); reading/literacy (M Ed); teaching (MAT). *Accreditation:* ASHA; NCATE. Part-time programs available. *Degree requirements:* For master's, comprehensive exam, thesis optional. *Entrance requirements:* For master's, GRE General Test or NTE (M Ed in gifted education or MS in speech/language pathology), MAT (M Ed in instructional management), minimum QPA of 3.0.

Missouri State University, Graduate College, College of Education, Department of Reading, Foundations, and Technology, Program in Literacy, Springfield, MO 65897. Offers MS Ed. Part-time programs available. *Students:* 1 (woman) full-time, 41 part-time (39 women); includes 1 minority (Black or African American, non-Hispanic/Latino). Average age 30. 17 applicants, 100% accepted, 6 enrolled. In 2013, 15 master's awarded. *Degree requirements:* For master's, comprehensive exam, thesis or alternative. *Entrance requirements:* For master's, GRE or minimum GPA of 3.0, teaching certificate. Additional exam requirements/recommendations for international students: Required—TOEFL (minimum score 550 paper-based; 79 iBT). *Application deadline:* For fall admission, 7/20 priority date for domestic students, 5/1 for international students; for spring admission, 12/20 for domestic students, 9/1 for international students. Applications are processed on a rolling basis. Application fee: $35 ($50 for international students). Electronic applications accepted. *Expenses:* Tuition, state resident: full-time $4500; part-time $250 per credit hour. Tuition, nonresident: full-time $9018; part-time $501 per credit hour. *Required fees:* $361 per semester. Tuition and fees vary according to course level, course load and program. *Financial support:* Federal Work-Study, institutionally sponsored loans, scholarships/grants, and unspecified assistantships available. Financial award application deadline: 3/31; financial award applicants required to submit FAFSA. *Unit head:* Dr. Deanne Camp, Program Director, 417-836-6983, E-mail: deannecamp@missouristate.edu. *Application contact:* Misty Stewart, Coordinator of Graduate Recruitment, 417-836-6079, Fax: 417-836-6200, E-mail: ericeckert@missouristate.edu. Website: http://education.missouristate.edu/rft/.

Monmouth University, The Graduate School, School of Education, West Long Branch, NJ 07764-1898. Offers applied behavioral analysis (Certificate); autism (Certificate); initial certification (MAT), including elementary level, K-12, secondary level; principal (MS Ed); principal/school administrator (MS Ed); reading specialist (MS Ed); school counseling (MS Ed); special education (MS Ed), including autism, learning disabilities teacher consultant, teacher of students with disabilities, teaching in inclusive settings;

speech-language pathology (MS Ed); student affairs and college counseling (MS Ed); teaching English to speakers of other languages (TESOL) (Certificate). *Accreditation:* NCATE. Part-time and evening/weekend programs available. *Faculty:* 15 full-time (11 women), 19 part-time/adjunct (17 women). *Students:* 125 full-time (97 women), 168 part-time (146 women); includes 38 minority (12 Black or African American, non-Hispanic/Latino; 5 Asian, non-Hispanic/Latino; 16 Hispanic/Latino; 5 Two or more races, non-Hispanic/Latino). Average age 28. 176 applicants, 90% accepted, 112 enrolled. In 2013, 147 master's awarded. *Entrance requirements:* For master's, GRE within last 5 years (for MS Ed in speech-language pathology), minimum GPA of 3.0 in major; 2 letters of recommendation (for some programs), resume, personal statement or essay (depending on degree program). Additional exam requirements/recommendations for international students: Required—TOEFL (minimum score 550 paper-based; 79 iBT), IELTS (minimum score 6), Michigan English Language Assessment Battery (minimum score 77). *Application deadline:* For fall admission, 7/15 priority date for domestic students, 7/1 for international students; for spring admission, 11/15 priority date for domestic students, 11/1 for international students. Applications are processed on a rolling basis. Application fee: $50. Electronic applications accepted. *Expenses: Tuition:* Part-time $1004 per credit hour. *Required fees:* $157 per semester. *Financial support:* In 2013–14, 191 students received support, including 159 fellowships (averaging $2,786 per year), 30 research assistantships (averaging $8,755 per year); career-related internships or fieldwork, scholarships/grants, and unspecified assistantships also available. Support available to part-time students. Financial award applicants required to submit FAFSA. *Faculty research:* Multicultural literacy, science and mathematics teaching strategies, teacher as reflective practitioner, children with disabilities. *Unit head:* Dr. Jason Barr, Program Director, 732-263-5238, Fax: 732-263-5277, E-mail: jbarr@monmouth.edu. *Application contact:* Lauren Vento-Cifelli, Associate Vice President of Undergraduate and Graduate Admission, 732-571-3452, Fax: 732-263-5123, E-mail: gradadm@monmouth.edu. Website: http://www.monmouth.edu/academics/schools/education/default.asp.

Montana State University Billings, College of Education, Department of Educational Theory and Practice, Billings, MT 59101-0298. Offers educational technology (M Ed); general curriculum (M Ed); interdisciplinary studies (M Ed); reading (M Ed); school counseling (M Ed); special education (MS Sp Ed), including special education generalist; special education (MS Sp Ed), including advanced studies; teaching (Certificate). Part-time programs available. Postbaccalaureate distance learning degree programs offered (minimal on-campus study). *Degree requirements:* For master's, thesis optional. *Entrance requirements:* For master's, GRE General Test or MAT, minimum GPA of 3.0 (undergraduate), 3.25 (graduate). *Application deadline:* For fall admission, 7/15 for international students; for spring admission, 12/1 for international students. Applications are processed on a rolling basis. Application fee: $40. *Expenses:* Tuition, state resident: full-time $2653.75; part-time $1718 per semester. Tuition, nonresident: full-time $7015; part-time $4640 per semester. *Required fees:* $2445; $444 per credit. *Financial support:* Teaching assistantships with partial tuition reimbursements, career-related internships or fieldwork, Federal Work-Study, institutionally sponsored loans, scholarships/grants, tuition waivers (partial), and unspecified assistantships available. Support available to part-time students. Financial award application deadline: 5/1; financial award applicants required to submit FAFSA. *Unit head:* Dr. Ken Miller, Chair, 406-657-2034, E-mail: kmiller@msubillings.edu. *Application contact:* David M. Sullivan, Graduate Studies Counselor, 406-657-2053, Fax: 406-657-2299, E-mail: dsullivan@msubillings.edu.

Montana State University Billings, College of Education, Department of Special Education, Counseling, Reading and Early Childhood, Option in Reading, Billings, MT 59101-0298. Offers M Ed. *Accreditation:* NCATE. Part-time programs available. *Degree requirements:* For master's, thesis or professional paper and/or field experience. *Entrance requirements:* For master's, GRE General Test or MAT, minimum GPA of 3.0 (undergraduate), 3.25 (graduate). *Application deadline:* Applications are processed on a rolling basis. Application fee: $40. *Expenses:* Tuition, state resident: full-time $2653.75; part-time $1718 per semester. Tuition, nonresident: full-time $7015; part-time $4640 per semester. *Required fees:* $2445; $444 per credit. *Financial support:* Teaching assistantships, career-related internships or fieldwork, Federal Work-Study, institutionally sponsored loans, scholarships/grants, tuition waivers (partial), and unspecified assistantships available. Support available to part-time students. Financial award application deadline: 5/1; financial award applicants required to submit FAFSA. *Unit head:* Sandra Rietz, Head, 406-657-2167, E-mail: srietz@msubillings.edu. *Application contact:* David M. Sullivan, Graduate Studies Counselor, 406-657-2053, Fax: 406-657-2299, E-mail: dsullivan@msubillings.edu.

Montclair State University, The Graduate School, College of Education and Human Services, Department of Early Childhood, Elementary and Literacy Education, Program in Reading, Montclair, NJ 07043-1624. Offers MA. Part-time and evening/weekend programs available. *Entrance requirements:* For master's, GRE General Test, interview, essay, 2 letters of recommendation. Additional exam requirements/recommendations for international students: Required—TOEFL (minimum score 83 iBT), IELTS (minimum score 6.5). Electronic applications accepted.

Montclair State University, The Graduate School, College of Humanities and Social Sciences, Department of English, Montclair, NJ 07043-1624. Offers elementary language arts/literacy (grades 5-8) (Certificate); English (MA); teaching writing (Certificate). Part-time and evening/weekend programs available. *Degree requirements:* For master's, thesis. *Entrance requirements:* For master's, GRE General Test, 2 letters of recommendation, essay. Additional exam requirements/recommendations for international students: Required—TOEFL (minimum score 83 iBT) or IELTS (minimum score 6.5). Electronic applications accepted. *Faculty research:* Modernism, Shakespeare, Victorian poetry, contemporary European film, nineteenth-century American literature.

Morehead State University, Graduate Programs, College of Education, Department of Curriculum and Instruction, Morehead, KY 40351. Offers curriculum and instruction (Ed S); elementary education (MA Ed), including elementary education, international education, middle school education, reading; secondary education (MA Ed); special education (MA Ed); teaching (MAT). Part-time and evening/weekend programs available. *Degree requirements:* For master's, comprehensive exam, thesis optional; for Ed S, thesis, oral exam. *Entrance requirements:* For master's, GRE General Test, minimum GPA of 2.75, teaching certificate; for Ed S, GRE General Test, interview, master's degree, minimum GPA of 3.5, work experience. Additional exam requirements/recommendations for international students: Required—TOEFL (minimum score 500 paper-based). Electronic applications accepted. *Faculty research:* Communicative competence of learning-disabled students, teaching social studies in elementary schools, ungraded primary school organization, study skills.

Morehead State University, Graduate Programs, College of Education, Department of Foundational and Graduate Studies in Education, Morehead, KY 40351. Offers adult and higher education (MA, Ed S); certified professional counselor (Ed S); counseling P-12 (MA); curriculum and instruction (Ed S); educational technology (MA Ed); instructional leadership (Ed S); school administration (MA); school counseling (Ed S); teacher leader business and marketing content (MA Ed); teacher leader business and marketing technology (MA Ed); teacher leader educational technology (MA Ed); teacher leader English (MA Ed); teacher leader gifted education (MA Ed); teacher leader IECE

certification (MA Ed); teacher leader interdisciplinary education P-5 (MA Ed); teacher leader middle grades (MA Ed); teacher leader non IECE certification (MA Ed); teacher leader reading/writing - non-certification (MA Ed); teacher leader reading/writing certification (MA Ed); teacher leader school communication - certification (MA Ed); teacher leader school communication - non-certification (MA Ed); teacher leader social studies (MA Ed); teacher leader special education (MA Ed). *Accreditation:* NCATE. Part-time and evening/weekend programs available. *Degree requirements:* For master's, thesis optional, oral and/or written comprehensive exams; for Ed S, thesis, oral exam. *Entrance requirements:* For master's, GRE General Test, minimum overall undergraduate GPA of 2.5; for Ed S, GRE General Test, interview, master's degree, minimum GPA of 3.5, work experience. Additional exam requirements/recommendations for international students: Required—TOEFL (minimum score 500 paper-based). Electronic applications accepted. *Faculty research:* Character education, school accountability, computer applications for school administrators.

Mount Mercy University, Program in Education, Cedar Rapids, IA 52402-4797. Offers reading (MA Ed); special education (MA Ed). *Entrance requirements:* For master's, minimum cumulative GPA of 3.0, 2 letters of recommendation, resume, valid teaching license. Additional exam requirements/recommendations for international students: Required—TOEFL (minimum score 570 paper-based; 88 iBT). Electronic applications accepted.

Mount St. Joseph University, Graduate Education Program, Cincinnati, OH 45233-1670. Offers adolescent to young adult education (MA); dyslexia (Certificate); inclusive early childhood education (MA); instructional leadership (MA); middle childhood education (MA); multicultural special education (MA); Pre-K special needs (Certificate); principal licensure (MA); reading (Certificate); reading science (MA). *Accreditation:* Teacher Education Accreditation Council. Part-time and evening/weekend programs available. *Faculty:* 10 full-time (7 women), 7 part-time/adjunct (6 women). *Students:* 28 full-time (25 women), 95 part-time (76 women); includes 27 minority (19 Black or African American, non-Hispanic/Latino; 6 Hispanic/Latino; 2 Two or more races, non-Hispanic/Latino). Average age 36. 73 applicants, 44% accepted, 30 enrolled. In 2013, 69 master's awarded. *Degree requirements:* For master's, research project, student teaching, clinical and field-based experiences. *Entrance requirements:* For master's, GRE, PRAXIS II in teaching content area (math or science), 2 letters of recommendation, interview, resume. Additional exam requirements/recommendations for international students: Required—TOEFL (minimum score 560 paper-based; 83 iBT). *Application deadline:* Applications are processed on a rolling basis. Application fee: $50. Electronic applications accepted. *Expenses: Tuition:* Full-time $18,400; part-time $575 per credit hour. *Required fees:* $450; $450 per year. Part-time tuition and fees vary according to course load, degree level and program. *Financial support:* Scholarships/grants available. Financial award applicants required to submit FAFSA. *Faculty research:* Foreign and second language learning problems/reading disabilities/hyperlexia, multicultural/bilingual special education, alternative educator licensure, science education, pedagogical content knowledge. *Unit head:* Dr. Mary West, Chair, 513-244-3263, Fax: 513-244-4867, E-mail: mary_west@mail.msj.edu. *Application contact:* Mary Brigham, Assistant Director of Graduate Recruitment, 513-244-4233, Fax: 513-244-4629, E-mail: mary_brigham@mail.msj.edu. Website: http://www.msj.edu/academics/graduate-programs/master-of-arts-initial-teacher-licensure-programs/.

Mount Saint Mary College, Division of Education, Newburgh, NY 12550-3494. Offers adolescence and special education (MS Ed); adolescence education (MS Ed); childhood and special education (MS Ed); childhood education (MS Ed); literacy (5-12) (Advanced Certificate); literacy (birth-6) (Advanced Certificate); literacy and special education (MS Ed); literacy/childhood (MS Ed); middle school (5-6) (MS Ed); middle school (7-9) (MS Ed); special education (1-6) (MS Ed); special education (7-12) (MS Ed). *Accreditation:* NCATE. Part-time and evening/weekend programs available. *Faculty:* 11 full-time (9 women), 9 part-time/adjunct (4 women). *Students:* 29 full-time (19 women), 142 part-time (117 women); includes 22 minority (5 Black or African American, non-Hispanic/Latino; 16 Hispanic/Latino; 1 Two or more races, non-Hispanic/Latino). Average age 29. 51 applicants, 65% accepted, 27 enrolled. In 2013, 72 master's awarded. *Application deadline:* Applications are processed on a rolling basis. Application fee: $45. Application fee is waived when completed online. *Expenses: Tuition:* Full-time $13,356; part-time $742 per credit. *Required fees:* $70 per semester. *Financial support:* In 2013–14, 69 students received support. Unspecified assistantships available. Financial award application deadline: 4/15; financial award applicants required to submit FAFSA. *Faculty research:* Learning and teaching styles, computers in special education, language development. *Unit head:* Dr. William Swart, Graduate Coordinator, 845-569-3149, Fax: 845-569-3535, E-mail: william.swart@msmc.edu. *Application contact:* Lisa Gallina, Director of Admissions for Graduate Programs and Adult Degree Completion, 845-569-3166, Fax: 845-569-3450, E-mail: lisa.gallina@msmc.edu. Website: http://www.msmc.edu/Academics/Graduate_Programs/Master_of_Science_in_Education.

Mount Saint Vincent University, Graduate Programs, Faculty of Education, Program in Literacy Education, Halifax, NS B3M 2J6, Canada. Offers M Ed, MA Ed, MA-R. Part-time and evening/weekend programs available. Postbaccalaureate distance learning degree programs offered (no on-campus study). *Degree requirements:* For master's, thesis (for some programs). *Entrance requirements:* For master's, minimum B average, 1 year of teaching experience, bachelor's degree in related field. Electronic applications accepted. *Faculty research:* Writing processes and instruction, assessment and evaluation of literacy education, critical literacy, early literacy development, gender and literacy.

Murray State University, College of Education, Department of Early Childhood and Elementary Education, Programs in Elementary Education/Reading and Writing, Murray, KY 42071. Offers elementary education (MA Ed, Ed S); reading and writing (MA Ed). *Accreditation:* NCATE. Part-time programs available. *Degree requirements:* For master's, comprehensive exam, thesis optional; for Ed S, comprehensive exam. *Entrance requirements:* For master's, minimum GPA of 2.5 for conditional admittance, 3.0 for unconditional; for Ed S, GRE General Test or MAT. Additional exam requirements/recommendations for international students: Required—TOEFL.

National Louis University, National College of Education, Chicago, IL 60603. Offers administration and supervision (M Ed, Ed D, CAS, Ed S); curriculum and instruction (M Ed, MS Ed, CAS); early childhood administration (M Ed, CAS); early childhood education (M Ed, MAT, MS Ed, CAS); education (Ed D); educational psychology/human learning and development (M Ed, MS Ed, CAS, Ed S); elementary education (MAT); interdisciplinary curriculum and instruction (M Ed); mathematics education (M Ed, MS Ed, CAS); reading and language (M Ed, MS Ed, CAS); school psychology (M Ed, Ed S); science education (M Ed, MS Ed, CAS); secondary education (MAT); special education (M Ed, MAT, CAS); technology in education (M Ed, CAS). *Accreditation:* NCATE. Part-time and evening/weekend programs available. *Degree requirements:* For doctorate, comprehensive exam, thesis/dissertation. *Entrance requirements:* For master's, MAT or GRE, minimum GPA of 3.0; for doctorate, GRE General Test, minimum GPA of 3.25, interview, resume, writing sample, 4 recommendations.

Additional exam requirements/recommendations for international students: Required—TOEFL (minimum score 550 paper-based; 79 iBT).

National University, Academic Affairs, School of Education, La Jolla, CA 92037-1011. Offers applied behavior analysis (Certificate); applied school leadership (MS); autism (Certificate); best practices (Certificate); e-teaching and learning (Certificate); early childhood education (Certificate); education (MA), including best practices (M Ed, MA), e-teaching and learning (M Ed, MA), education technology, teacher leadership (M Ed, MA), teaching and learning in a global society (M Ed, MA), teaching mathematics (M Ed, MA); education with preliminary multiple or single subject (M Ed), including best practices (M Ed, MA), e-teaching and learning (M Ed, MA), educational technology (M Ed, MA), teacher leadership (M Ed, MA), teaching and learning in a global society (M Ed, MA), teaching mathematics (M Ed, MA); educational administration (MS); educational and instructional technology (MS); educational counseling (MS); educational technology (Certificate); higher education administration (MS); innovative school leadership (MS); instructional leadership (MS); juvenile justice special education (MS); reading (Certificate); school psychology (MS); special education (MS), including deaf and hard-of-hearing, mild/moderate disabilities, moderate/severe disabilities; teacher leadership (Certificate); teaching (MA), including applied behavioral analysis, autism, best practices (M Ed, MA), e-teaching and learning (M Ed, MA), early childhood education, educational technology (M Ed, MA), reading, special education, teacher leadership (M Ed, MA), teaching and learning in a global society (M Ed, MA), teaching mathematics (M Ed, MA); teaching mathematics (Certificate). Part-time and evening/weekend programs available. Postbaccalaureate distance learning degree programs offered (no on-campus study). *Faculty:* 72 full-time (43 women), 287 part-time/adjunct (170 women). *Students:* 2,433 full-time (1,744 women), 2,017 part-time (1,371 women); includes 1,834 minority (358 Black or African American, non-Hispanic/Latino; 15 American Indian or Alaska Native, non-Hispanic/Latino; 250 Asian, non-Hispanic/Latino; 1,056 Hispanic/Latino; 29 Native Hawaiian or other Pacific Islander, non-Hispanic/Latino; 126 Two or more races, non-Hispanic/Latino), 1 international. Average age 34. 1,339 applicants, 100% accepted, 1035 enrolled. In 2013, 1,662 master's awarded. *Degree requirements:* For master's, thesis (for some programs). *Entrance requirements:* For master's, interview, minimum GPA of 2.5. Additional exam requirements/recommendations for international students: Required—TOEFL (minimum score 550 paper-based; 79 iBT), IELTS (minimum score 6). *Application deadline:* Applications are processed on a rolling basis. Application fee: $60 ($65 for international students). Electronic applications accepted. *Expenses: Tuition:* Full-time $13,824; part-time $1728 per course. One-time fee: $160. *Financial support:* Career-related internships or fieldwork, institutionally sponsored loans, scholarships/grants, and tuition waivers (partial) available. Support available to part-time students. Financial award application deadline: 6/30. *Faculty research:* Teacher education, special education, educational effectiveness, teaching abroad, school counseling. *Unit head:* School of Education, 800-628-8648, E-mail: soe@nu.edu. *Application contact:* Louis Cruz, Interim Vice President for Enrollment Services, 800-628-8648, E-mail: advisor@nu.edu.
Website: http://www.nu.edu/OurPrograms/SchoolOfEducation.html.

Nazareth College of Rochester, Graduate Studies, Department of Education, Program in Literacy Education, Rochester, NY 14618-3790. Offers MS Ed. *Accreditation:* Teacher Education Accreditation Council. Part-time and evening/weekend programs available. *Entrance requirements:* For master's, minimum GPA of 3.0.

New Jersey City University, Graduate Studies and Continuing Education, Debra Cannon Partridge Wolfe College of Education, Department of Literacy Education, Jersey City, NJ 07305-1597. Offers elementary school reading (MA); reading specialist (MA); secondary school reading (MA). Part-time and evening/weekend programs available. *Faculty:* 3 full-time (2 women), 1 (woman) part-time/adjunct. *Students:* 1 full-time (0 women), 34 part-time (30 women); includes 12 minority (5 Black or African American, non-Hispanic/Latino; 7 Hispanic/Latino). Average age 35. In 2013, 11 master's awarded. *Degree requirements:* For master's, comprehensive exam. *Entrance requirements:* Additional exam requirements/recommendations for international students: Required—TOEFL (minimum score 61 iBT). *Application deadline:* For fall admission, 8/1 priority date for domestic students; for spring admission, 12/1 for domestic students. Applications are processed on a rolling basis. Application fee: $0. *Expenses: Tuition, area resident:* Part-time $527.90 per credit. Tuition, nonresident: part-time $947.75 per credit. *Financial support:* Research assistantships and unspecified assistantships available. *Faculty research:* Reading clinic. *Unit head:* Dr. Mary McCullough, Chairperson, 201-200-3521, E-mail: mmccullough@njcu.edu. *Application contact:* Dr. William Bajor, Dean of Graduate Studies, 201-200-3409, Fax: 201-200-3411, E-mail: wbajor@njcu.edu.

Newman University, Master of Education Program, Wichita, KS 67213-2097. Offers building leadership (MS Ed); curriculum and instruction (MS Ed), including English as a second language, reading specialist; organizational leadership (MS Ed). *Accreditation:* NCATE. Part-time and evening/weekend programs available. Postbaccalaureate distance learning degree programs offered (no on-campus study). *Faculty:* 3 full-time (1 woman), 22 part-time/adjunct (all women). *Students:* 19 full-time (15 women), 498 part-time (407 women); includes 66 minority (19 Black or African American, non-Hispanic/Latino; 5 American Indian or Alaska Native, non-Hispanic/Latino; 10 Asian, non-Hispanic/Latino; 27 Hispanic/Latino; 1 Native Hawaiian or other Pacific Islander, non-Hispanic/Latino; 4 Two or more races, non-Hispanic/Latino). Average age 37. 67 applicants, 73% accepted, 35 enrolled. In 2013, 53 master's awarded. *Degree requirements:* For master's, thesis optional. *Entrance requirements:* For master's, 3 years' full-time teaching experience, minimum GPA of 3.0, writing sample, 2 letters of recommendation, evidence of teaching certification. Additional exam requirements/recommendations for international students: Required—TOEFL (minimum score 600 paper-based; 100 iBT). *Application deadline:* For fall admission, 8/15 priority date for domestic students, 7/15 priority date for international students; for spring admission, 1/10 priority date for domestic students, 11/15 priority date for international students. Applications are processed on a rolling basis. Application fee: $25 ($40 for international students). Electronic applications accepted. *Expenses:* Contact institution. *Financial support:* Application deadline: 8/15; applicants required to submit FAFSA. *Unit head:* Dr. Gina Marx, Director of Graduate Education, 316-942-4291 Ext. 2416, Fax: 316-942-4483, E-mail: marxg@newmanu.edu. *Application contact:* Linda Kay Sabala, Director of Graduate Admissions, 316-942-4291 Ext. 2230, Fax: 316-942-4483, E-mail: sabalal@newmanu.edu.
Website: http://www.newmanu.edu/studynu/graduate/master-science-education.

New York University, Steinhardt School of Culture, Education, and Human Development, Department of Teaching and Learning, Program in Literacy Education, New York, NY 10012-1019. Offers grades 5-12 (MA). *Accreditation:* Teacher Education Accreditation Council. Part-time programs available. *Faculty:* 1 (woman) full-time. *Students:* 8 full-time (5 women), 7 part-time (all women); includes 3 minority (1 Black or African American, non-Hispanic/Latino; 1 Asian, non-Hispanic/Latino; 1 Hispanic/Latino), 2 international. Average age 26. 52 applicants, 94% accepted, 11 enrolled. In 2013, 17 master's awarded. *Degree requirements:* For master's, thesis (for some programs), fieldwork. *Entrance requirements:* For master's, teacher certification. Additional exam requirements/recommendations for international students: Required—TOEFL (minimum score 100 iBT). *Application deadline:* For fall admission, 2/1 priority date for domestic and international students. Applications are processed on a rolling basis. Application fee: $75. Electronic applications accepted. *Expenses: Tuition:* Full-time $35,856; part-time $1494 per unit. *Required fees:* $1408; $64 per unit. $473 per term. Tuition and fees vary according to course load and program. *Financial support:* Career-related internships or fieldwork, Federal Work-Study, institutionally sponsored loans, scholarships/grants, and tuition waivers (partial) available. Support available to part-time students. Financial award application deadline: 2/1; financial award applicants required to submit FAFSA. *Faculty research:* Early literacy intervention and development, psycho and sociolinguistics, multicultural education, literacy assessment and instruction. *Unit head:* Prof. Kay Stahl, Director, 212-998-5204, Fax: 212-995-4049, E-mail: kay.stahl@nyu.edu. *Application contact:* Office of Graduate Admissions, 212-998-5030, Fax: 212-995-4328, E-mail: steinhardt.gradadmissions@nyu.edu.
Website: http://steinhardt.nyu.edu/teachlearn/literacy.

Niagara University, Graduate Division of Education, Concentration in Literacy Instruction, Niagara Falls, NY 14109. Offers MS Ed. Part-time programs available. *Students:* 22 full-time (all women), 25 part-time (21 women); includes 3 minority (1 Black or African American, non-Hispanic/Latino; 2 Hispanic/Latino). Average age 25. In 2013, 36 master's awarded. *Entrance requirements:* Additional exam requirements/recommendations for international students: Required—TOEFL (minimum score 550 paper-based, 79 iBT) or IELTS (minimum score 6). *Application deadline:* For fall admission, 8/1 for domestic students. Application fee: $30. Tuition and fees vary according to program. *Financial support:* Research assistantships with full and partial tuition reimbursements, teaching assistantships with full and partial tuition reimbursements, career-related internships or fieldwork, Federal Work-Study, scholarships/grants, and unspecified assistantships available. Financial award application deadline: 4/15. *Unit head:* Dr. Robin Erwin, Chair, 716-286-8551, E-mail: rerwin@niagara.edu. *Application contact:* Evan Pierce, Associate Director for Graduate Recruitment, 716-286-8769, Fax: 716-286-8170, E-mail: epierce@niagara.edu.
Website: http://www.niagara.edu/literacy-instruction.

North Carolina Agricultural and Technical State University, School of Graduate Studies, School of Education, Department of Curriculum and Instruction, Program in Reading Education, Greensboro, NC 27411. Offers MA Ed. *Accreditation:* NCATE. Part-time and evening/weekend programs available. *Degree requirements:* For master's, comprehensive exam, comprehensive portfolio. *Entrance requirements:* For master's, GRE General Test, minimum GPA of 3.0.

Northeastern Illinois University, College of Graduate Studies and Research, College of Education, Program in Literacy Education, Chicago, IL 60625-4699. Offers MA. Part-time and evening/weekend programs available. *Degree requirements:* For master's, comprehensive exam, thesis optional. *Entrance requirements:* For master's, previous course work in psychology or tests and measurements, minimum GPA of 2.75. Additional exam requirements/recommendations for international students: Required—TOEFL (minimum score 550 paper-based; 79 iBT). Electronic applications accepted. *Faculty research:* Early literacy, reading disabilities, cognitive processes, multicultural and linguistic diversity, use of literature in the classroom.

Northeastern State University, College of Education, Department of Curriculum and Instruction, Program in Reading, Tahlequah, OK 74464-2399. Offers M Ed. Part-time and evening/weekend programs available. *Faculty:* 20 full-time (15 women), 7 part-time/adjunct (2 women). *Students:* 3 full-time (all women), 73 part-time (all women); includes 24 minority (13 American Indian or Alaska Native, non-Hispanic/Latino; 1 Asian, non-Hispanic/Latino; 3 Hispanic/Latino; 7 Two or more races, non-Hispanic/Latino). Average age 37. In 2013, 57 master's awarded. *Degree requirements:* For master's, thesis. *Entrance requirements:* For master's, MAT or GRE, minimum GPA of 2.5. Additional exam requirements/recommendations for international students: Required—TOEFL. *Application deadline:* For fall admission, 6/1 priority date for domestic students. Applications are processed on a rolling basis. Application fee: $25. Electronic applications accepted. *Expenses:* Tuition, state resident: full-time $3029; part-time $168.25 per credit hour. Tuition, nonresident: full-time $7709; part-time $428.25 per credit hour. *Required fees:* $35.90 per credit hour. *Financial support:* Teaching assistantships and Federal Work-Study available. Financial award application deadline: 3/1. *Unit head:* Dr. Mindy Smith, Associate Professor, 918-449-6587, Fax: 918-458-2351, E-mail: smith071@nsuok.edu. *Application contact:* Margie Railey, Administrative Assistant, 918-456-5511 Ext. 2093, Fax: 918-458-2061, E-mail: railey@nsouk.edu.
Website: http://academics.nsuok.edu/education/GraduatePrograms/Reading.aspx.

Northern Illinois University, Graduate School, College of Education, Department of Literacy Education, De Kalb, IL 60115-2854. Offers curriculum and instruction (Ed D), including reading; literacy education (MS Ed). Part-time and evening/weekend programs available. *Faculty:* 12 full-time (10 women), 1 part-time/adjunct (0 women). *Students:* 7 full-time (all women), 115 part-time (110 women); includes 14 minority (3 Black or African American, non-Hispanic/Latino; 4 Asian, non-Hispanic/Latino; 7 Hispanic/Latino), 5 international. Average age 36. 28 applicants, 61% accepted, 4 enrolled. In 2013, 44 master's, 1 doctorate awarded. *Degree requirements:* For master's, comprehensive exam, thesis optional; for doctorate, thesis/dissertation, candidacy exam, dissertation defense. *Entrance requirements:* For master's, GRE General Test or MAT, minimum undergraduate GPA of 2.75; for doctorate, GRE General Test, minimum GPA of 2.75 (undergraduate), 3.2 (graduate). Additional exam requirements/recommendations for international students: Required—TOEFL (minimum score 550 paper-based). *Application deadline:* For fall admission, 3/1 priority date for domestic students, 5/1 for international students; for spring admission, 11/1 for domestic students, 10/1 for international students. Applications are processed on a rolling basis. Application fee: $40. Electronic applications accepted. *Financial support:* In 2013–14, 2 research assistantships with full tuition reimbursements, 17 teaching assistantships with full tuition reimbursements were awarded; fellowships with full tuition reimbursements, career-related internships or fieldwork, Federal Work-Study, scholarships/grants, tuition waivers (full), and staff assistantships also available. Support available to part-time students. Financial award applicants required to submit FAFSA. *Faculty research:* Early reading development, literacy for bilingual students, family literacy, expository writing, fluency. *Unit head:* Dr. Jennifer Berne, Chair, 815-753-8556, E-mail: ltcy@niu.edu. *Application contact:* Graduate School Office, 815-753-0395, E-mail: gradsch@niu.edu.
Website: http://www.cedu.niu.edu/ltcy/.

Northern Michigan University, College of Graduate Studies, College of Health Sciences and Professional Studies, School of Education, Leadership and Public Service, Marquette, MI 49855-5301. Offers administration and supervision (MAE, Ed S); elementary education (MAE); instruction (MAE); learning disabilities (MAE); public administration (MPA), including criminal justice administration, healthcare administration, human resource administration, public management, state and local government; reading education (MAE, Ed S), including literacy leadership (Ed S), reading (MAE), reading specialist (MAE); school guidance counseling (MAE); science education (MS); secondary education (MAE). *Accreditation:* Teacher Education Accreditation Council. Part-time programs available. Postbaccalaureate distance learning degree programs offered (no on-campus study). *Faculty:* 12 full-time (7 women), 3 part-time/adjunct (1 woman). *Students:* 25 full-time (16 women), 170 part-time (130 women); includes 12 minority (2 Black or African American, non-Hispanic/Latino; 5 American Indian or Alaska Native, non-Hispanic/Latino; 4 Hispanic/Latino; 1

Two or more races, non-Hispanic/Latino), 1 international. Average age 33. 39 applicants, 95% accepted, 35 enrolled. In 2013, 48 master's, 5 other advanced degrees awarded. *Degree requirements:* For master's, thesis (for some programs). *Entrance requirements:* For master's, minimum GPA of 3.0. Additional exam requirements/recommendations for international students: Required—TOEFL (minimum score 550 paper-based; 79 iBT), IELTS (minimum score 6.5). *Application deadline:* For fall admission, 7/1 priority date for domestic students; for winter admission, 11/15 for domestic students; for spring admission, 3/17 for domestic students. Applications are processed on a rolling basis. Application fee: $50. *Expenses:* Tuition, state resident: part-time $427 per credit. Tuition, nonresident: part-time $614.50 per credit. *Required fees:* $325 per semester. Tuition and fees vary according to course load and program. *Financial support:* In 2013–14, 2 research assistantships were awarded; career-related internships or fieldwork, Federal Work-Study, institutionally sponsored loans, and unspecified assistantships also available. Support available to part-time students. Financial award application deadline: 3/1. *Unit head:* Dr. Joseph Lubig, Associate Dean, School of Education, Leadership, and Public Service, 906-227-2780, Fax: 906-227-2764, E-mail: jlubig@nmu.edu. *Application contact:* Nancy E. Carter, Certification Counselor and Graduate Programs Coordinator, 906-227-1625, Fax: 906-227-2764, E-mail: ncarter@nmu.edu.
Website: http://www.nmu.edu/education/.

Northwestern Oklahoma State University, School of Professional Studies, Reading Specialist Program, Alva, OK 73717-2799. Offers M Ed. *Accreditation:* NCATE. Part-time programs available. *Degree requirements:* For master's, thesis optional, portfolio. *Entrance requirements:* For master's, GRE General Test or MAT, minimum GPA of 2.75.

Northwestern State University of Louisiana, Graduate Studies and Research, College of Education and Human Development, Programs in Educational Leadership and Instruction, Natchitoches, LA 71497. Offers counseling (Ed S); educational leadership (M Ed, Ed S); educational technology (Ed S); elementary teaching (Ed S); reading (Ed S); secondary teaching (Ed S); special education (Ed S). *Accreditation:* NASAD. *Degree requirements:* For master's, comprehensive exam, thesis (for some programs). *Entrance requirements:* For master's and Ed S, GRE General Test. Additional exam requirements/recommendations for international students: Required—TOEFL. Electronic applications accepted.

Northwest Missouri State University, Graduate School, College of Education and Human Services, Department of Professional Education, Program in Reading, Maryville, MO 64468-6001. Offers MS Ed. *Accreditation:* NCATE. Part-time programs available. *Degree requirements:* For master's, comprehensive exam. *Entrance requirements:* For master's, GRE General Test, minimum undergraduate GPA of 2.75, teaching certificate, writing sample. Additional exam requirements/recommendations for international students: Required—TOEFL (minimum score 550 paper-based).

Northwest Nazarene University, Graduate Studies, Program in Teacher Education, Nampa, ID 83686-5897. Offers curriculum and instruction (M Ed); educational leadership (M Ed, Ed D, Ed S); exceptional child (M Ed); reading education (M Ed). *Accreditation:* ACA (one or more programs are accredited); NCATE. Part-time programs available. Postbaccalaureate distance learning degree programs offered (no on-campus study). *Faculty:* 6 full-time (5 women), 29 part-time/adjunct (16 women). *Students:* 101 full-time (66 women), 98 part-time (74 women); includes 14 minority (1 Asian, non-Hispanic/Latino; 10 Hispanic/Latino; 3 Two or more races, non-Hispanic/Latino), 12 international. Average age 38. In 2013, 60 master's, 28 doctorates, 14 other advanced degrees awarded. *Degree requirements:* For master's, comprehensive exam (for some programs), action research project; for doctorate, thesis/dissertation; for Ed S, comprehensive exam (for some programs). *Entrance requirements:* For master's, minimum undergraduate GPA of 2.8 overall or 3.0 during final 30 semester credits, undergraduate degree; for doctorate, Ed S or equivalent; for Ed S, EDS - MEd required. Additional exam requirements/recommendations for international students: Recommended—TOEFL (minimum score 80 iBT). *Application deadline:* For fall admission, 9/1 for domestic students. Applications are processed on a rolling basis. Application fee: $50. *Expenses: Tuition:* Part-time $565 per credit. *Financial support:* In 2013–14, research assistantships (averaging $5,000 per year) were awarded. *Faculty research:* Action research, cooperative learning, accountability, institutional accreditation. *Unit head:* Dr. Paula Kellerer, Chair, 208-467-8729, Fax: 208-467-8562. *Application contact:* Lynette Kingsmore, Admissions Counselor, 208-467-8107, Fax: 208-467-8786, E-mail: lkingsmore@nnu.edu.
Website: http://www.nnu.edu/graded/.

Notre Dame College, Graduate Programs, South Euclid, OH 44121-4293. Offers mild/moderate needs (M Ed); reading (M Ed); security policy studies (MA, Graduate Certificate); technology (M Ed). Part-time and evening/weekend programs available. *Degree requirements:* For master's, thesis. *Entrance requirements:* For master's, GRE General Test, MAT, minimum undergraduate GPA of 2.75, valid teaching certificate, bachelor's degree in an education-related field from accredited college or university, official transcripts of most recent college work. *Faculty research:* Cognitive psychology, teaching critical thinking in the classroom.

Oakland University, Graduate Study and Lifelong Learning, School of Education and Human Services, Department of Reading and Language Arts, Rochester, MI 48309-4401. Offers advanced microcomputer applications (Certificate); reading (Certificate); reading and language arts (MAT); reading education (PhD); reading, language arts and literature (Certificate). *Accreditation:* Teacher Education Accreditation Council. *Faculty:* 10 full-time (6 women), 7 part-time/adjunct (all women). *Students:* 25 full-time (24 women), 100 part-time (96 women); includes 11 minority (8 Black or African American, non-Hispanic/Latino; 1 Asian, non-Hispanic/Latino; 1 Hispanic/Latino; 1 Two or more races, non-Hispanic/Latino), 4 international. Average age 35. 45 applicants, 69% accepted, 31 enrolled. In 2013, 101 master's, 5 doctorates awarded. *Degree requirements:* For doctorate, thesis/dissertation. *Entrance requirements:* For master's, minimum GPA of 3.0 for unconditional admission; for doctorate, MAT, minimum GPA of 3.0 for unconditional admission. *Application deadline:* For fall admission, 3/1 for domestic and international students. Application fee: $0. Electronic applications accepted. *Financial support:* Career-related internships or fieldwork, Federal Work-Study, institutionally sponsored loans, and tuition waivers (full) available. Financial award application deadline: 3/1; financial award applicants required to submit FAFSA. *Faculty research:* OSU-ARRA- Reading Recovery i3. *Total annual research expenditures:* $857,654. *Unit head:* Dr. Jane Cipielewski, Chair, 248-370-3065, Fax: 248-370-4367. *Application contact:* Dr. Toni Walters, Coordinator, 248-370-4205, Fax: 248-370-4367, E-mail: twalters@oakland.edu.

Ohio University, Graduate College, Gladys W. and David H. Patton College of Education and Human Services, Department of Teacher Education, Athens, OH 45701-2979. Offers adolescent to young adult education (M Ed); curriculum and instruction (M Ed, PhD); early childhood/special education (M Ed); intervention specialist/mild-moderate needs (M Ed); intervention specialist/moderate-intensive needs (M Ed); mathematics education (PhD); middle childhood education (M Ed); reading education (M Ed); social studies education (PhD). Part-time and evening/weekend programs available. *Degree requirements:* For master's, thesis or alternative; for doctorate, comprehensive exam, thesis/dissertation. *Entrance requirements:* For master's, GRE General Test or MAT (if GPA is below 2.9); for doctorate, GRE General Test, minimum GPA of 3.4, work experience. Additional exam requirements/recommendations for international students: Required—TOEFL (minimum score 550 paper-based; 80 iBT) or IELTS (minimum score 6.5). Electronic applications accepted. *Faculty research:* Cognition literacy, character education, teacher's education reform, disabilities.

Old Dominion University, Darden College of Education, Program in Literacy Leadership, Norfolk, VA 23529. Offers PhD. Part-time and evening/weekend programs available. *Faculty:* 13 full-time (9 women). *Students:* 1 (woman) full-time, 6 part-time (all women); includes 2 minority (both Black or African American, non-Hispanic/Latino). Average age 43. 3 applicants, 67% accepted, 2 enrolled. In 2013, 1 doctorate awarded. *Degree requirements:* For doctorate, comprehensive exam, thesis/dissertation. *Entrance requirements:* For doctorate, GRE, minimum GPA of 3.0, MS in reading or related degree, letters of recommendation. Additional exam requirements/recommendations for international students: Required—TOEFL (minimum score 600 paper-based). *Application deadline:* For fall admission, 6/1 for domestic students, 4/15 for international students; for winter admission, 11/1 for domestic students, 10/1 for international students; for spring admission, 11/1 for domestic students, 10/1 for international students; for summer admission, 2/1 for domestic and international students. Applications are processed on a rolling basis. Application fee: $50. Electronic applications accepted. *Expenses:* Tuition, state resident: full-time $9888; part-time $412 per credit. Tuition, nonresident: full-time $25,152; part-time $1048 per credit. *Required fees:* $59 per semester. One-time fee: $50. *Financial support:* In 2013–14, 1 teaching assistantship with full tuition reimbursement (averaging $15,000 per year) was awarded. *Faculty research:* Literacy for students with special needs, children's Reading First instruction, reading in the content area. *Total annual research expenditures:* $600,000. *Unit head:* Dr. Richard Overbaugh, Graduate Program Director, 757-683-3284, E-mail: roverbau@odu.edu. *Application contact:* William Heffelfinger, Director of Graduate Admissions, 757-683-5554, Fax: 757-683-3255, E-mail: gradadmit@odu.edu.
Website: http://education.odu.edu/eci/litphd/.

Old Dominion University, Darden College of Education, Program in Reading Education, Norfolk, VA 23529. Offers reading specialist (MS Ed). *Accreditation:* NCATE. Part-time and evening/weekend programs available. Postbaccalaureate distance learning degree programs offered (no on-campus study). *Faculty:* 7 full-time (6 women), 12 part-time/adjunct (11 women). *Students:* 1 (woman) full-time, 29 part-time (all women); includes 7 minority (all Black or African American, non-Hispanic/Latino). Average age 36. 33 applicants, 55% accepted, 18 enrolled. In 2013, 24 master's awarded. *Degree requirements:* For master's, thesis optional. *Entrance requirements:* For master's, GRE General Test or MAT, minimum GPA of 3.0 in major, 2.8 overall; teaching certificate. Additional exam requirements/recommendations for international students: Required—TOEFL. *Application deadline:* For fall admission, 6/1 for domestic students, 4/15 for international students; for spring admission, 11/1 for domestic students, 10/1 for international students; for summer admission, 3/1 for domestic students. Applications are processed on a rolling basis. Application fee: $50. Electronic applications accepted. *Expenses:* Tuition, state resident: full-time $9888; part-time $412 per credit. Tuition, nonresident: full-time $25,152; part-time $1048 per credit. *Required fees:* $59 per semester. One-time fee: $50. *Financial support:* In 2013–14, 7 students received support. Application deadline: 2/15; applicants required to submit FAFSA. *Faculty research:* Metacognition and reading, strategies for improving comprehension in reading science, reading in content areas, vocabulary instruction for adolescents, literacy with special needs children, Reading First instruction, reading in the content area, vocabulary, diversity and literacy. *Total annual research expenditures:* $150,000. *Unit head:* Dr. Tom Bean, Graduate Program Director, 757-683-3284, Fax: 757-683-5862, E-mail: tbean@odu.edu. *Application contact:* William Heffelfinger, Director of Graduate Admissions, 757-683-5554, Fax: 757-683-3255, E-mail: gradadmit@odu.edu.
Website: http://education.odu.edu/eci/reading/masters.shtml.

Olivet Nazarene University, Graduate School, Division of Education, Program in Reading Specialist, Bourbonnais, IL 60914. Offers MAE.

Our Lady of the Lake University of San Antonio, School of Professional Studies, Program in Curriculum and Instruction, San Antonio, TX 78207-4689. Offers bilingual education (M Ed); early childhood education (M Ed); English as a second language (M Ed); integrated math teaching (M Ed); integrated science teaching (M Ed); reading specialist (M Ed). Part-time and evening/weekend programs available. *Faculty:* 6 full-time (4 women), 3 part-time/adjunct (all women). *Students:* 4 full-time (all women), 84 part-time (72 women); includes 52 minority (2 Black or African American, non-Hispanic/Latino; 2 Asian, non-Hispanic/Latino; 48 Hispanic/Latino). Average age 40. 9 applicants, 56% accepted, 1 enrolled. In 2013, 8 master's awarded. *Degree requirements:* For master's, comprehensive exam. *Entrance requirements:* For master's, GRE General Test or MAT. Additional exam requirements/recommendations for international students: Required—TOEFL. *Application deadline:* For fall admission, 4/1 priority date for domestic and international students; for spring admission, 11/1 priority date for domestic and international students; for summer admission, 2/1 priority date for domestic students, 4/1 priority date for international students. Applications are processed on a rolling basis. Application fee: $25 ($50 for international students). Electronic applications accepted. *Expenses: Tuition:* Full-time $9120; part-time $760 per credit. *Required fees:* $698; $334 per trimester. Tuition and fees vary according to course load, degree level, campus/location and program. *Financial support:* Research assistantships, teaching assistantships, career-related internships or fieldwork, Federal Work-Study, institutionally sponsored loans, scholarships/grants, and tuition waivers (partial) available. Support available to part-time students. Financial award application deadline: 4/1. *Faculty research:* Professional educator to understand and meet the comprehensive needs of a diverse student population, life-long learners, innovative practices. *Unit head:* Dr. Jerrie Jackson, 210-434-6711 Ext. 2698, E-mail: jjackson@lake.ollusa.edu. *Application contact:* Graduate Admission, 210-431-3961, Fax: 210-431-4013, E-mail: gradadm@lake.ollusa.edu.
Website: http://www.ollusa.edu/s/1190/ollu-3-column-noads.aspx?sid=1190&gid=1&pgid=4173.

Pace University, School of Education, New York, NY 10038. Offers adolescent education (MST); childhood education (MST); early childhood development, learning and intervention (MST); educational leadership (MS Ed); educational technology studies (MS); inclusive adolescent education (MST); literacy (MS Ed); school business management (Certificate); special education (MS Ed). *Accreditation:* NCATE. Part-time and evening/weekend programs available. *Students:* 186 full-time (154 women), 441 part-time (315 women); includes 209 minority (89 Black or African American, non-Hispanic/Latino; 2 American Indian or Alaska Native, non-Hispanic/Latino; 30 Asian, non-Hispanic/Latino; 74 Hispanic/Latino; 1 Native Hawaiian or other Pacific Islander, non-Hispanic/Latino; 13 Two or more races, non-Hispanic/Latino), 7 international. Average age 29. 207 applicants, 71% accepted, 105 enrolled. In 2013, 296 master's, 25 other advanced degrees awarded. *Degree requirements:* For master's, internship. *Entrance requirements:* For master's, interview, teaching certificate. Additional exam requirements/recommendations for international students: Required—TOEFL. *Application deadline:* For fall admission, 8/1 priority date for domestic students, 6/1 for international students; for spring admission, 12/1 priority date for domestic students, 10/1 for international students. Applications are processed on a rolling basis. Application

fee: $70. Electronic applications accepted. *Expenses:* Contact institution. *Financial support:* Research assistantships, career-related internships or fieldwork, and Federal Work-Study available. Support available to part-time students. Financial award applicants required to submit FAFSA. *Faculty research:* Teacher education, technology in education, STEM, literacy education, special education. *Total annual research expenditures:* $1.3 million. *Unit head:* Dr. Andrea M. Spencer, Dean, School of Education, 914-773-3341, E-mail: aspencer@pace.edu. *Application contact:* Susan Ford-Goldschein, Director of Graduate Admissions, 212-346-1660, Fax: 212-346-1585, E-mail: gradnyc@pace.edu.
Website: http://www.pace.edu/school-of-education.

Park University, School of Graduate and Professional Studies, Kansas City, MO 54105. Offers adult education (M Ed); business and government leadership (Graduate Certificate); business, government, and global society (MPA); communication and leadership (MA); creative and life writing (Graduate Certificate); disaster and emergency management (MPA, Graduate Certificate); educational leadership (M Ed); finance (MBA, Graduate Certificate); general business (MBA); global business (Graduate Certificate); healthcare administration (MHA); healthcare services management and leadership (Graduate Certificate); international business (MBA); language and literacy (M Ed), including English for speakers of other languages, special reading teacher/ literacy coach; leadership of international healthcare organizations (Graduate Certificate); management information systems (MBA, Graduate Certificate); music performance (ADP, Graduate Certificate), including cello (MM, ADP), piano (MM, ADP), viola (MM, ADP), violin (MM, ADP); nonprofit and community services management (MPA); nonprofit leadership (Graduate Certificate); performance (MM), including cello (MM, ADP), piano (MM, ADP), viola (MM, ADP), violin (MM, ADP); public management (MPA); social work (MSW); teacher leadership (M Ed), including curriculum and assessment, instructional leader. Part-time and evening/weekend programs available. Postbaccalaureate distance learning degree programs offered (no on-campus study). *Students:* 862 full-time (482 women); includes 55 minority (30 Black or African American, non-Hispanic/Latino; 2 American Indian or Alaska Native, non-Hispanic/ Latino; 4 Asian, non-Hispanic/Latino; 14 Hispanic/Latino; 5 Two or more races, non-Hispanic/Latino), 141 international. Average age 34. 497 applicants, 62% accepted, 119 enrolled. In 2013, 281 master's, 14 other advanced degrees awarded. *Degree requirements:* For master's, comprehensive exam (for some programs), thesis (for some programs), internship (for some programs); exam (for some programs). *Entrance requirements:* For master's, GRE or GMAT (for some programs), teacher certification (for some M Ed programs), letters of recommendation, essay, resume (for some programs). Additional exam requirements/recommendations for international students: Required—TOEFL (minimum score 550 paper-based; 79 iBT), IELTS (minimum score 6). *Application deadline:* For fall admission, 8/1 priority date for domestic students, 7/15 priority date for international students; for spring admission, 1/1 priority date for domestic students, 11/1 priority date for international students. Applications are processed on a rolling basis. Application fee: $50 ($100 for international students). Electronic applications accepted. *Financial support:* In 2013–14, 2 research assistantships with full tuition reimbursements (averaging $15,760 per year) were awarded. Financial award applicants required to submit FAFSA. *Unit head:* Dr. Laurie Dipadova-Stocks, Dean of Graduate and Professional Studies, 816-559-5624, Fax: 816-472-1173, E-mail: ldipadovastocks@park.edu. *Application contact:* Judith Appollis, Director of Graduate Admissions and Internationalization, School of Graduate and Professional Studies, 816-559-5627, Fax: 816-472-1173, E-mail: gradschool@park.edu.
Website: http://www.park.edu/grad.

Penn State Harrisburg, Graduate School, School of Behavioral Sciences and Education, Middletown, PA 17057-4898. Offers applied behavior analysis (MA); applied clinical psychology (MA); applied psychological research (MA); community psychology and social change (MA); health education (M Ed); literacy education (M Ed); teaching and curriculum (M Ed, Certificate); training and development (M Ed). Part-time and evening/weekend programs available. *Financial support:* Career-related internships or fieldwork available. *Unit head:* Dr. Mukund S. Kulkarni, Chancellor, 717-948-6105, Fax: 717-948-6452, E-mail: msk5@psu.edu. *Application contact:* Robert W. Coffman, Jr., Director of Enrollment Management, Admissions, 717-948-6250, Fax: 717-948-6325, E-mail: ric1@psu.edu.
Website: http://harrisburg.psu.edu/behavioral-sciences-and-education/.

Pittsburg State University, Graduate School, College of Education, Department of Curriculum and Instruction, Pittsburg, KS 66762. Offers classroom reading teacher (MS); early childhood education (MS); elementary education (MS); reading (MS); reading specialist (MS); secondary education (MS); teaching (MAT). *Accreditation:* NCATE. *Degree requirements:* For master's, thesis or alternative. *Entrance requirements:* For master's, GRE or MAT.

Plymouth State University, College of Graduate Studies, Graduate Studies in Education, Program in Reading and Writing, Plymouth, NH 03264-1595. Offers M Ed. Part-time and evening/weekend programs available. *Degree requirements:* For master's, PRAXIS. *Entrance requirements:* For master's, GRE General Test or MAT, minimum GPA of 3.0.

Portland State University, Graduate Studies, School of Education, Department of Curriculum and Instruction, Portland, OR 97207-0751. Offers early childhood education (MA, MS); education (M Ed, MA, MS); educational leadership: curriculum and instruction (Ed D); educational media/school librarianship (MA, MS); elementary education (M Ed, MAT, MST); reading (MA, MS); secondary education (M Ed, MAT, MST). *Accreditation:* NCATE. Part-time programs available. *Faculty:* 22 full-time (15 women), 28 part-time/ adjunct (20 women). *Students:* 29 full-time (23 women), 162 part-time (123 women); includes 26 minority (3 Black or African American, non-Hispanic/Latino; 6 Asian, non-Hispanic/Latino; 13 Hispanic/Latino; 4 Two or more races, non-Hispanic/Latino), 6 international. Average age 36. 145 applicants, 69% accepted, 93 enrolled. In 2013, 257 master's, 5 doctorates awarded. *Degree requirements:* For master's, comprehensive exam, thesis or alternative; for doctorate, thesis/dissertation. *Entrance requirements:* For master's, California Basic Educational Skills Test, minimum GPA of 3.0 in upper-division course work or 2.75 overall. Additional exam requirements/recommendations for international students: Required—TOEFL (minimum score 550 paper-based). *Application deadline:* For fall admission, 4/1 for domestic and international students; for winter admission, 9/1 for domestic and international students; for spring admission, 11/1 for domestic and international students. Applications are processed on a rolling basis. Application fee: $50. *Expenses:* Tuition, state resident: full-time $9207; part-time $341 per credit. Tuition, nonresident: full-time $14,391; part-time $533 per credit. *Required fees:* $1263; $22 per credit. $98 per quarter. One-time fee: $150. Tuition and fees vary according to program. *Financial support:* In 2013–14, 1 research assistantship with full tuition reimbursement (averaging $6,248 per year), 2 teaching assistantships with full tuition reimbursements (averaging $7,755 per year) were awarded; career-related internships or fieldwork, Federal Work-Study, and institutionally sponsored loans also available. Support available to part-time students. Financial award application deadline: 3/1; financial award applicants required to submit FAFSA. *Faculty research:* Early literacy, characteristics of successful teachers of at-risk students, participation of women/minorities in technology courses, selection of cooperating teachers. *Total annual research expenditures:* $1 million. *Unit head:* Christine Chaille, Head, 503-725-4753,

Fax: 203-725-8475, E-mail: chaillec@pdx.edu. *Application contact:* Jake Fernandez, Department Assistant, 503-725-4756, Fax: 503-725-8475, E-mail: jifern@pdx.edu.
Website: http://www.ed.pdx.edu/ci/.

Providence College, Program in Literacy, Providence, RI 02918. Offers M Ed. Part-time and evening/weekend programs available. *Faculty:* 1 (woman) full-time, 11 part-time/adjunct (9 women). *Students:* 6 full-time (all women), 25 part-time (all women); includes 1 minority (Two or more races, non-Hispanic/Latino), 29 international. Average age 30. 1 applicant, 100% accepted, 1 enrolled. In 2013, 9 master's awarded. *Degree requirements:* For master's, comprehensive exam. *Entrance requirements:* For master's, GRE General Test. Additional exam requirements/recommendations for international students: Required—TOEFL (minimum score 550 paper-based; 80 iBT). *Application deadline:* For fall admission, 8/1 priority date for domestic and international students; for spring admission, 12/1 priority date for domestic and international students. Applications are processed on a rolling basis. Application fee: $55. *Expenses: Tuition:* Part-time $432 per credit. *Required fees:* $432 per credit. *Financial support:* Career-related internships or fieldwork, institutionally sponsored loans, and unspecified assistantships available. Support available to part-time students. Financial award application deadline: 8/1; financial award applicants required to submit FAFSA. *Unit head:* Dr. Beverly Paesano, Director, 401-865-1987, Fax: 401-865-1147, E-mail: bpaesano@providence.edu. *Application contact:* Rev. Mark D. Nowel, Dean of Undergraduate and Graduate Studies, 401-865-2649, Fax: 401-865-1496, E-mail: mnowel@providence.edu.
Website: http://www.providence.edu/professional-studies/graduate-degrees/Pages/master-education-literacy.aspx.

Purdue University, Graduate School, College of Education, Department of Curriculum and Instruction, West Lafayette, IN 47907. Offers agricultural and extension education (PhD, Ed S); agriculture and extension education (MS, MS Ed); art education (PhD); curriculum studies (MS Ed, PhD, Ed S); educational technology (MS Ed, PhD, Ed S); elementary education (MS Ed); family and consumer sciences education (MS Ed, PhD, Ed S); foreign language education (MS Ed, PhD, Ed S); industrial technology (PhD, Ed S); language arts (MS Ed, PhD, Ed S); literacy (MS Ed, PhD, Ed S); mathematics/ science education (MS, MS Ed, PhD, Ed S); social studies (MS Ed, PhD); social studies education (Ed S); vocational/industrial education (MS Ed, PhD, Ed S); vocational/ technical education (MS Ed, PhD, Ed S). *Accreditation:* NCATE. Part-time and evening/ weekend programs available. *Faculty:* 29 full-time (19 women), 33 part-time/adjunct (29 women). *Students:* 85 full-time (53 women), 271 part-time (195 women); includes 62 minority (19 Black or African American, non-Hispanic/Latino; 3 American Indian or Alaska Native, non-Hispanic/Latino; 13 Asian, non-Hispanic/Latino; 22 Hispanic/Latino; 1 Native Hawaiian or other Pacific Islander, non-Hispanic/Latino; 4 Two or more races, non-Hispanic/Latino), 41 international. Average age 36. 155 applicants, 71% accepted, 71 enrolled. In 2013, 60 master's, 20 doctorates awarded. *Degree requirements:* For master's, thesis optional; for doctorate, thesis/dissertation, oral and written exams; for Ed S, oral presentation, project. *Entrance requirements:* For master's, GRE General Test (if undergraduate GPA is below 3.0), minimum undergraduate GPA of 3.0 or equivalent; for doctorate, GRE General Test (minimum combined verbal and quantitative score of 1000, 300 for new scoring), minimum undergraduate GPA of 3.0 or equivalent; master's degree with minimum GPA of 3.0 or equivalent; for Ed S, GRE General Test (minimum combined verbal and quantitative score of 1000, 300 for new scoring), minimum undergraduate GPA of 3.0 or equivalent; master's degree. Additional exam requirements/recommendations for international students: Required—TOEFL (minimum score 550 paper-based; 77 iBT). *Application deadline:* For fall admission, 12/ 15 for domestic students, 3/1 for international students; for spring admission, 9/15 for domestic students, 8/1 for international students. Application fee: $60 ($75 for international students). Electronic applications accepted. *Financial support:* Fellowships with full tuition reimbursements, research assistantships with full tuition reimbursements, teaching assistantships with full tuition reimbursements, career-related internships or fieldwork, and tuition waivers (full) available. Support available to part-time students. Financial award application deadline: 3/1; financial award applicants required to submit FAFSA. *Faculty research:* Literacy acquisition and development, teacher beliefs and knowledge, recruitment and retention of underrepresented students, economic education, literacy discourse. *Unit head:* Dr. Phillip J. VanFossen, Head, 765-494-7935, Fax: 765-496-1622, E-mail: vanfoss@purdue.edu. *Application contact:* Cindy Blankenship, Graduate Contact, 765-494-2345, Fax: 765-494-5832, E-mail: prater0@purdue.edu.
Website: http://www.edci.purdue.edu/.

Queens College of the City University of New York, Division of Graduate Studies, Division of Education, Department of Elementary and Early Childhood Education, Program in Literacy, Flushing, NY 11367-1597. Offers MS Ed. Part-time programs available. *Degree requirements:* For master's, research project. *Entrance requirements:* For master's, minimum GPA of 3.0. Additional exam requirements/recommendations for international students: Required—TOEFL.

Queens University of Charlotte, Wayland H. Cato, Jr. School of Education, Charlotte, NC 28274-0002. Offers education in literacy (M Ed); elementary education (MAT); school administration (MSA). *Accreditation:* NCATE. Part-time and evening/weekend programs available. *Degree requirements:* For master's, comprehensive exam. *Entrance requirements:* For master's, GRE General Test. *Expenses:* Contact institution.

Quincy University, Program in Education, Quincy, IL 62301-2699. Offers curriculum and instruction (MS Ed), including bilingual/English as a second language; leadership (MS Ed); reading education (MS Ed); special education (MS Ed); teacher leader (MS Ed). Part-time and evening/weekend programs available. Postbaccalaureate distance learning degree programs offered (minimal on-campus study). *Students:* 62 full-time (39 women), 97 part-time (68 women); includes 43 minority (29 Black or African American, non-Hispanic/Latino; 1 American Indian or Alaska Native, non-Hispanic/ Latino; 4 Asian, non-Hispanic/Latino; 9 Hispanic/Latino). In 2013, 105 master's awarded. *Degree requirements:* For master's, comprehensive exam (for some programs), thesis optional. *Entrance requirements:* For master's, MAT or GRE. Additional exam requirements/recommendations for international students: Required— TOEFL (minimum score 550 paper-based; 79 iBT). *Application deadline:* Applications are processed on a rolling basis. Application fee: $25. Electronic applications accepted. *Expenses: Tuition:* Full-time $9600; part-time $400 per semester hour. *Required fees:* $720; $30 per semester hour. Tuition and fees vary according to course load and program. *Financial support:* Applicants required to submit FAFSA. *Unit head:* Dr. Kristen R. Anguiano, Director, 217-228-5432 Ext. 3119, E-mail: anguikr@quincy.edu. *Application contact:* Office of Admissions, 217-228-5210, Fax: 217-228-5479, E-mail: admissions@quincy.edu.
Website: http://www.quincy.edu/academics/graduate-programs/education.

Radford University, College of Graduate and Professional Studies, College of Education and Human Development, School of Teacher Education and Leadership, Program in Literacy Education, Radford, VA 24142. Offers MS. *Accreditation:* NCATE. Part-time and evening/weekend programs available. *Faculty:* 3 full-time (2 women), 1 (woman) part-time/adjunct. *Students:* 13 part-time (12 women). Average age 37. 2 applicants, 100% accepted, 1 enrolled. In 2013, 19 master's awarded. *Degree requirements:* For master's, comprehensive exam. *Entrance requirements:* For

master's, minimum GPA of 2.75; copy of teaching license; 2 letters of reference; personal essay; resume; official transcripts. Additional exam requirements/recommendations for international students: Required—TOEFL (minimum score 550 paper-based; 79 iBT). *Application deadline:* For fall admission, 2/15 priority date for domestic students, 12/1 for international students; for spring admission, 7/1 for international students. Applications are processed on a rolling basis. Application fee: $50. Electronic applications accepted. *Expenses:* Tuition, state resident: full-time $6800; part-time $283 per credit hour. Tuition, nonresident: full-time $15,610; part-time $627 per credit hour. *Required fees:* $2944; $123 per credit hour. Tuition and fees vary according to program. *Financial support:* Career-related internships or fieldwork, Federal Work-Study, institutionally sponsored loans, scholarships/grants, and unspecified assistantships available. Financial award application deadline: 3/1; financial award applicants required to submit FAFSA. *Faculty research:* Leading in reading: instructional leadership for student achievement. *Unit head:* Dr. Jennifer J. Powell, Coordinator, 540-831-5311, Fax: 540-831-5059, E-mail: jjones292@radford.edu. *Application contact:* Rebecca Conner, Director, Graduate Enrollment, 540-831-6296, Fax: 540-831-6061, E-mail: gradcollege@radford.edu.
Website: http://www.radford.edu/content/cehd/home/departments/STEL/programs/master-literacy.html.

Regent University, Graduate School, School of Education, Virginia Beach, VA 23464-9800. Offers adult education (Ed D, PhD); advanced educational leadership (Ed D, PhD); career switcher with licensure (M Ed), including alternative licensure; character education (Ed D, PhD); Christian education leadership (Ed D); Christian school administration (M Ed); curriculum and instruction (M Ed); distance education (Ed D, PhD); educational leadership (M Ed); educational leadership - special education (Ed S); educational psychology (Ed D); elementary education (M Ed); higher education (Ed D, PhD); higher education leadership and management (Ed D); K-12 school leadership (Ed D, PhD); leadership in mathematics education (M Ed); reading specialist (M Ed); special education (M Ed, Ed D, PhD); student affairs (M Ed); TESOL (M Ed), including adult education, PreK-12. *Accreditation:* Teacher Education Accreditation Council. Part-time and evening/weekend programs available. Postbaccalaureate distance learning degree programs offered (minimal on-campus study). *Faculty:* 25 full-time (12 women), 50 part-time/adjunct (31 women). *Students:* 100 full-time (78 women), 754 part-time (614 women); includes 225 minority (191 Black or African American, non-Hispanic/Latino; 1 American Indian or Alaska Native, non-Hispanic/Latino; 7 Asian, non-Hispanic/Latino; 26 Hispanic/Latino), 16 international. Average age 39. 487 applicants, 63% accepted, 233 enrolled. In 2013, 202 master's, 19 doctorates awarded. *Degree requirements:* For master's, thesis or alternative; for doctorate, comprehensive exam, thesis/dissertation. *Entrance requirements:* For master's, MAT, minimum undergraduate GPA of 2.75, writing sample, resume, recommendations, interview; for doctorate, GRE, writing sample, 3 years of relevant professional experience, master's-level paper, copies of published work, resume, transcripts, interview, recommendations. Additional exam requirements/recommendations for international students: Required—TOEFL (minimum score 577 paper-based). *Application deadline:* For fall admission, 4/1 priority date for domestic students; for spring admission, 10/15 priority date for domestic students. Applications are processed on a rolling basis. Application fee: $50. Electronic applications accepted. Tuition and fees vary according to course load and degree level. *Financial support:* Fellowships, career-related internships or fieldwork, scholarships/grants, tuition waivers (full and partial), and unspecified assistantships available. Support available to part-time students. Financial award application deadline: 4/1; financial award applicants required to submit FAFSA. *Faculty research:* Character development and discipline for children, education leadership development, diversity in schools, classroom management, technology in education settings. *Unit head:* Dr. Alan Arroyo, Dean, 757-352-4261, Fax: 757-352-4318, E-mail: alanarr@regent.edu. *Application contact:* Matthew Chadwick, Director of Enrollment Support Services, 800-373-5504, Fax: 757-352-4381, E-mail: admissions@regent.edu.
Website: http://www.regent.edu/education/.

Regis College, Department of Education, Weston, MA 02493. Offers elementary teacher (MAT); higher education leadership (Ed D); reading (MAT); special education (MAT). Part-time and evening/weekend programs available. *Degree requirements:* For master's, thesis. *Entrance requirements:* For master's, GRE or MAT. Additional exam requirements/recommendations for international students: Required—TOEFL. Electronic applications accepted. *Faculty research:* Reflective teaching, gender-based education, integrated teaching.

Regis University, College for Professional Studies, School of Education, Education Division, Denver, CO 80221-1099. Offers adult learning, training, and development (M Ed, Certificate); autism education (Certificate); curriculum, instruction, and assessment (M Ed); educational leadership (M Ed); gifted and talented education (M Ed); gifted/talented education (Certificate); initial licensure (M Ed); instructional technology (M Ed, Certificate); literacy (Certificate); reading (M Ed); school executive leadership (Certificate); space studies (M Ed). Program also offered in Henderson and Las Vegas (Summerlin), NV. *Accreditation:* Teacher Education Accreditation Council. Part-time and evening/weekend programs available. Postbaccalaureate distance learning degree programs offered (no on-campus study). *Degree requirements:* For master's, thesis. *Entrance requirements:* For master's, resume, minimum GPA of 2.75, criminal background check. Additional exam requirements/recommendations for international students: Required—TOEFL, TWE (minimum score 5). *Application deadline:* For fall admission, 7/23 priority date for domestic students; for winter admission, 9/17 priority date for domestic students; for spring admission, 12/3 priority date for domestic students. Applications are processed on a rolling basis. Application fee: $75. Electronic applications accepted. *Expenses:* Contact institution. *Financial support:* Federal Work-Study and scholarships/grants available. *Faculty research:* Issues of equity in the middle school classroom, professional learning communities, school reform, sociolinguistic and discursive obstacles to student integration, inclusive language arts curriculum. *Unit head:* Dr. Janna L. Oakes, Dean, 303-458-4302. *Application contact:* Information Contact, 303-458-4300, Fax: 303-964-5274, E-mail: masters@regis.edu.

Rhode Island College, School of Graduate Studies, Feinstein School of Education and Human Development, Department of Elementary Education, Providence, RI 02908-1991. Offers early childhood education (M Ed); elementary education (M Ed, MAT); reading (M Ed). *Accreditation:* NCATE. Part-time and evening/weekend programs available. *Faculty:* 11 full-time (9 women), 2 part-time/adjunct (both women). *Students:* 16 full-time (12 women), 51 part-time (49 women); includes 5 minority (1 Black or African American, non-Hispanic/Latino; 3 Hispanic/Latino; 1 Two or more races, non-Hispanic/Latino). Average age 37. In 2013, 29 master's awarded. *Degree requirements:* For master's, comprehensive exam (for some programs), comprehensive assessment. *Entrance requirements:* For master's, GRE General Test or MAT, PRAXIS II (elementary content knowledge), undergraduate transcripts; minimum undergraduate GPA of 3.0; 3 letters of recommendation. Additional exam requirements/recommendations for international students: Recommended—TOEFL (minimum score 550 paper-based; 79 iBT). *Application deadline:* For fall admission, 3/1 for domestic students; for spring admission, 11/1 for domestic students. Applications are processed on a rolling basis. Application fee: $50. *Expenses:* Tuition, state resident: full-time $8928; part-time $372 per credit hour. Tuition, nonresident: full-time $17,376; part-time $724 per credit hour. *Required fees:* $602; $22 per credit. $72 per term. *Financial support:* Teaching assistantships with full tuition reimbursements, Federal Work-Study, scholarships/grants, and health care benefits available. Support available to part-time students. Financial award application deadline: 5/15; financial award applicants required to submit FAFSA. *Unit head:* Dr. Patricia Cordeiro, Chair, 401-456-8016. *Application contact:* Graduate Studies, 401-456-8700.
Website: http://www.ric.edu/elementaryEducation/.

Rider University, Department of Graduate Education, Leadership and Counseling, Program in Reading/Language Arts, Lawrenceville, NJ 08648-3001. Offers reading specialist (Certificate); reading/language arts (MA). *Accreditation:* NCATE. Part-time and evening/weekend programs available. *Degree requirements:* For master's, comprehensive exam, research project. *Entrance requirements:* For master's, interview, resume. Additional exam requirements/recommendations for international students: Required—TOEFL (minimum score 550 paper-based). Electronic applications accepted. *Faculty research:* Ethnography in the reading/language arts process.

Rivier University, School of Graduate Studies, Department of Education, Nashua, NH 03060. Offers curriculum and instruction (M Ed); early childhood education (M Ed); educational administration (M Ed); educational studies (M Ed); elementary education (M Ed); elementary education and general special education (M Ed); emotional and behavioral disorders (M Ed); general social education (M Ed); leadership and learning (Ed D, CAGS); learning disabilities (M Ed); learning disabilities and reading (M Ed); mental health counseling (MA); reading (M Ed); school counseling (M Ed). Part-time and evening/weekend programs available. *Degree requirements:* For master's, comprehensive exam (for some programs), internships. *Entrance requirements:* For master's, GRE General Test or MAT.

Roberts Wesleyan College, Department of Teacher Education, Rochester, NY 14624-1997. Offers adolescence education (M Ed); childhood and special education (M Ed); literacy education (M Ed); special education online (M Ed). Part-time and evening/weekend programs available. *Faculty:* 10 full-time (7 women), 12 part-time/adjunct (6 women). *Students:* 37 full-time (29 women), 10 part-time (6 women); includes 16 minority (15 Black or African American, non-Hispanic/Latino; 1 Hispanic/Latino). Average age 33. 72 applicants, 63% accepted, 34 enrolled. In 2013, 20 master's awarded. *Degree requirements:* For master's, thesis. *Application deadline:* For fall admission, 6/1 for domestic and international students; for spring admission, 11/1 for domestic and international students; for summer admission, 3/1 for domestic and international students. Applications are processed on a rolling basis. Electronic applications accepted. Application fee is waived when completed online. *Expenses: Tuition:* Full-time $12,816; part-time $712 per credit hour. One-time fee: $300. Tuition and fees vary according to course load and program. *Financial support:* In 2013–14, 7 students received support. Career-related internships or fieldwork available. Financial award application deadline: 9/1; financial award applicants required to submit FAFSA. *Unit head:* Dr. Sharon Harris-Ewing, Chair, 585-594-6935, E-mail: harrisewing_sharon@roberts.edu. *Application contact:* Paul Ziegler, Director of Marketing and Recruitment for Teacher Education, 585-594-6146, Fax: 585-594-6108, E-mail: ziegler_paul@roberts.edu.
Website: https://www.roberts.edu/department-of-teacher-education.aspx.

Rockford University, Graduate Studies, Department of Education, Program in Reading, Rockford, IL 61108-2393. Offers MAT. Part-time and evening/weekend programs available. *Degree requirements:* For master's, thesis optional. *Entrance requirements:* For master's, GRE General Test, 3 letters of recommendation. Additional exam requirements/recommendations for international students: Required—TOEFL (minimum score 550 paper-based; 79 iBT). Electronic applications accepted.

Roger Williams University, Feinstein College of Arts and Sciences, Bristol, RI 02809. Offers clinical psychology (MA); education (MAT); forensic psychology (MA); literacy (MA). Part-time and evening/weekend programs available. Postbaccalaureate distance learning degree programs offered (minimal on-campus study). *Faculty:* 6 full-time (1 woman). *Students:* 38 full-time (31 women), 1 part-time (0 women); includes 5 minority (1 Black or African American, non-Hispanic/Latino; 1 Asian, non-Hispanic/Latino; 2 Hispanic/Latino; 1 Two or more races, non-Hispanic/Latino), 2 international. Average age 24. 109 applicants, 56% accepted, 18 enrolled. In 2013, 36 master's awarded. *Degree requirements:* For master's, thesis optional, internship. *Entrance requirements:* For master's, GRE, 3 letters of recommendation. Additional exam requirements/recommendations for international students: Required—TOEFL (minimum score 85 iBT), IELTS. *Application deadline:* Applications are processed on a rolling basis. Application fee: $50. Electronic applications accepted. *Expenses:* Contact institution. *Financial support:* In 2013–14, 39 students received support, including 5 research assistantships (averaging $5,000 per year). Financial award application deadline: 6/15; financial award applicants required to submit FAFSA. *Unit head:* Robert Eisinger, Dean, 401-254-3149, E-mail: reisinger@rwu.edu. *Application contact:* Jamie Grenon, Director of Graduate Admissions, 401-254-6000, Fax: 401-254-3557, E-mail: gradadmit@rwu.edu.
Website: http://www.rwu.edu/academics/schools/fcas/.

Roger Williams University, School of Education, Program in Literacy Education, Bristol, RI 02809. Offers literacy (MA). Part-time and evening/weekend programs available. *Faculty:* 5 full-time (4 women), 8 part-time/adjunct (7 women). *Students:* 35 part-time (31 women); includes 1 minority (Asian, non-Hispanic/Latino). Average age 33. 5 applicants, 60% accepted, 1 enrolled. In 2013, 9 master's awarded. *Degree requirements:* For master's, state-mandated exams. *Entrance requirements:* For master's, interview, teacher's certification, 2 recommendation letters, curriculum vitae/resume. Additional exam requirements/recommendations for international students: Recommended—TOEFL (minimum score 85 iBT), IELTS. *Application deadline:* Applications are processed on a rolling basis. Application fee: $50. Electronic applications accepted. *Expenses:* Contact institution. *Financial support:* Application deadline: 6/15; applicants required to submit FAFSA. *Faculty research:* Assessment of reading difficulties, action research in reading, comprehension and writing, student mediation techniques. *Unit head:* Dr. Susan Pasquarelli, Program Director, 401-254-3074, Fax: 401-254-3710, E-mail: spasquarelli@rwu.edu. *Application contact:* Jamie Grenon, Director of Graduate Admissions, 401-254-6000, Fax: 401-254-3557, E-mail: gradadmit@rwu.edu.
Website: http://www.rwu.edu/academics/departments/education.htm#literacygraduate.

Roosevelt University, Graduate Division, College of Education, Program in Language and Literacy, Chicago, IL 60605. Offers reading teacher education (MA).

Rowan University, Graduate School, College of Education, Department of Reading Education, Program in Reading Education, Glassboro, NJ 08028-1701. Offers MA. *Faculty:* 3 full-time (all women), 3 part-time/adjunct (all women). *Students:* 1 (woman) full-time, 60 part-time (59 women); includes 4 minority (2 Black or African American, non-Hispanic/Latino; 1 Asian, non-Hispanic/Latino; 1 Hispanic/Latino). Average age 32. In 2013, 41 master's awarded. *Expenses: Tuition, area resident:* Part-time $638 per credit. Tuition, state resident: full-time $5742. *Required fees:* $142 per credit. Tuition and fees vary according to course level and program. *Unit head:* Dr. Horacio Sosa, Dean, College of Graduate and Continuing Education, 856-256-4747, Fax: 856-256-

5638, E-mail: sosa@rowan.edu. *Application contact:* Admissions and Enrollment Services, 856-256-5145, Fax: 856-256-5637, E-mail: cgceadmissions@rowan.edu.

Rutgers, The State University of New Jersey, New Brunswick, Graduate School of Education, Department of Learning and Teaching, Program in Literacy Education, Piscataway, NJ 08854-8097. Offers Ed M, Ed D. Part-time programs available. Terminal master's awarded for partial completion of doctoral program. *Degree requirements:* For master's, comprehensive exam; for doctorate, thesis/dissertation, qualifying exam. *Entrance requirements:* For master's, GRE General Test, minimum undergraduate GPA of 3.0; for doctorate, GRE General Test, 2 years of teaching experience, certification, minimum graduate GPA of 3.5. Additional exam requirements/recommendations for international students: Required—TOEFL. Electronic applications accepted. *Faculty research:* Early childhood literacy development, discourse analysis-adult literacy.

Rutgers, The State University of New Jersey, New Brunswick, Graduate School of Education, Department of Learning and Teaching, Program in Reading Education, Piscataway, NJ 08854-8097. Offers Ed M. Part-time programs available. *Degree requirements:* For master's, comprehensive exam or paper. *Entrance requirements:* For master's, GRE General Test. Electronic applications accepted.

Rutgers, The State University of New Jersey, New Brunswick, Graduate School of Education, Doctoral Program in Education, New Brunswick, NJ 08901. Offers educational policy (PhD); educational psychology (PhD); literacy education (PhD); mathematics education (PhD). Part-time programs available. *Degree requirements:* For doctorate, thesis/dissertation, qualifying exam. *Entrance requirements:* For doctorate, GRE General Test, GRE Subject Test (mathematics education). Additional exam requirements/recommendations for international students: Required—TOEFL (minimum score 575 paper-based; 83 iBT). Electronic applications accepted. *Faculty research:* Literacy education, math education, educational psychology, educational policy, learning sciences.

Sacred Heart University, Graduate Programs, Isabelle Farrington College of Education, Department of Leadership/Literacy, Fairfield, CT 06825-1000. Offers literacy (CAS). *Faculty:* 12 full-time (5 women), 15 part-time/adjunct (8 women). *Students:* 86 part-time (75 women); includes 8 minority (2 Black or African American, non-Hispanic/Latino; 1 Asian, non-Hispanic/Latino; 4 Hispanic/Latino; 1 Two or more races, non-Hispanic/Latino). Average age 40. 188 applicants, 97% accepted, 152 enrolled. *Entrance requirements:* For degree, proof of teacher certification. Additional exam requirements/recommendations for international students: Required—PTE; Recommended—TOEFL (minimum score 570 paper-based; 80 iBT), IELTS (minimum score 6.5). *Application deadline:* Applications are processed on a rolling basis. Application fee: $60. *Expenses:* Tuition: Full-time $22,775; part-time $617 per credit. *Financial support:* Applicants required to submit FAFSA. *Unit head:* Dr. Jim Carl, Dean, 203-371-7800, E-mail: carlj@sacredheart.edu. *Application contact:* Kathy Dilks, Executive Director of Graduate Admissions, 203-365-7619, Fax: 203-365-4732, E-mail: gradstudies@sacredheart.edu.
Website: http://www.sacredheart.edu/academics/isabellefarringtoncollegeofeducation/.

Sage Graduate School, Esteves School of Education, Program in Childhood Education/Literacy, Troy, NY 12180-4115. Offers MS. Part-time and evening/weekend programs available. *Faculty:* 10 full-time (5 women), 33 part-time/adjunct (25 women). *Students:* 1 (woman) full-time, 9 part-time (7 women); includes 1 minority (Hispanic/Latino). Average age 25. 7 applicants, 29% accepted, 2 enrolled. In 2013, 7 master's awarded. *Degree requirements:* For master's, thesis optional. *Entrance requirements:* For master's, minimum GPA of 2.75, resume, 2 letters of recommendation, interview, assessment of writing skills. Additional exam requirements/recommendations for international students: Required—TOEFL (minimum score 550 paper-based). *Application deadline:* Applications are processed on a rolling basis. Application fee: $40. *Expenses:* Tuition: Full-time $11,880; part-time $660 per credit hour. *Financial support:* Fellowships, research assistantships, Federal Work-Study, scholarships/grants, and unspecified assistantships available. Support available to part-time students. Financial award application deadline: 3/1. *Unit head:* Dr. Lori Quigley, Dean, Esteves School of Education, 518-244-2326, Fax: 518-244-4571, E-mail: l.quigley@sage.edu. *Application contact:* Mary Grace Luibrand, Director, 518-244-4578, Fax: 518-244-4571, E-mail: luibrm@sage.edu.

Sage Graduate School, Esteves School of Education, Program in Literacy, Troy, NY 12180-4115. Offers MS Ed. *Accreditation:* NCATE. Part-time and evening/weekend programs available. *Faculty:* 10 full-time (6 women), 2 part-time/adjunct (both women). *Students:* 1 (woman) full-time, 9 part-time (7 women); includes 1 minority (Hispanic/Latino). Average age 28. 12 applicants, 75% accepted, 2 enrolled. In 2013, 16 master's awarded. *Entrance requirements:* For master's, minimum GPA of 2.75, resume, 2 letters of recommendation. Additional exam requirements/recommendations for international students: Required—TOEFL (minimum score 550 paper-based). *Application deadline:* Applications are processed on a rolling basis. Application fee: $40. *Expenses:* Tuition: Full-time $11,880; part-time $660 per credit hour. *Financial support:* Fellowships, research assistantships, Federal Work-Study, scholarships/grants, and unspecified assistantships available. Support available to part-time students. Financial award application deadline: 3/1; financial award applicants required to submit FAFSA. *Faculty research:* Literacy development in at-risk children. *Unit head:* Dr. Lori Quigley, Dean, Esteves School of Education, 518-244-2326, Fax: 518-244-4571, E-mail: l.quigley@sage.edu. *Application contact:* Dr. Ellen Adams, Department Chair, 518-244-2054, Fax: 518-244-2334, E-mail: adamse@sage.edu.

Sage Graduate School, Esteves School of Education, Program in Literacy/Childhood Special Education, Troy, NY 12180-4115. Offers MS Ed. *Accreditation:* NCATE. Part-time and evening/weekend programs available. *Faculty:* 10 full-time (5 women), 2 part-time/adjunct (both women). *Students:* 3 full-time (all women), 14 part-time (13 women); includes 1 minority (Two or more races, non-Hispanic/Latino). Average age 25. 22 applicants, 64% accepted, 11 enrolled. In 2013, 6 master's awarded. *Entrance requirements:* For master's, assessment of writing skills, minimum GPA of 2.75, resume, 2 letters of recommendation, interview with advisor. Additional exam requirements/recommendations for international students: Required—TOEFL (minimum score 550 paper-based). *Application deadline:* Applications are processed on a rolling basis. Application fee: $40. *Expenses:* Tuition: Full-time $11,880; part-time $660 per credit hour. *Financial support:* Fellowships, research assistantships, Federal Work-Study, scholarships/grants, and unspecified assistantships available. Support available to part-time students. Financial award application deadline: 3/1; financial award applicants required to submit FAFSA. *Faculty research:* Commonalities in the roles of reading specialists and resource/consultant teachers. *Unit head:* Dr. Lori Quigley, Dean, Esteves School of Education, 518-244-2326, Fax: 518-244-4571, E-mail: l.quigley@sage.edu. *Application contact:* Mary Grace Luibrand, Director, 518-244-4578, Fax: 518-244-2334, E-mail: luibrm@sage.edu.

Saginaw Valley State University, College of Education, Program in K-12 Literacy Specialist, University Center, MI 48710. Offers MAT. Part-time and evening/weekend programs available. *Students:* 1 (woman) full-time, 47 part-time (43 women); includes 2 minority (both Black or African American, non-Hispanic/Latino). Average age 33. 11 applicants, 100% accepted, 6 enrolled. In 2013, 20 master's awarded. *Degree requirements:* For master's, capstone course. *Entrance requirements:* For master's,

minimum GPA of 3.0. Additional exam requirements/recommendations for international students: Required—TOEFL (minimum score 550 paper-based; 79 iBT). *Application deadline:* For fall admission, 7/15 for international students; for winter admission, 11/15 for international students; for spring admission, 4/15 for international students. Applications are processed on a rolling basis. Application fee: $30 ($80 for international students). Electronic applications accepted. *Expenses:* Tuition, state resident: full-time $8933; part-time $496.30 per credit hour. Tuition, nonresident: full-time $16,806; part-time $933.65 per credit hour. *Required fees:* $263; $14.60 per credit hour. Tuition and fees vary according to degree level. *Financial support:* Federal Work-Study and scholarships/grants available. Support available to part-time students. Financial award applicants required to submit FAFSA. *Unit head:* Dr. Mary Harmon, Dean, 989-964-7107, Fax: 989-964-4563, E-mail: coeconnect@svsu.edu. *Application contact:* Jenna Briggs, Director, Graduate and International Admissions, 989-964-6096, Fax: 989-964-2788, E-mail: gradadm@svsu.edu.

Saginaw Valley State University, College of Education, Program in Reading Education, University Center, MI 48710. Offers MAT. *Accreditation:* NCATE. Part-time and evening/weekend programs available. *Students:* 19 part-time (18 women); includes 1 minority (Black or African American, non-Hispanic/Latino). Average age 36. In 2013, 20 master's awarded. *Degree requirements:* For master's, capstone course, practicum. *Entrance requirements:* For master's, minimum GPA of 3.0, teaching certificate. Additional exam requirements/recommendations for international students: Required—TOEFL (minimum score 550 paper-based; 79 iBT). *Application deadline:* For fall admission, 7/15 for international students; for winter admission, 11/15 for international students; for spring admission, 4/15 for international students. Applications are processed on a rolling basis. Application fee: $30 ($80 for international students). Electronic applications accepted. *Expenses:* Tuition, state resident: full-time $8933; part-time $496.30 per credit hour. Tuition, nonresident: full-time $16,806; part-time $933.65 per credit hour. *Required fees:* $263; $14.60 per credit hour. Tuition and fees vary according to degree level. *Financial support:* Federal Work-Study and scholarships/grants available. Support available to part-time students. Financial award applicants required to submit FAFSA. *Faculty research:* Pre-service, middle school, secondary teacher, literacy education. *Unit head:* Dr. Mary Harmon, Dean, 989-964-7107, Fax: 989-964-4563, E-mail: coeconnect@svsu.edu. *Application contact:* Jenna Briggs, Director, Graduate and International Admissions, 989-964-6096, Fax: 989-964-2788, E-mail: gradadm@svsu.edu.

St. Bonaventure University, School of Graduate Studies, School of Education, Literacy Programs, St. Bonaventure, NY 14778-2284. Offers adolescent literacy 5-12 (MS Ed); childhood literacy B-6 (MS Ed). Program offered in Olean and Buffalo Center (Hamburg, NY). *Accreditation:* NCATE. Part-time and evening/weekend programs available. *Faculty:* 2 full-time (both women), 1 (woman) part-time/adjunct. *Students:* 14 full-time (13 women), 14 part-time (13 women). Average age 29. 19 applicants, 100% accepted, 13 enrolled. In 2013, 27 master's awarded. *Degree requirements:* For master's, comprehensive exam, thesis optional, literacy coaching internship, portfolio. *Entrance requirements:* For master's, interview, writing sample, minimum undergraduate GPA of 3.0, two letters of recommendation, teaching certificate in matching area, transcripts. Additional exam requirements/recommendations for international students: Required—TOEFL (minimum score 550 paper-based; 80 iBT). *Application deadline:* For fall admission, 6/15 priority date for domestic students, 2/1 for international students; for spring admission, 11/15 priority date for domestic students, 7/1 for international students. Applications are processed on a rolling basis. Application fee: $0. Electronic applications accepted. *Financial support:* In 2013-14, 4 research assistantships with full and partial tuition reimbursements were awarded; Federal Work-Study, scholarships/grants, health care benefits, and unspecified assistantships also available. Support available to part-time students. Financial award application deadline: 4/15; financial award applicants required to submit FAFSA. *Unit head:* Dr. Karen M. Wieland, Program Director, 716-375-2369, Fax: 716-375-2360, E-mail: kwieland@sbu.edu. *Application contact:* Bruce Campbell, Director of Graduate Admissions, 716-375-2429, Fax: 716-375-4015, E-mail: gradsch@sbu.edu.
Website: http://www.sbu.edu/academics/schools/education/graduate-degrees-certificates/msed-in-childhood-literacy.

Saint Francis University, Graduate Education Program, Loretto, PA 15940-0600. Offers education (M Ed); leadership (M Ed); reading (M Ed). Part-time programs available. *Faculty:* 16 part-time/adjunct (8 women). *Students:* 5 full-time (4 women), 93 part-time (68 women); includes 1 minority (Black or African American, non-Hispanic/Latino). Average age 28. 15 applicants, 100% accepted, 15 enrolled. In 2013, 45 master's awarded. *Degree requirements:* For master's, comprehensive exam, thesis optional. *Entrance requirements:* For master's, GRE or MAT (if undergraduate GPA less than 3.0). Additional exam requirements/recommendations for international students: Required—TOEFL (minimum score 550 paper-based; 75 iBT), IELTS (minimum score 6.5), International Test of English Proficiency (minimum score 4). *Application deadline:* Applications are processed on a rolling basis. Application fee: $30. *Expenses:* Contact institution. *Financial support:* Applicants required to submit FAFSA. *Unit head:* Dr. Janette D. Kelly, Director, 814-472-3068, Fax: 814-472-3864, E-mail: jkelly@francis.edu. *Application contact:* Sherri L. Toth, Coordinator, 814-472-3058, Fax: 814-472-3864, E-mail: stoth@francis.edu.
Website: http://www.francis.edu/master-of-education/.

St. John Fisher College, Ralph C. Wilson Jr. School of Education, Program in Literacy Education, Rochester, NY 14618-3597. Offers literacy birth to grade 6 (MS); literacy grades 5 to 12 (MS). Part-time and evening/weekend programs available. *Faculty:* 3 full-time (all women), 5 part-time/adjunct (4 women). *Students:* 14 full-time (13 women), 41 part-time (34 women); includes 8 minority (5 Black or African American, non-Hispanic/Latino; 3 Hispanic/Latino). Average age 27. 38 applicants, 89% accepted, 20 enrolled. In 2013, 34 master's awarded. *Degree requirements:* For master's, capstone project, practicum. *Entrance requirements:* For master's, teacher certification, 2 letters of recommendation, personal statement, current resume. Additional exam requirements/recommendations for international students: Required—TOEFL (minimum score 575 paper-based; 80 iBT). *Application deadline:* Applications are processed on a rolling basis. Application fee: $30. Electronic applications accepted. *Expenses:* Tuition: Part-time $795 per credit hour. *Required fees:* $10 per credit hour. Tuition and fees vary according to course load, degree level and program. *Financial support:* In 2013-14, 18 students received support. Scholarships/grants available. Financial award applicants required to submit FAFSA. *Faculty research:* Adolescent use of new literacies (instant messaging), referral practices, at risk early literacy, new literacies (Internet, technology), equity in education. *Unit head:* Dr. Kathleen Broikou, Program Director, 585-385-8112, E-mail: kbroikou@sjfc.edu. *Application contact:* Jose Perales, Director of Graduate Admissions, 585-385-8067, E-mail: jperales@sjfc.edu.
Website: http://www.sjfc.edu/academics/education/departments/literacy/.

St. John's University, The School of Education, Department of Human Services and Counseling, Literacy Program, Queens, NY 11439. Offers literacy (PhD); literacy B-6 or 5-12 (Adv C); teaching literacy 5-12 (MS Ed); teaching literacy B-12 (MS Ed); teaching literacy B-6 (MS Ed); teaching literacy B-6 and children with disabilities (MS Ed). Part-time and evening/weekend programs available. *Students:* 32 full-time (30 women), 89 part-time (84 women); includes 33 minority (13 Black or African American, non-Hispanic/

Latino; 2 Asian, non-Hispanic/Latino; 17 Hispanic/Latino; 1 Two or more races, non-Hispanic/Latino), 1 international. Average age 30. 68 applicants, 94% accepted, 33 enrolled. In 2013, 33 master's, 4 doctorates, 3 other advanced degrees awarded. *Degree requirements:* For master's, comprehensive exam; for doctorate, thesis/dissertation, residency; for Adv C, 50-hour practicum, content specialty test in literacy. *Entrance requirements:* For master's, minimum GPA of 3.0, transcript, personal statement; for doctorate, MAT, GRE General Test (analytical), statement of goals, official transcripts showing conferral of degree, minimum GPA of 3.2, 2 letters of recommendation, resume, evidence of teaching experience, interview; for Adv C, master's degree, initial teaching certification, minimum GPA of 3.0. Additional exam requirements/recommendations for international students: Required—TOEFL (minimum score 600 paper-based; 100 iBT), IELTS (minimum score 5.5). *Application deadline:* For fall admission, 4/1 for domestic students, 4/1 priority date for international students; for spring admission, 11/1 priority date for international students. Applications are processed on a rolling basis. Application fee: $70. Electronic applications accepted. *Expenses: Tuition:* Full-time $19,800; part-time $1100 per credit. *Required fees:* $170 per semester. *Financial support:* Research assistantships, career-related internships or fieldwork, and scholarships/grants available. Support available to part-time students. Financial award application deadline: 3/1; financial award applicants required to submit FAFSA. *Faculty research:* Higher order reading comprehension development and instruction, children's literature theory and children's reading interests, critical comprehension development, early writing development at the primary level, self-efficacy with textbook formats, out of school time program effects for at-risk students, teacher training effects for low performing parochial school students. *Unit head:* Dr. E Francine Guastello, Chair, 718-990-1475, E-mail: guastelf@stjohns.edu. *Application contact:* Dr. Kelly K. Ronayne, Associate Dean of Graduate Admissions, 718-990-2304, Fax: 718-990-2343, E-mail: graded@stjohns.edu.

St. Joseph's College, Long Island Campus, Program in Literacy and Cognition, Patchogue, NY 11772-2399. Offers MA.

St. Joseph's College, New York, Graduate Programs, Program in Education, Field of Literacy and Cognition, Brooklyn, NY 11205-3688. Offers MA.

Saint Joseph's University, College of Arts and Sciences, Department of Education, Philadelphia, PA 19131-1395. Offers curriculum supervisor (Certificate); educational leadership (MS, Ed D); elementary education (MS, Certificate); elementary/middle school education (Certificate); instructional technology (MS, Certificate); principal certification (Certificate); professional education (MS); reading specialist (MS, Certificate); reading supervisor (Certificate); secondary education (MS, Certificate); special education (MS, Certificate); superintendent's letter of eligibility (Certificate); supervisor of special education (Certificate). Part-time and evening/weekend programs available. Postbaccalaureate distance learning degree programs offered (no on-campus study). *Faculty:* 32 full-time (25 women), 75 part-time/adjunct (53 women). *Students:* 91 full-time (81 women), 858 part-time (656 women); includes 133 minority (96 Black or African American, non-Hispanic/Latino; 3 American Indian or Alaska Native, non-Hispanic/Latino; 9 Asian, non-Hispanic/Latino; 20 Hispanic/Latino; 5 Native Hawaiian or other Pacific Islander, non-Hispanic/Latino), 16 international. Average age 31. 359 applicants, 77% accepted, 203 enrolled. In 2013, 363 master's, 9 doctorates, 1 other advanced degree awarded. *Entrance requirements:* For master's, 2 letters of recommendation, minimum GPA of 3.0, official transcripts, personal statement; for doctorate, GRE, master's degree from accredited institution, minimum graduate GPA of 3.5, computer competence, commitment to participate in cohort, interview with program director. Additional exam requirements/recommendations for international students: Required—TOEFL (minimum score 550 paper-based; 79 iBT), IELTS (minimum score 6.5). *Application deadline:* For fall admission, 7/15 priority date for domestic students, 4/15 for international students; for winter admission, 11/15 for domestic students, 1/15 for international students; for spring admission, 11/15 priority date for domestic students, 10/15 for international students. Applications are processed on a rolling basis. Application fee: $35. Electronic applications accepted. *Expenses:* Contact institution. *Financial support:* Unspecified assistantships available. Financial award applicants required to submit FAFSA. *Faculty research:* Factors predicting early mathematics skills for low income children, early child care and development, preschool quality. *Total annual research expenditures:* $229,264. *Unit head:* Dr. John Vacca, Associate Dean, Education, 610-660-3131, E-mail: gradstudies@sju.edu. *Application contact:* Elisabeth Woodward, Director of Marketing and Admissions, Graduate Arts and Sciences, 610-660-3131, Fax: 610-660-3230, E-mail: gradstudies@sju.edu.
Website: http://sju.edu/int/academics/cas/grad/education/index.html.

Saint Leo University, Graduate Studies in Education, Saint Leo, FL 33574-6665. Offers educational leadership (M Ed); exceptional student education (M Ed); instructional design (MS); instructional leadership (M Ed); reading (M Ed). Part-time and evening/weekend programs available. Postbaccalaureate distance learning degree programs offered (minimal on-campus study). *Faculty:* 10 full-time (8 women), 31 part-time/adjunct (23 women). *Students:* 680 full-time (554 women), 4 part-time (all women); includes 83 minority (51 Black or African American, non-Hispanic/Latino; 2 Asian, non-Hispanic/Latino; 27 Hispanic/Latino; 3 Two or more races, non-Hispanic/Latino), 4 international. Average age 36. In 2013, 295 master's awarded. *Degree requirements:* For master's, comprehensive exam, appropriate State of Florida certification tests. *Entrance requirements:* For master's, GRE (minimum score of 1000) or MAT (minimum score of 410) if undergraduate GPA for last 60 hours of coursework was below 3.0 (for M Ed), bachelor's degree with minimum GPA of 3.0 for last 60 hours of coursework from regionally-accredited college or university, 2 recommendations, resume, statement of professional goals, copy of valid teaching certificate (for M Ed). Additional exam requirements/recommendations for international students: Required—TOEFL (minimum score 550 paper-based; 80 iBT). *Application deadline:* For fall admission, 7/1 priority date for domestic students, 7/1 for international students; for winter admission, 7/1 for international students; for spring admission, 11/1 priority date for domestic students. Applications are processed on a rolling basis. Application fee: $80. Electronic applications accepted. *Expenses:* Contact institution. *Financial support:* In 2013–14, 618 students received support. Career-related internships or fieldwork, Federal Work-Study, scholarships/grants, and health care benefits available. Financial award application deadline: 3/1; financial award applicants required to submit FAFSA. *Faculty research:* The role of the school leader in data analysis of student achievement, teacher recruitment, teacher effectiveness. *Unit head:* Dr. Sharyn Disabato, Director of Graduate Education, 352-588-8309, Fax: 352-588-8861, E-mail: med@saintleo.edu. *Application contact:* Joshua Stagner, Director of Graduate Admission, 800-707-8846, Fax: 352-588-7873, E-mail: grad.admissions@saintleo.edu.
Website: http://www.saintleo.edu/admissions/graduate.aspx.

Saint Martin's University, Office of Graduate Studies, College of Education, Lacey, WA 98503. Offers administration (M Ed); English as a second language (M Ed); guidance and counseling (M Ed); reading (M Ed); special education (M Ed); teaching (MIT). *Accreditation:* Teacher Education Accreditation Council. Part-time and evening/weekend programs available. *Faculty:* 10 full-time (6 women), 15 part-time/adjunct (12 women). *Students:* 57 full-time (35 women), 52 part-time (38 women); includes 20 minority (7 Black or African American, non-Hispanic/Latino; 1 American Indian or Alaska Native, non-Hispanic/Latino; 2 Asian, non-Hispanic/Latino; 6 Hispanic/Latino; 1 Native Hawaiian or other Pacific Islander, non-Hispanic/Latino; 3 Two or more races, non-Hispanic/Latino). Average age 35. 63 applicants, 25% accepted, 13 enrolled. In 2013, 12 master's awarded. *Degree requirements:* For master's, comprehensive exam (for some programs), thesis or alternative, project or comprehensives. *Entrance requirements:* For master's, GRE General Test or MAT, three letters of recommendations; curriculum vitae. Additional exam requirements/recommendations for international students: Required—TOEFL (minimum score 550 paper-based; 79 iBT); Recommended—IELTS (minimum score 6.5). *Application deadline:* For fall admission, 4/1 priority date for domestic and international students; for spring admission, 11/1 priority date for domestic and international students. Applications are processed on a rolling basis. Application fee: $50. Electronic applications accepted. *Expenses: Tuition:* Part-time $990 per credit hour. Tuition and fees vary according to course level and program. *Financial support:* Career-related internships or fieldwork, Federal Work-Study, institutionally sponsored loans, and unspecified assistantships available. Support available to part-time students. Financial award application deadline: 3/1; financial award applicants required to submit FAFSA. *Faculty research:* Reader's theatre and reader/writer workshops, curriculum and assessment integration, gender and equity, classroom evaluations, organizational leadership. *Unit head:* Dr. Joyce Westgard, Dean, College of Education and Professional Psychology, 360-438-4509, Fax: 360-438-4486, E-mail: westgard@stmartin.edu. *Application contact:* Marie C. Boisvert, Administrative Assistant, 360-412-6145, E-mail: gradstudies@stmartin.edu.
Website: http://www.stmartin.edu/gradstudies.

Saint Mary's College of California, Kalmanovitz School of Education, Program in Montessori Education, Moraga, CA 94575. Offers reading and language arts (M Ed, MA).

Saint Mary's College of California, Kalmanovitz School of Education, Program in Reading Leadership, Moraga, CA 94575. Offers reading and language arts (M Ed, MA). Part-time and evening/weekend programs available. *Degree requirements:* For master's, thesis or alternative. *Entrance requirements:* For master's, interview, minimum GPA of 3.0.

St. Mary's University, Graduate School, Department of Teacher Education, Program in Reading, San Antonio, TX 78228-8507. Offers MA. Part-time programs available. Postbaccalaureate distance learning degree programs offered (no on-campus study). *Degree requirements:* For master's, comprehensive exam. *Entrance requirements:* For master's, GRE. Additional exam requirements/recommendations for international students: Required—TOEFL (minimum score 550 paper-based; 80 iBT). Electronic applications accepted.

Saint Mary's University of Minnesota, Schools of Graduate and Professional Programs, Graduate School of Education, Literacy Education Program, Winona, MN 55987-1399. Offers K-12 reading teacher (Certificate); literacy education (MA). *Unit head:* Rebecca Hopkins, Dean, 507-457-6620, E-mail: rhopkins@smumn.edu. *Application contact:* Denise Cichosz, Director of Admissions for Graduate and Professional Programs, 507-457-6629, E-mail: dcichosz@smumn.edu.
Website: http://www.smumn.edu/graduate-home/areas-of-study/graduate-school-of-education/ma-in-literacy-education.

Saint Michael's College, Graduate Programs, Program in Education, Colchester, VT 05439. Offers administration (M Ed, CAGS); arts in education (CAGS); curriculum and instruction (M Ed, CAGS); information technology (CAGS); reading (M Ed); special education (M Ed, CAGS); technology (M Ed). Part-time and evening/weekend programs available. *Degree requirements:* For master's, thesis. *Entrance requirements:* For master's, minimum GPA of 3.0. Electronic applications accepted. *Faculty research:* Integrative curriculum, moral and spiritual dimensions of education, learning styles, multiple intelligences, integrating technology into the curriculum.

Saint Peter's University, Graduate Programs in Education, Program in Special Education, Jersey City, NJ 07306-5997. Offers literacy (MA Ed). Part-time and evening/weekend programs available. *Degree requirements:* For master's, comprehensive exam. *Entrance requirements:* For master's, GRE or MAT. Additional exam requirements/recommendations for international students: Required—TOEFL. Electronic applications accepted.

Saint Peter's University, Graduate Programs in Education, Reading Program, Jersey City, NJ 07306-5997. Offers MA Ed. *Accreditation:* Teacher Education Accreditation Council. Part-time and evening/weekend programs available. *Degree requirements:* For master's, comprehensive exam. *Entrance requirements:* For master's, GRE or MAT. Additional exam requirements/recommendations for international students: Required—TOEFL. Electronic applications accepted.

St. Thomas Aquinas College, Division of Teacher Education, Sparkill, NY 10976. Offers adolescence education (MST); childhood and special education (MST); childhood education (MST); educational leadership (MS Ed); reading (MS Ed, PMC); special education (MS Ed, PMC); teaching (MS Ed), including elementary education, middle school education, secondary education. *Accreditation:* NCATE. Part-time and evening/weekend programs available. *Degree requirements:* For master's, comprehensive exam, comprehensive professional portfolio; for PMC, action research project. *Entrance requirements:* For master's, New York State Qualifying Exam, GRE General Test or minimum GPA of 3.0, teaching certificate; for PMC, GRE General Test or minimum GPA of 3.0. Electronic applications accepted. *Faculty research:* Computer applications in education, adolescent special education students, literacy development, inclusive practices for special education students.

St. Thomas University, School of Leadership Studies, Institute for Education, Miami Gardens, FL 33054-6459. Offers earth/space science (Certificate); educational administration (MS, Certificate); educational leadership (Ed D); elementary education (MS); ESOL (Certificate); gifted education (Certificate); instructional technology (MS, Certificate); professional/studies (Certificate); reading (MS, Certificate); special education (MS). Part-time and evening/weekend programs available. *Degree requirements:* For master's, comprehensive exam; for doctorate, comprehensive exam, thesis/dissertation. *Entrance requirements:* For master's, interview, minimum GPA of 3.0 or GRE; for doctorate, GRE or MAT. Additional exam requirements/recommendations for international students: Required—TOEFL (minimum score 550 paper-based; 79 iBT). Electronic applications accepted.

Saint Xavier University, Graduate Studies, School of Education, Chicago, IL 60655-3105. Offers counseling (MA); curriculum and instruction (MA); early childhood education (MA); educational administration (MA); elementary education (MA); individualized studies (MA), including educational technology, English as a second language (ESL), ISTEM (integrative science, technology, engineering, and math), science education; music education (MA); reading (MA); secondary education (MA); Spanish education (MA); special education (MA); teaching and leadership (MA). *Accreditation:* NCATE. Part-time and evening/weekend programs available. *Degree requirements:* For master's, thesis or project. *Entrance requirements:* For master's, minimum GPA of 3.0. *Expenses:* Contact institution.

Salem College, Department of Education, Winston-Salem, NC 27101. Offers art education (MAT); elementary education (M Ed, MAT); language and literacy (M Ed); middle school education (MAT); school counseling (M Ed); second language studies

(MAT); secondary education (MAT); special education (M Ed, MAT). *Accreditation:* NCATE. Part-time and evening/weekend programs available. Postbaccalaureate distance learning degree programs offered (minimal on-campus study). *Degree requirements:* For master's, practicum (MAT), project (M Ed), oral and written comprehensive exams. *Entrance requirements:* For master's, minimum GPA of 2.5. *Faculty research:* Content area reading strategies, literacy development, brain compatible instruction.

Salem State University, School of Graduate Studies, Program in Reading, Salem, MA 01970-5353. Offers M Ed. *Accreditation:* NCATE. Part-time and evening/weekend programs available. *Students:* 21 part-time (20 women). 2 applicants, 100% accepted, 2 enrolled. In 2013, 7 master's awarded. *Entrance requirements:* For master's, GRE or MAT. Additional exam requirements/recommendations for international students: Required—TOEFL (minimum score 550 paper-based; 80 iBT) or IELTS (minimum score 5.5). *Application deadline:* For fall admission, 5/1 for domestic students; for spring admission, 10/1 for domestic students. Applications are processed on a rolling basis. Application fee: $50. *Financial support:* Career-related internships or fieldwork, Federal Work-Study, scholarships/grants, and unspecified assistantships available. Support available to part-time students. Financial award application deadline: 5/1; financial award applicants required to submit FAFSA. *Application contact:* Dr. Lee A. Brossoit, Assistant Dean of Graduate Admissions, 978-542-6675, Fax: 978-542-7215, E-mail: lbrossoit@salemstate.edu.
Website: http://www.salemstate.edu/academics/schools/12624.php.

Salisbury University, Department of Education Specialties, Salisbury, MD 21801-6837. Offers curriculum and instruction (M Ed), including curriculum and instruction, post secondary track; educational leadership (M Ed); reading specialist (M Ed); secondary education (MAT). *Accreditation:* NCATE. Part-time programs available. *Degree requirements:* For master's, comprehensive exam (for some programs), thesis optional. *Application deadline:* For fall admission, 3/3 for domestic students; for spring admission, 10/1 for domestic students. *Expenses: Tuition, area resident:* Part-time $342 per credit hour. Tuition, state resident: part-time $342 per credit hour. Tuition, nonresident: part-time $631 per credit hour. *Required fees:* $76 per credit hour. Tuition and fees vary according to program. *Financial support:* Application deadline: 3/1.

Sam Houston State University, College of Education and Applied Science, Department of Language, Literacy, and Special Populations, Huntsville, TX 77341. Offers international literacy (M Ed); reading (M Ed, Ed D); special education (M Ed, MA). Part-time and evening/weekend programs available. *Faculty:* 26 full-time (22 women). *Students:* 44 full-time (38 women), 195 part-time (182 women); includes 85 minority (32 Black or African American, non-Hispanic/Latino; 5 Asian, non-Hispanic/Latino; 43 Hispanic/Latino; 5 Two or more races, non-Hispanic/Latino), 12 international. Average age 38. 129 applicants, 89% accepted, 54 enrolled. In 2013, 37 master's, 5 doctorates awarded. *Degree requirements:* For master's, comprehensive exam (for some programs), thesis optional, portfolio; for doctorate, comprehensive exam, thesis/dissertation. *Entrance requirements:* For master's, GRE General Test, minimum GPA of 2.5; for doctorate, GRE General Test. Additional exam requirements/recommendations for international students: Required—TOEFL (minimum score 550 paper-based; 79 iBT), IELTS (minimum score 6.5). *Application deadline:* For fall admission, 8/1 for domestic students, 6/25 for international students; for spring admission, 12/1 for domestic students, 11/12 for international students. Applications are processed on a rolling basis. Application fee: $45 ($75 for international students). Electronic applications accepted. *Financial support:* In 2013–14, 7 research assistantships (averaging $11,999 per year), 4 teaching assistantships (averaging $13,348 per year) were awarded. Financial award application deadline: 5/31; financial award applicants required to submit FAFSA. *Unit head:* Dr. Melinda Miller, Chair, 936-294-1357, Fax: 936-294-1131, E-mail: mmiller@shsu.edu. *Application contact:* Molly Doughtie, Advisor, 936-294-1105, E-mail: edu_mxd@shsu.edu.
Website: http://www.shsu.edu/~edu_lls/.

San Diego State University, Graduate and Research Affairs, College of Education, School of Teacher Education, Program in Reading Education, San Diego, CA 92182. Offers MA. *Accreditation:* NCATE. Part-time programs available. *Entrance requirements:* For master's, GRE General Test, letters of reference. Additional exam requirements/recommendations for international students: Required—TOEFL. Electronic applications accepted. *Faculty research:* Literacy, writing, reading/writing connection, class size reduction in reading, book clubs, evaluation instruments in reading/language arts.

San Francisco State University, Division of Graduate Studies, College of Education, Department of Elementary Education, Program in Language and Literacy Education, San Francisco, CA 94132-1722. Offers language and literacy education (MA); reading (Certificate); reading and language arts (Credential). *Unit head:* Dr. Debra Luna, Chair, 415-338-1562, E-mail: dluna@sfsu.edu. *Application contact:* Dr. Ali Borjian, MA Program Coordinator, 415-338-1838, E-mail: borjian@sfsu.edu.
Website: http://coe.sfsu.edu/eed/language-and-literacy-education.

San Francisco State University, Division of Graduate Studies, College of Liberal and Creative Arts, Department of English Language and Literature, San Francisco, CA 94132-1722. Offers composition (MA); immigrant literacies (Certificate); linguistics (MA); literature (MA); teaching English to speakers of other languages (MA); teaching of composition (Certificate); teaching post-secondary reading (Certificate). Part-time programs available. *Application deadline:* Applications are processed on a rolling basis. *Unit head:* Dr. Sugie Goen-Salter, Chair, 415-338-2264, E-mail: english@sfsu.edu. *Application contact:* Cynthia Losinsky, Administrative Support, Graduate Programs, 415-338-2660, E-mail: english@sfsu.edu.
Website: http://english.sfsu.edu/.

San Jose State University, Graduate Studies and Research, Connie L. Lurie College of Education, Department of Elementary Education, San Jose, CA 95192-0001. Offers curriculum and instruction (MA); reading (Certificate). *Accreditation:* NCATE. *Degree requirements:* For master's, thesis or alternative. Electronic applications accepted.

Seattle Pacific University, Master of Education in Curriculum and Instruction Program, Seattle, WA 98119-1997. Offers reading/language arts education (M Ed). *Accreditation:* NCATE. Part-time and evening/weekend programs available. *Students:* 1 (woman) full-time, 14 part-time (12 women); includes 6 minority (3 Asian, non-Hispanic/Latino; 2 Hispanic/Latino; 1 Two or more races, non-Hispanic/Latino). Average age 36. In 2013, 35 master's awarded. *Degree requirements:* For master's, comprehensive exam. *Entrance requirements:* For master's, GRE General Test or MAT, copy of teaching certificate, official transcript(s), resume, personal statement, two letters of recommendation. Additional exam requirements/recommendations for international students: Required—TOEFL (minimum score 550 paper-based). *Application deadline:* For fall admission, 8/15 priority date for domestic students, 7/1 for international students; for winter admission, 11/15 for domestic students; for spring admission, 2/15 priority date for domestic students, 3/1 for international students; for summer admission, 5/15 for domestic students. Applications are processed on a rolling basis. Application fee: $50. Electronic applications accepted. *Expenses:* Contact institution. *Financial support:* Applicants required to submit FAFSA. *Faculty research:* Educational technology, classroom environments, character education. *Unit head:* Dr. Tracy Williams, Chair, 206-281-2293, E-mail: williamst@spu.edu. *Application contact:* The Graduate Center, 206-281-2091.

Seattle Pacific University, Master of Education in Literacy Program, Seattle, WA 98119-1997. Offers M Ed. Part-time programs available. *Students:* 1 full-time (0 women), 14 part-time (13 women); includes 1 minority (Native Hawaiian or other Pacific Islander, non-Hispanic/Latino). Average age 30. 10 applicants, 50% accepted, 5 enrolled. In 2013, 9 master's awarded. *Degree requirements:* For master's, comprehensive exam. *Entrance requirements:* For master's, MAT or GRE (unless minimum undergraduate GPA of 3.4 or master's degree from accredited university), copy of teaching certificate, official transcript(s) from each college/university attended, personal statement (1-2 pages), two letters of recommendation, moral and character fitness policy form, resume. *Application deadline:* For fall admission, 8/15 for domestic students; for winter admission, 11/15 for domestic students; for spring admission, 2/15 for domestic students; for summer admission, 5/15 for domestic students. Applications are processed on a rolling basis. Application fee: $50. Electronic applications accepted. *Financial support:* Scholarships/grants available. Financial award applicants required to submit FAFSA. *Unit head:* Dr. Scott F. Beers, Chair, 206-281-2707, E-mail: sbeers@spu.edu. *Application contact:* The Graduate Center, 206-281-2091.
Website: http://spu.edu/academics/school-of-education/graduate-programs/masters-programs/literacy.

Seattle University, College of Education, Program in Literacy, Seattle, WA 98122-1090. Offers M Ed, Post-Master's Certificate. *Faculty:* 1 (woman) part-time/adjunct. *Students:* 11 part-time (all women); includes 2 minority (1 Asian, non-Hispanic/Latino; 1 Hispanic/Latino). Average age 31. 4 applicants, 100% accepted, 1 enrolled. In 2013, 6 other advanced degrees awarded. *Entrance requirements:* For master's, GRE, MAT or minimum GPA of 3.0, 1 year of K-12 teaching experience; for Post-Master's Certificate, GRE, MAT or minimum GPA of 3.0, master's degree, WA state teaching certification. Additional exam requirements/recommendations for international students: Required—TOEFL. *Application deadline:* For fall admission, 8/20 priority date for domestic students; for winter admission, 11/20 priority date for domestic students; for spring admission, 2/20 priority date for domestic students. Application fee: $55. *Financial support:* In 2013–14, 6 students received support. *Unit head:* Dr. Katherine Schlick Noe, Director, 206-296-5768, E-mail: kschlnoe@seattleu.edu. *Application contact:* Janet Shandley, Associate Dean of Graduate Admissions, 206-296-5900, Fax: 206-298-5656, E-mail: grad_admissions@seattleu.edu.

Shippensburg University of Pennsylvania, School of Graduate Studies, College of Education and Human Services, Department of Teacher Education, Shippensburg, PA 17257-2299. Offers curriculum and instruction (M Ed), including biology, early childhood education, elementary education, geography/earth science, history, mathematics, middle level education, modern languages; reading (M Ed). *Accreditation:* NCATE. Part-time and evening/weekend programs available. *Faculty:* 13 full-time (9 women), 2 part-time/adjunct (both women). *Students:* 6 full-time (all women), 72 part-time (61 women); includes 5 minority (1 Black or African American, non-Hispanic/Latino; 1 Asian, non-Hispanic/Latino; 2 Hispanic/Latino; 1 Two or more races, non-Hispanic/Latino), 1 international. Average age 30. 55 applicants, 60% accepted, 24 enrolled. In 2013, 63 master's awarded. *Degree requirements:* For master's, comprehensive exam (for some programs), thesis optional, practicum or internship; capstone seminar (for some programs). *Entrance requirements:* For master's, MAT or GRE (if GPA less than 2.75), interview, 3 letters of reference, questionnaire of teaching background and future goals. Additional exam requirements/recommendations for international students: Required—TOEFL (minimum score 580 paper-based); Recommended—IELTS (minimum score 6). *Application deadline:* For fall admission, 4/1 priority date for domestic students, 4/30 for international students; for spring admission, 9/1 priority date for domestic students, 9/30 for international students. Applications are processed on a rolling basis. Application fee: $45. Electronic applications accepted. *Expenses: Tuition, area resident:* Part-time $442 per credit. Tuition, state resident: part-time $442 per credit. Tuition, nonresident: part-time $663 per credit. *Required fees:* $127 per credit. *Financial support:* In 2013–14, 4 research assistantships with full tuition reimbursements (averaging $5,000 per year) were awarded; career-related internships or fieldwork, scholarships/grants, unspecified assistantships, and resident hall director and student payroll positions also available. Support available to part-time students. Financial award application deadline: 3/1; financial award applicants required to submit FAFSA. *Unit head:* Dr. Christine A. Royce, Chairperson, 717-477-1688, Fax: 717-477-4046, E-mail: caroyc@ship.edu. *Application contact:* Jeremy R. Goshorn, Assistant Dean of Graduate Admissions, 717-477-1231, Fax: 717-477-4016, E-mail: jrgoshorn@ship.edu.
Website: http://www.ship.edu/teacher/.

Siena Heights University, Graduate College, Adrian, MI 49221-1796. Offers clinical mental health counseling (MA); education leadership (Specialist); leadership (MA), including health care, higher education leadership, organizational; teacher education (MA), including early childhood, early childhood: Montessori-based, education leadership: principal, elementary education, K-12 reading, leadership: higher education, secondary education, K-12 reading, special education, K-12 cognitive impairment, special education, K-12 learning disabled. Part-time and evening/weekend programs available. *Faculty:* 37. *Students:* 9 full-time (7 women), 251 part-time (179 women). In 2013, 32 master's awarded. *Degree requirements:* For master's, thesis, presentation. *Entrance requirements:* For master's, minimum GPA of 3.0, current resume, essay, all post-secondary transcripts, 3 letters of reference, conviction disclosure form; copy of teaching certificate (for some education programs); for Specialist, master's degree, minimum GPA of 3.0, current resume, essay, all post-secondary transcripts, 3 letters of reference, conviction disclosure form; copy of teaching certificate (for some education programs). *Application deadline:* Applications are processed on a rolling basis. Application fee: $50. *Expenses: Tuition:* Part-time $535 per semester hour. *Required fees:* $130 per semester. *Financial support:* Career-related internships or fieldwork, Federal Work-Study, and resident assistantships available. Financial award application deadline: 9/1; financial award applicants required to submit FAFSA. *Unit head:* Dr. Linda S. Pettit, Dean, Graduate College, 517-264-7661, Fax: 517-264-7714, E-mail: lpettit@sienahts.edu.
Website: http://www.sienaheights.edu.

Simmons College, Graduate School of Library and Information Science, Boston, MA 02115. Offers archives management (MS, Certificate); children's literature (MA); digital stewardship (Certificate); instructional technology (Certificate); library and information science (MS, PhD); managerial leadership in the informational professions (PhD); school library teacher (MS, Certificate); writing for children (MFA); MA/MA; MA/MAT; MA/MFA; MS/MA. *Accreditation:* ALA (one or more programs are accredited). Part-time and evening/weekend programs available. Postbaccalaureate distance learning degree programs offered (no on-campus study). *Students:* 55 full-time (45 women), 716 part-time (585 women); includes 81 minority (19 Black or African American, non-Hispanic/Latino; 1 American Indian or Alaska Native, non-Hispanic/Latino; 14 Asian, non-Hispanic/Latino; 32 Hispanic/Latino; 15 Two or more races, non-Hispanic/Latino), 9 international. 430 applicants, 82% accepted, 207 enrolled. In 2013, 281 master's, 4 doctorates awarded. *Degree requirements:* For master's, thesis optional, capstone project experience; for doctorate, comprehensive exam, 36 credit hours (includes 3-credit dissertation). *Entrance requirements:* For doctorate, GRE, transcripts, personal

statement, resume, recommendations, master's degree. Additional exam requirements/recommendations for international students: Required—TOEFL (minimum score 550 paper-based; 79 iBT), IELTS (minimum score 7). *Application deadline:* For fall admission, 3/1 for domestic and international students; for spring admission, 9/1 for domestic and international students; for summer admission, 2/1 for domestic and international students. Applications are processed on a rolling basis. Application fee: $65. Electronic applications accepted. *Financial support:* In 2013–14, 67 students received support, including 5 fellowships with partial tuition reimbursements available (averaging $32,461 per year), 6 research assistantships (averaging $35,168 per year), 7 teaching assistantships with full and partial tuition reimbursements available (averaging $3,000 per year); scholarships/grants, tuition waivers, and unspecified assistantships also available. Financial award application deadline: 2/1; financial award applicants required to submit FAFSA. *Faculty research:* Archives and social justice, information-seeking behavior, information retrieval, organization of information, cultural heritage informatics. *Unit head:* Dr. Eileen G. Abels, Dean, 617-521-2869. *Application contact:* Sarah Petrakos, 617-521-2868, Fax: 617-521-3192, E-mail: gslisadm@simmons.edu.
Website: http://www.simmons.edu/gslis/.

Simmons College, School of Social Work, Boston, MA 02115. Offers assistive technology (MS Ed, Ed S); behavior analysis (MS, PhD, Ed S); education (MA, CAGS); language and literacy (MS Ed, Ed S); social work (MSW, PhD); special education (MS Ed), including moderate disabilities, severe disabilities; teaching (MAT), including elementary education, general education, high school education; teaching English as a second language (MA, CAGS); urban leadership (MSW); MSW/MBA. *Accreditation:* CSWE (one or more programs are accredited). Part-time programs available. Postbaccalaureate distance learning degree programs offered (no on-campus study). *Students:* 519 full-time (454 women), 703 part-time (604 women); includes 192 minority (61 Black or African American, non-Hispanic/Latino; 1 American Indian or Alaska Native, non-Hispanic/Latino; 35 Asian, non-Hispanic/Latino; 71 Hispanic/Latino; 2 Native Hawaiian or other Pacific Islander, non-Hispanic/Latino; 22 Two or more races, non-Hispanic/Latino), 16 international. 952 applicants, 66% accepted, 353 enrolled. In 2013, 159 master's, 2 doctorates awarded. Terminal master's awarded for partial completion of doctoral program. *Degree requirements:* For master's, thesis (for some programs); for doctorate, comprehensive exam (for some programs), thesis/dissertation (for some programs). *Entrance requirements:* For master's, GRE, MAT, MTEL (for different programs); for doctorate, GRE, BCBA Analyst Exam. Additional exam requirements/recommendations for international students: Required—TOEFL (minimum score 600 paper-based; 100 iBT). *Application deadline:* Applications are processed on a rolling basis. Application fee: $45. Electronic applications accepted. *Financial support:* Teaching assistantships and scholarships/grants available. *Unit head:* Dr. Stefan Krug, Dean, 617-521-3924. *Application contact:* Carlos D. Frontado, Director of Admissions, 617-521-3920, Fax: 617-521-3980, E-mail: ssw@simmons.edu.
Website: http://www.simmons.edu/ssw/.

Simon Fraser University, Office of Graduate Studies, Faculty of Education, Program in Languages, Cultures, and Literacies, Burnaby, BC V5A 1S6, Canada. Offers PhD. *Expenses: Tuition, area resident:* Full-time $5084 Canadian dollars. *Required fees:* $840 Canadian dollars.

Slippery Rock University of Pennsylvania, Graduate Studies (Recruitment), College of Education, Department of Elementary Education and Early Childhood, Slippery Rock, PA 16057-1383. Offers elementary education (M Ed), including K-12 reading specialist, math/science K-8, reading, reading specialist-instructional coach: literacy. *Accreditation:* NCATE. Part-time and evening/weekend programs available. Postbaccalaureate distance learning degree programs offered (no on-campus study). *Faculty:* 2 full-time (both women). *Students:* 4 full-time (all women), 23 part-time (all women); includes 1 minority (Black or African American, non-Hispanic/Latino). Average age 28. 47 applicants, 79% accepted, 11 enrolled. In 2013, 36 master's awarded. *Entrance requirements:* For master's, GRE General Test, MAT, minimum GPA of 3.0, resume, teaching certification, letters of recommendation, transcripts (depending on program). Additional exam requirements/recommendations for international students: Required—TOEFL (minimum score 550 paper-based; 80 iBT). *Application deadline:* For fall admission, 3/1 priority date for domestic students, 5/1 priority date for international students; for spring admission, 10/1 priority date for domestic students, 9/1 priority date for international students. Applications are processed on a rolling basis. Application fee: $25 ($30 for international students). Electronic applications accepted. *Expenses:* Tuition, state resident: full-time $7956; part-time $442 per credit. Tuition, nonresident: full-time $11,934; part-time $663 per credit. *Required fees:* $2896; $148 per credit. Tuition and fees vary according to degree level and program. *Financial support:* Career-related internships or fieldwork, Federal Work-Study, institutionally sponsored loans, scholarships/grants, tuition waivers (partial), and unspecified assistantships available. Support available to part-time students. Financial award application deadline: 5/1; financial award applicants required to submit FAFSA. *Unit head:* Dr. Suzanne Rose, Graduate Coordinator, 724-738-2042, Fax: 724-738-2779, E-mail: suzanne.rose@sru.edu. *Application contact:* Brandi Weber-Mortimer, Director of Graduate Admissions, 724-738-2051, Fax: 724-738-2146, E-mail: graduate.admissions@sru.edu.

Sojourner-Douglass College, Graduate Program, Baltimore, MD 21205-1814. Offers human services (MASS); public administration (MASS); urban education (reading) (MASS). Part-time and evening/weekend programs available. *Degree requirements:* For master's, comprehensive exam, written proposal oral defense. *Entrance requirements:* For master's, Graduate Examination.

Sonoma State University, School of Education, Rohnert Park, CA 94928. Offers curriculum, teaching, and learning (MA); early childhood education (MA); education (Ed D); educational administration (MA); multiple subject (Credential); reading and literacy (MA); single subject (Credential); special education (MA, Credential). *Accreditation:* NCATE. Part-time and evening/weekend programs available. *Faculty:* 11 full-time (9 women), 1 (woman) part-time/adjunct. *Students:* 162 full-time (119 women), 165 part-time (125 women); includes 61 minority (4 Black or African American, non-Hispanic/Latino; 1 American Indian or Alaska Native, non-Hispanic/Latino; 12 Asian, non-Hispanic/Latino; 29 Hispanic/Latino; 1 Native Hawaiian or other Pacific Islander, non-Hispanic/Latino; 14 Two or more races, non-Hispanic/Latino), 1 international. Average age 33. 314 applicants, 82% accepted, 75 enrolled. In 2013, 41 master's, 287 other advanced degrees awarded. *Degree requirements:* For master's, thesis or alternative. *Entrance requirements:* For master's, minimum GPA of 2.5. Additional exam requirements/recommendations for international students: Required—TOEFL (minimum score 500 paper-based). Application fee: $55. *Expenses:* Tuition, state resident: full-time $8500. Tuition, nonresident: full-time $12,964. *Required fees:* $1762. *Financial support:* In 2013–14, 1 research assistantship (averaging $1,876 per year) was awarded; fellowships, career-related internships or fieldwork, and Federal Work-Study also available. Support available to part-time students. Financial award application deadline: 3/2; financial award applicants required to submit FAFSA. *Unit head:* Dr. Carlos Ayala, Dean, 707-664-4412, E-mail: carlos.ayala@sonoma.edu. *Application contact:* Dr. Jennifer Mahdavi, Coordinator of Graduate Studies, 707-664-3311, E-mail: jennifer.mahdavi@sonoma.edu.
Website: http://www.sonoma.edu/education/.

Southeastern Louisiana University, College of Arts, Humanities and Social Sciences, Department of English, Hammond, LA 70402. Offers creative writing (MA); language and theory (MA); professional writing (MA). Part-time programs available. *Faculty:* 19 full-time (8 women), 1 part-time/adjunct (0 women). *Students:* 13 full-time (7 women), 21 part-time (17 women); includes 4 minority (1 Asian, non-Hispanic/Latino; 3 Hispanic/Latino), 1 international. Average age 29. 13 applicants, 54% accepted, 5 enrolled. In 2013, 15 master's awarded. *Degree requirements:* For master's, comprehensive exam, thesis optional. *Entrance requirements:* For master's, GRE General Test (minimum score of 850), bachelor's degree; minimum undergraduate GPA of 2.5; 24 hours of undergraduate English courses. Additional exam requirements/recommendations for international students: Required—TOEFL (minimum score 500 paper-based; 61 iBT), IELTS (minimum score 5.5). *Application deadline:* For fall admission, 7/15 priority date for domestic students, 6/1 priority date for international students; for spring admission, 12/1 priority date for domestic students, 10/1 priority date for international students. Applications are processed on a rolling basis. Application fee: $20 ($30 for international students). Electronic applications accepted. *Expenses:* Tuition, state resident: full-time $5047. Tuition, nonresident: full-time $17,066. *Required fees:* $1213. Tuition and fees vary according to degree level. *Financial support:* In 2013–14, 1 fellowship (averaging $10,800 per year), 7 research assistantships (averaging $6,900 per year), 1 teaching assistantship (averaging $9,000 per year) were awarded; career-related internships or fieldwork, Federal Work-Study, institutionally sponsored loans, scholarships/grants, and traineeships also available. Support available to part-time students. Financial award application deadline: 5/1; financial award applicants required to submit FAFSA. *Faculty research:* Creole studies, modernism, digital humanities, library studies, John Donne. *Total annual research expenditures:* $47,697. *Unit head:* Dr. David Hanson, Department Head, 985-549-2100, Fax: 985-549-5021, E-mail: dhanson@selu.edu. *Application contact:* Sandra Meyers, Graduate Admissions Analyst, 985-549-5620, Fax: 985-549-5632, E-mail: admissions@selu.edu.
Website: http://www.selu.edu/acad_research/depts/engl.

Southeastern Oklahoma State University, School of Education, Durant, OK 74701-0609. Offers math specialist (M Ed); reading specialist (M Ed); school administration (M Ed); school counseling (M Ed). *Accreditation:* NCATE. Part-time and evening/weekend programs available. *Degree requirements:* For master's, comprehensive exam, thesis optional, portfolio (M Ed). *Entrance requirements:* For master's, GRE General Test (for school counseling), minimum GPA of 3.0 in last 60 hours or 2.75 overall. Additional exam requirements/recommendations for international students: Required—TOEFL (minimum score 550 paper-based; 79 iBT). Electronic applications accepted.

Southern Adventist University, School of Education and Psychology, Collegedale, TN 37315-0370. Offers clinical mental health counseling (MS); inclusive education (MS Ed); instructional leadership (MS Ed); literacy education (MS Ed); outdoor teacher education (MS Ed); school counseling (MS). *Accreditation:* NCATE. Part-time and evening/weekend programs available. *Degree requirements:* For master's, comprehensive exam (for some programs), thesis optional, position paper (MS), portfolio (MS Ed in outdoor teacher education). *Entrance requirements:* For master's, interview (MS); 9 semester hours of upper-division course work in psychology or related field, including 1 course in psychology research or statistics; 9 semester hours of education (MS Ed). Additional exam requirements/recommendations for international students: Required—TOEFL (minimum score 600 paper-based; 100 iBT). Electronic applications accepted.

Southern Arkansas University–Magnolia, Graduate Programs, Magnolia, AR 71753. Offers agriculture (MS); business administration (MBA); computer and information sciences (MS); education (M Ed), including counseling and development, curriculum and instruction, educational administration and supervision, elementary education, reading, secondary education, TESOL; kinesiology (M Ed); library media and information specialist (M Ed); mental health and clinical counseling (MS); public administration (MPA); school counseling (M Ed); teaching (MAT). *Accreditation:* NCATE. Part-time and evening/weekend programs available. Postbaccalaureate distance learning degree programs offered. *Faculty:* 34 full-time (15 women), 8 part-time/adjunct (5 women). *Students:* 48 full-time (22 women), 269 part-time (167 women); includes 85 minority (78 Black or African American, non-Hispanic/Latino; 2 Asian, non-Hispanic/Latino; 2 Hispanic/Latino; 1 Native Hawaiian or other Pacific Islander, non-Hispanic/Latino; 2 Two or more races, non-Hispanic/Latino), 5 international. Average age 33. 149 applicants, 73% accepted, 109 enrolled. In 2013, 149 master's awarded. *Degree requirements:* For master's, comprehensive exam (for some programs), thesis optional. *Entrance requirements:* For master's, GRE, MAT or GMAT, minimum GPA of 2.5. Additional exam requirements/recommendations for international students: Required—TOEFL, IELTS. *Application deadline:* For fall admission, 7/10 for domestic and international students; for winter admission, 12/1 for domestic and international students; for spring admission, 12/1 for domestic and international students; for summer admission, 4/1 for domestic students. Applications are processed on a rolling basis. Application fee: $25 ($50 for international students). Electronic applications accepted. *Expenses:* Tuition, state resident: part-time $254 per credit hour. Tuition, nonresident: part-time $370 per credit hour. *Required fees:* $136 per credit hour. $259 per semester. Tuition and fees vary according to course load and program. *Financial support:* Career-related internships or fieldwork, Federal Work-Study, scholarships/grants, tuition waivers (full), and unspecified assistantships available. Financial award applicants required to submit FAFSA. *Faculty research:* Alternative certification for teachers, supervision of instruction, instructional leadership, counseling. *Unit head:* Dr. Kim Bloss, Dean, School of Graduate Studies, 870-235-4150, Fax: 870-235-5227, E-mail: kkbloss@saumag.edu. *Application contact:* Shrijana Malaka, Admissions Specialist, 870-235-4150, Fax: 870-235-5227, E-mail: smalakar@saumag.edu.
Website: http://www.saumag.edu/graduate.

Southern Connecticut State University, School of Graduate Studies, School of Education, Program in Reading, New Haven, CT 06515-1355. Offers MS, Diploma. Part-time and evening/weekend programs available. *Degree requirements:* For master's, thesis or alternative. *Entrance requirements:* For master's, interview, teaching certificate; for Diploma, master's degree. Electronic applications accepted.

Southern Illinois University Edwardsville, Graduate School, School of Education, Department of Curriculum and Instruction, Program in Literacy Education, Edwardsville, IL 62026-0001. Offers MS Ed. Part-time programs available. *Students:* 21 part-time (all women); includes 2 minority (1 Black or African American, non-Hispanic/Latino; 1 Hispanic/Latino). In 2013, 16 master's awarded. *Degree requirements:* For master's, comprehensive exam, research paper. *Entrance requirements:* Additional exam requirements/recommendations for international students: Required—TOEFL (minimum score 550 paper-based, 79 iBT), IELTS (minimum score 6.5), Michigan Test of English Language Proficiency or PTE. *Application deadline:* For fall admission, 7/18 for domestic students, 6/1 for international students; for spring admission, 12/12 for domestic students, 10/1 for international students; for summer admission, 4/24 for domestic students, 3/1 for international students. Applications are processed on a rolling basis. Application fee: $30. Electronic applications accepted. *Expenses:* Tuition, state resident: full-time $3551. Tuition, nonresident: full-time $8378. *Financial support:* Fellowships, research assistantships, teaching assistantships, institutionally sponsored loans, scholarships/grants, and unspecified assistantships available. Support available

to part-time students. Financial award application deadline: 3/1; financial award applicants required to submit FAFSA. *Unit head:* Dr. Stephanie McAndrews, Director, 618-650-3426, E-mail: smcandr@siue.edu. *Application contact:* Melissa K. Mace, Assistant Director of Graduate and International Recruitment, 618-650-2756, Fax: 618-650-3618, E-mail: mmace@siue.edu.
Website: http://www.siue.edu/education/ci/graduate/literacy.

Southern Illinois University Edwardsville, Graduate School, School of Education, Department of Curriculum and Instruction, Program in Literacy Specialist, Edwardsville, IL 62026. Offers Post-Master's Certificate. Part-time programs available. *Students:* 4 part-time (all women). 1 applicant, 100% accepted. In 2013, 2 Post-Master's Certificates awarded. *Entrance requirements:* Additional exam requirements/recommendations for international students: Required—TOEFL (minimum score 550 paper-based, 79 iBT), IELTS (minimum score 6.5), Michigan Test of English Language Proficiency or PTE. *Application deadline:* For fall admission, 7/18 for domestic students, 6/1 for international students; for spring admission, 12/12 for domestic students, 10/1 for international students; for summer admission, 4/24 for domestic students, 3/1 for international students. Applications are processed on a rolling basis. Application fee: $30. Electronic applications accepted. *Expenses:* Tuition, state resident: full-time $3551. Tuition, nonresident: full-time $8378. *Financial support:* Fellowships with full tuition reimbursements, research assistantships with full tuition reimbursements, teaching assistantships with full tuition reimbursements, institutionally sponsored loans, scholarships/grants, and unspecified assistantships available. Financial award application deadline: 3/1; financial award applicants required to submit FAFSA. *Unit head:* Dr. Stephanie McAndrews, Director, 618-650-3426, E-mail: smcandr@siue.edu. *Application contact:* Melissa K. Mace, Assistant Director of Graduate and International Recruitment, 618-650-2756, Fax: 618-650-3618, E-mail: mmace@siue.edu.
Website: http://www.siue.edu/education/ci/graduate/literacy/.

Southern Methodist University, Annette Caldwell Simmons School of Education and Human Development, Department of Teaching and Learning, Dallas, TX 75275. Offers bilingual/ESL education (MBE); education (M Ed, PhD); gifted education (MBE); reading and writing (M Ed); special education (M Ed). Part-time and evening/weekend programs available. Terminal master's awarded for partial completion of doctoral program. *Degree requirements:* For master's, comprehensive exam, minimum GPA of 3.0; for doctorate, thesis/dissertation, qualifying exams, major area paper, evidence of teaching competency, dissemination of research (e.g., conference presentation), professional portfolio. *Entrance requirements:* For master's, minimum GPA of 3.0 or GRE, 3 letters of recommendation; for doctorate, GRE, minimum GPA of 3.3, 3 years of full-time teaching, 3 letters of recommendation, interview. Additional exam requirements/recommendations for international students: Required—TOEFL. Electronic applications accepted. *Faculty research:* Reading intervention, mathematics intervention, bilingual education, new literacies.

Southern New Hampshire University, School of Education, Manchester, NH 03106-1045. Offers business education (M Ed); child development (M Ed); curriculum and instruction (M Ed), including education leadership, reading, special education, technology integration; education (M Ed); educational leadership (M Ed, Ed D); educational studies (M Ed); elementary education (M Ed); English (MAT); English for speakers of other languages (M Ed); reading and writing specialist (M Ed); school business administration (Certificate); secondary education (M Ed); special education (M Ed); technology integration specialist (M Ed). Part-time and evening/weekend programs available. Postbaccalaureate distance learning degree programs offered (no on-campus study). *Degree requirements:* For master's, comprehensive exam (for some programs), thesis or alternative. *Entrance requirements:* For master's, PRAXIS I, minimum GPA of 2.75. Additional exam requirements/recommendations for international students: Required—TOEFL (minimum score 550 paper-based). Electronic applications accepted. *Expenses:* Contact institution.

Southern Oregon University, Graduate Studies, School of Education, Ashland, OR 97520. Offers elementary education (MA Ed, MS Ed), including classroom teacher, early childhood, handicapped learner, reading, supervision; secondary education (MA Ed, MS Ed), including classroom teacher, handicapped learner, reading, supervision; teaching (MAT). Postbaccalaureate distance learning degree programs offered (minimal on-campus study). *Faculty:* 23 full-time (16 women), 21 part-time/adjunct (20 women). *Students:* 92 full-time (68 women), 118 part-time (88 women); includes 19 minority (1 Black or African American, non-Hispanic/Latino; 1 American Indian or Alaska Native, non-Hispanic/Latino; 2 Asian, non-Hispanic/Latino; 10 Hispanic/Latino; 5 Two or more races, non-Hispanic/Latino), 5 international. Average age 36. 22 applicants, 59% accepted, 12 enrolled. In 2013, 127 master's awarded. *Degree requirements:* For master's, thesis optional. *Entrance requirements:* For master's, GRE General Test, minimum cumulative GPA of 3.0 in the last 90 quarter credits (60 semester credits) of undergraduate coursework. Additional exam requirements/recommendations for international students: Required—TOEFL (minimum score 540 paper-based; 76 iBT), IELTS (minimum score 6), ELPT (minimum score 964) or ELS (minimum score 112). *Application deadline:* For fall admission, 7/31 priority date for domestic and international students; for winter admission, 11/15 priority date for domestic and international students; for spring admission, 1/7 priority date for domestic and international students. Applications are processed on a rolling basis. Application fee: $50. Electronic applications accepted. *Expenses:* Tuition, state resident: full-time $13,635; part-time $378.72 per credit hour. Tuition, nonresident: full-time $17,042; part-time $473.40 per credit hour. *Required fees:* $408 per quarter. *Financial support:* Research assistantships with partial tuition reimbursements, career-related internships or fieldwork, institutionally sponsored loans, scholarships/grants, and unspecified assistantships available. *Unit head:* Dr. Gerry McCain, Graduate Program Coordinator, 541-552-6934, E-mail: mccaing@sou.edu. *Application contact:* Kelly Moutsatson, Director of Admissions, 541-552-6411, Fax: 541-552-8403, E-mail: admissions@sou.edu.
Website: http://www.sou.edu/education/.

Southwestern Adventist University, Education Department, Keene, TX 76059. Offers curriculum and instruction with reading emphasis (M Ed); educational leadership (M Ed). Part-time and evening/weekend programs available. *Degree requirements:* For master's, thesis or alternative, professional paper. *Entrance requirements:* For master's, GRE General Test.

Southwest Minnesota State University, Department of Education, Marshall, MN 56258. Offers ESL (MS); math (MS); reading (MS); special education (MS), including developmental disabilities, early childhood education, emotional behavioral disorders, learning disabilities; teaching, learning and leadership (MS). Part-time and evening/weekend programs available. Postbaccalaureate distance learning degree programs offered (no on-campus study). *Entrance requirements:* Additional exam requirements/recommendations for international students: Required—TOEFL or IELTS; Recommended—TOEFL (minimum score 550 paper-based; 80 iBT), IELTS.

Spring Arbor University, School of Education, Spring Arbor, MI 49283-9799. Offers education (MAE); reading (MAR); special education (MSE). *Accreditation:* Teacher Education Accreditation Council. Part-time and evening/weekend programs available. Postbaccalaureate distance learning degree programs offered (minimal on-campus study). *Faculty:* 6 full-time (5 women), 13 part-time/adjunct (8 women). *Students:* 49 full-time (44 women), 175 part-time (141 women); includes 13 minority (10 Black or African American, non-Hispanic/Latino; 1 Asian, non-Hispanic/Latino; 2 Hispanic/Latino). Average age 36. In 2013, 54 master's awarded. *Degree requirements:* For master's, thesis. *Entrance requirements:* For master's, official transcripts from all institutions attended, including evidence of an earned bachelor's degree from regionally-accredited college or university with minimum cumulative GPA of 3.0 for the last two years of the bachelor's degree; two professional letters of recommendation. Additional exam requirements/recommendations for international students: Required—TOEFL (minimum score 600 paper-based). *Application deadline:* For fall admission, 9/1 priority date for domestic students; for winter admission, 2/1 priority date for domestic students; for spring admission, 2/1 priority date for domestic students. Applications are processed on a rolling basis. Application fee: $40. Electronic applications accepted. *Financial support:* Applicants required to submit FAFSA. *Unit head:* Dr. Linda Sherrill, Dean, 517-750-1200 Ext. 1562, Fax: 517-750-6629, E-mail: lsherril@arbor.edu. *Application contact:* James R. Weidman, Coordinator of Graduate Recruitment, 517-750-6523, Fax: 517-750-6629, E-mail: jimw@arbor.edu.
Website: http://www.arbor.edu/academics/school-of-education/.

State University of New York at Fredonia, Graduate Studies, College of Education, Program in Literacy, Fredonia, NY 14063-1136. Offers MS Ed. *Accreditation:* NCATE. Part-time and evening/weekend programs available. *Degree requirements:* For master's, thesis optional. *Expenses:* Tuition, state resident: full-time $7398; part-time $411 per credit hour. Tuition, nonresident: full-time $13,770; part-time $765 per credit hour. *Required fees:* $1143.90; $63.55 per credit hour. Tuition and fees vary according to course load.

State University of New York at New Paltz, Graduate School, School of Education, Department of Educational Studies, Program in Special Education, New Paltz, NY 12561. Offers adolescence special education (7-12) (MS Ed); adolescence special education and literacy education (MS Ed); childhood special education (1-6) (MS Ed); childhood special education and literacy education (MS Ed); early childhood special education (B-2) (MS Ed). *Accreditation:* NCATE. Part-time and evening/weekend programs available. *Faculty:* 6 full-time (4 women), 9 part-time/adjunct (all women). *Students:* 42 full-time (35 women), 35 part-time (24 women); includes 11 minority (1 Asian, non-Hispanic/Latino; 8 Hispanic/Latino; 2 Two or more races, non-Hispanic/Latino). Average age 27. 63 applicants, 73% accepted, 24 enrolled. In 2013, 43 master's awarded. *Degree requirements:* For master's, portfolio. *Entrance requirements:* For master's, minimum GPA of 3.0 (3.2 for special education and literacy programs), New York state teaching certificate. Additional exam requirements/recommendations for international students: Required—TOEFL (minimum score 550 paper-based; 80 iBT), IELTS (minimum score 6.5). *Application deadline:* For fall admission, 3/15 priority date for domestic students, 3/15 for international students; for spring admission, 11/1 for domestic and international students. Application fee: $50. Electronic applications accepted. *Expenses:* Tuition, state resident: full-time $9870; part-time $411 per credit. Tuition, nonresident: full-time $18,350; part-time $765 per credit. *Required fees:* $1213. Tuition and fees vary according to program. *Financial support:* Application deadline: 8/1. *Unit head:* Dr. Jane Sileo, Coordinator, 845-257-2835, E-mail: sileoj@newpaltz.edu. *Application contact:* Caroline Murphy, Graduate Admissions Advisor, 845-257-3285, E-mail: gradschool@newpaltz.edu.
Website: http://www.newpaltz.edu/edstudies/special_ed.html.

State University of New York at New Paltz, Graduate School, School of Education, Department of Elementary Education, New Paltz, NY 12561. Offers childhood education 1-6 (MS Ed, MST), including childhood education 1-6 (MST), early childhood B-2 (MS Ed), mathematics, science and technology (MS Ed), reading/literacy (MS Ed); literacy education 5-12 (MS Ed); literacy education and childhood special education (MS Ed); literacy education B-6 (MS Ed). *Accreditation:* NCATE. Part-time and evening/weekend programs available. *Faculty:* 11 full-time (10 women), 9 part-time/adjunct (8 women). *Students:* 51 full-time (47 women), 128 part-time (117 women); includes 13 minority (2 Black or African American, non-Hispanic/Latino; 11 Hispanic/Latino). Average age 27. 103 applicants, 89% accepted, 57 enrolled. In 2013, 96 master's awarded. *Degree requirements:* For master's, comprehensive exam (for some programs), portfolio. *Entrance requirements:* For master's, GRE or MAT (for MST), minimum GPA of 3.0 (3.2 for literacy and special education), New York state teaching certificate (for MS Ed). Additional exam requirements/recommendations for international students: Required—TOEFL (minimum score 550 paper-based; 80 iBT), IELTS (minimum score 6.5). *Application deadline:* For fall admission, 4/1 for domestic and international students; for spring admission, 11/15 for domestic and international students. Application fee: $50. Electronic applications accepted. *Expenses:* Tuition, state resident: full-time $9870; part-time $411 per credit. Tuition, nonresident: full-time $18,350; part-time $765 per credit. *Required fees:* $1213. Tuition and fees vary according to program. *Financial support:* Application deadline: 8/1. *Faculty research:* Multi-sensory teaching methods, volunteer tutoring programs for struggling readers, school readiness and transition, math/science/technology, university-school partnerships. *Unit head:* Dr. Andrea Noel, Chair, 845-257-2860, E-mail: noela@newpaltz.edu. *Application contact:* Caroline Murphy, Graduate Admissions Advisor, 845-257-3285, Fax: 845-257-3284, E-mail: gradschool@newpaltz.edu.
Website: http://www.newpaltz.edu/elementaryed/.

State University of New York at Oswego, Graduate Studies, School of Education, Department of Curriculum and Instruction, Oswego, NY 13126. Offers adolescence education (MST); art education (MAT); childhood education (MST); elementary education (MS Ed); literacy education (MS Ed); secondary education (MS Ed); special education (MS Ed). Part-time and evening/weekend programs available. *Degree requirements:* For master's, comprehensive exam (for some programs), thesis optional. *Entrance requirements:* For master's, GRE General Test, minimum GPA of 2.7, provisional teaching certificate. Additional exam requirements/recommendations for international students: Required—TOEFL (minimum score 560 paper-based). *Faculty research:* Classroom applications for microcomputers; classroom questioning, wait-time, and achievement; values clarification and academic achievement.

State University of New York at Plattsburgh, Division of Education, Health, and Human Services, Program in Teacher Education: Literacy Education, Plattsburgh, NY 12901-2681. Offers birth-grade 6 (MS Ed); grades 5-12 (MS Ed). *Accreditation:* Teacher Education Accreditation Council. Part-time and evening/weekend programs available. *Students:* 2 full-time (0 women), 4 part-time (2 women). Average age 28. *Entrance requirements:* For master's, minimum GPA of 2.75. Additional exam requirements/recommendations for international students: Required—TOEFL. *Application deadline:* For fall admission, 2/15 priority date for domestic students; for spring admission, 10/15 priority date for domestic students. Applications are processed on a rolling basis. Application fee: $75. *Financial support:* Federal Work-Study available. Support available to part-time students. Financial award application deadline: 4/15; financial award applicants required to submit FAFSA. *Faculty research:* Reading pedagogy, early childhood literacy, children's literature, integrated language arts. *Unit head:* Dr. Heidi Schnackenberg, Coordinator, 518-564-5143, E-mail: schnachl@plattsburgh.edu. *Application contact:* Betsy Kane, Director, Graduate Admissions, 518-564-4723, Fax: 518-564-4722, E-mail: bkane002@plattsburgh.edu.

Reading Education

State University of New York College at Cortland, Graduate Studies, School of Education, Program in Literacy Education, Cortland, NY 13045. Offers MS Ed. *Accreditation:* NCATE. Part-time and evening/weekend programs available. *Degree requirements:* For master's, one foreign language, comprehensive exam, thesis (for some programs). *Entrance requirements:* Additional exam requirements/ recommendations for international students: Required—TOEFL. *Expenses:* Tuition, state resident: full-time $9870; part-time $411 per credit hour. Tuition, nonresident: full-time $18,350; part-time $765 per credit hour. *Required fees:* $1458; $65 per credit hour.

State University of New York College at Geneseo, Graduate Studies, School of Education, Program in Literacy, Geneseo, NY 14454-1401. Offers MS Ed. Part-time and evening/weekend programs available. *Faculty:* 9 full-time (6 women), 1 (woman) part-time/adjunct. *Students:* 51 full-time (43 women), 56 part-time (49 women); includes 3 minority (1 Asian, non-Hispanic/Latino; 2 Hispanic/Latino), 1 international. Average age 25. 51 applicants, 100% accepted, 35 enrolled. In 2013, 78 master's awarded. *Degree requirements:* For master's, reading clinics, action research project. *Application deadline:* For fall admission, 3/1 priority date for domestic students; for spring admission, 10/1 for domestic students. Application fee: $50. *Expenses:* Tuition, state resident: full-time $8790; part-time $411 per credit hour. Tuition, nonresident: full-time $18,350; part-time $765 per credit hour. *Required fees:* $795; $32.90 per credit hour. *Financial support:* In 2013–14, 3 students received support. Scholarships/grants, health care benefits, tuition waivers (full), and unspecified assistantships available. Support available to part-time students. Financial award application deadline: 4/1; financial award applicants required to submit FAFSA. *Unit head:* Dr. Anjoo Sikka, Dean of School of Education, 585-245-5151, Fax: 585-245-5220, E-mail: sikka@geneseo.edu. *Application contact:* Tracy Peterson, Director of Student Success, 585-245-5443, Fax: 585-245-5220, E-mail: peterson@geneseo.edu.

State University of New York College at Oneonta, Graduate Education, Division of Education, Department of Elementary Education and Reading, Oneonta, NY 13820-4015. Offers childhood education (MS Ed); literacy education (MS Ed). *Accreditation:* NCATE. Part-time and evening/weekend programs available. *Entrance requirements:* For master's, GRE General Test.

State University of New York College at Potsdam, School of Education and Professional Studies, Program in Literacy, Potsdam, NY 13676. Offers literacy educator (MS Ed); literacy specialist (MS Ed), including birth-grade 6, grades 5-12. *Accreditation:* NCATE. Part-time programs available. Postbaccalaureate distance learning degree programs offered (minimal on-campus study). *Entrance requirements:* For master's, minimum GPA of 2.75 in last 60 hours of course work. Additional exam requirements/ recommendations for international students: Required—TOEFL (minimum score 550 paper-based; 80 iBT), IELTS (minimum score 6). Electronic applications accepted.

Sul Ross State University, Rio Grande College of Sul Ross State University, Alpine, TX 79832. Offers business administration (MBA); teacher education (M Ed), including bilingual education, counseling, educational diagnostics, elementary education, general education, reading, school administration, secondary education. Part-time and evening/ weekend programs available. Postbaccalaureate distance learning degree programs offered (no on-campus study). *Degree requirements:* For master's, comprehensive exam, thesis optional, minimum GPA of 3.0. *Entrance requirements:* For master's, GMAT or GRE General Test, minimum GPA of 2.5 in last 60 hours of undergraduate work. Additional exam requirements/recommendations for international students: Required—TOEFL.

Sul Ross State University, School of Professional Studies, Department of Teacher Education, Program in Reading Specialist, Alpine, TX 79832. Offers master reading teacher (Certificate); Texas reading specialist (M Ed). Part-time and evening/weekend programs available. *Degree requirements:* For master's, thesis optional. *Entrance requirements:* For master's, GMAT or GRE General Test, minimum GPA of 2.5 in last 60 hours of undergraduate work.

Syracuse University, School of Education, Program in Literacy Education: Birth-Grade 6, Syracuse, NY 13244. Offers MS. Part-time programs available. *Students:* 7 full-time (6 women), 5 part-time (all women). Average age 24. 13 applicants, 92% accepted, 6 enrolled. In 2013, 7 master's awarded. *Degree requirements:* For master's, thesis or alternative. *Entrance requirements:* For master's, New York state teacher certification or eligibility for certification. Additional exam requirements/recommendations for international students: Required—TOEFL (minimum score 100 iBT). *Application deadline:* For fall admission, 1/15 priority date for domestic and international students; for spring admission, 10/15 for domestic students, 10/15 priority date for international students. Applications are processed on a rolling basis. Application fee: $75. Electronic applications accepted. *Financial support:* Fellowships with full tuition reimbursements and teaching assistantships with full and partial tuition reimbursements available. Financial award application deadline: 1/1. *Faculty research:* Literacy, knowledge modeling, assessment, teaching of literature, writing. *Unit head:* Dr. Rachel Brown, Program Coordinator, 315-443-4755, E-mail: rfbrown@syr.edu. *Application contact:* Laurie Deyo, Graduate Recruiter, School of Education, 315-443-2505, E-mail: e-gradrcrt@syr.edu.
Website: http://soeweb.syr.edu/.

Syracuse University, School of Education, Program in Literacy Education: Grades 5-12, Syracuse, NY 13244. Offers MS. Part-time programs available. *Students:* 3 full-time (all women), 5 part-time (3 women). Average age 25. 9 applicants, 100% accepted, 3 enrolled. In 2013, 9 master's awarded. *Entrance requirements:* For master's, New York state teacher certification or eligibility. Additional exam requirements/recommendations for international students: Required—TOEFL (minimum score 100 iBT). *Application deadline:* For fall admission, 1/15 priority date for domestic and international students. Application fee: $75. Electronic applications accepted. *Financial support:* Fellowships with full tuition reimbursements and teaching assistantships with full and partial tuition reimbursements available. Financial award application deadline: 1/1. *Unit head:* Dr. Rachel Brown, Program Coordinator, 315-443-4755, E-mail: rfbrown@syr.edu. *Application contact:* Laurie Deyo, Graduate Recruiter, School of Education, 315-443-2505, E-mail: e-gradrcrt@syr.edu.
Website: http://soeweb.syr.edu/academic/reading_language_arts/graduate/masters/ literacy_ed_5_12/default.aspx.

Teachers College, Columbia University, Graduate Faculty of Education, Department of Curriculum and Teaching, Program in Literacy Specialist, New York, NY 10027-6696. Offers MA. *Faculty:* 6 full-time, 5 part-time/adjunct. *Students:* 37 full-time (all women), 47 part-time (42 women); includes 19 minority (9 Black or African American, non-Hispanic/ Latino; 6 Asian, non-Hispanic/Latino; 3 Hispanic/Latino; 1 Two or more races, non-Hispanic/Latino), 5 international. Average age 27. 82 applicants, 83% accepted, 20 enrolled. In 2013, 60 master's awarded. *Application deadline:* For fall admission, 1/15 priority date for domestic students; for spring admission, 11/1 for domestic students; for summer admission, 1/15 priority date for domestic students. Application fee: $65. Electronic applications accepted. *Financial support:* Applicants required to submit FAFSA. *Faculty research:* Teaching of reading and writing, staff development and school reform, reading in mathematics classrooms, cultural and critical perspectives on literacy education, literacy and the arts. *Unit head:* Prof. Lucy Calkins, Program Coordinator, 212-678-3931, E-mail: calkins@tc.columbia.edu. *Application contact:*

Elizabeth Puleio, Assistant Director of Admission, 212-678-3730, E-mail: eap2136@ tc.columbia.edu.
Website: http://www.tc.columbia.edu/c&t/literacy/.

Teachers College, Columbia University, Graduate Faculty of Education, Department of Health and Behavioral Studies, Program in Reading Specialist, New York, NY 10027. Offers MA. *Faculty:* 2 full-time, 3 part-time/adjunct. *Students:* 5 full-time (all women), 40 part-time (39 women); includes 11 minority (1 Black or African American, non-Hispanic/ Latino; 2 Asian, non-Hispanic/Latino; 7 Hispanic/Latino; 1 Two or more races, non-Hispanic/Latino), 1 international. Average age 28. 25 applicants, 72% accepted, 13 enrolled. In 2013, 26 master's awarded. *Degree requirements:* For master's, integrative project. *Application deadline:* For fall admission, 1/15 priority date for domestic students; for spring admission, 11/1 for domestic students; for summer admission, 1/15 for domestic students. Application fee: $65. Electronic applications accepted. *Financial support:* Application deadline: 2/1; applicants required to submit FAFSA. *Faculty research:* Reading and writing processes in children and adults, adult education and workplace literacy, early childhood education and mental health, learning disabilities. *Unit head:* Prof. Dolores Perin, Program Coordinator, 212-678-3943, E-mail: perin@ tc.edu. *Application contact:* Peter Shon, Assistant Director of Admission, 212-678-3305, Fax: 212-678-4171, E-mail: shon@exchange.tc.columbia.edu.
Website: http://www.tc.edu/hbs/reading-specialist/.

Tennessee Technological University, College of Graduate Studies, College of Education, Department of Curriculum and Instruction, Program in Exceptional Learning, Cookeville, TN 38505. Offers applied behavior analysis (PhD); literacy (PhD); program planning and evaluation (PhD); STEM education (PhD). Part-time and evening/weekend programs available. *Students:* 14 full-time (12 women), 22 part-time (16 women); includes 2 minority (1 Black or African American, non-Hispanic/Latino; 1 Two or more races, non-Hispanic/Latino), 1 international. 15 applicants, 47% accepted, 6 enrolled. In 2013, 1 doctorate awarded. *Degree requirements:* For doctorate, comprehensive exam, thesis/dissertation. *Entrance requirements:* For doctorate, GRE, minimum GPA of 3.0. Additional exam requirements/recommendations for international students: Required— TOEFL (minimum score 550 paper-based; 79 iBT), IELTS (minimum score 5.5), PTE (minimum score 53), or TOEIC (Test of English as an International Communication). *Application deadline:* For fall admission, 8/1 for domestic students, 5/1 for international students; for spring admission, 12/1 for domestic students, 10/1 for international students. Applications are processed on a rolling basis. Application fee: $35 ($40 for international students). Electronic applications accepted. *Expenses:* Tuition, state resident: full-time $9347; part-time $465 per credit hour. Tuition, nonresident: full-time $23,635; part-time $1152 per credit hour. *Financial support:* In 2013–14, 4 fellowships (averaging $8,000 per year), 10 research assistantships (averaging $12,000 per year), 1 teaching assistantship (averaging $12,000 per year) were awarded. Financial award application deadline: 4/1. *Unit head:* Dr. Lisa Zagumny, Director, 931-372-3078, Fax: 931-372-3517, E-mail: lzagumny@tntech.edu. *Application contact:* Shelia K. Kendrick, Coordinator of Graduate Studies, 931-372-3808, Fax: 931-372-3497, E-mail: skendrick@tntech.edu.
Website: https://www.tntech.edu/education/elphd/.

Tennessee Technological University, College of Graduate Studies, College of Education, Department of Curriculum and Instruction, Program in Reading, Cookeville, TN 38505. Offers MA, Ed S. *Accreditation:* NCATE. Part-time and evening/weekend programs available. *Faculty:* 2 full-time (both women). *Students:* 5 full-time (all women), 20 part-time (all women). Average age 27. 7 applicants, 100% accepted, 3 enrolled. In 2013, 24 master's, 6 other advanced degrees awarded. *Degree requirements:* For master's and Ed S, comprehensive exam, thesis or alternative. *Entrance requirements:* For master's and Ed S, MAT or GRE. Additional exam requirements/recommendations for international students: Required—TOEFL (minimum score 527 paper-based; 71 iBT), IELTS (minimum score 5.5), PTE (minimum score 48), or TOEIC (Test of English as an International Communication). *Application deadline:* For fall admission, 8/1 for domestic students, 5/1 for international students; for spring admission, 12/1 for domestic students, 10/1 for international students. Applications are processed on a rolling basis. Application fee: $35 ($40 for international students). Electronic applications accepted. *Expenses:* Tuition, state resident: full-time $9347; part-time $465 per credit hour. Tuition, nonresident: full-time $23,635; part-time $1152 per credit hour. *Financial support:* In 2013–14, fellowships (averaging $8,000 per year), 4 teaching assistantships (averaging $4,000 per year) were awarded; research assistantships and career-related internships or fieldwork also available. Financial award application deadline: 4/1. *Unit head:* Dr. Jeremy Wendt, Interim Chairperson, 931-372-3181, Fax: 931-372-6270, E-mail: jwendt@tntech.edu. *Application contact:* Shelia K. Kendrick, Coordinator of Graduate Studies, 931-372-3808, Fax: 931-372-3497, E-mail: skendrick@tntech.edu.

Texas A&M University–Commerce, Graduate School, College of Education and Human Services, Department of Curriculum and Instruction, Commerce, TX 75429-3011. Offers bilingual/ESL education (M Ed, MS); early childhood education (M Ed, MS); elementary education (M Ed, MS); reading (M Ed, MS); secondary education (M Ed, MS); supervision, curriculum and instruction: elementary education (Ed D). MS and M Ed programs in early childhood education offered jointly with Texas Woman's University and University of North Texas. Part-time programs available. Terminal master's awarded for partial completion of doctoral program. *Degree requirements:* For master's, comprehensive exam, thesis (for some programs); for doctorate, 2 foreign languages, thesis/dissertation, departmental qualifying exam. *Entrance requirements:* For master's and doctorate, GRE General Test. Electronic applications accepted. *Expenses:* Tuition, state resident: full-time $3630; part-time $2420 per year. Tuition, nonresident: full-time $9948; part-time $6632.16 per year. *Required fees:* $1006 per year. Tuition and fees vary according to course load. *Faculty research:* Literacy and learning, early childhood, preservice teacher education, technology.

Texas A&M University–Corpus Christi, Graduate Studies and Research, College of Education, Corpus Christi, TX 78412-5503. Offers counseling (MS, PhD), including counseling (MS); counselor education (PhD); curriculum and instruction (MS, Ed D); early childhood education (MS); educational administration (MS); educational leadership (Ed D); educational technology (MS); elementary education (MS); kinesiology (MS); reading (MS); secondary education (MS); special education (MS). Part-time and evening/weekend programs available. *Degree requirements:* For master's, comprehensive exam, thesis (for some programs); for doctorate, comprehensive exam, thesis/dissertation. *Entrance requirements:* For master's, GRE General Test. Additional exam requirements/recommendations for international students: Required—TOEFL. Electronic applications accepted.

Texas A&M University–Kingsville, College of Graduate Studies, College of Education, Department of Education, Program in Reading Specialization, Kingsville, TX 78363. Offers MS. Part-time and evening/weekend programs available. *Faculty:* 9 full-time (5 women), 4 part-time/adjunct (2 women). *Students:* 3 full-time (all women), 15 part-time (14 women); includes 14 minority (all Hispanic/Latino). Average age 32. 5 applicants, 100% accepted, 3 enrolled. *Degree requirements:* For master's, comprehensive exam, mini-thesis. *Entrance requirements:* For master's, GRE General Test, MAT, minimum GPA of 3.0. *Application deadline:* For fall admission, 6/1 for domestic students; for spring admission, 11/15 for domestic students. Applications are processed on a rolling basis. Application fee: $35 ($50 for international students). *Financial support:*

Application deadline: 5/15. *Faculty research:* Reading programs for preparing the handicapped, reading methods in elementary education, literature-based reading instruction. *Unit head:* Dr. Sue Mohrman, Director, 361-593-3203. *Application contact:* Dr. Alberto M. Olivares, Dean, College of Graduate Studies, 361-593-2808, Fax: 361-593-3412, E-mail: a-olivares@tamuk.edu.

Texas A&M University–San Antonio, Department of Curriculum and Kinesiology, San Antonio, TX 78224. Offers bilingual education (MA); early childhood education (M Ed); kinesiology (MS); reading (MS); special education (M Ed), including educational diagnostician, instructional specialist. Part-time and evening/weekend programs available. *Degree requirements:* For master's, comprehensive exam, thesis or alternative. *Entrance requirements:* For master's, MAT. Additional exam requirements/recommendations for international students: Required—TOEFL (minimum score 550 paper-based; 80 iBT), IELTS (minimum score 6). Electronic applications accepted.

Texas State University, Graduate School, College of Education, Department of Curriculum and Instruction, Program in Reading Education, San Marcos, TX 78666. Offers M Ed. Part-time and evening/weekend programs available. *Faculty:* 6 full-time (5 women). *Students:* 2 full-time (both women), 16 part-time (15 women); includes 2 minority (1 American Indian or Alaska Native, non-Hispanic/Latino; 1 Hispanic/Latino). Average age 34. 4 applicants, 75% accepted, 2 enrolled. In 2013, 8 master's awarded. *Degree requirements:* For master's, comprehensive exam, thesis optional. *Entrance requirements:* For master's, minimum GPA of 2.75 in last 60 hours of course work, teaching experience. Additional exam requirements/recommendations for international students: Required—TOEFL (minimum score 550 paper-based; 78 iBT). *Application deadline:* For fall admission, 6/15 priority date for domestic students, 6/1 for international students; for spring admission, 10/15 priority date for domestic students, 10/1 for international students. Applications are processed on a rolling basis. Application fee: $40 ($90 for international students). Electronic applications accepted. *Expenses:* Tuition, state resident: full-time $6663; part-time $278 per credit hour. Tuition, nonresident: full-time $15,159; part-time $632 per credit hour. *Required fees:* $1872; $54 per credit hour. $306 per term. Tuition and fees vary according to course load. *Financial support:* In 2013–14, 4 students received support. Research assistantships, teaching assistantships, career-related internships or fieldwork, Federal Work-Study, and institutionally sponsored loans available. Support available to part-time students. Financial award application deadline: 4/1; financial award applicants required to submit FAFSA. *Faculty research:* Reading comprehension, computer-assisted instruction. *Unit head:* Dr. Lori Czop Assaf, Graduate Advisor, 512-245-9163, Fax: 512-245-8365, E-mail: lc27@txstate.edu. *Application contact:* Dr. Andrea Golato, Dean of Graduate School, 512-245-2581, Fax: 512-245-8365, E-mail: gradcollege@txstate.edu. Website: http://www.education.txstate.edu/ci/degrees-programs/graduate/elementary-education.html.

Texas Tech University, Graduate School, College of Education, Department of Curriculum and Instruction, Lubbock, TX 79409-1071. Offers bilingual education (M Ed); curriculum and instruction (M Ed, PhD); elementary education (M Ed); language/literacy education (M Ed); multidisciplinary science (MS); secondary education (M Ed). *Accreditation:* NCATE. Part-time programs available. Postbaccalaureate distance learning degree programs offered (minimal on-campus study). *Faculty:* 27 full-time (21 women). *Students:* 49 full-time (40 women), 194 part-time (149 women); includes 74 minority (13 Black or African American, non-Hispanic/Latino; 6 Asian, non-Hispanic/Latino; 50 Hispanic/Latino; 5 Two or more races, non-Hispanic/Latino), 20 international. Average age 38. 105 applicants, 66% accepted, 46 enrolled. In 2013, 48 master's, 14 doctorates awarded. *Degree requirements:* For master's, comprehensive exam (for some programs), thesis optional; for doctorate, comprehensive exam, thesis/dissertation. *Entrance requirements:* For master's, bachelor's degree; resume; letter of intent; academic writing sample; 2 letters of recommendation; for doctorate, GRE, master's degree; resume; letter of intent; academic writing sample; 3 letters of recommendation. Additional exam requirements/recommendations for international students: Required—TOEFL (minimum score 550 paper-based; 79 iBT). *Application deadline:* For fall admission, 6/1 priority date for domestic students, 1/15 priority date for international students; for spring admission, 9/1 priority date for domestic students, 6/15 priority date for international students. Applications are processed on a rolling basis. Application fee: $60. Electronic applications accepted. *Expenses:* Tuition, state resident: full-time $6062; part-time $252.57 per credit hour. Tuition, nonresident: full-time $14,558; part-time $606.57 per credit hour. *Required fees:* $2655; $35 per credit hour. $907.50 per semester. Tuition and fees vary according to course load. *Financial support:* In 2013–14, 94 students received support, including 89 fellowships (averaging $2,276 per year), 14 research assistantships (averaging $5,226 per year), 6 teaching assistantships (averaging $4,517 per year); career-related internships or fieldwork, Federal Work-Study, institutionally sponsored loans, scholarships/grants, traineeships, health care benefits, and unspecified assistantships also available. Support available to part-time students. Financial award application deadline: 2/1; financial award applicants required to submit FAFSA. *Faculty research:* Teacher education, curriculum studies, bilingual education, science and math education, language and literacy education. *Total annual research expenditures:* $413,968. *Unit head:* Dr. Margaret Ann Price, Department Chair, Curriculum and Instruction, 806-834-4347, E-mail: peggie.price@ttu.edu. *Application contact:* Stephenie A. Jones, Administrative Assistant, 806-834-2751, Fax: 806-742-2179, E-mail: stephenie.a.jones@ttu.edu. Website: http://www.educ.ttu.edu.

Texas Woman's University, Graduate School, College of Professional Education, Department of Reading, Denton, TX 76201. Offers reading education (M Ed, MA, MS, Ed D, PhD). Part-time and evening/weekend programs available. *Faculty:* 7 full-time (all women), 12 part-time/adjunct (all women). *Students:* 81 part-time (78 women); includes 25 minority (12 Black or African American, non-Hispanic/Latino; 1 American Indian or Alaska Native, non-Hispanic/Latino; 1 Asian, non-Hispanic/Latino; 11 Hispanic/Latino). Average age 42. 36 applicants, 94% accepted, 26 enrolled. In 2013, 15 master's, 1 doctorate awarded. Terminal master's awarded for partial completion of doctoral program. *Degree requirements:* For master's, comprehensive exam, thesis (for some programs); for doctorate, comprehensive exam, thesis/dissertation. *Entrance requirements:* For master's, GRE General Test (preferred minimum score 143 [350 old version] Verbal, 138 [350 old version] Quantitative); for doctorate, GRE General Test (preferred minimum score 153 [500 old version] Verbal, 144 [500 old version] Quantitative), master's degree, minimum GPA of 3.5, on-site writing sample, interview, 3 letters of reference, curriculum vitae/resume, 1-2 page statement of professional experience and goals, 3 years of teaching experience. Additional exam requirements/recommendations for international students: Required—TOEFL (minimum score 550 paper-based; 79 iBT). *Application deadline:* For fall admission, 7/1 priority date for domestic students, 3/1 for international students; for spring admission, 12/1 priority date for domestic students, 7/1 for international students. Applications are processed on a rolling basis. Application fee: $50 ($75 for international students). Electronic applications accepted. *Expenses:* Tuition, state resident: full-time $4182; part-time $233.32 per credit hour. Tuition, nonresident: full-time $10,716; part-time $595.32 per credit hour. *Financial support:* In 2013–14, 16 students received support, including 1 research assistantship (averaging $5,767 per year); career-related internships or fieldwork, Federal Work-Study, institutionally sponsored loans, scholarships/grants, traineeships, health care benefits, and unspecified assistantships also available. Support available to

part-time students. Financial award application deadline: 3/1; financial award applicants required to submit FAFSA. *Faculty research:* Teacher change, home/school partnerships, literacy (middle grades), early literacy, language acquisitions, new literacies, multicultural education, children's literature, literacy leadership and coaching. *Total annual research expenditures:* $548,137. *Unit head:* Dr. Connie Briggs, Chair, 940-898-2230, Fax: 940-898-2224, E-mail: reading@twu.edu. *Application contact:* Dr. Samuel Wheeler, Assistant Director of Admissions, 940-898-3188, Fax: 940-898-3081, E-mail: wheelersr@twu.edu. Website: http://www.twu.edu/reading/.

Touro College, Graduate School of Education, New York, NY 10010. Offers education and special education (MS); education biology (MS); instructional technology (MS); mathematics education (MS); school leadership (MS); teaching English to speakers of other languages (MS); teaching literacy (MS). Part-time and evening/weekend programs available. Postbaccalaureate distance learning degree programs offered (no on-campus study). *Faculty:* 75 full-time, 131 part-time/adjunct. *Students:* 327 full-time (272 women), 2,454 part-time (2,103 women); includes 840 minority (333 Black or African American, non-Hispanic/Latino; 4 American Indian or Alaska Native, non-Hispanic/Latino; 139 Asian, non-Hispanic/Latino; 334 Hispanic/Latino; 8 Native Hawaiian or other Pacific Islander, non-Hispanic/Latino; 22 Two or more races, non-Hispanic/Latino), 4 international. 1,422 applicants, 50% accepted, 675 enrolled. In 2013, 6 master's awarded. *Entrance requirements:* Additional exam requirements/recommendations for international students: Required—TOEFL (minimum score 83 iBT), IELTS (minimum score 6.5). *Application deadline:* For fall admission, 8/26 for domestic students, 7/15 for international students; for spring admission, 12/31 for domestic students, 12/15 for international students. Applications are processed on a rolling basis. Application fee: $50. *Financial support:* Federal Work-Study available. Financial award applicants required to submit FAFSA. *Faculty research:* Equity assistance, language development, scholar communications, Latin American studies and cultural sensitivity, behavior management techniques and strategies in special education. *Unit head:* Dr. LaMar Miller, Dean, 212-463-0400 Ext. 5561, Fax: 212-462-4889, E-mail: lpmiller@touro.edu. *Application contact:* Natalie Arroyo, Admissions, 212-463-0400.

Towson University, Program in Reading, Towson, MD 21252-0001. Offers reading (M Ed); reading education (CAS). *Accreditation:* NCATE. Part-time and evening/weekend programs available. *Students:* 2 full-time (both women), 208 part-time (190 women); includes 27 minority (19 Black or African American, non-Hispanic/Latino; 1 American Indian or Alaska Native, non-Hispanic/Latino; 2 Asian, non-Hispanic/Latino; 5 Hispanic/Latino), 1 international. *Entrance requirements:* For master's, minimum GPA of 3.0, essay; for CAS, 3 letters of reference, portfolio, master's degree in reading or related field. *Application deadline:* Applications are processed on a rolling basis. Application fee: $45. Electronic applications accepted. *Financial support:* Application deadline: 4/1. *Unit head:* Dr. Barbara Laster, Graduate Program Co-Director, 410-704-2556, E-mail: reed@towson.edu. *Application contact:* Dr. Steve Mogge, Graduate Program Co-Director, 410-704-5771, E-mail: reed@towson.edu.

Trident University International, College of Education, Program in Education, Cypress, CA 90630. Offers adult education (MA Ed); aviation education (MA Ed); children's literacy development (MA Ed); e-learning (MA Ed); early childhood education (MA Ed); enrollment management (MA Ed); higher education (MA Ed); teaching and instruction (MA Ed); training and development (MA Ed). Part-time and evening/weekend programs available. Postbaccalaureate distance learning degree programs offered (no on-campus study). *Degree requirements:* For master's, capstone project with integrative paper. *Entrance requirements:* For master's, minimum GPA of 2.5 (students with GPA 3.0 or greater may transfer up to 30% of graduate level credits). Additional exam requirements/recommendations for international students: Required—TOEFL (minimum score 525 paper-based). Electronic applications accepted.

Trinity Washington University, School of Education, Washington, DC 20017-1094. Offers clinical mental health counseling (MA); early childhood education (MAT); educating for change (M Ed); educational administration (MSA); elementary education (MAT); reading (M Ed); school counseling (MA); secondary education (MAT), including English, social studies; special education (MAT). *Accreditation:* NCATE. Part-time and evening/weekend programs available. *Degree requirements:* For master's, thesis (for some programs), capstone project(s). *Entrance requirements:* For master's, PRAXIS I, minimum GPA of 2.8. Additional exam requirements/recommendations for international students: Required—TOEFL (minimum score 550 paper-based). *Application deadline:* For fall admission, 4/1 priority date for domestic students; for winter admission, 11/1 priority date for domestic students; for spring admission, 11/1 priority date for domestic students. Applications are processed on a rolling basis. Application fee: $40. *Expenses:* Tuition: Part-time $715 per credit. *Financial support:* Career-related internships or fieldwork, health care benefits, and unspecified assistantships available. Support available to part-time students. Financial award application deadline: 4/1; financial award applicants required to submit FAFSA. *Faculty research:* Technology, literacy, special education, organizations, inclusion models. *Unit head:* Dr. Janet Stocks, Dean, 202-884-9380, Fax: 202-884-9506, E-mail: stocksj@trinitydc.edu. *Application contact:* Erika Davis, Director of Admissions for School of Education, 202-884-9400, Fax: 202-884-9229, E-mail: daviser@trinitydc.edu. Website: http://www.trinitydc.edu/education/.

Troy University, Graduate School, College of Education, Program in Secondary Education, Troy, AL 36082. Offers 5th year biology (MS); 5th year computer science (MS); 5th year history (MS); 5th year language arts (MS); 5th year mathematics (MS); 5th year social science (MS); traditional biology (MS); traditional computer science (MS); traditional history (MS); traditional language arts (MS); traditional mathematics (MS); traditional social science (MS). *Accreditation:* NCATE. Part-time and evening/weekend programs available. *Faculty:* 2 full-time (1 woman). *Students:* 10 full-time (9 women), 21 part-time (14 women); includes 8 minority (6 Black or African American, non-Hispanic/Latino; 2 Hispanic/Latino). Average age 29. 15 applicants, 87% accepted, 6 enrolled. In 2013, 12 master's awarded. *Degree requirements:* For master's, comprehensive exam, thesis. *Entrance requirements:* For master's, GRE (minimum score of 850 on old exam or 290 on new exam), GMAT (minimum score of 380), or MAT (minimum score of 385), bachelor's degree; minimum undergraduate GPA of 2.5 or 3.0 on last 30 semester hours, letter of recommendation. Additional exam requirements/recommendations for international students: Required—TOEFL (minimum score 523 paper-based; 70 iBT), IELTS (minimum score 6). *Application deadline:* Applications are processed on a rolling basis. Application fee: $50. Electronic applications accepted. *Expenses:* Tuition, state resident: full-time $6084; part-time $338 per credit hour. Tuition, nonresident: full-time $12,168; part-time $676 per credit hour. *Required fees:* $630; $35 per credit hour. $50 per semester. *Financial support:* Career-related internships or fieldwork available. Support available to part-time students. Financial award applicants required to submit FAFSA. *Unit head:* Dr. Jan Oliver, Associate Professor, 334-670-3444, Fax: 334-670-3548, E-mail: oliver@troy.edu. *Application contact:* Brenda K. Campbell, Director of Graduate Admissions, 334-670-3178, Fax: 334-670-3733, E-mail: bcamp@troy.edu.

Troy University, Graduate School, College of Education, Program in Teacher Education-Multiple Levels, Troy, AL 36082. Offers art education (MS); gifted education (MS); instrumental (MS); physical education (MS); reading specialist (MS); vocal/choral (MS). Part-time and evening/weekend programs available. *Faculty:* 8 full-time (4

women). *Students:* 2 full-time (both women), 17 part-time (15 women); includes 3 minority (all Black or African American, non-Hispanic/Latino). Average age 30. 9 applicants, 89% accepted, 4 enrolled. In 2013, 19 master's awarded. *Degree requirements:* For master's, comprehensive exam, thesis. *Entrance requirements:* For master's, GRE (minimum score of 850 on old exam or 290 on new exam), GMAT (minimum score of 380), or MAT (minimum score of 385), bachelor's degree; minimum undergraduate GPA of 2.5 or 3.0 on last 30 semester hours, letter of recommendation. Additional exam requirements/recommendations for international students: Required—TOEFL (minimum score 523 paper-based; 70 iBT), IELTS (minimum score 6). *Application deadline:* Applications are processed on a rolling basis. Application fee: $50. Electronic applications accepted. *Expenses:* Tuition, state resident: full-time $6084; part-time $338 per credit hour. Tuition, nonresident: full-time $12,168; part-time $676 per credit hour. *Required fees:* $630; $35 per credit hour. $50 per semester. *Financial support:* Available to part-time students. Applicants required to submit FAFSA. *Unit head:* Dr. Charlotte S. Minnick, Director, Teacher Education, 334-670-3544, Fax: 334-670-3548, E-mail: csminnick@troy.edu. *Application contact:* Brenda K. Campbell, Director of Graduate Admissions, 334-670-3178, Fax: 334-670-3733, E-mail: bcamp@troy.edu.

Union College, Graduate Programs, Department of Education, Barbourville, KY 40906-1499. Offers elementary education (MA); health and physical education (MA); middle grades (MA); music education (MA); principalship (MA); reading specialist (MA); secondary education (MA); special education (MA). *Degree requirements:* For master's, thesis optional. *Entrance requirements:* For master's, GRE General Test, NTE.

University at Albany, State University of New York, School of Education, Department of Reading, Albany, NY 12222-0001. Offers MS, Ed D, CAS. Evening/weekend programs available. *Degree requirements:* For doctorate, one foreign language, thesis/dissertation. *Entrance requirements:* For doctorate, GRE General Test. Additional exam requirements/recommendations for international students: Required—TOEFL (minimum score 550 paper-based). Electronic applications accepted.

University at Buffalo, the State University of New York, Graduate School, Graduate School of Education, Department of Learning and Instruction, Buffalo, NY 14260. Offers biology education (Ed M, Certificate); chemistry education (Ed M, Certificate); childhood education (Ed M); childhood education with bilingual extension (Ed M); curriculum, instruction and the science of learning (PhD); early childhood education (Ed M); early childhood education with bilingual extension (birth-grade 2) (Ed M); earth science education (Ed M, Certificate); education studies (Ed M); educational technology and new literacies (Certificate); elementary education (Ed D); English education (Ed M, Certificate); English for speakers of other languages (Ed M); foreign and second language education (PhD); French education (Ed M, Certificate); German education (Ed M, Certificate); gifted education (Certificate); Latin education (Ed M, Certificate); literacy specialist (Ed M); literacy teaching and learning (Certificate); mathematics education (Ed M, Certificate); music education (Ed M, Certificate); physics education (Ed M, Certificate); science and the public (Ed M); social studies education (Ed M, Certificate); Spanish education (Ed M, Certificate); special education (PhD); teaching English to speakers of other languages (Ed M). Part-time and evening/weekend programs available. Postbaccalaureate distance learning degree programs offered (no on-campus study). *Faculty:* 31 full-time (23 women), 64 part-time/adjunct (53 women). *Students:* 275 full-time (215 women), 293 part-time (205 women); includes 35 minority (16 Black or African American, non-Hispanic/Latino; 5 American Indian or Alaska Native, non-Hispanic/Latino; 11 Asian, non-Hispanic/Latino; 3 Hispanic/Latino), 97 international. Average age 30. 544 applicants, 81% accepted, 246 enrolled. In 2013, 222 master's, 17 doctorates, 35 other advanced degrees awarded. *Degree requirements:* For master's, comprehensive exam; for doctorate, thesis/dissertation, research analysis exam, research experience component. *Entrance requirements:* For master's, content test in science and math, letters of reference; for doctorate, GRE General Test or MAT, interview, writing sample, letters of recommendation. Additional exam requirements/recommendations for international students: Required—TOEFL (minimum score 600 paper-based; 96 iBT). *Application deadline:* For fall admission, 2/1 priority date for domestic and international students; for spring admission, 11/15 priority date for domestic students, 10/1 for international students. Applications are processed on a rolling basis. Application fee: $50. Electronic applications accepted. *Financial support:* In 2013–14, 50 fellowships (averaging $8,589 per year), 31 research assistantships with tuition reimbursements (averaging $11,406 per year) were awarded; teaching assistantships, career-related internships or fieldwork, Federal Work-Study, institutionally sponsored loans, scholarships/grants, tuition waivers, and unspecified assistantships also available. Financial award application deadline: 2/28; financial award applicants required to submit FAFSA. *Faculty research:* Science assessment, foreign language teaching and learning, early learning, new literacies, gender and education. *Total annual research expenditures:* $1.7 million. *Unit head:* Dr. Suzanne Miller, Chair, 716-645-2455, Fax: 716-645-3161, E-mail: smiller@buffalo.edu. *Application contact:* Cathy Dimino, Admissions Assistant, 716-645-2110, Fax: 716-645-7937, E-mail: cadimino@buffalo.edu.
Website: http://gse.buffalo.edu/lai.

The University of Alabama at Birmingham, School of Education, Program in Reading, Birmingham, AL 35294. Offers MA Ed.

The University of Alabama in Huntsville, School of Graduate Studies, College of Liberal Arts, Department of English, Huntsville, AL 35899. Offers education (MA); English (MA); language arts (MA); reading specialist (MA); technical communications (Certificate). Part-time and evening/weekend programs available. *Faculty:* 16 full-time (8 women). *Students:* 15 full-time (12 women), 26 part-time (18 women); includes 7 minority (all Black or African American, non-Hispanic/Latino). Average age 32. 27 applicants, 56% accepted, 10 enrolled. In 2013, 20 master's, 3 other advanced degrees awarded. *Degree requirements:* For master's, one foreign language, comprehensive exam, thesis or alternative, oral and written exams. *Entrance requirements:* For master's and Certificate, GRE General Test, minimum GPA of 3.0. Additional exam requirements/recommendations for international students: Required—TOEFL (minimum score 500 paper-based; 80 iBT), IELTS (minimum score 6.5). *Application deadline:* For fall admission, 7/15 priority date for domestic students, 4/1 priority date for international students; for spring admission, 11/30 priority date for domestic students, 9/1 priority date for international students. Applications are processed on a rolling basis. Application fee: $50. Electronic applications accepted. *Expenses:* Tuition, state resident: full-time $8912; part-time $540 per credit hour. Tuition, nonresident: full-time $20,774; part-time $1252 per credit hour. *Required fees:* $148 per semester. One-time fee: $150. *Financial support:* In 2013–14, 10 students received support, including 7 teaching assistantships with full tuition reimbursements available (averaging $8,460 per year); career-related internships or fieldwork, Federal Work-Study, institutionally sponsored loans, scholarships/grants, health care benefits, tuition waivers (full and partial), and unspecified assistantships also available. Support available to part-time students. Financial award application deadline: 4/1; financial award applicants required to submit FAFSA. *Faculty research:* Fiction and identity, Shakespeare, science fiction, eighteenth-century literature, technical writing. *Total annual research expenditures:* $3,356. *Unit head:* Dr. Dan Schenker, Chair, 256-824-6320, Fax: 256-824-6949, E-mail: schenkd@uah.edu. *Application contact:* Kim Gray, Graduate Studies Admissions Coordinator, 256-824-6002, Fax: 256-824-6405, E-mail: deangrad@uah.edu.
Website: http://www.uah.edu/colleges/liberal/english/index.php.

University of Alaska Fairbanks, School of Education, Program in Education, Fairbanks, AK 99775. Offers curriculum and instruction (M Ed); education (M Ed, Graduate Certificate); elementary education (M Ed); language and literacy (M Ed); reading (M Ed); secondary education (M Ed); special education (M Ed). *Faculty:* 23 full-time (14 women), 1 part-time/adjunct (0 women). *Students:* 37 full-time (26 women), 78 part-time (54 women); includes 15 minority (6 American Indian or Alaska Native, non-Hispanic/Latino; 6 Hispanic/Latino; 3 Two or more races, non-Hispanic/Latino), 2 international. Average age 34. 37 applicants, 68% accepted, 19 enrolled. In 2013, 39 master's, 28 other advanced degrees awarded. *Degree requirements:* For master's, comprehensive exam, thesis, oral defense. *Entrance requirements:* Additional exam requirements/recommendations for international students: Required—TOEFL (minimum score 550 paper-based; 80 iBT). *Application deadline:* For fall admission, 5/1 for domestic students, 3/1 for international students; for spring admission, 10/15 for domestic students, 8/1 for international students. Applications are processed on a rolling basis. Application fee: $60. Electronic applications accepted. *Expenses:* Tuition, state resident: full-time $7254; part-time $403 per credit. Tuition, nonresident: full-time $14,814; part-time $823 per credit. Tuition and fees vary according to course level, course load and reciprocity agreements. *Financial support:* In 2013–14, 1 teaching assistantship with tuition reimbursement (averaging $11,011 per year) was awarded; fellowships with tuition reimbursements, research assistantships with tuition reimbursements, career-related internships or fieldwork, Federal Work-Study, scholarships/grants, health care benefits, and unspecified assistantships also available. Support available to part-time students. Financial award application deadline: 6/1; financial award applicants required to submit FAFSA. *Unit head:* Allan Morotti, Interim Dean, 907-474-7341, Fax: 907-474-5451, E-mail: uaf-soe-school@alaska.edu. *Application contact:* Libby Eddy, Director of Admissions, 907-474-7500, Fax: 907-474-7097, E-mail: admissions@uaf.edu.
Website: https://sites.google.com/a/alaska.edu/soe-graduate/.

The University of Arizona, College of Education, Department of Teaching, Learning and Sociocultural Studies, Program in Language, Reading and Culture, Tucson, AZ 85721. Offers MA, Ed D, PhD, Ed S. Part-time programs available. *Faculty:* 24 full-time (19 women), 1 (woman) part-time/adjunct. *Students:* 77 full-time (61 women), 45 part-time (35 women); includes 51 minority (6 Black or African American, non-Hispanic/Latino; 4 American Indian or Alaska Native, non-Hispanic/Latino; 3 Asian, non-Hispanic/Latino; 29 Hispanic/Latino; 9 Two or more races, non-Hispanic/Latino), 19 international. Average age 38. 41 applicants, 54% accepted, 10 enrolled. In 2013, 14 master's, 9 doctorates awarded. *Entrance requirements:* Additional exam requirements/recommendations for international students: Required—TOEFL (minimum score 550 paper-based; 79 iBT); Recommended—IELTS (minimum score 7). *Application deadline:* For fall admission, 2/1 for domestic and international students. Application fee: $75. Electronic applications accepted. *Expenses:* Tuition, state resident: full-time $11,526. Tuition, nonresident: full-time $27,398. *Financial support:* In 2013–14, 19 research assistantships with full tuition reimbursements (averaging $19,534 per year), 25 teaching assistantships with full tuition reimbursements (averaging $16,157 per year) were awarded. *Faculty research:* Literacy acquisition, sociocultural theory, indigenous education, heritage-language revitalization, the study of households and community settings, children's and adolescent literatures and literacy. *Total annual research expenditures:* $1.7 million. *Unit head:* Dr. Bruce Johnson, Department Head, 520-626-8700, E-mail: brucej@email.arizona.edu. *Application contact:* Information Contact, 520-621-1311, Fax: 520-621-1853, E-mail: lrcinfo@email.arizona.edu.

University of Arkansas at Little Rock, Graduate School, College of Education, Department of Teacher Education, Program in Reading Education, Little Rock, AR 72204-1099. Offers literacy coach (Graduate Certificate); reading (M Ed, Ed S). *Expenses:* Tuition, state resident: full-time $5690; part-time $284.50 per credit hour. Tuition, nonresident: full-time $13,030; part-time $651.50 per credit hour. *Required fees:* $1121; $672 per term. One-time fee: $40 full-time.

University of Bridgeport, School of Education, Department of Education, Bridgeport, CT 06604. Offers education (MS); educational management (Ed D, Diploma), including intermediate administrator or supervisor (Diploma), leadership (Ed D); elementary education (MS, Diploma), including early childhood education, elementary education; middle school education (MS); music education (MS); remedial reading and language arts (Diploma); secondary education (MS, Diploma), including computer specialist (Diploma), international education (Diploma), reading specialist, secondary education. Part-time and evening/weekend programs available. *Faculty:* 12 full-time (5 women), 108 part-time/adjunct (60 women). *Students:* 155 full-time (108 women), 139 part-time (98 women); includes 48 minority (22 Black or African American, non-Hispanic/Latino; 9 Asian, non-Hispanic/Latino; 15 Hispanic/Latino; 2 Two or more races, non-Hispanic/Latino), 2 international. Average age 30. 306 applicants, 55% accepted, 107 enrolled. In 2013, 153 master's, 16 other advanced degrees awarded. *Degree requirements:* For master's, final exam, final project, or thesis; for doctorate, comprehensive exam, thesis/dissertation; for Diploma, thesis or alternative, final project. *Entrance requirements:* For master's, minimum undergraduate QPA of 2.67; for doctorate, GRE, MAT; for Diploma, GRE General Test or MAT, minimum graduate QPA of 3.0. Additional exam requirements/recommendations for international students: Recommended—TOEFL (minimum score 550 paper-based; 80 iBT), IELTS (minimum score 6.5). *Application deadline:* For fall admission, 8/1 priority date for domestic and international students; for spring admission, 12/1 priority date for domestic and international students. Applications are processed on a rolling basis. Application fee: $50. Electronic applications accepted. *Expenses:* Contact institution. *Financial support:* In 2013–14, 120 students received support. Fellowships, research assistantships, teaching assistantships, career-related internships or fieldwork, Federal Work-Study, and institutionally sponsored loans available. Support available to part-time students. Financial award application deadline: 6/1; financial award applicants required to submit FAFSA. *Faculty research:* Self-concept, internship assessment, stress and situational development, follow-up of graduation, trend analysis. *Unit head:* Dr. Allen P. Cook, Dean, 203-576-4192, Fax: 203-576-4200, E-mail: acook@bridgeport.edu. *Application contact:* Leanne Proctor, Director of Graduate Admissions, 203-576-4552, Fax: 203-576-4941, E-mail: admit@bridgeport.edu.

The University of British Columbia, Faculty of Education, Program in Language and Literacy Education, Vancouver, BC V6T 1Z1, Canada. Offers library education (M Ed); literacy education (M Ed, MA, PhD); modern language education (M Ed, MA, PhD); teaching English as a second language (M Ed, MA, PhD). Part-time and evening/weekend programs available. *Degree requirements:* For master's, thesis (MA); for doctorate, thesis/dissertation. *Entrance requirements:* For master's and doctorate, minimum B+ average in last 2 years with minimum 2 courses at A standing. Additional exam requirements/recommendations for international students: Required—TOEFL (minimum score 580 paper-based; 92 iBT), TWE (minimum score 5). Electronic applications accepted. *Expenses: Tuition, area resident:* Full-time $8000 Canadian dollars. *Faculty research:* Language and literacy development, second language

acquisition, Asia Pacific language curriculum, children's literature, whole language instruction.

University of California, Riverside, Graduate Division, Graduate School of Education, Riverside, CA 92521-0102. Offers autism (M Ed); diversity and equity (M Ed); education specialist (Credential); education, society and culture (MA, PhD); educational psychology (MA, PhD); general education (M Ed); higher education administration and policy (M Ed, PhD); multiple subject (Credential); reading (M Ed); school psychology (PhD); single subject (Credential); special education (M Ed, MA, PhD); TESOL (M Ed). *Faculty:* 22 full-time (11 women), 14 part-time/adjunct (10 women). *Students:* 218 full-time (148 women); includes 95 minority (10 Black or African American, non-Hispanic/Latino; 30 Asian, non-Hispanic/Latino; 49 Hispanic/Latino; 6 Two or more races, non-Hispanic/Latino), 12 international. Average age 31. 236 applicants, 66% accepted, 78 enrolled. In 2013, 66 master's, 13 doctorates, 86 other advanced degrees awarded. Terminal master's awarded for partial completion of doctoral program. *Degree requirements:* For master's, thesis optional, comprehensive exams or thesis (MA), case study or analytical report (M Ed); for doctorate, thesis/dissertation, written and oral qualifying exams, college teaching practicum. *Entrance requirements:* For master's, GRE General Test (for MA), CBEST and CSET (for M Ed in general education only), UCR Extension TESOL certificate (for M Ed with TESOL emphasis only); for doctorate, GRE General Test, writing sample; for Credential, CBEST, CSET. Additional exam requirements/recommendations for international students: Required—TOEFL (minimum score 550 paper-based; 80 iBT), IELTS (minimum score 7). *Application deadline:* For fall admission, 9/1 for domestic students, 5/1 for international students; for winter admission, 11/15 for domestic students, 7/1 for international students; for spring admission, 3/1 for domestic students, 10/1 for international students. Applications are processed on a rolling basis. Application fee: $80 ($100 for international students). Electronic applications accepted. *Financial support:* In 2013–14, 58 students received support, including 31 fellowships with full tuition reimbursements available, 11 research assistantships with full tuition reimbursements available (averaging $14,691 per year), 5 teaching assistantships with full tuition reimbursements available (averaging $17,655 per year); career-related internships or fieldwork, Federal Work-Study, institutionally sponsored loans, scholarships/grants, and unspecified assistantships also available. Financial award application deadline: 1/5. *Faculty research:* Responsiveness to intervention, faculty core, response to intervention of English language learners, advanced modeling techniques, study on social capital, trust, and motivation. *Total annual research expenditures:* $1.9 million. *Unit head:* Prof. Douglas Mitchell, Interim Dean and Professor, 951-827-5802, Fax: 951-827-3942, E-mail: douglas.mitchell@ucr.edu. *Application contact:* Prof. Michael Orosco, Assistant Professor and Graduate Advisor of Admissions, 951-827-6362, Fax: 951-827-3291, E-mail: edgrad@ucr.edu. Website: http://www.education.ucr.edu/.

University of Central Arkansas, Graduate School, College of Education, Department of Early Childhood and Special Education, Program in Reading Education, Conway, AR 72035-0001. Offers MSE. *Accreditation:* NCATE. Part-time and evening/weekend programs available. Postbaccalaureate distance learning degree programs offered. *Degree requirements:* For master's, comprehensive exam, thesis optional. *Entrance requirements:* For master's, GRE General Test, minimum GPA of 2.7. Additional exam requirements/recommendations for international students: Required—TOEFL (minimum score 550 paper-based; 80 iBT).

University of Central Florida, College of Education and Human Performance, Education Doctoral Programs, Orlando, FL 32816. Offers communication sciences and disorders (PhD); counselor education (PhD); early childhood education (PhD); education (Ed D); elementary education (PhD); exceptional education (PhD); exercise physiology (PhD); higher education (PhD); hospitality education (PhD); instructional technology (PhD); mathematics education (PhD); reading education (PhD); science education (PhD); social science education (PhD); TESOL (PhD). *Students:* 137 full-time (94 women), 86 part-time (64 women); includes 45 minority (24 Black or African American, non-Hispanic/Latino; 5 Asian, non-Hispanic/Latino; 13 Hispanic/Latino; 3 Two or more races, non-Hispanic/Latino), 22 international. Average age 39. 132 applicants, 54% accepted, 54 enrolled. In 2013, 38 doctorates awarded. Application fee: $30. Electronic applications accepted. *Financial support:* In 2013–14, 84 students received support, including 38 fellowships with partial tuition reimbursements available (averaging $6,600 per year), 41 research assistantships with partial tuition reimbursements available (averaging $7,800 per year), 53 teaching assistantships with partial tuition reimbursements available (averaging $7,700 per year). *Unit head:* Dr. Edward Robinson, Director of Doctoral Programs, 407-823-6106, E-mail: edward.robinson@ucf.edu. *Application contact:* Barbara Rodriguez Lamas, Associate Director, Admissions and Student Services, 407-823-2766, Fax: 407-823-6442, E-mail: gradadmissions@ucf.edu.

Website: http://education.ucf.edu/departments.cfm.

University of Central Florida, College of Education and Human Performance, School of Teaching, Learning, and Leadership, Program in Reading Education, Orlando, FL 32816. Offers M Ed, Certificate. *Accreditation:* NCATE. Part-time and evening/weekend programs available. *Students:* 14 full-time (all women), 54 part-time (53 women); includes 18 minority (7 Black or African American, non-Hispanic/Latino; 2 Asian, non-Hispanic/Latino; 7 Hispanic/Latino; 2 Two or more races, non-Hispanic/Latino). Average age 31. 18 applicants, 100% accepted, 14 enrolled. In 2013, 30 master's awarded. *Degree requirements:* For master's, thesis or alternative. *Entrance requirements:* For master's, GRE General Test. Additional exam requirements/recommendations for international students: Required—TOEFL. *Application deadline:* For fall admission, 7/15 for domestic students; for spring admission, 12/1 for domestic students. Application fee: $30. Electronic applications accepted. *Financial support:* Career-related internships or fieldwork, Federal Work-Study, institutionally sponsored loans, tuition waivers (full), and unspecified assistantships available. Financial award application deadline: 3/1; financial award applicants required to submit FAFSA. *Unit head:* Dr. Karri J. Williams, Program Coordinator, 321-433-7922, E-mail: karri.williams@ucf.edu. *Application contact:* Barbara Rodriguez Lamas, Director, Admissions and Student Services, 407-823-2766, Fax: 407-823-6442, E-mail: gradadmissions@ucf.edu.

University of Central Missouri, The Graduate School, Warrensburg, MO 6409. Offers accountancy (MA); accounting (MBA); applied mathematics (MS); aviation safety (MA); biology (MS); business administration (MBA); career and technical education leadership (MS); college student personnel administration (MS); communication (MA); computer science (MS); counseling (MS); criminal justice (MS); educational leadership (Ed D); educational technology (MS); elementary and early childhood education (MSE); English (MA); environmental studies (MA); finance (MBA); history (MA); human services/educational technology (Ed S); human services/learning resources (Ed S); human services/professional counseling (Ed S); industrial hygiene (MS); industrial management (MS); information systems (MBA); information technology (MS); kinesiology (MS); library science and information services (MS); literacy education (MSE); marketing (MBA); mathematics (MS); music (MA); occupational safety management (MS); psychology (MS); rural family nursing (MS); school administration (MSE); social gerontology (MS); sociology (MA); special education (MSE); speech language pathology (MS); superintendency (Ed S); teaching (MAT); teaching English as a second language (MA); technology (MS); technology management (PhD); theatre (MA). Part-time programs

available. *Faculty:* 233. *Students:* 890 full-time (396 women), 1,486 part-time (1,001 women); includes 192 minority (97 Black or African American, non-Hispanic/Latino; 9 American Indian or Alaska Native, non-Hispanic/Latino; 32 Asian, non-Hispanic/Latino; 40 Hispanic/Latino; 3 Native Hawaiian or other Pacific Islander, non-Hispanic/Latino; 11 Two or more races, non-Hispanic/Latino), 539 international. Average age 31. 1,953 applicants, 75% accepted. In 2013, 719 master's, 58 other advanced degrees awarded. *Degree requirements:* For master's and Ed S, comprehensive exam (for some programs), thesis (for some programs). *Entrance requirements:* Additional exam requirements/recommendations for international students: Required—TOEFL (minimum score 550 paper-based; 79 iBT). *Application deadline:* For fall admission, 6/1 for domestic students; for spring admission, 10/1 for domestic and international students. Applications are processed on a rolling basis. Application fee: $30 ($75 for international students). Electronic applications accepted. *Expenses:* Tuition, state resident: full-time $7326; part-time $276.25 per credit hour. Tuition, nonresident: full-time $13,956; part-time $552.50 per credit hour. *Required fees:* $29 per credit hour. *Financial support:* In 2013–14, 118 students received support, including 271 research assistantships with full and partial tuition reimbursements available (averaging $7,500 per year), 109 teaching assistantships with full and partial tuition reimbursements available (averaging $7,500 per year); career-related internships or fieldwork, Federal Work-Study, scholarships/grants, and administrative and laboratory assistantships also available. Support available to part-time students. Financial award application deadline: 3/1; financial award applicants required to submit FAFSA. *Unit head:* Dr. Joseph Vaughn, Assistant Provost for Research/Dean, 660-543-4092, Fax: 660-543-4778, E-mail: vaughn@ucmo.edu. *Application contact:* Brittany Lawrence, Graduate Student Services Coordinator, 660-543-4621, Fax: 660-543-4778, E-mail: gradinfo@ucmo.edu. Website: http://www.ucmo.edu/graduate/.

University of Central Oklahoma, The Jackson College of Graduate Studies, College of Education and Professional Studies, Department of Advanced Professional and Special Services, Edmond, OK 73034-5209. Offers educational leadership (M Ed); library media education (M Ed); reading (M Ed); school counseling (M Ed); special education (M Ed), including mild/moderate disabilities, severe-profound/multiple disabilities, special education; speech-language pathology (MS). Part-time programs available. *Faculty:* 14 full-time (9 women), 16 part-time/adjunct (8 women). *Students:* 87 full-time (80 women), 298 part-time (251 women); includes 77 minority (32 Black or African American, non-Hispanic/Latino; 10 American Indian or Alaska Native, non-Hispanic/Latino; 2 Asian, non-Hispanic/Latino; 15 Hispanic/Latino; 18 Two or more races, non-Hispanic/Latino), 9 international. Average age 34. 147 applicants, 94% accepted, 89 enrolled. In 2013, 163 master's awarded. *Degree requirements:* For master's, comprehensive exam (for some programs), thesis (for some programs). *Entrance requirements:* For master's, GRE. Additional exam requirements/recommendations for international students: Required—TOEFL (minimum score 550 paper-based; 79 iBT), IELTS (minimum score 6.5). *Application deadline:* For fall admission, 7/1 for international students; for spring admission, 7/1 for international students. Applications are processed on a rolling basis. Application fee: $50. Electronic applications accepted. *Expenses:* Tuition, state resident: full-time $4137; part-time $206.85 per credit hour. Tuition, nonresident: full-time $10,359; part-time $517.95 per credit hour. *Required fees:* $481. Tuition and fees vary according to course load and program. *Financial support:* In 2013–14, 93 students received support, including 4 research assistantships with partial tuition reimbursements available (averaging $8,133 per year); teaching assistantships with partial tuition reimbursements available, career-related internships or fieldwork, scholarships/grants, tuition waivers (partial), and unspecified assistantships also available. Financial award application deadline: 3/31; financial award applicants required to submit FAFSA. *Faculty research:* Intellectual freedom, fair use copyright, technology integration, young adult literature, distance learning. *Unit head:* Dr. Patsy Couts, Chair, 405-974-3888, Fax: 405-974-3857, E-mail: pcouts@uco.edu. *Application contact:* Dr. Richard Bernard, Dean, Graduate College, 405-974-3493, Fax: 405-974-3852, E-mail: gradcoll@uco.edu. Website: http://www.uco.edu/ceps/dept/apss/.

University of Cincinnati, Graduate School, College of Education, Criminal Justice, and Human Services, Division of Teacher Education, Program in Reading/Literacy, Cincinnati, OH 45221. Offers M Ed, Ed D. *Accreditation:* NCATE. Part-time programs available. *Degree requirements:* For master's, thesis or alternative; for doctorate, thesis/dissertation. *Entrance requirements:* For master's, GRE General Test. Additional exam requirements/recommendations for international students: Required—TOEFL (minimum score 550 paper-based), TWE (minimum score 4.5), OEPT. Electronic applications accepted.

University of Colorado Denver, School of Education and Human Development, Teacher Education Programs, Denver, CO 80217. Offers elementary linguistically diverse education (MA); elementary math and science education (MA); elementary math education (MA); elementary reading and writing (MA); elementary science education (MA); secondary English education (MA); secondary linguistically diverse education (MA); secondary math education (MA); secondary reading and writing (MA); secondary science education (MA); special education (MA). *Accreditation:* NCATE. Part-time and evening/weekend programs available. *Students:* 269 full-time (208 women), 141 part-time (111 women); includes 55 minority (4 Black or African American, non-Hispanic/Latino; 1 American Indian or Alaska Native, non-Hispanic/Latino; 10 Asian, non-Hispanic/Latino; 39 Hispanic/Latino; 1 Two or more races, non-Hispanic/Latino), 7 international. Average age 31. 97 applicants, 81% accepted, 62 enrolled. In 2013, 180 master's awarded. *Degree requirements:* For master's, comprehensive exam. *Entrance requirements:* For master's, GRE or MAT (for those with GPA below 2.75), transcripts, resume, letters of recommendation. Additional exam requirements/recommendations for international students: Required—TOEFL (minimum score 537 paper-based; 75 iBT); Recommended—IELTS (minimum score 6.5). *Application deadline:* For fall admission, 4/15 priority date for domestic students, 4/1 for international students; for spring admission, 9/15 priority date for domestic students, 9/1 for international students. Applications are processed on a rolling basis. Application fee: $50 ($75 for international students). Electronic applications accepted. *Expenses:* Contact institution. *Financial support:* In 2013–14, 42 students received support. Fellowships, research assistantships, teaching assistantships, Federal Work-Study, institutionally sponsored loans, scholarships/grants, and traineeships available. Financial award application deadline: 4/1; financial award applicants required to submit FAFSA. *Faculty research:* Linguistically diverse education/ESL, elementary reading and writing, elementary teacher education, secondary teacher education, special education. *Unit head:* Cindy Gutierrez, Director, 303-315-4982, E-mail: cindy.gutierrez@ucdenver.edu. *Application contact:* Lori Sisneros, Student Services Center, 303-315-4979, E-mail: education@ucdenver.edu.

Website: http://www.ucdenver.edu/academics/colleges/SchoolOfEducation/Academics/MASTERS/Pages/default.aspx.

University of Connecticut, Graduate School, Neag School of Education, Department of Curriculum and Instruction, Program in Reading Education, Storrs, CT 06269. Offers MA, PhD, Post-Master's Certificate. *Accreditation:* NCATE. Terminal master's awarded for partial completion of doctoral program. *Degree requirements:* For master's, comprehensive exam, thesis or alternative; for doctorate, thesis/dissertation. *Entrance requirements:* For doctorate, GRE General Test. Additional exam requirements/

recommendations for international students: Required—TOEFL (minimum score 550 paper-based). Electronic applications accepted.

University of Dayton, Department of Teacher Education, Dayton, OH 45469-1300. Offers adolescence to young adult education (MS Ed); early childhood education (MS Ed); early childhood leadership and advocacy (MS Ed); interdisciplinary education studies (MS Ed); intervention specialist education, mild/moderate (MS Ed); literacy (MS Ed); middle childhood education (MS Ed); multi-age education (MS Ed); music education (MS Ed); teacher as leader (MS Ed); technology enhanced learning (MS Ed). Part-time and evening/weekend programs available. Postbaccalaureate distance learning degree programs offered (no on-campus study). *Faculty:* 19 full-time (13 women), 21 part-time/adjunct (18 women). *Students:* 69 full-time (57 women), 86 part-time (75 women); includes 16 minority (10 Black or African American, non-Hispanic/Latino; 2 Asian, non-Hispanic/Latino; 4 Hispanic/Latino), 10 international. Average age 31. 140 applicants, 54% accepted, 39 enrolled. In 2013, 93 master's awarded. *Degree requirements:* For master's, variable foreign language requirement, comprehensive exam (for some programs), thesis. *Entrance requirements:* For master's, GRE or MAT, minimum GPA of 2.75. Additional exam requirements/recommendations for international students: Required—TOEFL (minimum score 550 paper-based; 80 iBT), IELTS (minimum score 6.5). *Application deadline:* For fall admission, 3/1 for domestic students, 5/1 for international students; for winter admission, 7/1 for international students; for spring admission, 11/1 for international students. Applications are processed on a rolling basis. Application fee: $0 ($50 for international students). Electronic applications accepted. *Expenses:* Contact institution. *Financial support:* In 2013–14, 61 students received support, including 5 research assistantships with full tuition reimbursements available (averaging $8,720 per year), 3 teaching assistantships with full tuition reimbursements available (averaging $8,720 per year); career-related internships or fieldwork, institutionally sponsored loans, scholarships/grants, traineeships, health care benefits, and unspecified assistantships also available. Support available to part-time students. Financial award application deadline: 3/1; financial award applicants required to submit FAFSA. *Faculty research:* Diversity, literacy, art representation by young children, preservice teacher preparation. *Unit head:* Dr. Connie L. Bowman, Chair, 937-229-3305, E-mail: cbowman1@udayton.edu. *Application contact:* Gina Seiter, Graduate Program Advisor, 937-229-3103, E-mail: gseiter1@udayton.edu.

The University of Findlay, Office of Graduate Admissions, Findlay, OH 45840-3653. Offers athletic training (MAT); business (MBA), including health care management, hospitality management, organizational leadership, public management; education (MA Ed), including administration, children's literature, early childhood, human resource development, reading, science, special education, technology; environmental, safety and health management (MSEM); health informatics (MS); occupational therapy (MOT); pharmacy (Pharm D); physical therapy (DPT); physician assistant (MPA); rhetoric and writing (MA); teaching English to speakers of other languages (TESOL) and bilingual education (MA). Part-time and evening/weekend programs available. Postbaccalaureate distance learning degree programs offered (no on-campus study). *Faculty:* 209 full-time (98 women), 69 part-time/adjunct (38 women). *Students:* 551 full-time (332 women), 457 part-time (276 women); includes 77 minority (37 Black or African American, non-Hispanic/Latino; 1 American Indian or Alaska Native, non-Hispanic/Latino; 15 Asian, non-Hispanic/Latino; 23 Hispanic/Latino; 1 Native Hawaiian or other Pacific Islander, non-Hispanic/Latino), 135 international. Average age 28. 637 applicants, 66% accepted, 241 enrolled. In 2013, 267 master's, 91 doctorates awarded. *Degree requirements:* For master's, thesis, cumulative project, capstone project. *Entrance requirements:* For master's, GRE/GMAT, bachelor's degree from accredited institution, minimum undergraduate GPA of 2.5 in last 64 hours of course work; for doctorate, GRE, minimum cumulative GPA of 3.0. Additional exam requirements/recommendations for international students: Required—TOEFL (minimum score 80 iBT). *Application deadline:* Applications are processed on a rolling basis. Application fee: $25. Electronic applications accepted. *Expenses: Required fees:* $146 per semester. Tuition and fees vary according to degree level and program. *Financial support:* In 2013–14, 11 research assistantships with full and partial tuition reimbursements (averaging $4,000 per year), 10 teaching assistantships with full and partial tuition reimbursements (averaging $3,600 per year) were awarded; career-related internships or fieldwork, Federal Work-Study, health care benefits, and unspecified assistantships also available. Financial award application deadline: 4/1; financial award applicants required to submit FAFSA. *Unit head:* Christopher M. Harris, Director of Admissions, 419-434-4347, E-mail: harrisc1@findlay.edu. *Application contact:* Emily Ickes, Graduate Admissions Counselor, 419-434-6933, Fax: 419-434-4898, E-mail: ickese@findlay.edu.
Website: http://www.findlay.edu/admissions/graduate/Pages/default.aspx.

University of Florida, Graduate School, College of Education, School of Teaching and Learning, Gainesville, FL 32611. Offers curriculum and instruction (M Ed, MAE, Ed D, PhD, Ed S), including bilingual/ESOL specialization; elementary education (M Ed, MAE); English education (M Ed, MAE); mathematics education (M Ed, MAE); reading education (M Ed, MAE); science education (M Ed, MAE); social studies education (M Ed, MAE). *Accreditation:* NCATE. Part-time and evening/weekend programs available. Postbaccalaureate distance learning degree programs offered (no on-campus study). *Faculty:* 24 full-time (17 women), 12 part-time/adjunct (7 women). *Students:* 201 full-time (162 women), 325 part-time (255 women); includes 124 minority (36 Black or African American, non-Hispanic/Latino; 4 American Indian or Alaska Native, non-Hispanic/Latino; 10 Asian, non-Hispanic/Latino; 74 Hispanic/Latino), 47 international. Average age 34. 220 applicants, 55% accepted, 64 enrolled. In 2013, 215 master's, 15 doctorates, 14 other advanced degrees awarded. Terminal master's awarded for partial completion of doctoral program. *Degree requirements:* For master's, comprehensive exam (for some programs), thesis (for some programs); for doctorate, comprehensive exam (for some programs), thesis/dissertation (for some programs). *Entrance requirements:* For master's and doctorate, GRE General Test, minimum GPA of 3.0; for Ed S, GRE General Test. Additional exam requirements/recommendations for international students: Required—TOEFL (minimum score 550 paper-based; 80 iBT), IELTS (minimum score 6). *Application deadline:* For fall admission, 2/15 for domestic students, 12/1 for international students; for spring admission, 9/15 for domestic students, 3/1 for international students. Applications are processed on a rolling basis. Application fee: $30. Electronic applications accepted. *Expenses:* Tuition, state resident: full-time $12,640. Tuition, nonresident: full-time $30,000. *Financial support:* In 2013–14, 52 students received support, including 3 fellowships (averaging $2,365 per year), 20 research assistantships (averaging $11,715 per year), 58 teaching assistantships (averaging $8,410 per year); career-related internships or fieldwork and unspecified assistantships also available. Financial award applicants required to submit FAFSA. *Faculty research:* Early childhood, child and adolescents, diverse learners, race/ethnicity issues, teacher education, professional development, language and literacy development, policy development. *Unit head:* Elizabeth Bondy, PhD, Interim Director and Professor, 352-273-4242, Fax: 352-392-9193, E-mail: bondy@coe.ufl.edu. *Application contact:* Sevan Terzian, Graduate Coordinator, 352-273-4216, Fax: 352-392-9193, E-mail: sterzian@coe.ufl.edu.
Website: http://education.ufl.edu/school-teaching-learning/.

University of Georgia, College of Education, Department of Language and Literacy Education, Athens, GA 30602. Offers English education (M Ed, Ed S); language and literacy education (PhD); reading education (M Ed, Ed D, Ed S); teaching additional languages (M Ed, Ed S). *Accreditation:* NCATE. *Degree requirements:* For doctorate, variable foreign language requirement. *Entrance requirements:* For master's and Ed S, GRE General Test or MAT; for doctorate, GRE General Test. Additional exam requirements/recommendations for international students: Required—TOEFL (minimum score 550 paper-based). Electronic applications accepted. *Faculty research:* Comprehension, critical literacy, literacy and technology, vocabulary instruction, content area reading.

University of Guam, Office of Graduate Studies, School of Education, Program in Language and Literacy, Mangilao, GU 96923. Offers M Ed. Part-time programs available. *Degree requirements:* For master's, comprehensive oral and written exams, special project or thesis. *Entrance requirements:* For master's, GRE General Test. Additional exam requirements/recommendations for international students: Required—TOEFL.

University of Houston–Clear Lake, School of Education, Program in Curriculum and Instruction, Houston, TX 77058-1002. Offers curriculum and instruction (MS); early childhood education (MS); reading (MS); school library and information science (MS). Part-time and evening/weekend programs available. *Degree requirements:* For master's, thesis (for some programs). *Entrance requirements:* For master's, GRE or minimum GPA of 3.0 in last 60 hours. Additional exam requirements/recommendations for international students: Required—TOEFL (minimum score 550 paper-based). Electronic applications accepted.

University of Illinois at Chicago, Graduate College, College of Education, Department of Curriculum and Instruction, Chicago, IL 60607-7128. Offers curriculum studies (PhD); educational studies (M Ed); elementary education (M Ed); instructional leadership (M Ed); literacy, language and culture (M Ed, PhD); science education (M Ed); secondary education (M Ed). Part-time and evening/weekend programs available. *Faculty:* 20 full-time (10 women), 10 part-time/adjunct (8 women). *Students:* 124 full-time (89 women), 155 part-time (117 women); includes 117 minority (51 Black or African American, non-Hispanic/Latino; 19 Asian, non-Hispanic/Latino; 43 Hispanic/Latino; 4 Two or more races, non-Hispanic/Latino), 11 international. Average age 32. 154 applicants, 70% accepted, 74 enrolled. In 2013, 108 master's, 16 doctorates awarded. *Degree requirements:* For doctorate, thesis/dissertation. *Entrance requirements:* For master's, minimum GPA of 2.75; for doctorate, GRE General Test, minimum GPA of 2.75. Additional exam requirements/recommendations for international students: Required—TOEFL. *Application deadline:* For fall admission, 1/9 for domestic and international students; for spring admission, 10/1 for domestic and international students. Applications are processed on a rolling basis. Application fee: $40 ($50 for international students). Electronic applications accepted. *Expenses:* Tuition, state resident: full-time $11,066; part-time $3689 per term. Tuition, nonresident: full-time $23,064; part-time $7688 per term. *Required fees:* $3004; $1190 per term. Tuition and fees vary according to course level and program. *Financial support:* In 2013–14, 101 students received support, including 4 fellowships with full tuition reimbursements available; research assistantships with full tuition reimbursements available, teaching assistantships with full tuition reimbursements available, career-related internships or fieldwork, Federal Work-Study, institutionally sponsored loans, traineeships, tuition waivers (full), and unspecified assistantships also available. Support available to part-time students. Financial award application deadline: 3/1; financial award applicants required to submit FAFSA. *Faculty research:* Curriculum theory, curriculum development, research on teaching, curriculum and context, reading/literacy. *Total annual research expenditures:* $70,000. *Unit head:* Prof. Alfred Tatum, Associate Professor/Director/Chair, 312-413-3883, Fax: 312-996-8134, E-mail: atatum1@uic.edu.
Website: http://education.uic.edu.

University of Kentucky, Graduate School, College of Education, Department of Curriculum and Instruction, Lexington, KY 40506-0032. Offers curriculum and instruction (Ed D); elementary education (MA Ed); instructional system design (MS Ed); literacy (MA Ed); middle school education (MA Ed, MS Ed); secondary education (MA Ed, MS Ed). *Accreditation:* NCATE. *Degree requirements:* For master's, comprehensive exam, thesis optional; for doctorate, comprehensive exam, thesis/dissertation. *Entrance requirements:* For master's, GRE General Test, minimum undergraduate GPA of 2.75; for doctorate, GRE General Test, minimum graduate GPA of 3.0. Additional exam requirements/recommendations for international students: Required—TOEFL (minimum score 550 paper-based). Electronic applications accepted. *Faculty research:* Educational reform, multicultural education, classroom instructional practices, performance based assessment, primary school programs.

University of La Verne, College of Education and Organizational Leadership, Master's Program in Education, La Verne, CA 91750-4443. Offers advanced teaching skills (M Ed); education (special emphasis) (M Ed); educational leadership (M Ed); reading (M Ed). *Accreditation:* NCATE. Part-time programs available. *Faculty:* 7 full-time (4 women), 1 (woman) part-time/adjunct. *Students:* 42 full-time (34 women), 114 part-time (88 women); includes 71 minority (4 Black or African American, non-Hispanic/Latino; 7 Asian, non-Hispanic/Latino; 54 Hispanic/Latino; 6 Two or more races, non-Hispanic/Latino), 3 international. Average age 31. In 2013, 87 master's awarded. *Degree requirements:* For master's, thesis optional. *Entrance requirements:* For master's, California Basic Educational Skills Test, interview, writing sample, minimum GPA of 3.0, 3 letters of recommendation. Additional exam requirements/recommendations for international students: Required—TOEFL (minimum score 550 paper-based). *Application deadline:* Applications are processed on a rolling basis. Application fee: $50. *Expenses:* Contact institution. *Financial support:* Institutionally sponsored loans and unspecified assistantships available. Financial award application deadline: 3/2; financial award applicants required to submit FAFSA. *Unit head:* Lynn Stanton-Riggs, Chair, 909-448-4625, E-mail: lstanton-riggs@laverne.edu. *Application contact:* Christy Ranells, Program and Admission Specialist, 909-448-4644, Fax: 909-392-2744, E-mail: cranells@laverne.edu.
Website: http://www.laverne.edu/education/.

University of La Verne, College of Education and Organizational Leadership, Program in Reading, La Verne, CA 91750-4443. Offers reading (M Ed, Certificate); reading and language arts specialist (Credential). *Faculty:* 1 (woman) full-time, 3 part-time/adjunct (all women). *Students:* 1 (woman) full-time, 32 part-time (29 women); includes 13 minority (2 Black or African American, non-Hispanic/Latino; 2 Asian, non-Hispanic/Latino; 9 Hispanic/Latino). Average age 41. In 2013, 16 master's awarded. *Degree requirements:* For master's, thesis optional. *Entrance requirements:* For master's, MAT, California Basic Educational Skills Test, minimum GPA of 3.0, basic teaching credential, interview, 3 letters of reference. *Application deadline:* Applications are processed on a rolling basis. Application fee: $50. *Expenses:* Contact institution. *Financial support:* Institutionally sponsored loans, scholarships/grants, and unspecified assistantships available. Financial award application deadline: 3/2; financial award applicants required to submit FAFSA. *Unit head:* Lynn Stanton-Riggs, Chairperson, 909-448-4625, E-mail: lstanton-riggs@laverne.edu. *Application contact:* Christy Ranells, Program and Admission Specialist, 909-448-4644, Fax: 909-392-2744, E-mail: cranells@laverne.edu.
Website: http://www.laverne.edu/education/.

University of Louisiana at Monroe, Graduate School, College of Arts, Education, and Sciences, School of Education, Program in Curriculum and Instruction, Monroe, LA 71209-0001. Offers art education (M Ed); biology education (M Ed); chemistry education

(M Ed); curriculum and instruction (Ed D); early childhood education (M Ed); earth science education (M Ed); educational leadership (M Ed); elementary education (1-5) (M Ed); English as a second language (M Ed); English education (M Ed); family and consumer education (M Ed); French education (M Ed); history education (M Ed); math education (M Ed); middle school education (M Ed); music education (M Ed); reading education (K-12) (M Ed); Spanish education (M Ed); special education - academically gifted (M Ed); special education - early intervention (M Ed); special education - educational diagnostician (M Ed); special education - mild/moderate disabilities (M Ed); speech education (M Ed). *Accreditation:* NCATE. *Degree requirements:* For master's, comprehensive exam (for some programs), thesis; for doctorate, thesis/dissertation, internships. *Entrance requirements:* For master's, GRE General Test; for doctorate, GRE General Test, minimum undergraduate GPA of 2.75, graduate 3.25. Additional exam requirements/recommendations for international students: Required—TOEFL (minimum score 500 paper-based; 61 iBT). *Application deadline:* For fall admission, 8/24 priority date for domestic students, 7/1 for international students; for winter admission, 12/14 priority date for domestic students; for spring admission, 1/19 for domestic students, 11/1 for international students. Applications are processed on a rolling basis. Application fee: $20 ($30 for international students). Electronic applications accepted. *Expenses:* Tuition, state resident: full-time $6607. Tuition, nonresident: full-time $17,179. Full-time tuition and fees vary according to program. *Financial support:* Research assistantships, career-related internships or fieldwork, Federal Work-Study, and unspecified assistantships available. Financial award application deadline: 4/1; financial award applicants required to submit FAFSA. *Unit head:* Dr. Dorothy Schween, Director, 318-342-1268, Fax: 318-342-3131, E-mail: schween@ulm.edu. *Application contact:* Dr. Dorothy Schween, Director, 318-342-1268, Fax: 318-342-3131, E-mail: schween@ulm.edu.

University of Maine, Graduate School, College of Education and Human Development, Department of Teacher and Counselor Education, Orono, ME 04469. Offers counselor education (M Ed, MA, MS, CAS); early childhood teacher (CGS); education (PhD), including counselor education, literacy education, prevention and intervention studies; elementary education (M Ed, CAS); individualized education (M Ed); literacy education (M Ed, MS, CAS); response to intervention for behavior (CGS); secondary education (M Ed, MAT, CAS); social studies education (M Ed); special education (M Ed, CAS); teacher consultant in writing (CGS). Part-time programs available. *Students:* 147 full-time (118 women), 15 part-time (2 women); includes 8 minority (4 Black or African American, non-Hispanic/Latino; 2 American Indian or Alaska Native, non-Hispanic/Latino; 1 Hispanic/Latino; 1 Two or more races, non-Hispanic/Latino), 3 international. Average age 37. 100 applicants, 58% accepted, 50 enrolled. In 2013, 83 master's, 5 doctorates, 17 other advanced degrees awarded. *Degree requirements:* For master's, thesis (for some programs); for doctorate, comprehensive exam, thesis/dissertation. *Entrance requirements:* For master's, GRE General Test, MAT. Additional exam requirements/recommendations for international students: Required—TOEFL. *Application deadline:* For fall admission, 2/1 priority date for domestic students. Applications are processed on a rolling basis. Application fee: $65. Electronic applications accepted. *Expenses:* Tuition, state resident: full-time $7524. Tuition, nonresident: full-time $23,112. *Required fees:* $1970. *Financial support:* In 2013–14, 46 students received support, including 1 research assistantship (averaging $14,600 per year), 11 teaching assistantships (averaging $14,600 per year). Financial award application deadline: 3/1. *Unit head:* Dr. Janet Spector, Coordinator, 207-581-2459. *Application contact:* Scott G. Delcourt, Associate Dean of the Graduate School, 207-581-3291, Fax: 207-581-3232, E-mail: graduate@maine.edu.
Website: http://umaine.edu/edhd/.

University of Mary, School of Education and Behavioral Sciences, Department of Education, Bismarck, ND 58504-9652. Offers college teaching (M Ed); curriculum, instruction and assessment (M Ed); early childhood education (M Ed); early childhood special education (M Ed); elementary administration (M Ed); emotional disorders (M Ed); learning disabilities (M Ed); reading (M Ed); secondary administration (M Ed); special education strategist (M Ed). Part-time programs available. *Degree requirements:* For master's, portfolio or thesis. *Entrance requirements:* For master's, interview, letters of reference, minimum GPA of 2.5. Additional exam requirements/recommendations for international students: Required—TOEFL (minimum score 500 paper-based; 71 iBT). Electronic applications accepted. *Faculty research:* Innovative pedagogy in higher education, technology in education, content standards, children of poverty, children with diverse learning needs.

University of Maryland, College Park, Academic Affairs, College of Education, Department of Teaching, Learning, Policy and Leadership, College Park, MD 20742. Offers reading (M Ed, MA, PhD, CAGS); secondary education (M Ed, MA, Ed D, PhD, CAGS); teaching English to speakers of other languages (M Ed). *Accreditation:* NCATE. Part-time and evening/weekend programs available. Postbaccalaureate distance learning degree programs offered (no on-campus study). *Faculty:* 63 full-time (43 women), 20 part-time/adjunct (13 women). *Students:* 283 full-time (209 women), 188 part-time (151 women); includes 158 minority (58 Black or African American, non-Hispanic/Latino; 53 Asian, non-Hispanic/Latino; 23 Hispanic/Latino; 1 Native Hawaiian or other Pacific Islander, non-Hispanic/Latino; 23 Two or more races, non-Hispanic/Latino), 52 international. 482 applicants, 44% accepted, 126 enrolled. In 2013, 211 master's, 42 doctorates awarded. *Degree requirements:* For master's, comprehensive exam, seminar paper; for doctorate, comprehensive exam, thesis/dissertation, published paper, oral exam. *Entrance requirements:* For master's, GRE General Test or MAT, minimum GPA of 3.0, 3 letters of recommendation; for doctorate, GRE General Test or MAT, minimum undergraduate GPA of 3.0, graduate 3.5; 3 letters of recommendation. *Application deadline:* For fall admission, 2/1 priority date for domestic students, 9/1 priority date for international students; for spring admission, 9/1 for domestic students, 8/1 for international students. Applications are processed on a rolling basis. Application fee: $75. Electronic applications accepted. *Expenses:* Tuition, state resident: full-time $10,314; part-time $573 per credit hour. Tuition, nonresident: full-time $22,248; part-time $1236 per credit. *Required fees:* $1446; $403.15 per semester. Tuition and fees vary according to program. *Financial support:* In 2013–14, 11 fellowships with full and partial tuition reimbursements (averaging $22,271 per year), 7 research assistantships with tuition reimbursements (averaging $18,573 per year), 85 teaching assistantships with tuition reimbursements (averaging $17,609 per year) were awarded; Federal Work-Study and scholarships/grants also available. Support available to part-time students. Financial award applicants required to submit FAFSA. *Faculty research:* Teacher preparation, curriculum study, in-service education. *Total annual research expenditures:* $3.9 million. *Unit head:* Francine Hultgren, Interim Chair, 301-405-3117, E-mail: fh@umd.edu. *Application contact:* Dr. Charles A. Caramello, Dean of Graduate School, 301-405-0358, Fax: 301-314-9305, E-mail: ccaramel@umd.edu.

University of Massachusetts Amherst, Graduate School, College of Education, Program in Education, Amherst, MA 01003. Offers bilingual/English as a second language/multicultural education (M Ed, Ed S); child study and early education (M Ed); children, families and schools (Ed D, Ed S); early childhood and elementary teacher education (M Ed); educational leadership (M Ed); educational policy and leadership (Ed D); higher education (M Ed); international education (M Ed); language, literacy and culture (Ed D); learning, media and technology (M Ed, Ed S); mathematics, science, and learning technologies (Ed D); psychometric methods, educational statistics and research methods (Ed D); reading and writing (M Ed); school counselor education (M Ed, Ed S); school psychology (Ed S); science education (Ed S); secondary teacher education (M Ed); social justice education (M Ed, Ed D, Ed S); special education (M Ed, Ed D, Ed S); teacher education and school improvement (Ed D, Ed S). *Accreditation:* NCATE. Part-time programs available. Postbaccalaureate distance learning degree programs offered (minimal on-campus study). *Faculty:* 95 full-time (55 women). *Students:* 357 full-time (240 women), 264 part-time (194 women); includes 114 minority (41 Black or African American, non-Hispanic/Latino; 4 American Indian or Alaska Native, non-Hispanic/Latino; 10 Asian, non-Hispanic/Latino; 47 Hispanic/Latino; 12 Two or more races, non-Hispanic/Latino), 100 international. Average age 34. 761 applicants, 51% accepted, 200 enrolled. In 2013, 186 master's, 31 doctorates, 22 other advanced degrees awarded. Terminal master's awarded for partial completion of doctoral program. *Degree requirements:* For doctorate, comprehensive exam, thesis/dissertation. *Entrance requirements:* Additional exam requirements/recommendations for international students: Required—TOEFL (minimum score 550 paper-based; 80 iBT), IELTS (minimum score 6.5). *Application deadline:* For fall admission, 1/15 for domestic and international students. Applications are processed on a rolling basis. Application fee: $75. Electronic applications accepted. *Financial support:* Fellowships with full and partial tuition reimbursements, research assistantships with full and partial tuition reimbursements, teaching assistantships with full and partial tuition reimbursements, career-related internships or fieldwork, Federal Work-Study, scholarships/grants, traineeships, health care benefits, tuition waivers (full and partial), and unspecified assistantships available. Support available to part-time students. Financial award application deadline: 1/15; financial award applicants required to submit FAFSA. *Unit head:* Dr. Linda L. Griffin, Graduate Program Director, 413-545-6984, Fax: 413-545-1523. *Application contact:* Lindsay DeSantis, Supervisor of Admissions, 413-545-0722, Fax: 413-577-0010, E-mail: gradadm@grad.umass.edu.
Website: http://www.umass.edu/education/.

University of Massachusetts Lowell, Graduate School of Education, Lowell, MA 01854-2881. Offers administration, planning, and policy (CAGS); curriculum and instruction (M Ed, CAGS); educational administration (M Ed); language arts and literacy (Ed D); leadership in schooling (Ed D); math and science education (Ed D); reading and language (M Ed, CAGS). *Accreditation:* NCATE. Part-time and evening/weekend programs available. Postbaccalaureate distance learning degree programs offered (no on-campus study). Terminal master's awarded for partial completion of doctoral program. *Degree requirements:* For doctorate, thesis/dissertation. *Entrance requirements:* For master's, doctorate, and CAGS, GRE General Test. Additional exam requirements/recommendations for international students: Required—TOEFL. Electronic applications accepted.

University of Memphis, Graduate School, College of Education, Department of Instruction and Curriculum Leadership, Memphis, TN 38152. Offers early childhood education (MAT, MS, Ed D); elementary education (MAT); instruction and curriculum (MS, Ed D); instruction design and technology (MS, Ed D); middle grades education (MAT); reading (MS, Ed D); secondary education (MAT); special education (MAT, MS, Ed D). *Accreditation:* NCATE (one or more programs are accredited). Part-time programs available. *Faculty:* 30 full-time (18 women), 16 part-time/adjunct (10 women). *Students:* 55 full-time (44 women), 370 part-time (300 women); includes 169 minority (153 Black or African American, non-Hispanic/Latino; 5 American Indian or Alaska Native, non-Hispanic/Latino; 1 Asian, non-Hispanic/Latino; 6 Hispanic/Latino; 4 Two or more races, non-Hispanic/Latino), 7 international. Average age 35. 181 applicants, 84% accepted, 21 enrolled. In 2013, 137 master's, 10 doctorates awarded. Terminal master's awarded for partial completion of doctoral program. *Degree requirements:* For master's, comprehensive exam, thesis or alternative; for doctorate, comprehensive exam, thesis/dissertation. *Entrance requirements:* For master's, GRE General Test, minimum GPA of 2.5; for doctorate, GRE General Test, GRE Subject Test, 2 years of teaching experience. *Application deadline:* For fall admission, 8/1 for domestic students; for spring admission, 12/1 for domestic students. Applications are processed on a rolling basis. Application fee: $35 ($60 for international students). Electronic applications accepted. *Financial support:* In 2013–14, 635 students received support. Research assistantships with full tuition reimbursements available, teaching assistantships with full tuition reimbursements available, career-related internships or fieldwork, Federal Work-Study, institutionally sponsored loans, scholarships/grants, traineeships, and unspecified assistantships available. Support available to part-time students. Financial award application deadline: 2/15; financial award applicants required to submit FAFSA. *Faculty research:* Effective urban teachers, preparation and retention of urban teachers, technology utilization in schools, field-based teacher preparation programs, effective use of online instruction. *Unit head:* Dr. Sandra Cooley-Nichols, Interim Chair, 901-678-2365. *Application contact:* Dr. Sally Blake, Director of Graduate Studies, 901-678-4861.
Website: http://www.memphis.edu/icl/.

University of Miami, Graduate School, School of Education and Human Development, Department of Teaching and Learning, Program in Teaching and Learning, Coral Gables, FL 33124. Offers language and literacy learning in multilingual settings (PhD); science, technology, engineering and mathematics (PhD); special education (PhD). *Faculty:* 14 full-time (10 women), 9 part-time/adjunct (all women). *Students:* 24 full-time (21 women); includes 11 minority (3 Black or African American, non-Hispanic/Latino; 7 Hispanic/Latino; 1 Two or more races, non-Hispanic/Latino), 5 international. Average age 32. 29 applicants, 21% accepted, 5 enrolled. In 2013, 2 doctorates awarded. *Degree requirements:* For doctorate, thesis/dissertation, qualifying exam, electronic portfolio. *Entrance requirements:* For doctorate, GRE General Test. Additional exam requirements/recommendations for international students: Required—TOEFL (minimum score 550 paper-based; 80 iBT); Recommended—IELTS (minimum score 6.5). *Application deadline:* For fall admission, 2/15 for domestic students, 10/1 for international students. Application fee: $65. Electronic applications accepted. *Financial support:* In 2013–14, 24 students received support, including 11 research assistantships with full and partial tuition reimbursements available (averaging $18,900 per year), 8 teaching assistantships with full and partial tuition reimbursements available (averaging $18,900 per year). Financial award application deadline: 3/1; financial award applicants required to submit FAFSA. *Faculty research:* Teacher education, multicultural education, special education, second language acquisition, math and science education. *Unit head:* Dr. Elizabeth Harry, Department Chairperson and Program Director, 305-284-4961, Fax: 305-284-6998, E-mail: bharry@miami.edu. *Application contact:* Lois Heffernan, Graduate Admission Coordinator, 305-284-2167, Fax: 305-284-9395, E-mail: lheffernan@miami.edu.

University of Michigan–Flint, School of Education and Human Services, Department of Education, Flint, MI 48502-1950. Offers early childhood education (MA); educational technology (MA); elementary education with teaching certification (MA); literacy education (MA); special education (MA). Part-time programs available. *Faculty:* 14 full-time (12 women), 8 part-time/adjunct (4 women). *Students:* 27 full-time (24 women), 215 part-time (186 women); includes 22 minority (20 Black or African American, non-Hispanic/Latino; 2 American Indian or Alaska Native, non-Hispanic/Latino). Average age 35. 63 applicants, 86% accepted, 43 enrolled. In 2013, 91 master's awarded. *Entrance requirements:* For master's, BS with minimum GPA of 3.0. Additional exam requirements/recommendations for international students: Required—TOEFL (minimum score 560 paper-based; 84 iBT), IELTS (minimum score 6.5). *Application deadline:* For

fall admission, 8/1 priority date for domestic students, 5/1 priority date for international students; for winter admission, 11/15 priority date for domestic students, 9/15 priority date for international students; for spring admission, 3/15 priority date for domestic students, 1/15 priority date for international students. Application fee: $55. *Expenses:* Contact institution. *Financial support:* Federal Work-Study, scholarships/grants, and unspecified assistantships available. Support available to part-time students. Financial award application deadline: 6/1; financial award applicants required to submit FAFSA. *Unit head:* Dr. Beverly Schumer, Director, 810-424-5215, E-mail: bschumer@umflint.edu. *Application contact:* Beulah Alexander, Executive Secretary, 810-766-6879, Fax: 810-766-6891, E-mail: beulaha@umflint.edu.
Website: http://www.umflint.edu/education/graduate-programs.

University of Minnesota, Twin Cities Campus, Graduate School, College of Education and Human Development, Department of Curriculum and Instruction, Minneapolis, MN 55455-0213. Offers art education (M Ed, MA, PhD); children's literature (M Ed, MA, PhD); curriculum and instruction (MA, PhD); early childhood education (M Ed, PhD); elementary education (M Ed, MA, PhD); English education (MA, PhD); environmental education (M Ed); family education (M Ed, MA, Ed D, PhD); instructional systems and technology (M Ed, MA, PhD); language arts (MA, PhD); language immersion education (Certificate); literacy education (MA); mathematics education (MA, PhD); reading education (MA, PhD); science education (MA, PhD); second languages and cultures education (MA, PhD); social studies education (MA, PhD); teaching (M Ed), including Chinese, earth science, elementary special education, English, English as a second language, French, German, Hebrew, Japanese, life sciences, mathematics, middle school science, science, second languages and cultures, social studies, Spanish; technology enhanced learning (Certificate); writing education (M Ed, MA, PhD). *Faculty:* 29 full-time (16 women). *Students:* 425 full-time (301 women), 220 part-time (153 women); includes 85 minority (21 Black or African American, non-Hispanic/Latino; 6 American Indian or Alaska Native, non-Hispanic/Latino; 42 Asian, non-Hispanic/Latino; 16 Hispanic/Latino), 50 international. Average age 32. 551 applicants, 68% accepted, 340 enrolled. In 2013, 618 master's, 33 doctorates, 6 other advanced degrees awarded. Application fee: $75 ($95 for international students). *Financial support:* In 2013–14, 25 fellowships (averaging $28,500 per year), 23 research assistantships with full tuition reimbursements (averaging $8,082 per year), 81 teaching assistantships with full tuition reimbursements (averaging $9,974 per year) were awarded. *Faculty research:* Teaching and learning; quality of education; influence of cultural, linguistic, social, political, technological and economic factors on teaching, learning and educational research; relationship between educational practice and a democratic and just society. *Total annual research expenditures:* $272,048. *Unit head:* Dr. Nina Asher, Chair, 612-624-4772, Fax: 612-624-1357, E-mail: nasher@umn.edu. *Application contact:* Dr. Jennifer Engler, Assistant Dean, 612-626-2887, Fax: 612-626-7496, E-mail: engle009@umn.edu.
Website: http://www.cehd.umn.edu/ci.

University of Mississippi, Graduate School, School of Education, Department of Teacher Education, Oxford, MS 38677. Offers curriculum and instruction (MA); elementary education (M Ed, Ed D, Ed S); literacy education (M Ed); secondary education (M Ed, PhD, Ed S); special education (M Ed, PhD, Ed S). *Accreditation:* NCATE. *Faculty:* 42 full-time (29 women), 25 part-time/adjunct (22 women). *Students:* 70 full-time (59 women), 194 part-time (156 women); includes 67 minority (60 Black or African American, non-Hispanic/Latino; 1 Asian, non-Hispanic/Latino; 4 Hispanic/Latino; 2 Two or more races, non-Hispanic/Latino), 1 international. In 2013, 122 master's, 1 doctorate awarded. *Degree requirements:* For master's, thesis (for some programs); for doctorate, one foreign language, thesis/dissertation. *Entrance requirements:* For master's, GRE General Test, minimum GPA of 3.0; for doctorate, GRE General Test. Additional exam requirements/recommendations for international students: Required—TOEFL. *Application deadline:* For fall admission, 7/1 for domestic students; for spring admission, 10/1 for domestic students. Applications are processed on a rolling basis. Application fee: $40. *Financial support:* Scholarships/grants available. Financial award application deadline: 3/1; financial award applicants required to submit FAFSA. *Unit head:* Dr. Susan McClelland, Interim Chair, 662-915-7350. *Application contact:* Dr. Christy M. Wyandt, Associate Dean, 662-915-7474, Fax: 662-915-7577, E-mail: cwyandt@olemiss.edu.
Website: http://education.olemiss.edu/dco/teacher_education.html.

University of Missouri, Graduate School, College of Education, Department of Learning, Teaching and Curriculum, Columbia, MO 65211. Offers agricultural education (M Ed, PhD, Ed S); art education (M Ed, PhD, Ed S); business and office education (M Ed, PhD, Ed S); early childhood education (M Ed, PhD, Ed S); elementary education (M Ed, PhD, Ed S); English education (M Ed, PhD, Ed S); foreign language education (M Ed, PhD, Ed S); health education and promotion (M Ed, PhD); learning and instruction (M Ed); marketing education (M Ed, PhD, Ed S); mathematics education (M Ed, PhD, Ed S); music education (M Ed, PhD, Ed S); reading education (M Ed, PhD, Ed S); science education (M Ed, PhD, Ed S); social studies education (M Ed, PhD, Ed S); vocational education (M Ed, PhD, Ed S). Part-time programs available. *Faculty:* 26 full-time (16 women), 3 part-time/adjunct (2 women). *Students:* 186 full-time (143 women), 197 part-time (172 women); includes 19 minority (4 Black or African American, non-Hispanic/Latino; 4 Asian, non-Hispanic/Latino; 6 Hispanic/Latino; 5 Two or more races, non-Hispanic/Latino), 25 international. Average age 31. 288 applicants, 65% accepted, 160 enrolled. In 2013, 202 master's, 18 doctorates, 7 other advanced degrees awarded. Terminal master's awarded for partial completion of doctoral program. *Degree requirements:* For doctorate, thesis/dissertation. *Entrance requirements:* For master's and Ed S, GRE General Test or MAT, minimum GPA of 3.0; for doctorate, GRE General Test, minimum GPA of 3.0. Additional exam requirements/recommendations for international students: Required—TOEFL (minimum score 600 paper-based; 100 iBT). *Application deadline:* For fall admission, 12/1 priority date for domestic and international students. Applications are processed on a rolling basis. Application fee: $55 ($75 for international students). Electronic applications accepted. *Financial support:* Fellowships, research assistantships, teaching assistantships, institutionally sponsored loans, traineeships, health care benefits, and unspecified assistantships available. Support available to part-time students. *Faculty research:* Curriculum development and research, teacher education, art education, business and marketing, early childhood education, English education, literacy/reading education, mathematics education, music education, science education, social studies education. *Unit head:* Dr. James Tarr, Associate Division Director, 573-882-4034, E-mail: tarrj@missouri.edu. *Application contact:* Fran Colley, Academic Advisor, 573-882-6462, E-mail: colleyf@missouri.edu.
Website: http://education.missouri.edu/LTC/.

University of Missouri–Kansas City, School of Education, Kansas City, MO 64110-2499. Offers administration (Ed D); counseling and guidance (MA, Ed S), including mental health counseling (Ed S), school counseling (Ed S); counseling psychology (PhD); curriculum and instruction (MA, Ed S), including language and literacy (Ed S); education (PhD), including higher education administration, PK-12 education administration; educational administration (MA, Ed S), including advanced principal (Ed S), beginning principal (Ed S), district-level administration (Ed S); reading education (MA, Ed S); special education (MA). PhD in education offered through the School of Graduate Studies. *Accreditation:* NCATE. Part-time and evening/weekend programs available. *Faculty:* 44 full-time (34 women), 60 part-time/adjunct (45 women). *Students:* 206 full-time (145 women), 394 part-time (291 women); includes 154 minority (99 Black or African American, non-Hispanic/Latino; 13 Asian, non-Hispanic/Latino; 30 Hispanic/Latino; 1 Native Hawaiian or other Pacific Islander, non-Hispanic/Latino; 11 Two or more races, non-Hispanic/Latino), 16 international. Average age 32. 401 applicants, 48% accepted, 188 enrolled. In 2013, 156 master's, 9 doctorates, 24 other advanced degrees awarded. *Degree requirements:* For doctorate, thesis/dissertation, internship, practicum. *Entrance requirements:* For master's, GRE, minimum GPA of 2.75, 2 letters of reference, written statement of purpose; for doctorate, GRE, minimum GPA of 3.0; for Ed S, minimum GPA of 3.0. Additional exam requirements/recommendations for international students: Required—TOEFL (minimum score 550 paper-based; 80 iBT). *Application deadline:* For fall admission, 4/1 priority date for domestic and international students; for spring admission, 11/1 priority date for domestic and international students. Applications are processed on a rolling basis. Application fee: $45 ($50 for international students). *Expenses:* Tuition, state resident: full-time $6073; part-time $337.40 per credit hour. Tuition, nonresident: full-time $15,680; part-time $871.10 per credit hour. *Required fees:* $97.59 per credit hour. Full-time tuition and fees vary according to program. *Financial support:* In 2013–14, 12 research assistantships with partial tuition reimbursements (averaging $11,140 per year) were awarded; career-related internships or fieldwork, Federal Work-Study, institutionally sponsored loans, and tuition waivers (full and partial) also available. Support available to part-time students. Financial award application deadline: 3/1; financial award applicants required to submit FAFSA. *Faculty research:* Urban education, inquiry-based field study, theories of counseling and psychotherapy, school literacy, educational technology. *Unit head:* Dr. Wanda Blanchett, Dean, 816-235-2234, Fax: 816-235-5270, E-mail: education@umkc.edu. *Application contact:* Erica Hernandez-Scott, Student Recruiter, 816-235-1295, Fax: 816-235-5270, E-mail: hernandeze@umkc.edu.
Website: http://education.umkc.edu.

University of Missouri–St. Louis, College of Education, Division of Teaching and Learning, St. Louis, MO 63121. Offers autism studies (Certificate); elementary education (M Ed), including early childhood, general, reading; secondary education (M Ed), including curriculum and instruction, general, middle level education, reading, teaching English to speakers of other languages (TESOL); secondary school teaching (Certificate); special education (M Ed), including autism and developmental disabilities, cross-categorical disabilities, early childhood; teaching English to speakers of other languages (Certificate). Part-time and evening/weekend programs available. *Faculty:* 20 full-time (11 women), 1 (woman) part-time/adjunct. *Students:* 42 full-time (33 women), 578 part-time (442 women); includes 152 minority (101 Black or African American, non-Hispanic/Latino; 1 American Indian or Alaska Native, non-Hispanic/Latino; 20 Asian, non-Hispanic/Latino; 23 Hispanic/Latino; 7 Two or more races, non-Hispanic/Latino), 19 international. Average age 29. 245 applicants, 97% accepted, 166 enrolled. In 2013, 219 master's, 14 Certificates awarded. *Degree requirements:* For master's, comprehensive exam. *Entrance requirements:* Additional exam requirements/recommendations for international students: Recommended—TOEFL (minimum score 550 paper-based; 79 iBT), IELTS (minimum score 6.5). *Application deadline:* For fall admission, 7/1 priority date for domestic and international students; for spring admission, 12/1 priority date for domestic and international students. Application fee: $50 ($40 for international students). Electronic applications accepted. *Expenses:* Tuition, state resident: full-time $7364; part-time $409.10 per credit hour. Tuition, nonresident: full-time $19,162; part-time $1008.50 per credit hour. *Financial support:* Application deadline: 4/1; applicants required to submit FAFSA. *Unit head:* Dr. Patricia Kopetz, Chair, 314-516-5791. *Application contact:* 314-516-5458, Fax: 314-516-6996, E-mail: gadadm@umsl.edu.
Website: http://coe.umsl.edu/web/divisions/teach-learn/index.html.

University of Nebraska at Kearney, Graduate Programs, College of Education, Department of Teacher Education, Kearney, NE 68849-0001. Offers curriculum and instruction (MA Ed), including early childhood education, elementary education, English as a second language, instructional effectiveness, reading/special education, secondary education; instructional technology (MS Ed), including information technology, instructional technology, school librarian; reading PK-12 (MA Ed); special education (MA Ed), including advanced practitioner, gifted, mild/moderate. Part-time and evening/weekend programs available. *Degree requirements:* For master's, comprehensive exam, thesis optional. *Entrance requirements:* For master's, portfolio or GRE. Additional exam requirements/recommendations for international students: Required—TOEFL (minimum score 550 paper-based). Electronic applications accepted.

University of Nebraska at Omaha, Graduate Studies, College of Education, Department of Teacher Education, Program in Reading Education, Omaha, NE 68182. Offers MS. *Accreditation:* NCATE. Part-time and evening/weekend programs available. *Faculty:* 5 full-time (4 women). *Students:* 1 (woman) full-time, 102 part-time (91 women); includes 14 minority (4 Black or African American, non-Hispanic/Latino; 2 Asian, non-Hispanic/Latino; 5 Hispanic/Latino; 3 Two or more races, non-Hispanic/Latino). Average age 36. 7 applicants, 71% accepted, 3 enrolled. In 2013, 9 master's awarded. *Degree requirements:* For master's, comprehensive exam, thesis (for some programs). *Entrance requirements:* For master's, minimum GPA of 3.0, transcripts. Additional exam requirements/recommendations for international students: Required—TOEFL, IELTS, PTE. *Application deadline:* For fall admission, 8/1 priority date for domestic students; for spring admission, 12/1 priority date for domestic students; for summer admission, 6/1 for domestic students. Applications are processed on a rolling basis. Application fee: $45. Electronic applications accepted. *Financial support:* In 2013–14, 1 student received support, including 1 research assistantship with tuition reimbursement available; fellowships, teaching assistantships with tuition reimbursements available, Federal Work-Study, institutionally sponsored loans, scholarships/grants, tuition waivers (full), and unspecified assistantships also available. Support available to part-time students. Financial award application deadline: 3/1. *Unit head:* Dr. Sarah Edwards, Chairperson, 402-554-3512. *Application contact:* Dr. Wilma Kuhlman, Graduate Program Chair, 402-554-3926, E-mail: graduate@unomaha.edu.

University of Nevada, Reno, Graduate School, College of Education, Department of Educational Specialties, Program in Literacy Studies, Reno, NV 89557. Offers M Ed, MA, Ed D, PhD. Terminal master's awarded for partial completion of doctoral program. *Degree requirements:* For master's, thesis optional; for doctorate, thesis/dissertation. *Entrance requirements:* For master's, minimum GPA of 2.75; for doctorate, GRE General Test, minimum GPA of 3.0. Additional exam requirements/recommendations for international students: Required—TOEFL (minimum score 500 paper-based; 61 iBT), IELTS (minimum score 6). Electronic applications accepted. *Faculty research:* Cognitive language process, literacy.

University of New England, College of Arts and Sciences, Program in Education, Biddeford, ME 04005-9526. Offers advanced educational leadership (CAGS); career and technical education (MS Ed, CAGS); curriculum and instruction strategies (CAGS); curriculum and instruction strategy (MS Ed); educational leadership (MS Ed, CAGS); inclusion education (MS Ed); leadership, ethics and change (CAGS); literacy K-12 (MS Ed, CAGS); teaching methodologies (MS Ed). Part-time and evening/weekend programs available. Postbaccalaureate distance learning degree programs offered (no on-campus study). *Faculty:* 5 full-time (4 women), 17 part-time/adjunct (9 women). *Students:* 295 full-time (228 women), 233 part-time (175 women); includes 26 minority (19 Black or African American, non-Hispanic/Latino; 2 American Indian or Alaska Native,

non-Hispanic/Latino; 2 Asian, non-Hispanic/Latino; 2 Hispanic/Latino; 1 Two or more races, non-Hispanic/Latino). Average age 37. 289 applicants, 84% accepted, 189 enrolled. In 2013, 257 master's, 106 CAGSs awarded. *Degree requirements:* For master's, collaborative action research project, integrative seminar portfolio. *Entrance requirements:* For master's, teaching certificate, 2 years of teaching experience. *Application deadline:* For fall admission, 9/15 for domestic students; for spring admission, 1/15 for domestic students. Applications are processed on a rolling basis. Application fee: $40. Electronic applications accepted. *Financial support:* Application deadline: 5/1; applicants required to submit FAFSA. *Faculty research:* Distance learning, effective teaching, transition planning, adult learning. *Unit head:* Paulette St. Ours, Associate Dean, College of Arts and Sciences, 207-602-2400, E-mail: pstours@une.edu. *Application contact:* Dr. Cynthia Forrest, Vice President for Student Affairs, 207-221-4225, Fax: 207-523-1925, E-mail: gradadmissions@une.edu.
Website: http://www.une.edu/cas/education/msonline.cfm.

University of New Mexico, Graduate School, College of Education, Department of Language, Literacy and Sociocultural Studies, Program in Language, Literacy and Sociocultural Studies, Albuquerque, NM 87131. Offers American Indian education (MA); bilingual education (MA, PhD); educational linguistics (PhD); educational thought and sociocultural studies (MA, PhD); literacy/language arts (MA, PhD); social studies (MA); TESOL (MA, PhD). *Faculty:* 10 full-time (6 women), 3 part-time/adjunct (1 woman). *Students:* 63 full-time (48 women), 117 part-time (105 women); includes 96 minority (8 Black or African American, non-Hispanic/Latino; 16 American Indian or Alaska Native, non-Hispanic/Latino; 6 Asian, non-Hispanic/Latino; 62 Hispanic/Latino; 4 Two or more races, non-Hispanic/Latino), 20 international. Average age 39. 67 applicants, 63% accepted, 30 enrolled. In 2013, 30 master's, 8 doctorates awarded. *Degree requirements:* For master's, comprehensive exam, thesis optional; for doctorate, comprehensive exam, thesis/dissertation, research skills. *Entrance requirements:* For master's, letter of intent, 3 letters of recommendation, resume, BA/BS, department demographic form, transcripts; for doctorate, writing sample, letter of intent, 3 letters of recommendation, resume, BA/BS, MA, department demographic form, transcripts. Additional exam requirements/recommendations for international students: Required— TOEFL. *Application deadline:* For fall admission, 12/1 for domestic and international students; for spring admission, 9/15 for domestic and international students. Application fee: $50. Electronic applications accepted. *Financial support:* In 2013–14, 7 students received support, including 7 fellowships (averaging $3,170 per year), 1,318 teaching assistantships with tuition reimbursements available (averaging $3,789 per year); research assistantships, career-related internships or fieldwork, institutionally sponsored loans, scholarships/grants, and unspecified assistantships also available. Support available to part-time students. Financial award application deadline: 3/1; financial award applicants required to submit FAFSA. *Faculty research:* School reform, professional development, history of education, Native American education, politics of education, feminism and issues of sexual identity, critical race theory, bilingualism, literacy reading, adolescent literature, second language acquisition, critical theory and schooling, indigenous languages. *Unit head:* Dr. Lois M. Meyer, Chair, 505-277-7244, Fax: 505-277-8362, E-mail: lsmeyer@unm.edu. *Application contact:* Debra Schaffer, Administrative Assistant, 505-277-0437, Fax: 505-277-8362, E-mail: schaffer@unm.edu.
Website: http://coe.unm.edu/departments/department-of-language-literacy-and-sociocultural-studies/llss-program.html.

The University of North Carolina at Chapel Hill, Graduate School, School of Education, Program in Education, Chapel Hill, NC 27599. Offers culture, curriculum and change (MA, PhD); early childhood, intervention and literacy (MA, PhD); educational psychology, measurement and evaluation (MA, PhD). *Accreditation:* NCATE. *Degree requirements:* For master's, thesis; for doctorate, comprehensive exam, thesis/dissertation. *Entrance requirements:* For master's, GRE General Test, minimum GPA of 3.0 during last 2 years of undergraduates course work; for doctorate, GRE General Test, minimum GPA of 3.0 during last 2 years of undergraduate course work. Additional exam requirements/recommendations for international students: Required—TOEFL (minimum score 550 paper-based). Electronic applications accepted.

The University of North Carolina at Charlotte, The Graduate School, College of Education, Department of Reading and Elementary Education, Charlotte, NC 28223-0001. Offers elementary education (M Ed); reading, language and literacy (M Ed). Part-time and evening/weekend programs available. Postbaccalaureate distance learning degree programs offered (no on-campus study). *Faculty:* 27 full-time (15 women), 3 part-time/adjunct (2 women). *Students:* 16 full-time (15 women), 78 part-time (76 women); includes 12 minority (7 Black or African American, non-Hispanic/Latino; 1 American Indian or Alaska Native, non-Hispanic/Latino; 3 Hispanic/Latino; 1 Two or more races, non-Hispanic/Latino). Average age 31. 45 applicants, 91% accepted, 31 enrolled. In 2013, 10 master's awarded. *Degree requirements:* For master's, thesis or alternative. *Entrance requirements:* For master's, GRE or MAT. Additional exam requirements/recommendations for international students: Required—TOEFL (minimum score 557 paper-based; 83 iBT). *Application deadline:* For fall admission, 5/1 priority date for domestic students, 5/1 for international students; for spring admission, 10/1 priority date for domestic students, 10/1 for international students. Applications are processed on a rolling basis. Application fee: $75. Electronic applications accepted. *Expenses:* Tuition, state resident: full-time $3522. Tuition, nonresident: full-time $16,051. *Required fees:* $2585. Tuition and fees vary according to course load and program. *Financial support:* In 2013–14, 1 student received support, including 1 teaching assistantship (averaging $7,500 per year); career-related internships or fieldwork, institutionally sponsored loans, scholarships/grants, and unspecified assistantships also available. Support available to part-time students. Financial award application deadline: 4/1; financial award applicants required to submit FAFSA. *Total annual research expenditures:* $81,584. *Unit head:* Dr. Janice Hinson, Chair, 704-687-8019, Fax: 704-687-1631, E-mail: jhinso42@uncc.edu. *Application contact:* Kathy B. Giddings, Director of Graduate Admissions, 704-687-5503, Fax: 704-687-1668, E-mail: gradadm@uncc.edu.
Website: http://education.uncc.edu/reel.

The University of North Carolina at Greensboro, Graduate School, School of Education, Department of Curriculum and Instruction, Greensboro, NC 27412-5001. Offers college teaching and adult learning (Certificate); curriculum and instruction (M Ed), including chemistry education, elementary education, English as a second language, French education, instructional technology, mathematics education, middle grades education, reading education, science education, social studies education, Spanish education; curriculum and teaching (PhD), including higher education, teacher education and development; English as a second language (Certificate); higher education (M Ed); supervision (M Ed). *Accreditation:* NCATE. Part-time programs available. *Degree requirements:* For doctorate, thesis/dissertation. *Entrance requirements:* For master's and doctorate, GRE General Test. Additional exam requirements/recommendations for international students: Required—TOEFL. Electronic applications accepted. *Faculty research:* Community college literacy program, middle school mathematics/computer mathematics.

The University of North Carolina at Pembroke, Graduate Studies, School of Education, Program in Reading Education, Pembroke, NC 28372-1510. Offers MA Ed.

Accreditation: NCATE. Part-time and evening/weekend programs available. *Degree requirements:* For master's, comprehensive exam, thesis optional. *Entrance requirements:* For master's, GRE General Test or MAT, minimum GPA of 3.0 in major, 2.5 overall; teaching license; one year of teaching experience; three professional references. Additional exam requirements/recommendations for international students: Required—TOEFL.

The University of North Carolina Wilmington, Watson College of Education, Department of Early Childhood, Elementary, Middle, Literacy and Special Education, Wilmington, NC 28403-3297. Offers MAT. *Accreditation:* NCATE. Part-time and evening/weekend programs available. *Faculty:* 21 full-time (17 women). *Students:* 47 full-time (36 women), 13 part-time (11 women); includes 9 minority (5 Black or African American, non-Hispanic/Latino; 2 Hispanic/Latino; 2 Two or more races, non-Hispanic/Latino), 3 international. Average age 31. 36 applicants, 97% accepted, 33 enrolled. In 2013, 24 master's awarded. *Degree requirements:* For master's, comprehensive exam. *Entrance requirements:* For master's, GRE General Test, MAT, minimum B average in upper-division undergraduate course work. *Application deadline:* For fall admission, 6/1 for domestic students. Applications are processed on a rolling basis. Application fee: $60. *Expenses:* Tuition, state resident: full-time $4163. Tuition, nonresident: full-time $16,098. *Financial support:* Career-related internships or fieldwork, Federal Work-Study, and unspecified assistantships available. Support available to part-time students. Financial award application deadline: 3/15. *Unit head:* Dr. Tracy Hargrove, Chair, 910-962-3240, Fax: 910-962-3988, E-mail: hargrovet@uncw.edu. *Application contact:* Dr. Ron Vetter, Dean, Graduate School, 910-962-3224, Fax: 910-962-3787, E-mail: vetterr@uncw.edu.

University of North Dakota, Graduate School, College of Education and Human Development, Program in Reading Education, Grand Forks, ND 58202. Offers M Ed, MS. *Accreditation:* NCATE. Part-time programs available. Postbaccalaureate distance learning degree programs offered (minimal on-campus study). *Degree requirements:* For master's, comprehensive exam, thesis or alternative. *Entrance requirements:* For master's, minimum GPA of 3.0. Additional exam requirements/recommendations for international students: Required—TOEFL (minimum score 550 paper-based; 79 iBT), IELTS (minimum score 6.5). Electronic applications accepted. *Faculty research:* Whole language, multicultural education, child-focused learning, experiential science, cooperative learning.

University of Northern Colorado, Graduate School, College of Education and Behavioral Sciences, School of Teacher Education, Program in Reading, Greeley, CO 80639. Offers MA. *Accreditation:* NCATE. Part-time and evening/weekend programs available. Postbaccalaureate distance learning degree programs offered (no on-campus study). *Degree requirements:* For master's, comprehensive exam, thesis or alternative. *Entrance requirements:* For master's, GRE General Test (if undergraduate GPA less than 3.0), resume, letters of reference. Electronic applications accepted.

University of Northern Iowa, Graduate College, College of Education, Department of Curriculum and Instruction, MAE Program in Literacy Education, Cedar Falls, IA 50614. Offers MAE. Part-time and evening/weekend programs available. *Students:* 24 part-time (22 women); includes 1 minority (Asian, non-Hispanic/Latino). 5 applicants. In 2013, 6 master's awarded. *Degree requirements:* For master's, comprehensive exam, thesis or alternative. *Entrance requirements:* For master's, writing exam, minimum GPA of 3.0, two recommendations from professional educators. Additional exam requirements/recommendations for international students: Required—TOEFL (minimum score 500 paper-based; 61 iBT). *Application deadline:* For fall admission, 8/1 priority date for domestic students. Applications are processed on a rolling basis. Application fee: $50 ($70 for international students). Electronic applications accepted. *Financial support:* Career-related internships or fieldwork, Federal Work-Study, and tuition waivers (full and partial) available. Support available to part-time students. Financial award application deadline: 2/1. *Unit head:* Dr. Deborah Tidwell, Coordinator, 319-273-2983, Fax: 319-273-5886, E-mail: deborah.tidwell@uni.edu. *Application contact:* Laurie S. Russell, Record Analyst, 319-273-2623, Fax: 319-273-2885, E-mail: laurie.russell@uni.edu.
Website: http://www.grad.uni.edu/degrees/programs/programs/curriculum-and-instruction-literacy-education-mae.

University of North Florida, College of Education and Human Services, Department of Childhood Education, Jacksonville, FL 32224. Offers literacy K-12 (M Ed); professional education - elementary education (M Ed); TESOL K-12 (M Ed). *Accreditation:* NCATE. Part-time and evening/weekend programs available. *Faculty:* 10 full-time (8 women). *Students:* 11 full-time (10 women), 24 part-time (18 women); includes 6 minority (1 Black or African American, non-Hispanic/Latino; 1 Asian, non-Hispanic/Latino; 4 Hispanic/Latino), 1 international. Average age 33. 24 applicants, 79% accepted, 10 enrolled. In 2013, 21 master's awarded. *Entrance requirements:* For master's, GRE General Test, minimum GPA of 3.0 in last 60 hours, 3 letters of recommendation, interview. Additional exam requirements/recommendations for international students: Required—TOEFL (minimum score 500 paper-based). *Application deadline:* For fall admission, 7/1 priority date for domestic students, 5/1 for international students; for spring admission, 11/1 priority date for domestic students, 10/1 for international students. Application fee: $30. Electronic applications accepted. *Expenses:* Tuition, state resident: full-time $9794; part-time $408.10 per credit hour. Tuition, nonresident: full-time $22,383; part-time $932.61 per credit hour. *Required fees:* $2020; $84.20 per credit hour. Tuition and fees vary according to course load and program. *Financial support:* In 2013–14, 8 students received support, including 2 research assistantships (averaging $5,183 per year); Federal Work-Study, tuition waivers (partial), and unspecified assistantships also available. Support available to part-time students. Financial award application deadline: 4/1; financial award applicants required to submit FAFSA. *Faculty research:* The social context of and processes in learning, inter-disciplinary instruction, cross-cultural conflict resolution, the Vygotskian perspective on literacy diagnosis and instruction, performance poetry and teaching the language arts through drama. *Total annual research expenditures:* $2,158. *Unit head:* Dr. John Venn, Chair, 904-620-5352, Fax: 904-620-1025, E-mail: j.venn@unf.edu. *Application contact:* Dr. Amanda Pascale, Director, The Graduate School, 904-620-1360, Fax: 904-620-1362, E-mail: graduateschool@unf.edu.
Website: http://www.unf.edu/coehs/celt/.

University of North Texas, Robert B. Toulouse School of Graduate Studies, Denton, TN 76203-5017. Offers accounting (MS, PhD); applied anthropology (MA, MS); applied behavior analysis (Certificate); applied technology and performance improvement (M Ed, MS, PhD); art education (MA, PhD); art history (MA); art museum education (Certificate); arts leadership (Certificate); audiology (Au D); behavior analysis (MS); biochemistry and molecular biology (MS, PhD); biology (MA, MS, PhD); business (PhD); business computer information systems (PhD); chemistry (MS, PhD); clinical psychology (PhD); communication studies (MA, MS); computer engineering (MS); computer science (MS); computer science and engineering (PhD); counseling (M Ed, MS, PhD), including clinical mental health counseling (MS), college and university counseling (M Ed, MS), elementary school counseling (M Ed, MS), secondary school counseling (M Ed, MS), counseling psychology (PhD); creative writing (MA); criminal justice (MS); curriculum and instruction (M Ed, PhD), including curriculum studies (PhD), early childhood studies (PhD), language and literacy studies (PhD); decision sciences (MBA); design (MA, MFA), including fashion design (MFA), innovation studies, interior design (MFA); early

childhood studies (MS); economics (MS); educational leadership (M Ed, Ed D, PhD); educational psychology (MS), including family studies, gifted and talented (MS, PhD); human development, learning and cognition, research, measurement and evaluation; educational research (PhD), including gifted and talented (MS, PhD), human development and family studies, psychological aspects of sports and exercise, research, measurement and statistics; electrical engineering (MS); emergency management (MPA); engineering systems (MS); English (MA, PhD); environmental science (MS, PhD); experimental psychology (PhD); finance (MBA, MS, PhD); financial management (MPA); French (MA); health psychology and behavioral medicine (PhD); health services management (MBA); higher education (M Ed, Ed D, PhD); history (MA, MS, PhD), including European history (PhD), military history (PhD), United States history (PhD); hospitality management (MS); human resources management (MPA); information science (MS, PhD); information technologies (MBA); information technology and decision sciences (MS); interdisciplinary studies (MA, MS); international sustainable tourism (MS); jazz studies (MM); journalism (MA, MJ, Graduate Certificate), including interactive and virtual digital communication (Graduate Certificate), narrative journalism (Graduate Certificate); public relations (Graduate Certificate); kinesiology (MS); learning technologies (MS, PhD); library science (MS); local government management (MPA); logistics and supply chain management (MBA, PhD); long-term care, senior housing, and aging services (MA, MS); management science (PhD); marketing (MBA, PhD); materials science and engineering (MS, PhD); mathematics (MA, PhD); merchandising (MS); music (MA, MM Ed, PhD), including ethnomusicology (MA), music education (MM Ed, PhD), music theory (MA, PhD), musicology (MA, PhD), performance (MA); nonprofit management (MPA); operations and supply chain management (MBA); performance (MM, DMA); philosophy (MA, PhD); physics (MS, PhD); political science (MA, MS, PhD); public administration and management (PhD), including emergency management, nonprofit management, public financial management, urban management; radio, television and film (MA, MFA); recreation, event and sport management (MS); rehabilitation counseling (MS, Certificate); sociology (MA, MS, PhD); Spanish (MA); special education (M Ed, PhD), including autism intervention (PhD), emotional/behavioral disorders (PhD), mild/moderate disabilities (PhD); speech-language pathology (MA, MS); strategic management (MBA); studio art (MFA); taxation (MS); teaching (M Ed); MBA/MS; MS/MPH; MSES/MBA. Part-time and evening/weekend programs available. Postbaccalaureate distance learning degree programs offered. *Faculty:* 661 full-time (213 women), 240 part-time/adjunct (144 women). *Students:* 3,106 full-time (1,620 women), 3,543 part-time (2,221 women); includes 1,740 minority (533 Black or African American, non-Hispanic/Latino; 15 American Indian or Alaska Native, non-Hispanic/Latino; 286 Asian, non-Hispanic/Latino; 746 Hispanic/Latino; 3 Native Hawaiian or other Pacific Islander, non-Hispanic/Latino; 157 Two or more races, non-Hispanic/Latino), 1,145 international. Average age 32. 6,289 applicants, 43% accepted, 1751 enrolled. In 2013, 1,778 master's, 239 doctorates, 10 other advanced degrees awarded. Terminal master's awarded for partial completion of doctoral program. *Degree requirements:* For master's, variable foreign language requirement, comprehensive exam (for some programs), thesis (for some programs); for doctorate, variable foreign language requirement, comprehensive exam (for some programs), thesis/dissertation; for other advanced degree, variable foreign language requirement, comprehensive exam (for some programs). *Entrance requirements:* For master's and doctorate, GRE, GMAT. Additional exam requirements/recommendations for international students: Required—TOEFL (minimum score 550 paper-based; 79 iBT). *Application deadline:* For fall admission, 7/15 for domestic students, 3/15 for international students; for spring admission, 11/15 for domestic students, 9/15 for international students; for summer admission, 5/1 for domestic students. Applications are processed on a rolling basis. Application fee: $60. Electronic applications accepted. *Financial support:* Fellowships with partial tuition reimbursements, research assistantships with partial tuition reimbursements, teaching assistantships, career-related internships or fieldwork, Federal Work-Study, institutionally sponsored loans, scholarships/grants, health care benefits, and library assistantships available. Support available to part-time students. Financial award applicants required to submit FAFSA. *Unit head:* Mark Wardell, Dean, 940-565-2383, E-mail: mark.wardell@unt.edu. *Application contact:* Toulouse School of Graduate Studies, 940-565-2383, Fax: 940-565-2141, E-mail: gradsch@unt.edu. Website: http://tsgs.unt.edu/.

University of Oklahoma, Jeannine Rainbolt College of Education, Department of Instructional Leadership and Academic Curriculum, Norman, OK 73072. Offers communication, culture and pedagogy for Hispanic populations in educational settings (Graduate Certificate); instructional leadership and academic curriculum (M Ed, PhD), including bilingual education (PhD), early childhood education, elementary education, English education, instructional leadership, mathematics education, reading education, science education, science, technology, engineering and mathematics education (M Ed), secondary education, social studies education, teacher education (M Ed), world language education (M Ed). *Accreditation:* NCATE. Part-time and evening/weekend programs available. Postbaccalaureate distance learning degree programs offered (no on-campus study). *Faculty:* 22 full-time (15 women), 1 (woman) part-time/adjunct. *Students:* 64 full-time (49 women), 103 part-time (81 women); includes 33 minority (8 Black or African American, non-Hispanic/Latino; 9 American Indian or Alaska Native, non-Hispanic/Latino; 5 Asian, non-Hispanic/Latino; 4 Hispanic/Latino; 1 Native Hawaiian or other Pacific Islander, non-Hispanic/Latino; 6 Two or more races, non-Hispanic/Latino), 10 international. Average age 34. 50 applicants, 84% accepted, 36 enrolled. In 2013, 26 master's, 11 doctorates awarded. Terminal master's awarded for partial completion of doctoral program. *Degree requirements:* For master's, comprehensive exam (for some programs), thesis (for some programs); for doctorate, comprehensive exam, thesis/dissertation. *Entrance requirements:* For master's, essay; for doctorate, GRE, 3 recommendation letters; autobiography, statement of objectives; essay on chosen major; transcripts; writing sample. Additional exam requirements/recommendations for international students: Required—TOEFL (minimum score 79 iBT). *Application deadline:* For fall admission, 4/30 for domestic and international students; for spring admission, 10/31 for domestic and international students; for summer admission, 3/15 for domestic and international students. Applications are processed on a rolling basis. Application fee: $50 ($100 for international students). Electronic applications accepted. *Expenses:* Tuition, state resident: full-time $4205; part-time $175.20 per credit hour. Tuition, nonresident: full-time $16,205; part-time $675.20 per credit hour. *Required fees:* $2745; $103.85 per credit hour. $126.50 per semester. *Financial support:* In 2013–14, 98 students received support, including 10 research assistantships with partial tuition reimbursements available (averaging $10,671 per year), 7 teaching assistantships with partial tuition reimbursements available (averaging $10,753 per year); Federal Work-Study, institutionally sponsored loans, scholarships/grants, and unspecified assistantships also available. Support available to part-time students. Financial award application deadline: 6/1; financial award applicants required to submit FAFSA. *Total annual research expenditures:* $1 million. *Unit head:* Dr. Stacy Reeder, Chair/Graduate Liaison, 405-325-1498, Fax: 405-325-4061, E-mail: reeder@ou.edu. *Application contact:* Lynn Crussel, Graduate Programs Officer, 405-325-1498, Fax: 405-325-4061, E-mail: lcrussel@ou.edu. Website: http://education.ou.edu/departments/ilac.

University of Oklahoma Health Sciences Center, Graduate College, College of Allied Health, Department of Communication Sciences and Disorders, Oklahoma City, OK 73190. Offers audiology (MS, Au D, PhD); communication sciences and disorders (Certificate), including reading, speech-language pathology; education of the deaf (MS); speech-language pathology (MS, PhD). *Accreditation:* ASHA (one or more programs are accredited). Part-time programs available. *Faculty:* 15 full-time (12 women). *Students:* 72 full-time (67 women), 5 part-time (4 women); includes 12 minority (3 Asian, non-Hispanic/Latino; 1 Hispanic/Latino; 8 Two or more races, non-Hispanic/Latino). Average age 26. 181 applicants, 45% accepted, 30 enrolled. In 2013, 19 master's, 3 doctorates awarded. Terminal master's awarded for partial completion of doctoral program. *Degree requirements:* For master's, comprehensive exam, thesis optional; for doctorate, one foreign language, comprehensive exam, thesis/dissertation. *Entrance requirements:* For master's and doctorate, GRE General Test, 3 letters of recommendation. Additional exam requirements/recommendations for international students: Required—TOEFL (minimum score 550 paper-based). *Application deadline:* For fall admission, 2/1 for domestic students. Applications are processed on a rolling basis. Application fee: $50. *Expenses:* Tuition, state resident: full-time $3504; part-time $175.20 per credit hour. Tuition, nonresident: full-time $13,504; part-time $675.20 per credit hour. *Required fees:* $1545; $52.70 per credit hour. $245.25 per semester. Tuition and fees vary according to course load. *Financial support:* In 2013–14, 8 research assistantships (averaging $16,000 per year) were awarded; fellowships, career-related internships or fieldwork, Federal Work-Study, institutionally sponsored loans, and traineeships also available. Support available to part-time students. *Faculty research:* Event-related potentials, cleft palate, fluency disorders, language disorders, hearing and speech science. *Unit head:* Dr. Stephen Painton, Chair, 405-271-4214, E-mail: stephen-painton@ouhsc.edu. *Application contact:* Dr. Sarah Buckinghan, Graduate Liaison, 405-271-4214, Fax: 405-271-1153, E-mail: sarah-buckingham@ouhsc.edu.

University of Pennsylvania, Graduate School of Education, Division of Reading, Writing, and Literacy, Program in Language and Literacy, Philadelphia, PA 19104. Offers MS Ed. *Students:* 1 (woman) full-time, 1 (woman) part-time; includes 1 minority (Asian, non-Hispanic/Latino). 13 applicants, 54% accepted, 3 enrolled. In 2013, 4 master's awarded. *Unit head:* Dr. Andrew Porter, Dean, 215-898-7014. *Application contact:* 215-898-6415, Fax: 215-746-6884, E-mail: admissions@gse.upenn.edu. Website: http://www.gse.upenn.edu/rwl/ll.

University of Phoenix–Online Campus, College of Education, Phoenix, AZ 85034-7209. Offers administration and supervision (MAEd, Certificate); adult education and training (MAEd); curriculum and instruction (MAEd), including computer education, curriculum and instruction, English as a second language, language arts, mathematics, reading; early childhood education (MAEd); educational studies (MAEd); elementary teacher education (MAEd), including early childhood, elementary teacher education, high school middle level, middle level; principal licensure (Certificate); secondary teacher education (MAEd); special education (MAEd, Certificate); teacher education (MAEd), including middle level generalist; teacher education middle level mathematics (MAEd), including middle level mathematics; teacher education middle level science (MAEd), including middle level science; teacher education secondary mathematics (MAEd); teacher education secondary science (MAEd); teacher leadership (MAEd); teachers of English learners (Certificate); transition to teaching (Certificate), including elementary education, secondary education. *Accreditation:* Teacher Education Accreditation Council. Evening/weekend programs available. Postbaccalaureate distance learning degree programs offered. *Entrance requirements:* Additional exam requirements/recommendations for international students: Required—TOEFL, TOEIC (Test of English as an International Communication), Berlitz Online English Proficiency Exam, PTE, or IELTS. Electronic applications accepted. *Expenses:* Contact institution.

University of Phoenix–Phoenix Campus, College of Education, Tempe, AZ 85282-2371. Offers administration and supervision (MA Ed); adult education and training (MA Ed); curriculum and instruction reading (MA Ed); early childhood education (MA Ed); education studies (MA Ed); elementary teacher education (MA Ed); secondary teacher education (MA Ed); special education (MA Ed); teacher leadership (MA Ed). Evening/weekend programs available. Postbaccalaureate distance learning degree programs offered. *Entrance requirements:* Additional exam requirements/recommendations for international students: Required—TOEFL, TOEIC (Test of English as an International Communication), Berlitz Online English Proficiency Exam, PTE, or IELTS. Electronic applications accepted. *Expenses:* Contact institution.

University of Pittsburgh, School of Education, Department of Instruction and Learning, Program in Reading Education, Pittsburgh, PA 15260. Offers M Ed, Ed D, PhD. *Students:* 2 full-time (both women), 30 part-time (28 women); includes 4 minority (1 Black or African American, non-Hispanic/Latino; 1 Hispanic/Latino; 2 Two or more races, non-Hispanic/Latino). Average age 29. 28 applicants, 86% accepted, 15 enrolled. In 2013, 15 master's, 1 doctorate awarded. *Degree requirements:* For master's, thesis; for doctorate, thesis/dissertation. *Entrance requirements:* For master's, PRAXIS I; for doctorate, GRE General Test. Additional exam requirements/recommendations for international students: Required—TOEFL. *Application deadline:* For fall admission, 2/15 for domestic students. Application fee: $50. *Expenses:* Tuition, state resident: full-time $19,964; part-time $807 per credit. Tuition, nonresident: full-time $32,686; part-time $1337 per credit. *Required fees:* $740; $200. Tuition and fees vary according to program. *Financial support:* Application deadline: 3/15; applicants required to submit FAFSA. *Unit head:* Dr. Richard Donato, Chairman, 412-624-7248, Fax: 412-648-7081, E-mail: donato@pitt.edu. *Application contact:* Dr. Marjie Schermer, Graduate Enrollment Manager, 412-648-2230, Fax: 412-648-1899, E-mail: soeinfo@pitt.edu.

University of Portland, School of Education, Portland, OR 97203-5798. Offers education (MA, MAT); educational leadership (M Ed); English for speakers of other languages (M Ed); initial administrator licensure (M Ed); neuroeducation (Ed D); organizational leadership and development (Ed D); reading (M Ed); special education (M Ed). M Ed also available through the Graduate Outreach Program for teachers residing in the Oregon and Washington state areas. *Accreditation:* NCATE. Part-time and evening/weekend programs available. *Faculty:* 17 full-time (10 women), 12 part-time/adjunct (4 women). *Students:* 47 full-time (29 women), 214 part-time (155 women); includes 25 minority (1 Black or African American, non-Hispanic/Latino; 1 American Indian or Alaska Native, non-Hispanic/Latino; 8 Asian, non-Hispanic/Latino; 6 Hispanic/Latino; 6 Native Hawaiian or other Pacific Islander, non-Hispanic/Latino; 3 Two or more races, non-Hispanic/Latino), 63 international. Average age 32. In 2013, 96 master's awarded. *Entrance requirements:* For master's, minimum GPA of 3.0, teaching certificate, letters of recommendation, resume, statement of goals, official transcripts. Additional exam requirements/recommendations for international students: Required—TOEFL (minimum score 550 paper-based; 80 iBT), IELTS (minimum score 7). *Application deadline:* For fall admission, 7/15 priority date for domestic and international students; for spring admission, 12/15 priority date for domestic and international students. Applications are processed on a rolling basis. Application fee: $50. *Expenses:* Tuition: Part-time $1025 per credit hour. Tuition and fees vary according to program. *Financial support:* Federal Work-Study and scholarships/grants available. Support available to part-time students. Financial award application deadline: 3/1; financial award applicants required to submit FAFSA. *Faculty research:* Multicultural education, supervision/leadership. *Unit head:* Dr. Bruce Weitzel, Associate Dean, 503-943-7135,

E-mail: soed@up.edu. *Application contact:* Dr. Matt Baasten, Assistant to the Provost and Dean of the Graduate School, 503-943-7107, Fax: 503-943-7315, E-mail: baasten@up.edu.
Website: http://education.up.edu/default.aspx?cid-4318&pid-5590.

University of Rhode Island, Graduate School, College of Human Science and Services, School of Education, Kingston, RI 02881. Offers adult education (MA); education (PhD); elementary education (MA); music education (MM); reading education (MA); secondary education (MA); special education (MA); MS/PhD. *Accreditation:* NCATE. Part-time and evening/weekend programs available. *Faculty:* 16 full-time (9 women). *Students:* 64 full-time (48 women), 91 part-time (68 women); includes 17 minority (8 Black or African American, non-Hispanic/Latino; 2 American Indian or Alaska Native, non-Hispanic/Latino; 2 Asian, non-Hispanic/Latino; 3 Hispanic/Latino; 2 Two or more races, non-Hispanic/Latino), 6 international. In 2013, 47 master's, 11 doctorates awarded. *Degree requirements:* For master's, comprehensive exam (for some programs), thesis optional; for doctorate, comprehensive exam, thesis/dissertation. *Entrance requirements:* For master's, 2 letters of recommendation; interview (for special education applicants); for doctorate, GRE, 3 letters of recommendation, resume. Additional exam requirements/recommendations for international students: Required—TOEFL (minimum score 600 paper-based; 100 iBT). *Application deadline:* For fall admission, 1/31 for domestic and international students. Application fee: $65. Electronic applications accepted. *Expenses:* Tuition, state resident: full-time $11,532; part-time $641 per credit. Tuition, nonresident: full-time $23,606; part-time $1311 per credit. *Required fees:* $1388; $36 per credit. $35 per semester. One-time fee: $130. *Financial support:* In 2013–14, 2 research assistantships with full and partial tuition reimbursements (averaging $11,883 per year), 4 teaching assistantships with full and partial tuition reimbursements (averaging $8,488 per year) were awarded; career-related internships or fieldwork also available. Financial award application deadline: 1/31; financial award applicants required to submit FAFSA. *Total annual research expenditures:* $1.1 million. *Unit head:* Dr. David Byrd, Director, 401-874-5484, Fax: 401-874-5471, E-mail: dbyrd@uri.edu. *Application contact:* Graduate Admissions, 401-874-2872, E-mail: gradadm@etal.uri.edu.
Website: http://www.uri.edu/hss/education/.

University of Rio Grande, Graduate School, Rio Grande, OH 45674. Offers classroom teaching (M Ed), including fine arts, learning disabilities, mathematics, reading education. *Accreditation:* NCATE. Part-time and evening/weekend programs available. *Degree requirements:* For master's, final research project, portfolio. *Entrance requirements:* For master's, minimum GPA of 2.7 in major, 2.5 overall. Additional exam requirements/recommendations for international students: Required—TOEFL. *Faculty research:* Interagency collaboration, reading and mathematics, learning styles, college access, literacy.

University of St. Francis, College of Education, Joliet, IL 60435-6169. Offers educational leadership (MS, Ed D); elementary education (M Ed); higher education (MS); reading (MS); secondary education (M Ed), including English education, math education, science education, social studies education, visual arts education; special education (M Ed); teaching and learning (MS). *Accreditation:* NCATE. Part-time and evening/weekend programs available. Postbaccalaureate distance learning degree programs offered (no on-campus study). *Faculty:* 10 full-time (8 women), 34 part-time/adjunct (25 women). *Students:* 14 full-time (13 women), 250 part-time (183 women); includes 34 minority (20 Black or African American, non-Hispanic/Latino; 1 American Indian or Alaska Native, non-Hispanic/Latino; 13 Hispanic/Latino), 1 international. Average age 36. 133 applicants, 62% accepted, 71 enrolled. In 2013, 147 master's awarded. *Degree requirements:* For doctorate, thesis/dissertation. *Entrance requirements:* For doctorate, master's degree, IL Type 75 or Principal's endorsement, interview, minimum undergraduate GPA of 3.0, professional portfolio, letter of recommendation. Additional exam requirements/recommendations for international students: Required—TOEFL (minimum score 550 paper-based; 79 iBT), IELTS (minimum score 6.5). *Application deadline:* Applications are processed on a rolling basis. Application fee: $30. Electronic applications accepted. Application fee is waived when completed online. *Expenses:* Contact institution. *Financial support:* In 2013–14, 10 students received support. Scholarships/grants, tuition waivers (partial), and unspecified assistantships available. Support available to part-time students. Financial award applicants required to submit FAFSA. *Unit head:* Dr. John Gambro, Dean, 815-740-3829, Fax: 815-740-2264, E-mail: jgambro@stfrancis.edu. *Application contact:* Sandra Sloka, Director of Admissions for Graduate and Degree Completion Programs, 800-735-7500, Fax: 815-740-3431, E-mail: ssloka@stfrancis.edu.
Website: http://www.stfrancis.edu/academics/college-of-education/.

University of St. Thomas, Graduate Studies, School of Education, Department of Teacher Education, St. Paul, MN 55105-1096. Offers curriculum and instruction (MA), including elementary, individualized, K-12, secondary; elementary education (MA); English as a second language (MA); math education (Certificate); multicultural education (Certificate); reading (MA, Certificate), including elementary (MA), K-12 (MA). *Accreditation:* NCATE. Part-time and evening/weekend programs available. *Entrance requirements:* For master's, minimum GPA of 3.0 or MAT. Additional exam requirements/recommendations for international students: Required—TOEFL (minimum score 550 paper-based; 80 iBT). *Application deadline:* For fall admission, 6/1 for domestic students; for spring admission, 11/1 for domestic students. Applications are processed on a rolling basis. Application fee: $50. *Financial support:* Fellowships, research assistantships, institutionally sponsored loans, and scholarships/grants available. Support available to part-time students. Financial award applicants required to submit FAFSA. *Unit head:* Dr. Jan L. H. Frank, Chair, 651-962-4446, Fax: 651-962-4169, E-mail: jlhfrank@stthomas.edu. *Application contact:* Rosemary R. Barreto, Department Assistant, 651-962-4420, Fax: 651-962-4169, E-mail: barr7879@stthomas.edu.

University of St. Thomas, School of Education, Houston, TX 77006-4696. Offers all level education (M Ed); bilingual/dual language (M Ed); Catholic school teaching (M Ed); Catholic/private school leadership (M Ed); counselor education (M Ed); curriculum and instruction (M Ed); educational leadership (M Ed); elementary teaching (M Ed); English as a second language (M Ed); exceptionality/educational diagnostician (M Ed); exceptionality/special education (M Ed); generalist (M Ed); reading (M Ed); secondary teaching (M Ed). *Accreditation:* Teacher Education Accreditation Council. Part-time and evening/weekend programs available. Postbaccalaureate distance learning degree programs offered (no on-campus study). *Faculty:* 40 full-time (26 women), 43 part-time/adjunct (31 women). *Students:* 27 full-time (20 women), 1,091 part-time (981 women); includes 691 minority (247 Black or African American, non-Hispanic/Latino; 1 American Indian or Alaska Native, non-Hispanic/Latino; 44 Asian, non-Hispanic/Latino; 379 Hispanic/Latino; 2 Native Hawaiian or other Pacific Islander, non-Hispanic/Latino; 18 Two or more races, non-Hispanic/Latino), 28 international. Average age 36. 858 applicants, 83% accepted, 458 enrolled. In 2013, 454 master's awarded. *Degree requirements:* For master's, thesis, field experience. *Entrance requirements:* For master's, GRE or MAT if GPA is below 3.0, bachelor's degree; minimum GPA of 2.75 in bachelor's degree or last 60 credit hours; official transcripts from all institutions; goal statement of 250-300 words; 1 reference. Additional exam requirements/recommendations for international students: Required—TOEFL. *Application deadline:*

Applications are processed on a rolling basis. Application fee: $35. Electronic applications accepted. *Expenses:* Contact institution. *Financial support:* In 2013–14, 41 students received support. Federal Work-Study, scholarships/grants, and state work-study, institutional employment available. Support available to part-time students. Financial award application deadline: 4/15; financial award applicants required to submit FAFSA. *Faculty research:* Leadership, diversity, personality traits, second language acquisition. *Unit head:* Dr. Robert LeBlanc, Dean, 713-525-3540, Fax: 713-525-3871, E-mail: education@stthom.edu. *Application contact:* Rita Paredes, Administrative Assistant, 713-525-3442, Fax: 713-525-3871, E-mail: rparede@stthom.edu.
Website: http://www.stthom.edu/Academics/School_of_Education/Index.aqf.

University of San Diego, School of Leadership and Education Sciences, Department of Learning and Teaching, San Diego, CA 92110-2492. Offers curriculum and instruction (M Ed); special education (M Ed); special education with deaf and hard of hearing (M Ed); teaching (MAT); TESOL, literacy and culture (M Ed). Part-time and evening/weekend programs available. *Faculty:* 10 full-time (6 women), 46 part-time/adjunct (38 women). *Students:* 132 full-time (100 women), 52 part-time (43 women); includes 141 minority (1 Black or African American, non-Hispanic/Latino; 16 American Indian or Alaska Native, non-Hispanic/Latino; 30 Asian, non-Hispanic/Latino; 79 Hispanic/Latino; 1 Native Hawaiian or other Pacific Islander, non-Hispanic/Latino; 14 Two or more races, non-Hispanic/Latino), 4 international. Average age 29. 253 applicants, 85% accepted, 108 enrolled. In 2013, 94 master's awarded. *Degree requirements:* For master's, thesis (for some programs), international experience. *Entrance requirements:* For master's, California Basic Educational Skills Test, minimum GPA of 3.0. Additional exam requirements/recommendations for international students: Required—TOEFL (minimum score 580 paper-based; 83 iBT), TWE. *Application deadline:* For fall admission, 3/1 priority date for domestic and international students; for spring admission, 10/15 priority date for domestic and international students. Applications are processed on a rolling basis. Application fee: $45. Electronic applications accepted. *Expenses: Tuition:* Full-time $23,580; part-time $1310 per credit. *Required fees:* $350. *Financial support:* In 2013–14, 52 students received support. Career-related internships or fieldwork, Federal Work-Study, institutionally sponsored loans, and stipends available. Support available to part-time students. Financial award application deadline: 4/1; financial award applicants required to submit FAFSA. *Faculty research:* Action research methodology, cultural studies, instructional theories and practices, second language acquisition, school reform. *Unit head:* Dr. Heather Lattimer, Director, 619-260-7616, Fax: 619-260-8159, E-mail: hlattimer@sandiego.edu. *Application contact:* Monica Mahon, Associate Director of Graduate Admissions, 619-260-4524, Fax: 619-260-4158, E-mail: grads@sandiego.edu.
Website: http://www.sandiego.edu/soles/departments/learning-and-teaching/.

University of San Francisco, School of Education, Department of Learning and Instruction, San Francisco, CA 94117-1080. Offers digital technologies for teaching and learning (MA); learning and instruction (MA, Ed D); special education (MA, Ed D); teaching reading (MA). Part-time and evening/weekend programs available. *Faculty:* 7 full-time (4 women), 6 part-time/adjunct (4 women). *Students:* 76 full-time (59 women), 40 part-time (26 women); includes 35 minority (5 Black or African American, non-Hispanic/Latino; 2 American Indian or Alaska Native, non-Hispanic/Latino; 9 Asian, non-Hispanic/Latino; 16 Hispanic/Latino; 3 Two or more races, non-Hispanic/Latino), 5 international. Average age 39. 73 applicants, 86% accepted, 40 enrolled. In 2013, 14 master's, 7 doctorates awarded. *Degree requirements:* For doctorate, thesis/dissertation. *Application deadline:* For fall admission, 3/1 priority date for domestic and international students; for spring admission, 11/1 priority date for domestic and international students. Applications are processed on a rolling basis. Application fee: $55 ($65 for international students). Electronic applications accepted. *Expenses: Tuition:* Full-time $21,150; part-time $1175 per unit. Tuition and fees vary according to course load, campus/location and program. *Financial support:* In 2013–14, 14 students received support. Fellowships, research assistantships, and teaching assistantships available. Financial award application deadline: 3/2; financial award applicants required to submit FAFSA. *Unit head:* Dr. Patricia Busk, Chair, 415-422-6289. *Application contact:* Amy Fogliani, Associate Director of Graduate Outreach, 415-422-5467, E-mail: schoolofeducation@usfca.edu.

The University of Scranton, College of Graduate and Continuing Education, Department of Education, Program in Reading Education, Scranton, PA 18510. Offers MS. *Accreditation:* NCATE. Part-time and evening/weekend programs available. *Students:* 9 full-time (8 women), 3 part-time (all women). Average age 24. 10 applicants, 100% accepted. In 2013, 5 master's awarded. *Degree requirements:* For master's, comprehensive exam, thesis (for some programs), capstone experience. *Entrance requirements:* For master's, minimum GPA of 3.0. Additional exam requirements/recommendations for international students: Required—TOEFL (minimum score 500 paper-based), IELTS (minimum score 6). *Application deadline:* Applications are processed on a rolling basis. Application fee: $0. *Financial support:* Fellowships, teaching assistantships, career-related internships or fieldwork, Federal Work-Study, and unspecified assistantships available. Support available to part-time students. Financial award application deadline: 3/1. *Unit head:* Dr. Art Chambers, Director, 570-941-4668, Fax: 570-941-5515, E-mail: chambersa2@scranton.edu. *Application contact:* Joseph M. Roback, Director of Admissions, 570-941-4385, Fax: 570-941-5928, E-mail: robackj2@scranton.edu.

University of Sioux Falls, Fredrikson School of Education, Sioux Falls, SD 57105-1699. Offers educational administration (Ed S), including principal leadership, superintendent and district leadership; leadership in reading (M Ed); leadership in schools (M Ed); leadership in technology (M Ed); teaching (M Ed). Admission in summer only. *Accreditation:* NCATE. Part-time and evening/weekend programs available. *Degree requirements:* For master's, comprehensive exam (for some programs), research application project; for Ed S, comprehensive exam, portfolio. *Entrance requirements:* For master's, minimum GPA of 3.0, 1 year of teaching experience; for Ed S, minimum 3 years of teaching experience, minimum cumulative GPA of 3.5, 1 year of administrative experience. Additional exam requirements/recommendations for international students: Required—TOEFL. *Faculty research:* Reading, literacy, leadership.

University of South Alabama, Graduate School, College of Education, Department of Leadership and Teacher Education, Mobile, AL 36688-0002. Offers early childhood education (M Ed); educational administration (Ed S); educational leadership (M Ed); elementary education (M Ed); reading education (M Ed); science education (M Ed); secondary education (M Ed); special education (M Ed, Ed S). *Accreditation:* NCATE. Part-time programs available. *Faculty:* 17 full-time (11 women), 4 part-time/adjunct (all women). *Students:* 136 full-time (103 women), 78 part-time (67 women); includes 45 minority (40 Black or African American, non-Hispanic/Latino; 2 Asian, non-Hispanic/Latino; 1 Hispanic/Latino; 2 Two or more races, non-Hispanic/Latino). 90 applicants, 53% accepted, 45 enrolled. In 2013, 69 master's awarded. *Degree requirements:* For master's, comprehensive exam. *Entrance requirements:* For master's, GRE General Test or MAT, minimum GPA of 3.0. *Application deadline:* For fall admission, 7/15 priority date for domestic students, 6/15 priority date for international students; for spring admission, 12/1 priority date for domestic students, 11/1 priority date for international students. Applications are processed on a rolling basis. Application fee: $35. *Expenses:*

Tuition, state resident: full-time $8976; part-time $374 per credit hour. Tuition, nonresident: full-time $17,952; part-time $748 per credit hour. *Financial support:* Research assistantships and career-related internships or fieldwork available. Support available to part-time students. Financial award application deadline: 4/1. *Unit head:* Dr. Harold Dodge, Jr., Chair, 251-380-2894. *Application contact:* Dr. Abigail Baxter, Director of Graduate Studies, 251-380-2738, Fax: 251-380-2748, E-mail: abaxter@southalabama.edu.
Website: http://www.southalabama.edu/coe/lted.

University of South Carolina, The Graduate School, College of Education, Department of Instruction and Teacher Education, Program in Language and Literacy, Columbia, SC 29208. Offers M Ed, PhD. *Accreditation:* NCATE. *Degree requirements:* For master's, comprehensive exam; for doctorate, one foreign language, comprehensive exam, thesis/dissertation. *Entrance requirements:* For master's, GRE General Test, Miller Analogies Test, teaching certificate, resume, letters of reference, letter of intent; for doctorate, GRE General Test, Miller Analogies Test, resumé, letters of reference, letter of intent, interview. *Faculty research:* Remedial and compensatory education, metacognition and learning, literacy, learning, teacher change.

University of Southern Maine, College of Management and Human Service, School of Education and Human Development, Program in Literacy Education, Portland, ME 04104-9300. Offers applied literacy (MS Ed); English as a second language (MS Ed, CAS, Certificate); literacy (CAS); literacy education (MS Ed, Certificate). *Accreditation:* Teacher Education Accreditation Council. Part-time and evening/weekend programs available. *Faculty:* 15 full-time (9 women), 11 part-time/adjunct (8 women). *Students:* 5 full-time (all women), 51 part-time (47 women); includes 2 minority (1 Hispanic/Latino; 1 Two or more races, non-Hispanic/Latino), 1 international. Average age 38. 18 applicants, 89% accepted, 8 enrolled. In 2013, 19 master's, 20 CASs awarded. *Degree requirements:* For master's, comprehensive exam, thesis or alternative; for other advanced degree, thesis or alternative. *Entrance requirements:* For master's, teacher certification; for other advanced degree, master's degree. Additional exam requirements/recommendations for international students: Required—TOEFL (minimum score 550 paper-based; 79 iBT). *Application deadline:* For fall admission, 5/1 priority date for domestic students; for spring admission, 10/15 priority date for domestic students. Applications are processed on a rolling basis. Application fee: $65. Electronic applications accepted. *Expenses:* Tuition, state resident: part-time $380 per credit. Tuition, nonresident: part-time $1026 per credit. Part-time tuition and fees vary according to program. *Financial support:* Research assistantships, career-related internships or fieldwork, Federal Work-Study, institutionally sponsored loans, scholarships/grants, and unspecified assistantships available. Support available to part-time students. Financial award application deadline: 3/1; financial award applicants required to submit FAFSA. *Faculty research:* Teacher research in literacy, multiliteracies, learning to teach culturally and linguistically diverse students, motivation to read. *Unit head:* Dr. Andrea Stairs, Program Director, 207-780-5971, E-mail: astairs@usm.maine.edu. *Application contact:* Mary Sloan, Assistant Dean of Graduate Studies and Director of Graduate Admissions, 207-780-4812, E-mail: gradstudies@usm.maine.edu.
Website: http://usm.maine.edu/literacy-education/msed-literacy-education.

University of South Florida, College of Education, Department of Childhood Education, Tampa, FL 33620-9951. Offers early childhood education (M Ed, MA, PhD); elementary education (MA, MAT, PhD); reading/language arts (MA, PhD, Ed S). *Accreditation:* NCATE. Part-time and evening/weekend programs available. *Degree requirements:* For master's, comprehensive exam; for doctorate, comprehensive exam, thesis/dissertation, philosophies of inquiry; multiple research methods. *Entrance requirements:* For master's, GRE (if GPA less than 3.0), minimum GPA of 3.0 in last 60 hours of course work; for doctorate, GRE General Test, minimum GPA of 3.0 undergraduate, 3.5 graduate; interview; for Ed S, GRE General Test, interview. Additional exam requirements/recommendations for international students: Required—TOEFL (minimum score 550 paper-based). Electronic applications accepted. *Faculty research:* Evaluating interventions for struggling readers, prevention and intervention services for young children at risk for behavioral and mental health challenges, preservice teacher education and young adolescent middle school experience, art and inquiry-based approaches to teaching and learning, study of children's writing development.

University of South Florida, University College/Distance Education, Tampa, FL 33620-9951. *Unit head:* Kathy Barnes, Interdisciplinary Programs Coordinator, 813-974-8031, Fax: 813-974-7061, E-mail: barnesk@usf.edu. *Application contact:* Karen Tylinski, Metro Initiatives, 813-974-9943, Fax: 813-974-7061, E-mail: ktylinsk@usf.edu.
Website: http://uc.usf.edu/.

University of South Florida–St. Petersburg Campus, College of Education, St. Petersburg, FL 33701. Offers educational leadership development (M Ed); elementary education (MA), including math/science; English education (MA); middle grades STEM education (MS); reading education (MA). Part-time programs available. *Degree requirements:* For master's, comprehensive exam, practicum, internship, comprehensive portfolio. *Entrance requirements:* For master's, State of Florida General Knowledge Test (GKT), Florida Teaching Certificate (for non-initial certification programs), letters of recommendation. Additional exam requirements/recommendations for international students: Required—TOEFL (minimum score 550 paper-based; 79 iBT); Recommended—IELTS. Electronic applications accepted.

The University of Tennessee, Graduate School, College of Education, Health and Human Sciences, Program in Education, Knoxville, TN 37996. Offers art education (MS); counseling education (PhD); cultural studies in education (PhD); curriculum (MS, Ed S); curriculum, educational research and evaluation (Ed D, PhD); early childhood education (PhD); early childhood special education (MS); education of deaf and hard of hearing (MS); educational administration and policy studies (Ed D, PhD); educational administration and supervision (Ed S); educational psychology (Ed D, PhD); elementary education (MS, Ed S); elementary teaching (MS); English education (MS, Ed S); exercise science (PhD); foreign language/ESL education (MS, Ed S); instructional technology (MS, Ed D, PhD, Ed S); literacy, language and ESL education (PhD); literacy, language education, and ESL education (Ed D); mathematics education (MS, Ed S); modified and comprehensive special education (MS); reading education (MS, Ed S); school counseling (Ed S); school psychology (PhD, Ed S); science education (MS, Ed S); secondary teaching (MS); social foundations (MS); social science education (MS, Ed S); socio-cultural foundations of sports and education (PhD); special education (Ed S); teacher education (Ed D, PhD). *Accreditation:* NCATE. Part-time and evening/weekend programs available. *Degree requirements:* For master's and Ed S, thesis optional; for doctorate, variable foreign language requirement, thesis/dissertation. *Entrance requirements:* For master's, minimum GPA of 2.7; for doctorate and Ed S, GRE General Test, minimum GPA of 2.7. Additional exam requirements/recommendations for international students: Required—TOEFL. Electronic applications accepted. *Expenses:* Tuition, state resident: full-time $9540; part-time $531 per credit hour. Tuition, nonresident: full-time $27,728; part-time $1542 per credit hour. *Required fees:* $1404; $67 per credit hour.

The University of Texas at Austin, Graduate School, College of Education, Department of Curriculum and Instruction, Austin, TX 78712-1111. Offers bilingual/bicultural education (M Ed, MA, PhD); cultural studies in education (M Ed, MA, PhD); early childhood education (M Ed, MA, PhD); language and literacy studies (M Ed, PhD); learning technologies (M Ed, MA, PhD); physical education (M Ed, MA, PhD). Terminal master's awarded for partial completion of doctoral program. *Degree requirements:* For doctorate, thesis/dissertation. *Entrance requirements:* For master's and doctorate, GRE General Test. Electronic applications accepted.

The University of Texas at El Paso, Graduate School, College of Education, Department of Teacher Education, El Paso, TX 79968-0001. Offers education (MA); instruction (M Ed); reading education (M Ed); teaching, learning, and culture (PhD). Part-time and evening/weekend programs available. *Degree requirements:* For master's, thesis optional. *Entrance requirements:* For master's, GRE General Test, minimum GPA of 3.0. Additional exam requirements/recommendations for international students: Required—TOEFL. Electronic applications accepted.

The University of Texas at San Antonio, College of Education and Human Development, Department of Bicultural and Bilingual Studies, San Antonio, TX 78249-0617. Offers bicultural/bilingual studies (MA), including bicultural studies, bicultural/bilingual education; culture, literacy, and language (PhD); teaching English as a second language (MA). Part-time and evening/weekend programs available. *Faculty:* 17 full-time (11 women), 1 (woman) part-time/adjunct. *Students:* 49 full-time (42 women), 122 part-time (97 women); includes 105 minority (3 Black or African American, non-Hispanic/Latino; 7 Asian, non-Hispanic/Latino; 91 Hispanic/Latino; 4 Two or more races, non-Hispanic/Latino), 23 international. Average age 36. 59 applicants, 88% accepted, 26 enrolled. In 2013, 52 master's, 2 doctorates awarded. *Degree requirements:* For master's, one foreign language, comprehensive exam, thesis optional; for doctorate, one foreign language, comprehensive exam, thesis/dissertation. *Entrance requirements:* For master's, GRE General Test if GPA is less than 3.0 for last 60 hours, bachelor's degree with 18 credit hours in field of study or in another appropriate field of study; for doctorate, GRE General Test, resume or curriculum vitae, 3 letters of recommendation, statement of purpose. Additional exam requirements/recommendations for international students: Required—TOEFL (minimum score 550 paper-based; 79 iBT), IELTS (minimum score 6.5). *Application deadline:* For fall admission, 7/1 for domestic students, 4/1 for international students; for spring admission, 11/1 for domestic students, 9/1 for international students. Applications are processed on a rolling basis. Application fee: $45 ($80 for international students). Electronic applications accepted. *Expenses:* Tuition, state resident: full-time $4671. Tuition, nonresident: full-time $8708. *International tuition:* $17,415 full-time. *Required fees:* $1924.60. Tuition and fees vary according to course load and degree level. *Financial support:* In 2013–14, 19 students received support, including 7 fellowships with full tuition reimbursements available (averaging $27,315 per year), 9 research assistantships with full tuition reimbursements available (averaging $13,618 per year), 7 teaching assistantships with full tuition reimbursements available (averaging $11,000 per year). Financial award applicants required to submit FAFSA. *Faculty research:* Bilingualism and biliteracy development, second language teaching and learning, language minority education, Mexican American studies, transnationalism and immigration. *Unit head:* Dr. Belinda Bustos Flores, Chair, 210-458-4426, Fax: 210-458-5962, E-mail: belinda.flores@utsa.edu. *Application contact:* Armando Trujillo, Assistant Dean of the Graduate School, 210-458-5576, Fax: 210-458-5576, E-mail: armando.trujillo@utsa.edu.
Website: http://education.utsa.edu/bicultural-bilingual_studies.

The University of Texas at San Antonio, College of Education and Human Development, Department of Interdisciplinary Learning and Teaching, San Antonio, TX 78249-0617. Offers education (MA), including curriculum and instruction, early childhood and elementary education, instructional technology, reading and literacy, special education; interdisciplinary learning and teaching (PhD). Part-time and evening/weekend programs available. *Faculty:* 22 full-time (16 women), 1 (woman) part-time/adjunct. *Students:* 109 full-time (80 women), 272 part-time (221 women); includes 209 minority (24 Black or African American, non-Hispanic/Latino; 3 American Indian or Alaska Native, non-Hispanic/Latino; 12 Asian, non-Hispanic/Latino; 166 Hispanic/Latino; 4 Two or more races, non-Hispanic/Latino), 40 international. Average age 33. 178 applicants, 87% accepted, 80 enrolled. In 2013, 136 master's, 7 doctorates awarded. *Degree requirements:* For master's, comprehensive exam, thesis optional, 36 hours of course work without thesis (33 with thesis); for doctorate, comprehensive exam, thesis/dissertation, minimum of 60 semester credit hours. *Entrance requirements:* For master's, bachelor's degree with minimum GPA of 3.0 in last 60 hours of coursework; 18 hours of undergraduate coursework in education or related field; for doctorate, GRE, transcripts from all colleges and universities attended, professional vitae demonstrating experience in work environment where education was primary professional emphasis, 3 letters of recommendation, statement of purpose, minimum GPA of 3.5. Additional exam requirements/recommendations for international students: Required—TOEFL (minimum score 550 paper-based; 79 iBT), IELTS (minimum score 6.5). *Application deadline:* For fall admission, 7/1 for domestic students, 4/1 for international students; for spring admission, 11/1 for domestic students, 9/1 for international students. Applications are processed on a rolling basis. Application fee: $45 ($80 for international students). Electronic applications accepted. *Expenses:* Tuition, state resident: full-time $4671. Tuition, nonresident: full-time $8708. *International tuition:* $17,415 full-time. *Required fees:* $1924.60. Tuition and fees vary according to course load and degree level. *Financial support:* In 2013–14, 7 fellowships with partial tuition reimbursements (averaging $27,000 per year) were awarded; career-related internships or fieldwork, Federal Work-Study, and scholarships/grants also available. Support available to part-time students. *Faculty research:* Explorations of science, learning and teaching, family involvement in early childhood, culturally-responsive literacy instruction in diverse settings, STEM education, autism spectrum disorder. *Total annual research expenditures:* $5.9 million. *Unit head:* Dr. Maria R. Cortez, Department Chair, 210-458-5969, Fax: 210-458-7281, E-mail: mari.cortez@utsa.edu. *Application contact:* Erin Doran, Student Development Specialist, 210-458-7443, Fax: 210-458-7281, E-mail: erin.doran@utsa.edu.
Website: http://education.utsa.edu/interdisciplinary_learning_and_teaching/.

The University of Texas at Tyler, College of Education and Psychology, School of Education, Tyler, TX 75799-0001. Offers early childhood education (M Ed, MA); reading (M Ed, MA); special education (M Ed, MA). Part-time and evening/weekend programs available. *Degree requirements:* For master's, comprehensive exam, thesis (for some programs), research project. *Entrance requirements:* For master's, GRE General Test. Additional exam requirements/recommendations for international students: Required—TOEFL. Electronic applications accepted. *Faculty research:* Improving quality in childcare settings, play and creativity, teacher interactions, effects of modeling on early childhood teachers, biofeedback, literacy instruction.

The University of Texas of the Permian Basin, Office of Graduate Studies, School of Education, Program in Reading, Odessa, TX 79762-0001. Offers MA. *Degree requirements:* For master's, comprehensive exam (for some programs), thesis (for some programs). *Entrance requirements:* For master's, GRE General Test. Additional exam requirements/recommendations for international students: Required—TOEFL (minimum score 550 paper-based).

The University of Texas–Pan American, College of Education, Department of Curriculum and Instruction: Elementary and Secondary, Edinburg, TX 78539. Offers

bilingual education (M Ed); early childhood education (M Ed); elementary education (M Ed); reading (M Ed); secondary education (M Ed). Part-time programs available. *Degree requirements:* For master's, comprehensive exam, thesis optional. *Entrance requirements:* For master's, GRE. Additional exam requirements/recommendations for international students: Required—TOEFL, IELTS. *Expenses:* Tuition, state resident: full-time $5986; part-time $333 per credit hour. Tuition, nonresident: full-time $12,358; part-time $687 per credit hour. *Required fees:* $782. Tuition and fees vary according to program. *Faculty research:* Dual language instruction, literacy and technology, teacher education in diverse populations, mathematics and science education.

University of the Cumberlands, Graduate Programs in Education, Williamsburg, KY 40769-1372. Offers all grades (P-12) (M Ed); business and marketing (MA Ed, MAT); counselor education and supervision (Ed D); director of pupil personnel (Certificate); director of special education (Certificate); educational administration and supervision (Ed S); educational leadership (Ed D); elementary education (MA Ed, MAT); instructional leadership - principalship (MA Ed); instructional leadership - school principal (Certificate); middle school education (MA Ed, MAT); reading and writing (MA Ed); school counseling (MA Ed); school superintendent (Certificate); secondary education (MA Ed, MAT); special education (MAT); supervisor of instruction (Certificate); teacher leader (MA Ed). Part-time and evening/weekend programs available. Postbaccalaureate distance learning degree programs offered. *Degree requirements:* For master's, comprehensive exam. Electronic applications accepted.

University of the Incarnate Word, School of Graduate Studies and Research, Dreeben School of Education, Programs in Education, San Antonio, TX 78209-6397. Offers adult education (M Ed, MA); cross-cultural education (M Ed, MA); early childhood literacy (M Ed, MA); general education (M Ed, MA); higher education (PhD); instructional technology (M Ed, MA); international education and entrepreneurship (PhD); kinesiology (M Ed, MA); literacy (M Ed, MA); organizational leadership (PhD); organizational learning and learning (M Ed, MA); reading (M Ed, MA); special education (M Ed, MA); teacher leadership (M Ed, MA). Part-time and evening/weekend programs available. *Faculty:* 17 full-time (9 women), 6 part-time/adjunct (all women). *Students:* 23 full-time (13 women), 187 part-time (122 women); includes 114 minority (24 Black or African American, non-Hispanic/Latino; 1 American Indian or Alaska Native, non-Hispanic/Latino; 3 Asian, non-Hispanic/Latino; 85 Hispanic/Latino; 1 Two or more races, non-Hispanic/Latino), 30 international. Average age 41. 52 applicants, 67% accepted, 25 enrolled. In 2013, 12 master's, 14 doctorates awarded. *Degree requirements:* For master's, capstone; for doctorate, thesis/dissertation, qualifying exam. *Entrance requirements:* For master's, baccalaureate degree; minimum foundation GPA of 2.5; interview; for doctorate, master's degree; interview; supervised writing sample. Additional exam requirements/recommendations for international students: Required—TOEFL (minimum score 560 paper-based; 83 iBT). *Application deadline:* Applications are processed on a rolling basis. Application fee: $20. Electronic applications accepted. *Expenses: Tuition:* Part-time $815 per credit hour. *Required fees:* $86 per credit hour. One-time fee: $40 part-time. Tuition and fees vary according to degree level and program. *Financial support:* In 2013–14, 5 research assistantships were awarded; Federal Work-Study and scholarships/grants also available. Financial award applicants required to submit FAFSA. *Unit head:* Dr. Denise Staudt, Dean, Dreeben School of Education, 210-829-2762, E-mail: staudt@uiwtx.edu. *Application contact:* Andrea Cyterski-Acosta, Dean of Enrollment, 210-829-6005, Fax: 210-829-3921, E-mail: admis@uiwtx.edu.
Website: http://www.uiw.edu/education/index.htm.

University of Utah, Graduate School, College of Education, Department of Educational Psychology, Salt Lake City, UT 84112. Offers clinical mental health counseling (M Ed); counseling psychology (PhD); educational psychology (M Ed, MA, MS); elementary education (M Ed); instructional design and educational technology (M Ed); instructional design and technology (MS); learning and cognition (MS, PhD); reading and literacy (M Ed, MS, PhD); school counseling (M Ed); school psychology (M Ed, PhD); statistics (M Stat). *Accreditation:* APA (one or more programs are accredited). *Faculty:* 18 full-time (8 women), 20 part-time/adjunct (17 women). *Students:* 109 full-time (88 women), 108 part-time (68 women); includes 29 minority (2 Black or African American, non-Hispanic/Latino; 1 American Indian or Alaska Native, non-Hispanic/Latino; 7 Asian, non-Hispanic/Latino; 14 Hispanic/Latino; 1 Native Hawaiian or other Pacific Islander, non-Hispanic/Latino; 4 Two or more races, non-Hispanic/Latino), 7 international. Average age 32. 222 applicants, 35% accepted, 61 enrolled. In 2013, 51 master's, 10 doctorates awarded. *Degree requirements:* For master's, variable foreign language requirement, comprehensive exam (for some programs), thesis (for some programs), projects; for doctorate, variable foreign language requirement, comprehensive exam, thesis/dissertation, oral exam. *Entrance requirements:* For master's and doctorate, GRE General Test, minimum GPA of 3.0. Additional exam requirements/recommendations for international students: Required—TOEFL (minimum score 80 iBT). *Application deadline:* For fall admission, 4/1 for domestic and international students; for winter admission, 11/1 for domestic and international students; for spring admission, 3/15 for domestic and international students. Application fee: $55 ($65 for international students). Electronic applications accepted. *Expenses:* Contact institution. *Financial support:* In 2013–14, 81 students received support, including 29 fellowships with full and partial tuition reimbursements available (averaging $11,200 per year), 11 research assistantships with full and partial tuition reimbursements available (averaging $9,100 per year), 38 teaching assistantships with full and partial tuition reimbursements available (averaging $10,400 per year); career-related internships or fieldwork, Federal Work-Study, institutionally sponsored loans, scholarships/grants, health care benefits, and unspecified assistantships also available. Financial award application deadline: 4/1; financial award applicants required to submit FAFSA. *Faculty research:* Autism, computer technology and instruction, cognitive behavior, aging, group counseling. *Total annual research expenditures:* $441,375. *Unit head:* Dr. Anne E. Cook, Chair, 801-581-7148, Fax: 801-581-5566, E-mail: anne.cook@utah.edu. *Application contact:* JoLynn N. Yates, Academic Program Specialist, 801-581-7148, Fax: 801-581-5566, E-mail: jo.yates@utah.edu.
Website: http://www.ed.utah.edu/edps/.

University of Victoria, Faculty of Graduate Studies, Faculty of Education, Department of Curriculum and Instruction, Victoria, BC V8W 2Y2, Canada. Offers art education (M Ed, PhD); curriculum studies (M Ed, MA, PhD); early childhood education (M Ed, PhD); educational studies (PhD); language and literacy (M Ed, MA, PhD); mathematics (M Ed, MA, PhD); music education (M Ed, MA, PhD); science (M Ed, MA, PhD); social studies (M Ed, MA); social, cultural and foundational studies (MA, PhD); technology and environmental education (PhD). Part-time programs available. *Degree requirements:* For master's, thesis, project (M Ed); for doctorate, comprehensive exam, thesis/dissertation. *Entrance requirements:* For master's, minimum B average. Additional exam requirements/recommendations for international students: Required—TOEFL (minimum score 575 paper-based), IELTS (minimum score 7). Electronic applications accepted. *Faculty research:* Elementary and secondary English, language arts, curriculum theory and practice, educational media and technology, educational administration and leadership, history and philosophy of education.

University of Virginia, Curry School of Education, Department of Curriculum, Instruction, and Special Education, Program in Curriculum and Instruction, Charlottesville, VA 22903. Offers curriculum and instruction (M Ed, Ed S); elementary education (M Ed, Ed D); English (M Ed, Ed D); foreign language (M Ed); mathematics (M Ed, Ed D); reading (M Ed, Ed D, Ed S); science (Ed D); social studies (M Ed). *Students:* 42 full-time (30 women), 37 part-time (32 women); includes 4 minority (1 Black or African American, non-Hispanic/Latino; 2 Hispanic/Latino; 1 Two or more races, non-Hispanic/Latino), 1 international. Average age 31. 76 applicants, 74% accepted, 39 enrolled. In 2013, 84 master's, 3 doctorates, 23 other advanced degrees awarded. *Degree requirements:* For master's, comprehensive exam (for some programs); for doctorate, comprehensive exam, thesis/dissertation; for Ed S, comprehensive exam. *Entrance requirements:* For master's, doctorate, and Ed S, GRE General Test, 2 letters of recommendation. Additional exam requirements/recommendations for international students: Required—TOEFL (minimum score 600 paper-based; 90 iBT), IELTS (minimum score 7). *Application deadline:* Applications are processed on a rolling basis. Application fee: $60. Electronic applications accepted. *Expenses:* Tuition, state resident: part-time $334 per credit hour. Tuition, nonresident: part-time $1224 per credit hour. *Financial support:* Fellowships with tuition reimbursements, research assistantships with tuition reimbursements, and teaching assistantships with tuition reimbursements available. Financial award application deadline: 1/5; financial award applicants required to submit FAFSA. *Unit head:* Stephanie van Hover, Chair, 434-924-0841, E-mail: sdv2w@virginia.edu. *Application contact:* Karen Dwier, Information Contact, 434-924-0831, E-mail: kgd9g@virginia.edu.
Website: http://curry.virginia.edu/academics/areas-of-study/curriculum-teaching-learning.

University of Virginia, Curry School of Education, Program in Education, Charlottesville, VA 22903. Offers administration and supervision (PhD); applied developmental science (PhD); counselor education (PhD); curriculum and instruction (PhD); early childhood special education (MT); education evaluation (PhD); educational psychology (PhD); educational research (PhD); elementary education (MT); English education (MT, PhD); foreign language education (MT); higher education (PhD); instructional technology (PhD); kinesiology (MT, PhD); math education (PhD); reading education (PhD); research, statistics and evaluation (PhD); school psychology (PhD); science education (PhD); social studies education (MT, PhD); special education (PhD); world languages education (MT). *Students:* 474 full-time (379 women), 35 part-time (19 women); includes 89 minority (30 Black or African American, non-Hispanic/Latino; 1 American Indian or Alaska Native, non-Hispanic/Latino; 26 Asian, non-Hispanic/Latino; 19 Hispanic/Latino; 13 Two or more races, non-Hispanic/Latino), 21 international. Average age 26. 312 applicants, 49% accepted, 80 enrolled. In 2013, 137 master's, 38 doctorates awarded. *Degree requirements:* For master's, comprehensive exam (for some programs), field project; for doctorate, comprehensive exam, thesis/dissertation. *Entrance requirements:* For doctorate, GRE General Test. Additional exam requirements/recommendations for international students: Required—TOEFL (minimum score 600 paper-based; 90 iBT), IELTS (minimum score 7). *Application deadline:* Applications are processed on a rolling basis. Application fee: $60. Electronic applications accepted. *Expenses:* Tuition, state resident: part-time $334 per credit hour. Tuition, nonresident: part-time $1224 per credit hour. *Financial support:* Fellowships, research assistantships, and teaching assistantships available. Financial award application deadline: 1/5; financial award applicants required to submit FAFSA. *Unit head:* Robert C. Pianta, Dean, 434-924-3334, E-mail: pianta@virginia.edu. *Application contact:* Office of Admissions and Student Services, 434-924-0742, E-mail: curry-admissions@virginia.edu.
Website: http://curry.virginia.edu/teacher-education.

University of Washington, Graduate School, College of Education, Seattle, WA 98195. Offers curriculum and instruction (M Ed, Ed D, PhD), including educational technology, general curriculum (Ed D, PhD), language, literacy, and culture, mathematics education, multicultural education, reading and language arts education (Ed D), science education, social studies education, teaching and curriculum (M Ed); educational leadership and policy studies (M Ed, Ed D, PhD), including administration (Ed D), educational policy, organization, and leadership (M Ed, PhD), higher education, leadership for learning (Ed D), social and cultural foundations of education (M Ed, PhD); educational psychology (M Ed, PhD), including educational psychology (PhD), human development and cognition (M Ed), learning sciences, measurement, statistics and research design (M Ed), school psychology (M Ed); instructional leadership (M Ed); intercollegiate athletic leadership (M Ed); special education (M Ed, Ed D, PhD), including early childhood special education (M Ed), emotional and behavioral disabilities (M Ed), learning disabilities (M Ed), low-incidence disabilities (M Ed), severe disabilities (M Ed), special education (Ed D, PhD); teacher education (MIT). *Accreditation:* APA. Part-time and evening/weekend programs available. *Degree requirements:* For master's, thesis optional; for doctorate, thesis/dissertation. *Entrance requirements:* For master's and doctorate, GRE General Test, minimum GPA of 3.0. Additional exam requirements/recommendations for international students: Required—TOEFL. Electronic applications accepted. *Faculty research:* School restructuring/effective schools, special education interventions, literacy and writing, technology, school partnerships, teacher preparation.

University of West Florida, College of Professional Studies, School of Education, Program in Reading Education, Pensacola, FL 32514-5750. Offers M Ed. Part-time and evening/weekend programs available. *Degree requirements:* For master's, portfolio, teacher certification exams (general knowledge, professional, reading subject area). *Entrance requirements:* For master's, GRE (minimum score 450 verbal) or MAT (minimum score 396) if bachelor's GPA less than 3.0, state teaching certification; letter of intent; two professional references. Additional exam requirements/recommendations for international students: Required—TOEFL (minimum score 550 paper-based).

University of West Georgia, College of Education, Department of Learning and Teaching, Carrollton, GA 30118. Offers early childhood education (M Ed, Ed S); reading education (M Ed); special education (M Ed, Ed S). *Accreditation:* ACA; NCATE. Part-time and evening/weekend programs available. *Faculty:* 10 full-time (9 women), 3 part-time/adjunct (all women). *Students:* 50 full-time (44 women), 228 part-time (204 women); includes 112 minority (102 Black or African American, non-Hispanic/Latino; 6 Hispanic/Latino; 4 Two or more races, non-Hispanic/Latino), 2 international. Average age 34. 198 applicants, 57% accepted, 46 enrolled. In 2013, 73 master's, 31 Ed Ss awarded. *Degree requirements:* For master's and Ed S, comprehensive exam. *Entrance requirements:* For master's, undergraduate degree in early childhood, elementary (P-5), middle grades (4-8), special education; one year of teaching experience; minimum overall GPA of 2.7; clear and renewable level 4 teaching certificate; for Ed S, master's degree in early childhood or elementary education; minimum overall GPA of 3.0 in graduate work; level 5 teaching certificate. Additional exam requirements/recommendations for international students: Required—TOEFL (minimum score 523 paper-based; 69 iBT); Recommended—IELTS (minimum score 6). *Application deadline:* For fall admission, 7/21 for domestic students, 6/1 for international students; for spring admission, 1/30 for domestic students, 10/15 for international students. Applications are processed on a rolling basis. Application fee: $40. Electronic applications accepted. *Expenses:* Tuition, state resident: full-time $4600; part-time $192 per semester hour. Tuition, nonresident: full-time $17,880; part-time $745 per semester hour. *Required fees:* $1858; $46.34 per semester hour. $512 per semester. Tuition and fees vary according to course load, degree level, campus/location and program. *Financial support:* In 2013–14, 10 students received support, including 1 research assistantship with full

tuition reimbursement available (averaging $2,963 per year); scholarships/grants and unspecified assistantships also available. Support available to part-time students. Financial award application deadline: 4/1; financial award applicants required to submit FAFSA. *Faculty research:* Early childhood education, social justice, action research. *Total annual research expenditures:* $274,000. *Unit head:* Dr. Donna Harkins, Chair, 678-839-6066, Fax: 678-839-6063, E-mail: dharkins@westga.edu. *Application contact:* Dr. Jill Drake, Coordinator, Early Childhood Education, 678-839-6080, Fax: 678-839-6063, E-mail: jdrake@westga.edu.
Website: http://www.westga.edu/coeelce.

University of Wisconsin–Eau Claire, College of Education and Human Sciences, Program in Reading, Eau Claire, WI 54702-4004. Offers MST. Part-time programs available. *Faculty:* 5 full-time (3 women), 1 (woman) part-time/adjunct. *Students:* 5 part-time (all women). Average age 28. In 2013, 5 master's awarded. *Degree requirements:* For master's, comprehensive exam, portfolio with an oral examination. *Entrance requirements:* For master's, certification to teach. Additional exam requirements/recommendations for international students: Required—TOEFL (minimum score 79 iBT). *Application deadline:* For fall admission, 7/1 priority date for domestic students, 6/1 priority date for international students; for spring admission, 12/1 priority date for domestic students, 11/1 priority date for international students. Applications are processed on a rolling basis. Application fee: $56. *Expenses:* Tuition, state resident: full-time $7640; part-time $424.47 per credit. Tuition, nonresident: full-time $16,771; part-time $931.74 per credit. *Required fees:* $1146; $63.65 per credit. *Financial support:* Federal Work-Study and unspecified assistantships available. Financial award application deadline: 3/1; financial award applicants required to submit FAFSA. *Unit head:* Dr. Rose Battalio, Interim Chair, 715-836-2013, Fax: 715-836-4868, E-mail: battalrl@uwec.edu. *Application contact:* Nancy Amdahl, Graduate Dean Assistant, 715-836-2721, Fax: 715-836-2902, E-mail: graduate@uwec.edu.
Website: http://www.uwec.edu/ES/programs/readinglicensure.htm.

University of Wisconsin–Milwaukee, Graduate School, School of Education, Department of Curriculum and Instruction, Milwaukee, WI 53201-0413. Offers curriculum planning and instruction improvement (MS); early childhood education (MS); elementary education (MS); junior high/middle school education (MS); reading education (MS); secondary education (MS); teaching in an urban setting (MS). Part-time programs available. *Faculty:* 18 full-time (13 women). *Students:* 17 full-time (10 women), 46 part-time (42 women); includes 15 minority (7 Black or African American, non-Hispanic/Latino; 1 Asian, non-Hispanic/Latino; 7 Two or more races, non-Hispanic/Latino), 1 international. Average age 32. 35 applicants, 69% accepted, 11 enrolled. In 2013, 31 master's awarded. *Degree requirements:* For master's, thesis or alternative. *Entrance requirements:* Additional exam requirements/recommendations for international students: Required—TOEFL (minimum score 550 paper-based; 79 iBT), IELTS (minimum score 6.5). *Application deadline:* For fall admission, 1/1 priority date for domestic students; for spring admission, 9/1 for domestic students. Applications are processed on a rolling basis. Application fee: $56 ($96 for international students). Electronic applications accepted. *Financial support:* In 2013–14, 1 fellowship was awarded; research assistantships, teaching assistantships, career-related internships or fieldwork, health care benefits, unspecified assistantships, and project assistantships also available. Support available to part-time students. Financial award application deadline: 4/15; financial award applicants required to submit FAFSA. *Unit head:* Raquel Oxford, Department Chair, 414-229-4884, Fax: 414-229-5571, E-mail: roxford@uwm.edu. *Application contact:* General Information Contact, 414-229-4982, Fax: 414-229-6967, E-mail: gradschool@uwm.edu.
Website: http://www.uwm.edu/SOE/.

University of Wisconsin–Oshkosh, Graduate Studies, College of Education and Human Services, Department of Reading Education, Oshkosh, WI 54901. Offers MSE. Program offered jointly with University of Wisconsin–Green Bay. Part-time programs available. *Degree requirements:* For master's, thesis or alternative, reflective journey course. *Entrance requirements:* For master's, interview, teaching certificate, undergraduate degree in teacher education, letters of recommendation. Additional exam requirements/recommendations for international students: Required—TOEFL (minimum score 550 paper-based; 79 iBT). Electronic applications accepted. *Faculty research:* Writing and reading, assessment, learner-centered instruction, multicultural literature, family literacy.

University of Wisconsin–River Falls, Outreach and Graduate Studies, College of Education and Professional Studies, Department of Teacher Education, River Falls, WI 54022. Offers elementary education (MSE); professional development shared inquiry communities (MSE); reading (MSE). Part-time programs available. *Degree requirements:* For master's, comprehensive exam, thesis or alternative. *Entrance requirements:* For master's, minimum GPA of 2.75. Additional exam requirements/recommendations for international students: Required—TOEFL (minimum score 500 paper-based; 65 iBT), IELTS (minimum score 5.5). Electronic applications accepted.

University of Wisconsin–Stevens Point, College of Professional Studies, School of Education, Program in Education—General/Reading, Stevens Point, WI 54481-3897. Offers MSE. Part-time programs available. *Degree requirements:* For master's, comprehensive exam, thesis or alternative. *Entrance requirements:* For master's, minimum undergraduate GPA of 3.0, teacher certification, 2 years teaching experience, letters of recommendation. Additional exam requirements/recommendations for international students: Required—TOEFL (minimum score 523 paper-based). *Faculty research:* Reading strategies in the content areas, gifted education, curriculum and instruction, standards-based education.

University of Wisconsin–Superior, Graduate Division, Department of Teacher Education, Program in Teaching Reading, Superior, WI 54880-4500. Offers MSE. Part-time and evening/weekend programs available. *Faculty:* 3 full-time (all women). *Students:* 5 full-time (all women), 1 (woman) part-time. Average age 34. In 2013, 2 master's awarded. *Degree requirements:* For master's, comprehensive exam, thesis or alternative, research project. *Entrance requirements:* For master's, minimum GPA of 2.75, teaching certificate. *Application deadline:* For fall admission, 4/1 priority date for domestic students; for spring admission, 10/15 priority date for domestic students. Applications are processed on a rolling basis. Application fee: $56. Electronic applications accepted. *Expenses:* Tuition, state resident: full-time $4526; part-time $649.24 per credit. Tuition, nonresident: full-time $9091; part-time $1156.51 per credit. *Financial support:* Federal Work-Study and tuition waivers (partial) available. Support available to part-time students. Financial award application deadline: 4/15; financial award applicants required to submit FAFSA. *Unit head:* Dr. Wendy Kropid, Coordinator, 715-394-8240, E-mail: wkropid@uwsuper.edu. *Application contact:* Suzie Finckler, Student Status Examiner, 715-394-8295, Fax: 715-394-8371, E-mail: gradstudy@uwsuper.edu.
Website: http://www.uwsuper.edu/.

University of Wisconsin–Whitewater, School of Graduate Studies, College of Education and Professional Studies, Department of Curriculum and Instruction, Whitewater, WI 53190-1790. Offers professional development (MS), including bilingual education, challenging advanced learners, curriculum and instruction, educational leadership, health, human performance and recreation, health, physical education and coaching, information technologies and libraries, reading. *Accreditation:* NCATE. Part-time and evening/weekend programs available. Postbaccalaureate distance learning degree programs offered. *Degree requirements:* For master's, thesis or integrated project. *Entrance requirements:* Additional exam requirements/recommendations for international students: Required—TOEFL (minimum score 550 paper-based; 80 iBT), IELTS (minimum score 6). Electronic applications accepted. *Faculty research:* Hybrid of exercise physiology and psychology; gender equity; education, pedagogy, and technology; comprehensive school health education.

Ursuline College, School of Graduate Studies, Program in Education, Pepper Pike, OH 44124-4398. Offers art education (MA); early childhood education (MA); language arts education (MA); life science education (MA); math education (MA); middle school education (MA); social studies education (MA); special education (MA). *Accreditation:* NCATE. *Faculty:* 4 full-time (all women), 7 part-time/adjunct (5 women). *Students:* 18 full-time (16 women), 7 part-time (all women); includes 8 minority (4 Black or African American, non-Hispanic/Latino; 2 Asian, non-Hispanic/Latino; 2 Hispanic/Latino). Average age 34. 1 applicant, 100% accepted, 1 enrolled. In 2013, 25 master's awarded. *Degree requirements:* For master's, comprehensive exam. *Entrance requirements:* For master's, minimum undergraduate GPA of 3.0. Additional exam requirements/recommendations for international students: Required—TOEFL (minimum score 500 paper-based). *Application deadline:* For fall admission, 8/1 priority date for domestic students. Applications are processed on a rolling basis. Application fee: $25. *Expenses:* Contact institution. *Financial support:* In 2013–14, 1 student received support. Federal Work-Study available. Financial award application deadline: 3/1. *Unit head:* Dr. Edna West, Director, Master's Apprentice Program, 440-646-6134, Fax: 440-646-8328, E-mail: ewest@ursuline.edu. *Application contact:* Stephanie Pratt, Graduate Admission Coordinator, 440-646-8119, Fax: 440-684-6138, E-mail: graduateadmissions@ursuline.edu.

Vanderbilt University, Peabody College, Department of Teaching and Learning, Nashville, TN 37240-1001. Offers elementary education (M Ed); English language learners (M Ed); learning and instruction (M Ed); learning, diversity, and urban studies (M Ed); reading education (M Ed); secondary education (M Ed). *Accreditation:* NCATE. *Faculty:* 35 full-time (25 women), 20 part-time/adjunct (14 women). *Students:* 103 full-time (74 women), 44 part-time (39 women); includes 22 minority (8 Black or African American, non-Hispanic/Latino; 5 Asian, non-Hispanic/Latino; 5 Hispanic/Latino; 1 Native Hawaiian or other Pacific Islander, non-Hispanic/Latino; 3 Two or more races, non-Hispanic/Latino), 21 international. Average age 25. 264 applicants, 73% accepted, 57 enrolled. In 2013, 95 master's awarded. *Degree requirements:* For master's, comprehensive exam, thesis optional. *Entrance requirements:* For master's, GRE General Test, MAT. Additional exam requirements/recommendations for international students: Required—TOEFL (minimum score 550 paper-based; 80 iBT). *Application deadline:* For fall admission, 12/31 priority date for domestic and international students; for spring admission, 11/1 priority date for domestic and international students. Applications are processed on a rolling basis. Application fee: $0. Electronic applications accepted. *Financial support:* Fellowships with full and partial tuition reimbursements, research assistantships with full and partial tuition reimbursements, teaching assistantships with full and partial tuition reimbursements, Federal Work-Study, institutionally sponsored loans, scholarships/grants, tuition waivers (partial), and unspecified assistantships available. Support available to part-time students. Financial award application deadline: 1/15; financial award applicants required to submit FAFSA. *Faculty research:* Learning environments for mathematics of space and motion, visual programming tools for children's learning of basic science concepts, pathways for elementary and middle school children's learning about measurement and statistics, early reading intervention, professional development for ambitious mathematics teaching. *Unit head:* Dr. Rogers Hall, Chair, 615-322-8100, Fax: 615-322-8999, E-mail: rogers.hall@vanderbilt.edu. *Application contact:* Angela Saylor, Educational Coordinator, 615-322-8092, Fax: 615-322-8999, E-mail: angela.saylor@vanderbilt.edu.

Virginia Commonwealth University, Graduate School, School of Education, Program in Adult Learning, Richmond, VA 23284-9005. Offers adult literacy (M Ed); human resource development (M Ed); teaching and learning with technology (M Ed). *Accreditation:* NCATE. Part-time programs available. *Entrance requirements:* For master's, GRE General Test or MAT. Additional exam requirements/recommendations for international students: Required—TOEFL (minimum score 600 paper-based; 100 iBT). Electronic applications accepted. *Faculty research:* Adult development and learning, program planning and evaluation.

Virginia Commonwealth University, Graduate School, School of Education, Program in Reading, Richmond, VA 23284-9005. Offers reading (M Ed); reading specialist (Certificate). *Accreditation:* NCATE. *Degree requirements:* For master's, comprehensive exam. *Entrance requirements:* For master's, GRE General Test or MAT. Additional exam requirements/recommendations for international students: Required—TOEFL (minimum score 600 paper-based; 100 iBT). Electronic applications accepted.

Wagner College, Division of Graduate Studies, Department of Education, Program in Literacy (B-6), Staten Island, NY 10301-4495. Offers MS Ed. Part-time and evening/weekend programs available. *Degree requirements:* For master's, thesis. *Entrance requirements:* For master's, minimum GPA of 3.0, valid initial NY State Certificate or equivalent, interview, recommendations. Electronic applications accepted. *Expenses:* *Tuition:* Full-time $17,496; part-time $972 per credit. Tuition and fees vary according to course load.

Walden University, Graduate Programs, Richard W. Riley College of Education and Leadership, Minneapolis, MN 55401. *Accreditation:* NCATE. Part-time and evening/weekend programs available. Postbaccalaureate distance learning degree programs offered (minimal on-campus study). *Faculty:* 23 full-time (15 women), 830 part-time/adjunct (569 women). *Students:* 8,671 full-time (7,197 women), 2,122 part-time (1,735 women); includes 4,734 minority (3,802 Black or African American, non-Hispanic/Latino; 50 American Indian or Alaska Native, non-Hispanic/Latino; 136 Asian, non-Hispanic/Latino; 539 Hispanic/Latino; 35 Native Hawaiian or other Pacific Islander, non-Hispanic/Latino; 172 Two or more races, non-Hispanic/Latino), 73 international. Average age 40. 2,646 applicants, 96% accepted, 2074 enrolled. In 2013, 2,214 master's, 354 doctorates, 479 other advanced degrees awarded. *Degree requirements:* For doctorate, thesis/dissertation (for some programs), residency; for other advanced degree, residency (for some programs). *Entrance requirements:* For master's, bachelor's degree or higher; minimum GPA of 2.5; official transcripts; goal statement (for some programs); access to computer and Internet; for doctorate, master's degree or higher; three years of related professional or academic experience (preferred); minimum GPA of 3.0; goal statement and current resume (select programs); official transcripts; access to computer and Internet; for other advanced degree, relevant work experience; access to computer and Internet. Additional exam requirements/recommendations for international students: Required—TOEFL (minimum score 550 paper-based; 79 iBT), IELTS (minimum score 6.5), Michigan English Language Assessment Battery (minimum score 82), or PTE. *Application deadline:* Applications are processed on a rolling basis. Application fee: $0. Electronic applications accepted. *Expenses:* *Tuition:* Full-time $11,813.55; part-time $500 per credit. *Required fees:* $618.76. *Financial support:* In 2013–14, 1 fellowship was awarded; Federal Work-Study, scholarships/grants, unspecified assistantships, and family tuition reduction, active duty/veteran tuition reduction, group tuition reduction, interest-free payment plans, employee tuition reduction also available. Support available

to part-time students. Financial award applicants required to submit FAFSA. *Unit head:* Dr. Kate Steffens, Dean, 800-925-3368. *Application contact:* Jennifer Hall, Vice President of Enrollment Management, 866-4-WALDEN, E-mail: info@waldenu.edu. Website: http://www.waldenu.edu/colleges-schools/riley-college-of-education/.

Walla Walla University, Graduate School, School of Education and Psychology, College Place, WA 99324-1198. Offers counseling psychology (MA); curriculum and instruction (M Ed, MA, MAT); educational leadership (M Ed, MA, MAT); literacy instruction (M Ed, MA, MAT); students at risk (M Ed, MA, MAT); teaching (MAT). Part-time programs available. *Entrance requirements:* For master's, GRE General Test, minimum GPA of 2.75. Additional exam requirements/recommendations for international students: Required—TOEFL (minimum score 550 paper-based; 79 iBT). Electronic applications accepted. *Faculty research:* Admissions/retention, instructional psychology, moral development, teaching of reading.

Walsh University, Graduate Studies, Program in Education, North Canton, OH 44720-3396. Offers 21st-century technologies (MA Ed); leadership (MA Ed); reading literacy (MA Ed); traditional program (MA Ed). *Accreditation:* NCATE. Part-time and evening/weekend programs available. *Faculty:* 6 full-time (3 women), 10 part-time/adjunct (all women). *Students:* 13 full-time (10 women), 18 part-time (14 women), 1 international. Average age 32. 16 applicants, 100% accepted, 6 enrolled. In 2013, 46 master's awarded. *Degree requirements:* For master's, comprehensive exam (for some programs), thesis optional, action research project or comprehensive exam. *Entrance requirements:* For master's, MAT (minimum score 396) or GRE (minimum scores: verbal 145, quantitative 146, combined 291, writing 3.0), interview, minimum GPA of 3.0, writing sample, 3 recommendation forms, notarized affidavit of good moral character. Additional exam requirements/recommendations for international students: Required—TOEFL (minimum score 500 paper-based; 61 iBT). *Application deadline:* For fall admission, 7/15 priority date for domestic students. Applications are processed on a rolling basis. Application fee: $25. Electronic applications accepted. *Expenses: Tuition:* Full-time $10,890; part-time $605 per credit hour. *Required fees:* $100; $100. *Financial support:* In 2013–14, 41 students received support, including 3 research assistantships with partial tuition reimbursements available (averaging $12,355 per year), 5 teaching assistantships (averaging $4,734 per year); scholarships/grants, tuition waivers (partial), and unspecified assistantships also available. Support available to part-time students. Financial award application deadline: 12/31; financial award applicants required to submit FAFSA. *Faculty research:* Technology in education, strategies for working with children with special needs, reading literacy, whole brain teaching, hybrid learning, online teaching, global learning. *Unit head:* Dr. Gary Jacobs, Director, 330-490-7336, Fax: 330-490-7326, E-mail: gjacobs@walsh.edu. *Application contact:* Audra Dice, Graduate and Transfer Admissions Counselor, 330-490-7181, Fax: 330-244-4680, E-mail: adice@walsh.edu.

Washburn University, College of Arts and Sciences, Department of Education, Topeka, KS 66621. Offers curriculum and instruction (M Ed); educational leadership (M Ed); reading (M Ed); special education (M Ed). *Accreditation:* NCATE. Part-time programs available. *Faculty:* 7 full-time (5 women). *Students:* 32 part-time (21 women). Average age 33. In 2013, 9 master's awarded. *Degree requirements:* For master's, comprehensive exam, thesis or alternative, portfolio, comprehensive paper, or action research project. *Entrance requirements:* For master's, department exam, GRE General Test, or MAT, minimum GPA of 3.0 in graduate coursework or last 60 hours of undergraduate coursework. Additional exam requirements/recommendations for international students: Required—TOEFL (minimum score 80 iBT). *Application deadline:* For fall admission, 8/1 for domestic and international students; for spring admission, 11/1 for domestic and international students. Applications are processed on a rolling basis. *Expenses:* Tuition, state resident: full-time $5850; part-time $325 per credit hour. Tuition, nonresident: full-time $11,916; part-time $662 per credit hour. *Required fees:* $86; $43 per semester. Tuition and fees vary according to program. *Financial support:* Federal Work-Study, institutionally sponsored loans, and scholarships/grants available. Support available to part-time students. Financial award applicants required to submit FAFSA. *Faculty research:* Reading/literature/literacy, foundations, special education, diversity, teaching and technology. *Unit head:* Dr. Donna Lalonde, Interim Chairperson, 785-670-1943, Fax: 785-670-1046, E-mail: donna.lalonde@washburn.edu. *Application contact:* Tara Porter, Licensure Officer, 785-670-1434, Fax: 785-670-1046, E-mail: tara.porter@washburn.edu. Website: http://www.washburn.edu/academics/college-schools/arts-sciences/departments/education.

Washington State University, Graduate School, College of Education, Department of Teaching and Learning, Program in Literacy Education, Pullman, WA 99164. Offers Ed M, MA. *Degree requirements:* For master's, comprehensive exam (for some programs), thesis (for some programs), written or oral exam. *Entrance requirements:* For master's, minimum GPA of 3.0, letters of recommendation, transcripts, resume/curriculum vitae, personal statement. Additional exam requirements/recommendations for international students: Required—TOEFL (minimum score 550 paper-based; 80 iBT). Electronic applications accepted. *Faculty research:* Ideology of power in children's literature and the dissemination of this theory and pedagogy, gender and literacy, investigating the relationship between text processing and comprehension, understanding literacy and its instruction from a multi-dimensional perspective, the use of thematic units for promoting both literacy and concept development.

Washington State University Tri-Cities, Graduate Programs, Program in Education, Richland, WA 99352-1671. Offers educational leadership (Ed M, Ed D); literacy (Ed M); secondary certification (Ed M); teaching (MIT). Part-time programs available. *Degree requirements:* For master's, comprehensive exam, thesis or alternative; for doctorate, comprehensive exam, thesis/dissertation. *Entrance requirements:* For master's, GRE, minimum GPA of 3.0, Working with Youth form, Character and Fitness form, 3 letters of recommendation. Additional exam requirements/recommendations for international students: Required—TOEFL. Electronic applications accepted. *Faculty research:* Multicultural counseling, socio-cultural influences in schools, diverse learners, teacher education, K-12 educational leadership.

Wayne State University, College of Education, Division of Teacher Education, Detroit, MI 48202. Offers art education (M Ed), including art therapy; autism spectrum disorders (Certificate); bilingual/bicultural education (M Ed, Certificate); career and technical education (M Ed, Certificate); cognitive impairment (Certificate); curriculum and instruction (Ed D, PhD, Ed S), including art education (PhD), bilingual education (Ed D, Ed S), bilingual-bicultural education (PhD), career and technical education (MAT, Ed D, PhD, Ed S), early childhood education (MAT, Ed D, PhD, Ed S), elementary education, English as a second language (MAT, Ed D, Ed S), English education (MAT, Ed D, PhD, Ed S), foreign language education (MAT, PhD), K-12 curriculum, mathematics education (MAT, Ed D, PhD, Ed S), science education (MAT, Ed D, PhD, Ed S), secondary education, social studies education (MAT, Ed S), social studies education: secondary (Ed D, PhD); early childhood education (M Ed, Certificate); elementary education (M Ed, MAT), including children's literature (MAT), early childhood education (MAT, Ed D, PhD, Ed S), general elementary education (MAT); elementary or secondary education (MAT), including bilingual/bicultural education, English as a second language (MAT, Ed D, Ed S), mathematics education (MAT, Ed D, PhD, Ed S), science education (MAT, Ed D, PhD, Ed S), social studies education (MAT, Ed S); emotionally impaired (Certificate);

English as a second language (Certificate); English education (M Ed), including secondary; foreign language education (M Ed); K-12 reading specialist (Certificate); learning disabilities (Certificate); mathematics education (M Ed), including secondary; reading (M Ed, Ed S); reading, language and literature (Ed D); science education (M Ed), including secondary; secondary education (MAT), including art education (K-12), career and technical education (MAT, Ed D, PhD, Ed S), English education (MAT, Ed D, PhD, Ed S), foreign language education (MAT, PhD), kinesiology; social studies education (M Ed), including secondary; special education (M Ed, MAT, Ed D, PhD, Ed S); visual arts education (Certificate). Part-time programs available. *Faculty:* 36 full-time (25 women), 55 part-time/adjunct (43 women). *Students:* 218 full-time (163 women), 448 part-time (344 women); includes 218 minority (177 Black or African American, non-Hispanic/Latino; 2 American Indian or Alaska Native, non-Hispanic/Latino; 11 Asian, non-Hispanic/Latino; 19 Hispanic/Latino; 1 Native Hawaiian or other Pacific Islander, non-Hispanic/Latino; 8 Two or more races, non-Hispanic/Latino), 10 international. Average age 37. 258 applicants, 30% accepted, 52 enrolled. In 2013, 183 master's, 10 doctorates, 35 other advanced degrees awarded. *Degree requirements:* For master's, thesis, essay or project (for some M Ed programs), professional field experience (for MAT programs); for doctorate, thesis/dissertation. *Entrance requirements:* For master's, Michigan Basic Skills Test (MA in teaching), admission to the graduate school, verification of participation in group work with children and Michigan State Police Criminal Background check; for doctorate, minimum undergraduate GPA of 3.0, graduate 3.5; interview, curriculum vitae; references. Additional exam requirements/recommendations for international students: Required—TOEFL (minimum score 550 paper-based; 79 iBT), TWE (minimum score 5.5), Michigan English Language Assessment Battery (minimum score 85); Recommended—IELTS (minimum score 6.5). *Application deadline:* For fall admission, 6/1 priority date for domestic students, 5/1 priority date for international students; for winter admission, 10/1 priority date for domestic students, 9/1 priority date for international students; for spring admission, 2/1 priority date for domestic students, 1/1 priority date for international students. Applications are processed on a rolling basis. Application fee: $0. Electronic applications accepted. *Expenses:* Tuition, state resident: part-time $554.15 per credit. Tuition, nonresident: part-time $1200.35 per credit. *Required fees:* $42.15 per credit. $268.30 per semester. Tuition and fees vary according to course load and program. *Financial support:* In 2013–14, 83 students received support, including 1 fellowship (averaging $16,842 per year), 1 research assistantship with tuition reimbursement available (averaging $21,229 per year); career-related internships or fieldwork, Federal Work-Study, scholarships/grants, health care benefits, and unspecified assistantships also available. Support available to part-time students. Financial award application deadline: 3/31; financial award applicants required to submit FAFSA. *Faculty research:* Improving students' skill achievement in mathematics; improving elementary children's understanding of informational text; teachers' use of their pedagogical and mathematical knowledge in the interactive work of teaching; the intersection of identity construction in teaching and learning; identifying effective methods of literacy instruction and assessments for bilingual students in elementary language arts classrooms. *Total annual research expenditures:* $368,105. *Unit head:* Dr. Kathleen Crawford-McKinney, Assistant Dean, 313-577-0122. *Application contact:* Janice Green, Assistant Dean, 313-577-1605, E-mail: jwgreen@wayne.edu. Website: http://coe.wayne.edu/ted/index.php.

West Chester University of Pennsylvania, College of Education, Department of Literacy, West Chester, PA 19383. Offers literacy (Certificate); literacy coaching (Certificate); reading (M Ed, Teaching Certificate). Part-time programs available. *Faculty:* 9 full-time (8 women), 2 part-time/adjunct (1 woman). *Students:* 6 full-time (all women), 105 part-time (101 women); includes 2 minority (both Hispanic/Latino). Average age 28. 36 applicants, 100% accepted, 30 enrolled. In 2013, 67 master's, 2 Certificates awarded. *Degree requirements:* For master's, comprehensive exam, minimum GPA of 3.0; for other advanced degree, comprehensive exam. *Entrance requirements:* For master's, GRE or MAT if GPA is below 3.0, minimum GPA of 3.0, teaching certificate, two letters of reference. Additional exam requirements/recommendations for international students: Required—TOEFL (minimum score 550 paper-based; 80 iBT). *Application deadline:* For fall admission, 4/15 priority date for domestic students, 3/15 for international students; for spring admission, 10/15 priority date for domestic students, 9/1 for international students. Applications are processed on a rolling basis. Application fee: $45. Electronic applications accepted. *Expenses:* Tuition, state resident: full-time $7956; part-time $442 per credit. Tuition, nonresident: full-time $11,934; part-time $663 per credit. *Required fees:* $2134.20; $106.24 per credit. Tuition and fees vary according to campus/location and program. *Financial support:* Unspecified assistantships available. Support available to part-time students. Financial award application deadline: 2/15; financial award applicants required to submit FAFSA. *Faculty research:* Teaching and mentoring pre-service and in-service teachers to teach reading in urban settings. *Unit head:* Dr. Sunita Mayor, Chair, 610-436-2282, Fax: 610-436-3102, E-mail: smayor@wcupa.edu. *Application contact:* Dr. Kevin Flanigan, Graduate Coordinator, 610-430-5642, Fax: 610-436-3102, E-mail: kflanigan@wcupa.edu. Website: http://www.wcupa.edu/_academics/sch_sed.literacy/.

Western Connecticut State University, Division of Graduate Studies, School of Professional Studies, Department of Education and Educational Psychology, Reading Option, Danbury, CT 06810-6885. Offers MS. Part-time programs available. *Degree requirements:* For master's, thesis or research project, completion of program in 6 years. *Entrance requirements:* For master's, minimum GPA of 2.8, teaching certificate in elementary education. Additional exam requirements/recommendations for international students: Recommended—TOEFL (minimum score 550 paper-based; 79 iBT), IELTS (minimum score 6). *Faculty research:* Training guides for educators.

Western Illinois University, School of Graduate Studies, College of Education and Human Services, Department of Curriculum and Instruction, Program in Reading, Macomb, IL 61455-1390. Offers MS Ed. *Accreditation:* NCATE. Part-time programs available. *Students:* 1 (woman) full-time, 108 part-time (106 women); includes 6 minority (3 Black or African American, non-Hispanic/Latino; 1 Asian, non-Hispanic/Latino; 1 Hispanic/Latino; 1 Two or more races, non-Hispanic/Latino). Average age 33. In 2013, 33 master's awarded. *Degree requirements:* For master's, thesis or alternative. *Entrance requirements:* For master's, teacher certification. Additional exam requirements/recommendations for international students: Required—TOEFL (minimum score 550 paper-based; 80 iBT). *Application deadline:* Applications are processed on a rolling basis. Application fee: $30. Electronic applications accepted. *Financial support:* In 2013–14, 1 student received support, including 1 research assistantship with full tuition reimbursement available (averaging $7,544 per year). Financial award applicants required to submit FAFSA. *Unit head:* Dr. Anne Gregory, Chairperson, 309-298-1961. *Application contact:* Dr. Nancy Parsons, Assistant Director of Graduate Studies, 309-298-1806, Fax: 309-298-2345, E-mail: grad-office@wiu.edu. Website: http://wiu.edu/curriculum.

Western Kentucky University, Graduate Studies, College of Education and Behavioral Sciences, School of Teacher Education, Bowling Green, KY 42101. Offers elementary education (MAE, Ed S); exceptional education: learning and behavioral disorders (MAE); exceptional education: moderate and severe disabilities (MAE); instructional design (MS); interdisciplinary early childhood education (MAE); library media education

(MS); literacy education (MAE); middle grades education (MAE); secondary education (MAE, Ed S). Part-time and evening/weekend programs available. Postbaccalaureate distance learning degree programs offered (minimal on-campus study). *Degree requirements:* For master's, comprehensive exam. *Entrance requirements:* For master's, GRE General Test. Additional exam requirements/recommendations for international students: Required—TOEFL (minimum score 555 paper-based; 79 iBT). *Faculty research:* Teacher preparation in moderate/severe disabilities.

Western Michigan University, Graduate College, College of Education and Human Development, Department of Special Education and Literacy Studies, Kalamazoo, MI 49008. Offers literacy studies (MA); special education (MA, Ed D); teaching children with visual impairments (MA).

Western New Mexico University, Graduate Division, School of Education, Silver City, NM 88062-0680. Offers bilingual education (MAT); counseling (MA); educational leadership (MA); elementary education (MAT); reading (MAT); school psychology (MA); secondary education (MAT); special education (MAT); TESOL (teaching English to speakers of other languages) (MAT). *Accreditation:* NCATE. *Degree requirements:* For master's, comprehensive exam. *Entrance requirements:* For master's, GRE General Test, GRE Subject Test, minimum GPA of 3.2 in last 64 hours of undergraduate study. Additional exam requirements/recommendations for international students: Required—TOEFL (minimum score 550 paper-based). Electronic applications accepted.

Western State Colorado University, Graduate Programs in Education, Gunnison, CO 81231. Offers education administrator leadership (MA); reading leadership (MA); teacher leadership (MA). Postbaccalaureate distance learning degree programs offered (minimal on-campus study). *Degree requirements:* For master's, capstone.

Westfield State University, Division of Graduate and Continuing Education, Department of Education, Program in Reading, Westfield, MA 01086. Offers M Ed. *Accreditation:* NCATE. Part-time and evening/weekend programs available. *Degree requirements:* For master's, comprehensive exam, practicum. *Entrance requirements:* For master's, GRE General Test or MAT, minimum undergraduate GPA of 2.7.

Westminster College, Programs in Education, Program in Reading, New Wilmington, PA 16172-0001. Offers M Ed, Certificate. Part-time and evening/weekend programs available. *Degree requirements:* For master's, comprehensive exam, portfolio. *Entrance requirements:* For master's, minimum GPA of 3.0.

West Texas A&M University, College of Education and Social Sciences, Department of Education, Program in Reading Education, Canyon, TX 79016-0001. Offers M Ed. Part-time and evening/weekend programs available. *Degree requirements:* For master's, comprehensive exam. *Entrance requirements:* For master's, GRE General Test, interview with master's committee chairperson, state certification as a reading specialist with 3 years of teaching experience. Electronic applications accepted. *Faculty research:* Multicultural child and adolescent literature, bilingual, dual language, monolingual classrooms.

West Virginia University, College of Human Resources and Education, Department of Curriculum and Instruction/Literacy Studies, Program in Reading, Morgantown, WV 26506. Offers MA. *Accreditation:* NCATE. Part-time programs available. *Degree requirements:* For master's, thesis optional, content exams. *Entrance requirements:* For master's, minimum GPA of 2.75. Additional exam requirements/recommendations for international students: Required—TOEFL. Electronic applications accepted. *Faculty research:* Teacher education, current practices, protocol research, metacognitive studies.

Wheelock College, Graduate Programs, Division of Education, Boston, MA 02215-4176. Offers early childhood education (MS); education leadership (MS); elementary education (MS); language, literacy, and reading (MS); teaching students with moderate disabilities (MS). *Accreditation:* NCATE. Postbaccalaureate distance learning degree programs offered (minimal on-campus study). *Degree requirements:* For master's, comprehensive exam. *Entrance requirements:* Additional exam requirements/recommendations for international students: Required—TOEFL. Electronic applications accepted. *Faculty research:* Symbolic learning, emergent literacy, diversity inclusion, beginning reading language and culture, math education.

Widener University, School of Human Service Professions, Center for Education, Chester, PA 19013-5792. Offers adult education (M Ed); counseling in higher education (M Ed); counselor education (M Ed); early childhood education (M Ed); educational foundations (M Ed); educational leadership (M Ed); educational psychology (M Ed); elementary education (M Ed); English and language arts (M Ed); health education (M Ed); higher education leadership (Ed D); home and school visitor (M Ed); human sexuality (M Ed, PhD); mathematics education (M Ed); middle school education (M Ed); principalship (M Ed); reading and language arts (Ed D); reading education (M Ed); school administration (Ed D); science education (M Ed); social studies education (M Ed); special education (M Ed); technology education (M Ed). *Accreditation:* NCATE. Part-time and evening/weekend programs available. *Faculty:* 34 full-time (22 women), 37 part-time/adjunct (14 women). *Students:* 64 full-time (44 women), 209 part-time (146 women); includes 49 minority (39 Black or African American, non-Hispanic/Latino; 1 American Indian or Alaska Native, non-Hispanic/Latino; 4 Asian, non-Hispanic/Latino; 4 Hispanic/Latino; 1 Two or more races, non-Hispanic/Latino), 8 international. Average age 39. 139 applicants, 88% accepted. In 2013, 168 master's, 31 doctorates awarded. Terminal master's awarded for partial completion of doctoral program. *Degree requirements:* For doctorate, thesis/dissertation. *Entrance requirements:* For master's, minimum GPA of 2.5; for doctorate, GRE or MAT, minimum GPA of 2.0 (undergraduate), 3.5 (graduate). *Application deadline:* Applications are processed on a rolling basis. Application fee: $25 ($300 for international students). Electronic applications accepted. *Expenses:* Contact institution. *Financial support:* Career-related internships or fieldwork, tuition waivers (full and partial), and unspecified assistantships available. Support available to part-time students. Financial award application deadline: 5/1. *Faculty research:* Reading and cognition, adult education, technology education, educational leadership, special education. *Unit head:* Dr. Michael W. LeDoux, Associate Dean, 610-499-4294, Fax: 610-499-4623, E-mail: mwledoux@widener.edu. *Application contact:* Dr. Roberta Nolan, Director of Graduate Admissions, 610-499-4125, E-mail: rdnolan@widener.edu.

Wilkes University, College of Graduate and Professional Studies, School of Education, Wilkes-Barre, PA 18766-0002. Offers art and science of teaching (MS Ed); classroom technology (MS Ed); early childhood literacy (MS Ed); educational development and strategies (MS Ed); educational leadership (MS Ed); educational technology (Ed D); higher education administration (Ed D); instructional media (MS Ed); instructional technology (MS Ed); international school leadership (MS Ed); K-12 administration (Ed D); middle level education (MS Ed); online teaching (MS Ed); reading (MS Ed); school business leadership (MS Ed); secondary education (MS Ed), including biology, chemistry, English, history, mathematics; special education (MS Ed); teaching English as a second language (MS Ed); twenty-first century teaching and learning (MS Ed). Part-time and evening/weekend programs available. Postbaccalaureate distance learning degree programs offered (minimal on-campus study). *Students:* 46 full-time (37 women), 1,410 part-time (1,039 women); includes 67 minority (12 Black or African American, non-Hispanic/Latino; 2 American Indian or Alaska Native, non-Hispanic/Latino; 11 Asian, non-Hispanic/Latino; 28 Hispanic/Latino; 1 Native Hawaiian or other Pacific Islander, non-Hispanic/Latino; 13 Two or more races, non-Hispanic/Latino), 6 international. Average age 34. In 2013, 852 master's, 10 doctorates awarded. *Entrance requirements:* Additional exam requirements/recommendations for international students: Required—TOEFL (minimum score 550 paper-based; 79 iBT). *Application deadline:* Applications are processed on a rolling basis. Application fee: $45. Electronic applications accepted. *Expenses:* Contact institution. *Financial support:* Federal Work-Study and unspecified assistantships available. Financial award application deadline: 3/1; financial award applicants required to submit FAFSA. *Unit head:* Dr. Rhonda Waskiewicz, Interim Dean, Education, 570-408-4332, Fax: 570-408-7872, E-mail: rhonda.waskiewicz@wilkes.edu. *Application contact:* Joanne Thomas, Interim Director of Graduate Education, 570-408-4234, Fax: 570-408-7846, E-mail: joanne.thomas1@wilkes.edu.
Website: http://www.wilkes.edu/pages/383.asp.

Willamette University, Graduate School of Education, Salem, OR 97301-3931. Offers environmental literacy (M Ed); reading (M Ed); special education (M Ed); teaching (MAT). *Accreditation:* NCATE. Evening/weekend programs available. *Degree requirements:* For master's, leadership project (action research). *Entrance requirements:* For master's, California Basic Educational Skills Test, Multiple Subject Assessment for Teachers, PRAXIS, minimum GPA of 3.0, classroom experience, 2 letters of reference. Additional exam requirements/recommendations for international students: Recommended—TOEFL. Electronic applications accepted. *Expenses:* Contact institution. *Faculty research:* Educational leadership, multicultural education, middle school education, clinical supervision, educational technology.

William Paterson University of New Jersey, College of Education, Wayne, NJ 07470-8420. Offers curriculum and learning (M Ed); educational leadership (M Ed); reading (M Ed); special education and counseling services (M Ed), including counseling services, special education; teaching (MAT). *Accreditation:* NCATE. Part-time and evening/weekend programs available. Postbaccalaureate distance learning degree programs offered. *Faculty:* 33 full-time (8 women), 32 part-time/adjunct (9 women). *Students:* 118 full-time (92 women), 519 part-time (431 women); includes 134 minority (35 Black or African American, non-Hispanic/Latino; 1 American Indian or Alaska Native, non-Hispanic/Latino; 6 Asian, non-Hispanic/Latino; 86 Hispanic/Latino; 6 Two or more races, non-Hispanic/Latino). Average age 34. 439 applicants, 74% accepted, 240 enrolled. In 2013, 144 master's awarded. *Degree requirements:* For master's, comprehensive exam, thesis (for some programs), exit interview (for some programs), practicum/internship. *Entrance requirements:* For master's, GRE/MAT, minimum GPA of 2.75, teaching certificate. Additional exam requirements/recommendations for international students: Required—TOEFL (minimum score 550 paper-based; 79 iBT), IELTS (minimum score 6). *Application deadline:* For fall admission, 6/1 for domestic students, 5/1 for international students; for spring admission, 11/1 for domestic students, 10/1 for international students. Applications are processed on a rolling basis. Application fee: $50. Electronic applications accepted. *Financial support:* Research assistantships with full tuition reimbursements, career-related internships or fieldwork, Federal Work-Study, and unspecified assistantships available. Support available to part-time students. Financial award application deadline: 4/1; financial award applicants required to submit FAFSA. *Faculty research:* IPads in the classroom, characteristics of effective elementary teachers in language arts and mathematics, gender issues in science, after-school programs, middle class parents' roles and gentrifying school districts. *Unit head:* Dr. Candace Burns, Dean, 973-720-2137, Fax: 973-720-2955, E-mail: burnsc@wpunj.edu. *Application contact:* Liana Fornarotto, Assistant Director, Graduate Admissions, 973-720-3578, Fax: 973-720-2035, E-mail: fornarottol@wpunj.edu.
Website: http://www.wpunj.edu/coe.

Wilmington College, Department of Education, Wilmington, OH 45177. Offers reading (M Ed); special education (M Ed). Part-time programs available. *Degree requirements:* For master's, comprehensive exam. *Entrance requirements:* For master's, GRE or MAT, minimum GPA of 3.0, 2 letters of recommendation. Additional exam requirements/recommendations for international students: Required—TOEFL. *Faculty research:* Reading instruction, special education practices, conflict resolution in the schools, models of higher education for teachers.

Wilmington University, College of Education, New Castle, DE 19720-6491. Offers applied technology in education (M Ed); career and technical education (M Ed); educational leadership (Ed D); elementary and secondary school counseling (M Ed); elementary studies (M Ed); ESOL literacy (M Ed); higher education leadership (Ed D); instruction: gifted and talented (M Ed); instruction: teacher of reading (M Ed); instruction: teaching and learning (M Ed); organizational leadership (Ed D); school leadership (M Ed); secondary education (MAT); special education (M Ed). *Accreditation:* NCATE. Part-time and evening/weekend programs available. *Entrance requirements:* For master's, 2 letters of recommendation, interview. Additional exam requirements/recommendations for international students: Required—TOEFL (minimum score 500 paper-based). Electronic applications accepted.

Winthrop University, College of Education, Program in Reading Education, Rock Hill, SC 29733. Offers M Ed. *Accreditation:* NCATE. Part-time programs available. *Entrance requirements:* For master's, PRAXIS, South Carolina Class III Teaching Certificate, 1 year of teaching experience. Electronic applications accepted.

Worcester State University, Graduate Studies, Department of Education, Program in Reading, Worcester, MA 01602-2597. Offers M Ed, CAGS, Postbaccalaureate Certificate. Part-time and evening/weekend programs available. *Faculty:* 14 full-time (11 women), 22 part-time/adjunct (10 women). *Students:* 14 part-time (all women). Average age 34. 8 applicants, 88% accepted, 3 enrolled. In 2013, 1 master's, 2 CAGSs awarded. *Degree requirements:* For master's, comprehensive exam (for some programs), thesis optional. *Entrance requirements:* For master's, GRE General Test or MAT, teaching certificate. Additional exam requirements/recommendations for international students: Required—TOEFL (minimum score 500 paper-based; 61 iBT). *Application deadline:* For fall admission, 6/15 for domestic and international students; for spring admission, 4/1 for domestic and international students. Applications are processed on a rolling basis. Application fee: $40. Electronic applications accepted. *Expenses: Tuition, area resident:* Part-time $150 per credit. Tuition, state resident: part-time $150 per credit. Tuition, nonresident: part-time $150 per credit. *Required fees:* $114.50 per credit. *Financial support:* Career-related internships or fieldwork, scholarships/grants, and unspecified assistantships available. Financial award application deadline: 3/1; financial award applicants required to submit FAFSA. *Unit head:* Dr. Margaret Pray-Bouchard, Coordinator, 508-929-8840, Fax: 508-929-8164, E-mail: mbouchard@worcester.edu. *Application contact:* Sara Grady, Assistant Dean of Graduate and Continuing Education, 508-929-8787, Fax: 508-929-8100, E-mail: sara.grady@worcester.edu.

Xavier University, College of Social Sciences, Health and Education, School of Education, Department of Childhood Education and Literacy, Program in Children's Multicultural Literature, Cincinnati, OH 45207. Offers M Ed. Part-time programs available. *Faculty:* 2 part-time/adjunct (1 woman). In 2013, 4 master's awarded. *Degree requirements:* For master's, comprehensive exam, thesis, research project. *Entrance requirements:* For master's, GRE or MAT. Additional exam requirements/recommendations for international students: Required—TOEFL (minimum score 550 paper-based; 79 iBT). *Application deadline:* Applications are processed on a rolling basis. Application fee: $35. Electronic applications accepted. *Expenses: Tuition:* Part-

time $594 per credit hour. *Required fees:* $3 per semester. *Financial support:* Tuition waivers (partial) and unspecified assistantships available. Financial award applicants required to submit FAFSA. *Faculty research:* First-year teacher retention, teaching efficacy of science educators, adolescents' literacy practices, family resiliency, preparing culturally responsive teachers. *Unit head:* Dr. Cynthia Hayes Geer, Chair, 513-745-3262, Fax: 513-745-3504, E-mail: geer@xavier.edu. *Application contact:* Roger Bosse, Director of Graduate Studies, 513-745-3357, Fax: 513-745-1048, E-mail: bosse@xavier.edu.
Website: http://www.xavier.edu/multicultural-literature/.

Xavier University, College of Social Sciences, Health and Education, School of Education, Department of Childhood Education and Literacy, Program in Reading, Cincinnati, OH 45207. Offers M Ed. Part-time programs available. *Faculty:* 3 full-time (all women), 7 part-time/adjunct (6 women). *Students:* 35 part-time (32 women); includes 3 minority (1 Black or African American, non-Hispanic/Latino; 1 Asian, non-Hispanic/Latino; 1 Two or more races, non-Hispanic/Latino). Average age 32. 7 applicants, 100% accepted, 6 enrolled. In 2013, 23 master's awarded. *Degree requirements:* For master's, comprehensive exam, research project or thesis. *Entrance requirements:* For master's, GRE or MAT. Additional exam requirements/recommendations for international students: Required—TOEFL (minimum score 550 paper-based; 79 iBT). *Application deadline:* Applications are processed on a rolling basis. Application fee: $35. Electronic applications accepted. *Expenses: Tuition:* Part-time $594 per credit hour. *Required fees:* $3 per semester. *Financial support:* In 2013–14, 26 students received support. Unspecified assistantships available. Financial award applicants required to submit FAFSA. *Faculty research:* First-year teacher retention, teaching efficacy of science educators, adolescents' literacy practices, family resiliency, preparing culturally responsive teachers. *Unit head:* Dr. Cynthia Hayes Geer, Chair, 513-745-3262, Fax: 513-745-3504, E-mail: geer@xavier.edu. *Application contact:* Roger Bosse, Graduate Services Director, 513-745-3357, Fax: 513-745-1048, E-mail: bosse@xavier.edu.
Website: http://www.xavier.edu/reading/.

York College of Pennsylvania, Department of Education, York, PA 17405-7199. Offers educational leadership (M Ed); reading specialist (M Ed). Part-time and evening/weekend programs available. *Faculty:* 3 full-time (2 women), 8 part-time/adjunct (5 women). *Students:* 43 part-time (34 women); includes 1 minority (Hispanic/Latino). Average age 31. 15 applicants, 67% accepted, 7 enrolled. In 2013, 15 master's awarded. *Degree requirements:* For master's, comprehensive exam, thesis optional, portfolio. *Entrance requirements:* For master's, GRE, MAT or PRAXIS, letters of recommendation, portfolio. *Application deadline:* For fall admission, 7/15 priority date for domestic students; for spring admission, 11/15 priority date for domestic students; for summer admission, 4/15 priority date for domestic students. Applications are processed on a rolling basis. Application fee: $0. Electronic applications accepted. *Expenses: Tuition:* Full-time $12,870; part-time $715 per credit. *Required fees:* $1660; $360 per semester. Tuition and fees vary according to degree level. *Faculty research:* Mentoring, principal development, principal retention. *Unit head:* Dr. Philip Monteith, Director, 717-815-6406, E-mail: med@ycp.edu. *Application contact:* Irene Z. Altland, Administrative Assistant, 717-815-6406, Fax: 717-849-1629, E-mail: med@ycp.edu.
Website: http://www.ycp.edu/academics/academic-departments/education/.

Youngstown State University, Graduate School, Beeghly College of Education, Department of Teacher Education, Youngstown, OH 44555-0001. Offers adolescent/young adult education (MS Ed); content area concentration (MS Ed); early childhood education (MS Ed); educational technology (MS Ed); literacy (MS Ed); middle childhood education (MS Ed); special education (MS Ed), including gifted and talented education, special education. *Accreditation:* NCATE. Part-time and evening/weekend programs available. *Degree requirements:* For master's, comprehensive exam. *Entrance requirements:* For master's, GRE, MAT, or teaching certificate; minimum GPA of 2.7. Additional exam requirements/recommendations for international students: Required—TOEFL. *Faculty research:* Multicultural literacy, hands-on mathematics teaching, integrated instruction, reading comprehension, emergent curriculum.

Religious Education

Andover Newton Theological School, Graduate and Professional Programs, Newton Centre, MA 02459-2243. Offers divinity (M Div); religious education (MA); theological research (MA); theological studies (MA); theology (D Min). *Accreditation:* ACIPE; ATS. Part-time programs available. *Degree requirements:* For master's, comprehensive exam (for some programs), thesis (for some programs); for doctorate, comprehensive exam, thesis/dissertation. *Entrance requirements:* For doctorate, M Div or equivalent. Additional exam requirements/recommendations for international students: Required—TOEFL (minimum score 550 paper-based). Electronic applications accepted.

Andrews University, School of Graduate Studies, Seventh-day Adventist Theological Seminary, Program in Religious Education, Berrien Springs, MI 49104. Offers MA, Ed D, PhD, Ed S. Part-time programs available. *Faculty:* 3 full-time (1 woman). *Students:* 6 full-time (4 women), 9 part-time (7 women); includes 5 minority (1 Black or African American, non-Hispanic/Latino; 4 Hispanic/Latino), 10 international. Average age 38. 13 applicants, 38% accepted, 4 enrolled. In 2013, 5 master's, 2 doctorates awarded. Terminal master's awarded for partial completion of doctoral program. *Degree requirements:* For doctorate, thesis/dissertation. *Entrance requirements:* For master's, GRE Subject Test. Additional exam requirements/recommendations for international students: Required—TOEFL (minimum score 550 paper-based). *Application deadline:* For fall admission, 8/31 for domestic students. Applications are processed on a rolling basis. Application fee: $40. *Financial support:* Fellowships, research assistantships, teaching assistantships, and career-related internships or fieldwork available. Financial award application deadline: 6/1. *Faculty research:* Marriage and family, spiritual gifts and temperament. *Unit head:* Coordinator, 269-471-8618. *Application contact:* Monica Wringer, Supervisor of Graduate Admission, 800-253-2874, Fax: 269-471-6321, E-mail: graduate@andrews.edu.

Asbury Theological Seminary, Graduate and Professional Programs, Wilmore, KY 40390-1199. Offers MA, MAAS, MACE, MACL, MACM, MACP, MAMFC, MAMHC, MAPC, MASF, MAYM, Th M, PhD, Certificate. *Accreditation:* ATS. Part-time programs available. Postbaccalaureate distance learning degree programs offered (minimal on-campus study). *Faculty:* 64 full-time (10 women), 170 part-time/adjunct (31 women). *Students:* 675 full-time (237 women), 765 part-time (263 women); includes 237 minority (102 Black or African American, non-Hispanic/Latino; 9 American Indian or Alaska Native, non-Hispanic/Latino; 67 Asian, non-Hispanic/Latino; 42 Hispanic/Latino; 1 Native Hawaiian or other Pacific Islander, non-Hispanic/Latino; 16 Two or more races, non-Hispanic/Latino), 152 international. Average age 38. 603 applicants, 59% accepted, 244 enrolled. In 2013, 260 master's, 43 doctorates awarded. Terminal master's awarded for partial completion of doctoral program. *Degree requirements:* For master's, thesis (for some programs); for doctorate, thesis/dissertation, qualifying exam. *Entrance requirements:* For master's, minimum GPA of 2.75; for doctorate, minimum GPA of 3.0. Additional exam requirements/recommendations for international students: Required—TOEFL, IELTS. *Application deadline:* For fall admission, 8/15 for domestic students; for spring admission, 1/15 for domestic students; for summer admission, 5/15 for domestic students. Applications are processed on a rolling basis. Application fee: $50. Electronic applications accepted. *Expenses: Tuition:* Full-time $13,008; part-time $572 per credit hour. *Required fees:* $131 per semester. One-time fee: $50. *Financial support:* In 2013–14, 1,317 students received support. Career-related internships or fieldwork, Federal Work-Study, institutionally sponsored loans, and scholarships/grants available. Support available to part-time students. Financial award applicants required to submit FAFSA. *Unit head:* Dr. Douglas K. Matthews, Provost, 859-858-2206, Fax: 859-858-2025, E-mail: doug.matthews@asburyseminary.edu. *Application contact:* Kevin Bish, Vice President of Enrollment Management, 859-858-2211, Fax: 859-858-2287, E-mail: admissions.office@asburyseminary.edu.
Website: http://www.asburyseminary.edu.

Azusa Pacific University, Haggard Graduate School of Theology, Program in Pastoral Studies, Concentration in Christian Education in Youth Ministry, Azusa, CA 91702-7000. Offers MA. *Accreditation:* NCATE.

Baptist Bible College of Pennsylvania, Baptist Bible Seminary, Clarks Summit, PA 18411-1297. Offers Biblical apologetics (MA); church education (M Div, M Min); church planting (M Div, M Min); global ministry (M Div, M Min); leadership in communication (D Min); leadership in counseling and spiritual development (D Min); leadership in global ministry (D Min); leadership in pastoral ministry (D Min); leadership in theological studies (D Min); military chaplaincy (M Div); ministry (PhD); organizational leadership (M Min); outreach pastor (M Div, M Min); pastoral counseling (M Div, M Min); pastoral leadership (M Div, M Min); theology (Th M); worship ministries leadership (M Div, M Min); youth pastor (M Div, M Min). Part-time and evening/weekend programs available. Postbaccalaureate distance learning degree programs offered (minimal on-campus study). Terminal master's awarded for partial completion of doctoral program. *Degree requirements:* For master's, 2 foreign languages, thesis, oral exam (for M Div); for doctorate, 2 foreign languages, comprehensive exam (for some programs), thesis/dissertation, oral exam. *Entrance requirements:* For doctorate, Greek and Hebrew entrance exams (for PhD). Electronic applications accepted.

Baptist Bible College of Pennsylvania, Graduate Studies, Clarks Summit, PA 18411-1297. Offers Bible (MA); counseling (MA, MS); curriculum and instruction (M Ed); educational administration (M Ed); intercultural studies (MA); literature (MA); missions (MA); organizational leadership (MA); reading specialist (M Ed); secondary English/communications (M Ed); social entrepreneurship (MA); worldview studies (MA). MA in missions program available only for Association of Baptists for World Evangelism missionary personnel. Part-time and evening/weekend programs available. Postbaccalaureate distance learning degree programs offered (no on-campus study). *Entrance requirements:* Additional exam requirements/recommendations for international students: Required—TOEFL (minimum score 500 paper-based).

Baptist Theological Seminary at Richmond, Graduate and Professional Programs, Richmond, VA 23227. Offers Biblical interpretation (M Div); Christian education (M Div); Christian ministry (MCM); justice and peacebuilding (M Div, D Min); theological studies (MTS, Graduate Certificate); theology (D Min); youth and student ministries (M Div); M Div/MS; M Div/MSW. *Accreditation:* ATS. Part-time programs available. Postbaccalaureate distance learning degree programs offered (minimal on-campus study). *Faculty:* 9 full-time (2 women), 16 part-time/adjunct (6 women). *Students:* 60 full-time (27 women), 39 part-time (20 women); includes 10 minority (9 Black or African American, non-Hispanic/Latino; 1 Hispanic/Latino), 3 international. *Degree requirements:* For doctorate, one foreign language, comprehensive exam, thesis/dissertation, field study, independent study. *Entrance requirements:* For master's, BA/BS, 2 references, resume, official transcripts; for doctorate, MAT, M Div, 3 years of full-time ministry experience, minimum GPA of 2.75, 3 references, resume, official transcripts, writing sample, personal statement. Additional exam requirements/recommendations for international students: Required—TOEFL (minimum score 550 paper-based). *Application deadline:* For fall admission, 12/1 for domestic students, 5/1 for international students; for winter admission, 12/15 for domestic students, 9/1 for international students; for spring admission, 1/15 for domestic students, 10/1 for international students. Applications are processed on a rolling basis. Application fee: $35. *Financial support:* Teaching assistantships, scholarships/grants, and tuition waivers (partial) available. Financial award application deadline: 2/1. *Faculty research:* Biblical studies, pastoral care, church history, theology, ministry. *Unit head:* Dr. Ronald W. Crawford, President, 804-204-1201, Fax: 804-355-8182, E-mail: rcrawford@btsr.edu. *Application contact:* Tiffany Kellogg Pittman, Director of Admissions and Recruitment, 804-204-1208, E-mail: admissions@btsr.edu.

Biola University, Talbot School of Theology, La Mirada, CA 90639-0001. Offers adult/family ministry (MACE); Bible exposition (MA, Th M); Biblical and theological studies (MA); children's ministry (MACE); Christian education (M Div); Christian ministry and leadership (MA), including pastoral care and counseling, women's ministry; cross-cultural education ministry (MACE); educational studies (Ed D, PhD); evangelism and discipleship (M Div); general Christian education (MACE); Messianic Jewish studies (M Div, Certificate); missions and intercultural studies (M Div, Th M); New Testament (MA, Th M); Old Testament (MA); Old Testament and Semitics (Th M); pastoral and general ministry (M Div); pastoral care and counseling (M Div); philosophy (MA); spiritual formation (M Div); spiritual formation and soul care (MA); theology (Th M, D Min, Certificate); youth ministry (MACE). *Accreditation:* ATS. Part-time programs available. *Faculty:* 79. *Students:* 643 full-time (135 women), 540 part-time (147 women); includes 456 minority (42 Black or African American, non-Hispanic/Latino; 3 American Indian or Alaska Native, non-Hispanic/Latino; 379 Asian, non-Hispanic/Latino; 2 Native Hawaiian or other Pacific Islander, non-Hispanic/Latino; 30 Two or more races, non-Hispanic/Latino), 138 international. In 2013, 204 master's, 32 doctorates awarded. *Entrance requirements:* For master's, bachelor's degree from accredited college or university; minimum GPA of 2.6 (for M Di), 3.0 (for MA); for doctorate, M Div or MA. Additional exam requirements/recommendations for international students: Required—TOEFL (minimum score 600 paper-based; 88 iBT). *Application deadline:* For fall admission, 7/1 for domestic students, 6/1 for international students; for spring admission, 12/1 for domestic students. Applications are processed on a rolling basis.

Religious Education

Application fee: $55. Electronic applications accepted. *Financial support:* Scholarships/grants and unspecified assistantships available. Support available to part-time students. *Faculty research:* New Testament, Old Testament, spiritual formation, Christian education, theological studies. *Unit head:* Dr. Clint Arnold, Dean, 562-903-4816, Fax: 562-903-4748. *Application contact:* Graduate Admissions Office, 562-903-4752, E-mail: graduate.admissions@biola.edu.
Website: http://www.talbot.edu/.

Boston College, School of Theology and Ministry, Chestnut Hill, MA 02467-3800. Offers church leadership (MA); divinity (M Div); pastoral ministry (MA), including Hispanic ministry, liturgy and worship, pastoral care and counseling, spirituality; religious education (MA, PhD); sacred theology (STD, STL); social justice/social ministry (MA); spiritual direction (MA); theological studies (MTS); theology (Th M, PhD); youth ministry (MA); MA/MA; MS/MA; MSW/MA. *Accreditation:* Teacher Education Accreditation Council. Part-time programs available. *Degree requirements:* For doctorate, one foreign language, thesis/dissertation. *Entrance requirements:* For doctorate, GRE. Additional exam requirements/recommendations for international students: Required—TOEFL (minimum score 550 paper-based). Electronic applications accepted. *Faculty research:* Philosophy and practice of religious education, pastoral psychology, liturgical and spiritual theology, spiritual formation for the practice of ministry.

Brandeis University, Graduate School of Arts and Sciences, Teaching Program, Waltham, MA 02454-9110. Offers Jewish day school (MAT); public elementary education (MAT); secondary education (MAT), including Bible, biology, chemistry, Chinese, English, history, math, physics. *Degree requirements:* For master's, internship; research project. *Entrance requirements:* For master's, GRE General Test or MAT, official transcript(s), 3 letters of recommendation, resume, statement of purpose. Additional exam requirements/recommendations for international students: Required—TOEFL (minimum score 600 paper-based; 100 iBT), PTE (minimum score 68); Recommended—IELTS (minimum score 7). Electronic applications accepted. *Expenses:* Contact institution. *Faculty research:* Teacher education, education, teaching, elementary education, secondary education, Jewish education, English, history, biology, chemistry, physics, math, Chinese, Bible/Tanakh.

Brigham Young University, Graduate Studies, College of Religious Education, Provo, UT 84602-1001. Offers MA. *Faculty:* 48 full-time (4 women). *Students:* 12 full-time (0 women), 1 part-time (0 women); includes 1 minority (Hispanic/Latino). Average age 32. 6 applicants, 50% accepted, 3 enrolled. In 2013, 5 master's awarded. *Degree requirements:* For master's, thesis. *Entrance requirements:* For master's, GRE, minimum GPA of 3.0 in last 60 hours, letter of recommendation. *Application deadline:* For fall admission, 12/1 for domestic and international students. Application fee: $50. Electronic applications accepted. *Expenses: Tuition:* Full-time $6130; part-time $340 per credit hour. Tuition and fees vary according to program and student's religious affiliation. *Financial support:* In 2013–14, 3 students received support. Scholarships/grants available. *Unit head:* Dr. Brent L. Top, Dean, 801-422-2736, Fax: 801-422-0616, E-mail: brent_top@byu.edu. *Application contact:* Dr. Ray L. Huntington, Professor of Ancient Scripture, 801-422-3125, Fax: 801-422-0616, E-mail: ray_huntington@byu.edu.

Calvin Theological Seminary, Graduate and Professional Programs, Grand Rapids, MI 49546-4387. Offers Bible and theology (MA); divinity (M Div), including ancient near eastern languages and literature, contextual ministry, evangelism and teaching, history of Christianity, new church development, New Testament, Old Testament, pastoral care and leadership, preaching and worship, theological studies, youth and family ministries; educational ministry (MA); historical theology (PhD); missions and evangelism (MA); pastoral care (MA); philosophical and moral theology (PhD); systematic theology (PhD); theological studies (MTS); theology (Th M); worship (MA); youth and family ministries (MA). *Accreditation:* ACIPE; ATS. Part-time programs available. *Degree requirements:* For master's, variable foreign language requirement, thesis (for some programs); for doctorate, 4 foreign languages, comprehensive exam, thesis/dissertation. *Entrance requirements:* For doctorate, GRE General Test, Hebrew, Greek, and a modern foreign language. Additional exam requirements/recommendations for international students: Required—TOEFL (minimum score 550 paper-based), TWE (minimum score 4). Electronic applications accepted. *Faculty research:* Recent Trinity theory, Christian anthropology, Proverbs, reformed confessions, Paul's view of law.

Campbell University, Graduate and Professional Programs, Divinity School, Buies Creek, NC 27506. Offers Christian education (MA); divinity (M Div); ministry (D Min); M Div/MA; M Div/MBA. *Accreditation:* ATS. *Degree requirements:* For doctorate, final project. *Entrance requirements:* For master's, minimum GPA of 2.5; for doctorate, MAT, M Div, minimum graduate GPA of 3.0. Additional exam requirements/recommendations for international students: Required—TOEFL (minimum score 580 paper-based). *Expenses:* Contact institution. *Faculty research:* New Testament, theology, spiritual formation, Old Testament, Christian leadership.

Carolina Christian College, Program in Religious Education, Winston-Salem, NC 27102-0777. Offers Christian education (MRE); pastoral care (MRE). *Entrance requirements:* For master's, bachelor's degree from accredited institution, minimum undergraduate "B" average.

Claremont School of Theology, Graduate and Professional Programs, Program in Religion, Claremont, CA 91711-3199. Offers practical theology (PhD), including religious education, spiritual care and counseling; religion (PhD), including Hebrew Bible, New Testament and Christian origins, process studies, religion, ethics, and society; religion and theology (MA); religious education (MARE). *Accreditation:* ACIPE; ATS. Terminal master's awarded for partial completion of doctoral program. *Degree requirements:* For master's, thesis; for doctorate, 2 foreign languages, thesis/dissertation. *Entrance requirements:* For doctorate, GRE General Test. Additional exam requirements/recommendations for international students: Required—TOEFL. Electronic applications accepted.

Columbia International University, Columbia Graduate School, Columbia, SC 29230-3122. Offers Bible teaching (MABT); Christian higher education leadership (Ed D); Christian school educational leadership (Ed D); counseling (MACN); curriculum and instruction (M Ed), including Christian school guidance, English as a second language, learning disabilities, school technology; early childhood and elementary education (MAT); educational administration (M Ed); teaching English as a foreign language (Certificate); teaching English as a foreign language and intercultural studies (MATF). Part-time and evening/weekend programs available. *Degree requirements:* For master's, internships, professional project. *Entrance requirements:* For master's, Minnesota Multiphasic Personality Inventory, MAT, minimum GPA of 2.7. Additional exam requirements/recommendations for international students: Required—TOEFL. Electronic applications accepted.

Columbia International University, Seminary and School of Ministry, Columbia, SC 29230-3122. Offers academic ministries (M Div); bible exposition (M Div, MABE); biblical studies (Certificate); counseling ministries (Certificate); divinity (M Div); educational ministries (M Div, MAEM, Certificate); intercultural studies (M Div, MAIS, Certificate); leadership (D Min); member care (D Min); ministry (Certificate); missions (D Min); pastoral counseling and spiritual formation (M Div); preaching (D Min); theology (MA). *Accreditation:* ATS (one or more programs are accredited). Part-time and evening/weekend programs available. *Degree requirements:* For doctorate, comprehensive exam, thesis/dissertation. *Entrance requirements:* For doctorate, 3 years of ministerial experience, M Div. Additional exam requirements/recommendations for international students: Required—TOEFL. Electronic applications accepted.

Concordia University Chicago, College of Education, Program in Christian Education, River Forest, IL 60305-1499. Offers MA. *Entrance requirements:* Additional exam requirements/recommendations for international students: Required—TOEFL (minimum score 550 paper-based). Electronic applications accepted.

Concordia University, Nebraska, Graduate Programs in Education, Program in Parish Education, Seward, NE 68434-1556. Offers MPE. *Accreditation:* NCATE. Part-time and evening/weekend programs available. *Degree requirements:* For master's, thesis or alternative. *Entrance requirements:* For master's, GRE, MAT, or NTE, minimum GPA of 3.0, BS in education or equivalent.

Dallas Baptist University, Gary Cook School of Leadership, Program in Christian Education and Business Administration, Dallas, TX 75211-9299. Offers MA/MBA. Part-time and evening/weekend programs available. *Students:* 15 applicants, 80% accepted, 6 enrolled. *Entrance requirements:* Additional exam requirements/recommendations for international students: Required—TOEFL, IELTS. Application fee: $25. *Expenses: Tuition:* Full-time $13,410; part-time $745 per credit hour. *Required fees:* $300; $150 per semester. Tuition and fees vary according to degree level. *Financial support:* Federal Work-Study, institutionally sponsored loans, scholarships/grants, and tuition waivers available. Support available to part-time students. Financial award applicants required to submit FAFSA. *Unit head:* Dr. Judy Morris, Co-Director, 214-333-5246, Fax: 214-333-5115, E-mail: graduate@dbu.edu. *Application contact:* Kit P. Montgomery, Director of Graduate Programs, 214-333-5242, Fax: 214-333-5579, E-mail: graduate@dbu.edu.
Website: http://www3.dbu.edu/leadership/dual_degrees/mace_mba.asp.

Dallas Baptist University, Gary Cook School of Leadership, Program in Christian Education: Childhood Ministry, Dallas, TX 75211-9299. Offers MA, MA/MA. Part-time and evening/weekend programs available. *Entrance requirements:* For master's, minimum GPA of 3.0. Additional exam requirements/recommendations for international students: Required—TOEFL, IELTS. Application fee: $25. *Expenses: Tuition:* Full-time $13,410; part-time $745 per credit hour. *Required fees:* $300; $150 per semester. Tuition and fees vary according to degree level. *Financial support:* Federal Work-Study, institutionally sponsored loans, scholarships/grants, and tuition waivers (full and partial) available. Support available to part-time students. Financial award applicants required to submit FAFSA. *Unit head:* Jason Caillier, Acting Director, 214-333-5599, E-mail: graduate@dbu.edu. *Application contact:* Kit P. Montgomery, Director of Graduate Programs, 214-333-5242, Fax: 214-333-5579, E-mail: graduate@dbu.edu.
Website: http://www3.dbu.edu/leadership/childhoodministry.asp.

Dallas Baptist University, Gary Cook School of Leadership, Program in Christian Education: Student Ministry, Dallas, TX 75211-9299. Offers MA, MA/MA. Part-time and evening/weekend programs available. *Entrance requirements:* For master's, minimum GPA of 3.0. Additional exam requirements/recommendations for international students: Required—TOEFL, IELTS. Application fee: $25. *Expenses: Tuition:* Full-time $13,410; part-time $745 per credit hour. *Required fees:* $300; $150 per semester. Tuition and fees vary according to degree level. *Financial support:* Federal Work-Study, institutionally sponsored loans, scholarships/grants, and tuition waivers (full and partial) available. Support available to part-time students. Financial award applicants required to submit FAFSA. *Unit head:* Dr. Dwayne Ulmer, Director, 214-333-5246, Fax: 214-333-5115, E-mail: graduate@dbu.edu. *Application contact:* Kit P. Montgomery, Director of Graduate Programs, 214-333-5242, Fax: 214-333-5579, E-mail: graduate@dbu.edu.
Website: http://www3.dbu.edu/leadership/mace/macestudentministry.asp.

Dallas Theological Seminary, Graduate Programs, Dallas, TX 75204-6499. Offers adult education (Th M); apologetics (Th M); Bible backgrounds (Th M); Bible translation (Th M); Biblical and theological studies (Certificate); biblical counseling (MA); biblical exegesis and linguistics (MA); biblical exposition (PhD); biblical studies (MA); Biblical theology (Th M); children's education (Th M); Christian education (MA, D Min); Christian leadership (MA); cross-cultural ministries (MA); educational administration (Th M); educational leadership (Th M); evangelism and discipleship (Th M); exposition of Biblical books (Th M); family life education (Th M); general studies (Th M); Hebrew and cognate studies (Th M); hermeneutics (Th M); historical theology (Th M); homiletics (Th M); intercultural ministries (Th M); Jesus studies (Th M); leadership studies (Th M); media and communication (MA); media arts (Th M); ministry (D Min); ministry with women (Th M); New Testament studies (Th M, PhD); Old Testament studies (Th M, PhD); parachurch ministries (Th M); pastoral care and counseling (Th M); pastoral theology and practice (Th M); philosophy (Th M); sacred theology (STM); spiritual formation (Th M); systematic theology (Th M); teaching in Christian institutions (Th M); theological studies (PhD); urban ministries (Th M); worship studies (Th M); youth education (Th M). *Accreditation:* ATS (one or more programs are accredited). Part-time programs available. Postbaccalaureate distance learning degree programs offered (no on-campus study). *Faculty:* 66 full-time (4 women), 35 part-time/adjunct (8 women). *Students:* 901 full-time (252 women), 1,210 part-time (432 women); includes 552 minority (232 Black or African American, non-Hispanic/Latino; 5 American Indian or Alaska Native, non-Hispanic/Latino; 172 Asian, non-Hispanic/Latino; 104 Hispanic/Latino; 4 Native Hawaiian or other Pacific Islander, non-Hispanic/Latino; 35 Two or more races, non-Hispanic/Latino), 258 international. Average age 36. 978 applicants, 89% accepted, 607 enrolled. In 2013, 358 master's, 27 doctorates, 34 other advanced degrees awarded. *Degree requirements:* For master's, variable foreign language requirement, thesis (for some programs); for doctorate, 2 foreign languages, thesis/dissertation. *Entrance requirements:* For master's, GRE or MAT (if minimum undergraduate cumulative GPA is below 2.5 or undergraduate degree is unaccredited). Additional exam requirements/recommendations for international students: Required—TOEFL (minimum score 575 paper-based; 85 iBT), TWE. *Application deadline:* For fall admission, 7/1 for domestic students, 1/1 for international students; for winter admission, 11/1 for domestic students; for spring admission, 11/1 for domestic students. Applications are processed on a rolling basis. Application fee: $50. Electronic applications accepted. *Financial support:* In 2013–14, 1,042 students received support. Career-related internships or fieldwork, scholarships/grants, and tuition waivers (full and partial) available. Financial award application deadline: 2/28. *Unit head:* Dr. Mark L. Bailey, President, 214-887-5004, Fax: 214-887-5532. *Application contact:* Greg Hatteberg, Director of Admissions and Student Advising, 214-887-5040, Fax: 214-841-3664, E-mail: admissions@dts.edu.

Emmanuel Christian Seminary, Graduate and Professional Programs, Johnson City, TN 37601-9438. Offers Christian care and counseling (M Div); Christian education (M Div); Christian ministries (MCM); Christian ministry (M Div); Christian theology (M Div, MAR); church history (MAR); church history/historical theology (M Div); general studies (M Div); ministry (D Min); New Testament (M Div, MAR); Old Testament (M Div, MAR); urban ministry (M Div); world missions (M Div). *Accreditation:* ACIPE; ATS. Part-time programs available. Postbaccalaureate distance learning degree programs offered (minimal on-campus study). *Degree requirements:* For master's, 2 foreign languages, thesis or alternative, portfolio; for doctorate, thesis/dissertation. *Entrance requirements:* For master's, bachelor's degree from accredited undergraduate institution; for doctorate, M Div or equivalent. Additional exam requirements/recommendations for international students: Required—TOEFL. Electronic applications accepted. *Faculty research:* Theology of Old Testament prophets, spiritual formation for Christian leaders, history of

African churches and religions, social world of early Christianity, lay pastoral counseling, theology and art.

Felician College, Program in Religious Education, Lodi, NJ 07644-2117. Offers MA, Certificate. *Accreditation:* Teacher Education Accreditation Council. Part-time and evening/weekend programs available. Postbaccalaureate distance learning degree programs offered (no on-campus study). *Students:* 31 part-time (23 women); includes 6 minority (1 Black or African American, non-Hispanic/Latino; 3 Hispanic/Latino; 1 Native Hawaiian or other Pacific Islander, non-Hispanic/Latino; 1 Two or more races, non-Hispanic/Latino). Average age 48. *Degree requirements:* For master's, thesis. *Entrance requirements:* For master's, minimum GPA of 3.0, letter of recommendation. Additional exam requirements/recommendations for international students: Recommended—TOEFL (minimum score 550 paper-based). *Application deadline:* Applications are processed on a rolling basis. Application fee: $40. *Expenses: Tuition:* Part-time $945 per credit. *Required fees:* $317.50 per semester. *Financial support:* Scholarships/grants and tuition waivers (partial) available. *Faculty research:* Spirituality, race and ethnicity in religious settings. *Unit head:* Dr. Dolores M. Henchy, Director, 201-559-6053, Fax: 973-472-8936, E-mail: henchyd@felician.edu. *Application contact:* Michael Szarek, Assistant Vice-President for Graduate and International Enrollment Services, 201-559-6047, Fax: 201-559-6047, E-mail: adultandgraduate@felician.edu.

Fordham University, Graduate School of Religion and Religious Education, New York, NY 10458. Offers pastoral counseling and spiritual care (MA); pastoral ministry/spirituality/pastoral counseling (D Min); religion and religious education (MA); religious education (MS, PhD, PD); spiritual direction (Certificate). Part-time programs available. Terminal master's awarded for partial completion of doctoral program. *Degree requirements:* For master's, research paper; for doctorate, comprehensive exam, thesis/dissertation. *Entrance requirements:* For doctorate, MAT. Electronic applications accepted. *Expenses:* Contact institution. *Faculty research:* Spirituality and spiritual direction, pastoral care and counseling, adult family and community, growth and young adult.

Gardner-Webb University, School of Divinity, Boiling Springs, NC 28017. Offers biblical studies (M Div); Christian education and formation (M Div); intercultural studies (M Div); ministry (D Min); missiology (M Div); pastoral care and counseling (M Div); pastoral care and counseling/member care for missionaries (D Min); pastoral studies (M Div); M Div/MA; M Div/MBA. *Accreditation:* ACIPE; ATS. Part-time programs available. *Faculty:* 12 full-time (3 women), 4 part-time/adjunct (1 woman). *Students:* 150 full-time (83 women), 99 part-time (36 women); includes 113 minority (96 Black or African American, non-Hispanic/Latino; 7 Asian, non-Hispanic/Latino; 10 Hispanic/Latino). Average age 38. 134 applicants, 51% accepted, 63 enrolled. *Entrance requirements:* For master's, minimum GPA of 2.6; for doctorate, minimum GPA of 2.75. Additional exam requirements/recommendations for international students: Required—TOEFL (minimum score 500 paper-based; 61 iBT). *Application deadline:* Applications are processed on a rolling basis. Application fee: $40. Electronic applications accepted. *Expenses:* Contact institution. *Financial support:* Fellowships, institutionally sponsored loans, and unspecified assistantships available. Support available to part-time students. Financial award application deadline: 5/15. *Faculty research:* Jewish-Christian dialogue, Islam. *Unit head:* Dr. Robert W. Canoy, Sr., Dean, 704-406-4400, Fax: 704-406-3935, E-mail: rcanoy@gardner-webb.edu. *Application contact:* Kheresa Harmon, Director of Admissions, 704-406-3205, Fax: 704-406-3895, E-mail: kharmon@gardner-webb.edu.
Website: http://www.gardner-webb.edu/divinity.

Garrett-Evangelical Theological Seminary, Graduate and Professional Programs, Evanston, IL 60201-3298. Offers Bible and culture (PhD); Christian education (MA); Christian education and congregational studies (PhD); contemporary theology and culture (PhD); divinity (M Div); ethics, church, and society (MA); liturgical studies (PhD); ministry (D Min); music ministry (MA); pastoral care and counseling (MA); pastoral theology, personality, and culture (PhD); spiritual formation and evangelism (MA); theological studies (MTS); M Div/MSW. M Div/MSW offered jointly with Loyola University Chicago. *Accreditation:* ACIPE; ATS (one or more programs are accredited). Part-time programs available. *Degree requirements:* For master's, thesis (for some programs); for doctorate, thesis/dissertation. *Entrance requirements:* For doctorate, GRE (PhD). Additional exam requirements/recommendations for international students: Required—TOEFL (minimum score 560 paper-based). Electronic applications accepted.

George Fox University, George Fox Evangelical Seminary, Newberg, OR 97132-2697. Offers Biblical studies (M Div); Christian earthkeeping (M Div); Christian history and theology (M Div); clinical pastoral education and hospital chaplaincy (M Div); leadership and spiritual formation (D Min); military chaplaincy (M Div); ministry leadership (MA); pastoral studies (M Div); semiotics and future studies (M Div); spiritual formation (MA, Certificate); spiritual formation and discipleship (M Div); theological studies (MA). *Accreditation:* ACIPE; ATS. Part-time and evening/weekend programs available. Postbaccalaureate distance learning degree programs offered (minimal on-campus study). *Faculty:* 8 full-time (3 women), 23 part-time/adjunct (12 women). *Students:* 46 full-time (17 women), 332 part-time (117 women); includes 39 minority (11 Black or African American, non-Hispanic/Latino; 4 American Indian or Alaska Native, non-Hispanic/Latino; 14 Asian, non-Hispanic/Latino; 6 Hispanic/Latino; 1 Native Hawaiian or other Pacific Islander, non-Hispanic/Latino; 3 Two or more races, non-Hispanic/Latino), 6 international. Average age 40. 137 applicants, 96% accepted, 103 enrolled. In 2013, 14 master's, 40 doctorates, 8 other advanced degrees awarded. *Degree requirements:* For master's, thesis optional, internship; for doctorate, comprehensive exam (for some programs), thesis/dissertation, internship. *Entrance requirements:* For master's, resume, three references (one pastoral, one academic or professional, one personal), one official transcript from each college or university attended; for doctorate, resume, 3 references (1 professional, 1 academic, 1 personal), one official transcript from each college or university attended. Additional exam requirements/recommendations for international students: Required—TOEFL (minimum score 577 paper-based; 90 iBT). *Application deadline:* For fall admission, 7/1 for domestic and international students; for winter admission, 11/1 for domestic and international students; for spring admission, 4/1 for domestic and international students. Applications are processed on a rolling basis. Application fee: $40. Electronic applications accepted. *Expenses:* Contact institution. *Financial support:* Career-related internships or fieldwork and scholarships/grants available. Financial award application deadline: 5/1; financial award applicants required to submit FAFSA. *Unit head:* Dr. Chuck Conniry, Professor of Theology/Vice President and Dean, 503-554-6152, E-mail: cconniry@georgefox.edu. *Application contact:* Trenton Corvino, Graduate Admissions Counselor, 800-631-0921, Fax: 503-554-6122, E-mail: seminary@georgefox.edu.
Website: http://www.seminary.georgefox.edu/.

Georgian Court University, School of Arts and Sciences, Lakewood, NJ 08701-2697. Offers applied behavior analysis (MA); Catholic school leadership (Certificate); clinical mental health counseling (MA); holistic health studies (MA, Certificate); homeland security (MS); parish administration (Certificate); pastoral ministry (Certificate); professional counseling (Certificate); religious education (Certificate); school psychology (MA, Certificate); theology (MA, Certificate). Part-time and evening/weekend programs available. *Faculty:* 20 full-time (9 women), 9 part-time/adjunct (6 women). *Students:* 94 full-time (82 women), 134 part-time (117 women); includes 43 minority (13 Black or African American, non-Hispanic/Latino; 2 Asian, non-Hispanic/Latino; 25 Hispanic/Latino; 3 Two or more races, non-Hispanic/Latino), 1 international. In 2013, 60 master's awarded. *Degree requirements:* For master's, comprehensive exam (for some programs), thesis (for some programs). *Entrance requirements:* For master's, GRE, MAT, or NTE/PRAXIS, 3 letters of recommendation. Additional exam requirements/recommendations for international students: Required—TOEFL (minimum score 550 paper-based). *Application deadline:* For fall admission, 8/1 priority date for domestic students, 4/1 for international students; for spring admission, 1/1 priority date for domestic students, 7/1 for international students. Applications are processed on a rolling basis. Application fee: $40. Electronic applications accepted. *Expenses: Tuition:* Full-time $18,912; part-time $788 per credit. *Required fees:* $906. *Financial support:* Scholarships/grants, health care benefits, and unspecified assistantships available. Financial award application deadline: 4/15; financial award applicants required to submit FAFSA. *Unit head:* Dr. Rita Kipp, Dean, 732-987-2493, Fax: 732-987-2007. *Application contact:* Patrick Givens, Director of Graduate Admissions, 732-987-2736, Fax: 732-987-2084, E-mail: graduateadmissions@georgian.edu.
Website: http://www.georgian.edu/arts_sciences/index.htm.

Global University, Graduate School of Theology, Springfield, MO 65804. Offers biblical studies (MA); divinity (M Div); ministerial studies (MA), including education, leadership, missions, New Testament, Old Testament. Part-time and evening/weekend programs available. Postbaccalaureate distance learning degree programs offered (no on-campus study). *Degree requirements:* For master's, thesis (for some programs). *Entrance requirements:* For master's, minimum undergraduate GPA of 3.0. Electronic applications accepted. *Faculty research:* Higher education, cross-cultural missions.

Grand Rapids Theological Seminary of Cornerstone University, Graduate Programs, Grand Rapids, MI 49525-5897. Offers biblical counseling (MA); Biblical counseling (M Div); chaplaincy (M Div); Christian education (M Div, MA); intercultural studies (M Div, MA); New Testament (MA, Th M); Old Testament (MA, Th M); pastoral studies (M Div); systematic theology (MA); theology (Th M). *Accreditation:* ATS. Part-time programs available. Postbaccalaureate distance learning degree programs offered (minimal on-campus study). *Entrance requirements:* Additional exam requirements/recommendations for international students: Required—TOEFL (minimum score 577 paper-based; 90 iBT). Electronic applications accepted.

Gratz College, Graduate Programs, Program in Jewish Education, Melrose Park, PA 19027. Offers MA, Ed D, Certificate, MA/MA. Part-time and evening/weekend programs available. Postbaccalaureate distance learning degree programs offered. *Degree requirements:* For master's, one foreign language, internship. *Entrance requirements:* For master's, interview.

Hebrew College, Shoolman Graduate School of Jewish Education, Newton Centre, MA 02459. Offers early childhood Jewish education (Certificate); Jewish day school education (Certificate); Jewish education (MJ Ed); Jewish family education (Certificate); Jewish special education (Certificate); Jewish youth education, informal education and camping (Certificate). Part-time and evening/weekend programs available. Postbaccalaureate distance learning degree programs offered. *Degree requirements:* For master's, one foreign language. *Entrance requirements:* For master's, GRE, interview. Additional exam requirements/recommendations for international students: Required—TOEFL.

Hebrew Union College–Jewish Institute of Religion, School of Education, New York, NY 10012-1186. Offers MARE. Part-time programs available. *Degree requirements:* For master's, one foreign language, thesis. *Entrance requirements:* For master's, GRE, minimum 2 years of college-level Hebrew.

Institute for Creation Research, School of Biblical Apologetics, Dallas, TX 75229. Offers biblical education and apologetics (MCE); Christian school teaching (MCE); creation research (MCE); Genesis studies (MCE); sacred humanities (MCE). Part-time programs available. *Degree requirements:* For master's, comprehensive exam (for some programs), thesis (for some programs). *Entrance requirements:* For master's, minimum undergraduate GPA of 3.0, bachelor's degree in science or science education. *Faculty research:* Age of the earth, limits of variation, catastrophe, optimum methods for teaching.

Inter American University of Puerto Rico, Metropolitan Campus, Graduate Programs, Program in Christian Education, San Juan, PR 00919-1293. Offers PhD.

The Jewish Theological Seminary, William Davidson Graduate School of Jewish Education, New York, NY 10027-4649. Offers MA, Ed D. Offered in conjunction with Rabbinical School; H. L. Miller Cantorial School and College of Jewish Music; Teacher's College, Columbia University; and Union Theological Seminary. Part-time programs available. Postbaccalaureate distance learning degree programs offered (minimal on-campus study). *Degree requirements:* For master's, one foreign language, thesis optional; for doctorate, one foreign language, comprehensive exam, thesis/dissertation. *Entrance requirements:* For master's, GRE or MAT, 3 letters of recommendation; for doctorate, GRE or MAT, writing sample, 3 letters of recommendation. Additional exam requirements/recommendations for international students: Recommended—TOEFL.

Lancaster Theological Seminary, Graduate and Professional Programs, Lancaster, PA 17603-2812. Offers biblical studies (MAR); Christian education (MAR); Christianity and the arts (MAR); church history (MAR); congregational life (MAR); lay leadership (Certificate); theological studies (M Div); theology (D Min); theology and ethics (MAR). *Accreditation:* ACIPE; ATS. *Degree requirements:* For doctorate, thesis/dissertation.

La Salle University, School of Arts and Sciences, Program in Theological, Pastoral and Liturgical Studies, Philadelphia, PA 19141-1199. Offers Catholic studies (Th D); Christian spirituality (Th D); church ministry (Th D, Certificate); founder's studies (Th D); liturgy (Certificate); pastoral care (Certificate); pastoral studies (MA); religion (MA); religious education (Certificate); theological studies (MA, Certificate). Part-time and evening/weekend programs available. Postbaccalaureate distance learning degree programs offered (minimal on-campus study). *Faculty:* 1 full-time (0 women), 6 part-time/adjunct (2 women). *Students:* 46 part-time (25 women); includes 8 minority (3 Black or African American, non-Hispanic/Latino; 2 Asian, non-Hispanic/Latino; 3 Hispanic/Latino). Average age 48. 3 applicants, 100% accepted, 2 enrolled. In 2013, 8 master's awarded. *Degree requirements:* For doctorate, one foreign language, thesis/dissertation, evidence of basic reading and/or speaking knowledge of one of the following languages: a modern language other than English, Hebrew (biblical), Greek (biblical), or Latin (classical). *Entrance requirements:* For master's and Certificate, 26 credits in humanistic subjects, religion, theology, or ministry-related work; 2 letters of recommendation; statement of purpose; applications processed on rolling basis (Nov. 1 deadlien only applies to the ThD); for doctorate, master's degree in theology, religious studies, pastoral care, or similar field from accredited institution of higher education; professional resume; personal statement of interest in a doctoral degree; 2 letters of recommendation; personal on-campus interview. Additional exam requirements/recommendations for international students: Required—TOEFL (minimum score 550 paper-based). *Application deadline:* For fall admission, 8/15 priority date for domestic students, 8/15 for international students; for spring admission, 12/15 priority date for domestic students, 11/15 for international students; for summer admission, 4/24 for domestic students, 3/15 for international students. Applications are processed on a rolling basis. Application fee: $35. Electronic applications accepted. Application fee is waived when completed online. *Expenses: Tuition:* Full-time $20,750; part-time $695

per credit hour. *Required fees:* $300; $200 per year. Tuition and fees vary according to program. *Financial support:* In 2013–14, 6 students received support. Federal Work-Study, scholarships/grants, and tuition waivers (partial) available. Support available to part-time students. Financial award application deadline: 8/31; financial award applicants required to submit FAFSA. *Unit head:* Rev. Francis Berna, OFM, Director, 215-951-1346, Fax: 215-951-1665, E-mail: religion@lasalle.edu. *Application contact:* Paul J. Reilly, Assistant Vice President, Enrollment Services, 215-951-1946, Fax: 215-951-1462, E-mail: reilly@lasalle.edu.
Website: http://www.lasalle.edu/grad/index.php?section-theology&page-index.

La Sierra University, School of Religion, Riverside, CA 92515. Offers pastoral ministry (M Div); religion (MA); religious education (MA); religious studies (MA). Part-time programs available. *Degree requirements:* For master's, one foreign language, thesis or alternative. *Entrance requirements:* For master's, GRE General Test, minimum GPA of 3.0.

Liberty University, Liberty Baptist Theological Seminary, Lynchburg, VA 24515. Offers Biblical studies (M Div, MAR, MTS, Th M); church history (M Div, MAR, MTS, Th M); discipleship (D Min); discipleship and church ministry (M Div, MAR, MCM); evangelism and church planting (M Div, MAR, MCM, D Min); global studies (M Div, MA, MAR, MCM, Th M); homiletics (M Div, MAR, MCM, Th M, D Min); leadership (M Div, MAR, MCM, D Min); marketplace chaplaincy (M Div, MAR, MCM); ministry (D Min); pastoral counseling (M Div, MA, MAR, MCM, D Min), including addictions and recovery (MA), crisis response and trauma (MA), discipleship and church ministries (MA), leadership (MA), life coaching (MA), marketplace chaplaincy (MA), marriage and family (MA), military resilience (MA), pastoral counseling (MA); pastoral ministries (M Div, MAR, MCM); religious education (MRE); theology (M Div, MAR, MTS, Th M); theology and apologetics (PhD); worship (M Div, MAR, MCM, D Min). Part-time programs available. Postbaccalaureate distance learning degree programs offered (minimal on-campus study). *Students:* 2,953 full-time (776 women), 3,854 part-time (1,069 women); includes 2,136 minority (1,550 Black or African American, non-Hispanic/Latino; 27 American Indian or Alaska Native, non-Hispanic/Latino; 118 Asian, non-Hispanic/Latino; 289 Hispanic/Latino; 5 Native Hawaiian or other Pacific Islander, non-Hispanic/Latino; 147 Two or more races, non-Hispanic/Latino), 196 international. Average age 40. 5,986 applicants, 37% accepted, 1541 enrolled. In 2013, 2,130 master's, 72 doctorates awarded. *Degree requirements:* For master's, 2 foreign languages, thesis (for some programs); for doctorate, 2 foreign languages, thesis/dissertation. *Entrance requirements:* For master's, minimum undergraduate GPA of 2.0; for doctorate, GRE General Test or MAT, minimum graduate GPA of 3.0. Additional exam requirements/recommendations for international students: Required—TOEFL (minimum score 600 paper-based; 100 iBT). *Application deadline:* For fall admission, 6/1 for domestic students; for spring admission, 11/1 for domestic students. Applications are processed on a rolling basis. Application fee: $50. Electronic applications accepted. *Expenses:* Contact institution. *Financial support:* Teaching assistantships with tuition reimbursements, career-related internships or fieldwork, and Federal Work-Study available. Financial award applicants required to submit FAFSA. *Unit head:* Dr. David Hirschman, Acting Dean, 434-592.4140, Fax: 434-522-0415, E-mail: dwhirschman@liberty.edu. *Application contact:* Jay Bridge, Director of Graduate Admissions, 800-424-9595, Fax: 800-628-7977, E-mail: gradadmissions@liberty.edu.
Website: http://www.liberty.edu/seminary/.

Lincoln Christian Seminary, Graduate and Professional Programs, Lincoln, IL 62656-2167. Offers Bible and theology (MA); Christian ministries (MA); counseling (MA); divinity (M Div); leadership ministry (D Min); religious education (MRE). *Accreditation:* ACIPE; ATS. Part-time programs available. *Degree requirements:* For master's, 2 foreign languages, thesis; for doctorate, thesis/dissertation. *Entrance requirements:* For master's, minimum GPA of 2.5; for doctorate, M Div or equivalent. Additional exam requirements/recommendations for international students: Required—TOEFL (minimum score 550 paper-based). Electronic applications accepted.

Loyola Marymount University, School of Education, Department of Educational Support Services, Program in Catholic Inclusive Education, Los Angeles, CA 90045. Offers MA. Part-time programs available. *Faculty:* 12 full-time (6 women), 35 part-time/adjunct (26 women). *Degree requirements:* For master's, comprehensive exam. *Entrance requirements:* For master's, CBEST, CSET, full-time employment in Archdiocese of Los Angeles, 2 letters of recommendation, letter of intent. Additional exam requirements/recommendations for international students: Required—TOEFL (minimum score 600 paper-based; 100 iBT). *Application deadline:* For fall admission, 6/15 for domestic students; for spring admission, 11/15 for domestic students. Application fee: $50. Electronic applications accepted. *Financial support:* Scholarships/grants and unspecified assistantships available. Support available to part-time students. Financial award application deadline: 6/30; financial award applicants required to submit FAFSA. *Total annual research expenditures:* $132,233. *Unit head:* Dr. Brian P. Leung, Chair, 310-338-7313, E-mail: bleung@lmu.edu. *Application contact:* Chake H. Kouyoumjian, Associate Dean of Graduate Studies, 310-338-2721, E-mail: ckouyoum@lmu.edu.
Website: http://soe.lmu.edu/admissions/programs/sped/catholicinclusiveeducation/.

Loyola University Chicago, Institute of Pastoral Studies, Master of Arts in Pastoral Studies Program, Chicago, IL 60660. Offers healthcare (MA); religious education (MA); youth ministry (MA). *Accreditation:* ACIPE. Part-time programs available. Postbaccalaureate distance learning degree programs offered (no on-campus study). *Faculty:* 11 full-time (5 women). *Students:* 9 full-time (6 women), 73 part-time (54 women); includes 15 minority (6 Black or African American, non-Hispanic/Latino; 2 Asian, non-Hispanic/Latino; 7 Hispanic/Latino), 4 international. Average age 46. 30 applicants, 90% accepted, 17 enrolled. In 2013, 14 master's awarded. *Entrance requirements:* Additional exam requirements/recommendations for international students: Required—TOEFL. *Application deadline:* For fall admission, 8/1 priority date for domestic students; for spring admission, 12/1 for domestic students. Applications are processed on a rolling basis. Application fee: $50. Electronic applications accepted. *Expenses: Tuition:* Full-time $16,740; part-time $930 per credit. *Required fees:* $135 per semester. *Financial support:* Career-related internships or fieldwork, Federal Work-Study, institutionally sponsored loans, and scholarships/grants available. Support available to part-time students. Financial award application deadline: 3/1. *Faculty research:* Karl Rahner, Daniel Berrigan. *Unit head:* Dr. Heidi Russell, Director, 312-915-7476, Fax: 312-915-7410, E-mail: hrussell@luc.edu. *Application contact:* Rachel D. Gibbons, Assistant Director, 312-915-7450, Fax: 312-915-7410, E-mail: rgibbon@luc.edu.
Website: http://www.luc.edu/ips/academics/maps/index.shtml.

Maple Springs Baptist Bible College and Seminary, Graduate and Professional Programs, Capitol Heights, MD 20743. Offers biblical studies (MA, Certificate); Christian counseling (MA); church administration (MA); divinity (M Div); ministry (D Min); religious education (MRE).

Midwestern Baptist Theological Seminary, Graduate and Professional Programs, Kansas City, MO 64118-4697. Offers Christian education (MACE); Christian foundations (Graduate Certificate); church music (MCM); counseling (MA); ministry (D Ed Min, D Min); Old or New Testament studies (PhD); theology (M Div). *Accreditation:* ATS. Part-time programs available. Postbaccalaureate distance learning degree programs offered (minimal on-campus study). *Degree requirements:* For doctorate, thesis/dissertation. *Entrance requirements:* For doctorate, MAT. Electronic applications accepted. *Faculty research:* Ministerial studies, Biblical and theological studies, missions, counseling.

Moody Theological SeminaryMichigan, Graduate Programs, Plymouth, MI 48170. Offers Bible (Graduate Certificate); Christian education (MA); counseling psychology (MA); divinity (M Div); theological studies (MA). *Accreditation:* ATS. Part-time and evening/weekend programs available. *Degree requirements:* For master's, one foreign language, thesis. *Faculty research:* Judaism, cults, world religions.

Newman Theological College, Religious Education Programs, Edmonton, AB T6V 1H3, Canada. Offers Catholic school administration (CCSA); religious education (MRE, GDRE). Part-time programs available. Postbaccalaureate distance learning degree programs offered (no on-campus study). *Degree requirements:* For master's, thesis or alternative. *Entrance requirements:* For master's, 2 years of successful teaching experience, graduate diploma in religious education; for other advanced degree, bachelor's degree in education, teaching certificate. Additional exam requirements/recommendations for international students: Required—TOEFL (minimum score 560 paper-based; 86 iBT), IELTS (minimum score 6.5), TWE (minimum score 5).

New Orleans Baptist Theological Seminary, Graduate and Professional Programs, Division of Christian Education Ministries, New Orleans, LA 70126-4858. Offers Christian education (M Div, MACE, D Min, DEM, PhD). Evening/weekend programs available. Postbaccalaureate distance learning degree programs offered. *Degree requirements:* For master's, 2 foreign languages; for doctorate, 3 foreign languages, comprehensive exam, thesis/dissertation. *Entrance requirements:* For doctorate, GRE General Test.

Northeastern University, School of Education, Boston, MA 02115-5096. Offers curriculum, teaching, learning, and leadership (Ed D); elementary licensure (MAT); higher education administration (MAT, Ed D); Jewish education leadership (Ed D); learning and instruction (M Ed); organizational leadership studies (Ed D); secondary licensure (MAT); special education (M Ed). Part-time and evening/weekend programs available.

Oral Roberts University, School of Theology and Missions, Tulsa, OK 74171. Offers biblical literature (MA), including advanced languages, Judaic-Christian studies; Christian counseling (MA), including marriage and family therapy; divinity (M Div); missions (MA); practical theology (MA); theological/historical studies (MA); theology (D Min). *Accreditation:* ATS. Part-time programs available. Postbaccalaureate distance learning degree programs offered (minimal on-campus study). *Degree requirements:* For master's, thesis (for some programs), practicum/internship; for doctorate, thesis/dissertation, applied research project. *Entrance requirements:* For master's, GRE General Test or MAT, minimum GPA of 2.5; for doctorate, M Div, minimum GPA of 3.0, 3 years of full-time ministry experience. Additional exam requirements/recommendations for international students: Required—TOEFL (minimum score 550 paper-based; 79 iBT). Electronic applications accepted.

Pfeiffer University, Program in Practical Theology, Misenheimer, NC 28109-0960. Offers MA. Part-time and evening/weekend programs available. *Entrance requirements:* For master's, minimum GPA of 2.75.

Phillips Theological Seminary, Programs in Theology, Tulsa, OK 74116. Offers administration of church agencies (M Div); campus ministry (M Div); church-related social work (M Div); college and seminary teaching (M Div); global mission work (M Div); institutional chaplaincy (M Div); ministerial vocations in Christian education (M Div); ministry (D Min), including parish ministry, pastoral counseling, practices of ministry; ministry and culture (MAMC), including Christian education, congregational leadership, history and practice of Christian spirituality, theology, ethics, and culture; ministry of music (M Div); pastoral care and counseling (M Div); pastoral ministry (M Div); theological studies (MTS). *Accreditation:* ATS. Part-time programs available. Postbaccalaureate distance learning degree programs offered (minimal on-campus study). *Degree requirements:* For master's, thesis (for some programs); for doctorate, thesis/dissertation. *Entrance requirements:* For master's, minimum GPA of 2.5; for doctorate, M Div, minimum GPA of 3.0. *Faculty research:* Biblical studies, historical studies, theology and culture, practical theology, theology and film.

Pontifical Catholic University of Puerto Rico, College of Education, Program in Religious Education, Ponce, PR 00717-0777. Offers MRE.

Providence University College & Theological Seminary, Theological Seminary, Otterburne, MB R0A 1G0, Canada. Offers children's ministry (Certificate); Christian studies (MA, Certificate); counseling (MA); cross-cultural discipleship (Certificate); divinity (M Div); educational studies (MA), including counseling psychology, educational ministries, student development, teaching English to speakers of other languages, training teachers of English to speakers of other languages; global studies (MA); lay counseling (Diploma); ministry (D Min); teaching English to speakers of other languages (Certificate); theological studies (MA); training teacher of English to speakers of other languages (Certificate); youth ministry (Certificate). *Accreditation:* ATS. Part-time programs available. *Degree requirements:* For master's, variable foreign language requirement, thesis (for some programs); for doctorate, thesis/dissertation. *Entrance requirements:* Additional exam requirements/recommendations for international students: Recommended—TOEFL (minimum score 550 paper-based). *Faculty research:* Studies in Isaiah, theology of sin.

Reformed Theological Seminary–Jackson Campus, Graduate and Professional Programs, Jackson, MS 39209-3099. Offers Bible, theology, and missions (Certificate); biblical studies (MA); Christian education (M Div, MA); counseling (M Div); divinity (M Div, Diploma); marriage and family therapy (MA); ministry (D Min); missions (M Div, MA, D Min); New Testament (Th M); Old Testament (Th M); theological studies (MA); theology (Th M); M Div/MA. *Accreditation:* AAMFT/COAMFTE (one or more programs are accredited); ATS (one or more programs are accredited). *Degree requirements:* For master's, thesis (for some programs), fieldwork; for doctorate, 2 foreign languages, thesis/dissertation. *Entrance requirements:* For master's, minimum GPA of 2.6; for doctorate, minimum GPA of 3.0. Additional exam requirements/recommendations for international students: Required—TOEFL.

Regent University, Graduate School, School of Divinity, Virginia Beach, VA 23464-9800. Offers leadership and renewal (D Min), including Christian leadership and renewal, clinical pastoral education, community transformation, military ministry, ministry leadership coaching; practical theology (M Div, MA), including Biblical studies (M Div, MTS, PhD), chaplain ministry (M Div), Christian theology (M Div, MTS, PhD), church and ministry, history of Christianity (M Div, MTS), inter-cultural studies, interdisciplinary studies (M Div, MA, MTS), worship and renewal; renewal studies (PhD), including Biblical studies (M Div, MTS, PhD), Christian theology (M Div, MTS, PhD), history of global Christianity; theological studies (MTS), including Biblical studies (M Div, MTS, PhD), Christian theology (M Div, MTS, PhD), history of Christianity (M Div, MTS), interdisciplinary studies (M Div, MA, MTS). *Accreditation:* ACIPE; ATS. Part-time programs available. Postbaccalaureate distance learning degree programs offered (minimal on-campus study). *Faculty:* 20 full-time (3 women), 27 part-time/adjunct (3 women). *Students:* 83 full-time (40 women), 585 part-time (240 women); includes 325 minority (278 Black or African American, non-Hispanic/Latino; 5 American Indian or

Alaska Native, non-Hispanic/Latino; 15 Asian, non-Hispanic/Latino; 27 Hispanic/Latino), 33 international. Average age 42. 538 applicants, 58% accepted, 236 enrolled. In 2013, 111 master's, 10 doctorates awarded. *Degree requirements:* For master's, comprehensive exam, thesis or alternative, internship; for doctorate, thesis/dissertation or alternative. *Entrance requirements:* For master's, GRE General Test or MAT, minimum undergraduate GPA of 2.75, writing sample, clergy recommendation; for doctorate, M Div or theological master's degree; minimum graduate GPA of 3.5 (PhD), 3.0 (D Min); recommendations; writing sample; transcripts. Additional exam requirements/recommendations for international students: Required—TOEFL (minimum score 577 paper-based). *Application deadline:* For fall admission, 5/1 priority date for domestic students. Applications are processed on a rolling basis. Application fee: $50. Electronic applications accepted. *Expenses:* Contact institution. *Financial support:* Fellowships with full and partial tuition reimbursements, career-related internships or fieldwork, scholarships/grants, tuition waivers (full and partial), and unspecified assistantships available. Support available to part-time students. Financial award application deadline: 9/1; financial award applicants required to submit FAFSA. *Faculty research:* Greek and Hebrew, theology, spiritual formation, global missions and world Christianity, women's studies. *Unit head:* Dr. Amos Yong, Dean, 757-352-4412, Fax: 757-352-4636, E-mail: ayong@regent.edu. *Application contact:* Matthew Chadwick, Director of Enrollment Support Services, 800-373-5504, Fax: 757-352-4381, E-mail: admissions@regent.edu.
Website: http://www.regent.edu/acad/schdiv/home.shtml?r-home.cfm.

Regent University, Graduate School, School of Education, Virginia Beach, VA 23464-9800. Offers adult education (Ed D, PhD); advanced educational leadership (Ed D, PhD); career switcher with licensure (M Ed), including alternative licensure; character education (Ed D, PhD); Christian education leadership (Ed D); Christian school administration (M Ed); curriculum and instruction (M Ed); distance education (Ed D, PhD); educational leadership (M Ed); educational leadership - special education (Ed S); educational psychology (Ed D); elementary education (M Ed); higher education (Ed D, PhD); higher education leadership and management (Ed D); K-12 school leadership (Ed D, PhD); leadership in mathematics education (M Ed); reading specialist (M Ed); special education (M Ed, Ed D, PhD); student affairs (M Ed); TESOL (M Ed), including adult education, PreK-12. *Accreditation:* Teacher Education Accreditation Council. Part-time and evening/weekend programs available. Postbaccalaureate distance learning degree programs offered (minimal on-campus study). *Faculty:* 25 full-time (12 women), 50 part-time/adjunct (31 women). *Students:* 100 full-time (78 women), 754 part-time (614 women); includes 225 minority (191 Black or African American, non-Hispanic/Latino; 1 American Indian or Alaska Native, non-Hispanic/Latino; 7 Asian, non-Hispanic/Latino; 26 Hispanic/Latino), 16 international. Average age 39. 487 applicants, 63% accepted, 233 enrolled. In 2013, 202 master's, 19 doctorates awarded. *Degree requirements:* For master's, thesis or alternative; for doctorate, comprehensive exam, thesis/dissertation. *Entrance requirements:* For master's, MAT, minimum undergraduate GPA of 2.75, writing sample, resume, recommendations, interview; for doctorate, GRE, writing sample, 3 years of relevant professional experience, master's-level paper, copies of published work, resume, transcripts, interview, recommendations. Additional exam requirements/recommendations for international students: Required—TOEFL (minimum score 577 paper-based). *Application deadline:* For fall admission, 4/1 priority date for domestic students; for spring admission, 10/15 priority date for domestic students. Applications are processed on a rolling basis. Application fee: $50. Electronic applications accepted. Tuition and fees vary according to course load and degree level. *Financial support:* Fellowships, career-related internships or fieldwork, scholarships/grants, tuition waivers (full and partial), and unspecified assistantships available. Support available to part-time students. Financial award application deadline: 4/1; financial award applicants required to submit FAFSA. *Faculty research:* Character development and discipline for children, education leadership development, diversity in schools, classroom management, technology in education settings. *Unit head:* Dr. Alan Arroyo, Dean, 757-352-4261, Fax: 757-352-4318, E-mail: alanarr@regent.edu. *Application contact:* Matthew Chadwick, Director of Enrollment Support Services, 800-373-5504, Fax: 757-352-4381, E-mail: admissions@regent.edu.
Website: http://www.regent.edu/education/.

Rochester College, Center for Missional Leadership, Rochester Hills, MI 48307-2764. Offers MRE.

St. Augustine's Seminary of Toronto, Graduate and Professional Programs, Scarborough, ON M1M 1M3, Canada. Offers divinity (M Div); lay ministry (Diploma); religious education (MRE); theological studies (MTS, Diploma). *Accreditation:* ATS. Part-time and evening/weekend programs available. *Entrance requirements:* Additional exam requirements/recommendations for international students: Required—TOEFL (minimum score 580 paper-based), TWE (minimum score 5).

Saint Mary's University of Minnesota, Schools of Graduate and Professional Programs, Graduate School of Education, Institute for LaSallian Studies, Winona, MN 55987-1399. Offers LaSallian leadership (MA); LaSallian studies (MA). *Unit head:* Dr. Roxanne Eubank, Director, 612-728-5217, E-mail: reubank@smumn.edu. *Application contact:* Russell Kreager, Director of Admissions for Graduate and Professional Programs, 612-728-5207, Fax: 612-728-5121, E-mail: rkreager@smumn.edu.
Website: http://www.smumn.edu/graduate-home/areas-of-study/graduate-school-of-education/ma-in-lasallian-studies.

Saints Cyril and Methodius Seminary, Graduate and Professional Programs, Orchard Lake, MI 48324. Offers pastoral ministry (MAPM); religious education (MARE); theology (M Div, MA). *Accreditation:* ATS. Part-time programs available.

St. Vladimir's Orthodox Theological Seminary, Graduate School of Theology, Crestwood, NY 10707-1699. Offers general theological studies (MA); liturgical music (MA); religious education (MA); theology (M Div, M Th, D Min); M Div/MA. MA in general theological studies, M Div offered jointly with St. Nersess Seminary. *Accreditation:* ATS. Part-time programs available. *Degree requirements:* For master's, one foreign language, thesis, fieldwork; for doctorate, thesis/dissertation, fieldwork. *Entrance requirements:* For doctorate, M Div, minimum GPA of 3.0. Additional exam requirements/recommendations for international students: Required—TOEFL.

Shasta Bible College, Program in Biblical Counseling, Redding, CA 96002. Offers biblical counseling and Christian family life education (MA). Part-time programs available. *Degree requirements:* For master's, comprehensive exam (for some programs), thesis or alternative. *Entrance requirements:* For master's, minimum GPA of 2.5. Additional exam requirements/recommendations for international students: Required—TOEFL (minimum score 550 paper-based).

Southeastern Baptist Theological Seminary, Graduate and Professional Programs, Wake Forest, NC 27588-1889. Offers advanced biblical studies (M Div); Christian education (M Div, MACE); Christian ethics (PhD); Christian ministry (M Div); Christian planting (M Div); church music (MACM); counseling (MACO); evangelism (PhD); language (M Div); ministry (D Min); New Testament (PhD); Old Testament (PhD); philosophy (PhD); theology (Th M, PhD); women's studies (M Div). *Accreditation:* ACIPE; ATS (one or more programs are accredited). *Degree requirements:* For master's, thesis (for some programs), oral exam; for doctorate, thesis/dissertation, fieldwork. *Entrance requirements:* For master's, Cooperative English Test, minimum GPA of 2.0, M Div or equivalent (Th M); for doctorate, GRE General Test or MAT, Cooperative English Test, M Div or equivalent, 3 years of professional experience.

Southern Adventist University, School of Religion, Collegedale, TN 37315-0370. Offers Biblical and theological studies (MA); church leadership and management (M Min); church ministry and homiletics (M Min); evangelism and world mission (M Min); religious studies (MA). Part-time programs available. *Degree requirements:* For master's, comprehensive exam, thesis (for some programs). *Entrance requirements:* For master's, GRE. Additional exam requirements/recommendations for international students: Required—TOEFL (minimum score 600 paper-based). *Faculty research:* Biblical archaeology.

Southern Baptist Theological Seminary, School of Church Ministries, Louisville, KY 40280-0004. Offers Biblical counseling (M Div, MA); children's and family ministry (M Div, MA); Christian education (MA); Christian worship (PhD); church ministries (M Div); church music (MCM); college ministry (M Div, MA); discipleship and family ministry (M Div, MA); education (Ed D); family ministry (D Min, PhD); higher education (PhD); leadership (M Div, MA, D Min, PhD); ministry (D Ed Min); missions and ethnodoxology (M Div); women's leadership (M Div, MA); worship leadership (M Div, MA); worship leadership and church ministry (MA); youth and family ministry (M Div, MA). Part-time programs available. Postbaccalaureate distance learning degree programs offered (minimal on-campus study). *Degree requirements:* For doctorate, thesis/dissertation. *Entrance requirements:* For doctorate, GRE General Test, interview, M Div or MACE. Additional exam requirements/recommendations for international students: Required—TWE. *Faculty research:* Gerontology, creative teaching methods, faith development in children, faith development in youth, transformational learning.

Southern Evangelical Seminary, Graduate Programs, Matthews, NC 28105. Offers apologetics (MA, D Min, Certificate); Christian education (MA); church ministry (MA, Certificate); divinity (Certificate), including apologetics (M Div, Certificate); Islamic studies (MA, Certificate); Jewish studies (MA); philosophy (MA); philosophy of religion (PhD); religion (MA); theology (M Div), including apologetics (M Div, Certificate), Biblical studies; youth ministry (MA). Part-time and evening/weekend programs available. Postbaccalaureate distance learning degree programs offered. *Degree requirements:* For master's, thesis (for some programs); for doctorate, 2 foreign languages, comprehensive exam (for some programs), thesis/dissertation. *Entrance requirements:* Additional exam requirements/recommendations for international students: Required—TOEFL (minimum score 600 paper-based).

Southwestern Assemblies of God University, Thomas F. Harrison School of Graduate Studies, Program in Education, Waxahachie, TX 75165-5735. Offers Christian school administration (MS); curriculum development (MS); early education administration (M Ed); middle and secondary education (M Ed). *Degree requirements:* For master's, comprehensive written and oral exams. *Entrance requirements:* For master's, GRE General Test, minimum GPA of 2.5. Electronic applications accepted.

Southwestern Baptist Theological Seminary, School of Educational Ministries, Fort Worth, TX 76122-0000. Offers MA Comm, MACC, MACCM, MACE, MACSE, MAMFC, DEM, PhD, SPEM. Part-time and evening/weekend programs available. Terminal master's awarded for partial completion of doctoral program. *Degree requirements:* For master's, thesis; for doctorate, thesis/dissertation, statistics comprehensive exam. *Entrance requirements:* For doctorate, GRE or MAT, MACE or equivalent, minimum GPA of 3.0; for SPEM, 3 years of ministry experience after master's degree, MACE or equivalent. Additional exam requirements/recommendations for international students: Required—TOEFL, TWE. Electronic applications accepted.

Spertus Institute for Jewish Learning and Leadership, Graduate Programs, Program in Jewish Education, Chicago, IL 60605-1901. Offers MAJ Ed. Part-time and evening/weekend programs available. *Degree requirements:* For master's, one foreign language, thesis. *Entrance requirements:* For master's, bachelor of arts in Jewish studies.

Temple Baptist Seminary, Program in Theology, Chattanooga, TN 37404-3530. Offers biblical languages (M Div); Biblical studies (MABS); Christian education (MACE); English Bible language tools (M Div); theology (MM, D Min). Part-time and evening/weekend programs available. Postbaccalaureate distance learning degree programs offered (minimal on-campus study). *Degree requirements:* For doctorate, thesis/dissertation. *Entrance requirements:* For doctorate, minimum GPA of 3.0, M Div.

Towson University, Baltimore Hebrew Institute, Towson, MD 21252. Offers Jewish communal service (MAJCS, Postbaccalaureate Certificate); Jewish education (MAJE, Postbaccalaureate Certificate); Jewish studies (MAJS). *Students:* 6 full-time (5 women), 22 part-time (12 women); includes 3 minority (2 Black or African American, non-Hispanic/Latino; 1 American Indian or Alaska Native, non-Hispanic/Latino). *Entrance requirements:* For master's, bachelor's degree, minimum GPA of 3.0, letters of recommendation, statement of intent, sample of work, interview, resume; for Postbaccalaureate Certificate, bachelor's degree, minimum GPA of 3.0, statement of intent, sample of work, interview, 2 letters of recommendation, resume. Additional exam requirements/recommendations for international students: Required—TOEFL. *Application deadline:* Applications are processed on a rolling basis. Application fee: $45. Electronic applications accepted. *Unit head:* Dr. Hana Bor, Director, 410-704-5026, E-mail: hbor@towson.edu. *Application contact:* Alicia Arkell-Kleis, Information Contact, 410-704-6004, E-mail: grads@towson.edu.
Website: http://www.towson.edu/bhi/.

Trinity International University, Trinity Evangelical Divinity School, Deerfield, IL 60015-1284. Offers Biblical and Near Eastern archaeology and languages (MA); Christian studies (MA, Certificate); Christian thought (MA); church history (MA, Th M); congregational ministry: pastor-teacher (M Div); congregational ministry: team ministry (M Div); counseling ministries (MA); counseling psychology (MA); cross-cultural ministry (M Div); educational studies (PhD); evangelism (MA); history of Christianity in America (MA); intercultural studies (MA, PhD); leadership and ministry management (D Min); military chaplaincy (D Min); ministry (MA); mission and evangelism (Th M); missions and evangelism (D Min); New Testament (MA, Th M); Old Testament (Th M); Old Testament and Semitic languages (MA); pastoral care (M Div); pastoral care and counseling (D Min); pastoral counseling and psychology (Th M); pastoral theology (Th M); philosophy of religion (MA); preaching (D Min); religion (MA); research ministry (M Div); systematic theology (Th M); theological studies (PhD); urban ministry (MA). *Accreditation:* ATS (one or more programs are accredited). Part-time programs available. Postbaccalaureate distance learning degree programs offered (minimal on-campus study). *Degree requirements:* For master's, comprehensive exam, thesis, fieldwork; for doctorate, comprehensive exam (for some programs), thesis/dissertation; for Certificate, comprehensive exam, integrative papers. *Entrance requirements:* For master's, GRE, MAT, minimum cumulative undergraduate GPA of 3.0; for doctorate, GRE, minimum cumulative graduate GPA of 3.2; for Certificate, GRE, MAT, minimum undergraduate GPA of 2.5. Additional exam requirements/recommendations for international students: Required—TOEFL (minimum score 580 paper-based), TWE (minimum score 4). Electronic applications accepted.

Trinity Lutheran Seminary, Graduate and Professional Programs, Columbus, OH 43209-2334. Offers African American studies (MTS); Biblical studies (MTS, STM); Christian education (MA); Christian spirituality (STM); church in the world (MTS); church music (MA); divinity (M Div), including Bible in mission and ministry, Christian spirituality,

church in diverse world, leadership for missional church, youth and family ministry; general theological studies (MTS); mission and evangelism (STM); pastoral leadership/practice (STM); theological studies (STM); theology and ethics (MTS); youth and family ministry (MA); MSN/MTS; MTS/JD. *Accreditation:* ACIPE; ATS. Part-time programs available. *Faculty:* 11 full-time (5 women), 2 part-time/adjunct (both women). *Students:* 63 full-time (23 women), 53 part-time (23 women); includes 20 minority (19 Black or African American, non-Hispanic/Latino; 1 Asian, non-Hispanic/Latino), 1 international. Average age 35. 55 applicants, 93% accepted, 38 enrolled. In 2013, 27 master's awarded. *Degree requirements:* For master's, variable foreign language requirement, comprehensive exam (for some programs), thesis (for some programs), field experience (for some programs). *Entrance requirements:* For master's, BA or equivalent (MA, M Div, MTS); M Div, MTS, or equivalent (STM); audition (MACM). Additional exam requirements/recommendations for international students: Required—TOEFL. *Application deadline:* For fall admission, 7/15 priority date for domestic and international students. Applications are processed on a rolling basis. Application fee: $25. *Expenses: Tuition:* Full-time $14,370; part-time $479 per semester hour. One-time fee: $50. Part-time tuition and fees vary according to course load. *Financial support:* Career-related internships or fieldwork, Federal Work-Study, and scholarships/grants available. Support available to part-time students. Financial award application deadline: 5/1; financial award applicants required to submit FAFSA. *Unit head:* Dr. Brad A. Binau, Academic Dean, 614-235-4136 Ext. 4674, Fax: 614-384-4635, E-mail: bbinau@tlsohio.edu. *Application contact:* Laura Book, Director of Admissions, 614-235-4136 Ext. 4650, Fax: 866-610-8572, E-mail: lbook@tlsohio.edu.
Website: http://www.tlsohio.edu.

Unification Theological Seminary, Graduate Program, Main Campus, Barrytown, NY 12507. Offers divinity (M Div); ministry (D Min); religious education (MRE); religious studies (MA). Part-time and evening/weekend programs available. *Faculty:* 2 full-time (1 woman), 4 part-time/adjunct (0 women). *Students:* 38 full-time (7 women); includes 22 minority (15 Black or African American, non-Hispanic/Latino; 4 Asian, non-Hispanic/Latino; 3 Hispanic/Latino), 7 international. Average age 57. In 2013, 8 master's, 4 doctorates awarded. *Degree requirements:* For master's, one foreign language, thesis (for some programs); for doctorate, thesis/dissertation. *Entrance requirements:* For master's, bachelor's degree; for doctorate, M Div or equivalency. Additional exam requirements/recommendations for international students: Required—TOEFL (minimum score 450 paper-based; 45 iBT). *Application deadline:* For fall admission, 8/15 priority date for domestic students; for spring admission, 1/15 priority date for domestic students. Applications are processed on a rolling basis. Application fee: $30. Electronic applications accepted. *Expenses: Tuition:* Full-time $11,040; part-time $460 per credit. *Required fees:* $125 per semester. *Financial support:* In 2013–14, 4 students received support. Scholarships/grants available. Financial award application deadline: 6/15; financial award applicants required to submit FAFSA. *Faculty research:* Church leadership, church history, world religions, ecumenism, interfaith peace building, service-learning. *Unit head:* Dr. Kathy Winings, Vice-President for Academic Affairs, 845-752-3000 Ext. 228, Fax: 845-752-3014, E-mail: academics@uts.edu. *Application contact:* Drissa Kone, Interim Director of Admissions, 845-752-3000 Ext. 220, Fax: 845-752-3014, E-mail: d.kone@uts.edu.

Unification Theological Seminary, Graduate Program, New York Extension, New York, NY 10036. Offers divinity (M Div); religious education (MRE); religious studies (MA). Part-time and evening/weekend programs available. *Faculty:* 3 full-time (1 woman), 6 part-time/adjunct (0 women). *Students:* 34 full-time (11 women), 23 part-time (12 women); includes 22 minority (13 Black or African American, non-Hispanic/Latino; 6 Asian, non-Hispanic/Latino; 2 Hispanic/Latino; 1 Two or more races, non-Hispanic/Latino), 32 international. Average age 45. *Degree requirements:* For master's, variable foreign language requirement, thesis (for some programs). *Entrance requirements:* For master's, bachelor's degree. Additional exam requirements/recommendations for international students: Required—TOEFL (minimum score 450 paper-based; 45 iBT). *Application deadline:* For fall admission, 8/15 priority date for domestic students; for spring admission, 1/15 priority date for domestic students. Applications are processed on a rolling basis. Application fee: $30. Electronic applications accepted. *Expenses: Tuition:* Full-time $11,040; part-time $460 per credit. *Required fees:* $125 per semester. *Financial support:* In 2013–14, 57 students received support. Career-related internships or fieldwork, institutionally sponsored loans, scholarships/grants, and tuition waivers (partial) available. Support available to part-time students. Financial award application deadline: 6/15; financial award applicants required to submit FAFSA. *Faculty research:* Church history, world religions, ecumenism, interfaith peace building, service-learning. *Unit head:* Dr. Kathy Winings, Vice-President for Academic Affairs, 212-563-6647 Ext. 101, Fax: 212-563-6431, E-mail: academics@uts.edu. *Application contact:* Drissa Kone, Interim Director of Admissions, 845-752-3000 Ext. 220, Fax: 845-752-3014, E-mail: d.kone@uts.edu.

Union Presbyterian Seminary, Graduate and Professional Programs, Richmond, VA 23227-4597. Offers M Div, MACE, Th M, PhD, M Div/MACE. Part-time and evening/weekend programs available. Postbaccalaureate distance learning degree programs offered (minimal on-campus study). *Degree requirements:* For master's, oral and written exams. *Entrance requirements:* For master's, three references, transcripts, background check; for doctorate, GRE General Test, three references, transcripts, background check, statement of goals, essay. Additional exam requirements/recommendations for international students: Required—TOEFL (minimum score 550 paper-based), TWE (minimum score 4). Electronic applications accepted.

University of St. Michael's College, Faculty of Theology, Toronto, ON M5S 1J4, Canada. Offers Catholic leadership (MA); eastern Christian studies (Diploma); religious education (Diploma); theological studies (Diploma); theology (M Div, MA, MRE, MTS, D Min, PhD, Th D); theology and Jewish studies (MA). Th D offered jointly with University of Toronto. *Accreditation:* ATS (one or more programs are accredited). Part-time programs available. *Degree requirements:* For master's, thesis (for some programs), 1 foreign language (MA), 2 foreign languages (Th M); for doctorate, 3 foreign languages, comprehensive exam, thesis/dissertation; for other advanced degree, thesis optional. *Entrance requirements:* For master's, M Div or BA, course work in an ancient or modern language, minimum GPA of 3.3; for doctorate, MA in theology, Th M, or M Div with thesis, minimum GPA of 3.7; for other advanced degree, minimum GPA of 2.7. Additional exam requirements/recommendations for international students: Required—TOEFL (minimum score 600 paper-based). Electronic applications accepted. *Expenses:* Contact institution. *Faculty research:* Patristics, eastern Christianity, ecology and theology, ecumenism, Jewish Christian studies.

University of St. Thomas, Graduate Studies, The Saint Paul Seminary School of Divinity, St. Paul, MN 55105. Offers pastoral ministry (MAPM); religious education (MARE); theology (MA). *Accreditation:* ACIPE; ATS. Part-time and evening/weekend programs available. *Degree requirements:* For master's, one foreign language, comprehensive exam (for some programs), thesis (for some programs). *Entrance requirements:* For master's, GRE, 3 letters of recommendation, interview. Additional exam requirements/recommendations for international students: Required—TOEFL (minimum score 550 paper-based). *Application deadline:* For fall admission, 6/1 priority date for domestic students. Applications are processed on a rolling basis. Application fee: $40. Electronic applications accepted. *Expenses:* Contact institution. *Financial support:* Fellowships, research assistantships, institutionally sponsored loans, and scholarships/grants available. Support available to part-time students. Financial award application deadline: 4/1; financial award applicants required to submit FAFSA. *Faculty research:* Theological education. *Unit head:* Rev. Msgr. Aloysius R. Callaghan, Rector/Vice President, 651-962-5052, Fax: 651-962-5790, E-mail: arcallaghan@stthomas.edu. *Application contact:* Rev. Peter Williams, Vice Rector, 651-962-5775, Fax: 651-962-5790, E-mail: will2750@stthomas.edu.
Website: http://www.stthomas.edu/spssod/.

University of St. Thomas, School of Education, Houston, TX 77006-4696. Offers all level education (M Ed); bilingual/dual language (M Ed); Catholic school teaching (M Ed); Catholic/private school leadership (M Ed); counselor education (M Ed); curriculum and instruction (M Ed); educational leadership (M Ed); elementary teaching (M Ed); English as a second language (M Ed); exceptionality/educational diagnostician (M Ed); exceptionality/special education (M Ed); generalist (M Ed); reading (M Ed); secondary teaching (M Ed). *Accreditation:* Teacher Education Accreditation Council. Part-time and evening/weekend programs available. Postbaccalaureate distance learning degree programs offered (no on-campus study). *Faculty:* 40 full-time (26 women), 43 part-time/adjunct (31 women). *Students:* 27 full-time (20 women), 1,091 part-time (981 women); includes 691 minority (247 Black or African American, non-Hispanic/Latino; 1 American Indian or Alaska Native, non-Hispanic/Latino; 44 Asian, non-Hispanic/Latino; 379 Hispanic/Latino; 2 Native Hawaiian or other Pacific Islander, non-Hispanic/Latino; 18 Two or more races, non-Hispanic/Latino), 28 international. Average age 36. 858 applicants, 83% accepted, 458 enrolled. In 2013, 454 master's awarded. *Degree requirements:* For master's, thesis, field experience. *Entrance requirements:* For master's, GRE or MAT if GPA is below 3.0, bachelor's degree; minimum GPA of 2.75 in bachelor's degree or last 60 credit hours; official transcripts from all institutions; goal statement of 250-300 words; 1 reference. Additional exam requirements/recommendations for international students: Required—TOEFL. *Application deadline:* Applications are processed on a rolling basis. Application fee: $35. Electronic applications accepted. *Expenses:* Contact institution. *Financial support:* In 2013–14, 41 students received support. Federal Work-Study, scholarships/grants, and state work-study, institutional employment available. Support available to part-time students. Financial award application deadline: 4/15; financial award applicants required to submit FAFSA. *Faculty research:* Leadership, diversity, personality traits, second language acquisition. *Unit head:* Dr. Robert LeBlanc, Dean, 713-525-3540, Fax: 713-525-3871, E-mail: education@stthom.edu. *Application contact:* Rita Paredes, Administrative Assistant, 713-525-3442, Fax: 713-525-3871, E-mail: rparede@stthom.edu.
Website: http://www.stthom.edu/Academics/School_of_Education/Index.aqf.

University of San Francisco, School of Education, Catholic Educational Leadership Program, San Francisco, CA 94117-1080. Offers Catholic school leadership (MA, Ed D); Catholic school teaching (MA). *Faculty:* 2 full-time (1 woman), 3 part-time/adjunct (1 woman). *Students:* 12 full-time (5 women), 29 part-time (14 women); includes 6 minority (2 Black or African American, non-Hispanic/Latino; 1 Asian, non-Hispanic/Latino; 2 Hispanic/Latino; 1 Two or more races, non-Hispanic/Latino), 8 international. Average age 40. 20 applicants, 95% accepted, 11 enrolled. In 2013, 2 master's, 6 doctorates awarded. *Degree requirements:* For doctorate, thesis/dissertation. Application fee: $55 ($65 for international students). *Expenses: Tuition:* Full-time $21,150; part-time $1175 per unit. Tuition and fees vary according to course load, campus/location and program. *Financial support:* In 2013–14, 7 students received support. Fellowships, research assistantships, and teaching assistantships available. Financial award application deadline: 3/2; financial award applicants required to submit FAFSA. *Unit head:* Dr. Christopher Thomas, Chair, 415-422-2204. *Application contact:* Beth Teague, Associate Director of Graduate Outreach, 415-422-5467, E-mail: schoolofeducation@usfca.edu.
Website: http://www.soe.usfca.edu/departments/leadership/cel_index.html.

Walsh University, Graduate Studies, Master of Arts in Theology Program, North Canton, OH 44720-3396. Offers parish administration (MA); pastoral ministry (MA); religious education (MA). Part-time and evening/weekend programs available. *Faculty:* 3 full-time (0 women), 6 part-time/adjunct (1 woman). *Students:* 2 full-time (1 woman), 14 part-time (7 women). Average age 49. 5 applicants, 100% accepted, 5 enrolled. In 2013, 4 master's awarded. *Degree requirements:* For master's, thesis or alternative, culminating assignment. *Entrance requirements:* For master's, MAT or GRE (minimum scores: Verbal 145, Quantitative 146, Combined 291, Writing 3.0), minimum GPA of 3.0. Additional exam requirements/recommendations for international students: Required—TOEFL. *Application deadline:* For fall admission, 7/15 priority date for domestic students. Applications are processed on a rolling basis. Application fee: $25. Electronic applications accepted. *Expenses: Tuition:* Full-time $10,890; part-time $605 per credit hour. *Required fees:* $100; $100. *Financial support:* In 2013–14, 1 student received support, including 1 research assistantship (averaging $3,624 per year); scholarships/grants and unspecified assistantships also available. Financial award application deadline: 12/31; financial award applicants required to submit FAFSA. *Faculty research:* Virtue ethics, Biblical studies, early Christian theology, ancient philosophy, and fundamental doctrines such as the Trinity, the Incarnation, the Eucharist, theology and systematic theology; the confluence of theological anthropology and existential phenomenology, Anabaptist tradition, John Henry Newman, Second Temple period of Jewish history (539 BC to 70 AD), the relationship between material and spiritual being, evolutionary theory, and the phenomenology of the sacrament; Edith Stein. *Unit head:* Dr. Patrick Manning, Chair, 330-244-4922, Fax: 330-244-4955, E-mail: pmanning@walsh.edu. *Application contact:* Audra Dice, Graduate Admissions Counselor, 330-490-7181, Fax: 330-244-4925, E-mail: adice@walsh.edu.

Wesley Biblical Seminary, Graduate Programs, Jackson, MS 39206. Offers apologetics (MA); Biblical languages (M Div); Biblical literature (MA); Christian studies (MA); context and mission (M Div); honors research (M Div); interpretation (M Div); ministry (M Div); spiritual formation (M Div); teaching (M Div); theology (MA). *Accreditation:* ATS. Part-time programs available. *Degree requirements:* For master's, thesis. *Entrance requirements:* Additional exam requirements/recommendations for international students: Required—TOEFL. Electronic applications accepted. *Faculty research:* Patristics, missiology, culture, hermeneutics.

Wheaton College, Graduate School, Department of Christian Formation and Ministry, Wheaton, IL 60187-5593. Offers MA. Part-time programs available. *Degree requirements:* For master's, thesis or alternative. *Entrance requirements:* For master's, GRE General Test or MAT. Additional exam requirements/recommendations for international students: Required—TOEFL (minimum score 550 paper-based; 80 iBT), IELTS (minimum score 6.5). Electronic applications accepted.

Xavier University, College of Arts and Sciences, Department of Theology, Cincinnati, OH 45207. Offers health care mission integration (MA); theology (MA), including religious education, social and pastoral ministry, theology. Part-time and evening/weekend programs available. *Faculty:* 4 full-time (1 woman). *Students:* 11 part-time (6 women), 1 international. Average age 41. 5 applicants, 100% accepted, 3 enrolled. In 2013, 4 master's awarded. *Degree requirements:* For master's, final paper (or thesis) and defense. *Entrance requirements:* For master's, MAT or GRE, letters of recommendation; statement of reasons and goals for enrolling in program (1,000-2,000 words). Additional exam requirements/recommendations for international students: Required—TOEFL (minimum score 550 paper-based; 79 iBT). *Application deadline:*

Applications are processed on a rolling basis. Application fee: $35. Electronic applications accepted. *Expenses: Tuition:* Part-time $594 per credit hour. *Required fees:* $3 per semester. *Financial support:* In 2013–14, 2 students received support. Scholarships/grants and unspecified assistantships available. Financial award applicants required to submit FAFSA. *Faculty research:* Scripture, ethics, constructive theology, historical theology. *Unit head:* Dr. Sarah Melcher, Chair, 513-745-2043, Fax: 513-745-3215, E-mail: melcher@xavier.edu. *Application contact:* Roger Bosse, Graduate Services Director, 513-745-3357, Fax: 513-745-1048, E-mail: bosse@xavier.edu.
Website: http://www.xavier.edu/theology/.

Yeshiva University, Azrieli Graduate School of Jewish Education and Administration, New York, NY 10033-4391. Offers MS, Ed D, Specialist. Part-time and evening/weekend programs available. Terminal master's awarded for partial completion of doctoral program. *Degree requirements:* For master's, one foreign language, student teaching experience, comprehensive exam or thesis; for doctorate, one foreign language, comprehensive exam, thesis/dissertation, certifying exams, internship; for Specialist, one foreign language, comprehensive exam, certifying exams, internship. *Entrance requirements:* For master's, GRE General Test, BA in Jewish studies or equivalent; for doctorate and Specialist, GRE General Test, master's degree in Jewish education, 2 years of teaching experience. *Expenses:* Contact institution. *Faculty research:* Social patterns of American and Israeli Jewish population, special education, adult education, technology in education, return to religious values.

Science Education

Acadia University, Faculty of Professional Studies, School of Education, Program in Curriculum Studies, Wolfville, NS B4P 2R6, Canada. Offers cultural and media studies (M Ed); learning and technology (M Ed); science, math and technology (M Ed). Part-time programs available. *Degree requirements:* For master's, thesis optional. *Entrance requirements:* For master's, B Ed or the equivalent, minimum B average in undergraduate course work, 2 years of teaching experience. Additional exam requirements/recommendations for international students: Required—TOEFL (minimum score 580 paper-based; 93 iBT), IELTS (minimum score 6.5). *Faculty research:* Literacy development, postmodern philosophy and curriculum theory, historiography, philosophy of education, learning and technology.

Alabama State University, College of Education, Department of Curriculum and Instruction, Montgomery, AL 36101-0271. Offers early childhood education (M Ed, Ed S); elementary education (M Ed, Ed S); secondary education (M Ed, Ed S), including biology education, English language arts education (M Ed), history education, math education, music education (M Ed), reading education (M Ed), social science education; special education (M Ed). Part-time programs available. *Faculty:* 11 full-time (8 women), 13 part-time/adjunct (10 women). *Students:* 32 full-time (19 women), 162 part-time (136 women); includes 189 minority (187 Black or African American, non-Hispanic/Latino; 1 Hispanic/Latino; 1 Two or more races, non-Hispanic/Latino). Average age 33. 99 applicants, 45% accepted, 34 enrolled. In 2013, 74 master's, 20 Ed Ss awarded. *Degree requirements:* For master's, comprehensive exam, thesis optional; for Ed S, comprehensive exam, thesis. *Entrance requirements:* For master's, GRE General Test, MAT, writing competency test; for Ed S, writing competency test, GRE, MAT. Additional exam requirements/recommendations for international students: Required—TOEFL (minimum score 500 paper-based). *Application deadline:* For fall admission, 7/15 for domestic students; for spring admission, 12/15 for domestic students. Applications are processed on a rolling basis. Application fee: $25. *Expenses:* Tuition, state resident: full-time $7958; part-time $343 per credit hour. Tuition, nonresident: full-time $14,132; part-time $686 per credit hour. *Required fees:* $446 per term. One-time fee: $1784 full-time; $892 part-time. Tuition and fees vary according to course load. *Financial support:* In 2013–14, research assistantships (averaging $9,450 per year) were awarded. *Unit head:* Dr. Joyce Johnson, Acting Chairperson, 334-229-4485, Fax: 334-229-5603, E-mail: jjohnson@alasu.edu. *Application contact:* Dr. William Person, Dean of Graduate Studies, 334-229-4274, Fax: 334-229-4928, E-mail: wperson@alasu.edu.
Website: http://www.alasu.edu/academics/colleges—departments/college-of-education/curriculum—instruction/index.aspx.

Albany State University, College of Sciences and Health Professions, Albany, GA 31705-2717. Offers criminal justice (MS), including corrections, forensic science, law enforcement, public administration; mathematics education (M Ed); nursing (MSN), including RN to MSN family nurse practitioner, RN to MSN nurse educator; science education (M Ed). Part-time and evening/weekend programs available. Postbaccalaureate distance learning degree programs offered. *Degree requirements:* For master's, comprehensive exam, thesis. *Entrance requirements:* For master's, GRE or MAT, official transcript, letters of recommendations, pre-medical/certificate of immunizations. Electronic applications accepted.

Alverno College, School of Education, Milwaukee, WI 53234-3922. Offers adaptive education (MA); administrative leadership (MA); adult education and organizational development (MA); adult educational and instructional design (MA); adult educational and instructional technology (MA); global connections in the humanities (MA); instructional leadership (MA); instructional technology for K-12 settings (MA); professional development (MA); reading education (MA); reading education with adaptive education (MA); science education (MA); teaching in alternative schools (MA). *Accreditation:* NCATE. Part-time and evening/weekend programs available. *Faculty:* 7 full-time (all women), 26 part-time/adjunct (23 women). *Students:* 48 full-time (41 women), 89 part-time (83 women); includes 41 minority (24 Black or African American, non-Hispanic/Latino; 3 Asian, non-Hispanic/Latino;. 11 Hispanic/Latino; 3 Two or more races, non-Hispanic/Latino), 4 international. Average age 36. 89 applicants, 97% accepted, 59 enrolled. In 2013, 53 master's awarded. *Degree requirements:* For master's, presentation/defense of proposal, conference presentation of inquiry projects. *Entrance requirements:* For master's, bachelor's degree in related field, communication samples from work setting, 3 letters of recommendation. Additional exam requirements/recommendations for international students: Required—TOEFL. *Application deadline:* For fall admission, 7/15 priority date for domestic and international students; for spring admission, 12/15 priority date for domestic and international students. Applications are processed on a rolling basis. Application fee: $0. Electronic applications accepted. Application fee is waived when completed online. Tuition and fees vary according to program. *Financial support:* In 2013–14, 9 students received support. Federal Work-Study and scholarships/grants available. Support available to part-time students. Financial award application deadline: 4/15; financial award applicants required to submit FAFSA. *Faculty research:* Student self-assessment, self-reflection, integration of curriculum, identifying needs of students in strategic situations and designing appropriate classroom strategies. *Unit head:* Dr. Desiree Pointer-Mace, Associate Dean, Graduate Program, 414-382-6345, Fax: 414-382-6332, E-mail: desiree.pointer-mace@alverno.edu. *Application contact:* Mary Claire Jones, Senior Graduate Admissions Counselor, 414-382-6106, Fax: 414-382-6354, E-mail: maryclaire.jones@alverno.edu.

American University of Puerto Rico, Program in Education, Bayamón, PR 00960-2037. Offers art education (M Ed); elementary education 4-6 (M Ed); elementary education K-3 (M Ed); general science education (M Ed); physical education (M Ed); special education (M Ed). *Faculty:* 17 part-time/adjunct (7 women). *Students:* 55 full-time (42 women), 105 part-time (96 women); all minorities (all Hispanic/Latino). Average age 33. 120 applicants, 99% accepted, 81 enrolled. In 2013, 52 master's awarded.

Entrance requirements: For master's, EXADEP, GRE, or MAT, 2 letters of recommendation, minimum GPA of 2.5. *Application deadline:* For fall admission, 8/1 for domestic students; for winter admission, 10/18 for domestic students; for spring admission, 3/15 for domestic students. Applications are processed on a rolling basis. Application fee: $25. *Expenses: Tuition:* Part-time $240 per credit. Tuition and fees vary according to course load. *Unit head:* Dr. Jose A. Ramirez-Figueroa, Education and Technology Department Director/Chancellor, 787-620-2040 Ext. 2010, Fax: 787-620-2958, E-mail: jramirez@aupr.edu. *Application contact:* Keren I. Llanos-Figueroa, Information Contact, 787-620-2040 Ext. 2021, Fax: 787-785-7377, E-mail: oficnaadmisiones@aupr.edu.

Andrews University, School of Graduate Studies, College of Arts and Sciences, Department of Biology, Berrien Springs, MI 49104. Offers MAT, MS. *Faculty:* 9 full-time (3 women). *Students:* 3 full-time (2 women), 1 international. Average age 30. 7 applicants. In 2013, 2 master's awarded. *Degree requirements:* For master's, comprehensive exam, thesis. *Entrance requirements:* For master's, GRE Subject Test. Additional exam requirements/recommendations for international students: Required—TOEFL (minimum score 550 paper-based). *Application deadline:* Applications are processed on a rolling basis. Application fee: $40. *Financial support:* Fellowships, research assistantships, teaching assistantships, career-related internships or fieldwork, Federal Work-Study, and institutionally sponsored loans available. Financial award application deadline: 3/15. *Unit head:* Dr. Thomas Goodwin, Chairman, 269-471-3243. *Application contact:* Monica Wringer, Supervisor of Graduate Admission, 800-253-2874, Fax: 269-471-6321, E-mail: graduate@andrews.edu.

Andrews University, School of Graduate Studies, School of Education, Department of Teaching, Learning, and Curriculum, Berrien Springs, MI 49104. Offers curriculum and instruction (MA, Ed D, PhD, Ed S); elementary education (MAT); secondary education (MAT), including biology, education, English, English as a second language, French, history, physics; teacher education (MAT). *Faculty:* 7 full-time (4 women). *Students:* 16 full-time (11 women), 26 part-time (22 women); includes 14 minority (11 Black or African American, non-Hispanic/Latino; 1 Asian, non-Hispanic/Latino; 1 Hispanic/Latino; 1 Two or more races, non-Hispanic/Latino), 13 international. Average age 40. 33 applicants, 42% accepted, 3 enrolled. In 2013, 7 master's, 1 doctorate, 1 other advanced degree awarded. *Entrance requirements:* For master's, GRE Subject Test. Additional exam requirements/recommendations for international students: Required—TOEFL (minimum score 550 paper-based). *Application deadline:* For fall admission, 8/15 for domestic students. Applications are processed on a rolling basis. Application fee: $40. *Unit head:* Dr. Lee C. Davidson, Chair, 269-471-6364. *Application contact:* Monica Wringer, Supervisor of Graduate Admission, 800-253-2874, Fax: 269-471-6321, E-mail: graduate@andrews.edu.

Antioch University New England, Graduate School, Department of Education, Integrated Learning Program, Keene, NH 03431-3552. Offers early childhood education (M Ed); elementary education (M Ed), including arts and humanities, science and environmental education; special education (M Ed). *Degree requirements:* For master's, internship. *Entrance requirements:* For master's, previous course work or work experience in education. Additional exam requirements/recommendations for international students: Required—TOEFL (minimum score 550 paper-based). Electronic applications accepted. *Expenses:* Contact institution. *Faculty research:* Problem-based learning, place-based education, mathematics education, democratic classrooms, art education.

Antioch University New England, Graduate School, Department of Environmental Studies, Science Teacher Certification Program, Keene, NH 03431-3552. Offers MS. *Degree requirements:* For master's, practicum, seminar, student teaching. *Entrance requirements:* Additional exam requirements/recommendations for international students: Required—TOEFL (minimum score 550 paper-based). Electronic applications accepted.

Appalachian State University, Cratis D. Williams Graduate School, Department of Curriculum and Instruction, Boone, NC 28608. Offers curriculum specialist (MA); educational media (MA); elementary education (MA); middle grades education (MA), including language arts, mathematics, science, social studies. *Accreditation:* NCATE. Part-time and evening/weekend programs available. Postbaccalaureate distance learning degree programs offered (no on-campus study). *Degree requirements:* For master's, comprehensive exam, thesis or alternative. *Entrance requirements:* For master's, GRE General Test or MAT, 3 letters of recommendation. Additional exam requirements/recommendations for international students: Required—TOEFL (minimum score 570 paper-based; 79 iBT), IELTS (minimum score 6.5). Electronic applications accepted. *Faculty research:* Media literacy, elementary teaching, curriculum development, online learning environments.

Arcadia University, Graduate Studies, School of Education, Glenside, PA 19038-3295. Offers art education (M Ed); computer education (CAS); curriculum (CAS); curriculum studies (M Ed); early childhood education (M Ed, CAS), including individualized (M Ed), master teacher (M Ed), research in child development (M Ed); educational leadership (M Ed, Ed D, CAS); elementary education (M Ed, CAS); English education (MA Ed); environmental education (MA Ed, CAS); history education (MA Ed); instructional technology (M Ed); language arts (M Ed, CAS); library science (M Ed); mathematics education (M Ed, MA Ed, CAS); music education (MA Ed); psychology (MA Ed); reading (M Ed, CAS); science education (M Ed, CAS); secondary education (M Ed, CAS); special education (M Ed, Ed D, CAS); theater arts (MA Ed); written communication (MA Ed). *Accreditation:* NASAD. Part-time and evening/weekend programs available. Postbaccalaureate distance learning degree programs offered (minimal on-campus study). Electronic applications accepted. *Expenses:* Contact institution.

Science Education

Arkansas State University, Graduate School, College of Sciences and Mathematics, Department of Biological Sciences, Jonesboro, AR 72467. Offers biological sciences (MA); biology (MS); biology education (MSE, SCCT); biotechnology (PSM). Part-time programs available. *Faculty:* 22 full-time (7 women). *Students:* 10 full-time (5 women), 17 part-time (9 women); includes 3 minority (1 Black or African American, non-Hispanic/Latino; 1 American Indian or Alaska Native, non-Hispanic/Latino; 1 Hispanic/Latino). Average age 29. 26 applicants, 23% accepted, 6 enrolled. In 2013, 12 master's awarded. *Degree requirements:* For master's, comprehensive exam, thesis (for some programs); for SCCT, comprehensive exam. *Entrance requirements:* For master's, GRE General Test, appropriate bachelor's degree, letters of reference, interview, official transcripts, immunization records, statement of educational objectives and career goals, teaching certificate (MSE); for SCCT, GRE General Test or MAT, interview, master's degree, letters of reference, official transcript, personal statement, immunization records. Additional exam requirements/recommendations for international students: Required—TOEFL (minimum score 550 paper-based; 79 iBT), IELTS (minimum score 6), PTE (minimum score 56). *Application deadline:* For fall admission, 7/1 for domestic and international students; for spring admission, 11/15 for domestic students, 11/14 for international students. Applications are processed on a rolling basis. Application fee: $30 ($40 for international students). Electronic applications accepted. *Expenses:* Tuition, state resident: full-time $4284; part-time $238 per credit hour. Tuition, nonresident: full-time $8568; part-time $476 per credit hour. *International tuition:* $9268 full-time. *Required fees:* $1098; $61 per credit hour. $25 per term. Tuition and fees vary according to course load and program. *Financial support:* In 2013–14, 12 students received support. Research assistantships, career-related internships or fieldwork, scholarships/grants, and unspecified assistantships available. Financial award application deadline: 7/1; financial award applicants required to submit FAFSA. *Unit head:* Dr. Thomas Risch, Chair, 870-972-3082, Fax: 870-972-2638, E-mail: trisch@astate.edu. *Application contact:* Vickey Ring, Graduate Admissions Coordinator, 870-972-3029, Fax: 870-972-3857, E-mail: vickeyring@astate.edu.
Website: http://www.astate.edu/college/sciences-and-mathematics/departments/biology/index.dot.

Arkansas State University, Graduate School, College of Sciences and Mathematics, Department of Chemistry and Physics, Jonesboro, AR 72467. Offers chemistry (MS); chemistry education (MSE, SCCT). Part-time programs available. *Faculty:* 12 full-time (1 woman). *Students:* 7 part-time (3 women); includes 1 minority (Asian, non-Hispanic/Latino), 3 international. Average age 27. 11 applicants, 36% accepted, 2 enrolled. In 2013, 6 master's awarded. *Degree requirements:* For master's, comprehensive exam, thesis or alternative; for SCCT, comprehensive exam. *Entrance requirements:* For master's, GRE General Test or MAT, appropriate bachelor's degree, official transcript, immunization records, valid teaching certificate (for MSE); for SCCT, GRE General Test or MAT, interview, master's degree, official transcript, immunization records. Additional exam requirements/recommendations for international students: Required—TOEFL (minimum score 550 paper-based; 79 iBT), IELTS (minimum score 6), PTE (minimum score 56). *Application deadline:* For fall admission, 7/1 for domestic and international students; for spring admission, 11/15 for domestic students, 11/14 for international students. Applications are processed on a rolling basis. Application fee: $30 ($40 for international students). Electronic applications accepted. *Expenses:* Tuition, state resident: full-time $4284; part-time $238 per credit hour. Tuition, nonresident: full-time $8568; part-time $476 per credit hour. *International tuition:* $9268 full-time. *Required fees:* $1098; $61 per credit hour. $25 per term. Tuition and fees vary according to course load and program. *Financial support:* Teaching assistantships, career-related internships or fieldwork, scholarships/grants, and unspecified assistantships available. Financial award application deadline: 7/1; financial award applicants required to submit FAFSA. *Unit head:* Dr. William Burns, Chair, 870-972-3086, Fax: 870-972-3089, E-mail: wburns@astate.edu. *Application contact:* Vickey Ring, Graduate Admissions Coordinator, 870-972-3029, Fax: 870-972-3857, E-mail: vickeyring@astate.edu.
Website: http://www.astate.edu/college/sciences-and-mathematics/departments/chemistry-physics/index.dot.

Asbury University, School of Graduate and Professional Studies, Wilmore, KY 40390-1198. Offers biology: alternative certificate (MA Ed); chemistry: alternative certificate (MA Ed); English (MA Ed); English as a second language (MA Ed); ESL (MA Ed); French (MA Ed); Latin: alternative certificate (MA Ed); mathematics: alternative certificate (MA Ed); reading/writing endorsement (MA Ed); social studies (MA Ed); social work (MSW), including child and family services; Spanish (MA Ed); special education (MA Ed); special education: alternative certificate (MA Ed); teacher as leader endorsement (MA Ed). *Accreditation:* NCATE. Part-time programs available. *Degree requirements:* For master's, action research project, portfolio. *Entrance requirements:* For master's, PRAXIS/NTE, minimum GPA of 2.75, letters of recommendation. Additional exam requirements/recommendations for international students: Required—TOEFL (minimum score 550 paper-based). Electronic applications accepted.

Auburn University, Graduate School, College of Education, Department of Curriculum and Teaching, Auburn University, AL 36849. Offers business education (M Ed, MS, PhD); early childhood education (M Ed, MS, PhD, Ed S); elementary education (M Ed, MS, PhD, Ed S); foreign languages (M Ed, MS); music education (M Ed, MS, PhD, Ed S); postsecondary education (PhD); reading education (PhD, Ed S); secondary education (M Ed, MS, PhD, Ed S), including English language arts, mathematics, science, social studies. *Accreditation:* NASM (one or more programs are accredited); NCATE. Part-time programs available. *Faculty:* 29 full-time (21 women), 4 part-time/adjunct (all women). *Students:* 61 full-time (40 women), 153 part-time (108 women); includes 37 minority (32 Black or African American, non-Hispanic/Latino; 2 Asian, non-Hispanic/Latino; 3 Hispanic/Latino), 1 international. Average age 34. 150 applicants, 59% accepted, 74 enrolled. In 2013, 70 master's, 6 doctorates, 26 other advanced degrees awarded. *Degree requirements:* For master's, thesis (for some programs); for doctorate, thesis/dissertation; for Ed S, field project. *Entrance requirements:* For master's, doctorate, and Ed S, GRE General Test. *Application deadline:* For fall admission, 7/7 for domestic students; for spring admission, 11/24 for domestic students. Applications are processed on a rolling basis. Application fee: $50 ($60 for international students). Electronic applications accepted. *Expenses:* Tuition, state resident: full-time $8262; part-time $459 per credit hour. Tuition, nonresident: full-time $24,786; part-time $1377 per credit hour. Tuition and fees vary according to degree level and program. *Financial support:* Fellowships, teaching assistantships, career-related internships or fieldwork, and Federal Work-Study available. Support available to part-time students. Financial award application deadline: 3/15; financial award applicants required to submit FAFSA. *Faculty research:* Emerging literacy, reading attitudes, music for at-risk youth, portfolio assessment. *Unit head:* Dr. Kimberly Walls, Head, 334-844-4434. *Application contact:* Dr. George Flowers, Dean of the Graduate School, 334-844-2125.
Website: http://education.auburn.edu/academic_departments/curr/.

Auburn University at Montgomery, School of Education, Department of Foundations, Technology, and Secondary Education, Montgomery, AL 36124-4023. Offers instructional technology (M Ed); secondary education (M Ed, Ed S), including art education (M Ed), biology (M Ed), English language arts (M Ed), general science (M Ed), history (M Ed), mathematics (M Ed), social science (M Ed). *Accreditation:* NCATE. Part-time and evening/weekend programs available. *Faculty:* 6 full-time (2 women), 1 (woman) part-time/adjunct. *Students:* 47 full-time (22 women), 77 part-time (48 women); includes 30 minority (29 Black or African American, non-Hispanic/Latino; 1 Asian, non-Hispanic/Latino), 1 international. Average age 30. In 2013, 86 master's awarded. *Degree requirements:* For master's and Ed S, comprehensive exam, thesis optional. *Entrance requirements:* For master's, GRE General Test or MAT, certification, BS in teaching; for Ed S, GRE General Test or MAT, certification. *Application deadline:* Applications are processed on a rolling basis. Electronic applications accepted. *Expenses:* Tuition, state resident: full-time $5994; part-time $333 per credit hour. Tuition, nonresident: full-time $17,982; part-time $999 per credit hour. *Financial support:* Teaching assistantships, career-related internships or fieldwork, and scholarships/grants available. Support available to part-time students. Financial award application deadline: 3/1; financial award applicants required to submit FAFSA. *Unit head:* Dr. Sheila Austin, Dean, 334-244-3425, Fax: 334-244-3102, E-mail: saustin1@aum.edu. *Application contact:* Dr. Rhonda Morton, Associate Dean/Graduate Coordinator, 334-244-3287, Fax: 334-244-3978, E-mail: rmorton@aum.edu.
Website: http://www.education.aum.edu/departments/foundations-technology-and-secondary-education.

Aurora University, College of Arts and Sciences, Aurora, IL 60506-4892. Offers elementary math and science (MATL); life science (MATL); mathematics (MATL, MS). Part-time and evening/weekend programs available. *Entrance requirements:* Additional exam requirements/recommendations for international students: Required—TOEFL (minimum score 550 paper-based). Electronic applications accepted. *Expenses:* Contact institution.

Averett University, Master in Education Program, Danville, VA 24541-3692. Offers administration and supervision (M Ed); art (M Ed); biology (M Ed); chemistry (M Ed); curriculum and instruction (M Ed); early childhood (M Ed); English (M Ed); mathematics (M Ed); middle grades (M Ed); physical science (M Ed); reading specialist (M Ed); science (M Ed); special education (M Ed); special education learning disability (M Ed). Program offered on Danville Campus only. Part-time and evening/weekend programs available. *Faculty:* 4 full-time (3 women), 13 part-time/adjunct (8 women). *Students:* 43 full-time (35 women), 44 part-time (35 women); includes 7 minority (all Black or African American, non-Hispanic/Latino). *Degree requirements:* For master's, 30-credit core curriculum, minimum GPA of 3.0 throughout program, completion of degree requirements within six years from start of program. *Entrance requirements:* For master's, PRAXIS I, GRE, or MAT; writing proficiency test, minimum cumulative GPA of 3.0 over the last 60 hours of undergraduate study toward a baccalaureate degree, three letters of recommendation, Virginia teaching license (or eligibility). Additional exam requirements/recommendations for international students: Required—TOEFL (minimum score 600 paper-based; 100 iBT). *Application deadline:* Applications are processed on a rolling basis. Application fee: $100. *Expenses:* Contact institution. *Financial support:* Career-related internships or fieldwork, Federal Work-Study, and scholarships/grants available. Financial award application deadline: 4/1; financial award applicants required to submit FAFSA. *Unit head:* Wilfred Lawrence, Department Chair of Education, 434-791-5752, E-mail: priedel@averett.edu. *Application contact:* Christy Pack, Executive Director of Enrollment, 804-887-8612, E-mail: dpack@averett.edu.
Website: http://www.averett.edu/adultprograms/degrees/MEDtrad.php.

Ball State University, Graduate School, College of Sciences and Humanities, Department of Biology, Muncie, IN 47306-1099. Offers biology (MA, MAE, MS); biology education (Ed D). *Faculty:* 19 full-time (5 women). *Students:* 20 full-time (8 women), 23 part-time (14 women); includes 2 minority (both Hispanic/Latino), 6 international. Average age 24. 49 applicants, 80% accepted, 13 enrolled. In 2013, 18 master's awarded. *Degree requirements:* For doctorate, thesis/dissertation. *Entrance requirements:* For master's, GRE General Test; for doctorate, GRE General Test, minimum graduate GPA of 3.2. Application fee: $50. *Financial support:* In 2013–14, 29 students received support, including 33 teaching assistantships with full and partial tuition reimbursements available (averaging $11,907 per year); research assistantships with full tuition reimbursements available and career-related internships or fieldwork also available. Financial award application deadline: 3/1. *Faculty research:* Aquatics and fisheries, tumors, water and air pollution, developmental biology and genetics. *Unit head:* Dr. Kemuel Badger, Chairman, 765-285-8820, Fax: 765-285-8804, E-mail: kbadger@bsu.edu. *Application contact:* Dr. Robert Morris, Associate Provost for Research and Dean of the Graduate School, 765-285-1300, E-mail: rmorris@bsu.edu.
Website: http://cms.bsu.edu/Academics/CollegesandDepartments/Biology.aspx.

Benedictine University, Graduate Programs, Program in Science Content and Process, Lisle, IL 60532-0900. Offers MS. *Application deadline:* For fall admission, 9/1 for domestic students; for winter admission, 12/1 for domestic students; for spring admission, 2/15 for domestic students. Application fee: $40. *Expenses: Tuition:* Part-time $590 per credit hour. *Unit head:* Dr. Allison Wilson, Director, 630-829-6520, E-mail: awilson@ben.edu. *Application contact:* Kari Gibbons, Associate Vice President, Enrollment Center, 630-829-6200, Fax: 630-829-6584, E-mail: kgibbons@ben.edu.

Binghamton University, State University of New York, Graduate School, School of Education, Program in Adolescence Education, Vestal, NY 13850. Offers biology education (MAT, MS Ed); chemistry education (MAT, MS Ed); earth science education (MAT, MS Ed); English education (MAT, MS Ed); French education (MAT, MS Ed); literacy education (MS Ed); mathematical sciences education (MAT, MS Ed); physics (MAT, MS Ed); social studies (MAT, MS Ed); Spanish education (MAT, MS Ed). *Accreditation:* Teacher Education Accreditation Council. Part-time and evening/weekend programs available. *Students:* 48 full-time (29 women), 5 part-time (3 women); includes 7 minority (2 Black or African American, non-Hispanic/Latino; 3 Asian, non-Hispanic/Latino; 2 Hispanic/Latino), 1 international. Average age 26. 37 applicants, 86% accepted, 21 enrolled. In 2013, 34 master's awarded. *Entrance requirements:* For master's, GRE General Test. Additional exam requirements/recommendations for international students: Required—TOEFL (minimum score 550 paper-based; 80 iBT). *Application deadline:* For fall admission, 2/1 priority date for domestic and international students; for spring admission, 10/15 priority date for domestic and international students. Applications are processed on a rolling basis. Application fee: $75. Electronic applications accepted. *Financial support:* In 2013–14, 7 students received support, including 1 fellowship with partial tuition reimbursement available (averaging $4,500 per year); career-related internships or fieldwork, Federal Work-Study, institutionally sponsored loans, scholarships/grants, health care benefits, tuition waivers (full), and unspecified assistantships also available. Financial award application deadline: 2/15; financial award applicants required to submit FAFSA. *Unit head:* Dr. S. G. Grant, Dean of School of Education, 607-777-7329, E-mail: sggrant@binghamton.edu. *Application contact:* Kishan Zuber, Recruiting and Admissions Coordinator, 607-777-2151, Fax: 607-777-2501, E-mail: kzuber@binghamton.edu.

Biola University, School of Arts and Sciences, La Mirada, CA 90639-0001. Offers Christian apologetics (MA); science and religion (MA). Part-time and evening/weekend programs available. Postbaccalaureate distance learning degree programs offered (minimal on-campus study). *Faculty:* 23. *Students:* 30 full-time (9 women), 242 part-time (39 women); includes 38 minority (14 Black or African American, non-Hispanic/Latino; 2 American Indian or Alaska Native, non-Hispanic/Latino; 19 Asian, non-Hispanic/Latino; 3 Two or more races, non-Hispanic/Latino), 17 international. In 2013, 52 master's awarded. *Entrance requirements:* For master's, minimum GPA of 3.0, bachelor's degree from accredited college or university (in science-related field for science and religion

program). Additional exam requirements/recommendations for international students: Required—TOEFL (minimum score 600 paper-based; 100 iBT). *Application deadline:* For fall admission, 7/1 for domestic students, 6/1 for international students; for spring admission, 12/1 for domestic students. Applications are processed on a rolling basis. Application fee: $55. Electronic applications accepted. *Financial support:* Scholarships/grants and unspecified assistantships available. Support available to part-time students. Financial award applicants required to submit FAFSA. *Faculty research:* Apologetics, science and religion, intelligent design. *Application contact:* Graduate Admissions Office, 562-903-4752, E-mail: graduate.admissions@biola.edu.
Website: http://www.biola.edu/academics/sas/.

Bloomsburg University of Pennsylvania, School of Graduate Studies, College of Education, Department of Early Childhood and Adolescent Education, Program in Middle Level Education Grades 4-8, Bloomsburg, PA 17815-1301. Offers language arts (M Ed); math (M Ed); science (M Ed); social studies (M Ed). *Accreditation:* NCATE. *Faculty:* 14 full-time (6 women), 3 part-time/adjunct (2 women). In 2013, 2 master's awarded. *Degree requirements:* For master's, thesis optional, student teaching. *Entrance requirements:* For master's, MAT, GRE, or PRAXIS, minimum QPA of 3.0, teaching certificate, U.S. citizenship, related undergraduate coursework, professional liability insurance, recent TB test. Additional exam requirements/recommendations for international students: Required—TOEFL (minimum score 550 paper-based). *Application deadline:* Applications are processed on a rolling basis. Application fee: $35 ($60 for international students). Electronic applications accepted. *Expenses:* Tuition, state resident: full-time $7956; part-time $442 per credit. Tuition, nonresident: full-time $11,934; part-time $663 per credit. *Required fees:* $95.50 per credit. $55 per semester. Tuition and fees vary according to course load. *Financial support:* Unspecified assistantships available. *Unit head:* Dr. Tegan Kotarski, College of Education Graduate Coordinator, 570-389-3883, Fax: 570-389-5049, E-mail: tkotarsk@bloomu.edu. *Application contact:* Jennifer Richard, Administrative Assistant, 570-389-4015, Fax: 570-389-3054, E-mail: jrichard@bloomu.edu.
Website: http://www.bloomu.edu/gradschool/middle-level-education.

Boise State University, College of Arts and Sciences, Department of Geosciences, Boise, ID 83725-0399. Offers earth science (M E Sci); geology (MS, PhD); geophysics (MS, PhD); hydrology (MS). Part-time programs available. *Degree requirements:* For master's, thesis. *Entrance requirements:* For master's, GRE General Test, BS in related field, minimum GPA of 3.0; for doctorate, GRE General Test. Electronic applications accepted. *Faculty research:* Seismology, geothermal aquifers, sedimentation, tectonics, seismo-acoustic propagation.

Boston College, Graduate School of Arts and Sciences, Department of Chemistry, Chestnut Hill, MA 02467-3800. Offers biochemistry (PhD); inorganic chemistry (PhD); organic chemistry (PhD); physical chemistry (PhD); science education (MST). *Students:* 97 full-time (44 women); includes 7 minority (6 Asian, non-Hispanic/Latino; 1 Hispanic/Latino), 36 international. 216 applicants, 34% accepted, 22 enrolled. In 2013, 3 master's, 20 doctorates awarded. *Degree requirements:* For doctorate, thesis/dissertation, qualifying exam. *Entrance requirements:* For doctorate, GRE General Test, GRE Subject Test. Additional exam requirements/recommendations for international students: Required—TOEFL (minimum score 600 paper-based; 100 iBT), IELTS (minimum score 7). *Application deadline:* For fall admission, 1/2 for domestic and international students. Application fee: $70. Electronic applications accepted. *Financial support:* In 2013–14, fellowships with full tuition reimbursements (averaging $27,500 per year), research assistantships with full tuition reimbursements (averaging $27,500 per year), teaching assistantships with full tuition reimbursements (averaging $27,500 per year) were awarded; Federal Work-Study, health care benefits, and unspecified assistantships also available. Support available to part-time students. Financial award application deadline: 3/1; financial award applicants required to submit FAFSA. *Unit head:* Dr. Amir Hoveyda, Chairperson, 617-552-1735, E-mail: amir.hoveyda@bc.edu. *Application contact:* Dr. Marc Snapper, Graduate Program Director, 617-552-8096, Fax: 617-552-0833, E-mail: marc.snapper@bc.edu.
Website: http://www.bc.edu/schools/cas/chemistry/.

Bowling Green State University, Graduate College, College of Arts and Sciences, Department of Physics and Astronomy, Bowling Green, OH 43403. Offers geophysics (MS); physics (MAT, MS). *Degree requirements:* For master's, thesis or alternative. *Entrance requirements:* For master's, GRE General Test. Additional exam requirements/recommendations for international students: Required—TOEFL. Electronic applications accepted. *Faculty research:* Computational physics, solid-state physics, materials science, theoretical physics.

Bridgewater State University, School of Graduate Studies, School of Arts and Sciences, Department of Biological Sciences, Bridgewater, MA 02325-0001. Offers MAT. Part-time and evening/weekend programs available. *Entrance requirements:* For master's, GRE General Test.

Bridgewater State University, School of Graduate Studies, School of Arts and Sciences, Department of Physics, Bridgewater, MA 02325-0001. Offers MAT. *Accreditation:* NCATE. Part-time and evening/weekend programs available. *Entrance requirements:* For master's, GRE General Test.

Bridgewater State University, School of Graduate Studies, School of Arts and Sciences, Program in Physical Sciences, Bridgewater, MA 02325-0001. Offers MAT. *Accreditation:* NCATE. Part-time and evening/weekend programs available. *Entrance requirements:* For master's, GRE General Test.

Brigham Young University, Graduate Studies, College of Life Sciences, Department of Biology, Provo, UT 84602. Offers biological science education (MS); biology (MS, PhD). *Faculty:* 22 full-time (2 women). *Students:* 44 full-time (14 women); includes 7 minority (1 American Indian or Alaska Native, non-Hispanic/Latino; 3 Asian, non-Hispanic/Latino; 3 Hispanic/Latino). Average age 29. 26 applicants, 54% accepted, 14 enrolled. In 2013, 3 master's, 2 doctorates awarded. *Degree requirements:* For master's, comprehensive exam, thesis, prospectus, defense of research, defense of thesis; for doctorate, comprehensive exam, thesis/dissertation, prospectus, defense of research, defense of dissertation. *Entrance requirements:* For master's and doctorate, GRE General Test, GRE Subject Test (biology), minimum GPA of 3.0 for last 60 credit hours of course work. Additional exam requirements/recommendations for international students: Required—TOEFL (minimum score 580 paper-based; 85 iBT). *Application deadline:* For fall admission, 1/15 for domestic and international students. Application fee: $50. Electronic applications accepted. *Expenses:* Tuition: Full-time $6130; part-time $340 per credit hour. Tuition and fees vary according to program and student's religious affiliation. *Financial support:* In 2013–14, 39 students received support, including 5 fellowships with full and partial tuition reimbursements available (averaging $14,000 per year), 35 research assistantships with full and partial tuition reimbursements available (averaging $6,214 per year), 44 teaching assistantships with full and partial tuition reimbursements available (averaging $6,244 per year); career-related internships or fieldwork, institutionally sponsored loans, scholarships/grants, health care benefits, tuition waivers (full and partial), and unspecified assistantships also available. Financial award application deadline: 3/1; financial award applicants required to submit FAFSA. *Faculty research:* Systematics, bioinformatics, ecology, evolution. *Total annual research expenditures:* $1.3 million. *Unit head:* Dr. Dennis K. Shiozawa, Chair, 801-422-4972,

Fax: 801-422-0090, E-mail: dennis_shiozawa@byu.edu. *Application contact:* Gentri Glaittli, Graduate Secretary, 801-422-7137, Fax: 801-422-0090, E-mail: biogradsec@byu.edu.
Website: http://biology.byu.edu/.

Brooklyn College of the City University of New York, Division of Graduate Studies, School of Education, Program in Adolescence Education and Special Subjects, Brooklyn, NY 11210-2889. Offers adolescence science education (MAT); art teacher (MA); biology teacher (MA); chemistry teacher (MA); earth science teacher (MAT); English teacher (MA); French teacher (MA); health and nutrition sciences: health teacher (MS Ed); mathematics teacher (MA); music education (CAS); music teacher (MA); physical education teacher (MS Ed); physics teacher (MA); social studies teacher (MA); Spanish teacher (MA). Part-time and evening/weekend programs available. *Degree requirements:* For master's, comprehensive exam (for some programs), thesis (for some programs). *Entrance requirements:* For master's, LAST, previous course work in education, resume, 2 letters of recommendation, essay. Additional exam requirements/recommendations for international students: Required—TOEFL (minimum score 500 paper-based; 61 iBT). Electronic applications accepted. *Faculty research:* Interdisciplinary education, semiotics, discourse analysis, autobiography, teacher identity.

Brooklyn College of the City University of New York, Division of Graduate Studies, School of Education, Program in Childhood Education, Brooklyn, NY 11210-2889. Offers bilingual education (MS Ed); liberal arts (MS Ed); mathematics (MS Ed); science/environmental education (MS Ed). Part-time and evening/weekend programs available. *Entrance requirements:* For master's, LAST, interview, previous course work in education, writing sample, resume, 2 letters of recommendation. Additional exam requirements/recommendations for international students: Required—TOEFL (minimum score 500 paper-based; 61 iBT). Electronic applications accepted. *Faculty research:* Emotional intelligence, multiculturalism, arts immersion, the Holocaust.

Brooklyn College of the City University of New York, Division of Graduate Studies, School of Education, Program in Middle Childhood Education (Science), Brooklyn, NY 11210-2889. Offers biology (MA); chemistry (MA); earth science (MA); general science (MA); physics (MA). Part-time and evening/weekend programs available. *Entrance requirements:* For master's, LAST, interview, previous course work in education and mathematics, resume, 2 letters of recommendation, essay. Additional exam requirements/recommendations for international students: Required—TOEFL (minimum score 500 paper-based; 61 iBT). Electronic applications accepted. *Faculty research:* Geometric thinking, mastery of basic facts, problem-solving strategies, history of mathematics.

Brown University, Graduate School, Department of Education, Program in Teaching, Providence, RI 02912. Offers elementary education (MAT); English (MAT); history/social studies (MAT); science (MAT); secondary education (MAT). *Degree requirements:* For master's, student teaching, portfolio. *Entrance requirements:* For master's, GRE General Test, transcript, personal statement, 3 letters of recommendation, interview, writing sample (English applicants only). Additional exam requirements/recommendations for international students: Required—TOEFL (minimum score 577 paper-based). Electronic applications accepted. *Faculty research:* Literacy, English language learners, diversity, special education, biodiversity.

Buffalo State College, State University of New York, The Graduate School, Faculty of Natural and Social Sciences, Department of Biology, Buffalo, NY 14222-1095. Offers biology (MA); secondary education (MS Ed), including biology. Evening/weekend programs available. *Degree requirements:* For master's, thesis (for some programs), project. *Entrance requirements:* For master's, minimum GPA of 2.75. Additional exam requirements/recommendations for international students: Required—TOEFL (minimum score 550 paper-based).

Buffalo State College, State University of New York, The Graduate School, Faculty of Natural and Social Sciences, Department of Chemistry, Buffalo, NY 14222-1095. Offers chemistry (MA); secondary education (MS Ed), including chemistry. Part-time and evening/weekend programs available. *Degree requirements:* For master's, thesis (for some programs), project. *Entrance requirements:* For master's, minimum GPA of 2.6, New York teaching certificate (MS Ed). Additional exam requirements/recommendations for international students: Required—TOEFL (minimum score 550 paper-based).

Buffalo State College, State University of New York, The Graduate School, Faculty of Natural and Social Sciences, Department of Earth Science and Science Education, Buffalo, NY 14222-1095. Offers secondary education (MS Ed), including geoscience, science. *Accreditation:* NCATE. Part-time and evening/weekend programs available. *Degree requirements:* For master's, thesis or alternative, project. *Entrance requirements:* For master's, 36 undergraduate hours in mathematics and science. Additional exam requirements/recommendations for international students: Required—TOEFL (minimum score 550 paper-based).

Buffalo State College, State University of New York, The Graduate School, Faculty of Natural and Social Sciences, Department of Physics, Buffalo, NY 14222-1095. Offers secondary education physics (MS Ed). *Degree requirements:* For master's, project. *Entrance requirements:* For master's, minimum GPA of 2.5, New York State teaching certification. Additional exam requirements/recommendations for international students: Required—TOEFL (minimum score 550 paper-based).

California Baptist University, Program in Education, Riverside, CA 92504-3206. Offers educational leadership for faith-based institutions (MS); educational leadership for public institutions (MS); educational technology (MS); instructional computer applications (MS); international education (MS); leadership and adult learning (MS); leadership and organizational studies (MS); reading (MS); school counseling (MS); school psychology (MS); science education (MS); special education in mild/moderate disabilities (MS); special education in moderate/severe disabilities (MS); teaching (MS); teaching and learning (MS); TESOL (teachers of English to speakers of other languages) (MS). Part-time and evening/weekend programs available. Postbaccalaureate distance learning degree programs offered (minimal on-campus study). *Faculty:* 18 full-time (9 women), 8 part-time/adjunct (5 women). *Students:* 158 full-time (127 women), 228 part-time (179 women); includes 159 minority (27 Black or African American, non-Hispanic/Latino; 4 American Indian or Alaska Native, non-Hispanic/Latino; 13 Asian, non-Hispanic/Latino; 107 Hispanic/Latino; 1 Native Hawaiian or other Pacific Islander, non-Hispanic/Latino; 7 Two or more races, non-Hispanic/Latino), 2 international. Average age 33. 298 applicants, 74% accepted, 113 enrolled. In 2013, 70 master's awarded. *Degree requirements:* For master's, comprehensive exam, project, or thesis. *Entrance requirements:* For master's, minimum undergraduate GPA of 3.0; 18 semester units of prerequisite course work in education; three recommendations; 500-word essay; interview. Additional exam requirements/recommendations for international students: Required—TOEFL (minimum score 80 iBT). *Application deadline:* For fall admission, 8/1 priority date for domestic students, 7/1 for international students; for spring admission, 12/1 priority date for domestic students, 11/1 for international students. Applications are processed on a rolling basis. Application fee: $45. Electronic applications accepted. *Expenses:* Contact institution. *Financial support:* Institutionally sponsored loans available. Financial award applicants required to submit CSS PROFILE or FAFSA. *Faculty research:* Leadership development, complexity theory, faith and

learning, special education, social and philosophical contexts of education. *Unit head:* Dr. John Shoup, Dean, School of Education, 951-343-4205, Fax: 951-343-4516, E-mail: jshoup@calbaptist.edu. *Application contact:* Dr. Kathryn Norwood, Director, Master of Science Program in Education, 951-343-4760, E-mail: knorwood@calbaptist.edu. Website: http://www.calbaptist.edu/mastersined/.

California State University, Bakersfield, Division of Graduate Studies, School of Natural Sciences, Mathematics, and Engineering, Program in Geological Sciences, Bakersfield, CA 93311. Offers geological sciences (MS); hydrogeology (MS); petroleum geology (MS); science education (MS). Part-time and evening/weekend programs available. *Degree requirements:* For master's, thesis. *Entrance requirements:* For master's, GRE General Test, BS in geology. *Application deadline:* Applications are processed on a rolling basis. Application fee: $55. *Financial support:* Teaching assistantships, career-related internships or fieldwork, institutionally sponsored loans, and scholarships/grants available. *Unit head:* Dr. Dirk Baron, Department Chair, 661-664-3044, Fax: 661-664-2040, E-mail: dbaron@csub.edu. *Application contact:* Debbie Blowers, Assistant Director of Admissions, 661-664-3381, E-mail: dblowers@csub.edu.

California State University, Dominguez Hills, College of Education, Division of Graduate Education, Program in Curriculum and Instruction: Science Education, Carson, CA 90747-0001. Offers MA. Part-time and evening/weekend programs available. *Faculty:* 3 full-time (2 women). *Students:* 2 part-time (1 woman); includes 1 minority (Hispanic/Latino). Average age 29. In 2013, 1 master's awarded. *Degree requirements:* For master's, comprehensive exam. *Entrance requirements:* For master's, minimum GPA of 2.75. Additional exam requirements/recommendations for international students: Required—TOEFL. *Application deadline:* For fall admission, 6/1 for domestic students. Applications are processed on a rolling basis. Application fee: $55. *Expenses:* Tuition, state resident: full-time $6738. Tuition, nonresident: full-time $13,434. *Required fees:* $622. *Unit head:* Dr. Leena Furtado, Professor, 310-243-2743, E-mail: lfurtado@csudh.edu. *Application contact:* Admissions Office, 310-243-3530. Website: http://www4.csudh.edu/coe/programs/grad-prgs/curriculum/index.

California State University, Fullerton, Graduate Studies, College of Natural Science and Mathematics, Program in Science Education, Fullerton, CA 92834-9480. Offers teaching science (MAT). Part-time programs available. *Students:* 1. Average age 35. 1 applicant, 100% accepted. In 2013, 4 master's awarded. *Degree requirements:* For master's, project or thesis. *Entrance requirements:* For master's, diagnostic exam, minimum GPA of 2.5 in last 60 units of course work, teaching credential, bachelor's degree in science. Application fee: $55. *Financial support:* Teaching assistantships, career-related internships or fieldwork, Federal Work-Study, institutionally sponsored loans, and scholarships/grants available. Support available to part-time students. Financial award application deadline: 3/1; financial award applicants required to submit FAFSA. *Faculty research:* Earth and space science education. *Unit head:* Monica Azimioara, Director, 657-278-2817. *Application contact:* Admissions/Applications, 657-278-2731.

California State University, Long Beach, Graduate Studies, College of Natural Sciences and Mathematics, Department of Science Education, Long Beach, CA 90840. Offers MS.

California State University, Northridge, Graduate Studies, College of Education, Department of Secondary Education, Northridge, CA 91330. Offers educational technology (MA); English education (MA); mathematics education (MA); secondary science education (MA); teaching and learning (MA). *Accreditation:* NCATE. Part-time programs available. *Degree requirements:* For master's, thesis optional. *Entrance requirements:* For master's, GRE General Test or minimum GPA of 3.0. Additional exam requirements/recommendations for international students: Required—TOEFL.

California State University, San Bernardino, Graduate Studies, College of Education, Program in Teaching of Science, San Bernardino, CA 92407-2397. Offers MA. *Accreditation:* NCATE. *Students:* 1 (woman) full-time, 19 part-time (14 women); includes 9 minority (all Hispanic/Latino), 1 international. Average age 34. 13 applicants, 100% accepted, 12 enrolled. *Entrance requirements:* For master's, minimum GPA of 3.0. Application fee: $55. *Unit head:* Dr. Herbert Brunkhorst, Chair, 909-537-5613, Fax: 909-537-7119, E-mail: hkbrunkh@csusb.edu. *Application contact:* Dr. Jeffrey Thompson, Dean of Graduate Studies, 909-537-5058, E-mail: jthompso@csusb.edu.

Cambridge College, School of Education, Cambridge, MA 02138-5304. Offers autism specialist (M Ed); autism/behavior analyst (M Ed); behavior analyst (Post-Master's Certificate); behavioral management (M Ed); early childhood teacher (M Ed); education specialist in curriculum and instruction (CAGS); educational leadership (Ed D); elementary teacher (M Ed); English as a second language (M Ed, Certificate); general science (M Ed); health education (Post-Master's Certificate); health/family and consumer sciences (M Ed); history (M Ed); individualized (M Ed); information technology literacy (M Ed); instructional technology (M Ed); interdisciplinary studies (M Ed); library teacher (M Ed); literacy education (M Ed); mathematics (M Ed); mathematics specialist (Certificate); middle school mathematics and science (M Ed); school administration (M Ed, CAGS); school guidance counselor (M Ed); school nurse education (M Ed); school social worker/school adjustment counselor (M Ed); special education administrator (CAGS); special education/moderate disabilities (M Ed); teaching skills and methodologies (M Ed). Part-time and evening/weekend programs available. Postbaccalaureate distance learning degree programs offered (minimal on-campus study). *Degree requirements:* For master's, thesis, internship/practicum (licensure program only); for doctorate, thesis/dissertation; for other advanced degree, thesis. *Entrance requirements:* For master's, interview, resume, documentation of licensure, 2 professional references; for doctorate, official transcripts, interview, resume, documentation of licensure (if any), written personal statement/essay, portfolio of scholarly and professional work, qualifying assessment, 2 professional references, health insurance, immunizations form; for other advanced degree, official transcripts, interview, resume, documentation of licensure (if any), written personal statement/essay, 2 professional references, health insurance, immunizations form. Additional exam requirements/recommendations for international students: Required—TOEFL (minimum score 550 paper-based; 79 iBT), Michigan English Language Assessment Battery (minimum score 85); Recommended—IELTS (minimum score 6). Electronic applications accepted. *Expenses:* Contact institution. *Faculty research:* Adult education, accelerated learning, mathematics education, brain compatible learning, special education and law.

Caribbean University, Graduate School, Bayamón, PR 00960-0493. Offers administration and supervision (MA Ed); criminal justice (MA); curriculum and instruction (MA Ed, PhD), including elementary education (MA Ed), English education (MA Ed), history education (MA Ed), mathematics education (MA Ed), primary education (MA Ed), science education (MA Ed), Spanish education (MA Ed); educational technology in instructional systems (MA Ed); gerontology (MSN); human resources (MBA); museology, archiving and art history (MA Ed); neonatal pediatrics (MSN); physical education (MA Ed); special education (MA Ed). *Entrance requirements:* For master's, interview, minimum GPA of 2.5.

Carthage College, Division of Teacher Education, Kenosha, WI 53140. Offers classroom guidance and counseling (M Ed); creative arts (M Ed); gifted and talented children (M Ed); language arts (M Ed); modern language (M Ed); natural sciences (M Ed); reading (M Ed, Certificate); social sciences (M Ed); teacher leadership (M Ed). Part-time and evening/weekend programs available. *Degree requirements:* For master's, thesis optional. *Entrance requirements:* For master's, MAT, minimum B average, letters of reference.

Central Connecticut State University, School of Graduate Studies, School of Arts and Sciences, Department of Biology, New Britain, CT 06050-4010. Offers biological sciences (MA, MS), including anesthesia (MS), ecology and environmental sciences (MA), general biology (MA), health sciences (MS), professional education (MS); biology (Certificate). Part-time and evening/weekend programs available. *Faculty:* 4 full-time (0 women), 2 part-time/adjunct (both women). *Students:* 130 full-time (85 women), 34 part-time (23 women); includes 25 minority (9 Black or African American, non-Hispanic/Latino; 11 Asian, non-Hispanic/Latino; 3 Hispanic/Latino; 2 Two or more races, non-Hispanic/Latino), 1 international. Average age 30. 30 applicants, 67% accepted, 11 enrolled. In 2013, 46 master's, 10 other advanced degrees awarded. *Degree requirements:* For master's, comprehensive exam, thesis or alternative; for Certificate, qualifying exam. *Entrance requirements:* For master's and Certificate, minimum undergraduate GPA of 2.7, essay, letters of recommendation. Additional exam requirements/recommendations for international students: Required—TOEFL (minimum score 550 paper-based; 79 iBT). *Application deadline:* For fall admission, 6/1 for domestic students, 5/1 for international students; for spring admission, 11/1 for domestic and international students. Applications are processed on a rolling basis. Application fee: $50. Electronic applications accepted. Part-time tuition and fees vary according to degree level. *Financial support:* In 2013–14, 2 students received support, including 2 research assistantships; career-related internships or fieldwork, Federal Work-Study, scholarships/grants, and unspecified assistantships also available. Support available to part-time students. Financial award application deadline: 3/1; financial award applicants required to submit FAFSA. *Faculty research:* Environmental science, anesthesia, health sciences, zoology, animal behavior. *Unit head:* Dr. Douglas Carter, Chair, 860-832-2645, E-mail: carterd@ccsu.edu. *Application contact:* Patricia Gardner, Associate Director of Graduate Studies, 860-832-2350, Fax: 860-832-2362, E-mail: graduateadmissions@ccsu.edu.
Website: http://www.ccsu.edu/page.cfm?p=14516.

Central Connecticut State University, School of Graduate Studies, School of Arts and Sciences, Department of Physics and Earth Science, New Britain, CT 06050-4010. Offers natural sciences (MS); science education (Certificate). Part-time and evening/weekend programs available. *Faculty:* 2 full-time (1 woman). *Students:* 2 full-time (0 women), 5 part-time (4 women). Average age 30. 3 applicants, 100% accepted, 3 enrolled. In 2013, 4 master's awarded. *Degree requirements:* For master's, comprehensive exam, thesis or alternative; for Certificate, qualifying exam. *Entrance requirements:* For master's, minimum undergraduate GPA of 2.7. Additional exam requirements/recommendations for international students: Required—TOEFL (minimum score 550 paper-based; 79 iBT). *Application deadline:* For fall admission, 6/1 for domestic students, 5/1 for international students; for spring admission, 11/1 for domestic and international students. Applications are processed on a rolling basis. Application fee: $50. Electronic applications accepted. Part-time tuition and fees vary according to degree level. *Financial support:* In 2013–14, 1 student received support. Career-related internships or fieldwork, Federal Work-Study, scholarships/grants, and unspecified assistantships available. Support available to part-time students. Financial award application deadline: 3/1; financial award applicants required to submit FAFSA. *Faculty research:* Elementary/secondary science education, particle and solid states, weather patterns, planetary studies. *Unit head:* Dr. Mark Evans, Chair, 860-832-2930, E-mail: evansmaa@ccsu.edu. *Application contact:* Patricia Gardner, Associate Director of Graduate Studies, 860-832-2350, Fax: 860-832-2362, E-mail: graduateadmissions@ccsu.edu.
Website: http://www.physics.ccsu.edu/.

Central Michigan University, College of Graduate Studies, College of Science and Technology, Department of Chemistry, Mount Pleasant, MI 48859. Offers chemistry (MS); teaching chemistry (MA), including teaching college chemistry, teaching high school chemistry. Part-time programs available. *Degree requirements:* For master's, comprehensive exam, thesis or alternative. *Entrance requirements:* For master's, GRE. Electronic applications accepted. *Faculty research:* Analytical and organic-inorganic chemistry, biochemistry, catalysis, dendrimer and polymer studies, nanotechnology.

Chaminade University of Honolulu, Graduate Services, Program in Education, Honolulu, HI 96816-1578. Offers child development (M Ed); early childhood education (M Ed); educational leadership (M Ed); elementary education (MAT); instructional leadership (M Ed); Montessori education (M Ed); secondary education (MAT), including English, math, science, social studies; special education (MAT). Part-time and evening/weekend programs available. Postbaccalaureate distance learning degree programs offered (minimal on-campus study). *Degree requirements:* For master's, thesis or alternative. *Entrance requirements:* For master's, PRAXIS (for MAT only), minimum GPA of 2.75, 3 letters of recommendation. Additional exam requirements/recommendations for international students: Required—TOEFL (minimum score 550 paper-based). Electronic applications accepted. *Faculty research:* Peace and curriculum education.

Chatham University, Program in Education, Pittsburgh, PA 15232-2826. Offers early childhood education (MAT); elementary education (MAT); environmental education (K-12) (MAT); secondary art (MAT); secondary biology education (MAT); secondary chemistry education (MAT); secondary English education (MAT); secondary math education (MAT); secondary physics education (MAT); secondary social studies education (MAT); special education (MAT). *Faculty:* 1 (woman) full-time, 5 part-time/adjunct (4 women). *Students:* 19 full-time (15 women), 4 part-time (all women); includes 2 minority (1 Black or African American, non-Hispanic/Latino; 1 Asian, non-Hispanic/Latino), 2 international. Average age 28. 22 applicants, 73% accepted, 6 enrolled. In 2013, 20 master's awarded. *Degree requirements:* For master's, thesis, teaching experience. *Entrance requirements:* For master's, minimum GPA of 3.0, sample of written work, recommendation letters. Additional exam requirements/recommendations for international students: Required—TOEFL (minimum score 600 paper-based; 100 iBT), IELTS (minimum score 7), TWE. *Application deadline:* For fall admission, 4/1 priority date for domestic and international students; for spring admission, 11/1 priority date for domestic students, 10/1 priority date for international students. Applications are processed on a rolling basis. Application fee: $45. Electronic applications accepted. Application fee is waived when completed online. *Expenses: Tuition:* Full-time $14,886; part-time $827 per credit hour. One-time fee: $396 full-time. *Financial support:* Career-related internships or fieldwork available. Financial award applicants required to submit FAFSA. *Faculty research:* Gifted education, environmental education, technology in education, writing as learning, class size and achievement. *Unit head:* Dr. Edward Donovan, Director of Education Programs, 412-365-2773, E-mail: edonovan@chatham.edu. *Application contact:* Katie Noel, Assistant Director of Graduate Admission, 412-365-2758, Fax: 412-365-1609, E-mail: gradadmissions@chatham.edu.
Website: http://www.chatham.edu/mat.

Christopher Newport University, Graduate Studies, Department of Teacher Preparation, Newport News, VA 23606-3072. Offers art (PK-12) (MAT); biology (6-12) (MAT); chemistry (6-12) (MAT); computer science (6-12) (MAT); elementary (PK-6)

(MAT); English (6-12) (MAT); English as second language (PK-12) (MAT); French (PK-12) (MAT); history and social science (6-12) (MAT); mathematics (6-12) (MAT); music (PK-12) (MAT), including choral, instrumental; physics (6-12) (MAT); Spanish (PK-12) (MAT). Part-time programs available. *Faculty:* 15 full-time (7 women), 14 part-time/adjunct (13 women). *Students:* 74 full-time (64 women), 2 part-time (both women); includes 6 minority (4 Hispanic/Latino; 2 Two or more races, non-Hispanic/Latino). Average age 23. 90 applicants, 100% accepted, 67 enrolled. In 2013, 96 master's awarded. *Degree requirements:* For master's, comprehensive exam, thesis or alternative. *Entrance requirements:* For master's, PRAXIS I, minimum GPA of 3.0. Additional exam requirements/recommendations for international students: Required—TOEFL (minimum score 580 paper-based; 92 iBT). *Application deadline:* For fall admission, 4/1 for international students; for spring admission, 10/15 for domestic students, 10/1 for international students; for summer admission, 1/15 for domestic students, 3/1 for international students. Applications are processed on a rolling basis. Application fee: $50. Electronic applications accepted. *Expenses: Tuition, area resident:* Part-time $498 per credit hour. Tuition, state resident: part-time $498 per credit hour. Tuition, nonresident: part-time $899 per credit hour. *Financial support:* In 2013–14, 3 students received support, including 3 research assistantships with full tuition reimbursements available (averaging $2,000 per year); career-related internships or fieldwork, Federal Work-Study, and unspecified assistantships also available. Financial award application deadline: 3/1; financial award applicants required to submit FAFSA. *Faculty research:* Early literacy development, instructional innovations, professional teaching standards, multicultural issues, aesthetic education. *Total annual research expenditures:* $24,000. *Unit head:* Dr. Marsha Sprague, Director, 757-594-7388, Fax: 757-594-7803, E-mail: msprague@cnu.edu. *Application contact:* Lyn Sawyer, Associate Director, Graduate Admissions, 757-594-7544, Fax: 757-594-7649, E-mail: gradstdy@cnu.edu.

The Citadel, The Military College of South Carolina, Citadel Graduate College, School of Education, Program in Secondary Education, Charleston, SC 29409. Offers biology (MAT); English language arts (MAT); mathematics (MAT); mathematics education (MAE); physical education (MAT); social studies (MAT). *Accreditation:* NCATE. Part-time and evening/weekend programs available. *Faculty:* 10 full-time (6 women), 8 part-time/adjunct (3 women). *Students:* 14 full-time (9 women), 56 part-time (31 women); includes 9 minority (8 Black or African American, non-Hispanic/Latino; 1 Hispanic/Latino). Average age 30. In 2013, 24 master's awarded. *Degree requirements:* For master's, comprehensive exam, internship. *Entrance requirements:* For master's, GRE (minimum score 290; 900 on old scoring system) or MAT (minimum score 396), minimum undergraduate GPA of 2.5. Additional exam requirements/recommendations for international students: Required—TOEFL (minimum score 550 paper-based). *Application deadline:* Applications are processed on a rolling basis. Application fee: $30. Electronic applications accepted. *Expenses: Tuition, area resident:* Part-time $525 per credit hour. Tuition, state resident: part-time $525 per credit hour. Tuition, nonresident: part-time $865 per credit hour. *Financial support:* Career-related internships or fieldwork, health care benefits, and unspecified assistantships available. Support available to part-time students. Financial award application deadline: 7/1; financial award applicants required to submit FAFSA. *Unit head:* Dr. Kathryn A. Richardson-Jones, Coordinator, 843-953-3163, Fax: 843-953-7258, E-mail: kathryn.jones@citadel.edu. *Application contact:* Dr. Robert H. McNamara, Associate Provost, The Citadel Graduate College, 843-953-5089, Fax: 843-953-7630, E-mail: cgc@citadel.edu.
Website: http://www.citadel.edu/education/teacher-education/mat-master-of-arts-in-teaching.html.

City College of the City University of New York, Graduate School, School of Education, Department of Secondary Education, Program in Science Education, New York, NY 10031-9198. Offers MA. *Accreditation:* NCATE. *Entrance requirements:* For master's, Liberal Arts and Sciences Test (LAST), Content Specialty Test (CST). Additional exam requirements/recommendations for international students: Required—TOEFL.

Clarion University of Pennsylvania, Office of Transfer, Adult and Graduate Admissions, Master of Education Program, Clarion, PA 16214. Offers curriculum and instruction (M Ed); early childhood (M Ed); math education (M Ed); reading (M Ed); science education (M Ed); special education (M Ed); technology (M Ed). *Accreditation:* NCATE. Part-time programs available. Postbaccalaureate distance learning degree programs offered (no on-campus study). *Faculty:* 17 full-time (10 women). *Students:* 231 full-time (191 women), 535 part-time (448 women); includes 39 minority (12 Black or African American, non-Hispanic/Latino; 8 Asian, non-Hispanic/Latino; 11 Hispanic/Latino; 1 Native Hawaiian or other Pacific Islander, non-Hispanic/Latino; 7 Two or more races, non-Hispanic/Latino). Average age 31. 28 applicants, 75% accepted, 18 enrolled. In 2013, 99 master's awarded. *Degree requirements:* For master's, comprehensive exam, thesis, or portfolio. *Entrance requirements:* For master's, minimum QPA of 3.0. Additional exam requirements/recommendations for international students: Required—TOEFL (minimum score 550 paper-based; 80 iBT), IELTS (minimum score 7). *Application deadline:* For fall admission, 8/1 for domestic students, 4/15 for international students; for spring admission, 8/1 for domestic students, 9/15 for international students. Applications are processed on a rolling basis. Application fee: $40. Electronic applications accepted. *Expenses:* Tuition, state resident: part-time $442 per credit. Tuition, nonresident: part-time $451 per credit. *Required fees:* $142.40 per semester. One-time fee: $150 part-time. *Financial support:* In 2013–14, 8 research assistantships with full and partial tuition reimbursements (averaging $9,420 per year) were awarded; career-related internships or fieldwork also available. Support available to part-time students. Financial award application deadline: 3/1. *Unit head:* Ray Puller, Interim Dean, 814-393-2146, Fax: 514-393-2446, E-mail: rpuller@clarion.edu. *Application contact:* Susan Staub, Assistant Director, Graduate Programs, 814-393-2337, Fax: 814-393-2722, E-mail: gradstudies@clarion.edu.
Website: http://www.clarion.edu/25887/.

Clark Atlanta University, School of Education, Department of Curriculum, Atlanta, GA 30314. Offers special education general curriculum (MA); teaching math and science (MAT). Part-time programs available. *Faculty:* 2 full-time (1 woman), 1 (woman) part-time/adjunct. *Students:* 9 full-time (8 women), 3 part-time (1 woman); includes 11 minority (all Black or African American, non-Hispanic/Latino). Average age 28. 8 applicants, 88% accepted, 7 enrolled. In 2013, 4 master's awarded. *Degree requirements:* For master's, one foreign language, comprehensive exam. *Entrance requirements:* For master's, GRE General Test, minimum undergraduate GPA of 2.6. Additional exam requirements/recommendations for international students: Required—TOEFL (minimum score 500 paper-based; 61 iBT). *Application deadline:* For fall admission, 4/1 for domestic and international students; for spring admission, 11/1 for domestic and international students. Applications are processed on a rolling basis. Application fee: $40 ($55 for international students). *Expenses: Tuition:* Full-time $14,616; part-time $812 per credit hour. *Required fees:* $706; $353 per semester. *Financial support:* Career-related internships or fieldwork, Federal Work-Study, scholarships/grants, and unspecified assistantships available. Support available to part-time students. Financial award application deadline: 4/30; financial award applicants required to submit FAFSA. *Unit head:* Dr. Doris Terrell, Chairperson, 404-880-6336, E-mail: dterrell@cau.edu. *Application contact:* Michelle Clark-Davis, Graduate Program Admissions, 404-880-6605, E-mail: cauadmissions@cau.edu.
Website: http://www.cau.edu/School_of_Education_curriculum_dept.aspx.

Clemson University, Graduate School, College of Health, Education, and Human Development, Eugene T. Moore School of Education, Program in Secondary Education: Math and Science, Clemson, SC 29634. Offers MAT. *Accreditation:* NCATE. *Students:* 18 full-time (13 women); includes 1 minority (Black or African American, non-Hispanic/Latino). Average age 27. 4 applicants, 50% accepted, 1 enrolled. In 2013, 11 master's awarded. *Degree requirements:* For master's, digital portfolio. *Entrance requirements:* For master's, PRAXIS II. Additional exam requirements/recommendations for international students: Required—TOEFL; Recommended—IELTS. *Application deadline:* For fall admission, 4/1 for domestic students. Applications are processed on a rolling basis. Application fee: $70 ($80 for international students). Electronic applications accepted. *Expenses:* Contact institution. *Financial support:* In 2013–14, 4 students received support, including 12 fellowships with partial tuition reimbursements available (averaging $3,599 per year); institutionally sponsored loans, scholarships/grants, health care benefits, and unspecified assistantships also available. Financial award application deadline: 6/1; financial award applicants required to submit FAFSA. *Faculty research:* Science education, math education. *Unit head:* Dr. Michael J. Padilla, Director/Associate Dean, 864-656-4444, Fax: 864-656-0311, E-mail: padilla@clemson.edu. *Application contact:* Dr. David Fleming, Graduate Coordinator, 864-656-1881, Fax: 864-656-0311, E-mail: dflemin@clemson.edu.
Website: http://www.clemson.edu/hehd/departments/education/academics/graduate/MAT/secondary.html.

Clemson University, Graduate School, College of Health, Education, and Human Development, Eugene T. Moore School of Education, Program in Teaching and Learning, Clemson, SC 29634. Offers elementary education (M Ed); English education (M Ed); mathematics education (M Ed); science education (M Ed); social studies education (M Ed). *Students:* 6 full-time (5 women), 8 part-time (7 women), 3 international. Average age 28. 6 applicants, 100% accepted, 4 enrolled. In 2013, 9 master's awarded. *Entrance requirements:* For master's, GRE, baccalaureate degree from regionally-accredited institution, official transcripts, copy of valid teaching certificate, two letters of recommendation. *Financial support:* In 2013–14, 1 teaching assistantship (averaging $6,812 per year) was awarded. *Unit head:* Dr. Michael J. Padilla, Director/Associate Dean, 864-656-4444, Fax: 864-656-0311, E-mail: padilla@clemson.edu. *Application contact:* Dr. David Fleming, Graduate Programs Coordinator, 864-656-1881, Fax: 864-656-0311, E-mail: dflemin@clemson.edu.
Website: http://www.grad.clemson.edu/programs/Teaching-Learning/.

Cleveland State University, College of Graduate Studies, College of Education and Human Services, Department of Teacher Education, Cleveland, OH 44115. Offers art education (M Ed); early childhood education (M Ed); foreign language education (M Ed); mathematics and science education (M Ed); middle childhood education (M Ed); special education (M Ed), including mild/moderate disabilities, moderate/intensive disabilities; teaching English to speakers of other languages (M Ed). Part-time and evening/weekend programs available. *Faculty:* 20 full-time (12 women), 26 part-time/adjunct (20 women). *Students:* 108 full-time (78 women), 311 part-time (252 women); includes 103 minority (80 Black or African American, non-Hispanic/Latino; 2 Asian, non-Hispanic/Latino; 10 Hispanic/Latino; 1 Native Hawaiian or other Pacific Islander, non-Hispanic/Latino; 10 Two or more races, non-Hispanic/Latino), 52 international. Average age 32. 177 applicants, 55% accepted, 68 enrolled. In 2013, 192 master's awarded. *Degree requirements:* For master's, comprehensive exam (for some programs), thesis or alternative. *Entrance requirements:* For master's, GRE General Test or MAT, minimum GPA of 2.75. Additional exam requirements/recommendations for international students: Required—TOEFL (minimum score 525 paper-based), IELTS (minimum score 6). *Application deadline:* For fall admission, 7/15 priority date for domestic students. Applications are processed on a rolling basis. Application fee: $30. *Expenses:* Tuition, state resident: full-time $8335; part-time $521 per credit hour. Tuition, nonresident: full-time $15,670; part-time $979 per credit hour. *Required fees:* $50; $25 per semester. *Financial support:* In 2013–14, 12 research assistantships with full tuition reimbursements (averaging $3,480 per year) were awarded; tuition waivers (partial) and unspecified assistantships also available. *Faculty research:* Early literacy, professional development in reading, reading recovery, dual language, induction programs. *Total annual research expenditures:* $6.2 million. *Unit head:* Dr. Clifford T. Bennett, Chairperson, 216-523-7105, Fax: 216-687-5379, E-mail: c.t.bennett@csuohio.edu. *Application contact:* Deborah L. Brown, Interim Assistant Director, Graduate Admissions, 216-523-7572, E-mail: d.l.brown@csuohio.edu.
Website: http://www.csuohio.edu/cehs/departments/TE/te_dept.html.

The College at Brockport, State University of New York, School of Education and Human Services, Department of Education and Human Development, Program in Adolescence Education, Brockport, NY 14420-2997. Offers adolescence biology education (MS Ed); adolescence chemistry education (MS Ed); adolescence earth science education (MS Ed); adolescence English education (MS Ed); adolescence mathematics education (MS Ed); adolescence physics education (MS Ed); adolescence social studies education (MS Ed). *Accreditation:* NCATE. Part-time programs available. *Students:* 13 full-time (7 women), 47 part-time (28 women); includes 3 minority (1 Black or African American, non-Hispanic/Latino; 1 American Indian or Alaska Native, non-Hispanic/Latino; 1 Asian, non-Hispanic/Latino). 26 applicants, 88% accepted, 14 enrolled. In 2013, 27 master's awarded. *Degree requirements:* For master's, thesis or alternative. *Entrance requirements:* For master's, minimum GPA of 3.0, letters of recommendation; statement of objectives, current resume. Additional exam requirements/recommendations for international students: Required—TOEFL (minimum score 550 paper-based; 79 iBT), IELTS (minimum score 6.5). *Application deadline:* For fall admission, 3/15 priority date for domestic and international students; for spring admission, 10/15 priority date for domestic and international students; for summer admission, 3/15 priority date for domestic students, 3/13 priority date for international students. Application fee: $80. Electronic applications accepted. *Expenses:* Tuition, state resident: full-time $9870. Tuition, nonresident: full-time $18,350. *Required fees:* $1848. *Financial support:* Federal Work-Study, scholarships/grants, and unspecified assistantships available. Support available to part-time students. Financial award application deadline: 3/15; financial award applicants required to submit FAFSA. *Unit head:* Dr. Don Halquist, Chairperson, 585-395-5550, Fax: 585-395-2172, E-mail: dhalquis@brockport.edu. *Application contact:* Michael Harrison, Coordinator of Certification and Graduate Advisement, 585-395-2326, Fax: 585-395-2172, E-mail: mharriso@brockport.edu.
Website: http://www.brockport.edu/ehd/.

The College at Brockport, State University of New York, School of Education and Human Services, Department of Education and Human Development, Program in Adolescence Inclusive Generalist Education, Brockport, NY 14420-2997. Offers English (MS Ed); mathematics (MS Ed); science (MS Ed); social studies (MS Ed). *Students:* 30 full-time (18 women), 24 part-time (17 women); includes 6 minority (3 Black or African American, non-Hispanic/Latino; 2 Hispanic/Latino; 1 Two or more races, non-Hispanic/Latino). 16 applicants, 75% accepted, 8 enrolled. In 2013, 15 master's awarded. *Degree requirements:* For master's, thesis or alternative. *Entrance requirements:* For master's,

minimum GPA of 3.0, letters of recommendation, statement of objectives, academic major (or equivalent) in program discipline; current resume. Additional exam requirements/recommendations for international students: Required—TOEFL (minimum score 550 paper-based; 79 iBT), IELTS (minimum score 6.5). *Application deadline:* For fall admission, 3/15 priority date for domestic and international students; for spring admission, 10/15 priority date for domestic and international students; for summer admission, 3/15 for domestic and international students. Application fee: $80. Electronic applications accepted. *Expenses:* Tuition, state resident: full-time $9870. Tuition, nonresident: full-time $18,350. *Required fees:* $1848. *Financial support:* Federal Work-Study, scholarships/grants, and unspecified assistantships available. Support available to part-time students. Financial award application deadline: 3/15; financial award applicants required to submit FAFSA. *Unit head:* Dr. Don Halquist, Chairperson, 585-395-2205, Fax: 585-395-2171, E-mail: dhalquis@brockport.edu. *Application contact:* Michael Harrison, Coordinator of Certification and Graduate Advisement, 585-395-2326, Fax: 585-395-2172, E-mail: mharriso@brockport.edu.
Website: http://www.brockport.edu/ehd/.

College of Charleston, Graduate School, School of Education, Health, and Human Performance, Program in Science and Mathematics for Teachers, Charleston, SC 29424-0001. Offers M Ed. *Accreditation:* NCATE. Part-time and evening/weekend programs available. *Degree requirements:* For master's, capstone project. *Entrance requirements:* For master's, GRE or PRAXIS, 2 letters of recommendation, copy of teaching certificate. Additional exam requirements/recommendations for international students: Required—TOEFL (minimum score 81 iBT). Electronic applications accepted.

The College of William and Mary, School of Education, Program in Curriculum and Instruction, Williamsburg, VA 23187-8795. Offers elementary education (MA Ed); gifted education (MA Ed); literacy leadership (MA Ed); math specialist (MA Ed); secondary education (MA Ed), including English education, mathematics education, modern foreign languages education, science education, social studies education; special education (MA Ed), including collaborating master educator, general curriculum. *Accreditation:* NCATE. Part-time programs available. *Faculty:* 15 full-time (10 women), 44 part-time/adjunct (38 women). *Students:* 66 full-time (55 women), 27 part-time (26 women); includes 17 minority (4 Black or African American, non-Hispanic/Latino; 1 American Indian or Alaska Native, non-Hispanic/Latino; 3 Asian, non-Hispanic/Latino; 5 Hispanic/Latino; 4 Two or more races, non-Hispanic/Latino). Average age 28. 179 applicants, 72% accepted, 92 enrolled. In 2013, 76 master's awarded. *Degree requirements:* For master's, project. *Entrance requirements:* For master's, GRE or MAT, minimum GPA of 2.5. Additional exam requirements/recommendations for international students: Required—TOEFL, IELTS. *Application deadline:* For fall admission, 1/15 for domestic and international students; for spring admission, 10/1 for domestic and international students. Application fee: $50. Electronic applications accepted. *Expenses:* Tuition, state resident: full-time $7120; part-time $405 per credit hour. Tuition, nonresident: full-time $21,639; part-time $1050 per credit hour. *Required fees:* $4764. *Financial support:* In 2013–14, 49 students received support, including 6 research assistantships with full and partial tuition reimbursements available (averaging $8,269 per year); career-related internships or fieldwork, Federal Work-Study, institutionally sponsored loans, scholarships/grants, and unspecified assistantships also available. Financial award application deadline: 1/15; financial award applicants required to submit FAFSA. *Faculty research:* National Council of Teachers of Mathematics standards, counseling, self-concept and self-esteem, special education, curriculum development. *Unit head:* Dr. Mark Hofer, Area Coordinator, 757-221-1713, E-mail: mjhofe@wm.edu. *Application contact:* Dorothy Smith Osborne, Assistant Dean for Academic Programs and Student Services, 757-221-2317, Fax: 757-221-2293, E-mail: dsosbo@wm.edu.
Website: http://education.wm.edu.

The Colorado College, Education Department, Experienced Teacher Program, Colorado Springs, CO 80903-3294. Offers arts and humanities (MAT); integrated natural sciences (MAT); liberal arts (MAT); Southwest studies (MAT). Programs offered during summer only. Part-time programs available. *Degree requirements:* For master's, thesis, oral exam, 50-page paper. *Expenses:* Contact institution.

The Colorado College, Education Department, Program in Secondary Education, Colorado Springs, CO 80903-3294. Offers art teaching (K-12) (MAT); English teaching (MAT); foreign language teaching (MAT); mathematics teaching (MAT); music teaching (MAT); science teaching (MAT); social studies teaching (MAT). *Degree requirements:* For master's, thesis, internship. Electronic applications accepted.

Columbia University, College of Dental Medicine and Graduate School of Arts and Sciences, Programs in Dental Specialties, New York, NY 10027. Offers advanced education in general dentistry (Certificate); biomedical informatics (MA, PhD); endodontics (Certificate); orthodontics (MS, Certificate); periodontics (MS, Certificate); prosthodontics (MS, Certificate); science education (MA). *Degree requirements:* For master's, thesis, presentation of seminar. *Entrance requirements:* For master's, GRE General Test, DDS or equivalent. *Expenses:* Contact institution. *Faculty research:* Analysis of growth/form, pulpal microcirculation, implants, microbiology of oral environment, calcified tissues.

Columbus State University, Graduate Studies, College of Education and Health Professions, Department of Teacher Education, Columbus, GA 31907-5645. Offers accomplished teaching (M Ed); early childhood education (M Ed, MAT, Ed S); middle grades education (M Ed, MAT, Ed S); school library media (M Ed, MAT); secondary education (M Ed, MAT, Ed S), including English/language arts (M Ed, Ed S), general science (M Ed), mathematics (M Ed, Ed S), science (Ed S), social science (M Ed, Ed S); special education (M Ed, MAT, Ed S), including general curriculum (M Ed, MAT); teacher leadership (M Ed). *Accreditation:* NCATE. Part-time and evening/weekend programs available. Postbaccalaureate distance learning degree programs offered (minimal on-campus study). *Faculty:* 17 full-time (12 women), 31 part-time/adjunct (28 women). *Students:* 59 full-time (48 women), 190 part-time (150 women); includes 85 minority (68 Black or African American, non-Hispanic/Latino; 1 American Indian or Alaska Native, non-Hispanic/Latino; 6 Asian, non-Hispanic/Latino; 4 Hispanic/Latino; 6 Two or more races, non-Hispanic/Latino), 2 international. Average age 34. 132 applicants, 58% accepted, 50 enrolled. In 2013, 86 master's, 26 other advanced degrees awarded. *Degree requirements:* For master's, thesis, exit exam; for Ed S, thesis or alternative. *Entrance requirements:* For master's, GRE General Test, minimum undergraduate GPA of 2.75; for Ed S, GRE General Test, minimum undergraduate GPA of 2.75, graduate 3.0. Additional exam requirements/recommendations for international students: Required—TOEFL (minimum score 550 paper-based; 79 iBT). *Application deadline:* For fall admission, 6/30 for domestic students, 5/1 for international students; for spring admission, 11/1 for domestic and international students; for summer admission, 3/1 for domestic and international students. Applications are processed on a rolling basis. Application fee: $40. Electronic applications accepted. *Expenses:* Tuition, state resident: full-time $4572; part-time $382 per credit hour. Tuition, nonresident: full-time $18,292; part-time $1526 per credit hour. *Required fees:* $1800; $196 per credit hour. Tuition and fees vary according to campus/location and program. *Financial support:* In 2013–14, 173 students received support, including 12 research assistantships with partial tuition reimbursements available (averaging $3,000 per year); career-related internships or fieldwork, Federal Work-Study, institutionally sponsored loans, scholarships/grants, tuition waivers (partial), and unspecified assistantships also available. Support available to part-time students. Financial award application deadline: 5/1; financial award applicants required to submit FAFSA. *Unit head:* Dr. Deirdre Greer, Department Chair, 706-507-8034, Fax: 706-568-3134, E-mail: greer_deirdre@columbusstate.edu. *Application contact:* Kristin Williams, Director of International and Graduate Recruitment, 706-507-8848, Fax: 706-568-5091, E-mail: williams_kristin@columbusstate.edu.
Website: http://te.columbusstate.edu/.

Concordia University, College of Education, Portland, OR 97211-6099. Offers career and technical education (M Ed); curriculum and instruction (M Ed), including adolescent literacy, career and technical education, e-learning/technology education, early childhood education, English for speakers of other languages, English language development, environmental education, mathematics, methods and curriculum, reading, science, teacher leadership, the inclusive classroom; early childhood (MAT); education leadership (Ed D); educational administration (M Ed); elementary education (MAT); secondary education (MAT); special education (M Ed); teacher leadership (Ed D). Part-time programs available. Postbaccalaureate distance learning degree programs offered (no on-campus study). *Degree requirements:* For master's, comprehensive exam, work samples/portfolio. *Entrance requirements:* For master's, California Basic Educational Skills Test or PRAXIS I, minimum undergraduate GPA of 2.8, graduate 3.0; 2 letters of recommendation. Additional exam requirements/recommendations for international students: Required—TOEFL (minimum score 525 paper-based). Electronic applications accepted. *Faculty research:* Learner-centered classroom, brain-based learning, future of online learning.

Converse College, School of Education and Graduate Studies, Program in Middle Level Education, Spartanburg, SC 29302-0006. Offers language arts/English (MAT); mathematics (MAT); middle level education (M Ed); science (MAT); social studies (MAT).

Converse College, School of Education and Graduate Studies, Program in Secondary Education, Spartanburg, SC 29302-0006. Offers biology (MAT); chemistry (MAT); English (M Ed, MAT); mathematics (M Ed, MAT); natural sciences (M Ed); social sciences (M Ed, MAT). Part-time programs available. *Degree requirements:* For master's, capstone paper. *Entrance requirements:* For master's, NTE or PRAXIS II (M Ed), minimum GPA of 2.75, 2 recommendations. Electronic applications accepted.

Delaware State University, Graduate Programs, College of Education, Health and Public Policy, Program in Science Education, Dover, DE 19901-2277. Offers MA. Part-time and evening/weekend programs available. *Degree requirements:* For master's, comprehensive exam, thesis optional. *Entrance requirements:* For master's, GRE General Test, minimum GPA of 3.0 in major, 2.75 overall. Electronic applications accepted. *Faculty research:* Science reform in schools, inquiry science.

Delaware State University, Graduate Programs, Department of Biological Sciences, Program in Biology Education, Dover, DE 19901-2277. Offers MS. *Entrance requirements:* Additional exam requirements/recommendations for international students: Required—TOEFL (minimum score 550 paper-based).

Delaware State University, Graduate Programs, Department of Physics, Dover, DE 19901-2277. Offers applied optics (MS); optics (PhD); physics (MS); physics teaching (MS). Part-time and evening/weekend programs available. *Entrance requirements:* For master's, minimum GPA of 3.0 in major, 2.75 overall. Additional exam requirements/recommendations for international students: Required—TOEFL. Electronic applications accepted. *Faculty research:* Thermal properties of solids, nuclear physics, radiation damage in solids.

DePaul University, College of Science and Health, Chicago, IL 60614. Offers applied mathematics (MS); applied statistics (MS); biological sciences (MA, MS); chemistry (MS); mathematics education (MA); mathematics for teaching (MS); nursing (MS); nursing practice (DNP); physics (MS); psychology (MS); pure mathematics (MS); science education (MS); MA/PhD. *Faculty:* 66 full-time (40 women), 23 part-time/adjunct (21 women). *Students:* 485 full-time (338 women), 207 part-time (132 women); includes 198 minority (55 Black or African American, non-Hispanic/Latino; 1 American Indian or Alaska Native, non-Hispanic/Latino; 64 Asian, non-Hispanic/Latino; 53 Hispanic/Latino; 2 Native Hawaiian or other Pacific Islander, non-Hispanic/Latino; 23 Two or more races, non-Hispanic/Latino), 48 international. Average age 29. In 2013, 244 master's, 20 doctorates awarded. *Application deadline:* Applications are processed on a rolling basis. Application fee: $40. Electronic applications accepted. Tuition and fees vary according to course level, course load and degree level. *Financial support:* Applicants required to submit FAFSA. *Application contact:* Ann Spittle, Director of Graduate Admission, 773-325-7315, Fax: 312-476-3244, E-mail: graddepaul@depaul.edu.
Website: http://csh.depaul.edu/.

Drew University, Caspersen School of Graduate Studies, Program in Education, Madison, NJ 07940-1493. Offers biology (MAT); chemistry (MAT); English (MAT); French (MAT); Italian (MAT); math (MAT); physics (MAT); social studies (MAT); Spanish (MAT); theatre arts (MAT). Part-time programs available. *Degree requirements:* For master's, student teaching internship and seminar. *Entrance requirements:* For master's, transcripts, statement of purpose, three letters of recommendation. Additional exam requirements/recommendations for international students: Required—TOEFL. *Expenses:* Contact institution.

Duquesne University, School of Education, Department of Instruction and Leadership, Program in Secondary Education, Pittsburgh, PA 15282-0001. Offers biology (MS Ed); chemistry (MS Ed); English (MS Ed); K-12 education (MS Ed), including Latin; mathematics (MS Ed); physics (MS Ed); social studies (MS Ed). Part-time and evening/weekend programs available. *Faculty:* 4 full-time (2 women). *Students:* 44 full-time (23 women), 3 part-time (2 women); includes 7 minority (6 Black or African American, non-Hispanic/Latino; 1 Two or more races, non-Hispanic/Latino), 1 international. Average age 27. 43 applicants, 35% accepted, 15 enrolled. In 2013, 28 master's awarded. *Degree requirements:* For master's, thesis optional. *Entrance requirements:* For master's, letters of recommendation, letter of intent, interview, bachelor's degree. Additional exam requirements/recommendations for international students: Required—TOEFL (minimum score 550 paper-based), IELTS (minimum score 7). *Application deadline:* For fall admission, 9/1 for domestic students; for spring admission, 1/1 for domestic students. Applications are processed on a rolling basis. Application fee: $0. Electronic applications accepted. Application fee is waived when completed online. *Expenses: Tuition:* Full-time $18,162; part-time $1009 per credit. *Required fees:* $1728; $96 per credit. Tuition and fees vary according to program. *Financial support:* Research assistantships and Federal Work-Study available. Support available to part-time students. *Unit head:* Dr. Melissa Boston, Associate Professor and Director, 412-396-6109, E-mail: bostonm@duq.edu. *Application contact:* Michael Dolinger, Director of Student and Academic Services, 412-396-6647, Fax: 412-396-5585, E-mail: dolingerm@duq.edu.
Website: http://www.duq.edu/academics/schools/education/graduate-programs-education/ms-ed-secondary-education.

East Carolina University, Graduate School, College of Education, Department of Business and Information Technologies Education, Greenville, NC 27858-4353. Offers business education (MA Ed); elementary education (MAT); English education (MAT); family and consumer science (MAT); health education (MAT); Hispanic studies (MAT);

history education (MAT); marketing education (MA Ed); middle grades education (MAT); music education (MAT); physical education (MAT); science education (MAT); special education (MAT), including general curriculum; vocation education (MS). *Accreditation:* NCATE. Part-time and evening/weekend programs available. Postbaccalaureate distance learning degree programs offered (no on-campus study). *Degree requirements:* For master's, comprehensive exam, thesis optional. *Entrance requirements:* For master's, GRE or MAT, minimum GPA of 2.5, bachelor's degree in related field, teaching license (MA Ed). Additional exam requirements/recommendations for international students: Required—TOEFL. *Expenses:* Tuition, state resident: full-time $4223. Tuition, nonresident: full-time $16,540. *Required fees:* $2184.

East Carolina University, Graduate School, College of Education, Department of Mathematics, Science, and Instructional Technology Education, Greenville, NC 27858-4353. Offers computer-based instruction (Certificate); distance learning and administration (Certificate); instructional technology (MA Ed, MS); mathematics (MA Ed); performance improvement (Certificate); science education (MA, MA Ed); special endorsement in computer education (Certificate). Part-time and evening/weekend programs available. *Degree requirements:* For master's, comprehensive exam, thesis optional. *Entrance requirements:* For master's, GRE General Test or MAT, interview, minimum GPA of 2.5, bachelor's degree in related field, teaching license (MA Ed). Additional exam requirements/recommendations for international students: Required—TOEFL. *Expenses:* Tuition, state resident: full-time $4223. Tuition, nonresident: full-time $16,540. *Required fees:* $2184.

Eastern Connecticut State University, School of Education and Professional Studies/ Graduate Division, Program in Science Education, Willimantic, CT 06226-2295. Offers MS. *Accreditation:* NCATE. Part-time and evening/weekend programs available. *Degree requirements:* For master's, comprehensive exam or thesis. *Entrance requirements:* For master's, minimum GPA of 2.7, teaching certificate. Additional exam requirements/ recommendations for international students: Required—TOEFL (minimum score 550 paper-based).

Eastern Kentucky University, The Graduate School, College of Education, Department of Curriculum and Instruction, Program in Secondary and Higher Education, Richmond, KY 40475-3102. Offers secondary education (MA Ed), including agricultural education, art education, biological sciences education, business education, English education, geography education, history education, home economics education, industrial education, mathematical sciences education, physical education, school health education. *Accreditation:* NCATE. Part-time programs available. *Entrance requirements:* For master's, GRE General Test, minimum GPA of 2.5.

Eastern Michigan University, Graduate School, College of Arts and Sciences, Department of Biology, Ypsilanti, MI 48197. Offers cell and molecular biology (MS); community college biology teaching (MS); ecology and organismal biology (MS); general biology (MS); water resources (MS). Part-time and evening/weekend programs available. Postbaccalaureate distance learning degree programs offered (minimal on-campus study). *Faculty:* 19 full-time (4 women). *Students:* 11 full-time (6 women), 31 part-time (18 women); includes 3 minority (1 Black or African American, non-Hispanic/ Latino; 1 Asian, non-Hispanic/Latino; 1 Hispanic/Latino), 6 international. Average age 26. 56 applicants, 59% accepted, 20 enrolled. In 2013, 13 master's awarded. *Entrance requirements:* For master's, GRE General Test, GRE Subject Test. Additional exam requirements/recommendations for international students: Required—TOEFL. *Application deadline:* Applications are processed on a rolling basis. Application fee: $35. *Expenses:* Tuition, state resident: full-time $12,300; part-time $466 per credit hour. Tuition, nonresident: full-time $23,159; part-time $918 per credit hour. *Required fees:* $71 per credit hour. $46 per semester. One-time fee: $100. Tuition and fees vary according to course level and degree level. *Financial support:* Fellowships, research assistantships with full tuition reimbursements, teaching assistantships with full tuition reimbursements, career-related internships or fieldwork, Federal Work-Study, institutionally sponsored loans, scholarships/grants, tuition waivers (partial), and unspecified assistantships available. Support available to part-time students. Financial award applicants required to submit FAFSA. *Unit head:* Dr. Daniel Clemans, Department Head, 734-487-4242, Fax: 734-487-9235, E-mail: dclemans@emich.edu. *Application contact:* Dr. David Kass, Graduate Coordinator, 734-487-4242, Fax: 734-487-9235, E-mail: dkass@emich.edu.
Website: http://www.emich.edu/biology.

Eastern Michigan University, Graduate School, College of Arts and Sciences, Department of Geography and Geology, Program in Earth Science Education, Ypsilanti, MI 48197. Offers MS. *Students:* Average age 33. 1 applicant. In 2013, 3 master's awarded. Application fee: $35. *Expenses:* Tuition, state resident: full-time $12,300; part-time $466 per credit hour. Tuition, nonresident: full-time $23,159; part-time $918 per credit hour. *Required fees:* $71 per credit hour. $46 per semester. One-time fee: $100. Tuition and fees vary according to course level and degree level. *Unit head:* Dr. Richard Sambrook, Department Head, 734-487-0218, Fax: 734-487-6979, E-mail: rsambroo@emich.edu. *Application contact:* Dr. Thomas Kovacs, Program Advisor, 734-487-0218, Fax: 734-487-6979, E-mail: tkovacs@emich.edu.

Eastern Michigan University, Graduate School, College of Arts and Sciences, Department of Physics and Astronomy, Ypsilanti, MI 48197. Offers general science (MS); physics (MS); physics education (MS). Part-time and evening/weekend programs available. Postbaccalaureate distance learning degree programs offered (minimal on-campus study). *Faculty:* 9 full-time (2 women). *Students:* 2 full-time (1 woman), 13 part-time (4 women); includes 2 minority (1 Hispanic/Latino; 1 Two or more races, non-Hispanic/Latino), 1 international. Average age 28. 11 applicants, 73% accepted, 4 enrolled. In 2013, 3 master's awarded. *Entrance requirements:* Additional exam requirements/recommendations for international students: Required—TOEFL. *Application deadline:* Applications are processed on a rolling basis. Application fee: $35. *Expenses:* Tuition, state resident: full-time $12,300; part-time $466 per credit hour. Tuition, nonresident: full-time $23,159; part-time $918 per credit hour. *Required fees:* $71 per credit hour. $46 per semester. One-time fee: $100. Tuition and fees vary according to course level and degree level. *Financial support:* Fellowships, research assistantships with full tuition reimbursements, teaching assistantships with full tuition reimbursements, career-related internships or fieldwork, Federal Work-Study, institutionally sponsored loans, scholarships/grants, tuition waivers, and unspecified assistantships available. Support available to part-time students. Financial award applicants required to submit FAFSA. *Unit head:* Dr. Alexandria Oakes, Department Head, 734-487-4144, Fax: 734-487-0989, E-mail: aoakes@emich.edu. *Application contact:* Graduate Admissions, 734-487-2400, Fax: 734-487-6559, E-mail: graduate.admissions@emich.edu.
Website: http://www.emich.edu/physics/.

Eastern University, Graduate Education Programs, St. Davids, PA 19087-3696. Offers ESL program specialist (K-12) (Certificate); general supervisor (PreK-12) (Certificate); health and physical education (K-12) (Certificate); middle level (4-8) (Certificate); multicultural education (M Ed); pre K-4 (Certificate); pre K-4 with special education (Certificate); reading (M Ed); reading specialist (K-12) (Certificate); reading supervisor (K-12) (Certificate); school health services (M Ed); school health supervisor (Certificate); school nurse (Certificate); school principalship (K-12) (Certificate); secondary biology education (7-12) (Certificate); secondary chemistry education (7-12) (Certificate);

secondary communication education (7-12) (Certificate); secondary education (7-12) (Certificate); secondary English education (7-12) (Certificate); secondary math education (7-12) (Certificate); secondary social studies education (7-12) (Certificate); special education (M Ed); special education (7-12) (Certificate); special education (Pre K-8) (Certificate); special education supervisor (N-12) (Certificate); TESOL (M Ed); world language (Certificate), including French, Mandarin Chinese, Spanish. Part-time and evening/weekend programs available. Postbaccalaureate distance learning degree programs offered (no on-campus study). *Faculty:* 22 full-time (11 women), 26 part-time/ adjunct (18 women). *Students:* 77 full-time (58 women), 223 part-time (149 women); includes 112 minority (81 Black or African American, non-Hispanic/Latino; 1 American Indian or Alaska Native, non-Hispanic/Latino; 9 Asian, non-Hispanic/Latino; 18 Hispanic/ Latino; 1 Native Hawaiian or other Pacific Islander, non-Hispanic/Latino; 2 Two or more races, non-Hispanic/Latino), 7 international. Average age 34. 94 applicants, 100% accepted, 81 enrolled. In 2013, 120 master's awarded. *Entrance requirements:* For master's, minimum GPA of 2.5 (for M Ed); for Certificate, minimum GPA of 3.0 for certifications. Additional exam requirements/recommendations for international students: Required—TOEFL. *Application deadline:* For fall admission, 8/14 for domestic students; for spring admission, 12/20 for domestic students. Applications are processed on a rolling basis. Application fee: $35. Application fee is waived when completed online. *Expenses: Tuition:* Full-time $15,600; part-time $650 per credit. *Required fees:* $27.50 per semester. One-time fee: $50. Tuition and fees vary according to course load, degree level and program. *Financial support:* In 2013–14, 84 students received support, including 6 research assistantships with partial tuition reimbursements available (averaging $7,710 per year); scholarships/grants and unspecified assistantships also available. Financial award application deadline: 3/15; financial award applicants required to submit FAFSA. *Unit head:* Harry Gutelius, Associate Dean, 610-341-1729. *Application contact:* Michael Perpiglia, Associate Director of Enrollment, 610-341-5947, Fax: 484-581-1276, E-mail: mperpigl@eastern.edu.
Website: http://www.eastern.edu/academics/programs/loeb-school-education-0/ graduateprograms.

East Stroudsburg University of Pennsylvania, Graduate College, College of Arts and Sciences, Department of Biology, East Stroudsburg, PA 18301-2999. Offers M Ed, MS. Part-time and evening/weekend programs available. *Faculty:* 8 full-time (2 women). *Students:* 15 full-time (7 women), 4 part-time (1 woman); includes 1 minority (Two or more races, non-Hispanic/Latino), 1 international. Average age 28. 28 applicants, 68% accepted, 7 enrolled. In 2013, 9 master's awarded. *Degree requirements:* For master's, comprehensive exam, thesis or alternative. *Entrance requirements:* For master's, GRE, resume, undergraduate major in life science (or equivalent), completion of organic chemistry (minimum two semesters), 3 letters of recommendation, letter of intent. Additional exam requirements/recommendations for international students: Required—TOEFL (minimum score 560 paper-based; 83 iBT) or IELTS. *Application deadline:* For fall admission, 7/31 for domestic students, 6/30 priority date for international students; for spring admission, 11/30 for domestic students, 10/31 for international students. Applications are processed on a rolling basis. Application fee: $50. Electronic applications accepted. *Expenses:* Tuition, state resident: full-time $7956; part-time $442 per credit. Tuition, nonresident: full-time $11,934; part-time $663 per credit. *Required fees:* $2129; $118 per credit. *Financial support:* Research assistantships with full and partial tuition reimbursements, Federal Work-Study, and institutionally sponsored loans available. Financial award application deadline: 3/1; financial award applicants required to submit FAFSA. *Unit head:* Dr. Jane Huffman, Graduate Coordinator, 570-422-3725, Fax: 570-422-3724, E-mail: jhuffman@po-box.esu.edu. *Application contact:* Kevin Quintero, Graduate Admission Coordinator, 570-422-3536, Fax: 570-422-3711, E-mail: kquintero@esu.edu.
Website: http://www4.esu.edu/academics/departments/biology/graduate_programs/ index.cfm.

Elizabeth City State University, School of Mathematics, Science and Technology, Master of Science in Biology/Biological Science Program, Elizabeth City, NC 27909-7806. Offers biological sciences (MS); biology education (MS). Part-time and evening/ weekend programs available. *Faculty:* 8 full-time (1 woman), 1 (woman) part-time/ adjunct. *Students:* 3 full-time (1 woman), 17 part-time (11 women); includes 14 minority (12 Black or African American, non-Hispanic/Latino; 1 Asian, non-Hispanic/Latino; 1 Two or more races, non-Hispanic/Latino). Average age 30. 10 applicants, 70% accepted, 5 enrolled. In 2013, 10 master's awarded. *Degree requirements:* For master's, thesis. *Entrance requirements:* For master's, GRE, minimum GPA of 3.0, 3 letters of recommendation, 2 official transcripts from all undergraduate/graduate schools attended, typewritten one-page expository description of student educational preparation, research interests and career aspirations. Additional exam requirements/ recommendations for international students: Required—TOEFL (minimum score 550 paper-based, 80 iBT) or IELTS (minimum score 6.5). *Application deadline:* For fall admission, 7/15 priority date for domestic and international students; for spring admission, 11/15 priority date for domestic and international students; for summer admission, 3/15 priority date for domestic and international students. Applications are processed on a rolling basis. Application fee: $30. Electronic applications accepted. *Expenses:* Tuition, state resident: full-time $2916; part-time $364.48 per credit. Tuition, nonresident: full-time $14,199; part-time $1774.83 per credit. *Required fees:* $2972.23; $206.58 per credit. $571.06 per semester. *Financial support:* In 2013–14, 18 students received support. Scholarships/grants available. Financial award application deadline: 6/ 30; financial award applicants required to submit FAFSA. *Faculty research:* Apoptosis and cancer, plant bioengineering, development of biofuels, microbial degradation, developmental toxicology. *Unit head:* Dr. Gloria Payne, Chair, 252-335-3595, Fax: 252-335-3697, E-mail: gepayne@mail.ecsu.edu. *Application contact:* Dr. Paula S. Viltz, Interim Dean, School of Education & Psychology and Graduate Education, 252-335-3455, Fax: 252-335-3146, E-mail: psviltz@mail.ecsu.edu.

Elms College, Division of Education, Chicopee, MA 01013-2839. Offers early childhood education (MAT); education (M Ed, CAGS); elementary education (MAT); English as a second language (MAT); reading (MAT); secondary education (MAT), including biology education, English education, Spanish education; special education (MAT). Part-time and evening/weekend programs available. *Degree requirements:* For master's, thesis (for some programs). *Entrance requirements:* For master's, Massachusetts Educators Certification Test, minimum GPA of 3.0; for CAGS, master's degree in education. Additional exam requirements/recommendations for international students: Required—TOEFL.

Fairleigh Dickinson University, Metropolitan Campus, University College: Arts, Sciences, and Professional Studies, School of Natural Sciences, Program in Science, Teaneck, NJ 07666-1914. Offers MA. *Accreditation:* Teacher Education Accreditation Council.

Fitchburg State University, Division of Graduate and Continuing Education, Program in Science Education, Fitchburg, MA 01420-2697. Offers M Ed. *Accreditation:* NCATE. Part-time and evening/weekend programs available. *Entrance requirements:* Additional exam requirements/recommendations for international students: Required—TOEFL (minimum score 550 paper-based; 79 iBT). Electronic applications accepted.

Fitchburg State University, Division of Graduate and Continuing Education, Programs in Biology and Teaching Biology (Secondary Level), Fitchburg, MA 01420-2697. Offers

Science Education

MA, MAT, Certificate. *Accreditation:* NCATE. Part-time and evening/weekend programs available. *Entrance requirements:* Additional exam requirements/recommendations for international students: Required—TOEFL (minimum score 550 paper-based; 79 iBT). Electronic applications accepted.

Florida Agricultural and Mechanical University, Division of Graduate Studies, Research, and Continuing Education, College of Education, Program in Secondary Education and Foundation, Tallahassee, FL 32307-3200. Offers biology (M Ed); chemistry (MS Ed); English (MS Ed); history (MS Ed); math (MS Ed); physics (MS Ed). *Accreditation:* NCATE. *Degree requirements:* For master's, thesis (for some programs). *Entrance requirements:* For master's, GRE General Test, minimum GPA of 3.0. Additional exam requirements/recommendations for international students: Required—TOEFL.

Florida Atlantic University, Charles E. Schmidt College of Science, Department of Biological Sciences, Boca Raton, FL 33431-0991. Offers biology (MS, MST); business biotechnology (MS); environmental science (MS); integrative biology (PhD). Part-time programs available. *Faculty:* 36 full-time (7 women), 3 part-time/adjunct (1 woman). *Students:* 82 full-time (53 women), 63 part-time (37 women); includes 31 minority (3 Black or African American, non-Hispanic/Latino; 7 Asian, non-Hispanic/Latino; 18 Hispanic/Latino; 3 Two or more races, non-Hispanic/Latino), 15 international. Average age 30. 126 applicants, 20% accepted, 20 enrolled. In 2013, 32 master's, 15 doctorates awarded. *Degree requirements:* For master's, thesis (for some programs). *Entrance requirements:* For master's, GRE General Test, minimum GPA of 3.0. Additional exam requirements/recommendations for international students: Required—TOEFL (minimum score 500 paper-based; 61 iBT), IELTS (minimum score 6). *Application deadline:* For fall admission, 3/15 for domestic and international students; for spring admission, 10/1 for domestic and international students. Application fee: $30. *Expenses:* Tuition, state resident: full-time $6660; part-time $370 per credit hour. Tuition, nonresident: full-time $18,450; part-time $1025 per credit hour. Tuition and fees vary according to course load. *Financial support:* Fellowships, research assistantships, teaching assistantships with tuition reimbursements, career-related internships or fieldwork, and Federal Work-Study available. *Faculty research:* Ecology of the Everglades, molecular biology and biotechnology, marine biology. *Unit head:* Dr. Rodney K. Murphey, Chair, 561-297-3320, Fax: 561-297-2749. *Application contact:* Becky Dixon, Graduate Program Assistant, 561-297-3230.
Website: http://www.science.fau.edu/biology/.

Florida Atlantic University, Charles E. Schmidt College of Science, Department of Physics, Boca Raton, FL 33431-0991. Offers medical physics (MSMP); physics (MS, MST, PhD). Part-time programs available. *Faculty:* 5 full-time (1 woman), 3 part-time/adjunct (1 woman). *Students:* 21 full-time (4 women), 14 part-time (5 women); includes 5 minority (3 Black or African American, non-Hispanic/Latino; 1 Hispanic/Latino; 1 Two or more races, non-Hispanic/Latino), 18 international. Average age 31. 30 applicants, 33% accepted, 6 enrolled. In 2013, 8 master's awarded. *Degree requirements:* For master's, thesis; for doctorate, thesis/dissertation. *Entrance requirements:* For master's, GRE General Test, minimum GPA of 3.0; for doctorate, GRE General Test. Additional exam requirements/recommendations for international students: Required—TOEFL (minimum score 500 paper-based; 61 iBT), IELTS (minimum score 6). *Application deadline:* For fall admission, 7/1 for domestic students, 2/15 for international students; for spring admission, 11/1 for domestic students, 7/15 for international students. Applications are processed on a rolling basis. Application fee: $30. *Expenses:* Tuition, state resident: full-time $6660; part-time $370 per credit hour. Tuition, nonresident: full-time $18,450; part-time $1025 per credit hour. Tuition and fees vary according to course load. *Financial support:* Fellowships, research assistantships with tuition reimbursements, teaching assistantships with tuition reimbursements, Federal Work-Study, and unspecified assistantships available. *Faculty research:* Astrophysics, spectroscopy, mathematical physics, theory of metals, superconductivity. *Unit head:* Dr. Warner A. Miller, Chair, 561-297-3382, Fax: 561-297-2662, E-mail: wam@physics.fau.edu. *Application contact:* Dr. Wolfgang Tichy, Graduate Programs, 561-297-3353, Fax: 561-297-2662.
Website: http://physics.fau.edu/.

Florida Atlantic University, College of Education, Department of Teaching and Learning, Boca Raton, FL 33431-0991. Offers curriculum and instruction (M Ed), including art, biology, chemistry, English, French, German, mathematics, music, physics, Pre-K and primary education, reading, social sciences, Spanish; elementary education (M Ed); environmental education (M Ed); reading education (M Ed); social foundations of education (M Ed), including educational psychology, educational technology, multilingual education. *Accreditation:* NCATE. Part-time and evening/weekend programs available. *Faculty:* 16 full-time (12 women), 1 (woman) part-time/adjunct. *Students:* 56 full-time (46 women), 96 part-time (78 women); includes 39 minority (10 Black or African American, non-Hispanic/Latino; 6 Asian, non-Hispanic/Latino; 20 Hispanic/Latino; 3 Two or more races, non-Hispanic/Latino), 4 international. Average age 32. 101 applicants, 54% accepted, 42 enrolled. In 2013, 64 master's awarded. *Entrance requirements:* For master's, GRE General Test, minimum GPA of 3.0 in last 2 years of undergraduate course work. Additional exam requirements/recommendations for international students: Required—TOEFL (minimum score 500 paper-based; 61 iBT), IELTS (minimum score 6). *Application deadline:* For fall admission, 7/1 for domestic students, 2/15 for international students; for spring admission, 11/1 for domestic students, 7/15 for international students. Applications are processed on a rolling basis. Application fee: $30. *Expenses:* Tuition, state resident: full-time $6660; part-time $370 per credit hour. Tuition, nonresident: full-time $18,450; part-time $1025 per credit hour. Tuition and fees vary according to course load. *Financial support:* Fellowships with partial tuition reimbursements, research assistantships with partial tuition reimbursements, teaching assistantships with partial tuition reimbursements, career-related internships or fieldwork, scholarships/grants, and unspecified assistantships available. *Faculty research:* Technology, teaching English to speakers of other languages, math teaching, electronic portfolio assessment, global perspectives through social studies. *Unit head:* Dr. Barbara Ridener, Chairperson, 561-297-3588. *Application contact:* Dr. Eliah Watlington, Associate Dean, 561-296-8520, Fax: 261-297-2991, E-mail: ewatling@fau.edu.
Website: http://www.coe.fau.edu/academicdepartments/tl/.

Florida Institute of Technology, Graduate Programs, College of Science, Department of Education and Interdisciplinary Studies, Melbourne, FL 32901-6975. Offers computer education (MS); elementary science education (M Ed); environmental education (MS); interdisciplinary science (MS); mathematics education (MS, PhD, Ed S); science education (MS, PhD, Ed S), including informal science education (MS); teaching (MAT). Part-time and evening/weekend programs available. *Faculty:* 4 full-time (1 woman), 5 part-time/adjunct (2 women). *Students:* 47 full-time (29 women), 40 part-time (25 women); includes 10 minority (4 Black or African American, non-Hispanic/Latino; 4 Asian, non-Hispanic/Latino; 2 Hispanic/Latino), 48 international. Average age 32. 90 applicants, 63% accepted, 23 enrolled. In 2013, 16 master's awarded. Terminal master's awarded for partial completion of doctoral program. *Degree requirements:* For master's, comprehensive exam (for some programs), thesis optional; for doctorate, comprehensive exam, thesis/dissertation; for Ed S, comprehensive exam. *Entrance requirements:* For master's, minimum GPA of 3.0, resume, 3 letters of recommendation (elementary science education), statement of objectives; for doctorate, minimum GPA of 3.2, resume, 3 letters of recommendation, statement of objectives, 3 years of teaching experience (recommended); for Ed S, minimum GPA of 3.0, resume, 3 letters of recommendation, statement of objectives. Additional exam requirements/recommendations for international students: Required—TOEFL (minimum score 550 paper-based; 79 iBT). *Application deadline:* For fall admission, 4/1 for international students; for spring admission, 9/30 for international students. Applications are processed on a rolling basis. Electronic applications accepted. *Expenses: Tuition:* Full-time $20,214; part-time $1123 per credit. Tuition and fees vary according to campus/location. *Financial support:* In 2013–14, 2 teaching assistantships with full and partial tuition reimbursements (averaging $12,623 per year) were awarded; research assistantships with full and partial tuition reimbursements, career-related internships or fieldwork, institutionally sponsored loans, tuition waivers (partial), unspecified assistantships, and tuition remissions also available. Support available to part-time students. Financial award application deadline: 3/1; financial award applicants required to submit FAFSA. *Faculty research:* Measurement and evaluation, computers in education, educational technology. *Total annual research expenditures:* $644,517. *Unit head:* Dr. Kastro Hamed, Department Head, 321-674-8126, Fax: 321-674-7598, E-mail: khamed@fit.edu. *Application contact:* Cheryl A. Brown, Associate Director of Graduate Admissions, 321-674-7581, Fax: 321-723-9468, E-mail: cbrown@fit.edu.
Website: http://cos.fit.edu/education/.

Florida International University, College of Education, Department of Teaching and Learning, Miami, FL 33199. Offers art education (MA, MS); curriculum and instruction (MS, Ed D, PhD, Ed S), including curriculum development (MS), elementary education (MS), English education (MS), learning technologies (MS), mathematics education (MS), modern language education (MS), physical education (MS), science education (MS), social studies education (MS), special education (MS); early childhood education (MS); exceptional student education (Ed D); foreign language education (MS), including foreign language education, teaching English to speakers of other languages (TESOL); international/intercultural education (MS); language, literacy and culture (PhD); mathematics, science, and learning technologies (PhD); physical education (MS), including sport and fitness; reading education (MS). Part-time and evening/weekend programs available. *Degree requirements:* For doctorate, comprehensive exam, thesis/dissertation. *Entrance requirements:* For master's, GRE General Test, Florida General Knowledge Test or Florida College Level Academic Skills Test; for doctorate and Ed S, GRE General Test. Additional exam requirements/recommendations for international students: Required—TOEFL (minimum score 550 paper-based; 80 iBT), IELTS (minimum score 6.3). Electronic applications accepted.

Florida State University, The Graduate School, College of Arts and Sciences, Department of Biological Science, Masters in Science Teaching Program, Tallahassee, FL 32306. Offers community college science teaching (MST); secondary science teaching (MST). *Faculty:* 2 full-time (both women). *Students:* 4 full-time (2 women). Average age 27. 3 applicants, 67% accepted, 2 enrolled. In 2013, 4 master's awarded. *Degree requirements:* For master's, thesis or alternative, teacher work sample (action research). *Entrance requirements:* For master's, GRE. *Application deadline:* For fall admission, 7/1 for domestic students; for spring admission, 11/1 for domestic students; for summer admission, 3/1 for domestic students. Application fee: $30. Electronic applications accepted. *Expenses:* Tuition, state resident: part-time $403.51 per credit hour. Tuition, nonresident: part-time $1004.85 per credit hour. *Required fees:* $75.81 per credit hour. One-time fee: $20 part-time. Tuition and fees vary according to course load, campus/location and student level. *Faculty research:* Science and mathematics education, science and mathematics teacher preparation. *Total annual research expenditures:* $500,000. *Unit head:* Dr. Don R. Levitan, Chairman and Professor, Department of Biological Science, 850-644-4424, Fax: 850-645-8447, E-mail: levitan@bio.fsu.edu. *Application contact:* Erica M. Staehling, Director, Master's in Science Teaching Program, 850-644-1142, Fax: 850-644-0643, E-mail: staehling@bio.fsu.edu.
Website: http://bio.fsu.edu/osta/tpp.php.

Florida State University, The Graduate School, College of Education, School of Teacher Education, Tallahassee, FL 32306. Offers curriculum and instruction (MS, MST, PhD, Ed S), including early childhood education (MS, PhD, Ed S), elementary education (MS, PhD, Ed S), English education (MS, PhD, Ed S), English teaching (MST), exceptional student education (MST), foreign and second language education (MS, PhD, Ed S), foreign and second language teaching (MST), math education (MS, PhD, Ed S), math teaching (MST), reading education and language arts (MS, PhD, Ed S), science education (MS, PhD, Ed S), social science education (MS, PhD, Ed S), social science teaching (MST), special education (MS, PhD, Ed S), special education studies (MST), visual disabilities (MS, Ed S). Part-time programs available. *Faculty:* 30 full-time (20 women), 22 part-time/adjunct (18 women). *Students:* 183 full-time (151 women), 92 part-time (80 women); includes 47 minority (20 Black or African American, non-Hispanic/Latino; 3 American Indian or Alaska Native, non-Hispanic/Latino; 1 Asian, non-Hispanic/Latino; 20 Hispanic/Latino; 3 Two or more races, non-Hispanic/Latino), 61 international. Average age 30. 199 applicants, 79% accepted, 86 enrolled. In 2013, 119 master's, 9 doctorates, 4 other advanced degrees awarded. *Degree requirements:* For master's and Ed S, comprehensive exam, thesis optional; for doctorate, comprehensive exam, thesis/dissertation, preliminary exam, prospectus defense. *Entrance requirements:* For master's, doctorate, and Ed S, GRE General Test, minimum GPA of 3.0. Additional exam requirements/recommendations for international students: Required—TOEFL (minimum score 550 paper-based; 80 iBT). *Application deadline:* For fall admission, 7/1 for domestic and international students; for winter admission, 10/1 for domestic students, 11/1 for international students; for spring admission, 3/1 for domestic and international students. Applications are processed on a rolling basis. Application fee: $30. Electronic applications accepted. *Expenses:* Tuition, state resident: part-time $403.51 per credit hour. Tuition, nonresident: part-time $1004.85 per credit hour. *Required fees:* $75.81 per credit hour. One-time fee: $20 part-time. Tuition and fees vary according to course load, campus/location and student level. *Financial support:* In 2013–14, 113 students received support, including 55 research assistantships with full and partial tuition reimbursements available, 18 teaching assistantships with full and partial tuition reimbursements available; fellowships with full and partial tuition reimbursements available, career-related internships or fieldwork, scholarships/grants, health care benefits, and unspecified assistantships also available. Financial award application deadline: 1/15; financial award applicants required to submit FAFSA. *Faculty research:* Effective intervention and assessment strategies to improve reading skills; literacy teaching and learning through technology; understanding of student sense-making through instructions, especially STEM learning for all students; international education and consequences of globalization; support professional teacher development and adoption of effective/transformative practices. *Total annual research expenditures:* $1.3 million. *Unit head:* Dr. Sherry Southerland, Chair, 850-644-4880, Fax: 850-644-7736, E-mail: ssoutherland@admin.fsu.edu. *Application contact:* Dawn Matthews, Academic Support Assistant, 850-644-2122, Fax: 850-644-7736, E-mail: dmatthews@fsu.edu.
Website: http://www.coe.fsu.edu/STE.

Fresno Pacific University, Graduate Programs, School of Education, Division of Mathematics/Science/Computer Education, Program in Integrated Mathematics/Science Education, Fresno, CA 93702-4709. Offers MA Ed. Part-time and evening/weekend

programs available. *Students:* 9 part-time (5 women); includes 4 minority (all Hispanic/Latino). Average age 42. *Degree requirements:* For master's, thesis or alternative. *Entrance requirements:* Additional exam requirements/recommendations for international students: Required—TOEFL (minimum score 550 paper-based). *Application deadline:* For fall admission, 7/15 for domestic and international students; for spring admission, 11/15 for domestic and international students. Applications are processed on a rolling basis. Application fee: $90. *Expenses: Tuition:* Full-time $8910; part-time $495 per unit. *Required fees:* $270. Tuition and fees vary according to course load and program. *Financial support:* Scholarships/grants and tuition waivers (full and partial) available. Support available to part-time students. Financial award applicants required to submit FAFSA. *Unit head:* Dr. Dave Youngs, Program Director, 559-453-2244, Fax: 559-453-7106, E-mail: dyoungs@fresno.edu. *Application contact:* Amanda Krum-Stovall, Director of Graduate Admissions, 559-453-2016, E-mail: amanda.krum-stovall@fresno.edu.
Website: http://grad.fresno.edu/programs/master-arts-education-integrated-mathematicsscience-education-emphasis.

Georgia State University, College of Education, Department of Middle-Secondary Education and Instructional Technology, Atlanta, GA 30302-3083. Offers English education (M Ed, MAT); English speakers of other languages (MAT); instructional design and technology (MS); instructional technology (PhD), including alternative instructional delivery systems, consulting, instructional design, management, research; mathematics education (M Ed, MAT); middle level education (MAT); reading, language and literacy education (M Ed), including reading instruction; science education (MAT), including biology, broad field science, chemistry, earth science, physics; social studies education (M Ed, MAT), including economics (MAT), geography (MAT), history (MAT), political science (MAT); teaching and learning (PhD), including language and literacy, mathematics education, music education, science education, social studies, teaching and teacher education. *Accreditation:* NCATE. Part-time and evening/weekend programs available. Postbaccalaureate distance learning degree programs offered (minimal on-campus study). *Faculty:* 27 full-time (19 women). *Students:* 181 full-time (113 women), 203 part-time (145 women); includes 161 minority (127 Black or African American, non-Hispanic/Latino; 1 American Indian or Alaska Native, non-Hispanic/Latino; 10 Asian, non-Hispanic/Latino; 11 Hispanic/Latino; 1 Native Hawaiian or other Pacific Islander, non-Hispanic/Latino; 11 Two or more races, non-Hispanic/Latino), 9 international. Average age 36. 2 applicants, 50% accepted, 1 enrolled. In 2013, 213 master's, 17 doctorates awarded. *Degree requirements:* For master's, comprehensive exam (for some programs), thesis or alternative, exit portfolio; for doctorate, comprehensive exam, thesis/dissertation. *Entrance requirements:* For master's, GRE; GACE I (for initial teacher preparation degree programs), baccalaureate degree or equivalent, resume, goals statement, two letters of recommendation, minimum undergraduate GPA of 2.5; proof of initial teacher certification in the content area (for M Ed); for doctorate, GRE, resume, goals statement, writing sample, two letters of recommendation, minimum graduate GPA of 3.3, interview. Additional exam requirements/recommendations for international students: Required—TOEFL (minimum score 550 paper-based; 79 iBT) or IELTS (minimum score 6.5). *Application deadline:* For fall admission, 1/15 priority date for domestic and international students; for spring admission, 10/1 for domestic and international students. Application fee: $50. Electronic applications accepted. *Expenses: Tuition, area resident:* Full-time $4176; part-time $348 per credit hour. Tuition, state resident: full-time $14,544; part-time $1212 per credit hour. Tuition, nonresident: full-time $14,544; part-time $1212 per credit hour. Tuition and fees vary according to course load and program. *Financial support:* In 2013–14, fellowships with full tuition reimbursements (averaging $19,667 per year), research assistantships with full tuition reimbursements (averaging $5,436 per year), teaching assistantships with full tuition reimbursements (averaging $2,779 per year) were awarded; career-related internships or fieldwork, Federal Work-Study, scholarships/grants, health care benefits, tuition waivers (full and partial), and unspecified assistantships also available. Financial award application deadline: 3/15. *Faculty research:* Teacher education in language and literacy, mathematics, science, and social studies in urban middle and secondary school settings; learning technologies in school, community, and corporate settings; multicultural education and education for social justice; urban education; international education. *Unit head:* Dr. Dana L. Fox, Chair, 404-413-8060, Fax: 404-413-8063, E-mail: dfox@gsu.edu. *Application contact:* Bobbie Turner, Administrative Coordinator I, 404-413-8405, Fax: 404-413-8063, E-mail: bnturner@gsu.edu.
Website: http://msit.gsu.edu/msit_programs.htm.

Grambling State University, School of Graduate Studies and Research, College of Education, Department of Educational Leadership, Grambling, LA 71245. Offers developmental education (MS, Ed D, PMC), including curriculum and instructional design (Ed D), English (MS), guidance and counseling (MS), higher education administration and management (Ed D), mathematics (MS), reading (MS), science (MS), student development and personnel services (Ed D); educational leadership (M Ed). Part-time and evening/weekend programs available. *Faculty:* 10 full-time (7 women). *Students:* 19 full-time (13 women), 89 part-time (70 women); includes 83 minority (82 Black or African American, non-Hispanic/Latino; 1 Hispanic/Latino), 6 international. Average age 40. In 2013, 13 master's, 6 doctorates, 1 other advanced degree awarded. *Degree requirements:* For master's, comprehensive exam, thesis (for some programs); for doctorate, comprehensive exam, thesis/dissertation. *Entrance requirements:* For master's, GRE, minimum GPA of 2.5 on last degree; for doctorate, GRE (minimum score 1000, 500 on Verbal), master's degree, minimum GPA of 3.0 on last degree. Additional exam requirements/recommendations for international students: Required—TOEFL (minimum score 500 paper-based; 62 iBT). *Application deadline:* For fall admission, 7/1 for domestic and international students; for spring admission, 12/1 for domestic and international students; for summer admission, 5/1 for domestic and international students. Applications are processed on a rolling basis. Application fee: $20 ($30 for international students). Electronic applications accepted. *Financial support:* Research assistantships, health care benefits, tuition waivers (full), and unspecified assistantships available. Financial award application deadline: 5/31; financial award applicants required to submit FAFSA. *Unit head:* Dr. Olatunde Ogunyemi, Department Head, 318-274-2549, Fax: 318-274-6249, E-mail: ogunyemio@gram.edu. *Application contact:* Brenda Cooper, Administrative Assistant III, 318-274-2238, Fax: 318-274-6249, E-mail: cooper@gram.edu.
Website: http://www.gram.edu/academics/majors/education/departments/leadership/.

Hamline University, School of Education, St. Paul, MN 55104-1284. Offers education (MA Ed, Ed D); English as a second language (MA); literacy education (MA); natural science and environmental education (MA Ed); teaching (MAT). *Accreditation:* NCATE (one or more programs are accredited). Part-time and evening/weekend programs available. Postbaccalaureate distance learning degree programs offered (no on-campus study). *Faculty:* 19 full-time (14 women), 44 part-time/adjunct (38 women). *Students:* 107 full-time (75 women), 997 part-time (744 women); includes 71 minority (23 Black or African American, non-Hispanic/Latino; 4 American Indian or Alaska Native, non-Hispanic/Latino; 17 Asian, non-Hispanic/Latino; 21 Hispanic/Latino; 6 Two or more races, non-Hispanic/Latino), 10 international. Average age 33. 395 applicants, 74% accepted, 224 enrolled. In 2013, 221 master's, 13 doctorates awarded. *Degree requirements:* For master's, foreign language (for MA in English as a second language only); thesis or capstone project; for doctorate, comprehensive exam, thesis/dissertation. *Entrance requirements:* For master's, written essay, official transcripts, 2 letters of recommendation, minimum GPA of 3.0 from bachelor's work; for doctorate, personal statement, master's degree with minimum GPA of 3.0, 3 letters of recommendation, writing sample, interview. Additional exam requirements/recommendations for international students: Required—TOEFL (minimum score 550 paper-based; 80 iBT), TOEFL (625 paper-based, 107 iBT) or IELTS (minimum 7.5) for MA in ESL. *Application deadline:* Applications are processed on a rolling basis. Application fee: $0 ($100 for international students). Electronic applications accepted. *Financial support:* Career-related internships or fieldwork, Federal Work-Study, and scholarships/grants available. Support available to part-time students. Financial award applicants required to submit FAFSA. *Faculty research:* Adult basic education, service-learning, teacher dispositions, diversity, technology. *Unit head:* Dr. Nancy Sorenson, Dean, 651-523-2600, Fax: 651-523-2489, E-mail: nsorenson01@hamline.edu. *Application contact:* Shawn Skoog, Director of Graduate Recruitment and Admission, 651-523-2900, Fax: 651-523-3058, E-mail: sskoog03@hamline.edu.
Website: http://www.hamline.edu/education.

Hardin-Simmons University, Graduate School, Holland School of Sciences and Mathematics, Abilene, TX 79698-0001. Offers MS, DPT. Part-time programs available. *Faculty:* 3 full-time (1 woman). *Students:* 3 full-time (1 woman). Average age 27. In 2013, 6 master's awarded. *Degree requirements:* For master's, comprehensive exam, thesis or alternative, internship; for doctorate, comprehensive exam, thesis/dissertation or alternative. *Entrance requirements:* For master's, minimum undergraduate GPA of 3.0 in major, 2.7 overall; 2 semesters of course work each in biology, chemistry and geology; interview; writing sample; occupational experience; for doctorate, letters of recommendation, interview, writing sample. Additional exam requirements/recommendations for international students: Required—TOEFL (minimum score 550 paper-based; 75 iBT). *Application deadline:* For fall admission, 8/15 priority date for domestic students, 4/1 for international students; for spring admission, 1/5 priority date for domestic students, 9/1 for international students. Applications are processed on a rolling basis. Application fee: $50. *Expenses: Tuition:* Full-time $13,410; part-time $745 per credit hour. *Required fees:* $325; $110 per semester. Tuition and fees vary according to program. *Financial support:* In 2013–14, 5 students received support. Fellowships, career-related internships or fieldwork, and scholarships/grants available. Support available to part-time students. Financial award application deadline: 6/30; financial award applicants required to submit FAFSA. *Unit head:* Dr. Christopher McNair, Dean, 325-670-1401, Fax: 325-670-1385, E-mail: cmcnair@hsutx.edu. *Application contact:* Dr. Nancy Kucinski, Dean of Graduate Studies, 325-670-1298, Fax: 325-670-1564, E-mail: gradoff@hsutx.edu.
Website: http://www.hsutx.edu/academics/holland.

Harrison Middleton University, Graduate Program, Tempe, AZ 85282. Offers education (MA, Ed D); humanities (MA); imaginative literature (MA); interdisciplinary studies (DA); jurisprudence (MA); natural science (MA); philosophy and religion (MA); social science (MA). Part-time and evening/weekend programs available. Postbaccalaureate distance learning degree programs offered (no on-campus study). *Degree requirements:* For master's and doctorate, capstone project. *Entrance requirements:* For master's, interview; for doctorate, 2 academic letters of reference, interview, essay. Additional exam requirements/recommendations for international students: Required—TOEFL (minimum score 550 paper-based; 80 iBT). Electronic applications accepted. *Faculty research:* Japanese animation, educational leadership, war art, John Muir's wilderness.

Heritage University, Graduate Programs in Education, Program in Professional Studies, Toppenish, WA 98948-9599. Offers bilingual education/ESL (M Ed); biology (M Ed); English and literature (M Ed); reading/literacy (M Ed); special education (M Ed). Part-time and evening/weekend programs available. *Degree requirements:* For master's, comprehensive exam (for some programs), thesis (for some programs).

Hofstra University, School of Education, Programs in Teaching - Elementary and Early Childhood Education, Hempstead, NY 11549. Offers early childhood and childhood education (MS Ed); early childhood education (MA, MS Ed); educational technology (MA); elementary education (MS Ed); literacy (MA); math specialist (Advanced Certificate); math, science, technology (MA); multiculturalism (MA).

Hofstra University, School of Education, Programs in Teaching - Secondary Education, Hempstead, NY 11549. Offers business education (MS Ed); education technology (Advanced Certificate); English education (MA, MS Ed); foreign language and TESOL (MS Ed); foreign language education (MA, MS Ed), including French, German, Russian, Spanish; mathematics education (MA, MS Ed); science education (MA, MS Ed), including biology, chemistry, earth science, geology, physics; secondary education (Advanced Certificate); social studies education (MA, MS Ed); technology for learning (MA).

Hood College, Graduate School, Department of Education, Frederick, MD 21701-8575. Offers curriculum and instruction (MS), including early childhood education, elementary education, elementary school science and mathematics, secondary education, special education; educational leadership (MS, Certificate); reading specialization (MS); STEM (Certificate). *Accreditation:* NCATE. Part-time and evening/weekend programs available. *Faculty:* 4 full-time (3 women), 33 part-time/adjunct (25 women). *Students:* 1 (woman) full-time, 340 part-time (282 women); includes 59 minority (31 Black or African American, non-Hispanic/Latino; 1 American Indian or Alaska Native, non-Hispanic/Latino; 10 Asian, non-Hispanic/Latino; 13 Hispanic/Latino; 4 Two or more races, non-Hispanic/Latino). Average age 33. 97 applicants, 99% accepted, 86 enrolled. In 2013, 64 master's, 40 other advanced degrees awarded. *Degree requirements:* For master's, action research project, portfolio (reading). *Entrance requirements:* For master's, minimum GPA of 2.75, teaching certification. Additional exam requirements/recommendations for international students: Required—TOEFL (minimum score 575 paper-based; 89 iBT), IELTS (minimum score 6.5). *Application deadline:* For fall admission, 7/15 priority date for domestic students, 7/15 for international students; for spring admission, 12/1 priority date for domestic students, 12/1 for international students. Applications are processed on a rolling basis. Application fee: $35. Electronic applications accepted. Application fee is waived when completed online. *Expenses: Tuition:* Part-time $405 per credit. *Required fees:* $100 per semester. *Financial support:* In 2013–14, 1 student received support. Tuition waivers (partial) and unspecified assistantships available. Financial award applicants required to submit FAFSA. *Faculty research:* Leadership, action research, brain research, learning styles. *Unit head:* Dr. Ellen Koitz, Chairperson, 301-696-3466, Fax: 301-696-3597, E-mail: koitz@hood.edu. *Application contact:* Dr. Maria Green Cowles, Dean of Graduate School, 301-696-3811, Fax: 301-696-3597, E-mail: gofurther@hood.edu.
Website: http://www.hood.edu/academics/education/index.html.

Hunter College of the City University of New York, Graduate School, School of Arts and Sciences, Department of Geography, New York, NY 10065-5085. Offers analytical geography (MA); earth system science (MA); environmental and social issues (MA); geographic information science (Certificate); geographic information systems (MA); teaching earth science (MA). Part-time and evening/weekend programs available. *Faculty:* 5 full-time (2 women), 6 part-time/adjunct (0 women). *Students:* 2 full-time (both women), 55 part-time (26 women); includes 11 minority (1 Black or African American,

non-Hispanic/Latino; 5 Asian, non-Hispanic/Latino; 5 Hispanic/Latino), 3 international. Average age 33. 21 applicants, 71% accepted, 9 enrolled. In 2013, 12 master's, 4 other advanced degrees awarded. *Degree requirements:* For master's, comprehensive exam or thesis. *Entrance requirements:* For master's, GRE General Test, minimum B average in major, B- overall; 18 credits of course work in geography; 2 letters of recommendation; for Certificate, minimum B average in major, B- overall. Additional exam requirements/recommendations for international students: Required—TOEFL. *Application deadline:* For fall admission, 4/1 for domestic students; for spring admission, 11/1 for domestic students. Applications are processed on a rolling basis. Application fee: $125. *Financial support:* In 2013–14, 1 fellowship (averaging $3,000 per year), 2 research assistantships (averaging $10,000 per year), 10 teaching assistantships (averaging $6,000 per year) were awarded; career-related internships or fieldwork, Federal Work-Study, institutionally sponsored loans, and unspecified assistantships also available. Financial award application deadline: 3/1. *Faculty research:* Urban geography, economic geography, geographic information science, demographic methods, climate change. *Unit head:* Prof. Allan Frei, Chair, 212-772-5450, Fax: 212-772-5322, E-mail: afrei@hunter.cuny.edu. *Application contact:* Prof. Marianna Pavlovskaya, Graduate Adviser, 212-772-5320, Fax: 212-772-5268, E-mail: mpavlov@geo.hunter.cuny.edu. Website: http://www.geo.hunter.cuny.edu/.

Hunter College of the City University of New York, Graduate School, School of Education, Programs in Secondary Education, Concentration in Biology Education, New York, NY 10065-5085. Offers MA. *Accreditation:* NCATE. *Faculty:* 3 full-time (1 woman), 20 part-time/adjunct (9 women). *Students:* 1 (woman) full-time, 13 part-time (9 women); includes 7 minority (1 Black or African American, non-Hispanic/Latino; 5 Asian, non-Hispanic/Latino; 1 Hispanic/Latino), 1 international. Average age 31. 17 applicants, 71% accepted, 7 enrolled. In 2013, 6 master's awarded. *Degree requirements:* For master's, thesis, professional teaching portfolio, New York State Teacher Certification Exams, research project. *Entrance requirements:* For master's, minimum GPA of 2.8, 2 letters of reference, 21 credits of course work in biology. Additional exam requirements/recommendations for international students: Required—TOEFL, TWE. *Application deadline:* For fall admission, 4/1 for domestic students, 2/1 for international students; for spring admission, 11/1 for domestic students, 9/1 for international students. Application fee: $125. *Financial support:* Federal Work-Study and tuition waivers (partial) available. Support available to part-time students. *Unit head:* Dr. Steve Demeo, Program Advisor, 212-772-4776, E-mail: sdemeo@hunter.cuny.edu. *Application contact:* Milena Solo, Director for Graduate Admissions, 212-772-4482, E-mail: admissions@hunter.cuny.edu. Website: http://www.hunter.cuny.edu/school-of-education/programs/graduate/adolescent/science/biology.

Hunter College of the City University of New York, Graduate School, School of Education, Programs in Secondary Education, Concentration in Chemistry Education, New York, NY 10065-5085. Offers MA. *Accreditation:* NCATE. *Faculty:* 3 full-time (1 woman), 20 part-time/adjunct (9 women). *Students:* 9 part-time (7 women); includes 1 minority (Hispanic/Latino), 1 international. Average age 27. 10 applicants, 90% accepted, 3 enrolled. In 2013, 4 master's awarded. *Degree requirements:* For master's, thesis, professional teaching portfolio, New York State Teacher Certification Exam. *Entrance requirements:* For master's, minimum GPA of 2.8, 2 letters of reference, minimum of 29 credits in science and mathematics. *Application deadline:* For fall admission, 4/1 for domestic students, 2/1 for international students; for spring admission, 11/1 for domestic students, 9/1 for international students. Application fee: $125. *Financial support:* Federal Work-Study and tuition waivers (partial) available. Support available to part-time students. *Unit head:* Dr. Stephen DeMeo, Education Advisor, 212-772-4776, E-mail: sdemeo@patsy.hunter.cuny.edu. *Application contact:* Pamela Mills, Chemistry Department Advisor, 212-772-5331, E-mail: pam.mills@hunter.cuny.edu.
Website: http://www.hunter.cuny.edu/school-of-education/programs/graduate/adolescent/science/chemistry.

Illinois Institute of Technology, Graduate College, College of Science and Letters, Department of Mathematics and Science Education, Chicago, IL 60616. Offers collegiate mathematics education (PhD); mathematics education (MME, MS, PhD); science education (MS, MSE, PhD). *Degree requirements:* For master's, comprehensive exam (for some programs), thesis optional; for doctorate, comprehensive exam, thesis/dissertation. *Entrance requirements:* For master's, GRE General Test, minimum undergraduate GPA of 3.0; for doctorate, GRE General Test, minimum GPA of 3.0, 3 years of teaching experience. Additional exam requirements/recommendations for international students: Required—TOEFL (minimum score 523 paper-based; 70 iBT). Electronic applications accepted. *Faculty research:* Informal science/math education, curriculum development, integration of science/math disciplines and across disciplines, instructional methods, students' and teachers' conceptions of scientific/mathematical inquiry and the nature of science/math, instructional models, evaluation, and research design.

Indiana State University, College of Graduate and Professional Studies, College of Arts and Sciences, Department of Biology, Terre Haute, IN 47809. Offers ecology (PhD); life sciences (MS); microbiology (PhD); physiology (PhD); science education (MS). *Faculty:* 23 full-time (6 women), 1 (woman) part-time/adjunct. *Students:* 73 full-time (31 women), 15 part-time (6 women); includes 7 minority (6 Asian, non-Hispanic/Latino; 1 Hispanic/Latino), 17 international. Average age 26. 63 applicants, 65% accepted, 40 enrolled. In 2013, 9 master's, 5 doctorates awarded. *Degree requirements:* For master's, thesis (for some programs); for doctorate, comprehensive exam, thesis/dissertation. *Entrance requirements:* For master's and doctorate, GRE General Test. *Application deadline:* For fall admission, 7/1 priority date for domestic students; for spring admission, 11/1 priority date for domestic students. Applications are processed on a rolling basis. Application fee: $35. Electronic applications accepted. *Financial support:* In 2013–14, 9 research assistantships with partial tuition reimbursements (averaging $7,500 per year), 19 teaching assistantships with partial tuition reimbursements (averaging $8,000 per year) were awarded; Federal Work-Study, institutionally sponsored loans, and tuition waivers (partial) also available. Financial award application deadline: 3/1; financial award applicants required to submit FAFSA. *Unit head:* Dr. Arthur M. Halpern, Interim Chairperson, 812-237-2400. *Application contact:* Dr. Jay Gatrell, Dean, 800-444-GRAD, Fax: 812-237-8060, E-mail: jay.gatrell@indstate.edu.

Indiana State University, College of Graduate and Professional Studies, College of Arts and Sciences, Department of Science Education, Terre Haute, IN 47809. Offers MS. *Accreditation:* NCATE. *Degree requirements:* For master's, thesis optional. Electronic applications accepted.

Indiana Tech, Program in Science, Fort Wayne, IN 46803-1297. Offers MSE. Part-time and evening/weekend programs available. *Students:* 11 full-time (1 woman), 11 part-time (0 women); includes 2 minority (1 Asian, non-Hispanic/Latino; 1 Hispanic/Latino). Average age 36. *Entrance requirements:* For master's, BS in a technical field, minimum GPA of 2.5, one undergraduate course each in accounting and finance. *Application deadline:* Applications are processed on a rolling basis. Application fee: $25. Electronic applications accepted. *Expenses:* *Tuition:* Full-time $8910; part-time $495 per credit. Tuition and fees vary according to course load, degree level and program. *Financial support:* Applicants required to submit FAFSA. *Unit head:* David A. Aschliman, Dean of Engineering and Computer Sciences, 260-422-5561 Ext. 2102, E-mail: daaschliman@indianatech.edu.

Indiana University Bloomington, School of Education, Department of Curriculum and Instruction, Bloomington, IN 47405-7000. Offers art education (MS, Ed D, PhD); curriculum studies (Ed D, PhD); elementary education (MS, Ed D, PhD, Ed S); mathematics education (MS, Ed D, PhD); science education (MS, Ed D, PhD); secondary education (MS, Ed D, PhD); social studies education (MS, PhD); special education (PhD, Ed S). *Accreditation:* NCATE. Part-time and evening/weekend programs available. Terminal master's awarded for partial completion of doctoral program. *Degree requirements:* For doctorate, thesis/dissertation; for Ed S, comprehensive exam or project. *Entrance requirements:* For master's, doctorate, and Ed S, GRE General Test. Electronic applications accepted.

Indiana University Bloomington, University Graduate School, College of Arts and Sciences, Department of Biology, Bloomington, IN 47405. Offers biology teaching (MAT); biotechnology (MA); evolution, ecology, and behavior (MA, PhD); genetics (PhD); microbiology (MA, PhD); molecular, cellular, and developmental biology (PhD); plant sciences (MA, PhD); zoology (MA, PhD). *Faculty:* 58 full-time (15 women), 21 part-time/adjunct (6 women). *Students:* 166 full-time (94 women), 2 part-time (both women); includes 22 minority (8 Black or African American, non-Hispanic/Latino; 3 Asian, non-Hispanic/Latino; 10 Hispanic/Latino; 1 Two or more races, non-Hispanic/Latino), 47 international. Average age 27. 261 applicants, 23% accepted, 32 enrolled. In 2013, 17 master's, 20 doctorates awarded. Terminal master's awarded for partial completion of doctoral program. *Degree requirements:* For master's, thesis, oral defense; for doctorate, thesis/dissertation, oral defense. *Entrance requirements:* For master's and doctorate, GRE General Test. Additional exam requirements/recommendations for international students: Required—TOEFL (minimum score 100 iBT). *Application deadline:* For fall admission, 1/5 priority date for domestic students, 12/1 priority date for international students. Application fee: $55 ($65 for international students). Electronic applications accepted. *Financial support:* In 2013–14, fellowships with tuition reimbursements (averaging $24,000 per year), research assistantships with tuition reimbursements (averaging $21,000 per year), teaching assistantships with tuition reimbursements (averaging $22,000 per year) were awarded; scholarships/grants, traineeships, health care benefits, and unspecified assistantships also available. Financial award application deadline: 1/5. *Faculty research:* Evolution, ecology and behavior; microbiology; molecular biology and genetics; plant biology. *Unit head:* Dr. Clay Fuqua, Chair, 812-856-6005, Fax: 812-855-6082, E-mail: cfuqua@indiana.edu. *Application contact:* Tracey D. Stohr, Graduate Student Recruitment Coordinator, 812-856-6303, Fax: 812-855-6082, E-mail: gradbio@indiana.edu.
Website: http://www.bio.indiana.edu/.

Indiana University Bloomington, University Graduate School, College of Arts and Sciences, Department of Chemistry, Bloomington, IN 47405. Offers analytical chemistry (PhD); chemical biology (PhD); chemistry (MAT); inorganic chemistry (PhD); materials chemistry (PhD); organic chemistry (PhD); physical chemistry (PhD). *Faculty:* 42 full-time (4 women). *Students:* 189 full-time (80 women), 6 part-time (5 women); includes 17 minority (6 Black or African American, non-Hispanic/Latino; 7 Asian, non-Hispanic/Latino; 2 Hispanic/Latino; 2 Two or more races, non-Hispanic/Latino), 60 international. Average age 27. 220 applicants, 40% accepted, 19 enrolled. In 2013, 12 master's, 20 doctorates awarded. Terminal master's awarded for partial completion of doctoral program. *Degree requirements:* For master's, thesis; for doctorate, thesis/dissertation. *Entrance requirements:* For master's and doctorate, GRE General Test, GRE Subject Test. Additional exam requirements/recommendations for international students: Required—TOEFL. *Application deadline:* For fall admission, 1/15 priority date for domestic students, 12/1 for international students. Applications are processed on a rolling basis. Application fee: $55 ($65 for international students). Electronic applications accepted. *Financial support:* In 2013–14, 10 fellowships with full tuition reimbursements, 66 research assistantships with full tuition reimbursements, 108 teaching assistantships with full tuition reimbursements were awarded; Federal Work-Study and institutionally sponsored loans also available. *Faculty research:* Synthesis of complex natural products, organic reaction mechanisms, organic electrochemistry, transitive-metal chemistry, solid-state and surface chemistry. *Total annual research expenditures:* $7.7 million. *Unit head:* Dr. David Giedroc, Chairperson, 812-855-6239, E-mail: chemchair@indiana.edu. *Application contact:* Dalane Anderson, Admissions Coordinator, 812-855-2069, Fax: 812-855-8385, E-mail: chemgrad@indiana.edu.
Website: http://www.chem.indiana.edu/.

Instituto Tecnológico y de Estudios Superiores de Monterrey, Campus Monterrey, Graduate and Research Division, Program in Natural and Social Sciences, Monterrey, Mexico. Offers biotechnology (MS); chemistry (MS, PhD); communications (MS); education (MA). Part-time programs available. *Degree requirements:* For master's, one foreign language, thesis; for doctorate, one foreign language, thesis/dissertation. *Entrance requirements:* For master's, EXADEP; for doctorate, EXADEP, master's degree in related field. Additional exam requirements/recommendations for international students: Required—TOEFL. *Faculty research:* Cultural industries, mineral substances, bioremediation, food processing, CQ in industrial chemical processing.

Inter American University of Puerto Rico, Arecibo Campus, Programs in Education, Arecibo, PR 00614-4050. Offers administration and educational supervision (MA Ed); counseling and guidance (MA Ed); curriculum and teaching (MA Ed), including biology education, English as a second language, history education, math education, Spanish; elementary education (MA Ed). *Degree requirements:* For master's, comprehensive exam, thesis optional. *Entrance requirements:* For master's, GRE, EXADEP, bachelor's degree in education or teaching license (administration and supervision) or courses in education and psychology (counseling and guidance), minimum GPA of 2.5 in last 60 credits.

Inter American University of Puerto Rico, Barranquitas Campus, Program in Education, Barranquitas, PR 00794. Offers curriculum and teaching (M Ed), including biology education, English as a second language, history education, mathematics education, Spanish; educational leadership and management (MA); elementary education (M Ed); information and library service technology (M Ed); special education (MA). *Degree requirements:* For master's, comprehensive exam, thesis optional. *Entrance requirements:* For master's, EXADEP, letter of recommendation. Electronic applications accepted.

Inter American University of Puerto Rico, Metropolitan Campus, Graduate Programs, Program in Teaching of Science, San Juan, PR 00919-1293. Offers MA. *Degree requirements:* For master's, comprehensive exam. *Entrance requirements:* For master's, GRE or EXADEP, interview. Electronic applications accepted.

Inter American University of Puerto Rico, Ponce Campus, Graduate School, Mercedita, PR 00715-1602. Offers accounting (MBA); biology (M Ed); chemistry (M Ed); criminal justice (MA); elementary education (M Ed); English as a Second Language (M Ed); finance (MBA); history (M Ed); human resources (MBA); marketing (MBA); mathematics (M Ed); Spanish (M Ed). *Entrance requirements:* For master's, minimum GPA of 2.5.

Inter American University of Puerto Rico, San Germán Campus, Graduate Studies Center, Program in Science Education, San Germán, PR 00683-5008. Offers MA. Part-

time and evening/weekend programs available. *Faculty:* 8 full-time (6 women), 13 part-time/adjunct (7 women). *Students:* 15 full-time (14 women), 1 (woman) part-time; all minorities (all Hispanic/Latino). Average age 35. 3 applicants, 33% accepted, 1 enrolled. *Degree requirements:* For master's, comprehensive exam. *Entrance requirements:* For master's, GRE General Test or EXADEP, minimum GPA of 3.0. *Application deadline:* For fall admission, 4/30 priority date for domestic students; for spring admission, 11/15 for domestic students. Applications are processed on a rolling basis. Application fee: $31. *Expenses: Tuition:* Full-time $2424; part-time $202 per credit hour. *Required fees:* $260 per semester. Tuition and fees vary according to course level, course load, degree level and program. *Financial support:* Teaching assistantships and unspecified assistantships available. *Unit head:* Dr. Elba T. Irizarry, Director of Graduate Studies Center, 787-264-1912 Ext. 7357, Fax: 787-892-6350, E-mail: elbat@sg.inter.edu. *Application contact:* Dr. Elba T. Irizarry, Director of Graduate Studies Center, 787-264-1912 Ext. 7357, Fax: 787-892-6350, E-mail: elbat@sg.inter.edu.

Iona College, School of Arts and Science, Department of Education, New Rochelle, NY 10801-1890. Offers adolescence education: biology (MS Ed, MST); adolescence education: English (MS Ed, MST); adolescence education: Italian (MS Ed, MST); adolescence education: mathematics (MS Ed, MST); adolescence education: social studies (MS Ed, MST); adolescence education: Spanish (MS Ed, MST); adolescence special education 5-12 (MST); adolescence special education and literacy (MS Ed); childhood and special education (MST); childhood education (MST); early childhood and childhood (MST); educational leadership (MS Ed); literacy education: birth-grade 6 (MS Ed). *Accreditation:* NCATE. Part-time and evening/weekend programs available. *Faculty:* 11 full-time (9 women), 7 part-time/adjunct (6 women). *Students:* 34 full-time (25 women), 61 part-time (47 women); includes 5 minority (2 Asian, non-Hispanic/Latino; 3 Hispanic/Latino), 1 international. Average age 25. 27 applicants, 93% accepted, 16 enrolled. In 2013, 54 master's awarded. *Degree requirements:* For master's, thesis or alternative. *Entrance requirements:* For master's, minimum GPA of 3.0, NY State teaching certificate (for all MS Ed programs). Additional exam requirements/recommendations for international students: Required—TOEFL (minimum score 550 paper-based; 80 iBT), IELTS (minimum score 6.5). *Application deadline:* For fall admission, 8/1 priority date for domestic students, 5/1 priority date for international students; for spring admission, 1/1 priority date for domestic students, 9/1 priority date for international students. Applications are processed on a rolling basis. Application fee: $50. Electronic applications accepted. *Expenses: Tuition:* Part-time $948 per credit. *Required fees:* $235 per term. *Financial support:* In 2013–14, 84 students received support. Unspecified assistantships available. Support available to part-time students. Financial award application deadline: 4/15; financial award applicants required to submit FAFSA. *Faculty research:* Reading/writing, educational technology, administration, early literacy assessment, literacy development. *Unit head:* Margaret Smith, PhD, Chair, 914-633-2210, Fax: 914-633-2608, E-mail: msmith@iona.edu. *Application contact:* Veronica Jarek-Prinz, Director, Graduate Admissions, 914-633-2420, Fax: 914-633-2277, E-mail: vjarekprinz@iona.edu.
Website: http://www.iona.edu/Academics/School-of-Arts-Science/Departments/Education/Graduate-Programs.aspx.

Iowa State University of Science and Technology, Program in Science Education, Ames, IA 50011. Offers MAT. *Entrance requirements:* For master's, GRE, three letters of recommendation, undergraduate degree in sciences (preferred). Additional exam requirements/recommendations for international students: Required—TOEFL (minimum score 560 paper-based; 83 iBT), IELTS (minimum score 6.5). Electronic applications accepted.

Ithaca College, School of Humanities and Sciences, Program in Adolescence Education, Ithaca, NY 14850. Offers biology 7-12 (MAT); chemistry 7-12 (MAT); English 7-12 (MAT); French 7-12 (MAT); math 7-12 (MAT); physics 7-12 (MAT); social studies 7-12 (MAT); Spanish (MAT). Part-time programs available. *Faculty:* 31 full-time (11 women). *Students:* 12 full-time (4 women); includes 1 minority (Hispanic/Latino). Average age 24. 27 applicants, 81% accepted, 12 enrolled. In 2013, 7 master's awarded. *Degree requirements:* For master's, thesis or alternative, student teaching. *Entrance requirements:* For master's, minimum GPA of 3.0. Additional exam requirements/recommendations for international students: Required—TOEFL (minimum score 550 paper-based; 80 iBT). *Application deadline:* For fall admission, 2/15 priority date for domestic and international students; for spring admission, 12/1 for domestic and international students. Applications are processed on a rolling basis. Application fee: $40. Electronic applications accepted. *Expenses:* Contact institution. *Financial support:* In 2013–14, 7 students received support, including 7 teaching assistantships (averaging $9,781 per year); career-related internships or fieldwork, Federal Work-Study, scholarships/grants, and unspecified assistantships also available. Support available to part-time students. Financial award application deadline: 2/15; financial award applicants required to submit CSS PROFILE or FAFSA. *Faculty research:* Teacher preparation (elementary and secondary education), equity and social justice in education, language and literacy, multicultural education/sociocultural studies, reflective practice and teacher research. *Unit head:* Dr. Linda Hanrahan, Chair, 607-274-3143, Fax: 607-274-1263, E-mail: gps@ithaca.edu. *Application contact:* Gerard Turbide, Director, Office of Admission, 607-274-3143, Fax: 607-274-1263, E-mail: gps@ithaca.edu.
Website: http://www.ithaca.edu/gradprograms/education/programs/aded.

Jackson State University, Graduate School, College of Science, Engineering and Technology, Department of Physics, Atmospheric Sciences, and General Science, Jackson, MS 39217. Offers science and mathematics teaching (MST). Part-time and evening/weekend programs available. *Degree requirements:* For master's, comprehensive exam. *Entrance requirements:* For master's, GRE General Test. Additional exam requirements/recommendations for international students: Required—TOEFL (minimum score 520 paper-based; 67 iBT).

John Carroll University, Graduate School, Program in Integrated Science, University Heights, OH 44118-4581. Offers MA. Part-time programs available. *Degree requirements:* For master's, thesis optional. *Entrance requirements:* For master's, minimum GPA of 2.5, teachers license. Electronic applications accepted.

Kansas State University, Graduate School, College of Education, Department of Curriculum and Instruction, Manhattan, KS 66506. Offers career and technical education (Ed D, PhD); curriculum studies (Ed D, PhD); digital teaching and learning (MS); educational computing, design and online learning (MS); educational technology (Ed D, PhD); elementary/middle level curriculum and instruction (MS); English as a second language (MS); language/diversity education (Ed D, PhD); literacy education (Ed D, PhD); mathematics education (Ed D, PhD); middle level/secondary curriculum and instruction (MS); reading and language arts (MS); reading specialist endorsement (MS); science education (Ed D, PhD); social science education (Ed D, PhD); teacher education (Ed D, PhD); teacher leader/school improvement (MS, Ed D). *Accreditation:* NCATE. Part-time programs available. Postbaccalaureate distance learning degree programs offered (minimal on-campus study). *Faculty:* 18 full-time (13 women), 7 part-time/adjunct (4 women). *Students:* 39 full-time (23 women), 122 part-time (94 women); includes 19 minority (3 Black or African American, non-Hispanic/Latino; 2 Asian, non-Hispanic/Latino; 12 Hispanic/Latino; 2 Two or more races, non-Hispanic/Latino), 12 international. Average age 36. 80 applicants, 50% accepted, 34 enrolled. In 2013, 40 master's, 13 doctorates awarded. *Degree requirements:* For master's, comprehensive exam, portfolio, project, report or thesis; for doctorate, comprehensive exam, thesis/dissertation, preliminary exam. *Entrance requirements:* For master's, minimum GPA of 3.0, letters of recommendation; for doctorate, GRE, minimum GPA of 3.0, letters of recommendation, evidence of scholarly writing. Additional exam requirements/recommendations for international students: Required—TOEFL (minimum score 550 paper-based; 80 iBT). *Application deadline:* For fall admission, 3/1 priority date for domestic students, 2/1 priority date for international students; for spring admission, 10/1 priority date for domestic students, 8/1 priority date for international students. Applications are processed on a rolling basis. Application fee: $50 ($75 for international students). Electronic applications accepted. *Financial support:* In 2013–14, 1 research assistantship (averaging $16,900 per year), 8 teaching assistantships (averaging $12,466 per year) were awarded; career-related internships or fieldwork, institutionally sponsored loans, and scholarships/grants also available. Support available to part-time students. Financial award application deadline: 3/1; financial award applicants required to submit FAFSA. *Faculty research:* Literacy and technology, critical race theory and diversity, achievement gaps, school improvement, teacher education. *Total annual research expenditures:* $543,677. *Unit head:* Dr. Todd Goodson, Chair, 785-532-5904, Fax: 785-532-7304, E-mail: tgoodson@ksu.edu. *Application contact:* Dona Deam, Application Contact, 785-532-5595, Fax: 785-532-7304, E-mail: ddeam@ksu.edu.
Website: http://www.coe.k-state.edu/departments/edci/.

Kaplan University, Davenport Campus, School of Teacher Education, Davenport, IA 52807-2095. Offers education (M Ed); secondary education (M Ed); teaching and learning (MA); teaching literacy and language: grades 6-12 (MA); teaching literacy and language: grades K-6 (MA); teaching mathematics: grades 6-8 (MA); teaching mathematics: grades 9-12 (MA); teaching mathematics: grades K-5 (MA); teaching science: grades 6-12 (MA); teaching science: grades K-6 (MA); teaching students with special needs (MA); teaching with technology (MA). Part-time and evening/weekend programs available. Postbaccalaureate distance learning degree programs offered (no on-campus study). *Entrance requirements:* Additional exam requirements/recommendations for international students: Required—TOEFL (minimum score 550 paper-based; 80 iBT).

Kean University, College of Education, Program in Instruction and Curriculum, Union, NJ 07083. Offers bilingual/bicultural education (MA); classroom instruction (MA); earth science (MA); mathematics/science/computer education (MA); teaching (MA); teaching English as a second language (MA); world languages (Spanish) (MA). *Accreditation:* NCATE. Part-time programs available. *Faculty:* 22 full-time (12 women). *Students:* 16 full-time (10 women), 100 part-time (72 women); includes 57 minority (8 Black or African American, non-Hispanic/Latino; 3 Asian, non-Hispanic/Latino; 45 Hispanic/Latino; 1 Two or more races, non-Hispanic/Latino). Average age 35. 56 applicants, 100% accepted, 38 enrolled. In 2013, 42 master's awarded. *Degree requirements:* For master's, comprehensive exam, thesis (for some programs), two-semester advanced seminar. *Entrance requirements:* For master's, GRE General Test or MAT, PRAXIS, minimum GPA of 3.0, personal statement, professional resume/curriculum vitae, commitment to working with children, certification (for some programs). Additional exam requirements/recommendations for international students: Required—TOEFL (minimum score 550 paper-based; 79 iBT). *Application deadline:* For fall admission, 6/1 for domestic and international students; for spring admission, 12/1 for domestic and international students. Applications are processed on a rolling basis. Application fee: $75 ($150 for international students). Electronic applications accepted. *Expenses:* Tuition, state resident: full-time $12,099; part-time $589 per credit. Tuition, nonresident: full-time $16,399; part-time $722 per credit. *Required fees:* $3050; $139 per credit. Part-time tuition and fees vary according to course level, course load, degree level and program. *Financial support:* In 2013–14, 6 research assistantships with full tuition reimbursements (averaging $3,713 per year) were awarded; unspecified assistantships also available. Financial award applicants required to submit FAFSA. *Unit head:* Dr. Gail Verdi, Program Coordinator, 908-737-3908, E-mail: gverdi@kean.edu. *Application contact:* Ann-Marie Kay, Assistant Director for Graduate Admissions, 908-737-5922, Fax: 908-737-5925, E-mail: akay@kean.edu.
Website: http://grad.kean.edu/masters-programs/bilingualbicultural-education-instruction-and-curriculum.

Kutztown University of Pennsylvania, College of Education, Program in Secondary Education, Kutztown, PA 19530-0730. Offers biology (M Ed); curriculum and instruction (M Ed); English (M Ed); mathematics (M Ed); social studies (M Ed). *Accreditation:* NCATE. Part-time and evening/weekend programs available. *Faculty:* 6 full-time (2 women). *Students:* 34 full-time (17 women), 46 part-time (34 women); includes 4 minority (1 Asian, non-Hispanic/Latino; 3 Hispanic/Latino). Average age 31. 50 applicants, 70% accepted, 26 enrolled. In 2013, 31 master's awarded. *Degree requirements:* For master's, comprehensive exam, thesis optional. *Entrance requirements:* For master's, GRE General Test. Additional exam requirements/recommendations for international students: Required—TOEFL (minimum score 550 paper-based; 79 iBT). *Application deadline:* For fall admission, 8/1 priority date for domestic and international students; for spring admission, 12/1 priority date for domestic and international students. Applications are processed on a rolling basis. Application fee: $35. Electronic applications accepted. *Expenses: Tuition, area resident:* Part-time $442 per credit. Tuition, state resident: part-time $442 per credit. Tuition, nonresident: part-time $663 per credit. *Required fees:* $80 per credit. *Financial support:* Career-related internships or fieldwork, Federal Work-Study, scholarships/grants, and unspecified assistantships available. Financial award application deadline: 3/1; financial award applicants required to submit FAFSA. *Unit head:* Dr. Theresa Stahler, Chairperson, 610-683-4259, Fax: 610-683-1338, E-mail: stahler@kutztown.edu. *Application contact:* Kelly Hish, Admissions Clerk, 610-683-4200, Fax: 610-683-1393, E-mail: graduate@kutztown.edu.

Lake Forest College, Master of Arts in Teaching Program, Lake Forest, IL 60045. Offers elementary education (MAT); K-12 French (MAT); K-12 music (MAT); K-12 Spanish (MAT); K-12 visual art (MAT); secondary biology (MAT); secondary chemistry (MAT); secondary English (MAT); secondary history (MAT); secondary mathematics (MAT). *Degree requirements:* For master's, comprehensive exam, portfolio. *Entrance requirements:* For master's, GRE.

Laurentian University, School of Graduate Studies and Research, Programme in Science Communication, Sudbury, ON P3E 2C6, Canada. Offers G Dip.

Lawrence Technological University, College of Arts and Sciences, Southfield, MI 48075-1058. Offers computer science (MS); educational technology (MS); integrated science (MSE); science education (MSE); technical and professional communication (MS). Part-time and evening/weekend programs available. *Faculty:* 7 full-time (5 women), 14 part-time/adjunct (6 women). *Students:* 8 full-time (0 women), 74 part-time (38 women); includes 20 minority (12 Black or African American, non-Hispanic/Latino; 3 Asian, non-Hispanic/Latino; 1 Hispanic/Latino; 4 Two or more races, non-Hispanic/Latino), 12 international. Average age 35. 167 applicants, 47% accepted, 20 enrolled. In 2013, 26 master's awarded. *Degree requirements:* For master's, thesis (for some programs). *Entrance requirements:* Additional exam requirements/recommendations for international students: Required—TOEFL (minimum score 550 paper-based; 79 iBT). *Application deadline:* For fall admission, 8/1 priority date for domestic students, 5/29 for

international students; for spring admission, 12/1 priority date for domestic students, 10/15 for international students. Applications are processed on a rolling basis. Application fee: $50. Electronic applications accepted. *Expenses: Tuition:* Full-time $14,112; part-time $1008 per credit hour. *Required fees:* $519. One-time fee: $519 part-time. *Financial support:* In 2013–14, 9 students received support, including 1 research assistantship (averaging $9,000 per year); Federal Work-Study also available. Financial award application deadline: 4/1; financial award applicants required to submit FAFSA. *Unit head:* Dr. Hsiao-Ping Moore, Dean, 248-204-3500, Fax: 248-204-3518, E-mail: scidean@ltu.edu. *Application contact:* Jane Rohrback, Director of Admissions, 248-204-3160, Fax: 248-204-2228, E-mail: admissions@ltu.edu.
Website: http://www.ltu.edu/arts_sciences/graduate.asp.

Lebanon Valley College, Program in Science Education, Annville, PA 17003-1400. Offers MSE. Part-time and evening/weekend programs available. *Faculty:* 4 part-time/adjunct (2 women). *Students:* 22 part-time (13 women). Average age 36. In 2013, 8 master's awarded. *Degree requirements:* For master's, thesis. *Entrance requirements:* For master's, minimum GPA of 3.0, teacher certification. *Application deadline:* Applications are processed on a rolling basis. Application fee: $30. *Expenses:* Contact institution. *Financial support:* Application deadline: 5/1; applicants required to submit FAFSA. *Unit head:* Carrie Coryer, Director, 717-867-6190, Fax: 717-867-6018, E-mail: coryer@lvc.edu. *Application contact:* Lynnette Beidler, Administrative Assistant for MSE and STEM-Based Programs, 717-867-6482, Fax: 717-867-6018, E-mail: lbeidler@lvc.edu.
Website: http://www.lvc.edu/mse/.

Lehman College of the City University of New York, Division of Education, Department of Middle and High School Education, Program in Science Education, Bronx, NY 10468-1589. Offers MS Ed. *Accreditation:* NCATE.

Lesley University, School of Education, Cambridge, MA 02138-2790. Offers arts, community, and education (M Ed); autism studies (Certificate); curriculum and instruction (M Ed, CAGS); early childhood education (M Ed); ecological teaching and learning (MS); educational studies (PhD), including adult learning, educational leadership, individually designed; elementary education (M Ed); emergent technologies for educators (Certificate); ESLArts: language learning through the arts (M Ed); high school education (M Ed); individually designed (M Ed); integrated teaching through the arts (M Ed); literacy for K-8 classroom teachers (M Ed); mathematics education (M Ed); middle school education (M Ed); moderate disabilities (M Ed); online learning (Certificate); reading (CAGS); science in education (M Ed); severe disabilities (M Ed); special needs (CAGS); specialist teacher of reading (M Ed); teacher of visual art (M Ed); technology in education (M Ed, CAGS). *Accreditation:* Teacher Education Accreditation Council. Part-time and evening/weekend programs available. Postbaccalaureate distance learning degree programs offered (no on-campus study). *Faculty:* 40 full-time (30 women), 104 part-time/adjunct (77 women). *Students:* 453 full-time (381 women), 1,672 part-time (1,435 women); includes 284 minority (139 Black or African American, non-Hispanic/Latino; 11 American Indian or Alaska Native, non-Hispanic/Latino; 38 Asian, non-Hispanic/Latino; 58 Hispanic/Latino; 5 Native Hawaiian or other Pacific Islander, non-Hispanic/Latino; 33 Two or more races, non-Hispanic/Latino), 22 international. Average age 35. In 2013, 1,137 master's, 18 doctorates, 51 other advanced degrees awarded. *Degree requirements:* For master's, practicum; for doctorate, thesis/dissertation. *Entrance requirements:* For master's, Massachusetts Tests for Educator Licensure (MTEL), transcripts, statement of purpose, recommendations; interview (for special education); for doctorate, GRE General Test, transcripts, statement of purpose, recommendations, interview, master's degree, resume; for other advanced degree, interview, master's degree. Additional exam requirements/recommendations for international students: Required—TOEFL (minimum score 550 paper-based; 80 iBT). *Application deadline:* Applications are processed on a rolling basis. Application fee: $50. Electronic applications accepted. *Expenses: Tuition:* Part-time $900 per credit. *Financial support:* In 2013–14, 15 fellowships (averaging $3,600 per year) were awarded; career-related internships or fieldwork, Federal Work-Study, scholarships/grants, tuition waivers, and unspecified assistantships also available. Financial award application deadline: 4/15; financial award applicants required to submit FAFSA. *Faculty research:* Assessment in literacy, mathematics and science; autism spectrum disorders; instructional technology and online learning; multicultural education and English language learners. *Unit head:* Dr. Jack Gillette, Dean, 617-349-8401, Fax: 617-349-8607, E-mail: jgillett@lesley.edu. *Application contact:* Martha Sheehan, Director of Admissions, 888-LESLEYU, Fax: 617-349-8313, E-mail: info@lesley.edu.
Website: http://www.lesley.edu/soe.html.

Lewis University, College of Education, Program in Secondary Education, Romeoville, IL 60446. Offers biology (MA); chemistry (MA); English (MA); history (MA); math (MA); physics (MA); psychology and social science (MA). Part-time programs available. *Students:* 15 full-time (6 women), 15 part-time (9 women); includes 6 minority (2 Black or African American, non-Hispanic/Latino; 1 Asian, non-Hispanic/Latino; 3 Hispanic/Latino). Average age 30. *Entrance requirements:* For master's, departmental qualifying exam, writing exam, minimum GPA of 2.75, 2 letters of recommendation, interview. Additional exam requirements/recommendations for international students: Required—TOEFL (minimum score 550 paper-based; 80 iBT). *Application deadline:* For fall admission, 5/1 priority date for international students; for spring admission, 11/15 priority date for international students. Applications are processed on a rolling basis. Application fee: $40. Electronic applications accepted. *Financial support:* Federal Work-Study, scholarships/grants, and unspecified assistantships available. Financial award application deadline: 5/1; financial award applicants required to submit FAFSA. *Unit head:* Dr. Dorene Huvaere, Program Director, 815-838-0500 Ext. 5885, E-mail: huvaersdo@lewisu.edu. *Application contact:* Fran Welsh, Secretary, 815-838-0500 Ext. 5880, E-mail: welshfr@lewisu.edu.

Long Island University–LIU Post, College of Liberal Arts and Sciences, Department of Biology, Brookville, NY 11548-1300. Offers biology (MS); biology education (MS); genetic counseling (MS). Part-time and evening/weekend programs available. *Degree requirements:* For master's, thesis optional. *Entrance requirements:* For master's, GRE General Test, minimum GPA of 2.75 in major. Electronic applications accepted. *Faculty research:* Immunology, molecular biology, systematics, behavioral ecology, microbiology.

Long Island University–LIU Post, College of Liberal Arts and Sciences, Department of Earth and Environmental Science, Brookville, NY 11548-1300. Offers earth science (MS); earth science education (MS); environmental studies (MS).

Long Island University–LIU Post, School of Education, Department of Curriculum and Instruction, Brookville, NY 11548-1300. Offers adolescence education (MS); adolescence education: biology (MS); adolescence education: earth science (MS); adolescence education: English (MS); adolescence education: mathematics (MS); adolescence education: social studies (MS); adolescence education: Spanish (MS); art education (MS); bilingual education (MS); childhood education (MS); early childhood education (MS); middle childhood education (MS); music education (MS); teaching English to speakers of other languages (MS). Part-time and evening/weekend programs available. *Degree requirements:* For master's, comprehensive exam or thesis, student teaching. *Entrance requirements:* For master's, minimum GPA of 2.75 in major, 2.5 overall. Electronic applications accepted. *Faculty research:* Ethics and education, teaching strategies.

Louisiana Tech University, Graduate School, College of Education, Department of Curriculum, Instruction and Leadership, Ruston, LA 71272. Offers curriculum and instruction (M Ed, Ed D), including adult education (M Ed), early childhood (M Ed), English education (M Ed), mathematics education (M Ed), science education (M Ed), social studies education (M Ed), special education (M Ed); educational leadership (M Ed, Ed D). *Accreditation:* NCATE. Part-time programs available. *Degree requirements:* For doctorate, thesis/dissertation. *Entrance requirements:* For master's and doctorate, GRE General Test. *Application deadline:* For fall admission, 7/29 for domestic students; for spring admission, 2/3 for domestic students. Application fee: $20 ($30 for international students). *Financial support:* Fellowships, research assistantships, and teaching assistantships available. Financial award application deadline: 2/1. *Unit head:* Dr. Pauline Leonard, Head, 318-257-4609, Fax: 318-257-2379. *Application contact:* Dr. John Harrison, Associate Dean of Graduate Studies, 318-257-3229, Fax: 318-257-2379, E-mail: johnharrison@latech.edu.
Website: http://www.latech.edu/education/cil/.

Loyola University Chicago, School of Education, Program in Teaching and Learning, Chicago, IL 60660. Offers behavior intervention specialist (M Ed); elementary education (M Ed); English as a second language (Certificate); English language teaching and learning (M Ed); math education (M Ed); reading specialist (M Ed); reading teacher endorsement (Certificate); school technology (M Ed); science education (M Ed); secondary education (M Ed); special education (M Ed). *Accreditation:* NCATE. *Faculty:* 23 full-time (16 women), 49 part-time/adjunct (42 women). *Students:* 109. Average age 28. 104 applicants, 71% accepted, 44 enrolled. In 2013, 39 master's awarded. *Degree requirements:* For master's, comprehensive exam. *Entrance requirements:* For master's, Illinois Basic Skills Test, 3 letters of recommendation, minimum GPA of 3.0, resume. Additional exam requirements/recommendations for international students: Required—TOEFL (minimum score 550 paper-based; 79 iBT). *Application deadline:* For fall admission, 7/1 priority date for domestic and international students; for spring admission, 11/1 priority date for domestic and international students; for summer admission, 4/1 for domestic and international students. Applications are processed on a rolling basis. Application fee: $50. Electronic applications accepted. Application fee is waived when completed online. *Expenses: Tuition:* Full-time $16,740; part-time $930 per credit. *Required fees:* $135 per semester. *Financial support:* In 2013–14, 58 fellowships with partial tuition reimbursements were awarded; research assistantships, teaching assistantships, institutionally sponsored loans, scholarships/grants, and unspecified assistantships also available. Support available to part-time students. Financial award application deadline: 2/1; financial award applicants required to submit FAFSA. *Faculty research:* Positive behavior support, school reform, school improvement. *Unit head:* Dr. Ann Marie Ryan, Director, 312-915-7027, E-mail: aryan3@luc.edu. *Application contact:* Marie Rosin-Dittmar, Information Contact, 312-915-6800, E-mail: schleduc@luc.edu.

Loyola University Maryland, Graduate Programs, School of Education, Master of Arts in Teaching Program, Baltimore, MD 21210-2699. Offers elementary/middle education (MAT); secondary education (MAT); secondary education: biology (MAT); secondary education: chemistries (MAT); secondary education: earth science (MAT); secondary education: English (MAT); secondary education: mathematics (MAT); secondary education: physics (MAT). Part-time programs available. *Entrance requirements:* For master's, essay, 2 letters of recommendation, resume, transcipt. Additional exam requirements/recommendations for international students: Required—TOEFL (minimum score 550 paper-based).

Lynchburg College, Graduate Studies, School of Education and Human Development, M Ed Program in Science Education, Lynchburg, VA 24501-3199. Offers M Ed. Part-time and evening/weekend programs available. *Faculty:* 6 full-time (4 women), 1 part-time/adjunct (0 women). *Students:* 6 full-time (4 women), 5 part-time (4 women); includes 2 minority (both Two or more races, non-Hispanic/Latino). Average age 36. In 2013, 3 master's awarded. *Degree requirements:* For master's, comprehensive exam. *Entrance requirements:* For master's, GRE, minimum GPA of 3.0 (preferred), official transcripts (bachelor's, others as relevant), three letters of recommendation, career goals statement. Additional exam requirements/recommendations for international students: Required—TOEFL (minimum score 550 paper-based; 79 iBT), IELTS (minimum score 6.5). *Application deadline:* For fall admission, 7/31 for domestic students, 6/1 for international students; for spring admission, 11/30 for domestic students, 10/15 for international students. Applications are processed on a rolling basis. Application fee: $30. Electronic applications accepted. Application fee is waived when completed online. *Financial support:* Fellowships, research assistantships, Federal Work-Study, scholarships/grants, health care benefits, and unspecified assistantships available. Support available to part-time students. Financial award application deadline: 7/31; financial award applicants required to submit FAFSA. *Unit head:* Dr. Woody McKenzie, Associate Professor/Director of M Ed in Science Education, 434-544-8480, Fax: 434-544-8483, E-mail: mckenzie@lynchburg.edu. *Application contact:* Anne Pingstock, Executive Assistant, Graduate Studies, 434-544-8383, Fax: 434-544-8483, E-mail: gradstudies@lynchburg.edu.
Website: http://www.lynchburg.edu/master-education-science-education.

Lyndon State College, Graduate Programs in Education, Department of Natural Sciences, Lyndonville, VT 05851-0919. Offers science education (MST). Part-time programs available. *Degree requirements:* For master's, exam or major field project. *Entrance requirements:* Additional exam requirements/recommendations for international students: Recommended—TOEFL (minimum score 500 paper-based). *Faculty research:* Fern genetics, comparative butterfly research.

Manhattanville College, School of Education, Program in Middle Childhood/Adolescence Education (Grades 5-12), Purchase, NY 10577-2132. Offers biology (MAT); biology and special education (MPS); chemistry (MAT); chemistry and special education (MPS); English (MAT); English and special education (MPS); literacy and special education (MPS); literacy specialist (MPS); math and special education (MPS); mathematics (MAT); physics (MAT); social studies (MAT); social studies and special education (MPS); special education (MPS); teaching languages other than English (MAT), including French, Italian, Latin, Spanish. Part-time and evening/weekend programs available. *Degree requirements:* For master's, comprehensive exam or research project, field experience. *Entrance requirements:* For master's, minimum undergraduate GPA of 3.0, 2 letters of recommendation. Additional exam requirements/recommendations for international students: Required—TOEFL. Electronic applications accepted.

McNeese State University, Doré School of Graduate Studies, College of Science, Department of Chemistry, Program in Environmental and Chemical Sciences, Lake Charles, LA 70609. Offers chemistry (MS); chemistry/environmental science education (MS). Evening/weekend programs available. *Degree requirements:* For master's, comprehensive exam, thesis or alternative. *Entrance requirements:* For master's, GRE.

Michigan State University, The Graduate School, College of Natural Science and College of Education, Division of Science and Mathematics Education, East Lansing, MI 48824. Offers biological, physical and general science for teachers (MAT, MS), including

biological science (MS), general science (MAT), physical science (MS); mathematics education (MS, PhD).

Michigan Technological University, Graduate School, College of Sciences and Arts, Department of Cognitive and Learning Sciences, Houghton, MI 49931. Offers applied cognitive science and human factors (PhD); applied science education (MS). *Degree requirements:* For master's, comprehensive exam (for some programs), thesis (for some programs); for doctorate, comprehensive exam, thesis/dissertation. *Entrance requirements:* For master's and doctorate, GRE (recommended minimum score of 310 [1200 old version]), statement of purpose, official transcripts, 3 letters of recommendation, bachelor's/master's degree in a field related to cognitive science, human factors, or ergonomics, minimum GPA of 3.5 (recommended), resume/ curriculum vitae, writing sample (preferably related to the field of interest). Additional exam requirements/recommendations for international students: Required—TOEFL (minimum score 79 iBT) or IELTS. Electronic applications accepted. *Faculty research:* Cognitive engineering and decision-making, human-centered design, individual differences in human performance.

Middle Tennessee State University, College of Graduate Studies, College of Basic and Applied Sciences, Department of Aerospace, Murfreesboro, TN 37132. Offers aerospace education (M Ed); aviation administration (MS). Part-time and evening/ weekend programs available. Postbaccalaureate distance learning degree programs offered. *Faculty:* 4 full-time (1 woman). *Students:* 14 full-time (5 women), 20 part-time (2 women); includes 15 minority (6 Black or African American, non-Hispanic/Latino; 7 Asian, non-Hispanic/Latino; 1 Hispanic/Latino; 1 Two or more races, non-Hispanic/ Latino). 19 applicants, 63% accepted. In 2013, 11 master's awarded. *Degree requirements:* For master's, comprehensive exam, thesis optional. *Entrance requirements:* For master's, GRE General Test or MAT. Additional exam requirements/ recommendations for international students: Required—TOEFL (minimum score 525 paper-based; 71 iBT) or IELTS (minimum score 6). *Application deadline:* For fall admission, 6/1 for domestic and international students. Applications are processed on a rolling basis. Application fee: $25 ($30 for international students). Electronic applications accepted. *Financial support:* In 2013–14, 4 students received support. Tuition waivers available. Support available to part-time students. Financial award application deadline: 5/1. *Faculty research:* Unmanned vehicles, air traffic control. *Unit head:* Dr. Ron Ferrara, Interim Chair, 615-898-2788, Fax: 615-904-8273, E-mail: ron.ferrara@mtsu.edu. *Application contact:* Dr. Michael D. Allen, Vice Provost for Research and Dean, 615-898-2840, Fax: 615-904-8020, E-mail: michael.allen@mtsu.edu.

Middle Tennessee State University, College of Graduate Studies, Interdisciplinary Program in Mathematics and Science Education, Murfreesboro, TN 37132. Offers PhD. *Students:* 10 full-time (7 women), 25 part-time (12 women); includes 6 minority (3 Black or African American, non-Hispanic/Latino; 2 Asian, non-Hispanic/Latino; 1 Hispanic/ Latino). 22 applicants, 77% accepted. *Unit head:* Dr. Michael D. Allen, Vice Provost for Research and Dean, 615-898-2840, Fax: 615-904-8020, E-mail: michael.allen@ mtsu.edu. *Application contact:* Dr. Michael D. Allen, Vice Provost for Research and Dean, 615-898-2840, Fax: 615-904-8020, E-mail: michael.allen@mtsu.edu.

Mills College, Graduate Studies, School of Education, Oakland, CA 94613-1000. Offers child life in hospitals (MA); early childhood education (MA); education (MA), including art education, curriculum and instruction, elementary education, English education, foreign language education, mathematics education, science education, secondary education, social studies education, teaching; educational leadership (MA, Ed D). Part-time and evening/weekend programs available. *Faculty:* 10 full-time (7 women), 13 part-time/ adjunct (10 women). *Students:* 154 full-time (136 women), 54 part-time (47 women); includes 96 minority (32 Black or African American, non-Hispanic/Latino; 1 American Indian or Alaska Native, non-Hispanic/Latino; 23 Asian, non-Hispanic/Latino; 27 Hispanic/Latino; 1 Native Hawaiian or other Pacific Islander, non-Hispanic/Latino; 12 Two or more races, non-Hispanic/Latino), 2 international. Average age 25. 222 applicants, 89% accepted, 110 enrolled. In 2013, 96 master's, 38 doctorates awarded. Terminal master's awarded for partial completion of doctoral program. *Degree requirements:* For master's, comprehensive exam, thesis (for some programs); for doctorate, thesis/dissertation. *Entrance requirements:* For master's, statement of purpose, official transcript, 3 recommendations. Additional exam requirements/ recommendations for international students: Required—TOEFL (minimum score 550 paper-based; 80 iBT) or IELTS (minimum score 6). *Application deadline:* For fall admission, 12/31 priority date for domestic students, 12/15 for international students; for spring admission, 11/1 priority date for domestic students, 10/1 for international students. Applications are processed on a rolling basis. Application fee: $50. Electronic applications accepted. *Expenses: Tuition:* Full-time $29,860. *Required fees:* $1134. Part-time tuition and fees vary according to course load, degree level and program. *Financial support:* In 2013–14, 130 students received support, including 130 fellowships with full and partial tuition reimbursements available (averaging $7,565 per year); career-related internships or fieldwork and scholarships/grants also available. Support available to part-time students. Financial award application deadline: 2/1; financial award applicants required to submit FAFSA. *Faculty research:* Early childhood education, teacher preparation, educational leadership. *Total annual research expenditures:* $3.5 million. *Unit head:* Dr. Katherine Schultz, Department Head, 510-430-3384, Fax: 510-430-2159, E-mail: kschultz@mills.edu. *Application contact:* Shrim Bathey, Director of Graduate Admission, 510-430-3309, Fax: 510-430-2159, E-mail: grad-admission@mills.edu.
Website: http://www.mills.edu/education.

Minnesota State University Mankato, College of Graduate Studies, College of Science, Engineering and Technology, Department of Biological Sciences, Mankato, MN 56001. Offers biology (MS); biology education (MS); environmental sciences (MS). Part-time programs available. *Students:* 9 full-time (4 women), 24 part-time (11 women). *Degree requirements:* For master's, one foreign language, comprehensive exam, thesis or alternative. *Entrance requirements:* For master's, minimum GPA of 3.0 during previous 2 years of course work. Additional exam requirements/recommendations for international students: Required—TOEFL. *Application deadline:* For fall admission, 7/1 priority date for domestic students; for spring admission, 11/1 for domestic students. Applications are processed on a rolling basis. Application fee: $40. Electronic applications accepted. *Financial support:* Fellowships, research assistantships with full tuition reimbursements, teaching assistantships with full tuition reimbursements, career-related internships or fieldwork, Federal Work-Study, institutionally sponsored loans, and unspecified assistantships available. Support available to part-time students. Financial award application deadline: 3/15; financial award applicants required to submit FAFSA. *Faculty research:* Limnology, enzyme analysis, membrane engineering, converters. *Unit head:* Dr. Penny Knoblich, Graduate Coordinator, 507-389-5736. *Application contact:* 507-389-2321, E-mail: grad@mnsu.edu.

Minot State University, Graduate School, Program in Biological and Agricultural Sciences, Minot, ND 58707-0002. Offers science (MAT). *Degree requirements:* For master's, thesis. *Entrance requirements:* For master's, minimum GPA of 3.0 or GRE General Test, secondary teaching certificate. Additional exam requirements/ recommendations for international students: Required—TOEFL.

Mississippi College, Graduate School, School of Education, Department of Teacher Education and Leadership, Clinton, MS 39058. Offers art (M Ed); biological science

(M Ed); business education (M Ed); computer science (M Ed); dyslexia therapy (M Ed); educational leadership (M Ed, Ed D, Ed S); elementary education (M Ed, Ed S); English (M Ed); higher education administration (MS); mathematics (M Ed); secondary education (M Ed); social studies (history) (M Ed); teaching arts (M Ed). Part-time programs available. Postbaccalaureate distance learning degree programs offered (no on-campus study). *Degree requirements:* For master's, comprehensive exam, thesis optional. *Entrance requirements:* For master's, NTE. Additional exam requirements/ recommendations for international students: Recommended—TOEFL, IELTS. Electronic applications accepted.

Mississippi State University, College of Arts and Sciences, Department of Geosciences, Mississippi State, MS 39762. Offers applied meteorology (MS); broadcast meteorology (MS); earth and atmospheric science (PhD); environmental geoscience (MS); geography (MS); geology (MS); geospatial sciences (MS); professional meteorology/climatology (MS); teachers in geoscience (MS). Postbaccalaureate distance learning degree programs offered (no on-campus study). *Faculty:* 12 full-time (2 women), 1 part-time/adjunct (0 women). *Students:* 65 full-time (25 women), 249 part-time (115 women); includes 26 minority (6 Black or African American, non-Hispanic/ Latino; 1 American Indian or Alaska Native, non-Hispanic/Latino; 4 Asian, non-Hispanic/ Latino; 12 Hispanic/Latino; 3 Two or more races, non-Hispanic/Latino), 8 international. Average age 34. 321 applicants, 43% accepted, 113 enrolled. In 2013, 90 master's, 2 doctorates awarded. *Degree requirements:* For master's, thesis (for some programs), comprehensive oral or written exam; for doctorate, thesis/dissertation, comprehensive oral or written exam. *Entrance requirements:* For master's, GRE (for on-campus applicants), minimum undergraduate GPA of 2.75; for doctorate, completed thesis-based MS with background in one department emphasis area. Additional exam requirements/recommendations for international students: Required—TOEFL (minimum score 477 paper-based; 53 iBT); Recommended—IELTS (minimum score 4.5). *Application deadline:* For fall admission, 7/1 for domestic students, 5/1 for international students; for spring admission, 11/1 for domestic students, 9/1 for international students. Applications are processed on a rolling basis. Application fee: $60. Electronic applications accepted. *Financial support:* In 2013–14, 14 research assistantships with full tuition reimbursements (averaging $20,331 per year), 28 teaching assistantships with full tuition reimbursements (averaging $13,714 per year) were awarded; Federal Work-Study, institutionally sponsored loans, scholarships/grants, tuition waivers (partial), and unspecified assistantships also available. Financial award application deadline: 4/1; financial award applicants required to submit FAFSA. *Faculty research:* Climatology, hydrogeology, sedimentology, meteorology. *Total annual research expenditures:* $3.8 million. *Unit head:* Dr. William Cooke, Interim Department Head, 662-325-3915, Fax: 662-325-9423, E-mail: whc5@geosci.msstate.edu. *Application contact:* Dr. Mike Brown, Associate Professor/Graduate Coordinator, 662-325-3915, Fax: 662-325-9423, E-mail: tina@gesci.msstate.edu.
Website: http://www.geosciences.msstate.edu.

Missouri State University, Graduate College, College of Natural and Applied Sciences, Department of Physics, Astronomy, and Materials Science, Springfield, MO 65897. Offers materials science (MS); physics, astronomy, and materials science (MNAS); secondary education (MS Ed), including physics. Part-time programs available. *Faculty:* 11 full-time (0 women). *Students:* 13 full-time (1 woman), 6 part-time (0 women); includes 1 minority (Hispanic/Latino), 14 international. Average age 29. 15 applicants, 73% accepted, 7 enrolled. In 2013, 9 master's awarded. *Degree requirements:* For master's, comprehensive exam, thesis. *Entrance requirements:* For master's, GRE (MS, MNAS), minimum undergraduate GPA of 3.0 (MS and MNAS), 9-12 teaching certification (MS Ed). Additional exam requirements/recommendations for international students: Required—TOEFL (minimum score 550 paper-based; 79 iBT). *Application deadline:* For fall admission, 7/20 priority date for domestic students, 5/1 for international students; for spring admission, 12/20 priority date for domestic students, 9/1 for international students. Applications are processed on a rolling basis. Application fee: $35 ($50 for international students). Electronic applications accepted. *Expenses:* Tuition, state resident: full-time $4500; part-time $250 per credit hour. Tuition, nonresident: full-time $9018; part-time $501 per credit hour. *Required fees:* $361 per semester. Tuition and fees vary according to course level, course load and program. *Financial support:* In 2013–14, 1 research assistantship with full tuition reimbursement (averaging $10,128 per year), 10 teaching assistantships with full tuition reimbursements (averaging $10,128 per year) were awarded; Federal Work-Study, institutionally sponsored loans, scholarships/grants, and unspecified assistantships also available. Financial award application deadline: 3/31; financial award applicants required to submit FAFSA. *Faculty research:* Nanocomposites, ferroelectricity, infrared focal plane array sensors, biosensors, pulsating stars. *Unit head:* Dr. David Cornelison, Department Head, 417-836-4467, Fax: 417-836-6226, E-mail: physics@ missouristate.edu. *Application contact:* Misty Stewart, Coordinator of Graduate Recruitment, 417-836-6079, Fax: 417-836-6200, E-mail: mistystewart@ missouristate.edu.
Website: http://physics.missouristate.edu/.

Montclair State University, The Graduate School, College of Education and Human Services, Department of Secondary and Special Education, Program in Teaching in Subject Area, Montclair, NJ 07043-1624. Offers art (MAT); biology (MAT); chemistry (MAT); earth science (MAT); English (MAT); French (MAT); health and physical education (MAT); health education (MAT); mathematics (MAT); music (MAT); physical education (MAT); physical science (MAT); social studies (MAT); Spanish (MAT); teacher of English as a second language (MAT). *Degree requirements:* For master's, comprehensive exam, thesis or alternative. *Entrance requirements:* For master's, GRE General Test, interview, 2 letters of recommendation. Additional exam requirements/ recommendations for international students: Required—TOEFL (minimum score 83 iBT), IELTS (minimum score 6.5). Electronic applications accepted.

Montclair State University, The Graduate School, College of Science and Mathematics, Department of Biology and Molecular Biology, Montclair, NJ 07043-1624. Offers biology (MS), including biological science education, biology, ecology and evolution, physiology; molecular biology (MS, Certificate). Part-time and evening/ weekend programs available. *Degree requirements:* For master's, comprehensive exam, thesis or alternative. *Entrance requirements:* For master's, GRE General Test, 24 credits of course work in undergraduate biology, 2 letters of recommendation, teaching certificate (biology sciences education concentration); for Certificate, 2 letters of recommendation, essay. Additional exam requirements/recommendations for international students: Required—TOEFL (minimum score 83 iBT) or IELTS. Electronic applications accepted. *Faculty research:* Ecosystem biology, molecular biology, signal transduction, neuroscience, aquatic and coastal biology.

Montclair State University, The Graduate School, College of Science and Mathematics, Department of Mathematical Sciences, Program in Physical Science, Montclair, NJ 07043-1624. Offers MAT. *Degree requirements:* For master's, comprehensive exam. *Entrance requirements:* For master's, GRE General Test, interview, 2 letters of recommendation, essay. Additional exam requirements/ recommendations for international students: Required—TOEFL (minimum score 83 iBT), IELTS (minimum score 6.5). Electronic applications accepted. *Faculty research:* Teaching physics.

Morehead State University, Graduate Programs, College of Education, Department of Middle Grades and Secondary Education, Morehead, KY 40351. Offers business and marketing education (MAT); English/language arts 5-9 (MAT); French (MAT); health P-12 (MAT); mathematics 5-9 (MAT); physical education P-12 (MAT); science 5-9 (MAT); secondary biology (MAT); secondary chemistry (MAT); secondary earth science (MAT); secondary English (MAT); secondary math (MAT); secondary physics (MAT); secondary social studies (MAT); social studies 5-9 (MAT); Spanish (MAT). Part-time and evening/weekend programs available. *Degree requirements:* For master's, portfolio. *Entrance requirements:* For master's, GRE or PRAXIS II content exam, minimum overall undergraduate GPA of 2.5. Additional exam requirements/recommendations for international students: Required—TOEFL (minimum score 500 paper-based). Electronic applications accepted.

Morgan State University, School of Graduate Studies, School of Computer, Mathematical, and Natural Sciences, Department of Biology, Baltimore, MD 21251. Offers bioenvironmental science (PhD); biology (MS); science education (MS). *Degree requirements:* For master's, comprehensive exam, thesis. *Entrance requirements:* For master's, minimum GPA of 3.0.

Morgan State University, School of Graduate Studies, School of Education and Urban Studies, Department of Advanced Studies, Leadership and Policy, Program in Science Education, Baltimore, MD 21251. Offers MS, Ed D. *Entrance requirements:* Additional exam requirements/recommendations for international students: Required—TOEFL (minimum score 550 paper-based).

National Louis University, National College of Education, Chicago, IL 60603. Offers administration and supervision (M Ed, Ed D, CAS, Ed S); curriculum and instruction (M Ed, MS Ed, CAS); early childhood administration (M Ed, CAS); early childhood education (M Ed, MAT, MS Ed, CAS); education (Ed D); educational psychology/human learning and development (M Ed, MS Ed, CAS, Ed S); elementary education (MAT); interdisciplinary curriculum and instruction (M Ed); mathematics education (M Ed, MS Ed, CAS); reading and language (M Ed, MS Ed, CAS); school psychology (M Ed, Ed S); science education (M Ed, MS Ed, CAS); secondary education (MAT); special education (M Ed, MAT, CAS); technology in education (M Ed, CAS). *Accreditation:* NCATE. Part-time and evening/weekend programs available. *Degree requirements:* For doctorate, comprehensive exam, thesis/dissertation. *Entrance requirements:* For master's, MAT or GRE, minimum GPA of 3.0; for doctorate, GRE General Test, minimum GPA of 3.25, interview, resume, writing sample, 4 recommendations. Additional exam requirements/recommendations for international students: Required—TOEFL (minimum score 550 paper-based; 79 iBT).

New Mexico Institute of Mining and Technology, Graduate Studies, Master of Science for Teachers Interdepartmental Program, Socorro, NM 87801. Offers MST. *Degree requirements:* For master's, thesis optional. *Entrance requirements:* For master's, GRE General Test. Additional exam requirements/recommendations for international students: Required—TOEFL (minimum score 540 paper-based). Electronic applications accepted. *Expenses:* Tuition, state resident: full-time $5270; part-time $292.80 per credit hour. Tuition, nonresident: full-time $16,833; part-time $968.51 per credit hour. *Required fees:* $648. Part-time tuition and fees vary according to course load. *Faculty research:* Teaching secondary school science and/or mathematics.

New York Institute of Technology, School of Education, Department of Education, Old Westbury, NY 11568-8000. Offers adolescence education: mathematics (MS); adolescence education: science (MS); childhood education (MS); science, technology, engineering, and math education (Advanced Certificate); teaching 21st century skills (Advanced Certificate). Part-time and evening/weekend programs available. Postbaccalaureate distance learning degree programs offered (minimal on-campus study). *Faculty:* 1 (woman) full-time, 6 part-time/adjunct (3 women). *Students:* 13 full-time (11 women), 21 part-time (19 women); includes 7 minority (2 Black or African American, non-Hispanic/Latino; 3 Asian, non-Hispanic/Latino; 1 Hispanic/Latino; 1 Two or more races, non-Hispanic/Latino), 1 international. Average age 31. 32 applicants, 75% accepted, 13 enrolled. In 2013, 6 master's, 58 other advanced degrees awarded. *Entrance requirements:* Additional exam requirements/recommendations for international students: Required—TOEFL (minimum score 550 paper-based; 79 iBT), IELTS (minimum score 6). *Application deadline:* For fall admission, 7/1 priority date for domestic students, 6/1 for international students; for spring admission, 12/1 priority date for domestic students, 12/1 for international students. Applications are processed on a rolling basis. Application fee: $50. Electronic applications accepted. *Expenses: Tuition:* Full-time $18,900; part-time $1050 per credit. *Financial support:* Research assistantships with partial tuition reimbursements, career-related internships or fieldwork, scholarships/grants, health care benefits, tuition waivers (full and partial), and unspecified assistantships available. Support available to part-time students. Financial award applicants required to submit FAFSA. *Faculty research:* Evolving definition of new literacies and its impact on teaching and learning (twenty-first century skills), new literacies practices in teacher education, teachers' professional development, English language and literacy learning through mobile learning, teaching reading to culturally and linguistically diverse children. *Unit head:* Dr. Hui-Yin Hsu, Associate Professor, 516-686-1322, Fax: 516-686-7655, E-mail: hhsu02@nyit.edu. *Application contact:* Alice Dolitsky, Director, Graduate Admissions, 516-686-7520, Fax: 516-686-1116, E-mail: nyitgrad@nyit.edu.
Website: http://www.nyit.edu/education/departments.

New York University, Steinhardt School of Culture, Education, and Human Development, Department of Teaching and Learning, Clinically Rich Integrated Science Program (CRISP), New York, NY 10003. Offers biology (MA), including teaching biology grades 7-12; chemistry (MA), including teaching chemistry grades 7-12; physics (MA), including teaching physics grades 7-12. Part-time and evening/weekend programs available. *Faculty:* 4 full-time (3 women). *Students:* 22 full-time (14 women), 1 part-time (0 women); includes 8 minority (3 Black or African American, non-Hispanic/Latino; 3 Asian, non-Hispanic/Latino; 2 Hispanic/Latino), 2 international. Average age 27. 42 applicants, 64% accepted, 19 enrolled. In 2013, 9 master's awarded. *Degree requirements:* For master's, thesis (for some programs). *Entrance requirements:* Additional exam requirements/recommendations for international students: Required—TOEFL (minimum score 100 iBT). *Application deadline:* For fall admission, 2/1 priority date for domestic and international students; for spring admission, 10/1 for domestic and international students. Applications are processed on a rolling basis. Application fee: $75. Electronic applications accepted. *Expenses: Tuition:* Full-time $35,856; part-time $1494 per unit. *Required fees:* $1408; $64 per unit. $473 per term. Tuition and fees vary according to course load and program. *Financial support:* Career-related internships or fieldwork, Federal Work-Study, institutionally sponsored loans, scholarships/grants, and tuition waivers (partial) available. Support available to part-time students. Financial award application deadline: 2/1; financial award applicants required to submit FAFSA. *Faculty research:* Science curriculum development, gender and ethnicity, technology use, history and philosophy of school science, science in urban schools. *Unit head:* Dr. Pamela Fraser-Abder, Director, 212-998-5870, Fax: 212-995-4049. *Application contact:* 212-998-5030, Fax: 212-995-4328, E-mail: steinhardt.gradadmissions@nyu.edu.
Website: http://steinhardt.nyu.edu/teachlearn/crisp.

Niagara University, Graduate Division of Education, Concentration in Foundations of Teaching, Niagara Falls, NY 14109. Offers MS Ed. *Accreditation:* NCATE. Part-time programs available. *Students:* 1 (woman) full-time, 5 part-time (2 women). Average age 30. In 2013, 5 master's awarded. *Degree requirements:* For master's, thesis. *Entrance requirements:* For master's, GRE General Test or MAT. Additional exam requirements/recommendations for international students: Required—TOEFL (minimum score 550 paper-based, 79 iBT) or IELTS (minimum score 6). *Application deadline:* For fall admission, 8/1 for domestic students. Applications are processed on a rolling basis. Application fee: $30. *Expenses:* Contact institution. *Financial support:* Research assistantships with full and partial tuition reimbursements, teaching assistantships with full and partial tuition reimbursements, career-related internships or fieldwork, Federal Work-Study, scholarships/grants, and unspecified assistantships available. Financial award application deadline: 4/15; financial award applicants required to submit FAFSA. *Unit head:* Dr. Leticia Hahn, 716-286-8760, E-mail: lhahn@niagara.edu. *Application contact:* Dr. Debra A. Colley, Dean of Education, 716-286-8560, Fax: 716-286-8560, E-mail: dcolley@niagara.edu.
Website: http://www.niagara.edu/foundations-of-teaching-math-science-and-technology-education.

North Carolina Agricultural and Technical State University, School of Graduate Studies, College of Arts and Sciences, Department of Biology, Greensboro, NC 27411. Offers biology (MS); biology education (MAT). Part-time and evening/weekend programs available. *Degree requirements:* For master's, comprehensive exam, thesis (for some programs), qualifying exam. *Entrance requirements:* For master's, GRE General Test, personal statement. *Faculty research:* Physical ecology, cytochemistry, botany, parasitology, microbiology.

North Carolina State University, Graduate School, College of Education, Department of Mathematics, Science, and Technology Education, Program in Science Education, Raleigh, NC 27695. Offers M Ed, MS, PhD. *Accreditation:* NCATE. Part-time programs available. *Degree requirements:* For master's, thesis (for some programs), oral exam; for doctorate, one foreign language, thesis/dissertation, oral and written exams. *Entrance requirements:* For master's, GRE General Test or MAT, minimum GPA of 3.0; for doctorate, GRE General Test, minimum GPA of 3.0, interview. Electronic applications accepted. *Faculty research:* Teacher development, sociocultural issues in learning, student science misconceptions, technical applications to science teaching.

North Dakota State University, College of Graduate and Interdisciplinary Studies, College of Human Development and Education, School of Education, Fargo, ND 58108. Offers agricultural education (M Ed, MS), including agricultural education, agricultural extension education (MS); counseling (M Ed, MS, PhD); curriculum and instruction (M Ed, MS); education (PhD); educational leadership (M Ed, MS, Ed S); family and consumer sciences education (M Ed, MS); history education (M Ed, MS); institutional analysis (Ed D); mathematics education (M Ed, MS); music education (M Ed, MS); occupational and adult education (Ed D); science education (M Ed, MS). *Accreditation:* NCATE. Part-time and evening/weekend programs available. Postbaccalaureate distance learning degree programs offered (minimal on-campus study). *Faculty:* 25 full-time (11 women), 1 (woman) part-time/adjunct. *Students:* 110 full-time (82 women), 123 part-time (85 women); includes 14 minority (4 Black or African American, non-Hispanic/Latino; 4 American Indian or Alaska Native, non-Hispanic/Latino; 1 Native Hawaiian or other Pacific Islander, non-Hispanic/Latino; 5 Two or more races, non-Hispanic/Latino), 10 international. Average age 28. 57 applicants, 81% accepted, 42 enrolled. In 2013, 38 master's, 9 doctorates awarded. *Degree requirements:* For master's, comprehensive exam; for doctorate, thesis/dissertation; for Ed S, thesis. *Entrance requirements:* For degree, GRE General Test, master's degree, minimum GPA of 3.25. Additional exam requirements/recommendations for international students: Required—TOEFL. *Application deadline:* Applications are processed on a rolling basis. Application fee: $45 ($60 for international students). *Financial support:* Research assistantships, teaching assistantships, career-related internships or fieldwork, Federal Work-Study, institutionally sponsored loans, and tuition waivers (full) available. Financial award application deadline: 4/15. *Unit head:* Dr. William Martin, Chair, 701-231-7202, Fax: 701-231-7416, E-mail: william.martin@ndsu.edu. *Application contact:* Sonya Goergen, Marketing, Recruitment, and Public Relations Coordinator, 701-231-7033, Fax: 701-231-6524.
Website: http://www.ndsu.nodak.edu/school_of_education/.

North Dakota State University, College of Graduate and Interdisciplinary Studies, Program in STEM Education, Fargo, ND 58108. Offers PhD. In 2013, 1 doctorate awarded. Application fee: $35. Electronic applications accepted. *Unit head:* Dr. Donald Schwert, Director, 701-231-7496, Fax: 701-231-5924, E-mail: donald.schwert@ndsu.edu. *Application contact:* Sonya Goergen, Marketing, Recruitment, and Public Relations Coordinator, 701-231-7033, Fax: 701-231-6524.

Northeastern State University, College of Science and Health Professions, Department of Natural Sciences, Program in Science Education, Tahlequah, OK 74464-2399. Offers M Ed. Part-time and evening/weekend programs available. *Faculty:* 28 full-time (12 women), 1 part-time/adjunct (0 women). *Students:* 2 full-time (0 women), 21 part-time (14 women); includes 4 minority (2 American Indian or Alaska Native, non-Hispanic/Latino; 1 Native Hawaiian or other Pacific Islander, non-Hispanic/Latino; 1 Two or more races, non-Hispanic/Latino). Average age 35. In 2013, 3 master's awarded. *Entrance requirements:* For master's, MAT or GRE, minimum GPA of 2.5. *Application deadline:* For fall admission, 6/1 for domestic students. Application fee: $25. *Expenses:* Tuition, state resident: full-time $3029; part-time $168.25 per credit hour. Tuition, nonresident: full-time $7709; part-time $428.25 per credit hour. *Required fees:* $35.90 per credit hour. *Unit head:* Dr. April Adams, Chair, 918-456-5511 Ext. 3819. *Application contact:* Margie Railey, Administrative Assistant, 918-456-5511 Ext. 2093, Fax: 918-458-2061, E-mail: railey@nsouk.edu.
Website: http://academics.nsuok.edu/naturalsciences/Degrees/Graduate/MEdScienceEducation.aspx.

Northern Arizona University, Graduate College, College of Engineering, Forestry and Natural Sciences, Center for Science Teaching and Learning, Flagstaff, AZ 86011. Offers mathematics or science teaching (Certificate); science teaching and learning (MAST); teaching science (MAT). Part-time programs available. Postbaccalaureate distance learning degree programs offered (minimal on-campus study). *Faculty:* 7 full-time (3 women), 2 part-time/adjunct (both women). *Students:* 16 full-time (12 women), 4 part-time (3 women). Average age 31. 23 applicants, 83% accepted, 13 enrolled. In 2013, 11 master's, 3 other advanced degrees awarded. *Entrance requirements:* Additional exam requirements/recommendations for international students: Required—TOEFL (minimum score 550 paper-based; 80 iBT), IELTS (minimum score 7). *Application deadline:* For fall admission, 3/1 for international students; for spring admission, 9/15 for international students. Application fee: $65. *Financial support:* In 2013–14, 2 research assistantships (averaging $9,200 per year) were awarded; career-related internships or fieldwork, Federal Work-Study, and scholarships/grants also available. Financial award applicants required to submit FAFSA. *Unit head:* Max Dass, Director, 928-523-2066, E-mail: pradep.dass@nau.edu. *Application contact:* Ann Archuleta, Administrative Associate, 928-523-1709, E-mail: ann.archuleta@nau.edu.
Website: http://nau.edu/cefns/cstl/.

Northern Michigan University, College of Graduate Studies, College of Health Sciences and Professional Studies, School of Education, Leadership and Public Service, Program in Science Education, Marquette, MI 49855-5301. Offers MS.

Postbaccalaureate distance learning degree programs offered. *Expenses:* Tuition, state resident: part-time $427 per credit. Tuition, nonresident: part-time $614.50 per credit. *Required fees:* $325 per semester. Tuition and fees vary according to course load and program. *Unit head:* Rodney Clarken, Associate Dean, 906-227-1880, E-mail: rclarken@nmu.edu. *Application contact:* Dr. Cynthia A. Prosen, Dean of Graduate Studies and Research, 906-227-2300, Fax: 906-227-2315, E-mail: cprosen@nmu.edu.

Northwest Missouri State University, Graduate School, College of Arts and Sciences, Department of Natural Sciences, Program in Teaching: Science, Maryville, MO 64468-6001. Offers MS Ed. *Accreditation:* NCATE. Part-time programs available. *Degree requirements:* For master's, comprehensive exam, thesis optional. *Entrance requirements:* For master's, GRE General Test, minimum GPA of 2.75 in major, 2.5 overall; teaching certificate; writing sample. Additional exam requirements/recommendations for international students: Required—TOEFL (minimum score 550 paper-based).

Occidental College, Graduate Studies, Department of Education, Los Angeles, CA 90041-3314. Offers elementary education (MAT), including liberal studies; secondary education (MAT), including English and comparative literary studies, history, life science, mathematics, physical science, social science, Spanish. Part-time programs available. *Degree requirements:* For master's, comprehensive exam, synthesis paper. *Entrance requirements:* For master's, GRE General Test, minimum GPA of 3.0. Additional exam requirements/recommendations for international students: Required—TOEFL (minimum score 625 paper-based). *Expenses:* Contact institution. *Faculty research:* Preparing teacher-leaders, curriculum development.

Ohio University, Graduate College, College of Arts and Sciences, Department of Geological Sciences, Athens, OH 45701-2979. Offers environmental geochemistry (MS); environmental geology (MS); environmental/hydrology (MS); geology (MS); geology education (MS); geomorphology/surficial processes (MS); geophysics (MS); hydrogeology (MS); sedimentology (MS); structure/tectonics (MS). Part-time programs available. *Degree requirements:* For master's, thesis. *Entrance requirements:* Additional exam requirements/recommendations for international students: Required—TOEFL (minimum score 550 paper-based; 80 iBT) or IELTS (minimum score 6.5). Electronic applications accepted. *Faculty research:* Geoscience education, tectonics, fluvial geomorphology, invertebrate paleontology, mine/hydrology.

Old Dominion University, Darden College of Education, Programs in Secondary Education, Norfolk, VA 23529. Offers biology (MS Ed); chemistry (MS Ed); English (MS Ed); instructional technology (MS Ed); library science (MS Ed); secondary education (MS Ed). *Accreditation:* NCATE. Part-time and evening/weekend programs available. Postbaccalaureate distance learning degree programs offered (minimal on-campus study). *Faculty:* 13 full-time (7 women), 10 part-time/adjunct (7 women). *Students:* 74 full-time (56 women), 78 part-time (49 women); includes 25 minority (13 Black or African American, non-Hispanic/Latino; 6 Hispanic/Latino; 6 Two or more races, non-Hispanic/Latino). Average age 32. 75 applicants, 71% accepted, 53 enrolled. In 2013, 79 master's awarded. *Degree requirements:* For master's, comprehensive exam, thesis. *Entrance requirements:* For master's, GRE General Test or MAT, PRAXIS I (for licensure), minimum GPA of 2.8, teaching certificate. Additional exam requirements/recommendations for international students: Required—TOEFL. *Application deadline:* For fall admission, 6/1 for domestic and international students; for winter admission, 11/1 for domestic and international students; for spring admission, 3/1 for domestic and international students. Applications are processed on a rolling basis. Application fee: $50. Electronic applications accepted. *Expenses:* Tuition, state resident: full-time $9888; part-time $412 per credit. Tuition, nonresident: full-time $25,152; part-time $1048 per credit. *Required fees:* $59 per semester. One-time fee: $50. *Financial support:* In 2013–14, 56 students received support, including fellowships (averaging $15,000 per year), research assistantships with tuition reimbursements available (averaging $9,000 per year), teaching assistantships with tuition reimbursements available (averaging $15,000 per year). Financial award application deadline: 2/15; financial award applicants required to submit FAFSA. *Faculty research:* Use of technology, writing project for teachers, geography teaching, reading. *Unit head:* Dr. Robert Lucking, Graduate Program Director, 757-683-5545, Fax: 757-683-5862, E-mail: rlucking@odu.edu. *Application contact:* William Heffelfinger, Director of Graduate Admissions, 757-683-5554, Fax: 757-683-3255, E-mail: gradadmit@odu.edu. Website: http://education.odu.edu/eci/secondary/.

Oregon State University, College of Education, Program in Science Education, Corvallis, OR 97331. Offers MS, PhD. *Accreditation:* NCATE. Part-time programs available. Postbaccalaureate distance learning degree programs offered (no on-campus study). *Faculty:* 11 full-time (7 women), 1 part-time/adjunct (0 women). *Students:* 28 full-time (12 women), 16 part-time (14 women); includes 4 minority (2 Asian, non-Hispanic/Latino; 2 Hispanic/Latino), 2 international. Average age 35. 26 applicants, 62% accepted, 14 enrolled. In 2013, 12 master's, 5 doctorates awarded. *Degree requirements:* For doctorate, thesis/dissertation. *Entrance requirements:* For master's, minimum GPA of 3.0 in last 90 hours; for doctorate, GRE or MAT, minimum GPA of 3.0 in last 90 hours. Additional exam requirements/recommendations for international students: Required—TOEFL (minimum score 80 iBT), IELTS (minimum score 6.5). *Application deadline:* For fall admission, 6/1 for domestic students; for winter admission, 9/1 for domestic students; for spring admission, 12/1 for domestic students; for summer admission, 3/1 for domestic students. Application fee: $60. *Expenses:* Tuition, state resident: full-time $11,664; part-time $432 per credit hour. Tuition, nonresident: full-time $19,197; part-time $711 per credit hour. *Required fees:* $1446; $443 per quarter. One-time fee: $300. Tuition and fees vary according to course load and program. *Financial support:* Teaching assistantships, Federal Work-Study, and institutionally sponsored loans available. Support available to part-time students. Financial award application deadline: 2/1. *Faculty research:* Teacher thought processes, pedagogical content knowledge and teacher preparation. *Unit head:* Dr. Larry Flick, Dean, 541-737-3664, Fax: 541-737-8971, E-mail: larry.flick@oregonstate.edu. *Application contact:* Katherine Robertson, School-Based Education, E-mail: katherine.robertson@oregonstate.edu. Website: http://education.oregonstate.edu/academics.

Oregon State University, College of Education, Program in Teaching: Integrated Science Education, Corvallis, OR 97331. Offers MAT. Part-time programs available. *Faculty:* 3 full-time (2 women), 8 part-time/adjunct (6 women). *Students:* 1 part-time (0 women); minority (Hispanic/Latino). 11 applicants, 27% accepted, 1 enrolled. *Entrance requirements:* For master's, CBEST. Additional exam requirements/recommendations for international students: Required—TOEFL (minimum score 575 paper-based). *Expenses:* Tuition, state resident: full-time $11,664; part-time $432 per credit hour. Tuition, nonresident: full-time $19,197; part-time $711 per credit hour. *Required fees:* $1446; $443 per quarter. One-time fee: $300. Tuition and fees vary according to course load and program. *Unit head:* Dr. Carolyn Platt, Teacher Education Program Lead, 541-322-3120, E-mail: carolyn.platt@osucascades.edu.

Our Lady of the Lake University of San Antonio, School of Professional Studies, Program in Curriculum and Instruction, San Antonio, TX 78207-4689. Offers bilingual education (M Ed); early childhood education (M Ed); English as a second language (M Ed); integrated math teaching (M Ed); integrated science teaching (M Ed); reading specialist (M Ed). Part-time and evening/weekend programs available. *Faculty:* 6 full-time (4 women), 3 part-time/adjunct (all women). *Students:* 4 full-time (all women), 84 part-time (72 women); includes 52 minority (2 Black or African American, non-Hispanic/Latino; 2 Asian, non-Hispanic/Latino; 48 Hispanic/Latino). Average age 40. 9 applicants, 56% accepted, 1 enrolled. In 2013, 8 master's awarded. *Degree requirements:* For master's, comprehensive exam. *Entrance requirements:* For master's, GRE General Test or MAT. Additional exam requirements/recommendations for international students: Required—TOEFL. *Application deadline:* For fall admission, 4/1 priority date for domestic and international students; for spring admission, 11/1 priority date for domestic and international students; for summer admission, 2/1 priority date for domestic students, 4/1 priority date for international students. Applications are processed on a rolling basis. Application fee: $25 ($50 for international students). Electronic applications accepted. *Expenses:* Tuition: Full-time $9120; part-time $760 per credit. *Required fees:* $698; $334 per trimester. Tuition and fees vary according to course load, degree level, campus/location and program. *Financial support:* Research assistantships, teaching assistantships, career-related internships or fieldwork, Federal Work-Study, institutionally sponsored loans, scholarships/grants, and tuition waivers (partial) available. Support available to part-time students. Financial award application deadline: 4/1. *Faculty research:* Professional educator to understand and meet the comprehensive needs of a diverse student population, life-long learners, innovative practices. *Unit head:* Dr. Jerrie Jackson, 210-434-6711 Ext. 2698, E-mail: jjackson@lake.ollusa.edu. *Application contact:* Graduate Admission, 210-431-3961, Fax: 210-431-4013, E-mail: gradadm@lake.ollusa.edu. Website: http://www.ollusa.edu/s/1190/ollu-3-column-noads.aspx?sid=1190&gid=1&pgid=4173.

Our Lady of the Lake University of San Antonio, School of Professional Studies, Program in Intermediate Education, San Antonio, TX 78207-4689. Offers math/science education (M Ed); professional studies (M Ed). Part-time and evening/weekend programs available. *Faculty:* 6 full-time (4 women), 3 part-time/adjunct (all women). *Students:* 1 (woman) full-time; minority (Black or African American, non-Hispanic/Latino). Average age 50. 1 applicant, 100% accepted. In 2013, 1 master's awarded. *Degree requirements:* For master's, comprehensive exam. *Entrance requirements:* For master's, GRE General Test or MAT. Additional exam requirements/recommendations for international students: Required—TOEFL. *Application deadline:* For fall admission, 4/1 priority date for domestic and international students; for spring admission, 11/1 priority date for domestic and international students; for summer admission, 2/1 priority date for domestic and international students. Applications are processed on a rolling basis. Application fee: $25 ($50 for international students). Electronic applications accepted. *Expenses:* Tuition: Full-time $9120; part-time $760 per credit. *Required fees:* $698; $334 per trimester. Tuition and fees vary according to course load, degree level, campus/location and program. *Financial support:* Research assistantships, teaching assistantships, career-related internships or fieldwork, Federal Work-Study, institutionally sponsored loans, scholarships/grants, and tuition waivers (partial) available. Support available to part-time students. Financial award application deadline: 4/15. *Faculty research:* Professional educator to understand and meet the comprehensive needs of a diverse student population, life-long learners, innovative practices. *Unit head:* Dr. Jerrie Jackson, 210-434-6711 Ext. 2698, E-mail: jjackson@lake.ollusa.edu. *Application contact:* Graduate Admission, 210-431-3961, Fax: 210-431-4013, E-mail: gradadm@lake.ollusa.edu. Website: http://www.ollusa.edu/s/1190/ollu-3-column-noads.aspx?sid=1190&gid=1&pgid=3855.

Plymouth State University, College of Graduate Studies, Graduate Studies in Education, Program in Science, Plymouth, NH 03264-1595. Offers applied meteorology (MS); biology (MS); clinical mental health counseling (MS); environmental science and policy (MS); science education (MS).

Plymouth State University, College of Graduate Studies, Graduate Studies in Education, Program in Teaching, Plymouth, NH 03264-1595. Offers art education (MAT); science education (MAT). Evening/weekend programs available. *Degree requirements:* For master's, internship or teaching experience.

Portland State University, Graduate Studies, College of Liberal Arts and Sciences, Department of Geology, Portland, OR 97207-0751. Offers environmental sciences and resources (PhD); geology (MA, MS); science/geology (MAT, MST). Part-time programs available. *Faculty:* 9 full-time (0 women), 5 part-time/adjunct (3 women). *Students:* 19 full-time (13 women), 11 part-time (4 women); includes 4 minority (2 American Indian or Alaska Native, non-Hispanic/Latino; 2 Hispanic/Latino). Average age 33. 18 applicants, 44% accepted, 7 enrolled. In 2013, 14 master's awarded. *Degree requirements:* For master's, comprehensive exam, thesis, field comprehensive; for doctorate, thesis/dissertation, 2 years of residency. *Entrance requirements:* For master's, GRE General Test, GRE Subject Test, BA/BS in geology, minimum GPA of 3.0 in upper-division course work or 2.75 overall. Additional exam requirements/recommendations for international students: Required—TOEFL (minimum score 550 paper-based). *Application deadline:* 1/31 priority date for domestic and international students. Applications are processed on a rolling basis. Application fee: $50. *Expenses:* Tuition, state resident: full-time $9207; part-time $341 per credit. Tuition, nonresident: full-time $14,391; part-time $533 per credit. *Required fees:* $1263; $22 per credit. $98 per quarter. One-time fee: $150. Tuition and fees vary according to program. *Financial support:* In 2013–14, 5 research assistantships with full tuition reimbursements (averaging $10,301 per year), 7 teaching assistantships with full tuition reimbursements (averaging $14,998 per year) were awarded; career-related internships or fieldwork, Federal Work-Study, scholarships/grants, and unspecified assistantships also available. Support available to part-time students. Financial award application deadline: 3/1; financial award applicants required to submit FAFSA. *Faculty research:* Sediment transport, volcanic environmental geology, coastal and fluvial processes. *Total annual research expenditures:* $1.4 million. *Unit head:* Dr. Michael Cummings, Chair, 503-725-3395, Fax: 503-725-3025, E-mail: cummingsm@pdx.edu. *Application contact:* Nancy Eriksson, Office Coordinator, 503-725-3022, Fax: 503-725-3025, E-mail: nancye@pdx.edu. Website: http://www.geol.pdx.edu/.

Portland State University, Graduate Studies, College of Liberal Arts and Sciences, Interdisciplinary Programs in General Science, General Social Science, and General Arts and Letters, Portland, OR 97207-0751. Offers general arts and letters education (MAT, MST); general science education (MAT, MST); general social science education (MAT, MST). Part-time and evening/weekend programs available. *Students:* 7 full-time (5 women), 22 part-time (14 women); includes 6 minority (3 Hispanic/Latino; 1 Native Hawaiian or other Pacific Islander, non-Hispanic/Latino; 2 Two or more races, non-Hispanic/Latino). Average age 39. 11 applicants, 36% accepted, 3 enrolled. In 2013, 13 master's awarded. *Degree requirements:* For master's, variable foreign language requirement, written exam. *Entrance requirements:* For master's, minimum GPA of 3.0 in upper-division course work or 2.75 overall. Additional exam requirements/recommendations for international students: Required—TOEFL (minimum score 550 paper-based). *Application deadline:* For fall admission, 4/1 priority date for domestic students, 3/1 priority date for international students. Application fee: $50. *Expenses:* Tuition, state resident: full-time $9207; part-time $341 per credit. Tuition, nonresident: full-time $14,391; part-time $533 per credit. *Required fees:* $1263; $22 per credit. $98 per quarter. One-time fee: $150. Tuition and fees vary according to program. *Financial*

support: Federal Work-Study and unspecified assistantships available. Support available to part-time students. Financial award application deadline: 3/1; financial award applicants required to submit FAFSA. *Total annual research expenditures:* $462,166. *Unit head:* Robert Mercer, Associate Dean, 503-725-5059, Fax: 503-725-3693, E-mail: mercerr@pdx.edu. *Application contact:* 503-725-3511, Fax: 503-725-5525.

Portland State University, Graduate Studies, College of Liberal Arts and Sciences, Program in Environmental Sciences and Management, Portland, OR 97207-0751. Offers environmental management (MEM); environmental sciences/biology (PhD); environmental sciences/chemistry (PhD); environmental sciences/civil engineering (PhD); environmental sciences/geography (PhD); environmental sciences/geology (PhD); environmental sciences/physics (PhD); environmental studies (MS); science/environmental science (MST). Part-time programs available. *Faculty:* 14 full-time (6 women), 8 part-time/adjunct (4 women). *Students:* 46 full-time (26 women), 36 part-time (17 women); includes 12 minority (1 Black or African American, non-Hispanic/Latino; 2 American Indian or Alaska Native, non-Hispanic/Latino; 2 Asian, non-Hispanic/Latino; 3 Hispanic/Latino; 1 Native Hawaiian or other Pacific Islander, non-Hispanic/Latino; 3 Two or more races, non-Hispanic/Latino), 4 international. Average age 35. 30 applicants, 40% accepted, 9 enrolled. In 2013, 16 master's, 3 doctorates awarded. *Degree requirements:* For master's, thesis or alternative; for doctorate, variable foreign language requirement, comprehensive exam, thesis/dissertation, oral and qualifying exams. *Entrance requirements:* For master's, GRE General Test, 3 letters of recommendation; for doctorate, minimum GPA of 3.0 in upper-division course work or 2.75 overall. Additional exam requirements/recommendations for international students: Required—TOEFL (minimum score 550 paper-based). *Application deadline:* For fall admission, 2/1 for domestic and international students. Applications are processed on a rolling basis. Application fee: $50. *Expenses:* Tuition, state resident: full-time $9207; part-time $341 per credit. Tuition, nonresident: full-time $14,391; part-time $533 per credit. *Required fees:* $1263; $22 per credit. $98 per quarter. One-time fee: $150. Tuition and fees vary according to program. *Financial support:* In 2013–14, 3 research assistantships with full tuition reimbursements (averaging $12,463 per year), 15 teaching assistantships with full tuition reimbursements (averaging $15,000 per year) were awarded; Federal Work-Study, scholarships/grants, tuition waivers (partial), and unspecified assistantships also available. Support available to part-time students. Financial award application deadline: 3/1; financial award applicants required to submit FAFSA. *Faculty research:* Environmental aspects of biology, chemistry, civil engineering, geology, physics. *Total annual research expenditures:* $2.1 million. *Unit head:* Dr. Yangdong Pan, Chair, 503-725-4981, Fax: 503-725-3888, E-mail: pany@pdx.edu. *Application contact:* Dr. Robert Scheller, Chair, Graduate Admissions, 503-725-4982, Fax: 503-725-9040, E-mail: rmschell@pdx.edu.
Website: http://www.esr.pdx.edu/.

Purdue University, Graduate School, College of Education, Department of Curriculum and Instruction, West Lafayette, IN 47907. Offers agricultural and extension education (PhD, Ed S); agriculture and extension education (MS, MS Ed); art education (PhD); curriculum studies (MS Ed, PhD, Ed S); educational technology (MS Ed, PhD, Ed S); elementary education (MS Ed); family and consumer sciences education (MS Ed, PhD, Ed S); foreign language education (MS Ed, PhD, Ed S); industrial technology (PhD, Ed S); language arts (MS Ed, PhD, Ed S); literacy (MS Ed, PhD, Ed S); mathematics/science education (MS, MS Ed, PhD, Ed S); social studies (MS Ed, PhD); social studies education (Ed S); vocational/industrial education (MS Ed, PhD, Ed S); vocational/technical education (MS Ed, PhD, Ed S). *Accreditation:* NCATE. Part-time and evening/weekend programs available. *Faculty:* 29 full-time (19 women), 33 part-time/adjunct (29 women). *Students:* 85 full-time (53 women), 271 part-time (195 women); includes 62 minority (19 Black or African American, non-Hispanic/Latino; 3 American Indian or Alaska Native, non-Hispanic/Latino; 13 Asian, non-Hispanic/Latino; 22 Hispanic/Latino; 1 Native Hawaiian or other Pacific Islander, non-Hispanic/Latino; 4 Two or more races, non-Hispanic/Latino), 41 international. Average age 36. 155 applicants, 71% accepted, 71 enrolled. In 2013, 60 master's, 20 doctorates awarded. *Degree requirements:* For master's, thesis optional; for doctorate, thesis/dissertation, oral and written exams; for Ed S, oral presentation, project. *Entrance requirements:* For master's, GRE General Test (if undergraduate GPA is below 3.0), minimum undergraduate GPA of 3.0 or equivalent; for doctorate, GRE General Test (minimum combined verbal and quantitative score of 1000, 300 for new scoring), minimum undergraduate GPA of 3.0 or equivalent; master's degree with minimum GPA of 3.0 or equivalent; for Ed S, GRE General Test (minimum combined verbal and quantitative score of 1000, 300 for new scoring), minimum undergraduate GPA of 3.0 or equivalent; master's degree. Additional exam requirements/recommendations for international students: Required—TOEFL (minimum score 550 paper-based; 77 iBT). *Application deadline:* For fall admission, 12/15 for domestic students, 3/1 for international students; for spring admission, 9/15 for domestic students, 8/1 for international students. Application fee: $60 ($75 for international students). Electronic applications accepted. *Financial support:* Fellowships with full tuition reimbursements, research assistantships with full tuition reimbursements, teaching assistantships with full tuition reimbursements, career-related internships or fieldwork, and tuition waivers (full) available. Support available to part-time students. Financial award application deadline: 3/1; financial award applicants required to submit FAFSA. *Faculty research:* Literacy acquisition and development, teacher beliefs and knowledge, recruitment and retention of underrepresented students, economic education, literacy discourse. *Unit head:* Dr. Phillip J. VanFossen, Head, 765-494-7935, Fax: 765-496-1622, E-mail: vanfoss@purdue.edu. *Application contact:* Cindy Blankenship, Graduate Contact, 765-494-2345, Fax: 765-494-5832, E-mail: prater0@purdue.edu.
Website: http://www.edci.purdue.edu/.

Purdue University, Graduate School, College of Science, Department of Chemistry, West Lafayette, IN 47907. Offers analytical chemistry (MS, PhD); biochemistry (MS, PhD); chemical education (MS, PhD); inorganic chemistry (MS, PhD); organic chemistry (MS, PhD); physical chemistry (MS, PhD). *Faculty:* 36 full-time (12 women), 9 part-time/adjunct (1 woman). *Students:* 285 full-time (112 women), 28 part-time (11 women); includes 34 minority (15 Black or African American, non-Hispanic/Latino; 8 Asian, non-Hispanic/Latino; 8 Hispanic/Latino; 3 Two or more races, non-Hispanic/Latino), 106 international. Average age 26. 577 applicants, 25% accepted, 54 enrolled. In 2013, 10 master's, 56 doctorates awarded. Terminal master's awarded for partial completion of doctoral program. *Degree requirements:* For master's, thesis; for doctorate, comprehensive exam, thesis/dissertation. *Entrance requirements:* For master's and doctorate, minimum undergraduate GPA of 3.0. Additional exam requirements/recommendations for international students: Required—TOEFL (minimum score 550 paper-based; 77 iBT); Recommended—TWE. *Application deadline:* For fall admission, 2/15 priority date for domestic students, 1/1 for international students. Applications are processed on a rolling basis. Application fee: $60 ($75 for international students). Electronic applications accepted. *Financial support:* In 2013–14, 2 fellowships with partial tuition reimbursements (averaging $18,000 per year), 55 teaching assistantships with partial tuition reimbursements (averaging $18,000 per year) were awarded; research assistantships with partial tuition reimbursements and tuition waivers (partial) also available. Support available to part-time students. Financial award applicants required to submit FAFSA. *Unit head:* Dr. Paul B. Shepson, Head, 765-494-5203,

E-mail: pshepson@purdue.edu. *Application contact:* Betty L. Hatfield, Director of Graduate Admissions, 765-494-5208, E-mail: bettyh@purdue.edu.
Website: https://www.chem.purdue.edu/.

Purdue University Calumet, Graduate Studies Office, School of Engineering, Mathematics, and Science, Department of Biological Sciences, Hammond, IN 46323-2094. Offers biology (MS); biology teaching (MS); biotechnology (MS). *Entrance requirements:* For master's, GRE. Additional exam requirements/recommendations for international students: Required—TOEFL. Electronic applications accepted. *Faculty research:* Cell biology, molecular biology, genetics, microbiology, neurophysiology.

Queens College of the City University of New York, Division of Graduate Studies, Division of Education, Department of Secondary Education, Flushing, NY 11367-1597. Offers art (MS Ed); biology (MS Ed, AC); chemistry (MS Ed, AC); earth sciences (MS Ed, AC); English (MS Ed, AC); French (MS Ed, AC); Italian (MS Ed, AC); mathematics (MS Ed, AC); music (MS Ed, AC); physics (MS Ed, AC); social studies (MS Ed, AC); Spanish (MS Ed, AC). Part-time and evening/weekend programs available. *Degree requirements:* For master's, research project; for AC, thesis optional. *Entrance requirements:* For master's, minimum GPA of 3.0. Additional exam requirements/recommendations for international students: Required—TOEFL.

Quinnipiac University, School of Education, Program in Secondary Education, Hamden, CT 06518-1940. Offers biology (MAT); English (MAT); history/social studies (MAT); mathematics (MAT); Spanish (MAT). *Accreditation:* NCATE. *Faculty:* 14 full-time (7 women), 46 part-time/adjunct (27 women). *Students:* 44 full-time (37 women), 1 (woman) part-time; includes 2 minority (both Hispanic/Latino). 45 applicants, 93% accepted, 32 enrolled. In 2013, 32 master's awarded. *Entrance requirements:* For master's, PRAXIS I, minimum GPA of 2.67, interview. *Application deadline:* For fall admission, 4/1 priority date for domestic students. Applications are processed on a rolling basis. Application fee: $45. Electronic applications accepted. *Expenses: Tuition:* Part-time $920 per credit. *Required fees:* $37 per credit. *Financial support:* Career-related internships or fieldwork, tuition waivers (full and partial), and unspecified assistantships available. Support available to part-time students. Financial award application deadline: 6/1; financial award applicants required to submit FAFSA. *Faculty research:* Multicultural and urban education/leadership, challenges of teaching diverse learners, scholarship of teaching and learning, technology and teaching, humor and education. *Unit head:* Mordechai Gordon, Program Director, E-mail: mordechai.gordon@quinnipiac.edu. *Application contact:* Office of Graduate Admissions, 800-462-1944, Fax: 203-582-3443, E-mail: graduate@quinnipiac.edu.
Website: http://www.quinnipiac.edu/gradeducation.

Regis University, College for Professional Studies, School of Education, Education Division, Denver, CO 80221-1099. Offers adult learning, training, and development (M Ed, Certificate); autism education (Certificate); curriculum, instruction, and assessment (M Ed); educational leadership (M Ed); gifted and talented education (M Ed); gifted/talented education (Certificate); initial licensure (M Ed); instructional technology (M Ed, Certificate); literacy (Certificate); reading (M Ed); school executive leadership (Certificate); space studies (M Ed). Program also offered in Henderson and Las Vegas (Summerlin), NV. *Accreditation:* Teacher Education Accreditation Council. Part-time and evening/weekend programs available. Postbaccalaureate distance learning degree programs offered (no on-campus study). *Degree requirements:* For master's, thesis. *Entrance requirements:* For master's, resume, minimum GPA of 2.75, criminal background check. Additional exam requirements/recommendations for international students: Required—TOEFL, TWE (minimum score 5). *Application deadline:* For fall admission, 7/23 priority date for domestic students; for winter admission, 9/17 priority date for domestic students; for spring admission, 12/3 priority date for domestic students. Applications are processed on a rolling basis. Application fee: $75. Electronic applications accepted. *Expenses:* Contact institution. *Financial support:* Federal Work-Study and scholarships/grants available. *Faculty research:* Issues of equity in the middle school classroom, professional learning communities, school reform, sociolinguistic and discursive obstacles to student integration, inclusive language arts curriculum. *Unit head:* Dr. Janna L. Oakes, Dean, 303-458-4302. *Application contact:* Information Contact, 303-458-4300, Fax: 303-964-5274, E-mail: masters@regis.edu.

Regis University, Regis College, Denver, CO 80221-1099. Offers biomedical sciences (MS); education (MA). *Accreditation:* Teacher Education Accreditation Council. Part-time programs available. *Faculty:* 11 full-time (8 women), 24 part-time/adjunct (23 women). *Students:* 41 full-time (24 women), 52 part-time (47 women); includes 14 minority (2 Black or African American, non-Hispanic/Latino; 3 Asian, non-Hispanic/Latino; 9 Hispanic/Latino). Average age 38. 195 applicants, 100% accepted, 165 enrolled. In 2013, 36 master's awarded. *Degree requirements:* For master's, thesis (for some programs), capstone presentation. *Entrance requirements:* For master's, official transcript reflecting baccalaureate degree awarded from U.S.-based regionally-accredited college or university. Additional exam requirements/recommendations for international students: Required—TOEFL (minimum score 550 paper-based; 82 iBT). *Application deadline:* For fall admission, 4/15 priority date for domestic students, 7/1 priority date for international students; for spring admission, 12/15 priority date for domestic students. Applications are processed on a rolling basis. Application fee: $75. Electronic applications accepted. *Expenses:* Contact institution. *Financial support:* In 2013–14, 2 students received support. Federal Work-Study and scholarships/grants available. Financial award application deadline: 4/15; financial award applicants required to submit FAFSA. *Unit head:* Dr. Stephen Doty, Interim Academic Dean, 303-458-4040. *Application contact:* Sarah Engel, Director of Admissions, 303-458-4900, Fax: 303-964-5534, E-mail: regisadm@regis.edu.
Website: http://www.regis.edu/RC.aspx.

Rice University, Graduate Programs, Wiess School of Natural Sciences, Department of Physics and Astronomy, Houston, TX 77251-1892. Offers nanoscale physics (MS); physics and astronomy (PhD); science teaching (MST). Part-time programs available. *Degree requirements:* For master's, thesis (for some programs); for doctorate, thesis/dissertation, minimum B average. *Entrance requirements:* For master's, GRE General Test; for doctorate, GRE General Test, GRE Subject Test. Additional exam requirements/recommendations for international students: Required—TOEFL (minimum score 600 paper-based; 90 iBT). Electronic applications accepted. *Faculty research:* Optical physics; ultra cold atoms; membrane electr-statics, peptides, proteins and lipids; solar astrophysics; stellar activity; magnetic fields; young stars.

Rider University, Department of Graduate Education, Leadership and Counseling, Teacher Certification Program, Lawrenceville, NJ 08648-3001. Offers business education (Certificate); elementary education (Certificate); English as a second language (Certificate); English education (Certificate); mathematics education (Certificate); preschool to grade 3 (Certificate); science education (Certificate); social studies education (Certificate); world languages (Certificate), including French, German, Spanish. Part-time programs available. *Degree requirements:* For Certificate, internship, professional portfolio. *Entrance requirements:* For degree, PRAXIS, resume. Additional exam requirements/recommendations for international students: Required—TOEFL (minimum score 550 paper-based). Electronic applications accepted. *Faculty research:* Conceptual foundations for optimal development of creativity; creative theory, cognitive processes in mathematics learning, teacher collaboration.

Rowan University, Graduate School, College of Education, Department of Teacher Education, Glassboro, NJ 08028-1701. Offers bilingual/bicultural education (CGS); collaborative teaching (MST); educational technology (CGS); elementary education (MST); elementary school teaching (MA); ESL education (CGS); foreign language education (MST); music education (MA); science teaching (MST); secondary education (MST); subject matter teaching (MA); teacher leadership (M Ed); teaching and learning (CGS); theatre education (MST). *Accreditation:* NCATE. Part-time and evening/weekend programs available. *Faculty:* 7 full-time (5 women), 1 (woman) part-time/adjunct. *Students:* 35 full-time (22 women), 78 part-time (66 women); includes 23 minority (4 Black or African American, non-Hispanic/Latino; 3 Asian, non-Hispanic/Latino; 16 Hispanic/Latino). Average age 28. 58 applicants, 100% accepted, 37 enrolled. In 2013, 12 master's awarded. *Degree requirements:* For master's, comprehensive exam, thesis. *Entrance requirements:* For master's, GRE General Test, PRAXIS I, PRAXIS II, interview, minimum GPA of 2.8. Additional exam requirements/recommendations for international students: Required—TOEFL. *Application deadline:* For spring admission, 2/15 priority date for domestic students. Applications are processed on a rolling basis. Application fee: $65. Electronic applications accepted. *Expenses: Tuition, area resident:* Part-time $638 per credit. Tuition, state resident: full-time $5742. *Required fees:* $142 per credit. Tuition and fees vary according to course level and program. *Financial support:* Career-related internships or fieldwork, scholarships/grants, health care benefits, and unspecified assistantships available. Support available to part-time students. *Unit head:* Dr. Horacio Sosa, Dean, College of Graduate and Continuing Education, 856-256-4747, Fax: 856-256-5638, E-mail: sosa@rowan.edu. *Application contact:* Karen Haynes, Graduate Coordinator, 856-256-4052, Fax: 856-256-4436, E-mail: haynes@rowan.edu.

Rutgers, The State University of New Jersey, New Brunswick, Graduate School of Education, Department of Learning and Teaching, Program in Science Education, Piscataway, NJ 08854-8097. Offers Ed M, Ed D. Part-time programs available. Terminal master's awarded for partial completion of doctoral program. *Degree requirements:* For master's, comprehensive exam (for some programs); for doctorate, thesis/dissertation, qualifying exam. *Entrance requirements:* For master's, GRE General Test, minimum GPA of 3.0; for doctorate, GRE General Test, minimum GPA of 3.5. Additional exam requirements/recommendations for international students: Required—TOEFL. Electronic applications accepted.

Saginaw Valley State University, College of Education, Program in Natural Science Teaching, University Center, MI 48710. Offers elementary school (MAT); middle school (MAT); secondary school (MAT). *Accreditation:* NCATE. Part-time and evening/weekend programs available. *Students:* 1 (woman) part-time. Average age 43. In 2013, 8 master's awarded. *Degree requirements:* For master's, capstone course. *Entrance requirements:* For master's, minimum GPA of 3.0, teaching certificate. Additional exam requirements/recommendations for international students: Required—TOEFL (minimum score 550 paper-based; 79 iBT). *Application deadline:* For fall admission, 7/15 for international students; for winter admission, 11/15 for international students; for spring admission, 4/15 for international students. Applications are processed on a rolling basis. Application fee: $30 ($80 for international students). Electronic applications accepted. *Expenses:* Tuition, state resident: full-time $8933; part-time $496.30 per credit hour. Tuition, nonresident: full-time $16,806; part-time $933.65 per credit hour. *Required fees:* $263; $14.60 per credit hour. Tuition and fees vary according to degree level. *Financial support:* Federal Work-Study and scholarships/grants available. Support available to part-time students. Financial award applicants required to submit FAFSA. *Unit head:* Dr. Mary Harmon, Dean, 989-964-7107, Fax: 989-964-4563, E-mail: coeconnect@svsu.edu. *Application contact:* Jenna Briggs, Director, Graduate and International Admissions, 989-964-6096, Fax: 989-964-2788, E-mail: gradadm@svsu.edu.

St. John Fisher College, School of Arts and Sciences, Mathematics/Science/Technology Education Program, Rochester, NY 14618-3597. Offers MS. Part-time and evening/weekend programs available. *Faculty:* 3 full-time (0 women), 3 part-time/adjunct (1 woman). *Students:* 6 full-time (4 women), 21 part-time (14 women); includes 4 minority (1 American Indian or Alaska Native, non-Hispanic/Latino; 1 Asian, non-Hispanic/Latino; 1 Hispanic/Latino; 1 Two or more races, non-Hispanic/Latino). Average age 30. 10 applicants, 70% accepted, 6 enrolled. In 2013, 15 master's awarded. *Degree requirements:* For master's, thesis, capstone experience. *Entrance requirements:* For master's, 2 letters of recommendation, personal statement, current resume, interview, teaching certification. Additional exam requirements/recommendations for international students: Required—TOEFL (minimum score 575 paper-based; 80 iBT). *Application deadline:* Applications are processed on a rolling basis. Application fee: $30. Electronic applications accepted. *Expenses: Tuition:* Part-time $795 per credit hour. *Required fees:* $10 per credit hour. Tuition and fees vary according to course load, degree level and program. *Financial support:* In 2013–14, 2 students received support. Scholarships/grants available. Financial award applicants required to submit FAFSA. *Faculty research:* Mathematics education, science and technology education. *Unit head:* Dr. Bernard Ricca, Graduate Director, 585-899-3866, E-mail: bricca@sjfc.edu. *Application contact:* Jose Perales, Director of Graduate Admissions, 585-385-8067, E-mail: jperales@sjfc.edu.

Saint Xavier University, Graduate Studies, School of Education, Chicago, IL 60655-3105. Offers counseling (MA); curriculum and instruction (MA); early childhood education (MA); educational administration (MA); elementary education (MA); individualized studies (MA), including educational technology, English as a second language (ESL), ISTEM (integrative science, technology, engineering, and math), science education; music education (MA); reading (MA); secondary education (MA); Spanish education (MA); special education (MA); teaching and leadership (MA). *Accreditation:* NCATE. Part-time and evening/weekend programs available. *Degree requirements:* For master's, thesis or project. *Entrance requirements:* For master's, minimum GPA of 3.0. *Expenses:* Contact institution.

Salem State University, School of Graduate Studies, Program in Chemistry, Salem, MA 01970-5353. Offers MAT. Part-time and evening/weekend programs available. *Students:* 2 part-time (1 woman). *Entrance requirements:* For master's, GRE or MAT. Additional exam requirements/recommendations for international students: Required—TOEFL (minimum score 550 paper-based; 80 iBT) or IELTS (minimum score 5.5). *Application deadline:* For fall admission, 5/1 for domestic students; for spring admission, 10/1 for domestic students. Applications are processed on a rolling basis. Application fee: $50. *Financial support:* Career-related internships or fieldwork, Federal Work-Study, scholarships/grants, and unspecified assistantships available. Support available to part-time students. Financial award application deadline: 5/1; financial award applicants required to submit FAFSA. *Unit head:* Christine MacTaylor, Associate Professor, 978-542-6321, E-mail: cmactaylor@salemstate.edu. *Application contact:* Dr. Lee A. Brossoit, Assistant Dean of Graduate Admissions, 978-542-6673, Fax: 978-542-7215, E-mail: lbrossoit@salemstate.edu.
Website: https://www.salemstate.edu/academics/schools/1009.php.

Salem State University, School of Graduate Studies, Program in Middle School General Science, Salem, MA 01970-5353. Offers MAT. Part-time and evening/weekend programs available. *Students:* 2 full-time (both women), 3 part-time (all women). 2 applicants, 100% accepted, 2 enrolled. In 2013, 3 master's awarded. *Entrance requirements:* For master's, GRE or MAT. Additional exam requirements/recommendations for international students: Required—TOEFL (minimum score 550 paper-based; 80 iBT) or IELTS (minimum score 5.5). *Application deadline:* For fall admission, 5/1 for domestic students; for spring admission, 10/1 for domestic students. Applications are processed on a rolling basis. Application fee: $50. *Financial support:* Career-related internships or fieldwork, Federal Work-Study, scholarships/grants, and unspecified assistantships available. Support available to part-time students. Financial award application deadline: 5/1; financial award applicants required to submit FAFSA. *Application contact:* Dr. Lee A. Brossoit, Assistant Dean of Graduate Admissions, 978-542-6675, Fax: 978-542-7215, E-mail: lbrossoit@salemstate.edu.
Website: http://www.salemstate.edu/academics/schools/12196.php.

San Diego State University, Graduate and Research Affairs, College of Sciences, Department of Mathematics and Statistics, San Diego, CA 92182. Offers applied mathematics (MS); mathematics (MA); mathematics and science education (PhD); statistics (MS). PhD offered jointly wtih University of California, San Diego. Part-time programs available. *Degree requirements:* For doctorate, thesis/dissertation. *Entrance requirements:* For master's, GRE General Test; for doctorate, GRE, minimum GPA of 3.25 in last 30 undergraduate semester units, minimum graduate GPA of 3.5, MSE recommendation form, 3 letters of recommendation. Additional exam requirements/recommendations for international students: Required—TOEFL. Electronic applications accepted. *Faculty research:* Teacher education in mathematics.

San Jose State University, Graduate Studies and Research, College of Science, Program in Science Education, San Jose, CA 95192-0001. Offers natural science (MA). *Degree requirements:* For master's, project or thesis.

Shippensburg University of Pennsylvania, School of Graduate Studies, College of Education and Human Services, Department of Teacher Education, Shippensburg, PA 17257-2299. Offers curriculum and instruction (M Ed), including biology, early childhood education, elementary education, geography/earth science, history, mathematics, middle level education, modern languages; reading (M Ed). *Accreditation:* NCATE. Part-time and evening/weekend programs available. *Faculty:* 13 full-time (9 women), 2 part-time/adjunct (both women). *Students:* 6 full-time (all women), 72 part-time (61 women); includes 5 minority (1 Black or African American, non-Hispanic/Latino; 1 Asian, non-Hispanic/Latino; 2 Hispanic/Latino; 1 Two or more races, non-Hispanic/Latino), 1 international. Average age 30. 55 applicants, 60% accepted, 24 enrolled. In 2013, 63 master's awarded. *Degree requirements:* For master's, comprehensive exam (for some programs), thesis optional, practicum or internship; capstone seminar (for some programs). *Entrance requirements:* For master's, MAT or GRE (if GPA less than 2.75), interview, 3 letters of reference, questionnaire of teaching background and future goals. Additional exam requirements/recommendations for international students: Required—TOEFL (minimum score 580 paper-based); Recommended—IELTS (minimum score 6). *Application deadline:* For fall admission, 4/1 priority date for domestic students, 4/30 for international students; for spring admission, 9/1 priority date for domestic students, 9/30 for international students. Applications are processed on a rolling basis. Application fee: $45. Electronic applications accepted. *Expenses: Tuition, area resident:* Part-time $442 per credit. Tuition, state resident: part-time $442 per credit. Tuition, nonresident: part-time $663 per credit. *Required fees:* $127 per credit. *Financial support:* In 2013–14, 4 research assistantships with full tuition reimbursements (averaging $5,000 per year) were awarded; career-related internships or fieldwork, scholarships/grants, unspecified assistantships, and resident hall director and student payroll positions also available. Support available to part-time students. Financial award application deadline: 3/1; financial award applicants required to submit FAFSA. *Unit head:* Dr. Christine A. Royce, Chairperson, 717-477-1688, Fax: 717-477-4046, E-mail: caroyc@ship.edu. *Application contact:* Jeremy R. Goshorn, Assistant Dean of Graduate Admissions, 717-477-1231, Fax: 717-477-4016, E-mail: jrgoshorn@ship.edu.
Website: http://www.ship.edu/teacher/.

Shippensburg University of Pennsylvania, School of Graduate Studies, College of Education and Human Services, Master of Arts in Teaching in Science Education Program, Shippensburg, PA 17257-2299. Offers MAT. Part-time and evening/weekend programs available. *Students:* 4 part-time (2 women). Average age 36. 8 applicants, 75% accepted, 4 enrolled. *Degree requirements:* For master's, 12-week student teaching practicum (12 credits), two capstone projects which include professional portfolio and the results of a research project. *Entrance requirements:* For master's, Pre-Service Academic Performance Assessment (PAPA), PRAXIS II Subject Assessment, statement of intent summarizing motivations and goals for entering the teaching profession, two letters of recommendation. Additional exam requirements/recommendations for international students: Required—TOEFL (minimum score 580 paper-based); Recommended—IELTS (minimum score 6). *Application deadline:* For fall admission, 4/30 for international students; for spring admission, 9/30 for international students. Applications are processed on a rolling basis. Application fee: $45. Electronic applications accepted. *Expenses: Tuition, area resident:* Part-time $442 per credit. Tuition, state resident: part-time $442 per credit. Tuition, nonresident: part-time $663 per credit. *Required fees:* $127 per credit. *Financial support:* Research assistantships with tuition reimbursements, career-related internships or fieldwork, and resident hall director and student payroll positions available. Support available to part-time students. Financial award application deadline: 3/1; financial award applicants required to submit FAFSA. *Unit head:* Dr. Joseph W. Shane, Associate Professor of Chemistry and Science Education, 717-477-1572, Fax: 717-477-4048, E-mail: jwshan@ship.edu. *Application contact:* Jeremy R. Goshorn, Assistant Dean of Graduate Admissions, 717-477-1231, Fax: 717-477-4016, E-mail: jrgoshorn@ship.edu.
Website: http://www.ship.edu/scied/.

Slippery Rock University of Pennsylvania, Graduate Studies (Recruitment), College of Education, Department of Elementary Education and Early Childhood, Slippery Rock, PA 16057-1383. Offers elementary education (M Ed), including K-12 reading specialist, math/science K-8, reading, reading specialist-instructional coach: literacy. *Accreditation:* NCATE. Part-time and evening/weekend programs available. Postbaccalaureate distance learning degree programs offered (no on-campus study). *Faculty:* 2 full-time (both women). *Students:* 4 full-time (all women), 23 part-time (all women); includes 1 minority (Black or African American, non-Hispanic/Latino). Average age 28. 47 applicants, 79% accepted, 11 enrolled. In 2013, 36 master's awarded. *Entrance requirements:* For master's, GRE General Test, MAT, minimum GPA of 3.0, resume, teaching certification, letters of recommendation, transcripts (depending on program). Additional exam requirements/recommendations for international students: Required—TOEFL (minimum score 550 paper-based; 80 iBT). *Application deadline:* For fall admission, 3/1 priority date for domestic students, 5/1 priority date for international students; for spring admission, 10/1 priority date for domestic students, 9/1 priority date for international students. Applications are processed on a rolling basis. Application fee: $25 ($30 for international students). Electronic applications accepted. *Expenses:* Tuition, state resident: full-time $7956; part-time $442 per credit. Tuition, nonresident: full-time $11,934; part-time $663 per credit. *Required fees:* $2896; $148 per credit. Tuition and fees vary according to degree level and program. *Financial support:* Career-related internships or fieldwork, Federal Work-Study, institutionally sponsored loans, scholarships/grants, tuition waivers (partial), and unspecified assistantships available. Support available to part-time students. Financial award application deadline: 5/1; financial award applicants required to submit FAFSA. *Unit head:* Dr. Suzanne Rose,

Graduate Coordinator, 724-738-2042, Fax: 724-738-2779, E-mail: suzanne.rose@sru.edu. *Application contact:* Brandi Weber-Mortimer, Director of Graduate Admissions, 724-738-2051, Fax: 724-738-2146, E-mail: graduate.admissions@sru.edu.

Slippery Rock University of Pennsylvania, Graduate Studies (Recruitment), College of Education, Department of Secondary Education/Foundations of Education, Slippery Rock, PA 16057-1383. Offers educational leadership (M Ed); secondary education (M Ed), including English, math/science, social studies/history. *Accreditation:* NCATE. Part-time and evening/weekend programs available. *Faculty:* 12 full-time (5 women). *Students:* 48 full-time (24 women), 10 part-time (6 women). Average age 27. 50 applicants, 84% accepted, 29 enrolled. In 2013, 28 master's awarded. *Degree requirements:* For master's, comprehensive exam, thesis (for some programs). *Entrance requirements:* For master's, GRE General Test, MAT, minimum GPA of 2.8 or 3.0 (depending on program); copy of teaching certification and two letters of recommendation (for some programs). Additional exam requirements/recommendations for international students: Required—TOEFL (minimum score 550 paper-based; 80 iBT). *Application deadline:* For fall admission, 3/1 priority date for domestic students, 5/1 priority date for international students; for spring admission, 10/1 priority date for domestic students, 9/1 priority date for international students. Applications are processed on a rolling basis. Application fee: $25 ($30 for international students). Electronic applications accepted. *Expenses:* Tuition, state resident: full-time $7956; part-time $442 per credit. Tuition, nonresident: full-time $11,934; part-time $663 per credit. *Required fees:* $2896; $148 per credit. Tuition and fees vary according to degree level and program. *Financial support:* Career-related internships or fieldwork, Federal Work-Study, institutionally sponsored loans, scholarships/grants, tuition waivers (partial), and unspecified assistantships available. Support available to part-time students. Financial award application deadline: 5/1; financial award applicants required to submit FAFSA. *Unit head:* Dr. Jeffrey Lehman, Graduate Coordinator, 724-738-2311, Fax: 724-738-4987, E-mail: jeffrey.lehman@sru.edu. *Application contact:* Brandi Weber-Mortimer, Interim Director of Graduate Studies, 724-738-2051, Fax: 724-738-2146, E-mail: graduate.admissions@sru.edu.

Smith College, Graduate and Special Programs, Department of Education and Child Study, Program in Secondary Education, Northampton, MA 01063. Offers biological sciences education (MAT); chemistry education (MAT); English education (MAT); French education (MAT); geology education (MAT); government education (MAT); history education (MAT); mathematics education (MAT); physics education (MAT); Spanish education (MAT). Part-time programs available. *Faculty:* 6 full-time (4 women), 3 part-time/adjunct (2 women). *Students:* 4 full-time (3 women), 1 (woman) part-time, 2 international. Average age 33. 12 applicants, 92% accepted, 4 enrolled. In 2013, 6 master's awarded. *Entrance requirements:* Additional exam requirements/recommendations for international students: Required—TOEFL (minimum score 595 paper-based; 97 iBT). *Application deadline:* For fall admission, 4/1 for domestic students, 1/15 priority date for international students; for spring admission, 12/1 for domestic students. Application fee: $60. *Expenses:* Tuition: Full-time $32,160; part-time $1340 per credit. *Financial support:* In 2013–14, 5 students received support, including 2 fellowships with full tuition reimbursements available; career-related internships or fieldwork, institutionally sponsored loans, and scholarships/grants also available. Support available to part-time students. Financial award application deadline: 1/15; financial award applicants required to submit CSS PROFILE or FAFSA. *Unit head:* Rosetta Cohen, Graduate Student Advisor, 413-585-3266, E-mail: rcohen@smith.edu. *Application contact:* Ruth Morgan, Administrative Assistant, 413-585-3050, Fax: 413-585-3054, E-mail: gradstdy@smith.edu.
Website: http://www.smith.edu/educ/.

South Carolina State University, School of Graduate and Professional Studies, Department of Education, Orangeburg, SC 29117-0001. Offers early childhood and special education (M Ed); early childhood education (MAT); elementary education (M Ed, MAT); general science (MAT); mathematics (MAT); secondary education (M Ed), including biology education, business education, counselor education, English education, home economics education, industrial education, mathematics education, science education, social studies education; special education (M Ed), including emotionally handicapped, learning disabilities, mentally handicapped. *Accreditation:* NCATE. Part-time and evening/weekend programs available. *Faculty:* 9 full-time (3 women), 4 part-time/adjunct (3 women). *Students:* 32 full-time (26 women), 33 part-time (26 women); includes 63 minority (61 Black or African American, non-Hispanic/Latino; 2 Asian, non-Hispanic/Latino). Average age 31. 21 applicants, 100% accepted, 21 enrolled. In 2013, 15 master's awarded. *Degree requirements:* For master's, thesis optional, departmental qualifying exam. *Entrance requirements:* For master's, GRE General Test, NTE, interview, teaching certificate. *Application deadline:* For fall admission, 6/15 priority date for domestic students, 6/15 for international students; for spring admission, 11/1 for domestic and international students. Applications are processed on a rolling basis. Application fee: $25. Electronic applications accepted. *Expenses:* Tuition, state resident: full-time $8906; part-time $543 per credit hour. Tuition, nonresident: full-time $18,040; part-time $1051 per credit hour. *Financial support:* Fellowships, career-related internships or fieldwork, Federal Work-Study, and institutionally sponsored loans available. Financial award application deadline: 6/1. *Faculty research:* Critical thinking, child abuse, stress, test-taking skills, conflict resolution, mainstreaming. *Unit head:* Dr. Margaret Evelyn Fields, Interim Chair, 803-536-7098, Fax: 803-516-4568, E-mail: efields@scsu.edu. *Application contact:* Curtis Foskey, Coordinator of Graduate Studies, 803-536-8419, Fax: 803-536-8812, E-mail: cfoskey@scsu.edu.

Southern Connecticut State University, School of Graduate Studies, School of Arts and Sciences, Department of Science Education and Environmental Studies, New Haven, CT 06515-1355. Offers environmental education (MS); science education (MS, Diploma). *Accreditation:* NCATE. Part-time and evening/weekend programs available. *Degree requirements:* For master's, thesis or alternative. *Entrance requirements:* For master's, interview; for Diploma, master's degree. Electronic applications accepted.

Southern University and Agricultural and Mechanical College, Graduate School, Department of Science/Mathematics Education, Baton Rouge, LA 70813. Offers PhD. *Accreditation:* NCATE. *Degree requirements:* For doctorate, thesis/dissertation. *Entrance requirements:* For doctorate, GRE General Test. Additional exam requirements/recommendations for international students: Required—TOEFL (minimum score 525 paper-based). *Faculty research:* Performance assessment in science/mathematics education, equity in science/mathematics education, technology and distance learning, science/mathematics concept formation, cognitive themes, problem solving in science/mathematics education.

Southwestern Oklahoma State University, College of Arts and Sciences, Specialization in Natural Sciences, Weatherford, OK 73096-3098. Offers M Ed. Part-time programs available. *Degree requirements:* For master's, exam. *Entrance requirements:* For master's, GRE General Test or minimum undergraduate GPA of 3.0. Additional exam requirements/recommendations for international students: Required—TOEFL.

State University of New York at Fredonia, Graduate Studies, Department of Chemistry and Biochemistry, Fredonia, NY 14063-1136. Offers chemistry (MS); curriculum and instruction science education (MS Ed). Part-time and evening/weekend

programs available. *Degree requirements:* For master's, thesis optional. *Expenses:* Tuition, state resident: full-time $7398; part-time $411 per credit hour. Tuition, nonresident: full-time $13,770; part-time $765 per credit hour. *Required fees:* $1143.90; $63.55 per credit hour. Tuition and fees vary according to course load.

State University of New York at New Paltz, Graduate School, School of Education, Department of Elementary Education, New Paltz, NY 12561. Offers childhood education 1-6 (MS Ed, MST), including childhood education 1-6 (MST), early childhood B-2 (MS Ed), mathematics, science and technology (MS Ed), reading/literacy (MS Ed); literacy education 5-12 (MS Ed); literacy education and childhood special education (MS Ed); literacy education B-6 (MS Ed). *Accreditation:* NCATE. Part-time and evening/weekend programs available. *Faculty:* 11 full-time (10 women), 9 part-time/adjunct (8 women). *Students:* 51 full-time (47 women), 128 part-time (117 women); includes 13 minority (2 Black or African American, non-Hispanic/Latino; 11 Hispanic/Latino). Average age 27. 103 applicants, 89% accepted, 57 enrolled. In 2013, 96 master's awarded. *Degree requirements:* For master's, comprehensive exam (for some programs), portfolio. *Entrance requirements:* For master's, GRE or MAT (for MST), minimum GPA of 3.0 (3.2 for literacy and special education), New York state teaching certificate (for MS Ed). Additional exam requirements/recommendations for international students: Required—TOEFL (minimum score 550 paper-based; 80 iBT), IELTS (minimum score 6.5). *Application deadline:* For fall admission, 4/1 for domestic and international students; for spring admission, 11/15 for domestic and international students. Application fee: $50. Electronic applications accepted. *Expenses:* Tuition, state resident: full-time $9870; part-time $411 per credit. Tuition, nonresident: full-time $18,350; part-time $765 per credit. *Required fees:* $1213. Tuition and fees vary according to program. *Financial support:* Application deadline: 8/1. *Faculty research:* Multi-sensory teaching methods, volunteer tutoring programs for struggling readers, school readiness and transition, math/science/technology, university-school partnerships. *Unit head:* Dr. Andrea Noel, Chair, 845-257-2860, E-mail: noela@newpaltz.edu. *Application contact:* Caroline Murphy, Graduate Admissions Advisor, 845-257-3285, Fax: 845-257-3284, E-mail: gradschool@newpaltz.edu.
Website: http://www.newpaltz.edu/elementaryed/.

State University of New York at New Paltz, Graduate School, School of Education, Department of Secondary Education, New Paltz, NY 12561. Offers adolescence education: biology (MAT, MS Ed); adolescence education: chemistry (MAT, MS Ed); adolescence education: earth science (MAT, MS Ed); adolescence education: English (MAT, MS Ed); adolescence education: French (MAT, MS Ed); adolescence education: social studies (MAT, MS Ed); adolescence education: Spanish (MAT, MS Ed); second language education (MS Ed, AC), including second language education (MS Ed), teaching English language learners (AC). *Accreditation:* NCATE. Part-time and evening/weekend programs available. *Faculty:* 10 full-time (8 women), 15 part-time/adjunct (10 women). *Students:* 73 full-time (47 women), 52 part-time (39 women); includes 27 minority (2 Black or African American, non-Hispanic/Latino; 6 Asian, non-Hispanic/Latino; 16 Hispanic/Latino; 3 Two or more races, non-Hispanic/Latino), 1 international. Average age 29. 81 applicants, 84% accepted, 51 enrolled. In 2013, 85 master's awarded. *Degree requirements:* For master's, comprehensive exam (for some programs), portfolio. *Entrance requirements:* For master's, minimum GPA of 3.0, New York state teaching certificate (MS Ed). Additional exam requirements/recommendations for international students: Required—TOEFL (minimum score 550 paper-based; 80 iBT), IELTS (minimum score 6.5). *Application deadline:* For fall admission, 3/1 priority date for domestic students, 3/1 for international students; for spring admission, 10/1 priority date for domestic students, 10/1 for international students. Application fee: $50. Electronic applications accepted. *Expenses:* Tuition, state resident: full-time $9870; part-time $411 per credit. Tuition, nonresident: full-time $18,350; part-time $765 per credit. *Required fees:* $1213. Tuition and fees vary according to program. *Financial support:* Application deadline: 8/1. *Unit head:* Dr. Laura Dull, Chair, 845-257-2850, E-mail: dulll@newpaltz.edu. *Application contact:* Caroline Murphy, Graduate Admissions Advisor, 845-257-3285, Fax: 845-257-3284, E-mail: gradschool@newpaltz.edu.
Website: http://www.newpaltz.edu/secondaryed/.

State University of New York at Plattsburgh, Division of Education, Health, and Human Services, Program in Teacher Education: Adolescence, Plattsburgh, NY 12901-2681. Offers adolescence education (MST); biology 7-12 (MST); chemistry 7-12 (MST); earth science 7-12 (MST); English 7-12 (MST); French 7-12 (MST); mathematics 7-12 (MST); physics 7-12 (MST); social studies 7-12 (MST); Spanish 7-12 (MST). *Accreditation:* Teacher Education Accreditation Council. Part-time and evening/weekend programs available. *Students:* 75 full-time (47 women), 5 part-time (3 women); includes 10 minority (1 Black or African American, non-Hispanic/Latino; 4 Asian, non-Hispanic/Latino; 5 Hispanic/Latino), 1 international. Average age 25. *Entrance requirements:* For master's, minimum GPA of 2.75. Additional exam requirements/recommendations for international students: Required—TOEFL. *Application deadline:* For fall admission, 2/15 priority date for domestic students. Applications are processed on a rolling basis. Application fee: $75. *Financial support:* Application deadline: 4/15; applicants required to submit FAFSA. *Unit head:* Dr. Robert Ackland, Coordinator, 518-564-5131, E-mail: acklanrt@plattsburgh.edu. *Application contact:* Betsy Kane, Director, Graduate Admissions, 518-564-4723, Fax: 518-564-4722, E-mail: bkane002@plattsburgh.edu.

State University of New York at Plattsburgh, Faculty of Arts and Science, Program in Natural Science, Plattsburgh, NY 12901-2681. Offers MS, PSM. *Accreditation:* Teacher Education Accreditation Council. Part-time programs available. *Students:* 7 full-time (3 women), 2 part-time (both women), 1 international. Average age 30. *Entrance requirements:* For master's, GRE General Test (minimum score of 1200), bachelor's degree in science discipline, minimum GPA of 3.0. Additional exam requirements/recommendations for international students: Required—TOEFL. *Application deadline:* For fall admission, 2/15 priority date for domestic students; for spring admission, 10/15 priority date for domestic students. Applications are processed on a rolling basis. Application fee: $75. *Financial support:* Federal Work-Study available. Support available to part-time students. Financial award application deadline: 4/15; financial award applicants required to submit FAFSA. *Unit head:* Dr. Timothy B. Mihuc, Program Coordinator, 518-564-3039, Fax: 518-564-3036, E-mail: timothy.mihuc@plattsburgh.edu. *Application contact:* Betsy Kane, Director, Graduate Admissions, 518-564-4723, Fax: 518-564-4722, E-mail: bkane002@plattsburgh.edu.

State University of New York College at Cortland, Graduate Studies, School of Arts and Sciences, Programs in Adolescence Education, Cortland, NY 13045. Offers biology (MAT, MS Ed); chemistry (MAT, MS Ed); earth science (MAT, MS Ed); English (MAT, MS Ed); mathematics (MAT, MS Ed); physics (MAT, MS Ed); physics and mathematics (MS Ed); social studies (MS Ed), including geography, history. *Accreditation:* NCATE. Part-time and evening/weekend programs available. *Degree requirements:* For master's, one foreign language, comprehensive exam (for some programs), thesis (for some programs). *Entrance requirements:* For master's, GRE General Test. *Expenses:* Tuition, state resident: full-time $9870; part-time $411 per credit hour. Tuition, nonresident: full-time $18,350; part-time $765 per credit hour. *Required fees:* $1458; $65 per credit hour.

State University of New York College at Old Westbury, Program in Adolescent Education, Old Westbury, NY 11568-0210. Offers biology (MAT, MS); chemistry (MAT,

MS); English language arts (MAT, MS); math (MAT, MS); social studies (MAT, MS); Spanish (MAT, MS). Part-time and evening/weekend programs available. *Faculty:* 19 full-time (11 women), 6 part-time/adjunct (1 woman). *Students:* 33 full-time (20 women), 33 part-time (19 women); includes 16 minority (2 Black or African American, non-Hispanic/Latino; 4 Asian, non-Hispanic/Latino; 9 Hispanic/Latino; 1 Two or more races, non-Hispanic/Latino). 25 applicants, 84% accepted, 19 enrolled. In 2013, 29 master's awarded. *Entrance requirements:* For master's, Liberal Arts and Sciences Test, undergraduate degree with at least 30 semester hours of appropriate coursework as defined by the respective discipline; minimum cumulative undergraduate GPA of 3.0; two letters of recommendation (one from an academic source); essay. Additional exam requirements/recommendations for international students: Required—TOEFL (minimum score 550 paper-based); Recommended—IELTS. *Expenses:* Tuition, state resident: full-time $9370; part-time $390 per credit. Tuition, nonresident: full-time $16,680; part-time $695 per credit. *Required fees:* $45.85 per credit. $47 per term. *Application contact:* Philip D'Angelo, Graduate Admissions Office, 516-876-3073, E-mail: enroll@oldwestbury.edu.

State University of New York College at Potsdam, School of Education and Professional Studies, Program in Secondary Education, Potsdam, NY 13676. Offers English education (MST); mathematics education (MST); science education (MST), including biology, chemistry, earth science, physics; social studies education (MST). *Accreditation:* NCATE. *Degree requirements:* For master's, culminating experience. *Entrance requirements:* For master's, minimum GPA of 2.75 in last 60 hours of course work (3.0 for English program). Additional exam requirements/recommendations for international students: Required—TOEFL (minimum score 550 paper-based; 80 iBT), IELTS (minimum score 6). Electronic applications accepted.

Stony Brook University, State University of New York, Graduate School, College of Arts and Sciences, Department of Physics and Astronomy, Program in Physics, Stony Brook, NY 11794. Offers modern research instrumentation (MS); physics (MA, PhD); physics education (MAT). *Students:* 169 full-time (32 women), 1 part-time (0 women); includes 14 minority (2 Black or African American, non-Hispanic/Latino; 5 Asian, non-Hispanic/Latino; 6 Hispanic/Latino; 1 Two or more races, non-Hispanic/Latino), 5 international. *Degree requirements:* For doctorate, one foreign language, thesis/dissertation. *Entrance requirements:* For master's and doctorate, GRE General Test. Additional exam requirements/recommendations for international students: Required—TOEFL. *Application deadline:* For fall admission, 1/15 for domestic students; for spring admission, 10/1 for domestic students. Application fee: $100. *Expenses:* Tuition, state resident: full-time $9870; part-time $411 per credit. Tuition, nonresident: full-time $18,350; part-time $765 per credit. *Financial support:* Fellowships, research assistantships, and teaching assistantships available. Financial award application deadline: 2/1. *Unit head:* Dr. Laszlo Mihaly, Chair, 631-632-8100, Fax: 631-632-8176, E-mail: laszlo.mihaly@stonybrook.edu. *Application contact:* Sara Lutterbie, Coordinator, 631-632-8279, Fax: 631-632-8176, E-mail: sara.lutterbie@stonybrook.edu.

Stony Brook University, State University of New York, Graduate School, College of Arts and Sciences, Program in Science Education, Stony Brook, NY 11794. Offers PhD. *Students:* 32 part-time (23 women); includes 3 minority (all Black or African American, non-Hispanic/Latino). 21 applicants, 62% accepted, 12 enrolled. *Degree requirements:* For doctorate, comprehensive exam, thesis/dissertation. *Entrance requirements:* For doctorate, GRE. Additional exam requirements/recommendations for international students: Required—TOEFL (minimum score 550 paper-based; 90 iBT), IELTS (minimum score 6.5). *Application deadline:* For fall admission, 1/15 for domestic students; for spring admission, 10/1 for domestic students. Application fee: $100. *Expenses:* Tuition, state resident: full-time $9870; part-time $411 per credit. Tuition, nonresident: full-time $18,350; part-time $765 per credit. *Unit head:* Dr. Keith Sheppard, Director, 631-632-2989, Fax: 631-632-9791, E-mail: keith.sheppard@stonybrook.edu. *Application contact:* Melissa Jordan, Assistant Dean for Records and Admission, 631-632-9712, Fax: 631-632-7243, E-mail: graduate.school@sunysb.edu.
Website: http://www.stonybrook.edu/cesame/students/PhDSciEd/PhDSciEd.shtml.

Stony Brook University, State University of New York, School of Professional Development, Stony Brook, NY 11794. Offers biology (MAT); chemistry (MAT); coaching (Graduate Certificate); earth science (MAT); educational computing (Graduate Certificate); educational leadership (Advanced Certificate); English (MAT); environmental management (Graduate Certificate); French (MAT); German (MAT); higher education administration (MA, Certificate); human resource management (MS, Graduate Certificate); industrial management (Graduate Certificate); information systems management (Graduate Certificate); Italian (MAT); liberal studies (MA); mathematics (MAT); operations research (Graduate Certificate); physics (MAT); school district business leadership (Advanced Certificate); social science and the professions (MPS), including environmental management, human resource management; social studies (MAT); Spanish (MAT). Part-time and evening/weekend programs available. Postbaccalaureate distance learning degree programs offered. *Faculty:* 2 full-time (1 woman), 70 part-time/adjunct (30 women). *Students:* 241 full-time (135 women), 954 part-time (673 women); includes 209 minority (65 Black or African American, non-Hispanic/Latino; 2 American Indian or Alaska Native, non-Hispanic/Latino; 32 Asian, non-Hispanic/Latino; 104 Hispanic/Latino; 6 Two or more races, non-Hispanic/Latino), 7 international. Average age 28. 353 applicants, 92% accepted, 248 enrolled. In 2013, 312 master's, 131 other advanced degrees awarded. *Degree requirements:* For master's, one foreign language, thesis or alternative. *Application deadline:* For fall admission, 1/15 for domestic students; for spring admission, 10/1 for domestic students. Applications are processed on a rolling basis. Application fee: $100. *Expenses:* Tuition, state resident: full-time $9870; part-time $411 per credit. Tuition, nonresident: full-time $18,350; part-time $765 per credit. *Financial support:* Fellowships, research assistantships, teaching assistantships, and career-related internships or fieldwork available. Support available to part-time students. *Unit head:* Dr. Thomas Sexton, Interim Dean, 631-632-7181, Fax: 631-632-9046, E-mail: thomas.sexton@stonybrook.edu. *Application contact:* 631-632-7050 Ext. 1, E-mail: spd@stonybrook.edu.
Website: http://www.stonybrook.edu/spd/.

Syracuse University, College of Arts and Sciences, Program in College Science Teaching, Syracuse, NY 13244. Offers PhD. Part-time programs available. *Students:* 4 full-time (2 women), 3 part-time (2 women). Average age 39. 5 applicants, 60% accepted, 1 enrolled. In 2013, 1 doctorate awarded. *Degree requirements:* For doctorate, comprehensive exam, thesis/dissertation. *Entrance requirements:* For doctorate, GRE General Test, GRE Subject Test. Additional exam requirements/recommendations for international students: Required—TOEFL (minimum score 100 iBT). *Application deadline:* For fall admission, 2/1 priority date for domestic and international students. Applications are processed on a rolling basis. Application fee: $75. Electronic applications accepted. *Financial support:* Fellowships with full tuition reimbursements, research assistantships with full and partial tuition reimbursements, and teaching assistantships with full and partial tuition reimbursements available. Financial award application deadline: 1/1; financial award applicants required to submit FAFSA. *Unit head:* Dr. George M. Langford, Dean, 315-443-2201, E-mail: dean@cas.syr.edu. *Application contact:* Cynthia Daley, Information Contact, 315-443-2586, E-mail: cyndaley@syr.edu.
Website: http://sciteach.syr.edu/.

Syracuse University, School of Education, Emphasis in Biology Education, Syracuse, NY 13244. Offers MS. Part-time programs available. *Students:* 8 full-time (6 women); includes 2 minority (1 Black or African American, non-Hispanic/Latino; 1 Hispanic/Latino). Average age 31. 7 applicants, 71% accepted, 5 enrolled. In 2013, 3 master's awarded. *Entrance requirements:* For master's, GRE. Additional exam requirements/recommendations for international students: Required—TOEFL (minimum score 100 iBT). *Application deadline:* For fall admission, 1/15 priority date for domestic and international students. Applications are processed on a rolling basis. Application fee: $75. Electronic applications accepted. *Financial support:* Fellowships with full tuition reimbursements, teaching assistantships, scholarships/grants, and tuition waivers (partial) available. Financial award application deadline: 1/1; financial award applicants required to submit FAFSA. *Unit head:* Dr. John Tillotson, Program Director, 315-443-9137, E-mail: jwtillot@syr.edu. *Application contact:* Laurie Deyo, Graduate Recruiter, School of Education, 315-443-2505, E-mail: e-gradrcrt@syr.edu.
Website: http://soeweb.syr.edu/academic/teaching_and_leadership/graduate/masters/science_education/biology/default.aspx.

Syracuse University, School of Education, Emphasis in Chemistry Education, Syracuse, NY 13244. Offers MS. Part-time programs available. *Students:* 3 full-time (2 women), 1 international. Average age 31. 2 applicants, 50% accepted. In 2013, 2 master's awarded. *Entrance requirements:* For master's, GRE. Additional exam requirements/recommendations for international students: Required—TOEFL (minimum score 100 iBT). *Application deadline:* For fall admission, 1/15 priority date for domestic and international students. Applications are processed on a rolling basis. Application fee: $75. Electronic applications accepted. *Financial support:* Fellowships with full tuition reimbursements, teaching assistantships with full and partial tuition reimbursements, scholarships/grants, and tuition waivers (partial) available. Financial award application deadline: 1/1; financial award applicants required to submit FAFSA. *Unit head:* Dr. John Tillotson, Program Director, 315-443-9137, E-mail: jwtillot@syr.edu. *Application contact:* Laurie Deyo, Graduate Recruiter, School of Education, 315-443-2505, E-mail: e-gradrcrt@syr.edu.
Website: http://soeweb.syr.edu/academic/teaching_and_leadership/graduate/masters/science_education/chemistry/default.aspx.

Syracuse University, School of Education, Emphasis in Earth Science Education, Syracuse, NY 13244. Offers MS. Part-time programs available. *Students:* 4 full-time (3 women). Average age 27. 2 applicants, 50% accepted, 1 enrolled. In 2013, 1 master's awarded. *Entrance requirements:* For master's, GRE. Additional exam requirements/recommendations for international students: Required—TOEFL (minimum score 100 iBT). *Application deadline:* For fall admission, 1/15 priority date for domestic and international students. Applications are processed on a rolling basis. Application fee: $75. Electronic applications accepted. *Financial support:* Fellowships with full tuition reimbursements, teaching assistantships with full and partial tuition reimbursements, scholarships/grants, and tuition waivers (partial) available. Financial award application deadline: 1/1; financial award applicants required to submit FAFSA. *Unit head:* Dr. John Tillotson, Program Director, 315-443-9137, E-mail: jwtillot@syr.edu. *Application contact:* Laurie Deyo, Graduate Recruiter, School of Education, 315-443-2505, E-mail: e-gradrcrt@syr.edu.
Website: http://soeweb.syr.edu/academic/teaching_and_leadership/graduate/masters/science_education/earth_science/default.aspx.

Syracuse University, School of Education, Emphasis in Physics Education, Syracuse, NY 13244. Offers MS. Part-time programs available. *Students:* 1 full-time (0 women). Average age 23. *Entrance requirements:* For master's, GRE. Additional exam requirements/recommendations for international students: Required—TOEFL (minimum score 100 iBT). *Application deadline:* For fall admission, 1/15 priority date for domestic and international students. Applications are processed on a rolling basis. Application fee: $75. Electronic applications accepted. *Financial support:* Fellowships with full tuition reimbursements, teaching assistantships with full and partial tuition reimbursements, scholarships/grants, and tuition waivers (partial) available. Financial award application deadline: 1/1; financial award applicants required to submit FAFSA. *Unit head:* Dr. John Tillotson, Program Director, 315-443-9137, E-mail: jwtillot@syr.edu. *Application contact:* Laurie Deyo, Graduate Recruiter, School of Education, 315-443-2505, E-mail: e-gradrcrt@syr.edu.
Website: http://soeweb.syr.edu/academic/teaching_and_leadership/graduate/masters/science_education/physics/default.aspx.

Syracuse University, School of Education, Program in Science Education, Syracuse, NY 13244. Offers PhD. Part-time programs available. *Students:* 14 full-time (8 women), 4 part-time (3 women); includes 1 minority (Native Hawaiian or other Pacific Islander, non-Hispanic/Latino), 3 international. Average age 36. 9 applicants, 11% accepted, 1 enrolled. In 2013, 2 doctorates awarded. *Degree requirements:* For doctorate, comprehensive exam, thesis/dissertation. *Entrance requirements:* For doctorate, GRE General and Subject Tests, interview, master's degree. Additional exam requirements/recommendations for international students: Required—TOEFL (minimum score 100 iBT). *Application deadline:* For fall admission, 1/15 priority date for domestic and international students; for spring admission, 10/15 priority date for domestic and international students. Applications are processed on a rolling basis. Application fee: $75. Electronic applications accepted. *Financial support:* Fellowships with full tuition reimbursements, research assistantships with full and partial tuition reimbursements, and teaching assistantships with full and partial tuition reimbursements available. Financial award application deadline: 1/1. *Unit head:* Dr. John Tillotson, Coordinator, 315-443-9137, E-mail: jwtillot@syr.edu. *Application contact:* Laurie Deyo, Graduate Recruiter, School of Education, 315-443-2505, E-mail: e-gradrcrt@syr.edu.
Website: http://soeweb.syr.edu/.

Teachers College, Columbia University, Graduate Faculty of Education, Department of Math, Science and Technology, Programs in Science Education, New York, NY 10027. Offers Ed M, MA, MS, Ed D, Ed DCT, PhD. *Accreditation:* NCATE. Part-time and evening/weekend programs available. *Faculty:* 5 full-time, 5 part-time/adjunct. *Students:* 22 full-time (13 women), 83 part-time (51 women); includes 37 minority (15 Black or African American, non-Hispanic/Latino; 12 Asian, non-Hispanic/Latino; 8 Hispanic/Latino; 1 Native Hawaiian or other Pacific Islander, non-Hispanic/Latino; 1 Two or more races, non-Hispanic/Latino), 14 international. Average age 32. 73 applicants, 79% accepted, 23 enrolled. In 2013, 35 master's, 4 doctorates awarded. Terminal master's awarded for partial completion of doctoral program. *Degree requirements:* For master's, culminating paper; for doctorate, comprehensive exam, thesis/dissertation. *Entrance requirements:* For master's, bachelor's degree in one of the sciences or its equivalent with preferred minimum B+ average in courses within science; for doctorate, bachelor's degree in one of the sciences or its equivalent. *Application deadline:* For fall admission, 1/2 priority date for domestic students. Applications are processed on a rolling basis. Application fee: $65. Electronic applications accepted. *Financial support:* Fellowships, career-related internships or fieldwork, Federal Work-Study, institutionally sponsored loans, and tuition waivers (full and partial) available. Support available to part-time students. Financial award applicants required to submit FAFSA. *Faculty research:* Cell biology and physiological ecology of protozoa, teaching and learning of pre-college and college sciences, homelessness. *Total annual research expenditures:* $100,000. *Unit head:* Prof. Felicia Moore Mensah, Program Coordinator, 212-678-8316, E-mail:

moorefe@tc.columbia.edu. *Application contact:* Deanna Ghozati, Assistant Director of Admission, 212-678-4018, Fax: 212-678-4171, E-mail: ghozati@tc.edu.
Website: http://www.tc.edu/mst/scienceed/.

Temple University, College of Education, Department of Curriculum, Instruction, and Technology in Education, Philadelphia, PA 19122-6096. Offers career and technical education (Ed M), including business, computing, and information technology, industrial education, marketing education; middle grades education (Ed M), including math and language arts, math and science, science and language arts; secondary education (Ed M), including English, math, social studies; teaching English to speakers of other languages (MS Ed); urban education (Ed M). Part-time and evening/weekend programs available. *Students:* 66 full-time (48 women), 120 part-time (67 women); includes 50 minority (35 Black or African American, non-Hispanic/Latino; 1 American Indian or Alaska Native, non-Hispanic/Latino; 2 Asian, non-Hispanic/Latino; 7 Hispanic/Latino; 5 Two or more races, non-Hispanic/Latino), 1 international. 229 applicants, 41% accepted, 60 enrolled. In 2013, 41 master's awarded. Terminal master's awarded for partial completion of doctoral program. *Degree requirements:* For master's, thesis or alternative. *Entrance requirements:* Additional exam requirements/recommendations for international students: Required—TOEFL (minimum score 550 paper-based; 79 iBT). *Application deadline:* For fall admission, 4/1 for domestic students, 12/15 for international students; for spring admission, 10/1 for domestic students, 8/1 for international students. Application fee: $60. Electronic applications accepted. *Financial support:* Fellowships, research assistantships, and teaching assistantships available. Financial award application deadline: 1/15; financial award applicants required to submit FAFSA. *Faculty research:* Workforce development, vocational education, technical education, industrial education, professional development, literacy, classroom management, school communities, curriculum development, instruction, applied linguistics, crosslinguistic influence, bilingual education, oral proficiency, multilingualism. *Application contact:* Felicia Neuber, Enrollment Management, 215-204-8011, E-mail: educate@temple.edu.
Website: http://www.temple.edu/education/tl/.

Texas Christian University, College of Education, Program in Science Education, Fort Worth, TX 76129-0002. Offers M Ed, PhD. Part-time and evening/weekend programs available. *Students:* 6 full-time (all women), 12 part-time (9 women); includes 4 minority (2 Black or African American, non-Hispanic/Latino; 1 Asian, non-Hispanic/Latino; 1 Two or more races, non-Hispanic/Latino), 2 international. Average age 36. 6 applicants, 83% accepted, 5 enrolled. In 2013, 5 master's awarded. *Degree requirements:* For master's, comprehensive exam, thesis; for doctorate, comprehensive exam, thesis/dissertation. *Entrance requirements:* For doctorate, GRE or MAT. Additional exam requirements/recommendations for international students: Required—TOEFL (minimum score 550 paper-based; 80 iBT). *Application deadline:* For fall admission, 11/16 for domestic and international students; for winter admission, 2/1 for domestic and international students; for spring admission, 3/1 for domestic and international students. Application fee: $60. Electronic applications accepted. *Expenses: Tuition:* Part-time $1270 per credit hour. Tuition and fees vary according to course load and program. *Financial support:* Teaching assistantships with full tuition reimbursements, career-related internships or fieldwork, scholarships/grants, tuition waivers (partial), and unspecified assistantships available. Financial award application deadline: 2/1; financial award applicants required to submit FAFSA. *Unit head:* Dr. Jan Lacina, Associate Dean, 817-257-6786, E-mail: j.lacina@tcu.edu. *Application contact:* Lori Kimball, Administrative Program Specialist, 817-257-7661, E-mail: l.kimball@tcu.edu.
Website: http://www.coe.tcu.edu/graduate-students-graduate-programs.asp.

Texas State University, Graduate School, College of Science and Engineering, Interdisciplinary Studies Program in Elementary Mathematics, Science, and Technology, San Marcos, TX 78666. Offers MSIS. *Students:* 3 full-time (2 women); includes 1 minority (Hispanic/Latino), 1 international. Average age 24. 1 applicant, 100% accepted. In 2013, 2 master's awarded. *Degree requirements:* For master's, comprehensive exam, thesis optional. *Entrance requirements:* For master's, minimum GPA of 2.75 in the last 60 hours of undergraduate work. Additional exam requirements/recommendations for international students: Required—TOEFL (minimum score 550 paper-based; 78 iBT). *Application deadline:* For fall admission, 6/15 priority date for domestic students, 6/1 priority date for international students; for spring admission, 10/15 priority date for domestic students, 10/1 priority date for international students. Applications are processed on a rolling basis. Application fee: $40 ($90 for international students). Electronic applications accepted. *Expenses:* Tuition, state resident: full-time $6663; part-time $278 per credit hour. Tuition, nonresident: full-time $15,159; part-time $632 per credit hour. *Required fees:* $1872; $54 per credit hour. $306 per term. Tuition and fees vary according to course load. *Financial support:* In 2013–14, 1 student received support, including 1 teaching assistantship (averaging $11,568 per year); research assistantships, Federal Work-Study, institutionally sponsored loans, scholarships/grants, health care benefits, and unspecified assistantships also available. Support available to part-time students. Financial award application deadline: 4/1; financial award applicants required to submit FAFSA. *Unit head:* Dr. Sandra West Moody, Acting Dean, 512-245-3360, Fax: 512-245-8095, E-mail: sw04@txstate.edu. *Application contact:* Dr. Andrea Golato, Dean of Graduate School, 512-245-2581, Fax: 512-245-8365, E-mail: gradcollege@txstate.edu.

Texas Tech University, Graduate School, College of Education, Department of Curriculum and Instruction, Lubbock, TX 79409-1071. Offers bilingual education (M Ed); curriculum and instruction (M Ed, PhD); elementary education (M Ed); language/literacy education (M Ed); multidisciplinary science (MS); secondary education (M Ed). *Accreditation:* NCATE. Part-time programs available. Postbaccalaureate distance learning degree programs offered (minimal on-campus study). *Faculty:* 27 full-time (21 women). *Students:* 49 full-time (40 women), 194 part-time (149 women); includes 74 minority (13 Black or African American, non-Hispanic/Latino; 6 Asian, non-Hispanic/Latino; 50 Hispanic/Latino; 5 Two or more races, non-Hispanic/Latino), 20 international. Average age 38. 105 applicants, 66% accepted, 46 enrolled. In 2013, 48 master's, 14 doctorates awarded. *Degree requirements:* For master's, comprehensive exam (for some programs), thesis optional; for doctorate, comprehensive exam, thesis/dissertation. *Entrance requirements:* For master's, bachelor's degree; resume; letter of intent; academic writing sample; 2 letters of recommendation; for doctorate, GRE, master's degree; resume; letter of intent; academic writing sample; 3 letters of recommendation. Additional exam requirements/recommendations for international students: Required—TOEFL (minimum score 550 paper-based; 79 iBT). *Application deadline:* For fall admission, 6/1 priority date for domestic students, 1/15 priority date for international students; for spring admission, 9/1 priority date for domestic students, 6/15 priority date for international students. Applications are processed on a rolling basis. Application fee: $60. Electronic applications accepted. *Expenses:* Tuition, state resident: full-time $6062; part-time $252.57 per credit hour. Tuition, nonresident: full-time $14,558; part-time $606.57 per credit hour. *Required fees:* $2655; $35 per credit hour. $907.50 per semester. Tuition and fees vary according to course load. *Financial support:* In 2013–14, 94 students received support, including 89 fellowships (averaging $2,276 per year), 14 research assistantships (averaging $5,226 per year), 6 teaching assistantships (averaging $4,517 per year); career-related internships or fieldwork, Federal Work-Study, institutionally sponsored loans, scholarships/grants, traineeships, health care benefits, and unspecified assistantships also available. Support available to part-time students. Financial award application deadline: 2/1; financial award applicants required to submit FAFSA. *Faculty research:* Teacher education, curriculum studies, bilingual education, science and math education, language and literacy education. *Total annual research expenditures:* $413,968. *Unit head:* Dr. Margaret Ann Price, Department Chair, Curriculum and Instruction, 806-834-4347, E-mail: peggie.price@ttu.edu. *Application contact:* Stephenie A. Jones, Administrative Assistant, 806-834-2751, Fax: 806-742-2179, E-mail: stephenie.a.jones@ttu.edu.
Website: http://www.educ.ttu.edu.

Texas Tech University, Graduate School, Rawls College of Business Administration, Programs in Business Administration, Lubbock, TX 79409. Offers business administration (IMBA); general business (MBA); health organization management (MBA); STEM (MBA); JD/MBA; MBA/M Arch; MBA/MD; MBA/MS; MBA/Pharm D. Part-time and evening/weekend programs available. *Faculty:* 56 full-time (9 women), 1 part-time/adjunct (0 women). *Students:* 97 full-time (63 women), 296 part-time (88 women); includes 73 minority (21 Black or African American, non-Hispanic/Latino; 3 American Indian or Alaska Native, non-Hispanic/Latino; 30 Asian, non-Hispanic/Latino; 19 Hispanic/Latino), 19 international. Average age 31. 155 applicants, 79% accepted, 116 enrolled. In 2013, 225 master's awarded. *Degree requirements:* For master's, capstone course. *Entrance requirements:* For master's, GMAT, holistic review of academic credentials. Additional exam requirements/recommendations for international students: Required—TOEFL (minimum score 550 paper-based; 79 iBT). *Application deadline:* For fall admission, 6/1 priority date for domestic students, 1/15 for international students; for spring admission, 11/1 priority date for domestic students, 6/15 for international students; for summer admission, 4/15 for domestic students. Applications are processed on a rolling basis. Application fee: $60. Electronic applications accepted. *Expenses:* Tuition, state resident: full-time $6062; part-time $252.57 per credit hour. Tuition, nonresident: full-time $14,558; part-time $606.57 per credit hour. *Required fees:* $2655; $35 per credit hour. $907.50 per semester. Tuition and fees vary according to course load. *Financial support:* Research assistantships, teaching assistantships, Federal Work-Study, scholarships/grants, and unspecified assistantships available. Support available to part-time students. Financial award applicants required to submit FAFSA. *Unit head:* Dr. William J. Pasewark, Associate Dean, 806-742-3184, Fax: 806-742-3958, E-mail: w.pasewark@ttu.edu. *Application contact:* Terri Boston, Application Manager, 806-742-3184, Fax: 806-742-3958, E-mail: rawlsgrad@ttu.edu.
Website: http://mba.ba.ttu.edu/.

Touro College, Graduate School of Education, New York, NY 10010. Offers education and special education (MS); education biology (MS); instructional technology (MS); mathematics education (MS); school leadership (MS); teaching English to speakers of other languages (MS); teaching literacy (MS). Part-time and evening/weekend programs available. Postbaccalaureate distance learning degree programs offered (no on-campus study). *Faculty:* 75 full-time, 131 part-time/adjunct. *Students:* 327 full-time (272 women), 2,454 part-time (2,103 women); includes 840 minority (333 Black or African American, non-Hispanic/Latino; 4 American Indian or Alaska Native, non-Hispanic/Latino; 139 Asian, non-Hispanic/Latino; 334 Hispanic/Latino; 8 Native Hawaiian or other Pacific Islander, non-Hispanic/Latino; 22 Two or more races, non-Hispanic/Latino), 4 international. 1,422 applicants, 50% accepted, 675 enrolled. In 2013, 6 master's awarded. *Entrance requirements:* Additional exam requirements/recommendations for international students: Required—TOEFL (minimum score 83 iBT), IELTS (minimum score 6.5). *Application deadline:* For fall admission, 8/26 for domestic students, 7/15 for international students; for spring admission, 12/31 for domestic students, 12/15 for international students. Applications are processed on a rolling basis. Application fee: $50. *Financial support:* Federal Work-Study available. Financial award applicants required to submit FAFSA. *Faculty research:* Equity assistance, language development, scholar communications, Latin American studies and cultural sensitivity, behavior management techniques and strategies in special education. *Unit head:* Dr. LaMar Miller, Dean, 212-463-0400 Ext. 5561, Fax: 212-462-4889, E-mail: lpmiller@touro.edu. *Application contact:* Natalie Arroyo, Admissions, 212-463-0400.

Troy University, Graduate School, College of Education, Program in Postsecondary Education, Troy, AL 36082. Offers adult education (M Ed); biology (M Ed); criminal justice (M Ed); English (M Ed); foundations of education (M Ed); general science (M Ed); higher education administration (M Ed); history (M Ed); instructional technology (M Ed); mathematics (M Ed); music industry (M Ed); physical fitness (M Ed); political science (M Ed); public administration (M Ed); social science (M Ed); teaching English (M Ed). *Accreditation:* NCATE. Part-time and evening/weekend programs available. *Faculty:* 30 full-time (11 women), 8 part-time/adjunct (1 woman). *Students:* 17 full-time (13 women), 106 part-time (84 women); includes 55 minority (45 Black or African American, non-Hispanic/Latino; 3 Asian, non-Hispanic/Latino; 2 Hispanic/Latino; 5 Two or more races, non-Hispanic/Latino). Average age 34. 109 applicants, 83% accepted, 5 enrolled. In 2013, 130 master's awarded. *Degree requirements:* For master's, comprehensive exam (for some programs), thesis (for some programs), thesis or comprehensive exam. *Entrance requirements:* For master's, GRE (minimum score of 850 on old exam or 290 on new exam), GMAT (minimum score of 380), or MAT (minimum score of 385), bachelor's degree; minimum undergraduate GPA of 2.5 or 3.0 on last 30 semester hours, letter of recommendation. Additional exam requirements/recommendations for international students: Required—TOEFL (minimum score 523 paper-based; 70 iBT), IELTS (minimum score 6). *Application deadline:* Applications are processed on a rolling basis. Application fee: $50. Electronic applications accepted. *Expenses:* Tuition, state resident: full-time $6084; part-time $338 per credit hour. Tuition, nonresident: full-time $12,168; part-time $676 per credit hour. *Required fees:* $630; $35 per credit hour. $50 per semester. *Financial support:* Available to part-time students. Applicants required to submit FAFSA. *Unit head:* Dr. Jan Oliver, Associate Professor, 334-670-3444, Fax: 334-670-3474, E-mail: oliver@troy.edu. *Application contact:* Brenda K. Campbell, Director of Graduate Admissions, 334-670-3178, Fax: 334-670-3733, E-mail: bcamp@troy.edu.

Troy University, Graduate School, College of Education, Program in Secondary Education, Troy, AL 36082. Offers 5th year biology (MS); 5th year computer science (MS); 5th year history (MS); 5th year language arts (MS); 5th year mathematics (MS); 5th year social science (MS); traditional biology (MS); traditional computer science (MS); traditional history (MS); traditional language arts (MS); traditional mathematics (MS); traditional social science (MS). *Accreditation:* NCATE. Part-time and evening/weekend programs available. *Faculty:* 2 full-time (1 woman). *Students:* 10 full-time (9 women), 21 part-time (14 women); includes 8 minority (6 Black or African American, non-Hispanic/Latino; 2 Hispanic/Latino). Average age 29. 15 applicants, 87% accepted, 6 enrolled. In 2013, 12 master's awarded. *Degree requirements:* For master's, comprehensive exam, thesis. *Entrance requirements:* For master's, GRE (minimum score of 850 on old exam or 290 on new exam), GMAT (minimum score of 380), or MAT (minimum score of 385), bachelor's degree; minimum undergraduate GPA of 2.5 or 3.0 on last 30 semester hours, letter of recommendation. Additional exam requirements/recommendations for international students: Required—TOEFL (minimum score 523 paper-based; 70 iBT), IELTS (minimum score 6). *Application deadline:* Applications are processed on a rolling basis. Application fee: $50. Electronic applications accepted. *Expenses:* Tuition, state resident: full-time $6084; part-time $338 per credit hour. Tuition, nonresident: full-time $12,168; part-time $676 per credit hour. *Required fees:* $630; $35 per credit hour. $50 per semester. *Financial support:* Career-related internships or fieldwork available. Support available to part-time students. Financial award applicants required to submit

FAFSA. *Unit head:* Dr. Jan Oliver, Associate Professor, 334-670-3444, Fax: 334-670-3548, E-mail: oliver@troy.edu. *Application contact:* Brenda K. Campbell, Director of Graduate Admissions, 334-670-3178, Fax: 334-670-3733, E-mail: bcamp@troy.edu.

Tufts University, Graduate School of Arts and Sciences, Department of Education, Program in Education, Medford, MA 02155. Offers educational studies (MA); elementary education (MAT); middle and secondary education (MA, MAT); museum education (MA); secondary education (MA); STEM education (MS, PhD). *Faculty:* 13 full-time, 9 part-time/adjunct. *Students:* 85 full-time (72 women); includes 19 minority (4 Black or African American, non-Hispanic/Latino; 1 American Indian or Alaska Native, non-Hispanic/Latino; 3 Asian, non-Hispanic/Latino; 7 Hispanic/Latino; 4 Two or more races, non-Hispanic/Latino), 5 international. Average age 27. 154 applicants, 69% accepted, 50 enrolled. In 2013, 84 master's awarded. *Degree requirements:* For master's, thesis optional; for doctorate, thesis/dissertation. *Entrance requirements:* For master's and doctorate, GRE General Test. Additional exam requirements/recommendations for international students: Required—TOEFL (minimum score 550 paper-based; 80 iBT), IELTS (minimum score 6.5). *Application deadline:* For fall admission, 1/2 for domestic and international students; for spring admission, 10/15 for domestic students, 9/15 for international students. Applications are processed on a rolling basis. Application fee: $75. Electronic applications accepted. *Financial support:* Teaching assistantships with full and partial tuition reimbursements, Federal Work-Study, scholarships/grants, and tuition waivers (full and partial) available. Support available to part-time students. Financial award application deadline: 1/2. *Unit head:* Hammer David, Chair, 617-627-3244, Fax: 617-627-3901. *Application contact:* Patricia Romeo, Information Contact, 617-627-3244.

Tufts University, Graduate School of Arts and Sciences, Department of Physics and Astronomy, Medford, MA 02155. Offers astrophysics (MS, PhD); chemical physics (PhD); physics (MS, PhD); physics education (PhD). *Faculty:* 17 full-time, 2 part-time/adjunct. *Students:* 31 full-time (9 women), 13 international. Average age 27. 88 applicants, 25% accepted, 5 enrolled. In 2013, 4 doctorates awarded. Terminal master's awarded for partial completion of doctoral program. *Degree requirements:* For master's, thesis optional; for doctorate, thesis/dissertation. *Entrance requirements:* For master's and doctorate, GRE General Test. Additional exam requirements/recommendations for international students: Required—TOEFL (minimum score 550 paper-based; 80 iBT), IELTS (minimum score 6.5). *Application deadline:* For fall admission, 1/15 for domestic and international students; for spring admission, 10/15 for domestic students, 9/15 for international students. Applications are processed on a rolling basis. Application fee: $75. Electronic applications accepted. *Financial support:* Fellowships, research assistantships with full tuition reimbursements, teaching assistantships with full tuition reimbursements, Federal Work-Study, scholarships/grants, tuition waivers (partial), and unspecified assistantships available. Financial award application deadline: 1/15. *Unit head:* Roger Tobin, Chair, 617-627-3029. *Application contact:* Dr. William Oliver, Graduate Advisor, 617-627-3029.
Website: http://www.tufts.edu/as/physics/.

Union Graduate College, School of Education, Schenectady, NY 12308-3107. Offers biology (MAT); chemistry (MAT); Chinese (MAT); earth science (MAT); English (MA, MAT); English and history (MA); French (MAT); general science (MAT); German (MAT); history (MA); Latin (MAT); life sciences (MS); mathematics (MAT); mathematics and computer technology (MS); mentoring and teacher leadership (AC); middle childhood extension (AC); national board certification and teacher leadership (AC); physical sciences (MS); physics (MAT); social studies (MAT); Spanish (MAT); technology (MAT). *Accreditation:* Teacher Education Accreditation Council. *Faculty:* 3 full-time (1 woman), 56 part-time/adjunct (34 women). *Students:* 32 full-time (16 women), 27 part-time (22 women); includes 15 minority (1 Black or African American, non-Hispanic/Latino; 4 Asian, non-Hispanic/Latino; 6 Hispanic/Latino; 4 Two or more races, non-Hispanic/Latino), 1 international. Average age 32. In 2013, 25 master's, 11 other advanced degrees awarded. *Degree requirements:* For master's, thesis or project. *Entrance requirements:* For master's, minimum GPA of 3.0, letters of recommendation. Additional exam requirements/recommendations for international students: Required—TOEFL (minimum score 550 paper-based). *Application deadline:* Applications are processed on a rolling basis. Application fee: $60. Electronic applications accepted. *Expenses:* Contact institution. *Financial support:* Career-related internships or fieldwork, Federal Work-Study, scholarships/grants, health care benefits, and tuition waivers (partial) available. Support available to part-time students. Financial award applicants required to submit FAFSA. *Faculty research:* Transformative learning, science education, National Board Certification, teacher leadership, teacher quality. *Unit head:* Dr. Lynn Gelzheiser, Dean, 518-631-9870, Fax: 518-631-9901. *Application contact:* Nicki Foley, Assistant, 518-631-9871, Fax: 518-631-9903, E-mail: foleyn@uniongraduatecollege.edu.

Universidad Nacional Pedro Henriquez Urena, Graduate School, Santo Domingo, Dominican Republic. Offers agricultural diversity (MS), including horticultural/fruit production, tropical animal production; conservation of monuments and cultural assets (M Arch); ecology and environment (MS); environmental engineering (MEE); international relations (MA); natural resource management (MS); political science (MA); project optimization (MPM); project feasibility (MPM); project management (MPM); sanitation engineering (ME); science for teachers (MS); tropical Caribbean architecture (M Arch).

University at Albany, State University of New York, College of Arts and Sciences, Department of Mathematics and Statistics, Albany, NY 12222-0001. Offers mathematics (PhD); secondary teaching (MA); statistics (MA). *Degree requirements:* For doctorate, one foreign language, thesis/dissertation. *Entrance requirements:* For doctorate, GRE General Test. Additional exam requirements/recommendations for international students: Required—TOEFL (minimum score 550 paper-based). Electronic applications accepted.

University at Buffalo, the State University of New York, Graduate School, Graduate School of Education, Department of Learning and Instruction, Buffalo, NY 14260. Offers biology education (Ed M, Certificate); chemistry education (Ed M, Certificate); childhood education (Ed M); childhood education with bilingual extension (Ed M); curriculum, instruction and the science of learning (PhD); early childhood education (Ed M); early childhood education with bilingual extension (birth-grade 2) (Ed M); earth science education (Ed M, Certificate); education studies (Ed M); educational technology and new literacies (Certificate); elementary education (Ed D); English education (Ed M, Certificate); English for speakers of other languages (Ed M); foreign and second language education (PhD); French education (Ed M, Certificate); German education (Ed M, Certificate); gifted education (Certificate); Latin education (Ed M, Certificate); literacy specialist (Ed M); literacy teaching and learning (Certificate); mathematics education (Ed M, Certificate); music education (Ed M, Certificate); physics education (Ed M, Certificate); science and the public (Ed M); social studies education (Ed M, Certificate); Spanish education (Ed M, Certificate); special education (PhD); teaching English to speakers of other languages (Ed M). Part-time and evening/weekend programs available. Postbaccalaureate distance learning degree programs offered (no on-campus study). *Faculty:* 31 full-time (23 women), 64 part-time/adjunct (53 women). *Students:* 275 full-time (215 women), 293 part-time (205 women); includes 35 minority (16 Black or African American, non-Hispanic/Latino; 5 American Indian or Alaska Native, non-Hispanic/Latino; 11 Asian, non-Hispanic/Latino; 3 Hispanic/Latino), 97 international. Average age 30. 544 applicants, 81% accepted, 246 enrolled. In 2013, 222 master's, 17 doctorates, 35 other advanced degrees awarded. *Degree requirements:* For master's, comprehensive exam; for doctorate, thesis/dissertation, research analysis exam, research experience component. *Entrance requirements:* For master's, content test in science and math, letters of reference; for doctorate, GRE General Test or MAT, interview, writing sample, letters of recommendation. Additional exam requirements/recommendations for international students: Required—TOEFL (minimum score 600 paper-based; 96 iBT). *Application deadline:* For fall admission, 2/1 priority date for domestic and international students; for spring admission, 11/15 priority date for domestic students, 10/1 for international students. Applications are processed on a rolling basis. Application fee: $50. Electronic applications accepted. *Financial support:* In 2013–14, 50 fellowships (averaging $8,589 per year), 31 research assistantships with tuition reimbursements (averaging $11,406 per year) were awarded; teaching assistantships, career-related internships or fieldwork, Federal Work-Study, institutionally sponsored loans, scholarships/grants, tuition waivers, and unspecified assistantships also available. Financial award application deadline: 2/28; financial award applicants required to submit FAFSA. *Faculty research:* Science assessment, foreign language teaching and learning, early learning, new literacies, gender and education. *Total annual research expenditures:* $1.7 million. *Unit head:* Dr. Suzanne Miller, Chair, 716-645-2455, Fax: 716-645-3161, E-mail: smiller@buffalo.edu. *Application contact:* Cathy Dimino, Admissions Assistant, 716-645-2110, Fax: 716-645-7937, E-mail: cadimino@buffalo.edu.
Website: http://gse.buffalo.edu/lai.

The University of Alabama in Huntsville, School of Graduate Studies, College of Science, Department of Biological Sciences, Huntsville, AL 35899. Offers biology (MS); biotechnology science and engineering (PhD); education (MS). Part-time and evening/weekend programs available. *Faculty:* 11 full-time (1 woman). *Students:* 23 full-time (16 women), 14 part-time (10 women); includes 4 minority (1 Black or African American, non-Hispanic/Latino; 1 American Indian or Alaska Native, non-Hispanic/Latino; 1 Asian, non-Hispanic/Latino; 1 Two or more races, non-Hispanic/Latino), 6 international. Average age 30. 39 applicants, 44% accepted, 11 enrolled. In 2013, 9 master's awarded. *Degree requirements:* For master's, comprehensive exam, thesis or alternative, oral and written exams. *Entrance requirements:* For master's, GRE General Test, previous course work in biochemistry and organic chemistry, minimum GPA of 3.0. Additional exam requirements/recommendations for international students: Required—TOEFL (minimum score 550 paper-based; 80 iBT), IELTS (minimum score 6.5). *Application deadline:* For fall admission, 7/15 priority date for domestic students, 4/1 priority date for international students; for spring admission, 11/30 for domestic students, 9/1 priority date for international students. Applications are processed on a rolling basis. Application fee: $50. Electronic applications accepted. *Expenses:* Tuition, state resident: full-time $8912; part-time $540 per credit hour. Tuition, nonresident: full-time $20,774; part-time $1252 per credit hour. *Required fees:* $148 per semester. One-time fee: $150. *Financial support:* In 2013–14, 20 students received support, including 2 fellowships with full tuition reimbursements available (averaging $11,000 per year), 3 research assistantships (averaging $10,976 per year), 16 teaching assistantships with full and partial tuition reimbursements available (averaging $8,743 per year); career-related internships or fieldwork, Federal Work-Study, institutionally sponsored loans, scholarships/grants, health care benefits, tuition waivers (full and partial), and unspecified assistantships also available. Support available to part-time students. Financial award application deadline: 4/1; financial award applicants required to submit FAFSA. *Faculty research:* Physiology, microbiology, genomics and protemics, ecology and evolution, drug discovery. *Total annual research expenditures:* $1.1 million. *Unit head:* Dr. Debra M. Moriarity, Interim Chair, 256-824-6045, Fax: 256-824-6305, E-mail: moriard@uah.edu. *Application contact:* Kim Gray, Graduate Studies Admissions Manager, 256-824-6002, Fax: 256-824-6405, E-mail: deangrad@uah.edu.
Website: http://www.uah.edu/colleges/science/biology/.

The University of Alabama in Huntsville, School of Graduate Studies, College of Science, Department of Chemistry, Huntsville, AL 35899. Offers biotechnology science and engineering (PhD); chemistry (MS); education (MS); materials science (PhD). Part-time and evening/weekend programs available. *Faculty:* 11 full-time (2 women). *Students:* 8 full-time (1 woman), 3 part-time (all women); includes 2 minority (1 Black or African American, non-Hispanic/Latino; 1 Asian, non-Hispanic/Latino), 4 international. Average age 28. 13 applicants, 62% accepted, 3 enrolled. In 2013, 12 master's awarded. *Degree requirements:* For master's, comprehensive exam, thesis or alternative, oral and written exams. *Entrance requirements:* For master's, GRE General Test, minimum GPA of 3.0. Additional exam requirements/recommendations for international students: Required—TOEFL (minimum score 550 paper-based; 80 iBT), IELTS (minimum score 6.5). *Application deadline:* For fall admission, 7/15 priority date for domestic students, 4/1 priority date for international students; for spring admission, 11/30 priority date for domestic students, 9/1 priority date for international students. Applications are processed on a rolling basis. Application fee: $50. Electronic applications accepted. *Expenses:* Tuition, state resident: full-time $8912; part-time $540 per credit hour. Tuition, nonresident: full-time $20,774; part-time $1252 per credit hour. *Required fees:* $148 per semester. One-time fee: $150. *Financial support:* In 2013–14, 6 students received support, including 1 research assistantship (averaging $9,000 per year), 5 teaching assistantships with full tuition reimbursements available (averaging $11,619 per year); career-related internships or fieldwork, Federal Work-Study, institutionally sponsored loans, scholarships/grants, health care benefits, tuition waivers, and unspecified assistantships also available. Support available to part-time students. Financial award application deadline: 4/1; financial award applicants required to submit FAFSA. *Faculty research:* Natural products drug discovery, protein biochemistry, macromolecular biophysics, polymer synthesis, surface modification and analysis of materials. *Total annual research expenditures:* $873,881. *Unit head:* Dr. William Setzer, Chair, 256-824-6153, Fax: 256-824-6349, E-mail: setzerw@uah.edu. *Application contact:* Kim Gray, Graduate Studies Admissions Coordinator, 256-824-6002, Fax: 256-824-6405, E-mail: deangrad@uah.edu.
Website: http://chemistry.uah.edu.

The University of Alabama in Huntsville, School of Graduate Studies, College of Science, Department of Physics, Huntsville, AL 35899. Offers education (MS); optics and photonics technology (MS); physics (MS, PhD). Part-time and evening/weekend programs available. *Faculty:* 18 full-time (0 women). *Students:* 38 full-time (8 women), 19 part-time (6 women); includes 6 minority (1 Black or African American, non-Hispanic/Latino; 4 Asian, non-Hispanic/Latino; 1 Two or more races, non-Hispanic/Latino), 21 international. Average age 30. 44 applicants, 82% accepted, 13 enrolled. In 2013, 14 master's, 3 doctorates awarded. *Degree requirements:* For master's, comprehensive exam, thesis or alternative, oral and written exams; for doctorate, comprehensive exam, thesis/dissertation, oral and written exams. *Entrance requirements:* For master's and doctorate, GRE General Test, minimum GPA of 3.0. Additional exam requirements/recommendations for international students: Required—TOEFL (minimum score 550 paper-based; 80 iBT), IELTS (minimum score 6.5). *Application deadline:* For fall admission, 7/15 priority date for domestic students, 4/1 priority date for international students; for spring admission, 11/30 priority date for domestic students, 9/1 priority date for international students. Applications are processed on a rolling basis. Application fee: $50. Electronic applications accepted. *Expenses:* Tuition, state resident: full-time

$8912; part-time $540 per credit hour. Tuition, nonresident: full-time $20,774; part-time $1252 per credit hour. *Required fees:* $148 per semester. One-time fee: $150. *Financial support:* In 2013–14, 32 students received support, including 22 research assistantships with full and partial tuition reimbursements available (averaging $18,346 per year), 12 teaching assistantships with full and partial tuition reimbursements available (averaging $16,505 per year); career-related internships or fieldwork, Federal Work-Study, institutionally sponsored loans, scholarships/grants, health care benefits, and unspecified assistantships also available. Support available to part-time students. Financial award application deadline: 4/1; financial award applicants required to submit FAFSA. *Faculty research:* Space and solar physics, computational physics, optics, high energy astrophysics. *Total annual research expenditures:* $7 million. *Unit head:* Dr. Richard Lieu, Chair, 256-824-2859, Fax: 256-824-6873, E-mail: richard.lieu@uah.edu. *Application contact:* Kim Gray, Graduate Studies Admissions Coordinator, 256-824-6002, Fax: 256-824-6405, E-mail: deangrad@uah.edu.
Website: http://physics.uah.edu/.

University of Arkansas at Pine Bluff, School of Education, Pine Bluff, AR 71601-2799. Offers early childhood education (M Ed); secondary education (M Ed), including English education, mathematics education, physical education, science education, social studies education; teaching (MAT). *Accreditation:* NCATE. Part-time and evening/weekend programs available. *Degree requirements:* For master's, comprehensive exam. *Entrance requirements:* For master's, GRE, minimum GPA of 2.75, NTE or Standard Arkansas Teaching Certificate. *Faculty research:* Teacher certification, accreditation, assessment, standards, portfolio development, rehabilitation, technology.

The University of British Columbia, Faculty of Education, Department of Curriculum and Pedagogy, Vancouver, BC V6T 1Z4, Canada. Offers art education (M Ed, MA); business education (MA); curriculum studies (M Ed, MA, PhD); home economics education (M Ed, MA); math education (M Ed, MA); music education (M Ed, MA); physical education (M Ed, MA); science education (M Ed, MA); social studies education (M Ed, MA); technology studies education (M Ed, MA). Part-time programs available. Postbaccalaureate distance learning degree programs offered (no on-campus study). *Faculty:* 32 full-time (14 women), 1 (woman) part-time/adjunct. *Students:* 163 full-time, 134 part-time, 42 international. Average age 40. 160 applicants, 75% accepted, 97 enrolled. In 2013, 68 master's, 7 doctorates awarded. *Degree requirements:* For master's, thesis (MA); for doctorate, comprehensive exam, thesis/dissertation. *Entrance requirements:* Additional exam requirements/recommendations for international students: Required—TOEFL (minimum score 580 paper-based; 92 iBT), IELTS (minimum score 6.5). *Application deadline:* For fall admission, 12/1 for domestic and international students; for spring admission, 10/1 for domestic students, 9/1 for international students. Application fee: $90 Canadian dollars ($150 Canadian dollars for international students). Electronic applications accepted. *Expenses:* Contact institution. *Financial support:* In 2013–14, 10 fellowships with partial tuition reimbursements (averaging $16,000 per year), 11 research assistantships with partial tuition reimbursements (averaging $14,000 per year), 27 teaching assistantships with partial tuition reimbursements (averaging $14,000 per year) were awarded; tuition waivers (partial) also available. *Faculty research:* School subjects, teaching and learning. *Unit head:* Dr. Peter Grimmett, Head, 604-822-5422, Fax: 604-822-4714, E-mail: anna.ip@ubc.ca. *Application contact:* Basia Zurek, Graduate Programs Assistant, 604-822-5367, Fax: 604-822-4714, E-mail: edcp.grad@ubc.ca.
Website: http://www.edcp.educ.ubc.ca/.

University of California, Berkeley, Graduate Division, School of Education, Group in Science and Mathematics Education, Berkeley, CA 94720-1500. Offers PhD, MA/Credential. Electronic applications accepted.

University of California, Berkeley, Graduate Division, School of Education, Programs in Education, Berkeley, CA 94720-1500. Offers development in mathematics and science (MA); education in mathematics, science, and technology (MA, PhD); human development and education (MA, PhD); special education (PhD); MA/Credential; PhD/Credential; PhD/MA. Terminal master's awarded for partial completion of doctoral program. *Degree requirements:* For master's, exam or thesis; for doctorate, thesis/dissertation, oral qualifying exam. *Entrance requirements:* For master's and doctorate, GRE General Test, minimum GPA of 3.0 during last 2 years of undergraduate course work. Electronic applications accepted. *Faculty research:* Human development, social and moral educational psychology, developmental teacher preparation.

University of California, San Diego, Office of Graduate Studies, Program in Mathematics and Science Education, La Jolla, CA 92093. Offers PhD. Program offered jointly with San Diego State University. *Students:* 13 (6 women). In 2013, 5 doctorates awarded. *Degree requirements:* For doctorate, thesis/dissertation, teaching practicum. *Entrance requirements:* For doctorate, GRE General Test. Additional exam requirements/recommendations for international students: Required—TOEFL, IELTS. *Application deadline:* For fall admission, 1/7 for domestic students. Electronic applications accepted. *Expenses:* Tuition, state resident: full-time $11,220; part-time $1870 per quarter. Tuition, nonresident: full-time $26,322; part-time $4387 per quarter. *Required fees:* $519.50 per quarter. Part-time tuition and fees vary according to course load and program. *Financial support:* Scholarships/grants and stipends available. Financial award applicants required to submit FAFSA. *Faculty research:* Effective teaching of rational numbers, teacher development, development of number sense and estimation. *Unit head:* Gabriele Wienhausen, Co-Director, 858-534-2904, E-mail: gwienhausen@ucsd.edu. *Application contact:* Sherry Seethaler, Application Contact, 858-534-4656, E-mail: sseethaler@ucsd.edu.
Website: http://sci.sdsu.edu/CRMSE/msed/.

University of Central Florida, College of Education and Human Performance, Education Doctoral Programs, Orlando, FL 32816. Offers communication sciences and disorders (PhD); counselor education (PhD); early childhood education (PhD); education (Ed D); elementary education (PhD); exceptional education (PhD); exercise physiology (PhD); higher education (PhD); hospitality education (PhD); instructional technology (PhD); mathematics education (PhD); reading education (PhD); science education (PhD); social science education (PhD); TESOL (PhD). *Students:* 137 full-time (94 women), 86 part-time (64 women); includes 45 minority (24 Black or African American, non-Hispanic/Latino; 5 Asian, non-Hispanic/Latino; 13 Hispanic/Latino; 3 Two or more races, non-Hispanic/Latino), 22 international. Average age 39. 132 applicants, 54% accepted, 54 enrolled. In 2013, 38 doctorates awarded. Application fee: $30. Electronic applications accepted. *Financial support:* In 2013–14, 84 students received support, including 38 fellowships with partial tuition reimbursements available (averaging $6,600 per year), 41 research assistantships with partial tuition reimbursements available (averaging $7,800 per year), 53 teaching assistantships with partial tuition reimbursements available (averaging $7,700 per year). *Unit head:* Dr. Edward Robinson, Director of Doctoral Programs, 407-823-6106, E-mail: edward.robinson@ucf.edu. *Application contact:* Barbara Rodriguez Lamas, Associate Director, Admissions and Student Services, 407-823-2766, Fax: 407-823-6442, E-mail: gradadmissions@ucf.edu.
Website: http://education.ucf.edu/departments.cfm.

University of Central Florida, College of Education and Human Performance, School of Teaching, Learning, and Leadership, Program in K-8 Mathematics and Science Education, Orlando, FL 32816. Offers M Ed, Certificate. *Accreditation:* NCATE. *Students:* 14 part-time (11 women); includes 6 minority (1 Black or African American, non-Hispanic/Latino; 2 Asian, non-Hispanic/Latino; 3 Hispanic/Latino). Average age 31. 14 applicants, 71% accepted, 7 enrolled. In 2013, 8 master's awarded. Application fee: $30. *Unit head:* Dr. Juli K. Dixon, Program Coordinator, 407-823-4140, E-mail: juli.dixon@ucf.edu. *Application contact:* Barbara Rodriguez Lamas, Director, Admissions and Student Services, 407-823-2766, Fax: 407-823-6442, E-mail: gradadmissions@ucf.edu.

University of Chicago, Division of the Social Sciences, Committee on Conceptual and Historical Studies of Science, Chicago, IL 60637-1513. Offers PhD. *Degree requirements:* For doctorate, thesis/dissertation. *Entrance requirements:* For doctorate, GRE General Test, GRE Subject Test. Additional exam requirements/recommendations for international students: Required—TOEFL, IELTS (minimum score 7). Electronic applications accepted.

University of Cincinnati, Graduate School, College of Education, Criminal Justice, and Human Services, Division of Teacher Education, Cincinnati, OH 45221. Offers curriculum and instruction (M Ed, Ed D); deaf studies (Certificate); early childhood education (M Ed); middle childhood education (M Ed); postsecondary literacy instruction (Certificate); reading/literacy (M Ed, Ed D); secondary education (M Ed); special education (M Ed, Ed D); teaching English as a second language (M Ed, Ed D, Certificate); teaching science (MS). Part-time programs available. *Degree requirements:* For doctorate, thesis/dissertation. *Entrance requirements:* For master's, GRE General Test. Additional exam requirements/recommendations for international students: Required—TOEFL (minimum score 550 paper-based). Electronic applications accepted.

University of Colorado Denver, School of Education and Human Development, Program in Educational Leadership and Innovation, Denver, CO 80217-3364. Offers educational studies and research (PhD), including administrative leadership and policy, early childhood special education, math education, research, assessment and evaluation, science education, urban ecologies. Part-time and evening/weekend programs available. *Students:* 16 full-time (12 women), 12 part-time (9 women); includes 6 minority (2 Black or African American, non-Hispanic/Latino; 3 Asian, non-Hispanic/Latino; 1 Hispanic/Latino), 1 international. Average age 39. 16 applicants, 31% accepted, 4 enrolled. In 2013, 10 doctorates awarded. *Degree requirements:* For doctorate, comprehensive exam, thesis/dissertation, 75 credit hours (for PhD). *Entrance requirements:* For doctorate, GRE or equivalent, resume or curriculum vitae, letters of recommendation, master's degree or equivalent, completion of basic or advanced statistics course with minimum B grade. Additional exam requirements/recommendations for international students: Required—TOEFL (minimum score 537 paper-based; 75 iBT); Recommended—IELTS (minimum score 6.5). *Application deadline:* For fall admission, 5/1 priority date for domestic students, 4/15 priority date for international students. Applications are processed on a rolling basis. Application fee: $50 ($75 for international students). Electronic applications accepted. *Expenses:* Contact institution. *Financial support:* In 2013–14, 19 students received support. Fellowships, research assistantships, teaching assistantships, Federal Work-Study, institutionally sponsored loans, scholarships/grants, and traineeships available. Financial award application deadline: 4/1; financial award applicants required to submit FAFSA. *Faculty research:* Administrative leadership and policy studies, early childhood education, research in diversity, paraprofessionals in education, urban schools lab. *Unit head:* Dr. Deanna Sands, Associate Dean, Research and Professional Development, 303-315-4931, E-mail: deanna.sands@ucdenver.edu. *Application contact:* Student Services Center, 303-315-6300, Fax: 303-315-6311, E-mail: education@ucdenver.edu.
Website: http://www.ucdenver.edu/academics/colleges/SchoolOfEducation/Academics/Doctorate/Pages/PhD.aspx.

University of Colorado Denver, School of Education and Human Development, Teacher Education Programs, Denver, CO 80217. Offers elementary linguistically diverse education (MA); elementary math and science education (MA); elementary math education (MA); elementary reading and writing (MA); elementary science education (MA); secondary English education (MA); secondary linguistically diverse education (MA); secondary math education (MA); secondary reading and writing (MA); secondary science education (MA); special education (MA). *Accreditation:* NCATE. Part-time and evening/weekend programs available. *Students:* 269 full-time (208 women), 141 part-time (111 women); includes 55 minority (4 Black or African American, non-Hispanic/Latino; 1 American Indian or Alaska Native, non-Hispanic/Latino; 10 Asian, non-Hispanic/Latino; 39 Hispanic/Latino; 1 Two or more races, non-Hispanic/Latino), 7 international. Average age 31. 97 applicants, 81% accepted, 62 enrolled. In 2013, 180 master's awarded. *Degree requirements:* For master's, comprehensive exam. *Entrance requirements:* For master's, GRE or MAT (for those with GPA below 2.75), transcripts, resume, letters of recommendation. Additional exam requirements/recommendations for international students: Required—TOEFL (minimum score 537 paper-based; 75 iBT); Recommended—IELTS (minimum score 6.5). *Application deadline:* For fall admission, 4/15 priority date for domestic students, 4/1 for international students; for spring admission, 9/15 priority date for domestic students, 9/1 for international students. Applications are processed on a rolling basis. Application fee: $50 ($75 for international students). Electronic applications accepted. *Expenses:* Contact institution. *Financial support:* In 2013–14, 42 students received support. Fellowships, research assistantships, teaching assistantships, Federal Work-Study, institutionally sponsored loans, scholarships/grants, and traineeships available. Financial award application deadline: 4/1; financial award applicants required to submit FAFSA. *Faculty research:* Linguistically diverse education/ESL, elementary reading and writing, elementary teacher education, secondary teacher education, special education. *Unit head:* Cindy Gutierrez, Director, 303-315-4982, E-mail: cindy.gutierrez@ucdenver.edu. *Application contact:* Lori Sisneros, Student Services Center, 303-315-4979, E-mail: education@ucdenver.edu.
Website: http://www.ucdenver.edu/academics/colleges/SchoolOfEducation/Academics/MASTERS/Pages/default.aspx.

University of Connecticut, Graduate School, Neag School of Education, Department of Curriculum and Instruction, Program in Science Education, Storrs, CT 06269. Offers MA, PhD. *Accreditation:* NCATE. Terminal master's awarded for partial completion of doctoral program. *Degree requirements:* For master's, comprehensive exam, thesis or alternative; for doctorate, thesis/dissertation. *Entrance requirements:* For doctorate, GRE General Test. Additional exam requirements/recommendations for international students: Required—TOEFL (minimum score 550 paper-based). Electronic applications accepted.

The University of Findlay, Office of Graduate Admissions, Findlay, OH 45840-3653. Offers athletic training (MAT); business (MBA), including health care management, hospitality management, organizational leadership, public management; education (MA Ed), including administration, children's literature, early childhood, human resource development, reading, science, special education, technology; environmental, safety and health management (MSEM); health informatics (MS); occupational therapy (MOT); pharmacy (Pharm D); physical therapy (DPT); physician assistant (MPA); rhetoric and writing (MA); teaching English to speakers of other languages (TESOL) and bilingual education (MA). Part-time and evening/weekend programs available. Postbaccalaureate distance learning degree programs offered (no on-campus study). *Faculty:* 209 full-time (98 women), 69 part-time/adjunct (38 women). *Students:* 551 full-time (332 women), 457

part-time (276 women); includes 77 minority (37 Black or African American, non-Hispanic/Latino; 1 American Indian or Alaska Native, non-Hispanic/Latino; 15 Asian, non-Hispanic/Latino; 23 Hispanic/Latino; 1 Native Hawaiian or other Pacific Islander, non-Hispanic/Latino), 135 international. Average age 28. 637 applicants, 66% accepted, 241 enrolled. In 2013, 267 master's, 91 doctorates awarded. *Degree requirements:* For master's, thesis, cumulative project, capstone project. *Entrance requirements:* For master's, GRE/GMAT, bachelor's degree from accredited institution, minimum undergraduate GPA of 2.5 in last 64 hours of course work; for doctorate, GRE, minimum cumulative GPA of 3.0. Additional exam requirements/recommendations for international students: Required—TOEFL (minimum score 80 iBT). *Application deadline:* Applications are processed on a rolling basis. Application fee: $25. Electronic applications accepted. *Expenses: Required fees:* $146 per semester. Tuition and fees vary according to degree level and program. *Financial support:* In 2013–14, 11 research assistantships with full and partial tuition reimbursements (averaging $4,000 per year), 10 teaching assistantships with full and partial tuition reimbursements (averaging $3,600 per year) were awarded; career-related internships or fieldwork, Federal Work-Study, health care benefits, and unspecified assistantships also available. Financial award application deadline: 4/1; financial award applicants required to submit FAFSA. *Unit head:* Christopher M. Harris, Director of Admissions, 419-434-4347, E-mail: harrisc1@findlay.edu. *Application contact:* Emily Ickes, Graduate Admissions Counselor, 419-434-6933, Fax: 419-434-4898, E-mail: ickese@findlay.edu.
Website: http://www.findlay.edu/admissions/graduate/Pages/default.aspx.

University of Florida, Graduate School, College of Education, School of Teaching and Learning, Gainesville, FL 32611. Offers curriculum and instruction (M Ed, MAE, Ed D, PhD, Ed S), including bilingual/ESOL specialization; elementary education (M Ed, MAE); English education (M Ed, MAE); mathematics education (M Ed, MAE); reading education (M Ed, MAE); science education (M Ed, MAE); social studies education (M Ed, MAE). *Accreditation:* NCATE. Part-time and evening/weekend programs available. Postbaccalaureate distance learning degree programs offered (no on-campus study). *Faculty:* 24 full-time (17 women), 12 part-time/adjunct (7 women). *Students:* 201 full-time (162 women), 325 part-time (255 women); includes 124 minority (36 Black or African American, non-Hispanic/Latino; 4 American Indian or Alaska Native, non-Hispanic/Latino; 10 Asian, non-Hispanic/Latino; 74 Hispanic/Latino; 47 international. Average age 34. 220 applicants, 55% accepted, 64 enrolled. In 2013, 215 master's, 15 doctorates, 14 other advanced degrees awarded. Terminal master's awarded for partial completion of doctoral program. *Degree requirements:* For master's, comprehensive exam (for some programs), thesis (for some programs); for doctorate, comprehensive exam (for some programs), thesis/dissertation (for some programs). *Entrance requirements:* For master's and doctorate, GRE General Test, minimum GPA of 3.0; for Ed S, GRE General Test. Additional exam requirements/recommendations for international students: Required—TOEFL (minimum score 550 paper-based; 80 iBT), IELTS (minimum score 6). *Application deadline:* For fall admission, 2/15 for domestic students, 12/1 for international students; for spring admission, 9/15 for domestic students, 3/1 for international students. Applications are processed on a rolling basis. Application fee: $30. Electronic applications accepted. *Expenses:* Tuition, state resident: full-time $12,640. Tuition, nonresident: full-time $30,000. *Financial support:* In 2013–14, 52 students received support, including 3 fellowships (averaging $2,365 per year), 20 research assistantships (averaging $11,715 per year), 58 teaching assistantships (averaging $8,410 per year); career-related internships or fieldwork and unspecified assistantships also available. Financial award applicants required to submit FAFSA. *Faculty research:* Early childhood, child and adolescents, diverse learners, race/ethnicity issues, teacher education, professional development, language and literacy development, policy development. *Unit head:* Elizabeth Bondy, PhD, Interim Director and Professor, 352-273-4242, Fax: 352-392-9193, E-mail: bondy@coe.ufl.edu. *Application contact:* Sevan Terzian, Graduate Coordinator, 352-273-4216, Fax: 352-392-9193, E-mail: sterzian@coe.ufl.edu.
Website: http://education.ufl.edu/school-teaching-learning/.

University of Georgia, College of Education, Department of Mathematics and Science Education, Athens, GA 30602. Offers mathematics education (M Ed, Ed D, PhD, Ed S); science education (M Ed, Ed D, PhD, Ed S).

University of Illinois at Chicago, Graduate College, College of Education, Department of Curriculum and Instruction, Chicago, IL 60607-7128. Offers curriculum studies (PhD); educational studies (M Ed); elementary education (M Ed); instructional leadership (M Ed); literacy, language and culture (M Ed, PhD); science education (M Ed); secondary education (M Ed). Part-time and evening/weekend programs available. *Faculty:* 20 full-time (10 women), 10 part-time/adjunct (8 women). *Students:* 124 full-time (89 women), 155 part-time (117 women); includes 117 minority (51 Black or African American, non-Hispanic/Latino; 19 Asian, non-Hispanic/Latino; 43 Hispanic/Latino; 4 Two or more races, non-Hispanic/Latino), 11 international. Average age 32. 154 applicants, 70% accepted, 74 enrolled. In 2013, 108 master's, 16 doctorates awarded. *Degree requirements:* For doctorate, thesis/dissertation. *Entrance requirements:* For master's, minimum GPA of 2.75; for doctorate, GRE General Test, minimum GPA of 2.75. Additional exam requirements/recommendations for international students: Required—TOEFL. *Application deadline:* For fall admission, 1/9 for domestic and international students; for spring admission, 10/1 for domestic and international students. Applications are processed on a rolling basis. Application fee: $40 ($50 for international students). Electronic applications accepted. *Expenses:* Tuition, state resident: full-time $11,066; part-time $3689 per term. Tuition, nonresident: full-time $23,064; part-time $7688 per term. *Required fees:* $3004; $1190 per term. Tuition and fees vary according to course level and program. *Financial support:* In 2013–14, 101 students received support, including 4 fellowships with full tuition reimbursements available; research assistantships with full tuition reimbursements available, teaching assistantships with full tuition reimbursements available, career-related internships or fieldwork, Federal Work-Study, institutionally sponsored loans, traineeships, tuition waivers (full), and unspecified assistantships also available. Support available to part-time students. Financial award application deadline: 3/1; financial award applicants required to submit FAFSA. *Faculty research:* Curriculum theory, curriculum development, research on teaching, curriculum and context, reading/literacy. *Total annual research expenditures:* $70,000. *Unit head:* Prof. Alfred Tatum, Associate Professor/Director/Chair, 312-413-3883, Fax: 312-996-8134, E-mail: atatum1@uic.edu.
Website: http://education.uic.edu.

University of Illinois at Chicago, Graduate College, Program in Learning Sciences, Chicago, IL 60607-7128. Offers PhD. *Expenses:* Tuition, state resident: full-time $11,066; part-time $3689 per term. Tuition, nonresident: full-time $23,064; part-time $7688 per term. *Required fees:* $3004; $1190 per term. Tuition and fees vary according to course level and program. *Unit head:* Dr. Clark Hulse, Dean, 312-413-2550. *Application contact:* Receptionist, 312-413-2550, E-mail: gradcoll@uic.edu.

University of Illinois at Urbana–Champaign, Graduate College, College of Engineering, Department of Physics, Champaign, IL 61820. Offers physics (MS, PhD); teaching of physics (MS). *Students:* 254 (44 women). Application fee: $75 ($90 for international students). *Unit head:* Dr. Dale J. VanHarlingen, Head, 217-333-3760, Fax:

217-244-4293, E-mail: dvh@illinois.edu. *Application contact:* Melodee Jo Schweighart, Office Manager, 217-333-3645, Fax: 217-244-5073, E-mail: mschweig@illinois.edu.
Website: http://physics.illinois.edu/.

University of Illinois at Urbana–Champaign, Graduate College, College of Liberal Arts and Sciences, School of Chemical Sciences, Department of Chemistry, Champaign, IL 61820. Offers astrochemistry (PhD); chemical physics (PhD); chemistry (MA, MS, PhD); teaching of chemistry (MS); MS/JD; MS/MBA. *Students:* 305 (114 women). Application fee: $75 ($90 for international students). *Unit head:* Gregory S. Girolami, Head, 217-333-0711, Fax: 217-244-5943, E-mail: ggirolam@illinois.edu. *Application contact:* Karen York, Program Coordinator, 217-244-6425, Fax: 217-244-5943, E-mail: ksyork@illinois.edu.
Website: http://www.chemistry.illinois.edu/.

University of Illinois at Urbana–Champaign, Graduate College, College of Liberal Arts and Sciences, School of Earth, Society and Environment, Department of Geology, Champaign, IL 61820. Offers geology (MS, PhD); teaching of earth sciences (MS). *Students:* 35 (15 women). Terminal master's awarded for partial completion of doctoral program. Application fee: $75 ($90 for international students). *Unit head:* Thomas M. Johnson, Head, 217-244-2002, Fax: 217-244-4996, E-mail: tmjohnsn@illinois.edu. *Application contact:* Marilyn K. Whalen, Office Administrator, 217-333-3542, Fax: 217-244-4996, E-mail: mkt@illinois.edu.
Website: http://www.geology.illinois.edu/.

University of Indianapolis, Graduate Programs, School of Education, Indianapolis, IN 46227-3697. Offers art education (MAT); biology (MAT); chemistry (MAT); curriculum and instruction (MA); earth sciences (MAT); education (MA, MAT); educational leadership (MA); elementary education (MA); English (MAT); French (MAT); math (MAT); physical education (MAT); physics (MAT); secondary education (MA), including art education, education, English education, social studies education; social studies (MAT); Spanish (MAT). *Accreditation:* NCATE. Part-time and evening/weekend programs available. *Faculty:* 5 full-time (4 women), 2 part-time/adjunct (1 woman). *Students:* 19 full-time (9 women), 54 part-time (27 women); includes 13 minority (5 Black or African American, non-Hispanic/Latino; 1 Asian, non-Hispanic/Latino; 5 Hispanic/Latino; 2 Two or more races, non-Hispanic/Latino), 1 international. Average age 32. In 2013, 52 master's awarded. *Entrance requirements:* For master's, GRE Subject Test, PRAXIS I, minimum GPA of 2.5, 3 letters of recommendation, interview. Additional exam requirements/recommendations for international students: Required—TOEFL (minimum score 550 paper-based). *Application deadline:* Applications are processed on a rolling basis. Application fee: $50. *Expenses:* Tuition: Full-time $5436; part-time $810 per credit hour. *Financial support:* Federal Work-Study available. Financial award application deadline: 5/1; financial award applicants required to submit FAFSA. *Faculty research:* Assessment of teacher education, perceptions of prospective teachers by parents. *Unit head:* Dr. Kathy Moran, Dean, 317-788-3285, Fax: 317-788-3300, E-mail: kmoran@uindy.edu. *Application contact:* Jeni Kirby, Administrative Assistant, Teacher Education, 317-788-2113, E-mail: kirbyj@uindy.edu.
Website: http://education.uindy.edu/.

The University of Iowa, Graduate College, College of Education, Department of Teaching and Learning, Program in Education, Iowa City, IA 52242-1316. Offers art education (MA); developmental reading (MA); elementary education (MA); English education (MA, MAT); foreign and second language education (MAT); foreign language education (MA); foreign language/ESL education (PhD); language, literacy and culture (PhD); mathematics education (MA, MAT, PhD); music education (MM, PhD); science education (MA); secondary education (MA); social studies (MA, PhD). *Degree requirements:* For master's, thesis optional, exam; for doctorate, comprehensive exam, thesis/dissertation. *Entrance requirements:* For master's and doctorate, GRE General Test, minimum GPA of 3.0. Additional exam requirements/recommendations for international students: Required—TOEFL (minimum score 550 paper-based; 81 iBT). Electronic applications accepted.

University of Louisiana at Monroe, Graduate School, College of Arts, Education, and Sciences, School of Education, Program in Curriculum and Instruction, Monroe, LA 71209-0001. Offers art education (M Ed); biology education (M Ed); chemistry education (M Ed); curriculum and instruction (Ed D); early childhood education (M Ed); earth science education (M Ed); educational leadership (M Ed); elementary education (1-5) (M Ed); English as a second language (M Ed); English education (M Ed); family and consumer education (M Ed); French education (M Ed); history education (M Ed); math education (M Ed); middle school education (M Ed); music education (M Ed); reading education (K-12) (M Ed); Spanish education (M Ed); special education - academically gifted (M Ed); special education - early intervention (M Ed); special education - educational diagnostician (M Ed); special education - mild/moderate disabilities (M Ed); speech education (M Ed). *Accreditation:* NCATE. *Degree requirements:* For master's, comprehensive exam (for some programs), thesis; for doctorate, thesis/dissertation, internships. *Entrance requirements:* For master's, GRE General Test; for doctorate, GRE General Test, minimum undergraduate GPA of 2.75, graduate 3.25. Additional exam requirements/recommendations for international students: Required—TOEFL (minimum score 500 paper-based; 61 iBT). *Application deadline:* For fall admission, 8/24 priority date for domestic students, 7/1 for international students; for winter admission, 12/14 priority date for domestic students; for spring admission, 1/19 for domestic students, 11/1 for international students. Applications are processed on a rolling basis. Application fee: $20 ($30 for international students). Electronic applications accepted. *Expenses:* Tuition, state resident: full-time $6607. Tuition, nonresident: full-time $17,179. Full-time tuition and fees vary according to program. *Financial support:* Research assistantships, career-related internships or fieldwork, Federal Work-Study, and unspecified assistantships available. Financial award application deadline: 4/1; financial award applicants required to submit FAFSA. *Unit head:* Dr. Dorothy Schween, Director, 318-342-1268, Fax: 318-342-3131, E-mail: schween@ulm.edu. *Application contact:* Dr. Dorothy Schween, Director, 318-342-1268, Fax: 318-342-3131, E-mail: schween@ulm.edu.

University of Maine, Graduate School, College of Education and Human Development, Department of Exercise Science and STEM Education, Orono, ME 04469. Offers classroom technology integrationist (CGS); education data specialist (CGS); educational technology coordinator (CGS); kinesiology and physical education (M Ed, MS); science education (M Ed, MS); STEM education (PhD). Part-time and evening/weekend programs available. *Students:* 25 full-time (13 women), 28 part-time (16 women); includes 5 minority (2 Black or African American, non-Hispanic/Latino; 2 American Indian or Alaska Native, non-Hispanic/Latino; 1 Asian, non-Hispanic/Latino), 2 international. Average age 34. 19 applicants, 84% accepted, 12 enrolled. In 2013, 6 master's awarded. *Degree requirements:* For master's, thesis (for some programs); for doctorate, comprehensive exam, thesis/dissertation. *Entrance requirements:* For master's, GRE General Test, MAT; for doctorate, GRE General Test. Additional exam requirements/recommendations for international students: Required—TOEFL. *Application deadline:* For fall admission, 1/15 for domestic students. Applications are processed on a rolling basis. Application fee: $65. Electronic applications accepted. *Expenses:* Tuition, state resident: full-time $7524. Tuition, nonresident: full-time $23,112. *Required fees:* $1970. *Financial support:* In 2013–14, 13 students received support, including 2 teaching assistantships (averaging $14,600 per year). Financial

award application deadline: 3/1. *Faculty research:* Integration of technology in K-12 classrooms, instructional theory and practice in science, inquiry-based teaching, professional development, exercise science, adaptive physical education, neuromuscular function/dysfunction. *Unit head:* Dr. Janet Spector, Dean, 207-581-2441, Fax: 207-581-2423. *Application contact:* Scott G. Delcourt, Associate Dean of the Graduate School, 207-581-3291, Fax: 207-581-3232, E-mail: graduate@maine.edu.
Website: http://umaine.edu/edhd/.

University of Maryland, Baltimore County, Graduate School, College of Arts, Humanities and Social Sciences, Department of Education, Master of Arts in Education Program, Baltimore, MD 21250. Offers K-8 mathematics instructional leadership (MAE); K-8 science education (MAE); K-8 STEM education (MAE); secondary mathematics education (MAE); secondary science education (MAE); secondary STEM education (MAE). Part-time and evening/weekend programs available. Postbaccalaureate distance learning degree programs offered (no on-campus study). *Faculty:* 5 full-time (4 women), 5 part-time/adjunct (all women). *Students:* 1 (woman) full-time, 133 part-time (100 women); includes 15 minority (13 Black or African American, non-Hispanic/Latino; 2 Hispanic/Latino). Average age 32. 47 applicants, 96% accepted, 45 enrolled. In 2013, 41 master's awarded. *Degree requirements:* For master's, comprehensive exam (for some programs), thesis (for some programs). *Application deadline:* For fall admission, 6/1 for domestic students; for spring admission, 11/1 for domestic students. Electronic applications accepted. One-time fee: $200 full-time. *Financial support:* Application deadline: 3/1. *Unit head:* Dr. Eugene Schaffer, Director, 410-455-8423, Fax: 410-455-1880, E-mail: schaffer@umbc.edu.
Website: http://www.umbc.edu/education/mae.

University of Maryland, Baltimore County, Graduate School, College of Arts, Humanities and Social Sciences, Department of Education, Program in Teaching, Baltimore, MD 21250. Offers early childhood education (MAT); elementary education (MAT); secondary education (MAT), including art, biology, chemistry, dance, earth/space science, English, foreign language, mathematics, music, physics, social studies, theatre. Part-time and evening/weekend programs available. *Faculty:* 24 full-time (18 women), 25 part-time/adjunct (19 women). *Students:* 49 full-time (34 women), 35 part-time (23 women); includes 19 minority (9 Black or African American, non-Hispanic/Latino; 3 Asian, non-Hispanic/Latino; 6 Hispanic/Latino; 1 Two or more races, non-Hispanic/Latino). Average age 30. 40 applicants, 95% accepted, 35 enrolled. In 2013, 106 master's awarded. *Degree requirements:* For master's, comprehensive exam (for some programs), thesis (for some programs). *Entrance requirements:* For master's, PRAXIS I or SAT (minimum score of 1000), minimum GPA of 3.0. Additional exam requirements/recommendations for international students: Required—TOEFL. *Application deadline:* For fall admission, 6/1 for domestic students; for spring admission, 11/1 for domestic students. Applications are processed on a rolling basis. Application fee: $50. Electronic applications accepted. One-time fee: $200 full-time. *Financial support:* In 2013–14, 6 students received support, including teaching assistantships with full and partial tuition reimbursements available (averaging $12,000 per year); career-related internships or fieldwork, Federal Work-Study, scholarships/grants, tuition waivers, and unspecified assistantships also available. Financial award application deadline: 3/1. *Faculty research:* STEM teacher education, culturally sensitive pedagogy, ESOL/bilingual education, early childhood education, language, literacy and culture. *Unit head:* Dr. Susan M. Blunck, Graduate Program Director, 410-455-2869, Fax: 410-455-3986, E-mail: blunck@umbc.edu. *Application contact:* Dr. Susan M. Blunck, Graduate Program Director, 410-455-2869, Fax: 410-455-3986, E-mail: blunck@umbc.edu.
Website: http://www.umbc.edu/education/.

University of Massachusetts Amherst, Graduate School, College of Education, Program in Education, Amherst, MA 01003. Offers bilingual/English as a second language/multicultural education (M Ed, Ed S); child study and early education (M Ed); children, families and schools (Ed D, Ed S); early childhood and elementary teacher education (M Ed); educational leadership (M Ed); educational policy and leadership (Ed D); higher education (M Ed); international education (M Ed); language, literacy and culture (Ed D); learning, media and technology (M Ed, Ed S); mathematics, science, and learning technologies (Ed D); psychometric methods, educational statistics and research methods (Ed D); reading and writing (M Ed); school counselor education (M Ed, Ed S); school psychology (Ed S); science education (Ed S); secondary teacher education (M Ed); social justice education (M Ed, Ed D, Ed S); special education (M Ed, Ed D, Ed S); teacher education and school improvement (Ed D, Ed S). *Accreditation:* NCATE. Part-time programs available. Postbaccalaureate distance learning degree programs offered (minimal on-campus study). *Faculty:* 95 full-time (55 women). *Students:* 357 full-time (240 women), 264 part-time (194 women); includes 114 minority (41 Black or African American, non-Hispanic/Latino; 4 American Indian or Alaska Native, non-Hispanic/Latino; 10 Asian, non-Hispanic/Latino; 47 Hispanic/Latino; 12 Two or more races, non-Hispanic/Latino), 100 international. Average age 34. 761 applicants, 51% accepted, 200 enrolled. In 2013, 186 master's, 31 doctorates, 22 other advanced degrees awarded. Terminal master's awarded for partial completion of doctoral program. *Degree requirements:* For doctorate, comprehensive exam, thesis/dissertation. *Entrance requirements:* Additional exam requirements/recommendations for international students: Required—TOEFL (minimum score 550 paper-based; 80 iBT), IELTS (minimum score 6.5). *Application deadline:* For fall admission, 1/15 for domestic and international students. Applications are processed on a rolling basis. Application fee: $75. Electronic applications accepted. *Financial support:* Fellowships with full and partial tuition reimbursements, research assistantships with full and partial tuition reimbursements, teaching assistantships with full and partial tuition reimbursements, career-related internships or fieldwork, Federal Work-Study, scholarships/grants, traineeships, health care benefits, tuition waivers (full and partial), and unspecified assistantships available. Support available to part-time students. Financial award application deadline: 1/15; financial award applicants required to submit FAFSA. *Unit head:* Dr. Linda L. Griffin, Graduate Program Director, 413-545-6984, Fax: 413-545-1523. *Application contact:* Lindsay DeSantis, Supervisor of Admissions, 413-545-0722, Fax: 413-577-0010, E-mail: gradadm@grad.umass.edu.
Website: http://www.umass.edu/education/.

University of Massachusetts Lowell, Graduate School of Education, Lowell, MA 01854-2881. Offers administration, planning, and policy (CAGS); curriculum and instruction (M Ed, CAGS); educational administration (M Ed); language arts and literacy (Ed D); leadership in schooling (Ed D); math and science education (Ed D); reading and language (M Ed, CAGS). *Accreditation:* NCATE. Part-time and evening/weekend programs available. Postbaccalaureate distance learning degree programs offered (no on-campus study). Terminal master's awarded for partial completion of doctoral program. *Degree requirements:* For doctorate, thesis/dissertation. *Entrance requirements:* For master's, doctorate, and CAGS, GRE General Test. Additional exam requirements/recommendations for international students: Required—TOEFL. Electronic applications accepted.

University of Miami, Graduate School, School of Education and Human Development, Department of Teaching and Learning, Program in Teaching and Learning, Coral Gables, FL 33124. Offers language and literacy learning in multilingual settings (PhD); science, technology, engineering and mathematics (PhD); special education (PhD). *Faculty:* 14 full-time (10 women), 9 part-time/adjunct (all women). *Students:* 24 full-time (21 women); includes 11 minority (3 Black or African American, non-Hispanic/Latino; 7 Hispanic/Latino; 1 Two or more races, non-Hispanic/Latino), 5 international. Average age 32. 29 applicants, 21% accepted, 5 enrolled. In 2013, 2 doctorates awarded. *Degree requirements:* For doctorate, thesis/dissertation, qualifying exam, electronic portfolio. *Entrance requirements:* For doctorate, GRE General Test. Additional exam requirements/recommendations for international students: Required—TOEFL (minimum score 550 paper-based; 80 iBT); Recommended—IELTS (minimum score 6.5). *Application deadline:* For fall admission, 2/15 for domestic students, 10/1 for international students. Application fee: $65. Electronic applications accepted. *Financial support:* In 2013–14, 24 students received support, including 11 research assistantships with full and partial tuition reimbursements available (averaging $18,900 per year), 8 teaching assistantships with full and partial tuition reimbursements available (averaging $18,900 per year). Financial award application deadline: 3/1; financial award applicants required to submit FAFSA. *Faculty research:* Teacher education, multicultural education, special education, second language acquisition, math and science education. *Unit head:* Dr. Elizabeth Harry, Department Chairperson and Program Director, 305-284-4961, Fax: 305-284-6998, E-mail: bharry@miami.edu. *Application contact:* Lois Heffernan, Graduate Admission Coordinator, 305-284-2167, Fax: 305-284-9395, E-mail: lheffernan@miami.edu.

University of Michigan–Dearborn, College of Education, Health, and Human Services, Program in Science Education, Dearborn, MI 48126. Offers MS. *Accreditation:* Teacher Education Accreditation Council. Part-time and evening/weekend programs available. Postbaccalaureate distance learning degree programs offered (minimal on-campus study). *Faculty:* 2 full-time (1 woman), 1 (woman) part-time/adjunct. *Students:* 6 part-time (4 women). Average age 36. 3 applicants, 33% accepted, 1 enrolled. In 2013, 7 master's awarded. *Entrance requirements:* For master's, minimum GPA of 3.0, 3 letters of recommendation from supervisors or university faculty, proof of baccalaureate degree, valid teaching certificate, one-page statement of philosophy of teaching science, one-page statement of educational/career goals. Additional exam requirements/recommendations for international students: Required—TOEFL (minimum score 560 paper-based; 84 iBT), TWE. *Application deadline:* For fall admission, 8/1 priority date for domestic students, 5/1 priority date for international students; for winter admission, 12/1 priority date for domestic students, 9/1 priority date for international students; for spring admission, 4/1 priority date for domestic students, 1/1 priority date for international students. Applications are processed on a rolling basis. Application fee: $60. Electronic applications accepted. *Expenses:* Tuition, state resident: full-time $11,838; part-time $686 per credit hour. Tuition, nonresident: full-time $20,926; part-time $1206 per credit hour. *Required fees:* $760; $286 per semester. Tuition and fees vary according to course load and program. *Financial support:* Scholarships/grants available. Support available to part-time students. Financial award applicants required to submit FAFSA. *Faculty research:* Inquiry pedagogy. *Unit head:* Dr. Susan A. Everett, Program Coordinator, 313-593-5133, Fax: 313-593-4748, E-mail: everetts@umd.umich.edu. *Application contact:* Elizabeth Morden, Customer Service Assistant, 313-583-6333, Fax: 313-593-4748, E-mail: emorden@umd.umich.edu.
Website: http://cehhs.umd.umich.edu/cehhs_msse/.

University of Minnesota, Twin Cities Campus, Graduate School, College of Education and Human Development, Department of Curriculum and Instruction, Program in Teaching, Minneapolis, MN 55455-0213. Offers Chinese (M Ed); earth science (M Ed); elementary special education (M Ed); English (M Ed); English as a second language (M Ed); French (M Ed); German (M Ed); Hebrew (M Ed); Japanese (M Ed); life sciences (M Ed); mathematics (M Ed); middle school science (M Ed); science (M Ed); second languages and cultures (M Ed); social studies (M Ed); Spanish (M Ed). *Students:* 220 full-time (154 women), 83 part-time (60 women); includes 43 minority (10 Black or African American, non-Hispanic/Latino; 26 Asian, non-Hispanic/Latino; 7 Hispanic/Latino), 4 international. Average age 27. 261 applicants, 87% accepted, 222 enrolled. In 2013, 561 master's awarded. Application fee: $75 ($95 for international students). *Unit head:* Dr. Nina Asher, Chair, 612-624-1357, Fax: 612-624-8277, E-mail: nasher@umn.edu. *Application contact:* Dr. Jennifer Engler, Assistant Dean, 612-626-2887, Fax: 612-626-7496, E-mail: engle009@umn.edu.
Website: http://www.cehd.umn.edu/ci/.

University of Missouri, Graduate School, College of Education, Department of Learning, Teaching and Curriculum, Columbia, MO 65211. Offers agricultural education (M Ed, PhD, Ed S); art education (M Ed, PhD, Ed S); business and office education (M Ed, PhD, Ed S); early childhood education (M Ed, PhD, Ed S); elementary education (M Ed, PhD, Ed S); English education (M Ed, PhD, Ed S); foreign language education (M Ed, PhD, Ed S); health education and promotion (M Ed, PhD); learning and instruction (M Ed); marketing education (M Ed, PhD, Ed S); mathematics education (M Ed, PhD, Ed S); music education (M Ed, PhD, Ed S); reading education (M Ed, PhD, Ed S); science education (M Ed, PhD, Ed S); social studies education (M Ed, PhD, Ed S); vocational education (M Ed, PhD, Ed S). Part-time programs available. *Faculty:* 26 full-time (16 women), 3 part-time/adjunct (2 women). *Students:* 186 full-time (143 women), 197 part-time (172 women); includes 19 minority (4 Black or African American, non-Hispanic/Latino; 4 Asian, non-Hispanic/Latino; 6 Hispanic/Latino; 5 Two or more races, non-Hispanic/Latino), 25 international. Average age 31. 288 applicants, 65% accepted, 160 enrolled. In 2013, 202 master's, 18 doctorates, 7 other advanced degrees awarded. Terminal master's awarded for partial completion of doctoral program. *Degree requirements:* For doctorate, thesis/dissertation. *Entrance requirements:* For master's and Ed S, GRE General Test or MAT, minimum GPA of 3.0; for doctorate, GRE General Test, minimum GPA of 3.0. Additional exam requirements/recommendations for international students: Required—TOEFL (minimum score 600 paper-based; 100 iBT). *Application deadline:* For fall admission, 12/1 priority date for domestic and international students. Applications are processed on a rolling basis. Application fee: $55 ($75 for international students). Electronic applications accepted. *Financial support:* Fellowships, research assistantships, teaching assistantships, institutionally sponsored loans, traineeships, health care benefits, and unspecified assistantships available. Support available to part-time students. *Faculty research:* Curriculum development and research, teacher education, art education, business and marketing, early childhood education, English education, literacy/reading education, mathematics education, music education, science education, social studies education. *Unit head:* Dr. James Tarr, Associate Division Director, 573-882-4034, E-mail: tarrj@missouri.edu. *Application contact:* Fran Colley, Academic Advisor, 573-882-6462, E-mail: colleyf@missouri.edu.
Website: http://education.missouri.edu/LTC/.

University of Nebraska at Kearney, Graduate Programs, College of Natural and Social Sciences, Department of Biology, Kearney, NE 68849. Offers biology (MS); science/math education (MA Ed). Part-time and evening/weekend programs available. Postbaccalaureate distance learning degree programs offered (no on-campus study). *Degree requirements:* For master's, thesis optional. *Entrance requirements:* For master's, GRE, (for thesis option and for online program applicants if undergraduate GPA is below 2.75), letter of interest. Additional exam requirements/recommendations for international students: Required—TOEFL (minimum score 550 paper-based; 79 iBT). Electronic applications accepted. *Faculty research:* Pollution injury, molecular biology-viral gene expression, prairie range condition modeling, evolution of symbiotic nitrogen fixation.

University of New Hampshire, Graduate School, College of Engineering and Physical Sciences, Department of Chemistry, Durham, NH 03824. Offers chemistry (MS, MST, PhD); chemistry education (PhD). *Faculty:* 13 full-time (0 women). *Students:* 40 full-time (20 women), 20 part-time (10 women); includes 8 minority (1 Black or African American, non-Hispanic/Latino; 2 Asian, non-Hispanic/Latino; 3 Hispanic/Latino; 2 Two or more races, non-Hispanic/Latino), 23 international. Average age 27. 65 applicants, 38% accepted, 11 enrolled. In 2013, 5 master's, 1 doctorate awarded. Terminal master's awarded for partial completion of doctoral program. *Degree requirements:* For master's, thesis; for doctorate, one foreign language, thesis/dissertation. *Entrance requirements:* Additional exam requirements/recommendations for international students: Required—TOEFL (minimum score 550 paper-based; 80 iBT). *Application deadline:* For fall admission, 4/1 priority date for domestic students, 4/1 for international students; for spring admission, 12/1 for domestic students. Applications are processed on a rolling basis. Application fee: $65. Electronic applications accepted. *Expenses:* Tuition, state resident: full-time $13,500; part-time $750 per credit hour. Tuition, nonresident: full-time $26,200; part-time $1100 per credit hour. *Required fees:* $1741; $435.25 per term. Tuition and fees vary according to course level, course load, campus/location and program. *Financial support:* In 2013–14, 52 students received support, including 7 research assistantships, 41 teaching assistantships; fellowships, Federal Work-Study, scholarships/grants, and tuition waivers (full and partial) also available. Support available to part-time students. Financial award application deadline: 2/15. *Faculty research:* Analytical, physical, organic, and inorganic chemistry. *Unit head:* Dr. Chuck Zercher, Chairperson, 603-862-1550. *Application contact:* Cindi Rohwer, Administrative Assistant, 603-862-1795, E-mail: chem.dept@unh.edu.
Website: http://www.unh.edu/chemistry/.

University of New Haven, Graduate School, College of Arts and Sciences, Program in Environmental Sciences, West Haven, CT 06516-1916. Offers environmental ecology (MS); environmental geoscience (MS); environmental health and management (MS); environmental science (MS); environmental science education (MS); geographical information systems (MS, Certificate). Part-time and evening/weekend programs available. *Students:* 25 full-time (12 women), 20 part-time (11 women); includes 8 minority (3 Black or African American, non-Hispanic/Latino; 2 Asian, non-Hispanic/Latino; 3 Hispanic/Latino), 8 international. 42 applicants, 90% accepted, 14 enrolled. In 2013, 11 master's, 3 other advanced degrees awarded. *Degree requirements:* For master's, thesis optional, research project. *Entrance requirements:* Additional exam requirements/recommendations for international students: Required—TOEFL (minimum score 80 iBT), IELTS, PTE (minimum score 53). *Application deadline:* For fall admission, 5/31 for international students; for winter admission, 10/15 for international students; for spring admission, 1/15 for international students. Applications are processed on a rolling basis. Application fee: $75. Electronic applications accepted. Application fee is waived when completed online. *Expenses: Tuition:* Full-time $21,600; part-time $800 per credit hour. *Required fees:* $45 per trimester. *Financial support:* Research assistantships with partial tuition reimbursements, teaching assistantships with partial tuition reimbursements, career-related internships or fieldwork, Federal Work-Study, scholarships/grants, and unspecified assistantships available. Support available to part-time students. Financial award applicants required to submit FAFSA. *Faculty research:* Mapping and assessing geological and living resources in Long Island Sound, geology, San Salvador Island, Bahamas. *Unit head:* Dr. Roman Zajac, Coordinator, 203-932-7114, E-mail: rzajac@newhaven.edu. *Application contact:* Eloise Gormley, Director of Graduate Admissions, 203-932-7440, E-mail: gradinfo@newhaven.edu.
Website: http://www.newhaven.edu/4728/.

University of New Mexico, School of Medicine, Program in Biomedical Sciences, Program in University Science Teaching, Albuquerque, NM 87131-2039. Offers Certificate. In 2013, 1 Certificate awarded. *Unit head:* Dr. Sherry Rogers, Program Director, 505-272-0007, E-mail: srogers@salud.unm.edu. *Application contact:* Dr. Angela Wandinger-Ness, Coordinator, 505-272-1459, Fax: 505-272-8738, E-mail: awandinger@salud.unm.edu.

The University of North Carolina at Chapel Hill, Graduate School, School of Education, Program in Secondary Education, Chapel Hill, NC 27599. Offers English (Grades 9-12) (MAT); English as a second language (MAT); French (Grades K-12) (MAT); German (Grades K-12) (MAT); Japanese (Grades K-12) (MAT); Latin (Grades 9-12) (MAT); mathematics (Grades 9-12) (MAT); music (Grades K-12) (MAT); science (Grades 9-12) (MAT); social studies (Grades 9-12) (MAT); Spanish (Grades K-12) (MAT). *Accreditation:* NCATE. *Degree requirements:* For master's, comprehensive exam. *Entrance requirements:* For master's, GRE General Test, minimum GPA of 3.0 during last 2 years of undergraduate course work. Additional exam requirements/recommendations for international students: Required—TOEFL (minimum score 550 paper-based). Electronic applications accepted.

The University of North Carolina at Greensboro, Graduate School, School of Education, Department of Curriculum and Instruction, Greensboro, NC 27412-5001. Offers college teaching and adult learning (Certificate); curriculum and instruction (M Ed), including chemistry education, elementary education, English as a second language, French education, instructional technology, mathematics education, middle grades education, reading education, science education, social studies education, Spanish education; curriculum and teaching (PhD), including higher education, teacher education and development; English as a second language (Certificate); higher education (M Ed); supervision (M Ed). *Accreditation:* NCATE. Part-time programs available. *Degree requirements:* For doctorate, thesis/dissertation. *Entrance requirements:* For master's and doctorate, GRE General Test. Additional exam requirements/recommendations for international students: Required—TOEFL. Electronic applications accepted. *Faculty research:* Community college literacy program, middle school mathematics/computer mathematics.

The University of North Carolina at Pembroke, Graduate Studies, Department of Biology, Pembroke, NC 28372-1510. Offers science education (MA, MAT). Part-time and evening/weekend programs available. *Degree requirements:* For master's, thesis. *Entrance requirements:* For master's, GRE or MAT, minimum GPA of 3.0 in major or 2.5 overall.

University of Northern Colorado, Graduate School, College of Natural and Health Sciences, Department of Chemistry and Biochemistry, Greeley, CO 80639. Offers chemical education (MS, PhD); chemistry (MS). Part-time programs available. *Degree requirements:* For master's, comprehensive exam, thesis or alternative; for doctorate, comprehensive exam, thesis/dissertation. *Entrance requirements:* For master's, 3 letters of reference; for doctorate, GRE General Test, 3 letters of reference. Electronic applications accepted.

University of Northern Colorado, Graduate School, College of Natural and Health Sciences, School of Biological Sciences, Program in Biology Education, Greeley, CO 80639. Offers PhD. Part-time programs available. *Degree requirements:* For doctorate, comprehensive exam, thesis/dissertation. *Entrance requirements:* For doctorate, GRE General Test, 3 letters of recommendation. Electronic applications accepted.

University of Northern Iowa, Graduate College, College of Humanities, Arts and Sciences, MA Program in Science Education, Cedar Falls, IA 50614. Offers earth science education (MA); physics education (MA); science education (MA). *Students:* 3 full-time (2 women), 22 part-time (11 women); includes 1 minority (Two or more races, non-Hispanic/Latino). 1 applicant, 100% accepted, 1 enrolled. In 2013, 8 master's awarded. *Degree requirements:* For master's, comprehensive exam (for some programs), thesis or alternative. *Entrance requirements:* For master's, minimum GPA of 3.0. Additional exam requirements/recommendations for international students: Required—TOEFL (minimum score 500 paper-based; 61 iBT). *Application deadline:* For fall admission, 8/1 priority date for domestic students. Applications are processed on a rolling basis. Application fee: $50 ($70 for international students). Electronic applications accepted. *Financial support:* Application deadline: 2/1. *Unit head:* Dr. Dawn Del Carlo, Coordinator, 319-273-3296, Fax: 319-273-7140, E-mail: sciedgradcoord@uni.edu. *Application contact:* Laurie S. Russell, Record Analyst, 319-273-2623, Fax: 319-273-2885, E-mail: laurie.russell@uni.edu.
Website: http://www.uni.edu/science-ed/.

University of North Texas Health Science Center at Fort Worth, Graduate School of Biomedical Sciences, Fort Worth, TX 76107-2699. Offers anatomy and cell biology (MS, PhD); biochemistry and molecular biology (MS, PhD); biomedical sciences (MS, PhD); biotechnology (MS); forensic genetics (MS); integrative physiology (MS, PhD); medical science (MS); microbiology and immunology (MS, PhD); pharmacology (MS, PhD); science education (MS); DO/MS; DO/PhD. Terminal master's awarded for partial completion of doctoral program. *Degree requirements:* For master's, thesis; for doctorate, thesis/dissertation. *Entrance requirements:* For master's and doctorate, GRE General Test. Additional exam requirements/recommendations for international students: Required—TOEFL. *Expenses:* Contact institution. *Faculty research:* Alzheimer's disease, aging, eye diseases, cancer, cardiovascular disease.

University of Oklahoma, Jeannine Rainbolt College of Education, Department of Instructional Leadership and Academic Curriculum, Norman, OK 73072. Offers communication, culture and pedagogy for Hispanic populations in educational settings (Graduate Certificate); instructional leadership and academic curriculum (M Ed, PhD), including bilingual education (PhD), early childhood education, elementary education, English education, instructional leadership, mathematics education, reading education, science education, science, technology, engineering and mathematics education (M Ed), secondary education, social studies education, teacher education (M Ed), world language education (M Ed). *Accreditation:* NCATE. Part-time and evening/weekend programs available. Postbaccalaureate distance learning degree programs offered (no on-campus study). *Faculty:* 22 full-time (15 women), 1 (woman) part-time/adjunct. *Students:* 64 full-time (49 women), 103 part-time (81 women); includes 33 minority (8 Black or African American, non-Hispanic/Latino; 9 American Indian or Alaska Native, non-Hispanic/Latino; 5 Asian, non-Hispanic/Latino; 4 Hispanic/Latino; 1 Native Hawaiian or other Pacific Islander, non-Hispanic/Latino; 6 Two or more races, non-Hispanic/Latino), 10 international. Average age 34. 50 applicants, 84% accepted, 36 enrolled. In 2013, 26 master's, 11 doctorates awarded. Terminal master's awarded for partial completion of doctoral program. *Degree requirements:* For master's, comprehensive exam (for some programs), thesis (for some programs); for doctorate, comprehensive exam, thesis/dissertation. *Entrance requirements:* For master's, essay; for doctorate, GRE, 3 recommendation letters; autobiography, statement of objectives; essay on chosen major; transcripts; writing sample. Additional exam requirements/recommendations for international students: Required—TOEFL (minimum score 79 iBT). *Application deadline:* For fall admission, 4/30 for domestic and international students; for spring admission, 10/31 for domestic and international students; for summer admission, 3/15 for domestic and international students. Applications are processed on a rolling basis. Application fee: $50 ($100 for international students). Electronic applications accepted. *Expenses:* Tuition, state resident: full-time $4205; part-time $175.20 per credit hour. Tuition, nonresident: full-time $16,205; part-time $675.20 per credit hour. *Required fees:* $2745; $103.85 per credit hour. $126.50 per semester. *Financial support:* In 2013–14, 98 students received support, including 10 research assistantships with partial tuition reimbursements available (averaging $10,671 per year), 7 teaching assistantships with partial tuition reimbursements available (averaging $10,753 per year); Federal Work-Study, institutionally sponsored loans, scholarships/grants, and unspecified assistantships also available. Support available to part-time students. Financial award application deadline: 6/1; financial award applicants required to submit FAFSA. *Total annual research expenditures:* $1 million. *Unit head:* Dr. Stacy Reeder, Chair/Graduate Liaison, 405-325-1498, Fax: 405-325-4061, E-mail: reeder@ou.edu. *Application contact:* Lynn Crussel, Graduate Programs Officer, 405-325-1498, Fax: 405-325-4061, E-mail: lcrussel@ou.edu.
Website: http://education.ou.edu/departments/ilac.

University of Pennsylvania, Graduate School of Education, Medical Educators Program, Philadelphia, PA 19104. Offers MS Ed, Certificate. Program offered jointly with Perelman School of Medicine and The Children's Hospital of Philadelphia. *Students:* 21 part-time (13 women); includes 3 minority (1 Black or African American, non-Hispanic/Latino; 1 Asian, non-Hispanic/Latino; 1 Two or more races, non-Hispanic/Latino). 8 applicants, 75% accepted, 5 enrolled. *Unit head:* Dr. Andrew Porter, Dean, 215-898-7014. *Application contact:* Alyssa D'Alconzo, Associate Director, Admissions, 215-898-6415, Fax: 215-746-6884, E-mail: admissions@gse.upenn.edu.
Website: http://www.gse.upenn.edu/med-ed/.

University of Phoenix–Online Campus, College of Education, Phoenix, AZ 85034-7209. Offers administration and supervision (MAEd, Certificate); adult education and training (MAEd); curriculum and instruction (MAEd), including computer education, curriculum and instruction, English as a second language, language arts, mathematics, reading; early childhood education (MAEd); educational studies (MAEd); elementary teacher education (MAEd), including early childhood, elementary teacher education, high school middle level, middle level; principal licensure (Certificate); secondary teacher education (MAEd); special education (MAEd, Certificate); teacher education (MAEd), including middle level generalist; teacher education middle level mathematics (MAEd), including middle level mathematics; teacher education middle level science (MAEd), including middle level science; teacher education secondary mathematics (MAEd); teacher education secondary science (MAEd); teacher leadership (MAEd); teachers of English learners (Certificate); transition to teaching (Certificate), including elementary education, secondary education. *Accreditation:* Teacher Education Accreditation Council. Evening/weekend programs available. Postbaccalaureate distance learning degree programs offered. *Entrance requirements:* Additional exam requirements/recommendations for international students: Required—TOEFL, TOEIC (Test of English as an International Communication), Berlitz Online English Proficiency Exam, PTE, or IELTS. Electronic applications accepted. *Expenses:* Contact institution.

University of Pittsburgh, School of Education, Department of Instruction and Learning, Program in Secondary Education, Pittsburgh, PA 15260. Offers English/communications education (M Ed, MAT); foreign languages education (M Ed, MAT); mathematics education (M Ed, MAT, Ed D); science education (M Ed, MAT, Ed D); secondary education (PhD); social studies education (M Ed, MAT). Part-time and evening/weekend programs available. *Students:* 116 full-time (78 women), 47 part-time (36 women); includes 16 minority (4 Black or African American, non-Hispanic/Latino; 3 Asian, non-Hispanic/Latino; 5 Hispanic/Latino; 4 Two or more races, non-Hispanic/Latino), 29 international. Average age 30. 279 applicants, 66% accepted, 91 enrolled. In 2013, 113 master's, 8 doctorates awarded. *Degree requirements:* For master's, thesis; for

doctorate, thesis/dissertation. *Entrance requirements:* For master's, PRAXIS I; for doctorate, GRE General Test. Additional exam requirements/recommendations for international students: Required—TOEFL. *Application deadline:* For fall admission, 2/1 priority date for domestic students; for spring admission, 11/15 priority date for domestic students. Applications are processed on a rolling basis. Application fee: $50. Electronic applications accepted. *Expenses:* Tuition, state resident: full-time $19,964; part-time $807 per credit. Tuition, nonresident: full-time $32,686; part-time $1337 per credit. *Required fees:* $740; $200. Tuition and fees vary according to program. *Financial support:* Fellowships, teaching assistantships, career-related internships or fieldwork, Federal Work-Study, tuition waivers (partial), and unspecified assistantships available. Support available to part-time students. Financial award application deadline: 3/15; financial award applicants required to submit FAFSA. *Unit head:* Dr. Richard Donato, Chairman, 412-624-7248, Fax: 412-648-7081, E-mail: donato@pitt.edu. *Application contact:* Marianne L. Budziszewski, Director of Admissions and Enrollment Services, 412-648-2230, Fax: 412-648-1899, E-mail: soeinfo@pitt.edu.
Website: http://www.education.pitt.edu/.

University of Puerto Rico, Río Piedras Campus, College of Education, Program in Curriculum and Teaching, San Juan, PR 00931-3300. Offers biology education (M Ed); chemistry education (M Ed); curriculum and teaching (Ed D); history education (M Ed); mathematics education (M Ed); physics education (M Ed); Spanish education (M Ed). Part-time programs available. *Degree requirements:* For master's, thesis; for doctorate, thesis/dissertation, internship. *Entrance requirements:* For master's, PAEG or GRE, minimum GPA of 3.0, letter of recommendation; for doctorate, GRE or PAEG, master's degree, minimum GPA of 3.0, letter of recommendation (2), interview. *Faculty research:* Curriculum, math teaching.

University of St. Francis, College of Education, Joliet, IL 60435-6169. Offers educational leadership (MS, Ed D); elementary education (M Ed); higher education (MS); reading (MS); secondary education (M Ed), including English education, math education, science education, social studies education, visual arts education; special education (M Ed); teaching and learning (MS). *Accreditation:* NCATE. Part-time and evening/weekend programs available. Postbaccalaureate distance learning degree programs offered (no on-campus study). *Faculty:* 10 full-time (8 women), 34 part-time/adjunct (25 women). *Students:* 14 full-time (13 women), 250 part-time (183 women); includes 34 minority (20 Black or African American, non-Hispanic/Latino; 1 American Indian or Alaska Native, non-Hispanic/Latino; 13 Hispanic/Latino), 1 international. Average age 36. 133 applicants, 62% accepted, 71 enrolled. In 2013, 147 master's awarded. *Degree requirements:* For doctorate, thesis/dissertation. *Entrance requirements:* For doctorate, master's degree, IL Type 75 or Principal's endorsement, interview, minimum undergraduate GPA of 3.0, professional portfolio, letter of recommendation. Additional exam requirements/recommendations for international students: Required—TOEFL (minimum score 550 paper-based; 79 iBT), IELTS (minimum score 6.5). *Application deadline:* Applications are processed on a rolling basis. Application fee: $30. Electronic applications accepted. Application fee is waived when completed online. *Expenses:* Contact institution. *Financial support:* In 2013–14, 10 students received support. Scholarships/grants, tuition waivers (partial), and unspecified assistantships available. Support available to part-time students. Financial award applicants required to submit FAFSA. *Unit head:* Dr. John Gambro, Dean, 815-740-3829, Fax: 815-740-2264, E-mail: jgambro@stfrancis.edu. *Application contact:* Sandra Sloka, Director of Admissions for Graduate and Degree Completion Programs, 800-735-7500, Fax: 815-740-3431, E-mail: ssloka@stfrancis.edu.
Website: http://www.stfrancis.edu/academics/college-of-education/.

University of South Africa, College of Human Sciences, Pretoria, South Africa. Offers adult education (M Ed); African languages (MA, PhD); African politics (MA, PhD); Afrikaans (MA, PhD); ancient history (MA, PhD); ancient Near Eastern studies (MA, PhD); anthropology (MA, PhD); applied linguistics (MA); Arabic (MA, PhD); archaeology (MA); art history (MA); Biblical archaeology (MA); Biblical studies (M Th, D Th, PhD); Christian spirituality (M Th, D Th); church history (M Th, D Th); classical studies (MA, PhD); clinical psychology (MA); communication (MA, PhD); comparative education (M Ed, Ed D); consulting psychology (D Admin, D Com, PhD); curriculum studies (M Ed, Ed D); development studies (M Admin, MA, D Admin, PhD); didactics (M Ed, Ed D); education (M Tech); education management (M Ed, Ed D); educational psychology (M Ed); English (MA); environmental education (M Ed); French (MA, PhD); German (MA, PhD); Greek (MA); guidance and counseling (M Ed); health studies (MA, PhD), including health sciences education (MA), health services management (MA), medical and surgical nursing science (critical care general) (MA), midwifery and neonatal nursing science (MA), trauma and emergency care (MA); history (MA, PhD); history of education (Ed D); inclusive education (M Ed, Ed D); information and communications technology policy and regulation (MA); information science (MA, MIS, PhD); international politics (MA, PhD); Islamic studies (MA, PhD); Italian (MA, PhD); Judaica (MA, PhD); linguistics (MA, PhD); mathematical education (M Ed); mathematics education (MA); missiology (M Th, D Th); modern Hebrew (MA, PhD); musicology (MA, MMus, D Mus, PhD); natural science education (M Ed); New Testament (M Th, D Th); Old Testament (D Th); pastoral therapy (M Th, D Th); philosophy (MA); philosophy of education (M Ed, Ed D); politics (MA, PhD); Portuguese (MA, PhD); practical theology (M Th, D Th); psychology (MA, MS, PhD); psychology of education (M Ed, Ed D); public health (MA); religious studies (MA, D Th, PhD); Romance languages (MA); Russian (MA, PhD); Semitic languages (MA, PhD); social behavior studies in HIV/AIDS (MA); social science (mental health) (MA); social science in development studies (MA); social science in psychology (MA); social science in social work (MA); social science in sociology (MA); social work (MSW, DSW, PhD); socio-education (M Ed, Ed D); sociolinguistics (MA); sociology (MA, PhD); Spanish (MA, PhD); systematic theology (M Th, D Th); TESOL (teaching English to speakers of other languages) (MA); theological ethics (M Th, D Th); theory of literature (MA, PhD); urban ministries (D Th); urban ministry (M Th).

University of South Africa, Institute for Science and Technology Education, Pretoria, South Africa. Offers mathematics, science and technology education (M Sc, PhD).

University of South Alabama, Graduate School, College of Education, Department of Leadership and Teacher Education, Mobile, AL 36688-0002. Offers early childhood education (M Ed); educational administration (Ed S); educational leadership (M Ed); elementary education (M Ed); reading education (M Ed); science education (M Ed); secondary education (M Ed); special education (M Ed, Ed S). *Accreditation:* NCATE. Part-time programs available. *Faculty:* 17 full-time (11 women), 4 part-time/adjunct (all women). *Students:* 136 full-time (103 women), 78 part-time (67 women); includes 45 minority (40 Black or African American, non-Hispanic/Latino; 2 Asian, non-Hispanic/Latino; 1 Hispanic/Latino; 2 Two or more races, non-Hispanic/Latino). 90 applicants, 53% accepted, 45 enrolled. In 2013, 69 master's awarded. *Degree requirements:* For master's, comprehensive exam. *Entrance requirements:* For master's, GRE General Test or MAT, minimum GPA of 3.0. *Application deadline:* For fall admission, 7/15 priority date for domestic students, 6/15 priority date for international students; for spring admission, 12/1 priority date for domestic students, 11/1 priority date for international students. Applications are processed on a rolling basis. Application fee: $35. *Expenses:* Tuition, state resident: full-time $8976; part-time $374 per credit hour. Tuition, nonresident: full-time $17,952; part-time $748 per credit hour. *Financial support:* Research assistantships and career-related internships or fieldwork available. Support available to part-time students. Financial award application deadline: 4/1. *Unit head:* Dr. Harold Dodge, Jr., Chair, 251-380-2894. *Application contact:* Dr. Abigail Baxter, Director of Graduate Studies, 251-380-2738, Fax: 251-380-2748, E-mail: abaxter@southalabama.edu.
Website: http://www.southalabama.edu/coe/lted.

University of South Carolina, The Graduate School, College of Arts and Sciences, Department of Biological Sciences, Columbia, SC 29208. Offers biology (MS, PhD); biology education (IMA, MAT); ecology, evolution and organismal biology (MS, PhD); molecular, cellular, and developmental biology (MS, PhD). IMA and MAT offered in cooperation with the College of Education. Terminal master's awarded for partial completion of doctoral program. *Degree requirements:* For master's, one foreign language, thesis (for some programs); for doctorate, one foreign language, thesis/dissertation. *Entrance requirements:* For master's and doctorate, GRE General Test, minimum GPA of 3.0 in science. Electronic applications accepted. *Faculty research:* Marine ecology, population and evolutionary biology, molecular biology and genetics, development.

University of South Carolina, The Graduate School, College of Arts and Sciences, Department of Geography, Columbia, SC 29208. Offers geography (MA, MS, PhD); geography education (IMA). IMA and MAT offered in cooperation with the College of Education. Part-time programs available. *Degree requirements:* For master's, comprehensive exam, thesis (for some programs); for doctorate, comprehensive exam, thesis/dissertation. *Entrance requirements:* For master's, GRE General Test; for doctorate, GRE General Test, master's degree. Electronic applications accepted. *Faculty research:* Geographic information processing; economic, cultural, physical, and environmental geography.

University of South Carolina, The Graduate School, College of Education, Department of Instruction and Teacher Education, Program in Secondary Education, Columbia, SC 29208. Offers art education (IMA, MAT); business education (IMA, MAT); English (MAT); foreign language (MAT); health education (MAT); mathematics (MAT); science (IMA, MAT); secondary (Ed D); secondary education (MT, PhD); social studies (MAT); theatre and speech (MAT). IMA and MT offered jointly with the subject areas. *Accreditation:* NCATE. *Degree requirements:* For master's, comprehensive exam, thesis (for some programs), foreign language (MA); for doctorate, one foreign language, comprehensive exam, thesis/dissertation. *Entrance requirements:* For master's, GRE General Test or MAT, teaching certificate (IMA, M Ed), interview; for doctorate, GRE General Test or MAT, interview. *Faculty research:* Middle school programs, professional development, school collaboration.

University of Southern Mississippi, Graduate School, College of Science and Technology, Center for Science and Mathematics Education, Hattiesburg, MS 39406-0001. Offers MS, PhD. Part-time programs available. *Faculty:* 1 full-time (0 women), 1 (woman) part-time/adjunct. *Students:* 12 full-time (7 women), 28 part-time (18 women); includes 12 minority (9 Black or African American, non-Hispanic/Latino; 1 Asian, non-Hispanic/Latino; 1 Hispanic/Latino; 1 Two or more races, non-Hispanic/Latino), 5 international. Average age 37. 7 applicants, 100% accepted, 5 enrolled. In 2013, 2 master's, 10 doctorates awarded. *Degree requirements:* For master's, comprehensive exam, thesis or alternative; for doctorate, comprehensive exam, thesis/dissertation. *Entrance requirements:* For master's, GRE General Test, minimum GPA of 2.75 in last 60 hours; for doctorate, GRE General Test, minimum GPA of 3.5. Additional exam requirements/recommendations for international students: Required—TOEFL, IELTS. *Application deadline:* For fall admission, 3/15 priority date for domestic students, 3/15 for international students; for spring admission, 1/10 priority date for domestic and international students. Applications are processed on a rolling basis. Application fee: $50. *Financial support:* In 2013–14, 1 fellowship with full tuition reimbursement (averaging $21,000 per year), 1 research assistantship with full tuition reimbursement (averaging $14,500 per year), 8 teaching assistantships with full tuition reimbursements (averaging $8,400 per year) were awarded; Federal Work-Study, scholarships/grants, health care benefits, and unspecified assistantships also available. Financial award application deadline: 3/15; financial award applicants required to submit FAFSA. *Unit head:* Dr. Sherry Herron, Director, 601-266-4739, Fax: 601-266-4741. *Application contact:* Shonna Breland, Manager of Graduate School Admissions, 601-266-6567, Fax: 601-266-5138.
Website: http://www.usm.edu/graduateschool/table.php.

University of South Florida, College of Education, Department of Secondary Education, Tampa, FL 33620-9951. Offers English education (M Ed, MA, MAT, PhD); foreign language education/ESOL (M Ed, MA, MAT); instructional technology (M Ed, PhD, Ed S); mathematics education (M Ed, MA, MAT, PhD, Ed S); science education (M Ed, MA, MAT, PhD); second language acquisition/instructional technology (PhD); secondary education (M Ed, PhD); secondary education/TESOL (M Ed); social science education (M Ed, MA, MAT); teaching and learning in the content area (PhD). *Accreditation:* NCATE. Part-time and evening/weekend programs available. *Degree requirements:* For master's, variable foreign language requirement, comprehensive exam, project (for some programs); for doctorate, variable foreign language requirement, comprehensive exam, thesis/dissertation, philosophies of inquiry; multiple research methods. *Entrance requirements:* For master's, GRE General Test or General Knowledge Test, minimum GPA of 3.0; for doctorate, GRE General Test, minimum GPA of 3.5; for Ed S, GRE General Test. Additional exam requirements/recommendations for international students: Required—TOEFL (minimum score 550 paper-based; 79 iBT). Electronic applications accepted. *Faculty research:* English language learners/multicultural, social science education, mathematics education, science education, instructional technology.

University of South Florida–St. Petersburg Campus, College of Education, St. Petersburg, FL 33701. Offers educational leadership development (M Ed); elementary education (MA), including math/science; English education (MA); middle grades STEM education (MS); reading education (MA). Part-time programs available. *Degree requirements:* For master's, comprehensive exam, practicum, internship, comprehensive portfolio. *Entrance requirements:* For master's, State of Florida General Knowledge Test (GKT), Florida Teaching Certificate (for non-initial certification programs), letters of recommendation. Additional exam requirements/recommendations for international students: Required—TOEFL (minimum score 550 paper-based; 79 iBT); Recommended—IELTS. Electronic applications accepted.

The University of Tennessee, Graduate School, College of Education, Health and Human Sciences, Program in Education, Knoxville, TN 37996. Offers art education (MS); counseling education (PhD); cultural studies in education (PhD); curriculum (MS, Ed S); curriculum, educational research and evaluation (Ed D, PhD); early childhood education (PhD); early childhood special education (MS); education of deaf and hard of hearing (MS); educational administration and policy studies (Ed D, PhD); educational administration and supervision (Ed S); educational psychology (Ed D, PhD); elementary education (MS, Ed S); elementary teaching (MS); English education (MS, Ed S); exercise science (PhD); foreign language/ESL education (MS, Ed S); instructional technology (MS, Ed D, PhD, Ed S); literacy, language and ESL education (PhD); literacy, language education, and ESL education (Ed D); mathematics education (MS, Ed S); modified and comprehensive special education (MS); reading education (MS, Ed S); school counseling (Ed S); school psychology (PhD, Ed S); science education

(MS, Ed S); secondary teaching (MS); social foundations (MS); social science education (MS, Ed S); socio-cultural foundations of sports and education (PhD); special education (Ed S); teacher education (Ed D, PhD). *Accreditation:* NCATE. Part-time and evening/weekend programs available. *Degree requirements:* For master's and Ed S, thesis optional; for doctorate, variable foreign language requirement, thesis/dissertation. *Entrance requirements:* For master's, minimum GPA of 2.7; for doctorate and Ed S, GRE General Test, minimum GPA of 2.7. Additional exam requirements/recommendations for international students: Required—TOEFL. Electronic applications accepted. *Expenses:* Tuition, state resident: full-time $9540; part-time $531 per credit hour. Tuition, nonresident: full-time $27,728; part-time $1542 per credit hour. *Required fees:* $1404; $67 per credit hour.

The University of Texas at Dallas, School of Natural Sciences and Mathematics, Department of Science/Mathematics Education, Richardson, TX 75080. Offers mathematics education (MAT); science education (MAT). Part-time and evening/weekend programs available. Postbaccalaureate distance learning degree programs offered (minimal on-campus study). *Faculty:* 6 full-time (2 women). *Students:* 10 full-time (6 women), 27 part-time (19 women); includes 15 minority (3 Black or African American, non-Hispanic/Latino; 8 Asian, non-Hispanic/Latino; 3 Hispanic/Latino; 1 Two or more races, non-Hispanic/Latino). Average age 34. 27 applicants, 56% accepted, 11 enrolled. In 2013, 16 master's awarded. *Degree requirements:* For master's, thesis optional. *Entrance requirements:* For master's, GRE General Test, minimum GPA of 3.0 in upper-level coursework in field. Additional exam requirements/recommendations for international students: Required—TOEFL (minimum score 550 paper-based). *Application deadline:* For fall admission, 7/15 for domestic students, 5/1 priority date for international students; for spring admission, 11/15 for domestic students, 9/1 priority date for international students. Applications are processed on a rolling basis. Application fee: $50 ($100 for international students). Electronic applications accepted. *Expenses:* Tuition, state resident: full-time $11,940; part-time $663.33 per credit hour. Tuition, nonresident: full-time $21,606; part-time $1200.33 per credit hour. *Financial support:* In 2013–14, 27 students received support. Research assistantships with partial tuition reimbursements available, teaching assistantships with partial tuition reimbursements available, career-related internships or fieldwork, Federal Work-Study, institutionally sponsored loans, scholarships/grants, and unspecified assistantships available. Support available to part-time students. Financial award application deadline: 4/30; financial award applicants required to submit FAFSA. *Faculty research:* Innovative science/math education programs. *Unit head:* Dr. Mary L. Urquhart, Department Head, 972-883-2499, Fax: 972-883-6796, E-mail: scimathed@utdallas.edu. *Application contact:* Barbara Curry, Advisor, 972-883-4008, Fax: 972-883-6796, E-mail: barbc@utdallas.edu.
Website: http://www.utdallas.edu/scimathed/.

The University of Texas at El Paso, Graduate School, College of Science, Master of Arts in Teaching Science Program, El Paso, TX 79968-0001. Offers MAT. Part-time and evening/weekend programs available. *Degree requirements:* For master's, thesis optional. *Entrance requirements:* For master's, minimum GPA of 3.0. Additional exam requirements/recommendations for international students: Required—TOEFL; Recommended—IELTS. Electronic applications accepted.

The University of Texas–Pan American, College of Science and Mathematics, Department of Physics and Geology, Edinburg, TX 78539. Offers physics education (MSIS). *Degree requirements:* For master's, thesis optional. *Entrance requirements:* For master's, bachelor's degree, 16-18 hours of physics background. *Expenses:* Tuition, state resident: full-time $5986; part-time $333 per credit hour. Tuition, nonresident: full-time $12,358; part-time $687 per credit hour. *Required fees:* $782. Tuition and fees vary according to program. *Unit head:* Dr. Niklaos Dimakis, Interim Chair, 956-665-8761, E-mail: dimakis@utpa.edu. *Application contact:* Stephanie Ozuna, Graduate Recruiter, 956-665-3558, Fax: 956-665-2863, E-mail: ozunas@utpa.edu.
Website: http://portal.utpa.edu/utpa_main/daa_home/cosm_home/physics_home.

The University of Toledo, College of Graduate Studies, Judith Herb College of Education, Department of Curriculum and Instruction, Toledo, OH 43606-3390. Offers art education (ME); career and technical education (ME); career-technical education (Ed S); curriculum and instruction (ME, PhD, Ed S); early childhood education (PhD, Ed S); education and biology (MES); education and chemistry (MES); education and economics (MAE); education and English (MAE); education and French (MAE); education and geography (MAE); education and geology (MES); education and German (MAE); education and history (MAE); education and mathematics (MAE, MES); education and physics (MES); education and political science (MAE); education and sociology (MAE); education and Spanish (MAE); educational media (PhD); educational technology (ME); educational technology: virtual educator (Certificate); elementary education (PhD); English as a second language (MAE); gifted and talented (PhD); middle childhood education licensure (ME); music education (MME); secondary education (PhD); secondary education licensure (ME); special education (PhD, Ed S). *Accreditation:* NCATE. Part-time and evening/weekend programs available. *Faculty:* 41. *Students:* 53 full-time (30 women), 154 part-time (111 women); includes 21 minority (16 Black or African American, non-Hispanic/Latino; 4 Hispanic/Latino; 1 Two or more races, non-Hispanic/Latino), 21 international. Average age 34. 82 applicants, 79% accepted, 47 enrolled. In 2013, 80 master's, 5 doctorates awarded. *Degree requirements:* For master's, comprehensive exam, thesis or alternative; for doctorate, comprehensive exam, thesis/dissertation; for other advanced degree, thesis optional. *Entrance requirements:* For master's, doctorate, and other advanced degree, minimum cumulative GPA of 2.7 for all previous academic work, letters of recommendation. Additional exam requirements/recommendations for international students: Required—TOEFL (minimum score 550 paper-based; 80 iBT). *Application deadline:* For fall admission, 1/15 priority date for domestic and international students. Applications are processed on a rolling basis. Application fee: $45 ($75 for international students). Electronic applications accepted. *Financial support:* In 2013–14, 5 research assistantships with full and partial tuition reimbursements (averaging $13,200 per year), 11 teaching assistantships with full and partial tuition reimbursements (averaging $8,809 per year) were awarded; career-related internships or fieldwork, Federal Work-Study, institutionally sponsored loans, scholarships/grants, tuition waivers (full and partial), unspecified assistantships, and administrative assistantships also available. Support available to part-time students. *Unit head:* Dr. Joan Kaderavek, Chair, 419-530-5373, E-mail: eigh.chiarelott@utoledo.edu. *Application contact:* Graduate School Office, 419-530-4723, Fax: 419-530-4724, E-mail: grdsch@utnet.utoledo.edu.
Website: http://www.utoledo.edu/eduhshs/.

The University of Tulsa, Graduate School, College of Arts and Sciences, School of Urban Education, Program in Mathematics and Science Education, Tulsa, OK 74104-3189. Offers MSMSE. Part-time programs available. *Students:* 2 full-time (1 woman), 6 part-time (4 women), 1 international. Average age 31. 4 applicants, 100% accepted, 3 enrolled. In 2013, 1 master's awarded. *Entrance requirements:* For master's, GRE General Test. Additional exam requirements/recommendations for international students: Required—TOEFL (minimum score 577 paper-based), IELTS (minimum score 6.5). *Application deadline:* Applications are processed on a rolling basis. Application fee: $40. Electronic applications accepted. *Expenses: Tuition:* Full-time $19,566; part-time $1087 per credit hour. *Required fees:* $1690; $5 per credit hour. $160 per semester. Tuition and fees vary according to course load. *Financial support:* In 2013–14, 4 students received support, including 4 teaching assistantships with full and partial tuition reimbursements available (averaging $8,776 per year); fellowships with full and partial tuition reimbursements available, research assistantships, career-related internships or fieldwork, Federal Work-Study, scholarships/grants, health care benefits, tuition waivers (full and partial), and unspecified assistantships also available. Support available to part-time students. Financial award application deadline: 2/1; financial award applicants required to submit FAFSA. *Unit head:* Dr. Kara Gae Neal, Chair, 918-631-2238, Fax: 918-631-3721, E-mail: karagae-neal@utulsa.edu. *Application contact:* Dr. David Brown, Advisor, 918-631-2719, Fax: 918-631-2133, E-mail: david-brown@utulsa.edu.

University of Utah, Graduate School, College of Science, Department of Chemistry, Salt Lake City, UT 84112-0850. Offers chemistry (MS, PhD); science teacher education (MS). Part-time programs available. Postbaccalaureate distance learning degree programs offered. *Faculty:* 32 full-time (7 women), 9 part-time/adjunct (3 women). *Students:* 142 full-time (44 women), 26 part-time (8 women); includes 6 minority (1 Black or African American, non-Hispanic/Latino; 2 Asian, non-Hispanic/Latino; 2 Hispanic/Latino; 1 Two or more races, non-Hispanic/Latino), 49 international. Average age 27. 252 applicants, 39% accepted, 37 enrolled. In 2013, 28 master's, 27 doctorates awarded. Terminal master's awarded for partial completion of doctoral program. *Degree requirements:* For master's, thesis optional, 20 hours of course work, 10 hours of research; for doctorate, thesis/dissertation, 18 hours of course work, 14 hours of research. *Entrance requirements:* For master's and doctorate, GRE General Test, minimum GPA of 3.0. Additional exam requirements/recommendations for international students: Required—TOEFL (minimum score 620 paper-based; 105 iBT). *Application deadline:* For fall admission, 4/1 for domestic students, 2/1 for international students; for spring admission, 11/1 for domestic and international students. Application fee: $55 ($65 for international students). Electronic applications accepted. Application fee is waived when completed online. *Expenses:* Tuition, state resident: full-time $5259. Tuition, nonresident: full-time $18,569. *Required fees:* $841. Tuition and fees vary according to course load. *Financial support:* In 2013–14, 1 fellowship with tuition reimbursement (averaging $22,000 per year), 119 research assistantships with tuition reimbursements (averaging $22,500 per year), 55 teaching assistantships with tuition reimbursements (averaging $22,000 per year) were awarded; scholarships/grants and tuition waivers (full) also available. Financial award application deadline: 4/1; financial award applicants required to submit FAFSA. *Faculty research:* Analytical, biological, inorganic, materials, organic, physical and theoretical chemistry. *Total annual research expenditures:* $16.9 million. *Unit head:* Dr. Cynthia J. Burrows, Chair, 801-585-7290, Fax: 801-581-8433, E-mail: chair@chemistry.utah.edu. *Application contact:* Jo Hoovey, Graduate Coordinator, 801-581-4393, Fax: 801-581-5408, E-mail: jhoovey@chem.utah.edu.
Website: http://www.chem.utah.edu/.

University of Utah, Graduate School, College of Science, Department of Physics and Astronomy, Salt Lake City, UT 84112. Offers chemical physics (PhD); medical physics (MS, PhD); physics (MA, MS, PhD); physics teaching (PhD). Part-time programs available. *Faculty:* 32 full-time (4 women), 15 part-time/adjunct (0 women). *Students:* 76 full-time (23 women), 20 part-time (3 women); includes 6 minority (4 Asian, non-Hispanic/Latino; 2 Hispanic/Latino), 48 international. Average age 29. 141 applicants, 30% accepted, 17 enrolled. In 2013, 9 master's, 13 doctorates awarded. Terminal master's awarded for partial completion of doctoral program. *Degree requirements:* For master's, comprehensive exam (for some programs), thesis or alternative, teaching experience, departmental exam; for doctorate, comprehensive exam, thesis/dissertation, departmental qualifying exam. *Entrance requirements:* For master's and doctorate, GRE General Test, GRE Subject Test, minimum GPA of 3.0. Additional exam requirements/recommendations for international students: Required—TOEFL (minimum score 550 paper-based; 80 iBT). *Application deadline:* For fall admission, 4/1 priority date for domestic and international students. Applications are processed on a rolling basis. Application fee: $55 ($65 for international students). Electronic applications accepted. *Expenses:* Tuition, state resident: full-time $5259. Tuition, nonresident: full-time $18,569. *Required fees:* $841. Tuition and fees vary according to course load. *Financial support:* In 2013–14, 41 research assistantships with full tuition reimbursements (averaging $23,500 per year), 31 teaching assistantships with full tuition reimbursements (averaging $20,641 per year) were awarded; Federal Work-Study, institutionally sponsored loans, and scholarships/grants also available. Financial award application deadline: 2/15; financial award applicants required to submit FAFSA. *Faculty research:* High-energy, cosmic-ray, astrophysics, medical physics, condensed matter, relativity applied physics, biophysics, astronomy. *Total annual research expenditures:* $6.8 million. *Unit head:* Dr. Carleton DeTar, Chair, 801-581-3538, Fax: 801-581-4801, E-mail: detar@physics.utah.edu. *Application contact:* Jackie Hadley, Graduate Secretary, 801-581-6861, Fax: 801-581-4801, E-mail: jackie@physics.utah.edu.
Website: http://www.physics.utah.edu/.

University of Vermont, Graduate College, College of Arts and Sciences, Department of Biology, Burlington, VT 05405. Offers biology (MS, PhD); biology education (MST). *Faculty:* 17. *Students:* 38 (18 women); includes 4 minority (1 Asian, non-Hispanic/Latino; 3 Hispanic/Latino), 11 international. 55 applicants, 24% accepted, 8 enrolled. In 2013, 3 master's, 3 doctorates awarded. *Degree requirements:* For master's, thesis; for doctorate, thesis/dissertation. *Entrance requirements:* For master's and doctorate, GRE General Test. Additional exam requirements/recommendations for international students: Required—TOEFL (minimum score 550 paper-based; 80 iBT). *Application deadline:* For fall admission, 12/15 priority date for domestic students, 12/15 for international students. Applications are processed on a rolling basis. Application fee: $65. Electronic applications accepted. *Financial support:* Fellowships, research assistantships, and teaching assistantships available. Financial award application deadline: 3/1. *Unit head:* Dr. Jim Vigoreaux, Chairperson, 802-656-2922. *Application contact:* Dr. Judith Van Houten, Coordinator, 802-656-2922.

University of Victoria, Faculty of Graduate Studies, Faculty of Education, Department of Curriculum and Instruction, Victoria, BC V8W 2Y2, Canada. Offers art education (M Ed, PhD); curriculum studies (M Ed, MA, PhD); early childhood education (M Ed, PhD); educational studies (PhD); language and literacy (M Ed, MA, PhD); mathematics (M Ed, MA, PhD); music education (M Ed, MA, PhD); science (M Ed, MA, PhD); social studies (M Ed, MA); social, cultural and foundational studies (MA, PhD); technology and environmental education (PhD). Part-time programs available. *Degree requirements:* For master's, thesis, project (M Ed); for doctorate, comprehensive exam, thesis/dissertation. *Entrance requirements:* For master's, minimum B average. Additional exam requirements/recommendations for international students: Required—TOEFL (minimum score 575 paper-based), IELTS (minimum score 7). Electronic applications accepted. *Faculty research:* Elementary and secondary English, language arts, curriculum theory and practice, educational media and technology, educational administration and leadership, history and philosophy of education.

University of Virginia, College and Graduate School of Arts and Sciences, Department of Physics, Charlottesville, VA 22903. Offers physics (MA, MS, PhD); physics education (MAPE). *Faculty:* 31 full-time (3 women). *Students:* 91 full-time (18 women); includes 4 minority (all Asian, non-Hispanic/Latino), 65 international. Average age 26. 223 applicants, 33% accepted, 22 enrolled. In 2013, 9 master's, 9 doctorates awarded. *Degree requirements:* For master's, thesis (for some programs); for doctorate,

comprehensive exam, thesis/dissertation. *Entrance requirements:* For master's and doctorate, GRE General Test, GRE Subject Test, 2 or more letters of recommendation. Additional exam requirements/recommendations for international students: Required—TOEFL (minimum score 600 paper-based; 90 iBT), IELTS. *Application deadline:* For fall admission, 1/7 for domestic and international students. Applications are processed on a rolling basis. Application fee: $60. Electronic applications accepted. *Expenses:* Tuition, state resident: part-time $334 per credit hour. Tuition, nonresident: part-time $1224 per credit hour. *Financial support:* Fellowships, research assistantships, and teaching assistantships available. Financial award applicants required to submit FAFSA. *Unit head:* Joe Poon, Chair, 434-924-3781, Fax: 434-924-4576, E-mail: phys-chair@physics.virginia.edu. *Application contact:* Nilanga Liyanage, Director of Graduate Studies, 434-924-3781, Fax: 434-924-4576, E-mail: grad-info-request@physics.virginia.edu.
Website: http://www.phys.virginia.edu/.

University of Virginia, Curry School of Education, Department of Curriculum, Instruction, and Special Education, Program in Curriculum and Instruction, Charlottesville, VA 22903. Offers curriculum and instruction (M Ed, Ed S); elementary education (M Ed, Ed D); English (M Ed, Ed D); foreign language (M Ed); mathematics (M Ed, Ed D); reading (M Ed, Ed D, Ed S); science (Ed D); social studies (M Ed). *Students:* 42 full-time (30 women), 37 part-time (32 women); includes 4 minority (1 Black or African American, non-Hispanic/Latino; 2 Hispanic/Latino; 1 Two or more races, non-Hispanic/Latino), 1 international. Average age 31. 76 applicants, 74% accepted, 39 enrolled. In 2013, 84 master's, 3 doctorates, 23 other advanced degrees awarded. *Degree requirements:* For master's, comprehensive exam (for some programs); for doctorate, comprehensive exam, thesis/dissertation; for Ed S, comprehensive exam. *Entrance requirements:* For master's, doctorate, and Ed S, GRE General Test, 2 letters of recommendation. Additional exam requirements/recommendations for international students: Required—TOEFL (minimum score 600 paper-based; 90 iBT), IELTS (minimum score 7). *Application deadline:* Applications are processed on a rolling basis. Application fee: $60. Electronic applications accepted. *Expenses:* Tuition, state resident: part-time $334 per credit hour. Tuition, nonresident: part-time $1224 per credit hour. *Financial support:* Fellowships with tuition reimbursements, research assistantships with tuition reimbursements, and teaching assistantships with tuition reimbursements available. Financial award application deadline: 1/5; financial award applicants required to submit FAFSA. *Unit head:* Stephanie van Hover, Chair, 434-924-0841, E-mail: sdv2w@virginia.edu. *Application contact:* Karen Dwier, Information Contact, 434-924-0831, E-mail: kgd9g@virginia.edu.
Website: http://curry.virginia.edu/academics/areas-of-study/curriculum-teaching-learning.

University of Virginia, Curry School of Education, Program in Education, Charlottesville, VA 22903. Offers administration and supervision (PhD); applied developmental science (PhD); counselor education (PhD); curriculum and instruction (PhD); early childhood special education (MT); education evaluation (PhD); educational psychology (PhD); educational research (PhD); elementary education (MT); English education (MT, PhD); foreign language education (MT); higher education (PhD); instructional technology (PhD); kinesiology (MT, PhD); math education (PhD); reading education (PhD); research, statistics and evaluation (PhD); school psychology (PhD); science education (PhD); social studies education (MT, PhD); special education (PhD); world languages education (MT). *Students:* 474 full-time (379 women), 35 part-time (19 women); includes 89 minority (30 Black or African American, non-Hispanic/Latino; 1 American Indian or Alaska Native, non-Hispanic/Latino; 26 Asian, non-Hispanic/Latino; 19 Hispanic/Latino; 13 Two or more races, non-Hispanic/Latino), 21 international. Average age 26. 312 applicants, 49% accepted, 80 enrolled. In 2013, 137 master's, 38 doctorates awarded. *Degree requirements:* For master's, comprehensive exam (for some programs), field project; for doctorate, comprehensive exam, thesis/dissertation. *Entrance requirements:* For doctorate, GRE General Test. Additional exam requirements/recommendations for international students: Required—TOEFL (minimum score 600 paper-based; 90 iBT), IELTS (minimum score 7). *Application deadline:* Applications are processed on a rolling basis. Application fee: $60. Electronic applications accepted. *Expenses:* Tuition, state resident: part-time $334 per credit hour. Tuition, nonresident: part-time $1224 per credit hour. *Financial support:* Fellowships, research assistantships, and teaching assistantships available. Financial award application deadline: 1/5; financial award applicants required to submit FAFSA. *Unit head:* Robert C. Pianta, Dean, 434-924-3334, E-mail: pianta@virginia.edu. *Application contact:* Office of Admissions and Student Services, 434-924-0742, E-mail: curry-admissions@virginia.edu.
Website: http://curry.virginia.edu/teacher-education.

University of Washington, Graduate School, College of Education, Seattle, WA 98195. Offers curriculum and instruction (M Ed, Ed D, PhD), including educational technology, general curriculum (Ed D, PhD), language, literacy, and culture, mathematics education, multicultural education, reading and language arts education (Ed D), science education, social studies education, teaching and curriculum (M Ed); educational leadership and policy studies (M Ed, Ed D, PhD), including administration (Ed D), educational policy, organization, and leadership (M Ed, PhD), higher education, leadership for learning (Ed D), social and cultural foundations of education (M Ed, PhD); educational psychology (M Ed, PhD), including educational psychology (PhD), human development and cognition (M Ed), learning sciences, measurement, statistics and research design (M Ed), school psychology (M Ed); instructional leadership (M Ed); intercollegiate athletic leadership (M Ed); special education (M Ed, Ed D, PhD), including early childhood special education (M Ed), emotional and behavioral disabilities (M Ed), learning disabilities (M Ed), low-incidence disabilities (M Ed), severe disabilities (M Ed), special education (Ed D, PhD); teacher education (MIT). *Accreditation:* APA. Part-time and evening/weekend programs available. *Degree requirements:* For master's, thesis optional; for doctorate, thesis/dissertation. *Entrance requirements:* For master's and doctorate, GRE General Test, minimum GPA of 3.0. Additional exam requirements/recommendations for international students: Required—TOEFL. Electronic applications accepted. *Faculty research:* School restructuring/effective schools, special education interventions, literacy and writing, technology, school partnerships, teacher preparation.

University of Washington, Graduate School, Interdisciplinary Program in Biology for Teachers, Seattle, WA 98195. Offers MS. Part-time programs available. *Degree requirements:* For master's, research project and oral exam. *Entrance requirements:* For master's, GRE General Test, minimum GPA of 3.0, teaching certificate or professional teaching experience. Electronic applications accepted.

University of Washington, Tacoma, Graduate Programs, Program in Education, Tacoma, WA 98402-3100. Offers education (M Ed); educational administration (principal or program administrator certification) (M Ed); elementary education teacher certification (M Ed); elementary education/special education teacher certification (M Ed); secondary science or math teacher certification (M Ed). Part-time and evening/weekend programs available. *Degree requirements:* For master's, culminating project. *Entrance requirements:* For master's, WEST-B, WEST-E (teacher certification programs only), official sealed transcript from every college/university attended, personal goal statement, letters of recommendation, copy of valid teaching certificate. Additional exam requirements/recommendations for international students: Required—TOEFL (minimum score 580 paper-based; 92 iBT). Electronic applications accepted. *Faculty research:* Global learning communities for English/Chinese languages, evaluation of mathematics and reading intervention programs, response to intervention, school-wide behavioral and emotional support, mathematics education and culturally responsive mathematics education.

The University of West Alabama, School of Graduate Studies, College of Education, Departments of Instructional Leadership and Support/Curriculum and Instruction, Program in Secondary Education, Livingston, AL 35470. Offers biology (MAT); English language arts (MAT); history (MAT); mathematics (MAT); physical education (MAT); science (MAT); secondary education (M Ed); social science (MAT). Part-time and evening/weekend programs available. Postbaccalaureate distance learning degree programs offered (no on-campus study). *Faculty:* 20 full-time (4 women), 5 part-time/adjunct (2 women). *Students:* 210 (139 women); includes 86 minority (80 Black or African American, non-Hispanic/Latino; 2 Asian, non-Hispanic/Latino; 2 Hispanic/Latino; 2 Two or more races, non-Hispanic/Latino). 115 applicants, 86% accepted, 72 enrolled. In 2013, 61 master's awarded. *Degree requirements:* For master's, comprehensive exam, thesis optional. *Entrance requirements:* For master's, GRE General Test, MAT, minimum GPA of 2.75. Additional exam requirements/recommendations for international students: Required—TOEFL (minimum score 500 paper-based; 61 iBT). *Application deadline:* For fall admission, 8/12 priority date for domestic students; for spring admission, 3/24 for domestic students. Applications are processed on a rolling basis. Application fee: $25 ($50 for international students). Electronic applications accepted. Tuition and fees vary according to course load. *Financial support:* Teaching assistantships, career-related internships or fieldwork, Federal Work-Study, scholarships/grants, and unspecified assistantships available. Support available to part-time students. Financial award application deadline: 3/1; financial award applicants required to submit FAFSA. *Faculty research:* Integrated arts in the curriculum, moral development of children. *Unit head:* Dr. Esther Howard, Chair of Curriculum and Instruction, 205-652-3428, Fax: 205-652-3706, E-mail: ehoward@uwa.edu. *Application contact:* Dr. Kathy Chandler, Dean of Graduate Studies, 205-652-3421, Fax: 205-652-3706, E-mail: kchandler@uwa.edu.
Website: http://www.uwa.edu/highschool612.aspx.

University of West Florida, College of Arts and Sciences: Sciences, School of Allied Health and Life Sciences, Department of Biology, Pensacola, FL 32514-5750. Offers biological chemistry (MS); biology (MS); biology education (MST); biotechnology (MS); coastal zone studies (MS); environmental biology (MS). *Degree requirements:* For master's, thesis. *Entrance requirements:* For master's, GRE (minimum score: verbal 450, quantitative 550), official transcripts; BS in biology or related field; letter of interest; relevant past experience; three letters of recommendation from individuals who can evaluate applicant's academic ability. Additional exam requirements/recommendations for international students: Required—TOEFL (minimum score 550 paper-based).

University of West Florida, College of Professional Studies, Ed D Programs, Specialization in Curriculum and Instruction: Science and Social Sciences, Pensacola, FL 32514-5750. Offers Ed D. Part-time and evening/weekend programs available. *Degree requirements:* For doctorate, comprehensive exam, thesis/dissertation. *Entrance requirements:* For doctorate, GRE, MAT, or GMAT, letter of intent; writing sample; three letters of recommendation; two completed disposition assessment forms; written statement of goals; interview with admissions committee. Additional exam requirements/recommendations for international students: Required—TOEFL (minimum score 550 paper-based).

University of Wisconsin–Madison, Graduate School, School of Education, Department of Curriculum and Instruction, Madison, WI 53706-1380. Offers art education (MA); curriculum and instruction (MS, PhD); education and mathematics (MA); French education (MA); German education (MA); music education (MS); science education (MS); Spanish education (MA). *Accreditation:* NASM (one or more programs are accredited). *Degree requirements:* For doctorate, thesis/dissertation. Application fee: $56. *Expenses:* Tuition, state resident: full-time $10,728; part-time $790 per credit. Tuition, nonresident: full-time $24,054; part-time $1623 per credit. *Required fees:* $1130; $119 per credit. *Financial support:* Project assistantships available. *Unit head:* Dr. Beth Graue, Chair, 608-263-4600, E-mail: graue@education.wisc.edu. *Application contact:* 608-262-2433, Fax: 608-262-5134, E-mail: gradadmiss@mail.bascom.wisc.edu.
Website: http://www.education.wisc.edu/ci.

University of Wisconsin–River Falls, Outreach and Graduate Studies, College of Arts and Science, Program in Science, River Falls, WI 54022. Offers science education (MSE). Part-time programs available. *Degree requirements:* For master's, comprehensive exam, thesis or alternative. *Entrance requirements:* For master's, minimum GPA of 2.75. Additional exam requirements/recommendations for international students: Required—TOEFL (minimum score 500 paper-based; 65 iBT), IELTS (minimum score 5.5). Electronic applications accepted.

University of Wisconsin–Stevens Point, College of Letters and Science, Department of Biology, Stevens Point, WI 54481-3897. Offers MST. *Degree requirements:* For master's, thesis or alternative. *Entrance requirements:* For master's, minimum undergraduate GPA of 2.75 overall, 3.0 in biology; bachelor's degree; teacher's license.

University of Wyoming, College of Education, Science and Mathematics Teaching Center, Laramie, WY 82071. Offers MS, MST. *Degree requirements:* For master's, thesis. *Entrance requirements:* For master's, GRE General Test, minimum GPA of 3.0, writing sample, 3 letters of recommendation. Electronic applications accepted.

Ursuline College, School of Graduate Studies, Program in Education, Pepper Pike, OH 44124-4398. Offers art education (MA); early childhood education (MA); language arts education (MA); life science education (MA); math education (MA); middle school education (MA); social studies education (MA); special education (MA). *Accreditation:* NCATE. *Faculty:* 4 full-time (all women), 7 part-time/adjunct (5 women). *Students:* 18 full-time (16 women), 7 part-time (all women); includes 8 minority (4 Black or African American, non-Hispanic/Latino; 2 Asian, non-Hispanic/Latino; 2 Hispanic/Latino). Average age 34. 1 applicant, 100% accepted, 1 enrolled. In 2013, 25 master's awarded. *Degree requirements:* For master's, comprehensive exam. *Entrance requirements:* For master's, minimum undergraduate GPA of 3.0. Additional exam requirements/recommendations for international students: Required—TOEFL (minimum score 500 paper-based). *Application deadline:* For fall admission, 8/1 priority date for domestic students. Applications are processed on a rolling basis. Application fee: $25. *Expenses:* Contact institution. *Financial support:* In 2013–14, 1 student received support. Federal Work-Study available. Financial award application deadline: 3/1. *Unit head:* Dr. Edna West, Director, Master's Apprentice Program, 440-646-6134, Fax: 440-646-8328, E-mail: ewest@ursuline.edu. *Application contact:* Stephanie Pratt, Graduate Admission Coordinator, 440-646-8119, Fax: 440-684-6138, E-mail: graduateadmissions@ursuline.edu.

Vanderbilt University, Graduate School, Department of Physics and Astronomy, Nashville, TN 37240-1001. Offers astronomy (MS); health physics (MA); physics (MAT, MS, PhD). *Faculty:* 31 full-time (4 women). *Students:* 77 full-time (19 women); includes 14 minority (5 Black or African American, non-Hispanic/Latino; 1 Asian, non-Hispanic/Latino; 6 Hispanic/Latino; 2 Two or more races, non-Hispanic/Latino), 23 international.

Average age 27. 193 applicants, 16% accepted, 11 enrolled. In 2013, 7 master's, 11 doctorates awarded. *Degree requirements:* For master's, thesis; for doctorate, comprehensive exam, thesis/dissertation, final and qualifying exams. *Entrance requirements:* For master's, GRE General Test; for doctorate, GRE General Test, GRE Subject Test. Additional exam requirements/recommendations for international students: Required—TOEFL (minimum score 570 paper-based; 88 iBT). *Application deadline:* For fall admission, 1/15 for domestic and international students. Electronic applications accepted. *Financial support:* Fellowships with full and partial tuition reimbursements, research assistantships with full tuition reimbursements, teaching assistantships with full tuition reimbursements, career-related internships or fieldwork, Federal Work-Study, and institutionally sponsored loans available. Financial award application deadline: 1/15; financial award applicants required to submit CSS PROFILE or FAFSA. *Faculty research:* Experimental and theoretical physics, free electron laser, living-state physics, heavy-ion physics, nuclear structure. *Unit head:* Dr. Julia Velkovska, Director of Graduate Studies, 615-322-0656, Fax: 615-343-7263, E-mail: julia.velkovska@vanderbilt.edu. *Application contact:* Donald Pickert, Administrative Assistant, 615-343-1026, Fax: 615-343-7263, E-mail: donald.pickert@vanderbilt.edu. Website: http://www.vanderbilt.edu/physics/.

Wagner College, Division of Graduate Studies, Department of Education, Program in Secondary Education/Special Education, Staten Island, NY 10301-4495. Offers language arts (MS Ed); languages other than English (MS Ed); mathematics and technology (MS Ed); science and technology (MS Ed); social studies (MS Ed). Part-time and evening/weekend programs available. *Degree requirements:* For master's, thesis (for some programs). *Entrance requirements:* For master's, minimum GPA of 3.0, interview, recommendations. Electronic applications accepted. *Expenses: Tuition:* Full-time $17,496; part-time $972 per credit. Tuition and fees vary according to course load.

Walden University, Graduate Programs, Richard W. Riley College of Education and Leadership, Minneapolis, MN 55401. *Accreditation:* NCATE. Part-time and evening/weekend programs available. Postbaccalaureate distance learning degree programs offered (minimal on-campus study). *Faculty:* 23 full-time (15 women), 830 part-time/adjunct (569 women). *Students:* 8,671 full-time (7,197 women), 2,122 part-time (1,735 women); includes 4,734 minority (3,802 Black or African American, non-Hispanic/Latino; 50 American Indian or Alaska Native, non-Hispanic/Latino; 136 Asian, non-Hispanic/Latino; 539 Hispanic/Latino; 35 Native Hawaiian or other Pacific Islander, non-Hispanic/Latino; 172 Two or more races, non-Hispanic/Latino), 73 international. Average age 40. 2,646 applicants, 96% accepted, 2074 enrolled. In 2013, 2,214 master's, 354 doctorates, 479 other advanced degrees awarded. *Degree requirements:* For doctorate, thesis/dissertation (for some programs), residency; for other advanced degree, residency (for some programs). *Entrance requirements:* For master's, bachelor's degree or higher; minimum GPA of 2.5; official transcripts; goal statement (for some programs); access to computer and Internet; for doctorate, master's degree or higher; three years of related professional or academic experience (preferred); minimum GPA of 3.0; goal statement and current resume (select programs); official transcripts; access to computer and Internet; for other advanced degree, relevant work experience; access to computer and Internet. Additional exam requirements/recommendations for international students: Required—TOEFL (minimum score 550 paper-based; 79 iBT), IELTS (minimum score 6.5), Michigan English Language Assessment Battery (minimum score 82), or PTE. *Application deadline:* Applications are processed on a rolling basis. Application fee: $0. Electronic applications accepted. *Expenses: Tuition:* Full-time $11,813.55; part-time $500 per credit. *Required fees:* $618.76. *Financial support:* In 2013–14, 1 fellowship was awarded; Federal Work-Study, scholarships/grants, unspecified assistantships, and family tuition reduction, active duty/veteran tuition reduction, group tuition reduction, interest-free payment plans, employee tuition reduction also available. Support available to part-time students. Financial award applicants required to submit FAFSA. *Unit head:* Dr. Kate Steffens, Dean, 800-925-3368. *Application contact:* Jennifer Hall, Vice President of Enrollment Management, 866-4-WALDEN, E-mail: info@waldenu.edu. Website: http://www.waldenu.edu/colleges-schools/riley-college-of-education/.

Washington State University, Graduate School, College of Education, Department of Teaching and Learning, Program in Mathematics and Science Education, Pullman, WA 99164. Offers PhD. *Degree requirements:* For doctorate, comprehensive exam, thesis/dissertation, written and oral exam. *Entrance requirements:* For doctorate, GRE General Test, minimum GPA of 3.0, transcript showing all academic coursework, statement of purpose, current resume/curriculum vitae, letters of recommendation. Additional exam requirements/recommendations for international students: Required—TOEFL (minimum score 550 paper-based; 80 iBT). Electronic applications accepted. *Faculty research:* Student learning processes and the long-term development of mathematical understandings, assessment and learning of low-performing students (English language learners and special needs) in mathematics, mathematics instructional practices and professional development.

Wayland Baptist University, Graduate Programs, Program in Education, Plainview, TX 79072-6998. Offers education administration (M Ed); education diagnostics (M Ed); education literacy (M Ed); elementary certification (M Ed); English (M Ed); English as a second language (M Ed); higher education administration (M Ed); human resources (M Ed); instructional leadership (M Ed); instructional technology (M Ed); science education (M Ed); secondary certification (M Ed); social studies (M Ed); special education (M Ed). Part-time and evening/weekend programs available. Postbaccalaureate distance learning degree programs offered (no on-campus study). *Faculty:* 33 full-time (17 women), 28 part-time/adjunct (17 women). *Students:* 22 full-time (15 women), 316 part-time (189 women); includes 130 minority (48 Black or African American, non-Hispanic/Latino; 3 American Indian or Alaska Native, non-Hispanic/Latino; 71 Hispanic/Latino; 1 Native Hawaiian or other Pacific Islander, non-Hispanic/Latino; 7 Two or more races, non-Hispanic/Latino). Average age 39. 80 applicants, 96% accepted, 44 enrolled. In 2013, 170 master's awarded. *Degree requirements:* For master's, comprehensive exam, capstone course. *Entrance requirements:* For master's, GRE, GMAT or MAT. Additional exam requirements/recommendations for international students: Required—TOEFL (minimum score 500 paper-based; 61 iBT). *Application deadline:* Applications are processed on a rolling basis. Application fee: $50. Electronic applications accepted. *Expenses: Tuition:* Full-time $8190; part-time $455 per credit hour. *Required fees:* $970; $455 per credit hour. $485 per semester. *Financial support:* Federal Work-Study, institutionally sponsored loans, and scholarships/grants available. Support available to part-time students. Financial award application deadline: 5/1; financial award applicants required to submit FAFSA. *Unit head:* Dr. Jim Todd, Chairman, 806-291-1045, Fax: 806-291-1951. *Application contact:* Amanda Stanton, Coordinator of Graduate Studies, 806-291-3423, Fax: 806-291-1950, E-mail: stanton@wbu.edu.

Wayland Baptist University, Graduate Programs, Program in Multidisciplinary Science, Plainview, TX 79072-6998. Offers multidisciplinary science (MS); nursing (MS). Part-time and evening/weekend programs available. *Faculty:* 29 full-time (16 women), 1 (woman) part-time/adjunct. *Students:* 22 part-time (17 women); includes 8 minority (3 Black or African American, non-Hispanic/Latino; 5 Hispanic/Latino). Average age 41. 3 applicants, 67% accepted, 1 enrolled. *Degree requirements:* For master's, comprehensive exam. *Entrance requirements:* For master's, GRE or MAT. Additional exam requirements/recommendations for international students: Required—TOEFL (minimum score 500 paper-based; 61 iBT). *Application deadline:* Applications are processed on a rolling basis. Application fee: $50. Electronic applications accepted. *Expenses: Tuition:* Full-time $8190; part-time $455 per credit hour. *Required fees:* $970; $455 per credit hour. $485 per semester. *Financial support:* Federal Work-Study, institutionally sponsored loans, and scholarships/grants available. Support available to part-time students. Financial award application deadline: 5/1; financial award applicants required to submit FAFSA. *Unit head:* Dr. Herbert Grover, Chairman, Division of Mathematics and Science, 806-291-1115, Fax: 806-291-1968, E-mail: groverh@wbu.edu. *Application contact:* Amanda Stanton, Coordinator of Graduate Studies, 806-291-3423, Fax: 806-291-1950, E-mail: stanton@wbu.edu.

Wayne State College, School of Education and Counseling, Department of Educational Foundations and Leadership, Program in Curriculum and Instruction, Wayne, NE 68787. Offers alternative education (MSE); business and information technology education (MSE); communication arts education (MSE); early childhood education (MSE); elementary education (MSE); English as a second language (MSE); English education (MSE); family and consumer sciences education (MSE); industrial technology and vocational education (MSE); learning communities (MSE); mathematics education (MSE); music education (MSE); science education (MSE); social science education (MSE). *Accreditation:* NCATE. Part-time and evening/weekend programs available. *Degree requirements:* For master's, comprehensive exam, thesis optional. *Entrance requirements:* For master's, GRE General Test. Additional exam requirements/recommendations for international students: Required—TOEFL (minimum score 550 paper-based).

Wayne State University, College of Education, Division of Teacher Education, Detroit, MI 48202. Offers art education (M Ed), including art therapy; autism spectrum disorders (Certificate); bilingual/bicultural education (M Ed, Certificate); career and technical education (M Ed, Certificate); cognitive impairment (Certificate); curriculum and instruction (Ed D, PhD, Ed S), including art education (PhD), bilingual education (Ed D, Ed S), bilingual-bicultural education (PhD), career and technical education (MAT, Ed D, PhD, Ed S), early childhood education (MAT, Ed D, PhD, Ed S), elementary education, English as a second language (MAT, Ed D, Ed S), English education (MAT, Ed D, PhD, Ed S), foreign language education (MAT, PhD), K-12 curriculum, mathematics education (MAT, Ed D, PhD, Ed S), science education (MAT, Ed D, PhD, Ed S), secondary education, social studies education (MAT, Ed S), social studies education: secondary (Ed D, PhD); early childhood education (M Ed, Certificate); elementary education (M Ed, MAT), including children's literature (MAT), early childhood education (MAT, Ed D, PhD, Ed S), general elementary education (MAT); elementary or secondary education (MAT), including bilingual/bicultural education, English as a second language (MAT, Ed D, Ed S), mathematics education (MAT, Ed D, PhD, Ed S), science education (MAT, Ed D, PhD, Ed S), social studies education (MAT, Ed S); emotionally impaired (Certificate); English as a second language (Certificate); English education (M Ed), including secondary; foreign language education (M Ed); K-12 reading specialist (Certificate); learning disabilities (Certificate); mathematics education (M Ed), including secondary; reading (M Ed, Ed S); reading, language and literature (Ed D); science education (M Ed), including secondary; secondary education (MAT), including art education (K-12), career and technical education (MAT, Ed D, PhD, Ed S), English education (MAT, Ed D, PhD, Ed S), foreign language education (MAT, PhD), kinesiology; social studies education (M Ed), including secondary; special education (M Ed, MAT, Ed D, PhD, Ed S); visual arts education (Certificate). Part-time programs available. *Faculty:* 36 full-time (25 women), 55 part-time/adjunct (43 women). *Students:* 218 full-time (163 women), 448 part-time (344 women); includes 218 minority (177 Black or African American, non-Hispanic/Latino; 2 American Indian or Alaska Native, non-Hispanic/Latino; 11 Asian, non-Hispanic/Latino; 19 Hispanic/Latino; 1 Native Hawaiian or other Pacific Islander, non-Hispanic/Latino; 8 Two or more races, non-Hispanic/Latino), 10 international. Average age 37. 258 applicants, 30% accepted, 52 enrolled. In 2013, 183 master's, 10 doctorates, 35 other advanced degrees awarded. *Degree requirements:* For master's, thesis, essay or project (for some M Ed programs), professional field experience (for MAT programs); for doctorate, thesis/dissertation. *Entrance requirements:* For master's, Michigan Basic Skills Test (MA in teaching), admission to the graduate school, verification of participation in group work with children and Michigan State Police Criminal Background check; for doctorate, minimum undergraduate GPA of 3.0, graduate 3.5; interview, curriculum vitae; references. Additional exam requirements/recommendations for international students: Required—TOEFL (minimum score 550 paper-based; 79 iBT), TWE (minimum score 5.5), Michigan English Language Assessment Battery (minimum score 85); Recommended—IELTS (minimum score 6.5). *Application deadline:* For fall admission, 6/1 priority date for domestic students, 5/1 priority date for international students; for winter admission, 10/1 priority date for domestic students, 9/1 priority date for international students; for spring admission, 2/1 priority date for domestic students, 1/1 priority date for international students. Applications are processed on a rolling basis. Application fee: $0. Electronic applications accepted. *Expenses:* Tuition, state resident: part-time $554.15 per credit. Tuition, nonresident: part-time $1200.35 per credit. *Required fees:* $42.15 per credit. $268.30 per semester. Tuition and fees vary according to course load and program. *Financial support:* In 2013–14, 83 students received support, including 1 fellowship (averaging $16,842 per year), 1 research assistantship with tuition reimbursement available (averaging $21,229 per year); career-related internships or fieldwork, Federal Work-Study, scholarships/grants, health care benefits, and unspecified assistantships also available. Support available to part-time students. Financial award application deadline: 3/31; financial award applicants required to submit FAFSA. *Faculty research:* Improving students' skill achievement in mathematics; improving elementary children's understanding of informational text; teachers' use of their pedagogical and mathematical knowledge in the interactive work of teaching; the intersection of identity construction in teaching and learning; identifying effective methods of literacy instruction and assessments for bilingual students in elementary language arts classrooms. *Total annual research expenditures:* $368,105. *Unit head:* Dr. Kathleen Crawford-McKinney, Assistant Dean, 313-577-0122. *Application contact:* Janice Green, Assistant Dean, 313-577-1605, E-mail: jwgreen@wayne.edu. Website: http://coe.wayne.edu/ted/index.php.

Wayne State University, College of Liberal Arts and Sciences, Program in Multidisciplinary Science, Detroit, MI 48202. Offers MA. *Faculty:* 9 full-time (5 women), 1 part-time/adjunct (0 women). *Students:* 1 (woman) full-time, 5 part-time (3 women), 1 international. Average age 31. In 2013, 2 master's awarded. *Expenses:* Tuition, state resident: part-time $554.15 per credit. Tuition, nonresident: part-time $1200.35 per credit. *Required fees:* $42.15 per credit. $268.30 per semester. Tuition and fees vary according to course load and program. *Unit head:* Prof. Karur Padmanabhan, Director, 313-577-3005, E-mail: ad2639@wayne.edu. *Application contact:* Janet Hankin, Professor, 313-577-0841, E-mail: janet.hankin@wayne.edu. Website: http://www.clas.wayne.edu/mams/.

West Chester University of Pennsylvania, College of Arts and Sciences, Department of Physics, West Chester, PA 19383. Offers Teaching Certificate. *Students:* 2 full-time (0 women), 1 part-time (0 women); includes 1 minority (Two or more races, non-Hispanic/Latino). Average age 29. *Entrance requirements:* For degree, bachelor's degree or higher, minimum GPA of 3.0. Additional exam requirements/recommendations for international students: Required—TOEFL (minimum score 550 paper-based; 80 iBT).

Application deadline: For fall admission, 4/15 priority date for domestic students, 3/5 for international students; for spring admission, 10/15 priority date for domestic students, 9/1 for international students. Applications are processed on a rolling basis. Application fee: $45. Electronic applications accepted. *Expenses:* Tuition, state resident: full-time $7956; part-time $442 per credit. Tuition, nonresident: full-time $11,934; part-time $663 per credit. *Required fees:* $2134.20; $106.24 per credit. Tuition and fees vary according to campus/location and program. *Financial support:* Unspecified assistantships available. Support available to part-time students. Financial award application deadline: 2/15; financial award applicants required to submit FAFSA. *Unit head:* Dr. Anthony J. Nicastro, Chairperson, 610-436-2497, Fax: 610-436-3013. *Application contact:* Dr. Jeffrey J. Sudol, Graduate Coordinator, 610-436-2592, Fax: 610-436-3013, E-mail: jsudol@wcupa.edu.
Website: http://www.wcupa.edu/_ACADEMICS/SCH_CAS.PHY/.

Western Connecticut State University, Division of Graduate Studies, School of Professional Studies, Department of Education and Educational Psychology, Program in Secondary Education, Danbury, CT 06810-6885. Offers biology (MAT); mathematics (MAT). Part-time programs available. *Entrance requirements:* For master's, PRAXIS I Pre-Professional Skills Tests, PRAXIS II subject assessment(s), minimum combined undergraduate GPA of 2.8 or MAT (minimum score in 35th percentile). Additional exam requirements/recommendations for international students: Recommended—TOEFL (minimum score 550 paper-based; 79 iBT), IELTS (minimum score 6). *Faculty research:* Differentiated instruction, the transition of teacher learning, teacher retention, relationship building through the evaluation process and leadership development, culture development, differentiated instruction, scheduling, transitioning teacher learning and curriculum.

Western Governors University, Teachers College, Salt Lake City, UT 84107. Offers curriculum and instruction (MS); educational leadership (MS); educational studies (MA); educational studies (5-12) (MA), including mathematics; elementary education (K-8) (MAT, Postbaccalaureate Certificate); elementary education (PreK-8) (MAT); English language learning (K-12) (MA); instructional design (MAT); learning and technology (M Ed, MA); management and innovation (M Ed); mathematics (5-12) (MAT, Postbaccalaureate Certificate); mathematics (5-9) (MAT, Postbaccalaureate Certificate); mathematics education (5-12) (MA); mathematics education (5-9) (MA); mathematics education (K-6) (MA); measurement and evaluation (M Ed); science (5-12) (Postbaccalaureate Certificate); science (5-9) (MAT, Postbaccalaureate Certificate); science education (5-12) (MA), including biology, chemistry, geology, physics; science education (5-9) (MA); social science (5-12) (MAT, Postbaccalaureate Certificate); special education (MAT, MS). *Accreditation:* NCATE. Evening/weekend programs available. Postbaccalaureate distance learning degree programs offered (no on-campus study). *Degree requirements:* For master's, capstone project. *Entrance requirements:* For master's and Postbaccalaureate Certificate, Readiness Assessment, transcripts. Additional exam requirements/recommendations for international students: Required—TOEFL (minimum score 450 paper-based; 80 iBT). Electronic applications accepted. *Expenses:* Contact institution.

Western Michigan University, Graduate College, College of Arts and Sciences, Mallinson Institute for Science Education, Kalamazoo, MI 49008. Offers science education (MA, PhD); science education: biological sciences (PhD); science education: chemistry (PhD); science education: geosciences (PhD); science education: physical geography (PhD); science education: physics (PhD). *Degree requirements:* For doctorate, thesis/dissertation, oral and written exams. *Entrance requirements:* For master's, undergraduate degree in a science or science education, teacher certification (or appropriate education courses); for doctorate, GRE General Test, master's degree in a science or science education. Additional exam requirements/recommendations for international students: Recommended—TOEFL. Electronic applications accepted. *Faculty research:* History and philosophy of science, curriculum and instruction, science content learning, college science teaching and learning, social and cultural factors in science education.

Western Oregon University, Graduate Programs, College of Education, Division of Teacher Education, Program in Secondary Education, Monmouth, OR 97361-1394. Offers bilingual education (MS Ed); health (MS Ed); humanities (MAT, MS Ed); initial licensure (MAT); mathematics (MAT, MS Ed); science (MAT, MS Ed); social science (MAT, MS Ed). *Accreditation:* NCATE. Part-time and evening/weekend programs available. *Degree requirements:* For master's, thesis optional, written exam. *Entrance requirements:* For master's, minimum GPA of 3.0, teaching license. Additional exam requirements/recommendations for international students: Required—TOEFL (minimum score 550 paper-based; 79 iBT), IELTS (minimum score 6.5). *Faculty research:* Literacy, science in primary grades, geography education, retention, teacher burnout.

Western Washington University, Graduate School, College of Sciences and Technology, Program in Natural Science/Science Education, Bellingham, WA 98225-5996. Offers M Ed. Electronic applications accepted. *Faculty research:* Science education reform.

Widener University, School of Human Service Professions, Center for Education, Chester, PA 19013-5792. Offers adult education (M Ed); counseling in higher education (M Ed); counselor education (M Ed); early childhood education (M Ed); educational foundations (M Ed); educational leadership (M Ed); educational psychology (M Ed); elementary education (M Ed); English and language arts (M Ed); health education (M Ed); higher education leadership (Ed D); home and school visitor (M Ed); human sexuality (M Ed, PhD); mathematics education (M Ed); middle school education (M Ed); principalship (M Ed); reading and language arts (Ed D); reading education (M Ed); school administration (Ed D); science education (M Ed); social studies education (M Ed); special education (M Ed); technology education (M Ed). *Accreditation:* NCATE. Part-time and evening/weekend programs available. *Faculty:* 34 full-time (22 women), 37 part-time/adjunct (14 women). *Students:* 64 full-time (44 women), 209 part-time (146 women); includes 49 minority (39 Black or African American, non-Hispanic/Latino; 1 American Indian or Alaska Native, non-Hispanic/Latino; 4 Asian, non-Hispanic/Latino; 4 Hispanic/Latino; 1 Two or more races, non-Hispanic/Latino), 8 international. Average age 39. 139 applicants, 88% accepted. In 2013, 168 master's, 31 doctorates awarded. Terminal master's awarded for partial completion of doctoral program. *Degree requirements:* For doctorate, thesis/dissertation. *Entrance requirements:* For master's, minimum GPA of 2.5; for doctorate, GRE or MAT, minimum GPA of 2.0 (undergraduate), 3.5 (graduate). *Application deadline:* Applications are processed on a rolling basis. Application fee: $25 ($300 for international students). Electronic applications accepted. *Expenses:* Contact institution. *Financial support:* Career-related internships or fieldwork, tuition waivers (full and partial), and unspecified assistantships available. Support available to part-time students. Financial award application deadline: 5/1. *Faculty research:* Reading and cognition, adult education, technology education, educational leadership, special education. *Unit head:* Dr. Michael W. LeDoux, Associate Dean, 610-499-4294, Fax: 610-499-4623, E-mail: mwledoux@widener.edu. *Application contact:* Dr. Roberta Nolan, Director of Graduate Admissions, 610-499-4125, E-mail: rdnolan@widener.edu.

Wilkes University, College of Graduate and Professional Studies, School of Education, Wilkes-Barre, PA 18766-0002. Offers art and science of teaching (MS Ed); classroom technology (MS Ed); early childhood literacy (MS Ed); educational development and strategies (MS Ed); educational leadership (MS Ed); educational technology (Ed D); higher education administration (Ed D); instructional media (MS Ed); instructional technology (MS Ed); international school leadership (MS Ed); K-12 administration (Ed D); middle level education (MS Ed); online teaching (MS Ed); reading (MS Ed); school business leadership (MS Ed); secondary education (MS Ed), including biology, chemistry, English, history, mathematics; special education (MS Ed); teaching English as a second language (MS Ed); twenty-first century teaching and learning (MS Ed). Part-time and evening/weekend programs available. Postbaccalaureate distance learning degree programs offered (minimal on-campus study). *Students:* 46 full-time (37 women), 1,410 part-time (1,039 women); includes 67 minority (12 Black or African American, non-Hispanic/Latino; 2 American Indian or Alaska Native, non-Hispanic/Latino; 11 Asian, non-Hispanic/Latino; 28 Hispanic/Latino; 1 Native Hawaiian or other Pacific Islander, non-Hispanic/Latino; 13 Two or more races, non-Hispanic/Latino), 6 international. Average age 34. In 2013, 852 master's, 10 doctorates awarded. *Entrance requirements:* Additional exam requirements/recommendations for international students: Required—TOEFL (minimum score 550 paper-based; 79 iBT). *Application deadline:* Applications are processed on a rolling basis. Application fee: $45. Electronic applications accepted. *Expenses:* Contact institution. *Financial support:* Federal Work-Study and unspecified assistantships available. Financial award application deadline: 3/1; financial award applicants required to submit FAFSA. *Unit head:* Dr. Rhonda Waskiewicz, Interim Dean, Education, 570-408-4332, Fax: 570-408-7872, E-mail: rhonda.waskiewicz@wilkes.edu. *Application contact:* Joanne Thomas, Interim Director of Graduate Education, 570-408-4234, Fax: 570-408-7846, E-mail: joanne.thomas1@wilkes.edu.
Website: http://www.wilkes.edu/pages/383.asp.

Wright State University, School of Graduate Studies, College of Science and Mathematics, Department of Earth and Environmental Sciences, Program in Earth Science Education, Dayton, OH 45435. Offers MST. *Entrance requirements:* For master's, GRE General Test. Additional exam requirements/recommendations for international students: Required—TOEFL. *Faculty research:* Pedagogy.

Wright State University, School of Graduate Studies, College of Science and Mathematics, Department of Physics, Program in Physics Education, Dayton, OH 45435. Offers MST. Part-time and evening/weekend programs available. *Entrance requirements:* Additional exam requirements/recommendations for international students: Required—TOEFL. *Faculty research:* Pedagogy.

Wright State University, School of Graduate Studies, College of Science and Mathematics, Interdisciplinary Program in Science and Mathematics, Dayton, OH 45435. Offers MST.

Youngstown State University, Graduate School, College of Science, Technology, Engineering and Mathematics, Department of Chemistry, Youngstown, OH 44555-0001. Offers analytical chemistry (MS); biochemistry (MS); chemistry education (MS); inorganic chemistry (MS); organic chemistry (MS); physical chemistry (MS). Part-time programs available. *Degree requirements:* For master's, thesis. *Entrance requirements:* For master's, bachelor's degree in chemistry, minimum GPA of 2.7. Additional exam requirements/recommendations for international students: Required—TOEFL. *Faculty research:* Analysis of antioxidants, chromatography, defects and disorder in crystalline oxides, hydrogen bonding, novel organic and organometallic materials.

Social Sciences Education

Acadia University, Faculty of Professional Studies, School of Education, Program in Curriculum Studies, Wolfville, NS B4P 2R6, Canada. Offers cultural and media studies (M Ed); learning and technology (M Ed); science, math and technology (M Ed). Part-time programs available. *Degree requirements:* For master's, thesis optional. *Entrance requirements:* For master's, B Ed or the equivalent, minimum B average in undergraduate course work, 2 years of teaching experience. Additional exam requirements/recommendations for international students: Required—TOEFL (minimum score 580 paper-based; 93 iBT), IELTS (minimum score 6.5). *Faculty research:* Literacy development, postmodern philosophy and curriculum theory, historiography, philosophy of education, learning and technology.

Alabama State University, College of Education, Department of Curriculum and Instruction, Montgomery, AL 36101-0271. Offers early childhood education (M Ed, Ed S); elementary education (M Ed, Ed S); secondary education (M Ed, Ed S), including biology education, English language arts education (M Ed), history education, math education, music education (M Ed), reading education (M Ed), social science education; special education (M Ed). Part-time programs available. *Faculty:* 11 full-time (8 women), 13 part-time/adjunct (10 women). *Students:* 32 full-time (19 women), 162 part-time (136 women); includes 189 minority (187 Black or African American, non-Hispanic/Latino; 1 Hispanic/Latino; 1 Two or more races, non-Hispanic/Latino). Average age 33. 99 applicants, 45% accepted, 34 enrolled. In 2013, 74 master's, 20 Ed Ss awarded. *Degree requirements:* For master's, comprehensive exam, thesis optional; for Ed S, comprehensive exam, thesis. *Entrance requirements:* For master's, GRE General Test, MAT, writing competency test; for Ed S, writing competency test, GRE, MAT. Additional exam requirements/recommendations for international students: Required—TOEFL (minimum score 500 paper-based). *Application deadline:* For fall admission, 7/15 for domestic students; for spring admission, 12/15 for domestic students. Applications are processed on a rolling basis. Application fee: $25. *Expenses:* Tuition, state resident: full-time $7958; part-time $343 per credit hour. Tuition, nonresident: full-time $14,132; part-time $686 per credit hour. *Required fees:* $446 per term. One-time fee: $1784 full-time; $892 part-time. Tuition and fees vary according to course load. *Financial support:* In 2013–14, research assistantships (averaging $9,450 per year) were awarded. *Unit head:* Dr. Joyce Johnson, Acting Chairperson, 334-229-4485, Fax: 334-229-5603,

E-mail: jjohnson@alasu.edu. *Application contact:* Dr. William Person, Dean of Graduate Studies, 334-229-4274, Fax: 334-229-4928, E-mail: wperson@alasu.edu.
Website: http://www.alasu.edu/academics/colleges—departments/college-of-education/curriculum—instruction/index.aspx.

American Public University System, AMU/APU Graduate Programs, Charles Town, WV 25414. Offers accounting (MBA, MS); criminal justice (MA), including business administration, emergency and disaster management, general (MA, MS); educational leadership (M Ed); emergency and disaster management (MA); entrepreneurship (MBA); environmental policy and management (MS), including environmental planning, environmental sustainability, fish and wildlife management, general (MA, MS), global environmental management; finance (MBA); general (MBA); global business management (MBA); history (MA), including American history, ancient and classical history, European history, global history, public history; homeland security (MA), including business administration, counter-terrorism studies, criminal justice, cyber, emergency management and public health, intelligence studies, transportation security; homeland security resource allocation (MBA); humanities (MA); information technology (MS), including digital forensics, enterprise software development, information assurance and security, IT project management; information technology management (MBA); intelligence studies (MA), including criminal intelligence, cyber, general (MA, MS), homeland security, intelligence analysis, intelligence collection, intelligence management, intelligence operations, terrorism studies; international relations and conflict resolution (MA), including comparative and security issues, conflict resolution, international and transnational security issues, peacekeeping; legal studies (MA); management (MA), including defense management, general (MA, MS), human resource management, organizational leadership, public administration; marketing (MBA); military history (MA), including American military history, American Revolution, civil war, war since 1945, World War II; military studies (MA), including joint warfare, strategic leadership; national security studies (MA), including general (MA, MS), homeland security, regional security studies, security and intelligence analysis, terrorism studies; nonprofit management (MBA); political science (MA), including American politics and government, comparative government and development, general (MA, MS), international relations, public policy; psychology (MA), including general (MA, MS), maritime engineering management, reverse logistics management; public administration (MPA), including disaster management, environmental policy, health policy, human resources, national security, organizational management, security management; public health (MPH); reverse logistics management (MA); school counseling (M Ed); security management (MA); space studies (MS), including aerospace science, general (MA, MS), planetary science; sports and health sciences (MS); teaching (M Ed), including curriculum and instruction for elementary teachers, elementary reading, English language learners, instructional leadership, online learning, special education; transportation and logistics management (MA), including general (MA, MS), maritime engineering management, reverse logistics management. Programs offered via distance learning only. Part-time and evening/weekend programs available. Postbaccalaureate distance learning degree programs offered (no on-campus study). *Faculty:* 432 full-time (242 women), 1,722 part-time/adjunct (829 women). *Students:* 511 full-time (241 women), 10,947 part-time (4,294 women); includes 3,760 minority (2,058 Black or African American, non-Hispanic/Latino; 88 American Indian or Alaska Native, non-Hispanic/Latino; 293 Asian, non-Hispanic/Latino; 876 Hispanic/Latino; 91 Native Hawaiian or other Pacific Islander, non-Hispanic/Latino; 354 Two or more races, non-Hispanic/Latino), 134 international. Average age 36. In 2013, 3,323 master's awarded. *Degree requirements:* For master's, comprehensive exam or practicum. *Entrance requirements:* For master's, official transcript showing earned bachelor's degree from institution accredited by recognized accrediting body. Additional exam requirements/recommendations for international students: Required—TOEFL (minimum score 550 paper-based), IELTS (minimum score 6.5). *Application deadline:* Applications are processed on a rolling basis. Application fee: $0. Electronic applications accepted. *Expenses: Tuition:* Part-time $325 per semester hour. *Financial support:* Applicants required to submit FAFSA. *Faculty research:* Military history, criminal justice, management performance, national security. *Unit head:* Dr. Karan Powell, Executive Vice President and Provost, 877-468-6268, Fax: 304-724-3780. *Application contact:* Terry Grant, Vice President of Enrollment Management, 877-468-6268, Fax: 304-724-3780, E-mail: info@apus.edu.
Website: http://www.apus.edu.

Andrews University, School of Graduate Studies, School of Education, Department of Teaching, Learning, and Curriculum, Berrien Springs, MI 49104. Offers curriculum and instruction (MA, Ed D, PhD, Ed S); elementary education (MAT); secondary education (MAT), including biology, education, English, English as a second language, French, history, physics; teacher education (MAT). *Faculty:* 7 full-time (4 women). *Students:* 16 full-time (11 women), 26 part-time (22 women); includes 14 minority (11 Black or African American, non-Hispanic/Latino; 1 Asian, non-Hispanic/Latino; 1 Hispanic/Latino; 1 Two or more races, non-Hispanic/Latino), 13 international. Average age 40. 33 applicants, 42% accepted, 3 enrolled. In 2013, 7 master's, 1 doctorate, 1 other advanced degree awarded. *Entrance requirements:* For master's, GRE Subject Test. Additional exam requirements/recommendations for international students: Required—TOEFL (minimum score 550 paper-based). *Application deadline:* For fall admission, 8/15 for domestic students. Applications are processed on a rolling basis. Application fee: $40. *Unit head:* Dr. Lee C. Davidson, Chair, 269-471-6364. *Application contact:* Monica Wringer, Supervisor of Graduate Admission, 800-253-2874, Fax: 269-471-6321, E-mail: graduate@andrews.edu.

Appalachian State University, Cratis D. Williams Graduate School, Department of Curriculum and Instruction, Boone, NC 28608. Offers curriculum specialist (MA); educational media (MA); elementary education (MA); middle grades education (MA), including language arts, mathematics, science, social studies. *Accreditation:* NCATE. Part-time and evening/weekend programs available. Postbaccalaureate distance learning degree programs offered (no on-campus study). *Degree requirements:* For master's, comprehensive exam, thesis or alternative. *Entrance requirements:* For master's, GRE General Test or MAT, 3 letters of recommendation. Additional exam requirements/recommendations for international students: Required—TOEFL (minimum score 570 paper-based; 79 iBT), IELTS (minimum score 6.5). Electronic applications accepted. *Faculty research:* Media literacy, elementary teaching, curriculum development, online learning environments.

Arcadia University, Graduate Studies, School of Education, Glenside, PA 19038-3295. Offers art education (M Ed); computer education (CAS); curriculum (CAS); curriculum studies (M Ed); early childhood education (M Ed, CAS), including individualized (M Ed), master teacher (M Ed), research in child development (M Ed); educational leadership (M Ed, Ed D, CAS); elementary education (M Ed, CAS); English education (MA Ed); environmental education (MA Ed, CAS); history education (MA Ed); instructional technology (M Ed); language arts (M Ed, CAS); library science (M Ed); mathematics education (M Ed, MA Ed, CAS); music education (MA Ed); psychology (MA Ed); reading (M Ed, CAS); science education (M Ed, CAS); secondary education (M Ed, CAS); special education (M Ed, Ed D, CAS); theater arts (MA Ed); written communication (MA Ed). *Accreditation:* NASAD. Part-time and evening/weekend programs available. Postbaccalaureate distance learning degree programs offered (minimal on-campus study). Electronic applications accepted. *Expenses:* Contact institution.

Arkansas State University, Graduate School, College of Humanities and Social Sciences, Department of Criminology, Sociology, and Geography, Jonesboro, AR 72467. Offers criminal justice (MA); sociology (MA); sociology education (SCCT). Part-time programs available. *Faculty:* 9 full-time (5 women). *Students:* 5 full-time (2 women), 21 part-time (16 women); includes 8 minority (all Black or African American, non-Hispanic/Latino), 1 international. Average age 36. 22 applicants, 32% accepted, 6 enrolled. In 2013, 12 master's awarded. *Degree requirements:* For master's, one foreign language, comprehensive exam, thesis or alternative; for SCCT, comprehensive exam. *Entrance requirements:* For master's, GRE General Test or MAT, appropriate bachelor's degree, letters of recommendation, official transcripts, immunization records; for SCCT, GRE General Test or MAT, interview, master's degree, official transcript, immunization records. Additional exam requirements/recommendations for international students: Required—TOEFL (minimum score 550 paper-based; 79 iBT), IELTS (minimum score 6), PTE (minimum score 56). *Application deadline:* For fall admission, 4/1 for domestic and international students; for spring admission, 11/1 for domestic and international students. Applications are processed on a rolling basis. Application fee: $30 ($40 for international students). Electronic applications accepted. *Expenses:* Tuition, state resident: full-time $4284; part-time $238 per credit hour. Tuition, nonresident: full-time $8568; part-time $476 per credit hour. *International tuition:* $9268 full-time. *Required fees:* $1098; $61 per credit hour. $25 per term. Tuition and fees vary according to course load and program. *Financial support:* In 2013–14, 6 students received support. Career-related internships or fieldwork, scholarships/grants, and unspecified assistantships available. Financial award application deadline: 7/1; financial award applicants required to submit FAFSA. *Unit head:* Dr. William McLean, Interim Chair, 870-972-3705, Fax: 870-972-3694, E-mail: wmclean@astate.edu. *Application contact:* Vickey Ring, Graduate Admissions Coordinator, 870-972-3029, Fax: 870-972-3857, E-mail: vickeyring@astate.edu.
Website: http://www.astate.edu/college/humanities-and-social-sciences/departments/criminology-sociology-and-geography/.

Arkansas State University, Graduate School, College of Humanities and Social Sciences, Department of History, Jonesboro, AR 72467. Offers history (MA); history education (MSE, SCCT); social science education (MSE). Part-time programs available. *Faculty:* 13 full-time (7 women). *Students:* 3 full-time (1 woman), 26 part-time (12 women); includes 3 minority (2 Black or African American, non-Hispanic/Latino; 1 Hispanic/Latino). Average age 32. 24 applicants, 46% accepted, 9 enrolled. In 2013, 5 master's awarded. *Degree requirements:* For master's, comprehensive exam, thesis or alternative; for SCCT, comprehensive exam. *Entrance requirements:* For master's, GRE General Test or MAT, GMAT, appropriate bachelor's degree, letters of reference, official transcript, valid teaching certificate (for MSE), immunization records; for SCCT, GRE General Test or MAT, interview, master's degree, letters of reference, official transcript, immunization records. Additional exam requirements/recommendations for international students: Required—TOEFL (minimum score 550 paper-based; 79 iBT), IELTS (minimum score 6), PTE (minimum score 56). *Application deadline:* For fall admission, 7/1 for domestic and international students; for spring admission, 11/15 for domestic students, 11/14 for international students. Applications are processed on a rolling basis. Application fee: $30 ($40 for international students). Electronic applications accepted. *Expenses:* Tuition, state resident: full-time $4284; part-time $238 per credit hour. Tuition, nonresident: full-time $8568; part-time $476 per credit hour. *International tuition:* $9268 full-time. *Required fees:* $1098; $61 per credit hour. $25 per term. Tuition and fees vary according to course load and program. *Financial support:* In 2013–14, 8 students received support. Career-related internships or fieldwork, scholarships/grants, and unspecified assistantships available. Financial award application deadline: 7/1; financial award applicants required to submit FAFSA. *Unit head:* Dr. Joseph Key, Chair, 870-972-3046, Fax: 870-972-2880, E-mail: jkey@astate.edu. *Application contact:* Vickey Ring, Graduate Admissions Coordinator, 870-972-3029, Fax: 870-972-3857, E-mail: vickeyring@astate.edu.
Website: http://www.astate.edu/college/humanities-and-social-sciences/departments/history/.

Arkansas State University, Graduate School, College of Humanities and Social Sciences, Department of Political Science, Jonesboro, AR 72467. Offers political science (MA); political science education (SCCT); public administration (MPA). *Accreditation:* NASPAA (one or more programs are accredited). Part-time programs available. *Faculty:* 7 full-time (2 women). *Students:* 33 full-time (14 women), 113 part-time (65 women); includes 51 minority (43 Black or African American, non-Hispanic/Latino; 1 American Indian or Alaska Native, non-Hispanic/Latino; 1 Asian, non-Hispanic/Latino; 5 Hispanic/Latino; 1 Two or more races, non-Hispanic/Latino), 20 international. Average age 33. 167 applicants, 59% accepted, 64 enrolled. In 2013, 32 master's awarded. *Degree requirements:* For master's, comprehensive exam, thesis or alternative; for SCCT, comprehensive exam. *Entrance requirements:* For master's, GRE General Test or MAT, GMAT, appropriate bachelor's degree, letters of recommendation, official transcripts, immunization records, statement of purpose; for SCCT, GRE General Test or MAT, GMAT, interview, master's degree, official transcript, letters of recommendation, immunization records. Additional exam requirements/recommendations for international students: Required—TOEFL (minimum score 550 paper-based; 79 iBT), IELTS (minimum score 6), PTE (minimum score 56). *Application deadline:* For fall admission, 7/1 for domestic and international students; for spring admission, 11/15 for domestic students, 11/14 for international students. Applications are processed on a rolling basis. Application fee: $30 ($40 for international students). Electronic applications accepted. *Expenses:* Tuition, state resident: full-time $4284; part-time $238 per credit hour. Tuition, nonresident: full-time $8568; part-time $476 per credit hour. *International tuition:* $9268 full-time. *Required fees:* $1098; $61 per credit hour. $25 per term. Tuition and fees vary according to course load and program. *Financial support:* In 2013–14, 18 students received support. Teaching assistantships, career-related internships or fieldwork, scholarships/grants, and unspecified assistantships available. Financial award application deadline: 7/1; financial award applicants required to submit FAFSA. *Unit head:* Dr. William McLean, Chair, 870-972-3048, Fax: 870-972-2720, E-mail: wmclean@astate.edu. *Application contact:* Vickey Ring, Graduate Admissions Coordinator, 870-972-3029, Fax: 870-972-3857, E-mail: vickeyring@astate.edu.
Website: http://www.astate.edu/college/humanities-and-social-sciences/departments/political-science/.

Asbury University, School of Graduate and Professional Studies, Wilmore, KY 40390-1198. Offers biology: alternative certificate (MA Ed); chemistry: alternative certificate (MA Ed); English (MA Ed); English as a second language (MA Ed); ESL (MA Ed); French (MA Ed); Latin: alternative certificate (MA Ed); mathematics: alternative certificate (MA Ed); reading/writing endorsement (MA Ed); social studies (MA Ed); social work (MSW), including child and family services; Spanish (MA Ed); special education (MA Ed); special education: alternative certificate (MA Ed); teacher as leader endorsement (MA Ed). *Accreditation:* NCATE. Part-time programs available. *Degree requirements:* For master's, action research project, portfolio. *Entrance requirements:* For master's, PRAXIS/NTE, minimum GPA of 2.75, letters of recommendation. Additional exam requirements/recommendations for international students: Required—TOEFL (minimum score 550 paper-based). Electronic applications accepted.

Social Sciences Education

Auburn University, Graduate School, College of Education, Department of Curriculum and Teaching, Auburn University, AL 36849. Offers business education (M Ed, MS, PhD); early childhood education (M Ed, MS, PhD, Ed S); elementary education (M Ed, MS, PhD, Ed S); foreign languages (M Ed, MS); music education (M Ed, MS, PhD, Ed S); postsecondary education (PhD); reading education (PhD, Ed S); secondary education (M Ed, MS, PhD, Ed S), including English language arts, mathematics, science, social studies. *Accreditation:* NASM (one or more programs are accredited); NCATE. Part-time programs available. *Faculty:* 29 full-time (21 women), 4 part-time/adjunct (all women). *Students:* 61 full-time (40 women), 153 part-time (108 women); includes 37 minority (32 Black or African American, non-Hispanic/Latino; 2 Asian, non-Hispanic/Latino; 3 Hispanic/Latino), 1 international. Average age 34. 150 applicants, 59% accepted, 74 enrolled. In 2013, 70 master's, 6 doctorates, 26 other advanced degrees awarded. *Degree requirements:* For master's, thesis (for some programs); for doctorate, thesis/dissertation; for Ed S, field project. *Entrance requirements:* For master's, doctorate, and Ed S, GRE General Test. *Application deadline:* For fall admission, 7/7 for domestic students; for spring admission, 11/24 for domestic students. Applications are processed on a rolling basis. Application fee: $50 ($60 for international students). Electronic applications accepted. *Expenses:* Tuition, state resident: full-time $8262; part-time $459 per credit hour. Tuition, nonresident: full-time $24,786; part-time $1377 per credit hour. Tuition and fees vary according to degree level and program. *Financial support:* Fellowships, teaching assistantships, career-related internships or fieldwork, and Federal Work-Study available. Support available to part-time students. Financial award application deadline: 3/15; financial award applicants required to submit FAFSA. *Faculty research:* Emerging literacy, reading attitudes, music for at-risk youth, portfolio assessment. *Unit head:* Dr. Kimberly Walls, Head, 334-844-4434. *Application contact:* Dr. George Flowers, Dean of the Graduate School, 334-844-2125.
Website: http://education.auburn.edu/academic_departments/curr/.

Auburn University at Montgomery, School of Education, Department of Foundations, Technology, and Secondary Education, Montgomery, AL 36124-4023. Offers instructional technology (M Ed); secondary education (M Ed, Ed S), including art education (M Ed), biology (M Ed), English language arts (M Ed), general science (M Ed), history (M Ed), mathematics (M Ed), social science (M Ed). *Accreditation:* NCATE. Part-time and evening/weekend programs available. *Faculty:* 6 full-time (2 women), 1 (woman) part-time/adjunct. *Students:* 47 full-time (22 women), 77 part-time (48 women); includes 30 minority (29 Black or African American, non-Hispanic/Latino; 1 Asian, non-Hispanic/Latino), 1 international. Average age 30. In 2013, 86 master's awarded. *Degree requirements:* For master's and Ed S, comprehensive exam, thesis optional. *Entrance requirements:* For master's, GRE General Test or MAT, certification, BS in teaching; for Ed S, GRE General Test or MAT, certification. *Application deadline:* Applications are processed on a rolling basis. Electronic applications accepted. *Expenses:* Tuition, state resident: full-time $5994; part-time $333 per credit hour. Tuition, nonresident: full-time $17,982; part-time $999 per credit hour. *Financial support:* Teaching assistantships, career-related internships or fieldwork, and scholarships/grants available. Support available to part-time students. Financial award application deadline: 3/1; financial award applicants required to submit FAFSA. *Unit head:* Dr. Sheila Austin, Dean, 334-244-3425, Fax: 334-244-3102, E-mail: saustin1@aum.edu. *Application contact:* Dr. Rhonda Morton, Associate Dean/Graduate Coordinator, 334-244-3287, Fax: 334-244-3978, E-mail: rmorton@aum.edu.
Website: http://www.education.aum.edu/departments/foundations-technology-and-secondary-education.

Binghamton University, State University of New York, Graduate School, School of Education, Program in Adolescence Education, Vestal, NY 13850. Offers biology education (MAT, MS Ed); chemistry education (MAT, MS Ed); earth science education (MAT, MS Ed); English education (MAT, MS Ed); French education (MAT, MS Ed); literacy education (MS Ed); mathematical sciences education (MAT, MS Ed); physics (MAT, MS Ed); social studies (MAT, MS Ed); Spanish education (MAT, MS Ed). *Accreditation:* Teacher Education Accreditation Council. Part-time and evening/weekend programs available. *Students:* 48 full-time (29 women), 5 part-time (3 women); includes 7 minority (2 Black or African American, non-Hispanic/Latino; 3 Asian, non-Hispanic/Latino; 2 Hispanic/Latino), 1 international. Average age 26. 37 applicants, 86% accepted, 21 enrolled. In 2013, 34 master's awarded. *Entrance requirements:* For master's, GRE General Test. Additional exam requirements/recommendations for international students: Required—TOEFL (minimum score 550 paper-based; 80 iBT). *Application deadline:* For fall admission, 2/1 priority date for domestic and international students; for spring admission, 10/15 priority date for domestic and international students. Applications are processed on a rolling basis. Application fee: $75. Electronic applications accepted. *Financial support:* In 2013–14, 7 students received support, including 1 fellowship with partial tuition reimbursement available (averaging $4,500 per year); career-related internships or fieldwork, Federal Work-Study, institutionally sponsored loans, scholarships/grants, health care benefits, tuition waivers (full), and unspecified assistantships also available. Financial award application deadline: 2/15; financial award applicants required to submit FAFSA. *Unit head:* Dr. S. G. Grant, Dean of School of Education, 607-777-7329, E-mail: sggrant@binghamton.edu. *Application contact:* Kishan Zuber, Recruiting and Admissions Coordinator, 607-777-2151, Fax: 607-777-2501, E-mail: kzuber@binghamton.edu.

Bloomsburg University of Pennsylvania, School of Graduate Studies, College of Education, Department of Early Childhood and Adolescent Education, Program in Middle Level Education Grades 4-8, Bloomsburg, PA 17815-1301. Offers language arts (M Ed); math (M Ed); science (M Ed); social studies (M Ed). *Accreditation:* NCATE. *Faculty:* 14 full-time (6 women), 3 part-time/adjunct (2 women). In 2013, 2 master's awarded. *Degree requirements:* For master's, thesis optional, student teaching. *Entrance requirements:* For master's, MAT, GRE, or PRAXIS, minimum QPA of 3.0, teaching certificate, U.S. citizenship, related undergraduate coursework, professional liability insurance, recent TB test. Additional exam requirements/recommendations for international students: Required—TOEFL (minimum score 550 paper-based). *Application deadline:* Applications are processed on a rolling basis. Application fee: $35 ($60 for international students). Electronic applications accepted. *Expenses:* Tuition, state resident: full-time $7956; part-time $442 per credit. Tuition, nonresident: full-time $11,934; part-time $663 per credit. *Required fees:* $95.50 per credit. $55 per semester. Tuition and fees vary according to course load. *Financial support:* Unspecified assistantships available. *Unit head:* Dr. Tegan Kotarski, College of Education Graduate Coordinator, 570-389-3883, Fax: 570-389-5049, E-mail: tkotarsk@bloomu.edu. *Application contact:* Jennifer Richard, Administrative Assistant, 570-389-4015, Fax: 570-389-3054, E-mail: jrichard@bloomu.edu.
Website: http://www.bloomu.edu/gradschool/middle-level-education.

Bob Jones University, Graduate Programs, Greenville, SC 29614. Offers accountancy (MS); Bible (MA); Bible translation (MA); Biblical studies (Certificate); broadcast management (MS); business administration (MBA); church history (MA, PhD); church ministries (MA); church music (MM); cinema and video production (MA); counseling (MS); curriculum and instruction (Ed D); divinity (M Div); dramatic production (MA); educational leadership (MS, Ed D, Ed S); elementary education (M Ed, MAT); English (M Ed, MA, MAT); fine arts (MA); graphic design (MA); history (M Ed, MA); illustration (MA); interpretative speech (MA); mathematics (M Ed, MAT); medical missions (Certificate); ministry (MM, D Min); multi-categorical special education (M Ed, MAT); music (M Ed); New Testament interpretation (PhD); Old Testament interpretation (PhD); orchestral instrument performance (MM); organ performance (MM); pastoral studies (MA); personnel services (MS, Ed S); piano pedagogy (MM); piano performance (MM); platform arts (MA); radio and television broadcasting (MS); rhetoric and public address (MA); secondary education (M Ed); studio art (MA); teaching Bible (MA); theology (MA, PhD); voice performance (MM); youth ministries (MA); M Div/MM.

Bridgewater State University, School of Graduate Studies, School of Arts and Sciences, Department of History, Bridgewater, MA 02325-0001. Offers MAT. Part-time and evening/weekend programs available. *Entrance requirements:* For master's, GRE General Test.

Brooklyn College of the City University of New York, Division of Graduate Studies, School of Education, Program in Adolescence Education and Special Subjects, Brooklyn, NY 11210-2889. Offers adolescence science education (MAT); art teacher (MA); biology teacher (MA); chemistry teacher (MA); earth science teacher (MAT); English teacher (MA); French teacher (MA); health and nutrition sciences: health teacher (MS Ed); mathematics teacher (MA); music education (CAS); music teacher (MA); physical education teacher (MS Ed); physics teacher (MA); social studies teacher (MA); Spanish teacher (MA). Part-time and evening/weekend programs available. *Degree requirements:* For master's, comprehensive exam (for some programs), thesis (for some programs). *Entrance requirements:* For master's, LAST, previous course work in education, resume, 2 letters of recommendation, essay. Additional exam requirements/recommendations for international students: Required—TOEFL (minimum score 500 paper-based; 61 iBT). Electronic applications accepted. *Faculty research:* Interdisciplinary education, semiotics, discourse analysis, autobiography, teacher identity.

Brown University, Graduate School, Department of Education, Program in Teaching, Providence, RI 02912. Offers elementary education (MAT); English (MAT); history/social studies (MAT); science (MAT); secondary education (MAT). *Degree requirements:* For master's, student teaching, portfolio. *Entrance requirements:* For master's, GRE General Test, transcript, personal statement, 3 letters of recommendation, interview, writing sample (English applicants only). Additional exam requirements/recommendations for international students: Required—TOEFL (minimum score 577 paper-based). Electronic applications accepted. *Faculty research:* Literacy, English language learners, diversity, special education, biodiversity.

Buffalo State College, State University of New York, The Graduate School, Faculty of Natural and Social Sciences, Department of History and Social Studies, Buffalo, NY 14222-1095. Offers history (MA); secondary education (MS Ed), including social studies. Part-time and evening/weekend programs available. *Degree requirements:* For master's, one foreign language, thesis (for some programs), project (MS Ed). *Entrance requirements:* For master's, minimum GPA of 2.75, 30 hours in history (MA), 36 hours in history or social sciences (MS Ed). Additional exam requirements/recommendations for international students: Required—TOEFL (minimum score 550 paper-based).

California State University, Chico, Office of Graduate Studies, College of Behavioral and Social Sciences, Social Science Program, Chico, CA 95929-0722. Offers social science (MA); social science education (MA). *Degree requirements:* For master's, thesis or project. *Entrance requirements:* For master's, GRE General Test or MAT, two letters of recommendation, statement of purpose. Additional exam requirements/recommendations for international students: Required—TOEFL (minimum score 550 paper-based; 80 iBT), IELTS (minimum score 6.5), PTE (minimum score 59). Electronic applications accepted.

California State University, East Bay, Office of Academic Programs and Graduate Studies, College of Letters, Arts, and Social Sciences, Department of History, Hayward, CA 94542-3000. Offers history (MA); public history (MA); teaching (MA). Part-time and evening/weekend programs available. *Degree requirements:* For master's, one foreign language, comprehensive exam, project, thesis, or exam. *Entrance requirements:* For master's, GRE (strongly recommended), minimum GPA of 3.0 in field, 3.3 in history; 2 letters of recommendation; writing sample. Additional exam requirements/recommendations for international students: Required—TOEFL (minimum score 550 paper-based). Electronic applications accepted. *Faculty research:* Digital history, American women, early America, Native Americans, medieval colonial India.

California State University, Fresno, Division of Graduate Studies, College of Social Sciences, Department of History, Fresno, CA 93740-8027. Offers history-teaching option (MA); history-traditional track (MA). Part-time and evening/weekend programs available. *Degree requirements:* For master's, thesis or alternative. *Entrance requirements:* For master's, GRE General Test, minimum GPA of 3.0. Additional exam requirements/recommendations for international students: Required—TOEFL. Electronic applications accepted. *Faculty research:* International education, classical art history, improving teacher quality.

California State University, San Bernardino, Graduate Studies, College of Education, San Bernardino, CA 92407-2397. Offers bilingual/cross-cultural education (MA); curriculum and instruction (MA); educational administration (MA); educational leadership and curriculum (Ed D); educational psychology and counseling (MA, MS), including correctional and alternative education (MA), counseling and guidance (MS), rehabilitation counseling (MA); English as a second language (MA); general education (MA); history and English for secondary teachers (MA); instructional technology (MA); reading (MA); secondary education (MA); special education and rehabilitation counseling (MA), including rehabilitation counseling, special education; teaching of science (MA); vocational and career education (MA). *Accreditation:* NCATE. Part-time and evening/weekend programs available. *Students:* 217 full-time (172 women), 353 part-time (263 women); includes 283 minority (41 Black or African American, non-Hispanic/Latino; 1 American Indian or Alaska Native, non-Hispanic/Latino; 21 Asian, non-Hispanic/Latino; 204 Hispanic/Latino; 1 Native Hawaiian or other Pacific Islander, non-Hispanic/Latino; 15 Two or more races, non-Hispanic/Latino), 35 international. Average age 34. 349 applicants, 76% accepted, 207 enrolled. In 2013, 215 master's awarded. *Degree requirements:* For master's, comprehensive exam (for some programs), thesis (for some programs), advancement to candidacy. *Entrance requirements:* For master's, minimum GPA of 3.0 in education. *Application deadline:* For fall admission, 8/31 priority date for domestic students. Application fee: $55. *Financial support:* Career-related internships or fieldwork and Federal Work-Study available. Support available to part-time students. *Faculty research:* Multicultural education, brain-based learning, science education, social studies/global education. *Unit head:* Dr. Jay Fiene, Dean, 909-537-5600, Fax: 909-537-7011, E-mail: jfiene@csusb.edu. *Application contact:* Dr. Jeffrey Thompson, Dean of Graduate Studies, 909-537-5808, E-mail: jthompso@csusb.edu.

Cambridge College, School of Education, Cambridge, MA 02138-5304. Offers autism specialist (M Ed); autism/behavior analyst (M Ed); behavior analyst (Post-Master's Certificate); behavioral management (M Ed); early childhood teacher (M Ed); education specialist in curriculum and instruction (CAGS); educational leadership (Ed D); elementary teacher (M Ed); English as a second language (M Ed, Certificate); general science (M Ed); health education (Post-Master's Certificate); health/family and consumer sciences (M Ed); history (M Ed); individualized (M Ed); information technology literacy (M Ed); instructional technology (M Ed); interdisciplinary studies

(M Ed); library teacher (M Ed); literacy education (M Ed); mathematics (M Ed); mathematics specialist (Certificate); middle school mathematics and science (M Ed); school administration (M Ed, CAGS); school guidance counselor (M Ed); school nurse education (M Ed); school social worker/school adjustment counselor (M Ed); special education administrator (CAGS); special education/moderate disabilities (M Ed); teaching skills and methodologies (M Ed). Part-time and evening/weekend programs available. Postbaccalaureate distance learning degree programs offered (minimal on-campus study). *Degree requirements:* For master's, thesis, internship/practicum (licensure program only); for doctorate, thesis/dissertation; for other advanced degree, thesis. *Entrance requirements:* For master's, interview, resume, documentation of licensure, 2 professional references; for doctorate, official transcripts, interview, resume, documentation of licensure (if any), written personal statement/essay, portfolio of scholarly and professional work, qualifying assessment, 2 professional references, health insurance, immunizations form; for other advanced degree, official transcripts, interview, resume, documentation of licensure (if any), written personal statement/essay, 2 professional references, health insurance, immunizations form. Additional exam requirements/recommendations for international students: Required—TOEFL (minimum score 550 paper-based; 79 iBT), Michigan English Language Assessment Battery (minimum score 85); Recommended—IELTS (minimum score 6). Electronic applications accepted. *Expenses:* Contact institution. *Faculty research:* Adult education, accelerated learning, mathematics education, brain compatible learning, special education and law.

Campbell University, Graduate and Professional Programs, School of Education, Buies Creek, NC 27506. Offers administration (MSA); community counseling (MA); elementary education (M Ed); English education (M Ed); interdisciplinary studies (M Ed); mathematics education (M Ed); middle grades education (M Ed); physical education (M Ed); school counseling (M Ed); secondary education (M Ed); social science education (M Ed). *Accreditation:* NCATE. Part-time and evening/weekend programs available. *Degree requirements:* For master's, comprehensive exam. *Entrance requirements:* For master's, GRE General Test, minimum GPA of 2.7. *Faculty research:* Spiritual values and wellness issues in counseling, stress and professional burnout among counselors, thinking strategies, leadership, adaptive technology.

Caribbean University, Graduate School, Bayamón, PR 00960-0493. Offers administration and supervision (MA Ed); criminal justice (MA); curriculum and instruction (MA Ed, PhD), including elementary education (MA Ed), English education (MA Ed), history education (MA Ed), mathematics education (MA Ed), primary education (MA Ed), science education (MA Ed), Spanish education (MA Ed); educational technology in instructional systems (MA Ed); gerontology (MSN); human resources (MBA); museology, archiving and art history (MA Ed); neonatal pediatrics (MSN); physical education (MA Ed); special education (MA Ed). *Entrance requirements:* For master's, interview, minimum GPA of 2.5.

Carthage College, Division of Teacher Education, Kenosha, WI 53140. Offers classroom guidance and counseling (M Ed); creative arts (M Ed); gifted and talented children (M Ed); language arts (M Ed); modern language (M Ed); natural sciences (M Ed); reading (M Ed, Certificate); social sciences (M Ed); teacher leadership (M Ed). Part-time and evening/weekend programs available. *Degree requirements:* For master's, thesis optional. *Entrance requirements:* For master's, MAT, minimum B average, letters of reference.

Chadron State College, School of Professional and Graduate Studies, Department of Education, Chadron, NE 69337. Offers business (MA Ed); community counseling (MA Ed); educational administration (MS Ed, Sp Ed); elementary education (MS Ed); history (MA Ed); language and literature (MA Ed); secondary administration (MS Ed); secondary education (MS Ed). *Accreditation:* NCATE. Part-time and evening/weekend programs available. Postbaccalaureate distance learning degree programs offered. *Degree requirements:* For master's, thesis optional. *Entrance requirements:* For master's, GRE General Test, GRE Writing Test, minimum GPA of 2.75 or 12 graduate hours at CSC with minimum GPA of 3.25. Additional exam requirements/recommendations for international students: Required—TOEFL. Electronic applications accepted. *Faculty research:* Rural education, technology, mental health.

Chaminade University of Honolulu, Graduate Services, Program in Education, Honolulu, HI 96816-1578. Offers child development (M Ed); early childhood education (M Ed); educational leadership (M Ed); elementary education (MAT); instructional leadership (M Ed); Montessori education (M Ed); secondary education (MAT), including English, math, science, social studies; special education (MAT). Part-time and evening/weekend programs available. Postbaccalaureate distance learning degree programs offered (minimal on-campus study). *Degree requirements:* For master's, thesis or alternative. *Entrance requirements:* For master's, PRAXIS (for MAT only), minimum GPA of 2.75, 3 letters of recommendation. Additional exam requirements/recommendations for international students: Required—TOEFL (minimum score 550 paper-based). Electronic applications accepted. *Faculty research:* Peace and curriculum education.

Chatham University, Program in Education, Pittsburgh, PA 15232-2826. Offers early childhood education (MAT); elementary education (MAT); environmental education (K-12) (MAT); secondary art (MAT); secondary biology education (MAT); secondary chemistry education (MAT); secondary English education (MAT); secondary math education (MAT); secondary physics education (MAT); secondary social studies education (MAT); special education (MAT). *Faculty:* 1 (woman) full-time, 5 part-time/adjunct (4 women). *Students:* 19 full-time (15 women), 4 part-time (all women); includes 2 minority (1 Black or African American, non-Hispanic/Latino; 1 Asian, non-Hispanic/Latino), 2 international. Average age 28. 22 applicants, 73% accepted, 6 enrolled. In 2013, 20 master's awarded. *Degree requirements:* For master's, thesis, teaching experience. *Entrance requirements:* For master's, minimum GPA of 3.0, sample of written work, recommendation letters. Additional exam requirements/recommendations for international students: Required—TOEFL (minimum score 600 paper-based; 100 iBT), IELTS (minimum score 7), TWE. *Application deadline:* For fall admission, 4/1 priority date for domestic and international students; for spring admission, 11/1 priority date for domestic students, 10/1 priority date for international students. Applications are processed on a rolling basis. Application fee: $45. Electronic applications accepted. Application fee is waived when completed online. *Expenses: Tuition:* Full-time $14,886; part-time $827 per credit hour. One-time fee: $396 full-time. *Financial support:* Career-related internships or fieldwork available. Financial award applicants required to submit FAFSA. *Faculty research:* Gifted education, environmental education, technology in education, writing as learning, class size and achievement. *Unit head:* Dr. Edward Donovan, Director of Education Programs, 412-365-2773, E-mail: edonovan@chatham.edu. *Application contact:* Katie Noel, Assistant Director of Graduate Admission, 412-365-2758, Fax: 412-365-1609, E-mail: gradadmissions@chatham.edu.
Website: http://www.chatham.edu/mat.

Christopher Newport University, Graduate Studies, Department of Teacher Preparation, Newport News, VA 23606-3072. Offers art (PK-12) (MAT); biology (6-12) (MAT); chemistry (6-12) (MAT); computer science (6-12) (MAT); elementary (PK-6) (MAT); English (6-12) (MAT); English as second language (PK-12) (MAT); French (PK-12) (MAT); history and social science (6-12) (MAT); mathematics (6-12) (MAT); music (PK-12) (MAT), including choral, instrumental; physics (6-12) (MAT); Spanish (PK-12) (MAT). Part-time programs available. *Faculty:* 15 full-time (7 women), 14 part-time/adjunct (13 women). *Students:* 74 full-time (64 women), 2 part-time (both women); includes 6 minority (4 Hispanic/Latino; 2 Two or more races, non-Hispanic/Latino). Average age 23. 90 applicants, 100% accepted, 67 enrolled. In 2013, 96 master's awarded. *Degree requirements:* For master's, comprehensive exam, thesis or alternative. *Entrance requirements:* For master's, PRAXIS I, minimum GPA of 3.0. Additional exam requirements/recommendations for international students: Required—TOEFL (minimum score 580 paper-based; 92 iBT). *Application deadline:* For fall admission, 4/1 for international students; for spring admission, 10/15 for domestic students, 10/1 for international students; for summer admission, 1/15 for domestic students, 3/1 for international students. Applications are processed on a rolling basis. Application fee: $50. Electronic applications accepted. *Expenses: Tuition, area resident:* Part-time $498 per credit hour. Tuition, state resident: part-time $498 per credit hour. Tuition, nonresident: part-time $899 per credit hour. *Financial support:* In 2013–14, 3 students received support, including 3 research assistantships with full tuition reimbursements available (averaging $2,000 per year); career-related internships or fieldwork, Federal Work-Study, and unspecified assistantships also available. Financial award application deadline: 3/1; financial award applicants required to submit FAFSA. *Faculty research:* Early literacy development, instructional innovations, professional teaching standards, multicultural issues, aesthetic education. *Total annual research expenditures:* $24,000. *Unit head:* Dr. Marsha Sprague, Director, 757-594-7388, Fax: 757-594-7803, E-mail: msprague@cnu.edu. *Application contact:* Lyn Sawyer, Associate Director, Graduate Admissions, 757-594-7544, Fax: 757-594-7649, E-mail: gradstdy@cnu.edu.

The Citadel, The Military College of South Carolina, Citadel Graduate College, School of Education, Program in Secondary Education, Charleston, SC 29409. Offers biology (MAT); English language arts (MAT); mathematics (MAT); mathematics education (MAE); physical education (MAT); social studies (MAT). *Accreditation:* NCATE. Part-time and evening/weekend programs available. *Faculty:* 10 full-time (6 women), 8 part-time/adjunct (3 women). *Students:* 14 full-time (9 women), 56 part-time (31 women); includes 9 minority (8 Black or African American, non-Hispanic/Latino; 1 Hispanic/Latino). Average age 30. In 2013, 24 master's awarded. *Degree requirements:* For master's, comprehensive exam, internship. *Entrance requirements:* For master's, GRE (minimum score 290; 900 on old scoring system) or MAT (minimum score 396), minimum undergraduate GPA of 2.5. Additional exam requirements/recommendations for international students: Required—TOEFL (minimum score 550 paper-based). *Application deadline:* Applications are processed on a rolling basis. Application fee: $30. Electronic applications accepted. *Expenses: Tuition, area resident:* Part-time $525 per credit hour. Tuition, state resident: part-time $525 per credit hour. Tuition, nonresident: part-time $865 per credit hour. *Financial support:* Career-related internships or fieldwork, health care benefits, and unspecified assistantships available. Support available to part-time students. Financial award application deadline: 7/1; financial award applicants required to submit FAFSA. *Unit head:* Dr. Kathryn A. Richardson-Jones, Coordinator, 843-953-3163, Fax: 843-953-7258, E-mail: kathryn.jones@citadel.edu. *Application contact:* Dr. Robert H. McNamara, Associate Provost, The Citadel Graduate College, 843-953-5089, Fax: 843-953-7630, E-mail: cgc@citadel.edu.
Website: http://www.citadel.edu/education/teacher-education/mat-master-of-arts-in-teaching.html.

City College of the City University of New York, Graduate School, School of Education, Department of Secondary Education, New York, NY 10031-9198. Offers adolescent mathematics education (MA, AC); English education (MA); middle school mathematics education (MS); science education (MA); social studies education (AC). *Accreditation:* NCATE. *Entrance requirements:* For master's, Liberal Arts and Sciences Test (LAST), Content Specialty Test (CST). Additional exam requirements/recommendations for international students: Required—TOEFL.

Clemson University, Graduate School, College of Health, Education, and Human Development, Eugene T. Moore School of Education, Program in Teaching and Learning, Clemson, SC 29634. Offers elementary education (M Ed); English education (M Ed); mathematics education (M Ed); science education (M Ed); social studies education (M Ed). *Students:* 6 full-time (5 women), 8 part-time (7 women), 3 international. Average age 28. 6 applicants, 100% accepted, 4 enrolled. In 2013, 9 master's awarded. *Entrance requirements:* For master's, GRE, baccalaureate degree from regionally-accredited institution, official transcripts, copy of valid teaching certificate, two letters of recommendation. *Financial support:* In 2013–14, 1 teaching assistantship (averaging $6,812 per year) was awarded. *Unit head:* Dr. Michael J. Padilla, Director/Associate Dean, 864-656-4444, Fax: 864-656-0311, E-mail: padilla@clemson.edu. *Application contact:* Dr. David Fleming, Graduate Programs Coordinator, 864-656-1881, Fax: 864-656-0311, E-mail: dflemin@clemson.edu.
Website: http://www.grad.clemson.edu/programs/Teaching-Learning/.

The College at Brockport, State University of New York, School of Education and Human Services, Department of Education and Human Development, Program in Adolescence Education, Brockport, NY 14420-2997. Offers adolescence biology education (MS Ed); adolescence chemistry education (MS Ed); adolescence earth science education (MS Ed); adolescence English education (MS Ed); adolescence mathematics education (MS Ed); adolescence physics education (MS Ed); adolescence social studies education (MS Ed). *Accreditation:* NCATE. Part-time programs available. *Students:* 13 full-time (7 women), 47 part-time (28 women); includes 3 minority (1 Black or African American, non-Hispanic/Latino; 1 American Indian or Alaska Native, non-Hispanic/Latino; 1 Asian, non-Hispanic/Latino). 26 applicants, 88% accepted, 14 enrolled. In 2013, 27 master's awarded. *Degree requirements:* For master's, thesis or alternative. *Entrance requirements:* For master's, minimum GPA of 3.0, letters of recommendation; statement of objectives, current resume. Additional exam requirements/recommendations for international students: Required—TOEFL (minimum score 550 paper-based; 79 iBT), IELTS (minimum score 6.5). *Application deadline:* For fall admission, 3/15 priority date for domestic and international students; for spring admission, 10/15 priority date for domestic and international students; for summer admission, 3/15 priority date for domestic students, 3/13 priority date for international students. Application fee: $80. Electronic applications accepted. *Expenses:* Tuition, state resident: full-time $9870. Tuition, nonresident: full-time $18,350. *Required fees:* $1848. *Financial support:* Federal Work-Study, scholarships/grants, and unspecified assistantships available. Support available to part-time students. Financial award application deadline: 3/15; financial award applicants required to submit FAFSA. *Unit head:* Dr. Don Halquist, Chairperson, 585-395-5550, Fax: 585-395-2172, E-mail: dhalquis@brockport.edu. *Application contact:* Michael Harrison, Coordinator of Certification and Graduate Advisement, 585-395-2326, Fax: 585-395-2172, E-mail: mharriso@brockport.edu.
Website: http://www.brockport.edu/ehd/.

The College at Brockport, State University of New York, School of Education and Human Services, Department of Education and Human Development, Program in Adolescence Inclusive Generalist Education, Brockport, NY 14420-2997. Offers English (MS Ed); mathematics (MS Ed); science (MS Ed); social studies (MS Ed). *Students:* 30 full-time (18 women), 24 part-time (17 women); includes 6 minority (3 Black or African American, non-Hispanic/Latino; 2 Hispanic/Latino; 1 Two or more races, non-Hispanic/

Latino). 16 applicants, 75% accepted, 8 enrolled. In 2013, 15 master's awarded. *Degree requirements:* For master's, thesis or alternative. *Entrance requirements:* For master's, minimum GPA of 3.0, letters of recommendation, statement of objectives, academic major (or equivalent) in program discipline; current resume. Additional exam requirements/recommendations for international students: Required—TOEFL (minimum score 550 paper-based; 79 iBT), IELTS (minimum score 6.5). *Application deadline:* For fall admission, 3/15 priority date for domestic and international students; for spring admission, 10/15 priority date for domestic and international students; for summer admission, 3/15 for domestic and international students. Application fee: $80. Electronic applications accepted. *Expenses:* Tuition, state resident: full-time $9870. Tuition, nonresident: full-time $18,350. *Required fees:* $1848. *Financial support:* Federal Work-Study, scholarships/grants, and unspecified assistantships available. Support available to part-time students. Financial award application deadline: 3/15; financial award applicants required to submit FAFSA. *Unit head:* Dr. Don Halquist, Chairperson, 585-395-2205, Fax: 585-395-2171, E-mail: dhalquis@brockport.edu. *Application contact:* Michael Harrison, Coordinator of Certification and Graduate Advisement, 585-395-2326, Fax: 585-395-2172, E-mail: mharriso@brockport.edu.
Website: http://www.brockport.edu/ehd/.

College of St. Joseph, Graduate Programs, Division of Education, Program in Secondary Education, Rutland, VT 05701-3899. Offers English (M Ed); social studies (M Ed). Part-time and evening/weekend programs available. *Degree requirements:* For master's, comprehensive exam. *Entrance requirements:* For master's, PRAXIS I, official college transcripts; 2 letters of reference; minimum GPA of 3.0 (initial licensure) or 2.7 (nonlicensure); interview. Additional exam requirements/recommendations for international students: Required—TOEFL (minimum score 550 paper-based). Electronic applications accepted.

The College of William and Mary, School of Education, Program in Curriculum and Instruction, Williamsburg, VA 23187-8795. Offers elementary education (MA Ed); gifted education (MA Ed); literacy leadership (MA Ed); math specialist (MA Ed); secondary education (MA Ed), including English education, mathematics education, modern foreign languages education, science education, social studies education; special education (MA Ed), including collaborating master educator, general curriculum. *Accreditation:* NCATE. Part-time programs available. *Faculty:* 15 full-time (10 women), 44 part-time/adjunct (38 women). *Students:* 66 full-time (55 women), 27 part-time (26 women); includes 17 minority (4 Black or African American, non-Hispanic/Latino; 1 American Indian or Alaska Native, non-Hispanic/Latino; 3 Asian, non-Hispanic/Latino; 5 Hispanic/Latino; 4 Two or more races, non-Hispanic/Latino). Average age 28. 179 applicants, 72% accepted, 92 enrolled. In 2013, 76 master's awarded. *Degree requirements:* For master's, project. *Entrance requirements:* For master's, GRE or MAT, minimum GPA of 2.5. Additional exam requirements/recommendations for international students: Required—TOEFL, IELTS. *Application deadline:* For fall admission, 1/15 for domestic and international students; for spring admission, 10/1 for domestic and international students. Application fee: $50. Electronic applications accepted. *Expenses:* Tuition, state resident: full-time $7120; part-time $405 per credit hour. Tuition, nonresident: full-time $21,639; part-time $1050 per credit hour. *Required fees:* $4764. *Financial support:* In 2013–14, 49 students received support, including 6 research assistantships with full and partial tuition reimbursements available (averaging $8,269 per year); career-related internships or fieldwork, Federal Work-Study, institutionally sponsored loans, scholarships/grants, and unspecified assistantships also available. Financial award application deadline: 1/15; financial award applicants required to submit FAFSA. *Faculty research:* National Council of Teachers of Mathematics standards, counseling, self-concept and self-esteem, special education, curriculum development. *Unit head:* Dr. Mark Hofer, Area Coordinator, 757-221-1713, E-mail: mjhofe@wm.edu. *Application contact:* Dorothy Smith Osborne, Assistant Dean for Academic Programs and Student Services, 757-221-2317, Fax: 757-221-2293, E-mail: dsosbo@wm.edu.
Website: http://education.wm.edu.

The Colorado College, Education Department, Program in Secondary Education, Colorado Springs, CO 80903-3294. Offers art teaching (K-12) (MAT); English teaching (MAT); foreign language teaching (MAT); mathematics teaching (MAT); music teaching (MAT); science teaching (MAT); social studies teaching (MAT). *Degree requirements:* For master's, thesis, internship. Electronic applications accepted.

Columbus State University, Graduate Studies, College of Education and Health Professions, Department of Teacher Education, Columbus, GA 31907-5645. Offers accomplished teaching (M Ed); early childhood education (M Ed, MAT, Ed S); middle grades education (M Ed, MAT, Ed S); school library media (M Ed, MAT); secondary education (M Ed, MAT, Ed S), including English/language arts (M Ed, Ed S), general science (M Ed), mathematics (M Ed, Ed S), science (Ed S), social science (M Ed, Ed S); special education (M Ed, MAT, Ed S), including general curriculum (M Ed, MAT); teacher leadership (M Ed). *Accreditation:* NCATE. Part-time and evening/weekend programs available. Postbaccalaureate distance learning degree programs offered (minimal on-campus study). *Faculty:* 17 full-time (12 women), 31 part-time/adjunct (28 women). *Students:* 59 full-time (48 women), 190 part-time (150 women); includes 85 minority (68 Black or African American, non-Hispanic/Latino; 1 American Indian or Alaska Native, non-Hispanic/Latino; 6 Asian, non-Hispanic/Latino; 4 Hispanic/Latino; 6 Two or more races, non-Hispanic/Latino), 2 international. Average age 34. 132 applicants, 58% accepted, 50 enrolled. In 2013, 86 master's, 26 other advanced degrees awarded. *Degree requirements:* For master's, thesis, exit exam; for Ed S, thesis or alternative. *Entrance requirements:* For master's, GRE General Test, minimum undergraduate GPA of 2.75; for Ed S, GRE General Test, minimum undergraduate GPA of 2.75, graduate 3.0. Additional exam requirements/recommendations for international students: Required—TOEFL (minimum score 550 paper-based; 79 iBT). *Application deadline:* For fall admission, 6/30 for domestic students, 5/1 for international students; for spring admission, 11/1 for domestic and international students; for summer admission, 3/1 for domestic and international students. Applications are processed on a rolling basis. Application fee: $40. Electronic applications accepted. *Expenses:* Tuition, state resident: full-time $4572; part-time $382 per credit hour. Tuition, nonresident: full-time $18,292; part-time $1526 per credit hour. *Required fees:* $1800; $196 per credit hour. Tuition and fees vary according to campus/location and program. *Financial support:* In 2013–14, 173 students received support, including 12 research assistantships with partial tuition reimbursements available (averaging $3,000 per year); career-related internships or fieldwork, Federal Work-Study, institutionally sponsored loans, scholarships/grants, tuition waivers (partial), and unspecified assistantships also available. Support available to part-time students. Financial award application deadline: 5/1; financial award applicants required to submit FAFSA. *Unit head:* Dr. Deirdre Greer, Department Chair, 706-507-8034, Fax: 706-568-3134, E-mail: greer_deirdre@columbusstate.edu. *Application contact:* Kristin Williams, Director of International and Graduate Recruitment, 706-507-8848, Fax: 706-568-5091, E-mail: williams_kristin@columbusstate.edu.
Website: http://te.columbusstate.edu/.

Concord University, Graduate Studies, Athens, WV 24712-1000. Offers educational leadership and supervision (M Ed); geography (M Ed); health promotion (MA); reading specialist (M Ed); special education (M Ed); teaching (MAT). Part-time and evening/weekend programs available. Postbaccalaureate distance learning degree programs offered (no on-campus study). *Degree requirements:* For master's, thesis (for some programs). *Entrance requirements:* For master's, GRE or MAT, baccalaureate degree with minimum GPA of 2.5 from regionally-accredited institution; teaching license; 2 letters of recommendation; completed disposition assessment form. Electronic applications accepted.

Converse College, School of Education and Graduate Studies, Program in Middle Level Education, Spartanburg, SC 29302-0006. Offers language arts/English (MAT); mathematics (MAT); middle level education (M Ed); science (MAT); social studies (MAT).

Converse College, School of Education and Graduate Studies, Program in Secondary Education, Spartanburg, SC 29302-0006. Offers biology (MAT); chemistry (MAT); English (M Ed, MAT); mathematics (M Ed, MAT); natural sciences (M Ed); social sciences (M Ed, MAT). Part-time programs available. *Degree requirements:* For master's, capstone paper. *Entrance requirements:* For master's, NTE or PRAXIS II (M Ed), minimum GPA of 2.75, 2 recommendations. Electronic applications accepted.

Delta State University, Graduate Programs, College of Arts and Sciences, Division of Social Sciences and History, Program in Social Science Secondary Education, Cleveland, MS 38733-0001. Offers secondary education (M Ed), including social science. Part-time programs available. *Students:* 8 part-time (3 women); includes 2 minority (both Black or African American, non-Hispanic/Latino). Average age 34. 5 applicants, 100% accepted, 4 enrolled. In 2013, 12 master's awarded. *Degree requirements:* For master's, thesis or alternative. *Application deadline:* For fall admission, 8/1 priority date for domestic students; for spring admission, 12/1 priority date for domestic students. Applications are processed on a rolling basis. Application fee: $0. *Expenses:* Tuition, state resident: full-time $3006; part-time $334 per credit hour. Tuition, nonresident: full-time $3006; part-time $334 per credit hour. *Financial support:* Research assistantships, career-related internships or fieldwork, Federal Work-Study, and institutionally sponsored loans available. Support available to part-time students. Financial award application deadline: 6/1. *Unit head:* Dr. Paulette Miekle, Chair, 662-846-4065, Fax: 662-846-4016, E-mail: pmeikleyaw@deltastate.edu. *Application contact:* Dr. Beverly Moon, Dean of Graduate Studies, 662-846-4873, Fax: 662-846-4313, E-mail: grad-info@deltastate.edu.
Website: http://www.deltastate.edu/pages/4450.asp.

Drew University, Caspersen School of Graduate Studies, Program in Education, Madison, NJ 07940-1493. Offers biology (MAT); chemistry (MAT); English (MAT); French (MAT); Italian (MAT); math (MAT); physics (MAT); social studies (MAT); Spanish (MAT); theatre arts (MAT). Part-time programs available. *Degree requirements:* For master's, student teaching internship and seminar. *Entrance requirements:* For master's, transcripts, statement of purpose, three letters of recommendation. Additional exam requirements/recommendations for international students: Required—TOEFL. *Expenses:* Contact institution.

Duquesne University, School of Education, Department of Instruction and Leadership, Program in Secondary Education, Pittsburgh, PA 15282-0001. Offers biology (MS Ed); chemistry (MS Ed); English (MS Ed); K-12 education (MS Ed), including Latin; mathematics (MS Ed); physics (MS Ed); social studies (MS Ed). Part-time and evening/weekend programs available. *Faculty:* 4 full-time (2 women). *Students:* 44 full-time (23 women), 3 part-time (2 women); includes 7 minority (6 Black or African American, non-Hispanic/Latino; 1 Two or more races, non-Hispanic/Latino), 1 international. Average age 27. 43 applicants, 35% accepted, 15 enrolled. In 2013, 28 master's awarded. *Degree requirements:* For master's, thesis optional. *Entrance requirements:* For master's, letters of recommendation, letter of intent, interview, bachelor's degree. Additional exam requirements/recommendations for international students: Required—TOEFL (minimum score 550 paper-based), IELTS (minimum score 7). *Application deadline:* For fall admission, 9/1 for domestic students; for spring admission, 1/1 for domestic students. Applications are processed on a rolling basis. Application fee: $0. Electronic applications accepted. Application fee is waived when completed online. *Expenses: Tuition:* Full-time $18,162; part-time $1009 per credit. *Required fees:* $1728; $96 per credit. Tuition and fees vary according to program. *Financial support:* Research assistantships and Federal Work-Study available. Support available to part-time students. *Unit head:* Dr. Melissa Boston, Associate Professor and Director, 412-396-6109, E-mail: bostonm@duq.edu. *Application contact:* Michael Dolinger, Director of Student and Academic Services, 412-396-6647, Fax: 412-396-5585, E-mail: dolingerm@duq.edu.
Website: http://www.duq.edu/academics/schools/education/graduate-programs-education/ms-ed-secondary-education.

East Carolina University, Graduate School, College of Education, Department of Business and Information Technologies Education, Greenville, NC 27858-4353. Offers business education (MA Ed); elementary education (MAT); English education (MAT); family and consumer science (MAT); health education (MAT); Hispanic studies (MAT); history education (MAT); marketing education (MA Ed); middle grades education (MAT); music education (MAT); physical education (MAT); science education (MAT); special education (MAT), including general curriculum; vocation education (MS). *Accreditation:* NCATE. Part-time and evening/weekend programs available. Postbaccalaureate distance learning degree programs offered (no on-campus study). *Degree requirements:* For master's, comprehensive exam, thesis optional. *Entrance requirements:* For master's, GRE or MAT, minimum GPA of 2.5, bachelor's degree in related field, teaching license (MA Ed). Additional exam requirements/recommendations for international students: Required—TOEFL. *Expenses:* Tuition, state resident: full-time $4223. Tuition, nonresident: full-time $16,540. *Required fees:* $2184.

Eastern Kentucky University, The Graduate School, College of Education, Department of Curriculum and Instruction, Program in Secondary and Higher Education, Richmond, KY 40475-3102. Offers secondary education (MA Ed), including agricultural education, art education, biological sciences education, business education, English education, geography education, history education, home economics education, industrial education, mathematical sciences education, physical education, school health education. *Accreditation:* NCATE. Part-time programs available. *Entrance requirements:* For master's, GRE General Test, minimum GPA of 2.5.

Eastern University, Graduate Education Programs, St. Davids, PA 19087-3696. Offers ESL program specialist (K-12) (Certificate); general supervisor (PreK-12) (Certificate); health and physical education (K-12) (Certificate); middle level (4-8) (Certificate); multicultural education (M Ed); pre K-4 (Certificate); pre K-4 with special education (Certificate); reading (M Ed); reading specialist (K-12) (Certificate); reading supervisor (K-12) (Certificate); school health services (M Ed); school health supervisor (Certificate); school nurse (Certificate); school principalship (K-12) (Certificate); secondary biology education (7-12) (Certificate); secondary chemistry education (7-12) (Certificate); secondary communication education (7-12) (Certificate); secondary education (7-12) (Certificate); secondary English education (7-12) (Certificate); secondary math education (7-12) (Certificate); secondary social studies education (7-12) (Certificate); special education (M Ed); special education (7-12) (Certificate); special education (Pre K-8) (Certificate); special education supervisor (N-12) (Certificate); TESOL (M Ed); world language (Certificate), including French, Mandarin Chinese, Spanish. Part-time and evening/weekend programs available. Postbaccalaureate distance learning degree

programs offered (no on-campus study). *Faculty:* 22 full-time (11 women), 26 part-time/adjunct (18 women). *Students:* 77 full-time (58 women), 223 part-time (149 women); includes 112 minority (81 Black or African American, non-Hispanic/Latino; 1 American Indian or Alaska Native, non-Hispanic/Latino; 9 Asian, non-Hispanic/Latino; 18 Hispanic/Latino; 1 Native Hawaiian or other Pacific Islander, non-Hispanic/Latino; 2 Two or more races, non-Hispanic/Latino), 7 international. Average age 34. 94 applicants, 100% accepted, 81 enrolled. In 2013, 120 master's awarded. *Entrance requirements:* For master's, minimum GPA of 2.5 (for M Ed); for Certificate, minimum GPA of 3.0 for certifications. Additional exam requirements/recommendations for international students: Required—TOEFL. *Application deadline:* For fall admission, 8/14 for domestic students; for spring admission, 12/20 for domestic students. Applications are processed on a rolling basis. Application fee: $35. Application fee is waived when completed online. *Expenses: Tuition:* Full-time $15,600; part-time $650 per credit. *Required fees:* $27.50 per semester. One-time fee: $50. Tuition and fees vary according to course load, degree level and program. *Financial support:* In 2013–14, 84 students received support, including 6 research assistantships with partial tuition reimbursements available (averaging $7,710 per year); scholarships/grants and unspecified assistantships also available. Financial award application deadline: 3/15; financial award applicants required to submit FAFSA. *Unit head:* Harry Gutelius, Associate Dean, 610-341-1729. *Application contact:* Michael Perpiglia, Associate Director of Enrollment, 610-341-5947, Fax: 484-581-1276, E-mail: mperpigl@eastern.edu. Website: http://www.eastern.edu/academics/programs/loeb-school-education-0/graduateprograms.

East Stroudsburg University of Pennsylvania, Graduate College, College of Arts and Sciences, Department of History, East Stroudsburg, PA 18301-2999. Offers M Ed, MA. Part-time and evening/weekend programs available. *Faculty:* 7 full-time (3 women). *Students:* 13 full-time (5 women), 21 part-time (5 women); includes 6 minority (1 Black or African American, non-Hispanic/Latino; 1 Hispanic/Latino; 2 Native Hawaiian or other Pacific Islander, non-Hispanic/Latino; 2 Two or more races, non-Hispanic/Latino). Average age 28. 23 applicants, 78% accepted, 11 enrolled. In 2013, 5 master's awarded. *Degree requirements:* For master's, comprehensive exam, thesis, thesis defense. *Entrance requirements:* For master's, Commonwealth of Pennsylvania Department of Education Certification Requirements (M Ed). Additional exam requirements/recommendations for international students: Required—TOEFL (minimum score 560 paper-based; 83 iBT) or IELTS. *Application deadline:* For fall admission, 7/31 priority date for domestic students, 6/30 priority date for international students; for spring admission, 11/30 for domestic students, 10/31 for international students. Applications are processed on a rolling basis. Application fee: $50. Electronic applications accepted. *Expenses:* Tuition, state resident: full-time $7956; part-time $442 per credit. Tuition, nonresident: full-time $11,934; part-time $663 per credit. *Required fees:* $2129; $118 per credit. *Financial support:* Research assistantships with full and partial tuition reimbursements, Federal Work-Study, and institutionally sponsored loans available. Financial award application deadline: 3/1; financial award applicants required to submit FAFSA. *Unit head:* Dr. Martin Wilson, Graduate Coordinator, Fax: 570-422-3506. *Application contact:* Kevin Quintero, Graduate Admissions Coordinator, 570-422-3536, Fax: 570-422-2711, E-mail: kquintero@esu.edu.

East Stroudsburg University of Pennsylvania, Graduate College, College of Arts and Sciences, Department of Political Science, East Stroudsburg, PA 18301-2999. Offers M Ed, MA. Part-time and evening/weekend programs available. *Faculty:* 5 full-time (1 woman). *Students:* 22 full-time (5 women), 9 part-time (6 women); includes 8 minority (2 Black or African American, non-Hispanic/Latino; 5 Hispanic/Latino; 1 Native Hawaiian or other Pacific Islander, non-Hispanic/Latino), 4 international. Average age 26. 15 applicants, 60% accepted, 4 enrolled. In 2013, 16 master's awarded. *Degree requirements:* For master's, variable foreign language requirement, comprehensive exam, thesis or alternative. *Entrance requirements:* Additional exam requirements/recommendations for international students: Required—TOEFL (minimum score 560 paper-based; 83 iBT) or IELTS. *Application deadline:* For fall admission, 7/31 priority date for domestic students, 6/30 priority date for international students; for spring admission, 11/30 for domestic students, 10/31 for international students. Applications are processed on a rolling basis. Application fee: $50. Electronic applications accepted. *Expenses:* Tuition, state resident: full-time $7956; part-time $442 per credit. Tuition, nonresident: full-time $11,934; part-time $663 per credit. *Required fees:* $2129; $118 per credit. *Financial support:* Research assistantships with full and partial tuition reimbursements, Federal Work-Study, and institutionally sponsored loans available. Financial award application deadline: 3/1; financial award applicants required to submit FAFSA. *Unit head:* Dr. Ko Mishima, Graduate Coordinator, Fax: 570-422-3506. *Application contact:* Kevin Quintero, Graduate Admissions Coordinator, 570-422-3536, Fax: 570-422-2711, E-mail: kquintero@esu.edu. Website: http://www.esu.edu/pols/.

Emporia State University, Program in Social Sciences, Emporia, KS 66801-5415. Offers American history (MAT); anthropology (MAT); economics (MAT); geography (MAT); political science (MAT); social studies education (MAT); sociology (MAT); world history (MAT). *Accreditation:* NCATE. Part-time programs available. *Faculty:* 15 full-time (7 women). *Students:* 4 part-time (3 women). In 2013, 3 master's awarded. *Degree requirements:* For master's, comprehensive exam or thesis. *Entrance requirements:* For master's, appropriate bachelor's degree, teacher certification. Additional exam requirements/recommendations for international students: Required—TOEFL (minimum score 520 paper-based; 68 iBT). *Application deadline:* For fall admission, 8/15 priority date for domestic students. Applications are processed on a rolling basis. Application fee: $30 ($75 for international students). Electronic applications accepted. *Expenses: Tuition, area resident:* Part-time $220 per credit hour. Tuition, state resident: part-time $220 per credit hour. Tuition, nonresident: part-time $685 per credit hour. *Required fees:* $73 per credit hour. *Financial support:* Federal Work-Study, institutionally sponsored loans, health care benefits, and unspecified assistantships available. Financial award application deadline: 3/15; financial award applicants required to submit FAFSA. *Unit head:* Dr. Ellen Hansen, Chair, 620-341-5461, E-mail: ehansen@emporia.edu. *Application contact:* Dr. Christopher Lovett, Associate Professor, 620-341-5577, E-mail: clovett@emporia.edu.

Fayetteville State University, Graduate School, Programs in Middle Grades, Secondary and Special Education and Elementary Education, Fayetteville, NC 28301-4298. Offers biology (MA Ed); elementary education (MA Ed); history (MA Ed); mathematics (MA Ed); middle grades (MA Ed); political science (MA Ed); reading (MA Ed); sociology (MA Ed); special education (MA Ed), including behavioral-emotional handicaps, mentally handicapped, specific training disability. *Accreditation:* NCATE. Part-time and evening/weekend programs available. *Faculty:* 12 full-time (8 women), 4 part-time/adjunct (3 women). *Students:* 25 full-time (22 women), 49 part-time (45 women); includes 51 minority (48 Black or African American, non-Hispanic/Latino; 1 American Indian or Alaska Native, non-Hispanic/Latino; 2 Hispanic/Latino). Average age 35. 5 applicants, 100% accepted, 5 enrolled. In 2013, 29 master's awarded. *Degree requirements:* For master's, comprehensive exam, internship. *Application deadline:* For fall admission, 4/15 for domestic students; for spring admission, 10/15 for domestic students. Applications are processed on a rolling basis. Application fee: $40. Electronic applications accepted. *Faculty research:* Students with disabilities and selected leadership behaviors, new vision for professional development, gifted and talented

students, emotional and behavioral disabilities, professional development for high school biology teachers. *Unit head:* Dr. Kimberly Smith-Burton, Interim Chair, 910-672-1182, E-mail: cbarringerbrown@uncfsu.edu. *Application contact:* Katrina Hoffman, Graduate Admission Officer, 910-672-1374, Fax: 910-672-1470, E-mail: khoffma1@uncfsu.edu.

Fitchburg State University, Division of Graduate and Continuing Education, Programs in History and Teaching History (Secondary Level), Fitchburg, MA 01420-2697. Offers MA, MAT, Certificate. *Accreditation:* NCATE. Part-time and evening/weekend programs available. *Entrance requirements:* Additional exam requirements/recommendations for international students: Required—TOEFL (minimum score 550 paper-based; 79 iBT). Electronic applications accepted.

Florida Agricultural and Mechanical University, Division of Graduate Studies, Research, and Continuing Education, College of Education, Program in Secondary Education and Foundation, Tallahassee, FL 32307-3200. Offers biology (M Ed); chemistry (MS Ed); English (MS Ed); history (MS Ed); math (MS Ed); physics (MS Ed). *Accreditation:* NCATE. *Degree requirements:* For master's, thesis (for some programs). *Entrance requirements:* For master's, GRE General Test, minimum GPA of 3.0. Additional exam requirements/recommendations for international students: Required—TOEFL.

Florida Atlantic University, College of Education, Department of Teaching and Learning, Boca Raton, FL 33431-0991. Offers curriculum and instruction (M Ed), including art, biology, chemistry, English, French, German, mathematics, music, physics, Pre-K and primary education, reading, social sciences, Spanish; elementary education (M Ed); environmental education (M Ed); reading education (M Ed); social foundations of education (M Ed), including educational psychology, educational technology, multilingual education. *Accreditation:* NCATE. Part-time and evening/weekend programs available. *Faculty:* 16 full-time (12 women), 1 (woman) part-time/adjunct. *Students:* 56 full-time (46 women), 96 part-time (78 women); includes 39 minority (10 Black or African American, non-Hispanic/Latino; 6 Asian, non-Hispanic/Latino; 20 Hispanic/Latino; 3 Two or more races, non-Hispanic/Latino), 4 international. Average age 32. 101 applicants, 54% accepted, 42 enrolled. In 2013, 64 master's awarded. *Entrance requirements:* For master's, GRE General Test, minimum GPA of 3.0 in last 2 years of undergraduate course work. Additional exam requirements/recommendations for international students: Required—TOEFL (minimum score 500 paper-based; 61 iBT), IELTS (minimum score 6). *Application deadline:* For fall admission, 7/1 for domestic students, 2/15 for international students; for spring admission, 11/1 for domestic students, 7/15 for international students. Applications are processed on a rolling basis. Application fee: $30. *Expenses:* Tuition, state resident: full-time $6660; part-time $370 per credit hour. Tuition, nonresident: full-time $18,450; part-time $1025 per credit hour. Tuition and fees vary according to course load. *Financial support:* Fellowships with partial tuition reimbursements, research assistantships with partial tuition reimbursements, teaching assistantships with partial tuition reimbursements, career-related internships or fieldwork, scholarships/grants, and unspecified assistantships available. *Faculty research:* Technology, teaching English to speakers of other languages, math teaching, electronic portfolio assessment, global perspectives through social studies. *Unit head:* Dr. Barbara Ridener, Chairperson, 561-297-3588. *Application contact:* Dr. Eliah Watlington, Associate Dean, 561-296-8520, Fax: 261-297-2991, E-mail: ewatling@fau.edu. Website: http://www.coe.fau.edu/academicdepartments/tl/.

Florida International University, College of Education, Department of Teaching and Learning, Miami, FL 33199. Offers art education (MA, MS); curriculum and instruction (MS, Ed D, PhD, Ed S), including curriculum development (MS), elementary education (MS), English education (MS), learning technologies (MS), mathematics education (MS), modern language education (MS), physical education (MS), science education (MS), social studies education (MS), special education (MS); early childhood education (MS); exceptional student education (Ed D); foreign language education (MS), including foreign language education, teaching English to speakers of other languages (TESOL); international/intercultural education (MS); language, literacy and culture (PhD); mathematics, science, and learning technologies (PhD); physical education (MS), including sport and fitness; reading education (MS). Part-time and evening/weekend programs available. *Degree requirements:* For doctorate, comprehensive exam, thesis/dissertation. *Entrance requirements:* For master's, GRE General Test, Florida General Knowledge Test or Florida College Level Academic Skills Test; for doctorate and Ed S, GRE General Test. Additional exam requirements/recommendations for international students: Required—TOEFL (minimum score 550 paper-based; 80 iBT), IELTS (minimum score 6.3). Electronic applications accepted.

Florida State University, The Graduate School, College of Education, School of Teacher Education, Tallahassee, FL 32306. Offers curriculum and instruction (MS, MST, PhD, Ed S), including early childhood education (MS, PhD, Ed S), elementary education (MS, PhD, Ed S), English education (MS, PhD, Ed S), English teaching (MST), exceptional student education (MST), foreign and second language education (MS, PhD, Ed S), foreign and second language teaching (MST), math education (MS, PhD, Ed S), math teaching (MST), reading education and language arts (MS, PhD, Ed S), science education (MS, PhD, Ed S), social science education (MS, PhD, Ed S), social science teaching (MST), special education (MS, PhD, Ed S), special education studies (MST), visual disabilities (MS, Ed S). Part-time programs available. *Faculty:* 30 full-time (20 women), 22 part-time/adjunct (18 women). *Students:* 183 full-time (151 women), 92 part-time (80 women); includes 47 minority (20 Black or African American, non-Hispanic/Latino; 3 American Indian or Alaska Native, non-Hispanic/Latino; 1 Asian, non-Hispanic/Latino; 20 Hispanic/Latino; 3 Two or more races, non-Hispanic/Latino), 61 international. Average age 30. 199 applicants, 79% accepted, 86 enrolled. In 2013, 119 master's, 9 doctorates, 4 other advanced degrees awarded. *Degree requirements:* For master's and Ed S, comprehensive exam, thesis optional; for doctorate, comprehensive exam, thesis/dissertation, preliminary exam, prospectus defense. *Entrance requirements:* For master's, doctorate, and Ed S, GRE General Test, minimum GPA of 3.0. Additional exam requirements/recommendations for international students: Required—TOEFL (minimum score 550 paper-based; 80 iBT). *Application deadline:* For fall admission, 7/1 for domestic and international students; for winter admission, 10/1 for domestic students, 11/1 for international students; for spring admission, 3/1 for domestic and international students. Applications are processed on a rolling basis. Application fee: $30. Electronic applications accepted. *Expenses:* Tuition, state resident: part-time $403.51 per credit hour. Tuition, nonresident: part-time $1004.85 per credit hour. *Required fees:* $75.81 per credit hour. One-time fee: $20 part-time. Tuition and fees vary according to course load, campus/location and student level. *Financial support:* In 2013–14, 113 students received support, including 55 research assistantships with full and partial tuition reimbursements available, 18 teaching assistantships with full and partial tuition reimbursements available; fellowships with full and partial tuition reimbursements available, career-related internships or fieldwork, scholarships/grants, health care benefits, and unspecified assistantships also available. Financial award application deadline: 1/15; financial award applicants required to submit FAFSA. *Faculty research:* Effective intervention and assessment strategies to improve reading skills; literacy teaching and learning through technology; understanding of student sense-making through instructions, especially STEM learning for all students; international

education and consequences of globalization; support professional teacher development and adoption of effective/transformative practices. *Total annual research expenditures:* $1.3 million. *Unit head:* Dr. Sherry Southerland, Chair, 850-644-4880, Fax: 850-644-7736, E-mail: ssoutherland@admin.fsu.edu. *Application contact:* Dawn Matthews, Academic Support Assistant, 850-644-2122, Fax: 850-644-7736, E-mail: dmatthews@fsu.edu.
Website: http://www.coe.fsu.edu/STE.

Framingham State University, Continuing Education, Program in History, Framingham, MA 01701-9101. Offers M Ed.

Georgia Southern University, Jack N. Averitt College of Graduate Studies, College of Education, Department of Teaching and Learning, Program in Social Science Education, Statesboro, GA 30460. Offers MAT. *Accreditation:* NCATE. Part-time and evening/weekend programs available. *Students:* 2 part-time (1 woman). Average age 33. In 2013, 2 master's awarded. *Degree requirements:* For master's, portfolio, transition point assessments, exit assessment. *Entrance requirements:* For master's, GRE General Test or MAT; GACE Basic Skills and Content Assessments (for MAT), minimum cumulative GPA of 2.5. Additional exam requirements/recommendations for international students: Required—TOEFL (minimum score 550 paper-based; 80 iBT), IELTS (minimum score 6). *Application deadline:* For fall admission, 3/1 priority date for domestic and international students; for spring admission, 10/1 priority date for domestic students, 10/1 for international students. Applications are processed on a rolling basis. Application fee: $50. Electronic applications accepted. *Expenses:* Tuition, state resident: full-time $7068; part-time $270 per semester hour. Tuition, nonresident: full-time $26,446; part-time $1077 per semester hour. *Required fees:* $2092. *Financial support:* In 2013–14, 1 research assistantship with partial tuition reimbursement (averaging $7,200 per year), teaching assistantships with partial tuition reimbursements (averaging $7,200 per year) were awarded; Federal Work-Study, scholarships/grants, tuition waivers (partial), and unspecified assistantships also available. Support available to part-time students. Financial award application deadline: 4/15; financial award applicants required to submit FAFSA. *Faculty research:* Environmental issues. *Unit head:* Dr. Greg Chamblee, Program Coordinator, 912-478-5783, Fax: 912-478-0026, E-mail: gchamblee@georgiasouthern.edu. *Application contact:* Amanda Gilliland, Coordinator for Graduate Student Recruitment, 912-478-5384, Fax: 912-478-0740, E-mail: gradadmissions@georgiasouthern.edu.
Website: http://coe.georgiasouthern.edu/ger/.

Georgia State University, College of Education, Department of Middle-Secondary Education and Instructional Technology, Atlanta, GA 30302-3083. Offers English education (M Ed, MAT); English speakers of other languages (MAT); instructional design and technology (MS); instructional technology (PhD), including alternative instructional delivery systems, consulting, instructional design, management, research; mathematics education (M Ed, MAT); middle level education (MAT); reading, language and literacy education (M Ed), including reading instruction; science education (MAT), including biology, broad field science, chemistry, earth science, physics; social studies education (M Ed, MAT), including economics (MAT), geography (MAT), history (MAT), political science (MAT); teaching and learning (PhD), including language and literacy, mathematics education, music education, science education, social studies, teaching and teacher education. *Accreditation:* NCATE. Part-time and evening/weekend programs available. Postbaccalaureate distance learning degree programs offered (minimal on-campus study). *Faculty:* 27 full-time (19 women). *Students:* 181 full-time (113 women), 203 part-time (145 women); includes 161 minority (127 Black or African American, non-Hispanic/Latino; 1 American Indian or Alaska Native, non-Hispanic/Latino; 10 Asian, non-Hispanic/Latino; 11 Hispanic/Latino; 1 Native Hawaiian or other Pacific Islander, non-Hispanic/Latino; 11 Two or more races, non-Hispanic/Latino), 9 international. Average age 36. 2 applicants, 50% accepted, 1 enrolled. In 2013, 213 master's, 17 doctorates awarded. *Degree requirements:* For master's, comprehensive exam (for some programs), thesis or alternative, exit portfolio; for doctorate, comprehensive exam, thesis/dissertation. *Entrance requirements:* For master's, GRE; GACE I (for initial teacher preparation degree programs), baccalaureate degree or equivalent, resume, goals statement, two letters of recommendation, minimum undergraduate GPA of 2.5; proof of initial teacher certification in the content area (for M Ed); for doctorate, GRE, resume, goals statement, writing sample, two letters of recommendation, minimum graduate GPA of 3.3, interview. Additional exam requirements/recommendations for international students: Required—TOEFL (minimum score 550 paper-based; 79 iBT) or IELTS (minimum score 6.5). *Application deadline:* For fall admission, 1/15 priority date for domestic and international students; for spring admission, 10/1 for domestic and international students. Application fee: $50. Electronic applications accepted. *Expenses: Tuition, area resident:* Full-time $4176; part-time $348 per credit hour. Tuition, state resident: full-time $14,544; part-time $1212 per credit hour. Tuition, nonresident: full-time $14,544; part-time $1212 per credit hour. Tuition and fees vary according to course load and program. *Financial support:* In 2013–14, fellowships with full tuition reimbursements (averaging $19,667 per year), research assistantships with full tuition reimbursements (averaging $5,436 per year), teaching assistantships with full tuition reimbursements (averaging $2,779 per year) were awarded; career-related internships or fieldwork, Federal Work-Study, scholarships/grants, health care benefits, tuition waivers (full and partial), and unspecified assistantships also available. Financial award application deadline: 3/15. *Faculty research:* Teacher education in language and literacy, mathematics, science, and social studies in urban middle and secondary school settings; learning technologies in school, community, and corporate settings; multicultural education and education for social justice; urban education; international education. *Unit head:* Dr. Dana L. Fox, Chair, 404-413-8060, Fax: 404-413-8063, E-mail: dfox@gsu.edu. *Application contact:* Bobbie Turner, Administrative Coordinator I, 404-413-8405, Fax: 404-413-8063, E-mail: bnturner@gsu.edu.
Website: http://msit.gsu.edu/msit_programs.htm.

Grambling State University, School of Graduate Studies and Research, College of Arts and Sciences, Department of History and Geography, Grambling, LA 71245. Offers social sciences (MA). Part-time programs available. *Faculty:* 9 full-time (5 women). *Students:* 16 full-time (14 women), 39 part-time (30 women); all minorities (54 Black or African American, non-Hispanic/Latino; 1 Hispanic/Latino). Average age 34. *Degree requirements:* For master's, comprehensive exam (for some programs), thesis optional. *Entrance requirements:* For master's, GRE, minimum GPA of 3.0 on last degree. Additional exam requirements/recommendations for international students: Required—TOEFL (minimum score 500 paper-based; 62 iBT). *Application deadline:* For fall admission, 7/1 for domestic and international students; for spring admission, 12/1 for domestic and international students; for summer admission, 5/1 for domestic and international students. Applications are processed on a rolling basis. Application fee: $20 ($30 for international students). Electronic applications accepted. *Financial support:* Research assistantships, traineeships, health care benefits, tuition waivers (full), and unspecified assistantships available. Financial award application deadline: 5/31; financial award applicants required to submit FAFSA. *Unit head:* Dr. Roshunda L. Belton, Acting Department Head, 318-274-2738, Fax: 318-274-3260, E-mail: beltonr@gram.edu. *Application contact:* Katina Crowe-Fields, 318-274-2158, Fax: 318-274-7373, E-mail: croweks@gram.edu.
Website: http://www.gram.edu/academics/majors/arts%20and%20sciences/departments/history/curriculum/socscience%20master.php.

Harding University, Cannon-Clary College of Education, Searcy, AR 72149-0001. Offers advanced studies in teaching and learning (M Ed); art (MSE); behavioral science (MSE); counseling (MS, Ed S); early childhood special education (M Ed, MSE); education (MSE); educational leadership (M Ed, Ed S); elementary education (M Ed); English (MSE); French (MSE); history/social science (MSE); kinesiology (MSE); math (MSE); reading (M Ed); secondary education (M Ed); Spanish (MSE); teaching (MAT); teaching English as a second language (MSE). *Accreditation:* NCATE. Part-time and evening/weekend programs available. *Faculty:* 13 full-time (5 women), 42 part-time/adjunct (24 women). *Students:* 154 full-time (119 women), 393 part-time (270 women); includes 108 minority (81 Black or African American, non-Hispanic/Latino; 5 American Indian or Alaska Native, non-Hispanic/Latino; 5 Asian, non-Hispanic/Latino; 9 Hispanic/Latino; 8 Two or more races, non-Hispanic/Latino), 15 international. Average age 36. 187 applicants, 79% accepted, 135 enrolled. In 2013, 138 master's, 17 other advanced degrees awarded. *Degree requirements:* For master's, comprehensive exam (for some programs), thesis optional, portfolio(s); for Ed S, comprehensive exam, portfolio, project. *Entrance requirements:* For master's, GRE, MAT, PRAXIS; for Ed S, MAT or GRE. Additional exam requirements/recommendations for international students: Required—TOEFL (minimum score 550 paper-based; 79 iBT). *Application deadline:* For fall admission, 8/1 for domestic and international students; for spring admission, 1/1 for domestic and international students. Applications are processed on a rolling basis. Application fee: $35. *Expenses: Tuition:* Full-time $11,574; part-time $643 per credit hour. *Required fees:* $432; $24 per credit hour. Tuition and fees vary according to course load, degree level and program. *Financial support:* In 2013–14, 36 students received support. Unspecified assistantships available. *Faculty research:* Reading, comprehension, school violence, educational technology, behavior, college choice, differentiated instruction, brain-based teaching. *Unit head:* Dr. Clara Carroll, Chair, 501-279-4501, Fax: 501-279-4083, E-mail: ccarroll@harding.edu. *Application contact:* Information Contact, 501-279-4315, E-mail: gradstudiesedu@harding.edu.
Website: http://www.harding.edu/education.

Hofstra University, School of Education, Programs in Teaching - Secondary Education, Hempstead, NY 11549. Offers business education (MS Ed); education technology (Advanced Certificate); English education (MA, MS Ed); foreign language and TESOL (MS Ed); foreign language education (MA, MS Ed), including French, German, Russian, Spanish; mathematics education (MA, MS Ed); science education (MA, MS Ed), including biology, chemistry, earth science, geology, physics; secondary education (Advanced Certificate); social studies education (MA, MS Ed); technology for learning (MA).

Hunter College of the City University of New York, Graduate School, School of Education, Programs in Secondary Education, Concentration in Social Studies Education, New York, NY 10065-5085. Offers MA. *Accreditation:* NCATE. *Faculty:* 3 full-time (1 woman), 20 part-time/adjunct (9 women). *Students:* 7 full-time (1 woman), 37 part-time (20 women); includes 13 minority (7 Black or African American, non-Hispanic/Latino; 2 Asian, non-Hispanic/Latino; 4 Hispanic/Latino), 1 international. Average age 29. 50 applicants, 46% accepted, 10 enrolled. In 2013, 18 master's awarded. *Degree requirements:* For master's, thesis, professional teaching portfolio, New York State Teacher Certification Exam, research project. *Entrance requirements:* For master's, minimum GPA of 3.0 in history, 2.8 overall; 2 letters of reference; minimum of 30 credits in social studies areas. Additional exam requirements/recommendations for international students: Required—TOEFL, TWE. *Application deadline:* For fall admission, 4/1 for domestic students, 2/1 for international students; for spring admission, 11/1 for domestic students, 9/1 for international students. Applications are processed on a rolling basis. Application fee: $125. *Financial support:* Federal Work-Study and tuition waivers (partial) available. Support available to part-time students. *Unit head:* Dr. Debbie Sonu, Education Program Coordinator, 212-772-5445, E-mail: dsonu@hunter.cuny.edu. *Application contact:* Prof. Jonathan Rosenberg, History Department Program Coordinator, 212-772-5546, E-mail: jrosen8637@aol.com.
Website: http://www.hunter.cuny.edu/school-of-education/programs/graduate/adolescent/social-studies.

Indiana University Bloomington, School of Education, Department of Curriculum and Instruction, Bloomington, IN 47405-7000. Offers art education (MS, Ed D, PhD); curriculum studies (Ed D, PhD); elementary education (MS, Ed D, PhD, Ed S); mathematics education (MS, Ed D, PhD); science education (MS, Ed D, PhD); secondary education (MS, Ed D, PhD); social studies education (MS, PhD); special education (PhD, Ed S). *Accreditation:* NCATE. Part-time and evening/weekend programs available. Terminal master's awarded for partial completion of doctoral program. *Degree requirements:* For doctorate, thesis/dissertation; for Ed S, comprehensive exam or project. *Entrance requirements:* For master's, doctorate, and Ed S, GRE General Test. Electronic applications accepted.

Instituto Tecnologico de Santo Domingo, Graduate School, Area of Humanities and Social Sciences, Santo Domingo, Dominican Republic. Offers accounting (Certificate); adult education (Certificate); applied linguistics (MA); economics (MA); education (M Ed); educational psychology (MA, Certificate); gender and development (MA, Certificate); humanistic studies (MA); international marketing management (Certificate); international relations in the Caribbean basin (Certificate); intervention systems in family therapy (MA); linguistic and literary communication (Certificate); pedagogical support (MA); social science education (M Ed); sustainable human development (MA); terminal illness and death psychology (Certificate); youth and adult education (M Ed).

Inter American University of Puerto Rico, Arecibo Campus, Programs in Education, Arecibo, PR 00614-4050. Offers administration and educational supervision (MA Ed); counseling and guidance (MA Ed); curriculum and teaching (MA Ed), including biology education, English as a second language, history education, math education, Spanish; elementary education (MA Ed). *Degree requirements:* For master's, comprehensive exam, thesis optional. *Entrance requirements:* For master's, GRE, EXADEP, bachelor's degree in education or teaching license (administration and supervision) or courses in education and psychology (counseling and guidance), minimum GPA of 2.5 in last 60 credits.

Inter American University of Puerto Rico, Barranquitas Campus, Program in Education, Barranquitas, PR 00794. Offers curriculum and teaching (M Ed), including biology education, English as a second language, history education, mathematics education, Spanish; educational leadership and management (MA); elementary education (M Ed); information and library service technology (M Ed); special education (MA). *Degree requirements:* For master's, comprehensive exam, thesis optional. *Entrance requirements:* For master's, EXADEP, letter of recommendation. Electronic applications accepted.

Inter American University of Puerto Rico, Metropolitan Campus, Graduate Programs, Program in History Education, San Juan, PR 00919-1293. Offers MA.

Inter American University of Puerto Rico, Ponce Campus, Graduate School, Mercedita, PR 00715-1602. Offers accounting (MBA); biology (M Ed); chemistry (M Ed);

criminal justice (MA); elementary education (M Ed); English as a Second Language (M Ed); finance (MBA); history (M Ed); human resources (MBA); marketing (MBA); mathematics (M Ed); Spanish (M Ed). *Entrance requirements:* For master's, minimum GPA of 2.5.

Iona College, School of Arts and Science, Department of Education, New Rochelle, NY 10801-1890. Offers adolescence education: biology (MS Ed, MST); adolescence education: English (MS Ed, MST); adolescence education: Italian (MS Ed, MST); adolescence education: mathematics (MS Ed, MST); adolescence education: social studies (MS Ed, MST); adolescence education: Spanish (MS Ed, MST); adolescence special education 5-12 (MST); adolescence special education and literacy (MS Ed); childhood and special education (MST); childhood education (MST); early childhood and childhood (MST); educational leadership (MS Ed); literacy education: birth-grade 6 (MS Ed). *Accreditation:* NCATE. Part-time and evening/weekend programs available. *Faculty:* 11 full-time (9 women), 7 part-time/adjunct (6 women). *Students:* 34 full-time (25 women), 61 part-time (47 women); includes 5 minority (2 Asian, non-Hispanic/Latino; 3 Hispanic/Latino), 1 international. Average age 25. 27 applicants, 93% accepted, 16 enrolled. In 2013, 54 master's awarded. *Degree requirements:* For master's, thesis or alternative. *Entrance requirements:* For master's, minimum GPA of 3.0, NY State teaching certificate (for all MS Ed programs). Additional exam requirements/recommendations for international students: Required—TOEFL (minimum score 550 paper-based; 80 iBT), IELTS (minimum score 6.5). *Application deadline:* For fall admission, 8/1 priority date for domestic students, 5/1 priority date for international students; for spring admission, 1/1 priority date for domestic students, 9/1 priority date for international students. Applications are processed on a rolling basis. Application fee: $50. Electronic applications accepted. *Expenses: Tuition:* Part-time $948 per credit. *Required fees:* $235 per term. *Financial support:* In 2013–14, 84 students received support. Unspecified assistantships available. Support available to part-time students. Financial award application deadline: 4/15; financial award applicants required to submit FAFSA. *Faculty research:* Reading/writing, educational technology, administration, early literacy assessment, literacy development. *Unit head:* Margaret Smith, PhD, Chair, 914-633-2210, Fax: 914-633-2608, E-mail: msmith@iona.edu. *Application contact:* Veronica Jarek-Prinz, Director, Graduate Admissions, 914-633-2420, Fax: 914-633-2277, E-mail: vjarekprinz@iona.edu.
Website: http://www.iona.edu/Academics/School-of-Arts-Science/Departments/Education/Graduate-Programs.aspx.

Ithaca College, School of Humanities and Sciences, Program in Adolescence Education, Ithaca, NY 14850. Offers biology 7-12 (MAT); chemistry 7-12 (MAT); English 7-12 (MAT); French 7-12 (MAT); math 7-12 (MAT); physics 7-12 (MAT); social studies 7-12 (MAT); Spanish (MAT). Part-time programs available. *Faculty:* 31 full-time (11 women). *Students:* 12 full-time (4 women); includes 1 minority (Hispanic/Latino). Average age 24. 27 applicants, 81% accepted, 12 enrolled. In 2013, 7 master's awarded. *Degree requirements:* For master's, thesis or alternative, student teaching. *Entrance requirements:* For master's, minimum GPA of 3.0. Additional exam requirements/recommendations for international students: Required—TOEFL (minimum score 550 paper-based; 80 iBT). *Application deadline:* For fall admission, 2/15 priority date for domestic and international students; for spring admission, 12/1 for domestic and international students. Applications are processed on a rolling basis. Application fee: $40. Electronic applications accepted. *Expenses:* Contact institution. *Financial support:* In 2013–14, 7 students received support, including 7 teaching assistantships (averaging $9,781 per year); career-related internships or fieldwork, Federal Work-Study, scholarships/grants, and unspecified assistantships also available. Support available to part-time students. Financial award application deadline: 2/15; financial award applicants required to submit CSS PROFILE or FAFSA. *Faculty research:* Teacher preparation (elementary and secondary education), equity and social justice in education, language and literacy, multicultural education/sociocultural studies, reflective practice and teacher research. *Unit head:* Dr. Linda Hanrahan, Chair, 607-274-3143, Fax: 607-274-1263, E-mail: gps@ithaca.edu. *Application contact:* Gerard Turbide, Director, Office of Admission, 607-274-3143, Fax: 607-274-1263, E-mail: gps@ithaca.edu.
Website: http://www.ithaca.edu/gradprograms/education/programs/aded.

Kansas State University, Graduate School, College of Education, Department of Curriculum and Instruction, Manhattan, KS 66506. Offers career and technical education (Ed D, PhD); curriculum studies (Ed D, PhD); digital teaching and learning (MS); educational computing, design and online learning (MS); educational technology (Ed D, PhD); elementary/middle level curriculum and instruction (MS); English as a second language (MS); language/diversity education (Ed D, PhD); literacy education (Ed D, PhD); mathematics education (Ed D, PhD); middle level/secondary curriculum and instruction (MS); reading and language arts (MS); reading specialist endorsement (MS); science education (Ed D, PhD); social science education (Ed D, PhD); teacher education (Ed D, PhD); teacher leader/school improvement (MS, Ed D). *Accreditation:* NCATE. Part-time programs available. Postbaccalaureate distance learning degree programs offered (minimal on-campus study). *Faculty:* 18 full-time (13 women), 7 part-time/adjunct (4 women). *Students:* 39 full-time (23 women), 122 part-time (94 women); includes 19 minority (3 Black or African American, non-Hispanic/Latino; 2 Asian, non-Hispanic/Latino; 12 Hispanic/Latino; 2 Two or more races, non-Hispanic/Latino), 12 international. Average age 36. 80 applicants, 50% accepted, 34 enrolled. In 2013, 40 master's, 13 doctorates awarded. *Degree requirements:* For master's, comprehensive exam, portfolio, project, report or thesis; for doctorate, comprehensive exam, thesis/dissertation, preliminary exam. *Entrance requirements:* For master's, minimum GPA of 3.0, letters of recommendation; for doctorate, GRE, minimum GPA of 3.0, letters of recommendation, evidence of scholarly writing. Additional exam requirements/recommendations for international students: Required—TOEFL (minimum score 550 paper-based; 80 iBT). *Application deadline:* For fall admission, 3/1 priority date for domestic students, 2/1 priority date for international students; for spring admission, 10/1 priority date for domestic students, 8/1 priority date for international students. Applications are processed on a rolling basis. Application fee: $50 ($75 for international students). Electronic applications accepted. *Financial support:* In 2013–14, 1 research assistantship (averaging $16,900 per year), 8 teaching assistantships (averaging $12,466 per year) were awarded; career-related internships or fieldwork, institutionally sponsored loans, and scholarships/grants also available. Support available to part-time students. Financial award application deadline: 3/1; financial award applicants required to submit FAFSA. *Faculty research:* Literacy and technology, critical race theory and diversity, achievement gaps, school improvement, teacher education. *Total annual research expenditures:* $543,677. *Unit head:* Dr. Todd Goodson, Chair, 785-532-5904, Fax: 785-532-7304, E-mail: tgoodson@ksu.edu. *Application contact:* Dona Deam, Application Contact, 785-532-5595, Fax: 785-532-7304, E-mail: ddeam@ksu.edu.
Website: http://www.coe.k-state.edu/departments/edci/.

Kutztown University of Pennsylvania, College of Education, Program in Secondary Education, Kutztown, PA 19530-0730. Offers biology (M Ed); curriculum and instruction (M Ed); English (M Ed); mathematics (M Ed); social studies (M Ed). *Accreditation:* NCATE. Part-time and evening/weekend programs available. *Faculty:* 6 full-time (2 women). *Students:* 34 full-time (17 women), 46 part-time (34 women); includes 4 minority (1 Asian, non-Hispanic/Latino; 3 Hispanic/Latino). Average age 31. 50 applicants, 70% accepted, 26 enrolled. In 2013, 31 master's awarded. *Degree*

requirements: For master's, comprehensive exam, thesis optional. *Entrance requirements:* For master's, GRE General Test. Additional exam requirements/recommendations for international students: Required—TOEFL (minimum score 550 paper-based; 79 iBT). *Application deadline:* For fall admission, 8/1 priority date for domestic and international students; for spring admission, 12/1 priority date for domestic and international students. Applications are processed on a rolling basis. Application fee: $35. Electronic applications accepted. *Expenses: Tuition, area resident:* Part-time $442 per credit. Tuition, state resident: part-time $442 per credit. Tuition, nonresident: part-time $663 per credit. *Required fees:* $80 per credit. *Financial support:* Career-related internships or fieldwork, Federal Work-Study, scholarships/grants, and unspecified assistantships available. Financial award application deadline: 3/1; financial award applicants required to submit FAFSA. *Unit head:* Dr. Theresa Stahler, Chairperson, 610-683-4259, Fax: 610-683-1338, E-mail: stahler@kutztown.edu. *Application contact:* Kelly Hish, Admissions Clerk, 610-683-4200, Fax: 610-683-1393, E-mail: graduate@kutztown.edu.

Lake Forest College, Master of Arts in Teaching Program, Lake Forest, IL 60045. Offers elementary education (MAT); K-12 French (MAT); K-12 music (MAT); K-12 Spanish (MAT); K-12 visual art (MAT); secondary biology (MAT); secondary chemistry (MAT); secondary English (MAT); secondary history (MAT); secondary mathematics (MAT). *Degree requirements:* For master's, comprehensive exam, portfolio. *Entrance requirements:* For master's, GRE.

La Salle University, School of Arts and Sciences, Program in History, Philadelphia, PA 19141-1199. Offers American history (Certificate); European history (Certificate); history (MA); history for educators (MA); public history (MA); teaching advanced placement history (Certificate); world history (Certificate). Part-time programs available. *Faculty:* 5 full-time (1 woman), 1 (woman) part-time/adjunct. *Students:* 41 part-time (19 women); includes 8 minority (5 Black or African American, non-Hispanic/Latino; 2 Asian, non-Hispanic/Latino; 1 Two or more races, non-Hispanic/Latino). Average age 38. 16 applicants, 81% accepted, 5 enrolled. In 2013, 9 master's awarded. *Degree requirements:* For master's, thesis or comprehensive exam. *Entrance requirements:* For master's, GRE or MAT, 18 hours of undergraduate coursework in history or a related discipline with minimum GPA of 3.0; two letters of recommendation; brief personal statement (250 to 500 words); writing sample (preferably from an undergraduate research paper). Additional exam requirements/recommendations for international students: Required—TOEFL. *Application deadline:* For fall admission, 8/15 priority date for domestic students, 7/15 for international students; for spring admission, 12/15 priority date for domestic students, 11/15 for international students; for summer admission, 4/15 priority date for domestic students, 3/15 for international students. Applications are processed on a rolling basis. Application fee: $35. Electronic applications accepted. Application fee is waived when completed online. *Expenses: Tuition:* Full-time $20,750; part-time $695 per credit hour. *Required fees:* $300; $200 per year. Tuition and fees vary according to program. *Financial support:* In 2013–14, 3 students received support. Federal Work-Study, institutionally sponsored loans, and scholarships/grants available. Support available to part-time students. Financial award application deadline: 8/31; financial award applicants required to submit FAFSA. *Unit head:* Dr. George B. Stow, Director, 215-951-1097, E-mail: grahis@lasalle.edu. *Application contact:* Paul J. Reilly, Assistant Vice President, Enrollment Services, 215-951-1946, Fax: 215-951-1462, E-mail: reilly@lasalle.edu.
Website: http://www.lasalle.edu/grad/index.php?section-history&page-index.

Lehman College of the City University of New York, Division of Education, Department of Middle and High School Education, Program in Social Studies 7–12, Bronx, NY 10468-1589. Offers MA. *Accreditation:* NCATE. *Entrance requirements:* For master's, minimum GPA of 3.0 in social sciences, 2.7 overall.

Le Moyne College, Department of Education, Syracuse, NY 13214. Offers adolescent education (MS Ed, MST); adolescent education/special education (MS Ed, MST); adolescent English (MST), including grades 7-12 (MS Ed, MST); adolescent English/special education (MST), including grades 7-12 (MS Ed, MST); adolescent foreign language (MST), including grades 7-12 (MS Ed, MST); adolescent history (MST), including grades 7-12 (MS Ed, MST); childhood education (MS Ed); childhood education/special education (MS Ed); elementary education (MS Ed); general education (MS Ed); inclusive childhood education (MST); literacy education (MS Ed), including birth to grade 6, grades 5-12; school building leader (MS Ed); school building leadership (CAS); school district business leader (MS Ed, CAS); school district leader (MS Ed); school district leadership (CAS); secondary education (MS Ed); special education (MS Ed); students with disabilities-generalist (MS Ed), including grades 7-12 (MS Ed, MST); teaching English to speakers of other languages (MS Ed); urban studies (MS Ed). *Accreditation:* Teacher Education Accreditation Council. Part-time and evening/weekend programs available. *Faculty:* 8 full-time (5 women), 61 part-time/adjunct (38 women). *Students:* 24 full-time (20 women), 178 part-time (133 women); includes 22 minority (12 Black or African American, non-Hispanic/Latino; 1 American Indian or Alaska Native, non-Hispanic/Latino; 3 Asian, non-Hispanic/Latino; 6 Hispanic/Latino), 1 international. Average age 31. 248 applicants, 90% accepted, 86 enrolled. In 2013, 158 master's, 37 CASs awarded. *Degree requirements:* For master's, thesis. *Entrance requirements:* For master's, GRE General Test, bachelor's degree, 2 letters of recommendation, written statement, transcripts. Additional exam requirements/recommendations for international students: Required—TOEFL (minimum score 550 paper-based; 79 iBT). *Application deadline:* For fall admission, 4/1 priority date for domestic and international students; for spring admission, 10/1 priority date for domestic and international students; for summer admission, 3/1 priority date for domestic and international students. Applications are processed on a rolling basis. Application fee: $50. *Expenses:* Contact institution. *Financial support:* In 2013–14, 26 students received support. Career-related internships or fieldwork and health care benefits available. Support available to part-time students. Financial award applicants required to submit FAFSA. *Faculty research:* Minority teachers, special education, multiculturalism, literacy, technology, media literacy learning, autism, school district organization, service-learning, higher level problem solving, teacher leadership. *Unit head:* Dr. Suzanne L. Gilmour, Chair, Department of Education/Director of Graduate Education Programs, 315-445-4376, Fax: 315-445-4744, E-mail: gilmous@lemoyne.edu. *Application contact:* Kristen P. Trapasso, Senior Director of Enrollment Management, 315-445-4265, Fax: 315-445-6092, E-mail: trapaskp@lemoyne.edu.
Website: http://www.lemoyne.edu/education.

Lewis University, College of Education, Program in Secondary Education, Romeoville, IL 60446. Offers biology (MA); chemistry (MA); English (MA); history (MA); math (MA); physics (MA); psychology and social science (MA). Part-time programs available. *Students:* 15 full-time (6 women), 15 part-time (9 women); includes 6 minority (2 Black or African American, non-Hispanic/Latino; 1 Asian, non-Hispanic/Latino; 3 Hispanic/Latino). Average age 30. *Entrance requirements:* For master's, departmental qualifying exam, writing exam, minimum GPA of 2.75, 2 letters of recommendation, interview. Additional exam requirements/recommendations for international students: Required—TOEFL (minimum score 550 paper-based; 80 iBT). *Application deadline:* For fall admission, 5/1 priority date for international students; for spring admission, 11/15 priority date for international students. Applications are processed on a rolling basis. Application fee: $40. Electronic applications accepted. *Financial support:* Federal Work-Study,

scholarships/grants, and unspecified assistantships available. Financial award application deadline: 5/1; financial award applicants required to submit FAFSA. *Unit head:* Dr. Dorene Huvaere, Program Director, 815-838-0500 Ext. 5885, E-mail: huvaersdo@lewisu.edu. *Application contact:* Fran Welsh, Secretary, 815-838-0500 Ext. 5880, E-mail: welshfr@lewisu.edu.

Louisiana Tech University, Graduate School, College of Education, Department of Curriculum, Instruction and Leadership, Ruston, LA 71272. Offers curriculum and instruction (M Ed, Ed D), including adult education (M Ed), early childhood (M Ed), English education (M Ed), mathematics education (M Ed), science education (M Ed), social studies education (M Ed), special education (M Ed); educational leadership (M Ed, Ed D). *Accreditation:* NCATE. Part-time programs available. *Degree requirements:* For doctorate, thesis/dissertation. *Entrance requirements:* For master's and doctorate, GRE General Test. *Application deadline:* For fall admission, 7/29 for domestic students; for spring admission, 2/3 for domestic students. Application fee: $20 ($30 for international students). *Financial support:* Fellowships, research assistantships, and teaching assistantships available. Financial award application deadline: 2/1. *Unit head:* Dr. Pauline Leonard, Head, 318-257-4609, Fax: 318-257-2379. *Application contact:* Dr. John Harrison, Associate Dean of Graduate Studies, 318-257-3229, Fax: 318-257-2379, E-mail: johnharrison@latech.edu.
Website: http://www.latech.edu/education/cil/.

Manhattanville College, School of Education, Program in Middle Childhood/ Adolescence Education (Grades 5-12), Purchase, NY 10577-2132. Offers biology (MAT); biology and special education (MPS); chemistry (MAT); chemistry and special education (MPS); English (MAT); English and special education (MPS); literacy and special education (MPS); literacy specialist (MPS); math and special education (MPS); mathematics (MAT); physics (MAT); social studies (MAT); social studies and special education (MPS); special education (MPS); teaching languages other than English (MAT), including French, Italian, Latin, Spanish. Part-time and evening/weekend programs available. *Degree requirements:* For master's, comprehensive exam or research project, field experience. *Entrance requirements:* For master's, minimum undergraduate GPA of 3.0, 2 letters of recommendation. Additional exam requirements/ recommendations for international students: Required—TOEFL. Electronic applications accepted.

Michigan State University, The Graduate School, College of Social Science, Department of History, East Lansing, MI 48824. Offers history (MA, PhD); history-secondary school teaching (MA). *Entrance requirements:* Additional exam requirements/recommendations for international students: Required—TOEFL. Electronic applications accepted.

Mills College, Graduate Studies, School of Education, Oakland, CA 94613-1000. Offers child life in hospitals (MA); early childhood education (MA); education (MA), including art education, curriculum and instruction, elementary education, English education, foreign language education, mathematics education, science education, secondary education, social studies education, teaching; educational leadership (MA, Ed D). Part-time and evening/weekend programs available. *Faculty:* 10 full-time (7 women), 13 part-time/ adjunct (10 women). *Students:* 154 full-time (136 women), 54 part-time (47 women); includes 96 minority (32 Black or African American, non-Hispanic/Latino; 1 American Indian or Alaska Native, non-Hispanic/Latino; 23 Asian, non-Hispanic/Latino; 27 Hispanic/Latino; 1 Native Hawaiian or other Pacific Islander, non-Hispanic/Latino; 12 Two or more races, non-Hispanic/Latino), 2 international. Average age 25. 222 applicants, 89% accepted, 110 enrolled. In 2013, 96 master's, 38 doctorates awarded. Terminal master's awarded for partial completion of doctoral program. *Degree requirements:* For master's, comprehensive exam, thesis (for some programs); for doctorate, thesis/dissertation. *Entrance requirements:* For master's, statement of purpose, official transcript, 3 recommendations. Additional exam requirements/ recommendations for international students: Required—TOEFL (minimum score 550 paper-based; 80 iBT) or IELTS (minimum score 6). *Application deadline:* For fall admission, 12/31 priority date for domestic students, 12/15 for international students; for spring admission, 11/1 priority date for domestic students, 10/1 for international students. Applications are processed on a rolling basis. Application fee: $50. Electronic applications accepted. *Expenses: Tuition:* Full-time $29,860. *Required fees:* $1134. Part-time tuition and fees vary according to course load, degree level and program. *Financial support:* In 2013–14, 130 students received support, including 130 fellowships with full and partial tuition reimbursements available (averaging $7,565 per year); career-related internships or fieldwork and scholarships/grants also available. Support available to part-time students. Financial award application deadline: 2/1; financial award applicants required to submit FAFSA. *Faculty research:* Early childhood education, teacher preparation, educational leadership. *Total annual research expenditures:* $3.5 million. *Unit head:* Dr. Katherine Schultz, Department Head, 510-430-3384, Fax: 510-430-2159, E-mail: kschultz@mills.edu. *Application contact:* Shrim Bathey, Director of Graduate Admission, 510-430-3309, Fax: 510-430-2159, E-mail: grad-admission@mills.edu.
Website: http://www.mills.edu/education.

Minnesota State University Mankato, College of Graduate Studies, College of Social and Behavioral Sciences, Department of History, Mankato, MN 56001. Offers history (MA, MS); social studies (MAT). *Students:* 3 full-time (1 woman), 9 part-time (2 women). *Degree requirements:* For master's, one foreign language, comprehensive exam, thesis or alternative. *Entrance requirements:* For master's, minimum GPA of 3.0 during previous 2 years. Additional exam requirements/recommendations for international students: Required—TOEFL. *Application deadline:* For fall admission, 7/1 priority date for domestic students; for spring admission, 11/1 for domestic students. Applications are processed on a rolling basis. Application fee: $40. Electronic applications accepted. *Financial support:* Research assistantships, teaching assistantships with full tuition reimbursements, career-related internships or fieldwork, Federal Work-Study, institutionally sponsored loans, and unspecified assistantships available. Support available to part-time students. Financial award application deadline: 3/15. *Faculty research:* Charivaris, Lindbergh in the U.S., Dutch trade to South America in the seventeenth and eighteenth centuries. *Unit head:* Dr. Tao Peng, Graduate Coordinator, 507-389-1618. *Application contact:* 507-389-2321, E-mail: grad@mnsu.edu.
Website: http://sbs.mnsu.edu/history/.

Mississippi College, Graduate School, School of Education, Department of Teacher Education and Leadership, Clinton, MS 39058. Offers art (M Ed); biological science (M Ed); business education (M Ed); computer science (M Ed); dyslexia therapy (M Ed); educational leadership (M Ed, Ed D, Ed S); elementary education (M Ed, Ed S); English (M Ed); higher education administration (MS); mathematics (M Ed); secondary education (M Ed); social studies (history) (M Ed); teaching arts (M Ed). Part-time programs available. Postbaccalaureate distance learning degree programs offered (no on-campus study). *Degree requirements:* For master's, comprehensive exam, thesis optional. *Entrance requirements:* For master's, NTE. Additional exam requirements/ recommendations for international students: Recommended—TOEFL, IELTS. Electronic applications accepted.

Missouri State University, Graduate College, College of Humanities and Public Affairs, Department of History, Springfield, MO 65897. Offers history (MA); secondary education (MS Ed), including history, social science. Part-time programs available. *Faculty:* 20 full-time (7 women). *Students:* 12 full-time (4 women), 38 part-time (17 women); includes 3 minority (1 American Indian or Alaska Native, non-Hispanic/Latino; 1 Hispanic/Latino; 1 Two or more races, non-Hispanic/Latino). Average age 31. 17 applicants, 94% accepted, 8 enrolled. In 2013, 9 master's awarded. *Degree requirements:* For master's, comprehensive exam, thesis or alternative. *Entrance requirements:* For master's, minimum GPA of 2.75, 24 hours of undergraduate course work in history (MA), 9-12 teaching certification (MS Ed). Additional exam requirements/recommendations for international students: Required—TOEFL (minimum score 550 paper-based; 79 iBT). *Application deadline:* For fall admission, 7/20 priority date for domestic students, 5/1 for international students; for spring admission, 12/20 priority date for domestic students, 9/ 1 for international students. Applications are processed on a rolling basis. Application fee: $35 ($50 for international students). Electronic applications accepted. *Expenses:* Tuition, state resident: full-time $4500; part-time $250 per credit hour. Tuition, nonresident: full-time $9018; part-time $501 per credit hour. *Required fees:* $361 per semester. Tuition and fees vary according to course level, course load and program. *Financial support:* Federal Work-Study, scholarships/grants, and unspecified assistantships available. Support available to part-time students. Financial award application deadline: 3/31; financial award applicants required to submit FAFSA. *Faculty research:* U.S. history, Native American history, Latin American history, women's history, ancient Near East. *Unit head:* Dr. Kathleen Kennedy, Head, 417-836-5511, Fax: 417-836-5523, E-mail: history@missouristate.edu. *Application contact:* Misty Stewart, Coordinator of Graduate Recruitment, 417-836-6079, Fax: 417-836-6200, E-mail: mistystewart@missouristate.edu.
Website: http://history.missouristate.edu/.

Morehead State University, Graduate Programs, College of Education, Department of Foundational and Graduate Studies in Education, Morehead, KY 40351. Offers adult and higher education (MA, Ed S); certified professional counselor (Ed S); counseling P-12 (MA); curriculum and instruction (Ed S); educational technology (MA Ed); instructional leadership (Ed S); school administration (MA); school counseling (Ed S); teacher leader business and marketing content (MA Ed); teacher leader business and marketing technology (MA Ed); teacher leader educational technology (MA Ed); teacher leader English (MA Ed); teacher leader gifted education (MA Ed); teacher leader IECE certification (MA Ed); teacher leader interdisciplinary education P-5 (MA Ed); teacher leader middle grades (MA Ed); teacher leader non IECE certification (MA Ed); teacher leader reading/writing - non-certification (MA Ed); teacher leader reading/writing certification (MA Ed); teacher leader school communication - certification (MA Ed); teacher leader school communication - non-certification (MA Ed); teacher leader social studies (MA Ed); teacher leader special education (MA Ed). *Accreditation:* NCATE. Part-time and evening/weekend programs available. *Degree requirements:* For master's, thesis optional, oral and/or written comprehensive exams; for Ed S, thesis, oral exam. *Entrance requirements:* For master's, GRE General Test, minimum overall undergraduate GPA of 2.5; for Ed S, GRE General Test, interview, master's degree, minimum GPA of 3.5, work experience. Additional exam requirements/ recommendations for international students: Required—TOEFL (minimum score 500 paper-based). Electronic applications accepted. *Faculty research:* Character education, school accountability, computer applications for school administrators.

Morehead State University, Graduate Programs, College of Education, Department of Middle Grades and Secondary Education, Morehead, KY 40351. Offers business and marketing education (MAT); English/language arts 5-9 (MAT); French (MAT); health P-12 (MAT); mathematics 5-9 (MAT); physical education P-12 (MAT); science 5-9 (MAT); secondary biology (MAT); secondary chemistry (MAT); secondary earth science (MAT); secondary English (MAT); secondary math (MAT); secondary physics (MAT); secondary social studies (MAT); social studies 5-9 (MAT); Spanish (MAT). Part-time and evening/ weekend programs available. *Degree requirements:* For master's, portfolio. *Entrance requirements:* For master's, GRE or PRAXIS II content exam, minimum overall undergraduate GPA of 2.5. Additional exam requirements/recommendations for international students: Required—TOEFL (minimum score 500 paper-based). Electronic applications accepted.

New York University, Steinhardt School of Culture, Education, and Human Development, Department of Art and Art Professions, Program in Art Education, New York, NY 10003-5799. Offers art, education, and community practice (MA); teaching art and social studies (MA); teaching art, all grades (MA). *Accreditation:* Teacher Education Accreditation Council. Part-time programs available. *Faculty:* 2 full-time (1 woman). *Students:* 10 full-time (9 women), 12 part-time (9 women); includes 10 minority (1 Black or African American, non-Hispanic/Latino; 4 American Indian or Alaska Native, non-Hispanic/Latino; 3 Asian, non-Hispanic/Latino; 2 Hispanic/Latino), 4 international. Average age 35. 34 applicants, 94% accepted, 12 enrolled. In 2013, 14 master's awarded. *Degree requirements:* For master's, thesis (for some programs). *Entrance requirements:* For master's, portfolio. Additional exam requirements/recommendations for international students: Required—TOEFL (minimum score 100 iBT). *Application deadline:* For fall admission, 11/16 priority date for domestic and international students. Applications are processed on a rolling basis. Application fee: $75. Electronic applications accepted. *Expenses: Tuition:* Full-time $35,856; part-time $1494 per unit. *Required fees:* $1408; $64 per unit. $473 per term. Tuition and fees vary according to course load and program. *Financial support:* Career-related internships or fieldwork, Federal Work-Study, and tuition waivers (partial) available. Support available to part-time students. Financial award application deadline: 2/1; financial award applicants required to submit FAFSA. *Faculty research:* Multicultural aesthetic inquiry, urban art education, feminism, equity and social justice. *Unit head:* Prof. Dipti Desai, Director, 212-998-9022, Fax: 212-995-4320, E-mail: dd25@nyu.edu. *Application contact:* 212-998-5030, Fax: 212-995-4328, E-mail: steinhardt.gradadmissions@nyu.edu.
Website: http://steinhardt.nyu.edu/art/education.

New York University, Steinhardt School of Culture, Education, and Human Development, Department of Music and Performing Arts Professions, Program in Educational Theatre, New York, NY 10012. Offers educational theatre (Ed D, Advanced Certificate); educational theatre and English 7-12: dual certificate (MA); educational theatre and social studies 7-12: dual certificate (MA); educational theatre in colleges and communities (MA, PhD); educational theatre, all grades (MA). Part-time programs available. *Faculty:* 5 full-time (2 women). *Students:* 51 full-time (34 women), 36 part-time (24 women); includes 20 minority (10 Black or African American, non-Hispanic/Latino; 1 Asian, non-Hispanic/Latino; 7 Hispanic/Latino; 2 Two or more races, non-Hispanic/ Latino), 5 international. Average age 28. 66 applicants, 80% accepted, 25 enrolled. In 2013, 51 master's, 1 doctorate awarded. *Degree requirements:* For master's, thesis (for some programs); for doctorate, thesis/dissertation. *Entrance requirements:* For master's, audition; for doctorate, GRE General Test, interview; for Advanced Certificate, master's degree. Additional exam requirements/recommendations for international students: Required—TOEFL (minimum score 100 iBT). *Application deadline:* For fall admission, 12/1 priority date for domestic and international students; for spring admission, 10/1 for domestic and international students. Applications are processed on a rolling basis. Application fee: $75. Electronic applications accepted. *Expenses: Tuition:* Full-time $35,856; part-time $1494 per unit. *Required fees:* $1408; $64 per unit. $473 per term. Tuition and fees vary according to course load and program. *Financial support:* Teaching assistantships with partial tuition reimbursements, career-related internships or fieldwork, Federal Work-Study, institutionally sponsored loans, and scholarships/

grants available. Support available to part-time students. Financial award application deadline: 2/1; financial award applicants required to submit FAFSA. *Faculty research:* Theatre for young audiences, drama in education, applied theatre, arts education assessment, reflective praxis. *Unit head:* Prof. David Montgomery, Director, 212-998-5869, Fax: 212-995-4043, E-mail: dm635@nyu.edu. *Application contact:* 212-998-5030, Fax: 212-995-4328, E-mail: steinhardt.gradadmissions@nyu.edu.
Website: http://steinhardt.nyu.edu/music/edtheatre.

New York University, Steinhardt School of Culture, Education, and Human Development, Department of Teaching and Learning, Program in Social Studies Education, New York, NY 10003. Offers history, social studies, and global education (PhD); teaching art and social studies 7-12 (MA); teaching social studies 7-12 (MA). *Accreditation:* Teacher Education Accreditation Council. Part-time and evening/weekend programs available. *Faculty:* 3 full-time (2 women). *Students:* 5 full-time (3 women), 5 part-time (2 women); includes 4 minority (all Hispanic/Latino). Average age 27. 48 applicants, 88% accepted, 6 enrolled. In 2013, 23 master's awarded. *Degree requirements:* For master's, thesis (for some programs). *Entrance requirements:* Additional exam requirements/recommendations for international students: Required—TOEFL (minimum score 100 iBT). *Application deadline:* For fall admission, 2/1 priority date for domestic and international students; for spring admission, 10/1 for domestic and international students. Applications are processed on a rolling basis. Application fee: $75. Electronic applications accepted. *Expenses: Tuition:* Full-time $35,856; part-time $1494 per unit. *Required fees:* $1408; $64 per unit. $473 per term. Tuition and fees vary according to course load and program. *Financial support:* Career-related internships or fieldwork, Federal Work-Study, institutionally sponsored loans, scholarships/grants, and tuition waivers (partial) available. Support available to part-time students. Financial award application deadline: 2/1; financial award applicants required to submit FAFSA. *Faculty research:* Social studies education reform, ethnography and oral history, civic education, labor history and social studies curriculum, material culture. *Unit head:* 212-998-5460, Fax: 212-995-4049. *Application contact:* 212-998-5030, Fax: 212-995-4328, E-mail: steinhardt.gradadmissions@nyu.edu.
Website: http://steinhardt.nyu.edu/teachlearn/social_studies.

North Carolina State University, Graduate School, College of Education, Department of Curriculum and Instruction, Program in Social Studies Education, Raleigh, NC 27695. Offers M Ed. *Entrance requirements:* For master's, GRE or MAT, 3 letters of reference, interview, minimum GPA of 3.0.

North Dakota State University, College of Graduate and Interdisciplinary Studies, College of Human Development and Education, School of Education, Fargo, ND 58108. Offers agricultural education (M Ed, MS), including agricultural education, agricultural extension education (MS); counseling (M Ed, MS, PhD); curriculum and instruction (M Ed, MS); education (PhD); educational leadership (M Ed, MS, Ed S); family and consumer sciences education (M Ed, MS); history education (M Ed, MS); institutional analysis (Ed D); mathematics education (M Ed, MS); music education (M Ed, MS); occupational and adult education (Ed D); science education (M Ed, MS). *Accreditation:* NCATE. Part-time and evening/weekend programs available. Postbaccalaureate distance learning degree programs offered (minimal on-campus study). *Faculty:* 25 full-time (11 women), 1 (woman) part-time/adjunct. *Students:* 110 full-time (82 women), 123 part-time (85 women); includes 14 minority (4 Black or African American, non-Hispanic/Latino; 4 American Indian or Alaska Native, non-Hispanic/Latino; 1 Native Hawaiian or other Pacific Islander, non-Hispanic/Latino; 5 Two or more races, non-Hispanic/Latino), 10 international. Average age 28. 57 applicants, 81% accepted, 42 enrolled. In 2013, 38 master's, 9 doctorates awarded. *Degree requirements:* For master's, comprehensive exam; for doctorate, thesis/dissertation; for Ed S, thesis. *Entrance requirements:* For degree, GRE General Test, master's degree, minimum GPA of 3.25. Additional exam requirements/recommendations for international students: Required—TOEFL. *Application deadline:* Applications are processed on a rolling basis. Application fee: $45 ($60 for international students). *Financial support:* Research assistantships, teaching assistantships, career-related internships or fieldwork, Federal Work-Study, institutionally sponsored loans, and tuition waivers (full) available. Financial award application deadline: 4/15. *Unit head:* Dr. William Martin, Chair, 701-231-7202, Fax: 701-231-7416, E-mail: william.martin@ndsu.edu. *Application contact:* Sonya Goergen, Marketing, Recruitment, and Public Relations Coordinator, 701-231-7033, Fax: 701-231-6524.
Website: http://www.ndsu.nodak.edu/school_of_education/.

Northwest Missouri State University, Graduate School, College of Arts and Sciences, Department of Humanities and Social Sciences, Maryville, MO 64468-6001. Offers geographic information science (MS, Certificate); history (MA); teaching history (MS Ed). Part-time programs available. *Degree requirements:* For master's, comprehensive exam, thesis. *Entrance requirements:* For master's, GRE General Test, undergraduate major/minor in social studies/humanities, minimum undergraduate GPA of 2.5, writing sample. Additional exam requirements/recommendations for international students: Required—TOEFL (minimum score 550 paper-based).

Occidental College, Graduate Studies, Department of Education, Los Angeles, CA 90041-3314. Offers elementary education (MAT), including liberal studies; secondary education (MAT), including English and comparative literary studies, history, life science, mathematics, physical science, social science, Spanish. Part-time programs available. *Degree requirements:* For master's, comprehensive exam, synthesis paper. *Entrance requirements:* For master's, GRE General Test, minimum GPA of 3.0. Additional exam requirements/recommendations for international students: Required—TOEFL (minimum score 625 paper-based). *Expenses:* Contact institution. *Faculty research:* Preparing teacher-leaders, curriculum development.

Ohio University, Graduate College, Gladys W. and David H. Patton College of Education and Human Services, Department of Teacher Education, Athens, OH 45701-2979. Offers adolescent to young adult education (M Ed); curriculum and instruction (M Ed, PhD); early childhood/special education (M Ed); intervention specialist/mild-moderate needs (M Ed); intervention specialist/moderate-intensive needs (M Ed); mathematics education (PhD); middle childhood education (M Ed); reading education (M Ed); social studies education (PhD). Part-time and evening/weekend programs available. *Degree requirements:* For master's, thesis or alternative; for doctorate, comprehensive exam, thesis/dissertation. *Entrance requirements:* For master's, GRE General Test or MAT (if GPA is below 2.9); for doctorate, GRE General Test, minimum GPA of 3.4, work experience. Additional exam requirements/recommendations for international students: Required—TOEFL (minimum score 550 paper-based; 80 iBT) or IELTS (minimum score 6.5). Electronic applications accepted. *Faculty research:* Cognition literacy, character education, teacher's education reform, disabilities.

Plymouth State University, College of Graduate Studies, Graduate Studies in Education, Program in Heritage Studies, Plymouth, NH 03264-1595. Offers M Ed. Part-time and evening/weekend programs available. *Degree requirements:* For master's, internship. *Entrance requirements:* For master's, GRE General Test or MAT, minimum GPA of 3.0, resume.

Plymouth State University, College of Graduate Studies, Graduate Studies in Education, Program in Secondary Education, Plymouth, NH 03264-1595. Offers curriculum and instruction (M Ed); language education (M Ed); library media (M Ed); physical education (M Ed); social studies education (M Ed); special education (M Ed). Part-time and evening/weekend programs available. *Entrance requirements:* For master's, MAT.

Portland State University, Graduate Studies, College of Liberal Arts and Sciences, Interdisciplinary Programs in General Science, General Social Science, and General Arts and Letters, Portland, OR 97207-0751. Offers general arts and letters education (MAT, MST); general science education (MAT, MST); general social science education (MAT, MST). Part-time and evening/weekend programs available. *Students:* 7 full-time (5 women), 22 part-time (14 women); includes 6 minority (3 Hispanic/Latino; 1 Native Hawaiian or other Pacific Islander, non-Hispanic/Latino; 2 Two or more races, non-Hispanic/Latino). Average age 39. 11 applicants, 36% accepted, 3 enrolled. In 2013, 13 master's awarded. *Degree requirements:* For master's, variable foreign language requirement, written exam. *Entrance requirements:* For master's, minimum GPA of 3.0 in upper-division course work or 2.75 overall. Additional exam requirements/recommendations for international students: Required—TOEFL (minimum score 550 paper-based). *Application deadline:* For fall admission, 4/1 priority date for domestic students, 3/1 priority date for international students. Application fee: $50. *Expenses:* Tuition, state resident: full-time $9207; part-time $341 per credit. Tuition, nonresident: full-time $14,391; part-time $533 per credit. *Required fees:* $1263; $22 per credit. $98 per quarter. One-time fee: $150. Tuition and fees vary according to program. *Financial support:* Federal Work-Study and unspecified assistantships available. Support available to part-time students. Financial award application deadline: 3/1; financial award applicants required to submit FAFSA. *Total annual research expenditures:* $462,166. *Unit head:* Robert Mercer, Associate Dean, 503-725-5059, Fax: 503-725-3693, E-mail: mercerr@pdx.edu. *Application contact:* 503-725-3511, Fax: 503-725-5525.

Purdue University, Graduate School, College of Education, Department of Curriculum and Instruction, West Lafayette, IN 47907. Offers agricultural and extension education (PhD, Ed S); agriculture and extension education (MS, MS Ed); art education (PhD); curriculum studies (MS Ed, PhD, Ed S); educational technology (MS Ed, PhD, Ed S); elementary education (MS Ed); family and consumer sciences education (MS Ed, PhD, Ed S); foreign language education (MS Ed, PhD, Ed S); industrial technology (PhD, Ed S); language arts (MS Ed, PhD, Ed S); literacy (MS Ed, PhD, Ed S); mathematics/science education (MS, MS Ed, PhD, Ed S); social studies (MS Ed, PhD); social studies education (Ed S); vocational/industrial education (MS Ed, PhD, Ed S); vocational/technical education (MS Ed, PhD, Ed S). *Accreditation:* NCATE. Part-time and evening/weekend programs available. *Faculty:* 29 full-time (19 women), 33 part-time/adjunct (29 women). *Students:* 85 full-time (53 women), 271 part-time (195 women); includes 62 minority (19 Black or African American, non-Hispanic/Latino; 3 American Indian or Alaska Native, non-Hispanic/Latino; 13 Asian, non-Hispanic/Latino; 22 Hispanic/Latino; 1 Native Hawaiian or other Pacific Islander, non-Hispanic/Latino; 4 Two or more races, non-Hispanic/Latino), 41 international. Average age 36. 155 applicants, 71% accepted, 71 enrolled. In 2013, 60 master's, 20 doctorates awarded. *Degree requirements:* For master's, thesis optional; for doctorate, thesis/dissertation, oral and written exams; for Ed S, oral presentation, project. *Entrance requirements:* For master's, GRE General Test (if undergraduate GPA is below 3.0), minimum undergraduate GPA of 3.0 or equivalent; for doctorate, GRE General Test (minimum combined verbal and quantitative score of 1000, 300 for new scoring), minimum undergraduate GPA of 3.0 or equivalent; master's degree with minimum GPA of 3.0 or equivalent; for Ed S, GRE General Test (minimum combined verbal and quantitative score of 1000, 300 for new scoring), minimum undergraduate GPA of 3.0 or equivalent; master's degree. Additional exam requirements/recommendations for international students: Required—TOEFL (minimum score 550 paper-based; 77 iBT). *Application deadline:* For fall admission, 12/15 for domestic students, 3/1 for international students; for spring admission, 9/15 for domestic students, 8/1 for international students. Application fee: $60 ($75 for international students). Electronic applications accepted. *Financial support:* Fellowships with full tuition reimbursements, research assistantships with full tuition reimbursements, teaching assistantships with full tuition reimbursements, career-related internships or fieldwork, and tuition waivers (full) available. Support available to part-time students. Financial award application deadline: 3/1; financial award applicants required to submit FAFSA. *Faculty research:* Literacy acquisition and development, teacher beliefs and knowledge, recruitment and retention of underrepresented students, economic education, literacy discourse. *Unit head:* Dr. Phillip J. VanFossen, Head, 765-494-7935, Fax: 765-496-1622, E-mail: vanfoss@purdue.edu. *Application contact:* Cindy Blankenship, Graduate Contact, 765-494-2345, Fax: 765-494-5832, E-mail: prater0@purdue.edu.
Website: http://www.edci.purdue.edu/.

Queens College of the City University of New York, Division of Graduate Studies, Division of Education, Department of Secondary Education, Flushing, NY 11367-1597. Offers art (MS Ed); biology (MS Ed, AC); chemistry (MS Ed, AC); earth sciences (MS Ed, AC); English (MS Ed, AC); French (MS Ed, AC); Italian (MS Ed, AC); mathematics (MS Ed, AC); music (MS Ed, AC); physics (MS Ed, AC); social studies (MS Ed, AC); Spanish (MS Ed, AC). Part-time and evening/weekend programs available. *Degree requirements:* For master's, research project; for AC, thesis optional. *Entrance requirements:* For master's, minimum GPA of 3.0. Additional exam requirements/recommendations for international students: Required—TOEFL.

Quinnipiac University, School of Education, Program in Secondary Education, Hamden, CT 06518-1940. Offers biology (MAT); English (MAT); history/social studies (MAT); mathematics (MAT); Spanish (MAT). *Accreditation:* NCATE. *Faculty:* 14 full-time (7 women), 46 part-time/adjunct (27 women). *Students:* 44 full-time (37 women), 1 (woman) part-time; includes 2 minority (both Hispanic/Latino). 45 applicants, 93% accepted, 32 enrolled. In 2013, 32 master's awarded. *Entrance requirements:* For master's, PRAXIS I, minimum GPA of 2.67, interview. *Application deadline:* For fall admission, 4/1 priority date for domestic students. Applications are processed on a rolling basis. Application fee: $45. Electronic applications accepted. *Expenses: Tuition:* Part-time $920 per credit. *Required fees:* $37 per credit. *Financial support:* Career-related internships or fieldwork, tuition waivers (full and partial), and unspecified assistantships available. Support available to part-time students. Financial award application deadline: 6/1; financial award applicants required to submit FAFSA. *Faculty research:* Multicultural and urban education/leadership, challenges of teaching diverse learners, scholarship of teaching and learning, technology and teaching, humor and education. *Unit head:* Mordechai Gordon, Program Director, E-mail: mordechai.gordon@quinnipiac.edu. *Application contact:* Office of Graduate Admissions, 800-462-1944, Fax: 203-582-3443, E-mail: graduate@quinnipiac.edu.
Website: http://www.quinnipiac.edu/gradeducation.

Rhode Island College, School of Graduate Studies, Feinstein School of Education and Human Development, Department of Educational Studies, Providence, RI 02908-1991. Offers advanced studies in teaching and learning (M Ed); English (MAT); French (MAT); history (MAT); math (MAT); secondary education (MAT); Spanish (MAT); teaching English as a second language (M Ed). *Accreditation:* NCATE. Part-time and evening/weekend programs available. *Faculty:* 10 full-time (6 women), 7 part-time/adjunct (all women). *Students:* 4 full-time (3 women), 61 part-time (54 women); includes 2 minority (both Hispanic/Latino). Average age 37. In 2013, 27 master's awarded. *Degree*

requirements: For master's, capstone or comprehensive assessment. *Entrance requirements:* For master's, GRE or MAT (for most programs), minimum undergraduate GPA of 3.0; baccalaureate degree in English, French, history, math or Spanish; evaluation of content area knowledge; 3 letters of recommendation; interview. Additional exam requirements/recommendations for international students: Recommended—TOEFL (minimum score 550 paper-based; 79 iBT). *Application deadline:* For fall admission, 3/1 for domestic students; for spring admission, 11/1 for domestic students. Applications are processed on a rolling basis. Application fee: $50. *Expenses:* Tuition, state resident: full-time $8928; part-time $372 per credit hour. Tuition, nonresident: full-time $17,376; part-time $724 per credit hour. *Required fees:* $602; $22 per credit. $72 per term. *Financial support:* In 2013–14, 2 teaching assistantships with full tuition reimbursements (averaging $2,250 per year) were awarded; career-related internships or fieldwork, Federal Work-Study, scholarships/grants, health care benefits, and unspecified assistantships also available. Support available to part-time students. Financial award application deadline: 5/15; financial award applicants required to submit FAFSA. *Faculty research:* School administration, school/college articulation. *Unit head:* Dr. Paul Tiskus, Chair, 401-456-8170. *Application contact:* Graduate Studies, 401-456-8700.

Website: http://www.ric.edu/educationalStudies/.

Rider University, Department of Graduate Education, Leadership and Counseling, Teacher Certification Program, Lawrenceville, NJ 08648-3001. Offers business education (Certificate); elementary education (Certificate); English as a second language (Certificate); English education (Certificate); mathematics education (Certificate); preschool to grade 3 (Certificate); science education (Certificate); social studies education (Certificate); world languages (Certificate), including French, German, Spanish. Part-time programs available. *Degree requirements:* For Certificate, internship, professional portfolio. *Entrance requirements:* For degree, PRAXIS, resume. Additional exam requirements/recommendations for international students: Required—TOEFL (minimum score 550 paper-based). Electronic applications accepted. *Faculty research:* Conceptual foundations for optimal development of creativity; creative theory, cognitive processes in mathematics learning, teacher collaboration.

Rivier University, School of Graduate Studies, Department of History, Law and Government, Nashua, NH 03060. Offers social studies education (MAT).

Rutgers, The State University of New Jersey, New Brunswick, Graduate School of Education, Department of Educational Theory, Policy and Administration, Program in Social Studies Education, Piscataway, NJ 08854-8097. Offers Ed M, Ed D. Part-time and evening/weekend programs available. Terminal master's awarded for partial completion of doctoral program. *Degree requirements:* For master's, comprehensive exam; for doctorate, thesis/dissertation, qualifying exam. *Entrance requirements:* For master's and doctorate, GRE General Test. Additional exam requirements/recommendations for international students: Required—TOEFL. Electronic applications accepted. *Faculty research:* Academic freedom, equal educational opportunity, social studies curricula.

Sage Graduate School, Esteves School of Education, Program in Teaching, Troy, NY 12180-4115. Offers art education (MAT); English (MAT); mathematics (MAT); social studies (MAT). *Accreditation:* NASAD. Part-time and evening/weekend programs available. *Faculty:* 10 full-time (6 women), 6 part-time/adjunct (4 women). *Students:* 1 (woman) full-time, 12 part-time (10 women); includes 2 minority (1 Hispanic/Latino; 1 Two or more races, non-Hispanic/Latino). Average age 26. 13 applicants, 31% accepted, 1 enrolled. In 2013, 18 master's awarded. *Entrance requirements:* For master's, assessment of writing skills, minimum undergraduate GPA of 2.75 overall, 3.0 in content area; current resume; 2 letters of recommendation. Additional exam requirements/recommendations for international students: Required—TOEFL (minimum score 550 paper-based). *Application deadline:* For fall admission, 8/1 for domestic students. Applications are processed on a rolling basis. Application fee: $40. *Expenses: Tuition:* Full-time $11,880; part-time $660 per credit hour. *Financial support:* Fellowships, research assistantships, Federal Work-Study, scholarships/grants, and unspecified assistantships available. Support available to part-time students. Financial award application deadline: 3/1; financial award applicants required to submit FAFSA. *Unit head:* Dr. Lori Quigley, Dean, Esteves School of Education, 518-244-2326, Fax: 518-244-4571, E-mail: l.quigley@sage.edu. *Application contact:* Kelly Jones, Director, 518-244-2433, Fax: 518-244-6880, E-mail: jonesk4@sage.edu.

St. John Fisher College, Ralph C. Wilson Jr. School of Education, Program in Adolescence Education and Special Education, Rochester, NY 14618-3597. Offers adolescence education: English with special education (MS Ed); adolescence education: French with special education (MS Ed); adolescence education: social studies with special education (MS Ed); adolescence education: Spanish with special education (MS Ed). Part-time and evening/weekend programs available. *Faculty:* 4 full-time (2 women), 4 part-time/adjunct (all women). *Students:* 20 full-time (10 women), 27 part-time (21 women); includes 4 minority (1 Black or African American, non-Hispanic/Latino; 1 Asian, non-Hispanic/Latino; 1 Hispanic/Latino; 1 Two or more races, non-Hispanic/Latino). Average age 27. 45 applicants, 89% accepted, 28 enrolled. In 2013, 28 master's awarded. *Degree requirements:* For master's, field experiences, student teaching, LAST. *Entrance requirements:* For master's, 2 letters of recommendation, personal statement, current resume. Additional exam requirements/recommendations for international students: Required—TOEFL (minimum score 575 paper-based; 80 iBT). *Application deadline:* Applications are processed on a rolling basis. Application fee: $30. Electronic applications accepted. *Expenses: Tuition:* Part-time $795 per credit hour. *Required fees:* $10 per credit hour. Tuition and fees vary according to course load, degree level and program. *Financial support:* In 2013–14, 11 students received support. Scholarships/grants available. Financial award applicants required to submit FAFSA. *Faculty research:* Arts and humanities, urban schools, constructivist learning, at-risk students, mentoring. *Unit head:* Dr. Susan Schultz, Program Director, 585-385-7296, E-mail: sschultz@sjfc.edu. *Application contact:* Jose Perales, Director of Graduate Admissions, 585-385-8067, E-mail: jperales@sjfc.edu.

Website: http://www.sjfc.edu/academics/education/departments/ms-special-ed/options/initial-adolescence.dot.

Simmons College, School of Social Work, Boston, MA 02115. Offers assistive technology (MS Ed, Ed S); behavior analysis (MS, PhD, Ed S); education (MA, CAGS); language and literacy (MS Ed, Ed S); social work (MSW, PhD); special education (MS Ed), including moderate disabilities, severe disabilities; teaching (MAT), including elementary education, general education, high school education; teaching English as a second language (MA, CAGS); urban leadership (MSW); MSW/MBA. *Accreditation:* CSWE (one or more programs are accredited). Part-time programs available. Postbaccalaureate distance learning degree programs offered (no on-campus study). *Students:* 519 full-time (454 women), 703 part-time (604 women); includes 192 minority (61 Black or African American, non-Hispanic/Latino; 1 American Indian or Alaska Native, non-Hispanic/Latino; 35 Asian, non-Hispanic/Latino; 71 Hispanic/Latino; 2 Native Hawaiian or other Pacific Islander, non-Hispanic/Latino; 22 Two or more races, non-Hispanic/Latino), 16 international. 952 applicants, 66% accepted, 353 enrolled. In 2013, 159 master's, 2 doctorates awarded. Terminal master's awarded for partial completion of doctoral program. *Degree requirements:* For master's, thesis (for some programs); for doctorate, comprehensive exam (for some programs), thesis/dissertation (for some

programs). *Entrance requirements:* For master's, GRE, MAT, MTEL (for different programs); for doctorate, GRE, BCBA Analyst Exam. Additional exam requirements/recommendations for international students: Required—TOEFL (minimum score 600 paper-based; 100 iBT). *Application deadline:* Applications are processed on a rolling basis. Application fee: $45. Electronic applications accepted. *Financial support:* Teaching assistantships and scholarships/grants available. *Unit head:* Dr. Stefan Krug, Dean, 617-521-3924. *Application contact:* Carlos D. Frontado, Director of Admissions, 617-521-3920, Fax: 617-521-3980, E-mail: ssw@simmons.edu.

Website: http://www.simmons.edu/ssw/.

Slippery Rock University of Pennsylvania, Graduate Studies (Recruitment), College of Education, Department of Secondary Education/Foundations of Education, Slippery Rock, PA 16057-1383. Offers educational leadership (M Ed); secondary education (M Ed), including English, math/science, social studies/history. *Accreditation:* NCATE. Part-time and evening/weekend programs available. *Faculty:* 12 full-time (5 women). *Students:* 48 full-time (24 women), 10 part-time (6 women). Average age 27. 50 applicants, 84% accepted, 29 enrolled. In 2013, 28 master's awarded. *Degree requirements:* For master's, comprehensive exam, thesis (for some programs). *Entrance requirements:* For master's, GRE General Test, MAT, minimum GPA of 2.8 or 3.0 (depending on program); copy of teaching certification and two letters of recommendation (for some programs). Additional exam requirements/recommendations for international students: Required—TOEFL (minimum score 550 paper-based; 80 iBT). *Application deadline:* For fall admission, 3/1 priority date for domestic students, 5/1 priority date for international students; for spring admission, 10/1 priority date for domestic students, 9/1 priority date for international students. Applications are processed on a rolling basis. Application fee: $25 ($30 for international students). Electronic applications accepted. *Expenses:* Tuition, state resident: full-time $7956; part-time $442 per credit. Tuition, nonresident: full-time $11,934; part-time $663 per credit. *Required fees:* $2896; $148 per credit. Tuition and fees vary according to degree level and program. *Financial support:* Career-related internships or fieldwork, Federal Work-Study, institutionally sponsored loans, scholarships/grants, tuition waivers (partial), and unspecified assistantships available. Support available to part-time students. Financial award application deadline: 5/1; financial award applicants required to submit FAFSA. *Unit head:* Dr. Jeffrey Lehman, Graduate Coordinator, 724-738-2311, Fax: 724-738-4987, E-mail: jeffrey.lehman@sru.edu. *Application contact:* Brandi Weber-Mortimer, Interim Director of Graduate Studies, 724-738-2051, Fax: 724-738-2146, E-mail: graduate.admissions@sru.edu.

Smith College, Graduate and Special Programs, Department of Education and Child Study, Program in Secondary Education, Northampton, MA 01063. Offers biological sciences education (MAT); chemistry education (MAT); English education (MAT); French education (MAT); geology education (MAT); government education (MAT); history education (MAT); mathematics education (MAT); physics education (MAT); Spanish education (MAT). Part-time programs available. *Faculty:* 6 full-time (4 women), 3 part-time/adjunct (2 women). *Students:* 4 full-time (3 women), 1 (woman) part-time, 2 international. Average age 33. 12 applicants, 92% accepted, 4 enrolled. In 2013, 6 master's awarded. *Entrance requirements:* Additional exam requirements/recommendations for international students: Required—TOEFL (minimum score 595 paper-based; 97 iBT). *Application deadline:* For fall admission, 4/1 for domestic students, 1/15 priority date for international students; for spring admission, 12/1 for domestic students. Application fee: $60. *Expenses: Tuition:* Full-time $32,160; part-time $1340 per credit. *Financial support:* In 2013–14, 5 students received support, including 2 fellowships with full tuition reimbursements available; career-related internships or fieldwork, institutionally sponsored loans, and scholarships/grants also available. Support available to part-time students. Financial award application deadline: 1/15; financial award applicants required to submit CSS PROFILE or FAFSA. *Unit head:* Rosetta Cohen, Graduate Student Advisor, 413-585-3266, E-mail: rcohen@smith.edu. *Application contact:* Ruth Morgan, Administrative Assistant, 413-585-3050, Fax: 413-585-3054, E-mail: gradstdy@smith.edu.

Website: http://www.smith.edu/educ/.

Smith College, Graduate and Special Programs, Department of Government, Northampton, MA 01063. Offers MAT. Part-time programs available. *Students:* 2 full-time (1 woman), 1 international. Average age 26. 2 applicants, 100% accepted, 2 enrolled. In 2013, 1 master's awarded. *Entrance requirements:* Additional exam requirements/recommendations for international students: Required—TOEFL (minimum score 595 paper-based; 97 iBT). *Application deadline:* For fall admission, 4/1 for domestic students, 1/15 for international students; for spring admission, 12/1 for domestic students. Application fee: $60. *Expenses: Tuition:* Full-time $32,160; part-time $1340 per credit. *Financial support:* In 2013–14, 2 students received support, including 2 fellowships with full tuition reimbursements available; career-related internships or fieldwork, institutionally sponsored loans, and scholarships/grants also available. Support available to part-time students. Financial award application deadline: 1/15; financial award applicants required to submit CSS PROFILE or FAFSA. *Unit head:* Alice Hearst, Graduate Student Adviser, 413-585-3528, E-mail: ahearst@smith.edu. *Application contact:* Ruth Morgan, Administrative Assistant, 413-585-3050, Fax: 413-585-3054, E-mail: gradstdy@smith.edu.

Website: http://www.smith.edu/gov/.

South Carolina State University, School of Graduate and Professional Studies, Department of Education, Orangeburg, SC 29117-0001. Offers early childhood and special education (M Ed); early childhood education (MAT); elementary education (M Ed, MAT); general science (MAT); mathematics (MAT); secondary education (M Ed), including biology education, business education, counselor education, English education, home economics education, industrial education, mathematics education, science education, social studies education; special education (M Ed), including emotionally handicapped, learning disabilities, mentally handicapped. *Accreditation:* NCATE. Part-time and evening/weekend programs available. *Faculty:* 9 full-time (3 women), 4 part-time/adjunct (3 women). *Students:* 32 full-time (26 women), 33 part-time (26 women); includes 63 minority (61 Black or African American, non-Hispanic/Latino; 2 Asian, non-Hispanic/Latino). Average age 31. 21 applicants, 100% accepted, 21 enrolled. In 2013, 15 master's awarded. *Degree requirements:* For master's, thesis optional, departmental qualifying exam. *Entrance requirements:* For master's, GRE General Test, NTE, interview, teaching certificate. *Application deadline:* For fall admission, 6/15 priority date for domestic students, 6/15 for international students; for spring admission, 11/1 for domestic and international students. Applications are processed on a rolling basis. Application fee: $25. Electronic applications accepted. *Expenses:* Tuition, state resident: full-time $8906; part-time $543 per credit hour. Tuition, nonresident: full-time $18,040; part-time $1051 per credit hour. *Financial support:* Fellowships, career-related internships or fieldwork, Federal Work-Study, and institutionally sponsored loans available. Financial award application deadline: 6/1. *Faculty research:* Critical thinking, child abuse, stress, test-taking skills, conflict resolution, mainstreaming. *Unit head:* Dr. Margaret Evelyn Fields, Interim Chair, 803-536-7098, Fax: 803-516-4568, E-mail: efields@scsu.edu. *Application contact:* Curtis Foskey, Coordinator of Graduate Studies, 803-536-8419, Fax: 803-536-8812, E-mail: cfoskey@scsu.edu.

Southwestern Oklahoma State University, College of Arts and Sciences, Department of Social Sciences, Weatherford, OK 73096-3098. Offers M Ed. *Degree requirements:* For master's, exam. *Entrance requirements:* For master's, GRE General Test or minimum undergraduate GPA of 3.0. Additional exam requirements/recommendations for international students: Required—TOEFL.

Spring Hill College, Graduate Programs, Program in Liberal Arts, Mobile, AL 36608-1791. Offers fine arts (MLA); history and social science (MLA); leadership and ethics (MLA, Postbaccalaureate Certificate); literature (MLA); studio art (Postbaccalaureate Certificate). Part-time and evening/weekend programs available. *Faculty:* 3 full-time (0 women), 4 part-time/adjunct (1 woman). *Students:* 1 (woman) full-time, 26 part-time (19 women); includes 11 minority (9 Black or African American, non-Hispanic/Latino; 1 Hispanic/Latino; 1 Native Hawaiian or other Pacific Islander, non-Hispanic/Latino). Average age 35. In 2013, 16 master's, 6 other advanced degrees awarded. *Degree requirements:* For master's, capstone course, completion of program within 6 years of initial admittance. *Entrance requirements:* For master's, bachelor's degree with minimum undergraduate GPA of 3.0 or graduate/professional degree. Additional exam requirements/recommendations for international students: Required—TOEFL (minimum score 550 paper-based; 80 iBT), IELTS (minimum score 6.5), CPE or CAE (minimum score C), Michigan English Language Assessment Battery (minimum score 90). *Application deadline:* For fall admission, 8/1 priority date for domestic and international students; for spring admission, 12/1 priority date for domestic and international students. Applications are processed on a rolling basis. Application fee: $25 ($35 for international students). Electronic applications accepted. *Expenses:* Contact institution. *Financial support:* Applicants required to submit FAFSA. *Unit head:* Dr. Alexander R. Landi, Director, 251-380-3056, Fax: 251-460-2115, E-mail: landi@shc.edu. *Application contact:* Donna B. Tarasavage, Associate Director, Academic Affairs, 251-380-3067, Fax: 251-460-2182, E-mail: dtarasavage@shc.edu.
Website: http://www.shc.edu/grad/academics/liberal-arts.

State University of New York at New Paltz, Graduate School, School of Education, Department of Secondary Education, New Paltz, NY 12561. Offers adolescence education: biology (MAT, MS Ed); adolescence education: chemistry (MAT, MS Ed); adolescence education: earth science (MAT, MS Ed); adolescence education: English (MAT, MS Ed); adolescence education: French (MAT, MS Ed); adolescence education: social studies (MAT, MS Ed); adolescence education: Spanish (MAT, MS Ed); second language education (MS Ed, AC), including second language education (MS Ed), teaching English language learners (AC). *Accreditation:* NCATE. Part-time and evening/weekend programs available. *Faculty:* 10 full-time (8 women), 15 part-time/adjunct (10 women). *Students:* 73 full-time (47 women), 52 part-time (39 women); includes 27 minority (2 Black or African American, non-Hispanic/Latino; 6 Asian, non-Hispanic/Latino; 16 Hispanic/Latino; 3 Two or more races, non-Hispanic/Latino), 1 international. Average age 29. 81 applicants, 84% accepted, 51 enrolled. In 2013, 85 master's awarded. *Degree requirements:* For master's, comprehensive exam (for some programs), portfolio. *Entrance requirements:* For master's, minimum GPA of 3.0, New York state teaching certificate (MS Ed). Additional exam requirements/recommendations for international students: Required—TOEFL (minimum score 550 paper-based; 80 iBT), IELTS (minimum score 6.5). *Application deadline:* For fall admission, 3/1 priority date for domestic students, 3/1 for international students; for spring admission, 10/1 priority date for domestic students, 10/1 for international students. Application fee: $50. Electronic applications accepted. *Expenses:* Tuition, state resident: full-time $9870; part-time $411 per credit. Tuition, nonresident: full-time $18,350; part-time $765 per credit. *Required fees:* $1213. Tuition and fees vary according to program. *Financial support:* Application deadline: 8/1. *Unit head:* Dr. Laura Dull, Chair, 845-257-2850, E-mail: dulll@newpaltz.edu. *Application contact:* Caroline Murphy, Graduate Admissions Advisor, 845-257-3285, Fax: 845-257-3284, E-mail: gradschool@newpaltz.edu.
Website: http://www.newpaltz.edu/secondaryed/.

State University of New York at Plattsburgh, Division of Education, Health, and Human Services, Program in Teacher Education: Adolescence, Plattsburgh, NY 12901-2681. Offers adolescence education (MST); biology 7-12 (MST); chemistry 7-12 (MST); earth science 7-12 (MST); English 7-12 (MST); French 7-12 (MST); mathematics 7-12 (MST); physics 7-12 (MST); social studies 7-12 (MST); Spanish 7-12 (MST). *Accreditation:* Teacher Education Accreditation Council. Part-time and evening/weekend programs available. *Students:* 75 full-time (47 women), 5 part-time (3 women); includes 10 minority (1 Black or African American, non-Hispanic/Latino; 4 Asian, non-Hispanic/Latino; 5 Hispanic/Latino), 1 international. Average age 25. *Entrance requirements:* For master's, minimum GPA of 2.75. Additional exam requirements/recommendations for international students: Required—TOEFL. *Application deadline:* For fall admission, 2/15 priority date for domestic students. Applications are processed on a rolling basis. Application fee: $75. *Financial support:* Application deadline: 4/15; applicants required to submit FAFSA. *Unit head:* Dr. Robert Ackland, Coordinator, 518-564-5131, E-mail: acklanrt@plattsburgh.edu. *Application contact:* Betsy Kane, Director, Graduate Admissions, 518-564-4723, Fax: 518-564-4722, E-mail: bkane002@plattsburgh.edu.

State University of New York College at Cortland, Graduate Studies, School of Arts and Sciences, Programs in Adolescence Education, Cortland, NY 13045. Offers biology (MAT, MS Ed); chemistry (MAT, MS Ed); earth science (MAT, MS Ed); English (MAT, MS Ed); mathematics (MAT, MS Ed); physics (MAT, MS Ed); physics and mathematics (MS Ed); social studies (MS Ed), including geography, history. *Accreditation:* NCATE. Part-time and evening/weekend programs available. *Degree requirements:* For master's, one foreign language, comprehensive exam (for some programs), thesis (for some programs). *Entrance requirements:* For master's, GRE General Test. *Expenses:* Tuition, state resident: full-time $9870; part-time $411 per credit hour. Tuition, nonresident: full-time $18,350; part-time $765 per credit hour. *Required fees:* $1458; $65 per credit hour.

State University of New York College at Old Westbury, Program in Adolescent Education, Old Westbury, NY 11568-0210. Offers biology (MAT, MS); chemistry (MAT, MS); English language arts (MAT, MS); math (MAT, MS); social studies (MAT, MS); Spanish (MAT, MS). Part-time and evening/weekend programs available. *Faculty:* 19 full-time (11 women), 6 part-time/adjunct (1 woman). *Students:* 33 full-time (20 women), 33 part-time (19 women); includes 16 minority (2 Black or African American, non-Hispanic/Latino; 4 Asian, non-Hispanic/Latino; 9 Hispanic/Latino; 1 Two or more races, non-Hispanic/Latino). 25 applicants, 84% accepted, 19 enrolled. In 2013, 29 master's awarded. *Entrance requirements:* For master's, Liberal Arts and Sciences Test, undergraduate degree with at least 30 semester hours of appropriate coursework as defined by the respective discipline; minimum cumulative undergraduate GPA of 3.0; two letters of recommendation (one from an academic source); essay. Additional exam requirements/recommendations for international students: Required—TOEFL (minimum score 550 paper-based); Recommended—IELTS. *Expenses:* Tuition, state resident: full-time $9370; part-time $390 per credit. Tuition, nonresident: full-time $16,680; part-time $695 per credit. *Required fees:* $45.85 per credit. $47 per term. *Application contact:* Philip D'Angelo, Graduate Admissions Office, 516-876-3073, E-mail: enroll@oldwestbury.edu.

State University of New York College at Potsdam, School of Education and Professional Studies, Program in Secondary Education, Potsdam, NY 13676. Offers

English education (MST); mathematics education (MST); science education (MST), including biology, chemistry, earth science, physics; social studies education (MST). *Accreditation:* NCATE. *Degree requirements:* For master's, culminating experience. *Entrance requirements:* For master's, minimum GPA of 2.75 in last 60 hours of course work (3.0 for English program). Additional exam requirements/recommendations for international students: Required—TOEFL (minimum score 550 paper-based; 80 iBT), IELTS (minimum score 6). Electronic applications accepted.

Stony Brook University, State University of New York, School of Professional Development, Stony Brook, NY 11794. Offers biology (MAT); chemistry (MAT); coaching (Graduate Certificate); earth science (MAT); educational computing (Graduate Certificate); educational leadership (Advanced Certificate); English (MAT); environmental management (Graduate Certificate); French (MAT); German (MAT); higher education administration (MA, Certificate); human resource management (MS, Graduate Certificate); industrial management (Graduate Certificate); information systems management (Graduate Certificate); Italian (MAT); liberal studies (MA); mathematics (MAT); operations research (Graduate Certificate); physics (MAT); school district business leadership (Advanced Certificate); social science and the professions (MPS), including environmental management, human resource management; social studies (MAT); Spanish (MAT). Part-time and evening/weekend programs available. Postbaccalaureate distance learning degree programs offered. *Faculty:* 2 full-time (1 woman), 70 part-time/adjunct (30 women). *Students:* 241 full-time (135 women), 954 part-time (673 women); includes 209 minority (65 Black or African American, non-Hispanic/Latino; 2 American Indian or Alaska Native, non-Hispanic/Latino; 32 Asian, non-Hispanic/Latino; 104 Hispanic/Latino; 6 Two or more races, non-Hispanic/Latino), 7 international. Average age 28. 353 applicants, 92% accepted, 248 enrolled. In 2013, 312 master's, 131 other advanced degrees awarded. *Degree requirements:* For master's, one foreign language, thesis or alternative. *Application deadline:* For fall admission, 1/15 for domestic students; for spring admission, 10/1 for domestic students. Applications are processed on a rolling basis. Application fee: $100. *Expenses:* Tuition, state resident: full-time $9870; part-time $411 per credit. Tuition, nonresident: full-time $18,350; part-time $765 per credit. *Financial support:* Fellowships, research assistantships, teaching assistantships, and career-related internships or fieldwork available. Support available to part-time students. *Unit head:* Dr. Thomas Sexton, Interim Dean, 631-632-7181, Fax: 631-632-9046, E-mail: thomas.sexton@stonybrook.edu. *Application contact:* 631-632-7050 Ext. 1, E-mail: spd@stonybrook.edu.
Website: http://www.stonybrook.edu/spd/.

Syracuse University, School of Education, Program in Social Studies Education: Preparation 7-12, Syracuse, NY 13244. Offers MS. Part-time programs available. *Students:* 8 full-time (1 woman); all minorities (7 Black or African American, non-Hispanic/Latino; 1 American Indian or Alaska Native, non-Hispanic/Latino). Average age 26. 11 applicants, 73% accepted, 3 enrolled. In 2013, 6 master's awarded. *Degree requirements:* For master's, thesis or alternative. *Entrance requirements:* Additional exam requirements/recommendations for international students: Required—TOEFL (minimum score 100 iBT). *Application deadline:* For fall admission, 1/15 priority date for domestic and international students; for spring admission, 10/15 priority date for domestic and international students. Applications are processed on a rolling basis. Application fee: $75. Electronic applications accepted. *Financial support:* Fellowships with full tuition reimbursements and teaching assistantships with full and partial tuition reimbursements available. Financial award application deadline: 1/1; financial award applicants required to submit FAFSA. *Unit head:* Dr. Jeffery Mangram, Program Coordinator, 315-443-9077, E-mail: jamangra@syr.edu. *Application contact:* Laurie Deyo, Graduate Recruiter, School of Education, 315-443-2505, E-mail: e-gradrcrt@syr.edu.
Website: http://soeweb.syr.edu/.

Teachers College, Columbia University, Graduate Faculty of Education, Department of Arts and Humanities, Program in History and Education, New York, NY 10027-6696. Offers Ed M, MA, Ed D, PhD. *Faculty:* 3 full-time, 3 part-time/adjunct. *Students:* 3 full-time (2 women), 15 part-time (11 women); includes 7 minority (5 Black or African American, non-Hispanic/Latino; 1 Asian, non-Hispanic/Latino; 1 Two or more races, non-Hispanic/Latino), 2 international. Average age 32. 15 applicants, 67% accepted, 5 enrolled. In 2013, 3 master's, 2 doctorates awarded. *Degree requirements:* For master's, formal essay; for doctorate, 2 foreign languages, thesis/dissertation. *Entrance requirements:* For master's, GRE, sample of historical writing (Ed M); for doctorate, GRE, sample of historical writing. *Application deadline:* For fall admission, 1/15 priority date for domestic students. Application fee: $65. Electronic applications accepted. *Financial support:* Career-related internships or fieldwork, Federal Work-Study, institutionally sponsored loans, and tuition waivers (full and partial) available. Support available to part-time students. Financial award application deadline: 2/1. *Faculty research:* History of American education, urban areas, women, immigrants, African-Americans. *Unit head:* Prof. Cally Waite, Program Coordinator, 212-678-4138, E-mail: cwaite@tc.columbia.edu. *Application contact:* Thomas P. Rock, Director of Admissions, 212-678-3083, Fax: 212-678-4171, E-mail: rock@tc.edu.
Website: http://www.tc.columbia.edu/a&h/history-ed/.

Teachers College, Columbia University, Graduate Faculty of Education, Department of Arts and Humanities, Program in Social Studies Education, New York, NY 10027. Offers MA, Ed D, PhD. *Accreditation:* NCATE. Part-time and evening/weekend programs available. *Faculty:* 5 full-time, 4 part-time/adjunct. *Students:* 44 full-time (25 women), 48 part-time (29 women); includes 23 minority (7 Black or African American, non-Hispanic/Latino; 2 Asian, non-Hispanic/Latino; 9 Hispanic/Latino; 2 Native Hawaiian or other Pacific Islander, non-Hispanic/Latino; 3 Two or more races, non-Hispanic/Latino), 4 international. Average age 29. 79 applicants, 76% accepted, 31 enrolled. In 2013, 66 master's, 5 doctorates awarded. Terminal master's awarded for partial completion of doctoral program. *Degree requirements:* For master's, one foreign language, integrative project; New York State certification standards for study of language other than English; for doctorate, one foreign language, thesis/dissertation. *Entrance requirements:* For master's, GRE if GPA below 3.5 (recommended), minimum of 12 credits in history; for doctorate, GRE if GPA below 3.5 (recommended), at least 1-2 years of teaching experience, MA in social studies education or related content field. *Application deadline:* For fall admission, 1/15 priority date for domestic students; for spring admission, 11/1 for domestic students. Applications are processed on a rolling basis. Application fee: $65. Electronic applications accepted. *Financial support:* Fellowships, research assistantships, teaching assistantships, career-related internships or fieldwork, Federal Work-Study, institutionally sponsored loans, and tuition waivers (full and partial) available. Support available to part-time students. Financial award application deadline: 2/1. *Faculty research:* History of social studies education, social studies curriculum and teaching, women's history, gender and diversity issues in the classroom. *Unit head:* Prof. Bill Gaudelli, Program Coordinator, 212-678-3150, E-mail: gaudelli@exchange.tc.columbia.edu. *Application contact:* Thomas P. Rock, Director of Admissions, 212-678-3083, Fax: 212-678-4171, E-mail: rock@tc.edu.
Website: http://www.tc.columbia.edu/a%26h/socialstudies/.

Temple University, College of Education, Department of Curriculum, Instruction, and Technology in Education, Philadelphia, PA 19122-6096. Offers career and technical education (Ed M), including business, computing, and information technology, industrial

education, marketing education; middle grades education (Ed M), including math and language arts, math and science, science and language arts; secondary education (Ed M), including English, math, social studies; teaching English to speakers of other languages (MS Ed); urban education (Ed M). Part-time and evening/weekend programs available. *Students:* 66 full-time (48 women), 120 part-time (67 women); includes 50 minority (35 Black or African American, non-Hispanic/Latino; 1 American Indian or Alaska Native, non-Hispanic/Latino; 2 Asian, non-Hispanic/Latino; 7 Hispanic/Latino; 5 Two or more races, non-Hispanic/Latino), 1 international. 229 applicants, 41% accepted, 60 enrolled. In 2013, 41 master's awarded. Terminal master's awarded for partial completion of doctoral program. *Degree requirements:* For master's, thesis or alternative. *Entrance requirements:* Additional exam requirements/recommendations for international students: Required—TOEFL (minimum score 550 paper-based; 79 iBT). *Application deadline:* For fall admission, 4/1 for domestic students, 12/15 for international students; for spring admission, 10/1 for domestic students, 8/1 for international students. Application fee: $60. Electronic applications accepted. *Financial support:* Fellowships, research assistantships, and teaching assistantships available. Financial award application deadline: 1/15; financial award applicants required to submit FAFSA. *Faculty research:* Workforce development, vocational education, technical education, industrial education, professional development, literacy, classroom management, school communities, curriculum development, instruction, applied linguistics, crosslinguistic influence, bilingual education, oral proficiency, multilingualism. *Application contact:* Felicia Neuber, Enrollment Management, 215-204-8011, E-mail: educate@temple.edu.
Website: http://www.temple.edu/education/tl/.

Texas A&M University–Commerce, Graduate School, College of Humanities, Social Sciences and Arts, Department of History, Commerce, TX 75429-3011. Offers history (MA, MS); social sciences (M Ed, MS). Part-time programs available. *Degree requirements:* For master's, comprehensive exam, thesis (for some programs). *Entrance requirements:* For master's, GRE General Test. Electronic applications accepted. *Expenses:* Tuition, state resident: full-time $3630; part-time $2420 per year. Tuition, nonresident: full-time $9948; part-time $6632.16 per year. *Required fees:* $1006 per year. Tuition and fees vary according to course load. *Faculty research:* American foreign policy, colonial America, Texas politics, Medieval England.

Trinity Washington University, School of Education, Washington, DC 20017-1094. Offers clinical mental health counseling (MA); early childhood education (MAT); educating for change (M Ed); educational administration (MSA); elementary education (MAT); reading (M Ed); school counseling (MA); secondary education (MAT), including English, social studies; special education (MAT). *Accreditation:* NCATE. Part-time and evening/weekend programs available. *Degree requirements:* For master's, thesis (for some programs), capstone project(s). *Entrance requirements:* For master's, PRAXIS I, minimum GPA of 2.8. Additional exam requirements/recommendations for international students: Required—TOEFL (minimum score 550 paper-based). *Application deadline:* For fall admission, 4/1 priority date for domestic students; for winter admission, 11/1 priority date for domestic students; for spring admission, 11/1 priority date for domestic students. Applications are processed on a rolling basis. Application fee: $40. *Expenses: Tuition:* Part-time $715 per credit. *Financial support:* Career-related internships or fieldwork, health care benefits, and unspecified assistantships available. Support available to part-time students. Financial award application deadline: 4/1; financial award applicants required to submit FAFSA. *Faculty research:* Technology, literacy, special education, organizations, inclusion models. *Unit head:* Dr. Janet Stocks, Dean, 202-884-9380, Fax: 202-884-9506, E-mail: stocksj@trinitydc.edu. *Application contact:* Erika Davis, Director of Admissions for School of Education, 202-884-9400, Fax: 202-884-9229, E-mail: daviser@trinitydc.edu.
Website: http://www.trinitydc.edu/education/.

Troy University, Graduate School, College of Education, Program in Postsecondary Education, Troy, AL 36082. Offers adult education (M Ed); biology (M Ed); criminal justice (M Ed); English (M Ed); foundations of education (M Ed); general science (M Ed); higher education administration (M Ed); history (M Ed); instructional technology (M Ed); mathematics (M Ed); music industry (M Ed); physical fitness (M Ed); political science (M Ed); public administration (M Ed); social science (M Ed); teaching English (M Ed). *Accreditation:* NCATE. Part-time and evening/weekend programs available. *Faculty:* 30 full-time (11 women), 8 part-time/adjunct (1 woman). *Students:* 17 full-time (13 women), 106 part-time (84 women); includes 55 minority (45 Black or African American, non-Hispanic/Latino; 3 Asian, non-Hispanic/Latino; 2 Hispanic/Latino; 5 Two or more races, non-Hispanic/Latino). Average age 34. 109 applicants, 83% accepted, 5 enrolled. In 2013, 130 master's awarded. *Degree requirements:* For master's, comprehensive exam (for some programs), thesis (for some programs), thesis or comprehensive exam. *Entrance requirements:* For master's, GRE (minimum score of 850 on old exam or 290 on new exam), GMAT (minimum score of 380), or MAT (minimum score of 385), bachelor's degree; minimum undergraduate GPA of 2.5 or 3.0 on last 30 semester hours, letter of recommendation. Additional exam requirements/recommendations for international students: Required—TOEFL (minimum score 523 paper-based; 70 iBT), IELTS (minimum score 6). *Application deadline:* Applications are processed on a rolling basis. Application fee: $50. Electronic applications accepted. *Expenses:* Tuition, state resident: full-time $6084; part-time $338 per credit hour. Tuition, nonresident: full-time $12,168; part-time $676 per credit hour. *Required fees:* $630; $35 per credit hour. $50 per semester. *Financial support:* Available to part-time students. Applicants required to submit FAFSA. *Unit head:* Dr. Jan Oliver, Associate Professor, 334-670-3444, Fax: 334-670-3474, E-mail: oliver@troy.edu. *Application contact:* Brenda K. Campbell, Director of Graduate Admissions, 334-670-3178, Fax: 334-670-3733, E-mail: bcamp@troy.edu.

Troy University, Graduate School, College of Education, Program in Secondary Education, Troy, AL 36082. Offers 5th year biology (MS); 5th year computer science (MS); 5th year history (MS); 5th year language arts (MS); 5th year mathematics (MS); 5th year social science (MS); traditional biology (MS); traditional computer science (MS); traditional history (MS); traditional language arts (MS); traditional mathematics (MS); traditional social science (MS). *Accreditation:* NCATE. Part-time and evening/weekend programs available. *Faculty:* 2 full-time (1 woman). *Students:* 10 full-time (9 women), 21 part-time (14 women); includes 8 minority (6 Black or African American, non-Hispanic/Latino; 2 Hispanic/Latino). Average age 29. 15 applicants, 87% accepted, 6 enrolled. In 2013, 12 master's awarded. *Degree requirements:* For master's, comprehensive exam, thesis. *Entrance requirements:* For master's, GRE (minimum score of 850 on old exam or 290 on new exam), GMAT (minimum score of 380), or MAT (minimum score of 385), bachelor's degree; minimum undergraduate GPA of 2.5 or 3.0 on last 30 semester hours, letter of recommendation. Additional exam requirements/recommendations for international students: Required—TOEFL (minimum score 523 paper-based; 70 iBT), IELTS (minimum score 6). *Application deadline:* Applications are processed on a rolling basis. Application fee: $50. Electronic applications accepted. *Expenses:* Tuition, state resident: full-time $6084; part-time $338 per credit hour. Tuition, nonresident: full-time $12,168; part-time $676 per credit hour. *Required fees:* $630; $35 per credit hour. $50 per semester. *Financial support:* Career-related internships or fieldwork available. Support available to part-time students. Financial award applicants required to submit FAFSA. *Unit head:* Dr. Jan Oliver, Associate Professor, 334-670-3444, Fax: 334-670-3548, E-mail: oliver@troy.edu. *Application contact:* Brenda K. Campbell, Director of Graduate Admissions, 334-670-3178, Fax: 334-670-3733, E-mail: bcamp@troy.edu.

Union Graduate College, School of Education, Schenectady, NY 12308-3107. Offers biology (MAT); chemistry (MAT); Chinese (MAT); earth science (MAT); English (MA, MAT); English and history (MA); French (MAT); general science (MAT); German (MAT); history (MA); Latin (MAT); life sciences (MS); mathematics (MAT); mathematics and computer technology (MS); mentoring and teacher leadership (AC); middle childhood extension (AC); national board certification and teacher leadership (AC); physical sciences (MS); physics (MAT); social studies (MAT); Spanish (MAT); technology (MAT). *Accreditation:* Teacher Education Accreditation Council. *Faculty:* 3 full-time (1 woman), 56 part-time/adjunct (34 women). *Students:* 32 full-time (16 women), 27 part-time (22 women); includes 15 minority (1 Black or African American, non-Hispanic/Latino; 4 Asian, non-Hispanic/Latino; 6 Hispanic/Latino; 4 Two or more races, non-Hispanic/Latino), 1 international. Average age 32. In 2013, 25 master's, 11 other advanced degrees awarded. *Degree requirements:* For master's, thesis or project. *Entrance requirements:* For master's, minimum GPA of 3.0, letters of recommendation. Additional exam requirements/recommendations for international students: Required—TOEFL (minimum score 550 paper-based). *Application deadline:* Applications are processed on a rolling basis. Application fee: $60. Electronic applications accepted. *Expenses:* Contact institution. *Financial support:* Career-related internships or fieldwork, Federal Work-Study, scholarships/grants, health care benefits, and tuition waivers (partial) available. Support available to part-time students. Financial award applicants required to submit FAFSA. *Faculty research:* Transformative learning, science education, National Board Certification, teacher leadership, teacher quality. *Unit head:* Dr. Lynn Gelzheiser, Dean, 518-631-9870, Fax: 518-631-9901. *Application contact:* Nicki Foley, Assistant, 518-631-9871, Fax: 518-631-9903, E-mail: foleyn@uniongraduatecollege.edu.

University at Buffalo, the State University of New York, Graduate School, Graduate School of Education, Department of Learning and Instruction, Buffalo, NY 14260. Offers biology education (Ed M, Certificate); chemistry education (Ed M, Certificate); childhood education (Ed M); childhood education with bilingual extension (Ed M); curriculum, instruction and the science of learning (PhD); early childhood education (Ed M); early childhood education with bilingual extension (birth–grade 2) (Ed M); earth science education (Ed M, Certificate); education studies (Ed M); educational technology and new literacies (Certificate); elementary education (Ed D); English education (Ed M, Certificate); English for speakers of other languages (Ed M); foreign and second language education (PhD); French education (Ed M, Certificate); German education (Ed M, Certificate); gifted education (Certificate); Latin education (Ed M, Certificate); literacy specialist (Ed M); literacy teaching and learning (Certificate); mathematics education (Ed M, Certificate); music education (Ed M, Certificate); physics education (Ed M, Certificate); science and the public (Ed M); social studies education (Ed M, Certificate); Spanish education (Ed M, Certificate); special education (PhD); teaching English to speakers of other languages (Ed M). Part-time and evening/weekend programs available. Postbaccalaureate distance learning degree programs offered (no on-campus study). *Faculty:* 31 full-time (23 women), 64 part-time/adjunct (53 women). *Students:* 275 full-time (215 women), 293 part-time (205 women); includes 35 minority (16 Black or African American, non-Hispanic/Latino; 5 American Indian or Alaska Native, non-Hispanic/Latino; 11 Asian, non-Hispanic/Latino; 3 Hispanic/Latino), 97 international. Average age 30. 544 applicants, 81% accepted, 246 enrolled. In 2013, 222 master's, 17 doctorates, 35 other advanced degrees awarded. *Degree requirements:* For master's, comprehensive exam; for doctorate, thesis/dissertation, research analysis exam, research experience component. *Entrance requirements:* For master's, content test in science and math, letters of reference; for doctorate, GRE General Test or MAT, interview, writing sample, letters of recommendation. Additional exam requirements/recommendations for international students: Required—TOEFL (minimum score 600 paper-based; 96 iBT). *Application deadline:* For fall admission, 2/1 priority date for domestic and international students; for spring admission, 11/15 priority date for domestic students, 10/1 for international students. Applications are processed on a rolling basis. Application fee: $50. Electronic applications accepted. *Financial support:* In 2013–14, 50 fellowships (averaging $8,589 per year), 31 research assistantships with tuition reimbursements (averaging $11,406 per year) were awarded; teaching assistantships, career-related internships or fieldwork, Federal Work-Study, institutionally sponsored loans, scholarships/grants, tuition waivers, and unspecified assistantships also available. Financial award application deadline: 2/28; financial award applicants required to submit FAFSA. *Faculty research:* Science assessment, foreign language teaching and learning, early learning, new literacies, gender and education. *Total annual research expenditures:* $1.7 million. *Unit head:* Dr. Suzanne Miller, Chair, 716-645-2455, Fax: 716-645-3161, E-mail: smiller@buffalo.edu. *Application contact:* Cathy Dimino, Admissions Assistant, 716-645-2110, Fax: 716-645-7937, E-mail: cadimino@buffalo.edu.
Website: http://gse.buffalo.edu/lai.

The University of Alabama in Huntsville, School of Graduate Studies, College of Liberal Arts, Department of History, Huntsville, AL 35899. Offers education (MA); history (MA); social science (MA). Part-time and evening/weekend programs available. *Faculty:* 9 full-time (3 women). *Students:* 6 full-time (4 women), 13 part-time (10 women); includes 1 minority (Two or more races, non-Hispanic/Latino). Average age 30. 13 applicants, 85% accepted, 4 enrolled. In 2013, 2 master's awarded. *Degree requirements:* For master's, one foreign language, comprehensive exam, thesis or alternative, oral and written exams. *Entrance requirements:* For master's, GRE General Test, minimum GPA of 3.0, bachelor's degree in history or related area. Additional exam requirements/recommendations for international students: Required—TOEFL (minimum score 500 paper-based; 80 iBT), IELTS (minimum score 6.5). *Application deadline:* For fall admission, 7/15 priority date for domestic students, 4/1 priority date for international students; for spring admission, 11/30 priority date for domestic students, 9/1 priority date for international students. Applications are processed on a rolling basis. Application fee: $50. Electronic applications accepted. *Expenses:* Tuition, state resident: full-time $8912; part-time $540 per credit hour. Tuition, nonresident: full-time $20,774; part-time $1252 per credit hour. *Required fees:* $148 per semester. One-time fee: $150. *Financial support:* In 2013–14, 7 students received support, including 2 research assistantships with full tuition reimbursements available (averaging $10,896 per year); career-related internships or fieldwork, Federal Work-Study, institutionally sponsored loans, scholarships/grants, health care benefits, tuition waivers (full and partial), and unspecified assistantships also available. Support available to part-time students. Financial award application deadline: 4/1; financial award applicants required to submit FAFSA. *Faculty research:* Public history, history of the U.S. space program, military history, history of science and technology, women in history. *Unit head:* Dr. Stephen Waring, Chair, 256-824-6310, Fax: 256-824-6477, E-mail: warings@uah.edu. *Application contact:* Kim Gray, Graduate Studies Admissions Coordinator, 256-824-6002, Fax: 256-824-6405, E-mail: deangrad@uah.edu.
Website: http://www.uah.edu/colleges/liberal/history/.

University of Arkansas at Pine Bluff, School of Education, Pine Bluff, AR 71601-2799. Offers early childhood education (M Ed); secondary education (M Ed), including English education, mathematics education, physical education, science education, social studies education; teaching (MAT). *Accreditation:* NCATE. Part-time and evening/weekend programs available. *Degree requirements:* For master's, comprehensive exam. *Entrance requirements:* For master's, GRE, minimum GPA of 2.75, NTE or

Standard Arkansas Teaching Certificate. *Faculty research:* Teacher certification, accreditation, assessment, standards, portfolio development, rehabilitation, technology.

The University of British Columbia, Faculty of Education, Department of Curriculum and Pedagogy, Vancouver, BC V6T 1Z4, Canada. Offers art education (M Ed, MA); business education (MA); curriculum studies (M Ed, MA, PhD); home economics education (M Ed, MA); math education (M Ed, MA); music education (M Ed, MA); physical education (M Ed, MA); science education (M Ed, MA); social studies education (M Ed, MA); technology studies education (M Ed, MA). Part-time programs available. Postbaccalaureate distance learning degree programs offered (no on-campus study). *Faculty:* 32 full-time (14 women), 1 (woman) part-time/adjunct. *Students:* 163 full-time, 134 part-time, 42 international. Average age 40. 160 applicants, 75% accepted, 97 enrolled. In 2013, 68 master's, 7 doctorates awarded. *Degree requirements:* For master's, thesis (MA); for doctorate, comprehensive exam, thesis/dissertation. *Entrance requirements:* Additional exam requirements/recommendations for international students: Required—TOEFL (minimum score 580 paper-based; 92 iBT), IELTS (minimum score 6.5). *Application deadline:* For fall admission, 12/1 for domestic and international students; for spring admission, 10/1 for domestic students, 9/1 for international students. Application fee: $90 Canadian dollars ($150 Canadian dollars for international students). Electronic applications accepted. *Expenses:* Contact institution. *Financial support:* In 2013–14, 10 fellowships with partial tuition reimbursements (averaging $16,000 per year), 11 research assistantships with partial tuition reimbursements (averaging $14,000 per year), 27 teaching assistantships with partial tuition reimbursements (averaging $14,000 per year) were awarded; tuition waivers (partial) also available. *Faculty research:* School subjects, teaching and learning. *Unit head:* Dr. Peter Grimmett, Head, 604-822-5422, Fax: 604-822-4714, E-mail: anna.ip@ubc.ca. *Application contact:* Basia Zurek, Graduate Programs Assistant, 604-822-5367, Fax: 604-822-4714, E-mail: edcp.grad@ubc.ca.
Website: http://www.edcp.educ.ubc.ca/.

University of California, Santa Cruz, Division of Graduate Studies, Division of Social Sciences, Program in Social Documentation, Santa Cruz, CA 95064. Offers MA. *Entrance requirements:* For master's, resume or curriculum vitae, sample of documentary production work. Additional exam requirements/recommendations for international students: Required—TOEFL (minimum score 550 paper-based; 83 iBT); Recommended—IELTS (minimum score 8). Electronic applications accepted. *Faculty research:* Documentation of underrepresented areas of community life.

University of Central Florida, College of Education and Human Performance, Education Doctoral Programs, Orlando, FL 32816. Offers communication sciences and disorders (PhD); counselor education (PhD); early childhood education (PhD); education (Ed D); elementary education (PhD); exceptional education (PhD); exercise physiology (PhD); higher education (PhD); hospitality education (PhD); instructional technology (PhD); mathematics education (PhD); reading education (PhD); science education (PhD); social science education (PhD); TESOL (PhD). *Students:* 137 full-time (94 women), 86 part-time (64 women); includes 45 minority (24 Black or African American, non-Hispanic/Latino; 5 Asian, non-Hispanic/Latino; 13 Hispanic/Latino; 3 Two or more races, non-Hispanic/Latino), 22 international. Average age 39. 132 applicants, 54% accepted, 54 enrolled. In 2013, 38 doctorates awarded. Application fee: $30. Electronic applications accepted. *Financial support:* In 2013–14, 84 students received support, including 38 fellowships with partial tuition reimbursements available (averaging $6,600 per year), 41 research assistantships with partial tuition reimbursements available (averaging $7,800 per year), 53 teaching assistantships with partial tuition reimbursements available (averaging $7,700 per year). *Unit head:* Dr. Edward Robinson, Director of Doctoral Programs, 407-823-6106, E-mail: edward.robinson@ucf.edu. *Application contact:* Barbara Rodriguez Lamas, Associate Director, Admissions and Student Services, 407-823-2766, Fax: 407-823-6442, E-mail: gradadmissions@ucf.edu.
Website: http://education.ucf.edu/departments.cfm.

University of Central Florida, College of Education and Human Performance, School of Teaching, Learning, and Leadership, Orlando, FL 32816. Offers applied learning and instruction (MA, Certificate), including applied learning and instruction (MA), community college education (Certificate), gifted education (Certificate), global and comparative education (Certificate), initial teacher professional preparation (Certificate), urban education (Certificate); art education (M Ed, MAT), including teacher education (MAT), teacher leadership (M Ed); educational and instructional technology (MA, Certificate), including e-learning (Certificate), educational technology (Certificate), instructional design and technology (MA), instructional/educational technology (Certificate); educational leadership (Ed S); elementary education (M Ed, MA); English language arts education (M Ed, MAT), including teacher education (MAT), teacher leadership (M Ed); K-8 mathematics and science education (M Ed, Certificate); mathematics education (M Ed, MAT), including teacher education (MAT), teacher leadership (M Ed); reading education (M Ed, Certificate); science education (M Ed, MAT), including teacher education (MAT), teacher leadership (M Ed); social science education (M Ed, MAT), including teacher education (MAT), teacher leadership (M Ed); teacher leadership and educational leadership (M Ed, Ed S), including educational leadership (Ed S), teacher leadership (M Ed); teaching excellence (Certificate). Part-time and evening/weekend programs available. *Faculty:* 76 full-time (54 women), 75 part-time/adjunct (57 women). *Students:* 115 full-time (93 women), 476 part-time (364 women); includes 149 minority (49 Black or African American, non-Hispanic/Latino; 20 Asian, non-Hispanic/Latino; 69 Hispanic/Latino; 11 Two or more races, non-Hispanic/Latino), 8 international. Average age 31. 268 applicants, 79% accepted, 133 enrolled. In 2013, 212 master's, 48 other advanced degrees awarded. *Degree requirements:* For other advanced degree, thesis or alternative. *Entrance requirements:* For degree, GRE General Test, minimum GPA of 3.0. Additional exam requirements/recommendations for international students: Required—TOEFL. *Application deadline:* For fall admission, 7/15 for domestic students; for spring admission, 12/15 for domestic students. Application fee: $30. Electronic applications accepted. *Financial support:* In 2013–14, 8 students received support, including 5 research assistantships with partial tuition reimbursements available (averaging $7,300 per year), 3 teaching assistantships with partial tuition reimbursements available (averaging $7,000 per year); career-related internships or fieldwork, Federal Work-Study, institutionally sponsored loans, tuition waivers (partial), and unspecified assistantships also available. Financial award application deadline: 3/1; financial award applicants required to submit FAFSA. *Unit head:* Dr. Michael C. Hynes, Co-Director, 407-823-6076, E-mail: michael.hynes@ucf.edu. *Application contact:* Barbara Rodriguez Lamas, Director, Admissions and Student Services, 407-823-2766, Fax: 407-823-6442, E-mail: gradadmissions@ucf.edu.
Website: http://education.ucf.edu/departments.cfm.

University of Cincinnati, Graduate School, College of Education, Criminal Justice, and Human Services, Division of Teacher Education, Cincinnati, OH 45221. Offers curriculum and instruction (M Ed, Ed D); deaf studies (Certificate); early childhood education (M Ed); middle childhood education (M Ed); postsecondary literacy instruction (Certificate); reading/literacy (M Ed, Ed D); secondary education (M Ed); special education (M Ed, Ed D); teaching English as a second language (M Ed, Ed D, Certificate); teaching science (MS). Part-time programs available. *Degree requirements:* For doctorate, thesis/dissertation. *Entrance requirements:* For master's, GRE General

Test. Additional exam requirements/recommendations for international students: Required—TOEFL (minimum score 550 paper-based). Electronic applications accepted.

University of Connecticut, Graduate School, Neag School of Education, Department of Curriculum and Instruction, Program in History and Social Sciences Education, Storrs, CT 06269. Offers MA, PhD, Post-Master's Certificate. *Accreditation:* NCATE. Terminal master's awarded for partial completion of doctoral program. *Degree requirements:* For master's, comprehensive exam, thesis or alternative; for doctorate, thesis/dissertation. *Entrance requirements:* For doctorate, GRE General Test. Additional exam requirements/recommendations for international students: Required—TOEFL (minimum score 550 paper-based). Electronic applications accepted.

University of Florida, Graduate School, College of Education, School of Teaching and Learning, Gainesville, FL 32611. Offers curriculum and instruction (M Ed, MAE, Ed D, PhD, Ed S), including bilingual/ESOL specialization; elementary education (M Ed, MAE); English education (M Ed, MAE); mathematics education (M Ed, MAE); reading education (M Ed, MAE); science education (M Ed, MAE); social studies education (M Ed, MAE). *Accreditation:* NCATE. Part-time and evening/weekend programs available. Postbaccalaureate distance learning degree programs offered (no on-campus study). *Faculty:* 24 full-time (17 women), 12 part-time/adjunct (7 women). *Students:* 201 full-time (162 women), 325 part-time (255 women); includes 124 minority (36 Black or African American, non-Hispanic/Latino; 4 American Indian or Alaska Native, non-Hispanic/Latino; 10 Asian, non-Hispanic/Latino; 74 Hispanic/Latino), 47 international. Average age 34. 220 applicants, 55% accepted, 64 enrolled. In 2013, 215 master's, 15 doctorates, 14 other advanced degrees awarded. Terminal master's awarded for partial completion of doctoral program. *Degree requirements:* For master's, comprehensive exam (for some programs), thesis (for some programs); for doctorate, comprehensive exam (for some programs), thesis/dissertation (for some programs). *Entrance requirements:* For master's and doctorate, GRE General Test, minimum GPA of 3.0; for Ed S, GRE General Test. Additional exam requirements/recommendations for international students: Required—TOEFL (minimum score 550 paper-based; 80 iBT), IELTS (minimum score 6). *Application deadline:* For fall admission, 2/15 for domestic students, 12/1 for international students; for spring admission, 9/15 for domestic students, 3/1 for international students. Applications are processed on a rolling basis. Application fee: $30. Electronic applications accepted. *Expenses:* Tuition, state resident: full-time $12,640. Tuition, nonresident: full-time $30,000. *Financial support:* In 2013–14, 52 students received support, including 3 fellowships (averaging $2,365 per year), 20 research assistantships (averaging $11,715 per year), 58 teaching assistantships (averaging $8,410 per year); career-related internships or fieldwork and unspecified assistantships also available. Financial award applicants required to submit FAFSA. *Faculty research:* Early childhood, child and adolescents, diverse learners, race/ethnicity issues, teacher education, professional development, language and literacy development, policy development. *Unit head:* Elizabeth Bondy, PhD, Interim Director and Professor, 352-273-4242, Fax: 352-392-9193, E-mail: bondy@coe.ufl.edu. *Application contact:* Sevan Terzian, Graduate Coordinator, 352-273-4216, Fax: 352-392-9193, E-mail: sterzian@coe.ufl.edu.
Website: http://education.ufl.edu/school-teaching-learning/.

University of Georgia, College of Education, Department of Elementary and Social Studies Education, Athens, GA 30602. Offers early childhood education (M Ed, MAT, PhD, Ed S), including child and family development (MAT); elementary education (PhD); middle school education (M Ed, PhD, Ed S); social studies education (M Ed, Ed D, PhD, Ed S). *Entrance requirements:* For master's and Ed S, GRE General Test or MAT; for doctorate, GRE General Test. Electronic applications accepted.

University of Illinois at Chicago, Graduate College, Program in Learning Sciences, Chicago, IL 60607-7128. Offers PhD. *Expenses:* Tuition, state resident: full-time $11,066; part-time $3689 per term. Tuition, nonresident: full-time $23,064; part-time $7688 per term. *Required fees:* $3004; $1190 per term. Tuition and fees vary according to course level and program. *Unit head:* Dr. Clark Hulse, Dean, 312-413-2550. *Application contact:* Receptionist, 312-413-2550, E-mail: gradcoll@uic.edu.

University of Indianapolis, Graduate Programs, School of Education, Indianapolis, IN 46227-3697. Offers art education (MAT); biology (MAT); chemistry (MAT); curriculum and instruction (MA); earth sciences (MAT); education (MA, MAT); educational leadership (MA); elementary education (MA); English (MAT); French (MAT); math (MAT); physical education (MAT); physics (MAT); secondary education (MA), including art education, education, English education, social studies education; social studies (MAT); Spanish (MAT). *Accreditation:* NCATE. Part-time and evening/weekend programs available. *Faculty:* 5 full-time (4 women), 2 part-time/adjunct (1 woman). *Students:* 19 full-time (9 women), 54 part-time (27 women); includes 13 minority (5 Black or African American, non-Hispanic/Latino; 1 Asian, non-Hispanic/Latino; 5 Hispanic/Latino; 2 Two or more races, non-Hispanic/Latino), 1 international. Average age 32. In 2013, 52 master's awarded. *Entrance requirements:* For master's, GRE Subject Test, PRAXIS I, minimum GPA of 2.5, 3 letters of recommendation, interview. Additional exam requirements/recommendations for international students: Required—TOEFL (minimum score 550 paper-based). *Application deadline:* Applications are processed on a rolling basis. Application fee: $50. *Expenses: Tuition:* Full-time $5436; part-time $810 per credit hour. *Financial support:* Federal Work-Study available. Financial award application deadline: 5/1; financial award applicants required to submit FAFSA. *Faculty research:* Assessment of teacher education, perceptions of prospective teachers by parents. *Unit head:* Dr. Kathy Moran, Dean, 317-788-3285, Fax: 317-788-3300, E-mail: kmoran@uindy.edu. *Application contact:* Jeni Kirby, Administrative Assistant, Teacher Education, 317-788-2113, E-mail: kirbyj@uindy.edu.
Website: http://education.uindy.edu/.

The University of Iowa, Graduate College, College of Education, Department of Teaching and Learning, Program in Education, Iowa City, IA 52242-1316. Offers art education (MA); developmental reading (MA); elementary education (MA); English education (MA, MAT); foreign and second language education (MAT); foreign language education (MA); foreign language/ESL education (PhD); language, literacy and culture (PhD); mathematics education (MA, MAT, PhD); music education (MM, PhD); science education (MA); secondary education (MA); social studies (MA, PhD). *Degree requirements:* For master's, thesis optional, exam; for doctorate, comprehensive exam, thesis/dissertation. *Entrance requirements:* For master's and doctorate, GRE General Test, minimum GPA of 3.0. Additional exam requirements/recommendations for international students: Required—TOEFL (minimum score 550 paper-based; 81 iBT). Electronic applications accepted.

University of Louisiana at Monroe, Graduate School, College of Arts, Education, and Sciences, School of Education, Program in Curriculum and Instruction, Monroe, LA 71209-0001. Offers art education (M Ed); biology education (M Ed); chemistry education (M Ed); curriculum and instruction (Ed D); early childhood education (M Ed); earth science education (M Ed); educational leadership (M Ed); elementary education (1-5) (M Ed); English as a second language (M Ed); English education (M Ed); family and consumer education (M Ed); French education (M Ed); history education (M Ed); math education (M Ed); middle school education (M Ed); music education (M Ed); reading education (K-12) (M Ed); Spanish education (M Ed); special education - academically gifted (M Ed); special education - early intervention (M Ed); special education - educational diagnostician (M Ed); special education - mild/moderate disabilities (M Ed);

speech education (M Ed). *Accreditation:* NCATE. *Degree requirements:* For master's, comprehensive exam (for some programs), thesis; for doctorate, thesis/dissertation, internships. *Entrance requirements:* For master's, GRE General Test; for doctorate, GRE General Test, minimum undergraduate GPA of 2.75, graduate 3.25. Additional exam requirements/recommendations for international students: Required—TOEFL (minimum score 500 paper-based; 61 iBT). *Application deadline:* For fall admission, 8/24 priority date for domestic students, 7/1 for international students; for winter admission, 12/14 priority date for domestic students; for spring admission, 1/19 for domestic students, 11/1 for international students. Applications are processed on a rolling basis. Application fee: $20 ($30 for international students). Electronic applications accepted. *Expenses:* Tuition, state resident: full-time $6607. Tuition, nonresident: full-time $17,179. Full-time tuition and fees vary according to program. *Financial support:* Research assistantships, career-related internships or fieldwork, Federal Work-Study, and unspecified assistantships available. Financial award application deadline: 4/1; financial award applicants required to submit FAFSA. *Unit head:* Dr. Dorothy Schween, Director, 318-342-1268, Fax: 318-342-3131, E-mail: schween@ulm.edu. *Application contact:* Dr. Dorothy Schween, Director, 318-342-1268, Fax: 318-342-3131, E-mail: schween@ulm.edu.

University of Maine, Graduate School, College of Education and Human Development, Department of Teacher and Counselor Education, Orono, ME 04469. Offers counselor education (M Ed, MA, MS, CAS); early childhood teacher (CGS); education (PhD), including counselor education, literacy education, prevention and intervention studies; elementary education (M Ed, CAS); individualized education (M Ed); literacy education (M Ed, MS, CAS); response to intervention for behavior (CGS); secondary education (M Ed, MAT, CAS); social studies education (M Ed); special education (M Ed, CAS); teacher consultant in writing (CGS). Part-time programs available. *Students:* 147 full-time (118 women), 15 part-time (2 women); includes 8 minority (4 Black or African American, non-Hispanic/Latino; 2 American Indian or Alaska Native, non-Hispanic/Latino; 1 Hispanic/Latino; 1 Two or more races, non-Hispanic/Latino), 3 international. Average age 37. 100 applicants, 58% accepted, 50 enrolled. In 2013, 83 master's, 5 doctorates, 17 other advanced degrees awarded. *Degree requirements:* For master's, thesis (for some programs); for doctorate, comprehensive exam, thesis/dissertation. *Entrance requirements:* For master's, GRE General Test, MAT. Additional exam requirements/recommendations for international students: Required—TOEFL. *Application deadline:* For fall admission, 2/1 priority date for domestic students. Applications are processed on a rolling basis. Application fee: $65. Electronic applications accepted. *Expenses:* Tuition, state resident: full-time $7524. Tuition, nonresident: full-time $23,112. *Required fees:* $1970. *Financial support:* In 2013–14, 46 students received support, including 1 research assistantship (averaging $14,600 per year), 11 teaching assistantships (averaging $14,600 per year). Financial award application deadline: 3/1. *Unit head:* Dr. Janet Spector, Coordinator, 207-581-2459. *Application contact:* Scott G. Delcourt, Associate Dean of the Graduate School, 207-581-3291, Fax: 207-581-3232, E-mail: graduate@maine.edu.
Website: http://umaine.edu/edhd/.

University of Maryland, Baltimore County, Graduate School, College of Arts, Humanities and Social Sciences, Department of Education, Program in Teaching, Baltimore, MD 21250. Offers early childhood education (MAT); elementary education (MAT); secondary education (MAT), including art, biology, chemistry, dance, earth/space science, English, foreign language, mathematics, music, physics, social studies, theatre. Part-time and evening/weekend programs available. *Faculty:* 24 full-time (18 women), 25 part-time/adjunct (19 women). *Students:* 49 full-time (34 women), 35 part-time (23 women); includes 19 minority (9 Black or African American, non-Hispanic/Latino; 3 Asian, non-Hispanic/Latino; 6 Hispanic/Latino; 1 Two or more races, non-Hispanic/Latino). Average age 30. 40 applicants, 95% accepted, 35 enrolled. In 2013, 106 master's awarded. *Degree requirements:* For master's, comprehensive exam (for some programs), thesis (for some programs). *Entrance requirements:* For master's, PRAXIS I or SAT (minimum score of 1000), minimum GPA of 3.0. Additional exam requirements/recommendations for international students: Required—TOEFL. *Application deadline:* For fall admission, 6/1 for domestic students; for spring admission, 11/1 for domestic students. Applications are processed on a rolling basis. Application fee: $50. Electronic applications accepted. One-time fee: $200 full-time. *Financial support:* In 2013–14, 6 students received support, including teaching assistantships with full and partial tuition reimbursements available (averaging $12,000 per year); career-related internships or fieldwork, Federal Work-Study, scholarships/grants, tuition waivers, and unspecified assistantships also available. Financial award application deadline: 3/1. *Faculty research:* STEM teacher education, culturally sensitive pedagogy, ESOL/bilingual education, early childhood education, language, literacy and culture. *Unit head:* Dr. Susan M. Blunck, Graduate Program Director, 410-455-2869, Fax: 410-455-3986, E-mail: blunck@umbc.edu. *Application contact:* Dr. Susan M. Blunck, Graduate Program Director, 410-455-2869, Fax: 410-455-3986, E-mail: blunck@umbc.edu.
Website: http://www.umbc.edu/education/.

University of Minnesota, Twin Cities Campus, Graduate School, College of Education and Human Development, Department of Curriculum and Instruction, Program in Teaching, Minneapolis, MN 55455-0213. Offers Chinese (M Ed); earth science (M Ed); elementary special education (M Ed); English (M Ed); English as a second language (M Ed); French (M Ed); German (M Ed); Hebrew (M Ed); Japanese (M Ed); life sciences (M Ed); mathematics (M Ed); middle school science (M Ed); science (M Ed); second languages and cultures (M Ed); social studies (M Ed); Spanish (M Ed). *Students:* 220 full-time (154 women), 83 part-time (60 women); includes 43 minority (10 Black or African American, non-Hispanic/Latino; 26 Asian, non-Hispanic/Latino; 7 Hispanic/Latino), 4 international. Average age 27. 261 applicants, 87% accepted, 222 enrolled. In 2013, 561 master's awarded. Application fee: $75 ($95 for international students). *Unit head:* Dr. Nina Asher, Chair, 612-624-1357, Fax: 612-624-8277, E-mail: nasher@umn.edu. *Application contact:* Dr. Jennifer Engler, Assistant Dean, 612-626-2887, Fax: 612-626-7496, E-mail: engle009@umn.edu.
Website: http://www.cehd.umn.edu/ci/.

University of Missouri, Graduate School, College of Education, Department of Learning, Teaching and Curriculum, Columbia, MO 65211. Offers agricultural education (M Ed, PhD, Ed S); art education (M Ed, PhD, Ed S); business and office education (M Ed, PhD, Ed S); early childhood education (M Ed, PhD, Ed S); elementary education (M Ed, PhD, Ed S); English education (M Ed, PhD, Ed S); foreign language education (M Ed, PhD, Ed S); health education and promotion (M Ed, PhD); learning and instruction (M Ed); marketing education (M Ed, PhD, Ed S); mathematics education (M Ed, PhD, Ed S); music education (M Ed, PhD, Ed S); reading education (M Ed, PhD, Ed S); science education (M Ed, PhD, Ed S); social studies education (M Ed, PhD, Ed S); vocational education (M Ed, PhD, Ed S). Part-time programs available. *Faculty:* 26 full-time (16 women), 3 part-time/adjunct (2 women). *Students:* 186 full-time (143 women), 197 part-time (172 women); includes 19 minority (4 Black or African American, non-Hispanic/Latino; 4 Asian, non-Hispanic/Latino; 6 Hispanic/Latino; 5 Two or more races, non-Hispanic/Latino), 25 international. Average age 31. 288 applicants, 65% accepted, 160 enrolled. In 2013, 202 master's, 18 doctorates, 7 other advanced degrees awarded. Terminal master's awarded for partial completion of doctoral program. *Degree requirements:* For doctorate, thesis/dissertation. *Entrance requirements:* For master's and Ed S, GRE General Test or MAT, minimum GPA of 3.0; for doctorate, GRE General Test, minimum GPA of 3.0. Additional exam requirements/recommendations for international students: Required—TOEFL (minimum score 600 paper-based; 100 iBT). *Application deadline:* For fall admission, 12/1 priority date for domestic and international students. Applications are processed on a rolling basis. Application fee: $55 ($75 for international students). Electronic applications accepted. *Financial support:* Fellowships, research assistantships, teaching assistantships, institutionally sponsored loans, traineeships, health care benefits, and unspecified assistantships available. Support available to part-time students. *Faculty research:* Curriculum development and research, teacher education, art education, business and marketing, early childhood education, English education, literacy/reading education, mathematics education, music education, science education, social studies education. *Unit head:* Dr. James Tarr, Associate Division Director, 573-882-4034, E-mail: tarrj@missouri.edu. *Application contact:* Fran Colley, Academic Advisor, 573-882-6462, E-mail: colleyf@missouri.edu.
Website: http://education.missouri.edu/LTC/.

The University of North Carolina at Chapel Hill, Graduate School, School of Education, Program in Secondary Education, Chapel Hill, NC 27599. Offers English (Grades 9-12) (MAT); English as a second language (MAT); French (Grades K-12) (MAT); German (Grades K-12) (MAT); Japanese (Grades K-12) (MAT); Latin (Grades 9-12) (MAT); mathematics (Grades 9-12) (MAT); music (Grades K-12) (MAT); science (Grades 9-12) (MAT); social studies (Grades 9-12) (MAT); Spanish (Grades K-12) (MAT). *Accreditation:* NCATE. *Degree requirements:* For master's, comprehensive exam. *Entrance requirements:* For master's, GRE General Test, minimum GPA of 3.0 during last 2 years of undergraduate course work. Additional exam requirements/recommendations for international students: Required—TOEFL (minimum score 550 paper-based). Electronic applications accepted.

The University of North Carolina at Charlotte, The Graduate School, College of Liberal Arts and Sciences, Department of Sociology, Charlotte, NC 28223-0001. Offers health research (MA); mathematical sociology and quantitative methods (MA); organizations, occupations, and work (MA); political sociology (MA); race and gender (MA); social psychology (MA); social theory (MA); sociology of education (MA); stratification (MA). Part-time and evening/weekend programs available. *Faculty:* 16 full-time (10 women). *Students:* 10 full-time (3 women), 8 part-time (3 women); includes 4 minority (3 Black or African American, non-Hispanic/Latino; 1 Asian, non-Hispanic/Latino), 1 international. Average age 32. 11 applicants, 82% accepted, 7 enrolled. In 2013, 9 master's awarded. *Degree requirements:* For master's, thesis or comprehensive exam. *Entrance requirements:* For master's, GRE or MAT, minimum GPA of 3.0 in last 2 years, 2.75 overall. Additional exam requirements/recommendations for international students: Required—TOEFL (minimum score 557 paper-based; 83 iBT). *Application deadline:* For fall admission, 4/15 for domestic and international students; for spring admission, 10/1 for domestic and international students. Application fee: $75. Electronic applications accepted. *Expenses:* Tuition, state resident: full-time $3522. Tuition, nonresident: full-time $16,051. *Required fees:* $2585. Tuition and fees vary according to course load and program. *Financial support:* In 2013–14, 14 students received support, including 5 research assistantships (averaging $8,250 per year), 5 teaching assistantships (averaging $10,600 per year); career-related internships or fieldwork, institutionally sponsored loans, scholarships/grants, and unspecified assistantships also available. Support available to part-time students. Financial award application deadline: 4/1; financial award applicants required to submit FAFSA. *Faculty research:* Impact of race on high school course selection; income inequality within the United States and cross-nationally; small group interaction, nonverbal behaviors, identity, emotions, gender, and expectations; mathematical models of social processes. *Total annual research expenditures:* $400,908. *Unit head:* Dr. Lisa Walker, Chair, 704-687-7825, Fax: 704-687-3091, E-mail: lisa.walker@uncc.edu. *Application contact:* Kathy B. Giddings, Director of Graduate Admissions, 704-687-5503, Fax: 704-687-1668, E-mail: gradadm@uncc.edu.
Website: http://sociology.uncc.edu/.

The University of North Carolina at Greensboro, Graduate School, School of Education, Department of Curriculum and Instruction, Greensboro, NC 27412-5001. Offers college teaching and adult learning (Certificate); curriculum and instruction (M Ed), including chemistry education, elementary education, English as a second language, French education, instructional technology, mathematics education, middle grades education, reading education, science education, social studies education, Spanish education; curriculum and teaching (PhD), including higher education, teacher education and development; English as a second language (Certificate); higher education (M Ed); supervision (M Ed). *Accreditation:* NCATE. Part-time programs available. *Degree requirements:* For doctorate, thesis/dissertation. *Entrance requirements:* For master's and doctorate, GRE General Test. Additional exam requirements/recommendations for international students: Required—TOEFL. Electronic applications accepted. *Faculty research:* Community college literacy program, middle school mathematics/computer mathematics.

The University of North Carolina at Pembroke, Graduate Studies, Department of History, Program in Social Studies Education, Pembroke, NC 28372-1510. Offers MA, MAT. Part-time and evening/weekend programs available. *Degree requirements:* For master's, thesis optional. *Entrance requirements:* For master's, GRE or MAT, minimum GPA of 3.0 in major, 2.5 overall. Additional exam requirements/recommendations for international students: Required—TOEFL.

University of North Georgia, School of Education, Dahlonega, GA 30597. Offers art education (MAT); early childhood education (M Ed); English education (MAT); history education (MAT); math education (MAT); middle grades education (M Ed, MAT); physical education (MS); school leadership (Ed S); secondary education (M Ed), including English education, history education, mathematics education, physical education; teacher education (MAT). *Accreditation:* NCATE. Part-time and evening/weekend programs available. Postbaccalaureate distance learning degree programs offered (no on-campus study). *Degree requirements:* For master's, comprehensive exam, thesis optional. *Entrance requirements:* For master's, GRE or MAT, GACE, minimum GPA of 2.75; for Ed S, GRE General Test or MAT, 3 years of teaching experience, master's degree, minimum graduate GPA of 3.25, leadership position in the school. Additional exam requirements/recommendations for international students: Required—TOEFL (minimum score 550 paper-based; 79 iBT), IELTS (minimum score 6.5). Electronic applications accepted. *Faculty research:* Identification of professional development school structures supporting P-12 student achievement, impact of diverse field placement settings in teacher belief development among preservice teachers, use of inquiry methodology in social studies teaching with English language learners, use of instructional differentiation in the middle grades classroom, effects of international school placements on preservice teacher beliefs and attitudes.

University of Oklahoma, Jeannine Rainbolt College of Education, Department of Instructional Leadership and Academic Curriculum, Norman, OK 73072. Offers communication, culture and pedagogy for Hispanic populations in educational settings (Graduate Certificate); instructional leadership and academic curriculum (M Ed, PhD), including bilingual education (PhD), early childhood education, elementary education, English education, instructional leadership, mathematics education, reading education, science education, science, technology, engineering and mathematics education (M Ed), secondary education, social studies education, teacher education (M Ed), world

language education (M Ed). *Accreditation:* NCATE. Part-time and evening/weekend programs available. Postbaccalaureate distance learning degree programs offered (no on-campus study). *Faculty:* 22 full-time (15 women), 1 (woman) part-time/adjunct. *Students:* 64 full-time (49 women), 103 part-time (81 women); includes 33 minority (8 Black or African American, non-Hispanic/Latino; 9 American Indian or Alaska Native, non-Hispanic/Latino; 5 Asian, non-Hispanic/Latino; 4 Hispanic/Latino; 1 Native Hawaiian or other Pacific Islander, non-Hispanic/Latino; 6 Two or more races, non-Hispanic/Latino), 10 international. Average age 34. 50 applicants, 84% accepted, 36 enrolled. In 2013, 26 master's, 11 doctorates awarded. Terminal master's awarded for partial completion of doctoral program. *Degree requirements:* For master's, comprehensive exam (for some programs), thesis (for some programs); for doctorate, comprehensive exam, thesis/dissertation. *Entrance requirements:* For master's, essay; for doctorate, GRE, 3 recommendation letters; autobiography, statement of objectives; essay on chosen major; transcripts; writing sample. Additional exam requirements/recommendations for international students: Required—TOEFL (minimum score 79 iBT). *Application deadline:* For fall admission, 4/30 for domestic and international students; for spring admission, 10/31 for domestic and international students; for summer admission, 3/15 for domestic and international students. Applications are processed on a rolling basis. Application fee: $50 ($100 for international students). Electronic applications accepted. *Expenses:* Tuition, state resident: full-time $4205; part-time $175.20 per credit hour. Tuition, nonresident: full-time $16,205; part-time $675.20 per credit hour. *Required fees:* $2745; $103.85 per credit hour. $126.50 per semester. *Financial support:* In 2013–14, 98 students received support, including 10 research assistantships with partial tuition reimbursements available (averaging $10,671 per year), 7 teaching assistantships with partial tuition reimbursements available (averaging $10,753 per year); Federal Work-Study, institutionally sponsored loans, scholarships/grants, and unspecified assistantships also available. Support available to part-time students. Financial award application deadline: 6/1; financial award applicants required to submit FAFSA. *Total annual research expenditures:* $1 million. *Unit head:* Dr. Stacy Reeder, Chair/Graduate Liaison, 405-325-1498, Fax: 405-325-4061, E-mail: reeder@ou.edu. *Application contact:* Lynn Crussel, Graduate Programs Officer, 405-325-1498, Fax: 405-325-4061, E-mail: lcrussel@ou.edu. Website: http://education.ou.edu/departments/ilac.

University of Pittsburgh, School of Education, Department of Instruction and Learning, Program in Secondary Education, Pittsburgh, PA 15260. Offers English/communications education (M Ed, MAT); foreign languages education (M Ed, MAT); mathematics education (M Ed, MAT, Ed D); science education (M Ed, MAT, Ed D); secondary education (PhD); social studies education (M Ed, MAT). Part-time and evening/weekend programs available. *Students:* 116 full-time (78 women), 47 part-time (36 women); includes 16 minority (4 Black or African American, non-Hispanic/Latino; 3 Asian, non-Hispanic/Latino; 5 Hispanic/Latino; 4 Two or more races, non-Hispanic/Latino), 29 international. Average age 30. 279 applicants, 66% accepted, 91 enrolled. In 2013, 113 master's, 8 doctorates awarded. *Degree requirements:* For master's, thesis; for doctorate, thesis/dissertation. *Entrance requirements:* For master's, PRAXIS I; for doctorate, GRE General Test. Additional exam requirements/recommendations for international students: Required—TOEFL. *Application deadline:* For fall admission, 2/1 priority date for domestic students; for spring admission, 11/15 priority date for domestic students. Applications are processed on a rolling basis. Application fee: $50. Electronic applications accepted. *Expenses:* Tuition, state resident: full-time $19,964; part-time $807 per credit. Tuition, nonresident: full-time $32,686; part-time $1337 per credit. *Required fees:* $740; $200. Tuition and fees vary according to program. *Financial support:* Fellowships, teaching assistantships, career-related internships or fieldwork, Federal Work-Study, tuition waivers (partial), and unspecified assistantships available. Support available to part-time students. Financial award application deadline: 3/15; financial award applicants required to submit FAFSA. *Unit head:* Dr. Richard Donato, Chairman, 412-624-7248, Fax: 412-648-7081, E-mail: donato@pitt.edu. *Application contact:* Marianne L. Budziszewski, Director of Admissions and Enrollment Services, 412-648-2230, Fax: 412-648-1899, E-mail: soeinfo@pitt.edu. Website: http://www.education.pitt.edu/.

University of Puerto Rico, Río Piedras Campus, College of Education, Program in Curriculum and Teaching, San Juan, PR 00931-3300. Offers biology education (M Ed); chemistry education (M Ed); curriculum and teaching (Ed D); history education (M Ed); mathematics education (M Ed); physics education (M Ed); Spanish education (M Ed). Part-time programs available. *Degree requirements:* For master's, thesis; for doctorate, thesis/dissertation, internship. *Entrance requirements:* For master's, PAEG or GRE, minimum GPA of 3.0, letter of recommendation; for doctorate, GRE or PAEG, master's degree, minimum GPA of 3.0, letter of recommendation (2), interview. *Faculty research:* Curriculum, math teaching.

University of St. Francis, College of Education, Joliet, IL 60435-6169. Offers educational leadership (MS, Ed D); elementary education (M Ed); higher education (MS); reading (MS); secondary education (M Ed), including English education, math education, science education, social studies education, visual arts education; special education (M Ed); teaching and learning (MS). *Accreditation:* NCATE. Part-time and evening/weekend programs available. Postbaccalaureate distance learning degree programs offered (no on-campus study). *Faculty:* 10 full-time (8 women), 34 part-time/adjunct (25 women). *Students:* 14 full-time (13 women), 250 part-time (183 women); includes 34 minority (20 Black or African American, non-Hispanic/Latino; 1 American Indian or Alaska Native, non-Hispanic/Latino; 13 Hispanic/Latino), 1 international. Average age 36. 133 applicants, 62% accepted, 71 enrolled. In 2013, 147 master's awarded. *Degree requirements:* For doctorate, thesis/dissertation. *Entrance requirements:* For doctorate, master's degree, IL Type 75 or Principal's endorsement, interview, minimum undergraduate GPA of 3.0, professional portfolio, letter of recommendation. Additional exam requirements/recommendations for international students: Required—TOEFL (minimum score 550 paper-based; 79 iBT), IELTS (minimum score 6.5). *Application deadline:* Applications are processed on a rolling basis. Application fee: $30. Electronic applications accepted. Application fee is waived when completed online. *Expenses:* Contact institution. *Financial support:* In 2013–14, 10 students received support. Scholarships/grants, tuition waivers (partial), and unspecified assistantships available. Support available to part-time students. Financial award applicants required to submit FAFSA. *Unit head:* Dr. John Gambro, Dean, 815-740-3829, Fax: 815-740-2264, E-mail: jgambro@stfrancis.edu. *Application contact:* Sandra Sloka, Director of Admissions for Graduate and Degree Completion Programs, 800-735-7500, Fax: 815-740-3431, E-mail: ssloka@stfrancis.edu. Website: http://www.stfrancis.edu/academics/college-of-education/.

University of South Carolina, The Graduate School, College of Education, Department of Instruction and Teacher Education, Program in Secondary Education, Columbia, SC 29208. Offers art education (IMA, MAT); business education (IMA, MAT); English (MAT); foreign language (MAT); health education (MAT); mathematics (MAT); science (IMA, MAT); secondary (Ed D); secondary education (MT, PhD); social studies (MAT); theatre and speech (MAT). IMA and MT offered jointly with the subject areas. *Accreditation:* NCATE. *Degree requirements:* For master's, comprehensive exam, thesis (for some programs), foreign language (MA); for doctorate, one foreign language, comprehensive exam, thesis/dissertation. *Entrance requirements:* For master's, GRE General Test or MAT, teaching certificate (IMA, M Ed), interview; for doctorate, GRE

General Test or MAT, interview. *Faculty research:* Middle school programs, professional development, school collaboration.

University of Southern Mississippi, Graduate School, College of Education and Psychology, Department of Curriculum, Instruction, and Special Education, Hattiesburg, MS 39406-0001. Offers elementary education (M Ed, PhD, Ed S); instructional technology (MS, PhD); secondary education (MAT); special education (M Ed, PhD, Ed S). Part-time programs available. *Faculty:* 23 full-time (17 women), 3 part-time/adjunct (2 women). *Students:* 20 full-time (19 women), 59 part-time (49 women); includes 18 minority (14 Black or African American, non-Hispanic/Latino; 3 Hispanic/Latino; 1 Two or more races, non-Hispanic/Latino). Average age 36. 21 applicants, 95% accepted, 17 enrolled. In 2013, 22 master's, 3 doctorates, 13 other advanced degrees awarded. *Degree requirements:* For master's and Ed S, comprehensive exam, thesis (for some programs); for doctorate, comprehensive exam, thesis/dissertation. *Entrance requirements:* For master's, GRE General Test, MAT, minimum GPA of 3.0; for doctorate, GRE General Test, minimum GPA of 3.5; for Ed S, GRE General Test, MAT, minimum GPA of 3.25. Additional exam requirements/recommendations for international students: Required—TOEFL, IELTS. *Application deadline:* For fall admission, 3/1 priority date for domestic students, 3/1 for international students; for spring admission, 1/10 priority date for domestic and international students. Applications are processed on a rolling basis. Application fee: $50. *Financial support:* In 2013–14, 9 research assistantships with tuition reimbursements (averaging $18,316 per year), 2 teaching assistantships with full tuition reimbursements (averaging $8,500 per year) were awarded; Federal Work-Study, institutionally sponsored loans, scholarships/grants, health care benefits, tuition waivers (partial), and unspecified assistantships also available. Financial award application deadline: 3/15; financial award applicants required to submit FAFSA. *Faculty research:* Mathematical problem solving, integrative curriculum, writing process, teacher education models. *Total annual research expenditures:* $100,000. *Unit head:* Dr. Ravic P. Ringlaben, Chair, 601-266-4547, Fax: 601-266-4175. *Application contact:* David Daves, Director of Graduate Studies, 601-266-6005, Fax: 601-266-4548. Website: http://www.usm.edu/graduateschool/table.php.

University of South Florida, College of Education, Department of Secondary Education, Tampa, FL 33620-9951. Offers English education (M Ed, MA, MAT, PhD); foreign language education/ESOL (M Ed, MA, MAT); instructional technology (M Ed, PhD, Ed S); mathematics education (M Ed, MA, MAT, PhD, Ed S); science education (M Ed, MA, MAT, PhD); second language acquisition/instructional technology (PhD); secondary education (M Ed, PhD); secondary education/TESOL (M Ed); social science education (M Ed, MA, MAT); teaching and learning in the content area (PhD). *Accreditation:* NCATE. Part-time and evening/weekend programs available. *Degree requirements:* For master's, variable foreign language requirement, comprehensive exam, project (for some programs); for doctorate, variable foreign language requirement, comprehensive exam, thesis/dissertation, philosophies of inquiry; multiple research methods. *Entrance requirements:* For master's, GRE General Test or General Knowledge Test, minimum GPA of 3.0; for doctorate, GRE General Test, minimum GPA of 3.5; for Ed S, GRE General Test. Additional exam requirements/recommendations for international students: Required—TOEFL (minimum score 550 paper-based; 79 iBT). Electronic applications accepted. *Faculty research:* English language learners/multicultural, social science education, mathematics education, science education, instructional technology.

The University of Tennessee, Graduate School, College of Education, Health and Human Sciences, Program in Education, Knoxville, TN 37996. Offers art education (MS); counseling education (PhD); cultural studies in education (PhD); curriculum (MS, Ed S); curriculum, educational research and evaluation (Ed D, PhD); early childhood education (PhD); early childhood special education (MS); education of deaf and hard of hearing (MS); educational administration and policy studies (Ed D, PhD); educational administration and supervision (Ed S); educational psychology (Ed D, PhD); elementary education (MS, Ed S); elementary teaching (MS); English education (MS, Ed S); exercise science (PhD); foreign language/ESL education (MS, Ed S); instructional technology (MS, Ed D, PhD, Ed S); literacy, language and ESL education (PhD); literacy, language education, and ESL education (Ed D); mathematics education (MS, Ed S); modified and comprehensive special education (MS); reading education (MS, Ed S); school counseling (Ed S); school psychology (PhD, Ed S); science education (MS, Ed S); secondary teaching (MS); social foundations (MS); social science education (MS, Ed S); socio-cultural foundations of sports and education (PhD); special education (Ed S); teacher education (Ed D, PhD). *Accreditation:* NCATE. Part-time and evening/weekend programs available. *Degree requirements:* For master's and Ed S, thesis optional; for doctorate, variable foreign language requirement, thesis/dissertation. *Entrance requirements:* For master's, minimum GPA of 2.7; for doctorate and Ed S, GRE General Test, minimum GPA of 2.7. Additional exam requirements/recommendations for international students: Required—TOEFL. Electronic applications accepted. *Expenses:* Tuition, state resident: full-time $9540; part-time $531 per credit hour. Tuition, nonresident: full-time $27,728; part-time $1542 per credit hour. *Required fees:* $1404; $67 per credit hour.

The University of Toledo, College of Graduate Studies, Judith Herb College of Education, Department of Curriculum and Instruction, Toledo, OH 43606-3390. Offers art education (ME); career and technical education (ME); career-technical education (Ed S); curriculum and instruction (ME, PhD, Ed S); early childhood education (PhD, Ed S); education and biology (MES); education and chemistry (MES); education and economics (MAE); education and English (MAE); education and French (MAE); education and geography (MAE); education and geology (MES); education and German (MAE); education and history (MAE); education and mathematics (MAE, MES); education and physics (MES); education and political science (MAE); education and sociology (MAE); education and Spanish (MAE); educational media (PhD); educational technology (ME); educational technology: virtual educator (Certificate); elementary education (PhD); English as a second language (MAE); gifted and talented (PhD); middle childhood education licensure (ME); music education (MME); secondary education (PhD); secondary education licensure (ME); special education (PhD, Ed S). *Accreditation:* NCATE. Part-time and evening/weekend programs available. *Faculty:* 41. *Students:* 53 full-time (30 women), 154 part-time (111 women); includes 21 minority (16 Black or African American, non-Hispanic/Latino; 4 Hispanic/Latino; 1 Two or more races, non-Hispanic/Latino), 21 international. Average age 34. 82 applicants, 79% accepted, 47 enrolled. In 2013, 80 master's, 5 doctorates awarded. *Degree requirements:* For master's, comprehensive exam, thesis or alternative; for doctorate, comprehensive exam, thesis/dissertation; for other advanced degree, thesis optional. *Entrance requirements:* For master's, doctorate, and other advanced degree, minimum cumulative GPA of 2.7 for all previous academic work, letters of recommendation. Additional exam requirements/recommendations for international students: Required—TOEFL (minimum score 550 paper-based; 80 iBT). *Application deadline:* For fall admission, 1/15 priority date for domestic and international students. Applications are processed on a rolling basis. Application fee: $45 ($75 for international students). Electronic applications accepted. *Financial support:* In 2013–14, 5 research assistantships with full and partial tuition reimbursements (averaging $13,200 per year), 11 teaching assistantships with full and partial tuition reimbursements (averaging $8,809 per year) were awarded; career-related internships or fieldwork, Federal Work-Study,

institutionally sponsored loans, scholarships/grants, tuition waivers (full and partial), unspecified assistantships, and administrative assistantships also available. Support available to part-time students. *Unit head:* Dr. Joan Kaderavek, Chair, 419-530-5373, E-mail: eigh.chiarelott@utoledo.edu. *Application contact:* Graduate School Office, 419-530-4723, Fax: 419-530-4724, E-mail: grdsch@utnet.utoledo.edu.
Website: http://www.utoledo.edu/eduhshs/.

University of Victoria, Faculty of Graduate Studies, Faculty of Education, Department of Curriculum and Instruction, Victoria, BC V8W 2Y2, Canada. Offers art education (M Ed, PhD); curriculum studies (M Ed, MA, PhD); early childhood education (M Ed, PhD); educational studies (PhD); language and literacy (M Ed, MA, PhD); mathematics (M Ed, MA, PhD); music education (M Ed, MA, PhD); science (M Ed, MA, PhD); social studies (M Ed, MA); social, cultural and foundational studies (MA, PhD); technology and environmental education (PhD). Part-time programs available. *Degree requirements:* For master's, thesis, project (M Ed); for doctorate, comprehensive exam, thesis/dissertation. *Entrance requirements:* For master's, minimum B average. Additional exam requirements/recommendations for international students: Required—TOEFL (minimum score 575 paper-based), IELTS (minimum score 7). Electronic applications accepted. *Faculty research:* Elementary and secondary English, language arts, curriculum theory and practice, educational media and technology, educational administration and leadership, history and philosophy of education.

University of Virginia, Curry School of Education, Department of Curriculum, Instruction, and Special Education, Program in Curriculum and Instruction, Charlottesville, VA 22903. Offers curriculum and instruction (M Ed, Ed S); elementary education (M Ed, Ed D); English (M Ed, Ed D); foreign language (M Ed); mathematics (M Ed, Ed D); reading (M Ed, Ed D, Ed S); science (Ed D); social studies (M Ed). *Students:* 42 full-time (30 women), 37 part-time (32 women); includes 4 minority (1 Black or African American, non-Hispanic/Latino; 2 Hispanic/Latino; 1 Two or more races, non-Hispanic/Latino), 1 international. Average age 31. 76 applicants, 74% accepted, 39 enrolled. In 2013, 84 master's, 3 doctorates, 23 other advanced degrees awarded. *Degree requirements:* For master's, comprehensive exam (for some programs); for doctorate, comprehensive exam, thesis/dissertation; for Ed S, comprehensive exam. *Entrance requirements:* For master's, doctorate, and Ed S, GRE General Test, 2 letters of recommendation. Additional exam requirements/recommendations for international students: Required—TOEFL (minimum score 600 paper-based; 90 iBT), IELTS (minimum score 7). *Application deadline:* Applications are processed on a rolling basis. Application fee: $60. Electronic applications accepted. *Expenses:* Tuition, state resident: part-time $334 per credit hour. Tuition, nonresident: part-time $1224 per credit hour. *Financial support:* Fellowships with tuition reimbursements, research assistantships with tuition reimbursements, and teaching assistantships with tuition reimbursements available. Financial award application deadline: 1/5; financial award applicants required to submit FAFSA. *Unit head:* Stephanie van Hover, Chair, 434-924-0841, E-mail: sdv2w@virginia.edu. *Application contact:* Karen Dwier, Information Contact, 434-924-0831, E-mail: kgd9g@virginia.edu.
Website: http://curry.virginia.edu/academics/areas-of-study/curriculum-teaching-learning.

University of Virginia, Curry School of Education, Program in Education, Charlottesville, VA 22903. Offers administration and supervision (PhD); applied developmental science (PhD); counselor education (PhD); curriculum and instruction (PhD); early childhood special education (MT); education evaluation (PhD); educational psychology (PhD); educational research (PhD); elementary education (MT); English education (MT, PhD); foreign language education (MT); higher education (PhD); instructional technology (PhD); kinesiology (MT, PhD); math education (PhD); reading education (PhD); research, statistics and evaluation (PhD); school psychology (PhD); science education (PhD); social studies education (MT, PhD); special education (PhD); world languages education (MT). *Students:* 474 full-time (379 women), 35 part-time (19 women); includes 89 minority (30 Black or African American, non-Hispanic/Latino; 1 American Indian or Alaska Native, non-Hispanic/Latino; 26 Asian, non-Hispanic/Latino; 19 Hispanic/Latino; 13 Two or more races, non-Hispanic/Latino), 21 international. Average age 26. 312 applicants, 49% accepted, 80 enrolled. In 2013, 137 master's, 38 doctorates awarded. *Degree requirements:* For master's, comprehensive exam (for some programs), field project; for doctorate, comprehensive exam, thesis/dissertation. *Entrance requirements:* For doctorate, GRE General Test. Additional exam requirements/recommendations for international students: Required—TOEFL (minimum score 600 paper-based; 90 iBT), IELTS (minimum score 7). *Application deadline:* Applications are processed on a rolling basis. Application fee: $60. Electronic applications accepted. *Expenses:* Tuition, state resident: part-time $334 per credit hour. Tuition, nonresident: part-time $1224 per credit hour. *Financial support:* Fellowships, research assistantships, and teaching assistantships available. Financial award application deadline: 1/5; financial award applicants required to submit FAFSA. *Unit head:* Robert C. Pianta, Dean, 434-924-3334, E-mail: pianta@virginia.edu. *Application contact:* Office of Admissions and Student Services, 434-924-0742, E-mail: curry-admissions@virginia.edu.
Website: http://curry.virginia.edu/teacher-education.

University of Washington, Graduate School, College of Education, Seattle, WA 98195. Offers curriculum and instruction (M Ed, Ed D, PhD), including educational technology, general curriculum (Ed D, PhD), language, literacy, and culture, mathematics education, multicultural education, reading and language arts education (Ed D), science education, social studies education, teaching and curriculum (M Ed); educational leadership and policy studies (M Ed, Ed D, PhD), including administration (Ed D), educational policy, organization, and leadership (M Ed, PhD), higher education, leadership for learning (Ed D), social and cultural foundations of education (M Ed, PhD); educational psychology (M Ed, PhD), including educational psychology (PhD), human development and cognition (M Ed), learning sciences, measurement, statistics and research design (M Ed), school psychology (M Ed); instructional leadership (M Ed); intercollegiate athletic leadership (M Ed); special education (M Ed, Ed D, PhD), including early childhood special education (M Ed), emotional and behavioral disabilities (M Ed), learning disabilities (M Ed), low-incidence disabilities (M Ed), severe disabilities (M Ed), special education (Ed D, PhD); teacher education (MIT). *Accreditation:* APA. Part-time and evening/weekend programs available. *Degree requirements:* For master's, thesis optional; for doctorate, thesis/dissertation. *Entrance requirements:* For master's and doctorate, GRE General Test, minimum GPA of 3.0. Additional exam requirements/recommendations for international students: Required—TOEFL. Electronic applications accepted. *Faculty research:* School restructuring/effective schools, special education interventions, literacy and writing, technology, school partnerships, teacher preparation.

The University of West Alabama, School of Graduate Studies, College of Education, Departments of Instructional Leadership and Support/Curriculum and Instruction, Program in Secondary Education, Livingston, AL 35470. Offers biology (MAT); English language arts (MAT); history (MAT); mathematics (MAT); physical education (MAT); science (MAT); secondary education (M Ed); social science (MAT). Part-time and evening/weekend programs available. Postbaccalaureate distance learning degree programs offered (no on-campus study). *Faculty:* 20 full-time (4 women), 5 part-time/adjunct (2 women). *Students:* 210 (139 women); includes 86 minority (80 Black or African American, non-Hispanic/Latino; 2 Asian, non-Hispanic/Latino; 2 Hispanic/Latino; 2 Two or more races, non-Hispanic/Latino). 115 applicants, 86% accepted, 72 enrolled. In 2013, 61 master's awarded. *Degree requirements:* For master's, comprehensive exam, thesis optional. *Entrance requirements:* For master's, GRE General Test, MAT, minimum GPA of 2.75. Additional exam requirements/recommendations for international students: Required—TOEFL (minimum score 500 paper-based; 61 iBT). *Application deadline:* For fall admission, 8/12 priority date for domestic students; for spring admission, 3/24 for domestic students. Applications are processed on a rolling basis. Application fee: $25 ($50 for international students). Electronic applications accepted. Tuition and fees vary according to course load. *Financial support:* Teaching assistantships, career-related internships or fieldwork, Federal Work-Study, scholarships/grants, and unspecified assistantships available. Support available to part-time students. Financial award application deadline: 3/1; financial award applicants required to submit FAFSA. *Faculty research:* Integrated arts in the curriculum, moral development of children. *Unit head:* Dr. Esther Howard, Chair of Curriculum and Instruction, 205-652-3428, Fax: 205-652-3706, E-mail: ehoward@uwa.edu. *Application contact:* Dr. Kathy Chandler, Dean of Graduate Studies, 205-652-3421, Fax: 205-652-3706, E-mail: kchandler@uwa.edu.
Website: http://www.uwa.edu/highschool612.aspx.

University of West Florida, College of Professional Studies, Ed D Programs, Specialization in Curriculum and Instruction: Science and Social Sciences, Pensacola, FL 32514-5750. Offers Ed D. Part-time and evening/weekend programs available. *Degree requirements:* For doctorate, comprehensive exam, thesis/dissertation. *Entrance requirements:* For doctorate, GRE, MAT, or GMAT, letter of intent; writing sample; three letters of recommendation; two completed disposition assessment forms; written statement of goals; interview with admissions committee. Additional exam requirements/recommendations for international students: Required—TOEFL (minimum score 550 paper-based).

University of Wisconsin–River Falls, Outreach and Graduate Studies, College of Arts and Science, Department of History and Philosophy, River Falls, WI 54022. Offers social science education (MSE). Part-time programs available. *Degree requirements:* For master's, thesis (for some programs). *Entrance requirements:* For master's, minimum GPA of 2.75. Additional exam requirements/recommendations for international students: Required—TOEFL (minimum score 500 paper-based; 65 iBT), IELTS (minimum score 5.5). Electronic applications accepted. *Faculty research:* World War II, Hitler, modern China, women's history, immigration history.

Ursuline College, School of Graduate Studies, Program in Education, Pepper Pike, OH 44124-4398. Offers art education (MA); early childhood education (MA); language arts education (MA); life science education (MA); math education (MA); middle school education (MA); social studies education (MA); special education (MA). *Accreditation:* NCATE. *Faculty:* 4 full-time (all women), 7 part-time/adjunct (5 women). *Students:* 18 full-time (16 women), 7 part-time (all women); includes 8 minority (4 Black or African American, non-Hispanic/Latino; 2 Asian, non-Hispanic/Latino; 2 Hispanic/Latino). Average age 34. 1 applicant, 100% accepted, 1 enrolled. In 2013, 25 master's awarded. *Degree requirements:* For master's, comprehensive exam. *Entrance requirements:* For master's, minimum undergraduate GPA of 3.0. Additional exam requirements/recommendations for international students: Required—TOEFL (minimum score 500 paper-based). *Application deadline:* For fall admission, 8/1 priority date for domestic students. Applications are processed on a rolling basis. Application fee: $25. *Expenses:* Contact institution. *Financial support:* In 2013–14, 1 student received support. Federal Work-Study available. Financial award application deadline: 3/1. *Unit head:* Dr. Edna West, Director, Master's Apprentice Program, 440-646-6134, Fax: 440-646-8328, E-mail: ewest@ursuline.edu. *Application contact:* Stephanie Pratt, Graduate Admission Coordinator, 440-646-8119, Fax: 440-684-6138, E-mail: graduateadmissions@ursuline.edu.

Virginia Polytechnic Institute and State University, Graduate School, College of Liberal Arts and Human Sciences, Blacksburg, VA 24061. Offers career and technical education (MS Ed, Ed D, PhD, Ed S); communication (MA); counselor education (MA Ed, Ed D, PhD, Ed S); creative writing (MFA); curriculum and instruction (MA Ed, Ed D, PhD, Ed S); educational leadership and policy studies (MA Ed, Ed D, PhD, Ed S); educational research and evaluation (PhD); English (MA); foreign languages, cultures, and literatures (MA); higher education and student affairs (MA Ed); history (MA); human development (MS, PhD); material culture and public humanities (MA); philosophy (MA); political science (MA); rhetoric and writing (PhD); science and technology studies (MS, PhD); social, political, ethical, and cultural thought (PhD); sociology (MS, PhD); theater arts (MFA). *Faculty:* 410 full-time (211 women), 6 part-time/adjunct (5 women). *Students:* 688 full-time (464 women), 576 part-time (372 women); includes 243 minority (144 Black or African American, non-Hispanic/Latino; 3 American Indian or Alaska Native, non-Hispanic/Latino; 29 Asian, non-Hispanic/Latino; 48 Hispanic/Latino; 1 Native Hawaiian or other Pacific Islander, non-Hispanic/Latino; 18 Two or more races, non-Hispanic/Latino), 84 international. Average age 34. 1,054 applicants, 48% accepted, 374 enrolled. In 2013, 314 master's, 74 doctorates, 14 other advanced degrees awarded. *Degree requirements:* For master's, comprehensive exam (for some programs), thesis (for some programs); for doctorate, comprehensive exam (for some programs), thesis/dissertation (for some programs). *Entrance requirements:* For master's and doctorate, GRE/GMAT (may vary by department). Additional exam requirements/recommendations for international students: Required—TOEFL (minimum score 550 paper-based). *Application deadline:* For fall admission, 8/1 for domestic students, 4/1 for international students; for spring admission, 1/1 for domestic students, 9/1 for international students. Applications are processed on a rolling basis. Application fee: $75. Electronic applications accepted. *Expenses:* Tuition, state resident: full-time $11,185; part-time $621.50 per credit hour. Tuition, nonresident: full-time $22,146; part-time $1230.25 per credit hour. *Required fees:* $2442; $449.25 per semester. Tuition and fees vary according to course load, campus/location and program. *Financial support:* In 2013–14, 19 research assistantships with full tuition reimbursements (averaging $17,115 per year), 205 teaching assistantships with full tuition reimbursements (averaging $14,433 per year) were awarded. Financial award application deadline: 3/1; financial award applicants required to submit FAFSA. *Total annual research expenditures:* $6.8 million. *Unit head:* Joan Hirt, Interim Dean, 540-231-6779, Fax: 540-231-7157, E-mail: jbhirt@vt.edu. *Application contact:* Melissa Elliott, Executive Assistant, 540-231-6779, Fax: 540-231-7157, E-mail: elliott1@vt.edu.
Website: http://www.clahs.vt.edu/.

Wagner College, Division of Graduate Studies, Department of Education, Program in Secondary Education/Special Education, Staten Island, NY 10301-4495. Offers language arts (MS Ed); languages other than English (MS Ed); mathematics and technology (MS Ed); science and technology (MS Ed); social studies (MS Ed). Part-time and evening/weekend programs available. *Degree requirements:* For master's, thesis (for some programs). *Entrance requirements:* For master's, minimum GPA of 3.0, interview, recommendations. Electronic applications accepted. *Expenses: Tuition:* Full-time $17,496; part-time $972 per credit. Tuition and fees vary according to course load.

Wayland Baptist University, Graduate Programs, Program in Education, Plainview, TX 79072-6998. Offers education administration (M Ed); education diagnostics (M Ed); education literacy (M Ed); elementary certification (M Ed); English (M Ed); English as a second language (M Ed); higher education administration (M Ed); human resources

(M Ed); instructional leadership (M Ed); instructional technology (M Ed); science education (M Ed); secondary certification (M Ed); social studies (M Ed); special education (M Ed). Part-time and evening/weekend programs available. Postbaccalaureate distance learning degree programs offered (no on-campus study). *Faculty:* 33 full-time (17 women), 28 part-time/adjunct (17 women). *Students:* 22 full-time (15 women), 316 part-time (189 women); includes 130 minority (48 Black or African American, non-Hispanic/Latino; 3 American Indian or Alaska Native, non-Hispanic/Latino; 71 Hispanic/Latino; 1 Native Hawaiian or other Pacific Islander, non-Hispanic/Latino; 7 Two or more races, non-Hispanic/Latino). Average age 39. 80 applicants, 96% accepted, 44 enrolled. In 2013, 170 master's awarded. *Degree requirements:* For master's, comprehensive exam, capstone course. *Entrance requirements:* For master's, GRE, GMAT or MAT. Additional exam requirements/recommendations for international students: Required—TOEFL (minimum score 500 paper-based; 61 iBT). *Application deadline:* Applications are processed on a rolling basis. Application fee: $50. Electronic applications accepted. *Expenses: Tuition:* Full-time $8190; part-time $455 per credit hour. *Required fees:* $970; $455 per credit hour. $485 per semester. *Financial support:* Federal Work-Study, institutionally sponsored loans, and scholarships/grants available. Support available to part-time students. Financial award application deadline: 5/1; financial award applicants required to submit FAFSA. *Unit head:* Dr. Jim Todd, Chairman, 806-291-1045, Fax: 806-291-1951. *Application contact:* Amanda Stanton, Coordinator of Graduate Studies, 806-291-3423, Fax: 806-291-1950, E-mail: stanton@wbu.edu.

Wayne State College, School of Education and Counseling, Department of Educational Foundations and Leadership, Program in Curriculum and Instruction, Wayne, NE 68787. Offers alternative education (MSE); business and information technology education (MSE); communication arts education (MSE); early childhood education (MSE); elementary education (MSE); English as a second language (MSE); English education (MSE); family and consumer sciences education (MSE); industrial technology and vocational education (MSE); learning communities (MSE); mathematics education (MSE); music education (MSE); science education (MSE); social science education (MSE). *Accreditation:* NCATE. Part-time and evening/weekend programs available. *Degree requirements:* For master's, comprehensive exam, thesis optional. *Entrance requirements:* For master's, GRE General Test. Additional exam requirements/recommendations for international students: Required—TOEFL (minimum score 550 paper-based).

Wayne State University, College of Education, Division of Teacher Education, Detroit, MI 48202. Offers art education (M Ed), including art therapy; autism spectrum disorders (Certificate); bilingual/bicultural education (M Ed, Certificate); career and technical education (M Ed, Certificate); cognitive impairment (Certificate); curriculum and instruction (Ed D, PhD, Ed S), including art education (PhD), bilingual education (Ed D, Ed S), bilingual-bicultural education (PhD), career and technical education (MAT, Ed D, PhD, Ed S), early childhood education (MAT, Ed D, PhD, Ed S), elementary education, English as a second language (MAT, Ed D, Ed S), English education (MAT, Ed D, PhD, Ed S), foreign language education (MAT, PhD), K-12 curriculum, mathematics education (MAT, Ed D, PhD, Ed S), science education (MAT, Ed D, PhD, Ed S), secondary education, social studies education (MAT, Ed S), social studies education: secondary (Ed D, PhD); early childhood education (M Ed, Certificate); elementary education (M Ed, MAT), including children's literature (MAT), early childhood education (MAT, Ed D, PhD, Ed S), general elementary education (MAT); elementary or secondary education (MAT), including bilingual/bicultural education, English as a second language (MAT, Ed D, Ed S), mathematics education (MAT, Ed D, PhD, Ed S), science education (MAT, Ed D, PhD, Ed S), social studies education (MAT, Ed S); emotionally impaired (Certificate); English as a second language (Certificate); English education (M Ed), including secondary; foreign language education (M Ed); K-12 reading specialist (Certificate); learning disabilities (Certificate); mathematics education (M Ed), including secondary; reading (M Ed, Ed S); reading, language and literature (Ed D); science education (M Ed), including secondary; secondary education (MAT), including art education (K-12), career and technical education (MAT, Ed D, PhD, Ed S), English education (MAT, Ed D, PhD, Ed S), foreign language education (MAT, PhD), kinesiology; social studies education (M Ed), including secondary; special education (M Ed, MAT, Ed D, PhD, Ed S); visual arts education (Certificate). Part-time programs available. *Faculty:* 36 full-time (25 women), 55 part-time/adjunct (43 women). *Students:* 218 full-time (163 women), 448 part-time (344 women); includes 218 minority (177 Black or African American, non-Hispanic/Latino; 2 American Indian or Alaska Native, non-Hispanic/Latino; 11 Asian, non-Hispanic/Latino; 19 Hispanic/Latino; 1 Native Hawaiian or other Pacific Islander, non-Hispanic/Latino; 8 Two or more races, non-Hispanic/Latino), 10 international. Average age 37. 258 applicants, 30% accepted, 52 enrolled. In 2013, 183 master's, 10 doctorates, 35 other advanced degrees awarded. *Degree requirements:* For master's, thesis, essay or project (for some M Ed programs), professional field experience (for MAT programs); for doctorate, thesis/dissertation. *Entrance requirements:* For master's, Michigan Basic Skills Test (MA in teaching), admission to the graduate school, verification of participation in group work with children and Michigan State Police Criminal Background check; for doctorate, minimum undergraduate GPA of 3.0, graduate 3.5; interview, curriculum vitae; references. Additional exam requirements/recommendations for international students: Required—TOEFL (minimum score 550 paper-based; 79 iBT), TWE (minimum score 5.5), Michigan English Language Assessment Battery (minimum score 85); Recommended—IELTS (minimum score 6.5). *Application deadline:* For fall admission, 6/1 priority date for domestic students, 5/1 priority date for international students; for winter admission, 10/1 priority date for domestic students, 9/1 priority date for international students; for spring admission, 2/1 priority date for domestic students, 1/1 priority date for international students. Applications are processed on a rolling basis. Application fee: $0. Electronic applications accepted. *Expenses:* Tuition, state resident: part-time $554.15 per credit. Tuition, nonresident: part-time $1200.35 per credit. *Required fees:* $42.15 per credit. $268.30 per semester. Tuition and fees vary according to course load and program. *Financial support:* In 2013–14, 83 students received support, including 1 fellowship (averaging $16,842 per year), 1 research assistantship with tuition reimbursement available (averaging $21,229 per year); career-related internships or fieldwork, Federal Work-Study, scholarships/grants, health care benefits, and unspecified assistantships also available. Support available to part-time students. Financial award application deadline: 3/31; financial award applicants required to submit FAFSA. *Faculty research:* Improving students' skill achievement in mathematics; improving elementary children's understanding of informational text; teachers' use of their pedagogical and mathematical knowledge in the interactive work of teaching; the intersection of identity construction in teaching and learning; identifying effective methods of literacy instruction and assessments for bilingual students in elementary language arts classrooms. *Total annual research expenditures:* $368,105. *Unit head:* Dr. Kathleen Crawford-McKinney, Assistant Dean, 313-577-0122. *Application contact:* Janice Green, Assistant Dean, 313-577-1605, E-mail: jwgreen@wayne.edu.
Website: http://coe.wayne.edu/ted/index.php.

Wayne State University, College of Education, Division of Theoretical and Behavioral Foundations, Detroit, MI 48202. Offers counseling (M Ed, MA, Ed D, PhD, Ed S); education evaluation and research (M Ed, Ed D, PhD); educational psychology (M Ed, PhD), including learning and instruction sciences (PhD), school psychology (PhD); educational sociology (M Ed); history and philosophy of education (M Ed); rehabilitation counseling and community inclusion (MA); school and community psychology (MA); school psychology (Certificate). *Accreditation:* ACA (one or more programs are accredited); CORE (one or more programs are accredited). Evening/weekend programs available. *Students:* 239 full-time (199 women), 214 part-time (190 women); includes 181 minority (141 Black or African American, non-Hispanic/Latino; 2 American Indian or Alaska Native, non-Hispanic/Latino; 14 Asian, non-Hispanic/Latino; 10 Hispanic/Latino; 1 Native Hawaiian or other Pacific Islander, non-Hispanic/Latino; 13 Two or more races, non-Hispanic/Latino), 21 international. Average age 33. 271 applicants, 35% accepted, 62 enrolled. In 2013, 55 master's, 19 doctorates, 8 other advanced degrees awarded. *Degree requirements:* For master's, thesis (for some programs); for doctorate, thesis/dissertation. *Entrance requirements:* For master's, GRE; for doctorate, GRE, interview, minimum GPA of 3.0, curriculum vitae, references. Additional exam requirements/recommendations for international students: Required—TOEFL (minimum score 550 paper-based; 79 iBT), Michigan English Language Assessment Battery (minimum score 85); Recommended—IELTS (minimum score 6.5), TWE (minimum score 5.5). *Application deadline:* For fall admission, 6/1 priority date for domestic students, 5/1 priority date for international students; for winter admission, 10/1 priority date for domestic students, 9/1 priority date for international students; for spring admission, 2/1 priority date for domestic students, 1/1 priority date for international students. Applications are processed on a rolling basis. Application fee: $0. Electronic applications accepted. *Expenses:* Tuition, state resident: part-time $554.15 per credit. Tuition, nonresident: part-time $1200.35 per credit. *Required fees:* $42.15 per credit. $268.30 per semester. Tuition and fees vary according to course load and program. *Financial support:* In 2013–14, 83 students received support, including 2 research assistantships with tuition reimbursements available (averaging $16,508 per year); fellowships with tuition reimbursements available, teaching assistantships with tuition reimbursements available, scholarships/grants, health care benefits, and unspecified assistantships also available. Financial award application deadline: 3/31; financial award applicants required to submit FAFSA. *Faculty research:* Adolescents at risk, supervision of counseling. *Unit head:* Dr. Joanne Holbert, Interim Assistant Dean, 313-577-1691, E-mail: jholbert@wayne.edu. *Application contact:* Janice Green, Assistant Dean, 313-577-1605, E-mail: jwgreen@wayne.edu.
Website: http://coe.wayne.edu/tbf/index.php.

Webster University, School of Education, Department of Multidisciplinary Studies, St. Louis, MO 63119-3194. Offers education leadership (Ed S); educational technology (MAT); educational technology leadership (Ed S); mathematics (MA); multidisciplinary studies (MAT); school psychology (Ed S); school systems, superintendency and leadership (Ed S); social science (MAT); special education (MA). Part-time programs available. *Entrance requirements:* For master's, minimum GPA of 2.5. Additional exam requirements/recommendations for international students: Required—TOEFL. *Expenses: Tuition:* Full-time $11,610; part-time $645 per credit hour. Tuition and fees vary according to campus/location and program.

Western Governors University, Teachers College, Salt Lake City, UT 84107. Offers curriculum and instruction (MS); educational leadership (MS); educational studies (MA); educational studies (5-12) (MA), including mathematics; elementary education (K-8) (MAT, Postbaccalaureate Certificate); elementary education (PreK-8) (MAT); English language learning (K-12) (MA); instructional design (MAT); learning and technology (M Ed, MA); management and innovation (M Ed); mathematics (5-12) (MAT, Postbaccalaureate Certificate); mathematics (5-9) (MAT, Postbaccalaureate Certificate); mathematics education (5-12) (MA); mathematics education (5-9) (MA); mathematics education (K-6) (MA); measurement and evaluation (M Ed); science (5-12) (Postbaccalaureate Certificate); science (5-9) (MAT, Postbaccalaureate Certificate); science education (5-12) (MA), including biology, chemistry, geology, physics; science education (5-9) (MA); social science (5-12) (MAT, Postbaccalaureate Certificate); special education (MAT, MS). *Accreditation:* NCATE. Evening/weekend programs available. Postbaccalaureate distance learning degree programs offered (no on-campus study). *Degree requirements:* For master's, capstone project. *Entrance requirements:* For master's and Postbaccalaureate Certificate, Readiness Assessment, transcripts. Additional exam requirements/recommendations for international students: Required—TOEFL (minimum score 450 paper-based; 80 iBT). Electronic applications accepted. *Expenses:* Contact institution.

Western Oregon University, Graduate Programs, College of Education, Division of Teacher Education, Program in Secondary Education, Monmouth, OR 97361-1394. Offers bilingual education (MS Ed); health (MS Ed); humanities (MAT, MS Ed); initial licensure (MAT); mathematics (MAT, MS Ed); science (MAT, MS Ed); social science (MAT, MS Ed). *Accreditation:* NCATE. Part-time and evening/weekend programs available. *Degree requirements:* For master's, thesis optional, written exam. *Entrance requirements:* For master's, minimum GPA of 3.0, teaching license. Additional exam requirements/recommendations for international students: Required—TOEFL (minimum score 550 paper-based; 79 iBT), IELTS (minimum score 6.5). *Faculty research:* Literacy, science in primary grades, geography education, retention, teacher burnout.

Widener University, School of Human Service Professions, Center for Education, Chester, PA 19013-5792. Offers adult education (M Ed); counseling in higher education (M Ed); counselor education (M Ed); early childhood education (M Ed); educational foundations (M Ed); educational leadership (M Ed); educational psychology (M Ed); elementary education (M Ed); English and language arts (M Ed); health education (M Ed); higher education leadership (Ed D); home and school visitor (M Ed); human sexuality (M Ed, PhD); mathematics education (M Ed); middle school education (M Ed); principalship (M Ed); reading and language arts (Ed D); reading education (M Ed); school administration (Ed D); science education (M Ed); social studies education (M Ed); special education (M Ed); technology education (M Ed). *Accreditation:* NCATE. Part-time and evening/weekend programs available. *Faculty:* 34 full-time (22 women), 37 part-time/adjunct (14 women). *Students:* 64 full-time (44 women), 209 part-time (146 women); includes 49 minority (39 Black or African American, non-Hispanic/Latino; 1 American Indian or Alaska Native, non-Hispanic/Latino; 4 Asian, non-Hispanic/Latino; 4 Hispanic/Latino; 1 Two or more races, non-Hispanic/Latino), 8 international. Average age 39. 139 applicants, 88% accepted. In 2013, 168 master's, 31 doctorates awarded. Terminal master's awarded for partial completion of doctoral program. *Degree requirements:* For doctorate, thesis/dissertation. *Entrance requirements:* For master's, minimum GPA of 2.5; for doctorate, GRE or MAT, minimum GPA of 2.0 (undergraduate), 3.5 (graduate). *Application deadline:* Applications are processed on a rolling basis. Application fee: $25 ($300 for international students). Electronic applications accepted. *Expenses:* Contact institution. *Financial support:* Career-related internships or fieldwork, tuition waivers (full and partial), and unspecified assistantships available. Support available to part-time students. Financial award application deadline: 5/1. *Faculty research:* Reading and cognition, adult education, technology education, educational leadership, special education. *Unit head:* Dr. Michael W. LeDoux, Associate Dean, 610-499-4294, Fax: 610-499-4623, E-mail: mwledoux@widener.edu. *Application contact:* Dr. Roberta Nolan, Director of Graduate Admissions, 610-499-4125, E-mail: rdnolan@widener.edu.

Wilkes University, College of Graduate and Professional Studies, School of Education, Wilkes-Barre, PA 18766-0002. Offers art and science of teaching (MS Ed); classroom

technology (MS Ed); early childhood literacy (MS Ed); educational development and strategies (MS Ed); educational leadership (MS Ed); educational technology (Ed D); higher education administration (Ed D); instructional media (MS Ed); instructional technology (MS Ed); international school leadership (MS Ed); K-12 administration (Ed D); middle level education (MS Ed); online teaching (MS Ed); reading (MS Ed); school business leadership (MS Ed); secondary education (MS Ed), including biology, chemistry, English, history, mathematics; special education (MS Ed); teaching English as a second language (MS Ed); twenty-first century teaching and learning (MS Ed). Part-time and evening/weekend programs available. Postbaccalaureate distance learning degree programs offered (minimal on-campus study). *Students:* 46 full-time (37 women), 1,410 part-time (1,039 women); includes 67 minority (12 Black or African American, non-Hispanic/Latino; 2 American Indian or Alaska Native, non-Hispanic/Latino; 11 Asian, non-Hispanic/Latino; 28 Hispanic/Latino; 1 Native Hawaiian or other Pacific Islander, non-Hispanic/Latino; 13 Two or more races, non-Hispanic/Latino), 6 international. Average age 34. In 2013, 852 master's, 10 doctorates awarded. *Entrance requirements:* Additional exam requirements/recommendations for international students: Required—TOEFL (minimum score 550 paper-based; 79 iBT). *Application deadline:* Applications are processed on a rolling basis. Application fee: $45. Electronic applications accepted. *Expenses:* Contact institution. *Financial support:* Federal Work-Study and unspecified assistantships available. Financial award application deadline: 3/1; financial award applicants required to submit FAFSA. *Unit head:* Dr. Rhonda Waskiewicz, Interim Dean, Education, 570-408-4332, Fax: 570-408-7872, E-mail: rhonda.waskiewicz@wilkes.edu. *Application contact:* Joanne Thomas, Interim Director of Graduate Education, 570-408-4234, Fax: 570-408-7846, E-mail: joanne.thomas1@wilkes.edu.
Website: http://www.wilkes.edu/pages/383.asp.

William Carey University, School of Education, Hattiesburg, MS 39401-5499. Offers art education (M Ed); art of teaching (M Ed); elementary education (M Ed, Ed S); English education (M Ed); gifted education (M Ed); history and social science (M Ed);

mild/moderate disabilities (M Ed); secondary education (M Ed). *Accreditation:* NCATE. Part-time programs available. *Degree requirements:* For master's, comprehensive exam. *Entrance requirements:* For master's, GRE, MAT, minimum GPA of 2.5, Class A teacher's license. Additional exam requirements/recommendations for international students: Required—TOEFL (minimum score 550 paper-based).

Worcester State University, Graduate Studies, Program in History, Worcester, MA 01602-2597. Offers MA. Part-time programs available. *Faculty:* 3 full-time (2 women), 3 part-time/adjunct (1 woman). *Students:* 2 full-time (1 woman), 23 part-time (10 women); includes 1 minority (Hispanic/Latino), 1 international. Average age 34. 15 applicants, 100% accepted, 3 enrolled. In 2013, 11 master's awarded. *Degree requirements:* For master's, comprehensive exam (for some programs), thesis optional. *Entrance requirements:* For master's, GRE General Test or MAT, 18 undergraduate credits in history, including U.S. history and Western civilizations. Additional exam requirements/recommendations for international students: Required—TOEFL (minimum score 500 paper-based; 61 iBT). *Application deadline:* For fall admission, 6/15 for domestic and international students; for spring admission, 4/1 for domestic and international students. Applications are processed on a rolling basis. Application fee: $40. Electronic applications accepted. *Expenses: Tuition, area resident:* Part-time $150 per credit. Tuition, state resident: part-time $150 per credit. Tuition, nonresident: part-time $150 per credit. *Required fees:* $114.50 per credit. *Financial support:* In 2013–14, 2 students received support, including 2 research assistantships with full tuition reimbursements available (averaging $4,800 per year); career-related internships or fieldwork, scholarships/grants, and unspecified assistantships also available. Financial award application deadline: 3/1; financial award applicants required to submit FAFSA. *Faculty research:* Labor history, Middle East politics, American-Russian relations, American-East Asian relations. *Unit head:* Dr. Charlotte Haller, Coordinator, 508-929-8046, Fax: 508-929-8155, E-mail: challer1@worcester.edu. *Application contact:* Sara Grady, Assistant Dean of Graduate and Continuing Education, 508-929-8787, Fax: 508-929-8100, E-mail: sara.grady@worcester.edu.

Vocational and Technical Education

Alabama Agricultural and Mechanical University, School of Graduate Studies, School of Engineering and Technology, Department of Industrial Technology, Huntsville, AL 35811. Offers M Ed, MS. *Accreditation:* NCATE. Part-time and evening/weekend programs available. *Degree requirements:* For master's, comprehensive exam, thesis optional. *Entrance requirements:* For master's, GRE General Test. Additional exam requirements/recommendations for international students: Required—TOEFL (minimum score 500 paper-based; 61 iBT). Electronic applications accepted. *Faculty research:* Ionized gases, hypersonic flow, phenomenology, robotic systems development.

Alcorn State University, School of Graduate Studies, Department of Advanced Technologies, Alcorn State, MS 39096-7500. Offers workforce education leadership (MS).

Alcorn State University, School of Graduate Studies, School of Psychology and Education, Alcorn State, MS 39096-7500. Offers agricultural education (MS Ed); elementary education (MS Ed, Ed S); guidance and counseling (MS Ed); industrial education (MS Ed); secondary education (MS Ed), including health and physical education; special education (MS Ed). *Accreditation:* NCATE. *Degree requirements:* For master's, thesis optional.

Appalachian State University, Cratis D. Williams Graduate School, Department of Technology, Boone, NC 28608. Offers appropriate technology (MS); renewable energy engineering (MS). Part-time programs available. *Degree requirements:* For master's, comprehensive exam, thesis optional. *Entrance requirements:* For master's, GRE General Test, 3 letters of recommendation. Additional exam requirements/recommendations for international students: Required—TOEFL (minimum score 550 paper-based; 79 iBT), IELTS (minimum score 6.5). Electronic applications accepted. *Faculty research:* Wind power, biofuels, green construction, solar energy production.

Ball State University, Graduate School, College of Applied Science and Technology, Department of Industry and Technology, Muncie, IN 47306-1099. Offers MA, MAE. *Accreditation:* NCATE (one or more programs are accredited). *Faculty:* 4 full-time (1 woman). *Students:* 4 full-time (1 woman), 41 part-time (12 women); includes 4 minority (3 Black or African American, non-Hispanic/Latino; 1 Hispanic/Latino). Average age 38. In 2013, 20 master's awarded. Application fee: $25 ($35 for international students). *Financial support:* In 2013–14, 5 students received support, including 10 teaching assistantships with full tuition reimbursements available (averaging $10,771 per year). Financial award application deadline: 3/1. *Unit head:* Dr. Samuel Cotton, Chairperson, 765-285-5642, Fax: 765-285-2162, E-mail: scotton@bsu.edu. *Application contact:* Dr. Robert Morris, Associate Provost for Research and Dean of the Graduate School, 765-285-5723, Fax: 765-285-1328, E-mail: rmorris@bsu.edu.
Website: http://www.bsu.edu/cast/itech/.

Bowling Green State University, Graduate College, College of Technology, Program in Career and Technology Education, Bowling Green, OH 43403. Offers career and technology education (M Ed), including technology. Part-time programs available. *Degree requirements:* For master's, thesis or alternative. *Entrance requirements:* For master's, GRE General Test. Additional exam requirements/recommendations for international students: Required—TOEFL. Electronic applications accepted. *Faculty research:* Curriculum in technology education.

Buffalo State College, State University of New York, The Graduate School, Faculty of Applied Science and Education, Department of Educational Foundations, Program in Career and Technical Education, Buffalo, NY 14222-1095. Offers MS Ed. *Accreditation:* NCATE. Part-time and evening/weekend programs available. *Degree requirements:* For master's, thesis or project. *Entrance requirements:* For master's, minimum GPA of 2.5 in last 60 hours, New York teaching certificate. Additional exam requirements/recommendations for international students: Required—TOEFL (minimum score 550 paper-based).

Buffalo State College, State University of New York, The Graduate School, Faculty of Applied Science and Education, Department of Technology, Program in Technology Education, Buffalo, NY 14222-1095. Offers MS Ed. *Accreditation:* NCATE. *Degree requirements:* For master's, thesis or project. *Entrance requirements:* For master's, minimum GPA of 2.5 in last 60 hours, New York teaching certificate. Additional exam requirements/recommendations for international students: Required—TOEFL (minimum score 550 paper-based).

California Baptist University, Program in Education, Riverside, CA 92504-3206. Offers educational leadership for faith-based institutions (MS); educational leadership for public institutions (MS); educational technology (MS); instructional computer

applications (MS); international education (MS); leadership and adult learning (MS); leadership and organizational studies (MS); reading (MS); school counseling (MS); school psychology (MS); science education (MS); special education in mild/moderate disabilities (MS); special education in moderate/severe disabilities (MS); teaching (MS); teaching and learning (MS); TESOL (teachers of English to speakers of other languages) (MS). Part-time and evening/weekend programs available. Postbaccalaureate distance learning degree programs offered (minimal on-campus study). *Faculty:* 18 full-time (9 women), 8 part-time/adjunct (5 women). *Students:* 158 full-time (127 women), 228 part-time (179 women); includes 159 minority (27 Black or African American, non-Hispanic/Latino; 4 American Indian or Alaska Native, non-Hispanic/Latino; 13 Asian, non-Hispanic/Latino; 107 Hispanic/Latino; 1 Native Hawaiian or other Pacific Islander, non-Hispanic/Latino; 7 Two or more races, non-Hispanic/Latino), 2 international. Average age 33. 298 applicants, 74% accepted, 113 enrolled. In 2013, 70 master's awarded. *Degree requirements:* For master's, comprehensive exam, project, or thesis. *Entrance requirements:* For master's, minimum undergraduate GPA of 3.0; 18 semester units of prerequisite course work in education; three recommendations; 500-word essay; interview. Additional exam requirements/recommendations for international students: Required—TOEFL (minimum score 80 iBT). *Application deadline:* For fall admission, 8/1 priority date for domestic students, 7/1 for international students; for spring admission, 12/1 priority date for domestic students, 11/1 for international students. Applications are processed on a rolling basis. Application fee: $45. Electronic applications accepted. *Expenses:* Contact institution. *Financial support:* Institutionally sponsored loans available. Financial award applicants required to submit CSS PROFILE or FAFSA. *Faculty research:* Leadership development, complexity theory, faith and learning, special education, social and philosophical contexts of education. *Unit head:* Dr. John Shoup, Dean, School of Education, 951-343-4205, Fax: 951-343-4516, E-mail: jshoup@calbaptist.edu. *Application contact:* Dr. Kathryn Norwood, Director, Master of Science Program in Education, 951-343-4760, E-mail: knorwood@calbaptist.edu.
Website: http://www.calbaptist.edu/mastersined/.

California State University, Sacramento, Office of Graduate Studies, College of Education, Department of Special Education, Rehabilitation, and School Psychology, Sacramento, CA 95819. Offers school psychology (MA); special education (MA); vocational rehabilitation (MS). *Accreditation:* CORE. Part-time programs available. *Entrance requirements:* For master's, minimum GPA of 2.5. Additional exam requirements/recommendations for international students: Required—TOEFL. *Application deadline:* For fall admission, 3/1 for domestic and international students; for spring admission, 9/15 for domestic students, 9/30 for international students. Applications are processed on a rolling basis. Application fee: $55. Electronic applications accepted. *Financial support:* Career-related internships or fieldwork and Federal Work-Study available. Support available to part-time students. Financial award application deadline: 3/1; financial award applicants required to submit FAFSA. *Faculty research:* Reading and learning disabilities; vocational rehabilitation counseling issues and implementation; school-based crisis intervention; posttraumatic stress disorder; attention-deficit/hyperactivity disorder; school-based suicide prevention, intervention, and postvention; autism spectrum disorders; special education technology, strategies and assessment. *Unit head:* Bruce A. Ostertag, Chair, 916-278-5541, E-mail: ostertag@csus.edu. *Application contact:* Jose Martinez, Graduate Admissions Coordinator, 916-278-7871, E-mail: martinj@skymail.csus.edu.
Website: http://www.edweb.csus.edu/eds.

California State University, San Bernardino, Graduate Studies, College of Education, Program in Vocational and Career Education, San Bernardino, CA 92407-2397. Offers MA. *Accreditation:* NCATE. Part-time and evening/weekend programs available. *Students:* 6 full-time (3 women), 15 part-time (7 women); includes 7 minority (3 Black or African American, non-Hispanic/Latino; 1 Asian, non-Hispanic/Latino; 3 Hispanic/Latino). Average age 47. 21 applicants, 90% accepted, 13 enrolled. In 2013, 8 master's awarded. *Degree requirements:* For master's, thesis. *Entrance requirements:* For master's, minimum GPA of 3.0 in education, vocational teaching credential. *Application deadline:* For fall admission, 8/31 priority date for domestic students. Application fee: $55. *Financial support:* Career-related internships or fieldwork and Federal Work-Study available. Support available to part-time students. *Unit head:* Dr. Herbert Brunkhorst, Coordinator, Designated Subjects, 909-537-5613. *Application contact:* Dr. Jeffrey Thompson, Dean of Graduate Studies, 909-537-5058, E-mail: jthompso@csusb.edu.

California University of Pennsylvania, School of Graduate Studies and Research, College of Education and Human Services, Program in Technology Education,

California, PA 15419-1394. Offers M Ed. *Accreditation:* NCATE. Part-time and evening/weekend programs available. *Degree requirements:* For master's, comprehensive exam, thesis optional. *Entrance requirements:* For master's, MAT, minimum GPA of 3.0, teaching experience in industrial arts. Additional exam requirements/recommendations for international students: Required—TOEFL (minimum score 550 paper-based; 80 iBT). Electronic applications accepted. *Faculty research:* Curriculum, trends in technology, standards-based assessment.

Capella University, School of Business and Technology, Doctoral Programs in Technology, Minneapolis, MN 55402. Offers general information technology (PhD); global operations and supply chain management (DBA); information assurance and security (PhD); information technology education (PhD); information technology management (DBA, PhD).

Central Connecticut State University, School of Graduate Studies, School of Technology, Department of Technology Engineering Education, New Britain, CT 06050-4010. Offers MS, Certificate. Part-time and evening/weekend programs available. *Faculty:* 2 full-time (0 women). *Students:* 19 part-time (5 women). Average age 43. 1 applicant, 100% accepted. In 2013, 6 master's, 3 other advanced degrees awarded. *Degree requirements:* For master's, comprehensive exam, thesis or alternative; for Certificate, qualifying exam. *Entrance requirements:* For master's, minimum undergraduate GPA of 2.7. Additional exam requirements/recommendations for international students: Required—TOEFL (minimum score 550 paper-based; 79 iBT). *Application deadline:* For fall admission, 6/1 for domestic students, 5/1 for international students; for spring admission, 11/1 for domestic and international students. Applications are processed on a rolling basis. Application fee: $50. Electronic applications accepted. Part-time tuition and fees vary according to degree level. *Financial support:* In 2013–14, 1 research assistantship was awarded; career-related internships or fieldwork, Federal Work-Study, scholarships/grants, and unspecified assistantships also available. Support available to part-time students. Financial award application deadline: 3/1; financial award applicants required to submit FAFSA. *Faculty research:* Instruction, curriculum development, administration, occupational training. *Unit head:* Dr. James DeLaura, Chair, 860-832-1850, E-mail: delaura@ccsu.edu. *Application contact:* Patricia Gardner, Associate Director of Graduate Studies, 860-832-2350, Fax: 860-832-2362, E-mail: graduateadmissions@ccsu.edu.
Website: http://www.ccsu.edu/page.cfm?p=6498.

Central Washington University, Graduate Studies and Research, College of Education and Professional Studies, Department of Family and Consumer Sciences, Ellensburg, WA 98926. Offers career and technical education (MS); family and consumer sciences education (MS); family studies (MS). Part-time programs available. *Degree requirements:* For master's, thesis or alternative. *Entrance requirements:* For master's, minimum GPA of 3.0. Additional exam requirements/recommendations for international students: Required—TOEFL (minimum score 550 paper-based; 79 iBT). Electronic applications accepted.

Chicago State University, School of Graduate and Professional Studies, College of Education, Department of Technology and Education, Chicago, IL 60628. Offers secondary education (MAT); technology and education (MS Ed). Postbaccalaureate distance learning degree programs offered. *Degree requirements:* For master's, thesis optional. *Entrance requirements:* For master's, minimum GPA of 2.75.

Clarion University of Pennsylvania, Office of Transfer, Adult and Graduate Admissions, Master of Education Program, Clarion, PA 16214. Offers curriculum and instruction (M Ed); early childhood (M Ed); math education (M Ed); reading (M Ed); science education (M Ed); special education (M Ed); technology (M Ed). *Accreditation:* NCATE. Part-time programs available. Postbaccalaureate distance learning degree programs offered (no on-campus study). *Faculty:* 17 full-time (10 women). *Students:* 231 full-time (191 women), 535 part-time (448 women); includes 39 minority (12 Black or African American, non-Hispanic/Latino; 8 Asian, non-Hispanic/Latino; 11 Hispanic/Latino; 1 Native Hawaiian or other Pacific Islander, non-Hispanic/Latino; 7 Two or more races, non-Hispanic/Latino). Average age 31. 28 applicants, 75% accepted, 18 enrolled. In 2013, 99 master's awarded. *Degree requirements:* For master's, comprehensive exam, thesis, or portfolio. *Entrance requirements:* For master's, minimum QPA of 3.0. Additional exam requirements/recommendations for international students: Required—TOEFL (minimum score 550 paper-based; 80 iBT), IELTS (minimum score 7). *Application deadline:* For fall admission, 8/1 for domestic students, 4/15 for international students; for spring admission, 8/1 for domestic students, 9/15 for international students. Applications are processed on a rolling basis. Application fee: $40. Electronic applications accepted. *Expenses:* Tuition, state resident: part-time $442 per credit. Tuition, nonresident: part-time $451 per credit. *Required fees:* $142.40 per semester. One-time fee: $150 part-time. *Financial support:* In 2013–14, 8 research assistantships with full and partial tuition reimbursements (averaging $9,420 per year) were awarded; career-related internships or fieldwork also available. Support available to part-time students. Financial award application deadline: 3/1. *Unit head:* Ray Puller, Interim Dean, 814-393-2146, Fax: 514-393-2446, E-mail: rpuller@clarion.edu. *Application contact:* Susan Staub, Assistant Director, Graduate Programs, 814-393-2337, Fax: 814-393-2722, E-mail: gradstudies@clarion.edu.
Website: http://www.clarion.edu/25887/.

Colorado State University, Graduate School, College of Health and Human Sciences, School of Education, Fort Collins, CO 80523-1588. Offers adult education and training (M Ed); community college leadership (PhD); counseling and career development (M Ed); education and human resource studies (M Ed, PhD); educational leadership (M Ed, PhD); interdisciplinary studies (PhD); organizational performance and change (M Ed, PhD); student affairs in higher education (MS). *Accreditation:* ACA; Teacher Education Accreditation Council. Part-time and evening/weekend programs available. *Faculty:* 19 full-time (10 women). *Students:* 84 full-time (60 women), 545 part-time (356 women); includes 115 minority (26 Black or African American, non-Hispanic/Latino; 5 American Indian or Alaska Native, non-Hispanic/Latino; 13 Asian, non-Hispanic/Latino; 56 Hispanic/Latino; 15 Two or more races, non-Hispanic/Latino), 22 international. Average age 37. 475 applicants, 38% accepted, 147 enrolled. In 2013, 1,157 master's, 43 doctorates awarded. *Degree requirements:* For master's, comprehensive exam, thesis optional; for doctorate, comprehensive exam, thesis/dissertation, minimum of 60 credits. *Entrance requirements:* For master's and doctorate, GRE, minimum GPA of 3.0. Additional exam requirements/recommendations for international students: Required—TOEFL (minimum score 550 paper-based; 80 iBT), IELTS. *Application deadline:* For fall admission, 3/1 priority date for domestic and international students; for spring admission, 9/1 for domestic and international students. Applications are processed on a rolling basis. Application fee: $50. Electronic applications accepted. *Expenses:* Tuition, state resident: full-time $9075.40; part-time $504 per credit. Tuition, nonresident: full-time $22,248; part-time $1236 per credit. *Required fees:* $1819; $60 per credit. *Financial support:* In 2013–14, 7 students received support, including 1 research assistantship with partial tuition reimbursement available (averaging $16,135 per year), 6 teaching assistantships with partial tuition reimbursements available (averaging $10,106 per year); career-related internships or fieldwork, scholarships/grants, and unspecified assistantships also available. Financial award application deadline: 3/1; financial award applicants required to submit FAFSA. *Faculty research:* Issues in STEM education, diversity and multiculturalism, teacher education leadership, distance learning and

teaching. *Total annual research expenditures:* $498,539. *Unit head:* Dr. Daniel H. Robinson, Director, 970-491-6316, Fax: 970-491-1317, E-mail: dan.robinson@colostate.edu. *Application contact:* Kelli M. Clark, Academic Coordinator, 970-491-2093, Fax: 970-491-1317, E-mail: kelli.clark@colostate.edu.
Website: http://www.soe.chhs.colostate.edu/.

Concordia University, College of Education, Portland, OR 97211-6099. Offers career and technical education (M Ed); curriculum and instruction (M Ed), including adolescent literacy, career and technical education, e-learning/technology education, early childhood education, English for speakers of other languages, English language development, environmental education, mathematics, methods and curriculum, reading, science, teacher leadership, the inclusive classroom; early childhood (MAT); education leadership (Ed D); educational administration (M Ed); elementary education (MAT); secondary education (MAT); special education (M Ed); teacher leadership (Ed D). Part-time programs available. Postbaccalaureate distance learning degree programs offered (no on-campus study). *Degree requirements:* For master's, comprehensive exam, work samples/portfolio. *Entrance requirements:* For master's, California Basic Educational Skills Test or PRAXIS I, minimum undergraduate GPA of 2.8, graduate 3.0; 2 letters of recommendation. Additional exam requirements/recommendations for international students: Required—TOEFL (minimum score 525 paper-based). Electronic applications accepted. *Faculty research:* Learner-centered classroom, brain-based learning, future of online learning.

East Carolina University, Graduate School, College of Education, Department of Business and Information Technologies Education, Greenville, NC 27858-4353. Offers business education (MA Ed); elementary education (MAT); English education (MAT); family and consumer science (MAT); health education (MAT); Hispanic studies (MAT); history education (MAT); marketing education (MA Ed); middle grades education (MAT); music education (MAT); physical education (MAT); science education (MAT); special education (MAT), including general curriculum; vocation education (MS). *Accreditation:* NCATE. Part-time and evening/weekend programs available. Postbaccalaureate distance learning degree programs offered (no on-campus study). *Degree requirements:* For master's, comprehensive exam, thesis optional. *Entrance requirements:* For master's, GRE or MAT, minimum GPA of 2.5, bachelor's degree in related field, teaching license (MA Ed). Additional exam requirements/recommendations for international students: Required—TOEFL. *Expenses:* Tuition, state resident: full-time $4223. Tuition, nonresident: full-time $16,540. *Required fees:* $2184.

Eastern Kentucky University, The Graduate School, College of Business and Technology, Department of Technology, Program in Industrial Education, Richmond, KY 40475-3102. Offers occupational training and development (MS); technical administration (MS); technology education (MS). *Accreditation:* NCATE. Part-time programs available. *Entrance requirements:* For master's, GRE General Test, minimum GPA of 2.5.

Eastern Kentucky University, The Graduate School, College of Education, Department of Curriculum and Instruction, Program in Secondary and Higher Education, Richmond, KY 40475-3102. Offers secondary education (MA Ed), including agricultural education, art education, biological sciences education, business education, English education, geography education, history education, home economics education, industrial education, mathematical sciences education, physical education, school health education. *Accreditation:* NCATE. Part-time programs available. *Entrance requirements:* For master's, GRE General Test, minimum GPA of 2.5.

Eastern New Mexico University, Graduate School, College of Education and Technology, Department of Curriculum and Instruction, Portales, NM 88130. Offers bilingual education (M Ed); educational technology (M Ed); elementary education (M Ed); English as a second language (M Ed); pedagogy and learning (M Ed); professional technical education (M Ed); reading/literacy (M Ed). Part-time programs available. Postbaccalaureate distance learning degree programs offered (minimal on-campus study). *Degree requirements:* For master's, comprehensive exam, thesis optional. *Entrance requirements:* For master's, minimum GPA of 3.0, photocopy of teaching license, writing assessment, letter of recommendation. Additional exam requirements/recommendations for international students: Required—TOEFL (minimum score 550 paper-based; 79 iBT), IELTS (minimum score 6). Electronic applications accepted.

Fitchburg State University, Division of Graduate and Continuing Education, Program in Occupational Education, Fitchburg, MA 01420-2697. Offers M Ed. *Accreditation:* NCATE. Part-time and evening/weekend programs available. *Entrance requirements:* Additional exam requirements/recommendations for international students: Required—TOEFL (minimum score 550 paper-based; 79 iBT). Electronic applications accepted.

Fitchburg State University, Division of Graduate and Continuing Education, Program in Technology Education, Fitchburg, MA 01420-2697. Offers M Ed. *Accreditation:* NCATE. Part-time and evening/weekend programs available. *Entrance requirements:* Additional exam requirements/recommendations for international students: Required—TOEFL (minimum score 550 paper-based; 79 iBT). Electronic applications accepted.

Florida Agricultural and Mechanical University, Division of Graduate Studies, Research, and Continuing Education, College of Education, Department of Vocational Education, Tallahassee, FL 32307-3200. Offers business education (MBE); industrial education (M Ed, MS Ed). *Accreditation:* NCATE. *Degree requirements:* For master's, thesis (for some programs). *Entrance requirements:* For master's, GRE General Test, minimum GPA of 3.0. Additional exam requirements/recommendations for international students: Required—TOEFL.

The George Washington University, Graduate School of Education and Human Development, Department of Counseling and Human Development, Program in Career and Workforce Development, Washington, DC 20052. Offers Graduate Certificate. *Students:* 1 (woman) part-time. Average age 36. 4 applicants, 100% accepted. In 2013, 3 Graduate Certificates awarded. *Unit head:* Dr. Thomas R. Stowell, Co-Director, 202-994-6448, E-mail: tstowell@gwu.edu. *Application contact:* Sarah Lang, Director of Graduate Admissions, 202-994-1447, Fax: 202-994-7207, E-mail: slang@gwu.edu.
Website: http://gsehd.gwu.edu/career-and-workforce-development-certificate.

The George Washington University, Graduate School of Education and Human Development, Department of Counseling and Human Development, Program in Job Development and Placement, Washington, DC 20052. Offers Graduate Certificate. Postbaccalaureate distance learning degree programs offered. *Students:* 3 part-time (all women); includes 1 minority (Hispanic/Latino). Average age 28. 5 applicants, 100% accepted, 2 enrolled. In 2013, 7 Graduate Certificates awarded. *Financial support:* Fellowships available. *Unit head:* Dr. Kenneth C. Hergenrather, Director, 202-994-1334, E-mail: hergenkc@gwu.edu. *Application contact:* Sarah Lang, Director of Graduate Admissions, 202-994-1447, Fax: 202-994-7207, E-mail: slang@gwu.edu.
Website: http://gsehd.gwu.edu/programs/jdp/certificate.

Idaho State University, Office of Graduate Studies, College of Technology, Department of Human Resource Training and Development, Pocatello, ID 83209-8380. Offers MTD. Part-time and evening/weekend programs available. *Degree requirements:* For master's, comprehensive exam, thesis optional, statistical procedures. *Entrance requirements:* For master's, GRE or MAT, minimum GPA of 3.0 in upper-division

courses. Additional exam requirements/recommendations for international students: Required—TOEFL (minimum score 550 paper-based; 80 iBT). Electronic applications accepted. *Faculty research:* Learning styles, instructional methodology, leadership administration.

Indiana State University, College of Graduate and Professional Studies, College of Technology, Department of Industrial Technology Education, Terre Haute, IN 47809. Offers career and technical education (MS); human resource development (MS); technology education (MS); MA/MS. *Accreditation:* NCATE (one or more programs are accredited). *Entrance requirements:* For master's, bachelor's degree in industrial technology or related field. Additional exam requirements/recommendations for international students: Required—TOEFL. Electronic applications accepted.

Indiana University of Pennsylvania, School of Graduate Studies and Research, Eberly College of Business and Information Technology, Department of Technology Support and Training, Program in Business/Administrative, Indiana, PA 15705-1087. Offers M Ed. Part-time programs available. *Faculty:* 2 full-time (both women). *Students:* 1 part-time (0 women). Average age 47. 9 applicants, 11% accepted, 1 enrolled. In 2013, 1 master's awarded. *Degree requirements:* For master's, thesis optional. *Entrance requirements:* For master's, GMAT or GRE. Additional exam requirements/recommendations for international students: Required—TOEFL (minimum score 540 paper-based). *Application deadline:* Applications are processed on a rolling basis. Application fee: $50. Electronic applications accepted. *Expenses:* Tuition, state resident: full-time $3978; part-time $442 per credit. Tuition, nonresident: full-time $5967; part-time $663 per credit. *Required fees:* $2080; $115.55 per credit. $93 per semester. Tuition and fees vary according to degree level and program. *Financial support:* Career-related internships or fieldwork, Federal Work-Study, scholarships/grants, and unspecified assistantships available. Financial award application deadline: 4/15; financial award applicants required to submit FAFSA. *Unit head:* Dr. Lucinda Willis, Graduate Coordinator, 724-357-2061, E-mail: willisl@iup.edu.
Website: http://www.iup.edu/upper.aspx?id=89005.

Inter American University of Puerto Rico, Metropolitan Campus, Graduate Programs, Program in Occupational Education, San Juan, PR 00919-1293. Offers MA. *Degree requirements:* For master's, comprehensive exam. *Entrance requirements:* For master's, GRE or EXADEP, interview. Electronic applications accepted.

Iowa State University of Science and Technology, Program in Industrial Agriculture and Technology, Ames, IA 50011. Offers MS, PhD. *Entrance requirements:* For master's and doctorate, GRE General Test. Additional exam requirements/recommendations for international students: Required—TOEFL (minimum score 550 paper-based; 79 iBT), IELTS (minimum score 6.5). Electronic applications accepted. *Faculty research:* Industrial technology, technology education, training and development, technical education.

Jackson State University, Graduate School, College of Science, Engineering and Technology, Department of Technology, Jackson, MS 39217. Offers hazardous materials management (MS); technology education (MS Ed). Part-time and evening/weekend programs available. *Degree requirements:* For master's, comprehensive exam, thesis or alternative. *Entrance requirements:* For master's, GRE General Test. Additional exam requirements/recommendations for international students: Required—TOEFL (minimum score 520 paper-based; 67 iBT).

James Madison University, The Graduate School, College of Education, Adult Education Department, Program in Adult Education/Human Resource Development, Harrisonburg, VA 22807. Offers MS Ed. *Accreditation:* NCATE. Part-time and evening/weekend programs available. *Students:* 24 full-time (17 women), 11 part-time (10 women); includes 10 minority (5 Black or African American, non-Hispanic/Latino; 1 Asian, non-Hispanic/Latino; 2 Hispanic/Latino; 2 Two or more races, non-Hispanic/Latino), 2 international. Average age 27. In 2013, 14 master's awarded. *Entrance requirements:* For master's, GRE General Test. Additional exam requirements/recommendations for international students: Required—TOEFL. *Application deadline:* For fall admission, 5/1 priority date for domestic students; for spring admission, 9/1 priority date for domestic students. Applications are processed on a rolling basis. Application fee: $55. Electronic applications accepted. *Financial support:* In 2013–14, 18 students received support. 16 graduate assistantships (averaging $7530), 2 athletic assistantships (averaging $8837) available. Financial award application deadline: 3/1; financial award applicants required to submit FAFSA. *Unit head:* Dr. Diane Foucar-Szocki, Academic Unit Head, 540-568-6794. *Application contact:* Lynette M. Bible, Director of Graduate Admissions, 540-568-6395, Fax: 540-568-7860, E-mail: biblelm@jmu.edu.

Kansas State University, Graduate School, College of Education, Department of Curriculum and Instruction, Manhattan, KS 66506. Offers career and technical education (Ed D, PhD); curriculum studies (Ed D, PhD); digital teaching and learning (MS); educational computing, design and online learning (MS); educational technology (Ed D, PhD); elementary/middle level curriculum and instruction (MS); English as a second language (MS); language/diversity education (Ed D, PhD); literacy education (Ed D, PhD); mathematics education (Ed D, PhD); middle level/secondary curriculum and instruction (MS); reading and language arts (MS); reading specialist endorsement (MS); science education (Ed D, PhD); social science education (Ed D, PhD); teacher education (Ed D, PhD); teacher leader/school improvement (MS, Ed D). *Accreditation:* NCATE. Part-time programs available. Postbaccalaureate distance learning degree programs offered (minimal on-campus study). *Faculty:* 18 full-time (13 women), 7 part-time/adjunct (4 women). *Students:* 39 full-time (23 women), 122 part-time (94 women); includes 19 minority (3 Black or African American, non-Hispanic/Latino; 2 Asian, non-Hispanic/Latino; 12 Hispanic/Latino; 2 Two or more races, non-Hispanic/Latino), 12 international. Average age 36. 80 applicants, 50% accepted, 34 enrolled. In 2013, 40 master's, 13 doctorates awarded. *Degree requirements:* For master's, comprehensive exam, portfolio, project, report or thesis; for doctorate, comprehensive exam, thesis/dissertation, preliminary exam. *Entrance requirements:* For master's, minimum GPA of 3.0, letters of recommendation; for doctorate, GRE, minimum GPA of 3.0, letters of recommendation, evidence of scholarly writing. Additional exam requirements/recommendations for international students: Required—TOEFL (minimum score 550 paper-based; 80 iBT). *Application deadline:* For fall admission, 3/1 priority date for domestic students, 2/1 priority date for international students; for spring admission, 10/1 priority date for domestic students, 8/1 priority date for international students. Applications are processed on a rolling basis. Application fee: $50 ($75 for international students). Electronic applications accepted. *Financial support:* In 2013–14, 1 research assistantship (averaging $16,900 per year), 8 teaching assistantships (averaging $12,466 per year) were awarded; career-related internships or fieldwork, institutionally sponsored loans, and scholarships/grants also available. Support available to part-time students. Financial award application deadline: 3/1; financial award applicants required to submit FAFSA. *Faculty research:* Literacy and technology, critical race theory and diversity, achievement gaps, school improvement, teacher education. *Total annual research expenditures:* $543,677. *Unit head:* Dr. Todd Goodson, Chair, 785-532-5904, Fax: 785-532-7304, E-mail: tgoodson@ksu.edu. *Application contact:* Dona Deam, Application Contact, 785-532-5595, Fax: 785-532-7304, E-mail: ddeam@ksu.edu.
Website: http://www.coe.k-state.edu/departments/edci/.

Kansas State University, Graduate School, College of Education, Department of Educational Leadership, Manhattan, KS 66506. Offers adult, occupational and continuing education (MS, Ed D, PhD); educational leadership (MS, Ed D). *Accreditation:* NCATE. *Faculty:* 11 full-time (6 women), 3 part-time/adjunct (2 women). *Students:* 46 full-time (13 women), 206 part-time (106 women); includes 33 minority (14 Black or African American, non-Hispanic/Latino; 2 Asian, non-Hispanic/Latino; 12 Hispanic/Latino; 5 Two or more races, non-Hispanic/Latino), 4 international. Average age 39. 76 applicants, 72% accepted, 48 enrolled. In 2013, 94 master's, 7 doctorates awarded. *Degree requirements:* For master's, comprehensive exam; for doctorate, comprehensive exam, thesis/dissertation. *Entrance requirements:* For master's, minimum undergraduate GPA of 3.0; for doctorate, GRE General Test, minimum GPA of 3.0 in last 60 hours. Additional exam requirements/recommendations for international students: Required—TOEFL. *Application deadline:* For fall admission, 2/1 priority date for domestic and international students; for spring admission, 8/1 priority date for domestic and international students. Applications are processed on a rolling basis. Application fee: $50 ($75 for international students). Electronic applications accepted. *Financial support:* Career-related internships or fieldwork, institutionally sponsored loans, and scholarships/grants available. Support available to part-time students. Financial award application deadline: 3/1; financial award applicants required to submit FAFSA. *Faculty research:* Educational law, school finance, school facilities, organizational leadership, adult learning, distance learning/education. *Total annual research expenditures:* $7,569. *Unit head:* David C. Thompson, Head, 785-532-5535, Fax: 785-532-7304, E-mail: thomsond@ksu.edu. *Application contact:* Dona Deam, Applications Contact, 785-532-5595, Fax: 785-532-7304, E-mail: ddeam@ksu.edu.
Website: http://www.coe.k-state.edu/departments/edlea/index.html.

Kent State University, Graduate School of Education, Health, and Human Services, School of Teaching, Learning and Curriculum Studies, Program in Career Technical Teacher Education, Kent, OH 44242-0001. Offers M Ed. Part-time and evening/weekend programs available. *Faculty:* 2 full-time (0 women), 4 part-time/adjunct (2 women). *Students:* 36 part-time (17 women); includes 2 minority (both Black or African American, non-Hispanic/Latino). 16 applicants, 100% accepted. In 2013, 11 master's awarded. *Entrance requirements:* For master's, 2 letters of reference, goals statement. Additional exam requirements/recommendations for international students: Required—TOEFL (minimum score 550 paper-based; 80 iBT). *Application deadline:* Applications are processed on a rolling basis. Application fee: $30 ($60 for international students). Electronic applications accepted. *Financial support:* Research assistantships with full tuition reimbursements, Federal Work-Study, scholarships/grants, and unspecified assistantships available. Financial award application deadline: 4/1; financial award applicants required to submit FAFSA. *Faculty research:* Workforce education/development, adult education, training and organizational change. *Unit head:* Dr. Patrick O'Connor, Coordinator, 330-672-0689, E-mail: poconnor@kent.edu. *Application contact:* Nancy Miller, Academic Program Director, Office of Graduate Student Services, 330-672-2576, Fax: 330-672-9162, E-mail: ogs@kent.edu.

Louisiana State University and Agricultural & Mechanical College, Graduate School, College of Human Sciences and Education, School of Human Resource Education and Workforce Development, Baton Rouge, LA 70803. Offers agriculture and extension education and youth development (MS, PhD); career and technical education (MS, PhD); comprehensive vocational education (MS, PhD); extension and international education (MS, PhD); human resource and leadership development (MS, PhD); industrial education (MS); vocational agriculture education (MS, PhD); vocational business education (MS); vocational home economics education (MS). *Accreditation:* NCATE. Part-time programs available. *Faculty:* 10 full-time (5 women). *Students:* 46 full-time (28 women), 138 part-time (96 women); includes 65 minority (52 Black or African American, non-Hispanic/Latino; 2 American Indian or Alaska Native, non-Hispanic/Latino; 2 Asian, non-Hispanic/Latino; 6 Hispanic/Latino; 3 Two or more races, non-Hispanic/Latino), 6 international. Average age 35. 120 applicants, 62% accepted, 49 enrolled. In 2013, 23 master's, 14 doctorates awarded. Terminal master's awarded for partial completion of doctoral program. *Degree requirements:* For master's, thesis (for some programs); for doctorate, thesis/dissertation. *Entrance requirements:* For master's and doctorate, GRE General Test, minimum GPA of 3.0. Additional exam requirements/recommendations for international students: Required—TOEFL (minimum score 550 paper-based; 79 IBT), IELTS (minimum score 6.5), or PTE (minimum score 59). *Application deadline:* For fall admission, 1/25 priority date for domestic students, 5/15 for international students; for spring admission, 10/15 for international students. Applications are processed on a rolling basis. Application fee: $50 ($70 for international students). Electronic applications accepted. *Financial support:* In 2013–14, 85 students received support, including 4 fellowships with full and partial tuition reimbursements available (averaging $31,175 per year), 9 research assistantships with full and partial tuition reimbursements available (averaging $15,422 per year), 14 teaching assistantships with partial tuition reimbursements available (averaging $14,289 per year); career-related internships or fieldwork, Federal Work-Study, institutionally sponsored loans, health care benefits, tuition waivers (full and partial), and unspecified assistantships also available. Financial award application deadline: 3/1; financial award applicants required to submit FAFSA. *Faculty research:* Adult education, history and philosophy of vocational education, curriculum and instruction, career decision-making. *Total annual research expenditures:* $4,454. *Unit head:* Dr. Ed Holton, Director, 225-578-5748, Fax: 225-578-5755, E-mail: eholton@lsu.edu.
Website: http://www.lsu.edu/hrleader/.

Marshall University, Academic Affairs Division, College of Education and Professional Development, Programs in Adult and Technical Education, Huntington, WV 25755. Offers MS. *Accreditation:* NCATE. Evening/weekend programs available. *Students:* 34 full-time (21 women), 51 part-time (33 women); includes 8 minority (7 Black or African American, non-Hispanic/Latino; 1 Hispanic/Latino), 12 international. Average age 37. In 2013, 22 master's awarded. *Degree requirements:* For master's, thesis optional, comprehensive assessment. Application fee: $40. *Unit head:* Dr. Michael Cunningham, Program Coordinator, 304-746-1902, E-mail: mcunningham@marshall.edu. *Application contact:* Graduate Admission.

Middle Tennessee State University, College of Graduate Studies, College of Basic and Applied Sciences, Department of Engineering Technology and Industrial Studies, Murfreesboro, TN 37132. Offers engineering technology (MS). Part-time and evening/weekend programs available. Postbaccalaureate distance learning degree programs offered. *Faculty:* 10 full-time (1 woman). *Students:* 13 full-time (4 women), 16 part-time (1 woman); includes 8 minority (3 Black or African American, non-Hispanic/Latino; 3 Asian, non-Hispanic/Latino; 1 Hispanic/Latino; 1 Two or more races, non-Hispanic/Latino). 29 applicants, 62% accepted. In 2013, 5 master's awarded. *Degree requirements:* For master's, comprehensive exam. *Entrance requirements:* For master's, GRE. Additional exam requirements/recommendations for international students: Required—TOEFL (minimum score 525 paper-based; 71 iBT) or IELTS (minimum score 6). *Application deadline:* For fall admission, 6/1 for domestic and international students. Applications are processed on a rolling basis. Application fee: $25 ($30 for international students). Electronic applications accepted. *Financial support:* In 2013–14, 9 students received support. Tuition waivers available. Support available to part-time students. Financial award application deadline: 5/1; financial award applicants required to submit FAFSA. *Faculty research:* Solar energy, alternative fuels. *Unit head:*

Dr. Walter Boles, Chair, 615-898-2776, Fax: 615-898-5697, E-mail: walter.boles@mtsu.edu. *Application contact:* Dr. Michael D. Allen, Vice Provost for Research and Dean, 615-898-2840, Fax: 615-904-8020, E-mail: michael.allen@mtsu.edu.

Millersville University of Pennsylvania, College of Graduate and Professional Studies, School of Education, Department of Applied Engineering, Safety, and Technology, Millersville, PA 17551-0302. Offers technology education (M Ed). *Accreditation:* NCATE. Part-time and evening/weekend programs available. *Faculty:* 15 full-time (2 women), 8 part-time/adjunct (2 women). *Students:* 2 full-time (0 women), 7 part-time (0 women). Average age 26. 3 applicants, 67% accepted, 1 enrolled. In 2013, 3 master's awarded. *Degree requirements:* For master's, thesis optional. *Entrance requirements:* For master's, GRE or MAT (if GPA lower than 3.0), 3 letters of recommendation, official transcript, goal statement. Additional exam requirements/recommendations for international students: Required—TOEFL (minimum score 550 paper-based, 79 iBT) or IELTS (minimum score 6). *Application deadline:* For fall admission, 1/15 priority date for domestic and international students; for winter admission, 10/1 priority date for domestic and international students; for spring admission, 10/1 priority date for domestic and international students. Applications are processed on a rolling basis. Application fee: $40. Electronic applications accepted. *Expenses:* Tuition, state resident: full-time $7956; part-time $442 per credit. Tuition, nonresident: full-time $11,934; part-time $663 per credit. *Required fees:* $2196; $122 per credit. Tuition and fees vary according to course load. *Financial support:* In 2013–14, 5 students received support, including 5 research assistantships with full tuition reimbursements available (averaging $4,240 per year); institutionally sponsored loans and unspecified assistantships also available. Support available to part-time students. Financial award application deadline: 3/15; financial award applicants required to submit FAFSA. *Faculty research:* Artificial intelligence, humanoid robotics, STEM education, chemical dust explosions, accident investigations, augmented reality printing technology, systems integration microcontrollers, design-based education and thinking, solid-state metallic foams through oxide reduction, nanofibrous nonwoven carbon component, career identification and selection. *Unit head:* Dr. Barry G. David, Chair, 717-872-3327, Fax: 717-872-3318, E-mail: barry.david@millersville.edu. *Application contact:* Dr. Victor S. DeSantis, Dean of College of Graduate and Professional Studies/Associate Provost for Civic and Community Engagement, 717-872-3099, Fax: 717-872-3453, E-mail: victor.desantis@millersville.edu.
Website: http://www.millersville.edu/aest/.

Montana State University, College of Graduate Studies, College of Education, Health, and Human Development, Department of Education, Bozeman, MT 59717. Offers adult and higher education (Ed D); curriculum and instruction (M Ed, Ed D), including professional educator (M Ed), technology education (M Ed); education (M Ed), including adult and higher education, educational leadership, school counseling; educational leadership (Ed D, Ed S). *Accreditation:* Teacher Education Accreditation Council. Part-time programs available. Postbaccalaureate distance learning degree programs offered (minimal on-campus study). *Degree requirements:* For master's, comprehensive exam; for doctorate, comprehensive exam, thesis/dissertation. *Entrance requirements:* For master's, GRE, 3 letters of reference, essays, BA transcripts; for doctorate, GRE, MAT, 3 letters of reference, essay, BA and M Ed transcripts; for Ed S, PRAXIS. Additional exam requirements/recommendations for international students: Required—TOEFL (minimum score 550 paper-based). Electronic applications accepted. *Faculty research:* Critical literacy; standards-based education; school Improvement, organizational change, leadership in rural education, leadership in Indian education; student Learning; multicultural/culturally responsive education for social justice Native American indigenous education, community-centered education teacher preparation.

Morehead State University, Graduate Programs, College of Science and Technology, Department of Industrial and Engineering Technology, Morehead, KY 40351. Offers career and technical education (MS); engineering technology (MS). Part-time and evening/weekend programs available. *Degree requirements:* For master's, completion and defense of thesis or written and oral comprehensive exit exams. *Entrance requirements:* For master's, GRE, minimum undergraduate GPA of 3.0 in major. Additional exam requirements/recommendations for international students: Required—TOEFL (minimum score 500 paper-based). Electronic applications accepted.

Murray State University, College of Education, Department of Adolescent, Career and Special Education, Program in Industrial and Technical Education, Murray, KY 42071. Offers MS. *Accreditation:* NCATE. Part-time programs available. *Degree requirements:* For master's, thesis (for some programs), portfolio. *Entrance requirements:* For master's, GRE General Test. Additional exam requirements/recommendations for international students: Required—TOEFL.

Niagara University, Graduate Division of Education, Concentration in Foundations of Teaching, Niagara Falls, NY 14109. Offers MS Ed. *Accreditation:* NCATE. Part-time programs available. *Students:* 1 (woman) full-time, 5 part-time (2 women). Average age 30. In 2013, 5 master's awarded. *Degree requirements:* For master's, thesis. *Entrance requirements:* For master's, GRE General Test or MAT. Additional exam requirements/recommendations for international students: Required—TOEFL (minimum score 550 paper-based, 79 iBT) or IELTS (minimum score 6). *Application deadline:* For fall admission, 8/1 for domestic students. Applications are processed on a rolling basis. Application fee: $30. *Expenses:* Contact institution. *Financial support:* Research assistantships with full and partial tuition reimbursements, teaching assistantships with full and partial tuition reimbursements, career-related internships or fieldwork, Federal Work-Study, scholarships/grants, and unspecified assistantships available. Financial award application deadline: 4/15; financial award applicants required to submit FAFSA. *Unit head:* Dr. Leticia Hahn, 716-286-8760, E-mail: lhahn@niagara.edu. *Application contact:* Dr. Debra A. Colley, Dean of Education, 716-286-8560, Fax: 716-286-8560, E-mail: dcolley@niagara.edu.
Website: http://www.niagara.edu/foundations-of-teaching-math-science-and-technology-education.

North Carolina Agricultural and Technical State University, School of Graduate Studies, School of Technology, Department of Graphic Communication Systems and Technological Studies, Greensboro, NC 27411. Offers graphic communication systems (MSTM); technology education (MAT). *Accreditation:* NCATE (one or more programs are accredited). Part-time and evening/weekend programs available. *Degree requirements:* For master's, comprehensive exam, thesis or alternative, qualifying exam. *Entrance requirements:* For master's, GRE General Test, minimum GPA of 3.0.

North Dakota State University, College of Graduate and Interdisciplinary Studies, College of Human Development and Education, School of Education, Fargo, ND 58108. Offers agricultural education (M Ed, MS), including agricultural education, agricultural extension education (MS); counseling (M Ed, MS, PhD); curriculum and instruction (M Ed, MS); education (PhD); educational leadership (M Ed, MS, Ed S); family and consumer sciences education (M Ed, MS); history education (M Ed, MS); institutional analysis (Ed D); mathematics education (M Ed, MS); music education (M Ed, MS); occupational and adult education (Ed D); science education (M Ed, MS). *Accreditation:* NCATE. Part-time and evening/weekend programs available. Postbaccalaureate distance learning degree programs offered (minimal on-campus study). *Faculty:* 25 full-time (11 women), 1 (woman) part-time/adjunct. *Students:* 110 full-time (82 women), 123 part-time (85 women); includes 14 minority (4 Black or African American, non-Hispanic/

Latino; 4 American Indian or Alaska Native, non-Hispanic/Latino; 1 Native Hawaiian or other Pacific Islander, non-Hispanic/Latino; 5 Two or more races, non-Hispanic/Latino), 10 international. Average age 28. 57 applicants, 81% accepted, 42 enrolled. In 2013, 38 master's, 9 doctorates awarded. *Degree requirements:* For master's, comprehensive exam; for doctorate, thesis/dissertation; for Ed S, thesis. *Entrance requirements:* For degree, GRE General Test, master's degree, minimum GPA of 3.25. Additional exam requirements/recommendations for international students: Required—TOEFL. *Application deadline:* Applications are processed on a rolling basis. Application fee: $45 ($60 for international students). *Financial support:* Research assistantships, teaching assistantships, career-related internships or fieldwork, Federal Work-Study, institutionally sponsored loans, and tuition waivers (full) available. Financial award application deadline: 4/15. *Unit head:* Dr. William Martin, Chair, 701-231-7202, Fax: 701-231-7416, E-mail: william.martin@ndsu.edu. *Application contact:* Sonya Goergen, Marketing, Recruitment, and Public Relations Coordinator, 701-231-7033, Fax: 701-231-6524.
Website: http://www.ndsu.nodak.edu/school_of_education/.

Northern Arizona University, Graduate College, College of Education, Department of Educational Specialties, Flagstaff, AZ 86011. Offers autism spectrum disorders (Certificate); bilingual/multicultural education (M Ed), including bilingual education, ESL education; career and technical education (M Ed, Certificate); early childhood special education (M Ed); educational technology (M Ed, Certificate); special education (M Ed). *Faculty:* 32 full-time (21 women), 4 part-time/adjunct (all women). *Students:* 68 full-time (48 women), 158 part-time (119 women); includes 93 minority (6 Black or African American, non-Hispanic/Latino; 29 American Indian or Alaska Native, non-Hispanic/Latino; 4 Asian, non-Hispanic/Latino; 53 Hispanic/Latino; 1 Native Hawaiian or other Pacific Islander, non-Hispanic/Latino), 6 international. Average age 37. 66 applicants, 95% accepted, 38 enrolled. In 2013, 121 master's, 3 Certificates awarded. *Degree requirements:* For master's, comprehensive exam (for some programs), thesis (for some programs). *Entrance requirements:* For master's, minimum GPA of 3.0. Additional exam requirements/recommendations for international students: Required—TOEFL (minimum score 550 paper-based; 80 iBT), IELTS (minimum score 7). *Application deadline:* For fall admission, 3/1 for international students; for spring admission, 9/15 for international students. Applications are processed on a rolling basis. Application fee: $65. Electronic applications accepted. *Financial support:* In 2013–14, 9 teaching assistantships with full tuition reimbursements (averaging $9,698 per year) were awarded. Financial award applicants required to submit FAFSA. *Unit head:* Dr. Laura Sujo-Montes, Chair, 928-523-0892, Fax: 928-523-1929, E-mail: laura.sujo-montes@nau.edu. *Application contact:* Laura Cook, Coordinator, 928-523-5342, Fax: 928-523-8950, E-mail: laura.cook@nau.edu.
Website: http://nau.edu/coe/ed-specialties/.

Old Dominion University, Darden College of Education, Programs in Occupational and Technical Studies, Norfolk, VA 23529. Offers business and industry training (MS); career and technical education (MS, PhD); community college teaching (MS); human resources training (PhD); STEM education (MS); technology education (PhD). *Accreditation:* NCATE (one or more programs are accredited). Part-time and evening/weekend programs available. Postbaccalaureate distance learning degree programs offered (minimal on-campus study). *Faculty:* 6 full-time (2 women), 2 part-time/adjunct (both women). *Students:* 8 full-time (3 women), 41 part-time (21 women); includes 19 minority (13 Black or African American, non-Hispanic/Latino; 1 American Indian or Alaska Native, non-Hispanic/Latino; 1 Asian, non-Hispanic/Latino; 3 Hispanic/Latino; 1 Two or more races, non-Hispanic/Latino), 2 international. Average age 43. 12 applicants, 83% accepted, 10 enrolled. In 2013, 16 master's, 8 doctorates awarded. *Degree requirements:* For master's, comprehensive exam, thesis optional, writing exam, candidacy exam; for doctorate, comprehensive exam, thesis/dissertation, writing exam, candidacy exam. *Entrance requirements:* For master's, GRE General Test or MAT, minimum GPA of 2.8, 2 letters of reference; for doctorate, GRE, minimum GPA of 3.0, 3 letters of reference. Additional exam requirements/recommendations for international students: Required—TOEFL. *Application deadline:* For fall admission, 6/1 priority date for domestic students, 6/1 for international students; for winter admission, 11/1 priority date for domestic students, 11/1 for international students; for spring admission, 3/1 priority date for domestic students, 3/1 for international students. Applications are processed on a rolling basis. Application fee: $50. Electronic applications accepted. *Expenses:* Tuition, state resident: full-time $9888; part-time $412 per credit. Tuition, nonresident: full-time $25,152; part-time $1048 per credit. *Required fees:* $59 per semester. One-time fee: $50. *Financial support:* In 2013–14, 19 students received support, including fellowships with full tuition reimbursements available (averaging $15,000 per year), research assistantships with partial tuition reimbursements available (averaging $9,000 per year), 2 teaching assistantships with partial tuition reimbursements available (averaging $15,000 per year); career-related internships or fieldwork, scholarships/grants, tuition waivers (partial), and unspecified assistantships also available. Support available to part-time students. Financial award application deadline: 2/15; financial award applicants required to submit FAFSA. *Faculty research:* Training and development, marketing, technology, special populations, STEM education. *Total annual research expenditures:* $799,773. *Unit head:* Dr. Cynthia L. Tomovic, Graduate Program Director, 757-683-5228, Fax: 757-683-5228, E-mail: ctomovic@odu.edu. *Application contact:* William Heffelfinger, Director of Graduate Admissions, 757-683-5554, Fax: 757-683-3255, E-mail: gradadmit@odu.edu.
Website: http://education.odu.edu/ots/.

Penn State University Park, Graduate School, College of Education, Department of Learning and Performance Systems, State College, PA 16802. Offers adult education (M Ed, D Ed, PhD, Certificate); instructional systems (Certificate); learning, design, and technology (M Ed, MS, D Ed, PhD, Certificate); organization development and change (MPS); workforce education and development (M Ed, MS, PhD). *Unit head:* Dr. David H. Monk, Dean, 814-865-2523, Fax: 814-865-0555, E-mail: dhm6@psu.edu. *Application contact:* Cynthia E. Nicosia, Director, Graduate Enrollment Services, 814-865-1834, Fax: 814-863-4627, E-mail: cey1@psu.edu.
Website: http://www.ed.psu.edu/educ/lps/dept-lps.

Pittsburg State University, Graduate School, College of Technology, Department of Technology and Workforce Learning, Pittsburg, KS 66762. Offers career and technical education (MS); human resource development (MS); technology (MS), including printing management; workforce development and education (Ed S). *Degree requirements:* For master's, thesis or alternative.

Purdue University, Graduate School, College of Education, Department of Curriculum and Instruction, West Lafayette, IN 47907. Offers agricultural and extension education (PhD, Ed S); agriculture and extension education (MS, MS Ed); art education (PhD); curriculum studies (MS Ed, PhD, Ed S); educational technology (MS Ed, PhD, Ed S); elementary education (MS Ed); family and consumer sciences education (MS Ed, PhD, Ed S); foreign language education (MS Ed, PhD, Ed S); industrial technology (PhD, Ed S); language arts (MS Ed, PhD, Ed S); literacy (MS Ed, PhD, Ed S); mathematics/science education (MS, MS Ed, PhD, Ed S); social studies (MS Ed, PhD); social studies education (Ed S); vocational/industrial education (MS Ed, PhD, Ed S); vocational/technical education (MS Ed, PhD, Ed S). *Accreditation:* NCATE. Part-time and evening/weekend programs available. *Faculty:* 29 full-time (19 women), 33 part-time/adjunct (29

women). *Students:* 85 full-time (53 women), 271 part-time (195 women); includes 62 minority (19 Black or African American, non-Hispanic/Latino; 3 American Indian or Alaska Native, non-Hispanic/Latino; 13 Asian, non-Hispanic/Latino; 22 Hispanic/Latino; 1 Native Hawaiian or other Pacific Islander, non-Hispanic/Latino; 4 Two or more races, non-Hispanic/Latino), 41 international. Average age 36. 155 applicants, 71% accepted, 71 enrolled. In 2013, 60 master's, 20 doctorates awarded. *Degree requirements:* For master's, thesis optional; for doctorate, thesis/dissertation, oral and written exams; for Ed S, oral presentation, project. *Entrance requirements:* For master's, GRE General Test (if undergraduate GPA is below 3.0), minimum undergraduate GPA of 3.0 or equivalent; for doctorate, GRE General Test (minimum combined verbal and quantitative score of 1000, 300 for new scoring), minimum undergraduate GPA of 3.0 or equivalent; master's degree with minimum GPA of 3.0 or equivalent; for Ed S, GRE General Test (minimum combined verbal and quantitative score of 1000, 300 for new scoring), minimum undergraduate GPA of 3.0 or equivalent; master's degree. Additional exam requirements/recommendations for international students: Required—TOEFL (minimum score 550 paper-based; 77 iBT). *Application deadline:* For fall admission, 12/15 for domestic students, 3/1 for international students; for spring admission, 9/15 for domestic students, 8/1 for international students. Application fee: $60 ($75 for international students). Electronic applications accepted. *Financial support:* Fellowships with full tuition reimbursements, research assistantships with full tuition reimbursements, teaching assistantships with full tuition reimbursements, career-related internships or fieldwork, and tuition waivers (full) available. Support available to part-time students. Financial award application deadline: 3/1; financial award applicants required to submit FAFSA. *Faculty research:* Literacy acquisition and development, teacher beliefs and knowledge, recruitment and retention of underrepresented students, economic education, literacy discourse. *Unit head:* Dr. Phillip J. VanFossen, Head, 765-494-7935, Fax: 765-496-1622, E-mail: vanfoss@purdue.edu. *Application contact:* Cindy Blankenship, Graduate Contact, 765-494-2345, Fax: 765-494-5832, E-mail: prater0@purdue.edu.
Website: http://www.edci.purdue.edu/.

South Carolina State University, School of Graduate and Professional Studies, Department of Education, Orangeburg, SC 29117-0001. Offers early childhood and special education (M Ed); early childhood education (MAT); elementary education (M Ed, MAT); general science (MAT); mathematics (MAT); secondary education (M Ed), including biology education, business education, counselor education, English education, home economics education, industrial education, mathematics education, science education, social studies education; special education (M Ed), including emotionally handicapped, learning disabilities, mentally handicapped. *Accreditation:* NCATE. Part-time and evening/weekend programs available. *Faculty:* 9 full-time (3 women), 4 part-time/adjunct (3 women). *Students:* 32 full-time (26 women), 33 part-time (26 women); includes 63 minority (61 Black or African American, non-Hispanic/Latino; 2 Asian, non-Hispanic/Latino). Average age 31. 21 applicants, 100% accepted, 21 enrolled. In 2013, 15 master's awarded. *Degree requirements:* For master's, thesis optional, departmental qualifying exam. *Entrance requirements:* For master's, GRE General Test, NTE, interview, teaching certificate. *Application deadline:* For fall admission, 6/15 priority date for domestic students, 6/15 for international students; for spring admission, 11/1 for domestic and international students. Applications are processed on a rolling basis. Application fee: $25. Electronic applications accepted. *Expenses:* Tuition, state resident: full-time $8906; part-time $543 per credit hour. Tuition, nonresident: full-time $18,040; part-time $1051 per credit hour. *Financial support:* Fellowships, career-related internships or fieldwork, Federal Work-Study, and institutionally sponsored loans available. Financial award application deadline: 6/1. *Faculty research:* Critical thinking, child abuse, stress, test-taking skills, conflict resolution, mainstreaming. *Unit head:* Dr. Margaret Evelyn Fields, Interim Chair, 803-536-7098, Fax: 803-516-4568, E-mail: efields@scsu.edu. *Application contact:* Curtis Foskey, Coordinator of Graduate Studies, 803-536-8419, Fax: 803-536-8812, E-mail: cfoskey@scsu.edu.

Southern Illinois University Carbondale, Graduate School, College of Education and Human Services, Department of Workforce Education and Development, Carbondale, IL 62901-4701. Offers MS Ed, PhD. *Accreditation:* NCATE. Part-time programs available. *Faculty:* 15 full-time (6 women), 1 part-time/adjunct (0 women). *Students:* 66 full-time (33 women), 102 part-time (56 women); includes 55 minority (36 Black or African American, non-Hispanic/Latino; 1 American Indian or Alaska Native, non-Hispanic/Latino; 7 Asian, non-Hispanic/Latino; 11 Hispanic/Latino), 11 international. Average age 32. 61 applicants, 84% accepted, 35 enrolled. In 2013, 53 master's, 4 doctorates awarded. *Degree requirements:* For master's, thesis; for doctorate, thesis/dissertation. *Entrance requirements:* For master's, minimum GPA of 2.7; for doctorate, GRE General Test, minimum GPA of 3.25. Additional exam requirements/recommendations for international students: Required—TOEFL. *Application deadline:* Applications are processed on a rolling basis. Application fee: $50. *Financial support:* In 2013–14, 38 students received support, including 4 research assistantships with full tuition reimbursements available, 10 teaching assistantships with full tuition reimbursements available; fellowships with full tuition reimbursements available, career-related internships or fieldwork, Federal Work-Study, institutionally sponsored loans, tuition waivers (full), and unspecified assistantships also available. Support available to part-time students. *Faculty research:* Career education, technical training, curriculum development, competency-based instruction, impact of technology on workplace and workforce. *Unit head:* Dr. Keith Waugh, Chair, 618-453-3321, Fax: 618-453-1909, E-mail: ckwaugh@siu.edu. *Application contact:* Sandy McRoy, Office Manager, 618-453-1960, Fax: 618-453-1909, E-mail: smac59@siu.edu.
Website: http://wed.siu.edu/.

State University of New York at Oswego, Graduate Studies, School of Education, Department of Technology, Oswego, NY 13126. Offers MS Ed. *Accreditation:* NCATE. Part-time programs available. *Degree requirements:* For master's, thesis optional, departmental exam. *Entrance requirements:* For master's, provisional teaching certificate in technology education. Additional exam requirements/recommendations for international students: Required—TOEFL (minimum score 560 paper-based). *Faculty research:* Curriculum development, microcomputer applications.

State University of New York at Oswego, Graduate Studies, School of Education, Department of Vocational Teacher Preparation, Oswego, NY 13126. Offers agriculture (MS Ed); business and marketing (MS Ed); family and consumer sciences (MS Ed); health careers (MS Ed); technical education (MS Ed); trade education (MS Ed). *Accreditation:* NCATE. Part-time and evening/weekend programs available. *Degree requirements:* For master's, comprehensive exam, thesis or alternative. *Entrance requirements:* Additional exam requirements/recommendations for international students: Required—TOEFL (minimum score 560 paper-based).

Temple University, College of Education, Department of Curriculum, Instruction, and Technology in Education, Program in Career and Technical Education, Philadelphia, PA 19122-6096. Offers business, computing, and information technology (MS Ed); industrial education (MS Ed); marketing education (MS Ed). *Entrance requirements:* For master's, official transcripts, two professional letters of recommendation, professional resume. Electronic applications accepted.

Texas State University, Graduate School, College of Applied Arts, Interdisciplinary Studies Program in Occupational Education, San Marcos, TX 78666. Offers MAIS, MSIS. *Faculty:* 5 full-time (0 women), 1 part-time/adjunct (0 women). *Students:* 19 full-time (10 women), 30 part-time (19 women); includes 27 minority (9 Black or African American, non-Hispanic/Latino; 1 American Indian or Alaska Native, non-Hispanic/Latino; 1 Asian, non-Hispanic/Latino; 16 Hispanic/Latino), 2 international. Average age 41. 32 applicants, 84% accepted, 12 enrolled. In 2013, 7 master's awarded. *Degree requirements:* For master's, comprehensive exam, thesis optional. *Entrance requirements:* For master's, minimum GPA of 2.75 for undergraduate work, statement of personal goals. Additional exam requirements/recommendations for international students: Required—TOEFL (minimum score 550 paper-based; 78 iBT). *Application deadline:* For fall admission, 6/15 priority date for domestic students, 6/1 priority date for international students; for spring admission, 10/15 priority date for domestic students, 10/1 priority date for international students. Applications are processed on a rolling basis. Application fee: $40 ($90 for international students). Electronic applications accepted. *Expenses:* Tuition, state resident: full-time $6663; part-time $278 per credit hour. Tuition, nonresident: full-time $15,159; part-time $632 per credit hour. *Required fees:* $1872; $54 per credit hour. $306 per term. Tuition and fees vary according to course load. *Financial support:* In 2013–14, 38 students received support, including 2 research assistantships (averaging $13,200 per year), 1 teaching assistantship (averaging $11,570 per year); Federal Work-Study, institutionally sponsored loans, scholarships/grants, health care benefits, and unspecified assistantships also available. Support available to part-time students. Financial award application deadline: 4/1; financial award applicants required to submit FAFSA. *Unit head:* Dr. Matthew Eichler, Director, 512-245-2115, E-mail: me21@txstate.edu. *Application contact:* Dr. Andrea Golato, Dean of Graduate School, 512-245-2581, Fax: 512-245-8365, E-mail: gradcollege@txstate.edu.
Website: http://www.OCED.txstate.edu/.

Texas State University, Graduate School, College of Applied Arts, Program in Management of Technical Education, San Marcos, TX 78666. Offers M Ed. Part-time and evening/weekend programs available. *Faculty:* 2 full-time (1 woman), 1 part-time/adjunct (0 women). *Students:* 7 full-time (5 women), 9 part-time (6 women); includes 7 minority (3 Black or African American, non-Hispanic/Latino; 4 Hispanic/Latino). Average age 38. 11 applicants, 91% accepted, 8 enrolled. In 2013, 7 master's awarded. *Degree requirements:* For master's, comprehensive exam. *Entrance requirements:* For master's, minimum GPA of 2.75 in last 60 hours of course work. Additional exam requirements/recommendations for international students: Required—TOEFL (minimum score 550 paper-based; 78 iBT). *Application deadline:* For fall admission, 6/15 for domestic students, 6/1 for international students; for spring admission, 10/15 for domestic students, 10/1 for international students. Applications are processed on a rolling basis. Application fee: $40 ($90 for international students). Electronic applications accepted. *Expenses:* Tuition, state resident: full-time $6663; part-time $278 per credit hour. Tuition, nonresident: full-time $15,159; part-time $632 per credit hour. *Required fees:* $1872; $54 per credit hour. $306 per term. Tuition and fees vary according to course load. *Financial support:* In 2013–14, 8 students received support, including 2 research assistantships (averaging $11,815 per year); teaching assistantships, career-related internships or fieldwork, Federal Work-Study, and institutionally sponsored loans also available. Support available to part-time students. Financial award application deadline: 4/1; financial award applicants required to submit FAFSA. *Unit head:* Dr. Matthew Eichler, Graduate Advisor, 512-245-2115, E-mail: me21@txstate.edu. *Application contact:* Dr. Andrea Golato, Dean of the Graduate College, 512-245-2581, Fax: 512-245-8365, E-mail: gradcollege@txstate.edu.
Website: http://www.owls.txstate.edu/graduate-degrees/management-technical-education.html.

The University of Akron, Graduate School, College of Education, Department of Educational Foundations and Leadership, Akron, OH 44325. Offers higher education administration (MA, MS); principalship (MA, MS); teaching and training technical professionals (MS). *Accreditation:* NCATE. *Faculty:* 20 full-time (17 women), 48 part-time/adjunct (30 women). *Students:* 52 full-time (34 women), 192 part-time (140 women); includes 36 minority (31 Black or African American, non-Hispanic/Latino; 1 Asian, non-Hispanic/Latino; 3 Hispanic/Latino; 1 Two or more races, non-Hispanic/Latino), 13 international. Average age 35. 113 applicants, 86% accepted, 60 enrolled. In 2013, 81 master's awarded. Terminal master's awarded for partial completion of doctoral program. *Degree requirements:* For master's, written comprehensive exam or portfolio assessment. *Entrance requirements:* For master's, GRE, minimum GPA of 2.75, statement of purpose. Additional exam requirements/recommendations for international students: Required—TOEFL (minimum score 550 paper-based; 79 iBT). *Application deadline:* Applications are processed on a rolling basis. Application fee: $40 ($60 for international students). Electronic applications accepted. *Expenses:* Tuition, state resident: full-time $7430; part-time $412.80 per credit hour. Tuition, nonresident: full-time $12,722; part-time $706.80 per credit hour. *Required fees:* $53 per credit hour. $12 per semester. Tuition and fees vary according to course load and program. *Financial support:* In 2013–14, 4 research assistantships with full tuition reimbursements, 16 teaching assistantships with full tuition reimbursements were awarded. *Faculty research:* K-12 education law, K-12 education leadership, higher education leadership, postsecondary technical education, diversity of learned (K-16 U.S. and international). *Total annual research expenditures:* $78,289. *Unit head:* Dr. Sharon Kruse, Chair, 330-972-8177, E-mail: skruse@uakron.edu.
Website: http://www.uakron.edu/education/academic-programs/EFL/index.dot.

University of Arkansas, Graduate School, College of Education and Health Professions, Department of Rehabilitation, Human Resources and Communication Disorders, Program in Human Resource and Workforce Development Education, Fayetteville, AR 72701-1201. Offers M Ed, Ed D. Part-time and evening/weekend programs available. Postbaccalaureate distance learning degree programs offered. Electronic applications accepted.

The University of British Columbia, Faculty of Education, Department of Curriculum and Pedagogy, Vancouver, BC V6T 1Z4, Canada. Offers art education (M Ed, MA); business education (MA); curriculum studies (M Ed, MA, PhD); home economics education (M Ed, MA); math education (M Ed, MA); music education (M Ed, MA); physical education (M Ed, MA); science education (M Ed, MA); social studies education (M Ed, MA); technology studies education (M Ed, MA). Part-time programs available. Postbaccalaureate distance learning degree programs offered (no on-campus study). *Faculty:* 32 full-time (14 women), 1 (woman) part-time/adjunct. *Students:* 163 full-time, 134 part-time, 42 international. Average age 40. 160 applicants, 75% accepted, 97 enrolled. In 2013, 68 master's, 7 doctorates awarded. *Degree requirements:* For master's, thesis (MA); for doctorate, comprehensive exam, thesis/dissertation. *Entrance requirements:* Additional exam requirements/recommendations for international students: Required—TOEFL (minimum score 580 paper-based; 92 iBT), IELTS (minimum score 6.5). *Application deadline:* For fall admission, 12/1 for domestic and international students; for spring admission, 10/1 for domestic students, 9/1 for international students. Application fee: $90 Canadian dollars ($150 Canadian dollars for international students). Electronic applications accepted. *Expenses:* Contact institution. *Financial support:* In 2013–14, 10 fellowships with partial tuition reimbursements (averaging $16,000 per year), 11 research assistantships with partial tuition

reimbursements (averaging $14,000 per year), 27 teaching assistantships with partial tuition reimbursements (averaging $14,000 per year) were awarded; tuition waivers (partial) also available. *Faculty research:* School subjects, teaching and learning. *Unit head:* Dr. Peter Grimmett, Head, 604-822-5422, Fax: 604-822-4714, E-mail: anna.ip@ubc.ca. *Application contact:* Basia Zurek, Graduate Programs Assistant, 604-822-5367, Fax: 604-822-4714, E-mail: edcp.grad@ubc.ca.
Website: http://www.edcp.educ.ubc.ca/.

University of Central Florida, College of Education and Human Performance, Department of Educational and Human Sciences, Program in Career and Technical Education, Orlando, FL 32816. Offers MA. *Accreditation:* NCATE. Part-time and evening/weekend programs available. *Students:* 13 full-time (10 women), 38 part-time (28 women); includes 18 minority (11 Black or African American, non-Hispanic/Latino; 2 Asian, non-Hispanic/Latino; 4 Hispanic/Latino; 1 Two or more races, non-Hispanic/Latino). Average age 41. 14 applicants, 93% accepted, 9 enrolled. In 2013, 16 master's awarded. *Entrance requirements:* For master's, GRE General Test. Additional exam requirements/recommendations for international students: Required—TOEFL. *Application deadline:* For fall admission, 7/15 for domestic students; for spring admission, 12/1 for domestic students. Electronic applications accepted. *Financial support:* Fellowships with partial tuition reimbursements, research assistantships with partial tuition reimbursements, teaching assistantships with partial tuition reimbursements, career-related internships or fieldwork, Federal Work-Study, institutionally sponsored loans, tuition waivers (partial), and unspecified assistantships available. Financial award application deadline: 3/1; financial award applicants required to submit FAFSA. *Unit head:* Dr. Jo Ann M. Whiteman, Program Coordinator, 407-823-2848, E-mail: joann.whiteman@ucf.edu. *Application contact:* Barbara Rodriguez Lamas, Director, Admissions and Student Services, 407-823-2766, Fax: 407-823-6442, E-mail: gradadmissions@ucf.edu.

University of Central Missouri, The Graduate School, Warrensburg, MO 6409. Offers accountancy (MA); accounting (MBA); applied mathematics (MS); aviation safety (MA); biology (MS); business administration (MBA); career and technical education leadership (MS); college student personnel administration (MS); communication (MA); computer science (MS); counseling (MS); criminal justice (MS); educational leadership (Ed D); educational technology (MS); elementary and early childhood education (MSE); English (MA); environmental studies (MA); finance (MBA); history (MA); human services/educational technology (Ed S); human services/learning resources (Ed S); human services/professional counseling (Ed S); industrial hygiene (MS); industrial management (MS); information systems (MBA); information technology (MS); kinesiology (MS); library science and information services (MS); literacy education (MSE); marketing (MBA); mathematics (MS); music (MA); occupational safety management (MS); psychology (MS); rural family nursing (MS); school administration (MSE); social gerontology (MS); sociology (MA); special education (MSE); speech language pathology (MS); superintendency (Ed S); teaching (MAT); teaching English as a second language (MA); technology (MS); technology management (PhD); theatre (MA). Part-time programs available. *Faculty:* 233. *Students:* 890 full-time (396 women), 1,486 part-time (1,001 women); includes 192 minority (97 Black or African American, non-Hispanic/Latino; 9 American Indian or Alaska Native, non-Hispanic/Latino; 32 Asian, non-Hispanic/Latino; 40 Hispanic/Latino; 3 Native Hawaiian or other Pacific Islander, non-Hispanic/Latino; 11 Two or more races, non-Hispanic/Latino), 539 international. Average age 31. 1,953 applicants, 75% accepted. In 2013, 719 master's, 58 other advanced degrees awarded. *Degree requirements:* For master's and Ed S, comprehensive exam (for some programs), thesis (for some programs). *Entrance requirements:* Additional exam requirements/recommendations for international students: Required—TOEFL (minimum score 550 paper-based; 79 iBT). *Application deadline:* For fall admission, 6/1 for domestic students; for spring admission, 10/1 for domestic and international students. Applications are processed on a rolling basis. Application fee: $30 ($75 for international students). Electronic applications accepted. *Expenses:* Tuition, state resident: full-time $7326; part-time $276.25 per credit hour. Tuition, nonresident: full-time $13,956; part-time $552.50 per credit hour. *Required fees:* $29 per credit hour. *Financial support:* In 2013–14, 118 students received support, including 271 research assistantships with full and partial tuition reimbursements available (averaging $7,500 per year), 109 teaching assistantships with full and partial tuition reimbursements available (averaging $7,500 per year); career-related internships or fieldwork, Federal Work-Study, scholarships/grants, and administrative and laboratory assistantships also available. Support available to part-time students. Financial award application deadline: 3/1; financial award applicants required to submit FAFSA. *Unit head:* Dr. Joseph Vaughn, Assistant Provost for Research/Dean, 660-543-4092, Fax: 660-543-4778, E-mail: vaughn@ucmo.edu. *Application contact:* Brittany Lawrence, Graduate Student Services Coordinator, 660-543-4621, Fax: 660-543-4778, E-mail: gradinfo@ucmo.edu.
Website: http://www.ucmo.edu/graduate/.

University of Georgia, College of Education, Department of Career and Information Studies, Athens, GA 30602. Offers learning, design, and technology (M Ed, PhD, Ed S), including instructional design and development (M Ed, Ed S), instructional technology (M Ed), learning, design, and technology (M Ed), school library media (M Ed, Ed S); workforce education (M Ed, MAT, Ed D, PhD, Ed S), including business education (MAT), family and consumer sciences education (MAT), health science and technology education (MAT), marketing education (MAT), technology education (MAT), trade and industry education (MAT). *Accreditation:* NCATE. *Entrance requirements:* For master's, GRE General Test, MAT; for doctorate, GRE General Test; for Ed S, GRE General Test or MAT. Electronic applications accepted.

University of Idaho, College of Graduate Studies, College of Education, Department of Curriculum and Instruction, Moscow, ID 83844-3082. Offers curriculum and instruction (M Ed, Ed S); industrial technology education (M Ed). *Faculty:* 24 full-time, 2 part-time/adjunct. *Students:* 10 full-time, 44 part-time. Average age 39. In 2013, 51 master's awarded. *Entrance requirements:* For master's, minimum GPA of 2.8. Additional exam requirements/recommendations for international students: Required—TOEFL (minimum score 550 paper-based). *Application deadline:* For fall admission, 8/1 for domestic students; for spring admission, 12/15 for domestic students. Applications are processed on a rolling basis. Application fee: $60. Electronic applications accepted. *Expenses:* Tuition, state resident: full-time $5596; part-time $363 per credit hour. Tuition, nonresident: full-time $18,672; part-time $1089 per credit hour. *Financial support:* Research assistantships and teaching assistantships available. Financial award applicants required to submit FAFSA. *Unit head:* Dr. Paul H. Gathercoal, Chair, 208-885-6587. *Application contact:* Stephanie Thomas, Graduate Recruitment Coordinator, 208-885-4001, Fax: 208-885-4406, E-mail: gadms@uidaho.edu.
Website: http://www.uidaho.edu/ed/ci.

University of Illinois at Urbana–Champaign, Graduate College, College of Education, Department of Human Resource Education, Champaign, IL 61820. Offers Ed M, MS, Ed D, PhD, CAS, MBA/M Ed. Part-time and evening/weekend programs available. Postbaccalaureate distance learning degree programs offered. *Students:* 48 full-time (21 women), 118 part-time (81 women); includes 30 minority (19 Black or African American, non-Hispanic/Latino; 6 Asian, non-Hispanic/Latino; 5 Hispanic/Latino), 38 international. Application fee: $75 ($90 for international students). *Unit head:* James D. Anderson, Head, 217-333-7404, Fax: 217-244-5632, E-mail: janders@illinois.edu. *Application*

contact: Laura Ketchum, Business Manager, 217-333-2155, Fax: 217-244-5632, E-mail: ketchum@illinois.edu.
Website: http://education.illinois.edu/hre/index.html.

University of Maryland Eastern Shore, Graduate Programs, Department of Technology, Princess Anne, MD 21853-1299. Offers career and technology education (M Ed). Part-time and evening/weekend programs available. *Degree requirements:* For master's, comprehensive exam, seminar paper. *Entrance requirements:* For master's, PRAXIS, writing sample. Additional exam requirements/recommendations for international students: Required—TOEFL (minimum score 80 iBT). Electronic applications accepted. *Faculty research:* Doppler Radar study.

University of Minnesota, Twin Cities Campus, Graduate School, College of Education and Human Development, Department of Organizational Leadership, Policy and Development, Minneapolis, MN 55455-0213. Offers adult education (M Ed, MA, Ed D, PhD, Certificate); agricultural, food and environmental education (M Ed, MA, Ed D, PhD); business and industry education (M Ed, MA, Ed D, PhD); business education (M Ed); comparative and international development education (MA, PhD); disability policy and services (Certificate); educational administration (MA, Ed D, PhD); evaluation studies (MA, PhD); higher education (MA, PhD); human resource development (M Ed, MA, Ed D, PhD, Certificate); marketing education (M Ed); postsecondary administration (Ed D); program evaluation (Certificate); school-to-work (Certificate); staff development (Certificate); teacher leadership (M Ed); technical education (Certificate); technology education (M Ed, MA); work and human resource education (M Ed, MA, Ed D, PhD); youth development leadership (M Ed). *Faculty:* 29 full-time (12 women). *Students:* 229 full-time (149 women), 352 part-time (227 women); includes 108 minority (46 Black or African American, non-Hispanic/Latino; 7 American Indian or Alaska Native, non-Hispanic/Latino; 36 Asian, non-Hispanic/Latino; 19 Hispanic/Latino), 62 international. Average age 38. 416 applicants, 63% accepted, 132 enrolled. In 2013, 84 master's, 56 doctorates, 120 other advanced degrees awarded. Application fee: $75 ($95 for international students). *Financial support:* In 2013–14, 2 fellowships (averaging $26,250 per year), 41 research assistantships with full tuition reimbursements (averaging $9,917 per year), 17 teaching assistantships with full tuition reimbursements (averaging $9,447 per year) were awarded. *Faculty research:* Organizational change in schools, universities, and other organizations; international education and development; program evaluation to facilitate organizational reform; international human resource development and change; interactions of gender and race/ethnicity on learning and leadership; development of initiatives to develop intercultural sensitivity and global awareness; leadership theory and development in educational, work-based, and other organizations. Total annual research expenditures: $836,434. *Unit head:* Dr. Rebecca Ropers-Huilman, Chair, 612-624-1006, Fax: 612-624-3377, E-mail: ropers@umn.edu. *Application contact:* Dr. Jennifer Engler, Assistant Dean, 612-626-2887, Fax: 612-626-7496, E-mail: engle009@umn.edu.
Website: http://www.cehd.umn.edu/olpd/.

University of Missouri, Graduate School, College of Education, Department of Learning, Teaching and Curriculum, Columbia, MO 65211. Offers agricultural education (M Ed, PhD, Ed S); art education (M Ed, PhD, Ed S); business and office education (M Ed, PhD, Ed S); early childhood education (M Ed, PhD, Ed S); elementary education (M Ed, PhD, Ed S); English education (M Ed, PhD, Ed S); foreign language education (M Ed, PhD, Ed S); health education and promotion (M Ed, PhD); learning and instruction (M Ed); marketing education (M Ed, PhD, Ed S); mathematics education (M Ed, PhD, Ed S); music education (M Ed, PhD, Ed S); reading education (M Ed, PhD, Ed S); science education (M Ed, PhD, Ed S); social studies education (M Ed, PhD, Ed S); vocational education (M Ed, PhD, Ed S). Part-time programs available. *Faculty:* 26 full-time (16 women), 3 part-time/adjunct (2 women). *Students:* 186 full-time (143 women), 197 part-time (172 women); includes 19 minority (4 Black or African American, non-Hispanic/Latino; 4 Asian, non-Hispanic/Latino; 6 Hispanic/Latino; 5 Two or more races, non-Hispanic/Latino), 25 international. Average age 31. 288 applicants, 65% accepted, 160 enrolled. In 2013, 202 master's, 18 doctorates, 7 other advanced degrees awarded. Terminal master's awarded for partial completion of doctoral program. *Degree requirements:* For doctorate, thesis/dissertation. *Entrance requirements:* For master's and Ed S, GRE General Test or MAT, minimum GPA of 3.0; for doctorate, GRE General Test, minimum GPA of 3.0. Additional exam requirements/recommendations for international students: Required—TOEFL (minimum score 600 paper-based; 100 iBT). *Application deadline:* For fall admission, 12/1 priority date for domestic and international students. Applications are processed on a rolling basis. Application fee: $55 ($75 for international students). Electronic applications accepted. *Financial support:* Fellowships, research assistantships, teaching assistantships, institutionally sponsored loans, traineeships, health care benefits, and unspecified assistantships available. Support available to part-time students. *Faculty research:* Curriculum development and research, teacher education, art education, business and marketing, early childhood education, English education, literacy/reading education, mathematics education, music education, science education, social studies education. *Unit head:* Dr. James Tarr, Associate Division Director, 573-882-4034, E-mail: tarrj@missouri.edu. *Application contact:* Fran Colley, Academic Advisor, 573-882-6462, E-mail: colleyf@missouri.edu.
Website: http://education.missouri.edu/LTC/.

University of Nebraska–Lincoln, Graduate College, College of Education and Human Sciences, Department of Teaching, Learning and Teacher Education, Lincoln, NE 68588. Offers adult and continuing education (MA); educational studies (Ed D, PhD), including special education (Ed D); teaching, learning and teacher education (M Ed, MA, MST, Ed D, PhD); vocational and adult education (M Ed, MA). *Accreditation:* NCATE. *Degree requirements:* For master's, thesis optional. *Entrance requirements:* Additional exam requirements/recommendations for international students: Required—TOEFL (minimum score 550 paper-based). Electronic applications accepted. *Faculty research:* Teacher education, instructional leadership, literacy education, technology, improvement of school curriculum.

University of New England, College of Arts and Sciences, Program in Education, Biddeford, ME 04005-9526. Offers advanced educational leadership (CAGS); career and technical education (MS Ed, CAGS); curriculum and instruction strategies (CAGS); curriculum and instruction strategy (MS Ed); educational leadership (MS Ed, CAGS); inclusion education (MS Ed); leadership, ethics and change (CAGS); literacy K-12 (MS Ed, CAGS); teaching methodologies (MS Ed). Part-time and evening/weekend programs available. Postbaccalaureate distance learning degree programs offered (no on-campus study). *Faculty:* 5 full-time (4 women), 17 part-time/adjunct (9 women). *Students:* 295 full-time (228 women), 233 part-time (175 women); includes 26 minority (19 Black or African American, non-Hispanic/Latino; 2 American Indian or Alaska Native, non-Hispanic/Latino; 2 Asian, non-Hispanic/Latino; 2 Hispanic/Latino; 1 Two or more races, non-Hispanic/Latino). Average age 37. 289 applicants, 84% accepted, 189 enrolled. In 2013, 257 master's, 106 CAGSs awarded. *Degree requirements:* For master's, collaborative action research project, integrative seminar portfolio. *Entrance requirements:* For master's, teaching certificate, 2 years of teaching experience. *Application deadline:* For fall admission, 9/15 for domestic students; for spring admission, 1/15 for domestic students. Applications are processed on a rolling basis. Application fee: $40. Electronic applications accepted. *Financial support:* Application deadline: 5/1; applicants required to submit FAFSA. *Faculty research:* Distance learning,

effective teaching, transition planning, adult learning. *Unit head:* Paulette St. Ours, Associate Dean, College of Arts and Sciences, 207-602-2400, E-mail: pstours@une.edu. *Application contact:* Dr. Cynthia Forrest, Vice President for Student Affairs, 207-221-4225, Fax: 207-523-1925, E-mail: gradadmissions@une.edu.
Website: http://www.une.edu/cas/education/msonline.cfm.

University of Northern Iowa, Graduate College, College of Humanities, Arts and Sciences, Department of Technology, Doctor of Technology Program, Cedar Falls, IA 50614. Offers DT. *Students:* 8 full-time (1 woman), 9 part-time (5 women); includes 1 minority (Black or African American, non-Hispanic/Latino), 8 international. 13 applicants, 85% accepted, 8 enrolled. In 2013, 2 doctorates awarded. Application fee: $50 ($70 for international students). *Unit head:* Dr. Julie Zhang, Coordinator, 319-273-2596, Fax: 319-273-5818, E-mail: julie.zhang@uni.edu. *Application contact:* Laurie S. Russell, Record Analyst, 319-273-2623, Fax: 319-273-2885, E-mail: laurie.russell@uni.edu.
Website: http://www.uni.edu/tech/DT.

University of Northern Iowa, Graduate College, College of Humanities, Arts and Sciences, Department of Technology, Master of Science in Technology Program, Cedar Falls, IA 50614. Offers MS. *Students:* 7 full-time (0 women), 26 part-time (2 women); includes 1 minority (Black or African American, non-Hispanic/Latino), 8 international. 25 applicants, 60% accepted, 8 enrolled. In 2013, 8 master's awarded. Application fee: $50 ($70 for international students). *Unit head:* Dr. Mohammed F. Fahmy, Department Head, 319-273-2758, Fax: 319-273-5818, E-mail: mohammed.fahmy@uni.edu. *Application contact:* Laurie S. Russell, Record Analyst, 319-273-2623, Fax: 319-273-2885, E-mail: laurie.russell@uni.edu.
Website: http://www.uni.edu/tech/masters-program.

University of North Texas, Robert B. Toulouse School of Graduate Studies, Denton, TN 76203-5017. Offers accounting (MS, PhD); applied anthropology (MA, MS); applied behavior analysis (Certificate); applied technology and performance improvement (M Ed, MS, PhD); art education (MA, PhD); art history (MA); art museum education (Certificate); arts leadership (Certificate); audiology (Au D); behavior analysis (MS); biochemistry and molecular biology (MS, PhD); biology (MA, MS, PhD); business (PhD); business computer information systems (PhD); chemistry (MS, PhD); clinical psychology (PhD); communication studies (MA, MS); computer engineering (MS); computer science (MS); computer science and engineering (PhD); counseling (M Ed, MS, PhD), including clinical mental health counseling (MS), college and university counseling (M Ed, MS), elementary school counseling (M Ed, MS), secondary school counseling (M Ed, MS); counseling psychology (PhD); creative writing (MA); criminal justice (MS); curriculum and instruction (M Ed, PhD), including curriculum studies (PhD), early childhood studies (PhD), language and literacy studies (PhD); decision sciences (MBA); design (MA, MFA), including fashion design (MFA), innovation studies, interior design (MFA); early childhood studies (MS); economics (MS); educational leadership (M Ed, Ed D, PhD); educational psychology (MS), including family studies, gifted and talented (MS, PhD), human development, learning and cognition, research, measurement and evaluation; educational research (PhD), including gifted and talented (MS, PhD), human development and family studies, psychological aspects of sports and exercise, research, measurement and statistics; electrical engineering (MS); emergency management (MPA); engineering systems (MS); English (MA, PhD); environmental science (MS, PhD); experimental psychology (PhD); finance (MBA, MS, PhD); financial management (MPA); French (MA); health psychology and behavioral medicine (PhD); health services management (MBA); higher education (M Ed, Ed D, PhD); history (MA, MS, PhD), including European history (PhD), military history (PhD), United States history (PhD); hospitality management (MS); human resources management (MPA); information science (MS, PhD); information technologies (MBA); information technology and decision sciences (MS); interdisciplinary studies (MA, MS); international sustainable tourism (MS); jazz studies (MM); journalism (MA, MJ, Graduate Certificate), including interactive and virtual digital communication (Graduate Certificate), narrative journalism (Graduate Certificate), public relations (Graduate Certificate); kinesiology (MS); learning technologies (MS, PhD); library science (MS); local government management (MPA); logistics and supply chain management (MBA, PhD); long-term care, senior housing, and aging services (MA, MS); management science (PhD); marketing (MBA, PhD); materials science and engineering (MS, PhD); mathematics (MA, PhD); merchandising (MS); music (MA, MM Ed, PhD), including ethnomusicology (MA), music education (MM Ed, PhD), music theory (MA, PhD), musicology (MA, PhD), performance (MA); nonprofit management (MPA); operations and supply chain management (MBA); performance (MM, DMA); philosophy (MA, PhD); physics (MS, PhD); political science (MA, MS, PhD); public administration and management (PhD), including emergency management, nonprofit management, public financial management, urban management; radio, television and film (MA, MFA); recreation, event and sport management (MS); rehabilitation counseling (MS, Certificate); sociology (MA, MS, PhD); Spanish (MA); special education (M Ed, PhD), including autism intervention (PhD), emotional/behavioral disorders (PhD), mild/moderate disabilities (PhD); speech-language pathology (MA, MS); strategic management (MBA); studio art (MFA); taxation (MS); teaching (M Ed); MBA/MS; MS/MPH; MSES/MBA. Part-time and evening/weekend programs available. Postbaccalaureate distance learning degree programs offered. *Faculty:* 661 full-time (213 women), 240 part-time/adjunct (144 women). *Students:* 3,106 full-time (1,620 women), 3,543 part-time (2,221 women); includes 1,740 minority (533 Black or African American, non-Hispanic/Latino; 15 American Indian or Alaska Native, non-Hispanic/Latino; 286 Asian, non-Hispanic/Latino; 746 Hispanic/Latino; 3 Native Hawaiian or other Pacific Islander, non-Hispanic/Latino; 157 Two or more races, non-Hispanic/Latino), 1,145 international. Average age 32. 6,289 applicants, 43% accepted, 1751 enrolled. In 2013, 1,778 master's, 239 doctorates, 10 other advanced degrees awarded. Terminal master's awarded for partial completion of doctoral program. *Degree requirements:* For master's, variable foreign language requirement, comprehensive exam (for some programs), thesis (for some programs); for doctorate, variable foreign language requirement, comprehensive exam (for some programs), thesis/dissertation; for other advanced degree, variable foreign language requirement, comprehensive exam (for some programs). *Entrance requirements:* For master's and doctorate, GRE, GMAT. Additional exam requirements/recommendations for international students: Required—TOEFL (minimum score 550 paper-based; 79 iBT). *Application deadline:* For fall admission, 7/15 for domestic students, 3/15 for international students; for spring admission, 11/15 for domestic students, 9/15 for international students; for summer admission, 5/1 for domestic students. Applications are processed on a rolling basis. Application fee: $60. Electronic applications accepted. *Financial support:* Fellowships with partial tuition reimbursements, research assistantships with partial tuition reimbursements, teaching assistantships, career-related internships or fieldwork, Federal Work-Study, institutionally sponsored loans, scholarships/grants, health care benefits, and library assistantships available. Support available to part-time students. Financial award applicants required to submit FAFSA. *Unit head:* Mark Wardell, Dean, 940-565-2383, E-mail: mark.wardell@unt.edu. *Application contact:* Toulouse School of Graduate Studies, 940-565-2383, Fax: 940-565-2141, E-mail: gradsch@unt.edu.
Website: http://tsgs.unt.edu/.

University of Phoenix–Phoenix Campus, College of Education, Tempe, AZ 85282-2371. Offers administration and supervision (MA Ed); adult education and training (MA Ed); curriculum and instruction reading (MA Ed); early childhood education (MA Ed); education studies (MA Ed); elementary teacher education (MA Ed); secondary teacher education (MA Ed); special education (MA Ed); teacher leadership (MA Ed). Evening/weekend programs available. Postbaccalaureate distance learning degree programs offered. *Entrance requirements:* Additional exam requirements/recommendations for international students: Required—TOEFL, TOEIC (Test of English as an International Communication), Berlitz Online English Proficiency Exam, PTE, or IELTS. Electronic applications accepted. *Expenses:* Contact institution.

University of South Africa, Institute for Science and Technology Education, Pretoria, South Africa. Offers mathematics, science and technology education (M Sc, PhD).

University of Southern Mississippi, Graduate School, College of Education and Psychology, Department of Technology Education, Hattiesburg, MS 39406-0001. Offers business technology education (MS); instructional technology (MS); technical occupational education (MS). Part-time programs available. *Faculty:* 6 full-time (3 women). *Students:* 4 full-time (3 women), 22 part-time (15 women); includes 6 minority (5 Black or African American, non-Hispanic/Latino; 1 Hispanic/Latino), 3 international. Average age 38. 5 applicants, 100% accepted, 4 enrolled. In 2013, 2 master's awarded. *Degree requirements:* For master's, comprehensive exam, thesis (for some programs). *Entrance requirements:* For master's, GRE General Test, MAT, minimum GPA of 2.75 in last 60 hours. Additional exam requirements/recommendations for international students: Required—TOEFL. *Application deadline:* For fall admission, 3/1 priority date for domestic students, 3/1 for international students. Applications are processed on a rolling basis. Application fee: $50. *Financial support:* In 2013–14, 2 research assistantships with full tuition reimbursements (averaging $9,000 per year), 1 teaching assistantship with full tuition reimbursement (averaging $10,000 per year) were awarded; Federal Work-Study also available. Financial award application deadline: 3/15; financial award applicants required to submit FAFSA. *Faculty research:* Occupational competency, professional development for vocational-technical. *Total annual research expenditures:* $166,068. *Unit head:* Dr. Edward C. Mann, Chair, 601-266-4446, Fax: 601-266-5957, E-mail: edward.mann@usm.edu. *Application contact:* Shonna Breland, Manager of Graduate Admissions, 601-266-6563, Fax: 601-266-5138.
Website: http://www.usm.edu/technologyeducation.

University of South Florida, College of Education, Department of Adult, Career and Higher Education, Tampa, FL 33620-9951. Offers adult education (MA, Ed D, PhD, Ed S); career and technical education (MA); career and workforce education (PhD); higher education/community college teaching (MA, Ed D, PhD); vocational education (Ed S). Part-time programs available. Postbaccalaureate distance learning degree programs offered (minimal on-campus study). *Degree requirements:* For master's, comprehensive exam; for doctorate, comprehensive exam, thesis/dissertation, philosophies of inquiry; multiple research methods; for Ed S, comprehensive exam, thesis. *Entrance requirements:* For master's, minimum GPA of 3.0 in last 60 hours of course work; for doctorate and Ed S, GRE General Test, GRE Writing Test. Additional exam requirements/recommendations for international students: Required—TOEFL (minimum score 500 paper-based; 91 iBT). Electronic applications accepted. *Faculty research:* Community college leadership; integration of academic, career and technical education; competency-based education; continuing education administration; adult learning and development.

The University of Texas at Tyler, College of Business and Technology, School of Human Resource Development and Technology, Tyler, TX 75799-0001. Offers human resource development (MS, PhD); industrial management (MS). Part-time and evening/weekend programs available. Postbaccalaureate distance learning degree programs offered (no on-campus study). *Degree requirements:* For master's, comprehensive exam. *Entrance requirements:* For master's, GRE General Test or MAT. Additional exam requirements/recommendations for international students: Required—TOEFL. Electronic applications accepted. *Faculty research:* Human resource development.

The University of Toledo, College of Graduate Studies, Judith Herb College of Education, Department of Curriculum and Instruction, Toledo, OH 43606-3390. Offers art education (ME); career and technical education (ME); career-technical education (Ed S); curriculum and instruction (ME, PhD, Ed S); early childhood education (PhD, Ed S); education and biology (MES); education and chemistry (MES); education and economics (MAE); education and English (MAE); education and French (MAE); education and geography (MAE); education and geology (MES); education and German (MAE); education and history (MAE); education and mathematics (MAE, MES); education and physics (MES); education and political science (MAE); education and sociology (MAE); education and Spanish (MAE); educational media (PhD); educational technology (ME); educational technology: virtual educator (Certificate); elementary education (PhD); English as a second language (MAE); gifted and talented (PhD); middle childhood education licensure (ME); music education (MME); secondary education (PhD); secondary education licensure (ME); special education (PhD, Ed S). *Accreditation:* NCATE. Part-time and evening/weekend programs available. *Faculty:* 41. *Students:* 53 full-time (30 women), 154 part-time (111 women); includes 21 minority (16 Black or African American, non-Hispanic/Latino; 4 Hispanic/Latino; 1 Two or more races, non-Hispanic/Latino), 21 international. Average age 34. 82 applicants, 79% accepted, 47 enrolled. In 2013, 80 master's, 5 doctorates awarded. *Degree requirements:* For master's, comprehensive exam, thesis or alternative; for doctorate, comprehensive exam, thesis/dissertation; for other advanced degree, thesis optional. *Entrance requirements:* For master's, doctorate, and other advanced degree, minimum cumulative GPA of 2.7 for all previous academic work, letters of recommendation. Additional exam requirements/recommendations for international students: Required—TOEFL (minimum score 550 paper-based; 80 iBT). *Application deadline:* For fall admission, 1/15 priority date for domestic and international students. Applications are processed on a rolling basis. Application fee: $45 ($75 for international students). Electronic applications accepted. *Financial support:* In 2013–14, 5 research assistantships with full and partial tuition reimbursements (averaging $13,200 per year), 11 teaching assistantships with full and partial tuition reimbursements (averaging $8,809 per year) were awarded; career-related internships or fieldwork, Federal Work-Study, institutionally sponsored loans, scholarships/grants, tuition waivers (full and partial), unspecified assistantships, and administrative assistantships also available. Support available to part-time students. *Unit head:* Dr. Joan Kaderavek, Chair, 419-530-5373, E-mail: eigh.chiarelott@utoledo.edu. *Application contact:* Graduate School Office, 419-530-4723, Fax: 419-530-4724, E-mail: grdsch@utnet.utoledo.edu.
Website: http://www.utoledo.edu/eduhshs/.

University of Victoria, Faculty of Graduate Studies, Faculty of Education, Department of Curriculum and Instruction, Victoria, BC V8W 2Y2, Canada. Offers art education (M Ed, PhD); curriculum studies (M Ed, MA, PhD); early childhood education (M Ed, PhD); educational studies (PhD); language and literacy (M Ed, MA, PhD); mathematics (M Ed, MA, PhD); music education (M Ed, MA, PhD); science (M Ed, MA, PhD); social studies (M Ed, MA); social, cultural and foundational studies (MA, PhD); technology and environmental education (PhD). Part-time programs available. *Degree requirements:* For master's, thesis, project (M Ed); for doctorate, comprehensive exam, thesis/dissertation. *Entrance requirements:* For master's, minimum B average. Additional exam requirements/recommendations for international students: Required—TOEFL (minimum score 575 paper-based), IELTS (minimum score 7). Electronic applications accepted. *Faculty research:* Elementary and secondary English, language arts, curriculum theory

and practice, educational media and technology, educational administration and leadership, history and philosophy of education.

University of West Florida, College of Professional Studies, Department of Applied Science, Technology and Administration, Pensacola, FL 32514-5750. Offers career and technical education (M Ed); curriculum and instruction (Ed S); curriculum and instruction: instructional technology (Ed D); educational leadership (M Ed), including education and training management; instructional technology (M Ed), including educational leadership, instructional technology. *Entrance requirements:* For master's, GRE, GMAT, or MAT, letter of intent, names of references. Additional exam requirements/recommendations for international students: Required—TOEFL (minimum score 550 paper-based). Electronic applications accepted.

University of Wisconsin–Stout, Graduate School, School of Education, Program in Career and Technical Education, Menomonie, WI 54751. Offers MS, Ed S. Part-time programs available. *Degree requirements:* For master's and Ed S, thesis. *Entrance requirements:* For master's, minimum GPA of 2.75; for Ed S, minimum GPA of 3.25. Additional exam requirements/recommendations for international students: Required—TOEFL (minimum score 500 paper-based; 61 iBT). Electronic applications accepted. *Faculty research:* Needs assessment, task analysis, instructional development, learning technologies.

University of Wisconsin–Stout, Graduate School, School of Education, Program in Industrial/Technology Education, Menomonie, WI 54751. Offers MS. Part-time programs available. *Degree requirements:* For master's, thesis. *Entrance requirements:* For master's, minimum GPA of 2.75. Additional exam requirements/recommendations for international students: Required—TOEFL (minimum score 500 paper-based; 61 iBT). Electronic applications accepted. *Faculty research:* Gender equity, instructional design, cognitive processes, socio-cultural impacts.

Utah State University, School of Graduate Studies, College of Engineering, Department of Engineering and Technology Education, Logan, UT 84322. Offers industrial technology (MS). Part-time and evening/weekend programs available. *Degree requirements:* For master's, thesis optional. *Entrance requirements:* For master's, GRE General Test, MAT, minimum GPA of 3.0 in last 30 hours of course work. Additional exam requirements/recommendations for international students: Required—TOEFL. *Faculty research:* Computer-aided design drafting, technology and the public school, materials, electronics, aviation.

Valley City State University, Online Master of Education Program, Valley City, ND 58072. Offers elementary education (M Ed); English education (M Ed); library and information technologies (M Ed); teaching and technology (M Ed); teaching English language learners (ELL) (M Ed); technology education (M Ed). *Accreditation:* NCATE. Part-time and evening/weekend programs available. Postbaccalaureate distance learning degree programs offered (no on-campus study). *Faculty:* 21 full-time (14 women), 7 part-time/adjunct (all women). *Students:* 2 full-time (both women), 151 part-time (102 women); includes 10 minority (1 Black or African American, non-Hispanic/Latino; 3 Asian, non-Hispanic/Latino; 2 Hispanic/Latino; 4 Two or more races, non-Hispanic/Latino), 1 international. Average age 34. 27 applicants, 93% accepted, 21 enrolled. In 2013, 45 master's awarded. *Degree requirements:* For master's, action research report, comprehensive portfolio. *Entrance requirements:* For master's, GRE, MAT, PRAXIS II or National Teaching Board for Professional Standards (if GPA is less than 3.0). Additional exam requirements/recommendations for international students: Required—TOEFL (minimum score 525 paper-based; 71 iBT); Recommended—IELTS (minimum score 5.5). *Application deadline:* For fall admission, 7/19 priority date for domestic and international students; for spring admission, 12/13 priority date for domestic and international students; for summer admission, 5/9 priority date for domestic and international students. Applications are processed on a rolling basis. Application fee: $35. Electronic applications accepted. *Expenses:* Contact institution. *Financial support:* In 2013–14, 24 students received support. Scholarships/grants and tuition waivers (full and partial) available. Financial award application deadline: 5/15; financial award applicants required to submit FAFSA. *Faculty research:* Academically at-risk students in higher education, communication pedagogy and technology, gender communication, computer-mediated communication, creativity in music, STEM education in K-12. *Total annual research expenditures:* $26,000. *Unit head:* Dr. Gary Thompson, Dean, 701-845-7197, E-mail: gary.thompson@vcsu.edu. *Application contact:* Misty Lindgren, Graduate Studies, 701-845-7303, Fax: 701-845-7190, E-mail: misty.lindgren@vcsu.edu.
Website: http://www.vcsu.edu/graduate.

Virginia Polytechnic Institute and State University, Graduate School, College of Liberal Arts and Human Sciences, Blacksburg, VA 24061. Offers career and technical education (MS Ed, Ed D, PhD, Ed S); communication (MA); counselor education (MA Ed, Ed D, PhD, Ed S); creative writing (MFA); curriculum and instruction (MA Ed, Ed D, PhD, Ed S); educational leadership and policy studies (MA Ed, Ed D, PhD, Ed S); educational research and evaluation (PhD); English (MA); foreign languages, cultures, and literatures (MA); higher education and student affairs (MA Ed); history (MA); human development (MS, PhD); material culture and public humanities (MA); philosophy (MA); political science (MA); rhetoric and writing (PhD); science and technology studies (MS, PhD); social, political, ethical, and cultural thought (PhD); sociology (MS, PhD); theater arts (MFA). *Faculty:* 410 full-time (211 women), 6 part-time/adjunct (5 women). *Students:* 688 full-time (464 women), 576 part-time (372 women); includes 243 minority (144 Black or African American, non-Hispanic/Latino; 3 American Indian or Alaska Native, non-Hispanic/Latino; 29 Asian, non-Hispanic/Latino; 48 Hispanic/Latino; 1 Native Hawaiian or other Pacific Islander, non-Hispanic/Latino; 18 Two or more races, non-Hispanic/Latino), 84 international. Average age 34. 1,054 applicants, 48% accepted, 374 enrolled. In 2013, 314 master's, 74 doctorates, 14 other advanced degrees awarded. *Degree requirements:* For master's, comprehensive exam (for some programs), thesis (for some programs); for doctorate, comprehensive exam (for some programs), thesis/dissertation (for some programs). *Entrance requirements:* For master's and doctorate, GRE/GMAT (may vary by department). Additional exam requirements/recommendations for international students: Required—TOEFL (minimum score 550 paper-based). *Application deadline:* For fall admission, 8/1 for domestic students, 4/1 for international students; for spring admission, 1/1 for domestic students, 9/1 for international students. Applications are processed on a rolling basis. Application fee: $75. Electronic applications accepted. *Expenses:* Tuition, state resident: full-time $11,185; part-time $621.50 per credit hour. Tuition, nonresident: full-time $22,146; part-time $1230.25 per credit hour. *Required fees:* $2442; $449.25 per semester. Tuition and fees vary according to course load, campus/location and program. *Financial support:* In 2013–14, 19 research assistantships with full tuition reimbursements (averaging $17,115 per year), 205 teaching assistantships with full tuition reimbursements (averaging $14,433 per year) were awarded. Financial award application deadline: 3/1; financial award applicants required to submit FAFSA. *Total annual research expenditures:* $6.8 million. *Unit head:* Joan Hirt, Interim Dean, 540-231-6779, Fax: 540-231-7157, E-mail: jbhirt@vt.edu. *Application contact:* Melissa Elliott, Executive Assistant, 540-231-6779, Fax: 540-231-7157, E-mail: elliott1@vt.edu.
Website: http://www.clahs.vt.edu/.

Virginia Polytechnic Institute and State University, VT Online, Blacksburg, VA 24061. Offers advanced transportation systems (Certificate); aerospace engineering (MS); agricultural and life sciences (MSLFS); business information systems (Graduate Certificate); career and technical education (MS); civil engineering (MS); computer engineering (M Eng, MS); decision support systems (Graduate Certificate); eLearning leadership (MA); electrical engineering (M Eng, MS); engineering administration (MEA); environmental engineering (Certificate); environmental politics and policy (Graduate Certificate); environmental sciences and engineering (MS); foundations of political analysis (Graduate Certificate); health product risk management (Graduate Certificate); industrial and systems engineering (MS); information policy and society (Graduate Certificate); information security (Graduate Certificate); information technology (MIT); instructional technology (MA); integrative STEM education (MA Ed); liberal arts (Graduate Certificate); life sciences: health product risk management (MS); natural resources (MNR, Graduate Certificate); networking (Graduate Certificate); nonprofit and nongovernmental organization management (Graduate Certificate); ocean engineering (MS); political science (MA); security studies (Graduate Certificate); software development (Graduate Certificate). *Expenses:* Tuition, state resident: full-time $11,185; part-time $621.50 per credit hour. Tuition, nonresident: full-time $22,146; part-time $1230.25 per credit hour. *Required fees:* $2442; $449.25 per semester. Tuition and fees vary according to course load, campus/location and program.

Virginia State University, School of Graduate Studies, Research, and Outreach, School of Liberal Arts and Education, Department of Graduate Professional Education Programs, Program in Career and Technical Studies, Petersburg, VA 23806-0001. Offers M Ed, MS, CAGS. *Degree requirements:* For master's, thesis (for some programs).

Washington State University, Graduate School, College of Education, Department of Teaching and Learning, Program in Language, Literacy and Technology, Pullman, WA 99164. Offers PhD. *Degree requirements:* For doctorate, comprehensive exam, thesis/dissertation, written and oral exam. *Entrance requirements:* For doctorate, minimum GPA of 3.0, letters of recommendation, transcripts, resume/curriculum vitae, personal statement, writing sample. Additional exam requirements/recommendations for international students: Required—TOEFL (minimum score 550 paper-based; 80 iBT). Electronic applications accepted. *Faculty research:* Learning environments, critical sociolinguistics, language policy, language education, differentiated instruction; literacy and technology, bilingual literacies.

Wayne State College, School of Education and Counseling, Department of Educational Foundations and Leadership, Program in Curriculum and Instruction, Wayne, NE 68787. Offers alternative education (MSE); business and information technology education (MSE); communication arts education (MSE); early childhood education (MSE); elementary education (MSE); English as a second language (MSE); English education (MSE); family and consumer sciences education (MSE); industrial technology and vocational education (MSE); learning communities (MSE); mathematics education (MSE); music education (MSE); science education (MSE); social science education (MSE). *Accreditation:* NCATE. Part-time and evening/weekend programs available. *Degree requirements:* For master's, comprehensive exam, thesis optional. *Entrance requirements:* For master's, GRE General Test. Additional exam requirements/recommendations for international students: Required—TOEFL (minimum score 550 paper-based).

Wayne State University, College of Education, Division of Teacher Education, Detroit, MI 48202. Offers art education (M Ed), including art therapy; autism spectrum disorders (Certificate); bilingual/bicultural education (M Ed, Certificate); career and technical education (M Ed, Certificate); cognitive impairment (Certificate); curriculum and instruction (Ed D, PhD, Ed S), including art education (PhD), bilingual education (Ed D, Ed S), bilingual-bicultural education (PhD), career and technical education (MAT, Ed D, PhD, Ed S), early childhood education (MAT, Ed D, PhD, Ed S), elementary education, English as a second language (MAT, Ed D, Ed S), English education (MAT, Ed D, PhD, Ed S), foreign language education (MAT, PhD), K-12 curriculum, mathematics education (MAT, Ed D, PhD, Ed S), science education (MAT, Ed D, PhD, Ed S), secondary education, social studies education (MAT, Ed S), social studies education: secondary (Ed D, PhD); early childhood education (M Ed, Certificate); elementary education (M Ed, MAT), including children's literature (MAT), early childhood education (MAT, Ed D, PhD, Ed S), general elementary education (MAT); elementary or secondary education (MAT), including bilingual/bicultural education, English as a second language (MAT, Ed D, Ed S), mathematics education (MAT, Ed D, PhD, Ed S), science education (MAT, Ed D, PhD, Ed S), social studies education (MAT, Ed S); emotionally impaired (Certificate); English as a second language (Certificate); English education (M Ed), including secondary; foreign language education (M Ed); K-12 reading specialist (Certificate); learning disabilities (Certificate); mathematics education (M Ed), including secondary; reading (M Ed, Ed S); reading, language and literature (Ed D); science education (M Ed), including secondary; secondary education (MAT), including art education (K-12), career and technical education (MAT, Ed D, PhD, Ed S), English education (MAT, Ed D, PhD, Ed S), foreign language education (MAT, PhD), kinesiology; social studies education (M Ed), including secondary; special education (M Ed, MAT, Ed D, PhD, Ed S); visual arts education (Certificate). Part-time programs available. *Faculty:* 36 full-time (25 women), 55 part-time/adjunct (43 women). *Students:* 218 full-time (163 women), 448 part-time (344 women); includes 218 minority (177 Black or African American, non-Hispanic/Latino; 2 American Indian or Alaska Native, non-Hispanic/Latino; 11 Asian, non-Hispanic/Latino; 19 Hispanic/Latino; 1 Native Hawaiian or other Pacific Islander, non-Hispanic/Latino; 8 Two or more races, non-Hispanic/Latino), 10 international. Average age 37. 258 applicants, 30% accepted, 52 enrolled. In 2013, 183 master's, 10 doctorates, 35 other advanced degrees awarded. *Degree requirements:* For master's, thesis, essay or project (for some M Ed programs), professional field experience (for MAT programs); for doctorate, thesis/dissertation. *Entrance requirements:* For master's, Michigan Basic Skills Test (MA in teaching), admission to the graduate school, verification of participation in group work with children and Michigan State Police Criminal Background check; for doctorate, minimum undergraduate GPA of 3.0, graduate 3.5; interview, curriculum vitae; references. Additional exam requirements/recommendations for international students: Required—TOEFL (minimum score 550 paper-based; 79 iBT), TWE (minimum score 5.5), Michigan English Language Assessment Battery (minimum score 85); Recommended—IELTS (minimum score 6.5). *Application deadline:* For fall admission, 6/1 priority date for domestic students, 5/1 priority date for international students; for winter admission, 10/1 priority date for domestic students, 9/1 priority date for international students; for spring admission, 2/1 priority date for domestic students, 1/1 priority date for international students. Applications are processed on a rolling basis. Application fee: $0. Electronic applications accepted. *Expenses:* Tuition, state resident: part-time $554.15 per credit. Tuition, nonresident: part-time $1200.35 per credit. *Required fees:* $42.15 per credit. $268.30 per semester. Tuition and fees vary according to course load and program. *Financial support:* In 2013–14, 83 students received support, including 1 fellowship (averaging $16,842 per year), 1 research assistantship with tuition reimbursement available (averaging $21,229 per year); career-related internships or fieldwork, Federal Work-Study, scholarships/grants, health care benefits, and unspecified assistantships also available. Support available to part-time students. Financial award application deadline: 3/31; financial award applicants required to submit FAFSA. *Faculty research:* Improving students' skill achievement in mathematics; improving elementary children's understanding of informational text; teachers' use of their pedagogical and mathematical

knowledge in the interactive work of teaching; the intersection of identity construction in teaching and learning; identifying effective methods of literacy instruction and assessments for bilingual students in elementary language arts classrooms. *Total annual research expenditures:* $368,105. *Unit head:* Dr. Kathleen Crawford-McKinney, Assistant Dean, 313-577-0122. *Application contact:* Janice Green, Assistant Dean, 313-577-1605, E-mail: jwgreen@wayne.edu.
Website: http://coe.wayne.edu/ted/index.php.

Western Michigan University, Graduate College, College of Education and Human Development, Department of Family and Consumer Sciences, Program in Career and Technical Education, Kalamazoo, MI 49008. Offers MA. *Accreditation:* NCATE.

Westfield State University, Division of Graduate and Continuing Education, Department of Education, Program in Occupational Education, Westfield, MA 01086. Offers M Ed, CAGS. *Accreditation:* NCATE. Part-time and evening/weekend programs available. *Degree requirements:* For master's, comprehensive exam. *Entrance requirements:* For master's, GRE General Test or MAT, minimum undergraduate GPA of 2.7.

Wilmington University, College of Education, New Castle, DE 19720-6491. Offers applied technology in education (M Ed); career and technical education (M Ed); educational leadership (Ed D); elementary and secondary school counseling (M Ed); elementary studies (M Ed); ESOL literacy (M Ed); higher education leadership (Ed D); instruction: gifted and talented (M Ed); instruction: teacher of reading (M Ed); instruction: teaching and learning (M Ed); organizational leadership (Ed D); school leadership (M Ed); secondary education (MAT); special education (M Ed). *Accreditation:* NCATE. Part-time and evening/weekend programs available. *Entrance requirements:* For master's, 2 letters of recommendation, interview. Additional exam requirements/recommendations for international students: Required—TOEFL (minimum score 500 paper-based). Electronic applications accepted.

Wright State University, School of Graduate Studies, College of Education and Human Services, Department of Educational Leadership, Programs in Educational Leadership, Dayton, OH 45435. Offers curriculum and instruction: teacher leader (MA); educational administrative specialist: teacher leader (M Ed); educational administrative specialist: vocational education administration (M Ed, MA); student affairs in higher education-administration (M Ed, MA). *Accreditation:* NCATE. *Degree requirements:* For master's, thesis (for some programs). *Entrance requirements:* For master's, GRE General Test, MAT. Additional exam requirements/recommendations for international students: Required—TOEFL.

Wright State University, School of Graduate Studies, College of Education and Human Services, Department of Teacher Education, Programs in Workforce Education, Dayton, OH 45435. Offers career, technology and vocational education (M Ed, MA); computer/technology education (M Ed, MA); library/media (M Ed, MA); vocational education (M Ed, MA). *Accreditation:* NCATE. *Degree requirements:* For master's, thesis (for some programs). *Entrance requirements:* For master's, GRE General Test, MAT. Additional exam requirements/recommendations for international students: Required—TOEFL.

ACADEMIC AND PROFESSIONAL PROGRAMS IN LAW

Section 27
Law

This section contains a directory of institutions offering graduate work in law. Additional information about programs listed in the directory may be obtained by writing directly to the dean of a graduate school or chair of a department at the address given in the directory.

For programs offering related work, see also in this book *Business Administration and Management* and *Social Work*. In the other guides in this series:

Graduate Programs in the Humanities, Arts & Social Sciences
See *Criminology and Forensics; Public, Regional, and Industrial Affairs; Economics;* and *Political Science and International Affairs*

Graduate Programs in the Physical Sciences, Mathematics, Agricultural Sciences, the Environment & Natural Resources
See *Environmental Sciences and Management*

Graduate Programs in Engineering & Applied Sciences
See *Management of Engineering and Technology*

CONTENTS

Program Directories

Environmental Law	1542
Health Law	1543
Intellectual Property Law	1545
Law	1547
Legal and Justice Studies	1567

Environmental Law

Baylor University, School of Law, Waco, TX 76798-7288. Offers administrative practice (JD); business litigation (JD); business transactions (JD); criminal practice (JD); estate planning (JD); general civil litigation (JD); healthcare (JD); intellectual property (JD); law (JD); real estate and natural resources (JD); JD/M Tax; JD/MBA; JD/MPPA. *Accreditation:* ABA. *Faculty:* 30 full-time (7 women), 45 part-time/adjunct (5 women). *Students:* 371 full-time (163 women), 8 part-time (2 women); includes 71 minority (6 Black or African American, non-Hispanic/Latino; 9 American Indian or Alaska Native, non-Hispanic/Latino; 14 Asian, non-Hispanic/Latino; 28 Hispanic/Latino; 14 Two or more races, non-Hispanic/Latino). Average age 24. 2,226 applicants, 37% accepted, 86 enrolled. In 2013, 176 doctorates awarded. *Entrance requirements:* For doctorate, LSAT. Additional exam requirements/recommendations for international students: Recommended—TOEFL. *Application deadline:* For fall admission, 3/1 for domestic and international students; for spring admission, 11/1 for domestic and international students; for summer admission, 2/1 for domestic and international students. Applications are processed on a rolling basis. Application fee: $0. Electronic applications accepted. Application fee is waived when completed online. *Expenses:* Contact institution. *Financial support:* In 2013–14, 296 students received support. Career-related internships or fieldwork and scholarships/grants available. Financial award application deadline: 3/1; financial award applicants required to submit FAFSA. *Unit head:* Dr. Bradley J. B. Toben, Dean, 254-710-1911, Fax: 254-710-2316. *Application contact:* Nicole Neeley, Assistant Dean of Admissions, 254-710-1911, Fax: 254-710-2316, E-mail: nicole_neeley@baylor.edu.
Website: http://www.baylor.edu/law.

Chapman University, School of Law, Orange, CA 92866. Offers advocacy and dispute resolution (JD); entertainment and media law (LL M); entertainment law (JD); environmental, land use, and real estate (JD); international law (JD); law (JD); prosecutorial science (LL M); tax law (JD); taxation (LL M); trial advocacy (LL M); JD/MBA; JD/MFA. *Accreditation:* ABA. Part-time and evening/weekend programs available. *Faculty:* 47 full-time (19 women), 35 part-time/adjunct (4 women). *Students:* 483 full-time (241 women), 71 part-time (28 women); includes 164 minority (5 Black or African American, non-Hispanic/Latino; 1 American Indian or Alaska Native, non-Hispanic/Latino; 84 Asian, non-Hispanic/Latino; 47 Hispanic/Latino; 1 Native Hawaiian or other Pacific Islander, non-Hispanic/Latino; 26 Two or more races, non-Hispanic/Latino), 76 international. Average age 26. 1,691 applicants, 51% accepted, 157 enrolled. In 2013, 36 master's, 187 doctorates awarded. *Entrance requirements:* For doctorate, LSAT, minimum undergraduate GPA of 2.75. Additional exam requirements/recommendations for international students: Required—TOEFL (minimum score 600 paper-based; 80 iBT). *Application deadline:* For fall admission, 4/15 priority date for domestic students. Applications are processed on a rolling basis. Application fee: $65. Electronic applications accepted. *Expenses:* Contact institution. *Financial support:* Fellowships, Federal Work-Study, and scholarships/grants available. Financial award applicants required to submit FAFSA. *Unit head:* Dr. Tom Campbell, Dean, 714-628-2500. *Application contact:* Karman Hsu, Assistant Dean of Admissions and Diversity Initiatives, 877-CHAPLAW, E-mail: mvargas@chapman.edu.
Website: http://www.chapman.edu/law/.

Florida State University, College of Law, Tallahassee, FL 32306-1601. Offers American law for foreign lawyers (LL M); environmental law and policy (LL M); law (JM, JD); JD/MBA; JD/MPA; JD/MS; JD/MSP; JD/MSW. *Accreditation:* ABA. *Faculty:* 57 full-time (26 women), 25 part-time/adjunct (6 women). *Students:* 661 full-time (283 women), 53 part-time (27 women); includes 161 minority (61 Black or African American, non-Hispanic/Latino; 11 American Indian or Alaska Native, non-Hispanic/Latino; 20 Asian, non-Hispanic/Latino; 65 Hispanic/Latino; 1 Native Hawaiian or other Pacific Islander, non-Hispanic/Latino; 3 Two or more races, non-Hispanic/Latino), 8 international. Average age 23. 2,022 applicants, 42% accepted, 170 enrolled. In 2013, 9 master's, 237 doctorates awarded. Terminal master's awarded for partial completion of doctoral program. *Degree requirements:* For master's, comprehensive exam (for some programs). *Entrance requirements:* For master's, one graduate-level standardized test (for JM), JD or equivalent degree (for LL M programs); for doctorate, LSAT. Additional exam requirements/recommendations for international students: Required—TOEFL (minimum score 600 paper-based; 100 iBT). *Application deadline:* For fall admission, 4/1 priority date for domestic and international students. Applications are processed on a rolling basis. Application fee: $30. Electronic applications accepted. *Expenses:* Contact institution. *Financial support:* In 2013–14, 300 students received support, including 55 research assistantships (averaging $1,183 per year), 11 teaching assistantships (averaging $1,835 per year); scholarships/grants and unspecified assistantships also available. Financial award application deadline: 3/1; financial award applicants required to submit FAFSA. *Faculty research:* Business law, environmental and land use law, international law, criminal law. *Total annual research expenditures:* $134,160. *Unit head:* Donald J. Weidner, Dean, 850-644-3400, Fax: 850-644-5487, E-mail: dweidner@law.fsu.edu. *Application contact:* Jennifer L. Kessinger, Director of Admissions and Records, 850-644-3787, Fax: 850-644-7284, E-mail: jkessing@law.fsu.edu.
Website: http://www.law.fsu.edu/.

Golden Gate University, School of Law, San Francisco, CA 94105-2968. Offers environmental law (LL M); intellectual property law (LL M); international legal studies (LL M, SJD); law (JD); taxation (LL M); U. S. legal studies (LL M); JD/MBA; JD/PhD. *Accreditation:* ABA. Part-time and evening/weekend programs available. *Degree requirements:* For doctorate, thesis/dissertation (for some programs). *Entrance requirements:* For doctorate, LSAT (for JD). Additional exam requirements/recommendations for international students: Required—TOEFL (minimum score 600 paper-based). Electronic applications accepted. *Expenses:* Contact institution. *Faculty research:* International law, intellectual property law, environmental law, real estate, civil rights.

Lehigh University, College of Arts and Sciences, Program in Environmental Initiative, Bethlehem, PA 18015. Offers environmental law and policy (Graduate Certificate); environmental policy design (MA). Part-time programs available. *Students:* 8 full-time (4 women), 2 part-time (both women); includes 1 minority (Hispanic/Latino), 1 international. Average age 26. 12 applicants, 83% accepted, 3 enrolled. In 2013, 6 master's awarded. *Degree requirements:* For master's, thesis or additional course work. *Entrance requirements:* For master's, GRE, minimum GPA of 2.75, 3.0 for last two undergraduate semesters, essay, 2 letters of recommendation. Additional exam requirements/recommendations for international students: Required—TOEFL (minimum score 85 iBT). *Application deadline:* For fall admission, 1/15 for domestic and international students; for spring admission, 12/1 for domestic and international students. Applications are processed on a rolling basis. Application fee: $75. Electronic applications accepted. *Financial support:* In 2013–14, 6 students received support, including 1 teaching assistantship with full tuition reimbursement available (averaging $18,850 per year); scholarships/grants, tuition waivers (partial), and community

fellowship and tuition remission (from College of Arts and Sciences) also available. Financial award application deadline: 1/15. *Faculty research:* Dissolved organic carbon in freshwater ecosystems, environmental law, politics, sustainability, policy (national and local), environmental justice, land use law and planning, paleoclimatology, global hydrology, sea levels and impact on risk management. *Unit head:* Dr. Donald P. Morris, Director, 610-758-5175, E-mail: dpm2@lehigh.edu. *Application contact:* Cassandra L. Petroski, Academic Coordinator, 610-758-4281, Fax: 610-758-6232, E-mail: cap211@lehigh.edu.
Website: http://ei.cas2.lehigh.edu/.

Lewis & Clark College, Lewis & Clark Law School, Portland, OR 97219. Offers environmental and natural resources law (LL M); law (JD). *Accreditation:* ABA. Part-time and evening/weekend programs available. *Entrance requirements:* For doctorate, LSAT. Additional exam requirements/recommendations for international students: Recommended—TOEFL (minimum score 600 paper-based). Electronic applications accepted. *Expenses:* Contact institution.

Pace University, Pace Law School, White Plains, NY 10603. Offers comparative legal studies (LL M); environmental law (LL M, SJD), including climate change (LL M), land use and sustainability (LL M); law (JD); JD/LL M; JD/MA; JD/MBA; JD/MEM; JD/MPA; JD/MS. JD/MA offered jointly with Sarah Lawrence College; JD/MEM offered jointly with Yale University School of Forestry and Environmental Studies. *Accreditation:* ABA. Part-time programs available. *Degree requirements:* For master's, writing sample; for doctorate, thesis/dissertation (for some programs), extensive thesis proposal (for SJD). *Entrance requirements:* For doctorate, LSAT (for JD). Additional exam requirements/recommendations for international students: Required—TOEFL (minimum score 600 paper-based); Recommended—TWE. Electronic applications accepted. *Expenses:* Contact institution. *Faculty research:* Reform of energy regulations, international law, land use law, prosecutorial misconduct, corporation law, international sale of goods.

Thomas M. Cooley Law School, JD and LL M Programs, Lansing, MI 48901-3038. Offers administrative law (public law) (JD); business transactions (JD); Canadian law practice (JD); Constitutional law and civil rights (public law) (JD); corporate law and finance (LL M); environmental law (public law) (JD); general practice (JD), including solo and small firm; homeland and national security law (LL M); insurance law (LL M); intellectual property (JD); intellectual property law (LL M); international law (JD); litigation (JD); self-directed (LL M, JD); tax law (LL M); taxation (JD); U.S. legal studies for foreign attorneys (LL M); JD/MBA; JD/MPA; JD/MSW. *Accreditation:* ABA. Part-time and evening/weekend programs available. Postbaccalaureate distance learning degree programs offered (no on-campus study). *Degree requirements:* For master's, thesis optional; for doctorate, minimum of 3 credits of clinical experience. *Entrance requirements:* For master's, JD or LL B; for doctorate, LSAT. Additional exam requirements/recommendations for international students: Required—TOEFL (for U.S. legal studies for foreign attorneys LL M program). Electronic applications accepted. *Faculty research:* Wrongful convictions, civil rights, environmental law, litigation techniques, data mining, intellectual property, practical and skills-based legal education.

University of Calgary, Faculty of Law, Programs in Natural Resources, Energy and Environmental Law, Calgary, AB T2N 1N4, Canada. Offers LL M, Postbaccalaureate Certificate. Part-time and evening/weekend programs available. *Degree requirements:* For master's, thesis optional. *Entrance requirements:* For master's, JD or LL B. Additional exam requirements/recommendations for international students: Required—TOEFL (minimum score 100 iBT), IELTS (minimum score 7). Electronic applications accepted. *Faculty research:* Natural resources law and regulations; environmental law, ethics and policies; oil and gas and energy law; water and municipal law; Aboriginal law.

University of Colorado Denver, School of Public Affairs, Program in Public Affairs and Administration, Denver, CO 80127. Offers public administration (MPA), including domestic violence, emergency management and homeland security, environmental policy, management and law, homeland security and defense, local government, nonprofit management, public administration; public affairs (PhD). *Accreditation:* NASPAA. Part-time and evening/weekend programs available. Postbaccalaureate distance learning degree programs offered (no on-campus study). *Students:* 268 full-time (168 women), 162 part-time (100 women); includes 60 minority (8 Black or African American, non-Hispanic/Latino; 6 American Indian or Alaska Native, non-Hispanic/Latino; 9 Asian, non-Hispanic/Latino; 34 Hispanic/Latino; 1 Native Hawaiian or other Pacific Islander, non-Hispanic/Latino; 2 Two or more races, non-Hispanic/Latino), 31 international. Average age 34. 293 applicants, 64% accepted, 109 enrolled. In 2013, 133 master's, 3 doctorates awarded. *Degree requirements:* For master's, thesis or alternative, 36-39 credit hours; for doctorate, comprehensive exam, thesis/dissertation, minimum of 66 semester hours, including at least 30 hours of dissertation. *Entrance requirements:* For master's, GRE, GMAT or LSAT, resume, essay, transcripts, recommendations; for doctorate, GRE, resume, essay, transcripts, recommendations. Additional exam requirements/recommendations for international students: Required—TOEFL (minimum score 550 paper-based; 80 iBT); Recommended—IELTS (minimum score 6.5). *Application deadline:* For fall admission, 2/1 priority date for domestic students, 1/15 priority date for international students; for spring admission, 10/15 priority date for domestic students, 10/1 priority date for international students. Application fee: $50 ($75 for international students). Electronic applications accepted. *Expenses:* Contact institution. *Financial support:* In 2013–14, 54 students received support. Fellowships with partial tuition reimbursements available, research assistantships with partial tuition reimbursements available, teaching assistantships with partial tuition reimbursements available, Federal Work-Study, institutionally sponsored loans, scholarships/grants, traineeships, and unspecified assistantships available. Financial award application deadline: 4/1; financial award applicants required to submit FAFSA. *Faculty research:* Housing, education and the social and economic issues of vulnerable populations; nonprofit governance and management; education finance, effectiveness and reform; P-20 education initiatives; municipal government accountability. *Unit head:* Dr. Christine Martell, Director of MPA Program, 303-315-2716, Fax: 303-315-2229, E-mail: christine.martell@ucdenver.edu. *Application contact:* Dawn Savage, Student Services Coordinator, 303-315-2743, Fax: 303-315-2229, E-mail: dawn.savage@ucdenver.edu.
Website: http://www.ucdenver.edu/academics/colleges/SPA/Academics/programs/PublicAffairsAdmin/Pages/index.aspx.

University of Florida, Levin College of Law, Gainesville, FL 32611. Offers comparative law (LL M); environmental law (LL M); international taxation (LL M); law (JD); taxation (LL M, SJD). *Accreditation:* ABA. *Faculty:* 77 full-time (37 women), 36 part-time/adjunct (10 women). *Students:* 1,072 full-time (452 women); includes 283 minority (69 Black or African American, non-Hispanic/Latino; 13 American Indian or Alaska Native, non-Hispanic/Latino; 45 Asian, non-Hispanic/Latino; 115 Hispanic/Latino; 41 Two or more races, non-Hispanic/Latino), 37 international. Average age 24. 2,686 applicants, 33%

accepted, 284 enrolled. In 2013, 356 doctorates awarded. *Entrance requirements:* For doctorate, LSAT (for JD). *Application deadline:* For fall admission, 3/15 for domestic and international students. Applications are processed on a rolling basis. Application fee: $30. Electronic applications accepted. *Expenses:* Tuition, state resident: full-time $12,640. Tuition, nonresident: full-time $30,000. *Financial support:* In 2013–14, 446 students received support, including 42 research assistantships (averaging $9,261 per year); Federal Work-Study, institutionally sponsored loans, scholarships/grants, health care benefits, and unspecified assistantships also available. Financial award application deadline: 3/15; financial award applicants required to submit FAFSA. *Faculty research:* Environmental and land use law, taxation, dispute resolution, family law, Constitutional law. *Unit head:* Robert Jerry, Dean, 352-273-0600, Fax: 352-392-8727, E-mail: jerryr@law.ufl.edu. *Application contact:* Michelle Adorno, Assistant Dean for Admissions, 352-273-0890, Fax: 352-392-4087, E-mail: madorno@law.ufl.edu. Website: http://www.law.ufl.edu/.

University of Houston, Law Center, Houston, TX 77204-6060. Offers energy, environment, and natural resources (LL M); health law (LL M); intellectual property and information law (LL M); international law (LL M); .law (LL M, JD); tax law (LL M). *Accreditation:* ABA. Part-time and evening/weekend programs available. *Entrance requirements:* For doctorate, LSAT. Additional exam requirements/recommendations for international students: Required—TOEFL (minimum score 600 paper-based; 100 iBT). Electronic applications accepted. *Expenses:* Contact institution. *Faculty research:* Health law, international, tax, environmental/energy, information law/intellectual property.

University of Idaho, College of Law, Moscow, ID 83844-2321. Offers business law and entrepreneurship (JD); law (JD); litigation and alternative dispute resolution (JD); Native American law (JD); natural resources and environmental law (JD). *Accreditation:* ABA. *Faculty:* 31 full-time, 7 part-time/adjunct. *Students:* 314 full-time, 8 part-time. Average age 29. *Entrance requirements:* For doctorate, LSAT, Law School Admission Council Credential Assembly Service (CAS) Report. Additional exam requirements/recommendations for international students: Required—TOEFL. *Application deadline:* For fall admission, 2/15 for domestic students. Applications are processed on a rolling basis. Application fee: $50 ($60 for international students). Electronic applications accepted. *Expenses:* Tuition, state resident: full-time $5596; part-time $363 per credit hour. Tuition, nonresident: full-time $18,672; part-time $1089 per credit hour. *Financial support:* Career-related internships or fieldwork, Federal Work-Study, and institutionally sponsored loans available. Financial award applicants required to submit FAFSA. *Faculty research:* Transboundary river governance, tribal protection and stewardship, regional water issues, environmental law. *Unit head:* Michael Satz, Jr., Dean, 208-885-4977, E-mail: uilaw@uidaho.edu. *Application contact:* Carole Wells, Interim Director of Admissions, 208-885-2300, Fax: 208-885-2252, E-mail: lawadmit@uidaho.edu. Website: http://www.uidaho.edu/law/.

University of Pittsburgh, School of Law, Master of Studies in Law Program, Pittsburgh, PA 15260. Offers business law (MSL), including commercial law, corporate law, general business law, international business, tax law; Constitutional law (MSL); criminal law and justice (MSL); disabilities law (MSL); dispute resolution (MSL); education law (MSL); elder and estate planning law (MSL); employment and labor law (MSL); energy law (MSL); environment and real estate law (MSL); family law (MSL); health law (MSL); intellectual property and technology (MSL); international and comparative law (MSL); jurisprudence (MSL); personal injury and civil litigation (MSL); regulatory law (MSL); self-designed (MSL); sports and entertainment law (MSL). Part-time programs available. *Faculty:* 43 full-time (16 women), 110 part-time/adjunct (31 women). *Students:* 4 full-time (all women), 6 part-time (4 women); includes 7 minority (4 Black or African American, non-Hispanic/Latino; 2 Asian, non-Hispanic/Latino; 1 Native Hawaiian or other Pacific Islander, non-Hispanic/Latino). Average age 29. 11 applicants, 73% accepted, 7 enrolled. In 2013, 5 master's awarded. *Entrance requirements:* Additional exam requirements/recommendations for international students: Required—TOEFL (minimum

score 600 paper-based; 100 iBT). *Application deadline:* For fall admission, 6/30 for domestic students, 5/1 for international students. Applications are processed on a rolling basis. Application fee: $0. *Expenses:* Tuition, state resident: full-time $19,964; part-time $807 per credit. Tuition, nonresident: full-time $32,686; part-time $1337 per credit. *Required fees:* $740; $200. Tuition and fees vary according to program. *Faculty research:* Law, health law, business law, contracts, intellectual property, environmental law. *Unit head:* Prof. Alan Meisel, Director, 412-648-1384, Fax: 412-648-2649, E-mail: meisel@pitt.edu. *Application contact:* Bethann Pischke, Administrative Coordinator, 412-648-7120, Fax: 412-648-2649, E-mail: pischke@pitt.edu. Website: http://www.law.pitt.edu/academics/msl.

University of Pittsburgh, School of Law, Program in Environmental Law, Science and Policy, Pittsburgh, PA 15260. Offers Certificate. *Faculty:* 39 full-time (15 women), 112 part-time/adjunct (26 women). *Students:* 23 full-time (11 women). *Expenses:* Tuition, state resident: full-time $19,964; part-time $807 per credit. Tuition, nonresident: full-time $32,686; part-time $1337 per credit. *Required fees:* $740; $200. Tuition and fees vary according to program. *Unit head:* Emily Collins, Director, 412-648-8549, Fax: 412-648-1992, E-mail: eac50@pitt.edu. *Application contact:* Charmaine McCall, Assistant Dean of Admissions and Financial Aid, 412-648-1413, Fax: 412-648-1318, E-mail: cmccall@pitt.edu.

The University of Tulsa, College of Law, Tulsa, OK 74104. Offers American Indian and indigenous law (LL M); American law for foreign lawyers (LL M); energy and natural resources law (LL M); energy law (MJ); health law (Certificate); Indian law (MJ); law (JD); Native American law (Certificate); resources, energy, and environmental law (Certificate); JD/M Tax; JD/MA; JD/MBA; JD/MS. *Accreditation:* ABA. Part-time programs available. Postbaccalaureate distance learning degree programs offered (no on-campus study). *Faculty:* 27 full-time (12 women), 17 part-time/adjunct (6 women). *Students:* 278 full-time (132 women), 89 part-time (45 women); includes 114 minority (20 Black or African American, non-Hispanic/Latino; 63 American Indian or Alaska Native, non-Hispanic/Latino; 4 Asian, non-Hispanic/Latino; 9 Hispanic/Latino; 18 Two or more races, non-Hispanic/Latino), 5 international. Average age 28. 1,226 applicants, 37% accepted, 83 enrolled. In 2013, 4 master's, 1 doctorate awarded. *Degree requirements:* For master's, thesis optional. *Entrance requirements:* For master's, JD from an ABA-approved U.S. law school or a JD equivalent from non-U.S. university; for doctorate, LSAT, BS or BA from 4-year regionally-accredited college/university; for Certificate, BS or BA from 4-year regionally-accredited college/university. Additional exam requirements/recommendations for international students: Required—TOEFL (minimum score 570 paper-based; 90 iBT), IELTS (minimum score 6.5). *Application deadline:* For fall admission, 2/1 priority date for domestic and international students; for spring admission, 12/5 priority date for domestic and international students. Applications are processed on a rolling basis. Application fee: $30. Electronic applications accepted. *Expenses:* Contact institution. *Financial support:* In 2013–14, 196 students received support. Career-related internships or fieldwork, Federal Work-Study, and scholarships/grants available. Support available to part-time students. Financial award application deadline: 8/1; financial award applicants required to submit FAFSA. *Faculty research:* International law, Native American law, criminal law, commercial speech, copyright law. *Unit head:* Janet Levit, Dean, 918-631-2400, Fax: 918-631-3126, E-mail: janet-levit@utulsa.edu. *Application contact:* April M. Fox, Assistant Dean of Admissions and Financial Aid, 918-631-2406, Fax: 918-631-3630, E-mail: april-fox@utulsa.edu. Website: http://www.utulsa.edu/law/.

Vermont Law School, Graduate and Professional Programs, Environmental Law Center, South Royalton, VT 05068-0096. Offers energy law (LL M); energy regulation and law (MERL); environmental law (LL M); environmental law and policy (MELP); JD/MELP. Part-time programs available. *Entrance requirements:* Additional exam requirements/recommendations for international students: Required—TOEFL. *Faculty research:* Environment and technology; takings; international environmental law; interaction among science, law, and environmental policy; air pollution.

Health Law

Baylor University, School of Law, Waco, TX 76798-7288. Offers administrative practice (JD); business litigation (JD); business transactions (JD); criminal practice (JD); estate planning (JD); general civil litigation (JD); healthcare (JD); intellectual property (JD); law (JD); real estate and natural resources (JD); JD/M Tax; JD/MBA; JD/MPPA. *Accreditation:* ABA. *Faculty:* 30 full-time (7 women), 45 part-time/adjunct (5 women). *Students:* 371 full-time (163 women), 8 part-time (2 women); includes 71 minority (6 Black or African American, non-Hispanic/Latino; 9 American Indian or Alaska Native, non-Hispanic/Latino; 14 Asian, non-Hispanic/Latino; 28 Hispanic/Latino; 14 Two or more races, non-Hispanic/Latino). Average age 24; 2,226 applicants, 37% accepted, 86 enrolled. In 2013, 176 doctorates awarded. *Entrance requirements:* For doctorate, LSAT. Additional exam requirements/recommendations for international students: Recommended—TOEFL. *Application deadline:* For fall admission, 3/1 for domestic and international students; for spring admission, 11/1 for domestic and international students; for summer admission, 2/1 for domestic and international students. Applications are processed on a rolling basis. Application fee: $0. Electronic applications accepted. Application fee is waived when completed online. *Expenses:* Contact institution. *Financial support:* In 2013–14, 296 students received support. Career-related internships or fieldwork and scholarships/grants available. Financial award application deadline: 3/1; financial award applicants required to submit FAFSA. *Unit head:* Dr. Bradley J. B. Toben, Dean, 254-710-1911, Fax: 254-710-2316. *Application contact:* Nicole Neeley, Assistant Dean of Admissions, 254-710-1911, Fax: 254-710-2316, E-mail: nicole_neeley@baylor.edu. Website: http://www.baylor.edu/law.

Boston University, School of Public Health, Health Law, Bioethics and Human Rights Department, Boston, MA 02215. Offers MPH. Part-time and evening/weekend programs available. *Faculty:* 5 full-time, 16 part-time/adjunct. *Students:* 10 full-time (all women), 7 part-time (6 women); includes 1 minority (Asian, non-Hispanic/Latino). Average age 26. 86 applicants, 56% accepted, 9 enrolled. *Entrance requirements:* For master's, GRE, MCAT, LSAT, GMAT, DAT. Additional exam requirements/recommendations for international students: Required—TOEFL (minimum score 600 paper-based; 100 iBT) or IELTS (minimum score 6). *Application deadline:* For fall admission, 2/1 priority date for domestic and international students; for spring admission, 10/15 priority date for domestic and international students. Applications are processed on a rolling basis. Application fee: $115. Electronic applications accepted. *Expenses: Tuition:* Full-time $43,970; part-time $1374 per credit hour. *Required fees:* $60 per semester. Tuition and fees vary according to class time, course level and program. *Financial support:* In

2013–14, 1 fellowship was awarded; career-related internships or fieldwork, Federal Work-Study, institutionally sponsored loans, scholarships/grants, and tuition waivers (partial) also available. Support available to part-time students. Financial award application deadline: 3/1; financial award applicants required to submit FAFSA. *Unit head:* Prof. George Annas, Chair, 617-638-4626, E-mail: hld@bu.edu. *Application contact:* LePhan Quan, Associate Director of Admissions, 617-638-4640, Fax: 617-638-5299, E-mail: asksph@bu.edu. Website: http://sph.bu.edu.

Cleveland State University, Cleveland-Marshall College of Law, Cleveland, OH 44115. Offers business law (JD); civil litigation and dispute resolution (JD); criminal law (JD); employment labor law (JD); health care compliance (Certificate); health law (Certificate); international and comparative law (JD); law (LL M, MLS); JD/MAES; JD/MBA; JD/MPA; JD/MSES; JD/MUPDD. *Accreditation:* ABA. Part-time and evening/weekend programs available. *Faculty:* 37 full-time (16 women), 40 part-time/adjunct (11 women). *Students:* 307 full-time (129 women), 158 part-time (79 women); includes 86 minority (40 Black or African American, non-Hispanic/Latino; 3 American Indian or Alaska Native, non-Hispanic/Latino; 14 Asian, non-Hispanic/Latino; 21 Hispanic/Latino; 8 Two or more races, non-Hispanic/Latino), 9 international. Average age 28. 1,655 applicants, 38% accepted, 173 enrolled. In 2013, 1 master's, 155 doctorates, 4 Certificates awarded. *Degree requirements:* For master's, thesis for graduates of U.S. law schools (for LL M); 30 credits, 6 in required courses (for MLS); for doctorate, 90 credits (41 in required courses). *Entrance requirements:* For master's, JD or LL B (for LL M); bachelor's degree (for MLS); for doctorate, LSAT, bachelor's degree. Additional exam requirements/recommendations for international students: Required—TOEFL (minimum score 600 paper-based, 100 iBT) or IELTS (minimum score 7) for LL.M. *Application deadline:* For fall admission, 5/1 for domestic and international students. Applications are processed on a rolling basis. Application fee: $0. Electronic applications accepted. *Expenses:* Contact institution. *Financial support:* In 2013–14, 162 students received support, including 18 fellowships (averaging $2,500 per year), 25 research assistantships, 8 teaching assistantships with partial tuition reimbursements available (averaging $7,328 per year); career-related internships or fieldwork, Federal Work-Study, scholarships/grants, tuition waivers (full and partial), and unspecified assistantships also available. Support available to part-time students. Financial award application deadline: 5/1; financial award applicants required to submit FAFSA. *Faculty research:* Health law, international law, Constitutional law, criminal law, business law. *Unit head:* Craig M. Boise, Dean, 216-687-2300, Fax: 216-687-6881, E-mail: c.boise@csuohio.edu.

Health Law

Application contact: Christopher Lucak, Assistant Dean for Admissions, 216-687-4692, Fax: 216-687-6881, E-mail: c.lucak@csuohio.edu. Website: http://www.law.csuohio.edu/.

DePaul University, College of Law, Chicago, IL 60604-2287. Offers health law (LL M); intellectual property law (LL M); international law (LL M); law (JD); taxation (LL M); JD/MA; JD/MBA; JD/MPS; JD/MS. *Accreditation:* ABA. Part-time and evening/weekend programs available. *Faculty:* 52 full-time (23 women), 53 part-time/adjunct (23 women). In 2013, 25 master's, 287 doctorates awarded. *Entrance requirements:* For doctorate, LSAT, LSAC applicant evaluation/letter of recommendation, personal statement, resume. Additional exam requirements/recommendations for international students: Required—TOEFL (minimum score 577 paper-based; 90 iBT), IELTS (minimum score 6.5). *Application deadline:* For fall admission, 3/1 for domestic and international students. Applications are processed on a rolling basis. Electronic applications accepted. *Expenses:* Contact institution. *Financial support:* Application deadline: 3/1; applicants required to submit FAFSA. *Unit head:* Gregory Mark, Dean, 312-362-5595, E-mail: gmark@depaul.edu. *Application contact:* Michael S. Burns, Director of Law Admission/Associate Dean, 312-362-6831, Fax: 312-362-5280, E-mail: lawinfo@depaul.edu. Website: http://www.law.depaul.edu.

Georgetown University, Law Center, Washington, DC 20001. Offers global health law (LL M); individualized study (LL M); international business and economic law (LL M); law (JD, SJD); national security law (LL M); securities and financial regulation (LL M); taxation (LL M); JD/LL M; JD/MA; JD/MBA; JD/MPH; JD/PhD. *Accreditation:* ABA. Part-time and evening/weekend programs available. *Degree requirements:* For master's, thesis; for doctorate, thesis/dissertation (for some programs). *Entrance requirements:* For master's, JD, LL B, or first law degree earned in country of origin; for doctorate, LSAT (for JD). Additional exam requirements/recommendations for international students: Required—TOEFL. *Expenses:* Contact institution. *Faculty research:* Constitutional law, legal history, jurisprudence.

Loyola University Chicago, School of Law, Chicago, IL 60611. Offers advocacy (LL M); business law (LL M, MJ); child and family law (LL M); children's law and policy (MJ); health law (LL M, MJ); health law and policy (D Law, SJD); international law (LL M); law (JD); rule of law development (LL M); tax law (LL M); JD/MA; JD/MBA; JD/MSW; MJ/MSW. MJ in business law offered in partnership with Concord Law School. *Accreditation:* ABA. Part-time and evening/weekend programs available. Postbaccalaureate distance learning degree programs offered (minimal on-campus study). *Faculty:* 48 full-time (16 women), 174 part-time/adjunct (98 women). *Students:* 851 full-time (461 women), 271 part-time (206 women); includes 333 minority (142 Black or African American, non-Hispanic/Latino; 3 American Indian or Alaska Native, non-Hispanic/Latino; 55 Asian, non-Hispanic/Latino; 98 Hispanic/Latino; 2 Native Hawaiian or other Pacific Islander, non-Hispanic/Latino; 33 Two or more races, non-Hispanic/Latino), 33 international. Average age 31. 3,333 applicants, 51% accepted, 213 enrolled. In 2013, 144 master's, 282 doctorates awarded. *Entrance requirements:* For doctorate, LSAT. Additional exam requirements/recommendations for international students: Required—TOEFL (minimum score 550 paper-based; 79 iBT), IELTS (minimum score 6.5). *Application deadline:* For fall admission, 3/1 for domestic and international students. Applications are processed on a rolling basis. Application fee: $0. Electronic applications accepted. *Expenses:* Contact institution. *Financial support:* In 2013–14, 676 students received support, including 72 fellowships; Federal Work-Study and scholarships/grants also available. Financial award application deadline: 3/1; financial award applicants required to submit FAFSA. *Unit head:* Pamela Bloomquist, Assistant Dean for Admission and Financial Assistance, Law School, 312-915-7170, Fax: 312-915-7906, E-mail: ploom@luc.edu. *Application contact:* Ron Martin, Associate Director, Graduate and Professional Enrollment Management Operations, 312-915-8951, E-mail: rmarti7@luc.edu. Website: http://www.luc.edu/law/.

Nova Southeastern University, Shepard Broad Law Center, Fort Lauderdale, FL 33314. Offers education law (MS); employment law (MS); health law (MS); law (JD); JD/MBA; JD/MS; JD/MURP. JD/MURP offered jointly with Florida Atlantic University. *Accreditation:* ABA. Part-time and evening/weekend programs available. Postbaccalaureate distance learning degree programs offered (minimal on-campus study). *Faculty:* 65 full-time (33 women), 96 part-time/adjunct (35 women). *Students:* 726 full-time (379 women), 324 part-time (233 women); includes 443 minority (127 Black or African American, non-Hispanic/Latino; 2 American Indian or Alaska Native, non-Hispanic/Latino; 41 Asian, non-Hispanic/Latino; 262 Hispanic/Latino; 1 Native Hawaiian or other Pacific Islander, non-Hispanic/Latino; 10 Two or more races, non-Hispanic/Latino), 11 international. Average age 28. 1,692 applicants, 49% accepted, 339 enrolled. In 2013, 61 master's, 303 doctorates awarded. *Degree requirements:* For master's, capstone research project; for doctorate, thesis/dissertation, rigorous upper-level writing requirement fulfilled through seminar paper or law journal article. *Entrance requirements:* For master's, regionally-accredited undergraduate degree and at least 2 years??? experience in the field of business or health care for the Employment Law and Health Care programs; for doctorate, LSAT. Additional exam requirements/recommendations for international students: Recommended—TOEFL, IELTS, TWE. *Application deadline:* For fall admission, 5/1 priority date for domestic and international students. Applications are processed on a rolling basis. Application fee: $53. Electronic applications accepted. *Expenses:* Contact institution. *Financial support:* In 2013–14, 325 students received support, including 17 fellowships (averaging $1,382 per year); Federal Work-Study, scholarships/grants, tuition waivers (partial), and unspecified assistantships also available. Support available to part-time students. Financial award application deadline: 4/15; financial award applicants required to submit FAFSA. *Faculty research:* Legal issues in family law, civil rights, business associations, criminal law, law and popular culture. *Unit head:* Elena Langan, Dean, 954-262-6100, Fax: 954-262-6317, E-mail: langane@nsu.law.nova.edu. *Application contact:* William Perez, Assistant Dean of Admissions, 954-262-6121, Fax: 954-262-3844, E-mail: perezw@nsu.law.nova.edu. Website: http://www.nsulaw.nova.edu/.

Quinnipiac University, School of Law, Hamden, CT 06518. Offers health law (LL M); law (JD); JD/MBA. *Accreditation:* ABA. Part-time and evening/weekend programs available. *Faculty:* 33 full-time (11 women), 33 part-time/adjunct (9 women). *Students:* 252 full-time (142 women), 80 part-time (45 women); includes 44 minority (17 Black or African American, non-Hispanic/Latino; 6 American Indian or Alaska Native, non-Hispanic/Latino; 13 Asian, non-Hispanic/Latino; 8 Hispanic/Latino). Average age 25. 1,063 applicants, 53% accepted, 84 enrolled. In 2013, 148 doctorates awarded. *Entrance requirements:* For doctorate, LSAT. Additional exam requirements/recommendations for international students: Recommended—TOEFL. *Application deadline:* For fall admission, 3/1 priority date for domestic and international students. Applications are processed on a rolling basis. Application fee: $65. Electronic applications accepted. *Expenses:* Contact institution. *Financial support:* In 2013–14, 225 students received support, including 32 fellowships (averaging $1,560 per year), 70 research assistantships (averaging $2,160 per year); career-related internships or fieldwork, Federal Work-Study, and scholarships/grants also available. Support available to part-time students. Financial award application deadline: 4/15; financial

award applicants required to submit FAFSA. *Faculty research:* Tax, health, public interest, corporate law, dispute resolution, intellectual property. *Unit head:* Jennifer Brown, Dean, 203-582-3200, Fax: 203-582-3209, E-mail: ladm@quinnipiac.edu. *Application contact:* Edwin Wilkes, Associate Vice-President/Dean of Law School Admissions, 203-582-3400, Fax: 203-582-3339, E-mail: ladm@quinnipiac.edu. Website: http://law.quinnipiac.edu/.

Seton Hall University, School of Law, Newark, NJ 07102-5210. Offers health law (LL M, JD); intellectual property (LL M, JD); law (MSJ); JD/MADIR; JD/MBA; MD/JD; MD/MSJ. MD/JD, MD/MSJ offered jointly with University of Medicine and Dentistry of New Jersey. *Accreditation:* ABA. Part-time and evening/weekend programs available. *Degree requirements:* For master's, thesis optional. *Entrance requirements:* For master's, professional experience, letters of recommendation; for doctorate, LSAT, active LSDAS registration, letters of recommendation. Additional exam requirements/recommendations for international students: Recommended—TOEFL. Electronic applications accepted. *Expenses:* Contact institution. *Faculty research:* Health law, intellectual property law, science and the law, international law and employment/labor law.

Southern Illinois University Carbondale, School of Law, Program in Legal Studies, Carbondale, IL 62901-4701. Offers general law (MLS); health law and policy (MLS). *Students:* 5 full-time (2 women), 7 part-time (4 women), 1 international. 10 applicants, 70% accepted, 7 enrolled. In 2013, 6 master's awarded. *Application fee:* $50. *Unit head:* Lisa David, Admissions Coordinator, 618-453-8767, E-mail: ldavid@law.siu.edu.

Suffolk University, Law School, Boston, MA 02108. Offers business law and financial services (JD); civil litigation (JD); global law and technology (LL M); health and biomedical law (JD); intellectual property law (JD); international law (JD); JD/MBA; JD/MPA; JD/MSCJ; JD/MSF; JD/MSIE. *Accreditation:* ABA. Part-time and evening/weekend programs available. *Faculty:* 73 full-time (34 women), 54 part-time/adjunct (14 women). *Students:* 1,074 full-time (575 women), 504 part-time (248 women); includes 351 minority (101 Black or African American, non-Hispanic/Latino; 3 American Indian or Alaska Native, non-Hispanic/Latino; 96 Asian, non-Hispanic/Latino; 132 Hispanic/Latino; 19 Two or more races, non-Hispanic/Latino), 65 international. Average age 27. 2,390 applicants, 77% accepted, 450 enrolled. In 2013, 516 doctorates awarded. *Degree requirements:* For master's, legal writing. *Entrance requirements:* For master's, 2 letters of recommendation, resume, personal statement; for doctorate, LSAT, LSDAS, dean's certification, recommendation. Additional exam requirements/recommendations for international students: Required—TOEFL (minimum score 600 paper-based; 100 iBT). *Application deadline:* For fall admission, 3/1 for domestic and international students. Applications are processed on a rolling basis. Application fee: $60. Electronic applications accepted. *Expenses:* Contact institution. *Financial support:* Career-related internships or fieldwork, Federal Work-Study, institutionally sponsored loans, and scholarships/grants available. Support available to part-time students. Financial award application deadline: 3/1; financial award applicants required to submit FAFSA. *Faculty research:* Civil law, international law, health/biomedical law, business and finance, intellectual property. *Unit head:* Camille A. Nelson, Dean of Suffolk University Law School, 617-573-8144, Fax: 617-523-1367, E-mail: gellis@suffolk.edu. *Application contact:* Jennifer Sims, Assistant Dean for Admissions and Financial Aid, 617-573-8144, Fax: 617-523-1367, E-mail: ilawadm@suffolk.edu. Website: http://www.law.suffolk.edu/.

Syracuse University, College of Arts and Sciences, Program in Medicolegal Death Investigation, Syracuse, NY 13244. Offers CAS. Part-time programs available. *Entrance requirements:* Additional exam requirements/recommendations for international students: Required—TOEFL (minimum score 100 iBT). *Application deadline:* For fall admission, 2/15 priority date for domestic and international students; for summer admission, 2/15 priority date for domestic students, 2/15 for international students. Applications are processed on a rolling basis. Application fee: $75. Electronic applications accepted. *Unit head:* Dr. Michael M. Sponsler, Professor of Chemistry/Director of Curricular Programs for the Forensic and National Security Sciences Institute, 315-443-4880, E-mail: sponsler@syr.edu. *Application contact:* Same as above. Website: http://forensics.syr.edu/index.html.

Union Graduate College, Center for Bioethics and Clinical Leadership, Schenectady, NY 12308-3107. Offers bioethics (MS); clinical ethics (AC); clinical leadership in health management (MS); health, policy and law (AC); research ethics (AC). Part-time and evening/weekend programs available. Postbaccalaureate distance learning degree programs offered (minimal on-campus study). *Faculty:* 2 full-time (0 women), 9 part-time/adjunct (7 women). *Students:* 2 full-time (both women), 59 part-time (39 women); includes 17 minority (3 Black or African American, non-Hispanic/Latino; 8 Asian, non-Hispanic/Latino; 2 Hispanic/Latino; 4 Two or more races, non-Hispanic/Latino), 4 international. Average age 36. In 2013, 19 master's, 3 other advanced degrees awarded. *Entrance requirements:* For master's, letters of recommendation. Additional exam requirements/recommendations for international students: Required—TOEFL (minimum score 550 paper-based). *Application deadline:* Applications are processed on a rolling basis. Electronic applications accepted. *Expenses:* Contact institution. *Financial support:* Federal Work-Study, scholarships/grants, health care benefits, and tuition waivers (partial) available. Support available to part-time students. Financial award applicants required to submit FAFSA. *Faculty research:* Bioethics education, clinical ethics consultation, research ethics, history of biomedical ethics, international bioethics/research ethics. *Unit head:* Dr. Sean Philpott, Director, 518-631-9860, Fax: 518-631-9903, E-mail: philpotts@uniongraduatecollege.edu. *Application contact:* Ann Nolte, Assistant Director, 518-631-9860, Fax: 518-631-9903, E-mail: noltea@uniongraduatecollege.edu.

Université de Sherbrooke, Faculty of Law, Sherbrooke, QC J1K 2R1, Canada. Offers alternative dispute resolution (LL M, Diploma); business law (Diploma); common law (JD); criminal and penal law (Diploma); health law (LL M, Diploma); international law (LL M); law (LL D); legal management (Diploma); notarial law (Diploma); transnational law (Diploma). Part-time and evening/weekend programs available. *Degree requirements:* For master's, thesis; for Diploma, one foreign language. *Entrance requirements:* For master's and Diploma, LL B. Electronic applications accepted.

University of California, San Diego, Office of Graduate Studies, Program in Health Policy and Law, La Jolla, CA 92093. Offers MAS. Program offered jointly with School of Medicine and California Western School of Law. Part-time programs available. *Students:* 36 part-time (26 women); includes 14 minority (2 Black or African American, non-Hispanic/Latino; 6 Asian, non-Hispanic/Latino; 6 Hispanic/Latino). 26 applicants, 77% accepted, 15 enrolled. In 2013, 12 master's awarded. *Entrance requirements:* For master's, appropriate medical, healthcare, legal or related degree; minimum GPA of 3.0 in final two years of study; minimum 3 years of relevant work experience or equivalent. Additional exam requirements/recommendations for international students: Required—TOEFL, IELTS. *Application deadline:* For fall admission, 4/7 for domestic students. Applications are processed on a rolling basis. Application fee: $80 ($100 for international students). Electronic applications accepted. *Expenses:* Tuition, state resident: full-time $11,220; part-time $1870 per quarter. Tuition, nonresident: full-time $26,322; part-time $4387 per quarter. *Required fees:* $519.50 per quarter. Part-time tuition and fees vary according to course load and program. *Financial support:* Scholarships/grants available. *Unit head:* Gerard Manecke, Program Co-Director, 619-543-3164, E-mail:

gmanecke@ucsd.edu. *Application contact:* Jenna Lucius, Program Coordinator, 858-534-9162, E-mail: healthlaw@ucsd.edu.
Website: http://hlaw.ucsd.edu/.

University of Denver, University College, Denver, CO 80208. Offers arts and culture (MLS, Certificate), including art, literature, and culture, arts development and program management (Certificate), creative writing; environmental policy and management (MAS, Certificate), including energy and sustainability (Certificate), environmental assessment of nuclear power (Certificate), environmental health and safety (Certificate), environmental management, natural resource management (Certificate); geographic information systems (MAS, Certificate); global affairs (MLS, Certificate), including translation studies, world history and culture; healthcare leadership (MPH, Certificate), including healthcare policy, law, and ethics, medical and healthcare information technologies, strategic management of healthcare; information and communications technology (MCIS, Certificate), including database design and administration (Certificate), geographic information systems (MCIS), information security systems security (Certificate), information systems security (MCIS), project management (MCIS, MPS, Certificate), software design and administration (Certificate), software design and programming (MCIS), technology management, telecommunications technology (MCIS), Web design and development; leadership and organizations (MPS, Certificate), including human capital in organizations, philanthropic leadership, project management (MCIS, MPS, Certificate), strategic innovation and change; organizational and professional communication (MPS, Certificate), including alternative dispute resolution, organizational communication, organizational development and training, public relations and marketing; security management (MAS, Certificate), including emergency planning and response, information security (MAS), organizational security; strategic human resource management (MPS, Certificate), including global human resources (MPS), human resource management and development (MPS). Part-time and evening/weekend programs available. Postbaccalaureate distance learning degree programs offered (no on-campus study). *Faculty:* 139 part-time/adjunct (61 women). *Students:* 49 full-time (16 women), 1,297 part-time (732 women); includes 272 minority (92 Black or African American, non-Hispanic/Latino; 5 American Indian or Alaska Native, non-Hispanic/Latino; 30 Asian, non-Hispanic/Latino; 114 Hispanic/Latino; 3 Native Hawaiian or other Pacific Islander, non-Hispanic/Latino; 28 Two or more races, non-Hispanic/Latino), 92 international. Average age 35. 542 applicants, 95% accepted, 362 enrolled. In 2013, 374 master's, 128 other advanced degrees awarded. *Degree requirements:* For master's, capstone project. *Entrance requirements:* For master's, transcripts, two letters of recommendation, personal statement, resume. Additional exam requirements/recommendations for international students: Required—TOEFL (minimum score 550 paper-based; 80 iBT). *Application deadline:* For fall admission, 7/18 priority date for domestic students, 5/2 priority date for international students; for winter admission, 10/24 priority date for domestic students, 9/19 priority date for international students; for spring admission, 2/1 for domestic students, 12/14 for international students; for summer admission, 4/18 priority date for domestic students, 3/7 priority date for international students. Applications are processed on a rolling basis. Application fee: $75. Electronic applications accepted. *Expenses:* Contact institution. *Financial support:* In 2013–14, 28 students received support. Applicants required to submit FAFSA. *Unit head:* Dr. Michael McGuire, Interim Dean, 303-871-3518, E-mail: mmcguire@du.edu. *Application contact:* Information Contact, 303-871-2291, E-mail: ucoladm@du.edu.
Website: http://www.universitycollege.du.edu/.

University of Houston, Law Center, Houston, TX 77204-6060. Offers energy, environment, and natural resources (LL M); health law (LL M); intellectual property and information law (LL M); international law (LL M); law (LL M, JD); tax law (LL M). *Accreditation:* ABA. Part-time and evening/weekend programs available. *Entrance requirements:* For doctorate, LSAT. Additional exam requirements/recommendations for international students: Required—TOEFL (minimum score 600 paper-based; 100 iBT). Electronic applications accepted. *Expenses:* Contact institution. *Faculty research:* Health law, international, tax, environmental/energy, information law/intellectual property.

The University of Manchester, School of Law, Manchester, United Kingdom. Offers bioethics and medical jurisprudence (PhD); criminology (M Phil, PhD); law (M Phil, PhD).

University of Pittsburgh, School of Law, Master of Studies in Law Program, Pittsburgh, PA 15260. Offers business law (MSL), including commercial law, corporate law, general business law, international business, tax law; Constitutional law (MSL); criminal law and justice (MSL); disabilities law (MSL); dispute resolution (MSL); education law (MSL); elder and estate planning law (MSL); employment and labor law (MSL); energy law (MSL); environment and real estate law (MSL); family law (MSL); health law (MSL); intellectual property and technology (MSL); international and comparative law (MSL); jurisprudence (MSL); personal injury and civil litigation (MSL); regulatory law (MSL); self-designed (MSL); sports and entertainment law (MSL). Part-time programs available. *Faculty:* 43 full-time (16 women), 110 part-time/adjunct (31 women). *Students:* 4 full-time (all women), 6 part-time (4 women); includes 7 minority (4 Black or African American, non-Hispanic/Latino; 2 Asian, non-Hispanic/Latino; 1 Native Hawaiian or other Pacific Islander, non-Hispanic/Latino). Average age 29. 11 applicants, 73% accepted, 7 enrolled. In 2013, 5 master's awarded. *Entrance requirements:* Additional exam requirements/recommendations for international students: Required—TOEFL (minimum score 600 paper-based; 100 iBT). *Application deadline:* For fall admission, 6/30 for domestic students, 5/1 for international students. Applications are processed on a rolling basis. Application fee: $0. *Expenses:* Tuition, state resident: full-time $19,964; part-time $807 per credit. Tuition, nonresident: full-time $32,686; part-time $1337 per credit. *Required fees:* $740; $200. Tuition and fees vary according to program. *Faculty research:* Law, health law, business law, contracts, intellectual property, environmental law. *Unit head:* Prof. Alan Meisel, Director, 412-648-1384, Fax: 412-648-2649, E-mail: meisel@pitt.edu. *Application contact:* Bethann Pischke, Administrative Coordinator, 412-648-7120, Fax: 412-648-2649, E-mail: pischke@pitt.edu.
Website: http://www.law.pitt.edu/academics/msl.

University of Pittsburgh, School of Law, Program in Health Law, Pittsburgh, PA 15260. Offers Certificate. *Faculty:* 39 full-time (15 women), 112 part-time/adjunct (26 women). *Students:* 23 full-time (9 women). *Application deadline:* For spring admission, 7/31 for domestic students. Applications are processed on a rolling basis. *Expenses:* Tuition, state resident: full-time $19,964; part-time $807 per credit. Tuition, nonresident: full-time $32,686; part-time $1337 per credit. *Required fees:* $740; $200. Tuition and fees vary according to program. *Unit head:* Prof. Alan Meisel, Professor/Director, 412-648-1384, Fax: 412-648-2649, E-mail: meisel@pitt.edu. *Application contact:* Bethann Pischke, Program Administrator, 412-648-7120, Fax: 412-648-2649, E-mail: pischke@pitt.edu.

The University of Tulsa, College of Law, Tulsa, OK 74104. Offers American Indian and indigenous law (LL M); American law for foreign lawyers (LL M); energy and natural resources law (LL M); energy law (MJ); health law (Certificate); Indian law (MJ); law (JD); Native American law (Certificate); resources, energy, and environmental law (Certificate); JD/M Tax; JD/MA; JD/MBA; JD/MS. *Accreditation:* ABA. Part-time programs available. Postbaccalaureate distance learning degree programs offered (no on-campus study). *Faculty:* 27 full-time (12 women), 17 part-time/adjunct (6 women). *Students:* 278 full-time (132 women), 89 part-time (45 women); includes 114 minority (20 Black or African American, non-Hispanic/Latino; 63 American Indian or Alaska Native, non-Hispanic/Latino; 4 Asian, non-Hispanic/Latino; 9 Hispanic/Latino; 18 Two or more races, non-Hispanic/Latino), 5 international. Average age 28. 1,226 applicants, 37% accepted, 83 enrolled. In 2013, 4 master's, 1 doctorate awarded. *Degree requirements:* For master's, thesis optional. *Entrance requirements:* For master's, JD from an ABA-approved U.S. law school or a JD equivalent from non-U.S. university; for doctorate, LSAT, BS or BA from 4-year regionally-accredited college/university; for Certificate, BS or BA from 4-year regionally-accredited college/university. Additional exam requirements/recommendations for international students: Required—TOEFL (minimum score 570 paper-based; 90 iBT), IELTS (minimum score 6.5). *Application deadline:* For fall admission, 2/1 priority date for domestic and international students; for spring admission, 12/5 priority date for domestic and international students. Applications are processed on a rolling basis. Application fee: $30. Electronic applications accepted. *Expenses:* Contact institution. *Financial support:* In 2013–14, 196 students received support. Career-related internships or fieldwork, Federal Work-Study, and scholarships/grants available. Support available to part-time students. Financial award application deadline: 8/1; financial award applicants required to submit FAFSA. *Faculty research:* International law, Native American law, criminal law, commercial speech, copyright law. *Unit head:* Janet Levit, Dean, 918-631-2400, Fax: 918-631-3126, E-mail: janet-levit@utulsa.edu. *Application contact:* April M. Fox, Assistant Dean of Admissions and Financial Aid, 918-631-2406, Fax: 918-631-3630, E-mail: april-fox@utulsa.edu.
Website: http://www.utulsa.edu/law/.

Widener University, School of Law at Wilmington, Wilmington, DE 19803-0474. Offers corporate law and finance (LL M); health law (LL M, MJ, D Law); juridical science (SJD); law (JD). *Accreditation:* ABA. Part-time programs available. *Faculty:* 58 full-time (23 women), 42 part-time/adjunct (15 women). *Students:* 692 full-time (313 women), 103 part-time (72 women); includes 174 minority (94 Black or African American, non-Hispanic/Latino; 10 American Indian or Alaska Native, non-Hispanic/Latino; 26 Asian, non-Hispanic/Latino; 34 Hispanic/Latino; 10 Two or more races, non-Hispanic/Latino), 10 international. Average age 26. 2,376 applicants, 39% accepted, 351 enrolled. In 2013, 28 master's, 269 doctorates awarded. *Degree requirements:* For doctorate, thesis/dissertation (for some programs). *Entrance requirements:* For master's, GMAT. *Application deadline:* For fall admission, 5/15 for domestic students; for spring admission, 12/1 for domestic students. Applications are processed on a rolling basis. Application fee: $60. *Expenses:* *Tuition:* Full-time $30,000; part-time $950 per credit. *Financial support:* Career-related internships or fieldwork, Federal Work-Study, institutionally sponsored loans, and scholarships/grants available. Support available to part-time students. Financial award application deadline: 2/15; financial award applicants required to submit FAFSA. *Unit head:* Linda L. Ammons, Dean, 302-477-2100, Fax: 302-477-2282, E-mail: llammons@widener.edu. *Application contact:* Barbara L. Ayars, Assistant Dean of Admissions, 302-477-2210, Fax: 302-477-2224, E-mail: barbara.l.ayars@law.widener.edu.
Website: http://law.widener.edu/.

Xavier University, College of Social Sciences, Health and Education, School of Nursing, Nursing Program, Cincinnati, OH 45207. Offers clinical nurse leader (MSN); education (MSN); forensic nursing (MSN); healthcare law (MSN); informatics (MSN); nursing administration (MSN); school nursing (MSN); MSN/M Ed; MSN/MBA; MSN/MS. *Faculty:* 16 full-time (15 women), 9 part-time/adjunct (all women). *Students:* 66 full-time (56 women), 170 part-time (162 women); includes 35 minority (17 Black or African American, non-Hispanic/Latino; 2 American Indian or Alaska Native, non-Hispanic/Latino; 5 Asian, non-Hispanic/Latino; 10 Hispanic/Latino; 1 Native Hawaiian or other Pacific Islander, non-Hispanic/Latino). Average age 37. 103 applicants, 66% accepted, 86 enrolled. In 2013, 78 master's awarded. *Expenses:* *Tuition:* Part-time $594 per credit hour. *Required fees:* $3 per semester. *Financial support:* In 2013–14, 68 students received support. *Unit head:* Dr. Susan M. Schmidt, Director, School of Nursing, 513-745-3814, E-mail: schmidt@xavier.edu. *Application contact:* Marilyn Volk Gomez, Director of Nursing Student Services, 513-745-4392, Fax: 513-745-1087, E-mail: gomez@xavier.edu.
Website: http://www.xavier.edu/msn/.

Intellectual Property Law

Baylor University, School of Law, Waco, TX 76798-7288. Offers administrative practice (JD); business litigation (JD); business transactions (JD); criminal practice (JD); estate planning (JD); general civil litigation (JD); healthcare (JD); intellectual property (JD); law (JD); real estate and natural resources (JD); JD/M Tax; JD/MBA; JD/MPPA. *Accreditation:* ABA. *Faculty:* 30 full-time (7 women), 45 part-time/adjunct (5 women). *Students:* 371 full-time (163 women), 8 part-time (2 women); includes 71 minority (6 Black or African American, non-Hispanic/Latino; 9 American Indian or Alaska Native, non-Hispanic/Latino; 14 Asian, non-Hispanic/Latino; 28 Hispanic/Latino; 14 Two or more races, non-Hispanic/Latino). Average age 24. 2,226 applicants, 37% accepted, 86 enrolled. In 2013, 176 doctorates awarded. *Entrance requirements:* For doctorate, LSAT. Additional exam requirements/recommendations for international students: Recommended—TOEFL. *Application deadline:* For fall admission, 3/1 for domestic and international students; for spring admission, 11/1 for domestic and international students; for summer admission, 2/1 for domestic and international students. Applications are processed on a rolling basis. Application fee: $0. Electronic applications accepted. Application fee is waived when completed online. *Expenses:* Contact institution. *Financial support:* In 2013–14, 296 students received support. Career-related internships or fieldwork and scholarships/grants available. Financial award application deadline: 3/1; financial award applicants required to submit FAFSA. *Unit head:* Dr. Bradley J. B. Toben, Dean, 254-710-1911, Fax: 254-710-2316. *Application*

contact: Nicole Neeley, Assistant Dean of Admissions, 254-710-1911, Fax: 254-710-2316, E-mail: nicole_neeley@baylor.edu.
Website: http://www.baylor.edu/law.

Boston University, School of Law, Boston, MA 02215. Offers American law (LL M); banking (LL M); intellectual property law (LL M); international business law (LL M); law (JD); taxation (LL M); JD/LL M; JD/MA; JD/MBA; JD/MPH; JD/MS; JD/MSW. *Accreditation:* ABA. *Faculty:* 48 full-time (19 women), 91 part-time/adjunct (26 women). *Students:* 842 full-time (462 women), 118 part-time (54 women); includes 206 minority (19 Black or African American, non-Hispanic/Latino; 1 American Indian or Alaska Native, non-Hispanic/Latino; 83 Asian, non-Hispanic/Latino; 77 Hispanic/Latino; 26 Two or more races, non-Hispanic/Latino), 157 international. Average age 27. 4,584 applicants, 35% accepted, 220 enrolled. In 2013, 183 master's, 272 doctorates awarded. *Degree requirements:* For master's, thesis (for some programs); for doctorate, thesis/dissertation, research project resulting in a paper. *Entrance requirements:* For master's, JD; for doctorate, LSAT. Additional exam requirements/recommendations for international students: Required—TOEFL (minimum score 600 paper-based; 100 iBT). *Application deadline:* For fall admission, 4/1 for domestic and international students. Applications are processed on a rolling basis. Application fee: $80. Electronic applications accepted. *Expenses: Tuition:* Full-time $43,970; part-time $1374 per credit hour. *Required fees:* $60 per semester. Tuition and fees vary according to class time, course level and program. *Financial support:* In 2013–14, 600 students received support. Career-related internships or fieldwork, Federal Work-Study, institutionally sponsored loans, and scholarships/grants available. Financial award application deadline: 3/1; financial award applicants required to submit FAFSA. *Faculty research:* Health law, tax, intellectual property, Constitutional law, corporate law, business organizations and financial law, international law, and family law. *Unit head:* Maureen A. O'Rourke, Dean, 617-353-3112, Fax: 617-353-7400, E-mail: lawdean@bu.edu. *Application contact:* Alissa Leonard, Director of Admissions and Financial Aid, 617-353-3100, Fax: 617-353-0578, E-mail: bulawadm@bu.edu.
Website: http://www.bu.edu/law/.

Case Western Reserve University, School of Law, Cleveland, OH 44106. Offers intellectual property (LL M); international business law (LL M); international criminal law (LL M); law (JD, SJD); U.S. legal studies (LL M); JD/MA; JD/MBA; JD/MD; JD/MPH; JD/MS; JD/MSSA. *Accreditation:* ABA. *Faculty:* 39 full-time (14 women), 43 part-time/adjunct (12 women). *Students:* 501 full-time (231 women), 6 part-time (3 women); includes 87 minority (35 Black or African American, non-Hispanic/Latino; 3 American Indian or Alaska Native, non-Hispanic/Latino; 30 Asian, non-Hispanic/Latino; 15 Hispanic/Latino; 1 Native Hawaiian or other Pacific Islander, non-Hispanic/Latino; 3 Two or more races, non-Hispanic/Latino), 123 international. Average age 24. 1,200 applicants, 49% accepted, 100 enrolled. In 2013, 78 master's, 229 doctorates awarded. *Entrance requirements:* For doctorate, LSAT, LSDAS. Additional exam requirements/recommendations for international students: Required—TOEFL. *Application deadline:* For fall admission, 4/1 priority date for domestic and international students. Applications are processed on a rolling basis. Application fee: $40. Electronic applications accepted. Application fee is waived when completed online. *Expenses:* Contact institution. *Financial support:* In 2013–14, 450 students received support. Career-related internships or fieldwork, Federal Work-Study, institutionally sponsored loans, and scholarships/grants available. Financial award application deadline: 5/1; financial award applicants required to submit FAFSA. *Unit head:* Jessica Berg, Interim Co-Dean, 216-368-3283. *Application contact:* Kelli Curtis, Assistant Dean for Admissions, 216-368-3600, Fax: 216-368-0185, E-mail: lawadmissions@case.edu.
Website: http://law.case.edu/.

DePaul University, College of Law, Chicago, IL 60604-2287. Offers health law (LL M); intellectual property law (LL M); international law (LL M); law (JD); taxation (LL M); JD/MA; JD/MBA; JD/MPS; JD/MS. *Accreditation:* ABA. Part-time and evening/weekend programs available. *Faculty:* 52 full-time (23 women), 53 part-time/adjunct (23 women). In 2013, 25 master's, 287 doctorates awarded. *Entrance requirements:* For doctorate, LSAT, LSAC applicant evaluation/letter of recommendation, personal statement, resume. Additional exam requirements/recommendations for international students: Required—TOEFL (minimum score 577 paper-based; 90 iBT), IELTS (minimum score 6.5). *Application deadline:* For fall admission, 3/1 for domestic and international students. Applications are processed on a rolling basis. Electronic applications accepted. *Expenses:* Contact institution. *Financial support:* Application deadline: 3/1; applicants required to submit FAFSA. *Unit head:* Gregory Mark, Dean, 312-362-5595, E-mail: gmark@depaul.edu. *Application contact:* Michael S. Burns, Director of Law Admission/Associate Dean, 312-362-6831, Fax: 312-362-5280, E-mail: lawinfo@depaul.edu.
Website: http://www.law.depaul.edu.

Fordham University, School of Law, New York, NY 10023. Offers banking, corporate and finance law (LL M); intellectual property and information law (LL M); international business and trade law (LL M); law (JD); JD/MA; JD/MBA; JD/MSW. *Accreditation:* ABA. Part-time and evening/weekend programs available. *Entrance requirements:* For doctorate, LSAT. Additional exam requirements/recommendations for international students: Required—TOEFL. Electronic applications accepted. *Expenses:* Contact institution. *Faculty research:* Intellectual property, business law, international law.

Golden Gate University, School of Law, San Francisco, CA 94105-2968. Offers environmental law (LL M); intellectual property law (LL M); international legal studies (LL M, SJD); law (JD); taxation (LL M); U. S. legal studies (LL M); JD/MBA; JD/PhD. *Accreditation:* ABA. Part-time and evening/weekend programs available. *Degree requirements:* For doctorate, thesis/dissertation (for some programs). *Entrance requirements:* For doctorate, LSAT (for JD). Additional exam requirements/recommendations for international students: Required—TOEFL (minimum score 600 paper-based). Electronic applications accepted. *Expenses:* Contact institution. *Faculty research:* International law, intellectual property law, environmental law, real estate, civil rights.

John Marshall Law School, Graduate and Professional Programs, Chicago, IL 60604-3968. Offers employee benefits (LL M, MS); estate planning (LL M); global legal studies (LL M); information technology (MS); information technology and privacy law (LL M); intellectual property (LL M, MS); international business and trade (LL M); law (JD); real estate (LL M, MS); taxation (LL M, MS); trial advocacy (LL M); JD/LL M; JD/MA; JD/MBA; JD/MPA. JD/MBA offered jointly with Dominican University; JD/MA and JD/MPA with Roosevelt University. *Accreditation:* ABA. Part-time and evening/weekend programs available. *Faculty:* 71 full-time (26 women), 132 part-time/adjunct (49 women). *Students:* 1,045 full-time (512 women), 421 part-time (211 women); includes 403 minority (152 Black or African American, non-Hispanic/Latino; 8 American Indian or Alaska Native, non-Hispanic/Latino; 89 Asian, non-Hispanic/Latino; 138 Hispanic/Latino; 3 Native Hawaiian or other Pacific Islander, non-Hispanic/Latino; 13 Two or more races, non-Hispanic/Latino), 57 international. Average age 27. 2,694 applicants, 73% accepted, 419 enrolled. In 2013, 81 master's, 445 doctorates awarded. *Degree requirements:* For master's, 24 credits; for doctorate, 90 credits. *Entrance requirements:* For master's, JD; for doctorate, LSAT. Additional exam requirements/recommendations for international students: Required—TOEFL. *Application deadline:* For fall admission, 3/1 priority date for domestic and international students; for spring admission, 10/15 priority date for domestic and international students. Applications are processed on a rolling basis. Application fee: $0. Electronic applications accepted. *Expenses:* Contact institution. *Financial support:* In 2013–14, 1,275 students received support. Scholarships/grants and tuition waivers (full and partial) available. Support available to part-time students. Financial award application deadline: 4/1; financial award applicants required to submit FAFSA. *Unit head:* John Corkery, Dean, 312-427-2737. *Application contact:* William B. Powers, Associate Dean of Admission and Student Affairs, 800-537-4280, Fax: 312-427-5136, E-mail: admission@jmls.edu.

Michigan State University College of Law, Professional Program, East Lansing, MI 48824-1300. Offers American legal system (LL M, MJ); global food law (LL M, MJ); intellectual property (LL M, MJ); law (JD). *Accreditation:* ABA. Part-time programs available. *Faculty:* 58 full-time (25 women), 90 part-time/adjunct (21 women). *Students:* 823 full-time (352 women), 175 part-time (77 women); includes 218 minority (74 Black or African American, non-Hispanic/Latino; 19 American Indian or Alaska Native, non-Hispanic/Latino; 45 Asian, non-Hispanic/Latino; 46 Hispanic/Latino; 4 Native Hawaiian or other Pacific Islander, non-Hispanic/Latino; 30 Two or more races, non-Hispanic/Latino), 112 international. Average age 26. 2,673 applicants, 50% accepted, 270 enrolled. In 2013, 39 master's, 301 doctorates awarded. *Entrance requirements:* For doctorate, LSAT. Additional exam requirements/recommendations for international students: Required—TOEFL (minimum score 600 paper-based). *Application deadline:* For fall admission, 4/30 priority date for domestic students, 7/1 priority date for international students. Applications are processed on a rolling basis. Application fee: $60. Electronic applications accepted. *Expenses:* Contact institution. *Financial support:* In 2013–14, 490 students received support. Career-related internships or fieldwork, Federal Work-Study, scholarships/grants, and tuition waivers (full and partial) available. Support available to part-time students. Financial award application deadline: 4/15; financial award applicants required to submit FAFSA. *Faculty research:* International, Constitutional, health, tax and environmental law; intellectual property, trial practice, corporate law. *Unit head:* Joan W. Howarth, Dean/Professor of Law, 517-432-6993, Fax: 517-432-6801, E-mail: howarth@law.msu.edu. *Application contact:* Charles Roboski, Assistant Dean of Admissions, 517-432-0222, Fax: 517-432-0098, E-mail: roboski@law.msu.edu.
Website: http://www.law.msu.edu/.

Montclair State University, The Graduate School, College of Humanities and Social Sciences, MA Program in Law and Governance, Montclair, NJ 07043-1624. Offers conflict management and peace studies (MA); governance, compliance and regulation (MA); intellectual property (MA); law and governance (MA); legal management (MA). Part-time and evening/weekend programs available. *Degree requirements:* For master's, thesis or comprehensive exam. *Entrance requirements:* For master's, GRE General Test, minimum cumulative GPA of 2.75 for undergraduate work, 2 letters of recommendation, essay. Additional exam requirements/recommendations for international students: Required—TOEFL (minimum score 83 iBT) or IELTS (minimum score 6.5). Electronic applications accepted.

Santa Clara University, School of Law, Santa Clara, CA 95053. Offers high technology law (Certificate); intellectual property law (LL M); international and comparative law (LL M); international high tech law (Certificate); international law (Certificate); law (JD); public interest and social justice law (Certificate); United States law (LL M); JD/MBA; MSIS/JD. LL M in United States law for non-U.S. attorneys only. *Accreditation:* ABA. Part-time and evening/weekend programs available. *Faculty:* 72 full-time (36 women), 33 part-time/adjunct (18 women). *Students:* 756 full-time (354 women), 85 part-time (53 women); includes 339 minority (14 Black or African American, non-Hispanic/Latino; 1 American Indian or Alaska Native, non-Hispanic/Latino; 182 Asian, non-Hispanic/Latino; 100 Hispanic/Latino; 5 Native Hawaiian or other Pacific Islander, non-Hispanic/Latino; 37 Two or more races, non-Hispanic/Latino), 47 international. Average age 28. 2,791 applicants, 58% accepted, 295 enrolled. In 2013, 23 master's, 323 Certificates awarded. *Degree requirements:* For master's, comprehensive exam, thesis; for doctorate, comprehensive exam, thesis/dissertation, 86 units. *Entrance requirements:* For master's and doctorate, LSAT, transcript, personal statement, letters of recommendation. *Application deadline:* For fall admission, 2/1 priority date for domestic and international students. Applications are processed on a rolling basis. Application fee: $75. Electronic applications accepted. *Expenses:* Contact institution. *Financial support:* In 2013–14, 449 students received support. Career-related internships or fieldwork, Federal Work-Study, and scholarships/grants available. Support available to part-time students. Financial award application deadline: 2/1; financial award applicants required to submit FAFSA. *Faculty research:* Intellectual property, international human rights, privacy rights, wrongful convictions, shareholder and firm governance. *Unit head:* Donald Polden, Dean, 408-554-4362. *Application contact:* Jeannette Leach, Director of Admissions, 408-554-5048.
Website: http://law.scu.edu/.

Suffolk University, Law School, Boston, MA 02108. Offers business law and financial services (JD); civil litigation (JD); global law and technology (LL M); health and biomedical law (JD); intellectual property law (JD); international law (JD); JD/MBA; JD/MPA; JD/MSCJ; JD/MSF; JD/MSIE. *Accreditation:* ABA. Part-time and evening/weekend programs available. *Faculty:* 73 full-time (34 women), 54 part-time/adjunct (14 women). *Students:* 1,074 full-time (575 women), 504 part-time (248 women); includes 351 minority (101 Black or African American, non-Hispanic/Latino; 3 American Indian or Alaska Native, non-Hispanic/Latino; 96 Asian, non-Hispanic/Latino; 132 Hispanic/Latino; 19 Two or more races, non-Hispanic/Latino), 65 international. Average age 27. 2,390 applicants, 77% accepted, 450 enrolled. In 2013, 516 doctorates awarded. *Degree requirements:* For master's, legal writing. *Entrance requirements:* For master's, 2 letters of recommendation, resume, personal statement; for doctorate, LSAT, LSDAS, dean's certification, recommendation. Additional exam requirements/recommendations for international students: Required—TOEFL (minimum score 600 paper-based; 100 iBT). *Application deadline:* For fall admission, 3/1 for domestic and international students. Applications are processed on a rolling basis. Application fee: $60. Electronic applications accepted. *Expenses:* Contact institution. *Financial support:* Career-related internships or fieldwork, Federal Work-Study, institutionally sponsored loans, and scholarships/grants available. Support available to part-time students. Financial award application deadline: 3/1; financial award applicants required to submit FAFSA. *Faculty research:* Civil law, international law, health/biomedical law, business and finance, intellectual property. *Unit head:* Camille A. Nelson, Dean of Suffolk University Law School, 617-573-8144, Fax: 617-523-1367, E-mail: gellis@suffolk.edu. *Application contact:* Jennifer Sims, Assistant Dean for Admissions and Financial Aid, 617-573-8144, Fax: 617-523-1367, E-mail: ilawadm@suffolk.edu.
Website: http://www.law.suffolk.edu/.

Thomas M. Cooley Law School, JD and LL M Programs, Lansing, MI 48901-3038. Offers administrative law (public law) (JD); business transactions (JD); Canadian law practice (JD); Constitutional law and civil rights (public law) (JD); corporate law and finance (LL M); environmental law (public law) (JD); general practice (JD), including solo and small firm; homeland and national security law (LL M); insurance law (LL M); intellectual property (JD); intellectual property law (LL M); international law (JD); litigation (JD); self-directed (LL M, JD); tax law (LL M); taxation (JD); U.S. legal studies for foreign attorneys (LL M); JD/MBA; JD/MPA; JD/MSW. *Accreditation:* ABA. Part-time

and evening/weekend programs available. Postbaccalaureate distance learning degree programs offered (no on-campus study). *Degree requirements:* For master's, thesis optional; for doctorate, minimum of 3 credits of clinical experience. *Entrance requirements:* For master's, JD or LL B; for doctorate, LSAT. Additional exam requirements/recommendations for international students: Required—TOEFL (for U.S. legal studies for foreign attorneys LL M program). Electronic applications accepted. *Faculty research:* Wrongful convictions, civil rights, environmental law, litigation techniques, data mining, intellectual property, practical and skills-based legal education.

University of Houston, Law Center, Houston, TX 77204-6060. Offers energy, environment, and natural resources (LL M); health law (LL M); intellectual property and information law (LL M); international law (LL M); law (LL M, JD); tax law (LL M). *Accreditation:* ABA. Part-time and evening/weekend programs available. *Entrance requirements:* For doctorate, LSAT. Additional exam requirements/recommendations for international students: Required—TOEFL (minimum score 600 paper-based; 100 iBT). Electronic applications accepted. *Expenses:* Contact institution. *Faculty research:* Health law, international, tax, environmental/energy, information law/intellectual property.

University of Pittsburgh, School of Law, Master of Studies in Law Program, Pittsburgh, PA 15260. Offers business law (MSL), including commercial law, corporate law, general business law, international business, tax law; Constitutional law (MSL); criminal law and justice (MSL); disabilities law (MSL); dispute resolution (MSL); education law (MSL); elder and estate planning law (MSL); employment and labor law (MSL); energy law (MSL); environment and real estate law (MSL); family law (MSL); health law (MSL); intellectual property and technology (MSL); international and comparative law (MSL); jurisprudence (MSL); personal injury and civil litigation (MSL); regulatory law (MSL); self-designed (MSL); sports and entertainment law (MSL). Part-time programs available. *Faculty:* 43 full-time (16 women), 110 part-time/adjunct (31 women). *Students:* 4 full-time (all women), 6 part-time (4 women); includes 7 minority (4 Black or African American, non-Hispanic/Latino; 2 Asian, non-Hispanic/Latino; 1 Native Hawaiian or other Pacific Islander, non-Hispanic/Latino). Average age 29. 11 applicants, 73% accepted, 7 enrolled. In 2013, 5 master's awarded. *Entrance requirements:* Additional exam requirements/recommendations for international students: Required—TOEFL (minimum score 600 paper-based; 100 iBT). *Application deadline:* For fall admission, 6/30 for domestic students, 5/1 for international students. Applications are processed on a rolling basis. Application fee: $0. *Expenses:* Tuition, state resident: full-time $19,964; part-time $807 per credit. Tuition, nonresident: full-time $32,686; part-time $1337 per credit. *Required fees:* $740; $200. Tuition and fees vary according to program. *Faculty research:* Law, health law, business law, contracts, intellectual property, environmental law. *Unit head:* Prof. Alan Meisel, Director, 412-648-1384, Fax: 412-648-2649, E-mail: meisel@pitt.edu. *Application contact:* Bethann Pischke, Administrative Coordinator, 412-648-7120, Fax: 412-648-2649, E-mail: pischke@pitt.edu.
Website: http://www.law.pitt.edu/academics/msl.

University of Pittsburgh, School of Law, Program in Intellectual Property and Technology Law, Pittsburgh, PA 15260. Offers Certificate. *Faculty:* 3 full-time (0 women), 10 part-time/adjunct (2 women). *Students:* 41 full-time (15 women). *Expenses:* Tuition, state resident: full-time $19,964; part-time $807 per credit. Tuition, nonresident: full-time $32,686; part-time $1337 per credit. *Required fees:* $740; $200. Tuition and fees vary according to program. *Faculty research:* Patent, copyright, trademark, cyberspace, biotechnology. *Unit head:* Prof. Michael Madison, Professor and Interim Director, 412-648-7855, E-mail: madison@pitt.edu. *Application contact:* Charmaine

McCall, Assistant Dean of Admissions and Financial Aid, 412-648-1413, Fax: 412-648-1318, E-mail: cmccall@pitt.edu.
Website: http://www.law.pitt.edu/academics/programs/ip/index.html.

University of San Francisco, School of Law, Master of Law Program, San Francisco, CA 94117-1080. Offers intellectual property and technology law (LL M); international transactions and comparative law (LL M). *Faculty:* 25 full-time (18 women), 61 part-time/adjunct (22 women). *Students:* 13 full-time (8 women), 4 part-time (2 women); includes 1 minority (Black or African American, non-Hispanic/Latino), 13 international. Average age 28. 122 applicants, 77% accepted, 14 enrolled. In 2013, 12 master's awarded. *Entrance requirements:* For master's, law degree from U.S. or foreign school (intellectual property and technology law); law degree from foreign school (international transactions and comparative law). Application fee: $60. *Expenses: Tuition:* Full-time $21,150; part-time $1175 per unit. Tuition and fees vary according to course load, campus/location and program. *Financial support:* In 2013–14, 6 students received support. *Unit head:* Constance De La Vega, Director, 650-728-6658. *Application contact:* Julianne Traylor, Program Assistant, 415-422-6658, E-mail: masterlaws@usfca.edu.
Website: http://www.usfca.edu/law/llm/.

University of Washington, Graduate School, School of Law, Seattle, WA 98195-3020. Offers Asian law (LL M, PhD); intellectual property law and policy (LL M); law (JD); law of sustainable international development (LL M); taxation (LL M); JD/LL M; JD/MA; JD/MAIS; JD/MBA; JD/MPA; JD/MS; JD/PhD. *Accreditation:* ABA. *Degree requirements:* For master's, thesis; for doctorate, thesis/dissertation (for some programs). *Entrance requirements:* For master's, language proficiency (LL M in Asian law); for doctorate, LSAT (for JD). Additional exam requirements/recommendations for international students: Required—TOEFL. *Expenses:* Contact institution. *Faculty research:* Asian, international and comparative law, intellectual property law, health law, environmental law, taxation.

Yeshiva University, Benjamin N. Cardozo School of Law, New York, NY 10003-4301. Offers comparative legal thought (LL M); dispute resolution and advocacy (LL M); general studies (LL M); intellectual property law (LL M); law (JD). *Accreditation:* ABA. *Faculty:* 62 full-time (24 women), 100 part-time/adjunct (40 women). *Students:* 1,047 full-time (558 women), 97 part-time (47 women); includes 278 minority (59 Black or African American, non-Hispanic/Latino; 89 Asian, non-Hispanic/Latino; 106 Hispanic/Latino; 1 Native Hawaiian or other Pacific Islander, non-Hispanic/Latino; 23 Two or more races, non-Hispanic/Latino), 85 international. Average age 24. 3,006 applicants, 43% accepted, 244 enrolled. In 2013, 67 master's, 398 doctorates awarded. *Entrance requirements:* For doctorate, LSAT, 2 letters of recommendation. *Application deadline:* For fall admission, 4/1 priority date for domestic students; for spring admission, 12/1 priority date for domestic students. Applications are processed on a rolling basis. Application fee: $75. Electronic applications accepted. *Expenses:* Contact institution. *Financial support:* In 2013–14, 751 students received support, including 67 research assistantships, 38 teaching assistantships; career-related internships or fieldwork, Federal Work-Study, institutionally sponsored loans, scholarships/grants, health care benefits, and tuition waivers (full and partial) also available. Support available to part-time students. Financial award application deadline: 3/1; financial award applicants required to submit FAFSA. *Faculty research:* Corporate and commercial law, intellectual property law, criminal law and litigation, Constitutional law, legal theory and jurisprudence. *Unit head:* David G. Martinidez, Dean of Admissions, 212-790-0274, Fax: 212-790-0482, E-mail: lawinfo@yu.edu.
Website: http://www.cardozo.yu.edu/.

Law

Albany Law School, Professional Program, Albany, NY 12208-3494. Offers LL M, JD, JD/MBA, JD/MPA, JD/MRP, JD/MS, JD/MSW. JD/MBA offered jointly with The College of Saint Rose, The Sage Colleges, Union Graduate College, and University at Albany, State University of New York; JD/MPA, JD/MRP, and JD/MSW offered jointly with University at Albany, State University of New York. *Accreditation:* ABA. Part-time programs available. *Entrance requirements:* For master's, GRE or LSAT; for doctorate, LSAT. Additional exam requirements/recommendations for international students: Recommended—TOEFL (minimum score 600 paper-based). *Expenses:* Contact institution. *Faculty research:* Federal tax, Constitutional law, secured transactions, international law, American politics.

Alliant International University–San Francisco, San Francisco Law School, JD Program, San Francisco, CA 94133-1221. Offers JD. Part-time and evening/weekend programs available. *Faculty:* 2 full-time (1 woman), 15 part-time/adjunct (3 women). *Students:* 61 full-time (29 women), 5 part-time (1 woman); includes 25 minority (3 Black or African American, non-Hispanic/Latino; 1 American Indian or Alaska Native, non-Hispanic/Latino; 7 Asian, non-Hispanic/Latino; 10 Hispanic/Latino; 4 Two or more races, non-Hispanic/Latino). Average age 34. 54 applicants, 50% accepted, 18 enrolled. In 2013, 11 doctorates awarded. *Entrance requirements:* For doctorate, LSAT, personal statement, interview. *Application deadline:* For fall admission, 7/1 for domestic and international students. Applications are processed on a rolling basis. Application fee: $75. Electronic applications accepted. *Financial support:* Application deadline: 2/15; applicants required to submit FAFSA. *Unit head:* Jane Gamp, Dean, 415-626-5550, Fax: 415-626-5584, E-mail: admissions@alliant.edu. *Application contact:* Margaret Havey, Director of Admissions, 415-626-5550, E-mail: admissions@alliant.edu.
Website: http://www.alliant.edu/sfls/sfls-program-and-coursework/index.php.

American University, Washington College of Law, Washington, DC 20016-8181. Offers advocacy (LL M); arbitration (Certificate); human rights and the law (Certificate); international legal studies (LL M, Certificate); judicial sciences (SJD); law (JD); law and government (LL M); JD/MA; JD/MBA; JD/MPP; JD/MS; LL M/MBA; LL M/MPA; LL M/MPP. *Accreditation:* ABA. Part-time and evening/weekend programs available. *Faculty:* 95 full-time (45 women), 161 part-time/adjunct (49 women). *Students:* 1,277 full-time (757 women), 428 part-time (227 women); includes 433 minority (96 Black or African American, non-Hispanic/Latino; 1 American Indian or Alaska Native, non-Hispanic/Latino; 101 Asian, non-Hispanic/Latino; 203 Hispanic/Latino; 2 Native Hawaiian or other Pacific Islander, non-Hispanic/Latino; 30 Two or more races, non-Hispanic/Latino), 195 international. Average age 26. 6,324 applicants, 28% accepted, 316 enrolled. In 2013, 142 master's, 512 doctorates awarded. *Entrance requirements:* For doctorate, LSAT, transcript, letters of recommendation. Application fee: $0. *Expenses:* Contact institution. *Financial support:* Fellowships with full tuition reimbursements, career-related internships or fieldwork, Federal Work-Study, institutionally sponsored loans, and tuition waivers (full and partial) available. Support available to part-time students. Financial award application deadline: 3/1; financial award applicants required to submit FAFSA. *Unit head:* Claudio Grossman, Dean, 202-274-4004, Fax: 202-274-4005, E-mail:

grossman@wcl.american.edu. *Application contact:* Akira Shiroma, Assistant Dean of Admissions, 202-274-4101, Fax: 202-274-4107, E-mail: shiroma@wcl.american.edu.
Website: http://www.wcl.american.edu/.

The American University in Cairo, School of Global Affairs and Public Policy, Department of Law, Cairo, Egypt. Offers international and comparative law (LL M); international human rights law (MA). Tuition and fees vary according to course level, course load and program.

American University of Armenia, Graduate Programs, Yerevan, Armenia. Offers business administration (MBA); computer and information science (MS), including business management, design and manufacturing, energy (ME, MS), industrial engineering and systems management; economics (MS); industrial engineering and systems management (ME), including business, computer aided design/manufacturing, energy (ME, MS), information technology; law (LL M); political science and international affairs (MPSIA); public health (MPH); teaching English as a foreign language (MA). Part-time and evening/weekend programs available. *Faculty:* 30 full-time (10 women), 42 part-time/adjunct (13 women). *Students:* 398 full-time (272 women), 138 part-time (84 women). Average age 24. 351 applicants, 77% accepted, 247 enrolled. In 2013, 215 master's awarded. *Degree requirements:* For master's, thesis (for some programs), capstone/project. *Entrance requirements:* For master's, GRE, GMAT, or LSAT. Additional exam requirements/recommendations for international students: Recommended—TOEFL (minimum score 79 iBT), IELTS (minimum score 6.5). *Application deadline:* For fall admission, 3/31 for domestic and international students; for spring admission, 12/20 for domestic and international students. Applications are processed on a rolling basis. Application fee: $30 ($70 for international students). *Expenses: Tuition:* Full-time $2683; part-time $122 per credit. Full-time tuition and fees vary according to program. *Financial support:* In 2013–14, 199 students received support. Teaching assistantships with partial tuition reimbursements available, career-related internships or fieldwork, institutionally sponsored loans, scholarships/grants, unspecified assistantships, and tuition assistance, institutionally-sponsored work study available. Support available to part-time students. Financial award application deadline: 6/30. *Faculty research:* Microfinance, finance (rural/development, international, corporate), firm life cycle theory, TESOL, language proficiency testing, public policy, administrative law, economic development, cryptography, artificial intelligence, energy efficiency/renewable energy, computer-aided design/manufacturing, health financing, tuberculosis control, mother/child health, preventive ophthalmology, post-earthquake psychopathological investigations, tobacco control, environmental health risk assessments. *Total annual research expenditures:* $465,763. *Unit head:* Dr. Dennis Leavens, Provost, 374 10512526, E-mail: provost@aua.am. *Application contact:* Karine Satamyan, Admissions Coordinator, 374-10324040, E-mail: grad@aua.am.
Website: http://www.aua.am.

The American University of Paris, Graduate Programs, Paris, France. Offers cross-cultural and sustainable business management (MA); cultural translation (MA); global communications (MA); global communications and civil society (MA); international

affairs (MA); international affairs, conflict resolution and civil society development (MA); Middle East and Islamic studies (MA); Middle East and Islamic studies and international affairs (MA); public policy and international affairs (MA); public policy and international law (MA). *Faculty:* 17 full-time (4 women), 12 part-time/adjunct (4 women). *Students:* 86 full-time (70 women), 92 part-time (75 women). *Degree requirements:* For master's, thesis (for some programs). *Entrance requirements:* For master's, minimum undergraduate GPA of 3.0. Additional exam requirements/recommendations for international students: Recommended—TOEFL, IELTS. *Application deadline:* For fall admission, 4/15 priority date for international students; for spring admission, 11/15 priority date for international students. Applications are processed on a rolling basis. Application fee: $75. Electronic applications accepted. *Expenses: Tuition:* Full-time 12,990 euros; part-time 812 euros per credit. *Required fees:* 890 euros per year. One-time fee: 510 euros. *Financial support:* In 2013–14, 86 students received support. Scholarships/grants available. Financial award applicants required to submit FAFSA. *Unit head:* Oliver Feltham, Associate Dean of Graduate Studies, 33 1 40 62 06 67, E-mail: ofeltham@aup.edu. *Application contact:* International Admissions Counselor, 33 1 40 62 07 20, Fax: 33 1 47 05 34 32, E-mail: admissions@aup.edu.
Website: http://www.aup.edu/academics/graduate.

Appalachian School of Law, Professional Program in Law, Grundy, VA 24614. Offers JD. *Accreditation:* ABA. *Entrance requirements:* For doctorate, LSAT, bachelor's degree from accredited institution. Electronic applications accepted. *Faculty research:* Natural resources, alternative dispute resolution, Constitutional law, professional ethics, intellectual property.

Arizona State University at the Tempe campus, Sandra Day O'Connor College of Law, Tempe, AZ 85287-7906. Offers biotechnology and genomics (LL M); global legal studies (LL M); law (JD); law (customized) (LL M); legal studies (MLS); patent practice (MLS); tribal policy, law and government (LL M); JD/MBA; JD/MD; JD/PhD. JD/MD offered jointly with Mayo Medical School. *Accreditation:* ABA. *Faculty:* 61 full-time (24 women), 64 part-time/adjunct (14 women). *Students:* 578 full-time (238 women), 45 part-time (23 women); includes 137 minority (17 Black or African American, non-Hispanic/Latino; 16 American Indian or Alaska Native, non-Hispanic/Latino; 20 Asian, non-Hispanic/Latino; 64 Hispanic/Latino; 20 Two or more races, non-Hispanic/Latino), 16 international. Average age 28. 1,595 applicants, 39% accepted, 128 enrolled. In 2013, 27 master's, 204 doctorates awarded. *Degree requirements:* For doctorate, papers. *Entrance requirements:* For master's, bachelor's degree and JD (for LL M); for doctorate, LSAT, bachelor's degree. Additional exam requirements/recommendations for international students: Required—TOEFL (minimum score 550 paper-based; 80 iBT). *Application deadline:* For fall admission, 2/1 priority date for domestic and international students. Applications are processed on a rolling basis. Application fee: $65. Electronic applications accepted. *Expenses:* Contact institution. *Financial support:* Research assistantships, teaching assistantships, career-related internships or fieldwork, Federal Work-Study, institutionally sponsored loans, scholarships/grants, tuition waivers (full and partial), and unspecified assistantships available. Financial award application deadline: 3/15; financial award applicants required to submit FAFSA. *Faculty research:* Emerging technologies and the law, Indian law, law and philosophy, international law, intellectual property. *Total annual research expenditures:* $1.7 million. *Unit head:* Douglas Sylvester, Dean/Professor, 480-965-6188, Fax: 480-965-6521, E-mail: douglas.sylvester@asu.edu. *Application contact:* Chitra Damania, Director of Operations, 480-965-1474, Fax: 480-727-7930, E-mail: law.admissions@asu.edu.
Website: http://www.law.asu.edu/.

Atlanta's John Marshall Law School, JD and LL M Programs, Atlanta, GA 30309. Offers American legal studies (LL M); employment law (LL M); law (JD). *Accreditation:* ABA. Part-time and evening/weekend programs available. Postbaccalaureate distance learning degree programs offered (minimal on-campus study). *Entrance requirements:* For master's, JD from accredited law school or bar admission; for doctorate, LSAT, LSDAS report, personal statement, two letters of reference. Additional exam requirements/recommendations for international students: Required—TOEFL. Electronic applications accepted. *Faculty research:* Tort reform, terrorism and the use of the U.S. military, Title VII's referral and deferral scheme, public utilities, eminent domain and land use regulations, recent films and their visions of law in Western society.

Ave Maria School of Law, School of Law, Naples, FL 34119. Offers JD. *Accreditation:* ABA. *Faculty:* 29 full-time (11 women), 13 part-time/adjunct (3 women). *Students:* 315 full-time (154 women), 4 part-time (2 women); includes 91 minority (18 Black or African American, non-Hispanic/Latino; 6 American Indian or Alaska Native, non-Hispanic/Latino; 4 Asian, non-Hispanic/Latino; 60 Hispanic/Latino; 1 Native Hawaiian or other Pacific Islander, non-Hispanic/Latino; 2 Two or more races, non-Hispanic/Latino), 3 international. Average age 26. 815 applicants, 71% accepted, 117 enrolled. In 2013, 159 doctorates awarded. *Entrance requirements:* For doctorate, LSAT, 2 letters of recommendation, LSDAS, personal statement. Additional exam requirements/recommendations for international students: Required—TOEFL (minimum score 600 paper-based). *Application deadline:* For fall admission, 4/1 priority date for domestic and international students. Applications are processed on a rolling basis. Application fee: $50. Electronic applications accepted. Application fee is waived when completed online. *Expenses: Tuition:* Full-time $37,950; part-time $1897.50 per credit. *Required fees:* $703 per semester. *Financial support:* In 2013–14, 176 students received support. Career-related internships or fieldwork, Federal Work-Study, and scholarships/grants available. Financial award application deadline: 6/1; financial award applicants required to submit FAFSA. *Faculty research:* International law, immigration, religious freedom, litigation, military law. *Unit head:* Eugene R. Milhizer, President/Dean, 239-687-5300. *Application contact:* Monique McCarthy, Associate Dean for Admissions, 239-687-5420, Fax: 239-352-2890, E-mail: info@avemarialaw.edu.
Website: http://www.avemarialaw.edu/.

Barry University, Dwayne O. Andreas School of Law, Orlando, FL 32807. Offers JD, JD/MS. *Accreditation:* ABA. *Entrance requirements:* For doctorate, LSAT.

Baylor University, School of Law, Waco, TX 76798-7288. Offers administrative practice (JD); business litigation (JD); business transactions (JD); criminal practice (JD); estate planning (JD); general civil litigation (JD); healthcare (JD); intellectual property (JD); law (JD); real estate and natural resources (JD); JD/M Tax; JD/MBA; JD/MPPA. *Accreditation:* ABA. *Faculty:* 30 full-time (7 women), 45 part-time/adjunct (5 women). *Students:* 371 full-time (163 women), 8 part-time (2 women); includes 71 minority (6 Black or African American, non-Hispanic/Latino; 9 American Indian or Alaska Native, non-Hispanic/Latino; 14 Asian, non-Hispanic/Latino; 28 Hispanic/Latino; 14 Two or more races, non-Hispanic/Latino). Average age 24. 2,226 applicants, 37% accepted, 86 enrolled. In 2013, 176 doctorates awarded. *Entrance requirements:* For doctorate, LSAT. Additional exam requirements/recommendations for international students: Recommended—TOEFL. *Application deadline:* For fall admission, 3/1 for domestic and international students; for spring admission, 11/1 for domestic and international students; for summer admission, 2/1 for domestic and international students. Applications are processed on a rolling basis. Application fee: $0. Electronic applications accepted. Application fee is waived when completed online. *Expenses:* Contact institution. *Financial support:* In 2013–14, 296 students received support. Career-related internships or fieldwork and scholarships/grants available. Financial award application deadline: 3/1; financial award applicants required to submit FAFSA. *Unit head:* Dr. Bradley J. B. Toben, Dean, 254-710-1911, Fax: 254-710-2316. *Application contact:* Nicole Neeley, Assistant Dean of Admissions, 254-710-1911, Fax: 254-710-2316, E-mail: nicole_neeley@baylor.edu.
Website: http://www.baylor.edu/law.

Belmont University, College of Law, Nashville, TN 37212-3757. Offers JD. *Faculty:* 20 full-time, 9 part-time/adjunct. *Students:* 296 full-time (164 women); includes 42 minority (20 Black or African American, non-Hispanic/Latino; 1 American Indian or Alaska Native, non-Hispanic/Latino; 1 Asian, non-Hispanic/Latino; 8 Hispanic/Latino; 1 Native Hawaiian or other Pacific Islander, non-Hispanic/Latino; 11 Two or more races, non-Hispanic/Latino), 1 international. Average age 26. 301 applicants, 60% accepted, 89 enrolled. *Entrance requirements:* For doctorate, LSAT. Additional exam requirements/recommendations for international students: Required—TOEFL. *Application deadline:* For fall admission, 7/31 priority date for domestic students, 7/30 priority date for international students. Applications are processed on a rolling basis. Electronic applications accepted. *Financial support:* Applicants required to submit FAFSA. *Unit head:* Jeff Kinsler, Dean, 615-460-6320, E-mail: jeff.kinsler@belmont.edu. *Application contact:* David Mee, Dean of Enrollment Services, 615-460-6785, Fax: 615-460-5434, E-mail: david.mee@belmont.edu.
Website: http://www.belmont.edu/law/.

Boston College, Law School, Newton, MA 02459. Offers JD, JD/MA, JD/MBA, JD/MSW. *Accreditation:* ABA. *Entrance requirements:* For doctorate, LSAT. Additional exam requirements/recommendations for international students: Required—TOEFL. Electronic applications accepted. *Expenses:* Contact institution. *Faculty research:* Commercial law, labor law, legal history, comparative law, international law, business law, intellectual property law, tax law, environmental law.

Boston University, School of Law, Boston, MA 02215. Offers American law (LL M); banking (LL M); intellectual property law (LL M); international business law (LL M); law (JD); taxation (LL M); JD/LL M; JD/MA; JD/MBA; JD/MPH; JD/MS; JD/MSW. *Accreditation:* ABA. *Faculty:* 48 full-time (19 women), 91 part-time/adjunct (26 women). *Students:* 842 full-time (462 women), 118 part-time (54 women); includes 206 minority (19 Black or African American, non-Hispanic/Latino; 1 American Indian or Alaska Native, non-Hispanic/Latino; 83 Asian, non-Hispanic/Latino; 77 Hispanic/Latino; 26 Two or more races, non-Hispanic/Latino), 157 international. Average age 27. 4,584 applicants, 35% accepted, 220 enrolled. In 2013, 183 master's, 272 doctorates awarded. *Degree requirements:* For master's, thesis (for some programs); for doctorate, thesis/dissertation, research project resulting in a paper. *Entrance requirements:* For master's, JD; for doctorate, LSAT. Additional exam requirements/recommendations for international students: Required—TOEFL (minimum score 600 paper-based; 100 iBT). *Application deadline:* For fall admission, 4/1 for domestic and international students. Applications are processed on a rolling basis. Application fee: $80. Electronic applications accepted. *Expenses: Tuition:* Full-time $43,970; part-time $1374 per credit hour. *Required fees:* $60 per semester. Tuition and fees vary according to class time, course level and program. *Financial support:* In 2013–14, 600 students received support. Career-related internships or fieldwork, Federal Work-Study, institutionally sponsored loans, and scholarships/grants available. Financial award application deadline: 3/1; financial award applicants required to submit FAFSA. *Faculty research:* Health law, tax, intellectual property, Constitutional law, corporate law, business organizations and financial law, international law, and family law. *Unit head:* Maureen A. O'Rourke, Dean, 617-353-3112, Fax: 617-353-7400, E-mail: lawdean@bu.edu. *Application contact:* Alissa Leonard, Director of Admissions and Financial Aid, 617-353-3100, Fax: 617-353-0578, E-mail: bulawadm@bu.edu.
Website: http://www.bu.edu/law/.

Brigham Young University, Graduate Studies, J. Reuben Clark Law School, Provo, UT 84602-8000. Offers LL M, JD, JD/M Acc, JD/M Ed, JD/MBA, JD/MPA. *Accreditation:* ABA. *Faculty:* 39 full-time (13 women), 46 part-time/adjunct (10 women). *Students:* 424 full-time (164 women), 4 part-time (1 woman); includes 66 minority (6 Black or African American, non-Hispanic/Latino; 3 American Indian or Alaska Native, non-Hispanic/Latino; 15 Asian, non-Hispanic/Latino; 26 Hispanic/Latino; 8 Native Hawaiian or other Pacific Islander, non-Hispanic/Latino; 8 Two or more races, non-Hispanic/Latino), 13 international. Average age 27. 610 applicants, 36% accepted, 139 enrolled. In 2013, 6 master's, 151 doctorates awarded. *Entrance requirements:* For doctorate, LSAT. Additional exam requirements/recommendations for international students: Recommended—TOEFL (minimum score 590 paper-based; 96 iBT), IELTS (minimum score 7). *Application deadline:* For fall admission, 6/30 priority date for domestic students. Applications are processed on a rolling basis. Application fee: $50. Electronic applications accepted. *Expenses:* Contact institution. *Financial support:* In 2013–14, 211 students received support, including 159 fellowships (averaging $6,108 per year); research assistantships, teaching assistantships, career-related internships or fieldwork, institutionally sponsored loans, scholarships/grants, and health care benefits also available. Financial award application deadline: 6/1; financial award applicants required to submit FAFSA. *Faculty research:* International law, federal taxation, real property law, Constitutional law, business organization law. *Unit head:* James R. Rasband, Dean, 801-422-6383, Fax: 801-422-0389, E-mail: rasbandj@law.byu.edu. *Application contact:* Marie Kulbeth, Admissions Director, 801-422-4277, Fax: 801-422-0389, E-mail: kulbethm@law.byu.edu.
Website: http://www.law2.byu.edu/.

Brooklyn Law School, Graduate and Professional Programs, Brooklyn, NY 11201-3798. Offers LL M, JD, JD/MA, JD/MBA, JD/MS, JD/MUP. JD/MBA offered jointly with Bernard M. Baruch College of the City University of New York; JD/MS with Pratt Institute; JD/MUP with Hunter College of the City University of New York; and JD/MA with Brooklyn College of the City University of New York. *Accreditation:* ABA. Part-time and evening/weekend programs available. *Entrance requirements:* For doctorate, LSAT, dean's certification, 2 faculty letters of evaluation. Additional exam requirements/recommendations for international students: Required—TOEFL and TWE (required for Foreign Trained Lawyers Program); Recommended—TOEFL (minimum score 600 paper-based; 100 iBT), TWE. Electronic applications accepted. *Faculty research:* Civil procedure, securities regulation, family law, corporate finance, international business and law, health law.

California Western School of Law, Graduate and Professional Programs, San Diego, CA 92101-3090. Offers law (LL M, JD); JD/MBA; JD/MSW; JD/PhD; MCL/LL M. JD/MSW and JD/MBA offered jointly with San Diego State University; JD/PhD with University of California, San Diego. *Accreditation:* ABA. Part-time programs available. *Entrance requirements:* For doctorate, LSAT. Additional exam requirements/recommendations for international students: Required—TOEFL. Electronic applications accepted. *Faculty research:* Biotechnology, child and family law, international law, labor and employment law, sports law.

Campbell University, Graduate and Professional Programs, Norman Adrian Wiggins School of Law, Buies Creek, NC 27506. Offers JD, JD/MPA. Dual degree offered in partnership with North Carolina State University. *Accreditation:* ABA. *Entrance requirements:* For doctorate, LSAT, interview. Additional exam requirements/recommendations for international students: Recommended—TOEFL. Electronic applications accepted. *Expenses:* Contact institution. *Faculty research:* Interdisciplinary

approaches to legal problems, management and planning for lawyers, church/state constitutional problems, basic research in substantive legal areas.

Capital University, Law School, Columbus, OH 43215-3200. Offers LL M, MT, JD, JD/LL M, JD/MBA, JD/MSA, JD/MSN, JD/MTS. *Accreditation:* ABA. Part-time and evening/weekend programs available. *Degree requirements:* For master's, thesis or alternative. *Entrance requirements:* For master's, previous course work in accounting, business law, and taxation; for doctorate, LSAT, LSDAS. Additional exam requirements/recommendations for international students: Required—TOEFL. Electronic applications accepted. *Expenses:* Contact institution. *Faculty research:* Dispute resolution, remedies, taxation, commercial law, election law.

Case Western Reserve University, School of Law, Cleveland, OH 44106. Offers intellectual property (LL M); international business law (LL M); international criminal law (LL M); law (JD, SJD); U.S. legal studies (LL M); JD/MA; JD/MBA; JD/MD; JD/MPH; JD/MS; JD/MSSA. *Accreditation:* ABA. *Faculty:* 39 full-time (14 women), 43 part-time/adjunct (12 women). *Students:* 501 full-time (231 women), 6 part-time (3 women); includes 87 minority (35 Black or African American, non-Hispanic/Latino; 3 American Indian or Alaska Native, non-Hispanic/Latino; 30 Asian, non-Hispanic/Latino; 15 Hispanic/Latino; 1 Native Hawaiian or other Pacific Islander, non-Hispanic/Latino; 3 Two or more races, non-Hispanic/Latino; 123 international. Average age 24. 1,200 applicants, 49% accepted, 100 enrolled. In 2013, 78 master's, 229 doctorates awarded. *Entrance requirements:* For doctorate, LSAT, LSDAS. Additional exam requirements/recommendations for international students: Required—TOEFL. *Application deadline:* For fall admission, 4/1 priority date for domestic and international students. Applications are processed on a rolling basis. Application fee: $40. Electronic applications accepted. Application fee is waived when completed online. *Expenses:* Contact institution. *Financial support:* In 2013–14, 450 students received support. Career-related internships or fieldwork, Federal Work-Study, institutionally sponsored loans, and scholarships/grants available. Financial award application deadline: 5/1; financial award applicants required to submit FAFSA. *Unit head:* Jessica Berg, Interim Co-Dean, 216-368-3283. *Application contact:* Kelli Curtis, Assistant Dean for Admissions, 216-368-3600, Fax: 216-368-0185, E-mail: lawadmissions@case.edu.
Website: http://law.case.edu/.

The Catholic University of America, Columbus School of Law, Washington, DC 20064. Offers JD, JD/JCL, JD/MA, JD/MLS, JD/MSW. *Accreditation:* ABA. Part-time and evening/weekend programs available. *Faculty:* 46 full-time (21 women), 3 part-time/adjunct (1 woman). *Students:* 401 full-time (221 women), 211 part-time (99 women); includes 80 minority (33 Black or African American, non-Hispanic/Latino; 1 American Indian or Alaska Native, non-Hispanic/Latino; 22 Asian, non-Hispanic/Latino; 23 Hispanic/Latino; 1 Two or more races, non-Hispanic/Latino; 6 international. Average age 26. 1,869 applicants, 55% accepted, 161 enrolled. *Entrance requirements:* For doctorate, LSAT. Additional exam requirements/recommendations for international students: Required—TOEFL (minimum score 600 paper-based; 100 iBT). *Application deadline:* For fall admission, 3/16 priority date for domestic students, 3/16 for international students. Applications are processed on a rolling basis. Application fee: $65. Electronic applications accepted. Application fee is waived when completed online. *Expenses:* Contact institution. *Financial support:* In 2013–14, 318 students received support. Career-related internships or fieldwork, Federal Work-Study, institutionally sponsored loans, and scholarships/grants available. Support available to part-time students. Financial award application deadline: 8/15; financial award applicants required to submit FAFSA. *Unit head:* Daniel F. Attridge, Dean, 202-319-5139, Fax: 202-319-5473. *Application contact:* Shani J. P. Butts, Director of Admissions, 202-319-5151, Fax: 202-319-6285, E-mail: butts@law.edu.
Website: http://www.law.edu/.

Central European University, Graduate Studies, Department of Legal Studies, Budapest, Hungary. Offers comparative Constitutional law (LL M); human rights (LL M, MA); international business law (LL M); law and economics (LL M, MA); legal studies (SJD). *Faculty:* 9 full-time (4 women), 16 part-time/adjunct (3 women). *Students:* 98 full-time (54 women). Average age 27. 324 applicants, 32% accepted, 67 enrolled. In 2013, 47 master's awarded. Terminal master's awarded for partial completion of doctoral program. *Degree requirements:* For master's, one foreign language, thesis; for doctorate, one foreign language, comprehensive exam, thesis/dissertation. *Entrance requirements:* For master's and doctorate, LSAT. Additional exam requirements/recommendations for international students: Required—TOEFL (minimum score 570 paper-based); Recommended—IELTS (minimum score 6.5). *Application deadline:* For fall admission, 1/24 for domestic and international students. Application fee: $40. Electronic applications accepted. *Expenses:* Contact institution. *Financial support:* In 2013–14, 77 students received support, including 77 fellowships with full and partial tuition reimbursements available (averaging $6,100 per year); career-related internships or fieldwork, institutionally sponsored loans, scholarships/grants, and tuition waivers (full and partial) also available. Financial award application deadline: 1/5. *Faculty research:* Institutional, constitutional and human rights in European Union law; biomedical law and reproductive rights; data protection law; Islamic banking and finance. *Unit head:* Dr. Renata Uitz, Head of Department, 36 1 327-3201, Fax: 361-327-3198, E-mail: legalst@ceu.hu. *Application contact:* Andrea Jenei, Department Coordinator, 361-327-3205, Fax: 361-327-3198, E-mail: jeneia@ceu.hu.
Website: http://legal.ceu.hu/.

Champlain College, Graduate Studies, Burlington, VT 05402-0670. Offers business (MBA); digital forensic management (MS); digital forensic science (MS); early childhood education (M Ed); emergent media (MFA, MS); health care administration (MS); law (MS); managing innovation and information technology (MS); mediation and applied conflict studies (MS). MS in emergent media program held in Shanghai. Part-time programs available. Postbaccalaureate distance learning degree programs offered (no on-campus study). *Faculty:* 13 full-time (2 women), 34 part-time/adjunct (14 women). *Students:* 303 full-time (191 women), 104 part-time (58 women); includes 38 minority (21 Black or African American, non-Hispanic/Latino; 8 Asian, non-Hispanic/Latino; 7 Hispanic/Latino; 2 Two or more races, non-Hispanic/Latino; 4 international. Average age 37. In 2013, 169 master's awarded. *Degree requirements:* For master's, capstone project. *Entrance requirements:* Additional exam requirements/recommendations for international students: Required—TOEFL (minimum score 550 paper-based; 80 iBT). *Application deadline:* For fall admission, 8/1 priority date for domestic and international students; for spring admission, 1/1 priority date for domestic and international students. Applications are processed on a rolling basis. Electronic applications accepted. *Expenses:* Tuition: Full-time $18,456; part-time $769 per credit. Tuition and fees vary according to program. *Financial support:* Applicants required to submit FAFSA. *Unit head:* Dr. Donald Haggerty, Associate Provost of Graduate Studies, 802-865-6496, Fax: 802-865-6447, E-mail: haggerty@champlain.edu. *Application contact:* Matt Manz, Assistant Director, Graduate Admission, 800-383-6603, E-mail: mmanz@champlain.edu.
Website: http://www.champlain.edu/academics/graduate-studies.

Chapman University, School of Law, Orange, CA 92866. Offers advocacy and dispute resolution (JD); entertainment and media law (LL M); entertainment law (JD); environmental, land use, and real estate (JD); international law (JD); law (JD); prosecutorial science (LL M); tax law (JD); taxation (LL M); trial advocacy (LL M); JD/

MBA; JD/MFA. *Accreditation:* ABA. Part-time and evening/weekend programs available. *Faculty:* 47 full-time (19 women), 35 part-time/adjunct (4 women). *Students:* 483 full-time (241 women), 71 part-time (28 women); includes 164 minority (5 Black or African American, non-Hispanic/Latino; 1 American Indian or Alaska Native, non-Hispanic/Latino; 84 Asian, non-Hispanic/Latino; 47 Hispanic/Latino; 1 Native Hawaiian or other Pacific Islander, non-Hispanic/Latino; 26 Two or more races, non-Hispanic/Latino), 76 international. Average age 26. 1,691 applicants, 51% accepted, 157 enrolled. In 2013, 36 master's, 187 doctorates awarded. *Entrance requirements:* For doctorate, LSAT, minimum undergraduate GPA of 2.75. Additional exam requirements/recommendations for international students: Required—TOEFL (minimum score 600 paper-based; 80 iBT). *Application deadline:* For fall admission, 4/15 priority date for domestic students. Applications are processed on a rolling basis. Application fee: $65. Electronic applications accepted. *Expenses:* Contact institution. *Financial support:* Fellowships, Federal Work-Study, and scholarships/grants available. Financial award applicants required to submit FAFSA. *Unit head:* Dr. Tom Campbell, Dean, 714-628-2500. *Application contact:* Karman Hsu, Assistant Dean of Admissions and Diversity Initiatives, 877-CHAPLAW, E-mail: mvargas@chapman.edu.
Website: http://www.chapman.edu/law/.

Charlotte School of Law, Professional Program, Charlotte, NC 28204. Offers JD. *Accreditation:* ABA.

City University of New York School of Law, Professional Program, Long Island City, NY 11101-4356. Offers JD. *Accreditation:* ABA. *Faculty:* 52 full-time (34 women), 5 part-time/adjunct (2 women). *Students:* 375 full-time (229 women), 3 part-time (1 woman); includes 160 minority (30 Black or African American, non-Hispanic/Latino; 1 American Indian or Alaska Native, non-Hispanic/Latino; 46 Asian, non-Hispanic/Latino; 68 Hispanic/Latino; 1 Native Hawaiian or other Pacific Islander, non-Hispanic/Latino; 14 Two or more races, non-Hispanic/Latino), 10 international. Average age 27. 1,512 applicants, 30% accepted, 104 enrolled. In 2013, 138 doctorates awarded. *Entrance requirements:* For doctorate, LSAT, CAS Report, bachelor's degree. Additional exam requirements/recommendations for international students: Recommended—TOEFL. *Application deadline:* For fall admission, 5/15 priority date for domestic students. Applications are processed on a rolling basis. Application fee: $60. Electronic applications accepted. *Financial support:* In 2013–14, 101 students received support, including 35 fellowships (averaging $12,760 per year), 56 research assistantships (averaging $1,319 per year); career-related internships or fieldwork, Federal Work-Study, scholarships/grants, and tuition waivers (partial) also available. Financial award application deadline: 5/1; financial award applicants required to submit FAFSA. *Unit head:* Michelle J. Anderson, Dean/Professor of Law, 718-340-4201, Fax: 718-340-4482. *Application contact:* Helena Quon, Assistant Dean for Enrollment Management/Director of Admissions, 718-340-4210, Fax: 718-340-4435, E-mail: admissions@law.cuny.edu.
Website: http://www.law.cuny.edu/.

Cleveland State University, Cleveland-Marshall College of Law, Cleveland, OH 44115. Offers business law (JD); civil litigation and dispute resolution (JD); criminal law (JD); employment labor law (JD); health care compliance (Certificate); health law (Certificate); international and comparative law (JD); law (LL M, MLS); JD/MAES; JD/MBA; JD/MPA; JD/MSES; JD/MUPDD. *Accreditation:* ABA. Part-time and evening/weekend programs available. *Faculty:* 37 full-time (16 women), 40 part-time/adjunct (11 women). *Students:* 307 full-time (129 women), 158 part-time (79 women); includes 86 minority (40 Black or African American, non-Hispanic/Latino; 3 American Indian or Alaska Native, non-Hispanic/Latino; 14 Asian, non-Hispanic/Latino; 21 Hispanic/Latino; 8 Two or more races, non-Hispanic/Latino), 9 international. Average age 28. 1,655 applicants, 38% accepted, 173 enrolled. In 2013, 1 master's, 155 doctorates, 4 Certificates awarded. *Degree requirements:* For master's, thesis for graduates of U.S. law schools (for LL M); 30 credits, 6 in required courses (for MLS); for doctorate, 90 credits (41 in required courses). *Entrance requirements:* For master's, JD or LL B (for LL M); bachelor's degree (for MLS); for doctorate, LSAT, bachelor's degree. Additional exam requirements/recommendations for international students: Required—TOEFL (minimum score 600 paper-based, 100 iBT) or IELTS (minimum score 7) for LL.M. *Application deadline:* For fall admission, 5/1 for domestic and international students. Applications are processed on a rolling basis. Application fee: $0. Electronic applications accepted. *Expenses:* Contact institution. *Financial support:* In 2013–14, 162 students received support, including 18 fellowships (averaging $2,500 per year), 25 research assistantships, 8 teaching assistantships with partial tuition reimbursements available (averaging $7,328 per year); career-related internships or fieldwork, Federal Work-Study, scholarships/grants, tuition waivers (full and partial), and unspecified assistantships also available. Support available to part-time students. Financial award application deadline: 5/1; financial award applicants required to submit FAFSA. *Faculty research:* Health law, international law, Constitutional law, criminal law, business law. *Unit head:* Craig M. Boise, Dean, 216-687-2300, Fax: 216-687-6881, E-mail: c.boise@csuohio.edu. *Application contact:* Christopher Lucak, Assistant Dean for Admissions, 216-687-4692, Fax: 216-687-6881, E-mail: c.lucak@csuohio.edu.
Website: http://www.law.csuohio.edu/.

Cleveland State University, College of Graduate Studies, Maxine Goodman Levin College of Urban Affairs, Program in Urban Studies, Cleveland, OH 44115. Offers community and neighborhood development (MS); economic development (MS); law and public policy (MS); public finance (MS); urban economic development (Certificate); urban policy analysis (MS); urban real estate development (MS); urban real estate development and finance (Certificate). Part-time and evening/weekend programs available. *Faculty:* 21 full-time (10 women), 11 part-time/adjunct (3 women). *Students:* 5 full-time (1 woman), 8 part-time (2 women); includes 1 minority (Black or African American, non-Hispanic/Latino). Average age 34. 21 applicants, 29% accepted, 4 enrolled. In 2013, 8 master's awarded. *Degree requirements:* For master's, thesis or alternative, exit project. *Entrance requirements:* For master's, GRE General Test (minimum score: verbal and quantitative combined 40th percentile, analytical writing 4.0), minimum GPA of 3.0. Additional exam requirements/recommendations for international students: Required—TOEFL (minimum score 525 paper-based; 65 iBT), IELTS or ITEP. *Application deadline:* For fall admission, 1/15 priority date for domestic students, 1/15 for international students. Applications are processed on a rolling basis. Application fee: $30. Electronic applications accepted. *Expenses:* Tuition, state resident: full-time $8335; part-time $521 per credit hour. Tuition, nonresident: full-time $15,670; part-time $979 per credit hour. *Required fees:* $50; $25 per semester. *Financial support:* In 2013–14, 4 students received support, including 3 research assistantships with full and partial tuition reimbursements available (averaging $7,200 per year), 1 teaching assistantship with full and partial tuition reimbursement available (averaging $7,200 per year); career-related internships or fieldwork, scholarships/grants, traineeships, and unspecified assistantships also available. Support available to part-time students. Financial award application deadline: 3/1; financial award applicants required to submit FAFSA. *Faculty research:* Environmental issues, economic development, urban and public policy, public management. *Unit head:* Dr. Brian Mikelbank, Director, 216-875-9980, Fax: 216-687-9342, E-mail: b.mikelbank@csuohio.edu. *Application contact:* David Arrighi, Graduate Academic Advisor, 216-523-7522, Fax: 216-687-5398, E-mail: urbanprograms@csuohio.edu.
Website: http://urban.csuohio.edu/academics/graduate/msus/.

Law

The College of William and Mary, William and Mary Law School, Williamsburg, VA 23187-8795. Offers LL M, JD, JD/MA, JD/MBA, JD/MPP. *Accreditation:* ABA. *Faculty:* 44 full-time (19 women), 54 part-time/adjunct (16 women). *Students:* 667 full-time (334 women), 16 part-time (8 women); includes 95 minority (40 Black or African American, non-Hispanic/Latino; 17 Asian, non-Hispanic/Latino; 20 Hispanic/Latino; 1 Native Hawaiian or other Pacific Islander, non-Hispanic/Latino; 17 Two or more races, non-Hispanic/Latino), 62 international. Average age 25. 6,106 applicants, 31% accepted, 286 enrolled. In 2013, 27 master's, 219 doctorates awarded. *Degree requirements:* For doctorate, major paper. *Entrance requirements:* For master's, LL B, references; for doctorate, LSAT, baccalaureate degree, references. Additional exam requirements/recommendations for international students: Required—TOEFL (minimum score 600 paper-based; 100 iBT). *Application deadline:* For fall admission, 3/1 priority date for domestic and international students. Application fee: $50. Electronic applications accepted. *Expenses:* Contact institution. *Financial support:* In 2013–14, 566 students received support, including 167 fellowships with partial tuition reimbursements available (averaging $4,000 per year), 94 research assistantships (averaging $1,326 per year), 49 teaching assistantships (averaging $2,808 per year); career-related internships or fieldwork, scholarships/grants, and unspecified assistantships also available. Financial award application deadline: 2/15; financial award applicants required to submit FAFSA. *Faculty research:* Constitutional law, criminal law, corporate law, international law, legal skills/trial advocacy. *Total annual research expenditures:* $53,285. *Unit head:* Davison M. Douglas, Dean/Professor, 757-221-3790, Fax: 757-221-3261, E-mail: dmdoug@wm.edu. *Application contact:* Faye F. Shealy, Associate Dean for Admission, 757-221-3785, Fax: 757-221-3261, E-mail: ffshea@wm.edu.
Website: http://law.wm.edu/.

Columbia University, School of Law, New York, NY 10027. Offers LL M, JD, JSD, JD/M Phil, JD/MA, JD/MBA, JD/MFA, JD/MIA, JD/MPA, JD/MPH, JD/MSW. *Accreditation:* ABA. *Entrance requirements:* For doctorate, LSAT (for JD). Electronic applications accepted. *Expenses:* Contact institution. *Faculty research:* Human rights, law and philosophy, corporate governance, regulation of the workplace, death penalty.

Concord Law School, Program in Law, Los Angeles, CA 90024. Offers EJD, JD. Part-time and evening/weekend programs available. Postbaccalaureate distance learning degree programs offered (no on-campus study). *Degree requirements:* For doctorate, comprehensive exam. *Entrance requirements:* For doctorate, online admissions test. Additional exam requirements/recommendations for international students: Required—TOEFL (minimum score 520 paper-based). Electronic applications accepted.

Cornell University, Cornell Law School, Ithaca, NY 14853-4901. Offers LL M, JD, JSD, JD/DESS, JD/LL M, JD/MA, JD/MBA, JD/MILR, JD/MLLP, JD/MLP, JD/MPA, JD/MRP, JD/Maitrise en Droit, JD/PhD. JD/MLLP offered jointly with Humboldt University, Berlin; JD/DESS offered jointly with Institut d'etudes Politiques de Paris ("Sciences Po") and Paris I. *Accreditation:* ABA. *Entrance requirements:* For doctorate, LSAT (for JD). Electronic applications accepted. *Expenses:* Contact institution. *Faculty research:* International law, Constitutional law, corporate laws, public interest law, feminist legal theory.

Cornell University, Graduate School, Graduate Field in the Law School, Ithaca, NY 14853. Offers JSD. *Faculty:* 37 full-time (11 women). *Students:* 14 full-time (9 women); includes 1 minority (Black or African American, non-Hispanic/Latino), 12 international. Average age 31. 4 applicants, 100% accepted, 4 enrolled. In 2013, 2 doctorates awarded. *Entrance requirements:* For doctorate, JD, LL M, or equivalent; 2 letters of recommendation. Additional exam requirements/recommendations for international students: Required—TOEFL (minimum score 550 paper-based). *Application deadline:* For fall admission, 5/1 for domestic students. Application fee: $95. Electronic applications accepted. *Expenses:* Contact institution. *Financial support:* In 2013–14, 10 students received support, including 10 fellowships with full tuition reimbursements available; research assistantships with full tuition reimbursements available, teaching assistantships with full tuition reimbursements available, institutionally sponsored loans, scholarships/grants, health care benefits, tuition waivers (full and partial), and unspecified assistantships also available. Financial award applicants required to submit FAFSA. *Faculty research:* International economic integration (World Trade Organization and European Union), international commercial arbitration, feminist jurisprudence, human rights. *Unit head:* Director of Graduate Studies, 607-255-5141. *Application contact:* Graduate Field Assistant, 607-255-5141, E-mail: gradlaw@law.mail.cornell.edu.
Website: http://www.gradschool.cornell.edu/fields.php?id-89&a-2.

Creighton University, School of Law, Omaha, NE 68178. Offers MS, JD, Certificate, JD/MA, JD/MBA, JD/MS. *Accreditation:* ABA. Part-time programs available. *Faculty:* 34 full-time (11 women), 16 part-time/adjunct (5 women). *Students:* 382 full-time (137 women), 11 part-time (2 women); includes 47 minority (16 Black or African American, non-Hispanic/Latino; 1 American Indian or Alaska Native, non-Hispanic/Latino; 13 Asian, non-Hispanic/Latino; 7 Hispanic/Latino; 10 Two or more races, non-Hispanic/Latino), 8 international. Average age 25. 763 applicants, 75% accepted, 139 enrolled. In 2013, 128 doctorates awarded. *Entrance requirements:* For doctorate, LSAT, bachelor's degree. Additional exam requirements/recommendations for international students: Recommended—TOEFL (minimum score 600 paper-based). *Application deadline:* For fall admission, 5/1 priority date for domestic and international students; for summer admission, 4/1 priority date for domestic and international students. Applications are processed on a rolling basis. Application fee: $50. Electronic applications accepted. Application fee is waived when completed online. *Expenses:* Contact institution. *Financial support:* In 2013–14, 199 students received support. Career-related internships or fieldwork, institutionally sponsored loans, and scholarships/grants available. Support available to part-time students. Financial award application deadline: 7/1; financial award applicants required to submit FAFSA. *Faculty research:* Conflict of laws, international law, evidence, cyber warfare, Constitutional law. *Unit head:* Marianne B. Culhane, Dean and Professor of Law, 402-280-2874, Fax: 402-280-3161. *Application contact:* Andrea D. Bashara, Assistant Dean, 402-280-2586, Fax: 402-280-3161, E-mail: bashara@creighton.edu.
Website: http://www.creighton.edu/law.

Dalhousie University, Faculty of Graduate Studies, Dalhousie Law School, Halifax, NS B3H 4H9, Canada. Offers LL M, JSD, LL B/MBA, LL B/MLIS, LL B/MPA. Part-time programs available. *Degree requirements:* For master's, thesis or alternative; for doctorate, thesis/dissertation. *Entrance requirements:* For master's, LL B; for doctorate, LL M. Additional exam requirements/recommendations for international students: Required—1 of 5 approved tests: TOEFL, IELTS, CANTEST, CAEL, Michigan English Language Assessment Battery. Electronic applications accepted. *Expenses:* Contact institution. *Faculty research:* Marine and environmental law, health law, the family law program.

DePaul University, College of Law, Chicago, IL 60604-2287. Offers health law (LL M); intellectual property law (LL M); international law (LL M); law (JD); taxation (LL M); JD/MA; JD/MBA; JD/MPS; JD/MS. *Accreditation:* ABA. Part-time and evening/weekend programs available. *Faculty:* 52 full-time (23 women), 53 part-time/adjunct (23 women). In 2013, 25 master's, 287 doctorates awarded. *Entrance requirements:* For doctorate, LSAT, LSAC applicant evaluation/letter of recommendation, personal statement, resume. Additional exam requirements/recommendations for international students: Required—TOEFL (minimum score 577 paper-based; 90 iBT), IELTS (minimum score 6.5). *Application deadline:* For fall admission, 3/1 for domestic and international students. Applications are processed on a rolling basis. Electronic applications accepted. *Expenses:* Contact institution. *Financial support:* Application deadline: 3/1; applicants required to submit FAFSA. *Unit head:* Gregory Mark, Dean, 312-362-5595, E-mail: gmark@depaul.edu. *Application contact:* Michael S. Burns, Director of Law Admission/Associate Dean, 312-362-6831, Fax: 312-362-5280, E-mail: lawinfo@depaul.edu.
Website: http://www.law.depaul.edu.

Drake University, Law School, Des Moines, IA 50311-4505. Offers LL M, JD, JD/MA, JD/MBA, JD/MPA, JD/MS, JD/MSW, JD/Pharm D. JD/MA and JD/MS offered jointly with Iowa State University of Science and Technology; JD/MSW with The University of Iowa. *Accreditation:* ABA. *Faculty:* 30 full-time (10 women), 1 (woman) part-time/adjunct. *Students:* 365 full-time (163 women), 10 part-time (6 women); includes 44 minority (18 Black or African American, non-Hispanic/Latino; 6 Asian, non-Hispanic/Latino; 17 Hispanic/Latino; 3 Two or more races, non-Hispanic/Latino), 5 international. Average age 26. 1,009 applicants, 55% accepted, 142 enrolled. In 2013, 5 master's, 140 doctorates awarded. *Degree requirements:* For doctorate, 2 internships. *Entrance requirements:* For doctorate, LSAT, LSDAS report. Additional exam requirements/recommendations for international students: Required—TOEFL (minimum score 560 paper-based), TWE. *Application deadline:* For fall admission, 4/1 priority date for domestic and international students. Applications are processed on a rolling basis. Application fee: $40. Electronic applications accepted. *Expenses:* Contact institution. *Financial support:* In 2013–14, 20 research assistantships (averaging $757 per year), 6 teaching assistantships (averaging $2,142 per year) were awarded; career-related internships or fieldwork, Federal Work-Study, institutionally sponsored loans, scholarships/grants, and tuition waivers (full and partial) also available. Support available to part-time students. Financial award application deadline: 3/1; financial award applicants required to submit FAFSA. *Faculty research:* Constitutional law, environmental law, agricultural law, computers and the law, bioethics and health law. *Unit head:* Alan Vestal, Dean, 515-271-3985, Fax: 515-271-4118, E-mail: alan.vestal@drake.edu. *Application contact:* Jason Allen, Director of Admission, 515-271-2040, Fax: 515-271-2530, E-mail: jason.allen@drake.edu.
Website: http://www.law.drake.edu/.

Duke University, School of Law, Durham, NC 27708. Offers LL M, MJS, MLS, JD, SJD, JD/AM, JD/LL M, JD/MA, JD/MBA, JD/MEM, JD/MPP, JD/MS, JD/MTS, JD/PhD, MD/JD. LL M and SJD offered only to international students; MJS offered only to sitting judges. *Accreditation:* ABA. *Faculty:* 56 full-time (18 women), 32 part-time/adjunct (10 women). *Students:* 647 full-time (285 women); includes 172 minority (47 Black or African American, non-Hispanic/Latino; 84 Asian, non-Hispanic/Latino; 39 Hispanic/Latino; 2 Native Hawaiian or other Pacific Islander, non-Hispanic/Latino), 33 international. Average age 24. 5,014 applicants, 19% accepted, 209 enrolled. In 2013, 133 master's, 244 doctorates awarded. *Degree requirements:* For doctorate, thesis/dissertation (for some programs). *Entrance requirements:* For doctorate, LSAT (for JD). Additional exam requirements/recommendations for international students: Required—TOEFL (minimum score 600 paper-based). *Application deadline:* For fall admission, 2/15 for domestic and international students. Applications are processed on a rolling basis. Application fee: $70. Electronic applications accepted. *Expenses:* Contact institution. *Financial support:* In 2013–14, 542 students received support. Institutionally sponsored loans and scholarships/grants available. Financial award application deadline: 3/15; financial award applicants required to submit FAFSA. *Faculty research:* International and comparative law; constitutional and public law; intellectual property, science and technology; business, finance, and corporate law; environmental law and policy. *Unit head:* David F. Levi, Dean/Professor of Law, 919-613-7001, Fax: 919-613-7158. *Application contact:* William J. Hoye, Associate Dean for Admissions and Student Affairs, 919-613-7020, Fax: 919-613-7257, E-mail: hoye@law.duke.edu.
Website: http://www.law.duke.edu/.

Duquesne University, Bayer School of Natural and Environmental Sciences, Program in Forensic Science and Law, Pittsburgh, PA 15282-0001. Offers MS. *Faculty:* 4 full-time (2 women), 13 part-time/adjunct (7 women). *Students:* 10 full-time (6 women); includes 1 minority (Hispanic/Latino). Average age 22. In 2013, 10 master's awarded. *Degree requirements:* For master's, comprehensive exam. *Entrance requirements:* For master's, SAT or ACT, 1 recommendation form; minimum total QPA of 3.0, 2.5 in math and science. *Application deadline:* For fall admission, 7/1 for domestic and international students. Applications are processed on a rolling basis. Application fee: $50. Electronic applications accepted. *Expenses: Tuition:* Full-time $18,162; part-time $1009 per credit. *Required fees:* $1728; $96 per credit. Tuition and fees vary according to program. *Financial support:* In 2013–14, 10 students received support. Career-related internships or fieldwork and unspecified assistantships available. Financial award application deadline: 5/1. *Faculty research:* Extraction protocols, mass spectrometry, synthetic fiber analysis, synthetic polymer characterization, trace analysis, amplification of DNA, methods for labeling DNA, construction of a genetic profile, experiential exploration of mitochondrial DNA, the Y-chromosome, and amelogenin. *Total annual research expenditures:* $115,510. *Unit head:* Dr. Federick W. Fochtman, Director, 412-396-6373, Fax: 412-396-1402, E-mail: fochtman@duq.edu. *Application contact:* Valerie L. Lijewski, Academic Advisor, 412-396-1084, Fax: 412-396-1402, E-mail: lijewski@duq.edu.
Website: http://www.duq.edu/academics/schools/natural-and-environmental-sciences/academic-programs/forensic-science-and-law.

Duquesne University, School of Law, Pittsburgh, PA 15282-0700. Offers American law for foreign lawyers (LL M); law (JD); JD/M Div; JD/MBA; JD/MS; JD/MSEM. JD/M Div offered jointly with Pittsburgh Theological Seminary. *Accreditation:* ABA. Part-time and evening/weekend programs available. *Faculty:* 27 full-time (9 women), 39 part-time/adjunct (12 women). *Students:* 351 full-time (164 women), 140 part-time (65 women); includes 36 minority (6 Black or African American, non-Hispanic/Latino; 2 American Indian or Alaska Native, non-Hispanic/Latino; 9 Asian, non-Hispanic/Latino; 11 Hispanic/Latino; 8 Two or more races, non-Hispanic/Latino), 4 international. Average age 26. 689 applicants, 64% accepted, 147 enrolled. In 2013, 2 master's, 205 doctorates awarded. *Entrance requirements:* For doctorate, LSAT. Additional exam requirements/recommendations for international students: Required—TOEFL. *Application deadline:* For fall admission, 3/1 priority date for domestic students. Applications are processed on a rolling basis. Application fee: $60. Electronic applications accepted. *Expenses:* Contact institution. *Financial support:* In 2013–14, 267 students received support. Research assistantships, teaching assistantships, career-related internships or fieldwork, Federal Work-Study, scholarships/grants, and tuition waivers (partial) available. Support available to part-time students. Financial award application deadline: 5/31; financial award applicants required to submit FAFSA. *Faculty research:* Constitutional law, law and religion, intellectual property and patents, neuroscience and law, civil and criminal law and procedure, feminist perspective on environmental law. *Total annual research expenditures:* $100,000. *Unit head:* Ken Gormley, Dean, 412-396-6300, Fax: 412-396-6659, E-mail: lawadmissions@duq.edu. *Application contact:* Office of Admissions, 412-396-6296, Fax: 412-396-6659, E-mail: lawadmissions@duq.edu.
Website: http://www.duq.edu/academics/schools/law.

Elon University, Program in Law, Elon, NC 27244-2010. Offers JD. *Accreditation:* ABA. *Faculty:* 17 full-time (4 women), 30 part-time/adjunct (7 women). *Students:* 294 full-time (143 women); includes 54 minority (33 Black or African American, non-Hispanic/Latino; 8 American Indian or Alaska Native, non-Hispanic/Latino; 5 Asian, non-Hispanic/Latino; 8 Hispanic/Latino), 1 international. Average age 26. 694 applicants, 68% accepted, 107 enrolled. *Entrance requirements:* For doctorate, LSAT, LSDAS. Additional exam requirements/recommendations for international students: Required—TOEFL (minimum score 550 paper-based; 79 iBT). *Application deadline:* For fall admission, 6/30 for domestic students; for spring admission, 4/1 priority date for domestic students. Applications are processed on a rolling basis. Application fee: $50. Electronic applications accepted. *Expenses:* Contact institution. *Financial support:* In 2013–14, 275 students received support. Federal Work-Study and scholarships/grants available. Financial award applicants required to submit FAFSA. *Faculty research:* Quality of life and job satisfaction, civil procedure, damages, assessment for development of instruments, psychological types. *Unit head:* George Johnson, Dean, 336-279-9201, E-mail: gjohnson8@elon.edu. *Application contact:* Alan Woodlief, Associate Dean of School of Law/Director of Law School Admissions, 336-279-9203, E-mail: awoodlief@elon.edu.
Website: http://www.elon.edu/law.

Emory University, School of Law, Atlanta, GA 30322-2770. Offers LL M, JD, Certificate, JD/Certificate, JD/LL M, JD/M Div, JD/MA, JD/MBA, JD/MPH, JD/MTS, JD/PhD. *Accreditation:* ABA. *Faculty:* 64 full-time (32 women), 44 part-time/adjunct (11 women). *Students:* 892 full-time (439 women), 50 part-time (33 women); includes 263 minority (83 Black or African American, non-Hispanic/Latino; 1 American Indian or Alaska Native, non-Hispanic/Latino; 88 Asian, non-Hispanic/Latino; 65 Hispanic/Latino; 1 Native Hawaiian or other Pacific Islander, non-Hispanic/Latino; 25 Two or more races, non-Hispanic/Latino), 93 international. Average age 24. 3,876 applicants, 32% accepted, 231 enrolled. In 2013, 270 doctorates, 37 Certificates awarded. *Entrance requirements:* For doctorate, LSAT, 2 letters of recommendation. Additional exam requirements/recommendations for international students: Required—TOEFL (minimum score 600 paper-based). *Application deadline:* For fall admission, 3/1 for domestic and international students. Applications are processed on a rolling basis. Application fee: $80. Electronic applications accepted. *Expenses:* Contact institution. *Financial support:* In 2013–14, 623 students received support, including 67 fellowships (averaging $9,000 per year), 57 research assistantships (averaging $9,880 per year); career-related internships or fieldwork, Federal Work-Study, institutionally sponsored loans, scholarships/grants, and tuition waivers (full and partial) also available. Financial award application deadline: 3/1; financial award applicants required to submit FAFSA. *Faculty research:* Law and economics, law and religion, international law, human rights, feminism and legal theory. *Total annual research expenditures:* $201,645. *Unit head:* Robert Schapiro, Dean, 404-712-8815, Fax: 404-727-0866, E-mail: david.partlett@emory.edu. *Application contact:* Ethan Rosenzweig, Assistant Dean for Admission, 404-727-6802, Fax: 404-727-2477, E-mail: lawinfo@law.emory.edu.

Facultad de derecho Eugenio María de Hostos, School of Law, Mayagüez, PR 00681. Offers JD. *Entrance requirements:* For doctorate, EXADEP, LSAT, 2 letters of recommendation.

Faulkner University, Thomas Goode Jones School of Law, Montgomery, AL 36109-3398. Offers JD. *Accreditation:* ABA. *Entrance requirements:* For doctorate, LSAT. Additional exam requirements/recommendations for international students: Recommended—TOEFL. Electronic applications accepted.

Florida Agricultural and Mechanical University, College of Law, Tallahassee, FL 32307-3200. Offers JD. *Accreditation:* ABA. Part-time and evening/weekend programs available. *Entrance requirements:* For doctorate, LSAT, LSDAS, 2 letters of recommendation. Additional exam requirements/recommendations for international students: Required—TOEFL. *Expenses:* Contact institution.

Florida Coastal School of Law, Professional Program, Jacksonville, FL 32256. Offers JD. *Accreditation:* ABA. Part-time programs available. *Entrance requirements:* For doctorate, LSAT. Additional exam requirements/recommendations for international students: Recommended—TOEFL (minimum score 600 paper-based). Electronic applications accepted. *Expenses:* Contact institution. *Faculty research:* Law and business, law technology and intellectual property, juvenile justice and family law, constitutional law, labor law.

Florida International University, College of Law, Miami, FL 33199. Offers JD, JD/MA, JD/MIB. *Accreditation:* ABA. Part-time and evening/weekend programs available. *Entrance requirements:* For doctorate, LSAT, 3 letters of recommendation. Additional exam requirements/recommendations for international students: Recommended—TOEFL. Electronic applications accepted. *Expenses:* Contact institution.

Florida State University, College of Law, Tallahassee, FL 32306-1601. Offers American law for foreign lawyers (LL M); environmental law and policy (LL M); law (JM, JD); JD/MBA; JD/MPA; JD/MS; JD/MSP; JD/MSW. *Accreditation:* ABA. *Faculty:* 57 full-time (26 women), 25 part-time/adjunct (6 women). *Students:* 661 full-time (283 women), 53 part-time (27 women); includes 161 minority (61 Black or African American, non-Hispanic/Latino; 11 American Indian or Alaska Native, non-Hispanic/Latino; 20 Asian, non-Hispanic/Latino; 65 Hispanic/Latino; 1 Native Hawaiian or other Pacific Islander, non-Hispanic/Latino; 3 Two or more races, non-Hispanic/Latino), 8 international. Average age 23. 2,022 applicants, 42% accepted, 170 enrolled. In 2013, 9 master's, 237 doctorates awarded. Terminal master's awarded for partial completion of doctoral program. *Degree requirements:* For master's, comprehensive exam (for some programs). *Entrance requirements:* For master's, one graduate-level standardized test (for JM), JD or equivalent degree (for LL M programs); for doctorate, LSAT. Additional exam requirements/recommendations for international students: Required—TOEFL (minimum score 600 paper-based; 100 iBT). *Application deadline:* For fall admission, 4/1 priority date for domestic and international students. Applications are processed on a rolling basis. Application fee: $30. Electronic applications accepted. *Expenses:* Contact institution. *Financial support:* In 2013–14, 300 students received support, including 55 research assistantships (averaging $1,183 per year), 11 teaching assistantships (averaging $1,835 per year); scholarships/grants and unspecified assistantships also available. Financial award application deadline: 3/1; financial award applicants required to submit FAFSA. *Faculty research:* Business law, environmental and land use law, international law, criminal law. *Total annual research expenditures:* $134,160. *Unit head:* Donald J. Weidner, Dean, 850-644-3400, Fax: 850-644-5487, E-mail: dweidner@law.fsu.edu. *Application contact:* Jennifer L. Kessinger, Director of Admissions and Records, 850-644-3787, Fax: 850-644-7284, E-mail: jkessing@law.fsu.edu.
Website: http://www.law.fsu.edu/.

Fordham University, School of Law, New York, NY 10023. Offers banking, corporate and finance law (LL M); intellectual property and information law (LL M); international business and trade law (LL M); law (JD); JD/MA; JD/MBA; JD/MSW. *Accreditation:* ABA. Part-time and evening/weekend programs available. *Entrance requirements:* For doctorate, LSAT. Additional exam requirements/recommendations for international students: Required—TOEFL. Electronic applications accepted. *Expenses:* Contact institution. *Faculty research:* Intellectual property, business law, international law.

Friends University, Graduate School, Wichita, KS 67213. Offers business law (MBL); Christian ministry (MACM); family therapy (MSFT); global (MBA), including accounting, business law, change management, health care leadership, management information systems, supply chain management and logistics; health care leadership (MHCL); management information systems (MMIS); operations management (MSOM); professional (MBA), including accounting, business law, change management, health care leadership, management information systems, supply chain management and logistics; teaching (MAT). Part-time and evening/weekend programs available. Postbaccalaureate distance learning degree programs offered (no on-campus study). *Faculty:* 18 full-time (8 women), 62 part-time/adjunct (28 women). *Students:* 161 full-time (111 women), 408 part-time (258 women); includes 157 minority (68 Black or African American, non-Hispanic/Latino; 7 American Indian or Alaska Native, non-Hispanic/Latino; 28 Asian, non-Hispanic/Latino; 18 Hispanic/Latino; 1 Native Hawaiian or other Pacific Islander, non-Hispanic/Latino; 35 Two or more races, non-Hispanic/Latino). Average age 36. 371 applicants, 90% accepted, 178 enrolled. In 2013, 432 master's awarded. *Degree requirements:* For master's, research project. *Entrance requirements:* For master's, bachelor's degree from accredited institution, official transcripts, interview with program director, letter(s) of recommendation. Additional exam requirements/recommendations for international students: Required—TOEFL (minimum score 560 paper-based). *Application deadline:* Applications are processed on a rolling basis. Application fee: $35 ($50 for international students). Electronic applications accepted. *Expenses:* Tuition: Part-time $631 per credit hour. Tuition and fees vary according to program. *Financial support:* In 2013–14, 30 students received support. Applicants required to submit FAFSA. *Unit head:* Dr. David Hofmeister, Dean of the Graduate School, 800-794-6945 Ext. 5858, Fax: 316-295-5040, E-mail: david_hofmeister@friends.edu. *Application contact:* Rachel Steiner, Manager, Graduate Recruiting Services, 800-794-6945, Fax: 316-295-5872, E-mail: rachel_steiner@friends.edu.
Website: http://www.friends.edu/.

George Mason University, School of Law, Arlington, VA 22201. Offers intellectual property (LL M); law (JD); law and economics (LL M); JD/MA; JD/MPP; JD/PhD. *Accreditation:* ABA. Part-time programs available. *Faculty:* 33 full-time (9 women), 92 part-time/adjunct (25 women). *Students:* 363 full-time (166 women), 157 part-time (71 women); includes 98 minority (18 Black or African American, non-Hispanic/Latino; 43 Asian, non-Hispanic/Latino; 22 Hispanic/Latino; 15 Two or more races, non-Hispanic/Latino), 10 international. 2,160 applicants, 35% accepted, 149 enrolled. In 2013, 4 master's, 255 doctorates awarded. *Entrance requirements:* For master's, JD or international equivalent; for doctorate, LSAT, baccalaureate degree. Additional exam requirements/recommendations for international students: Required—TOEFL or IELTS (for LL M applicants only). *Application deadline:* For fall admission, 4/1 for domestic and international students. Applications are processed on a rolling basis. Application fee: $0. Electronic applications accepted. *Expenses:* Contact institution. *Financial support:* In 2013–14, 3 fellowships with full tuition reimbursements (averaging $40,737 per year) were awarded; research assistantships, career-related internships or fieldwork, scholarships/grants, and tuition waivers (partial) also available. Support available to part-time students. *Faculty research:* Law and economics; infrastructure protection, including homeland and national security; intellectual property. *Unit head:* Daniel D. Polsby, Dean, 703-993-8006, Fax: 703-993-8088. *Application contact:* Alison H. Price, Associate Dean/Director of Admission, 703-993-8010, Fax: 703-993-8088, E-mail: lawadmit@gmu.edu.
Website: http://www.law.gmu.edu/.

Georgetown University, Graduate School of Arts and Sciences, Department of Government, Washington, DC 20057. Offers American government (MA, PhD); comparative government (PhD); conflict resolution (MA); democracy and governance (MA); international law and government (MA); international relations (PhD); political theory (PhD); MA/PhD. Terminal master's awarded for partial completion of doctoral program. *Degree requirements:* For master's, one foreign language, comprehensive exam; for doctorate, one foreign language, comprehensive exam, thesis/dissertation. *Entrance requirements:* For master's, GRE General Test, minimum B average; for doctorate, GRE General Test, MA. Additional exam requirements/recommendations for international students: Required—TOEFL. *Faculty research:* Western Europe, Latin America, the Middle East, political theory, international relations and law, methodology, American politics and institutions.

Georgetown University, Law Center, Washington, DC 20001. Offers global health law (LL M); individualized study (LL M); international business and economic law (LL M); law (JD, SJD); national security law (LL M); securities and financial regulation (LL M); taxation (LL M); JD/LL M; JD/MA; JD/MBA; JD/MPH; JD/PhD. *Accreditation:* ABA. Part-time and evening/weekend programs available. *Degree requirements:* For master's, thesis; for doctorate, thesis/dissertation (for some programs). *Entrance requirements:* For master's, JD, LL B, or first law degree earned in country of origin; for doctorate, LSAT (for JD). Additional exam requirements/recommendations for international students: Required—TOEFL. *Expenses:* Contact institution. *Faculty research:* Constitutional law, legal history, jurisprudence.

The George Washington University, Law School, Washington, DC 20052. Offers LL M, JD, SJD, JD/MA, JD/MBA, JD/MPA, JD/MPH, LL M/MA, LL M/MPH. *Accreditation:* ABA. Part-time and evening/weekend programs available. *Faculty:* 90 full-time (37 women). *Students:* 1,554 full-time (766 women), 413 part-time (155 women); includes 476 minority (147 Black or African American, non-Hispanic/Latino; 12 American Indian or Alaska Native, non-Hispanic/Latino; 202 Asian, non-Hispanic/Latino; 109 Hispanic/Latino; 2 Native Hawaiian or other Pacific Islander, non-Hispanic/Latino; 4 Two or more races, non-Hispanic/Latino), 180 international. Average age 28. 284 applicants, 100% accepted, 231 enrolled. In 2013, 210 master's, 616 doctorates awarded. *Degree requirements:* For doctorate, thesis/dissertation (for some programs). *Entrance requirements:* For master's, JD or equivalent; for doctorate, LSAT (for JD), LL M or equivalent (for SJD). *Application deadline:* For fall admission, 3/1 for domestic students. Applications are processed on a rolling basis. Application fee: $75. *Expenses:* Contact institution. *Financial support:* Research assistantships, career-related internships or fieldwork, Federal Work-Study, institutionally sponsored loans, scholarships/grants, and tuition waivers (full and partial) available. Support available to part-time students. Financial award application deadline: 3/1; financial award applicants required to submit CSS PROFILE or FAFSA. *Unit head:* Blake D. Morant, Dean, 202-994-6261, Fax: 202-994-5157. *Application contact:* Sophia Sim, Assistant Dean of Admissions and Financial Aid, 202-994-7230, Fax: 202-739-0624, E-mail: ssim@law.gwu.edu.
Website: http://www.law.gwu.edu/.

Georgia State University, College of Law, Atlanta, GA 30302-4037. Offers JD, JD/MA, JD/MBA, JD/MCRP, JD/MHA, JD/MPA, JD/MSHA. *Accreditation:* ABA. Part-time and evening/weekend programs available. *Faculty:* 38 full-time (15 women). *Students:* 654 full-time (294 women), 19 part-time (5 women); includes 174 minority (78 Black or African American, non-Hispanic/Latino; 5 American Indian or Alaska Native, non-Hispanic/Latino; 49 Asian, non-Hispanic/Latino; 32 Hispanic/Latino; 3 Native Hawaiian or other Pacific Islander, non-Hispanic/Latino; 7 Two or more races, non-Hispanic/Latino), 4 international. Average age 28. 2,010 applicants, 28% accepted, 194 enrolled. In 2013, 200 doctorates awarded. *Entrance requirements:* For doctorate, LSAT. Additional exam requirements/recommendations for international students:

Recommended—TOEFL. *Application deadline:* For fall admission, 3/15 for domestic students, 3/15 priority date for international students. Applications are processed on a rolling basis. Application fee: $50. Electronic applications accepted. *Expenses:* Contact institution. *Financial support:* In 2013–14, research assistantships with full and partial tuition reimbursements (averaging $2,500 per year), teaching assistantships (averaging $2,500 per year) were awarded; scholarships/grants, tuition waivers, and unspecified assistantships also available. Financial award application deadline: 4/1; financial award applicants required to submit FAFSA. *Faculty research:* Health law; land use, urban planning and environmental law; intellectual property; criminal law and procedure; Constitutional law. *Unit head:* Dr. Steven J. Kaminshine, Dean, College of Law, 404-413-9035, Fax: 404-413-9227, E-mail: skaminshine@gsu.edu. *Application contact:* Dr. Cheryl Jester-George, Senior Director of Admissions, 404-413-9004, Fax: 404-413-9203, E-mail: cjgeorge@gsu.edu.
Website: http://law.gsu.edu/.

Golden Gate University, School of Law, San Francisco, CA 94105-2968. Offers environmental law (LL M); intellectual property law (LL M); international legal studies (LL M, SJD); law (JD); taxation (LL M); U. S. legal studies (LL M); JD/MBA; JD/PhD. *Accreditation:* ABA. Part-time and evening/weekend programs available. *Degree requirements:* For doctorate, thesis/dissertation (for some programs). *Entrance requirements:* For doctorate, LSAT (for JD). Additional exam requirements/recommendations for international students: Required—TOEFL (minimum score 600 paper-based). Electronic applications accepted. *Expenses:* Contact institution. *Faculty research:* International law, intellectual property law, environmental law, real estate, civil rights.

Gonzaga University, School of Law, Spokane, WA 99220-3528. Offers JD, JD/M Acc, JD/MBA. *Accreditation:* ABA. Part-time programs available. *Faculty:* 32 full-time (15 women), 19 part-time/adjunct (7 women). *Students:* 383 full-time (171 women), 4 part-time (1 woman); includes 114 minority (3 Black or African American, non-Hispanic/Latino; 10 American Indian or Alaska Native, non-Hispanic/Latino; 12 Asian, non-Hispanic/Latino; 81 Hispanic/Latino; 1 Native Hawaiian or other Pacific Islander, non-Hispanic/Latino; 7 Two or more races, non-Hispanic/Latino), 8 international. Average age 27. In 2013, 161 doctorates awarded. *Degree requirements:* For doctorate, experiential learning. *Entrance requirements:* For doctorate, LSAT. *Application deadline:* For fall admission, 4/15 priority date for domestic students. Applications are processed on a rolling basis. Application fee: $50. Electronic applications accepted. *Expenses:* Contact institution. *Financial support:* Career-related internships or fieldwork, Federal Work-Study, institutionally sponsored loans, and scholarships/grants available. Support available to part-time students. Financial award application deadline: 2/1; financial award applicants required to submit FAFSA. *Faculty research:* Environmental law, business law, public interest law, tax law. *Unit head:* Earl Martin, Dean, 509-328-4220 Ext. 3700. *Application contact:* Susan Lee, Director of Admissions, 509-323-5532, Fax: 509-323-3857, E-mail: admissions@lawschool.gonzaga.edu.
Website: http://www.law.gonzaga.edu/.

Hamline University, School of Law, St. Paul, MN 55104-1284. Offers LL M, MSL, JD, JD/MANM, JD/MAOL, JD/MAPA, JD/MBA, JD/MFA. JD/MAOL offered jointly with St. Catherine University. *Accreditation:* ABA. Part-time and evening/weekend programs available. *Faculty:* 33 full-time (16 women), 34 part-time/adjunct (20 women). *Students:* 306 full-time (163 women), 133 part-time (79 women); includes 71 minority (15 Black or African American, non-Hispanic/Latino; 7 American Indian or Alaska Native, non-Hispanic/Latino; 23 Asian, non-Hispanic/Latino; 21 Hispanic/Latino; 5 Two or more races, non-Hispanic/Latino), 10 international. Average age 30. 690 applicants, 63% accepted, 88 enrolled. In 2013, 1 master's, 185 doctorates awarded. *Entrance requirements:* For master's, GMAT, GRE or LSAT, 2 letters of recommendation; for doctorate, LSAT, 2 letters of recommendation. Additional exam requirements/recommendations for international students: Required—TOEFL (minimum score 100 iBT). *Application deadline:* For fall admission, 5/1 for domestic students, 8/1 priority date for international students. Applications are processed on a rolling basis. Application fee: $0 ($50 for international students). Electronic applications accepted. *Expenses:* Contact institution. *Financial support:* In 2013–14, 316 students received support, including 18 fellowships (averaging $2,200 per year); career-related internships or fieldwork, Federal Work-Study, and scholarships/grants also available. Support available to part-time students. Financial award applicants required to submit FAFSA. *Faculty research:* Alternative dispute resolution, intellectual property, health law/bio ethic, business law, ethics/public law. *Unit head:* Jean F. Holloway, Dean, 651-523-2968, Fax: 651-523-2435, E-mail: jholloway01@hamline.edu. *Application contact:* Emily Dunsworth, Director of Admissions, 800-388-3688, Fax: 651-523-3064, E-mail: edunsworth01@hamline.edu.
Website: http://www.hamline.edu/law/.

Harvard University, Law School, Graduate Programs in Law, Cambridge, MA 02138. Offers LL M, SJD. *Degree requirements:* For master's, thesis optional; for doctorate, thesis/dissertation. *Entrance requirements:* Additional exam requirements/recommendations for international students: Required—TOEFL. *Expenses: Tuition:* Full-time $38,888. *Required fees:* $958. Tuition and fees vary according to campus/location, program and student level. *Faculty research:* Corporation finance, national and international law, legal ethics, family law, criminal law, administrative law, constitutional law.

Harvard University, Law School, Professional Programs in Law, Cambridge, MA 02138. Offers international and comparative law (JD); law and business (JD); law and government (JD); law and social change (JD); law, science and technology (JD); JD/MALD; JD/MBA; JD/MPH; JD/MPP; JD/PhD. *Accreditation:* ABA. *Degree requirements:* For doctorate, 3rd-year paper. *Entrance requirements:* For doctorate, LSAT. *Expenses: Tuition:* Full-time $38,888. *Required fees:* $958. Tuition and fees vary according to campus/location, program and student level. *Faculty research:* Constitutional law, voting rights law, cyber law.

Hofstra University, School of Law, Hempstead, NY 11549. Offers American legal studies (LL M); family law (LL M); law (JD); JD/MBA. *Accreditation:* ABA.

Howard University, School of Law, Washington, DC 20008. Offers LL M, JD, JD/MBA. *Accreditation:* ABA. *Degree requirements:* For master's, one foreign language, thesis; for doctorate, thesis/dissertation (for some programs). *Entrance requirements:* For doctorate, LSAT. Additional exam requirements/recommendations for international students: Required—TOEFL. Electronic applications accepted. *Expenses:* Contact institution. *Faculty research:* Criminal law, family law, telecommunications, religion, antitrust.

Humphreys College, Laurence Drivon School of Law, Stockton, CA 95207-3896. Offers JD. Part-time and evening/weekend programs available. *Entrance requirements:* For doctorate, LSAT, minimum GPA of 2.5. Electronic applications accepted.

Illinois Institute of Technology, Chicago-Kent College of Law, Chicago, IL 60661-3691. Offers family law (LL M); financial services (LL M); international intellectual property (LL M); law (JD); taxation (LL M); U.S., international, and transnational law (LL M); JD/LL M; JD/MBA; JD/MPA; JD/MPH; JD/MS. *Accreditation:* ABA. Part-time and evening/weekend programs available. *Faculty:* 71 full-time (27 women), 154 part-time/adjunct (40 women). *Students:* 856 full-time (403 women), 137 part-time (63 women); includes 230 minority (44 Black or African American, non-Hispanic/Latino; 56 Asian, non-Hispanic/Latino; 108 Hispanic/Latino; 2 Native Hawaiian or other Pacific Islander, non-Hispanic/Latino; 20 Two or more races, non-Hispanic/Latino), 115 international. Average age 27. 2,676 applicants, 55% accepted, 282 enrolled. In 2013, 106 master's, 286 doctorates awarded. Terminal master's awarded for partial completion of doctoral program. *Entrance requirements:* For master's, 1st degree in law or certified license to practice law; for doctorate, LSAT. Additional exam requirements/recommendations for international students: Required—TOEFL (minimum score 600 paper-based; 100 iBT); Recommended—IELTS (minimum score 7). *Application deadline:* For fall admission, 3/15 priority date for domestic students, 2/1 priority date for international students. Applications are processed on a rolling basis. Application fee: $0 ($75 for international students). Electronic applications accepted. *Expenses:* Contact institution. *Financial support:* In 2013–14, 742 students received support. Career-related internships or fieldwork, Federal Work-Study, institutionally sponsored loans, scholarships/grants, and tuition waivers (full) available. Support available to part-time students. Financial award application deadline: 3/15; financial award applicants required to submit FAFSA. *Faculty research:* Constitutional law, bioethics, environmental law, intellectual property. *Total annual research expenditures:* $217,995. *Unit head:* Harold J. Krent, Dean, 312-906-5010, Fax: 312-906-5335, E-mail: hkrent@kentlaw.iit.edu. *Application contact:* Nicole Vilches, Assistant Dean, 312-906-5020, Fax: 312-906-5274, E-mail: admissions@kentlaw.iit.edu.
Website: http://www.kentlaw.iit.edu/.

Indiana University Bloomington, Maurer School of Law, Bloomington, IN 47405-7000. Offers comparative law (MCL); juridical science (SJD); law (LL M, JD); law and social sciences (PhD); legal studies (Certificate); JD/MA; JD/MBA; JD/MLS; JD/MPA; JD/MS; JD/MSES. PhD offered through University Graduate School. *Accreditation:* ABA. *Faculty:* 72 full-time (28 women), 14 part-time/adjunct (4 women). *Students:* 691 full-time (308 women), 51 part-time (19 women); includes 108 minority (32 Black or African American, non-Hispanic/Latino; 2 American Indian or Alaska Native, non-Hispanic/Latino; 30 Asian, non-Hispanic/Latino; 38 Hispanic/Latino; 6 Two or more races, non-Hispanic/Latino), 149 international. Average age 26. 695 applicants, 45% accepted, 205 enrolled. In 2013, 73 master's, 233 doctorates awarded. *Degree requirements:* For master's, thesis or practicum; for doctorate, thesis/dissertation (for some programs), research seminar (for JD). *Entrance requirements:* For master's, LSAT, 3 letters of recommendation, law degree or license to practice; for doctorate, LSAT. Additional exam requirements/recommendations for international students: Required—TOEFL (minimum score 560 paper-based; 80 iBT). *Application deadline:* For fall admission, 3/1 priority date for domestic and international students. Applications are processed on a rolling basis. Application fee: $55 ($65 for international students). Electronic applications accepted. *Financial support:* In 2013–14, 301 students received support, including 278 fellowships (averaging $16,000 per year), 1 research assistantship (averaging $15,217 per year), 2 teaching assistantships (averaging $14,000 per year); career-related internships or fieldwork, Federal Work-Study, institutionally sponsored loans, scholarships/grants, health care benefits, and unspecified assistantships also available. Financial award application deadline: 3/1; financial award applicants required to submit FAFSA. *Faculty research:* Environmental risk assessment and policy analysis, information privacy and security, judicial independence, accountability, ethics. *Total annual research expenditures:* $1.4 million. *Unit head:* Hannah Buxbaum, Interim Dean, 812-855-8886, E-mail: hbuxbaum@indiana.edu. *Application contact:* Will Schaad, Director of Graduate Admissions, 812-856-7217, E-mail: wschaad@indiana.edu.
Website: http://www.law.indiana.edu/.

Indiana University–Purdue University Indianapolis, Robert H. McKinney School of Law, Indianapolis, IN 46202-2896. Offers LL M, JD, SJD, JD/M Phil, JD/MBA, JD/MHA, JD/MLS, JD/MPA, JD/MPH, JD/MSW. *Accreditation:* ABA. *Faculty:* 1 (woman) full-time. *Students:* 850 full-time (382 women), 123 part-time (44 women); includes 138 minority (59 Black or African American, non-Hispanic/Latino; 1 American Indian or Alaska Native, non-Hispanic/Latino; 27 Asian, non-Hispanic/Latino; 23 Hispanic/Latino; 28 Two or more races, non-Hispanic/Latino), 116 international. Average age 28. 353 applicants, 90% accepted, 242 enrolled. In 2013, 67 master's, 265 doctorates awarded. *Entrance requirements:* Additional exam requirements/recommendations for international students: Required—TOEFL. Application fee: $55 ($65 for international students). *Financial support:* Fellowships, research assistantships with full and partial tuition reimbursements, Federal Work-Study, institutionally sponsored loans, and scholarships/grants available. Support available to part-time students. Financial award applicants required to submit FAFSA. *Unit head:* Andrew R. Klein, Dean. *Application contact:* Patricia Kinney, Assistant Dean of Admissions, 317-274-2459, E-mail: pkkinney@iupui.edu.
Website: http://mckinneylaw.iu.edu/.

Instituto Tecnológico y de Estudios Superiores de Monterrey, Campus Ciudad de México, School of Humanities and Social Sciences, Ciudad de Mexico, Mexico. Offers LL B. Part-time and evening/weekend programs available. *Entrance requirements:* For degree, Instituto entrance exam. Additional exam requirements/recommendations for international students: Required—TOEFL. *Faculty research:* Law; politics; international relations.

Inter American University of Puerto Rico School of Law, Professional Program, San Juan, PR 00936-8351. Offers JD. *Accreditation:* ABA. Part-time and evening/weekend programs available. *Entrance requirements:* For doctorate, LSAT, PAEG, minimum GPA of 2.5. *Expenses:* Contact institution.

John F. Kennedy University, School of Law, Pleasant Hill, CA 94523-4817. Offers JD. Part-time and evening/weekend programs available. *Entrance requirements:* For doctorate, LSAT, interview. Additional exam requirements/recommendations for international students: Required—TOEFL. *Expenses:* Contact institution.

John Marshall Law School, Graduate and Professional Programs, Chicago, IL 60604-3968. Offers employee benefits (LL M, MS); estate planning (LL M); global legal studies (LL M); information technology (MS); information technology and privacy law (LL M); intellectual property (LL M, MS); international business and trade (LL M); law (JD); real estate (LL M, MS); taxation (LL M, MS); trial advocacy (LL M); JD/LL M; JD/MA; JD/MBA; JD/MPA. JD/MBA offered jointly with Dominican University; JD/MA and JD/MPA with Roosevelt University. *Accreditation:* ABA. Part-time and evening/weekend programs available. *Faculty:* 71 full-time (26 women), 132 part-time/adjunct (49 women). *Students:* 1,045 full-time (512 women), 421 part-time (211 women); includes 403 minority (152 Black or African American, non-Hispanic/Latino; 8 American Indian or Alaska Native, non-Hispanic/Latino; 89 Asian, non-Hispanic/Latino; 138 Hispanic/Latino; 3 Native Hawaiian or other Pacific Islander, non-Hispanic/Latino; 13 Two or more races, non-Hispanic/Latino), 57 international. Average age 27. 2,694 applicants, 73% accepted, 419 enrolled. In 2013, 81 master's, 445 doctorates awarded. *Degree requirements:* For master's, 24 credits; for doctorate, 90 credits. *Entrance requirements:* For master's, JD; for doctorate, LSAT. Additional exam requirements/recommendations for international students: Required—TOEFL. *Application deadline:* For fall admission, 3/1 priority date for domestic and international students; for spring admission, 10/15 priority date for domestic and international students. Applications are processed on a rolling basis. Application fee: $0. Electronic applications accepted. *Expenses:* Contact institution. *Financial support:* In 2013–14, 1,275 students received support. Scholarships/grants and tuition waivers (full and partial) available. Support available to

part-time students. Financial award application deadline: 4/1; financial award applicants required to submit FAFSA. *Unit head:* John Corkery, Dean, 312-427-2737. *Application contact:* William B. Powers, Associate Dean of Admission and Student Affairs, 800-537-4280, Fax: 312-427-5136, E-mail: admission@jmls.edu.

The Judge Advocate General's School, U.S. Army, Graduate Programs, Charlottesville, VA 22903-1781. Offers military law (LL M). Only active duty military lawyers attend this school. *Accreditation:* ABA. *Degree requirements:* For master's, thesis optional. *Entrance requirements:* For master's, active duty military lawyer, international military officer, or DOD civilian attorney, JD or LL B. *Faculty research:* Criminal law, administrative and civil law, contract law, international law, legal research and writing.

Kaplan University, Davenport Campus, School of Criminal Justice, Davenport, IA 52807-2095. Offers corrections (MSCJ); global issues in criminal justice (MSCJ); law (MSCJ); leadership and executive management (MSCJ); policing (MSCJ). Part-time and evening/weekend programs available. Postbaccalaureate distance learning degree programs offered (no on-campus study). *Entrance requirements:* Additional exam requirements/recommendations for international students: Required—TOEFL (minimum score 550 paper-based; 80 iBT). Electronic applications accepted.

Lewis & Clark College, Lewis & Clark Law School, Portland, OR 97219. Offers environmental and natural resources law (LL M); law (JD). *Accreditation:* ABA. Part-time and evening/weekend programs available. *Entrance requirements:* For doctorate, LSAT. Additional exam requirements/recommendations for international students: Recommended—TOEFL (minimum score 600 paper-based). Electronic applications accepted. *Expenses:* Contact institution.

Liberty University, School of Law, Lynchburg, VA 24515. Offers JD. *Accreditation:* ABA. *Students:* 204 full-time (79 women), 1 part-time (0 women); includes 28 minority (13 Black or African American, non-Hispanic/Latino; 2 American Indian or Alaska Native, non-Hispanic/Latino; 10 Hispanic/Latino; 3 Two or more races, non-Hispanic/Latino), 6 international. Average age 27. 302 applicants, 26% accepted, 71 enrolled. *Entrance requirements:* For doctorate, LSAT, 2 letters of recommendation, interview, subscription to LSDAS. Additional exam requirements/recommendations for international students: Required—TOEFL (minimum score 600 paper-based; 100 iBT). *Application deadline:* For fall admission, 6/1 for domestic students. *Expenses: Tuition:* Full-time $9630; part-time $535 per credit hour. *Required fees:* $175 per term. One-time fee: $50. Tuition and fees vary according to course load, degree level, campus/location and program. *Unit head:* Mathew D. Staver, Dean, 434-592-5300, Fax: 434-592-5400, E-mail: law@liberty.edu. *Application contact:* Joleen Thaxton, Assistant Director of Admissions, 434-592-5300, Fax: 434-592-5400, E-mail: lawadmissions@liberty.edu.

Lincoln Memorial University, Duncan School of Law, Harrogate, TN 37752-1901. Offers JD. Part-time programs available. *Entrance requirements:* For doctorate, LSAT. Additional exam requirements/recommendations for international students: Required—TOEFL (minimum score 500 paper-based). Electronic applications accepted. *Expenses:* Contact institution.

Louisiana State University and Agricultural & Mechanical College, Paul M. Hebert Law Center, Baton Rouge, LA 70803. Offers LL M, JD. *Accreditation:* ABA; SACS. *Degree requirements:* For master's, thesis. *Entrance requirements:* For doctorate, LSAT. Additional exam requirements/recommendations for international students: Required—TOEFL (minimum score 600 paper-based; 100 iBT). Electronic applications accepted. *Expenses:* Contact institution.

Loyola Marymount University, College of Business Administration, MBA/JD Program, Los Angeles, CA 90045-2659. Offers MBA/JD. Part-time programs available. *Faculty:* 66 full-time (18 women), 6 part-time/adjunct (0 women). *Students:* 7 full-time (0 women), 1 (woman) part-time; includes 2 minority (1 Asian, non-Hispanic/Latino; 1 Hispanic/Latino). Average age 27. 6 applicants, 100% accepted, 4 enrolled. *Entrance requirements:* Additional exam requirements/recommendations for international students: Required—TOEFL (minimum score 600 paper-based; 100 iBT). *Application deadline:* For fall admission, 7/1 for domestic students; for spring admission, 6/30 for domestic students. Application fee: $75. Electronic applications accepted. *Expenses:* Contact institution. *Financial support:* In 2013–14, 3 students received support. Scholarships/grants and unspecified assistantships available. Financial award application deadline: 6/30; financial award applicants required to submit FAFSA. *Unit head:* Dr. Dennis Draper, Dean, 310-338-7504, E-mail: ddraper@lmu.edu. *Application contact:* Chake H. Kouyoumjian, Associate Dean of the Graduate Division, 310-338-2721, E-mail: ckouyoum@lmu.edu.
Website: http://www.lls.edu/academics/degreesoffered/jdmbaprogram/.

Loyola Marymount University, Loyola Law School Los Angeles, Los Angeles, CA 90015. Offers foreign-trained attorneys (LL M); law (JD); taxation (LL M); JD/LL M; JD/MBA. *Accreditation:* ABA. Part-time and evening/weekend programs available. *Degree requirements:* For master's and doctorate, comprehensive exam. *Entrance requirements:* For master's, JD; for doctorate, LSAT. Electronic applications accepted.

Loyola University Chicago, School of Law, Chicago, IL 60611. Offers advocacy (LL M); business law (LL M, MJ); child and family law (LL M); children's law and policy (MJ); health law (LL M, MJ); health law and policy (D Law, SJD); international law (LL M); law (JD); rule of law development (LL M); tax law (LL M); JD/MA; JD/MBA; JD/MSW; MJ/MSW. MJ in business law offered in partnership with Concord Law School. *Accreditation:* ABA. Part-time and evening/weekend programs available. Postbaccalaureate distance learning degree programs offered (minimal on-campus study). *Faculty:* 48 full-time (16 women), 174 part-time/adjunct (98 women). *Students:* 851 full-time (461 women), 271 part-time (206 women); includes 333 minority (142 Black or African American, non-Hispanic/Latino; 3 American Indian or Alaska Native, non-Hispanic/Latino; 55 Asian, non-Hispanic/Latino; 98 Hispanic/Latino; 2 Native Hawaiian or other Pacific Islander, non-Hispanic/Latino; 33 Two or more races, non-Hispanic/Latino), 33 international. Average age 31. 3,333 applicants, 51% accepted, 213 enrolled. In 2013, 144 master's, 282 doctorates awarded. *Entrance requirements:* For doctorate, LSAT. Additional exam requirements/recommendations for international students: Required—TOEFL (minimum score 550 paper-based; 79 iBT), IELTS (minimum score 6.5). *Application deadline:* For fall admission, 3/1 for domestic and international students. Applications are processed on a rolling basis. Application fee: $0. Electronic applications accepted. *Expenses:* Contact institution. *Financial support:* In 2013–14, 676 students received support, including 72 fellowships; Federal Work-Study and scholarships/grants also available. Financial award application deadline: 3/1; financial award applicants required to submit FAFSA. *Unit head:* Pamela Bloomquist, Assistant Dean for Admission and Financial Assistance, Law School, 312-915-7170, Fax: 312-915-7906, E-mail: ploom@luc.edu. *Application contact:* Ron Martin, Associate Director, Graduate and Professional Enrollment Management Operations, 312-915-8951, E-mail: rmarti7@luc.edu.
Website: http://www.luc.edu/law/.

Loyola University New Orleans, College of Law, New Orleans, LA 70118. Offers LL M, JD, JD/MBA, JD/MPA, JD/MURP. *Accreditation:* ABA. Part-time and evening/weekend programs available. *Faculty:* 44 full-time (23 women), 26 part-time/adjunct (8 women). *Students:* 407 full-time (196 women), 355 part-time (167 women); includes 186 minority (66 Black or African American, non-Hispanic/Latino; 10 American Indian or Alaska Native, non-Hispanic/Latino; 23 Asian, non-Hispanic/Latino; 82 Hispanic/Latino; 1 Native Hawaiian or other Pacific Islander, non-Hispanic/Latino; 4 Two or more races, non-Hispanic/Latino), 8 international. Average age 27. 1,291 applicants, 70% accepted, 204 enrolled. In 2013, 255 doctorates awarded. *Entrance requirements:* For doctorate, LSAT, letters of recommendation, interview, resume, personal statement, bachelor's degree from accredited college/university. Additional exam requirements/recommendations for international students: Recommended—TOEFL (minimum score 550 paper-based). *Application deadline:* For fall admission, 2/1 priority date for domestic and international students. Applications are processed on a rolling basis. Application fee: $40. Electronic applications accepted. *Expenses:* Contact institution. *Financial support:* Research assistantships, teaching assistantships, career-related internships or fieldwork, and scholarships/grants available. Support available to part-time students. Financial award application deadline: 5/1; financial award applicants required to submit FAFSA. *Faculty research:* Louisiana civil code, international law, commercial law, comparative law. *Unit head:* Dr. Maria Lopez, Dean, 504-861-5575, Fax: 504-861-5772, E-mail: ladmit@loyno.edu. *Application contact:* Forrest Stanford, Associate Dean for Admissions and Financial Aid, 504-861-5575, Fax: 504-861-5772, E-mail: ladmit@loyno.edu.
Website: http://www.loyno.edu/law/.

Marquette University, Law School, Milwaukee, WI 53201-1881. Offers JD, JD/Certificate, JD/MA, JD/MBA. *Accreditation:* ABA. Part-time and evening/weekend programs available. *Faculty:* 40 full-time (17 women), 30 part-time/adjunct (18 women). *Students:* 602 full-time (242 women), 93 part-time (46 women); includes 132 minority (42 Black or African American, non-Hispanic/Latino; 4 American Indian or Alaska Native, non-Hispanic/Latino; 20 Asian, non-Hispanic/Latino; 44 Hispanic/Latino; 1 Native Hawaiian or other Pacific Islander, non-Hispanic/Latino; 21 Two or more races, non-Hispanic/Latino), 3 international. Average age 26. 1,458 applicants, 72% accepted, 209 enrolled. In 2013, 235 doctorates awarded. *Entrance requirements:* For doctorate, LSAT, subscription to LSAC's Credential Assembly Service. Additional exam requirements/recommendations for international students: Required—TOEFL. *Application deadline:* For fall admission, 4/1 for domestic students. Applications are processed on a rolling basis. Application fee: $50. Electronic applications accepted. *Expenses:* Contact institution. *Financial support:* Career-related internships or fieldwork, Federal Work-Study, and scholarships/grants available. Support available to part-time students. Financial award application deadline: 3/1; financial award applicants required to submit FAFSA. *Faculty research:* Constitutional law, sports law, dispute resolution, intellectual property, legal ethics. *Total annual research expenditures:* $311,587. *Unit head:* Joseph D. Kearney, Dean, 414-288-7090, Fax: 414-288-6403, E-mail: joseph.kearney@marquette.edu. *Application contact:* Joseph D. Kearney, Dean, 414-288-7090, Fax: 414-288-6403, E-mail: joseph.kearney@marquette.edu.
Website: http://law.marquette.edu/.

Massachusetts School of Law at Andover, Professional Program, Andover, MA 01810. Offers JD. Part-time and evening/weekend programs available. *Entrance requirements:* For doctorate, Massachusetts School of Law Aptitude Test (MSLAT), interview. Additional exam requirements/recommendations for international students: Recommended—TOEFL. Electronic applications accepted.

McGill University, Faculty of Graduate and Postdoctoral Studies, Faculty of Law, Department of Law, Montréal, QC H3A 2T5, Canada. Offers LL M, DCL.

McGill University, Faculty of Graduate and Postdoctoral Studies, Faculty of Law, Institute of Air and Space Law, Montréal, QC H3A 2T5, Canada. Offers LL M, DCL, Graduate Certificate.

McGill University, Faculty of Graduate and Postdoctoral Studies, Faculty of Law, Institute of Comparative Law, Montréal, QC H3A 2T5, Canada. Offers LL M, DCL, Graduate Certificate.

Mercer University, Walter F. George School of Law, Macon, GA 31207. Offers JD, JD/MBA. *Accreditation:* ABA. Part-time programs available. *Entrance requirements:* For doctorate, LSAT. Electronic applications accepted. *Expenses:* Contact institution. *Faculty research:* Legal ethics, environmental law, employment discrimination, statutory law, legal writing.

Michigan State University College of Law, Professional Program, East Lansing, MI 48824-1300. Offers American legal system (LL M, MJ); global food law (LL M, MJ); intellectual property (LL M, MJ); law (JD). *Accreditation:* ABA. Part-time programs available. *Faculty:* 58 full-time (25 women), 90 part-time/adjunct (21 women). *Students:* 823 full-time (352 women), 175 part-time (77 women); includes 218 minority (74 Black or African American, non-Hispanic/Latino; 19 American Indian or Alaska Native, non-Hispanic/Latino; 45 Asian, non-Hispanic/Latino; 46 Hispanic/Latino; 4 Native Hawaiian or other Pacific Islander, non-Hispanic/Latino; 30 Two or more races, non-Hispanic/Latino), 112 international. Average age 26. 2,673 applicants, 50% accepted, 270 enrolled. In 2013, 39 master's, 301 doctorates awarded. *Entrance requirements:* For doctorate, LSAT. Additional exam requirements/recommendations for international students: Required—TOEFL (minimum score 600 paper-based). *Application deadline:* For fall admission, 4/30 priority date for domestic students, 7/1 priority date for international students. Applications are processed on a rolling basis. Application fee: $60. Electronic applications accepted. *Expenses:* Contact institution. *Financial support:* In 2013–14, 490 students received support. Career-related internships or fieldwork, Federal Work-Study, scholarships/grants, and tuition waivers (full and partial) available. Support available to part-time students. Financial award application deadline: 4/15; financial award applicants required to submit FAFSA. *Faculty research:* International, Constitutional, health, tax and environmental law; intellectual property, trial practice, corporate law. *Unit head:* Joan W. Howarth, Dean/Professor of Law, 517-432-6993, Fax: 517-432-6801, E-mail: howarth@law.msu.edu. *Application contact:* Charles Roboski, Assistant Dean of Admissions, 517-432-0222, Fax: 517-432-0098, E-mail: roboski@law.msu.edu.
Website: http://www.law.msu.edu/.

Mississippi College, School of Law, Jackson, MS 39201. Offers civil law studies (Certificate); law (JD); JD/MBA. *Accreditation:* ABA. *Degree requirements:* For doctorate, thesis/dissertation. *Entrance requirements:* For doctorate, LSAT, LDAS report. Additional exam requirements/recommendations for international students: Recommended—TOEFL, IELTS. Electronic applications accepted. *Expenses:* Contact institution.

Montclair State University, The Graduate School, College of Humanities and Social Sciences, MA Program in Law and Governance, Montclair, NJ 07043-1624. Offers conflict management and peace studies (MA); governance, compliance and regulation (MA); intellectual property (MA); law and governance (MA); legal management (MA). Part-time and evening/weekend programs available. *Degree requirements:* For master's, thesis or comprehensive exam. *Entrance requirements:* For master's, GRE General Test, minimum cumulative GPA of 2.75 for undergraduate work, 2 letters of recommendation, essay. Additional exam requirements/recommendations for international students: Required—TOEFL (minimum score 83 iBT) or IELTS (minimum score 6.5). Electronic applications accepted.

New England Law–Boston, Professional Program, Boston, MA 02116-5687. Offers advanced legal studies (LL M); law (JD). *Accreditation:* ABA. Part-time and evening/

weekend programs available. *Faculty:* 42 full-time (16 women), 85 part-time/adjunct (38 women). *Students:* 676 full-time (394 women), 288 part-time (162 women); includes 229 minority (64 Black or African American, non-Hispanic/Latino; 3 American Indian or Alaska Native, non-Hispanic/Latino; 43 Asian, non-Hispanic/Latino; 73 Hispanic/Latino; 1 Native Hawaiian or other Pacific Islander, non-Hispanic/Latino; 45 Two or more races, non-Hispanic/Latino), 14 international. Average age 26. 2,934 applicants, 72% accepted, 385 enrolled. In 2013, 342 doctorates awarded. *Entrance requirements:* For doctorate, LSAT, LSDAS. Additional exam requirements/recommendations for international students: Required—TOEFL (minimum score 600 paper-based; 100 iBT). *Application deadline:* For fall admission, 3/15 for domestic students. Applications are processed on a rolling basis. Application fee: $65. Electronic applications accepted. *Expenses: Tuition:* Full-time $42,490. Tuition and fees vary according to class time, course load and degree level. *Financial support:* In 2013–14, 484 students received support, including 80 fellowships (averaging $3,500 per year); scholarships/grants and tuition waivers (full and partial) also available. Financial award application deadline: 3/24; financial award applicants required to submit FAFSA. *Unit head:* John F. O'Brien, Dean, 617-422-7221, Fax: 617-422-7333. *Application contact:* Michelle L'Etoile, Director of Admissions, 617-422-7210, Fax: 617-422-7201, E-mail: admit@nesl.edu.

New York Law School, Graduate Programs, New York, NY 10013. Offers American business law (LL M); financial services (LL M); law (JD); mental disability law (MA); real estate (LL M); taxation (LL M); JD/MA; JD/MBA. JD/MBA offered jointly with Bernard M. Baruch College of the City University of New York; JD/MA in forensic psychology offered jointly with John Jay College of Criminal Justice of the City University of New York. *Accreditation:* ABA. Part-time and evening/weekend programs available. *Faculty:* 79 full-time (31 women), 103 part-time/adjunct (44 women). *Students:* 891 full-time (453 women), 415 part-time (212 women); includes 411 minority (95 Black or African American, non-Hispanic/Latino; 1 American Indian or Alaska Native, non-Hispanic/Latino; 96 Asian, non-Hispanic/Latino; 194 Hispanic/Latino; 3 Native Hawaiian or other Pacific Islander, non-Hispanic/Latino; 22 Two or more races, non-Hispanic/Latino), 42 international. Average age 27. 3,484 applicants, 59% accepted, 341 enrolled. In 2013, 33 master's, 562 doctorates awarded. *Entrance requirements:* For master's, JD (for LL M); for doctorate, LSAT, undergraduate degree, letter of recommendation, resume, essay/personal statement. Additional exam requirements/recommendations for international students: Required—TOEFL (minimum score 600 paper-based; 100 iBT). *Application deadline:* For fall admission, 7/1 priority date for domestic and international students. Applications are processed on a rolling basis. Application fee: $0. Electronic applications accepted. *Expenses: Tuition:* Full-time $47,600; part-time $36,680 per year. *Required fees:* $1640; $1200. Part-time tuition and fees vary according to course load, degree level and student level. *Financial support:* In 2013–14, 495 students received support, including 142 fellowships (averaging $3,000 per year), 46 research assistantships (averaging $4,615 per year), 29 teaching assistantships (averaging $4,379 per year); career-related internships or fieldwork, Federal Work-Study, institutionally sponsored loans, and scholarships/grants also available. Support available to part-time students. Financial award application deadline: 7/1; financial award applicants required to submit FAFSA. *Faculty research:* Immigration law, corporate law, civil rights, family law, international law. *Unit head:* Anthony W. Crowell, Dean and President, 212-431-2840, Fax: 212-219-3752, E-mail: acrowell@nyls.edu. *Application contact:* Adam Barrett, Associate Dean of Admissions and Financial Aid, 212-431-2888, Fax: 212-966-1522, E-mail: admissions@nyls.edu.
Website: http://www.nyls.edu.

New York University, School of Law, New York, NY 10012-1019. Offers law (LL M, JD, JSD); law and business (Advanced Certificate); taxation (MSL, Advanced Certificate); JD/JD; JD/LL B; JD/MA; JD/MBA; JD/MPA; JD/MPP; JD/MSW; JD/MUP; JD/PhD. *Accreditation:* ABA. Part-time programs available. Postbaccalaureate distance learning degree programs offered. *Faculty:* 137 full-time (44 women), 68 part-time/adjunct (18 women). *Students:* 1,418 full-time (619 women); includes 394 minority (80 Black or African American, non-Hispanic/Latino; 1 American Indian or Alaska Native, non-Hispanic/Latino; 165 Asian, non-Hispanic/Latino; 120 Hispanic/Latino; 28 Two or more races, non-Hispanic/Latino), 69 international. 5,730 applicants, 437 enrolled. In 2013, 532 master's, 537 doctorates awarded. *Entrance requirements:* For doctorate, LSAT (for JD). *Application deadline:* For fall admission, 2/15 for domestic students. Application fee: $85. Electronic applications accepted. *Expenses:* Contact institution. *Financial support:* Fellowships, research assistantships, teaching assistantships, career-related internships or fieldwork, Federal Work-Study, scholarships/grants, and loan repayment assistance available. Financial award application deadline: 4/15; financial award applicants required to submit FAFSA. *Faculty research:* International law, environmental law, corporate law, globalization of law, philosophy of law. *Unit head:* Trevor Morrison, Dean, 212-998-6000, Fax: 212-995-3150. *Application contact:* Kenneth J. Kleinrock, Assistant Dean for Admissions, 212-998-6060, Fax: 212-995-4527.
Website: http://www.law.nyu.edu/.

North Carolina Central University, School of Law, Durham, NC 27707. Offers JD, JD/MLS. *Accreditation:* ABA. Part-time and evening/weekend programs available. *Entrance requirements:* For doctorate, LSAT, LSDAS. Additional exam requirements/recommendations for international students: Required—TOEFL. *Expenses:* Contact institution.

Northeastern University, School of Law, Boston, MA 02115-5005. Offers JD, JD/MA, JD/MBA, JD/MELP, JD/MPH, JD/MS, JD/MSA/MBA. JD/MPH offered jointly with Tufts University; JD/MSA/MBA with Graduate School of Professional Accounting; JD/MS with Program in Law and Public Policy; JD/MELP with Vermont Law School; and JD/MA with Brandeis University. *Accreditation:* ABA. *Degree requirements:* For doctorate, recommendation of faculty, 103 quarter hours of academic credit, four quarters of cooperative work under the supervision of an attorney, fulfillment of the public interest graduation requirement, rigorous writing requirement. *Entrance requirements:* For doctorate, LSAT, personal statement; resume; two recommendations; current CAS report (including transcripts from all academic institutions attended). Additional exam requirements/recommendations for international students: Recommended—TOEFL (minimum score 600 paper-based; 100 iBT). Electronic applications accepted. *Expenses:* Contact institution. *Faculty research:* Human rights, health, criminal, corporate/finance, international.

Northern Illinois University, College of Law, De Kalb, IL 60115-2854. Offers JD. *Accreditation:* ABA. Part-time programs available. *Faculty:* 22 full-time (11 women). *Students:* 264 full-time (122 women), 40 part-time (22 women); includes 74 minority (22 Black or African American, non-Hispanic/Latino; 3 American Indian or Alaska Native, non-Hispanic/Latino; 16 Asian, non-Hispanic/Latino; 25 Hispanic/Latino; 2 Native Hawaiian or other Pacific Islander, non-Hispanic/Latino; 6 Two or more races, non-Hispanic/Latino), 1 international. Average age 28. 621 applicants, 68% accepted, 100 enrolled. In 2013, 116 doctorates awarded. *Entrance requirements:* For doctorate, LSAT. Additional exam requirements/recommendations for international students: Required—TOEFL. *Application deadline:* For fall admission, 4/1 priority date for domestic and international students. Applications are processed on a rolling basis. Electronic applications accepted. Application fee is waived when completed online. *Expenses:* Contact institution. *Financial support:* In 2013–14, 1 research assistantship, 7 teaching assistantships were awarded; career-related internships or fieldwork, Federal Work-Study, tuition waivers (full and partial), and unspecified assistantships also available. Support available to part-time students. Financial award application deadline: 3/1; financial award applicants required to submit FAFSA. *Faculty research:* Criminal practice, intellectual property, environmental law, taxation. *Unit head:* Jennifer L. Rosato, Dean, 815-753-1380, Fax: 815-753-8552, E-mail: jrosato@niu.edu. *Application contact:* Sarah Scarpelli, Director of Admissions and Financial Aid, 815-753-8535, Fax: 815-753-5680, E-mail: lawadm@niu.edu.
Website: http://law.niu.edu/.

Northern Kentucky University, Chase College of Law, Highland Heights, KY 41099. Offers JD, JD/MBA, JD/MBI, JD/MHI. *Accreditation:* ABA. Part-time and evening/weekend programs available. *Faculty:* 36 full-time (16 women), 25 part-time/adjunct (11 women). *Students:* 332 full-time (135 women), 171 part-time (64 women); includes 44 minority (20 Black or African American, non-Hispanic/Latino; 4 American Indian or Alaska Native, non-Hispanic/Latino; 9 Asian, non-Hispanic/Latino; 10 Hispanic/Latino; 1 Native Hawaiian or other Pacific Islander, non-Hispanic/Latino). Average age 27. 681 applicants, 70% accepted, 154 enrolled. In 2013, 160 doctorates awarded. *Entrance requirements:* For doctorate, LSAT. Additional exam requirements/recommendations for international students: Required—TOEFL. *Application deadline:* For fall admission, 4/1 priority date for domestic and international students. Applications are processed on a rolling basis. Application fee: $40. Electronic applications accepted. *Expenses:* Contact institution. *Financial support:* In 2013–14, 193 students received support, including 22 fellowships (averaging $3,000 per year), 58 research assistantships (averaging $2,000 per year); career-related internships or fieldwork, Federal Work-Study, scholarships/grants, and unspecified assistantships also available. Support available to part-time students. Financial award application deadline: 3/1; financial award applicants required to submit FAFSA. *Faculty research:* Business law, Constitutional law, criminal law, environmental law, law and technology. *Unit head:* Jeffrey A. Standen, Dean and Professor of Law, 859-572-6406, Fax: 859-572-6183, E-mail: jstanden@nku.edu. *Application contact:* Ashley Folger Gray, Director of Admissions, 859-572-5841, Fax: 859-572-6081, E-mail: graya4@nku.edu.
Website: http://chaselaw.nku.edu.

Northwestern University, Law School, Chicago, IL 60611-3069. Offers international human rights (LL M); law (JD); law and business (LL M); tax (LL M in Tax); JD/LL M; JD/MBA; JD/PhD; LL M/Certificate. Executive LL M programs offered in Madrid (Spain), Seoul (South Korea), and Tel Aviv (Israel). *Accreditation:* ABA. *Entrance requirements:* For master's, law degree or equivalent, letter of recommendation, resume; for doctorate, LSAT, 1 letter of recommendation, resume. Additional exam requirements/recommendations for international students: Required—TOEFL. Electronic applications accepted. *Expenses:* Contact institution. *Faculty research:* Constitutional law, corporate law, international law, law and social policy, ethical studies.

Nova Southeastern University, Shepard Broad Law Center, Fort Lauderdale, FL 33314. Offers education law (MS); employment law (MS); health law (MS); law (JD); JD/MBA; JD/MS; JD/MURP. JD/MURP offered jointly with Florida Atlantic University. *Accreditation:* ABA. Part-time and evening/weekend programs available. Postbaccalaureate distance learning degree programs offered (minimal on-campus study). *Faculty:* 65 full-time (33 women), 96 part-time/adjunct (35 women). *Students:* 726 full-time (379 women), 324 part-time (233 women); includes 443 minority (127 Black or African American, non-Hispanic/Latino; 2 American Indian or Alaska Native, non-Hispanic/Latino; 41 Asian, non-Hispanic/Latino; 262 Hispanic/Latino; 1 Native Hawaiian or other Pacific Islander, non-Hispanic/Latino; 10 Two or more races, non-Hispanic/Latino), 11 international. Average age 28. 1,692 applicants, 49% accepted, 339 enrolled. In 2013, 61 master's, 303 doctorates awarded. *Degree requirements:* For master's, capstone research project; for doctorate, thesis/dissertation, rigorous upper-level writing requirement fulfilled through seminar paper or law journal article. *Entrance requirements:* For master's, regionally-accredited undergraduate degree and at least 2 years??? experience in the field of business or health care for the Employment Law and Health Care programs; for doctorate, LSAT. Additional exam requirements/recommendations for international students: Recommended—TOEFL, IELTS, TWE. *Application deadline:* For fall admission, 5/1 priority date for domestic and international students. Applications are processed on a rolling basis. Application fee: $53. Electronic applications accepted. *Expenses:* Contact institution. *Financial support:* In 2013–14, 325 students received support, including 17 fellowships (averaging $1,382 per year); Federal Work-Study, scholarships/grants, tuition waivers (partial), and unspecified assistantships also available. Support available to part-time students. Financial award application deadline: 4/15; financial award applicants required to submit FAFSA. *Faculty research:* Legal issues in family law, civil rights, business associations, criminal law, law and popular culture. *Unit head:* Elena Langan, Dean, 954-262-6100, Fax: 954-262-6317, E-mail: langane@nsu.law.nova.edu. *Application contact:* William Perez, Assistant Dean of Admissions, 954-262-6121, Fax: 954-262-3844, E-mail: perezw@nsu.law.nova.edu.
Website: http://www.nsulaw.nova.edu/.

Ohio Northern University, Claude W. Pettit College of Law, Ada, OH 45810-1599. Offers LL M, JD. *Accreditation:* ABA. *Faculty:* 23 full-time (10 women), 10 part-time/adjunct (4 women). *Students:* 248 full-time (112 women), 3 part-time (1 woman); includes 31 minority (19 Black or African American, non-Hispanic/Latino; 1 American Indian or Alaska Native, non-Hispanic/Latino; 2 Asian, non-Hispanic/Latino; 4 Hispanic/Latino; 5 Two or more races, non-Hispanic/Latino), 14 international. Average age 26. 515 applicants, 47% accepted, 93 enrolled. In 2013, 11 master's, 101 doctorates awarded. *Entrance requirements:* For doctorate, LSAT. Additional exam requirements/recommendations for international students: Required—TOEFL. *Application deadline:* Applications are processed on a rolling basis. Electronic applications accepted. *Expenses:* Contact institution. *Financial support:* Career-related internships or fieldwork, Federal Work-Study, institutionally sponsored loans, and scholarships/grants available. Financial award applicants required to submit FAFSA. *Faculty research:* Constitutional law, environmental law, business law and taxation, criminal law, public interest law, death penalty for women and juveniles, international human rights, sports violence. *Unit head:* Dr. Richard Bales, Dean, 419-772-3051, Fax: 419-772-3051, E-mail: r-bales@onu.edu. *Application contact:* Chad Vondenhuevel, Director of Law Admissions, 419-772-2213, Fax: 419-772-2213, E-mail: c-condenhuevel@onu.edu.
Website: http://www.law.onu.edu/.

The Ohio State University, Moritz College of Law, Columbus, OH 43210. Offers LL M, MSL, JD, JD/MA, JD/MBA, JD/MD, JD/MHA, JD/MPH. *Accreditation:* ABA. Electronic applications accepted. *Expenses:* Contact institution. *Faculty research:* Alternative dispute resolution, law and policy, clinical programs, criminal law, intellectual property, cyberlaw.

Oklahoma City University, School of Law, Oklahoma City, OK 73106-1402. Offers LL M, JD, JD/MBA. *Accreditation:* ABA. Part-time programs available. *Faculty:* 33 full-time (14 women), 30 part-time/adjunct (5 women). *Students:* 840 full-time (379 women), 100 part-time (55 women); includes 247 minority (45 Black or African American, non-Hispanic/Latino; 45 American Indian or Alaska Native, non-Hispanic/Latino; 22 Asian, non-Hispanic/Latino; 65 Hispanic/Latino; 70 Two or more races, non-Hispanic/Latino), 2 international. Average age 29. 602 applicants, 76% accepted, 162 enrolled. In 2013, 169 doctorates awarded. *Entrance requirements:* For doctorate, LSAT, bachelor's degree

from accredited undergraduate institution (except for OCU students admitted through the Oxford plan). Additional exam requirements/recommendations for international students: Required—TOEFL (minimum score 100 iBT). *Application deadline:* For fall admission, 8/1 for domestic and international students. Application fee: $50. Electronic applications accepted. *Expenses:* Contact institution. *Financial support:* Career-related internships or fieldwork, Federal Work-Study, institutionally sponsored loans, scholarships/grants, and tuition waivers available. Support available to part-time students. Financial award application deadline: 3/1; financial award applicants required to submit FAFSA. *Faculty research:* Family law, environmental law, consumer law, alternative dispute resolution, criminal law and procedure. *Unit head:* Dr. Valerie K. Couch, Dean, 405-208-5440, Fax: 405-208-6041, E-mail: vcouch@okcu.edu. *Application contact:* Dr. Laurie W. Jones, Associate Dean of Admissions, Law School, 405-208-5354, Fax: 405-208-5814, E-mail: ljones@okcu.edu.
Website: http://www.okcu.edu/law/.

Pace University, Pace Law School, White Plains, NY 10603. Offers comparative legal studies (LL M); environmental law (LL M, SJD), including climate change (LL M), land use and sustainability (LL M); law (JD); JD/LL M; JD/MA; JD/MBA; JD/MEM; JD/MPA; JD/MS. JD/MA offered jointly with Sarah Lawrence College; JD/MEM offered jointly with Yale University School of Forestry and Environmental Studies. *Accreditation:* ABA. Part-time programs available. *Degree requirements:* For master's, writing sample; for doctorate, thesis/dissertation (for some programs), extensive thesis proposal (for SJD). *Entrance requirements:* For doctorate, LSAT (for JD). Additional exam requirements/recommendations for international students: Required—TOEFL (minimum score 600 paper-based); Recommended—TWE. Electronic applications accepted. *Expenses:* Contact institution. *Faculty research:* Reform of energy regulations, international law, land use law, prosecutorial misconduct, corporation law, international sale of goods.

Penn State Dickinson School of Law, Graduate and Professional Programs, University Park, PA 16802-1017. Offers LL M, JD, SJD. *Accreditation:* ABA. *Faculty:* 53 full-time (22 women), 26 part-time/adjunct (9 women). *Students:* 573 full-time (253 women); includes 71 minority (30 Black or African American, non-Hispanic/Latino; 3 American Indian or Alaska Native, non-Hispanic/Latino; 10 Asian, non-Hispanic/Latino; 14 Hispanic/Latino; 14 Two or more races, non-Hispanic/Latino), 120 international. In 2013, 47 master's awarded. *Entrance requirements:* For doctorate, LSAT. Additional exam requirements/recommendations for international students: Required—TOEFL. *Application deadline:* Applications are processed on a rolling basis. Application fee: $60. Electronic applications accepted. *Financial support:* Applicants required to submit FAFSA. *Faculty research:* International law, dispute resolution, international affairs, business law, science and technology, energy law and policy. *Unit head:* James W. Houck, Interim Dean, 814-865-4294, E-mail: jwh32@psu.edu. *Application contact:* Amanda DiPolvere, Assistant Dean, Admissions and Financial Aid, 814-865-8978, E-mail: admissions@law.psu.edu.
Website: http://law.psu.edu/.

Pepperdine University, School of Law, Juris Doctor Program, Malibu, CA 90263. Offers JD, JD/MBA. *Accreditation:* ABA. *Students:* 598 full-time (293 women), 4 part-time (2 women); includes 167 minority (22 Black or African American, non-Hispanic/Latino; 1 American Indian or Alaska Native, non-Hispanic/Latino; 53 Asian, non-Hispanic/Latino; 57 Hispanic/Latino; 1 Native Hawaiian or other Pacific Islander, non-Hispanic/Latino; 33 Two or more races, non-Hispanic/Latino), 13 international. In 2013, 212 doctorates awarded. *Entrance requirements:* For doctorate, LSAT, 2 letters of recommendation, resume, personal statement, registration with the Credential Assembly Service (CAS). Additional exam requirements/recommendations for international students: Required—TOEFL. *Application deadline:* For fall admission, 3/1 priority date for domestic and international students. Applications are processed on a rolling basis. Application fee: $60. *Expenses:* Contact institution. *Financial support:* Federal Work-Study, institutionally sponsored loans, and scholarships/grants available. Financial award application deadline: 4/1; financial award applicants required to submit FAFSA. *Unit head:* Dr. Deanell Tacha, Dean, School of Law, 310-506-4621. *Application contact:* Shannon Phillips, Director of Admissions and Records, 310-506-4631, Fax: 310-506-4266, E-mail: shannon.phillips@pepperdine.edu.
Website: http://law.pepperdine.edu/academics/juris-doctor/.

Pontifical Catholic University of Puerto Rico, School of Law, Ponce, PR 00717-0777. Offers JD. *Accreditation:* ABA. Part-time and evening/weekend programs available. *Entrance requirements:* For doctorate, LSAT, PAEG, 3 letters of recommendation.

Pontificia Universidad Catolica Madre y Maestra, Graduate School, Faculty of Social and Administrative Sciences, Santiago, Dominican Republic. Offers business administration (MBA), including business development, finance, international business, management skills (M Mgmt, MBA), marketing, operations, strategic cost management, strategy, tourist destination planning and management; law (LL M), including civil law, corporate business law, criminal law, international relations, real estate law; management (M Mgmt), including higher financial management, insurance program administration, management skills (M Mgmt, MBA); psychology (MA), including clinical child and adolescent psychology, forensic psychology; strategic human resources (EMBA).

Queen's University at Kingston, Faculty of Law, Kingston, ON K7L 3N6, Canada. Offers LL M, JD, JD/MBA, JD/MIR, JD/MPA. Part-time programs available. *Degree requirements:* For master's, thesis. *Entrance requirements:* For doctorate, LSAT, minimum 2 years of college. Additional exam requirements/recommendations for international students: Required—TOEFL, TWE. *Faculty research:* Labor relations law, tax law and policy, criminal law and policy, critical legal theories, international legal relations.

Quinnipiac University, School of Law, Hamden, CT 06518. Offers health law (LL M); law (JD); JD/MBA. *Accreditation:* ABA. Part-time and evening/weekend programs available. *Faculty:* 33 full-time (11 women), 33 part-time/adjunct (9 women). *Students:* 252 full-time (142 women), 80 part-time (45 women); includes 44 minority (17 Black or African American, non-Hispanic/Latino; 6 American Indian or Alaska Native, non-Hispanic/Latino; 13 Asian, non-Hispanic/Latino; 8 Hispanic/Latino). Average age 25. 1,063 applicants, 53% accepted, 84 enrolled. In 2013, 148 doctorates awarded. *Entrance requirements:* For doctorate, LSAT. Additional exam requirements/recommendations for international students: Recommended—TOEFL. *Application deadline:* For fall admission, 3/1 priority date for domestic and international students. Applications are processed on a rolling basis. Application fee: $65. Electronic applications accepted. *Expenses:* Contact institution. *Financial support:* In 2013–14, 225 students received support, including 32 fellowships (averaging $1,560 per year), 70 research assistantships (averaging $2,160 per year); career-related internships or fieldwork, Federal Work-Study, and scholarships/grants also available. Support available to part-time students. Financial award application deadline: 4/15; financial award applicants required to submit FAFSA. *Faculty research:* Tax, health, public interest, corporate law, dispute resolution, intellectual property. *Unit head:* Jennifer Brown, Dean, 203-582-3200, Fax: 203-582-3209, E-mail: ladm@quinnipiac.edu. *Application contact:* Edwin Wilkes, Associate Vice-President/Dean of Law School Admissions, 203-582-3400, Fax: 203-582-3339, E-mail: ladm@quinnipiac.edu.
Website: http://law.quinnipiac.edu/.

Regent University, Graduate School, School of Law, Virginia Beach, VA 23464. Offers American legal studies (LL M); human rights (LL M); law (MA, JD); JD/MA; JD/MBA. *Accreditation:* ABA. Part-time programs available. *Faculty:* 25 full-time (7 women), 56 part-time/adjunct (17 women). *Students:* 342 full-time (179 women), 72 part-time (47 women); includes 56 minority (15 Black or African American, non-Hispanic/Latino; 9 American Indian or Alaska Native, non-Hispanic/Latino; 16 Asian, non-Hispanic/Latino; 16 Hispanic/Latino), 63 international. Average age 28. 615 applicants, 53% accepted, 87 enrolled. In 2013, 138 doctorates awarded. *Entrance requirements:* For doctorate, LSAT, minimum undergraduate GPA of 2.75, 3 letters of recommendation, resume. Additional exam requirements/recommendations for international students: Required—TOEFL (minimum score 600 paper-based). *Application deadline:* For fall admission, 3/1 for domestic students. Applications are processed on a rolling basis. Application fee: $50. Electronic applications accepted. *Expenses:* Contact institution. *Financial support:* Career-related internships or fieldwork, scholarships/grants, and tuition waivers (full and partial) available. Support available to part-time students. Financial award application deadline: 2/1; financial award applicants required to submit FAFSA. *Faculty research:* Family law, Constitutional law, law and culture, evidence and practice, intellectual property. *Unit head:* Jeffrey Brauch, Dean, 757-352-4040, Fax: 757-352-4595, E-mail: jeffbra@regent.edu. *Application contact:* Matthew Chadwick, Director of Enrollment Support Services, 800-373-5504, Fax: 757-352-4381, E-mail: admissions@regent.edu.
Website: http://www.regent.edu/acad/schlaw/admissions/abouthome.cfm.

Roger Williams University, School of Law, Bristol, RI 02809-5171. Offers JD, JD/MLRHR, JD/MMA, JD/MS, JD/MSCJ. JD/MMA and JD/MLRHR offered jointly with University of Rhode Island; JD/MSCJ with School of Justice Studies. *Accreditation:* ABA. Part-time programs available. *Faculty:* 32 full-time (18 women), 44 part-time/adjunct (15 women). *Students:* 420 full-time (214 women); includes 79 minority (15 Black or African American, non-Hispanic/Latino; 1 American Indian or Alaska Native, non-Hispanic/Latino; 4 Asian, non-Hispanic/Latino; 49 Hispanic/Latino; 10 Two or more races, non-Hispanic/Latino), 6 international. Average age 26. 1,018 applicants, 72% accepted, 111 enrolled. In 2013, 174 doctorates awarded. *Entrance requirements:* For doctorate, LSAT. Additional exam requirements/recommendations for international students: Required—TOEFL (minimum score 600 paper-based; 100 iBT). *Application deadline:* For fall admission, 4/1 priority date for domestic and international students. Applications are processed on a rolling basis. Application fee: $60. Electronic applications accepted. *Expenses:* Tuition: Full-time $6939; part-time $2313 per course. *Required fees:* $1147; $871 per term. *Financial support:* In 2013–14, 276 students received support, including 11 fellowships (averaging $1,157 per year), 30 research assistantships (averaging $1,226 per year); career-related internships or fieldwork, Federal Work-Study, and scholarships/grants also available. Support available to part-time students. Financial award application deadline: 3/31; financial award applicants required to submit FAFSA. *Faculty research:* Civil rights, admiralty, labor, intellectual property, international and comparative law. *Unit head:* David A. Logan, Dean, 401-254-4500, Fax: 401-254-3525, E-mail: dlogan@rwu.edu. *Application contact:* Michael W. Donnelly-Boylen, Assistant Dean of Admissions, 800-633-2727, Fax: 401-254-4516, E-mail: mdonnelly-boylen@rwu.edu.
Website: http://law.rwu.edu.

Rutgers, The State University of New Jersey, Camden, School of Law, Camden, NJ 08102. Offers JD, JD/DO, JD/MA, JD/MBA, JD/MCRP, JD/MD, JD/MPA, JD/MPH, JD/MS, JD/MSW, JD/MCRP, JD/MA, JD/MPA, JD/MSW, JD/MS offered jointly with Rutgers, The State University of New Jersey, New Brunswick; JD/MPA, JD/MD, JD/DO with University of Medicine and Dentistry of New Jersey. *Accreditation:* ABA. Part-time and evening/weekend programs available. *Entrance requirements:* For doctorate, LSAT. Additional exam requirements/recommendations for international students: Recommended—TOEFL. Electronic applications accepted. *Expenses:* Contact institution. *Faculty research:* International law, commercial law, public law, health law, constitutional law, jurisprudence.

Rutgers, The State University of New Jersey, Newark, School of Law, Newark, NJ 07102-3094. Offers JD, JD/MA, JD/MBA, JD/MCRP, JD/MD, JD/MSW, JD/PhD. JD/MCRP, JD/PhD offered jointly with Rutgers, The State University of New Jersey, New Brunswick. *Accreditation:* ABA. Part-time and evening/weekend programs available. *Entrance requirements:* For doctorate, LSAT. *Expenses:* Contact institution. *Faculty research:* Civil rights and liberties, women and the law, international human rights and world order, corporate law, employment law.

St. John's University, School of Law, Program in International and Comparative Sports Law, Queens, NY 11439. Offers LL M. Program offered jointly with the Instituto Superior de Derecho y Economia (ISDE) in Madrid, Spain. *Students:* 18 full-time (5 women); includes 10 minority (3 Black or African American, non-Hispanic/Latino; 1 Asian, non-Hispanic/Latino; 4 Hispanic/Latino; 2 Two or more races, non-Hispanic/Latino), 6 international. Average age 29. 30 applicants, 67% accepted, 15 enrolled. In 2013, 9 master's awarded. *Degree requirements:* For master's, thesis, practicum, seminar. *Entrance requirements:* For master's, resume, 2 letters of recommendation, writing sample, personal statement, interview, transcript, proficiency in English. Additional exam requirements/recommendations for international students: Required—TOEFL (minimum score 600 paper-based; 22 iBT), IELTS (minimum score 7), TWE (minimum score 5). *Application deadline:* For fall admission, 4/1 priority date for domestic and international students. Application fee: $100. *Expenses:* Contact institution. *Unit head:* Jeffrey K. Walker, Associate Dean for Transnational Programs, 718-990-8335, E-mail: walkerj@stjohns.edu. *Application contact:* Robert Harrison, Associate Dean of Admissions and Financial Services, 718-990-6474, Fax: 718-990-6699, E-mail: lawinfo@stjohns.edu.
Website: http://www.stjohns.edu/law/programs-and-majors/international-and-comparative-sports-law-llm.

St. John's University, School of Law, Program in Law, Queens, NY 11439. Offers JD, JD/LL M, MA/JD, MBA/JD. Part-time and evening/weekend programs available. *Students:* 671 full-time (303 women), 132 part-time (68 women); includes 224 minority (42 Black or African American, non-Hispanic/Latino; 72 Asian, non-Hispanic/Latino; 87 Hispanic/Latino; 3 Native Hawaiian or other Pacific Islander, non-Hispanic/Latino; 20 Two or more races, non-Hispanic/Latino), 15 international. Average age 25. 2,519 applicants, 57% accepted, 255 enrolled. In 2013, 309 doctorates awarded. *Entrance requirements:* For doctorate, LSAT, personal statement, CAS Report, 2 letters of recommendation, bachelor's degree. Additional exam requirements/recommendations for international students: Required—TOEFL (minimum score 600 paper-based; 100 iBT), IELTS (minimum score 5.5). *Application deadline:* For fall admission, 4/1 priority date for domestic and international students. Applications are processed on a rolling basis. Application fee: $60. Electronic applications accepted. *Expenses:* Contact institution. *Unit head:* Michael Simons, Dean, 718-990-6602, Fax: 718-990-6694, E-mail: simonsm@stjohns.edu. *Application contact:* Robert Harrison, Associate Dean of Admissions and Financial Services, 718-990-6474, Fax: 718-990-6699, E-mail: lawinfo@stjohns.edu.
Website: http://www.stjohns.edu/law/programs-and-majors/juris-doctor.

Saint Joseph's University, College of Arts and Sciences, Department of Criminal Justice, Philadelphia, PA 19131-1395. Offers administration/police executive (MS); behavior analysis (MS, Post-Master's Certificate); criminal justice (MS, Post-Master's Certificate); criminology (MS); federal law (MS); intelligence and crime (MS); probation,

parole, and corrections (MS). Part-time and evening/weekend programs available. Postbaccalaureate distance learning degree programs offered (no on-campus study). *Faculty:* 2 full-time (both women), 20 part-time/adjunct (4 women). *Students:* 44 full-time (32 women), 475 part-time (319 women); includes 189 minority (125 Black or African American, non-Hispanic/Latino; 2 American Indian or Alaska Native, non-Hispanic/Latino; 8 Asian, non-Hispanic/Latino; 36 Hispanic/Latino; 2 Native Hawaiian or other Pacific Islander, non-Hispanic/Latino; 16 Two or more races, non-Hispanic/Latino), 1 international. Average age 33. 270 applicants, 70% accepted, 144 enrolled. In 2013, 226 master's, 21 other advanced degrees awarded. *Degree requirements:* For master's, thesis. *Entrance requirements:* For master's, GRE General Test or minimum GPA of 3.0, 2 letters of recommendation, personal statement, resume, official transcripts. Additional exam requirements/recommendations for international students: Required—TOEFL (minimum score 550 paper-based; 80 iBT). *Application deadline:* For fall admission, 7/15 priority date for domestic students, 4/15 for international students; for winter admission, 1/15 for international students; for spring admission, 11/15 priority date for domestic students, 10/15 for international students. Applications are processed on a rolling basis. Application fee: $35. Electronic applications accepted. *Expenses: Tuition:* Part-time $786 per credit hour. Tuition and fees vary according to degree level and program. *Financial support:* Career-related internships or fieldwork and unspecified assistantships available. Financial award applicants required to submit FAFSA. *Faculty research:* Early response, community preparedness, cyber bullying. *Total annual research expenditures:* $119,650. *Unit head:* Cheralynn Ewing, Director, 610-660-1294, E-mail: cewing@sju.edu. *Application contact:* Elisabeth Woodward, Director of Marketing and Admissions, Graduate Arts and Sciences, 610-660-3131, Fax: 610-660-3131, E-mail: gradstudies@sju.edu.
Website: http://www.sju.edu/majors-programs/graduate-arts-sciences/masters/criminal-justice-ms.

Saint Louis University, School of Law, St. Louis, MO 63108. Offers LL M, JD. *Accreditation:* ABA. Part-time and evening/weekend programs available. *Degree requirements:* For master's, thesis (for some programs). *Entrance requirements:* For master's, JD or equivalent; for doctorate, LSAT, letters of recommendation, resume, personal statement, LSDAS. Additional exam requirements/recommendations for international students: Required—TOEFL (minimum score 590 paper-based). Electronic applications accepted. *Expenses:* Contact institution. *Faculty research:* Health law, employment law, international comparative law, lawyering skills (clinical).

St. Mary's University, School of Law, San Antonio, TX 78228-8602. Offers JD, JD/MA, JD/MBA, JD/MPA, JD/MS. *Accreditation:* ABA. *Entrance requirements:* For doctorate, LSAT. Additional exam requirements/recommendations for international students: Required—TOEFL (minimum score 600 paper-based). Electronic applications accepted. *Expenses:* Contact institution. *Faculty research:* Ethics, church and state, exclusionary rule, civil rights, tort law.

St. Thomas University, School of Law, Miami Gardens, FL 33054-6459. Offers international human rights (LL M); international taxation (LL M); law (JD); JD/MBA; JD/MS. *Accreditation:* ABA. Postbaccalaureate distance learning degree programs offered (no on-campus study). *Degree requirements:* For master's, thesis (international taxation). *Entrance requirements:* For doctorate, LSAT. Electronic applications accepted. *Expenses:* Contact institution.

Samford University, Cumberland School of Law, Birmingham, AL 35229. Offers MCL, JD, JD/M Acc, JD/M Div, JD/MATS, JD/MBA, JD/MPA, JD/MPH, JD/MS, JD/MSEM. JD/MPH, JD/MPA offered jointly with The University of Alabama at Birmingham. *Accreditation:* ABA. *Faculty:* 22 full-time (7 women), 17 part-time/adjunct (6 women). *Students:* 417 full-time (185 women), 9 part-time (7 women); includes 47 minority (19 Black or African American, non-Hispanic/Latino; 11 Asian, non-Hispanic/Latino; 12 Hispanic/Latino; 5 Two or more races, non-Hispanic/Latino). Average age 25. 713 applicants, 81% accepted, 172 enrolled. In 2013, 1 master's, 146 doctorates awarded. *Degree requirements:* For master's, thesis. *Entrance requirements:* For doctorate, LSAT. Additional exam requirements/recommendations for international students: Required—TOEFL (minimum score 550 paper-based). *Application deadline:* For fall admission, 2/28 priority date for domestic and international students. Applications are processed on a rolling basis. Application fee: $50. Electronic applications accepted. *Expenses:* Contact institution. *Financial support:* In 2013–14, 204 students received support. Career-related internships or fieldwork, Federal Work-Study, institutionally sponsored loans, and scholarships/grants available. Financial award application deadline: 3/1; financial award applicants required to submit FAFSA. *Faculty research:* Constitutional law (commerce clause), law and literature, legal history, law and ethics, evidence. *Unit head:* John L. Carroll, Dean, 205-726-2704, Fax: 205-726-4107, E-mail: jlcarrol@samford.edu. *Application contact:* Ken England, Director of Admissions and Administration, 205-726-2887, Fax: 205-726-4457, E-mail: law.admissions@samford.edu.
Website: http://cumberland.samford.edu/.

San Joaquin College of Law, Law Program, Clovis, CA 93612-1312. Offers JD. Part-time and evening/weekend programs available. *Entrance requirements:* For doctorate, LSAT.

Santa Clara University, School of Law, Santa Clara, CA 95053. Offers high technology law (Certificate); intellectual property law (LL M); international and comparative law (LL M); international high tech law (Certificate); international law (Certificate); law (JD); public interest and social justice law (Certificate); United States law (LL M); JD/MBA; MSIS/JD. LL M in United States law for non-U.S. attorneys only. *Accreditation:* ABA. Part-time and evening/weekend programs available. *Faculty:* 72 full-time (36 women), 33 part-time/adjunct (18 women). *Students:* 756 full-time (354 women), 85 part-time (53 women); includes 339 minority (14 Black or African American, non-Hispanic/Latino; 1 American Indian or Alaska Native, non-Hispanic/Latino; 182 Asian, non-Hispanic/Latino; 100 Hispanic/Latino; 5 Native Hawaiian or other Pacific Islander, non-Hispanic/Latino; 37 Two or more races, non-Hispanic/Latino), 47 international. Average age 28. 2,791 applicants, 58% accepted, 295 enrolled. In 2013, 23 master's, 323 Certificates awarded. *Degree requirements:* For master's, comprehensive exam, thesis; for doctorate, comprehensive exam, thesis/dissertation, 86 units. *Entrance requirements:* For master's and doctorate, LSAT, transcript, personal statement, letters of recommendation. *Application deadline:* For fall admission, 2/1 priority date for domestic and international students. Applications are processed on a rolling basis. Application fee: $75. Electronic applications accepted. *Expenses:* Contact institution. *Financial support:* In 2013–14, 449 students received support. Career-related internships or fieldwork, Federal Work-Study, and scholarships/grants available. Support available to part-time students. Financial award application deadline: 2/1; financial award applicants required to submit FAFSA. *Faculty research:* Intellectual property, international human rights, privacy rights, wrongful convictions, shareholder and firm governance. *Unit head:* Donald Polden, Dean, 408-554-4362. *Application contact:* Jeannette Leach, Director of Admissions, 408-554-5048.
Website: http://law.scu.edu/.

Seattle University, School of Law, Seattle, WA 98122-4340. Offers JD, JD/MATL, JD/MBA, JD/MCJ, JD/MIB, JD/MPA, JD/MSAL, JD/MSF, JD/MSL. *Accreditation:* ABA. Part-time programs available. *Entrance requirements:* For doctorate, LSAT. Additional exam requirements/recommendations for international students: Required—TOEFL (minimum score 600 paper-based; 100 iBT). Electronic applications accepted. *Expenses:* Contact institution. *Faculty research:* Race, postcolonial theory, and U.S. civil rights; secrecy and democratic decisions; linguistic features of police culture and the coercive impact of police officer swearing in police-citizen interaction; the imprisoned parent: differential power in same-sex families based on legal and cultural understandings of parentage; theology in public reason and legal discourse: a case for the preferential option for the poor.

Seton Hall University, School of Law, Newark, NJ 07102-5210. Offers health law (LL M, JD); intellectual property (LL M, JD); law (MSJ); JD/MADIR; JD/MBA; MD/JD; MD/MSJ. MD/JD, MD/MSJ offered jointly with University of Medicine and Dentistry of New Jersey. *Accreditation:* ABA. Part-time and evening/weekend programs available. *Degree requirements:* For master's, thesis optional. *Entrance requirements:* For master's, professional experience, letters of recommendation; for doctorate, LSAT, active LSDAS registration, letters of recommendation. Additional exam requirements/recommendations for international students: Recommended—TOEFL. Electronic applications accepted. *Expenses:* Contact institution. *Faculty research:* Health law, intellectual property law, science and the law, international law and employment/labor law.

Southern Illinois University Carbondale, School of Law, Carbondale, IL 62901-6804. Offers general law (LL M); health law and policy (LL M); law (JD); legal studies (MLS), including general law, health law and policy; JD/M Acc; JD/MBA; JD/MD; JD/MPA; JD/MSW; JD/PhD. *Accreditation:* ABA. Part-time programs available. *Faculty:* 23 full-time (11 women), 12 part-time/adjunct (6 women). *Students:* 5 full-time (2 women), 7 part-time (4 women), 1 international. Average age 27. 10 applicants, 70% accepted, 7 enrolled. In 2013, 6 master's awarded. *Entrance requirements:* For doctorate, LSAT. Additional exam requirements/recommendations for international students: Required—TOEFL (minimum score 600 paper-based). *Application deadline:* For fall admission, 3/1 for domestic and international students. Applications are processed on a rolling basis. Application fee: $50. Electronic applications accepted. *Expenses:* Contact institution. *Financial support:* In 2013–14, 326 students received support. Career-related internships or fieldwork, Federal Work-Study, institutionally sponsored loans, scholarships/grants, and health care benefits available. Support available to part-time students. Financial award application deadline: 4/1; financial award applicants required to submit FAFSA. *Faculty research:* Health care, criminal, environmental, and international law; tort reform. *Unit head:* Michael Ruiz, Assistant Dean, 618-453-8763, Fax: 618-453-8769, E-mail: mikeruiz@siu.edu. *Application contact:* Lisa David, Admissions Coordinator, 618-453-8767, Fax: 618-453-8769, E-mail: ldavid@law.siu.edu.
Website: http://www.law.siu.edu/.

Southern Methodist University, Dedman College of Humanities and Sciences, Department of Economics, Dallas, TX 75205. Offers applied economics (MA); applied economics and predictive analytics (MS); economics (PhD); law and economics (MA). Part-time and evening/weekend programs available. Terminal master's awarded for partial completion of doctoral program. *Degree requirements:* For master's, thesis, oral qualifying exam; for doctorate, thesis/dissertation, written exams. *Entrance requirements:* For master's, GRE General Test or GMAT, 12 hours of course work in economics, minimum GPA of 3.0, previous course work in calculus and statistics; for doctorate, GRE General Test, minimum GPA of 3.0; 3 semesters of course work in calculus; 1 semester each of course work in statistics and linear algebra. Additional exam requirements/recommendations for international students: Required—TOEFL (minimum score 550 paper-based). Electronic applications accepted. *Faculty research:* Economic theory, game theory, econometrics, international trade, labor.

Southern Methodist University, Dedman School of Law, Dallas, TX 75275-0110. Offers law (JD, SJD); law (for foreign law school graduates) (LL M); law (general) (LL M); taxation (LL M); JD/MA; JD/MBA. *Accreditation:* ABA. Part-time and evening/weekend programs available. *Degree requirements:* For master's, thesis optional; for doctorate, thesis/dissertation (for some programs), 30 hours of public service (for JD). *Entrance requirements:* For master's, JD; for doctorate, LSAT (for JD). Additional exam requirements/recommendations for international students: Required—TOEFL (minimum score 575 paper-based; 91 iBT). Electronic applications accepted. *Expenses:* Contact institution. *Faculty research:* Corporate law, intellectual property, international law, commercial law, dispute resolution.

Southern University and Agricultural and Mechanical College, Southern University Law Center, Baton Rouge, LA 70813. Offers JD. *Accreditation:* ABA. Part-time and evening/weekend programs available. *Entrance requirements:* For doctorate, LSAT. Additional exam requirements/recommendations for international students: Recommended—TOEFL. Electronic applications accepted. *Expenses:* Contact institution. *Faculty research:* Civil law, comparative law, constitutional law, civil rights law.

South Texas College of Law, Professional Program, Houston, TX 77002-7000. Offers JD. *Accreditation:* ABA. Part-time and evening/weekend programs available. *Degree requirements:* For doctorate, completion of 90 hours within 7 years of enrollment. *Entrance requirements:* For doctorate, LSAT (taken within last 4 years), degree from accredited 4-year institution. Electronic applications accepted.

Southwestern Law School, Graduate Programs, Los Angeles, CA 90010. Offers entertainment and media law (LL M); individualized studies (LL M); law (JD). *Accreditation:* ABA. Part-time and evening/weekend programs available. Postbaccalaureate distance learning degree programs offered. *Faculty:* 52 full-time (20 women), 28 part-time/adjunct (6 women). *Students:* 686 full-time (384 women), 397 part-time (211 women); includes 336 minority (50 Black or African American, non-Hispanic/Latino; 7 American Indian or Alaska Native, non-Hispanic/Latino; 158 Asian, non-Hispanic/Latino; 121 Hispanic/Latino), 7 international. Average age 27. *Entrance requirements:* For master's, JD; for doctorate, LSAT, LSDAS. Additional exam requirements/recommendations for international students: Required—TOEFL. *Application deadline:* For fall admission, 4/1 priority date for domestic and international students. Applications are processed on a rolling basis. Application fee: $60. Electronic applications accepted. *Expenses: Tuition:* Full-time $45,180; part-time $30,120 per year. *Required fees:* $200 per year. *Financial support:* Research assistantships, career-related internships or fieldwork, Federal Work-Study, institutionally sponsored loans, scholarships/grants, and tuition waivers (full and partial) available. Support available to part-time students. Financial award application deadline: 4/1; financial award applicants required to submit FAFSA. *Faculty research:* International trade and law, mediation/arbitration, land use and urban planning, antitrust law, entertainment and media law. *Unit head:* Susan Westerberg Prager, Dean, 213-738-6710, Fax: 213-383-1688. *Application contact:* Lisa Gear, Assistant Dean of Admissions, 213-738-6834, Fax: 213-383-1688, E-mail: admissions@swlaw.edu.

Stanford University, Law School, Stanford, CA 94305-8610. Offers JSM, MLS, JD, JSD, JD/MA, JD/MBA, JD/MPP, JD/MS, JD/PhD. *Accreditation:* ABA. *Degree requirements:* For doctorate, thesis/dissertation (for some programs). *Entrance requirements:* For doctorate, LSAT (for JD). Electronic applications accepted. *Expenses:* Contact institution.

Stetson University, College of Law, Gulfport, FL 33707-3299. Offers advocacy (LL M); elder law (LL M); international law (LL M); law (JD); JD/MBA. *Accreditation:* ABA. Part-time and evening/weekend programs available. Postbaccalaureate distance learning degree programs offered (minimal on-campus study). *Faculty:* 50 full-time (26 women), 68 part-time/adjunct (21 women). *Students:* 881 full-time (447 women), 111 part-time (55 women); includes 219 minority (42 Black or African American, non-Hispanic/Latino; 2 American Indian or Alaska Native, non-Hispanic/Latino; 24 Asian, non-Hispanic/Latino; 120 Hispanic/Latino; 1 Native Hawaiian or other Pacific Islander, non-Hispanic/Latino; 30 Two or more races, non-Hispanic/Latino), 28 international. Average age 28. 2,068 applicants, 44% accepted, 267 enrolled. In 2013, 25 master's, 322 doctorates awarded. *Entrance requirements:* For doctorate, LSAT. Additional exam requirements/recommendations for international students: Required—TOEFL (minimum score 600 paper-based, 100 iBT) or IELTS (minimum score 7). *Application deadline:* For fall admission, 5/15 for domestic and international students; for spring admission, 9/1 for domestic students. Applications are processed on a rolling basis. Application fee: $55. Electronic applications accepted. *Expenses:* Contact institution. *Financial support:* In 2013–14, 329 students received support, including 13 fellowships (averaging $1,640 per year), 104 research assistantships (averaging $1,017 per year), 39 teaching assistantships (averaging $1,017 per year); Federal Work-Study and scholarships/grants also available. Financial award application deadline: 5/15; financial award applicants required to submit FAFSA. *Faculty research:* Advocacy and legal communication, law and higher education, elder law, international law including biodiversity and Caribbean law, veterans law and policy. *Unit head:* Dr. Christopher M. Pietruszkiewicz, Dean/Professor of Law, 727-562-7809, Fax: 727-562-6428, E-mail: cmp@law.stetson.edu. *Application contact:* Laura Zuppo, Assistant Dean of Admissions and Financial Planning, 727-562-7802, Fax: 727-343-0136, E-mail: lawadmit@law.stetson.edu.
Website: http://www.law.stetson.edu/.

Suffolk University, Law School, Boston, MA 02108. Offers business law and financial services (JD); civil litigation (JD); global law and technology (LL M); health and biomedical law (JD); intellectual property law (JD); international law (JD); JD/MBA; JD/MPA; JD/MSCJ; JD/MSF; JD/MSIE. *Accreditation:* ABA. Part-time and evening/weekend programs available. *Faculty:* 73 full-time (34 women), 54 part-time/adjunct (14 women). *Students:* 1,074 full-time (575 women), 504 part-time (248 women); includes 351 minority (101 Black or African American, non-Hispanic/Latino; 3 American Indian or Alaska Native, non-Hispanic/Latino; 96 Asian, non-Hispanic/Latino; 132 Hispanic/Latino; 19 Two or more races, non-Hispanic/Latino), 65 international. Average age 27. 2,390 applicants, 77% accepted, 450 enrolled. In 2013, 516 doctorates awarded. *Degree requirements:* For master's, legal writing. *Entrance requirements:* For master's, 2 letters of recommendation, resume, personal statement; for doctorate, LSAT, LSDAS, dean's certification, recommendation. Additional exam requirements/recommendations for international students: Required—TOEFL (minimum score 600 paper-based; 100 iBT). *Application deadline:* For fall admission, 3/1 for domestic and international students. Applications are processed on a rolling basis. Application fee: $60. Electronic applications accepted. *Expenses:* Contact institution. *Financial support:* Career-related internships or fieldwork, Federal Work-Study, institutionally sponsored loans, and scholarships/grants available. Support available to part-time students. Financial award application deadline: 3/1; financial award applicants required to submit FAFSA. *Faculty research:* Civil law, international law, health/biomedical law, business and finance, intellectual property. *Unit head:* Camille A. Nelson, Dean of Suffolk University Law School, 617-573-8144, Fax: 617-523-1367, E-mail: gellis@suffolk.edu. *Application contact:* Jennifer Sims, Assistant Dean for Admissions and Financial Aid, 617-573-8144, Fax: 617-523-1367, E-mail: ilawadm@suffolk.edu.
Website: http://www.law.suffolk.edu/.

Syracuse University, College of Law, Syracuse, NY 13244-1030. Offers JD, JD/MA, JD/MBA, JD/MLS, JD/MPA, JD/MPS, JD/MS, JD/MS Acct, JD/MSW, JD/PhD. *Accreditation:* ABA. Part-time programs available. *Faculty:* 45 full-time (14 women), 29 part-time/adjunct (11 women). *Students:* 615 full-time (259 women), 5 part-time (2 women); includes 115 minority (18 Black or African American, non-Hispanic/Latino; 1 American Indian or Alaska Native, non-Hispanic/Latino; 38 Asian, non-Hispanic/Latino; 44 Hispanic/Latino; 14 Two or more races, non-Hispanic/Latino), 29 international. Average age 25. 1,865 applicants, 59% accepted, 206 enrolled. In 2013, 205 doctorates awarded. *Entrance requirements:* For doctorate, LSAT. Additional exam requirements/recommendations for international students: Required—TOEFL (minimum score 600 paper-based), TWE. *Application deadline:* For fall admission, 4/1 priority date for domestic and international students. Applications are processed on a rolling basis. Application fee: $70. Electronic applications accepted. *Expenses:* Contact institution. *Financial support:* In 2013–14, 487 students received support. Fellowships, research assistantships, career-related internships or fieldwork, Federal Work-Study, institutionally sponsored loans, scholarships/grants, and tuition waivers (partial) available. Support available to part-time students. Financial award application deadline: 2/15; financial award applicants required to submit FAFSA. *Faculty research:* Interdisciplinary legal studies, law and technology, international law, advocacy training, family law. *Unit head:* Hannah Arterian, Dean, 315-443-2524, Fax: 315-443-4213. *Application contact:* Nikki Laubenstein, Director of Admissions, 315-443-1962, Fax: 315-443-9568, E-mail: admissions@law.syr.edu.
Website: http://www.law.syr.edu/.

Taft Law School, Graduate Programs, Santa Ana, CA 92704-6954. Offers American jurisprudence (LL M); law (JD); taxation (LL M).

Temple University, James E. Beasley School of Law, Philadelphia, PA 19122. Offers law (JD); legal education (SJD); taxation (LL M); transnational law (LL M); trial advocacy (LL M); JD/LL M; JD/MBA. *Accreditation:* ABA. Part-time and evening/weekend programs available. *Entrance requirements:* For doctorate, LSAT (for JD). Additional exam requirements/recommendations for international students: Recommended—TOEFL. Electronic applications accepted. *Expenses:* Contact institution. *Faculty research:* Evidence, gender issues, health care law, immigration law, and intellectual property law.

Texas A&M University, School of Law, College Station, TX 77843. Offers JD. *Faculty:* 56. *Students:* 734 full-time (355 women), 36 part-time (17 women); includes 209 minority (52 Black or African American, non-Hispanic/Latino; 3 American Indian or Alaska Native, non-Hispanic/Latino; 26 Asian, non-Hispanic/Latino; 105 Hispanic/Latino; 23 Two or more races, non-Hispanic/Latino), 3 international. Average age 30. *Entrance requirements:* For doctorate, CAS/LSAT. *Application deadline:* For fall admission, 5/31 for domestic students. Application fee: $55. *Expenses:* Tuition, state resident: full-time $4078; part-time $226.55 per credit hour. Tuition, nonresident: full-time $10,450; part-time $580.55 per credit hour. *Required fees:* $2328; $278.50 per credit hour. $642.45 per semester. *Unit head:* Dr. Andrew Morriss, Dean, 817-212-4000. *Application contact:* Law School Admissions, 817-212-4040, E-mail: law-admissions@law.tamu.edu.
Website: http://law.tamu.edu/.

Texas Southern University, Thurgood Marshall School of Law, Houston, TX 77004-4584. Offers JD. *Accreditation:* ABA. *Faculty:* 39 full-time (20 women), 15 part-time/adjunct (9 women). *Students:* 530 full-time (294 women), 2 part-time (0 women); includes 455 minority (254 Black or African American, non-Hispanic/Latino; 6 American Indian or Alaska Native, non-Hispanic/Latino; 31 Asian, non-Hispanic/Latino; 164 Hispanic/Latino), 2 international. Average age 28. 252 applicants, 100% accepted, 200 enrolled. In 2013, 161 doctorates awarded. *Entrance requirements:* For doctorate, LSAT. *Application deadline:* For fall admission, 4/1 for domestic and international students. Applications are processed on a rolling basis. Application fee: $55. Electronic applications accepted. *Expenses:* Contact institution. *Financial support:* In 2013–14, 75 students received support. Research assistantships, teaching assistantships, career-related internships or fieldwork, scholarships/grants, tuition waivers (partial), and unspecified assistantships available. Financial award application deadline: 4/1; financial award applicants required to submit FAFSA. *Faculty research:* Sports law, civil rights and minors, international economics regulation, contracts principle, standards of judicial review. *Unit head:* Dr. Dannye Holley, Dean, 713-313-7388, Fax: 713-313-1049, E-mail: dholley@tsulaw.edu. *Application contact:* Pearly Pendenque, Administrative Assistant, 713-313-1076 Ext. 1, E-mail: ppendeque@tsulaw.tsu.edu.
Website: http://www.tsulaw.edu/.

Texas Tech University, School of Law, Lubbock, TX 79409-0004. Offers law (JD); United States legal studies (LL M); JD/M Engr; JD/MBA; JD/MD; JD/MPA; JD/MS; JD/MSA. *Accreditation:* ABA. *Faculty:* 30 full-time (8 women). *Students:* 629 full-time (294 women), 9 part-time (6 women); includes 175 minority (14 Black or African American, non-Hispanic/Latino; 3 American Indian or Alaska Native, non-Hispanic/Latino; 36 Asian, non-Hispanic/Latino; 85 Hispanic/Latino; 1 Native Hawaiian or other Pacific Islander, non-Hispanic/Latino; 36 Two or more races, non-Hispanic/Latino), 19 international. Average age 25. 1,485 applicants, 50% accepted, 218 enrolled. In 2013, 238 doctorates awarded. *Entrance requirements:* For doctorate, LSAT. Additional exam requirements/recommendations for international students: Required—TOEFL (minimum score 550 paper-based; 79 iBT), IELTS (minimum score 6.5), TOEFL (minimum score 600 paper-based; 100 iBT) or IELTS (minimum score 7) for LL M. *Application deadline:* For fall admission, 2/15 priority date for domestic and international students. Applications are processed on a rolling basis. Application fee: $50. Electronic applications accepted. *Expenses:* Contact institution. *Financial support:* In 2013–14, 380 students received support, including 193 fellowships (averaging $6,504 per year), 43 research assistantships (averaging $375 per year), 51 teaching assistantships (averaging $1,012 per year); Federal Work-Study, scholarships/grants, and tuition waivers also available. Financial award application deadline: 4/15; financial award applicants required to submit FAFSA. *Faculty research:* Emerging technologies law, criminal law, military law and policy, energy law, estate planning/tax. *Total annual research expenditures:* $112,589. *Unit head:* Darby Dickerson, Dean/Professor of Law, 806-834-5421, Fax: 806-742-4014, E-mail: darby.dickerson@ttu.edu. *Application contact:* Stephen M. Perez, Assistant Dean for Admissions and Financial Aid, 806-834-5024, E-mail: admissions.law@ttu.edu.
Website: http://www.law.ttu.edu/.

Texas Wesleyan University, School of Law, Fort Worth, TX 76102. Offers JD. *Accreditation:* ABA. Part-time and evening/weekend programs available. *Entrance requirements:* For doctorate, LSAT, LSDAS report, 2 letters of recommendation. Additional exam requirements/recommendations for international students: Required—TOEFL. Electronic applications accepted. *Expenses:* Contact institution.

Thomas Jefferson School of Law, Graduate and Professional Programs, San Diego, CA 92110-2905. Offers JD. JD/MBA offered in partnership with San Diego State University. *Accreditation:* ABA. Part-time and evening/weekend programs available. *Entrance requirements:* For doctorate, LSAT. Additional exam requirements/recommendations for international students: Required—TOEFL. Electronic applications accepted. *Faculty research:* Tenant's rights, fetal rights/medical ethics, bilateral treaties/international law, sexual harassment and gender treatment.

Thomas M. Cooley Law School, JD and LL M Programs, Lansing, MI 48901-3038. Offers administrative law (public law) (JD); business transactions (JD); Canadian law practice (JD); Constitutional law and civil rights (public law) (JD); corporate law and finance (LL M); environmental law (public law) (JD); general practice (JD), including solo and small firm; homeland and national security law (LL M); insurance law (LL M); intellectual property (JD); intellectual property law (LL M); international law (JD); litigation (JD); self-directed (LL M, JD); tax law (LL M); taxation (JD); U.S. legal studies for foreign attorneys (LL M); JD/MBA; JD/MPA; JD/MSW. *Accreditation:* ABA. Part-time and evening/weekend programs available. Postbaccalaureate distance learning degree programs offered (no on-campus study). *Degree requirements:* For master's, thesis optional; for doctorate, minimum of 3 credits of clinical experience. *Entrance requirements:* For master's, JD or LL B; for doctorate, LSAT. Additional exam requirements/recommendations for international students: Required—TOEFL (for U.S. legal studies for foreign attorneys LL M program). Electronic applications accepted. *Faculty research:* Wrongful convictions, civil rights, environmental law, litigation techniques, data mining, intellectual property, practical and skills-based legal education.

Touro College, Jacob D. Fuchsberg Law Center, Central Islip, NY 11743. Offers general law (LL M); law (JD); U.S. legal studies (LL M); JD/MBA; JD/MPA; JD/MSW. JD/MBA offered with Long Island University, C.W. Post Campus or Dowling College; JD/MPA offered with Long Island University, C.W. Post Campus; JD/MSW offered with Stony Brook University, State University of New York. *Accreditation:* ABA. Part-time and evening/weekend programs available. *Entrance requirements:* For doctorate, LSAT. *Application deadline:* Applications are processed on a rolling basis. Application fee: $60. *Expenses:* Contact institution. *Financial support:* Fellowships, career-related internships or fieldwork, and Federal Work-Study available. Support available to part-time students. Financial award application deadline: 5/1. *Faculty research:* Business law, civil rights, international law, criminal justice. *Unit head:* Patricia E. Salkin, Dean, 631-761-7100. *Application contact:* Office of Admissions, 631-761-7010, E-mail: admissions@tourolaw.edu.
Website: http://www.tourolaw.edu/.

Trine University, Program in Criminal Justice, Angola, IN 46703-1764. Offers emergency management (MS); forensic psychology (MS); law (MS); public administration (MS). *Unit head:* Barbara E. Molargik-Fitch, JD, Director, Master of Science with a Major in Criminal Justice, 260-203-2693, Fax: 260-203-2965, E-mail: molargik-fitchb@trine.edu. *Application contact:* Dr. Earl D. Brooks, II, President.
Website: http://www.trine.edu/academics/majors-and-minors/graduate/criminal-justice/index.aspx.

Trinity International University, Trinity Law School, Santa Ana, CA 92705. Offers JD. Part-time and evening/weekend programs available. *Entrance requirements:* For doctorate, LSAT. Additional exam requirements/recommendations for international students: Required—TOEFL (minimum score 580 paper-based). *Expenses:* Contact institution.

Tufts University, The Fletcher School of Law and Diplomacy, Medford, MA 02155. Offers LL M, MA, MALD, MIB, PhD, DVM/MA, JD/MALD, MALD/MA, MALD/MBA, MALD/MS, MD/MA. Postbaccalaureate distance learning degree programs offered (minimal on-campus study). *Faculty:* 43 full-time, 42 part-time/adjunct. *Students:* 615 full-time (310 women), 12 part-time (5 women); includes 116 minority (17 Black or African American, non-Hispanic/Latino; 50 Asian, non-Hispanic/Latino; 27 Hispanic/Latino; 22 Two or more races, non-Hispanic/Latino), 211 international. Average age 31.

Law

In 2013, 313 master's, 12 doctorates awarded. *Degree requirements:* For master's, one foreign language, thesis; for doctorate, one foreign language, comprehensive exam, thesis/dissertation, dissertation defense. *Entrance requirements:* For master's and doctorate, GMAT or GRE General Test. Additional exam requirements/recommendations for international students: Required—TOEFL (minimum score 600 paper-based; 100 iBT), IELTS (minimum score 7). *Application deadline:* For fall admission, 1/10 for domestic and international students; for spring admission, 10/15 for domestic and international students. Application fee: $80. Electronic applications accepted. *Expenses:* Contact institution. *Financial support:* Career-related internships or fieldwork, Federal Work-Study, institutionally sponsored loans, scholarships/grants, and tuition waivers (partial) available. Financial award application deadline: 1/10; financial award applicants required to submit FAFSA. *Faculty research:* Negotiation and conflict resolution, international organizations, international business and economic law, security studies, development economics. *Unit head:* Dr. James Stavridis, Dean, 617-627-3050, Fax: 617-627-3712. *Application contact:* Laurie A. Hurley, Director of Admissions and Financial Aid, 617-627-3040, E-mail: fletcheradmissions@tufts.edu. Website: http://www.fletcher.tufts.edu.

Tulane University, School of Law, New Orleans, LA 70118. Offers admiralty (LL M); American business law (LL M); energy and environment (LL M); international and comparative law (LL M); law (LL M, JD, SJD); JD/M Acct; JD/MA; JD/MBA; JD/MHA; JD/MPH; JD/MS; JD/MSW. *Accreditation:* ABA. *Degree requirements:* For doctorate, thesis/dissertation (for some programs). *Entrance requirements:* For doctorate, LSAT (for JD). Additional exam requirements/recommendations for international students: Required—TOEFL (minimum score 575 paper-based). Electronic applications accepted. *Expenses:* Contact institution. *Faculty research:* Civil law.

Universidad Autonoma de Guadalajara, Graduate Programs, Guadalajara, Mexico. Offers administrative law and justice (LL M); advertising and corporate communications (MA); architecture (M Arch); business (MBA); computational science (MCC); education (Ed M, Ed D); English-Spanish translation (MA); entrepreneurship and management (MBA); integrated management of digital animation (MA); international business (MIB); international corporate law (LL M); internet technologies (MS); manufacturing systems (MMS); occupational health (MS); philosophy (MA, PhD); power electronics (MS); quality systems (MQS); renewable energy (MS); social evaluation of projects (MBA); strategic market research (MBA); tax law (MA); teaching mathematics (MA).

Universidad Central del Este, Law School, San Pedro de Macoris, Dominican Republic. Offers JD.

Universidad Iberoamericana, Graduate School, Santo Domingo D.N., Dominican Republic. Offers business administration (MBA, PMBA); constitutional law (LL M); dentistry (DMD); educational management (MA); integrated marketing communication (MA); psychopedagogical intervention (M Ed); real estate law (LL M); strategic management of human talent (MM).

Université de Montréal, Faculty of Law, Montréal, QC H3C 3J7, Canada. Offers business law (DESS); common law (North America) (JD); international law (DESS); law (LL M, LL D, DDN, DESS, LL B); tax law (LL M). Part-time programs available. *Degree requirements:* For master's, thesis; for doctorate, thesis/dissertation, project; for other advanced degree, thesis (for some programs). Electronic applications accepted. *Faculty research:* Legal theory; constitutional, private, and public law.

Université de Sherbrooke, Faculty of Law, Sherbrooke, QC J1K 2R1, Canada. Offers alternative dispute resolution (LL M, Diploma); business law (Diploma); common law (JD); criminal and penal law (Diploma); health law (LL M, Diploma); international law (LL M); law (LL D); legal management (Diploma); notarial law (Diploma); transnational law (Diploma). Part-time and evening/weekend programs available. *Degree requirements:* For master's, thesis; for Diploma, one foreign language. *Entrance requirements:* For master's and Diploma, LL B. Electronic applications accepted.

Université du Québec à Montréal, Graduate Programs, Program in Social and Labor Law, Montréal, QC H3C 3P8, Canada. Offers Certificate.

Université Laval, Faculty of Law, Programs in Law, Québec, QC G1K 7P4, Canada. Offers environment, sustainable development and food safety (LL M); international and transnational law (LL M, Diploma); law (LL M, LL D); law of business (LL M, Diploma). Part-time programs available. Terminal master's awarded for partial completion of doctoral program. *Degree requirements:* For master's, thesis (for some programs); for doctorate, thesis/dissertation. *Entrance requirements:* For master's, doctorate, and Diploma, knowledge of French and English. Electronic applications accepted.

University at Buffalo, the State University of New York, Graduate School, Law School, Buffalo, NY 14260. Offers criminal law (LL M); general law (LL M); law (JD); JD/MA; JD/MBA; JD/MLS; JD/MPH; JD/MSW; JD/MUP; JD/PhD; JD/Pharm D. *Accreditation:* ABA. *Faculty:* 61 full-time (26 women), 109 part-time/adjunct (36 women). *Students:* 616 full-time (290 women), 3 part-time (2 women); includes 102 minority (25 Black or African American, non-Hispanic/Latino; 34 Asian, non-Hispanic/Latino; 25 Hispanic/Latino; 18 Two or more races, non-Hispanic/Latino), 25 international. Average age 26. 1,148 applicants, 53% accepted, 198 enrolled. In 2013, 235 doctorates awarded. *Entrance requirements:* For master's, JD; for doctorate, LSAT. Additional exam requirements/recommendations for international students: Required—TOEFL (minimum score 88 iBT) or IELTS. *Application deadline:* For fall admission, 3/1 priority date for domestic and international students. Applications are processed on a rolling basis. Application fee: $75. Electronic applications accepted. *Expenses:* Contact institution. *Financial support:* In 2013–14, 314 students received support. Career-related internships or fieldwork, Federal Work-Study, institutionally sponsored loans, scholarships/grants, tuition waivers (full and partial), and unspecified assistantships available. Financial award application deadline: 3/1; financial award applicants required to submit FAFSA. *Faculty research:* Criminal law, environmental law, international law, human rights. Total annual research expenditures: $287,070. *Unit head:* Dr. Makau Mutua, Dean, 716-645-2311, Fax: 716-645-2064, E-mail: mutua@buffalo.edu. *Application contact:* Lillie V. Wiley-Upshaw, Vice Dean for Admissions and Student Life, 716-645-2907, Fax: 716-645-6676, E-mail: law-admissions@buffalo.edu. Website: http://www.law.buffalo.edu/.

The University of Akron, School of Law, Akron, OH 44325. Offers intellectual property law (LL M); law (JD); JD/LL M; JD/M Tax; JD/MAP; JD/MBA; JD/MPA. *Accreditation:* ABA. Part-time and evening/weekend programs available. *Faculty:* 38 full-time (16 women), 16 part-time/adjunct (2 women). *Students:* 293 full-time (127 women), 192 part-time (81 women); includes 59 minority (19 Black or African American, non-Hispanic/Latino; 2 American Indian or Alaska Native, non-Hispanic/Latino; 19 Asian, non-Hispanic/Latino; 9 Hispanic/Latino; 10 Two or more races, non-Hispanic/Latino), 3 international. Average age 28. 1,446 applicants, 50% accepted, 165 enrolled. In 2013, 175 doctorates awarded. *Entrance requirements:* For doctorate, LSAT, LSDAS. Additional exam requirements/recommendations for international students: Required—TOEFL (minimum score 650 paper-based; 115 iBT). *Application deadline:* For fall admission, 3/1 priority date for domestic and international students. Applications are processed on a rolling basis. Application fee: $0. Electronic applications accepted. *Expenses:* Contact institution. *Financial support:* In 2013–14, 264 students received support. Career-related internships or fieldwork, scholarships/grants, and tuition waivers (full and partial) available. Support available to part-time students. Financial award

applicants required to submit FAFSA. *Faculty research:* Intellectual property; law and science; trust and elder law, including taxation and retirement benefits; professional responsibility and judicial ethics; Constitutional law, theory, and process. *Unit head:* Martin H. Belsky, Dean, 330-972-6359, Fax: 330-258-2343, E-mail: belsky@uakron.edu. *Application contact:* Lauri S. File, Assistant Dean of Admission and Financial Aid, 330-972-7331, Fax: 330-258-2343, E-mail: lfile@uakron.edu. Website: http://www.uakron.edu/law/index.dot.

The University of Alabama, School of Law, Tuscaloosa, AL 35487. Offers business transactions (LL M); comparative law (LL M, JSD); law (JD, JSD); taxation (LL M in Tax); JD/MBA. *Accreditation:* ABA. *Faculty:* 56 full-time (24 women), 51 part-time/adjunct (13 women). *Students:* 466 full-time (192 women), 148 part-time (57 women); includes 93 minority (60 Black or African American, non-Hispanic/Latino; 2 American Indian or Alaska Native, non-Hispanic/Latino; 9 Asian, non-Hispanic/Latino; 13 Hispanic/Latino; 9 Two or more races, non-Hispanic/Latino), 1 international. 2,038 applicants, 29% accepted, 217 enrolled. In 2013, 167 doctorates awarded. *Degree requirements:* For master's, 24 hours, exams; for doctorate, 90 hours, including 3 hours of professional skills, 1 seminar, and 36 required hours. *Entrance requirements:* For master's, LSAT, undergraduate degree in law, letters of recommendation; for doctorate, LSAT, undergraduate degree, letter of recommendation, resume. Additional exam requirements/recommendations for international students: Required—TOEFL, IELTS. *Application deadline:* Applications are processed on a rolling basis. Application fee: $40. Electronic applications accepted. *Expenses:* Contact institution. *Financial support:* Applicants required to submit FAFSA. *Faculty research:* Public interest law, Constitutional law, civil rights, international law, tax law. *Unit head:* Claude R. Arrington, Associate Dean for Academic Affairs, 205-348-6557, Fax: 205-348-3077, E-mail: carrington@law.ua.edu. *Application contact:* Martha Griffith, Assistant Director for Admissions, 205-348-7945, Fax: 205-348-3917, E-mail: mgriffith@law.ua.edu. Website: http://www.law.ua.edu/.

University of Alberta, Faculty of Law, Edmonton, AB T6G 2E1, Canada. Offers LL M, PhD. Part-time programs available. *Degree requirements:* For master's, thesis. *Entrance requirements:* For master's, minimum GPA of 3.0, curriculum vitae, 3 letters of recommendation; for doctorate, LSAT. Additional exam requirements/recommendations for international students: Required—TOEFL (minimum score 600 paper-based). Electronic applications accepted. *Faculty research:* Health law, environmental law, native law issues, constitutional law, human rights.

The University of Arizona, James E. Rogers College of Law, Tucson, AZ 85721-0176. Offers indigenous peoples law and policy (LL M); international trade and business law (LL M); law (JD); JD/MA; JD/MBA; JD/MPA; JD/PhD. *Accreditation:* ABA. *Degree requirements:* For doctorate, publishable paper. *Entrance requirements:* For doctorate, LSAT, LSDAS, resume, 2 letters of recommendation. Additional exam requirements/recommendations for international students: Required—TOEFL. Electronic applications accepted. *Expenses:* Contact institution. *Faculty research:* Tax law, employment law, corporate law, torts, trial practice and skills, constitutional law, Indian law, family law, estates and trusts.

University of Arkansas, School of Law, Fayetteville, AR 72701. Offers agricultural law (LL M); law (JD). *Accreditation:* ABA. *Entrance requirements:* For doctorate, LSAT. *Expenses:* Contact institution.

University of Arkansas at Little Rock, William H. Bowen School of Law, Little Rock, AR 72202-5142. Offers JD, JD/MPS. *Accreditation:* ABA. Part-time and evening/weekend programs available. *Entrance requirements:* For doctorate, LSAT. Electronic applications accepted. *Expenses:* Contact institution. *Faculty research:* Employment discrimination, uniform commercial code, Arkansas legal history, scientific evidence, mediation.

University of Baltimore, School of Law, Baltimore, MD 21201. Offers law (JD); law of the United States (LL M); taxation (LL M); JD/LL M; JD/MBA; JD/MPA; JD/MS; JD/PhD. JD/MS offered jointly with Division of Criminology, Criminal Justice, and Social Policy; JD/PhD with University of Maryland, Baltimore. *Accreditation:* ABA. Part-time and evening/weekend programs available. *Faculty:* 54 full-time (18 women), 45 part-time/adjunct (12 women). *Students:* 654 full-time (325 women), 325 part-time (150 women); includes 254 minority (121 Black or African American, non-Hispanic/Latino; 1 American Indian or Alaska Native, non-Hispanic/Latino; 51 Asian, non-Hispanic/Latino; 53 Hispanic/Latino; 1 Native Hawaiian or other Pacific Islander, non-Hispanic/Latino; 27 Two or more races, non-Hispanic/Latino), 4 international. Average age 27. 1,352 applicants, 63% accepted, 287 enrolled. In 2013, 310 doctorates awarded. *Entrance requirements:* For doctorate, LSAT. *Application deadline:* For fall admission, 4/1 priority date for domestic and international students. Applications are processed on a rolling basis. Application fee: $60. Electronic applications accepted. *Expenses:* Contact institution. *Financial support:* In 2013–14, 257 students received support. Research assistantships, teaching assistantships, career-related internships or fieldwork, Federal Work-Study, institutionally sponsored loans, and scholarships/grants available. Support available to part-time students. Financial award application deadline: 4/1; financial award applicants required to submit FAFSA. *Faculty research:* Plain view doctrine, statute of limitations, bankruptcy, family law, international and comparative law, Constitutional law. *Unit head:* Ronald Weich, Dean, 410-837-4458. *Application contact:* Jeffrey L. Zavrotny, Assistant Dean for Admissions, 410-837-5809, Fax: 410-837-4188, E-mail: jzavrotny@ubalt.edu. Website: http://law.ubalt.edu/.

The University of British Columbia, Faculty of Law, Vancouver, BC V6T 1Z1, Canada. Offers LL M, LL M CL, PhD. Part-time programs available. *Degree requirements:* For master's, variable foreign language requirement, thesis, seminar; for doctorate, variable foreign language requirement, comprehensive exam, thesis/dissertation, seminar. *Entrance requirements:* For master's, LL B or JD, thesis proposal, 3 letters of reference; for doctorate, LL B or JD, LL M, thesis proposal, 3 letters of reference. Additional exam requirements/recommendations for international students: Required—TOEFL (minimum score 600 paper-based; 100 iBT), IELTS (minimum score 7). Electronic applications accepted. *Expenses:* Tuition, area resident: Full-time $8000 Canadian dollars. *Faculty research:* Aboriginal rights/native law, Asian legal studies, criminal law, environmental law, international law, corporate, human rights, intellectual property, dispute resolution, entertainment.

University of Calgary, Faculty of Law, Calgary, AB T2N 1N4, Canada. Offers LL M, JD, Postbaccalaureate Certificate. *Entrance requirements:* For doctorate, LSAT. Additional exam requirements/recommendations for international students: Required—TOEFL (minimum score 600 paper-based; 100 iBT). *Expenses:* Contact institution.

University of California, Berkeley, Graduate Division, Haas School of Business and School of Law, Concurrent JD/MBA Program, Berkeley, CA 94720-1500. Offers JD/MBA. *Accreditation:* AACSB; ABA. *Students:* 1 (woman) full-time; minority (Two or more races, non-Hispanic/Latino). Average age 29. *Entrance requirements:* Additional exam requirements/recommendations for international students: Required—TOEFL (minimum score 570 paper-based; 68 iBT). *Application deadline:* For fall admission, 10/16 for domestic and international students; for winter admission, 1/8 for domestic and international students; for spring admission, 3/12 for domestic and international students. Application fee: $200. Electronic applications accepted. *Financial support:*

Application deadline: 3/1; applicants required to submit FAFSA. *Faculty research:* Accounting, business and public policy, economic analysis and public policy, entrepreneurship, finance, management of organizations, marketing, operations and information technology management, real estate. *Unit head:* Julia Hwang, Director, MBA Program, 510-642-1405, Fax: 510-643-6659, E-mail: julia_hwang@haas.berkeley.edu. *Application contact:* Office of Admissions, 510-642-1405, Fax: 510-643-6659, E-mail: admissions@boalt.berkeley.edu.
Website: http://mba.haas.berkeley.edu/academics/concurrentdegrees.html.

University of California, Berkeley, School of Law, Berkeley, CA 94720-7200. Offers jurisprudence and social policy (PhD); law (LL M, JD, JSD); JD/MA; JD/MBA; JD/MCP; JD/MJ; JD/MPP; JD/MSW. *Accreditation:* ABA. Terminal master's awarded for partial completion of doctoral program. *Degree requirements:* For master's, thesis; for doctorate, variable foreign language requirement, thesis/dissertation (for some programs). *Entrance requirements:* For master's and doctorate, letters of recommendation. Additional exam requirements/recommendations for international students: Required—TOEFL. *Expenses:* Contact institution. *Faculty research:* Law and technology; social justice; environmental law; business, law and economics; international/comparative law.

University of California, Davis, School of Law, Davis, CA 95616-5201. Offers LL M, JD, JD/MA, JD/MBA. *Accreditation:* ABA. *Faculty:* 57 full-time (28 women), 16 part-time/ adjunct (5 women). *Students:* 499 full-time (252 women); includes 188 minority (7 Black or African American, non-Hispanic/Latino; 117 Asian, non-Hispanic/Latino; 42 Hispanic/ Latino; 22 Two or more races, non-Hispanic/Latino), 20 international. Average age 24. 2,420 applicants, 52% accepted, 142 enrolled. In 2013, 33 master's, 196 doctorates awarded. *Entrance requirements:* For doctorate, LSAT. Additional exam requirements/ recommendations for international students: Required—TOEFL. *Application deadline:* For fall admission, 2/1 priority date for domestic students, 2/1 for international students. Applications are processed on a rolling basis. Electronic applications accepted. *Expenses:* Contact institution. *Financial support:* In 2013–14, 368 students received support, including 6 research assistantships with partial tuition reimbursements available, 35 teaching assistantships with partial tuition reimbursements available; Federal Work-Study, institutionally sponsored loans, scholarships/grants, and health care benefits also available. Financial award application deadline: 3/2; financial award applicants required to submit FAFSA. *Faculty research:* International law, intellectual property, immigration, environmental law, public interest law. *Unit head:* Kevin R. Johnson, Dean, 530-752-0243, Fax: 530-752-7279, E-mail: krjohnson@ucdavis.edu. *Application contact:* Kristen Mercado, JD, Director, Admissions, 530-752-6477, Fax: 530-754-8371, E-mail: admissions@law.ucdavis.edu.
Website: http://www.law.ucdavis.edu/.

University of California, Hastings College of the Law, Graduate Programs, San Francisco, CA 94102-4978. Offers LL M, MSL, JD. *Accreditation:* ABA. *Entrance requirements:* For doctorate, LSAT. Electronic applications accepted.

University of California, Irvine, School of Law, Irvine, CA 92697. Offers JD. *Degree requirements:* For doctorate, project. *Application deadline:* For fall admission, 3/15 for domestic students. Application fee: $0. *Unit head:* Erwin Chemerinsky, Dean, 949-824-7722, E-mail: echemerinsky@law.uci.edu.
Website: http://www.law.uci.edu/.

University of California, Los Angeles, School of Law, Los Angeles, CA 90095. Offers LL M, JD, SJD, JD/MA, JD/MBA, JD/MPH, JD/MPP, JD/MSW, JD/MURP, JD/PhD. *Accreditation:* ABA. *Entrance requirements:* For doctorate, LSAT (for JD). Additional exam requirements/recommendations for international students: Required—TOEFL for LL M. Electronic applications accepted. *Expenses:* Contact institution. *Faculty research:* Business law and policy; critical race studies, entertainment; media, and intellectual property law; law and philosophy; public interest law and policy.

University of California, San Diego, Office of Graduate Studies, Program in Health Policy and Law, La Jolla, CA 92093. Offers MAS. Program offered jointly with School of Medicine and California Western School of Law. Part-time programs available. *Students:* 36 part-time (26 women); includes 14 minority (2 Black or African American, non-Hispanic/Latino; 6 Asian, non-Hispanic/Latino; 6 Hispanic/Latino). 26 applicants, 77% accepted, 15 enrolled. In 2013, 12 master's awarded. *Entrance requirements:* For master's, appropriate medical, healthcare, legal or related degree; minimum GPA of 3.0 in final two years of study; minimum 3 years of relevant work experience or equivalent. Additional exam requirements/recommendations for international students: Required—TOEFL, IELTS. *Application deadline:* For fall admission, 4/7 for domestic students. Applications are processed on a rolling basis. Application fee: $80 ($100 for international students). Electronic applications accepted. *Expenses:* Tuition, state resident: full-time $11,220; part-time $1870 per quarter. Tuition, nonresident: full-time $26,322; part-time $4387 per quarter. *Required fees:* $519.50 per quarter. Part-time tuition and fees vary according to course load and program. *Financial support:* Scholarships/grants available. *Unit head:* Gerard Manecke, Program Co-Director, 619-543-3164, E-mail: gmanecke@ucsd.edu. *Application contact:* Jenna Lucius, Program Coordinator, 858-534-9162, E-mail: healthlaw@ucsd.edu.
Website: http://hlaw.ucsd.edu/.

University of Chicago, The Law School, Chicago, IL 60637. Offers LL M, MCL, DCL, JD, JSD, JD/AM, JD/MBA, JD/MPP. *Accreditation:* ABA. *Faculty:* 65 full-time (20 women), 38 part-time/adjunct (14 women). *Students:* 612 full-time (263 women); includes 158 minority (37 Black or African American, non-Hispanic/Latino; 56 Asian, non-Hispanic/Latino; 51 Hispanic/Latino; 14 Two or more races, non-Hispanic/Latino), 27 international. Average age 24. 4,271 applicants, 20% accepted, 196 enrolled. In 2013, 69 master's, 215 doctorates awarded. *Entrance requirements:* For doctorate, LSAT (for JD). Additional exam requirements/recommendations for international students: Required—TOEFL (minimum score 104 iBT). *Application deadline:* For fall admission, 2/1 priority date for domestic students. Applications are processed on a rolling basis. Application fee: $75. Electronic applications accepted. *Expenses:* Contact institution. *Financial support:* In 2013–14, 392 students received support. Fellowships, research assistantships, career-related internships or fieldwork, institutionally sponsored loans, and scholarships/grants available. Financial award application deadline: 3/1; financial award applicants required to submit FAFSA. *Unit head:* Michael Schill, Dean, 773-702-9494, Fax: 773-834-4409. *Application contact:* Ann K. Perry, Associate Dean of Admissions and Financial Aid, 773-834-4425, Fax: 773-834-0942, E-mail: admissions@law.uchicago.edu.
Website: http://www.law.uchicago.edu/.

University of Cincinnati, College of Law, Cincinnati, OH 45221-0040. Offers JD, JD/ MA, JD/MBA, JD/MCP, JD/MSW. *Accreditation:* ABA. *Faculty:* 32 full-time (18 women), 34 part-time/adjunct (7 women). *Students:* 352 full-time (150 women), 2 part-time (1 woman); includes 48 minority (22 Black or African American, non-Hispanic/Latino; 1 American Indian or Alaska Native, non-Hispanic/Latino; 11 Asian, non-Hispanic/Latino; 10 Hispanic/Latino; 4 Two or more races, non-Hispanic/Latino), 5 international. Average age 25. 1,007 applicants, 61% accepted, 100 enrolled. In 2013, 149 doctorates awarded. *Entrance requirements:* For doctorate, LSAT. Additional exam requirements/ recommendations for international students: Required—TOEFL (minimum score 520 paper-based; 68 iBT). *Application deadline:* For fall admission, 3/15 priority date for

domestic and international students. Applications are processed on a rolling basis. Application fee: $35. Electronic applications accepted. *Expenses:* Contact institution. *Financial support:* Fellowships, research assistantships, career-related internships or fieldwork, Federal Work-Study, scholarships/grants, tuition waivers (full and partial), and unspecified assistantships available. Financial award application deadline: 3/15; financial award applicants required to submit FAFSA. *Faculty research:* International human rights, corporate law, intellectual property law, criminal law, law and psychiatry. *Unit head:* Louis D. Bilionis, Dean, 513-556-0121, Fax: 513-556-2391, E-mail: louis.bilionis@uc.edu. *Application contact:* Al Watson, Senior Assistant Dean and Director of Admissions, 513-556-0077, Fax: 513-556-2391, E-mail: alfred.watson@uc.edu.
Website: http://www.law.uc.edu/.

University of Colorado Boulder, School of Law, Boulder, CO 80309-0401. Offers JD, JD/MBA, JD/MPA, JD/MS, JD/PhD. *Accreditation:* ABA. *Faculty:* 38 full-time (15 women). *Students:* 503 full-time (227 women), 12 part-time (4 women); includes 106 minority (15 Black or African American, non-Hispanic/Latino; 8 American Indian or Alaska Native, non-Hispanic/Latino; 22 Asian, non-Hispanic/Latino; 53 Hispanic/Latino; 2 Native Hawaiian or other Pacific Islander, non-Hispanic/Latino; 6 Two or more races, non-Hispanic/Latino), 3 international. Average age 27. 906 applicants, 99% accepted, 187 enrolled. In 2013, 175 doctorates awarded. *Entrance requirements:* For doctorate, LSAT, minimum undergraduate GPA of 2.75. *Application deadline:* For fall admission, 2/ 15 for domestic students. Applications are processed on a rolling basis. Application fee: $50 ($60 for international students). Electronic applications accepted. *Expenses:* Contact institution. *Financial support:* In 2013–14, 914 students received support, including 658 fellowships (averaging $8,484 per year), 12 teaching assistantships with full and partial tuition reimbursements available (averaging $2,033 per year); institutionally sponsored loans, scholarships/grants, health care benefits, and unspecified assistantships also available. Financial award applicants required to submit FAFSA. *Faculty research:* Law and society, law, Constitutional law, business/corporate law, international and comparative law. *Total annual research expenditures:* $1.5 million.
Website: http://www.colorado.edu/law/.

University of Connecticut, School of Law, Hartford, CT 06105. Offers JD, JD/LL M, JD/MBA, JD/MLS, JD/MPA, JD/MPH, JD/MSW. *Accreditation:* ABA. Part-time programs available. *Degree requirements:* For doctorate, extensive research paper. *Entrance requirements:* For doctorate, LSAT, undergraduate degree. Additional exam requirements/recommendations for international students: Required—TOEFL. Electronic applications accepted. *Expenses:* Contact institution. *Faculty research:* International law, intellectual property, human rights, taxation, energy and environmental law.

University of Dayton, School of Law, Dayton, OH 45469-2772. Offers LL M, MSL, JD, JD/M Ed, JD/MBA, JD/MS Ed. *Accreditation:* ABA. *Faculty:* 34 full-time (17 women), 29 part-time/adjunct (9 women). *Students:* 333 full-time (147 women); includes 55 minority (25 Black or African American, non-Hispanic/Latino; 9 Asian, non-Hispanic/Latino; 11 Hispanic/Latino; 10 Two or more races, non-Hispanic/Latino), 9 international. Average age 27. 1,044 applicants, 70% accepted, 115 enrolled. In 2013, 1 master's, 147 doctorates awarded. *Entrance requirements:* For master's, GRE, GMAT, MSL; for doctorate, LSAT, accredited bachelor's degree or foreign equivalent. Additional exam requirements/recommendations for international students: Recommended—TOEFL (minimum score 550 paper-based; 80 iBT). *Application deadline:* For fall admission, 5/1 priority date for domestic and international students; for spring admission, 3/1 for domestic and international students; for summer admission, 2/1 for domestic students, 3/1 priority date for international students. Applications are processed on a rolling basis. Application fee: $0 ($50 for international students). Electronic applications accepted. *Expenses:* Contact institution. *Financial support:* In 2013–14, 187 students received support. Career-related internships or fieldwork, institutionally sponsored loans, scholarships/grants, and tuition waivers (partial) available. Financial award application deadline: 3/1; financial award applicants required to submit FAFSA. *Faculty research:* Cybercrime, social media law, disability law, environmental law, intellectual property. *Unit head:* Paul McGreal, Dean, 937-229-3795, Fax: 937-229-2469. *Application contact:* Claire Schrader, Assistant Dean and Executive Director of Enrollment Management and Marketing, 937-229-3555, Fax: 937-229-4194, E-mail: lawinfo@udayton.edu.
Website: http://www.udayton.edu/law.

University of Denver, Morgridge College of Education, Denver, CO 80208. Offers child, family and school psychology (MA, PhD, Ed S); counseling psychology (MA, PhD); curriculum and instruction (MA, Ed D, PhD); curriculum instruction and teaching (Certificate); early childhood special education (MA); educational leadership and policy studies (MA, Ed D, PhD, Certificate); higher education (MA, Ed D, PhD); law librarianship (Certificate); library and information science (MLIS); research methods and statistics (MA, PhD). *Accreditation:* ALA; APA (one or more programs are accredited). Part-time and evening/weekend programs available. Postbaccalaureate distance learning degree programs offered (no on-campus study). *Faculty:* 35 full-time (21 women), 63 part-time/adjunct (43 women). *Students:* 435 full-time (332 women), 414 part-time (297 women); includes 194 minority (45 Black or African American, non-Hispanic/Latino; 9 American Indian or Alaska Native, non-Hispanic/Latino; 16 Asian, non-Hispanic/Latino; 96 Hispanic/Latino; 2 Native Hawaiian or other Pacific Islander, non-Hispanic/Latino; 26 Two or more races, non-Hispanic/Latino), 14 international. Average age 32. 672 applicants, 61% accepted, 193 enrolled. In 2013, 248 master's, 30 doctorates, 130 other advanced degrees awarded. Terminal master's awarded for partial completion of doctoral program. *Degree requirements:* For master's, comprehensive exam; for doctorate, 2 foreign languages, comprehensive exam, thesis/ dissertation. *Entrance requirements:* For master's and doctorate, GRE General Test or GMAT. Additional exam requirements/recommendations for international students: Required—TOEFL (minimum score 550 paper-based; 80 iBT). *Application deadline:* Applications are processed on a rolling basis. Application fee: $65. Electronic applications accepted. *Financial support:* In 2013–14, 706 students received support, including 54 research assistantships with full and partial tuition reimbursements available (averaging $15,599 per year), 77 teaching assistantships with full and partial tuition reimbursements available (averaging $12,804 per year); career-related internships or fieldwork, Federal Work-Study, institutionally sponsored loans, scholarships/grants, and unspecified assistantships also available. Support available to part-time students. Financial award application deadline: 2/15; financial award applicants required to submit FAFSA. *Faculty research:* Principal and teacher preparation, development and assessments, gifted education, service-learning, early childhood, mathematics education, access to higher education. *Total annual research expenditures:* $6.3 million. *Unit head:* Dr. Karen Riley, Interim Dean, 303-871-3665, E-mail: karen.riley@du.edu. *Application contact:* Jodi Dye, Assistant Director of Admissions, 303-871-2510, E-mail: jodi.dye@du.edu.
Website: http://morgridge.du.edu/.

University of Denver, Sturm College of Law, JD Program, Denver, CO 80208. Offers JD. *Accreditation:* ABA. Part-time and evening/weekend programs available. *Students:* 864 full-time (441 women), 21 part-time (10 women); includes 137 minority (18 Black or African American, non-Hispanic/Latino; 5 American Indian or Alaska Native, non-Hispanic/Latino; 17 Asian, non-Hispanic/Latino; 67 Hispanic/Latino; 30 Two or more

races, non-Hispanic/Latino), 6 international. Average age 27. 1,812 applicants, 55% accepted, 305 enrolled. In 2013, 263 doctorates awarded. *Entrance requirements:* For doctorate, LSAT. Additional exam requirements/recommendations for international students: Required—TOEFL (minimum score 587 paper-based; 95 iBT). *Application deadline:* For fall admission, 3/1 priority date for domestic students. Applications are processed on a rolling basis. Application fee: $65. Electronic applications accepted. *Financial support:* In 2013–14, 417 students received support. Career-related internships or fieldwork, Federal Work-Study, institutionally sponsored loans, scholarships/grants, unspecified assistantships, and tutorships available. Support available to part-time students. Financial award application deadline: 2/15; financial award applicants required to submit FAFSA. *Faculty research:* Lawyering skills, international and legal studies, natural resources law (domestic and international), transportation law, public interest law, business and commercial law. *Unit head:* Martin Katz, Dean, 303-871-6103, Fax: 303-871-6992, E-mail: martin.katz@du.edu. *Application contact:* Yvonne Cherena-Pacheco, Associate Director of Admissions, 303-871-6135, Fax: 303-871-6992, E-mail: admissions@law.du.edu.
Website: http://www.law.du.edu/.

University of Denver, Sturm College of Law, Programs in Environmental and Natural Resources Law and Policy, Denver, CO 80208. Offers environmental and natural resources law and policy (LL M); natural resources law and policy (Certificate); resources law studies (MRLS). *Students:* 17 full-time (9 women), 21 part-time (9 women); includes 6 minority (2 Black or African American, non-Hispanic/Latino; 1 American Indian or Alaska Native, non-Hispanic/Latino; 1 Asian, non-Hispanic/Latino; 2 Hispanic/Latino), 8 international. Average age 35. 30 applicants, 60% accepted, 13 enrolled. In 2013, 37 master's awarded. *Degree requirements:* For master's, internship. *Entrance requirements:* For master's, bachelor's degree (for MRLS), JD (for LL M), transcripts, two letters of recommendation. Additional exam requirements/recommendations for international students: Required—TOEFL (minimum score 550 paper-based; 80 iBT). *Application deadline:* For fall admission, 8/1 priority date for domestic students, 6/5 priority date for international students; for spring admission, 12/15 priority date for domestic students, 11/5 priority date for international students. Applications are processed on a rolling basis. Application fee: $50. Electronic applications accepted. *Financial support:* In 2013–14, 3 students received support. Federal Work-Study, institutionally sponsored loans, scholarships/grants, and unspecified assistantships available. Support available to part-time students. Financial award application deadline: 2/15; financial award applicants required to submit FAFSA. *Unit head:* Don Smith, Director, 303-871-6052, E-mail: dcsmith@law.du.edu. *Application contact:* Lucy Daberkow, Assistant Director of Graduate Programs, 303-871-6324, Fax: 303-871-6711, E-mail: ldaberkow@law.du.edu.
Website: http://www.law.du.edu/index.php/enrgp/degrees.

University of Detroit Mercy, School of Law, Detroit, MI 48226. Offers JD, JD/LL B, JD/MBA. *Accreditation:* ABA. Part-time programs available. *Entrance requirements:* For doctorate, LSAT. *Expenses:* Contact institution.

University of Florida, Graduate School, College of Journalism and Communications, Gainesville, FL 32611. Offers advertising (M Adv); global strategic commication (MAMC); international/intercultural communications (MAMC); journalism (MAMC); mass communication (MAMC, PhD); mass communication law (MAMC); public relations (MAMC); social media (MAMC); telecommunication (MAMC); Web design and online communication (MAMC); JD/MAMC; JD/PhD. *Accreditation:* ACEJMC (one or more programs are accredited). Part-time programs available. Postbaccalaureate distance learning degree programs offered. *Faculty:* 33 full-time (17 women), 3 part-time/adjunct (2 women). *Students:* 175 full-time (131 women), 164 part-time (113 women); includes 75 minority (29 Black or African American, non-Hispanic/Latino; 1 American Indian or Alaska Native, non-Hispanic/Latino; 9 Asian, non-Hispanic/Latino; 36 Hispanic/Latino), 87 international. Average age 30. 544 applicants, 36% accepted, 88 enrolled. In 2013, 52 master's, 17 doctorates awarded. *Degree requirements:* For master's, comprehensive exam (for some programs), thesis; for doctorate, comprehensive exam (for some programs), thesis/dissertation. *Entrance requirements:* For master's and doctorate, GRE General Test, minimum GPA of 3.0. Additional exam requirements/recommendations for international students: Required—TOEFL (minimum score 550 paper-based; 80 iBT), IELTS (minimum score 6). *Application deadline:* For fall admission, 1/15 for domestic and international students; for spring admission, 7/15 for domestic and international students. Applications are processed on a rolling basis. Application fee: $30. Electronic applications accepted. *Expenses:* Tuition, state resident: full-time $12,640. Tuition, nonresident: full-time $30,000. *Financial support:* In 2013–14, 70 students received support, including 7 fellowships with full and partial tuition reimbursements available (averaging $20,535 per year), 9 research assistantships with full tuition reimbursements available (averaging $9,174 per year), 76 teaching assistantships with full tuition reimbursements available (averaging $8,580 per year); career-related internships or fieldwork, Federal Work-Study, institutionally sponsored loans, and unspecified assistantships also available. Support available to part-time students. Financial award application deadline: 3/15; financial award applicants required to submit FAFSA. *Faculty research:* Health communication, international/cross-cultural communication, political communication, ethics, persuasion/message development. *Unit head:* Diane McFarlin, Dean, 352-392-0466, Fax: 352-392-1794, E-mail: dmcfarlin@ufl.edu. *Application contact:* Debbie M. Treise, PhD, Senior Associate Dean, Division of Graduate Studies and Research, 352-392-6557, E-mail: dtreise@jou.ufl.edu.
Website: http://www.jou.ufl.edu/.

University of Florida, Levin College of Law, Gainesville, FL 32611. Offers comparative law (LL M); environmental law (LL M); international taxation (LL M); law (JD); taxation (LL M, SJD). *Accreditation:* ABA. *Faculty:* 77 full-time (37 women), 36 part-time/adjunct (10 women). *Students:* 1,072 full-time (452 women); includes 283 minority (69 Black or African American, non-Hispanic/Latino; 13 American Indian or Alaska Native, non-Hispanic/Latino; 45 Asian, non-Hispanic/Latino; 115 Hispanic/Latino; 41 Two or more races, non-Hispanic/Latino), 37 international. Average age 24. 2,686 applicants, 33% accepted, 284 enrolled. In 2013, 356 doctorates awarded. *Entrance requirements:* For doctorate, LSAT (for JD). *Application deadline:* For fall admission, 3/15 for domestic and international students. Applications are processed on a rolling basis. Application fee: $30. Electronic applications accepted. *Expenses:* Tuition, state resident: full-time $12,640. Tuition, nonresident: full-time $30,000. *Financial support:* In 2013–14, 446 students received support, including 42 research assistantships (averaging $9,261 per year); Federal Work-Study, institutionally sponsored loans, scholarships/grants, health care benefits, and unspecified assistantships also available. Financial award application deadline: 3/15; financial award applicants required to submit FAFSA. *Faculty research:* Environmental and land use law, taxation, dispute resolution, family law, Constitutional law. *Unit head:* Robert Jerry, Dean, 352-273-0600, Fax: 352-392-8727, E-mail: jerryr@law.ufl.edu. *Application contact:* Michelle Adorno, Assistant Dean for Admissions, 352-273-0890, Fax: 352-392-4087, E-mail: madorno@law.ufl.edu.
Website: http://www.law.ufl.edu/.

University of Georgia, School of Law, Athens, GA 30602. Offers LL M, JD, JD/M Acc, JD/MBA. *Accreditation:* ABA. *Degree requirements:* For master's, thesis. *Entrance requirements:* For doctorate, LSAT. Additional exam requirements/recommendations for international students: Required—TOEFL (minimum score 600 paper-based). Electronic applications accepted. *Expenses:* Contact institution.

University of Hawaii at Manoa, William S. Richardson School of Law, Honolulu, HI 96822-2328. Offers LL M, JD, Graduate Certificate, JD/Certificate, JD/MA, JD/MBA, JD/MLI Sc, JD/MS, JD/MURP, JD/PhD. *Accreditation:* ABA. *Degree requirements:* For doctorate, 6 semesters of full-time residency. *Entrance requirements:* For doctorate, LSAT. Additional exam requirements/recommendations for international students: Required—TOEFL. *Expenses:* Contact institution. *Faculty research:* Law of the sea, Asian and Pacific comparative law, native Hawaiian rights, environmental law.

University of Houston, Law Center, Houston, TX 77204-6060. Offers energy, environment, and natural resources (LL M); health law (LL M); intellectual property and information law (LL M); international law (LL M); law (LL M, JD); tax law (LL M). *Accreditation:* ABA. Part-time and evening/weekend programs available. *Entrance requirements:* For doctorate, LSAT. Additional exam requirements/recommendations for international students: Required—TOEFL (minimum score 600 paper-based; 100 iBT). Electronic applications accepted. *Expenses:* Contact institution. *Faculty research:* Health law, international, tax, environmental/energy, information law/intellectual property.

University of Idaho, College of Law, Moscow, ID 83844-2321. Offers business law and entrepreneurship (JD); law (JD); litigation and alternative dispute resolution (JD); Native American law (JD); natural resources and environmental law (JD). *Accreditation:* ABA. *Faculty:* 31 full-time, 7 part-time/adjunct. *Students:* 314 full-time, 8 part-time. Average age 29. *Entrance requirements:* For doctorate, LSAT, Law School Admission Council Credential Assembly Service (CAS) Report. Additional exam requirements/recommendations for international students: Required—TOEFL. *Application deadline:* For fall admission, 2/15 for domestic students. Applications are processed on a rolling basis. Application fee: $50 ($60 for international students). Electronic applications accepted. *Expenses:* Tuition, state resident: full-time $5596; part-time $363 per credit hour. Tuition, nonresident: full-time $18,672; part-time $1089 per credit hour. *Financial support:* Career-related internships or fieldwork, Federal Work-Study, and institutionally sponsored loans available. Financial award applicants required to submit FAFSA. *Faculty research:* Transboundary river governance, tribal protection and stewardship, regional water issues, environmental law. *Unit head:* Michael Satz, Jr., Dean, 208-885-4977, E-mail: uilaw@uidaho.edu. *Application contact:* Carole Wells, Interim Director of Admissions, 208-885-2300, Fax: 208-885-2252, E-mail: lawadmit@uidaho.edu.
Website: http://www.uidaho.edu/law/.

University of Illinois at Urbana–Champaign, College of Law, Champaign, IL 61820. Offers LL M, MCL, JD, JSD, JD/DVM, JD/MBA, JD/MCS, JD/MHRIR, JD/MS, JD/MUP, MAS/JD, MD/JD. *Accreditation:* ABA. *Students:* 646. *Expenses:* Contact institution. *Unit head:* Bruce Smith, Dean, 217-244-8446, Fax: 217-244-1478, E-mail: smithb@illinois.edu. *Application contact:* Christine Renshaw, Assistant Director, 217-244-1476, Fax: 217-244-1478, E-mail: renshaw@illinois.edu.
Website: http://www.law.illinois.edu/.

The University of Iowa, College of Law, Iowa City, IA 52242. Offers LL M, JD, SJD, JD/MA, JD/MBA, JD/MD, JD/MHA, JD/MPH, JD/MS, JD/PhD. *Accreditation:* ABA. *Faculty:* 43 full-time (16 women), 17 part-time/adjunct (4 women). *Students:* 419 full-time (177 women), 2 part-time (1 woman); includes 71 minority (13 Black or African American, non-Hispanic/Latino; 21 Asian, non-Hispanic/Latino; 23 Hispanic/Latino; 1 Native Hawaiian or other Pacific Islander, non-Hispanic/Latino; 13 Two or more races, non-Hispanic/Latino), 12 international. Average age 25. 792 applicants, 52% accepted, 93 enrolled. In 2013, 2 master's, 190 doctorates awarded. *Entrance requirements:* For doctorate, LSAT. Additional exam requirements/recommendations for international students: Required—TOEFL. *Application deadline:* For fall admission, 5/1 priority date for domestic students, 3/1 priority date for international students. Applications are processed on a rolling basis. Application fee: $0 ($100 for international students). Electronic applications accepted. *Expenses:* Contact institution. *Financial support:* In 2013–14, 424 students received support, including 424 fellowships with full and partial tuition reimbursements available (averaging $20,333 per year), 150 research assistantships with partial tuition reimbursements available (averaging $2,175 per year); career-related internships or fieldwork, Federal Work-Study, scholarships/grants, and health care benefits also available. Financial award applicants required to submit FAFSA. *Faculty research:* International and comparative law, business law, intellectual property law, competition law, Constitutional law. *Total annual research expenditures:* $288,699. *Unit head:* Gail Agrawal, Dean, 319-335-9034, E-mail: gail-agrawal@uiowa.edu. *Application contact:* Collins Byrd, Assistant Dean of Admissions, 319-335-9095, Fax: 319-335-9646, E-mail: law-admissions@uiowa.edu.
Website: http://www.law.uiowa.edu/.

The University of Kansas, School of Law, Lawrence, KS 66045-7608. Offers JD, JD/MA, JD/MBA, JD/MHSA, JD/MPA, JD/MS, JD/MSW, JD/MUP. *Accreditation:* ABA. *Faculty:* 41 full-time (19 women), 21 part-time/adjunct (7 women). *Students:* 371 full-time (163 women), 20 part-time (3 women); includes 57 minority (17 Black or African American, non-Hispanic/Latino; 4 American Indian or Alaska Native, non-Hispanic/Latino; 8 Asian, non-Hispanic/Latino; 19 Hispanic/Latino; 9 Two or more races, non-Hispanic/Latino), 21 international. Average age 25. 860 applicants, 57% accepted, 106 enrolled. In 2013, 173 doctorates awarded. *Entrance requirements:* For doctorate, LSAT, 2 letters of recommendation. Additional exam requirements/recommendations for international students: Required—TOEFL. *Application deadline:* For fall admission, 5/1 for domestic and international students. Applications are processed on a rolling basis. Application fee: $55. Electronic applications accepted. *Expenses:* Contact institution. *Financial support:* In 2013–14, 5 fellowships (averaging $1,804 per year), 49 research assistantships (averaging $534 per year), 9 teaching assistantships (averaging $991 per year) were awarded; career-related internships or fieldwork, Federal Work-Study, institutionally sponsored loans, and scholarships/grants also available. Financial award application deadline: 2/15; financial award applicants required to submit FAFSA. *Faculty research:* International law, business law, criminal law, elder law, law and public policy. *Unit head:* Stephen W. Mazza, Dean, 785-864-4550, Fax: 785-864-5054. *Application contact:* Steven Freedman, Assistant Dean for Admissions, 866-220-3654, E-mail: admitlaw@ku.edu.
Website: http://www.law.ku.edu/.

University of Kentucky, College of Law, Lexington, KY 40506-0048. Offers JD, JD/MA, JD/MBA, JD/MPA. *Accreditation:* ABA. *Entrance requirements:* For doctorate, LSAT, LSDAS. Additional exam requirements/recommendations for international students: Required—TOEFL. Electronic applications accepted. *Expenses:* Contact institution. *Faculty research:* Health law, education law, advocacy, business law, white collar crime, international trade law, corporate mergers, taxation of Internet transactions.

University of La Verne, College of Law, Ontario, CA 91764. Offers JD. Part-time and evening/weekend programs available. *Entrance requirements:* For doctorate, LSAT. Additional exam requirements/recommendations for international students: Recommended—TOEFL. Electronic applications accepted. *Expenses:* Contact institution.

University of Louisville, Louis D. Brandeis School of Law, Louisville, KY 40208. Offers JD, JD/M Div, JD/MAH, JD/MAPS, JD/MBA, JD/MSSW, JD/MUP. *Accreditation:* ABA.

Part-time programs available. *Faculty:* 28 full-time (12 women), 16 part-time/adjunct (6 women). *Students:* 363 full-time (164 women), 20 part-time (13 women); includes 16 minority (7 Black or African American, non-Hispanic/Latino; 1 Asian, non-Hispanic/Latino; 4 Hispanic/Latino; 4 Two or more races, non-Hispanic/Latino). Average age 26. 749 applicants, 66% accepted, 129 enrolled. In 2013, 129 doctorates awarded. *Degree requirements:* For doctorate, 30 work hours of pro bono service. *Entrance requirements:* For doctorate, LSAT. Additional exam requirements/recommendations for international students: Required—TOEFL (minimum score 550 paper-based). *Application deadline:* For fall admission, 4/15 for domestic and international students. Applications are processed on a rolling basis. Application fee: $50. Electronic applications accepted. *Expenses:* Contact institution. *Financial support:* In 2013–14, 184 students received support. Fellowships, research assistantships, teaching assistantships, career-related internships or fieldwork, scholarships/grants, and tuition waivers (partial) available. Support available to part-time students. Financial award application deadline: 6/1; financial award applicants required to submit FAFSA. *Faculty research:* Intellectual property, environmental law, corporate law, taxation, health law, disability law. *Unit head:* Susan Duncan, Dean, 502-852-6373, Fax: 502-852-0862, E-mail: susan.duncan@louisville.edu. *Application contact:* Henry M. Cantu, Assistant Dean for Admission, 502-852-6365, Fax: 502-852-8971, E-mail: lawadmissions@louisville.edu.
Website: http://www.law.louisville.edu/.

The University of Manchester, School of Law, Manchester, United Kingdom. Offers bioethics and medical jurisprudence (PhD); criminology (M Phil, PhD); law (M Phil, PhD).

University of Manitoba, Faculty of Graduate Studies, Faculty of Law, Winnipeg, MB R3T 2N2, Canada. Offers LL M. *Degree requirements:* For master's, thesis. *Entrance requirements:* For master's, LL B, minimum GPA of 3.0. Additional exam requirements/recommendations for international students: Required—TOEFL (minimum score 600 paper-based). Electronic applications accepted. *Faculty research:* Constitutional law, alternative dispute resolution, human rights law, international trade law, corporate law.

University of Maryland, Baltimore, Francis King Carey School of Law, Baltimore, MD 21201. Offers LL M, JD, JD/MA, JD/MBA, JD/MCP, JD/MPH, JD/MPM, JD/MPP, JD/MS, JD/MSN, JD/MSW, JD/PhD, JD/Pharm D. *Accreditation:* ABA. Part-time and evening/weekend programs available. *Faculty:* 66 full-time (33 women), 59 part-time/adjunct (16 women). *Students:* 648 full-time (357 women), 185 part-time (82 women); includes 308 minority (88 Black or African American, non-Hispanic/Latino; 2 American Indian or Alaska Native, non-Hispanic/Latino; 100 Asian, non-Hispanic/Latino; 81 Hispanic/Latino; 37 Two or more races, non-Hispanic/Latino), 19 international. Average age 27. 2,755 applicants, 44% accepted, 206 enrolled. In 2013, 3 master's, 290 doctorates awarded. *Degree requirements:* For master's, thesis; for doctorate, writing certification. *Entrance requirements:* For doctorate, LSAT, LSDAS. Additional exam requirements/recommendations for international students: Required—TOEFL (minimum score 550 paper-based; 80 iBT). *Application deadline:* For fall admission, 4/1 priority date for domestic and international students. Applications are processed on a rolling basis. Application fee: $70. Electronic applications accepted. *Expenses:* Contact institution. *Financial support:* In 2013–14, 288 students received support, including 28 fellowships (averaging $4,000 per year); Federal Work-Study, institutionally sponsored loans, and scholarships/grants also available. Support available to part-time students. Financial award application deadline: 3/1; financial award applicants required to submit FAFSA. *Faculty research:* Environmental regulation, health care policy, intellectual property, civil rights and race history and policy, international and comparative law. *Total annual research expenditures:* $6.2 million. *Unit head:* Phoebe A. Haddon, Dean/Professor, 410-706-7214, Fax: 410-706-4045, E-mail: phaddon@law.umaryland.edu. *Application contact:* Susan Krinsky, Associate Dean for Student Services, 410-706-3492, Fax: 410-706-1793, E-mail: admissions@law.umaryland.edu.
Website: http://www.law.umaryland.edu/.

University of Maryland, College Park, Academic Affairs, Robert H. Smith School of Business, Program in Business Management/Law, College Park, MD 20742. Offers JD/MBA. *Accreditation:* AACSB. *Students:* 3 full-time (0 women), 1 part-time (0 women); includes 2 minority (1 Black or African American, non-Hispanic/Latino; 1 Hispanic/Latino). 6 applicants, 33% accepted, 1 enrolled. *Entrance requirements:* Additional exam requirements/recommendations for international students: Required—TOEFL. *Application deadline:* For fall admission, 12/15 for domestic and international students; for spring admission, 11/30 for domestic students, 6/1 for international students. Applications are processed on a rolling basis. Application fee: $75. *Expenses:* Tuition, state resident: full-time $10,314; part-time $573 per credit hour. Tuition, nonresident: full-time $22,248; part-time $1236 per credit. *Required fees:* $1446; $403.15 per semester. Tuition and fees vary according to program. *Financial support:* In 2013–14, 1 fellowship (averaging $10,000 per year), 1 teaching assistantship (averaging $16,078 per year) were awarded. Financial award applicants required to submit FAFSA. *Unit head:* Dr. Anand Anandalingam, Dean, 301-405-2308, E-mail: ganand@umd.edu. *Application contact:* Dr. Charles A. Caramello, Dean of Graduate School, 301-405-0358, Fax: 301-314-9305, E-mail: ccaramel@umd.edu.

University of Maryland, College Park, Academic Affairs, School of Public Policy, Joint Program in Public Policy/Law, College Park, MD 20742. Offers JD/MPM. *Students:* 1 full-time (0 women), 2 part-time (0 women). 18 applicants, 28% accepted. *Application deadline:* For fall admission, 4/1 for domestic students, 2/1 for international students; for spring admission, 10/15 for domestic students, 6/1 for international students. Applications are processed on a rolling basis. Application fee: $75. Electronic applications accepted. *Expenses:* Tuition, state resident: full-time $10,314; part-time $573 per credit hour. Tuition, nonresident: full-time $22,248; part-time $1236 per credit. *Required fees:* $1446; $403.15 per semester. Tuition and fees vary according to program. *Financial support:* In 2013–14, 2 teaching assistantships (averaging $14,000 per year) were awarded. Financial award applicants required to submit FAFSA. *Unit head:* Dr. Donald Kettl, Dean, 301-405-6356, E-mail: kettl@umd.edu. *Application contact:* Dr. Charles A. Caramello, Dean of Graduate School, 301-405-0358, Fax: 301-314-9305, E-mail: ccaramel@umd.edu.

University of Massachusetts Dartmouth, Graduate School, University of Massachusetts School of Law –Dartmouth, Dartmouth, MA 02747. Offers JD. Part-time and evening/weekend programs available. *Faculty:* 18 full-time (9 women), 20 part-time/adjunct (9 women). *Students:* 155 full-time (77 women), 99 part-time (56 women); includes 66 minority (22 Black or African American, non-Hispanic/Latino; 11 Asian, non-Hispanic/Latino; 24 Hispanic/Latino; 9 Two or more races, non-Hispanic/Latino), 3 international. Average age 30. 490 applicants, 68% accepted, 78 enrolled. In 2013, 103 doctorates awarded. *Entrance requirements:* For doctorate, LSAT, CAS report, 2 letters of recommendation or evaluations, resume, statement of intent. Additional exam requirements/recommendations for international students: Recommended—TOEFL (minimum score 533 paper-based; 72 iBT). *Application deadline:* For fall admission, 6/30 priority date for domestic students, 5/30 priority date for international students. Applications are processed on a rolling basis. Application fee: $50. Electronic applications accepted. *Expenses:* Contact institution. *Financial support:* In 2013–14, 135 students received support. Scholarships/grants, tuition waivers (full and partial), and summer stipends available. Support available to part-time students. Financial award application deadline: 4/15; financial award applicants required to submit FAFSA. *Faculty research:* Domestic drones and privacy rights, freedom of information law, Constitutionality of gay marriage, surveillance and third-party privacy, cyber crime. *Unit head:* Mary Lu Bilek, Dean, University of Massachusetts School of Law - Dartmouth, 508-985-1149, Fax: 508-985-1104, E-mail: mbilek@umassd.edu. *Application contact:* David Pallozzi, Assistant Dean of Admissions, 508-985-1118, Fax: 508-985-1175, E-mail: dpallozzi@umassd.edu.
Website: http://www.umassd.edu/law.

University of Memphis, Cecil C. Humphreys School of Law, Memphis, TN 38103-2189. Offers JD, JD/MA, JD/MBA, JD/MPH. *Accreditation:* ABA. Part-time programs available. *Faculty:* 20 full-time (9 women), 25 part-time/adjunct (11 women). *Students:* 339 full-time (126 women), 20 part-time (8 women); includes 63 minority (48 Black or African American, non-Hispanic/Latino; 5 American Indian or Alaska Native, non-Hispanic/Latino; 4 Asian, non-Hispanic/Latino; 6 Hispanic/Latino). Average age 25. 612 applicants, 48% accepted, 111 enrolled. In 2013, 1,274 doctorates awarded. *Entrance requirements:* For doctorate, LSAT, CAS report, letters of recommendation, or evaluations. Additional exam requirements/recommendations for international students: Required—TOEFL. *Application deadline:* For fall admission, 3/15 priority date for domestic and international students. Applications are processed on a rolling basis. Application fee: $25 ($40 for international students). Electronic applications accepted. *Expenses:* Contact institution. *Financial support:* In 2013–14, 139 students received support, including 4 fellowships with full and partial tuition reimbursements available (averaging $3,000 per year), 24 research assistantships with full tuition reimbursements available (averaging $3,000 per year), 2 teaching assistantships (averaging $3,000 per year); career-related internships or fieldwork, Federal Work-Study, scholarships/grants, and tuition waivers (partial) also available. Support available to part-time students. Financial award application deadline: 5/1; financial award applicants required to submit FAFSA. *Faculty research:* Legal education, shareholder rights, tort law, evidence law, employment law. *Total annual research expenditures:* $41,000. *Unit head:* Peter V. Letsou, Dean, 901-678-2421, Fax: 901-678-5210, E-mail: pvletsou@memphis.edu. *Application contact:* Dr. Sue Ann McClellan, Assistant Dean for Law Admissions, Recruiting and Scholarships, 901-678-5403, Fax: 901-678-0741, E-mail: smcclell@memphis.edu.
Website: http://www.memphis.edu/law/.

University of Miami, Graduate School, School of Law, Coral Gables, FL 33124-8087. Offers business and financial, international, employment, labor and immigration law, litigation specialization (Certificate); employment, labor and immigration law (JD); estate planning (LL M); international law (LL M), including general international law, inter-American law, international arbitration, U.S. transnational law for foreign lawyers; law (JD); ocean and coastal law (LL M); real property development (real estate) (LL M); taxation (LL M); JD/LL M; JD/LL M/MBA; JD/MA; JD/MBA; JD/MD; JD/MM; JD/MPH; JD/MPS; JD/MS Ed; JD/PhD. *Accreditation:* ABA. *Faculty:* 82 full-time (42 women), 108 part-time/adjunct (36 women). *Students:* 1,176 full-time (521 women); includes 402 minority (79 Black or African American, non-Hispanic/Latino; 7 American Indian or Alaska Native, non-Hispanic/Latino; 31 Asian, non-Hispanic/Latino; 266 Hispanic/Latino; 1 Native Hawaiian or other Pacific Islander, non-Hispanic/Latino; 18 Two or more races, non-Hispanic/Latino), 38 international. Average age 24. 3,300 applicants, 53% accepted, 308 enrolled. In 2013, 430 doctorates awarded. *Entrance requirements:* For doctorate, LSAT, 2 letters of recommendation. Additional exam requirements/recommendations for international students: Required—TOEFL (minimum score 580 paper-based; 92 iBT). *Application deadline:* For fall admission, 1/6 priority date for domestic and international students. Applications are processed on a rolling basis. Application fee: $60. Electronic applications accepted. *Expenses:* Contact institution. *Financial support:* Fellowships, research assistantships, career-related internships or fieldwork, Federal Work-Study, institutionally sponsored loans, scholarships/grants, and unspecified assistantships available. Financial award application deadline: 3/1; financial award applicants required to submit FAFSA. *Faculty research:* National security law, international finance, Internet law/law of electronic commerce, law of the seas, art law/cultural heritage law. *Unit head:* Michael Goodnight, Associate Dean of Admissions and Enrollment Management, 305-284-2527, Fax: 305-284-3084, E-mail: mgoodnig@law.miami.edu. *Application contact:* Therese Lambert, Director of Student Recruitment, 305-284-6746, Fax: 305-284-3084, E-mail: tlambert@law.miami.edu.
Website: http://www.law.miami.edu/.

University of Michigan, Law School, Ann Arbor, MI 48109-1215. Offers comparative law (MCL); international tax (LL M); law (LL M, JD, SJD); JD/MA; JD/MBA; JD/MHSA; JD/MPH; JD/MPP; JD/MS; JD/MSI; JD/MSW; JD/MUP; JD/PhD. *Accreditation:* ABA. *Faculty:* 94 full-time (33 women), 52 part-time/adjunct (12 women). *Students:* 1,055 full-time (479 women); includes 236 minority (36 Black or African American, non-Hispanic/Latino; 3 American Indian or Alaska Native, non-Hispanic/Latino; 101 Asian, non-Hispanic/Latino; 56 Hispanic/Latino; 40 Two or more races, non-Hispanic/Latino), 33 international. 4,875 applicants, 27% accepted, 315 enrolled. In 2013, 34 master's, 399 doctorates awarded. *Entrance requirements:* For doctorate, LSAT. Additional exam requirements/recommendations for international students: Required—TOEFL. *Application deadline:* For fall admission, 2/15 for domestic students. Applications are processed on a rolling basis. Application fee: $75. Electronic applications accepted. *Expenses:* Contact institution. *Financial support:* In 2013–14, 759 students received support. Career-related internships or fieldwork, Federal Work-Study, institutionally sponsored loans, and scholarships/grants available. Financial award applicants required to submit FAFSA. *Unit head:* Mark D. West, Dean, 734-764-1358. *Application contact:* Sarah C. Zearfoss, Assistant Dean and Director of Admissions, 734-764-0537, Fax: 734-647-3218, E-mail: law.jd.admissions@umich.edu.
Website: http://www.law.umich.edu/.

University of Minnesota, Twin Cities Campus, Law School, Minneapolis, MN 55455. Offers LL M, JD, JD/MA, JD/MBA, JD/MBS, JD/MD, JD/MHA, JD/MPA, JD/MPH, JD/MPP, JD/MS, JD/MSST, JD/MURP, JD/PhD. *Accreditation:* ABA. *Faculty:* 67 full-time (27 women), 112 part-time/adjunct (45 women). *Students:* 721 full-time (307 women), 12 part-time (8 women); includes 150 minority (21 Black or African American, non-Hispanic/Latino; 6 American Indian or Alaska Native, non-Hispanic/Latino; 64 Asian, non-Hispanic/Latino; 14 Hispanic/Latino; 45 Two or more races, non-Hispanic/Latino), 70 international. Average age 25. 2,946 applicants, 31% accepted, 221 enrolled. In 2013, 48 master's, 274 doctorates awarded. *Entrance requirements:* For doctorate, LSAT. Additional exam requirements/recommendations for international students: Required—TOEFL. *Application deadline:* For fall admission, 4/1 for domestic students. Applications are processed on a rolling basis. Application fee: $75. Electronic applications accepted. *Expenses:* Contact institution. *Financial support:* In 2013–14, 584 students received support. Fellowships, research assistantships, teaching assistantships, career-related internships or fieldwork, Federal Work-Study, institutionally sponsored loans, scholarships/grants, and tuition waivers (partial) available. Financial award application deadline: 5/1; financial award applicants required to submit FAFSA. *Faculty research:* International and comparative law; law, science, and technology; criminal justice; law and business. *Unit head:* David Wippman, Dean, 612-625-4841. *Application contact:* Nick Wallace, Director of Admissions, 612-625-0718, Fax: 612-625-2011, E-mail: umnlsadm@umn.edu.
Website: http://www.law.umn.edu/.

University of Mississippi, School of Law, Oxford, MS 38677. Offers air and space law (LL M); law (JD); JD/MBA. *Accreditation:* ABA. *Faculty:* 28 full-time (11 women), 7 part-time/adjunct (2 women). *Students:* 438 full-time (171 women), 6 part-time (1 woman); includes 87 minority (63 Black or African American, non-Hispanic/Latino; 4 American Indian or Alaska Native, non-Hispanic/Latino; 5 Asian, non-Hispanic/Latino; 11 Hispanic/Latino; 4 Two or more races, non-Hispanic/Latino). Average age 24. In 2013, 188 doctorates awarded. *Entrance requirements:* For doctorate, LSAT, LSDAS. Additional exam requirements/recommendations for international students: Required—TOEFL. *Application deadline:* For fall admission, 4/1 for domestic students. Application fee: $40. *Expenses:* Contact institution. *Financial support:* Fellowships, research assistantships, teaching assistantships, career-related internships or fieldwork, Federal Work-Study, institutionally sponsored loans, and scholarships/grants available. Support available to part-time students. Financial award application deadline: 3/1; financial award applicants required to submit FAFSA. *Unit head:* Dr. Ira Richard Gershon, Dean, 662-915-6900, Fax: 662-915-6895, E-mail: igershon@olemiss.edu. *Application contact:* Cary Lee Cluck, Assistant Dean for Admissions, 662-915-6815, Fax: 662-915-7577, E-mail: clee@olemiss.edu.

University of Missouri, School of Law, Columbia, MO 65211. Offers dispute resolution (LL M); law (JD); JD/MA; JD/MBA; JD/MPA. *Accreditation:* ABA. *Entrance requirements:* For doctorate, LSAT. Additional exam requirements/recommendations for international students: Required—TOEFL. *Application deadline:* For fall admission, 3/1 priority date for domestic students. Applications are processed on a rolling basis. *Expenses:* Contact institution. *Financial support:* Fellowships, Federal Work-Study, and institutionally sponsored loans available. Financial award application deadline: 3/1; financial award applicants required to submit FAFSA. *Unit head:* Gary Myers, Dean, 573-882-3246, E-mail: myers@missouri.edu. *Application contact:* Lisa E. Key, Assistant Dean for Career Development and Student Services, 573-884-2949, E-mail: keye@missouri.edu.
Website: http://www.law.missouri.edu/.

University of Missouri–Kansas City, School of Law, Kansas City, MO 64110-2499. Offers law (LL M, JD), including general (LL M), taxation (LL M); JD/LL M; JD/MBA; JD/MPA; LL M/MPA. *Accreditation:* ABA. Part-time programs available. *Faculty:* 36 full-time (15 women), 9 part-time/adjunct (5 women). *Students:* 458 full-time (186 women), 51 part-time (18 women); includes 66 minority (24 Black or African American, non-Hispanic/Latino; 2 American Indian or Alaska Native, non-Hispanic/Latino; 10 Asian, non-Hispanic/Latino; 25 Hispanic/Latino; 5 Two or more races, non-Hispanic/Latino), 17 international. Average age 28. 665 applicants, 57% accepted, 203 enrolled. In 2013, 33 master's, 159 doctorates awarded. *Degree requirements:* For master's, thesis (for general). *Entrance requirements:* For master's, LSAT, minimum GPA of 3.0 (for general), 2.7 (for taxation); for doctorate, LSAT. Additional exam requirements/recommendations for international students: Required—TOEFL (minimum score 550 paper-based; 80 iBT). *Application deadline:* For fall admission, 3/1 priority date for domestic and international students. Applications are processed on a rolling basis. Application fee: $50. Electronic applications accepted. *Expenses:* Contact institution. *Financial support:* In 2013–14, 21 teaching assistantships with partial tuition reimbursements (averaging $2,570 per year) were awarded; career-related internships or fieldwork, Federal Work-Study, institutionally sponsored loans, scholarships/grants, and tuition waivers (full and partial) also available. Support available to part-time students. Financial award application deadline: 3/1; financial award applicants required to submit FAFSA. *Faculty research:* Family and children's issues, litigation, estate planning, urban law, business, tax entrepreneurial law. *Unit head:* Ellen Y. Suni, Dean, 816-235-1007, Fax: 816-235-5276, E-mail: sunie@umkc.edu. *Application contact:* Lydia Dagenais, Director of Law School Admissions, 816-235-1677, Fax: 816-235-5276, E-mail: dagenaisl@umkc.edu.
Website: http://www.law.umkc.edu/.

The University of Montana, School of Law, Missoula, MT 59812-0002. Offers JD, JD/MBA, JD/MPA. *Accreditation:* ABA. *Degree requirements:* For doctorate, oral presentation, paper. *Entrance requirements:* For doctorate, LSAT. *Expenses:* Contact institution. *Faculty research:* Legal education curriculum, business and probate law reform, rules of civil procedure reform, tribal courts, women's issues.

University of Nebraska–Lincoln, College of Law, Lincoln, NE 68583-0902. Offers law (JD); legal studies (MLS); space and telecommunications law (LL M); JD/MA; JD/MBA; JD/MCRP; JD/MPA; JD/PhD. *Accreditation:* ABA. *Entrance requirements:* For doctorate, LSAT. Electronic applications accepted. *Expenses:* Contact institution. *Faculty research:* Law and medicine, constitutional law, criminal procedure, international trade.

University of Nevada, Las Vegas, William S. Boyd School of Law, Las Vegas, NV 89154-1003. Offers JD, JD/MBA, JD/MSW, JD/PhD. *Accreditation:* ABA. Part-time and evening/weekend programs available. *Entrance requirements:* For doctorate, LSAT, resume, personal statement, letter of recommendation, LSDAS report. *Application deadline:* For fall admission, 3/15 for domestic and international students. Applications are processed on a rolling basis. Application fee: $50. Electronic applications accepted. *Expenses:* Contact institution. *Financial support:* Career-related internships or fieldwork and scholarships/grants available. Support available to part-time students. Financial award application deadline: 2/1; financial award applicants required to submit FAFSA. *Faculty research:* Civil procedure, Constitutional law, federal courts, professional responsibility, juvenile justice. *Total annual research expenditures:* $8,620. *Unit head:* John V. White, Dean, 702-895-3671, Fax: 702-895-1095. *Application contact:* Elizabeth M. Karl, Admissions and Records Assistant III, 702-895-2424, Fax: 702-895-2414, E-mail: elizabeth.karl@unlv.edu.
Website: http://www.law.unlv.edu/.

University of New Hampshire, School of Law, Concord, NH 03301. Offers intellectual property (Diploma); intellectual property, commerce and technology (LL M, MIP); law (JD); JD/MIP. Diploma awarded as part of Intellectual Property Summer Institute. *Accreditation:* ABA. *Entrance requirements:* For doctorate, LSAT. Additional exam requirements/recommendations for international students: Required—TOEFL (minimum score 600 paper-based). *Application deadline:* For fall admission, 5/1 priority date for domestic students. Applications are processed on a rolling basis. Electronic applications accepted. *Expenses:* Contact institution. *Financial support:* Application deadline: 4/15. *Faculty research:* Legal applications of artificial intelligence, intellectual property. *Unit head:* John T. Broderick, Jr., Dean, 603-228-1541, Fax: 603-228-1074, E-mail: john.broderick@law.unh.edu. *Application contact:* Robin Ingli, Assistant Dean for Admissions, 603-513-5300, Fax: 603-513-5234, E-mail: robin.ingli@law.unh.edu.
Website: http://law.unh.edu/.

University of New Mexico, School of Law, Albuquerque, NM 87131-0001. Offers JD, JD/M Acct, JD/MA, JD/MBA, JD/MPA, JD/MS, JD/PhD. *Accreditation:* ABA. *Faculty:* 33 full-time (16 women), 27 part-time/adjunct (16 women). *Students:* 344 full-time (171 women), 1 (woman) part-time; includes 160 minority (4 Black or African American, non-Hispanic/Latino; 30 American Indian or Alaska Native, non-Hispanic/Latino; 9 Asian, non-Hispanic/Latino; 117 Hispanic/Latino). 640 applicants, 40% accepted, 119 enrolled. In 2013, 114 doctorates awarded. *Degree requirements:* For doctorate, advanced writing piece, clinic. *Entrance requirements:* For doctorate, LSAT, bachelor's degree. Additional exam requirements/recommendations for international students: Required—TOEFL (minimum score 600 paper-based; 100 iBT). *Application deadline:* For fall admission, 2/15 priority date for domestic and international students. Applications are processed on a rolling basis. Application fee: $50. Electronic applications accepted. *Expenses:* Contact institution. *Financial support:* In 2013–14, 155 students received support, including 4 research assistantships with full tuition reimbursements available (averaging $5,000 per year); career-related internships or fieldwork, Federal Work-Study, and scholarships/grants also available. Financial award application deadline: 3/1; financial award applicants required to submit FAFSA. *Faculty research:* Clinical legal education, international law, Indian law, natural resources and environmental law, Constitutional law. *Unit head:* David Herring, Dean, 505-277-4700, Fax: 505-277-9558, E-mail: herring@law.unm.edu. *Application contact:* Jeffery Dubinski-Neessen, Assistant Dean for Admissions and Financial Aid, 505-277-0959, Fax: 505-277-9958, E-mail: neessen@law.unm.edu.
Website: http://lawschool.unm.edu/.

The University of North Carolina at Chapel Hill, School of Law, Chapel Hill, NC 27599-3380. Offers JD, JD/MAMC, JD/MAPPS, JD/MASA, JD/MBA, JD/MPA, JD/MPH, JD/MRP, JD/MSIS, JD/MSLS, JD/MSW. JD/MAPPS offered jointly with Duke University. *Accreditation:* ABA. *Faculty:* 53 full-time (23 women), 53 part-time/adjunct (11 women). *Students:* 720 full-time (352 women); includes 183 minority (50 Black or African American, non-Hispanic/Latino; 7 American Indian or Alaska Native, non-Hispanic/Latino; 39 Asian, non-Hispanic/Latino; 49 Hispanic/Latino; 38 Two or more races, non-Hispanic/Latino), 1 international. Average age 25. 1,484 applicants, 45% accepted, 237 enrolled. In 2013, 246 doctorates awarded. *Entrance requirements:* For doctorate, LSAT. Additional exam requirements/recommendations for international students: Required—TOEFL (minimum score 650 paper-based; 100 iBT). *Application deadline:* For fall admission, 3/1 for domestic and international students. Applications are processed on a rolling basis. Application fee: $75. Electronic applications accepted. *Expenses:* Contact institution. *Financial support:* In 2013–14, 502 students received support. Career-related internships or fieldwork, Federal Work-Study, and scholarships/grants available. Financial award application deadline: 3/1; financial award applicants required to submit FAFSA. *Faculty research:* Corporate and banking law, environmental policy, state and U.S. Constitutional law, health law policy, immigration law and civil rights. *Unit head:* John C. Boger, Dean and Professor, 919-962-4417, Fax: 919-962-1170. *Application contact:* Michael J. States, JD, Assistant Dean for Admissions, 919-962-5109, Fax: 919-843-7939, E-mail: law_admission@unc.edu.
Website: http://www.law.unc.edu/.

University of North Dakota, School of Law, Grand Forks, ND 58202. Offers JD. *Accreditation:* ABA. *Entrance requirements:* For doctorate, LSAT. *Expenses:* Contact institution.

University of Notre Dame, Law School, Notre Dame, IN 46556-0780. Offers human rights (LL M, JSD); international and comparative law (LL M); law (JD). *Accreditation:* ABA. *Faculty:* 58 full-time (19 women), 50 part-time/adjunct (22 women). *Students:* 548 full-time (245 women); includes 128 minority (30 Black or African American, non-Hispanic/Latino; 4 American Indian or Alaska Native, non-Hispanic/Latino; 30 Asian, non-Hispanic/Latino; 56 Hispanic/Latino; 8 Two or more races, non-Hispanic/Latino), 40 international. 2,614 applicants, 28% accepted, 163 enrolled. In 2013, 19 master's, 184 doctorates awarded. *Degree requirements:* For master's, thesis, 1-year residency; for doctorate, thesis/dissertation, 2-year residency (for JSD). *Entrance requirements:* For doctorate, LSAT (for JD), LL M (for JSD). Additional exam requirements/recommendations for international students: Required—TOEFL. *Application deadline:* For fall admission, 3/15 for domestic and international students; for winter admission, 3/15 for domestic students. Applications are processed on a rolling basis. Application fee: $75. Electronic applications accepted. *Expenses:* Contact institution. *Financial support:* In 2013–14, 368 students received support, including 368 fellowships with tuition reimbursements available (averaging $18,866 per year); research assistantships, teaching assistantships, career-related internships or fieldwork, Federal Work-Study, institutionally sponsored loans, scholarships/grants, health care benefits, unspecified assistantships, and university dormitory rector assistantships also available. Financial award application deadline: 2/28; financial award applicants required to submit FAFSA. *Unit head:* Nell Jessup Newton, Dean, 574-631-6789, Fax: 574-631-8400, E-mail: nell.newton@nd.edu. *Application contact:* Jacob Baska, Director of Admissions and Financial Aid, 574-631-6626, Fax: 574-631-5474, E-mail: lawadmit@nd.edu.
Website: http://www.law.nd.edu/.

University of Oklahoma, College of Law, Norman, OK 73019. Offers LL M, JD, JD/MA, JD/MBA, JD/MPH, JD/MS. *Accreditation:* ABA. Postbaccalaureate distance learning degree programs offered (minimal on-campus study). *Faculty:* 45 full-time (17 women), 15 part-time/adjunct (4 women). *Students:* 481 full-time (213 women), 14 part-time (9 women); includes 118 minority (26 Black or African American, non-Hispanic/Latino; 59 American Indian or Alaska Native, non-Hispanic/Latino; 13 Asian, non-Hispanic/Latino; 18 Hispanic/Latino; 2 Two or more races, non-Hispanic/Latino), 13 international. Average age 24. 943 applicants, 41% accepted, 143 enrolled. In 2013, 14 master's, 184 doctorates awarded. *Entrance requirements:* For master's, JD or equivalent; for doctorate, LSAT. Additional exam requirements/recommendations for international students: Required—TOEFL (minimum score 550 paper-based, 79 iBT for LL M; 600 paper-based, 100 iBT for JD). *Application deadline:* For fall admission, 3/15 for domestic and international students. Applications are processed on a rolling basis. Application fee: $50. Electronic applications accepted. *Expenses:* Contact institution. *Financial support:* In 2013–14, 421 students received support. Career-related internships or fieldwork, Federal Work-Study, institutionally sponsored loans, scholarships/grants, and tuition waivers (full and partial) available. Financial award application deadline: 6/1; financial award applicants required to submit FAFSA. *Unit head:* Joseph Harroz, Jr., Dean, 405-325-4884, Fax: 405-325-7712, E-mail: jharroz@ou.edu. *Application contact:* Vicki Ferguson, Admissions Coordinator, 405-325-4728, Fax: 405-325-0502, E-mail: admissions@law.ou.edu.
Website: http://www.law.ou.edu/.

University of Oregon, School of Law, Eugene, OR 97403. Offers MA, MS, JD, JD/MBA, JD/MS. *Accreditation:* ABA. *Entrance requirements:* For doctorate, LSAT. *Expenses:* Contact institution.

University of Ottawa, Faculty of Graduate and Postdoctoral Studies, Faculty of Law, Ottawa, ON K1N 6N5, Canada. Offers LL M, LL D. Part-time and evening/weekend programs available. *Degree requirements:* For master's, thesis or alternative; for doctorate, thesis/dissertation. *Entrance requirements:* For master's, minimum B average, LL B; for doctorate, LL M, minimum B+ average. Electronic applications accepted. *Faculty research:* International law, human rights law, family law.

University of Pennsylvania, Law School, Philadelphia, PA 19104. Offers LL CM, LL M, JD, SJD, JD/AM, JD/DMD, JD/LL M, JD/MA, JD/MBA, JD/MBE, JD/MCP, JD/MD, JD/MES, JD/MPA, JD/MPH, JD/MS, JD/MS Ed, JD/MSE, JD/MSSP, JD/MSW, JD/PhD. JD/LL M offered jointly with Hong Kong University. *Accreditation:* ABA. *Faculty:* 63 full-time (18 women), 68 part-time/adjunct (24 women). *Students:* 786 full-time (363 women); includes 226 minority (53 Black or African American, non-Hispanic/Latino; 2 American Indian or Alaska Native, non-Hispanic/Latino; 101 Asian, non-Hispanic/Latino; 45 Hispanic/Latino; 1 Native Hawaiian or other Pacific Islander, non-Hispanic/Latino; 24 Two or more races, non-Hispanic/Latino), 24 international. Average age 24. 5,283 applicants, 17% accepted, 251 enrolled. In 2013, 114 master's, 259 doctorates awarded. *Degree requirements:* For master's, thesis optional; for doctorate, thesis/

dissertation. *Entrance requirements:* For master's, prior law degree (for LL M); for doctorate, LSAT (for JD), LL M (for SJD). Additional exam requirements/recommendations for international students: Recommended—TOEFL (minimum score 600 paper-based; 100 iBT), IELTS (minimum score 7). *Application deadline:* For fall admission, 3/1 for domestic students, 2/1 for international students. Applications are processed on a rolling basis. Application fee: $80. Electronic applications accepted. *Expenses:* Contact institution. *Financial support:* In 2013–14, 406 students received support, including 2 teaching assistantships (averaging $3,500 per year); fellowships, research assistantships, career-related internships or fieldwork, Federal Work-Study, institutionally sponsored loans, and scholarships/grants also available. Financial award application deadline: 3/1; financial award applicants required to submit FAFSA. *Faculty research:* Administrative law and regulation, business and corporate law, civil procedure, Constitutional law, criminal law, environmental law, health law, intellectual property and technology law, international and comparative law, law and economics, legal history, philosophy, tax law and policy. *Total annual research expenditures:* $983,532. *Unit head:* Michael A. Fitts, Dean, 215-898-7463, Fax: 215-573-2025. *Application contact:* Renee Post, Associate Dean of Admissions and Financial Aid, 215-898-7400, Fax: 215-898-9606, E-mail: contactadmissions@law.upenn.edu.
Website: http://www.law.upenn.edu/.

University of Pittsburgh, Katz Graduate School of Business, MBA/Juris Doctor Program, Pittsburgh, PA 15260. Offers MBA/JD. *Faculty:* 61 full-time (15 women), 21 part-time/adjunct (5 women). *Students:* 23 full-time (10 women), 1 (woman) part-time; includes 3 minority (2 Black or African American, non-Hispanic/Latino; 1 Hispanic/Latino), 4 international. Average age 37. 17 applicants, 88% accepted, 10 enrolled. *Entrance requirements:* Additional exam requirements/recommendations for international students: Required—TOEFL (minimum score 600 paper-based; 100 iBT) or IELTS. *Application deadline:* For fall admission, 4/1 priority date for domestic students, 2/1 priority date for international students. Application fee: $50. Electronic applications accepted. *Expenses:* Tuition, state resident: full-time $19,964; part-time $807 per credit. Tuition, nonresident: full-time $32,686; part-time $1337 per credit. *Required fees:* $740; $200. Tuition and fees vary according to program. *Financial support:* In 2013–14, 11 students received support. Career-related internships or fieldwork and scholarships/grants available. Financial award application deadline: 2/1. *Faculty research:* Accounting systems/financial reporting, corporate finance, shopper marketing/consumer behavior, management information systems, organizational behavior and entrepreneurship. *Unit head:* Tim Robison, Assistant Dean, 412-648-1700, Fax: 412-648-1659, E-mail: trobison@katz.pitt.edu. *Application contact:* Thomas Keller, Director of MBA Admissions, 412-648-1700, Fax: 412-648-1659, E-mail: mba@katz.pitt.edu.
Website: http://www.business.pitt.edu/katz/mba/academics/programs/mba-jd.php.

University of Pittsburgh, School of Law, Certificate Program in International and Comparative Law, Pittsburgh, PA 15260. Offers Certificate. *Faculty:* 39 full-time (15 women), 126 part-time/adjunct (37 women). *Students:* 33 full-time (18 women); includes 7 minority (2 Black or African American, non-Hispanic/Latino; 2 Asian, non-Hispanic/Latino; 1 Hispanic/Latino; 2 Two or more races, non-Hispanic/Latino). Average age 24. *Expenses:* Tuition, state resident: full-time $19,964; part-time $807 per credit. Tuition, nonresident: full-time $32,686; part-time $1337 per credit. *Required fees:* $740; $200. Tuition and fees vary according to program. *Unit head:* Prof. Ronald A. Brand, Director, Center for International Legal Education, 412-648-7023, Fax: 412-648-2648, E-mail: rbrand@pitt.edu. *Application contact:* Gina Huggins, Program Administrator, 412-648-2023, Fax: 412-648-2648, E-mail: cile@pitt.edu.

University of Pittsburgh, School of Law, John P. Gismondi Civil Litigation Certificate Program, Pittsburgh, PA 15260. Offers Certificate. *Faculty:* 9 full-time (6 women), 30 part-time/adjunct (2 women). *Students:* 57 full-time (20 women). *Expenses:* Tuition, state resident: full-time $19,964; part-time $807 per credit. Tuition, nonresident: full-time $32,686; part-time $1337 per credit. *Required fees:* $740; $200. Tuition and fees vary according to program. *Unit head:* Martha Mannix, Clinical Associate Professor of Law/Director, 412-648-1390, Fax: 412-648-1947, E-mail: mmannix@pitt.edu. *Application contact:* Charmaine McCall, Assistant Dean of Admissions and Financial Aid, 412-648-1413, Fax: 412-648-1318, E-mail: cmccall@pitt.edu.

University of Pittsburgh, School of Law, LL M Program for Foreign Lawyers, Pittsburgh, PA 15260. Offers LL M. Program offered to international students only. Part-time programs available. *Faculty:* 39 full-time (15 women), 126 part-time/adjunct (37 women). *Students:* 12 full-time (6 women), 5 part-time (1 woman); includes 1 minority (Hispanic/Latino), 16 international. Average age 25. 57 applicants, 70% accepted, 17 enrolled. In 2013, 16 master's awarded. *Degree requirements:* For master's, seminar paper. *Entrance requirements:* For master's, law degree from foreign university. Additional exam requirements/recommendations for international students: Required—TOEFL (minimum score 600 paper-based; 100 iBT); Recommended—IELTS (minimum score 7). *Application deadline:* For fall admission, 3/31 priority date for international students. Applications are processed on a rolling basis. Application fee: $0 ($55 for international students). *Expenses:* Contact institution. *Financial support:* In 2013–14, 9 students received support, including 7 fellowships with partial tuition reimbursements available (averaging $15,000 per year); career-related internships or fieldwork and scholarships/grants also available. *Faculty research:* International arbitration, private international law, Islamic law, environmental criminal and comparative law. *Unit head:* Prof. Ronald A. Brand, Director, Center for International Legal Education, 412-648-7023, Fax: 412-648-2648, E-mail: rbrand@pitt.edu. *Application contact:* Gina Huggins, Program Administrator, 412-648-7023, Fax: 412-648-2648, E-mail: cile@pitt.edu.
Website: http://www.law.pitt.edu/academics/international-lawyers-programs/llm.

University of Pittsburgh, School of Law, Professional Programs in Law, Pittsburgh, PA 15260. Offers JD, JD/MA, JD/MAM, JD/MBA, JD/MID, JD/MPA, JD/MPH, JD/MPIA, JD/MSPPM, JD/MSW. *Accreditation:* ABA. *Faculty:* 39 full-time (15 women), 112 part-time/adjunct (26 women). *Students:* 590 full-time (251 women), 3 part-time (0 women); includes 113 minority (62 Black or African American, non-Hispanic/Latino; 3 American Indian or Alaska Native, non-Hispanic/Latino; 24 Asian, non-Hispanic/Latino; 16 Hispanic/Latino; 8 Two or more races, non-Hispanic/Latino), 14 international. 1,487 applicants, 50% accepted, 174 enrolled. In 2013, 222 doctorates awarded. *Entrance requirements:* For doctorate, LSAT. Additional exam requirements/recommendations for international students: Required—TOEFL. *Application deadline:* For fall admission, 4/1 for domestic students. Applications are processed on a rolling basis. Application fee: $65. Electronic applications accepted. *Expenses:* Contact institution. *Financial support:* In 2013–14, 375 students received support, including 36 research assistantships (averaging $5,440 per year), 13 teaching assistantships (averaging $1,200 per year); career-related internships or fieldwork, Federal Work-Study, scholarships/grants, and unspecified assistantships also available. Financial award application deadline: 3/1; financial award applicants required to submit FAFSA. *Faculty research:* Civil and criminal justice, Constitutional law, health law, international law, law and society. *Total annual research expenditures:* $397,636. *Unit head:* William M. Carter, Jr., Dean, 412-648-1401, Fax: 412-648-2647, E-mail: william.carter@law.pitt.edu. *Application contact:* Charmaine McCall, Assistant Dean of Admissions and Financial Aid, 412-648-1413, Fax: 412-648-1318, E-mail: cmccall@pitt.edu.
Website: http://www.law.pitt.edu/.

University of Puerto Rico, Río Piedras Campus, School of Law, San Juan, PR 00931-3349. Offers LL M, JD. *Accreditation:* ABA. Part-time and evening/weekend programs available. *Entrance requirements:* For master's, LSAT, minimum GPA of 3.0, letter of recommendation; for doctorate, GMAT, GRE, LSAT, EXADEP, minimum GPA of 3.0. Additional exam requirements/recommendations for international students: Required—TOEFL. *Faculty research:* Civil code; Puerto Rico constitutional law; professional behavior, rules and regulations; international law; expert testimony.

University of Richmond, School of Law, Richmond, VA 23173. Offers JD, JD/MA, JD/MBA, JD/MHA, JD/MPA, JD/MS, JD/MSW, JD/MURP. JD/MSW, JD/MHA, JD/MPA offered jointly with Virginia Commonwealth University; JD/MURP with Virginia Commonwealth University; JD/MA with Department of History; JD/MS with Department of Biology. *Accreditation:* ABA. *Entrance requirements:* For doctorate, LSAT. Electronic applications accepted. *Expenses:* Contact institution.

University of St. Thomas, Graduate Studies, School of Law, Minneapolis, MN 55403-2015. Offers law (JD); organizational ethics and compliance (LL M, MSL); U.S. law (LL M); JD/MA; JD/MBA; JD/MSW. *Accreditation:* ABA. *Faculty:* 33 full-time (10 women), 76 part-time/adjunct (26 women). *Students:* 401 full-time (180 women), 4 part-time (2 women); includes 50 minority (8 Black or African American, non-Hispanic/Latino; 2 American Indian or Alaska Native, non-Hispanic/Latino; 9 Asian, non-Hispanic/Latino; 22 Hispanic/Latino; 1 Native Hawaiian or other Pacific Islander, non-Hispanic/Latino; 8 Two or more races, non-Hispanic/Latino), 6 international. Average age 27. 716 applicants, 72% accepted, 114 enrolled. In 2013, 158 doctorates awarded. *Degree requirements:* For doctorate, mentor externship, public service. *Entrance requirements:* For doctorate, LSAT, 2 letters of recommendation. Additional exam requirements/recommendations for international students: Required—TOEFL (minimum score 550 paper-based), IELTS (minimum score 6.5), or Michigan English Language Assessment Battery (minimum score 80). *Application deadline:* For fall admission, 7/1 priority date for domestic and international students. Applications are processed on a rolling basis. Application fee: $0. Electronic applications accepted. *Financial support:* In 2013–14, 357 students received support. Scholarships/grants available. Financial award application deadline: 7/1; financial award applicants required to submit FAFSA. *Faculty research:* Constitutional law (executive powers and First Amendment); banking, securities, and financial markets; law, religion, and jurisprudence; international law, development and dispute resolution; formation of professional identity, values, and skills. *Unit head:* Robert K. Vischer, Dean, 651-962-4880, Fax: 651-962-4881, E-mail: rkvischer@stthomas.edu. *Application contact:* Cari Haaland, Assistant Dean for Admissions and International Programs, 651-962-4895, Fax: 651-962-4876, E-mail: lawschool@stthomas.edu.
Website: http://www.stthomas.edu/law/.

University of San Diego, School of Law, San Diego, CA 92110. Offers business and corporate law (LL M); comparative law (LL M); general studies (LL M); international law (LL M); law (JD); taxation (LL M, Diploma); JD/IMBA; JD/MA; JD/MBA. *Accreditation:* ABA. Part-time and evening/weekend programs available. *Faculty:* 48 full-time (16 women), 67 part-time/adjunct (24 women). *Students:* 708 full-time (357 women), 155 part-time (73 women); includes 269 minority (18 Black or African American, non-Hispanic/Latino; 4 American Indian or Alaska Native, non-Hispanic/Latino; 127 Asian, non-Hispanic/Latino; 98 Hispanic/Latino; 3 Native Hawaiian or other Pacific Islander, non-Hispanic/Latino; 19 Two or more races, non-Hispanic/Latino), 33 international. Average age 27. 2,844 applicants, 48% accepted, 243 enrolled. In 2013, 63 master's, 316 doctorates awarded. *Entrance requirements:* For master's, JD, LL B or equivalent from an ABA-accredited law school; for doctorate, LSAT, bachelor's degree, registration with the Credential Assemble Service (CAS). Additional exam requirements/recommendations for international students: Required—TOEFL (minimum score 600 paper-based; 100 iBT). *Application deadline:* For fall admission, 2/1 priority date for domestic students. Applications are processed on a rolling basis. Application fee: $50. Electronic applications accepted. *Expenses:* Contact institution. *Financial support:* In 2013–14, 610 students received support. Career-related internships or fieldwork, Federal Work-Study, institutionally sponsored loans, and scholarships/grants available. Support available to part-time students. Financial award application deadline: 3/1; financial award applicants required to submit FAFSA. *Faculty research:* Corporate law, children's advocacy, Constitutional and criminal law, international and comparative law, public interest law, intellectual property and tax law. *Unit head:* Dr. Stephen C. Ferruolo, Dean, 619-260-4527, E-mail: lawdean@sandiego.edu. *Application contact:* Jorge Garcia, Assistant Dean, JD Admissions, 619-260-4528, Fax: 619-260-2218, E-mail: jdinfo@sandiego.edu.
Website: http://www.sandiego.edu/law/.

University of San Francisco, School of Law, San Francisco, CA 94117-1080. Offers law (LL M, JD), including intellectual property and technology law (LL M), international transactions and comparative law (LL M), taxation (LL M); JD/MBA. *Accreditation:* ABA. Part-time and evening/weekend programs available. *Faculty:* 15 full-time (8 women), 61 part-time/adjunct (22 women). *Students:* 473 full-time (256 women), 103 part-time (52 women); includes 251 minority (39 Black or African American, non-Hispanic/Latino; 3 American Indian or Alaska Native, non-Hispanic/Latino; 74 Asian, non-Hispanic/Latino; 88 Hispanic/Latino; 1 Native Hawaiian or other Pacific Islander, non-Hispanic/Latino; 46 Two or more races, non-Hispanic/Latino), 16 international. Average age 26. 2,961 applicants, 50% accepted, 178 enrolled. In 2013, 12 master's, 204 doctorates awarded. *Entrance requirements:* For doctorate, LSAT, minimum undergraduate GPA of 3.2. *Application deadline:* For fall admission, 4/1 for domestic students. Applications are processed on a rolling basis. *Expenses:* Contact institution. *Financial support:* In 2013–14, 246 students received support. Career-related internships or fieldwork, Federal Work-Study, and institutionally sponsored loans available. Support available to part-time students. Financial award application deadline: 3/2; financial award applicants required to submit FAFSA. *Unit head:* John Trasvia, Dean, 415-422-6304. *Application contact:* Alan P. Guerrero, Director of Admissions, 415-422-2975, E-mail: lawadmissions@usfca.edu.
Website: http://www.law.usfca.edu/.

University of Saskatchewan, College of Graduate Studies and Research, College of Law, Saskatoon, SK S7N 5A2, Canada. Offers LL M, JD. Part-time programs available. *Degree requirements:* For master's, thesis. *Entrance requirements:* For master's, LL B; for doctorate, LSAT. Additional exam requirements/recommendations for international students: Required—TOEFL. *Expenses: Tuition, area resident:* Full-time $3585 Canadian dollars; part-time $585 Canadian dollars per course. Tuition, nonresident: part-time $877 Canadian dollars per course. *International tuition:* $5377 Canadian dollars full-time. *Required fees:* $889.51 Canadian dollars. *Faculty research:* Cooperative, native/aboriginal, constitutional, commercial, consumer, and natural resource law; criminal justice; human rights.

University of South Africa, College of Law, Pretoria, South Africa. Offers correctional services management (M Tech); criminology (MA, PhD); law (LL M, LL D); penology (MA, PhD); police science (MA, PhD); policing (M Tech); security risk management (M Tech); social science in criminology (MA).

University of South Carolina, School of Law, Columbia, SC 29208. Offers JD, JD/IMBA, JD/M Acc, JD/MCJ, JD/MEERM, JD/MHA, JD/MHR, JD/MIBS, JD/MPA, JD/MSEL, JD/MSW. *Accreditation:* ABA. *Degree requirements:* For doctorate, thesis/

dissertation. *Entrance requirements:* For doctorate, LSAT. *Expenses:* Contact institution.

The University of South Dakota, Graduate School, School of Law, Vermillion, SD 57069-2390. Offers JD, JD/MA, JD/MBA, JD/MP Acc, JD/MPA, JD/MS. *Accreditation:* ABA. Part-time programs available. *Entrance requirements:* For doctorate, LSAT. Additional exam requirements/recommendations for international students: Required—TOEFL (minimum score 600 paper-based). Electronic applications accepted. *Expenses:* Contact institution. *Faculty research:* Indian law, skills training, international law, family law, evidence.

University of Southern California, Graduate School, Gould School of Law, Los Angeles, CA 90089. Offers comparative law for foreign attorneys (MCL); law (JD); law for foreign-educated attorneys (LL M); JD/MA; JD/MBA; JD/MBT; JD/MPA; JD/MPP; JD/MRED; JD/MS; JD/MSW; JD/PhD; JD/Pharm D. *Accreditation:* ABA. *Entrance requirements:* For doctorate, LSAT. Additional exam requirements/recommendations for international students: Required—TOEFL. *Faculty research:* Intellectual property law, tax law, criminal law, law and philosophy, law and history.

University of Southern Maine, University of Maine School of Law, Portland, ME 04102. Offers JD, JD/MBA. *Accreditation:* ABA. Part-time programs available. *Faculty:* 23 full-time (8 women), 16 part-time/adjunct (4 women). *Students:* 253 full-time (124 women), 14 part-time (4 women); includes 26 minority (7 Black or African American, non-Hispanic/Latino; 4 American Indian or Alaska Native, non-Hispanic/Latino; 7 Asian, non-Hispanic/Latino; 6 Hispanic/Latino; 2 Native Hawaiian or other Pacific Islander, non-Hispanic/Latino), 5 international. Average age 28. 788 applicants, 45% accepted, 86 enrolled. In 2013, 96 doctorates awarded. *Entrance requirements:* For doctorate, LSAT. Additional exam requirements/recommendations for international students: Required—TOEFL. *Application deadline:* For fall admission, 4/15 for domestic students, 3/1 for international students. Applications are processed on a rolling basis. Application fee: $50. Electronic applications accepted. Application fee is waived when completed online. *Expenses:* Contact institution. *Financial support:* In 2013–14, 129 students received support, including 22 fellowships (averaging $2,840 per year), 25 research assistantships (averaging $2,000 per year), 7 teaching assistantships (averaging $2,000 per year); Federal Work-Study and scholarships/grants also available. Financial award application deadline: 2/15; financial award applicants required to submit FAFSA. *Faculty research:* Commercial law aspects of intellectual property; domestic violence; race, gender, and law; environmental law and climate change; bankruptcy and predatory lending. *Unit head:* Peter R. Pitegoff, Dean, 207-780-4344, Fax: 207-780-4239. *Application contact:* Alison Beyea, Director of Admissions, 207-780-4341, Fax: 207-780-4239, E-mail: lawadmissions@maine.edu.
Website: http://mainelaw.maine.edu/.

The University of Tennessee, College of Law, Knoxville, TN 37996-1810. Offers business transactions (JD); law (JD); trial advocacy and dispute resolution (JD); JD/MBA; JD/MPH; JD/MPPA. *Accreditation:* ABA. *Faculty:* 47 full-time (24 women), 47 part-time/adjunct (17 women). *Students:* 442 full-time (184 women); includes 91 minority (47 Black or African American, non-Hispanic/Latino; 2 American Indian or Alaska Native, non-Hispanic/Latino; 15 Asian, non-Hispanic/Latino; 17 Hispanic/Latino; 2 Native Hawaiian or other Pacific Islander, non-Hispanic/Latino; 8 Two or more races, non-Hispanic/Latino). Average age 23. 806 applicants, 51% accepted, 15 enrolled. In 2013, 166 doctorates awarded. *Entrance requirements:* For doctorate, LSAT. Additional exam requirements/recommendations for international students: Recommended—TOEFL. *Application deadline:* For fall admission, 2/1 priority date for domestic and international students. Applications are processed on a rolling basis. Application fee: $15. Electronic applications accepted. *Expenses:* Contact institution. *Financial support:* In 2013–14, 219 students received support, including 10 research assistantships with full tuition reimbursements available (averaging $30,833 per year); career-related internships or fieldwork, Federal Work-Study, institutionally sponsored loans, scholarships/grants, and unspecified assistantships also available. Support available to part-time students. Financial award application deadline: 3/1; financial award applicants required to submit FAFSA. *Faculty research:* Legal expert systems, medical malpractice remedies, professional ethics, insanity defense. *Unit head:* Dr. Karen R. Britton, Director of Admissions, Financial Aid and Career Services, 865-974-4131, Fax: 865-974-1572, E-mail: lawadmit@utk.edu. *Application contact:* Janet S. Hatcher, Admissions and Financial Aid Advisor, 865-974-4131, Fax: 865-974-1572, E-mail: hatcher@utk.edu.
Website: http://www.law.utk.edu/.

The University of Texas at Austin, Graduate School, College of Liberal Arts, Teresa Lozano Long Institute of Latin American Studies, Austin, TX 78712-1111. Offers cultural politics of Afro-Latin and indigenous peoples (MA); development studies (MA); environmental studies (MA); human rights (MA); Latin American and international law (LL M); JD/MA; MA/MA; MBA/MA; MP Aff/MA; MSCRP/MA. LL M offered jointly with The University of Texas School of Law. *Entrance requirements:* For master's, GRE General Test.

The University of Texas at Austin, School of Law, Austin, TX 78705-3224. Offers LL M, JD, JD/MA, JD/MBA, JD/MGPS, JD/MP Aff, JD/MSCRP. *Accreditation:* ABA. *Faculty:* 87 full-time (32 women), 84 part-time/adjunct (26 women). *Students:* 1,093 full-time (491 women); includes 317 minority (45 Black or African American, non-Hispanic/Latino; 3 American Indian or Alaska Native, non-Hispanic/Latino; 63 Asian, non-Hispanic/Latino; 164 Hispanic/Latino; 42 Two or more races, non-Hispanic/Latino), 19 international. Average age 24. 4,188 applicants, 28% accepted, 319 enrolled. In 2013, 50 master's, 373 doctorates awarded. *Entrance requirements:* For doctorate, LSAT, minimum GPA of 2.2. *Application deadline:* For fall admission, 11/1 for domestic students; for spring admission, 3/1 for domestic students. Application fee: $70. Electronic applications accepted. *Expenses:* Contact institution. *Financial support:* In 2013–14, 792 students received support, including 5 fellowships (averaging $54,896 per year), 200 research assistantships (averaging $23,379 per year), 36 teaching assistantships (averaging $20,000 per year); career-related internships or fieldwork, scholarships/grants, and tuition waivers (full) also available. Financial award application deadline: 3/15; financial award applicants required to submit FAFSA. *Faculty research:* Constitutional law, corporate law, environmental law, employment and labor law, intellectual property law. *Unit head:* Ward Farnsworth, Dean, 512-232-1120, Fax: 512-471-6987, E-mail: wfarnsworth@law.utexas.edu. *Application contact:* School of Law Admissions, 512-232-1200, Fax: 512-471-2765, E-mail: admissions@law.utexas.edu.
Website: http://www.utexas.edu/law/.

The University of Texas at Dallas, School of Economic, Political and Policy Sciences, Program in Political Science, Richardson, TX 75080. Offers Constitutional law (MA); legislative studies (MA); political science (MA, PhD). Part-time and evening/weekend programs available. *Faculty:* 12 full-time (2 women). *Students:* 31 full-time (13 women), 15 part-time (7 women); includes 12 minority (5 Black or African American, non-Hispanic/Latino; 1 American Indian or Alaska Native, non-Hispanic/Latino; 3 Asian, non-Hispanic/Latino; 2 Hispanic/Latino; 1 Two or more races, non-Hispanic/Latino), 6 international. Average age 31. 57 applicants, 47% accepted, 15 enrolled. In 2013, 15 master's, 4 doctorates awarded. Terminal master's awarded for partial completion of doctoral program. *Degree requirements:* For master's, thesis optional, independent study; for doctorate, thesis/dissertation, practicum research. *Entrance requirements:* For master's, GRE (minimum combined verbal and quantitative score of 1100), minimum undergraduate GPA of 3.0; for doctorate, GRE (minimum combined verbal and quantitative score of 1200, writing 4.5), minimum undergraduate GPA of 3.2. Additional exam requirements/recommendations for international students: Required—TOEFL (minimum score 550 paper-based). *Application deadline:* For fall admission, 7/15 for domestic students, 5/1 priority date for international students; for spring admission, 11/15 for domestic students, 9/1 priority date for international students. Applications are processed on a rolling basis. Application fee: $50 ($100 for international students). Electronic applications accepted. *Expenses:* Tuition, state resident: full-time $11,940; part-time $663.33 per credit hour. Tuition, nonresident: full-time $21,606; part-time $1200.33 per credit hour. *Financial support:* In 2013–14, 36 students received support, including 2 research assistantships with partial tuition reimbursements available (averaging $16,800 per year), 16 teaching assistantships with partial tuition reimbursements available (averaging $12,050 per year); career-related internships or fieldwork, Federal Work-Study, institutionally sponsored loans, and scholarships/grants also available. Support available to part-time students. Financial award application deadline: 4/30; financial award applicants required to submit FAFSA. *Faculty research:* Terrorism and democratic stability, redistricting and representation, trust and social exchange, how economic ideas impact political thought and public policy. *Unit head:* Dr. Robert C. Lowry, Program Head, 972-883-6720, Fax: 972-883-2735, E-mail: robert.lowry@utdallas.edu. *Application contact:* Cheryl Berry, Graduate Program Administrator, 972-883-2932, Fax: 972-883-2735, E-mail: politicalscience@utdallas.edu.
Website: http://www.utdallas.edu/epps/political-science/.

University of the District of Columbia, David A. Clarke School of Law, Washington, DC 20008. Offers clinical teaching and social justice (LL M); law (JD). *Accreditation:* ABA. Part-time and evening/weekend programs available. *Degree requirements:* For doctorate, 90 credits, advanced legal writing. *Entrance requirements:* For doctorate, LSAT. Additional exam requirements/recommendations for international students: Recommended—TOEFL. Electronic applications accepted. *Expenses:* Contact institution. *Faculty research:* HIV law, juvenile law, legislative law, community development, small business, immigration and human rights.

University of the Pacific, McGeorge School of Law, Sacramento, CA 95817. Offers advocacy (JD); criminal justice (JD); experiential law teaching (LL M); intellectual property (JD); international legal studies (JD); international water resources law (LL M, JSD); law (JD); public law and policy (JD); public policy and law (LL M); tax (JD); transnational business practice (LL M); U.S. law and policy (LL M), including public law and policy, U.S. law; water resources law (LL M), including international law, U.S. law; JD/MBA; JD/MPPA. *Accreditation:* ABA. Part-time and evening/weekend programs available. *Faculty:* 38 full-time (16 women), 32 part-time/adjunct (8 women). *Students:* 486 full-time (242 women), 179 part-time (79 women); includes 215 minority (17 Black or African American, non-Hispanic/Latino; 14 American Indian or Alaska Native, non-Hispanic/Latino; 108 Asian, non-Hispanic/Latino; 75 Hispanic/Latino; 1 Two or more races, non-Hispanic/Latino), 17 international. Average age 28. 1,558 applicants, 65% accepted, 162 enrolled. In 2013, 37 master's, 308 doctorates awarded. *Degree requirements:* For master's, thesis (for some programs); for doctorate, thesis/dissertation (for some programs). *Entrance requirements:* For master's, JD; for doctorate, LSAT (for JD), LL M (for JSD). Additional exam requirements/recommendations for international students: Required—TOEFL (minimum score 600 paper-based; 100 iBT). *Application deadline:* For fall admission, 3/15 priority date for domestic students. Applications are processed on a rolling basis. Application fee: $50. Electronic applications accepted. *Expenses:* Contact institution. *Financial support:* Fellowships, research assistantships, teaching assistantships, career-related internships or fieldwork, Federal Work-Study, institutionally sponsored loans, and scholarships/grants available. Support available to part-time students. Financial award applicants required to submit FAFSA. *Faculty research:* International legal studies, public policy and law, advocacy, intellectual property law, taxation, criminal law. *Unit head:* Francis Jay Mootz, III, Dean, 916-739-7151, E-mail: jmootz@pacific.edu. *Application contact:* 916-739-7105, Fax: 916-739-7301, E-mail: mcgeorge@pacific.edu.
Website: http://www.mcgeorge.edu/.

The University of Toledo, College of Law, Toledo, OH 43606. Offers JD, JD/MACJ, JD/MBA, JD/MD, JD/MPA, JD/MSE. *Accreditation:* ABA. Part-time and evening/weekend programs available. *Faculty:* 27 full-time (12 women), 18 part-time/adjunct (4 women). *Students:* 284 full-time (107 women), 78 part-time (34 women); includes 55 minority (23 Black or African American, non-Hispanic/Latino; 2 American Indian or Alaska Native, non-Hispanic/Latino; 11 Asian, non-Hispanic/Latino; 9 Hispanic/Latino; 10 Two or more races, non-Hispanic/Latino), 2 international. Average age 27. 749 applicants, 59% accepted, 108 enrolled. In 2013, 123 doctorates awarded. *Degree requirements:* For doctorate, 89 credits (mix of required and elective courses). *Entrance requirements:* For doctorate, LSAT, bachelor's degree. Additional exam requirements/recommendations for international students: Recommended—TOEFL (minimum score 600 paper-based; 100 iBT). *Application deadline:* For fall admission, 7/31 priority date for domestic students, 7/31 for international students. Applications are processed on a rolling basis. Application fee: $0. Electronic applications accepted. Application fee is waived when completed online. *Expenses:* Contact institution. *Financial support:* In 2013–14, 176 students received support, including 12 research assistantships (averaging $622 per year), 23 teaching assistantships; career-related internships or fieldwork, Federal Work-Study, and scholarships/grants also available. Support available to part-time students. Financial award application deadline: 8/1; financial award applicants required to submit FAFSA. *Faculty research:* Generation skipping transfer tax; land reform in Guatemala; international securities regulation; preemption doctrine in health reform jurisprudence; appellate jurisdiction over non-final decisions; sentencing, reasonableness/review/purpose; lender misconduct in bankruptcy cases; Constitutional history, ex post facto clause. *Total annual research expenditures:* $104,000. *Unit head:* Daniel J. Steinbock, Dean, 419-530-2379, Fax: 419-530-4526, E-mail: daniel.steinbock@utoledo.edu. *Application contact:* Brian Miller, Assistant Dean of Law Admissions, 419-530-4131, Fax: 419-530-4345, E-mail: law.admissions@utoledo.edu.
Website: http://www.utoledo.edu/law/.

University of Toronto, School of Graduate Studies, Faculty of Law and School of Graduate Studies, Graduate Programs in Law, Toronto, ON M5S 1A1, Canada. Offers LL M, MSL, SJD. *Degree requirements:* For master's, thesis (for some programs); for doctorate, thesis/dissertation. *Entrance requirements:* Additional exam requirements/recommendations for international students: Required—TOEFL (minimum score 600 paper-based; 100 iBT), TWE (minimum score 5). Electronic applications accepted.

University of Toronto, School of Graduate Studies, Faculty of Law, Professional Program in Law, Toronto, ON M5S 1A1, Canada. Offers JD, JD/Certificate, JD/MA, JD/MBA, JD/MI, JD/MSW, JD/PhD. *Entrance requirements:* For doctorate, LSAT. *Expenses:* Contact institution.

The University of Tulsa, College of Law, Tulsa, OK 74104. Offers American Indian and indigenous law (LL M); American law for foreign lawyers (LL M); energy and natural resources law (LL M); energy law (MJ); health law (Certificate); Indian law (MJ); law (JD); Native American law (Certificate); resources, energy, and environmental law (Certificate); JD/M Tax; JD/MA; JD/MBA; JD/MS. *Accreditation:* ABA. Part-time programs available. Postbaccalaureate distance learning degree programs offered (no

on-campus study). *Faculty:* 27 full-time (12 women), 17 part-time/adjunct (6 women). *Students:* 278 full-time (132 women), 89 part-time (45 women); includes 114 minority (20 Black or African American, non-Hispanic/Latino; 63 American Indian or Alaska Native, non-Hispanic/Latino; 4 Asian, non-Hispanic/Latino; 9 Hispanic/Latino; 18 Two or more races, non-Hispanic/Latino), 5 international. Average age 28. 1,226 applicants, 37% accepted, 83 enrolled. In 2013, 4 master's, 1 doctorate awarded. *Degree requirements:* For master's, thesis optional. *Entrance requirements:* For master's, JD from an ABA-approved U.S. law school or a JD equivalent from non-U.S. university; for doctorate, LSAT, BS or BA from 4-year regionally-accredited college/university; for Certificate, BS or BA from 4-year regionally-accredited college/university. Additional exam requirements/recommendations for international students: Required—TOEFL (minimum score 570 paper-based; 90 iBT), IELTS (minimum score 6.5). *Application deadline:* For fall admission, 2/1 priority date for domestic and international students; for spring admission, 12/5 priority date for domestic and international students. Applications are processed on a rolling basis. Application fee: $30. Electronic applications accepted. *Expenses:* Contact institution. *Financial support:* In 2013–14, 196 students received support. Career-related internships or fieldwork, Federal Work-Study, and scholarships/grants available. Support available to part-time students. Financial award application deadline: 8/1; financial award applicants required to submit FAFSA. *Faculty research:* International law, Native American law, criminal law, commercial speech, copyright law. *Unit head:* Janet Levit, Dean, 918-631-2400, Fax: 918-631-3126, E-mail: janet-levit@utulsa.edu. *Application contact:* April M. Fox, Assistant Dean of Admissions and Financial Aid, 918-631-2406, Fax: 918-631-3630, E-mail: april-fox@utulsa.edu.
Website: http://www.utulsa.edu/law/.

University of Utah, S. J. Quinney College of Law, Salt Lake City, UT 84112-0730. Offers LL M, JD, JD/MBA, JD/MPA, JD/MPP, JD/MSW. *Accreditation:* ABA. *Faculty:* 29 full-time (11 women), 25 part-time/adjunct (7 women). *Students:* 360 full-time (139 women), 4 part-time (1 woman); includes 28 minority (2 Black or African American, non-Hispanic/Latino; 2 American Indian or Alaska Native, non-Hispanic/Latino; 8 Asian, non-Hispanic/Latino; 15 Hispanic/Latino; 1 Native Hawaiian or other Pacific Islander, non-Hispanic/Latino), 3 international. Average age 29. 716 applicants, 45% accepted, 142 enrolled. In 2013, 1 master's, 146 doctorates awarded. *Entrance requirements:* For doctorate, LSAT, bachelor's degree from accredited college/university. Additional exam requirements/recommendations for international students: Required—TOEFL (minimum score 600 paper-based; 100 iBT). *Application deadline:* For fall admission, 2/15 for domestic and international students. Applications are processed on a rolling basis. Application fee: $60. Electronic applications accepted. *Expenses:* Contact institution. *Financial support:* In 2013–14, 213 students received support, including 167 fellowships with full and partial tuition reimbursements available (averaging $3,837 per year), 20 research assistantships with partial tuition reimbursements available (averaging $6,525 per year); career-related internships or fieldwork, Federal Work-Study, institutionally sponsored loans, and scholarships/grants also available. Financial award application deadline: 4/1; financial award applicants required to submit FAFSA. *Faculty research:* Environmental law, intellectual property, international law, criminal law, business law. *Total annual research expenditures:* $743,903. *Unit head:* Reyes Aguilar, Associate Dean of Admissions and Financial Aid, 801-581-6833, Fax: 801-581-6897, E-mail: reyes.aguilar@utah.edu. *Application contact:* Susan Baca, Operations Manager for Admissions and Financial Aid, 801-581-7479, Fax: 801-581-6897, E-mail: susan.baca@law.utah.edu.
Website: http://www.law.utah.edu.

University of Victoria, Faculty of Law, Victoria, BC V8W 2Y2, Canada. Offers LL M, JD, PhD, MBA/JD, MPA/JD. Part-time programs available. *Degree requirements:* For master's, thesis; for doctorate, thesis/dissertation (for some programs), major research paper (for JD). *Entrance requirements:* For master's, LL B or JD; for doctorate, LSAT (for JD), LL B or JD (for PhD); minimum 3 years of full-time study or part-time equivalent leading toward a bachelor's degree (for JD). Additional exam requirements/recommendations for international students: Required—TOEFL (minimum score 600 paper-based; 100 iBT). Electronic applications accepted. *Expenses:* Contact institution. *Faculty research:* Environmental law and policy, international law, alternative dispute resolution, intellectual property law, Aboriginal law.

University of Virginia, School of Law, Charlottesville, VA 22903-1789. Offers LL M, JD, SJD, JD/MA, JD/MBA, JD/MP, JD/MPH, JD/MS, JD/MUEP. JD/MA in international relations offered jointly with The Johns Hopkins University. *Accreditation:* ABA. *Faculty:* 80 full-time (24 women), 5 part-time/adjunct (2 women). *Students:* 1,117 full-time (482 women); includes 227 minority (61 Black or African American, non-Hispanic/Latino; 1 American Indian or Alaska Native, non-Hispanic/Latino; 89 Asian, non-Hispanic/Latino; 42 Hispanic/Latino; 34 Two or more races, non-Hispanic/Latino), 70 international. Average age 25. 6,529 applicants, 20% accepted, 404 enrolled. In 2013, 43 master's, 366 doctorates awarded. *Degree requirements:* For doctorate, thesis/dissertation (for some programs), oral exam (for SJD). *Entrance requirements:* For master's, 2 letters of recommendation; personal statement; for doctorate, LSAT (for JD). Additional exam requirements/recommendations for international students: Required—TOEFL. *Application deadline:* For fall admission, 3/1 priority date for domestic students, 3/2 for international students. Applications are processed on a rolling basis. Application fee: $75. Electronic applications accepted. *Expenses:* Contact institution. *Financial support:* Fellowships, career-related internships or fieldwork, Federal Work-Study, and institutionally sponsored loans available. Financial award application deadline: 3/1; financial award applicants required to submit FAFSA. *Unit head:* Paul G. Mahoney, Jr., Dean, 434-924-7351, Fax: 434-982-2128, E-mail: lawadmit@virginia.edu. *Application contact:* Anne M. Richard, Senior Assistant Dean for Admissions, 434-243-1456, Fax: 434-982-2128, E-mail: lawadmit@virginia.edu.
Website: http://www.law.virginia.edu/.

University of Washington, Graduate School, School of Law, Seattle, WA 98195-3020. Offers Asian law (LL M, PhD); intellectual property law and policy (LL M); law (JD); law of sustainable international development (LL M); taxation (LL M); JD/LL M; JD/MA; JD/MAIS; JD/MBA; JD/MPA; JD/MS; JD/PhD. *Accreditation:* ABA. *Degree requirements:* For master's, thesis; for doctorate, thesis/dissertation (for some programs). *Entrance requirements:* For master's, language proficiency (LL M in Asian law); for doctorate, LSAT (for JD). Additional exam requirements/recommendations for international students: Required—TOEFL. *Expenses:* Contact institution. *Faculty research:* Asian, international and comparative law, intellectual property law, health law, environmental law, taxation.

The University of Western Ontario, Faculty of Law, London, ON N6A 5B8, Canada. Offers LL M, MLS, JD, Diploma. *Entrance requirements:* For master's, B+ average in BA, sample of legal academic writing; for doctorate, LSAT. Additional exam requirements/recommendations for international students: Required—TOEFL. *Expenses:* Contact institution. *Faculty research:* Taxation, administrative law, torts, drug and alcohol law and policy, property.

University of Wisconsin–Madison, Law School, Madison, WI 53706-1399. Offers LL M, JD, SJD. *Accreditation:* ABA. Part-time programs available. *Faculty:* 70 full-time (38 women), 52 part-time/adjunct (18 women). *Students:* 699 full-time (306 women), 50 part-time (16 women); includes 135 minority (35 Black or African American, non-Hispanic/Latino; 9 American Indian or Alaska Native, non-Hispanic/Latino; 24 Asian, non-Hispanic/Latino; 42 Hispanic/Latino; 3 Native Hawaiian or other Pacific Islander, non-Hispanic/Latino; 22 Two or more races, non-Hispanic/Latino), 113 international. Average age 26. 1,653 applicants, 45% accepted, 237 enrolled. In 2013, 49 master's, 258 doctorates awarded. *Degree requirements:* For master's, thesis (for some programs); for doctorate, thesis/dissertation (for some programs). *Entrance requirements:* For doctorate, LSAT (for JD). Additional exam requirements/recommendations for international students: Required—TOEFL. *Application deadline:* For fall admission, 4/1 for domestic students, 3/1 for international students. Applications are processed on a rolling basis. Application fee: $56. Electronic applications accepted. *Expenses:* Contact institution. *Financial support:* In 2013–14, 342 students received support, including 59 fellowships with partial tuition reimbursements available (averaging $15,644 per year), 4 research assistantships with full tuition reimbursements available (averaging $9,732 per year); career-related internships or fieldwork, Federal Work-Study, institutionally sponsored loans, scholarships/grants, health care benefits, tuition waivers (partial), and unspecified assistantships also available. Support available to part-time students. Financial award application deadline: 4/1; financial award applicants required to submit FAFSA. *Unit head:* Margaret Raymond, Dean, 608-262-0618, Fax: 608-262-5485. *Application contact:* Rebecca L. Scheller, Assistant Dean for Admissions and Financial Aid, 608-262-5914, Fax: 608-263-3190, E-mail: admissions@law.wisc.edu.
Website: http://www.law.wisc.edu/.

University of Wyoming, College of Law, Laramie, WY 82071. Offers JD, JD/MPA. *Accreditation:* ABA. *Entrance requirements:* For doctorate, LSAT. Additional exam requirements/recommendations for international students: Required—TOEFL. Electronic applications accepted. *Expenses:* Contact institution. *Faculty research:* Environmental, public land, constitutional, securities law, criminal law.

Valparaiso University, School of Law, Valparaiso, IN 46383-4945. Offers LL M, JD, JD/MA, JD/MALS, JD/MBA, JD/MS, JD/MSSA. *Accreditation:* ABA. Part-time programs available. *Faculty:* 44 full-time (18 women), 21 part-time/adjunct (9 women). *Students:* 501 full-time (253 women), 15 part-time (6 women); includes 188 minority (86 Black or African American, non-Hispanic/Latino; 4 American Indian or Alaska Native, non-Hispanic/Latino; 15 Asian, non-Hispanic/Latino; 67 Hispanic/Latino; 2 Native Hawaiian or other Pacific Islander, non-Hispanic/Latino; 14 Two or more races, non-Hispanic/Latino), 4 international. 1,188 applicants, 81% accepted, 208 enrolled. *Entrance requirements:* For doctorate, LSAT. Additional exam requirements/recommendations for international students: Required—TOEFL (minimum score 600 paper-based; 95 iBT), IELTS (minimum score 7), completion of approved English Program, or LSAT. *Application deadline:* For fall admission, 6/1 priority date for domestic students. Applications are processed on a rolling basis. Application fee: $0. Electronic applications accepted. *Expenses:* Contact institution. *Financial support:* In 2013–14, 171 students received support, including 7 fellowships (averaging $2,400 per year), 22 research assistantships, 18 teaching assistantships (averaging $2,400 per year); career-related internships or fieldwork, Federal Work-Study, institutionally sponsored loans, scholarships/grants, and tuition waivers (partial) also available. Support available to part-time students. Financial award application deadline: 3/1; financial award applicants required to submit FAFSA. *Faculty research:* International law, jurisprudence, Constitutional law, animal law. *Total annual research expenditures:* $122,000. *Unit head:* Prof. Ivan Bodensteiner, Interim Dean, 219-465-7834, Fax: 219-465-7872, E-mail: ivan.bodensteiner@valpo.edu. *Application contact:* Adam Greathouse, Assistant Director of Admissions, 219-465-7821, Fax: 219-465-7975, E-mail: law.admissions@valpo.edu.
Website: http://www.valpo.edu/law/.

Vanderbilt University, Vanderbilt Law School, Nashville, TN 37203. Offers law (LL M, JD); law and economics (PhD); JD/M Div; JD/MA; JD/MBA; JD/MD; JD/MPP; JD/MTS; JD/PhD; LL M/MA. *Accreditation:* ABA. *Degree requirements:* For doctorate, comprehensive exam (for some programs), thesis/dissertation (for some programs), 72 hours of coursework and research (for PhD). *Entrance requirements:* For master's, foreign law degree; for doctorate, GRE (for PhD), LSAT, advanced undergraduate economics (for PhD). Additional exam requirements/recommendations for international students: Required—TOEFL. Electronic applications accepted. *Expenses:* Contact institution.

Vermont Law School, Graduate and Professional Programs, Professional Program, South Royalton, VT 05068-0096. Offers JD, JD/MELP. *Accreditation:* ABA. *Entrance requirements:* For doctorate, LSAT, LSDAS/registration, resume. Additional exam requirements/recommendations for international students: Required—TOEFL (minimum score 600 paper-based). Electronic applications accepted. *Expenses:* Contact institution. *Faculty research:* Environmental law, national security, law and medicine.

Villanova University, School of Law, Program in Law, Villanova, PA 19085-1699. Offers JD, JD/LL M, JD/MBA. *Faculty:* 54 full-time (28 women), 60 part-time/adjunct (18 women). *Students:* 594 full-time (291 women); includes 92 minority (17 Black or African American, non-Hispanic/Latino; 3 American Indian or Alaska Native, non-Hispanic/Latino; 26 Asian, non-Hispanic/Latino; 32 Hispanic/Latino; 1 Native Hawaiian or other Pacific Islander, non-Hispanic/Latino; 13 Two or more races, non-Hispanic/Latino), 2 international. 1,472 applicants, 55% accepted, 157 enrolled. In 2013, 245 doctorates awarded. *Entrance requirements:* For doctorate, LSAT. *Application deadline:* For fall admission, 4/1 for domestic and international students. Applications are processed on a rolling basis. Application fee: $75. Electronic applications accepted. *Expenses:* Contact institution. *Financial support:* In 2013–14, 389 students received support, including 29 research assistantships, 7 teaching assistantships; career-related internships or fieldwork, Federal Work-Study, and scholarships/grants also available. Financial award application deadline: 3/15; financial award applicants required to submit FAFSA. *Faculty research:* Business law; international law (public and private); tax law; criminal law, procedure, and sentencing; law and religion. *Unit head:* John Y. Gotanda, Dean/Professor of Law, 610-519-7007, Fax: 610-519-6472, E-mail: gotanda@law.villanova.edu. *Application contact:* Bayrex Marti, Executive Director, Admissions and Financial Aid, 610-519-7010, Fax: 610-519-6291, E-mail: admissions@law.villanova.edu.
Website: http://www.law.villanova.edu/.

Wake Forest University, School of Law, Winston-Salem, NC 27109. Offers LL M, JD, SJD, JD/M Div, JD/MA, JD/MBA. LL M for foreign law graduates in American law. *Accreditation:* ABA. *Entrance requirements:* For doctorate, LSAT (for JD). Additional exam requirements/recommendations for international students: Required—TOEFL. Electronic applications accepted. *Expenses:* Contact institution. *Faculty research:* Constitutional law, family law, land use planning, torts, taxation.

Walden University, Graduate Programs, School of Public Policy and Administration, Minneapolis, MN 55401. Offers criminal justice (MPA, MPP, MS, Graduate Certificate), including emergency management (MS, PhD), general program (MS, PhD), homeland security and policy coordination (MS, PhD), law and public policy (MS, PhD), policy analysis (MS, PhD), public management and leadership (MS, PhD), self-designed (MS), terrorism, mediation, and peace (MS, PhD); criminal justice leadership and executive management (MS), including emergency management (MS, PhD), general program (MS, PhD), homeland security and policy coordination (MS, PhD), law and public policy (MS, PhD), policy analysis (MS, PhD), public management and leadership (MS, PhD),

self-designed, terrorism, mediation, and peace (MS, PhD); emergency management (MPA, MPP, MS), including criminal justice (MS, PhD), general program (MS, PhD), homeland security (MS), public management and leadership (MS, PhD), terrorism and emergency management (MS); general program (MPA, MPP); government management (Graduate Certificate); health policy (MPA, MPP); homeland security (Graduate Certificate); homeland security and policy coordination (MPA, MPP); international nongovernmental organizations (MPA, MPP); law and public policy (MPA, MPP); local government management for sustainable communities (MPA, MPP); nonprofit management (Graduate Certificate); nonprofit management and leadership (MPA, MPP, MS); policy analysis (MPA); public management and leadership (MPA, MPP, Graduate Certificate); public policy (Graduate Certificate); public policy and administration (PhD), including criminal justice (MS, PhD), emergency management (MS, PhD), general program (MS, PhD), health policy, homeland security and policy coordination (MS, PhD), international nongovernmental organizations, law and public policy (MS, PhD), local government management for sustainable communities, nonprofit management and leadership, policy analysis (MS, PhD), public management and leadership (MS, PhD), terrorism, mediation, and peace (MS, PhD); strategic planning and public policy (Graduate Certificate); terrorism, mediation, and peace (MPA, MPP). Part-time and evening/weekend programs available. Postbaccalaureate distance learning degree programs offered (minimal on-campus study). *Faculty:* 10 full-time (4 women), 123 part-time/adjunct (55 women). *Students:* 1,029 full-time (640 women), 1,601 part-time (981 women); includes 1,579 minority (1,326 Black or African American, non-Hispanic/Latino; 18 American Indian or Alaska Native, non-Hispanic/Latino; 39 Asian, non-Hispanic/Latino; 127 Hispanic/Latino; 3 Native Hawaiian or other Pacific Islander, non-Hispanic/Latino; 66 Two or more races, non-Hispanic/Latino), 27 international. Average age 42. 566 applicants, 93% accepted, 412 enrolled. In 2013, 257 master's, 44 doctorates, 18 other advanced degrees awarded. *Degree requirements:* For doctorate, thesis/dissertation, residency. *Entrance requirements:* For master's, bachelor's degree or higher; minimum GPA of 2.5; official transcripts; goal statement (for some programs); access to computer and Internet; for doctorate, master's degree or higher; three years of related professional or academic experience (preferred); minimum GPA of 3.0; goal statement and current resume (select programs); official transcripts; access to computer and Internet; for Graduate Certificate, relevant work experience; access to computer and Internet. Additional exam requirements/recommendations for international students: Required—TOEFL (minimum score 550 paper-based; 79 iBT), IELTS (minimum score 6.5), Michigan English Language Assessment Battery (minimum score 82), or PTE. *Application deadline:* Applications are processed on a rolling basis. Application fee: $0. Electronic applications accepted. *Expenses: Tuition:* Full-time $11,813.55; part-time $500 per credit. *Required fees:* $618.76. *Financial support:* Fellowships, Federal Work-Study, scholarships/grants, unspecified assistantships, and family tuition reduction, active duty/veteran tuition reduction, group tuition reduction, interest-free payment plans, employee tuition reduction available. Support available to part-time students. Financial award applicants required to submit FAFSA. *Unit head:* Dr. Mark Gordon, Associate Dean, 800-925-3368. *Application contact:* Jennifer Hall, Vice President of Enrollment Management, 866-4-WALDEN, E-mail: info@waldenu.edu.
Website: http://www.waldenu.edu/programs/colleges-schools/public-policy-and-administration.

Washburn University, School of Law, Topeka, KS 66621. Offers global legal studies (LL M); law (MSL, JD). *Accreditation:* ABA. *Entrance requirements:* For doctorate, LSAT. Additional exam requirements/recommendations for international students: Recommended—TOEFL (minimum score 550 paper-based). *Application deadline:* For fall admission, 4/1 priority date for domestic and international students; for spring admission, 11/1 priority date for domestic and international students. Applications are processed on a rolling basis. Application fee: $40. Electronic applications accepted. Application fee is waived when completed online. *Expenses:* Contact institution. *Financial support:* Career-related internships or fieldwork and scholarships/grants available. Financial award applicants required to submit FAFSA. *Faculty research:* Constitutional law, family law, energy law, banking and securities law, oil and gas. *Unit head:* Thomas J. Romig, Dean, 785-670-1662, Fax: 785-670-3249, E-mail: thomas.romig@washburn.edu. *Application contact:* Yolanda Ingram, Director of Admissions, 785-670-1185, Fax: 785-670-1120, E-mail: yolanda.ingram@washburn.edu.
Website: http://washburnlaw.edu/.

Washington and Lee University, School of Law, Lexington, VA 24450. Offers law (JD); U.S. law (LL M). *Accreditation:* ABA. *Faculty:* 40 full-time (15 women), 42 part-time/adjunct (11 women). *Students:* 422 full-time (203 women); includes 71 minority (35 Black or African American, non-Hispanic/Latino; 15 Asian, non-Hispanic/Latino; 16 Hispanic/Latino; 5 Two or more races, non-Hispanic/Latino), 4 international. Average age 24. 2,409 applicants, 38% accepted, 111 enrolled. In 2013, 141 doctorates awarded. *Entrance requirements:* For doctorate, LSAT. Additional exam requirements/recommendations for international students: Required—TOEFL (minimum score 600 paper-based; 100 iBT). *Application deadline:* For fall admission, 3/1 priority date for domestic and international students. Applications are processed on a rolling basis. Application fee: $0. Electronic applications accepted. *Expenses: Tuition:* Full-time $43,570. *Required fees:* $1157. *Financial support:* In 2013–14, 396 students received support. Fellowships, research assistantships, career-related internships or fieldwork, Federal Work-Study, institutionally sponsored loans, and scholarships/grants available. Financial award application deadline: 2/15; financial award applicants required to submit FAFSA. *Faculty research:* Criminal law, corporate law, experiential education, international and comparative law, public interest law. *Unit head:* Nora V. Demleitner, Dean, 540-458-8502, Fax: 540-458-8488, E-mail: demleitnern@wlu.edu. *Application contact:* Shawn McShay, Assistant Dean of Admissions, 540-458-8503, Fax: 540-458-8586, E-mail: mcshays@wlu.edu.
Website: http://law.wlu.edu/.

Washington University in St. Louis, School of Law, St. Louis, MO 63130-4899. Offers LL M, MJS, JD, JSD, JD/MA, JD/MBA, JD/MHA, JD/MS, JD/MSW, JD/PhD. *Accreditation:* ABA. *Entrance requirements:* For doctorate, LSAT (for JD). Electronic applications accepted. *Expenses:* Contact institution. *Faculty research:* International law, environmental law, employment discrimination, reproductive rights, bankruptcy and white-collar crime.

Wayne State University, Law School, Detroit, MI 48202. Offers corporate and finance law (LL M); labor and employment law (LL M); law (JD); taxation (LL M); United States law (LL M); JD/MA; JD/MADR; JD/MBA. *Accreditation:* ABA. Part-time and evening/weekend programs available. *Faculty:* 35 full-time (16 women), 21 part-time/adjunct (7 women). *Students:* 418 full-time (178 women), 82 part-time (48 women); includes 75 minority (40 Black or African American, non-Hispanic/Latino; 3 American Indian or Alaska Native, non-Hispanic/Latino; 18 Asian, non-Hispanic/Latino; 11 Hispanic/Latino; 3 Two or more races, non-Hispanic/Latino), 13 international. Average age 27. 807 applicants, 48% accepted, 139 enrolled. In 2013, 2 master's, 172 doctorates awarded. *Degree requirements:* For master's, essay. *Entrance requirements:* For master's, admission to the Graduate School, JD from ABA-accredited institution and member institution of the AALS; for doctorate, LSAT, LDAS report, bachelor's degree from accredited institution, personal statement, transcripts from all U.S. undergraduate schools attended and an analysis and summary of the transcripts; letter of recommendation (up to two are accepted). Additional exam requirements/recommendations for international students: Required—TOEFL (minimum score 600 paper-based), Michigan English Language Assessment Battery (minimum score 85); Recommended—IELTS (minimum score 6.5). *Application deadline:* For fall admission, 5/15 for domestic and international students. Application fee: $0. Electronic applications accepted. *Expenses:* Contact institution. *Financial support:* Scholarships/grants available. Support available to part-time students. Financial award application deadline: 3/31; financial award applicants required to submit FAFSA. *Faculty research:* Public interest law, tax law, international law, environmental law, health law. *Unit head:* Jocelyn Benson, Dean, 313-577-3933. *Application contact:* Marcia McDonald, Director of Admissions, 313-577-3937, Fax: 313-993-8129, E-mail: marcia.mcdonald2@wayne.edu.
Website: http://law.wayne.edu/.

Wayne State University, School of Library and Information Science, Detroit, MI 48202. Offers academic libraries (MLIS); archival administration (MLIS, Certificate); general librarianship (MLIS); health sciences librarianship (MLIS); information management for librarians (Certificate); information science (MLIS); law librarianship (MLIS); library and information science (Spec); organization of information (MLIS); public libraries (MLIS); public library services to children and young adults (MLIS, Certificate); records management (MLIS); references services (MLIS); school library media specialist endorsement (MLIS); special libraries (MLIS); urban libraries (MLIS); MLIS/MA. *Accreditation:* ALA (one or more programs are accredited). Part-time and evening/weekend programs available. Postbaccalaureate distance learning degree programs offered (no on-campus study). *Faculty:* 13 full-time (9 women), 17 part-time/adjunct (13 women). *Students:* 112 full-time (80 women), 372 part-time (296 women); includes 65 minority (26 Black or African American, non-Hispanic/Latino; 11 Asian, non-Hispanic/Latino; 18 Hispanic/Latino; 10 Two or more races, non-Hispanic/Latino), 2 international. Average age 33. 275 applicants, 61% accepted, 109 enrolled. In 2013, 179 master's, 42 other advanced degrees awarded. *Entrance requirements:* For master's and other advanced degree, GRE or MAT (if undergraduate GPA is between 2.5 and 2.99), minimum undergraduate GPA of 3.0 or graduate degree, personal statement, resume or curriculum vitae. Additional exam requirements/recommendations for international students: Required—TOEFL (minimum score 550 paper-based; 79 iBT); Recommended—IELTS (minimum score 6.5), TWE (minimum score 5.5). *Application deadline:* For fall admission, 7/1 for domestic students, 5/1 priority date for international students; for winter admission, 10/1 for domestic students, 9/1 priority date for international students; for spring admission, 3/15 for domestic students, 1/1 priority date for international students. Applications are processed on a rolling basis. Application fee: $0. Electronic applications accepted. *Expenses:* Contact institution. *Financial support:* In 2013–14, 65 students received support. Fellowships with tuition reimbursements available, research assistantships with tuition reimbursements available, institutionally sponsored loans, scholarships/grants, and unspecified assistantships available. Support available to part-time students. Financial award application deadline: 3/31; financial award applicants required to submit FAFSA. *Faculty research:* Library services, information management issues, digital content management, library/community engagement, archives and preservation. *Unit head:* Dr. Stephen Bajjaly, Associate Dean and Professor, 313-577-0350, Fax: 313-577-7563, E-mail: bajjaly@wayne.edu. *Application contact:* Matthew Fredericks, Academic Services Officer I, 313-577-2446, Fax: 313-577-7563, E-mail: mfredericks@wayne.edu.
Website: http://slis.wayne.edu/.

Western New England University, School of Law, Springfield, MA 01119. Offers estate planning/elder law (LL M); law (JD). *Accreditation:* ABA. Part-time and evening/weekend programs available. *Faculty:* 27 full-time (14 women). *Students:* 234 full-time (119 women), 174 part-time (96 women); includes 77 minority (36 Black or African American, non-Hispanic/Latino; 6 American Indian or Alaska Native, non-Hispanic/Latino; 11 Asian, non-Hispanic/Latino; 22 Hispanic/Latino; 2 Native Hawaiian or other Pacific Islander, non-Hispanic/Latino). Average age 29. 719 applicants, 83% accepted, 120 enrolled. In 2013, 24 master's, 135 doctorates awarded. *Entrance requirements:* For master's, official law school transcript, resume; for doctorate, LSAT, two letters of recommendation, personal statement. *Application deadline:* For fall admission, 3/15 priority date for domestic students. Applications are processed on a rolling basis. Application fee: $50. Electronic applications accepted. *Expenses:* Contact institution. *Financial support:* Career-related internships or fieldwork, Federal Work-Study, institutionally sponsored loans, and scholarships/grants available. Support available to part-time students. Financial award application deadline: 4/15; financial award applicants required to submit FAFSA. *Unit head:* Eric Gouvin, Dean/Professor, 413-796-2031, E-mail: eric.gouvin@law.wne.edu. *Application contact:* Michael A. Johnson, Associate Dean for Law Student Affairs and Enroll Plan, 413-782-1406, Fax: 413-796-2067, E-mail: admissions@law.wne.edu.
Website: http://www.law.wne.edu/.

Western State College of Law at Argosy University, Professional Program, Fullerton, CA 92831-3000. Offers JD. *Accreditation:* ABA. Part-time and evening/weekend programs available. *Faculty:* 28 full-time (15 women), 33 part-time/adjunct (10 women). *Students:* 280 full-time (143 women), 151 part-time (79 women); includes 188 minority (28 Black or African American, non-Hispanic/Latino; 6 American Indian or Alaska Native, non-Hispanic/Latino; 64 Asian, non-Hispanic/Latino; 89 Hispanic/Latino; 1 Two or more races, non-Hispanic/Latino), 5 international. Average age 28. 1,020 applicants, 57% accepted, 103 enrolled. In 2013, 122 doctorates awarded. *Entrance requirements:* For doctorate, LSAT, 2 letters of recommendation. Additional exam requirements/recommendations for international students: Required—TOEFL (minimum score 550 paper-based; 80 iBT). *Application deadline:* For fall admission, 6/1 for domestic and international students; for spring admission, 12/1 for domestic and international students. Applications are processed on a rolling basis. Application fee: $60. Electronic applications accepted. *Expenses: Tuition:* Full-time $40,400; part-time $13,500 per term. *Required fees:* $245 per term. *Financial support:* In 2013–14, 8 fellowships (averaging $5,400 per year) were awarded; career-related internships or fieldwork, Federal Work-Study, and scholarships/grants also available. Support available to part-time students. Financial award application deadline: 9/15; financial award applicants required to submit FAFSA. *Faculty research:* Criminal law and practice, entrepreneurship, teaching effectiveness and student success, learning theory and legal education. *Application contact:* Gloria Switzer, Assistant Dean of Admission, 714-459-1101, Fax: 714-441-1748, E-mail: adm@wsulaw.edu.
Website: http://www.wsulaw.edu/.

West Virginia University, College of Law, Morgantown, WV 26506-6130. Offers JD, JD/MBA, JD/MPA. *Accreditation:* ABA. Part-time programs available. *Entrance requirements:* For doctorate, LSAT. Additional exam requirements/recommendations for international students: Required—TOEFL. Electronic applications accepted. *Expenses:* Contact institution. *Faculty research:* Constitutional law, public interest law, corporate law, environment and natural resources innocence project, professional skills, leadership, intellectual property, entrepreneurship, labor, sustainable development, family law, IR human rights, immigration.

Whittier College, Whittier Law School, Costa Mesa, CA 92626. Offers law (JD). *Accreditation:* ABA. Part-time and evening/weekend programs available. *Faculty:* 26 full-

time (12 women), 17 part-time/adjunct (8 women). *Students:* 169 full-time (85 women), 52 part-time (32 women); includes 189 minority (9 Black or African American, non-Hispanic/Latino; 79 Asian, non-Hispanic/Latino; 46 Hispanic/Latino; 26 Native Hawaiian or other Pacific Islander, non-Hispanic/Latino; 29 Two or more races, non-Hispanic/Latino), 2 international. Average age 28. 1,520 applicants, 46% accepted, 140 enrolled. *Entrance requirements:* For doctorate, LSAT. Additional exam requirements/recommendations for international students: Required—TOEFL (minimum score 600 paper-based). *Application deadline:* For fall admission, 6/1 priority date for domestic students, 3/15 priority date for international students; for spring admission, 11/1 priority date for domestic and international students. Applications are processed on a rolling basis. Application fee: $50. Electronic applications accepted. *Expenses:* Contact institution. *Financial support:* In 2013–14, 313 students received support. Federal Work-Study, scholarships/grants, and unspecified assistantships available. Financial award application deadline: 5/1; financial award applicants required to submit FAFSA. *Faculty research:* Intellectual property, international law, health law, children's rights. *Total annual research expenditures:* $164,629. *Unit head:* Penelope Bryan, Dean, 714-444-4141 Ext. 111, Fax: 714-444-0855. *Application contact:* Tom McColl, Director of Admissions, 714-444-4141 Ext. 123, Fax: 714-444-0250.
Website: http://www.law.whittier.edu/.

Widener University, School of Human Service Professions, Institute for Graduate Clinical Psychology, Law-Psychology Program, Chester, PA 19013-5792. Offers JD/Psy D. *Faculty:* 15 full-time (6 women), 18 part-time/adjunct (10 women). *Students:* 1 full-time (0 women), 1 (woman) part-time. Average age 23. 21 applicants, 19% accepted. *Application deadline:* For fall admission, 2/1 for domestic students. Applications are processed on a rolling basis. Application fee: $60. Electronic applications accepted. *Expenses:* Tuition: Full-time $30,000; part-time $950 per credit. *Financial support:* In 2013–14, 12 students received support. Research assistantships, career-related internships or fieldwork, Federal Work-Study, institutionally sponsored loans, and scholarships/grants available. Financial award application deadline: 5/31. *Unit head:* Dr. Amiram Elwork, Director, 610-499-1206, Fax: 610-499-4625, E-mail: amiram.elwork@widener.edu. *Application contact:* Maureen A. Brennan, Admissions Coordinator, 610-499-1206, Fax: 610-499-4625, E-mail: maureen.a.brennan@widener.edu.

Widener University, School of Law at Harrisburg, Harrisburg, PA 17106-9381. Offers JD. *Accreditation:* ABA. Part-time programs available. *Faculty:* 26 full-time (12 women), 18 part-time/adjunct (6 women). *Students:* 286 full-time (133 women), 2 part-time (1 woman); includes 46 minority (16 Black or African American, non-Hispanic/Latino; 4 American Indian or Alaska Native, non-Hispanic/Latino; 8 Asian, non-Hispanic/Latino; 17 Hispanic/Latino; 1 Two or more races, non-Hispanic/Latino). Average age 25. *Entrance requirements:* For doctorate, LSAT. *Application deadline:* For fall admission, 5/15 for domestic students. Applications are processed on a rolling basis. Application fee: $60. Electronic applications accepted. *Expenses:* Contact institution. *Financial support:* Fellowships, research assistantships, career-related internships or fieldwork, Federal Work-Study, institutionally sponsored loans, and scholarships/grants available. Support available to part-time students. Financial award application deadline: 2/15; financial award applicants required to submit FAFSA. *Faculty research:* Health law, toxic torts, Constitutional law, intellectual property, corporate law. *Unit head:* Linda L. Ammons, Dean, 302-477-2100, Fax: 302-477-2282, E-mail: llammons@widener.edu. *Application contact:* Barbara L. Ayars, Assistant Dean of Admissions, 302-477-2210, Fax: 302-477-2224, E-mail: barbara.l.ayars@law.widener.edu.
Website: http://www.law.widener.edu/.

Widener University, School of Law at Wilmington, Wilmington, DE 19803-0474. Offers corporate law and finance (LL M); health law (LL M, MJ, D Law); juridical science (SJD); law (JD). *Accreditation:* ABA. Part-time programs available. *Faculty:* 58 full-time (23 women), 42 part-time/adjunct (15 women). *Students:* 692 full-time (313 women), 103 part-time (72 women); includes 174 minority (94 Black or African American, non-Hispanic/Latino; 10 American Indian or Alaska Native, non-Hispanic/Latino; 26 Asian, non-Hispanic/Latino; 34 Hispanic/Latino; 10 Two or more races, non-Hispanic/Latino), 10 international. Average age 26. 2,376 applicants, 39% accepted, 351 enrolled. In 2013, 28 master's, 269 doctorates awarded. *Degree requirements:* For doctorate, thesis/dissertation (for some programs). *Entrance requirements:* For master's, GMAT. *Application deadline:* For fall admission, 5/15 for domestic students; for spring admission, 12/1 for domestic students. Applications are processed on a rolling basis. Application fee: $60. *Expenses:* Tuition: Full-time $30,000; part-time $950 per credit. *Financial support:* Career-related internships or fieldwork, Federal Work-Study, institutionally sponsored loans, and scholarships/grants available. Support available to part-time students. Financial award application deadline: 2/15; financial award applicants required to submit FAFSA. *Unit head:* Linda L. Ammons, Dean, 302-477-2100, Fax: 302-477-2282, E-mail: llammons@widener.edu. *Application contact:* Barbara L. Ayars, Assistant Dean of Admissions, 302-477-2210, Fax: 302-477-2224, E-mail: barbara.l.ayars@law.widener.edu.
Website: http://law.widener.edu/.

Willamette University, College of Law, Salem, OR 97301-3922. Offers LL M, JD, JD/MBA. *Accreditation:* ABA. Part-time programs available. *Degree requirements:* For master's, thesis; for doctorate, thesis/dissertation. *Entrance requirements:* For

doctorate, LSAT. Additional exam requirements/recommendations for international students: Required—TOEFL (minimum score 600 paper-based; 100 iBT); Recommended—IELTS (minimum score 7.5). Electronic applications accepted. Application fee is waived when completed online. *Expenses:* Contact institution. *Faculty research:* Dispute resolution, international law, business law, law and government, sustainability.

William Mitchell College of Law, Professional Program, St. Paul, MN 55105-3076. Offers LL M, JD. *Accreditation:* ABA. Part-time and evening/weekend programs available. *Faculty:* 34 full-time (15 women), 187 part-time/adjunct (84 women). *Students:* 553 full-time (282 women), 260 part-time (132 women); includes 117 minority (26 Black or African American, non-Hispanic/Latino; 5 American Indian or Alaska Native, non-Hispanic/Latino; 36 Asian, non-Hispanic/Latino; 21 Hispanic/Latino; 2 Native Hawaiian or other Pacific Islander, non-Hispanic/Latino; 27 Two or more races, non-Hispanic/Latino), 9 international. Average age 28. 885 applicants, 71% accepted, 236 enrolled. In 2013, 325 doctorates awarded. *Entrance requirements:* For doctorate, LSAT. Additional exam requirements/recommendations for international students: Required—TOEFL (minimum score 100 iBT). *Application deadline:* For fall admission, 8/1 for domestic and international students; for spring admission, 12/1 for domestic and international students. Applications are processed on a rolling basis. Application fee: $0. Electronic applications accepted. *Expenses:* Tuition: Full-time $37,320; part-time $27,050 per year. *Required fees:* $220; $220. *Financial support:* In 2013–14, 817 students received support, including 80 research assistantships (averaging $1,296 per year); Federal Work-Study and scholarships/grants also available. Financial award application deadline: 4/15; financial award applicants required to submit FAFSA. *Faculty research:* Child protection, domestic violence, elder law, intellectual property law, preventive detention and post-release civil commitment. *Unit head:* Eric S. Janus, President/Dean, 651-290-6310, Fax: 651-290-6426. *Application contact:* Julie Ekkers, Assistant Dean of Admissions, 651-290-6476, Fax: 651-290-7535, E-mail: admissions@wmitchell.edu.
Website: http://www.wmitchell.edu/.

Yale University, Yale Law School, New Haven, CT 06520-8215. Offers LL M, MSL, JD, JSD, PhD, JD/MA, JD/MAR, JD/MBA, JD/MD, JD/MES, JD/PhD. *Accreditation:* ABA. *Faculty:* 70 full-time, 41 part-time/adjunct. *Students:* 625 full-time (288 women). Average age 24. 2,684 applicants, 9% accepted, 199 enrolled. In 2013, 21 master's, 9 doctorates awarded. *Entrance requirements:* For doctorate, LSAT (for JD). Additional exam requirements/recommendations for international students: Required—TOEFL (minimum score 600 paper-based). *Application deadline:* For fall admission, 2/28 for domestic students. Applications are processed on a rolling basis. Application fee: $60. Electronic applications accepted. *Expenses:* Contact institution. *Financial support:* Application deadline: 3/15; applicants required to submit FAFSA. *Unit head:* Robert Post, Dean, 203-432-1660. *Application contact:* Asha Rangappa, Associate Dean, 203-432-4995, E-mail: admissions.law@yale.edu.
Website: http://www.law.yale.edu/.

Yeshiva University, Benjamin N. Cardozo School of Law, New York, NY 10003-4301. Offers comparative legal thought (LL M); dispute resolution and advocacy (LL M); general studies (LL M); intellectual property law (LL M); law (JD). *Accreditation:* ABA. *Faculty:* 62 full-time (24 women), 100 part-time/adjunct (40 women). *Students:* 1,047 full-time (558 women), 97 part-time (47 women); includes 278 minority (59 Black or African American, non-Hispanic/Latino; 89 Asian, non-Hispanic/Latino; 106 Hispanic/Latino; 1 Native Hawaiian or other Pacific Islander, non-Hispanic/Latino; 23 Two or more races, non-Hispanic/Latino), 85 international. Average age 24. 3,006 applicants, 43% accepted, 244 enrolled. In 2013, 67 master's, 398 doctorates awarded. *Entrance requirements:* For doctorate, LSAT, 2 letters of recommendation. *Application deadline:* For fall admission, 4/1 priority date for domestic students; for spring admission, 12/1 priority date for domestic students. Applications are processed on a rolling basis. Application fee: $75. Electronic applications accepted. *Expenses:* Contact institution. *Financial support:* In 2013–14, 751 students received support, including 67 research assistantships, 38 teaching assistantships; career-related internships or fieldwork, Federal Work-Study, institutionally sponsored loans, scholarships/grants, health care benefits, and tuition waivers (full and partial) also available. Support available to part-time students. Financial award application deadline: 3/1; financial award applicants required to submit FAFSA. *Faculty research:* Corporate and commercial law, intellectual property law, criminal law and litigation, Constitutional law, legal theory and jurisprudence. *Unit head:* David G. Martinidez, Dean of Admissions, 212-790-0274, Fax: 212-790-0482, E-mail: lawinfo@yu.edu.
Website: http://www.cardozo.yu.edu/.

York University, Faculty of Graduate Studies, Atkinson Faculty of Liberal and Professional Studies, Program in Public Policy, Administration and Law, Toronto, ON M3J 1P3, Canada. Offers MPPAL.

York University, Faculty of Graduate Studies, Osgoode Hall Law School, Toronto, ON M3J 1P3, Canada. Offers LL M, JD, PhD. Part-time and evening/weekend programs available. *Degree requirements:* For master's, thesis; for doctorate, comprehensive exam, thesis/dissertation. *Entrance requirements:* For doctorate, LSAT. Electronic applications accepted.

Legal and Justice Studies

American Public University System, AMU/APU Graduate Programs, Charles Town, WV 25414. Offers accounting (MBA, MS); criminal justice (MA), including business administration, emergency and disaster management, general (MA, MS); educational leadership (M Ed); emergency and disaster management (MA); entrepreneurship (MBA); environmental policy and management (MS), including environmental planning, environmental sustainability, fish and wildlife management, general (MA, MS); global environmental management; finance (MBA); general (MBA); global business management (MBA); history (MA), including American history, ancient and classical history, European history, global history, public history; homeland security (MA), including business administration, counter-terrorism studies, criminal justice, cyber, emergency management and public health, intelligence studies, transportation security; homeland security resource allocation (MBA); humanities (MA); information technology (MS), including digital forensics, enterprise software development, information assurance and security, IT project management; information technology management (MBA); intelligence studies (MA), including criminal intelligence, cyber, general (MA, MS), homeland security, intelligence analysis, intelligence collection, intelligence management, intelligence operations, terrorism studies; international relations and conflict resolution (MA), including comparative and security issues, conflict resolution,

international and transnational security issues, peacekeeping; legal studies (MA); management (MA), including defense management, general (MA, MS), human resource management, organizational leadership, public administration; marketing (MBA); military history (MA), including American military history, American Revolution, civil war, war since 1945, World War II; military studies (MA), including joint warfare, strategic leadership; national security studies (MA), including general (MA, MS), homeland security, regional security studies, security and intelligence analysis, terrorism studies; nonprofit management (MBA); political science (MA), including American politics and government, comparative government and development, general (MA, MS), international relations, public policy; psychology (MA), including general (MA, MS), maritime engineering management, reverse logistics management; public administration (MPA), including disaster management, environmental policy, health policy, human resources, national security, organizational management, security management; public health (MPH); reverse logistics management (MA); school counseling (M Ed); security management (MA); space studies (MS), including aerospace science, general (MA, MS), planetary science; sports and health sciences (MS); teaching (M Ed), including curriculum and instruction for elementary teachers, elementary reading, English language learners, instructional leadership, online learning, special education;

transportation and logistics management (MA), including general (MA, MS), maritime engineering management, reverse logistics management. Programs offered via distance learning only. Part-time and evening/weekend programs available. Postbaccalaureate distance learning degree programs offered (no on-campus study). *Faculty:* 432 full-time (242 women), 1,722 part-time/adjunct (829 women). *Students:* 511 full-time (241 women), 10,947 part-time (4,294 women); includes 3,760 minority (2,058 Black or African American, non-Hispanic/Latino; 88 American Indian or Alaska Native, non-Hispanic/Latino; 293 Asian, non-Hispanic/Latino; 876 Hispanic/Latino; 91 Native Hawaiian or other Pacific Islander, non-Hispanic/Latino; 354 Two or more races, non-Hispanic/Latino), 134 international. Average age 36. In 2013, 3,323 master's awarded. *Degree requirements:* For master's, comprehensive exam or practicum. *Entrance requirements:* For master's, official transcript showing earned bachelor's degree from institution accredited by recognized accrediting body. Additional exam requirements/recommendations for international students: Required—TOEFL (minimum score 550 paper-based), IELTS (minimum score 6.5). *Application deadline:* Applications are processed on a rolling basis. Application fee: $0. Electronic applications accepted. *Expenses: Tuition:* Part-time $325 per semester hour. *Financial support:* Applicants required to submit FAFSA. *Faculty research:* Military history, criminal justice, management performance, national security. *Unit head:* Dr. Karan Powell, Executive Vice President and Provost, 877-468-6268, Fax: 304-724-3780. *Application contact:* Terry Grant, Vice President of Enrollment Management, 877-468-6268, Fax: 304-724-3780, E-mail: info@apus.edu.
Website: http://www.apus.edu.

American University, Washington College of Law, Washington, DC 20016-8181. Offers advocacy (LL M); arbitration (Certificate); human rights and the law (Certificate); international legal studies (LL M, Certificate); judicial sciences (SJD); law (JD); law and government (LL M); JD/MA; JD/MBA; JD/MPP; JD/MS; LL M/MBA; LL M/MPA; LL M/MPP. *Accreditation:* ABA. Part-time and evening/weekend programs available. *Faculty:* 95 full-time (45 women), 161 part-time/adjunct (49 women). *Students:* 1,277 full-time (757 women), 428 part-time (227 women); includes 433 minority (96 Black or African American, non-Hispanic/Latino; 1 American Indian or Alaska Native, non-Hispanic/Latino; 101 Asian, non-Hispanic/Latino; 203 Hispanic/Latino; 2 Native Hawaiian or other Pacific Islander, non-Hispanic/Latino; 30 Two or more races, non-Hispanic/Latino), 195 international. Average age 26. 6,324 applicants, 28% accepted, 316 enrolled. In 2013, 142 master's, 512 doctorates awarded. *Entrance requirements:* For doctorate, LSAT, transcript, letters of recommendation. Application fee: $0. *Expenses:* Contact institution. *Financial support:* Fellowships with full tuition reimbursements, career-related internships or fieldwork, Federal Work-Study, institutionally sponsored loans, and tuition waivers (full and partial) available. Support available to part-time students. Financial award application deadline: 3/1; financial award applicants required to submit FAFSA. *Unit head:* Claudio Grossman, Dean, 202-274-4004, Fax: 202-274-4005, E-mail: grossman@wcl.american.edu. *Application contact:* Akira Shiroma, Assistant Dean of Admissions, 202-274-4101, Fax: 202-274-4107, E-mail: shiroma@wcl.american.edu.
Website: http://www.wcl.american.edu/.

Arizona State University at the Tempe campus, College of Liberal Arts and Sciences, School of Justice and Social Inquiry, Tempe, AZ 85287-4902. Offers African American diaspora studies (Graduate Certificate); gender studies (PhD, Graduate Certificate); justice studies (MS, PhD); socio-economic justice (Graduate Certificate); PhD/JD. Part-time programs available. Terminal master's awarded for partial completion of doctoral program. *Degree requirements:* For master's, thesis or alternative, interactive Program of Study (iPOS) submitted before completing 50 percent of required credit hours; for doctorate, comprehensive exam, thesis/dissertation, interactive Program of Study (iPOS) submitted before completing 50 percent of required credit hours. *Entrance requirements:* For master's, GRE or LSAT, minimum GPA of 3.0 or equivalent in last 2 years of work leading to bachelor's degree; for doctorate, GRE or LSAT (for justice studies program), minimum GPA of 3.0 or equivalent in last 2 years of work leading to bachelor's degree. Additional exam requirements/recommendations for international students: Required—TOEFL (minimum score 80 iBT), TOEFL, IELTS, or PTE. Electronic applications accepted.

Arizona State University at the Tempe campus, New College of Interdisciplinary Arts and Sciences, Program in Social Justice and Human Rights, Phoenix, AZ 85069-7100. Offers MA. Fall admission only. Part-time and evening/weekend programs available. *Degree requirements:* For master's, thesis or applied project, interactive Program of Study (iPOS) submitted before completing 50 percent of required credit hours. *Entrance requirements:* For master's, GRE, minimum GPA of 3.0 or equivalent in last 2 years of work leading to bachelor's degree, 2 letters of recommendation, official transcripts, writing sample, personal statement, resume. Additional exam requirements/recommendations for international students: Required—TOEFL (minimum score 80 iBT), TOEFL, IELTS, or PTE. Electronic applications accepted. *Faculty research:* Social movements, violence against women, globalization, innovative uses of human rights law, environmental ethics, social justice and art, women and international development, slavery, genocide, metropolitan studies, urban culture and social space, fair trade, citizenship; immigration.

Arizona State University at the Tempe campus, Sandra Day O'Connor College of Law, Tempe, AZ 85287-7906. Offers biotechnology and genomics (LL M); global legal studies (LL M); law (JD); law (customized) (LL M); legal studies (MLS); patent practice (MLS); tribal policy, law and government (LL M); JD/MBA; JD/MD; JD/PhD. JD/MD offered jointly with Mayo Medical School. *Accreditation:* ABA. *Faculty:* 61 full-time (24 women), 64 part-time/adjunct (14 women). *Students:* 578 full-time (238 women), 45 part-time (23 women); includes 137 minority (17 Black or African American, non-Hispanic/Latino; 16 American Indian or Alaska Native, non-Hispanic/Latino; 20 Asian, non-Hispanic/Latino; 64 Hispanic/Latino; 20 Two or more races, non-Hispanic/Latino), 16 international. Average age 28. 1,595 applicants, 39% accepted, 128 enrolled. In 2013, 27 master's, 204 doctorates awarded. *Degree requirements:* For doctorate, papers. *Entrance requirements:* For master's, bachelor's degree and JD (for LL M); for doctorate, LSAT, bachelor's degree. Additional exam requirements/recommendations for international students: Required—TOEFL (minimum score 550 paper-based; 80 iBT). *Application deadline:* For fall admission, 2/1 priority date for domestic and international students. Applications are processed on a rolling basis. Application fee: $65. Electronic applications accepted. *Expenses:* Contact institution. *Financial support:* Research assistantships, teaching assistantships, career-related internships or fieldwork, Federal Work-Study, institutionally sponsored loans, scholarships/grants, tuition waivers (full and partial), and unspecified assistantships available. Financial award application deadline: 3/15; financial award applicants required to submit FAFSA. *Faculty research:* Emerging technologies and the law, Indian law, law and philosophy, international law, intellectual property. *Total annual research expenditures:* $1.7 million. *Unit head:* Douglas Sylvester, Dean/Professor, 480-965-6188, Fax: 480-965-6521, E-mail: douglas.sylvester@asu.edu. *Application contact:* Chitra Damania, Director of Operations, 480-965-1474, Fax: 480-727-7930, E-mail: law.admissions@asu.edu.
Website: http://www.law.asu.edu/.

Auburn University at Montgomery, School of Sciences, Department of Justice and Public Safety, Montgomery, AL 36124-4023. Offers criminal studies (MSJPS); homeland security (MSJPS); homeland security and emergency management (MS); legal studies (MSJPS); organizational leadership (MSJPS); paralegal (Certificate). Part-time and evening/weekend programs available. *Faculty:* 4 full-time (1 woman), 3 part-time/adjunct (0 women). *Students:* 15 full-time (10 women), 53 part-time (35 women); includes 28 minority (27 Black or African American, non-Hispanic/Latino; 1 Asian, non-Hispanic/Latino). Average age 33. In 2013, 29 master's awarded. *Degree requirements:* For master's, comprehensive exam, thesis optional. *Entrance requirements:* For master's, GRE General Test or MAT. *Application deadline:* Applications are processed on a rolling basis. Electronic applications accepted. *Expenses:* Tuition, state resident: full-time $5994; part-time $333 per credit hour. Tuition, nonresident: full-time $17,982; part-time $999 per credit hour. *Financial support:* Career-related internships or fieldwork and scholarships/grants available. Support available to part-time students. Financial award application deadline: 3/1; financial award applicants required to submit FAFSA. *Faculty research:* Law enforcement, corrections, juvenile justice. *Unit head:* Dr. Ralph Ioimo, Head, 334-244-3691, Fax: 334-244-3244, E-mail: rioimo@aum.edu. *Application contact:* Jennifer Fuller, Administrative Associate, 334-244-3692, Fax: 334-244-3244, E-mail: jfuller@aum.edu.
Website: http://sciences.aum.edu/departments/justice-and-public-safety.

Binghamton University, State University of New York, Graduate School, School of Arts and Sciences, Program in Social, Political, Ethical and Legal Philosophy, Vestal, NY 13850. Offers MA, PhD. *Students:* 19 full-time (10 women), 16 part-time (3 women); includes 9 minority (1 Black or African American, non-Hispanic/Latino; 1 American Indian or Alaska Native, non-Hispanic/Latino; 6 Hispanic/Latino; 1 Native Hawaiian or other Pacific Islander, non-Hispanic/Latino), 4 international. Average age 31. 39 applicants, 41% accepted, 7 enrolled. In 2013, 6 master's, 3 doctorates awarded. Application fee: $75. *Financial support:* In 2013–14, 25 students received support, including 23 teaching assistantships with full tuition reimbursements available (averaging $15,000 per year); career-related internships or fieldwork, Federal Work-Study, institutionally sponsored loans, scholarships/grants, health care benefits, tuition waivers (full and partial), and unspecified assistantships also available. Financial award application deadline: 2/15; financial award applicants required to submit FAFSA. *Unit head:* Dr. Max Pensky, Chairperson, 607-777-4163, E-mail: mpensky@binghamton.edu. *Application contact:* Kishan Zuber, Recruiting and Admissions Coordinator, 607-777-2151, Fax: 607-777-2501, E-mail: kzuber@binghamton.edu.
Website: http://philosophy.binghamton.edu.

Boston University, School of Public Health, Health Law, Bioethics and Human Rights Department, Boston, MA 02215. Offers MPH. Part-time and evening/weekend programs available. *Faculty:* 5 full-time, 16 part-time/adjunct. *Students:* 10 full-time (all women), 7 part-time (6 women); includes 1 minority (Asian, non-Hispanic/Latino). Average age 26. 86 applicants, 56% accepted, 9 enrolled. *Entrance requirements:* For master's, GRE, MCAT, LSAT, GMAT, DAT. Additional exam requirements/recommendations for international students: Required—TOEFL (minimum score 600 paper-based; 100 iBT) or IELTS (minimum score 6). *Application deadline:* For fall admission, 2/1 priority date for domestic and international students; for spring admission, 10/15 priority date for domestic and international students. Applications are processed on a rolling basis. Application fee: $115. Electronic applications accepted. *Expenses: Tuition:* Full-time $43,970; part-time $1374 per credit hour. *Required fees:* $60 per semester. Tuition and fees vary according to class time, course level and program. *Financial support:* In 2013–14, 1 fellowship was awarded; career-related internships or fieldwork, Federal Work-Study, institutionally sponsored loans, scholarships/grants, and tuition waivers (partial) also available. Support available to part-time students. Financial award application deadline: 3/1; financial award applicants required to submit FAFSA. *Unit head:* Prof. George Annas, Chair, 617-638-4626, E-mail: hld@bu.edu. *Application contact:* LePhan Quan, Associate Director of Admissions, 617-638-4640, Fax: 617-638-5299, E-mail: asksph@bu.edu.
Website: http://sph.bu.edu.

Brock University, Faculty of Graduate Studies, Faculty of Social Sciences, Program in Social Justice and Equity Studies, St. Catharines, ON L2S 3A1, Canada. Offers MA. Part-time programs available. *Degree requirements:* For master's, thesis optional. *Entrance requirements:* For master's, honors degree. Additional exam requirements/recommendations for international students: Required—TOEFL (minimum score 550 paper-based; 80 iBT), IELTS (minimum score 6.5), TWE (minimum score 4). Electronic applications accepted. *Faculty research:* Social inequality, social movements, gender, racism, environmental justice.

California University of Pennsylvania, School of Graduate Studies and Research, Department of Professional Studies, California, PA 15419-1394. Offers legal studies (MS), including homeland security, law and public policy. Part-time and evening/weekend programs available. Postbaccalaureate distance learning degree programs offered (no on-campus study). *Degree requirements:* For master's, thesis optional. *Entrance requirements:* For master's, interview, minimum QPA of 3.0. Additional exam requirements/recommendations for international students: Required—TOEFL (minimum score 550 paper-based; 80 iBT). Electronic applications accepted. *Faculty research:* Ethics in political practice, ethics and law, law and morality, St. Thomas Aquinas and crime, police policy.

Capital University, School of Nursing, Columbus, OH 43209-2394. Offers administration (MSN); legal studies (MSN); theological studies (MSN); JD/MSN; MBA/MSN; MSN/MTS. *Accreditation:* AACN. Part-time and evening/weekend programs available. *Degree requirements:* For master's, thesis or alternative. *Entrance requirements:* For master's, BSN, current RN license, minimum GPA of 3.0, undergraduate courses in statistics and research. Additional exam requirements/recommendations for international students: Required—TOEFL (minimum score 550 paper-based). *Expenses:* Contact institution. *Faculty research:* Bereavement, wellness/health promotion, emergency cardiac care, critical thinking, complementary and alternative healthcare.

Carleton University, Faculty of Graduate Studies, Faculty of Public Affairs and Management, Department of Law, Ottawa, ON K1S 5B6, Canada. Offers conflict resolution (Certificate); legal studies (MA). *Degree requirements:* For master's, thesis. *Entrance requirements:* For master's, honors degree. Additional exam requirements/recommendations for international students: Required—TOEFL. *Faculty research:* Legal and social theory; women, law, and gender relations; law, crime, and social order; political economy of law; international law.

Case Western Reserve University, School of Law, Cleveland, OH 44106. Offers intellectual property (LL M); international business law (LL M); international criminal law (LL M); law (JD, SJD); U.S. legal studies (LL M); JD/MA; JD/MBA; JD/MD; JD/MPH; JD/MS; JD/MSSA. *Accreditation:* ABA. *Faculty:* 39 full-time (14 women), 43 part-time/adjunct (12 women). *Students:* 501 full-time (231 women), 6 part-time (3 women); includes 87 minority (35 Black or African American, non-Hispanic/Latino; 3 American Indian or Alaska Native, non-Hispanic/Latino; 30 Asian, non-Hispanic/Latino; 15 Hispanic/Latino; 1 Native Hawaiian or other Pacific Islander, non-Hispanic/Latino; 3 Two or more races, non-Hispanic/Latino), 123 international. Average age 24. 1,200 applicants, 49% accepted, 100 enrolled. In 2013, 78 master's, 229 doctorates awarded. *Entrance requirements:* For doctorate, LSAT, LSDAS. Additional exam requirements/recommendations for international students: Required—TOEFL. *Application deadline:* For fall admission, 4/1 priority date for domestic and international students. Applications

are processed on a rolling basis. Application fee: $40. Electronic applications accepted. Application fee is waived when completed online. *Expenses:* Contact institution. *Financial support:* In 2013–14, 450 students received support. Career-related internships or fieldwork, Federal Work-Study, institutionally sponsored loans, and scholarships/grants available. Financial award application deadline: 5/1; financial award applicants required to submit FAFSA. *Unit head:* Jessica Berg, Interim Co-Dean, 216-368-3283. *Application contact:* Kelli Curtis, Assistant Dean for Admissions, 216-368-3600, Fax: 216-368-0185, E-mail: lawadmissions@case.edu.
Website: http://law.case.edu/.

The Catholic University of America, School of Canon Law, Washington, DC 20064. Offers JCD, JCL, JD/JCL. Part-time programs available. *Faculty:* 4 full-time (0 women), 4 part-time/adjunct (1 woman). *Students:* 41 full-time (4 women), 38 part-time (6 women); includes 9 minority (5 Asian, non-Hispanic/Latino; 2 Hispanic/Latino; 2 Two or more races, non-Hispanic/Latino), 10 international. Average age 39. 44 applicants, 86% accepted, 29 enrolled. *Degree requirements:* For doctorate, 2 foreign languages, thesis/dissertation, fluency in canonical Latin. *Entrance requirements:* For doctorate, GRE General Test, minimum A- average, JCL. Additional exam requirements/recommendations for international students: Required—TOEFL (minimum score 580 paper-based). *Application deadline:* For fall admission, 8/1 priority date for domestic students, 7/15 for international students; for spring admission, 12/1 priority date for domestic students, 10/15 for international students. Applications are processed on a rolling basis. Application fee: $55. Electronic applications accepted. *Expenses: Tuition:* Full-time $38,500; part-time $1490 per credit hour. *Required fees:* $400; $1525 per credit hour. One-time fee: $425. Tuition and fees vary according to program. *Financial support:* Fellowships, research assistantships, teaching assistantships, Federal Work-Study, scholarships/grants, tuition waivers (full and partial), and unspecified assistantships available. Financial award application deadline: 2/1; financial award applicants required to submit FAFSA. *Faculty research:* Ecclesiology and the Sacrament of Orders, procedural law, temporal goods, matrimonial jurisprudence, sacramental and liturgical law. *Unit head:* Rev. Robert Kaslyn, SJ, Dean, 202-319-5492, Fax: 202-319-4187, E-mail: cua-canonlaw@cua.edu. *Application contact:* Andrew Woodall, Director of Graduate Admissions, 202-319-5057, Fax: 202-319-6533, E-mail: cua-admissions@cua.edu.
Website: http://canonlaw.cua.edu.

Central European University, Graduate Studies, Department of Legal Studies, Budapest, Hungary. Offers comparative Constitutional law (LL M); human rights (LL M, MA); international business law (LL M); law and economics (LL M, MA); legal studies (SJD). *Faculty:* 9 full-time (4 women), 16 part-time/adjunct (3 women). *Students:* 98 full-time (54 women). Average age 27. 324 applicants, 32% accepted, 67 enrolled. In 2013, 47 master's awarded. Terminal master's awarded for partial completion of doctoral program. *Degree requirements:* For master's, one foreign language, thesis; for doctorate, one foreign language, comprehensive exam, thesis/dissertation. *Entrance requirements:* For master's and doctorate, LSAT. Additional exam requirements/recommendations for international students: Required—TOEFL (minimum score 570 paper-based); Recommended—IELTS (minimum score 6.5). *Application deadline:* For fall admission, 1/24 for domestic and international students. Application fee: $40. Electronic applications accepted. *Expenses:* Contact institution. *Financial support:* In 2013–14, 77 students received support, including 77 fellowships with full and partial tuition reimbursements available (averaging $6,100 per year); career-related internships or fieldwork, institutionally sponsored loans, scholarships/grants, and tuition waivers (full and partial) also available. Financial award application deadline: 1/5. *Faculty research:* Institutional, constitutional and human rights in European Union law; biomedical law and reproductive rights; data protection law; Islamic banking and finance. *Unit head:* Dr. Renata Uitz, Head of Department, 36 1 327-3201, Fax: 361-327-3198, E-mail: legalst@ceu.hu. *Application contact:* Andrea Jenei, Department Coordinator, 361-327-3205, Fax: 361-327-3198, E-mail: jeneia@ceu.hu.
Website: http://legal.ceu.hu/.

Columbia University, Graduate School of Arts and Sciences, New York, NY 10027. Offers African-American studies (MA); American studies (MA); anthropology (MA, PhD); art history and archaeology (MA, PhD); astronomy (PhD); biological sciences (PhD); biotechnology (MA); chemical physics (PhD); chemistry (PhD); classical studies (MA, PhD); classics (MA, PhD); climate and society (MA); earth and environmental sciences (PhD); East Asia: regional studies (MA); East Asian languages and cultures (MA, PhD); ecology, evolution and environmental biology (MA), including conservation biology; ecology, evolution, and environmental biology (PhD), including ecology and evolutionary biology, evolutionary primatology; economics (PhD); English and comparative literature (MA, PhD); French and Romance philology (MA, PhD); Germanic languages (MA, PhD); global French studies (MA); Hispanic cultural studies (MA); history (PhD); history and literature (MA); human rights studies (MA); Islamic studies (MA); Italian (MA, PhD); Japanese pedagogy (MA); Jewish studies (MA); Latin America and the Caribbean: regional studies (MA); Latin American and Iberian cultures (PhD); mathematics (MA, PhD), including finance (MA); medieval and Renaissance studies (MA); Middle Eastern, South Asian, and African studies (MA, PhD); modern art: critical and curatorial studies (MA); modern European studies (MA); museum anthropology (MA); music (DMA, PhD); oral history (MA); philosophical foundations of physics (MA); philosophy (MA, PhD); physics (PhD); political science (MA, PhD); psychology (PhD); quantitative methods in the social sciences (MA); religion (MA, PhD); Russia, Eurasia and East Europe: regional studies (MA); Russian translation (MA); Slavic cultures (MA); Slavic languages (MA, PhD); sociology (MA, PhD); South Asian studies (MA); statistics (MA, PhD); theatre (PhD); JD/PhD; MA/MS; MD/PhD; MPA/MA. Dual-degree programs require admission to both Graduate School of Arts and Sciences and another Columbia school. Part-time and evening/weekend programs available. *Faculty:* 808 full-time (310 women). *Students:* 2,755 full-time, 354 part-time; includes 493 minority (80 Black or African American, non-Hispanic/Latino; 6 American Indian or Alaska Native, non-Hispanic/Latino; 215 Asian, non-Hispanic/Latino; 135 Hispanic/Latino; 3 Native Hawaiian or other Pacific Islander, non-Hispanic/Latino; 54 Two or more races, non-Hispanic/Latino), 1,433 international. 12,949 applicants, 19% accepted, 998 enrolled. In 2013, 969 master's, 461 doctorates awarded. Terminal master's awarded for partial completion of doctoral program. *Degree requirements:* For master's, thesis (for some programs); for doctorate, comprehensive exam, thesis/dissertation. *Entrance requirements:* For master's and doctorate, GRE General Test, GRE Subject Test (for some programs). Application fee: $105. Electronic applications accepted. *Financial support:* Application deadline: 12/15. *Faculty research:* Humanities, natural sciences, social sciences. *Unit head:* Carlos J. Alonso, Dean of the Graduate School of Arts and Sciences, 212-854-5177. *Application contact:* GSAS Office of Admissions, 212-854-8903, E-mail: gsas-admissions@columbia.edu.
Website: http://gsas.columbia.edu/.

Fielding Graduate University, Graduate Programs, School of Human and Organization Development, Santa Barbara, CA 93105-3814. Offers comprehensive evidence-based coaching (Certificate); evidence based coaching for education leadership (Certificate); evidence based coaching for organization leadership (Certificate); evidence based coaching for personal development (Certificate); human and organizational systems (PhD), including aging, culture and society, information society and knowledge organizations, transformative learning for social justice; human development (PhD), including aging, culture and society, information society and knowledge organizations, transformative learning for social justice; leadership and management effectiveness (Certificate); leadership for sustainability (Certificate); nonprofit leadership (Certificate); organization consulting (Certificate); organizational development and leadership (MA). Postbaccalaureate distance learning degree programs offered (minimal on-campus study). *Faculty:* 19 full-time (11 women), 38 part-time/adjunct (20 women). *Students:* 321 full-time (225 women), 135 part-time (101 women); includes 103 minority (55 Black or African American, non-Hispanic/Latino; 3 American Indian or Alaska Native, non-Hispanic/Latino; 12 Asian, non-Hispanic/Latino; 23 Hispanic/Latino; 1 Native Hawaiian or other Pacific Islander, non-Hispanic/Latino; 9 Two or more races, non-Hispanic/Latino), 1 international. Average age 49. 106 applicants, 96% accepted, 70 enrolled. In 2013, 35 master's, 58 doctorates, 60 other advanced degrees awarded. Terminal master's awarded for partial completion of doctoral program. *Degree requirements:* For master's, thesis or alternative; for doctorate, comprehensive exam, thesis/dissertation. *Entrance requirements:* For master's and Certificate, BA from regionally-accredited institution or equivalent; for doctorate, BA or MA from regionally-accredited institution or equivalent. *Application deadline:* For fall admission, 3/1 for domestic and international students; for spring admission, 9/1 for domestic and international students. Application fee: $75. Electronic applications accepted. *Expenses:* Contact institution. *Financial support:* In 2013–14, 35 students received support, including 1 research assistantship (averaging $1,600 per year); scholarships/grants, health care benefits, and unspecified assistantships also available. Support available to part-time students. Financial award applicants required to submit FAFSA. *Unit head:* Dr. Mario Borunda, Dean, 805-898-2940, Fax: 805-687-9793, E-mail: mborunda@fielding.edu. *Application contact:* Kathy Wells, Admission Counselor, 800-340-1099 Ext. 4098, Fax: 805-687-9793, E-mail: hodadmissions@fielding.edu.
Website: http://www.fielding.edu/programs/hod/default.aspx.

The George Washington University, College of Professional Studies, Paralegal Studies Programs, Washington, DC 20052. Offers MPS, Graduate Certificate. *Students:* 11 full-time (9 women), 149 part-time (131 women); includes 71 minority (51 Black or African American, non-Hispanic/Latino; 2 American Indian or Alaska Native, non-Hispanic/Latino; 2 Asian, non-Hispanic/Latino; 10 Hispanic/Latino; 6 Two or more races, non-Hispanic/Latino), 1 international. Average age 39. 94 applicants, 87% accepted, 51 enrolled. In 2013, 87 master's, 12 other advanced degrees awarded. *Application deadline:* For fall admission, 7/15 for domestic and international students; for spring admission, 10/1 for domestic and international students. Electronic applications accepted. *Unit head:* Toni Marsh, Director, 202-994-2844, E-mail: marsht01@gwu.edu. *Application contact:* Analisa Encinas, Paralegal Studies Program Representative, 703-248-6011, E-mail: aencinas@gwu.edu.
Website: http://nearyou.gwu.edu/plx/.

The George Washington University, College of Professional Studies, Program in Law Firm Management, Washington, DC 20052. Offers MPS, Graduate Certificate. Program offered in partnership with The Hildebrandt Institute and held in Alexandria, VA. Postbaccalaureate distance learning degree programs offered. *Students:* 24 part-time (16 women); includes 5 minority (3 Black or African American, non-Hispanic/Latino; 1 Hispanic/Latino; 1 Two or more races, non-Hispanic/Latino), 1 international. Average age 40. 19 applicants, 100% accepted, 13 enrolled. In 2013, 10 master's, 12 other advanced degrees awarded. *Entrance requirements:* For master's, resume, 2 references. Additional exam requirements/recommendations for international students: Required—TOEFL. *Application deadline:* For fall admission, 4/1 for domestic and international students. Electronic applications accepted. *Unit head:* Kathleen M. Burke, Dean, 202-994-9711. *Application contact:* Kristin Williams, Assistant Vice President for Graduate and Special Enrollment Management, 202-994-0467, Fax: 202-994-0371, E-mail: ksw@gwu.edu.
Website: http://nearyou.gwu.edu/lawfirm/.

Golden Gate University, School of Law, San Francisco, CA 94105-2968. Offers environmental law (LL M); intellectual property law (LL M); international legal studies (LL M, SJD); law (JD); taxation (LL M); U. S. legal studies (LL M); JD/MBA; JD/PhD. *Accreditation:* ABA. Part-time and evening/weekend programs available. *Degree requirements:* For doctorate, thesis/dissertation (for some programs). *Entrance requirements:* For doctorate, LSAT (for JD). Additional exam requirements/recommendations for international students: Required—TOEFL (minimum score 600 paper-based). Electronic applications accepted. *Expenses:* Contact institution. *Faculty research:* International law, intellectual property law, environmental law, real estate, civil rights.

Governors State University, College of Arts and Sciences, Program in Political and Justice Studies, University Park, IL 60484. Offers MA. Part-time and evening/weekend programs available. *Degree requirements:* For master's, thesis or alternative. *Entrance requirements:* For master's, bachelor's degree in related field.

Harrison Middleton University, Graduate Program, Tempe, AZ 85282. Offers education (MA, Ed D); humanities (MA); imaginative literature (MA); interdisciplinary studies (DA); jurisprudence (MA); natural science (MA); philosophy and religion (MA); social science (MA). Part-time and evening/weekend programs available. Postbaccalaureate distance learning degree programs offered (no on-campus study). *Degree requirements:* For master's and doctorate, capstone project. *Entrance requirements:* For master's, interview; for doctorate, 2 academic letters of reference, interview, essay. Additional exam requirements/recommendations for international students: Required—TOEFL (minimum score 550 paper-based; 80 iBT). Electronic applications accepted. *Faculty research:* Japanese animation, educational leadership, war art, John Muir's wilderness.

Harvard University, Law School, Professional Programs in Law, Cambridge, MA 02138. Offers international and comparative law (JD); law and business (JD); law and government (JD); law and social change (JD); law, science and technology (JD); JD/MALD; JD/MBA; JD/MPH; JD/MPP; JD/PhD. *Accreditation:* ABA. *Degree requirements:* For doctorate, 3rd-year paper. *Entrance requirements:* For doctorate, LSAT. *Expenses: Tuition:* Full-time $38,888. *Required fees:* $958. Tuition and fees vary according to campus/location, program and student level. *Faculty research:* Constitutional law, voting rights law, cyber law.

Hodges University, Graduate Programs, Naples, FL 34119. Offers business administration (MBA); clinical mental health counseling (MS); criminal justice (MS); education (MPS); information systems management (MIS); legal studies (MS); management (MSM); public administration (MPA). Part-time and evening/weekend programs available. Postbaccalaureate distance learning degree programs offered (no on-campus study). *Faculty:* 17 full-time (5 women), 5 part-time/adjunct (3 women). *Students:* 20 full-time (13 women), 182 part-time (131 women); includes 75 minority (18 Black or African American, non-Hispanic/Latino; 1 American Indian or Alaska Native, non-Hispanic/Latino; 7 Asian, non-Hispanic/Latino; 48 Hispanic/Latino; 1 Two or more races, non-Hispanic/Latino). Average age 35. 58 applicants, 100% accepted, 58 enrolled. In 2013, 88 master's awarded. *Degree requirements:* For master's, comprehensive exam (for some programs), thesis (for some programs). *Entrance requirements:* For master's, in-house entrance exam. Additional exam requirements/recommendations for international students: Recommended—TOEFL. *Application deadline:* Applications are processed on a rolling basis. Application fee: $50. Electronic

applications accepted. *Financial support:* In 2013–14, 153 students received support. Federal Work-Study and scholarships/grants available. Financial award application deadline: 7/9; financial award applicants required to submit FAFSA. *Unit head:* Dr. Jeanette Brock, President, 239-513-1122, Fax: 239-598-6253, E-mail: jbrock@hodges.edu. *Application contact:* Christy Saunders, Director of Admissions, 239-513-1122, Fax: 239-598-6253, E-mail: csaunders@hodges.edu.

Hofstra University, School of Law, Hempstead, NY 11549. Offers American legal studies (LL M); family law (LL M); law (JD); JD/MBA. *Accreditation:* ABA.

Hollins University, Graduate Programs, Program in Liberal Studies, Roanoke, VA 24020. Offers humanities (MALS); interdisciplinary studies (MALS); justice and legal studies (MALS); liberal studies (CAS); social science (MALS); visual and performing arts (MALS). Part-time and evening/weekend programs available. *Degree requirements:* For master's, thesis. *Entrance requirements:* For master's, letters of recommendation, interview. Additional exam requirements/recommendations for international students: Required—TOEFL (minimum score 550 paper-based; 79 iBT). Electronic applications accepted. *Faculty research:* Elderly blacks, film, feminist economics, US voting patterns, Wagner, diversity.

John Jay College of Criminal Justice of the City University of New York, Graduate Studies, Programs in Criminal Justice, New York, NY 10019-1093. Offers criminal justice (MA, PhD); criminology and deviance (PhD); forensic psychology (PhD); forensic science (PhD); law and philosophy (PhD); organizational behavior (PhD); public policy (PhD). Part-time and evening/weekend programs available. Terminal master's awarded for partial completion of doctoral program. *Degree requirements:* For master's, thesis or alternative; for doctorate, one foreign language, thesis/dissertation. *Entrance requirements:* For master's, GRE General Test, minimum B average; for doctorate, GRE General Test. Additional exam requirements/recommendations for international students: Required—TOEFL (minimum score 500 paper-based).

John Marshall Law School, Graduate and Professional Programs, Chicago, IL 60604-3968. Offers employee benefits (LL M, MS); estate planning (LL M); global legal studies (LL M); information technology (MS); information technology and privacy law (LL M); intellectual property (LL M, MS); international business and trade (LL M); law (JD); real estate (LL M, MS); taxation (LL M, MS); trial advocacy (LL M); JD/LL M; JD/MA; JD/MBA; JD/MPA. JD/MBA offered jointly with Dominican University; JD/MA and JD/MPA with Roosevelt University. *Accreditation:* ABA. Part-time and evening/weekend programs available. *Faculty:* 71 full-time (26 women), 132 part-time/adjunct (49 women). *Students:* 1,045 full-time (512 women), 421 part-time (211 women); includes 403 minority (152 Black or African American, non-Hispanic/Latino; 8 American Indian or Alaska Native, non-Hispanic/Latino; 89 Asian, non-Hispanic/Latino; 138 Hispanic/Latino; 3 Native Hawaiian or other Pacific Islander, non-Hispanic/Latino; 13 Two or more races, non-Hispanic/Latino), 57 international. Average age 27. 2,694 applicants, 73% accepted, 419 enrolled. In 2013, 81 master's, 445 doctorates awarded. *Degree requirements:* For master's, 24 credits; for doctorate, 90 credits. *Entrance requirements:* For master's, JD; for doctorate, LSAT. Additional exam requirements/recommendations for international students: Required—TOEFL. *Application deadline:* For fall admission, 3/1 priority date for domestic and international students; for spring admission, 10/15 priority date for domestic and international students. Applications are processed on a rolling basis. Application fee: $0. Electronic applications accepted. *Expenses:* Contact institution. *Financial support:* In 2013–14, 1,275 students received support. Scholarships/grants and tuition waivers (full and partial) available. Support available to part-time students. Financial award application deadline: 4/1; financial award applicants required to submit FAFSA. *Unit head:* John Corkery, Dean, 312-427-2737. *Application contact:* William B. Powers, Associate Dean of Admission and Student Affairs, 800-537-4280, Fax: 312-427-5136, E-mail: admission@jmls.edu.

Kaplan University, Davenport Campus, School of Legal Studies, Davenport, IA 52807-2095. Offers health care delivery (MS); pathway to paralegal (Postbaccalaureate Certificate); state and local government (MS). Part-time and evening/weekend programs available. Postbaccalaureate distance learning degree programs offered (no on-campus study). *Entrance requirements:* Additional exam requirements/recommendations for international students: Required—TOEFL (minimum score 550 paper-based; 80 iBT).

Loyola University Chicago, Institute of Pastoral Studies, Master of Arts in Social Justice and Community Development Program, Chicago, IL 60660. Offers MA, MSW/MA. *Degree requirements:* For master's, internship. *Entrance requirements:* Additional exam requirements/recommendations for international students: Required—TOEFL. *Expenses: Tuition:* Full-time $16,740; part-time $930 per credit. *Required fees:* $135 per semester. *Unit head:* Dr. Melissa Browning, Graduate Program Director, 312-915-7453, Fax: 312-915-7410, E-mail: mbrowning@luc.edu. *Application contact:* Rachel D. Gibbons, Assistant Director, 312-915-7450, Fax: 312-915-7410, E-mail: rgibbon@luc.edu.

Marlboro College, Graduate and Professional Studies, Program in Teaching for Social Justice, Brattleboro, VT 05301. Offers MAT. Evening/weekend programs available. *Faculty:* 6 part-time/adjunct (4 women). *Students:* 8 full-time (5 women); includes 2 minority (both Asian, non-Hispanic/Latino). Average age 30. 19 applicants, 53% accepted, 6 enrolled. In 2013, 12 master's awarded. *Degree requirements:* For master's, 32 credits including teaching internship and portfolio. *Entrance requirements:* For master's, letter of intent, 2 letters of recommendation, transcripts, interview. Additional exam requirements/recommendations for international students: Required—TOEFL (minimum scores 577 paper-based, 90 iBT) or IELTS (minimum score 7). *Application deadline:* For fall admission, 7/1 priority date for domestic and international students; for winter admission, 11/1 priority date for domestic and international students. Applications are processed on a rolling basis. Electronic applications accepted. *Expenses: Tuition:* Part-time $685 per credit. Tuition and fees vary according to course load and program. *Financial support:* Applicants required to submit FAFSA. *Unit head:* Janaki Natarajan, Degree Chair, 802-258-9209, Fax: 802-258-9201, E-mail: admissions@gradschool.marlboro.edu. *Application contact:* Matthew Livingston, Director of Admissions, 802-258-9209, Fax: 802-258-9201, E-mail: mlivingston@marlboro.edu.
Website: https://www.marlboro.edu/academics/graduate/teach.

Marygrove College, Graduate Division, Program in Social Justice, Detroit, MI 48221-2599. Offers MA.

Marymount University, School of Business Administration, Program in Legal Administration, Arlington, VA 22207-4299. Offers legal administration (MA); paralegal studies (Certificate). Part-time and evening/weekend programs available. *Faculty:* 1 full-time (0 women), 3 part-time/adjunct (0 women). *Students:* 1 (woman) full-time, 10 part-time (8 women); includes 7 minority (4 Black or African American, non-Hispanic/Latino; 1 Asian, non-Hispanic/Latino; 1 Hispanic/Latino; 1 Native Hawaiian or other Pacific Islander, non-Hispanic/Latino). Average age 31. In 2013, 11 master's, 12 other advanced degrees awarded. *Degree requirements:* For master's, thesis or alternative. *Entrance requirements:* For master's, GMAT or GRE General Test, resume; for Certificate, resume. Additional exam requirements/recommendations for international students: Required—TOEFL (minimum score 600 paper-based; 96 iBT), IELTS (minimum score 6.5). *Application deadline:* For fall admission, 7/1 priority date for domestic students, 7/1 for international students; for spring admission, 11/15 for domestic and international students. *Expenses: Tuition:* Part-time $850 per credit. *Required fees:* $10 per credit. One-time fee: $200 part-time. Tuition and fees vary according to program. *Financial support:* Career-related internships or fieldwork, Federal Work-Study, scholarships/grants, and unspecified assistantships available. Support available to part-time students. Financial award applicants required to submit FAFSA. *Unit head:* Susan Ninassi, Director, 703-284-5934, Fax: 703-527-3830, E-mail: susanne.ninassi@marymount.edu. *Application contact:* Francesca Reed, Director, Graduate Admissions, 703-284-5901, Fax: 703-527-3815, E-mail: grad.admissions@marymount.edu.
Website: http://www.marymount.edu/academics/programs/legalAdmin.

Michigan State University College of Law, Professional Program, East Lansing, MI 48824-1300. Offers American legal system (LL M, MJ); global food law (LL M, MJ); intellectual property (LL M, MJ); law (JD). *Accreditation:* ABA. Part-time programs available. *Faculty:* 58 full-time (25 women), 90 part-time/adjunct (21 women). *Students:* 823 full-time (352 women), 175 part-time (77 women); includes 218 minority (74 Black or African American, non-Hispanic/Latino; 19 American Indian or Alaska Native, non-Hispanic/Latino; 45 Asian, non-Hispanic/Latino; 46 Hispanic/Latino; 4 Native Hawaiian or other Pacific Islander, non-Hispanic/Latino; 30 Two or more races, non-Hispanic/Latino), 112 international. Average age 26. 2,673 applicants, 50% accepted, 270 enrolled. In 2013, 39 master's, 301 doctorates awarded. *Entrance requirements:* For doctorate, LSAT. Additional exam requirements/recommendations for international students: Required—TOEFL (minimum score 600 paper-based). *Application deadline:* For fall admission, 4/30 priority date for domestic students, 7/1 priority date for international students. Applications are processed on a rolling basis. Application fee: $60. Electronic applications accepted. *Expenses:* Contact institution. *Financial support:* In 2013–14, 490 students received support. Career-related internships or fieldwork, Federal Work-Study, scholarships/grants, and tuition waivers (full and partial) available. Support available to part-time students. Financial award application deadline: 4/15; financial award applicants required to submit FAFSA. *Faculty research:* International, Constitutional, health, tax and environmental law; intellectual property, trial practice, corporate law. *Unit head:* Joan W. Howarth, Dean/Professor of Law, 517-432-6993, Fax: 517-432-6801, E-mail: howarth@law.msu.edu. *Application contact:* Charles Roboski, Assistant Dean of Admissions, 517-432-0222, Fax: 517-432-0098, E-mail: roboski@law.msu.edu.
Website: http://www.law.msu.edu/.

Mississippi College, Graduate School, College of Arts and Sciences, School of Humanities and Social Sciences, Department of History, Political Science, Administration of Justice, and Paralegal Studies, Clinton, MS 39058. Offers administration of justice (MSS); history (M Ed, MA, MSS); paralegal studies (Certificate); political science (MSS); social sciences (M Ed, MSS). Part-time programs available. *Degree requirements:* For master's, one foreign language, comprehensive exam, thesis (for some programs). *Entrance requirements:* For master's, GRE or NTE, minimum GPA of 2.5. Additional exam requirements/recommendations for international students: Recommended—TOEFL, IELTS. Electronic applications accepted.

Montclair State University, The Graduate School, College of Humanities and Social Sciences, Paralegal Studies Certificate Program, Montclair, NJ 07043-1624. Offers Certificate. Part-time and evening/weekend programs available. *Entrance requirements:* For degree, 2 letters of recommendation, essay. Additional exam requirements/recommendations for international students: Required—TOEFL (minimum score 83 iBT) or IELTS. Electronic applications accepted.

National University, Academic Affairs, School of Professional Studies, La Jolla, CA 92037-1011. Offers criminal justice (MCJ); digital cinema (MFA); digital journalism (MA); juvenile justice (MS); professional screen writing (MFA); public administration (MPA), including human resource management, organizational leadership, public finance. Part-time and evening/weekend programs available. Postbaccalaureate distance learning degree programs offered (no on-campus study). *Faculty:* 14 full-time (6 women), 28 part-time/adjunct (8 women). *Students:* 265 full-time (140 women), 130 part-time (69 women); includes 233 minority (90 Black or African American, non-Hispanic/Latino; 3 American Indian or Alaska Native, non-Hispanic/Latino; 23 Asian, non-Hispanic/Latino; 92 Hispanic/Latino; 8 Native Hawaiian or other Pacific Islander, non-Hispanic/Latino; 17 Two or more races, non-Hispanic/Latino), 4 international. Average age 37. 89 applicants, 100% accepted, 70 enrolled. *Degree requirements:* For master's, thesis (for some programs). *Entrance requirements:* For master's, interview, minimum GPA of 2.5. Additional exam requirements/recommendations for international students: Required—TOEFL (minimum score 550 paper-based; 79 iBT), IELTS (minimum score 6). *Application deadline:* Applications are processed on a rolling basis. Application fee: $60 ($65 for international students). Electronic applications accepted. *Expenses: Tuition:* Full-time $13,824; part-time $1728 per course. One-time fee: $160. *Financial support:* Career-related internships or fieldwork, institutionally sponsored loans, scholarships/grants, and tuition waivers (partial) available. Support available to part-time students. Financial award application deadline: 6/30; financial award applicants required to submit FAFSA. *Unit head:* School of Professional Studies, 800-628-8648, E-mail: sops@nu.edu. *Application contact:* Louis Cruz, Interim Vice President for Enrollment Services, 800-628-8648, E-mail: advisor@nu.edu.
Website: http://www.nu.edu/OurPrograms/School-of-Professional-Studies.html.

New York University, Graduate School of Arts and Science and School of Law, Institute for Law and Society, New York, NY 10012-1019. Offers MA, PhD, JD/MA, JD/PhD. *Faculty:* 3 full-time (1 woman). *Students:* 4 full-time (3 women), 2 part-time (0 women), 1 international. Average age 36. In 2013, 1 doctorate awarded. *Degree requirements:* For doctorate, one foreign language, thesis/dissertation. *Entrance requirements:* Additional exam requirements/recommendations for international students: Required—TOEFL. Application fee: $95. *Expenses: Tuition:* Full-time $35,856; part-time $1494 per unit. *Required fees:* $1408; $64 per unit. $473 per term. Tuition and fees vary according to course load and program. *Financial support:* Fellowships with tuition reimbursements, teaching assistantships with tuition reimbursements, career-related internships or fieldwork, Federal Work-Study, institutionally sponsored loans, scholarships/grants, health care benefits, and unspecified assistantships available. Financial award applicants required to submit FAFSA. *Faculty research:* Politics of law, law and social policy, law in comparative global perspective, rights and social movements. *Unit head:* Jo Dixon, Director of Graduate Studies, 212-998-8040. *Application contact:* Roberta Popik, Associate Dean for Graduate Enrollment Services, 212-998-8050, Fax: 212-995-4557, E-mail: gsas.admissions@nyu.edu.

New York University, School of Continuing and Professional Studies, The Preston Robert Tisch Center for Hospitality, Tourism, and Sports Management, Program in Sports Business, New York, NY 10012-1019. Offers global sports media (MS); professional and collegiate sports operations (MS); sports business (Advanced Certificate); sports law (MS); sports marketing and sales (MS). Part-time and evening/weekend programs available. *Faculty:* 8 full-time (3 women), 24 part-time/adjunct (7 women). *Students:* 75 full-time (27 women), 56 part-time (17 women); includes 23 minority (8 Black or African American, non-Hispanic/Latino; 6 Asian, non-Hispanic/Latino; 7 Hispanic/Latino; 2 Two or more races, non-Hispanic/Latino), 39 international. Average age 26. 136 applicants, 79% accepted, 59 enrolled. In 2013, 32 master's, 5 other advanced degrees awarded. *Degree requirements:* For master's, thesis. *Entrance requirements:* For master's, bachelor's degree, resume with relevant professional work,

internship or volunteer experience, two letters of recommendation, statement of purpose. Additional exam requirements/recommendations for international students: Required—TOEFL (minimum score 600 paper-based; 100 iBT), IELTS (minimum score 7). *Application deadline:* For fall admission, 2/1 priority date for domestic and international students; for spring admission, 10/15 priority date for domestic students, 8/15 priority date for international students. Applications are processed on a rolling basis. Application fee: $150. Electronic applications accepted. *Expenses: Tuition:* Full-time $35,856; part-time $1494 per unit. *Required fees:* $1408; $64 per unit. $473 per term. Tuition and fees vary according to course load and program. *Financial support:* In 2013–14, 51 students received support, including 50 fellowships (averaging $3,118 per year); scholarships/grants also available. Support available to part-time students. Financial award application deadline: 2/15. *Faculty research:* Implications of college football's bowl coalition series from a legal, economic, and academic perspective; social history of sports. *Unit head:* Bjorn Hanson, Division Dean and Clinical Professor, 212-998-7100. *Application contact:* Admissions Office, 212-998-7100, E-mail: scps.gradadmissions@nyu.edu.
Website: http://www.scps.nyu.edu/areas-of-study/tisch/graduate-programs/ms-sports-business/.

Northeastern University, College of Social Sciences and Humanities, Boston, MA 02115. Offers criminology and criminal justice (MSCJ); criminology and justice policy (PhD); economics (MA, PhD); English (MA, PhD); law and public policy (MS, PhD); political science (MA, PhD); public administration (MPA); public history (MA); sociology (MA, PhD); urban and regional policy (MS); world history (MA, PhD). *Degree requirements:* For doctorate, variable foreign language requirement, comprehensive exam, thesis/dissertation. *Entrance requirements:* For master's and doctorate, GRE. Additional exam requirements/recommendations for international students: Required—TOEFL, IELTS. Electronic applications accepted.

Nova Southeastern University, Shepard Broad Law Center, Fort Lauderdale, FL 33314. Offers education law (MS); employment law (MS); health law (MS); law (JD); JD/MBA; JD/MS; JD/MURP. JD/MURP offered jointly with Florida Atlantic University. *Accreditation:* ABA. Part-time and evening/weekend programs available. Postbaccalaureate distance learning degree programs offered (minimal on-campus study). *Faculty:* 65 full-time (33 women), 96 part-time/adjunct (35 women). *Students:* 726 full-time (379 women), 324 part-time (233 women); includes 443 minority (127 Black or African American, non-Hispanic/Latino; 2 American Indian or Alaska Native, non-Hispanic/Latino; 41 Asian, non-Hispanic/Latino; 262 Hispanic/Latino; 1 Native Hawaiian or other Pacific Islander, non-Hispanic/Latino; 10 Two or more races, non-Hispanic/Latino), 11 international. Average age 28. 1,692 applicants, 49% accepted, 339 enrolled. In 2013, 61 master's, 303 doctorates awarded. *Degree requirements:* For master's, capstone research project; for doctorate, thesis/dissertation, rigorous upper-level writing requirement fulfilled through seminar paper or law journal article. *Entrance requirements:* For master's, regionally-accredited undergraduate degree and at least 2 years experience in the field of business or health care for the Employment Law and Health Care programs; for doctorate, LSAT. Additional exam requirements/recommendations for international students: Recommended—TOEFL, IELTS, TWE. *Application deadline:* For fall admission, 5/1 priority date for domestic and international students. Applications are processed on a rolling basis. Application fee: $53. Electronic applications accepted. *Expenses:* Contact institution. *Financial support:* In 2013–14, 325 students received support, including 17 fellowships (averaging $1,382 per year); Federal Work-Study, scholarships/grants, tuition waivers (partial), and unspecified assistantships also available. Support available to part-time students. Financial award application deadline: 4/15; financial award applicants required to submit FAFSA. *Faculty research:* Legal issues in family law, civil rights, business associations, criminal law, law and popular culture. *Unit head:* Elena Langan, Dean, 954-262-6100, Fax: 954-262-6317, E-mail: langane@nsu.law.nova.edu. *Application contact:* William Perez, Assistant Dean of Admissions, 954-262-6121, Fax: 954-262-3844, E-mail: perezw@nsu.law.nova.edu.
Website: http://www.nsulaw.nova.edu/.

Oklahoma City University, Meinders School of Business, Program in Energy Legal Studies, Oklahoma City, OK 73106-1402. Offers MS. Part-time and evening/weekend programs available. Postbaccalaureate distance learning degree programs offered (no on-campus study). *Students:* 99 part-time (50 women); includes 17 minority (4 Black or African American, non-Hispanic/Latino; 8 American Indian or Alaska Native, non-Hispanic/Latino; 3 Asian, non-Hispanic/Latino; 2 Two or more races, non-Hispanic/Latino). Average age 33. 29 applicants, 90% accepted, 20 enrolled. *Entrance requirements:* For master's, GRE/GMAT, bachelor's degree from accredited institution, minimum GPA of 3.0, essay, recommendation letters, professional resume. Additional exam requirements/recommendations for international students: Required—TOEFL (minimum score 550 paper-based; 80 iBT). *Application deadline:* Applications are processed on a rolling basis. Application fee: $50. Electronic applications accepted. *Expenses: Tuition:* Full-time $16,848; part-time $936 per credit hour. Tuition and fees vary according to course load, degree level and program. *Financial support:* Career-related internships or fieldwork, Federal Work-Study, institutionally sponsored loans, scholarships/grants, and tuition waivers available. Support available to part-time students. Financial award applicants required to submit FAFSA. *Unit head:* Dr. Steve Agee, Dean, 405-208-5275, Fax: 405-208-5008, E-mail: sagee@okcu.edu. *Application contact:* Heidi Puckett, Director of Graduate Admission, 800-633-7242, Fax: 405-208-5356, E-mail: gadmissions@okcu.edu.

Pace University, Pace Law School, White Plains, NY 10603. Offers comparative legal studies (LL M); environmental law (LL M, SJD), including climate change (LL M), land use and sustainability (LL M); law (JD); JD/LL M; JD/MA; JD/MBA; JD/MEM; JD/MPA; JD/MS. JD/MA offered jointly with Sarah Lawrence College; JD/MEM offered jointly with Yale University School of Forestry and Environmental Studies. *Accreditation:* ABA. Part-time programs available. *Degree requirements:* For master's, writing sample; for doctorate, thesis/dissertation (for some programs), extensive thesis proposal (for SJD). *Entrance requirements:* For doctorate, LSAT (for JD). Additional exam requirements/recommendations for international students: Required—TOEFL (minimum score 600 paper-based); Recommended—TWE. Electronic applications accepted. *Expenses:* Contact institution. *Faculty research:* Reform of energy regulations, international law, land use law, prosecutorial misconduct, corporation law, international sale of goods.

Prairie View A&M University, College of Juvenile Justice and Psychology, Prairie View, TX 77446-0519. Offers clinical adolescent psychology (PhD); juvenile forensic psychology (MSJFP); juvenile justice (MSJJ, PhD). Part-time and evening/weekend programs available. *Faculty:* 6 full-time (3 women), 4 part-time/adjunct (2 women). *Students:* 45 full-time (39 women), 27 part-time (21 women); includes 5 minority (3 Black or African American, non-Hispanic/Latino; 2 Hispanic/Latino), 4 international. Average age 26. 110 applicants, 35% accepted, 28 enrolled. In 2013, 11 master's, 13 doctorates awarded. *Degree requirements:* For master's, comprehensive exam (for some programs), thesis (for some programs); for doctorate, comprehensive exam, thesis/dissertation. *Entrance requirements:* For master's, GRE, minimum GPA of 2.75; for doctorate, GRE, previous course work in clinical adolescent psychology, minimum GPA of 3.5. Additional exam requirements/recommendations for international students: Required—TOEFL. *Application deadline:* For fall admission, 7/1 for domestic and international students; for spring admission, 11/1 for domestic and international students. Applications are processed on a rolling basis. Application fee: $50. *Expenses:* Tuition, state resident: full-time $3776; part-time $209.77 per credit hour. Tuition, nonresident: full-time $10,183; part-time $565.77 per credit hour. *Required fees:* $2037; $446.50 per credit hour. *Financial support:* In 2013–14, 23 students received support, including 12 research assistantships (averaging $15,000 per year), 11 teaching assistantships (averaging $20,000 per year); career-related internships or fieldwork, Federal Work-Study, institutionally sponsored loans, tuition waivers (full and partial), and unspecified assistantships also available. Support available to part-time students. Financial award application deadline: 3/1; financial award applicants required to submit FAFSA. *Faculty research:* Juvenile justice, juvenile forensic psychology, teen court, graduate education, capital punishment. *Total annual research expenditures:* $2,888. *Unit head:* Dr. Dennis E. Daniels, Interim Dean, 936-261-5205, Fax: 936-261-5252, E-mail: dedaniels@pvamu.edu. *Application contact:* Sandy Siegmund, Executive Secretary, Graduate Program, 936-261-5234, Fax: 936-261-5249, E-mail: sisiegmund@pvamu.edu.

Prescott College, Graduate Programs, Program in Humanities, Prescott, AZ 86301. Offers humanities (MA); social justice and human rights (MA); student-directed independent study (MA). Part-time programs available. Postbaccalaureate distance learning degree programs offered (minimal on-campus study). *Degree requirements:* For master's, thesis, fieldwork or internship, practicum. *Entrance requirements:* For master's, 2 letters of recommendation, resume, essay. Additional exam requirements/recommendations for international students: Required—TOEFL (minimum score 500 paper-based). Electronic applications accepted.

Queen's University at Kingston, School of Graduate Studies, Faculty of Arts and Sciences, Department of Sociology, Kingston, ON K7L 3N6, Canada. Offers communication and Information technology (MA, PhD); feminist sociology (MA, PhD); socio-legal studies (MA, PhD); sociological theory (MA, PhD). Part-time programs available. *Degree requirements:* For master's, thesis; for doctorate, comprehensive exam, thesis/dissertation. *Entrance requirements:* For master's, honors bachelors degree in sociology; for doctorate, honors bachelors degree, masters degree in sociology. Additional exam requirements/recommendations for international students: Required—TOEFL. *Faculty research:* Social change and modernization, social control, deviance and criminology, surveillance.

Regent University, Graduate School, School of Law, Virginia Beach, VA 23464. Offers American legal studies (LL M); human rights (LL M); law (MA, JD); JD/MA; JD/MBA. *Accreditation:* ABA. Part-time programs available. *Faculty:* 25 full-time (7 women), 56 part-time/adjunct (17 women). *Students:* 342 full-time (179 women), 72 part-time (47 women); includes 56 minority (15 Black or African American, non-Hispanic/Latino; 9 American Indian or Alaska Native, non-Hispanic/Latino; 16 Asian, non-Hispanic/Latino; 16 Hispanic/Latino), 63 international. Average age 28. 615 applicants, 53% accepted, 87 enrolled. In 2013, 138 doctorates awarded. *Entrance requirements:* For doctorate, LSAT, minimum undergraduate GPA of 2.75, 3 letters of recommendation, resume. Additional exam requirements/recommendations for international students: Required—TOEFL (minimum score 600 paper-based). *Application deadline:* For fall admission, 3/1 for domestic students. Applications are processed on a rolling basis. Application fee: $50. Electronic applications accepted. *Expenses:* Contact institution. *Financial support:* Career-related internships or fieldwork, scholarships/grants, and tuition waivers (full and partial) available. Support available to part-time students. Financial award application deadline: 2/1; financial award applicants required to submit FAFSA. *Faculty research:* Family law, Constitutional law, law and culture, evidence and practice, intellectual property. *Unit head:* Jeffrey Brauch, Dean, 757-352-4040, Fax: 757-352-4595, E-mail: jeffbra@regent.edu. *Application contact:* Matthew Chadwick, Director of Enrollment Support Services, 800-373-5504, Fax: 757-352-4381, E-mail: admissions@regent.edu.
Website: http://www.regent.edu/acad/schlaw/admissions/abouthome.cfm.

Rutgers, The State University of New Jersey, New Brunswick, Graduate School-New Brunswick, Department of Political Science, Piscataway, NJ 08854-8097. Offers American politics (PhD); comparative politics (PhD); international relations (PhD); political theory (PhD); public law (PhD); women and politics (PhD). *Degree requirements:* For doctorate, one foreign language, comprehensive exam, thesis/dissertation. *Entrance requirements:* For doctorate, GRE General Test. Additional exam requirements/recommendations for international students: Required—TOEFL.

St. John's University, College of Professional Studies, Department of Criminal Justice and Legal Studies, Queens, NY 11439. Offers criminal justice leadership (MPS). Part-time and evening/weekend programs available. Postbaccalaureate distance learning degree programs offered (no on-campus study). *Students:* 27 full-time (10 women), 40 part-time (13 women); includes 35 minority (11 Black or African American, non-Hispanic/Latino; 3 Asian, non-Hispanic/Latino; 19 Hispanic/Latino; 1 Native Hawaiian or other Pacific Islander, non-Hispanic/Latino; 1 Two or more races, non-Hispanic/Latino), 1 international. Average age 29. 50 applicants, 78% accepted, 25 enrolled. In 2013, 21 master's awarded. *Degree requirements:* For master's, comprehensive exam, thesis optional, capstone project. *Entrance requirements:* For master's, bachelor's degree from regionally-accredited college or university, minimum overall GPA of 3.0, 2 letters of recommendation, 300-word essay. Additional exam requirements/recommendations for international students: Required—TOEFL (minimum score 600 paper-based; 100 iBT), IELTS (minimum score 5.5). *Application deadline:* For fall admission, 5/1 priority date for domestic and international students; for spring admission, 11/1 priority date for domestic and international students. Applications are processed on a rolling basis. Application fee: $70. Electronic applications accepted. *Expenses: Tuition:* Full-time $19,800; part-time $1100 per credit. *Required fees:* $170 per semester. *Financial support:* Research assistantships available. *Faculty research:* Fire litigation, forensic psychology, organized crime, probation and parole, leadership studies, criminal justice ethics and integration control. *Unit head:* Jeffrey Grossman, Chair, 718-990-7436, E-mail: grossmaj@stjohns.edu. *Application contact:* Robert Medrano, Director of Graduate Admission, 718-990-1601, Fax: 718-990-5686, E-mail: gradhelp@stjohns.edu.
Website: http://www.stjohns.edu/academics/schools-and-colleges/college-professional-studies/programs-and-majors.

St. John's University, St. John's College of Liberal Arts and Sciences, Program in Global Development and Social Justice, Queens, NY 11439. Offers MA. Program offered jointly with Unicaritas. Part-time and evening/weekend programs available. Postbaccalaureate distance learning degree programs offered (minimal on-campus study). *Students:* 49 part-time (34 women); includes 28 minority (14 Black or African American, non-Hispanic/Latino; 3 Asian, non-Hispanic/Latino; 10 Hispanic/Latino; 1 Two or more races, non-Hispanic/Latino), 2 international. Average age 34. 101 applicants, 60% accepted, 26 enrolled. In 2013, 18 master's awarded. *Degree requirements:* For master's, capstone project. *Entrance requirements:* For master's, 2 letters of recommendation, personal essay, proficiency in English. Additional exam requirements/recommendations for international students: Required—TOEFL (minimum score 600 paper-based; 100 iBT), IELTS (minimum score 5.5). *Application deadline:* For fall admission, 4/1 priority date for domestic and international students; for spring admission, 11/1 priority date for domestic and international students. Applications are processed on a rolling basis. Application fee: $70. Electronic applications accepted. *Expenses: Tuition:* Full-time $19,800; part-time $1100 per credit. *Required fees:* $170

per semester. *Unit head:* Dr. Barrett Brenton, Director of the Center for Global Development, 718-990-5662, E-mail: brentonb@stjohns.edu. *Application contact:* Robert Medrano, Director of Graduate Admissions, 718-990-1601, Fax: 718-990-5686, E-mail: gradhelp@stjohns.edu.
Website: http://www.stjohns.edu/academics/schools-and-colleges/st-johns-college-liberal-arts-and-sciences/programs-and-majors/global-development-and-social-jus.

St. John's University, School of Law, Program in Transnational Legal Practice, Queens, NY 11439. Offers LL M. *Students:* 18 full-time (4 women), all international. Average age 27. 68 applicants, 65% accepted, 9 enrolled. In 2013, 4 master's awarded. *Entrance requirements:* For master's, resume, 2 letters of recommendation, writing sample, interview, transcript, personal statement. Additional exam requirements/recommendations for international students: Required—TOEFL (minimum score 600 paper-based; 22 iBT), IELTS (minimum score 7), TWE (minimum score 5). *Application deadline:* For fall admission, 4/1 priority date for domestic and international students. Applications are processed on a rolling basis. Application fee: $100. Electronic applications accepted. *Expenses:* Contact institution. *Unit head:* Jeffrey K. Walker, Associate Dean for Transnational Programs, 718-990-8358, E-mail: walkerj@stjohns.edu. *Application contact:* Robert Harrison, Associate Dean of Admissions and Financial Services, 718-990-6474, Fax: 718-990-6699, E-mail: lawinfo@stjohns.edu.
Website: http://www.stjohns.edu/academics/graduate/law/academics/llm/tlp.

St. John's University, School of Law, Program in U.S. Legal Studies for Foreign Law School Graduates, Queens, NY 11439. Offers LL M. Part-time programs available. *Students:* 16 full-time (8 women), 8 part-time (5 women); includes 11 minority (3 Black or African American, non-Hispanic/Latino; 1 American Indian or Alaska Native, non-Hispanic/Latino; 3 Asian, non-Hispanic/Latino; 4 Hispanic/Latino), 6 international. Average age 35. 58 applicants, 64% accepted, 16 enrolled. In 2013, 11 master's awarded. *Entrance requirements:* For master's, law degree from non-U.S. law school, resume, 2 letters of recommendation, writing sample, interview, personal statement. Additional exam requirements/recommendations for international students: Required—TWE, TOEFL (minimum score 600 paper-based, 100 iBT) or IELTS (minimum score 7). *Application deadline:* For fall admission, 4/1 priority date for domestic and international students. Applications are processed on a rolling basis. Application fee: $100. Electronic applications accepted. *Expenses:* Contact institution. *Unit head:* Jeffrey K. Walker, Associate Dean for Transnational Programs, 718-990-8335, E-mail: walkerj@stjohns.edu. *Application contact:* Robert Harrison, Associate Dean of Admissions and Financial Services, 718-990-6474, Fax: 718-990-6699, E-mail: lawinfo@stjohns.edu.
Website: http://www.stjohns.edu/academics/graduate/law/academics/llm/usls.

Saint Leo University, Graduate Studies in Criminal Justice, Saint Leo, FL 33574-6665. Offers correction (MS); criminal justice (MS); critical incident management (MS); cybersecurity (MS); forensic psychology (MS); forensic science (MS); legal studies (MS). Part-time and evening/weekend programs available. Postbaccalaureate distance learning degree programs offered (minimal on-campus study). *Faculty:* 11 full-time (4 women), 16 part-time/adjunct (3 women). *Students:* 651 full-time (376 women), 7 part-time (6 women); includes 345 minority (276 Black or African American, non-Hispanic/Latino; 3 American Indian or Alaska Native, non-Hispanic/Latino; 7 Asian, non-Hispanic/Latino; 51 Hispanic/Latino; 8 Two or more races, non-Hispanic/Latino), 1 international. Average age 38. In 2013, 292 master's awarded. *Degree requirements:* For master's, comprehensive project. *Entrance requirements:* For master's, bachelor's degree with minimum GPA of 3.0 from regionally-accredited college or university. Additional exam requirements/recommendations for international students: Required—TOEFL (minimum score 550 paper-based; 80 iBT). *Application deadline:* For fall admission, 7/1 priority date for domestic and international students; for spring admission, 11/1 priority date for domestic and international students. Applications are processed on a rolling basis. Application fee: $80. Electronic applications accepted. *Expenses:* Contact institution. *Financial support:* In 2013–14, 18 students received support. Federal Work-Study, scholarships/grants, and health care benefits available. Financial award application deadline: 3/1; financial award applicants required to submit FAFSA. *Unit head:* Dr. Robert Diemer, Director of Graduate Studies in Criminal Justice, 352-588-8974, Fax: 352-588-8289, E-mail: robert.diemer@saintleo.edu. *Application contact:* Joshua Stagner, Director of Graduate Admission, 800-707-8846, Fax: 352-588-7873, E-mail: grad.admissions@saintleo.edu.
Website: http://www.saintleo.edu/academics/graduate/criminal-justice.aspx.

San Francisco State University, Division of Graduate Studies, College of Education, Department of Equity, Leadership Studies, and Instructional Technologies, Program in Equity and Social Justice in Education, San Francisco, CA 94132-1722. Offers MA. *Unit head:* Dr. David Hemphill, Interim Chair, 415-338-1653, E-mail: hemphill@sfsu.edu. *Application contact:* Dr. Doris Flowers, Graduate Coordinator, 415-338-2614, E-mail: dflowers@sfsu.edu.
Website: http://coe.sfsu.edu/elsit.

Simon Fraser University, Office of Graduate Studies, Faculty of Arts and Social Sciences, School of Criminology, Burnaby, BC V5A 1S6, Canada. Offers applied legal studies (MA); criminology (MA, PhD). *Faculty:* 33 full-time (11 women). *Students:* 148 full-time (103 women), 2 part-time (both women). 143 applicants, 45% accepted, 53 enrolled. In 2013, 30 master's, 8 doctorates awarded. *Degree requirements:* For master's, thesis or alternative, practicum; for doctorate, thesis/dissertation. *Entrance requirements:* For master's, minimum GPA of 3.0 (on scale of 4.33), or 3.33 based on last 60 credits of undergraduate courses; for doctorate, minimum GPA of 3.5 (on scale of 4.33). Additional exam requirements/recommendations for international students: Recommended—TOEFL (minimum score 580 paper-based; 93 iBT), IELTS (minimum score 7), TWE (minimum score 5). *Application deadline:* For fall admission, 2/1 for domestic and international students; for spring admission, 2/1 for domestic students. Application fee: $90 ($125 for international students). Electronic applications accepted. *Expenses: Tuition, area resident:* Full-time $5084 Canadian dollars. *Required fees:* $840 Canadian dollars. *Financial support:* In 2013–14, 31 students received support, including 24 fellowships (averaging $6,250 per year), teaching assistantships (averaging $5,608 per year); research assistantships, career-related internships or fieldwork, Federal Work-Study, and scholarships/grants also available. *Faculty research:* Media and crime, feminist jurisprudence, policy evaluation, forensic entomology, restorative justice. *Unit head:* Dr. Williamson Glackman, Director, 778-782-4147, Fax: 778-782-4140, E-mail: crim-grad-chair@sfu.ca. *Application contact:* Alexis Vanderveen, Graduate Secretary, 778-782-4762, Fax: 778-782-4140, E-mail: crimgrad@sfu.ca.
Website: http://www.sfu.ca/criminology/.

Southern Illinois University Carbondale, School of Law, Program in Legal Studies, Carbondale, IL 62901-4701. Offers general law (MLS); health law and policy (MLS). *Students:* 5 full-time (2 women), 7 part-time (4 women), 1 international. 10 applicants, 70% accepted, 7 enrolled. In 2013, 6 master's awarded. Application fee: $50. *Unit head:* Lisa David, Admissions Coordinator, 618-453-8767, E-mail: ldavid@law.siu.edu.

Southern New Hampshire University, School of Business, Manchester, NH 03106-1045. Offers accounting (MBA, MS, Graduate Certificate); accounting finance (MS); accounting/auditing (MS); accounting/forensic accounting (MS); accounting/taxation (MS); athletic administration (MBA, Graduate Certificate); business administration (IMBA, MBA, Certificate, Graduate Certificate), including accounting (Certificate), business administration (MBA), business information systems (Graduate Certificate), human resource management (Certificate); corporate social responsibility (MBA); entrepreneurship (MBA); finance (MBA, MS, Graduate Certificate); finance/corporate finance (MS); finance/investments and securities (MS); forensic accounting (MBA); healthcare informatics (MBA); healthcare management (MBA); human resource management (Graduate Certificate); information technology (MS, Graduate Certificate); information technology management (MBA); international business (Graduate Certificate); international business and information technology (Graduate Certificate); international finance (Graduate Certificate); international sport management (Graduate Certificate); justice studies (MBA); leadership of nonprofit organizations (Graduate Certificate); marketing (MBA, MS, Graduate Certificate); operations and project management (MS); operations and supply chain management (MBA, Graduate Certificate); organizational leadership (MS); project management (MBA, Graduate Certificate); Six Sigma (MBA); Six Sigma quality (Graduate Certificate); social media marketing (MBA); sport management (MBA, MS, Graduate Certificate); sustainability and environmental compliance (MBA); workplace conflict management (MBA); MBA/Certificate. *Accreditation:* ACBSP. Part-time and evening/weekend programs available. Postbaccalaureate distance learning degree programs offered (no on-campus study). Terminal master's awarded for partial completion of doctoral program. *Degree requirements:* For master's, one foreign language, comprehensive exam (for some programs), thesis or alternative. *Entrance requirements:* For master's, minimum GPA of 2.5. Additional exam requirements/recommendations for international students: Required—TOEFL (minimum score 500 paper-based). Electronic applications accepted.

Taft Law School, Graduate Programs, Santa Ana, CA 92704-6954. Offers American jurisprudence (LL M); law (JD); taxation (LL M).

Temple University, James E. Beasley School of Law, Philadelphia, PA 19122. Offers law (JD); legal education (SJD); taxation (LL M); transnational law (LL M); trial advocacy (LL M); JD/LL M; JD/MBA. *Accreditation:* ABA. Part-time and evening/weekend programs available. *Entrance requirements:* For doctorate, LSAT (for JD). Additional exam requirements/recommendations for international students: Recommended—TOEFL. Electronic applications accepted. *Expenses:* Contact institution. *Faculty research:* Evidence, gender issues, health care law, immigration law, and intellectual property law.

Texas State University, Graduate School, College of Liberal Arts, Department of Political Science, Program in Legal Studies, San Marcos, TX 78666. Offers MA. *Faculty:* 5 full-time (2 women). *Students:* 33 full-time (21 women), 32 part-time (24 women); includes 31 minority (10 Black or African American, non-Hispanic/Latino; 2 American Indian or Alaska Native, non-Hispanic/Latino; 19 Hispanic/Latino). Average age 32. 31 applicants, 65% accepted, 17 enrolled. In 2013, 28 master's awarded. *Degree requirements:* For master's, comprehensive exam. *Entrance requirements:* For master's, GRE General Test (minimum score 900, 4 analytical preferred) or LSAT, minimum GPA of 2.75 in last 60 hours of undergraduate work. Additional exam requirements/recommendations for international students: Required—TOEFL (minimum score 550 paper-based; 78 iBT). *Application deadline:* For fall admission, 6/15 priority date for domestic students, 6/1 priority date for international students; for spring admission, 10/15 priority date for domestic students, 10/1 priority date for international students. Applications are processed on a rolling basis. Application fee: $90 ($140 for international students). Electronic applications accepted. *Expenses:* Tuition, state resident: full-time $6663; part-time $278 per credit hour. Tuition, nonresident: full-time $15,159; part-time $632 per credit hour. *Required fees:* $1872; $54 per credit hour. $306 per term. Tuition and fees vary according to course load. *Financial support:* In 2013–14, 50 students received support, including 3 research assistantships (averaging $11,640 per year), 1 teaching assistantship (averaging $11,280 per year); Federal Work-Study, institutionally sponsored loans, scholarships/grants, health care benefits, and unspecified assistantships also available. Financial award application deadline: 4/1; financial award applicants required to submit FAFSA. *Unit head:* Dr. Lynn Crossett, Graduate Advisor, 512-245-2233, Fax: 512-245-7815, E-mail: th10@txstate.edu. *Application contact:* Dr. Andrea Golato, Dean of Graduate School, 512-245-2581, Fax: 512-245-8365, E-mail: gradcollege@txstate.edu.
Website: http://www.polisci.txstate.edu/.

Thomas M. Cooley Law School, JD and LL M Programs, Lansing, MI 48901-3038. Offers administrative law (public law) (JD); business transactions (JD); Canadian law practice (JD); Constitutional law and civil rights (public law) (JD); corporate law and finance (LL M); environmental law (public law) (JD); general practice (JD), including solo and small firm; homeland and national security law (LL M); insurance law (LL M); intellectual property (JD); intellectual property law (LL M); international law (JD); litigation (JD); self-directed (LL M, JD); tax law (LL M); taxation (JD); U.S. legal studies for foreign attorneys (LL M); JD/MBA; JD/MPA; JD/MSW. *Accreditation:* ABA. Part-time and evening/weekend programs available. Postbaccalaureate distance learning degree programs offered (no on-campus study). *Degree requirements:* For master's, thesis optional; for doctorate, minimum of 3 credits of clinical experience. *Entrance requirements:* For master's, JD or LL B; for doctorate, LSAT. Additional exam requirements/recommendations for international students: Required—TOEFL (for U.S. legal studies for foreign attorneys LL M program). Electronic applications accepted. *Faculty research:* Wrongful convictions, civil rights, environmental law, litigation techniques, data mining, intellectual property, practical and skills-based legal education.

Touro College, Jacob D. Fuchsberg Law Center, Central Islip, NY 11743. Offers general law (LL M); law (JD); U.S. legal studies (LL M); JD/MBA; JD/MPA; JD/MSW. JD/MBA offered with Long Island University, C.W. Post Campus or Dowling College; JD/MPA offered with Long Island University, C.W. Post Campus; JD/MSW offered with Stony Brook University, State University of New York. *Accreditation:* ABA. Part-time and evening/weekend programs available. *Entrance requirements:* For doctorate, LSAT. *Application deadline:* Applications are processed on a rolling basis. Application fee: $60. *Expenses:* Contact institution. *Financial support:* Fellowships, career-related internships or fieldwork, and Federal Work-Study available. Support available to part-time students. Financial award application deadline: 5/1. *Faculty research:* Business law, civil rights, international law, criminal justice. *Unit head:* Patricia E. Salkin, Dean, 631-761-7100. *Application contact:* Office of Admissions, 631-761-7010, E-mail: admissions@tourolaw.edu.
Website: http://www.tourolaw.edu/.

Trident University International, College of Health Sciences, Program in Health Sciences, Cypress, CA 90630. Offers clinical research administration (MS, Certificate); emergency and disaster management (MS, Certificate); environmental health science (Certificate); health care administration (PhD); health care management (MS), including health informatics; health education (MS, Certificate); health informatics (Certificate); health sciences (PhD); international health (MS); international health: educator or researcher option (PhD); international health: practitioner option (PhD); law and expert witness studies (MS, Certificate); public health (MS); quality assurance (Certificate). Part-time and evening/weekend programs available. Postbaccalaureate distance learning degree programs offered (no on-campus study). *Degree requirements:* For doctorate, comprehensive exam, thesis/dissertation, defense of dissertation. *Entrance requirements:* For master's, minimum GPA of 2.5 (students with GPA 3.0 or greater may transfer up to 30% of graduate level credits); for doctorate, minimum GPA of 3.4, curriculum vitae, course work in research methods or statistics. Additional exam

requirements/recommendations for international students: Required—TOEFL. Electronic applications accepted.

Universidad Autonoma de Guadalajara, Graduate Programs, Guadalajara, Mexico. Offers administrative law and justice (LL M); advertising and corporate communications (MA); architecture (M Arch); business (MBA); computational science (MCC); education (Ed M, Ed D); English-Spanish translation (MA); entrepreneurship and management (MBA); integrated management of digital animation (MA); international business (MIB); international corporate law (LL M); internet technologies (MS); manufacturing systems (MMS); occupational health (MS); philosophy (MA, PhD); power electronics (MS); quality systems (MQS); renewable energy (MS); social evaluation of projects (MBA); strategic market research (MBA); tax law (MA); teaching mathematics (MA).

Université Laval, Faculty of Law, Program in Notarial Law, Québec, QC G1K 7P4, Canada. Offers Diploma. Part-time programs available. *Entrance requirements:* For degree, knowledge of French. Electronic applications accepted.

University of Baltimore, Graduate School, The Yale Gordon College of Liberal Arts, Program in Legal and Ethical Studies, Baltimore, MD 21201-5779. Offers MA. Part-time and evening/weekend programs available. *Degree requirements:* For master's, thesis optional. *Entrance requirements:* For master's, minimum GPA of 3.0. Additional exam requirements/recommendations for international students: Required—TOEFL (minimum score 550 paper-based). Electronic applications accepted. *Faculty research:* Morality in law and economics, religion in lawmaking, comparative legal history, law and social change, critical issues in constitutional law, theories of justice.

University of Calgary, Faculty of Law, Programs in Natural Resources, Energy and Environmental Law, Calgary, AB T2N 1N4, Canada. Offers LL M, Postbaccalaureate Certificate. Part-time and evening/weekend programs available. *Degree requirements:* For master's, thesis optional. *Entrance requirements:* For master's, JD or LL B. Additional exam requirements/recommendations for international students: Required—TOEFL (minimum score 100 iBT), IELTS (minimum score 7). Electronic applications accepted. *Faculty research:* Natural resources law and regulations; environmental law, ethics and policies; oil and gas and energy law; water and municipal law; Aboriginal law.

University of California, Berkeley, School of Law, Program in Jurisprudence and Social Policy, Berkeley, CA 94720-1500. Offers PhD. *Degree requirements:* For doctorate, one foreign language, thesis/dissertation, oral qualifying exam. *Entrance requirements:* For doctorate, GRE General Test, sample of written work, letters of recommendation. Electronic applications accepted. *Expenses:* Contact institution. *Faculty research:* Law and philosophy, legal history, law and economics, law and political science, law and sociology.

University of California, San Diego, Office of Graduate Studies, Program in Health Policy and Law, La Jolla, CA 92093. Offers MAS. Program offered jointly with School of Medicine and California Western School of Law. Part-time programs available. *Students:* 36 part-time (26 women); includes 14 minority (2 Black or African American, non-Hispanic/Latino; 6 Asian, non-Hispanic/Latino; 6 Hispanic/Latino). 26 applicants, 77% accepted, 15 enrolled. In 2013, 12 master's awarded. *Entrance requirements:* For master's, appropriate medical, healthcare, legal or related degree; minimum GPA of 3.0 in final two years of study; minimum 3 years of relevant work experience or equivalent. Additional exam requirements/recommendations for international students: Required—TOEFL, IELTS. *Application deadline:* For fall admission, 4/7 for domestic students. Applications are processed on a rolling basis. Application fee: $80 ($100 for international students). Electronic applications accepted. *Expenses:* Tuition, state resident: full-time $11,220; part-time $1870 per quarter. Tuition, nonresident: full-time $26,322; part-time $4387 per quarter. *Required fees:* $519.50 per quarter. Part-time tuition and fees vary according to course load and program. *Financial support:* Scholarships/grants available. *Unit head:* Gerard Manecke, Program Co-Director, 619-543-3164, E-mail: gmanecke@ucsd.edu. *Application contact:* Jenna Lucius, Program Coordinator, 858-534-9162, E-mail: healthlaw@ucsd.edu.
Website: http://hlaw.ucsd.edu/.

University of Charleston, Executive Master of Forensic Accounting Program, Charleston, WV 25304-1099. Offers EMFA. Part-time programs available. Postbaccalaureate distance learning degree programs offered (minimal on-campus study). *Students:* 4 full-time (2 women). Average age 45. In 2013, 8 master's awarded. *Degree requirements:* For master's, capstone project with mock trial testimony. *Entrance requirements:* Additional exam requirements/recommendations for international students: Required—TOEFL. *Application deadline:* Applications are processed on a rolling basis. Application fee: $50. Electronic applications accepted. *Financial support:* In 2013–14, 1 student received support. Applicants required to submit FAFSA. *Unit head:* Dr. Scott Bellamy, Dean of the School of Business, 304-357-4373, E-mail: scottbellamy@ucwv.edu. *Application contact:* Robert Rufus, Program Coordinator, 304-522-8770, E-mail: mfa@ucwv.edu.
Website: http://www.ucwv.edu/Forensic-Accounting/.

University of Denver, Sturm College of Law, Program in Legal Administration, Denver, CO 80208. Offers MSLA, Certificate. Part-time and evening/weekend programs available. *Students:* 10 full-time (8 women), 27 part-time (18 women); includes 9 minority (6 Black or African American, non-Hispanic/Latino; 1 Hispanic/Latino; 2 Two or more races, non-Hispanic/Latino). Average age 36. 21 applicants, 100% accepted, 14 enrolled. In 2013, 10 master's, 1 Certificate awarded. *Degree requirements:* For master's, internship. *Entrance requirements:* For master's, GRE General Test, GMAT, or LSAT. Additional exam requirements/recommendations for international students: Required—TOEFL (minimum score 570 paper-based; 88 iBT). *Application deadline:* Applications are processed on a rolling basis. Application fee: $65. Electronic applications accepted. *Financial support:* In 2013–14, 15 students received support. Career-related internships or fieldwork, Federal Work-Study, scholarships/grants, and unspecified assistantships available. Support available to part-time students. Financial award application deadline: 2/15; financial award applicants required to submit FAFSA. *Unit head:* Hope Kentnor, Director, 303-871-6308, Fax: 303-871-6333, E-mail: hope.kentor@law.du.edu. *Application contact:* Lucy Daberkow, Assistant Director of Graduate Programs, 303-871-6324, Fax: 303-871-6378, E-mail: ldaberkow@law.du.edu.
Website: http://www.law.du.edu/index.php/msla.

University of Illinois at Springfield, Graduate Programs, College of Public Affairs and Administration, Program in Legal Studies, Springfield, IL 62703-5407. Offers MA. Part-time and evening/weekend programs available. Postbaccalaureate distance learning degree programs offered (no on-campus study). *Faculty:* 4 full-time (all women). *Students:* 6 full-time (5 women), 46 part-time (29 women); includes 19 minority (12 Black or African American, non-Hispanic/Latino; 1 American Indian or Alaska Native, non-Hispanic/Latino; 2 Hispanic/Latino; 4 Two or more races, non-Hispanic/Latino). Average age 38. 48 applicants, 38% accepted, 19 enrolled. In 2013, 7 master's awarded. *Degree requirements:* For master's, thesis or seminar. *Entrance requirements:* For master's, minimum undergraduate GPA of 3.0 (for on-campus program), 3.25 (for online program); demonstration of writing ability. Additional exam requirements/recommendations for international students: Required—TOEFL (minimum score 600 paper-based; 100 iBT). *Application deadline:* Applications are processed on a rolling basis. Application fee: $60 ($75 for international students). Electronic applications

accepted. *Expenses:* Tuition, state resident: full-time $7440. Tuition, nonresident: full-time $15,744. *Required fees:* $2985.60. *Financial support:* In 2013–14, fellowships with full tuition reimbursements (averaging $9,900 per year), research assistantships with full tuition reimbursements (averaging $9,550 per year), teaching assistantships with full tuition reimbursements (averaging $9,700 per year) were awarded; career-related internships or fieldwork, Federal Work-Study, scholarships/grants, health care benefits, and unspecified assistantships also available. Support available to part-time students. Financial award application deadline: 11/15; financial award applicants required to submit FAFSA. *Unit head:* Kathryn E. Eisenhart, JD, Program Administrator, 217-206-7882, Fax: 217-206-7807, E-mail: keise1@uis.edu. *Application contact:* Dr. Lynn Pardie, Office of Graduate Studies, 800-252-8533, Fax: 217-206-7623, E-mail: lpard1@uis.edu.
Website: http://www.uis.edu/legalstudies/.

University of Massachusetts Lowell, College of Fine Arts, Humanities and Social Sciences, School of Criminology and Justice Studies, Lowell, MA 01854-2881. Offers MA, PhD. Part-time and evening/weekend programs available. *Degree requirements:* For master's, thesis optional. *Entrance requirements:* For master's, GRE General Test or MAT. Electronic applications accepted. *Faculty research:* Family violence, criminal justice management, corrections, policing, delinquency.

University of Mississippi, Graduate School, School of Applied Sciences, Department of Legal Studies, Oxford, MS 38677. Offers MS. *Faculty:* 14 full-time (5 women), 5 part-time/adjunct (2 women). *Students:* 28 full-time (13 women), 27 part-time (9 women); includes 18 minority (16 Black or African American, non-Hispanic/Latino; 2 Two or more races, non-Hispanic/Latino), 2 international. In 2013, 15 master's awarded. Application fee: $40. *Unit head:* Dr. Eric Lambert, Interim Chair, 662-915-7902, Fax: 662-915-7981, E-mail: eglambert@olemiss.edu. *Application contact:* Dr. Christy M. Wyandt, Associate Dean, 662-915-7474, Fax: 662-915-7577, E-mail: cwyandt@olemiss.edu.
Website: http://www.olemiss.edu/depts/legalstudies/.

University of Nebraska–Lincoln, College of Law, Program in Legal Studies, Lincoln, NE 68588. Offers MLS. *Entrance requirements:* For master's, GRE or LSAT. Additional exam requirements/recommendations for international students: Required—TOEFL (minimum score 600 paper-based). Electronic applications accepted.

University of Nevada, Reno, Graduate School, College of Liberal Arts, School of Social Research and Justice Studies, Program in Judicial Studies, Reno, NV 89557. Offers MJS, PhD. Offered jointly with the National Judicial College and the National Council of Juvenile and Family Court Judges. Part-time programs available. Terminal master's awarded for partial completion of doctoral program. *Degree requirements:* For master's, thesis; for doctorate, thesis/dissertation. *Entrance requirements:* For master's and doctorate, sitting judge, law degree from an accredited school. Additional exam requirements/recommendations for international students: Required—TOEFL (minimum score 500 paper-based; 61 iBT), IELTS (minimum score 6). Electronic applications accepted. *Expenses:* Contact institution. *Faculty research:* Jury research, capital punishment, expert testimony, environmental law, medical issues.

University of New Hampshire, Graduate School, College of Liberal Arts, Program in Justice Studies, Durham, NH 03824. Offers MA. Program offered in summer only. Part-time programs available. *Faculty:* 2 full-time (1 woman). *Students:* 9 full-time (7 women), 4 part-time (3 women). Average age 24. In 2013, 12 master's awarded. *Degree requirements:* For master's, thesis optional. *Entrance requirements:* For master's, GRE. Additional exam requirements/recommendations for international students: Required—TOEFL (minimum score 550 paper-based; 80 iBT); Recommended—TWE. *Application deadline:* For fall admission, 3/1 for domestic students, 3/1 priority date for international students. Applications are processed on a rolling basis. Application fee: $65. Electronic applications accepted. *Expenses:* Tuition, state resident: full-time $13,500; part-time $750 per credit hour. Tuition, nonresident: full-time $26,200; part-time $1100 per credit hour. *Required fees:* $1741; $435.25 per term. Tuition and fees vary according to course level, course load, campus/location and program. *Financial support:* In 2013–14, 3 students received support, including 3 teaching assistantships; fellowships, research assistantships, career-related internships or fieldwork, Federal Work-Study, scholarships/grants, and tuition waivers (full and partial) also available. Support available to part-time students. Financial award application deadline: 3/1. *Unit head:* Dr. Ellen Cohn, Chairperson, 603-862-3197, E-mail: ellen.cohn@unh.edu. *Application contact:* Deborah Briand, Administrative Assistant, 603-862-1716, E-mail: justice.studies@unh.edu.
Website: http://www.unh.edu/justice-studies/.

University of Pennsylvania, Wharton School, Legal Studies and Business Ethics Department, Philadelphia, PA 19104. Offers MBA, PhD.

University of Pittsburgh, School of Law, Master of Studies in Law Program, Pittsburgh, PA 15260. Offers business law (MSL), including commercial law, corporate law, general business law, international business, tax law; Constitutional law (MSL); criminal law and justice (MSL); disabilities law (MSL); dispute resolution (MSL); education law (MSL); elder and estate planning law (MSL); employment and labor law (MSL); energy law (MSL); environment and real estate law (MSL); family law (MSL); health law (MSL); intellectual property and technology (MSL); international and comparative law (MSL); jurisprudence (MSL); personal injury and civil litigation (MSL); regulatory law (MSL); self-designed (MSL); sports and entertainment law (MSL). Part-time programs available. *Faculty:* 43 full-time (16 women), 110 part-time/adjunct (31 women). *Students:* 4 full-time (all women), 6 part-time (4 women); includes 7 minority (4 Black or African American, non-Hispanic/Latino; 2 Asian, non-Hispanic/Latino; 1 Native Hawaiian or other Pacific Islander, non-Hispanic/Latino). Average age 29. 11 applicants, 73% accepted, 7 enrolled. In 2013, 5 master's awarded. *Entrance requirements:* Additional exam requirements/recommendations for international students: Required—TOEFL (minimum score 600 paper-based; 100 iBT). *Application deadline:* For fall admission, 6/30 for domestic students, 5/1 for international students. Applications are processed on a rolling basis. Application fee: $0. *Expenses:* Tuition, state resident: full-time $19,964; part-time $807 per credit. Tuition, nonresident: full-time $32,686; part-time $1337 per credit. *Required fees:* $740; $200. Tuition and fees vary according to program. *Faculty research:* Law, health law, business law, contracts, intellectual property, environmental law. *Unit head:* Prof. Alan Meisel, Director, 412-648-1384, Fax: 412-648-2649, E-mail: meisel@pitt.edu. *Application contact:* Bethann Pischke, Administrative Coordinator, 412-648-7120, Fax: 412-648-2649, E-mail: pischke@pitt.edu.
Website: http://www.law.pitt.edu/academics/msl.

University of Pittsburgh, School of Law, Program in Health Law, Pittsburgh, PA 15260. Offers Certificate. *Faculty:* 39 full-time (15 women), 112 part-time/adjunct (26 women). *Students:* 23 full-time (9 women). *Application deadline:* For spring admission, 7/31 for domestic students. Applications are processed on a rolling basis. *Expenses:* Tuition, state resident: full-time $19,964; part-time $807 per credit. Tuition, nonresident: full-time $32,686; part-time $1337 per credit. *Required fees:* $740; $200. Tuition and fees vary according to program. *Unit head:* Prof. Alan Meisel, Professor/Director, 412-648-1384, Fax: 412-648-2649, E-mail: meisel@pitt.edu. *Application contact:* Bethann Pischke, Program Administrator, 412-648-7120, Fax: 412-648-2649, E-mail: pischke@pitt.edu.

University of San Diego, School of Law, San Diego, CA 92110. Offers business and corporate law (LL M); comparative law (LL M); general studies (LL M); international law

(LL M); law (JD); taxation (LL M, Diploma); JD/IMBA; JD/MA; JD/MBA. *Accreditation:* ABA. Part-time and evening/weekend programs available. *Faculty:* 48 full-time (16 women), 67 part-time/adjunct (24 women). *Students:* 708 full-time (357 women), 155 part-time (73 women); includes 269 minority (18 Black or African American, non-Hispanic/Latino; 4 American Indian or Alaska Native, non-Hispanic/Latino; 127 Asian, non-Hispanic/Latino; 98 Hispanic/Latino; 3 Native Hawaiian or other Pacific Islander, non-Hispanic/Latino; 19 Two or more races, non-Hispanic/Latino), 33 international. Average age 27. 2,844 applicants, 48% accepted, 243 enrolled. In 2013, 63 master's, 316 doctorates awarded. *Entrance requirements:* For master's, JD, LL B or equivalent from an ABA-accredited law school; for doctorate, LSAT, bachelor's degree, registration with the Credential Assemble Service (CAS). Additional exam requirements/recommendations for international students: Required—TOEFL (minimum score 600 paper-based; 100 iBT). *Application deadline:* For fall admission, 2/1 priority date for domestic students. Applications are processed on a rolling basis. Application fee: $50. Electronic applications accepted. *Expenses:* Contact institution. *Financial support:* In 2013–14, 610 students received support. Career-related internships or fieldwork, Federal Work-Study, institutionally sponsored loans, and scholarships/grants available. Support available to part-time students. Financial award application deadline: 3/1; financial award applicants required to submit FAFSA. *Faculty research:* Corporate law, children's advocacy, Constitutional and criminal law, international and comparative law, public interest law, intellectual property and tax law. *Unit head:* Dr. Stephen C. Ferruolo, Dean, 619-260-4527, E-mail: lawdean@sandiego.edu. *Application contact:* Jorge Garcia, Assistant Dean, JD Admissions, 619-260-4528, Fax: 619-260-2218, E-mail: jdinfo@sandiego.edu.
Website: http://www.sandiego.edu/law/.

University of South Florida, University College/Distance Education, Tampa, FL 33620-9951. *Unit head:* Kathy Barnes, Interdisciplinary Programs Coordinator, 813-974-8031, Fax: 813-974-7061, E-mail: barnesk@usf.edu. *Application contact:* Karen Tylinski, Metro Initiatives, 813-974-9943, Fax: 813-974-7061, E-mail: ktylinsk@usf.edu.
Website: http://uc.usf.edu/.

University of the District of Columbia, David A. Clarke School of Law, Washington, DC 20008. Offers clinical teaching and social justice (LL M); law (JD). *Accreditation:* ABA. Part-time and evening/weekend programs available. *Degree requirements:* For doctorate, 90 credits, advanced legal writing. *Entrance requirements:* For doctorate, LSAT. Additional exam requirements/recommendations for international students: Recommended—TOEFL. Electronic applications accepted. *Expenses:* Contact institution. *Faculty research:* HIV law, juvenile law, legislative law, community development, small business, immigration and human rights.

University of the Pacific, McGeorge School of Law, Sacramento, CA 95817. Offers advocacy (JD); criminal justice (JD); experiential law teaching (LL M); intellectual property (JD); international legal studies (JD); international water resources law (LL M, JSD); law (JD); public law and policy (JD); public policy and law (LL M); tax (JD); transnational business practice (LL M); U.S. law and policy (LL M), including public law and policy, U.S. law; water resources law (LL M), including international law, U.S. law; JD/MBA; JD/MPPA. *Accreditation:* ABA. Part-time and evening/weekend programs available. *Faculty:* 38 full-time (16 women), 32 part-time/adjunct (8 women). *Students:* 486 full-time (242 women), 179 part-time (79 women); includes 215 minority (17 Black or African American, non-Hispanic/Latino; 14 American Indian or Alaska Native, non-Hispanic/Latino; 108 Asian, non-Hispanic/Latino; 75 Hispanic/Latino; 1 Two or more races, non-Hispanic/Latino), 17 international. Average age 28. 1,558 applicants, 65% accepted, 162 enrolled. In 2013, 37 master's, 308 doctorates awarded. *Degree requirements:* For master's, thesis (for some programs); for doctorate, thesis/dissertation (for some programs). *Entrance requirements:* For master's, JD; for doctorate, LSAT (for JD), LL M (for JSD). Additional exam requirements/recommendations for international students: Required—TOEFL (minimum score 600 paper-based; 100 iBT). *Application deadline:* For fall admission, 3/15 priority date for domestic students. Applications are processed on a rolling basis. Application fee: $50. Electronic applications accepted. *Expenses:* Contact institution. *Financial support:* Fellowships, research assistantships, teaching assistantships, career-related internships or fieldwork, Federal Work-Study, institutionally sponsored loans, and scholarships/grants available. Support available to part-time students. Financial award applicants required to submit FAFSA. *Faculty research:* International legal studies, public policy and law, advocacy, intellectual property law, taxation, criminal law. *Unit head:* Francis Jay Mootz, III, Dean, 916-739-7151, E-mail: jmootz@pacific.edu. *Application contact:* 916-739-7105, Fax: 916-739-7301, E-mail: mcgeorge@pacific.edu.
Website: http://www.mcgeorge.edu/.

University of the Sacred Heart, Graduate Programs, Program in Systems of Justice, San Juan, PR 00914-0383. Offers human rights and anti-discriminatory processes (MASJ); mediation and transformation of conflicts (MASJ).

University of Washington, Graduate School, School of Law, Seattle, WA 98195-3020. Offers Asian law (LL M, PhD); intellectual property law and policy (LL M); law (JD); law of sustainable international development (LL M); taxation (LL M); JD/LL M; JD/MA; JD/MAIS; JD/MBA; JD/MPA; JD/MS; JD/PhD. *Accreditation:* ABA. *Degree requirements:* For master's, thesis; for doctorate, thesis/dissertation (for some programs). *Entrance requirements:* For master's, language proficiency (LL M in Asian law); for doctorate, LSAT (for JD). Additional exam requirements/recommendations for international students: Required—TOEFL. *Expenses:* Contact institution. *Faculty research:* Asian, international and comparative law, intellectual property law, health law, environmental law, taxation.

University of Windsor, Faculty of Graduate Studies, Faculty of Arts and Social Sciences, Department of Communication Studies, Windsor, ON N9B 3P4, Canada. Offers communication and social justice (MA). *Degree requirements:* For master's, thesis. *Entrance requirements:* For master's, writing sample/media production or multimedia portfolio. Additional exam requirements/recommendations for international students: Required—TOEFL (minimum score 600 paper-based). Electronic applications accepted. *Faculty research:* Sociology of news, media ownership and control, communication networks and social movements, issues of media representation.

Valparaiso University, Graduate School, Program in Legal Studies and Principles, Valparaiso, IN 46383. Offers Certificate. Part-time and evening/weekend programs

available. *Entrance requirements:* Additional exam requirements/recommendations for international students: Required—TOEFL (minimum score 550 paper-based; 80 iBT), IELTS (minimum score 6). *Application deadline:* Applications are processed on a rolling basis. Application fee: $30 ($50 for international students). Electronic applications accepted. *Expenses: Tuition:* Full-time $10,350; part-time $575 per credit hour. *Required fees:* $378; $101 per term. Tuition and fees vary according to course load and program. *Financial support:* Available to part-time students. Applicants required to submit FAFSA. *Unit head:* Dr. Jennifer A. Ziegler, Dean, Graduate School and Continuing Education, 219-464-5313, Fax: 219-464-5381, E-mail: jennifer.ziegler@valpo.edu. *Application contact:* Jessica Choquette, Graduate Admissions Specialist, 219-464-5313, Fax: 219-464-5381, E-mail: jessica.choquette@valpo.edu.
Website: http://www.valpo.edu/grad/programs/lawcert.php.

Vermont Law School, Graduate and Professional Programs, Environmental Law Center, South Royalton, VT 05068-0096. Offers energy law (LL M); energy regulation and law (MERL); environmental law (LL M); environmental law and policy (MELP); JD/MELP. Part-time programs available. *Entrance requirements:* Additional exam requirements/recommendations for international students: Required—TOEFL. *Faculty research:* Environment and technology; takings; international environmental law; interaction among science, law, and environmental policy; air pollution.

Washburn University, School of Law, Topeka, KS 66621. Offers global legal studies (LL M); law (MSL, JD). *Accreditation:* ABA. *Entrance requirements:* For doctorate, LSAT. Additional exam requirements/recommendations for international students: Recommended—TOEFL (minimum score 550 paper-based). *Application deadline:* For fall admission, 4/1 priority date for domestic and international students; for spring admission, 11/1 priority date for domestic and international students. Applications are processed on a rolling basis. Application fee: $40. Electronic applications accepted. Application fee is waived when completed online. *Expenses:* Contact institution. *Financial support:* Career-related internships or fieldwork and scholarships/grants available. Financial award applicants required to submit FAFSA. *Faculty research:* Constitutional law, family law, energy law, banking and securities law, oil and gas. *Unit head:* Thomas J. Romig, Dean, 785-670-1662, Fax: 785-670-3249, E-mail: thomas.romig@washburn.edu. *Application contact:* Yolanda Ingram, Director of Admissions, 785-670-1185, Fax: 785-670-1120, E-mail: yolanda.ingram@washburn.edu.
Website: http://washburnlaw.edu/.

Weber State University, College of Social and Behavioral Sciences, Program in Criminal Justice, Ogden, UT 84408-1001. Offers MCJ. Part-time and evening/weekend programs available. *Faculty:* 4 full-time (0 women), 2 part-time/adjunct (1 woman). *Students:* 6 full-time (4 women), 12 part-time (8 women); includes 3 minority (1 Hispanic/Latino; 2 Two or more races, non-Hispanic/Latino). Average age 33. 13 applicants, 100% accepted, 13 enrolled. In 2013, 21 master's awarded. *Entrance requirements:* For master's, GRE General Test, resume. Additional exam requirements/recommendations for international students: Required—TOEFL. *Application deadline:* Applications are processed on a rolling basis. Application fee: $60 ($90 for international students). *Expenses:* Tuition, state resident: full-time $7118; part-time $253 per credit hour. Tuition, nonresident: full-time $12,480; part-time $634 per credit hour. *Required fees:* $34.33; $34.33 per credit hour. $257 per semester. Full-time tuition and fees vary according to course load. *Financial support:* In 2013–14, 3 students received support, including 3 research assistantships (averaging $1,000 per year). *Unit head:* Dr. Bruce Bayley, Chair, 801-626-8134, Fax: 801-626-6145, E-mail: bbayley@weber.edu. *Application contact:* Faye Medd, Secretary, 801-626-6369, Fax: 801-626-6146, E-mail: fmedd@weber.edu.

Webster University, College of Arts and Sciences, Department of Behavioral and Social Sciences, Program in Legal Studies, St. Louis, MO 63119-3194. Offers MA. Part-time and evening/weekend programs available. *Degree requirements:* For master's, thesis optional. *Entrance requirements:* Additional exam requirements/recommendations for international students: Required—TOEFL. *Expenses: Tuition:* Full-time $11,610; part-time $645 per credit hour. Tuition and fees vary according to campus/location and program. *Faculty research:* Intellectual property rights, emerging torts, death penalty, juvenile justice, confidentiality issues in banking.

Webster University, College of Arts and Sciences, Department of Behavioral and Social Sciences, Program in Patent Practice, St. Louis, MO 63119-3194. Offers MS. Part-time and evening/weekend programs available. *Entrance requirements:* Additional exam requirements/recommendations for international students: Required—TOEFL. *Expenses: Tuition:* Full-time $11,610; part-time $645 per credit hour. Tuition and fees vary according to campus/location and program. *Faculty research:* Intellectual property rights, emerging torts, death penalty, juvenile justice, confidentiality issues in banking.

West Virginia University, Eberly College of Arts and Sciences, School of Applied Social Sciences, Division of Public Administration, Morgantown, WV 26506. Offers legal studies (MLS); public administration (MPA); JD/MPA; MSW/MPA. *Accreditation:* NASPAA. Part-time programs available. *Degree requirements:* For master's, internship. *Entrance requirements:* For master's, GRE General Test, minimum GPA of 2.75. Additional exam requirements/recommendations for international students: Required—TOEFL. Electronic applications accepted. *Faculty research:* Public management and organization, conflict resolution, work satisfaction, health administration, social policy and welfare.

Wilfrid Laurier University, Faculty of Graduate and Postdoctoral Studies, School of International Policy and Governance, Global Governance Program, Waterloo, ON N2L 3C5, Canada. Offers conflict and security (PhD); global environment (PhD); global justice and human rights (PhD); global political economy (PhD); global social governance (PhD); multilateral institutions and diplomacy (PhD). Offered jointly with University of Waterloo. *Degree requirements:* For doctorate, thesis/dissertation. *Entrance requirements:* For doctorate, MA in political science, history, economics, international development studies, international peace studies, globalization studies, environmental studies or related field with minimum A-. Additional exam requirements/recommendations for international students: Required—TOEFL (minimum score 89 iBT). Electronic applications accepted. *Faculty research:* Global political economy, global environment, conflict and security, global justice and human rights, multilateral institutions and diplomacy.

ACADEMIC AND PROFESSIONAL PROGRAMS IN LIBRARY AND INFORMATION STUDIES

Section 28
Library and Information Studies

This section contains a directory of institutions offering graduate work in library and information studies, followed by in-depth entries submitted by institutions that chose to prepare detailed program descriptions. Additional information about programs listed in the directory but not augmented by an in-depth entry may be obtained by writing directly to the dean of a graduate school or chair of a department at the address given in the directory.

For programs offering related work, see also in this book *Education.* In another guide in this series:

Graduate Programs in Engineering & Applied Sciences
See *Computer Science and Information Technology*

CONTENTS

Program Directories

Archives/Archival Administration	1578
Information Studies	1580
Library Science	1586

Displays and Close-Ups

Pratt Institute	1582, 1597
Syracuse University	1583, 1599
University of Kentucky	1593, 1601

Archives/Archival Administration

Claremont Graduate University, Graduate Programs, School of Arts and Humanities, Department of History, Claremont, CA 91711-6160. Offers Africana history (Certificate); American studies and U.S. history (MA, PhD); archival studies (MA); early modern studies (MA, PhD); European studies (MA, PhD); oral history (MA, PhD); MBA/MA; MBA/PhD. *Faculty:* 4 full-time (2 women), 1 part-time/adjunct (0 women). *Students:* 42 full-time (20 women), 22 part-time (9 women); includes 21 minority (1 Black or African American, non-Hispanic/Latino; 7 Asian, non-Hispanic/Latino; 8 Hispanic/Latino; 1 Native Hawaiian or other Pacific Islander, non-Hispanic/Latino; 4 Two or more races, non-Hispanic/Latino), 1 international. Average age 37. In 2013, 6 master's, 4 doctorates, 1 other advanced degree awarded. Terminal master's awarded for partial completion of doctoral program. *Entrance requirements:* For master's and doctorate, GRE General Test. Additional exam requirements/recommendations for international students: Required—TOEFL (minimum score 550 paper-based; 80 iBT). *Application deadline:* For fall admission, 2/1 priority date for domestic and international students. Applications are processed on a rolling basis. Application fee: $80. Electronic applications accepted. *Expenses: Tuition:* Full-time $40,560; part-time $1690 per credit. *Required fees:* $275 per semester. Tuition and fees vary according to program. *Financial support:* Fellowships, research assistantships, Federal Work-Study, institutionally sponsored loans, and scholarships/grants available. Support available to part-time students. Financial award application deadline: 2/15; financial award applicants required to submit FAFSA. *Faculty research:* Intellectual and social history, cultural studies, gender studies, Western history, Chicano history. *Unit head:* Joshua Goode, Chair, 909-607-7430, E-mail: joshua.goode@cgu.edu. *Application contact:* Susan Hampson, Admissions Coordinator, 909-607-1278, E-mail: humanities@cgu.edu. Website: http://www.cgu.edu/pages/369.asp.

Clayton State University, School of Graduate Studies, College of Information and Mathematical Sciences, Program in Archival Studies, Morrow, GA 30260-0285. Offers MAS. Postbaccalaureate distance learning degree programs offered (no on-campus study). *Entrance requirements:* For master's, GRE, 2 official transcripts; 3 letters of recommendation; statement of purpose. Additional exam requirements/recommendations for international students: Required—TOEFL (minimum score 550 paper-based). Electronic applications accepted.

Columbia University, School of Continuing Education, Program in Information and Archive Management, New York, NY 10027. Offers MS. Part-time programs available. *Entrance requirements:* For master's, minimum undergraduate GPA of 3.0. Additional exam requirements/recommendations for international students: Required—American Language Program placement test. Electronic applications accepted. *Faculty research:* Library science technology, information systems.

Drexel University, Antoinette Westphal College of Media Arts and Design, Program in Museum Leadership, Philadelphia, PA 19104-2875. Offers MS. Offered in partnership with the Academy of Natural Sciences of Drexel University. Part-time programs available. Postbaccalaureate distance learning degree programs offered (minimal on-campus study). *Degree requirements:* For master's, practicum.

Drexel University, College of Computing and Informatics, Master of Science in Library and Information Science Program, Philadelphia, PA 19104-2875. Offers archival studies (MS); competitive intelligence and knowledge management (MS); digital libraries (MS); library and information services (MS); school library media (MS); youth services (MS). Part-time and evening/weekend programs available. Postbaccalaureate distance learning degree programs offered (no on-campus study). *Faculty:* 31 full-time (20 women), 24 part-time/adjunct (15 women). *Students:* 136 full-time (99 women), 282 part-time (234 women); includes 55 minority (26 Black or African American, non-Hispanic/Latino; 4 American Indian or Alaska Native, non-Hispanic/Latino; 12 Asian, non-Hispanic/Latino; 13 Hispanic/Latino), 12 international. Average age 34. 277 applicants, 90% accepted, 116 enrolled. In 2013, 234 master's awarded. *Entrance requirements:* For master's, GRE General Test. Additional exam requirements/recommendations for international students: Required—TOEFL (minimum score 600 paper-based; 100 iBT). *Application deadline:* For fall admission, 8/1 for domestic and international students; for spring admission, 2/1 for domestic and international students. Applications are processed on a rolling basis. Electronic applications accepted. *Expenses:* Contact institution. *Financial support:* In 2013–14, 217 students received support, including 227 fellowships with partial tuition reimbursements available (averaging $22,500 per year); institutionally sponsored loans and scholarships/grants also available. Support available to part-time students. Financial award application deadline: 3/1; financial award applicants required to submit FAFSA. *Faculty research:* Library and information resources and services, knowledge organization and representation, information retrieval/information visualization/bibliometrics, information needs and behaviors, digital libraries. *Unit head:* Dr. David E. Fenske, Dean/Professor of Information Science, 215-895-2475, Fax: 215-895-6378, E-mail: fenske@drexel.edu. *Application contact:* Matthew Lechtenberg, Graduate Admissions Manager, 215-895-1951, Fax: 215-895-2303, E-mail: ml333@drexel.edu. Website: http://cci.drexel.edu/academics/graduate-programs/ms-in-library-information-science.aspx.

East Tennessee State University, School of Graduate Studies, School of Continuing Studies and Academic Outreach, Johnson City, TN 37614. Offers archival studies (MALS, Postbaccalaureate Certificate); gender and diversity (MALS); regional and community studies (MALS); strategic leadership (MPS); training and development (MPS). Part-time programs available. Postbaccalaureate distance learning degree programs offered (no on-campus study). *Faculty:* 4 full-time (all women), 2 part-time/adjunct (1 woman). *Students:* 20 full-time (14 women), 41 part-time (33 women); includes 8 minority (2 Black or African American, non-Hispanic/Latino; 1 Asian, non-Hispanic/Latino; 2 Hispanic/Latino; 3 Two or more races, non-Hispanic/Latino), 2 international. Average age 39. 42 applicants, 50% accepted, 19 enrolled. In 2013, 11 master's, 5 other advanced degrees awarded. *Degree requirements:* For master's, comprehensive exam, thesis optional, professional project. *Entrance requirements:* For master's, GRE General Test, minimum GPA of 2.75, professional portfolio, three letters of recommendation, interview, writing sample; for Postbaccalaureate Certificate, minimum GPA of 2.5, three letters of recommendation, interview. Additional exam requirements/recommendations for international students: Required—TOEFL (minimum score 550 paper-based; 79 iBT). *Application deadline:* For fall admission, 6/1 for domestic students, 4/30 for international students; for spring admission, 11/1 for domestic students, 9/30 for international students. Application fee: $35 ($45 for international students). Electronic applications accepted. *Expenses:* Tuition, state resident: full-time $7900; part-time $395 per credit hour. Tuition, nonresident: full-time $21,960; part-time $1098 per credit hour. *Required fees:* $1345; $84 per credit hour. *Financial support:* In 2013–14, 14 students received support, including 3 research assistantships with full tuition reimbursements available (averaging $6,000 per year), 1 teaching assistantship with full tuition reimbursement available (averaging $9,000 per year); institutionally sponsored loans, scholarships/grants, tuition waivers, and unspecified assistantships also available. Financial award application deadline: 7/1; financial award applicants required to submit FAFSA. *Faculty research:* Appalachian studies, women's and gender studies, interdisciplinary theory, regional and Southern cultures. *Unit head:* Dr. Rick E. Osborn, Dean, 423-439-4223, Fax: 423-439-7091, E-mail: osbornr@etsu.edu. *Application contact:* Mary Duncan, Graduate Specialist, 423-439-4302, Fax: 423-439-5624, E-mail: duncanm@etsu.edu. Website: http://www.etsu.edu/academicaffairs/scs/.

Emporia State University, School of Library and Information Management, Emporia, KS 66801-5415. Offers archives studies (Certificate); library and information management (MLS, PhD, Certificate). *Accreditation:* ALA (one or more programs are accredited). Part-time and evening/weekend programs available. Postbaccalaureate distance learning degree programs offered (minimal on-campus study). *Faculty:* 9 full-time (5 women). *Students:* 92 full-time (68 women), 225 part-time (188 women); includes 32 minority (1 Black or African American, non-Hispanic/Latino; 6 Asian, non-Hispanic/Latino; 13 Hispanic/Latino; 1 Native Hawaiian or other Pacific Islander, non-Hispanic/Latino; 11 Two or more races, non-Hispanic/Latino), 4 international. 138 applicants, 80% accepted, 77 enrolled. In 2013, 139 master's, 3 doctorates, 12 other advanced degrees awarded. *Degree requirements:* For master's, comprehensive exam, thesis optional; for doctorate, thesis/dissertation. *Entrance requirements:* For master's, GRE General Test, interview, minimum undergraduate GPA of 3.0, letters of recommendation; for doctorate, GRE General Test, interview, minimum graduate GPA of 3.5. Additional exam requirements/recommendations for international students: Required—TOEFL (minimum score 520 paper-based; 68 iBT). *Application deadline:* For fall admission, 8/15 priority date for domestic students. Applications are processed on a rolling basis. Application fee: $30 ($75 for international students). Electronic applications accepted. *Expenses: Tuition, area resident:* Part-time $220 per credit hour. Tuition, state resident: part-time $220 per credit hour. Tuition, nonresident: part-time $685 per credit hour. *Required fees:* $73 per credit hour. *Financial support:* In 2013–14, 12 research assistantships with full tuition reimbursements (averaging $7,200 per year) were awarded; Federal Work-Study, institutionally sponsored loans, and unspecified assistantships also available. Financial award application deadline: 3/15; financial award applicants required to submit FAFSA. *Unit head:* Dr. Gwen Alexander, Dean, 620-341-5203, Fax: 620-341-5233, E-mail: galexan1@emporia.edu. *Application contact:* Candace Boardman, Director, Kansas MLS Program, 620-341-6159, E-mail: cboardma@emporia.edu. Website: http://www.emporia.edu/las/index.html.

Long Island University–LIU Post, College of Information and Computer Science, Palmer School of Library and Information Science, Brookville, NY 11548-1300. Offers archives and records management (Certificate); information studies (PhD); library and information science (MS); library media specialist (MS); public library management (Certificate). *Accreditation:* ALA (one or more programs are accredited). Part-time and evening/weekend programs available. Postbaccalaureate distance learning degree programs offered (minimal on-campus study). *Degree requirements:* For master's, thesis optional, internship; for doctorate, thesis/dissertation, qualifying exam. *Entrance requirements:* For master's, GRE or MAT, minimum undergraduate GPA of 3.0, resume. Electronic applications accepted. *Faculty research:* Information retrieval, digital libraries, scientometric and infometric studies, preservation/archiving and electronic records.

Middle Tennessee State University, College of Graduate Studies, College of Liberal Arts, Department of History, Murfreesboro, TN 37132. Offers archival management (Graduate Certificate); history (MA); public history (PhD). Part-time and evening/weekend programs available. Postbaccalaureate distance learning degree programs offered. *Faculty:* 28 full-time (13 women), 7 part-time/adjunct (3 women). *Students:* 30 full-time (20 women), 72 part-time (51 women); includes 10 minority (5 Black or African American, non-Hispanic/Latino; 3 Hispanic/Latino; 2 Two or more races, non-Hispanic/Latino). 65 applicants, 86% accepted. *Degree requirements:* For master's, one foreign language, comprehensive exam, thesis optional; for doctorate, one foreign language, comprehensive exam, thesis/dissertation. *Entrance requirements:* For master's and doctorate, GRE. Additional exam requirements/recommendations for international students: Required—TOEFL (minimum score 525 paper-based; 71 iBT) or IELTS (minimum score 6). *Application deadline:* For fall admission, 6/1 for domestic and international students. Applications are processed on a rolling basis. Application fee: $25 ($30 for international students). Electronic applications accepted. *Financial support:* In 2013–14, 27 students received support. Tuition waivers available. Support available to part-time students. Financial award application deadline: 5/1; financial award applicants required to submit FAFSA. *Faculty research:* Historic preservation, public history. *Unit head:* Dr. James Beeby, Chair, 615-898-2536, Fax: 615-898-5881. *Application contact:* Dr. Michael D. Allen, Dean and Vice Provost for Research, 615-898-2840, Fax: 615-904-8020, E-mail: michael.allen@mtsu.edu.

Montclair State University, The Graduate School, College of the Arts, Department of Art and Design, Program in Fine Art, Montclair, NJ 07043-1624. Offers museum management (MA); studio (MA). Part-time and evening/weekend programs available. *Degree requirements:* For master's, project. *Entrance requirements:* For master's, GRE or MAT, 2 letters of recommendation, essay. Electronic applications accepted.

New York University, Graduate School of Arts and Science, Department of History, New York, NY 10012-1019. Offers African diaspora (PhD); African history (PhD); archival management (Advanced Certificate); Atlantic history (PhD); French studies/history (PhD); Hebrew and Judaic studies/history (PhD); history (MA, PhD), including Europe (PhD), Latin America and the Caribbean (PhD), United States (PhD), women's history (MA); Middle Eastern history (MA); Middle Eastern studies/history (PhD); public history (Advanced Certificate); world history (MA); JD/MA; MA/Advanced Certificate. Part-time programs available. *Faculty:* 43 full-time (19 women). *Students:* 120 full-time (76 women), 45 part-time (33 women); includes 33 minority (13 Black or African American, non-Hispanic/Latino; 1 American Indian or Alaska Native, non-Hispanic/Latino; 3 Asian, non-Hispanic/Latino; 10 Hispanic/Latino; 6 Two or more races, non-Hispanic/Latino), 38 international. Average age 29. 447 applicants, 30% accepted, 37 enrolled. In 2013, 23 master's, 11 doctorates, 1 other advanced degree awarded. Terminal master's awarded for partial completion of doctoral program. *Degree requirements:* For master's, seminar paper; for doctorate, one foreign language, thesis/dissertation, oral and written exams; for Advanced Certificate, internship. *Entrance requirements:* For master's, GRE General Test, minimum GPA of 3.0, writing sample; for doctorate, GRE. Additional exam requirements/recommendations for international students: Required—TOEFL. *Application deadline:* For fall admission, 12/18 for domestic and international students. Application fee: $95. *Expenses: Tuition:* Full-time $35,856; part-time $1494 per unit. *Required fees:* $1408; $64 per unit. $473 per term. Tuition and fees vary according to course load and program. *Financial support:* Fellowships with tuition reimbursements, research assistantships, teaching

assistantships with tuition reimbursements, career-related internships or fieldwork, Federal Work-Study, institutionally sponsored loans, scholarships/grants, health care benefits, and unspecified assistantships available. Financial award application deadline: 12/18; financial award applicants required to submit FAFSA. *Faculty research:* African, East Asian, medieval, early modern, and modern European history; U.S. history; African and African diaspora; Latin American history; Atlantic world. *Unit head:* Barbara Weinstein, Chair, 212-998-8600, Fax: 212-995-4017, E-mail: history.admissions@nyu.edu. *Application contact:* Kostis Smyrlis, Director of Graduate Studies, 212-998-8600, Fax: 212-995-4017, E-mail: history.admissions@nyu.edu.
Website: http://history.as.nyu.edu/.

New York University, Tisch School of the Arts, Program in Moving Image Archiving and Preservation, New York, NY 10012-1019. Offers MA. *Faculty:* 2 full-time, 4 part-time/adjunct. *Students:* 20 full-time (10 women), 4 part-time (3 women); includes 7 minority (2 Asian, non-Hispanic/Latino; 4 Hispanic/Latino; 1 Two or more races, non-Hispanic/Latino), 2 international. Average age 28. 32 applicants, 53% accepted, 12 enrolled. In 2013, 6 master's awarded. *Degree requirements:* For master's, internship. *Entrance requirements:* For master's, GRE. Additional exam requirements/recommendations for international students: Required—TOEFL or IELTS. *Application deadline:* For fall admission, 12/1 for domestic and international students. Application fee: $60. Electronic applications accepted. *Expenses: Tuition:* Full-time $35,856; part-time $1494 per unit. *Required fees:* $1408; $64 per unit. $473 per term. Tuition and fees vary according to course load and program. *Financial support:* In 2013–14, 11 students received support, including 5 fellowships with full and partial tuition reimbursements available; tuition waivers (partial) also available. Financial award application deadline: 2/15. *Unit head:* Richard Allen, Head, 212-998-1618. *Application contact:* Dan Sandford, Director of Graduate Admissions, 212-998-1918, Fax: 212-995-4060, E-mail: tisch.gradadmissions@nyu.edu.
Website: http://www.cinema.tisch.nyu.edu/.

Pratt Institute, School of Information and Library Science, New York, NY 10011. Offers archives (Adv C); library and information science (MS, Adv C); library and information science: library media specialist (MS); library media specialist (Adv C); museum libraries (Adv C); JD/MS. *Accreditation:* ALA. Part-time programs available. *Faculty:* 9 full-time (4 women), 26 part-time/adjunct (13 women). *Students:* 134 full-time (108 women), 91 part-time (72 women); includes 47 minority (17 Black or African American, non-Hispanic/Latino; 10 Asian, non-Hispanic/Latino; 19 Hispanic/Latino; 1 Native Hawaiian or other Pacific Islander, non-Hispanic/Latino), 1 international. Average age 30. 197 applicants, 94% accepted, 77 enrolled. In 2013, 134 master's, 3 other advanced degrees awarded. *Degree requirements:* For master's, thesis. *Entrance requirements:* Additional exam requirements/recommendations for international students: Required—TOEFL (minimum score 600 paper-based; 100 iBT). *Application deadline:* For fall admission, 1/5 for domestic and international students; for spring admission, 10/1 for domestic and international students. Application fee: $50 ($90 for international students). Electronic applications accepted. *Expenses:* Contact institution. *Financial support:* Career-related internships or fieldwork, Federal Work-Study, institutionally sponsored loans, scholarships/grants, health care benefits, and unspecified assistantships available. Support available to part-time students. Financial award application deadline: 2/1; financial award applicants required to submit FAFSA. *Faculty research:* Development of urban libraries and information centers, medical and law librarianship, information management. *Unit head:* Dr. Tula Giannini, Dean, 212-647-7682, E-mail: giannini@pratt.edu. *Application contact:* Young Hah, Director of Graduate Admissions, 718-636-3683, Fax: 718-399-4242, E-mail: yhah@pratt.edu.
Website: https://www.pratt.edu/academics/information-and-library-sciences/.
See Display on page 1582 and Close-Up on page 1597.

Simmons College, Graduate School of Library and Information Science, Boston, MA 02115. Offers archives management (MS, Certificate); children's literature (MA); digital stewardship (Certificate); instructional technology (Certificate); library and information science (MS, PhD); managerial leadership in the informational professions (PhD); school library teacher (MS, Certificate); writing for children (MFA); MA/MA; MA/MAT; MA/MFA; MS/MA. *Accreditation:* ALA (one or more programs are accredited). Part-time and evening/weekend programs available. Postbaccalaureate distance learning degree programs offered (no on-campus study). *Students:* 55 full-time (45 women), 716 part-time (585 women); includes 81 minority (19 Black or African American, non-Hispanic/Latino; 1 American Indian or Alaska Native, non-Hispanic/Latino; 14 Asian, non-Hispanic/Latino; 32 Hispanic/Latino; 15 Two or more races, non-Hispanic/Latino), 9 international. 430 applicants, 82% accepted, 207 enrolled. In 2013, 281 master's, 4 doctorates awarded. *Degree requirements:* For master's, thesis optional, capstone project experience; for doctorate, comprehensive exam, 36 credit hours (includes 3-credit dissertation). *Entrance requirements:* For doctorate, GRE, transcripts, personal statement, resume, recommendations, master's degree. Additional exam requirements/recommendations for international students: Required—TOEFL (minimum score 550 paper-based; 79 iBT), IELTS (minimum score 7). *Application deadline:* For fall admission, 3/1 for domestic and international students; for spring admission, 9/1 for domestic and international students; for summer admission, 2/1 for domestic and international students. Applications are processed on a rolling basis. Application fee: $65. Electronic applications accepted. *Financial support:* In 2013–14, 67 students received support, including 5 fellowships with partial tuition reimbursements available (averaging $32,461 per year), 6 research assistantships (averaging $35,168 per year), 7 teaching assistantships with full and partial tuition reimbursements available (averaging $3,000 per year); scholarships/grants, tuition waivers, and unspecified assistantships also available. Financial award application deadline: 2/1; financial award applicants required to submit FAFSA. *Faculty research:* Archives and social justice, information-seeking behavior, information retrieval, organization of information, cultural heritage informatics. *Unit head:* Dr. Eileen G. Abels, Dean, 617-521-2869. *Application contact:* Sarah Petrakos, 617-521-2868, Fax: 617-521-3192, E-mail: gslisadm@simmons.edu.
Website: http://www.simmons.edu/gslis/.

The University of British Columbia, Faculty of Arts, School of Library, Archival and Information Studies, Master of Archival Studies Program, Vancouver, BC V6T 1Z1, Canada. Offers MAS. *Degree requirements:* For master's, thesis optional. *Entrance requirements:* For master's, minimum B+ average or minimum GPA of 3.3 in undergraduate upper-division courses. Additional exam requirements/recommendations for international students: Required—TOEFL (minimum score 600 paper-based; 100 iBT). Electronic applications accepted. *Expenses: Tuition, area resident:* Full-time $8000 Canadian dollars. *Faculty research:* Diplomatics, electronic record, appraisal, descriptive standards, preservation.

The University of British Columbia, Faculty of Arts, School of Library, Archival and Information Studies, PhD Program in Library, Archival and Information Studies, Vancouver, BC V6T 1Z1, Canada. Offers PhD. *Degree requirements:* For doctorate, thesis/dissertation. *Entrance requirements:* For doctorate, GRE, minimum GPA of 3.3 in MAS or MLIS (other master's degrees may be considered). Additional exam requirements/recommendations for international students: Required—TOEFL (minimum score 600 paper-based; 100 iBT). Electronic applications accepted. *Expenses: Tuition, area resident:* Full-time $8000 Canadian dollars. *Faculty research:* Computer systems/

database design; library and archival management; archival description and organization; children's literature and youth services; interactive information retrieval.

University of California, Los Angeles, Graduate Division, Graduate School of Education and Information Studies, Department of Information Studies, Los Angeles, CA 90095-1521. Offers archival studies (MLIS); informatics (MLIS); information studies (PhD); library and information science (Certificate); library studies (MLIS); moving image archive studies (MA); rare books, print and visual culture (MLIS); MBA/MLIS; MLIS/MA. *Accreditation:* ALA (one or more programs are accredited). *Faculty:* 10 full-time (6 women), 14 part-time/adjunct (9 women). *Students:* 114 full-time (79 women), 11 part-time (8 women); includes 50 minority (9 Black or African American, non-Hispanic/Latino; 1 American Indian or Alaska Native, non-Hispanic/Latino; 19 Asian, non-Hispanic/Latino; 18 Hispanic/Latino; 2 Native Hawaiian or other Pacific Islander, non-Hispanic/Latino; 1 Two or more races, non-Hispanic/Latino), 6 international. Average age 27. 165 applicants, 62% accepted, 51 enrolled. In 2013, 80 master's, 7 doctorates, 1 other advanced degree awarded. Terminal master's awarded for partial completion of doctoral program. *Degree requirements:* For master's, thesis or alternative, professional portfolio; for doctorate, thesis/dissertation, oral and written qualifying exams. *Entrance requirements:* For master's, GRE General Test, previous course work in statistics; for doctorate, GRE General Test, previous course work in statistics, 2 samples of research writing in English. Additional exam requirements/recommendations for international students: Required—TOEFL (minimum score 560 paper-based; 87 iBT), IELTS (minimum score 7). *Application deadline:* For fall admission, 12/10 for domestic and international students. Applications are processed on a rolling basis. Application fee: $80 ($100 for international students). Electronic applications accepted. *Financial support:* In 2013–14, 47 students received support, including 47 fellowships with full and partial tuition reimbursements available (averaging $14,045 per year), 7 research assistantships with partial tuition reimbursements available (averaging $30,155 per year), 8 teaching assistantships with partial tuition reimbursements available (averaging $20,656 per year); career-related internships or fieldwork, Federal Work-Study, institutionally sponsored loans, scholarships/grants, and unspecified assistantships also available. Financial award application deadline: 3/1; financial award applicants required to submit FAFSA. *Faculty research:* Digital libraries, archives and electronic records, interface design, cultural informatics, preservation/conservation, access. *Unit head:* Dr. Gregory H. Leazer, Associate Professor and Chair, 310-825-8799, E-mail: gleazer@ucla.edu. *Application contact:* Susan S. Abler, Student Affairs Officer, 310-825-5269, Fax: 310-206-4460, E-mail: abler@gseis.ucla.edu.
Website: http://is.gseis.ucla.edu/.

University of California, Los Angeles, Graduate Division, School of Theater, Film and Television, Interdepartmental Program in Moving Image Archive Studies, Los Angeles, CA 90095. Offers MA. *Degree requirements:* For master's, comprehensive exam, thesis. *Entrance requirements:* For master's, bachelor's degree; minimum undergraduate GPA of 3.0 (or its equivalent if letter grade system not used); writing sample. Additional exam requirements/recommendations for international students: Required—TOEFL. Electronic applications accepted.

University of California, Riverside, Graduate Division, Department of History, Riverside, CA 92521-0102. Offers archival management (MA); historic preservation (MA); history (MA, PhD); museum curatorship (MA). Part-time programs available. *Faculty:* 28 full-time (12 women). *Students:* 79 full-time (34 women); includes 18 minority (2 Black or African American, non-Hispanic/Latino; 2 American Indian or Alaska Native, non-Hispanic/Latino; 7 Asian, non-Hispanic/Latino; 6 Hispanic/Latino; 1 Native Hawaiian or other Pacific Islander, non-Hispanic/Latino), 1 international. Average age 31. 69 applicants, 29% accepted, 9 enrolled. In 2013, 22 master's, 3 doctorates awarded. Terminal master's awarded for partial completion of doctoral program. *Degree requirements:* For master's, one foreign language, comprehensive exam, internship report and oral exams, or thesis; for doctorate, 2 foreign languages, thesis/dissertation, qualifying exams. *Entrance requirements:* For master's and doctorate, GRE General Test, minimum GPA of 3.2. Additional exam requirements/recommendations for international students: Required—TOEFL (minimum score 550 paper-based; 80 iBT). *Application deadline:* For fall admission, 12/15 priority date for domestic and international students. Applications are processed on a rolling basis. Application fee: $80 ($100 for international students). Electronic applications accepted. *Financial support:* In 2013–14, 56 students received support, including fellowships with full tuition reimbursements available (averaging $10,129 per year), research assistantships with partial tuition reimbursements available (averaging $16,169 per year), teaching assistantships with partial tuition reimbursements available (averaging $17,310 per year); career-related internships or fieldwork, Federal Work-Study, institutionally sponsored loans, scholarships/grants, traineeships, health care benefits, tuition waivers (full and partial), and unspecified assistantships also available. Financial award application deadline: 12/15; financial award applicants required to submit FAFSA. *Faculty research:* Native American history, United States, public history, Europe, Latin America. *Unit head:* Dr. Thomas Cogswell, Chair, 951-827-1437, Fax: 951-827-5299, E-mail: history@ucr.edu. *Application contact:* Graduate Admissions, 951-827-3313, Fax: 951-827-2238, E-mail: grdadmis@ucr.edu.
Website: http://history.ucr.edu/.

University of Manitoba, Faculty of Graduate Studies, Faculty of Arts, Department of History, Winnipeg, MB R3T 2N2, Canada. Offers archival studies (MA); history (MA, PhD). MA offered jointly with The University of Winnipeg. *Degree requirements:* For master's, thesis; for doctorate, one foreign language, thesis/dissertation.

University of Massachusetts Boston, Office of Graduate Studies, College of Liberal Arts, Program in History, Boston, MA 02125-3393. Offers archival methods (MA); historical archaeology (MA); history (MA). Part-time and evening/weekend programs available. *Degree requirements:* For master's, thesis, oral exam. *Entrance requirements:* For master's, minimum GPA of 2.75. *Faculty research:* European intellectual history, American labor and social history in 19th century, colonial American Revolution, Afro-American Cold War.

University of Michigan, Horace H. Rackham School of Graduate Studies, School of Information, Ann Arbor, MI 48109-1285. Offers archives and records management (MSI); health informatics (MS); human computer interaction (MSI); information (PhD); information analysis and retrieval (MSI); information economics for management (MSI); library and information science (MSI); preservation of information (MSI); school library media (MSI); social computing (MSI). *Accreditation:* ALA (one or more programs are accredited). *Entrance requirements:* For master's and doctorate, GRE General Test. Additional exam requirements/recommendations for international students: Required—TOEFL (minimum score 600 paper-based; 100 iBT). Electronic applications accepted. Tuition and fees vary according to course level, course load, degree level, program and student level.

University of Oklahoma, College of Arts and Sciences, School of Library and Information Studies, Program in Library and Information Studies, Norman, OK 73019-0390. Offers MLIS, Graduate Certificate, M Ed/MLIS, MBA/MLIS. Part-time and evening/weekend programs available. Postbaccalaureate distance learning degree programs offered. *Students:* 60 full-time (47 women), 121 part-time (97 women); includes 32 minority (8 Black or African American, non-Hispanic/Latino; 13 American Indian or Alaska Native, non-Hispanic/Latino; 4 Asian, non-Hispanic/Latino; 3 Hispanic/Latino; 4

Two or more races, non-Hispanic/Latino), 3 international. Average age 33. 38 applicants, 87% accepted, 27 enrolled. In 2013, 60 master's awarded. *Degree requirements:* For master's, comprehensive exam (MLIS). *Entrance requirements:* For master's, GRE, minimum GPA of 3.2 in last 60 hours or 3.0 overall. Additional exam requirements/recommendations for international students: Required—TOEFL (minimum score 550 paper-based; 79 iBT). *Application deadline:* For fall admission, 3/1 priority date for domestic students, 4/1 for international students; for spring admission, 10/15 for domestic students, 9/1 for international students. Application fee: $40 ($90 for international students). Electronic applications accepted. *Expenses:* Tuition, state resident: full-time $4205; part-time $175.20 per credit hour. Tuition, nonresident: full-time $16,205; part-time $675.20 per credit hour. *Required fees:* $2745; $103.85 per credit hour. $126.50 per semester. *Financial support:* Federal Work-Study, scholarships/grants, health care benefits, and unspecified assistantships available. Support available to part-time students. Financial award application deadline: 6/1; financial award applicants required to submit FAFSA. *Faculty research:* Equity of access, information services to special populations, information use in the digital age, library services and materials for young people, pluralization of archival theory and education. *Unit head:* Cecelia Brown, Director, 405-325-3921, Fax: 405-325-7648, E-mail: cbrown@ou.edu. *Application contact:* Maggie Ryan, Coordinator of Admissions, 405-325-3921, Fax: 405-325-7648, E-mail: mryan@ou.edu.

University of South Carolina, The Graduate School, College of Arts and Sciences, Department of History, Program in Public History, Columbia, SC 29208. Offers archive management (MA); historic preservation (MA); museum administration (MA); museum management (Certificate); MLIS/MA. *Degree requirements:* For master's, one foreign language, thesis, internship. *Entrance requirements:* For master's, GRE General Test, writing sample. Additional exam requirements/recommendations for international students: Required—TOEFL. Electronic applications accepted. *Faculty research:* Museum studies, historic preservation, archives administration.

University of Wisconsin–Milwaukee, Graduate School, School of Information Studies, Milwaukee, WI 53201-0413. Offers advanced studies in library and information science (CAS); archives and records administration (CAS); digital libraries (Certificate); information studies (MLIS, PhD); MLIS/MA; MLIS/MM; MLIS/MS. *Accreditation:* ALA (one or more programs are accredited). Part-time programs available. *Faculty:* 22 full-time (11 women). *Students:* 140 full-time (109 women), 254 part-time (196 women); includes 33 minority (12 Black or African American, non-Hispanic/Latino; 1 American Indian or Alaska Native, non-Hispanic/Latino; 1 Asian, non-Hispanic/Latino; 4 Hispanic/Latino; 15 Two or more races, non-Hispanic/Latino), 24 international. Average age 34. 221 applicants, 79% accepted, 94 enrolled. In 2013, 238 master's awarded. *Entrance requirements:* For master's, GRE General Test or MAT; for doctorate, GRE. Additional exam requirements/recommendations for international students: Required—TOEFL (minimum score 550 paper-based), IELTS (minimum score 6.5). *Application deadline:* For fall admission, 1/1 priority date for domestic students; for spring admission, 9/1 for domestic students. Applications are processed on a rolling basis. Application fee: $56 ($96 for international students). Electronic applications accepted. *Financial support:* In 2013–14, 4 teaching assistantships were awarded; fellowships, research assistantships, career-related internships or fieldwork, Federal Work-Study, health care benefits, unspecified assistantships, and project assistantships also available. Support available to part-time students. Financial award application deadline: 4/15; financial award applicants required to submit FAFSA. *Total annual research expenditures:* $298,170. *Unit head:* Wooseob Jeong, Interim Dean/Associate Professor, 414-229-6167, E-mail: wjj8612@uwm.edu. *Application contact:* Hur-Li Lee, Representative, 414-229-6838, E-mail: hurli@uwm.edu.
Website: http://www.uwm.edu/Dept/SLIS/.

Wayne State University, College of Liberal Arts and Sciences, Department of History, Detroit, MI 48202. Offers Africa (PhD); America (PhD); archival administration (Graduate Certificate); Asia (PhD); Europe (PhD); gender (PhD); history (MA); labor (PhD); science and technology (PhD); world history (PhD, Graduate Certificate); JD/MA; M Ed/MA; MLIS/MA. Evening/weekend programs available. *Faculty:* 22 full-time (9 women). *Students:* 28 full-time (12 women), 23 part-time (7 women); includes 5 minority (3 Black or African American, non-Hispanic/Latino; 1 Hispanic/Latino; 1 Two or more races, non-Hispanic/Latino), 2 international. Average age 40. 67 applicants, 30% accepted, 10 enrolled. In 2013, 9 master's, 3 doctorates awarded. *Degree requirements:* For master's, one foreign language, thesis (for some programs), final oral exam on thesis or essay and seminar; for doctorate, 2 foreign languages, thesis/dissertation, qualifying exam in 4 fields of history. *Entrance requirements:* For master's, GRE General Test, minimum undergraduate GPA of 3.25 in history, 3.0 overall; at least 18 credits in history and related subjects at the advanced undergraduate level, foreign language; letter of intent; research paper; at least two letters of recommendation from former instructors; must meet admissions requirements for 2nd program if applying for joint degree program; for doctorate, GRE General Test, minimum GPA of 3.0; letter of intent; research paper; at least three letters of recommendation from former professors; apply by February 15 for fall admission only; for Graduate Certificate, baccalaureate degree from accredited college or university; minimum GPA of 3.0, 3.25 in a minimum of eighteen semester credits in history and related subjects at the advanced undergraduate level. Additional exam requirements/recommendations for international students: Required—TOEFL (minimum score 550 paper-based; 79 iBT), TWE (minimum score 5.5), Michigan English Language Assessment Battery (minimum score 85); Recommended—IELTS (minimum score 6.5). *Application deadline:* For fall admission, 2/1 for domestic and international students; for winter admission, 11/1 for domestic students, 10/1 priority date for international students; for spring admission, 3/15 for domestic students, 1/1 priority date for international students. Applications are processed on a rolling basis. Application fee: $0. Electronic applications accepted. *Expenses:* Tuition, state resident: part-time $554.15 per credit. Tuition, nonresident: part-time $1200.35 per credit. *Required fees:* $42.15 per credit. $268.30 per semester. Tuition and fees vary according to course load and program. *Financial support:* In 2013–14, 16 students received support, including 1 fellowship with tuition reimbursement available (averaging $16,842 per year), 6 teaching assistantships with tuition reimbursements available (averaging $16,508 per year); research assistantships with tuition reimbursements available, institutionally sponsored loans, scholarships/grants, health care benefits, and unspecified assistantships also available. Financial award application deadline: 3/31; financial award applicants required to submit FAFSA. *Faculty research:* Labor and working class history, urban history, citizenship and politics, gender and women's history. *Unit head:* Dr. Marc W. Kruman, Chair, 313-577-2525, Fax: 313-577-6987, E-mail: mkruman@wayne.edu. *Application contact:* Dr. Gayle McCreedy, Academic Service Officer, 313-577-2592, Fax: 313-577-6987, E-mail: g.mccreedy@wayne.edu.
Website: http://clasweb.clas.wayne.edu/history.

Wayne State University, School of Library and Information Science, Detroit, MI 48202. Offers academic libraries (MLIS); archival administration (MLIS, Certificate); general librarianship (MLIS); health sciences librarianship (MLIS); information management for librarians (Certificate); information science (MLIS); law librarianship (MLIS); library and information science (Spec); organization of information (MLIS); public libraries (MLIS); public library services to children and young adults (MLIS, Certificate); records management (MLIS); references services (MLIS); school library media specialist endorsement (MLIS); special libraries (MLIS); urban libraries (MLIS); MLIS/MA. *Accreditation:* ALA (one or more programs are accredited). Part-time and evening/weekend programs available. Postbaccalaureate distance learning degree programs offered (no on-campus study). *Faculty:* 13 full-time (9 women), 17 part-time/adjunct (13 women). *Students:* 112 full-time (80 women), 372 part-time (296 women); includes 65 minority (26 Black or African American, non-Hispanic/Latino; 11 Asian, non-Hispanic/Latino; 18 Hispanic/Latino; 10 Two or more races, non-Hispanic/Latino), 2 international. Average age 33. 275 applicants, 61% accepted, 109 enrolled. In 2013, 179 master's, 42 other advanced degrees awarded. *Entrance requirements:* For master's and other advanced degree, GRE or MAT (if undergraduate GPA is between 2.5 and 2.99), minimum undergraduate GPA of 3.0 or graduate degree, personal statement, resume or curriculum vitae. Additional exam requirements/recommendations for international students: Required—TOEFL (minimum score 550 paper-based; 79 iBT); Recommended—IELTS (minimum score 6.5), TWE (minimum score 5.5). *Application deadline:* For fall admission, 7/1 for domestic students, 5/1 priority date for international students; for winter admission, 10/1 for domestic students, 9/1 priority date for international students; for spring admission, 3/15 for domestic students, 1/1 priority date for international students. Applications are processed on a rolling basis. Application fee: $0. Electronic applications accepted. *Expenses:* Contact institution. *Financial support:* In 2013–14, 65 students received support. Fellowships with tuition reimbursements available, research assistantships with tuition reimbursements available, institutionally sponsored loans, scholarships/grants, and unspecified assistantships available. Support available to part-time students. Financial award application deadline: 3/31; financial award applicants required to submit FAFSA. *Faculty research:* Library services, information management issues, digital content management, library/community engagement, archives and preservation. *Unit head:* Dr. Stephen Bajjaly, Associate Dean and Professor, 313-577-0350, Fax: 313-577-7563, E-mail: bajjaly@wayne.edu. *Application contact:* Matthew Fredericks, Academic Services Officer I, 313-577-2446, Fax: 313-577-7563, E-mail: mfredericks@wayne.edu.
Website: http://slis.wayne.edu/.

Information Studies

The Catholic University of America, School of Arts and Sciences, Department of Library and Information Science, Washington, DC 20064. Offers MSLS, JD/MSLS, MSLS/MA, MSLS/MS. *Accreditation:* ALA (one or more programs are accredited). Part-time programs available. *Faculty:* 8 full-time (6 women), 14 part-time/adjunct (7 women). *Students:* 11 full-time (7 women), 159 part-time (121 women); includes 66 minority (33 Black or African American, non-Hispanic/Latino; 10 Asian, non-Hispanic/Latino; 14 Hispanic/Latino; 9 Two or more races, non-Hispanic/Latino), 3 international. Average age 34. 97 applicants, 60% accepted, 34 enrolled. In 2013, 105 master's awarded. *Degree requirements:* For master's, comprehensive exam. *Entrance requirements:* For master's, statement of purpose, official copies of academic transcripts, three letters of recommendation, interview. Additional exam requirements/recommendations for international students: Required—TOEFL (minimum score 580 paper-based). *Application deadline:* For fall admission, 8/1 priority date for domestic students, 7/15 for international students; for spring admission, 11/1 priority date for domestic students, 10/15 for international students. Applications are processed on a rolling basis. Application fee: $55. Electronic applications accepted. *Expenses:* Contact institution. *Financial support:* Fellowships, research assistantships, teaching assistantships, Federal Work-Study, scholarships/grants, tuition waivers (full and partial), and unspecified assistantships available. Financial award application deadline: 2/1; financial award applicants required to submit FAFSA. *Faculty research:* Digital collections, library and information science education, information design and architecture, information system design and evaluation. *Total annual research expenditures:* $474. *Unit head:* Dr. William Kules, Chair, 202-319-5876, E-mail: kules@cua.edu. *Application contact:* Andrew Woodall, Director of Graduate Admissions, 202-319-5057, Fax: 202-319-6533, E-mail: cua-admissions@cua.edu.
Website: http://slis.cua.edu/.

Central Connecticut State University, School of Graduate Studies, School of Arts and Sciences, Department of Information Design, New Britain, CT 06050-4010. Offers graphic information design (MA). Part-time and evening/weekend programs available. *Faculty:* 3 full-time (1 woman). *Students:* 8 full-time (6 women), 9 part-time (8 women); includes 2 minority (1 Black or African American, non-Hispanic/Latino; 1 Asian, non-Hispanic/Latino), 2 international. Average age 36. 9 applicants, 78% accepted, 5 enrolled. In 2013, 5 master's awarded. *Degree requirements:* For master's, thesis or alternative. *Entrance requirements:* For master's, portfolio, minimum undergraduate GPA of 3.0, essay. Additional exam requirements/recommendations for international students: Required—TOEFL (minimum score 550 paper-based; 79 iBT). *Application deadline:* For fall admission, 6/1 for domestic students, 5/1 for international students; for spring admission, 11/1 for domestic and international students. Applications are processed on a rolling basis. Application fee: $50. Electronic applications accepted. Part-time tuition and fees vary according to degree level. *Financial support:* In 2013–14, 3 research assistantships were awarded; career-related internships or fieldwork, Federal Work-Study, scholarships/grants, and unspecified assistantships also available. Support available to part-time students. Financial award application deadline: 3/1; financial award applicants required to submit FAFSA. *Unit head:* Dr. Eleanor Thornton, Chair, 860-832-2564, E-mail: thorntone@ccsu.edu. *Application contact:* Patricia Gardner, Associate Director of Graduate Studies, 860-832-2350, Fax: 860-832-2362, E-mail: graduateadmissions@ccsu.edu.
Website: http://www.design.ccsu.edu/.

Columbia University, School of Continuing Education, Program in Information and Archive Management, New York, NY 10027. Offers MS. Part-time programs available. *Entrance requirements:* For master's, minimum undergraduate GPA of 3.0. Additional exam requirements/recommendations for international students: Required—American

Language Program placement test. Electronic applications accepted. *Faculty research:* Library science technology, information systems.

Cornell University, Graduate School, Graduate Fields of Arts and Sciences, Field of Information Science, Ithaca, NY 14853-0001. Offers cognition (PhD); human computer interaction (PhD); information science (PhD); information systems (PhD); social aspects of information (PhD). *Faculty:* 42 full-time (13 women). *Students:* 52 full-time (21 women); includes 9 minority (1 Black or African American, non-Hispanic/Latino; 6 Asian, non-Hispanic/Latino; 2 Two or more races, non-Hispanic/Latino, 30 international. Average age 26. 214 applicants, 26% accepted, 32 enrolled. In 2013, 1 doctorate awarded. *Degree requirements:* For doctorate, comprehensive exam, thesis/dissertation. *Entrance requirements:* For doctorate, GRE General Test, 3 letters of recommendation. Additional exam requirements/recommendations for international students: Required—TOEFL (minimum score 550 paper-based; 77 iBT). *Application deadline:* For fall admission, 1/1 for domestic students. Application fee: $95. Electronic applications accepted. *Financial support:* In 2013–14, 24 students received support, including 5 fellowships with full tuition reimbursements available, 13 research assistantships with full tuition reimbursements available, 6 teaching assistantships with full tuition reimbursements available; institutionally sponsored loans, scholarships/grants, tuition waivers (full and partial), and unspecified assistantships also available. Financial award applicants required to submit FAFSA. *Faculty research:* Digital libraries, game theory, data mining, human-computer interaction, computational linguistics. *Unit head:* Director of Graduate Studies, 607-255-5925. *Application contact:* Graduate Field Assistant, 607-255-5925, E-mail: info@infosci.cornell.edu.
Website: http://www.gradschool.cornell.edu/fields.php?id-9A&a-2.

Dalhousie University, Faculty of Management, School of Information Management, Halifax, NS B3H 3J5, Canada. Offers MIM, MLIS, LL B/MLIS, MBA/MLIS, MLIS/MPA, MLIS/MREM. *Accreditation:* ALA (one or more programs are accredited). Part-time programs available. *Degree requirements:* For master's, one foreign language, thesis optional. *Entrance requirements:* For master's, resume, interview. Additional exam requirements/recommendations for international students: Required—TOEFL, IELTS, CANTEST, CAEL, or Michigan English Language Assessment Battery. Electronic applications accepted. *Faculty research:* Information-seeking behavior, electronic text design, browsing in digital environments, information diffusion among scientists.

Dominican University, Graduate School of Library and Information Science, River Forest, IL 60305-1099. Offers knowledge management (Certificate); library and information science (MLIS, PhD); professional studies (MA); special studies (CSS); MBA/MLIS; MLIS/M Div; MLIS/MA; MLIS/MM. MLIS/M Div offered jointly with McCormick Theological Seminary, MLIS/MA with Loyola University Chicago, MLIS/MM with Northwestern University. *Accreditation:* ALA (one or more programs are accredited). Part-time and evening/weekend programs available. Postbaccalaureate distance learning degree programs offered (minimal on-campus study). *Faculty:* 13 full-time (7 women), 11 part-time/adjunct (7 women). *Students:* 97 full-time (76 women), 225 part-time (181 women); includes 61 minority (23 Black or African American, non-Hispanic/Latino; 1 American Indian or Alaska Native, non-Hispanic/Latino; 7 Asian, non-Hispanic/Latino; 29 Hispanic/Latino; 1 Two or more races, non-Hispanic/Latino), 3 international. Average age 34. 140 applicants, 69% accepted, 68 enrolled. In 2013, 194 master's, 5 doctorates awarded. *Degree requirements:* For doctorate, thesis/dissertation. *Entrance requirements:* For master's, minimum GPA of 3.0, GRE General Test, or MAT; for doctorate, MLIS or related MA, minimum GPA of 3.0, GRE General Test or MAT. Additional exam requirements/recommendations for international students: Required—TOEFL. *Application deadline:* For fall admission, 6/1 priority date for domestic students; for winter admission, 3/1 priority date for domestic students; for spring admission, 10/1 priority date for domestic students. Applications are processed on a rolling basis. Application fee: $25. *Expenses:* Contact institution. *Financial support:* In 2013–14, 158 students received support. Fellowships, research assistantships, career-related internships or fieldwork, Federal Work-Study, scholarships/grants, and tuition waivers (partial) available. Support available to part-time students. Financial award application deadline: 4/15; financial award applicants required to submit FAFSA. *Faculty research:* Productivity and the information environment, bibliometrics, library history, subject access, library materials and services for children. *Unit head:* Dr. Kate Marek, Acting Dean, 708-524-6648, Fax: 708-524-6657, E-mail: kmarek@dom.edu. *Application contact:* Anne Hurley, Director of Graduate Admissions, 708-524-6829, E-mail: ahurley@dom.edu.
Website: http://gslis.dom.edu/.

Drexel University, College of Computing and Informatics, Master of Science in Information Systems Program, Philadelphia, PA 19104-2875. Offers MSIS. Part-time and evening/weekend programs available. Postbaccalaureate distance learning degree programs offered (no on-campus study). *Faculty:* 31 full-time (20 women), 24 part-time/adjunct (15 women). *Students:* 33 full-time (13 women), 140 part-time (47 women); includes 52 minority (26 Black or African American, non-Hispanic/Latino; 22 Asian, non-Hispanic/Latino; 4 Hispanic/Latino), 20 international. Average age 32. 120 applicants, 68% accepted, 53 enrolled. In 2013, 56 master's awarded. *Entrance requirements:* For master's, GRE General Test. Additional exam requirements/recommendations for international students: Required—TOEFL (minimum score 600 paper-based; 100 iBT). *Application deadline:* For fall admission, 8/1 for domestic and international students; for spring admission, 2/1 for domestic and international students. Applications are processed on a rolling basis. Electronic applications accepted. *Expenses:* Contact institution. *Financial support:* In 2013–14, 25 students received support, including 44 fellowships with partial tuition reimbursements available (averaging $22,500 per year); institutionally sponsored loans, scholarships/grants, and tuition waivers (partial) also available. Support available to part-time students. Financial award applicants required to submit FAFSA. *Faculty research:* Information retrieval/information visualization/bibliometrics, human-computer interaction, digital libraries, databases, text/data mining. *Unit head:* Dr. David E. Fenske, Dean/Professor of Information Science, 215-895-2475, Fax: 215-895-6378, E-mail: fenske@drexel.edu. *Application contact:* Matthew Lechtenberg, Graduate Admissions Manager, 215-895-1951, Fax: 215-895-2303, E-mail: ml333@drexel.edu.
Website: http://cci.drexel.edu/academics/graduate-programs/ms-in-information-systems.aspx.

Emporia State University, School of Library and Information Management, Emporia, KS 66801-5415. Offers archives studies (Certificate); library and information management (MLS, PhD, Certificate). *Accreditation:* ALA (one or more programs are accredited). Part-time and evening/weekend programs available. Postbaccalaureate distance learning degree programs offered (minimal on-campus study). *Faculty:* 9 full-time (5 women). *Students:* 92 full-time (68 women), 225 part-time (188 women); includes 32 minority (1 Black or African American, non-Hispanic/Latino; 6 Asian, non-Hispanic/Latino; 13 Hispanic/Latino; 1 Native Hawaiian or other Pacific Islander, non-Hispanic/Latino; 11 Two or more races, non-Hispanic/Latino), 4 international. 138 applicants, 80% accepted, 77 enrolled. In 2013, 139 master's, 3 doctorates, 12 other advanced degrees awarded. *Degree requirements:* For master's, comprehensive exam, thesis optional; for doctorate, thesis/dissertation. *Entrance requirements:* For master's, GRE General Test, interview, minimum undergraduate GPA of 3.0, letters of recommendation; for doctorate, GRE General Test, interview, minimum graduate GPA

of 3.5. Additional exam requirements/recommendations for international students: Required—TOEFL (minimum score 520 paper-based; 68 iBT). *Application deadline:* For fall admission, 8/15 priority date for domestic students. Applications are processed on a rolling basis. Application fee: $30 ($75 for international students). Electronic applications accepted. *Expenses: Tuition, area resident:* Part-time $220 per credit hour. Tuition, state resident: part-time $220 per credit hour. Tuition, nonresident: part-time $685 per credit hour. *Required fees:* $73 per credit hour. *Financial support:* In 2013–14, 12 research assistantships with full tuition reimbursements (averaging $7,200 per year) were awarded; Federal Work-Study, institutionally sponsored loans, and unspecified assistantships also available. Financial award application deadline: 3/15; financial award applicants required to submit FAFSA. *Unit head:* Dr. Gwen Alexander, Dean, 620-341-5203, Fax: 620-341-5233, E-mail: galexan1@emporia.edu. *Application contact:* Candace Boardman, Director, Kansas MLS Program, 620-341-6159, E-mail: cboardma@emporia.edu.
Website: http://www.emporia.edu/las/index.html.

Florida State University, The Graduate School, College of Communication and Information, School of Information, Tallahassee, FL 32306-2100. Offers general information studies (MA); information studies (Specialist); information technology (MS); library and information studies (PhD). *Accreditation:* ALA (one or more programs are accredited). Part-time and evening/weekend programs available. Postbaccalaureate distance learning degree programs offered (no on-campus study). *Faculty:* 31 full-time (18 women), 11 part-time/adjunct (5 women). *Students:* 108 full-time (82 women), 305 part-time (230 women); includes 99 minority (36 Black or African American, non-Hispanic/Latino; 20 Asian, non-Hispanic/Latino; 34 Hispanic/Latino; 9 Two or more races, non-Hispanic/Latino). Average age 35. 195 applicants, 78% accepted, 103 enrolled. In 2013, 166 master's, 4 doctorates, 4 other advanced degrees awarded. Terminal master's awarded for partial completion of doctoral program. *Degree requirements:* For master's, thesis optional, minimum GPA of 3.0, 36 hours (MSLIS); 32 hours (MSIT); for doctorate, comprehensive exam, thesis/dissertation, dissertation defense, manuscript clearance, minimum GPA of 3.0; for Specialist, minimum GPA of 3.0; 30 hours. *Entrance requirements:* For master's, GRE (recommended minimum percentile of 50 on each of the verbal and quantitative portions and writing score of 4.0), minimum GPA of 3.0 on last 2 years of baccalaureate degree, resume, statement of goals, two letters of recommendation, official transcripts from every college-level institution attended; for doctorate, GRE (recommended minimum percentile of 50 on each of the verbal and quantitative portions and writing score of 4.0), minimum GPA of 3.0 on last degree program, resume, 3 letters of recommendation, personal/goals statement, writing sample, brief digital video, official transcripts from all college-level institutions attended; for Specialist, GRE (recommended minimum percentile of 50 on each of the verbal and quantitative portions and writing score of 4.0), minimum graduate GPA of 3.2, resume, statement of goals, 2 letters of recommendation, writing sample, official transcripts from every college-level institution attended. Additional exam requirements/recommendations for international students: Required—TOEFL (minimum score 585 paper-based; 94 iBT), IELTS (minimum score 6.5). *Application deadline:* For fall admission, 7/1 for domestic and international students; for spring admission, 11/1 for domestic and international students. Applications are processed on a rolling basis. Application fee: $30. Electronic applications accepted. *Expenses:* Contact institution. *Financial support:* In 2013–14, 54 students received support, including 7 fellowships with full tuition reimbursements available (averaging $16,000 per year), 24 research assistantships with full tuition reimbursements available (averaging $16,000 per year), 23 teaching assistantships with full tuition reimbursements available (averaging $16,000 per year); career-related internships or fieldwork, Federal Work-Study, scholarships/grants, health care benefits, tuition waivers, and unspecified assistantships also available. Financial award application deadline: 3/1; financial award applicants required to submit FAFSA. *Faculty research:* Needs assessment, social informatics, usability analysis, human information behavior, youth services. *Total annual research expenditures:* $2 million. *Unit head:* Dr. Kathleen Burnett, Interim Director and Professor, 850-644-8124, Fax: 850-644-9763, E-mail: kathleen.burnett@cci.fsu.edu. *Application contact:* Graduate Student Services, 850-645-3280, Fax: 850-644-9763, E-mail: slisgradadmissions@admin.fsu.edu.
Website: http://slis.fsu.edu/.

Long Island University–Hudson at Westchester, Program in Library and Information Science, Purchase, NY 10577. Offers MS. Part-time and evening/weekend programs available.

Long Island University–LIU Post, College of Information and Computer Science, Palmer School of Library and Information Science, Brookville, NY 11548-1300. Offers archives and records management (Certificate); information studies (PhD); library and information science (MS); library media specialist (MS); public library management (Certificate). *Accreditation:* ALA (one or more programs are accredited). Part-time and evening/weekend programs available. Postbaccalaureate distance learning degree programs offered (minimal on-campus study). *Degree requirements:* For master's, thesis optional, internship; for doctorate, thesis/dissertation, qualifying exam. *Entrance requirements:* For master's, GRE or MAT, minimum undergraduate GPA of 3.0, resume. Electronic applications accepted. *Faculty research:* Information retrieval, digital libraries, scientometric and infometric studies, preservation/archiving and electronic records.

Louisiana State University and Agricultural & Mechanical College, Graduate School, College of Human Sciences and Education, School of Library and Information Science, Baton Rouge, LA 70803. Offers MLIS. *Accreditation:* ALA. Part-time and evening/weekend programs available. Postbaccalaureate distance learning degree programs offered (no on-campus study). *Faculty:* 10 full-time (8 women). *Students:* 56 full-time (45 women), 83 part-time (69 women); includes 17 minority (9 Black or African American, non-Hispanic/Latino; 1 American Indian or Alaska Native, non-Hispanic/Latino; 1 Asian, non-Hispanic/Latino; 4 Hispanic/Latino; 2 Two or more races, non-Hispanic/Latino), 1 international. Average age 32. 42 applicants, 83% accepted, 21 enrolled. In 2013, 62 master's awarded. *Degree requirements:* For master's, comprehensive exam, thesis optional. *Entrance requirements:* For master's, GRE General Test, minimum GPA of 3.0. Additional exam requirements/recommendations for international students: Required—TOEFL (minimum score 550 paper-based; 79 IBT), IELTS (minimum score 6.5), or PTE (minimum score 59). *Application deadline:* For fall admission, 1/25 priority date for domestic students, 5/15 for international students; for spring admission, 10/15 for international students. Applications are processed on a rolling basis. Application fee: $50 ($70 for international students). Electronic applications accepted. *Financial support:* In 2013–14, 97 students received support, including 10 fellowships (averaging $20,000 per year), 6 research assistantships with partial tuition reimbursements available (averaging $13,000 per year), 14 teaching assistantships with partial tuition reimbursements available (averaging $12,630 per year); career-related internships or fieldwork, Federal Work-Study, institutionally sponsored loans, scholarships/grants, health care benefits, and unspecified assistantships also available. Support available to part-time students. Financial award applicants required to submit FAFSA. *Faculty research:* Information retrieval, management, collection development, public libraries. *Total annual research expenditures:* $21,404. *Unit head:* Dr. Beth M. Paskoff, Dean, 225-578-3158, Fax: 225-578-4581, E-mail: bpaskoff@lsu.edu.

SECTION 28: LIBRARY AND INFORMATION STUDIES

Information Studies

Application contact: LaToya Joseph, Administrative Assistant, 225-578-3150, Fax: 225-578-4581, E-mail: lcjoseph@lsu.edu. Website: http://slis.lsu.edu/.

Mansfield University of Pennsylvania, Graduate Studies, Program in School Library and Information Technologies, Mansfield, PA 16933. Offers library science (M Ed). Part-time and evening/weekend programs available. Postbaccalaureate distance learning degree programs offered. *Degree requirements:* For master's, comprehensive exam, thesis optional. *Entrance requirements:* For master's, minimum GPA of 3.0. Additional exam requirements/recommendations for international students: Required—TOEFL (minimum score 550 paper-based). Electronic applications accepted. *Expenses:* Contact institution.

McGill University, Faculty of Graduate and Postdoctoral Studies, Faculty of Education, School of Information Studies, Montréal, QC H3A 2T5, Canada. Offers MLIS, PhD, Certificate, Diploma. *Accreditation:* ALA (one or more programs are accredited).

Metropolitan State University, College of Management, St. Paul, MN 55106-5000. Offers business administration (MBA, DBA); database administration (Graduate Certificate); healthcare information technology management (Graduate Certificate); information assurance security (Graduate Certificate); management information systems (MMIS); MIS generalist (Graduate Certificate); MIS systems analysis and design (Graduate Certificate); project management (Graduate Certificate); public and nonprofit administration (MPNA). Part-time and evening/weekend programs available. *Degree requirements:* For master's, thesis optional, computer language (MMIS). *Entrance requirements:* For master's, GMAT (for MBA), resume. Additional exam requirements/recommendations for international students: Required—TOEFL (minimum score 550 paper-based). Electronic applications accepted. *Expenses:* Tuition, state resident: full-time $5548. Tuition, nonresident: full-time $10,929. *Faculty research:* Yugoslav economic system, workers' cooperatives, participative management and job enrichment, global business systems.

North Carolina Central University, School of Library and Information Sciences, Durham, NC 27707-3129. Offers MIS, MLS. *Accreditation:* ALA (one or more programs are accredited). Part-time and evening/weekend programs available. *Degree requirements:* For master's, one foreign language, thesis, research paper, or project. *Entrance requirements:* For master's, GRE, 90 hours in liberal arts. Additional exam requirements/recommendations for international students: Required—TOEFL. *Faculty research:* African-American resources, planning and evaluation, analysis of economic and physical resources, geography of information, artificial intelligence.

Pratt Institute, School of Information and Library Science, New York, NY 10011. Offers archives (Adv C); library and information science (MS, Adv C); library and information science: library media specialist (MS); library media specialist (Adv C); museum libraries (Adv C); JD/MS. *Accreditation:* ALA. Part-time programs available. *Faculty:* 9 full-time (4 women), 26 part-time/adjunct (13 women). *Students:* 134 full-time (108 women), 91 part-time (72 women); includes 47 minority (17 Black or African American, non-Hispanic/Latino; 10 Asian, non-Hispanic/Latino; 19 Hispanic/Latino; 1 Native Hawaiian or other Pacific Islander, non-Hispanic/Latino), 1 international. Average age 30. 197 applicants, 94% accepted, 77 enrolled. In 2013, 134 master's, 3 other advanced degrees awarded. *Degree requirements:* For master's, thesis. *Entrance requirements:* Additional exam requirements/recommendations for international students: Required—TOEFL (minimum score 600 paper-based; 100 iBT). *Application deadline:* For fall admission, 1/5 for domestic and international students; for spring admission, 10/1 for domestic and international students. Application fee: $50 ($90 for international students). Electronic applications accepted. *Expenses:* Contact institution. *Financial support:* Career-related internships or fieldwork, Federal Work-Study, institutionally sponsored loans, scholarships/grants, health care benefits, and unspecified assistantships available. Support available to part-time students. Financial award application deadline: 2/1; financial award applicants required to submit FAFSA. *Faculty research:* Development of urban libraries and information centers, medical and law librarianship, information management. *Unit head:* Dr. Tula Giannini, Dean, 212-647-7682, E-mail: giannini@pratt.edu. *Application contact:* Young Hah, Director of Graduate Admissions, 718-636-3683, Fax: 718-399-4242, E-mail: yhah@pratt.edu. Website: https://www.pratt.edu/academics/information-and-library-sciences/.
See Display on this page and Close-Up on page 1597.

Queens College of the City University of New York, Division of Graduate Studies, Social Science Division, Graduate School of Library and Information Studies, Flushing, NY 11367-1597. Offers MLS, AC. *Accreditation:* ALA (one or more programs are accredited). Part-time and evening/weekend programs available. *Degree requirements:* For master's, thesis; for AC, thesis optional. *Entrance requirements:* For master's, minimum GPA of 3.0; for AC, master's degree or equivalent. Additional exam requirements/recommendations for international students: Required—TOEFL.

Queen's University at Kingston, School of Graduate Studies, Faculty of Arts and Sciences, Department of Sociology, Kingston, ON K7L 3N6, Canada. Offers communication and Information technology (MA, PhD); feminist sociology (MA, PhD); socio-legal studies (MA, PhD); sociological theory (MA, PhD). Part-time programs available. *Degree requirements:* For master's, thesis; for doctorate, comprehensive exam, thesis/dissertation. *Entrance requirements:* For master's, honors bachelors degree in sociology; for doctorate, honors bachelors degree, masters degree in sociology. Additional exam requirements/recommendations for international students: Required—TOEFL. *Faculty research:* Social change and modernization, social control, deviance and criminology, surveillance.

Rutgers, The State University of New Jersey, New Brunswick, School of Communication, Information and Library Studies, Program in Communication and Information Studies, Piscataway, NJ 08854-8097. Offers MCIS. Part-time programs available. *Entrance requirements:* For master's, GRE General Test. Additional exam requirements/recommendations for international students: Required—TOEFL. Electronic applications accepted. *Faculty research:* Communication processes and systems, information process and systems, human information and communication behavior.

Rutgers, The State University of New Jersey, New Brunswick, School of Communication, Information and Library Studies, Program in Communication, Library and Information Science and Media Studies, Piscataway, NJ 08854-8097. Offers PhD. Part-time programs available. *Degree requirements:* For doctorate, comprehensive exam, thesis/dissertation, qualifying exams. *Entrance requirements:* For doctorate, GRE General Test, proficiency in statistics. Additional exam requirements/recommendations for international students: Required—TOEFL (minimum score 600 paper-based). Electronic applications accepted. *Faculty research:* Information science, media studies.

St. Catherine University, Graduate Programs, Program in Library and Information Science, St. Paul, MN 55105. Offers MLIS. *Accreditation:* ALA. Part-time and evening/weekend programs available. *Degree requirements:* For master's, microcomputer competency. *Entrance requirements:* For master's, GRE or MAT, minimum GPA of 3.2 or GRE. Additional exam requirements/recommendations for international students: Required—Michigan English Language Assessment Battery or TOEFL (minimum score 600 paper-based; 100 iBT).

St. John's University, St. John's College of Liberal Arts and Sciences, Division of Library and Information Science, Queens, NY 11439. Offers MLS, Adv C, MA/MLS, MS/MLS. *Accreditation:* ALA (one or more programs are accredited). Part-time and evening/weekend programs available. Postbaccalaureate distance learning degree programs offered (no on-campus study). *Students:* 33 full-time (29 women), 31 part-time (28 women); includes 16 minority (3 Black or African American, non-Hispanic/Latino; 4 Asian, non-Hispanic/Latino; 8 Hispanic/Latino; 1 Two or more races, non-Hispanic/Latino), 1 international. Average age 31. 70 applicants, 83% accepted, 27 enrolled. In 2013, 35 master's awarded. *Degree requirements:* For master's, comprehensive exam, portfolio. *Entrance requirements:* For master's, interview, minimum GPA of 3.0, 2 letters of recommendation, bachelor's degree, personal statement, transcript. Additional exam requirements/recommendations for international students: Required—TOEFL (minimum score 600 paper-based; 100 iBT), IELTS (minimum score 5.5). *Application deadline:* For fall admission, 5/1 priority date for domestic and international students; for spring admission, 11/1 priority date for domestic and international students. Applications are processed on a rolling basis. Application fee: $70. Electronic applications accepted. *Expenses:* Contact institution. *Financial support:* Research assistantships, career-related internships or fieldwork, and scholarships/grants available. Support available to part-time students. Financial award application deadline: 3/1; financial award applicants required to submit FAFSA. *Faculty research:* Indexes and metatags, information use and users, competitive intelligence, knowledge management, database theory, young adult and children services, school media services, archives, oral history. *Unit head:* Dr. Jeffery E. Olson, Director, 718-990-5705, E-mail: olsonj@stjohns.edu. *Application contact:* Robert Medrano, Director of Graduate Admissions, 718-990-1601, Fax: 718-990-5686, E-mail: gradhelp@stjohns.edu.

San Jose State University, Graduate Studies and Research, College of Applied Sciences and Arts, School of Library and Information Science, San Jose, CA 95192-0001. Offers MLIS, PhD. *Accreditation:* ALA (one or more programs are accredited). Part-time and evening/weekend programs available. *Degree requirements:* For master's, comprehensive exam. *Entrance requirements:* Additional exam requirements/recommendations for international students: Required—TOEFL (minimum score 600 paper-based). Electronic applications accepted. *Faculty research:* Evaluation of information services online, search strategy, organizational behavior.

Simmons College, Graduate School of Library and Information Science, Boston, MA 02115. Offers archives management (MS, Certificate); children's literature (MA); digital stewardship (Certificate); instructional technology (Certificate); library and information science (MS, PhD); managerial leadership in the informational professions (PhD); school library teacher (MS, Certificate); writing for children (MFA); MA/MA; MA/MAT; MA/MFA; MS/MA. *Accreditation:* ALA (one or more programs are accredited). Part-time and evening/weekend programs available. Postbaccalaureate distance learning degree programs offered (no on-campus study). *Students:* 55 full-time (45 women), 716 part-time (585 women); includes 81 minority (19 Black or African American, non-Hispanic/Latino; 1 American Indian or Alaska Native, non-Hispanic/Latino; 14 Asian, non-Hispanic/Latino; 32 Hispanic/Latino; 15 Two or more races, non-Hispanic/Latino), 9 international. 430 applicants, 82% accepted, 207 enrolled. In 2013, 281 master's, 4 doctorates awarded. *Degree requirements:* For master's, thesis optional, capstone project experience; for doctorate, comprehensive exam, 36 credit hours (includes 3-credit dissertation). *Entrance requirements:* For doctorate, GRE, transcripts, personal statement, resume, recommendations, master's degree. Additional exam requirements/recommendations for international students: Required—TOEFL (minimum score 550 paper-based; 79 iBT), IELTS (minimum score 7). *Application deadline:* For fall admission, 3/1 for domestic and international students; for spring admission, 9/1 for domestic and international students; for summer admission, 2/1 for domestic and international students. Applications are processed on a rolling basis. Application fee:

$65. Electronic applications accepted. *Financial support:* In 2013–14, 67 students received support, including 5 fellowships with partial tuition reimbursements available (averaging $32,461 per year), 6 research assistantships (averaging $35,168 per year), 7 teaching assistantships with full and partial tuition reimbursements available (averaging $3,000 per year); scholarships/grants, tuition waivers, and unspecified assistantships also available. Financial award application deadline: 2/1; financial award applicants required to submit FAFSA. *Faculty research:* Archives and social justice, information-seeking behavior, information retrieval, organization of information, cultural heritage informatics. *Unit head:* Dr. Eileen G. Abels, Dean, 617-521-2869. *Application contact:* Sarah Petrakos, 617-521-2868, Fax: 617-521-3192, E-mail: gslisadm@simmons.edu. Website: http://www.simmons.edu/gslis/.

Southern Connecticut State University, School of Graduate Studies, School of Education, Department of Information and Library Science, New Haven, CT 06515-1355. Offers information studies (Diploma); library science (MLS); JD/MLS; MLS/MA; MLS/MS. *Accreditation:* ALA. Part-time and evening/weekend programs available. Postbaccalaureate distance learning degree programs offered (no on-campus study). *Degree requirements:* For master's and Diploma, thesis or alternative. *Entrance requirements:* For master's, GRE General Test, interview, minimum QPA of 2.7, introductory computer science course; for Diploma, master's degree in library science or information science. Electronic applications accepted.

Syracuse University, School of Information Studies, Program in Information Management, Syracuse, NY 13244. Offers MS, DPS. Part-time and evening/weekend programs available. Postbaccalaureate distance learning degree programs offered (minimal on-campus study). *Students:* 225 full-time (102 women), 72 part-time (20 women); includes 46 minority (15 Black or African American, non-Hispanic/Latino; 1 American Indian or Alaska Native, non-Hispanic/Latino; 10 Asian, non-Hispanic/Latino; 14 Hispanic/Latino; 6 Two or more races, non-Hispanic/Latino), 170 international. Average age 27. 842 applicants, 40% accepted, 127 enrolled. In 2013, 142 master's awarded. *Degree requirements:* For doctorate, thesis/dissertation. *Entrance requirements:* For master's and doctorate, GRE General Test. Additional exam requirements/recommendations for international students: Required—TOEFL (minimum score 100 iBT). *Application deadline:* For fall admission, 1/15 priority date for domestic and international students; for spring admission, 10/15 priority date for domestic and international students. Applications are processed on a rolling basis. Application fee: $75. Electronic applications accepted. *Financial support:* Fellowships with full tuition reimbursements, research assistantships with partial tuition reimbursements, teaching assistantships with partial tuition reimbursements, and scholarships/grants available. Financial award application deadline: 1/1; financial award applicants required to submit FAFSA. *Unit head:* Art Thomas, Program Director, 315-443-2911, Fax: 315-443-6886, E-mail: igrad@syr.edu. *Application contact:* Susan Corieri, Director of Enrollment Management, 315-443-2575, E-mail: ischool@syr.edu. Website: http://ischool.syr.edu/.

See Display below and Close-Up on page 1599.

Universidad del Turabo, Graduate Programs, Programs in Education, Program in Library Service and Information Technology, Gurabo, PR 00778-3030. Offers M Ed.

Université de Montréal, Faculty of Arts and Sciences, School of Library and Information Sciences, Montréal, QC H3C 3J7, Canada. Offers information sciences (MIS, PhD). *Accreditation:* ALA (one or more programs are accredited). *Degree requirements:* For master's, thesis optional. *Entrance requirements:* For master's, interview, master's degree in library and information science or equivalent. Electronic applications accepted.

University at Albany, State University of New York, College of Computing and Information, Department of Information Studies, Albany, NY 12222-0001. Offers

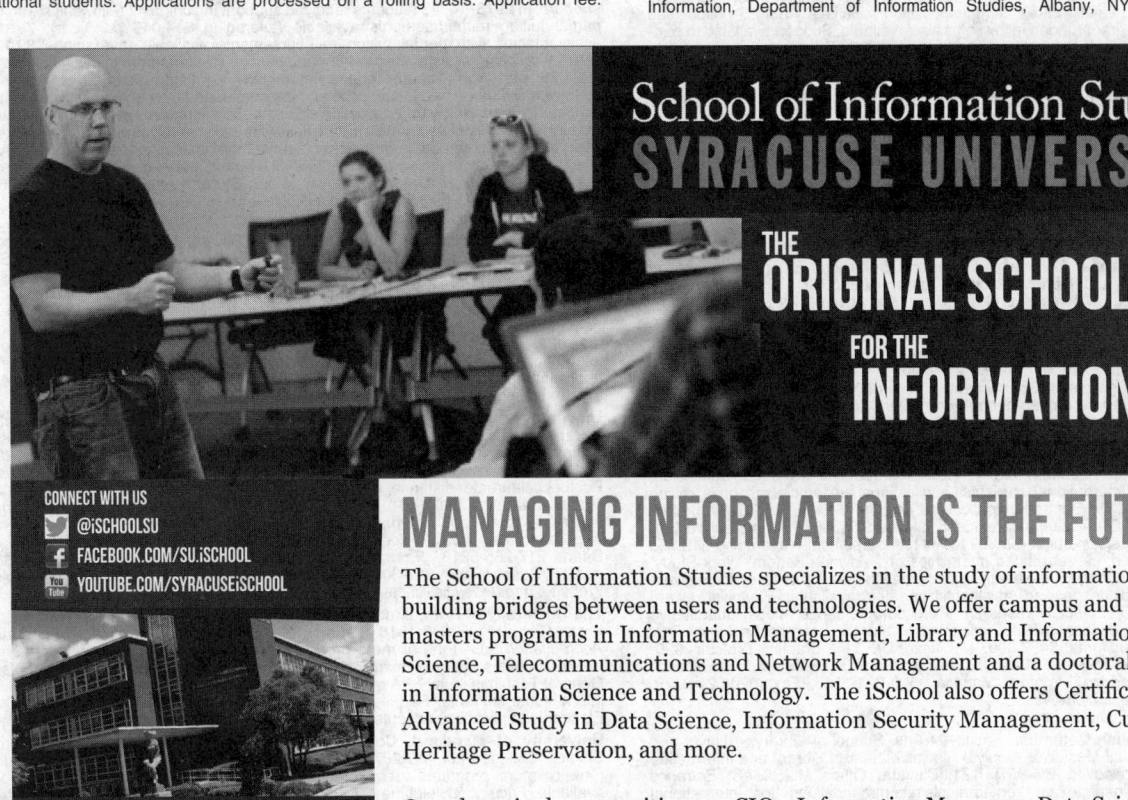

information science (MS, CAS). *Faculty research:* Electronic information across technologies system dynamics modeling archives, records administration.

University at Buffalo, the State University of New York, Graduate School, Graduate School of Education, Department of Library and Information Studies, Buffalo, NY 14260. Offers library and information studies (MLS, Certificate); library media specialist (MLS). *Accreditation:* ALA (one or more programs are accredited). Part-time programs available. Postbaccalaureate distance learning degree programs offered (no on-campus study). *Faculty:* 11 full-time (9 women), 20 part-time/adjunct (16 women). *Students:* 55 full-time (39 women), 149 part-time (123 women); includes 15 minority (9 Black or African American, non-Hispanic/Latino; 4 Asian, non-Hispanic/Latino; 2 Hispanic/Latino). Average age 32. 155 applicants, 92% accepted, 87 enrolled. In 2013, 102 master's, 1 other advanced degree awarded. *Degree requirements:* For master's, thesis optional; for Certificate, thesis. *Entrance requirements:* For master's, letters of recommendation. Additional exam requirements/recommendations for international students: Required—TOEFL (minimum score 550 paper-based; 79 iBT). *Application deadline:* For fall admission, 4/1 priority date for domestic and international students; for spring admission, 10/15 priority date for domestic students, 10/15 for international students. Applications are processed on a rolling basis. Application fee: $50. Electronic applications accepted. *Financial support:* In 2013–14, 17 fellowships (averaging $2,776 per year), 4 research assistantships with tuition reimbursements (averaging $9,000 per year) were awarded; teaching assistantships, career-related internships or fieldwork, Federal Work-Study, institutionally sponsored loans, scholarships/grants, tuition waivers, and unspecified assistantships also available. Support available to part-time students. Financial award application deadline: 3/1; financial award applicants required to submit FAFSA. *Faculty research:* Information-seeking behavior, thesauri, impact of technology, questioning behaviors, educational informatics. *Total annual research expenditures:* $20,068. *Unit head:* Dr. Heidi Julien, Chair, 716-645-1474, Fax: 716-645-3775, E-mail: heidijul@buffalo.edu. *Application contact:* Pat Glinski, Admissions Assistant, 716-645-2110, Fax: 716-645-7937, E-mail: gse-info@buffalo.edu.
Website: http://www.gse.buffalo.edu/lis/.

The University of Alabama, Graduate School, College of Communication and Information Sciences, School of Library and Information Studies, Tuscaloosa, AL 35487. Offers book arts (MFA); library and information studies (MLIS, PhD). *Accreditation:* ALA (one or more programs are accredited). Part-time and evening/weekend programs available. Postbaccalaureate distance learning degree programs offered (minimal on-campus study). *Faculty:* 8 full-time (3 women), 2 part-time/adjunct (1 woman). *Students:* 69 full-time (55 women), 193 part-time (155 women); includes 26 minority (12 Black or African American, non-Hispanic/Latino; 2 Asian, non-Hispanic/Latino; 8 Hispanic/Latino; 4 Two or more races, non-Hispanic/Latino), 3 international. Average age 33. 141 applicants, 77% accepted, 85 enrolled. In 2013, 121 master's awarded. *Degree requirements:* For master's, comprehensive exam (for some programs), thesis optional; for doctorate, comprehensive exam, thesis/dissertation. *Entrance requirements:* For master's, GRE General Test or MAT, minimum GPA of 3.0; for doctorate, GRE. Additional exam requirements/recommendations for international students: Required—TOEFL. *Application deadline:* For fall admission, 7/1 priority date for domestic and international students; for spring admission, 11/1 priority date for domestic and international students. Applications are processed on a rolling basis. Application fee: $50 ($60 for international students). Electronic applications accepted. *Expenses:* Tuition, state resident: full-time $9450. Tuition, nonresident: full-time $23,950. *Financial support:* In 2013–14, 64 students received support, including 3 fellowships with full tuition reimbursements available (averaging $15,000 per year), 18 research assistantships with full and partial tuition reimbursements available (averaging $6,183 per year), 12 teaching assistantships with full and partial tuition reimbursements available (averaging $6,183 per year); career-related internships or fieldwork, scholarships/grants, health care benefits, tuition waivers (full), unspecified assistantships, and 15 grant-funded fellowships also available. Support available to part-time students. Financial award application deadline: 3/15. *Faculty research:* Library administration, user services, digital libraries, book arts, evaluation. *Unit head:* Dr. Heidi Julien, Director and Professor, 205-348-4610, Fax: 205-348-3746, E-mail: hjulien@slis.ua.edu. *Application contact:* Beth Riggs, Assistant to the Director, 205-348-1527, Fax: 205-348-3746, E-mail: briggs@slis.ua.edu.
Website: http://www.slis.ua.edu/.

University of Alberta, Faculty of Graduate Studies and Research, School of Library and Information Studies, Edmonton, AB T6G 2E1, Canada. Offers MLIS. *Accreditation:* ALA. *Entrance requirements:* Additional exam requirements/recommendations for international students: Required—TOEFL, Canadian Academic English Language Assessment. Electronic applications accepted. *Faculty research:* Intellectual freedom, materials for children and young adults, library classification, multi-media literacy.

The University of Arizona, College of Social and Behavioral Sciences, School of Information Resources and Library Science, Tucson, AZ 85721. Offers MA, PhD. *Accreditation:* ALA (one or more programs are accredited). Part-time programs available. *Faculty:* 9 full-time (7 women). *Students:* 81 full-time (61 women), 125 part-time (110 women); includes 56 minority (2 Black or African American, non-Hispanic/Latino; 2 American Indian or Alaska Native, non-Hispanic/Latino; 2 Asian, non-Hispanic/Latino; 32 Hispanic/Latino; 18 Two or more races, non-Hispanic/Latino), 4 international. Average age 36. 139 applicants, 62% accepted, 44 enrolled. In 2013, 84 master's, 2 doctorates awarded. *Degree requirements:* For master's, proficiency in disk operating system (DOS); for doctorate, thesis/dissertation. *Entrance requirements:* For master's and doctorate, GRE General Test, 3 letters of recommendation, resume. Additional exam requirements/recommendations for international students: Required—TOEFL (minimum score 550 paper-based; 79 iBT). *Application deadline:* For spring admission, 9/1 for domestic and international students. Applications are processed on a rolling basis. Application fee: $75. Electronic applications accepted. *Expenses:* Tuition, state resident: full-time $11,526. Tuition, nonresident: full-time $27,398. *Financial support:* In 2013–14, 9 teaching assistantships with full tuition reimbursements (averaging $19,700 per year) were awarded; career-related internships or fieldwork, Federal Work-Study, institutionally sponsored loans, scholarships/grants, health care benefits, tuition waivers (full and partial), and unspecified assistantships also available. Financial award application deadline: 3/1. *Faculty research:* Microcomputer applications; quantitative methods systems; information transfer, planning, evaluation, and technology. *Total annual research expenditures:* $457,000. *Unit head:* Dr. Jana Bradley, Director, 520-621-3565, Fax: 520-621-3279, E-mail: janabrad@email.arizona.edu. *Application contact:* Geraldine Fragoso, Program Manager, 520-621-3565, Fax: 520-621-3279, E-mail: gfragoso@email.arizona.edu.
Website: http://www.sirls.arizona.edu/.

The University of British Columbia, Faculty of Arts, School of Library, Archival and Information Studies, Dual Master of Archival Studies/Master of Library and Information Studies Program, Vancouver, BC V6T 1Z1, Canada. Offers MLIS/MAS. *Entrance requirements:* Additional exam requirements/recommendations for international students: Required—TOEFL (minimum score 600 paper-based; 100 iBT). Electronic applications accepted. *Expenses: Tuition, area resident:* Full-time $8000 Canadian dollars. *Faculty research:* Computer systems/database design, information-seeking behaviour, archives and records management, children's literature and services, digital libraries and archives.

The University of British Columbia, Faculty of Arts, School of Library, Archival and Information Studies, Master of Library and Information Studies Program, Vancouver, BC V6T 1Z1, Canada. Offers MLIS. Part-time programs available. *Degree requirements:* For master's, thesis optional. *Entrance requirements:* For master's, minimum GPA of 3.3 in undergraduate upper-division courses. Additional exam requirements/recommendations for international students: Required—TOEFL (minimum score 600 paper-based; 100 iBT). Electronic applications accepted. *Expenses: Tuition, area resident:* Full-time $8000 Canadian dollars. *Faculty research:* Computer systems/database design; digital libraries; metadata/classification; human-computer interaction; children's literature and services.

The University of British Columbia, Faculty of Arts, School of Library, Archival and Information Studies, PhD Program in Library, Archival and Information Studies, Vancouver, BC V6T 1Z1, Canada. Offers PhD. *Degree requirements:* For doctorate, thesis/dissertation. *Entrance requirements:* For doctorate, GRE, minimum GPA of 3.3 in MAS or MLIS (other master's degrees may be considered). Additional exam requirements/recommendations for international students: Required—TOEFL (minimum score 600 paper-based; 100 iBT). Electronic applications accepted. *Expenses: Tuition, area resident:* Full-time $8000 Canadian dollars. *Faculty research:* Computer systems/database design; library and archival management; archival description and organization; children's literature and youth services; interactive information retrieval.

University of California, Berkeley, Graduate Division, School of Information Management and Systems, Berkeley, CA 94720-1500. Offers MIMS, PhD. *Degree requirements:* For doctorate, thesis/dissertation, qualifying exam. *Entrance requirements:* For master's, GRE General Test, minimum GPA of 3.0, previous course work in java or C programming, 3 letters of recommendation; for doctorate, GRE General Test, minimum GPA of 3.0. Additional exam requirements/recommendations for international students: Required—TOEFL. *Faculty research:* Information retrieval research, design and evaluation of information systems, work practice-based design of information systems, economics of information, intellectual property law.

University of California, Los Angeles, Graduate Division, Graduate School of Education and Information Studies, Department of Information Studies, Los Angeles, CA 90095-1521. Offers archival studies (MLIS); informatics (MLIS); information studies (PhD); library and information science (Certificate); library studies (MLIS); moving image archive studies (MA); rare books, print and visual culture (MLIS); MBA/MLIS; MLIS/MA. *Accreditation:* ALA (one or more programs are accredited). *Faculty:* 10 full-time (6 women), 14 part-time/adjunct (9 women). *Students:* 114 full-time (79 women), 11 part-time (8 women); includes 50 minority (9 Black or African American, non-Hispanic/Latino; 1 American Indian or Alaska Native, non-Hispanic/Latino; 19 Asian, non-Hispanic/Latino; 18 Hispanic/Latino; 2 Native Hawaiian or other Pacific Islander, non-Hispanic/Latino; 1 Two or more races, non-Hispanic/Latino), 6 international. Average age 27. 165 applicants, 62% accepted, 51 enrolled. In 2013, 80 master's, 7 doctorates, 1 other advanced degree awarded. Terminal master's awarded for partial completion of doctoral program. *Degree requirements:* For master's, thesis or alternative, professional portfolio; for doctorate, thesis/dissertation, oral and written qualifying exams. *Entrance requirements:* For master's, GRE General Test, previous course work in statistics; for doctorate, GRE General Test, previous course work in statistics, 2 samples of research writing in English. Additional exam requirements/recommendations for international students: Required—TOEFL (minimum score 560 paper-based; 87 iBT), IELTS (minimum score 7). *Application deadline:* For fall admission, 12/10 for domestic and international students. Applications are processed on a rolling basis. Application fee: $80 ($100 for international students). Electronic applications accepted. *Financial support:* In 2013–14, 47 students received support, including 47 fellowships with full and partial tuition reimbursements available (averaging $14,045 per year), 7 research assistantships with partial tuition reimbursements available (averaging $30,155 per year), 8 teaching assistantships with partial tuition reimbursements available (averaging $20,656 per year); career-related internships or fieldwork, Federal Work-Study, institutionally sponsored loans, scholarships/grants, and unspecified assistantships also available. Financial award application deadline: 3/1; financial award applicants required to submit FAFSA. *Faculty research:* Digital libraries, archives and electronic records, interface design, cultural informatics, preservation/conservation, access. *Unit head:* Dr. Gregory H. Leazer, Associate Professor and Chair, 310-825-8799, E-mail: gleazer@ucla.edu. *Application contact:* Susan S. Abler, Student Affairs Officer, 310-825-5269, Fax: 310-206-4460, E-mail: abler@gseis.ucla.edu.
Website: http://is.gseis.ucla.edu/.

University of Hawaii at Manoa, Graduate Division, College of Natural Sciences, Department of Information and Computer Sciences, Library and Information Science Program, Honolulu, HI 96822-2233. Offers advanced library and information science (Graduate Certificate); library and information science (MLI Sc). *Accreditation:* ALA (one or more programs are accredited). Part-time programs available. *Degree requirements:* For master's, comprehensive exam, thesis optional. *Entrance requirements:* For master's, GRE General Test. Additional exam requirements/recommendations for international students: Required—TOEFL (minimum score 600 paper-based). Electronic applications accepted. *Faculty research:* Information behavior, evaluation of electronic information sources, online learning, history of libraries, information literacy.

University of Illinois at Urbana–Champaign, Graduate College, Graduate School of Library and Information Science, Champaign, IL 61820. Offers bioinformatics (MS); digital libraries (CAS); library and information science (MS, PhD, CAS). *Accreditation:* ALA (one or more programs are accredited). Part-time programs available. Postbaccalaureate distance learning degree programs offered (minimal on-campus study). *Students:* 596 (461 women). *Entrance requirements:* For degree, master's degree in library and information science or related field with minimum GPA of 3.0. Application fee: $75 ($90 for international students). *Unit head:* Allen Renear, Interim Dean, 217-265-5216, Fax: 217-244-3302, E-mail: renear@illinois.edu. *Application contact:* Susan Weiss, 217-300-6646, Fax: 217-244-3302, E-mail: sweiss1@illinois.edu.
Website: http://www.lis.illinois.edu.

The University of Iowa, Graduate College, School of Library and Information Science, Iowa City, IA 52242-1316. Offers MA, PhD, MA/Certificate, PhD/Certificate. *Accreditation:* ALA (one or more programs are accredited). *Degree requirements:* For master's, thesis optional, exam, portfolio. *Entrance requirements:* For master's, GRE General Test, minimum GPA of 3.0. Additional exam requirements/recommendations for international students: Required—TOEFL (minimum score 550 paper-based; 81 iBT). Electronic applications accepted.

University of Maryland, College Park, Academic Affairs, College of Information Studies, College Park, MD 20742. Offers MIM, MLS, PhD, MA/MLS. *Accreditation:* ALA (one or more programs are accredited). Part-time and evening/weekend programs available. *Faculty:* 31 full-time (17 women), 28 part-time/adjunct (19 women). *Students:* 282 full-time (169 women), 187 part-time (129 women); includes 62 minority (25 Black or African American, non-Hispanic/Latino; 20 Asian, non-Hispanic/Latino; 10 Hispanic/Latino; 7 Two or more races, non-Hispanic/Latino), 119 international. 850 applicants, 50% accepted, 205 enrolled. In 2013, 180 master's, 2 doctorates awarded. Terminal

master's awarded for partial completion of doctoral program. *Degree requirements:* For master's, thesis optional; for doctorate, comprehensive exam, thesis/dissertation, 1-year residency. *Entrance requirements:* For master's and doctorate, GRE General Test, minimum GPA of 3.0, 3 letters of recommendation. Additional exam requirements/recommendations for international students: Required—TOEFL. *Application deadline:* For fall admission, 12/1 for domestic students, 11/1 for international students. Applications are processed on a rolling basis. Application fee: $75. Electronic applications accepted. *Expenses:* Tuition, state resident: full-time $10,314; part-time $573 per credit hour. Tuition, nonresident: full-time $22,248; part-time $1236 per credit. *Required fees:* $1446; $403.15 per semester. Tuition and fees vary according to program. *Financial support:* In 2013–14, 16 fellowships with full and partial tuition reimbursements (averaging $20,296 per year), 4 research assistantships (averaging $17,479 per year), 91 teaching assistantships (averaging $16,264 per year) were awarded; career-related internships or fieldwork, Federal Work-Study, scholarships/grants, and tuition waivers (full and partial) also available. Support available to part-time students. Financial award application deadline: 2/1; financial award applicants required to submit FAFSA. *Total annual research expenditures:* $2.8 million. *Unit head:* Dr. Jennifer Preece, Dean, 301-405-2036, Fax: 301-314-9145, E-mail: preece@umd.edu. *Application contact:* Dr. Charles A. Caramello, Dean of Graduate School, 301-405-0358, Fax: 301-314-9305, E-mail: ccaramel@umd.edu.

University of Michigan, Horace H. Rackham School of Graduate Studies, School of Information, Ann Arbor, MI 48109-1285. Offers archives and records management (MSI); health informatics (MS); human computer interaction (MSI); information (PhD); information analysis and retrieval (MSI); information economics for management (MSI); library and information science (MSI); preservation of information (MSI); school library media (MSI); social computing (MSI). *Accreditation:* ALA (one or more programs are accredited). *Entrance requirements:* For master's and doctorate, GRE General Test. Additional exam requirements/recommendations for international students: Required—TOEFL (minimum score 600 paper-based; 100 iBT). Electronic applications accepted. Tuition and fees vary according to course level, course load, degree level, program and student level.

University of Missouri, Graduate School, College of Education, School of Information Science and Learning Technologies, Columbia, MO 65211. Offers educational technology (M Ed, Ed S); information science and learning technology (PhD); library science (MA). *Accreditation:* ALA (one or more programs are accredited). Part-time and evening/weekend programs available. *Faculty:* 16 full-time (11 women), 1 (woman) part-time/adjunct. *Students:* 94 full-time (67 women), 258 part-time (178 women); includes 20 minority (8 Black or African American, non-Hispanic/Latino; 2 Asian, non-Hispanic/Latino; 7 Hispanic/Latino; 3 Two or more races, non-Hispanic/Latino), 15 international. Average age 35. 122 applicants, 81% accepted, 74 enrolled. In 2013, 140 master's, 7 doctorates, 22 other advanced degrees awarded. *Entrance requirements:* For master's, GRE General Test or MAT, minimum GPA of 3.0. Additional exam requirements/recommendations for international students: Required—TOEFL (minimum score 540 paper-based; 76 iBT). *Application deadline:* For fall admission, 2/15 priority date for domestic and international students; for winter admission, 9/15 priority date for domestic and international students; for spring admission, 3/1 priority date for domestic students. Applications are processed on a rolling basis. Application fee: $55 ($75 for international students). Electronic applications accepted. *Financial support:* Fellowships, teaching assistantships, scholarships/grants, health care benefits, and unspecified assistantships available. Support available to part-time students. *Faculty research:* Problem-based learning, technology usability in classrooms, computer-based performance support tools for children and youth with learning disabilities and/or emotional/behavioral disorders, engineering education collaboration environment, effectiveness of activities designed to recruit and retain women in engineering and science. *Unit head:* Dr. Joi L. Moore, Associate Division Director, 573-884-2877, E-mail: morrejoi@missouri.edu. *Application contact:* Amy Adam, Academic Advisor, 573-884-1391, E-mail: adamae@missouri.edu. Website: http://education.missouri.edu/SISLT/.

The University of North Carolina at Chapel Hill, Graduate School, School of Information and Library Science, Chapel Hill, NC 27599. Offers data curation (PMC); information and library science (PhD); information science (MSIS); library science (MSLS). *Accreditation:* ALA (one or more programs are accredited). Part-time programs available. Terminal master's awarded for partial completion of doctoral program. *Degree requirements:* For master's, comprehensive exam, paper or project; for doctorate, comprehensive exam, thesis/dissertation. *Entrance requirements:* For master's and doctorate, GRE General Test. Additional exam requirements/recommendations for international students: Required—TOEFL (minimum score 625 paper-based). Electronic applications accepted. *Faculty research:* Information retrieval and management, digital libraries, management of information resources, archives and records management, health informatics.

The University of North Carolina at Greensboro, Graduate School, School of Education, Department of Library and Information Studies, Greensboro, NC 27412-5001. Offers MLIS. *Accreditation:* ALA. Part-time and evening/weekend programs available. Postbaccalaureate distance learning degree programs offered (no on-campus study). *Degree requirements:* For master's, portfolio. *Entrance requirements:* For master's, GRE General Test. Additional exam requirements/recommendations for international students: Required—TOEFL (minimum score 550 paper-based), IELTS (minimum score 6.5). Electronic applications accepted. *Faculty research:* Library history, gender studies, children's literature, web design, homeless, technical services.

University of Oklahoma, College of Arts and Sciences, School of Library and Information Studies, Program in Library and Information Studies, Norman, OK 73019-0390. Offers MLIS, Graduate Certificate, M Ed/MLIS, MBA/MLIS. Part-time and evening/weekend programs available. Postbaccalaureate distance learning degree programs offered. *Students:* 60 full-time (47 women), 121 part-time (97 women); includes 32 minority (8 Black or African American, non-Hispanic/Latino; 13 American Indian or Alaska Native, non-Hispanic/Latino; 4 Asian, non-Hispanic/Latino; 3 Hispanic/Latino; 4 Two or more races, non-Hispanic/Latino), 3 international. Average age 33. 38 applicants, 87% accepted, 27 enrolled. In 2013, 60 master's awarded. *Degree requirements:* For master's, comprehensive exam (MLIS). *Entrance requirements:* For master's, GRE, minimum GPA of 3.2 in last 60 hours or 3.0 overall. Additional exam requirements/recommendations for international students: Required—TOEFL (minimum score 550 paper-based; 79 iBT). *Application deadline:* For fall admission, 3/1 priority date for domestic students, 4/1 for international students; for spring admission, 10/15 for domestic students, 9/1 for international students. Application fee: $40 ($90 for international students). Electronic applications accepted. *Expenses:* Tuition, state resident: full-time $4205; part-time $175.20 per credit hour. Tuition, nonresident: full-time $16,205; part-time $675.20 per credit hour. *Required fees:* $2745; $103.85 per credit hour. $126.50 per semester. *Financial support:* Federal Work-Study, scholarships/grants, health care benefits, and unspecified assistantships available. Support available to part-time students. Financial award application deadline: 6/1; financial award applicants required to submit FAFSA. *Faculty research:* Equity of access, information services to special populations, information use in the digital age, library services and materials for young people, pluralization of archival theory and education. *Unit head:* Cecelia Brown, Director, 405-325-3921, Fax: 405-325-7648, E-mail: cbrown@ou.edu. *Application contact:* Maggie Ryan, Coordinator of Admissions, 405-325-3921, Fax: 405-325-7648, E-mail: mryan@ou.edu.

University of Pittsburgh, School of Information Sciences, Library and Information Science Program, Pittsburgh, PA 15260. Offers library and information science (MLIS, PhD). *Accreditation:* ALA (one or more programs are accredited). Part-time and evening/weekend programs available. Postbaccalaureate distance learning degree programs offered (minimal on-campus study). *Faculty:* 14 full-time (7 women), 12 part-time/adjunct (7 women). *Students:* 107 full-time (84 women), 87 part-time (66 women); includes 29 minority (15 Black or African American, non-Hispanic/Latino; 2 Asian, non-Hispanic/Latino; 10 Hispanic/Latino; 2 Two or more races, non-Hispanic/Latino), 18 international. 231 applicants, 82% accepted, 187 enrolled. In 2013, 128 master's, 3 doctorates awarded. *Degree requirements:* For master's, thesis optional; for doctorate, comprehensive exam, thesis/dissertation. *Entrance requirements:* For master's, GRE General Test or MAT, bachelor's degree from accredited university; minimum GPA of 3.0; for doctorate, GRE General Test, minimum GPA of 3.5. Additional exam requirements/recommendations for international students: Required—TOEFL (minimum score 550 paper-based; 80 iBT). *Application deadline:* For fall admission, 1/15 priority date for domestic and international students. Applications are processed on a rolling basis. Application fee: $50. Electronic applications accepted. *Expenses:* Contact institution. *Financial support:* Fellowships with full tuition reimbursements, research assistantships with full and partial tuition reimbursements, teaching assistantships with full and partial tuition reimbursements, career-related internships or fieldwork, scholarships/grants, health care benefits, tuition waivers (full and partial), and unspecified assistantships available. Financial award application deadline: 1/15; financial award applicants required to submit FAFSA. *Faculty research:* Archives, children's resources and services, digital libraries, cyberscholarship and citizen science. *Unit head:* Prof. Sheila Corrall, Chair, 412-624-9317, Fax: 412-624-5231, E-mail: scorrall@sis.pitt.edu. *Application contact:* Brandi Liskey Belleau, Student Services Specialist, 412-648-3108, Fax: 412-624-5231, E-mail: lisinq@sis.pitt.edu. Website: http://www.ischool.pitt.edu/lis.

University of Puerto Rico, Río Piedras Campus, Graduate School of Information Sciences and Technologies, San Juan, PR 00931-3300. Offers administration of academic libraries (PMC); administration of public libraries (PMC); administration of special libraries (PMC); consultant in information services (PMC); documents and files administration (Post-Graduate Certificate); electronic information resources analyst (Post-Graduate Certificate); information science (MIS); librarianship and information services (MLS); school librarian (Post-Graduate Certificate); school librarian distance education mode (Post-Graduate Certificate); specialist in legal information (PMC). *Accreditation:* ALA. Part-time programs available. *Degree requirements:* For master's, comprehensive exam, thesis, portfolio. *Entrance requirements:* For master's, PAEG, GRE, interview, minimum GPA of 3.0, 3 letters of recommendation; for other advanced degree, PAEG, GRE, minimum GPA of 3.0, IST master's degree. *Faculty research:* Investigating the users needs and preferences for a specialized environmental library.

University of Rhode Island, Graduate School, College of Arts and Sciences, Graduate School of Library and Information Studies, Kingston, RI 02881. Offers MLIS, MLIS/MA, MLIS/MPA. *Accreditation:* ALA (one or more programs are accredited). Part-time programs available. *Faculty:* 4 full-time (all women). *Students:* 29 full-time (19 women), 70 part-time (57 women); includes 5 minority (1 Black or African American, non-Hispanic/Latino; 3 American Indian or Alaska Native, non-Hispanic/Latino; 1 Hispanic/Latino), 1 international. In 2013, 58 master's awarded. *Degree requirements:* For master's, comprehensive exam. *Entrance requirements:* For master's, GRE or MAT (if undergraduate GPA less than 3.0), 2 letters of recommendation. Additional exam requirements/recommendations for international students: Required—TOEFL (minimum score 550 paper-based). *Application deadline:* For fall admission, 6/15 for domestic students, 2/1 for international students; for spring admission, 10/15 for domestic students, 7/15 for international students. Application fee: $65. Electronic applications accepted. *Expenses:* Tuition, state resident: full-time $11,532; part-time $641 per credit. Tuition, nonresident: full-time $23,606; part-time $1311 per credit. *Required fees:* $1388; $36 per credit. $35 per semester. One-time fee: $130. *Financial support:* Application deadline: 1/15; applicants required to submit FAFSA. *Unit head:* Dr. Valerie Karno, Director, Graduate School of Library and Information Studies, 401-874-4682, Fax: 401-874-4127, E-mail: karno@uri.edu. *Application contact:* GSLIS Student Services Office, 401-874-2872, Fax: 401-874-5787, E-mail: stefaniemetko@mail.uri.edu. Website: http://www.uri.edu/artsci/lsc/.

University of South Carolina, The Graduate School, College of Mass Communications and Information Studies, School of Library and Information Science, Columbia, SC 29208. Offers MLIS, PhD, Certificate, Specialist, MLIS/MA. *Accreditation:* ALA (one or more programs are accredited). Part-time programs available. Postbaccalaureate distance learning degree programs offered (no on-campus study). *Degree requirements:* For master's, end of program portfolio; for doctorate, comprehensive exam, thesis/dissertation. *Entrance requirements:* For master's and other advanced degree, GRE General Test or MAT; for doctorate, GTE, writing sample. Additional exam requirements/recommendations for international students: Required—TOEFL (minimum score 570 paper-based; 75 iBT). Electronic applications accepted. *Faculty research:* Information technology management, distance education, library services for children and young adults, special libraries.

University of South Florida, College of Arts and Sciences, School of Information, Tampa, FL 33620-9951. Offers library and information science (MA), including youth services and school librarianship. *Accreditation:* ALA. Part-time and evening/weekend programs available. Postbaccalaureate distance learning degree programs offered (minimal on-campus study). *Faculty:* 14 full-time (8 women), 12 part-time/adjunct (8 women). *Students:* 68 full-time (59 women), 150 part-time (124 women); includes 45 minority (15 Black or African American, non-Hispanic/Latino; 1 American Indian or Alaska Native, non-Hispanic/Latino; 4 Asian, non-Hispanic/Latino; 22 Hispanic/Latino; 3 Two or more races, non-Hispanic/Latino), 2 international. Average age 35. 98 applicants, 73% accepted, 41 enrolled. In 2013, 117 master's awarded. *Degree requirements:* For master's, comprehensive exam, thesis optional. *Entrance requirements:* For master's, minimum GPA of 3.25 in upper-division course work, 3.5 in a completed master's degree program, or GRE; statement of purpose and goals, academic writing sample, three letters of recommendation. Additional exam requirements/recommendations for international students: Required—TOEFL (minimum score 550 paper-based; 79 iBT) or IELTS (minimum score 6.5). *Application deadline:* For fall admission, 6/1 for domestic students, 1/2 for international students; for spring admission, 10/15 for domestic students, 6/1 for international students. Applications are processed on a rolling basis. Application fee: $30. Electronic applications accepted. *Financial support:* Unspecified assistantships available. Financial award application deadline: 6/30. *Faculty research:* Youth services in libraries, community engagement and libraries, information architecture, biomedical informatics, health informatics. *Total annual research expenditures:* $49,361. *Unit head:* Dr. Jim Andrews, Director and Associate Professor, 813-974-2108, Fax: 813-974-6840, E-mail: jimandrews@usf.edu.

Information Studies

Application contact: Dr. Diane Austin, Assistant Director, 813-974-6364, Fax: 813-974-6840, E-mail: dianeaustin@usf.edu.
Website: http://si.usf.edu/.

University of South Florida, University College/Distance Education, Tampa, FL 33620-9951. *Unit head:* Kathy Barnes, Interdisciplinary Programs Coordinator, 813-974-8031, Fax: 813-974-7061, E-mail: barnesk@usf.edu. *Application contact:* Karen Tylinski, Metro Initiatives, 813-974-9943, Fax: 813-974-7061, E-mail: ktylinsk@usf.edu.
Website: http://uc.usf.edu/.

The University of Texas at Austin, Graduate School, School of Information, Austin, TX 78712-1111. Offers MSIS, PhD, MSIS/MA. *Accreditation:* ALA (one or more programs are accredited). Part-time programs available. *Degree requirements:* For doctorate, 2 foreign languages, thesis/dissertation. *Entrance requirements:* For master's and doctorate, GRE General Test. Electronic applications accepted. *Faculty research:* Information retrieval and artificial intelligence, library history and administration, classification and cataloguing.

University of Toronto, School of Graduate Studies, Faculty of Information Studies, Toronto, ON M5S 1A1, Canada. Offers information (MI, PhD); museum studies (MM St); JD/MI. *Accreditation:* ALA (one or more programs are accredited). Part-time programs available. *Degree requirements:* For master's, thesis optional; for doctorate, thesis/dissertation, oral exam/thesis defense. *Entrance requirements:* For master's, 2 letters of reference; for doctorate, 3 letters of reference, minimum B+ average. Additional exam requirements/recommendations for international students: Required—TOEFL (minimum score 600 paper-based; 100 iBT), IELTS (minimum score 8), TWE (minimum score 5.5), or Michigan English Language Assessment Battery (minimum score 95). Electronic applications accepted. *Expenses:* Contact institution.

The University of Western Ontario, Faculty of Graduate Studies, Faculty of Information and Media Studies, Programs in Library and Information Science, London, ON N6A 5B8, Canada. Offers MLIS, PhD. Program conducted on a trimester basis. *Accreditation:* ALA (one or more programs are accredited). Part-time and evening/weekend programs available. *Degree requirements:* For doctorate, comprehensive exam, thesis/dissertation. *Entrance requirements:* For master's, honors degree, minimum B average during previous 2 years of course work; for doctorate, MLIS or equivalent. Additional exam requirements/recommendations for international students: Required—TOEFL (minimum score 625 paper-based), TWE (minimum score 5). Electronic applications accepted. *Faculty research:* Information, individuals, and society; information systems, policy, power, and institutions.

University of Wisconsin–Madison, Graduate School, College of Letters and Science, School of Library and Information Studies, Madison, WI 53706-1380. Offers MA, PhD. *Accreditation:* ALA (one or more programs are accredited). Part-time programs available. *Degree requirements:* For doctorate, comprehensive exam, thesis/dissertation. Electronic applications accepted. *Expenses:* Tuition, state resident: full-time $10,728; part-time $790 per credit. Tuition, nonresident: full-time $24,054; part-time $1623 per credit. *Required fees:* $1130; $119 per credit. *Faculty research:* Intellectual freedom, children's literature, print culture history, information systems design and evaluation, school library media centers.

University of Wisconsin–Milwaukee, Graduate School, School of Information Studies, Milwaukee, WI 53201-0413. Offers advanced studies in library and information science (CAS); archives and records administration (CAS); digital libraries (Certificate); information studies (MLIS, PhD); MLIS/MA; MLIS/MM; MLIS/MS. *Accreditation:* ALA (one or more programs are accredited). Part-time programs available. *Faculty:* 22 full-time (11 women). *Students:* 140 full-time (109 women), 254 part-time (196 women); includes 33 minority (12 Black or African American, non-Hispanic/Latino; 1 American Indian or Alaska Native, non-Hispanic/Latino; 1 Asian, non-Hispanic/Latino; 4 Hispanic/Latino; 15 Two or more races, non-Hispanic/Latino), 24 international. Average age 34. 221 applicants, 79% accepted, 94 enrolled. In 2013, 238 master's awarded. *Entrance requirements:* For master's, GRE General Test or MAT; for doctorate, GRE. Additional exam requirements/recommendations for international students: Required—TOEFL (minimum score 550 paper-based), IELTS (minimum score 6.5). *Application deadline:* For fall admission, 1/1 priority date for domestic students; for spring admission, 9/1 for domestic students. Applications are processed on a rolling basis. Application fee: $56 ($96 for international students). Electronic applications accepted. *Financial support:* In 2013–14, 4 teaching assistantships were awarded; fellowships, research assistantships, career-related internships or fieldwork, Federal Work-Study, health care benefits, unspecified assistantships, and project assistantships also available. Support available to part-time students. Financial award application deadline: 4/15; financial award applicants required to submit FAFSA. *Total annual research expenditures:* $298,170. *Unit head:* Wooseob Jeong, Interim Dean/Associate Professor, 414-229-6167, E-mail: wjj8612@uwm.edu. *Application contact:* Hur-Li Lee, Representative, 414-229-6838, E-mail: hurli@uwm.edu.
Website: http://www.uwm.edu/Dept/SLIS/.

Valdosta State University, Program in Library and Information Science, Valdosta, GA 31698. Offers MLIS. *Accreditation:* ALA. Postbaccalaureate distance learning degree programs offered (minimal on-campus study). *Faculty:* 6 full-time (3 women), 4 part-time/adjunct (3 women). *Students:* 12 full-time (6 women), 145 part-time (113 women); includes 34 minority (21 Black or African American, non-Hispanic/Latino; 2 American Indian or Alaska Native, non-Hispanic/Latino; 1 Asian, non-Hispanic/Latino; 2 Hispanic/Latino; 1 Native Hawaiian or other Pacific Islander, non-Hispanic/Latino; 7 Two or more races, non-Hispanic/Latino), 1 international. Average age 25. 58 applicants, 55% accepted, 28 enrolled. In 2013, 69 master's awarded. *Degree requirements:* For master's, comprehensive exam. *Entrance requirements:* For master's, two essays, resume, three recommendations. Additional exam requirements/recommendations for international students: Required—TOEFL (minimum score 523 paper-based). *Application deadline:* For fall admission, 4/15 for domestic and international students. Application fee: $35. *Expenses:* Tuition, state resident: full-time $4140; part-time $230 per credit hour. Tuition, nonresident: full-time $14,904; part-time $828 per credit hour. *Required fees:* $995 per semester. Tuition and fees vary according to course load. *Financial support:* In 2013–14, 4 students received support, including 4 research assistantships with full tuition reimbursements available (averaging $3,652 per year); institutionally sponsored loans, scholarships/grants, and unspecified assistantships also available. Support available to part-time students. Financial award application deadline: 7/1; financial award applicants required to submit FAFSA. *Unit head:* Dr. Linda Most, Assistant Director, 229-245-3732, Fax: 229-333-5862, E-mail: lrmost@valdosta.edu. *Application contact:* Jessica Powers, Admissions Specialist, 229-333-5694, Fax: 229-245-3853, E-mail: jldevane@valdosta.edu.
Website: http://www.valdosta.edu/academics/graduate-school/our-programs/library-and-information-science.php.

Wayne State University, School of Library and Information Science, Detroit, MI 48202. Offers academic libraries (MLIS); archival administration (MLIS, Certificate); general librarianship (MLIS); health sciences librarianship (MLIS); information management for librarians (Certificate); information science (MLIS); law librarianship (MLIS); library and information science (Spec); organization of information (MLIS); public libraries (MLIS); public library services to children and young adults (MLIS, Certificate); records management (MLIS); references services (MLIS); school library media specialist endorsement (MLIS); special libraries (MLIS); urban libraries (MLIS); MLIS/MA. *Accreditation:* ALA (one or more programs are accredited). Part-time and evening/weekend programs available. Postbaccalaureate distance learning degree programs offered (no on-campus study). *Faculty:* 13 full-time (9 women), 17 part-time/adjunct (13 women). *Students:* 112 full-time (80 women), 372 part-time (296 women); includes 65 minority (26 Black or African American, non-Hispanic/Latino; 11 Asian, non-Hispanic/Latino; 18 Hispanic/Latino; 10 Two or more races, non-Hispanic/Latino), 2 international. Average age 33. 275 applicants, 61% accepted, 109 enrolled. In 2013, 179 master's, 42 other advanced degrees awarded. *Entrance requirements:* For master's and other advanced degree, GRE or MAT (if undergraduate GPA is between 2.5 and 2.99), minimum undergraduate GPA of 3.0 or graduate degree, personal statement, resume or curriculum vitae. Additional exam requirements/recommendations for international students: Required—TOEFL (minimum score 550 paper-based; 79 iBT); Recommended—IELTS (minimum score 6.5), TWE (minimum score 5.5). *Application deadline:* For fall admission, 7/1 for domestic students, 5/1 priority date for international students; for winter admission, 10/1 for domestic students, 9/1 priority date for international students; for spring admission, 3/15 for domestic students, 1/1 priority date for international students. Applications are processed on a rolling basis. Application fee: $0. Electronic applications accepted. *Expenses:* Contact institution. *Financial support:* In 2013–14, 65 students received support. Fellowships with tuition reimbursements available, research assistantships with tuition reimbursements available, institutionally sponsored loans, scholarships/grants, and unspecified assistantships available. Support available to part-time students. Financial award application deadline: 3/31; financial award applicants required to submit FAFSA. *Faculty research:* Library services, information management issues, digital content management, library/community engagement, archives and preservation. *Unit head:* Dr. Stephen Bajjaly, Associate Dean and Professor, 313-577-0350, Fax: 313-577-7563, E-mail: bajjaly@wayne.edu. *Application contact:* Matthew Fredericks, Academic Services Officer I, 313-577-2446, Fax: 313-577-7563, E-mail: mfredericks@wayne.edu.
Website: http://slis.wayne.edu/.

Library Science

Appalachian State University, Cratis D. Williams Graduate School, Department of Leadership and Educational Studies, Boone, NC 28608. Offers educational administration (Ed S); educational media (MA); higher education (MA, Ed S); library science (MLS); school administration (MSA). Part-time and evening/weekend programs available. Postbaccalaureate distance learning degree programs offered (no on-campus study). *Degree requirements:* For master's and Ed S, comprehensive exam, thesis optional. *Entrance requirements:* For master's and Ed S, GRE or MAT, 3 letters of recommendation. Additional exam requirements/recommendations for international students: Required—TOEFL (minimum score 570 paper-based; 79 iBT), IELTS (minimum score 6.5). Electronic applications accepted. *Faculty research:* Brain, learning and meditation; leadership of teaching and learning.

Azusa Pacific University, School of Education, Department of Advanced Studies, Program in School Librarianship, Azusa, CA 91702-7000. Offers MA.

Azusa Pacific University, School of Education, Department of Advanced Studies, Program in Teacher Librarian Services, Azusa, CA 91702-7000. Offers Credential. Postbaccalaureate distance learning degree programs offered (no on-campus study).

The Catholic University of America, School of Arts and Sciences, Department of Library and Information Science, Washington, DC 20064. Offers MSLS, JD/MSLS, MSLS/MA, MSLS/MS. *Accreditation:* ALA (one or more programs are accredited). Part-time programs available. *Faculty:* 8 full-time (6 women), 14 part-time/adjunct (7 women). *Students:* 11 full-time (7 women), 159 part-time (121 women); includes 66 minority (33 Black or African American, non-Hispanic/Latino; 10 Asian, non-Hispanic/Latino; 14 Hispanic/Latino; 9 Two or more races, non-Hispanic/Latino), 3 international. Average age 34. 97 applicants, 60% accepted, 34 enrolled. In 2013, 105 master's awarded. *Degree requirements:* For master's, comprehensive exam. *Entrance requirements:* For master's, statement of purpose, official copies of academic transcripts, three letters of recommendation, interview. Additional exam requirements/recommendations for international students: Required—TOEFL (minimum score 580 paper-based). *Application deadline:* For fall admission, 8/1 priority date for domestic students, 7/15 for international students; for spring admission, 11/1 priority date for domestic students, 10/15 for international students. Applications are processed on a rolling basis. Application fee: $55. Electronic applications accepted. *Expenses:* Contact institution. *Financial support:* Fellowships, research assistantships, teaching assistantships, Federal Work-Study, scholarships/grants, tuition waivers (full and partial), and unspecified assistantships available. Financial award application deadline: 2/1; financial award applicants required to submit FAFSA. *Faculty research:* Digital collections, library and information science education, information design and architecture, information system design and evaluation. *Total annual research expenditures:* $474. *Unit head:* Dr. William Kules, Chair, 202-319-5876, E-mail: kules@cua.edu. *Application contact:* Andrew Woodall, Director of Graduate Admissions, 202-319-5057, Fax: 202-319-6533, E-mail: cua-admissions@cua.edu.
Website: http://slis.cua.edu/.

Chicago State University, School of Graduate and Professional Studies, College of Education, Department of Reading, Elementary Education, Library Information and Media Studies, Program in Library Information and Media Studies, Chicago, IL 60628. Offers MS Ed. *Entrance requirements:* For master's, minimum GPA of 2.75.

Clarion University of Pennsylvania, Office of Transfer, Adult and Graduate Admissions, Online Certificate Programs, Clarion, PA 16214. Offers family nurse practitioner (Post-Master's Certificate); library science (CAS); nurse educator (Post-Master's Certificate); public relations (Certificate). *Accreditation:* ALA (one or more programs are accredited at the [master's] level). Part-time programs available. Postbaccalaureate distance learning degree programs offered (no on-campus study).

Faculty: 34 full-time (20 women). *Students:* 15 part-time (12 women); includes 1 minority (Black or African American, non-Hispanic/Latino). Average age 35. 16 applicants, 100% accepted, 7 enrolled. In 2013, 12 CASs awarded. *Entrance requirements:* Additional exam requirements/recommendations for international students: Required—TOEFL (minimum score 550 paper-based; 80 iBT), IELTS (minimum score 7). *Application deadline:* For fall admission, 8/1 priority date for domestic students, 4/15 priority date for international students; for spring admission, 12/1 priority date for domestic students, 9/15 priority date for international students. Applications are processed on a rolling basis. Application fee: $40. Electronic applications accepted. *Expenses:* Tuition, state resident: part-time $442 per credit. Tuition, nonresident: part-time $451 per credit. *Required fees:* $142.40 per semester. One-time fee: $150 part-time. *Financial support:* Research assistantships available. Financial award application deadline: 3/1. *Unit head:* Dr. William Buchanan, Chair, Library Science, 814-393-2271, Fax: 814-393-2150. *Application contact:* Michelle Ritzler, Assistant Director, Graduate Programs, 814-393-2337, Fax: 814-393-2722, E-mail: gradstudies@clarion.edu.
Website: http://www.clarion.edu/991/.

Clarion University of Pennsylvania, Office of Transfer, Adult and Graduate Admissions, Online Master of Science Programs, Clarion, PA 16214. Offers library science (MSLS); mass media arts and journalism (MS). Part-time programs available. Postbaccalaureate distance learning degree programs offered (no on-campus study). *Faculty:* 23 full-time (14 women). *Students:* 124 full-time (96 women), 396 part-time (330 women); includes 48 minority (16 Black or African American, non-Hispanic/Latino; 7 American Indian or Alaska Native, non-Hispanic/Latino; 8 Asian, non-Hispanic/Latino; 9 Hispanic/Latino; 1 Native Hawaiian or other Pacific Islander, non-Hispanic/Latino; 7 Two or more races, non-Hispanic/Latino), 4 international. Average age 32. 227 applicants, 85% accepted, 136 enrolled. In 2013, 184 master's awarded. *Degree requirements:* For master's, comprehensive exam, thesis or alternative. *Entrance requirements:* For master's, minimum QPA of 3.0. Additional exam requirements/recommendations for international students: Required—TOEFL (minimum score 600 paper-based; 100 iBT), IELTS (minimum score 7.5). *Application deadline:* For fall admission, 8/1 priority date for domestic students, 4/15 priority date for international students; for spring admission, 12/1 priority date for domestic students, 9/15 priority date for international students. Applications are processed on a rolling basis. Application fee: $40. Electronic applications accepted. *Expenses:* Tuition, state resident: part-time $442 per credit. Tuition, nonresident: part-time $451 per credit. *Required fees:* $142.40 per semester. One-time fee: $150 part-time. *Financial support:* In 2013–14, 12 research assistantships with full and partial tuition reimbursements (averaging $9,240 per year) were awarded. Support available to part-time students. Financial award application deadline: 3/1. *Unit head:* Dr. Myrna Kuehn, Chair, 814-393-2245, Fax: 814-393-2186. *Application contact:* Michelle Ritzler, Assistant Director, Graduate Programs, 814-393-2337, Fax: 814-393-2030, E-mail: gradstudies@clarion.edu.
Website: http://www.clarion.edu/991/.

Dalhousie University, Faculty of Management, School of Information Management, Halifax, NS B3H 3J5, Canada. Offers MIM, MLIS, LL B/MLIS, MBA/MLIS, MLIS/MPA, MLIS/MREM. *Accreditation:* ALA (one or more programs are accredited). Part-time programs available. *Degree requirements:* For master's, one foreign language, thesis optional. *Entrance requirements:* For master's, resume, interview. Additional exam requirements/recommendations for international students: Required—TOEFL, IELTS, CANTEST, CAEL, or Michigan English Language Assessment Battery. Electronic applications accepted. *Faculty research:* Information-seeking behavior, electronic text design, browsing in digital environments, information diffusion among scientists.

Dominican University, Graduate School of Library and Information Science, River Forest, IL 60305-1099. Offers knowledge management (Certificate); library and information science (MLIS, PhD); professional studies (MA); special studies (CSS); MBA/MLIS; MLIS/M Div; MLIS/MA; MLIS/MM. MLIS/M Div offered jointly with McCormick Theological Seminary, MLIS/MA with Loyola University Chicago, MLIS/MM with Northwestern University. *Accreditation:* ALA (one or more programs are accredited). Part-time and evening/weekend programs available. Postbaccalaureate distance learning degree programs offered (minimal on-campus study). *Faculty:* 13 full-time (7 women), 11 part-time/adjunct (7 women). *Students:* 97 full-time (76 women), 225 part-time (181 women); includes 61 minority (23 Black or African American, non-Hispanic/Latino; 1 American Indian or Alaska Native, non-Hispanic/Latino; 7 Asian, non-Hispanic/Latino; 29 Hispanic/Latino; 1 Two or more races, non-Hispanic/Latino), 3 international. Average age 34. 140 applicants, 69% accepted, 68 enrolled. In 2013, 194 master's, 5 doctorates awarded. *Degree requirements:* For doctorate, thesis/dissertation. *Entrance requirements:* For master's, minimum GPA of 3.0, GRE General Test, or MAT; for doctorate, MLIS or related MA, minimum GPA of 3.0, GRE General Test or MAT. Additional exam requirements/recommendations for international students: Required—TOEFL. *Application deadline:* For fall admission, 6/1 priority date for domestic students; for winter admission, 3/1 priority date for domestic students; for spring admission, 10/1 priority date for domestic students. Applications are processed on a rolling basis. Application fee: $25. *Expenses:* Contact institution. *Financial support:* In 2013–14, 158 students received support. Fellowships, research assistantships, career-related internships or fieldwork, Federal Work-Study, scholarships/grants, and tuition waivers (partial) available. Support available to part-time students. Financial award application deadline: 4/15; financial award applicants required to submit FAFSA. *Faculty research:* Productivity and the information environment, bibliometrics, library history, subject access, library materials and services for children. *Unit head:* Dr. Kate Marek, Acting Dean, 708-524-6648, Fax: 708-524-6657, E-mail: kmarek@dom.edu. *Application contact:* Anne Hurley, Director of Graduate Admissions, 708-524-6829, E-mail: ahurley@dom.edu.
Website: http://gslis.dom.edu/.

Drexel University, College of Computing and Informatics, Philadelphia, PA 19104-2875. Offers MS, MSIS, MSSE, PhD, Advanced Certificate, Certificate, PMC. *Accreditation:* ALA (one or more programs are accredited). Part-time and evening/weekend programs available. Postbaccalaureate distance learning degree programs offered (no on-campus study). *Faculty:* 31 full-time (20 women), 24 part-time/adjunct (15 women). *Students:* 234 full-time (131 women), 582 part-time (339 women); includes 151 minority (63 Black or African American, non-Hispanic/Latino; 5 American Indian or Alaska Native, non-Hispanic/Latino; 54 Asian, non-Hispanic/Latino; 29 Hispanic/Latino), 87 international. Average age 34. 555 applicants, 73% accepted, 220 enrolled. In 2013, 327 master's, 9 doctorates, 27 other advanced degrees awarded. *Degree requirements:* For doctorate, thesis/dissertation. *Entrance requirements:* For master's and doctorate, GRE General Test. Additional exam requirements/recommendations for international students: Required—TOEFL (minimum score 600 paper-based; 100 iBT). *Application deadline:* For fall admission, 9/1 for domestic and international students; for spring admission, 3/4 for domestic students, 2/15 for international students. Applications are processed on a rolling basis. Electronic applications accepted. *Expenses:* Contact institution. *Financial support:* In 2013–14, 282 students received support, including 279 fellowships with partial tuition reimbursements available (averaging $22,500 per year), 34 research assistantships with full tuition reimbursements available (averaging $22,500 per year), 2 teaching assistantships with full tuition reimbursements available (averaging $22,250 per year); career-related internships or fieldwork, institutionally sponsored loans, scholarships/grants, traineeships, health care benefits, tuition waivers (partial), and unspecified assistantships also available. Support available to part-time students. Financial award application deadline: 3/1; financial award applicants required to submit FAFSA. *Faculty research:* Information retrieval/information visualization/bibliometrics, human-computer interaction, digital libraries, databases, text/data mining. *Total annual research expenditures:* $2 million. *Unit head:* Dr. David E. Fenske, Dean/Professor of Information Science, 215-895-2475, Fax: 215-895-6378, E-mail: fenske@drexel.edu. *Application contact:* Matthew Lechtenberg, Graduate Admissions Manager, 215-895-1951, Fax: 215-895-2303, E-mail: ml333@drexel.edu.
Website: http://cci.drexel.edu/.

East Carolina University, Graduate School, College of Education, Department of Library Science, Greenville, NC 27858-4353. Offers MLS. *Accreditation:* NCATE. Part-time and evening/weekend programs available. Postbaccalaureate distance learning degree programs offered (no on-campus study). *Degree requirements:* For master's, comprehensive exam, thesis optional. *Entrance requirements:* For master's, GRE General Test or MAT, interview, minimum GPA of 2.5, bachelor's degree in related field, teaching license (MA Ed). Additional exam requirements/recommendations for international students: Required—TOEFL. *Expenses:* Tuition, state resident: full-time $4223. Tuition, nonresident: full-time $16,540. *Required fees:* $2184.

Eastern Kentucky University, The Graduate School, College of Education, Department of Curriculum and Instruction, Richmond, KY 40475-3102. Offers elementary education (MA Ed), including early elementary education, reading; library science (MA Ed); music education (MA Ed); secondary and higher education (MA Ed), including secondary education; teaching (MAT). *Accreditation:* NCATE. Part-time programs available. *Degree requirements:* For master's, portfolio is part of exam. *Entrance requirements:* For master's, GRE General Test, PRAXIS II (KY), minimum GPA of 2.5. *Faculty research:* Technology in education, reading instruction, e-portfolios, induction to teacher education, dispositions of teachers.

East Tennessee State University, School of Graduate Studies, College of Education, Department of Curriculum and Instruction, Johnson City, TN 37614. Offers educational media and educational technology (M Ed), including educational communications and technology, school library media; elementary education (M Ed); reading (MA), including reading education, storytelling; school library professional (Post-Master's Certificate); secondary education (M Ed), including classroom technology, secondary education (M Ed, MAT); storytelling (Postbaccalaureate Certificate); teacher education with multiple levels (MAT), including elementary education, middle grades education, secondary education (M Ed, MAT). *Accreditation:* NCATE. Part-time and evening/weekend programs available. Postbaccalaureate distance learning degree programs offered (no on-campus study). *Faculty:* 25 full-time (18 women), 12 part-time/adjunct (8 women). *Students:* 66 full-time (50 women), 97 part-time (85 women); includes 5 minority (3 Black or African American, non-Hispanic/Latino; 2 Two or more races, non-Hispanic/Latino), 2 international. Average age 31. 144 applicants, 57% accepted, 70 enrolled. In 2013, 83 master's, 5 other advanced degrees awarded. *Degree requirements:* For master's, comprehensive exam, thesis optional, student teaching, practicum; for other advanced degree, field work (school library); culminating experience (storytelling). *Entrance requirements:* For master's, GRE, SAT, ACT, PRAXIS, minimum GPA of 3.0; for other advanced degree, master's degree, TN teaching license (for school library professional Post-Master's Certificate); three letters of recommendation (for storytelling Postbaccalaureate Certificate). Additional exam requirements/recommendations for international students: Required—TOEFL (minimum score 550 paper-based; 79 iBT). *Application deadline:* For fall admission, 6/1 for domestic students, 4/30 for international students; for spring admission, 11/1 for domestic students, 4/30 for international students. Application fee: $35 ($45 for international students). Electronic applications accepted. *Expenses:* Tuition, state resident: full-time $7900; part-time $395 per credit hour. Tuition, nonresident: full-time $21,960; part-time $1098 per credit hour. *Required fees:* $1345; $84 per credit hour. *Financial support:* In 2013–14, 43 students received support, including 6 research assistantships with full tuition reimbursements available (averaging $6,000 per year), 10 teaching assistantships with full tuition reimbursements available (averaging $6,000 per year); career-related internships or fieldwork, institutionally sponsored loans, scholarships/grants, and unspecified assistantships also available. Financial award application deadline: 7/1; financial award applicants required to submit FAFSA. *Faculty research:* Critical thinking; curriculum development in reading, math, and science education; cultural diversity; cognitive processes; effective teaching strategies. *Unit head:* Dr. Rhona Hurwitz, Chair, 423-439-7598, Fax: 423-439-8362, E-mail: hurwitz@etsu.edu. *Application contact:* Fiona Goodyear, Graduate Specialist, 423-439-6148, Fax: 423-439-5624, E-mail: goodyear@etsu.edu.
Website: http://www.etsu.edu/coe/cuai/.

Emporia State University, School of Library and Information Management, Emporia, KS 66801-5415. Offers archives studies (Certificate); library and information management (MLS, PhD, Certificate). *Accreditation:* ALA (one or more programs are accredited). Part-time and evening/weekend programs available. Postbaccalaureate distance learning degree programs offered (minimal on-campus study). *Faculty:* 9 full-time (5 women). *Students:* 92 full-time (68 women), 225 part-time (188 women); includes 32 minority (1 Black or African American, non-Hispanic/Latino; 6 Asian, non-Hispanic/Latino; 13 Hispanic/Latino; 1 Native Hawaiian or other Pacific Islander, non-Hispanic/Latino; 11 Two or more races, non-Hispanic/Latino), 4 international. 138 applicants, 80% accepted, 77 enrolled. In 2013, 139 master's, 3 doctorates, 12 other advanced degrees awarded. *Degree requirements:* For master's, comprehensive exam, thesis optional; for doctorate, thesis/dissertation. *Entrance requirements:* For master's, GRE General Test, interview, minimum undergraduate GPA of 3.0, letters of recommendation; for doctorate, GRE General Test, interview, minimum graduate GPA of 3.5. Additional exam requirements/recommendations for international students: Required—TOEFL (minimum score 520 paper-based; 68 iBT). *Application deadline:* For fall admission, 8/15 priority date for domestic students. Applications are processed on a rolling basis. Application fee: $30 ($75 for international students). Electronic applications accepted. *Expenses: Tuition, area resident:* Part-time $220 per credit hour. Tuition, state resident: part-time $220 per credit hour. Tuition, nonresident: part-time $685 per credit hour. *Required fees:* $73 per credit hour. *Financial support:* In 2013–14, 12 research assistantships with full tuition reimbursements (averaging $7,200 per year) were awarded; Federal Work-Study, institutionally sponsored loans, and unspecified assistantships also available. Financial award application deadline: 3/15; financial award applicants required to submit FAFSA. *Unit head:* Dr. Gwen Alexander, Dean, 620-341-5203, Fax: 620-341-5233, E-mail: galexan1@emporia.edu. *Application contact:* Candace Boardman, Director, Kansas MLS Program, 620-341-6159, E-mail: cboardma@emporia.edu.
Website: http://www.emporia.edu/las/index.html.

Florida State University, The Graduate School, College of Communication and Information, School of Information, Tallahassee, FL 32306-2100. Offers general information studies (MA); information studies (Specialist); information technology (MS); library and information studies (PhD). *Accreditation:* ALA (one or more programs are accredited). Part-time and evening/weekend programs available. Postbaccalaureate distance learning degree programs offered (no on-campus study). *Faculty:* 31 full-time (18 women), 11 part-time/adjunct (5 women). *Students:* 108 full-time (82 women), 305

part-time (230 women); includes 99 minority (36 Black or African American, non-Hispanic/Latino; 20 Asian, non-Hispanic/Latino; 34 Hispanic/Latino; 9 Two or more races, non-Hispanic/Latino). Average age 35. 195 applicants, 78% accepted, 103 enrolled. In 2013, 166 master's, 4 doctorates, 4 other advanced degrees awarded. Terminal master's awarded for partial completion of doctoral program. *Degree requirements:* For master's, thesis optional, minimum GPA of 3.0, 36 hours (MSLIS); 32 hours (MSIT); for doctorate, comprehensive exam, thesis/dissertation, dissertation defense, manuscript clearance, minimum GPA of 3.0; for Specialist, minimum GPA of 3.0; 30 hours. *Entrance requirements:* For master's, GRE (recommended minimum percentile of 50 on each of the verbal and quantitative portions and writing score of 4.0), minimum GPA of 3.0 on last 2 years of baccalaureate degree, resume, statement of goals, two letters of recommendation, official transcripts from every college-level institution attended; for doctorate, GRE (recommended minimum percentile of 50 on each of the verbal and quantitative portions and writing score of 4.0), minimum GPA of 3.0 on last degree program, resume, 3 letters of recommendation, personal/goals statement, writing sample, brief digital video, official transcripts from all college-level institutions attended; for Specialist, GRE (recommended minimum percentile of 50 on each of the verbal and quantitative portions and writing score of 4.0), minimum graduate GPA of 3.2, resume, statement of goals, 2 letters of recommendation, writing sample, official transcripts from every college-level institution attended. Additional exam requirements/recommendations for international students: Required—TOEFL (minimum score 585 paper-based; 94 iBT), IELTS (minimum score 6.5). *Application deadline:* For fall admission, 7/1 for domestic and international students; for spring admission, 11/1 for domestic and international students. Applications are processed on a rolling basis. Application fee: $30. Electronic applications accepted. *Expenses:* Contact institution. *Financial support:* In 2013–14, 54 students received support, including 7 fellowships with full tuition reimbursements available (averaging $16,000 per year), 24 research assistantships with full tuition reimbursements available (averaging $16,000 per year), 23 teaching assistantships with full tuition reimbursements available (averaging $16,000 per year); career-related internships or fieldwork, Federal Work-Study, scholarships/grants, health care benefits, tuition waivers, and unspecified assistantships also available. Financial award application deadline: 3/1; financial award applicants required to submit FAFSA. *Faculty research:* Needs assessment, social informatics, usability analysis, human information behavior, youth services. *Total annual research expenditures:* $2 million. *Unit head:* Dr. Kathleen Burnett, Interim Director and Professor, 850-644-8124, Fax: 850-644-9763, E-mail: kathleen.burnett@cci.fsu.edu. *Application contact:* Graduate Student Services, 850-645-3280, Fax: 850-644-9763, E-mail: slisgradadmissions@admin.fsu.edu.
Website: http://slis.fsu.edu/.

Indiana University Bloomington, School of Informatics and Computing, Department of Information and Library Science, Bloomington, IN 47405-3907. Offers information architecture (Graduate Certificate); information science (MIS, PhD); library and information science (Sp LIS); library science (MLS); JD/MLS; MIS/MA; MLS/MA; MPA/MIS; MPA/MLS. *Accreditation:* ALA (one or more programs are accredited). Part-time programs available. *Faculty:* 16 full-time (7 women). *Students:* 146 full-time (101 women), 63 part-time (46 women); includes 20 minority (6 Black or African American, non-Hispanic/Latino; 1 American Indian or Alaska Native, non-Hispanic/Latino; 4 Asian, non-Hispanic/Latino; 4 Hispanic/Latino; 5 Two or more races, non-Hispanic/Latino), 29 international. Average age 29. 242 applicants, 80% accepted, 71 enrolled. In 2013, 170 master's, 4 doctorates, 1 other advanced degree awarded. *Degree requirements:* For doctorate, thesis/dissertation. *Entrance requirements:* For master's and doctorate, GRE General Test, 3 letters of reference. Additional exam requirements/recommendations for international students: Required—TOEFL (minimum score 600 paper-based; 100 iBT). *Application deadline:* For fall admission, 5/15 priority date for domestic students, 12/1 priority date for international students; for spring admission, 10/15 priority date for domestic students, 9/1 priority date for international students. Applications are processed on a rolling basis. Application fee: $55 ($65 for international students). Electronic applications accepted. *Expenses:* Contact institution. *Financial support:* Fellowships with full and partial tuition reimbursements, research assistantships with full and partial tuition reimbursements, career-related internships or fieldwork, Federal Work-Study, institutionally sponsored loans, scholarships/grants, tuition waivers (partial), and unspecified assistantships available. Support available to part-time students. Financial award application deadline: 1/15. *Faculty research:* Scholarly communication, interface design, library and management policy, computer-mediated communication, information retrieval. *Unit head:* Dr. Howard Rosenbaum, Associate Dean for Graduate Studies, E-mail: hrosenba@indiana.edu. *Application contact:* Rhonda Spencer, Director of Admissions, 812-855-2018, Fax: 812-855-6166, E-mail: slis@indiana.edu.
Website: http://ils.indiana.edu/.

Indiana University–Purdue University Indianapolis, School of Informatics and Computing, Department of Information and Library Science, Indianapolis, IN 46202-2896. Offers MLS. Part-time and evening/weekend programs available. *Faculty:* 3 full-time (2 women). *Students:* 43 full-time (32 women), 120 part-time (98 women); includes 13 minority (7 Black or African American, non-Hispanic/Latino; 2 Asian, non-Hispanic/Latino; 1 Hispanic/Latino; 3 Two or more races, non-Hispanic/Latino). Average age 34. 48 applicants, 90% accepted, 30 enrolled. In 2013, 73 master's awarded. *Entrance requirements:* For master's, GRE General Test. Additional exam requirements/recommendations for international students: Required—TOEFL (minimum score 600 paper-based). *Application deadline:* For fall admission, 7/15 priority date for domestic students; for spring admission, 11/15 priority date for domestic students. Applications are processed on a rolling basis. Application fee: $55 ($65 for international students). *Financial support:* Teaching assistantships, career-related internships or fieldwork, Federal Work-Study, institutionally sponsored loans, and scholarships/grants available. Support available to part-time students. *Unit head:* Dr. Rachel Applegate, Chair, 317-278-2395, E-mail: rapplega@iupui.edu. *Application contact:* Elizabeth Bunge, Graduate Admissions Coordinator, 317-278-9200, E-mail: ebunge@iupui.edu.
Website: http://soic.iupui.edu/departments/lis/.

Indiana University–Purdue University Indianapolis, School of Public and Environmental Affairs, Indianapolis, IN 46202. Offers criminal justice and public safety (MS); homeland security and emergency management (Graduate Certificate); library management (Graduate Certificate); nonprofit management (Graduate Certificate); public affairs (MPA); public management (Graduate Certificate); social entrepreneurship: nonprofit and public benefit organizations (Graduate Certificate); JD/MPA; MLS/NMC; MLS/PMC; MPA/MA. *Accreditation:* CAHME (one or more programs are accredited); NASPAA. Part-time and evening/weekend programs available. Postbaccalaureate distance learning degree programs offered (no on-campus study). *Entrance requirements:* For master's, GRE General Test, GMAT or LSAT, minimum GPA of 3.0 (preferred). Additional exam requirements/recommendations for international students: Required—TOEFL (minimum score 93 iBT), IELTS (minimum score 6.5). Electronic applications accepted. *Faculty research:* Nonprofit and public management, public policy, urban policy, sustainability policy, disaster preparedness and recovery, vehicular safety, homicide, offender rehabilitation and re-entry.

Instituto Tecnológico y de Estudios Superiores de Monterrey, Campus Irapuato, Graduate Programs, Irapuato, Mexico. Offers administration (MBA); administration of information technology (MAIT); administration of telecommunications (MAT); architecture (M Arch); computer science (MCS); education (M Ed); educational administration (MEA); educational innovation and technology (DEIT); educational technology (MET); electronic commerce (MBA); environmental administration and planning (MEAP); environmental systems (MES); finances (MBA); humanistic studies (MHS); international management for Latin American executives (MIMLAE); library and information science (MLIS); manufacturing quality management (MMQM); marketing research (MBA).

Inter American University of Puerto Rico, Barranquitas Campus, Program in Education, Barranquitas, PR 00794. Offers curriculum and teaching (M Ed), including biology education, English as a second language, history education, mathematics education, Spanish; educational leadership and management (MA); elementary education (M Ed); information and library service technology (M Ed); special education (MA). *Degree requirements:* For master's, comprehensive exam, thesis optional. *Entrance requirements:* For master's, EXADEP, letter of recommendation. Electronic applications accepted.

Inter American University of Puerto Rico, San Germán Campus, Graduate Studies Center, Program in Library Sciences, San Germán, PR 00683-5008. Offers MLS. Part-time and evening/weekend programs available. *Faculty:* 9 full-time (6 women), 13 part-time/adjunct (7 women). *Students:* 16 full-time (14 women), 2 part-time (both women); all minorities (all Hispanic/Latino). Average age 34. 10 applicants, 40% accepted, 4 enrolled. In 2013, 2 master's awarded. *Degree requirements:* For master's, comprehensive exam. *Entrance requirements:* For master's, GRE General Test or EXADEP, minimum GPA of 3.0. *Application deadline:* For fall admission, 4/30 priority date for domestic students; for spring admission, 11/15 for domestic students. Applications are processed on a rolling basis. Application fee: $31. *Expenses: Tuition:* Full-time $2424; part-time $202 per credit hour. *Required fees:* $260 per semester. Tuition and fees vary according to course level, course load, degree level and program. *Financial support:* Teaching assistantships, Federal Work-Study, and unspecified assistantships available. *Unit head:* Dr. Elba T. Irizarry, Director of Graduate Studies Center, 787-264-1912 Ext. 7357, Fax: 787-892-6350, E-mail: elbat@sg.inter.edu. *Application contact:* Dr. Elba T. Irizarry, Director of Graduate Studies Center, 787-264-1912 Ext. 7357, Fax: 787-892-6350, E-mail: elbat@sg.inter.edu.

Kent State University, College of Communication and Information, School of Library and Information Science, Kent, OH 44242-0001. Offers MLIS. *Accreditation:* ALA. *Degree requirements:* For master's, thesis optional. *Entrance requirements:* For master's, GRE General Test, minimum GPA of 2.75.

Kutztown University of Pennsylvania, College of Education, Program in Library Science, Kutztown, PA 19530-0730. Offers MLS. Part-time and evening/weekend programs available. *Faculty:* 6 full-time (5 women). *Students:* 16 part-time (14 women). Average age 33. 12 applicants, 75% accepted, 6 enrolled. In 2013, 9 master's awarded. *Degree requirements:* For master's, comprehensive exam. *Entrance requirements:* For master's, GRE General Test. Additional exam requirements/recommendations for international students: Required—TOEFL (minimum score 550 paper-based; 79 iBT). *Application deadline:* For fall admission, 8/1 priority date for domestic and international students; for spring admission, 12/1 priority date for domestic and international students. Applications are processed on a rolling basis. Application fee: $35. Electronic applications accepted. *Expenses: Tuition, area resident:* Part-time $442 per credit. Tuition, state resident: part-time $442 per credit. Tuition, nonresident: part-time $663 per credit. *Required fees:* $80 per credit. *Financial support:* Career-related internships or fieldwork, Federal Work-Study, scholarships/grants, and unspecified assistantships available. Financial award application deadline: 3/1; financial award applicants required to submit FAFSA. *Unit head:* Dr. Andrea Harmer, Chairperson, 610-683-4301, Fax: 610-683-1326, E-mail: harmer@kutztown.edu. *Application contact:* Kelly Hish, Admissions Clerk, 610-683-4200, Fax: 610-683-1393, E-mail: graduate@kutztown.edu.

Long Island University–Hudson at Westchester, Program in Library and Information Science, Purchase, NY 10577. Offers MS. Part-time and evening/weekend programs available.

Long Island University–LIU Post, College of Information and Computer Science, Palmer School of Library and Information Science, Brookville, NY 11548-1300. Offers archives and records management (Certificate); information studies (PhD); library and information science (MS); library media specialist (MS); public library management (Certificate). *Accreditation:* ALA (one or more programs are accredited). Part-time and evening/weekend programs available. Postbaccalaureate distance learning degree programs offered (minimal on-campus study). *Degree requirements:* For master's, thesis optional, internship; for doctorate, thesis/dissertation, qualifying exam. *Entrance requirements:* For master's, GRE or MAT, minimum undergraduate GPA of 3.0, resume. Electronic applications accepted. *Faculty research:* Information retrieval, digital libraries, scientometric and infometric studies, preservation/archiving and electronic records.

Louisiana State University and Agricultural & Mechanical College, Graduate School, College of Human Sciences and Education, School of Library and Information Science, Baton Rouge, LA 70803. Offers MLIS. *Accreditation:* ALA. Part-time and evening/weekend programs available. Postbaccalaureate distance learning degree programs offered (no on-campus study). *Faculty:* 10 full-time (8 women). *Students:* 56 full-time (45 women), 83 part-time (69 women); includes 17 minority (9 Black or African American, non-Hispanic/Latino; 1 American Indian or Alaska Native, non-Hispanic/Latino; 1 Asian, non-Hispanic/Latino; 4 Hispanic/Latino; 2 Two or more races, non-Hispanic/Latino), 1 international. Average age 32. 42 applicants, 83% accepted, 21 enrolled. In 2013, 62 master's awarded. *Degree requirements:* For master's, comprehensive exam, thesis optional. *Entrance requirements:* For master's, GRE General Test, minimum GPA of 3.0. Additional exam requirements/recommendations for international students: Required—TOEFL (minimum score 550 paper-based; 79 IBT), IELTS (minimum score 6.5), or PTE (minimum score 59). *Application deadline:* For fall admission, 1/25 priority date for domestic students, 5/15 for international students; for spring admission, 10/15 for international students. Applications are processed on a rolling basis. Application fee: $50 ($70 for international students). Electronic applications accepted. *Financial support:* In 2013–14, 97 students received support, including 10 fellowships (averaging $20,000 per year), 6 research assistantships with partial tuition reimbursements available (averaging $13,000 per year), 14 teaching assistantships with partial tuition reimbursements available (averaging $12,630 per year); career-related internships or fieldwork, Federal Work-Study, institutionally sponsored loans, scholarships/grants, health care benefits, and unspecified assistantships also available. Support available to part-time students. Financial award applicants required to submit FAFSA. *Faculty research:* Information retrieval, management, collection development, public libraries. *Total annual research expenditures:* $21,404. *Unit head:* Dr. Beth M. Paskoff, Dean, 225-578-3158, Fax: 225-578-4581, E-mail: bpaskoff@lsu.edu. *Application contact:* LaToya Joseph, Administrative Assistant, 225-578-3150, Fax: 225-578-4581, E-mail: lcjoseph@lsu.edu.
Website: http://slis.lsu.edu/.

Mansfield University of Pennsylvania, Graduate Studies, Program in School Library and Information Technologies, Mansfield, PA 16933. Offers library science (M Ed). Part-time and evening/weekend programs available. Postbaccalaureate distance learning

degree programs offered. *Degree requirements:* For master's, comprehensive exam, thesis optional. *Entrance requirements:* For master's, minimum GPA of 3.0. Additional exam requirements/recommendations for international students: Required—TOEFL (minimum score 550 paper-based). Electronic applications accepted. *Expenses:* Contact institution.

McDaniel College, Graduate and Professional Studies, Program in School Librarianship, Westminster, MD 21157-4390. Offers MS. Part-time and evening/weekend programs available. *Degree requirements:* For master's, comprehensive exam, thesis optional. *Entrance requirements:* For master's, GRE General Test, MAT, or NTE/PRAXIS I, 3 letters of reference. Additional exam requirements/recommendations for international students: Required—TOEFL.

McGill University, Faculty of Graduate and Postdoctoral Studies, Faculty of Education, School of Information Studies, Montréal, QC H3A 2T5, Canada. Offers MLIS, PhD, Certificate, Diploma. *Accreditation:* ALA (one or more programs are accredited).

McNeese State University, Doré School of Graduate Studies, Burton College of Education, Office of Student Teaching and Professional Education Services, Program in School Librarian, Lake Charles, LA 70609. Offers Postbaccalaureate Certificate. *Entrance requirements:* For degree, PRAXIS, 2 letters of recommendation, autobiography.

North Carolina Central University, School of Library and Information Sciences, Durham, NC 27707-3129. Offers MIS, MLS. *Accreditation:* ALA (one or more programs are accredited). Part-time and evening/weekend programs available. *Degree requirements:* For master's, one foreign language, thesis, research paper, or project. *Entrance requirements:* For master's, GRE, 90 hours in liberal arts. Additional exam requirements/recommendations for international students: Required—TOEFL. *Faculty research:* African-American resources, planning and evaluation, analysis of economic and physical resources, geography of information, artificial intelligence.

Old Dominion University, Darden College of Education, Program in Elementary/Middle Education, Norfolk, VA 23529. Offers elementary education (MS Ed); instructional technology (MS Ed); library science (MS Ed); middle school education (MS Ed). *Accreditation:* NCATE. Part-time and evening/weekend programs available. Postbaccalaureate distance learning degree programs offered (no on-campus study). *Faculty:* 20 full-time (15 women), 31 part-time/adjunct (26 women). *Students:* 157 full-time (152 women), 91 part-time (77 women); includes 46 minority (17 Black or African American, non-Hispanic/Latino; 3 Asian, non-Hispanic/Latino; 17 Hispanic/Latino; 1 Native Hawaiian or other Pacific Islander, non-Hispanic/Latino; 8 Two or more races, non-Hispanic/Latino), 1 international. Average age 31. 291 applicants, 50% accepted, 123 enrolled. In 2013, 142 master's awarded. *Degree requirements:* For master's, comprehensive exam. *Entrance requirements:* For master's, GRE General Test or MAT; PRAXIS I, SAT or ACT, minimum GPA of 2.8. Additional exam requirements/recommendations for international students: Required—TOEFL (minimum score 600 paper-based). *Application deadline:* For fall admission, 6/1 priority date for domestic students; for winter admission, 11/1 priority date for domestic students; for spring admission, 3/1 priority date for domestic students. Applications are processed on a rolling basis. Application fee: $50. Electronic applications accepted. *Expenses:* Tuition, state resident: full-time $9888; part-time $412 per credit. Tuition, nonresident: full-time $25,152; part-time $1048 per credit. *Required fees:* $59 per semester. One-time fee: $50. *Financial support:* In 2013–14, 180 students received support. Application deadline: 2/15; applicants required to submit FAFSA. *Faculty research:* Education pre-K to 6, school librarianship. *Unit head:* Dr. Charlene Fleener, Graduate Program Director, 757-683-3284, Fax: 757-683-5862, E-mail: cfleener@odu.edu. *Application contact:* William Heffelfinger, Director of Graduate Admissions, 757-683-5554, Fax: 757-683-3255, E-mail: gradadmit@odu.edu.
Website: http://education.odu.edu/eci/.

Old Dominion University, Darden College of Education, Programs in Secondary Education, Norfolk, VA 23529. Offers biology (MS Ed); chemistry (MS Ed); English (MS Ed); instructional technology (MS Ed); library science (MS Ed); secondary education (MS Ed). *Accreditation:* NCATE. Part-time and evening/weekend programs available. Postbaccalaureate distance learning degree programs offered (minimal on-campus study). *Faculty:* 13 full-time (7 women), 10 part-time/adjunct (7 women). *Students:* 74 full-time (56 women), 78 part-time (49 women); includes 25 minority (13 Black or African American, non-Hispanic/Latino; 6 Hispanic/Latino; 6 Two or more races, non-Hispanic/Latino). Average age 32. 75 applicants, 71% accepted, 53 enrolled. In 2013, 79 master's awarded. *Degree requirements:* For master's, comprehensive exam, thesis. *Entrance requirements:* For master's, GRE General Test or MAT, PRAXIS I (for licensure), minimum GPA of 2.8, teaching certificate. Additional exam requirements/recommendations for international students: Required—TOEFL. *Application deadline:* For fall admission, 6/1 for domestic and international students; for winter admission, 11/1 for domestic and international students; for spring admission, 3/1 for domestic and international students. Applications are processed on a rolling basis. Application fee: $50. Electronic applications accepted. *Expenses:* Tuition, state resident: full-time $9888; part-time $412 per credit. Tuition, nonresident: full-time $25,152; part-time $1048 per credit. *Required fees:* $59 per semester. One-time fee: $50. *Financial support:* In 2013–14, 56 students received support, including fellowships (averaging $15,000 per year), research assistantships with tuition reimbursements available (averaging $9,000 per year), teaching assistantships with tuition reimbursements available (averaging $15,000 per year). Financial award application deadline: 2/15; financial award applicants required to submit FAFSA. *Faculty research:* Use of technology, writing project for teachers, geography teaching, reading. *Unit head:* Dr. Robert Lucking, Graduate Program Director, 757-683-5545, Fax: 757-683-5862, E-mail: rlucking@odu.edu. *Application contact:* William Heffelfinger, Director of Graduate Admissions, 757-683-5554, Fax: 757-683-3255, E-mail: gradadmit@odu.edu.
Website: http://education.odu.edu/eci/secondary/.

Olivet Nazarene University, Graduate School, Division of Education, Program in Library Information Specialist, Bourbonnais, IL 60914. Offers MAE.

Pratt Institute, School of Information and Library Science, New York, NY 10011. Offers archives (Adv C); library and information science (MS, Adv C); library and information science: library media specialist (MS); library media specialist (Adv C); museum libraries (Adv C); JD/MS. *Accreditation:* ALA. Part-time programs available. *Faculty:* 9 full-time (4 women), 26 part-time/adjunct (13 women). *Students:* 134 full-time (108 women), 91 part-time (72 women); includes 47 minority (17 Black or African American, non-Hispanic/Latino; 10 Asian, non-Hispanic/Latino; 19 Hispanic/Latino; 1 Native Hawaiian or other Pacific Islander, non-Hispanic/Latino), 1 international. Average age 30. 197 applicants, 94% accepted, 77 enrolled. In 2013, 134 master's, 3 other advanced degrees awarded. *Degree requirements:* For master's, thesis. *Entrance requirements:* Additional exam requirements/recommendations for international students: Required—TOEFL (minimum score 600 paper-based; 100 iBT). *Application deadline:* For fall admission, 1/5 for domestic and international students; for spring admission, 10/1 for domestic and international students. Application fee: $50 ($90 for international students). Electronic applications accepted. *Expenses:* Contact institution. *Financial support:* Career-related internships or fieldwork, Federal Work-Study, institutionally sponsored loans, scholarships/grants, health care benefits, and unspecified assistantships available. Support available to part-time students. Financial award application deadline: 2/1; financial award applicants required to submit FAFSA. *Faculty research:* Development of urban libraries and information centers, medical and law librarianship, information management. *Unit head:* Dr. Tula Giannini, Dean, 212-647-7682, E-mail: giannini@pratt.edu. *Application contact:* Young Hah, Director of Graduate Admissions, 718-636-3683, Fax: 718-399-4242, E-mail: yhah@pratt.edu.
Website: https://www.pratt.edu/academics/information-and-library-sciences/.

See Display on page 1582 and Close-Up on page 1597.

Queens College of the City University of New York, Division of Graduate Studies, Social Science Division, Graduate School of Library and Information Studies, Flushing, NY 11367-1597. Offers MLS, AC. *Accreditation:* ALA (one or more programs are accredited). Part-time and evening/weekend programs available. *Degree requirements:* For master's, thesis; for AC, thesis optional. *Entrance requirements:* For master's, minimum GPA of 3.0; for AC, master's degree or equivalent. Additional exam requirements/recommendations for international students: Required—TOEFL.

Rowan University, Graduate School, College of Education, Department of Special Educational Services/Instruction, Glassboro, NJ 08028-1701. Offers counseling in educational settings (MA); educational services (Ed S); higher education administration (MA); principal preparation (CAGS); school administration (MA); school and public librarianship (MA); school nursing (Postbaccalaureate Certificate); school psychology (MA, Ed S); supervisor (CAGS). *Accreditation:* NCATE. Part-time and evening/weekend programs available. *Faculty:* 22 full-time (15 women), 18 part-time/adjunct (12 women). *Students:* 117 full-time (93 women), 211 part-time (154 women); includes 64 minority (42 Black or African American, non-Hispanic/Latino; 1 American Indian or Alaska Native, non-Hispanic/Latino; 5 Asian, non-Hispanic/Latino; 14 Hispanic/Latino; 2 Two or more races, non-Hispanic/Latino), 3 international. Average age 31. 127 applicants, 94% accepted, 76 enrolled. In 2013, 109 master's, 31 other advanced degrees awarded. *Degree requirements:* For master's, comprehensive exam, thesis; for other advanced degree, thesis or alternative. *Entrance requirements:* For master's and other advanced degree, GRE General Test. Additional exam requirements/recommendations for international students: Required—TOEFL. *Application deadline:* Applications are processed on a rolling basis. Application fee: $65. Electronic applications accepted. *Expenses: Tuition, area resident:* Part-time $638 per credit. Tuition, state resident: full-time $5742. *Required fees:* $142 per credit. Tuition and fees vary according to course level and program. *Financial support:* Career-related internships or fieldwork, Federal Work-Study, scholarships/grants, and unspecified assistantships available. Support available to part-time students. *Unit head:* Dr. Horacio Sosa, Dean, College of Graduate and Continuing Education, 856-256-4747, Fax: 856-256-5638, E-mail: sosa@rowan.edu. *Application contact:* Admissions and Enrollment Services, 856-256-5145, Fax: 856-256-5637, E-mail: haynes@rowan.edu.

Rutgers, The State University of New Jersey, New Brunswick, School of Communication, Information and Library Studies, Department of Library and Information Science, Piscataway, NJ 08854-8097. Offers MLS. *Accreditation:* ALA. Part-time programs available. Postbaccalaureate distance learning degree programs offered (no on-campus study). *Entrance requirements:* For master's, GRE General Test. Additional exam requirements/recommendations for international students: Required—TOEFL. Electronic applications accepted. *Faculty research:* Information science, library services, management of information services.

Rutgers, The State University of New Jersey, New Brunswick, School of Communication, Information and Library Studies, Program in Communication, Information and Library Science and Media Studies, Piscataway, NJ 08854-8097. Offers PhD. Part-time programs available. *Degree requirements:* For doctorate, comprehensive exam, thesis/dissertation, qualifying exams. *Entrance requirements:* For doctorate, GRE General Test, proficiency in statistics. Additional exam requirements/recommendations for international students: Required—TOEFL (minimum score 600 paper-based). Electronic applications accepted. *Faculty research:* Information science, media studies.

St. Catherine University, Graduate Programs, Program in Library and Information Science, St. Paul, MN 55105. Offers MLIS. *Accreditation:* ALA. Part-time and evening/weekend programs available. *Degree requirements:* For master's, microcomputer competency. *Entrance requirements:* For master's, GRE or MAT, minimum GPA of 3.2 or GRE. Additional exam requirements/recommendations for international students: Required—Michigan English Language Assessment Battery or TOEFL (minimum score 600 paper-based; 100 iBT).

St. John's University, St. John's College of Liberal Arts and Sciences, Division of Library and Information Science, Queens, NY 11439. Offers MLS, Adv C, MA/MLS, MS/MLS. *Accreditation:* ALA (one or more programs are accredited). Part-time and evening/weekend programs available. Postbaccalaureate distance learning degree programs offered (no on-campus study). *Students:* 33 full-time (29 women), 31 part-time (28 women); includes 16 minority (3 Black or African American, non-Hispanic/Latino; 4 Asian, non-Hispanic/Latino; 8 Hispanic/Latino; 1 Two or more races, non-Hispanic/Latino), 1 international. Average age 31. 70 applicants, 83% accepted, 27 enrolled. In 2013, 35 master's awarded. *Degree requirements:* For master's, comprehensive exam, portfolio. *Entrance requirements:* For master's, interview, minimum GPA of 3.0, 2 letters of recommendation, bachelor's degree, personal statement, transcript. Additional exam requirements/recommendations for international students: Required—TOEFL (minimum score 600 paper-based; 100 iBT), IELTS (minimum score 5.5). *Application deadline:* For fall admission, 5/1 priority date for domestic and international students; for spring admission, 11/1 priority date for domestic and international students. Applications are processed on a rolling basis. Application fee: $70. Electronic applications accepted. *Expenses:* Contact institution. *Financial support:* Research assistantships, career-related internships or fieldwork, and scholarships/grants available. Support available to part-time students. Financial award application deadline: 3/1; financial award applicants required to submit FAFSA. *Faculty research:* Indexes and metatags, information use and users, competitive intelligence, knowledge management, database theory, young adult and children services, school media services, archives, oral history. *Unit head:* Dr. Jeffery E. Olson, Director, 718-990-5705, E-mail: olsonj@stjohns.edu. *Application contact:* Robert Medrano, Director of Graduate Admissions, 718-990-1601, Fax: 718-990-5686, E-mail: gradhelp@stjohns.edu.

Sam Houston State University, College of Education and Applied Science, Department of Library Science, Huntsville, TX 77341. Offers MLS. Part-time and evening/weekend programs available. *Faculty:* 5 full-time (all women), 2 part-time/adjunct (1 woman). *Students:* 3 full-time (all women), 157 part-time (151 women); includes 79 minority (14 Black or African American, non-Hispanic/Latino; 2 Asian, non-Hispanic/Latino; 61 Hispanic/Latino; 2 Two or more races, non-Hispanic/Latino), 4 international. Average age 37. 114 applicants, 99% accepted, 62 enrolled. In 2013, 55 master's awarded. *Degree requirements:* For master's, portfolio. *Entrance requirements:* For master's, GRE General Test, minimum GPA of 2.8. Additional exam requirements/recommendations for international students: Required—TOEFL (minimum score 550 paper-based; 79 iBT), IELTS (minimum score 6.5). *Application deadline:* For fall admission, 8/1 for domestic students, 6/25 for international students; for spring admission, 12/1 for domestic students, 11/12 for international students. Applications are processed on a rolling basis. Application fee: $45 ($75 for international students).

Library Science

Electronic applications accepted. *Financial support:* Career-related internships or fieldwork, Federal Work-Study, institutionally sponsored loans, scholarships/grants, and tuition waivers (partial) available. Support available to part-time students. Financial award application deadline: 5/31; financial award applicants required to submit FAFSA. *Unit head:* Dr. Holly Weimar, Acting Chair, 936-294-1151, Fax: 936-294-1153, E-mail: haw001@shsu.edu. *Application contact:* Molly Doughtie, Advisor, 936-294-1105, E-mail: edu_mxd@shsu.edu.
Website: http://www.shsu.edu/~lis_www/.

San Jose State University, Graduate Studies and Research, College of Applied Sciences and Arts, School of Library and Information Science, San Jose, CA 95192-0001. Offers MLIS, PhD. *Accreditation:* ALA (one or more programs are accredited). Part-time and evening/weekend programs available. *Degree requirements:* For master's, comprehensive exam. *Entrance requirements:* Additional exam requirements/recommendations for international students: Required—TOEFL (minimum score 600 paper-based). Electronic applications accepted. *Faculty research:* Evaluation of information services online, search strategy, organizational behavior.

Simmons College, Graduate School of Library and Information Science, Boston, MA 02115. Offers archives management (MS, Certificate); children's literature (MA); digital stewardship (Certificate); instructional technology (Certificate); library and information science (MS, PhD); managerial leadership in the informational professions (PhD); school library teacher (MS, Certificate); writing for children (MFA); MA/MA; MA/MAT; MA/MFA; MS/MA. *Accreditation:* ALA (one or more programs are accredited). Part-time and evening/weekend programs available. Postbaccalaureate distance learning degree programs offered (no on-campus study). *Students:* 55 full-time (45 women), 716 part-time (585 women); includes 81 minority (19 Black or African American, non-Hispanic/Latino; 1 American Indian or Alaska Native, non-Hispanic/Latino; 14 Asian, non-Hispanic/Latino; 32 Hispanic/Latino; 15 Two or more races, non-Hispanic/Latino), 9 international. 430 applicants, 82% accepted, 207 enrolled. In 2013, 281 master's, 4 doctorates awarded. *Degree requirements:* For master's, thesis optional, capstone project experience; for doctorate, comprehensive exam, 36 credit hours (includes 3-credit dissertation). *Entrance requirements:* For doctorate, GRE, transcripts, personal statement, resume, recommendations, master's degree. Additional exam requirements/recommendations for international students: Required—TOEFL (minimum score 550 paper-based; 79 iBT), IELTS (minimum score 7). *Application deadline:* For fall admission, 3/1 for domestic and international students; for spring admission, 9/1 for domestic and international students; for summer admission, 2/1 for domestic and international students. Applications are processed on a rolling basis. Application fee: $65. Electronic applications accepted. *Financial support:* In 2013–14, 67 students received support, including 5 fellowships with partial tuition reimbursements available (averaging $32,461 per year), 6 research assistantships (averaging $35,168 per year), 7 teaching assistantships with full and partial tuition reimbursements available (averaging $3,000 per year); scholarships/grants, tuition waivers, and unspecified assistantships also available. Financial award application deadline: 2/1; financial award applicants required to submit FAFSA. *Faculty research:* Archives and social justice, information-seeking behavior, information retrieval, organization of information, cultural heritage informatics. *Unit head:* Dr. Eileen G. Abels, Dean, 617-521-2869. *Application contact:* Sarah Petrakos, 617-521-2868, Fax: 617-521-3192, E-mail: gslisadm@simmons.edu.
Website: http://www.simmons.edu/gslis/.

Southern Arkansas University–Magnolia, Graduate Programs, Magnolia, AR 71753. Offers agriculture (MS); business administration (MBA); computer and information sciences (MS); education (M Ed), including counseling and development, curriculum and instruction, educational administration and supervision, elementary education, reading, secondary education, TESOL; kinesiology (M Ed); library media and information specialist (M Ed); mental health and clinical counseling (MS); public administration (MPA); school counseling (M Ed); teaching (MAT). *Accreditation:* NCATE. Part-time and evening/weekend programs available. Postbaccalaureate distance learning degree programs offered. *Faculty:* 34 full-time (15 women), 8 part-time/adjunct (5 women). *Students:* 48 full-time (22 women), 269 part-time (167 women); includes 85 minority (78 Black or African American, non-Hispanic/Latino; 2 Asian, non-Hispanic/Latino; 2 Hispanic/Latino; 1 Native Hawaiian or other Pacific Islander, non-Hispanic/Latino; 2 Two or more races, non-Hispanic/Latino), 5 international. Average age 33. 149 applicants, 73% accepted, 109 enrolled. In 2013, 149 master's awarded. *Degree requirements:* For master's, comprehensive exam (for some programs), thesis optional. *Entrance requirements:* For master's, GRE, MAT or GMAT, minimum GPA of 2.5. Additional exam requirements/recommendations for international students: Required—TOEFL, IELTS. *Application deadline:* For fall admission, 7/10 for domestic and international students; for winter admission, 12/1 for domestic and international students; for spring admission, 12/1 for domestic and international students; for summer admission, 4/1 for domestic students. Applications are processed on a rolling basis. Application fee: $25 ($50 for international students). Electronic applications accepted. *Expenses:* Tuition, state resident: part-time $254 per credit hour. Tuition, nonresident: part-time $370 per credit hour. *Required fees:* $136 per credit hour. $259 per semester. Tuition and fees vary according to course load and program. *Financial support:* Career-related internships or fieldwork, Federal Work-Study, scholarships/grants, tuition waivers (full), and unspecified assistantships available. Financial award applicants required to submit FAFSA. *Faculty research:* Alternative certification for teachers, supervision of instruction, instructional leadership, counseling. *Unit head:* Dr. Kim Bloss, Dean, School of Graduate Studies, 870-235-4150, Fax: 870-235-5227, E-mail: kkbloss@saumag.edu. *Application contact:* Shrijana Malaka, Admissions Specialist, 870-235-4150, Fax: 870-235-5227, E-mail: smalakar@saumag.edu.
Website: http://www.saumag.edu/graduate.

Southern Connecticut State University, School of Graduate Studies, School of Education, Department of Information and Library Science, New Haven, CT 06515-1355. Offers information studies (Diploma); library science (MLS); JD/MLS; MLS/MA; MLS/MS. *Accreditation:* ALA. Part-time and evening/weekend programs available. Postbaccalaureate distance learning degree programs offered (no on-campus study). *Degree requirements:* For master's and Diploma, thesis or alternative. *Entrance requirements:* For master's, GRE General Test, interview, minimum QPA of 2.7, introductory computer science course; for Diploma, master's degree in library science or information science. Electronic applications accepted.

Syracuse University, School of Information Studies, Program in Library and Information Science, Syracuse, NY 13244. Offers MS. *Accreditation:* ALA. Part-time and evening/weekend programs available. Postbaccalaureate distance learning degree programs offered (minimal on-campus study). *Students:* 66 full-time (44 women), 67 part-time (56 women); includes 18 minority (6 Black or African American, non-Hispanic/Latino; 5 Asian, non-Hispanic/Latino; 5 Hispanic/Latino; 2 Two or more races, non-Hispanic/Latino), 9 international. Average age 30. 172 applicants, 92% accepted, 63 enrolled. In 2013, 56 master's awarded. *Degree requirements:* For master's, fieldwork or research paper. *Entrance requirements:* For master's, GRE General Test. Additional exam requirements/recommendations for international students: Required—TOEFL (minimum score 100 iBT). *Application deadline:* For fall admission, 1/1 priority date for domestic and international students; for spring admission, 10/15 priority date for domestic and international students. Applications are processed on a rolling basis.

Application fee: $75. Electronic applications accepted. *Financial support:* Fellowships with full tuition reimbursements available. Financial award application deadline: 1/1; financial award applicants required to submit FAFSA. *Unit head:* Prof. Jill Hurst-Wahl, Program Director, 315-443-2911, E-mail: igrad@syr.edu. *Application contact:* Susan Corieri, Director of Enrollment Management, 315-443-2575, E-mail: ischool@syr.edu.
Website: http://ischool.syr.edu.

See Display on page 1583 and Close-Up on page 1599.

Tennessee Technological University, College of Graduate Studies, College of Education, Department of Curriculum and Instruction, Program in Library Science, Cookeville, TN 38505. Offers MA. Part-time and evening/weekend programs available. *Students:* 9 full-time (7 women), 5 part-time (all women); includes 2 minority (1 Hispanic/Latino; 1 Two or more races, non-Hispanic/Latino), 1 international. 7 applicants, 100% accepted, 5 enrolled. In 2013, 2 master's awarded. *Degree requirements:* For master's, comprehensive exam, thesis or alternative. *Entrance requirements:* For master's, MAT or GRE. Additional exam requirements/recommendations for international students: Required—TOEFL (minimum score 527 paper-based; 71 iBT), IELTS (minimum score 5.5), PTE (minimum score 48), or TOEIC (Test of English as an International Communication). *Application deadline:* For fall admission, 8/1 for domestic students, 5/1 for international students; for spring admission, 12/1 for domestic students, 10/1 for international students. Applications are processed on a rolling basis. Application fee: $35 ($40 for international students). Electronic applications accepted. *Expenses:* Tuition, state resident: full-time $9347; part-time $465 per credit hour. Tuition, nonresident: full-time $23,635; part-time $1152 per credit hour. *Financial support:* In 2013–14, research assistantships (averaging $4,000 per year), 2 teaching assistantships (averaging $4,000 per year) were awarded. Financial award application deadline: 4/1. *Unit head:* Dr. Jeremy Wendt, Interim Chairperson, 931-372-3181, Fax: 931-372-6270, E-mail: jwendt@tntech.edu. *Application contact:* Shelia K. Kendrick, Coordinator of Graduate Studies, 931-372-3808, Fax: 931-372-3497, E-mail: skendrick@tntech.edu.

Texas Woman's University, Graduate School, College of Professional Education, School of Library and Information Studies, Denton, TX 76201. Offers library science (MA, MLS, PhD). *Accreditation:* ALA (one or more programs are accredited). Part-time and evening/weekend programs available. Postbaccalaureate distance learning degree programs offered (minimal on-campus study). *Faculty:* 12 full-time (10 women), 6 part-time/adjunct (3 women). *Students:* 76 full-time (70 women), 351 part-time (333 women); includes 127 minority (34 Black or African American, non-Hispanic/Latino; 4 American Indian or Alaska Native, non-Hispanic/Latino; 9 Asian, non-Hispanic/Latino; 80 Hispanic/Latino). Average age 36. 120 applicants, 75% accepted, 69 enrolled. In 2013, 152 master's, 3 doctorates awarded. *Degree requirements:* For master's, comprehensive exam, thesis or alternative; for doctorate, comprehensive exam, thesis/dissertation. *Entrance requirements:* For master's, GRE (preferred), GMAT, MCAT, MAT, 3 letters of recommendation, 2-page statement of intent, resume; for doctorate, GRE (preferred), GMAT, MCAT, MAT, curriculum vitae/resume, 3 letters of reference, essay. Additional exam requirements/recommendations for international students: Required—TOEFL (minimum score 550 paper-based; 79 iBT). *Application deadline:* For fall admission, 2/15 priority date for domestic students, 2/15 for international students. Applications are processed on a rolling basis. Application fee: $50 ($75 for international students). Electronic applications accepted. *Expenses:* Tuition, state resident: full-time $4182; part-time $233.32 per credit hour. Tuition, nonresident: full-time $10,716; part-time $595.32 per credit hour. *Financial support:* In 2013–14, 89 students received support, including 15 research assistantships (averaging $10,079 per year), teaching assistantships (averaging $10,079 per year); career-related internships or fieldwork, Federal Work-Study, institutionally sponsored loans, scholarships/grants, traineeships, health care benefits, and unspecified assistantships also available. Support available to part-time students. Financial award application deadline: 3/1; financial award applicants required to submit FAFSA. *Faculty research:* Children's literature, health information, information needs analysis, school library leadership, library management and assessment. *Total annual research expenditures:* $180,157. *Unit head:* Dr. Ling Hwey Jeng, Director, 940-898-2602, Fax: 940-898-2611, E-mail: slis@twu.edu. *Application contact:* Dr. Samuel Wheeler, Assistant Director of Admissions, 940-898-3188, Fax: 940-898-3081, E-mail: wheelersr@twu.edu.
Website: http://www.twu.edu/slis/.

Trevecca Nazarene University, Graduate Education Program, Nashville, TN 37210-2877. Offers curriculum, assessment, and instruction K-12 (M Ed); educational leadership (M Ed); English language learners (PreK-12) (M Ed); leadership and professional practice (Ed D); library and information science (MLI Sc); teacher leader (M Ed); teaching (MAE, MAT), including teaching 7-12 (MAT), teaching K-6 (MAT); visual impairments special education (M Ed). *Accreditation:* NCATE. Part-time and evening/weekend programs available. Postbaccalaureate distance learning degree programs offered. *Faculty:* 19 full-time (17 women), 14 part-time/adjunct (5 women). *Students:* 186 full-time (137 women), 134 part-time (94 women); includes 93 minority (87 Black or African American, non-Hispanic/Latino; 1 American Indian or Alaska Native, non-Hispanic/Latino; 2 Asian, non-Hispanic/Latino; 1 Hispanic/Latino; 1 Native Hawaiian or other Pacific Islander, non-Hispanic/Latino; 1 Two or more races, non-Hispanic/Latino), 2 international. In 2013, 201 master's, 40 doctorates awarded. *Degree requirements:* For master's, comprehensive exam, exit assessment/e-portfolio; for doctorate, thesis/dissertation, proposal study, symposium presentation. *Entrance requirements:* For master's, GRE with minimum score of 378 or MAT with minimum score of 290, ACT with minimum score of 22 or SAT with minimum score of 1020 (for MAT programs only); PRAXIS (for MAT and MAE programs), minimum GPA of 2.7, official transcript from regionally accredited institution, 3+ years successful teaching experience (Teacher Leader and Education Leadership majors), technology pre-assessment written requirements (some majors); for doctorate, GRE or MAT, minimum GPA of 3.4, official transcript from regionally-accredited institution, resume, writing sample, interview, reference forms. Additional exam requirements/recommendations for international students: Required—TOEFL (minimum score 550 paper-based). *Application deadline:* Applications are processed on a rolling basis. *Expenses:* Contact institution. *Financial support:* Applicants required to submit FAFSA. *Unit head:* Dr. Suzie Harris, Dean, School of Education/Director of Graduate Education Programs, 615-248-1201, Fax: 615-248-1597, E-mail: admissions_ged@trevecca.edu. *Application contact:* 615-248-1529, E-mail: cll@trevecca.edu.
Website: http://www.trevecca.edu/academics/schools-colleges/education/.

Universidad del Turabo, Graduate Programs, Programs in Education, Program in Administration of School Libraries, Gurabo, PR 00778-3030. Offers M Ed, Certificate.

Universidad del Turabo, Graduate Programs, Programs in Education, Program in Library Service and Information Technology, Gurabo, PR 00778-3030. Offers M Ed.

Université de Montréal, Faculty of Arts and Sciences, School of Library and Information Sciences, Montréal, QC H3C 3J7, Canada. Offers information sciences (MIS, PhD). *Accreditation:* ALA (one or more programs are accredited). *Degree requirements:* For master's, thesis optional. *Entrance requirements:* For master's, interview, master's degree in library and information science or equivalent. Electronic applications accepted.

University at Buffalo, the State University of New York, Graduate School, Graduate School of Education, Department of Library and Information Studies, Buffalo, NY 14260. Offers library and information studies (MLS, Certificate); library media specialist (MLS). *Accreditation:* ALA (one or more programs are accredited). Part-time programs available. Postbaccalaureate distance learning degree programs offered (no on-campus study). *Faculty:* 11 full-time (9 women), 20 part-time/adjunct (16 women). *Students:* 55 full-time (39 women), 149 part-time (123 women); includes 15 minority (9 Black or African American, non-Hispanic/Latino; 4 Asian, non-Hispanic/Latino; 2 Hispanic/Latino). Average age 32. 155 applicants, 92% accepted, 87 enrolled. In 2013, 102 master's, 1 other advanced degree awarded. *Degree requirements:* For master's, thesis optional; for Certificate, thesis. *Entrance requirements:* For master's, letters of recommendation. Additional exam requirements/recommendations for international students: Required—TOEFL (minimum score 550 paper-based; 79 iBT). *Application deadline:* For fall admission, 4/1 priority date for domestic and international students; for spring admission, 10/15 priority date for domestic students, 10/15 for international students. Applications are processed on a rolling basis. Application fee: $50. Electronic applications accepted. *Financial support:* In 2013–14, 17 fellowships (averaging $2,776 per year), 4 research assistantships with tuition reimbursements (averaging $9,000 per year) were awarded; teaching assistantships, career-related internships or fieldwork, Federal Work-Study, institutionally sponsored loans, scholarships/grants, tuition waivers, and unspecified assistantships also available. Support available to part-time students. Financial award application deadline: 3/1; financial award applicants required to submit FAFSA. *Faculty research:* Information-seeking behavior, thesauri, impact of technology, questioning behaviors, educational informatics. *Total annual research expenditures:* $20,068. *Unit head:* Dr. Heidi Julien, Chair, 716-645-1474, Fax: 716-645-3775, E-mail: heidijul@buffalo.edu. *Application contact:* Pat Glinski, Admissions Assistant, 716-645-2110, Fax: 716-645-7937, E-mail: gse-info@buffalo.edu. Website: http://www.gse.buffalo.edu/lis/.

The University of Alabama, Graduate School, College of Communication and Information Sciences, School of Library and Information Studies, Tuscaloosa, AL 35487. Offers book arts (MFA); library and information studies (MLIS, PhD). *Accreditation:* ALA (one or more programs are accredited). Part-time and evening/weekend programs available. Postbaccalaureate distance learning degree programs offered (minimal on-campus study). *Faculty:* 8 full-time (3 women), 2 part-time/adjunct (1 woman). *Students:* 69 full-time (55 women), 193 part-time (155 women); includes 26 minority (12 Black or African American, non-Hispanic/Latino; 2 Asian, non-Hispanic/Latino; 8 Hispanic/Latino; 4 Two or more races, non-Hispanic/Latino), 3 international. Average age 33. 141 applicants, 77% accepted, 85 enrolled. In 2013, 121 master's awarded. *Degree requirements:* For master's, comprehensive exam (for some programs), thesis optional; for doctorate, comprehensive exam, thesis/dissertation. *Entrance requirements:* For master's, GRE General Test or MAT, minimum GPA of 3.0; for doctorate, GRE. Additional exam requirements/recommendations for international students: Required—TOEFL. *Application deadline:* For fall admission, 7/1 priority date for domestic and international students; for spring admission, 11/1 priority date for domestic and international students. Applications are processed on a rolling basis. Application fee: $50 ($60 for international students). Electronic applications accepted. *Expenses:* Tuition, state resident: full-time $9450. Tuition, nonresident: full-time $23,950. *Financial support:* In 2013–14, 64 students received support, including 3 fellowships with full tuition reimbursements available (averaging $15,000 per year), 18 research assistantships with full and partial tuition reimbursements available (averaging $6,183 per year), 12 teaching assistantships with full and partial tuition reimbursements available (averaging $6,183 per year); career-related internships or fieldwork, scholarships/grants, health care benefits, tuition waivers (full), unspecified assistantships, and 15 grant-funded fellowships also available. Support available to part-time students. Financial award application deadline: 3/15. *Faculty research:* Library administration, user services, digital libraries, book arts, evaluation. *Unit head:* Dr. Heidi Julien, Director and Professor, 205-348-4610, Fax: 205-348-3746, E-mail: hjulien@slis.ua.edu. *Application contact:* Beth Riggs, Assistant to the Director, 205-348-1527, Fax: 205-348-3746, E-mail: briggs@slis.ua.edu. Website: http://www.slis.ua.edu/.

University of Alberta, Faculty of Graduate Studies and Research, School of Library and Information Studies, Edmonton, AB T6G 2E1, Canada. Offers MLIS. *Accreditation:* ALA. *Entrance requirements:* Additional exam requirements/recommendations for international students: Required—TOEFL, Canadian Academic English Language Assessment. Electronic applications accepted. *Faculty research:* Intellectual freedom, materials for children and young adults, library classification, multi-media literacy.

The University of Arizona, College of Social and Behavioral Sciences, School of Information Resources and Library Science, Tucson, AZ 85721. Offers MA, PhD. *Accreditation:* ALA (one or more programs are accredited). Part-time programs available. *Faculty:* 9 full-time (7 women). *Students:* 81 full-time (61 women), 125 part-time (110 women); includes 56 minority (2 Black or African American, non-Hispanic/Latino; 2 American Indian or Alaska Native, non-Hispanic/Latino; 2 Asian, non-Hispanic/Latino; 32 Hispanic/Latino; 18 Two or more races, non-Hispanic/Latino), 4 international. Average age 36. 139 applicants, 62% accepted, 44 enrolled. In 2013, 84 master's, 2 doctorates awarded. *Degree requirements:* For master's, proficiency in disk operating system (DOS); for doctorate, thesis/dissertation. *Entrance requirements:* For master's and doctorate, GRE General Test, 3 letters of recommendation, resume. Additional exam requirements/recommendations for international students: Required—TOEFL (minimum score 550 paper-based; 79 iBT). *Application deadline:* For spring admission, 9/1 for domestic and international students. Applications are processed on a rolling basis. Application fee: $75. Electronic applications accepted. *Expenses:* Tuition, state resident: full-time $11,526. Tuition, nonresident: full-time $27,398. *Financial support:* In 2013–14, 9 teaching assistantships with full tuition reimbursements (averaging $19,700 per year) were awarded; career-related internships or fieldwork, Federal Work-Study, institutionally sponsored loans, scholarships/grants, health care benefits, tuition waivers (full and partial), and unspecified assistantships also available. Financial award application deadline: 3/1. *Faculty research:* Microcomputer applications; quantitative methods systems; information transfer, planning, evaluation, and technology. *Total annual research expenditures:* $457,000. *Unit head:* Dr. Jana Bradley, Director, 520-621-3565, Fax: 520-621-3279, E-mail: janabrad@email.arizona.edu. *Application contact:* Geraldine Fragoso, Program Manager, 520-621-3565, Fax: 520-621-3279, E-mail: gfragoso@email.arizona.edu. Website: http://www.sirls.arizona.edu/.

The University of British Columbia, Faculty of Arts, School of Library, Archival and Information Studies, Dual Master of Archival Studies/Master of Library and Information Studies Program, Vancouver, BC V6T 1Z1, Canada. Offers MLIS/MAS. *Entrance requirements:* Additional exam requirements/recommendations for international students: Required—TOEFL (minimum score 600 paper-based; 100 iBT). Electronic applications accepted. *Expenses:* Tuition, area resident: Full-time $8000 Canadian dollars. *Faculty research:* Computer systems/database design, information-seeking behaviour, archives and records management, children's literature and services, digital libraries and archives.

The University of British Columbia, Faculty of Arts, School of Library, Archival and Information Studies, Master of Library and Information Studies Program, Vancouver, BC V6T 1Z1, Canada. Offers MLIS. Part-time programs available. *Degree requirements:* For master's, thesis optional. *Entrance requirements:* For master's, minimum GPA of 3.3 in undergraduate upper-division courses. Additional exam requirements/recommendations for international students: Required—TOEFL (minimum score 600 paper-based; 100 iBT). Electronic applications accepted. *Expenses: Tuition, area resident:* Full-time $8000 Canadian dollars. *Faculty research:* Computer systems/database design; digital libraries; metadata/classification; human-computer interaction; children's literature and services.

The University of British Columbia, Faculty of Arts, School of Library, Archival and Information Studies, PhD Program in Library, Archival and Information Studies, Vancouver, BC V6T 1Z1, Canada. Offers PhD. *Degree requirements:* For doctorate, thesis/dissertation. *Entrance requirements:* For doctorate, GRE, minimum GPA of 3.3 in MAS or MLIS (other master's degrees may be considered). Additional exam requirements/recommendations for international students: Required—TOEFL (minimum score 600 paper-based; 100 iBT). Electronic applications accepted. *Expenses: Tuition, area resident:* Full-time $8000 Canadian dollars. *Faculty research:* Computer systems/database design; library and archival management; archival description and organization; children's literature and youth services; interactive information retrieval.

University of California, Los Angeles, Graduate Division, Graduate School of Education and Information Studies, Department of Information Studies, Los Angeles, CA 90095-1521. Offers archival studies (MLIS); informatics (MLIS); information studies (PhD); library and information science (Certificate); library studies (MLIS); moving image archive studies (MA); rare books, print and visual culture (MLIS); MBA/MLIS; MLIS/MA. *Accreditation:* ALA (one or more programs are accredited). *Faculty:* 10 full-time (6 women), 14 part-time/adjunct (9 women). *Students:* 114 full-time (79 women), 11 part-time (8 women); includes 50 minority (9 Black or African American, non-Hispanic/Latino; 1 American Indian or Alaska Native, non-Hispanic/Latino; 19 Asian, non-Hispanic/Latino; 18 Hispanic/Latino; 2 Native Hawaiian or other Pacific Islander, non-Hispanic/Latino; 1 Two or more races, non-Hispanic/Latino), 6 international. Average age 27. 165 applicants, 62% accepted, 51 enrolled. In 2013, 80 master's, 7 doctorates, 1 other advanced degree awarded. Terminal master's awarded for partial completion of doctoral program. *Degree requirements:* For master's, thesis or alternative, professional portfolio; for doctorate, thesis/dissertation, oral and written qualifying exams. *Entrance requirements:* For master's, GRE General Test, previous course work in statistics; for doctorate, GRE General Test, previous course work in statistics, 2 samples of research writing in English. Additional exam requirements/recommendations for international students: Required—TOEFL (minimum score 560 paper-based; 87 iBT), IELTS (minimum score 7). *Application deadline:* For fall admission, 12/10 for domestic and international students. Applications are processed on a rolling basis. Application fee: $80 ($100 for international students). Electronic applications accepted. *Financial support:* In 2013–14, 47 students received support, including 47 fellowships with full and partial tuition reimbursements available (averaging $14,045 per year), 7 research assistantships with partial tuition reimbursements available (averaging $30,155 per year), 8 teaching assistantships with partial tuition reimbursements available (averaging $20,656 per year); career-related internships or fieldwork, Federal Work-Study, institutionally sponsored loans, scholarships/grants, and unspecified assistantships also available. Financial award application deadline: 3/1; financial award applicants required to submit FAFSA. *Faculty research:* Digital libraries, archives and electronic records, interface design, cultural informatics, preservation/conservation, access. *Unit head:* Dr. Gregory H. Leazer, Associate Professor and Chair, 310-825-8799, E-mail: gleazer@ucla.edu. *Application contact:* Susan S. Abler, Student Affairs Officer, 310-825-5269, Fax: 310-206-4460, E-mail: abler@gseis.ucla.edu. Website: http://is.gseis.ucla.edu/.

University of Central Arkansas, Graduate School, College of Education, Department of Leadership Studies, Program in Library Media and Information Technology, Conway, AR 72035-0001. Offers MS. Part-time and evening/weekend programs available. Postbaccalaureate distance learning degree programs offered (minimal on-campus study). *Degree requirements:* For master's, comprehensive exam. *Entrance requirements:* For master's, GRE General Test, minimum GPA of 2.7. Additional exam requirements/recommendations for international students: Required—TOEFL (minimum score 550 paper-based). Electronic applications accepted.

University of Central Missouri, The Graduate School, Warrensburg, MO 6409. Offers accountancy (MA); accounting (MBA); applied mathematics (MS); aviation safety (MA); biology (MS); business administration (MBA); career and technical education leadership (MS); college student personnel administration (MS); communication (MA); computer science (MS); counseling (MS); criminal justice (MS); educational leadership (Ed D); educational technology (MS); elementary and early childhood education (MSE); English (MA); environmental studies (MA); finance (MBA); history (MA); human services/educational technology (Ed S); human services/learning resources (Ed S); human services/professional counseling (Ed S); industrial hygiene (MS); industrial management (MS); information systems (MBA); information technology (MS); kinesiology (MS); library science and information services (MS); literacy education (MSE); marketing (MBA); mathematics (MS); music (MA); occupational safety management (MS); psychology (MS); rural family nursing (MS); school administration (MSE); social gerontology (MS); sociology (MA); special education (MSE); speech language pathology (MS); superintendency (Ed S); teaching (MAT); teaching English as a second language (MA); technology (MS); technology management (PhD); theatre (MA). Part-time programs available. *Faculty:* 233. *Students:* 890 full-time (396 women), 1,486 part-time (1,001 women); includes 192 minority (97 Black or African American, non-Hispanic/Latino; 9 American Indian or Alaska Native, non-Hispanic/Latino; 32 Asian, non-Hispanic/Latino; 40 Hispanic/Latino; 3 Native Hawaiian or other Pacific Islander, non-Hispanic/Latino; 11 Two or more races, non-Hispanic/Latino), 539 international. Average age 31. 1,953 applicants, 75% accepted. In 2013, 719 master's, 58 other advanced degrees awarded. *Degree requirements:* For master's and Ed S, comprehensive exam (for some programs), thesis (for some programs). *Entrance requirements:* Additional exam requirements/recommendations for international students: Required—TOEFL (minimum score 550 paper-based; 79 iBT). *Application deadline:* For fall admission, 6/1 for domestic students; for spring admission, 10/1 for domestic and international students. Applications are processed on a rolling basis. Application fee: $30 ($75 for international students). Electronic applications accepted. *Expenses:* Tuition, state resident: full-time $7326; part-time $276.25 per credit hour. Tuition, nonresident: full-time $13,956; part-time $552.50 per credit hour. *Required fees:* $29 per credit hour. *Financial support:* In 2013–14, 118 students received support, including 271 research assistantships with full and partial tuition reimbursements available (averaging $7,500 per year), 109 teaching assistantships with full and partial tuition reimbursements available (averaging $7,500 per year); career-related internships or fieldwork, Federal Work-Study, scholarships/grants, and administrative and laboratory assistantships also available. Support available to part-time students. Financial award application deadline: 3/1; financial award applicants required to submit FAFSA. *Unit head:* Dr. Joseph Vaughn, Assistant Provost for Research/Dean, 660-543-4092, Fax: 660-543-4778, E-mail: vaughn@

ucmo.edu. *Application contact:* Brittany Lawrence, Graduate Student Services Coordinator, 660-543-4621, Fax: 660-543-4778, E-mail: gradinfo@ucmo.edu.
Website: http://www.ucmo.edu/graduate/.

University of Central Oklahoma, The Jackson College of Graduate Studies, College of Education and Professional Studies, Department of Advanced Professional and Special Services, Edmond, OK 73034-5209. Offers educational leadership (M Ed); library media education (M Ed); reading (M Ed); school counseling (M Ed); special education (M Ed), including mild/moderate disabilities, severe-profound/multiple disabilities, special education; speech-language pathology (MS). Part-time programs available. *Faculty:* 14 full-time (9 women), 16 part-time/adjunct (8 women). *Students:* 87 full-time (80 women), 298 part-time (251 women); includes 77 minority (32 Black or African American, non-Hispanic/Latino; 10 American Indian or Alaska Native, non-Hispanic/Latino; 2 Asian, non-Hispanic/Latino; 15 Hispanic/Latino; 18 Two or more races, non-Hispanic/Latino), 9 international. Average age 34. 147 applicants, 94% accepted, 89 enrolled. In 2013, 163 master's awarded. *Degree requirements:* For master's, comprehensive exam (for some programs), thesis (for some programs). *Entrance requirements:* For master's, GRE. Additional exam requirements/recommendations for international students: Required—TOEFL (minimum score 550 paper-based; 79 iBT), IELTS (minimum score 6.5). *Application deadline:* For fall admission, 7/1 for international students; for spring admission, 7/1 for international students. Applications are processed on a rolling basis. Application fee: $50. Electronic applications accepted. *Expenses:* Tuition, state resident: full-time $4137; part-time $206.85 per credit hour. Tuition, nonresident: full-time $10,359; part-time $517.95 per credit hour. *Required fees:* $481. Tuition and fees vary according to course load and program. *Financial support:* In 2013–14, 93 students received support, including 4 research assistantships with partial tuition reimbursements available (averaging $8,133 per year); teaching assistantships with partial tuition reimbursements available, career-related internships or fieldwork, scholarships/grants, tuition waivers (partial), and unspecified assistantships also available. Financial award application deadline: 3/31; financial award applicants required to submit FAFSA. *Faculty research:* Intellectual freedom, fair use copyright, technology integration, young adult literature, distance learning. *Unit head:* Dr. Patsy Couts, Chair, 405-974-3888, Fax: 405-974-3857, E-mail: pcouts@uco.edu. *Application contact:* Dr. Richard Bernard, Dean, Graduate College, 405-974-3493, Fax: 405-974-3852, E-mail: gradcoll@uco.edu.
Website: http://www.uco.edu/ceps/dept/apss/.

University of Denver, Morgridge College of Education, Denver, CO 80208. Offers child, family and school psychology (MA, PhD, Ed S); counseling psychology (MA, PhD); curriculum and instruction (MA, Ed D, PhD); curriculum instruction and teaching (Certificate); early childhood special education (MA); educational leadership and policy studies (MA, Ed D, PhD, Certificate); higher education (MA, Ed D, PhD); law librarianship (Certificate); library and information science (MLIS); research methods and statistics (MA, PhD). *Accreditation:* ALA; APA (one or more programs are accredited). Part-time and evening/weekend programs available. Postbaccalaureate distance learning degree programs offered (no on-campus study). *Faculty:* 35 full-time (21 women), 63 part-time/adjunct (43 women). *Students:* 435 full-time (332 women), 414 part-time (297 women); includes 194 minority (45 Black or African American, non-Hispanic/Latino; 9 American Indian or Alaska Native, non-Hispanic/Latino; 16 Asian, non-Hispanic/Latino; 96 Hispanic/Latino; 2 Native Hawaiian or other Pacific Islander, non-Hispanic/Latino; 26 Two or more races, non-Hispanic/Latino), 14 international. Average age 32. 672 applicants, 61% accepted, 193 enrolled. In 2013, 248 master's, 30 doctorates, 130 other advanced degrees awarded. Terminal master's awarded for partial completion of doctoral program. *Degree requirements:* For master's, comprehensive exam; for doctorate, 2 foreign languages, comprehensive exam, thesis/dissertation. *Entrance requirements:* For master's and doctorate, GRE General Test or GMAT. Additional exam requirements/recommendations for international students: Required—TOEFL (minimum score 550 paper-based; 80 iBT). *Application deadline:* Applications are processed on a rolling basis. Application fee: $65. Electronic applications accepted. *Financial support:* In 2013–14, 706 students received support, including 54 research assistantships with full and partial tuition reimbursements available (averaging $15,599 per year), 77 teaching assistantships with full and partial tuition reimbursements available (averaging $12,804 per year); career-related internships or fieldwork, Federal Work-Study, institutionally sponsored loans, scholarships/grants, and unspecified assistantships also available. Support available to part-time students. Financial award application deadline: 2/15; financial award applicants required to submit FAFSA. *Faculty research:* Principal and teacher preparation, development and assessments, gifted education, service-learning, early childhood, mathematics education, access to higher education. *Total annual research expenditures:* $6.3 million. *Unit head:* Dr. Karen Riley, Interim Dean, 303-871-3665, E-mail: karen.riley@du.edu. *Application contact:* Jodi Dye, Assistant Director of Admissions, 303-871-2510, E-mail: jodi.dye@du.edu.
Website: http://morgridge.du.edu/.

University of Hawaii at Manoa, Graduate Division, College of Natural Sciences, Department of Information and Computer Sciences, Library and Information Science Program, Honolulu, HI 96822-2233. Offers advanced library and information science (Graduate Certificate); library and information science (MLI Sc). *Accreditation:* ALA (one or more programs are accredited). Part-time programs available. *Degree requirements:* For master's, comprehensive exam, thesis optional. *Entrance requirements:* For master's, GRE General Test. Additional exam requirements/recommendations for international students: Required—TOEFL (minimum score 600 paper-based). Electronic applications accepted. *Faculty research:* Information behavior, evaluation of electronic information sources, online learning, history of libraries, information literacy.

University of Houston–Clear Lake, School of Education, Program in Curriculum and Instruction, Houston, TX 77058-1002. Offers curriculum and instruction (MS); early childhood education (MS); reading (MS); school library and information science (MS). Part-time and evening/weekend programs available. *Degree requirements:* For master's, thesis (for some programs). *Entrance requirements:* For master's, GRE or minimum GPA of 3.0 in last 60 hours. Additional exam requirements/recommendations for international students: Required—TOEFL (minimum score 550 paper-based). Electronic applications accepted.

University of Illinois at Urbana–Champaign, Graduate College, Graduate School of Library and Information Science, Champaign, IL 61820. Offers bioinformatics (MS); digital libraries (CAS); library and information science (MS, PhD, CAS). *Accreditation:* ALA (one or more programs are accredited). Part-time programs available. Postbaccalaureate distance learning degree programs offered (minimal on-campus study). *Students:* 596 (461 women). *Entrance requirements:* For degree, master's degree in library and information science or related field with minimum GPA of 3.0. Application fee: $75 ($90 for international students). *Unit head:* Allen Renear, Interim Dean, 217-265-5216, Fax: 217-244-3302, E-mail: renear@illinois.edu. *Application contact:* Susan Weiss, 217-300-6646, Fax: 217-244-3302, E-mail: sweiss1@illinois.edu.
Website: http://www.lis.illinois.edu.

The University of Iowa, Graduate College, School of Library and Information Science, Iowa City, IA 52242-1316. Offers MA, PhD, MA/Certificate, PhD/Certificate. *Accreditation:* ALA (one or more programs are accredited). *Degree requirements:* For master's, thesis optional, exam, portfolio. *Entrance requirements:* For master's, GRE General Test, minimum GPA of 3.0. Additional exam requirements/recommendations for international students: Required—TOEFL (minimum score 550 paper-based; 81 iBT). Electronic applications accepted.

University of Kentucky, Graduate School, College of Communication and Information, Program in Library and Information Science, Lexington, KY 40506-0032. Offers MA, MSLS. *Accreditation:* ALA (one or more programs are accredited). Part-time programs available. *Degree requirements:* For master's, variable foreign language requirement, comprehensive exam. *Entrance requirements:* For master's, GRE General Test, minimum undergraduate GPA of 2.75. Additional exam requirements/recommendations for international students: Required—TOEFL (minimum score 550 paper-based). *Faculty research:* Information retrieval systems, information-seeking behavior, organizational behavior, computer cataloging, library resource sharing.

See Display on next page and Close-Up on page 1601.

University of Maryland, College Park, Academic Affairs, Program in History, Library, and Information Services, College Park, MD 20742. Offers MA/MLS. *Students:* 16 full-time (12 women), 3 part-time (1 woman); includes 4 minority (1 Black or African American, non-Hispanic/Latino; 1 Asian, non-Hispanic/Latino; 2 Hispanic/Latino). 28 applicants, 54% accepted, 8 enrolled. *Entrance requirements:* Additional exam requirements/recommendations for international students: Required—TOEFL. *Application deadline:* For fall admission, 12/15 for domestic and international students. Applications are processed on a rolling basis. Application fee: $75. Electronic applications accepted. *Expenses:* Tuition, state resident: full-time $10,314; part-time $573 per credit hour. Tuition, nonresident: full-time $22,248; part-time $1236 per credit. *Required fees:* $1446; $403.15 per semester. Tuition and fees vary according to program. *Financial support:* In 2013–14, 15 teaching assistantships (averaging $16,604 per year) were awarded. Financial award applicants required to submit FAFSA. *Unit head:* Dr. David Sicilia, Associate Professor/Associate Director, 301-405-4628, E-mail: dsicilia@umd.edu. *Application contact:* Dr. Charles A. Caramello, Dean of Graduate School, 301-405-0358, Fax: 301-314-9305.

University of Michigan, Horace H. Rackham School of Graduate Studies, School of Information, Ann Arbor, MI 48109-1285. Offers archives and records management (MSI); health informatics (MS); human computer interaction (MSI); information (PhD); information analysis and retrieval (MSI); information economics for management (MSI); library and information science (MSI); preservation of information (MSI); school library media (MSI); social computing (MSI). *Accreditation:* ALA (one or more programs are accredited). *Entrance requirements:* For master's and doctorate, GRE General Test. Additional exam requirements/recommendations for international students: Required—TOEFL (minimum score 600 paper-based; 100 iBT). Electronic applications accepted. Tuition and fees vary according to course level, course load, degree level, program and student level.

University of Missouri, Graduate School, College of Education, School of Information Science and Learning Technologies, Columbia, MO 65211. Offers educational technology (M Ed, Ed S); information science and learning technology (PhD); library science (MA). *Accreditation:* ALA (one or more programs are accredited). Part-time and evening/weekend programs available. *Faculty:* 16 full-time (11 women), 1 (woman) part-time/adjunct. *Students:* 94 full-time (67 women), 258 part-time (178 women); includes 20 minority (8 Black or African American, non-Hispanic/Latino; 2 Asian, non-Hispanic/Latino; 7 Hispanic/Latino; 3 Two or more races, non-Hispanic/Latino), 15 international. Average age 35. 122 applicants, 81% accepted, 74 enrolled. In 2013, 140 master's, 7 doctorates, 22 other advanced degrees awarded. *Entrance requirements:* For master's, GRE General Test or MAT, minimum GPA of 3.0. Additional exam requirements/recommendations for international students: Required—TOEFL (minimum score 540 paper-based; 76 iBT). *Application deadline:* For fall admission, 2/15 priority date for domestic and international students; for winter admission, 9/15 priority date for domestic and international students; for spring admission, 3/1 priority date for domestic students. Applications are processed on a rolling basis. Application fee: $55 ($75 for international students). Electronic applications accepted. *Financial support:* Fellowships, teaching assistantships, scholarships/grants, health care benefits, and unspecified assistantships available. Support available to part-time students. *Faculty research:* Problem-based learning, technology usability in classrooms, computer-based performance support tools for children and youth with learning disabilities and/or emotional/behavioral disorders, engineering education collaboration environment, effectiveness of activities designed to recruit and retain women in engineering and science. *Unit head:* Dr. Joi L. Moore, Associate Division Director, 573-884-2877, E-mail: morrejoi@missouri.edu. *Application contact:* Amy Adam, Academic Advisor, 573-884-1391, E-mail: adamae@missouri.edu.
Website: http://education.missouri.edu/SISLT/.

University of Nebraska at Kearney, Graduate Programs, College of Education, Department of Teacher Education, Kearney, NE 68849-0001. Offers curriculum and instruction (MA Ed), including early childhood education, elementary education, English as a second language, instructional effectiveness, reading/special education, secondary education; instructional technology (MS Ed), including information technology, instructional technology, school librarian; reading PK-12 (MA Ed); special education (MA Ed), including advanced practitioner, gifted, mild/moderate. Part-time and evening/weekend programs available. *Degree requirements:* For master's, comprehensive exam, thesis optional. *Entrance requirements:* For master's, portfolio or GRE. Additional exam requirements/recommendations for international students: Required—TOEFL (minimum score 550 paper-based). Electronic applications accepted.

The University of North Carolina at Chapel Hill, Graduate School, School of Information and Library Science, Chapel Hill, NC 27599. Offers data curation (PMC); information and library science (PhD); information science (MSIS); library science (MSLS). *Accreditation:* ALA (one or more programs are accredited). Part-time programs available. Terminal master's awarded for partial completion of doctoral program. *Degree requirements:* For master's, comprehensive exam, paper or project; for doctorate, comprehensive exam, thesis/dissertation. *Entrance requirements:* For master's and doctorate, GRE General Test. Additional exam requirements/recommendations for international students: Required—TOEFL (minimum score 625 paper-based). Electronic applications accepted. *Faculty research:* Information retrieval and management, digital libraries, management of information resources, archives and records management, health informatics.

The University of North Carolina at Greensboro, Graduate School, School of Education, Department of Library and Information Studies, Greensboro, NC 27412-5001. Offers MLIS. *Accreditation:* ALA. Part-time and evening/weekend programs available. Postbaccalaureate distance learning degree programs offered (no on-campus study). *Degree requirements:* For master's, portfolio. *Entrance requirements:* For master's, GRE General Test. Additional exam requirements/recommendations for international students: Required—TOEFL (minimum score 550 paper-based), IELTS (minimum score 6.5). Electronic applications accepted. *Faculty research:* Library history, gender studies, children's literature, web design, homeless, technical services.

University of Northern Colorado, Graduate School, College of Education and Behavioral Sciences, Department of Educational Technology, Program in School Library Education, Greeley, CO 80639. Offers MA. Part-time programs available. Electronic applications accepted.

University of North Texas, Robert B. Toulouse School of Graduate Studies, Denton, TN 76203-5017. Offers accounting (MS, PhD); applied anthropology (MA, MS); applied behavior analysis (Certificate); applied technology and performance improvement (M Ed, MS, PhD); art education (MA, PhD); art history (MA); art museum education (Certificate); arts leadership (Certificate); audiology (Au D); behavior analysis (MS); biochemistry and molecular biology (MS, PhD); biology (MA, MS, PhD); business (PhD); business computer information systems (PhD); chemistry (MS, PhD); clinical psychology (PhD); communication studies (MA, MS); computer engineering (MS); computer science (MS); computer science and engineering (PhD); counseling (M Ed, MS, PhD), including clinical mental health counseling (MS), college and university counseling (M Ed, MS), elementary school counseling (M Ed, MS), secondary school counseling (M Ed, MS); counseling psychology (PhD); creative writing (MA); criminal justice (MS); curriculum and instruction (M Ed, PhD), including curriculum studies (PhD), early childhood studies (PhD), language and literacy studies (PhD); decision sciences (MBA); design (MA, MFA), including fashion design (MFA), innovation studies, interior design (MFA); early childhood studies (MS); economics (MS); educational leadership (M Ed, Ed D, PhD); educational psychology (MS), including family studies, gifted and talented (MS, PhD), human development, learning and cognition, research, measurement and evaluation; educational research (PhD), including gifted and talented (MS, PhD), human development and family studies, psychological aspects of sports and exercise, research, measurement and statistics; electrical engineering (MS); emergency management (MPA); engineering systems (MS); English (MA, PhD); environmental science (MS, PhD); experimental psychology (PhD); finance (MBA, MS, PhD); financial management (MPA); French (MA); health psychology and behavioral medicine (PhD); health services management (MBA); higher education (M Ed, Ed D, PhD); history (MA, MS, PhD), including European history (PhD), military history (PhD), United States history (PhD); hospitality management (MS); human resources management (MPA); information science (MS, PhD); information technologies (MBA); information technology and decision sciences (MS); interdisciplinary studies (MA, MS); international sustainable tourism (MS); jazz studies (MM); journalism (MA, MJ, Graduate Certificate), including interactive and virtual digital communication (Graduate Certificate), narrative journalism (Graduate Certificate), public relations (Graduate Certificate); kinesiology (MS); learning technologies (MS, PhD); library science (MS); local government management (MPA); logistics and supply chain management (MBA, PhD); long-term care, senior housing, and aging services (MA, MS); management science (PhD); marketing (MBA, PhD); materials science and engineering (MS, PhD); mathematics (MA, PhD); merchandising (MS); music (MA, MM Ed, PhD), including ethnomusicology (MA), music education (MM Ed, PhD), music theory (MA, PhD), musicology (MA, PhD), performance (MA); nonprofit management (MPA); operations and supply chain management (MBA); performance (MM, DMA); philosophy (MA, PhD); physics (MS, PhD); political science (MA, MS, PhD); public administration and management (PhD), including emergency management, nonprofit management, public financial management, urban management; radio, television and film (MA, MFA); recreation, event and sport management (MS); rehabilitation counseling (MS, Certificate); sociology (MA, MS, PhD); Spanish (MA); special education (M Ed, PhD), including autism intervention (PhD), emotional/behavioral disorders (PhD), mild/moderate disabilities (PhD); speech-language pathology (MA, MS); strategic management (MBA); studio art (MFA); taxation (MS); teaching (M Ed); MBA/MS; MS/MPH; MSES/MBA. Part-time and evening/weekend programs available. Postbaccalaureate distance learning degree programs offered. *Faculty:* 661 full-time (213 women), 240 part-time/adjunct (144 women). *Students:* 3,106 full-time (1,620 women), 3,543 part-time (2,221 women); includes 1,740 minority (533 Black or African American, non-Hispanic/Latino; 15 American Indian or Alaska Native, non-Hispanic/Latino; 286 Asian, non-Hispanic/Latino; 746 Hispanic/Latino; 3 Native Hawaiian or other Pacific Islander, non-Hispanic/Latino; 157 Two or more races, non-Hispanic/Latino), 1,145 international. Average age 32. 6,289 applicants, 43% accepted, 1751 enrolled. In 2013, 1,778 master's, 239 doctorates, 10 other advanced degrees awarded. Terminal master's awarded for partial completion of doctoral program. *Degree requirements:* For master's, variable foreign language requirement, comprehensive exam (for some programs), thesis (for some programs); for doctorate, variable foreign language requirement, comprehensive exam (for some programs), thesis/dissertation; for other advanced degree, variable foreign language requirement, comprehensive exam (for some programs). *Entrance requirements:* For master's and doctorate, GRE, GMAT. Additional exam requirements/recommendations for international students: Required—TOEFL (minimum score 550 paper-based; 79 iBT). *Application deadline:* For fall admission, 7/15 for domestic students, 3/15 for international students; for spring admission, 11/15 for domestic students, 9/15 for international students; for summer admission, 5/1 for domestic students. Applications are processed on a rolling basis. Application fee: $60. Electronic applications accepted. *Financial support:* Fellowships with partial tuition reimbursements, research assistantships with partial tuition reimbursements, teaching assistantships, career-related internships or fieldwork, Federal Work-Study, institutionally sponsored loans, scholarships/grants, health care benefits, and library assistantships available. Support available to part-time students. Financial award applicants required to submit FAFSA. *Unit head:* Mark Wardell, Dean, 940-565-2383, E-mail: mark.wardell@unt.edu. *Application contact:* Toulouse School of Graduate Studies, 940-565-2383, Fax: 940-565-2141, E-mail: gradsch@unt.edu. Website: http://tsgs.unt.edu/.

University of Oklahoma, College of Arts and Sciences, School of Library and Information Studies, Program in Library and Information Studies, Norman, OK 73019-0390. Offers MLIS, Graduate Certificate, M Ed/MLIS, MBA/MLIS. Part-time and evening/weekend programs available. Postbaccalaureate distance learning degree programs offered. *Students:* 60 full-time (47 women), 121 part-time (97 women); includes 32 minority (8 Black or African American, non-Hispanic/Latino; 13 American Indian or Alaska Native, non-Hispanic/Latino; 4 Asian, non-Hispanic/Latino; 3 Hispanic/Latino; 4 Two or more races, non-Hispanic/Latino), 3 international. Average age 33. 38 applicants, 87% accepted, 27 enrolled. In 2013, 60 master's awarded. *Degree requirements:* For master's, comprehensive exam (MLIS). *Entrance requirements:* For master's, GRE, minimum GPA of 3.2 in last 60 hours or 3.0 overall. Additional exam requirements/recommendations for international students: Required—TOEFL (minimum score 550 paper-based; 79 iBT). *Application deadline:* For fall admission, 3/1 priority date for domestic students, 4/1 for international students; for spring admission, 10/15 for domestic students, 9/1 for international students. Application fee: $40 ($90 for international students). Electronic applications accepted. *Expenses:* Tuition, state resident: full-time $4205; part-time $175.20 per credit hour. Tuition, nonresident: full-time $16,205; part-time $675.20 per credit hour. *Required fees:* $2745; $103.85 per credit hour. $126.50 per semester. *Financial support:* Federal Work-Study, scholarships/grants, health care benefits, and unspecified assistantships available. Support available to part-time students. Financial award application deadline: 6/1; financial award applicants required to submit FAFSA. *Faculty research:* Equity of access, information services to special populations, information use in the digital age, library services and materials for young people, pluralization of archival theory and education. *Unit head:* Cecelia Brown, Director, 405-325-3921, Fax: 405-325-7648, E-mail: cbrown@ou.edu. *Application contact:* Maggie Ryan, Coordinator of Admissions, 405-325-3921, Fax: 405-325-7648, E-mail: mryan@ou.edu.

Library Science

University of Pittsburgh, School of Information Sciences, Library and Information Science Program, Pittsburgh, PA 15260. Offers library and information science (MLIS, PhD). *Accreditation:* ALA (one or more programs are accredited). Part-time and evening/weekend programs available. Postbaccalaureate distance learning degree programs offered (minimal on-campus study). *Faculty:* 14 full-time (7 women), 12 part-time/adjunct (7 women). *Students:* 107 full-time (84 women), 87 part-time (66 women); includes 29 minority (15 Black or African American, non-Hispanic/Latino; 2 Asian, non-Hispanic/Latino; 10 Hispanic/Latino; 2 Two or more races, non-Hispanic/Latino), 18 international. 231 applicants, 82% accepted, 187 enrolled. In 2013, 128 master's, 3 doctorates awarded. *Degree requirements:* For master's, thesis optional; for doctorate, comprehensive exam, thesis/dissertation. *Entrance requirements:* For master's, GRE General Test or MAT, bachelor's degree from accredited university; minimum GPA of 3.0; for doctorate, GRE General Test, minimum GPA of 3.5. Additional exam requirements/recommendations for international students: Required—TOEFL (minimum score 550 paper-based; 80 iBT). *Application deadline:* For fall admission, 1/15 priority date for domestic and international students. Applications are processed on a rolling basis. Application fee: $50. Electronic applications accepted. *Expenses:* Contact institution. *Financial support:* Fellowships with full tuition reimbursements, research assistantships with full and partial tuition reimbursements, teaching assistantships with full and partial tuition reimbursements, career-related internships or fieldwork, scholarships/grants, health care benefits, tuition waivers (full and partial), and unspecified assistantships available. Financial award application deadline: 1/15; financial award applicants required to submit FAFSA. *Faculty research:* Archives, children's resources and services, digital libraries, cyberscholarship and citizen science. *Unit head:* Prof. Sheila Corrall, Chair, 412-624-9317, Fax: 412-624-5231, E-mail: scorrall@sis.pitt.edu. *Application contact:* Brandi Liskey Belleau, Student Services Specialist, 412-648-3108, Fax: 412-624-5231, E-mail: lisinq@sis.pitt.edu. Website: http://www.ischool.pitt.edu/lis.

University of Puerto Rico, Río Piedras Campus, Graduate School of Information Sciences and Technologies, San Juan, PR 00931-3300. Offers administration of academic libraries (PMC); administration of public libraries (PMC); administration of special libraries (PMC); consultant in information services (PMC); documents and files administration (Post-Graduate Certificate); electronic information resources analyst (Post-Graduate Certificate); information science (MIS); librarianship and information services (MLS); school librarian (Post-Graduate Certificate); school librarian distance education mode (Post-Graduate Certificate); specialist in legal information (PMC). *Accreditation:* ALA. Part-time programs available. *Degree requirements:* For master's, comprehensive exam, thesis, portfolio. *Entrance requirements:* For master's, PAEG, GRE, interview, minimum GPA of 3.0, 3 letters of recommendation; for other advanced degree, PAEG, GRE, minimum GPA of 3.0, IST master's degree. *Faculty research:* Investigating the users needs and preferences for a specialized environmental library.

University of Rhode Island, Graduate School, College of Arts and Sciences, Graduate School of Library and Information Studies, Kingston, RI 02881. Offers MLIS, MLIS/MA, MLIS/MPA. *Accreditation:* ALA (one or more programs are accredited). Part-time programs available. *Faculty:* 4 full-time (all women). *Students:* 29 full-time (19 women), 70 part-time (57 women); includes 5 minority (1 Black or African American, non-Hispanic/Latino; 3 American Indian or Alaska Native, non-Hispanic/Latino; 1 Hispanic/Latino), 1 international. In 2013, 58 master's awarded. *Degree requirements:* For master's, comprehensive exam. *Entrance requirements:* For master's, GRE or MAT (if undergraduate GPA less than 3.0), 2 letters of recommendation. Additional exam requirements/recommendations for international students: Required—TOEFL (minimum score 550 paper-based). *Application deadline:* For fall admission, 6/15 for domestic students, 2/1 for international students; for spring admission, 10/15 for domestic students, 7/15 for international students. Application fee: $65. Electronic applications accepted. *Expenses:* Tuition, state resident: full-time $11,532; part-time $641 per credit. Tuition, nonresident: full-time $23,606; part-time $1311 per credit. *Required fees:* $1388; $36 per credit. $35 per semester. One-time fee: $130. *Financial support:* Application deadline: 1/15; applicants required to submit FAFSA. *Unit head:* Dr. Valerie Karno, Director, Graduate School of Library and Information Studies, 401-874-4682, Fax: 401-874-4127, E-mail: karno@uri.edu. *Application contact:* GSLIS Student Services Office, 401-874-2872, Fax: 401-874-5787, E-mail: stefaniemetko@mail.uri.edu.
Website: http://www.uri.edu/artsci/lsc/.

University of South Carolina, The Graduate School, College of Mass Communications and Information Studies, School of Library and Information Science, Columbia, SC 29208. Offers MLIS, PhD, Certificate, Specialist, MLIS/MA. *Accreditation:* ALA (one or more programs are accredited). Part-time programs available. Postbaccalaureate distance learning degree programs offered (no on-campus study). *Degree requirements:* For master's, end of program portfolio; for doctorate, comprehensive exam, thesis/dissertation. *Entrance requirements:* For master's and other advanced degree, GRE General Test or MAT; for doctorate, GTE, writing sample. Additional exam requirements/recommendations for international students: Required—TOEFL (minimum score 570 paper-based; 75 iBT). Electronic applications accepted. *Faculty research:* Information technology management, distance education, library services for children and young adults, special libraries.

University of Southern Mississippi, Graduate School, College of Education and Psychology, School of Library and Information Science, Hattiesburg, MS 39406-0001. Offers MLIS. *Accreditation:* ALA. Part-time and evening/weekend programs available. Postbaccalaureate distance learning degree programs offered (minimal on-campus study). *Faculty:* 8 full-time (7 women), 1 part-time/adjunct (0 women). *Students:* 30 full-time (24 women), 111 part-time (90 women); includes 22 minority (17 Black or African American, non-Hispanic/Latino; 5 Two or more races, non-Hispanic/Latino), 3 international. Average age 36. 27 applicants, 96% accepted, 22 enrolled. In 2013, 56 master's awarded. *Degree requirements:* For master's, comprehensive exam, thesis. *Entrance requirements:* For master's, GRE General Test, minimum GPA of 3.0. Additional exam requirements/recommendations for international students: Required—TOEFL, IELTS. *Application deadline:* For fall admission, 3/15 priority date for domestic students, 3/15 for international students; for spring admission, 1/10 priority date for domestic and international students. Applications are processed on a rolling basis. Application fee: $50. Electronic applications accepted. *Financial support:* In 2013–14, 8 students received support, including 6 research assistantships with full tuition reimbursements available (averaging $7,200 per year), 1 teaching assistantship with full tuition reimbursement available (averaging $7,200 per year); fellowships with tuition reimbursements available, career-related internships or fieldwork, Federal Work-Study, institutionally sponsored loans, scholarships/grants, health care benefits, and unspecified assistantships also available. Financial award application deadline: 3/15; financial award applicants required to submit FAFSA. *Faculty research:* Printing, library history, children's literature, telecommunications, management. *Total annual research expenditures:* $14,185. *Unit head:* Dr. Melanie J. Norton, Director, 601-266-4228, Fax: 601-266-5774. *Application contact:* Shonna Breland, Manager of Graduate Admissions, 601-266-6563, Fax: 601-266-5138.
Website: http://www.usm.edu/graduateschool/table.php.

University of South Florida, College of Arts and Sciences, School of Information, Tampa, FL 33620-9951. Offers library and information science (MA), including youth services and school librarianship. *Accreditation:* ALA. Part-time and evening/weekend programs available. Postbaccalaureate distance learning degree programs offered (minimal on-campus study). *Faculty:* 14 full-time (8 women), 12 part-time/adjunct (8 women). *Students:* 68 full-time (59 women), 150 part-time (124 women); includes 45 minority (15 Black or African American, non-Hispanic/Latino; 1 American Indian or Alaska Native, non-Hispanic/Latino; 4 Asian, non-Hispanic/Latino; 22 Hispanic/Latino; 3 Two or more races, non-Hispanic/Latino), 2 international. Average age 35. 98 applicants, 73% accepted, 41 enrolled. In 2013, 117 master's awarded. *Degree requirements:* For master's, comprehensive exam, thesis optional. *Entrance requirements:* For master's, minimum GPA of 3.25 in upper-division course work, 3.5 in a completed master's degree program, or GRE; statement of purpose and goals, academic writing sample, three letters of recommendation. Additional exam requirements/recommendations for international students: Required—TOEFL (minimum score 550 paper-based; 79 iBT) or IELTS (minimum score 6.5). *Application deadline:* For fall admission, 6/1 for domestic students, 1/2 for international students; for spring admission, 10/15 for domestic students, 6/1 for international students. Applications are processed on a rolling basis. Application fee: $30. Electronic applications accepted. *Financial support:* Unspecified assistantships available. Financial award application deadline: 6/30. *Faculty research:* Youth services in libraries, community engagement and libraries, information architecture, biomedical informatics, health informatics. *Total annual research expenditures:* $49,361. *Unit head:* Dr. Jim Andrews, Director and Associate Professor, 813-974-2108, Fax: 813-974-6840, E-mail: jimandrews@usf.edu. *Application contact:* Dr. Diane Austin, Assistant Director, 813-974-6364, Fax: 813-974-6840, E-mail: dianeaustin@usf.edu.
Website: http://si.usf.edu/.

University of South Florida, University College/Distance Education, Tampa, FL 33620-9951. *Unit head:* Kathy Barnes, Interdisciplinary Programs Coordinator, 813-974-8031, Fax: 813-974-7061, E-mail: barnesk@usf.edu. *Application contact:* Karen Tylinski, Metro Initiatives, 813-974-9943, Fax: 813-974-7061, E-mail: ktylinsk@usf.edu.
Website: http://uc.usf.edu/.

University of Washington, Graduate School, The Information School, Seattle, WA 98195. Offers information management (MSIM); information science (PhD); library and information science (MLIS). *Accreditation:* ALA (one or more programs are accredited). Part-time and evening/weekend programs available. Postbaccalaureate distance learning degree programs offered (minimal on-campus study). *Faculty:* 39 full-time (17 women), 26 part-time/adjunct (14 women). *Students:* 344 full-time (214 women), 247 part-time (193 women); includes 110 minority (16 Black or African American, non-Hispanic/Latino; 11 American Indian or Alaska Native, non-Hispanic/Latino; 49 Asian, non-Hispanic/Latino; 31 Hispanic/Latino; 3 Native Hawaiian or other Pacific Islander, non-Hispanic/Latino), 159 international. Average age 32. 1,173 applicants, 46% accepted, 256 enrolled. In 2013, 227 master's, 7 doctorates awarded. Terminal master's awarded for partial completion of doctoral program. *Degree requirements:* For master's, comprehensive exam (for some programs), thesis optional, capstone project; for doctorate, comprehensive exam, thesis/dissertation. *Entrance requirements:* For master's, GRE General Test, GMAT; for doctorate, GRE General Test. Additional exam requirements/recommendations for international students: Required—TOEFL (minimum score 580 paper-based; 92 iBT), IELTS (minimum score 7). *Application deadline:* For fall admission, 12/1 priority date for domestic and international students. Application fee: $85. Electronic applications accepted. *Expenses:* Contact institution. *Financial support:* In 2013–14, 88 students received support, including 16 fellowships with full tuition reimbursements available (averaging $7,445 per year), 25 research assistantships with full and partial tuition reimbursements available (averaging $18,590 per year), 24 teaching assistantships with full and partial tuition reimbursements available (averaging $18,563 per year); career-related internships or fieldwork, Federal Work-Study, institutionally sponsored loans, scholarships/grants, health care benefits, tuition waivers (full and partial), and assistantships (14 awards averaging $15,401) also available. Support available to part-time students. Financial award application deadline: 1/15; financial award applicants required to submit FAFSA. *Faculty research:* Human/computer interaction, information policy and ethics, knowledge organization, information literacy and access, data science, information assurance and cyber security, digital youth, information architecture, project management, systems analyst, user experience design. *Unit head:* Dr. Harry Bruce, Dean, 206-616-0985, E-mail: harryb@uw.edu. *Application contact:* Kari Brothers, Admissions Counselor, 206-616-5541, Fax: 206-616-3152, E-mail: kari683@uw.edu. Website: http://ischool.uw.edu/.

The University of Western Ontario, Faculty of Graduate Studies, Faculty of Information and Media Studies, Programs in Library and Information Science, London, ON N6A 5B8, Canada. Offers MLIS, PhD. Program conducted on a trimester basis. *Accreditation:* ALA (one or more programs are accredited). Part-time and evening/weekend programs available. *Degree requirements:* For doctorate, comprehensive exam, thesis/dissertation. *Entrance requirements:* For master's, honors degree, minimum B average during previous 2 years of course work; for doctorate, MLIS or equivalent. Additional exam requirements/recommendations for international students: Required—TOEFL (minimum score 625 paper-based), TWE (minimum score 5). Electronic applications accepted. *Faculty research:* Information, individuals, and society; information systems, policy, power, and institutions.

University of Wisconsin–Eau Claire, College of Education and Human Sciences, Program in Secondary Education, Eau Claire, WI 54702-4004. Offers professional development (ME-PD), including library science, professional development. Part-time programs available. Postbaccalaureate distance learning degree programs offered (minimal on-campus study). *Faculty:* 5 full-time (3 women), 1 (woman) part-time/adjunct. *Students:* 1 full-time (0 women), 17 part-time (13 women); includes 1 minority (Black or African American, non-Hispanic/Latino), 1 international. Average age 31. 6 applicants, 83% accepted, 3 enrolled. In 2013, 8 master's awarded. *Degree requirements:* For master's, comprehensive exam, thesis, research paper, portfolio or written exam; oral exam. *Entrance requirements:* For master's, certification to teach, minimum GPA of 2.75. Additional exam requirements/recommendations for international students: Required—TOEFL (minimum score 79 iBT). *Application deadline:* For fall admission, 7/1 priority date for domestic students, 6/1 priority date for international students; for spring admission, 12/1 priority date for domestic students, 11/1 priority date for international students. Applications are processed on a rolling basis. Application fee: $56. *Expenses:* Tuition, state resident: full-time $7640; part-time $424.47 per credit. Tuition, nonresident: full-time $16,771; part-time $931.74 per credit. *Required fees:* $1146; $63.65 per credit. *Financial support:* In 2013–14, 1 student received support. Federal Work-Study and unspecified assistantships available. Financial award application deadline: 3/1; financial award applicants required to submit FAFSA. *Unit head:* Dr. Rose Battalio, Interim Chair, 715-836-2013, Fax: 715-836-4868, E-mail: battalrl@uwec.edu. *Application contact:* Nancy Amdahl, Graduate Dean Assistant, 715-836-2721, Fax: 715-836-2902, E-mail: graduate@uwec.edu.
Website: http://www.uwec.edu/ES/programs/graduateprograms.htm.

University of Wisconsin–Madison, Graduate School, College of Letters and Science, School of Library and Information Studies, Madison, WI 53706-1380. Offers MA, PhD. *Accreditation:* ALA (one or more programs are accredited). Part-time programs available. *Degree requirements:* For doctorate, comprehensive exam, thesis/dissertation. Electronic applications accepted. *Expenses:* Tuition, state resident: full-time $10,728; part-time $790 per credit. Tuition, nonresident: full-time $24,054; part-time $1623 per credit. *Required fees:* $1130; $119 per credit. *Faculty research:* Intellectual freedom, children's literature, print culture history, information systems design and evaluation, school library media centers.

University of Wisconsin–Milwaukee, Graduate School, School of Information Studies, Milwaukee, WI 53201-0413. Offers advanced studies in library and information science (CAS); archives and records administration (CAS); digital libraries (Certificate); information studies (MLIS, PhD); MLIS/MA; MLIS/MM; MLIS/MS. *Accreditation:* ALA (one or more programs are accredited). Part-time programs available. *Faculty:* 22 full-time (11 women). *Students:* 140 full-time (109 women), 254 part-time (196 women); includes 33 minority (12 Black or African American, non-Hispanic/Latino; 1 American Indian or Alaska Native, non-Hispanic/Latino; 1 Asian, non-Hispanic/Latino; 4 Hispanic/Latino; 15 Two or more races, non-Hispanic/Latino), 24 international. Average age 34. 221 applicants, 79% accepted, 94 enrolled. In 2013, 238 master's awarded. *Entrance requirements:* For master's, GRE General Test or MAT; for doctorate, GRE. Additional exam requirements/recommendations for international students: Required—TOEFL (minimum score 550 paper-based), IELTS (minimum score 6.5). *Application deadline:* For fall admission, 1/1 priority date for domestic students; for spring admission, 9/1 for domestic students. Applications are processed on a rolling basis. Application fee: $56 ($96 for international students). Electronic applications accepted. *Financial support:* In 2013–14, 4 teaching assistantships were awarded; fellowships, research assistantships, career-related internships or fieldwork, Federal Work-Study, health care benefits, unspecified assistantships, and project assistantships also available. Support available to part-time students. Financial award application deadline: 4/15; financial award applicants required to submit FAFSA. *Total annual research expenditures:* $298,170. *Unit head:* Wooseob Jeong, Interim Dean/Associate Professor, 414-229-6167, E-mail: wjj8612@uwm.edu. *Application contact:* Hur-Li Lee, Representative, 414-229-6838, E-mail: hurli@uwm.edu.
Website: http://www.uwm.edu/Dept/SLIS/.

University of Wisconsin–Whitewater, School of Graduate Studies, College of Education and Professional Studies, Department of Curriculum and Instruction, Whitewater, WI 53190-1790. Offers professional development (MS), including bilingual education, challenging advanced learners, curriculum and instruction, educational leadership, health, human performance and recreation, health, physical education and coaching, information technologies and libraries, reading. *Accreditation:* NCATE. Part-time and evening/weekend programs available. Postbaccalaureate distance learning degree programs offered. *Degree requirements:* For master's, thesis or integrated project. *Entrance requirements:* Additional exam requirements/recommendations for international students: Required—TOEFL (minimum score 550 paper-based; 80 iBT), IELTS (minimum score 6). Electronic applications accepted. *Faculty research:* Hybrid of exercise physiology and psychology; gender equity; education, pedagogy, and technology; comprehensive school health education.

Valdosta State University, Program in Library and Information Science, Valdosta, GA 31698. Offers MLIS. *Accreditation:* ALA. Postbaccalaureate distance learning degree programs offered (minimal on-campus study). *Faculty:* 6 full-time (3 women), 4 part-time/adjunct (3 women). *Students:* 12 full-time (6 women), 145 part-time (113 women); includes 34 minority (21 Black or African American, non-Hispanic/Latino; 2 American Indian or Alaska Native, non-Hispanic/Latino; 1 Asian, non-Hispanic/Latino; 2 Hispanic/Latino; 1 Native Hawaiian or other Pacific Islander, non-Hispanic/Latino; 7 Two or more races, non-Hispanic/Latino), 1 international. Average age 25. 58 applicants, 55% accepted, 28 enrolled. In 2013, 69 master's awarded. *Degree requirements:* For master's, comprehensive exam. *Entrance requirements:* For master's, two essays, resume, three recommendations. Additional exam requirements/recommendations for international students: Required—TOEFL (minimum score 523 paper-based). *Application deadline:* For fall admission, 4/15 for domestic and international students. Application fee: $35. *Expenses:* Tuition, state resident: full-time $4140; part-time $230 per credit hour. Tuition, nonresident: full-time $14,904; part-time $828 per credit hour. *Required fees:* $995 per semester. Tuition and fees vary according to course load. *Financial support:* In 2013–14, 4 students received support, including 4 research assistantships with full tuition reimbursements available (averaging $3,652 per year); institutionally sponsored loans, scholarships/grants, and unspecified assistantships also available. Support available to part-time students. Financial award application deadline: 7/1; financial award applicants required to submit FAFSA. *Unit head:* Dr. Linda Most, Assistant Director, 229-245-3732, Fax: 229-333-5862, E-mail: lrmost@valdosta.edu. *Application contact:* Jessica Powers, Admissions Specialist, 229-333-5694, Fax: 229-245-3853, E-mail: jldevane@valdosta.edu.
Website: http://www.valdosta.edu/academics/graduate-school/our-programs/library-and-information-science.php.

Valley City State University, Online Master of Education Program, Valley City, ND 58072. Offers elementary education (M Ed); English education (M Ed); library and information technologies (M Ed); teaching and technology (M Ed); teaching English language learners (ELL) (M Ed); technology education (M Ed). *Accreditation:* NCATE. Part-time and evening/weekend programs available. Postbaccalaureate distance learning degree programs offered (no on-campus study). *Faculty:* 21 full-time (14 women), 7 part-time/adjunct (all women). *Students:* 2 full-time (both women), 151 part-time (102 women); includes 10 minority (1 Black or African American, non-Hispanic/Latino; 3 Asian, non-Hispanic/Latino; 2 Hispanic/Latino; 4 Two or more races, non-Hispanic/Latino), 1 international. Average age 34. 27 applicants, 93% accepted, 21 enrolled. In 2013, 45 master's awarded. *Degree requirements:* For master's, action research report, comprehensive portfolio. *Entrance requirements:* For master's, GRE, MAT, PRAXIS II or National Teaching Board for Professional Standards (if GPA is less than 3.0). Additional exam requirements/recommendations for international students: Required—TOEFL (minimum score 525 paper-based; 71 iBT); Recommended—IELTS (minimum score 5.5). *Application deadline:* For fall admission, 7/19 priority date for domestic and international students; for spring admission, 12/13 priority date for domestic and international students; for summer admission, 5/9 priority date for domestic and international students. Applications are processed on a rolling basis. Application fee: $35. Electronic applications accepted. *Expenses:* Contact institution. *Financial support:* In 2013–14, 24 students received support. Scholarships/grants and tuition waivers (full and partial) available. Financial award application deadline: 5/15; financial award applicants required to submit FAFSA. *Faculty research:* Academically at-risk students in higher education, communication pedagogy and technology, gender communication, computer-mediated communication, creativity in music, STEM education in K-12. *Total annual research expenditures:* $26,000. *Unit head:* Dr. Gary Thompson, Dean, 701-845-7197, E-mail: gary.thompson@vcsu.edu. *Application contact:* Misty Lindgren, Graduate Studies, 701-845-7303, Fax: 701-845-7190, E-mail: misty.lindgren@vcsu.edu.
Website: http://www.vcsu.edu/graduate.

Wayne State University, School of Library and Information Science, Detroit, MI 48202. Offers academic libraries (MLIS); archival administration (MLIS, Certificate); general librarianship (MLIS); health sciences librarianship (MLIS); information management for librarians (Certificate); information science (MLIS); law librarianship (MLIS); library and information science (Spec); organization of information (MLIS); public libraries (MLIS); public library services to children and young adults (MLIS, Certificate); records management (MLIS); references services (MLIS); school library media specialist endorsement (MLIS); special libraries (MLIS); urban libraries (MLIS); MLIS/MA. *Accreditation:* ALA (one or more programs are accredited). Part-time and evening/weekend programs available. Postbaccalaureate distance learning degree programs offered (no on-campus study). *Faculty:* 13 full-time (9 women), 17 part-time/adjunct (13 women). *Students:* 112 full-time (80 women), 372 part-time (296 women); includes 65 minority (26 Black or African American, non-Hispanic/Latino; 11 Asian, non-Hispanic/Latino; 18 Hispanic/Latino; 10 Two or more races, non-Hispanic/Latino), 2 international. Average age 33. 275 applicants, 61% accepted, 109 enrolled. In 2013, 179 master's, 42 other advanced degrees awarded. *Entrance requirements:* For master's and other advanced degree, GRE or MAT (if undergraduate GPA is between 2.5 and 2.99), minimum undergraduate GPA of 3.0 or graduate degree, personal statement, resume or curriculum vitae. Additional exam requirements/recommendations for international students: Required—TOEFL (minimum score 550 paper-based; 79 iBT); Recommended—IELTS (minimum score 6.5), TWE (minimum score 5.5). *Application deadline:* For fall admission, 7/1 for domestic students, 5/1 priority date for international students; for winter admission, 10/1 for domestic students, 9/1 priority date for international students; for spring admission, 3/15 for domestic students, 1/1 priority date for international students. Applications are processed on a rolling basis. Application fee: $0. Electronic applications accepted. *Financial support:* In 2013–14, 65 students received support. Fellowships with tuition reimbursements available, research assistantships with tuition reimbursements available, institutionally sponsored loans, scholarships/grants, and unspecified assistantships available. Support available to part-time students. Financial award application deadline: 3/31; financial award applicants required to submit FAFSA. *Faculty research:* Library services, information management issues, digital content management, library/community engagement, archives and preservation. *Unit head:* Dr. Stephen Bajjaly, Associate Dean and Professor, 313-577-0350, Fax: 313-577-7563, E-mail: bajjaly@wayne.edu. *Application contact:* Matthew Fredericks, Academic Services Officer I, 313-577-2446, Fax: 313-577-7563, E-mail: mfredericks@wayne.edu.
Website: http://slis.wayne.edu/.

Wright State University, School of Graduate Studies, College of Education and Human Services, Department of Teacher Education, Programs in Workforce Education, Dayton, OH 45435. Offers career, technology and vocational education (M Ed, MA); computer/technology education (M Ed, MA); library/media (M Ed, MA); vocational education (M Ed, MA). *Accreditation:* NCATE. *Degree requirements:* For master's, thesis (for some programs). *Entrance requirements:* For master's, GRE General Test, MAT. Additional exam requirements/recommendations for international students: Required—TOEFL.

PRATT INSTITUTE
School of Information and Library Science

Programs of Study

Distinguished as the only ALA-accredited graduate school of information and library science based in Manhattan and the oldest library and information science (LIS) school in North America, Pratt's School of Information and Library Science (SILS) was established in 1890 and has been continuously accredited since 1923, when accreditation was first introduced to the field. The Archives program is ranked 11th in the country by *U.S. News & World Report*.

Building upon Pratt's national reputation as a leading school in art and design, Pratt brings creativity and innovation to library science education to offer students exciting and cutting-edge programs and courses from archives and digital libraries, to special libraries and school library media.

In addition to the 36-credit Master of Science in Library and Information Science (M.S.L.I.S.) degree, Pratt offers three joint-degree programs, one with Pratt's History of Art Department (M.S.L.I.S./M.S. in history of art, 60 credits), one with Pratt's Digital Arts M.F.A. (M.S.L.I.S./M.F.A. in digital arts, 75 credits), and one with the Brooklyn Law School (M.S.L.I.S./J.D., 86 credits); a 12-credit Archives Certificate Program within the M.S.L.I.S.; a 12-credit Museum Libraries Certificate; and an M.S. with Library Media Specialist certification.

The School of Information and Library Science prepares students for leadership positions in the information professions, including special opportunities in arts and humanities librarianship for students pursuing careers in academic and research libraries, art and museum libraries, and archives and special collections. The program combines a core curriculum (information professions, information services and sources, information technologies, and knowledge organization) with elective courses, such as advanced Web design, digital libraries, human information behavior, information architecture, information policy, and projects in digital archives. Some courses are taught on location in museums and libraries, such as the New York Public Library, the Watson Library, and the Metropolitan Museum of Art. Other courses are held on the Brooklyn Campus in the Pratt Library, and students in the library and media specialist (LMS) studies program take courses in the Art and Design Education Department. SILS maintains a dean's office in North Hall. Students carry out practicum internships at many of New York's leading cultural institutions. Students may choose from a number of program concentrations, depending on their interests and career goals, including business, cultural informatics, digital technology and knowledge organization, legal and health information, library media specialist studies, management and leadership, public urban libraries, and reference and information literacy.

The master's program may be completed in as little as two semesters and one summer and must be completed within four years of enrollment. Courses are offered in the evening, during the day, and on Saturday and Sunday to accommodate students who work.

Research Facilities

The program's teaching and research facilities occupy the entire sixth floor of a seven-story facility in its home at 144 West 14th Street, Manhattan, in a beautifully restored landmark building, designated the Pratt Manhattan Center (PMC). Here, students find faculty and staff offices, smart classrooms, large computer labs, an elegant conference room, and the student cyber place. The fifth-floor computer lab adds to SILS resources, and a separate scanning lab supports digital library projects. The fourth floor is home to the PMC library, containing extensive LIS collections of books, journals, and full-text online databases. Special SILS events and lectures are held in a 150-person lecture hall adjoining the second-floor gallery space. This rich complex of facilities, all with wireless access and convenient to students and faculty members, adds greatly to effective operations and enhances the learning environment.

Financial Aid

Financial aid awards are offered through a variety of institutional, state, and federally funded programs. These include Graduate Scholarships awarded by departments to incoming students on the basis of merit, endowed and restricted scholarships for continuing students, and student employment. Assistantships are awarded on a competitive basis to continuing students in all departments. Special alumni-sponsored fellowships are also available.

Cost of Study

In 2014–15, tuition is $1,229 per credit for the M.S.L.I.S. degree, and student fees are approximately $1,866 per year. The cost of books and supplies varies widely among the different programs.

Living and Housing Costs

Housing is available for single students on the Brooklyn Campus. The cost averages $16,572 (room and board $20,588) per year. The Office of Residential Life maintains listings of off-campus housing to help students find suitable accommodations.

Student Group

Graduate students at Pratt are drawn from all parts of the United States (thirty-eight states) and fifty-three other countries. The SILS graduate program average age is 30, with most students working full-time while taking M.S.L.I.S. courses. The employment outlook for Pratt graduates is bright. At present, more than 95 percent of the graduates obtain positions in a broad range of work environments from academic libraries and museums, to special libraries, including those in the corporate, business, and medical fields. The growth potential of the job market is seemingly unlimited. Job opportunities have been increasing for graduates of the information and library science program.

Location

Pratt-SILS is headquartered in the heart of Manhattan. Here, most SILS courses are offered at times convenient to those students who wish to work and pursue their M.S.L.I.S. The main campus of Pratt Institute is located in the Clinton Hill section of Brooklyn. Some courses are offered there to support programs such as the joint degree with Brooklyn Law School and program courses in urban librarianship at Brooklyn Public Library. In Manhattan, courses are taught at Cornell Medical Center for health sciences specialization and the New York Public Library/Research Libraries for special collections.

SILS students enjoy the advantages of New York's position as a world center for the information professions. Students also benefit from the wealth of professional experience and expertise that complements their formal study. A vast variety of cultural and recreational activities are available in the neighborhood, in Brooklyn, in the city, and in the region. Pratt has a park-like campus in a quiet neighborhood of Victorian buildings set in the midst of one of the most vibrant cities in the world.

Pratt Institute

The Institute

A private, nonsectarian institute of higher education, Pratt was founded in 1887 by industrialist and philanthropist Charles Pratt. Changing with the requirements of the professions for which it educates, Pratt today prepares a student body of approximately 4,600 undergraduate and graduate students for a wide range of careers in architecture and planning, design and fine arts, and information science.

Applying

The deadline for applications and all supporting materials, including portfolio, is January 5. Applicants should complete the application process online. Early submission of applications with all necessary credentials is highly desirable. For applicants who intend to file for financial aid, applications and all supporting documents should be received no later than January 5 for the fall semester and October 1 for the spring semester. Applications received after these dates are considered if openings exist in a particular program.

Correspondence and Information

Graduate Admissions Office
Pratt Institute
200 Willoughby Avenue
Brooklyn, New York 11205
Phone: 718-636-3514
      800-331-0834 (toll-free)
Fax: 718-399-4242
Website: http://www.pratt.edu/admissions

School of Information and Library Science
Pratt Institute
144 West 14th Street, 6th Floor
New York, New York 10011
Phone: 212-647-7682
E-mail: infosils@pratt.edu
Website: http://www.pratt.edu/academics/information-and-library-sciences

THE FACULTY

Tula Giannini, Dean; Ph.D., Bryn Mawr.
Selenay Aytac, Visiting Assistant Professor; Ph.D., LIU, C.W. Post.
Virginia L. Bartow, Visiting Assistant Professor; M.L.S., Columbia.
Carrie Banks, Visiting Assistant Professor; M.L.S. CUNY, Queens.
Johanna Bauman, Visiting Assistant Professor, M.L.S. CUNY, Queens.
Jason Baumann, Visiting Assistant Professor; M.L.S., CUNY, Queens.

John Berry, Visiting Professor; M.L.S., Simmons.
Helen-Ann Brown-Epstein, Visiting Assistant Professor; M.L.S., Maryland, College Park.
Charles Cuykendall, Carter, Visiting Instructor; M.S.L.I.S., LIU.
Gilok Choi, Assistant Professor; Ph.D., Texas at Austin.
Anthony Cocciolo, Assistant Professor; Ed.D., Columbia.
Anthony M. Cucchiara, Visiting Assistant Professor; M.L.S., Pratt.
Deirdre Donohue, Visiting Assistant Professor; M.L.S., Pratt.
Judith Freeman, Visiting Professor; M.L.S., Rutgers.
Nancy Friedland, Visiting Associate Professor; M.L.S., Rutgers.
Barbara Genco, Visiting Associate Professor; M.L.S., Pratt.
Sharareh Goldsmith, Visiting Assistant Professor; M.L.S., Pratt.
Joshua Hadro, Instructor; M.L.S., Pratt.
Alexis Hagadorn, Visiting Assistant Professor; M.L.S., Columbia.
Susan Hamson, Visiting Assistant Professor; Ph.D., Temple.
Jessica Lee Hochman, Assistant Professor; Ph.D., Columbia.
David Alan Hollander, Visiting Assistant Professor; J.D., Fordham.
Jennifer Hubert-Swan, Visiting Assistant Professor; M.L.S. Wayne State (Michigan).
Michael Inman, Visiting Assistant Professor; M.L.S., Pratt.
Elizabeth Johnston, Instructor; M.L.S., Pratt.
Jesse Karp, Instructor; M.L.S., Pratt.
Matthew Knutzen, Assistant Professor; M.F.A., Pratt.
Elizabeth Kroski, Visiting Assistant Professor; M.S.L.I.S., LIU.
Irene Lopatovska, Assistant Professor; M.L.S., North Texas.
Amy Lucker, Visiting Assistant Professor; M.S.L.I.S., Simmons College.
Laura Lutz, Visiting Assistant Professor; M.L.S., Arizona.
Craig MacDonald, Assistant Professor; Ph.D., Information Studies, Drexel.
Susan L. Malbin, Visiting Instructor; Ph.D., Brandeis.
David Marcinkowski, Visiting Associate Professor; M.A., New School.
Hillias Martin, Visiting Assistant Professor; M.L.I.S., Pratt.
Seoud M. Matta, Dean Emeritus; D.L.S., Columbia.
Abigail Meisterman, Visiting Instructor; M.L.S., CUNY, Queens.
Jacob Nadal, Visiting Assistant Professor; M.L.S., Indiana Bloomington.
Elena Dana Neacsu, Visiting Assistant Professor; M.L.S., CUNY, Queens.
Lisa Norberg, Visiting Assistant Professor; M.L.S., Indiana.
Lea Osborne, Visiting Assistant Professor; M.S.L., LIU.
Maria Cristina Pattuelli, Assistant Professor; Ph.D., North Carolina at Chapel Hill.
Alexa Pearse, Visiting Assistant Professor; M.L.S., LIU, C.W. Post.
Slava Polishchuk, Visiting Assistant Professor; M.F.A., CUNY, Brooklyn.
Deborah Rabina, Assistant Professor; Ph.D., Rutgers.
Lee Robinson, Visiting Associate Professor; M.L.S., Columbia.
Pamela Rollo, Visiting Professor; M.L.S., Columbia.
Caroline Romans, Visiting Professor; M.L.S., Drexel.
Charles Rubenstein, Professor; Ph.D., Polytechnic of NYU.
Kenneth Soehner, Visiting Associate Professor; M.L.S., Columbia.
Christopher Sula, Assistant Professor; Ph.D., CUNY Graduate Center.
Kyle Triplett, Visiting Instructor; M.S.L.I.S., Pratt.
Brooke Watkins, Visiting Assistant Professor; M.L.S., Pratt.
Christopher Weller, Visiting Instructor; M.L.S., Pratt.

© Bob Handelman

© Bob Handelman

SYRACUSE UNIVERSITY

School of Information Studies
Master of Science in Information Management
Master of Science in Library and Information Science
Master of Science in Telecommunications and Network Management

Programs of Study

The Syracuse University School of Information Studies (iSchool) offers M.S. degree programs in three areas to prepare students for a growing number of dynamic careers that involve the management and use of information. Master's students in the iSchool obtain specialized skills in areas such as digital librarianship, data science, global enterprise technologies, social media, virtual environments, databases, information security and IT governance, information and communication technologies, wireless networks, mobile and web applications, and telecommunications technologies. Students can earn M.S. degrees on campus or online with limited residency requirements. *Note:* The Telecommunications and Network Management program offers a hybrid campus and online option but no fully online program.

Ranked number one in information systems by *U.S. News & World Report,* the iSchool offers an M.S. in information management (IM), which requires the completion of 42 credit hours. Each student completes course work in management approaches and strategies, user information needs, technological infrastructures, and elective subjects. There is also an exit requirement. The program provides an integrated approach to the effective management and use of information and communication technologies within organizations. Many IM students concurrently pursue a Certificate of Advanced Study in information security management or data science.

The iSchool also offers a 30-credit executive track for the M.S. in information management, geared toward midcareer professionals looking to advance their organizations and their job prospects. This track can be completed online or on campus.

Accredited by the American Library Association (ALA), the M.S. in library and information science (LIS) program requires the completion of 36 credit hours. The program is dedicated to educating students to become leaders in the evolution of the library and information profession. LIS students work with interdisciplinary faculty advisers to plan their programs of study, which may include course work in other academic areas. The program offers a concentration in school media (ranked third in the 2013 *U.S. News & World Report* rankings) and certificates of advanced study in digital libraries and school media, as well as a certificate in cultural heritage preservation and data science.

The M.S. in telecommunications and network management (TNM) requires the completion of 36 credit hours. It provides an integrated approach to the effective management, operation, and implementation of telecommunication systems, including voice, data, and wireless networks, within organizations. Faculty members engage students in research and classroom lessons in a wide variety of areas, including international telecommunications policy and Internet governance, information assurance/security, e-collaboration, enterprise architecture, wireless systems, information policy, information systems management, online retrieval systems, project management, strategic planning, and telecommunications management. Many TNM students also pursue a Certificate of Advanced Study in information systems and telecommunications management.

All three degree programs focus on employing technology and digital tools to find, evaluate, organize, and use information for the betterment of people. Graduates of the iSchool at Syracuse work in a broad range of managerial and technical positions in business, government, education, health care, and other fields.

The iSchool also offers two doctoral-level programs: a research-oriented Ph.D. in information science and technology for those individuals interested in becoming researchers, professors, and consultants (i.e., more theoretically oriented positions) and the Doctorate of Professional Studies in information management, a part-time distance-learning executive degree program for working professionals who are interested in the applied aspects of the information field.

The iSchool's Certificates of Advanced Study have broad appeal and attract students across disciplines. Options include information security management, information systems and telecommunications management, e-government management and leadership, cultural heritage and preservation, school media, and data science. These certificates can be earned on campus or online, and provide a valuable development opportunity both for emerging and experienced professionals in the information field.

Research Facilities

Ranked as one of the most connected campuses by Princeton Review/forbes.com and a 2010 Campus Technology Innovator award recipient, Syracuse University offers wireless capabilities from most buildings and public spaces on campus and provides students with hundreds of computer workstations in public clusters. The School of Information Studies is located in a recently renovated building, Hinds Hall, in the heart of the University's Main Campus Quad. The facility features the latest technologies and innovative instructional and meeting spaces to encourage collaborative and interactive learning. The iSchool's research and development centers, which have achieved national and international distinction, allow students to apply classroom lessons to authentic problems, sometimes using technologies that have not yet made it to market.

The University's library system includes collections of 3.1 million volumes, more than 24,000 online and print journals, and extensive collections of microforms, maps, images, music scores, videos, rare books, and manuscripts. Many of these resources can be accessed from academic and residence hall computer clusters.

Among its special collections is the Belfer Audio Laboratory and Archive, which contains more than 340,000 historical sound recordings in all formats, including a collection of 22,000 cylinder records, the largest held by any private institution in North America.

Financial Aid

Fellowships, scholarships, and assistantships are available to full-time students both on campus and online. The most prestigious and competitive are Syracuse University graduate fellowships, which include a scholarship and a stipend for the academic year. University scholarships provide 24 credit hours of tuition, and graduate assistantships provide tuition and a stipend for the academic year. Syracuse also offers fellowships through the McNair Scholars program and Graduate Education for Minorities (GEM) program. Tuition scholarships and other small scholarships are available to part-time students.

Loans are available through the University financial aid office. For Federal Work-Study Program contracts, students work through the University student employment office. Financial aid is awarded according to federal financial need guidelines.

Cost of Study

Tuition for 2014–15 is $1,341 per graduate credit hour.

Living and Housing Costs

Academic-year living expenses are about $17,870 for single students. The University has residence hall rooms and on-campus apartments for single and married graduate students. Many graduate students choose to live off campus.

Student Group

Syracuse University has about 18,000 students, including about 4,500 graduate students. Approximately 650 graduate students are enrolled in the School of Information Studies. Thirty percent are international students, with the remainder coming from all parts of the United States. Students have diverse backgrounds, with undergraduate majors in the liberal arts, natural sciences, fine arts, business administration, computer science, and engineering. They participate in more than 300 student groups and extracurricular activities, including Women in Information Technology, Information Studies Graduate Organization, Black and Latino Information Studies Support, and chapters of national information and library associations.

Student Outcomes

Career opportunities for graduates of the programs are excellent. Information management graduates find lucrative professional positions in a wide variety of organizations, with responsibilities ranging from information systems analysis, database design, and consulting, to risk assessment, social media strategy, and systems management. Library and information science graduates not only work in library settings, but they also hold professional positions in corporations, media and communications outlets, museums, government agencies, and universities. Telecommunications and network management graduates find success in four main sectors of industry: information systems positions within organizations requiring data and voice network management and strategies; telecommunications organizations involved in voice, data, or video transmissions; large voice and data network communication vendors such as Cisco and Nortel; and large consulting companies.

Location

The Syracuse metropolitan area is home to more than a half million people and is the commercial, industrial, medical, and cultural center of central New York State. The 200-acre Main Campus is spacious and attractive, and new University facilities extend the campus into the heart of downtown Syracuse, which is only a 20-minute walk from the University. Winters are snowy and summers are pleasant. Lake Ontario, the Finger Lakes, and the Adirondack and Catskill Mountains are nearby. Boston, Toronto, New York, and Philadelphia are within a 5-hour drive.

The School

The School of Information Studies is a leading center for innovative graduate programs in information fields. The school's focus on information users and understanding user information needs sets it apart from other institutions that offer computer science, management, and related programs. The interdisciplinary faculty combines expertise in information science, telecommunications, public administration, education, school media, business management and management information systems, social science, design, linguistics, computer science, library science, and communications. The iSchool also offers unique undergraduate degree programs in information management and technology, and systems and information science.

Applying

Applicants for the master's degree programs must have a bachelor's degree from an accredited undergraduate institution and an academic record that is satisfactory for admission to the graduate school. Two letters of recommendation, a resume, and an essay on academic plans and professional goals are also required.

Syracuse University

Applicants for the master's degree and doctoral programs are required to submit scores from the Graduate Record Examinations (GRE). Whenever possible, an interview is recommended. International students should plan to take the Test of English as a Foreign Language (TOEFL); a score of at least 90 on the internet-based test is expected. Students interested in University fellowships must apply by January 8. Other financial aid applicants must submit all materials by February 1.

For additional information, please visit the School of Information Studies website, http://ischool.syr.edu or e-mail iGrad@syr.edu. Follow the School on Facebook or Twitter at http://facebook.com/su.ischool and http://twitter.com/ischoolsu. Videos about the School can be found at http://www.youtube.com/user/syracuseischool.

Correspondence and Information

School of Information Studies
343 Hinds Hall
Syracuse University
Syracuse, New York 13244-4100
United States
Phone: 315-443-2911
E-mail: iGrad@syr.edu
Websites: http://ischool.syr.edu
http://facebook.com/su.ischool (Facebook)
http://twitter.com/ischoolsu (Twitter)

THE FACULTY AND THEIR RESEARCH

Marilyn Arnone, Research Associate Professor; Ph.D. (instructional design, development, and evaluation), Syracuse. Information literacy education, children's learning and curiosity in interactive multimedia environments.

Bahram Attaie, Assistant Professor of Practice. Microsoft and Cisco certification, business information technology, networking and database programming for the corporate world.

Carlos E. Caicedo, Assistant Professor; Ph.D. (telecommunications), Pittsburgh. Security in future data environments, spectrum trading markets and technology, security management, telecommunication and network systems management.

Kevin Crowston, Professor; Ph.D. (information technologies), MIT. Organizational implications of technology, free/libre open source software development, coordination in distributed teams, ICT in real estate.

Jason Dedrick, Associate Professor; Ph.D. (management information systems), California, Irvine. Globalization of information technology, national technology policy, offshoring of knowledge work, personal computing industry, green information technologies.

Michael D'Eredita, Assistant Professor; Ph.D. (experimental/cognitive psychology), Syracuse. Enterprise skill acquisition, collective expertise, virtual apprenticeship, organizational behavior, collaboration.

David Dischiave, Assistant Professor of Practice; M.S. (computer information technology), Regis. Systems analysis and design, database management and design, project management, computer hardware and operating system architecture.

Susan Dischiave, Assistant Professor of Practice; M.B.A. (business administration), Le Moyne. Enterprise systems analysis and design, database management and design, application development.

Renee Franklin, Assistant Professor; Ph.D. (information studies), Florida State. School library media, intellectual freedom in K–12 schools, increasing the level of participation of underrepresented ethnic groups in library and information science education.

Paul Gandel, Professor; Ph.D. (information studies), Syracuse. Digital libraries; digital services; information organization and retrieval; information technology and development; information, organizations, and society knowledge.

Martha A. Garcia-Murillo, Associate Professor; Ph.D. (international political economy and telecommunications), USC. Digital divide, economics of the information industry, information and communications policy and regulations.

Robert Heckman, Senior Associate Dean; Ph.D. (information systems), Pittsburgh. Strategy and planning for information resources, teaching and learning strategies for professionals, collaboration in virtual communities and teams, open source software development.

Jeff Hemsley, Assistant Professor: Ph.D. (information sciences), Washington. Power as it relates to information asymmetries, computer-medicated social networks in the context of politics or social movements.

Jill Hurst-Wahl, Assistant Professor of Practice; M.L.S., Maryland. Digitization, digital libraries, copyright, online social networking, web 2.0, virtual worlds.

Michelle Lynn Kaarst-Brown, Associate Professor; Ph.D. (organizational theory and management information systems), York. Information technology culture, strategic alignment of information technology with business strategy, perceptions of risk and opportunity in IT adoption, influences on IT governance, Internet-based business.

Bruce Kingma, Professor and Associate Provost for Innovation and Entrepreneurship; Ph.D. (economics), Rochester. Economics of online education, digital libraries, scholarly publishing, library and nonprofit management.

Barbara Kwasnik, Professor; Ph.D. (library and information studies), Rutgers. Classification research, knowledge representation and organization, research methods, information-related behavior.

R. David Lankes, Associate Professor; Ph.D. (information transfer), Syracuse. Participatory librarianship, digital reference, digital libraries, credibility.

Kenneth Lavender, Assistant Professor of Practice; Ph.D. (English), California, Santa Barbara. Digital reference, rare books, archives, preservation of cultural heritage, distance education pedagogy, context of information services.

Elizabeth D. Liddy, Dean and Trustee Professor; Ph.D. (information transfer), Syracuse. Indexing, data mining, natural-language processing, information retrieval.

Ian MacInnes, Associate Dean for Academic Affairs; Ph.D. (political economy and public policy), USC. Electronic commerce, competition policy, information technology and globalization, public policy, standardization, network economics, microeconomics.

Nancy McCracken, Research Associate Professor; Ph.D. (computer and information science), Syracuse. Computational linguistics, natural language processing, data mining, information extraction and retrieval, question answering, knowledge representation.

Lee McKnight, Associate Professor; Ph.D. (political science, communication, and international relations), MIT. Wireless grids, nomadicity, social networking of devices, Internet economics and policy, national and international technology policy.

David Molta, Assistant Dean, Technology Integration; M.P.A., North Texas. Mobile and wireless information systems; interoperability and performance testing; impact of mobile communications technologies on individuals, organizations, and society.

Milton L. Mueller, Professor; Ph.D. (telecommunication), Pennsylvania. Internet governance, telecommunication policy, transnational civil society, global governance institutions in communication and information, digital identity, digital convergence.

Scott Nicholson, Associate Professor; Ph.D. (information studies), North Texas. Gaming in libraries, evaluation and assessment of library services, data mining for libraries, web search tools.

Michael Nilan, Associate Professor; Ph.D. (communication research), Washington (Seattle). Virtual communities, cognitive behavior, information seeking and using, information system design and evaluation, user-based research methods.

Megan Oakleaf, Assistant Professor; Ph.D. (information and library science), North Carolina at Chapel Hill. Evolution and assessment of information services, outcomes-based assessment, evidence-based decision making, digital reference, digital libraries, information services.

Carsten Osterlund, Associate Professor; Ph.D. (organization studies and behavioral policy science), MIT. Medical informatics, documenting work, distributed work, organizational implications of information technology, indoor tracking systems, qualitative research techniques.

Joon S. Park, Associate Professor; Ph.D. (information technology and information security), George Mason. Information and systems security; security policies, models, mechanisms, evaluation, survivability, and applications.

Jian Qin, Associate Professor; Ph.D. (library and information science), Illinois at Urbana-Champaign. Knowledge organization, information organization, information technology applications in managing knowledge and information.

Jeffrey Rubin, Assistant Professor of Practice; M.S. (telecommunications and network management), Syracuse. Managing websites, e-business, content management systems, information architecture, designing Internet services, web analytics.

Jeff Saltz, Professor of Practice; Ph.D. (information systems), NJIT. Analyzing and visualizing large datasets, experiential learning and teaching, investigating startup ecosystems.

Steven B. Sawyer, Associate Professor; D.B.A. (management information systems), Boston. Social informatics, design and development of information systems, project management, role of information and communication technologies relative to organizational and social change.

Carl Schramm, Professor; Ph.D. (labor economics and industrial relations), Wisconsin. Entrepreneurship, innovation and economic growth.

Bryan Semaan, Assistant Professor; Ph.D. (information and computer science), California, Irvine. How people appropriate and are shaped by interactive and collaborative technologies.

Ruth V. Small, Meredith Professor; Ph.D. (instructional design, development, and evaluation), Syracuse. Motivational aspects of information literacy, design and use of information and information technologies in education, role of school media specialist, information components of inventive thinking.

Jeffrey Stanton, Associate Dean for Research and Doctoral Programs; Ph.D. (information studies), Connecticut. Organizational psychology and data collection; behavioral information security; statistical models to predict attitudes, motivation, and behavior; interactions between people and technology.

Zixiang (Alex) Tan, Associate Professor; Ph.D. (telecommunications management and policy), Rutgers. Telecommunications policy and regulations, new technology development and applications, industry restructure and competition.

Arthur Thomas, Assistant Professor of Practice; Ph.D. (research and evaluation/instructional systems design and management), SUNY at Buffalo. Performance improvement, project management, data networking engineering, instructional design, information systems management.

Howard Turtle, Associate Research Professor; Ph.D. (computer science), Massachusetts Amherst. Design and implementation of retrieval systems, operating system support for large databases, text representation techniques, automatic classification, text and data mining, and automated inference techniques.

Murali Venkatesh, Associate Professor; Ph.D. (management), Indiana. Civic network design, group-based decision support systems, sociological analyses of administrative documents, human-computer interaction, telecommunications.

Carlos Villalba, Assistant Professor of Practice; Ph.D. candidate (instructional design, development, and evaluation), Syracuse. Oracle database administration, IT security, open source application development, search engine optimization, e-commerce.

Jun Wang, Assistant Research Professor; Ph.D. (library and information science), Illinois at Urbana-Champaign. Human computation, machine learning, computational neuroscience, computational language evolution.

Ozgur Yilmazel, Assistant Research Professor; Ph.D. (electrical engineering), Syracuse. Natural language processing, information retrieval, text categorization, software engineering.

Bei Yu, Assistant Professor; Ph.D. (library and information science), Illinois at Urbana-Champaign. Text classification and analysis, natural language processing, political linguistics, language and social behavior, automated language extraction and classification development.

Ping Zhang, Professor; Ph.D. (information systems), Texas at Austin. Human computer interaction, information management, intellectual development of information-related fields.

The iSchool is located on the Main Campus Quad in the heart of the Syracuse University campus.

UNIVERSITY OF KENTUCKY

Program in Library and Information Science

Programs of Study

The University of Kentucky's School of Library and Information Science (UK SLIS) offers the only ALA-accredited master's degree program in Kentucky. The program includes a wide array of courses for students who choose to pursue a master's degree. UK SLIS is a member of the iSchools organization, a collective of information schools dedicated to advancing the information field in the twenty-first century.

The M.S. degree is a 36-hour program including required core courses for general preparation and electives customized to the students' interests. Course tracks include: school library certification, health information, information systems, academic libraries, public libraries, youth services and literature, and others. Students complete a program portfolio in their final semester.

Licensed school teachers can earn a school library certification as they work toward the master's degree. Certification and master's courses are combined for a total of 36 credit hours.

SLIS students can also elect to complete an additional certificate program in distance education, which is offered online. The graduate certificate requires students to complete 12 hours of coursework, at least 6 of which will count toward the M.S. degree. More information about the certificate is available at http://www.uky.edu/DistanceLearning/DEGCP.

Students can complete all course work online, with no required face-to-face meetings. Students taking only online courses are charged in-state (resident) tuition rates, which are significantly lower than out-of-state tuition rates. Students may also opt to complete the program with a mix of online and face-to-face courses, with the program's required core courses (600, 601, 602, and 603) being offered in both online and face-to-face formats.

Students at UK SLIS can apply to participate in an alternative spring-break program, spending a week interning at the Library of Congress, the National Library of Medicine, or the National Archives. The program offers students an excellent opportunity for real-world application of the theory learned in classes. The school also supports a study-abroad program. While abroad, students examine how librarians and other information professionals serve their patrons in other cultural contexts.

Research Facilities

The University's Library System, one of the nation's top research libraries, contains more than 3.7 million volumes and 26,000 linear feet of manuscripts. In addition, UK serves as a Regional Depository of the Federal Depository Library Program.

Financial Aid

All applicants are encouraged to submit the FAFSA form. In addition, assistantships and scholarships are available through the program. Information on assistantships is available online at http://www.research.uky.edu/gs/StudentFunding/funding.html.

Information on program scholarships is available at http://ci.uky.edu/lis/content/funding-your-education.

Cost of Study

Students taking only online courses are charged in-state tuition. Information about tuition charges and fees can be found online at http://www.uky.edu/registrar/tuition-fees.

Living and Housing Costs

Students who choose to pursue their degree on campus can apply for a limited number of efficiency, one-bedroom, and two-bedroom apartments designated for graduate student and family housing. Additional information is available at http://www.uky.edu/Housing/graduate.

Student Group

UK SLIS has several active student groups. LISSO coordinates social activities for distance and face-to-face students. The school is also home to a student chapter of the American Library Association (UK ALA) and a student group of the Special Library Association (SLA).

The Faculty and Their Research

Members of the University of Kentucky SLIS faculty are a varied group with a wide range of interests. Complete faculty profiles are available online at http://ci.uky.edu/lis/content/faculty.

Location

The University is located in Lexington, Kentucky, a metropolitan area with a population of approximately 300,000. Lexington is located in the heart of the famous Bluegrass region of central Kentucky, about 85 miles from both Louisville, Kentucky, and Cincinnati, Ohio. Lexington has numerous theaters, concert halls, and restaurants and more than 400 horse farms—the city is often referred to as the Horse Capital of the World. There are many opportunities for outdoor recreation, including a readily accessible network of state parks with opportunities for hiking and canoeing. In addition, the University has recreational facilities and offers a variety of artistic presentations. Lexington's downtown area is within walking distance of the University campus.

The University

The University of Kentucky was established in 1865 as the Agricultural and Mechanical College of the Kentucky University. Today, it is a public, research-extensive, land-grant university with an enrollment of more than 29,000 and an annual budget of $2.7 billion. The University is also Kentucky's ninth-largest organization. The University has more than eighty national rankings for academic excellence, and it ranks tenth in the nation among all universities for the number of start-up companies formed per $10 million in research spending.

Applying

The application deadline is July 15 for the fall term, November 15 for the spring term, and March 15 for the summer term. Applicants must apply to the University of Kentucky Graduate School. Requirements include: a completed application for admission (available online), one official transcript from each previous school attended (an undergraduate GPA of at least 3.0 is required), an official score report of GRE results (requirements: 150 verbal and either 140 quantitative or 4.0 analytical), a personal statement, and three recommendations. Additional information regarding application to the Graduate School can be found at http://www.rgs.uky.edu/gs.

For additional details, applicants may contact Ashley DeWitt at ashdewitt@uky.edu or sign up to receive LIS News, a newsletter for prospective students, at http://ci.uky.edu/lis/content/subscribe.

Correspondence and Information

Ashley DeWitt, Lecturer
School of Library and Information Science
University of Kentucky
320 Lucille Little Fine Arts Library
Lexington, Kentucky 40506-0224
Phone: 859-218-2290
Fax: 859-257-4205
E-mail: ashdewitt@uky.edu
Website: http://ci.uky.edu/lis/

Participants in the 2014 alternative spring break program at UK.

Students using technology to connect and share their research at the 2014 Student Conference.

ACADEMIC AND PROFESSIONAL PROGRAMS IN PHYSICAL EDUCATION, SPORTS, AND RECREATION

Section 29
Leisure Studies and Recreation

This section contains a directory of institutions offering graduate work in leisure studies and recreation. Additional information about programs listed in the directory may be obtained by writing directly to the dean of a graduate school or chair of a department at the address given in the directory.

In the other guides in this series:

Graduate Programs in the Humanities, Arts & Social Sciences
See *Performing Arts*

Graduate Programs in the Physical Sciences, Mathematics, Agricultural Sciences, the Environment & Natural Resources
See *Natural Resources*

CONTENTS

Program Directories

Leisure Studies 1606
Recreation and Park Management 1608

Leisure Studies

Bowling Green State University, Graduate College, College of Education and Human Development, School of Human Movement, Sport, and Leisure Studies, Bowling Green, OH 43403. Offers developmental kinesiology (M Ed); recreation and leisure (M Ed); sport administration (M Ed). Part-time programs available. *Degree requirements:* For master's, thesis or alternative. *Entrance requirements:* For master's, GRE General Test, minimum GPA of 2.7. Additional exam requirements/recommendations for international students: Required—TOEFL. Electronic applications accepted. *Faculty research:* Teacher-learning process, travel and tourism, sport marketing and management, exercise physiology and sport psychology, life-span motor development.

California State University, Long Beach, Graduate Studies, College of Health and Human Services, Department of Recreation and Leisure Studies, Long Beach, CA 90840. Offers recreation administration (MS). Part-time programs available. *Degree requirements:* For master's, comprehensive exam or thesis. *Entrance requirements:* For master's, GRE General Test. Electronic applications accepted.

The College at Brockport, State University of New York, School of Health and Human Performance, Department of Recreation and Leisure Studies, Brockport, NY 14420-2997. Offers recreation and leisure service management (MS). Part-time programs available. *Faculty:* 4 full-time (3 women), 1 (woman) part-time/adjunct. *Students:* 4 full-time (3 women), 5 part-time (0 women); includes 1 minority (Black or African American, non-Hispanic/Latino). In 2013, 11 master's awarded. *Degree requirements:* For master's, thesis or alternative. *Entrance requirements:* For master's, minimum GPA of 3.0, letters of recommendation, written critical analysis; statement of objectives. Additional exam requirements/recommendations for international students: Required—TOEFL (minimum score 550 paper-based; 79 iBT). *Application deadline:* For fall admission, 5/30 for domestic and international students; for spring admission, 11/15 for domestic and international students. Application fee: $50. Electronic applications accepted. *Expenses:* Tuition, state resident: full-time $9870. Tuition, nonresident: full-time $18,350. *Required fees:* $1848. *Financial support:* In 2013–14, 1 fellowship with full tuition reimbursement (averaging $3,750 per year) was awarded; Federal Work-Study, scholarships/grants, and unspecified assistantships also available. Support available to part-time students. Financial award application deadline: 3/15; financial award applicants required to submit FAFSA. *Faculty research:* Leisure service delivery systems; therapeutic recreation; international issues in recreation and leisure; tourism; customer service, customer behavior and perceived value/satisfaction; leisure motivation among Baby Boomers. *Unit head:* Arthur Graham, Chairperson, 585-395-2643, Fax: 585-395-5246, E-mail: jfrater@brockport.edu. *Application contact:* Dr. Lynda Sperazza, Graduate Director, 585-395-5490, Fax: 585-395-5246, E-mail: lsperazza@brockport.edu.
Website: http://www.brockport.edu/leisure/grad.html.

Dalhousie University, Faculty of Health Professions, School of Health and Human Performance, Program in Leisure Studies, Halifax, NS B3H 1T8, Canada. Offers MA. Part-time programs available. *Degree requirements:* For master's, thesis. *Entrance requirements:* For master's, minimum GPA of 3.3. Additional exam requirements/recommendations for international students: Required—TOEFL, IELTS, CANTEST, CAEL, or Michigan English Language Assessment Battery. Electronic applications accepted. *Faculty research:* Leisure and lifestyles of social groups such as older adults, women, and persons with health problems or disabilities; historical analysis of leisure; sport and leisure administration.

East Carolina University, Graduate School, College of Health and Human Performance, Department of Recreation and Leisure Studies, Greenville, NC 27858-4353. Offers aquatic therapy (Certificate); biofeedback (Certificate); recreation and park administration (MS), including generalist, recreational sports management; recreational therapy administration (MS). Part-time and evening/weekend programs available. Postbaccalaureate distance learning degree programs offered (minimal on-campus study). *Degree requirements:* For master's, comprehensive exam, thesis optional. *Entrance requirements:* For master's, GRE General Test or MAT. Additional exam requirements/recommendations for international students: Required—TOEFL. *Expenses:* Tuition, state resident: full-time $4223. Tuition, nonresident: full-time $16,540. *Required fees:* $2184. *Faculty research:* Therapeutic recreation, stress and coping behavior, medicine carrying capacity, choice behavior, tourism preferences.

Howard University, Graduate School, Department of Health, Human Performance and Leisure Studies, Washington, DC 20059-0002. Offers exercise physiology (MS); health education (MS); sports studies (MS), including sociology of sports, sports management; urban recreation (MS), including leisure studies. Part-time and evening/weekend programs available. *Degree requirements:* For master's, comprehensive exam, thesis. *Entrance requirements:* For master's, BS in human performance or related field. Additional exam requirements/recommendations for international students: Recommended—TOEFL. Electronic applications accepted. *Faculty research:* Health promotion, cardiovascular hypertension, physical activity, sport and human rights issues.

Indiana University Bloomington, School of Public Health, Department of Recreation, Park, and Tourism Studies, Bloomington, IN 47405-7000. Offers leisure behavior (PhD); outdoor recreation (MS); park and public lands management (MS); recreation administration (MS); recreational sports administration (MS); recreational therapy (MS); tourism management (MS). *Faculty:* 16 full-time (5 women), 1 (woman) part-time/adjunct. *Students:* 43 full-time (21 women), 9 part-time (6 women); includes 6 minority (2 Black or African American, non-Hispanic/Latino; 2 Hispanic/Latino; 2 Two or more races, non-Hispanic/Latino), 17 international. Average age 31. 47 applicants, 81% accepted, 18 enrolled. In 2013, 21 master's, 4 doctorates awarded. Terminal master's awarded for partial completion of doctoral program. *Degree requirements:* For master's, thesis optional; for doctorate, comprehensive exam, thesis/dissertation. *Entrance requirements:* For master's, GRE General Test, minimum GPA of 2.8; for doctorate, GRE General Test, minimum GPA of 3.0 (undergraduate), 3.5 (graduate). Additional exam requirements/recommendations for international students: Required—TOEFL (minimum score 550 paper-based; 80 iBT). *Application deadline:* For fall admission, 1/1 priority date for international students; for spring admission, 9/1 priority date for international students. Applications are processed on a rolling basis. Application fee: $55 ($65 for international students). Electronic applications accepted. *Financial support:* In 2013–14, 19 students received support. Fellowships, research assistantships, teaching assistantships with partial tuition reimbursements available, career-related internships or fieldwork, Federal Work-Study, institutionally sponsored loans, scholarships/grants, health care benefits, tuition waivers (partial), unspecified assistantships, and fee remissions available. Support available to part-time students. Financial award application deadline: 3/1; financial award applicants required to submit FAFSA. *Faculty research:* Leisure counseling, gerontology, special populations, planning and development. *Unit head:* Dr. Bryan McCormick, Chair, 812-855-3482,

E-mail: bmccormi@indiana.edu. *Application contact:* Program Office, 812-855-4711, Fax: 812-855-3998, E-mail: recpark@indiana.edu.
Website: http://www.publichealth.indiana.edu/departments/recreation-park-tourism-studies/index.shtml.

Murray State University, College of Health Sciences and Human Services, Department of Wellness and Therapeutic Sciences, Program in Exercise and Leisure Studies, Murray, KY 42071. Offers MS. Part-time programs available. *Degree requirements:* For master's, thesis optional. *Entrance requirements:* For master's, GRE General Test or MAT. Additional exam requirements/recommendations for international students: Required—TOEFL. *Faculty research:* Exercise and cancer recovery.

Penn State University Park, Graduate School, College of Health and Human Development, Department of Recreation, Park and Tourism Management, State College, PA 16802. Offers M Ed, MS, PhD. *Unit head:* Dr. Ann C. Crouter, Dean, 814-865-1420, Fax: 814-865-3282, E-mail: ac1@psu.edu. *Application contact:* Cynthia E. Nicosia, Director, Graduate Enrollment Services, 814-865-1834, Fax: 814-863-4627, E-mail: cey1@psu.edu.
Website: http://www.hhdev.psu.edu/rptm.

Prescott College, Graduate Programs, Program in Adventure Education/Wilderness Leadership, Prescott, AZ 86301. Offers adventure education (MA); adventure-based environmental education (MA); student-directed concentrations (MA). Part-time programs available. Postbaccalaureate distance learning degree programs offered (minimal on-campus study). *Degree requirements:* For master's, thesis, fieldwork or internship, practicum. *Entrance requirements:* For master's, 2 letters of recommendation, resume. Additional exam requirements/recommendations for international students: Required—TOEFL (minimum score 500 paper-based). Electronic applications accepted.

San Francisco State University, Division of Graduate Studies, College of Health and Social Sciences, Department of Recreation, Parks, and Tourism, San Francisco, CA 94132-1722. Offers MS. Part-time programs available. *Application deadline:* Applications are processed on a rolling basis. *Financial support:* Career-related internships or fieldwork available. *Unit head:* Dr. Patrick Tierney, Chair, 415-338-2030, E-mail: ptierney@sfsu.edu. *Application contact:* Prof. Jackson Wilson, Graduate Coordinator, 415-338-1487, E-mail: wilsonj@sfsu.edu.
Website: http://recdept.sfsu.edu/.

Southeast Missouri State University, School of Graduate Studies, Department of Health, Human Performance and Recreation, Cape Girardeau, MO 63701-4799. Offers nutrition and exercise science (MS). Part-time and evening/weekend programs available. *Faculty:* 6 full-time (2 women), 2 part-time/adjunct (0 women). *Students:* 23 full-time (12 women), 7 part-time (6 women); includes 2 minority (1 Black or African American, non-Hispanic/Latino; 1 Hispanic/Latino), 12 international. Average age 24. 29 applicants, 86% accepted, 15 enrolled. In 2013, 4 master's awarded. *Degree requirements:* For master's, comprehensive exam, thesis optional, internship. *Entrance requirements:* For master's, GRE General Test (minimum combined score of 950), minimum undergraduate GPA of 3.0, minimum B grade in prerequisite courses. Additional exam requirements/recommendations for international students: Required—TOEFL (minimum score 550 paper-based; 79 iBT), IELTS (minimum score 6), PTE (minimum score 53). *Application deadline:* For fall admission, 8/1 for domestic students, 5/1 for international students; for spring admission, 11/21 for domestic students, 10/1 for international students; for summer admission, 5/15 for domestic students. Applications are processed on a rolling basis. Application fee: $30 ($40 for international students). Electronic applications accepted. *Expenses:* Tuition, state resident: full-time $5139; part-time $285.50 per credit hour. Tuition, nonresident: full-time $9099; part-time $505.50 per credit hour. *Financial support:* In 2013–14, 18 students received support. Career-related internships or fieldwork, Federal Work-Study, scholarships/grants, traineeships, tuition waivers (full), and unspecified assistantships available. Financial award application deadline: 6/30; financial award applicants required to submit FAFSA. *Faculty research:* Blood lipids, body composition assessment, exercise testing, perceptual responses to physical activity, sport governance, youth sports participation. *Unit head:* Dr. Joe Pujol, Chairperson, 573-651-2664, E-mail: jpujol@semo.edu. *Application contact:* Alisa Aleen McFerron, Assistant Director of Admissions for Operations, 573-651-5937, E-mail: amcferron@semo.edu.
Website: http://www.semo.edu/health/.

Southern Connecticut State University, School of Graduate Studies, School of Health and Human Services, Department of Recreation and Leisure Studies, New Haven, CT 06515-1355. Offers MS. Part-time and evening/weekend programs available. *Degree requirements:* For master's, thesis or alternative. *Entrance requirements:* For master's, interview, minimum undergraduate QPA of 3.0 in graduate major field or 2.5 overall. Electronic applications accepted.

Temple University, School of Tourism and Hospitality Management, Program in Tourism and Sport, Philadelphia, PA 19122-6096. Offers PhD. *Unit head:* Dr. Elizabeth H. Barber, Associate Dean, 215-204-8701, Fax: 215-204-8705, E-mail: betsyb@temple.edu. *Application contact:* Michael J. Usino, Senior Associate Director of Recruitment, 215-204-3103, Fax: 215-204-8705, E-mail: musino@temple.edu.
Website: http://sthm.temple.edu/cms/main/phd/.

Texas State University, Graduate School, College of Education, Department of Health and Human Performance, Program in Recreation and Leisure Services, San Marcos, TX 78666. Offers MSRLS. *Faculty:* 4 full-time (3 women), 1 (woman) part-time/adjunct. *Students:* 45 full-time (31 women), 24 part-time (8 women); includes 29 minority (10 Black or African American, non-Hispanic/Latino; 1 Asian, non-Hispanic/Latino; 16 Hispanic/Latino; 2 Two or more races, non-Hispanic/Latino), 2 international. Average age 27. 43 applicants, 86% accepted, 27 enrolled. In 2013, 24 master's awarded. *Degree requirements:* For master's, comprehensive exam, thesis optional. *Entrance requirements:* For master's, GRE General Test, minimum GPA of 2.75 in last 60 hours of course work. Additional exam requirements/recommendations for international students: Required—TOEFL (minimum score 550 paper-based; 78 iBT). *Application deadline:* For fall admission, 6/15 priority date for domestic students, 6/1 for international students; for spring admission, 10/15 priority date for domestic students, 10/1 for international students. Applications are processed on a rolling basis. Application fee: $40 ($90 for international students). Electronic applications accepted. *Expenses:* Tuition, state resident: full-time $6663; part-time $278 per credit hour. Tuition, nonresident: full-time $15,159; part-time $632 per credit hour. *Required fees:* $1872; $54 per credit hour. $306 per term. Tuition and fees vary according to course load. *Financial support:* In 2013–14, 33 students received support, including 10 research assistantships (averaging $11,983 per year), 5 teaching assistantships (averaging $12,263 per year). Financial award application deadline: 4/1; financial award applicants required to submit FAFSA. *Unit head:* Dr. Janet Hodges, Graduate Advisor, 512-245-

7482, Fax: 512-245-8678, E-mail: jh223@txstate.edu. *Application contact:* Dr. Andrea Golato, Dean of the Graduate College, 512-245-2581, Fax: 512-245-8365, E-mail: gradcollege@txstate.edu.
Website: http://www.hhp.txstate.edu/Degree-Plans/Graduate.html.

Universidad Metropolitana, School of Education, Program in Managing Recreation and Sports Services, San Juan, PR 00928-1150. Offers M Ed. Part-time programs available. *Degree requirements:* For master's, thesis or alternative. *Entrance requirements:* For master's, EXADEP, interview. Electronic applications accepted.

Université du Québec à Trois-Rivières, Graduate Programs, Program in Leisure, Culture and Tourism Sciences, Trois-Rivières, QC G9A 5H7, Canada. Offers MA, DESS. Part-time programs available. *Degree requirements:* For master's, thesis optional. *Entrance requirements:* For master's, appropriate bachelor's degree, proficiency in French.

University of Connecticut, Graduate School, Neag School of Education, Department of Kinesiology, Program in Sport Management and Sociology, Storrs, CT 06269. Offers MA, PhD. Terminal master's awarded for partial completion of doctoral program. *Degree requirements:* For master's, comprehensive exam, thesis or alternative; for doctorate, thesis/dissertation. *Entrance requirements:* For doctorate, GRE General Test. Additional exam requirements/recommendations for international students: Required—TOEFL (minimum score 550 paper-based). Electronic applications accepted.

University of Georgia, College of Education, Department of Counseling and Human Development Services, Athens, GA 30602. Offers college student affairs administration (M Ed, PhD); counseling and student personnel (PhD); counseling psychology (PhD); professional counseling (M Ed); professional school counseling (Ed S); recreation and leisure studies (M Ed, MA, PhD). *Accreditation:* ACA (one or more programs are accredited); APA (one or more programs are accredited); NCATE. *Degree requirements:* For master's, thesis (MA); for doctorate, variable foreign language requirement, thesis/dissertation. *Entrance requirements:* For master's, GRE General Test or MAT; for doctorate, GRE General Test. Electronic applications accepted.

University of Illinois at Urbana–Champaign, Graduate College, College of Applied Health Sciences, Department of Recreation, Sport and Tourism, Champaign, IL 61820. Offers MS, PhD. Part-time programs available. Postbaccalaureate distance learning degree programs offered (no on-campus study). *Students:* 110 (61 women). *Application fee:* $75 ($90 for international students). *Unit head:* Laurence Chalip, Head, 217-333-4410, Fax: 217-244-1935, E-mail: lchalip@illinois.edu. *Application contact:* Karen D. Bickers, Office Support Specialist, 217-333-4410, Fax: 217-244-1935, E-mail: kbickers@illinois.edu.
Website: http://www.rst.illinois.edu.

The University of Iowa, Graduate College, College of Liberal Arts and Sciences, Department of Health and Human Physiology, Iowa City, IA 52242-1316. Offers athletic training (MS); clinical exercise physiology (MS); health and human physiology (PhD); leisure studies (MA, PhD), including recreational sport management (PhD), therapeutic recreation (MA). *Degree requirements:* For master's, thesis optional, exam; for doctorate, comprehensive exam, thesis/dissertation. *Entrance requirements:* For master's and doctorate, GRE General Test, minimum GPA of 3.0. Additional exam requirements/recommendations for international students: Required—TOEFL (minimum score 600 paper-based; 100 iBT). Electronic applications accepted.

University of Memphis, Graduate School, College of Education, Department of Health and Sport Sciences, Memphis, TN 38152. Offers clinical nutrition (MS); exercise and sport science (MS); health promotion (MS); physical education teacher education (MS), including teacher education; sport and leisure commerce (MS). Part-time and evening/weekend programs available. *Faculty:* 22 full-time (8 women), 3 part-time/adjunct (2 women). *Students:* 83 full-time (51 women), 28 part-time (23 women); includes 37 minority (29 Black or African American, non-Hispanic/Latino; 6 Asian, non-Hispanic/Latino; 2 Two or more races, non-Hispanic/Latino), 7 international. Average age 27. 86 applicants, 67% accepted, 29 enrolled. In 2013, 35 master's awarded. *Degree requirements:* For master's, comprehensive exam, thesis. *Entrance requirements:* For master's, GRE General Test or GMAT (for sport and leisure commerce). *Application deadline:* For fall admission, 5/1 priority date for domestic students; for spring admission, 11/1 for domestic students. Applications are processed on a rolling basis. Application fee: $35 ($60 for international students). *Financial support:* In 2013–14, 59 students received support. Research assistantships with full tuition reimbursements available, teaching assistantships with full tuition reimbursements available, career-related internships or fieldwork, Federal Work-Study, scholarships/grants, tuition waivers (partial), and unspecified assistantships available. Financial award application deadline: 2/15; financial award applicants required to submit FAFSA. *Faculty research:* Sport marketing and consumer analysis, health psychology, smoking cessation, psychosocial aspects of cardiovascular disease, global health promotion. *Unit head:* Linda H. Clemens, Interim Chair, 901-678-2324, Fax: 901-678-3591, E-mail: lhclemns@memphis.edu. *Application contact:* Dr. Kenneth Ward, Graduate Studies Coordinator, 901-678-1714, E-mail: kdward@memphis.edu.
Website: http://coe.memphis.edu/hss/.

University of Minnesota, Twin Cities Campus, Graduate School, College of Education and Human Development, School of Kinesiology, Division of Recreation, Park, and Leisure Studies, Minneapolis, MN 55455-0213. Offers M Ed, MA, PhD. Part-time programs available. *Students:* 1 part-time (0 women). Average age 37. In 2013, 2 master's awarded. Terminal master's awarded for partial completion of doctoral program. *Degree requirements:* For master's, thesis (for some programs), final oral exam; for doctorate, thesis/dissertation, preliminary written/oral exam, final oral exam. *Entrance requirements:* For master's, GRE or MAT, minimum GPA of 3.0; for doctorate, GRE or MAT, minimum GPA of 3.0, writing sample. *Application deadline:* For fall admission, 7/15 for domestic students; for spring admission, 12/15 for domestic students. Applications are processed on a rolling basis. Application fee: $75 ($95 for international students). *Financial support:* Fellowships, research assistantships, teaching assistantships, career-related internships or fieldwork, Federal Work-Study, institutionally sponsored loans, and tuition waivers (full and partial) available. Support available to part-time students. *Unit head:* Dr. Li Li Ji, Director, 612-642-9809, Fax: 612-626-7700, E-mail: llji@umn.edu. *Application contact:* Dr. Jennifer Engler, Assistant Dean, 612-626-2887, Fax: 612-626-7496, E-mail: engle009@umn.edu.
Website: http://www.cehd.umn.edu/kin/recreation.

University of Mississippi, Graduate School, School of Applied Sciences, Department of Health, Exercise Science, and Recreation Management, Oxford, MS 38677. Offers exercise science (MS); health and kinesiology (PhD); health promotion (MS); park and recreation management (MA). *Faculty:* 9 full-time (3 women), 3 part-time/adjunct (1 woman). *Students:* 45 full-time (23 women), 14 part-time (9 women); includes 11 minority (8 Black or African American, non-Hispanic/Latino; 1 Asian, non-Hispanic/Latino; 2 Hispanic/Latino), 5 international. In 2013, 19 master's, 1 doctorate awarded. *Degree requirements:* For master's, thesis (for some programs); for doctorate, thesis/dissertation. *Entrance requirements:* For master's, GRE General Test, minimum GPA of 3.0; for doctorate, GRE General Test. Additional exam requirements/recommendations for international students: Required—TOEFL. *Application deadline:* For fall admission, 4/1 for domestic students; for spring admission, 10/1 for domestic students. Applications

are processed on a rolling basis. *Financial support:* Scholarships/grants available. Financial award application deadline: 3/1; financial award applicants required to submit FAFSA. *Unit head:* Dr. Scott G. Owens, Chair, 662-915-5844, Fax: 662-915-5525, E-mail: dbramlett@olemiss.edu. *Application contact:* Dr. Christy M. Wyandt, Associate Dean, 662-915-7474, Fax: 662-915-7577, E-mail: cwyandt@olemiss.edu.

University of Nebraska at Kearney, Graduate Programs, College of Education, Department of Health, Physical Education, Recreation, and Leisure Studies, Kearney, NE 68849-0001. Offers general physical education (MA Ed), including recreation and leisure, sports administration; physical education exercise science (MA Ed); physical education master teacher (MA Ed), including pedagogy, special populations. Part-time and evening/weekend programs available. *Degree requirements:* For master's, comprehensive exam, thesis optional. *Entrance requirements:* For master's, GRE General Test, personal statement. Additional exam requirements/recommendations for international students: Required—TOEFL (minimum score 550 paper-based). Electronic applications accepted. *Faculty research:* Ergonomic aids, nutrition, motor development, sports pedagogy, applied behavior analysis.

University of South Alabama, Graduate School, College of Education, Department of Health, Physical Education and Leisure Services, Mobile, AL 36688-0002. Offers exercise science (MS); health education (M Ed); physical education (M Ed); therapeutic recreation (MS). *Accreditation:* NCATE (one or more programs are accredited). Part-time programs available. *Faculty:* 4 full-time (1 woman), 2 part-time/adjunct (0 women). *Students:* 34 full-time (16 women), 5 part-time (1 woman); includes 12 minority (9 Black or African American, non-Hispanic/Latino; 3 Two or more races, non-Hispanic/Latino), 4 international. 36 applicants, 61% accepted, 18 enrolled. In 2013, 16 master's awarded. *Degree requirements:* For master's, comprehensive exam. *Entrance requirements:* For master's, GRE General Test or MAT. *Application deadline:* For fall admission, 7/15 priority date for domestic students, 6/15 priority date for international students; for spring admission, 12/1 priority date for domestic students, 11/1 priority date for international students. Applications are processed on a rolling basis. Application fee: $35. *Expenses:* Tuition, state resident: full-time $8976; part-time $374 per credit hour. Tuition, nonresident: full-time $17,952; part-time $748 per credit hour. *Financial support:* In 2013–14, 10 teaching assistantships were awarded; career-related internships or fieldwork also available. Support available to part-time students. Financial award application deadline: 4/1. *Unit head:* Dr. Frederick M. Scaffidi, Chair, 251-460-7131. *Application contact:* Dr. Abigail Baxter, Director of Graduate Studies, 251-460-7131.

University of Southern Mississippi, Graduate School, College of Health, School of Human Performance and Recreation, Hattiesburg, MS 39406-0001. Offers human performance (MS, PhD), including exercise physiology (PhD), human performance (MS), physical education (MS); interscholastic athletic administration (MS); recreation and leisure management (MS); sport administration (MS); sport and coaching education (MS); sport management (MS). Part-time and evening/weekend programs available. *Faculty:* 13 full-time (5 women). *Students:* 60 full-time (20 women), 43 part-time (9 women); includes 19 minority (13 Black or African American, non-Hispanic/Latino; 1 American Indian or Alaska Native, non-Hispanic/Latino; 2 Hispanic/Latino; 3 Two or more races, non-Hispanic/Latino), 4 international. Average age 29. 62 applicants, 77% accepted, 38 enrolled. In 2013, 39 master's, 1 doctorate awarded. *Degree requirements:* For master's, comprehensive exam, thesis optional; for doctorate, comprehensive exam, thesis/dissertation. *Entrance requirements:* For master's, GRE General Test, minimum GPA of 2.75 in last 60 hours; for doctorate, GRE General Test, minimum GPA of 3.5. Additional exam requirements/recommendations for international students: Required—TOEFL, IELTS. *Application deadline:* For fall admission, 3/1 priority date for domestic students, 3/1 for international students; for spring admission, 1/10 priority date for domestic and international students. Applications are processed on a rolling basis. Application fee: $50. Electronic applications accepted. *Financial support:* In 2013–14, 1 fellowship (averaging $16,000 per year), 6 research assistantships with full tuition reimbursements (averaging $7,492 per year), 5 teaching assistantships with full tuition reimbursements (averaging $7,330 per year) were awarded; career-related internships or fieldwork, Federal Work-Study, institutionally sponsored loans, scholarships/grants, health care benefits, and unspecified assistantships also available. Financial award application deadline: 3/15; financial award applicants required to submit FAFSA. *Faculty research:* Exercise physiology, health behaviors, resource management, activity interaction, site development. *Unit head:* Dr. Frederick Green, Director, 601-266-5379, Fax: 601-266-4445. *Application contact:* Dr. Trenton Gould, Graduate Coordinator, 601-266-5379, Fax: 601-266-4445.
Website: http://www.usm.edu/graduateschool/table.php.

The University of Tennessee, Graduate School, College of Education, Health and Human Sciences, Department of Exercise, Sport, and Leisure Studies, Knoxville, TN 37996. Offers exercise science (MS, PhD), including biomechanics/sports medicine, exercise physiology; recreation and leisure studies (MS); sport management (MS); sport studies (MS, PhD); therapeutic recreation (MS). Part-time and evening/weekend programs available. *Degree requirements:* For master's, thesis optional. *Entrance requirements:* For master's, minimum GPA of 2.7. Additional exam requirements/recommendations for international students: Required—TOEFL. Electronic applications accepted. *Expenses:* Tuition, state resident: full-time $9540; part-time $531 per credit hour. Tuition, nonresident: full-time $27,728; part-time $1542 per credit hour. *Required fees:* $1404; $67 per credit hour.

The University of Toledo, College of Graduate Studies, College of Health Sciences, Department of Health and Recreation Professions, Toledo, OH 43606-3390. Offers health education (PhD); recreation and leisure studies (MA). Part-time programs available. *Faculty:* 12. *Students:* 36 full-time (30 women), 38 part-time (20 women); includes 14 minority (10 Black or African American, non-Hispanic/Latino; 1 Asian, non-Hispanic/Latino; 2 Hispanic/Latino; 1 Two or more races, non-Hispanic/Latino), 2 international. Average age 28. 41 applicants, 80% accepted, 26 enrolled. In 2013, 10 master's, 3 doctorates awarded. *Degree requirements:* For master's, comprehensive exam, thesis; for doctorate, thesis/dissertation. *Entrance requirements:* For master's and doctorate, minimum cumulative GPA of 2.7 for all previous academic work, letters of recommendation. Additional exam requirements/recommendations for international students: Required—TOEFL (minimum score 550 paper-based; 80 iBT). *Application deadline:* For fall admission, 1/15 priority date for domestic and international students. Applications are processed on a rolling basis. Application fee: $45 ($75 for international students). Electronic applications accepted. *Financial support:* In 2013–14, 1 research assistantship with full and partial tuition reimbursement (averaging $9,000 per year), 17 teaching assistantships with full and partial tuition reimbursements (averaging $11,588 per year) were awarded; career-related internships or fieldwork, Federal Work-Study, institutionally sponsored loans, scholarships/grants, tuition waivers (full and partial), unspecified assistantships, and administrative assistantships also available. Support available to part-time students. Financial award applicants required to submit FAFSA. *Unit head:* Dr. Joseph Dake, Chair, 419-530-2767, E-mail: joseph.dake@utoledo.edu. *Application contact:* Graduate School Office, 419-530-4723, Fax: 419-530-4724, E-mail: grdsch@utnet.utoledo.edu.
Website: http://www.utoledo.edu/eduhshs/.

University of Utah, Graduate School, College of Health, Department of Parks, Recreation, and Tourism, Salt Lake City, UT 84112. Offers M Phil, MS, PhD. Part-time

programs available. *Faculty:* 8 full-time (4 women), 6 part-time/adjunct (2 women). *Students:* 31 full-time (20 women), 20 part-time (11 women); includes 2 minority (1 Black or African American, non-Hispanic/Latino; 1 Hispanic/Latino), 5 international. Average age 32. 26 applicants, 50% accepted, 10 enrolled. In 2013, 13 master's, 5 doctorates awarded. Terminal master's awarded for partial completion of doctoral program. *Degree requirements:* For master's, comprehensive exam, thesis or alternative; for doctorate, comprehensive exam, thesis/dissertation. *Entrance requirements:* For master's, GRE General Test, minimum GPA of 3.0; for doctorate, GRE General Test, minimum GPA of 3.2. Additional exam requirements/recommendations for international students: Required—TOEFL (minimum score 500 paper-based). *Application deadline:* For fall admission, 3/1 for domestic students, 2/15 for international students; for spring admission, 10/1 for domestic students. Application fee: $55 ($65 for international students). Electronic applications accepted. *Expenses:* Tuition, state resident: full-time $5259. Tuition, nonresident: full-time $18,569. *Required fees:* $841. Tuition and fees vary according to course load. *Financial support:* In 2013–14, 3 research assistantships with full tuition reimbursements, 8 teaching assistantships with full tuition reimbursements were awarded; career-related internships or fieldwork, scholarships/grants, health care benefits, and unspecified assistantships also available. Financial award application deadline: 2/15; financial award applicants required to submit FAFSA. *Faculty research:* Therapeutic recreation, community and youth sport, outdoor recreation, protected area management, sustainable tourism and youth development. *Total annual research expenditures:* $39,469. *Unit head:* Dr. Kelly S. Bricker, Chair, 801-585-6503, E-mail: kelly.bricker@health.utah.edu. *Application contact:* Dr. Jim Sibthorp, Director of Graduate Studies, 801-581-5940, Fax: 801-581-4930, E-mail: jim.sibthorp@health.utah.edu.
Website: http://www.health.utah.edu/prt/.

University of Victoria, Faculty of Graduate Studies, Faculty of Education, School of Exercise Science, Physical, and Health Education, Victoria, BC V8W 2Y2, Canada. Offers coaching studies (co-operative education) (M Ed); kinesiology (M Sc, MA); leisure service administration (MA); physical education (MA). Part-time programs available. *Degree requirements:* For master's, comprehensive exam (for some programs), thesis (for some programs). *Entrance requirements:* For master's, minimum B average. Additional exam requirements/recommendations for international students: Required—TOEFL (minimum score 575 paper-based), IELTS (minimum score 7). Electronic applications accepted. *Faculty research:* Children and exercise, mental skills in sports, teaching effectiveness, neural control of human movement, physical performance and health.

University of Waterloo, Graduate Studies, Faculty of Applied Health Sciences, Department of Recreation and Leisure Studies, Waterloo, ON N2L 3G1, Canada. Offers MA, PhD. Part-time programs available. *Degree requirements:* For master's, thesis; for doctorate, comprehensive exam, thesis/dissertation. *Entrance requirements:* For master's, honors degree, minimum B average, writing sample, resume; for doctorate, GRE (recommended), master's degree, minimum B average, writing sample, resumé. Additional exam requirements/recommendations for international students: Required—TOEFL, TWE. Electronic applications accepted. *Faculty research:* Tourism, leisure behavior, special populations, leisure service management, outdoor resources, aging, health and well-being, work and health.

University of West Florida, College of Professional Studies, Department of Health, Leisure, and Exercise Science, Program in Health, Leisure, and Exercise Science, Pensacola, FL 32514-5750. Offers exercise science (MS); physical education (MS). Part-time and evening/weekend programs available. *Degree requirements:* For master's, thesis or alternative. *Entrance requirements:* For master's, GRE or MAT, official transcripts; minimum GPA of 3.0; letter of intent; two personal references; work experience. Additional exam requirements/recommendations for international students: Required—TOEFL (minimum score 550 paper-based). Electronic applications accepted.

Recreation and Park Management

Acadia University, Faculty of Professional Studies, School of Recreation Management and Community Development, Wolfville, NS B4P 2R6, Canada. Offers MR. *Degree requirements:* For master's, thesis. *Entrance requirements:* Additional exam requirements/recommendations for international students: Required—TOEFL (minimum score 630 paper-based; 93 iBT), IELTS (minimum score 6.5).

Arizona State University at the Tempe campus, College of Public Programs, School of Community Resources and Development, Phoenix, AZ 85004-0685. Offers community resources and development (PhD); nonprofit leadership and management (Graduate Certificate); nonprofit studies (MNpS); recreation and tourism studies (MS). *Accreditation:* ACSP. Part-time and evening/weekend programs available. Terminal master's awarded for partial completion of doctoral program. *Degree requirements:* For master's, thesis or alternative, interactive Program of Study (iPOS) submitted before completing 50 percent of required credit hours; for doctorate, comprehensive exam, thesis/dissertation, interactive Program of Study (iPOS) submitted before completing 50 percent of required credit hours. *Entrance requirements:* For master's and doctorate, GRE, minimum GPA of 3.0 or equivalent in last 2 years of work leading to bachelor's degree. Additional exam requirements/recommendations for international students: Required—TOEFL (minimum score 80 iBT), TOEFL, IELTS, or PTE. Electronic applications accepted. *Expenses:* Contact institution.

Aurora University, George Williams College, Aurora, IL 60506-4892. Offers MS. Part-time and evening/weekend programs available. *Entrance requirements:* Additional exam requirements/recommendations for international students: Required—TOEFL (minimum score 550 paper-based). Electronic applications accepted.

Bowling Green State University, Graduate College, College of Education and Human Development, School of Human Movement, Sport, and Leisure Studies, Bowling Green, OH 43403. Offers developmental kinesiology (M Ed); recreation and leisure (M Ed); sport administration (M Ed). Part-time programs available. *Degree requirements:* For master's, thesis or alternative. *Entrance requirements:* For master's, GRE General Test, minimum GPA of 2.7. Additional exam requirements/recommendations for international students: Required—TOEFL. Electronic applications accepted. *Faculty research:* Teacher-learning process, travel and tourism, sport marketing and management, exercise physiology and sport psychology, life-span motor development.

Brigham Young University, Graduate Studies, Marriott School of Management, Department of Recreation Management and Youth Leadership, Provo, UT 84602. Offers youth and family recreation (MS). *Degree requirements:* For master's, thesis, oral defense. *Entrance requirements:* For master's, GRE General Test, minimum GPA of 3.0 in last 60 hours. Additional exam requirements/recommendations for international students: Required—TOEFL (minimum score 580 paper-based; 85 iBT), IELTS (minimum score 7). Electronic applications accepted. *Expenses:* Contact institution. *Faculty research:* Family recreation, adolescent development, leisure behavior, families with child with disability inclusive and adaptive recreation.

California State University, Chico, Office of Graduate Studies, College of Communication and Education, Department of Recreation, Hospitality and Parks Management, Chico, CA 95929-0722. Offers recreation administration (MA). Part-time programs available. *Degree requirements:* For master's, thesis or alternative, thesis or plan. *Entrance requirements:* For master's, GRE General Test, 3 letters of recommendation, statement of purpose, resume. Additional exam requirements/recommendations for international students: Required—TOEFL (minimum score 550 paper-based; 80 iBT), IELTS (minimum score 6.5). Electronic applications accepted.

California State University, East Bay, Office of Academic Programs and Graduate Studies, College of Education and Allied Studies, Department of Hospitality, Recreation and Tourism, Hayward, CA 94542-3000. Offers recreation and tourism (MS). Part-time and evening/weekend programs available. Postbaccalaureate distance learning degree programs offered (no on-campus study). *Degree requirements:* For master's, thesis optional. *Entrance requirements:* For master's, minimum GPA of 2.75; 2 years' related work experience; 3 letters of recommendation; resume; baccalaureate degree. Additional exam requirements/recommendations for international students: Required—TOEFL (minimum score 550 paper-based). Electronic applications accepted. *Faculty research:* Leisure, online vs. face-to-face (F2F) learning, risk management, leadership, tourism consumer behavior.

California State University, Long Beach, Graduate Studies, College of Health and Human Services, Department of Recreation and Leisure Studies, Long Beach, CA 90840. Offers recreation administration (MS). Part-time programs available. *Degree requirements:* For master's, comprehensive exam or thesis. *Entrance requirements:* For master's, GRE General Test. Electronic applications accepted.

California State University, Northridge, Graduate Studies, College of Health and Human Development, Department of Recreation and Tourism Management, Northridge, CA 91330. Offers hospitality and tourism (MS); recreational sport management/campus recreation (MS). *Degree requirements:* For master's, thesis (for some programs). *Entrance requirements:* For master's, GRE (if cumulative undergraduate GPA less than 3.0). Additional exam requirements/recommendations for international students: Required—TOEFL.

California State University, Northridge, Graduate Studies, The Tseng College of Extended Learning, Northridge, CA 91330. Offers business administration (Graduate Certificate); health administration (MPA); health education (MPH); knowledge management (MKM); music industry administration (MA); nonprofit-sector management (Graduate Certificate); public administration (MPA); public sector management and leadership (MPA); social work (MSW); taxation (MS); tourism, hospitality and recreation management (MS). *Entrance requirements:* For master's, GRE (if cumulative undergraduate GPA less than 3.0).

California State University, Sacramento, Office of Graduate Studies, College of Health and Human Services, Department of Recreation, Parks and Tourism Administration, Sacramento, CA 95819. Offers MS. Part-time programs available. *Degree requirements:* For master's, thesis or project; writing proficiency exam. *Entrance requirements:* Additional exam requirements/recommendations for international students: Required—TOEFL. *Application deadline:* For fall admission, 3/1 for domestic and international students; for spring admission, 9/30 for international students. Applications are processed on a rolling basis. Application fee: $55. Electronic applications accepted. *Financial support:* Research assistantships, teaching assistantships, career-related internships or fieldwork, and Federal Work-Study available. Support available to part-time students. Financial award application deadline: 3/1; financial award applicants required to submit FAFSA. *Unit head:* Greg Shaw, Chair, 916-278-2936, E-mail: shaw@csus.edu. *Application contact:* Jose Martinez, Graduate Admissions Supervisor, 916-278-7871, E-mail: martinj@skymail.csus.edu.
Website: http://www.csus.edu/hhs/rpta.

Central Michigan University, Central Michigan University Global Campus, Program in Administration, Mount Pleasant, MI 48859. Offers acquisitions administration (MSA, Certificate); engineering management administration (MSA, Certificate); general administration (MSA, Certificate); health services administration (MSA, Certificate); human resources administration (MSA, Certificate); information resource management (MSA); information resource management administration (Certificate); international administration (MSA, Certificate); leadership (MSA, Certificate); philanthropy and fundraising administration (MSA, Certificate); public administration (MSA, Certificate); recreation and park administration (MSA); research administration (MSA, Certificate). Part-time and evening/weekend programs available. Postbaccalaureate distance learning degree programs offered (no on-campus study). *Students:* Average age 38. *Entrance requirements:* For master's, minimum GPA of 2.7 in major. *Application deadline:* Applications are processed on a rolling basis. Application fee: $50. Electronic applications accepted. *Financial support:* Scholarships/grants available. Support available to part-time students. Financial award applicants required to submit FAFSA. *Unit head:* Dr. Patricia Chase, Director, 989-774-1845, E-mail: chase1pb@cmich.edu. *Application contact:* 877-268-4636, E-mail: cmuglobal@cmich.edu.

Clemson University, Graduate School, College of Health, Education, and Human Development, Department of Parks, Recreation, and Tourism Management, Clemson, SC 29634. Offers MS, PhD. Part-time programs available. Postbaccalaureate distance learning degree programs offered (no on-campus study). *Faculty:* 19 full-time (8 women), 1 (woman) part-time/adjunct. *Students:* 49 full-time (27 women), 44 part-time (26 women); includes 10 minority (4 Black or African American, non-Hispanic/Latino; 2 Hispanic/Latino; 4 Two or more races, non-Hispanic/Latino), 20 international. Average age 28. 69 applicants, 67% accepted, 35 enrolled. In 2013, 11 master's, 8 doctorates awarded. *Median time to degree:* Of those who began their doctoral program in fall 2005, 100% received their degree in 8 years or less. *Degree requirements:* For master's, thesis (for some programs); for doctorate, thesis/dissertation. *Entrance requirements:* For master's, GRE (for on-campus thesis MS), minimum undergraduate GPA of 3.0; for doctorate, GRE General Test, minimum graduate GPA of 3.0. Additional exam requirements/recommendations for international students: Required—TOEFL. *Application deadline:* For fall admission, 5/1 priority date for domestic students; for spring admission, 10/1 for domestic students. Applications are processed on a rolling

basis. Application fee: $70 ($80 for international students). Electronic applications accepted. *Financial support:* In 2013–14, 48 students received support, including 1 fellowship with full and partial tuition reimbursement available (averaging $3,000 per year), 2 research assistantships with partial tuition reimbursements available (averaging $11,752 per year), 32 teaching assistantships with partial tuition reimbursements available (averaging $17,275 per year); career-related internships or fieldwork, scholarships/grants, health care benefits, tuition waivers (partial), and unspecified assistantships also available. Support available to part-time students. Financial award application deadline: 1/15; financial award applicants required to submit FAFSA. *Faculty research:* Recreation resource management, leisure behavior, therapeutic recreation, community leisure. *Total annual research expenditures:* $422,028. *Unit head:* Dr. Brett A. Wright, Chair, 864-656-3036, Fax: 864-656-2226, E-mail: wright@clemson.edu. *Application contact:* Dr. Denise M. Anderson, Graduate Coordinator, 864-656-5679, Fax: 864-656-2226, E-mail: dander2@clemson.edu.
Website: http://www.hehd.clemson.edu/prtm/.

The College at Brockport, State University of New York, School of Health and Human Performance, Department of Recreation and Leisure Studies, Brockport, NY 14420-2997. Offers recreation and leisure service management (MS). Part-time programs available. *Faculty:* 4 full-time (3 women), 1 (woman) part-time/adjunct. *Students:* 4 full-time (3 women), 5 part-time (0 women); includes 1 minority (Black or African American, non-Hispanic/Latino). In 2013, 11 master's awarded. *Degree requirements:* For master's, thesis or alternative. *Entrance requirements:* For master's, minimum GPA of 3.0, letters of recommendation, written critical analysis; statement of objectives. Additional exam requirements/recommendations for international students: Required—TOEFL (minimum score 550 paper-based; 79 iBT). *Application deadline:* For fall admission, 5/30 for domestic and international students; for spring admission, 11/15 for domestic and international students. Application fee: $50. Electronic applications accepted. *Expenses:* Tuition, state resident: full-time $9870. Tuition, nonresident: full-time $18,350. *Required fees:* $1848. *Financial support:* In 2013–14, 1 fellowship with full tuition reimbursement (averaging $3,750 per year) was awarded; Federal Work-Study, scholarships/grants, and unspecified assistantships also available. Support available to part-time students. Financial award application deadline: 3/15; financial award applicants required to submit FAFSA. *Faculty research:* Leisure service delivery systems; therapeutic recreation; international issues in recreation and leisure; tourism; customer service, customer behavior and perceived value/satisfaction; leisure motivation among Baby Boomers. *Unit head:* Arthur Graham, Chairperson, 585-395-2643, Fax: 585-395-5246, E-mail: jfrater@brockport.edu. *Application contact:* Dr. Lynda Sperazza, Graduate Director, 585-395-5490, Fax: 585-395-5246, E-mail: lsperazza@brockport.edu.
Website: http://www.brockport.edu/leisure/grad.html.

Colorado State University, Graduate School, Warner College of Natural Resources, Department of Human Dimensions of Natural Resources, Fort Collins, CO 80523-1480. Offers MS, PhD. Part-time programs available. Postbaccalaureate distance learning degree programs offered. *Faculty:* 11 full-time (3 women). *Students:* 58 full-time (31 women), 50 part-time (32 women); includes 13 minority (2 Black or African American, non-Hispanic/Latino; 1 Asian, non-Hispanic/Latino; 8 Hispanic/Latino; 2 Two or more races, non-Hispanic/Latino), 14 international. Average age 31. 103 applicants, 93% accepted, 68 enrolled. In 2013, 18 master's, 4 doctorates awarded. Terminal master's awarded for partial completion of doctoral program. *Degree requirements:* For master's, comprehensive exam, thesis; for doctorate, comprehensive exam, thesis/dissertation. *Entrance requirements:* For master's, GRE General Test, minimum GPA of 3.0, 3 letters of recommendation, statement of interest; for doctorate, GRE General Test (combined minimum score of 1000 on the Verbal and Quantitative sections), minimum GPA of 3.0, 3 letters of recommendation, copy of master's thesis or professional paper, interview, statement of interest. Additional exam requirements/recommendations for international students: Required—TOEFL (minimum score 550 paper-based; 80 iBT). *Application deadline:* For fall admission, 2/1 priority date for domestic students, 2/1 for international students. Application fee: $50. Electronic applications accepted. *Expenses:* Tuition, state resident: full-time $9075.40; part-time $504 per credit. Tuition, nonresident: full-time $22,248; part-time $1236 per credit. *Required fees:* $1819; $60 per credit. *Financial support:* In 2013–14, 10 students received support, including 3 research assistantships with tuition reimbursements available (averaging $9,446 per year), 7 teaching assistantships with tuition reimbursements available (averaging $12,137 per year); career-related internships or fieldwork, Federal Work-Study, scholarships/grants, traineeships, and unspecified assistantships also available. Support available to part-time students. Financial award application deadline: 2/15; financial award applicants required to submit FAFSA. *Faculty research:* International tourism, wilderness preservation, resource interpretation, human dimensions in natural resources, protected areas management. *Total annual research expenditures:* $634,242. *Unit head:* Dr. Michael J. Manfredo, Head, 970-491-6591, Fax: 970-491-2255, E-mail: michael.manfredo@colostate.edu. *Application contact:* Jacqie Hasan, Graduate Contact, 970-491-6591, Fax: 970-491-2255, E-mail: jacqie.hasan@colostate.edu.
Website: http://warnercnr.colostate.edu/hdnr-home.

Delta State University, Graduate Programs, College of Education, Division of Health, Physical Education, and Recreation, Cleveland, MS 38733-0001. Offers health, physical education, and recreation (M Ed); sport and human performance (MS). Part-time and evening/weekend programs available. *Faculty:* 5 full-time (1 woman), 1 part-time/adjunct (0 women). *Students:* 37 full-time (12 women), 13 part-time (4 women); includes 15 minority (11 Black or African American, non-Hispanic/Latino; 1 Hispanic/Latino; 3 Two or more races, non-Hispanic/Latino), 4 international. Average age 27. 35 applicants, 91% accepted, 29 enrolled. In 2013, 11 master's awarded. *Degree requirements:* For master's, thesis optional. *Entrance requirements:* For master's, GRE General Test or MAT, Class A teaching certificate. *Application deadline:* For fall admission, 8/1 priority date for domestic students; for spring admission, 12/1 priority date for domestic students. Applications are processed on a rolling basis. Application fee: $0. *Expenses:* Tuition, state resident: full-time $3006; part-time $334 per credit hour. Tuition, nonresident: full-time $3006; part-time $334 per credit hour. *Financial support:* In 2013–14, research assistantships (averaging $4,000 per year) were awarded; career-related internships or fieldwork, Federal Work-Study, and institutionally sponsored loans also available. Support available to part-time students. Financial award application deadline: 6/1. *Faculty research:* Blood pressure, body fat, power and reaction time, learning disorders for athletes, effects of walking. *Unit head:* Tim Colbert, Chair, 662-846-4555, Fax: 662-846-4571. *Application contact:* Dr. Albert Nylander, Dean of Graduate Studies, 662-846-4875, Fax: 662-846-4313, E-mail: grad-info@deltastate.edu.
Website: http://www.deltastate.edu/pages/2963.asp.

East Carolina University, Graduate School, College of Health and Human Performance, Department of Recreation and Leisure Studies, Greenville, NC 27858-4353. Offers aquatic therapy (Certificate); biofeedback (Certificate); recreation and park administration (MS), including generalist, recreational sports management; recreational therapy administration (MS). Part-time and evening/weekend programs available. Postbaccalaureate distance learning degree programs offered (minimal on-campus study). *Degree requirements:* For master's, comprehensive exam, thesis optional. *Entrance requirements:* For master's, GRE General Test or MAT. Additional exam requirements/recommendations for international students: Required—TOEFL.

Expenses: Tuition, state resident: full-time $4223. Tuition, nonresident: full-time $16,540. *Required fees:* $2184. *Faculty research:* Therapeutic recreation, stress and coping behavior, medicine carrying capacity, choice behavior, tourism preferences.

Eastern Kentucky University, The Graduate School, College of Health Sciences, Department of Recreation and Park Administration, Richmond, KY 40475-3102. Offers MS. Part-time programs available. *Degree requirements:* For master's, comprehensive exam, thesis optional. *Entrance requirements:* For master's, GRE General Test, MAT, minimum GPA of 2.5. *Faculty research:* Marketing, at risk youth, outdoor education, event planning, TR in schools.

Eastern Washington University, Graduate Studies, College of Arts, Letters and Education, Department of Physical Education, Health and Recreation, Cheney, WA 99004-2431. Offers exercise science (MS); sports and recreation administration (MS). *Faculty:* 17 full-time (7 women), 5 part-time/adjunct (2 women). *Students:* 26 full-time (10 women), 8 part-time (3 women); includes 7 minority (3 Black or African American, non-Hispanic/Latino; 1 American Indian or Alaska Native, non-Hispanic/Latino; 2 Asian, non-Hispanic/Latino; 1 Hispanic/Latino). Average age 29. 64 applicants, 38% accepted, 21 enrolled. In 2013, 14 master's awarded. *Degree requirements:* For master's, comprehensive exam, thesis or alternative. *Entrance requirements:* For master's, minimum GPA of 3.0. *Application deadline:* For fall admission, 4/1 priority date for domestic students; for spring admission, 1/15 for domestic students. Applications are processed on a rolling basis. Application fee: $50. *Financial support:* In 2013–14, 10 teaching assistantships with partial tuition reimbursements (averaging $6,624 per year) were awarded; career-related internships or fieldwork, Federal Work-Study, institutionally sponsored loans, and scholarships/grants also available. Support available to part-time students. Financial award application deadline: 2/1; financial award applicants required to submit FAFSA. *Unit head:* John Cogley, Chair, 509-359-2486, E-mail: john.cogley@mail.ewu.edu. *Application contact:* Dr. Jeni McNeal, Professor of Physical Education, Health and Recreation, 509-359-2872, Fax: 509-359-4833, E-mail: jeni_mcneal@hotmail.com.

Florida Agricultural and Mechanical University, Division of Graduate Studies, Research, and Continuing Education, College of Education, Department of Health, Physical Education, and Recreation, Tallahassee, FL 32307-3200. Offers M Ed, MS Ed. *Accreditation:* NCATE. Part-time and evening/weekend programs available. *Degree requirements:* For master's, thesis optional. *Entrance requirements:* For master's, GRE General Test, minimum GPA of 3.0. Additional exam requirements/recommendations for international students: Required—TOEFL. *Faculty research:* Administration/curriculum, work behavior, psychology.

Florida International University, College of Education, Department of Leadership and Professional Studies, Miami, FL 33199. Offers adult education and human resource development (MS, Ed D); counseling (MS), including rehabilitation counseling, school counseling; counselor education (MS), including clinical mental health counseling; educational administration and supervision (Ed D); educational leadership (MS, Certificate, Ed S); higher education (Ed D); higher education administration (MS); recreation and sport management (MS), including recreation and sport management, recreational therapy; school psychology (Ed S); urban education (MS), including instruction in urban settings, learning technologies, multicultural/bilingual, multicultural/TESOL, urban education. Part-time and evening/weekend programs available. *Degree requirements:* For doctorate, thesis/dissertation. *Entrance requirements:* For master's, minimum GPA of 3.0; for doctorate and other advanced degree, GRE General Test. Additional exam requirements/recommendations for international students: Required—TOEFL (minimum score 550 paper-based; 80 iBT), IELTS (minimum score 6.3). Electronic applications accepted.

Florida State University, The Graduate School, College of Education, Department of Sport Management, Tallahassee, FL 32306. Offers MS, PhD, Certificate, JD/MS. *Faculty:* 9 full-time (3 women), 3 part-time/adjunct (1 woman). *Students:* 113 full-time (34 women), 40 part-time (11 women); includes 26 minority (17 Black or African American, non-Hispanic/Latino; 8 Hispanic/Latino; 1 Two or more races, non-Hispanic/Latino), 33 international. Average age 28. 165 applicants, 67% accepted, 54 enrolled. In 2013, 62 master's, 4 doctorates awarded. *Degree requirements:* For master's and Certificate, comprehensive exam, thesis optional; for doctorate, comprehensive exam, thesis/dissertation. *Entrance requirements:* For master's, doctorate, and Certificate, GRE General Test, minimum GPA of 3.0. Additional exam requirements/recommendations for international students: Required—TOEFL (minimum score 550 paper-based; 80 iBT). *Application deadline:* For fall admission, 7/1 for domestic and international students; for winter admission, 11/1 for domestic and international students; for spring admission, 3/1 for domestic and international students. Application fee: $30. Electronic applications accepted. *Expenses:* Tuition, state resident: part-time $403.51 per credit hour. Tuition, nonresident: part-time $1004.85 per credit hour. *Required fees:* $75.81 per credit hour. One-time fee: $20 part-time. Tuition and fees vary according to course load, campus/location and student level. *Financial support:* In 2013–14, 3 students received support, including 1 research assistantship with full and partial tuition reimbursement available, 93 teaching assistantships with full and partial tuition reimbursements available; fellowships with full and partial tuition reimbursements available, career-related internships or fieldwork, Federal Work-Study, scholarships/grants, health care benefits, and unspecified assistantships also available. Financial award application deadline: 1/15; financial award applicants required to submit FAFSA. *Faculty research:* Sport marketing, gender issues in sport, finances in sport industry, coaching. *Unit head:* Dr. Jeffrey D. James, Chair, 850-644-9214, Fax: 850-644-0975, E-mail: jdjames@fsu.edu. *Application contact:* Dr. Thomas F. McMorrow, Academic Specialist, 850-644-0577, Fax: 850-644-0975, E-mail: tmcmorrow@admin.fsu.edu.
Website: http://www.coe.fsu.edu/SM/.

Frostburg State University, Graduate School, College of Education, Program in Parks and Recreational Management, Frostburg, MD 21532-1099. Offers MS. Part-time and evening/weekend programs available. *Degree requirements:* For master's, thesis. *Entrance requirements:* For master's, resume. Additional exam requirements/recommendations for international students: Required—TOEFL. Electronic applications accepted. *Expenses:* Tuition, area resident: Part-time $340 per credit hour. Tuition, state resident: part-time $340 per credit hour. Tuition, nonresident: part-time $437 per credit hour.

George Mason University, College of Education and Human Development, School of Recreation, Health and Tourism, Manassas, VA 20110. Offers exercise, fitness, and health promotion (MS); sport and recreation studies (MS). *Faculty:* 31 full-time (12 women), 67 part-time/adjunct (37 women). *Students:* 24 full-time (16 women), 25 part-time (10 women); includes 13 minority (7 Black or African American, non-Hispanic/Latino; 5 Hispanic/Latino; 1 Two or more races, non-Hispanic/Latino), 1 international. Average age 27. 60 applicants, 77% accepted, 24 enrolled. In 2013, 19 master's awarded. *Degree requirements:* For master's, thesis (for some programs). *Entrance requirements:* For master's, GRE General Test or MAT, 3 letters of recommendation; official transcripts; expanded goals statement; undergraduate course in statistics and minimum GPA of 3.0 in last 60 credit hours and overall (for MS in sport and recreation studies); baccalaureate degree related to kinesiology, exercise science or athletic training (for MS in exercise, fitness and health promotion). Additional exam requirements/recommendations for international students: Required—TOEFL (minimum

score 575 paper-based; 88 iBT), IELTS (minimum score 6.5), PTE. *Application deadline:* For fall admission, 4/1 priority date for domestic students; for spring admission, 11/1 priority date for domestic students. Application fee: $65 ($80 for international students). Electronic applications accepted. *Expenses:* Tuition, state resident: full-time $9350; part-time $390 per credit. Tuition, nonresident: full-time $25,754; part-time $1073 per credit. *Required fees:* $2688; $112 per credit. *Financial support:* In 2013–14, 10 students received support, including 10 research assistantships with full and partial tuition reimbursements available (averaging $10,484 per year); career-related internships or fieldwork, Federal Work-Study, scholarships/grants, unspecified assistantships, and health care benefits (for full-time research or teaching assistantship recipients) also available. Support available to part-time students. Financial award application deadline: 3/1; financial award applicants required to submit FAFSA. *Faculty research:* Informing policy; promoting economic development; advocating stewardship of natural resources; improving the quality of life of individuals, families, and communities at the local, national and international levels. *Total annual research expenditures:* $1.5 million. *Unit head:* David Wiggins, Director, 703-993-2057, Fax: 703-993-2025, E-mail: dwiggin1@gmu.edu. *Application contact:* Lindsey Olson, Office Assistant, 703-993-2098, Fax: 703-993-2025, E-mail: lolson7@gmu.edu. Website: http://rht.gmu.edu/.

Georgia College & State University, Graduate School, College of Health Sciences, Department of Kinesiology, Milledgeville, GA 31061. Offers health promotion (M Ed); human performance (M Ed); outdoor education (M Ed); physical education (MAT). *Accreditation:* NCATE (one or more programs are accredited). Part-time and evening/weekend programs available. *Students:* 31 full-time (14 women), 13 part-time (12 women); includes 11 minority (all Black or African American, non-Hispanic/Latino), 1 international. Average age 26. In 2013, 25 master's awarded. *Degree requirements:* For master's, comprehensive exam, thesis optional. *Entrance requirements:* For master's, GRE General Test or MAT, minimum GPA of 2.75 in upper-level undergraduate courses, 2 letters of reference. Additional exam requirements/recommendations for international students: Recommended—TOEFL (minimum score 550 paper-based; 79 iBT). *Application deadline:* For fall admission, 7/1 priority date for domestic students, 4/1 priority date for international students; for spring admission, 11/15 priority date for domestic students, 9/1 priority date for international students. Applications are processed on a rolling basis. Application fee: $40. Electronic applications accepted. *Financial support:* In 2013–14, 26 research assistantships with full tuition reimbursements were awarded; career-related internships or fieldwork and unspecified assistantships also available. Support available to part-time students. Financial award applicants required to submit FAFSA. *Unit head:* Dr. Lisa Griffin, Chair, 478-445-4072, Fax: 478-445-4074, E-mail: lisa.griffin@gcsu.edu. *Application contact:* 800-342-0471, E-mail: grad-admit@gcsu.edu.

Hardin-Simmons University, Graduate School, Irvin School of Education, Department of Fitness and Sport Sciences, Program in Kinesiology, Sport, and Recreation, Abilene, TX 79698-0001. Offers M Ed. Part-time programs available. *Faculty:* 6 full-time (2 women), 1 part-time/adjunct (0 women). *Students:* 12 full-time (7 women), 22 part-time (7 women); includes 10 minority (2 Black or African American, non-Hispanic/Latino; 1 Asian, non-Hispanic/Latino; 7 Hispanic/Latino). Average age 24. 17 applicants, 94% accepted, 13 enrolled. In 2013, 10 master's awarded. *Degree requirements:* For master's, comprehensive exam, thesis optional, internship, project. *Entrance requirements:* For master's, minimum undergraduate GPA of 3.0 in major, 2.7 overall; interview; writing sample; letters of recommendation; resume. Additional exam requirements/recommendations for international students: Required—TOEFL (minimum score 550 paper-based; 75 iBT). *Application deadline:* For fall admission, 8/15 priority date for domestic students, 4/1 for international students; for spring admission, 1/5 priority date for domestic students, 9/1 for international students. Applications are processed on a rolling basis. Application fee: $50. *Expenses: Tuition:* Full-time $13,410; part-time $745 per credit hour. *Required fees:* $325; $110 per semester. Tuition and fees vary according to program. *Financial support:* In 2013–14, 10 students received support, including 15 fellowships (averaging $1,333 per year); career-related internships or fieldwork, scholarships/grants, and recreation assistantships also available. Support available to part-time students. Financial award application deadline: 6/30; financial award applicants required to submit FAFSA. *Unit head:* Dr. Robert Moore, Director, 325-670-1265, Fax: 325-670-1218, E-mail: bemoore@hsutx.edu. *Application contact:* Dr. Nancy Kucinski, Dean of Graduate Studies, 325-670-1298, Fax: 325-670-1564, E-mail: gradoff@hsutx.edu.
Website: http://www.hsutx.edu/academics/irvin/graduate/kinesiology.

Indiana University Bloomington, School of Public Health, Department of Recreation, Park, and Tourism Studies, Bloomington, IN 47405-7000. Offers leisure behavior (PhD); outdoor recreation (MS); park and public lands management (MS); recreation administration (MS); recreational sports administration (MS); recreational therapy (MS); tourism management (MS). *Faculty:* 16 full-time (5 women), 1 (woman) part-time/adjunct. *Students:* 43 full-time (21 women), 9 part-time (6 women); includes 6 minority (2 Black or African American, non-Hispanic/Latino; 2 Hispanic/Latino; 2 Two or more races, non-Hispanic/Latino), 17 international. Average age 31. 47 applicants, 81% accepted, 18 enrolled. In 2013, 21 master's, 4 doctorates awarded. Terminal master's awarded for partial completion of doctoral program. *Degree requirements:* For master's, thesis optional; for doctorate, comprehensive exam, thesis/dissertation. *Entrance requirements:* For master's, GRE General Test, minimum GPA of 2.8; for doctorate, GRE General Test, minimum GPA of 3.0 (undergraduate), 3.5 (graduate). Additional exam requirements/recommendations for international students: Required—TOEFL (minimum score 550 paper-based; 80 iBT). *Application deadline:* For fall admission, 1/1 priority date for international students; for spring admission, 9/1 priority date for international students. Applications are processed on a rolling basis. Application fee: $55 ($65 for international students). Electronic applications accepted. *Financial support:* In 2013–14, 19 students received support. Fellowships, research assistantships, teaching assistantships with partial tuition reimbursements available, career-related internships or fieldwork, Federal Work-Study, institutionally sponsored loans, scholarships/grants, health care benefits, tuition waivers (partial), unspecified assistantships, and fee remissions available. Support available to part-time students. Financial award application deadline: 3/1; financial award applicants required to submit FAFSA. *Faculty research:* Leisure counseling, gerontology, special populations, planning and development. *Unit head:* Dr. Bryan McCormick, Chair, 812-855-3482, E-mail: bmccormi@indiana.edu. *Application contact:* Program Office, 812-855-4711, Fax: 812-855-3998, E-mail: recpark@indiana.edu.
Website: http://www.publichealth.indiana.edu/departments/recreation-park-tourism-studies/index.shtml.

Iona College, Hagan School of Business, Department of Marketing and International Business, New Rochelle, NY 10801-1890. Offers international business (AC, PMC); marketing (MBA); sports and entertainment management (AC). Part-time and evening/weekend programs available. *Faculty:* 2 full-time (both women), 1 (woman) part-time/adjunct. *Students:* 17 full-time (9 women), 24 part-time (16 women); includes 4 minority (2 Black or African American, non-Hispanic/Latino; 2 Hispanic/Latino), 5 international. Average age 27. 15 applicants, 100% accepted, 9 enrolled. In 2013, 28 master's, 114 other advanced degrees awarded. *Entrance requirements:* For master's, GMAT, 2 letters of recommendation, minimum GPA of 3.0; for other advanced degree, GMAT,

minimum GPA of 3.0. Additional exam requirements/recommendations for international students: Required—TOEFL (minimum score 550 paper-based; 80 iBT), IELTS (minimum score 6.5). *Application deadline:* For fall admission, 8/15 priority date for domestic students, 8/1 priority date for international students; for winter admission, 11/15 priority date for domestic students, 11/1 priority date for international students; for spring admission, 2/15 priority date for domestic students, 2/1 priority date for international students; for summer admission, 5/15 for domestic students, 5/1 priority date for international students. Applications are processed on a rolling basis. Application fee: $50. Electronic applications accepted. *Expenses:* Contact institution. *Financial support:* In 2013–14, 23 students received support. Scholarships/grants, tuition waivers (partial), and unspecified assistantships available. Support available to part-time students. Financial award application deadline: 4/15; financial award applicants required to submit FAFSA. *Faculty research:* Business ethics, international retailing, mega-marketing, consumer behavior and consumer confidence. *Unit head:* Dr. Frederica E. Rudell, Chair, 914-637-2748, E-mail: frudell@iona.edu. *Application contact:* Cameron Hudson, Director of MBA Admissions, 914-633-2288, Fax: 914-637-2708, E-mail: chudson@iona.edu.
Website: http://www.iona.edu/Academics/Hagan-School-of-Business/Departments/Marketing/Graduate-Programs.aspx.

Kent State University, Graduate School of Education, Health, and Human Services, School of Foundations, Leadership and Administration, Sports Recreation and Management Program, Kent, OH 44242-0001. Offers sport and recreation management (MA); sports studies (MA). *Faculty:* 10 full-time (5 women), 14 part-time/adjunct (6 women). *Students:* 42 full-time (12 women), 18 part-time (8 women); includes 12 minority (9 Black or African American, non-Hispanic/Latino; 1 Asian, non-Hispanic/Latino; 2 Native Hawaiian or other Pacific Islander, non-Hispanic/Latino), 9 international. 80 applicants, 60% accepted. In 2013, 23 master's awarded. *Degree requirements:* For master's, thesis optional. *Entrance requirements:* For master's, GRE if undergraduate GPA below 3.0, goals statement, 2 letters of recommendation. Additional exam requirements/recommendations for international students: Required—TOEFL (minimum score 550 paper-based; 80 iBT). Application fee: $30 ($60 for international students). *Financial support:* In 2013–14, 7 research assistantships (averaging $8,500 per year) were awarded; teaching assistantships, Federal Work-Study, scholarships/grants, and unspecified assistantships also available. *Unit head:* Mark Lyberger, Coordinator, 330-672-0228, E-mail: mlyberge@kent.edu. *Application contact:* Nancy Miller, Academic Program Director, Office of Graduate Student Services, 330-672-2576, Fax: 330-672-9162, E-mail: ogs@kent.edu.

Lehman College of the City University of New York, School of Natural and Social Sciences, Department of Health Sciences, Program in Recreation, Bronx, NY 10468-1589. Offers recreation education (MA, MS Ed). Part-time and evening/weekend programs available. *Degree requirements:* For master's, comprehensive exam, thesis or alternative. *Entrance requirements:* For master's, minimum GPA of 2.7. *Faculty research:* Therapeutic recreation philosophy, curriculum, current approaches to treatment, impact of societal trends, ethical issues.

Liberty University, School of Education, Lynchburg, VA 24515. Offers administration and supervision (M Ed); curriculum and instruction (Ed D, Ed S); early childhood education (M Ed); educational leadership (Ed D, Ed S); educational technology and online instruction (M Ed); elementary education (M Ed, MAT); English (M Ed); gifted education (M Ed); history (M Ed); leadership (M Ed); math specialist (M Ed); middle grades (M Ed, MAT); outdoor adventure sport (MS); reading specialist (M Ed); school counseling (M Ed); secondary education (MAT); special education (M Ed, MAT); sport management (MS), including administration, outdoor recreation, sport management, tourism; sports administration (MS); student service (M Ed); teaching and learning (M Ed); tourism (MS). *Accreditation:* NCATE. Part-time programs available. Postbaccalaureate distance learning degree programs offered (minimal on-campus study). *Students:* 2,241 full-time (1,639 women), 4,413 part-time (3,240 women); includes 2,052 minority (1,588 Black or African American, non-Hispanic/Latino; 37 American Indian or Alaska Native, non-Hispanic/Latino; 67 Asian, non-Hispanic/Latino; 173 Hispanic/Latino; 37 Native Hawaiian or other Pacific Islander, non-Hispanic/Latino; 150 Two or more races, non-Hispanic/Latino), 15 international. Average age 37. 6,185 applicants, 43% accepted, 1603 enrolled. In 2013, 1,256 master's, 117 doctorates, 470 other advanced degrees awarded. *Degree requirements:* For doctorate, comprehensive exam, thesis/dissertation. *Entrance requirements:* For master's, GRE General Test or MAT (if taken in or before 1999), 2 letters of recommendation, minimum undergraduate GPA of 3.0, curriculum vitae; for doctorate and Ed S, GRE General Test or MAT (if taken before 1999), minimum master's GPA of 3.0, 3 years of teaching experience. Additional exam requirements/recommendations for international students: Required—TOEFL (minimum score 600 paper-based; 100 iBT). *Application deadline:* For fall admission, 6/1 for domestic students; for spring admission, 11/1 for domestic students. Applications are processed on a rolling basis. Application fee: $50. Electronic applications accepted. *Expenses:* Contact institution. *Financial support:* Federal Work-Study and tuition waivers (partial) available. *Faculty research:* Self-determination, character education, bibliotherapy, learning styles, distance education. *Unit head:* Dr. Karen L. Parker, Dean, 434-582-2195, Fax: 434-582-2468, E-mail: kparker@liberty.edu. *Application contact:* Jay Bridge, Director of Graduate Admissions, 800-424-9595, Fax: 800-628-7977, E-mail: gradadmissions@liberty.edu.
Website: http://www.liberty.edu/academics/education/graduate/.

Loyola Marymount University, College of Liberal Arts, Program in Yoga Studies, Los Angeles, CA 90045. Offers MA. *Faculty:* 1 full-time (0 women), 3 part-time/adjunct (0 women). *Students:* 21 full-time (16 women); includes 7 minority (1 Asian, non-Hispanic/Latino; 6 Hispanic/Latino). Average age 40. 35 applicants, 69% accepted, 20 enrolled. *Degree requirements:* For master's, comprehensive exam, thesis. *Entrance requirements:* For master's, bachelor's degree, official transcripts, two-page letter of intent, two letters of recommendation. Additional exam requirements/recommendations for international students: Required—TOEFL (minimum score 600 paper-based; 100 iBT). *Application deadline:* Applications are processed on a rolling basis. Application fee: $50. *Financial support:* In 2013–14, 16 students received support, including 1 research assistantship (averaging $720 per year). Financial award application deadline: 6/30; financial award applicants required to submit FAFSA. *Unit head:* Dr. Christopher Key Chapple, Director, 310-338-2846, E-mail: cchapple@lmu.edu. *Application contact:* Chake H. Kouyoumjian, Associate Dean of the Graduate Division, 310-338-2721, E-mail: ckouyoum@lmu.edu.
Website: http://bellarmine.lmu.edu/yoga/.

Michigan State University, The Graduate School, College of Agriculture and Natural Resources, Department of Community, Agriculture, Recreation, and Resource Studies, East Lansing, MI 48824. Offers MS, PhD. *Entrance requirements:* Additional exam requirements/recommendations for international students: Required—TOEFL. Electronic applications accepted.

Middle Tennessee State University, College of Graduate Studies, College of Behavioral and Health Sciences, Department of Health and Human Performance, Program in Health, Physical Education and Recreation, Murfreesboro, TN 37132. Offers health and human performance (MS); leisure and sport management (MS). Part-time and evening/weekend programs available. Postbaccalaureate distance learning degree

programs offered. *Faculty:* 24 full-time (9 women), 5 part-time/adjunct (3 women). *Students:* 26 full-time (15 women), 40 part-time (23 women); includes 20 minority (15 Black or African American, non-Hispanic/Latino; 1 Asian, non-Hispanic/Latino; 3 Hispanic/Latino; 1 Two or more races, non-Hispanic/Latino). 87 applicants, 61% accepted. In 2013, 31 master's awarded. *Degree requirements:* For master's, comprehensive exam, thesis optional. *Entrance requirements:* For master's, GRE. Additional exam requirements/recommendations for international students: Required—TOEFL (minimum score 525 paper-based; 71 iBT) or IELTS (minimum score 6). *Application deadline:* For fall admission, 6/1 for domestic and international students. Applications are processed on a rolling basis. Application fee: $25 ($30 for international students). *Financial support:* In 2013–14, 14 students received support. Tuition waivers available. Support available to part-time students. Financial award application deadline: 5/1. *Faculty research:* Kinesiometrics, leisure behavior, health, lifestyles. *Unit head:* Dr. Harold D. Whiteside, Interim Dean, 615-898-2900, Fax: 615-494-7704, E-mail: harold.whiteside@mtsu.edu. *Application contact:* Dr. Michael D. Allen, Vice Provost for Research and Dean, 615-898-2840, Fax: 615-904-8020, E-mail: michael.allen@mtsu.edu.

Naropa University, Graduate Programs, Program in Transpersonal Counseling Psychology, Concentration in Wilderness Therapy, Boulder, CO 80302-6697. Offers MA. *Faculty:* 5 full-time (3 women), 4 part-time/adjunct (3 women). *Students:* 24 full-time (14 women), 10 part-time (8 women); includes 2 minority (both Hispanic/Latino). Average age 29. 29 applicants, 55% accepted, 13 enrolled. In 2013, 16 master's awarded. *Degree requirements:* For master's, internship, counseling practicum. *Entrance requirements:* For master's, in-person interview, outdoor experience, course work in psychology, resume, letter of interest, 2 letters of recommendation, transcripts, confidential medical record form, 10-day wilderness trip. Additional exam requirements/recommendations for international students: Required—TOEFL (minimum score 600 paper-based; 80 iBT). *Application deadline:* For fall admission, 1/13 priority date for domestic students, 1/15 priority date for international students. Applications are processed on a rolling basis. Application fee: $60. Electronic applications accepted. *Expenses:* Tuition: Full-time $16,848; part-time $936 per credit. *Required fees:* $335 per semester. *Financial support:* In 2013–14, 13 students received support, including 3 research assistantships with partial tuition reimbursements available (averaging $6,417 per year); career-related internships or fieldwork, Federal Work-Study, scholarships/grants, tuition waivers (partial), and unspecified assistantships also available. Support available to part-time students. Financial award application deadline: 3/1; financial award applicants required to submit FAFSA. *Unit head:* Dr. MacAndrew Jack, Director, Graduate School of Psychology, 303-245-4752, E-mail: mjack@naropa.edu. *Application contact:* Office of Admissions, 303-546-3572, Fax: 303-546-3583, E-mail: admissions@naropa.edu.
Website: http://www.naropa.edu/academics/gsp/grad/transpersonal-counseling-psychology-ma/wilderness-therapy/index.php.

New England College, Program in Sports and Recreation Management: Coaching, Henniker, NH 03242-3293. Offers MS. *Entrance requirements:* For master's, resume, 2 letters of reference.

North Carolina Central University, College of Behavioral and Social Sciences, Department of Physical Education and Recreation, Durham, NC 27707-3129. Offers athletic administration (MS); physical education (MS); recreation administration (MS); therapeutic recreation (MS). Part-time and evening/weekend programs available. *Degree requirements:* For master's, one foreign language, comprehensive exam, thesis. *Entrance requirements:* For master's, GRE, minimum GPA of 3.0 in major, 2.5 overall. Additional exam requirements/recommendations for international students: Required—TOEFL. *Faculty research:* Physical activity patterns of children with disabilities, physical fitness test of North Carolina school children, exercise physiology, motor learning/development.

North Carolina State University, Graduate School, College of Natural Resources, Department of Parks, Recreation and Tourism Management, Raleigh, NC 27695. Offers natural resource management (MPRTM, MS); park and recreation management (MPRTM, MS); parks, recreation and tourism management (PhD); recreational sport management (MPRTM, MS); spatial information science (MPRTM, MS); tourism policy and development (MPRTM, MS). *Degree requirements:* For master's, thesis (for some programs); for doctorate, thesis/dissertation. *Entrance requirements:* For master's and doctorate, GRE General Test. Additional exam requirements/recommendations for international students: Required—TOEFL. Electronic applications accepted. *Faculty research:* Tourism policy and development, spatial information systems, natural resource management, recreational sports management, park and recreation management.

Northwest Missouri State University, Graduate School, College of Education and Human Services, Department of Health and Human Services, Maryville, MO 64468-6001. Offers applied health science (MS); health and physical education (MS Ed); recreation (MS). *Accreditation:* NCATE. Part-time programs available. *Degree requirements:* For master's, comprehensive exam. *Entrance requirements:* For master's, GRE General Test, minimum undergraduate GPA of 2.75, teaching certificate, writing sample. Additional exam requirements/recommendations for international students: Required—TOEFL (minimum score 550 paper-based).

Ohio University, Graduate College, Gladys W. and David H. Patton College of Education and Human Services, Department of Recreation and Sport Pedagogy, Program in Recreation Studies, Athens, OH 45701-2979. Offers MS. Part-time programs available. *Degree requirements:* For master's, thesis or alternative. *Entrance requirements:* For master's, GRE. Additional exam requirements/recommendations for international students: Required—TOEFL (minimum score 550 paper-based; 80 iBT) or IELTS (minimum score 6.5). Electronic applications accepted. *Faculty research:* Recreation, leisure studies, physical education, national parks.

Penn State University Park, Graduate School, College of Health and Human Development, Department of Recreation, Park and Tourism Management, State College, PA 16802. Offers M Ed, MS, PhD. *Unit head:* Dr. Ann C. Crouter, Dean, 814-865-1420, Fax: 814-865-3282, E-mail: ac1@psu.edu. *Application contact:* Cynthia E. Nicosia, Director, Graduate Enrollment Services, 814-865-1834, Fax: 814-863-4627, E-mail: cey1@psu.edu.
Website: http://www.hhdev.psu.edu/rptm.

Purdue University, Graduate School, College of Health and Human Sciences, Department of Health and Kinesiology, West Lafayette, IN 47907. Offers athletic training education administration (MS, PhD); biomechanics (MS, PhD); exercise physiology (MS, PhD); health education (MS, PhD); history/philosophy of sport (MS, PhD); motor control and development (MS, PhD); physical education pedagogy (PhD); physical education teacher education (MS); recreation and sport management (MS, PhD); sport and exercise psychology (MS, PhD). Part-time programs available. *Faculty:* 16 full-time (8 women), 20 part-time/adjunct (3 women). *Students:* 43 full-time (29 women), 21 part-time (11 women); includes 6 minority (2 Black or African American, non-Hispanic/Latino; 1 American Indian or Alaska Native, non-Hispanic/Latino; 1 Asian, non-Hispanic/Latino; 2 Two or more races, non-Hispanic/Latino), 12 international. Average age 28. 103 applicants, 32% accepted, 16 enrolled. In 2013, 15 master's, 8 doctorates awarded. *Degree requirements:* For master's, thesis optional; for doctorate, comprehensive exam, thesis/dissertation, qualifying examination, preliminary examination. *Entrance requirements:* For master's, GRE General Test (minimum score 1000 combined verbal and quantitative), minimum undergraduate GPA of 3.0 or equivalent; for doctorate, GRE General Test (minimum score 1100 combined verbal and quantitative), minimum undergraduate GPA of 3.0 or equivalent; master's degree with minimum GPA of 3.25 (recommended). Additional exam requirements/recommendations for international students: Required—TOEFL (minimum score 77 iBT); Recommended—TWE. *Application deadline:* For fall admission, 4/30 for domestic and international students; for spring admission, 10/15 for domestic and international students. Applications are processed on a rolling basis. Application fee: $60 ($75 for international students). Electronic applications accepted. *Financial support:* Fellowships with partial tuition reimbursements, research assistantships with partial tuition reimbursements, teaching assistantships with partial tuition reimbursements, and Federal Work-Study available. Support available to part-time students. Financial award applicants required to submit FAFSA. *Faculty research:* Wellness, motivation, teaching effectiveness, learning and development. *Unit head:* Dr. Timothy P. Gavin, Head of the Graduate Program, 765-494-3178, Fax: 765-494-1239, E-mail: gavin1@purdue.edu. *Application contact:* Lisa Duncan, Graduate Contact, 765-494-3162, E-mail: llduncan@purdue.edu.
Website: http://www.purdue.edu/hhs/hk/.

San Francisco State University, Division of Graduate Studies, College of Health and Social Sciences, Department of Recreation, Parks, and Tourism, San Francisco, CA 94132-1722. Offers MS. Part-time programs available. *Application deadline:* Applications are processed on a rolling basis. *Financial support:* Career-related internships or fieldwork available. *Unit head:* Dr. Patrick Tierney, Chair, 415-338-2030, E-mail: ptierney@sfsu.edu. *Application contact:* Prof. Jackson Wilson, Graduate Coordinator, 415-338-1487, E-mail: wilsonj@sfsu.edu.
Website: http://recdept.sfsu.edu/.

San Jose State University, Graduate Studies and Research, College of Applied Sciences and Arts, Department of Hospitality, Recreation and Tourism Management, San Jose, CA 95192-0001. Offers recreation (MS). Electronic applications accepted.

Slippery Rock University of Pennsylvania, Graduate Studies (Recruitment), College of Health, Environment, and Science, Department of Parks, Recreation, and Environmental Education, Slippery Rock, PA 16057-1383. Offers environmental education (M Ed); parks and resource management (MS). Part-time and evening/weekend programs available. Postbaccalaureate distance learning degree programs offered (no on-campus study). *Faculty:* 2 full-time (0 women), 3 part-time/adjunct (2 women). *Students:* 19 full-time (11 women), 79 part-time (44 women); includes 5 minority (1 Black or African American, non-Hispanic/Latino; 2 Hispanic/Latino; 2 Two or more races, non-Hispanic/Latino), 2 international. Average age 31. 70 applicants, 90% accepted, 38 enrolled. In 2013, 45 master's awarded. *Degree requirements:* For master's, comprehensive exam (for some programs), thesis (for some programs). *Entrance requirements:* For master's, GRE General Test, MAT, minimum GPA of 2.75. Additional exam requirements/recommendations for international students: Required—TOEFL (minimum score 550 paper-based; 80 iBT). *Application deadline:* For fall admission, 3/1 priority date for domestic students, 5/1 priority date for international students; for spring admission, 10/1 priority date for domestic students, 9/1 priority date for international students. Applications are processed on a rolling basis. Application fee: $25 ($30 for international students). Electronic applications accepted. *Expenses:* Tuition, state resident: full-time $7956; part-time $442 per credit. Tuition, nonresident: full-time $11,934; part-time $663 per credit. *Required fees:* $2896; $148 per credit. Tuition and fees vary according to degree level and program. *Financial support:* Career-related internships or fieldwork, Federal Work-Study, institutionally sponsored loans, scholarships/grants, and tuition waivers (partial) available. Support available to part-time students. Financial award application deadline: 5/1; financial award applicants required to submit FAFSA. *Unit head:* Dr. Daniel Dziubek, Graduate Coordinator, 724-738-2958, Fax: 724-738-2938, E-mail: daniel.dziubek@sru.edu. *Application contact:* Brandi Weber-Mortimer, Director of Graduate Admissions, 724-738-2051, Fax: 724-738-2146, E-mail: graduate.admissions@sru.edu.

South Dakota State University, Graduate School, College of Education and Human Sciences, Department of Health, Physical Education and Recreation, Brookings, SD 57007. Offers MS. Part-time programs available. *Degree requirements:* For master's, thesis, oral and written exams. *Entrance requirements:* Additional exam requirements/recommendations for international students: Required—TOEFL (minimum score 550 paper-based; 71 iBT). *Faculty research:* Effective teaching behaviors in physical education, sports nutrition, muscle/bone interaction, hormonal response to exercise.

Southern Adventist University, School of Business and Management, Collegedale, TN 37315-0370. Offers accounting (MBA); church administration (MSA); church and nonprofit leadership (MBA); financial management (MFM); healthcare administration (MBA); management (MBA); marketing management (MBA); outdoor education (MSA). Part-time and evening/weekend programs available. Postbaccalaureate distance learning degree programs offered (no on-campus study). *Entrance requirements:* For master's, GMAT. Additional exam requirements/recommendations for international students: Required—TOEFL (minimum score 600 paper-based; 100 iBT). Electronic applications accepted.

Southern Connecticut State University, School of Graduate Studies, School of Health and Human Services, Department of Recreation and Leisure Studies, New Haven, CT 06515-1355. Offers MS. Part-time and evening/weekend programs available. *Degree requirements:* For master's, thesis or alternative. *Entrance requirements:* For master's, interview, minimum undergraduate QPA of 3.0 in graduate major field or 2.5 overall. Electronic applications accepted.

Southern Illinois University Carbondale, Graduate School, College of Education and Human Services, Department of Health Education and Recreation, Program in Recreation, Carbondale, IL 62901-4701. Offers MS Ed. Part-time programs available. *Faculty:* 5 full-time (2 women). *Students:* 17 full-time (7 women), 17 part-time (6 women); includes 7 minority (4 Black or African American, non-Hispanic/Latino; 1 American Indian or Alaska Native, non-Hispanic/Latino; 1 Asian, non-Hispanic/Latino; 1 Hispanic/Latino), 5 international. Average age 26. 16 applicants, 81% accepted, 12 enrolled. In 2013, 14 master's awarded. *Degree requirements:* For master's, thesis. *Entrance requirements:* For master's, minimum GPA of 2.7. Additional exam requirements/recommendations for international students: Required—TOEFL. *Application deadline:* Applications are processed on a rolling basis. Application fee: $50. *Financial support:* In 2013–14, 15 students received support, including 4 research assistantships with full tuition reimbursements available, 4 teaching assistantships with full tuition reimbursements available; fellowships with full tuition reimbursements available, career-related internships or fieldwork, Federal Work-Study, institutionally sponsored loans, and tuition waivers (full) also available. Support available to part-time students. Financial award application deadline: 2/1. *Faculty research:* Leisure across the life span, outdoor recreation, recreation therapy, leisure service administration. *Unit head:* Dr. Stephen L. Brown, Chair, 618-453-2777, Fax: 618-453-1829, E-mail: slbrown@siu.edu.
Website: http://ehs.siu.edu/her/graduate/recreation/index.php.

Recreation and Park Management

Southern University and Agricultural and Mechanical College, Graduate School, College of Education, Program in Leisure and Recreation Studies, Baton Rouge, LA 70813. Offers therapeutic recreation (MS). *Degree requirements:* For master's, comprehensive exam, thesis optional. *Entrance requirements:* For master's, GMAT or GRE General Test. Additional exam requirements/recommendations for international students: Required—TOEFL (minimum score 525 paper-based).

Southwestern Oklahoma State University, College of Professional and Graduate Studies, School of Behavioral Sciences and Education, Specialization in Parks and Recreation Management, Weatherford, OK 73096-3098. Offers M Ed.

Springfield College, Graduate Programs, Programs in Sport Management and Recreation, Springfield, MA 01109-3797. Offers recreational management (M Ed, MS); sport management (M Ed, MS); therapeutic recreational management (M Ed, MS). Part-time programs available. *Faculty:* 8 full-time, 2 part-time/adjunct. *Students:* 36 full-time. 43 applicants, 77% accepted, 21 enrolled. In 2013, 14 master's awarded. *Degree requirements:* For master's, comprehensive exam, research project. *Entrance requirements:* Additional exam requirements/recommendations for international students: Required—TOEFL (minimum score 550 paper-based); Recommended—IELTS (minimum score 6). *Application deadline:* For fall admission, 1/15 for domestic and international students; for winter admission, 11/1 for international students; for spring admission, 11/1 for domestic and international students. Applications are processed on a rolling basis. Application fee: $50. Electronic applications accepted. *Expenses: Tuition:* Full-time $13,620; part-time $908 per credit. *Financial support:* Fellowships with partial tuition reimbursements, teaching assistantships with partial tuition reimbursements, career-related internships or fieldwork, Federal Work-Study, institutionally sponsored loans, and unspecified assistantships available. Financial award application deadline: 3/1; financial award applicants required to submit FAFSA. *Unit head:* Dr. Kevin McAllister, Director, 413-748-3476, Fax: 413-748-3685, E-mail: kmcallister@springfieldcollege.edu. *Application contact:* Evelyn Cohen, Associate Director of Graduate Admissions, 413-748-3479, Fax: 413-748-3694, E-mail: ecohen@springfieldcollege.edu.

State University of New York College at Cortland, Graduate Studies, School of Professional Studies, Department of Recreation and Leisure Studies, Cortland, NY 13045. Offers MS, MS Ed. Part-time and evening/weekend programs available. *Degree requirements:* For master's, comprehensive exam, thesis (for some programs). *Entrance requirements:* Additional exam requirements/recommendations for international students: Required—TOEFL. *Expenses:* Tuition, state resident: full-time $9870; part-time $411 per credit hour. Tuition, nonresident: full-time $18,350; part-time $765 per credit hour. *Required fees:* $1458; $65 per credit hour.

Temple University, College of Health Professions and Social Work, Department of Rehabilitation Sciences, Program in Therapeutic Recreation, Philadelphia, PA 19122. Offers recreation therapy (MS). Part-time programs available. *Faculty:* 17 full-time (14 women). *Students:* 13 full-time (12 women), 4 part-time (all women); includes 1 minority (Hispanic/Latino), 1 international. 23 applicants, 65% accepted, 9 enrolled. In 2013, 3 master's awarded. *Degree requirements:* For master's, comprehensive exam, thesis optional, practicum project. *Entrance requirements:* For master's, GRE or MAT, 2 letters of reference, statement of goals, minimum GPA of 3.0, resume. Additional exam requirements/recommendations for international students: Required—TOEFL (minimum score 550 paper-based; 79 iBT). *Application deadline:* For fall admission, 5/1 for domestic students, 4/1 for international students; for spring admission, 10/15 for domestic students, 8/1 for international students. Applications are processed on a rolling basis. Application fee: $60. Electronic applications accepted. *Financial support:* Career-related internships or fieldwork and Federal Work-Study available. Financial award application deadline: 1/15. *Faculty research:* Participation, community inclusion, disability issues, leisure/recreation, occupation, quality of life, adaptive equipment and technology. *Unit head:* Dr. Mark Salzer, 215-204-7879, E-mail: mark.salzer@temple.edu. *Application contact:* Jacquee Lukawski, 215-707-4875, E-mail: jacquee.lukawski@temple.edu.
Website: http://chpsw.temple.edu/rs/home.

Temple University, School of Tourism and Hospitality Management, Program in Sport Business, Philadelphia, PA 19122-6096. Offers athletics administration (MS); recreation and event management (MS); sport analytics (MS); sport marketing and promotions (MS). Part-time programs available. *Faculty:* 12 full-time (2 women), 3 part-time/adjunct (1 woman). *Students:* 19 full-time (10 women), 7 part-time (4 women); includes 2 minority (both Black or African American, non-Hispanic/Latino). 54 applicants, 54% accepted, 20 enrolled. *Degree requirements:* For master's, thesis optional, internship or project. *Entrance requirements:* For master's, GRE General Test, GMAT, or MAT, bachelor's degree or equivalent with minimum GPA of 3.0, 500-word essay, 2 letters of recommendation, resume. Additional exam requirements/recommendations for international students: Required—TOEFL (minimum score 550 paper-based; 79 iBT), IELTS (minimum score 6.5). *Application deadline:* For fall admission, 3/1 priority date for domestic students, 1/15 priority date for international students; for spring admission, 8/15 priority date for domestic students, 6/30 priority date for international students. Applications are processed on a rolling basis. Application fee: $60. Electronic applications accepted. *Expenses:* Contact institution. *Financial support:* In 2013–14, 1 teaching assistantship with full tuition reimbursement (averaging $18,000 per year) was awarded. Financial award application deadline: 3/1; financial award applicants required to submit FAFSA. *Faculty research:* Industrial/organization management, corporate social responsibility, diversity/inclusion, sport/recreation for persons with disabilities, youth sport development, sport pricing, sport consumer behavior, marketing/advertising assessment, facility design and operation, participant sport behavior, mass participant sport events, brand evaluation, sport marketing communication, sport economics, recreation programming and assessment, non-profit development and management. *Unit head:* Dr. Joris Drayer, Associate Professor/Director of Programs in Sport and Recreation, 215-204-8701, Fax: 215-204-8705, E-mail: joris.drayer@temple.edu. *Application contact:* Michael J. Usino, Senior Associate Director of Recruitment, 215-204-3103, Fax: 215-204-8705, E-mail: musino@temple.edu.
Website: http://sthm.temple.edu/grad/explore-ma-sports.html.

Texas A&M University, College of Agriculture and Life Sciences, Department of Recreation, Park and Tourism Sciences, College Station, TX 77843. Offers recreation and resources development (MRRD); recreation, park, and tourism sciences (MS, PhD). *Faculty:* 19. *Students:* 61 full-time (34 women), 19 part-time (10 women); includes 10 minority (6 Black or African American, non-Hispanic/Latino; 3 Asian, non-Hispanic/Latino; 1 Hispanic/Latino), 29 international. Average age 33. 23 applicants, 96% accepted, 21 enrolled. In 2013, 14 master's, 9 doctorates awarded. *Degree requirements:* For master's, thesis (for some programs), internship and professional paper (M Agr); for doctorate, thesis/dissertation. *Entrance requirements:* For master's and doctorate, GRE General Test. Additional exam requirements/recommendations for international students: Required—TOEFL. *Application deadline:* For fall admission, 4/15 priority date for domestic students; for spring admission, 10/15 priority date for domestic students. Applications are processed on a rolling basis. Application fee: $50 ($75 for international students). Electronic applications accepted. *Expenses:* Tuition, state resident: full-time $4078; part-time $226.55 per credit hour. Tuition, nonresident: full-time $10,450; part-time $580.55 per credit hour. *Required fees:* $2328; $278.50 per credit hour. $642.45 per semester. *Financial support:* Fellowships, research assistantships, teaching assistantships, career-related internships or fieldwork, institutionally sponsored loans, and scholarships/grants available. Financial award application deadline: 4/15; financial award applicants required to submit FAFSA. *Faculty research:* Administration and tourism, outdoor recreation, commercial recreation, environmental law, system planning. *Unit head:* Dr. Gary Ellis, Department Head, 979-845-7324, E-mail: gellis@ag.tamu.edu. *Application contact:* Dr. James Petrick, Associate Department Head, 979-854-8806, E-mail: jpetrick@tamu.edu.
Website: http://rpts.tamu.edu/.

Texas State University, Graduate School, College of Education, Department of Health and Human Performance, Program in Recreation and Leisure Services, San Marcos, TX 78666. Offers MSRLS. *Faculty:* 4 full-time (3 women), 1 (woman) part-time/adjunct. *Students:* 45 full-time (31 women), 24 part-time (8 women); includes 29 minority (10 Black or African American, non-Hispanic/Latino; 1 Asian, non-Hispanic/Latino; 16 Hispanic/Latino; 2 Two or more races, non-Hispanic/Latino), 2 international. Average age 27. 43 applicants, 86% accepted, 27 enrolled. In 2013, 24 master's awarded. *Degree requirements:* For master's, comprehensive exam, thesis optional. *Entrance requirements:* For master's, GRE General Test, minimum GPA of 2.75 in last 60 hours of course work. Additional exam requirements/recommendations for international students: Required—TOEFL (minimum score 550 paper-based; 78 iBT). *Application deadline:* For fall admission, 6/15 priority date for domestic students, 6/1 for international students; for spring admission, 10/15 priority date for domestic students, 10/1 for international students. Applications are processed on a rolling basis. Application fee: $40 ($90 for international students). Electronic applications accepted. *Expenses:* Tuition, state resident: full-time $6663; part-time $278 per credit hour. Tuition, nonresident: full-time $15,159; part-time $632 per credit hour. *Required fees:* $1872; $54 per credit hour. $306 per term. Tuition and fees vary according to course load. *Financial support:* In 2013–14, 33 students received support, including 10 research assistantships (averaging $11,983 per year), 5 teaching assistantships (averaging $12,263 per year). Financial award application deadline: 4/1; financial award applicants required to submit FAFSA. *Unit head:* Dr. Janet Hodges, Graduate Advisor, 512-245-7482, Fax: 512-245-8678, E-mail: jh223@txstate.edu. *Application contact:* Dr. Andrea Golato, Dean of the Graduate College, 512-245-2581, Fax: 512-245-8365, E-mail: gradcollege@txstate.edu.
Website: http://www.hhp.txstate.edu/Degree-Plans/Graduate.html.

Universidad Metropolitana, School of Education, Program in Managing Recreation and Sports Services, San Juan, PR 00928-1150. Offers M Ed. Part-time programs available. *Degree requirements:* For master's, thesis or alternative. *Entrance requirements:* For master's, EXADEP, interview. Electronic applications accepted.

University of Alberta, Faculty of Graduate Studies and Research, Department of Physical Education and Recreation, Edmonton, AB T6G 2E1, Canada. Offers physical education (M Sc); recreation and physical education (MA, PhD). Part-time programs available. Terminal master's awarded for partial completion of doctoral program. *Degree requirements:* For master's, thesis (for some programs); for doctorate, thesis/dissertation. *Entrance requirements:* For master's, bachelor's degree in related field; for doctorate, master's degree in related field with thesis. Additional exam requirements/recommendations for international students: Required—TOEFL. *Faculty research:* Motivation and adherence to physical ability, performance enhancement, adapted physical activity, exercise physiology, sport administration, tourism.

University of Arkansas, Graduate School, College of Education and Health Professions, Department of Health, Human Performance and Recreation, Program in Recreation and Sports Management, Fayetteville, AR 72701-1201. Offers M Ed, Ed D. *Degree requirements:* For master's, thesis optional; for doctorate, thesis/dissertation. *Entrance requirements:* For doctorate, GRE General Test. Electronic applications accepted.

University of Florida, Graduate School, College of Health and Human Performance, Department of Tourism, Recreation and Sport Management, Gainesville, FL 32611. Offers health and human performance (PhD), including recreation, parks and tourism (MS, PhD), sport management; recreation, parks and tourism (MS), including natural resource recreation, recreation, parks and tourism (MS, PhD), therapeutic recreation, tourism; sport management (MS); JD/MS; MSM/MS. *Faculty:* 7 full-time (5 women). *Students:* 64 full-time (27 women), 13 part-time (4 women); includes 11 minority (7 Black or African American, non-Hispanic/Latino; 1 Asian, non-Hispanic/Latino; 3 Hispanic/Latino), 27 international. Average age 27. 15 applicants, 40% accepted, 1 enrolled. In 2013, 51 master's, 4 doctorates awarded. *Degree requirements:* For master's, comprehensive exam (for some programs), thesis (for some programs); for doctorate, comprehensive exam, thesis/dissertation. *Entrance requirements:* For master's and doctorate, GRE General Test, minimum GPA of 3.0. Additional exam requirements/recommendations for international students: Required—TOEFL (minimum score 550 paper-based; 80 iBT), IELTS (minimum score 6). *Application deadline:* For fall admission, 3/1 for domestic students, 12/1 for international students; for spring admission, 10/15 for domestic students, 5/1 for international students. Applications are processed on a rolling basis. Application fee: $30. Electronic applications accepted. *Expenses:* Tuition, state resident: full-time $12,640. Tuition, nonresident: full-time $30,000. *Financial support:* In 2013–14, 27 students received support, including 10 research assistantships (averaging $15,850 per year), 20 teaching assistantships (averaging $11,840 per year); career-related internships or fieldwork, Federal Work-Study, and unspecified assistantships also available. Financial award application deadline: 2/1; financial award applicants required to submit FAFSA. *Faculty research:* Hospitality, natural resource management, sport management, tourism. *Unit head:* Michael Sagas, PhD, Department Chair and Professor, 352-294-1640, Fax: 352-392-7588, E-mail: msagas@hhp.ufl.edu. *Application contact:* Stephen M. Holland, PhD, Professor/Graduate Coordinator, 352-294-1669, Fax: 352-392-7588, E-mail: sholland@hhp.ufl.edu.
Website: http://www.hhp.ufl.edu/trsm/.

University of Idaho, College of Graduate Studies, College of Education, Department of Movement Sciences, Moscow, ID 83844-2401. Offers athletic training (MSAT, DAT); movement and leisure sciences (MS); physical education (M Ed). *Faculty:* 14 full-time, 1 part-time/adjunct. *Students:* 63 full-time, 14 part-time. Average age 31. In 2013, 17 master's, 2 doctorates awarded. *Degree requirements:* For doctorate, thesis/dissertation. *Entrance requirements:* For master's, minimum GPA of 2.8; for doctorate, minimum undergraduate GPA of 2.8, graduate 3.0. *Application deadline:* For fall admission, 8/1 for domestic students; for spring admission, 12/15 for domestic students. Applications are processed on a rolling basis. Application fee: $60. Electronic applications accepted. *Expenses:* Tuition, state resident: full-time $5596; part-time $363 per credit hour. Tuition, nonresident: full-time $18,672; part-time $1089 per credit hour. *Financial support:* Research assistantships and teaching assistantships available. Financial award applicants required to submit FAFSA. *Unit head:* Dr. Philip W. Scruggs, Chair, 208-885-7921, E-mail: movementsciences@uidaho.edu. *Application contact:* Stephanie Thomas, Graduate Recruitment Coordinator, 208-885-4001, Fax: 208-885-4406, E-mail: gadms@uidaho.edu.
Website: http://www.uidaho.edu/ed/movementsciences.

The University of Iowa, Graduate College, College of Liberal Arts and Sciences, Department of Health and Human Physiology, Iowa City, IA 52242-1316. Offers athletic training (MS); clinical exercise physiology (MS); health and human physiology (PhD); leisure studies (MA, PhD), including recreational sport management (PhD), therapeutic recreation (MA). *Degree requirements:* For master's, thesis optional, exam; for doctorate, comprehensive exam, thesis/dissertation. *Entrance requirements:* For master's and doctorate, GRE General Test, minimum GPA of 3.0. Additional exam requirements/recommendations for international students: Required—TOEFL (minimum score 600 paper-based; 100 iBT). Electronic applications accepted.

University of Manitoba, Faculty of Graduate Studies, Faculty of Kinesiology and Recreation Management, Winnipeg, MB R3T 2N2, Canada. Offers kinesiology and recreation (M Sc, MA).

University of Minnesota, Twin Cities Campus, Graduate School, College of Education and Human Development, School of Kinesiology, Division of Recreation, Park, and Leisure Studies, Minneapolis, MN 55455-0213. Offers M Ed, MA, PhD. Part-time programs available. *Students:* 1 part-time (0 women). Average age 37. In 2013, 2 master's awarded. Terminal master's awarded for partial completion of doctoral program. *Degree requirements:* For master's, thesis (for some programs), final oral exam; for doctorate, thesis/dissertation, preliminary written/oral exam, final oral exam. *Entrance requirements:* For master's, GRE or MAT, minimum GPA of 3.0; for doctorate, GRE or MAT, minimum GPA of 3.0, writing sample. *Application deadline:* For fall admission, 7/15 for domestic students; for spring admission, 12/15 for domestic students. Applications are processed on a rolling basis. Application fee: $75 ($95 for international students). *Financial support:* Fellowships, research assistantships, teaching assistantships, career-related internships or fieldwork, Federal Work-Study, institutionally sponsored loans, and tuition waivers (full and partial) available. Support available to part-time students. *Unit head:* Dr. Li Li Ji, Director, 612-642-9809, Fax: 612-626-7700, E-mail: llji@umn.edu. *Application contact:* Dr. Jennifer Engler, Assistant Dean, 612-626-2887, Fax: 612-626-7496, E-mail: engle009@umn.edu.
Website: http://www.cehd.umn.edu/kin/recreation.

University of Mississippi, Graduate School, School of Applied Sciences, Department of Health, Exercise Science, and Recreation Management, Oxford, MS 38677. Offers exercise science (MS); health and kinesiology (PhD); health promotion (MS); park and recreation management (MA). *Faculty:* 9 full-time (3 women), 3 part-time/adjunct (1 woman). *Students:* 45 full-time (23 women), 14 part-time (9 women); includes 11 minority (8 Black or African American, non-Hispanic/Latino; 1 Asian, non-Hispanic/Latino; 2 Hispanic/Latino), 5 international. In 2013, 19 master's, 1 doctorate awarded. *Degree requirements:* For master's, thesis (for some programs); for doctorate, thesis/dissertation. *Entrance requirements:* For master's, GRE General Test, minimum GPA of 3.0; for doctorate, GRE General Test. Additional exam requirements/recommendations for international students: Required—TOEFL. *Application deadline:* For fall admission, 4/1 for domestic students; for spring admission, 10/1 for domestic students. Applications are processed on a rolling basis. *Financial support:* Scholarships/grants available. Financial award application deadline: 3/1; financial award applicants required to submit FAFSA. *Unit head:* Dr. Scott G. Owens, Chair, 662-915-5844, Fax: 662-915-5525, E-mail: dbramlett@olemiss.edu. *Application contact:* Dr. Christy M. Wyandt, Associate Dean, 662-915-7474, Fax: 662-915-7577, E-mail: cwyandt@olemiss.edu.

University of Missouri, Graduate School, School of Natural Resources, Department of Parks, Recreation and Tourism, Columbia, MO 65211. Offers MS. *Faculty:* 6 full-time (3 women), 1 part-time/adjunct (0 women). *Students:* 12 full-time (6 women), 1 part-time (0 women); includes 1 minority (Hispanic/Latino), 2 international. Average age 29. 12 applicants, 58% accepted, 6 enrolled. In 2013, 3 master's awarded. *Entrance requirements:* For master's, GRE General Test, minimum GPA of 3.0. Additional exam requirements/recommendations for international students: Required—TOEFL (minimum score 500 paper-based; 61 iBT). *Application deadline:* Applications are processed on a rolling basis. Application fee: $55 ($75 for international students). Electronic applications accepted. *Financial support:* Research assistantships, teaching assistantships, institutionally sponsored loans, and scholarships/grants available. *Faculty research:* Rural and cultural tourism, agriculture entrepreneurship, marketing research in commercial recreation, therapeutic recreation, social aspects of natural resource management, education and outreach, human dimensions of natural resource management with an emphasis in the social psychological aspects of outdoor recreation. *Unit head:* Dr. David Vaught, Department Chair, 573-882-9517, E-mail: vaughtdr@missouri.edu. *Application contact:* Dr. Mark Morgan, Director of Graduate Studies, 573-882-9525, E-mail: morganm@missouri.edu.
Website: http://www.snr.missouri.edu/prt/academics/graduate-program.php.

The University of Montana, Graduate School, College of Forestry and Conservation, Missoula, MT 59812-0002. Offers ecosystem management (MEM, MS); fish and wildlife biology (PhD); forestry (MS, PhD); recreation management (MS); resource conservation (MS); wildlife biology (MS). *Degree requirements:* For doctorate, thesis/dissertation. *Entrance requirements:* For master's and doctorate, GRE General Test. Additional exam requirements/recommendations for international students: Required—TOEFL (minimum score 575 paper-based).

University of Nebraska at Omaha, Graduate Studies, College of Education, School of Health, Physical Education, and Recreation, Omaha, NE 68182. Offers athletic training (MA); exercise science (PhD); health, physical education, and recreation (MA, MS). Part-time and evening/weekend programs available. *Faculty:* 15 full-time (7 women). *Students:* 54 full-time (24 women), 32 part-time (9 women); includes 8 minority (2 Asian, non-Hispanic/Latino; 3 Hispanic/Latino; 3 Two or more races, non-Hispanic/Latino), 4 international. Average age 28. 79 applicants, 51% accepted, 22 enrolled. In 2013, 27 master's awarded. *Degree requirements:* For master's, comprehensive exam, thesis (for some programs). *Entrance requirements:* For master's, GRE; entrance exam, minimum GPA of 3.0, official transcripts, statement of purpose, 2 letters of recommendation; for doctorate, GRE, minimum GPA of 3.2, official transcripts, statement of purpose, 3 letters of recommendation, resume, writing sample. Additional exam requirements/recommendations for international students: Required—TOEFL, IELTS, PTE. *Application deadline:* For fall admission, 7/1 priority date for domestic students; for spring admission, 11/1 priority date for domestic students; for summer admission, 2/1 for domestic students. Applications are processed on a rolling basis. Application fee: $45. Electronic applications accepted. *Financial support:* In 2013–14, 19 students received support, including 12 research assistantships with tuition reimbursements available, 7 teaching assistantships with tuition reimbursements available; fellowships, Federal Work-Study, institutionally sponsored loans, scholarships/grants, tuition waivers (full), and unspecified assistantships also available. Support available to part-time students. Financial award application deadline: 3/1; financial award applicants required to submit FAFSA. *Unit head:* Dr. Daniel Blanke, Director, 402-554-2670. *Application contact:* Dr. Kris Berg, Graduate Program Chair, 402-554-2670, E-mail: graduate@unomaha.edu.

University of New Brunswick Fredericton, School of Graduate Studies, Faculty of Kinesiology, Fredericton, NB E3B 5A3, Canada. Offers exercise and sport science (M Sc); sport and recreation management (MBA); sport and recreation studies (MA). Part-time programs available. *Faculty:* 14 full-time (6 women), 1 part-time/adjunct (0 women). *Students:* 27 full-time (13 women), 5 part-time (1 woman). In 2013, 9 master's awarded. *Degree requirements:* For master's, thesis (for some programs). *Entrance requirements:* For master's, GMAT (minimum score of 550 for sport and recreation management program), minimum GPA of 3.0, written statement of research goals and interests. Additional exam requirements/recommendations for international students: Required—TOEFL (minimum score 92 iBT), IELTS (minimum score 7). *Application deadline:* For winter admission, 1/31 for domestic students; for spring admission, 3/31 for domestic students. Applications are processed on a rolling basis. Application fee: $50 Canadian dollars. Electronic applications accepted. *Financial support:* In 2013–14, 31 research assistantships, 61 teaching assistantships were awarded; fellowships with tuition reimbursements, career-related internships or fieldwork, and scholarships/grants also available. *Unit head:* Dr. Usha Kuruganti, Acting Director of Graduate Studies, 506-447-3101, Fax: 506-453-3511, E-mail: ukurugan@unb.ca. *Application contact:* Leslie Harquail, Graduate Secretary, 506-453-4575, Fax: 506-453-3511, E-mail: harquail@unb.ca.
Website: http://go.unb.ca/gradprograms.

University of New Hampshire, Graduate School, School of Health and Human Services, Department of Recreation Management and Policy, Durham, NH 03824. Offers recreation administration (MS); therapeutic recreation (MS). Part-time programs available. *Faculty:* 5 full-time (4 women). *Students:* 6 full-time (2 women), 6 part-time (4 women); includes 2 minority (1 Asian, non-Hispanic/Latino; 1 Hispanic/Latino), 1 international. Average age 28. 17 applicants, 59% accepted, 7 enrolled. In 2013, 7 master's awarded. *Degree requirements:* For master's, thesis optional. *Entrance requirements:* For master's, GRE. Additional exam requirements/recommendations for international students: Required—TOEFL (minimum score 550 paper-based; 80 iBT); Recommended—TWE. *Application deadline:* For fall admission, 6/1 priority date for domestic students, 4/1 priority date for international students; for spring admission, 12/1 for domestic students. Applications are processed on a rolling basis. Application fee: $65. Electronic applications accepted. *Expenses:* Tuition, state resident: full-time $13,500; part-time $750 per credit hour. Tuition, nonresident: full-time $26,200; part-time $1100 per credit hour. *Required fees:* $1741; $435.25 per term. Tuition and fees vary according to course level, course load, campus/location and program. *Financial support:* In 2013–14, 5 students received support, including 5 teaching assistantships; fellowships and research assistantships also available. *Unit head:* Dr. Janet Sable, Chairperson, 603-862-3401. *Application contact:* Linda Noon, Administrative Assistant, 603-862-2391, E-mail: rmp.graduate@unh.edu.
Website: http://chhs.unh.edu/rmp/index.

The University of North Carolina at Greensboro, Graduate School, School of Health and Human Performance, Department of Recreation, Tourism, and Hospitality Management, Greensboro, NC 27412-5001. Offers parks and recreation management (MS). *Degree requirements:* For master's, thesis. *Entrance requirements:* For master's, GRE General Test. Additional exam requirements/recommendations for international students: Required—TOEFL. Electronic applications accepted.

University of North Texas, Robert B. Toulouse School of Graduate Studies, Denton, TN 76203-5017. Offers accounting (MS, PhD); applied anthropology (MA, MS); applied behavior analysis (Certificate); applied technology and performance improvement (M Ed, MS, PhD); art education (MA, PhD); art history (MA); art museum education (Certificate); arts leadership (Certificate); audiology (Au D); behavior analysis (MS); biochemistry and molecular biology (MS, PhD); biology (MA, MS, PhD); business (PhD); business computer information systems (PhD); chemistry (MS, PhD); clinical psychology (PhD); communication studies (MA, MS); computer engineering (MS); computer science (MS); computer science and engineering (PhD); counseling (M Ed, MS, PhD), including clinical mental health counseling (MS), college and university counseling (M Ed, MS), elementary school counseling (M Ed, MS), secondary school counseling (M Ed, MS); counseling psychology (PhD); creative writing (MA); criminal justice (MS); curriculum and instruction (M Ed, PhD), including curriculum studies (PhD), early childhood studies (PhD), language and literacy studies (PhD); decision sciences (MBA); design (MA, MFA), including fashion design (MFA), innovation studies, interior design (MFA); early childhood studies (MS); economics (MS); educational leadership (M Ed, Ed D, PhD); educational psychology (MS), including family studies, gifted and talented (MS, PhD), human development, learning and cognition, research, measurement and evaluation; educational research (PhD), including gifted and talented (MS, PhD), human development and family studies, psychological aspects of sports and exercise, research, measurement and statistics; electrical engineering (MS); emergency management (MPA); engineering systems (MS); English (MA, PhD); environmental science (MS, PhD); experimental psychology (PhD); finance (MBA, MS, PhD); financial management (MPA); French (MA); health psychology and behavioral medicine (PhD); health services management (MBA); higher education (M Ed, Ed D, PhD); history (MA, MS, PhD), including European history (PhD), military history (PhD), United States history (PhD); hospitality management (MS); human resources management (MPA); information science (MS, PhD); information technologies (MBA); information technology and decision sciences (MS); interdisciplinary studies (MA, MS); international sustainable tourism (MS); jazz studies (MM); journalism (MA, MJ, Graduate Certificate), including interactive and virtual digital communication (Graduate Certificate), narrative journalism (Graduate Certificate), public relations (Graduate Certificate); kinesiology (MS); learning technologies (MS, PhD); library science (MS); local government management (MPA); logistics and supply chain management (MBA, PhD); long-term care, senior housing, and aging services (MA, MS); management science (PhD); marketing (MBA, PhD); materials science and engineering (MS, PhD); mathematics (MA, PhD); merchandising (MS); music (MA, MM Ed, PhD), including ethnomusicology (MA), music education (MM Ed, PhD), music theory (MA, PhD), musicology (MA, PhD), performance (MA); nonprofit management (MPA); operations and supply chain management (MBA); performance (MM, DMA); philosophy (MA, PhD); physics (MS, PhD); political science (MA, MS, PhD); public administration and management (PhD), including emergency management, nonprofit management, public financial management, urban management; radio, television and film (MA, MFA); recreation, event and sport management (MS); rehabilitation counseling (MS, Certificate); sociology (MA, MS, PhD); Spanish (MA); special education (M Ed, PhD), including autism intervention (PhD), emotional/behavioral disorders (PhD), mild/moderate disabilities (PhD); speech-language pathology (MA, MS); strategic management (MBA); studio art (MFA); taxation (MS); teaching (M Ed); MBA/MS; MS/MPH; MSES/MBA. Part-time and evening/weekend programs available. Postbaccalaureate distance learning degree programs offered. *Faculty:* 661 full-time (213 women), 240 part-time/adjunct (144 women). *Students:* 3,106 full-time (1,620 women), 3,543 part-time (2,221 women); includes 1,740 minority (533 Black or African American, non-Hispanic/Latino; 15 American Indian or Alaska Native, non-Hispanic/Latino; 286 Asian, non-Hispanic/Latino; 746 Hispanic/Latino; 3 Native Hawaiian or other Pacific Islander, non-Hispanic/Latino; 157 Two or more races, non-Hispanic/Latino), 1,145 international. Average age 32. 6,289 applicants, 43% accepted, 1751 enrolled. In 2013, 1,778 master's, 239 doctorates, 10 other advanced degrees awarded. Terminal master's awarded for partial completion of doctoral program. *Degree requirements:* For master's, variable foreign language requirement, comprehensive exam (for some programs), thesis (for some programs); for doctorate, variable foreign language requirement, comprehensive exam (for some programs), thesis/dissertation; for other advanced degree, variable foreign language requirement, comprehensive exam (for some programs). *Entrance requirements:* For master's and doctorate, GRE, GMAT. Additional exam requirements/recommendations

for international students: Required—TOEFL (minimum score 550 paper-based; 79 iBT). *Application deadline:* For fall admission, 7/15 for domestic students, 3/15 for international students; for spring admission, 11/15 for domestic students, 9/15 for international students; for summer admission, 5/1 for domestic students. Applications are processed on a rolling basis. Application fee: $60. Electronic applications accepted. *Financial support:* Fellowships with partial tuition reimbursements, research assistantships with partial tuition reimbursements, teaching assistantships, career-related internships or fieldwork, Federal Work-Study, institutionally sponsored loans, scholarships/grants, health care benefits, and library assistantships available. Support available to part-time students. Financial award applicants required to submit FAFSA. *Unit head:* Mark Wardell, Dean, 940-565-2383, E-mail: mark.wardell@unt.edu. *Application contact:* Toulouse School of Graduate Studies, 940-565-2383, Fax: 940-565-2141, E-mail: gradsch@unt.edu.
Website: http://tsgs.unt.edu/.

University of Rhode Island, Graduate School, College of Human Science and Services, Department of Kinesiology, Kingston, RI 02881. Offers cultural studies of sport and physical culture (MS); exercise science (MS); physical education pedagogy (MS); psychosocial/behavioral aspects of physical activity (MS). *Accreditation:* NCATE. Part-time programs available. *Faculty:* 17 full-time (11 women). *Students:* 13 full-time (8 women), 5 part-time (2 women); includes 4 minority (1 Black or African American, non-Hispanic/Latino; 1 American Indian or Alaska Native, non-Hispanic/Latino; 2 Hispanic/Latino). In 2013, 12 master's awarded. *Degree requirements:* For master's, thesis optional. *Entrance requirements:* For master's, GRE, 2 letters of recommendation. Additional exam requirements/recommendations for international students: Required—TOEFL (minimum score 550 paper-based). *Application deadline:* For fall admission, 7/15 for domestic students, 2/1 for international students; for spring admission, 11/15 for domestic students, 7/15 for international students. Application fee: $65. Electronic applications accepted. *Expenses:* Tuition, state resident: full-time $11,532; part-time $641 per credit. Tuition, nonresident: full-time $23,606; part-time $1311 per credit. *Required fees:* $1388; $36 per credit. $35 per semester. One-time fee: $130. *Financial support:* In 2013–14, 5 teaching assistantships with full and partial tuition reimbursements (averaging $9,903 per year) were awarded. Financial award application deadline: 7/15; financial award applicants required to submit FAFSA. *Faculty research:* Strength training and older adults, interventions to promote a healthy lifestyle as well as analysis of the psychosocial outcomes of those interventions, effects of exercise and nutrition on skeletal muscle of aging healthy adults with CVD and other metabolic related diseases, physical activity and fitness of deaf children and youth. *Total annual research expenditures:* $51,804. *Unit head:* Dr. Deborah Riebe, Chair, 401-874-5444, Fax: 401-874-4215, E-mail: debriebe@uri.edu. *Application contact:* Dr. Matthew Delmonico, Graduate Program Director, 401-874-5440, E-mail: delmonico@uri.edu.
Website: http://www.uri.edu/hss/.

University of South Alabama, Graduate School, College of Education, Department of Health, Physical Education and Leisure Services, Mobile, AL 36688-0002. Offers exercise science (MS); health education (M Ed); physical education (M Ed); therapeutic recreation (MS). *Accreditation:* NCATE (one or more programs are accredited). Part-time programs available. *Faculty:* 4 full-time (1 woman), 2 part-time/adjunct (0 women). *Students:* 34 full-time (16 women), 5 part-time (1 woman); includes 12 minority (9 Black or African American, non-Hispanic/Latino; 3 Two or more races, non-Hispanic/Latino), 4 international. 36 applicants, 61% accepted, 18 enrolled. In 2013, 16 master's awarded. *Degree requirements:* For master's, comprehensive exam. *Entrance requirements:* For master's, GRE General Test or MAT. *Application deadline:* For fall admission, 7/15 priority date for domestic students, 6/15 priority date for international students; for spring admission, 12/1 priority date for domestic students, 11/1 priority date for international students. Applications are processed on a rolling basis. Application fee: $35. *Expenses:* Tuition, state resident: full-time $8976; part-time $374 per credit hour. Tuition, nonresident: full-time $17,952; part-time $748 per credit hour. *Financial support:* In 2013–14, 10 teaching assistantships were awarded; career-related internships or fieldwork also available. Support available to part-time students. Financial award application deadline: 4/1. *Unit head:* Dr. Frederick M. Scaffidi, Chair, 251-460-7131. *Application contact:* Dr. Abigail Baxter, Director of Graduate Studies, 251-460-7131.

University of Southern Mississippi, Graduate School, College of Health, School of Human Performance and Recreation, Hattiesburg, MS 39406-0001. Offers human performance (MS, PhD), including exercise physiology (PhD), human performance (MS), physical education (MS); interscholastic athletic administration (MS); recreation and leisure management (MS); sport administration (MS); sport and coaching education (MS); sport management (MS). Part-time and evening/weekend programs available. *Faculty:* 13 full-time (5 women). *Students:* 60 full-time (20 women), 43 part-time (9 women); includes 19 minority (13 Black or African American, non-Hispanic/Latino; 1 American Indian or Alaska Native, non-Hispanic/Latino; 2 Hispanic/Latino; 3 Two or more races, non-Hispanic/Latino), 4 international. Average age 29. 62 applicants, 77% accepted, 38 enrolled. In 2013, 39 master's, 1 doctorate awarded. *Degree requirements:* For master's, comprehensive exam, thesis optional; for doctorate, comprehensive exam, thesis/dissertation. *Entrance requirements:* For master's, GRE General Test, minimum GPA of 2.75 in last 60 hours; for doctorate, GRE General Test, minimum GPA of 3.5. Additional exam requirements/recommendations for international students: Required—TOEFL, IELTS. *Application deadline:* For fall admission, 3/1 priority date for domestic students, 3/1 for international students; for spring admission, 1/10 priority date for domestic and international students. Applications are processed on a rolling basis. Application fee: $50. Electronic applications accepted. *Financial support:* In 2013–14, 1 fellowship (averaging $16,000 per year), 6 research assistantships with full tuition reimbursements (averaging $7,492 per year), 5 teaching assistantships with full tuition reimbursements (averaging $7,330 per year) were awarded; career-related internships or fieldwork, Federal Work-Study, institutionally sponsored loans, scholarships/grants, health care benefits, and unspecified assistantships also available. Financial award application deadline: 3/15; financial award applicants required to submit FAFSA. *Faculty research:* Exercise physiology, health behaviors, resource management, activity interaction, site development. *Unit head:* Dr. Frederick Green, Director, 601-266-5379, Fax: 601-266-4445. *Application contact:* Dr. Trenton Gould, Graduate Coordinator, 601-266-5379, Fax: 601-266-4445.
Website: http://www.usm.edu/graduateschool/table.php.

The University of Tennessee, Graduate School, College of Education, Health and Human Sciences, Department of Exercise, Sport, and Leisure Studies, Knoxville, TN 37996. Offers exercise science (MS, PhD), including biomechanics/sports medicine, exercise physiology; recreation and leisure studies (MS); sport management (MS); sport studies (MS, PhD); therapeutic recreation (MS). Part-time and evening/weekend programs available. *Degree requirements:* For master's, thesis optional. *Entrance requirements:* For master's, minimum GPA of 2.7. Additional exam requirements/recommendations for international students: Required—TOEFL. Electronic applications accepted. *Expenses:* Tuition, state resident: full-time $9540; part-time $531 per credit hour. Tuition, nonresident: full-time $27,728; part-time $1542 per credit hour. *Required fees:* $1404; $67 per credit hour.

The University of Toledo, College of Graduate Studies, College of Health Sciences, Department of Health and Recreation Professions, Toledo, OH 43606-3390. Offers health education (PhD); recreation and leisure studies (MA). Part-time programs available. *Faculty:* 12. *Students:* 36 full-time (30 women), 38 part-time (20 women); includes 14 minority (10 Black or African American, non-Hispanic/Latino; 1 Asian, non-Hispanic/Latino; 2 Hispanic/Latino; 1 Two or more races, non-Hispanic/Latino), 2 international. Average age 28. 41 applicants, 80% accepted, 26 enrolled. In 2013, 10 master's, 3 doctorates awarded. *Degree requirements:* For master's, comprehensive exam, thesis; for doctorate, thesis/dissertation. *Entrance requirements:* For master's and doctorate, minimum cumulative GPA of 2.7 for all previous academic work, letters of recommendation. Additional exam requirements/recommendations for international students: Required—TOEFL (minimum score 550 paper-based; 80 iBT). *Application deadline:* For fall admission, 1/15 priority date for domestic and international students. Applications are processed on a rolling basis. Application fee: $45 ($75 for international students). Electronic applications accepted. *Financial support:* In 2013–14, 1 research assistantship with full and partial tuition reimbursement (averaging $9,000 per year), 17 teaching assistantships with full and partial tuition reimbursements (averaging $11,588 per year) were awarded; career-related internships or fieldwork, Federal Work-Study, institutionally sponsored loans, scholarships/grants, tuition waivers (full and partial), unspecified assistantships, and administrative assistantships also available. Support available to part-time students. Financial award applicants required to submit FAFSA. *Unit head:* Dr. Joseph Dake, Chair, 419-530-2767, E-mail: joseph.dake@utoledo.edu. *Application contact:* Graduate School Office, 419-530-4723, Fax: 419-530-4724, E-mail: grdsch@utnet.utoledo.edu.
Website: http://www.utoledo.edu/eduhshs/.

University of Utah, Graduate School, College of Health, Department of Parks, Recreation, and Tourism, Salt Lake City, UT 84112. Offers M Phil, MS, PhD. Part-time programs available. *Faculty:* 8 full-time (4 women), 6 part-time/adjunct (2 women). *Students:* 31 full-time (20 women), 20 part-time (11 women); includes 2 minority (1 Black or African American, non-Hispanic/Latino; 1 Hispanic/Latino), 5 international. Average age 32. 26 applicants, 50% accepted, 10 enrolled. In 2013, 13 master's, 5 doctorates awarded. Terminal master's awarded for partial completion of doctoral program. *Degree requirements:* For master's, comprehensive exam, thesis or alternative; for doctorate, comprehensive exam, thesis/dissertation. *Entrance requirements:* For master's, GRE General Test, minimum GPA of 3.0; for doctorate, GRE General Test, minimum GPA of 3.2. Additional exam requirements/recommendations for international students: Required—TOEFL (minimum score 500 paper-based). *Application deadline:* For fall admission, 3/1 for domestic students, 2/15 for international students; for spring admission, 10/1 for domestic students. Application fee: $55 ($65 for international students). Electronic applications accepted. *Expenses:* Tuition, state resident: full-time $5259. Tuition, nonresident: full-time $18,569. *Required fees:* $841. Tuition and fees vary according to course load. *Financial support:* In 2013–14, 3 research assistantships with full tuition reimbursements, 8 teaching assistantships with full tuition reimbursements were awarded; career-related internships or fieldwork, scholarships/grants, health care benefits, and unspecified assistantships also available. Financial award application deadline: 2/15; financial award applicants required to submit FAFSA. *Faculty research:* Therapeutic recreation, community and sport, outdoor recreation, protected area management, sustainable tourism and youth development. *Total annual research expenditures:* $39,469. *Unit head:* Dr. Kelly S. Bricker, Chair, 801-585-6503, E-mail: kelly.bricker@health.utah.edu. *Application contact:* Dr. Jim Sibthorp, Director of Graduate Studies, 801-581-5940, Fax: 801-581-4930, E-mail: jim.sibthorp@health.utah.edu.
Website: http://www.health.utah.edu/prt/.

University of Waterloo, Graduate Studies, Faculty of Applied Health Sciences, Department of Recreation and Leisure Studies, Waterloo, ON N2L 3G1, Canada. Offers MA, PhD. Part-time programs available. *Degree requirements:* For master's, thesis; for doctorate, comprehensive exam, thesis/dissertation. *Entrance requirements:* For master's, honors degree, minimum B average, writing sample, resume; for doctorate, GRE (recommended), master's degree, minimum B average, writing sample, resumé. Additional exam requirements/recommendations for international students: Required—TOEFL, TWE. Electronic applications accepted. *Faculty research:* Tourism, leisure behavior, special populations, leisure service management, outdoor resources, aging, health and well-being, work and health.

University of Wisconsin–La Crosse, Graduate Studies, College of Science and Health, Department of Recreation Management and Therapeutic Recreation, La Crosse, WI 54601-3742. Offers recreation management (MS); therapeutic recreation (MS). Part-time programs available. *Faculty:* 10 full-time (5 women), 2 part-time/adjunct (1 woman). *Students:* 33 full-time (24 women), 3 part-time (1 woman); includes 4 minority (1 Black or African American, non-Hispanic/Latino; 2 Asian, non-Hispanic/Latino; 1 Hispanic/Latino), 1 international. Average age 26. 34 applicants, 88% accepted, 16 enrolled. In 2013, 22 master's awarded. *Degree requirements:* For master's, thesis or alternative, project or internship. *Entrance requirements:* Additional exam requirements/recommendations for international students: Required—TOEFL (minimum score 550 paper-based; 79 iBT). *Application deadline:* For fall admission, 3/15 priority date for domestic students. Applications are processed on a rolling basis. Electronic applications accepted. *Financial support:* Research assistantships with partial tuition reimbursements, Federal Work-Study, scholarships/grants, health care benefits, and tuition waivers (partial) available. Support available to part-time students. Financial award application deadline: 3/15; financial award applicants required to submit FAFSA. *Unit head:* Dr. Jearold Holland, Program Director, 608-785-8214, Fax: 608-785-8206, E-mail: jholland@uwlax.edu. *Application contact:* Corey Sjoquist, Director of Admissions, 608-785-8939, E-mail: admissions@uwlax.edu.
Website: http://www.uwlax.edu/sah/rmtr/.

University of Wisconsin–Milwaukee, Graduate School, College of Health Sciences, Department of Occupational Science and Technology, Milwaukee, WI 53201-0413. Offers ergonomics (Certificate); occupational therapy (MS); therapeutic recreation (Certificate). *Accreditation:* AOTA. *Faculty:* 11 full-time (6 women), 1 (woman) part-time/adjunct. *Students:* 45 full-time (37 women), 4 part-time (3 women); includes 4 minority (2 Asian, non-Hispanic/Latino; 2 Two or more races, non-Hispanic/Latino), 1 international. Average age 27. 54 applicants, 24% accepted, 11 enrolled. In 2013, 33 master's awarded. *Degree requirements:* For master's, thesis or alternative. *Entrance requirements:* Additional exam requirements/recommendations for international students: Required—TOEFL (minimum score 550 paper-based; 79 iBT), IELTS (minimum score 6.5). *Application deadline:* For fall admission, 1/1 priority date for domestic students; for spring admission, 9/1 for domestic students. Applications are processed on a rolling basis. Application fee: $45 ($75 for international students). *Financial support:* Fellowships, research assistantships, teaching assistantships, and unspecified assistantships available. Support available to part-time students. Financial award application deadline: 4/15. *Unit head:* Carol Haertlein Sells, Department Chair, 414-229-6933, E-mail: chaert@uwm.edu. *Application contact:* Roger O. Smith, General Information Contact, 414-229-6697, Fax: 414-229-6697, E-mail: smithro@uwm.edu.
Website: http://www4.uwm.edu/chs/academics/occupational_therapy/.

Utah State University, School of Graduate Studies, College of Natural Resources, Department of Environment and Society, Logan, UT 84322. Offers bioregional planning (MS); geography (MA, MS); human dimensions of ecosystem science and management

(MS, PhD); recreation resource management (MS, PhD). *Degree requirements:* For master's, comprehensive exam, thesis (for some programs). *Entrance requirements:* For master's and doctorate, GRE General Test, minimum GPA of 3.0. Additional exam requirements/recommendations for international students: Required—TOEFL. Electronic applications accepted. *Faculty research:* Geographic information systems/ geographic and environmental education, bioregional planning, natural resource and environmental policy, outdoor recreation and tourism, natural resource and environmental management.

Virginia Commonwealth University, Graduate School, School of Education, Program in Sport Leadership, Richmond, VA 23284-9005. Offers MS. *Entrance requirements:* For master's, GRE General Test or MAT. Additional exam requirements/recommendations for international students: Required—TOEFL (minimum score 600 paper-based; 100 iBT). Electronic applications accepted.

Western Illinois University, School of Graduate Studies, College of Education and Human Services, Department of Recreation, Park, and Tourism Administration, Macomb, IL 61455-1390. Offers MS. Part-time programs available. *Students:* 22 full-time (10 women), 11 part-time (5 women); includes 3 minority (1 Black or African American, non-Hispanic/Latino; 1 Asian, non-Hispanic/Latino; 1 Hispanic/Latino), 4 international. Average age 31. In 2013, 24 master's awarded. *Degree requirements:* For master's, thesis or alternative. *Entrance requirements:* Additional exam requirements/ recommendations for international students: Required—TOEFL (minimum score 550 paper-based; 80 iBT). *Application deadline:* Applications are processed on a rolling basis. Application fee: $30. Electronic applications accepted. *Financial support:* In 2013–14, 17 students received support, including 15 research assistantships with full tuition reimbursements available (averaging $7,544 per year), 2 teaching assistantships with tuition reimbursements available (averaging $8,688 per year). Financial award applicants required to submit FAFSA. *Unit head:* Dr. Dan Yoder, Interim Chairperson, 309-298-1967. *Application contact:* Dr. Nancy Parsons, Assistant Director of Graduate Studies, 309-298-1806, Fax: 309-298-2345, E-mail: grad-office@wiu.edu. Website: http://www.wiu.edu/rpta.

Western Kentucky University, Graduate Studies, College of Health and Human Services, Department of Kinesiology, Recreation and Sport, Bowling Green, KY 42101. Offers athletic administration and coaching (MS); physical education (MS); recreation and sport administration (MS). Part-time and evening/weekend programs available. Postbaccalaureate distance learning degree programs offered. *Degree requirements:* For master's, comprehensive exam, thesis optional. *Entrance requirements:* For master's, GRE General Test, minimum GPA of 2.75. Additional exam requirements/ recommendations for international students: Required—TOEFL (minimum score 555 paper-based; 79 iBT). *Faculty research:* Orthopedic rehabilitation, fitness center coordination, heat acclimation, biomechanical and physiological parameters.

West Virginia University, Davis College of Agriculture, Forestry and Consumer Sciences, Division of Forestry, Program in Recreation, Parks and Tourism Resources, Morgantown, WV 26506. Offers MS. Part-time programs available. *Degree requirements:* For master's, thesis (for some programs). *Entrance requirements:* For master's, GRE, minimum GPA of 3.0. Additional exam requirements/recommendations for international students: Required—TOEFL. *Faculty research:* Attitudes, use patterns and impacts of outdoor recreation in West Virginia.

Winona State University, College of Education, Department of Education Leadership, Winona, MN 55987. Offers educational leadership (Ed S), including general superintendency, K-12 principalship; general school leadership (MS); K-12 principalship (MS); outdoor education/adventure-based leadership (MS); sports management (MS); teacher leadership (MS). *Accreditation:* NCATE. Part-time and evening/weekend programs available. *Degree requirements:* For master's, comprehensive exam, thesis optional; for Ed S, thesis optional.

Wright State University, School of Graduate Studies, College of Education and Human Services, Department of Health, Physical Education, and Recreation, Dayton, OH 45435. Offers M Ed, MA. *Accreditation:* NCATE. *Degree requirements:* For master's, comprehensive exam, thesis (for some programs). *Entrance requirements:* For master's, GRE General Test, MAT. Additional exam requirements/recommendations for international students: Required—TOEFL. *Faculty research:* Motor learning, motor development, exercise physiology, adapted physical education.

Section 30
Physical Education and Kinesiology

This section contains a directory of institutions offering graduate work in physical education and kinesiology. Additional information about programs listed in the directory may be obtained by writing directly to the dean of a graduate school or chair of a department at the address given in the directory.

For programs offering related work, see also in this book *Business Administration and Management, Education,* and *Sports Management.* In another guide in this series:

Graduate Programs in the Humanities, Arts & Social Sciences
See *Performing Arts*

CONTENTS

Program Directories

Athletic Training and Sports Medicine 1618
Exercise and Sports Science 1623
Kinesiology and Movement Studies 1641
Physical Education 1653

Athletic Training and Sports Medicine

Adrian College, Graduate Programs, Adrian, MI 49221-2575. Offers accounting (MS); athletic training (MS); criminal justice (MA). *Faculty:* 11 part-time/adjunct (3 women). *Students:* 9 full-time (3 women); includes 1 minority (Black or African American, non-Hispanic/Latino). Average age 23. 9 applicants, 100% accepted, 6 enrolled. In 2013, 2 master's awarded. *Degree requirements:* For master's, comprehensive exam (for some programs), thesis (for some programs), thesis, internship or practicum with corresponding in-depth paper and/or presentation. *Entrance requirements:* For master's, appropriate undergraduate degree, minimum cumulative and major GPA of 3.0, personal statement. *Application deadline:* For fall admission, 8/1 priority date for domestic and international students. Applications are processed on a rolling basis. Application fee: $0. *Expenses: Tuition:* Full-time $5880; part-time $490 per credit hour. *Required fees:* $550; $275 per semester. *Financial support:* Scholarships/grants and tuition waivers (full and partial) available. Financial award application deadline: 3/1; financial award applicants required to submit FAFSA. *Unit head:* Dr. Paul Rupert, Dean, Graduate Studies, 517-264-3931, E-mail: prupert@adrian.edu. *Application contact:* Melissa Woolsey, Admissions Counselor, 800-877-2246, E-mail: mwoolsey@adrian.edu.

Armstrong State University, School of Graduate Studies, Program in Sports Medicine, Savannah, GA 31419-1997. Offers sports health sciences (MSSM); strength and conditioning (Certificate). Part-time programs available. *Faculty:* 3 full-time (0 women), 1 part-time/adjunct (0 women). *Students:* 2 full-time (1 woman), 26 part-time (17 women); includes 4 minority (all Black or African American, non-Hispanic/Latino). Average age 25. 34 applicants, 56% accepted, 11 enrolled. In 2013, 10 master's awarded. *Degree requirements:* For master's, comprehensive exam, thesis optional, project. *Entrance requirements:* For master's, GRE General Test, MAT, GMAT, minimum GPA of 2.7, letter of intent. Additional exam requirements/recommendations for international students: Required—TOEFL (minimum score 523 paper-based). *Application deadline:* For fall admission, 6/1 priority date for domestic students, 5/1 priority date for international students; for spring admission, 11/15 priority date for domestic students, 9/15 priority date for international students; for summer admission, 4/15 for domestic students, 9/15 for international students. Application fee: $30. *Expenses:* Tuition, state resident: part-time $201 per credit hour. Tuition, nonresident: part-time $745 per credit hour. *Required fees:* $310 per semester. Tuition and fees vary according to course load, campus/location and program. *Financial support:* In 2013–14, research assistantships with full tuition reimbursements (averaging $5,000 per year) were awarded; scholarships/grants, tuition waivers (full), and unspecified assistantships also available. Financial award application deadline: 3/15; financial award applicants required to submit FAFSA. *Unit head:* Dr. James Streater, Department Head, 912-921-2548, Fax: 912-344-3490, E-mail: sandy.streater@armstrong.edu. *Application contact:* Bryan Riemann, Graduate Coordinator, 912-344-2934, Fax: 912-344-3490, E-mail: brian.riemann@armstrong.edu.
Website: http://www.armstrong.edu/Majors/degree/sports_medicine1.

A.T. Still University, Arizona School of Health Sciences, Mesa, AZ 85206. Offers advanced occupational therapy (MS); advanced physician assistant studies (MS); athletic training (MS); audiology (Au D); health sciences (DHSc); human movement (MS); occupational therapy (MS, DOT); physical therapy (DPT); physician assistant (MS); transitional audiology (Au D); transitional physical therapy (DPT). *Accreditation:* AOTA (one or more programs are accredited); ASHA. Part-time and evening/weekend programs available. Postbaccalaureate distance learning degree programs offered (minimal on-campus study). *Faculty:* 47 full-time (27 women), 279 part-time/adjunct (173 women). *Students:* 531 full-time (354 women), 865 part-time (547 women); includes 315 minority (79 Black or African American, non-Hispanic/Latino; 10 American Indian or Alaska Native, non-Hispanic/Latino; 114 Asian, non-Hispanic/Latino; 83 Hispanic/Latino; 6 Native Hawaiian or other Pacific Islander, non-Hispanic/Latino; 23 Two or more races, non-Hispanic/Latino), 82 international. Average age 36. 3,325 applicants, 14% accepted, 329 enrolled. In 2013, 252 master's, 370 doctorates awarded. *Degree requirements:* For master's, thesis (for some programs); for doctorate, thesis/dissertation (for some programs). *Entrance requirements:* For master's, GRE General Test; for doctorate, GRE, Evaluation of Practicing Audiologists Capabilities (Au D), Physical Therapist Evaluation Tool (DPT), current state licensure, master's degree or equivalent (Au D). Additional exam requirements/recommendations for international students: Required—TOEFL (minimum score 550 paper-based; 80 iBT). *Application deadline:* For fall admission, 8/1 for domestic and international students. Applications are processed on a rolling basis. Application fee: $70. Electronic applications accepted. *Expenses:* Contact institution. *Financial support:* In 2013–14, 151 students received support. Federal Work-Study and scholarships/grants available. Financial award application deadline: 5/1; financial award applicants required to submit FAFSA. *Faculty research:* Pediatric sport-related concussion, adolescent athlete health-related quality of life; geriatric and pediatric well-being, pain management for participation, practice-based research network, BMI and dental caries. *Total annual research expenditures:* $174,826. *Unit head:* Dr. Randy Danielsen, Dean, 480-219-6000, Fax: 480-219-6110, E-mail: rdanielsen@atsu.edu. *Application contact:* Donna Sparks, Associate Director, Admissions Processing, 660-626-2117, Fax: 660-626-2969, E-mail: admissions@atsu.edu.
Website: http://www.atsu.edu/ashs.

Barry University, School of Human Performance and Leisure Sciences, Programs in Movement Science, Specialization in Athletic Training, Miami Shores, FL 33161-6695. Offers MS. Part-time and evening/weekend programs available. *Degree requirements:* For master's, comprehensive exam, project or thesis. *Entrance requirements:* For master's, GRE General Test, minimum GPA of 3.0. Electronic applications accepted. *Faculty research:* Pain management, prevention and injury analysis, low energy static magnetic field therapy, upper extremity biomechanics.

Bloomsburg University of Pennsylvania, School of Graduate Studies, College of Science and Technology, Department of Exercise Science and Athletics, Bloomsburg, PA 17815-1301. Offers clinical athletic training (MS); exercise science (MS). *Faculty:* 6 full-time (1 woman). *Students:* 1 full-time (0 women), 55 part-time (33 women); includes 11 minority (5 Black or African American, non-Hispanic/Latino; 1 Asian, non-Hispanic/Latino; 3 Hispanic/Latino; 2 Two or more races, non-Hispanic/Latino), 1 international. Average age 24. 74 applicants, 65% accepted, 27 enrolled. In 2013, 20 master's awarded. *Degree requirements:* For master's, thesis optional, practical clinical experience. *Entrance requirements:* For master's, GRE, minimum QPA of 3.0, related undergraduate coursework. Additional exam requirements/recommendations for international students: Required—TOEFL (minimum score 550 paper-based; 79 iBT). *Application deadline:* Applications are processed on a rolling basis. Application fee: $35 ($60 for international students). Electronic applications accepted. *Expenses:* Tuition, state resident: full-time $7956; part-time $442 per credit. Tuition, nonresident: full-time $11,934; part-time $663 per credit. *Required fees:* $95.50 per credit. $55 per semester.

Tuition and fees vary according to course load. *Financial support:* Unspecified assistantships available. *Unit head:* Dr. Timothy McConnell, Chairperson, 570-389-4376, Fax: 570-389-5047, E-mail: tmconne@bloomu.edu. *Application contact:* Jennifer Richard, Administrative Assistant, 570-389-4015, Fax: 570-389-3054, E-mail: jrichard@bloomu.edu.
Website: http://www.bloomu.edu/exercise_science.

Boston University, College of Health and Rehabilitation Sciences: Sargent College, Department of Physical Therapy and Athletic Training, Boston, MA 02215. Offers physical therapy (DPT); rehabilitation sciences (PhD). *Accreditation:* APTA (one or more programs are accredited). *Faculty:* 13 full-time (10 women), 26 part-time/adjunct (12 women). *Students:* 139 full-time (100 women), 25 part-time (21 women); includes 29 minority (17 Asian, non-Hispanic/Latino; 7 Hispanic/Latino; 5 Two or more races, non-Hispanic/Latino), 6 international. Average age 27. 836 applicants, 17% accepted, 37 enrolled. In 2013, 72 doctorates awarded. *Degree requirements:* For doctorate, comprehensive exam and thesis (for PhD). *Entrance requirements:* For doctorate, GRE General Test, master's degree (for PhD), bachelor's degree (for DPT). Additional exam requirements/recommendations for international students: Required—TOEFL (minimum score 550 paper-based). *Application deadline:* For fall admission, 1/7 priority date for domestic and international students. Applications are processed on a rolling basis. Application fee: $120. Electronic applications accepted. *Expenses: Tuition:* Full-time $43,970; part-time $1374 per credit hour. *Required fees:* $60 per semester. Tuition and fees vary according to class time, course level and program. *Financial support:* In 2013–14, 120 students received support, including 113 fellowships (averaging $10,000 per year), 6 teaching assistantships (averaging $3,000 per year); career-related internships or fieldwork, Federal Work-Study, institutionally sponsored loans, scholarships/grants, and tuition waivers (partial) also available. Financial award application deadline: 4/15; financial award applicants required to submit FAFSA. *Faculty research:* Gait, balance, motor control, dynamic systems analysis, spinal cord injury. *Total annual research expenditures:* $1.5 million. *Unit head:* Dr. Melanie Matthies, Department Chair, 617-353-2724, E-mail: pt@bu.edu. *Application contact:* Sharon Sankey, Director, Student Services, 617-353-2713, Fax: 617-353-7500, E-mail: ssankey@bu.edu.
Website: http://www.bu.edu/sargent/.

Brigham Young University, Graduate Studies, College of Life Sciences, Department of Exercise Sciences, Provo, UT 84602. Offers athletic training (MS); exercise physiology (MS, PhD); exercise science (MS); health promotion (MS, PhD); physical medicine and rehabilitation (PhD). *Faculty:* 20 full-time (3 women), 1 part-time/adjunct (0 women). *Students:* 45 full-time (20 women), 2 part-time (1 woman); includes 4 minority (2 Asian, non-Hispanic/Latino; 2 Two or more races, non-Hispanic/Latino). Average age 28. 23 applicants, 48% accepted, 8 enrolled. In 2013, 13 master's, 1 doctorate awarded. *Degree requirements:* For master's, thesis, oral defense; for doctorate, comprehensive exam, thesis/dissertation, oral defense, oral and written exams. *Entrance requirements:* For master's, GRE General Test, minimum GPA of 3.2 in last 60 hours of course work; for doctorate, GRE General Test, minimum GPA of 3.5 in last 60 hours of course work. Additional exam requirements/recommendations for international students: Required—TOEFL (minimum score 580 paper-based; 85 iBT), IELTS (minimum score 7). *Application deadline:* For fall admission, 2/1 for domestic and international students. Application fee: $50. Electronic applications accepted. *Expenses: Tuition:* Full-time $6130; part-time $340 per credit hour. Tuition and fees vary according to program and student's religious affiliation. *Financial support:* In 2013–14, 36 students received support, including 24 research assistantships with partial tuition reimbursements available (averaging $2,600 per year), 19 teaching assistantships with partial tuition reimbursements available (averaging $3,350 per year); fellowships, career-related internships or fieldwork, institutionally sponsored loans, scholarships/grants, tuition waivers (partial), unspecified assistantships, and 10 PhD full tuition scholarships also available. Financial award application deadline: 3/1. *Faculty research:* Injury prevention and rehabilitation, human skeletal muscle adaptation, cardiovascular health and fitness, lifestyle modification and health promotion. *Total annual research expenditures:* $22,117. *Unit head:* Dr. Gary Mack, Chair, 801-422-2466, Fax: 801-422-0555, E-mail: gary_mack@byu.edu. *Application contact:* Dr. William J. Myrer, Graduate Coordinator, 801-422-2690, Fax: 801-422-0555, E-mail: bill_myrer@byu.edu.
Website: http://exsc.byu.edu/.

California Baptist University, Program in Athletic Training, Riverside, CA 92504-3206. Offers MS. Part-time programs available. *Faculty:* 3 full-time (all women). *Students:* 39 full-time (31 women), 2 part-time (1 woman); includes 16 minority (3 Black or African American, non-Hispanic/Latino; 4 Asian, non-Hispanic/Latino; 9 Hispanic/Latino). Average age 25. 1 applicant, 100% accepted, 1 enrolled. In 2013, 18 master's awarded. *Degree requirements:* For master's, 53-56 units of core courses; at least 900 cumulative hours of Athletic Training Clinical Education courses. *Entrance requirements:* For master's, minimum GPA of 2.75; three recommendations; comprehensive essay; current resume; CPR professional Rescuer Certification; 150 hours of clinical observation; interview. Additional exam requirements/recommendations for international students: Required—TOEFL (minimum score 80 iBT). *Application deadline:* For fall admission, 8/1 priority date for domestic students, 7/1 for international students; for spring admission, 12/1 priority date for domestic students, 11/1 for international students. Applications are processed on a rolling basis. Application fee: $45. Electronic applications accepted. *Expenses:* Contact institution. *Financial support:* Applicants required to submit CSS PROFILE or FAFSA. *Faculty research:* Eating disorders, nutrition, public health, manual therapies. *Unit head:* Dr. Chuck Sands, Dean of the College of Allied Health, 951-343-4619, E-mail: csands@calbaptist.edu. *Application contact:* Dr. Nicole MacDonald, Director, Athletic Training Program, 951-343-4379, E-mail: nmacdona@calbaptist.edu.
Website: http://www.calbaptist.edu/at/.

California State University, Long Beach, Graduate Studies, College of Health and Human Services, Department of Kinesiology, Long Beach, CA 90840. Offers adapted physical education (MA); coaching and student athlete development (MA); exercise physiology and nutrition (MS); exercise science (MS); individualized studies (MA); kinesiology (MA); pedagogical studies (MA); sport and exercise psychology (MS); sport management (MA); sports medicine and injury studies (MS). Part-time programs available. *Degree requirements:* For master's, oral and written comprehensive exams or thesis. *Entrance requirements:* For master's, GRE General Test, minimum GPA of 2.75 during previous 2 years of course work. Electronic applications accepted. *Faculty research:* Pulmonary functioning, feedback and practice structure, strength training, history and politics of sports, special population research issues.

California University of Pennsylvania, School of Graduate Studies and Research, College of Education and Human Services, Department of Health Science, California, PA 15419-1394. Offers athletic training (MS). *Degree requirements:* For master's, comprehensive exam, thesis. *Entrance requirements:* For master's, minimum GPA of

3.0. Additional exam requirements/recommendations for international students: Required—TOEFL (minimum score 550 paper-based; 80 iBT). *Faculty research:* Exercise physiology, pedagogy, athletic training, biomechanical engineering, case studies in injury and athletic medicine.

The College of St. Scholastica, Graduate Studies, Department of Athletic Training, Duluth, MN 55811-4199. Offers MS. Part-time programs available. Postbaccalaureate distance learning degree programs offered. *Faculty:* 2 full-time (1 woman), 1 (woman) part-time/adjunct. *Students:* 29 full-time (24 women); includes 1 minority (Hispanic/Latino). Average age 23. 36 applicants, 64% accepted, 16 enrolled. In 2013, 10 master's awarded. *Entrance requirements:* Additional exam requirements/recommendations for international students: Required—TOEFL. *Application deadline:* For spring admission, 1/15 priority date for domestic and international students. Applications are processed on a rolling basis. Application fee: $0. Electronic applications accepted. Application fee is waived when completed online. Tuition and fees vary according to course load, program and student level. *Financial support:* Scholarships/grants available. Support available to part-time students. Financial award applicants required to submit FAFSA. *Unit head:* Dr. Beth Domholt, Vice President for Academic Affairs, 218-723-6012, Fax: 218-723-6278, E-mail: bdomhold@css.edu. *Application contact:* Lindsay Lahti, Director of Graduate and Extended Studies Recruitment, 218-723-2240, Fax: 218-733-2275, E-mail: llahti@css.edu.
Website: http://www.css.edu/Graduate/Masters-Doctoral-and-Professional-Programs/Areas-of-Study/MS-Athletic-Training.html.

East Carolina University, Graduate School, College of Health and Human Performance, Department of Health Education and Promotion, Greenville, NC 27858-4353. Offers athletic training (MS); environmental health (MS); health education (MA, MA Ed). *Accreditation:* NCATE. *Degree requirements:* For master's, comprehensive exam, thesis optional. *Entrance requirements:* For master's, GRE General Test or MAT. Additional exam requirements/recommendations for international students: Required—TOEFL. *Expenses:* Tuition, state resident: full-time $4223. Tuition, nonresident: full-time $16,540. *Required fees:* $2184. *Faculty research:* Community health education, worksite health promotion, school health education, environmental health.

Eastern Michigan University, Graduate School, College of Health and Human Services, School of Health Promotion and Human Performance, Programs in Exercise Physiology, Ypsilanti, MI 48197. Offers exercise physiology (MS); sports medicine-biomechanics (MS); sports medicine-corporate adult fitness (MS); sports medicine-exercise physiology (MS). Part-time and evening/weekend programs available. *Students:* 13 full-time (9 women), 36 part-time (12 women); includes 12 minority (5 Black or African American, non-Hispanic/Latino; 1 American Indian or Alaska Native, non-Hispanic/Latino; 2 Asian, non-Hispanic/Latino; 2 Hispanic/Latino; 2 Two or more races, non-Hispanic/Latino), 3 international. Average age 29. 46 applicants, 74% accepted, 18 enrolled. In 2013, 29 master's awarded. *Degree requirements:* For master's, comprehensive exam, thesis or 450-hour internship. *Entrance requirements:* Additional exam requirements/recommendations for international students: Required—TOEFL. *Application deadline:* For fall admission, 8/1 for domestic students, 5/1 for international students; for winter admission, 12/1 for domestic students, 10/1 for international students; for spring admission, 3/15 for domestic students, 3/1 for international students. Application fee: $35. *Expenses:* Tuition, state resident: full-time $12,300; part-time $466 per credit hour. Tuition, nonresident: full-time $23,159; part-time $918 per credit hour. *Required fees:* $71 per credit hour. $46 per semester. One-time fee: $100. Tuition and fees vary according to course level and degree level. *Unit head:* Dr. Christopher Herman, Director, 734-487-2815, Fax: 734-487-2024, E-mail: cherman2@emich.edu. *Application contact:* Dr. Stephen McGregor, Program Coordinator, 734-487-2820, Fax: 734-487-2024, E-mail: stephen.mcgregor@emich.edu.

Eastern Michigan University, Graduate School, College of Health and Human Services, School of Health Promotion and Human Performance, Programs in Orthotics and Prosthetics, Ypsilanti, MI 48197. Offers orthotics (Graduate Certificate); orthotics/prosthetics (MS); prosthetics (Graduate Certificate). *Students:* 36 full-time (21 women), 3 part-time (2 women); includes 5 minority (2 Black or African American, non-Hispanic/Latino; 1 American Indian or Alaska Native, non-Hispanic/Latino; 2 Hispanic/Latino). Average age 27. 33 applicants, 67% accepted, 19 enrolled. In 2013, 21 master's awarded. *Degree requirements:* For master's, comprehensive exam, thesis or project, 500 hours of clinicals. *Entrance requirements:* For master's, MAT. Additional exam requirements/recommendations for international students: Required—TOEFL. *Application deadline:* For fall admission, 5/1 for domestic and international students. Applications are processed on a rolling basis. Application fee: $35. *Expenses:* Tuition, state resident: full-time $12,300; part-time $466 per credit hour. Tuition, nonresident: full-time $23,159; part-time $918 per credit hour. *Required fees:* $71 per credit hour. $46 per semester. One-time fee: $100. Tuition and fees vary according to course level and degree level. *Financial support:* Fellowships, research assistantships with full tuition reimbursements, teaching assistantships with full tuition reimbursements, career-related internships or fieldwork, Federal Work-Study, institutionally sponsored loans, scholarships/grants, tuition waivers (partial), and unspecified assistantships available. Support available to part-time students. Financial award applicants required to submit FAFSA. *Unit head:* Dr. Christopher Herman, Director, 734-487-2815, Fax: 734-487-2024, E-mail: cherman2@emich.edu. *Application contact:* Dr. Wendy Fischl Beattie, Program Coordinator, 734-487-2814, Fax: 734-487-2024, E-mail: wbeattie@emich.edu.

East Stroudsburg University of Pennsylvania, Graduate College, College of Health Sciences, Department of Athletic Training, East Stroudsburg, PA 18301-2999. Offers MS. Part-time and evening/weekend programs available. Postbaccalaureate distance learning degree programs offered. *Faculty:* 6 full-time (2 women), 1 part-time/adjunct (0 women). *Students:* 43 full-time (24 women), 1 part-time (0 women); includes 11 minority (2 Black or African American, non-Hispanic/Latino; 1 Asian, non-Hispanic/Latino; 7 Hispanic/Latino; 1 Two or more races, non-Hispanic/Latino). Average age 23. 103 applicants, 67% accepted, 43 enrolled. In 2013, 28 master's awarded. *Entrance requirements:* For master's, GRE. Additional exam requirements/recommendations for international students: Required—TOEFL (minimum score 560 paper-based; 83 iBT) or IELTS. *Application deadline:* For fall admission, 7/31 for domestic students, 6/30 for international students; for spring admission, 10/30 for domestic students, 10/31 for international students. Applications are processed on a rolling basis. Application fee: $50. Electronic applications accepted. *Expenses:* Tuition, state resident: full-time $7956; part-time $442 per credit. Tuition, nonresident: full-time $11,934; part-time $663 per credit. *Required fees:* $2129; $118 per credit. *Financial support:* Research assistantships with full and partial tuition reimbursements available. *Unit head:* John Hauth, Chair, 570-422-3231, E-mail: jhauth@esu.edu. *Application contact:* Kevin Quintero, Graduate Admissions Coordinator, 570-422-3536, Fax: 570-422-2711, E-mail: kquintero@esu.edu.

Florida International University, College of Nursing and Health Sciences, Department of Athletic Training, Miami, FL 33199. Offers MS. *Degree requirements:* For master's, 800 clinical education hours. *Entrance requirements:* For master's, bachelor's degree from accredited institution; minimum GPA of 3.0 overall and in last 60 credits of upper-division courses of the bachelor's degree; three letters of recommendation; resume; personal statement of professional/educational goals. Additional exam requirements/recommendations for international students: Required—TOEFL (minimum score 550

paper-based; 80 iBT). Electronic applications accepted. *Expenses:* Contact institution. *Faculty research:* Continuing professional education, leadership styles and outcomes, professionalism and professional image.

Gannon University, School of Graduate Studies, Morosky College of Health Professions and Sciences, School of Health Professions, Program in Athletic Training, Erie, PA 16541-0001. Offers MAT. Part-time and evening/weekend programs available. *Entrance requirements:* Additional exam requirements/recommendations for international students: Required—TOEFL (minimum score 79 iBT). *Application deadline:* Applications are processed on a rolling basis. Application fee: $25. Electronic applications accepted. *Expenses:* Tuition: Full-time $15,930; part-time $885 per credit. *Required fees:* $430; $18 per credit. Tuition and fees vary according to course load, degree level and program. *Application contact:* Kara Morgan, Director of Graduate Admissions, 814-871-5831, Fax: 814-871-5827, E-mail: graduate@gannon.edu.

Georgia State University, College of Education, Department of Kinesiology and Health, Program in Sports Medicine, Atlanta, GA 30302-3083. Offers MS. *Degree requirements:* For master's, comprehensive exam. *Entrance requirements:* For master's, GRE General Test, minimum GPA of 2.5. *Application deadline:* For fall admission, 5/1 for domestic students; for spring admission, 10/1 for domestic students. Application fee: $50. *Expenses:* Tuition, area resident: Full-time $4176; part-time $348 per credit hour. Tuition, state resident: full-time $14,544; part-time $1212 per credit hour. Tuition, nonresident: full-time $14,544; part-time $1212 per credit hour. Tuition and fees vary according to course load and program. *Financial support:* Research assistantships available. *Faculty research:* Athletic training. *Unit head:* Dr. Jacalyn Lund, Chair, 404-413-8051, E-mail: jlund@gsu.edu. *Application contact:* Dr. Shelley Linens, Program Coordinator, 404-413-8366, E-mail: slinens@gsu.edu.
Website: http://education.gsu.edu/KIN/kh_sportsMed_MS.html.

Humboldt State University, Academic Programs, College of Professional Studies, Department of Kinesiology and Recreation Administration, Arcata, CA 95521-8299. Offers athletic training education (MS); exercise science/wellness management (MS); pre-physical therapy (MS); teaching/coaching (MS). *Degree requirements:* For master's, thesis or alternative. *Entrance requirements:* For master's, GMAT, minimum GPA of 2.5. Additional exam requirements/recommendations for international students: Required—TOEFL. *Faculty research:* Human performance, adapted physical education, physical therapy.

Indiana State University, College of Graduate and Professional Studies, College of Nursing, Health and Human Services, Department of Athletic Training, Terre Haute, IN 47809. Offers MS. *Degree requirements:* For master's, thesis or alternative. *Entrance requirements:* For master's, GRE General Test. Electronic applications accepted.

Indiana University Bloomington, School of Public Health, Department of Kinesiology, Bloomington, IN 47405. Offers applied sport science (MS); athletic administration/sport management (MS); athletic training (MS); biomechanics (MS); ergonomics (MS); exercise physiology (MS); human performance (PhD), including biomechanics, exercise physiology, motor learning/control, sport management; motor learning/control (MS); physical activity (MPH); physical activity, fitness and wellness (MS). Part-time programs available. *Faculty:* 26 full-time (9 women). *Students:* 128 full-time (45 women), 16 part-time (6 women); includes 20 minority (11 Black or African American, non-Hispanic/Latino; 2 American Indian or Alaska Native, non-Hispanic/Latino; 3 Asian, non-Hispanic/Latino; 3 Hispanic/Latino; 1 Two or more races, non-Hispanic/Latino), 28 international. Average age 28. 174 applicants, 57% accepted, 48 enrolled. In 2013, 56 master's, 8 doctorates awarded. Terminal master's awarded for partial completion of doctoral program. *Degree requirements:* For master's, thesis optional; for doctorate, variable foreign language requirement, comprehensive exam, thesis/dissertation. *Entrance requirements:* For master's, GRE General Test, minimum GPA of 2.8; for doctorate, GRE General Test, minimum graduate GPA of 3.5, undergraduate 3.0. Additional exam requirements/recommendations for international students: Required—TOEFL (minimum score 80 iBT). *Application deadline:* For fall admission, 1/1 priority date for international students; for spring admission, 9/1 priority date for international students. Applications are processed on a rolling basis. Application fee: $55 ($65 for international students). *Financial support:* Fellowships, research assistantships with full tuition reimbursements, teaching assistantships with full tuition reimbursements, career-related internships or fieldwork, Federal Work-Study, institutionally sponsored loans, scholarships/grants, health care benefits, tuition waivers (partial), unspecified assistantships, and fee remissions available. Support available to part-time students. Financial award application deadline: 3/1; financial award applicants required to submit FAFSA. *Faculty research:* Exercise physiology and biochemistry, sports biomechanics, human motor control, adaptation of fitness and exercise to special populations. *Unit head:* Dr. David M. Koceja, Chairperson, 812-855-5523, Fax: 812-855-3193, E-mail: koceja@indiana.edu. *Application contact:* Kristine M. Wasson, Administrative Assistant for Graduate Studies, 812-855-5523, Fax: 812-855-3193, E-mail: ktanksle@indiana.edu.
Website: http://www.publichealth.indiana.edu/departments/kinesiology/index.shtml.

Inter American University of Puerto Rico, Metropolitan Campus, Graduate Programs, Program in Physical Education, San Juan, PR 00919-1293. Offers teaching of physical education (MA); training and sport performance (MA). *Degree requirements:* For master's, comprehensive exam. *Entrance requirements:* For master's, GRE or EXADEP, interview. Electronic applications accepted.

Kent State University, Graduate School of Education, Health, and Human Services, School of Health Sciences, Program in Exercise Physiology, Kent, OH 44242-0001. Offers athletic training (MS); exercise physiology (PhD). *Faculty:* 11 full-time (6 women), 1 part-time/adjunct (0 women). *Students:* 38 full-time (19 women), 22 part-time (12 women); includes 4 minority (3 Asian, non-Hispanic/Latino; 1 Native Hawaiian or other Pacific Islander, non-Hispanic/Latino), 3 international. 59 applicants, 47% accepted. In 2013, 21 master's, 3 doctorates awarded. *Degree requirements:* For doctorate, comprehensive exam, thesis/dissertation. *Entrance requirements:* For master's, GRE, 2 letters of reference, goals statement; for doctorate, GRE, 2 letters of reference, goals statement, minimum master's-level GPA of 3.0. Additional exam requirements/recommendations for international students: Required—TOEFL (minimum score 550 paper-based; 80 iBT). Application fee: $30 ($60 for international students). *Financial support:* In 2013–14, 9 research assistantships (averaging $11,222 per year), 5 teaching assistantships (averaging $9,600 per year) were awarded; Federal Work-Study, scholarships/grants, and unspecified assistantships also available. *Unit head:* Ellen Glickman, Coordinator, 330-672-2930, E-mail: eglickma@kent.edu. *Application contact:* Nancy Miller, Academic Program Director, Office of Graduate Student Services, 330-672-2576, Fax: 330-672-9162, E-mail: ogs@kent.edu.

Lenoir-Rhyne University, Graduate Programs, School of Health, Exercise and Sport Science, Hickory, NC 28601. Offers athletic training (MS).

Long Island University–LIU Brooklyn, School of Health Professions, Division of Sports Sciences, Brooklyn, NY 11201-8423. Offers adapted physical education (MS); athletic training and sports sciences (MS); exercise physiology (MS); health sciences (MS). Part-time and evening/weekend programs available. *Entrance requirements:* For master's, 2 letters of recommendation. Additional exam requirements/recommendations for international students: Required—TOEFL (minimum score 500 paper-based). Electronic applications accepted.

Athletic Training and Sports Medicine

Manchester University, Graduate Programs, Program in Athletic Training, North Manchester, IN 46962-1225. Offers MAT. *Faculty:* 6 part-time/adjunct (1 woman). *Students:* 12 full-time (9 women). 32 applicants, 75% accepted, 12 enrolled. In 2013, 4 master's awarded. *Degree requirements:* For master's, 51 semester hours; minimum cumulative GPA of 3.0, 2.0 in each required course; completion of all required didactic and clinical courses. *Entrance requirements:* For master's, baccalaureate degree from regionally-accredited institution; minimum cumulative undergraduate GPA of 3.0; certification in first aid and CPR; letters of recommendation. Additional exam requirements/recommendations for international students: Required—TOEFL (minimum score 550 paper-based; 79 iBT). *Application deadline:* For fall admission, 2/1 priority date for domestic students. Applications are processed on a rolling basis. Electronic applications accepted. *Financial support:* In 2013–14, 12 students received support, including 12 fellowships (averaging $6,750 per year). Financial award application deadline: 5/1; financial award applicants required to submit FAFSA. *Unit head:* Mark Huntington, Associate Dean for Academic Affairs/Director, 260-982-5033, E-mail: mwhuntington@manchester.edu. *Application contact:* Dr. Mark Huntington, Associate Dean for Academic Affairs, 260-982-5033, E-mail: mwhuntington@manchester.edu. Website: http://graduateprograms.manchester.edu/AT/index.htm.

Marshall University, Academic Affairs Division, College of Health Professions, School of Kinesiology, Program in Athletic Training, Huntington, WV 25755. Offers MS. *Students:* 8 full-time (6 women). Average age 23. *Entrance requirements:* For master's, GRE. *Unit head:* Dr. Gary McIlvain, Interim Chair, 304-696-2930, E-mail: mcilvain@marshall.edu. *Application contact:* Information Contact, 304-746-1900, Fax: 304-746-1902, E-mail: services@marshall.edu.

Missouri State University, Graduate College, College of Health and Human Services, Department of Sports Medicine and Athletic Training, Springfield, MO 65897. Offers athletic training (MS). Part-time programs available. *Faculty:* 4 full-time (1 woman), 2 part-time/adjunct (0 women). *Students:* 7 full-time (4 women), 7 part-time (6 women); includes 3 minority (1 American Indian or Alaska Native, non-Hispanic/Latino; 1 Asian, non-Hispanic/Latino; 1 Hispanic/Latino), 1 international. 11 applicants, 64% accepted, 6 enrolled. *Degree requirements:* For master's, comprehensive exam, thesis or alternative. *Entrance requirements:* For master's, GRE, current Professional Rescuer and AED certification, BOC certification, licensure as an athletic trainer, minimum undergraduate GPA of 3.0. Additional exam requirements/recommendations for international students: Required—TOEFL (minimum score 550 paper-based; 79 iBT). *Application deadline:* For fall admission, 2/1 for domestic and international students. Application fee: $35 ($50 for international students). *Expenses:* Tuition, state resident: full-time $4500; part-time $250 per credit hour. Tuition, nonresident: full-time $9018; part-time $501 per credit hour. *Required fees:* $361 per semester. Tuition and fees vary according to course level, course load and program. *Financial support:* In 2013–14, 8 teaching assistantships with full tuition reimbursements (averaging $8,324 per year) were awarded; Federal Work-Study, institutionally sponsored loans, and unspecified assistantships also available. *Unit head:* Dr. Tona Hetzler, Head, 417-836-8924, Fax: 417-836-8554, E-mail: tonahetzler@missouristate.edu. *Application contact:* Misty Stewart, Coordinator of Graduate Recruitment, 417-836-6079, Fax: 417-836-6200, E-mail: mistystewart@missouristate.edu. Website: http://sportsmed.missouristate.edu/.

Montana State University Billings, College of Allied Health Professions, Department of Health and Human Performance, Program in Athletic Training, Billings, MT 59101-0298. Offers MS. *Expenses:* Tuition, state resident: full-time $2653.75; part-time $1718 per semester. Tuition, nonresident: full-time $7015; part-time $4640 per semester. *Required fees:* $2445; $444 per credit. *Unit head:* Suzette Nynas, director, 406-657-2351, E-mail: snynas@msubillings.edu. *Application contact:* David M. Sullivan, Graduate Studies Counselor, 406-657-2053, Fax: 406-657-2299, E-mail: dsullivan@msubillings.edu.

North Dakota State University, College of Graduate and Interdisciplinary Studies, College of Human Development and Education, Department of Health, Nutrition, and Exercise Sciences, Fargo, ND 58108. Offers athletic training (MS); dietetics (MS); exercise science (MS); nutrition science (MS); sport pedagogy (MS); sports recreation management (MS). Part-time and evening/weekend programs available. Postbaccalaureate distance learning degree programs offered (no on-campus study). *Faculty:* 17 full-time (14 women). *Students:* 54 full-time (30 women), 18 part-time (8 women); includes 5 minority (2 Hispanic/Latino; 3 Two or more races, non-Hispanic/Latino), 2 international. Average age 28. 27 applicants, 78% accepted, 16 enrolled. In 2013, 23 master's awarded. *Degree requirements:* For master's, thesis (for some programs). *Entrance requirements:* For master's, minimum GPA of 3.0. Additional exam requirements/recommendations for international students: Required—TOEFL (minimum score 525 paper-based; 71 iBT). *Application deadline:* For fall admission, 3/1 priority date for domestic and international students. Applications are processed on a rolling basis. Application fee: $35. Electronic applications accepted. *Financial support:* In 2013–14, 18 teaching assistantships with full tuition reimbursements (averaging $6,500 per year) were awarded. Financial award application deadline: 3/31. *Faculty research:* Biomechanics, sport specialization, recreation, nutrition, athletic training. *Unit head:* Dr. Margaret Fitzgerald, Head, 701-231-7474, Fax: 701-231-8872, E-mail: margaret.fitzgerald@ndsu.edu. *Application contact:* Dr. Gary Liguori, Graduate Coordinator, 701-231-7474, Fax: 701-231-6524. Website: http://www.ndsu.edu/hnes/.

Ohio University, Graduate College, College of Health Sciences and Professions, School of Applied Health Sciences and Wellness, Program in Athletic Training, Athens, OH 45701-2979. Offers MS. *Entrance requirements:* For master's, GRE. Additional exam requirements/recommendations for international students: Required—TOEFL (minimum score 550 paper-based; 80 iBT) or IELTS (minimum score 7.5). *Faculty research:* Athletic training, heart, injuries, health, muscles, exercise, sport.

Plymouth State University, College of Graduate Studies, Graduate Studies in Education, Program in Athletic Training, Plymouth, NH 03264-1595. Offers MS. Part-time and evening/weekend programs available. *Entrance requirements:* For master's, MAT, GRE General Test.

Saint Louis University, Graduate Education, Doisy College of Health Sciences, Department of Physical Therapy, St. Louis, MO 63103-2097. Offers athletic training (MAT); physical therapy (DPT). *Accreditation:* APTA. Part-time programs available. *Entrance requirements:* Additional exam requirements/recommendations for international students: Required—TOEFL (minimum score 525 paper-based; 55 iBT). Electronic applications accepted. *Faculty research:* Patellofemoral pain and associated risk factors; prevalence of disordered eating in physical therapy students; effects of selected interventions for children with cerebral palsy on gait and posture: hippotherapy, ankle strengthening, supported treadmill training, spirituality in physical therapy/patient care, risk factors for exercise-related leg pain in running athletes.

Seton Hall University, School of Health and Medical Sciences, Program in Athletic Training, South Orange, NJ 07079-2697. Offers MS. *Degree requirements:* For master's, research project. *Entrance requirements:* Additional exam requirements/recommendations for international students: Required—TOEFL. Electronic applications accepted. *Faculty research:* Electrotherapy.

Shenandoah University, School of Health Professions, Division of Athletic Training, Winchester, VA 22601-5195. Offers athletic training (MS); performing arts medicine (Certificate). *Faculty:* 3 full-time (all women), 3 part-time/adjunct (1 woman). *Students:* 27 full-time (15 women), 4 part-time (all women); includes 7 minority (4 Black or African American, non-Hispanic/Latino; 2 Asian, non-Hispanic/Latino; 1 Hispanic/Latino). Average age 26. In 2013, 10 master's, 1 other advanced degree awarded. *Degree requirements:* For master's, comprehensive exam, thesis, clinical field experience. *Entrance requirements:* For master's, GRE General Test, minimum GPA of 2.8, interview, athletic experience, 3 letters of recommendation, essay. Additional exam requirements/recommendations for international students: Required—TOEFL (minimum score 550 paper-based; 79 iBT), IELTS (minimum score 6.5), Sakae Institute of Study Abroad (SISA) test (minimum score 15). *Application deadline:* For fall admission, 5/1 for domestic and international students; for summer admission, 5/1 for domestic and international students. Application fee: $30. Electronic applications accepted. *Expenses:* Contact institution. *Financial support:* In 2013–14, 4 students received support. Application deadline: 3/15; applicants required to submit FAFSA. *Faculty research:* Clinical outcomes following cryotherapy, prediction of athletic injuries, functional movement assessment in athletes, biomechanical changes after functional taping, performing arts. *Unit head:* Rose A. Schmieg, PhD, Director, 540-545-7385, Fax: 540-545-7387, E-mail: rschmieg@su.edu. *Application contact:* Andrew Woodall, Executive Director of Recruitment and Admissions, 540-665-4581, Fax: 540-665-4627, E-mail: admit@su.edu. Website: http://www.athletic-training.su.edu.

Springfield College, Graduate Programs, Programs in Exercise Science and Sport Studies, Springfield, MA 01109-3797. Offers athletic training (MS); exercise physiology (MS), including clinical exercise physiology, science and research; exercise science and sport studies (PhD); health promotion and disease prevention (MS); sport psychology (MS). Part-time programs available. *Faculty:* 17 full-time, 2 part-time/adjunct. *Students:* 85 full-time. Average age 30. 138 applicants, 59% accepted, 48 enrolled. In 2013, 27 master's awarded. Terminal master's awarded for partial completion of doctoral program. *Degree requirements:* For master's, comprehensive exam, research project or thesis; for doctorate, comprehensive exam, thesis/dissertation. *Entrance requirements:* For master's and doctorate, GRE General Test. Additional exam requirements/recommendations for international students: Required—TOEFL (minimum score 550 paper-based); Recommended—IELTS (minimum score 6). *Application deadline:* For fall admission, 1/15 for domestic and international students; for winter admission, 11/1 for domestic and international students; for spring admission, 11/1 for domestic and international students. Application fee: $50. Electronic applications accepted. *Expenses:* Tuition: Full-time $13,620; part-time $908 per credit. *Financial support:* Fellowships with partial tuition reimbursements, teaching assistantships with partial tuition reimbursements, career-related internships or fieldwork, Federal Work-Study, institutionally sponsored loans, and unspecified assistantships available. Financial award application deadline: 3/1; financial award applicants required to submit FAFSA. *Unit head:* Dr. Tracey Matthews, Director, 413-748-3397, E-mail: tmatthews@springfieldcollege.edu. *Application contact:* Evelyn Cohen, Associate Director of Graduate Admissions, 413-748-3479, Fax: 413-748-3694, E-mail: ecohen@springfieldcollege.edu.

Stephen F. Austin State University, Graduate School, College of Education, Department of Kinesiology and Health Science, Nacogdoches, TX 75962. Offers athletic training (MS); kinesiology (M Ed). *Degree requirements:* For master's, comprehensive exam. *Entrance requirements:* For master's, GRE General Test. Additional exam requirements/recommendations for international students: Required—TOEFL.

Temple University, College of Health Professions and Social Work, Department of Kinesiology, Philadelphia, PA 19122. Offers athletic training (MS, PhD); behavioral sciences (Ed M); curriculum and instruction (MS); integrated exercise physiology (PhD); integrative exercise physiology (MS); kinesiology (MS); psychology of movement (MS); somatic sciences (PhD). Part-time programs available. *Faculty:* 15 full-time (7 women). *Students:* 49 full-time (30 women), 8 part-time (5 women); includes 6 minority (2 Black or African American, non-Hispanic/Latino; 1 Asian, non-Hispanic/Latino; 2 Hispanic/Latino; 1 Two or more races, non-Hispanic/Latino), 6 international. 100 applicants, 33% accepted, 18 enrolled. In 2013, 15 master's, 6 doctorates awarded. Terminal master's awarded for partial completion of doctoral program. *Degree requirements:* For master's, thesis, final project; for doctorate, comprehensive exam, thesis/dissertation. *Entrance requirements:* For master's, GRE General Test or MAT, minimum undergraduate GPA of 3.0, 3 letters of reference, statement of goals, interview, resume; for doctorate, GRE General Test, minimum undergraduate GPA of 3.0, 3 letters of reference, statement of goals, interview, resume. Additional exam requirements/recommendations for international students: Required—TOEFL (minimum score 550 paper-based; 79 iBT). *Application deadline:* For fall admission, 1/15 for domestic students, 12/15 for international students; for spring admission, 10/1 for domestic students, 8/1 for international students. Applications are processed on a rolling basis. Application fee: $60. Electronic applications accepted. *Financial support:* In 2013–14, 4 research assistantships with full and partial tuition reimbursements (averaging $16,459 per year), 24 teaching assistantships with full and partial tuition reimbursements (averaging $15,966 per year) were awarded; fellowships, career-related internships or fieldwork, Federal Work-Study, scholarships/grants, tuition waivers, and unspecified assistantships also available. Financial award application deadline: 1/15. *Faculty research:* Exercise physiology, athletic training, motor neuroscience, exercise and sports psychology. *Total annual research expenditures:* $318,204. *Unit head:* Dr. John Jeka, Department Chair, 214-204-4405, Fax: 215-204-4414, E-mail: jjeka@temple.edu. *Application contact:* Megan P. Mannal DiMarco, 215-204-7503, E-mail: megan.dimarco@temple.edu. Website: http://chpsw.temple.edu/kinesiology/home.

Texas A&M University, College of Education and Human Development, Department of Health and Kinesiology, College Station, TX 77843. Offers athletic training (MS); health education (M Ed, MS, Ed D, PhD); kinesiology (MS, PhD); sport management (MS). Part-time programs available. *Faculty:* 38. *Students:* 206 full-time (113 women), 71 part-time (38 women); includes 81 minority (35 Black or African American, non-Hispanic/Latino; 8 Asian, non-Hispanic/Latino; 33 Hispanic/Latino; 5 Two or more races, non-Hispanic/Latino), 43 international. Average age 29. 167 applicants, 71% accepted, 79 enrolled. In 2013, 68 master's, 16 doctorates awarded. *Degree requirements:* For master's, thesis (for some programs); for doctorate, comprehensive exam, thesis/dissertation. *Entrance requirements:* For master's and doctorate, GRE General Test. Additional exam requirements/recommendations for international students: Required—TOEFL. *Application deadline:* Applications are processed on a rolling basis. Application fee: $50 ($75 for international students). Electronic applications accepted. *Expenses:* Tuition, state resident: full-time $4078; part-time $226.55 per credit hour. Tuition, nonresident: full-time $10,450; part-time $580.55 per credit hour. *Required fees:* $2328; $278.50 per credit hour. $642.45 per semester. *Financial support:* Fellowships with partial tuition reimbursements, research assistantships, teaching assistantships, career-related internships or fieldwork, and institutionally sponsored loans available. Financial award application deadline: 2/15; financial award applicants required to submit FAFSA. *Unit head:* Dr. Richard Kreider, Head, 979-845-1333, Fax: 979-847-8987, E-mail:

rkreider@hlkn.tamu.edu. *Application contact:* Christina Escamilla, Senior Academic Advisor I, 979-845-4530, E-mail: cescamil@tamu.edu.
Website: http://hlknweb.tamu.edu/.

Texas State University, Graduate School, College of Education, Department of Health and Human Performance, Program in Athletic Training, San Marcos, TX 78666. Offers MS. *Faculty:* 4 full-time (1 woman). *Students:* 24 full-time (16 women), 2 part-time (1 woman); includes 5 minority (all Hispanic/Latino), 3 international. Average age 24. 44 applicants, 59% accepted, 10 enrolled. In 2013, 4 master's awarded. *Degree requirements:* For master's, comprehensive exam, thesis optional. *Entrance requirements:* For master's, athletic trainer certification or eligibility for certification exam. Additional exam requirements/recommendations for international students: Required—TOEFL (minimum score 550 paper-based; 78 iBT). *Application deadline:* For fall admission, 6/15 for domestic students, 6/1 for international students; for spring admission, 10/15 for domestic students, 10/1 for international students. Application fee: $40 ($90 for international students). *Expenses:* Tuition, state resident: full-time $6663; part-time $278 per credit hour. Tuition, nonresident: full-time $15,159; part-time $632 per credit hour. *Required fees:* $1872; $54 per credit hour. $306 per term. Tuition and fees vary according to course load. *Financial support:* In 2013–14, 9 students received support, including 12 research assistantships (averaging $12,966 per year), 12 teaching assistantships (averaging $12,972 per year). *Unit head:* Dr. Luzita Vela, Coordinator, 512-245-1971, E-mail: lv19@txstate.edu. *Application contact:* Dr. Andrea Golato, Dean of the Graduate College, 512-245-2581, Fax: 512-245-8365, E-mail: gradcollege@txstate.edu.
Website: http://www.hhp.txstate.edu/Degree-Plans/Graduate.html.

Texas Tech University Health Sciences Center, School of Allied Health Sciences, Program in Athletic Training, Lubbock, TX 79430. Offers MAT. *Faculty:* 3 full-time (2 women). *Students:* 49 full-time (29 women); includes 19 minority (8 Black or African American, non-Hispanic/Latino; 1 American Indian or Alaska Native, non-Hispanic/Latino; 1 Asian, non-Hispanic/Latino; 4 Hispanic/Latino; 5 Two or more races, non-Hispanic/Latino). Average age 24. 75 applicants, 33% accepted, 25 enrolled. In 2013, 22 master's awarded. *Entrance requirements:* Additional exam requirements/recommendations for international students: Required—TOEFL, IELTS. *Application deadline:* For fall admission, 10/15 priority date for domestic students; for spring admission, 2/1 priority date for domestic students. Applications are processed on a rolling basis. Application fee: $40. Electronic applications accepted. *Financial support:* Career-related internships or fieldwork, institutionally sponsored loans, and scholarships/grants available. Financial award applicants required to submit FAFSA. *Unit head:* Dr. LesLee Taylor, Program Director, 806-743-3237, Fax: 806-743-2189, E-mail: leslee.taylor@ttuhsc.edu. *Application contact:* Lindsay Johnson, Associate Dean for Admissions and Student Affairs, 806-743-3220, Fax: 806-743-2994, E-mail: lindsay.johnson@ttuhsc.edu.
Website: http://www.ttuhsc.edu/sah/mat/.

United States Sports Academy, Graduate Programs, Program in Sports Medicine, Daphne, AL 36526-7055. Offers MSS. Part-time programs available. Postbaccalaureate distance learning degree programs offered (no on-campus study). *Degree requirements:* For master's, comprehensive exam, thesis optional. *Entrance requirements:* For master's, GRE General Test, GMAT, or MAT, minimum GPA of 2.5, 3 letters of recommendation, resume. Additional exam requirements/recommendations for international students: Required—TOEFL (minimum score 500 paper-based). Electronic applications accepted. *Faculty research:* Psychiatric aspects of injury rehabilitation, geriatric exercises and mobility.

Universidad del Turabo, Graduate Programs, Programs in Education, Program in Athletic Training, Gurabo, PR 00778-3030. Offers MPHE.

University of Arkansas, Graduate School, College of Education and Health Professions, Department of Health, Human Performance and Recreation, Program in Athletic Training, Fayetteville, AR 72701-1201. Offers MAT. Electronic applications accepted.

University of Central Oklahoma, The Jackson College of Graduate Studies, College of Education and Professional Studies, Department of Kinesiology and Health Studies, Edmond, OK 73034-5209. Offers athletic training (MS); wellness management (MS), including exercise science, health studies. *Faculty:* 5 full-time (4 women), 8 part-time/adjunct (3 women). *Students:* 31 full-time (20 women), 43 part-time (23 women); includes 26 minority (10 Black or African American, non-Hispanic/Latino; 3 American Indian or Alaska Native, non-Hispanic/Latino; 1 Asian, non-Hispanic/Latino; 6 Hispanic/Latino; 6 Two or more races, non-Hispanic/Latino), 10 international. Average age 27. 41 applicants, 95% accepted, 22 enrolled. In 2013, 18 master's awarded. *Degree requirements:* For master's, comprehensive exam (for some programs), thesis (for some programs). *Entrance requirements:* For master's, GRE. Additional exam requirements/recommendations for international students: Required—TOEFL (minimum score 550 paper-based; 79 iBT), IELTS (minimum score 6.5). *Application deadline:* For fall admission, 12/15 priority date for domestic students, 7/1 for international students; for spring admission, 11/1 for international students. Application fee: $50. Electronic applications accepted. *Expenses:* Tuition, state resident: full-time $4137; part-time $206.85 per credit hour. Tuition, nonresident: full-time $10,359; part-time $517.95 per credit hour. *Required fees:* $481. Tuition and fees vary according to course load and program. *Financial support:* In 2013–14, 23 students received support, including 8 research assistantships with partial tuition reimbursements available (averaging $3,189 per year), 1 teaching assistantship with partial tuition reimbursement available (averaging $2,958 per year); career-related internships or fieldwork, scholarships/grants, tuition waivers (partial), and unspecified assistantships also available. Financial award application deadline: 3/31. *Unit head:* Dr. Debra T. Traywick, Chair, 405-974-5363, Fax: 405-974-3805, E-mail: dtraywick@uco.edu. *Application contact:* Dr. Richard Bernard, Dean, Graduate College, 405-974-3493, Fax: 405-974-3852, E-mail: gradcoll@uco.edu.
Website: http://www.ucogradat.net.

University of Colorado Colorado Springs, College of Letters, Arts and Sciences, Master of Sciences Program, Colorado Springs, CO 80933-7150. Offers biology (M Sc); chemistry (M Sc); health promotion (M Sc); mathematics (M Sc); physics (M Sc); sports medicine (M Sc), including strength and conditioning; sports nutrition (M Sc). Part-time programs available. *Students:* 50 full-time (36 women), 35 part-time (23 women); includes 12 minority (1 Black or African American, non-Hispanic/Latino; 1 American Indian or Alaska Native, non-Hispanic/Latino; 3 Asian, non-Hispanic/Latino; 5 Hispanic/Latino; 2 Two or more races, non-Hispanic/Latino), 11 international. Average age 29. 122 applicants, 47% accepted, 36 enrolled. In 2013, 37 master's awarded. *Degree requirements:* For master's, thesis or alternative. *Entrance requirements:* For master's, minimum GPA of 2.75. Additional exam requirements/recommendations for international students: Required—TOEFL (minimum score 525 paper-based). *Application deadline:* For fall admission, 3/1 priority date for domestic students; for spring admission, 12/1 for domestic students. Applications are processed on a rolling basis. Application fee: $60 ($75 for international students). Electronic applications accepted. *Expenses:* Contact institution. *Financial support:* In 2013–14, 21 students received support, including 21 fellowships (averaging $2,600 per year); research assistantships, teaching assistantships, career-related internships or fieldwork, Federal Work-Study, and

scholarships/grants also available. Support available to part-time students. Financial award application deadline: 3/1; financial award applicants required to submit FAFSA. *Faculty research:* Biomechanics and physiology of elite athletic training, genetic engineering in yeast and bacteria including phage display and DNA repair, immunology and cell biology, synthetic organic chemistry. *Total annual research expenditures:* $38,075. *Unit head:* Dr. Peter A. Braza, Dean, 719-255-4550, Fax: 719-255-4200, E-mail: pbraza@uccs.edu. *Application contact:* Taryn Bailey, Graduate Recruitment Specialist, 719-255-3702, Fax: 719-255-3037, E-mail: gradinfo@uccs.edu.

The University of Findlay, Office of Graduate Admissions, Findlay, OH 45840-3653. Offers athletic training (MAT); business (MBA), including health care management, hospitality management, organizational leadership, public management; education (MA Ed), including administration, children's literature, early childhood, human resource development, reading, science, special education, technology; environmental, safety and health management (MSEM); health informatics (MS); occupational therapy (MOT); pharmacy (Pharm D); physical therapy (DPT); physician assistant (MPA); rhetoric and writing (MA); teaching English to speakers of other languages (TESOL) and bilingual education (MA). Part-time and evening/weekend programs available. Postbaccalaureate distance learning degree programs offered (no on-campus study). *Faculty:* 209 full-time (98 women), 69 part-time/adjunct (38 women). *Students:* 551 full-time (332 women), 457 part-time (276 women); includes 77 minority (37 Black or African American, non-Hispanic/Latino; 1 American Indian or Alaska Native, non-Hispanic/Latino; 15 Asian, non-Hispanic/Latino; 23 Hispanic/Latino; 1 Native Hawaiian or other Pacific Islander, non-Hispanic/Latino; 135 international. Average age 28. 637 applicants, 66% accepted, 241 enrolled. In 2013, 267 master's, 91 doctorates awarded. *Degree requirements:* For master's, thesis, cumulative project, capstone project. *Entrance requirements:* For master's, GRE/GMAT, bachelor's degree from accredited institution, minimum undergraduate GPA of 2.5 in last 64 hours of course work; for doctorate, GRE, minimum cumulative GPA of 3.0. Additional exam requirements/recommendations for international students: Required—TOEFL (minimum score 80 iBT). *Application deadline:* Applications are processed on a rolling basis. Application fee: $25. Electronic applications accepted. *Expenses: Required fees:* $146 per semester. Tuition and fees vary according to degree level and program. *Financial support:* In 2013–14, 11 research assistantships with full and partial tuition reimbursements (averaging $4,000 per year), 10 teaching assistantships with full and partial tuition reimbursements (averaging $3,600 per year) were awarded; career-related internships or fieldwork, Federal Work-Study, health care benefits, and unspecified assistantships also available. Financial award application deadline: 4/1; financial award applicants required to submit FAFSA. *Unit head:* Christopher M. Harris, Director of Admissions, 419-434-4347, E-mail: harrisc1@findlay.edu. *Application contact:* Emily Ickes, Graduate Admissions Counselor, 419-434-6933, Fax: 419-434-4898, E-mail: ickese@findlay.edu.
Website: http://www.findlay.edu/admissions/graduate/Pages/default.aspx.

University of Florida, Graduate School, College of Health and Human Performance, Department of Applied Physiology and Kinesiology, Gainesville, FL 32611. Offers athletic training/sport medicine (MS); biobehavioral science (MS); clinical exercise physiology (MS); health and human performance (PhD), including applied physiology and kinesiology, biobehavioral science, exercise physiology; human performance (MS). *Faculty:* 18 full-time (3 women), 3 part-time/adjunct (1 woman). *Students:* 73 full-time (32 women), 6 part-time (3 women); includes 9 minority (1 Black or African American, non-Hispanic/Latino; 3 Asian, non-Hispanic/Latino; 5 Hispanic/Latino), 18 international. Average age 27. 163 applicants, 23% accepted, 21 enrolled. In 2013, 23 master's, 8 doctorates awarded. *Degree requirements:* For master's, comprehensive exam, thesis (for some programs); for doctorate, comprehensive exam, thesis/dissertation. *Entrance requirements:* For master's and doctorate, GRE General Test, minimum GPA of 3.0. Additional exam requirements/recommendations for international students: Required—TOEFL (minimum score 550 paper-based; 80 iBT), IELTS (minimum score 6). *Application deadline:* For fall admission, 6/1 priority date for domestic students, 6/1 for international students; for spring admission, 9/15 for domestic and international students. Applications are processed on a rolling basis. Application fee: $30. Electronic applications accepted. *Expenses:* Tuition, state resident: full-time $12,640. Tuition, nonresident: full-time $30,000. *Financial support:* In 2013–14, 55 students received support, including 18 research assistantships (averaging $17,260 per year), 41 teaching assistantships (averaging $12,166 per year); unspecified assistantships also available. Financial award application deadline: 2/1; financial award applicants required to submit FAFSA. *Faculty research:* Cardiovascular disease; basic mechanisms that underlie exercise-induced changes in the body at the organ, tissue, cellular and molecular level; development of rehabilitation techniques for regaining motor control after stroke or as a consequence of Parkinson's disease; maintaining optimal health and delaying age-related declines in physiological function; psychomotor mechanisms impacting health and performance across the life span. *Unit head:* Michael Delp, PhD, Professor and Chair, 352-392-0584 Ext. 1338, E-mail: mdelp@hhp.ufl.edu. *Application contact:* Evangelos A. Christou, PhD, Associate Professor and Graduate Coordinator, 352-294-1719 Ext. 1270, E-mail: eachristou@hhp.ufl.edu.
Website: http://apk.hhp.ufl.edu/.

University of Idaho, College of Graduate Studies, College of Education, Department of Movement Sciences, Moscow, ID 83844-2401. Offers athletic training (MSAT, DAT); movement and leisure sciences (MS); physical education (M Ed). *Faculty:* 14 full-time, 1 part-time/adjunct. *Students:* 63 full-time, 14 part-time. Average age 31. In 2013, 17 master's, 2 doctorates awarded. *Degree requirements:* For doctorate, thesis/dissertation. *Entrance requirements:* For master's, minimum GPA of 2.8; for doctorate, minimum undergraduate GPA of 2.8, graduate 3.0. *Application deadline:* For fall admission, 8/1 for domestic students; for spring admission, 12/15 for domestic students. Applications are processed on a rolling basis. Application fee: $60. Electronic applications accepted. *Expenses:* Tuition, state resident: full-time $5596; part-time $363 per credit hour. Tuition, nonresident: full-time $18,672; part-time $1089 per credit hour. *Financial support:* Research assistantships and teaching assistantships available. Financial award applicants required to submit FAFSA. *Unit head:* Dr. Philip W. Scruggs, Chair, 208-885-7921, E-mail: movementsciences@uidaho.edu. *Application contact:* Stephanie Thomas, Graduate Recruitment Coordinator, 208-885-4001, Fax: 208-885-4406, E-mail: gadms@uidaho.edu.
Website: http://www.uidaho.edu/ed/movementsciences.

The University of Iowa, Graduate College, College of Liberal Arts and Sciences, Department of Health and Human Physiology, Iowa City, IA 52242-1316. Offers athletic training (MS); clinical exercise physiology (MS); health and human physiology (PhD); leisure studies (MA, PhD), including recreational sport management (PhD), therapeutic recreation (MA). *Degree requirements:* For master's, thesis optional, exam; for doctorate, comprehensive exam, thesis/dissertation. *Entrance requirements:* For master's and doctorate, GRE General Test, minimum GPA of 3.0. Additional exam requirements/recommendations for international students: Required—TOEFL (minimum score 600 paper-based; 100 iBT). Electronic applications accepted.

University of Kentucky, Graduate School, College of Health Sciences, Division of Athletic Training, Lexington, KY 40506-0032. Offers MS.

University of Miami, Graduate School, School of Education and Human Development, Department of Kinesiology and Sport Sciences, Program in Exercise Physiology, Coral

Gables, FL 33124. Offers exercise physiology (MS Ed, PhD); strength and conditioning (MS Ed). Part-time and evening/weekend programs available. *Faculty:* 4 full-time (1 woman). *Students:* 52 full-time (25 women), 6 part-time (3 women); includes 20 minority (4 Black or African American, non-Hispanic/Latino; 1 Asian, non-Hispanic/Latino; 13 Hispanic/Latino; 2 Two or more races, non-Hispanic/Latino), 8 international. Average age 27. 68 applicants, 35% accepted, 24 enrolled. In 2013, 20 master's awarded. Terminal master's awarded for partial completion of doctoral program. *Degree requirements:* For master's, comprehensive exam (for some programs), thesis optional, special project; for doctorate, thesis/dissertation, qualifying exam. *Entrance requirements:* For master's and doctorate, GRE General Test. Additional exam requirements/recommendations for international students: Required—TOEFL (minimum score 550 paper-based; 80 iBT); Recommended—IELTS (minimum score 6.5). *Application deadline:* For fall admission, 10/1 for international students; for spring admission, 10/1 for international students. Applications are processed on a rolling basis. Application fee: $65. Electronic applications accepted. *Financial support:* In 2013–14, 36 students received support. Health care benefits and unspecified assistantships available. Support available to part-time students. Financial award application deadline: 3/1; financial award applicants required to submit FAFSA. *Faculty research:* Women's health, cardiovascular health, aging, metabolism, obesity. *Unit head:* Dr. Arlette Perry, Department Chairperson, 305-284-3024, Fax: 305-284-5168, E-mail: aperry@miami.edu. *Application contact:* Lois Heffernan, Graduate Admissions Coordinator, 305-284-2167, Fax: 305-284-9395, E-mail: lheffernan@miami.edu.
Website: http://www.education.miami.edu/career/graduate.asp.

University of Miami, Graduate School, School of Education and Human Development, Department of Kinesiology and Sport Sciences, Program in Sports Medicine, Coral Gables, FL 33124. Offers athletic training (MS Ed). Part-time and evening/weekend programs available. *Faculty:* 2 full-time (1 woman). In 2013, 1 master's awarded. *Degree requirements:* For master's, thesis optional, special project. *Entrance requirements:* For master's, GRE General Test. Additional exam requirements/recommendations for international students: Required—TOEFL (minimum score 550 paper-based; 80 iBT); Recommended—IELTS (minimum score 6.5). *Application deadline:* Applications are processed on a rolling basis. Application fee: $65. Electronic applications accepted. *Financial support:* Available to part-time students. Application deadline: 3/1; applicants required to submit FAFSA. *Faculty research:* Care, prevention, and treatment of athletic injuries. *Unit head:* Dr. Kysha Harriell, Professor, 305-284-3201, Fax: 305-284-5168, E-mail: kharriell@miami.edu. *Application contact:* Lois Heffernan, Graduate Admissions Coordinator, 305-284-2167, Fax: 305-284-9395, E-mail: lheffernan@miami.edu.

University of Nebraska at Omaha, Graduate Studies, College of Education, School of Health, Physical Education, and Recreation, Omaha, NE 68182. Offers athletic training (MA); exercise science (PhD); health, physical education, and recreation (MA, MS). Part-time and evening/weekend programs available. *Faculty:* 15 full-time (7 women). *Students:* 54 full-time (24 women), 32 part-time (9 women); includes 8 minority (2 Asian, non-Hispanic/Latino; 3 Hispanic/Latino; 3 Two or more races, non-Hispanic/Latino), 4 international. Average age 28. 79 applicants, 51% accepted, 22 enrolled. In 2013, 27 master's awarded. *Degree requirements:* For master's, comprehensive exam, thesis (for some programs). *Entrance requirements:* For master's, GRE; entrance exam, minimum GPA of 3.0, official transcripts, statement of purpose, 2 letters of recommendation; for doctorate, GRE, minimum GPA of 3.2, official transcripts, statement of purpose, 3 letters of recommendation, resume, writing sample. Additional exam requirements/recommendations for international students: Required—TOEFL, IELTS, PTE. *Application deadline:* For fall admission, 7/1 priority date for domestic students; for spring admission, 11/1 priority date for domestic students; for summer admission, 2/1 for domestic students. Applications are processed on a rolling basis. Application fee: $45. Electronic applications accepted. *Financial support:* In 2013–14, 19 students received support, including 12 research assistantships with tuition reimbursements available, 7 teaching assistantships with tuition reimbursements available; fellowships, Federal Work-Study, institutionally sponsored loans, scholarships/grants, tuition waivers (full), and unspecified assistantships also available. Support available to part-time students. Financial award application deadline: 3/1; financial award applicants required to submit FAFSA. *Unit head:* Dr. Daniel Blanke, Director, 402-554-2670. *Application contact:* Dr. Kris Berg, Graduate Program Chair, 402-554-2670, E-mail: graduate@unomaha.edu.

The University of North Carolina at Chapel Hill, Graduate School, College of Arts and Sciences, Department of Exercise and Sport Science, Chapel Hill, NC 27599. Offers athletic training (MA); exercise physiology (MA); sport administration (MA). *Degree requirements:* For master's, comprehensive exam, thesis. *Entrance requirements:* For master's, GRE General Test, minimum GPA of 3.0. Additional exam requirements/recommendations for international students: Required—TOEFL (minimum score 550 paper-based). Electronic applications accepted. *Faculty research:* Mild head injury in sport, endocrine system's response to exercise, obesity and children, effect of aerobic exercise on cerebral bloodflow in elderly population.

University of Northern Iowa, Graduate College, College of Education, School of Health, Physical Education, and Leisure Services, MS Program in Athletic Training, Cedar Falls, IA 50614. Offers MS. Part-time and evening/weekend programs available. *Students:* 10 full-time (7 women), 1 part-time (0 women), 1 international. 26 applicants, 77% accepted, 7 enrolled. In 2013, 3 master's awarded. *Degree requirements:* For master's, comprehensive exam. *Entrance requirements:* Additional exam requirements/recommendations for international students: Required—TOEFL (minimum score 550 paper-based; 79 iBT). *Application deadline:* For fall admission, 4/1 priority date for international students; for winter admission, 10/1 priority date for international students. Applications are processed on a rolling basis. Application fee: $50 ($70 for international students). Electronic applications accepted. *Financial support:* Unspecified assistantships available. Financial award application deadline: 2/1; financial award applicants required to submit FAFSA. *Unit head:* Dr. Todd Evans, Coordinator, 319-273-6152, Fax: 319-273-5958, E-mail: todd.evans@uni.edu. *Application contact:* Laurie S. Russell, Record Analyst, 319-273-2623, Fax: 319-273-6792, E-mail: laurie.russell@uni.edu.
Website: http://www.uni.edu/coe/departments/school-health-physical-education-leisure-services/athletic-training/post-professional-m-0.

University of Pittsburgh, School of Health and Rehabilitation Sciences, Master's Programs in Health and Rehabilitation Sciences, Pittsburgh, PA 15260. Offers health and rehabilitation sciences (MS), including health care supervision and management, health information systems, occupational therapy, physical therapy, rehabilitation counseling, rehabilitation science and technology, sports medicine, wellness and human performance. *Accreditation:* APTA. Part-time and evening/weekend programs available. *Faculty:* 63 full-time (37 women), 4 part-time/adjunct (2 women). *Students:* 117 full-time (70 women), 44 part-time (27 women); includes 18 minority (8 Black or African American, non-Hispanic/Latino; 1 American Indian or Alaska Native, non-Hispanic/Latino; 6 Asian, non-Hispanic/Latino; 3 Hispanic/Latino), 52 international. Average age 30. 368 applicants, 57% accepted, 96 enrolled. In 2013, 90 master's awarded. *Degree requirements:* For master's, comprehensive exam (for some programs), thesis optional. *Entrance requirements:* For master's, minimum GPA of 3.0. Additional exam requirements/recommendations for international students: Required—TOEFL (minimum score 550 paper-based; 80 iBT), IELTS (minimum score 6.5). *Application deadline:* For fall admission, 3/1 for international students; for spring admission, 9/1 for international students. Applications are processed on a rolling basis. Application fee: $50. Electronic applications accepted. *Expenses:* Contact institution. *Financial support:* In 2013–14, 3 fellowships (averaging $20,460 per year) were awarded; Federal Work-Study, institutionally sponsored loans, scholarships/grants, traineeships, and unspecified assistantships also available. Financial award applicants required to submit FAFSA. *Faculty research:* Assistive technology, seating and wheeled mobility, cellular neurophysiology, low back syndrome, augmentative communication. *Total annual research expenditures:* $8.1 million. *Unit head:* Dr. Clifford E. Brubaker, Dean, 412-383-6560, Fax: 412-383-6535, E-mail: cliffb@pitt.edu. *Application contact:* Jessica Maguire, Director of Admissions, 412-383-6557, Fax: 412-383-6535, E-mail: maguire@pitt.edu.
Website: http://www.shrs.pitt.edu/.

University of South Florida, Morsani College of Medicine and Graduate School, Graduate Programs in Medical Sciences, Tampa, FL 33620-9951. Offers aging and neuroscience (MSMS); allergy, immunology and infectious disease (PhD); anatomy (MSMS, PhD); athletic training (MSMS); bioinformatics and computational biology (MSBCB); biotechnology (MSB); clinical and translational research (MSMS, PhD); health informatics (MSHI, MSMS); health science (MSMS); interdisciplinary medical sciences (MSMS); medical microbiology and immunology (MSMS); metabolic and nutritional medicine (MSMS); molecular medicine (MSMS, PhD); molecular pharmacology and physiology (PhD); neurology (PhD); pathology and laboratory medicine (PhD); pharmacology and therapeutics (PhD); physiology and biophysics (PhD); women's health (MSMS). *Students:* 336 full-time (182 women), 39 part-time (21 women); includes 170 minority (45 Black or African American, non-Hispanic/Latino; 54 Asian, non-Hispanic/Latino; 59 Hispanic/Latino; 2 Native Hawaiian or other Pacific Islander, non-Hispanic/Latino; 10 Two or more races, non-Hispanic/Latino), 17 international. Average age 26. 1,066 applicants, 44% accepted, 250 enrolled. In 2013, 191 master's, 12 doctorates awarded. Terminal master's awarded for partial completion of doctoral program. *Degree requirements:* For master's, comprehensive exam, thesis; for doctorate, comprehensive exam, thesis/dissertation. *Entrance requirements:* For master's, GRE General Test or GMAT, bachelor's degree or equivalent from regionally-accredited university with minimum GPA of 3.0 in upper-division sciences coursework; prerequisites in general biology, general chemistry, general physics, organic chemistry, quantitative analysis, and integral and differential calculus; for doctorate, GRE General Test (minimum score of 600 quantitative), bachelor's degree from regionally-accredited university with minimum GPA of 3.0 in upper-division sciences coursework; 3 letters of recommendation; personal interview; 1-2 page personal statement; prerequisites in biology, chemistry, physics, organic chemistry, quantitative analysis, and integral/differential calculus. Additional exam requirements/recommendations for international students: Required—TOEFL (minimum score 550 paper-based; 79 iBT) or IELTS (minimum score 6.5). *Application deadline:* For fall admission, 2/15 for domestic students, 1/2 for international students. Application fee: $30. *Expenses:* Contact institution. *Faculty research:* Anatomy, biochemistry, cancer biology, cardiovascular disease, cell biology, immunology, microbiology, molecular biology, neuroscience, pharmacology, physiology. *Unit head:* Dr. Michael Barber, Professor and Associate Dean for Graduate and Postdoctoral Affairs, 813-974-9908, Fax: 813-974-4317, E-mail: mbarber@health.usf.edu. *Application contact:* Dr. Eric Bennett, Graduate Director, PhD Program in Medical Sciences, 813-974-1545, Fax: 813-974-4317, E-mail: esbennet@health.usf.edu.
Website: http://health.usf.edu/nocms/medicine/graduatestudies/.

The University of Tennessee, Graduate School, College of Education, Health and Human Sciences, Department of Exercise, Sport, and Leisure Studies, Program in Exercise Science, Knoxville, TN 37996. Offers biomechanics/sports medicine (MS, PhD); exercise physiology (MS, PhD). *Accreditation:* CEPH (one or more programs are accredited). Part-time programs available. *Degree requirements:* For master's, thesis optional. *Entrance requirements:* For master's, minimum GPA of 2.7. Additional exam requirements/recommendations for international students: Required—TOEFL. Electronic applications accepted. *Expenses:* Tuition, state resident: full-time $9540; part-time $531 per credit hour. Tuition, nonresident: full-time $27,728; part-time $1542 per credit hour. *Required fees:* $1404; $67 per credit hour.

The University of Tennessee at Chattanooga, Graduate School, College of Health, Education and Professional Studies, Department of Health and Human Performance, Chattanooga, TN 37403. Offers athletic training (MSAT); health and human performance (MS). *Faculty:* 5 full-time (3 women). *Students:* 37 full-time (24 women), 2 part-time (1 woman); includes 4 minority (2 Black or African American, non-Hispanic/Latino; 1 Hispanic/Latino; 1 Two or more races, non-Hispanic/Latino). Average age 24. 5 applicants, 60% accepted, 2 enrolled. In 2013, 22 master's awarded. *Degree requirements:* For master's, thesis or alternative, clinical rotations. *Entrance requirements:* For master's, GRE General Test or MAT, minimum GPA of 2.75 overall or 3.0 in last 60 hours; CPR and First Aid certification. Additional exam requirements/recommendations for international students: Required—TOEFL (minimum score 550 paper-based; 79 iBT), IELTS (minimum score 6). *Application deadline:* For fall admission, 6/13 priority date for domestic students, 6/1 for international students; for spring admission, 10/15 priority date for domestic students, 10/1 for international students. Applications are processed on a rolling basis. Application fee: $30 ($35 for international students). Electronic applications accepted. *Financial support:* In 2013–14, 6 research assistantships with tuition reimbursements (averaging $5,320 per year), 2 teaching assistantships with tuition reimbursements (averaging $3,432 per year) were awarded; career-related internships or fieldwork, scholarships/grants, and unspecified assistantships also available. Support available to part-time students. *Faculty research:* Therapeutic exercise, lumbar spine biomechanics, physical activity epidemiology, functional rehabilitation outcomes, metabolic health. *Unit head:* Dr. Gary Liguori, Department Head, 423-425-4196, Fax: 423-425-4457, E-mail: gary-liguori@utc.edu. *Application contact:* Dr. J. Randy Walker, Interim Dean of Graduate Studies, 423-425-4478, Fax: 423-425-5223, E-mail: randy-walker@utc.edu.
Website: https://www.utc.edu/Academic/HealthAndHumanPerformance/.

University of Wisconsin–La Crosse, Graduate Studies, College of Science and Health, Department of Exercise and Sport Science, Program in Human Performance, La Crosse, WI 54601-3742. Offers applied sport science (MS); human performance (MS); strength and conditioning (MS). Part-time programs available. *Students:* 14 full-time (4 women), 7 part-time (3 women); includes 2 minority (1 Black or African American, non-Hispanic/Latino; 1 American Indian or Alaska Native, non-Hispanic/Latino). Average age 24. 40 applicants, 53% accepted, 13 enrolled. In 2013, 10 master's awarded. *Degree requirements:* For master's, comprehensive exam (for some programs), thesis optional. *Entrance requirements:* For master's, GRE, course work in anatomy, physiology, biomechanics, and exercise physiology. Additional exam requirements/recommendations for international students: Required—TOEFL (minimum score 550 paper-based; 79 iBT). *Application deadline:* For fall admission, 2/1 priority date for domestic and international students. Electronic applications accepted. *Financial support:* Federal Work-Study, scholarships/grants, health care benefits, and tuition waivers (partial) available. Support available to part-time students. Financial award application deadline: 3/15; financial award applicants required to submit FAFSA. *Faculty research:* Anaerobic metabolism, power development, strength training, biomechanics, athletic performance. *Unit head:* Dr. Glenn Wright, Director, 608-785-8689, Fax: 608-785-8172,

E-mail: wright.glen@uwlax.edu. *Application contact:* Corey Sjoquist, Director of Admissions, 608-785-8939, E-mail: admissions@uwlax.edu.
Website: http://www.uwlax.edu/sah/ess/hp/.

Virginia Commonwealth University, Graduate School, School of Education, Department of Health and Human Performance, Program in Athletic Training, Richmond, VA 23284-9005. Offers MSAT. Electronic applications accepted.

Weber State University, Jerry and Vickie Moyes College of Education, Program in Athletic Training, Ogden, UT 84408-1001. Offers MSAT. Part-time programs available. *Faculty:* 5 full-time (3 women). *Students:* 31 full-time (17 women), 1 (woman) part-time; includes 2 minority (both Hispanic/Latino), 3 international. Average age 32. 33 applicants, 55% accepted, 14 enrolled. In 2013, 14 master's awarded. *Degree requirements:* For master's, thesis. *Entrance requirements:* For master's, GRE (if GPA less than 3.0), physical, immunizations. Additional exam requirements/recommendations for international students: Required—TOEFL (minimum score 550 paper-based). *Application deadline:* For fall admission, 2/1 priority date for domestic and international students. Applications are processed on a rolling basis. Application fee: $60 ($90 for international students). *Expenses:* Tuition, state resident: full-time $7118; part-time $253 per credit hour. Tuition, nonresident: full-time $12,480; part-time $634 per credit hour. *Required fees:* $34.33; $34.33 per credit hour. $257 per semester. Full-time tuition and fees vary according to course load. *Financial support:* In 2013–14, 25 students received support. Application deadline: 4/1; applicants required to submit FAFSA. *Faculty research:* Pedagogy, heat illness, electrical stimulation. *Unit head:* Dr. Valerie W. Herzog, Program Director, 801-626-7675, Fax: 801-626-6228, E-mail: valerieherzog@weber.edu.
Website: http://www.weber.edu/athletictraining.

West Chester University of Pennsylvania, College of Health Sciences, Department of Kinesiology, West Chester, PA 19383. Offers adapted physical education (Certificate); exercise and sport physiology (MS), including athletic training, exercise and sport physiology; general physical education (MS); sport management and athletics (MPA). Part-time and evening/weekend programs available. Postbaccalaureate distance learning degree programs offered (no on-campus study). *Faculty:* 6 full-time (5 women). *Students:* 25 full-time (13 women), 10 part-time (4 women); includes 5 minority (1 Black or African American, non-Hispanic/Latino; 1 Asian, non-Hispanic/Latino; 2 Hispanic/Latino; 1 Two or more races, non-Hispanic/Latino), 1 international. Average age 27. 33 applicants, 97% accepted, 18 enrolled. In 2013, 15 master's, 6 other advanced degrees awarded. *Degree requirements:* For master's, thesis or report (for MS); 2 internships, capstone course including research project or thesis (for MPA). *Entrance requirements:* For master's, GRE (for MS), 2 letters of recommendation, transcripts, and statement of professional goals (for MS); 2 letters of reference, resume, and career goal statement (for MPA). Additional exam requirements/recommendations for international students: Required—TOEFL (minimum score 550 paper-based; 80 iBT). *Application deadline:* For fall admission, 4/15 priority date for domestic students, 3/15 for international students; for spring admission, 10/15 priority date for domestic students, 9/1 for international students. Applications are processed on a rolling basis. Application fee: $45. Electronic applications accepted. *Expenses:* Tuition, state resident: full-time $7956; part-time $442 per credit. Tuition, nonresident: full-time $11,934; part-time $663 per credit. *Required fees:* $2134.20; $106.24 per credit. Tuition and fees vary according to campus/location and program. *Financial support:* Unspecified assistantships available. Support available to part-time students. Financial award application deadline: 2/15; financial award applicants required to submit FAFSA. *Faculty research:* Metabolism during exercise, biomechanics, rating of perceived exertion, motor learning. *Unit head:* Dr. Frank Fry, Chair/Graduate Coordinator for the MS in General Physical Education Program, 610-436-2610, Fax: 610-436-2860, E-mail: ffry@wcupa.edu. *Application contact:* Dr. David Stearne, Graduate Coordinator for the Exercise and Sport Physiology Programs, 610-436-2347, Fax: 610-436-2860, E-mail: dstearne@wcupa.edu.
Website: http://www.wcupa.edu/_academics/sch_shs.hpe/.

Western Michigan University, Graduate College, College of Education and Human Development, Department of Health, Physical Education and Recreation, Kalamazoo, MI 49008. Offers exercise and sports medicine (MS), including athletic training, exercise physiology; physical education (MA), including coaching sport performance, pedagogy, special physical education, sport management.

West Virginia University, School of Physical Education, Morgantown, WV 26506. Offers athletic coaching education (MS); athletic training (MS); physical education/teacher education (MS, PhD), including curriculum and instruction (PhD), motor behavior (PhD), physical education supervision (PhD); sport and exercise psychology (PhD); sport management (MS). *Degree requirements:* For doctorate, comprehensive exam, thesis/dissertation, oral exam. *Entrance requirements:* For master's, GRE or MAT, minimum GPA of 3.0; for doctorate, GRE General Test or MAT, minimum GPA of 3.5. Additional exam requirements/recommendations for international students: Required—TOEFL (minimum score 550 paper-based). Electronic applications accepted. *Faculty research:* Sport psychosociology, teacher education, exercise psychology, counseling.

West Virginia Wesleyan College, Department of Exercise Science, Buckhannon, WV 26201. Offers athletic training (MS).

Exercise and Sports Science

American Public University System, AMU/APU Graduate Programs, Charles Town, WV 25414. Offers accounting (MBA, MS); criminal justice (MA), including business administration, emergency and disaster management, general (MA, MS); educational leadership (M Ed); emergency and disaster management (MA); entrepreneurship (MBA); environmental policy and management (MS), including environmental planning, environmental sustainability, fish and wildlife management, general (MA, MS), global environmental management; finance (MBA); general (MBA); global business management (MBA); history (MA), including American history, ancient and classical history, European history, global history, public history; homeland security (MA), including business administration, counter-terrorism studies, criminal justice, cyber, emergency management and public health, intelligence studies, transportation security; homeland security resource allocation (MBA); humanities (MA); information technology (MS), including digital forensics, enterprise software development, information assurance and security, IT project management; information technology management (MBA); intelligence studies (MA), including criminal intelligence, cyber, general (MA, MS), homeland security, intelligence analysis, intelligence collection, intelligence management, intelligence operations, terrorism studies; international relations and conflict resolution (MA), including comparative and security issues, conflict resolution, international and transnational security issues, peacekeeping; legal studies (MA); management (MA), including defense management, general (MA, MS), human resource management, organizational leadership, public administration; marketing (MBA); military history (MA), including American military history, American Revolution, civil war, war since 1945, World War II; military studies (MA), including joint warfare, strategic leadership; national security studies (MA), including general (MA, MS), homeland security, regional security studies, security and intelligence analysis, terrorism studies; nonprofit management (MBA); political science (MA), including American politics and government, comparative government and development, general (MA, MS), international relations, public policy; psychology (MA), including general (MA, MS), maritime engineering management, reverse logistics management; public administration (MPA), including disaster management, environmental policy, health policy, human resources, national security, organizational management, security management; public health (MPH); reverse logistics management (MA); school counseling (M Ed); security management (MA); space studies (MS), including aerospace science, general (MA, MS), planetary science; sports and health sciences (MS); teaching (M Ed), including curriculum and instruction for elementary teachers, elementary reading, English language learners, instructional leadership, online learning, special education; transportation and logistics management (MA), including general (MA, MS), maritime engineering management, reverse logistics management. Programs offered via distance learning only. Part-time and evening/weekend programs available. Postbaccalaureate distance learning degree programs offered (no on-campus study). *Faculty:* 432 full-time (242 women), 1,722 part-time/adjunct (829 women). *Students:* 511 full-time (241 women), 10,947 part-time (4,294 women); includes 3,760 minority (2,058 Black or African American, non-Hispanic/Latino; 88 American Indian or Alaska Native, non-Hispanic/Latino; 293 Asian, non-Hispanic/Latino; 876 Hispanic/Latino; 91 Native Hawaiian or other Pacific Islander, non-Hispanic/Latino; 354 Two or more races, non-Hispanic/Latino), 134 international. Average age 36. In 2013, 3,323 master's awarded. *Degree requirements:* For master's, comprehensive exam or practicum. *Entrance requirements:* For master's, official transcript showing earned bachelor's degree from institution accredited by recognized accrediting body. Additional exam requirements/recommendations for international students: Required—TOEFL (minimum score 550 paper-based), IELTS (minimum score 6.5). *Application deadline:* Applications are processed on a rolling basis. Application fee: $0. Electronic applications accepted. *Expenses: Tuition:* Part-time $325 per semester hour. *Financial support:* Applicants required to submit FAFSA. *Faculty research:* Military history, criminal justice, management performance, national security. *Unit head:* Dr. Karan Powell, Executive Vice President and Provost, 877-468-6268, Fax: 304-724-3780. *Application contact:* Terry Grant, Vice President of Enrollment Management, 877-468-6268, Fax: 304-724-3780, E-mail: info@apus.edu.
Website: http://www.apus.edu.

American University, College of Arts and Sciences, Washington, DC 20016-8012. Offers addiction and addictive behavior (Certificate); anthropology (PhD); applied microeconomics (Certificate); applied statistics (Certificate); art history (MA); arts management (MA, Certificate); Asian studies (Certificate); audio production (Certificate); audio technology (MA); behavior, cognition, and neuroscience (PhD); bilingual education (MA, Certificate); biology (MA, MS); chemistry (MS); clinical psychology (PhD); computer science (MS, Certificate); creative writing (MFA); curriculum and instruction (M Ed, Certificate); economics (MA, PhD); environmental assessment (Certificate); environmental science (MS); ethics, peace, and global affairs (MA); gender analysis in economics (Certificate); health promotion management (MS); history (MA, PhD); international arts management (Certificate); international economic relations (Certificate); international economics (MA); international training and education (MA); literature (MA); mathematics (MA); North American studies (Certificate); nutrition education (MS, Certificate); philosophy (MA); professional science: biotechnology (MS); professional science: environmental assessment (MS); professional science: quantitative analysis (MS); psychobiology of healing (Certificate); psychology (MA); psychology: general (PhD); public anthropology (MA, Certificate); public sociology (Certificate); social research (Certificate); sociology (MA); Spanish: Latin American studies (MA); special education: learning disabilities (MA); statistics (MS); studio art (MFA); teaching (MAT); teaching English as a foreign language (MA); teaching: early childhood (Certificate); teaching: elementary (Certificate); teaching: ESOL (Certificate); teaching: secondary (Certificate); technology in arts management (Certificate); TESOL (MA); translation: French (Certificate); translation: Russian (Certificate); translation: Spanish (Certificate); women's, gender, and sexuality studies (Certificate). Part-time and evening/weekend programs available. Postbaccalaureate distance learning degree programs offered (no on-campus study). *Faculty:* 358 full-time (187 women), 254 part-time/adjunct (127 women). *Students:* 627 full-time (411 women), 416 part-time (300 women); includes 206 minority (91 Black or African American, non-Hispanic/Latino; 5 American Indian or Alaska Native, non-Hispanic/Latino; 32 Asian, non-Hispanic/Latino; 64 Hispanic/Latino; 1 Native Hawaiian or other Pacific Islander, non-Hispanic/Latino; 13 Two or more races, non-Hispanic/Latino), 124 international. Average age 29. 1,672 applicants, 52% accepted, 361 enrolled. In 2013, 382 master's, 38 doctorates, 33 other advanced degrees awarded. Terminal master's awarded for partial completion of doctoral program. *Degree requirements:* For master's, comprehensive exam (for some programs), thesis (for some programs); for doctorate, comprehensive exam (for some programs), thesis/dissertation. *Entrance requirements:* For master's, GRE, minimum GPA of 3.0 in last 60 credit hours, letter of recommendation, statement of purpose, resume, unofficial transcript; for doctorate, GRE, minimum GPA of 3.0 for all graduate work, letter of recommendation, statement of purpose, resume, unofficial transcript. Additional exam requirements/recommendations for international students: Required—TOEFL (minimum score 600 paper-based; 100 iBT), IELTS (minimum score 7). *Application deadline:* For fall admission, 2/1 for domestic students; for spring admission, 10/1 for domestic students. Applications are processed on a rolling basis. Application fee: $55. Electronic applications accepted. *Expenses: Tuition:* Full-time $25,920; part-time $1482 per credit hour. *Required fees:* $430. Tuition and fees vary according to course load and program. *Financial support:* Fellowships, research assistantships with full and partial tuition reimbursements, teaching assistantships with full and partial tuition reimbursements, career-related internships or fieldwork, Federal Work-Study, institutionally sponsored loans, scholarships/grants, traineeships, tuition waivers (full and partial), and unspecified assistantships available. Support available to part-time students. Financial award applicants required to submit FAFSA. *Unit head:* Dr. Peter Starr, Dean, 202-885-2446, Fax: 202-885-2429, E-mail: pstarr@american.edu.

Application contact: Kathleen Clowery, Associate Director, Graduate Enrollment Management, 202-885-3621, Fax: 202-885-1505, E-mail: clowery@american.edu.
Website: http://www.american.edu/cas/.

Appalachian State University, Cratis D. Williams Graduate School, Department of Health, Leisure, and Exercise Science, Boone, NC 28608. Offers exercise science (MS), including clinical exercise physiology, research, strength and conditioning. *Degree requirements:* For master's, comprehensive exam, thesis optional. *Entrance requirements:* For master's, GRE General Test, 3 letters of recommendation. Additional exam requirements/recommendations for international students: Required—TOEFL (minimum score 570 paper-based; 79 iBT), IELTS (minimum score 6.5). Electronic applications accepted. *Faculty research:* Exercise immunology, biomechanics, exercise and chronic disease, muscle damage, strength and conditioning.

Arizona State University at the Tempe campus, College of Nursing and Health Innovation, Phoenix, AZ 85004. Offers advanced nursing practice (DNP); child/family mental health nurse practitioner (Graduate Certificate); clinical research management (MS); community and public health practice (Graduate Certificate); community health (MS); exercise and wellness (MS), including exercise and wellness; family nurse practitioner (Graduate Certificate); healthcare innovation (MHI); international health for healthcare (Graduate Certificate); kinesiology (MS, PhD); nursing (MS, Graduate Certificate); nursing and healthcare innovation (PhD); nutrition (MS); physical activity nutrition and wellness (PhD), including physical activity, nutrition and wellness; public health (MPH); regulatory science and health safety (MS). *Accreditation:* AACN. Postbaccalaureate distance learning degree programs offered (minimal on-campus study). *Degree requirements:* For master's, comprehensive exam (for some programs), thesis (for some programs), interactive Program of Study (iPOS) submitted before completing 50 percent of required credit hours; for doctorate, comprehensive exam, thesis/dissertation, interactive Program of Study (iPOS) submitted before completing 50 percent of required credit hours. *Entrance requirements:* For master's and doctorate, GRE, minimum GPA of 3.0 or equivalent in last 2 years of work leading to bachelor's degree. Additional exam requirements/recommendations for international students: Required—TOEFL (minimum score 80 iBT), TOEFL, IELTS, or PTE. Electronic applications accepted. *Expenses:* Contact institution.

Arkansas State University, Graduate School, College of Education and Behavioral Science, Department of Health, Physical Education, and Sport Sciences, Jonesboro, AR 72467. Offers exercise science (MS); physical education (MSE, SCCT); sports administration (MS). Part-time programs available. *Faculty:* 9 full-time (3 women). *Students:* 20 full-time (5 women), 35 part-time (11 women); includes 19 minority (13 Black or African American, non-Hispanic/Latino; 5 Hispanic/Latino; 1 Two or more races, non-Hispanic/Latino), 8 international. Average age 26. 53 applicants, 70% accepted, 29 enrolled. In 2013, 18 master's awarded. *Degree requirements:* For master's, comprehensive exam, thesis or alternative; for SCCT, comprehensive exam. *Entrance requirements:* For master's, GRE General Test or MAT, appropriate bachelor's degree, official transcripts, immunization records, statement of goals, letters of recommendation; for SCCT, GRE General Test or MAT, interview, master's degree, official transcript, immunization records. Additional exam requirements/recommendations for international students: Required—TOEFL (minimum score 550 paper-based; 79 iBT), IELTS (minimum score 6), PTE (minimum score 56). *Application deadline:* For fall admission, 7/1 for domestic and international students; for spring admission, 11/15 for domestic students, 11/14 for international students. Applications are processed on a rolling basis. Application fee: $30 ($40 for international students). Electronic applications accepted. *Expenses:* Tuition, state resident: full-time $4284; part-time $238 per credit hour. Tuition, nonresident: full-time $8568; part-time $476 per credit hour. *International tuition:* $9268 full-time. *Required fees:* $1098; $61 per credit hour. $25 per term. Tuition and fees vary according to course load and program. *Financial support:* In 2013–14, 18 students received support. Teaching assistantships, career-related internships or fieldwork, scholarships/grants, and unspecified assistantships available. Financial award application deadline: 7/1; financial award applicants required to submit FAFSA. *Unit head:* Dr. Jim Stillwell, Chair, 870-972-3066, Fax: 870-972-3096, E-mail: jstillwel@astate.edu. *Application contact:* Vickey Ring, Graduate Admissions Coordinator, 870-972-3029, Fax: 870-972-3857, E-mail: vickeyring@astate.edu.
Website: http://www.astate.edu/college/education/departments/health-physical-educations-and-sport-sciences/index.dot.

Armstrong State University, School of Graduate Studies, Program in Sports Medicine, Savannah, GA 31419-1997. Offers sports health sciences (MSSM); strength and conditioning (Certificate). Part-time programs available. *Faculty:* 3 full-time (0 women), 1 part-time/adjunct (0 women). *Students:* 2 full-time (1 woman), 26 part-time (17 women); includes 4 minority (all Black or African American, non-Hispanic/Latino). Average age 25. 34 applicants, 56% accepted, 11 enrolled. In 2013, 10 master's awarded. *Degree requirements:* For master's, comprehensive exam, MAT, thesis optional, project. *Entrance requirements:* For master's, GRE General Test, MAT, GMAT, minimum GPA of 2.7, letter of intent. Additional exam requirements/recommendations for international students: Required—TOEFL (minimum score 523 paper-based). *Application deadline:* For fall admission, 6/1 priority date for domestic students, 5/1 priority date for international students; for spring admission, 11/15 priority date for domestic students, 9/15 priority date for international students; for summer admission, 4/15 for domestic students, 9/15 for international students. Application fee: $30. *Expenses:* Tuition, state resident: part-time $201 per credit hour. Tuition, nonresident: part-time $745 per credit hour. *Required fees:* $310 per semester. Tuition and fees vary according to course load, campus/location and program. *Financial support:* In 2013–14, research assistantships with full tuition reimbursements (averaging $5,000 per year) were awarded; scholarships/grants, tuition waivers (full), and unspecified assistantships also available. Financial award application deadline: 3/15; financial award applicants required to submit FAFSA. *Unit head:* Dr. James Streater, Department Head, 912-921-2548, Fax: 912-344-3490, E-mail: sandy.streater@armstrong.edu. *Application contact:* Bryan Riemann, Graduate Coordinator, 912-344-2934, Fax: 912-344-3490, E-mail: brian.riemann@armstrong.edu.
Website: http://www.armstrong.edu/Majors/degree/sports_medicine1.

Ashland University, Dwight Schar College of Education, Department of Sport Sciences, Ashland, OH 44805-3702. Offers adapted physical education (M Ed); applied exercise science (M Ed); sport education (M Ed); sport management (M Ed). Part-time programs available. *Degree requirements:* For master's, practicum, inquiry seminar, thesis, or internship. *Entrance requirements:* For master's, teaching certificate or license, bachelor's degree, minimum cumulative GPA of 2.75. Additional exam requirements/recommendations for international students: Required—TOEFL. *Faculty research:* Coaching, legal issues, strength and conditioning, sport management rating of perceived exertion, youth fitness, geriatric exercise science.

Auburn University, Graduate School, College of Education, Department of Kinesiology, Auburn University, AL 36849. Offers exercise science (M Ed, MS, PhD); health promotion (M Ed, MS); kinesiology (PhD); physical education/teacher education (M Ed, MS, Ed D, Ed S). *Accreditation:* NCATE. Part-time programs available. *Faculty:* 19 full-time (9 women). *Students:* 89 full-time (43 women), 21 part-time (9 women); includes 17 minority (15 Black or African American, non-Hispanic/Latino; 1 Asian, non-Hispanic/Latino; 1 Hispanic/Latino), 5 international. Average age 26. 136 applicants, 71% accepted, 60 enrolled. In 2013, 38 master's, 10 doctorates awarded. *Degree requirements:* For master's, thesis (for some programs); for doctorate, thesis/dissertation; for Ed S, exam, field project. *Entrance requirements:* For master's, GRE General Test; for doctorate and Ed S, GRE General Test, interview, master's degree. *Application deadline:* For fall admission, 7/7 for domestic students; for spring admission, 11/24 for domestic students. Applications are processed on a rolling basis. Application fee: $50 ($60 for international students). Electronic applications accepted. *Expenses:* Tuition, state resident: full-time $8262; part-time $459 per credit hour. Tuition, nonresident: full-time $24,786; part-time $1377 per credit hour. Tuition and fees vary according to degree level and program. *Financial support:* Research assistantships, teaching assistantships, and Federal Work-Study available. Support available to part-time students. Financial award application deadline: 3/15; financial award applicants required to submit FAFSA. *Faculty research:* Biomechanics, exercise physiology, motor skill learning, school health, curriculum development. *Unit head:* Dr. Mary E. Rudisill, Head, 334-844-1458. *Application contact:* Dr. George Flowers, Dean of the Graduate School, 334-844-2125.

Austin Peay State University, College of Graduate Studies, College of Behavioral and Health Sciences, Department of Health and Human Performance, Clarksville, TN 37044. Offers health leadership (MS). Part-time and evening/weekend programs available. Postbaccalaureate distance learning degree programs offered (no on-campus study). *Faculty:* 6 full-time (3 women). *Students:* 15 full-time (6 women), 30 part-time (21 women); includes 14 minority (13 Black or African American, non-Hispanic/Latino; 1 Hispanic/Latino). Average age 27. 41 applicants, 90% accepted, 32 enrolled. In 2013, 32 master's awarded. *Degree requirements:* For master's, comprehensive exam, thesis optional. *Entrance requirements:* For master's, GRE General Test, 3 letters of recommendation, minimum undergraduate GPA of 2.5. Additional exam requirements/recommendations for international students: Required—TOEFL (minimum score 500 paper-based). *Application deadline:* For fall admission, 8/5 priority date for domestic students. Applications are processed on a rolling basis. Application fee: $25. Electronic applications accepted. *Expenses:* Tuition, state resident: full-time $7500; part-time $375 per credit hour. Tuition, nonresident: full-time $20,800; part-time $1040 per credit hour. *Required fees:* $1284; $64.20 per credit hour. *Financial support:* In 2013–14, research assistantships with full tuition reimbursements (averaging $6,500 per year) were awarded; career-related internships or fieldwork, Federal Work-Study, institutionally sponsored loans, scholarships/grants, and unspecified assistantships also available. Support available to part-time students. Financial award application deadline: 3/1; financial award applicants required to submit FAFSA. *Unit head:* Dr. Marcy Maurer, Chair, 931-221-6105, Fax: 931-221-7040, E-mail: maurerm@apsu.edu. *Application contact:* June D. Lee, Graduate Coordinator, 800-859-4723, Fax: 931-221-7641, E-mail: gradadmissions@apsu.edu.
Website: http://www.apsu.edu/hhp/.

Ball State University, Graduate School, College of Applied Science and Technology, Interdepartmental Program in Human Bioenergetics, Muncie, IN 47306-1099. Offers PhD. *Students:* 10 part-time (2 women), 1 international. 7 applicants, 43% accepted, 2 enrolled. In 2013, 1 doctorate awarded. *Degree requirements:* For doctorate, thesis/dissertation. *Entrance requirements:* For doctorate, GRE General Test, interview, minimum graduate GPA of 3.2, resume. Application fee: $50. *Financial support:* In 2013–14, 8 students received support, including 8 research assistantships with full tuition reimbursements available (averaging $17,359 per year), 13 teaching assistantships with full tuition reimbursements available (averaging $10,800 per year). Financial award application deadline: 3/1. *Unit head:* Dr. Scott Trappe, Director, 765-285-1145, Fax: 765-285-8596, E-mail: strappe@bsu.edu. *Application contact:* Dr. Robert Morris, Associate Provost for Research and Dean of the Graduate School, 765-285-5723, Fax: 765-285-1328, E-mail: rmorris@bsu.edu.
Website: http://cms.bsu.edu/Academics/CentersandInstitutes/HPL/GraduatePrograms/HumanBioenergetics.aspx.

Barry University, School of Human Performance and Leisure Sciences, Programs in Movement Science, Specialization in Exercise Science, Miami Shores, FL 33161-6695. Offers MS. *Degree requirements:* For master's, comprehensive exam, thesis. *Entrance requirements:* For master's, GRE, minimum GPA of 3.0. Electronic applications accepted. *Faculty research:* Physiological adaptations to exercise.

Baylor University, Graduate School, School of Education, Department of Health, Human Performance and Recreation, Waco, TX 76798. Offers community health education (MPH); exercise physiology (MS Ed); kinesiology, exercise nutrition and health promotion (PhD); sport management (MS Ed); sport pedagogy (MS Ed). *Accreditation:* NCATE. Part-time programs available. *Faculty:* 13 full-time (5 women), 3 part-time/adjunct (1 woman). *Students:* 79 full-time (40 women), 28 part-time (14 women); includes 26 minority (9 Black or African American, non-Hispanic/Latino; 1 American Indian or Alaska Native, non-Hispanic/Latino; 3 Asian, non-Hispanic/Latino; 8 Hispanic/Latino; 5 Two or more races, non-Hispanic/Latino), 9 international. 30 applicants, 87% accepted. In 2013, 48 master's awarded. *Degree requirements:* For master's, comprehensive exam, thesis optional; for doctorate, comprehensive exam, thesis/dissertation. *Entrance requirements:* For master's and doctorate, GRE General Test. Additional exam requirements/recommendations for international students: Required—TOEFL. *Application deadline:* For fall admission, 2/1 priority date for domestic students, 2/1 for international students; for spring admission, 10/1 for domestic and international students. Applications are processed on a rolling basis. Application fee: $25. Electronic applications accepted. *Expenses: Tuition:* Full-time $25,866; part-time $1437 per credit hour. *Required fees:* $2736; $152 per credit hour. Tuition and fees vary according to course load and program. *Financial support:* In 2013–14, 35 students received support, including 1 research assistantship with tuition reimbursement available, 33 teaching assistantships with tuition reimbursements available; career-related internships or fieldwork, Federal Work-Study, institutionally sponsored loans, tuition waivers (partial), and unspecified assistantships also available. Financial award application deadline: 2/1. *Faculty research:* Behavior change theory, nutrition and enzyme therapy, exercise testing, health planning, sport management. *Unit head:* Dr. Jeffrey Petersen, Graduate Program Director, 254-710-4007, Fax: 254-710-3527, E-mail: jeffrey_petersen@baylor.edu. *Application contact:* Kathy Mirick, Administrative Assistant, 254-710-3526, Fax: 254-710-3527, E-mail: kathy_mirick@baylor.edu.
Website: http://www.baylor.edu/HHPR/.

Benedictine University, Graduate Programs, Program in Clinical Exercise Physiology, Lisle, IL 60532-0900. Offers MS. Part-time programs available. *Students:* 22 part-time (16 women); includes 5 minority (1 Black or African American, non-Hispanic/Latino; 1 American Indian or Alaska Native, non-Hispanic/Latino; 3 Hispanic/Latino). 24 applicants, 75% accepted, 11 enrolled. In 2013, 10 master's awarded. *Entrance requirements:* Additional exam requirements/recommendations for international students: Required—TOEFL (minimum score 550 paper-based). *Application deadline:* For fall admission, 9/1 for domestic students; for winter admission, 12/1 for domestic students; for spring admission, 2/15 for domestic students. Applications are processed on a rolling basis. Application fee: $40. Electronic applications accepted. *Expenses: Tuition:* Part-time $590 per credit hour. *Financial support:* Career-related internships or fieldwork and health care benefits available. Support available to part-time students. *Faculty research:* Protein synthesis cell signaling control, aging. *Unit head:* Dr. Allison

Wilson, Director of New Faculty Mentoring Program, 630-829-6520, E-mail: awilson@ben.edu. *Application contact:* Kari Gibbons, Associate Vice President, Enrollment Center, 630-829-6200, Fax: 630-829-6584, E-mail: kgibbons@ben.edu.

Bloomsburg University of Pennsylvania, School of Graduate Studies, College of Science and Technology, Department of Exercise Science and Athletics, Bloomsburg, PA 17815-1301. Offers clinical athletic training (MS); exercise science (MS). *Faculty:* 6 full-time (1 woman). *Students:* 1 full-time (0 women), 55 part-time (33 women); includes 11 minority (5 Black or African American, non-Hispanic/Latino; 1 Asian, non-Hispanic/Latino; 3 Hispanic/Latino; 2 Two or more races, non-Hispanic/Latino), 1 international. Average age 24. 74 applicants, 65% accepted, 27 enrolled. In 2013, 20 master's awarded. *Degree requirements:* For master's, thesis optional, practical clinical experience. *Entrance requirements:* For master's, GRE, minimum QPA of 3.0, related undergraduate coursework. Additional exam requirements/recommendations for international students: Required—TOEFL (minimum score 550 paper-based; 79 iBT). *Application deadline:* Applications are processed on a rolling basis. Application fee: $35 ($60 for international students). Electronic applications accepted. *Expenses:* Tuition, state resident: full-time $7956; part-time $442 per credit. Tuition, nonresident: full-time $11,934; part-time $663 per credit. *Required fees:* $95.50 per credit. $55 per semester. Tuition and fees vary according to course load. *Financial support:* Unspecified assistantships available. *Unit head:* Dr. Timothy McConnell, Chairperson, 570-389-4376, Fax: 570-389-5047, E-mail: tmconne@bloomu.edu. *Application contact:* Jennifer Richard, Administrative Assistant, 570-389-4015, Fax: 570-389-3054, E-mail: jrichard@bloomu.edu.
Website: http://www.bloomu.edu/exercise_science.

Boise State University, College of Education, Department of Kinesiology, Boise, ID 83725-0399. Offers exercise and sports studies (MS); kinesiology (MK); physical education (MS). Part-time programs available. *Degree requirements:* For master's, thesis. *Entrance requirements:* For master's, minimum GPA of 3.0. Electronic applications accepted.

Brigham Young University, Graduate Studies, College of Life Sciences, Department of Exercise Sciences, Provo, UT 84602. Offers athletic training (MS); exercise physiology (MS, PhD); exercise science (MS); health promotion (MS, PhD); physical medicine and rehabilitation (PhD). *Faculty:* 20 full-time (3 women), 1 part-time/adjunct (0 women). *Students:* 45 full-time (20 women), 2 part-time (1 woman); includes 4 minority (2 Asian, non-Hispanic/Latino; 2 Two or more races, non-Hispanic/Latino). Average age 28. 23 applicants, 48% accepted, 8 enrolled. In 2013, 13 master's, 1 doctorate awarded. *Degree requirements:* For master's, thesis, oral defense; for doctorate, comprehensive exam, thesis/dissertation, oral defense, oral and written exams. *Entrance requirements:* For master's, GRE General Test, minimum GPA of 3.2 in last 60 hours of course work; for doctorate, GRE General Test, minimum GPA of 3.5 in last 60 hours of course work. Additional exam requirements/recommendations for international students: Required—TOEFL (minimum score 580 paper-based; 85 iBT), IELTS (minimum score 7). *Application deadline:* For fall admission, 2/1 for domestic and international students. Application fee: $50. Electronic applications accepted. *Expenses:* Tuition: Full-time $6130; part-time $340 per credit hour. Tuition and fees vary according to program and student's religious affiliation. *Financial support:* In 2013–14, 36 students received support, including 24 research assistantships with partial tuition reimbursements available (averaging $2,600 per year), 19 teaching assistantships with partial tuition reimbursements available (averaging $3,350 per year); fellowships, career-related internships or fieldwork, institutionally sponsored loans, scholarships/grants, tuition waivers (partial), unspecified assistantships, and 10 PhD full tuition scholarships also available. Financial award application deadline: 3/1. *Faculty research:* Injury prevention and rehabilitation, human skeletal muscle adaptation, cardiovascular health and fitness, lifestyle modification and health promotion. *Total annual research expenditures:* $22,117. *Unit head:* Dr. Gary Mack, Chair, 801-422-2466, Fax: 801-422-0555, E-mail: gary_mack@byu.edu. *Application contact:* Dr. William J. Myrer, Graduate Coordinator, 801-422-2690, Fax: 801-422-0555, E-mail: bill_myrer@byu.edu.
Website: http://exsc.byu.edu/.

Brooklyn College of the City University of New York, Division of Graduate Studies, Department of Physical Education and Exercise Science, Brooklyn, NY 11210-2889. Offers exercise science and rehabilitation (MS); physical education (MS), including sports management. Part-time programs available. *Degree requirements:* For master's, comprehensive exam or thesis. *Entrance requirements:* For master's, previous course work in physical education and education, minimum GPA of 3.0, 2 letters of recommendation, essay. Additional exam requirements/recommendations for international students: Required—TOEFL (minimum score 500 paper-based; 61 iBT). Electronic applications accepted. *Faculty research:* Exercise physiology, motor learning, sports psychology, women in athletics.

California Baptist University, Program in Kinesiology, Riverside, CA 92504-3206. Offers exercise science (MS); physical education pedagogy (MS); sport management (MS). Part-time programs available. *Faculty:* 7 full-time (4 women), 3 part-time/adjunct (1 woman). *Students:* 27 full-time (8 women), 23 part-time (8 women); includes 19 minority (10 Black or African American, non-Hispanic/Latino; 2 Asian, non-Hispanic/Latino; 5 Hispanic/Latino; 2 Two or more races, non-Hispanic/Latino), 6 international. Average age 27. 64 applicants, 66% accepted, 25 enrolled. In 2013, 41 master's awarded. *Degree requirements:* For master's, comprehensive exam (for some programs), comprehensive exam or research thesis. *Entrance requirements:* For master's, minimum undergraduate GPA of 2.75; 12 units of kinesiology prerequisites; three recommendations; 500-word essay; resume; interview. Additional exam requirements/recommendations for international students: Required—TOEFL (minimum score 80 iBT). *Application deadline:* For fall admission, 8/1 priority date for domestic students, 7/1 for international students; for spring admission, 12/1 priority date for domestic students, 11/1 for international students. Applications are processed on a rolling basis. Application fee: $45. Electronic applications accepted. *Expenses:* Contact institution. *Financial support:* In 2013–14, 3 students received support, including 3 fellowships (averaging $8,100 per year). Financial award applicants required to submit CSS PROFILE or FAFSA. *Faculty research:* Physical education pedagogy, exercise management and prevention of cardiovascular and metabolic diseases, sport management, immune function, carbohydrate oxidation. *Unit head:* Dr. Chuck Sands, Dean, College of Allied Health, 951-343-4619, E-mail: csands@calbaptist.edu. *Application contact:* Dr. Sean Sullivan, Chair, Department of Kinesiology, 951-343-4528, Fax: 951-343-5095, E-mail: ssullivan@calbaptist.edu.
Website: http://www.calbaptist.edu/mskin/.

California Baptist University, Program in Public Health, Riverside, CA 92504-3206. Offers food, nutrition and health (MPH); health policy and administration (MPH); physical activity (MPH). Part-time and evening/weekend programs available. *Degree requirements:* For master's, capstone project; practicum. *Entrance requirements:* For master's, minimum undergraduate GPA of 2.75, bachelor's degree transcripts, three recommendations, 500-word essay, resume, interview. Additional exam requirements/recommendations for international students: Required—TOEFL (minimum score 80 iBT). *Application deadline:* For fall admission, 8/1 priority date for domestic students, 7/1 for international students; for spring admission, 12/1 priority date for domestic students, 11/1 for international students. Applications are processed on a rolling basis. Application

fee: $45. Electronic applications accepted. *Expenses:* Contact institution. *Financial support:* Applicants required to submit CSS PROFILE or FAFSA. *Unit head:* Dr. Chuck Sands, Dean, College of Allied Health, 951-343-4619, E-mail: csands@calbaptist.edu. *Application contact:* Dr. Wayne Fletcher, Chair, Department of Health Sciences, 951-552-8724, E-mail: wfletcher@calbaptist.edu.
Website: http://www.calbaptist.edu/explore-cbu/schools-colleges/college-allied-health/health-sciences/master-public-health/.

California State University, Fresno, Division of Graduate Studies, College of Health and Human Services, Department of Kinesiology, Fresno, CA 93740-8027. Offers exercise science (MA); sport psychology (MA). Part-time and evening/weekend programs available. *Degree requirements:* For master's, thesis or alternative. *Entrance requirements:* For master's, GRE General Test, minimum GPA of 2.7. Additional exam requirements/recommendations for international students: Required—TOEFL. Electronic applications accepted. *Faculty research:* Refugee education, homeless, geriatrics, fitness.

California State University, Long Beach, Graduate Studies, College of Health and Human Services, Department of Kinesiology, Long Beach, CA 90840. Offers adapted physical education (MA); coaching and student athlete development (MA); exercise physiology and nutrition (MS); exercise science (MS); individualized studies (MA); kinesiology (MA); pedagogical studies (MA); sport and exercise psychology (MS); sport management (MA); sports medicine and injury studies (MS). Part-time programs available. *Degree requirements:* For master's, oral and written comprehensive exams or thesis. *Entrance requirements:* For master's, GRE General Test, minimum GPA of 2.75 during previous 2 years of course work. Electronic applications accepted. *Faculty research:* Pulmonary functioning, feedback and practice structure, strength training, history and politics of sports, special population research issues.

California University of Pennsylvania, School of Graduate Studies and Research, College of Education and Human Services, Program in Exercise Science and Health Promotion, California, PA 15419-1394. Offers performance enhancement and injury prevention (MS); rehabilitation science (MS); sport psychology (MS); wellness and fitness (MS). Part-time and evening/weekend programs available. Postbaccalaureate distance learning degree programs offered (no on-campus study). *Degree requirements:* For master's, comprehensive exam, thesis optional. *Entrance requirements:* For master's, minimum QPA of 3.0. Additional exam requirements/recommendations for international students: Required—TOEFL (minimum score 550 paper-based; 80 iBT). Electronic applications accepted. *Expenses:* Contact institution. *Faculty research:* Reducing obesity in children, sport performance, creating unique biomechanical assessment techniques, Web-based training for fitness professionals, Webcams.

Central Connecticut State University, School of Graduate Studies, School of Education and Professional Studies, Department of Physical Education and Human Performance, New Britain, CT 06050-4010. Offers physical education (MS, Certificate). Part-time and evening/weekend programs available. *Faculty:* 4 full-time (1 woman), 2 part-time/adjunct (1 woman). *Students:* 15 full-time (6 women), 29 part-time (10 women); includes 4 minority (2 Black or African American, non-Hispanic/Latino; 1 American Indian or Alaska Native, non-Hispanic/Latino; 1 Two or more races, non-Hispanic/Latino), 1 international. Average age 26. 20 applicants, 60% accepted, 8 enrolled. In 2013, 10 master's, 5 other advanced degrees awarded. *Degree requirements:* For master's, comprehensive exam, thesis or alternative; for Certificate, qualifying exam. *Entrance requirements:* For master's, minimum GPA of 2.7, bachelor's degree in physical education (preferred). Additional exam requirements/recommendations for international students: Required—TOEFL (minimum score 550 paper-based; 79 iBT). *Application deadline:* For fall admission, 6/1 for domestic students, 5/1 for international students; for spring admission, 11/1 for domestic and international students. Applications are processed on a rolling basis. Application fee: $50. Electronic applications accepted. Part-time tuition and fees vary according to degree level. *Financial support:* In 2013–14, 3 students received support, including 3 research assistantships; career-related internships or fieldwork, Federal Work-Study, scholarships/grants, and unspecified assistantships also available. Support available to part-time students. Financial award application deadline: 3/1; financial award applicants required to submit FAFSA. *Faculty research:* Exercise science, athletic training, preparation of physical education for schools. *Unit head:* Dr. Kimberly Kostelis, Chair, 860-832-2155, E-mail: kostelisk@ccsu.edu. *Application contact:* Patricia Gardner, Associate Director of Graduate Studies, 860-832-2350, Fax: 860-832-2362, E-mail: graduateadmissions@ccsu.edu.
Website: http://www.ccsu.edu/page.cfm?p=1357.

Central Michigan University, College of Graduate Studies, The Herbert H. and Grace A. Dow College of Health Professions, Department of Physical Education and Sport, Mount Pleasant, MI 48859. Offers sport administration (MA). Part-time and evening/weekend programs available. *Degree requirements:* For master's, thesis or alternative. *Entrance requirements:* For master's, GRE (recommended). Electronic applications accepted. *Faculty research:* Athletic administration and sport management, performance enhancing substance use in sport, computer applications for sport managers, mental skill development for ultimate performance, teaching methods.

Central Michigan University, College of Graduate Studies, The Herbert H. and Grace A. Dow College of Health Professions, School of Health Sciences, Mount Pleasant, MI 48859. Offers exercise science (MA); health administration (DHA). Part-time and evening/weekend programs available. Postbaccalaureate distance learning degree programs offered (no on-campus study). *Degree requirements:* For doctorate, comprehensive exam, thesis/dissertation. *Entrance requirements:* For doctorate, accredited master's or doctoral degree, 5 years of related work experience. Electronic applications accepted. *Faculty research:* Exercise science.

Central Washington University, Graduate Studies and Research, College of Education and Professional Studies, Department of Nutrition, Exercise and Health Services, Ellensburg, WA 98926. Offers exercise science (MS); nutrition (MS). Part-time programs available. *Degree requirements:* For master's, thesis or alternative. *Entrance requirements:* For master's, GRE, minimum GPA of 3.0; writing sample (for exercise students). Additional exam requirements/recommendations for international students: Required—TOEFL (minimum score 550 paper-based; 79 iBT). Electronic applications accepted.

Cleveland State University, College of Graduate Studies, College of Education and Human Services, Department of Health, Physical Education, Recreation and Dance, Cleveland, OH 44115. Offers community health education (M Ed); exercise science (M Ed); human performance (M Ed); physical education pedagogy (M Ed); public health (MPH); school health education (M Ed); sport and exercise psychology (M Ed); sports management (M Ed). Part-time programs available. *Faculty:* 7 full-time (4 women), 3 part-time/adjunct (2 women). *Students:* 49 full-time (31 women), 79 part-time (46 women); includes 32 minority (25 Black or African American, non-Hispanic/Latino; 2 Asian, non-Hispanic/Latino; 5 Hispanic/Latino), 7 international. Average age 35. 103 applicants, 72% accepted, 35 enrolled. In 2013, 40 master's awarded. *Degree requirements:* For master's, comprehensive exam, thesis optional. *Entrance requirements:* For master's, GRE General Test or MAT (if undergraduate GPA less than 2.75), minimum undergraduate GPA of 2.75. Additional exam requirements/

recommendations for international students: Required—TOEFL (minimum score 525 paper-based), IELTS (minimum score 6). *Application deadline:* For fall admission, 7/15 priority date for domestic students; for spring admission, 12/15 priority date for domestic students. Applications are processed on a rolling basis. Application fee: $30. Electronic applications accepted. *Expenses:* Tuition, state resident: full-time $8335; part-time $521 per credit hour. Tuition, nonresident: full-time $15,670; part-time $979 per credit hour. *Required fees:* $50; $25 per semester. *Financial support:* In 2013–14, 6 research assistantships with full and partial tuition reimbursements (averaging $3,480 per year), 1 teaching assistantship with full and partial tuition reimbursement (averaging $3,480 per year) were awarded; career-related internships or fieldwork, tuition waivers (full), and unspecified assistantships also available. Financial award application deadline: 3/15. *Faculty research:* Bone density, marketing fitness centers, motor development of disabled, online learning and survey research. *Unit head:* Dr. Sheila M. Patterson, Chairperson, 216-687-4870, Fax: 216-687-5410, E-mail: s.m.patterson@csuohio.edu. *Application contact:* Deborah L. Brown, Interim Assistant Director, Graduate Admissions, 216-523-7572, Fax: 216-687-5400, E-mail: d.l.brown@csuohio.edu.
Website: http://www.csuohio.edu/cehs/departments/HPERD/hperd_dept.html.

College of Saint Elizabeth, Department of Foods and Nutrition, Morristown, NJ 07960-6989. Offers dietetic internship (Certificate); dietetics verification (Certificate); nutrition (MS); sports nutrition and wellness (Certificate). *Accreditation:* AND. Part-time programs available. *Faculty:* 3 full-time (all women), 1 (woman) part-time/adjunct. *Students:* 7 full-time (6 women), 42 part-time (39 women); includes 5 minority (1 Asian, non-Hispanic/Latino; 4 Hispanic/Latino). Average age 30. In 2013, 11 master's, 18 other advanced degrees awarded. *Entrance requirements:* For master's, minimum cumulative undergraduate GPA of 3.0. Additional exam requirements/recommendations for international students: Required—TOEFL. *Application deadline:* Applications are processed on a rolling basis. Application fee: $35. Electronic applications accepted. *Expenses: Tuition:* Full-time $19,152; part-time $1064 per credit. *Financial support:* Tuition waivers (partial) and unspecified assistantships available. Support available to part-time students. Financial award application deadline: 3/15; financial award applicants required to submit FAFSA. *Faculty research:* Medical nutrition intervention, public policy, obesity, hunger and food security, osteoporosis, nutrition and exercise. *Unit head:* Dr. Marie Boyle, Program Chair, 973-290-4127, Fax: 973-290-4167, E-mail: mboyle01@cse.edu. *Application contact:* Deborah S. Cobo, Associate Director of Graduate Admission, 973-290-4194, Fax: 973-290-4710, E-mail: dscobo@cse.edu.

The College of St. Scholastica, Graduate Studies, Department of Exercise Physiology, Duluth, MN 55811-4199. Offers MA. Part-time programs available. *Faculty:* 3 full-time (0 women). *Students:* 25 full-time (16 women), 1 part-time (0 women); includes 1 minority (Two or more races, non-Hispanic/Latino), 2 international. Average age 24. 57 applicants, 75% accepted, 32 enrolled. In 2013, 18 master's awarded. *Degree requirements:* For master's, thesis (for some programs). *Entrance requirements:* Additional exam requirements/recommendations for international students: Required—TOEFL (minimum score 550 paper-based; 79 iBT). *Application deadline:* For fall admission, 4/2 priority date for domestic students, 4/2 for international students; for spring admission, 11/15 priority date for domestic students, 11/15 for international students. Applications are processed on a rolling basis. Application fee: $0. Electronic applications accepted. Application fee is waived when completed online. Tuition and fees vary according to course load, program and student level. *Financial support:* In 2013–14, 17 students received support. Scholarships/grants available. Support available to part-time students. Financial award applicants required to submit FAFSA. *Faculty research:* Cardiovascular and metabolic responses, cardiorespiratory effects, orthostatic intolerance, lower extremity asymmetry. *Unit head:* Dr. Larry Birnbaum, Director, 218-723-6297, Fax: 218-723-5991. *Application contact:* Lindsay Lahti, Director of Graduate and Extended Studies Recruitment, 218-733-2240, Fax: 218-733-2275, E-mail: gradstudies@css.edu.
Website: http://www.css.edu/Graduate/Masters-Doctoral-and-Professional-Programs/Areas-of-Study/MS-Exercise-Physiology.html.

Colorado State University, Graduate School, College of Health and Human Sciences, Department of Health and Exercise Science, Fort Collins, CO 80523-1582. Offers exercise science and nutrition (MS); health and exercise science (MS); human bioenergetics (PhD). *Faculty:* 14 full-time (3 women). *Students:* 29 full-time (18 women), 10 part-time (3 women), 1 international. Average age 29. 27 applicants, 48% accepted, 11 enrolled. In 2013, 4 master's, 1 doctorate awarded. *Degree requirements:* For master's, thesis; for doctorate, comprehensive exam, thesis/dissertation, mentored teaching. *Entrance requirements:* For master's and doctorate, GRE General Test, minimum GPA of 3.0. *Application deadline:* For fall admission, 1/31 priority date for domestic and international students; for spring admission, 9/30 priority date for domestic and international students. Application fee: $50. Electronic applications accepted. *Expenses:* Tuition, state resident: full-time $9075.40; part-time $504 per credit. Tuition, nonresident: full-time $22,248; part-time $1236 per credit. *Required fees:* $1819; $60 per credit. *Financial support:* In 2013–14, 30 students received support, including 1 fellowship (averaging $19,632 per year), 8 research assistantships with full tuition reimbursements available (averaging $14,263 per year), 21 teaching assistantships with full tuition reimbursements available (averaging $12,951 per year). Financial award application deadline: 1/31; financial award applicants required to submit FAFSA. *Faculty research:* Chronic disease, aging, neuromuscular function, cardiovascular function. *Total annual research expenditures:* $1.7 million. *Unit head:* Dr. Richard Gay Israel, Department Head, 970-491-3785, Fax: 970-491-0216, E-mail: richard.israel@colostate.edu. *Application contact:* Dr. Matthew Hickey, Department Operations, 970-491-5727, Fax: 970-491-0445, E-mail: matthew.hickey@colostate.edu.
Website: http://www.hes.chhs.colostate.edu/.

Columbus State University, Graduate Studies, College of Education and Health Professions, Department of Health, Physical Education and Exercise Science, Columbus, GA 31907-5645. Offers exercise science (MS); health and physical education (M Ed). Part-time and evening/weekend programs available. *Faculty:* 6 full-time (3 women). *Students:* 25 full-time (10 women), 14 part-time (9 women); includes 17 minority (15 Black or African American, non-Hispanic/Latino; 2 Hispanic/Latino), 1 international. Average age 28. 23 applicants, 70% accepted, 12 enrolled. In 2013, 20 master's awarded. *Degree requirements:* For master's, thesis optional. *Entrance requirements:* For master's, GRE, minimum undergraduate GPA of 2.75. Additional exam requirements/recommendations for international students: Required—TOEFL (minimum score 550 paper-based; 79 iBT). *Application deadline:* For fall admission, 5/1 for domestic students, 4/1 for international students; for spring admission, 11/1 for domestic and international students; for summer admission, 2/1 for domestic students, 3/1 for international students. Application fee: $40. *Expenses:* Tuition, state resident: full-time $4572; part-time $382 per credit hour. Tuition, nonresident: full-time $18,292; part-time $1526 per credit hour. *Required fees:* $1800; $196 per credit hour. Tuition and fees vary according to campus/location and program. *Financial support:* In 2013–14, 30 students received support, including 18 research assistantships (averaging $3,000 per year). *Unit head:* Dr. Tara Underwood, Chair, 706-568-2485, E-mail: underwood_tara@columbusstate.edu. *Application contact:* Kristin Williams, Director of International and Graduate Admissions, 706-507-8848, Fax: 706-568-5091, E-mail: williams_kristin@columbusstate.edu.
Website: http://hpex.columbusstate.edu/.

Concordia University, School of Graduate Studies, Faculty of Arts and Science, Department of Exercise Science, Montréal, QC H3G 1M8, Canada. Offers M Sc.

Concordia University Chicago, College of Graduate and Innovative Programs, Program in Human Services, River Forest, IL 60305-1499. Offers human services (MA), including administration, exercise science. Part-time and evening/weekend programs available. *Degree requirements:* For master's, comprehensive exam, thesis. *Entrance requirements:* For master's, minimum GPA of 2.9. Additional exam requirements/recommendations for international students: Required—TOEFL (minimum score 550 paper-based). Electronic applications accepted.

Concordia University, St. Paul, College of Education and Science, St. Paul, MN 55104-5494. Offers curriculum and instruction (MA Ed), including K-12 reading; differentiated instruction (MA Ed); early childhood education (MA Ed); educational leadership (MA Ed); educational technology (MA Ed); exercise science (MA); family life education (MA); K-12 principal licensure (Ed S); K-12 reading (Certificate); special education (MA Ed, Certificate), including autism spectrum disorder (MA Ed), emotional and behavioral disorders (MA Ed), learning disabilities (MA Ed); sports management (MA); superintendent (Ed S). *Accreditation:* NCATE. Part-time and evening/weekend programs available. Postbaccalaureate distance learning degree programs offered (minimal on-campus study). *Faculty:* 12 full-time (7 women), 92 part-time/adjunct (49 women). *Students:* 915 full-time (659 women), 64 part-time (53 women); includes 99 minority (47 Black or African American, non-Hispanic/Latino; 5 American Indian or Alaska Native, non-Hispanic/Latino; 18 Asian, non-Hispanic/Latino; 15 Hispanic/Latino; 2 Native Hawaiian or other Pacific Islander, non-Hispanic/Latino; 12 Two or more races, non-Hispanic/Latino), 24 international. Average age 34. 664 applicants, 67% accepted, 411 enrolled. In 2013, 275 master's, 69 other advanced degrees awarded. *Degree requirements:* For master's, thesis (for some programs). *Entrance requirements:* For master's, official transcripts from regionally-accredited institution stating the conferral of a bachelor's degree with minimum cumulative GPA of 3.0; personal statement; professional resume; practitioner in field through work or volunteerism; resume. Additional exam requirements/recommendations for international students: Recommended—TOEFL (minimum score 547 paper-based; 78 iBT), IELTS (minimum score 6). *Application deadline:* For fall admission, 8/1 for domestic and international students; for spring admission, 12/1 for domestic and international students; for summer admission, 5/1 for domestic and international students. Applications are processed on a rolling basis. Application fee: $50. Electronic applications accepted. *Expenses: Tuition:* Full-time $6200; part-time $425 per credit. Tuition and fees vary according to degree level and program. *Financial support:* Applicants required to submit FAFSA. *Unit head:* Dr. Donald Helmstetter, Dean, 651-641-8227, Fax: 651-641-8807, E-mail: helmstetter@csp.edu. *Application contact:* Kimberly Craig, Director of Graduate and Cohort Admission, 651-603-6223, Fax: 651-603-6320, E-mail: craig@csp.edu.

Delaware State University, Graduate Programs, College of Education, Health and Public Policy, Department of Sport Sciences, Dover, DE 19901-2277. Offers sport administration (MS). *Entrance requirements:* Additional exam requirements/recommendations for international students: Required—TOEFL (minimum score 550 paper-based). Electronic applications accepted.

Delta State University, Graduate Programs, College of Education, Division of Health, Physical Education, and Recreation, Cleveland, MS 38733-0001. Offers health, physical education, and recreation (M Ed); sport and human performance (MS). Part-time and evening/weekend programs available. *Faculty:* 5 full-time (1 woman), 1 part-time/adjunct (0 women). *Students:* 37 full-time (12 women), 13 part-time (4 women); includes 15 minority (11 Black or African American, non-Hispanic/Latino; 1 Hispanic/Latino; 3 Two or more races, non-Hispanic/Latino), 4 international. Average age 27. 35 applicants, 91% accepted, 29 enrolled. In 2013, 11 master's awarded. *Degree requirements:* For master's, thesis optional. *Entrance requirements:* For master's, GRE General Test or MAT, Class A teaching certificate. *Application deadline:* For fall admission, 8/1 priority date for domestic students; for spring admission, 12/1 priority date for domestic students. Applications are processed on a rolling basis. Application fee: $0. *Expenses:* Tuition, state resident: full-time $3006; part-time $334 per credit hour. Tuition, nonresident: full-time $3006; part-time $334 per credit hour. *Financial support:* In 2013–14, research assistantships (averaging $4,000 per year) were awarded; career-related internships or fieldwork, Federal Work-Study, and institutionally sponsored loans also available. Support available to part-time students. Financial award application deadline: 6/1. *Faculty research:* Blood pressure, body fat, power and reaction time, learning disorders for athletes, effects of walking. *Unit head:* Tim Colbert, Chair, 662-846-4555, Fax: 662-846-4571. *Application contact:* Dr. Albert Nylander, Dean of Graduate Studies, 662-846-4875, Fax: 662-846-4313, E-mail: grad-info@deltastate.edu.
Website: http://www.deltastate.edu/pages/2963.asp.

East Carolina University, Graduate School, College of Health and Human Performance, Department of Kinesiology, Greenville, NC 27858-4353. Offers adapted physical education (MA Ed, MS); bioenergetics and exercise science (PhD); biomechanics (MS); exercise physiology (MS); physical activity promotion (MS); physical education (MA Ed, MAT); physical education clinical supervision (Certificate); physical education pedagogy (MA Ed, MS); sport and exercise psychology (MS); sport management (Certificate). *Degree requirements:* For master's, comprehensive exam, thesis optional; for doctorate, comprehensive exam, thesis/dissertation. *Entrance requirements:* For master's, GRE General Test or MAT; for doctorate, GRE. Additional exam requirements/recommendations for international students: Required—TOEFL. *Expenses:* Tuition, state resident: full-time $4223. Tuition, nonresident: full-time $16,540. *Required fees:* $2184. *Faculty research:* Diabetes metabolism, pediatric obesity, biomechanics of arthritis, physical activity measurement.

Eastern Illinois University, Graduate School, College of Education and Professional Studies, Department of Kinesiology and Sports Studies, Charleston, IL 61920-3099. Offers MS. Part-time programs available. *Expenses: Tuition, area resident:* Part-time $283 per credit hour. Tuition, state resident: part-time $283 per credit hour. Tuition, nonresident: part-time $679 per credit hour.

Eastern Michigan University, Graduate School, College of Health and Human Services, School of Health Promotion and Human Performance, Programs in Exercise Physiology, Ypsilanti, MI 48197. Offers exercise physiology (MS); sports medicine-biomechanics (MS); sports medicine-corporate adult fitness (MS); sports medicine-exercise physiology (MS). Part-time and evening/weekend programs available. *Students:* 13 full-time (9 women), 36 part-time (12 women); includes 12 minority (5 Black or African American, non-Hispanic/Latino; 1 American Indian or Alaska Native, non-Hispanic/Latino; 2 Asian, non-Hispanic/Latino; 2 Hispanic/Latino; 2 Two or more races, non-Hispanic/Latino), 3 international. Average age 29. 46 applicants, 74% accepted, 18 enrolled. In 2013, 29 master's awarded. *Degree requirements:* For master's, comprehensive exam, thesis or 450-hour internship. *Entrance requirements:* Additional exam requirements/recommendations for international students: Required—TOEFL. *Application deadline:* For fall admission, 8/1 for domestic students, 5/1 for international students; for winter admission, 12/1 for domestic students, 10/1 for international students; for spring admission, 3/15 for domestic students, 3/1 for international students. Application fee: $35. *Expenses:* Tuition, state resident: full-time $12,300; part-time $466 per credit hour. Tuition, nonresident: full-time $23,159; part-time $918 per credit hour. *Required fees:* $71 per credit hour. $46 per semester. One-time fee: $100. Tuition and

fees vary according to course level and degree level. *Unit head:* Dr. Christopher Herman, Director, 734-487-2815, Fax: 734-487-2024, E-mail: cherman2@emich.edu. *Application contact:* Dr. Stephen McGregor, Program Coordinator, 734-487-2820, Fax: 734-487-2024, E-mail: stephen.mcgregor@emich.edu.

Eastern New Mexico University, Graduate School, College of Education and Technology, Department of Health and Physical Education, Portales, NM 88130. Offers physical education (MS), including sport administration, sport science. Part-time programs available. *Degree requirements:* For master's, comprehensive exam, thesis optional. *Entrance requirements:* For master's, minimum GPA of 3.0, 15 hours of leveling courses without bachelor's degree in physical education, two references. Additional exam requirements/recommendations for international students: Required— TOEFL (minimum score 550 paper-based; 79 iBT), IELTS (minimum score 6). Electronic applications accepted.

Eastern Washington University, Graduate Studies, College of Arts, Letters and Education, Department of Physical Education, Health and Recreation, Cheney, WA 99004-2431. Offers exercise science (MS); sports and recreation administration (MS). *Faculty:* 17 full-time (7 women), 5 part-time/adjunct (2 women). *Students:* 26 full-time (10 women), 8 part-time (3 women); includes 7 minority (3 Black or African American, non-Hispanic/Latino; 1 American Indian or Alaska Native, non-Hispanic/Latino; 2 Asian, non-Hispanic/Latino; 1 Hispanic/Latino). Average age 29. 64 applicants, 38% accepted, 21 enrolled. In 2013, 14 master's awarded. *Degree requirements:* For master's, comprehensive exam, thesis or alternative. *Entrance requirements:* For master's, minimum GPA of 3.0. *Application deadline:* For fall admission, 4/1 priority date for domestic students; for spring admission, 1/15 for domestic students. Applications are processed on a rolling basis. *Application fee:* $50. *Financial support:* In 2013–14, 10 teaching assistantships with partial tuition reimbursements (averaging $6,624 per year) were awarded; career-related internships or fieldwork, Federal Work-Study, institutionally sponsored loans, and scholarships/grants also available. Support available to part-time students. Financial award application deadline: 2/1; financial award applicants required to submit FAFSA. *Unit head:* John Cogley, Chair, 509-359-2486, E-mail: john.cogley@mail.ewu.edu. *Application contact:* Dr. Jeni McNeal, Professor of Physical Education, Health and Recreation, 509-359-2872, Fax: 509-359-4833, E-mail: jeni_mcneal@hotmail.com.

East Stroudsburg University of Pennsylvania, Graduate College, College of Health Sciences, Department of Exercise Science, East Stroudsburg, PA 18301-2999. Offers cardiac rehabilitation and exercise science (MS). Part-time and evening/weekend programs available. Postbaccalaureate distance learning degree programs offered. *Faculty:* 7 full-time (2 women). *Students:* 48 full-time (28 women), 2 part-time (1 woman); includes 11 minority (6 Black or African American, non-Hispanic/Latino; 3 Hispanic/Latino; 2 Two or more races, non-Hispanic/Latino), 1 international. Average age 23. 114 applicants, 75% accepted, 54 enrolled. In 2013, 38 master's awarded. *Degree requirements:* For master's, comprehensive exam, thesis or alternative, computer literacy. *Entrance requirements:* Additional exam requirements/recommendations for international students: Required—TOEFL (minimum score 560 paper-based; 83 iBT) or IELTS. *Application deadline:* For fall admission, 3/1 priority date for domestic and international students; for spring admission, 11/30 for domestic students, 10/31 for international students. Applications are processed on a rolling basis. *Application fee:* $50. Electronic applications accepted. *Expenses:* Tuition, state resident: full-time $7956; part-time $442 per credit. Tuition, nonresident: full-time $11,934; part-time $663 per credit. *Required fees:* $2129; $118 per credit. *Financial support:* Research assistantships with full and partial tuition reimbursements, Federal Work-Study, and institutionally sponsored loans available. Financial award application deadline: 3/1. *Unit head:* Dr. Shala Davis, Graduate Coordinator, 570-422-3302, Fax: 570-422-3616, E-mail: sdavis@po-box.esu.edu. *Application contact:* Kevin Quintero, Graduate Admissions Coordinator, 570-422-3536, Fax: 570-422-2711, E-mail: kquintero@esu.edu.

East Tennessee State University, School of Graduate Studies, College of Education, Department of Exercise and Sport Science, Johnson City, TN 37614. Offers exercise and sport science (MA); sport physiology and performance (PhD), including sport performance, sport physiology. Part-time and evening/weekend programs available. *Faculty:* 9 full-time (3 women), 5 part-time/adjunct (1 woman). *Students:* 44 full-time (8 women), 1 part-time (0 women); includes 3 minority (2 Black or African American, non-Hispanic/Latino; 1 Two or more races, non-Hispanic/Latino), 5 international. 57 applicants, 63% accepted, 34 enrolled. In 2013, 9 master's awarded. *Degree requirements:* For master's, comprehensive exam, thesis or internship; for doctorate, comprehensive exam, thesis/dissertation, two semesters of full-time residency. *Entrance requirements:* For master's, GRE General Test, undergraduate degree in related field; minimum GPA of 2.7; resume; three references; essay explaining goals and reasons for pursuing degree; for doctorate, GRE General Test, curriculum vitae or resume; four letters of recommendation (minimum of two from previous college professors); interview. Additional exam requirements/recommendations for international students: Required—TOEFL (minimum score 550 paper-based; 79 iBT). *Application deadline:* For fall admission, 6/1 for domestic students, 4/30 for international students; for spring admission, 11/1 for domestic students, 9/30 for international students. *Application fee:* $35 ($45 for international students). Electronic applications accepted. *Expenses:* Tuition, state resident: full-time $7900; part-time $395 per credit hour. Tuition, nonresident: full-time $21,960; part-time $1098 per credit hour. *Required fees:* $1345; $84 per credit hour. *Financial support:* In 2013–14, 9 fellowships with full tuition reimbursements (averaging $17,250 per year), 6 research assistantships (averaging $6,000 per year), 1 teaching assistantship (averaging $6,000 per year) were awarded; career-related internships or fieldwork, institutionally sponsored loans, scholarships/grants, and unspecified assistantships also available. Financial award application deadline: 7/1; financial award applicants required to submit FAFSA. *Unit head:* Dr. Mike Ramsey, Chair, 423-439-4375, E-mail: ramseym@etsu.edu. *Application contact:* Linda Raines, Graduate Specialist, 423-439-6158, Fax: 423-439-5624, E-mail: raineslt@etsu.edu.
Website: http://www.etsu.edu/coe/exss/.

Fairmont State University, Programs in Education, Fairmont, WV 26554. Offers digital media, new literacies and learning (M Ed); education (MAT); exercise science, fitness and wellness (M Ed); online learning (M Ed); professional studies (M Ed); reading (M Ed); special education (M Ed). *Accreditation:* NCATE. Part-time and evening/weekend programs available. Postbaccalaureate distance learning degree programs offered. *Faculty:* 18 part-time/adjunct (11 women). *Students:* 75 full-time (55 women), 120 part-time (96 women); includes 11 minority (5 Black or African American, non-Hispanic/Latino; 2 American Indian or Alaska Native, non-Hispanic/Latino; 1 Asian, non-Hispanic/Latino; 1 Hispanic/Latino; 2 Two or more races, non-Hispanic/Latino), 1 international. Average age 32. 69 applicants, 86% accepted, 45 enrolled. In 2013, 82 master's awarded. *Entrance requirements:* For master's, GRE. Additional exam requirements/recommendations for international students: Required—TOEFL. *Application deadline:* For fall admission, 5/1 for domestic and international students. Applications are processed on a rolling basis. *Application fee:* $40. *Expenses:* Tuition, state resident: full-time $6404; part-time $349 per credit hour. Tuition, nonresident: full-time $13,694; part-time $754 per credit hour. Part-time tuition and fees vary according to

course load. *Financial support:* In 2013–14, 30 students received support. *Unit head:* Dr. Carolyn Crislip-Tacy, Interim Dean, School of Education, 304-367-4143, Fax: 304-367-4599, E-mail: carolyn.crislip-tacy@fairmontstate.edu. *Application contact:* Jack Kirby, Director of Graduate Studies, 304-367-4101, E-mail: jack.kirby@fairmontstate.edu.
Website: http://www.fairmontstate.edu/graduatestudies/default.asp.

Florida Atlantic University, College of Education, Department of Exercise Science and Health Promotion, Boca Raton, FL 33431-0991. Offers MS. Part-time and evening/weekend programs available. *Faculty:* 5 full-time (1 woman), 1 (woman) part-time/adjunct. *Students:* 46 full-time (20 women), 17 part-time (9 women); includes 22 minority (6 Black or African American, non-Hispanic/Latino; 1 Asian, non-Hispanic/Latino; 14 Hispanic/Latino; 1 Two or more races, non-Hispanic/Latino), 4 international. Average age 28. 76 applicants, 43% accepted, 22 enrolled. In 2013, 20 master's awarded. *Degree requirements:* For master's, comprehensive exam, thesis optional. *Entrance requirements:* For master's, GRE General Test, minimum GPA of 3.0 during last 60 hours of course work. Additional exam requirements/recommendations for international students: Required—TOEFL (minimum score 500 paper-based; 61 iBT), IELTS (minimum score 6). *Application deadline:* For fall admission, 7/1 priority date for domestic students, 2/15 for international students; for spring admission, 11/1 priority date for domestic students, 7/15 for international students. Applications are processed on a rolling basis. *Application fee:* $30. *Expenses:* Tuition, state resident: full-time $6660; part-time $370 per credit hour. Tuition, nonresident: full-time $18,450; part-time $1025 per credit hour. Tuition and fees vary according to course load. *Financial support:* Research assistantships with partial tuition reimbursements, teaching assistantships with partial tuition reimbursements, and career-related internships or fieldwork available. *Faculty research:* Pulmonary limitations during exercise, metabolism regulation, determinants of performance, age-related change in functional mobility and geriatric exercise, behavioral change aimed at promoting active lifestyles. *Unit head:* Dr. Sue Graves, Chair, 954-236-1261, Fax: 954-236-1259. *Application contact:* Dr. Joseph A. O'Kroy, Graduate Coordinator, 954-236-1266, Fax: 954-236-1259, E-mail: okroy@fau.edu.
Website: http://www.coe.fau.edu/academicdepartments/eshp/.

Florida State University, The Graduate School, College of Human Sciences, Department of Nutrition, Food and Exercise Sciences, Tallahassee, FL 32306-1493. Offers exercise physiology (MS, PhD); nutrition and food science (MS, PhD), including clinical nutrition (MS), food science, human nutrition (PhD), nutrition education and health promotion (MS), nutrition science (MS); sports nutrition (MS); sports sciences (MS). Part-time programs available. *Faculty:* 19 full-time (12 women). *Students:* 102 full-time (55 women), 17 part-time (13 women); includes 21 minority (7 Black or African American, non-Hispanic/Latino; 3 Asian, non-Hispanic/Latino; 2 Hispanic/Latino; 9 Two or more races, non-Hispanic/Latino), 24 international. Average age 26. 168 applicants, 51% accepted, 43 enrolled. In 2013, 29 master's, 3 doctorates awarded. *Degree requirements:* For master's, comprehensive exam (for some programs), thesis optional; for doctorate, thesis/dissertation. *Entrance requirements:* For master's, GRE General Test, minimum upper-division GPA of 3.0; for doctorate, GRE General Test, minimum upper-division GPA of 3.0. MS. Additional exam requirements/recommendations for international students: Required—TOEFL (minimum score 550 paper-based; 80 iBT). *Application deadline:* For fall admission, 7/1 for domestic and international students; for spring admission, 11/1 for domestic and international students. Applications are processed on a rolling basis. *Application fee:* $30. Electronic applications accepted. *Expenses:* Tuition, state resident: part-time $403.51 per credit hour. Tuition, nonresident: part-time $1004.85 per credit hour. *Required fees:* $75.81 per credit hour. One-time fee: $20 part-time. Tuition and fees vary according to course load, campus/location and student level. *Financial support:* In 2013–14, 54 students received support, including 3 fellowships with partial tuition reimbursements available (averaging $2,362 per year), 21 research assistantships with full tuition reimbursements available (averaging $3,902 per year), 42 teaching assistantships with full tuition reimbursements available (averaging $10,993 per year); career-related internships or fieldwork, Federal Work-Study, institutionally sponsored loans, scholarships/grants, and unspecified assistantships also available. Financial award application deadline: 2/1; financial award applicants required to submit FAFSA. *Faculty research:* Body composition, functional food, chronic disease and aging response; food safety, food allergy, and safety/quality detection methods; sports nutrition, energy and human performance; strength training, functional performance, cardiovascular physiology, sarcopenia. *Total annual research expenditures:* $497,515. *Unit head:* Dr. Bahram H. Arjmandi, Professor/Chair, 850-645-1517, Fax: 850-645-5000, E-mail: barjmandi@fsu.edu. *Application contact:* Ann R. Smith, Office Administrator, 850-644-1828, Fax: 850-645-5000, E-mail: asmith@fsu.edu.
Website: http://www.chs.fsu.edu/Departments/Nutrition-Food-Exercise-Sciences.

Gannon University, School of Graduate Studies, Morosky College of Health Professions and Sciences, School of Health Professions, Program in Sport and Exercise Science, Erie, PA 16541-0001. Offers human performance (MS). Part-time and evening/weekend programs available. *Students:* 3 full-time (1 woman), 3 part-time (all women). Average age 31. 19 applicants, 74% accepted, 6 enrolled. *Degree requirements:* For master's, thesis (for some programs), internship (for some programs). *Entrance requirements:* For master's, minimum GPA of 2.75 for external applicants, minimum GPA of 3.0 for internal applicants, prerequisite coursework. Additional exam requirements/recommendations for international students: Required—TOEFL (minimum score 79 iBT). *Application deadline:* Applications are processed on a rolling basis. *Application fee:* $25. Electronic applications accepted. *Expenses:* Tuition: Full-time $15,930; part-time $885 per credit. *Required fees:* $430; $18 per credit. Tuition and fees vary according to course load, degree level and program. *Unit head:* Dr. Jason Willow, Chair, 814-871-7788, E-mail: willow001@gannon.edu. *Application contact:* Kara Morgan, Director of Graduate Admissions, 814-871-5831, Fax: 814-871-5827, E-mail: graduate@gannon.edu.

Gardner-Webb University, Graduate School, Department of Physical Education, Wellness, and Sport Studies, Boiling Springs, NC 28017. Offers sport science and pedagogy (MA). Part-time and evening/weekend programs available. *Students:* 26 part-time (12 women); includes 8 minority (7 Black or African American, non-Hispanic/Latino; 1 American Indian or Alaska Native, non-Hispanic/Latino). Average age 25. 39 applicants, 59% accepted, 17 enrolled. In 2013, 3 master's awarded. *Degree requirements:* For master's, comprehensive exam. *Entrance requirements:* For master's, GRE General Test or NTE, PRAXIS, minimum GPA of 2.5. *Application deadline:* For fall admission, 8/1 priority date for domestic students. Applications are processed on a rolling basis. *Application fee:* $40. Electronic applications accepted. *Expenses:* Tuition: Full-time $7200; part-time $400 per credit hour. Tuition and fees vary according to course load and program. *Financial support:* Unspecified assistantships available. *Unit head:* Dr. Ken Baker, Chair, 704-406-4481, Fax: 704-406-4739. *Application contact:* Office of Graduate Admissions, 877-498-4723, Fax: 704-406-3895, E-mail: gradinfo@gardner-webb.edu.

George Mason University, College of Education and Human Development, School of Recreation, Health and Tourism, Manassas, VA 20110. Offers exercise, fitness, and health promotion (MS); sport and recreation studies (MS). *Faculty:* 31 full-time (12

women), 67 part-time/adjunct (37 women). *Students:* 24 full-time (16 women), 25 part-time (10 women); includes 13 minority (7 Black or African American, non-Hispanic/Latino; 5 Hispanic/Latino; 1 Two or more races, non-Hispanic/Latino), 1 international. Average age 27. 60 applicants, 77% accepted, 24 enrolled. In 2013, 19 master's awarded. *Degree requirements:* For master's, thesis (for some programs). *Entrance requirements:* For master's, GRE General Test or MAT, 3 letters of recommendation; official transcripts; expanded goals statement; undergraduate course in statistics and minimum GPA of 3.0 in last 60 credit hours and overall (for MS in sport and recreation studies); baccalaureate degree related to kinesiology, exercise science or athletic training (for MS in exercise, fitness and health promotion). Additional exam requirements/recommendations for international students: Required—TOEFL (minimum score 575 paper-based; 88 iBT), IELTS (minimum score 6.5), PTE. *Application deadline:* For fall admission, 4/1 priority date for domestic students; for spring admission, 11/1 priority date for domestic students. Application fee: $65 ($80 for international students). Electronic applications accepted. *Expenses:* Tuition, state resident: full-time $9350; part-time $390 per credit. Tuition, nonresident: full-time $25,754; part-time $1073 per credit. *Required fees:* $2688; $112 per credit. *Financial support:* In 2013–14, 10 students received support, including 10 research assistantships with full and partial tuition reimbursements available (averaging $10,484 per year); career-related internships or fieldwork, Federal Work-Study, scholarships/grants, unspecified assistantships, and health care benefits (for full-time research or teaching assistantship recipients) also available. Support available to part-time students. Financial award application deadline: 3/1; financial award applicants required to submit FAFSA. *Faculty research:* Informing policy; promoting economic development; advocating stewardship of natural resources; improving the quality of life of individuals, families, and communities at the local, national and international levels. *Total annual research expenditures:* $1.5 million. *Unit head:* David Wiggins, Director, 703-993-2057, Fax: 703-993-2025, E-mail: dwiggin1@gmu.edu. *Application contact:* Lindsey Olson, Office Assistant, 703-993-2098, Fax: 703-993-2025, E-mail: lolson7@gmu.edu. Website: http://rht.gmu.edu/.

The George Washington University, School of Public Health and Health Services, Department of Exercise Science, Washington, DC 20052. Offers MS. *Faculty:* 10 full-time (6 women). *Students:* 29 full-time (20 women), 4 part-time (3 women); includes 4 minority (2 Black or African American, non-Hispanic/Latino; 2 Asian, non-Hispanic/Latino), 2 international. Average age 25. 29 applicants, 97% accepted. In 2013, 17 master's awarded. *Degree requirements:* For master's, comprehensive exam, thesis. *Entrance requirements:* For master's, GRE General Test or MAT. Additional exam requirements/recommendations for international students: Required—TOEFL. *Application deadline:* For fall admission, 4/15 priority date for domestic students, 4/15 for international students; for spring admission, 11/1 for domestic and international students. Applications are processed on a rolling basis. Application fee: $75. *Financial support:* In 2013–14, 12 students received support. Tuition waivers available. Financial award application deadline: 2/15. *Faculty research:* Fitness and cardiac rehabilitation, exercise testing, women in exercise. *Unit head:* Dr. Loretta DiPietro, Chair, 202-994-4910, Fax: 202-994-1420, E-mail: esclxd@gwumc.edu. *Application contact:* Jane Smith, Director of Admissions, 202-994-0248, Fax: 202-994-1860, E-mail: sphhsinfo@gwumc.edu.

Georgia College & State University, Graduate School, College of Health Sciences, Department of Kinesiology, Milledgeville, GA 31061. Offers health promotion (M Ed); human performance (M Ed); outdoor education (M Ed); physical education (MAT). *Accreditation:* NCATE (one or more programs are accredited). Part-time and evening/weekend programs available. *Students:* 31 full-time (14 women), 13 part-time (12 women); includes 11 minority (all Black or African American, non-Hispanic/Latino), 1 international. Average age 26. In 2013, 25 master's awarded. *Degree requirements:* For master's, comprehensive exam, thesis optional. *Entrance requirements:* For master's, GRE General Test or MAT, minimum GPA of 2.75 in upper-level undergraduate courses, 2 letters of reference. Additional exam requirements/recommendations for international students: Recommended—TOEFL (minimum score 550 paper-based; 79 iBT). *Application deadline:* For fall admission, 7/1 priority date for domestic students, 4/1 priority date for international students; for spring admission, 11/15 priority date for domestic students, 9/1 priority date for international students. Applications are processed on a rolling basis. Application fee: $40. Electronic applications accepted. *Financial support:* In 2013–14, 26 research assistantships with full tuition reimbursements were awarded; career-related internships or fieldwork and unspecified assistantships also available. Support available to part-time students. Financial award applicants required to submit FAFSA. *Unit head:* Dr. Lisa Griffin, Chair, 478-445-4072, Fax: 478-445-4074, E-mail: lisa.griffin@gcsu.edu. *Application contact:* 800-342-0471, E-mail: grad-admit@gcsu.edu.

Georgia State University, College of Education, Department of Kinesiology and Health, Program in Exercise Science, Atlanta, GA 30302-3083. Offers MS. *Degree requirements:* For master's, comprehensive exam. *Entrance requirements:* For master's, GRE General Test, minimum GPA of 2.5. *Application deadline:* For fall admission, 5/1 for domestic students; for spring admission, 10/1 for domestic students. Application fee: $50. *Expenses: Tuition, area resident:* Full-time $4176; part-time $348 per credit hour. Tuition, state resident: full-time $14,544; part-time $1212 per credit hour. Tuition, nonresident: full-time $14,544; part-time $1212 per credit hour. Tuition and fees vary according to course load and program. *Financial support:* Research assistantships available. *Faculty research:* Aging, exercise metabolism, biomechanics and ergonomics, blood pressure regulation, exercise performance. *Unit head:* Dr. Jacalyn Lea Lund, Chair, 404-413-8051, E-mail: jlund@gsu.edu. *Application contact:* Dr. Christopher Ingalls, Program Coordinator, 404-413-8377, E-mail: cingalls@gsu.edu. Website: http://education.gsu.edu/KIN/kh_M.S._exerciseScience.html.

Hofstra University, School of Education, Programs in Physical and Health Education, Hempstead, NY 11549. Offers adventure education (Advanced Certificate); health education (MS), including PK-12 teaching certification; physical education (MA, MS), including adventure education, curriculum (MA), strength and conditioning; sport science (MS), including adventure education (MA, MS), strength and conditioning (MA, MS).

Howard University, Graduate School, Department of Health, Human Performance and Leisure Studies, Washington, DC 20059-0002. Offers exercise physiology (MS); health education (MS); sports studies (MS), including sociology of sports, sports management; urban recreation (MS), including leisure studies. Part-time and evening/weekend programs available. *Degree requirements:* For master's, comprehensive exam, thesis. *Entrance requirements:* For master's, BS in human performance or related field. Additional exam requirements/recommendations for international students: Recommended—TOEFL. Electronic applications accepted. *Faculty research:* Health promotion, cardiovascular hypertension, physical activity, sport and human rights issues.

Humboldt State University, Academic Programs, College of Professional Studies, Department of Kinesiology and Recreation Administration, Arcata, CA 95521-8299. Offers athletic training education (MS); exercise science/wellness management (MS); pre-physical therapy (MS); teaching/coaching (MS). *Degree requirements:* For master's, thesis or alternative. *Entrance requirements:* For master's, GMAT, minimum GPA of 2.5. Additional exam requirements/recommendations for international students: Required—TOEFL. *Faculty research:* Human performance, adapted physical education, physical therapy.

Indiana State University, College of Graduate and Professional Studies, College of Nursing, Health and Human Services, Department of Physical Education, Terre Haute, IN 47809. Offers adult fitness (MA, MS); coaching (MA, MS); exercise science (MA, MS). *Degree requirements:* For master's, thesis (for some programs). *Entrance requirements:* For master's, minor in physical education. Electronic applications accepted. *Faculty research:* Exercise science.

Indiana University Bloomington, School of Public Health, Department of Kinesiology, Bloomington, IN 47405. Offers applied sport science (MS); athletic administration/sport management (MS); athletic training (MS); biomechanics (MS); ergonomics (MS); exercise physiology (MS); human performance (PhD), including biomechanics, exercise physiology, motor learning/control, sport management; motor learning/control (MS); physical activity (MPH); physical activity, fitness and wellness (MS). Part-time programs available. *Faculty:* 26 full-time (9 women). *Students:* 128 full-time (45 women), 16 part-time (6 women); includes 20 minority (11 Black or African American, non-Hispanic/Latino; 2 American Indian or Alaska Native, non-Hispanic/Latino; 3 Asian, non-Hispanic/Latino; 3 Hispanic/Latino; 1 Two or more races, non-Hispanic/Latino), 28 international. Average age 28. 174 applicants, 57% accepted, 48 enrolled. In 2013, 56 master's, 8 doctorates awarded. Terminal master's awarded for partial completion of doctoral program. *Degree requirements:* For master's, thesis optional; for doctorate, variable foreign language requirement, comprehensive exam, thesis/dissertation. *Entrance requirements:* For master's, GRE General Test, minimum GPA of 2.8; for doctorate, GRE General Test, minimum graduate GPA of 3.5, undergraduate 3.0. Additional exam requirements/recommendations for international students: Required—TOEFL (minimum score 80 iBT). *Application deadline:* For fall admission, 1/1 priority date for international students; for spring admission, 9/1 priority date for international students. Applications are processed on a rolling basis. Application fee: $55 ($65 for international students). *Financial support:* Fellowships, research assistantships with full tuition reimbursements, teaching assistantships with full tuition reimbursements, career-related internships or fieldwork, Federal Work-Study, institutionally sponsored loans, scholarships/grants, health care benefits, tuition waivers (partial), unspecified assistantships, and fee remissions available. Support available to part-time students. Financial award application deadline: 3/1; financial award applicants required to submit FAFSA. *Faculty research:* Exercise physiology and biochemistry, sports biomechanics, human motor control, adaptation of fitness and exercise to special populations. *Unit head:* Dr. David M. Koceja, Chairperson, 812-855-5523, Fax: 812-855-3193, E-mail: koceja@indiana.edu. *Application contact:* Kristine M. Wasson, Administrative Assistant for Graduate Studies, 812-855-5523, Fax: 812-855-3193, E-mail: ktanksle@indiana.edu. Website: http://www.publichealth.indiana.edu/departments/kinesiology/index.shtml.

Indiana University of Pennsylvania, School of Graduate Studies and Research, College of Health and Human Services, Department of Health and Physical Education, MS Program in Sport Science/Exercise Science, Indiana, PA 15705-1087. Offers MS. Part-time programs available. *Faculty:* 8 full-time (4 women). *Students:* 14 full-time (5 women), 2 part-time (both women); includes 2 minority (1 Black or African American, non-Hispanic/Latino; 1 Asian, non-Hispanic/Latino). Average age 24. 41 applicants, 59% accepted, 13 enrolled. In 2013, 12 master's awarded. *Degree requirements:* For master's, thesis optional. *Entrance requirements:* For master's, 2 letters of recommendation. Additional exam requirements/recommendations for international students: Required—TOEFL (minimum score 540 paper-based). *Application deadline:* Applications are processed on a rolling basis. Application fee: $50. Electronic applications accepted. *Expenses:* Tuition, state resident: full-time $3978; part-time $442 per credit. Tuition, nonresident: full-time $5967; part-time $663 per credit. *Required fees:* $2080; $115.55 per credit. $93 per semester. Tuition and fees vary according to degree level and program. *Financial support:* In 2013–14, 7 research assistantships with full and partial tuition reimbursements (averaging $4,949 per year) were awarded; fellowships, career-related internships or fieldwork, scholarships/grants, and unspecified assistantships also available. Support available to part-time students. Financial award application deadline: 4/15; financial award applicants required to submit FAFSA. *Unit head:* Dr. Madeline Bayles, Coordinator, 724-357-7835, E-mail: mpbayles@iup.edu. *Application contact:* Paula Stossel, Assistant Dean for Administration, 724-357-4511, E-mail: graduate-admissions@iup.edu. Website: http://www.iup.edu/page.aspx?id-12277.

Indiana University of Pennsylvania, School of Graduate Studies and Research, College of Health and Human Services, Department of Health and Physical Education, Program in Sports Science/Sport Studies, Indiana, PA 15705-1087. Offers MS. Part-time programs available. *Faculty:* 8 full-time (4 women). *Students:* 7 full-time (3 women); includes 2 minority (both Black or African American, non-Hispanic/Latino). Average age 24. 7 applicants, 57% accepted, 4 enrolled. In 2013, 8 master's awarded. *Degree requirements:* For master's, thesis optional. *Entrance requirements:* Additional exam requirements/recommendations for international students: Required—TOEFL (minimum score 540 paper-based). *Application deadline:* Applications are processed on a rolling basis. Application fee: $50. Electronic applications accepted. *Expenses:* Tuition, state resident: full-time $3978; part-time $442 per credit. Tuition, nonresident: full-time $5967; part-time $663 per credit. *Required fees:* $2080; $115.55 per credit. $93 per semester. Tuition and fees vary according to degree level and program. *Financial support:* In 2013–14, 3 research assistantships with full and partial tuition reimbursements (averaging $2,147 per year) were awarded; career-related internships or fieldwork, Federal Work-Study, scholarships/grants, and unspecified assistantships also available. Support available to part-time students. Financial award application deadline: 4/15; financial award applicants required to submit FAFSA. *Unit head:* Dr. Elaine Blair, Chairperson, 724-357-2770, E-mail: eblair@iup.edu. Website: http://www.iup.edu/grad/sportscience/default.aspx.

Inter American University of Puerto Rico, Metropolitan Campus, Graduate Programs, Program in Physical Education, San Juan, PR 00919-1293. Offers teaching of physical education (MA); training and sport performance (MA). *Degree requirements:* For master's, comprehensive exam. *Entrance requirements:* For master's, GRE or EXADEP, interview. Electronic applications accepted.

Iowa State University of Science and Technology, Program in Diet and Exercise, Ames, IA 50011. Offers MS. *Entrance requirements:* For master's, GRE, minimum GPA of 3.5, 3 letters of recommendation. Additional exam requirements/recommendations for international students: Required—TOEFL (minimum score 550 paper-based; 79 iBT), IELTS (minimum score 6.5). Electronic applications accepted.

Ithaca College, School of Health Sciences and Human Performance, Program in Exercise and Sport Sciences, Ithaca, NY 14850. Offers MS. Part-time programs available. *Faculty:* 11 full-time (5 women). *Students:* 22 full-time (16 women), 8 part-time (5 women); includes 1 minority (Hispanic/Latino), 3 international. Average age 23. 105 applicants, 45% accepted, 19 enrolled. In 2013, 16 master's awarded. *Degree requirements:* For master's, comprehensive exam (for some programs), thesis optional. *Entrance requirements:* For master's, GRE General Test, minimum GPA of 3.0. Additional exam requirements/recommendations for international students: Required—TOEFL (minimum score 550 paper-based; 80 iBT). *Application deadline:* For fall admission, 3/1 priority date for domestic and international students. Applications are

processed on a rolling basis. Application fee: $40. Electronic applications accepted. Tuition and fees vary according to program. *Financial support:* In 2013–14, 25 students received support, including 25 teaching assistantships (averaging $12,486 per year); career-related internships or fieldwork, Federal Work-Study, scholarships/grants, and unspecified assistantships also available. Support available to part-time students. Financial award application deadline: 3/1; financial award applicants required to submit CSS PROFILE or FAFSA. *Faculty research:* Coach and athlete behavior and performance, strength and conditioning for athletes, exercise physiology across the age spectrum, psychophysiology, sport psychology, expert performance. *Unit head:* Dr. Jeff Ives, Chairperson, 607-274-3143, Fax: 607-274-1263, E-mail: gps@ithaca.edu. *Application contact:* Gerard Turbide, Director, Office of Admission, 607-274-3143, Fax: 607-274-1263, E-mail: gps@ithaca.edu.
Website: http://www.ithaca.edu/gps/gradprograms/ess.

Kean University, College of Education, Program in Exercise Science, Union, NJ 07083. Offers MS. Part-time programs available. *Faculty:* 18 full-time (12 women). *Students:* 11 full-time (6 women), 14 part-time (8 women); includes 6 minority (2 Black or African American, non-Hispanic/Latino; 3 Hispanic/Latino; 1 Two or more races, non-Hispanic/Latino). Average age 27. 18 applicants, 100% accepted, 6 enrolled. In 2013, 9 master's awarded. *Degree requirements:* For master's, comprehensive exam, thesis, research component. *Entrance requirements:* For master's, GRE General Test, minimum B average in undergraduate prerequisites; minimum cumulative GPA of 3.0; official transcripts from all institutions attended; two letters of recommendation; personal statement; professional resume/curriculum vitae. Additional exam requirements/recommendations for international students: Required—TOEFL (minimum score 550 paper-based; 79 iBT). *Application deadline:* For fall admission, 6/1 for domestic and international students; for spring admission, 12/1 for domestic and international students. Applications are processed on a rolling basis. Application fee: $75 ($150 for international students). Electronic applications accepted. *Expenses:* Tuition, state resident: full-time $12,099; part-time $589 per credit. Tuition, nonresident: full-time $16,399; part-time $722 per credit. *Required fees:* $3050; $139 per credit. Part-time tuition and fees vary according to course level, course load, degree level and program. *Financial support:* In 2013–14, 7 research assistantships with full tuition reimbursements (averaging $3,713 per year) were awarded; unspecified assistantships also available. Financial award applicants required to submit FAFSA. *Unit head:* Dr. Walter D. Andzel, Program Coordinator, 908-737-0662, E-mail: wandzel@kean.edu. *Application contact:* Steven Koch, Admissions Counselor, 908-737-5924, Fax: 908-737-5925, E-mail: skoch@kean.edu.
Website: http://grad.kean.edu/masters-programs/exercise-science.

Kennesaw State University, College of Health and Human Services, Program in Applied Exercise and Health Science, Kennesaw, GA 30144-5591. Offers MS. Part-time and evening/weekend programs available. *Students:* 11 full-time (8 women), 3 part-time (1 woman); includes 1 minority (American Indian or Alaska Native, non-Hispanic/Latino). Average age 25. 22 applicants, 50% accepted, 3 enrolled. In 2013, 10 master's awarded. *Entrance requirements:* For master's, GRE, resume. Additional exam requirements/recommendations for international students: Required—TOEFL (minimum score 550 paper-based; 80 iBT), IELTS (minimum score 6). *Application deadline:* For fall admission, 3/1 for domestic and international students; for winter admission, 10/1 for domestic and international students; for spring admission, 3/1 for domestic and international students. Applications are processed on a rolling basis. Application fee: $60. Electronic applications accepted. *Expenses:* Tuition, state resident: full-time $4806; part-time $267 per semester hour. Tuition, nonresident: full-time $17,298; part-time $961 per semester hour. *Required fees:* $1834; $784.50 per semester. *Financial support:* In 2013–14, 2 research assistantships (averaging $8,000 per year) were awarded. Financial award application deadline: 4/1; financial award applicants required to submit FAFSA. *Unit head:* Dr. Cherilyn McLester, Program Director, 678-797-2651, E-mail: cmclest1@kennesaw.edu. *Application contact:* Dr. Cherilyn McLester, Program Director, 678-797-2651, E-mail: cmclest1@kennesaw.edu.

Kent State University, Graduate School of Education, Health, and Human Services, School of Foundations, Leadership and Administration, Sports Recreation and Management Program, Kent, OH 44242-0001. Offers sport and recreation management (MA); sports studies (MA). *Faculty:* 10 full-time (5 women), 14 part-time/adjunct (6 women). *Students:* 42 full-time (12 women), 18 part-time (8 women); includes 12 minority (9 Black or African American, non-Hispanic/Latino; 1 Asian, non-Hispanic/Latino; 2 Native Hawaiian or other Pacific Islander, non-Hispanic/Latino), 9 international. 80 applicants, 60% accepted. In 2013, 23 master's awarded. *Degree requirements:* For master's, thesis optional. *Entrance requirements:* For master's, GRE if undergraduate GPA below 3.0, goals statement, 2 letters of recommendation. Additional exam requirements/recommendations for international students: Required—TOEFL (minimum score 550 paper-based; 80 iBT). Application fee: $30 ($60 for international students). *Financial support:* In 2013–14, 7 research assistantships (averaging $8,500 per year) were awarded; teaching assistantships, Federal Work-Study, scholarships/grants, and unspecified assistantships also available. *Unit head:* Mark Lyberger, Coordinator, 330-672-0228, E-mail: mlyberge@kent.edu. *Application contact:* Nancy Miller, Academic Program Director, Office of Graduate Student Services, 330-672-2576, Fax: 330-672-9162, E-mail: ogs@kent.edu.

Kent State University, Graduate School of Education, Health, and Human Services, School of Health Sciences, Program in Exercise Physiology, Kent, OH 44242-0001. Offers athletic training (MS); exercise physiology (PhD). *Faculty:* 11 full-time (6 women), 1 part-time/adjunct (0 women). *Students:* 38 full-time (19 women), 22 part-time (12 women); includes 4 minority (3 Asian, non-Hispanic/Latino; 1 Native Hawaiian or other Pacific Islander, non-Hispanic/Latino), 3 international. 59 applicants, 47% accepted. In 2013, 21 master's, 3 doctorates awarded. *Degree requirements:* For doctorate, comprehensive exam, thesis/dissertation. *Entrance requirements:* For master's, GRE, 2 letters of reference, goals statement; for doctorate, GRE, 2 letters of reference, goals statement, minimum master's-level GPA of 3.0. Additional exam requirements/recommendations for international students: Required—TOEFL (minimum score 550 paper-based; 80 iBT). Application fee: $30 ($60 for international students). *Financial support:* In 2013–14, 9 research assistantships (averaging $11,222 per year), 5 teaching assistantships (averaging $9,600 per year) were awarded; Federal Work-Study, scholarships/grants, and unspecified assistantships also available. *Unit head:* Ellen Glickman, Coordinator, 330-672-2930, E-mail: eglickma@kent.edu. *Application contact:* Nancy Miller, Academic Program Director, Office of Graduate Student Services, 330-672-2576, Fax: 330-672-9162, E-mail: ogs@kent.edu.

Lakehead University, Graduate Studies, School of Kinesiology, Thunder Bay, ON P7B 5E1, Canada. Offers kinesiology (M Sc); kinesiology and gerontology (M Sc). Part-time programs available. *Degree requirements:* For master's, thesis. *Entrance requirements:* For master's, minimum B average. Additional exam requirements/recommendations for international students: Required—TOEFL. *Faculty research:* Social psychology and physical education, sport history, sports medicine, exercise physiology, gerontology.

Liberty University, School of Education, Lynchburg, VA 24515. Offers administration and supervision (M Ed); curriculum and instruction (Ed D, Ed S); early childhood education (M Ed); educational leadership (Ed D, Ed S); educational technology and online instruction (M Ed); elementary education (M Ed, MAT); English (M Ed); gifted education (M Ed); history (M Ed); leadership (M Ed); math specialist (M Ed); middle grades (M Ed, MAT); outdoor adventure sport (MS); reading specialist (M Ed); school counseling (M Ed); secondary education (MAT); special education (M Ed, MAT); sport management (MS), including administration, outdoor recreation, sport management, tourism; sports administration (MS); student service (M Ed); teaching and learning (M Ed); tourism (MS). *Accreditation:* NCATE. Part-time programs available. Postbaccalaureate distance learning degree programs offered (minimal on-campus study). *Students:* 2,241 full-time (1,639 women), 4,413 part-time (3,240 women); includes 2,052 minority (1,588 Black or African American, non-Hispanic/Latino; 37 American Indian or Alaska Native, non-Hispanic/Latino; 67 Asian, non-Hispanic/Latino; 173 Hispanic/Latino; 37 Native Hawaiian or other Pacific Islander, non-Hispanic/Latino; 150 Two or more races, non-Hispanic/Latino), 15 international. Average age 37. 6,185 applicants, 43% accepted, 1603 enrolled. In 2013, 1,256 master's, 117 doctorates, 470 other advanced degrees awarded. *Degree requirements:* For doctorate, comprehensive exam, thesis/dissertation. *Entrance requirements:* For master's, GRE General Test or MAT (if taken in or before 1999), 2 letters of recommendation, minimum undergraduate GPA of 3.0, curriculum vitae; for doctorate and Ed S, GRE General Test or MAT (if taken before 1999), minimum master's GPA of 3.0, 3 years of teaching experience. Additional exam requirements/recommendations for international students: Required—TOEFL (minimum score 600 paper-based; 100 iBT). *Application deadline:* For fall admission, 6/1 for domestic students; for spring admission, 11/1 for domestic students. Applications are processed on a rolling basis. Application fee: $50. Electronic applications accepted. *Expenses:* Contact institution. *Financial support:* Federal Work-Study and tuition waivers (partial) available. *Faculty research:* Self-determination, character education, bibliotherapy, learning styles, distance education. *Unit head:* Dr. Karen L. Parker, Dean, 434-582-2195, Fax: 434-582-2468, E-mail: kparker@liberty.edu. *Application contact:* Jay Bridge, Director of Graduate Admissions, 800-424-9595, Fax: 800-628-7977, E-mail: gradadmissions@liberty.edu.
Website: http://www.liberty.edu/academics/education/graduate/.

Life University, Program in Sport Health Science, Marietta, GA 30060-2903. Offers chiropractic sport science (MS); clinical nutrition (MS); exercise sport science (MS); nutrition and sport health science (MS); sport coaching (MS); sport injury management (MS). Part-time programs available. *Degree requirements:* For master's, comprehensive exam (for some programs), thesis optional. *Entrance requirements:* For master's, GRE General Test or MAT, minimum GPA of 3.0, 3 letters of recommendation. Additional exam requirements/recommendations for international students: Required—TOEFL (minimum score 500 paper-based). Electronic applications accepted.

Lipscomb University, Program in Exercise and Nutrition Science, Nashville, TN 37204-3951. Offers MS. Part-time and evening/weekend programs available. *Faculty:* 5 full-time (3 women). *Students:* 22 full-time (17 women), 32 part-time (24 women); includes 6 minority (5 Black or African American, non-Hispanic/Latino; 1 Asian, non-Hispanic/Latino), 3 international. Average age 27. 31 applicants, 52% accepted, 14 enrolled. In 2013, 11 master's awarded. *Degree requirements:* For master's, comprehensive exam (for some programs), thesis optional. *Entrance requirements:* For master's, GRE (minimum score of 800), minimum GPA of 2.75 on all undergraduate work; 2 letters of recommendation; resume. Additional exam requirements/recommendations for international students: Required—TOEFL (minimum score 570 paper-based). *Application deadline:* For fall admission, 6/1 for domestic students; for spring admission, 12/1 for domestic students. Applications are processed on a rolling basis. Application fee: $50 ($75 for international students). Electronic applications accepted. *Expenses: Tuition:* Full-time $15,570; part-time $865 per credit hour. Tuition and fees vary according to degree level and program. *Financial support:* Unspecified assistantships available. Financial award applicants required to submit FAFSA. *Unit head:* Dr. Karen Robichaud, Director, 615-966-5602, E-mail: karen.robichaud@lipscomb.edu. *Application contact:* Barbara Blackman, Coordinator of Graduate Studies, 615-966-6287, Fax: 615-966-7619, E-mail: graduatestudies@lipscomb.edu.
Website: http://www.lipscomb.edu/kinesiology/graduate-programs.

Logan University, College of Health Sciences, Chesterfield, MO 63017. Offers nutrition and human performance (MS); sports science and rehabilitation (MS). Part-time programs available. Postbaccalaureate distance learning degree programs offered (no on-campus study). *Faculty:* 10 full-time (3 women), 15 part-time/adjunct (8 women). *Students:* 19 full-time (9 women), 63 part-time (31 women); includes 12 minority (2 Black or African American, non-Hispanic/Latino; 5 Asian, non-Hispanic/Latino; 3 Hispanic/Latino; 2 Two or more races, non-Hispanic/Latino), 1 international. Average age 32. In 2013, 82 master's awarded. *Degree requirements:* For master's, comprehensive exam. *Entrance requirements:* For master's, GRE or National Board of Chiropractic Examiners test, minimum GPA of 2.5; specific undergraduate coursework based on program of interest. Additional exam requirements/recommendations for international students: Required—TOEFL (minimum score 79 iBT). *Application deadline:* For fall admission, 7/15 priority date for domestic and international students; for winter admission, 11/15 priority date for domestic and international students; for spring admission, 3/15 priority date for domestic students, 3/15 for international students. Applications are processed on a rolling basis. Application fee: $50. Electronic applications accepted. *Expenses:* Contact institution. *Financial support:* Federal Work-Study and scholarships/grants available. Support available to part-time students. Financial award applicants required to submit FAFSA. *Faculty research:* Ankle injury prevention in high school athletes, low back pain in college football players, short arc banding and low back pain, the effects of enzymes on inflammatory blood markers, gait analysis in high school and college athletes. *Unit head:* Dr. Sherri Cole, Vice President, Academic Affairs, 636-227-2100 Ext. 2702, Fax: 636-207-2431, E-mail: sherri.cole@logan.edu. *Application contact:* Stacey Till, Director of Admissions, 636-227-2100 Ext. 1749, Fax: 636-207-2425, E-mail: admissions@logan.edu.
Website: http://www.logan.edu.

Long Island University–LIU Brooklyn, School of Health Professions, Division of Sports Sciences, Brooklyn, NY 11201-8423. Offers adapted physical education (MS); athletic training and sports sciences (MS); exercise physiology (MS); health sciences (MS). Part-time and evening/weekend programs available. *Entrance requirements:* For master's, 2 letters of recommendation. Additional exam requirements/recommendations for international students: Required—TOEFL (minimum score 500 paper-based). Electronic applications accepted.

Louisiana Tech University, Graduate School, College of Education, Department of Kinesiology, Ruston, LA 71272. Offers administration of sport and physical activity (MS); sports performance (MS). *Accreditation:* NCATE. Part-time programs available. *Degree requirements:* For master's, thesis or alternative. *Entrance requirements:* For master's, GRE General Test. *Application deadline:* For fall admission, 7/29 for domestic students; for spring admission, 2/3 for domestic students. Application fee: $20 ($30 for international students). *Financial support:* Fellowships and research assistantships available. Financial award application deadline: 2/1. *Unit head:* Dr. Lanie Dornier, Head, 318-257-4432, Fax: 318-257-2379. *Application contact:* Dr. Cathy Stockton, Associate Dean of Graduate Studies, 318-257-3229, Fax: 318-257-2379, E-mail: cstock@latech.edu.
Website: http://www.latech.edu/education/kinesiology/.

Exercise and Sports Science

Manhattanville College, School of Education, Program in Physical Education and Sport Pedagogy, Purchase, NY 10577-2132. Offers MAT. Part-time and evening/weekend programs available. *Entrance requirements:* For master's, interview, bachelor's degree from accredited institution, minimum undergraduate GPA of 3.0. Additional exam requirements/recommendations for international students: Required—TOEFL. Electronic applications accepted.

Marshall University, Academic Affairs Division, College of Health Professions, School of Kinesiology, Program in Exercise Science, Huntington, WV 25755. Offers MS. *Students:* 16 full-time (9 women), 2 part-time (0 women); includes 2 minority (both Black or African American, non-Hispanic/Latino). Average age 28. In 2013, 20 master's awarded. *Degree requirements:* For master's, thesis optional, comprehensive assessment. *Entrance requirements:* For master's, GRE General Test. Application fee: $40. *Unit head:* Dr. Gary McIlvain, Chair, 304-696-2930, E-mail: mcilvain2@marshall.edu. *Application contact:* Information Contact, 304-746-1900, Fax: 304-746-1902, E-mail: services@marshall.edu.

Marywood University, Academic Affairs, College of Health and Human Services, Department of Nutrition and Dietetics, Program in Sports Nutrition and Exercise Science, Scranton, PA 18509-1598. Offers MS. *Entrance requirements:* Additional exam requirements/recommendations for international students: Required—TOEFL (minimum score 550 paper-based; 79 iBT). *Application deadline:* For fall admission, 4/1 priority date for domestic students, 3/31 priority date for international students; for spring admission, 11/1 priority date for domestic students, 8/31 priority date for international students. Applications are processed on a rolling basis. Application fee: $35. Electronic applications accepted. *Expenses: Tuition:* Part-time $775 per credit. Tuition and fees vary according to degree level. *Financial support:* Career-related internships or fieldwork, scholarships/grants, and unspecified assistantships available. Support available to part-time students. Financial award application deadline: 6/30; financial award applicants required to submit FAFSA. *Faculty research:* Lung function studies (pulmonary diffusing capacity of nitric oxide). *Unit head:* Dr. Lee Harrison, Chairperson, 570-348-6211 Ext. 2303, E-mail: harrisonl@marywood.edu. *Application contact:* Tammy Manka, Assistant Director of Graduate Admissions, 866-279-9663, E-mail: tmanka@marywood.edu.
Website: http://www.marywood.edu/nutrition/graduate-programs/sports-nutrition/.

McDaniel College, Graduate and Professional Studies, Program in Exercise Science and Physical Education, Westminster, MD 21157-4390. Offers MS. Part-time and evening/weekend programs available. *Degree requirements:* For master's, comprehensive exam, thesis optional. *Entrance requirements:* For master's, 3 letters of reference. Additional exam requirements/recommendations for international students: Required—TOEFL.

McNeese State University, Doré School of Graduate Studies, Burton College of Education, Department of Health and Human Performance, Lake Charles, LA 70609. Offers exercise physiology (MS); health promotion (MS); nutrition and wellness (MS). *Accreditation:* NCATE. Evening/weekend programs available. *Entrance requirements:* For master's, GRE, undergraduate major or minor in health and human performance or related field of study.

Memorial University of Newfoundland, School of Graduate Studies, School of Human Kinetics and Recreation, St. John's, NL A1C 5S7, Canada. Offers administration, curriculum and supervision (MPE); biomechanics/ergonomics (MS Kin); exercise and work physiology (MS Kin); sport psychology (MS Kin). Part-time programs available. *Degree requirements:* For master's, thesis optional, seminars, thesis presentations. *Entrance requirements:* For master's, bachelor's degree in a related field, minimum B average. Electronic applications accepted. *Faculty research:* Administration, sociology of sports, kinesiology, physiology/recreation.

Mercyhurst University, Graduate Studies, Program in Exercise Science, Erie, PA 16546. Offers MS. *Degree requirements:* For master's, comprehensive exam. *Entrance requirements:* For master's, GRE, resume, essay, three professional references, transcripts from accredited institution. Additional exam requirements/recommendations for international students: Required—TOEFL. Application fee is waived when completed online.

Miami University, College of Education, Health and Society, Department of Kinesiology and Health, Oxford, OH 45056. Offers MS. *Students:* 54 full-time (22 women), 6 part-time (4 women); includes 8 minority (4 Black or African American, non-Hispanic/Latino; 2 Asian, non-Hispanic/Latino; 2 Two or more races, non-Hispanic/Latino), 2 international. Average age 25. In 2013, 26 master's awarded. *Entrance requirements:* For master's, GRE or MAT. Additional exam requirements/recommendations for international students: Recommended—TOEFL (minimum score 80 iBT), IELTS (minimum score 6.5), TSE (minimum score 54). *Application deadline:* For fall admission, 2/1 priority date for domestic and international students. Applications are processed on a rolling basis. Application fee: $50. Electronic applications accepted. *Expenses:* Tuition, state resident: full-time $12,634; part-time $526 per credit hour. Tuition, nonresident: full-time $27,892; part-time $1162 per credit hour. Part-time tuition and fees vary according to course load, campus/location and program. *Financial support:* Research assistantships with full tuition reimbursements, teaching assistantships with full tuition reimbursements, Federal Work-Study, health care benefits, and unspecified assistantships available. Financial award application deadline: 2/1; financial award applicants required to submit FAFSA. *Unit head:* Dr. Helaine Alessio, Chair, 513-529-2700, E-mail: alessih@miamioh.edu. *Application contact:* 513-529-2700, E-mail: knhdept@miamioh.edu.
Website: http://www.MiamiOH.edu/KNH.

Middle Tennessee State University, College of Graduate Studies, College of Behavioral and Health Sciences, Department of Health and Human Performance, Program in Exercise Science, Murfreesboro, TN 37132. Offers MS. Part-time and evening/weekend programs available. Postbaccalaureate distance learning degree programs offered. *Faculty:* 24 full-time (9 women), 5 part-time/adjunct (3 women). *Students:* 7 full-time (3 women), 14 part-time (6 women); includes 6 minority (5 Black or African American, non-Hispanic/Latino; 1 Hispanic/Latino). 28 applicants, 82% accepted. In 2013, 13 master's awarded. *Degree requirements:* For master's, comprehensive exam, thesis optional. *Entrance requirements:* For master's, GRE. Additional exam requirements/recommendations for international students: Required—TOEFL (minimum score 525 paper-based; 71 iBT) or IELTS (minimum score 6). *Application deadline:* For fall admission, 6/1 for domestic and international students. Applications are processed on a rolling basis. Application fee: $25 ($30 for international students). *Financial support:* Application deadline: 5/1. *Faculty research:* Kinesiometrics, leisure behavior, health, lifestyles. *Unit head:* Dr. Harold D. Whiteside, Interim Dean, 615-898-2900, Fax: 615-494-7704, E-mail: harold.whiteside@mtsu.edu. *Application contact:* Dr. Michael D. Allen, Vice Provost for Research and Dean, 615-898-2840, Fax: 615-904-8020, E-mail: michael.allen@mtsu.edu.

Middle Tennessee State University, College of Graduate Studies, College of Behavioral and Health Sciences, Department of Health and Human Performance, Program in Human Performance, Murfreesboro, TN 37132. Offers PhD. Part-time and evening/weekend programs available. Postbaccalaureate distance learning degree programs offered. *Faculty:* 24 full-time (9 women), 5 part-time/adjunct (3 women).

Students: 19 full-time (4 women), 29 part-time (18 women); includes 15 minority (7 Black or African American, non-Hispanic/Latino; 6 Asian, non-Hispanic/Latino; 2 Two or more races, non-Hispanic/Latino). 29 applicants, 76% accepted. In 2013, 5 doctorates awarded. *Degree requirements:* For doctorate, comprehensive exam, thesis/dissertation. *Entrance requirements:* For doctorate, GRE. Additional exam requirements/recommendations for international students: Required—TOEFL (minimum score 525 paper-based; 71 iBT) or IELTS (minimum score 6). *Application deadline:* For fall admission, 6/1 for domestic and international students. Applications are processed on a rolling basis. Application fee: $25 ($30 for international students). *Financial support:* In 2013–14, 15 students received support. Tuition waivers available. Support available to part-time students. Financial award application deadline: 5/1. *Faculty research:* Kinesiometrics, leisure behavior, health/lifestyles. *Unit head:* Dr. Steve Estes, Chair, 615-898-2906, Fax: 615-494-5020, E-mail: steve.estes@mtsu.edu. *Application contact:* Dr. Michael D. Allen, Vice Provost for Research and Dean, 615-898-2840, Fax: 615-904-8020, E-mail: michael.allen@mtsu.edu.

Midwestern State University, Graduate School, Robert D. and Carol Gunn College of Health Sciences and Human Services, Department of Athletic Training and Exercise Physiology, Wichita Falls, TX 76308. Offers exercise physiology (MS). Part-time programs available. *Degree requirements:* For master's, comprehensive exam, thesis optional. *Entrance requirements:* For master's, GRE General Test or MAT. Additional exam requirements/recommendations for international students: Required—TOEFL (minimum score 550 paper-based). *Application deadline:* For fall admission, 7/1 priority date for domestic students, 4/1 for international students; for spring admission, 11/1 priority date for domestic students, 8/1 for international students. Applications are processed on a rolling basis. Application fee: $35 ($50 for international students). Electronic applications accepted. *Expenses:* Tuition, state resident: full-time $3627; part-time $201.50 per credit hour. Tuition, nonresident: full-time $10,899; part-time $605.50 per credit hour. *Required fees:* $1357. *Financial support:* Teaching assistantships with partial tuition reimbursements, career-related internships or fieldwork, Federal Work-Study, institutionally sponsored loans, scholarships/grants, tuition waivers (partial), and unspecified assistantships available. Support available to part-time students. Financial award application deadline: 3/1; financial award applicants required to submit FAFSA. *Faculty research:* Exercise adherence, muscular tissue remodeling during hypertrophy, student engagement and success, operational paradigms of the exercise sciences. *Unit head:* Dr. Benito Velasquez, Chair, 940-397-4829, Fax: 940-397-4901, E-mail: benito.velasquez@mwsu.edu.
Website: http://www.mwsu.edu/academics/hs2/atep/index.

Mississippi State University, College of Education, Department of Kinesiology, Mississippi State, MS 39762. Offers exercise physiology (MS); sport administration (MS); sport pedagogy (MS). Part-time programs available. Postbaccalaureate distance learning degree programs offered (minimal on-campus study). *Faculty:* 6 full-time (1 woman). *Students:* 44 full-time (12 women), 11 part-time (4 women); includes 6 minority (3 Black or African American, non-Hispanic/Latino; 2 Hispanic/Latino; 1 Two or more races, non-Hispanic/Latino), 4 international. Average age 25. 98 applicants, 35% accepted, 23 enrolled. In 2013, 36 master's awarded. *Degree requirements:* For master's, comprehensive exam, thesis optional. *Entrance requirements:* For master's, GRE General Test, minimum GPA of 2.75 on undergraduate work from four-year accredited institution, 3.0 graduate. Additional exam requirements/recommendations for international students: Required—TOEFL (minimum score 550 paper-based; 79 iBT); Recommended—IELTS (minimum score 6.5). *Application deadline:* For fall admission, 7/1 for domestic students, 5/1 for international students; for spring admission, 11/1 for domestic students, 9/1 for international students. Applications are processed on a rolling basis. Application fee: $60. Electronic applications accepted. *Financial support:* In 2013–14, 7 teaching assistantships (averaging $8,772 per year) were awarded; career-related internships or fieldwork, Federal Work-Study, institutionally sponsored loans, and unspecified assistantships also available. Financial award application deadline: 4/1; financial award applicants required to submit FAFSA. *Faculty research:* Static balance and stepping performance of older adults, organizational justice, public health, strength training and recovery drinks, high risk drinking perceptions and behaviors. *Unit head:* Dr. Stanley Brown, Professor and Department Head, 662-325-2963, Fax: 662-325-4525, E-mail: spb107@msstate.edu. *Application contact:* Dr. Adam Love, Graduate Coordinator, 662-325-2963, Fax: 662-325-4525, E-mail: adam.love@msstate.edu.
Website: http://www.kinesiology.msstate.edu/.

Montclair State University, The Graduate School, College of Education and Human Services, Department of Exercise Science and Physical Education, Nutrition and Exercise Science Certificate Program, Montclair, NJ 07043-1624. Offers Certificate. Electronic applications accepted.

Montclair State University, The Graduate School, College of Education and Human Services, Department of Exercise Science and Physical Education, Program in Exercise Science and Physical Education, Montclair, NJ 07043-1624. Offers exercise science (MA); sports administration and coaching (MA); teaching and supervision in physical education (MA). Part-time and evening/weekend programs available. *Degree requirements:* For master's, comprehensive exam, thesis or alternative. *Entrance requirements:* For master's, GRE General Test, essay, 2 letters of recommendation. Additional exam requirements/recommendations for international students: Required—TOEFL (minimum score 83 iBT), IELTS (minimum score 6.5). Electronic applications accepted.

Morehead State University, Graduate Programs, College of Science and Technology, Department of Health, Wellness and Human Performance, Morehead, KY 40351. Offers health/physical education (MA). *Accreditation:* NCATE. Part-time and evening/weekend programs available. *Degree requirements:* For master's, comprehensive exam, thesis, oral exam, written core exam. *Entrance requirements:* For master's, GRE General Test or MAT, minimum GPA of 2.5; undergraduate major/minor in health, physical education, or recreation. Additional exam requirements/recommendations for international students: Required—TOEFL (minimum score 500 paper-based). Electronic applications accepted. *Faculty research:* Child growth and performance, instructional strategies, outdoor leadership qualities, exercise science, athletic training.

Murray State University, College of Health Sciences and Human Services, Department of Wellness and Therapeutic Sciences, Program in Exercise and Leisure Studies, Murray, KY 42071. Offers MS. Part-time programs available. *Degree requirements:* For master's, thesis optional. *Entrance requirements:* For master's, GRE General Test or MAT. Additional exam requirements/recommendations for international students: Required—TOEFL. *Faculty research:* Exercise and cancer recovery.

New Mexico Highlands University, Graduate Studies, College of Arts and Sciences, Department of Exercise and Sport Sciences, Las Vegas, NM 87701. Offers human performance and sport (MA), including human performance and sport sciences, sports administration, teacher education. Part-time programs available. *Faculty:* 5 full-time (2 women). *Students:* 22 full-time (10 women), 28 part-time (8 women); includes 35 minority (13 Black or African American, non-Hispanic/Latino; 1 American Indian or Alaska Native, non-Hispanic/Latino; 1 Asian, non-Hispanic/Latino; 19 Hispanic/Latino; 1 Two or more races, non-Hispanic/Latino), 3 international. Average age 31. 18 applicants, 83% accepted, 13 enrolled. In 2013, 22 master's awarded. *Degree requirements:* For master's, comprehensive exam, thesis or alternative. *Entrance*

requirements: For master's, minimum undergraduate GPA of 3.0. Additional exam requirements/recommendations for international students: Required—TOEFL (minimum score 540 paper-based). *Application deadline:* For fall admission, 8/1 priority date for domestic students. Applications are processed on a rolling basis. Application fee: $15. *Expenses:* Tuition, state resident: full-time $4278; part-time $178 per credit hour. Tuition, nonresident: full-time $6716; part-time $281 per credit hour. One-time fee: $15. *Financial support:* Career-related internships or fieldwork, Federal Work-Study, institutionally sponsored loans, scholarships/grants, tuition waivers (partial), and unspecified assistantships available. Support available to part-time students. Financial award application deadline: 3/1; financial award applicants required to submit FAFSA. *Faculty research:* Child obesity and physical inactivity, body composition and fitness assessment, motor development, sport marketing, sport finance. *Unit head:* Dr. Yongseek Kim, Department Head, 505-454-3490, E-mail: ykim@nmhu.edu. *Application contact:* Diane Trujillo, Administrative Assistant, Graduate Studies, 505-454-3266, Fax: 505-426-2117, E-mail: dtrujillo@nmhu.edu.

North Dakota State University, College of Graduate and Interdisciplinary Studies, College of Human Development and Education, Department of Health, Nutrition, and Exercise Sciences, Fargo, ND 58108. Offers athletic training (MS); dietetics (MS); exercise science (MS); nutrition science (MS); sport pedagogy (MS); sports recreation management (MS). Part-time and evening/weekend programs available. Postbaccalaureate distance learning degree programs offered (no on-campus study). *Faculty:* 17 full-time (14 women). *Students:* 54 full-time (30 women), 18 part-time (8 women); includes 5 minority (2 Hispanic/Latino; 3 Two or more races, non-Hispanic/Latino), 2 international. Average age 28. 27 applicants, 78% accepted, 16 enrolled. In 2013, 23 master's awarded. *Degree requirements:* For master's, thesis (for some programs). *Entrance requirements:* For master's, minimum GPA of 3.0. Additional exam requirements/recommendations for international students: Required—TOEFL (minimum score 525 paper-based; 71 iBT). *Application deadline:* For fall admission, 3/1 priority date for domestic and international students. Applications are processed on a rolling basis. Application fee: $35. Electronic applications accepted. *Financial support:* In 2013–14, 18 teaching assistantships with full tuition reimbursements (averaging $6,500 per year) were awarded. Financial award application deadline: 3/31. *Faculty research:* Biomechanics, sport specialization, recreation, nutrition, athletic training. *Unit head:* Dr. Margaret Fitzgerald, Head, 701-231-7474, Fax: 701-231-8872, E-mail: margaret.fitzgerald@ndsu.edu. *Application contact:* Dr. Gary Liguori, Graduate Coordinator, 701-231-7474, Fax: 701-231-6524. Website: http://www.ndsu.edu/hnes/.

Northeastern Illinois University, College of Graduate Studies and Research, College of Education, Program in Exercise Science, Chicago, IL 60625-4699. Offers MS. *Degree requirements:* For master's, thesis optional, internship. *Entrance requirements:* For master's, 21 hours of undergraduate course work in science, minimum GPA of 2.75.

Northeastern University, Bouvé College of Health Sciences, Boston, MA 02115-5096. Offers audiology (Au D); biotechnology (MS); counseling psychology (MS, PhD, CAGS); counseling/school psychology (PhD); exercise physiology (MS), including exercise physiology, public health; health informatics (MS); nursing (MS, PhD, CAGS), including acute care (MS), administration (MS), anesthesia (MS), primary care (MS), psychiatric mental health (MS); pharmaceutical sciences (PhD); pharmaceutics and drug delivery systems (MS); pharmacology (MS); physical therapy (DPT); physician assistant (MS); school psychology (PhD, CAGS); school/counseling psychology (PhD); speech language pathology (MS); urban public health (MPH); MS/MBA. *Accreditation:* ACPE (one or more programs are accredited). Part-time and evening/weekend programs available. *Degree requirements:* For doctorate, thesis/dissertation (for some programs); for CAGS, comprehensive exam.

Northern Michigan University, College of Graduate Studies, College of Health Sciences and Professional Studies, School of Health and Human Performance, Marquette, MI 49855-5301. Offers exercise science (MS). Part-time programs available. *Faculty:* 12 full-time (6 women). *Students:* 31. Average age 26. 35 applicants, 86% accepted, 16 enrolled. In 2013, 9 master's awarded. *Degree requirements:* For master's, submission of two scholarly papers or thesis. *Entrance requirements:* For master's, minimum GPA of 3.0 plus relevant major or 9-10 credits of course work in human anatomy/physiology, exercise physiology, physics, biomechanics, nutrition. Additional exam requirements/recommendations for international students: Required—TOEFL (minimum score 550 paper-based; 79 iBT), IELTS (minimum score 6.6). *Application deadline:* For fall admission, 2/15 priority date for domestic and international students; for winter admission, 11/15 for domestic students; for spring admission, 3/17 for domestic students. Applications are processed on a rolling basis. Application fee: $50. Electronic applications accepted. *Expenses:* Tuition, state resident: part-time $427 per credit. Tuition, nonresident: part-time $614.50 per credit. *Required fees:* $325 per semester. Tuition and fees vary according to course load and program. *Financial support:* In 2013–14, 7 teaching assistantships with full tuition reimbursements (averaging $8,848 per year) were awarded; career-related internships or fieldwork, Federal Work-Study, institutionally sponsored loans, and unspecified assistantships also available. Support available to part-time students. Financial award application deadline: 3/1. *Faculty research:* Physiology of rock climbing and cross country ski racing, physical activity behaviors of children, exercise training and cancer treatment, normobaric hypoxia, concussion. *Unit head:* Dr. Brian Cherry, Assistant Provost of Graduate Education and Research, 906-227-2300, E-mail: graduate@nmu.edu. *Application contact:* Dr. Randall L. Jensen, Coordinator, 906-227-2130, E-mail: rajensen@nmu.edu. Website: http://www.nmu.edu/hper/.

Oakland University, Graduate Study and Lifelong Learning, School of Health Sciences, Program in Exercise Science, Rochester, MI 48309-4401. Offers MS, Certificate. *Faculty:* 3 full-time (1 woman). *Students:* 33 full-time (20 women), 27 part-time (18 women); includes 9 minority (6 Black or African American, non-Hispanic/Latino; 2 Asian, non-Hispanic/Latino; 1 Two or more races, non-Hispanic/Latino), 5 international. Average age 32. 54 applicants, 54% accepted, 19 enrolled. In 2013, 5 master's awarded. *Degree requirements:* For master's, thesis (for some programs). *Entrance requirements:* For master's, minimum GPA of 3.0 for unconditional admission. Additional exam requirements/recommendations for international students: Required—TOEFL (minimum score 550 paper-based). *Application deadline:* For fall admission, 7/15 priority date for domestic students, 5/1 priority date for international students; for winter admission, 12/1 priority date for domestic students, 9/1 priority date for international students; for spring admission, 3/15 priority date for domestic students. Applications are processed on a rolling basis. Application fee: $0. Electronic applications accepted. *Expenses:* Contact institution. *Financial support:* Federal Work-Study, institutionally sponsored loans, and tuition waivers (full) available. Financial award application deadline: 3/1; financial award applicants required to submit FAFSA. *Unit head:* Dr. Brian Goslin, Director, 248-370-4038, Fax: 248-370-4227, E-mail: goslin@oakland.edu. *Application contact:* Christina J. Grabowski, Associate Director of Graduate Study and Lifelong Learning, 248-370-3167, Fax: 248-370-4114, E-mail: grabowsk@oakland.edu.

Ohio University, Graduate College, College of Arts and Sciences, Department of Biological Sciences, Athens, OH 45701-2979. Offers biological sciences (MS, PhD); cell biology and physiology (MS, PhD); ecology and evolutionary biology (MS, PhD); exercise physiology and muscle biology (MS, PhD); microbiology (MS, PhD);

neuroscience (MS, PhD). Terminal master's awarded for partial completion of doctoral program. *Degree requirements:* For master's, comprehensive exam, thesis, 1 quarter of teaching experience; for doctorate, comprehensive exam, thesis/dissertation, 2 quarters of teaching experience. *Entrance requirements:* For master's, GRE General Test, names of three faculty members whose research interests most closely match the applicant's interest; for doctorate, GRE General Test, essay concerning prior training, research interest and career goals, plus names of three faculty members whose research interests most closely match the applicant's interest. Additional exam requirements/recommendations for international students: Required—TOEFL (minimum score 620 paper-based; 105 iBT) or IELTS (minimum score 7.5). Electronic applications accepted. *Faculty research:* Ecology and evolutionary biology, exercise physiology and muscle biology, neurobiology, cell biology, physiology.

Ohio University, Graduate College, College of Health Sciences and Professions, School of Applied Health Sciences and Wellness, Program in Physiology of Exercise, Athens, OH 45701-2979. Offers MS. *Degree requirements:* For master's, thesis or alternative. *Entrance requirements:* For master's, GRE, minimum GPA of 3.0. Additional exam requirements/recommendations for international students: Required—TOEFL (minimum score 550 paper-based; 80 iBT) or IELTS (minimum score 6.5). Electronic applications accepted. *Faculty research:* Blood pressure, heart rate, health skeleton, muscles, training.

Oklahoma City University, Petree College of Arts and Sciences, Oklahoma City, OK 73106-1402. Offers creative writing (MFA); education (M Ed), including applied behavioral studies, early childhood education, elementary education; exercise and sports science (MS); liberal arts (MLA), including general studies, leadership/management; mass communications (MA); religion (M Rel); sociology and justice studies (MA, MS), including applied sociology (MA), criminology (MS); teaching English to speakers of other languages (MA). Part-time and evening/weekend programs available. *Faculty:* 22 full-time (10 women), 13 part-time/adjunct (7 women). *Students:* 186 full-time (144 women), 79 part-time (59 women); includes 54 minority (26 Black or African American, non-Hispanic/Latino; 7 American Indian or Alaska Native, non-Hispanic/Latino; 1 Asian, non-Hispanic/Latino; 9 Hispanic/Latino; 11 Two or more races, non-Hispanic/Latino), 124 international. Average age 32. 142 applicants, 71% accepted, 67 enrolled. In 2013, 100 master's awarded. *Degree requirements:* For master's, capstone/practicum. *Entrance requirements:* For master's, bachelor's degree from accredited institution with minimum GPA of 3.0, essay, recommendation letters. Additional exam requirements/recommendations for international students: Required—TOEFL (minimum score 550 paper-based; 80 iBT). *Application deadline:* Applications are processed on a rolling basis. Application fee: $50. Electronic applications accepted. *Expenses:* Tuition: Full-time $16,848; part-time $936 per credit hour. Tuition and fees vary according to course load, degree level and program. *Financial support:* Federal Work-Study, institutionally sponsored loans, scholarships/grants, and tuition waivers available. Support available to part-time students. Financial award application deadline: 6/1; financial award applicants required to submit FAFSA. *Unit head:* Dr. Mark Davies, Dean, 405-208-5281, Fax: 405-208-5447, E-mail: mdavies@okcu.edu. *Application contact:* Heidi Puckett, Director of Graduate Admissions, 800-633-7242, Fax: 405-208-5356, E-mail: gadmissions@okcu.edu. Website: http://www.okcu.edu/petree/.

Old Dominion University, Darden College of Education, Program in Physical Education, Exercise and Wellness Emphasis, Norfolk, VA 23529. Offers MS Ed. Part-time and evening/weekend programs available. *Faculty:* 7 full-time (2 women). *Students:* 18 full-time (8 women), 5 part-time (4 women); includes 4 minority (2 Black or African American, non-Hispanic/Latino; 1 Asian, non-Hispanic/Latino; 1 Hispanic/Latino), 1 international. Average age 27. 27 applicants, 48% accepted, 11 enrolled. In 2013, 16 master's awarded. *Degree requirements:* For master's, comprehensive exam, thesis or alternative, internship, research project. *Entrance requirements:* For master's, GRE, minimum GPA of 2.8 overall, 3.0 in major. Additional exam requirements/recommendations for international students: Required—TOEFL (minimum score 550 paper-based; 79 iBT). *Application deadline:* For fall admission, 3/1 for domestic students; for spring admission, 11/1 for domestic students. Application fee: $50. *Expenses:* Tuition, state resident: full-time $9888; part-time $412 per credit. Tuition, nonresident: full-time $25,152; part-time $1048 per credit. *Required fees:* $59 per semester. One-time fee: $50. *Financial support:* In 2013–14, 1 research assistantship (averaging $9,000 per year), 2 teaching assistantships (averaging $9,000 per year) were awarded; unspecified assistantships also available. Financial award application deadline: 4/15. *Faculty research:* Diabetes, exercise prescription, gait and balance, lower extremity biomechanics, vascular function. *Total annual research expenditures:* $581,000. *Unit head:* Dr. Lynn Ridinger, Graduate Program Director, 757-683-4353, E-mail: lridinge@odu.edu. *Application contact:* William Heffelfinger, Director of Graduate Admissions, 757-683-5554, Fax: 757-683-3255, E-mail: gradadmit@odu.edu. Website: http://education.odu.edu/esper/academics/exsci/graduate.shtml.

Oregon State University, College of Public Health and Human Sciences, Program in Exercise and Sport Science, Corvallis, OR 97331. Offers exercise physiology (MS, PhD); movement studies in disability (MS, PhD); neuromechanics (MS, PhD); physical activity and public health (MS, PhD); physical education and teacher education (MS); sport and exercise psychology (MS, PhD). Part-time programs available. *Faculty:* 12 full-time (5 women), 1 (woman) part-time/adjunct. *Students:* 47 full-time (28 women), 7 part-time (3 women); includes 6 minority (2 Asian, non-Hispanic/Latino; 2 Hispanic/Latino; 2 Two or more races, non-Hispanic/Latino), 4 international. Average age 28. 127 applicants, 18% accepted, 23 enrolled. In 2013, 16 master's, 8 doctorates awarded. Terminal master's awarded for partial completion of doctoral program. *Median time to degree:* Of those who began their doctoral program in fall 2005, 86% received their degree in 8 years or less. *Degree requirements:* For master's, thesis; for doctorate, thesis/dissertation. *Entrance requirements:* For master's and doctorate, GRE, minimum GPA of 3.0 in last 90 hours. Additional exam requirements/recommendations for international students: Required—TOEFL (minimum score 80 iBT), IELTS (minimum score 6.5). *Application deadline:* For fall admission, 12/1 for domestic students. Application fee: $60. *Expenses:* Tuition, state resident: full-time $11,664; part-time $432 per credit hour. Tuition, nonresident: full-time $19,197; part-time $711 per credit hour. *Required fees:* $1446; $443 per quarter. One-time fee: $300. Tuition and fees vary according to course load and program. *Financial support:* Research assistantships, teaching assistantships, career-related internships or fieldwork, Federal Work-Study, and institutionally sponsored loans available. Support available to part-time students. Financial award application deadline: 2/1. *Faculty research:* Motor control, sports medicine, exercise physiology, sport psychology, biomechanics. *Unit head:* Dr. Tony Wilcox, Co-Director of the School of Biological and Population Health Sciences, 541-737-2643. *Application contact:* Debi Rothermund, Exercise and Sports Science Advisor, 541-737-3324, E-mail: debi.rothermund@oregonstate.edu. Website: http://health.oregonstate.edu/degrees/graduate/exercise-sport-science.

Purdue University, Graduate School, College of Health and Human Sciences, Department of Health and Kinesiology, West Lafayette, IN 47907. Offers athletic training education administration (MS, PhD); biomechanics (MS, PhD); exercise physiology (MS, PhD); health education (MS, PhD); history/philosophy of sport (MS, PhD); motor control and development (MS, PhD); physical education pedagogy (PhD); physical education

teacher education (MS); recreation and sport management (MS, PhD); sport and exercise psychology (MS, PhD). Part-time programs available. *Faculty:* 16 full-time (8 women), 20 part-time/adjunct (3 women). *Students:* 43 full-time (29 women), 21 part-time (11 women); includes 6 minority (2 Black or African American, non-Hispanic/Latino; 1 American Indian or Alaska Native, non-Hispanic/Latino; 1 Asian, non-Hispanic/Latino; 2 Two or more races, non-Hispanic/Latino), 12 international. Average age 28. 103 applicants, 32% accepted, 16 enrolled. In 2013, 15 master's, 8 doctorates awarded. *Degree requirements:* For master's, thesis optional; for doctorate, comprehensive exam, thesis/dissertation, qualifying examination, preliminary examination. *Entrance requirements:* For master's, GRE General Test (minimum score 1000 combined verbal and quantitative), minimum undergraduate GPA of 3.0 or equivalent; for doctorate, GRE General Test (minimum score 1100 combined verbal and quantitative), minimum undergraduate GPA of 3.0 or equivalent; master's degree with minimum GPA of 3.25 (recommended). Additional exam requirements/recommendations for international students: Required—TOEFL (minimum score 77 iBT); Recommended—TWE. *Application deadline:* For fall admission, 4/30 for domestic and international students; for spring admission, 10/15 for domestic and international students. Applications are processed on a rolling basis. Application fee: $60 ($75 for international students). Electronic applications accepted. *Financial support:* Fellowships with partial tuition reimbursements, research assistantships with partial tuition reimbursements, teaching assistantships with partial tuition reimbursements, and Federal Work-Study available. Support available to part-time students. Financial award applicants required to submit FAFSA. *Faculty research:* Wellness, motivation, teaching effectiveness, learning and development. *Unit head:* Dr. Timothy P. Gavin, Head of the Graduate Program, 765-494-3178, Fax: 765-494-1239, E-mail: gavin1@purdue.edu. *Application contact:* Lisa Duncan, Graduate Contact, 765-494-3162, E-mail: llduncan@purdue.edu. Website: http://www.purdue.edu/hhs/hk/.

Queens College of the City University of New York, Division of Graduate Studies, Mathematics and Natural Sciences Division, Department of Family, Nutrition and Exercise Sciences, Flushing, NY 11367-1597. Offers home economics (MS Ed); physical education and exercise sciences (MS Ed). Part-time and evening/weekend programs available. *Degree requirements:* For master's, research project. *Entrance requirements:* For master's, minimum GPA of 3.0. Additional exam requirements/recommendations for international students: Required—TOEFL.

Queen's University at Kingston, School of Graduate Studies, School of Kinesiology and Health Studies, Kingston, ON K7L 3N6, Canada. Offers applied exercise science (PhD); biomechanics/ergonomics (M Sc); exercise physiology (M Sc); social psychology of sport and exercise rehabilitation (MA); sociology of sport (MA). Part-time programs available. *Degree requirements:* For master's, thesis (for some programs); for doctorate, comprehensive exam, thesis/dissertation. *Entrance requirements:* For master's and doctorate, minimum B+ average. Additional exam requirements/recommendations for international students: Required—TOEFL. Electronic applications accepted. *Faculty research:* Expert performance ergonomics, obesity research, pregnancy and exercise, gender and sport participation.

Rowan University, Graduate School, College of Education, Department of Health and Exercise Science, Glassboro, NJ 08028-1701. Offers MA. *Faculty:* 2 full-time (both women), 2 part-time/adjunct (both women). *Students:* 66 part-time (55 women); includes 8 minority (4 Black or African American, non-Hispanic/Latino; 1 American Indian or Alaska Native, non-Hispanic/Latino; 1 Asian, non-Hispanic/Latino; 2 Hispanic/Latino). Average age 35. 32 applicants, 100% accepted, 21 enrolled. In 2013, 5 master's awarded. *Degree requirements:* For master's, comprehensive exam, thesis. *Entrance requirements:* For master's, GRE General Test, GRE Subject Test, interview, minimum GPA of 2.8. Additional exam requirements/recommendations for international students: Required—TOEFL. *Application deadline:* For fall admission, 9/15 for domestic and international students; for spring admission, 2/15 for domestic and international students. Applications are processed on a rolling basis. Application fee: $65. Electronic applications accepted. *Expenses: Tuition, area resident:* Part-time $638 per credit. Tuition, state resident: full-time $5742. *Required fees:* $142 per credit. Tuition and fees vary according to course level and program. *Financial support:* Career-related internships or fieldwork, Federal Work-Study, and unspecified assistantships available. Support available to part-time students. *Unit head:* Richard Fopeano, Chair, 856-256-4500 Ext. 3740, E-mail: fopeano@rowan.edu. *Application contact:* Admissions and Enrollment Services, 856-256-5435, Fax: 856-256-5637, E-mail: cgceadmissions@rowan.edu.

Sacred Heart University, Graduate Programs, College of Health Professions, Program in Exercise Science and Nutrition, Fairfield, CT 06825-1000. Offers MS. Part-time and evening/weekend programs available. *Faculty:* 3 full-time (2 women). *Students:* 19 full-time (13 women); includes 4 minority (1 Black or African American, non-Hispanic/Latino; 2 Asian, non-Hispanic/Latino; 1 Hispanic/Latino), 1 international. Average age 26. 46 applicants, 83% accepted, 14 enrolled. In 2013, 7 master's awarded. *Entrance requirements:* For master's, bachelor's degree in related major, minimum GPA of 3.0, anatomy and physiology (with labs), exercise physiology, nutrition, statistics or health/exercise-specific research methods course, kinesiology (preferred). Additional exam requirements/recommendations for international students: Required—PTE; Recommended—TOEFL (minimum score 570 paper-based; 80 iBT), IELTS (minimum score 6.5). *Application deadline:* Applications are processed on a rolling basis. Application fee: $60. *Expenses: Tuition:* Full-time $22,775; part-time $617 per credit. *Financial support:* Career-related internships or fieldwork, institutionally sponsored loans, health care benefits, and unspecified assistantships available. Financial award applicants required to submit FAFSA. *Unit head:* Dr. Beau Greer, Director, 203-396-8064, E-mail: greerb@sacredheart.edu. *Application contact:* Kathy Dilks, Executive Director of Graduate Admissions, 203-396-8259, Fax: 203-365-4732, E-mail: gradstudies@sacredheart.edu. Website: http://www.sacredheart.edu/academics/collegeofhealthprofessions/academicprograms/exercisescience/masterofscienceinexercisesciencenutrition/.

St. Cloud State University, School of Graduate Studies, School of Health and Human Services, Department of Kinesiology, St. Cloud, MN 56301-4498. Offers exercise science (MS); sports management (MS). *Degree requirements:* For master's, thesis or alternative. *Entrance requirements:* For master's, GRE General Test, minimum overall GPA of 2.75 in previous undergraduate and graduate records or in last half of undergraduate work. Additional exam requirements/recommendations for international students: Required—Michigan English Language Assessment Battery; Recommended—TOEFL (minimum score 550 paper-based; 79 iBT), IELTS (minimum score 6.5). Electronic applications accepted.

Saint Mary's College of California, School of Liberal Arts, Department of Kinesiology, Moraga, CA 94575. Offers sport management (MA); sport studies (MA). Part-time programs available. *Degree requirements:* For master's, thesis or special project. *Entrance requirements:* For master's, minimum GPA of 2.75, BA in physical education or related field, or professional experience. Electronic applications accepted. *Expenses:* Contact institution. *Faculty research:* Moral development in sport, applied motor learning, achievement motivation, sport history.

San Diego State University, Graduate and Research Affairs, College of Health and Human Services, School of Exercise and Nutritional Sciences, Program in Exercise Physiology, San Diego, CA 92182. Offers MS, MS/MS. *Degree requirements:* For master's, thesis. *Entrance requirements:* For master's, GRE General Test, 2 letters of reference. Additional exam requirements/recommendations for international students: Required—TOEFL. Electronic applications accepted.

San Francisco State University, Division of Graduate Studies, College of Health and Social Sciences, Department of Kinesiology, San Francisco, CA 94132-1722. Offers exercise physiology (MS); movement science (MS); physical activity: social scientific perspectives (MS). *Application deadline:* Applications are processed on a rolling basis. *Unit head:* Dr. Mi-Sook Kim, Chair, 415-338-2244, E-mail: kimms@sfsu.edu. *Application contact:* Prof. Marialice Kern, Graduate Coordinator, 415-338-1491, E-mail: mkern@sfsu.edu. Website: http://kin.sfsu.edu/.

Smith College, Graduate and Special Programs, Department of Exercise and Sport Studies, Northampton, MA 01063. Offers MS. Part-time programs available. *Faculty:* 4 full-time (2 women), 1 part-time/adjunct (0 women). *Students:* 17 full-time (15 women), 1 (woman) part-time. Average age 26. 20 applicants, 45% accepted, 6 enrolled. In 2013, 7 master's awarded. *Degree requirements:* For master's, thesis or special studies. *Entrance requirements:* Additional exam requirements/recommendations for international students: Required—TOEFL (minimum score 595 paper-based; 97 iBT). *Application deadline:* For fall admission, 4/1 for domestic students, 1/15 for international students; for spring admission, 12/1 for domestic students. Application fee: $60. *Expenses: Tuition:* Full-time $32,160; part-time $1340 per credit. *Financial support:* In 2013–14, 18 students received support, including 1 fellowship with full tuition reimbursement available, 9 teaching assistantships with full tuition reimbursements available (averaging $13,370 per year); career-related internships or fieldwork, institutionally sponsored loans, and scholarships/grants also available. Support available to part-time students. Financial award application deadline: 1/15; financial award applicants required to submit CSS PROFILE or FAFSA. *Faculty research:* Women in sport, perceived exertion, motor programming, race in sport, stress management. *Unit head:* Lynn Oberbillig, Graduate Student Adviser, 413-585-2701, E-mail: loberbil@smith.edu. *Application contact:* Ruth Morgan, Administrative Assistant, 413-585-3050, Fax: 413-585-3054, E-mail: rmorgan@smith.edu. Website: http://www.smith.edu/ess/.

Southeast Missouri State University, School of Graduate Studies, Department of Health, Human Performance and Recreation, Cape Girardeau, MO 63701-4799. Offers nutrition and exercise science (MS). Part-time and evening/weekend programs available. *Faculty:* 6 full-time (2 women), 2 part-time/adjunct (0 women). *Students:* 23 full-time (12 women), 7 part-time (6 women); includes 2 minority (1 Black or African American, non-Hispanic/Latino; 1 Hispanic/Latino), 12 international. Average age 24. 29 applicants, 86% accepted, 15 enrolled. In 2013, 4 master's awarded. *Degree requirements:* For master's, comprehensive exam, thesis optional, internship. *Entrance requirements:* For master's, GRE General Test (minimum combined score of 950), minimum undergraduate GPA of 3.0, minimum B grade in prerequisite courses. Additional exam requirements/recommendations for international students: Required—TOEFL (minimum score 550 paper-based; 79 iBT), IELTS (minimum score 6), PTE (minimum score 53). *Application deadline:* For fall admission, 8/1 for domestic students, 5/1 for international students; for spring admission, 11/21 for domestic students, 10/1 for international students; for summer admission, 5/15 for domestic students. Applications are processed on a rolling basis. Application fee: $30 ($40 for international students). Electronic applications accepted. *Expenses:* Tuition, state resident: full-time $5139; part-time $285.50 per credit hour. Tuition, nonresident: full-time $9099; part-time $505.50 per credit hour. *Financial support:* In 2013–14, 18 students received support. Career-related internships or fieldwork, Federal Work-Study, scholarships/grants, traineeships, tuition waivers (full), and unspecified assistantships available. Financial award application deadline: 6/30; financial award applicants required to submit FAFSA. *Faculty research:* Blood lipids, body composition assessment, exercise testing, perceptual responses to physical activity, sport governance, youth sports participation. *Unit head:* Dr. Joe Pujol, Chairperson, 573-651-2664, E-mail: jpujol@semo.edu. *Application contact:* Alisa Aleen McFerron, Assistant Director of Admissions for Operations, 573-651-5937, E-mail: amcferron@semo.edu. Website: http://www.semo.edu/health/.

Southern Connecticut State University, School of Graduate Studies, School of Education, Department of Exercise Science, New Haven, CT 06515-1355. Offers human performance (MS); physical education (MS); school health education (MS); sport psychology (MS). Part-time and evening/weekend programs available. *Degree requirements:* For master's, thesis or alternative. *Entrance requirements:* For master's, interview. Electronic applications accepted.

Southern Illinois University Edwardsville, Graduate School, School of Education, Department of Kinesiology and Health Education, Program in Exercise Physiology, Edwardsville, IL 62026. Offers MS. Part-time and evening/weekend programs available. *Students:* 24 full-time (13 women), 30 part-time (17 women); includes 12 minority (7 Black or African American, non-Hispanic/Latino; 1 American Indian or Alaska Native, non-Hispanic/Latino; 3 Asian, non-Hispanic/Latino; 1 Two or more races, non-Hispanic/Latino), 3 international. 7 applicants, 100% accepted. In 2013, 25 master's awarded. *Degree requirements:* For master's, thesis (for some programs), internship. *Entrance requirements:* Additional exam requirements/recommendations for international students: Required—TOEFL (minimum score 550 paper-based, 79 iBT), IELTS (minimum score 6.5), Michigan Test of English Language Proficiency or PTE. *Application deadline:* For fall admission, 7/18 for domestic students, 6/1 for international students; for spring admission, 12/12 for domestic students, 10/1 for international students; for summer admission, 4/24 for domestic students, 3/1 for international students. Applications are processed on a rolling basis. Application fee: $30. Electronic applications accepted. *Expenses:* Tuition, state resident: full-time $3551. Tuition, nonresident: full-time $8378. *Financial support:* Career-related internships or fieldwork, institutionally sponsored loans, scholarships/grants, and unspecified assistantships available. Financial award application deadline: 3/1; financial award applicants required to submit FAFSA. *Unit head:* Dr. Erik Kirk, Program Director, 618-650-2718, E-mail: ekirk@siue.edu. *Application contact:* Melissa K. Mace, Assistant Director of Graduate and International Recruitment, 618-650-2756, Fax: 618-650-3618, E-mail: mmace@siue.edu. Website: http://www.siue.edu/education/khe/.

Southern Utah University, Program in Sports Conditioning, Cedar City, UT 84720-2498. Offers MS. Part-time programs available. Postbaccalaureate distance learning degree programs offered (minimal on-campus study). *Students:* 11 full-time (0 women), 25 part-time (11 women); includes 6 minority (1 Black or African American, non-Hispanic/Latino; 2 American Indian or Alaska Native, non-Hispanic/Latino; 1 Hispanic/Latino; 2 Native Hawaiian or other Pacific Islander, non-Hispanic/Latino). Average age 28. 10 applicants, 80% accepted, 2 enrolled. In 2013, 11 master's awarded. *Entrance requirements:* For master's, GRE or MAT. Additional exam requirements/recommendations for international students: Required—TOEFL (minimum score 550 paper-based, 79 iBT) or IELTS (minimum score 6). *Application deadline:* For fall admission, 7/15 for domestic and international students; for spring admission, 10/15 for domestic and international students; for summer admission, 2/15 for domestic and

international students. Applications are processed on a rolling basis. Application fee: $60 ($65 for international students). Electronic applications accepted. *Expenses:* Contact institution. *Unit head:* Dr. Deb Hill, Dean, 435-865-8628, Fax: 435-865-8485, E-mail: hilld@suu.edu. *Application contact:* Joan Anderson, Administrative Assistant, 435-586-7816, Fax: 435-865-8057, E-mail: anderson_j@suu.edu. Website: http://www.suu.edu/prostu/majors/ed/sportsconditioning.html.

Springfield College, Graduate Programs, Programs in Exercise Science and Sport Studies, Springfield, MA 01109-3797. Offers athletic training (MS); exercise physiology (MS), including clinical exercise physiology, science and research; exercise science and sport studies (PhD); health promotion and disease prevention (MS); sport psychology (MS). Part-time programs available. *Faculty:* 17 full-time, 2 part-time/adjunct. *Students:* 85 full-time. Average age 30. 138 applicants, 59% accepted, 48 enrolled. In 2013, 27 master's awarded. Terminal master's awarded for partial completion of doctoral program. *Degree requirements:* For master's, comprehensive exam, research project or thesis; for doctorate, comprehensive exam, thesis/dissertation. *Entrance requirements:* For master's and doctorate, GRE General Test. Additional exam requirements/recommendations for international students: Required—TOEFL (minimum score 550 paper-based); Recommended—IELTS (minimum score 6). *Application deadline:* For fall admission, 1/15 for domestic and international students; for winter admission, 11/1 for domestic and international students; for spring admission, 11/1 for domestic and international students. Application fee: $50. Electronic applications accepted. *Expenses:* Tuition: Full-time $13,620; part-time $908 per credit. *Financial support:* Fellowships with partial tuition reimbursements, teaching assistantships with partial tuition reimbursements, career-related internships or fieldwork, Federal Work-Study, institutionally sponsored loans, and unspecified assistantships available. Financial award application deadline: 3/1; financial award applicants required to submit FAFSA. *Unit head:* Dr. Tracey Matthews, Director, 413-748-3397, E-mail: tmatthews@springfieldcollege.edu. *Application contact:* Evelyn Cohen, Associate Director of Graduate Admissions, 413-748-3479, Fax: 413-748-3694, E-mail: ecohen@springfieldcollege.edu.

State University of New York College at Cortland, Graduate Studies, School of Professional Studies, Department of Exercise Science and Sport Studies, Cortland, NY 13045. Offers MS. *Expenses:* Tuition, state resident: full-time $9870; part-time $411 per credit hour. Tuition, nonresident: full-time $18,350; part-time $765 per credit hour. *Required fees:* $1458; $65 per credit hour.

Syracuse University, School of Education, Program in Exercise Science, Syracuse, NY 13244. Offers MS. Part-time programs available. *Students:* 21 full-time (10 women), 1 (woman) part-time; includes 2 minority (both Two or more races, non-Hispanic/Latino), 1 international. Average age 24. 26 applicants, 69% accepted, 10 enrolled. In 2013, 9 master's awarded. *Degree requirements:* For master's, thesis or alternative. *Entrance requirements:* For master's, GRE, resume. Additional exam requirements/recommendations for international students: Required—TOEFL (minimum score 100 iBT). *Application deadline:* For fall admission, 1/15 priority date for domestic and international students; for spring admission, 10/15 priority date for domestic and international students. Applications are processed on a rolling basis. Application fee: $75. Electronic applications accepted. *Financial support:* Fellowships, research assistantships with full and partial tuition reimbursements, and teaching assistantships with full and partial tuition reimbursements available. Financial award application deadline: 1/1. *Faculty research:* Bone density, obesity in females, cardiovascular functioning, attitudes toward physical education, sports management and psychology. *Unit head:* Dr. Tom Brutsaert, Chair, 315-443-9696, E-mail: tdbrutsa@syr.edu. *Application contact:* Laurie Deyo, Graduate Recruiter, School of Education, 315-443-2505, E-mail: e-gradrcrt@syr.edu. Website: http://soeweb.syr.edu/exsci/exercisescience.html.

Temple University, College of Health Professions and Social Work, Department of Kinesiology, Philadelphia, PA 19122. Offers athletic training (MS, PhD); behavioral sciences (Ed M); curriculum and instruction (MS); integrated exercise physiology (PhD); integrative exercise physiology (MS); kinesiology (MS); psychology of movement (MS); somatic sciences (PhD). Part-time programs available. *Faculty:* 15 full-time (7 women). *Students:* 49 full-time (30 women), 8 part-time (5 women); includes 6 minority (2 Black or African American, non-Hispanic/Latino; 1 Asian, non-Hispanic/Latino; 2 Hispanic/Latino; 1 Two or more races, non-Hispanic/Latino), 6 international. 100 applicants, 33% accepted, 18 enrolled. In 2013, 15 master's, 6 doctorates awarded. Terminal master's awarded for partial completion of doctoral program. *Degree requirements:* For master's, thesis, final project; for doctorate, comprehensive exam, thesis/dissertation. *Entrance requirements:* For master's, GRE General Test or MAT, minimum undergraduate GPA of 3.0, 3 letters of reference, statement of goals, interview, resume; for doctorate, GRE General Test, minimum undergraduate GPA of 3.0, 3 letters of reference, statement of goals, interview, resume. Additional exam requirements/recommendations for international students: Required—TOEFL (minimum score 550 paper-based; 79 iBT). *Application deadline:* For fall admission, 1/15 for domestic students, 12/15 for international students; for spring admission, 10/1 for domestic students, 8/1 for international students. Applications are processed on a rolling basis. Application fee: $60. Electronic applications accepted. *Financial support:* In 2013–14, 4 research assistantships with full and partial tuition reimbursements (averaging $16,459 per year), 24 teaching assistantships with full and partial tuition reimbursements (averaging $15,966 per year) were awarded; fellowships, career-related internships or fieldwork, Federal Work-Study, scholarships/grants, tuition waivers, and unspecified assistantships also available. Financial award application deadline: 1/15. *Faculty research:* Exercise physiology, athletic training, motor neuroscience, exercise and sports psychology. *Total annual research expenditures:* $318,204. *Unit head:* Dr. John Jeka, Department Chair, 214-204-4405, Fax: 215-204-4414, E-mail: jjeka@temple.edu. *Application contact:* Megan P. Mannal DiMarco, 215-204-7503, E-mail: megan.dimarco@temple.edu. Website: http://chpsw.temple.edu/kinesiology/home.

Tennessee State University, The School of Graduate Studies and Research, College of Health Sciences, Department of Human Performance and Sports Sciences, Nashville, TN 37209-1561. Offers exercise science (MA Ed); sport administration (MA Ed). *Degree requirements:* For master's, thesis optional. *Entrance requirements:* For master's, GRE General Test or MAT.

Texas A&M University–Commerce, Graduate School, College of Education and Human Services, Department of Health and Human Performance, Commerce, TX 75429-3011. Offers exercise physiology (MS); health and human performance (M Ed); health promotion (MS); health, kinesiology and sports studies (Ed D); motor performance (MS); sport studies (MS). Part-time programs available. *Degree requirements:* For master's, comprehensive exam, thesis (for some programs). *Entrance requirements:* For master's, GRE General Test. Electronic applications accepted. *Expenses:* Tuition, state resident: full-time $3630; part-time $2420 per year. Tuition, nonresident: full-time $9948; part-time $6632.16 per year. *Required fees:* $1006 per year. Tuition and fees vary according to course load. *Faculty research:* Teaching, physical fitness.

Texas State University, Graduate School, College of Education, Department of Health and Human Performance, San Marcos, TX 78666. Offers athletic training (MS); exercise

science (MS); health education (M Ed); physical education (M Ed); recreation and leisure services (MSRLS). Part-time and evening/weekend programs available. *Faculty:* 11 full-time (3 women). *Students:* 27 full-time (19 women), 9 part-time (3 women); includes 10 minority (3 Black or African American, non-Hispanic/Latino; 6 Hispanic/Latino; 1 Two or more races, non-Hispanic/Latino). Average age 26. 39 applicants, 67% accepted, 19 enrolled. In 2013, 12 master's awarded. *Degree requirements:* For master's, comprehensive exam, thesis optional. *Entrance requirements:* For master's, minimum GPA of 2.75 in last 60 hours of course work. Additional exam requirements/recommendations for international students: Required—TOEFL (minimum score 550 paper-based; 78 iBT). *Application deadline:* For fall admission, 6/15 priority date for domestic students, 6/1 for international students; for spring admission, 10/15 priority date for domestic students, 10/1 for international students. Applications are processed on a rolling basis. Application fee: $40 ($90 for international students). Electronic applications accepted. *Expenses:* Tuition, state resident: full-time $6663; part-time $278 per credit hour. Tuition, nonresident: full-time $15,159; part-time $632 per credit hour. *Required fees:* $1872; $54 per credit hour. $306 per term. Tuition and fees vary according to course load. *Financial support:* In 2013–14, 24 students received support, including 1 research assistantship (averaging $12,680 per year), 14 teaching assistantships (averaging $12,780 per year); career-related internships or fieldwork, Federal Work-Study, and institutionally sponsored loans also available. Support available to part-time students. Financial award application deadline: 4/1; financial award applicants required to submit FAFSA. *Unit head:* Dr. Karen Meaney, Graduate Advisor, 512-245-2952, Fax: 512-245-8678, E-mail: km66@txstate.edu. *Application contact:* Dr. Andrea Golato, Dean of the Graduate College, 512-245-2581, Fax: 512-245-8365, E-mail: gradcollege@txstate.edu. Website: http://www.hhp.txstate.edu/.

Texas Tech University, Graduate School, College of Arts and Sciences, Department of Health, Exercise and Sport Sciences, Lubbock, TX 79409-3011. Offers exercise and sport sciences (MS). Part-time and evening/weekend programs available. *Faculty:* 17 full-time (9 women), 1 (woman) part-time/adjunct. *Students:* 53 full-time (27 women), 18 part-time (3 women); includes 16 minority (7 Black or African American, non-Hispanic/Latino; 2 Asian, non-Hispanic/Latino; 6 Hispanic/Latino; 1 Two or more races, non-Hispanic/Latino), 6 international. Average age 25. 62 applicants, 71% accepted, 31 enrolled. In 2013, 40 master's awarded. *Degree requirements:* For master's, comprehensive exam (for some programs), thesis (for some programs). *Entrance requirements:* For master's, GRE, letter of intent, 3 letters of recommendation (preferably from academic professors), minimum GPA of 3.0 in the last 60 hours. Additional exam requirements/recommendations for international students: Required—TOEFL (minimum score 550 paper-based; 79 iBT). *Application deadline:* For fall admission, 6/1 priority date for domestic students, 1/15 priority date for international students; for spring admission, 9/1 priority date for domestic students, 6/15 priority date for international students. Applications are processed on a rolling basis. Application fee: $60. Electronic applications accepted. *Expenses:* Tuition, state resident: full-time $6062; part-time $252.57 per credit hour. Tuition, nonresident: full-time $14,558; part-time $606.57 per credit hour. *Required fees:* $2655; $35 per credit hour. $907.50 per semester. Tuition and fees vary according to course load. *Financial support:* In 2013–14, 43 students received support, including 7 fellowships (averaging $8,758 per year), 5 research assistantships (averaging $4,036 per year), 33 teaching assistantships (averaging $4,400 per year); career-related internships or fieldwork, scholarships/grants, health care benefits, and unspecified assistantships also available. Financial award application deadline: 8/1; financial award applicants required to submit FAFSA. *Faculty research:* Sport management, exercise physiology, strength and conditioning, motor behavior, pedagogy, sport psychology. *Total annual research expenditures:* $257,966. *Unit head:* Dr. Melanie Hart, Interim Chair/Vice Provost, 806-834-6584, E-mail: melanie.hart@ttu.edu. *Application contact:* Dr. Anna Tacon, Graduate Coordinator, 806-834-4783, E-mail: anna.tacon@ttu.edu. Website: http://www.depts.ttu.edu/hess/.

Texas Woman's University, Graduate School, College of Health Sciences, Department of Kinesiology, Denton, TX 76201. Offers adapted physical education (MS, PhD); biomechanics (MS, PhD); coaching (MS); exercise physiology (MS, PhD); pedagogy (MS); sport management (MS, PhD). Part-time and evening/weekend programs available. *Faculty:* 11 full-time (5 women), 3 part-time/adjunct (2 women). *Students:* 48 full-time (35 women), 105 part-time (70 women); includes 42 minority (26 Black or African American, non-Hispanic/Latino; 2 American Indian or Alaska Native, non-Hispanic/Latino; 5 Asian, non-Hispanic/Latino; 9 Hispanic/Latino), 16 international. Average age 30. 51 applicants, 69% accepted, 25 enrolled. In 2013, 55 master's, 3 doctorates awarded. Terminal master's awarded for partial completion of doctoral program. *Degree requirements:* For master's, comprehensive exam, thesis or alternative; for doctorate, comprehensive exam, thesis/dissertation, qualifying exam. *Entrance requirements:* For master's, GRE General Test (biomechanics emphasis only), 2 letters of reference, curriculum vitae, interview (adapted physical education emphasis only); for doctorate, GRE General Test (biomechanics emphasis only), interview, 3 letters of reference, curriculum vitae. Additional exam requirements/recommendations for international students: Required—TOEFL (minimum score 550 paper-based; 79 iBT). *Application deadline:* For fall admission, 7/1 priority date for domestic students, 3/1 for international students; for spring admission, 11/1 priority date for domestic students, 7/1 for international students. Applications are processed on a rolling basis. Application fee: $50 ($75 for international students). Electronic applications accepted. *Expenses:* Tuition, state resident: full-time $4182; part-time $233.32 per credit hour. Tuition, nonresident: full-time $10,716; part-time $595.32 per credit hour. *Financial support:* In 2013–14, 46 students received support, including 7 research assistantships (averaging $10,659 per year), 14 teaching assistantships (averaging $10,659 per year); career-related internships or fieldwork, Federal Work-Study, institutionally sponsored loans, scholarships/grants, traineeships, health care benefits, and unspecified assistantships also available. Support available to part-time students. Financial award application deadline: 3/1; financial award applicants required to submit FAFSA. *Faculty research:* Exercise and Type 2 diabetes risk, bone mineral density and exercise in special populations, obesity in children, factors influencing sport consumer behavior and loyalty, roles and responsibilities of paraeducators in adapted physical education. *Total annual research expenditures:* $200,485. *Unit head:* Dr. Charlotte (Barney) Sanborn, Chair, 940-898-2575, Fax: 940-898-2581, E-mail: dnichols@twu.edu. *Application contact:* Dr. Samuel Wheeler, Assistant Director of Admissions, 940-898-3188, Fax: 940-898-3081, E-mail: wheelersr@twu.edu. Website: http://www.twu.edu/kinesiology/.

Texas Woman's University, Graduate School, College of Health Sciences, Department of Nutrition and Food Sciences, Program in Exercise and Sports Nutrition, Denton, TX 76201. Offers MS. Part-time programs available. *Students:* 8 full-time (6 women), 2 part-time (both women); includes 4 minority (1 Black or African American, non-Hispanic/Latino; 1 Asian, non-Hispanic/Latino; 2 Hispanic/Latino). Average age 27. 2 applicants, 50% accepted, 1 enrolled. In 2013, 3 master's awarded. *Degree requirements:* For master's, comprehensive exam, thesis or alternative. *Entrance requirements:* For master's, GRE General Test (preferred minimum score 153 [500 old version] Verbal, 140 [400 old version] Quantitative), 9 hours each of chemistry, nutrition, and kinesiology; 3 hours of human physiology; minimum GPA of 3.0 in last 60 hours; resume; 2 letters of

recommendation. Additional exam requirements/recommendations for international students: Required—TOEFL (minimum score 550 paper-based; 79 iBT). *Application deadline:* For fall admission, 7/1 priority date for domestic students, 3/1 for international students; for spring admission, 11/1 priority date for domestic students, 7/1 for international students. Applications are processed on a rolling basis. Application fee: $50 ($75 for international students). Electronic applications accepted. *Expenses:* Tuition, state resident: full-time $4182; part-time $233.32 per credit hour. Tuition, nonresident: full-time $10,716; part-time $595.32 per credit hour. *Financial support:* In 2013–14, 8 students received support, including 6 research assistantships (averaging $11,520 per year), teaching assistantships (averaging $11,520 per year); career-related internships or fieldwork, Federal Work-Study, institutionally sponsored loans, scholarships/grants, traineeships, health care benefits, and unspecified assistantships also available. Support available to part-time students. Financial award application deadline: 3/1; financial award applicants required to submit FAFSA. *Faculty research:* Metabolism of lipoproteins, bone metabolism, osteoporosis, adult and childhood obesity. *Unit head:* Dr. Gay James, Interim Program Director, 940-898-2636, Fax: 940-898-2634, E-mail: nutrfdsci@twu.edu. *Application contact:* Dr. Samuel Wheeler, Assistant Director of Admissions, 940-898-3188, Fax: 940-898-3081, E-mail: wheelersr@twu.edu.
Website: http://www.twu.edu/nutrition-food-sciences/.

Troy University, Graduate School, College of Education, Program in Postsecondary Education, Troy, AL 36082. Offers adult education (M Ed); biology (M Ed); criminal justice (M Ed); English (M Ed); foundations of education (M Ed); general science (M Ed); higher education administration (M Ed); history (M Ed); instructional technology (M Ed); mathematics (M Ed); music industry (M Ed); physical fitness (M Ed); political science (M Ed); public administration (M Ed); social science (M Ed); teaching English (M Ed). *Accreditation:* NCATE. Part-time and evening/weekend programs available. *Faculty:* 30 full-time (11 women), 8 part-time/adjunct (1 woman). *Students:* 17 full-time (13 women), 106 part-time (84 women); includes 55 minority (45 Black or African American, non-Hispanic/Latino; 3 Asian, non-Hispanic/Latino; 2 Hispanic/Latino; 5 Two or more races, non-Hispanic/Latino). Average age 34. 109 applicants, 83% accepted, 5 enrolled. In 2013, 130 master's awarded. *Degree requirements:* For master's, comprehensive exam (for some programs), thesis (for some programs), thesis or comprehensive exam. *Entrance requirements:* For master's, GRE (minimum score of 850 on old exam or 290 on new exam), GMAT (minimum score of 380), or MAT (minimum score of 385), bachelor's degree; minimum undergraduate GPA of 2.5 or 3.0 on last 30 semester hours, letter of recommendation. Additional exam requirements/recommendations for international students: Required—TOEFL (minimum score 523 paper-based; 70 iBT), IELTS (minimum score 6). *Application deadline:* Applications are processed on a rolling basis. Application fee: $50. Electronic applications accepted. *Expenses:* Tuition, state resident: full-time $6084; part-time $338 per credit hour. Tuition, nonresident: full-time $12,168; part-time $676 per credit hour. *Required fees:* $630; $35 per credit hour. $50 per semester. *Financial support:* Available to part-time students. Applicants required to submit FAFSA. *Unit head:* Dr. Jan Oliver, Associate Professor, 334-670-3444, Fax: 334-670-3474, E-mail: oliver@troy.edu. *Application contact:* Brenda K. Campbell, Director of Graduate Admissions, 334-670-3178, Fax: 334-670-3733, E-mail: bcamp@troy.edu.

United States Sports Academy, Graduate Programs, Program in Sports Fitness and Health, Daphne, AL 36526-7055. Offers MSS. Part-time programs available. Postbaccalaureate distance learning degree programs offered (no on-campus study). *Degree requirements:* For master's, comprehensive exam, thesis optional. *Entrance requirements:* For master's, GRE General Test, GMAT, or MAT, minimum GPA of 2.5, 3 letters of recommendation, resume. Additional exam requirements/recommendations for international students: Required—TOEFL (minimum score 500 paper-based). Electronic applications accepted. *Faculty research:* Exercise physiology, conditioning.

United States Sports Academy, Graduate Programs, Program in Sport Studies, Daphne, AL 36526-7055. Offers MSS. Part-time programs available. Postbaccalaureate distance learning degree programs offered (no on-campus study). *Degree requirements:* For master's, comprehensive exam, thesis optional. *Entrance requirements:* For master's, GRE General Test, GMAT, or MAT, minimum GPA of 2.5, 3 letters of recommendation, resume. Additional exam requirements/recommendations for international students: Required—TOEFL (minimum score 500 paper-based). Electronic applications accepted.

University at Buffalo, the State University of New York, Graduate School, School of Public Health and Health Professions, Department of Exercise and Nutrition Sciences, Buffalo, NY 14260. Offers exercise science (MS, PhD); nutrition (MS, Advanced Certificate). Part-time programs available. *Faculty:* 11 full-time (2 women), 3 part-time/adjunct (2 women). *Students:* 72 full-time (45 women), 2 part-time (1 woman); includes 13 minority (2 Black or African American, non-Hispanic/Latino; 11 Asian, non-Hispanic/Latino), 17 international. Average age 24. 136 applicants, 45% accepted, 33 enrolled. In 2013, 35 master's, 3 doctorates, 17 other advanced degrees awarded. *Degree requirements:* For master's, comprehensive exam or thesis; for doctorate, comprehensive exam, thesis/dissertation. *Entrance requirements:* For master's, doctorate, and Advanced Certificate, GRE General Test, minimum GPA of 3.0. Additional exam requirements/recommendations for international students: Required—TOEFL (minimum score 550 paper-based; 79 iBT), IELTS (minimum score 6.5). *Application deadline:* For fall admission, 4/1 for domestic students, 3/1 for international students; for spring admission, 8/15 for international students. Applications are processed on a rolling basis. Application fee: $50. Electronic applications accepted. *Financial support:* In 2013–14, 14 students received support, including 1 research assistantship with full tuition reimbursement available (averaging $15,000 per year), 11 teaching assistantships with full and partial tuition reimbursements available (averaging $6,980 per year); tuition waivers (full) and Fulbright Scholarship also available. Financial award application deadline: 3/15; financial award applicants required to submit FAFSA. *Faculty research:* Cardiovascular disease-diet and exercise, respiratory control and muscle function, plasticity of connective and neural tissue, exercise nutrition, diet and cancer. *Unit head:* Dr. Gaspar Farkas, Interim Chair, 716-829-6756, Fax: 716-829-2428, E-mail: farkas@buffalo.edu. *Application contact:* Dr. John Wilson, Director of Graduate Studies, 716-829-5596, Fax: 716-829-2428, E-mail: phhpadv@buffalo.edu.
Website: http://sphhp.buffalo.edu/exercise-and-nutrition-sciences.html.

The University of Akron, Graduate School, College of Health Professions, School of Sport Science and Wellness Education, Program in Exercise Physiology/Adult Fitness, Akron, OH 44325. Offers MA, MS. *Students:* 42 full-time (20 women), 33 part-time (18 women); includes 13 minority (10 Black or African American, non-Hispanic/Latino; 1 Asian, non-Hispanic/Latino; 2 Two or more races, non-Hispanic/Latino), 1 international. Average age 28. 47 applicants, 87% accepted, 27 enrolled. In 2013, 29 master's awarded. *Degree requirements:* For master's, comprehensive exam, thesis optional. *Entrance requirements:* For master's, minimum GPA of 2.75, two letters of recommendation, statement of purpose. Additional exam requirements/recommendations for international students: Required—TOEFL (minimum score 550 paper-based; 79 iBT). *Application deadline:* Applications are processed on a rolling basis. Application fee: $40 ($60 for international students). Electronic applications accepted. *Expenses:* Tuition, state resident: full-time $7430; part-time $412.80 per credit hour. Tuition, nonresident: full-time $12,722; part-time $706.80 per credit hour. *Required fees:* $53 per credit hour. $12 per semester. Tuition and fees vary according to course load and program. *Unit head:* Dr. Victor Pinheiro, Department Chair, 330-972-6055, E-mail: victor@uakron.edu. *Application contact:* Dr. Ron Otterstetter, Program Contact, 330-972-7738.

The University of Akron, Graduate School, College of Health Professions, School of Sport Science and Wellness Education, Program in Sports Science/Coaching, Akron, OH 44325. Offers MA, MS. *Students:* 68 full-time (10 women), 11 part-time (5 women); includes 21 minority (all Black or African American, non-Hispanic/Latino), 1 international. Average age 26. 51 applicants, 86% accepted, 35 enrolled. In 2013, 42 master's awarded. *Degree requirements:* For master's, comprehensive exam, thesis optional. *Entrance requirements:* For master's, minimum GPA of 2.75, three letters of recommendation, statement of purpose. Additional exam requirements/recommendations for international students: Required—TOEFL (minimum score 550 paper-based; 79 iBT). *Application deadline:* Applications are processed on a rolling basis. Application fee: $40 ($60 for international students). Electronic applications accepted. *Expenses:* Tuition, state resident: full-time $7430; part-time $412.80 per credit hour. Tuition, nonresident: full-time $12,722; part-time $706.80 per credit hour. *Required fees:* $53 per credit hour. $12 per semester. Tuition and fees vary according to course load and program. *Unit head:* Dr. Victor Pinheiro, Department Chair, 330-972-6055, E-mail: victor@uakron.edu. *Application contact:* Dr. Alan Kornspan, Program Contact, 330-972-8145.

The University of Alabama, Graduate School, College of Education, Department of Kinesiology, Tuscaloosa, AL 35487-0312. Offers alternative sport pedagogy (MA); exercise science (MA, PhD); human performance (MA); sport management (MA); sport pedagogy (MA, PhD). Part-time programs available. *Faculty:* 8 full-time (1 woman). *Students:* 58 full-time (18 women), 29 part-time (15 women); includes 15 minority (9 Black or African American, non-Hispanic/Latino; 1 Asian, non-Hispanic/Latino; 2 Hispanic/Latino; 3 Two or more races, non-Hispanic/Latino), 7 international. Average age 30. 74 applicants, 74% accepted, 32 enrolled. In 2013, 26 master's, 4 doctorates awarded. *Degree requirements:* For master's, comprehensive exam, thesis optional; for doctorate, comprehensive exam, thesis/dissertation. *Entrance requirements:* For master's and doctorate, GRE, MAT, minimum GPA of 3.0. Additional exam requirements/recommendations for international students: Required—TOEFL. *Application deadline:* Applications are processed on a rolling basis. Application fee: $50 ($60 for international students). Electronic applications accepted. *Expenses:* Tuition, state resident: full-time $9450. Tuition, nonresident: full-time $23,950. *Financial support:* In 2013–14, 14 students received support, including 26 teaching assistantships with full and partial tuition reimbursements available (averaging $12,366 per year); fellowships and research assistantships also available. Financial award applicants required to submit FAFSA. *Faculty research:* Race, gender and sexuality in sports; physical education teacher socialization; disability sports; physical activity and health; environmental physiology. *Unit head:* Dr. Matt Curtner-Smith, Department Head and Professor, 205-348-9209, Fax: 205-348-0867, E-mail: msmith@bamaed.ua.edu. *Application contact:* Dr. Kathy S. Wetzel, Assistant Dean for Student Services, 205-348-1154, Fax: 205-348-0080, E-mail: kwetzel@bamaed.ua.edu.
Website: http://education.ua.edu/academics/kine/.

The University of Alabama at Birmingham, School of Education, Program in Physical Education, Birmingham, AL 35294. Offers exercise physiology (MA Ed); physical education with teacher certification (MA Ed). Evening/weekend programs available. *Degree requirements:* For master's, thesis optional. *Entrance requirements:* For master's, GRE General Test, MAT, or NTE, minimum GPA of 3.0. Electronic applications accepted.

University of Alberta, Faculty of Graduate Studies and Research, Department of Physical Education and Recreation, Edmonton, AB T6G 2E1, Canada. Offers physical education (M Sc); recreation and physical education (MA, PhD). Part-time programs available. Terminal master's awarded for partial completion of doctoral program. *Degree requirements:* For master's, thesis (for some programs); for doctorate, thesis/dissertation. *Entrance requirements:* For master's, bachelor's degree in related field; for doctorate, master's degree in related field with thesis. Additional exam requirements/recommendations for international students: Required—TOEFL. *Faculty research:* Motivation and adherence to physical ability, performance enhancement, adapted physical activity, exercise physiology, sport administration, tourism.

University of California, Davis, Graduate Studies, Graduate Group in Exercise Science, Davis, CA 95616. Offers MS. *Degree requirements:* For master's, thesis. *Entrance requirements:* For master's, GRE, minimum GPA of 3.25. Additional exam requirements/recommendations for international students: Required—TOEFL (minimum score 550 paper-based). Electronic applications accepted.

University of Central Florida, College of Education and Human Performance, Department of Child, Family and Community Sciences, Program in Sport and Exercise Science, Orlando, FL 32816. Offers MS. Part-time and evening/weekend programs available. *Students:* 48 full-time (23 women), 20 part-time (4 women); includes 17 minority (7 Black or African American, non-Hispanic/Latino; 10 Hispanic/Latino), 3 international. Average age 26. 96 applicants, 56% accepted, 26 enrolled. In 2013, 33 master's awarded. *Entrance requirements:* For master's, GRE General Test. Additional exam requirements/recommendations for international students: Required—TOEFL. *Application deadline:* For fall admission, 7/15 for domestic students; for spring admission, 12/1 for domestic students. Application fee: $30. Electronic applications accepted. *Financial support:* In 2013–14, 7 students received support, including 4 research assistantships with partial tuition reimbursements available (averaging $7,000 per year), 8 teaching assistantships with partial tuition reimbursements available (averaging $5,000 per year); career-related internships or fieldwork, Federal Work-Study, institutionally sponsored loans, tuition waivers (partial), and unspecified assistantships also available. Financial award application deadline: 3/1; financial award applicants required to submit FAFSA. *Unit head:* Dr. Jeffrey Stout, Chair, 407-823-0211, E-mail: jeffrey.stout@ucf.edu. *Application contact:* Barbara Rodriguez Lamas, Director, Admissions and Student Support, 407-823-2766, Fax: 407-823-6442, E-mail: gradadmissions@ucf.edu.

University of Central Florida, College of Education and Human Performance, Education Doctoral Programs, Orlando, FL 32816. Offers communication sciences and disorders (PhD); counselor education (PhD); early childhood education (PhD); education (Ed D); elementary education (PhD); exceptional education (PhD); exercise physiology (PhD); higher education (PhD); hospitality education (PhD); instructional technology (PhD); mathematics education (PhD); reading education (PhD); science education (PhD); social science education (PhD); TESOL (PhD). *Students:* 137 full-time (94 women), 86 part-time (64 women); includes 45 minority (24 Black or African American, non-Hispanic/Latino; 5 Asian, non-Hispanic/Latino; 13 Hispanic/Latino; 3 Two or more races, non-Hispanic/Latino), 22 international. Average age 39. 132 applicants, 54% accepted, 54 enrolled. In 2013, 38 doctorates awarded. Application fee: $30. Electronic applications accepted. *Financial support:* In 2013–14, 84 students received support, including 38 fellowships with partial tuition reimbursements available (averaging $6,600 per year), 41 research assistantships with partial tuition reimbursements available (averaging $7,800 per year), 53 teaching assistantships with partial tuition reimbursements available (averaging $7,700 per year). *Unit head:* Dr. Edward Robinson, Director of Doctoral Programs, 407-823-6106, E-mail: edward.robinson@

ucf.edu. *Application contact:* Barbara Rodriguez Lamas, Associate Director, Admissions and Student Services, 407-823-2766, Fax: 407-823-6442, E-mail: gradadmissions@ucf.edu.
Website: http://education.ucf.edu/departments.cfm.

University of Central Oklahoma, The Jackson College of Graduate Studies, College of Education and Professional Studies, Department of Kinesiology and Health Studies, Edmond, OK 73034-5209. Offers athletic training (MS); wellness management (MS), including exercise science, health studies. *Faculty:* 5 full-time (4 women), 8 part-time/adjunct (3 women). *Students:* 31 full-time (20 women), 43 part-time (23 women); includes 26 minority (10 Black or African American, non-Hispanic/Latino; 3 American Indian or Alaska Native, non-Hispanic/Latino; 1 Asian, non-Hispanic/Latino; 6 Hispanic/Latino; 6 Two or more races, non-Hispanic/Latino), 10 international. Average age 27. 41 applicants, 95% accepted, 22 enrolled. In 2013, 18 master's awarded. *Degree requirements:* For master's, comprehensive exam (for some programs), thesis (for some programs). *Entrance requirements:* For master's, GRE. Additional exam requirements/recommendations for international students: Required—TOEFL (minimum score 550 paper-based; 79 iBT), IELTS (minimum score 6.5). *Application deadline:* For fall admission, 12/15 priority date for domestic students, 7/1 for international students; for spring admission, 11/1 for international students. Application fee: $50. Electronic applications accepted. *Expenses:* Tuition, state resident: full-time $4137; part-time $206.85 per credit hour. Tuition, nonresident: full-time $10,359; part-time $517.95 per credit hour. *Required fees:* $481. Tuition and fees vary according to course load and program. *Financial support:* In 2013–14, 23 students received support, including 8 research assistantships with partial tuition reimbursements available (averaging $3,189 per year), 1 teaching assistantship with partial tuition reimbursement available (averaging $2,958 per year); career-related internships or fieldwork, scholarships/grants, tuition waivers (partial), and unspecified assistantships also available. Financial award application deadline: 3/31. *Unit head:* Dr. Debra T. Traywick, Chair, 405-974-5363, Fax: 405-974-3805, E-mail: dtraywick@uco.edu. *Application contact:* Dr. Richard Bernard, Dean, Graduate College, 405-974-3493, Fax: 405-974-3852, E-mail: gradcoll@uco.edu.
Website: http://www.ucogradat.net.

University of Connecticut, Graduate School, Neag School of Education, Department of Kinesiology, Program in Exercise Science, Storrs, CT 06269. Offers MA, PhD. Terminal master's awarded for partial completion of doctoral program. *Degree requirements:* For master's, comprehensive exam, thesis or alternative; for doctorate, thesis/dissertation. *Entrance requirements:* For doctorate, GRE General Test. Additional exam requirements/recommendations for international students: Required—TOEFL (minimum score 550 paper-based). Electronic applications accepted.

University of Dayton, Department of Health and Sport Science, Dayton, OH 45469-1300. Offers exercise science (MS Ed); physical therapy (DPT). Part-time programs available. *Faculty:* 17 full-time (8 women). *Students:* 119 full-time (76 women), 6 part-time (5 women); includes 4 minority (2 Black or African American, non-Hispanic/Latino; 2 Asian, non-Hispanic/Latino), 7 international. Average age 25. 150 applicants, 45% accepted, 38 enrolled. In 2013, 3 master's, 33 doctorates awarded. *Degree requirements:* For master's, thesis; for doctorate, thesis/dissertation or alternative, research project. *Entrance requirements:* For master's, GRE General Test, MAT, minimum GPA of 2.75; for doctorate, GRE General Test, bachelor's degree from accredited college or university; minimum GPA of 3.0, across all schools attended; 80 observation hours; science prerequisites of human anatomy/physiology, general biology, general chemistry, general physics, and exercise physiology. Additional exam requirements/recommendations for international students: Required—TOEFL (minimum score 550 paper-based; 80 iBT). *Application deadline:* For fall admission, 2/15 priority date for domestic students, 5/1 priority date for international students; for winter admission, 7/1 for international students; for spring admission, 11/1 priority date for international students. Applications are processed on a rolling basis. Application fee: $0 ($50 for international students). Electronic applications accepted. *Expenses: Tuition:* Full-time $10,296; part-time $858 per credit hour. *Required fees:* $50; $25. *Financial support:* In 2013–14, 1 research assistantship with full tuition reimbursement (averaging $8,720 per year), 10 teaching assistantships with full tuition reimbursements (averaging $8,720 per year) were awarded; career-related internships or fieldwork, institutionally sponsored loans, health care benefits, and unspecified assistantships also available. Financial award application deadline: 3/1; financial award applicants required to submit FAFSA. *Faculty research:* Energy expenditure, strength, training, teaching nutrition and calcium intake for children and families in Head Start; motion analysis of human gait, pediatric physical therapy, arm function of breast cancer survivors, predicting injury in athletes, neurological rehab in persons with multiple sclerosis. *Unit head:* Dr. Lloyd Laubach, Chair, 937-229-4240, Fax: 937-229-4244, E-mail: llaubach1@udayton.edu. *Application contact:* Laura Greger, Administrative Assistant, 937-229-4225, E-mail: lgreger1@udayton.edu.

University of Florida, Graduate School, College of Health and Human Performance, Department of Applied Physiology and Kinesiology, Gainesville, FL 32611. Offers athletic training/sport medicine (MS); biobehavioral science (MS); clinical exercise physiology (MS); health and human performance (PhD), including applied physiology and kinesiology, biobehavioral science, exercise physiology; human performance (MS). *Faculty:* 18 full-time (3 women), 3 part-time/adjunct (1 woman). *Students:* 73 full-time (32 women), 6 part-time (3 women); includes 9 minority (1 Black or African American, non-Hispanic/Latino; 3 Asian, non-Hispanic/Latino; 5 Hispanic/Latino), 18 international. Average age 27. 163 applicants, 23% accepted, 21 enrolled. In 2013, 23 master's, 8 doctorates awarded. *Degree requirements:* For master's, comprehensive exam, thesis (for some programs); for doctorate, comprehensive exam, thesis/dissertation. *Entrance requirements:* For master's and doctorate, GRE General Test, minimum GPA of 3.0. Additional exam requirements/recommendations for international students: Required—TOEFL (minimum score 550 paper-based; 80 iBT), IELTS (minimum score 6). *Application deadline:* For fall admission, 6/1 priority date for domestic students, 6/1 for international students; for spring admission, 9/15 for domestic and international students. Applications are processed on a rolling basis. Application fee: $30. Electronic applications accepted. *Expenses:* Tuition, state resident: full-time $12,640. Tuition, nonresident: full-time $30,000. *Financial support:* In 2013–14, 55 students received support, including 18 research assistantships (averaging $17,260 per year), 41 teaching assistantships (averaging $12,166 per year); unspecified assistantships also available. Financial award application deadline: 2/1; financial award applicants required to submit FAFSA. *Faculty research:* Cardiovascular disease; basic mechanisms that underlie exercise-induced changes in the body at the organ, tissue, cellular and molecular level; development of rehabilitation techniques for regaining motor control after stroke or as a consequence of Parkinson's disease; maintaining optimal health and delaying age-related declines in physiological function; psychomotor mechanisms impacting health and performance across the life span. *Unit head:* Michael Delp, PhD, Professor and Chair, 352-392-0584 Ext. 1338, E-mail: mdelp@hhp.ufl.edu. *Application contact:* Evangelos A. Christou, PhD, Associate Professor and Graduate Coordinator, 352-294-1719 Ext. 1270, E-mail: eachristou@hhp.ufl.edu.
Website: http://apk.hhp.ufl.edu/.

University of Houston, College of Liberal Arts and Social Sciences, Department of Health and Human Performance, Houston, TX 77204. Offers exercise science (MS); human nutrition (MS); human space exploration sciences (MS); kinesiology (PhD); physical education (M Ed). *Accreditation:* NCATE (one or more programs are accredited). Part-time and evening/weekend programs available. *Degree requirements:* For master's, comprehensive exam (for some programs), thesis (for some programs); for doctorate, comprehensive exam, thesis/dissertation, qualifying exam, candidacy paper. *Entrance requirements:* For master's, GRE (minimum 35th percentile on each section), minimum cumulative GPA of 3.0; for doctorate, GRE (minimum 35th percentile on each section), minimum cumulative GPA of 3.3. Additional exam requirements/recommendations for international students: Required—TOEFL (minimum score 550 paper-based; 79 iBT). Electronic applications accepted. *Faculty research:* Biomechanics, exercise physiology, obesity, nutrition, space exploration science.

University of Houston–Clear Lake, School of Human Sciences and Humanities, Programs in Human Sciences, Houston, TX 77058-1002. Offers behavioral sciences (MA), including criminology, cross cultural studies, general psychology, sociology; clinical psychology (MA); criminology (MA); cross cultural studies (MA); family therapy (MA); fitness and human performance (MA); school psychology (MA). *Accreditation:* AAMFT/COAMFTE. Part-time and evening/weekend programs available. Postbaccalaureate distance learning degree programs offered (minimal on-campus study). *Degree requirements:* For master's, thesis or alternative. *Entrance requirements:* For master's, GRE General Test. Additional exam requirements/recommendations for international students: Required—TOEFL (minimum score 550 paper-based). Electronic applications accepted. *Faculty research:* Smoking cessation, adolescent sexuality, white collar crime, serial murder, human factors/human computer interaction.

The University of Iowa, Graduate College, College of Liberal Arts and Sciences, Department of Health and Human Physiology, Iowa City, IA 52242-1316. Offers athletic training (MS); clinical exercise physiology (MS); health and human physiology (PhD); leisure studies (MA, PhD), including recreational sport management (PhD), therapeutic recreation (MA). *Degree requirements:* For master's, thesis optional, exam; for doctorate, comprehensive exam, thesis/dissertation. *Entrance requirements:* For master's and doctorate, GRE General Test, minimum GPA of 3.0. Additional exam requirements/recommendations for international students: Required—TOEFL (minimum score 600 paper-based; 100 iBT). Electronic applications accepted.

University of Kentucky, Graduate School, College of Education, Department of Kinesiology and Health Promotion, Lexington, KY 40506-0032. Offers exercise science (PhD); health promotion (MS, Ed D); kinesiology (MS); physical education training (Ed D). Terminal master's awarded for partial completion of doctoral program. *Degree requirements:* For master's, comprehensive exam, thesis optional; for doctorate, comprehensive exam, thesis/dissertation. *Entrance requirements:* For master's, GRE General Test, minimum undergraduate GPA of 2.75; for doctorate, GRE General Test, minimum graduate GPA of 3.0. Additional exam requirements/recommendations for international students: Required—TOEFL (minimum score 550 paper-based). Electronic applications accepted.

University of Lethbridge, School of Graduate Studies, Lethbridge, AB T1K 3M4, Canada. Offers accounting (MScM); addictions counseling (M Sc); agricultural biotechnology (M Sc); agricultural studies (M Sc, MA); anthropology (MA); archaeology (M Sc, MA); art (MA, MFA); biochemistry (M Sc); biological sciences (M Sc); biomolecular science (PhD); biosystems and biodiversity (PhD); Canadian studies (MA); chemistry (M Sc); computer science (M Sc); computer science and geographical information science (M Sc); counseling (MC); counseling psychology (M Ed); dramatic arts (MA); earth, space, and physical science (PhD); economics (MA); education (MA); educational leadership (M Ed); English (MA); environmental science (M Sc); evolution and behavior (PhD); exercise science (M Sc); finance (MScM); French (MA); French/German (MA); French/Spanish (MA); general education (M Ed); general management (MScM); geography (M Sc, MA); German (MA); health sciences (M Sc); human resource management and labour relations (MScM); individualized multidisciplinary (M Sc, MA); information systems (MScM); international management (MScM); kinesiology (M Sc, MA); marketing (MScM); mathematics (M Sc); modern languages (MA); music (M Mus, MA); Native American studies (MA); neuroscience (M Sc, PhD); new media (MA, MFA); nursing (M Sc); philosophy (MA); physics (M Sc); policy and strategy (MScM); political science (MA); psychology (M Sc, MA); religious studies (MA); sociology (MA); theatre and dramatic arts (MFA); theoretical and computational science (PhD); urban and regional studies (MA); women and gender studies (MA). Part-time and evening/weekend programs available. *Degree requirements:* For doctorate, comprehensive exam, thesis/dissertation. *Entrance requirements:* For master's, GMAT (for M Sc in management), bachelor's degree in related field, minimum GPA of 3.0 during previous 20 graded semester courses, 2 years teaching or related experience (M Ed); for doctorate, master's degree, minimum graduate GPA of 3.5. Additional exam requirements/recommendations for international students: Required—TOEFL. Application fee: $60 Canadian dollars. *Financial support:* Fellowships, research assistantships, teaching assistantships, scholarships/grants, health care benefits, and unspecified assistantships available. *Faculty research:* Movement and brain plasticity, gibberellin physiology, photosynthesis, carbon cycling, molecular properties of main-group ring components. *Application contact:* School of Graduate Studies, 403-329-2793, Fax: 403-332-5239, E-mail: sgsinquiries@uleth.ca.
Website: http://www.uleth.ca/graduatestudies/.

University of Louisiana at Monroe, Graduate School, College of Health and Pharmaceutical Sciences, Department of Kinesiology, Monroe, LA 71209-0001. Offers applied exercise physiology (MS); clinical exercise physiology (MS); sports, fitness and recreation (MS). Part-time and evening/weekend programs available. Postbaccalaureate distance learning degree programs offered (minimal on-campus study). *Degree requirements:* For master's, comprehensive exam, thesis, 6-hour internship. *Entrance requirements:* For master's, GRE General Test. Additional exam requirements/recommendations for international students: Required—TOEFL (minimum score 500 paper-based; 61 iBT). *Application deadline:* For fall admission, 8/24 priority date for domestic students, 7/1 for international students; for winter admission, 12/14 priority date for domestic students; for spring admission, 1/19 for domestic students, 11/1 for international students. Applications are processed on a rolling basis. Application fee: $20 ($30 for international students). Electronic applications accepted. *Expenses:* Tuition, state resident: full-time $6607. Tuition, nonresident: full-time $17,179. Full-time tuition and fees vary according to program. *Financial support:* Research assistantships, career-related internships or fieldwork, Federal Work-Study, and unspecified assistantships available. Financial award application deadline: 4/1; financial award applicants required to submit FAFSA. *Faculty research:* Cardiovascular disease risk factors; exercise and immunological system; attitude, exercise, and the aged. *Unit head:* Dr. Ken Alford, Director, 318-342-1306, E-mail: alford@ulm.edu. *Application contact:* Dr. Tommie Church, Director of Graduate Studies, 318-342-1321, E-mail: church@ulm.edu.
Website: http://www.ulm.edu/kinesiology/.

University of Louisville, Graduate School, College of Education and Human Development, Department of Health and Sport Sciences, Louisville, KY 40292-0001. Offers community health education (M Ed); exercise physiology (MS); health and physical education (MAT); sport administration (MS). Part-time and evening/weekend

programs available. *Students:* 54 full-time (22 women), 11 part-time (9 women); includes 12 minority (6 Black or African American, non-Hispanic/Latino; 1 American Indian or Alaska Native, non-Hispanic/Latino; 1 Asian, non-Hispanic/Latino; 3 Hispanic/Latino; 1 Two or more races, non-Hispanic/Latino), 3 international. Average age 27. 91 applicants, 70% accepted, 40 enrolled. In 2013, 16 master's awarded. *Entrance requirements:* For master's, GRE General Test. Additional exam requirements/recommendations for international students: Required—TOEFL (minimum score 560 paper-based; 83 iBT). Application fee: $60. Electronic applications accepted. *Expenses:* Tuition, state resident: full-time $10,788; part-time $599 per credit hour. Tuition, nonresident: full-time $22,446; part-time $1247 per credit hour. *Required fees:* $196. Tuition and fees vary according to program and reciprocity agreements. *Financial support:* Fellowships, research assistantships, teaching assistantships, career-related internships or fieldwork, Federal Work-Study, scholarships/grants, health care benefits, and unspecified assistantships available. Financial award application deadline: 6/1; financial award applicants required to submit FAFSA. *Faculty research:* Impact of sports and sport marketing on society, factors associated with school and community health, cardiac and pulmonary rehabilitation, impact of participation in activities on student retention and graduation, strength and conditioning. *Unit head:* Dr. Anita Moorman, Chair, 502-852-0553, Fax: 502-852-4534, E-mail: amm@louisville.edu. *Application contact:* Libby Leggett, Director, Graduate Admissions, 502-852-3101, Fax: 502-852-6536, E-mail: gradadm@louisville.edu.
Website: http://www.louisville.edu/education/departments/hss.

University of Maine, Graduate School, College of Education and Human Development, Department of Exercise Science and STEM Education, Orono, ME 04469. Offers classroom technology integrationist (CGS); education data specialist (CGS); educational technology coordinator (CGS); kinesiology and physical education (M Ed, MS); science education (M Ed, MS); STEM education (PhD). Part-time and evening/weekend programs available. *Students:* 25 full-time (13 women), 28 part-time (16 women); includes 5 minority (2 Black or African American, non-Hispanic/Latino; 2 American Indian or Alaska Native, non-Hispanic/Latino; 1 Asian, non-Hispanic/Latino), 2 international. Average age 34. 19 applicants, 84% accepted, 12 enrolled. In 2013, 6 master's awarded. *Degree requirements:* For master's, thesis (for some programs); for doctorate, comprehensive exam, thesis/dissertation. *Entrance requirements:* For master's, GRE General Test, MAT; for doctorate, GRE General Test. Additional exam requirements/recommendations for international students: Required—TOEFL. *Application deadline:* For fall admission, 1/15 for domestic students. Applications are processed on a rolling basis. Application fee: $65. Electronic applications accepted. *Expenses:* Tuition, state resident: full-time $7524. Tuition, nonresident: full-time $23,112. *Required fees:* $1970. *Financial support:* In 2013–14, 13 students received support, including 2 teaching assistantships (averaging $14,600 per year). Financial award application deadline: 3/1. *Faculty research:* Integration of technology in K-12 classrooms, instructional theory and practice in science, inquiry-based teaching, professional development, exercise science, adaptive physical education, neuromuscular function/dysfunction. *Unit head:* Dr. Janet Spector, Dean, 207-581-2441, Fax: 207-581-2423. *Application contact:* Scott G. Delcourt, Associate Dean of the Graduate School, 207-581-3291, Fax: 207-581-3232, E-mail: graduate@maine.edu.
Website: http://umaine.edu/edhd/.

University of Mary Hardin-Baylor, Graduate Studies in Exercise Science, Belton, TX 76513. Offers exercise science (MS Ed); sport administration (MS Ed). Part-time and evening/weekend programs available. *Faculty:* 7 full-time (2 women). *Students:* 10 full-time (6 women), 14 part-time (3 women); includes 5 minority (2 Black or African American, non-Hispanic/Latino; 3 Hispanic/Latino). Average age 27. 15 applicants, 73% accepted, 10 enrolled. In 2013, 8 master's awarded. *Degree requirements:* For master's, comprehensive exam. *Entrance requirements:* For master's, minimum GPA of 3.0. Additional exam requirements/recommendations for international students: Required—TOEFL (minimum score 550 paper-based; 80 iBT), IELTS (minimum score 6). *Application deadline:* For fall admission, 6/15 priority date for international students; for spring admission, 10/15 priority date for international students. Application fee: $35 ($135 for international students). *Expenses: Tuition:* Full-time $14,130; part-time $785 per credit hour. *Required fees:* $1350; $75 per credit hour. $50 per term. *Financial support:* Federal Work-Study, unspecified assistantships, and scholarships (for some active duty military personnel only) available. Support available to part-time students. Financial award application deadline: 6/1; financial award applicants required to submit FAFSA. *Unit head:* Dr. Colin Wilborn, Dean, Graduate School/Program Director, Master of Science in Education in Exercise Science Program/Associate Professor of Exercise Sport Science, 254-295-4488, E-mail: cwilborn@umhb.edu. *Application contact:* Melissa Ford, Director of Graduate Admissions, 254-295-4020, Fax: 254-295-5038, E-mail: mford@umhb.edu.
Website: http://www.graduate.umhb.edu/exss.

University of Memphis, Graduate School, College of Education, Department of Health and Sport Sciences, Memphis, TN 38152. Offers clinical nutrition (MS); exercise and sport science (MS); health promotion (MS); physical education teacher education (MS), including teacher education; sport and leisure commerce (MS). Part-time and evening/weekend programs available. *Faculty:* 22 full-time (8 women), 3 part-time/adjunct (2 women). *Students:* 83 full-time (51 women), 28 part-time (23 women); includes 37 minority (29 Black or African American, non-Hispanic/Latino; 6 Asian, non-Hispanic/Latino; 2 Two or more races, non-Hispanic/Latino), 7 international. Average age 27. 86 applicants, 67% accepted, 29 enrolled. In 2013, 35 master's awarded. *Degree requirements:* For master's, comprehensive exam, thesis. *Entrance requirements:* For master's, GRE General Test or GMAT (for sport and leisure commerce). *Application deadline:* For fall admission, 5/1 priority date for domestic students; for spring admission, 11/1 for domestic students. Applications are processed on a rolling basis. Application fee: $35 ($60 for international students). *Financial support:* In 2013–14, 59 students received support. Research assistantships with full tuition reimbursements available, teaching assistantships with full tuition reimbursements available, career-related internships or fieldwork, Federal Work-Study, scholarships/grants, tuition waivers (partial), and unspecified assistantships available. Financial award application deadline: 2/15; financial award applicants required to submit FAFSA. *Faculty research:* Sport marketing and consumer analysis, health psychology, smoking cessation, psychosocial aspects of cardiovascular disease, global health promotion. *Unit head:* Linda H. Clemens, Interim Chair, 901-678-2324, Fax: 901-678-3591, E-mail: lhclemns@memphis.edu. *Application contact:* Dr. Kenneth Ward, Graduate Studies Coordinator, 901-678-1714, E-mail: kdward@memphis.edu.
Website: http://coe.memphis.edu/hss/.

University of Miami, Graduate School, School of Education and Human Development, Department of Kinesiology and Sport Sciences, Program in Exercise Physiology, Coral Gables, FL 33124. Offers exercise physiology (MS Ed, PhD); strength and conditioning (MS Ed). Part-time and evening/weekend programs available. *Faculty:* 4 full-time (1 woman). *Students:* 52 full-time (25 women), 6 part-time (3 women); includes 20 minority (4 Black or African American, non-Hispanic/Latino; 1 Asian, non-Hispanic/Latino; 13 Hispanic/Latino; 2 Two or more races, non-Hispanic/Latino), 8 international. Average age 27. 68 applicants, 35% accepted, 24 enrolled. In 2013, 20 master's awarded. Terminal master's awarded for partial completion of doctoral program. *Degree requirements:* For master's, comprehensive exam (for some programs), thesis optional, special project; for doctorate, thesis/dissertation, qualifying exam. *Entrance requirements:* For master's and doctorate, GRE General Test. Additional exam requirements/recommendations for international students: Required—TOEFL (minimum score 550 paper-based; 80 iBT); Recommended—IELTS (minimum score 6.5). *Application deadline:* For fall admission, 10/1 for international students; for spring admission, 10/1 for international students. Applications are processed on a rolling basis. Application fee: $65. Electronic applications accepted. *Financial support:* In 2013–14, 36 students received support. Health care benefits and unspecified assistantships available. Support available to part-time students. Financial award application deadline: 3/1; financial award applicants required to submit FAFSA. *Faculty research:* Women's health, cardiovascular health, aging, metabolism, obesity. *Unit head:* Dr. Arlette Perry, Department Chairperson, 305-284-3024, Fax: 305-284-5168, E-mail: aperry@miami.edu. *Application contact:* Lois Heffernan, Graduate Admissions Coordinator, 305-284-2167, Fax: 305-284-9395, E-mail: lheffernan@miami.edu.
Website: http://www.education.miami.edu/career/graduate.asp.

University of Minnesota, Twin Cities Campus, Graduate School, College of Education and Human Development, School of Kinesiology, Minneapolis, MN 55455-0213. Offers adapted physical education (MA, PhD); biomechanics (MA); biomechanics and neural control (PhD); coaching (Certificate); developmental adapted physical education (M Ed); exercise physiology (MA, PhD); human factors/ergonomics (MA, PhD); international/comparative sport (MA, PhD); kinesiology (M Ed, MA, MS, PhD); leisure services/management (MA, PhD); motor development (MA, PhD); motor learning/control (MA, PhD); outdoor education/recreation (MA, PhD); physical education (M Ed); recreation, park, and leisure studies (M Ed, MA, PhD); sport and exercise science (M Ed); sport management (M Ed, MA, PhD); sport psychology (MA, PhD); sport sociology (MA, PhD); therapeutic recreation (MA, PhD). Part-time programs available. *Faculty:* 14 full-time (6 women). *Students:* 140 full-time (51 women), 52 part-time (19 women); includes 18 minority (9 Black or African American, non-Hispanic/Latino; 1 American Indian or Alaska Native, non-Hispanic/Latino; 4 Asian, non-Hispanic/Latino; 4 Hispanic/Latino), 25 international. Average age 29. 172 applicants, 51% accepted, 77 enrolled. In 2013, 89 master's, 11 doctorates, 13 other advanced degrees awarded. Terminal master's awarded for partial completion of doctoral program. *Degree requirements:* For master's, final oral exam; for doctorate, thesis/dissertation, preliminary written/oral exam, final oral exam. *Entrance requirements:* For master's, GRE or MAT, minimum GPA of 3.0; for doctorate, GRE or MAT, minimum GPA of 3.0, writing sample. Application fee: $75 ($95 for international students). *Financial support:* In 2013–14, 3 fellowships (averaging $22,667 per year), 8 research assistantships with full tuition reimbursements (averaging $849 per year), 41 teaching assistantships with full tuition reimbursements (averaging $12,766 per year) were awarded; career-related internships or fieldwork, Federal Work-Study, institutionally sponsored loans, and tuition waivers (full and partial) also available. Support available to part-time students. *Faculty research:* Exercise physiology; biochemical, molecular and nutritional aspects of exercise; sport training and performance; sport and exercise psychology; behavioral aspects of physical activity; youth sport science; gender and sport sociology; sports management; sports policy, marketing and law; motor development and disabilities; movement perception and action; movement neuroscience. *Total annual research expenditures:* $472,507. *Unit head:* Dr. Li Li Ji, Director, 612-624-9809, Fax: 612-626-7700, E-mail: llji@umn.edu. *Application contact:* Dr. Jennifer Engler, Assistant Dean, 612-626-2887, Fax: 612-626-7496, E-mail: engle009@umn.edu.

University of Mississippi, Graduate School, School of Applied Sciences, Department of Health, Exercise Science, and Recreation Management, Oxford, MS 38677. Offers exercise science (MS); health and kinesiology (PhD); health promotion (MS); park and recreation management (MA). *Faculty:* 9 full-time (3 women), 3 part-time/adjunct (1 woman). *Students:* 45 full-time (23 women), 14 part-time (9 women); includes 11 minority (8 Black or African American, non-Hispanic/Latino; 1 Asian, non-Hispanic/Latino; 2 Hispanic/Latino), 5 international. In 2013, 19 master's, 1 doctorate awarded. *Degree requirements:* For master's, thesis (for some programs); for doctorate, thesis/dissertation. *Entrance requirements:* For master's, GRE General Test, minimum GPA of 3.0; for doctorate, GRE General Test. Additional exam requirements/recommendations for international students: Required—TOEFL. *Application deadline:* For fall admission, 4/1 for domestic students; for spring admission, 10/1 for domestic students. Applications are processed on a rolling basis. *Financial support:* Scholarships/grants available. Financial award application deadline: 3/1; financial award applicants required to submit FAFSA. *Unit head:* Dr. Scott G. Owens, Chair, 662-915-5844, Fax: 662-915-5525, E-mail: dbramlett@olemiss.edu. *Application contact:* Dr. Christy M. Wyandt, Associate Dean, 662-915-7474, Fax: 662-915-7577, E-mail: cwyandt@olemiss.edu.

University of Missouri, Graduate School, College of Human Environmental Sciences, Department of Nutrition and Exercise Physiology, Columbia, MO 65211. Offers exercise physiology (MA, PhD); nutritional sciences (MS, PhD). *Faculty:* 10 full-time (7 women). *Students:* 8 full-time (4 women), 11 part-time (6 women), 3 international. Average age 27. 20 applicants, 25% accepted, 1 enrolled. In 2013, 6 master's awarded. *Degree requirements:* For doctorate, thesis/dissertation. *Entrance requirements:* For master's and doctorate, GRE General Test, minimum GPA of 3.0. Additional exam requirements/recommendations for international students: Required—TOEFL (minimum score 500 paper-based; 61 iBT). *Application deadline:* For fall admission, 12/31 priority date for domestic and international students. Applications are processed on a rolling basis. Application fee: $55 ($75 for international students). Electronic applications accepted. *Financial support:* Fellowships with full and partial tuition reimbursements, research assistantships with full and partial tuition reimbursements, teaching assistantships with full and partial tuition reimbursements, institutionally sponsored loans, scholarships/grants, health care benefits, and unspecified assistantships available. Support available to part-time students. *Faculty research:* Fitness and wellness; body composition research; child care provider workforce development; childhood overweight: etiology and outcomes; development during infancy and early childhood; regulation and organization of glycolysis; metabolomics; diabetes and smooth muscle metabolism; lipid metabolism and lipotoxicity - mitochondrial dysfunction in diabetes, atherosclerosis, and cell phenotype transformation; magnetic resonance measures of cellular metabolism; smooth muscle physiology/pathophysiology. *Unit head:* Dr. Chris Hardin, Department Chair, 573-882-4288, E-mail: hardinc@missouri.edu. *Application contact:* Tammy Conrad, Academic Advisor, 573-882-1144, E-mail: conradt@missouri.edu.
Website: http://ns.missouri.edu/.

The University of Montana, Graduate School, Phyllis J. Washington College of Education and Human Sciences, Department of Health and Human Performance, Missoula, MT 59812-0002. Offers exercise science (MS); health and human performance (MS); health promotion (MS). Part-time programs available. *Entrance requirements:* For master's, GRE General Test. Additional exam requirements/recommendations for international students: Required—TOEFL. *Faculty research:* Exercise physiology, performance psychology, nutrition, pre-employment physical screening, program evaluation.

University of Nebraska at Kearney, Graduate Programs, College of Education, Department of Health, Physical Education, Recreation, and Leisure Studies, Kearney, NE 68849-0001. Offers general physical education (MA Ed), including recreation and leisure, sports administration; physical education exercise science (MA Ed); physical

education master teacher (MA Ed), including pedagogy, special populations. Part-time and evening/weekend programs available. *Degree requirements:* For master's, comprehensive exam, thesis optional. *Entrance requirements:* For master's, GRE General Test, personal statement. Additional exam requirements/recommendations for international students: Required—TOEFL (minimum score 550 paper-based). Electronic applications accepted. *Faculty research:* Ergonomic aids, nutrition, motor development, sports pedagogy, applied behavior analysis.

University of Nebraska at Omaha, Graduate Studies, College of Education, School of Health, Physical Education, and Recreation, Omaha, NE 68182. Offers athletic training (MA); exercise science (PhD); health, physical education, and recreation (MA, MS). Part-time and evening/weekend programs available. *Faculty:* 15 full-time (7 women). *Students:* 54 full-time (24 women), 32 part-time (9 women); includes 8 minority (2 Asian, non-Hispanic/Latino; 3 Hispanic/Latino; 3 Two or more races, non-Hispanic/Latino), 4 international. Average age 28. 79 applicants, 51% accepted, 22 enrolled. In 2013, 27 master's awarded. *Degree requirements:* For master's, comprehensive exam, thesis (for some programs). *Entrance requirements:* For master's, GRE; entrance exam, minimum GPA of 3.0, official transcripts, statement of purpose, 2 letters of recommendation; for doctorate, GRE, minimum GPA of 3.2, official transcripts, statement of purpose, 3 letters of recommendation, resume, writing sample. Additional exam requirements/recommendations for international students: Required—TOEFL, IELTS, PTE. *Application deadline:* For fall admission, 7/1 priority date for domestic students; for spring admission, 11/1 priority date for domestic students; for summer admission, 2/1 for domestic students. Applications are processed on a rolling basis. Application fee: $45. Electronic applications accepted. *Financial support:* In 2013–14, 19 students received support, including 12 research assistantships with tuition reimbursements available, 7 teaching assistantships with tuition reimbursements available; fellowships, Federal Work-Study, institutionally sponsored loans, scholarships/grants, tuition waivers (full), and unspecified assistantships also available. Support available to part-time students. Financial award application deadline: 3/1; financial award applicants required to submit FAFSA. *Unit head:* Dr. Daniel Blanke, Director, 402-554-2670. *Application contact:* Dr. Kris Berg, Graduate Program Chair, 402-554-2670, E-mail: graduate@unomaha.edu.

University of Nebraska–Lincoln, Graduate College, College of Education and Human Sciences, Department of Nutrition and Health Sciences, Lincoln, NE 68588. Offers community nutrition and health promotion (MS); nutrition (MS, PhD); nutrition and exercise (MS); nutrition and health sciences (MS, PhD). *Degree requirements:* For master's, thesis optional. *Entrance requirements:* For master's, GRE General Test. Additional exam requirements/recommendations for international students: Required—TOEFL (minimum score 550 paper-based). Electronic applications accepted. *Faculty research:* Foods/food service administration, community nutrition science, diet-health relationships.

University of Nevada, Las Vegas, Graduate College, School of Allied Health Sciences, Department of Kinesiology, Las Vegas, NV 89154-3034. Offers exercise physiology (MS); kinesiology (PhD). Part-time programs available. *Faculty:* 8 full-time (3 women), 2 part-time/adjunct (1 woman). *Students:* 38 full-time (12 women), 16 part-time (8 women); includes 13 minority (1 Black or African American, non-Hispanic/Latino; 1 Asian, non-Hispanic/Latino; 7 Hispanic/Latino; 4 Two or more races, non-Hispanic/Latino), 2 international. Average age 27. 44 applicants, 80% accepted, 21 enrolled. In 2013, 18 master's awarded. *Degree requirements:* For master's, comprehensive exam (for some programs), thesis (for some programs). *Entrance requirements:* For master's, GRE General Test. Additional exam requirements/recommendations for international students: Required—TOEFL (minimum score 550 paper-based; 80 iBT), IELTS (minimum score 7). *Application deadline:* For fall admission, 6/15 for domestic students, 5/1 for international students; for spring admission, 11/15 for domestic students, 10/1 for international students. Application fee: $60 ($95 for international students). Electronic applications accepted. *Expenses:* Tuition, state resident: full-time $4752; part-time $264 per credit. Tuition, nonresident: full-time $18,662; part-time $554.50 per credit. *International tuition:* $18,952 full-time. *Required fees:* $532; $12 per credit. $266 per semester. One-time fee: $35. Tuition and fees vary according to course load and program. *Financial support:* In 2013–14, 29 students received support, including 12 research assistantships with partial tuition reimbursements available (averaging $10,840 per year), 17 teaching assistantships with partial tuition reimbursements available (averaging $8,924 per year); institutionally sponsored loans, scholarships/grants, health care benefits, and unspecified assistantships also available. Financial award application deadline: 3/1. *Faculty research:* Biomechanics of gait, factors in motor skill acquisition and performance, nutritional supplements and performance, lipoprotein chemistry, body composition methods. *Total annual research expenditures:* $149,898. *Unit head:* Richard Tandy, Chair/Professor, 702-895-5080, E-mail: dick.tandy@unlv.edu. *Application contact:* Graduate College Admissions Evaluator, 702-895-3320, Fax: 702-895-4180, E-mail: gradcollege@unlv.edu. Website: http://kinesiology.unlv.edu/.

University of New Brunswick Fredericton, School of Graduate Studies, Faculty of Kinesiology, Fredericton, NB E3B 5A3, Canada. Offers exercise and sport science (M Sc); sport and recreation management (MBA); sport and recreation studies (MA). Part-time programs available. *Faculty:* 14 full-time (6 women), 1 part-time/adjunct (0 women). *Students:* 27 full-time (13 women), 5 part-time (1 woman). In 2013, 9 master's awarded. *Degree requirements:* For master's, thesis (for some programs). *Entrance requirements:* For master's, GMAT (minimum score of 550 for sport and recreation management program), minimum GPA of 3.0, written statement of research goals and interests. Additional exam requirements/recommendations for international students: Required—TOEFL (minimum score 92 iBT), IELTS (minimum score 7). *Application deadline:* For winter admission, 1/31 for domestic students; for spring admission, 3/31 for domestic students. Applications are processed on a rolling basis. Application fee: $50 Canadian dollars. Electronic applications accepted. *Financial support:* In 2013–14, 31 research assistantships, 61 teaching assistantships were awarded; fellowships with tuition reimbursements, career-related internships or fieldwork, and scholarships/grants also available. *Unit head:* Dr. Usha Kuruganti, Acting Director of Graduate Studies, 506-447-3101, Fax: 506-453-3511, E-mail: ukurugan@unb.ca. *Application contact:* Leslie Harquail, Graduate Secretary, 506-453-4575, Fax: 506-453-3511, E-mail: harquail@unb.ca. Website: http://go.unb.ca/gradprograms.

University of New Mexico, Graduate School, College of Education, Department of Health, Exercise and Sports Sciences, Program in Physical Education, Albuquerque, NM 87131-2039. Offers adapted physical education (MS); curriculum and instruction (MS); exercise science (MS); generalist (MS); sports administration (MS). Part-time programs available. *Faculty:* 6 full-time (3 women). *Students:* 53 full-time (19 women), 27 part-time (14 women); includes 32 minority (3 Black or African American, non-Hispanic/Latino; 3 American Indian or Alaska Native, non-Hispanic/Latino; 2 Asian, non-Hispanic/Latino; 22 Hispanic/Latino; 2 Two or more races, non-Hispanic/Latino), 12 international. Average age 28. 48 applicants, 65% accepted, 23 enrolled. In 2013, 22 master's awarded. Terminal master's awarded for partial completion of doctoral program. *Degree requirements:* For master's, comprehensive exam, thesis optional. *Entrance requirements:* For master's, GRE, 3 letters of reference, minimum cumulative GPA of 3.0 in last 2 years of bachelor's degree, letter of intent. Additional exam

requirements/recommendations for international students: Required—TOEFL (minimum score 550 paper-based). *Application deadline:* For fall admission, 3/1 priority date for domestic students; for spring admission, 11/1 priority date for domestic students. Application fee: $50. Electronic applications accepted. *Financial support:* In 2013–14, 57 students received support, including 1 fellowship (averaging $2,290 per year), 1 teaching assistantship with full tuition reimbursement available (averaging $11,294 per year); career-related internships or fieldwork, Federal Work-Study, institutionally sponsored loans, scholarships/grants, health care benefits, tuition waivers, and unspecified assistantships also available. Financial award application deadline: 3/1; financial award applicants required to submit FAFSA. *Faculty research:* Physical education pedagogy, sports psychology, sports administration, cardiac rehabilitation, sports physiology, physical fitness assessment, exercise prescription. *Total annual research expenditures:* $17,400. *Unit head:* Dr. Todd Seidler, Chair, 505-277-2783, Fax: 505-277-6227, E-mail: tseidler@unm.edu. *Application contact:* Monica Lopez, Department Office, 505-277-5151, Fax: 505-277-6227, E-mail: mllopez@unm.edu. Website: http://coe.unm.edu/departments/hess/pe-teacher-education.html.

University of New Mexico, Graduate School, College of Education, Department of Health, Exercise and Sports Sciences, Program in Physical Education, Sports and Exercise Science, Albuquerque, NM 87131-2039. Offers curriculum and instruction (PhD); exercise science (PhD); sports administration (PhD). Part-time programs available. *Faculty:* 18 full-time (10 women). *Students:* 26 full-time (9 women), 17 part-time (5 women); includes 11 minority (3 Black or African American, non-Hispanic/Latino; 1 Asian, non-Hispanic/Latino; 6 Hispanic/Latino; 1 Native Hawaiian or other Pacific Islander, non-Hispanic/Latino), 7 international. Average age 34. 25 applicants, 36% accepted, 5 enrolled. In 2013, 4 doctorates awarded. *Degree requirements:* For doctorate, comprehensive exam, thesis/dissertation, inquiry skills, 24 credits in supporting area. *Entrance requirements:* For doctorate, GRE, letter of intent, 3 letters of reference, minimum cumulative GPA of 3.0 in last 2 years of bachelor's degree. Additional exam requirements/recommendations for international students: Required—TOEFL (minimum score 550 paper-based). *Application deadline:* For fall admission, 3/1 priority date for domestic students; for spring admission, 11/1 priority date for domestic students. Application fee: $50. Electronic applications accepted. *Financial support:* In 2013–14, 33 students received support, including 3 fellowships (averaging $2,290 per year), 16 teaching assistantships with full tuition reimbursements available (averaging $10,987 per year); career-related internships or fieldwork, Federal Work-Study, institutionally sponsored loans, scholarships/grants, health care benefits, tuition waivers, and unspecified assistantships also available. Financial award application deadline: 3/1; financial award applicants required to submit FAFSA. *Faculty research:* Facility risk management, physical education pedagogy practices, physiological adaptations to exercise, physiological adaptations to heat, sport leadership. *Total annual research expenditures:* $17,400. *Unit head:* Dr. Todd Seidler, Chair, 505-277-2783, Fax: 505-277-6227, E-mail: tseidler@unm.edu. *Application contact:* Monica Lopez, Program Office, 505-277-5151, Fax: 505-277-6227, E-mail: mllopez@unm.edu. Website: http://coe.unm.edu/departments/hess/pe-teacher-education/physical-education-sports-and-exercise-science-phd.html.

University of North Alabama, College of Education, Department of Health, Physical Education, and Recreation, Florence, AL 35632-0001. Offers health and human performance (MS), including exercise science, kinesiology, wellness and health promotion; secondary education (MA Ed), including physical education (P-12). Part-time and evening/weekend programs available. *Faculty:* 5 full-time (2 women). *Students:* 21 full-time (11 women), 7 part-time (2 women); includes 3 minority (2 Black or African American, non-Hispanic/Latino; 1 Two or more races, non-Hispanic/Latino), 3 international. Average age 27. 30 applicants, 90% accepted, 22 enrolled. In 2013, 3 master's awarded. *Degree requirements:* For master's, comprehensive exam (for some programs), thesis optional. *Entrance requirements:* For master's, MAT or GRE, 3 letters of recommendation, essay. Additional exam requirements/recommendations for international students: Required—TOEFL (minimum score 550 paper-based; 79 iBT), IELTS (minimum score 6). *Application deadline:* For fall admission, 7/1 for domestic and international students; for spring admission, 12/1 for domestic and international students. Applications are processed on a rolling basis. Application fee: $25 ($50 for international students). Electronic applications accepted. *Expenses:* Tuition, state resident: full-time $4968; part-time $3312 per year. Tuition, nonresident: full-time $9936; part-time $6624 per year. *Required fees:* $970; $60.33 per credit. $362 per semester. *Financial support:* Application deadline: 4/1; applicants required to submit FAFSA. *Unit head:* Dr. Thomas E. Coates, Chair, 256-765-4377. *Application contact:* Russ Darracott, Graduate Admissions Counselor, 256-765-4447, E-mail: erdarracott@una.edu. Website: http://www.una.edu/hper/docs/HPERThesisGuideliens.pdf.

The University of North Carolina at Chapel Hill, Graduate School, College of Arts and Sciences, Department of Exercise and Sport Science, Chapel Hill, NC 27599. Offers athletic training (MA); exercise physiology (MA); sport administration (MA). *Degree requirements:* For master's, comprehensive exam, thesis. *Entrance requirements:* For master's, GRE General Test, minimum GPA of 3.0. Additional exam requirements/recommendations for international students: Required—TOEFL (minimum score 550 paper-based). Electronic applications accepted. *Faculty research:* Mild head injury in sport, endocrine system's response to exercise, obesity and children, effect of aerobic exercise on cerebral bloodflow in elderly population.

The University of North Carolina at Charlotte, The Graduate School, College of Health and Human Services, Department of Kinesiology, Charlotte, NC 28223-0001. Offers clinical exercise physiology (Postbaccalaureate Certificate); kinesiology (MS). Part-time programs available. *Faculty:* 12 full-time (5 women). *Students:* 13 full-time (8 women), 18 part-time (12 women); includes 7 minority (5 Black or African American, non-Hispanic/Latino; 1 American Indian or Alaska Native, non-Hispanic/Latino; 1 Hispanic/Latino). Average age 24. 38 applicants, 84% accepted, 15 enrolled. In 2013, 6 master's awarded. *Degree requirements:* For master's, thesis or practicum. *Entrance requirements:* For master's, GRE or MAT. Additional exam requirements/recommendations for international students: Required—TOEFL (minimum score 557 paper-based; 83 iBT). *Application deadline:* For fall admission, 5/1 priority date for domestic students, 5/1 for international students; for spring admission, 10/1 priority date for domestic students, 10/1 for international students. Applications are processed on a rolling basis. Application fee: $75. Electronic applications accepted. *Expenses:* Tuition, state resident: full-time $3522. Tuition, nonresident: full-time $16,051. *Required fees:* $2585. Tuition and fees vary according to course load and program. *Financial support:* In 2013–14, 7 students received support, including 2 research assistantships (averaging $4,785 per year), 5 teaching assistantships (averaging $8,720 per year); career-related internships or fieldwork, institutionally sponsored loans, scholarships/grants, traineeships, and unspecified assistantships also available. Support available to part-time students. Financial award application deadline: 4/1; financial award applicants required to submit FAFSA. *Faculty research:* Biodynamics, systems physiology. *Total annual research expenditures:* $85,878. *Unit head:* Dr. Scott E. Gordon, Chair, 704-687-0855, Fax: 704-687-3180, E-mail: scott.gordon@uncc.edu. *Application contact:* Kathy B. Giddings, Director of Graduate Admissions, 704-687-5503, Fax: 704-687-1668, E-mail: gradadm@uncc.edu. Website: http://kinesiology.uncc.edu/.

Exercise and Sports Science

The University of North Carolina at Greensboro, Graduate School, School of Health and Human Performance, Department of Exercise and Sports Science, Greensboro, NC 27412-5001. Offers M Ed, MS, Ed D, PhD. *Degree requirements:* For master's, thesis (for some programs); for doctorate, thesis/dissertation. *Entrance requirements:* For master's and doctorate, GRE General Test. Additional exam requirements/recommendations for international students: Required—TOEFL. Electronic applications accepted.

University of Northern Colorado, Graduate School, College of Natural and Health Sciences, School of Sport and Exercise Science, Greeley, CO 80639. Offers exercise science (MS, PhD); sport administration (MS, PhD); sport pedagogy (MS, PhD). Part-time and evening/weekend programs available. *Degree requirements:* For master's, comprehensive exam; for doctorate, comprehensive exam, thesis/dissertation. *Entrance requirements:* For master's, 2 letters of recommendation, resume; for doctorate, GRE General Test, 3 letters of recommendation, resume. Electronic applications accepted.

University of North Florida, Brooks College of Health, Department of Clinical and Applied Movement Sciences, Jacksonville, FL 32224. Offers exercise science and chronic disease (MSH); physical therapy (DPT). *Accreditation:* APTA. Part-time and evening/weekend programs available. *Faculty:* 14 full-time (8 women), 2 part-time/adjunct (0 women). *Students:* 86 full-time (50 women), 2 part-time (both women); includes 22 minority (3 Black or African American, non-Hispanic/Latino; 3 Asian, non-Hispanic/Latino; 11 Hispanic/Latino; 5 Two or more races, non-Hispanic/Latino). Average age 25. 464 applicants, 9% accepted, 30 enrolled. In 2013, 28 doctorates awarded. *Degree requirements:* For master's, internship. *Entrance requirements:* For master's, GRE General Test, minimum GPA of 3.0 in last 60 hours, volunteer/observation experience. Additional exam requirements/recommendations for international students: Required—TOEFL (minimum score 500 paper-based). *Application deadline:* For fall admission, 2/15 for domestic students, 1/15 for international students. Application fee: $30. Electronic applications accepted. *Expenses:* Tuition, state resident: full-time $9794; part-time $408.10 per credit hour. Tuition, nonresident: full-time $22,383; part-time $932.61 per credit hour. *Required fees:* $2020; $84.20 per credit hour. Tuition and fees vary according to course load and program. *Financial support:* In 2013–14, 29 students received support. Teaching assistantships, career-related internships or fieldwork, Federal Work-Study, scholarships/grants, and tuition waivers (partial) available. Support available to part-time students. Financial award application deadline: 4/1; financial award applicants required to submit FAFSA. *Faculty research:* Clinical outcomes related to orthopedic physical therapy interventions, instructional multimedia in physical therapy education, effect of functional electrical stimulation orthostatic hypotension in acute complete spinal cord injury individuals. *Total annual research expenditures:* $123,734. *Unit head:* Dr. Joel Beam, Chair, 904-620-1424, E-mail: jbeam@unf.edu. *Application contact:* Beth Dibble, Program Director, 904-620-2418, E-mail: ptadmissions@unf.edu.
Website: http://www.unf.edu/brooks/movement_science/.

University of Oklahoma, College of Arts and Sciences, Department of Health and Exercise Science, Norman, OK 73019. Offers exercise physiology (PhD); health promotion (MS). *Faculty:* 10 full-time (4 women). *Students:* 43 full-time (21 women), 9 part-time (6 women); includes 9 minority (2 Black or African American, non-Hispanic/Latino; 1 American Indian or Alaska Native, non-Hispanic/Latino; 1 Hispanic/Latino; 5 Two or more races, non-Hispanic/Latino), 9 international. Average age 27. 49 applicants, 57% accepted, 27 enrolled. In 2013, 9 master's, 5 doctorates awarded. *Degree requirements:* For master's, comprehensive exam (for some programs), thesis, minimum GPA of 3.0; for doctorate, comprehensive exam, thesis/dissertation, minimum GPA of 3.0. *Entrance requirements:* For master's and doctorate, GRE, letters of recommendation, interview. Additional exam requirements/recommendations for international students: Required—TOEFL (minimum score 79 iBT). *Application deadline:* For fall and spring admission, 2/1 for domestic and international students. Application fee: $50 ($100 for international students). Electronic applications accepted. *Expenses:* Tuition, state resident: full-time $4205; part-time $175.20 per credit hour. Tuition, nonresident: full-time $16,205; part-time $675.20 per credit hour. *Required fees:* $2745; $103.85 per credit hour. $126.50 per semester. *Financial support:* In 2013–14, 49 students received support, including 46 teaching assistantships with partial tuition reimbursements available (averaging $12,543 per year); health care benefits, tuition waivers (full), and unspecified assistantships also available. Financial award application deadline: 6/1; financial award applicants required to submit FAFSA. *Faculty research:* Aging and muscle wasting; osteoporosis and bone loss; multiple sclerosis; tobacco use prevention; diet, obesity, and nutrition; behavioral change and lifestyle intervention; cardiovascular adjustment to exercise and aging; neural aspects of muscle function; pain; functional physical performance. *Total annual research expenditures:* $90,383. *Unit head:* Dr. Michael G. Bemben, Professor/Chair, 405-325-2717, Fax: 405-325-0594, E-mail: mgbemben@ou.edu. *Application contact:* Dr. Travis Beck, Graduate Liaison, 405-325-1378, Fax: 405-325-0594, E-mail: tbeck@ou.edu.
Website: http://cas.ou.edu/hes.

University of Pittsburgh, School of Education, Department of Health and Physical Activity, Program in Developmental Movement, Pittsburgh, PA 15260. Offers MS. *Students:* 3 full-time (0 women), 1 (woman) part-time; includes 1 minority (Black or African American, non-Hispanic/Latino), 1 international. Average age 25. 2 applicants, 100% accepted, 1 enrolled. In 2013, 2 master's awarded. *Degree requirements:* For master's, thesis. *Entrance requirements:* Additional exam requirements/recommendations for international students: Required—TOEFL. *Application deadline:* For fall admission, 2/1 for domestic students. Application fee: $50. Electronic applications accepted. *Expenses:* Tuition, state resident: full-time $19,964; part-time $807 per credit. Tuition, nonresident: full-time $32,686; part-time $1337 per credit. *Required fees:* $740; $200. Tuition and fees vary according to program. *Financial support:* Traineeships and unspecified assistantships available. Financial award application deadline: 3/1; financial award applicants required to submit FAFSA. *Unit head:* Dr. John M. Jakicic, Chair, 412-648-8914, E-mail: jjakicic@pitt.edu. *Application contact:* Greg Donahue, Graduate Enrollment Manager, 412-648-2230, Fax: 412-648-1899, E-mail: soeinfo@pitt.edu.

University of Pittsburgh, School of Education, Department of Health and Physical Activity, Program in Exercise Physiology, Pittsburgh, PA 15260. Offers MS, PhD. *Students:* 47 full-time (32 women), 17 part-time (13 women); includes 9 minority (2 Black or African American, non-Hispanic/Latino; 2 Asian, non-Hispanic/Latino; 5 Hispanic/Latino), 5 international. Average age 28. 58 applicants, 78% accepted, 31 enrolled. In 2013, 26 master's, 9 doctorates awarded. *Entrance requirements:* Additional exam requirements/recommendations for international students: Required—TOEFL (minimum score 550 paper-based; 80 iBT). *Application deadline:* Applications are processed on a rolling basis. Application fee: $50. Electronic applications accepted. *Expenses:* Tuition, state resident: full-time $19,964; part-time $807 per credit. Tuition, nonresident: full-time $32,686; part-time $1337 per credit. *Required fees:* $740; $200. Tuition and fees vary according to program. *Unit head:* Dr. John M. Jakicic, Chair, 412-648-8914, E-mail: jjakicic@pitt.edu. *Application contact:* Greg Donahue, Graduate Enrollment Manager, 412-648-2230, Fax: 412-648-1899, E-mail: soeinfo@pitt.edu.

University of Puerto Rico, Mayagüez Campus, Graduate Studies, College of Arts and Sciences, Department of Physical Education, Mayagüez, PR 00681-9000. Offers kinesiology (MA), including biomechanics, education, exercise physiology, sports training. Part-time programs available. *Faculty:* 18 full-time (7 women), 1 (woman) part-time/adjunct. *Students:* 19 full-time (9 women), 4 part-time (2 women). 14 applicants, 64% accepted, 7 enrolled. In 2013, 2 master's awarded. *Degree requirements:* For master's, thesis optional. *Entrance requirements:* For master's, EXADEP, minimum GPA of 2.5. *Application deadline:* For fall admission, 2/15 for domestic and international students; for spring admission, 9/15 for domestic and international students. Applications are processed on a rolling basis. *Expenses: Tuition, area resident:* Full-time $2466; part-time $822 per year. *International tuition:* $6371 full-time. *Required fees:* $1095; $1095. Tuition and fees vary according to course level, course load and reciprocity agreements. *Financial support:* In 2013–14, 10 students received support, including 10 teaching assistantships (averaging $9,489 per year); fellowships with full tuition reimbursements available, institutionally sponsored loans, and unspecified assistantships also available. *Unit head:* Dr. Margarita Fernandez, Interim Director, 787-832-4040 Ext. 3841, Fax: 787-833-4825, E-mail: margarita.fernandez1@upr.edu. *Application contact:* Aracelys Gonzalez, Secretary, 787-832-4040 Ext. 2008, E-mail: aracelis.gonzalez23@upr.edu.
Website: http://ece.uprm.edu/artssciences/edfi/descrip.htm.

University of Puerto Rico, Río Piedras Campus, College of Education, Program in Exercise Sciences, San Juan, PR 00931-3300. Offers MS. *Entrance requirements:* For master's, PAEG or GRE, minimum GPA of 3.0.

University of Rhode Island, Graduate School, College of Human Science and Services, Department of Kinesiology, Kingston, RI 02881. Offers cultural studies of sport and physical culture (MS); exercise science (MS); physical education pedagogy (MS); psychosocial/behavioral aspects of physical activity (MS). *Accreditation:* NCATE. Part-time programs available. *Faculty:* 17 full-time (11 women). *Students:* 13 full-time (8 women), 5 part-time (2 women); includes 4 minority (1 Black or African American, non-Hispanic/Latino; 1 American Indian or Alaska Native, non-Hispanic/Latino; 2 Hispanic/Latino). In 2013, 12 master's awarded. *Degree requirements:* For master's, thesis optional. *Entrance requirements:* For master's, GRE, 2 letters of recommendation. Additional exam requirements/recommendations for international students: Required—TOEFL (minimum score 550 paper-based). *Application deadline:* For fall admission, 7/15 for domestic students, 2/1 for international students; for spring admission, 11/15 for domestic students, 7/15 for international students. Application fee: $65. Electronic applications accepted. *Expenses:* Tuition, state resident: full-time $11,532; part-time $641 per credit. Tuition, nonresident: full-time $23,606; part-time $1311 per credit. *Required fees:* $1388; $36 per credit. $35 per semester. One-time fee: $130. *Financial support:* In 2013–14, 5 teaching assistantships with full and partial tuition reimbursements (averaging $9,903 per year) were awarded. Financial award application deadline: 7/15; financial award applicants required to submit FAFSA. *Faculty research:* Strength training and older adults, interventions to promote a healthy lifestyle as well as analysis of the psychosocial outcomes of those interventions, effects of exercise and nutrition on skeletal muscle of aging healthy adults with CVD and other metabolic related diseases, physical activity and fitness of deaf children and youth. *Total annual research expenditures:* $51,804. *Unit head:* Dr. Deborah Riebe, Chair, 401-874-5444, Fax: 401-874-4215, E-mail: debriebe@uri.edu. *Application contact:* Dr. Matthew Delmonico, Graduate Program Director, 401-874-5440, E-mail: delmonico@uri.edu.
Website: http://www.uri.edu/hss/.

University of South Alabama, Graduate School, College of Education, Department of Health, Physical Education and Leisure Services, Mobile, AL 36688-0002. Offers exercise science (MS); health education (M Ed); physical education (M Ed); therapeutic recreation (MS). *Accreditation:* NCATE (one or more programs are accredited). Part-time programs available. *Faculty:* 4 full-time (1 woman), 2 part-time/adjunct (0 women). *Students:* 34 full-time (16 women), 5 part-time (1 woman); includes 12 minority (9 Black or African American, non-Hispanic/Latino; 3 Two or more races, non-Hispanic/Latino), 4 international. 36 applicants, 61% accepted, 18 enrolled. In 2013, 16 master's awarded. *Degree requirements:* For master's, comprehensive exam. *Entrance requirements:* For master's, GRE General Test or MAT. *Application deadline:* For fall admission, 7/15 priority date for domestic students, 6/15 priority date for international students; for spring admission, 12/1 priority date for domestic students, 11/1 priority date for international students. Applications are processed on a rolling basis. Application fee: $35. *Expenses:* Tuition, state resident: full-time $8976; part-time $374 per credit hour. Tuition, nonresident: full-time $17,952; part-time $748 per credit hour. *Financial support:* In 2013–14, 10 teaching assistantships were awarded; career-related internships or fieldwork also available. Support available to part-time students. Financial award application deadline: 4/1. *Unit head:* Dr. Frederick M. Scaffidi, Chair, 251-460-7131. *Application contact:* Dr. Abigail Baxter, Director of Graduate Studies, 251-460-7131.

University of South Carolina, The Graduate School, Arnold School of Public Health, Department of Exercise Science, Columbia, SC 29208. Offers MS, DPT, PhD. Part-time programs available. *Degree requirements:* For master's, comprehensive exam, thesis (for some programs), project; for doctorate, comprehensive exam, thesis/dissertation. *Entrance requirements:* For master's and doctorate, GRE General Test. Additional exam requirements/recommendations for international students: Required—TOEFL (minimum score 570 paper-based). Electronic applications accepted. *Faculty research:* Effects of acute and chronic exercise on human function and health, motor control.

The University of South Dakota, Graduate School, School of Education, Division of Kinesiology and Sport Science, Vermillion, SD 57069-2390. Offers MA. *Accreditation:* NCATE. Part-time programs available. *Degree requirements:* For master's, comprehensive exam, thesis or alternative. *Entrance requirements:* For master's, GRE General Test, MAT, minimum GPA of 2.7. Additional exam requirements/recommendations for international students: Required—TOEFL (minimum score 550 paper-based; 79 iBT). Electronic applications accepted.

University of Southern Mississippi, Graduate School, College of Health, School of Human Performance and Recreation, Hattiesburg, MS 39406-0001. Offers human performance (MS, PhD), including exercise physiology (PhD), human performance (MS); physical education (MS); interscholastic athletic administration (MS); recreation and leisure management (MS); sport administration (MS); sport and coaching education (MS); sport management (MS). Part-time and evening/weekend programs available. *Faculty:* 13 full-time (5 women). *Students:* 60 full-time (20 women), 43 part-time (9 women); includes 19 minority (13 Black or African American, non-Hispanic/Latino; 1 American Indian or Alaska Native, non-Hispanic/Latino; 2 Hispanic/Latino; 3 Two or more races, non-Hispanic/Latino), 4 international. Average age 29. 62 applicants, 77% accepted, 38 enrolled. In 2013, 39 master's, 1 doctorate awarded. *Degree requirements:* For master's, comprehensive exam, thesis optional; for doctorate, comprehensive exam, thesis/dissertation. *Entrance requirements:* For master's, GRE General Test, minimum GPA of 2.75 in last 60 hours; for doctorate, GRE General Test, minimum GPA of 3.5. Additional exam requirements/recommendations for international students: Required—TOEFL, IELTS. *Application deadline:* For fall admission, 3/1 priority date for domestic students, 3/1 for international students; for spring admission, 1/10 priority date for domestic and international students. Applications are processed on a rolling basis. Application fee: $50. Electronic applications accepted. *Financial support:* In 2013–14, 1 fellowship (averaging $16,000 per year), 6 research assistantships with full tuition reimbursements (averaging $7,492 per year), 5 teaching assistantships with full tuition

reimbursements (averaging $7,330 per year) were awarded; career-related internships or fieldwork, Federal Work-Study, institutionally sponsored loans, scholarships/grants, health care benefits, and unspecified assistantships also available. Financial award application deadline: 3/15; financial award applicants required to submit FAFSA. *Faculty research:* Exercise physiology, health behaviors, resource management, activity interaction, site development. *Unit head:* Dr. Frederick Green, Director, 601-266-5379, Fax: 601-266-4445. *Application contact:* Dr. Trenton Gould, Graduate Coordinator, 601-266-5379, Fax: 601-266-4445.
Website: http://www.usm.edu/graduateschool/table.php.

University of South Florida, College of Education, School of Physical Education and Exercise Science, Tampa, FL 33620-9951. Offers exercise science (MA); physical education teacher preparation (MA). Part-time and evening/weekend programs available. Postbaccalaureate distance learning degree programs offered (no on-campus study). *Degree requirements:* For master's, comprehensive exam, thesis optional. *Entrance requirements:* For master's, GRE General Test, minimum GPA of 3.0 in last 60 hours of coursework. Additional exam requirements/recommendations for international students: Required—TOEFL (minimum score 500 paper-based). Electronic applications accepted. *Faculty research:* Physical education pedagogy, active gaming, exercise motivation, heat stress research, strength and nutrition research, physical activity risk management.

The University of Tennessee, Graduate School, College of Education, Health and Human Sciences, Department of Exercise, Sport, and Leisure Studies, Program in Exercise Science, Knoxville, TN 37996. Offers biomechanics/sports medicine (MS, PhD); exercise physiology (MS, PhD). *Accreditation:* CEPH (one or more programs are accredited). Part-time programs available. *Degree requirements:* For master's, thesis optional. *Entrance requirements:* For master's, minimum GPA of 2.7. Additional exam requirements/recommendations for international students: Required—TOEFL. Electronic applications accepted. *Expenses:* Tuition, state resident: full-time $9540; part-time $531 per credit hour. Tuition, nonresident: full-time $27,728; part-time $1542 per credit hour. *Required fees:* $1404; $67 per credit hour.

The University of Tennessee, Graduate School, College of Education, Health and Human Sciences, Program in Education, Knoxville, TN 37996. Offers art education (MS); counseling education (PhD); cultural studies in education (PhD); curriculum (MS, Ed S); curriculum, educational research and evaluation (Ed D, PhD); early childhood education (PhD); early childhood special education (MS); education of deaf and hard of hearing (MS); educational administration and policy studies (Ed D, PhD); educational administration and supervision (Ed S); educational psychology (Ed D, PhD); elementary education (MS, Ed S); elementary teaching (MS); English education (MS, Ed S); exercise science (PhD); foreign language/ESL education (MS, Ed S); instructional technology (MS, Ed D, PhD, Ed S); literacy, language and ESL education (PhD); literacy, language education, and ESL education (Ed D); mathematics education (MS, Ed S); modified and comprehensive special education (MS); reading education (MS, Ed S); school counseling (Ed S); school psychology (PhD, Ed S); science education (MS, Ed S); secondary teaching (MS); social foundations (MS); social science education (MS, Ed S); socio-cultural foundations of sports and education (PhD); special education (Ed S); teacher education (Ed D, PhD). *Accreditation:* NCATE. Part-time and evening/weekend programs available. *Degree requirements:* For master's and Ed S, thesis optional; for doctorate, variable foreign language requirement, thesis/dissertation. *Entrance requirements:* For master's, minimum GPA of 2.7; for doctorate and Ed S, GRE General Test, minimum GPA of 2.7. Additional exam requirements/recommendations for international students: Required—TOEFL. Electronic applications accepted. *Expenses:* Tuition, state resident: full-time $9540; part-time $531 per credit hour. Tuition, nonresident: full-time $27,728; part-time $1542 per credit hour. *Required fees:* $1404; $67 per credit hour.

The University of Texas at Arlington, Graduate School, College of Education and Health Professions, Department of Kinesiology, Arlington, TX 76019. Offers exercise science (MS). *Degree requirements:* For master's, 36 hours with at least 21 hours in kinesiology. *Entrance requirements:* For master's, GRE (minimum quantitative score of 144 [500 on old scale] and verbal of 153 [500 on old scale]), undergraduate and/or graduate course work in exercise science, kinesiology, or physical education (preferred); minimum GPA of 3.0 overall and/or in last 60 undergraduate hours; 3 letters of reference.

The University of Texas at Austin, Graduate School, College of Education, Department of Kinesiology and Health Education, Austin, TX 78712-1111. Offers behavioral health (PhD); exercise and sport psychology (M Ed, MA); exercise science (M Ed, MS, PhD); health education (M Ed, MS, Ed D, PhD). Part-time programs available. Terminal master's awarded for partial completion of doctoral program. *Degree requirements:* For master's, thesis (for some programs); for doctorate, thesis/dissertation. *Entrance requirements:* For master's and doctorate, GRE General Test. Additional exam requirements/recommendations for international students: Required—TOEFL. Electronic applications accepted. *Faculty research:* Health promotion, human performance and exercise biochemistry, motor behavior and biomechanics, sport management, aging and pediatric development.

The University of Texas at Brownsville, Graduate Studies, College of Education, Brownsville, TX 78520-4991. Offers bilingual education (M Ed); counseling and guidance (M Ed); curriculum and instruction (M Ed); early childhood education (M Ed); educational leadership (M Ed); educational technology (M Ed); exercise science (MS); special education (M Ed). Part-time and evening/weekend programs available. Postbaccalaureate distance learning degree programs offered (no on-campus study). *Faculty:* 51 full-time (28 women). *Students:* 60 full-time (43 women), 496 part-time (363 women); includes 467 minority (4 Black or African American, non-Hispanic/Latino; 1 American Indian or Alaska Native, non-Hispanic/Latino; 10 Asian, non-Hispanic/Latino; 451 Hispanic/Latino; 1 Native Hawaiian or other Pacific Islander, non-Hispanic/Latino), 12 international. 161 applicants, 67% accepted, 81 enrolled. In 2013, 142 master's awarded. *Degree requirements:* For master's, comprehensive exam (for some programs), thesis optional, electronic portfolio. *Entrance requirements:* For master's, GRE General Test, curriculum vitae or resume, teaching certificate. Additional exam requirements/recommendations for international students: Required—TOEFL (minimum score 550 paper-based; 77 iBT). *Application deadline:* For fall admission, 7/1 priority date for domestic students, 7/1 for international students; for spring admission, 12/1 priority date for domestic students, 12/1 for international students. Applications are processed on a rolling basis. Application fee: $30. Electronic applications accepted. *Expenses:* Tuition, state resident: full-time $3444; part-time $1148 per semester. Tuition, nonresident: full-time $9816. *Required fees:* $1018; $221 per credit hour. $401 per semester. *Financial support:* In 2013–14, 136 students received support, including 6 research assistantships (averaging $10,000 per year); career-related internships or fieldwork, Federal Work-Study, scholarships/grants, tuition waivers (partial), and unspecified assistantships also available. Support available to part-time students. Financial award application deadline: 3/1; financial award applicants required to submit FAFSA. *Unit head:* Dr. Miguel Angel Escotet, Dean, 956-882-7220, Fax: 956-882-7431, E-mail: miguel.escotet@utb.edu. *Application contact:* Mari E. Stevens, Graduate Studies Specialist, 956-882-6587, Fax: 956-882-7279, E-mail: mari.stevens@utb.edu.
Website: http://www.utb.edu/vpaa/coe/Pages/default.aspx.

University of the Pacific, College of the Pacific, Department of Health, Exercise and Sport Science, Stockton, CA 95211-0197. Offers MA. *Faculty:* 10 full-time (4 women), 1 (woman) part-time/adjunct. *Students:* 16 part-time (8 women); includes 7 minority (1 Black or African American, non-Hispanic/Latino; 1 Asian, non-Hispanic/Latino; 4 Hispanic/Latino; 1 Two or more races, non-Hispanic/Latino), 1 international. Average age 25. 29 applicants, 55% accepted, 10 enrolled. In 2013, 3 master's awarded. *Degree requirements:* For master's, comprehensive exam (for some programs), thesis (for some programs). *Entrance requirements:* For master's, GRE General Test. Additional exam requirements/recommendations for international students: Required—TOEFL (minimum score 475 paper-based). *Application deadline:* For fall admission, 3/1 priority date for domestic students; for spring admission, 10/1 for domestic students. Applications are processed on a rolling basis. Application fee: $75. *Financial support:* In 2013–14, 7 teaching assistantships were awarded; institutionally sponsored loans also available. Support available to part-time students. Financial award application deadline: 3/1; financial award applicants required to submit FAFSA. *Unit head:* Dr. Peter J. Schroeder, Chairperson, 209-946-2704, E-mail: pschroeder@pacific.edu. *Application contact:* Information Contact, 209-946-2261.

The University of Toledo, College of Graduate Studies, College of Health Sciences, Department of Kinesiology, Toledo, OH 43606-3390. Offers exercise science (MSES, PhD). Part-time programs available. *Faculty:* 11. *Students:* 44 full-time (22 women), 4 part-time (2 women); includes 2 minority (both Asian, non-Hispanic/Latino), 4 international. Average age 26. 37 applicants, 54% accepted, 18 enrolled. In 2013, 12 master's awarded. *Degree requirements:* For master's, comprehensive exam, thesis; for doctorate, comprehensive exam, thesis/dissertation. *Entrance requirements:* For master's and doctorate, minimum cumulative GPA of 2.7 for all previous academic work, letters of recommendation. Additional exam requirements/recommendations for international students: Required—TOEFL (minimum score 550 paper-based; 80 iBT). *Application deadline:* For fall admission, 1/15 priority date for domestic and international students. Applications are processed on a rolling basis. Application fee: $45 ($75 for international students). Electronic applications accepted. *Financial support:* In 2013–14, 20 teaching assistantships with full and partial tuition reimbursements (averaging $13,232 per year) were awarded; career-related internships or fieldwork, Federal Work-Study, institutionally sponsored loans, scholarships/grants, tuition waivers (full and partial), and unspecified assistantships also available. *Unit head:* Dr. Barry Scheuermann, Chair, 419-530-2692. *Application contact:* Graduate School Office, 419-530-4723, Fax: 419-530-4724, E-mail: grdsch@utnet.utoledo.edu.
Website: http://www.utoledo.edu/eduhshs/.

University of Utah, Graduate School, College of Health, Department of Exercise and Sport Science, Salt Lake City, UT 84112. Offers MS, PhD. *Faculty:* 10 full-time (4 women), 17 part-time/adjunct (12 women). *Students:* 87 full-time (44 women), 24 part-time (8 women); includes 10 minority (4 Black or African American, non-Hispanic/Latino; 1 Asian, non-Hispanic/Latino; 5 Two or more races, non-Hispanic/Latino), 4 international. Average age 30. 115 applicants, 48% accepted, 47 enrolled. In 2013, 23 master's, 5 doctorates awarded. Terminal master's awarded for partial completion of doctoral program. *Degree requirements:* For master's, comprehensive exam, thesis (for some programs); for doctorate, comprehensive exam, thesis/dissertation. *Entrance requirements:* For master's, GRE, curriculum vitae, 2 letters of recommendation, 500-word statement of intent, minimum GPA of 3.0; for doctorate, GRE, curriculum vitae, 3 letters of recommendation, 800-word statement of intent, minimum GPA of 3.0. Additional exam requirements/recommendations for international students: Required—TOEFL (minimum score 500 paper-based; 61 iBT). *Application deadline:* For fall admission, 12/1 for domestic and international students. Application fee: $55 ($65 for international students). Electronic applications accepted. *Expenses:* Tuition, state resident: full-time $5259. Tuition, nonresident: full-time $18,569. *Required fees:* $841. Tuition and fees vary according to course load. *Financial support:* In 2013–14, 61 students received support, including 1 fellowship with full and partial tuition reimbursement available (averaging $14,000 per year), 29 research assistantships with full and partial tuition reimbursements available (averaging $13,000 per year), 31 teaching assistantships with full and partial tuition reimbursements available (averaging $12,000 per year); career-related internships or fieldwork, scholarships/grants, traineeships, health care benefits, and unspecified assistantships also available. Financial award application deadline: 4/15; financial award applicants required to submit FAFSA. *Faculty research:* Exercise physiology, psychosocial aspects of sports and physical education, special physical education, elementary/secondary physical education, sport medicine education. *Total annual research expenditures:* $382,095. *Unit head:* Dr. James C. Hannon, Chair, 801-581-7646, Fax: 801-581-7558, E-mail: james.hannon@hsc.utah.edu. *Application contact:* Dr. Maria Newton, Director of Graduate Studies, 801-581-4729, Fax: 801-581-7558, E-mail: maria.newton@health.utah.edu.
Website: http://www.health.utah.edu/ess/.

University of West Florida, College of Professional Studies, Department of Health, Leisure, and Exercise Science, Program in Health, Leisure, and Exercise Science, Pensacola, FL 32514-5750. Offers exercise science (MS); physical education (MS). Part-time and evening/weekend programs available. *Degree requirements:* For master's, thesis or alternative. *Entrance requirements:* For master's, GRE or MAT, official transcripts; minimum GPA of 3.0; letter of intent; two personal references; work experience. Additional exam requirements/recommendations for international students: Required—TOEFL (minimum score 550 paper-based). Electronic applications accepted.

University of West Florida, College of Professional Studies, Department of Research and Advanced Studies, Pensacola, FL 32514-5750. Offers administration (MSA), including acquisition and contract administration, biomedical/pharmaceutical, criminal justice administration, database administration, education leadership, healthcare administration, human performance technology, leadership, nursing administration, public administration, software engineering and administration; college student personnel administration (M Ed), including college personnel administration, guidance and counseling; curriculum and instruction (M Ed, Ed S); educational leadership (M Ed); middle and secondary level education and ESOL (M Ed). Part-time and evening/weekend programs available. *Entrance requirements:* For master's, GRE or MAT, official transcripts; minimum undergraduate GPA of 3.0; letter of intent; three letters of recommendation; resume. Additional exam requirements/recommendations for international students: Required—TOEFL (minimum score 550 paper-based).

University of West Florida, College of Professional Studies, Program in Administration, Pensacola, FL 32514-5750. Offers acquisition and contract administration (MSA); database administration (MSA); health care administration (MSA); human performance technology (MSA); leadership (MSA); public administration (MSA); software engineering administration (MSA). Part-time and evening/weekend programs available. Postbaccalaureate distance learning degree programs offered (no on-campus study). *Entrance requirements:* For master's, GRE General Test, letter of intent, names of references. Additional exam requirements/recommendations for international students: Required—TOEFL (minimum score 550 paper-based).

University of Wisconsin–La Crosse, Graduate Studies, College of Science and Health, Department of Exercise and Sport Science, Program in Clinical Exercise Physiology, La Crosse, WI 54601-3742. Offers MS. *Students:* 15 full-time (9 women);

includes 2 minority (1 Asian, non-Hispanic/Latino; 1 Two or more races, non-Hispanic/Latino). Average age 23. 42 applicants, 45% accepted, 15 enrolled. In 2013, 17 master's awarded. *Degree requirements:* For master's, thesis optional. *Entrance requirements:* Additional exam requirements/recommendations for international students: Required—TOEFL (minimum score 550 paper-based; 79 iBT). *Application deadline:* For fall admission, 2/1 priority date for domestic and international students. Electronic applications accepted. *Financial support:* Federal Work-Study, scholarships/grants, health care benefits, and tuition waivers (partial) available. Support available to part-time students. Financial award application deadline: 3/15; financial award applicants required to submit FAFSA. *Unit head:* Dr. John Porcari, Director, 608-785-8684, Fax: 608-785-8686, E-mail: porcari.john@uwlax.edu. *Application contact:* Corey Sjoquist, Director of Admissions, 608-785-8939, E-mail: admissions@uwlax.edu.
Website: http://www.uwlax.edu/sah/ess/cep/.

University of Wisconsin–La Crosse, Graduate Studies, College of Science and Health, Department of Exercise and Sport Science, Program in Human Performance, La Crosse, WI 54601-3742. Offers applied sport science (MS); human performance (MS); strength and conditioning (MS). Part-time programs available. *Students:* 14 full-time (4 women), 7 part-time (3 women); includes 2 minority (1 Black or African American, non-Hispanic/Latino; 1 American Indian or Alaska Native, non-Hispanic/Latino). Average age 24. 40 applicants, 53% accepted, 13 enrolled. In 2013, 10 master's awarded. *Degree requirements:* For master's, comprehensive exam (for some programs), thesis optional. *Entrance requirements:* For master's, GRE, course work in anatomy, physiology, biomechanics, and exercise physiology. Additional exam requirements/recommendations for international students: Required—TOEFL (minimum score 550 paper-based; 79 iBT). *Application deadline:* For fall admission, 2/1 priority date for domestic and international students. Electronic applications accepted. *Financial support:* Federal Work-Study, scholarships/grants, health care benefits, and tuition waivers (partial) available. Support available to part-time students. Financial award application deadline: 3/15; financial award applicants required to submit FAFSA. *Faculty research:* Anaerobic metabolism, power development, strength training, biomechanics, athletic performance. *Unit head:* Dr. Glenn Wright, Director, 608-785-8689, Fax: 608-785-8172, E-mail: wright.glen@uwlax.edu. *Application contact:* Corey Sjoquist, Director of Admissions, 608-785-8939, E-mail: admissions@uwlax.edu.
Website: http://www.uwlax.edu/sah/ess/hp/.

University of Wisconsin–Whitewater, School of Graduate Studies, College of Education and Professional Studies, Department of Curriculum and Instruction, Whitewater, WI 53190-1790. Offers professional development (MS), including bilingual education, challenging advanced learners, curriculum and instruction, educational leadership, health, human performance and recreation, health, physical education and coaching, information technologies and libraries, reading. *Accreditation:* NCATE. Part-time and evening/weekend programs available. Postbaccalaureate distance learning degree programs offered. *Degree requirements:* For master's, thesis or integrated project. *Entrance requirements:* Additional exam requirements/recommendations for international students: Required—TOEFL (minimum score 550 paper-based; 80 iBT), IELTS (minimum score 6). Electronic applications accepted. *Faculty research:* Hybrid of exercise physiology and psychology; gender equity; education, pedagogy, and technology; comprehensive school health education.

University of Wyoming, College of Health Sciences, Division of Kinesiology and Health, Laramie, WY 82071. Offers MS. *Accreditation:* NCATE. Part-time programs available. Postbaccalaureate distance learning degree programs offered (no on-campus study). *Degree requirements:* For master's, comprehensive exam (for some programs), thesis (for some programs). *Entrance requirements:* For master's, GRE General Test, minimum GPA of 3.0. Additional exam requirements/recommendations for international students: Required—TOEFL. Electronic applications accepted. *Faculty research:* Teacher effectiveness, effects of exercising on heart function, physiological responses of overtraining, psychological benefits of physical activity, health behavior.

Virginia Commonwealth University, Graduate School, School of Education, Department of Health and Human Performance, Program in Health and Movement Sciences, Richmond, VA 23284-9005. Offers MS. *Entrance requirements:* For master's, GRE or MAT. Additional exam requirements/recommendations for international students: Required—TOEFL (minimum score 600 paper-based; 100 iBT). Electronic applications accepted.

Virginia Polytechnic Institute and State University, Graduate School, College of Agriculture and Life Sciences, Blacksburg, VA 24061. Offers agricultural and applied economics (MS); agricultural and life sciences (MS); animal and poultry science (MS, PhD); crop and soil environmental sciences (MS, PhD); dairy science (MS); entomology (PhD); horticulture (MS, PhD); human nutrition, foods and exercise (MS, PhD); life sciences (MS, PhD); plant pathology, physiology and weed science (PhD). *Faculty:* 234 full-time (66 women), 1 (woman) part-time/adjunct. *Students:* 347 full-time (188 women), 80 part-time (53 women); includes 53 minority (19 Black or African American, non-Hispanic/Latino; 1 American Indian or Alaska Native, non-Hispanic/Latino; 19 Asian, non-Hispanic/Latino; 7 Hispanic/Latino; 7 Two or more races, non-Hispanic/Latino), 106 international. Average age 29. 410 applicants, 35% accepted, 111 enrolled. In 2013, 80 master's, 44 doctorates awarded. *Degree requirements:* For master's, comprehensive exam (for some programs), thesis (for some programs); for doctorate, comprehensive exam (for some programs), thesis/dissertation (for some programs). *Entrance requirements:* For master's and doctorate, GRE/GMAT (may vary by department). Additional exam requirements/recommendations for international students: Required—TOEFL (minimum score 550 paper-based). *Application deadline:* For fall admission, 8/1 for domestic students, 4/1 for international students; for spring admission, 1/1 for domestic students, 9/1 for international students. Applications are processed on a rolling basis. Application fee: $75. Electronic applications accepted. *Expenses:* Tuition, state resident: full-time $11,185; part-time $621.50 per credit hour. Tuition, nonresident: full-time $22,146; part-time $1230.25 per credit hour. *Required fees:* $2442; $449.25 per semester. Tuition and fees vary according to course load, campus/location and program. *Financial support:* In 2013–14, 1 fellowship with full tuition reimbursement (averaging $19,278 per year), 232 research assistantships with full tuition reimbursements (averaging $19,370 per year), 83 teaching assistantships with full tuition reimbursements (averaging $18,677 per year) were awarded. Financial award application deadline: 3/1; financial award applicants required to submit FAFSA. *Total annual research expenditures:* $44.3 million. *Unit head:* Dr. Alan L. Grant, Dean, 540-231-4152, Fax: 540-231-4163, E-mail: algrant@vt.edu. *Application contact:* Sheila Norman, Administrative Assistant, 540-231-4152, Fax: 540-231-4163, E-mail: snorman@vt.edu.
Website: http://www.cals.vt.edu/.

Wake Forest University, Graduate School of Arts and Sciences, Department of Health and Exercise Science, Winston-Salem, NC 27109. Offers MS. *Degree requirements:* For master's, one foreign language, thesis. *Entrance requirements:* For master's, GRE General Test, resume. Additional exam requirements/recommendations for international students: Required—TOEFL (minimum score 79 iBT). Electronic applications accepted. *Faculty research:* Cardiac rehabilitation, biomechanics, health psychology, exercise physiology.

Washington State University, Graduate School, College of Pharmacy, Pullman, WA 99164. Offers dietetics, nutrition, and exercise physiology (MS); pharmacy (PhD, Pharm D). *Accreditation:* ACPE (one or more programs are accredited). *Degree requirements:* For master's, comprehensive exam, thesis, oral exam; for doctorate, comprehensive exam, thesis/dissertation, oral exam (for PhD). *Entrance requirements:* For master's, GRE General Test, minimum GPA of 3.0, interview; for doctorate, GRE General Test, minimum GPA of 3.0, interview, minimum 60 hours of documented pharmacy experience. *Faculty research:* Hormonal carcinogenesis, drug metabolism/transport, toxicology of chlorinated compounds, alcohol effects on immune system, effects of cocaine on neuronal function.

Wayne State College, Department of Health, Human Performance and Sport, Wayne, NE 68787. Offers exercise science (MSE); organizational management (MS), including sport management. Part-time and evening/weekend programs available. *Degree requirements:* For master's, comprehensive exam, thesis optional. *Entrance requirements:* For master's, GRE General Test, minimum GPA of 3.0. Additional exam requirements/recommendations for international students: Required—TOEFL (minimum score 550 paper-based). Electronic applications accepted.

Wayne State University, College of Education, Division of Kinesiology, Health and Sports Studies, Detroit, MI 48202. Offers adapted physical education (Certificate); coaching (Certificate); elementary physical education (Certificate); exercise and sport science (M Ed); health education (M Ed, Certificate); kinesiology (M Ed, PhD), including exercise and sport science (PhD), physical education pedagogy (PhD); physical education (M Ed); secondary physical education (Certificate); sports administration (MA); wellness clinician/research (M Ed). Part-time programs available. *Students:* 42 full-time (27 women), 78 part-time (38 women); includes 43 minority (35 Black or African American, non-Hispanic/Latino; 1 Asian, non-Hispanic/Latino; 5 Hispanic/Latino; 2 Two or more races, non-Hispanic/Latino), 5 international. Average age 30. 120 applicants, 48% accepted, 30 enrolled. In 2013, 32 master's awarded. *Degree requirements:* For master's, thesis (for some programs); for doctorate, thesis/dissertation. *Entrance requirements:* For master's and doctorate, minimum undergraduate GPA of 3.0, undergraduate degree directly relating to the field of specialization being applied for, or undergraduate degree accompanied by extensive educational background in a closely-related field. Additional exam requirements/recommendations for international students: Required—TOEFL (minimum score 79 iBT), TWE (minimum score 5.5), Michigan English Language Assessment Battery (minimum score 85); Recommended—IELTS (minimum score 6.5). *Application deadline:* For fall admission, 6/1 priority date for domestic students, 5/1 priority date for international students; for winter admission, 10/1 priority date for domestic students, 9/1 priority date for international students; for spring admission, 2/1 priority date for domestic students, 1/1 priority date for international students. Applications are processed on a rolling basis. Application fee: $0. Electronic applications accepted. *Expenses:* Tuition, state resident: part-time $554.15 per credit. Tuition, nonresident: part-time $1200.35 per credit. *Required fees:* $42.15 per credit. $268.30 per semester. Tuition and fees vary according to course load and program. *Financial support:* In 2013–14, 22 students received support, including 4 fellowships with tuition reimbursements available (averaging $13,050 per year), 5 research assistantships with tuition reimbursements available (averaging $16,508 per year); career-related internships or fieldwork, Federal Work-Study, scholarships/grants, health care benefits, and unspecified assistantships also available. Support available to part-time students. Financial award application deadline: 3/31; financial award applicants required to submit FAFSA. *Faculty research:* Exercise and sport science, nutrition and physical activity interventions, school and community health, obesity prevention. *Total annual research expenditures:* $1.3 million. *Unit head:* Dr. Nate McCaughtry, Assistant Dean, Division of Kinesiology, Health and Sport Studies/Director, Center for School Health, 313-577-0014, Fax: 313-577-5002, E-mail: aj4391@wayne.edu. *Application contact:* Janice Green, Assistant Dean, 313-577-1605, E-mail: jwgreen@wayne.edu.
Website: http://coe.wayne.edu/kinesiology/index.php.

West Chester University of Pennsylvania, College of Health Sciences, Department of Kinesiology, West Chester, PA 19383. Offers adapted physical education (Certificate); exercise and sport physiology (MS), including athletic training, exercise and sport physiology; general physical education (MS); sport management and athletics (MPA). Part-time and evening/weekend programs available. Postbaccalaureate distance learning degree programs offered (no on-campus study). *Faculty:* 6 full-time (5 women). *Students:* 25 full-time (13 women), 10 part-time (4 women); includes 5 minority (1 Black or African American, non-Hispanic/Latino; 1 Asian, non-Hispanic/Latino; 2 Hispanic/Latino; 1 Two or more races, non-Hispanic/Latino), 1 international. Average age 27. 33 applicants, 97% accepted, 18 enrolled. In 2013, 15 master's, 6 other advanced degrees awarded. *Degree requirements:* For master's, thesis or report (for MS); 2 internships, capstone course including research project or thesis (for MPA). *Entrance requirements:* For master's, GRE (for MS), 2 letters of recommendation, transcripts, and statement of professional goals (for MS); 2 letters of reference, resume, and career goal statement (for MPA). Additional exam requirements/recommendations for international students: Required—TOEFL (minimum score 550 paper-based; 80 iBT). *Application deadline:* For fall admission, 4/15 priority date for domestic students, 3/15 for international students; for spring admission, 10/15 priority date for domestic students, 9/1 for international students. Applications are processed on a rolling basis. Application fee: $45. Electronic applications accepted. *Expenses:* Tuition, state resident: full-time $7956; part-time $442 per credit. Tuition, nonresident: full-time $11,934; part-time $663 per credit. *Required fees:* $2134.20; $106.24 per credit. Tuition and fees vary according to campus/location and program. *Financial support:* Unspecified assistantships available. Support available to part-time students. Financial award application deadline: 2/15; financial award applicants required to submit FAFSA. *Faculty research:* Metabolism during exercise, biomechanics, rating of perceived exertion, motor learning. *Unit head:* Dr. Frank Fry, Chair/Graduate Coordinator for the MS in General Physical Education Program, 610-436-2610, Fax: 610-436-2860, E-mail: ffry@wcupa.edu. *Application contact:* Dr. David Stearne, Graduate Coordinator for the Exercise and Sport Physiology Programs, 610-436-2347, Fax: 610-436-2860, E-mail: dstearne@wcupa.edu.
Website: http://www.wcupa.edu/_academics/sch_shs.hpe/.

Western Michigan University, Graduate College, College of Education and Human Development, Department of Health, Physical Education and Recreation, Kalamazoo, MI 49008. Offers exercise and sports medicine (MS), including athletic training, exercise physiology; physical education (MA), including coaching sport performance, pedagogy, special physical education, sport management.

Western Washington University, Graduate School, College of Humanities and Social Sciences, Department of Physical Education, Health, and Recreation, Bellingham, WA 98225-5996. Offers exercise science (MS); sport psychology (MS). Part-time programs available. *Degree requirements:* For master's, thesis. *Entrance requirements:* For master's, GRE General Test, minimum GPA of 3.0 in last 60 semester hours or last 90 quarter hours. Additional exam requirements/recommendations for international students: Required—TOEFL (minimum score 567 paper-based). Electronic applications accepted. *Faculty research:* Spinal motor control, biomechanics/kinesiology, biomechanics of aging, mobility of older adults, fall prevention, exercise interventions and function, magnesium and inspiratory muscle training (IMT).

West Texas A&M University, College of Nursing and Health Sciences, Department of Sports and Exercise Sciences, Canyon, TX 79016-0001. Offers sport management (MS); sports and exercise sciences (MS). Part-time and evening/weekend programs available. *Degree requirements:* For master's, comprehensive exam, thesis optional. *Entrance requirements:* For master's, GRE General Test. Additional exam requirements/recommendations for international students: Required—TOEFL (minimum score 550 paper-based). Electronic applications accepted. *Faculty research:* American government, public administration, state and local government, international politics.

West Virginia University, School of Medicine, Graduate Programs at the Health Sciences Center, Interdisciplinary Graduate Programs in Biomedical Sciences, Exercise Physiology Program, Morgantown, WV 26506. Offers MS, PhD, MD/PhD. *Degree requirements:* For doctorate, comprehensive exam, thesis/dissertation. *Entrance requirements:* For doctorate, GRE General Test, minimum GPA of 3.0. Additional exam requirements/recommendations for international students: Required—TOEFL. Electronic applications accepted. *Faculty research:* Cardiovascular function in health and disease, circulatory adaptations to exercise training, aging, microgravity, muscle adaptation and injury.

West Virginia University, School of Physical Education, Morgantown, WV 26506. Offers athletic coaching education (MS); athletic training (MS); physical education/teacher education (MS, PhD), including curriculum and instruction (PhD), motor behavior (PhD), physical education supervision (PhD); sport and exercise psychology (PhD); sport management (MS). *Degree requirements:* For doctorate, comprehensive exam, thesis/dissertation, oral exam. *Entrance requirements:* For master's, GRE or MAT, minimum GPA of 3.0; for doctorate, GRE General Test or MAT, minimum GPA of 3.5. Additional exam requirements/recommendations for international students: Required—TOEFL (minimum score 550 paper-based). Electronic applications accepted. *Faculty research:* Sport psychosociology, teacher education, exercise psychology, counseling.

Wichita State University, Graduate School, College of Education, Department of Human Performance Studies, Wichita, KS 67260. Offers exercise science (M Ed). Part-time programs available. *Unit head:* Dr. Mike Rogers, Chairperson, 316-978-3340, Fax: 316-978-3302, E-mail: mike.rogers@wichita.edu. *Application contact:* Jordan Oleson, Admissions Coordinator, 316-978-3095, Fax: 316-978-3253, E-mail: jordan.oleson@wichita.edu.
Website: http://www.wichita.edu/.

William Paterson University of New Jersey, College of Science and Health, Wayne, NJ 07470-8420. Offers biotechnology (MS); communication disorders (MS); exercise and sports studies (MS); general biology (MS); nursing (MSN); nursing practice (DNP). Part-time and evening/weekend programs available. *Faculty:* 29 full-time (10 women), 10 part-time/adjunct (1 woman). *Students:* 67 full-time (56 women), 160 part-time (138 women); includes 76 minority (19 Black or African American, non-Hispanic/Latino; 26 Asian, non-Hispanic/Latino; 29 Hispanic/Latino; 2 Two or more races, non-Hispanic/Latino). Average age 35. 490 applicants, 33% accepted, 83 enrolled. In 2013, 51 master's awarded. *Degree requirements:* For master's, comprehensive exam (for some programs), thesis (for some programs), non-thesis internship/practicum (for some programs). *Entrance requirements:* For master's, GRE/MAT, minimum GPA of 2.75; for doctorate, GRE/MAT, minimum GPA of 3.3. Additional exam requirements/recommendations for international students: Required—TOEFL (minimum score 550 paper-based; 79 iBT), IELTS (minimum score 6). *Application deadline:* For fall admission, 6/1 for domestic students, 5/1 for international students; for spring admission, 11/1 for domestic students, 10/1 for international students. Applications are processed on a rolling basis. Application fee: $50. Electronic applications accepted. *Financial support:* Research assistantships with full tuition reimbursements, career-related internships or fieldwork, and unspecified assistantships available. Support available to part-time students. Financial award application deadline: 4/1; financial award applicants required to submit FAFSA. *Faculty research:* Human biomechanics, autism, nanomaterials, health and environment, red-tide causing algae. *Unit head:* Dr. Kenneth Wolf, Dean, 973-720-2194, E-mail: wolfk@wpunj.edu. *Application contact:* Christina Aiello, Assistant Director, Graduate Admissions, 973-720-2506, Fax: 973-720-2035, E-mail: aielloc@wpunj.edu.
Website: http://www.wpunj.edu/cosh.

Kinesiology and Movement Studies

Arizona State University at the Tempe campus, College of Nursing and Health Innovation, Phoenix, AZ 85004. Offers advanced nursing practice (DNP); child/family mental health nurse practitioner (Graduate Certificate); clinical research management (MS); community and public health practice (Graduate Certificate); community health (MS); exercise and wellness (MS), including exercise and wellness; family nurse practitioner (Graduate Certificate); healthcare innovation (MHI); international health for healthcare (Graduate Certificate); kinesiology (MS, PhD); nursing (MS, Graduate Certificate); nursing and healthcare innovation (PhD); nutrition (MS); physical activity nutrition and wellness (PhD), including physical activity, nutrition and wellness; public health (MPH); regulatory science and health safety (MS). *Accreditation:* AACN. Postbaccalaureate distance learning degree programs offered (minimal on-campus study). *Degree requirements:* For master's, comprehensive exam (for some programs), thesis (for some programs), interactive Program of Study (iPOS) submitted before completing 50 percent of required credit hours; for doctorate, comprehensive exam, thesis/dissertation, interactive Program of Study (iPOS) submitted before completing 50 percent of required credit hours. *Entrance requirements:* For master's and doctorate, GRE, minimum GPA of 3.0 or equivalent in last 2 years of work leading to bachelor's degree. Additional exam requirements/recommendations for international students: Required—TOEFL (minimum score 80 iBT), TOEFL, IELTS, or PTE. Electronic applications accepted. *Expenses:* Contact institution.

A.T. Still University, Arizona School of Health Sciences, Mesa, AZ 85206. Offers advanced occupational therapy (MS); advanced physician assistant studies (MS); athletic training (MS); audiology (Au D); health sciences (DHSc); human movement (MS); occupational therapy (MS, DOT); physical therapy (DPT); physician assistant (MS); transitional audiology (Au D); transitional physical therapy (DPT). *Accreditation:* AOTA (one or more programs are accredited); ASHA. Part-time and evening/weekend programs available. Postbaccalaureate distance learning degree programs offered (minimal on-campus study). *Faculty:* 47 full-time (27 women), 279 part-time/adjunct (173 women). *Students:* 531 full-time (354 women), 865 part-time (547 women); includes 315 minority (79 Black or African American, non-Hispanic/Latino; 10 American Indian or Alaska Native, non-Hispanic/Latino; 114 Asian, non-Hispanic/Latino; 83 Hispanic/Latino; 6 Native Hawaiian or other Pacific Islander, non-Hispanic/Latino; 23 Two or more races, non-Hispanic/Latino), 82 international. Average age 36. 3,325 applicants, 14% accepted, 329 enrolled. In 2013, 252 master's, 370 doctorates awarded. *Degree requirements:* For master's, thesis (for some programs); for doctorate, thesis/dissertation (for some programs). *Entrance requirements:* For master's, GRE General Test; for doctorate, GRE, Evaluation of Practicing Audiologists Capabilities (Au D), Physical Therapist Evaluation Tool (DPT), current state licensure, master's degree or equivalent (Au D). Additional exam requirements/recommendations for international students: Required—TOEFL (minimum score 550 paper-based; 80 iBT). *Application deadline:* For fall admission, 8/1 for domestic and international students. Applications are processed on a rolling basis. Application fee: $70. Electronic applications accepted. *Expenses:* Contact institution. *Financial support:* In 2013–14, 151 students received support. Federal Work-Study and scholarships/grants available. Financial award application deadline: 5/1; financial award applicants required to submit FAFSA. *Faculty research:* Pediatric sport-related concussion, adolescent athlete health-related quality of life; geriatric and pediatric well-being, pain management for participation, practice-based research network, BMI and dental caries. *Total annual research expenditures:* $174,826. *Unit head:* Dr. Randy Danielsen, Dean, 480-219-6000, Fax: 480-219-6110, E-mail: rdanielsen@atsu.edu. *Application contact:* Donna Sparks, Associate Director, Admissions Processing, 660-626-2117, Fax: 660-626-2969, E-mail: admissions@atsu.edu.
Website: http://www.atsu.edu/ashs.

Auburn University, Graduate School, College of Education, Department of Kinesiology, Auburn University, AL 36849. Offers exercise science (M Ed, MS, PhD); health promotion (M Ed, MS); kinesiology (PhD); physical education/teacher education (M Ed, MS, Ed D, Ed S). *Accreditation:* NCATE. Part-time programs available. *Faculty:* 19 full-time (9 women). *Students:* 89 full-time (43 women), 21 part-time (9 women); includes 17 minority (15 Black or African American, non-Hispanic/Latino; 1 Asian, non-Hispanic/Latino; 1 Hispanic/Latino), 5 international. Average age 26. 136 applicants, 71% accepted, 60 enrolled. In 2013, 38 master's, 10 doctorates awarded. *Degree requirements:* For master's, thesis (for some programs); for doctorate, thesis/dissertation; for Ed S, exam, field project. *Entrance requirements:* For master's, GRE General Test; for doctorate and Ed S, GRE General Test, interview, master's degree. *Application deadline:* For fall admission, 7/7 for domestic students; for spring admission, 11/24 for domestic students. Applications are processed on a rolling basis. Application fee: $50 ($60 for international students). Electronic applications accepted. *Expenses:* Tuition, state resident: full-time $8262; part-time $459 per credit hour. Tuition, nonresident: full-time $24,786; part-time $1377 per credit hour. Tuition and fees vary according to degree level and program. *Financial support:* Research assistantships, teaching assistantships, and Federal Work-Study available. Support available to part-time students. Financial award application deadline: 3/15; financial award applicants required to submit FAFSA. *Faculty research:* Biomechanics, exercise physiology, motor skill learning, school health, curriculum development. *Unit head:* Dr. Mary E. Rudisill, Head, 334-844-1458. *Application contact:* Dr. George Flowers, Dean of the Graduate School, 334-844-2125.

Barry University, School of Human Performance and Leisure Sciences, Programs in Movement Science, General Movement Science Program, Miami Shores, FL 33161-6695. Offers MS.

Barry University, School of Human Performance and Leisure Sciences, Programs in Movement Science, Specialization in Biomechanics, Miami Shores, FL 33161-6695. Offers MS. *Entrance requirements:* For master's, GRE General Test, minimum GPA of 3.0. Electronic applications accepted. *Faculty research:* Upper extremity biomechanics, orthopedic biomechanics.

Baylor University, Graduate School, School of Education, Department of Health, Human Performance and Recreation, Waco, TX 76798. Offers community health education (MPH); exercise physiology (MS Ed); kinesiology, exercise nutrition and health promotion (PhD); sport management (MS Ed); sport pedagogy (MS Ed). *Accreditation:* NCATE. Part-time programs available. *Faculty:* 13 full-time (5 women), 3 part-time/adjunct (1 woman). *Students:* 79 full-time (40 women), 28 part-time (14 women); includes 26 minority (9 Black or African American, non-Hispanic/Latino; 1 American Indian or Alaska Native, non-Hispanic/Latino; 3 Asian, non-Hispanic/Latino; 8 Hispanic/Latino; 5 Two or more races, non-Hispanic/Latino), 9 international. 30 applicants, 87% accepted. In 2013, 48 master's awarded. *Degree requirements:* For master's, comprehensive exam, thesis optional; for doctorate, comprehensive exam, thesis/dissertation. *Entrance requirements:* For master's and doctorate, GRE General Test. Additional exam requirements/recommendations for international students: Required—TOEFL. *Application deadline:* For fall admission, 2/1 priority date for domestic students, 2/1 for international students; for spring admission, 10/1 for domestic and international students. Applications are processed on a rolling basis. Application fee: $25. Electronic applications accepted. *Expenses: Tuition:* Full-time $25,866; part-time $1437 per credit hour. *Required fees:* $2736; $152 per credit hour. Tuition and fees vary according to course load and program. *Financial support:* In 2013–14, 35 students received support, including 1 research assistantship with tuition reimbursement available, 33 teaching assistantships with tuition reimbursements available; career-related internships or fieldwork, Federal Work-Study, institutionally sponsored loans, tuition waivers (partial), and unspecified assistantships also available. Financial award application deadline: 2/1. *Faculty research:* Behavior change theory, nutrition and enzyme therapy, exercise testing, health planning, sport management. *Unit head:* Dr. Jeffrey Petersen, Graduate Program Director, 254-710-4007, Fax: 254-710-3527, E-mail: jeffrey_petersen@baylor.edu. *Application contact:* Kathy Mirick, Administrative Assistant, 254-710-3526, Fax: 254-710-3527, E-mail: kathy_mirick@baylor.edu.
Website: http://www.baylor.edu/HHPR/.

Boise State University, College of Education, Department of Kinesiology, Boise, ID 83725-0399. Offers exercise and sports studies (MS); kinesiology (MK); physical education (MS). Part-time programs available. *Degree requirements:* For master's, thesis. *Entrance requirements:* For master's, minimum GPA of 3.0. Electronic applications accepted.

Bowling Green State University, Graduate College, College of Education and Human Development, School of Human Movement, Sport, and Leisure Studies, Bowling Green, OH 43403. Offers developmental kinesiology (M Ed); recreation and leisure (M Ed); sport administration (M Ed). Part-time programs available. *Degree requirements:* For master's, thesis or alternative. *Entrance requirements:* For master's, GRE General Test,

minimum GPA of 2.7. Additional exam requirements/recommendations for international students: Required—TOEFL. Electronic applications accepted. *Faculty research:* Teacher-learning process, travel and tourism, sport marketing and management, exercise physiology and sport psychology, life-span motor development.

California Polytechnic State University, San Luis Obispo, College of Science and Mathematics, Department of Kinesiology, San Luis Obispo, CA 93407. Offers MS. Part-time programs available. *Faculty:* 5 full-time (4 women), 1 (woman) part-time/adjunct. *Students:* 7 full-time (4 women), 10 part-time (5 women); includes 3 minority (1 Asian, non-Hispanic/Latino; 1 Hispanic/Latino; 1 Two or more races, non-Hispanic/Latino). Average age 25. 26 applicants, 73% accepted, 7 enrolled. In 2013, 9 master's awarded. *Degree requirements:* For master's, comprehensive exam (for some programs), thesis (for some programs). *Entrance requirements:* For master's, minimum GPA of 2.75 in last 90 quarter units of course work; letters of recommendation. Additional exam requirements/recommendations for international students: Required—TOEFL (minimum score 550 paper-based) or IELTS (minimum score 6). *Application deadline:* For fall admission, 4/1 for domestic students, 11/30 for international students; for winter admission, 9/1 for domestic students, 6/30 for international students. Applications are processed on a rolling basis. Application fee: $55. Electronic applications accepted. *Financial support:* Fellowships, research assistantships, teaching assistantships, career-related internships or fieldwork, Federal Work-Study, and scholarships/grants available. Support available to part-time students. Financial award application deadline: 3/2; financial award applicants required to submit FAFSA. *Faculty research:* Biomechanics, motor learning and control, physiology of exercise, commercial fitness, cardiac rehabilitation. *Unit head:* Dr. Kris Jankovitz, Graduate Coordinator, 805-756-2534, Fax: 805-756-7273, E-mail: kjankovi@calpoly.edu. *Application contact:* Dr. James Maraviglia, Associate Vice Provost for Marketing and Enrollment Development, 805-756-2311, Fax: 805-756-5400, E-mail: admissions@calpoly.edu.
Website: http://www.kinesiology.calpoly.edu/degrees/ms/index.html.

California State Polytechnic University, Pomona, Academic Affairs, College of Science, Program in Kinesiology, Pomona, CA 91768-2557. Offers MS. Part-time programs available. *Students:* 4 full-time (2 women), 10 part-time (8 women); includes 9 minority (4 Asian, non-Hispanic/Latino; 4 Hispanic/Latino; 1 Two or more races, non-Hispanic/Latino), 1 international. Average age 29. 6 applicants, 17% accepted. In 2013, 10 master's awarded. *Degree requirements:* For master's, thesis or alternative. *Application deadline:* For fall admission, 5/1 priority date for domestic students; for winter admission, 10/15 priority date for domestic students; for spring admission, 1/20 priority date for domestic students. Applications are processed on a rolling basis. Application fee: $55. Electronic applications accepted. *Expenses:* Tuition, state resident: full-time $6738. Tuition, nonresident: full-time $12,690. *Required fees:* $878; $248 per credit hour. *Financial support:* Federal Work-Study and institutionally sponsored loans available. Support available to part-time students. Financial award application deadline: 3/2; financial award applicants required to submit FAFSA. *Unit head:* Dr. Ken Hansen, Graduate Coordinator, 909-869-4638, E-mail: kahansen@csupomona.edu. *Application contact:* Deborah L. Brandon, Executive Director, Admissions and Outreach, 909-869-3427, Fax: 909-869-5315, E-mail: dlbrandon@csupomona.edu.
Website: http://www.csupomona.edu/~kin/programs.html.

California State University, Chico, Office of Graduate Studies, College of Communication and Education, Department of Kinesiology, Chico, CA 95929-0722. Offers MA. Part-time programs available. *Degree requirements:* For master's, thesis, project, or comprehensive examination. *Entrance requirements:* For master's, GRE General Test, 2 letters of recommendation, statement of purpose. Additional exam requirements/recommendations for international students: Required—TOEFL (minimum score 550 paper-based; 80 iBT), IELTS (minimum score 6.5), PTE (minimum score 59). Electronic applications accepted.

California State University, Fresno, Division of Graduate Studies, College of Health and Human Services, Department of Kinesiology, Fresno, CA 93740-8027. Offers exercise science (MA); sport psychology (MA). Part-time and evening/weekend programs available. *Degree requirements:* For master's, thesis or alternative. *Entrance requirements:* For master's, GRE General Test, minimum GPA of 2.7. Additional exam requirements/recommendations for international students: Required—TOEFL. Electronic applications accepted. *Faculty research:* Refugee education, homeless, geriatrics, fitness.

California State University, Long Beach, Graduate Studies, College of Health and Human Services, Department of Kinesiology, Long Beach, CA 90840. Offers adapted physical education (MA); coaching and student athlete development (MA); exercise physiology and nutrition (MS); exercise science (MS); individualized studies (MA); kinesiology (MA); pedagogical studies (MA); sport and exercise psychology (MS); sport management (MA); sports medicine and injury studies (MS). Part-time programs available. *Degree requirements:* For master's, oral and written comprehensive exams or thesis. *Entrance requirements:* For master's, GRE General Test, minimum GPA of 2.75 during previous 2 years of course work. Electronic applications accepted. *Faculty research:* Pulmonary functioning, feedback and practice structure, strength training, history and politics of sports, special population research issues.

California State University, Los Angeles, Graduate Studies, College of Health and Human Services, Department of Kinesiology and Nutritional Sciences, Los Angeles, CA 90032-8530. Offers nutritional science (MS); physical education and kinesiology (MA, MS). *Accreditation:* AND. Part-time and evening/weekend programs available. *Faculty:* 6 full-time (3 women), 1 part-time/adjunct (0 women). *Students:* 69 full-time (65 women), 50 part-time (36 women); includes 64 minority (3 Black or African American, non-Hispanic/Latino; 30 Asian, non-Hispanic/Latino; 25 Hispanic/Latino; 1 Native Hawaiian or other Pacific Islander, non-Hispanic/Latino; 5 Two or more races, non-Hispanic/Latino), 8 international. Average age 31. 138 applicants, 24% accepted, 23 enrolled. In 2013, 60 master's awarded. *Degree requirements:* For master's, comprehensive exam, project or thesis. *Entrance requirements:* For master's, minimum GPA of 2.75. Additional exam requirements/recommendations for international students: Required—TOEFL (minimum score 500 paper-based). *Application deadline:* For fall admission, 5/1 for domestic and international students. Applications are processed on a rolling basis. Application fee: $55. *Financial support:* Federal Work-Study available. Support available to part-time students. Financial award application deadline: 3/1. *Unit head:* Dr. Nazareth Khodiguian, Chair, 323-343-4650, Fax: 323-343-6482, E-mail: nkhodig@calstatela.edu. *Application contact:* Dr. Larry Fritz, Dean of Graduate Studies, 323-343-3820, Fax: 323-343-5653, E-mail: lfritz@calstatela.edu.
Website: http://www.calstatela.edu/dept/pe/.

California State University, Northridge, Graduate Studies, College of Health and Human Development, Department of Kinesiology, Northridge, CA 91330. Offers MS. Part-time and evening/weekend programs available. *Degree requirements:* For master's, thesis or alternative. *Entrance requirements:* For master's, GRE General Test or minimum GPA of 3.0, 3 letters of recommendation. Additional exam requirements/recommendations for international students: Required—TOEFL.

Canisius College, Graduate Division, School of Education and Human Services, Department of Kinesiology, Buffalo, NY 14208-1098. Offers physical education (MS Ed); physical education birth -12 (MS Ed). Part-time and evening/weekend programs available. Postbaccalaureate distance learning degree programs offered (minimal on-campus study). *Faculty:* 10 full-time (1 woman), 9 part-time/adjunct (3 women). *Students:* 33 full-time (12 women), 81 part-time (32 women); includes 12 minority (6 Black or African American, non-Hispanic/Latino; 4 Hispanic/Latino; 2 Two or more races, non-Hispanic/Latino), 7 international. Average age 30. 45 applicants, 76% accepted, 22 enrolled. In 2013, 89 master's awarded. *Degree requirements:* For master's, research project. *Entrance requirements:* For master's, official college and/or university transcript(s) showing completion of a bachelor's degree from accredited institution with evidence of teaching certification (not for initial certification candidates); two letters of recommendation; minimum cumulative undergraduate GPA of 2.7. Additional exam requirements/recommendations for international students: Required—TOEFL (minimum score 550 paper-based, 80 iBT), IELTS (minimum score 6.5), or CAEL (minimum score 70). *Application deadline:* Applications are processed on a rolling basis. Application fee: $25. Electronic applications accepted. Application fee is waived when completed online. *Expenses: Tuition:* Part-time $750 per credit hour. *Financial support:* Career-related internships or fieldwork, Federal Work-Study, scholarships/grants, tuition waivers (partial), and unspecified assistantships available. Support available to part-time students. Financial award application deadline: 4/30; financial award applicants required to submit FAFSA. *Faculty research:* Culturally congruent pedagogy in physical education, information processing and perceptual styles of athletes, qualities of effective coaches. *Unit head:* Dr. Timothy M. Sawicki, Associate Professor, Kinesiology, 716-888-8262, Fax: 716-888-8445, E-mail: sawickit@canisius.edu. *Application contact:* Julie A. Zulewski, Director of Graduate Admissions, 716-888-2548, Fax: 716-888-3195, E-mail: zulewskj@canisius.edu.
Website: http://www.canisius.edu/graduate/.

Columbia University, College of Physicians and Surgeons, Programs in Occupational Therapy, New York, NY 10032. Offers movement science (Ed D), including occupational therapy; occupational therapy (professional) (MS); occupational therapy administration or education (post-professional) (MS); MPH/MS. *Accreditation:* AOTA. *Degree requirements:* For master's, project, 6 months of fieldwork, thesis (for post-professional students); for doctorate, comprehensive exam, thesis/dissertation. *Entrance requirements:* For master's, undergraduate course work in anatomy, physiology, statistics, psychology, social sciences, humanities, English composition; NBCOT eligibility; for doctorate, NBCOT certification, MS. Additional exam requirements/recommendations for international students: Required—TOEFL (minimum score 100 iBT), TWE (minimum score 4). Electronic applications accepted. *Expenses:* Contact institution. *Faculty research:* Community mental health, developmental tasks of late life, infant play, cognition, obesity, motor learning.

Dalhousie University, Faculty of Health Professions, School of Health and Human Performance, Program in Kinesiology, Halifax, NS B3H 3J5, Canada. Offers M Sc. Part-time programs available. *Degree requirements:* For master's, thesis. *Entrance requirements:* Additional exam requirements/recommendations for international students: Required—TOEFL, IELTS, CANTEST, CAEL, or Michigan English Language Assessment Battery. Electronic applications accepted. *Faculty research:* Sport science, fitness, neuromuscular physiology, biomechanics, ergonomics, sport psychology.

Dallas Baptist University, Dorothy M. Bush College of Education, Program in Kinesiology, Dallas, TX 75211-9299. Offers M Ed. *Entrance requirements:* For master's, GRE General Test, minimum GPA of 3.0. Additional exam requirements/recommendations for international students: Required—TOEFL, IELTS. Application fee: $25. *Expenses: Tuition:* Full-time $13,410; part-time $745 per credit hour. *Required fees:* $300; $150 per semester. Tuition and fees vary according to degree level. *Financial support:* Federal Work-Study, institutionally sponsored loans, scholarships/grants, and tuition waivers (full and partial) available. Support available to part-time students. Financial award applicants required to submit FAFSA. *Unit head:* Dr. Ray Galloway, Director, 214-333-5414, Fax: 214-333-5306, E-mail: rayg@dbu.edu. *Application contact:* Kit Montgomery, Director of Graduate Programs, 214-333-5242, Fax: 214-333-5579, E-mail: graduate@dbu.edu.
Website: http://www3.dbu.edu/graduate/kinesiology.asp.

East Carolina University, Graduate School, College of Health and Human Performance, Department of Kinesiology, Greenville, NC 27858-4353. Offers adapted physical education (MA Ed, MS); bioenergetics and exercise science (PhD); biomechanics (MS); exercise physiology (MS); physical activity promotion (MS); physical education (MA Ed, MAT); physical education clinical supervision (Certificate); physical education pedagogy (MA Ed, MS); sport and exercise psychology (MS); sport management (Certificate). *Degree requirements:* For master's, comprehensive exam, thesis optional; for doctorate, comprehensive exam, thesis/dissertation. *Entrance requirements:* For master's, GRE General Test or MAT; for doctorate, GRE. Additional exam requirements/recommendations for international students: Required—TOEFL. *Expenses:* Tuition, state resident: full-time $4223. Tuition, nonresident: full-time $16,540. *Required fees:* $2184. *Faculty research:* Diabetes metabolism, pediatric obesity, biomechanics of arthritis, physical activity measurement.

Eastern Illinois University, Graduate School, College of Education and Professional Studies, Department of Kinesiology and Sports Studies, Charleston, IL 61920-3099. Offers MS. Part-time programs available. *Expenses: Tuition, area resident:* Part-time $283 per credit hour. Tuition, state resident: part-time $283 per credit hour. Tuition, nonresident: part-time $679 per credit hour.

Eastern Michigan University, Graduate School, College of Health and Human Services, School of Health Promotion and Human Performance, Programs in Exercise Physiology, Ypsilanti, MI 48197. Offers exercise physiology (MS); sports medicine-biomechanics (MS); sports medicine-corporate adult fitness (MS); sports medicine-exercise physiology (MS). Part-time and evening/weekend programs available. *Students:* 13 full-time (9 women), 36 part-time (12 women); includes 12 minority (5 Black or African American, non-Hispanic/Latino; 1 American Indian or Alaska Native, non-Hispanic/Latino; 2 Asian, non-Hispanic/Latino; 2 Hispanic/Latino; 2 Two or more races, non-Hispanic/Latino), 3 international. Average age 29. 46 applicants, 74% accepted, 18 enrolled. In 2013, 29 master's awarded. *Degree requirements:* For master's, comprehensive exam, thesis or 450-hour internship. *Entrance requirements:* Additional exam requirements/recommendations for international students: Required—TOEFL. *Application deadline:* For fall admission, 8/1 for domestic students, 5/1 for international students; for winter admission, 12/1 for domestic students, 10/1 for international students; for spring admission, 3/15 for domestic students, 3/1 for international students. Application fee: $35. *Expenses:* Tuition, state resident: full-time $12,300; part-time $466 per credit hour. Tuition, nonresident: full-time $23,159; part-time $918 per credit hour. *Required fees:* $71 per credit hour. $46 per semester. One-time fee: $100. Tuition and fees vary according to course level and degree level. *Unit head:* Dr. Christopher Herman, Director, 734-487-2815, Fax: 734-487-2024, E-mail: cherman2@emich.edu. *Application contact:* Dr. Stephen McGregor, Program Coordinator, 734-487-2820, Fax: 734-487-2024, E-mail: stephen.mcgregor@emich.edu.

East Tennessee State University, School of Graduate Studies, College of Education, Department of Kinesiology, Sport and Recreation Management, Johnson City, TN 37614. Offers sport management (MA). Part-time and evening/weekend programs available. *Faculty:* 12 full-time (1 woman), 4 part-time/adjunct (1 woman). *Students:* 90

full-time (31 women), 8 part-time (3 women); includes 8 minority (5 Black or African American, non-Hispanic/Latino; 1 Hispanic/Latino; 2 Two or more races, non-Hispanic/Latino), 5 international. Average age 25. 32 applicants, 81% accepted, 19 enrolled. In 2013, 35 master's awarded. Terminal master's awarded for partial completion of doctoral program. *Degree requirements:* For master's, comprehensive exam, thesis or internship. *Entrance requirements:* For master's, GRE General Test or GMAT, undergraduate degree in related field; minimum GPA of 2.7; resume; three references; essay explaining goals and reasons for pursuing degree. Additional exam requirements/recommendations for international students: Required—TOEFL (minimum score 550 paper-based; 79 iBT). *Application deadline:* For fall admission, 6/1 for domestic students, 4/30 for international students; for spring admission, 11/1 for domestic students, 9/30 for international students. Application fee: $35 ($45 for international students). Electronic applications accepted. *Expenses:* Tuition, state resident: full-time $7900; part-time $395 per credit hour. Tuition, nonresident: full-time $21,960; part-time $1098 per credit hour. *Required fees:* $1345; $84 per credit hour. *Financial support:* In 2013–14, 34 students received support, including 7 teaching assistantships with full tuition reimbursements available (averaging $6,000 per year); career-related internships or fieldwork, institutionally sponsored loans, scholarships/grants, and unspecified assistantships also available. Financial award application deadline: 7/1; financial award applicants required to submit FAFSA. *Faculty research:* Methods of training for individual and team sports, enhancing acute sport performance, fatigue management in athletes, risk management, facilities management, motorsport. *Unit head:* Dr. Christopher Ayers, Chair, 423-439-4265, Fax: 423-439-7560, E-mail: ayersc@etsu.edu. *Application contact:* Linda Raines, Graduate Specialist, 423-439-6158, Fax: 423-439-5624, E-mail: raineslt@etsu.edu.
Website: http://www.etsu.edu/coe/ksrm/default.aspx.

Fresno Pacific University, Graduate Programs, Program in Kinesiology, Fresno, CA 93702-4709. Offers MA. *Faculty:* 3 full-time. *Students:* 31 full-time (14 women), 8 part-time (2 women); includes 17 minority (8 Black or African American, non-Hispanic/Latino; 3 American Indian or Alaska Native, non-Hispanic/Latino; 1 Asian, non-Hispanic/Latino; 5 Hispanic/Latino). Average age 30. In 2013, 65 master's awarded. *Entrance requirements:* Additional exam requirements/recommendations for international students: Required—TOEFL (minimum score 550 paper-based). *Application deadline:* For fall admission, 7/15 for domestic and international students; for spring admission, 11/15 for domestic and international students. *Expenses: Tuition:* Full-time $8910; part-time $495 per unit. *Required fees:* $270. Tuition and fees vary according to course load and program. *Unit head:* Dr. Jim Ave, Program Director, 559-453-7186, Fax: 559-453-7182, E-mail: jimave@fresno.edu. *Application contact:* Amanda Krum-Stovall, Director of Graduate Admissions, 559-453-2016, E-mail: amanda.krum-stovall@fresno.edu.
Website: http://grad.fresno.edu/programs/master-arts-kinesiology.

Georgia College & State University, Graduate School, College of Health Sciences, Department of Kinesiology, Milledgeville, GA 31061. Offers health promotion (M Ed); human performance (M Ed); outdoor education (M Ed); physical education (MAT). *Accreditation:* NCATE (one or more programs are accredited). Part-time and evening/weekend programs available. *Students:* 31 full-time (14 women), 13 part-time (12 women); includes 11 minority (all Black or African American, non-Hispanic/Latino), 1 international. Average age 26. In 2013, 25 master's awarded. *Degree requirements:* For master's, comprehensive exam, thesis optional. *Entrance requirements:* For master's, GRE General Test or MAT, minimum GPA of 2.75 in upper-level undergraduate courses, 2 letters of reference. Additional exam requirements/recommendations for international students: Recommended—TOEFL (minimum score 550 paper-based; 79 iBT). *Application deadline:* For fall admission, 7/1 priority date for domestic students, 4/1 priority date for international students; for spring admission, 11/15 priority date for domestic students, 9/1 priority date for international students. Applications are processed on a rolling basis. Application fee: $40. Electronic applications accepted. *Financial support:* In 2013–14, 26 research assistantships with full tuition reimbursements were awarded; career-related internships or fieldwork and unspecified assistantships also available. Support available to part-time students. Financial award applicants required to submit FAFSA. *Unit head:* Dr. Lisa Griffin, Chair, 478-445-4072, Fax: 478-445-4074, E-mail: lisa.griffin@gcsu.edu. *Application contact:* 800-342-0471, E-mail: grad-admit@gcsu.edu.

Georgia Southern University, Jack N. Averitt College of Graduate Studies, College of Health and Human Sciences, Department of Health and Kinesiology, Program in Kinesiology, Statesboro, GA 30460. Offers MS. *Students:* 67 full-time (39 women), 42 part-time (11 women); includes 15 minority (9 Black or African American, non-Hispanic/Latino; 1 Asian, non-Hispanic/Latino; 3 Hispanic/Latino; 2 Two or more races, non-Hispanic/Latino), 5 international. Average age 26. 139 applicants, 40% accepted, 33 enrolled. In 2013, 68 master's awarded. *Expenses:* Tuition, state resident: full-time $7068; part-time $270 per semester hour. Tuition, nonresident: full-time $26,446; part-time $1077 per semester hour. *Required fees:* $2092. *Financial support:* In 2013–14, 29 students received support. *Unit head:* Dr. Barry Joyner, Chair, 912-478-0495, Fax: 912-478-0381, E-mail: joyner@georgiasouthern.edu. *Application contact:* Amanda Gilliland, Coordinator for Graduate Student Recruitment, 912-478-5384, Fax: 912-478-0740, E-mail: gradadmissions@georgiasouthern.edu.

Georgia State University, College of Education, Department of Kinesiology and Health, Program in Kinesiology, Atlanta, GA 30302-3083. Offers PhD. *Degree requirements:* For doctorate, comprehensive exam, thesis/dissertation. *Entrance requirements:* For doctorate, GRE General Test or MAT, minimum GPA of 3.3. *Application deadline:* For fall admission, 3/1 for domestic students; for spring admission, 10/1 for domestic students. Application fee: $50. *Expenses: Tuition, area resident:* Full-time $4176; part-time $348 per credit hour. Tuition, state resident: full-time $14,544; part-time $1212 per credit hour. Tuition, nonresident: full-time $14,544; part-time $1212 per credit hour. Tuition and fees vary according to course load and program. *Financial support:* Research assistantships and teaching assistantships available. *Faculty research:* Aging, exercise metabolism, biomechanics and ergonomics, blood pressure regulation, exercise performance. *Unit head:* Dr. Jacalyn Lea Lund, Chair, 404-413-8051, E-mail: jlund@gsu.edu. *Application contact:* Dr. Christopher Ingalls, Program Coordinator, 404-413-8377, E-mail: cingalls@gsu.edu.
Website: http://education.gsu.edu/KIN/kh_PhD_Kinesiology.html.

Hardin-Simmons University, Graduate School, Irvin School of Education, Department of Fitness and Sport Sciences, Program in Kinesiology, Sport, and Recreation, Abilene, TX 79698-0001. Offers M Ed. Part-time programs available. *Faculty:* 6 full-time (2 women), 1 part-time/adjunct (0 women). *Students:* 12 full-time (7 women), 22 part-time (7 women); includes 10 minority (2 Black or African American, non-Hispanic/Latino; 1 Asian, non-Hispanic/Latino; 7 Hispanic/Latino). Average age 24. 17 applicants, 94% accepted, 13 enrolled. In 2013, 10 master's awarded. *Degree requirements:* For master's, comprehensive exam, thesis optional, internship, project. *Entrance requirements:* For master's, minimum undergraduate GPA of 3.0 in major, 2.7 overall; interview; writing sample; letters of recommendation; resume. Additional exam requirements/recommendations for international students: Required—TOEFL (minimum score 550 paper-based; 75 iBT). *Application deadline:* For fall admission, 8/15 priority date for domestic students, 4/1 for international students; for spring admission, 1/5 priority date for domestic students, 9/1 for international students. Applications are processed on a rolling basis. Application fee: $50. *Expenses: Tuition:* Full-time $13,410; part-time $745 per credit hour. *Required fees:* $325; $110 per semester. Tuition and fees vary according to program. *Financial support:* In 2013–14, 10 students received support, including 15 fellowships (averaging $1,333 per year); career-related internships or fieldwork, scholarships/grants, and recreation assistantships also available. Support available to part-time students. Financial award application deadline: 6/30; financial award applicants required to submit FAFSA. *Unit head:* Dr. Robert Moore, Director, 325-670-1265, Fax: 325-670-1218, E-mail: bemoore@hsutx.edu. *Application contact:* Dr. Nancy Kucinski, Dean of Graduate Studies, 325-670-1298, Fax: 325-670-1564, E-mail: gradoff@hsutx.edu.
Website: http://www.hsutx.edu/academics/irvin/graduate/kinesiology.

Humboldt State University, Academic Programs, College of Professional Studies, Department of Kinesiology and Recreation Administration, Arcata, CA 95521-8299. Offers athletic training education (MS); exercise science/wellness management (MS); pre-physical therapy (MS); teaching/coaching (MS). *Degree requirements:* For master's, thesis or alternative. *Entrance requirements:* For master's, GMAT, minimum GPA of 2.5. Additional exam requirements/recommendations for international students: Required—TOEFL. *Faculty research:* Human performance, adapted physical education, physical therapy.

Indiana University Bloomington, School of Public Health, Department of Kinesiology, Bloomington, IN 47405. Offers applied sport science (MS); athletic administration/sport management (MS); athletic training (MS); biomechanics (MS); ergonomics (MS); exercise physiology (MS); human performance (PhD), including biomechanics, exercise physiology, motor learning/control, sport management; motor learning/control (MS); physical activity (MPH); physical activity, fitness and wellness (MS). Part-time programs available. *Faculty:* 26 full-time (9 women). *Students:* 128 full-time (45 women), 16 part-time (6 women); includes 20 minority (11 Black or African American, non-Hispanic/Latino; 2 American Indian or Alaska Native, non-Hispanic/Latino; 3 Asian, non-Hispanic/Latino; 3 Hispanic/Latino; 1 Two or more races, non-Hispanic/Latino), 28 international. Average age 28. 174 applicants, 57% accepted, 48 enrolled. In 2013, 56 master's, 8 doctorates awarded. Terminal master's awarded for partial completion of doctoral program. *Degree requirements:* For master's, thesis optional; for doctorate, variable foreign language requirement, comprehensive exam, thesis/dissertation. *Entrance requirements:* For master's, GRE General Test, minimum GPA of 2.8; for doctorate, GRE General Test, minimum graduate GPA of 3.5, undergraduate 3.0. Additional exam requirements/recommendations for international students: Required—TOEFL (minimum score 80 iBT). *Application deadline:* For fall admission, 1/1 priority date for international students; for spring admission, 9/1 priority date for international students. Applications are processed on a rolling basis. Application fee: $55 ($65 for international students). *Financial support:* Fellowships, research assistantships with full tuition reimbursements, teaching assistantships with full tuition reimbursements, career-related internships or fieldwork, Federal Work-Study, institutionally sponsored loans, scholarships/grants, health care benefits, tuition waivers (partial), unspecified assistantships, and fee remissions available. Support available to part-time students. Financial award application deadline: 3/1; financial award applicants required to submit FAFSA. *Faculty research:* Exercise physiology and biochemistry, sports biomechanics, human motor control, adaptation of fitness and exercise to special populations. *Unit head:* Dr. David M. Koceja, Chairperson, 812-855-5523, Fax: 812-855-3193, E-mail: koceja@indiana.edu. *Application contact:* Kristine M. Wasson, Administrative Assistant for Graduate Studies, 812-855-5523, Fax: 812-855-3193, E-mail: ktanksle@indiana.edu.
Website: http://www.publichealth.indiana.edu/departments/kinesiology/index.shtml.

Inter American University of Puerto Rico, San Germán Campus, Graduate Studies Center, Program in Health and Physical Education, San Germán, PR 00683-5008. Offers MA. Part-time and evening/weekend programs available. *Faculty:* 12 full-time (7 women), 27 part-time/adjunct (17 women). *Students:* 20 full-time (9 women), 2 part-time (1 woman); all minorities (all Hispanic/Latino). Average age 29. 7 applicants, 86% accepted, 5 enrolled. In 2013, 8 master's awarded. *Degree requirements:* For master's, comprehensive exam. *Entrance requirements:* For master's, GRE General Test or EXADEP, minimum GPA of 3.0. *Application deadline:* For fall admission, 4/30 priority date for domestic students; for spring admission, 11/15 for domestic students. Applications are processed on a rolling basis. Application fee: $31. *Expenses: Tuition:* Full-time $2424; part-time $202 per credit hour. *Required fees:* $260 per semester. Tuition and fees vary according to course level, course load, degree level and program. *Financial support:* Teaching assistantships available. *Unit head:* Dr. Elba T. Irizarry, Director of Graduate Studies Center, 787-264-1912 Ext. 7357, Fax: 787-892-6350, E-mail: elbat@sg.inter.edu. *Application contact:* Dr. Elba T. Irizarry, Director of Graduate Studies Center, 787-264-1912 Ext. 7357, Fax: 787-892-6350, E-mail: elbat@sg.inter.edu.

Iowa State University of Science and Technology, Department of Kinesiology, Ames, IA 50011. Offers MS, PhD. *Entrance requirements:* For master's and doctorate, GRE General Test. Additional exam requirements/recommendations for international students: Required—TOEFL (minimum score 560 paper-based; 79 iBT), IELTS (minimum score 6.5). Electronic applications accepted.

James Madison University, The Graduate School, College of Health and Behavioral Studies, Department of Kinesiology, Harrisonburg, VA 22807. Offers MS. Part-time and evening/weekend programs available. *Faculty:* 12 full-time (5 women), 2 part-time/adjunct (0 women). *Students:* 69 full-time (39 women), 11 part-time (7 women); includes 9 minority (3 Black or African American, non-Hispanic/Latino; 1 Asian, non-Hispanic/Latino; 3 Hispanic/Latino; 1 Native Hawaiian or other Pacific Islander, non-Hispanic/Latino; 1 Two or more races, non-Hispanic/Latino), 1 international. Average age 27. In 2013, 47 master's awarded. *Degree requirements:* For master's, thesis or alternative. *Entrance requirements:* For master's, GRE General Test. Additional exam requirements/recommendations for international students: Required—TOEFL. *Application deadline:* For fall admission, 5/1 priority date for domestic students; for spring admission, 9/1 priority date for domestic students. Applications are processed on a rolling basis. Application fee: $55. Electronic applications accepted. *Financial support:* In 2013–14, 43 students received support, including 14 teaching assistantships with full tuition reimbursements available (averaging $8,837 per year); Federal Work-Study and 10 athletic assistantships (averaging $8837), 5 service assistantships (averaging $7530), 14 graduate assistantships (averaging $7530) also available. Financial award application deadline: 3/1; financial award applicants required to submit FAFSA. *Unit head:* Dr. Christopher J. Womack, Academic Unit Head, 540-568-6145, E-mail: womackex@jmu.edu. *Application contact:* Dr. M. Kent Todd, Graduate Coordinator, 540-568-3947, E-mail: toddmk@jmu.edu.

Kansas State University, Graduate School, College of Human Ecology, Department of Human Nutrition, Manhattan, KS 66506. Offers human nutrition (MS, PhD); nutritional sciences (PhD); public health nutrition (PhD); public health physical activity (PhD); sensory analysis and consumer behavior (PhD). Part-time programs available. *Faculty:* 17 full-time (10 women), 11 part-time/adjunct (3 women). *Students:* 19 full-time (11 women), 5 part-time (3 women); includes 3 minority (2 Asian, non-Hispanic/Latino; 1 Hispanic/Latino), 13 international. Average age 30. 34 applicants, 21% accepted, 5 enrolled. In 2013, 3 doctorates awarded. *Degree requirements:* For master's, thesis or alternative, residency; for doctorate, thesis/dissertation, residency. *Entrance*

requirements: For master's, GRE General Test, minimum undergraduate GPA of 3.0; for doctorate, GRE General Test, minimum graduate GPA of 3.0. Additional exam requirements/recommendations for international students: Required—TOEFL (minimum score 550 paper-based; 79 iBT), IELTS (minimum score 6.5). *Application deadline:* For fall admission, 2/1 priority date for domestic and international students; for spring admission, 8/1 priority date for domestic and international students. Applications are processed on a rolling basis. Application fee: $50 ($75 for international students). Electronic applications accepted. *Financial support:* In 2013–14, 15 students received support, including 18 research assistantships (averaging $20,000 per year), 4 teaching assistantships with tuition reimbursements available (averaging $11,671 per year); career-related internships or fieldwork, Federal Work-Study, institutionally sponsored loans, scholarships/grants, health care benefits, and tuition waivers (full) also available. Support available to part-time students. Financial award application deadline: 3/1; financial award applicants required to submit FAFSA. *Faculty research:* Biochemical and molecular nutrition, public health nutrition, human and clinical nutrition, sensory analysis and consumer behavior. *Total annual research expenditures:* $809,805. *Unit head:* Dr. Mark Haub, Head, 785-532-5508, Fax: 785-532-3132, E-mail: nutrgrad@ksu.edu. *Application contact:* Janet Finney, Senior Administrative Specialist, 785-532-5508, Fax: 785-532-3132, E-mail: nutrgrad@ksu.edu.
Website: http://www.he.k-state.edu/hn/.

Kansas State University, Graduate School, College of Human Ecology, Department of Kinesiology, Manhattan, KS 66506. Offers MS. Part-time programs available. *Faculty:* 8 full-time (3 women), 1 part-time/adjunct (0 women). *Students:* 19 full-time (7 women), 4 part-time (1 woman); includes 6 minority (4 Hispanic/Latino; 1 Native Hawaiian or other Pacific Islander, non-Hispanic/Latino; 1 Two or more races, non-Hispanic/Latino). Average age 25. 23 applicants, 30% accepted, 5 enrolled. In 2013, 11 master's awarded. *Degree requirements:* For master's, thesis optional. *Entrance requirements:* For master's, GRE General Test, bachelor's degree in kinesiology or exercise science, minimum GPA of 3.0. Additional exam requirements/recommendations for international students: Required—TOEFL. *Application deadline:* For fall admission, 2/1 priority date for domestic and international students; for spring admission, 8/1 priority date for domestic and international students. Applications are processed on a rolling basis. Application fee: $50 ($75 for international students). Electronic applications accepted. *Financial support:* In 2013–14, 9 teaching assistantships (averaging $10,000 per year) were awarded; tuition waivers (full) also available. Financial award application deadline: 3/1; financial award applicants required to submit FAFSA. *Faculty research:* Exercise physiology, vascular function, cardiorespiratory disease, physical inactivity, exercise adherence and compliance, public health/physical activity. *Total annual research expenditures:* $326,230. *Unit head:* Prof. David Dzewaltowski, Head, 785-532-6765, Fax: 785-532-6486, E-mail: dadx@ksu.edu. *Application contact:* Prof. Thomas J. Barstow, Graduate Program Coordinator, 785-532-0712, Fax: 785-532-6486, E-mail: tbarsto@ksu.edu.
Website: http://www.k-state.edu/kines/.

Lakehead University, Graduate Studies, School of Kinesiology, Thunder Bay, ON P7B 5E1, Canada. Offers kinesiology (M Sc); kinesiology and gerontology (M Sc). Part-time programs available. *Degree requirements:* For master's, thesis. *Entrance requirements:* For master's, minimum B average. Additional exam requirements/recommendations for international students: Required—TOEFL. *Faculty research:* Social psychology and physical education, sport history, sports medicine, exercise physiology, gerontology.

Lamar University, College of Graduate Studies, College of Education and Human Development, Department of Health and Kinesiology, Beaumont, TX 77710. Offers kinesiology (MS). *Degree requirements:* For master's, comprehensive exam (for some programs), thesis optional. *Entrance requirements:* For master's, GRE General Test, minimum GPA of 2.5. Additional exam requirements/recommendations for international students: Required—TOEFL. *Faculty research:* Motor learning, exercise physiology, pedagogy.

Louisiana State University and Agricultural & Mechanical College, Graduate School, College of Human Sciences and Education, Department of Kinesiology, Baton Rouge, LA 70803. Offers MS, PhD. PhD offered jointly with Louisiana State University in Shreveport. *Faculty:* 24 full-time (9 women), 1 part-time/adjunct (0 women). *Students:* 65 full-time (29 women), 42 part-time (19 women); includes 19 minority (8 Black or African American, non-Hispanic/Latino; 6 Hispanic/Latino; 5 Two or more races, non-Hispanic/Latino), 4 international. Average age 25. 88 applicants, 68% accepted, 24 enrolled. In 2013, 27 master's, 5 doctorates awarded. Terminal master's awarded for partial completion of doctoral program. *Degree requirements:* For master's, thesis (for some programs); for doctorate, one foreign language, thesis/dissertation, residency. *Entrance requirements:* For master's and doctorate, GRE General Test, minimum GPA of 3.0. Additional exam requirements/recommendations for international students: Required—TOEFL (minimum score 550 paper-based; 79 IBT), IELTS (minimum score 6.5), or PTE (minimum score 59). *Application deadline:* For fall admission, 1/25 priority date for domestic students, 5/15 for international students; for spring admission, 10/15 for international students. Applications are processed on a rolling basis. Application fee: $50 ($70 for international students). Electronic applications accepted. *Financial support:* In 2013–14, 81 students received support, including 2 fellowships with full and partial tuition reimbursements available (averaging $28,599 per year), 1 research assistantship with full and partial tuition reimbursement available (averaging $16,000 per year), 31 teaching assistantships with full and partial tuition reimbursements available (averaging $9,968 per year); career-related internships or fieldwork, Federal Work-Study, health care benefits, tuition waivers (full and partial), and unspecified assistantships also available. Financial award applicants required to submit FAFSA. *Faculty research:* Physical activity promotion in schools, wellness centers, hospitals and sports settings, healthy aging, rehabilitation studies. *Total annual research expenditures:* $196,230. *Unit head:* Dr. Melinda Solmon, Chair, 225-578-2036, Fax: 225-578-3680, E-mail: msolmo1@lsu.edu. *Application contact:* Dr. Chad Seifried, Graduate Advisor, 225-578-2208, Fax: 225-578-2267, E-mail: cseifried@lsu.edu.
Website: http://uiswcmsweb.prod.lsu.edu/kinesiology/.

McGill University, Faculty of Graduate and Postdoctoral Studies, Faculty of Education, Department of Kinesiology and Physical Education, Montréal, QC H3A 2T5, Canada. Offers M Sc, MA, PhD, Certificate, Diploma.

McMaster University, School of Graduate Studies, Faculty of Social Sciences, Department of Kinesiology, Hamilton, ON L8S 4M2, Canada. Offers human biodynamics (M Sc, PhD). *Degree requirements:* For master's, thesis. *Entrance requirements:* For master's, minimum B+ average in undergraduate course work. Additional exam requirements/recommendations for international students: Required—TOEFL (minimum score 580 paper-based). *Faculty research:* Motor learning and control, neuromuscular physiology, exercise rehabilitation, cellular responses to exercise, management.

Memorial University of Newfoundland, School of Graduate Studies, School of Human Kinetics and Recreation, St. John's, NL A1C 5S7, Canada. Offers administration, curriculum and supervision (MPE); biomechanics/ergonomics (MS Kin); exercise and work physiology (MS Kin); sport psychology (MS Kin). Part-time programs available. *Degree requirements:* For master's, thesis optional, seminars, thesis presentations. *Entrance requirements:* For master's, bachelor's degree in a related field, minimum B average. Electronic applications accepted. *Faculty research:* Administration, sociology of sports, kinesiology, physiology/recreation.

Michigan State University, The Graduate School, College of Education, Department of Kinesiology, East Lansing, MI 48824. Offers MS, PhD. *Entrance requirements:* Additional exam requirements/recommendations for international students: Required—TOEFL. Electronic applications accepted.

Mississippi College, Graduate School, School of Education, Department of Kinesiology, Clinton, MS 39058. Offers athletic administration (MS). *Degree requirements:* For master's, comprehensive exam, thesis optional. *Entrance requirements:* For master's, GRE, GMAT, or PRAXIS, minimum GPA of 2.5. Additional exam requirements/recommendations for international students: Recommended—TOEFL, IELTS. Electronic applications accepted.

Mississippi State University, College of Education, Department of Kinesiology, Mississippi State, MS 39762. Offers exercise physiology (MS); sport administration (MS); sport pedagogy (MS). Part-time programs available. Postbaccalaureate distance learning degree programs offered (minimal on-campus study). *Faculty:* 6 full-time (1 woman). *Students:* 44 full-time (12 women), 11 part-time (4 women); includes 6 minority (3 Black or African American, non-Hispanic/Latino; 2 Hispanic/Latino; 1 Two or more races, non-Hispanic/Latino), 4 international. Average age 25. 98 applicants, 35% accepted, 23 enrolled. In 2013, 36 master's awarded. *Degree requirements:* For master's, comprehensive exam, thesis optional. *Entrance requirements:* For master's, GRE General Test, minimum GPA of 2.75 on undergraduate work from four-year accredited institution, 3.0 graduate. Additional exam requirements/recommendations for international students: Required—TOEFL (minimum score 550 paper-based; 79 iBT); Recommended—IELTS (minimum score 6.5). *Application deadline:* For fall admission, 7/1 for domestic students, 5/1 for international students; for spring admission, 11/1 for domestic students, 9/1 for international students. Applications are processed on a rolling basis. Application fee: $60. Electronic applications accepted. *Financial support:* In 2013–14, 7 teaching assistantships (averaging $8,772 per year) were awarded; career-related internships or fieldwork, Federal Work-Study, institutionally sponsored loans, and unspecified assistantships also available. Financial award application deadline: 4/1; financial award applicants required to submit FAFSA. *Faculty research:* Static balance and stepping performance of older adults, organizational justice, public health, strength training and recovery drinks, high risk drinking perceptions and behaviors. *Unit head:* Dr. Stanley Brown, Professor and Department Head, 662-325-2963, Fax: 662-325-4525, E-mail: spb107@msstate.edu. *Application contact:* Dr. Adam Love, Graduate Coordinator, 662-325-2963, Fax: 662-325-4525, E-mail: adam.love@msstate.edu.
Website: http://www.kinesiology.msstate.edu/.

Missouri State University, Graduate College, College of Health and Human Services, Department of Kinesiology, Springfield, MO 65897. Offers health promotion and wellness management (MS); secondary education (MS Ed), including physical education. Part-time programs available. *Faculty:* 14 full-time (6 women). *Students:* 14 full-time (6 women), 17 part-time (10 women); includes 1 minority (Hispanic/Latino), 7 international. Average age 28. 15 applicants, 93% accepted, 7 enrolled. In 2013, 7 master's awarded. *Degree requirements:* For master's, comprehensive exam, thesis or alternative. *Entrance requirements:* For master's, GRE (MS), minimum GPA of 2.8 (MS); 9-12 teaching certification (MS Ed). Additional exam requirements/recommendations for international students: Required—TOEFL (minimum score 550 paper-based; 79 iBT). *Application deadline:* For fall admission, 7/20 priority date for domestic students, 5/1 for international students; for spring admission, 12/20 priority date for domestic students, 9/1 for international students. Applications are processed on a rolling basis. Application fee: $35 ($50 for international students). Electronic applications accepted. *Expenses:* Tuition, state resident: full-time $4500; part-time $250 per credit hour. Tuition, nonresident: full-time $9018; part-time $501 per credit hour. *Required fees:* $361 per semester. Tuition and fees vary according to course level, course load and program. *Financial support:* In 2013–14, 7 teaching assistantships with full tuition reimbursements (averaging $9,097 per year) were awarded; Federal Work-Study, institutionally sponsored loans, scholarships/grants, and unspecified assistantships also available. Financial award application deadline: 3/31; financial award applicants required to submit FAFSA. *Unit head:* Dr. Sarah McCallister, Acting Head, 417-836-6582, Fax: 417-836-5371, E-mail: sarahmccallister@missouristate.edu. *Application contact:* Misty Stewart, Coordinator of Graduate Admissions and Recruitment, 417-836-6079, Fax: 417-836-6200, E-mail: mistystewart@missouristate.edu.
Website: http://www.missouristate.edu/kinesiology/.

New York University, Steinhardt School of Culture, Education, and Human Development, Department of Physical Therapy, New York, NY 10010-5615. Offers orthopedic physical therapy (Advanced Certificate); physical therapy (MA, DPT, PhD), including pathokinesiology (MA). *Accreditation:* APTA (one or more programs are accredited). Part-time programs available. *Faculty:* 10 full-time (5 women), 15 part-time/adjunct (6 women). *Students:* 116 full-time (82 women), 9 part-time (6 women); includes 41 minority (8 Black or African American, non-Hispanic/Latino; 14 Asian, non-Hispanic/Latino; 15 Hispanic/Latino; 2 Native Hawaiian or other Pacific Islander, non-Hispanic/Latino; 2 Two or more races, non-Hispanic/Latino), 15 international. Average age 29. 496 applicants, 19% accepted, 48 enrolled. In 2013, 4 master's, 42 doctorates, 3 other advanced degrees awarded. *Degree requirements:* For master's, thesis (for some programs); for doctorate, thesis/dissertation. *Entrance requirements:* For master's, physical therapy certificate; for doctorate, GRE General Test, interview, physical therapy certificate. Additional exam requirements/recommendations for international students: Required—TOEFL (minimum score 100 iBT). *Application deadline:* For fall admission, 12/1 priority date for domestic and international students; for spring admission, 10/1 for domestic and international students. Applications are processed on a rolling basis. Application fee: $75. Electronic applications accepted. *Expenses: Tuition:* Full-time $35,856; part-time $1494 per unit. *Required fees:* $1408; $64 per unit. $473 per term. Tuition and fees vary according to course load and program. *Financial support:* Fellowships with full and partial tuition reimbursements, research assistantships with full and partial tuition reimbursements, career-related internships or fieldwork, Federal Work-Study, scholarships/grants, tuition waivers (partial), and unspecified assistantships available. Support available to part-time students. Financial award application deadline: 2/1; financial award applicants required to submit FAFSA. *Faculty research:* Motor learning and control, neuromuscular disorders, biomechanics and ergonomics, movement analysis, pathomechanics. *Unit head:* Prof. Mitchell Batavia, Chairperson, 212-998-9400, Fax: 212-995-4190, E-mail: mitchell.batavia@nyu.edu. *Application contact:* 212-998-5030, Fax: 212-995-4328, E-mail: steinhardt.gradadmissions@nyu.edu.
Website: http://steinhardt.nyu.edu/pt.

Northeastern State University, College of Education, Department of Health and Kinesiology, Tahlequah, OK 74464-2399. Offers MS. Part-time and evening/weekend programs available. *Faculty:* 17 full-time (12 women), 7 part-time/adjunct (2 women). *Students:* 11 full-time (4 women), 22 part-time (7 women); includes 13 minority (9 American Indian or Alaska Native, non-Hispanic/Latino; 1 Hispanic/Latino; 3 Two or more races, non-Hispanic/Latino), 4 international. Average age 27. In 2013, 15 master's awarded. *Entrance requirements:* For master's, MAT or GRE, minimum GPA of 2.5. Additional exam requirements/recommendations for international students: Required—

TOEFL. *Application deadline:* For fall admission, 6/1 for domestic and international students; for winter admission, 11/1 for domestic and international students; for spring admission, 3/1 for domestic students, 2/1 for international students. Applications are processed on a rolling basis. Application fee: $25. Electronic applications accepted. *Expenses:* Tuition, state resident: full-time $3029; part-time $168.25 per credit hour. Tuition, nonresident: full-time $7709; part-time $428.25 per credit hour. *Required fees:* $35.90 per credit hour. *Unit head:* Dr. Mark Giese, Chair, 918-456-5511 Ext. 3950. *Application contact:* Margie Railey, Administrative Assistant, 918-456-5511 Ext. 2093, Fax: 918-458-2061, E-mail: railey@nsouk.edu.
Website: http://academics.nsuok.edu/education/DegreePrograms/GraduatePrograms/HealthandKinesiology.aspx.

Northwestern University, Fienberg School of Medicine, Department of Physical Therapy and Human Movement Sciences, Chicago, IL 60611-2814. Offers neuroscience (PhD), including movement and rehabilitation science; physical therapy (DPT); DPT/PhD. *Accreditation:* APTA. *Degree requirements:* For doctorate, synthesis research project. *Entrance requirements:* For doctorate, GRE General Test (for DPT), baccalaureate degree with minimum GPA of 3.0 in required course work (DPT). Additional exam requirements/recommendations for international students: Required—TOEFL. Electronic applications accepted. *Expenses:* Contact institution. *Faculty research:* Motor control, robotics, neuromuscular imaging, student performance (academic/professional), clinical outcomes.

The Ohio State University, Graduate School, College of Education and Human Ecology, Department of Human Sciences, Columbus, OH 43210. Offers consumer sciences (MS, PhD); human development and family science (PhD); human nutrition (MS, PhD); kinesiology (MA, PhD). Part-time programs available. *Faculty:* 65. *Students:* 97 full-time (77 women), 4 part-time (3 women); includes 14 minority (5 Black or African American, non-Hispanic/Latino; 6 Asian, non-Hispanic/Latino; 3 Hispanic/Latino), 40 international. Average age 29. In 2013, 13 master's, 21 doctorates awarded. *Degree requirements:* For master's, thesis optional; for doctorate, thesis/dissertation. *Entrance requirements:* For master's and doctorate, GRE. Additional exam requirements/recommendations for international students: Required—TOEFL (minimum score 550 paper-based; 79 iBT), Michigan English Language Assessment Battery (minimum score 82); Recommended—IELTS (minimum score 7). *Application deadline:* For fall admission, 12/1 priority date for domestic and international students; for winter admission, 12/1 for domestic students, 11/1 for international students; for spring admission, 3/1 for domestic students, 2/1 for international students. Applications are processed on a rolling basis. Application fee: $60 ($70 for international students). Electronic applications accepted. *Financial support:* Fellowships with tuition reimbursements, research assistantships with tuition reimbursements, teaching assistantships with tuition reimbursements, Federal Work-Study, and institutionally sponsored loans available. Support available to part-time students. *Unit head:* Earl Harrison, Chair, 614-292-8189, E-mail: harrison.304@osu.edu. *Application contact:* Graduate Admissions, 614-292-6031, Fax: 614-292-3656, E-mail: gradadmissions@osu.edu.
Website: http://ehe.osu.edu/human-sciences/.

Old Dominion University, Darden College of Education, Program in Human Movement Science, Norfolk, VA 23529. Offers PhD. *Faculty:* 8 full-time (3 women). *Students:* 8 full-time (6 women), 3 part-time (2 women); includes 1 minority (Black or African American, non-Hispanic/Latino). Average age 33. 8 applicants, 75% accepted, 6 enrolled. In 2013, 1 doctorate awarded. *Degree requirements:* For doctorate, comprehensive exam, thesis/dissertation. *Entrance requirements:* For doctorate, GRE, minimum GPA of 3.0. Additional exam requirements/recommendations for international students: Required—TOEFL. *Application deadline:* For fall admission, 1/15 for domestic students; for spring admission, 2/1 for domestic and international students. Application fee: $50. Electronic applications accepted. *Expenses:* Tuition, state resident: full-time $9888; part-time $412 per credit. Tuition, nonresident: full-time $25,152; part-time $1048 per credit. *Required fees:* $59 per semester. One-time fee: $50. *Financial support:* In 2013–14, 6 students received support, including 2 fellowships with full tuition reimbursements available (averaging $15,000 per year), 6 teaching assistantships with full tuition reimbursements available (averaging $15,000 per year); career-related internships or fieldwork, scholarships/grants, and unspecified assistantships also available. Financial award application deadline: 5/1. *Faculty research:* Biomechanics, exercise physiology, sport management, recreation management. *Total annual research expenditures:* $10,000. *Unit head:* Dr. Lynn Ridinger, Graduate Program Director, 757-683-4353, Fax: 757-683-4270, E-mail: lridinge@odu.edu. *Application contact:* Alice McAdory, Director of Admissions, 757-683-3685, Fax: 757-683-3255, E-mail: gradadmit@odu.edu.
Website: http://education.odu.edu/esper/academics/phd/.

Oregon State University, College of Public Health and Human Sciences, Program in Exercise and Sport Science, Corvallis, OR 97331. Offers exercise physiology (MS, PhD); movement studies in disability (MS, PhD); neuromechanics (MS, PhD); physical activity and public health (MS, PhD); physical education and teacher education (MS); sport and exercise psychology (MS, PhD). Part-time programs available. *Faculty:* 12 full-time (5 women), 1 (woman) part-time/adjunct. *Students:* 47 full-time (28 women), 7 part-time (3 women); includes 6 minority (2 Asian, non-Hispanic/Latino; 2 Hispanic/Latino; 2 Two or more races, non-Hispanic/Latino), 4 international. Average age 28. 127 applicants, 18% accepted, 23 enrolled. In 2013, 16 master's, 8 doctorates awarded. Terminal master's awarded for partial completion of doctoral program. *Median time to degree:* Of those who began their doctoral program in fall 2005, 86% received their degree in 8 years or less. *Degree requirements:* For master's, thesis; for doctorate, thesis/dissertation. *Entrance requirements:* For master's and doctorate, GRE, minimum GPA of 3.0 in last 90 hours. Additional exam requirements/recommendations for international students: Required—TOEFL (minimum score 80 iBT), IELTS (minimum score 6.5). *Application deadline:* For fall admission, 12/1 for domestic students. Application fee: $60. *Expenses:* Tuition, state resident: full-time $11,664; part-time $432 per credit hour. Tuition, nonresident: full-time $19,197; part-time $711 per credit hour. *Required fees:* $1446; $443 per quarter. One-time fee: $300. Tuition and fees vary according to course load and program. *Financial support:* Research assistantships, teaching assistantships, career-related internships or fieldwork, Federal Work-Study, and institutionally sponsored loans available. Support available to part-time students. Financial award application deadline: 2/1. *Faculty research:* Motor control, sports medicine, exercise physiology, sport psychology, biomechanics. *Unit head:* Dr. Tony Wilcox, Co-Director of the School of Biological and Population Health Sciences, 541-737-2643. *Application contact:* Debi Rothermund, Exercise and Sports Science Advisor, 541-737-3324, E-mail: debi.rothermund@oregonstate.edu.
Website: http://health.oregonstate.edu/degrees/graduate/exercise-sport-science.

Penn State University Park, Graduate School, College of Health and Human Development, Department of Kinesiology, State College, PA 16802. Offers MS, PhD, Certificate. *Unit head:* Dr. Ann C. Crouter, Dean, 814-865-1420, Fax: 814-865-3282, E-mail: ac1@psu.edu. *Application contact:* Cynthia E. Nicosia, Director, Graduate Enrollment Services, 814-865-1834, Fax: 814-863-4627, E-mail: cey1@psu.edu.
Website: http://www.hhdev.psu.edu/kines.

Purdue University, Graduate School, College of Health and Human Sciences, Department of Health and Kinesiology, West Lafayette, IN 47907. Offers athletic training education administration (MS, PhD); biomechanics (MS, PhD); exercise physiology (MS, PhD); health education (MS, PhD); history/philosophy of sport (MS, PhD); motor control and development (MS, PhD); physical education pedagogy (PhD); physical education teacher education (MS); recreation and sport management (MS, PhD); sport and exercise psychology (MS, PhD). Part-time programs available. *Faculty:* 16 full-time (8 women), 20 part-time/adjunct (3 women). *Students:* 43 full-time (29 women), 21 part-time (11 women); includes 6 minority (2 Black or African American, non-Hispanic/Latino; 1 American Indian or Alaska Native, non-Hispanic/Latino; 1 Asian, non-Hispanic/Latino; 2 Two or more races, non-Hispanic/Latino), 12 international. Average age 28. 103 applicants, 32% accepted, 16 enrolled. In 2013, 15 master's, 8 doctorates awarded. *Degree requirements:* For master's, thesis optional; for doctorate, comprehensive exam, thesis/dissertation, qualifying examination, preliminary examination. *Entrance requirements:* For master's, GRE General Test (minimum score 1000 combined verbal and quantitative), minimum undergraduate GPA of 3.0 or equivalent; for doctorate, GRE General Test (minimum score 1100 combined verbal and quantitative), minimum undergraduate GPA of 3.0 or equivalent; master's degree with minimum GPA of 3.25 (recommended). Additional exam requirements/recommendations for international students: Required—TOEFL (minimum score 77 iBT); Recommended—TWE. *Application deadline:* For fall admission, 4/30 for domestic and international students; for spring admission, 10/15 for domestic and international students. Applications are processed on a rolling basis. Application fee: $60 ($75 for international students). Electronic applications accepted. *Financial support:* Fellowships with partial tuition reimbursements, research assistantships with partial tuition reimbursements, teaching assistantships with partial tuition reimbursements, and Federal Work-Study available. Support available to part-time students. Financial award applicants required to submit FAFSA. *Faculty research:* Wellness, motivation, teaching effectiveness, learning and development. *Unit head:* Dr. Timothy P. Gavin, Head of the Graduate Program, 765-494-3178, Fax: 765-494-1239, E-mail: gavin1@purdue.edu. *Application contact:* Lisa Duncan, Graduate Contact, 765-494-3162, E-mail: llduncan@purdue.edu.
Website: http://www.purdue.edu/hhs/hk/.

Saint Mary's College of California, School of Liberal Arts, Department of Kinesiology, Moraga, CA 94575. Offers sport management (MA); sport studies (MA). Part-time programs available. *Degree requirements:* For master's, thesis or special project. *Entrance requirements:* For master's, minimum GPA of 2.75, BA in physical education or related field, or professional experience. Electronic applications accepted. *Expenses:* Contact institution. *Faculty research:* Moral development in sport, applied motor learning, achievement motivation, sport history.

Sam Houston State University, College of Education and Applied Science, Department of Health and Kinesiology, Huntsville, TX 77341. Offers health (MA); kinesiology (MA). Part-time and evening/weekend programs available. *Faculty:* 11 full-time (5 women). *Students:* 34 full-time (14 women), 29 part-time (19 women); includes 18 minority (10 Black or African American, non-Hispanic/Latino; 1 Asian, non-Hispanic/Latino; 7 Hispanic/Latino), 12 international. Average age 28. 48 applicants, 98% accepted, 23 enrolled. In 2013, 28 master's awarded. *Degree requirements:* For master's, comprehensive exam, thesis optional. *Entrance requirements:* For master's, GRE, MAT. Additional exam requirements/recommendations for international students: Required—TOEFL (minimum score 550 paper-based; 79 iBT), IELTS (minimum score 6.5). *Application deadline:* For fall admission, 8/1 for domestic students, 6/25 for international students; for spring admission, 12/1 for domestic students, 11/12 for international students. Applications are processed on a rolling basis. Application fee: $45 ($75 for international students). Electronic applications accepted. *Financial support:* In 2013–14, 1 research assistantship (averaging $7,658 per year), 2 teaching assistantships (averaging $7,200 per year) were awarded; career-related internships or fieldwork, Federal Work-Study, institutionally sponsored loans, scholarships/grants, tuition waivers (partial), and unspecified assistantships also available. Support available to part-time students. Financial award application deadline: 5/31; financial award applicants required to submit FAFSA. *Unit head:* Dr. Michael Lacourse, Dean, 936-294-2300, Fax: 936-294-3891, E-mail: mlacourse@shsu.edu. *Application contact:* Dr. Bill Hyman, Professor and Graduate Coordinator, 936-294-1212, E-mail: hpe_wvh@shsu.edu.
Website: http://www.shsu.edu/~hpe_www/.

San Diego State University, Graduate and Research Affairs, College of Health and Human Services, School of Exercise and Nutritional Sciences, Program in Kinesiology, San Diego, CA 92182. Offers MA. *Degree requirements:* For master's, thesis. *Entrance requirements:* For master's, GRE General Test, 2 letters of reference. Additional exam requirements/recommendations for international students: Required—TOEFL. Electronic applications accepted.

San Francisco State University, Division of Graduate Studies, College of Health and Social Sciences, Department of Kinesiology, San Francisco, CA 94132-1722. Offers exercise physiology (MS); movement science (MS); physical activity: social scientific perspectives (MS). *Application deadline:* Applications are processed on a rolling basis. *Unit head:* Dr. Mi-Sook Kim, Chair, 415-338-2244, E-mail: kimms@sfsu.edu. *Application contact:* Prof. Marialice Kern, Graduate Coordinator, 415-338-1491, E-mail: mkern@sfsu.edu.
Website: http://kin.sfsu.edu/.

San Jose State University, Graduate Studies and Research, College of Applied Sciences and Arts, Department of Kinesiology, San Jose, CA 95192-0001. Offers MA. *Degree requirements:* For master's, comprehensive exam. *Entrance requirements:* For master's, bachelor's degree in physical education. Electronic applications accepted.

Sarah Lawrence College, Graduate Studies, Program in Dance/Movement Therapy, Bronxville, NY 10708-5999. Offers MS. *Degree requirements:* For master's, thesis, practicum. *Application deadline:* For fall admission, 3/1 priority date for domestic students. *Unit head:* Cathy Appel, Director. *Application contact:* Emanual Lomax, 914-395-2371, E-mail: elomax@sarahlawrence.edu.
Website: https://www.slc.edu/movement-therapy/.

Simon Fraser University, Office of Graduate Studies, Faculty of Science, Department of Biomedical Physiology and Kinesiology, Burnaby, BC V5A 1S6, Canada. Offers M Sc, PhD. *Faculty:* 21 full-time (4 women). *Students:* 50 full-time (28 women). 11 applicants, 91% accepted, 7 enrolled. In 2013, 11 master's, 2 doctorates awarded. *Degree requirements:* For master's, thesis, thesis proposal; for doctorate, comprehensive exam, thesis/dissertation, dissertation proposal, seminar presentations. *Entrance requirements:* For master's, minimum GPA of 3.0 (on scale of 4.33), or 3.33 based on last 60 credits of undergraduate courses; for doctorate, minimum GPA of 3.5 (on scale of 4.33). Additional exam requirements/recommendations for international students: Recommended—TOEFL (minimum score 580 paper-based; 93 iBT), IELTS (minimum score 7), TWE (minimum score 5). *Application deadline:* For fall admission, 1/15 for domestic and international students; for winter admission, 8/31 for domestic and international students; for spring admission, 1/15 for domestic and international students. Applications are processed on a rolling basis. Application fee: $90 ($125 for international students). Electronic applications accepted. *Expenses: Tuition, area resident:* Full-time $5084 Canadian dollars. *Required fees:* $840 Canadian dollars. *Financial support:* In 2013–14, 24 students received support, including 19 fellowships (averaging $6,250 per year), teaching assistantships (averaging $5,608 per year);

research assistantships and scholarships/grants also available. *Faculty research:* Cardiovascular physiology, chronic disease, environmental physiology, neuromechanics, neuroscience. *Unit head:* Dr. Angela Brooks-Wilson, Graduate Chair, 778-782-3889, Fax: 778-782-3040, E-mail: bpk-grad-chair@sfu.ca. *Application contact:* Susie Nugent, Graduate Secretary, 778-782-4061, Fax: 778-782-3040, E-mail: bpk-grad-sec@sfu.ca.
Website: http://www.sfu.ca/bpk.html.

Sonoma State University, School of Science and Technology, Department of Kinesiology, Rohnert Park, CA 94928. Offers adapted physical education (MA); interdisciplinary (MA); interdisciplinary pre-occupational therapy (MA); lifetime physical activity (MA), including coach education, fitness and wellness; physical education (MA); pre-physical therapy (MA). Part-time programs available. *Faculty:* 5 full-time (3 women). *Students:* 1 full-time (0 women), 11 part-time (3 women); includes 2 minority (1 Hispanic/Latino; 1 Two or more races, non-Hispanic/Latino). Average age 29. *Degree requirements:* For master's, thesis, oral exam. *Entrance requirements:* For master's, minimum GPA of 2.8. Additional exam requirements/recommendations for international students: Required—TOEFL (minimum score 500 paper-based). *Application deadline:* For fall admission, 11/30 for domestic students; for spring admission, 9/1 for domestic students. Applications are processed on a rolling basis. Application fee: $55. *Expenses:* Tuition, state resident: full-time $8500. Tuition, nonresident: full-time $12,964. *Required fees:* $1762. *Financial support:* Career-related internships or fieldwork available. Financial award application deadline: 3/2; financial award applicants required to submit FAFSA. *Unit head:* Dr. Elaine McHugh, Chair, 707-664-2660, E-mail: elaine.mchugh@sonoma.edu. *Application contact:* Dr. Lauren Morimoto, Graduate Coordinator, 707-664-2479, E-mail: morimoto@sonoma.edu.
Website: http://www.sonoma.edu/kinesiology/.

Southeastern Louisiana University, College of Nursing and Health Sciences, Department of Kinesiology and Health Studies, Hammond, LA 70402. Offers health and kinesiology (MA), including exercise science, health promotion and exercise science, health studies, kinesiology. *Accreditation:* NCATE. Part-time programs available. *Faculty:* 10 full-time (4 women). *Students:* 26 full-time (13 women), 17 part-time (9 women); includes 10 minority (7 Black or African American, non-Hispanic/Latino; 2 Asian, non-Hispanic/Latino; 1 Hispanic/Latino), 1 international. Average age 28. 38 applicants, 66% accepted, 12 enrolled. In 2013, 21 master's awarded. *Degree requirements:* For master's, comprehensive exam (for some programs), thesis (for some programs). *Entrance requirements:* For master's, GRE General Test (minimum score 800), undergraduate human anatomy and physiology course. Additional exam requirements/recommendations for international students: Required—TOEFL (minimum score 500 paper-based; 61 iBT). *Application deadline:* For fall admission, 7/15 priority date for domestic students, 6/1 priority date for international students; for spring admission, 12/1 priority date for domestic students, 10/1 priority date for international students. Applications are processed on a rolling basis. Application fee: $20 ($30 for international students). Electronic applications accepted. *Expenses:* Tuition, state resident: full-time $5047. Tuition, nonresident: full-time $17,066. *Required fees:* $1213. Tuition and fees vary according to degree level. *Financial support:* In 2013–14, 3 fellowships (averaging $10,800 per year), 4 research assistantships (averaging $8,425 per year), 5 teaching assistantships (averaging $8,540 per year) were awarded; career-related internships or fieldwork, Federal Work-Study, institutionally sponsored loans, scholarships/grants, and unspecified assistantships also available. Support available to part-time students. Financial award application deadline: 5/1; financial award applicants required to submit FAFSA. *Faculty research:* Exercise endocrinology, perceptions of exercise intensity and pain, spirituality and health, alternative health practices, use of podcasting and other technology to promote healthy behaviors. *Unit head:* Dr. Edward Hebert, Department Head, 985-549-2129, Fax: 985-549-5119, E-mail: ehebert@selu.edu. *Application contact:* Sandra Meyers, Graduate Admissions Analyst, 985-549-5620, Fax: 985-549-5632, E-mail: admissions@selu.edu.
Website: http://www.selu.edu/acad_research/depts/kin_hs.

Southern Arkansas University–Magnolia, Graduate Programs, Magnolia, AR 71753. Offers agriculture (MS); business administration (MBA); computer and information sciences (MS); education (M Ed), including counseling and development, curriculum and instruction, educational administration and supervision, elementary education, reading, secondary education, TESOL; kinesiology (M Ed); library media and information specialist (M Ed); mental health and clinical counseling (MS); public administration (MPA); school counseling (M Ed); teaching (MAT). *Accreditation:* NCATE. Part-time and evening/weekend programs available. Postbaccalaureate distance learning degree programs offered. *Faculty:* 34 full-time (15 women), 8 part-time/adjunct (5 women). *Students:* 48 full-time (22 women), 269 part-time (167 women); includes 85 minority (78 Black or African American, non-Hispanic/Latino; 2 Asian, non-Hispanic/Latino; 2 Hispanic/Latino; 1 Native Hawaiian or other Pacific Islander, non-Hispanic/Latino; 2 Two or more races, non-Hispanic/Latino), 5 international. Average age 33. 149 applicants, 73% accepted, 109 enrolled. In 2013, 149 master's awarded. *Degree requirements:* For master's, comprehensive exam (for some programs), thesis optional. *Entrance requirements:* For master's, GRE, MAT or GMAT, minimum GPA of 2.5. Additional exam requirements/recommendations for international students: Required—TOEFL, IELTS. *Application deadline:* For fall admission, 7/10 for domestic and international students; for winter admission, 12/1 for domestic and international students; for spring admission, 12/1 for domestic and international students; for summer admission, 4/1 for domestic students. Applications are processed on a rolling basis. Application fee: $25 ($50 for international students). Electronic applications accepted. *Expenses:* Tuition, state resident: part-time $254 per credit hour. Tuition, nonresident: part-time $370 per credit hour. *Required fees:* $136 per credit hour. $259 per semester. Tuition and fees vary according to course load and program. *Financial support:* Career-related internships or fieldwork, Federal Work-Study, scholarships/grants, tuition waivers (full), and unspecified assistantships available. Financial award applicants required to submit FAFSA. *Faculty research:* Alternative certification for teachers, supervision of instruction, instructional leadership, counseling. *Unit head:* Dr. Kim Bloss, Dean, School of Graduate Studies, 870-235-4150, Fax: 870-235-5227, E-mail: kkbloss@saumag.edu. *Application contact:* Shrijana Malaka, Admissions Specialist, 870-235-4150, Fax: 870-235-5227, E-mail: smalakar@saumag.edu.
Website: http://www.saumag.edu/graduate.

Southern Illinois University Carbondale, Graduate School, College of Education and Human Services, Department of Kinesiology, Carbondale, IL 62901-4701. Offers physical education (MS Ed). Part-time programs available. *Faculty:* 6 full-time (2 women). *Students:* 42 full-time (19 women), 30 part-time (10 women); includes 12 minority (10 Black or African American, non-Hispanic/Latino; 1 Asian, non-Hispanic/Latino; 1 Hispanic/Latino), 8 international. Average age 25. 35 applicants, 54% accepted, 12 enrolled. In 2013, 19 master's awarded. *Degree requirements:* For master's, thesis. *Entrance requirements:* For master's, GRE, minimum GPA of 2.7. Additional exam requirements/recommendations for international students: Required—TOEFL. *Application deadline:* Applications are processed on a rolling basis. Application fee: $50. *Financial support:* In 2013–14, 17 students received support, including 10 teaching assistantships; fellowships, research assistantships, career-related internships or fieldwork, Federal Work-Study, institutionally sponsored loans, and tuition waivers (full) also available. Support available to part-time students. *Faculty research:* Caffeine and exercise effects, ground reaction forces in walking and running, social psychology of sports. *Unit head:* Dr. E. William Vogler, Chairperson, 618-536-2431, E-mail: wvogler@siu.edu. *Application contact:* Lori Johnson, Graduate Program Assistant, 618-453-3134, E-mail: lorij20@siu.edu.
Website: http://kin.ehs.siu.edu/.

Southern Illinois University Edwardsville, Graduate School, School of Education, Department of Kinesiology and Health Education, Program in Physical Education and Sport Pedagogy, Edwardsville, IL 62026. Offers MS Ed. Part-time and evening/weekend programs available. *Students:* 1 full-time (0 women), 13 part-time (7 women); includes 2 minority (1 Black or African American, non-Hispanic/Latino; 1 Hispanic/Latino). 3 applicants, 100% accepted. In 2013, 8 master's awarded. *Degree requirements:* For master's, comprehensive exam (for some programs), thesis (for some programs). *Entrance requirements:* Additional exam requirements/recommendations for international students: Required—TOEFL (minimum score 550 paper-based, 79 iBT), IELTS (minimum score 6.5), Michigan Test of English Language Proficiency or PTE. *Application deadline:* For fall admission, 7/18 for domestic students, 6/1 for international students; for spring admission, 12/12 for domestic students, 9/1 for international students; for summer admission, 4/24 for domestic students, 3/1 for international students. Applications are processed on a rolling basis. Application fee: $30. Electronic applications accepted. *Expenses:* Tuition, state resident: full-time $3551. Tuition, nonresident: full-time $8378. *Financial support:* Institutionally sponsored loans, scholarships/grants, and unspecified assistantships available. Financial award application deadline: 3/1; financial award applicants required to submit FAFSA. *Unit head:* Dr. Erik Kirk, Program Director, 618-650-2718, E-mail: ekirk@siue.edu. *Application contact:* Melissa K. Mace, Assistant Director of Graduate and International Recruitment, 618-650-2756, Fax: 618-650-3618, E-mail: mmace@siue.edu.
Website: http://www.siue.edu/education/khe/.

Southwestern Oklahoma State University, College of Professional and Graduate Studies, School of Behavioral Sciences and Education, Specialization in Kinesiology, Weatherford, OK 73096-3098. Offers M Ed. Part-time programs available. *Degree requirements:* For master's, exam. *Entrance requirements:* For master's, GRE General Test or minimum undergraduate GPA of 3.0. Additional exam requirements/recommendations for international students: Required—TOEFL.

Stephen F. Austin State University, Graduate School, College of Education, Department of Kinesiology and Health Science, Nacogdoches, TX 75962. Offers athletic training (MS); kinesiology (M Ed). *Degree requirements:* For master's, comprehensive exam. *Entrance requirements:* For master's, GRE General Test. Additional exam requirements/recommendations for international students: Required—TOEFL.

Teachers College, Columbia University, Graduate Faculty of Education, Department of Biobehavioral Studies, Program in Motor Learning/Movement Science, New York, NY 10027-6696. Offers Ed M, MA, Ed D. Part-time and evening/weekend programs available. *Faculty:* 1 full-time, 3 part-time/adjunct. *Students:* 15 full-time (8 women), 54 part-time (36 women); includes 25 minority (10 Black or African American, non-Hispanic/Latino; 5 Asian, non-Hispanic/Latino; 10 Hispanic/Latino), 11 international. Average age 30. 37 applicants, 73% accepted, 17 enrolled. In 2013, 24 master's, 3 doctorates awarded. Terminal master's awarded for partial completion of doctoral program. *Degree requirements:* For master's, integrative paper; for doctorate, thesis/dissertation, teaching assistantship. *Application deadline:* For fall admission, 1/2 priority date for domestic students; for spring admission, 11/1 for domestic students. Applications are processed on a rolling basis. Application fee: $65. Electronic applications accepted. *Financial support:* Teaching assistantships, career-related internships or fieldwork, Federal Work-Study, institutionally sponsored loans, traineeships, and tuition waivers (full and partial) available. Support available to part-time students. Financial award application deadline: 2/1. *Faculty research:* Motor control, analysis of tasks, biomechanical aspect of learning, skill acquisition, recovery of motor behavior. *Unit head:* Prof. Andrew Gordon, Program Coordinator, 212-678-3325, E-mail: agordona@tc.edu. *Application contact:* Morgan Oakes, Assistant Director of Admission, 212-678-3710, Fax: 212-678-4171, E-mail: tcinfo@tc.edu.
Website: http://www.tc.columbia.edu/bbs/Movement/.

Temple University, College of Health Professions and Social Work, Department of Kinesiology, Philadelphia, PA 19122. Offers athletic training (MS, PhD); behavioral sciences (Ed M); curriculum and instruction (MS); integrated exercise physiology (PhD); integrative exercise physiology (MS); kinesiology (MS); psychology of movement (MS); somatic sciences (PhD). Part-time programs available. *Faculty:* 15 full-time (7 women). *Students:* 49 full-time (30 women), 8 part-time (5 women); includes 6 minority (2 Black or African American, non-Hispanic/Latino; 1 Asian, non-Hispanic/Latino; 2 Hispanic/Latino; 1 Two or more races, non-Hispanic/Latino), 6 international. 100 applicants, 33% accepted, 18 enrolled. In 2013, 15 master's, 6 doctorates awarded. Terminal master's awarded for partial completion of doctoral program. *Degree requirements:* For master's, thesis, final project; for doctorate, comprehensive exam, thesis/dissertation. *Entrance requirements:* For master's, GRE General Test or MAT, minimum undergraduate GPA of 3.0, 3 letters of reference, statement of goals, interview, resume; for doctorate, GRE General Test, minimum undergraduate GPA of 3.0, 3 letters of reference, statement of goals, interview, resume. Additional exam requirements/recommendations for international students: Required—TOEFL (minimum score 550 paper-based; 79 iBT). *Application deadline:* For fall admission, 1/15 for domestic students, 12/15 for international students; for spring admission, 10/1 for domestic students, 8/1 for international students. Applications are processed on a rolling basis. Application fee: $60. Electronic applications accepted. *Financial support:* In 2013–14, 4 research assistantships with full and partial tuition reimbursements (averaging $16,459 per year), 24 teaching assistantships with full and partial tuition reimbursements (averaging $15,966 per year) were awarded; fellowships, career-related internships or fieldwork, Federal Work-Study, scholarships/grants, tuition waivers, and unspecified assistantships also available. Financial award application deadline: 1/15. *Faculty research:* Exercise physiology, athletic training, motor neuroscience, exercise and sports psychology. *Total annual research expenditures:* $318,204. *Unit head:* Dr. John Jeka, Department Chair, 214-204-4405, Fax: 215-204-4414, E-mail: jjeka@temple.edu. *Application contact:* Megan P. Mannal DiMarco, 215-204-7503, E-mail: megan.dimarco@temple.edu.
Website: http://chpsw.temple.edu/kinesiology/home.

Tennessee Technological University, College of Graduate Studies, College of Education, Department of Exercise Science, Physical Education and Wellness, Cookeville, TN 38505. Offers adapted physical education (MA); elementary/middle school physical education (MA); lifetime wellness (MA); sport management (MA). *Accreditation:* NCATE. Part-time programs available. Postbaccalaureate distance learning degree programs offered (no on-campus study). *Faculty:* 7 full-time (0 women). *Students:* 10 full-time (0 women), 38 part-time (11 women); includes 5 minority (all Black or African American, non-Hispanic/Latino). Average age 27. 38 applicants, 58% accepted, 20 enrolled. In 2013, 23 master's awarded. *Degree requirements:* For master's, comprehensive exam, thesis or alternative. *Entrance requirements:* For master's, MAT or GRE. Additional exam requirements/recommendations for international students: Required—TOEFL (minimum score 527 paper-based; 71 iBT), IELTS (minimum score 5.5), PTE (minimum score 48), or TOEIC (Test of English as an

International Communication). *Application deadline:* For fall admission, 8/1 for domestic students, 5/1 for international students; for spring admission, 12/1 for domestic students, 10/1 for international students. Applications are processed on a rolling basis. Application fee: $35 ($40 for international students). Electronic applications accepted. *Expenses:* Tuition, state resident: full-time $9347; part-time $465 per credit hour. Tuition, nonresident: full-time $23,635; part-time $1152 per credit hour. *Financial support:* In 2013–14, fellowships (averaging $8,000 per year), 3 research assistantships (averaging $4,000 per year), 4 teaching assistantships (averaging $4,000 per year) were awarded; career-related internships or fieldwork also available. Financial award application deadline: 4/1. *Unit head:* Dr. John Steven Smith, Interim Chairperson, 931-372-3467, Fax: 931-372-6319, E-mail: jssmith@tntech.edu. *Application contact:* Shelia K. Kendrick, Coordinator of Graduate Studies, 931-372-3808, Fax: 931-372-3497, E-mail: skendrick@tntech.edu.

Texas A&M University, College of Education and Human Development, Department of Health and Kinesiology, College Station, TX 77843. Offers athletic training (MS); health education (M Ed, MS, Ed D, PhD); kinesiology (MS, PhD); sport management (MS). Part-time programs available. *Faculty:* 38. *Students:* 206 full-time (113 women), 71 part-time (38 women); includes 81 minority (35 Black or African American, non-Hispanic/Latino; 8 Asian, non-Hispanic/Latino; 33 Hispanic/Latino; 5 Two or more races, non-Hispanic/Latino), 43 international. Average age 29. 167 applicants, 71% accepted, 79 enrolled. In 2013, 68 master's, 16 doctorates awarded. *Degree requirements:* For master's, thesis (for some programs); for doctorate, comprehensive exam, thesis/dissertation. *Entrance requirements:* For master's and doctorate, GRE General Test. Additional exam requirements/recommendations for international students: Required—TOEFL. *Application deadline:* Applications are processed on a rolling basis. Application fee: $50 ($75 for international students). Electronic applications accepted. *Expenses:* Tuition, state resident: full-time $4078; part-time $226.55 per credit hour. Tuition, nonresident: full-time $10,450; part-time $580.55 per credit hour. *Required fees:* $2328; $278.50 per credit hour. $642.45 per semester. *Financial support:* Fellowships with partial tuition reimbursements, research assistantships, teaching assistantships, career-related internships or fieldwork, and institutionally sponsored loans available. Financial award application deadline: 2/15; financial award applicants required to submit FAFSA. *Unit head:* Dr. Richard Kreider, Head, 979-845-1333, Fax: 979-847-8987, E-mail: rkreider@hlkn.tamu.edu. *Application contact:* Christina Escamilla, Senior Academic Advisor I, 979-845-4530, E-mail: cescamil@tamu.edu.
Website: http://hlknweb.tamu.edu/.

Texas A&M University–Commerce, Graduate School, College of Education and Human Services, Department of Health and Human Performance, Commerce, TX 75429-3011. Offers exercise physiology (MS); health and human performance (M Ed); health promotion (MS); health, kinesiology and sports studies (Ed D); motor performance (MS); sport studies (MS). Part-time programs available. *Degree requirements:* For master's, comprehensive exam, thesis (for some programs). *Entrance requirements:* For master's, GRE General Test. Electronic applications accepted. *Expenses:* Tuition, state resident: full-time $3630; part-time $2420 per year. Tuition, nonresident: full-time $9948; part-time $6632.16 per year. *Required fees:* $1006 per year. Tuition and fees vary according to course load. *Faculty research:* Teaching, physical fitness.

Texas A&M University–Corpus Christi, Graduate Studies and Research, College of Education, Corpus Christi, TX 78412-5503. Offers counseling (MS, PhD), including counseling (MS), counselor education (PhD); curriculum and instruction (MS, Ed D); early childhood education (MS); educational administration (MS); educational leadership (Ed D); educational technology (MS); elementary education (MS); kinesiology (MS); reading (MS); secondary education (MS); special education (MS). Part-time and evening/weekend programs available. *Degree requirements:* For master's, comprehensive exam, thesis (for some programs); for doctorate, comprehensive exam, thesis/dissertation. *Entrance requirements:* For master's, GRE General Test. Additional exam requirements/recommendations for international students: Required—TOEFL. Electronic applications accepted.

Texas A&M University–Kingsville, College of Graduate Studies, College of Education, Department of Health and Kinesiology, Kingsville, TX 78363. Offers MA, MS. Part-time programs available. *Faculty:* 4 full-time (0 women). *Students:* 16 full-time (7 women), 15 part-time (11 women); includes 15 minority (1 Black or African American, non-Hispanic/Latino; 12 Hispanic/Latino; 2 Two or more races, non-Hispanic/Latino), 4 international. Average age 26. 16 applicants, 94% accepted, 11 enrolled. In 2013, 7 master's awarded. *Degree requirements:* For master's, comprehensive exam, thesis or alternative. *Entrance requirements:* For master's, GRE General Test, minimum GPA of 3.0. *Application deadline:* For fall admission, 6/1 for domestic students; for spring admission, 11/15 for domestic students. Applications are processed on a rolling basis. Application fee: $35 ($50 for international students). *Financial support:* Teaching assistantships, Federal Work-Study, institutionally sponsored loans, and tuition waivers (partial) available. Financial award application deadline: 5/15. *Faculty research:* Body composition, electromyography. *Unit head:* Dr. Mike Daniel, Head, 361-593-2301, E-mail: m-daniel@tamuk.edu. *Application contact:* Dr. Alberto M. Olivares, Dean, College of Graduate Studies, 361-593-2808, Fax: 361-593-3412, E-mail: a-olivares@tamuk.edu.

Texas A&M University–San Antonio, Department of Curriculum and Kinesiology, San Antonio, TX 78224. Offers bilingual education (MA); early childhood education (M Ed); kinesiology (MS); reading (MS); special education (M Ed), including educational diagnostician, instructional specialist. Part-time and evening/weekend programs available. *Degree requirements:* For master's, comprehensive exam, thesis or alternative. *Entrance requirements:* For master's, MAT. Additional exam requirements/recommendations for international students: Required—TOEFL (minimum score 550 paper-based; 80 iBT), IELTS (minimum score 6). Electronic applications accepted.

Texas Christian University, Harris College of Nursing and Health Sciences, Department of Kinesiology, Fort Worth, TX 76129-0002. Offers MS. Part-time programs available. *Faculty:* 9 full-time (5 women). *Students:* 11 full-time (4 women), 7 part-time (4 women); includes 3 minority (1 Black or African American, non-Hispanic/Latino; 2 Hispanic/Latino). Average age 24. 16 applicants, 88% accepted, 7 enrolled. In 2013, 3 master's awarded. *Degree requirements:* For master's, thesis. *Entrance requirements:* For master's, GRE General Test, course work in kinesiology. Additional exam requirements/recommendations for international students: Required—TOEFL. *Application deadline:* For fall admission, 3/1 for domestic and international students; for spring admission, 12/1 for domestic and international students. Applications are processed on a rolling basis. Application fee: $60. *Expenses: Tuition:* Part-time $1270 per credit hour. Tuition and fees vary according to course load and program. *Financial support:* In 2013–14, 11 students received support, including 8 research assistantships with full tuition reimbursements available (averaging $8,000 per year), 3 teaching assistantships; unspecified assistantships also available. Financial award application deadline: 3/1. *Faculty research:* Exercise physiology, motor control, sport psychology, nutrition and disease. *Unit head:* Dr. Joel Mitchell, Chair, 817-257-7665, E-mail: j.mitchell@tcu.edu. *Application contact:* Admissions, TCU Graduate Studies Office, 817-257-7515, Fax: 817-257-7484, E-mail: frogmail@tcu.edu.
Website: http://www.kinesiology.tcu.edu.

Texas Woman's University, Graduate School, College of Health Sciences, Department of Kinesiology, Denton, TX 76201. Offers adapted physical education (MS, PhD); biomechanics (MS, PhD); coaching (MS); exercise physiology (MS, PhD); pedagogy (MS); sport management (MS, PhD). Part-time and evening/weekend programs available. *Faculty:* 11 full-time (5 women), 3 part-time/adjunct (2 women). *Students:* 48 full-time (35 women), 105 part-time (70 women); includes 42 minority (26 Black or African American, non-Hispanic/Latino; 2 American Indian or Alaska Native, non-Hispanic/Latino; 5 Asian, non-Hispanic/Latino; 9 Hispanic/Latino), 16 international. Average age 30. 51 applicants, 69% accepted, 25 enrolled. In 2013, 55 master's, 3 doctorates awarded. Terminal master's awarded for partial completion of doctoral program. *Degree requirements:* For master's, comprehensive exam, thesis or alternative; for doctorate, comprehensive exam, thesis/dissertation, qualifying exam. *Entrance requirements:* For master's, GRE General Test (biomechanics emphasis only), 2 letters of reference, curriculum vitae, interview (adapted physical education emphasis only); for doctorate, GRE General Test (biomechanics emphasis only), interview, 3 letters of reference, curriculum vitae. Additional exam requirements/recommendations for international students: Required—TOEFL (minimum score 550 paper-based; 79 iBT). *Application deadline:* For fall admission, 7/1 priority date for domestic students, 3/1 for international students; for spring admission, 11/1 priority date for domestic students, 7/1 for international students. Applications are processed on a rolling basis. Application fee: $50 ($75 for international students). Electronic applications accepted. *Expenses:* Tuition, state resident: full-time $4182; part-time $233.32 per credit hour. Tuition, nonresident: full-time $10,716; part-time $595.32 per credit hour. *Financial support:* In 2013–14, 46 students received support, including 7 research assistantships (averaging $10,659 per year), 14 teaching assistantships (averaging $10,659 per year); career-related internships or fieldwork, Federal Work-Study, institutionally sponsored loans, scholarships/grants, traineeships, health care benefits, and unspecified assistantships also available. Support available to part-time students. Financial award application deadline: 3/1; financial award applicants required to submit FAFSA. *Faculty research:* Exercise and Type 2 diabetes risk, bone mineral density and exercise in special populations, obesity in children, factors influencing sport consumer behavior and loyalty, roles and responsibilities of paraeducators in adapted physical education. *Total annual research expenditures:* $200,485. *Unit head:* Dr. Charlotte (Barney) Sanborn, Chair, 940-898-2575, Fax: 940-898-2581, E-mail: dnichols@twu.edu. *Application contact:* Dr. Samuel Wheeler, Assistant Director of Admissions, 940-898-3188, Fax: 940-898-3081, E-mail: wheelersr@twu.edu.
Website: http://www.twu.edu/kinesiology/.

Towson University, Program in Kinesiology, Towson, MD 21252-0001. Offers MS. *Students:* 22 part-time (9 women); includes 1 minority (Black or African American, non-Hispanic/Latino). *Entrance requirements:* For master's, minimum GPA of 3.0; undergraduate degree in physical education or post-baccalaureate teacher certification in physical education; certification/licensure to teach physical education or minimum of 3 years of full-time physical education teaching experience; essay; 2 recommendation forms. *Application deadline:* Applications are processed on a rolling basis. Application fee: $45. Electronic applications accepted. *Unit head:* Dr. Martha James, Graduate Program Director, 410-704-3169, E-mail: mjames@towson.edu. *Application contact:* Alicia Arkell-Kleis, Information Contact, 410-704-6004, Fax: 410-704-4675, E-mail: grads@towson.edu.
Website: http://grad.towson.edu/program/master/knes-ms/.

Université de Montréal, Department of Kinesiology, Montréal, QC H3C 3J7, Canada. Offers kinesiology (M Sc, DESS); physical activity (M Sc, PhD). *Degree requirements:* For master's, one foreign language, thesis (for some programs); for doctorate, one foreign language, thesis/dissertation, general exam. Electronic applications accepted. *Faculty research:* Physiology of exercise, psychology of sports, biomechanics, dance, sociology of sports.

Université de Sherbrooke, Faculty of Physical Education and Sports, Program in Physical Education, Sherbrooke, QC J1K 2R1, Canada. Offers kinanthropology (M Sc); physical activity (Diploma). *Degree requirements:* For master's, thesis. *Entrance requirements:* For master's, minimum GPA of 2.7; for Diploma, bachelor's degree in physical education. *Faculty research:* Physical fitness, nutrition, human factors, sociology, teaching.

Université du Québec à Montréal, Graduate Programs, Program in Human Movement Studies, Montréal, QC H3C 3P8, Canada. Offers M Sc. Part-time programs available. *Degree requirements:* For master's, thesis optional. *Entrance requirements:* For master's, appropriate bachelor's degree or equivalent and proficiency in French.

Université Laval, Faculty of Medicine, Graduate Programs in Medicine, Programs in Kinesiology, Québec, QC G1K 7P4, Canada. Offers M Sc, PhD. Terminal master's awarded for partial completion of doctoral program. *Degree requirements:* For master's, thesis; for doctorate, comprehensive exam, thesis/dissertation. *Entrance requirements:* For master's and doctorate, French exam, knowledge of French, comprehension of written English. Electronic applications accepted.

The University of Alabama, Graduate School, College of Education, Department of Kinesiology, Tuscaloosa, AL 35487-0312. Offers alternative sport pedagogy (MA); exercise science (MA, PhD); human performance (MA); sport management (MA); sport pedagogy (MA, PhD). Part-time programs available. *Faculty:* 8 full-time (1 woman). *Students:* 58 full-time (18 women), 29 part-time (15 women); includes 15 minority (9 Black or African American, non-Hispanic/Latino; 1 Asian, non-Hispanic/Latino; 2 Hispanic/Latino; 3 Two or more races, non-Hispanic/Latino), 7 international. Average age 30. 74 applicants, 74% accepted, 32 enrolled. In 2013, 26 master's, 4 doctorates awarded. *Degree requirements:* For master's, comprehensive exam, thesis optional; for doctorate, comprehensive exam, thesis/dissertation. *Entrance requirements:* For master's and doctorate, GRE, MAT, minimum GPA of 3.0. Additional exam requirements/recommendations for international students: Required—TOEFL. *Application deadline:* Applications are processed on a rolling basis. Application fee: $50 ($60 for international students). Electronic applications accepted. *Expenses:* Tuition, state resident: full-time $9450. Tuition, nonresident: full-time $23,950. *Financial support:* In 2013–14, 14 students received support, including 26 teaching assistantships with full and partial tuition reimbursements available (averaging $12,366 per year); fellowships and research assistantships also available. Financial award applicants required to submit FAFSA. *Faculty research:* Race, gender and sexuality in sports; physical education teacher socialization; disability sports; physical activity and health; environmental physiology. *Unit head:* Dr. Matt Curtner-Smith, Department Head and Professor, 205-348-9209, Fax: 205-348-0867, E-mail: msmith@bamaed.ua.edu. *Application contact:* Dr. Kathy S. Wetzel, Assistant Dean for Student Services, 205-348-1154, Fax: 205-348-0080, E-mail: kwetzel@bamaed.ua.edu.
Website: http://education.ua.edu/academics/kine/.

University of Arkansas, Graduate School, College of Education and Health Professions, Department of Health, Human Performance and Recreation, Program in Kinesiology, Fayetteville, AR 72701-1201. Offers MS, PhD. *Degree requirements:* For doctorate, thesis/dissertation. *Entrance requirements:* For doctorate, GRE General Test. Electronic applications accepted.

Kinesiology and Movement Studies

The University of British Columbia, Faculty of Education, School of Human Kinetics, Vancouver, BC V6T 1Z1, Canada. Offers M Sc, MA, MHK, PhD. Part-time programs available. *Degree requirements:* For master's, thesis (for some programs); for doctorate, comprehensive exam, thesis/dissertation. *Entrance requirements:* For doctorate, thesis-based master's degree. Additional exam requirements/recommendations for international students: Required—TOEFL (minimum score 550 paper-based), IELTS. Electronic applications accepted. *Expenses: Tuition, area resident:* Full-time $8000 Canadian dollars. *Faculty research:* Exercise physiology, biomechanics, motor learning, natural sciences, socio-managerial.

University of Calgary, Faculty of Graduate Studies, Faculty of Kinesiology, Calgary, AB T2N 1N4, Canada. Offers M Kin, M Sc, PhD. *Degree requirements:* For master's, thesis (M Sc); for doctorate, thesis/dissertation. *Entrance requirements:* Additional exam requirements/recommendations for international students: Required—TOEFL. Electronic applications accepted. *Faculty research:* Load acting on the human body, muscle mechanics and physiology, optimizing high performance athlete performance, eye movement in sports, analysis of body composition.

University of Central Arkansas, Graduate School, College of Health and Behavioral Sciences, Department of Kinesiology, Conway, AR 72035-0001. Offers MS. Part-time programs available. *Degree requirements:* For master's, comprehensive exam, thesis optional. *Entrance requirements:* For master's, GRE General Test, minimum GPA of 2.7. Additional exam requirements/recommendations for international students: Required—TOEFL (minimum score 550 paper-based; 80 iBT). Electronic applications accepted.

University of Central Missouri, The Graduate School, Warrensburg, MO 6409. Offers accountancy (MA); accounting (MBA); applied mathematics (MS); aviation safety (MA); biology (MS); business administration (MBA); career and technical education leadership (MS); college student personnel administration (MS); communication (MA); computer science (MS); counseling (MS); criminal justice (MS); educational leadership (Ed D); educational technology (MS); elementary and early childhood education (MSE); English (MA); environmental studies (MA); finance (MBA); history (MA); human services/ educational technology (Ed S); human services/learning resources (Ed S); human services/professional counseling (Ed S); industrial hygiene (MS); industrial management (MS); information systems (MBA); information technology (MS); kinesiology (MS); library science and information services (MS); literacy education (MSE); marketing (MBA); mathematics (MS); music (MA); occupational safety management (MS); psychology (MS); rural family nursing (MS); school administration (MSE); social gerontology (MS); sociology (MA); special education (MSE); speech language pathology (MS); superintendency (Ed S); teaching (MAT); teaching English as a second language (MA); technology (MS); technology management (PhD); theatre (MA). Part-time programs available. *Faculty:* 233. *Students:* 890 full-time (396 women), 1,486 part-time (1,001 women); includes 192 minority (97 Black or African American, non-Hispanic/Latino; 9 American Indian or Alaska Native, non-Hispanic/Latino; 32 Asian, non-Hispanic/Latino; 40 Hispanic/Latino; 3 Native Hawaiian or other Pacific Islander, non-Hispanic/Latino; 11 Two or more races, non-Hispanic/Latino), 539 international. Average age 31. 1,953 applicants, 75% accepted. In 2013, 719 master's, 58 other advanced degrees awarded. *Degree requirements:* For master's and Ed S, comprehensive exam (for some programs), thesis (for some programs). *Entrance requirements:* Additional exam requirements/recommendations for international students: Required—TOEFL (minimum score 550 paper-based; 79 iBT). *Application deadline:* For fall admission, 6/1 for domestic students; for spring admission, 10/1 for domestic and international students. Applications are processed on a rolling basis. Application fee: $30 ($75 for international students). Electronic applications accepted. *Expenses:* Tuition, state resident: full-time $7326; part-time $276.25 per credit hour. Tuition, nonresident: full-time $13,956; part-time $552.50 per credit hour. *Required fees:* $29 per credit hour. *Financial support:* In 2013–14, 118 students received support, including 271 research assistantships with full and partial tuition reimbursements available (averaging $7,500 per year), 109 teaching assistantships with full and partial tuition reimbursements available (averaging $7,500 per year); career-related internships or fieldwork, Federal Work-Study, scholarships/ grants, and administrative and laboratory assistantships also available. Support available to part-time students. Financial award application deadline: 3/1; financial award applicants required to submit FAFSA. *Unit head:* Dr. Joseph Vaughn, Assistant Provost for Research/Dean, 660-543-4092, Fax: 660-543-4778, E-mail: vaughn@ ucmo.edu. *Application contact:* Brittany Lawrence, Graduate Student Services Coordinator, 660-543-4621, Fax: 660-543-4778, E-mail: gradinfo@ucmo.edu.
Website: http://www.ucmo.edu/graduate/.

University of Colorado Boulder, Graduate School, College of Arts and Sciences, Department of Integrative Physiology, Boulder, CO 80309. Offers MS, PhD. *Faculty:* 23 full-time (8 women). *Students:* 68 full-time (35 women), 6 part-time (1 woman); includes 12 minority (3 Asian, non-Hispanic/Latino; 7 Hispanic/Latino; 2 Two or more races, non-Hispanic/Latino), 2 international. Average age 26. 83 applicants, 28% accepted, 20 enrolled. In 2013, 24 master's, 7 doctorates awarded. Terminal master's awarded for partial completion of doctoral program. *Degree requirements:* For master's, comprehensive exam, thesis or alternative; for doctorate, thesis/dissertation. *Entrance requirements:* For master's, GRE General Test, minimum undergraduate GPA of 2.75. *Application deadline:* For fall admission, 1/15 for domestic students, 12/15 for international students. Applications are processed on a rolling basis. Application fee: $50 ($60 for international students). Electronic applications accepted. *Financial support:* In 2013–14, 184 students received support, including 28 fellowships (averaging $8,335 per year), 38 research assistantships with full and partial tuition reimbursements available (averaging $17,566 per year), 47 teaching assistantships with full and partial tuition reimbursements available (averaging $26,509 per year); institutionally sponsored loans, scholarships/grants, health care benefits, and unspecified assistantships also available. Financial award application deadline: 2/1; financial award applicants required to submit FAFSA. *Faculty research:* Aging/gerontology, human physiology, nervous system, neurophysiology, physiological controls and systems. *Total annual research expenditures:* $7.6 million.
Website: http://www.colorado.edu/intphys/.

University of Delaware, College of Arts and Sciences, Interdisciplinary Program in Biomechanics and Movement Science, Newark, DE 19716. Offers MS, PhD. Part-time programs available. Terminal master's awarded for partial completion of doctoral program. *Degree requirements:* For master's, thesis; for doctorate, thesis/dissertation. *Entrance requirements:* For master's and doctorate, GRE General Test, minimum undergraduate GPA of 3.0. Additional exam requirements/recommendations for international students: Required—TOEFL (minimum score 550 paper-based). Electronic applications accepted. *Faculty research:* Muscle modeling, gait, motor control, human movement.

University of Delaware, College of Health Sciences, Department of Kinesiology and Applied Physiology, Newark, DE 19716. Offers MS, PhD.

University of Florida, Graduate School, College of Health and Human Performance, Department of Applied Physiology and Kinesiology, Gainesville, FL 32611. Offers athletic training/sport medicine (MS); biobehavioral science (MS); clinical exercise physiology (MS); health and human performance (PhD), including applied physiology and kinesiology, biobehavioral science, exercise physiology; human performance (MS). *Faculty:* 18 full-time (3 women), 3 part-time/adjunct (1 woman). *Students:* 73 full-time (32 women), 6 part-time (3 women); includes 9 minority (1 Black or African American, non-Hispanic/Latino; 3 Asian, non-Hispanic/Latino; 5 Hispanic/Latino), 18 international. Average age 27. 163 applicants, 23% accepted, 21 enrolled. In 2013, 23 master's, 8 doctorates awarded. *Degree requirements:* For master's, comprehensive exam, thesis (for some programs); for doctorate, comprehensive exam, thesis/dissertation. *Entrance requirements:* For master's and doctorate, GRE General Test, minimum GPA of 3.0. Additional exam requirements/recommendations for international students: Required—TOEFL (minimum score 550 paper-based; 80 iBT), IELTS (minimum score 6). *Application deadline:* For fall admission, 6/1 priority date for domestic students, 6/1 for international students; for spring admission, 9/15 for domestic and international students. Applications are processed on a rolling basis. Application fee: $30. Electronic applications accepted. *Expenses:* Tuition, state resident: full-time $12,640. Tuition, nonresident: full-time $30,000. *Financial support:* In 2013–14, 55 students received support, including 18 research assistantships (averaging $17,260 per year), 41 teaching assistantships (averaging $12,166 per year); unspecified assistantships also available. Financial award application deadline: 2/1; financial award applicants required to submit FAFSA. *Faculty research:* Cardiovascular disease; basic mechanisms that underlie exercise-induced changes in the body at the organ, tissue, cellular and molecular level; development of rehabilitation techniques for regaining motor control after stroke or as a consequence of Parkinson's disease; maintaining optimal health and delaying age-related declines in physiological function; psychomotor mechanisms impacting health and performance across the life span. *Unit head:* Michael Delp, PhD, Professor and Chair, 352-392-0584 Ext. 1338, E-mail: mdelp@hhp.ufl.edu. *Application contact:* Evangelos A. Christou, PhD, Associate Professor and Graduate Coordinator, 352-294-1719 Ext. 1270, E-mail: eachristou@hhp.ufl.edu.
Website: http://apk.hhp.ufl.edu/.

University of Georgia, College of Education, Department of Kinesiology, Athens, GA 30602. Offers MS, PhD. *Entrance requirements:* For master's, GRE General Test or MAT; for doctorate, GRE General Test. Additional exam requirements/ recommendations for international students: Required—TOEFL. Electronic applications accepted.

University of Hawaii at Manoa, Graduate Division, College of Education, Department of Kinesiology and Rehabilitation Science, Honolulu, HI 96822. Offers kinesiology (MS). Part-time programs available. *Degree requirements:* For master's, thesis optional. *Entrance requirements:* For master's, GRE General Test. Additional exam requirements/ recommendations for international students: Required—TOEFL (minimum score 540 paper-based; 76 iBT), IELTS (minimum score 5).

University of Hawaii at Manoa, Graduate Division, College of Education, PhD in Education Program, Honolulu, HI 96822. Offers curriculum and instruction (PhD); educational administration (PhD); educational foundations (PhD); educational policy studies (PhD); educational technology (PhD); exceptionalities (PhD); kinesiology (PhD). Part-time and evening/weekend programs available. *Degree requirements:* For doctorate, thesis/dissertation. *Entrance requirements:* For doctorate, GRE General Test, sample of written work. Additional exam requirements/recommendations for international students: Required—TOEFL (minimum score 600 paper-based; 100 iBT), IELTS (minimum score 7).

University of Houston, College of Liberal Arts and Social Sciences, Department of Health and Human Performance, Houston, TX 77204. Offers exercise science (MS); human nutrition (MS); human space exploration sciences (MS); kinesiology (PhD); physical education (M Ed). *Accreditation:* NCATE (one or more programs are accredited). Part-time and evening/weekend programs available. *Degree requirements:* For master's, comprehensive exam (for some programs), thesis (for some programs); for doctorate, comprehensive exam, thesis/dissertation, qualifying exam, candidacy paper. *Entrance requirements:* For master's, GRE (minimum 35th percentile on each section), minimum cumulative GPA of 3.0; for doctorate, GRE (minimum 35th percentile on each section), minimum cumulative GPA of 3.3. Additional exam requirements/ recommendations for international students: Required—TOEFL (minimum score 550 paper-based; 79 iBT). Electronic applications accepted. *Faculty research:* Biomechanics, exercise physiology, obesity, nutrition, space exploration science.

University of Illinois at Chicago, Graduate College, College of Applied Health Sciences, Program in Kinesiology, Chicago, IL 60607-7128. Offers MS, PhD. Part-time programs available. *Students:* 41 full-time (26 women), 9 part-time (8 women); includes 13 minority (3 Black or African American, non-Hispanic/Latino; 3 Asian, non-Hispanic/ Latino; 5 Hispanic/Latino; 2 Two or more races, non-Hispanic/Latino), 12 international. Average age 29. 135 applicants, 74% accepted, 13 enrolled. In 2013, 10 master's, 5 doctorates awarded. *Degree requirements:* For master's, thesis. *Entrance requirements:* For master's, GRE General Test, minimum GPA of 2.75. Additional exam requirements/ recommendations for international students: Required—TOEFL. *Application deadline:* For fall admission, 1/1 for domestic and international students. Application fee: $40 ($50 for international students). Electronic applications accepted. *Expenses:* Tuition, state resident: full-time $11,066; part-time $3689 per term. Tuition, nonresident: full-time $23,064; part-time $7688 per term. *Required fees:* $3004; $1190 per term. Tuition and fees vary according to course level and program. *Financial support:* Fellowships with full tuition reimbursements, research assistantships with full tuition reimbursements, teaching assistantships with full tuition reimbursements, career-related internships or fieldwork, Federal Work-Study, traineeships, tuition waivers (full), and unspecified assistantships available. Financial award application deadline: 3/1; financial award applicants required to submit FAFSA. *Faculty research:* Mitochondrial biogenesis, glucocorticoid lipid metabolism, at-risk youth, motor control. *Unit head:* Charles B. Walter, Department Head and Professor, 312-355-1713, E-mail: cwalter@uic.edu. *Application contact:* Receptionist, 312-413-2550, E-mail: gradcoll@uic.edu.
Website: http://www.ahs.uic.edu/kn/.

University of Illinois at Urbana–Champaign, Graduate College, College of Applied Health Sciences, Department of Kinesiology and Community Health, Champaign, IL 61820. Offers community health (MS, MSPH, PhD); kinesiology (MS, PhD); public health (MPH); rehabilitation (MS); PhD/MPH. *Students:* 138 (83 women). Application fee: $75 ($90 for international students). *Unit head:* Wojciech Chodzko-Zajko, Head, 217-244-0823, Fax: 217-244-7322, E-mail: wojtek@illinois.edu. *Application contact:* Julie Jenkins, Office Administrator, 217-333-1083, Fax: 217-244-7322, E-mail: jjenkns@ illinois.edu.
Website: http://www.kch.illinois.edu/.

University of Kentucky, Graduate School, College of Education, Department of Kinesiology and Health Promotion, Lexington, KY 40506-0032. Offers exercise science (PhD); health promotion (MS, Ed D); kinesiology (MS); physical education training (Ed D). Terminal master's awarded for partial completion of doctoral program. *Degree requirements:* For master's, comprehensive exam, thesis optional; for doctorate, comprehensive exam, thesis/dissertation. *Entrance requirements:* For master's, GRE General Test, minimum undergraduate GPA of 2.75; for doctorate, GRE General Test, minimum graduate GPA of 3.0. Additional exam requirements/recommendations for international students: Required—TOEFL (minimum score 550 paper-based). Electronic applications accepted.

University of Lethbridge, School of Graduate Studies, Lethbridge, AB T1K 3M4, Canada. Offers accounting (MScM); addictions counseling (M Sc); agricultural biotechnology (M Sc); agricultural studies (M Sc, MA); anthropology (MA); archaeology (M Sc, MA); art (MA, MFA); biochemistry (M Sc); biological sciences (M Sc); biomolecular science (PhD); biosystems and biodiversity (PhD); Canadian studies (MA); chemistry (M Sc); computer science (M Sc); computer science and geographical information science (M Sc); counseling (MC); counseling psychology (M Ed); dramatic arts (MA); earth, space, and physical science (PhD); economics (MA); education (MA); educational leadership (M Ed); English (MA); environmental science (M Sc); evolution and behavior (PhD); exercise science (M Sc); finance (MScM); French (MA); French/German (MA); French/Spanish (MA); general education (M Ed); general management (MScM); geography (M Sc, MA); German (MA); health sciences (M Sc); human resource management and labour relations (MScM); individualized multidisciplinary (M Sc, MA); information systems (MScM); international management (MScM); kinesiology (M Sc, MA); marketing (MScM); mathematics (M Sc); modern languages (MA); music (M Mus, MA); Native American studies (MA); neuroscience (M Sc, PhD); new media (MA, MFA); nursing (M Sc); philosophy (MA); physics (M Sc); policy and strategy (MScM); political science (MA); psychology (M Sc, MA); religious studies (MA); sociology (MA); theatre and dramatic arts (MFA); theoretical and computational science (PhD); urban and regional studies (MA); women and gender studies (MA). Part-time and evening/weekend programs available. *Degree requirements:* For doctorate, comprehensive exam, thesis/dissertation. *Entrance requirements:* For master's, GMAT (for M Sc in management), bachelor's degree in related field, minimum GPA of 3.0 during previous 20 graded semester courses, 2 years teaching or related experience (M Ed); for doctorate, master's degree, minimum graduate GPA of 3.5. Additional exam requirements/recommendations for international students: Required—TOEFL. Application fee: $60 Canadian dollars. *Financial support:* Fellowships, research assistantships, teaching assistantships, scholarships/grants, health care benefits, and unspecified assistantships available. *Faculty research:* Movement and brain plasticity, gibberellin physiology, photosynthesis, carbon cycling, molecular properties of main-group ring components. *Application contact:* School of Graduate Studies, 403-329-2793, Fax: 403-332-5239, E-mail: sgsinquiries@uleth.ca.
Website: http://www.uleth.ca/graduatestudies/.

University of Maine, Graduate School, College of Education and Human Development, Department of Exercise Science and STEM Education, Orono, ME 04469. Offers classroom technology integrationist (CGS); education data specialist (CGS); educational technology coordinator (CGS); kinesiology and physical education (M Ed, MS); science education (M Ed, MS); STEM education (PhD). Part-time and evening/weekend programs available. *Students:* 25 full-time (13 women), 28 part-time (16 women); includes 5 minority (2 Black or African American, non-Hispanic/Latino; 2 American Indian or Alaska Native, non-Hispanic/Latino; 1 Asian, non-Hispanic/Latino), 2 international. Average age 34. 19 applicants, 84% accepted, 12 enrolled. In 2013, 6 master's awarded. *Degree requirements:* For master's, thesis (for some programs); for doctorate, comprehensive exam, thesis/dissertation. *Entrance requirements:* For master's, GRE General Test, MAT; for doctorate, GRE General Test. Additional exam requirements/recommendations for international students: Required—TOEFL. *Application deadline:* For fall admission, 1/15 for domestic students. Applications are processed on a rolling basis. Application fee: $65. Electronic applications accepted. *Expenses:* Tuition, state resident: full-time $7524. Tuition, nonresident: full-time $23,112. *Required fees:* $1970. *Financial support:* In 2013–14, 13 students received support, including 2 teaching assistantships (averaging $14,600 per year). Financial award application deadline: 3/1. *Faculty research:* Integration of technology in K-12 classrooms, instructional theory and practice in science, inquiry-based teaching, professional development, exercise science, adaptive physical education, neuromuscular function/dysfunction. *Unit head:* Dr. Janet Spector, Dean, 207-581-2441, Fax: 207-581-2423. *Application contact:* Scott G. Delcourt, Associate Dean of the Graduate School, 207-581-3291, Fax: 207-581-3232, E-mail: graduate@maine.edu.
Website: http://umaine.edu/edhd/.

University of Manitoba, Faculty of Graduate Studies, Faculty of Kinesiology and Recreation Management, Winnipeg, MB R3T 2N2, Canada. Offers kinesiology and recreation (M Sc, MA).

University of Maryland, College Park, Academic Affairs, School of Public Health, Department of Kinesiology, College Park, MD 20742. Offers MA, PhD. Part-time and evening/weekend programs available. *Faculty:* 28 full-time (8 women), 13 part-time/adjunct (2 women). *Students:* 45 full-time (18 women), 8 part-time (3 women); includes 7 minority (2 Black or African American, non-Hispanic/Latino; 1 Asian, non-Hispanic/Latino; 4 Hispanic/Latino), 14 international. 52 applicants, 12% accepted, 6 enrolled. In 2013, 4 master's, 5 doctorates awarded. *Degree requirements:* For master's, thesis optional; for doctorate, thesis/dissertation. *Entrance requirements:* For master's, GRE General Test, minimum GPA of 3.0, 3 letters of recommendation; for doctorate, GRE General Test, minimum GPA of 3.5, 3 letters of recommendation. *Application deadline:* For fall admission, 1/15 for domestic and international students; for spring admission, 10/1 for domestic students, 6/1 for international students. Applications are processed on a rolling basis. Application fee: $75. Electronic applications accepted. *Expenses:* Tuition, state resident: full-time $10,314; part-time $573 per credit hour. Tuition, nonresident: full-time $22,248; part-time $1236 per credit. *Required fees:* $1446; $403.15 per semester. Tuition and fees vary according to program. *Financial support:* In 2013–14, 11 fellowships with full and partial tuition reimbursements (averaging $31,168 per year), 2 research assistantships (averaging $16,124 per year), 21 teaching assistantships (averaging $15,920 per year) were awarded; career-related internships or fieldwork, Federal Work-Study, and scholarships/grants also available. Support available to part-time students. Financial award applicants required to submit CSS PROFILE or FAFSA. *Faculty research:* Sports, biophysical and professional studies, cognitive motor behavior, exercise physiology. *Total annual research expenditures:* $1.1 million. *Unit head:* Bradley Hatfield, Chair, 301-405-2450, Fax: 301-405-5578, E-mail: bhatfiel@umd.edu. *Application contact:* Dr. Charles A. Caramello, Dean of Graduate School, 301-405-0358, Fax: 301-314-9305, E-mail: ccaramel@umd.edu.

University of Massachusetts Amherst, Graduate School, School of Public Health and Health Sciences, Department of Kinesiology, Amherst, MA 01003. Offers MS, PhD. Part-time programs available. *Faculty:* 21 full-time (8 women). *Students:* 35 full-time (19 women), 8 part-time (3 women); includes 6 minority (1 Black or African American, non-Hispanic/Latino; 1 Asian, non-Hispanic/Latino; 4 Hispanic/Latino), 4 international. Average age 27. 86 applicants, 17% accepted, 13 enrolled. In 2013, 7 master's, 4 doctorates awarded. Terminal master's awarded for partial completion of doctoral program. *Degree requirements:* For master's, comprehensive exam (for some programs), thesis optional; for doctorate, comprehensive exam, thesis/dissertation. *Entrance requirements:* For master's and doctorate, GRE General Test. Additional exam requirements/recommendations for international students: Required—TOEFL (minimum score 550 paper-based; 80 iBT), IELTS (minimum score 6.5). *Application deadline:* For fall admission, 2/1 for domestic and international students. Applications are processed on a rolling basis. Application fee: $75. Electronic applications accepted. *Financial support:* Fellowships with full and partial tuition reimbursements, research assistantships with full and partial tuition reimbursements, teaching assistantships with full and partial tuition reimbursements, career-related internships or fieldwork, Federal Work-Study, scholarships/grants, traineeships, health care benefits, tuition waivers (full and partial), and unspecified assistantships available. Support available to part-time students. Financial award application deadline: 2/1; financial award applicants required to submit FAFSA. *Unit head:* Dr. Graham Caldwell, Graduate Program Director, 413-545-6070, Fax: 413-545-2906. *Application contact:* Lindsay DeSantis, Supervisor of Admissions, 413-545-0722, Fax: 413-577-0010, E-mail: gradadm@grad.umass.edu.
Website: http://www.umass.edu/sphhs/kinesiology/.

University of Michigan, Horace H. Rackham School of Graduate Studies, School of Kinesiology, Ann Arbor, MI 48109. Offers kinesiology (MS, PhD); sport management (AM). *Faculty:* 30 full-time (13 women). *Students:* 72 full-time (34 women); includes 32 minority (3 Black or African American, non-Hispanic/Latino; 22 Asian, non-Hispanic/Latino; 5 Hispanic/Latino; 2 Two or more races, non-Hispanic/Latino). 166 applicants, 42% accepted, 31 enrolled. In 2013, 17 master's, 11 doctorates awarded. Terminal master's awarded for partial completion of doctoral program. *Degree requirements:* For master's, thesis (for some programs); for doctorate, comprehensive exam, thesis/dissertation, oral defense of dissertation. *Entrance requirements:* For master's and doctorate, GRE General Test. Additional exam requirements/recommendations for international students: Required—TOEFL. *Application deadline:* For fall admission, 1/15 priority date for domestic students, 1/15 for international students. Applications are processed on a rolling basis. Application fee: $60 ($75 for international students). Electronic applications accepted. *Expenses:* Contact institution. *Financial support:* In 2013–14, 9 fellowships, 10 research assistantships, 8 teaching assistantships were awarded; Federal Work-Study, scholarships/grants, health care benefits, and unspecified assistantships also available. Financial award application deadline: 1/15. *Faculty research:* Motor development, exercise physiology, biomechanics, sport medicine, sport management. *Unit head:* Dr. Ketra L. Armstrong, Associate Dean for Graduate Programs and Faculty Affairs, 734-647-3027, Fax: 734-647-2808, E-mail: ketra@umich.edu. *Application contact:* Charlene F. Ruloff, Graduate Program Coordinator, 734-764-1343, Fax: 734-647-2808, E-mail: cruloff@umich.edu.
Website: http://www.kines.umich.edu/.

University of Minnesota, Twin Cities Campus, Graduate School, College of Education and Human Development, School of Kinesiology, Division of Kinesiology, Minneapolis, MN 55455-0213. Offers M Ed, MA, MS, PhD. Part-time programs available. *Students:* 140 full-time (51 women), 51 part-time (19 women); includes 18 minority (9 Black or African American, non-Hispanic/Latino; 1 American Indian or Alaska Native, non-Hispanic/Latino; 4 Asian, non-Hispanic/Latino; 4 Hispanic/Latino), 25 international. Average age 27. 172 applicants, 51% accepted, 77 enrolled. In 2013, 87 master's, 11 doctorates awarded. Terminal master's awarded for partial completion of doctoral program. *Degree requirements:* For master's, thesis (for some programs), final oral exam; for doctorate, thesis/dissertation, preliminary written/oral exam, final oral exam. *Entrance requirements:* For master's, GRE or MAT, minimum GPA of 3.0; for doctorate, GRE or MAT, minimum GPA of 3.0, writing sample. *Application deadline:* Applications are processed on a rolling basis. Application fee: $75 ($95 for international students). *Financial support:* Fellowships, research assistantships, teaching assistantships, career-related internships or fieldwork, Federal Work-Study, institutionally sponsored loans, and tuition waivers (full and partial) available. Support available to part-time students. *Unit head:* Dr. Li Li Ji, Director, 612-624-9809, Fax: 612-626-7700, E-mail: llji@umn.edu. *Application contact:* Dr. Jennifer Engler, Assistant Dean, 612-626-2887, Fax: 612-626-7496, E-mail: engle009@umn.edu.
Website: http://www.cehd.umn.edu/kin/kinesiology.

University of Mississippi, Graduate School, School of Applied Sciences, Department of Health, Exercise Science, and Recreation Management, Oxford, MS 38677. Offers exercise science (MS); health and kinesiology (PhD); health promotion (MS); park and recreation management (MA). *Faculty:* 9 full-time (3 women), 3 part-time/adjunct (1 woman). *Students:* 45 full-time (23 women), 14 part-time (9 women); includes 11 minority (8 Black or African American, non-Hispanic/Latino; 1 Asian, non-Hispanic/Latino; 2 Hispanic/Latino), 5 international. In 2013, 19 master's, 1 doctorate awarded. *Degree requirements:* For master's, thesis (for some programs); for doctorate, thesis/dissertation. *Entrance requirements:* For master's, GRE General Test, minimum GPA of 3.0; for doctorate, GRE General Test. Additional exam requirements/recommendations for international students: Required—TOEFL. *Application deadline:* For fall admission, 4/1 for domestic students; for spring admission, 10/1 for domestic students. Applications are processed on a rolling basis. *Financial support:* Scholarships/grants available. Financial award application deadline: 3/1; financial award applicants required to submit FAFSA. *Unit head:* Dr. Scott G. Owens, Chair, 662-915-5844, Fax: 662-915-5525, E-mail: dbramlett@olemiss.edu. *Application contact:* Dr. Christy M. Wyandt, Associate Dean, 662-915-7474, Fax: 662-915-7577, E-mail: cwyandt@olemiss.edu.

University of Nevada, Las Vegas, Graduate College, School of Allied Health Sciences, Department of Kinesiology, Las Vegas, NV 89154-3034. Offers exercise physiology (MS); kinesiology (PhD). Part-time programs available. *Faculty:* 8 full-time (3 women), 2 part-time/adjunct (1 woman). *Students:* 38 full-time (12 women), 16 part-time (8 women); includes 13 minority (1 Black or African American, non-Hispanic/Latino; 1 Asian, non-Hispanic/Latino; 7 Hispanic/Latino; 4 Two or more races, non-Hispanic/Latino), 2 international. Average age 27. 44 applicants, 80% accepted, 21 enrolled. In 2013, 18 master's awarded. *Degree requirements:* For master's, comprehensive exam (for some programs), thesis (for some programs). *Entrance requirements:* For master's, GRE General Test. Additional exam requirements/recommendations for international students: Required—TOEFL (minimum score 550 paper-based; 80 iBT), IELTS (minimum score 7). *Application deadline:* For fall admission, 6/15 for domestic students, 5/1 for international students; for spring admission, 11/15 for domestic students, 10/1 for international students. Application fee: $60 ($95 for international students). Electronic applications accepted. *Expenses:* Tuition, state resident: full-time $4752; part-time $264 per credit. Tuition, nonresident: full-time $18,662; part-time $554.50 per credit. *International tuition:* $18,952 full-time. *Required fees:* $532; $12 per credit. $266 per semester. One-time fee: $35. Tuition and fees vary according to course load and program. *Financial support:* In 2013–14, 29 students received support, including 12 research assistantships with partial tuition reimbursements available (averaging $10,840 per year), 17 teaching assistantships with partial tuition reimbursements available (averaging $8,924 per year); institutionally sponsored loans, scholarships/grants, health care benefits, and unspecified assistantships also available. Financial award application deadline: 3/1. *Faculty research:* Biomechanics of gait, factors in motor skill acquisition and performance, nutritional supplements and performance, lipoprotein chemistry, body composition methods. *Total annual research expenditures:* $149,898. *Unit head:* Richard Tandy, Chair/Professor, 702-895-5080, E-mail: dick.tandy@unlv.edu. *Application contact:* Graduate College Admissions Evaluator, 702-895-3320, Fax: 702-895-4180, E-mail: gradcollege@unlv.edu.
Website: http://kinesiology.unlv.edu/.

University of New Hampshire, Graduate School, School of Health and Human Services, Department of Kinesiology, Durham, NH 03824. Offers adapted physical education (Postbaccalaureate Certificate); kinesiology (MS). Part-time programs available. *Faculty:* 14 full-time (4 women). *Students:* 3 full-time (2 women), 9 part-time (4 women); includes 2 minority (1 Hispanic/Latino; 1 Two or more races, non-Hispanic/Latino). Average age 27. 29 applicants, 48% accepted, 11 enrolled. In 2013, 4 master's

awarded. *Degree requirements:* For master's, thesis or alternative. *Entrance requirements:* For master's, GRE General Test. Additional exam requirements/recommendations for international students: Required—TOEFL (minimum score 550 paper-based; 80 iBT). *Application deadline:* For fall admission, 6/1 priority date for domestic students, 4/1 for international students; for spring admission, 12/1 for domestic students. Applications are processed on a rolling basis. Application fee: $65. *Expenses:* Tuition, state resident: full-time $13,500; part-time $750 per credit hour. Tuition, nonresident: full-time $26,200; part-time $1100 per credit hour. *Required fees:* $1741; $435.25 per term. Tuition and fees vary according to course level, course load, campus/location and program. *Financial support:* In 2013–14, 5 students received support, including 4 teaching assistantships; fellowships, research assistantships, career-related internships or fieldwork, Federal Work-Study, scholarships/grants, and tuition waivers (full and partial) also available. Support available to part-time students. Financial award application deadline: 2/15. *Faculty research:* Exercise specialist, sports studies, special physical education, pediatric exercises and motor behavior. *Unit head:* Dr. Ron Croce, Chairperson, 603-862-2080. *Application contact:* Stephanie McAdams, Administrative Assistant, 603-862-2071, E-mail: kinesiology.dept@unh.edu.
Website: http://chhs.unh.edu/kin/index.

University of North Alabama, College of Education, Department of Health, Physical Education, and Recreation, Florence, AL 35632-0001. Offers health and human performance (MS), including exercise science, kinesiology, wellness and health promotion; secondary education (MA Ed), including physical education (P-12). Part-time and evening/weekend programs available. *Faculty:* 5 full-time (2 women). *Students:* 21 full-time (11 women), 7 part-time (2 women); includes 3 minority (2 Black or African American, non-Hispanic/Latino; 1 Two or more races, non-Hispanic/Latino), 3 international. Average age 27. 30 applicants, 90% accepted, 22 enrolled. In 2013, 3 master's awarded. *Degree requirements:* For master's, comprehensive exam (for some programs), thesis optional. *Entrance requirements:* For master's, MAT or GRE, 3 letters of recommendation, essay. Additional exam requirements/recommendations for international students: Required—TOEFL (minimum score 550 paper-based; 79 iBT), IELTS (minimum score 6). *Application deadline:* For fall admission, 7/1 for domestic and international students; for spring admission, 12/1 for domestic and international students. Applications are processed on a rolling basis. Application fee: $25 ($50 for international students). Electronic applications accepted. *Expenses:* Tuition, state resident: full-time $4968; part-time $3312 per year. Tuition, nonresident: full-time $9936; part-time $6624 per year. *Required fees:* $970; $60.33 per credit. $362 per semester. *Financial support:* Application deadline: 4/1; applicants required to submit FAFSA. *Unit head:* Dr. Thomas E. Coates, Chair, 256-765-4377. *Application contact:* Russ Darracott, Graduate Admissions Counselor, 256-765-4447, E-mail: erdarracott@una.edu.
Website: http://www.una.edu/hper/docs/HPERThesisGuideliens.pdf.

The University of North Carolina at Chapel Hill, School of Medicine and Graduate School, Graduate Programs in Medicine, Chapel Hill, NC 27599. Offers allied health sciences (MPT, MS, Au D, DPT, PhD), including human movement science (MS, PhD), occupational science (MS, PhD), physical therapy (MPT, MS, DPT), rehabilitation counseling and psychology (MS), speech and hearing sciences (MS, Au D, PhD); biochemistry and biophysics (MS, PhD); bioinformatics and computational biology (PhD); biomedical engineering (MS, PhD); cell and developmental biology (PhD); cell and molecular physiology (PhD); genetics and molecular biology (PhD); microbiology and immunology (MS, PhD), including immunology, microbiology; neurobiology (PhD); pathology and laboratory medicine (PhD), including experimental pathology; pharmacology (PhD); MD/PhD. Postbaccalaureate distance learning degree programs offered. Terminal master's awarded for partial completion of doctoral program. *Degree requirements:* For master's, comprehensive exam; for doctorate, thesis/dissertation. Electronic applications accepted. *Expenses:* Contact institution.

The University of North Carolina at Chapel Hill, School of Medicine and Graduate School, Graduate Programs in Medicine, Department of Allied Health Sciences, Curriculum in Human Movement Science, Chapel Hill, NC 27599. Offers PhD. *Degree requirements:* For doctorate, comprehensive exam, thesis/dissertation or alternative. *Entrance requirements:* For doctorate, GRE General Test, curriculum vitae, minimum GPA of 3.0. Additional exam requirements/recommendations for international students: Required—TOEFL (minimum score 550 paper-based). Electronic applications accepted. *Faculty research:* Orthopaedics, neuromuscular, biomedical endocrinology, postural control developmental disabilities.

The University of North Carolina at Chapel Hill, School of Medicine and Graduate School, Graduate Programs in Medicine, Department of Allied Health Sciences, Program in Human Movement Science, Chapel Hill, NC 27599. Offers PhD. *Entrance requirements:* Additional exam requirements/recommendations for international students: Required—TOEFL (minimum score 550 paper-based). Electronic applications accepted.

The University of North Carolina at Charlotte, The Graduate School, College of Health and Human Services, Department of Kinesiology, Charlotte, NC 28223-0001. Offers clinical exercise physiology (Postbaccalaureate Certificate); kinesiology (MS). Part-time programs available. *Faculty:* 12 full-time (5 women). *Students:* 13 full-time (8 women), 18 part-time (12 women); includes 7 minority (5 Black or African American, non-Hispanic/Latino; 1 American Indian or Alaska Native, non-Hispanic/Latino; 1 Hispanic/Latino). Average age 24. 38 applicants, 84% accepted, 15 enrolled. In 2013, 6 master's awarded. *Degree requirements:* For master's, thesis or practicum. *Entrance requirements:* For master's, GRE or MAT. Additional exam requirements/recommendations for international students: Required—TOEFL (minimum score 557 paper-based; 83 iBT). *Application deadline:* For fall admission, 5/1 priority date for domestic students, 5/1 for international students; for spring admission, 10/1 priority date for domestic students, 10/1 for international students. Applications are processed on a rolling basis. Application fee: $75. Electronic applications accepted. *Expenses:* Tuition, state resident: full-time $3522. Tuition, nonresident: full-time $16,051. *Required fees:* $2585. Tuition and fees vary according to course load and program. *Financial support:* In 2013–14, 7 students received support, including 2 research assistantships (averaging $4,785 per year), 5 teaching assistantships (averaging $8,720 per year); career-related internships or fieldwork, institutionally sponsored loans, scholarships/grants, traineeships, and unspecified assistantships also available. Support available to part-time students. Financial award application deadline: 4/1; financial award applicants required to submit FAFSA. *Faculty research:* Biodynamics, systems physiology. *Total annual research expenditures:* $85,878. *Unit head:* Dr. Scott E. Gordon, Chair, 704-687-0855, Fax: 704-687-3180, E-mail: scott.gordon@uncc.edu. *Application contact:* Kathy B. Giddings, Director of Graduate Admissions, 704-687-5503, Fax: 704-687-1668, E-mail: gradadm@uncc.edu.
Website: http://kinesiology.uncc.edu/.

The University of North Carolina at Pembroke, Graduate Studies, School of Education, Pembroke, NC 28372-1510. Offers counseling (MA Ed), including clinical mental health counseling, professional school counseling; elementary education (MA Ed); health, physical education, and recreation (MA), including physical education; middle grades education (MA Ed, MAT); reading education (MA Ed); school administration (MSA). *Accreditation:* NCATE. Part-time and evening/weekend programs available. *Degree requirements:* For master's, comprehensive exam (for some programs), thesis optional. *Entrance requirements:* For master's, GRE General Test or MAT, minimum GPA of 3.0 in major, 2.5 overall. Additional exam requirements/recommendations for international students: Required—TOEFL.

University of North Dakota, Graduate School, College of Education and Human Development, Department of Kinesiology, Grand Forks, ND 58202. Offers MS. Part-time programs available. *Degree requirements:* For master's, thesis or alternative, final or comprehensive examination. *Entrance requirements:* For master's, GRE General Test, minimum GPA of 3.0. Additional exam requirements/recommendations for international students: Required—TOEFL (minimum score 550 paper-based; 79 iBT), IELTS (minimum score 6.5). Electronic applications accepted. *Faculty research:* Exercise physiology, exercise biomechanics, anatomy and physiology, exercise psychology.

University of Northern Iowa, Graduate College, College of Education, School of Health, Physical Education, and Leisure Services, MA Program in Physical Education, Cedar Falls, IA 50614. Offers kinesiology (MA); physical education (MA); teaching/coaching (MA). Part-time and evening/weekend programs available. *Students:* 22 full-time (7 women), 18 part-time (6 women); includes 1 minority (Hispanic/Latino), 4 international. 22 applicants, 91% accepted, 13 enrolled. In 2013, 13 master's awarded. *Degree requirements:* For master's, comprehensive exam, thesis or alternative. *Entrance requirements:* For master's, minimum GPA of 3.0. Additional exam requirements/recommendations for international students: Required—TOEFL (minimum score 500 paper-based; 61 iBT). *Application deadline:* For fall admission, 8/1 priority date for domestic students. Applications are processed on a rolling basis. Application fee: $50 ($70 for international students). Electronic applications accepted. *Financial support:* Career-related internships or fieldwork, Federal Work-Study, and tuition waivers (full and partial) available. Support available to part-time students. Financial award application deadline: 2/1. *Unit head:* Dr. Doris Corbett, Director, 319-273-6475, Fax: 319-273-5958, E-mail: doris.corbett@uni.edu. *Application contact:* Laurie S. Russell, Record Analyst, 319-273-2623, Fax: 319-273-2885, E-mail: laurie.russell@uni.edu.
Website: http://www.grad.uni.edu/degrees-programs/programs/physical-education-ma.

University of North Texas, Robert B. Toulouse School of Graduate Studies, Denton, TN 76203-5017. Offers accounting (MS, PhD); applied anthropology (MA, MS); applied behavior analysis (Certificate); applied technology and performance improvement (M Ed, MS, PhD); art education (MA, PhD); art history (MA); art museum education (Certificate); arts leadership (Certificate); audiology (Au D); behavior analysis (MS); biochemistry and molecular biology (MS, PhD); biology (MA, MS, PhD); business (PhD); business computer information systems (PhD); chemistry (MS, PhD); clinical psychology (PhD); communication studies (MA, MS); computer engineering (MS); computer science (MS); computer science and engineering (PhD); counseling (M Ed, MS, PhD), including clinical mental health counseling (MS), college and university counseling (M Ed, MS), elementary school counseling (M Ed, MS), secondary school counseling (M Ed, MS); counseling psychology (PhD); creative writing (MA); criminal justice (MS); curriculum and instruction (M Ed, PhD), including curriculum studies (PhD), early childhood studies (PhD), language and literacy studies (PhD); decision sciences (MBA); design (MA, MFA), including fashion design (MFA), innovation studies, interior design (MFA); early childhood studies (MS); economics (MS); educational leadership (M Ed, Ed D, PhD); educational psychology (MS), including family studies, gifted and talented (MS, PhD), human development, learning and cognition, research, measurement and evaluation; educational research (PhD), including gifted and talented (MS, PhD), human development and family studies, psychological aspects of sports and exercise, research, measurement and statistics; electrical engineering (MS); emergency management (MPA); engineering systems (MS); English (MA, PhD); environmental science (MS, PhD); experimental psychology (PhD); finance (MBA, MS, PhD); financial management (MPA); French (MA); health psychology and behavioral medicine (PhD); health services management (MBA); higher education (M Ed, Ed D, PhD); history (MA, MS, PhD), including European history (PhD), military history (PhD), United States history (PhD); hospitality management (MS); human resources management (MPA); information science (MS, PhD); information technologies (MBA); information technology and decision sciences (MS); interdisciplinary studies (MA, MS); international sustainable tourism (MS); jazz studies (MM); journalism (MA, MJ, Graduate Certificate), including interactive and virtual digital communication (Graduate Certificate), narrative journalism (Graduate Certificate), public relations (Graduate Certificate); kinesiology (MS); learning technologies (MS, PhD); library science (MS); local government management (MPA); logistics and supply chain management (MBA, PhD); long-term care, senior housing, and aging services (MA, MS); management science (PhD); marketing (MBA, PhD); materials science and engineering (MS, PhD); mathematics (MA, PhD); merchandising (MS); music (MA, MM Ed, PhD), including ethnomusicology (MA), music education (MM Ed, PhD), music theory (MA, PhD), musicology (MA, PhD), performance (MA); nonprofit management (MPA); operations and supply chain management (MBA); performance (MM, DMA); philosophy (MA, PhD); physics (MS, PhD); political science (MA, MS, PhD); public administration and management (PhD), including emergency management, nonprofit management, public financial management, urban management; radio, television and film (MA, MFA); recreation, event and sport management (MS); rehabilitation counseling (MS, Certificate); sociology (MA, MS, PhD); Spanish (MA); special education (M Ed, PhD), including autism intervention (PhD), emotional/behavioral disorders (PhD), mild/moderate disabilities (PhD); speech-language pathology (MA, MS); strategic management (MBA); studio art (MFA); taxation (MS); teaching (M Ed); MBA/MS; MS/MPH; MSES/MBA. Part-time and evening/weekend programs available. Postbaccalaureate distance learning degree programs offered. *Faculty:* 661 full-time (213 women), 240 part-time/adjunct (144 women). *Students:* 3,106 full-time (1,620 women), 3,543 part-time (2,221 women); includes 1,740 minority (533 Black or African American, non-Hispanic/Latino; 15 American Indian or Alaska Native, non-Hispanic/Latino; 286 Asian, non-Hispanic/Latino; 746 Hispanic/Latino; 3 Native Hawaiian or other Pacific Islander, non-Hispanic/Latino; 157 Two or more races, non-Hispanic/Latino), 1,145 international. Average age 32. 6,289 applicants, 43% accepted, 1751 enrolled. In 2013, 1,778 master's, 239 doctorates, 10 other advanced degrees awarded. Terminal master's awarded for partial completion of doctoral program. *Degree requirements:* For master's, variable foreign language requirement, comprehensive exam (for some programs), thesis (for some programs); for doctorate, variable foreign language requirement, comprehensive exam (for some programs), thesis/dissertation; for other advanced degree, variable foreign language requirement, comprehensive exam (for some programs). *Entrance requirements:* For master's and doctorate, GRE, GMAT. Additional exam requirements/recommendations for international students: Required—TOEFL (minimum score 550 paper-based; 79 iBT). *Application deadline:* For fall admission, 7/15 for domestic students, 3/15 for international students; for spring admission, 11/15 for domestic students, 9/15 for international students; for summer admission, 5/1 for domestic students. Applications are processed on a rolling basis. Application fee: $60. Electronic applications accepted. *Financial support:* Fellowships with partial tuition reimbursements, research assistantships with partial tuition reimbursements, teaching assistantships, career-related internships or fieldwork, Federal Work-Study, institutionally sponsored loans, scholarships/grants, health care benefits, and library assistantships available. Support available to part-time students. Financial award applicants required to submit FAFSA.

Unit head: Mark Wardell, Dean, 940-565-2383, E-mail: mark.wardell@unt.edu. *Application contact:* Toulouse School of Graduate Studies, 940-565-2383, Fax: 940-565-2141, E-mail: gradsch@unt.edu. Website: http://tsgs.unt.edu/.

University of Ottawa, Faculty of Graduate and Postdoctoral Studies, Faculty of Health Sciences, School of Human Kinetics, Ottawa, ON K1N 6N5, Canada. Offers MA. *Degree requirements:* For master's, thesis or alternative. *Entrance requirements:* For master's, honors degree or equivalent, minimum B average. Electronic applications accepted. *Faculty research:* Psychosocial sciences, physical and health administration of sport and physical activity, intervention and consultation in sport, physical activity and health.

University of Puerto Rico, Mayagüez Campus, Graduate Studies, College of Arts and Sciences, Department of Physical Education, Mayagüez, PR 00681-9000. Offers kinesiology (MA), including biomechanics, education, exercise physiology, sports training. Part-time programs available. *Faculty:* 18 full-time (7 women), 1 (woman) part-time/adjunct. *Students:* 19 full-time (9 women), 4 part-time (2 women). 14 applicants, 64% accepted, 7 enrolled. In 2013, 2 master's awarded. *Degree requirements:* For master's, thesis optional. *Entrance requirements:* For master's, EXADEP, minimum GPA of 2.5. *Application deadline:* For fall admission, 2/15 for domestic and international students; for spring admission, 9/15 for domestic and international students. Applications are processed on a rolling basis. *Expenses: Tuition, area resident:* Full-time $2466; part-time $822 per year. *International tuition:* $6371 full-time. *Required fees:* $1095; $1095. Tuition and fees vary according to course level, course load and reciprocity agreements. *Financial support:* In 2013–14, 10 students received support, including 10 teaching assistantships (averaging $9,489 per year); fellowships with full tuition reimbursements available, institutionally sponsored loans, and unspecified assistantships also available. *Unit head:* Dr. Margarita Fernandez, Interim Director, 787-832-4040 Ext. 3841, Fax: 787-833-4825, E-mail: margarita.fernandez1@upr.edu. *Application contact:* Aracelys Gonzalez, Secretary, 787-832-4040 Ext. 2008, E-mail: aracelis.gonzalez23@upr.edu. Website: http://ece.uprm.edu/artssciences/edfi/descrip.htm.

University of Regina, Faculty of Graduate Studies and Research, Faculty of Kinesiology and Health Studies, Regina, SK S4S 0A2, Canada. Offers M Sc, PhD. *Faculty:* 18 full-time (7 women), 34 part-time/adjunct (7 women). *Students:* 24 full-time (14 women), 11 part-time (6 women). 12 applicants, 83% accepted. In 2013, 1 master's, 1 doctorate awarded. *Degree requirements:* For master's, thesis; for doctorate, thesis/ dissertation. *Entrance requirements:* For doctorate, writing sample. Additional exam requirements/recommendations for international students: Required—TOEFL (minimum score 580 paper-based; 80 iBT), IELTS (minimum score 6.5). *Application deadline:* Applications are processed on a rolling basis. Application fee: $100. Electronic applications accepted. *Expenses: Tuition, area resident:* Full-time $4338 Canadian dollars. *International tuition:* $7338 Canadian dollars full-time. *Required fees:* $449.25 Canadian dollars. *Financial support:* In 2013–14, 4 fellowships (averaging $6,500 per year), 8 teaching assistantships (averaging $2,399 per year) were awarded; research assistantships and scholarships/grants also available. Financial award application deadline: 6/15. *Faculty research:* Social psychology of physical activity and health, social science of physical activity and recreation, recreation and leisure, sport management, exercise science. *Unit head:* Dr. Craig Chamberlin, Dean, 306-585-4535, Fax: 306-585-5441, E-mail: shanthi.johnson@uregina.ca. *Application contact:* Dr. Shanthi Johnson, Graduate Program Coordinator, 306-585-3180, Fax: 306-585-5693, E-mail: shanthi.johnson@uregina.ca.

University of Saskatchewan, College of Graduate Studies and Research, College of Kinesiology, Saskatoon, SK S7N 5A2, Canada. Offers M Sc, PhD, Diploma. *Degree requirements:* For master's, thesis; for doctorate, thesis/dissertation. *Entrance requirements:* Additional exam requirements/recommendations for international students: Required—TOEFL. *Expenses: Tuition, area resident:* Full-time $3585 Canadian dollars; part-time $585 Canadian dollars per course. Tuition, nonresident: part-time $877 Canadian dollars per course. *International tuition:* $5377 Canadian dollars full-time. *Required fees:* $889.51 Canadian dollars.

The University of South Dakota, Graduate School, School of Education, Division of Kinesiology and Sport Science, Vermillion, SD 57069-2390. Offers MA. *Accreditation:* NCATE. Part-time programs available. *Degree requirements:* For master's, comprehensive exam, thesis or alternative. *Entrance requirements:* For master's, GRE General Test, MAT, minimum GPA of 2.7. Additional exam requirements/ recommendations for international students: Required—TOEFL (minimum score 550 paper-based; 79 iBT). Electronic applications accepted.

University of Southern California, Graduate School, Herman Ostrow School of Dentistry, Division of Biokinesiology and Physical Therapy, Los Angeles, CA 90089. Offers biokinesiology (MS, PhD); physical therapy (DPT). *Accreditation:* APTA (one or more programs are accredited). *Degree requirements:* For master's, comprehensive exam; for doctorate, thesis/dissertation. *Entrance requirements:* For master's and doctorate, GRE (minimum combined score 1200, verbal 600, quantitative 600). Additional exam requirements/recommendations for international students: Required— TOEFL. Electronic applications accepted. *Expenses:* Contact institution. *Faculty research:* Exercise and aging biomechanics, musculoskeletal biomechanics, exercise and hormones related to muscle wasting, computational neurorehabilitation, motor behavior and neurorehabilitation, motor development, infant motor performance.

The University of Tennessee, Graduate School, College of Education, Health and Human Sciences, Department of Exercise, Sport, and Leisure Studies, Program in Exercise Science, Knoxville, TN 37996. Offers biomechanics/sports medicine (MS, PhD); exercise physiology (MS, PhD). *Accreditation:* CEPH (one or more programs are accredited). Part-time programs available. *Degree requirements:* For master's, thesis optional. *Entrance requirements:* For master's, minimum GPA of 2.7. Additional exam requirements/recommendations for international students: Required—TOEFL. Electronic applications accepted. *Expenses:* Tuition, state resident: full-time $9540; part-time $531 per credit hour. Tuition, nonresident: full-time $27,728; part-time $1542 per credit hour. *Required fees:* $1404; $67 per credit hour.

The University of Texas at Austin, Graduate School, College of Education, Department of Kinesiology and Health Education, Austin, TX 78712-1111. Offers behavioral health (PhD); exercise and sport psychology (M Ed, MA); exercise science (M Ed, MS, PhD); health education (M Ed, MS, Ed D, PhD). Part-time programs available. Terminal master's awarded for partial completion of doctoral program. *Degree requirements:* For master's, thesis (for some programs); for doctorate, thesis/ dissertation. *Entrance requirements:* For master's and doctorate, GRE General Test. Additional exam requirements/recommendations for international students: Required— TOEFL. Electronic applications accepted. *Faculty research:* Health promotion, human performance and exercise biochemistry, motor behavior and biomechanics, sport management, aging and pediatric development.

The University of Texas at El Paso, Graduate School, College of Health Sciences, Department of Kinesiology, El Paso, TX 79968-0001. Offers MS. Part-time and evening/ weekend programs available. Postbaccalaureate distance learning degree programs offered (no on-campus study). *Degree requirements:* For master's, thesis optional. *Entrance requirements:* For master's, GRE. Additional exam requirements/

recommendations for international students: Required—TOEFL; Recommended— IELTS. Electronic applications accepted.

The University of Texas at San Antonio, College of Education and Human Development, Department of Kinesiology, Health, and Nutrition, San Antonio, TX 78249-0617. Offers dietetics studies (MSD); health and kinesiology (MS). Part-time and evening/weekend programs available. *Faculty:* 17 full-time (7 women), 1 part-time/ adjunct (0 women). *Students:* 65 full-time (38 women), 66 part-time (29 women); includes 88 minority (12 Black or African American, non-Hispanic/Latino; 4 Asian, non-Hispanic/Latino; 71 Hispanic/Latino; 1 Two or more races, non-Hispanic/Latino), 9 international. Average age 28. 79 applicants, 95% accepted, 45 enrolled. In 2013, 48 master's awarded. *Degree requirements:* For master's, comprehensive exam, thesis optional. *Entrance requirements:* For master's, bachelor's degree with minimum GPA of 3.0 in last 60 hours of coursework; resume; statement of purpose; two letters of recommendation. Additional exam requirements/recommendations for international students: Required—TOEFL (minimum score 550 paper-based; 79 iBT), IELTS (minimum score 6.5). *Application deadline:* For fall admission, 7/1 for domestic students, 4/1 for international students; for spring admission, 11/1 for domestic students, 9/1 for international students; for summer admission, 4/1 for domestic students, 3/1 for international students. Applications are processed on a rolling basis. Application fee: $45 ($80 for international students). Electronic applications accepted. *Expenses:* Tuition, state resident: full-time $4671. Tuition, nonresident: full-time $8708. *International tuition:* $17,415 full-time. *Required fees:* $1924.60. Tuition and fees vary according to course load and degree level. *Faculty research:* Motor behavior, motor skills, exercise and nutrition, athlete efficacy, diabetes prevention. *Unit head:* Dr. Wan Xiang Yao, Chair, 210-458-6224, Fax: 210-452-5873, E-mail: wanxiang.yao@utsa.edu. *Application contact:* Dr. Alberto Cordova, Graduate Advisor of Record, 210-458-6226, Fax: 210-458-5873, E-mail: alberto.cordova@utsa.edu. Website: http://education.utsa.edu/health_and_kinesiology.

The University of Texas at Tyler, College of Nursing and Health Sciences, Department of Health and Kinesiology, Tyler, TX 75799-0001. Offers health and kinesiology (M Ed, MA); health sciences (MS); kinesiology (MS). *Accreditation:* Teacher Education Accreditation Council. Part-time programs available. Postbaccalaureate distance learning degree programs offered. *Degree requirements:* For master's, comprehensive exam (for some programs), thesis (for some programs). *Entrance requirements:* Additional exam requirements/recommendations for international students: Required— TOEFL. Electronic applications accepted. *Faculty research:* Osteoporosis, muscle soreness, economy of locomotion, adoption of rehabilitation programs, effect of inactivity and aging on muscle blood vessels, territoriality.

The University of Texas of the Permian Basin, Office of Graduate Studies, College of Arts and Sciences, Department of Kinesiology, Odessa, TX 79762-0001. Offers MS. Part-time and evening/weekend programs available. Postbaccalaureate distance learning degree programs offered (no on-campus study). *Degree requirements:* For master's, comprehensive exam (for some programs), thesis (for some programs). *Entrance requirements:* For master's, GRE General Test, minimum GPA of 2.5. Additional exam requirements/recommendations for international students: Required— TOEFL (minimum score 550 paper-based).

The University of Texas–Pan American, College of Education, Department of Health and Kinesiology, Edinburg, TX 78539. Offers MS. Part-time and evening/weekend programs available. Postbaccalaureate distance learning degree programs offered (no on-campus study). *Degree requirements:* For master's, comprehensive exam, thesis optional, oral exam. *Entrance requirements:* For master's, minimum GPA of 3.0 in last 60 hours. *Expenses:* Tuition, state resident: full-time $5986; part-time $333 per credit hour. Tuition, nonresident: full-time $12,358; part-time $687 per credit hour. *Required fees:* $782. Tuition and fees vary according to program. *Faculty research:* History, physiology of exercise, fitness levels, Mexican American children, winter tourist profiles, sports psychology.

University of the Incarnate Word, School of Graduate Studies and Research, Dreeben School of Education, Programs in Education, San Antonio, TX 78209-6397. Offers adult education (M Ed, MA); cross-cultural education (M Ed, MA); early childhood literacy (M Ed, MA); general education (M Ed, MA); higher education (PhD); instructional technology (M Ed, MA); international education and entrepreneurship (PhD); kinesiology (M Ed, MA); literacy (M Ed, MA); organizational leadership (PhD); organizational learning and learning (M Ed, MA); reading (M Ed, MA); special education (M Ed, MA); teacher leadership (M Ed, MA). Part-time and evening/weekend programs available. *Faculty:* 17 full-time (9 women), 6 part-time/adjunct (all women). *Students:* 23 full-time (13 women), 187 part-time (122 women); includes 114 minority (24 Black or African American, non-Hispanic/Latino; 1 American Indian or Alaska Native, non-Hispanic/ Latino; 3 Asian, non-Hispanic/Latino; 85 Hispanic/Latino; 1 Two or more races, non-Hispanic/Latino), 30 international. Average age 41. 52 applicants, 67% accepted, 25 enrolled. In 2013, 12 master's, 14 doctorates awarded. *Degree requirements:* For master's, capstone; for doctorate, thesis/dissertation, qualifying exam. *Entrance requirements:* For master's, baccalaureate degree; minimum foundation GPA of 2.5; interview; for doctorate, master's degree; interview; supervised writing sample. Additional exam requirements/recommendations for international students: Required— TOEFL (minimum score 560 paper-based; 83 iBT). *Application deadline:* Applications are processed on a rolling basis. Application fee: $20. Electronic applications accepted. *Expenses:* Tuition: Part-time $815 per credit hour. *Required fees:* $86 per credit hour. One-time fee: $40 part-time. Tuition and fees vary according to degree level and program. *Financial support:* In 2013–14, 5 research assistantships were awarded; Federal Work-Study and scholarships/grants also available. Financial award applicants required to submit FAFSA. *Unit head:* Dr. Denise Staudt, Dean, Dreeben School of Education, 210-829-2762, E-mail: staudt@uiwtx.edu. *Application contact:* Andrea Cyterski-Acosta, Dean of Enrollment, 210-829-6005, Fax: 210-829-3921, E-mail: admis@uiwtx.edu. Website: http://www.uiw.edu/education/index.htm.

University of the Incarnate Word, School of Graduate Studies and Research, School of Nursing and Health Professions, Programs in Kinesiology, San Antonio, TX 78209-6397. Offers MS. Part-time and evening/weekend programs available. *Faculty:* 4 full-time (2 women), 1 (woman) part-time/adjunct. *Students:* 7 full-time (2 women), 13 part-time (11 women); includes 12 minority (1 Black or African American, non-Hispanic/ Latino; 11 Hispanic/Latino). Average age 27. 16 applicants, 75% accepted, 5 enrolled. In 2013, 4 master's awarded. *Degree requirements:* For master's, capstone. *Entrance requirements:* For master's, GRE, master's and baccalaureate degrees in kinesiology or related field; teacher certification in physical education or other teaching field plus athletic coaching experience, or letter of recommendation from professional in field. Additional exam requirements/recommendations for international students: Required— TOEFL (minimum score 560 paper-based; 83 iBT). *Application deadline:* Applications are processed on a rolling basis. Application fee: $20. Electronic applications accepted. *Expenses:* Tuition: Part-time $815 per credit hour. *Required fees:* $86 per credit hour. One-time fee: $40 part-time. Tuition and fees vary according to degree level and program. *Financial support:* Federal Work-Study and scholarships/grants available. *Unit head:* Dr. William Carleton, Chair, 210-829-3966, Fax: 210-829-3174, E-mail:

carleton@uiwtx.edu. *Application contact:* Andrea Cyterski-Acosta, Dean of Enrollment, 210-829-6005, Fax: 210-829-3921, E-mail: admis@uiwtx.edu.
Website: http://www.uiw.edu/gradstudies/documents/mskinesiology.pdf.

University of Victoria, Faculty of Graduate Studies, Faculty of Education, School of Exercise Science, Physical, and Health Education, Victoria, BC V8W 2Y2, Canada. Offers coaching studies (co-operative education) (M Ed); kinesiology (M Sc, MA); leisure service administration (MA); physical education (MA). Part-time programs available. *Degree requirements:* For master's, comprehensive exam (for some programs), thesis (for some programs). *Entrance requirements:* For master's, minimum B average. Additional exam requirements/recommendations for international students: Required—TOEFL (minimum score 575 paper-based), IELTS (minimum score 7). Electronic applications accepted. *Faculty research:* Children and exercise, mental skills in sports, teaching effectiveness, neural control of human movement, physical performance and health.

University of Virginia, Curry School of Education, Department of Human Services, Program in Health and Physical Education, Charlottesville, VA 22903. Offers M Ed, Ed D. *Students:* 42 full-time (25 women), 7 part-time (3 women); includes 1 minority (Asian, non-Hispanic/Latino), 1 international. Average age 26. 32 applicants, 53% accepted, 6 enrolled. In 2013, 39 master's, 1 doctorate awarded. *Entrance requirements:* For master's and doctorate, GRE General Test, 2 letters of recommendation. Additional exam requirements/recommendations for international students: Required—TOEFL (minimum score 600 paper-based; 90 iBT), IELTS (minimum score 7). *Application deadline:* Applications are processed on a rolling basis. Application fee: $60. Electronic applications accepted. *Expenses:* Tuition, state resident: part-time $334 per credit hour. Tuition, nonresident: part-time $1224 per credit hour. *Financial support:* Applicants required to submit FAFSA. *Unit head:* Arthur L. Weltman, Chair, Kinesiology, 434-924-6191, E-mail: alw2v@virginia.edu. *Application contact:* Lynn Renfroe, Information Contact, 434-924-6254, E-mail: ldr9t@virginia.edu.
Website: http://curry.virginia.edu/academics/degrees/bachelor-master-in-teaching/b-mt-in-health-physical-education.

University of Virginia, Curry School of Education, Program in Education, Charlottesville, VA 22903. Offers administration and supervision (PhD); applied developmental science (PhD); counselor education (PhD); curriculum and instruction (PhD); early childhood special education (MT); education evaluation (PhD); educational psychology (PhD); educational research (PhD); elementary education (MT); English education (MT, PhD); foreign language education (MT); higher education (PhD); instructional technology (PhD); kinesiology (MT, PhD); math education (PhD); reading education (PhD); research, statistics and evaluation (PhD); school psychology (PhD); science education (PhD); social studies education (MT, PhD); special education (PhD); world languages education (MT). *Students:* 474 full-time (379 women), 35 part-time (19 women); includes 89 minority (30 Black or African American, non-Hispanic/Latino; 1 American Indian or Alaska Native, non-Hispanic/Latino; 26 Asian, non-Hispanic/Latino; 19 Hispanic/Latino; 13 Two or more races, non-Hispanic/Latino), 21 international. Average age 26. 312 applicants, 49% accepted, 80 enrolled. In 2013, 137 master's, 38 doctorates awarded. *Degree requirements:* For master's, comprehensive exam (for some programs), field project; for doctorate, comprehensive exam, thesis/dissertation. *Entrance requirements:* For doctorate, GRE General Test. Additional exam requirements/recommendations for international students: Required—TOEFL (minimum score 600 paper-based; 90 iBT), IELTS (minimum score 7). *Application deadline:* Applications are processed on a rolling basis. Application fee: $60. Electronic applications accepted. *Expenses:* Tuition, state resident: part-time $334 per credit hour. Tuition, nonresident: part-time $1224 per credit hour. *Financial support:* Fellowships, research assistantships, and teaching assistantships available. Financial award application deadline: 1/5; financial award applicants required to submit FAFSA. *Unit head:* Robert C. Pianta, Dean, 434-924-3334, E-mail: pianta@virginia.edu. *Application contact:* Office of Admissions and Student Services, 434-924-0742, E-mail: curry-admissions@virginia.edu.
Website: http://curry.virginia.edu/teacher-education.

University of Waterloo, Graduate Studies, Faculty of Applied Health Sciences, Department of Kinesiology, Waterloo, ON N2L 3G1, Canada. Offers M Sc, PhD. Part-time programs available. *Degree requirements:* For master's, thesis; for doctorate, comprehensive exam, thesis/dissertation. *Entrance requirements:* For master's, honors degree, minimum B average, writing sample; for doctorate, GRE (recommended), master's degree, minimum B average, writing sample. Additional exam requirements/recommendations for international students: Required—TOEFL, TWE. Electronic applications accepted. *Faculty research:* Work physiology, biomechanics and neural control of human movement, psychomotor learning and performance, aging, health and well-being, work and health.

The University of Western Ontario, Faculty of Graduate Studies, Health Sciences Division, School of Kinesiology, London, ON N6A 5B8, Canada. Offers M Sc, MA, PhD. *Degree requirements:* For master's, thesis optional; for doctorate, comprehensive exam, thesis/dissertation. *Entrance requirements:* For doctorate, MA in physical education or kinesiology. Additional exam requirements/recommendations for international students: Required—Michigan English Language Assessment Battery, TOEFL or IELTS. *Faculty research:* Exercise physiology/biochemistry, sports injuries, sport psychology, sport history, sport philosophy.

University of Windsor, Faculty of Graduate Studies, Faculty of Human Kinetics, Windsor, ON N9B 3P4, Canada. Offers MHK. Part-time programs available. *Degree requirements:* For master's, thesis optional. *Entrance requirements:* For master's, minimum B average. Additional exam requirements/recommendations for international students: Required—TOEFL (minimum score 600 paper-based). Electronic applications accepted. *Faculty research:* Movement sciences, sport and lifestyle management, historical and sociological studies of sport.

University of Wisconsin–Madison, Graduate School, School of Education, Department of Kinesiology, Madison, WI 53706-1380. Offers kinesiology (MS, PhD); occupational therapy (MS, PhD). *Accreditation:* AOTA. *Degree requirements:* For doctorate, thesis/dissertation. *Entrance requirements:* For master's and doctorate, GRE General Test. Application fee: $56. Electronic applications accepted. *Expenses:* Tuition, state resident: full-time $10,728; part-time $790 per credit. Tuition, nonresident: full-time $24,054; part-time $1623 per credit. *Required fees:* $1130; $119 per credit. *Financial support:* Fellowships with full tuition reimbursements, research assistantships with full tuition reimbursements, teaching assistantships with full tuition reimbursements, and project assistantships available. *Unit head:* Dr. Dorothy Edwards, Chair, 608-262-1654, E-mail: dfedwards@education.wisc.edu. *Application contact:* 608-262-2433, Fax: 608-262-5134, E-mail: gradadmiss@mail.bascom.wisc.edu.
Website: http://www.education.wisc.edu/kinesiology.

University of Wisconsin–Milwaukee, Graduate School, College of Health Sciences, Program in Kinesiology, Milwaukee, WI 53201-0413. Offers MS. Part-time programs available. *Faculty:* 8 full-time (4 women), 1 part-time/adjunct (0 women). *Students:* 12 full-time (8 women), 7 part-time (3 women); includes 2 minority (1 Asian, non-Hispanic/Latino; 1 Two or more races, non-Hispanic/Latino). Average age 27. 43 applicants, 44% accepted, 7 enrolled. In 2013, 13 master's awarded. *Degree requirements:* For master's, comprehensive exam, thesis optional. *Entrance requirements:* For master's, GRE General Test. Additional exam requirements/recommendations for international students: Required—TOEFL (minimum score 550 paper-based; 79 iBT), IELTS (minimum score 6.5). *Application deadline:* For fall admission, 1/1 priority date for domestic students; for spring admission, 9/1 for domestic students. Applications are processed on a rolling basis. Application fee: $56 ($96 for international students). *Financial support:* In 2013–14, 2 fellowships, 7 teaching assistantships were awarded; research assistantships, career-related internships or fieldwork, unspecified assistantships, and project assistantships also available. Support available to part-time students. Financial award application deadline: 4/15. *Unit head:* Kristian O'Connor, Department Chair, 414-229-2680, E-mail: krisocon@uwm.edu. *Application contact:* Roger O. Smith, General Information Contact, 414-229-6697, Fax: 414-229-6697, E-mail: smithro@uwm.edu.
Website: http://www4.uwm.edu/chs/academics/kinesiology/kinesiology_masters/.

University of Wyoming, College of Health Sciences, Division of Kinesiology and Health, Laramie, WY 82071. Offers MS. *Accreditation:* NCATE. Part-time programs available. Postbaccalaureate distance learning degree programs offered (no on-campus study). *Degree requirements:* For master's, comprehensive exam (for some programs), thesis (for some programs). *Entrance requirements:* For master's, GRE General Test, minimum GPA of 3.0. Additional exam requirements/recommendations for international students: Required—TOEFL. Electronic applications accepted. *Faculty research:* Teacher effectiveness, effects of exercising on heart function, physiological responses of overtraining, psychological benefits of physical activity, health behavior.

Washington University in St. Louis, School of Medicine, Interdisciplinary Program in Movement Science, St. Louis, MO 63130-4899. Offers PhD. *Degree requirements:* For doctorate, thesis/dissertation. *Entrance requirements:* For doctorate, GRE General Test. Electronic applications accepted.

Wayne State University, College of Education, Division of Kinesiology, Health and Sports Studies, Detroit, MI 48202. Offers adapted physical education (Certificate); coaching (Certificate); elementary physical education (Certificate); exercise and sport science (M Ed); health education (M Ed, Certificate); kinesiology (M Ed, PhD), including exercise and sport science (PhD), physical education pedagogy (PhD); physical education (M Ed); secondary physical education (Certificate); sports administration (MA); wellness clinician/research (M Ed). Part-time programs available. *Students:* 42 full-time (27 women), 78 part-time (38 women); includes 43 minority (35 Black or African American, non-Hispanic/Latino; 1 Asian, non-Hispanic/Latino; 5 Hispanic/Latino; 2 Two or more races, non-Hispanic/Latino), 5 international. Average age 30. 120 applicants, 48% accepted, 30 enrolled. In 2013, 32 master's awarded. *Degree requirements:* For master's, thesis (for some programs); for doctorate, thesis/dissertation. *Entrance requirements:* For master's and doctorate, minimum undergraduate GPA of 3.0, undergraduate degree directly relating to the field of specialization being applied for, or undergraduate degree accompanied by extensive educational background in a closely-related field. Additional exam requirements/recommendations for international students: Required—TOEFL (minimum score 79 iBT), TWE (minimum score 5.5), Michigan English Language Assessment Battery (minimum score 85); Recommended—IELTS (minimum score 6.5). *Application deadline:* For fall admission, 6/1 priority date for domestic students, 5/1 priority date for international students; for winter admission, 10/1 priority date for domestic students, 9/1 priority date for international students; for spring admission, 2/1 priority date for domestic students, 1/1 priority date for international students. Applications are processed on a rolling basis. Application fee: $0. Electronic applications accepted. *Expenses:* Tuition, state resident: part-time $554.15 per credit. Tuition, nonresident: part-time $1200.35 per credit. *Required fees:* $42.15 per credit. $268.30 per semester. Tuition and fees vary according to course load and program. *Financial support:* In 2013–14, 22 students received support, including 4 fellowships with tuition reimbursements available (averaging $13,050 per year), 5 research assistantships with tuition reimbursements available (averaging $16,508 per year); career-related internships or fieldwork, Federal Work-Study, scholarships/grants, health care benefits, and unspecified assistantships also available. Support available to part-time students. Financial award application deadline: 3/31; financial award applicants required to submit FAFSA. *Faculty research:* Exercise and sport science, nutrition and physical activity interventions, school and community health, obesity prevention. *Total annual research expenditures:* $1.3 million. *Unit head:* Dr. Nate McCaughtry, Assistant Dean, Division of Kinesiology, Health and Sport Studies/Director, Center for School Health, 313-577-0014, Fax: 313-577-5002, E-mail: aj4391@wayne.edu. *Application contact:* Janice Green, Assistant Dean, 313-577-1605, E-mail: jwgreen@wayne.edu.
Website: http://coe.wayne.edu/kinesiology/index.php.

Wayne State University, College of Education, Division of Teacher Education, Detroit, MI 48202. Offers art education (M Ed), including art therapy; autism spectrum disorders (Certificate); bilingual/bicultural education (M Ed, Certificate); career and technical education (M Ed, Certificate); cognitive impairment (Certificate); curriculum and instruction (Ed D, PhD, Ed S), including art education (PhD), bilingual education (Ed D, Ed S), bilingual-bicultural education (PhD), career and technical education (MAT, Ed D, PhD, Ed S), early childhood education (MAT, Ed D, PhD, Ed S), elementary education, English as a second language (MAT, Ed D, Ed S), English education (MAT, Ed D, PhD, Ed S), foreign language education (MAT, PhD), K-12 curriculum, mathematics education (MAT, Ed D, PhD, Ed S), science education (MAT, Ed D, PhD, Ed S), secondary education, social studies education (MAT, Ed S), social studies education: secondary (Ed D, PhD); early childhood education (M Ed, Certificate); elementary education (M Ed, MAT), including children's literature (MAT), early childhood education (MAT, Ed D, PhD, Ed S), general elementary education (MAT); elementary or secondary education (MAT), including bilingual/bicultural education, English as a second language (MAT, Ed D, Ed S), mathematics education (MAT, Ed D, PhD, Ed S), science education (MAT, Ed D, PhD, Ed S), social studies education (MAT, Ed S); emotionally impaired (Certificate); English as a second language (Certificate); English education (M Ed), including secondary; foreign language education (M Ed); K-12 reading specialist (Certificate); learning disabilities (Certificate); mathematics education (M Ed), including secondary; reading (M Ed, Ed S); reading, language and literature (Ed D); science education (M Ed), including secondary; secondary education (MAT), including art education (K-12), career and technical education (MAT, Ed D, PhD, Ed S), English education (MAT, Ed D, PhD, Ed S), foreign language education (MAT, PhD), kinesiology; social studies education (M Ed), including secondary; special education (M Ed, MAT, Ed D, PhD, Ed S); visual arts education (Certificate). Part-time programs available. *Faculty:* 36 full-time (25 women), 55 part-time/adjunct (43 women). *Students:* 218 full-time (163 women), 448 part-time (344 women); includes 218 minority (177 Black or African American, non-Hispanic/Latino; 2 American Indian or Alaska Native, non-Hispanic/Latino; 11 Asian, non-Hispanic/Latino; 19 Hispanic/Latino; 1 Native Hawaiian or other Pacific Islander, non-Hispanic/Latino; 8 Two or more races, non-Hispanic/Latino), 10 international. Average age 37. 258 applicants, 30% accepted, 52 enrolled. In 2013, 183 master's, 10 doctorates, 35 other advanced degrees awarded. *Degree requirements:* For master's, thesis, essay or project (for some M Ed programs), professional field experience (for MAT programs); for doctorate, thesis/dissertation. *Entrance requirements:* For master's, Michigan Basic Skills Test (MA in teaching), admission to the graduate school, verification of participation in group work with children and Michigan State Police Criminal Background check; for doctorate, minimum

undergraduate GPA of 3.0, graduate 3.5; interview, curriculum vitae; references. Additional exam requirements/recommendations for international students: Required—TOEFL (minimum score 550 paper-based; 79 iBT), TWE (minimum score 5.5), Michigan English Language Assessment Battery (minimum score 85); Recommended—IELTS (minimum score 6.5). *Application deadline:* For fall admission, 6/1 priority date for domestic students, 5/1 priority date for international students; for winter admission, 10/1 priority date for domestic students, 9/1 priority date for international students; for spring admission, 2/1 priority date for domestic students, 1/1 priority date for international students. Applications are processed on a rolling basis. Application fee: $0. Electronic applications accepted. *Expenses:* Tuition, state resident: part-time $554.15 per credit. Tuition, nonresident: part-time $1200.35 per credit. *Required fees:* $42.15 per credit. $268.30 per semester. Tuition and fees vary according to course load and program. *Financial support:* In 2013–14, 83 students received support, including 1 fellowship (averaging $16,842 per year), 1 research assistantship with tuition reimbursement available (averaging $21,229 per year); career-related internships or fieldwork, Federal Work-Study, scholarships/grants, health care benefits, and unspecified assistantships also available. Support available to part-time students. Financial award application deadline: 3/31; financial award applicants required to submit FAFSA. *Faculty research:* Improving students' skill achievement in mathematics; improving elementary children's understanding of informational text; teachers' use of their pedagogical and mathematical knowledge in the interactive work of teaching; the intersection of identity construction in teaching and learning; identifying effective methods of literacy instruction and assessments for bilingual students in elementary language arts classrooms. *Total annual research expenditures:* $368,105. *Unit head:* Dr. Kathleen Crawford-McKinney, Assistant Dean, 313-577-0122. *Application contact:* Janice Green, Assistant Dean, 313-577-1605, E-mail: jwgreen@wayne.edu.
Website: http://coe.wayne.edu/ted/index.php.

West Chester University of Pennsylvania, College of Health Sciences, Department of Kinesiology, West Chester, PA 19383. Offers adapted physical education (Certificate); exercise and sport physiology (MS), including athletic training, exercise and sport physiology; general physical education (MS); sport management and athletics (MPA). Part-time and evening/weekend programs available. Postbaccalaureate distance learning degree programs offered (no on-campus study). *Faculty:* 6 full-time (5 women). *Students:* 25 full-time (13 women), 10 part-time (4 women); includes 5 minority (1 Black or African American, non-Hispanic/Latino; 1 Asian, non-Hispanic/Latino; 2 Hispanic/Latino; 1 Two or more races, non-Hispanic/Latino), 1 international. Average age 27. 33 applicants, 97% accepted, 18 enrolled. In 2013, 15 master's, 6 other advanced degrees awarded. *Degree requirements:* For master's, thesis or report (for MS); 2 internships, capstone course including research project or thesis (for MPA). *Entrance requirements:* For master's, GRE (for MS), 2 letters of recommendation, transcripts, and statement of professional goals (for MS); 2 letters of reference, resume, and career goal statement (for MPA). Additional exam requirements/recommendations for international students: Required—TOEFL (minimum score 550 paper-based; 80 iBT). *Application deadline:* For fall admission, 4/15 priority date for domestic students, 3/15 for international students; for spring admission, 10/15 priority date for domestic students, 9/1 for international students. Applications are processed on a rolling basis. Application fee: $45. Electronic applications accepted. *Expenses:* Tuition, state resident: full-time $7956; part-time $442 per credit. Tuition, nonresident: full-time $11,934; part-time $663 per credit. *Required fees:* $2134.20; $106.24 per credit. Tuition and fees vary according to campus/location and program. *Financial support:* Unspecified assistantships available. Support available to part-time students. Financial award application deadline: 2/15; financial award applicants required to submit FAFSA. *Faculty research:* Metabolism during exercise, biomechanics, rating of perceived exertion, motor learning. *Unit head:* Dr. Frank Fry, Chair/Graduate Coordinator for the MS in General Physical Education Program, 610-436-2610, Fax: 610-436-2860, E-mail: ffry@wcupa.edu. *Application contact:* Dr. David Stearne, Graduate Coordinator for the Exercise and Sport Physiology Programs, 610-436-2347, Fax: 610-436-2860, E-mail: dstearne@wcupa.edu.
Website: http://www.wcupa.edu/_academics/sch_shs.hpe/.

Western Illinois University, School of Graduate Studies, College of Education and Human Services, Department of Kinesiology, Program in Kinesiology, Macomb, IL 61455-1390. Offers MS. Part-time programs available. *Students:* 31 full-time (14 women), 2 part-time (1 woman); includes 1 minority (Black or African American, non-Hispanic/Latino), 4 international. Average age 24. In 2013, 13 master's awarded. *Entrance requirements:* For master's, minimum GPA of 3.0. Additional exam requirements/recommendations for international students: Required—TOEFL (minimum score 550 paper-based; 80 iBT). *Application deadline:* Applications are processed on a rolling basis. Application fee: $30. Electronic applications accepted. *Financial support:* In 2013–14, 19 students received support, including 14 research assistantships with full tuition reimbursements available (averaging $7,544 per year), 5 teaching assistantships with full tuition reimbursements available (averaging $8,688 per year). Financial award applicants required to submit FAFSA. *Unit head:* Dr. Janet Wigglesworth, Chairperson, 309-298-1981. *Application contact:* Dr. Nancy Parsons, Associate Provost and Director of Graduate Studies, 309-298-1806, Fax: 309-298-2345, E-mail: grad-office@wiu.edu.
Website: http://wiu.edu/kinesiology.

Wilfrid Laurier University, Faculty of Graduate and Postdoctoral Studies, Faculty of Science, Department of Kinesiology and Physical Education, Waterloo, ON N2L 3C5, Canada. Offers physical activity and health (M Sc). *Degree requirements:* For master's, thesis. *Entrance requirements:* For master's, honours degree in kinesiology, health, physical education with a minimum B+ in kinesiology and health-related courses. Additional exam requirements/recommendations for international students: Required—TOEFL (minimum score 89 iBT). Electronic applications accepted. *Faculty research:* Biomechanics, health, exercise physiology, motor control, sport psychology.

York University, Faculty of Graduate Studies, Faculty of Health, Program in Kinesiology and Health Science, Toronto, ON M3J 1P3, Canada. Offers M Sc, MA, PhD. Part-time programs available. *Degree requirements:* For master's, thesis or alternative; for doctorate, comprehensive exam, thesis/dissertation. Electronic applications accepted.

Physical Education

Adams State University, The Graduate School, Department of Human Performance and Physical Education, Alamosa, CO 81101. Offers MA. *Accreditation:* Teacher Education Accreditation Council. Part-time programs available. *Degree requirements:* For master's, comprehensive exam. *Entrance requirements:* For master's, GRE General Test or MAT, minimum undergraduate GPA of 2.75.

Adelphi University, Ruth S. Ammon School of Education, Program in Physical Education and Human Performance Science, Garden City, NY 11530-0701. Offers aging (Certificate); physical/educational human performance science (MA). Part-time and evening/weekend programs available. *Students:* 40 full-time (21 women), 37 part-time (16 women); includes 12 minority (4 Black or African American, non-Hispanic/Latino; 1 Asian, non-Hispanic/Latino; 7 Hispanic/Latino), 1 international. Average age 28. In 2013, 30 master's awarded. *Degree requirements:* For master's, internship. *Entrance requirements:* For master's, 3 letters of recommendation, resume. Additional exam requirements/recommendations for international students: Required—TOEFL (minimum score 550 paper-based; 80 iBT). *Application deadline:* For fall admission, 4/1 for international students; for spring admission, 11/1 for international students. Applications are processed on a rolling basis. Application fee: $50. Electronic applications accepted. *Expenses: Tuition:* Full-time $32,530; part-time $1010 per credit. *Required fees:* $1150. Tuition and fees vary according to degree level and program. *Financial support:* Career-related internships or fieldwork, Federal Work-Study, tuition waivers (full), and unspecified assistantships available. Financial award application deadline: 2/15; financial award applicants required to submit FAFSA. *Faculty research:* Physical education for the handicapped, sport sociology, sport pedagogy. *Unit head:* Dr. Ronald Feingold, Chair, 516-877-4764, E-mail: feingold@adelphi.edu. *Application contact:* Christine Murphy, Director of Admissions, 516-877-3050, Fax: 516-877-3039, E-mail: graduateadmissions@adelphi.edu.

Alabama Agricultural and Mechanical University, School of Graduate Studies, School of Education, Area in Health and Physical Education, Huntsville, AL 35811. Offers physical education (M Ed, MS). Part-time and evening/weekend programs available. *Degree requirements:* For master's, comprehensive exam. *Entrance requirements:* For master's, GRE General Test. Additional exam requirements/recommendations for international students: Required—TOEFL (minimum score 500 paper-based; 61 iBT). Electronic applications accepted. *Faculty research:* Cardiorespiratory assessment.

Alabama State University, College of Education, Department of Health, Physical Education, and Recreation, Montgomery, AL 36101-0271. Offers health education (M Ed); physical education (M Ed). Part-time programs available. *Faculty:* 4 full-time (all women), 1 part-time/adjunct (0 women). *Students:* 5 full-time (2 women), 8 part-time (3 women); includes 12 minority (all Black or African American, non-Hispanic/Latino). Average age 27. 20 applicants, 55% accepted, 9 enrolled. In 2013, 6 master's awarded. *Degree requirements:* For master's, comprehensive exam. *Entrance requirements:* For master's, GRE General Test, MAT, writing competency test. Additional exam requirements/recommendations for international students: Required—TOEFL (minimum score 500 paper-based). *Application deadline:* For fall admission, 7/15 for domestic students; for spring admission, 12/15 for domestic students. Applications are processed on a rolling basis. Application fee: $10. *Expenses:* Tuition, state resident: full-time $7958; part-time $343 per credit hour. Tuition, nonresident: full-time $14,132; part-time $686 per credit hour. *Required fees:* $446 per term. One-time fee: $1784 full-time; $892 part-time. Tuition and fees vary according to course load. *Financial support:* In 2013–14, research assistantships (averaging $9,450 per year) were awarded. *Faculty research:* Risk factors for heart disease in the college-age population, cardiovascular reactivity for the Cold Pressor Test. *Unit head:* Dr. Doris Screws, Chair, 334-229-4504, Fax: 334-229-4928, E-mail: dscrews@alasu.edu. *Application contact:* Dr. William Person, Dean of Graduate Studies, 334-229-4274, Fax: 334-229-4928, E-mail: wperson@alasu.edu.
Website: http://www.alasu.edu/academics/colleges—departments/college-of-education/health-physical-education—recreation/index.aspx.

Albany State University, College of Education, Albany, GA 31705-2717. Offers early childhood education (M Ed); education specialist (Ed S); educational leadership and administration (M Ed); health, physical education and recreation (M Ed); middle grades education (M Ed); school counseling (M Ed); special education (M Ed). *Accreditation:* NCATE. Part-time and evening/weekend programs available. Postbaccalaureate distance learning degree programs offered (minimal on-campus study). *Degree requirements:* For master's, comprehensive exam, internship, GACE Content Exam. *Entrance requirements:* For master's, GRE or MAT. Electronic applications accepted. *Faculty research:* GACE preparation, STEM (science, technology, engineering, and mathematics), technology education, special education, professional teacher development, health implications liberation philosophy, NET-Q, learning community, disabled or at-risk students.

Alcorn State University, School of Graduate Studies, School of Psychology and Education, Alcorn State, MS 39096-7500. Offers agricultural education (MS Ed); elementary education (MS Ed, Ed S); guidance and counseling (MS Ed); industrial education (MS Ed); secondary education (MS Ed), including health and physical education; special education (MS Ed). *Accreditation:* NCATE. *Degree requirements:* For master's, thesis optional.

American University of Puerto Rico, Program in Education, Bayamón, PR 00960-2037. Offers art education (M Ed); elementary education 4-6 (M Ed); elementary education K-3 (M Ed); general science education (M Ed); physical education (M Ed); special education (M Ed). *Faculty:* 17 part-time/adjunct (7 women). *Students:* 55 full-time (42 women), 105 part-time (96 women); all minorities (all Hispanic/Latino). Average age 33. 120 applicants, 99% accepted, 81 enrolled. In 2013, 52 master's awarded. *Entrance requirements:* For master's, EXADEP, GRE, or MAT, 2 letters of recommendation, minimum GPA of 2.5. *Application deadline:* For fall admission, 8/1 for domestic students; for winter admission, 10/18 for domestic students; for spring admission, 3/15 for domestic students. Applications are processed on a rolling basis. Application fee: $25. *Expenses: Tuition:* Part-time $240 per credit. Tuition and fees vary according to course load. *Unit head:* Dr. Jose A. Ramirez-Figueroa, Education and Technology Department Director/Chancellor, 787-620-2040 Ext. 2010, Fax: 787-620-2958, E-mail: jramirez@aupr.edu. *Application contact:* Keren I. Llanos-Figueroa, Information Contact, 787-620-2040 Ext. 2021, Fax: 787-785-7377, E-mail: oficnaadmisiones@aupr.edu.

Arizona State University at the Tempe campus, Mary Lou Fulton Teachers College, Program in Curriculum and Instruction, Phoenix, AZ 85069. Offers curriculum and instruction (M Ed, MA, PhD); elementary education (M Ed); physical education (MPE); secondary education (M Ed). Part-time and evening/weekend programs available. Postbaccalaureate distance learning degree programs offered (minimal on-campus study). Terminal master's awarded for partial completion of doctoral program. *Degree requirements:* For master's, thesis or alternative, applied project, interactive Program of

Physical Education

Study (iPOS) submitted before completing 50 percent of required credit hours; for doctorate, comprehensive exam, thesis/dissertation, interactive Program of Study (iPOS) submitted before completing 50 percent of required credit hours. *Entrance requirements:* For master's, GRE or GMAT (for some programs), minimum GPA of 3.0 or equivalent in last 2 years of work leading to bachelor's degree, 3 letters of recommendation, personal statement describing research and career goals, curriculum vitae or resume, IVP fingerprint clearance card (for those seeking Arizona certification); for doctorate, GRE or GMAT (depending on program), minimum GPA of 3.0 or equivalent in last 2 years of work leading to bachelor's degree, 3 letters of recommendation, personal statement describing research and career goals, curriculum vitae or resume. Additional exam requirements/recommendations for international students: Required—TOEFL, IELTS, or PTE. Electronic applications accepted. *Expenses:* Contact institution. *Faculty research:* Early childhood, media and computers, elementary education, secondary education, English education, bilingual education, language and literacy, science education, engineering education, exercise and wellness education.

Arkansas State University, Graduate School, College of Education and Behavioral Science, Department of Health, Physical Education, and Sport Sciences, Jonesboro, AR 72467. Offers exercise science (MS); physical education (MSE, SCCT); sports administration (MS). Part-time programs available. *Faculty:* 9 full-time (3 women). *Students:* 20 full-time (5 women), 35 part-time (11 women); includes 19 minority (13 Black or African American, non-Hispanic/Latino; 5 Hispanic/Latino; 1 Two or more races, non-Hispanic/Latino), 8 international. Average age 26. 53 applicants, 70% accepted, 29 enrolled. In 2013, 18 master's awarded. *Degree requirements:* For master's, comprehensive exam, thesis or alternative; for SCCT, comprehensive exam. *Entrance requirements:* For master's, GRE General Test or MAT, appropriate bachelor's degree, official transcripts, immunization records, statement of goals, letters of recommendation; for SCCT, GRE General Test or MAT, interview, master's degree, official transcript, immunization records. Additional exam requirements/recommendations for international students: Required—TOEFL (minimum score 550 paper-based; 79 iBT), IELTS (minimum score 6), PTE (minimum score 56). *Application deadline:* For fall admission, 7/1 for domestic and international students; for spring admission, 11/15 for domestic students, 11/14 for international students. Applications are processed on a rolling basis. Application fee: $30 ($40 for international students). Electronic applications accepted. *Expenses:* Tuition, state resident: full-time $4284; part-time $238 per credit hour. Tuition, nonresident: full-time $8568; part-time $476 per credit hour. *International tuition:* $9268 full-time. *Required fees:* $1098; $61 per credit hour. $25 per term. Tuition and fees vary according to course load and program. *Financial support:* In 2013–14, 18 students received support. Teaching assistantships, career-related internships or fieldwork, scholarships/grants, and unspecified assistantships available. Financial award application deadline: 7/1; financial award applicants required to submit FAFSA. *Unit head:* Dr. Jim Stillwell, Chair, 870-972-3066, Fax: 870-972-3096, E-mail: jstillwel@astate.edu. *Application contact:* Vickey Ring, Graduate Admissions Coordinator, 870-972-3029, Fax: 870-972-3857, E-mail: vickeyring@astate.edu.
Website: http://www.astate.edu/college/education/departments/health-physical-educations-and-sport-sciences/index.dot.

Arkansas Tech University, College of Education, Russellville, AR 72801. Offers college student personnel (MS); elementary education (M Ed); instructional improvement (M Ed); instructional technology (M Ed); physical education (M Ed); teaching (MAT). *Accreditation:* NCATE. Part-time and evening/weekend programs available. Postbaccalaureate distance learning degree programs offered (no on-campus study). *Students:* 58 full-time (39 women), 304 part-time (240 women); includes 76 minority (58 Black or African American, non-Hispanic/Latino; 3 American Indian or Alaska Native, non-Hispanic/Latino; 4 Asian, non-Hispanic/Latino; 8 Hispanic/Latino; 3 Two or more races, non-Hispanic/Latino), 2 international. Average age 32. In 2013, 130 master's awarded. *Degree requirements:* For master's, comprehensive exam, thesis optional, action research project. *Entrance requirements:* Additional exam requirements/recommendations for international students: Required—TOEFL (minimum score 550 paper-based; 79 iBT), IELTS (minimum score 6.5). *Application deadline:* For fall admission, 3/1 priority date for domestic students, 5/1 priority date for international students; for spring admission, 10/1 priority date for domestic and international students. Applications are processed on a rolling basis. Application fee: $25 ($75 for international students). Electronic applications accepted. *Expenses:* Tuition, state resident: full-time $5976; part-time $249 per credit hour. Tuition, nonresident: full-time $11,952; part-time $498 per credit hour. *Required fees:* $411 per semester. Tuition and fees vary according to course load. *Financial support:* In 2013–14, research assistantships with full tuition reimbursements (averaging $4,800 per year), teaching assistantships with full tuition reimbursements (averaging $4,800 per year) were awarded; career-related internships or fieldwork, Federal Work-Study, scholarships/grants, health care benefits, and unspecified assistantships also available. Support available to part-time students. Financial award application deadline: 4/15; financial award applicants required to submit FAFSA. *Unit head:* Dr. Sherry Field, Dean, 479-968-0418, E-mail: sfield@atu.edu. *Application contact:* Dr. Mary B. Gunter, Dean of Graduate College, 479-968-0398, Fax: 479-964-0542, E-mail: gradcollege@atu.edu.
Website: http://www.atu.edu/education/.

Ashland University, Dwight Schar College of Education, Department of Sport Sciences, Ashland, OH 44805-3702. Offers adapted physical education (M Ed); applied exercise science (M Ed); sport education (M Ed); sport management (M Ed). Part-time programs available. *Degree requirements:* For master's, practicum, inquiry seminar, thesis, or internship. *Entrance requirements:* For master's, teaching certificate or license, bachelor's degree, minimum cumulative GPA of 2.75. Additional exam requirements/recommendations for international students: Required—TOEFL. *Faculty research:* Coaching, legal issues, strength and conditioning, sport management rating of perceived exertion, youth fitness, geriatric exercise science.

Auburn University, Graduate School, College of Education, Department of Kinesiology, Auburn University, AL 36849. Offers exercise science (M Ed, MS, PhD); health promotion (M Ed, MS); kinesiology (PhD); physical education/teacher education (M Ed, MS, Ed D, Ed S). *Accreditation:* NCATE. Part-time programs available. *Faculty:* 19 full-time (9 women). *Students:* 89 full-time (43 women), 21 part-time (9 women); includes 17 minority (15 Black or African American, non-Hispanic/Latino; 1 Asian, non-Hispanic/Latino; 1 Hispanic/Latino), 5 international. Average age 26. 136 applicants, 71% accepted, 60 enrolled. In 2013, 38 master's, 10 doctorates awarded. *Degree requirements:* For master's, thesis (for some programs); for doctorate, thesis/dissertation; for Ed S, exam, field project. *Entrance requirements:* For master's, GRE General Test; for doctorate and Ed S, GRE General Test, interview, master's degree. *Application deadline:* For fall admission, 7/7 for domestic students; for spring admission, 11/24 for domestic students. Applications are processed on a rolling basis. Application fee: $50 ($60 for international students). Electronic applications accepted. *Expenses:* Tuition, state resident: full-time $8262; part-time $459 per credit hour. Tuition, nonresident: full-time $24,786; part-time $1377 per credit hour. Tuition and fees vary according to degree level and program. *Financial support:* Research assistantships, teaching assistantships, and Federal Work-Study available. Support available to part-time students. Financial award application deadline: 3/15; financial award applicants required to submit FAFSA. *Faculty research:* Biomechanics, exercise physiology, motor skill learning, school health, curriculum development. *Unit head:* Dr. Mary E. Rudisill, Head, 334-844-1458. *Application contact:* Dr. George Flowers, Dean of the Graduate School, 334-844-2125.

Azusa Pacific University, School of Education, Department of Advanced Studies, Program in Physical Education, Azusa, CA 91702-7000. Offers M Ed. Evening/weekend programs available. *Degree requirements:* For master's, core exams, oral exam, oral presentation. *Entrance requirements:* For master's, BA in physical education or 12 units of course work in education, minimum GPA of 3.0.

Ball State University, Graduate School, College of Applied Science and Technology, School of Physical Education, Muncie, IN 47306-1099. Offers MA, MAE, MS, PhD. *Faculty:* 12 full-time (2 women), 4 part-time/adjunct (1 woman). *Students:* 39 full-time (16 women), 79 part-time (23 women); includes 4 minority (3 Black or African American, non-Hispanic/Latino; 1 Hispanic/Latino), 6 international. Average age 24. 84 applicants, 35% accepted, 18 enrolled. In 2013, 74 master's, 1 doctorate awarded. *Degree requirements:* For doctorate, thesis/dissertation. *Entrance requirements:* For master's, resume; for doctorate, GRE General Test, minimum graduate GPA of 3.2. Application fee: $50. *Financial support:* In 2013–14, 78 students received support, including 20 teaching assistantships with full tuition reimbursements available (averaging $11,080 per year); research assistantships also available. Financial award application deadline: 3/1. *Unit head:* Dr. Mitchell Whaley, Director, 765-285-5818, Fax: 765-285-8254, E-mail: mwhaley@bsu.edu. *Application contact:* Dr. Robert Morris, Associate Provost for Research and Dean of the Graduate School, 765-285-5723, Fax: 765-285-1328, E-mail: rmorris@bsu.edu.
Website: http://cms.bsu.edu/Academics/CollegesandDepartments/PhysicalEducation.aspx.

Baylor University, Graduate School, School of Education, Department of Health, Human Performance and Recreation, Waco, TX 76798. Offers community health education (MPH); exercise physiology (MS Ed); kinesiology, exercise nutrition and health promotion (PhD); sport management (MS Ed); sport pedagogy (MS Ed). *Accreditation:* NCATE. Part-time programs available. *Faculty:* 13 full-time (5 women), 3 part-time/adjunct (1 woman). *Students:* 79 full-time (40 women), 28 part-time (14 women); includes 26 minority (9 Black or African American, non-Hispanic/Latino; 1 American Indian or Alaska Native, non-Hispanic/Latino; 3 Asian, non-Hispanic/Latino; 8 Hispanic/Latino; 5 Two or more races, non-Hispanic/Latino), 9 international. 30 applicants, 87% accepted. In 2013, 48 master's awarded. *Degree requirements:* For master's, comprehensive exam, thesis optional; for doctorate, comprehensive exam, thesis/dissertation. *Entrance requirements:* For master's and doctorate, GRE General Test. Additional exam requirements/recommendations for international students: Required—TOEFL. *Application deadline:* For fall admission, 2/1 priority date for domestic students, 2/1 for international students; for spring admission, 10/1 for domestic and international students. Applications are processed on a rolling basis. Application fee: $25. Electronic applications accepted. *Expenses: Tuition:* Full-time $25,866; part-time $1437 per credit hour. *Required fees:* $2736; $152 per credit hour. Tuition and fees vary according to course load and program. *Financial support:* In 2013–14, 35 students received support, including 1 research assistantship with tuition reimbursement available, 33 teaching assistantships with tuition reimbursements available; career-related internships or fieldwork, Federal Work-Study, institutionally sponsored loans, tuition waivers (partial), and unspecified assistantships also available. Financial award application deadline: 2/1. *Faculty research:* Behavior change theory, nutrition and enzyme therapy, exercise testing, health planning, sport management. *Unit head:* Dr. Jeffrey Petersen, Graduate Program Director, 254-710-4007, Fax: 254-710-3527, E-mail: jeffrey_petersen@baylor.edu. *Application contact:* Kathy Mirick, Administrative Assistant, 254-710-3526, Fax: 254-710-3527, E-mail: kathy_mirick@baylor.edu.
Website: http://www.baylor.edu/HHPR/.

Boise State University, College of Education, Department of Kinesiology, Boise, ID 83725-0399. Offers exercise and sports studies (MS); kinesiology (MK); physical education (MS). Part-time programs available. *Degree requirements:* For master's, thesis. *Entrance requirements:* For master's, minimum GPA of 3.0. Electronic applications accepted.

Bridgewater State University, School of Graduate Studies, School of Education and Allied Studies, Department of Movement Arts, Health Promotion, and Leisure Studies, Program in Physical Education, Bridgewater, MA 02325-0001. Offers MS. Part-time and evening/weekend programs available. *Degree requirements:* For master's, thesis or alternative. *Entrance requirements:* For master's, GRE General Test.

Brigham Young University, Graduate Studies, David O. McKay School of Education, Department of Teacher Education, Provo, UT 84602. Offers integrative science-technology-engineering-mathematics (STEM) (MA); literacy education (MA); physical education teacher education (MA); teacher education (MA). *Faculty:* 27 full-time (14 women). *Students:* 15 full-time (9 women). Average age 33. In 2013, 7 master's awarded. *Degree requirements:* For master's, thesis. *Entrance requirements:* For master's, GRE General Test, minimum 1 year of teaching experience (preferred), minimum GPA of 3.25 in last 60 hours of course work. Additional exam requirements/recommendations for international students: Recommended—TOEFL. *Application deadline:* For fall admission, 2/1 for domestic and international students; for winter admission, 2/1 for domestic and international students; for spring admission, 3/15 for domestic students; for summer admission, 2/1 priority date for domestic and international students. Application fee: $50. Electronic applications accepted. *Expenses: Tuition:* Full-time $6130; part-time $340 per credit hour. Tuition and fees vary according to program and student's religious affiliation. *Financial support:* In 2013–14, 13 students received support. Scholarships/grants and tuition waivers (full and partial) available. *Faculty research:* Literacy education, stem education, teacher development and education, physical education teacher education. *Unit head:* Dr. Michael O. Tunnell, Chair, 801-422-3497, Fax: 801-422-0652, E-mail: mike_tunnell@byu.edu. *Application contact:* Dr. Janet R. Young, Associate Chair/Graduate Coordinator, 801-422-4979, Fax: 801-422-0652, E-mail: janet_young@byu.edu.
Website: http://education.byu.edu/ted/.

Brooklyn College of the City University of New York, Division of Graduate Studies, Department of Physical Education and Exercise Science, Brooklyn, NY 11210-2889. Offers exercise science and rehabilitation (MS); physical education (MS), including sports management. Part-time programs available. *Degree requirements:* For master's, comprehensive exam or thesis. *Entrance requirements:* For master's, previous course work in physical education and education, minimum GPA of 3.0, 2 letters of recommendation, essay. Additional exam requirements/recommendations for international students: Required—TOEFL (minimum score 500 paper-based; 61 iBT). Electronic applications accepted. *Faculty research:* Exercise physiology, motor learning, sports psychology, women in athletics.

Brooklyn College of the City University of New York, Division of Graduate Studies, School of Education, Program in Adolescence Education and Special Subjects, Brooklyn, NY 11210-2889. Offers adolescence science education (MAT); art teacher (MA); biology teacher (MA); chemistry teacher (MA); earth science teacher (MAT); English teacher (MA); French teacher (MA); health and nutrition sciences: health teacher (MS Ed); mathematics teacher (MA); music education (CAS); music teacher

(MA); physical education teacher (MS Ed); physics teacher (MA); social studies teacher (MA); Spanish teacher (MA). Part-time and evening/weekend programs available. *Degree requirements:* For master's, comprehensive exam (for some programs), thesis (for some programs). *Entrance requirements:* For master's, LAST, previous course work in education, resume, 2 letters of recommendation, essay. Additional exam requirements/recommendations for international students: Required—TOEFL (minimum score 500 paper-based; 61 iBT). Electronic applications accepted. *Faculty research:* Interdisciplinary education, semiotics, discourse analysis, autobiography, teacher identity.

California Baptist University, Program in Kinesiology, Riverside, CA 92504-3206. Offers exercise science (MS); physical education pedagogy (MS); sport management (MS). Part-time programs available. *Faculty:* 7 full-time (4 women), 3 part-time/adjunct (1 woman). *Students:* 27 full-time (8 women), 23 part-time (8 women); includes 19 minority (10 Black or African American, non-Hispanic/Latino; 2 Asian, non-Hispanic/Latino; 5 Hispanic/Latino; 2 Two or more races, non-Hispanic/Latino), 6 international. Average age 27. 64 applicants, 66% accepted, 25 enrolled. In 2013, 41 master's awarded. *Degree requirements:* For master's, comprehensive exam (for some programs), comprehensive exam or research thesis. *Entrance requirements:* For master's, minimum undergraduate GPA of 2.75; 12 units of kinesiology prerequisites; three recommendations; 500-word essay; resume; interview. Additional exam requirements/recommendations for international students: Required—TOEFL (minimum score 80 iBT). *Application deadline:* For fall admission, 8/1 priority date for domestic students, 7/1 for international students; for spring admission, 12/1 priority date for domestic students, 11/1 for international students. Applications are processed on a rolling basis. Application fee: $45. Electronic applications accepted. *Expenses:* Contact institution. *Financial support:* In 2013–14, 3 students received support, including 3 fellowships (averaging $8,100 per year). Financial award applicants required to submit CSS PROFILE or FAFSA. *Faculty research:* Physical education pedagogy, exercise management and prevention of cardiovascular and metabolic diseases, sport management, immune function, carbohydrate oxidation. *Unit head:* Dr. Chuck Sands, Dean, College of Allied Health, 951-343-4619, E-mail: csands@calbaptist.edu. *Application contact:* Dr. Sean Sullivan, Chair, Department of Kinesiology, 951-343-4528, Fax: 951-343-5095, E-mail: ssullivan@calbaptist.edu.
Website: http://www.calbaptist.edu/mskin/.

California State University, Dominguez Hills, College of Health, Human Services and Nursing, Program in Physical Education Administration, Carson, CA 90747-0001. Offers MA. Part-time programs available. *Faculty:* 1 full-time (0 women). *Students:* 1 full-time (0 women), 19 part-time (3 women); includes 13 minority (9 Black or African American, non-Hispanic/Latino; 3 Hispanic/Latino; 1 Two or more races, non-Hispanic/Latino), 3 international. Average age 31. 12 applicants, 75% accepted, 7 enrolled. In 2013, 8 master's awarded. *Degree requirements:* For master's, comprehensive exam. *Entrance requirements:* For master's, minimum GPA of 2.75. Additional exam requirements/recommendations for international students: Required—TOEFL, IELTS. *Application deadline:* For fall admission, 6/1 for domestic students. Applications are processed on a rolling basis. Application fee: $55. *Expenses:* Tuition, state resident: full-time $6738. Tuition, nonresident: full-time $13,434. *Required fees:* $622. *Faculty research:* Teaching pedagogy, physical activity. *Unit head:* Dr. Michael Ernst, Chair, 310-243-3761, E-mail: mernst@csudh.edu. *Application contact:* 310-243-3600.
Website: http://www.csudh.edu/cps/dkr.htm.

California State University, East Bay, Office of Academic Programs and Graduate Studies, College of Education and Allied Studies, Department of Kinesiology, Hayward, CA 94542-3000. Offers MS. *Degree requirements:* For master's, exam or thesis. *Entrance requirements:* For master's, BA in kinesiology or related discipline, minimum major course work GPA of 3.0. Additional exam requirements/recommendations for international students: Required—TOEFL (minimum score 550 paper-based). Electronic applications accepted. *Faculty research:* Physiology, psychology of sport/movement, skill acquisition, cultural influence on physical activity.

California State University, Fullerton, Graduate Studies, College of Health and Human Development, Department of Kinesiology, Fullerton, CA 92834-9480. Offers MS. Part-time programs available. *Students:* 44 full-time (20 women), 54 part-time (22 women); includes 42 minority (2 Black or African American, non-Hispanic/Latino; 1 American Indian or Alaska Native, non-Hispanic/Latino; 8 Asian, non-Hispanic/Latino; 27 Hispanic/Latino; 1 Native Hawaiian or other Pacific Islander, non-Hispanic/Latino; 3 Two or more races, non-Hispanic/Latino), 3 international. Average age 27. 99 applicants, 60% accepted, 41 enrolled. In 2013, 37 master's awarded. *Degree requirements:* For master's, project or thesis. *Entrance requirements:* For master's, minimum GPA of 3.0 in field, 2.5 overall. Application fee: $55. *Financial support:* Career-related internships or fieldwork, Federal Work-Study, institutionally sponsored loans, and scholarships/grants available. Support available to part-time students. Financial award application deadline: 3/1; financial award applicants required to submit FAFSA. *Unit head:* Dr. Stephen Walk, Head, 657-278-3320. *Application contact:* Admissions/Applications, 657-278-2371.

California State University, Long Beach, Graduate Studies, College of Health and Human Services, Department of Kinesiology, Long Beach, CA 90840. Offers adapted physical education (MA); coaching and student athlete development (MA); exercise physiology and nutrition (MS); exercise science (MS); individualized studies (MA); kinesiology (MA); pedagogical studies (MA); sport and exercise psychology (MS); sport management (MA); sports medicine and injury studies (MS). Part-time programs available. *Degree requirements:* For master's, oral and written comprehensive exams or thesis. *Entrance requirements:* For master's, GRE General Test, minimum GPA of 2.75 during previous 2 years of course work. Electronic applications accepted. *Faculty research:* Pulmonary functioning, feedback and practice structure, strength training, history and politics of sports, special population research issues.

California State University, Los Angeles, Graduate Studies, College of Health and Human Services, Department of Kinesiology and Nutritional Sciences, Los Angeles, CA 90032-8530. Offers nutritional science (MS); physical education and kinesiology (MA, MS). *Accreditation:* AND. Part-time and evening/weekend programs available. *Faculty:* 6 full-time (3 women), 1 part-time/adjunct (0 women). *Students:* 69 full-time (65 women), 50 part-time (36 women); includes 64 minority (3 Black or African American, non-Hispanic/Latino; 30 Asian, non-Hispanic/Latino; 25 Hispanic/Latino; 1 Native Hawaiian or other Pacific Islander, non-Hispanic/Latino; 5 Two or more races, non-Hispanic/Latino), 8 international. Average age 31. 138 applicants, 24% accepted, 23 enrolled. In 2013, 60 master's awarded. *Degree requirements:* For master's, comprehensive exam, project or thesis. *Entrance requirements:* For master's, minimum GPA of 2.75. Additional exam requirements/recommendations for international students: Required—TOEFL (minimum score 500 paper-based). *Application deadline:* For fall admission, 5/1 for domestic and international students. Applications are processed on a rolling basis. Application fee: $55. *Financial support:* Federal Work-Study available. Support available to part-time students. Financial award application deadline: 3/1. *Unit head:* Dr. Nazareth Khodiguian, Chair, 323-343-4650, Fax: 323-343-6482, E-mail: nkhodig@calstatela.edu. *Application contact:* Dr. Larry Fritz, Dean of Graduate Studies, 323-343-3820, Fax: 323-343-5653, E-mail: lfritz@calstatela.edu.
Website: http://www.calstatela.edu/dept/pe/.

California State University, Sacramento, Office of Graduate Studies, College of Health and Human Services, Department of Kinesiology and Health Science, Sacramento, CA 95819. Offers MS. *Accreditation:* APTA. Part-time programs available. *Degree requirements:* For master's, thesis or project; writing proficiency exam. *Entrance requirements:* Additional exam requirements/recommendations for international students: Required—TOEFL. *Application deadline:* For fall admission, 1/28 for domestic students, 3/1 for international students; for spring admission, 9/30 for international students. Applications are processed on a rolling basis. Application fee: $55. Electronic applications accepted. *Financial support:* Research assistantships, teaching assistantships, career-related internships or fieldwork, and Federal Work-Study available. Support available to part-time students. Financial award application deadline: 3/1; financial award applicants required to submit FAFSA. *Unit head:* Steve Gray, Interim Department Chair, 916-278-6192, E-mail: graysw@saclink.csus.edu. *Application contact:* Jose Martinez, Graduate Admissions Supervisor, 916-278-7871, E-mail: martinj@skymail.csus.edu.
Website: http://www.csus.edu/hhs/khs.

California State University, Stanislaus, College of Education, Program in Education (MA), Turlock, CA 95382. Offers curriculum and instruction (MA), including education technology, elementary education, multilingual education, physical education, reading, secondary education, special education; school administration (MA); school counseling (MA). Part-time and evening/weekend programs available. *Degree requirements:* For master's, comprehensive exam (for some programs), thesis (for some programs). *Entrance requirements:* For master's, MAT, GRE, or CBEST (varies by concentration), 3 letters of recommendation, personal statement. Additional exam requirements/recommendations for international students: Required—TOEFL (minimum score 550 paper-based). Electronic applications accepted. *Faculty research:* Children's perspectives on historical events, method elementary schools dual language education, K-12 reading programs.

Campbell University, Graduate and Professional Programs, School of Education, Buies Creek, NC 27506. Offers administration (MSA); community counseling (MA); elementary education (M Ed); English education (M Ed); interdisciplinary studies (M Ed); mathematics education (M Ed); middle grades education (M Ed); physical education (M Ed); school counseling (M Ed); secondary education (M Ed); social science education (M Ed). *Accreditation:* NCATE. Part-time and evening/weekend programs available. *Degree requirements:* For master's, comprehensive exam. *Entrance requirements:* For master's, GRE General Test, minimum GPA of 2.7. *Faculty research:* Spiritual values and wellness issues in counseling, stress and professional burnout among counselors, thinking strategies, leadership, adaptive technology.

Canisius College, Graduate Division, School of Education and Human Services, Department of Kinesiology, Buffalo, NY 14208-1098. Offers physical education (MS Ed); physical education birth -12 (MS Ed). Part-time and evening/weekend programs available. Postbaccalaureate distance learning degree programs offered (minimal on-campus study). *Faculty:* 10 full-time (1 woman), 9 part-time/adjunct (3 women). *Students:* 33 full-time (12 women), 81 part-time (32 women); includes 12 minority (6 Black or African American, non-Hispanic/Latino; 4 Hispanic/Latino; 2 Two or more races, non-Hispanic/Latino), 7 international. Average age 30. 45 applicants, 76% accepted, 22 enrolled. In 2013, 89 master's awarded. *Degree requirements:* For master's, research project. *Entrance requirements:* For master's, official college and/or university transcript(s) showing completion of a bachelor's degree from accredited institution with evidence of teaching certification (not for initial certification candidates); two letters of recommendation; minimum cumulative undergraduate GPA of 2.7. Additional exam requirements/recommendations for international students: Required—TOEFL (minimum score 550 paper-based, 80 iBT), IELTS (minimum score 6.5), or CAEL (minimum score 70). *Application deadline:* Applications are processed on a rolling basis. Application fee: $25. Electronic applications accepted. Application fee is waived when completed online. *Expenses: Tuition:* Part-time $750 per credit hour. *Financial support:* Career-related internships or fieldwork, Federal Work-Study, scholarships/grants, tuition waivers (partial), and unspecified assistantships available. Support available to part-time students. Financial award application deadline: 4/30; financial award applicants required to submit FAFSA. *Faculty research:* Culturally congruent pedagogy in physical education, information processing and perceptual styles of athletes, qualities of effective coaches. *Unit head:* Dr. Timothy M. Sawicki, Associate Professor, Kinesiology, 716-888-8262, Fax: 716-888-8445, E-mail: sawickit@canisius.edu. *Application contact:* Julie A. Zulewski, Director of Graduate Admissions, 716-888-2548, Fax: 716-888-3195, E-mail: zulewskj@canisius.edu.
Website: http://www.canisius.edu/graduate/.

Canisius College, Graduate Division, School of Education and Human Services, Office of Professional Studies, Buffalo, NY 14208-1098. Offers applied nutrition (MS, Certificate); community and school health (MS); health and human performance (MS); health information technology (MS); respiratory care (MS). Postbaccalaureate distance learning degree programs offered (no on-campus study). *Faculty:* 17 part-time/adjunct (11 women). *Students:* 51 full-time (35 women), 37 part-time (26 women); includes 16 minority (8 Black or African American, non-Hispanic/Latino; 1 American Indian or Alaska Native, non-Hispanic/Latino; 7 Hispanic/Latino), 2 international. Average age 32. 98 applicants, 57% accepted, 24 enrolled. In 2013, 29 master's awarded. *Entrance requirements:* Additional exam requirements/recommendations for international students: Required—TOEFL (minimum score 550 paper-based, 80 iBT), IELTS (minimum score 6.5), or CAEL (minimum score 70). *Application deadline:* Applications are processed on a rolling basis. Application fee: $25. Electronic applications accepted. Application fee is waived when completed online. *Expenses: Tuition:* Part-time $750 per credit hour. *Financial support:* Career-related internships or fieldwork, Federal Work-Study, scholarships/grants, and unspecified assistantships available. Support available to part-time students. Financial award application deadline: 4/30; financial award applicants required to submit FAFSA. *Faculty research:* Nutrition, community and school health; community and health; health and human performance applied; nutrition and respiratory care. *Unit head:* Dr. Khalid Bibi, Executive Director, 716-888-8296. *Application contact:* Julie A. Zulewski, Director of Graduate Admission, 716-888-2548, Fax: 716-888-3195, E-mail: zulewskj@canisius.edu.
Website: http://www.canisius.edu/graduate/.

Caribbean University, Graduate School, Bayamón, PR 00960-0493. Offers administration and supervision (MA Ed); criminal justice (MA); curriculum and instruction (MA Ed, PhD), including elementary education (MA Ed), English education (MA Ed), history education (MA Ed), mathematics education (MA Ed), primary education (MA Ed), science education (MA Ed), Spanish education (MA Ed); educational technology in instructional systems (MA Ed); gerontology (MSN); human resources (MBA); museology, archiving and art history (MA Ed); neonatal pediatrics (MSN); physical education (MA Ed); special education (MA Ed). *Entrance requirements:* For master's, interview, minimum GPA of 2.5.

Central Connecticut State University, School of Graduate Studies, School of Education and Professional Studies, Department of Physical Education and Human Performance, New Britain, CT 06050-4010. Offers physical education (MS, Certificate). Part-time and evening/weekend programs available. *Faculty:* 4 full-time (1 woman), 2 part-time/adjunct (1 woman). *Students:* 15 full-time (6 women), 29 part-time (10 women);

includes 4 minority (2 Black or African American, non-Hispanic/Latino; 1 American Indian or Alaska Native, non-Hispanic/Latino; 1 Two or more races, non-Hispanic/Latino), 1 international. Average age 26. 20 applicants, 60% accepted, 8 enrolled. In 2013, 10 master's, 5 other advanced degrees awarded. *Degree requirements:* For master's, comprehensive exam, thesis or alternative; for Certificate, qualifying exam. *Entrance requirements:* For master's, minimum GPA of 2.7, bachelor's degree in physical education (preferred). Additional exam requirements/recommendations for international students: Required—TOEFL (minimum score 550 paper-based; 79 iBT). *Application deadline:* For fall admission, 6/1 for domestic students, 5/1 for international students; for spring admission, 11/1 for domestic and international students. Applications are processed on a rolling basis. Application fee: $50. Electronic applications accepted. Part-time tuition and fees vary according to degree level. *Financial support:* In 2013–14, 3 students received support, including 3 research assistantships; career-related internships or fieldwork, Federal Work-Study, scholarships/grants, and unspecified assistantships also available. Support available to part-time students. Financial award application deadline: 3/1; financial award applicants required to submit FAFSA. *Faculty research:* Exercise science, athletic training, preparation of physical education for schools. *Unit head:* Dr. Kimberly Kostelis, Chair, 860-832-2155, E-mail: kostelisk@ccsu.edu. *Application contact:* Patricia Gardner, Associate Director of Graduate Studies, 860-832-2350, Fax: 860-832-2362, E-mail: graduateadmissions@ccsu.edu.
Website: http://www.ccsu.edu/page.cfm?p=1357.

Central Washington University, Graduate Studies and Research, College of Education and Professional Studies, Department of Physical Education, School and Public Health, Ellensburg, WA 98926. Offers athletic administration (MS); health and physical education (MS). Part-time programs available. *Degree requirements:* For master's, comprehensive exam, thesis or alternative. *Entrance requirements:* For master's, minimum GPA of 3.0. Additional exam requirements/recommendations for international students: Required—TOEFL (minimum score 550 paper-based; 79 iBT), IELTS. Electronic applications accepted.

Chicago State University, School of Graduate and Professional Studies, College of Education, Department of Health, Physical Education and Recreation, Chicago, IL 60628. Offers physical education (MS Ed). Part-time and evening/weekend programs available. Postbaccalaureate distance learning degree programs offered. *Degree requirements:* For master's, thesis optional. *Entrance requirements:* For master's, minimum GPA of 2.75. *Faculty research:* Sports psychology, recreation and leisure studies administration.

The Citadel, The Military College of South Carolina, Citadel Graduate College, Department of Health, Exercise, and Sport Science, Charleston, SC 29409. Offers health, exercise, and sport science (MS); physical education (MAT). *Accreditation:* NCATE. Part-time and evening/weekend programs available. *Faculty:* 10 full-time (4 women). *Students:* 9 full-time (5 women), 29 part-time (16 women); includes 7 minority (all Black or African American, non-Hispanic/Latino), 2 international. Average age 26. In 2013, 25 master's awarded. *Degree requirements:* For master's, comprehensive exam, thesis optional. *Entrance requirements:* For master's, GRE (minimum score 900) or MAT (minimum score 396), minimum undergraduate GPA of 2.5, 3 letters of recommendation, resume detailing previous work experience (for MS only). Additional exam requirements/recommendations for international students: Required—TOEFL (minimum score 550 paper-based; 79 iBT). *Application deadline:* Applications are processed on a rolling basis. Application fee: $30. Electronic applications accepted. *Expenses: Tuition, area resident:* Part-time $525 per credit hour. Tuition, state resident: part-time $525 per credit hour. Tuition, nonresident: part-time $865 per credit hour. *Financial support:* Career-related internships or fieldwork, health care benefits, and unspecified assistantships available. Support available to part-time students. Financial award application deadline: 7/1; financial award applicants required to submit FAFSA. *Faculty research:* Risk management in sport and physical activity programs, school-wide physical activity programs, exercise intervention among HIV-infected individuals, factors influencing motor skill in SC physical education programs, effect of mouthpiece use on human performance. *Unit head:* Dr. Harry D. Davakos, Department Head, 843-953-5060, Fax: 843-953-6798, E-mail: harry.davakos@citadel.edu. *Application contact:* Dr. Robert H. McNamara, Associate Provost, The Citadel Graduate College, 843-953-5089, Fax: 843-953-7630, E-mail: cgc@citadel.edu.
Website: http://www.citadel.edu/hess/index.htm.

The Citadel, The Military College of South Carolina, Citadel Graduate College, School of Education, Program in Secondary Education, Charleston, SC 29409. Offers biology (MAT); English language arts (MAT); mathematics (MAT); mathematics education (MAE); physical education (MAT); social studies (MAT). *Accreditation:* NCATE. Part-time and evening/weekend programs available. *Faculty:* 10 full-time (6 women), 8 part-time/adjunct (3 women). *Students:* 14 full-time (9 women), 56 part-time (31 women); includes 9 minority (8 Black or African American, non-Hispanic/Latino; 1 Hispanic/Latino). Average age 30. In 2013, 24 master's awarded. *Degree requirements:* For master's, comprehensive exam, internship. *Entrance requirements:* For master's, GRE (minimum score 290; 900 on old scoring system) or MAT (minimum score 396), minimum undergraduate GPA of 2.5. Additional exam requirements/recommendations for international students: Required—TOEFL (minimum score 550 paper-based). *Application deadline:* Applications are processed on a rolling basis. Application fee: $30. Electronic applications accepted. *Expenses: Tuition, area resident:* Part-time $525 per credit hour. Tuition, state resident: part-time $525 per credit hour. Tuition, nonresident: part-time $865 per credit hour. *Financial support:* Career-related internships or fieldwork, health care benefits, and unspecified assistantships available. Support available to part-time students. Financial award application deadline: 7/1; financial award applicants required to submit FAFSA. *Unit head:* Dr. Kathryn A. Richardson-Jones, Coordinator, 843-953-3163, Fax: 843-953-7258, E-mail: kathryn.jones@citadel.edu. *Application contact:* Dr. Robert H. McNamara, Associate Provost, The Citadel Graduate College, 843-953-5089, Fax: 843-953-7630, E-mail: cgc@citadel.edu.
Website: http://www.citadel.edu/education/teacher-education/mat-master-of-arts-in-teaching.html.

Cleveland State University, College of Graduate Studies, College of Education and Human Services, Department of Health, Physical Education, Recreation and Dance, Cleveland, OH 44115. Offers community health education (M Ed); exercise science (M Ed); human performance (M Ed); physical education pedagogy (M Ed); public health (MPH); school health education (M Ed); sport and exercise psychology (M Ed); sports management (M Ed). Part-time programs available. *Faculty:* 7 full-time (4 women), 3 part-time/adjunct (2 women). *Students:* 49 full-time (31 women), 79 part-time (46 women); includes 32 minority (25 Black or African American, non-Hispanic/Latino; 2 Asian, non-Hispanic/Latino; 5 Hispanic/Latino), 7 international. Average age 35. 103 applicants, 72% accepted, 35 enrolled. In 2013, 40 master's awarded. *Degree requirements:* For master's, comprehensive exam, thesis optional. *Entrance requirements:* For master's, GRE General Test or MAT (if undergraduate GPA less than 2.75), minimum undergraduate GPA of 2.75. Additional exam requirements/recommendations for international students: Required—TOEFL (minimum score 525 paper-based), IELTS (minimum score 6). *Application deadline:* For fall admission, 7/15 priority date for domestic students; for spring admission, 12/15 priority date for domestic students. Applications are processed on a rolling basis. Application fee: $30. Electronic applications accepted. *Expenses:* Tuition, state resident: full-time $8335; part-time $521 per credit hour. Tuition, nonresident: full-time $15,670; part-time $979 per credit hour. *Required fees:* $50; $25 per semester. *Financial support:* In 2013–14, 6 research assistantships with full and partial tuition reimbursements (averaging $3,480 per year), 1 teaching assistantship with full and partial tuition reimbursement (averaging $3,480 per year) were awarded; career-related internships or fieldwork, tuition waivers (full), and unspecified assistantships also available. Financial award application deadline: 3/15. *Faculty research:* Bone density, marketing fitness centers, motor development of disabled, online learning and survey research. *Unit head:* Dr. Sheila M. Patterson, Chairperson, 216-687-4870, Fax: 216-687-5410, E-mail: s.m.patterson@csuohio.edu. *Application contact:* Deborah L. Brown, Interim Assistant Director, Graduate Admissions, 216-523-7572, Fax: 216-687-5400, E-mail: d.l.brown@csuohio.edu.
Website: http://www.csuohio.edu/cehs/departments/HPERD/hperd_dept.html.

The College at Brockport, State University of New York, School of Health and Human Performance, Department of Kinesiology, Sports Studies and Physical Education, Brockport, NY 14420-2997. Offers adapted physical education (AGC); physical education (MS Ed), including adapted physical education, athletic administration, teacher education/pedagogy. Part-time programs available. *Faculty:* 8 full-time (2 women), 2 part-time/adjunct (0 women). *Students:* 34 full-time (19 women), 24 part-time (12 women); includes 5 minority (4 Black or African American, non-Hispanic/Latino; 1 Asian, non-Hispanic/Latino), 2 international. 34 applicants, 97% accepted, 25 enrolled. In 2013, 41 master's awarded. *Degree requirements:* For master's, thesis or alternative. *Entrance requirements:* For master's, minimum GPA of 3.0; statement of objectives. Additional exam requirements/recommendations for international students: Required—TOEFL (minimum score 550 paper-based; 79 iBT), IELTS (minimum score 6.5). *Application deadline:* For fall admission, 4/15 priority date for domestic and international students; for spring admission, 11/15 priority date for domestic and international students. Application fee: $80. Electronic applications accepted. *Expenses:* Tuition, state resident: full-time $9870. Tuition, nonresident: full-time $18,350. *Required fees:* $1848. *Financial support:* In 2013–14, 11 teaching assistantships with full tuition reimbursements (averaging $7,000 per year) were awarded; Federal Work-Study, scholarships/grants, and unspecified assistantships also available. Support available to part-time students. Financial award application deadline: 3/15; financial award applicants required to submit FAFSA. *Faculty research:* Athletic administration, adapted physical education, physical education curriculum, physical education teaching/coaching, children's physical activity. *Unit head:* Dr. Susan C. Petersen, Chairperson, 585-395-5332, Fax: 585-395-2771, E-mail: spetersen@brockport.edu. *Application contact:* Dr. Cathy Houston-Wilson, Graduate Program Director, 585-395-5352, Fax: 585-395-2771, E-mail: chouston@brockport.edu.
Website: http://www.brockport.edu/pes/grad/gradtoc.html.

The College of New Jersey, Graduate Studies, School of Nursing, Health and Exercise Science, Department of Health and Exercise Science, Program in Health Education, Ewing, NJ 08628. Offers health (MAT); physical education (M Ed). *Accreditation:* NCATE. Part-time programs available. *Degree requirements:* For master's, comprehensive exam. *Entrance requirements:* For master's, GRE, minimum GPA of 3.0 in field or 2.75 overall. Additional exam requirements/recommendations for international students: Required—TOEFL. Electronic applications accepted.

The College of New Jersey, Graduate Studies, School of Nursing, Health and Exercise Science, Department of Health and Exercise Science, Program in Physical Education, Ewing, NJ 08628. Offers M Ed, MAT. Part-time programs available. *Degree requirements:* For master's, comprehensive exam. *Entrance requirements:* For master's, GRE, minimum GPA of 2.75 overall or 3.0 in field. Additional exam requirements/recommendations for international students: Required—TOEFL. Electronic applications accepted.

Colorado State University–Pueblo, College of Education, Engineering and Professional Studies, Education Program, Pueblo, CO 81001-4901. Offers art education (M Ed); foreign language education (M Ed); health and physical education (M Ed); instructional technology (M Ed); linguistically diverse education (M Ed); music education (M Ed); special education (M Ed). *Accreditation:* Teacher Education Accreditation Council. Part-time programs available. *Degree requirements:* For master's, portfolio. *Entrance requirements:* For master's, 3 recommendations, teaching license. Additional exam requirements/recommendations for international students: Required—TOEFL (minimum score 500 paper-based). Electronic applications accepted. *Faculty research:* Portfolio assessment, math education, science education.

Columbus State University, Graduate Studies, College of Education and Health Professions, Department of Health, Physical Education and Exercise Science, Columbus, GA 31907-5645. Offers exercise science (MS); health and physical education (M Ed). Part-time and evening/weekend programs available. *Faculty:* 6 full-time (3 women). *Students:* 25 full-time (10 women), 14 part-time (9 women); includes 17 minority (15 Black or African American, non-Hispanic/Latino; 2 Hispanic/Latino), 1 international. Average age 28. 23 applicants, 70% accepted, 12 enrolled. In 2013, 20 master's awarded. *Degree requirements:* For master's, thesis optional. *Entrance requirements:* For master's, GRE, minimum undergraduate GPA of 2.75. Additional exam requirements/recommendations for international students: Required—TOEFL (minimum score 550 paper-based; 79 iBT). *Application deadline:* For fall admission, 5/1 for domestic students, 4/1 for international students; for spring admission, 11/1 for domestic and international students; for summer admission, 2/1 for domestic students, 3/1 for international students. Application fee: $40. *Expenses:* Tuition, state resident: full-time $4572; part-time $382 per credit hour. Tuition, nonresident: full-time $18,292; part-time $1526 per credit hour. *Required fees:* $1800; $196 per credit hour. Tuition and fees vary according to campus/location and program. *Financial support:* In 2013–14, 30 students received support, including 18 research assistantships (averaging $3,000 per year). *Unit head:* Dr. Tara Underwood, Chair, 706-568-2485, E-mail: underwood_tara@columbusstate.edu. *Application contact:* Kristin Williams, Director of International and Graduate Admissions, 706-507-8848, Fax: 706-568-5091, E-mail: williams_kristin@columbusstate.edu.
Website: http://hpex.columbusstate.edu/.

Concordia University, School of Arts and Sciences, Irvine, CA 92612-3299. Offers coaching and athletic administration (MA). Part-time and evening/weekend programs available. Postbaccalaureate distance learning degree programs offered (no on-campus study). *Faculty:* 7 full-time (1 woman), 27 part-time/adjunct (2 women). *Students:* 524 full-time (132 women), 309 part-time (76 women); includes 145 minority (81 Black or African American, non-Hispanic/Latino; 1 American Indian or Alaska Native, non-Hispanic/Latino; 8 Asian, non-Hispanic/Latino; 30 Hispanic/Latino; 1 Native Hawaiian or other Pacific Islander, non-Hispanic/Latino; 24 Two or more races, non-Hispanic/Latino), 2 international. Average age 34. 419 applicants, 93% accepted, 333 enrolled. In 2013, 286 master's awarded. *Degree requirements:* For master's, culminating project. *Entrance requirements:* For master's, official college/university transcript(s); signed statement of intent. Additional exam requirements/recommendations for international students: Required—TOEFL (minimum score 550 paper-based; 79 iBT). *Application deadline:* For fall admission, 8/10 for domestic students, 6/1 for international students; for spring admission, 2/15 for domestic students, 10/1 for international students.

Application fee: $50 ($125 for international students). Electronic applications accepted. *Expenses:* Contact institution. *Financial support:* In 2013–14, 19 students received support. Tuition waivers (full and partial) and unspecified assistantships available. Financial award applicants required to submit FAFSA. *Unit head:* Dr. Timothy Preuss, Dean, 949-214-3286, E-mail: tim.preuss@cui.edu. *Application contact:* Jon O'Neill, Associate Director of Graduate Admissions, 949-214-3577, Fax: 949-214-3577, E-mail: jon.oneill@cui.edu.
Website: http://www.cui.edu.

Delta State University, Graduate Programs, College of Education, Division of Health, Physical Education, and Recreation, Cleveland, MS 38733-0001. Offers health, physical education, and recreation (M Ed); sport and human performance (MS). Part-time and evening/weekend programs available. *Faculty:* 5 full-time (1 woman), 1 part-time/adjunct (0 women). *Students:* 37 full-time (12 women), 13 part-time (4 women); includes 15 minority (11 Black or African American, non-Hispanic/Latino; 1 Hispanic/Latino; 3 Two or more races, non-Hispanic/Latino), 4 international. Average age 27. 35 applicants, 91% accepted, 29 enrolled. In 2013, 11 master's awarded. *Degree requirements:* For master's, thesis optional. *Entrance requirements:* For master's, GRE General Test or MAT, Class A teaching certificate. *Application deadline:* For fall admission, 8/1 priority date for domestic students; for spring admission, 12/1 priority date for domestic students. Applications are processed on a rolling basis. Application fee: $0. *Expenses:* Tuition, state resident: full-time $3006; part-time $334 per credit hour. Tuition, nonresident: full-time $3006; part-time $334 per credit hour. *Financial support:* In 2013–14, research assistantships (averaging $4,000 per year) were awarded; career-related internships or fieldwork, Federal Work-Study, and institutionally sponsored loans also available. Support available to part-time students. Financial award application deadline: 6/1. *Faculty research:* Blood pressure, body fat, power and reaction time, learning disorders for athletes, effects of walking. *Unit head:* Tim Colbert, Chair, 662-846-4555, Fax: 662-846-4571. *Application contact:* Dr. Albert Nylander, Dean of Graduate Studies, 662-846-4875, Fax: 662-846-4313, E-mail: grad-info@deltastate.edu.
Website: http://www.deltastate.edu/pages/2963.asp.

East Carolina University, Graduate School, College of Education, Department of Business and Information Technologies Education, Greenville, NC 27858-4353. Offers business education (MA Ed); elementary education (MAT); English education (MAT); family and consumer science (MAT); health education (MAT); Hispanic studies (MAT); history education (MAT); marketing education (MA Ed); middle grades education (MAT); music education (MAT); physical education (MAT); science education (MAT); special education (MAT), including general curriculum; vocation education (MS). *Accreditation:* NCATE. Part-time and evening/weekend programs available. Postbaccalaureate distance learning degree programs offered (no on-campus study). *Degree requirements:* For master's, comprehensive exam, thesis optional. *Entrance requirements:* For master's, GRE or MAT, minimum GPA of 2.5, bachelor's degree in related field, teaching license (MA Ed). Additional exam requirements/recommendations for international students: Required—TOEFL. *Expenses:* Tuition, state resident: full-time $4223. Tuition, nonresident: full-time $16,540. *Required fees:* $2184.

East Carolina University, Graduate School, College of Health and Human Performance, Department of Kinesiology, Greenville, NC 27858-4353. Offers adapted physical education (MA Ed, MS); bioenergetics and exercise science (PhD); biomechanics (MS); exercise physiology (MS); physical activity promotion (MS); physical education (MA Ed, MAT); physical education clinical supervision (Certificate); physical education pedagogy (MA Ed, MS); sport and exercise psychology (MS); sport management (Certificate). *Degree requirements:* For master's, comprehensive exam, thesis optional; for doctorate, comprehensive exam, thesis/dissertation. *Entrance requirements:* For master's, GRE General Test or MAT; for doctorate, GRE. Additional exam requirements/recommendations for international students: Required—TOEFL. *Expenses:* Tuition, state resident: full-time $4223. Tuition, nonresident: full-time $16,540. *Required fees:* $2184. *Faculty research:* Diabetes metabolism, pediatric obesity, biomechanics of arthritis, physical activity measurement.

Eastern Kentucky University, The Graduate School, College of Education, Department of Curriculum and Instruction, Program in Secondary and Higher Education, Richmond, KY 40475-3102. Offers secondary education (MA Ed), including agricultural education, art education, biological sciences education, business education, English education, geography education, history education, home economics education, industrial education, mathematical sciences education, physical education, school health education. *Accreditation:* NCATE. Part-time programs available. *Entrance requirements:* For master's, GRE General Test, minimum GPA of 2.5.

Eastern Kentucky University, The Graduate School, College of Health Sciences, Department of Exercise and Sport Science, Richmond, KY 40475-3102. Offers exercise and sport science (MS); exercise and wellness (MS); sports administration (MS). Part-time programs available. *Entrance requirements:* For master's, GRE General Test (minimum score 700 verbal and quantitative), minimum GPA of 2.5 (for most), minimum GPA of 3.0 (analytical writing). *Faculty research:* Nutrition and exercise.

Eastern Michigan University, Graduate School, College of Health and Human Services, School of Health Promotion and Human Performance, Programs in Physical Education, Ypsilanti, MI 48197. Offers adapted physical education (MS); physical education pedagogy (MS). Part-time and evening/weekend programs available. Postbaccalaureate distance learning degree programs offered (minimal on-campus study). *Students:* 7 part-time (1 woman). Average age 32. 1 applicant, 100% accepted. *Degree requirements:* For master's, thesis or independent study project and comprehensive exams. *Entrance requirements:* Additional exam requirements/recommendations for international students: Required—TOEFL. *Application deadline:* For fall admission, 8/1 for domestic students, 5/1 for international students; for winter admission, 12/1 for domestic students, 10/1 for international students; for spring admission, 4/15 for domestic students, 3/1 for international students. Applications are processed on a rolling basis. Application fee: $35. *Expenses:* Tuition, state resident: full-time $12,300; part-time $466 per credit hour. Tuition, nonresident: full-time $23,159; part-time $918 per credit hour. *Required fees:* $71 per credit hour. $46 per semester. One-time fee: $100. Tuition and fees vary according to course level and degree level. *Financial support:* Fellowships, research assistantships with full tuition reimbursements, teaching assistantships with full tuition reimbursements, career-related internships or fieldwork, Federal Work-Study, institutionally sponsored loans, scholarships/grants, tuition waivers (partial), and unspecified assistantships available. Support available to part-time students. Financial award applicants required to submit FAFSA. *Unit head:* Dr. Christopher Herman, Director, 734-487-2815, Fax: 734-487-2024, E-mail: cherman2@emich.edu. *Application contact:* Dr. Roberta Faust, Program Coordinator, 734-487-7120 Ext. 2745, Fax: 734-487-2024, E-mail: rfaust@emich.edu.

Eastern New Mexico University, Graduate School, College of Education and Technology, Department of Health and Physical Education, Portales, NM 88130. Offers physical education (MS), including sport administration, sport science. Part-time programs available. *Degree requirements:* For master's, comprehensive exam, thesis optional. *Entrance requirements:* For master's, minimum GPA of 3.0, 15 hours of leveling courses without bachelor's degree in physical education, two references. Additional exam requirements/recommendations for international students: Required—

TOEFL (minimum score 550 paper-based; 79 iBT), IELTS (minimum score 6). Electronic applications accepted.

Eastern University, Graduate Education Programs, St. Davids, PA 19087-3696. Offers ESL program specialist (K-12) (Certificate); general supervisor (PreK-12) (Certificate); health and physical education (K-12) (Certificate); middle level (4-8) (Certificate); multicultural education (M Ed); pre K-4 (Certificate); pre K-4 with special education (Certificate); reading (M Ed); reading specialist (K-12) (Certificate); reading supervisor (K-12) (Certificate); school health services (M Ed); school health supervisor (Certificate); school nurse (Certificate); school principalship (K-12) (Certificate); secondary biology education (7-12) (Certificate); secondary chemistry education (7-12) (Certificate); secondary communication education (7-12) (Certificate); secondary education (7-12) (Certificate); secondary English education (7-12) (Certificate); secondary math education (7-12) (Certificate); secondary social studies education (7-12) (Certificate); special education (M Ed); special education (7-12) (Certificate); special education (Pre K-8) (Certificate); special education supervisor (N-12) (Certificate); TESOL (M Ed); world language (Certificate), including French, Mandarin Chinese, Spanish. Part-time and evening/weekend programs available. Postbaccalaureate distance learning degree programs offered (no on-campus study). *Faculty:* 22 full-time (11 women), 26 part-time/adjunct (18 women). *Students:* 77 full-time (58 women), 223 part-time (149 women); includes 112 minority (81 Black or African American, non-Hispanic/Latino; 1 American Indian or Alaska Native, non-Hispanic/Latino; 9 Asian, non-Hispanic/Latino; 18 Hispanic/Latino; 1 Native Hawaiian or other Pacific Islander, non-Hispanic/Latino; 2 Two or more races, non-Hispanic/Latino), 7 international. Average age 34. 94 applicants, 100% accepted, 81 enrolled. In 2013, 120 master's awarded. *Entrance requirements:* For master's, minimum GPA of 2.5 (for M Ed); for Certificate, minimum GPA of 3.0 for certifications. Additional exam requirements/recommendations for international students: Required—TOEFL. *Application deadline:* For fall admission, 8/14 for domestic students; for spring admission, 12/20 for domestic students. Applications are processed on a rolling basis. Application fee: $35. Application fee is waived when completed online. *Expenses:* Tuition: Full-time $15,600; part-time $650 per credit. *Required fees:* $27.50 per semester. One-time fee: $50. Tuition and fees vary according to course load, degree level and program. *Financial support:* In 2013–14, 84 students received support, including 6 research assistantships with partial tuition reimbursements available (averaging $7,710 per year); scholarships/grants and unspecified assistantships also available. Financial award application deadline: 3/15; financial award applicants required to submit FAFSA. *Unit head:* Harry Gutelius, Associate Dean, 610-341-1729. *Application contact:* Michael Perpiglia, Associate Director of Enrollment, 610-341-5947, Fax: 484-581-1276, E-mail: mperpigl@eastern.edu.
Website: http://www.eastern.edu/academics/programs/loeb-school-education-0/graduateprograms.

Eastern Washington University, Graduate Studies, College of Arts, Letters and Education, Department of Physical Education, Health and Recreation, Cheney, WA 99004-2431. Offers exercise science (MS); sports and recreation administration (MS). *Faculty:* 17 full-time (7 women), 5 part-time/adjunct (2 women). *Students:* 26 full-time (10 women), 8 part-time (3 women); includes 7 minority (3 Black or African American, non-Hispanic/Latino; 1 American Indian or Alaska Native, non-Hispanic/Latino; 2 Asian, non-Hispanic/Latino; 1 Hispanic/Latino). Average age 29. 64 applicants, 38% accepted, 21 enrolled. In 2013, 14 master's awarded. *Degree requirements:* For master's, comprehensive exam, thesis or alternative. *Entrance requirements:* For master's, minimum GPA of 3.0. *Application deadline:* For fall admission, 4/1 priority date for domestic students; for spring admission, 1/15 for domestic students. Applications are processed on a rolling basis. Application fee: $50. *Financial support:* In 2013–14, 10 teaching assistantships with partial tuition reimbursements (averaging $6,624 per year) were awarded; career-related internships or fieldwork, Federal Work-Study, institutionally sponsored loans, and scholarships/grants also available. Support available to part-time students. Financial award application deadline: 2/1; financial award applicants required to submit FAFSA. *Unit head:* John Cogley, Chair, 509-359-2486, E-mail: john.cogley@mail.ewu.edu. *Application contact:* Dr. Jeni McNeal, Professor of Physical Education, Health and Recreation, 509-359-2872, Fax: 509-359-4833, E-mail: jeni_mcneal@hotmail.com.

East Stroudsburg University of Pennsylvania, Graduate College, College of Health Sciences, Department of Exercise Science, East Stroudsburg, PA 18301-2999. Offers cardiac rehabilitation and exercise science (MS). Part-time and evening/weekend programs available. Postbaccalaureate distance learning degree programs offered. *Faculty:* 7 full-time (2 women). *Students:* 48 full-time (28 women), 2 part-time (1 woman); includes 11 minority (6 Black or African American, non-Hispanic/Latino; 3 Hispanic/Latino; 2 Two or more races, non-Hispanic/Latino), 1 international. Average age 23. 114 applicants, 75% accepted, 54 enrolled. In 2013, 38 master's awarded. *Degree requirements:* For master's, comprehensive exam, thesis or alternative, computer literacy. *Entrance requirements:* Additional exam requirements/recommendations for international students: Required—TOEFL (minimum score 560 paper-based; 83 iBT) or IELTS. *Application deadline:* For fall admission, 3/1 priority date for domestic and international students; for spring admission, 11/30 for domestic students, 10/31 for international students. Applications are processed on a rolling basis. Application fee: $50. Electronic applications accepted. *Expenses:* Tuition, state resident: full-time $7956; part-time $442 per credit. Tuition, nonresident: full-time $11,934; part-time $663 per credit. *Required fees:* $2129; $118 per credit. *Financial support:* Research assistantships with full and partial tuition reimbursements, Federal Work-Study, and institutionally sponsored loans available. Financial award application deadline: 3/1. *Unit head:* Dr. Shala Davis, Graduate Coordinator, 570-422-3302, Fax: 570-422-3616, E-mail: sdavis@po-box.esu.edu. *Application contact:* Kevin Quintero, Graduate Admissions Coordinator, 570-422-3536, Fax: 570-422-2711, E-mail: kquintero@esu.edu.

East Texas Baptist University, Master of Education Program, Marshall, TX 75670-1498. Offers curriculum and instruction (M Ed); sports and exercise leadership (M Ed); teacher certification (M Ed). Part-time programs available. *Entrance requirements:* For master's, GRE. Additional exam requirements/recommendations for international students: Required—TOEFL (minimum score 550 paper-based; 79 iBT). Electronic applications accepted. *Expenses:* Contact institution.

Emporia State University, Department of Health, Physical Education and Recreation, Emporia, KS 66801-5415. Offers physical education (MS). Part-time programs available. Postbaccalaureate distance learning degree programs offered (no on-campus study). *Faculty:* 17 full-time (11 women), 1 (woman) part-time/adjunct. *Students:* 29 full-time (11 women), 163 part-time (74 women); includes 24 minority (10 Black or African American, non-Hispanic/Latino; 2 American Indian or Alaska Native, non-Hispanic/Latino; 2 Asian, non-Hispanic/Latino; 5 Hispanic/Latino; 1 Native Hawaiian or other Pacific Islander, non-Hispanic/Latino; 4 Two or more races, non-Hispanic/Latino), 3 international. 61 applicants, 85% accepted, 34 enrolled. In 2013, 71 master's awarded. *Degree requirements:* For master's, comprehensive exam or thesis. *Entrance requirements:* For master's, bachelor's degree in physical education, health, and recreation; letters of recommendation. Additional exam requirements/recommendations for international students: Required—TOEFL (minimum score 520 paper-based; 68 iBT). *Application deadline:* For fall admission, 8/15 priority date for domestic students. Applications are

processed on a rolling basis. Application fee: $30 ($75 for international students). Electronic applications accepted. *Expenses: Tuition, area resident:* Part-time $220 per credit hour. Tuition, state resident: part-time $220 per credit hour. Tuition, nonresident: part-time $685 per credit hour. *Required fees:* $73 per credit hour. *Financial support:* In 2013–14, 1 research assistantship (averaging $7,200 per year), 5 teaching assistantships with full tuition reimbursements (averaging $7,200 per year) were awarded; career-related internships or fieldwork, Federal Work-Study, institutionally sponsored loans, health care benefits, and unspecified assistantships also available. Financial award application deadline: 3/15; financial award applicants required to submit FAFSA. *Unit head:* Dr. Shawna Shane, Interim Chair, 620-341-5848, E-mail: sshane@emporia.edu. *Application contact:* Mary Sewell, Admissions Coordinator, 800-950-GRAD, Fax: 620-341-5909, E-mail: msewell@emporia.edu.
Website: http://www.emporia.edu/hper/.

Florida Agricultural and Mechanical University, Division of Graduate Studies, Research, and Continuing Education, College of Education, Department of Health, Physical Education, and Recreation, Tallahassee, FL 32307-3200. Offers M Ed, MS Ed. *Accreditation:* NCATE. Part-time and evening/weekend programs available. *Degree requirements:* For master's, thesis optional. *Entrance requirements:* For master's, GRE General Test, minimum GPA of 3.0. Additional exam requirements/recommendations for international students: Required—TOEFL. *Faculty research:* Administration/curriculum, work behavior, psychology.

Florida International University, College of Education, Department of Teaching and Learning, Miami, FL 33199. Offers art education (MA, MS); curriculum and instruction (MS, Ed D, PhD, Ed S), including curriculum development (MS); elementary education (MS), English education (MS), learning technologies (MS), mathematics education (MS), modern language education (MS), physical education (MS), science education (MS), social studies education (MS), special education (MS); early childhood education (MS); exceptional student education (Ed D); foreign language education (MS), including foreign language education, teaching English to speakers of other languages (TESOL); international/intercultural education (MS); language, literacy and culture (PhD); mathematics, science, and learning technologies (PhD); physical education (MS), including sport and fitness; reading education (MS). Part-time and evening/weekend programs available. *Degree requirements:* For doctorate, comprehensive exam, thesis/dissertation. *Entrance requirements:* For master's, GRE General Test, Florida General Knowledge Test or Florida College Level Academic Skills Test; for doctorate and Ed S, GRE General Test. Additional exam requirements/recommendations for international students: Required—TOEFL (minimum score 550 paper-based; 80 iBT), IELTS (minimum score 6.3). Electronic applications accepted.

Florida State University, The Graduate School, College of Education, Department of Sport Management, Tallahassee, FL 32306. Offers MS, PhD, Certificate, JD/MS. *Faculty:* 9 full-time (3 women), 3 part-time/adjunct (1 woman). *Students:* 113 full-time (34 women), 40 part-time (11 women); includes 26 minority (17 Black or African American, non-Hispanic/Latino; 8 Hispanic/Latino; 1 Two or more races, non-Hispanic/Latino), 33 international. Average age 28. 165 applicants, 67% accepted, 54 enrolled. In 2013, 62 master's, 4 doctorates awarded. *Degree requirements:* For master's and Certificate, comprehensive exam, thesis optional; for doctorate, comprehensive exam, thesis/dissertation. *Entrance requirements:* For master's, doctorate, and Certificate, GRE General Test, minimum GPA of 3.0. Additional exam requirements/recommendations for international students: Required—TOEFL (minimum score 550 paper-based; 80 iBT). *Application deadline:* For fall admission, 7/1 for domestic and international students; for winter admission, 11/1 for domestic and international students; for spring admission, 3/1 for domestic and international students. Application fee: $30. Electronic applications accepted. *Expenses:* Tuition, state resident: part-time $403.51 per credit hour. Tuition, nonresident: part-time $1004.85 per credit hour. *Required fees:* $75.81 per credit hour. One-time fee: $20 part-time. Tuition and fees vary according to course load, campus/location and student level. *Financial support:* In 2013–14, 3 students received support, including 1 research assistantship with full and partial tuition reimbursement available, 93 teaching assistantships with full and partial tuition reimbursements available; fellowships with full and partial tuition reimbursements available, career-related internships or fieldwork, Federal Work-Study, scholarships/grants, health care benefits, and unspecified assistantships also available. Financial award application deadline: 1/15; financial award applicants required to submit FAFSA. *Faculty research:* Sport marketing, gender issues in sport, finances in sport industry, coaching. *Unit head:* Dr. Jeffrey D. James, Chair, 850-644-9214, Fax: 850-644-0975, E-mail: jdjames@fsu.edu. *Application contact:* Dr. Thomas F. McMorrow, Academic Specialist, 850-644-0577, Fax: 850-644-0975, E-mail: tmcmorrow@admin.fsu.edu.
Website: http://www.coe.fsu.edu/SM/.

Fort Hays State University, Graduate School, College of Health and Life Sciences, Department of Health and Human Performance, Hays, KS 67601-4099. Offers MS. Part-time programs available. *Degree requirements:* For master's, comprehensive exam, thesis optional. *Entrance requirements:* For master's, GRE General Test or MAT. Additional exam requirements/recommendations for international students: Required—TOEFL (minimum score 550 paper-based). Electronic applications accepted. *Faculty research:* Isoproterenol hydrochloride and exercise, dehydrogenase and high-density lipoprotein levels in athletics, venous blood parameters to adipose fat.

Gardner-Webb University, Graduate School, Department of Physical Education, Wellness, and Sport Studies, Boiling Springs, NC 28017. Offers sport science and pedagogy (MA). Part-time and evening/weekend programs available. *Students:* 26 part-time (12 women); includes 8 minority (7 Black or African American, non-Hispanic/Latino; 1 American Indian or Alaska Native, non-Hispanic/Latino). Average age 25. 39 applicants, 59% accepted, 17 enrolled. In 2013, 3 master's awarded. *Degree requirements:* For master's, comprehensive exam. *Entrance requirements:* For master's, GRE General Test or NTE, PRAXIS, minimum GPA of 2.5. *Application deadline:* For fall admission, 8/1 priority date for domestic students. Applications are processed on a rolling basis. Application fee: $40. Electronic applications accepted. *Expenses: Tuition:* Full-time $7200; part-time $400 per credit hour. Tuition and fees vary according to course load and program. *Financial support:* Unspecified assistantships available. *Unit head:* Dr. Ken Baker, Chair, 704-406-4481, Fax: 704-406-4739. *Application contact:* Office of Graduate Admissions, 877-498-4723, Fax: 704-406-3895, E-mail: gradinfo@gardner-webb.edu.

Georgia College & State University, Graduate School, College of Health Sciences, Department of Kinesiology, Milledgeville, GA 31061. Offers health promotion (M Ed); human performance (M Ed); outdoor education (M Ed); physical education (MAT). *Accreditation:* NCATE (one or more programs are accredited). Part-time and evening/weekend programs available. *Students:* 31 full-time (14 women), 13 part-time (12 women); includes 11 minority (all Black or African American, non-Hispanic/Latino), 1 international. Average age 26. In 2013, 25 master's awarded. *Degree requirements:* For master's, comprehensive exam, thesis optional. *Entrance requirements:* For master's, GRE General Test or MAT, minimum GPA of 2.75 in upper-level undergraduate courses, 2 letters of reference. Additional exam requirements/recommendations for international students: Recommended—TOEFL (minimum score 550 paper-based; 79 iBT). *Application deadline:* For fall admission, 7/1 priority date for domestic students, 4/1 priority date for international students; for spring admission, 11/15 priority date for

domestic students, 9/1 priority date for international students. Applications are processed on a rolling basis. Application fee: $40. Electronic applications accepted. *Financial support:* In 2013–14, 26 research assistantships with full tuition reimbursements were awarded; career-related internships or fieldwork and unspecified assistantships also available. Support available to part-time students. Financial award applicants required to submit FAFSA. *Unit head:* Dr. Lisa Griffin, Chair, 478-445-4072, Fax: 478-445-4074, E-mail: lisa.griffin@gcsu.edu. *Application contact:* 800-342-0471, E-mail: grad-admit@gcsu.edu.

Georgia Regents University, The Graduate School, College of Education, Program in Health and Physical Education, Augusta, GA 30912. Offers M Ed. *Entrance requirements:* For master's, GRE, MAT, minimum GPA of 2.5.

Georgia Southwestern State University, Graduate Studies, School of Education, Americus, GA 31709-4693. Offers early childhood education (M Ed, Ed S); health and physical education (M Ed); middle grades education (M Ed, Ed S); reading (M Ed); secondary education (M Ed); special education (M Ed). *Accreditation:* NCATE. *Degree requirements:* For master's, comprehensive exam. *Entrance requirements:* For master's, GRE General Test or MAT, minimum GPA of 2.5; for Ed S, GRE General Test or MAT, minimum graduate GPA of 3.25, M Ed from accredited college or university, 3 years teaching experience. Electronic applications accepted.

Georgia State University, College of Education, Department of Kinesiology and Health, Program in Health and Physical Education, Atlanta, GA 30302-3083. Offers M Ed. Part-time and evening/weekend programs available. *Degree requirements:* For master's, comprehensive exam. *Entrance requirements:* For master's, GRE General Test, minimum GPA of 2.5. *Application deadline:* For fall admission, 5/1 for domestic students; for spring admission, 10/1 for domestic students. Application fee: $50. *Expenses: Tuition, area resident:* Full-time $4176; part-time $348 per credit hour. Tuition, state resident: full-time $14,544; part-time $1212 per credit hour. Tuition, nonresident: full-time $14,544; part-time $1212 per credit hour. Tuition and fees vary according to course load and program. *Financial support:* Teaching assistantships and career-related internships or fieldwork available. *Faculty research:* Exercise science, teacher behavior. *Unit head:* Dr. Jacalyn Lea Lund, Chair, 404-413-8051, E-mail: jlund@gsu.edu. *Application contact:* Dr. Rachel Gurvitch, Program Coordinator, 404-413-8374, E-mail: rgurvitch@gsu.edu.
Website: http://education.gsu.edu/KIN/kh_programs.htm.

Henderson State University, Graduate Studies, Teachers College, Department of Health, Physical Education, Recreation and Athletic Training, Arkadelphia, AR 71999-0001. Offers sports administration (MS). Part-time programs available. *Faculty:* 4 full-time (1 woman), 1 (woman) part-time/adjunct. *Students:* 6 full-time (3 women), 36 part-time (14 women); includes 15 minority (11 Black or African American, non-Hispanic/Latino; 1 Hispanic/Latino; 3 Two or more races, non-Hispanic/Latino). Average age 25. 16 applicants, 100% accepted, 16 enrolled. In 2013, 22 master's awarded. *Entrance requirements:* For master's, GRE General Test or MAT, minimum GPA of 2.7 as an undergraduate student. Additional exam requirements/recommendations for international students: Required—TOEFL (minimum score 600 paper-based); Recommended—IELTS (minimum score 6.5). *Application deadline:* For fall admission, 8/1 priority date for domestic students, 6/30 priority date for international students; for spring admission, 1/1 priority date for domestic students, 11/30 priority date for international students. Applications are processed on a rolling basis. Application fee: $25 ($75 for international students). *Expenses:* Tuition, state resident: full-time $4284; part-time $238 per credit hour. Tuition, nonresident: full-time $8802; part-time $489 per credit hour. Tuition and fees vary according to course load and campus/location. *Financial support:* In 2013–14, 10 teaching assistantships with partial tuition reimbursements (averaging $4,000 per year) were awarded; scholarships/grants and unspecified assistantships also available. *Unit head:* Dr. Lynn Glover-Stanley, Chair, 870-230-5200, E-mail: stanlel@hsu.edu. *Application contact:* Dr. Ken Taylor, Graduate Dean, 870-230-5126, Fax: 870-230-5479, E-mail: taylorke@hsu.edu.
Website: http://www.hsu.edu/hper/.

Hofstra University, School of Education, Programs in Physical and Health Education, Hempstead, NY 11549. Offers adventure education (Advanced Certificate); health education (MS), including PK-12 teaching certification; physical education (MA, MS), including adventure education, curriculum (MA), strength and conditioning; sport science (MS), including adventure education (MA, MS), strength and conditioning (MA, MS).

Howard University, Graduate School, Department of Health, Human Performance and Leisure Studies, Washington, DC 20059-0002. Offers exercise physiology (MS); health education (MS); sports studies (MS), including sociology of sports, sports management; urban recreation (MS), including leisure studies. Part-time and evening/weekend programs available. *Degree requirements:* For master's, comprehensive exam, thesis. *Entrance requirements:* For master's, BS in human performance or related field. Additional exam requirements/recommendations for international students: Recommended—TOEFL. Electronic applications accepted. *Faculty research:* Health promotion, cardiovascular hypertension, physical activity, sport and human rights issues.

Humboldt State University, Academic Programs, College of Professional Studies, Department of Kinesiology and Recreation Administration, Arcata, CA 95521-8299. Offers athletic training education (MS); exercise science/wellness management (MS); pre-physical therapy (MS); teaching/coaching (MS). *Degree requirements:* For master's, thesis or alternative. *Entrance requirements:* For master's, GMAT, minimum GPA of 2.5. Additional exam requirements/recommendations for international students: Required—TOEFL. *Faculty research:* Human performance, adapted physical education, physical therapy.

Idaho State University, Office of Graduate Studies, College of Education, Department of Sports Science and Physical Education, Pocatello, ID 83209-8105. Offers physical education (MPE). Part-time programs available. *Degree requirements:* For master's, comprehensive exam (for some programs), thesis optional, internship, oral defense of dissertation, or written exams. *Entrance requirements:* For master's, MAT or GRE General Test, minimum GPA of 3.0 in upper division classes. Additional exam requirements/recommendations for international students: Required—TOEFL (minimum score 550 paper-based; 80 iBT). Electronic applications accepted. *Faculty research:* Gender and diversity; concussion awareness/sports medicine; legal aspects of athletic health care; sports psychology; exercise physiology; sports management and leadership; adapted activities; fitness, wellness, and nutrition; coaching perspectives; critical features of athletic activities.

Illinois State University, Graduate School, College of Applied Science and Technology, School of Kinesiology and Recreation, Normal, IL 61790-2200. Offers health education (MS); physical education (MS). *Degree requirements:* For master's, thesis or alternative. *Entrance requirements:* For master's, GRE General Test, minimum GPA of 2.6 in last 60 hours of course work. *Faculty research:* Influences on positive youth development through sport, country-wide health fitness project, graduate practicum in athletic training, perceived exertion and self-selected intensity during resistance exercise in younger and older.

Indiana State University, College of Graduate and Professional Studies, College of Nursing, Health and Human Services, Department of Physical Education, Terre Haute,

IN 47809. Offers adult fitness (MA, MS); coaching (MA, MS); exercise science (MA, MS). *Degree requirements:* For master's, thesis (for some programs). *Entrance requirements:* For master's, minor in physical education. Electronic applications accepted. *Faculty research:* Exercise science.

Indiana University Bloomington, School of Public Health, Department of Kinesiology, Bloomington, IN 47405. Offers applied sport science (MS); athletic administration/sport management (MS); athletic training (MS); biomechanics (MS); ergonomics (MS); exercise physiology (MS); human performance (PhD), including biomechanics, exercise physiology, motor learning/control, sport management; motor learning/control (MS); physical activity (MPH); physical activity, fitness and wellness (MS). Part-time programs available. *Faculty:* 26 full-time (9 women). *Students:* 128 full-time (45 women), 16 part-time (6 women); includes 20 minority (11 Black or African American, non-Hispanic/Latino; 2 American Indian or Alaska Native, non-Hispanic/Latino; 3 Asian, non-Hispanic/Latino; 3 Hispanic/Latino; 1 Two or more races, non-Hispanic/Latino), 28 international. Average age 28. 174 applicants, 57% accepted, 48 enrolled. In 2013, 56 master's, 8 doctorates awarded. Terminal master's awarded for partial completion of doctoral program. *Degree requirements:* For master's, thesis optional; for doctorate, variable foreign language requirement, comprehensive exam, thesis/dissertation. *Entrance requirements:* For master's, GRE General Test, minimum GPA of 2.8; for doctorate, GRE General Test, minimum graduate GPA of 3.5, undergraduate 3.0. Additional exam requirements/recommendations for international students: Required—TOEFL (minimum score 80 iBT). *Application deadline:* For fall admission, 1/1 priority date for international students; for spring admission, 9/1 priority date for international students. Applications are processed on a rolling basis. Application fee: $55 ($65 for international students). *Financial support:* Fellowships, research assistantships with full tuition reimbursements, teaching assistantships with full tuition reimbursements, career-related internships or fieldwork, Federal Work-Study, institutionally sponsored loans, scholarships/grants, health care benefits, tuition waivers (partial), unspecified assistantships, and fee remissions available. Support available to part-time students. Financial award application deadline: 3/1; financial award applicants required to submit FAFSA. *Faculty research:* Exercise physiology and biochemistry, sports biomechanics, human motor control, adaptation of fitness and exercise to special populations. *Unit head:* Dr. David M. Koceja, Chairperson, 812-855-5523, Fax: 812-855-3193, E-mail: koceja@indiana.edu. *Application contact:* Kristine M. Wasson, Administrative Assistant for Graduate Studies, 812-855-5523, Fax: 812-855-3193, E-mail: ktanksle@indiana.edu. Website: http://www.publichealth.indiana.edu/departments/kinesiology/index.shtml.

Indiana University of Pennsylvania, School of Graduate Studies and Research, College of Health and Human Services, Department of Health and Physical Education, Program in Health and Physical Education, Indiana, PA 15705-1087. Offers M Ed. Part-time programs available. *Faculty:* 8 full-time (4 women). *Students:* 12 full-time (9 women), 3 part-time (1 woman); includes 2 minority (both Black or African American, non-Hispanic/Latino). Average age 26. 8 applicants, 75% accepted, 4 enrolled. In 2013, 20 master's awarded. *Entrance requirements:* Additional exam requirements/recommendations for international students: Required—TOEFL (minimum score 540 paper-based). *Application deadline:* Applications are processed on a rolling basis. Application fee: $50. Electronic applications accepted. *Expenses:* Tuition, state resident: full-time $3978; part-time $442 per credit. Tuition, nonresident: full-time $5967; part-time $663 per credit. *Required fees:* $2080; $115.55 per credit. $93 per semester. Tuition and fees vary according to degree level and program. *Financial support:* In 2013–14, 6 research assistantships with full and partial tuition reimbursements (averaging $5,440 per year) were awarded; career-related internships or fieldwork, Federal Work-Study, scholarships/grants, and unspecified assistantships also available. Support available to part-time students. Financial award application deadline: 4/15; financial award applicants required to submit FAFSA. *Unit head:* Dr. Keri Kulik, Coordinator, 724-357-5656, E-mail: kskulik@iup.edu. Website: http://www.iup.edu/grad/healthphysed/default.aspx.

Indiana University–Purdue University Indianapolis, School of Physical Education and Tourism Management, Indianapolis, IN 46202-2896. Offers physical education (MS). *Faculty:* 4 full-time (2 women). *Students:* 18 full-time (9 women), 8 part-time (7 women); includes 1 minority (Black or African American, non-Hispanic/Latino), 2 international. Average age 28. 31 applicants, 58% accepted, 17 enrolled. In 2013, 14 master's awarded. Application fee: $55 ($65 for international students). *Financial support:* Career-related internships or fieldwork, Federal Work-Study, institutionally sponsored loans, and scholarships/grants available. Support available to part-time students. *Unit head:* Dr. James M. Gladden, Dean, E-mail: jamglad@iupui.edu. Website: http://petm.iupui.edu/.

Inter American University of Puerto Rico, Metropolitan Campus, Graduate Programs, Program in Physical Education, San Juan, PR 00919-1293. Offers teaching of physical education (MA); training and sport performance (MA). *Degree requirements:* For master's, comprehensive exam. *Entrance requirements:* For master's, GRE or EXADEP, interview. Electronic applications accepted.

Inter American University of Puerto Rico, San Germán Campus, Graduate Studies Center, Program in Health and Physical Education, San Germán, PR 00683-5008. Offers MA. Part-time and evening/weekend programs available. *Faculty:* 12 full-time (7 women), 27 part-time/adjunct (17 women). *Students:* 20 full-time (9 women), 2 part-time (1 woman); all minorities (all Hispanic/Latino). Average age 29. 7 applicants, 86% accepted, 5 enrolled. In 2013, 8 master's awarded. *Degree requirements:* For master's, comprehensive exam. *Entrance requirements:* For master's, GRE General Test or EXADEP, minimum GPA of 3.0. *Application deadline:* For fall admission, 4/30 priority date for domestic students; for spring admission, 11/15 for domestic students. Applications are processed on a rolling basis. Application fee: $31. *Expenses:* Tuition: Full-time $2424; part-time $202 per credit hour. *Required fees:* $260 per semester. Tuition and fees vary according to course level, course load, degree level and program. *Financial support:* Teaching assistantships available. *Unit head:* Dr. Elba T. Irizarry, Director of Graduate Studies Center, 787-264-1912 Ext. 7357, Fax: 787-892-6350, E-mail: elbat@sg.inter.edu. *Application contact:* Dr. Elba T. Irizarry, Director of Graduate Studies Center, 787-264-1912 Ext. 7357, Fax: 787-892-6350, E-mail: elbat@sg.inter.edu.

Ithaca College, School of Health Sciences and Human Performance, Program in Physical Education, Ithaca, NY 14850. Offers MS. Part-time programs available. *Faculty:* 7 full-time (5 women). In 2013, 1 master's awarded. *Degree requirements:* For master's, thesis optional. *Entrance requirements:* For master's, minimum GPA of 3.0. Additional exam requirements/recommendations for international students: Required—TOEFL (minimum score 550 paper-based; 80 iBT). *Application deadline:* For fall admission, 3/1 priority date for domestic and international students; for spring admission, 12/1 for domestic and international students. Applications are processed on a rolling basis. Application fee: $40. Electronic applications accepted. *Expenses:* Contact institution. *Financial support:* Career-related internships or fieldwork, Federal Work-Study, scholarships/grants, and unspecified assistantships available. Support available to part-time students. Financial award application deadline: 3/1; financial award applicants required to submit CSS PROFILE or FAFSA. *Faculty research:* Needs assessment evaluation of health education programs, minority health (includes diversity), employee health assessment and program planning, youth at risk/families,

multicultural/international health, program planning/health behaviors, sexuality education in the family and school setting, parent-teacher and student-teacher relationships, attitude/interest/motivation, teaching effectiveness, student learning/achievement. *Unit head:* Dr. Srijana Bajracharya, Chairperson, 607-274-3143, Fax: 607-274-1263, E-mail: gps@ithaca.edu. *Application contact:* Gerard Turbide, Director, Office of Admission, 607-274-3143, Fax: 607-274-1263, E-mail: gps@ithaca.edu. Website: http://www.ithaca.edu/gps/gradprograms/hppe/programs/physed.

Jackson State University, Graduate School, College of Education and Human Development, Department of Health, Physical Education and Recreation, Jackson, MS 39217. Offers MS Ed. *Accreditation:* NCATE. Part-time and evening/weekend programs available. *Degree requirements:* For master's, comprehensive exam, thesis or alternative. *Entrance requirements:* For master's, GRE General Test. Additional exam requirements/recommendations for international students: Required—TOEFL (minimum score 520 paper-based; 67 iBT).

Jacksonville State University, College of Graduate Studies and Continuing Education, College of Education and Professional Studies, Program in Physical Education, Jacksonville, AL 36265-1602. Offers MS Ed, Ed S. *Accreditation:* NCATE. Part-time and evening/weekend programs available. *Degree requirements:* For master's, comprehensive exam, thesis (for some programs). *Entrance requirements:* For master's, GRE General Test or MAT. Additional exam requirements/recommendations for international students: Required—TOEFL (minimum score 61 iBT). Electronic applications accepted.

Kent State University, Graduate School of Education, Health, and Human Services, School of Teaching, Learning and Curriculum Studies, Program in Physical Education, Kent, OH 44242-0001. Offers M Ed. *Unit head:* Dr. Steve Mitchell, Coordinator, 330-672-0229, E-mail: smitchel@kent.edu. *Application contact:* Nancy Miller, Academic Program Coordinator, Office of Graduate Student Services, 330-672-2576, Fax: 330-672-9162, E-mail: ogs@kent.edu. Website: http://www.kent.edu/ehhs/pep/.

Lindenwood University, Graduate Programs, School of Education, St. Charles, MO 63301-1695. Offers education (MA); educational administration (MA, Ed D, Ed S); human performance (MS); instructional leadership (Ed D, Ed S); library media (MA); professional counseling (MA); school administration (Ed S); school counseling (MA); teaching (MA); teaching English to speakers of other languages (MA). Part-time and evening/weekend programs available. Postbaccalaureate distance learning degree programs offered (no on-campus study). *Faculty:* 50 full-time (33 women), 228 part-time/adjunct (136 women). *Students:* 454 full-time (352 women), 1,772 part-time (1,351 women); includes 637 minority (545 Black or African American, non-Hispanic/Latino; 9 American Indian or Alaska Native, non-Hispanic/Latino; 9 Asian, non-Hispanic/Latino; 42 Hispanic/Latino; 32 Two or more races, non-Hispanic/Latino), 32 international. Average age 36. 644 applicants, 71% accepted, 401 enrolled. In 2013, 564 master's, 35 doctorates, 83 other advanced degrees awarded. *Degree requirements:* For master's, thesis (for some programs), minimum GPA of 3.0; for doctorate, thesis/dissertation, minimum GPA of 3.0; for Ed S, comprehensive exam, project, minimum GPA of 3.0. *Entrance requirements:* For master's, interview, minimum GPA of 3.0, writing sample, letter of recommendation; for doctorate, GRE, minimum graduate GPA of 3.4, resume, interview, writing sample, 4 letters of recommendation; for Ed S, master's degree in education, relevant work experience. Additional exam requirements/recommendations for international students: Required—TOEFL (minimum score 550 paper-based; 80 iBT). *Application deadline:* For fall admission, 8/26 priority date for domestic and international students; for spring admission, 1/27 priority date for domestic and international students. Applications are processed on a rolling basis. Application fee: $30 ($100 for international students). Electronic applications accepted. *Expenses:* Tuition: Full-time $14,800; part-time $428 per credit hour. *Required fees:* $350. Tuition and fees vary according to course level and course load. *Financial support:* In 2013–14, 385 students received support. Career-related internships or fieldwork, Federal Work-Study, institutionally sponsored loans, scholarships/grants, tuition waivers (partial), and unspecified assistantships available. Financial award application deadline: 6/30; financial award applicants required to submit FAFSA. *Unit head:* Dr. Cynthia Bice, Dean, 636-949-4618, Fax: 636-949-4197, E-mail: cbice@lindenwood.edu. *Application contact:* Brett Barger, Dean of Evening Admissions and Extension Campuses, 636-949-4934, Fax: 636-949-4109, E-mail: adultadmissions@lindenwood.edu.

Long Island University–LIU Brooklyn, School of Health Professions, Division of Sports Sciences, Brooklyn, NY 11201-8423. Offers adapted physical education (MS); athletic training and sports sciences (MS); exercise physiology (MS); health sciences (MS). Part-time and evening/weekend programs available. *Entrance requirements:* For master's, 2 letters of recommendation. Additional exam requirements/recommendations for international students: Required—TOEFL (minimum score 500 paper-based). Electronic applications accepted.

Longwood University, College of Graduate and Professional Studies, College of Education and Human Services, Farmville, VA 23909. Offers education (MS), including algebra and middle school math, counselor education, elementary and middle school math, elementary education, elementary education initial licensure, health and physical education, school librarianship, special education general curriculum, special education initial licensure; social work and communication sciences and disorders (MS). *Accreditation:* NCATE. Part-time and evening/weekend programs available. *Faculty:* 28 full-time (15 women), 9 part-time/adjunct (7 women). *Students:* 86 full-time (80 women), 187 part-time (173 women); includes 38 minority (26 Black or African American, non-Hispanic/Latino; 1 Asian, non-Hispanic/Latino; 5 Hispanic/Latino; 1 Native Hawaiian or other Pacific Islander, non-Hispanic/Latino; 5 Two or more races, non-Hispanic/Latino). 98 applicants, 89% accepted, 85 enrolled. In 2013, 132 master's awarded. *Degree requirements:* For master's, comprehensive exam (for some programs), thesis optional, professional portfolio, internship, clinical experience, or practicum. *Entrance requirements:* For master's, bachelor's degree from regionally-accredited institution, 2 recommendations, 500-word personal essay, official transcripts, minimum GPA of 2.75, valid teaching license (for some programs), passing Praxis I scores for initial teaching licensure programs. Additional exam requirements/recommendations for international students: Required—TOEFL (minimum score 570 paper-based), IELTS (minimum score 6.5). *Application deadline:* For fall admission, 5/1 priority date for domestic students; for spring admission, 10/1 priority date for domestic students; for summer admission, 2/1 priority date for domestic students. Applications are processed on a rolling basis. Application fee: $50. Electronic applications accepted. *Expenses:* Tuition, state resident: full-time $7506; part-time $327 per credit hour. Tuition, nonresident: full-time $17,100; part-time $837 per credit hour. Tuition and fees vary according to course load and campus/location. *Financial support:* Career-related internships or fieldwork and Federal Work-Study available. Financial award applicants required to submit FAFSA. *Unit head:* Dr. Peggy L. Tarpley, Chair of the Department of Education and Special Education, 434-395-2337, E-mail: tarpleypl@longwood.edu. *Application contact:* College of Graduate and Professional Studies, 434-395-2380, Fax: 434-395-2750, E-mail: graduate@longwood.edu. Website: http://www.longwood.edu/cehs/.

Louisiana Tech University, Graduate School, College of Education, Department of Kinesiology, Ruston, LA 71272. Offers administration of sport and physical activity (MS);

sports performance (MS). *Accreditation:* NCATE. Part-time programs available. *Degree requirements:* For master's, thesis or alternative. *Entrance requirements:* For master's, GRE General Test. *Application deadline:* For fall admission, 7/29 for domestic students; for spring admission, 2/3 for domestic students. Application fee: $20 ($30 for international students). *Financial support:* Fellowships and research assistantships available. Financial award application deadline: 2/1. *Unit head:* Dr. Lanie Dornier, Head, 318-257-4432, Fax: 318-257-2379. *Application contact:* Dr. Cathy Stockton, Associate Dean of Graduate Studies, 318-257-3229, Fax: 318-257-2379, E-mail: cstock@latech.edu.
Website: http://www.latech.edu/education/kinesiology/.

Massachusetts College of Liberal Arts, Graduate Programs, North Adams, MA 01247-4100. Offers business (MBA); educational administration (M Ed); educational leadership (CAGS); instruction and curriculum (M Ed); instructional technology (M Ed); physical education and health (M Ed); reading (M Ed); special education (M Ed). Part-time and evening/weekend programs available. *Degree requirements:* For master's, thesis. *Entrance requirements:* For master's, writing sample.

McDaniel College, Graduate and Professional Studies, Program in Exercise Science and Physical Education, Westminster, MD 21157-4390. Offers MS. Part-time and evening/weekend programs available. *Degree requirements:* For master's, comprehensive exam, thesis optional. *Entrance requirements:* For master's, 3 letters of reference. Additional exam requirements/recommendations for international students: Required—TOEFL.

McGill University, Faculty of Graduate and Postdoctoral Studies, Faculty of Education, Department of Kinesiology and Physical Education, Montréal, QC H3A 2T5, Canada. Offers M Sc, MA, PhD, Certificate, Diploma.

Memorial University of Newfoundland, School of Graduate Studies, School of Human Kinetics and Recreation, St. John's, NL A1C 5S7, Canada. Offers administration, curriculum and supervision (MPE); biomechanics/ergonomics (MS Kin); exercise and work physiology (MS Kin); sport psychology (MS Kin). Part-time programs available. *Degree requirements:* For master's, thesis optional, seminars, thesis presentations. *Entrance requirements:* For master's, bachelor's degree in a related field, minimum B average. Electronic applications accepted. *Faculty research:* Administration, sociology of sports, kinesiology, physiology/recreation.

Middle Tennessee State University, College of Graduate Studies, College of Behavioral and Health Sciences, Department of Health and Human Performance, Program in Health, Physical Education and Recreation, Murfreesboro, TN 37132. Offers health and human performance (MS); leisure and sport management (MS). Part-time and evening/weekend programs available. Postbaccalaureate distance learning degree programs offered. *Faculty:* 24 full-time (9 women), 5 part-time/adjunct (3 women). *Students:* 26 full-time (15 women), 40 part-time (23 women); includes 20 minority (15 Black or African American, non-Hispanic/Latino; 1 Asian, non-Hispanic/Latino; 3 Hispanic/Latino; 1 Two or more races, non-Hispanic/Latino). 87 applicants, 61% accepted. In 2013, 31 master's awarded. *Degree requirements:* For master's, comprehensive exam, thesis optional. *Entrance requirements:* For master's, GRE. Additional exam requirements/recommendations for international students: Required—TOEFL (minimum score 525 paper-based; 71 iBT) or IELTS (minimum score 6). *Application deadline:* For fall admission, 6/1 for domestic and international students. Applications are processed on a rolling basis. Application fee: $25 ($30 for international students). *Financial support:* In 2013–14, 14 students received support. Tuition waivers available. Support available to part-time students. Financial award application deadline: 5/1. *Faculty research:* Kinesiometrics, leisure behavior, health, lifestyles. *Unit head:* Dr. Harold D. Whiteside, Interim Dean, 615-898-2900, Fax: 615-494-7704, E-mail: harold.whiteside@mtsu.edu. *Application contact:* Dr. Michael D. Allen, Vice Provost for Research and Dean, 615-898-2840, Fax: 615-904-8020, E-mail: michael.allen@mtsu.edu.

Minnesota State University Mankato, College of Graduate Studies, College of Allied Health and Nursing, Department of Human Performance, Mankato, MN 56001. Offers MA, MS. Part-time programs available. *Students:* 64 full-time (29 women), 40 part-time (21 women). *Degree requirements:* For master's, comprehensive exam, thesis. *Entrance requirements:* For master's, minimum GPA of 3.0 during previous 2 years. Additional exam requirements/recommendations for international students: Required—TOEFL. *Application deadline:* For fall admission, 3/1 priority date for domestic and international students. Applications are processed on a rolling basis. Application fee: $40. *Financial support:* Research assistantships with full tuition reimbursements, teaching assistantships with full tuition reimbursements, career-related internships or fieldwork, Federal Work-Study, institutionally sponsored loans, and unspecified assistantships available. Support available to part-time students. Financial award application deadline: 3/15; financial award applicants required to submit FAFSA. *Faculty research:* Exercise physiology. *Unit head:* Dr. Cindra Kamphoff, Graduate Coordinator, 507-389-6313. *Application contact:* 507-389-2321, E-mail: grad@mnsu.edu.
Website: http://ahn.mnsu.edu/hp/.

Mississippi State University, College of Education, Department of Kinesiology, Mississippi State, MS 39762. Offers exercise physiology (MS); sport administration (MS); sport pedagogy (MS). Part-time programs available. Postbaccalaureate distance learning degree programs offered (minimal on-campus study). *Faculty:* 6 full-time (1 woman). *Students:* 44 full-time (12 women), 11 part-time (4 women); includes 6 minority (3 Black or African American, non-Hispanic/Latino; 2 Hispanic/Latino; 1 Two or more races, non-Hispanic/Latino), 4 international. Average age 25. 98 applicants, 35% accepted, 23 enrolled. In 2013, 36 master's awarded. *Degree requirements:* For master's, comprehensive exam, thesis optional. *Entrance requirements:* For master's, GRE General Test, minimum GPA of 2.75 on undergraduate work from four-year accredited institution, 3.0 graduate. Additional exam requirements/recommendations for international students: Required—TOEFL (minimum score 550 paper-based; 79 iBT); Recommended—IELTS (minimum score 6.5). *Application deadline:* For fall admission, 7/1 for domestic students, 5/1 for international students; for spring admission, 11/1 for domestic students, 9/1 for international students. Applications are processed on a rolling basis. Application fee: $60. Electronic applications accepted. *Financial support:* In 2013–14, 7 teaching assistantships (averaging $8,772 per year) were awarded; career-related internships or fieldwork, Federal Work-Study, institutionally sponsored loans, and unspecified assistantships also available. Financial award application deadline: 4/1; financial award applicants required to submit FAFSA. *Faculty research:* Static balance and stepping performance of older adults, organizational justice, public health, strength training and recovery drinks, high risk drinking perceptions and behaviors. *Unit head:* Dr. Stanley Brown, Professor and Department Head, 662-325-2963, Fax: 662-325-4525, E-mail: spb107@msstate.edu. *Application contact:* Dr. Adam Love, Graduate Coordinator, 662-325-2963, Fax: 662-325-4525, E-mail: adam.love@msstate.edu.
Website: http://www.kinesiology.msstate.edu/.

Missouri State University, Graduate College, College of Health and Human Services, Department of Kinesiology, Springfield, MO 65897. Offers health promotion and wellness management (MS); secondary education (MS Ed), including physical education. Part-time programs available. *Faculty:* 14 full-time (6 women). *Students:* 14 full-time (6 women), 17 part-time (10 women); includes 1 minority (Hispanic/Latino), 7 international. Average age 28. 15 applicants, 93% accepted, 7 enrolled. In 2013, 7 master's awarded. *Degree requirements:* For master's, comprehensive exam, thesis or alternative. *Entrance requirements:* For master's, GRE (MS), minimum GPA of 2.8 (MS); 9-12 teaching certification (MS Ed). Additional exam requirements/recommendations for international students: Required—TOEFL (minimum score 550 paper-based; 79 iBT). *Application deadline:* For fall admission, 7/20 priority date for domestic students, 5/1 for international students; for spring admission, 12/20 priority date for domestic students, 9/1 for international students. Applications are processed on a rolling basis. Application fee: $35 ($50 for international students). Electronic applications accepted. *Expenses:* Tuition, state resident: full-time $4500; part-time $250 per credit hour. Tuition, nonresident: full-time $9018; part-time $501 per credit hour. *Required fees:* $361 per semester. Tuition and fees vary according to course level, course load and program. *Financial support:* In 2013–14, 7 teaching assistantships with full tuition reimbursements (averaging $9,097 per year) were awarded; Federal Work-Study, institutionally sponsored loans, scholarships/grants, and unspecified assistantships also available. Financial award application deadline: 3/31; financial award applicants required to submit FAFSA. *Unit head:* Dr. Sarah McCallister, Acting Head, 417-836-6582, Fax: 417-836-5371, E-mail: sarahmccallister@missouristate.edu. *Application contact:* Misty Stewart, Coordinator of Graduate Admissions and Recruitment, 417-836-6079, Fax: 417-836-6200, E-mail: mistystewart@missouristate.edu.
Website: http://www.missouristate.edu/kinesiology/.

Montclair State University, The Graduate School, College of Education and Human Services, Department of Exercise Science and Physical Education, Program in Exercise Science and Physical Education, Montclair, NJ 07043-1624. Offers exercise science (MA); sports administration and coaching (MA); teaching and supervision in physical education (MA). Part-time and evening/weekend programs available. *Degree requirements:* For master's, comprehensive exam, thesis or alternative. *Entrance requirements:* For master's, GRE General Test, essay, 2 letters of recommendation. Additional exam requirements/recommendations for international students: Required—TOEFL (minimum score 83 iBT), IELTS (minimum score 6.5). Electronic applications accepted.

Montclair State University, The Graduate School, College of Education and Human Services, Department of Exercise Science and Physical Education, Program in Teaching Physical Education, Montclair, NJ 07043-1624. Offers MAT. *Degree requirements:* For master's, comprehensive exam, thesis or alternative. *Entrance requirements:* For master's, GRE General Test, interview, essay, 2 letters of recommendation. Additional exam requirements/recommendations for international students: Required—TOEFL (minimum score 83 iBT), IELTS (minimum score 6.5). Electronic applications accepted.

Montclair State University, The Graduate School, College of Education and Human Services, Department of Secondary and Special Education, Program in Teaching in Subject Area, Montclair, NJ 07043-1624. Offers art (MAT); biology (MAT); chemistry (MAT); earth science (MAT); English (MAT); French (MAT); health and physical education (MAT); health education (MAT); mathematics (MAT); music (MAT); physical education (MAT); physical science (MAT); social studies (MAT); Spanish (MAT); teacher of English as a second language (MAT). *Degree requirements:* For master's, comprehensive exam, thesis or alternative. *Entrance requirements:* For master's, GRE General Test, interview, 2 letters of recommendation. Additional exam requirements/recommendations for international students: Required—TOEFL (minimum score 83 iBT), IELTS (minimum score 6.5). Electronic applications accepted.

Morehead State University, Graduate Programs, College of Education, Department of Middle Grades and Secondary Education, Morehead, KY 40351. Offers business and marketing education (MAT); English/language arts 5-9 (MAT); French (MAT); health P-12 (MAT); mathematics 5-9 (MAT); physical education P-12 (MAT); science 5-9 (MAT); secondary biology (MAT); secondary chemistry (MAT); secondary earth science (MAT); secondary English (MAT); secondary math (MAT); secondary physics (MAT); secondary social studies (MAT); social studies 5-9 (MAT); Spanish (MAT). Part-time and evening/weekend programs available. *Degree requirements:* For master's, portfolio. *Entrance requirements:* For master's, GRE or PRAXIS II content exam, minimum overall undergraduate GPA of 2.5. Additional exam requirements/recommendations for international students: Required—TOEFL (minimum score 500 paper-based). Electronic applications accepted.

Morehead State University, Graduate Programs, College of Science and Technology, Department of Health, Wellness and Human Performance, Morehead, KY 40351. Offers health/physical education (MA). *Accreditation:* NCATE. Part-time and evening/weekend programs available. *Degree requirements:* For master's, comprehensive exam, thesis, oral exam, written core exam. *Entrance requirements:* For master's, GRE General Test or MAT, minimum GPA of 2.5; undergraduate major/minor in health, physical education, or recreation. Additional exam requirements/recommendations for international students: Required—TOEFL (minimum score 500 paper-based). Electronic applications accepted. *Faculty research:* Child growth and performance, instructional strategies, outdoor leadership qualities, exercise science, athletic training.

Murray State University, College of Education, Department of Adolescent, Career and Special Education, Murray, KY 42071. Offers health, physical education, and recreation (MA), including physical education; industrial and technical education (MS); middle school education (MA Ed, Ed S); secondary education (MA Ed, Ed S); special education (MA Ed), including advanced learning behavior disorders, learning disabilities, moderate/severe disorders. *Accreditation:* NCATE. Part-time programs available. *Entrance requirements:* Additional exam requirements/recommendations for international students: Required—TOEFL.

North Carolina Agricultural and Technical State University, School of Graduate Studies, School of Education, Department of Human Performance and Leisure Studies, Greensboro, NC 27411. Offers physical education (MAT, MS). *Accreditation:* NCATE. Part-time and evening/weekend programs available. *Degree requirements:* For master's, comprehensive exam, thesis or alternative, qualifying exam. *Entrance requirements:* For master's, GRE General Test or MAT.

North Carolina Central University, College of Behavioral and Social Sciences, Department of Physical Education and Recreation, Durham, NC 27707-3129. Offers athletic administration (MS); physical education (MS); recreation administration (MS); therapeutic recreation (MS). Part-time and evening/weekend programs available. *Degree requirements:* For master's, one foreign language, comprehensive exam, thesis. *Entrance requirements:* For master's, GRE, minimum GPA of 3.0 in major, 2.5 overall. Additional exam requirements/recommendations for international students: Required—TOEFL. *Faculty research:* Physical activity patterns of children with disabilities, physical fitness test of North Carolina school children, exercise physiology, motor learning/development.

Northern Illinois University, Graduate School, College of Education, Department of Kinesiology and Physical Education, De Kalb, IL 60115-2854. Offers physical education (MS Ed); sport management (MS). Part-time and evening/weekend programs available. *Faculty:* 21 full-time (12 women). *Students:* 66 full-time (22 women), 55 part-time (24 women); includes 29 minority (15 Black or African American, non-Hispanic/Latino; 3 Asian, non-Hispanic/Latino; 8 Hispanic/Latino; 3 Two or more races, non-Hispanic/

Latino), 4 international. Average age 26. 91 applicants, 63% accepted, 36 enrolled. In 2013, 52 master's awarded. *Degree requirements:* For master's, comprehensive exam, thesis optional. *Entrance requirements:* For master's, GRE General Test, minimum GPA of 2.75, undergraduate major in related area. Additional exam requirements/recommendations for international students: Required—TOEFL (minimum score 550 paper-based). *Application deadline:* For fall admission, 6/1 for domestic students, 5/1 for international students; for spring admission, 11/1 for domestic students, 10/1 for international students. Applications are processed on a rolling basis. Application fee: $40. Electronic applications accepted. *Financial support:* In 2013–14, 6 research assistantships with full tuition reimbursements, 33 teaching assistantships with full tuition reimbursements were awarded; fellowships with full tuition reimbursements, career-related internships or fieldwork, Federal Work-Study, scholarships/grants, tuition waivers (full), and unspecified assistantships also available. Support available to part-time students. Financial award applicants required to submit FAFSA. *Faculty research:* Leadership in athletic training, motor development, dance education, gait analysis, fat phobia. *Unit head:* Dr. Paul Carpenter, Chair, 815-753-8284, Fax: 815-753-1413, E-mail: knpe@niu.edu. *Application contact:* Dr. Laurie Zittel, Director, Graduate Studies, 815-753-1425, E-mail: lzape@niu.edu.
Website: http://cedu.niu.edu/knpe/.

Northwest Missouri State University, Graduate School, College of Education and Human Services, Department of Health and Human Services, Maryville, MO 64468-6001. Offers applied health science (MS); health and physical education (MS Ed); recreation (MS). *Accreditation:* NCATE. Part-time programs available. *Degree requirements:* For master's, comprehensive exam. *Entrance requirements:* For master's, GRE General Test, minimum undergraduate GPA of 2.75, teaching certificate, writing sample. Additional exam requirements/recommendations for international students: Required—TOEFL (minimum score 550 paper-based).

The Ohio State University, Graduate School, College of Education and Human Ecology, Department of Human Sciences, Columbus, OH 43210. Offers consumer sciences (MS, PhD); human development and family science (PhD); human nutrition (MS, PhD); kinesiology (MA, PhD). Part-time programs available. *Faculty:* 65. *Students:* 97 full-time (77 women), 4 part-time (3 women); includes 14 minority (5 Black or African American, non-Hispanic/Latino; 6 Asian, non-Hispanic/Latino; 3 Hispanic/Latino), 40 international. Average age 29. In 2013, 13 master's, 21 doctorates awarded. *Degree requirements:* For master's, thesis optional; for doctorate, thesis/dissertation. *Entrance requirements:* For master's and doctorate, GRE. Additional exam requirements/recommendations for international students: Required—TOEFL (minimum score 550 paper-based; 79 iBT), Michigan English Language Assessment Battery (minimum score 82); Recommended—IELTS (minimum score 7). *Application deadline:* For fall admission, 12/1 priority date for domestic and international students; for winter admission, 12/1 for domestic students, 11/1 for international students; for spring admission, 3/1 for domestic students, 2/1 for international students. Applications are processed on a rolling basis. Application fee: $60 ($70 for international students). Electronic applications accepted. *Financial support:* Fellowships with tuition reimbursements, research assistantships with tuition reimbursements, teaching assistantships with tuition reimbursements, Federal Work-Study, and institutionally sponsored loans available. Support available to part-time students. *Unit head:* Earl Harrison, Chair, 614-292-8189, E-mail: harrison.304@osu.edu. *Application contact:* Graduate Admissions, 614-292-6031, Fax: 614-292-3656, E-mail: gradadmissions@osu.edu.
Website: http://ehe.osu.edu/human-sciences/.

Ohio University, Graduate College, Gladys W. and David H. Patton College of Education and Human Services, Department of Recreation and Sport Pedagogy, Program in Coaching Education, Athens, OH 45701-2979. Offers MS. *Entrance requirements:* For master's, GRE. Additional exam requirements/recommendations for international students: Required—TOEFL (minimum score 550 paper-based; 80 iBT) or IELTS (minimum score 6.5). Electronic applications accepted. *Faculty research:* Sports, physical activity, athletes.

Old Dominion University, Darden College of Education, Program in Physical Education, Norfolk, VA 23529. Offers curriculum and instruction (MS Ed); exercise and wellness (MS Ed); physical education (MS Ed); sport management (MS Ed). Part-time and evening/weekend programs available. *Faculty:* 15 full-time (5 women), 2 part-time/adjunct (1 woman). *Students:* 74 full-time (37 women), 45 part-time (20 women); includes 20 minority (14 Black or African American, non-Hispanic/Latino; 3 Hispanic/Latino; 3 Two or more races, non-Hispanic/Latino), 5 international. Average age 26. 105 applicants, 72% accepted, 55 enrolled. In 2013, 50 master's awarded. *Degree requirements:* For master's, comprehensive exam, thesis or alternative, internship, research project. *Entrance requirements:* For master's, GRE General Test, minimum GPA of 2.8. Additional exam requirements/recommendations for international students: Required—TOEFL (minimum score 500 paper-based). *Application deadline:* For fall admission, 3/1 for domestic students; for spring admission, 11/1 for domestic students. Applications are processed on a rolling basis. Application fee: $50. *Expenses:* Tuition, state resident: full-time $9888; part-time $412 per credit. Tuition, nonresident: full-time $25,152; part-time $1048 per credit. *Required fees:* $59 per semester. One-time fee: $50. *Financial support:* In 2013–14, 1 fellowship (averaging $1,500 per year), 2 research assistantships with partial tuition reimbursements (averaging $9,000 per year), 5 teaching assistantships with tuition reimbursements (averaging $9,000 per year) were awarded; career-related internships or fieldwork and scholarships/grants also available. Financial award application deadline: 4/15; financial award applicants required to submit FAFSA. *Faculty research:* Exercise physiology, nutrition and sports, sport management, biomechanics, physical education. *Total annual research expenditures:* $183,251. *Unit head:* Chair, 757-683-4995, Fax: 757-683-4270. *Application contact:* William Heffelfinger, Director of Graduate Admissions, 757-683-5554, Fax: 757-683-3255, E-mail: gradadmit@odu.edu.
Website: http://education.odu.edu/esper/.

Oregon State University, College of Public Health and Human Sciences, Program in Exercise and Sport Science, Corvallis, OR 97331. Offers exercise physiology (MS, PhD); movement studies in disability (MS, PhD); neuromechanics (MS, PhD); physical activity and public health (MS, PhD); physical education and teacher education (MS); sport and exercise psychology (MS, PhD). Part-time programs available. *Faculty:* 12 full-time (5 women), 1 (woman) part-time/adjunct. *Students:* 47 full-time (28 women), 7 part-time (3 women); includes 6 minority (2 Asian, non-Hispanic/Latino; 2 Hispanic/Latino; 2 Two or more races, non-Hispanic/Latino), 4 international. Average age 28. 127 applicants, 18% accepted, 23 enrolled. In 2013, 16 master's, 8 doctorates awarded. Terminal master's awarded for partial completion of doctoral program. *Median time to degree:* Of those who began their doctoral program in fall 2005, 86% received their degree in 8 years or less. *Degree requirements:* For master's, thesis; for doctorate, thesis/dissertation. *Entrance requirements:* For master's and doctorate, GRE, minimum GPA of 3.0 in last 90 hours. Additional exam requirements/recommendations for international students: Required—TOEFL (minimum score 80 iBT), IELTS (minimum score 6.5). *Application deadline:* For fall admission, 12/1 for domestic students. Application fee: $60. *Expenses:* Tuition, state resident: full-time $11,664; part-time $432 per credit hour. Tuition, nonresident: full-time $19,197; part-time $711 per credit hour. *Required fees:* $1446; $443 per quarter. One-time fee: $300. Tuition and fees vary according to course load and program. *Financial support:* Research assistantships, teaching assistantships, career-related internships or fieldwork, Federal Work-Study, and institutionally sponsored loans available. Support available to part-time students. Financial award application deadline: 2/1. *Faculty research:* Motor control, sports medicine, exercise physiology, sport psychology, biomechanics. *Unit head:* Dr. Tony Wilcox, Co-Director of the School of Biological and Population Health Sciences, 541-737-2643. *Application contact:* Debi Rothermund, Exercise and Sports Science Advisor, 541-737-3324, E-mail: debi.rothermund@oregonstate.edu.
Website: http://health.oregonstate.edu/degrees/graduate/exercise-sport-science.

Pittsburg State University, Graduate School, College of Education, Department of Health, Physical Education and Recreation, Pittsburg, KS 66762. Offers physical education (MS). *Degree requirements:* For master's, thesis or alternative. *Faculty research:* Personality of athletes, fitness activities for children, aerobic conditioning, fitness evaluation.

Plymouth State University, College of Graduate Studies, Graduate Studies in Education, Program in Secondary Education, Plymouth, NH 03264-1595. Offers curriculum and instruction (M Ed); language education (M Ed); library media (M Ed); physical education (M Ed); social studies education (M Ed); special education (M Ed). Part-time and evening/weekend programs available. *Entrance requirements:* For master's, MAT.

Prairie View A&M University, College of Education, Department of Health and Human Performance, Prairie View, TX 77446-0519. Offers health education (M Ed, MS); physical education (M Ed, MS). *Accreditation:* NCATE. Part-time and evening/weekend programs available. *Faculty:* 1 (woman) full-time, 2 part-time/adjunct (0 women). *Students:* 18 full-time (10 women), 14 part-time (7 women); includes 27 minority (24 Black or African American, non-Hispanic/Latino; 3 Hispanic/Latino), 1 international. Average age 31. 36 applicants, 100% accepted. In 2013, 12 master's awarded. *Entrance requirements:* For master's, GRE General Test. Additional exam requirements/recommendations for international students: Required—TOEFL. *Application deadline:* For fall admission, 7/1 priority date for domestic students, 7/1 for international students; for spring admission, 11/1 for domestic and international students. Applications are processed on a rolling basis. Application fee: $50. *Expenses:* Tuition, state resident: full-time $3776; part-time $209.77 per credit hour. Tuition, nonresident: full-time $10,183; part-time $565.77 per credit hour. *Required fees:* $2037; $446.50 per credit hour. *Financial support:* In 2013–14, 8 fellowships with tuition reimbursements (averaging $1,200 per year), 10 research assistantships with tuition reimbursements (averaging $15,000 per year) were awarded; teaching assistantships with tuition reimbursements, career-related internships or fieldwork, Federal Work-Study, and institutionally sponsored loans also available. Support available to part-time students. Financial award application deadline: 4/1. *Unit head:* Dr. Patricia Hoffman-Miller, Interim Department Head, 936-261-3530, Fax: 936-261-3617, E-mail: phmiller@pvamu.edu. *Application contact:* Dr. William H. Parker, Dean of Graduate School, 936-261-3500, Fax: 936-261-3529, E-mail: whparker@pvamu.edu.

Purdue University, Graduate School, College of Health and Human Sciences, Department of Health and Kinesiology, West Lafayette, IN 47907. Offers athletic training education administration (MS, PhD); biomechanics (MS, PhD); exercise physiology (MS, PhD); health education (MS, PhD); history/philosophy of sport (MS, PhD); motor control and development (MS, PhD); physical education pedagogy (PhD); physical education teacher education (MS); recreation and sport management (MS, PhD); sport and exercise psychology (MS, PhD). Part-time programs available. *Faculty:* 16 full-time (8 women), 20 part-time/adjunct (3 women). *Students:* 43 full-time (29 women), 21 part-time (11 women); includes 6 minority (2 Black or African American, non-Hispanic/Latino; 1 American Indian or Alaska Native, non-Hispanic/Latino; 1 Asian, non-Hispanic/Latino; 2 Two or more races, non-Hispanic/Latino), 12 international. Average age 28. 103 applicants, 32% accepted, 16 enrolled. In 2013, 15 master's, 8 doctorates awarded. *Degree requirements:* For master's, thesis optional; for doctorate, comprehensive exam, thesis/dissertation, qualifying examination, preliminary examination. *Entrance requirements:* For master's, GRE General Test (minimum score 1000 combined verbal and quantitative), minimum undergraduate GPA of 3.0 or equivalent; for doctorate, GRE General Test (minimum score 1100 combined verbal and quantitative), minimum undergraduate GPA of 3.0 or equivalent; master's degree with minimum GPA of 3.25 (recommended). Additional exam requirements/recommendations for international students: Required—TOEFL (minimum score 77 iBT); Recommended—TWE. *Application deadline:* For fall admission, 4/30 for domestic and international students; for spring admission, 10/15 for domestic and international students. Applications are processed on a rolling basis. Application fee: $60 ($75 for international students). Electronic applications accepted. *Financial support:* Fellowships with partial tuition reimbursements, research assistantships with partial tuition reimbursements, teaching assistantships with partial tuition reimbursements, and Federal Work-Study available. Support available to part-time students. Financial award applicants required to submit FAFSA. *Faculty research:* Wellness, motivation, teaching effectiveness, learning and development. *Unit head:* Dr. Timothy P. Gavin, Head of the Graduate Program, 765-494-3178, Fax: 765-494-1239, E-mail: gavin1@purdue.edu. *Application contact:* Lisa Duncan, Graduate Contact, 765-494-3162, E-mail: llduncan@purdue.edu.
Website: http://www.purdue.edu/hhs/hk/.

Rhode Island College, School of Graduate Studies, Feinstein School of Education and Human Development, Department of Health and Physical Education, Providence, RI 02908-1991. Offers health education (M Ed); physical education (CGS). *Accreditation:* NCATE. Part-time and evening/weekend programs available. *Faculty:* 2 full-time (1 woman), 1 part-time/adjunct (0 women). *Students:* 9 part-time (all women); includes 1 minority (Native Hawaiian or other Pacific Islander, non-Hispanic/Latino). Average age 42. In 2013, 2 master's awarded. *Degree requirements:* For master's, comprehensive assessment. *Entrance requirements:* For master's, GRE General Test or MAT, undergraduate transcripts; minimum undergraduate GPA of 3.0; 3 letters of recommendation; for CGS, GRE or MAT (for most programs), undergraduate transcripts; minimum undergraduate GPA of 3.0; 3 letters of recommendation. Additional exam requirements/recommendations for international students: Recommended—TOEFL (minimum score 550 paper-based; 79 iBT). *Application deadline:* For fall admission, 3/1 for domestic students; for spring admission, 11/1 for domestic students. Applications are processed on a rolling basis. Application fee: $50. *Expenses:* Tuition, state resident: full-time $8928; part-time $372 per credit hour. Tuition, nonresident: full-time $17,376; part-time $724 per credit hour. *Required fees:* $602; $22 per credit. $72 per term. *Financial support:* Teaching assistantships with full tuition reimbursements, Federal Work-Study, scholarships/grants, health care benefits, and unspecified assistantships available. Support available to part-time students. Financial award application deadline: 5/15; financial award applicants required to submit FAFSA. *Unit head:* Dr. Robin Auld, Chair, 401-456-8046. *Application contact:* Graduate Studies, 401-456-8700.
Website: http://www.ric.edu/healthPhysicalEducation/.

Salem State University, School of Graduate Studies, Program in Physical Education, Salem, MA 01970-5353. Offers M Ed. Part-time and evening/weekend programs available. *Students:* 15 part-time (6 women); includes 2 minority (both Hispanic/Latino).

2 applicants, 100% accepted, 1 enrolled. In 2013, 5 master's awarded. *Entrance requirements:* For master's, GRE or MAT. Additional exam requirements/recommendations for international students: Required—TOEFL (minimum score 550 paper-based; 80 iBT) or IELTS (minimum score 5.5). *Application deadline:* For fall admission, 5/1 for domestic students; for spring admission, 10/1 for domestic students. Applications are processed on a rolling basis. Application fee: $50. *Financial support:* Career-related internships or fieldwork, Federal Work-Study, scholarships/grants, and unspecified assistantships available. Support available to part-time students. Financial award application deadline: 5/1; financial award applicants required to submit FAFSA. *Application contact:* Dr. Lee A. Brossoit, Assistant Dean of Graduate Admissions, 978-542-6675, Fax: 978-542-7215, E-mail: lbrossoit@salemstate.edu.
Website: http://www.salemstate.edu/academics/schools/12614.php.

Slippery Rock University of Pennsylvania, Graduate Studies (Recruitment), College of Education, Department of Physical Education, Slippery Rock, PA 16057-1383. Offers adapted physical activity (MS). *Faculty:* 3 full-time (1 woman). *Students:* 20 full-time (14 women), 3 part-time (all women); includes 5 minority (2 Black or African American, non-Hispanic/Latino; 2 Hispanic/Latino; 1 Two or more races, non-Hispanic/Latino). Average age 24. 29 applicants, 83% accepted, 14 enrolled. In 2013, 12 master's awarded. *Degree requirements:* For master's, internship. *Entrance requirements:* For master's, GRE General Test, MAT, minimum GPA of 2.75, two letters of recommendation, essay, official transcripts. Additional exam requirements/recommendations for international students: Required—TOEFL (minimum score 550 paper-based; 80 iBT). *Application deadline:* For fall admission, 3/1 priority date for domestic students, 5/1 priority date for international students; for spring admission, 10/1 priority date for domestic students. Application fee: $25 ($30 for international students). Electronic applications accepted. *Expenses:* Tuition, state resident: full-time $7956; part-time $442 per credit. Tuition, nonresident: full-time $11,934; part-time $663 per credit. *Required fees:* $2896; $148 per credit. Tuition and fees vary according to degree level and program. *Financial support:* Career-related internships or fieldwork, Federal Work-Study, institutionally sponsored loans, scholarships/grants, tuition waivers (partial), and unspecified assistantships available. Support available to part-time students. Financial award application deadline: 5/1; financial award applicants required to submit FAFSA. *Unit head:* Dr. Robert Arnhold, Graduate Coordinator, 724-738-2847, Fax: 724-738-2921, E-mail: robert.arnhold@sru.edu. *Application contact:* Angela Barrett, Director of Graduate Admissions, 724-738-2051, Fax: 724-738-2146, E-mail: graduate.admissions@sru.edu.

Sonoma State University, School of Science and Technology, Department of Kinesiology, Rohnert Park, CA 94928. Offers adapted physical education (MA); interdisciplinary (MA); interdisciplinary pre-occupational therapy (MA); lifetime physical activity (MA), including coach education, fitness and wellness; physical education (MA); pre-physical therapy (MA). Part-time programs available. *Faculty:* 5 full-time (3 women). *Students:* 1 full-time (0 women), 11 part-time (3 women); includes 2 minority (1 Hispanic/Latino; 1 Two or more races, non-Hispanic/Latino). Average age 29. *Degree requirements:* For master's, thesis, oral exam. *Entrance requirements:* For master's, minimum GPA of 2.8. Additional exam requirements/recommendations for international students: Required—TOEFL (minimum score 500 paper-based). *Application deadline:* For fall admission, 11/30 for domestic students; for spring admission, 9/1 for domestic students. Applications are processed on a rolling basis. Application fee: $55. *Expenses:* Tuition, state resident: full-time $8500. Tuition, nonresident: full-time $12,964. *Required fees:* $1762. *Financial support:* Career-related internships or fieldwork available. Financial award application deadline: 3/2; financial award applicants required to submit FAFSA. *Unit head:* Dr. Elaine McHugh, Chair, 707-664-2660, E-mail: elaine.mchugh@sonoma.edu. *Application contact:* Dr. Lauren Morimoto, Graduate Coordinator, 707-664-2479, E-mail: morimoto@sonoma.edu.
Website: http://www.sonoma.edu/kinesiology/.

South Dakota State University, Graduate School, College of Education and Human Sciences, Department of Health, Physical Education and Recreation, Brookings, SD 57007. Offers MS. Part-time programs available. *Degree requirements:* For master's, thesis, oral and written exams. *Entrance requirements:* Additional exam requirements/recommendations for international students: Required—TOEFL (minimum score 550 paper-based; 71 iBT). *Faculty research:* Effective teaching behaviors in physical education, sports nutrition, muscle/bone interaction, hormonal response to exercise.

Southern Connecticut State University, School of Graduate Studies, School of Education, Department of Exercise Science, New Haven, CT 06515-1355. Offers human performance (MS); physical education (MS); school health education (MS); sport psychology (MS). Part-time and evening/weekend programs available. *Degree requirements:* For master's, thesis or alternative. *Entrance requirements:* For master's, interview. Electronic applications accepted.

Southern Illinois University Carbondale, Graduate School, College of Education and Human Services, Department of Kinesiology, Carbondale, IL 62901-4701. Offers physical education (MS Ed). Part-time programs available. *Faculty:* 6 full-time (2 women). *Students:* 42 full-time (19 women), 30 part-time (10 women); includes 12 minority (10 Black or African American, non-Hispanic/Latino; 1 Asian, non-Hispanic/Latino; 1 Hispanic/Latino), 8 international. Average age 25. 35 applicants, 54% accepted, 12 enrolled. In 2013, 19 master's awarded. *Degree requirements:* For master's, thesis. *Entrance requirements:* For master's, GRE, minimum GPA of 2.7. Additional exam requirements/recommendations for international students: Required—TOEFL. *Application deadline:* Applications are processed on a rolling basis. Application fee: $50. *Financial support:* In 2013–14, 17 students received support, including 10 teaching assistantships; fellowships, research assistantships, career-related internships or fieldwork, Federal Work-Study, institutionally sponsored loans, and tuition waivers (full) also available. Support available to part-time students. *Faculty research:* Caffeine and exercise effects, ground reaction forces in walking and running, social psychology of sports. *Unit head:* Dr. E. William Vogler, Chairperson, 618-536-2431, E-mail: wvogler@siu.edu. *Application contact:* Lori Johnson, Graduate Program Assistant, 618-453-3134, E-mail: lorij20@siu.edu.
Website: http://kin.ehs.siu.edu/.

Southern Illinois University Edwardsville, Graduate School, School of Education, Department of Kinesiology and Health Education, Program in Physical Education and Sport Pedagogy, Edwardsville, IL 62026. Offers MS Ed. Part-time and evening/weekend programs available. *Students:* 1 full-time (0 women), 13 part-time (7 women); includes 2 minority (1 Black or African American, non-Hispanic/Latino; 1 Hispanic/Latino). 3 applicants, 100% accepted. In 2013, 8 master's awarded. *Degree requirements:* For master's, comprehensive exam (for some programs), thesis (for some programs). *Entrance requirements:* Additional exam requirements/recommendations for international students: Required—TOEFL (minimum score 550 paper-based, 79 iBT), IELTS (minimum score 6.5), Michigan Test of English Language Proficiency or PTE. *Application deadline:* For fall admission, 7/18 for domestic students, 6/1 for international students; for spring admission, 12/12 for domestic students, 9/1 for international students; for summer admission, 4/24 for domestic students, 3/1 for international students. Applications are processed on a rolling basis. Application fee: $30. Electronic applications accepted. *Expenses:* Tuition, state resident: full-time $3551. Tuition, nonresident: full-time $8378. *Financial support:* Institutionally sponsored loans, scholarships/grants, and unspecified assistantships available. Financial award application deadline: 3/1; financial award applicants required to submit FAFSA. *Unit head:* Dr. Erik Kirk, Program Director, 618-650-2718, E-mail: ekirk@siue.edu. *Application contact:* Melissa K. Mace, Assistant Director of Graduate and International Recruitment, 618-650-2756, Fax: 618-650-3618, E-mail: mmace@siue.edu.
Website: http://www.siue.edu/education/khe/.

Springfield College, Graduate Programs, Programs in Physical Education, Springfield, MA 01109-3797. Offers adapted physical education (M Ed, MPE, MS); advanced level coaching (M Ed, MPE, MS); athletic administration (M Ed, MPE, MS); general physical education (PhD, CAGS); health education licensure (MPE, MS); health education licensure program (M Ed); physical education licensure (MPE, MS); physical education licensure program (M Ed); teaching and administration (MS). Part-time programs available. *Faculty:* 33 full-time, 5 part-time/adjunct. *Students:* 52 full-time. 44 applicants, 86% accepted, 26 enrolled. In 2013, 22 master's, 4 doctorates awarded. *Degree requirements:* For master's, comprehensive exam, thesis (for some programs). *Entrance requirements:* For master's and doctorate, GRE General Test. Additional exam requirements/recommendations for international students: Required—TOEFL (minimum score 550 paper-based); Recommended—IELTS (minimum score 6). *Application deadline:* For fall admission, 1/15 priority date for domestic students, 1/15 for international students; for winter admission, 11/1 for domestic and international students; for spring admission, 11/1 for domestic and international students. Applications are processed on a rolling basis. Application fee: $50. Electronic applications accepted. *Expenses: Tuition:* Full-time $13,620; part-time $908 per credit. *Financial support:* Fellowships with partial tuition reimbursements, teaching assistantships with partial tuition reimbursements, career-related internships or fieldwork, Federal Work-Study, institutionally sponsored loans, and unspecified assistantships available. Financial award application deadline: 3/1; financial award applicants required to submit FAFSA. *Unit head:* Dr. Michelle Moosbrugger, Director, 413-748-3486, E-mail: mmoosbrugger@springfieldcollege.edu. *Application contact:* Evelyn Cohen, Associate Director of Graduate Admissions, 413-748-3479, Fax: 413-748-3694, E-mail: ecohen@springfieldcollege.edu.

State University of New York College at Cortland, Graduate Studies, School of Professional Studies, Department of Physical Education, Cortland, NY 13045. Offers adapted physical education (MS Ed); coaching pedagogy (MS Ed); physical education leadership (MS Ed). Part-time and evening/weekend programs available. *Entrance requirements:* Additional exam requirements/recommendations for international students: Required—TOEFL. *Expenses:* Tuition, state resident: full-time $9870; part-time $411 per credit hour. Tuition, nonresident: full-time $18,350; part-time $765 per credit hour. *Required fees:* $1458; $65 per credit hour.

Stony Brook University, State University of New York, School of Professional Development, Stony Brook, NY 11794. Offers biology (MAT); chemistry (MAT); coaching (Graduate Certificate); earth science (MAT); educational computing (Graduate Certificate); educational leadership (Advanced Certificate); English (MAT); environmental management (Graduate Certificate); French (MAT); German (MAT); higher education administration (MA, Certificate); human resource management (MS, Graduate Certificate); industrial management (Graduate Certificate); information systems management (Graduate Certificate); Italian (MAT); liberal studies (MA); mathematics (MAT); operations research (Graduate Certificate); physics (MAT); school district business leadership (Advanced Certificate); social science and the professions (MPS), including environmental management, human resource management; social studies (MAT); Spanish (MAT). Part-time and evening/weekend programs available. Postbaccalaureate distance learning degree programs offered. *Faculty:* 2 full-time (1 woman), 70 part-time/adjunct (30 women). *Students:* 241 full-time (135 women), 954 part-time (673 women); includes 209 minority (65 Black or African American, non-Hispanic/Latino; 2 American Indian or Alaska Native, non-Hispanic/Latino; 32 Asian, non-Hispanic/Latino; 104 Hispanic/Latino; 6 Two or more races, non-Hispanic/Latino), 7 international. Average age 28. 353 applicants, 92% accepted, 248 enrolled. In 2013, 312 master's, 131 other advanced degrees awarded. *Degree requirements:* For master's, one foreign language, thesis or alternative. *Application deadline:* For fall admission, 1/15 for domestic students; for spring admission, 10/1 for domestic students. Applications are processed on a rolling basis. Application fee: $100. *Expenses:* Tuition, state resident: full-time $9870; part-time $411 per credit. Tuition, nonresident: full-time $18,350; part-time $765 per credit. *Financial support:* Fellowships, research assistantships, teaching assistantships, and career-related internships or fieldwork available. Support available to part-time students. *Unit head:* Dr. Thomas Sexton, Interim Dean, 631-632-7181, Fax: 631-632-9046, E-mail: thomas.sexton@stonybrook.edu. *Application contact:* 631-632-7050 Ext. 1, E-mail: spd@stonybrook.edu.
Website: http://www.stonybrook.edu/spd/.

Sul Ross State University, School of Professional Studies, Department of Physical Education, Alpine, TX 79832. Offers M Ed. Part-time programs available. *Entrance requirements:* For master's, GMAT or GRE General Test, minimum GPA of 2.5 in last 60 hours of undergraduate work.

Tarleton State University, College of Graduate Studies, College of Education, Department of Kinesiology, Stephenville, TX 76402. Offers physical education (M Ed). Part-time and evening/weekend programs available. *Faculty:* 5 full-time (2 women). *Students:* 14 full-time (6 women), 39 part-time (16 women); includes 10 minority (5 Black or African American, non-Hispanic/Latino; 1 Asian, non-Hispanic/Latino; 2 Hispanic/Latino; 2 Two or more races, non-Hispanic/Latino), 1 international. Average age 25. 24 applicants, 92% accepted, 19 enrolled. In 2013, 28 master's awarded. *Degree requirements:* For master's, comprehensive exam, thesis optional. *Entrance requirements:* For master's, GRE General Test, minimum GPA of 3.0. Additional exam requirements/recommendations for international students: Required—TOEFL (minimum score 550 paper-based; 80 iBT). *Application deadline:* For fall admission, 8/15 priority date for domestic students; for spring admission, 1/7 for domestic students. Applications are processed on a rolling basis. Application fee: $30 ($130 for international students). Electronic applications accepted. *Expenses:* Tuition, state resident: full-time $3312; part-time $184 per credit hour. Tuition, nonresident: full-time $9144; part-time $508 per credit hour. *Required fees:* $1916. Tuition and fees vary according to course load and campus/location. *Financial support:* Research assistantships, teaching assistantships with partial tuition reimbursements, career-related internships or fieldwork, Federal Work-Study, and institutionally sponsored loans available. Support available to part-time students. Financial award application deadline: 5/1; financial award applicants required to submit FAFSA. *Unit head:* Dr. Kayla Peak, Head, 254-968-9377, Fax: 254-968-9824, E-mail: peak@tarleton.edu. *Application contact:* Information Contact, 254-968-9104, Fax: 254-968-9670, E-mail: gradoffice@tarleton.edu.
Website: http://www.tarleton.edu/kinesiology/index.html.

Teachers College, Columbia University, Graduate Faculty of Education, Department of Biobehavioral Studies, Program in Curriculum and Teaching in Physical Education, New York, NY 10027-6696. Offers Ed M, MA, Ed D. Part-time and evening/weekend programs available. *Faculty:* 2 full-time, 2 part-time/adjunct. *Students:* 4 full-time (2 women), 16 part-time (7 women); includes 8 minority (5 Black or African American, non-Hispanic/Latino; 2 Hispanic/Latino; 1 Two or more races, non-Hispanic/Latino), 2 international. Average age 32. 7 applicants, 86% accepted, 4 enrolled. In 2013, 7

master's, 1 doctorate awarded. Terminal master's awarded for partial completion of doctoral program. *Degree requirements:* For master's, integrative paper; for doctorate, thesis/dissertation. *Entrance requirements:* For doctorate, writing sample, prior formal training and/or teaching experience in physical education. *Application deadline:* For fall admission, 1/15 priority date for domestic students; for spring admission, 11/1 for domestic students. Applications are processed on a rolling basis. Application fee: $65. *Financial support:* Career-related internships or fieldwork, Federal Work-Study, institutionally sponsored loans, and tuition waivers (full and partial) available. Support available to part-time students. Financial award application deadline: 2/1. *Faculty research:* Analysis of teaching, teacher performance, program development, data bank project in physical education. *Unit head:* Prof. Stephen Silverman, Program Coordinator, 212-678-3324, E-mail: ss928@columbia.edu. *Application contact:* Morgan Oakes, Assistant Counselor, 212-678-3710, Fax: 212-678-4171, E-mail: tcinfo@tc.edu.

Temple University, College of Health Professions and Social Work, Department of Kinesiology, Philadelphia, PA 19122. Offers athletic training (MS, PhD); behavioral sciences (Ed M); curriculum and instruction (MS); integrated exercise physiology (PhD); integrative exercise physiology (MS); kinesiology (MS); psychology of movement (MS); somatic sciences (PhD). Part-time programs available. *Faculty:* 15 full-time (7 women). *Students:* 49 full-time (30 women), 8 part-time (5 women); includes 6 minority (2 Black or African American, non-Hispanic/Latino; 1 Asian, non-Hispanic/Latino; 2 Hispanic/Latino; 1 Two or more races, non-Hispanic/Latino), 6 international. 100 applicants, 33% accepted, 18 enrolled. In 2013, 15 master's, 6 doctorates awarded. Terminal master's awarded for partial completion of doctoral program. *Degree requirements:* For master's, thesis, final project; for doctorate, comprehensive exam, thesis/dissertation. *Entrance requirements:* For master's, GRE General Test or MAT, minimum undergraduate GPA of 3.0, 3 letters of reference, statement of goals, interview, resume; for doctorate, GRE General Test, minimum undergraduate GPA of 3.0, 3 letters of reference, statement of goals, interview, resume. Additional exam requirements/recommendations for international students: Required—TOEFL (minimum score 550 paper-based; 79 iBT). *Application deadline:* For fall admission, 1/15 for domestic students, 12/15 for international students; for spring admission, 10/1 for domestic students, 8/1 for international students. Applications are processed on a rolling basis. Application fee: $60. Electronic applications accepted. *Financial support:* In 2013–14, 4 research assistantships with full and partial tuition reimbursements (averaging $16,459 per year), 24 teaching assistantships with full and partial tuition reimbursements (averaging $15,966 per year) were awarded; fellowships, career-related internships or fieldwork, Federal Work-Study, scholarships/grants, tuition waivers, and unspecified assistantships also available. Financial award application deadline: 1/15. *Faculty research:* Exercise physiology, athletic training, motor neuroscience, exercise and sports psychology. *Total annual research expenditures:* $318,204. *Unit head:* Dr. John Jeka, Department Chair, 214-204-4405, Fax: 215-204-4414, E-mail: jjeka@temple.edu. *Application contact:* Megan P. Mannal DiMarco, 215-204-7503, E-mail: megan.dimarco@temple.edu.
Website: http://chpsw.temple.edu/kinesiology/home.

Tennessee State University, The School of Graduate Studies and Research, College of Health Sciences, Department of Human Performance and Sports Sciences, Nashville, TN 37209-1561. Offers exercise science (MA Ed); sport administration (MA Ed). *Degree requirements:* For master's, thesis optional. *Entrance requirements:* For master's, GRE General Test or MAT.

Tennessee Technological University, College of Graduate Studies, College of Education, Department of Exercise Science, Physical Education and Wellness, Cookeville, TN 38505. Offers adapted physical education (MA); elementary/middle school physical education (MA); lifetime wellness (MA); sport management (MA). *Accreditation:* NCATE. Part-time programs available. Postbaccalaureate distance learning degree programs offered (no on-campus study). *Faculty:* 7 full-time (0 women). *Students:* 10 full-time (0 women), 38 part-time (11 women); includes 5 minority (all Black or African American, non-Hispanic/Latino). Average age 27. 38 applicants, 58% accepted, 20 enrolled. In 2013, 23 master's awarded. *Degree requirements:* For master's, comprehensive exam, thesis or alternative. *Entrance requirements:* For master's, MAT or GRE. Additional exam requirements/recommendations for international students: Required—TOEFL (minimum score 527 paper-based; 71 iBT), IELTS (minimum score 5.5), PTE (minimum score 48), or TOEIC (Test of English as an International Communication). *Application deadline:* For fall admission, 8/1 for domestic students, 5/1 for international students; for spring admission, 12/1 for domestic students, 10/1 for international students. Applications are processed on a rolling basis. Application fee: $35 ($40 for international students). Electronic applications accepted. *Expenses:* Tuition, state resident: full-time $9347; part-time $465 per credit hour. Tuition, nonresident: full-time $23,635; part-time $1152 per credit hour. *Financial support:* In 2013–14, fellowships (averaging $8,000 per year), 3 research assistantships (averaging $4,000 per year), 4 teaching assistantships (averaging $4,000 per year) were awarded; career-related internships or fieldwork also available. Financial award application deadline: 4/1. *Unit head:* Dr. John Steven Smith, Interim Chairperson, 931-372-3467, Fax: 931-372-6319, E-mail: jssmith@tntech.edu. *Application contact:* Shelia K. Kendrick, Coordinator of Graduate Studies, 931-372-3808, Fax: 931-372-3497, E-mail: skendrick@tntech.edu.

Texas A&M University–Commerce, Graduate School, College of Education and Human Services, Department of Health and Human Performance, Commerce, TX 75429-3011. Offers exercise physiology (MS); health and human performance (M Ed); health promotion (MS); health, kinesiology and sports studies (Ed D); motor performance (MS); sport studies (MS). Part-time programs available. *Degree requirements:* For master's, comprehensive exam, thesis (for some programs). *Entrance requirements:* For master's, GRE General Test. Electronic applications accepted. *Expenses:* Tuition, state resident: full-time $3630; part-time $2420 per year. Tuition, nonresident: full-time $9948; part-time $6632.16 per year. *Required fees:* $1006 per year. Tuition and fees vary according to course load. *Faculty research:* Teaching, physical fitness.

Texas Southern University, College of Education, Department of Health and Kinesiology, Houston, TX 77004-4584. Offers health education (MS); human performance (MS). Part-time and evening/weekend programs available. *Faculty:* 3 full-time (0 women), 2 part-time/adjunct (1 woman). *Students:* 32 full-time (15 women), 19 part-time (12 women); includes 49 minority (45 Black or African American, non-Hispanic/Latino; 4 Hispanic/Latino), 1 international. Average age 30. 31 applicants, 55% accepted, 12 enrolled. In 2013, 22 master's awarded. *Degree requirements:* For master's, comprehensive exam, thesis optional. *Entrance requirements:* For master's, GRE General Test, minimum GPA of 2.5. Additional exam requirements/recommendations for international students: Required—TOEFL. *Application deadline:* For fall admission, 7/1 for domestic and international students; for spring admission, 11/1 for domestic and international students. Applications are processed on a rolling basis. Application fee: $50 ($75 for international students). Electronic applications accepted. *Financial support:* Teaching assistantships, scholarships/grants, and unspecified assistantships available. Support available to part-time students. Financial award application deadline: 5/1. *Unit head:* Dr. Dwalah Fisher, Interim Chair, 713-313-7272, E-mail: fisher_dl@tsu.edu. *Application contact:* Dr. Gregory Maddox, Interim Dean of the Graduate School, 713-313-7011 Ext. 4410, Fax: 713-639-1876, E-mail: maddox_gh@tsu.edu.
Website: http://www.tsu.edu/academics/colleges__schools/College_of_Education/Departments/default.php.

Texas State University, Graduate School, College of Education, Department of Health and Human Performance, Program in Physical Education, San Marcos, TX 78666. Offers M Ed. Part-time and evening/weekend programs available. *Faculty:* 8 full-time (3 women). *Students:* 17 full-time (8 women), 10 part-time (7 women); includes 12 minority (4 Black or African American, non-Hispanic/Latino; 7 Hispanic/Latino; 1 Two or more races, non-Hispanic/Latino). Average age 27. 12 applicants, 58% accepted, 6 enrolled. In 2013, 22 master's awarded. *Degree requirements:* For master's, comprehensive exam, thesis optional. *Entrance requirements:* For master's, GRE General Test, minimum GPA of 2.75 in last 60 hours of course work. Additional exam requirements/recommendations for international students: Required—TOEFL (minimum score 550 paper-based; 78 iBT). *Application deadline:* For fall admission, 6/15 priority date for domestic students, 6/1 for international students; for spring admission, 10/15 priority date for domestic students, 10/1 for international students. Applications are processed on a rolling basis. Application fee: $40 ($90 for international students). Electronic applications accepted. *Expenses:* Tuition, state resident: full-time $6663; part-time $278 per credit hour. Tuition, nonresident: full-time $15,159; part-time $632 per credit hour. *Required fees:* $1872; $54 per credit hour. $306 per term. Tuition and fees vary according to course load. *Financial support:* In 2013–14, 17 students received support, including 1 research assistantship (averaging $10,950 per year), 6 teaching assistantships (averaging $12,030 per year); career-related internships or fieldwork, Federal Work-Study, and institutionally sponsored loans also available. Support available to part-time students. Financial award application deadline: 4/1; financial award applicants required to submit FAFSA. *Faculty research:* AIDS education, employee wellness, isometric strength evaluation. *Unit head:* Dr. Karen Meaney, Graduate Advisor, 512-245-2952, Fax: 512-245-8678, E-mail: km66@txstate.edu. *Application contact:* Dr. Andrea Golato, Head, 512-245-2581, Fax: 512-245-8365, E-mail: gradcollege@txstate.edu.
Website: http://www.hhp.txstate.edu/Degree-Plans/Graduate.html.

Texas Woman's University, Graduate School, College of Health Sciences, Department of Kinesiology, Denton, TX 76201. Offers adapted physical education (MS, PhD); biomechanics (MS, PhD); coaching (MS); exercise physiology (MS, PhD); pedagogy (MS); sport management (MS, PhD). Part-time and evening/weekend programs available. *Faculty:* 11 full-time (5 women), 3 part-time/adjunct (2 women). *Students:* 48 full-time (35 women), 105 part-time (70 women); includes 42 minority (26 Black or African American, non-Hispanic/Latino; 2 American Indian or Alaska Native, non-Hispanic/Latino; 5 Asian, non-Hispanic/Latino; 9 Hispanic/Latino), 16 international. Average age 30. 51 applicants, 69% accepted, 25 enrolled. In 2013, 55 master's, 3 doctorates awarded. Terminal master's awarded for partial completion of doctoral program. *Degree requirements:* For master's, comprehensive exam, thesis or alternative; for doctorate, comprehensive exam, thesis/dissertation, qualifying exam. *Entrance requirements:* For master's, GRE General Test (biomechanics emphasis only), 2 letters of reference, curriculum vitae, interview (adapted physical education emphasis only); for doctorate, GRE General Test (biomechanics emphasis only), interview, 3 letters of reference, curriculum vitae. Additional exam requirements/recommendations for international students: Required—TOEFL (minimum score 550 paper-based; 79 iBT). *Application deadline:* For fall admission, 7/1 priority date for domestic students, 3/1 for international students; for spring admission, 11/1 priority date for domestic students, 7/1 for international students. Applications are processed on a rolling basis. Application fee: $50 ($75 for international students). Electronic applications accepted. *Expenses:* Tuition, state resident: full-time $4182; part-time $233.32 per credit hour. Tuition, nonresident: full-time $10,716; part-time $595.32 per credit hour. *Financial support:* In 2013–14, 46 students received support, including 7 research assistantships (averaging $10,659 per year), 14 teaching assistantships (averaging $10,659 per year); career-related internships or fieldwork, Federal Work-Study, institutionally sponsored loans, scholarships/grants, traineeships, health care benefits, and unspecified assistantships also available. Support available to part-time students. Financial award application deadline: 3/1; financial award applicants required to submit FAFSA. *Faculty research:* Exercise and Type 2 diabetes risk, bone mineral density and exercise in special populations, obesity in children, factors influencing sport consumer behavior and loyalty, roles and responsibilities of paraeducators in adapted physical education. *Total annual research expenditures:* $200,485. *Unit head:* Dr. Charlotte (Barney) Sanborn, Chair, 940-898-2575, Fax: 940-898-2581, E-mail: dnichols@twu.edu. *Application contact:* Dr. Samuel Wheeler, Assistant Director of Admissions, 940-898-3188, Fax: 940-898-3081, E-mail: wheelersr@twu.edu.
Website: http://www.twu.edu/kinesiology/.

Troy University, Graduate School, College of Education, Program in Teacher Education-Multiple Levels, Troy, AL 36082. Offers art education (MS); gifted education (MS); instrumental (MS); physical education (MS); reading specialist (MS); vocal/choral (MS). Part-time and evening/weekend programs available. *Faculty:* 8 full-time (4 women). *Students:* 2 full-time (both women), 17 part-time (15 women); includes 3 minority (all Black or African American, non-Hispanic/Latino). Average age 30. 9 applicants, 89% accepted, 4 enrolled. In 2013, 19 master's awarded. *Degree requirements:* For master's, comprehensive exam, thesis. *Entrance requirements:* For master's, GRE (minimum score of 850 on old exam or 290 on new exam), GMAT (minimum score of 380), or MAT (minimum score of 385), bachelor's degree; minimum undergraduate GPA of 2.5 or 3.0 on last 30 semester hours, letter of recommendation. Additional exam requirements/recommendations for international students: Required—TOEFL (minimum score 523 paper-based; 70 iBT), IELTS (minimum score 6). *Application deadline:* Applications are processed on a rolling basis. Application fee: $50. Electronic applications accepted. *Expenses:* Tuition, state resident: full-time $6084; part-time $338 per credit hour. Tuition, nonresident: full-time $12,168; part-time $676 per credit hour. *Required fees:* $630; $35 per credit hour. $50 per semester. *Financial support:* Available to part-time students. Applicants required to submit FAFSA. *Unit head:* Dr. Charlotte S. Minnick, Director, Teacher Education, 334-670-3544, Fax: 334-670-3548, E-mail: csminnick@troy.edu. *Application contact:* Brenda K. Campbell, Director of Graduate Admissions, 334-670-3178, Fax: 334-670-3733, E-mail: bcamp@troy.edu.

Union College, Graduate Programs, Department of Education, Barbourville, KY 40906-1499. Offers elementary education (MA); health and physical education (MA); middle grades (MA); music education (MA); principalship (MA); reading specialist (MA); secondary education (MA); special education (MA). *Degree requirements:* For master's, thesis optional. *Entrance requirements:* For master's, GRE General Test, NTE.

United States Sports Academy, Graduate Programs, Program in Sports Coaching, Daphne, AL 36526-7055. Offers MSS. Part-time programs available. Postbaccalaureate distance learning degree programs offered (no on-campus study). *Degree requirements:* For master's, comprehensive exam, thesis optional. *Entrance requirements:* For master's, GRE General Test, GMAT, or MAT, minimum GPA of 2.5, 3 letters of recommendation, resume. Additional exam requirements/recommendations for international students: Required—TOEFL (minimum score 500 paper-based). Electronic

applications accepted. *Faculty research:* Effect of attentional skill on sports performance, survey of coaching qualifications, coaching certification.

Universidad del Turabo, Graduate Programs, Programs in Education, Program in Coaching, Gurabo, PR 00778-3030. Offers MPHE.

Universidad Metropolitana, School of Education, Program in Teaching of Physical Education, San Juan, PR 00928-1150. Offers teaching of adult physical education (M Ed); teaching of elementary physical education (M Ed); teaching of secondary physical education (M Ed). *Degree requirements:* For master's, thesis or alternative. *Entrance requirements:* For master's, EXADEP, interview. Electronic applications accepted.

Université de Montréal, Department of Kinesiology, Montréal, QC H3C 3J7, Canada. Offers kinesiology (M Sc, DESS); physical activity (M Sc, PhD). *Degree requirements:* For master's, one foreign language, thesis (for some programs); for doctorate, one foreign language, thesis/dissertation, general exam. Electronic applications accepted. *Faculty research:* Physiology of exercise, psychology of sports, biomechanics, dance, sociology of sports.

Université de Sherbrooke, Faculty of Physical Education and Sports, Program in Physical Education, Sherbrooke, QC J1K 2R1, Canada. Offers kinanthropology (M Sc); physical activity (Diploma). *Degree requirements:* For master's, thesis. *Entrance requirements:* For master's, minimum GPA of 2.7; for Diploma, bachelor's degree in physical education. *Faculty research:* Physical fitness, nutrition, human factors, sociology, teaching.

Université du Québec à Trois-Rivières, Graduate Programs, Program in Physical Education, Trois-Rivières, QC G9A 5H7, Canada. Offers M Sc. Part-time programs available. *Degree requirements:* For master's, thesis. *Entrance requirements:* For master's, appropriate bachelor's degree, proficiency in French.

The University of Akron, Graduate School, College of Health Professions, School of Sport Science and Wellness Education, Program in Sports Science/Coaching, Akron, OH 44325. Offers MA, MS. *Students:* 68 full-time (10 women), 11 part-time (5 women); includes 21 minority (all Black or African American, non-Hispanic/Latino), 1 international. Average age 26. 51 applicants, 86% accepted, 35 enrolled. In 2013, 42 master's awarded. *Degree requirements:* For master's, comprehensive exam, thesis optional. *Entrance requirements:* For master's, minimum GPA of 2.75, three letters of recommendation, statement of purpose. Additional exam requirements/recommendations for international students: Required—TOEFL (minimum score 550 paper-based; 79 iBT). *Application deadline:* Applications are processed on a rolling basis. Application fee: $40 ($60 for international students). Electronic applications accepted. *Expenses:* Tuition, state resident: full-time $7430; part-time $412.80 per credit hour. Tuition, nonresident: full-time $12,722; part-time $706.80 per credit hour. *Required fees:* $53 per credit hour. $12 per semester. Tuition and fees vary according to course load and program. *Unit head:* Dr. Victor Pinheiro, Department Chair, 330-972-6055, E-mail: victor@uakron.edu. *Application contact:* Dr. Alan Kornspan, Program Contact, 330-972-8145.

The University of Alabama, Graduate School, College of Education, Department of Kinesiology, Tuscaloosa, AL 35487-0312. Offers alternative sport pedagogy (MA); exercise science (MA, PhD); human performance (MA); sport management (MA); sport pedagogy (MA, PhD). Part-time programs available. *Faculty:* 8 full-time (1 woman). *Students:* 58 full-time (18 women), 29 part-time (15 women); includes 15 minority (9 Black or African American, non-Hispanic/Latino; 1 Asian, non-Hispanic/Latino; 2 Hispanic/Latino; 3 Two or more races, non-Hispanic/Latino), 7 international. Average age 30. 74 applicants, 74% accepted, 32 enrolled. In 2013, 26 master's, 4 doctorates awarded. *Degree requirements:* For master's, comprehensive exam, thesis optional; for doctorate, comprehensive exam, thesis/dissertation. *Entrance requirements:* For master's and doctorate, GRE, MAT, minimum GPA of 3.0. Additional exam requirements/recommendations for international students: Required—TOEFL. *Application deadline:* Applications are processed on a rolling basis. Application fee: $50 ($60 for international students). Electronic applications accepted. *Expenses:* Tuition, state resident: full-time $9450. Tuition, nonresident: full-time $23,950. *Financial support:* In 2013–14, 14 students received support, including 26 teaching assistantships with full and partial tuition reimbursements available (averaging $12,366 per year); fellowships and research assistantships also available. Financial award applicants required to submit FAFSA. *Faculty research:* Race, gender and sexuality in sports; physical education teacher socialization; disability sports; physical activity and health; environmental physiology. *Unit head:* Dr. Matt Curtner-Smith, Department Head and Professor, 205-348-9209, Fax: 205-348-0867, E-mail: msmith@bamaed.ua.edu. *Application contact:* Dr. Kathy S. Wetzel, Assistant Dean for Student Services, 205-348-1154, Fax: 205-348-0080, E-mail: kwetzel@bamaed.ua.edu.
Website: http://education.ua.edu/academics/kine/.

The University of Alabama at Birmingham, School of Education, Program in Physical Education, Birmingham, AL 35294. Offers exercise physiology (MA Ed); physical education with teacher certification (MA Ed). Evening/weekend programs available. *Degree requirements:* For master's, thesis optional. *Entrance requirements:* For master's, GRE General Test, MAT, or NTE, minimum GPA of 3.0. Electronic applications accepted.

University of Alberta, Faculty of Graduate Studies and Research, Department of Physical Education and Recreation, Edmonton, AB T6G 2E1, Canada. Offers physical education (M Sc); recreation and physical education (MA, PhD). Part-time programs available. Terminal master's awarded for partial completion of doctoral program. *Degree requirements:* For master's, thesis (for some programs); for doctorate, thesis/dissertation. *Entrance requirements:* For master's, bachelor's degree in related field; for doctorate, master's degree in related field with thesis. Additional exam requirements/recommendations for international students: Required—TOEFL. *Faculty research:* Motivation and adherence to physical ability, performance enhancement, adapted physical activity, exercise physiology, sport administration, tourism.

University of Arkansas, Graduate School, College of Education and Health Professions, Department of Health, Human Performance and Recreation, Program in Physical Education, Fayetteville, AR 72701-1201. Offers M Ed, MAT. *Degree requirements:* For master's, thesis optional. Electronic applications accepted.

University of Arkansas at Pine Bluff, School of Education, Pine Bluff, AR 71601-2799. Offers early childhood education (M Ed); secondary education (M Ed), including English education, mathematics education, physical education, science education, social studies education; teaching (MAT). *Accreditation:* NCATE. Part-time and evening/weekend programs available. *Degree requirements:* For master's, comprehensive exam. *Entrance requirements:* For master's, GRE, minimum GPA of 2.75, NTE or Standard Arkansas Teaching Certificate. *Faculty research:* Teacher certification, accreditation, assessment, standards, portfolio development, rehabilitation, technology.

The University of British Columbia, Faculty of Education, Department of Curriculum and Pedagogy, Vancouver, BC V6T 1Z4, Canada. Offers art education (M Ed, MA); business education (MA); curriculum studies (M Ed, MA, PhD); home economics education (M Ed, MA); math education (M Ed, MA); music education (M Ed, MA); physical education (M Ed, MA); science education (M Ed, MA); social studies education (M Ed, MA); technology studies education (M Ed, MA). Part-time programs available. Postbaccalaureate distance learning degree programs offered (no on-campus study). *Faculty:* 32 full-time (14 women), 1 (woman) part-time/adjunct. *Students:* 163 full-time, 134 part-time, 42 international. Average age 40. 160 applicants, 75% accepted, 97 enrolled. In 2013, 68 master's, 7 doctorates awarded. *Degree requirements:* For master's, thesis (MA); for doctorate, comprehensive exam, thesis/dissertation. *Entrance requirements:* Additional exam requirements/recommendations for international students: Required—TOEFL (minimum score 580 paper-based; 92 iBT), IELTS (minimum score 6.5). *Application deadline:* For fall admission, 12/1 for domestic and international students; for spring admission, 10/1 for domestic students, 9/1 for international students. Application fee: $90 Canadian dollars ($150 Canadian dollars for international students). Electronic applications accepted. *Expenses:* Contact institution. *Financial support:* In 2013–14, 10 fellowships with partial tuition reimbursements (averaging $16,000 per year), 11 research assistantships with partial tuition reimbursements (averaging $14,000 per year), 27 teaching assistantships with partial tuition reimbursements (averaging $14,000 per year) were awarded; tuition waivers (partial) also available. *Faculty research:* School subjects, teaching and learning. *Unit head:* Dr. Peter Grimmett, Head, 604-822-5422, Fax: 604-822-4714, E-mail: anna.ip@ubc.ca. *Application contact:* Basia Zurek, Graduate Programs Assistant, 604-822-5367, Fax: 604-822-4714, E-mail: edcp.grad@ubc.ca.
Website: http://www.edcp.educ.ubc.ca/.

University of Dayton, Department of Health and Sport Science, Dayton, OH 45469-1300. Offers exercise science (MS Ed); physical therapy (DPT). Part-time programs available. *Faculty:* 17 full-time (8 women). *Students:* 119 full-time (76 women), 6 part-time (5 women); includes 4 minority (2 Black or African American, non-Hispanic/Latino; 2 Asian, non-Hispanic/Latino), 7 international. Average age 25. 150 applicants, 45% accepted, 38 enrolled. In 2013, 3 master's, 33 doctorates awarded. *Degree requirements:* For master's, thesis; for doctorate, thesis/dissertation or alternative, research project. *Entrance requirements:* For master's, GRE General Test, MAT, minimum GPA of 2.75; for doctorate, GRE General Test, bachelor's degree from accredited college or university; minimum GPA of 3.0, across all schools attended; 80 observation hours; science prerequisites of human anatomy/physiology, general biology, general chemistry, general physics, and exercise physiology. Additional exam requirements/recommendations for international students: Required—TOEFL (minimum score 550 paper-based; 80 iBT). *Application deadline:* For fall admission, 2/15 priority date for domestic students, 5/1 priority date for international students; for winter admission, 7/1 for international students; for spring admission, 11/1 priority date for international students. Applications are processed on a rolling basis. Application fee: $0 ($50 for international students). Electronic applications accepted. *Expenses: Tuition:* Full-time $10,296; part-time $858 per credit hour. *Required fees:* $50; $25. *Financial support:* In 2013–14, 1 research assistantship with full tuition reimbursement (averaging $8,720 per year), 10 teaching assistantships with full tuition reimbursements (averaging $8,720 per year) were awarded; career-related internships or fieldwork, institutionally sponsored loans, health care benefits, and unspecified assistantships also available. Financial award application deadline: 3/1; financial award applicants required to submit FAFSA. *Faculty research:* Energy expenditure, strength, training, teaching nutrition and calcium intake for children and families in Head Start; motion analysis of human gait, pediatric physical therapy, arm function of breast cancer survivors, predicting injury in athletes, neurological rehab in persons with multiple sclerosis. *Unit head:* Dr. Lloyd Laubach, Chair, 937-229-4240, Fax: 937-229-4244, E-mail: llaubach1@udayton.edu. *Application contact:* Laura Greger, Administrative Assistant, 937-229-4225, E-mail: lgreger1@udayton.edu.

University of Florida, Graduate School, College of Health and Human Performance, Department of Applied Physiology and Kinesiology, Gainesville, FL 32611. Offers athletic training/sport medicine (MS); biobehavioral science (MS); clinical exercise physiology (MS); health and human performance (PhD), including applied physiology and kinesiology, biobehavioral science, exercise physiology; human performance (MS). *Faculty:* 18 full-time (3 women), 3 part-time/adjunct (1 woman). *Students:* 73 full-time (32 women), 6 part-time (3 women); includes 9 minority (1 Black or African American, non-Hispanic/Latino; 3 Asian, non-Hispanic/Latino; 5 Hispanic/Latino), 18 international. Average age 27. 163 applicants, 23% accepted, 21 enrolled. In 2013, 23 master's, 8 doctorates awarded. *Degree requirements:* For master's, comprehensive exam, thesis (for some programs); for doctorate, comprehensive exam, thesis/dissertation. *Entrance requirements:* For master's and doctorate, GRE General Test, minimum GPA of 3.0. Additional exam requirements/recommendations for international students: Required—TOEFL (minimum score 550 paper-based; 80 iBT), IELTS (minimum score 6). *Application deadline:* For fall admission, 6/1 priority date for domestic students, 6/1 for international students; for spring admission, 9/15 for domestic and international students. Applications are processed on a rolling basis. Application fee: $30. Electronic applications accepted. *Expenses:* Tuition, state resident: full-time $12,640. Tuition, nonresident: full-time $30,000. *Financial support:* In 2013–14, 55 students received support, including 18 research assistantships (averaging $17,260 per year), 41 teaching assistantships (averaging $12,166 per year); unspecified assistantships also available. Financial award application deadline: 2/1; financial award applicants required to submit FAFSA. *Faculty research:* Cardiovascular disease; basic mechanisms that underlie exercise-induced changes in the body at the organ, tissue, cellular and molecular level; development of rehabilitation techniques for regaining motor control after stroke or as a consequence of Parkinson's disease; maintaining optimal health and delaying age-related declines in physiological function; psychomotor mechanisms impacting health and performance across the life span. *Unit head:* Michael Delp, PhD, Professor and Chair, 352-392-0584 Ext. 1338, E-mail: mdelp@hhp.ufl.edu. *Application contact:* Evangelos A. Christou, PhD, Associate Professor and Graduate Coordinator, 352-294-1719 Ext. 1270, E-mail: eachristou@hhp.ufl.edu.
Website: http://apk.hhp.ufl.edu/.

University of Georgia, College of Education, Department of Kinesiology, Athens, GA 30602. Offers MS, PhD. *Entrance requirements:* For master's, GRE General Test or MAT; for doctorate, GRE General Test. Additional exam requirements/recommendations for international students: Required—TOEFL. Electronic applications accepted.

University of Houston, College of Liberal Arts and Social Sciences, Department of Health and Human Performance, Houston, TX 77204. Offers exercise science (MS); human nutrition (MS); human space exploration sciences (MS); kinesiology (PhD); physical education (M Ed). *Accreditation:* NCATE (one or more programs are accredited). Part-time and evening/weekend programs available. *Degree requirements:* For master's, comprehensive exam (for some programs), thesis (for some programs); for doctorate, comprehensive exam, thesis/dissertation, qualifying exam, candidacy paper. *Entrance requirements:* For master's, GRE (minimum 35th percentile on each section), minimum cumulative GPA of 3.0; for doctorate, GRE (minimum 35th percentile on each section), minimum cumulative GPA of 3.3. Additional exam requirements/recommendations for international students: Required—TOEFL (minimum score 550 paper-based; 79 iBT). Electronic applications accepted. *Faculty research:* Biomechanics, exercise physiology, obesity, nutrition, space exploration science.

University of Idaho, College of Graduate Studies, College of Education, Department of Movement Sciences, Moscow, ID 83844-2401. Offers athletic training (MSAT, DAT); movement and leisure sciences (MS); physical education (M Ed). *Faculty:* 14 full-time, 1 part-time/adjunct. *Students:* 63 full-time, 14 part-time. Average age 31. In 2013, 17 master's, 2 doctorates awarded. *Degree requirements:* For doctorate, thesis/dissertation. *Entrance requirements:* For master's, minimum GPA of 2.8; for doctorate, minimum undergraduate GPA of 2.8, graduate 3.0. *Application deadline:* For fall admission, 8/1 for domestic students; for spring admission, 12/15 for domestic students. Applications are processed on a rolling basis. Application fee: $60. Electronic applications accepted. *Expenses:* Tuition, state resident: full-time $5596; part-time $363 per credit hour. Tuition, nonresident: full-time $18,672; part-time $1089 per credit hour. *Financial support:* Research assistantships and teaching assistantships available. Financial award applicants required to submit FAFSA. *Unit head:* Dr. Philip W. Scruggs, Chair, 208-885-7921, E-mail: movementsciences@uidaho.edu. *Application contact:* Stephanie Thomas, Graduate Recruitment Coordinator, 208-885-4001, Fax: 208-885-4406, E-mail: gadms@uidaho.edu.
Website: http://www.uidaho.edu/ed/movementsciences.

University of Indianapolis, Graduate Programs, School of Education, Indianapolis, IN 46227-3697. Offers art education (MAT); biology (MAT); chemistry (MAT); curriculum and instruction (MA); earth sciences (MAT); education (MA, MAT); educational leadership (MA); elementary education (MA); English (MAT); French (MAT); math (MAT); physical education (MAT); physics (MAT); secondary education (MA), including art education, education, English education, social studies education; social studies (MAT); Spanish (MAT). *Accreditation:* NCATE. Part-time and evening/weekend programs available. *Faculty:* 5 full-time (4 women), 2 part-time/adjunct (1 woman). *Students:* 19 full-time (9 women), 54 part-time (27 women); includes 13 minority (5 Black or African American, non-Hispanic/Latino; 1 Asian, non-Hispanic/Latino; 5 Hispanic/Latino; 2 Two or more races, non-Hispanic/Latino), 1 international. Average age 32. In 2013, 52 master's awarded. *Entrance requirements:* For master's, GRE Subject Test, PRAXIS I, minimum GPA of 2.5, 3 letters of recommendation, interview. Additional exam requirements/recommendations for international students: Required—TOEFL (minimum score 550 paper-based). *Application deadline:* Applications are processed on a rolling basis. Application fee: $50. *Expenses: Tuition:* Full-time $5436; part-time $810 per credit hour. *Financial support:* Federal Work-Study available. Financial award application deadline: 5/1; financial award applicants required to submit FAFSA. *Faculty research:* Assessment of teacher education, perceptions of prospective teachers by parents. *Unit head:* Dr. Kathy Moran, Dean, 317-788-3285, Fax: 317-788-3300, E-mail: kmoran@uindy.edu. *Application contact:* Jeni Kirby, Administrative Assistant, Teacher Education, 317-788-2113, E-mail: kirbyj@uindy.edu.
Website: http://education.uindy.edu/.

The University of Kansas, Graduate Studies, School of Education, Department of Health, Sport, and Exercise Sciences, Lawrence, KS 66045. Offers health and physical education (MS Ed, Ed D, PhD). *Accreditation:* NCATE. Part-time and evening/weekend programs available. *Faculty:* 21. *Students:* 56 full-time (20 women), 25 part-time (12 women); includes 7 minority (3 Black or African American, non-Hispanic/Latino; 2 American Indian or Alaska Native, non-Hispanic/Latino; 1 Asian, non-Hispanic/Latino; 1 Hispanic/Latino), 3 international. Average age 28. 59 applicants, 53% accepted, 19 enrolled. In 2013, 20 master's, 3 doctorates awarded. *Degree requirements:* For master's, comprehensive exam (for some programs), thesis (for some programs); for doctorate, variable foreign language requirement, comprehensive exam, thesis/dissertation. *Entrance requirements:* For master's, GRE General Test (minimum score 1000, 450 verbal, 450 quantitative, 4.0 analytical), minimum GPA of 3.0; for doctorate, GRE General Test (minimum score 1100, verbal 500, quantitative 500, analytical 4.5), minimum graduate GPA of 3.5, undergraduate 3.0. Additional exam requirements/recommendations for international students: Required—TOEFL (minimum score 570 paper-based). *Application deadline:* For fall admission, 3/15 priority date for domestic students; for spring admission, 10/15 priority date for domestic students. Applications are processed on a rolling basis. Application fee: $55 ($65 for international students). Electronic applications accepted. *Financial support:* Research assistantships with full and partial tuition reimbursements and teaching assistantships with full and partial tuition reimbursements available. Financial award application deadline: 4/1. *Faculty research:* Exercise and sport psychology, obesity prevention, sexuality health, sport ethics, skeletal muscle cell signaling and performance. *Unit head:* Dr. Joseph Weir, Chair, 785-864-0784, Fax: 785-864-3343, E-mail: joseph.weir@ku.edu. *Application contact:* Linda Faust, Graduate Admissions Coordinator, 785-864-0783, Fax: 785-864-3343, E-mail: lfaust@ku.edu.
Website: http://hses.soe.ku.edu/.

University of Louisville, Graduate School, College of Education and Human Development, Department of Health and Sport Sciences, Louisville, KY 40292-0001. Offers community health education (M Ed); exercise physiology (MS); health and physical education (MAT); sport administration (MS). Part-time and evening/weekend programs available. *Students:* 54 full-time (22 women), 11 part-time (9 women); includes 12 minority (6 Black or African American, non-Hispanic/Latino; 1 American Indian or Alaska Native, non-Hispanic/Latino; 1 Asian, non-Hispanic/Latino; 3 Hispanic/Latino; 1 Two or more races, non-Hispanic/Latino), 3 international. Average age 27. 91 applicants, 70% accepted, 40 enrolled. In 2013, 16 master's awarded. *Entrance requirements:* For master's, GRE General Test. Additional exam requirements/recommendations for international students: Required—TOEFL (minimum score 560 paper-based; 83 iBT). Application fee: $60. Electronic applications accepted. *Expenses:* Tuition, state resident: full-time $10,788; part-time $599 per credit hour. Tuition, nonresident: full-time $22,446; part-time $1247 per credit hour. *Required fees:* $196. Tuition and fees vary according to program and reciprocity agreements. *Financial support:* Fellowships, research assistantships, teaching assistantships, career-related internships or fieldwork, Federal Work-Study, scholarships/grants, health care benefits, and unspecified assistantships available. Financial award application deadline: 6/1; financial award applicants required to submit FAFSA. *Faculty research:* Impact of sports and sport marketing on society, factors associated with school and community health, cardiac and pulmonary rehabilitation, impact of participation in activities on student retention and graduation, strength and conditioning. *Unit head:* Dr. Anita Moorman, Chair, 502-852-0553, Fax: 502-852-4534, E-mail: amm@louisville.edu. *Application contact:* Libby Leggett, Director, Graduate Admissions, 502-852-3101, Fax: 502-852-6536, E-mail: gradadm@louisville.edu.
Website: http://www.louisville.edu/education/departments/hss.

University of Maine, Graduate School, College of Education and Human Development, Department of Exercise Science and STEM Education, Orono, ME 04469. Offers classroom technology integrationist (CGS); education data specialist (CGS); educational technology coordinator (CGS); kinesiology and physical education (M Ed, MS); science education (M Ed, MS); STEM education (PhD). Part-time and evening/weekend programs available. *Students:* 25 full-time (13 women), 28 part-time (16 women); includes 5 minority (2 Black or African American, non-Hispanic/Latino; 2 American Indian or Alaska Native, non-Hispanic/Latino; 1 Asian, non-Hispanic/Latino), 2 international. Average age 34. 19 applicants, 84% accepted, 12 enrolled. In 2013, 6 master's awarded. *Degree requirements:* For master's, thesis (for some programs); for doctorate, comprehensive exam, thesis/dissertation. *Entrance requirements:* For

master's, GRE General Test, MAT; for doctorate, GRE General Test. Additional exam requirements/recommendations for international students: Required—TOEFL. *Application deadline:* For fall admission, 1/15 for domestic students. Applications are processed on a rolling basis. Application fee: $65. Electronic applications accepted. *Expenses:* Tuition, state resident: full-time $7524. Tuition, nonresident: full-time $23,112. *Required fees:* $1970. *Financial support:* In 2013–14, 13 students received support, including 2 teaching assistantships (averaging $14,600 per year). Financial award application deadline: 3/1. *Faculty research:* Integration of technology in K-12 classrooms, instructional theory and practice in science, inquiry-based teaching, professional development, exercise science, adaptive physical education, neuromuscular function/dysfunction. *Unit head:* Dr. Janet Spector, Dean, 207-581-2441, Fax: 207-581-2423. *Application contact:* Scott G. Delcourt, Associate Dean of the Graduate School, 207-581-3291, Fax: 207-581-3232, E-mail: graduate@maine.edu.
Website: http://umaine.edu/edhd/.

University of Manitoba, Faculty of Graduate Studies, Faculty of Kinesiology and Recreation Management, Winnipeg, MB R3T 2N2, Canada. Offers kinesiology and recreation (M Sc, MA).

University of Memphis, Graduate School, College of Education, Department of Health and Sport Sciences, Memphis, TN 38152. Offers clinical nutrition (MS); exercise and sport science (MS); health promotion (MS); physical education teacher education (MS), including teacher education; sport and leisure commerce (MS). Part-time and evening/weekend programs available. *Faculty:* 22 full-time (8 women), 3 part-time/adjunct (2 women). *Students:* 83 full-time (51 women), 28 part-time (23 women); includes 37 minority (29 Black or African American, non-Hispanic/Latino; 6 Asian, non-Hispanic/Latino; 2 Two or more races, non-Hispanic/Latino), 7 international. Average age 27. 86 applicants, 67% accepted, 29 enrolled. In 2013, 35 master's awarded. *Degree requirements:* For master's, comprehensive exam, thesis. *Entrance requirements:* For master's, GRE General Test or GMAT (for sport and leisure commerce). *Application deadline:* For fall admission, 5/1 priority date for domestic students; for spring admission, 11/1 for domestic students. Applications are processed on a rolling basis. Application fee: $35 ($60 for international students). *Financial support:* In 2013–14, 59 students received support. Research assistantships with full tuition reimbursements available, teaching assistantships with full tuition reimbursements available, career-related internships or fieldwork, Federal Work-Study, scholarships/grants, tuition waivers (partial), and unspecified assistantships available. Financial award application deadline: 2/15; financial award applicants required to submit FAFSA. *Faculty research:* Sport marketing and consumer analysis, health psychology, smoking cessation, psychosocial aspects of cardiovascular disease, global health promotion. *Unit head:* Linda H. Clemens, Interim Chair, 901-678-2324, Fax: 901-678-3591, E-mail: lhclemns@memphis.edu. *Application contact:* Dr. Kenneth Ward, Graduate Studies Coordinator, 901-678-1714, E-mail: kdward@memphis.edu.
Website: http://coe.memphis.edu/hss/.

University of Minnesota, Twin Cities Campus, Graduate School, College of Education and Human Development, School of Kinesiology, Minneapolis, MN 55455-0213. Offers adapted physical education (MA, PhD); biomechanics (MA); biomechanics and neural control (PhD); coaching (Certificate); developmental adapted physical education (M Ed); exercise physiology (MA, PhD); human factors/ergonomics (MA, PhD); international/comparative sport (MA, PhD); kinesiology (M Ed, MA, MS, PhD); leisure services/management (MA, PhD); motor development (MA, PhD); motor learning/control (MA, PhD); outdoor education/recreation (MA, PhD); physical education (M Ed); recreation, park, and leisure studies (M Ed, MA, PhD); sport and exercise science (M Ed); sport management (M Ed, MA, PhD); sport psychology (MA, PhD); sport sociology (MA, PhD); therapeutic recreation (MA, PhD). Part-time programs available. *Faculty:* 14 full-time (6 women). *Students:* 140 full-time (51 women), 52 part-time (19 women); includes 18 minority (9 Black or African American, non-Hispanic/Latino; 1 American Indian or Alaska Native, non-Hispanic/Latino; 4 Asian, non-Hispanic/Latino; 4 Hispanic/Latino), 25 international. Average age 29. 172 applicants, 51% accepted, 77 enrolled. In 2013, 89 master's, 11 doctorates, 13 other advanced degrees awarded. Terminal master's awarded for partial completion of doctoral program. *Degree requirements:* For master's, final oral exam; for doctorate, thesis/dissertation, preliminary written/oral exam, final oral exam. *Entrance requirements:* For master's, GRE or MAT, minimum GPA of 3.0; for doctorate, GRE or MAT, minimum GPA of 3.0, writing sample. Application fee: $75 ($95 for international students). *Financial support:* In 2013–14, 3 fellowships (averaging $22,667 per year), 8 research assistantships with full tuition reimbursements (averaging $849 per year), 41 teaching assistantships with full tuition reimbursements (averaging $12,766 per year) were awarded; career-related internships or fieldwork, Federal Work-Study, institutionally sponsored loans, and tuition waivers (full and partial) also available. Support available to part-time students. *Faculty research:* Exercise physiology; biochemical, molecular and nutritional aspects of exercise; sport training and performance; sport and exercise psychology; behavioral aspects of physical activity; youth sport science; gender and sport sociology; sports management; sports policy, marketing and law; motor development and disabilities; movement perception and action; movement neuroscience. *Total annual research expenditures:* $472,507. *Unit head:* Dr. Li Li Ji, Director, 612-624-9809, Fax: 612-626-7700, E-mail: llji@umn.edu. *Application contact:* Dr. Jennifer Engler, Assistant Dean, 612-626-2887, Fax: 612-626-7496, E-mail: engle009@umn.edu.

The University of Montana, Graduate School, Phyllis J. Washington College of Education and Human Sciences, Department of Health and Human Performance, Missoula, MT 59812-0002. Offers exercise science (MS); health and human performance (MS); health promotion (MS). Part-time programs available. *Entrance requirements:* For master's, GRE General Test. Additional exam requirements/recommendations for international students: Required—TOEFL. *Faculty research:* Exercise physiology, performance psychology, nutrition, pre-employment physical screening, program evaluation.

University of Nebraska at Kearney, Graduate Programs, College of Education, Department of Health, Physical Education, Recreation, and Leisure Studies, Kearney, NE 68849-0001. Offers general physical education (MA Ed), including recreation and leisure, sports administration; physical education exercise science (MA Ed); physical education master teacher (MA Ed), including pedagogy, special populations. Part-time and evening/weekend programs available. *Degree requirements:* For master's, comprehensive exam, thesis optional. *Entrance requirements:* For master's, GRE General Test, personal statement. Additional exam requirements/recommendations for international students: Required—TOEFL (minimum score 550 paper-based). Electronic applications accepted. *Faculty research:* Ergonomic aids, nutrition, motor development, sports pedagogy, applied behavior analysis.

University of Nebraska at Omaha, Graduate Studies, College of Education, School of Health, Physical Education, and Recreation, Omaha, NE 68182. Offers athletic training (MA); exercise science (PhD); health, physical education, and recreation (MA, MS). Part-time and evening/weekend programs available. *Faculty:* 15 full-time (7 women). *Students:* 54 full-time (24 women), 32 part-time (9 women); includes 8 minority (2 Asian, non-Hispanic/Latino; 3 Hispanic/Latino; 3 Two or more races, non-Hispanic/Latino), 4 international. Average age 28. 79 applicants, 51% accepted, 22 enrolled. In 2013, 27 master's awarded. *Degree requirements:* For master's, comprehensive exam, thesis (for

some programs). *Entrance requirements:* For master's, GRE; entrance exam, minimum GPA of 3.0, official transcripts, statement of purpose, 2 letters of recommendation; for doctorate, GRE, minimum GPA of 3.2, official transcripts, statement of purpose, 3 letters of recommendation, resume, writing sample. Additional exam requirements/recommendations for international students: Required—TOEFL, IELTS, PTE. *Application deadline:* For fall admission, 7/1 priority date for domestic students; for spring admission, 11/1 priority date for domestic students; for summer admission, 2/1 for domestic students. Applications are processed on a rolling basis. Application fee: $45. Electronic applications accepted. *Financial support:* In 2013–14, 19 students received support, including 12 research assistantships with tuition reimbursements available, 7 teaching assistantships with tuition reimbursements available; fellowships, Federal Work-Study, institutionally sponsored loans, scholarships/grants, tuition waivers (full), and unspecified assistantships also available. Support available to part-time students. Financial award application deadline: 3/1; financial award applicants required to submit FAFSA. *Unit head:* Dr. Daniel Blanke, Director, 402-554-2670. *Application contact:* Dr. Kris Berg, Graduate Program Chair, 402-554-2670, E-mail: graduate@unomaha.edu.

University of New Brunswick Fredericton, School of Graduate Studies, Faculty of Kinesiology, Fredericton, NB E3B 5A3, Canada. Offers exercise and sport science (M Sc); sport and recreation management (MBA); sport and recreation studies (MA). Part-time programs available. *Faculty:* 14 full-time (6 women), 1 part-time/adjunct (0 women). *Students:* 27 full-time (13 women), 5 part-time (1 woman). In 2013, 9 master's awarded. *Degree requirements:* For master's, thesis (for some programs). *Entrance requirements:* For master's, GMAT (minimum score of 550 for sport and recreation management program), minimum GPA of 3.0, written statement of research goals and interests. Additional exam requirements/recommendations for international students: Required—TOEFL (minimum score 92 iBT), IELTS (minimum score 7). *Application deadline:* For winter admission, 1/31 for domestic students; for spring admission, 3/31 for domestic students. Applications are processed on a rolling basis. Application fee: $50 Canadian dollars. Electronic applications accepted. *Financial support:* In 2013–14, 31 research assistantships, 61 teaching assistantships were awarded; fellowships with tuition reimbursements, career-related internships or fieldwork, and scholarships/grants also available. *Unit head:* Dr. Usha Kuruganti, Acting Director of Graduate Studies, 506-447-3101, Fax: 506-453-3511, E-mail: ukurugan@unb.ca. *Application contact:* Leslie Harquail, Graduate Secretary, 506-453-4575, Fax: 506-453-3511, E-mail: harquail@unb.ca.
Website: http://go.unb.ca/gradprograms.

University of New Hampshire, Graduate School, School of Health and Human Services, Department of Kinesiology, Durham, NH 03824. Offers adapted physical education (Postbaccalaureate Certificate); kinesiology (MS). Part-time programs available. *Faculty:* 14 full-time (4 women). *Students:* 3 full-time (2 women), 9 part-time (4 women); includes 2 minority (1 Hispanic/Latino; 1 Two or more races, non-Hispanic/Latino). Average age 27. 29 applicants, 48% accepted, 11 enrolled. In 2013, 4 master's awarded. *Degree requirements:* For master's, thesis or alternative. *Entrance requirements:* For master's, GRE General Test. Additional exam requirements/recommendations for international students: Required—TOEFL (minimum score 550 paper-based; 80 iBT). *Application deadline:* For fall admission, 6/1 priority date for domestic students, 4/1 for international students; for spring admission, 12/1 for domestic students. Applications are processed on a rolling basis. Application fee: $65. *Expenses:* Tuition, state resident: full-time $13,500; part-time $750 per credit hour. Tuition, nonresident: full-time $26,200; part-time $1100 per credit hour. *Required fees:* $1741; $435.25 per term. Tuition and fees vary according to course level, course load, campus/location and program. *Financial support:* In 2013–14, 5 students received support, including 4 teaching assistantships; fellowships, research assistantships, career-related internships or fieldwork, Federal Work-Study, scholarships/grants, and tuition waivers (full and partial) also available. Support available to part-time students. Financial award application deadline: 2/15. *Faculty research:* Exercise specialist, sports studies, special physical education, pediatric exercises and motor behavior. *Unit head:* Dr. Ron Croce, Chairperson, 603-862-2080. *Application contact:* Stephanie McAdams, Administrative Assistant, 603-862-2071, E-mail: kinesiology.dept@unh.edu.
Website: http://chhs.unh.edu/kin/index.

University of New Mexico, Graduate School, College of Education, Department of Health, Exercise and Sports Sciences, Program in Physical Education, Albuquerque, NM 87131-2039. Offers adapted physical education (MS); curriculum and instruction (MS); exercise science (MS); generalist (MS); sports administration (MS). Part-time programs available. *Faculty:* 6 full-time (3 women). *Students:* 53 full-time (19 women), 27 part-time (14 women); includes 32 minority (3 Black or African American, non-Hispanic/Latino; 3 American Indian or Alaska Native, non-Hispanic/Latino; 2 Asian, non-Hispanic/Latino; 22 Hispanic/Latino; 2 Two or more races, non-Hispanic/Latino), 12 international. Average age 28. 48 applicants, 65% accepted, 23 enrolled. In 2013, 22 master's awarded. Terminal master's awarded for partial completion of doctoral program. *Degree requirements:* For master's, comprehensive exam, thesis optional. *Entrance requirements:* For master's, GRE, 3 letters of reference, minimum cumulative GPA of 3.0 in last 2 years of bachelor's degree, letter of intent. Additional exam requirements/recommendations for international students: Required—TOEFL (minimum score 550 paper-based). *Application deadline:* For fall admission, 3/1 priority date for domestic students; for spring admission, 11/1 priority date for domestic students. Application fee: $50. Electronic applications accepted. *Financial support:* In 2013–14, 57 students received support, including 1 fellowship (averaging $2,290 per year), 1 teaching assistantship with full tuition reimbursement available (averaging $11,294 per year); career-related internships or fieldwork, Federal Work-Study, institutionally sponsored loans, scholarships/grants, health care benefits, tuition waivers, and unspecified assistantships also available. Financial award application deadline: 3/1; financial award applicants required to submit FAFSA. *Faculty research:* Physical education pedagogy, sports psychology, sports administration, cardiac rehabilitation, sports physiology, physical fitness assessment, exercise prescription. *Total annual research expenditures:* $17,400. *Unit head:* Dr. Todd Seidler, Chair, 505-277-2783, Fax: 505-277-6227, E-mail: tseidler@unm.edu. *Application contact:* Monica Lopez, Department Office, 505-277-5151, Fax: 505-277-6227, E-mail: mllopez@unm.edu.
Website: http://coe.unm.edu/departments/hess/pe-teacher-education.html.

University of New Mexico, Graduate School, College of Education, Department of Health, Exercise and Sports Sciences, Program in Physical Education, Sports and Exercise Science, Albuquerque, NM 87131-2039. Offers curriculum and instruction (PhD); exercise science (PhD); sports administration (PhD). Part-time programs available. *Faculty:* 18 full-time (10 women). *Students:* 26 full-time (9 women), 17 part-time (5 women); includes 11 minority (3 Black or African American, non-Hispanic/Latino; 1 Asian, non-Hispanic/Latino; 6 Hispanic/Latino; 1 Native Hawaiian or other Pacific Islander, non-Hispanic/Latino), 7 international. Average age 34. 25 applicants, 36% accepted, 5 enrolled. In 2013, 4 doctorates awarded. *Degree requirements:* For doctorate, comprehensive exam, thesis/dissertation, inquiry skills, 24 credits in supporting area. *Entrance requirements:* For doctorate, GRE, letter of intent, 3 letters of reference, minimum cumulative GPA of 3.0 in last 2 years of bachelor's degree. Additional exam requirements/recommendations for international students: Required—TOEFL (minimum score 550 paper-based). *Application deadline:* For fall admission, 3/1 priority date for domestic students; for spring admission, 11/1 priority date for domestic students. Application fee: $50. Electronic applications accepted. *Financial support:* In 2013–14, 33 students received support, including 3 fellowships (averaging $2,290 per year), 16 teaching assistantships with full tuition reimbursements available (averaging $10,987 per year); career-related internships or fieldwork, Federal Work-Study, institutionally sponsored loans, scholarships/grants, health care benefits, tuition waivers, and unspecified assistantships also available. Financial award application deadline: 3/1; financial award applicants required to submit FAFSA. *Faculty research:* Facility risk management, physical education pedagogy practices, physiological adaptations to exercise, physiological adaptations to heat, sport leadership. *Total annual research expenditures:* $17,400. *Unit head:* Dr. Todd Seidler, Chair, 505-277-2783, Fax: 505-277-6227, E-mail: tseidler@unm.edu. *Application contact:* Monica Lopez, Program Office, 505-277-5151, Fax: 505-277-6227, E-mail: mllopez@unm.edu.
Website: http://coe.unm.edu/departments/hess/pe-teacher-education/physical-education-sports-and-exercise-science-phd.html.

University of North Alabama, College of Education, Department of Health, Physical Education, and Recreation, Florence, AL 35632-0001. Offers health and human performance (MS), including exercise science, kinesiology, wellness and health promotion; secondary education (MA Ed), including physical education (P-12). Part-time and evening/weekend programs available. *Faculty:* 5 full-time (2 women). *Students:* 21 full-time (11 women), 7 part-time (2 women); includes 3 minority (2 Black or African American, non-Hispanic/Latino; 1 Two or more races, non-Hispanic/Latino), 3 international. Average age 27. 30 applicants, 90% accepted, 22 enrolled. In 2013, 3 master's awarded. *Degree requirements:* For master's, comprehensive exam (for some programs), thesis optional. *Entrance requirements:* For master's, MAT or GRE, 3 letters of recommendation, essay. Additional exam requirements/recommendations for international students: Required—TOEFL (minimum score 550 paper-based; 79 iBT), IELTS (minimum score 6). *Application deadline:* For fall admission, 7/1 for domestic and international students; for spring admission, 12/1 for domestic and international students. Applications are processed on a rolling basis. Application fee: $25 ($50 for international students). Electronic applications accepted. *Expenses:* Tuition, state resident: full-time $4968; part-time $3312 per year. Tuition, nonresident: full-time $9936; part-time $6624 per year. *Required fees:* $970; $60.33 per credit. $362 per semester. *Financial support:* Application deadline: 4/1; applicants required to submit FAFSA. *Unit head:* Dr. Thomas E. Coates, Chair, 256-765-4377. *Application contact:* Russ Darracott, Graduate Admissions Counselor, 256-765-4447, E-mail: erdarracott@una.edu.
Website: http://www.una.edu/hper/docs/HPERThesisGuideliens.pdf.

The University of North Carolina at Chapel Hill, Graduate School, College of Arts and Sciences, Department of Exercise and Sport Science, Chapel Hill, NC 27599. Offers athletic training (MA); exercise physiology (MA); sport administration (MA). *Degree requirements:* For master's, comprehensive exam, thesis. *Entrance requirements:* For master's, GRE General Test, minimum GPA of 3.0. Additional exam requirements/recommendations for international students: Required—TOEFL (minimum score 550 paper-based). Electronic applications accepted. *Faculty research:* Mild head injury in sport, endocrine system's response to exercise, obesity and children, effect of aerobic exercise on cerebral bloodflow in elderly population.

The University of North Carolina at Pembroke, Graduate Studies, School of Education, Department of Health, Physical Education, and Recreation, Pembroke, NC 28372-1510. Offers physical education (MA). Part-time and evening/weekend programs available. *Degree requirements:* For master's, comprehensive exam, thesis optional. *Entrance requirements:* For master's, MAT or GRE, minimum GPA of 3.0 in major, 2.5 overall. Additional exam requirements/recommendations for international students: Required—TOEFL.

University of Northern Colorado, Graduate School, College of Natural and Health Sciences, School of Sport and Exercise Science, Greeley, CO 80639. Offers exercise science (MS, PhD); sport administration (MS, PhD); sport pedagogy (MS, PhD). Part-time and evening/weekend programs available. *Degree requirements:* For master's, comprehensive exam; for doctorate, comprehensive exam, thesis/dissertation. *Entrance requirements:* For master's, 2 letters of recommendation, resume; for doctorate, GRE General Test, 3 letters of recommendation, resume. Electronic applications accepted.

University of Northern Iowa, Graduate College, College of Education, School of Health, Physical Education, and Leisure Services, MA Program in Physical Education, Cedar Falls, IA 50614. Offers kinesiology (MA); physical education (MA); teaching/coaching (MA). Part-time and evening/weekend programs available. *Students:* 22 full-time (7 women), 18 part-time (6 women); includes 1 minority (Hispanic/Latino), 4 international. 22 applicants, 91% accepted, 13 enrolled. In 2013, 13 master's awarded. *Degree requirements:* For master's, comprehensive exam, thesis or alternative. *Entrance requirements:* For master's, minimum GPA of 3.0. Additional exam requirements/recommendations for international students: Required—TOEFL (minimum score 500 paper-based; 61 iBT). *Application deadline:* For fall admission, 8/1 priority date for domestic students. Applications are processed on a rolling basis. Application fee: $50 ($70 for international students). Electronic applications accepted. *Financial support:* Career-related internships or fieldwork, Federal Work-Study, and tuition waivers (full and partial) available. Support available to part-time students. Financial award application deadline: 2/1. *Unit head:* Dr. Doris Corbett, Director, 319-273-6475, Fax: 319-273-5958, E-mail: doris.corbett@uni.edu. *Application contact:* Laurie S. Russell, Record Analyst, 319-273-2623, Fax: 319-273-2885, E-mail: laurie.russell@uni.edu.
Website: http://www.grad.uni.edu/degrees-programs/programs/physical-education-ma.

University of North Georgia, School of Education, Dahlonega, GA 30597. Offers art education (MAT); early childhood education (M Ed); English education (MAT); history education (MAT); math education (MAT); middle grades education (M Ed, MAT); physical education (MS); school leadership (Ed S); secondary education (M Ed), including English education, history education, mathematics education, physical education; teacher education (MAT). *Accreditation:* NCATE. Part-time and evening/weekend programs available. Postbaccalaureate distance learning degree programs offered (no on-campus study). *Degree requirements:* For master's, comprehensive exam, thesis optional. *Entrance requirements:* For master's, GRE or MAT, GACE, minimum GPA of 2.75; for Ed S, GRE General Test or MAT, 3 years of teaching experience, master's degree, minimum graduate GPA of 3.25, leadership position in the school. Additional exam requirements/recommendations for international students: Required—TOEFL (minimum score 550 paper-based; 79 iBT), IELTS (minimum score 6.5). Electronic applications accepted. *Faculty research:* Identification of professional development school structures supporting P-12 student achievement, impact of diverse field placement settings in teacher belief development among preservice teachers, use of inquiry methodology in social studies teaching with English language learners, use of instructional differentiation in the middle grades classroom, effects of international school placements on preservice teacher beliefs and attitudes.

University of Puerto Rico, Mayagüez Campus, Graduate Studies, College of Arts and Sciences, Department of Physical Education, Mayagüez, PR 00681-9000. Offers kinesiology (MA), including biomechanics, education, exercise physiology, sports training. Part-time programs available. *Faculty:* 18 full-time (7 women), 1 (woman) part-time/adjunct. *Students:* 19 full-time (9 women), 4 part-time (2 women). 14 applicants,

64% accepted, 7 enrolled. In 2013, 2 master's awarded. *Degree requirements:* For master's, thesis optional. *Entrance requirements:* For master's, EXADEP, minimum GPA of 2.5. *Application deadline:* For fall admission, 2/15 for domestic and international students; for spring admission, 9/15 for domestic and international students. Applications are processed on a rolling basis. *Expenses: Tuition, area resident:* Full-time $2466; part-time $822 per year. *International tuition:* $6371 full-time. *Required fees:* $1095; $1095. Tuition and fees vary according to course level, course load and reciprocity agreements. *Financial support:* In 2013–14, 10 students received support, including 10 teaching assistantships (averaging $9,489 per year); fellowships with full tuition reimbursements available, institutionally sponsored loans, and unspecified assistantships also available. *Unit head:* Dr. Margarita Fernandez, Interim Director, 787-832-4040 Ext. 3841, Fax: 787-833-4825, E-mail: margarita.fernandez1@upr.edu. *Application contact:* Aracelys Gonzalez, Secretary, 787-832-4040 Ext. 2008, E-mail: aracelis.gonzalez23@upr.edu.
Website: http://ece.uprm.edu/artssciences/edfi/descrip.htm.

University of Rhode Island, Graduate School, College of Human Science and Services, Department of Kinesiology, Kingston, RI 02881. Offers cultural studies of sport and physical culture (MS); exercise science (MS); physical education pedagogy (MS); psychosocial/behavioral aspects of physical activity (MS). *Accreditation:* NCATE. Part-time programs available. *Faculty:* 17 full-time (11 women). *Students:* 13 full-time (8 women), 5 part-time (2 women); includes 4 minority (1 Black or African American, non-Hispanic/Latino; 1 American Indian or Alaska Native, non-Hispanic/Latino; 2 Hispanic/Latino). In 2013, 12 master's awarded. *Degree requirements:* For master's, thesis optional. *Entrance requirements:* For master's, GRE, 2 letters of recommendation. Additional exam requirements/recommendations for international students: Required—TOEFL (minimum score 550 paper-based). *Application deadline:* For fall admission, 7/15 for domestic students, 2/1 for international students; for spring admission, 11/15 for domestic students, 7/15 for international students. Application fee: $65. Electronic applications accepted. *Expenses:* Tuition, state resident: full-time $11,532; part-time $641 per credit. Tuition, nonresident: full-time $23,606; part-time $1311 per credit. *Required fees:* $1388; $36 per credit. $35 per semester. One-time fee: $130. *Financial support:* In 2013–14, 5 teaching assistantships with full and partial tuition reimbursements (averaging $9,903 per year) were awarded. Financial award application deadline: 7/15; financial award applicants required to submit FAFSA. *Faculty research:* Strength training and older adults, interventions to promote a healthy lifestyle as well as analysis of the psychosocial outcomes of those interventions, effects of exercise and nutrition on skeletal muscle of aging healthy adults with CVD and other metabolic related diseases, physical activity and fitness of deaf children and youth. *Total annual research expenditures:* $51,804. *Unit head:* Dr. Deborah Riebe, Chair, 401-874-5444, Fax: 401-874-4215, E-mail: debriebe@uri.edu. *Application contact:* Dr. Matthew Delmonico, Graduate Program Director, 401-874-5440, E-mail: delmonico@uri.edu.
Website: http://www.uri.edu/hss/.

University of South Alabama, Graduate School, College of Education, Department of Health, Physical Education and Leisure Services, Mobile, AL 36688-0002. Offers exercise science (MS); health education (M Ed); physical education (M Ed); therapeutic recreation (MS). *Accreditation:* NCATE (one or more programs are accredited). Part-time programs available. *Faculty:* 4 full-time (1 woman), 2 part-time/adjunct (0 women). *Students:* 34 full-time (16 women), 5 part-time (1 woman); includes 12 minority (9 Black or African American, non-Hispanic/Latino; 3 Two or more races, non-Hispanic/Latino), 4 international. 36 applicants, 61% accepted, 18 enrolled. In 2013, 16 master's awarded. *Degree requirements:* For master's, comprehensive exam. *Entrance requirements:* For master's, GRE General Test or MAT. *Application deadline:* For fall admission, 7/15 priority date for domestic students, 6/15 priority date for international students; for spring admission, 12/1 priority date for domestic students, 11/1 priority date for international students. Applications are processed on a rolling basis. Application fee: $35. *Expenses:* Tuition, state resident: full-time $8976; part-time $374 per credit hour. Tuition, nonresident: full-time $17,952; part-time $748 per credit hour. *Financial support:* In 2013–14, 10 teaching assistantships were awarded; career-related internships or fieldwork also available. Support available to part-time students. Financial award application deadline: 4/1. *Unit head:* Dr. Frederick M. Scaffidi, Chair, 251-460-7131. *Application contact:* Dr. Abigail Baxter, Director of Graduate Studies, 251-460-7131.

University of South Carolina, The Graduate School, College of Education, Department of Physical Education, Columbia, SC 29208. Offers IMA, MAT, MS, PhD. Part-time programs available. *Degree requirements:* For master's, comprehensive exam, thesis (for some programs); for doctorate, comprehensive exam, thesis/dissertation. *Entrance requirements:* For master's, GRE General Test, or Miller Analogies Test, writing sample, letter of intent, letters of recommendation; for doctorate, GRE General Test or Miller Analogies Test, writing sample, interview, letter of intent, letters of recommendation. *Faculty research:* Teaching/learning processes, anthropometric measurement, growth and development, motor development.

University of Southern Mississippi, Graduate School, College of Health, School of Human Performance and Recreation, Hattiesburg, MS 39406-0001. Offers human performance (MS, PhD), including exercise physiology (PhD), human performance (MS), physical education (MS); interscholastic athletic administration (MS); recreation and leisure management (MS); sport administration (MS); sport and coaching education (MS); sport management (MS). Part-time and evening/weekend programs available. *Faculty:* 13 full-time (5 women). *Students:* 60 full-time (20 women), 43 part-time (9 women); includes 19 minority (13 Black or African American, non-Hispanic/Latino; 1 American Indian or Alaska Native, non-Hispanic/Latino; 2 Hispanic/Latino; 3 Two or more races, non-Hispanic/Latino), 4 international. Average age 29. 62 applicants, 77% accepted, 38 enrolled. In 2013, 39 master's, 1 doctorate awarded. *Degree requirements:* For master's, comprehensive exam, thesis optional; for doctorate, comprehensive exam, thesis/dissertation. *Entrance requirements:* For master's, GRE General Test, minimum GPA of 2.75 in last 60 hours; for doctorate, GRE General Test, minimum GPA of 3.5. Additional exam requirements/recommendations for international students: Required—TOEFL, IELTS. *Application deadline:* For fall admission, 3/1 priority date for domestic students, 3/1 for international students; for spring admission, 1/10 priority date for domestic and international students. Applications are processed on a rolling basis. Application fee: $50. Electronic applications accepted. *Financial support:* In 2013–14, 1 fellowship (averaging $16,000 per year), 6 research assistantships with full tuition reimbursements (averaging $7,492 per year), 5 teaching assistantships with full tuition reimbursements (averaging $7,330 per year) were awarded; career-related internships or fieldwork, Federal Work-Study, institutionally sponsored loans, scholarships/grants, health care benefits, and unspecified assistantships also available. Financial award application deadline: 3/15; financial award applicants required to submit FAFSA. *Faculty research:* Exercise physiology, health behaviors, resource management, activity interaction, site development. *Unit head:* Dr. Frederick Green, Director, 601-266-5379, Fax: 601-266-4445. *Application contact:* Dr. Trenton Gould, Graduate Coordinator, 601-266-5379, Fax: 601-266-4445.
Website: http://www.usm.edu/graduateschool/table.php.

University of South Florida, College of Education, School of Physical Education and Exercise Science, Tampa, FL 33620-9951. Offers exercise science (MA); physical education teacher preparation (MA). Part-time and evening/weekend programs available. Postbaccalaureate distance learning degree programs offered (no on-campus study). *Degree requirements:* For master's, comprehensive exam, thesis optional. *Entrance requirements:* For master's, GRE General Test, minimum GPA of 3.0 in last 60 hours of coursework. Additional exam requirements/recommendations for international students: Required—TOEFL (minimum score 500 paper-based). Electronic applications accepted. *Faculty research:* Physical education pedagogy, active gaming, exercise motivation, heat stress research, strength and nutrition research, physical activity risk management.

The University of Tennessee at Chattanooga, Graduate School, College of Health, Education and Professional Studies, Department of Health and Human Performance, Chattanooga, TN 37403. Offers athletic training (MSAT); health and human performance (MS). *Faculty:* 5 full-time (3 women). *Students:* 37 full-time (24 women), 2 part-time (1 woman); includes 4 minority (2 Black or African American, non-Hispanic/Latino; 1 Hispanic/Latino; 1 Two or more races, non-Hispanic/Latino). Average age 24. 5 applicants, 60% accepted, 2 enrolled. In 2013, 22 master's awarded. *Degree requirements:* For master's, thesis or alternative, clinical rotations. *Entrance requirements:* For master's, GRE General Test or MAT, minimum GPA of 2.75 overall or 3.0 in last 60 hours; CPR and First Aid certification. Additional exam requirements/recommendations for international students: Required—TOEFL (minimum score 550 paper-based; 79 iBT), IELTS (minimum score 6). *Application deadline:* For fall admission, 6/13 priority date for domestic students, 6/1 for international students; for spring admission, 10/15 priority date for domestic students, 10/1 for international students. Applications are processed on a rolling basis. Application fee: $30 ($35 for international students). Electronic applications accepted. *Financial support:* In 2013–14, 6 research assistantships with tuition reimbursements (averaging $5,320 per year), 2 teaching assistantships with tuition reimbursements (averaging $3,432 per year) were awarded; career-related internships or fieldwork, scholarships/grants, and unspecified assistantships also available. Support available to part-time students. *Faculty research:* Therapeutic exercise, lumbar spine biomechanics, physical activity epidemiology, functional rehabilitation outcomes, metabolic health. *Unit head:* Dr. Gary Liguori, Department Head, 423-425-4196, Fax: 423-425-4457, E-mail: gary-liguori@utc.edu. *Application contact:* Dr. J. Randy Walker, Interim Dean of Graduate Studies, 423-425-4478, Fax: 423-425-5223, E-mail: randy-walker@utc.edu.
Website: https://www.utc.edu/Academic/HealthAndHumanPerformance/.

The University of Tennessee at Martin, Graduate Programs, College of Education, Health and Behavioral Sciences, Program in Teaching, Martin, TN 38238-1000. Offers curriculum and instruction (MS Ed), including 7-12, K-6; initial licensure (MS Ed), including elementary, secondary; initial licensure K-12 (MS Ed), including physical education, special education; interdisciplinary (MS Ed). Part-time programs available. *Students:* 20 full-time (14 women), 88 part-time (65 women); includes 9 minority (8 Black or African American, non-Hispanic/Latino; 1 Two or more races, non-Hispanic/Latino). 78 applicants, 64% accepted, 33 enrolled. In 2013, 32 master's awarded. *Degree requirements:* For master's, comprehensive exam. *Entrance requirements:* For master's, GRE General Test, minimum GPA of 2.5. Additional exam requirements/recommendations for international students: Required—TOEFL (minimum score 525 paper-based; 71 iBT). *Application deadline:* For fall admission, 7/29 priority date for domestic students, 7/29 for international students; for spring admission, 12/12 priority date for domestic students, 12/12 for international students. Applications are processed on a rolling basis. Application fee: $30 ($130 for international students). Electronic applications accepted. *Financial support:* Research assistantships with full tuition reimbursements, teaching assistantships with full tuition reimbursements, career-related internships or fieldwork, scholarships/grants, and unspecified assistantships available. Financial award application deadline: 3/1. *Faculty research:* Special education, science/math/technology, school reform, reading. *Unit head:* Dr. Gail Stephens, Interim Dean, 731-881-7127, Fax: 731-881-7975, E-mail: gstephe6@utm.edu. *Application contact:* Jolene L. Cunningham, Student Services Specialist, 731-881-7012, Fax: 731-881-7499, E-mail: jcunningham@utm.edu.

The University of Texas at Austin, Graduate School, College of Education, Department of Curriculum and Instruction, Austin, TX 78712-1111. Offers bilingual/bicultural education (M Ed, MA, PhD); cultural studies in education (M Ed, MA, PhD); early childhood education (M Ed, MA, PhD); language and literacy studies (M Ed, PhD); learning technologies (M Ed, MA, PhD); physical education (M Ed, MA, PhD). Terminal master's awarded for partial completion of doctoral program. *Degree requirements:* For doctorate, thesis/dissertation. *Entrance requirements:* For master's and doctorate, GRE General Test. Electronic applications accepted.

The University of Toledo, College of Graduate Studies, Judith Herb College of Education, Department of Early Childhood, Physical and Special Education, Toledo, OH 43606-3390. Offers early childhood education (ME); physical education (ME); special education (ME). Part-time programs available. *Faculty:* 25. *Students:* 9 full-time (all women), 89 part-time (80 women); includes 16 minority (13 Black or African American, non-Hispanic/Latino; 3 Hispanic/Latino), 1 international. Average age 32. 28 applicants, 75% accepted, 16 enrolled. In 2013, 47 master's awarded. *Degree requirements:* For master's, thesis. *Entrance requirements:* For master's, minimum cumulative GPA of 2.7 for all previous academic work, letters of recommendation. Additional exam requirements/recommendations for international students: Required—TOEFL (minimum score 550 paper-based; 80 iBT). *Application deadline:* For fall admission, 1/15 priority date for domestic and international students. Applications are processed on a rolling basis. Application fee: $45 ($75 for international students). Electronic applications accepted. *Financial support:* In 2013–14, 3 teaching assistantships with full and partial tuition reimbursements (averaging $4,500 per year) were awarded; career-related internships or fieldwork, Federal Work-Study, institutionally sponsored loans, scholarships/grants, tuition waivers (full and partial), unspecified assistantships, and administrative assistantships also available. Support available to part-time students. *Unit head:* Dr. Richard Welsch, Chair, 419-530-7736, E-mail: richard.welsch@utoledo.edu. *Application contact:* Graduate School Office, 419-530-4723, Fax: 419-530-4724, E-mail: grdsch@utnet.utoledo.edu.
Website: http://www.utoledo.edu/eduhshs/.

University of Toronto, School of Graduate Studies, Faculty of Physical Education and Health, Toronto, ON M5S 1A1, Canada. Offers M Sc, PhD. *Degree requirements:* For master's, thesis, oral defense of thesis; for doctorate, comprehensive exam, defense of thesis. *Entrance requirements:* For master's, background in physical education and health, minimum B+ average in final year of undergraduate study, 2 letters of reference, resume, 2 writing samples; for doctorate, master's degree with successful defense of thesis, background in exercise sciences, minimum A- average, 2 letters of reference. Additional exam requirements/recommendations for international students: Required—TOEFL (minimum score 580 paper-based; 93 iBT), TWE (minimum score 5). Electronic applications accepted.

University of Victoria, Faculty of Graduate Studies, Faculty of Education, School of Exercise Science, Physical, and Health Education, Victoria, BC V8W 2Y2, Canada. Offers coaching studies (co-operative education) (M Ed); kinesiology (M Sc, MA); leisure service administration (MA); physical education (MA). Part-time programs available. *Degree requirements:* For master's, comprehensive exam (for some programs), thesis (for some programs). *Entrance requirements:* For master's, minimum B average.

Physical Education

Additional exam requirements/recommendations for international students: Required—TOEFL (minimum score 575 paper-based), IELTS (minimum score 7). Electronic applications accepted. *Faculty research:* Children and exercise, mental skills in sports, teaching effectiveness, neural control of human movement, physical performance and health.

University of Virginia, Curry School of Education, Department of Human Services, Program in Health and Physical Education, Charlottesville, VA 22903. Offers M Ed, Ed D. *Students:* 42 full-time (25 women), 7 part-time (3 women); includes 1 minority (Asian, non-Hispanic/Latino), 1 international. Average age 26. 32 applicants, 53% accepted, 6 enrolled. In 2013, 39 master's, 1 doctorate awarded. *Entrance requirements:* For master's and doctorate, GRE General Test, 2 letters of recommendation. Additional exam requirements/recommendations for international students: Required—TOEFL (minimum score 600 paper-based; 90 iBT), IELTS (minimum score 7). *Application deadline:* Applications are processed on a rolling basis. Application fee: $60. Electronic applications accepted. *Expenses:* Tuition, state resident: part-time $334 per credit hour. Tuition, nonresident: part-time $1224 per credit hour. *Financial support:* Applicants required to submit FAFSA. *Unit head:* Arthur L. Weltman, Chair, Kinesiology, 434-924-6191, E-mail: alw2v@virginia.edu. *Application contact:* Lynn Renfroe, Information Contact, 434-924-6254, E-mail: ldr9t@virginia.edu. Website: http://curry.virginia.edu/academics/degrees/bachelor-master-in-teaching/b-mt-in-health-physical-education.

University of Washington, Graduate School, College of Education, Seattle, WA 98195. Offers curriculum and instruction (M Ed, Ed D, PhD), including educational technology, general curriculum (Ed D, PhD), language, literacy, and culture, mathematics education, multicultural education, reading and language arts education (Ed D), science education, social studies education, teaching and curriculum (M Ed); educational leadership and policy studies (M Ed, Ed D, PhD), including administration (Ed D), educational policy, organization, and leadership (M Ed, PhD), higher education, leadership for learning (Ed D), social and cultural foundations of education (M Ed, PhD); educational psychology (M Ed, PhD), including educational psychology (PhD), human development and cognition (M Ed), learning sciences, measurement, statistics and research design (M Ed), school psychology (M Ed); instructional leadership (M Ed); intercollegiate athletic leadership (M Ed); special education (M Ed, Ed D, PhD), including early childhood special education (M Ed), emotional and behavioral disabilities (M Ed), learning disabilities (M Ed), low-incidence disabilities (M Ed), severe disabilities (M Ed), special education (Ed D, PhD); teacher education (MIT). *Accreditation:* APA. Part-time and evening/weekend programs available. *Degree requirements:* For master's, thesis optional; for doctorate, thesis/dissertation. *Entrance requirements:* For master's and doctorate, GRE General Test, minimum GPA of 3.0. Additional exam requirements/recommendations for international students: Required—TOEFL. Electronic applications accepted. *Faculty research:* School restructuring/effective schools, special education interventions, literacy and writing, technology, school partnerships, teacher preparation.

The University of West Alabama, School of Graduate Studies, College of Education, Departments of Instructional Leadership and Support/Curriculum and Instruction, Program in Secondary Education, Livingston, AL 35470. Offers biology (MAT); English language arts (MAT); history (MAT); mathematics (MAT); physical education (MAT); science (MAT); secondary education (M Ed); social science (MAT). Part-time and evening/weekend programs available. Postbaccalaureate distance learning degree programs offered (no on-campus study). *Faculty:* 20 full-time (4 women), 5 part-time/adjunct (2 women). *Students:* 210 (139 women); includes 86 minority (80 Black or African American, non-Hispanic/Latino; 2 Asian, non-Hispanic/Latino; 2 Hispanic/Latino; 2 Two or more races, non-Hispanic/Latino). 115 applicants, 86% accepted, 72 enrolled. In 2013, 61 master's awarded. *Degree requirements:* For master's, comprehensive exam, thesis optional. *Entrance requirements:* For master's, GRE General Test, MAT, minimum GPA of 2.75. Additional exam requirements/recommendations for international students: Required—TOEFL (minimum score 500 paper-based; 61 iBT). *Application deadline:* For fall admission, 8/12 priority date for domestic students; for spring admission, 3/24 for domestic students. Applications are processed on a rolling basis. Application fee: $25 ($50 for international students). Electronic applications accepted. Tuition and fees vary according to course load. *Financial support:* Teaching assistantships, career-related internships or fieldwork, Federal Work-Study, scholarships/grants, and unspecified assistantships available. Support available to part-time students. Financial award application deadline: 3/1; financial award applicants required to submit FAFSA. *Faculty research:* Integrated arts in the curriculum, moral development of children. *Unit head:* Dr. Esther Howard, Chair of Curriculum and Instruction, 205-652-3428, Fax: 205-652-3706, E-mail: ehoward@uwa.edu. *Application contact:* Dr. Kathy Chandler, Dean of Graduate Studies, 205-652-3421, Fax: 205-652-3706, E-mail: kchandler@uwa.edu. Website: http://www.uwa.edu/highschool612.aspx.

University of West Florida, College of Professional Studies, Department of Health, Leisure, and Exercise Science, Program in Health, Leisure, and Exercise Science, Pensacola, FL 32514-5750. Offers exercise science (MS); physical education (MS). Part-time and evening/weekend programs available. *Degree requirements:* For master's, thesis or alternative. *Entrance requirements:* For master's, GRE or MAT, official transcripts; minimum GPA of 3.0; letter of intent; two personal references; work experience. Additional exam requirements/recommendations for international students: Required—TOEFL (minimum score 550 paper-based). Electronic applications accepted.

University of West Florida, College of Professional Studies, Ed D Programs, Specialization in Curriculum and Instruction: Physical Education and Health, Pensacola, FL 32514-5750. Offers Ed D. Part-time and evening/weekend programs available. *Degree requirements:* For doctorate, comprehensive exam, thesis/dissertation. *Entrance requirements:* For doctorate, GRE, MAT, or GMAT, letter of intent; writing sample; three letters of recommendation; two completed disposition assessment forms; written statement of goals; interview with admissions committee. Additional exam requirements/recommendations for international students: Required—TOEFL (minimum score 550 paper-based).

University of Wisconsin–La Crosse, Graduate Studies, College of Science and Health, Department of Exercise and Sport Science, Program in Physical Education Teaching, La Crosse, WI 54601-3742. Offers adapted physical education (MS); adventure education (MS); physical education teaching (MS). Part-time and evening/weekend programs available. *Students:* 16 full-time (4 women), 1 international. Average age 24. 25 applicants, 60% accepted, 13 enrolled. In 2013, 24 master's awarded. *Degree requirements:* For master's, thesis optional. *Entrance requirements:* For master's, minimum GPA of 3.0 during previous 2 years, 2.85 overall; BA in physical education. Additional exam requirements/recommendations for international students: Required—TOEFL (minimum score 550 paper-based; 79 iBT). *Application deadline:* Applications are processed on a rolling basis. Electronic applications accepted. *Financial support:* Federal Work-Study, scholarships/grants, health care benefits, and tuition waivers (partial) available. Support available to part-time students. Financial award application deadline: 3/15; financial award applicants required to submit FAFSA. *Unit head:* Dr. Jeff Steffen, Director, 608-785-6535, E-mail: steffen.jeff@uwlax.edu.

Application contact: Corey Sjoquist, Director of Admissions, 608-785-8939, E-mail: admissions@uwlax.edu. Website: http://www.uwlax.edu/sah/ess/pe/.

University of Wisconsin–Whitewater, School of Graduate Studies, College of Education and Professional Studies, Department of Curriculum and Instruction, Whitewater, WI 53190-1790. Offers professional development (MS), including bilingual education, challenging advanced learners, curriculum and instruction, educational leadership, health, human performance and recreation, health, physical education and coaching, information technologies and libraries, reading. *Accreditation:* NCATE. Part-time and evening/weekend programs available. Postbaccalaureate distance learning degree programs offered. *Degree requirements:* For master's, thesis or integrated project. *Entrance requirements:* Additional exam requirements/recommendations for international students: Required—TOEFL (minimum score 550 paper-based; 80 iBT), IELTS (minimum score 6). Electronic applications accepted. *Faculty research:* Hybrid of exercise physiology and psychology; gender equity; education, pedagogy, and technology; comprehensive school health education.

University of Wyoming, College of Health Sciences, Division of Kinesiology and Health, Laramie, WY 82071. Offers MS. *Accreditation:* NCATE. Part-time programs available. Postbaccalaureate distance learning degree programs offered (no on-campus study). *Degree requirements:* For master's, comprehensive exam (for some programs), thesis (for some programs). *Entrance requirements:* For master's, GRE General Test, minimum GPA of 3.0. Additional exam requirements/recommendations for international students: Required—TOEFL. Electronic applications accepted. *Faculty research:* Teacher effectiveness, effects of exercising on heart function, physiological responses of overtraining, psychological benefits of physical activity, health behavior.

Utah State University, School of Graduate Studies, Emma Eccles Jones College of Education and Human Services, Department of Health, Physical Education and Recreation, Logan, UT 84322. Offers M Ed, MS. Part-time and evening/weekend programs available. Postbaccalaureate distance learning degree programs offered (minimal on-campus study). *Degree requirements:* For master's, thesis (for some programs). *Entrance requirements:* For master's, GRE General Test or MAT, minimum GPA of 3.0. Additional exam requirements/recommendations for international students: Required—TOEFL. *Faculty research:* Sport psychology intervention, motor learning biomechanics, pedagogy, physiology.

Virginia Commonwealth University, Graduate School, School of Education, Department of Health and Human Performance, Richmond, VA 23284-9005. Offers athletic training (MSAT); health and movement sciences (MS); rehabilitation and movement science (PhD). *Entrance requirements:* For master's, GRE General Test or MAT. Additional exam requirements/recommendations for international students: Required—TOEFL (minimum score 600 paper-based; 100 iBT); Recommended—IELTS (minimum score 6.5). Electronic applications accepted.

Virginia Commonwealth University, Graduate School, School of Education, Program in Teaching and Learning, Richmond, VA 23284-9005. Offers early and elementary education (MT); health and physical education (MT); secondary 6-12 education (MT); secondary education (Certificate). *Accreditation:* NCATE. Part-time programs available. *Entrance requirements:* For master's, GRE General Test or MAT. Additional exam requirements/recommendations for international students: Required—TOEFL (minimum score 600 paper-based; 100 iBT). Electronic applications accepted.

Wayne State College, Department of Health, Human Performance and Sport, Wayne, NE 68787. Offers exercise science (MSE); organizational management (MS), including sport management. Part-time and evening/weekend programs available. *Degree requirements:* For master's, comprehensive exam, thesis optional. *Entrance requirements:* For master's, GRE General Test, minimum GPA of 3.0. Additional exam requirements/recommendations for international students: Required—TOEFL (minimum score 550 paper-based). Electronic applications accepted.

Wayne State University, College of Education, Division of Kinesiology, Health and Sports Studies, Detroit, MI 48202. Offers adapted physical education (Certificate); coaching (Certificate); elementary physical education (Certificate); exercise and sport science (M Ed); health education (M Ed, Certificate); kinesiology (M Ed, PhD), including exercise and sport science (PhD), physical education pedagogy (PhD); physical education (M Ed); secondary physical education (Certificate); sports administration (MA); wellness clinician/research (M Ed). Part-time programs available. *Students:* 42 full-time (27 women), 78 part-time (38 women); includes 43 minority (35 Black or African American, non-Hispanic/Latino; 1 Asian, non-Hispanic/Latino; 5 Hispanic/Latino; 2 Two or more races, non-Hispanic/Latino), 5 international. Average age 30. 120 applicants, 48% accepted, 30 enrolled. In 2013, 32 master's awarded. *Degree requirements:* For master's, thesis (for some programs); for doctorate, thesis/dissertation. *Entrance requirements:* For master's and doctorate, minimum undergraduate GPA of 3.0, undergraduate degree directly relating to the field of specialization being applied for, or undergraduate degree accompanied by extensive educational background in a closely-related field. Additional exam requirements/recommendations for international students: Required—TOEFL (minimum score 79 iBT), TWE (minimum score 5.5), Michigan English Language Assessment Battery (minimum score 85); Recommended—IELTS (minimum score 6.5). *Application deadline:* For fall admission, 6/1 priority date for domestic students, 5/1 priority date for international students; for winter admission, 10/1 priority date for domestic students, 9/1 priority date for international students; for spring admission, 2/1 priority date for domestic students, 1/1 priority date for international students. Applications are processed on a rolling basis. Application fee: $0. Electronic applications accepted. *Expenses:* Tuition, state resident: part-time $554.15 per credit. Tuition, nonresident: part-time $1200.35 per credit. *Required fees:* $42.15 per credit. $268.30 per semester. Tuition and fees vary according to course load and program. *Financial support:* In 2013–14, 22 students received support, including 4 fellowships with tuition reimbursements available (averaging $13,050 per year), 5 research assistantships with tuition reimbursements available (averaging $16,508 per year); career-related internships or fieldwork, Federal Work-Study, scholarships/grants, health care benefits, and unspecified assistantships also available. Support available to part-time students. Financial award application deadline: 3/31; financial award applicants required to submit FAFSA. *Faculty research:* Exercise and sport science, nutrition and physical activity interventions, school and community health, obesity prevention. *Total annual research expenditures:* $1.3 million. *Unit head:* Dr. Nate McCaughtry, Assistant Dean, Division of Kinesiology, Health and Sport Studies/Director, Center for School Health, 313-577-0014, Fax: 313-577-5002, E-mail: aj4391@wayne.edu. *Application contact:* Janice Green, Assistant Dean, 313-577-1605, E-mail: jwgreen@wayne.edu. Website: http://coe.wayne.edu/kinesiology/index.php.

West Chester University of Pennsylvania, College of Health Sciences, Department of Kinesiology, West Chester, PA 19383. Offers adapted physical education (Certificate); exercise and sport physiology (MS), including athletic training, exercise and sport physiology; general physical education (MS); sport management and athletics (MPA). Part-time and evening/weekend programs available. Postbaccalaureate distance learning degree programs offered (no on-campus study). *Faculty:* 6 full-time (5 women). *Students:* 25 full-time (13 women), 10 part-time (4 women); includes 5 minority (1 Black or African American, non-Hispanic/Latino; 1 Asian, non-Hispanic/Latino; 2 Hispanic/

Latino; 1 Two or more races, non-Hispanic/Latino), 1 international. Average age 27. 33 applicants, 97% accepted, 18 enrolled. In 2013, 15 master's, 6 other advanced degrees awarded. *Degree requirements:* For master's, thesis or report (for MS); 2 internships, capstone course including research project or thesis (for MPA). *Entrance requirements:* For master's, GRE (for MS), 2 letters of recommendation, transcripts, and statement of professional goals (for MS); 2 letters of reference, resume, and career goal statement (for MPA). Additional exam requirements/recommendations for international students: Required—TOEFL (minimum score 550 paper-based; 80 iBT). *Application deadline:* For fall admission, 4/15 priority date for domestic students, 3/15 for international students; for spring admission, 10/15 priority date for domestic students, 9/1 for international students. Applications are processed on a rolling basis. Application fee: $45. Electronic applications accepted. *Expenses:* Tuition, state resident: full-time $7956; part-time $442 per credit. Tuition, nonresident: full-time $11,934; part-time $663 per credit. *Required fees:* $2134.20; $106.24 per credit. Tuition and fees vary according to campus/location and program. *Financial support:* Unspecified assistantships available. Support available to part-time students. Financial award application deadline: 2/15; financial award applicants required to submit FAFSA. *Faculty research:* Metabolism during exercise, biomechanics, rating of perceived exertion, motor learning. *Unit head:* Dr. Frank Fry, Chair/Graduate Coordinator for the MS in General Physical Education Program, 610-436-2610, Fax: 610-436-2860, E-mail: ffry@wcupa.edu. *Application contact:* Dr. David Stearne, Graduate Coordinator for the Exercise and Sport Physiology Programs, 610-436-2347, Fax: 610-436-2860, E-mail: dstearne@wcupa.edu.
Website: http://www.wcupa.edu/_academics/sch_shs.hpe/.

Western Carolina University, Graduate School, College of Education and Allied Professions, School of Teaching and Learning, Cullowhee, NC 28723. Offers community college and higher education (MA Ed), including community college administration, community college teaching; comprehensive education (MA Ed, MAT); educational leadership (MA Ed, MSA, Ed D, Ed S), including educational leadership (MSA, Ed D, Ed S), educational supervision (MA Ed); teaching (MA Ed, MAT), including comprehensive education (MA Ed), physical education (MA Ed), teaching (MAT). *Accreditation:* NCATE. Part-time and evening/weekend programs available. Postbaccalaureate distance learning degree programs offered. *Degree requirements:* For master's, comprehensive exam; for doctorate, comprehensive exam, thesis/dissertation. *Entrance requirements:* For master's, GRE, appropriate undergraduate degree, 3 letters of recommendation; for doctorate, GRE General Test, minimum graduate GPA of 3.5, appropriate master's degree; for other advanced degree, GRE General Test, minimum graduate GPA of 3.5, work experience, appropriate master's degree. Additional exam requirements/recommendations for international students: Required—TOEFL (minimum score 550 paper-based; 79 iBT). *Faculty research:* Educational leadership, special education, rural education, organizational theory and practice, interinstitutional partnership, program evaluation.

Western Kentucky University, Graduate Studies, College of Health and Human Services, Department of Kinesiology, Recreation and Sport, Bowling Green, KY 42101. Offers athletic administration and coaching (MS); physical education (MS); recreation and sport administration (MS). Part-time and evening/weekend programs available. Postbaccalaureate distance learning degree programs offered. *Degree requirements:* For master's, comprehensive exam, thesis optional. *Entrance requirements:* For master's, GRE General Test, minimum GPA of 2.75. Additional exam requirements/recommendations for international students: Required—TOEFL (minimum score 555 paper-based; 79 iBT). *Faculty research:* Orthopedic rehabilitation, fitness center coordination, heat acclimation, biomechanical and physiological parameters.

Western Michigan University, Graduate College, College of Education and Human Development, Department of Health, Physical Education and Recreation, Kalamazoo, MI 49008. Offers exercise and sports medicine (MS), including athletic training, exercise physiology; physical education (MA), including coaching sport performance, pedagogy, special physical education, sport management.

Western Washington University, Graduate School, College of Humanities and Social Sciences, Department of Physical Education, Health, and Recreation, Bellingham, WA 98225-5996. Offers exercise science (MS); sport psychology (MS). Part-time programs available. *Degree requirements:* For master's, thesis. *Entrance requirements:* For master's, GRE General Test, minimum GPA of 3.0 in last 60 semester hours or last 90 quarter hours. Additional exam requirements/recommendations for international students: Required—TOEFL (minimum score 567 paper-based). Electronic applications accepted. *Faculty research:* Spinal motor control, biomechanics/kinesiology, biomechanics of aging, mobility of older adults, fall prevention, exercise interventions and function, magnesium and inspiratory muscle training (IMT).

Westfield State University, Division of Graduate and Continuing Education, Department of Movement Science, Sport, and Leisure, Westfield, MA 01086. Offers physical education (M Ed). Part-time and evening/weekend programs available. *Degree requirements:* For master's, comprehensive exam. *Entrance requirements:* For master's, GRE General Test or MAT, minimum GPA of 2.7.

West Virginia University, School of Physical Education, Morgantown, WV 26506. Offers athletic coaching education (MS); athletic training (MS); physical education/teacher education (MS, PhD), including curriculum and instruction (PhD), motor behavior (PhD), physical education supervision (PhD); sport and exercise psychology (PhD); sport management (MS). *Degree requirements:* For doctorate, comprehensive exam, thesis/dissertation, oral exam. *Entrance requirements:* For master's, GRE or MAT, minimum GPA of 3.0; for doctorate, GRE General Test or MAT, minimum GPA of 3.5. Additional exam requirements/recommendations for international students: Required—TOEFL (minimum score 550 paper-based). Electronic applications accepted. *Faculty research:* Sport psychosociology, teacher education, exercise psychology, counseling.

Wilfrid Laurier University, Faculty of Graduate and Postdoctoral Studies, Faculty of Science, Department of Kinesiology and Physical Education, Waterloo, ON N2L 3C5, Canada. Offers physical activity and health (M Sc). *Degree requirements:* For master's, thesis. *Entrance requirements:* For master's, honours degree in kinesiology, health, physical education with a minimum B+ in kinesiology and health-related courses. Additional exam requirements/recommendations for international students: Required—TOEFL (minimum score 89 iBT). Electronic applications accepted. *Faculty research:* Biomechanics, health, exercise physiology, motor control, sport psychology.

William Woods University, Graduate and Adult Studies, Fulton, MO 65251-1098. Offers administration (M Ed, Ed S); athletic/activities administration (M Ed); curriculum and instruction (M Ed, Ed S); educational leadership (Ed D); equestrian education (M Ed); health management (MBA); human resources (MBA); leadership (MBA); marketing, advertising, and public relations (MBA); teaching and technology (M Ed). Part-time and evening/weekend programs available. *Faculty:* 231 part-time/adjunct (87 women). *Students:* 418 full-time (276 women), 716 part-time (433 women); includes 51 minority (34 Black or African American, non-Hispanic/Latino; 4 American Indian or Alaska Native, non-Hispanic/Latino; 5 Asian, non-Hispanic/Latino; 3 Hispanic/Latino; 5 Two or more races, non-Hispanic/Latino), 4 international. Average age 35. In 2013, 507 master's, 8 doctorates, 143 other advanced degrees awarded. *Degree requirements:* For master's, capstone course (MBA), action research (M Ed); for Ed S, field experience. *Entrance requirements:* Additional exam requirements/recommendations for international students: Required—TOEFL (minimum score 550 paper-based). *Application deadline:* Applications are processed on a rolling basis. Application fee: $0. Electronic applications accepted. *Expenses:* Contact institution. *Financial support:* Institutionally sponsored loans available. Financial award applicants required to submit FAFSA. *Unit head:* Dr. Michael Westerfield, Vice President and Dean of the Graduate College, 573-592-4383, Fax: 573-592-1164. *Application contact:* Jessica Brush, Director of Operations, 573-592-4227, Fax: 573-592-1164, E-mail: jessica.brush@williamwoods.ede.
Website: http://www.williamwoods.edu/evening_programs/index.asp.

Wingate University, Thayer School of Education, Wingate, NC 28174-0159. Offers community college leadership (Ed D); educational leadership (MA Ed, Ed D); elementary education (MA Ed, MAT); health and physical education (MA Ed); sport administration (MA Ed). *Accreditation:* NCATE. Part-time and evening/weekend programs available. *Degree requirements:* For master's, portfolio. *Entrance requirements:* For master's, GRE General Test or MAT, teaching certificate (MA Ed).

Winthrop University, College of Education, Program in Physical Education, Rock Hill, SC 29733. Offers MS. Part-time programs available. *Degree requirements:* For master's, comprehensive exam, thesis optional. *Entrance requirements:* For master's, GRE General Test or PRAXIS. Electronic applications accepted.

Wright State University, School of Graduate Studies, College of Education and Human Services, Department of Health, Physical Education, and Recreation, Dayton, OH 45435. Offers M Ed, MA. *Accreditation:* NCATE. *Degree requirements:* For master's, comprehensive exam, thesis (for some programs). *Entrance requirements:* For master's, GRE General Test, MAT. Additional exam requirements/recommendations for international students: Required—TOEFL. *Faculty research:* Motor learning, motor development, exercise physiology, adapted physical education.

Section 31
Sports Management

This section contains a directory of institutions offering graduate work in sports management. Additional information about programs listed in the directory may be obtained by writing directly to the dean of a graduate school or chair of a department at the address given in the directory.

For programs offering related work, see also in this book *Business Administration and Management, Education,* and *Physical Education and Kinesiology.*

CONTENTS

Program Directory
Sports Management   1672

Sports Management

Angelo State University, College of Graduate Studies, College of Education, Department of Kinesiology, San Angelo, TX 76909. Offers coaching, sport, recreation and fitness administration (M Ed). Part-time and evening/weekend programs available. *Degree requirements:* For master's, comprehensive exam. *Entrance requirements:* Additional exam requirements/recommendations for international students: Required—TOEFL or IELTS. Electronic applications accepted.

Arkansas State University, Graduate School, College of Education and Behavioral Science, Department of Health, Physical Education, and Sport Sciences, Jonesboro, AR 72467. Offers exercise science (MS); physical education (MSE, SCCT); sports administration (MS). Part-time programs available. *Faculty:* 9 full-time (3 women). *Students:* 20 full-time (5 women), 35 part-time (11 women); includes 19 minority (13 Black or African American, non-Hispanic/Latino; 5 Hispanic/Latino; 1 Two or more races, non-Hispanic/Latino), 8 international. Average age 26. 53 applicants, 70% accepted, 29 enrolled. In 2013, 18 master's awarded. *Degree requirements:* For master's, comprehensive exam, thesis or alternative; for SCCT, comprehensive exam. *Entrance requirements:* For master's, GRE General Test or MAT, appropriate bachelor's degree, official transcripts, immunization records, statement of goals, letters of recommendation; for SCCT, GRE General Test or MAT, interview, master's degree, official transcript, immunization records. Additional exam requirements/recommendations for international students: Required—TOEFL (minimum score 550 paper-based; 79 iBT), IELTS (minimum score 6), PTE (minimum score 56). *Application deadline:* For fall admission, 7/1 for domestic and international students; for spring admission, 11/15 for domestic students, 11/14 for international students. Applications are processed on a rolling basis. Application fee: $30 ($40 for international students). Electronic applications accepted. *Expenses:* Tuition, state resident: full-time $4284; part-time $238 per credit hour. Tuition, nonresident: full-time $8568; part-time $476 per credit hour. *International tuition:* $9268 full-time. *Required fees:* $1098; $61 per credit hour. $25 per term. Tuition and fees vary according to course load and program. *Financial support:* In 2013–14, 18 students received support. Teaching assistantships, career-related internships or fieldwork, scholarships/grants, and unspecified assistantships available. Financial award application deadline: 7/1; financial award applicants required to submit FAFSA. *Unit head:* Dr. Jim Stillwell, Chair, 870-972-3066, Fax: 870-972-3096, E-mail: jstillwel@astate.edu. *Application contact:* Vickey Ring, Graduate Admissions Coordinator, 870-972-3029, Fax: 870-972-3857, E-mail: vickeyring@astate.edu.
Website: http://www.astate.edu/college/education/departments/health-physical-educations-and-sport-sciences/index.dot.

Ashland University, Dwight Schar College of Education, Department of Sport Sciences, Ashland, OH 44805-3702. Offers adapted physical education (M Ed); applied exercise science (M Ed); sport education (M Ed); sport management (M Ed). Part-time programs available. *Degree requirements:* For master's, practicum, inquiry seminar, thesis, or internship. *Entrance requirements:* For master's, teaching certificate or license, bachelor's degree, minimum cumulative GPA of 2.75. Additional exam requirements/recommendations for international students: Required—TOEFL. *Faculty research:* Coaching, legal issues, strength and conditioning, sport management rating of perceived exertion, youth fitness, geriatric exercise science.

Augustana College, Sports Administration and Leadership Program, Sioux Falls, SD 57197. Offers MA. Part-time programs available. *Faculty:* 4 full-time (all women), 1 part-time/adjunct (0 women). *Students:* 1 full-time (0 women), 17 part-time (6 women); includes 1 minority (Hispanic/Latino), 1 international. Average age 25. 7 applicants, 100% accepted, 7 enrolled. In 2013, 6 master's awarded. *Degree requirements:* For master's, thesis or alternative. *Entrance requirements:* For master's, minimum cumulative undergraduate GPA of 3.0 for last 60 semester hours; appropriate bachelor's degree; 2-3 page essay discussing academic interests, education goals, and plans for graduate study. Additional exam requirements/recommendations for international students: Required—TOEFL (minimum score 550 paper-based). *Application deadline:* For fall admission, 6/1 priority date for domestic and international students. Applications are processed on a rolling basis. Application fee: $50. Electronic applications accepted. *Financial support:* In 2013–14, 11 students received support, including 9 teaching assistantships with full tuition reimbursements available (averaging $4,500 per year). Financial award application deadline: 3/1; financial award applicants required to submit FAFSA. *Unit head:* Dr. Sherry Barkley, Sports Administration and Leadership Master's Program Director, 605-274-4312, E-mail: sherry.barkley@augie.edu. *Application contact:* Nancy Wright, Administrative Assistant, Graduate Education, 605-274-4043, Fax: 605-274-4450, E-mail: graduate@augie.edu.
Website: http://www.augie.edu/academics/graduate-education/sal.

Barry University, School of Human Performance and Leisure Sciences, Program in Sport Management, Miami Shores, FL 33161-6695. Offers MS. Part-time and evening/weekend programs available. *Degree requirements:* For master's, comprehensive exam, project or thesis. *Entrance requirements:* For master's, GMAT or GRE General Test, minimum GPA of 3.0. Electronic applications accepted. *Faculty research:* Economic impact of professional sports, sport marketing.

Barry University, School of Human Performance and Leisure Sciences and Andreas School of Business, Program in Sport Management and Business Administration, Miami Shores, FL 33161-6695. Offers MS/MBA. Part-time and evening/weekend programs available. Electronic applications accepted. *Faculty research:* Economic impact of professional sports, sport marketing.

Baylor University, Graduate School, School of Education, Department of Health, Human Performance and Recreation, Waco, TX 76798. Offers community health education (MPH); exercise physiology (MS Ed); kinesiology, exercise nutrition and health promotion (PhD); sport management (MS Ed); sport pedagogy (MS Ed). *Accreditation:* NCATE. Part-time programs available. *Faculty:* 13 full-time (5 women), 3 part-time/adjunct (1 woman). *Students:* 79 full-time (40 women), 28 part-time (14 women); includes 26 minority (9 Black or African American, non-Hispanic/Latino; 1 American Indian or Alaska Native, non-Hispanic/Latino; 3 Asian, non-Hispanic/Latino; 8 Hispanic/Latino; 5 Two or more races, non-Hispanic/Latino), 9 international. 30 applicants, 87% accepted. In 2013, 48 master's awarded. *Degree requirements:* For master's, comprehensive exam, thesis optional; for doctorate, comprehensive exam, thesis/dissertation. *Entrance requirements:* For master's and doctorate, GRE General Test. Additional exam requirements/recommendations for international students: Required—TOEFL. *Application deadline:* For fall admission, 2/1 priority date for domestic students, 2/1 for international students; for spring admission, 10/1 for domestic and international students. Applications are processed on a rolling basis. Application fee: $25. Electronic applications accepted. *Expenses:* Tuition: Full-time $25,866; part-time $1437 per credit hour. *Required fees:* $2736; $152 per credit hour. Tuition and fees vary according to course load and program. *Financial support:* In 2013–14, 35 students received support, including 1 research assistantship with tuition reimbursement

available, 33 teaching assistantships with tuition reimbursements available; career-related internships or fieldwork, Federal Work-Study, institutionally sponsored loans, tuition waivers (partial), and unspecified assistantships also available. Financial award application deadline: 2/1. *Faculty research:* Behavior change theory, nutrition and enzyme therapy, exercise testing, health planning, sport management. *Unit head:* Dr. Jeffrey Petersen, Graduate Program Director, 254-710-4007, Fax: 254-710-3527, E-mail: jeffrey_petersen@baylor.edu. *Application contact:* Kathy Mirick, Administrative Assistant, 254-710-3526, Fax: 254-710-3527, E-mail: kathy_mirick@baylor.edu.
Website: http://www.baylor.edu/HHPR/.

Belhaven University, School of Business, Jackson, MS 39202-1789. Offers business administration (MBA); health administration (MBA); human resources (MBA, MSL); leadership (MBA); public administration (MPA); sports administration (MBA). MBA program also offered in Houston, TX, Memphis, TN and Orlando, FL. Part-time and evening/weekend programs available. Postbaccalaureate distance learning degree programs offered. *Faculty:* 21 full-time (4 women), 34 part-time/adjunct (12 women). *Students:* 166 full-time (112 women), 688 part-time (460 women); includes 576 minority (540 Black or African American, non-Hispanic/Latino; 2 American Indian or Alaska Native, non-Hispanic/Latino; 2 Asian, non-Hispanic/Latino; 26 Hispanic/Latino; 6 Two or more races, non-Hispanic/Latino). Average age 36. 325 applicants, 72% accepted, 185 enrolled. In 2013, 189 master's awarded. *Degree requirements:* For master's, comprehensive exam (for some programs), thesis (for some programs). *Entrance requirements:* For master's, GMAT, GRE General Test or MAT, minimum GPA of 2.8. *Application deadline:* Applications are processed on a rolling basis. Application fee: $25. Electronic applications accepted. *Financial support:* Applicants required to submit FAFSA. *Unit head:* Dr. Ralph Mason, Dean, 601-968-8949, Fax: 601-968-8951, E-mail: cmason@belhaven.edu. *Application contact:* Dr. Audrey Kelleher, Vice President of Adult and Graduate Marketing and Development, 407-804-1424, Fax: 407-620-5210, E-mail: akelleher@belhaven.edu.
Website: http://www.belhaven.edu/campuses/index.htm.

Belmont University, College of Arts and Sciences, Nashville, TN 37212-3757. Offers education (M Ed); English (MA); special education (MA); sport administration (MSA); teaching (MAT). Part-time and evening/weekend programs available. *Faculty:* 29 full-time (21 women), 24 part-time/adjunct (12 women). *Students:* 144 full-time (97 women), 63 part-time (49 women); includes 26 minority (9 Black or African American, non-Hispanic/Latino; 1 Asian, non-Hispanic/Latino; 8 Hispanic/Latino; 8 Two or more races, non-Hispanic/Latino), 3 international. Average age 29. 201 applicants, 57% accepted, 81 enrolled. *Degree requirements:* For master's, comprehensive exam (for some programs), thesis (for some programs). *Entrance requirements:* For master's, GRE, GMAT, MAT. Additional exam requirements/recommendations for international students: Required—TOEFL. *Application deadline:* For fall admission, 8/1 for domestic students; for spring admission, 12/1 for domestic students. Applications are processed on a rolling basis. Application fee: $50. Electronic applications accepted. *Expenses:* Contact institution. *Financial support:* In 2013–14, 50 students received support. Fellowships with partial tuition reimbursements available, teaching assistantships with partial tuition reimbursements available, Federal Work-Study, institutionally sponsored loans, scholarships/grants, tuition waivers (partial), and unspecified assistantships available. Financial award application deadline: 4/15; financial award applicants required to submit FAFSA. *Unit head:* Dr. Bryce Sullivan, Dean, 615-460-6437, Fax: 615-385-5084, E-mail: bryce.sullivan@belmont.edu. *Application contact:* David Mee, Dean of Enrollment Services, 615-460-6785, Fax: 615-460-5434, E-mail: david.mee@belmont.edu.

Bowling Green State University, Graduate College, College of Education and Human Development, School of Human Movement, Sport, and Leisure Studies, Bowling Green, OH 43403. Offers developmental kinesiology (M Ed); recreation and leisure (M Ed); sport administration (M Ed). Part-time programs available. *Degree requirements:* For master's, thesis or alternative. *Entrance requirements:* For master's, GRE General Test, minimum GPA of 2.7. Additional exam requirements/recommendations for international students: Required—TOEFL. Electronic applications accepted. *Faculty research:* Teacher-learning process, travel and tourism, sport marketing and management, exercise physiology and sport psychology, life-span motor development.

Brooklyn College of the City University of New York, Division of Graduate Studies, Department of Physical Education and Exercise Science, Brooklyn, NY 11210-2889. Offers exercise science and rehabilitation (MS); physical education (MS), including sports management. Part-time programs available. *Degree requirements:* For master's, comprehensive exam or thesis. *Entrance requirements:* For master's, previous course work in physical education and education, minimum GPA of 3.0, 2 letters of recommendation, essay. Additional exam requirements/recommendations for international students: Required—TOEFL (minimum score 500 paper-based; 61 iBT). Electronic applications accepted. *Faculty research:* Exercise physiology, motor learning, sports psychology, women in athletics.

California Baptist University, Program in Kinesiology, Riverside, CA 92504-3206. Offers exercise science (MS); physical education pedagogy (MS); sport management (MS). Part-time programs available. *Faculty:* 7 full-time (4 women), 3 part-time/adjunct (1 woman). *Students:* 27 full-time (8 women), 23 part-time (8 women); includes 19 minority (10 Black or African American, non-Hispanic/Latino; 2 Asian, non-Hispanic/Latino; 5 Hispanic/Latino; 2 Two or more races, non-Hispanic/Latino), 6 international. Average age 27. 64 applicants, 66% accepted, 25 enrolled. In 2013, 41 master's awarded. *Degree requirements:* For master's, comprehensive exam (for some programs), comprehensive exam or research thesis. *Entrance requirements:* For master's, minimum undergraduate GPA of 2.75; 12 units of kinesiology prerequisites; three recommendations; 500-word essay; resume; interview. Additional exam requirements/recommendations for international students: Required—TOEFL (minimum score 80 iBT). *Application deadline:* For fall admission, 8/1 priority date for domestic students, 7/1 for international students; for spring admission, 12/1 priority date for domestic students, 11/1 for international students. Applications are processed on a rolling basis. Application fee: $45. Electronic applications accepted. *Expenses:* Contact institution. *Financial support:* In 2013–14, 3 students received support, including 3 fellowships (averaging $8,100 per year). Financial award applicants required to submit CSS PROFILE or FAFSA. *Faculty research:* Physical education pedagogy, exercise management and prevention of cardiovascular and metabolic diseases, sport management, immune function, carbohydrate oxidation. *Unit head:* Dr. Chuck Sands, Dean, College of Allied Health, 951-343-4619, E-mail: csands@calbaptist.edu. *Application contact:* Dr. Sean Sullivan, Chair, Department of Kinesiology, 951-343-4528, Fax: 951-343-5095, E-mail: ssullivan@calbaptist.edu.
Website: http://www.calbaptist.edu/mskin/.

California State University, Long Beach, Graduate Studies, College of Health and Human Services, Department of Kinesiology, Long Beach, CA 90840. Offers adapted physical education (MA); coaching and student athlete development (MA); exercise physiology and nutrition (MS); exercise science (MS); individualized studies (MA); kinesiology (MA); pedagogical studies (MA); sport and exercise psychology (MS); sport management (MA); sports medicine and injury studies (MS). Part-time programs available. *Degree requirements:* For master's, oral and written comprehensive exams or thesis. *Entrance requirements:* For master's, GRE General Test, minimum GPA of 2.75 during previous 2 years of course work. Electronic applications accepted. *Faculty research:* Pulmonary functioning, feedback and practice structure, strength training, history and politics of sports, special population research issues.

California University of Management and Sciences, Graduate Programs, Anaheim, CA 92801. Offers business administration (MBA, DBA); computer information systems (MS); economics (MS); international business (MS); sports management (MS).

California University of Pennsylvania, School of Graduate Studies and Research, College of Education and Human Services, Program in Sport Management Studies, California, PA 15419-1394. Offers intercollegiate athletic administration (MS); sport management (MS); sports counseling (MS). Postbaccalaureate distance learning degree programs offered.

Canisius College, Graduate Division, School of Education and Human Services, Program in Sport Administration, Buffalo, NY 14208-1098. Offers MSA. Postbaccalaureate distance learning degree programs offered (no on-campus study). *Faculty:* 2 full-time (0 women), 9 part-time/adjunct (1 woman). *Students:* 65 full-time (26 women), 105 part-time (32 women); includes 28 minority (16 Black or African American, non-Hispanic/Latino; 1 American Indian or Alaska Native, non-Hispanic/Latino; 5 Asian, non-Hispanic/Latino; 4 Hispanic/Latino; 2 Two or more races, non-Hispanic/Latino), 8 international. Average age 27. 78 applicants, 79% accepted, 37 enrolled. In 2013, 111 master's awarded. *Entrance requirements:* For master's, transcripts, essay, minimum GPA of 2.7, resume, BA. Additional exam requirements/recommendations for international students: Required—TOEFL (minimum score 550 paper-based, 80 iBT), IELTS (minimum score 6.5), or CAEL (minimum score 70). *Application deadline:* Applications are processed on a rolling basis. Application fee: $25. Electronic applications accepted. Application fee is waived when completed online. *Expenses: Tuition:* Part-time $750 per credit hour. *Financial support:* Career-related internships or fieldwork, Federal Work-Study, scholarships/grants, and unspecified assistantships available. Support available to part-time students. Financial award application deadline: 4/30; financial award applicants required to submit FAFSA. *Unit head:* Dr. Shawn O'Rourke, Associate Dean, 716-888-3179, E-mail: orourke1@canisius.edu. *Application contact:* Julie A. Zulewski, Director of Graduate Recruitment and Admissions, 716-888-2548, Fax: 716-888-3195, E-mail: zulewskj@canisius.edu.
Website: http://www.canisius.edu/graduate/.

Cardinal Stritch University, College of Arts and Sciences, Program in Sport Management, Milwaukee, WI 53217-3985. Offers MS.

Central Michigan University, Central Michigan University Global Campus, Program in Sport Administration, Mount Pleasant, MI 48859. Offers MA. Part-time and evening/weekend programs available. *Entrance requirements:* For master's, minimum GPA of 3.0. *Unit head:* Scott J. Smith, Director, 989-774-6525, E-mail: smith5sj@cmich.edu. *Application contact:* 877-268-4636, E-mail: cmuglobal@cmich.edu.

Central Michigan University, College of Graduate Studies, The Herbert H. and Grace A. Dow College of Health Professions, Department of Physical Education and Sport, Mount Pleasant, MI 48859. Offers sport administration (MA). Part-time and evening/weekend programs available. *Degree requirements:* For master's, thesis or alternative. *Entrance requirements:* For master's, GRE (recommended). Electronic applications accepted. *Faculty research:* Athletic administration and sport management, performance enhancing substance use in sport, computer applications for sport managers, mental skill development for ultimate performance, teaching methods.

Central Michigan University, College of Graduate Studies, Interdisciplinary Administration Programs, Mount Pleasant, MI 48859. Offers acquisitions administration (MSA, Graduate Certificate); general administration (MSA, Graduate Certificate); health services administration (MSA, Graduate Certificate); human resource administration (Graduate Certificate); human resources administration (MSA); information resource management (MSA, Graduate Certificate); international administration (MSA, Graduate Certificate); leadership (MSA, Graduate Certificate); public administration (MSA, Graduate Certificate); research administration (Graduate Certificate); sport administration (MSA). *Accreditation:* AACSB. Part-time and evening/weekend programs available. Postbaccalaureate distance learning degree programs offered (no on-campus study). *Degree requirements:* For master's, thesis or alternative. *Entrance requirements:* For master's, bachelor's degree with minimum GPA of 2.7. Electronic applications accepted. *Faculty research:* Interdisciplinary studies in acquisitions administration, health services administration, sport administration, recreation and park administration, and international administration.

Central Washington University, Graduate Studies and Research, College of Education and Professional Studies, Department of Physical Education, School and Public Health, Ellensburg, WA 98926. Offers athletic administration (MS); health and physical education (MS). Part-time programs available. *Degree requirements:* For master's, comprehensive exam, thesis or alternative. *Entrance requirements:* For master's, minimum GPA of 3.0. Additional exam requirements/recommendations for international students: Required—TOEFL (minimum score 550 paper-based; 79 iBT), IELTS. Electronic applications accepted.

Cleveland State University, College of Graduate Studies, College of Education and Human Services, Department of Health, Physical Education, Recreation and Dance, Cleveland, OH 44115. Offers community health education (M Ed); exercise science (M Ed); human performance (M Ed); physical education pedagogy (M Ed); public health (MPH); school health education (M Ed); sport and exercise psychology (M Ed); sports management (M Ed). Part-time programs available. *Faculty:* 7 full-time (4 women), 3 part-time/adjunct (2 women). *Students:* 49 full-time (31 women), 79 part-time (46 women); includes 32 minority (25 Black or African American, non-Hispanic/Latino; 2 Asian, non-Hispanic/Latino; 5 Hispanic/Latino), 7 international. Average age 35. 103 applicants, 72% accepted, 35 enrolled. In 2013, 40 master's awarded. *Degree requirements:* For master's, comprehensive exam, thesis optional. *Entrance requirements:* For master's, GRE General Test or MAT (if undergraduate GPA less than 2.75), minimum undergraduate GPA of 2.75. Additional exam requirements/recommendations for international students: Required—TOEFL (minimum score 525 paper-based), IELTS (minimum score 6). *Application deadline:* For fall admission, 7/15 priority date for domestic students; for spring admission, 12/15 priority date for domestic students. Applications are processed on a rolling basis. Application fee: $30. Electronic applications accepted. *Expenses: Tuition:* state resident: full-time $8335; part-time $521 per credit hour. Tuition, nonresident: full-time $15,670; part-time $979 per credit hour. *Required fees:* $50; $25 per semester. *Financial support:* In 2013–14, 6 research assistantships with full and partial tuition reimbursements (averaging $3,480 per year), 1 teaching assistantship with full and partial tuition reimbursement (averaging $3,480 per year) were awarded; career-related internships or fieldwork, tuition waivers (full), and

unspecified assistantships also available. Financial award application deadline: 3/15. *Faculty research:* Bone density, marketing fitness centers, motor development of disabled, online learning and survey research. *Unit head:* Dr. Sheila M. Patterson, Chairperson, 216-687-4870, Fax: 216-687-5410, E-mail: s.m.patterson@csuohio.edu. *Application contact:* Deborah L. Brown, Interim Assistant Director, Graduate Admissions, 216-523-7572, Fax: 216-687-5400, E-mail: d.l.brown@csuohio.edu.
Website: http://www.csuohio.edu/cehs/departments/HPERD/hperd_dept.html.

Coker College, Program in College Athletic Administration, Hartsville, SC 29550. Offers MS. Part-time programs available. Postbaccalaureate distance learning degree programs offered (no on-campus study). *Faculty:* 5 part-time/adjunct (2 women). *Students:* 3 full-time (2 women), 25 part-time (9 women); includes 6 minority (4 Black or African American, non-Hispanic/Latino; 2 Hispanic/Latino). Average age 30. 20 applicants, 65% accepted, 13 enrolled. *Degree requirements:* For master's, comprehensive exam, portfolio. *Entrance requirements:* For master's, GRE or GMAT, minimum overall GPA of 2.85 in bachelor's program, official transcripts, resume, three letters of recommendation. *Application deadline:* Applications are processed on a rolling basis. Application fee: $25. Electronic applications accepted. *Expenses: Tuition:* Part-time $520 per credit hour. *Financial support:* In 2013–14, 3 students received support. Unspecified assistantships available. Financial award application deadline: 6/30; financial award applicants required to submit FAFSA. *Unit head:* Dr. Karen Hamilton, Coordinator, 843-383-8112, E-mail: khamilton@coker.edu. *Application contact:* Benjamin Beetch, Manager of Special Program Marketing, 843-857-4226, E-mail: bbeetch@coker.edu.
Website: http://www.coker.edu/masters.html.

The College at Brockport, State University of New York, School of Health and Human Performance, Department of Kinesiology, Sports Studies and Physical Education, Brockport, NY 14420-2997. Offers adapted physical education (AGC); physical education (MS Ed), including adapted physical education, athletic administration, teacher education/pedagogy. Part-time programs available. *Faculty:* 8 full-time (2 women), 2 part-time/adjunct (0 women). *Students:* 34 full-time (19 women), 24 part-time (12 women); includes 5 minority (4 Black or African American, non-Hispanic/Latino; 1 Asian, non-Hispanic/Latino), 2 international. 34 applicants, 97% accepted, 25 enrolled. In 2013, 41 master's awarded. *Degree requirements:* For master's, thesis or alternative. *Entrance requirements:* For master's, minimum GPA of 3.0; statement of objectives. Additional exam requirements/recommendations for international students: Required—TOEFL (minimum score 550 paper-based; 79 iBT), IELTS (minimum score 6.5). *Application deadline:* For fall admission, 4/15 priority date for domestic and international students; for spring admission, 11/15 priority date for domestic and international students. Application fee: $80. Electronic applications accepted. *Expenses:* Tuition, state resident: full-time $9870. Tuition, nonresident: full-time $18,350. *Required fees:* $1848. *Financial support:* In 2013–14, 11 teaching assistantships with full tuition reimbursements (averaging $7,000 per year) were awarded; Federal Work-Study, scholarships/grants, and unspecified assistantships also available. Support available to part-time students. Financial award application deadline: 3/15; financial award applicants required to submit FAFSA. *Faculty research:* Athletic administration, adapted physical education, physical education curriculum, physical education teaching/coaching, children's physical activity. *Unit head:* Dr. Susan C. Petersen, Chairperson, 585-395-5332, Fax: 585-395-2771, E-mail: speterse@brockport.edu. *Application contact:* Dr. Cathy Houston-Wilson, Graduate Program Director, 585-395-5352, Fax: 585-395-2771, E-mail: chouston@brockport.edu.
Website: http://www.brockport.edu/pes/grad/gradtoc.html.

Columbia University, School of Continuing Education, Program in Sports Management, New York, NY 10027. Offers MS. Part-time programs available. *Entrance requirements:* For master's, minimum GPA of 3.0, 2 letters of recommendation, professional resume. Electronic applications accepted.

Concordia University, School of Arts and Sciences, Irvine, CA 92612-3299. Offers coaching and athletic administration (MA). Part-time and evening/weekend programs available. Postbaccalaureate distance learning degree programs offered (no on-campus study). *Faculty:* 7 full-time (1 woman), 27 part-time/adjunct (2 women). *Students:* 524 full-time (132 women), 309 part-time (76 women); includes 145 minority (81 Black or African American, non-Hispanic/Latino; 1 American Indian or Alaska Native, non-Hispanic/Latino; 8 Asian, non-Hispanic/Latino; 30 Hispanic/Latino; 1 Native Hawaiian or other Pacific Islander, non-Hispanic/Latino; 24 Two or more races, non-Hispanic/Latino), 2 international. Average age 34. 419 applicants, 93% accepted, 333 enrolled. In 2013, 286 master's awarded. *Degree requirements:* For master's, culminating project. *Entrance requirements:* For master's, official college/university transcript(s); signed statement of intent. Additional exam requirements/recommendations for international students: Required—TOEFL (minimum score 550 paper-based; 79 iBT). *Application deadline:* For fall admission, 8/10 for domestic students, 6/1 for international students; for spring admission, 2/15 for domestic students, 10/1 for international students. Application fee: $50 ($125 for international students). Electronic applications accepted. *Expenses:* Contact institution. *Financial support:* In 2013–14, 19 students received support. Tuition waivers (full and partial) and unspecified assistantships available. Financial award applicants required to submit FAFSA. *Unit head:* Dr. Timothy Preuss, Dean, 949-214-3286, E-mail: tim.preuss@cui.edu. *Application contact:* Jon O'Neill, Associate Director of Graduate Admissions, 949-214-3577, Fax: 949-214-3577, E-mail: jon.oneill@cui.edu.
Website: http://www.cui.edu.

Concordia University, St. Paul, College of Education and Science, St. Paul, MN 55104-5494. Offers curriculum and instruction (MA Ed), including K-12 reading; differentiated instruction (MA Ed); early childhood education (MA Ed); educational leadership (MA Ed); educational technology (MA Ed); exercise science (MA); family life education (MA); K-12 principal licensure (Ed S); K-12 reading (Certificate); special education (MA Ed, Certificate), including autism spectrum disorder (MA Ed), emotional and behavioral disorders (MA Ed), learning disabilities (MA Ed); sports management (MA); superintendent (Ed S). *Accreditation:* NCATE. Part-time and evening/weekend programs available. Postbaccalaureate distance learning degree programs offered (minimal on-campus study). *Faculty:* 12 full-time (7 women), 92 part-time/adjunct (49 women). *Students:* 915 full-time (659 women), 64 part-time (53 women); includes 99 minority (47 Black or African American, non-Hispanic/Latino; 5 American Indian or Alaska Native, non-Hispanic/Latino; 18 Asian, non-Hispanic/Latino; 15 Hispanic/Latino; 2 Native Hawaiian or other Pacific Islander, non-Hispanic/Latino; 12 Two or more races, non-Hispanic/Latino), 24 international. Average age 34. 664 applicants, 67% accepted, 411 enrolled. In 2013, 275 master's, 69 other advanced degrees awarded. *Degree requirements:* For master's, thesis (for some programs). *Entrance requirements:* For master's, official transcripts from regionally-accredited institution stating the conferral of a bachelor's degree with minimum cumulative GPA of 3.0; personal statement; professional resume; practitioner in field through work or volunteerism; resume. Additional exam requirements/recommendations for international students: Recommended—TOEFL (minimum score 547 paper-based; 78 iBT), IELTS (minimum score 6). *Application deadline:* For fall admission, 8/1 for domestic and international students; for spring admission, 12/1 for domestic and international students; for summer admission, 5/1 for domestic and international students. Applications are processed on a

rolling basis. Application fee: $50. Electronic applications accepted. *Expenses: Tuition:* Full-time $6200; part-time $425 per credit. Tuition and fees vary according to degree level and program. *Financial support:* Applicants required to submit FAFSA. *Unit head:* Dr. Donald Helmstetter, Dean, 651-641-8227, Fax: 651-641-8807, E-mail: helmstetter@csp.edu. *Application contact:* Kimberly Craig, Director of Graduate and Cohort Admission, 651-603-6223, Fax: 651-603-6320, E-mail: craig@csp.edu.

Defiance College, Program in Business Administration, Defiance, OH 43512-1610. Offers criminal justice (MBA); health care (MBA); leadership (MBA); sport management (MBA). Part-time and evening/weekend programs available. *Degree requirements:* For master's, thesis. *Entrance requirements:* For master's, minimum GPA of 2.5. Additional exam requirements/recommendations for international students: Recommended—TOEFL.

DePaul University, Charles H. Kellstadt Graduate School of Business, Chicago, IL 60604. Offers accountancy (M Acc, MS, MSA); applied economics (MBA); banking (MBA); behavioral finance (MBA); brand and product management (MBA); business development (MBA); business information technology (MS); business strategy and decision-making (MBA); computational finance (MS); consumer insights (MBA); corporate finance (MBA); economic policy analysis (MS); entrepreneurship (MBA, MS); finance (MBA, MS); financial analysis (MBA); general business (MBA); health sector management (MBA); hospitality leadership (MBA); hospitality leadership and operational performance (MS); human resource management (MBA); human resources (MS); investment management (MBA); leadership and change management (MBA); management accounting (MBA); marketing (MBA, MS); marketing analysis (MS); marketing strategy and planning (MBA); operations management (MBA); organizational diversity (MBA); real estate (MS); real estate finance and investment (MBA); revenue management (MBA); sports management (MBA); strategic global marketing (MBA); strategy, execution and valuation (MBA); sustainable management (MBA, MS); taxation (MS); wealth management (MS); JD/MBA. *Accreditation:* AACSB. Part-time and evening/weekend programs available. Postbaccalaureate distance learning degree programs offered (no on-campus study). *Faculty:* 81 full-time (20 women), 45 part-time/adjunct (8 women). *Students:* 1,238 full-time (605 women), 617 part-time (223 women); includes 295 minority (71 Black or African American, non-Hispanic/Latino; 129 Asian, non-Hispanic/Latino; 74 Hispanic/Latino; 4 Native Hawaiian or other Pacific Islander, non-Hispanic/Latino; 17 Two or more races, non-Hispanic/Latino), 462 international. Average age 29. In 2013, 911 master's awarded. *Entrance requirements:* For master's, GMAT, 2 letters of recommendation, resume, essay, official transcripts. Additional exam requirements/recommendations for international students: Required—TOEFL (minimum score 550 paper-based; 80 iBT). *Application deadline:* For fall admission, 7/1 for domestic students, 6/1 for international students; for winter admission, 10/1 for domestic students, 9/1 for international students; for spring admission, 2/1 for domestic students, 1/1 for international students. Applications are processed on a rolling basis. Application fee: $60. Electronic applications accepted. *Expenses:* Contact institution. *Financial support:* Application deadline: 4/1; applicants required to submit FAFSA. *Unit head:* Robert T. Ryan, Assistant Dean and Director, 312-362-8810, Fax: 312-362-6677, E-mail: rryan1@depaul.edu. *Application contact:* James Parker, Director of Recruitment and Admission, 312-362-8810, Fax: 312-362-6677, E-mail: kgsb@depaul.edu.
Website: http://kellstadt.depaul.edu.

Dowling College, Graduate Programs in Education, Oakdale, NY 11769-1999. Offers adolescence education with middle childhood extension (MS); childhood and early childhood education (MS); childhood and gifted education (MS); childhood education (1-6) (MS); computers in education (AC); early childhood education (B-2) (MS); educational administration (Ed D); educational technology leadership (MS); educational technology specialist (AC); gifted education (AC); literacy education (MS, AC), including 5-12 (MS), B-12 (MS); literacy education (MS), including B-6; school building leader (AC); school district business leader (MBA, AC); school district leader (AC); special education (MS), including autism, severe disabilities; sport management (MS). *Accreditation:* NCATE. Part-time and evening/weekend programs available. Postbaccalaureate distance learning degree programs offered (minimal on-campus study). *Faculty:* 44 full-time (24 women), 17 part-time/adjunct (8 women). *Students:* 183 full-time (124 women), 314 part-time (231 women); includes 51 minority (19 Black or African American, non-Hispanic/Latino; 1 American Indian or Alaska Native, non-Hispanic/Latino; 3 Asian, non-Hispanic/Latino; 26 Hispanic/Latino; 2 Native Hawaiian or other Pacific Islander, non-Hispanic/Latino). Average age 32. 174 applicants, 80% accepted, 82 enrolled. In 2013, 198 master's, 33 doctorates, 48 other advanced degrees awarded. *Degree requirements:* For master's and AC, comprehensive exam; for doctorate, thesis/dissertation. *Entrance requirements:* For master's, minimum GPA of 3.0; for doctorate, GRE, master's degree; for AC, teaching certificate. Additional exam requirements/recommendations for international students: Required—TOEFL (minimum score 550 paper-based). *Application deadline:* For fall admission, 9/1 priority date for domestic students; for winter admission, 1/1 priority date for domestic students; for spring admission, 2/1 priority date for domestic students. Applications are processed on a rolling basis. Application fee: $50. Electronic applications accepted. *Expenses: Tuition:* Full-time $22,731; part-time $1029 per credit. *Required fees:* $956; $956. *Financial support:* Career-related internships or fieldwork and Federal Work-Study available. Support available to part-time students. Financial award application deadline: 6/30; financial award applicants required to submit FAFSA. *Faculty research:* Natural readers, Korean styles and learning strategies, mothers of children with disabilities, computers in instruction, cultural background and organizational roadblocks to problem solving. *Unit head:* Dr. Robert Manley, Dean, 631-244-3447, E-mail: manleyr@dowling.edu. *Application contact:* Mary Boullianne, Director of Admissions, 631-244-3274, Fax: 631-244-1059, E-mail: boulliam@dowling.edu.

Dowling College, School of Business, Oakdale, NY 11769. Offers aviation management (MBA, Certificate); corporate finance (MBA, Certificate); health care management (MBA); human resource management (Certificate); information systems management (MBA); management and leadership (MBA); marketing (Certificate); project management (Certificate); public management (MBA); school district business leader (MBA); sport, event and entertainment management (Certificate); JD/MBA. Part-time and evening/weekend programs available. Postbaccalaureate distance learning degree programs offered (minimal on-campus study). *Faculty:* 7 full-time (2 women), 43 part-time/adjunct (7 women). *Students:* 183 full-time (79 women), 299 part-time (142 women); includes 137 minority (84 Black or African American, non-Hispanic/Latino; 14 Asian, non-Hispanic/Latino; 20 Hispanic/Latino; 19 Native Hawaiian or other Pacific Islander, non-Hispanic/Latino). Average age 32. 360 applicants, 58% accepted, 127 enrolled. In 2013, 235 master's, 15 other advanced degrees awarded. *Degree requirements:* For master's, comprehensive exam, thesis optional. *Entrance requirements:* For master's, minimum GPA of 2.8, 2 letters of recommendation, courses or seminar in accounting and finance, resume. Additional exam requirements/recommendations for international students: Required—TOEFL (minimum score 550 paper-based). *Application deadline:* For fall admission, 9/1 priority date for domestic students; for winter admission, 1/1 priority date for domestic students; for spring admission, 2/1 priority date for domestic students. Applications are processed on a rolling basis. Application fee: $50. Electronic applications accepted. *Expenses: Tuition:* Full-time $22,731; part-time $1029 per credit. *Required fees:* $956; $956. *Financial support:* Career-related internships or fieldwork and Federal Work-Study available. Support available to part-time students. Financial award application deadline: 6/30; financial award applicants required to submit FAFSA. *Faculty research:* International finance, computer applications, labor relations, executive development. *Unit head:* Dr. Elana Zolfo, Dean, 631-244-3266, Fax: 631-244-1018, E-mail: zolfoe@dowling.edu. *Application contact:* Mary Boullianne, Dean of Admissions, 631-244-3274, Fax: 631-244-1059, E-mail: boulliam@dowling.edu.

Drexel University, Goodwin College of Professional Studies, School of Technology and Professional Studies, Philadelphia, PA 19104-2875. Offers construction management (MS); creativity and innovation (MS); engineering technology (MS); food science (MS); hospitality management (MS); professional studies: creativity studies (MS); professional studies: e-learning leadership (MS); professional studies: homeland security management (MS); project management (MS); property management (MS); sport management (MS). Part-time and evening/weekend programs available. *Entrance requirements:* Additional exam requirements/recommendations for international students: Required—TOEFL, IELTS. Electronic applications accepted. Application fee is waived when completed online.

Duquesne University, School of Leadership and Professional Advancement, Pittsburgh, PA 15282-0001. Offers leadership (MS), including business ethics, community leadership, global leadership, health care, information technology, leadership, liberal studies, professional administration, sports leadership. Part-time and evening/weekend programs available. Postbaccalaureate distance learning degree programs offered (no on-campus study). *Faculty:* 15 full-time (7 women), 64 part-time/adjunct (26 women). *Students:* 213 full-time (106 women), 170 part-time (86 women); includes 89 minority (59 Black or African American, non-Hispanic/Latino; 2 American Indian or Alaska Native, non-Hispanic/Latino; 7 Asian, non-Hispanic/Latino; 9 Hispanic/Latino; 1 Native Hawaiian or other Pacific Islander, non-Hispanic/Latino; 11 Two or more races, non-Hispanic/Latino), 9 international. Average age 36. 204 applicants, 56% accepted, 103 enrolled. In 2013, 140 master's awarded. *Degree requirements:* For master's, capstone course. *Entrance requirements:* For master's, professional work experience, 500-word essay, resume, interview. Additional exam requirements/recommendations for international students: Required—TOEFL (minimum score 80 iBT). *Application deadline:* Applications are processed on a rolling basis. Application fee: $0. Electronic applications accepted. Application fee is waived when completed online. *Expenses: Tuition:* Full-time $18,162; part-time $1009 per credit. *Required fees:* $1728; $96 per credit. Tuition and fees vary according to program. *Financial support:* Scholarships/grants available. Financial award applicants required to submit FAFSA. *Unit head:* Dr. Dorothy Bassett, Dean, 412-396-2141, Fax: 412-396-4711, E-mail: bassettd@duq.edu. *Application contact:* Marianne Leister, Director of Student Services, 412-396-4933, Fax: 412-396-5072, E-mail: leister@duq.edu.
Website: http://www.duq.edu/academics/schools/leadership-and-professional-advancement.

East Carolina University, Graduate School, College of Health and Human Performance, Department of Kinesiology, Greenville, NC 27858-4353. Offers adapted physical education (MA Ed, MS); bioenergetics and exercise science (PhD); biomechanics (MS); exercise physiology (MS); physical activity promotion (MS); physical education (MA Ed, MAT); physical education clinical supervision (Certificate); physical education pedagogy (MA Ed, MS); sport and exercise psychology (MS); sport management (Certificate). *Degree requirements:* For master's, comprehensive exam, thesis optional; for doctorate, comprehensive exam, thesis/dissertation. *Entrance requirements:* For master's, GRE General Test or MAT; for doctorate, GRE. Additional exam requirements/recommendations for international students: Required—TOEFL. *Expenses:* Tuition, state resident: full-time $4223. Tuition, nonresident: full-time $16,540. *Required fees:* $2184. *Faculty research:* Diabetes metabolism, pediatric obesity, biomechanics of arthritis, physical activity measurement.

East Carolina University, Graduate School, College of Health and Human Performance, Department of Recreation and Leisure Studies, Greenville, NC 27858-4353. Offers aquatic therapy (Certificate); biofeedback (Certificate); recreation and park administration (MS), including generalist, recreational sports management; recreational therapy administration (MS). Part-time and evening/weekend programs available. Postbaccalaureate distance learning degree programs offered (minimal on-campus study). *Degree requirements:* For master's, comprehensive exam, thesis optional. *Entrance requirements:* For master's, GRE General Test or MAT. Additional exam requirements/recommendations for international students: Required—TOEFL. *Expenses:* Tuition, state resident: full-time $4223. Tuition, nonresident: full-time $16,540. *Required fees:* $2184. *Faculty research:* Therapeutic recreation, stress and coping behavior, medicine carrying capacity, choice behavior, tourism preferences.

Eastern Kentucky University, The Graduate School, College of Health Sciences, Department of Exercise and Sport Science, Richmond, KY 40475-3102. Offers exercise and sport science (MS); exercise and wellness (MS); sports administration (MS). Part-time programs available. *Entrance requirements:* For master's, GRE General Test (minimum score 700 verbal and quantitative), minimum GPA of 2.5 (for most), minimum GPA of 3.0 (analytical writing). *Faculty research:* Nutrition and exercise.

Eastern Michigan University, Graduate School, College of Health and Human Services, School of Health Promotion and Human Performance, Program in Sports Management, Ypsilanti, MI 48197. Offers MS. Part-time and evening/weekend programs available. *Students:* 15 full-time (7 women), 41 part-time (15 women); includes 11 minority (9 Black or African American, non-Hispanic/Latino; 2 Hispanic/Latino). Average age 27. 50 applicants, 72% accepted, 25 enrolled. In 2013, 24 master's awarded. *Degree requirements:* For master's, comprehensive exams or thesis. *Entrance requirements:* For master's, minimum GPA of 2.75. Additional exam requirements/recommendations for international students: Required—TOEFL. *Application deadline:* For fall admission, 8/1 for domestic students, 5/1 for international students; for winter admission, 12/1 for domestic students, 10/1 for international students; for spring admission, 4/15 for domestic students, 3/1 for international students. Applications are processed on a rolling basis. Application fee: $35. *Expenses:* Tuition, state resident: full-time $12,300; part-time $466 per credit hour. Tuition, nonresident: full-time $23,159; part-time $918 per credit hour. *Required fees:* $71 per credit hour. $46 per semester. One-time fee: $100. Tuition and fees vary according to course level and degree level. *Financial support:* Fellowships, research assistantships with full tuition reimbursements, teaching assistantships with full tuition reimbursements, career-related internships or fieldwork, Federal Work-Study, institutionally sponsored loans, scholarships/grants, tuition waivers (partial), and unspecified assistantships available. Support available to part-time students. Financial award applicants required to submit FAFSA. *Unit head:* Dr. Christopher Herman, Coordinator, 734-487-2185, Fax: 734-487-2024, E-mail: cherman2@emich.edu. *Application contact:* Dr. Brenda Riemer, Graduate Program Coordinator, 734-487-7120 Ext. 2745, Fax: 734-487-2024, E-mail: briemer@emich.edu.

Eastern New Mexico University, Graduate School, College of Education and Technology, Department of Health and Physical Education, Portales, NM 88130. Offers physical education (MS), including sport administration, sport science. Part-time programs available. *Degree requirements:* For master's, comprehensive exam, thesis optional. *Entrance requirements:* For master's, minimum GPA of 3.0, 15 hours of leveling courses without bachelor's degree in physical education, two references. Additional exam requirements/recommendations for international students: Required—

TOEFL (minimum score 550 paper-based; 79 iBT), IELTS (minimum score 6). Electronic applications accepted.

Eastern Washington University, Graduate Studies, College of Arts, Letters and Education, Department of Physical Education, Health and Recreation, Cheney, WA 99004-2431. Offers exercise science (MS); sports and recreation administration (MS). *Faculty:* 17 full-time (7 women), 5 part-time/adjunct (2 women). *Students:* 26 full-time (10 women), 8 part-time (3 women); includes 7 minority (3 Black or African American, non-Hispanic/Latino; 1 American Indian or Alaska Native, non-Hispanic/Latino; 2 Asian, non-Hispanic/Latino; 1 Hispanic/Latino). Average age 29. 64 applicants, 38% accepted, 21 enrolled. In 2013, 14 master's awarded. *Degree requirements:* For master's, comprehensive exam, thesis or alternative. *Entrance requirements:* For master's, minimum GPA of 3.0. *Application deadline:* For fall admission, 4/1 priority date for domestic students; for spring admission, 1/15 for domestic students. Applications are processed on a rolling basis. Application fee: $50. *Financial support:* In 2013–14, 10 teaching assistantships with partial tuition reimbursements (averaging $6,624 per year) were awarded; career-related internships or fieldwork, Federal Work-Study, institutionally sponsored loans, and scholarships/grants also available. Support available to part-time students. Financial award application deadline: 2/1; financial award applicants required to submit FAFSA. *Unit head:* John Cogley, Chair, 509-359-2486, E-mail: john.cogley@mail.ewu.edu. *Application contact:* Dr. Jeni McNeal, Professor of Physical Education, Health and Recreation, 509-359-2872, Fax: 509-359-4833, E-mail: jeni_mcneal@hotmail.com.

East Stroudsburg University of Pennsylvania, Graduate College, College of Business and Management, Department of Sport Management, East Stroudsburg, PA 18301-2999. Offers management and leadership (MS); sports management (MS). Part-time and evening/weekend programs available. Postbaccalaureate distance learning degree programs offered. *Faculty:* 3 full-time (0 women). *Students:* 22 full-time (8 women), 8 part-time (1 woman); includes 6 minority (2 Black or African American, non-Hispanic/Latino; 1 Hispanic/Latino; 1 Native Hawaiian or other Pacific Islander, non-Hispanic/Latino; 2 Two or more races, non-Hispanic/Latino). Average age 24. 35 applicants, 66% accepted, 14 enrolled. In 2013, 14 master's awarded. *Degree requirements:* For master's, comprehensive exam. *Entrance requirements:* For master's, GRE and/or GMAT. Additional exam requirements/recommendations for international students: Required—TOEFL (minimum score 560 paper-based; 83 iBT) or IELTS. *Application deadline:* For fall admission, 7/31 priority date for domestic students, 6/30 priority date for international students; for spring admission, 11/30 for domestic students, 10/31 for international students. Applications are processed on a rolling basis. Application fee: $50. Electronic applications accepted. *Expenses:* Tuition, state resident: full-time $7956; part-time $442 per credit. Tuition, nonresident: full-time $11,934; part-time $663 per credit. *Required fees:* $2129; $118 per credit. *Financial support:* Research assistantships, Federal Work-Study, and unspecified assistantships available. Financial award application deadline: 3/1; financial award applicants required to submit FAFSA. *Unit head:* Dr. Robert Fleischman, Graduate Coordinator, 570-422-3316, Fax: 570-422-3824, E-mail: bfleischman@po-box.esu.edu. *Application contact:* Kevin Quintero, Graduate Admissions Coordinator, 570-422-3536, Fax: 570-422-2711, E-mail: kquintero@esu.edu.

East Tennessee State University, School of Graduate Studies, College of Education, Department of Kinesiology, Sport and Recreation Management, Johnson City, TN 37614. Offers sport management (MA). Part-time and evening/weekend programs available. *Faculty:* 12 full-time (1 woman), 4 part-time/adjunct (1 woman). *Students:* 90 full-time (31 women), 8 part-time (3 women); includes 8 minority (5 Black or African American, non-Hispanic/Latino; 1 Hispanic/Latino; 2 Two or more races, non-Hispanic/Latino), 5 international. Average age 25. 32 applicants, 81% accepted, 19 enrolled. In 2013, 35 master's awarded. Terminal master's awarded for partial completion of doctoral program. *Degree requirements:* For master's, comprehensive exam, thesis or internship. *Entrance requirements:* For master's, GRE General Test or GMAT, undergraduate degree in related field; minimum GPA of 2.7; resume; three references; essay explaining goals and reasons for pursuing degree. Additional exam requirements/recommendations for international students: Required—TOEFL (minimum score 550 paper-based; 79 iBT). *Application deadline:* For fall admission, 6/1 for domestic students, 4/30 for international students; for spring admission, 11/1 for domestic students, 9/30 for international students. Application fee: $35 ($45 for international students). Electronic applications accepted. *Expenses:* Tuition, state resident: full-time $7900; part-time $395 per credit hour. Tuition, nonresident: full-time $21,960; part-time $1098 per credit hour. *Required fees:* $1345; $84 per credit hour. *Financial support:* In 2013–14, 34 students received support, including 7 teaching assistantships with full tuition reimbursements available (averaging $6,000 per year); career-related internships or fieldwork, institutionally sponsored loans, scholarships/grants, and unspecified assistantships also available. Financial award application deadline: 7/1; financial award applicants required to submit FAFSA. *Faculty research:* Methods of training for individual and team sports, enhancing acute sport performance, fatigue management in athletes, risk management, facilities management, motorsport. *Unit head:* Dr. Christopher Ayers, Chair, 423-439-4265, Fax: 423-439-7560, E-mail: ayersc@etsu.edu. *Application contact:* Linda Raines, Graduate Specialist, 423-439-6158, Fax: 423-439-5624, E-mail: rainesl@etsu.edu.
Website: http://www.etsu.edu/coe/ksrm/default.aspx.

Endicott College, Van Loan School of Graduate and Professional Studies, Program in Athletic Administration, Beverly, MA 01915-2096. Offers M Ed. Part-time and evening/weekend programs available. *Faculty:* 3 full-time (all women), 9 part-time/adjunct (1 woman). *Students:* 21 full-time (5 women), 37 part-time (4 women); includes 5 minority (1 Black or African American, non-Hispanic/Latino; 1 Asian, non-Hispanic/Latino; 1 Hispanic/Latino; 2 Two or more races, non-Hispanic/Latino), 2 international. Average age 29. 27 applicants, 96% accepted, 22 enrolled. In 2013, 56 master's awarded. *Degree requirements:* For master's, thesis, practicum. *Entrance requirements:* For master's, GRE or MAT, two letters of recommendation. Additional exam requirements/recommendations for international students: Required—TOEFL. *Application deadline:* Applications are processed on a rolling basis. Application fee: $50. Electronic applications accepted. *Expenses:* Contact institution. *Financial support:* Applicants required to submit FAFSA. *Unit head:* Richard Benedetto, Associate Dean of Graduate School, 978-232-2744, Fax: 978-232-3000, E-mail: rbenedet@endicott.edu. *Application contact:* Dr. Mary Huegel, Vice President and Dean of the School of Graduate and Professional Studies, 978-232-2084, Fax: 978-232-3000, E-mail: mhuegel@endicott.edu.

Fairleigh Dickinson University, College at Florham, Anthony J. Petrocelli College of Continuing Studies, Program in Sports Administration, Madison, NJ 07940-1099. Offers MSA.

Fairleigh Dickinson University, Metropolitan Campus, Anthony J. Petrocelli College of Continuing Studies, Department of Sports Administration, Program in Sports Administration, Teaneck, NJ 07666-1914. Offers MSA.

Florida Atlantic University, College of Business, Department of Management, Boca Raton, FL 33431-0991. Offers business administration (Exec MBA, MBA); entrepreneurship (MBA); health administration (MBA, MHA, MS); international business (MBA); management (PhD); sports management (MBA). *Faculty:* 22 full-time (10 women), 11 part-time/adjunct (6 women). *Students:* 267 full-time (120 women), 397 part-time (194 women); includes 279 minority (92 Black or African American, non-Hispanic/Latino; 31 Asian, non-Hispanic/Latino; 147 Hispanic/Latino; 9 Two or more races, non-Hispanic/Latino), 37 international. Average age 32. 551 applicants, 50% accepted, 216 enrolled. In 2013, 255 master's, 7 doctorates awarded. *Entrance requirements:* For master's, GMAT or GRE General Test, minimum GPA of 3.0 in last 60 hours of course work. Additional exam requirements/recommendations for international students: Required—TOEFL (minimum score 600 paper-based; 61 iBT), IELTS (minimum score 6). *Application deadline:* For fall admission, 7/25 for domestic students, 2/15 for international students; for spring admission, 12/10 for domestic students, 7/15 for international students. Applications are processed on a rolling basis. Application fee: $30. Electronic applications accepted. *Expenses:* Tuition, state resident: full-time $6660; part-time $370 per credit hour. Tuition, nonresident: full-time $18,450; part-time $1025 per credit hour. Tuition and fees vary according to course load. *Financial support:* Research assistantships with full tuition reimbursements, career-related internships or fieldwork, tuition waivers (partial), and unspecified assistantships available. *Faculty research:* Sports administration, healthcare, policy, finance, real estate, senior living. *Unit head:* Dr. Peggy Golden, Chair, 561-297-2675, E-mail: golden@fau.edu. *Application contact:* Dr. Marcy Krugel, Graduate Adviser, 561-297-3633, Fax: 561-297-1315, E-mail: krugel@fau.edu.
Website: http://business.fau.edu/departments/management/index.aspx.

Florida International University, College of Education, Department of Leadership and Professional Studies, Miami, FL 33199. Offers adult education and human resource development (MS, Ed D); counseling (MS), including rehabilitation counseling, school counseling; counselor education (MS), including clinical mental health counseling; educational administration and supervision (Ed D); educational leadership (MS, Certificate, Ed S); higher education (Ed D); higher education administration (MS); recreation and sport management (MS), including recreation and sport management, recreational therapy; school psychology (Ed S); urban education (MS), including instruction in urban settings, learning technologies, multicultural/bilingual, multicultural/TESOL, urban education. Part-time and evening/weekend programs available. *Degree requirements:* For doctorate, thesis/dissertation. *Entrance requirements:* For master's, minimum GPA of 3.0; for doctorate and other advanced degree, GRE General Test. Additional exam requirements/recommendations for international students: Required—TOEFL (minimum score 550 paper-based; 80 iBT), IELTS (minimum score 6.3). Electronic applications accepted.

Florida International University, College of Education, Department of Teaching and Learning, Miami, FL 33199. Offers art education (MA, MS); curriculum and instruction (MS, Ed D, PhD, Ed S), including curriculum development (MS), elementary education (MS), English education (MS), learning technologies (MS), mathematics education (MS), modern language education (MS), physical education (MS), science education (MS), social studies education (MS), special education (MS); early childhood education (MS); exceptional student education (Ed D); foreign language education (MS), including foreign language education, teaching English to speakers of other languages (TESOL); international/intercultural education (MS); language, literacy and culture (PhD); mathematics, science, and learning technologies (PhD); physical education (MS), including sport and fitness; reading education (MS). Part-time and evening/weekend programs available. *Degree requirements:* For doctorate, comprehensive exam, thesis/dissertation. *Entrance requirements:* For master's, GRE General Test, Florida General Knowledge Test or Florida College Level Academic Skills Test; for doctorate and Ed S, GRE General Test. Additional exam requirements/recommendations for international students: Required—TOEFL (minimum score 550 paper-based; 80 iBT), IELTS (minimum score 6.3). Electronic applications accepted.

Florida State University, The Graduate School, College of Education, Department of Sport Management, Tallahassee, FL 32306. Offers MS, PhD, Certificate, JD/MS. *Faculty:* 9 full-time (3 women), 3 part-time/adjunct (1 woman). *Students:* 113 full-time (34 women), 40 part-time (11 women); includes 26 minority (17 Black or African American, non-Hispanic/Latino; 8 Hispanic/Latino; 1 Two or more races, non-Hispanic/Latino), 33 international. Average age 28. 165 applicants, 67% accepted, 54 enrolled. In 2013, 62 master's, 4 doctorates awarded. *Degree requirements:* For master's and Certificate, comprehensive exam, thesis optional; for doctorate, comprehensive exam, thesis/dissertation. *Entrance requirements:* For master's, doctorate, and Certificate, GRE General Test, minimum GPA of 3.0. Additional exam requirements/recommendations for international students: Required—TOEFL (minimum score 550 paper-based; 80 iBT). *Application deadline:* For fall admission, 7/1 for domestic and international students; for winter admission, 11/1 for domestic and international students; for spring admission, 3/1 for domestic and international students. Application fee: $30. Electronic applications accepted. *Expenses:* Tuition, state resident: part-time $403.51 per credit hour. Tuition, nonresident: part-time $1004.85 per credit hour. *Required fees:* $75.81 per credit hour. One-time fee: $20 part-time. Tuition and fees vary according to course load, campus/location and student level. *Financial support:* In 2013–14, 3 students received support, including 1 research assistantship with full and partial tuition reimbursement available, 93 teaching assistantships with full and partial tuition reimbursements available; fellowships with full and partial tuition reimbursements available, career-related internships or fieldwork, Federal Work-Study, scholarships/grants, health care benefits, and unspecified assistantships also available. Financial award application deadline: 1/15; financial award applicants required to submit FAFSA. *Faculty research:* Sport marketing, gender issues in sport, finances in sport industry, coaching. *Unit head:* Dr. Jeffrey D. James, Chair, 850-644-9214, Fax: 850-644-0975, E-mail: jdjames@fsu.edu. *Application contact:* Dr. Thomas F. McMorrow, Academic Specialist, 850-644-0577, Fax: 850-644-0975, E-mail: tmcmorrow@admin.fsu.edu.
Website: http://www.coe.fsu.edu/SM/.

Franklin Pierce University, Graduate Studies, Rindge, NH 03461-0060. Offers curriculum and instruction (M Ed); emerging network technologies (Graduate Certificate); energy and sustainability studies (MBA); health administration (MBA, Graduate Certificate); human resource management (MBA, Graduate Certificate); information technology (MBA); information technology management (MS); leadership (MBA, DA); nursing (MS); physical therapy (DPT); physician assistant studies (MPAS); special education (M Ed); sports management (MBA). *Accreditation:* APTA. Part-time programs available. Postbaccalaureate distance learning degree programs offered (no on-campus study). *Degree requirements:* For master's, concentrated original research projects; student teaching; fieldwork and/or internship; leadership project; PRAXIS I and II (for M Ed); for doctorate, concentrated original research projects, clinical fieldwork and/or internship, leadership project. *Entrance requirements:* For master's, minimum GPA of 2.5, 3 letters of recommendation; competencies in accounting, economics, statistics, and computer skills through life experience or undergraduate coursework (for MBA); certification/e-portfolio, minimum C grade in all education courses (for M Ed); license to practice as RN (for MS in nursing); for doctorate, GRE, BA/BS, 3 letters of recommendation, personal mission statement, interview, writing sample, minimum cumulative GPA of 2.8, master's degree (for DA); 80 hours of observation/work in PT settings, completion of anatomy, chemistry, physics, and statistics, minimum GPA of 3.0 (for DPT). Additional exam requirements/recommendations for international students: Required—TOEFL (minimum score 550 paper-based; 61 iBT). Electronic applications accepted. *Faculty research:* Evidence-based practice in sports physical therapy, human

resource management in economic crisis, leadership in nursing, innovation in sports facility management, differentiated learning and understanding by design.

George Mason University, College of Education and Human Development, School of Recreation, Health and Tourism, Manassas, VA 20110. Offers exercise, fitness, and health promotion (MS); sport and recreation studies (MS). *Faculty:* 31 full-time (12 women), 67 part-time/adjunct (37 women). *Students:* 24 full-time (16 women), 25 part-time (10 women); includes 13 minority (7 Black or African American, non-Hispanic/Latino; 5 Hispanic/Latino; 1 Two or more races, non-Hispanic/Latino), 1 international. Average age 27. 60 applicants, 77% accepted, 24 enrolled. In 2013, 19 master's awarded. *Degree requirements:* For master's, thesis (for some programs). *Entrance requirements:* For master's, GRE General Test or MAT, 3 letters of recommendation; official transcripts; expanded goals statement; undergraduate course in statistics and minimum GPA of 3.0 in last 60 credit hours and overall (for MS in sport and recreation studies); baccalaureate degree related to kinesiology, exercise science or athletic training (for MS in exercise, fitness and health promotion). Additional exam requirements/recommendations for international students: Required—TOEFL (minimum score 575 paper-based; 88 iBT), IELTS (minimum score 6.5), PTE. *Application deadline:* For fall admission, 4/1 priority date for domestic students; for spring admission, 11/1 priority date for domestic students. Application fee: $65 ($80 for international students). Electronic applications accepted. *Expenses:* Tuition, state resident: full-time $9350; part-time $390 per credit. Tuition, nonresident: full-time $25,754; part-time $1073 per credit. *Required fees:* $2688; $112 per credit. *Financial support:* In 2013–14, 10 students received support, including 10 research assistantships with full and partial tuition reimbursements available (averaging $10,484 per year); career-related internships or fieldwork, Federal Work-Study, scholarships/grants, unspecified assistantships, and health care benefits (for full-time research or teaching assistantship recipients) also available. Support available to part-time students. Financial award application deadline: 3/1; financial award applicants required to submit FAFSA. *Faculty research:* Informing policy; promoting economic development; advocating stewardship of natural resources; improving the quality of life of individuals, families, and communities at the local, national and international levels. *Total annual research expenditures:* $1.5 million. *Unit head:* David Wiggins, Director, 703-993-2057, Fax: 703-993-2025, E-mail: dwiggin1@gmu.edu. *Application contact:* Lindsey Olson, Office Assistant, 703-993-2098, Fax: 703-993-2025, E-mail: lolson7@gmu.edu.
Website: http://rht.gmu.edu/.

Georgetown University, Graduate School of Arts and Sciences, School of Continuing Studies, Washington, DC 20057. Offers American studies (MALS); Catholic studies (MALS); classical civilizations (MALS); emergency and disaster management (MPS); ethics and the professions (MALS); human resources management (MPS); humanities (MALS); individualized study (MALS); international affairs (MALS); Islam and Muslim-Christian relations (MALS); journalism (MPS); liberal studies (DLS); literature and society (MALS); medieval and early modern European studies (MALS); public relations and corporate communications (MPS); real estate (MPS); religious studies (MALS); social and public policy (MALS); sports industry management (MPS); systems engineering management (MPS); technology management (MPS); the theory and practice of American democracy (MALS); urban and regional planning (MPS); visual culture (MALS). MPS in systems engineering management offered in conjunction with Stevens Institute of Technology. *Entrance requirements:* Additional exam requirements/recommendations for international students: Required—TOEFL.

The George Washington University, School of Business, Department of Tourism and Hospitality Management, Washington, DC 20052. Offers event and meeting management (MTA); event management (Professional Certificate); hospitality management (MTA, Professional Certificate); sport management (MTA); sports business management (Professional Certificate); sustainable tourism destination management (MTA); tourism administration (MTA); tourism and hospitality management (MBA); tourism destination management (Professional Certificate). Part-time programs available. Postbaccalaureate distance learning degree programs offered. *Faculty:* 2 full-time (1 woman). *Students:* 99 full-time (79 women), 58 part-time (45 women); includes 32 minority (24 Black or African American, non-Hispanic/Latino; 4 Asian, non-Hispanic/Latino; 3 Hispanic/Latino; 1 Two or more races, non-Hispanic/Latino), 63 international. Average age 28. 124 applicants, 71% accepted, 52 enrolled. In 2013, 68 master's awarded. *Degree requirements:* For master's, comprehensive exam, thesis. *Entrance requirements:* For master's, GRE General Test. Additional exam requirements/recommendations for international students: Required—TOEFL. *Application deadline:* For fall admission, 4/1 priority date for domestic students; for spring admission, 10/1 for domestic students. Applications are processed on a rolling basis. Application fee: $75. *Financial support:* In 2013–14, 32 students received support. Fellowships, teaching assistantships, career-related internships or fieldwork, Federal Work-Study, institutionally sponsored loans, and tuition waivers (partial) available. Financial award application deadline: 4/1. *Faculty research:* Tourism policy, tourism impact forecasting, geotourism. *Unit head:* Larry Yu, Director, 202-994-6380, E-mail: lyu@gwu.edu. *Application contact:* Kristin Williams, Assistant Vice President for Graduate and Special Enrollment Management, 202-994-0467, Fax: 202-994-0371, E-mail: ksw@gwu.edu.
Website: http://business.gwu.edu/tourism/.

Georgia Southern University, Jack N. Averitt College of Graduate Studies, College of Health and Human Sciences, Department of Health and Kinesiology, Program in Sport Management, Statesboro, GA 30460. Offers MS. Part-time programs available. *Students:* 3 full-time (0 women), 34 part-time (14 women); includes 10 minority (7 Black or African American, non-Hispanic/Latino; 1 Asian, non-Hispanic/Latino; 2 Two or more races, non-Hispanic/Latino). Average age 27. 42 applicants, 50% accepted, 8 enrolled. In 2013, 9 master's awarded. *Degree requirements:* For master's, terminal exam. *Entrance requirements:* For master's, GMAT, GRE, resume. Additional exam requirements/recommendations for international students: Required—TOEFL (minimum score 550 paper-based; 80 iBT), IELTS (minimum score 6). *Application deadline:* For fall admission, 3/1 priority date for domestic and international students; for spring admission, 10/1 priority date for domestic students, 10/1 for international students. Applications are processed on a rolling basis. Application fee: $50. Electronic applications accepted. *Expenses:* Tuition, state resident: full-time $7068; part-time $270 per semester hour. Tuition, nonresident: full-time $26,446; part-time $1077 per semester hour. *Required fees:* $2092. *Financial support:* In 2013–14, 1 student received support. Career-related internships or fieldwork, Federal Work-Study, scholarships/grants, and tuition waivers (partial) available. Support available to part-time students. Financial award application deadline: 4/15; financial award applicants required to submit FAFSA. *Faculty research:* Outsourcing sport marketing, international integration of North American sports, sport law, sport financing, sport economics. *Unit head:* Dr. Jim McMillan, Program Coordinator, 912-478-1926, Fax: 912-478-0386, E-mail: jmcmillan@georgiasouthern.edu. *Application contact:* Amanda Gilliland, Coordinator for Graduate Student Recruitment, 912-478-5384, Fax: 912-478-0740, E-mail: gradadmissions@georgiasouthern.edu.

Georgia State University, College of Education, Department of Kinesiology and Health, Program in Sports Administration, Atlanta, GA 30302-3083. Offers MS. *Degree requirements:* For master's, comprehensive exam. *Entrance requirements:* For master's, GRE General Test, minimum GPA of 2.5. *Application deadline:* For fall admission, 5/1 for domestic students; for spring admission, 10/1 for domestic students. Application fee: $50. *Expenses: Tuition, area resident:* Full-time $4176; part-time $348 per credit hour. Tuition, state resident: full-time $14,544; part-time $1212 per credit hour. Tuition, nonresident: full-time $14,544; part-time $1212 per credit hour. Tuition and fees vary according to course load and program. *Financial support:* Research assistantships available. *Faculty research:* Sports marketing. *Unit head:* Dr. Jacalyn Lea Lund, Chair, 404-413-8051, E-mail: jlund@gsu.edu. *Application contact:* Kaila Muecke, Academic Ambassador, 404-413-8360, E-mail: khambassador@gsu.edu.
Website: http://education.gsu.edu/KIN/kh_Sports_Admin_MS.html.

Gonzaga University, School of Education, Program in Sports and Athletic Administration, Spokane, WA 99258. Offers MASPAA. Part-time and evening/weekend programs available. Postbaccalaureate distance learning degree programs offered (no on-campus study). *Faculty:* 5 full-time (3 women), 3 part-time/adjunct (0 women). *Students:* 7 full-time (0 women), 49 part-time (16 women); includes 14 minority (2 Black or African American, non-Hispanic/Latino; 2 Asian, non-Hispanic/Latino; 9 Hispanic/Latino; 1 Two or more races, non-Hispanic/Latino), 2 international. Average age 28. 82 applicants, 68% accepted, 39 enrolled. In 2013, 20 master's awarded. *Degree requirements:* For master's, comprehensive exam. *Entrance requirements:* Additional exam requirements/recommendations for international students: Required—TOEFL. *Application deadline:* For fall admission, 2/10 priority date for domestic students. Application fee: $50. Electronic applications accepted. *Expenses:* Contact institution. *Financial support:* Application deadline: 2/1; applicants required to submit FAFSA. *Unit head:* Dr. Roger Park, Director of Graduate Program, 509-313-3482, E-mail: park@gonzaga.edu. *Application contact:* Julie McCulloh, Dean of Admissions, 509-323-6592, Fax: 509-323-5780, E-mail: mcculloh@gu.gonzaga.edu.

Grambling State University, School of Graduate Studies and Research, College of Education, Department of Kinesiology, Sport and Leisure Studies, Grambling, LA 71245. Offers sports administration (MS). Part-time programs available. *Faculty:* 3 full-time (1 woman). *Students:* 55 full-time (21 women), 30 part-time (14 women); includes 81 minority (all Black or African American, non-Hispanic/Latino), 1 international. Average age 28. In 2013, 42 master's awarded. *Degree requirements:* For master's, comprehensive exam. *Entrance requirements:* For master's, GRE General Test, minimum GPA of 2.5 on last degree. Additional exam requirements/recommendations for international students: Required—TOEFL (minimum score 500 paper-based; 62 iBT). *Application deadline:* For fall admission, 7/1 for domestic and international students; for spring admission, 12/1 for domestic and international students; for summer admission, 5/1 for domestic and international students. Applications are processed on a rolling basis. Application fee: $20 ($30 for international students). Electronic applications accepted. *Financial support:* Research assistantships, career-related internships or fieldwork, health care benefits, tuition waivers (full and partial), and unspecified assistantships available. Financial award application deadline: 5/31; financial award applicants required to submit FAFSA. *Faculty research:* Administrative relations and organization, measuring human performance, sport history from ancient times through current date, learning dynamics of personality and sports selection. *Unit head:* Dr. Willie Daniel, Department Head, 318-274-2294, Fax: 318-274-6053, E-mail: danielw@gram.edu. *Application contact:* Sheila Griffin, Administrative Assistant III, 318-274-2438, Fax: 318-274-6053, E-mail: griffins@gram.edu.
Website: http://www.gram.edu/academics/majors/education/departments/kinesiology/.

Hardin-Simmons University, Graduate School, Kelley College of Business, Abilene, TX 79698-0001. Offers business administration (MBA); sports management (MBA). *Accreditation:* ACBSP. Part-time and evening/weekend programs available. *Faculty:* 10 full-time (3 women). *Students:* 16 full-time (9 women), 13 part-time (6 women); includes 8 minority (2 Black or African American, non-Hispanic/Latino; 5 Hispanic/Latino; 1 Two or more races, non-Hispanic/Latino), 5 international. Average age 27. 5 applicants, 100% accepted, 5 enrolled. In 2013, 16 master's awarded. *Degree requirements:* For master's, thesis or alternative. *Entrance requirements:* For master's, GMAT, minimum GPA of 3.0 in upper-level course work, resume, interview. Additional exam requirements/recommendations for international students: Required—TOEFL (minimum score 600 paper-based; 75 iBT). *Application deadline:* For fall admission, 8/15 priority date for domestic students, 4/1 for international students; for spring admission, 1/5 priority date for domestic students, 9/1 for international students. Applications are processed on a rolling basis. Application fee: $50. *Expenses: Tuition:* Full-time $13,410; part-time $745 per credit hour. *Required fees:* $325; $110 per semester. Tuition and fees vary according to program. *Financial support:* In 2013–14, 16 students received support, including 1 fellowship (averaging $1,500 per year); scholarships/grants also available. Support available to part-time students. Financial award application deadline: 6/30; financial award applicants required to submit FAFSA. *Unit head:* Dr. Nancy Kucinski, Dean of Graduate Studies, 325-670-1298, Fax: 325-670-1564, E-mail: gradoff@hsutx.edu. *Application contact:* Dr. Nancy Kucinski, Dean of Graduate Studies, 325-670-1298, Fax: 325-670-1564, E-mail: gradoff@hsutx.edu.
Website: http://www.hsutx.edu/academics/kelley/graduate/mba.

Henderson State University, Graduate Studies, Teachers College, Department of Health, Physical Education, Recreation and Athletic Training, Arkadelphia, AR 71999-0001. Offers sports administration (MS). Part-time programs available. *Faculty:* 4 full-time (1 woman), 1 (woman) part-time/adjunct. *Students:* 6 full-time (3 women), 36 part-time (14 women); includes 15 minority (11 Black or African American, non-Hispanic/Latino; 1 Hispanic/Latino; 3 Two or more races, non-Hispanic/Latino). Average age 25. 16 applicants, 100% accepted, 16 enrolled. In 2013, 22 master's awarded. *Entrance requirements:* For master's, GRE General Test or MAT, minimum GPA of 2.7 as an undergraduate student. Additional exam requirements/recommendations for international students: Required—TOEFL (minimum score 600 paper-based); Recommended—IELTS (minimum score 6.5). *Application deadline:* For fall admission, 8/1 priority date for domestic students, 6/30 priority date for international students; for spring admission, 1/1 priority date for domestic students, 11/30 priority date for international students. Applications are processed on a rolling basis. Application fee: $25 ($75 for international students). *Expenses:* Tuition, state resident: full-time $4284; part-time $238 per credit hour. Tuition, nonresident: full-time $8802; part-time $489 per credit hour. Tuition and fees vary according to course load and campus/location. *Financial support:* In 2013–14, 10 teaching assistantships with partial tuition reimbursements (averaging $4,000 per year) were awarded; scholarships/grants and unspecified assistantships also available. *Unit head:* Dr. Lynn Glover-Stanley, Chair, 870-230-5200, E-mail: stanlel@hsu.edu. *Application contact:* Dr. Ken Taylor, Graduate Dean, 870-230-5126, Fax: 870-230-5479, E-mail: taylorke@hsu.edu.
Website: http://www.hsu.edu/hper/.

Hofstra University, Frank G. Zarb School of Business, Programs in Management and General Business, Hempstead, NY 11549. Offers business administration (MBA), including health services management, management, sports and entertainment management; general management (Advanced Certificate); human resource management (MS, Advanced Certificate).

Holy Names University, Graduate Division, Department of Business, Oakland, CA 94619-1699. Offers energy and environment management (MBA); finance (MBA); management and leadership (MBA); marketing (MBA); sports management (MBA). Part-time and evening/weekend programs available. *Faculty:* 4 full-time, 12 part-time/adjunct.

Students: 23 full-time (14 women), 20 part-time (12 women); includes 30 minority (19 Black or African American, non-Hispanic/Latino; 4 Asian, non-Hispanic/Latino; 7 Hispanic/Latino), 4 international. Average age 32. 35 applicants, 31% accepted, 7 enrolled. In 2013, 30 master's awarded. *Entrance requirements:* For master's, minimum undergraduate GPA of 2.6 overall, 3.0 in major; two recommendations (letter or form) from previous professors or current or previous work supervisors, 1-3 page personal statement, resume. Additional exam requirements/recommendations for international students: Required—TOEFL (minimum score 550 paper-based; 79 iBT). *Application deadline:* For fall admission, 8/1 priority date for domestic students, 7/15 for international students; for spring admission, 12/1 priority date for domestic students, 12/1 for international students; for summer admission, 5/1 priority date for domestic students, 5/1 for international students. Applications are processed on a rolling basis. Application fee: $65. Electronic applications accepted. Application fee is waived when completed online. *Expenses: Tuition:* Part-time $866 per unit. *Financial support:* Career-related internships or fieldwork, Federal Work-Study, scholarships/grants, and unspecified assistantships available. Support available to part-time students. Financial award application deadline: 3/2; financial award applicants required to submit FAFSA. *Faculty research:* Business ethics, sustainable economics, accounting models, cross-cultural management, diversity in organizations. *Unit head:* Dr. Hector Saez, MBA Program Director, 510-436-1622, E-mail: saez@hnu.edu. *Application contact:* 800-430-1321, Fax: 510-436-1325, E-mail: graduateadmissions@hnu.edu.
Website: http://www.hnu.edu.

Howard University, Graduate School, Department of Health, Human Performance and Leisure Studies, Washington, DC 20059-0002. Offers exercise physiology (MS); health education (MS); sports studies (MS), including sociology of sports, sports management; urban recreation (MS), including leisure studies. Part-time and evening/weekend programs available. *Degree requirements:* For master's, comprehensive exam, thesis. *Entrance requirements:* For master's, BS in human performance or related field. Additional exam requirements/recommendations for international students: Recommended—TOEFL. Electronic applications accepted. *Faculty research:* Health promotion, cardiovascular hypertension, physical activity, sport and human rights issues.

Indiana State University, College of Graduate and Professional Studies, College of Nursing, Health and Human Services, Department of Physical Education, Terre Haute, IN 47809. Offers adult fitness (MA, MS); coaching (MA, MS); exercise science (MA, MS). *Degree requirements:* For master's, thesis (for some programs). *Entrance requirements:* For master's, minor in physical education. Electronic applications accepted. *Faculty research:* Exercise science.

Indiana State University, College of Graduate and Professional Studies, College of Nursing, Health and Human Services, Department of Recreation and Sport Management, Terre Haute, IN 47809. Offers MA, MS. *Degree requirements:* For master's, comprehensive exam (for some programs), thesis (for some programs). *Entrance requirements:* For master's, GRE General Test, undergraduate major in related field. Electronic applications accepted.

Indiana University Bloomington, School of Public Health, Department of Kinesiology, Bloomington, IN 47405. Offers applied sport science (MS); athletic administration/sport management (MS); athletic training (MS); biomechanics (MS); ergonomics (MS); exercise physiology (MS); human performance (PhD), including biomechanics, exercise physiology, motor learning/control, sport management; motor learning/control (MS); physical activity (MPH); physical activity, fitness and wellness (MS). Part-time programs available. *Faculty:* 26 full-time (9 women). *Students:* 128 full-time (45 women), 16 part-time (6 women); includes 20 minority (11 Black or African American, non-Hispanic/Latino; 2 American Indian or Alaska Native, non-Hispanic/Latino; 3 Asian, non-Hispanic/Latino; 3 Hispanic/Latino; 1 Two or more races, non-Hispanic/Latino), 28 international. Average age 28. 174 applicants, 57% accepted, 48 enrolled. In 2013, 56 master's, 8 doctorates awarded. Terminal master's awarded for partial completion of doctoral program. *Degree requirements:* For master's, thesis optional; for doctorate, variable foreign language requirement, comprehensive exam, thesis/dissertation. *Entrance requirements:* For master's, GRE General Test, minimum GPA of 2.8; for doctorate, GRE General Test, minimum graduate GPA of 3.5, undergraduate 3.0. Additional exam requirements/recommendations for international students: Required—TOEFL (minimum score 80 iBT). *Application deadline:* For fall admission, 1/1 priority date for international students; for spring admission, 9/1 priority date for international students. Applications are processed on a rolling basis. Application fee: $55 ($65 for international students). *Financial support:* Fellowships, research assistantships with full tuition reimbursements, teaching assistantships with full tuition reimbursements, career-related internships or fieldwork, Federal Work-Study, institutionally sponsored loans, scholarships/grants, health care benefits, tuition waivers (partial), unspecified assistantships, and fee remissions available. Support available to part-time students. Financial award application deadline: 3/1; financial award applicants required to submit FAFSA. *Faculty research:* Exercise physiology and biochemistry, sports biomechanics, human motor control, adaptation of fitness and exercise to special populations. *Unit head:* Dr. David M. Koceja, Chairperson, 812-855-5523, Fax: 812-855-3193, E-mail: koceja@indiana.edu. *Application contact:* Kristine M. Wasson, Administrative Assistant for Graduate Studies, 812-855-5523, Fax: 812-855-3193, E-mail: ktanksle@indiana.edu.
Website: http://www.publichealth.indiana.edu/departments/kinesiology/index.shtml.

Indiana University Bloomington, School of Public Health, Department of Recreation, Park, and Tourism Studies, Bloomington, IN 47405-7000. Offers leisure behavior (PhD); outdoor recreation (MS); park and public lands management (MS); recreation administration (MS); recreational sports administration (MS); recreational therapy (MS); tourism management (MS). *Faculty:* 16 full-time (5 women), 1 (woman) part-time/adjunct. *Students:* 43 full-time (21 women), 9 part-time (6 women); includes 6 minority (2 Black or African American, non-Hispanic/Latino; 2 Hispanic/Latino; 2 Two or more races, non-Hispanic/Latino), 17 international. Average age 31. 47 applicants, 81% accepted, 18 enrolled. In 2013, 21 master's, 4 doctorates awarded. Terminal master's awarded for partial completion of doctoral program. *Degree requirements:* For master's, thesis optional; for doctorate, comprehensive exam, thesis/dissertation. *Entrance requirements:* For master's, GRE General Test, minimum GPA of 2.8; for doctorate, GRE General Test, minimum GPA of 3.0 (undergraduate), 3.5 (graduate). Additional exam requirements/recommendations for international students: Required—TOEFL (minimum score 550 paper-based; 80 iBT). *Application deadline:* For fall admission, 1/1 priority date for international students; for spring admission, 9/1 priority date for international students. Applications are processed on a rolling basis. Application fee: $55 ($65 for international students). Electronic applications accepted. *Financial support:* In 2013–14, 19 students received support. Fellowships, research assistantships, teaching assistantships with partial tuition reimbursements available, career-related internships or fieldwork, Federal Work-Study, institutionally sponsored loans, scholarships/grants, health care benefits, tuition waivers (partial), unspecified assistantships, and fee remissions available. Support available to part-time students. Financial award application deadline: 3/1; financial award applicants required to submit FAFSA. *Faculty research:* Leisure counseling, gerontology, special populations, planning and development. *Unit head:* Dr. Bryan McCormick, Chair, 812-855-3482, E-mail: bmccormi@indiana.edu. *Application contact:* Program Office, 812-855-4711, Fax: 812-855-3998, E-mail: recpark@indiana.edu.
Website: http://www.publichealth.indiana.edu/departments/recreation-park-tourism-studies/index.shtml.

Indiana University of Pennsylvania, School of Graduate Studies and Research, College of Health and Human Services, Department of Health and Physical Education, Program in Sport Science/Sport Management, Indiana, PA 15705-1087. Offers MS. *Faculty:* 8 full-time (4 women). *Students:* 16 full-time (4 women), 4 part-time (3 women); includes 1 minority (Black or African American, non-Hispanic/Latino), 3 international. Average age 25. 20 applicants, 65% accepted, 10 enrolled. In 2013, 12 master's awarded. *Degree requirements:* For master's, thesis or internship. *Entrance requirements:* Additional exam requirements/recommendations for international students: Required—TOEFL (minimum score 540 paper-based). Application fee: $50. *Expenses:* Tuition, state resident: full-time $3978; part-time $442 per credit. Tuition, nonresident: full-time $5967; part-time $663 per credit. *Required fees:* $2080; $115.55 per credit. $93 per semester. Tuition and fees vary according to degree level and program. *Financial support:* In 2013–14, 3 research assistantships with full and partial tuition reimbursements (averaging $3,053 per year) were awarded. Financial award application deadline: 4/15; financial award applicants required to submit FAFSA. *Unit head:* Dr. Robert Kostelnik, Chairperson, 724-357-7645, E-mail: bkostel@iup.edu.
Website: http://www.iup.edu/grad/sportscience/default.aspx.

Iona College, Hagan School of Business, Department of Marketing and International Business, New Rochelle, NY 10801-1890. Offers international business (AC, PMC); marketing (MBA); sports and entertainment management (AC). Part-time and evening/weekend programs available. *Faculty:* 2 full-time (both women), 1 (woman) part-time/adjunct. *Students:* 17 full-time (9 women), 24 part-time (16 women); includes 4 minority (2 Black or African American, non-Hispanic/Latino; 2 Hispanic/Latino), 5 international. Average age 27. 15 applicants, 100% accepted, 9 enrolled. In 2013, 28 master's, 114 other advanced degrees awarded. *Entrance requirements:* For master's, GMAT, 2 letters of recommendation, minimum GPA of 3.0; for other advanced degree, GMAT, minimum GPA of 3.0. Additional exam requirements/recommendations for international students: Required—TOEFL (minimum score 550 paper-based; 80 iBT), IELTS (minimum score 6.5). *Application deadline:* For fall admission, 8/15 priority date for domestic students, 8/1 priority date for international students; for winter admission, 11/15 priority date for domestic students, 11/1 priority date for international students; for spring admission, 2/15 priority date for domestic students, 2/1 priority date for international students; for summer admission, 5/15 for domestic students, 5/1 priority date for international students. Applications are processed on a rolling basis. Application fee: $50. Electronic applications accepted. *Expenses:* Contact institution. *Financial support:* In 2013–14, 23 students received support. Scholarships/grants, tuition waivers (partial), and unspecified assistantships available. Support available to part-time students. Financial award application deadline: 4/15; financial award applicants required to submit FAFSA. *Faculty research:* Business ethics, international retailing, mega-marketing, consumer behavior and consumer confidence. *Unit head:* Dr. Frederica E. Rudell, Chair, 914-637-2748, E-mail: frudell@iona.edu. *Application contact:* Cameron Hudson, Director of MBA Admissions, 914-633-2288, Fax: 914-637-2708, E-mail: chudson@iona.edu.
Website: http://www.iona.edu/Academics/Hagan-School-of-Business/Departments/Marketing/Graduate-Programs.aspx.

Jacksonville University, School of Education, Jacksonville, FL 32211. Offers educational leadership (M Ed); instructional leadership and organizational development (M Ed); sport management and leadership (M Ed). Part-time and evening/weekend programs available. *Degree requirements:* For master's, comprehensive exam. *Entrance requirements:* For master's, GRE General Test, minimum GPA of 3.0. Additional exam requirements/recommendations for international students: Required—TOEFL (minimum score 550 paper-based), TWE. *Expenses:* Contact institution.

Kansas Wesleyan University, Program in Business Administration, Salina, KS 67401-6196. Offers business administration (MBA); sports management (MBA). Part-time and evening/weekend programs available. *Entrance requirements:* For master's, GMAT, minimum graduate GPA of 3.0 or undergraduate GPA of 3.25.

Kent State University, Graduate School of Education, Health, and Human Services, School of Foundations, Leadership and Administration, Sports Recreation and Management Program, Kent, OH 44242-0001. Offers sport and recreation management (MA); sports studies (MA). *Faculty:* 10 full-time (5 women), 14 part-time/adjunct (6 women). *Students:* 42 full-time (12 women), 18 part-time (8 women); includes 12 minority (9 Black or African American, non-Hispanic/Latino; 1 Asian, non-Hispanic/Latino; 2 Native Hawaiian or other Pacific Islander, non-Hispanic/Latino), 9 international. 80 applicants, 60% accepted. In 2013, 23 master's awarded. *Degree requirements:* For master's, thesis optional. *Entrance requirements:* For master's, GRE if undergraduate GPA below 3.0, goals statement, 2 letters of recommendation. Additional exam requirements/recommendations for international students: Required—TOEFL (minimum score 550 paper-based; 80 iBT). Application fee: $30 ($60 for international students). *Financial support:* In 2013–14, 7 research assistantships (averaging $8,500 per year) were awarded; teaching assistantships, Federal Work-Study, scholarships/grants, and unspecified assistantships also available. *Unit head:* Mark Lyberger, Coordinator, 330-672-0228, E-mail: mlyberge@kent.edu. *Application contact:* Nancy Miller, Academic Program Director, Office of Graduate Student Services, 330-672-2576, Fax: 330-672-9162, E-mail: ogs@kent.edu.

Lasell College, Graduate and Professional Studies in Sport Management, Newton, MA 02466-2709. Offers sport hospitality management (MS, Graduate Certificate); sport leadership (MS, Graduate Certificate); sport non-profit management (MS, Graduate Certificate). Part-time programs available. Postbaccalaureate distance learning degree programs offered (no on-campus study). *Faculty:* 2 full-time (0 women), 6 part-time/adjunct (5 women). *Students:* 13 full-time (4 women), 42 part-time (16 women); includes 17 minority (11 Black or African American, non-Hispanic/Latino; 3 American Indian or Alaska Native, non-Hispanic/Latino; 2 Hispanic/Latino; 1 Two or more races, non-Hispanic/Latino). Average age 30. 34 applicants, 62% accepted, 11 enrolled. In 2013, 11 master's awarded. *Entrance requirements:* For master's and Graduate Certificate, bachelor's degree from an accredited institution. Additional exam requirements/recommendations for international students: Required—TOEFL (minimum score 550 paper-based; 79 iBT), IELTS. *Application deadline:* For fall admission, 8/31 priority date for domestic students, 6/30 priority date for international students; for spring admission, 12/31 priority date for domestic students, 10/31 priority date for international students. Applications are processed on a rolling basis. Electronic applications accepted. *Expenses: Tuition:* Part-time $575 per credit. *Required fees:* $80 per semester. *Financial support:* Available to part-time students. Application deadline: 8/31; applicants required to submit FAFSA. *Unit head:* Dr. Joan Dolamore, Dean of Graduate and Professional Studies, 617-243-2485, Fax: 617-243-2450, E-mail: gradinfo@lasell.edu. *Application contact:* Adrienne Franciosi, Director of Graduate Admission, 617-243-2214, Fax: 617-243-2450, E-mail: gradinfo@lasell.edu.
Website: http://www.lasell.edu/Academics/Graduate-and-Professional-Studies/MS-in-Sport-Management-.html.

Sports Management

Lewis University, College of Arts and Sciences, Program in Organizational Leadership, Romeoville, IL 60446. Offers coaching (MA); higher education/student services (MA); non-for-profit management (MA); organizational management (MA); public administration (MA); training and development (MA). Part-time and evening/weekend programs available. Postbaccalaureate distance learning degree programs offered (no on-campus study). *Students:* 24 full-time (21 women), 200 part-time (152 women); includes 87 minority (60 Black or African American, non-Hispanic/Latino; 2 American Indian or Alaska Native, non-Hispanic/Latino; 4 Asian, non-Hispanic/Latino; 20 Hispanic/Latino; 1 Two or more races, non-Hispanic/Latino), 1 international. Average age 36. *Entrance requirements:* For master's, bachelor's degree, at least 24 years of age, minimum of 3 years of work experience, minimum GPA of 3.0, letter of recommendation. Additional exam requirements/recommendations for international students: Required—TOEFL (minimum score 550 paper-based; 80 iBT). *Application deadline:* For fall admission, 5/1 priority date for international students; for spring admission, 11/15 priority date for international students. Applications are processed on a rolling basis. Application fee: $40. Electronic applications accepted. *Financial support:* Tuition waivers and unspecified assistantships available. Financial award application deadline: 5/1; financial award applicants required to submit FAFSA. *Unit head:* Dr. Keith Lavine, Chair of Organizational Leadership, 815-838-0500, E-mail: lavineke@lewisu.edu. *Application contact:* Julie Branchaw, Assistant Director, Graduate and Adult Admission, 815-836-5574, Fax: 815-836-5578, E-mail: branchju@lewisu.edu.

Liberty University, School of Education, Lynchburg, VA 24515. Offers administration and supervision (M Ed); curriculum and instruction (Ed D, Ed S); early childhood education (M Ed); educational leadership (Ed D, Ed S); educational technology and online instruction (M Ed); elementary education (M Ed, MAT); English (M Ed); gifted education (M Ed); history (M Ed); leadership (M Ed); math specialist (M Ed); middle grades (M Ed, MAT); outdoor adventure sport (MS); reading specialist (M Ed); school counseling (M Ed); secondary education (MAT); special education (M Ed, MAT); sport management (MS), including administration, outdoor recreation, sport management, tourism; sports administration (MS); student service (M Ed); teaching and learning (M Ed); tourism (MS). *Accreditation:* NCATE. Part-time programs available. Postbaccalaureate distance learning degree programs offered (minimal on-campus study). *Students:* 2,241 full-time (1,639 women), 4,413 part-time (3,240 women); includes 2,052 minority (1,588 Black or African American, non-Hispanic/Latino; 37 American Indian or Alaska Native, non-Hispanic/Latino; 67 Asian, non-Hispanic/Latino; 173 Hispanic/Latino; 37 Native Hawaiian or other Pacific Islander, non-Hispanic/Latino; 150 Two or more races, non-Hispanic/Latino), 15 international. Average age 37. 6,185 applicants, 43% accepted, 1603 enrolled. In 2013, 1,256 master's, 117 doctorates, 470 other advanced degrees awarded. *Degree requirements:* For doctorate, comprehensive exam, thesis/dissertation. *Entrance requirements:* For master's, GRE General Test or MAT (if taken in or before 1999), 2 letters of recommendation, minimum undergraduate GPA of 3.0, curriculum vitae; for doctorate and Ed S, GRE General Test or MAT (if taken before 1999), minimum master's GPA of 3.0, 3 years of teaching experience. Additional exam requirements/recommendations for international students: Required—TOEFL (minimum score 600 paper-based; 100 iBT). *Application deadline:* For fall admission, 6/1 for domestic students; for spring admission, 11/1 for domestic students. Applications are processed on a rolling basis. Application fee: $50. Electronic applications accepted. *Expenses:* Contact institution. *Financial support:* Federal Work-Study and tuition waivers (partial) available. *Faculty research:* Self-determination, character education, bibliotherapy, learning styles, distance education. *Unit head:* Dr. Karen L. Parker, Dean, 434-582-2195, Fax: 434-582-2468, E-mail: kparker@liberty.edu. *Application contact:* Jay Bridge, Director of Graduate Admissions, 800-424-9595, Fax: 800-628-7977, E-mail: gradadmissions@liberty.edu.
Website: http://www.liberty.edu/academics/education/graduate/.

Lindenwood University, Graduate Programs, School of Business and Entrepreneurship, St. Charles, MO 63301-1695. Offers accountancy (MA); accounting (MBA); business administration (MBA); entrepreneurial studies (MBA); finance (MBA, MS); human resource management (MBA); international business (MBA); leadership (MA); management (MBA); marketing (MBA, MS); public management (MBA); sport management (MA); supply chain management (MBA). *Accreditation:* ACBSP. Part-time and evening/weekend programs available. Postbaccalaureate distance learning degree programs offered (no on-campus study). *Faculty:* 18 full-time (8 women), 33 part-time/adjunct (8 women). *Students:* 292 full-time (130 women), 111 part-time (46 women); includes 59 minority (42 Black or African American, non-Hispanic/Latino; 5 American Indian or Alaska Native, non-Hispanic/Latino; 1 Asian, non-Hispanic/Latino; 5 Hispanic/Latino; 6 Two or more races, non-Hispanic/Latino), 112 international. Average age 29. 212 applicants, 51% accepted, 102 enrolled. In 2013, 221 master's awarded. *Degree requirements:* For master's, comprehensive exam (for some programs), thesis (for some programs), minimum GPA of 3.0. *Entrance requirements:* For master's, interview, minimum GPA of 3.0, letter of recommendation. Additional exam requirements/recommendations for international students: Required—TOEFL (minimum score 550 paper-based; 80 iBT). *Application deadline:* For fall admission, 8/12 priority date for domestic and international students; for winter admission, 1/6 priority date for domestic and international students; for spring admission, 3/10 priority date for domestic and international students; for summer admission, 5/27 priority date for domestic and international students. Applications are processed on a rolling basis. Application fee: $30 ($100 for international students). Electronic applications accepted. *Expenses: Tuition:* Full-time $14,800; part-time $428 per credit hour. *Required fees:* $350. Tuition and fees vary according to course level and course load. *Financial support:* In 2013–14, 268 students received support. Career-related internships or fieldwork, Federal Work-Study, institutionally sponsored loans, scholarships/grants, tuition waivers (partial), and unspecified assistantships available. Financial award application deadline: 6/30; financial award applicants required to submit FAFSA. *Unit head:* Roger Ellis, Dean, 636-949-4839, E-mail: rellis@lindenwood.edu. *Application contact:* Brett Barger, Dean of Evening Admissions and Extension Campuses, 636-949-4934, Fax: 636-949-4109, E-mail: adultadmissions@lindenwood.edu.
Website: http://www.lindenwood.edu.

Lipscomb University, Graduate School of Business, Nashville, TN 37204-3951. Offers accountancy (M Acc); accounting (MBA); conflict management (MBA); distributive (general) (MBA); financial services (MBA); health care informatics (MBA); healthcare management (MBA); human resources (MHR); information security (MBA); leadership (MBA); nonprofit management (MBA); professional accountancy (Certificate); sports management (MBA); strategic human resources (MBA); sustainability (MBA); MBA/MS. *Accreditation:* ACBSP. Part-time and evening/weekend programs available. *Faculty:* 12 full-time (1 woman), 12 part-time/adjunct (2 women). *Students:* 90 full-time (44 women), 104 part-time (51 women); includes 28 minority (24 Black or African American, non-Hispanic/Latino; 3 Hispanic/Latino; 1 Two or more races, non-Hispanic/Latino), 6 international. Average age 33. 145 applicants, 79% accepted, 69 enrolled. In 2013, 98 master's, 1 other advanced degree awarded. *Entrance requirements:* For master's, GMAT, transcripts, interview, 2 references, resume. Additional exam requirements/recommendations for international students: Required—TOEFL (minimum score 570 paper-based). *Application deadline:* For fall admission, 6/15 for domestic students, 2/1 for international students; for winter admission, 6/1 for international students; for spring admission, 11/15 for domestic students. Applications are processed on a rolling basis. Application fee: $50 ($75 for international students). Electronic applications accepted. *Expenses:* Contact institution. *Financial support:* Career-related internships or fieldwork, scholarships/grants, tuition waivers (partial), and unspecified assistantships available. Support available to part-time students. Financial award application deadline: 7/1; financial award applicants required to submit FAFSA. *Faculty research:* Impact of spirituality on organization commitment, women in corporate leadership, psychological empowerment, training. *Unit head:* Joe Ivey, Associate Dean of Graduate Business Programs, 615-966-6229, Fax: 615-966-1818, E-mail: joe.ivey@lipscomb.edu. *Application contact:* Lisa Shacklett, Assistant Dean of Enrollment and Marketing, 615-966-5968, E-mail: lisa.shacklett@lipscomb.edu.
Website: http://www.lipscomb.edu/business/Graduate-Programs.

Lock Haven University of Pennsylvania, College of Business, Information Systems and Human Services, Lock Haven, PA 17745-2390. Offers clinical mental health counseling (MS); sport science (MS). Postbaccalaureate distance learning degree programs offered (no on-campus study). *Degree requirements:* For master's, thesis. *Entrance requirements:* For master's, minimum undergraduate GPA of 3.0. Additional exam requirements/recommendations for international students: Required—TOEFL. *Application deadline:* Applications are processed on a rolling basis. Application fee: $25. Electronic applications accepted. *Expenses: Tuition, area resident:* Part-time $442 per credit hour. Tuition, state resident: part-time $442 per credit hour. Tuition, nonresident: part-time $663 per credit hour. *Required fees:* $208.45 per credit hour. Tuition and fees vary according to program. *Financial support:* Unspecified assistantships available. Financial award application deadline: 8/1. *Unit head:* Dr. Stephen Neun, Dean, 570-484-2136, E-mail: spn207@lhup.edu. *Application contact:* Lucas A. Fanning, Assistant to the Dean, 570-484-2169, Fax: 570-484-2734, E-mail: laf1158@lhup.edu.
Website: http://www.lhup.edu/colleges/Business_Information/.

Lynn University, College of Business and Management, Boca Raton, FL 33431-5598. Offers aviation management (MBA); financial valuation and investment management (MBA); hospitality management (MBA); international business (MBA); marketing (MBA); mass communication and media management (MBA); sports and athletics administration (MBA). Part-time and evening/weekend programs available. Postbaccalaureate distance learning degree programs offered. *Faculty:* 16 full-time (6 women), 8 part-time/adjunct (3 women). *Students:* 181 full-time (95 women), 83 part-time (37 women); includes 41 minority (22 Black or African American, non-Hispanic/Latino; 1 Asian, non-Hispanic/Latino; 17 Hispanic/Latino; 1 Two or more races, non-Hispanic/Latino), 77 international. Average age 28. 137 applicants, 100% accepted, 107 enrolled. In 2013, 149 master's awarded. *Degree requirements:* For master's, projects. *Entrance requirements:* For master's, GMAT or GRE, bachelor's degree from accredited institution, minimum undergraduate GPA of 2.5, resume, 2 letters of recommendation. Additional exam requirements/recommendations for international students: Required—TOEFL (minimum score 550 paper-based). *Application deadline:* Applications are processed on a rolling basis. Application fee: $45. Electronic applications accepted. *Expenses: Tuition:* Full-time $23,760; part-time $660 per credit. *Required fees:* $300; $50 per term. Tuition and fees vary according to degree level and program. *Financial support:* Career-related internships or fieldwork, Federal Work-Study, institutionally sponsored loans, scholarships/grants, tuition waivers (full and partial), and unspecified assistantships available. Support available to part-time students. Financial award application deadline: 8/1; financial award applicants required to submit FAFSA. *Faculty research:* Labor relations, dynamic balance in leisure-time skills, ethics in athletics, hotel development. *Unit head:* Dr. Ralph Norcio, Senior Associate Dean, 561-237-7010, Fax: 561-237-7014, E-mail: rnorcio@lynn.edu. *Application contact:* Steven Pruitt, Director of Graduate and Undergraduate Evening Admission, 561-237-7834, Fax: 561-237-7100, E-mail: spruitt@lynn.edu.
Website: http://www.lynn.edu/academics/colleges/business-and-management.

Manhattanville College, School of Business, Program in Sport Business Management, Purchase, NY 10577-2132. Offers MS. Part-time and evening/weekend programs available. *Degree requirements:* For master's, internship or work experience. *Entrance requirements:* Additional exam requirements/recommendations for international students: Required—TOEFL.

Marquette University, Graduate School, College of Professional Studies, Milwaukee, WI 53201-1881. Offers criminal justice administration (MLS, Certificate); dispute resolution (MDR, MLS); health care administration (MLS); leadership studies (Certificate); non-profit sector administration (MLS); public service (MAPS, MLS); sports leadership (MLS). Part-time and evening/weekend programs available. Postbaccalaureate distance learning degree programs offered (no on-campus study). *Faculty:* 3 full-time (2 women), 25 part-time/adjunct (11 women). *Students:* 29 full-time (14 women), 109 part-time (61 women); includes 28 minority (17 Black or African American, non-Hispanic/Latino; 2 American Indian or Alaska Native, non-Hispanic/Latino; 2 Asian, non-Hispanic/Latino; 5 Hispanic/Latino; 2 Two or more races, non-Hispanic/Latino), 1 international. Average age 36. 81 applicants, 81% accepted, 36 enrolled. In 2013, 42 master's, 18 Certificates awarded. *Degree requirements:* For master's, comprehensive exam (for some programs). *Entrance requirements:* For master's, GRE General Test (preferred), GMAT, or LSAT, official transcripts from all current and previous colleges/universities except Marquette, three letters of recommendation, statement of purpose. Additional exam requirements/recommendations for international students: Required—TOEFL. *Application deadline:* Applications are processed on a rolling basis. Electronic applications accepted. *Financial support:* In 2013–14, 9 students received support, including 8 fellowships with full tuition reimbursements available (averaging $16,247 per year). Financial award application deadline: 2/15. *Unit head:* Dr. Robert Deahl, Dean/Assistant Professor, 414-288-3156. *Application contact:* Eva Soeka, Director and Associate Professor, 414-288-5535.

Marquette University, Graduate School of Management, Executive MBA Program, Milwaukee, WI 53201-1881. Offers economics (MBA); finance (MBA); human resources (MBA); international business (MBA); management information systems (MBA); marketing (MBA); operations and supply chain management (MBA); sports business (MBA). *Accreditation:* AACSB. *Students:* 38 full-time (12 women), 1 international. Average age 36. 36 applicants. In 2013, 21 master's awarded. *Degree requirements:* For master's, international trip. *Entrance requirements:* For master's, GMAT or GRE, two letters of recommendation, official transcripts from current and previous colleges/universities. Additional exam requirements/recommendations for international students: Required—TOEFL (minimum score 550 paper-based; 88 iBT), IELTS (minimum score 6.5), PTE. *Application deadline:* For fall admission, 2/15 for domestic and international students. Application fee: $50. Electronic applications accepted. *Expenses:* Contact institution. *Financial support:* Application deadline: 2/15. *Faculty research:* International trade and finance, customer relationship management, consumer satisfaction, customer service. *Unit head:* Dr. Mark Eppli, Dean, 414-288-5724. *Application contact:* Dr. Jeanne Simmons, Associate Dean, 414-288-7145.
Website: http://www.busadm.mu.edu/emba/.

Marquette University, Graduate School of Management, Program in Business Administration, Milwaukee, WI 53201-1881. Offers business administration (MBA); economics (MBA); entrepreneurship (Certificate); finance (MBA); human resources (MBA); international business (MBA); management information systems (MBA);

marketing (MBA); operations and supply chain management (MBA); sports business (MBA); JD/MBA; MBA/MA; MBA/MSN. *Accreditation:* AACSB. Part-time and evening/weekend programs available. *Students:* 28 full-time (13 women), 265 part-time (66 women); includes 20 minority (7 Black or African American, non-Hispanic/Latino; 8 Asian, non-Hispanic/Latino; 5 Hispanic/Latino), 11 international. Average age 31. 185 applicants. In 2013, 129 master's, 2 other advanced degrees awarded. *Degree requirements:* For Certificate, business plan. *Entrance requirements:* For master's, GMAT or GRE, letters of recommendation. Additional exam requirements/recommendations for international students: Required—TOEFL (minimum score 550 paper-based; 88 iBT), IELTS (minimum score 6.5), PTE. *Application deadline:* For fall admission, 2/15 for domestic and international students. Applications are processed on a rolling basis. Application fee: $50. Electronic applications accepted. *Financial support:* In 2013–14, 4 fellowships, 11 teaching assistantships were awarded; research assistantships, Federal Work-Study, institutionally sponsored loans, scholarships/grants, and tuition waivers (full and partial) also available. Support available to part-time students. Financial award application deadline: 2/15. *Faculty research:* Ethics in the professions, services marketing, technology impact on decision-making, mentoring. *Unit head:* Dr. Mark Eppli, Dean, 414-288-5724. *Application contact:* Dr. Jeanne Simmons, Associate Dean, 414-288-7145.
Website: http://business.marquette.edu/academics/mba.

Marshall University, Academic Affairs Division, College of Health Professions, School of Kinesiology, Program in Sport Administration, Huntington, WV 25755. Offers MS. *Students:* 21 full-time (8 women), 5 part-time (1 woman); includes 3 minority (1 Black or African American, non-Hispanic/Latino; 1 American Indian or Alaska Native, non-Hispanic/Latino; 1 Two or more races, non-Hispanic/Latino). Average age 25. In 2013, 7 master's awarded. *Degree requirements:* For master's, thesis optional, comprehensive assessment. *Entrance requirements:* For master's, GRE General Test. Application fee: $40. *Unit head:* Dr. Jennifer Mak, Director, 304-696-2927, E-mail: mak@marshall.edu. *Application contact:* Information Contact, 304-746-1900, Fax: 304-746-1902, E-mail: services@marshall.edu.

Maryville University of Saint Louis, The John E. Simon School of Business, St. Louis, MO 63141-7299. Offers accounting (MBA, PGC); management (MBA, PGC); marketing (MBA, PGC); process and project management (MBA, PGC); sport and entertainment management (MBA, PGC). *Accreditation:* ACBSP. Part-time and evening/weekend programs available. *Faculty:* 5 full-time (3 women), 14 part-time/adjunct (4 women). *Students:* 21 full-time (12 women), 85 part-time (41 women); includes 22 minority (8 Black or African American, non-Hispanic/Latino; 2 Asian, non-Hispanic/Latino; 7 Hispanic/Latino; 5 Two or more races, non-Hispanic/Latino), 3 international. Average age 31. In 2013, 39 master's awarded. *Entrance requirements:* For master's, GMAT (unless applicant possesses undergraduate business degree with minimum cumulative GPA of 3.0, or has completed master's degree from accredited university or one early access course prior to undergraduate degree). Additional exam requirements/recommendations for international students: Required—TOEFL (minimum score 85 iBT). *Application deadline:* Applications are processed on a rolling basis. Application fee: $40 ($60 for international students). Electronic applications accepted. Application fee is waived when completed online. *Expenses: Tuition:* Full-time $23,812; part-time $728 per credit hour. *Required fees:* $395 per year. Tuition and fees vary according to course load, degree level and program. *Financial support:* Career-related internships or fieldwork, Federal Work-Study, tuition waivers (partial), and campus employment available. Financial award application deadline: 3/1; financial award applicants required to submit FAFSA. *Faculty research:* International business, e-marketing, strategic planning, interpersonal management skills, financial analysis. *Unit head:* Dr. Pamela Horwitz, Dean, 314-529-9418, Fax: 314-529-9975, E-mail: horwitz@maryville.edu. *Application contact:* Kathy Dougherty, Director of MBA Programs, 314-529-9382, Fax: 314-529-9975, E-mail: business@maryville.edu.
Website: http://www.maryville.edu/bu/business-administration-masters/.

Mercyhurst University, Graduate Studies, Program in Organizational Leadership, Erie, PA 16546. Offers accounting (MS); entrepreneurship (MS); higher education administration (MS); human resources (MS); nonprofit management (MS); organizational leadership (Certificate); sports leadership (MS). Part-time and evening/weekend programs available. *Degree requirements:* For master's, thesis. *Entrance requirements:* For master's, GRE General Test or MAT, interview, resume, essay, three professional references, transcripts. Additional exam requirements/recommendations for international students: Required—TOEFL. Electronic applications accepted. *Faculty research:* Leadership training, organizational communication, leadership pedagogy.

Messiah College, Program in Higher Education, Mechanicsburg, PA 17055. Offers college athletics management (MA); self-designed concentration (MA); student affairs (MA). Part-time programs available. Electronic applications accepted. *Expenses: Tuition:* Part-time $595 per credit hour. *Required fees:* $30 per course. *Faculty research:* College athletics management, assessment and student learning outcomes, the life and legacy of Ernest L. Boyer, common learning, student affairs practice.

Millersville University of Pennsylvania, College of Graduate and Professional Studies, School of Education, Department of Wellness and Sport Sciences, Millersville, PA 17551-0302. Offers sport management (M Ed), including athletic coaching, athletic management. Part-time and evening/weekend programs available. *Faculty:* 10 full-time (3 women), 2 part-time/adjunct (0 women). *Students:* 8 full-time (3 women), 26 part-time (9 women); includes 2 minority (both Hispanic/Latino), 1 international. Average age 27. 19 applicants, 74% accepted, 10 enrolled. In 2013, 21 master's awarded. *Degree requirements:* For master's, comprehensive exam, thesis optional. *Entrance requirements:* For master's, GRE, MAT, or GMAT, 3 letters of recommendation, goal statement, official transcripts. Additional exam requirements/recommendations for international students: Required—TOEFL (minimum score 550 paper-based, 79 iBT) or IELTS (minimum score 6). *Application deadline:* For fall admission, 1/15 priority date for domestic and international students; for winter admission, 10/1 priority date for domestic and international students; for spring admission, 10/1 priority date for domestic and international students. Applications are processed on a rolling basis. Application fee: $40. Electronic applications accepted. *Expenses:* Tuition, state resident: full-time $7956; part-time $442 per credit. Tuition, nonresident: full-time $11,934; part-time $663 per credit. *Required fees:* $2196; $122 per credit. Tuition and fees vary according to course load. *Financial support:* In 2013–14, 12 students received support, including 12 research assistantships with full tuition reimbursements available (averaging $5,233 per year); institutionally sponsored loans and unspecified assistantships also available. Support available to part-time students. Financial award application deadline: 3/15; financial award applicants required to submit FAFSA. *Faculty research:* Childhood health and wellness issues, using technology for monitoring physical activity, global public health and sport issues, gender and sport, leadership self-efficacy. *Unit head:* Dr. Daniel J. Keefer, Chair, 717-872-2182, Fax: 717-871-2393, E-mail: daniel.keefer@millersville.edu. *Application contact:* Dr. Victor S. DeSantis, Dean of College of Graduate and Professional Studies/Associate Provost for Civic and Community Engagement, 717-872-3099, Fax: 717-872-3453, E-mail: victor.desantis@millersville.edu.
Website: http://www.millersville.edu/wssd/.

Misericordia University, College of Professional Studies and Social Sciences, Master of Business Administration Program, Dallas, PA 18612-1098. Offers accounting (MBA); human resources (MBA); management (MBA); sport management (MBA). Part-time and evening/weekend programs available. Postbaccalaureate distance learning degree programs offered (no on-campus study). *Faculty:* 4 full-time (2 women), 5 part-time/adjunct (2 women). *Students:* 100 part-time (53 women); includes 1 minority (Black or African American, non-Hispanic/Latino), 1 international. Average age 33. In 2013, 32 master's awarded. *Entrance requirements:* For master's, GMAT, MAT, GRE (50th percentile or higher), or minimum undergraduate GPA of 3.0, interview. Additional exam requirements/recommendations for international students: Required—TOEFL. *Application deadline:* Applications are processed on a rolling basis. Application fee: $35. Electronic applications accepted. Application fee is waived when completed online. *Expenses: Tuition:* Full-time $14,450; part-time $680 per credit. Tuition and fees vary according to degree level. *Financial support:* In 2013–14, 68 students received support. Scholarships/grants and unspecified assistantships available. Support available to part-time students. Financial award applicants required to submit FAFSA. *Unit head:* Dr. Timothy Kearney, Chair of Business Department, 570-674-1487, E-mail: tkearney@misericordia.edu. *Application contact:* David Pasquini, Assistant Director of Admissions, 570-674-8183, Fax: 570-674-6232, E-mail: dpasquin@misericordia.edu.
Website: http://www.misericordia.edu/mba.

Mississippi State University, College of Education, Department of Kinesiology, Mississippi State, MS 39762. Offers exercise physiology (MS); sport administration (MS); sport pedagogy (MS). Part-time programs available. Postbaccalaureate distance learning degree programs offered (minimal on-campus study). *Faculty:* 6 full-time (1 woman). *Students:* 44 full-time (12 women), 11 part-time (4 women); includes 6 minority (3 Black or African American, non-Hispanic/Latino; 2 Hispanic/Latino; 1 Two or more races, non-Hispanic/Latino), 4 international. Average age 25. 98 applicants, 35% accepted, 23 enrolled. In 2013, 36 master's awarded. *Degree requirements:* For master's, comprehensive exam, thesis optional. *Entrance requirements:* For master's, GRE General Test, minimum GPA of 2.75 on undergraduate work from four-year accredited institution, 3.0 graduate. Additional exam requirements/recommendations for international students: Required—TOEFL (minimum score 550 paper-based; 79 iBT); Recommended—IELTS (minimum score 6.5). *Application deadline:* For fall admission, 7/1 for domestic students, 5/1 for international students; for spring admission, 11/1 for domestic students, 9/1 for international students. Applications are processed on a rolling basis. Application fee: $60. Electronic applications accepted. *Financial support:* In 2013–14, 7 teaching assistantships (averaging $8,772 per year) were awarded; career-related internships or fieldwork, Federal Work-Study, institutionally sponsored loans, and unspecified assistantships also available. Financial award application deadline: 4/1; financial award applicants required to submit FAFSA. *Faculty research:* Static balance and stepping performance of older adults, organizational justice, public health, strength training and recovery drinks, high risk drinking perceptions and behaviors. *Unit head:* Dr. Stanley Brown, Professor and Department Head, 662-325-2963, Fax: 662-325-4525, E-mail: spb107@msstate.edu. *Application contact:* Dr. Adam Love, Graduate Coordinator, 662-325-2963, Fax: 662-325-4525, E-mail: adam.love@msstate.edu.
Website: http://www.kinesiology.msstate.edu/.

Missouri State University, Graduate College, Interdisciplinary Program in Administrative Studies, Springfield, MO 65897. Offers applied communication (MS); criminal justice (MS); environmental management (MS); homeland security (MS); project management (MS); sports management (MS). Part-time and evening/weekend programs available. Postbaccalaureate distance learning degree programs offered (no on-campus study). *Students:* 14 full-time (9 women), 67 part-time (31 women); includes 3 minority (1 Hispanic/Latino; 2 Two or more races, non-Hispanic/Latino), 4 international. Average age 32. 31 applicants, 87% accepted, 22 enrolled. In 2013, 30 master's awarded. *Degree requirements:* For master's, comprehensive exam, thesis or alternative. *Entrance requirements:* For master's, GRE, GMAT, 3 years of work experience. Additional exam requirements/recommendations for international students: Required—TOEFL (minimum score 550 paper-based; 79 iBT). *Application deadline:* For fall admission, 7/20 priority date for domestic students; for spring admission, 12/20 priority date for domestic students. Applications are processed on a rolling basis. Application fee: $35 ($50 for international students). Electronic applications accepted. *Expenses:* Tuition, state resident: full-time $4500; part-time $250 per credit hour. Tuition, nonresident: full-time $9018; part-time $501 per credit hour. *Required fees:* $361 per semester. Tuition and fees vary according to course level, course load and program. *Financial support:* Career-related internships or fieldwork, Federal Work-Study, institutionally sponsored loans, scholarships/grants, and unspecified assistantships available. Support available to part-time students. Financial award application deadline: 3/31; financial award applicants required to submit FAFSA. *Unit head:* Dr. Gerald Masterson, Program Coordinator, 417-836-5251, Fax: 417-836-6888, E-mail: msas@missouristate.edu. *Application contact:* Misty Stewart, Coordinator of Graduate Recruitment, 417-836-6079, Fax: 417-836-6200, E-mail: mistystewart@missouristate.edu.
Website: http://msas.missouristate.edu.

Missouri Western State University, Program in Applied Science, St. Joseph, MO 64507-2294. Offers chemistry (MAS); engineering technology management (MAS); human factors and usability testing (MAS); industrial life science (MAS); information technology management (MAS); sport and fitness management (MAS). Part-time programs available. *Students:* 38 full-time (11 women), 24 part-time (10 women); includes 7 minority (4 Black or African American, non-Hispanic/Latino; 1 Asian, non-Hispanic/Latino; 1 Hispanic/Latino; 1 Two or more races, non-Hispanic/Latino), 21 international. Average age 28. 60 applicants, 90% accepted, 37 enrolled. In 2013, 15 master's awarded. *Entrance requirements:* Additional exam requirements/recommendations for international students: Recommended—TOEFL (minimum score 500 paper-based; 61 iBT), IELTS (minimum score 5.5). *Application deadline:* For fall admission, 7/15 for domestic students, 6/15 for international students; for spring admission, 10/1 for domestic students, 10/15 for international students. Applications are processed on a rolling basis. Application fee: $45 ($50 for international students). Electronic applications accepted. *Expenses:* Tuition, state resident: full-time $6019; part-time $300.96 per credit hour. Tuition, nonresident: full-time $11,194; part-time $559.71 per credit hour. *Required fees:* $542; $99 per credit hour. $176 per semester. Tuition and fees vary according to course load and program. *Financial support:* Scholarships/grants and unspecified assistantships available. Support available to part-time students. *Unit head:* Dr. Benjamin D. Caldwell, Dean of the Graduate School, 816-271-4394, Fax: 816-271-4525, E-mail: graduate@missouriwestern.edu. *Application contact:* Dr. Benjamin D. Caldwell, Dean of the Graduate School, 816-271-4394, Fax: 816-271-4525, E-mail: graduate@missouriwestern.edu.

Montclair State University, The Graduate School, College of Education and Human Services, Department of Exercise Science and Physical Education, Program in Exercise Science and Physical Education, Montclair, NJ 07043-1624. Offers exercise science (MA); sports administration and coaching (MA); teaching and supervision in physical education (MA). Part-time and evening/weekend programs available. *Degree requirements:* For master's, comprehensive exam, thesis or alternative. *Entrance requirements:* For master's, GRE General Test, essay, 2 letters of recommendation. Additional exam requirements/recommendations for international students: Required—TOEFL (minimum score 83 iBT), IELTS (minimum score 6.5). Electronic applications accepted.

Sports Management

Morehead State University, Graduate Programs, College of Business and Public Affairs, School of Business Administration, Morehead, KY 40351. Offers business administration (MBA); information systems (MSIS); sport management (MA). Part-time and evening/weekend programs available. *Entrance requirements:* For master's, GRE or GMAT. Additional exam requirements/recommendations for international students: Required—TOEFL (minimum score 500 paper-based). Electronic applications accepted.

National University, Academic Affairs, School of Business and Management, La Jolla, CA 92037-1011. Offers accountancy (Certificate); business administration (GMBA, MBA), including financial management (MBA), human resource management (MBA), integrated marketing communications (MBA), international business (MBA), management accounting (MBA), marketing (MBA), mobile marketing and social media (MBA), organizational leadership (MA, MBA), professional golf management (MBA); global management (MGM); human resource management (MA), including organizational development and change, organizational leadership (MA, MBA); international business (Certificate); management information systems (MS); organizational leadership (MS), including community development; sustainability management (MS). Part-time and evening/weekend programs available. Postbaccalaureate distance learning degree programs offered (no on-campus study). *Faculty:* 30 full-time (8 women), 88 part-time/adjunct (25 women). *Students:* 688 full-time (357 women), 331 part-time (161 women); includes 453 minority (105 Black or African American, non-Hispanic/Latino; 2 American Indian or Alaska Native, non-Hispanic/Latino; 143 Asian, non-Hispanic/Latino; 162 Hispanic/Latino; 13 Native Hawaiian or other Pacific Islander, non-Hispanic/Latino; 28 Two or more races, non-Hispanic/Latino), 165 international. Average age 33. 286 applicants, 100% accepted, 217 enrolled. In 2013, 641 master's awarded. *Degree requirements:* For master's, thesis (for some programs). *Entrance requirements:* For master's, interview, minimum GPA of 2.5. Additional exam requirements/recommendations for international students: Required—TOEFL (minimum score 550 paper-based; 79 iBT), IELTS (minimum score 6). *Application deadline:* Applications are processed on a rolling basis. Application fee: $60 ($65 for international students). Electronic applications accepted. *Expenses: Tuition:* Full-time $13,824; part-time $1728 per course. One-time fee: $160. *Financial support:* Career-related internships or fieldwork, scholarships/grants, and tuition waivers (partial) available. Support available to part-time students. Financial award application deadline: 6/30; financial award applicants required to submit FAFSA. *Unit head:* School of Business and Management, 800-628-8648, Fax: 858-642-8719, E-mail: sobm@nu.edu. *Application contact:* Louis Cruz, Interim Vice President for Enrollment Services, 800-628-8648, E-mail: advisor@nu.edu.
Website: http://www.nu.edu/OurPrograms/SchoolOfBusinessAndManagement.html.

Neumann University, Program in Sports Management, Aston, PA 19014-1298. Offers MS. Part-time programs available. *Degree requirements:* For master's, thesis or alternative, experiential component. Electronic applications accepted.

New England College, Program in Sports and Recreation Management: Coaching, Henniker, NH 03242-3293. Offers MS. *Entrance requirements:* For master's, resume, 2 letters of reference.

New Mexico Highlands University, Graduate Studies, College of Arts and Sciences, Department of Exercise and Sport Sciences, Las Vegas, NM 87701. Offers human performance and sport (MA), including human performance and sport sciences, sports administration, teacher education. Part-time programs available. *Faculty:* 5 full-time (2 women). *Students:* 22 full-time (10 women), 28 part-time (8 women); includes 35 minority (13 Black or African American, non-Hispanic/Latino; 1 American Indian or Alaska Native, non-Hispanic/Latino; 1 Asian, non-Hispanic/Latino; 19 Hispanic/Latino; 1 Two or more races, non-Hispanic/Latino), 3 international. Average age 31. 18 applicants, 83% accepted, 13 enrolled. In 2013, 22 master's awarded. *Degree requirements:* For master's, comprehensive exam, thesis or alternative. *Entrance requirements:* For master's, minimum undergraduate GPA of 3.0. Additional exam requirements/recommendations for international students: Required—TOEFL (minimum score 540 paper-based). *Application deadline:* For fall admission, 8/1 priority date for domestic students. Applications are processed on a rolling basis. Application fee: $15. *Expenses:* Tuition, state resident: full-time $4278; part-time $178 per credit hour. Tuition, nonresident: full-time $6716; part-time $281 per credit hour. One-time fee: $15. *Financial support:* Career-related internships or fieldwork, Federal Work-Study, institutionally sponsored loans, scholarships/grants, tuition waivers (partial), and unspecified assistantships available. Support available to part-time students. Financial award application deadline: 3/1; financial award applicants required to submit FAFSA. *Faculty research:* Child obesity and physical inactivity, body composition and fitness assessment, motor development, sport marketing, sport finance. *Unit head:* Dr. Yongseek Kim, Department Head, 505-454-3490, E-mail: ykim@nmhu.edu. *Application contact:* Diane Trujillo, Administrative Assistant, Graduate Studies, 505-454-3266, Fax: 505-426-2117, E-mail: dtrujillo@nmhu.edu.

New York University, School of Continuing and Professional Studies, The Preston Robert Tisch Center for Hospitality, Tourism, and Sports Management, Program in Sports Business, New York, NY 10012-1019. Offers global sports media (MS); professional and collegiate sports operations (MS); sports business (Advanced Certificate); sports law (MS); sports marketing and sales (MS). Part-time and evening/weekend programs available. *Faculty:* 8 full-time (3 women), 24 part-time/adjunct (7 women). *Students:* 75 full-time (27 women), 56 part-time (17 women); includes 23 minority (8 Black or African American, non-Hispanic/Latino; 6 Asian, non-Hispanic/Latino; 7 Hispanic/Latino; 2 Two or more races, non-Hispanic/Latino), 39 international. Average age 26. 136 applicants, 79% accepted, 59 enrolled. In 2013, 32 master's, 5 other advanced degrees awarded. *Degree requirements:* For master's, thesis. *Entrance requirements:* For master's, bachelor's degree, resume with relevant professional work, internship or volunteer experience, two letters of recommendation, statement of purpose. Additional exam requirements/recommendations for international students: Required—TOEFL (minimum score 600 paper-based; 100 iBT), IELTS (minimum score 7). *Application deadline:* For fall admission, 2/1 priority date for domestic and international students; for spring admission, 10/15 priority date for domestic students, 8/15 priority date for international students. Applications are processed on a rolling basis. Application fee: $150. Electronic applications accepted. *Expenses: Tuition:* Full-time $35,856; part-time $1494 per unit. *Required fees:* $1408; $64 per unit. $473 per term. Tuition and fees vary according to course load and program. *Financial support:* In 2013–14, 51 students received support, including 50 fellowships (averaging $3,118 per year); scholarships/grants also available. Support available to part-time students. Financial award application deadline: 2/15. *Faculty research:* Implications of college football's bowl coalition series from a legal, economic, and academic perspective; social history of sports. *Unit head:* Bjorn Hanson, Division Dean and Clinical Professor, 212-998-7100. *Application contact:* Admissions Office, 212-998-7100, E-mail: scps.gradadmissions@nyu.edu.
Website: http://www.scps.nyu.edu/areas-of-study/tisch/graduate-programs/ms-sports-business/.

North Carolina Central University, College of Behavioral and Social Sciences, Department of Physical Education and Recreation, Durham, NC 27707-3129. Offers athletic administration (MS); physical education (MS); recreation administration (MS); therapeutic recreation (MS). Part-time and evening/weekend programs available. *Degree requirements:* For master's, one foreign language, comprehensive exam, thesis. *Entrance requirements:* For master's, GRE, minimum GPA of 3.0 in major, 2.5 overall. Additional exam requirements/recommendations for international students: Required—TOEFL. *Faculty research:* Physical activity patterns of children with disabilities, physical fitness test of North Carolina school children, exercise physiology, motor learning/development.

North Carolina State University, Graduate School, College of Natural Resources, Department of Parks, Recreation and Tourism Management, Raleigh, NC 27695. Offers natural resource management (MPRTM, MS); park and recreation management (MPRTM, MS); parks, recreation and tourism management (PhD); recreational sport management (MPRTM, MS); spatial information science (MPRTM, MS); tourism policy and development (MPRTM, MS). *Degree requirements:* For master's, thesis (for some programs); for doctorate, thesis/dissertation. *Entrance requirements:* For master's and doctorate, GRE General Test. Additional exam requirements/recommendations for international students: Required—TOEFL. Electronic applications accepted. *Faculty research:* Tourism policy and development, spatial information systems, natural resource management, recreational sports management, park and recreation management.

North Central College, Graduate and Continuing Studies Programs, Program in Leadership Studies, Naperville, IL 60566-7063. Offers higher education leadership (MLD); professional leadership (MLD); social entrepreneurship (MLD); sports leadership (MLD). Part-time and evening/weekend programs available. *Faculty:* 9 full-time (1 woman), 16 part-time/adjunct (9 women). *Students:* 42 full-time (24 women), 24 part-time (8 women); includes 16 minority (10 Black or African American, non-Hispanic/Latino; 6 Hispanic/Latino), 4 international. Average age 28. 104 applicants, 51% accepted, 23 enrolled. In 2013, 36 master's awarded. *Degree requirements:* For master's, thesis optional, project. *Entrance requirements:* For master's, interview. Additional exam requirements/recommendations for international students: Required—TOEFL (minimum score 570 paper-based; 90 iBT). *Application deadline:* For fall admission, 8/15 for domestic students; for winter admission, 12/1 for domestic students; for spring admission, 2/1 for domestic students. Applications are processed on a rolling basis. Application fee: $25. *Expenses:* Contact institution. *Financial support:* In 2013–14, 1 student received support. Scholarships/grants available. Support available to part-time students. *Unit head:* Dr. Thomas Cavenagh, Program Coordinator, Leadership Studies, 630-637-5285. *Application contact:* Wendy Kulpinski, Director of Graduate and Continuing Education Admission, 630-637-5808, Fax: 630-637-5844, E-mail: wekulpinski@noctrl.edu.

North Dakota State University, College of Graduate and Interdisciplinary Studies, College of Human Development and Education, Department of Health, Nutrition, and Exercise Sciences, Fargo, ND 58108. Offers athletic training (MS); dietetics (MS); exercise science (MS); nutrition science (MS); sport pedagogy (MS); sports recreation management (MS). Part-time and evening/weekend programs available. Postbaccalaureate distance learning degree programs offered (no on-campus study). *Faculty:* 17 full-time (14 women). *Students:* 54 full-time (30 women), 18 part-time (8 women); includes 5 minority (2 Hispanic/Latino; 3 Two or more races, non-Hispanic/Latino), 2 international. Average age 28. 27 applicants, 78% accepted, 16 enrolled. In 2013, 23 master's awarded. *Degree requirements:* For master's, thesis (for some programs). *Entrance requirements:* For master's, minimum GPA of 3.0. Additional exam requirements/recommendations for international students: Required—TOEFL (minimum score 525 paper-based; 71 iBT). *Application deadline:* For fall admission, 3/1 priority date for domestic and international students. Applications are processed on a rolling basis. Application fee: $35. Electronic applications accepted. *Financial support:* In 2013–14, 18 teaching assistantships with full tuition reimbursements (averaging $6,500 per year) were awarded. Financial award application deadline: 3/31. *Faculty research:* Biomechanics, sport specialization, recreation, nutrition, athletic training. *Unit head:* Dr. Margaret Fitzgerald, Head, 701-231-7474, Fax: 701-231-8872, E-mail: margaret.fitzgerald@ndsu.edu. *Application contact:* Dr. Gary Liguori, Graduate Coordinator, 701-231-7474, Fax: 701-231-6524.
Website: http://www.ndsu.edu/hnes/.

Northern Illinois University, Graduate School, College of Education, Department of Kinesiology and Physical Education, De Kalb, IL 60115-2854. Offers physical education (MS Ed); sport management (MS). Part-time and evening/weekend programs available. *Faculty:* 21 full-time (12 women). *Students:* 66 full-time (22 women), 55 part-time (24 women); includes 29 minority (15 Black or African American, non-Hispanic/Latino; 3 Asian, non-Hispanic/Latino; 8 Hispanic/Latino; 3 Two or more races, non-Hispanic/Latino), 4 international. Average age 26. 91 applicants, 63% accepted, 36 enrolled. In 2013, 52 master's awarded. *Degree requirements:* For master's, comprehensive exam, thesis optional. *Entrance requirements:* For master's, GRE General Test, minimum GPA of 2.75, undergraduate major in related area. Additional exam requirements/recommendations for international students: Required—TOEFL (minimum score 550 paper-based). *Application deadline:* For fall admission, 6/1 for domestic students, 5/1 for international students; for spring admission, 11/1 for domestic students, 10/1 for international students. Applications are processed on a rolling basis. Application fee: $40. Electronic applications accepted. *Financial support:* In 2013–14, 6 research assistantships with full tuition reimbursements, 33 teaching assistantships with full tuition reimbursements were awarded; fellowships with full tuition reimbursements, career-related internships or fieldwork, Federal Work-Study, scholarships/grants, tuition waivers (full), and unspecified assistantships also available. Support available to part-time students. Financial award applicants required to submit FAFSA. *Faculty research:* Leadership in athletic training, motor development, dance education, gait analysis, fat phobia. *Unit head:* Dr. Paul Carpenter, Chair, 815-753-8284, Fax: 815-753-1413, E-mail: knpe@niu.edu. *Application contact:* Dr. Laurie Zittel, Director, Graduate Studies, 815-753-1425, E-mail: lzape@niu.edu.
Website: http://cedu.niu.edu/knpe/.

Northern State University, MS Ed Program in Sport Performance and Leadership, Aberdeen, SD 57401-7198. Offers MS Ed. Part-time programs available. *Faculty:* 4 full-time (2 women), 1 (woman) part-time/adjunct. *Students:* 12 full-time (3 women), 5 part-time (3 women). Average age 25. 17 applicants, 53% accepted, 7 enrolled. In 2013, 8 master's awarded. *Degree requirements:* For master's, comprehensive exam, thesis optional. *Entrance requirements:* For master's, minimum GPA of 2.75. Additional exam requirements/recommendations for international students: Required—TOEFL (minimum score 550 paper-based; 78 iBT), IELTS (minimum score 6). *Application deadline:* Applications are processed on a rolling basis. Application fee: $35. Electronic applications accepted. *Expenses:* Tuition, state resident: full-time $3634. Tuition, nonresident: full-time $7690. One-time fee: $35 full-time. Part-time tuition and fees vary according to course load, degree level, campus/location and reciprocity agreements. *Financial support:* In 2013–14, 4 students received support, including 16 teaching assistantships (averaging $6,478 per year); career-related internships or fieldwork, Federal Work-Study, institutionally sponsored loans, scholarships/grants, and unspecified assistantships also available. Support available to part-time students. Financial award application deadline: 3/1; financial award applicants required to submit FAFSA. *Unit head:* Dr. Constance Geier, Dean of Education, 605-626-2558, Fax: 605-626-7190, E-mail: connie.geier@northern.edu. *Application contact:* Tammy K. Griffith,

Program Assistant, 605-626-2558, Fax: 605-626-7190, E-mail: tammy.griffith@northern.edu.

Northwestern University, School of Professional Studies, Program in Sports Administration, Evanston, IL 60208. Offers MA.

Ohio University, Graduate College, College of Business, Department of Sports Administration, Athens, OH 45701-2979. Offers athletic administration (MS); sports administration (MSA). Part-time and evening/weekend programs available. Postbaccalaureate distance learning degree programs offered (minimal on-campus study). *Degree requirements:* For master's, 11-week internship. *Entrance requirements:* For master's, interview. Additional exam requirements/recommendations for international students: Required—TOEFL (minimum score 600 paper-based; 100 iBT) or IELTS (minimum score 7.5). Electronic applications accepted. *Faculty research:* Sport management, sport marketing, sports and technology, career development.

Ohio University, Graduate College, Gladys W. and David H. Patton College of Education and Human Services, Department of Recreation and Sport Pedagogy, Program in Coaching Education, Athens, OH 45701-2979. Offers MS. *Entrance requirements:* For master's, GRE. Additional exam requirements/recommendations for international students: Required—TOEFL (minimum score 550 paper-based; 80 iBT) or IELTS (minimum score 6.5). Electronic applications accepted. *Faculty research:* Sports, physical activity, athletes.

Old Dominion University, Darden College of Education, Program in Physical Education, Sport Management Emphasis, Norfolk, VA 23529. Offers MS Ed. Part-time and evening/weekend programs available. Postbaccalaureate distance learning degree programs offered (no on-campus study). *Faculty:* 5 full-time (2 women), 1 part-time/adjunct (0 women). *Students:* 24 full-time (10 women), 34 part-time (13 women); includes 14 minority (11 Black or African American, non-Hispanic/Latino; 3 Hispanic/Latino), 1 international. Average age 26. 63 applicants, 70% accepted, 36 enrolled. In 2013, 15 master's awarded. *Degree requirements:* For master's, comprehensive exam, thesis or alternative, internship, research project. *Entrance requirements:* For master's, GRE, GMAT, or MAT, minimum GPA of 2.8 overall, 3.0 in major. Additional exam requirements/recommendations for international students: Required—TOEFL (minimum score 500 paper-based). *Application deadline:* For fall admission, 3/1 for domestic students; for spring admission, 11/1 for domestic students. Application fee: $50. *Expenses:* Tuition, state resident: full-time $9888; part-time $412 per credit. Tuition, nonresident: full-time $25,152; part-time $1048 per credit. *Required fees:* $59 per semester. One-time fee: $50. *Financial support:* In 2013–14, 1 student received support, including 1 teaching assistantship (averaging $9,000 per year); unspecified assistantships also available. Financial award application deadline: 4/15; financial award applicants required to submit FAFSA. *Faculty research:* Leadership, consumer behavior in sport, sport finance, sport marketing, sport involvement. *Total annual research expenditures:* $50,000. *Unit head:* Dr. Lynn Ridinger, Graduate Program Director, 757-683-4353, Fax: 757-683-4270, E-mail: lridinge@odu.edu. *Application contact:* William Heffelfinger, Director of Graduate Admissions, 757-683-5554, Fax: 757-683-3255, E-mail: gradadmit@odu.edu.
Website: http://education.odu.edu/esper/academics/sportsman/graduate/graduate.shtml.

Purdue University, Graduate School, College of Health and Human Sciences, Department of Health and Kinesiology, West Lafayette, IN 47907. Offers athletic training education administration (MS, PhD); biomechanics (MS, PhD); exercise physiology (MS, PhD); health education (MS, PhD); history/philosophy of sport (MS, PhD); motor control and development (MS, PhD); physical education pedagogy (PhD); physical education teacher education (MS); recreation and sport management (MS, PhD); sport and exercise psychology (MS, PhD). Part-time programs available. *Faculty:* 16 full-time (8 women), 20 part-time/adjunct (3 women). *Students:* 43 full-time (29 women), 21 part-time (11 women); includes 6 minority (2 Black or African American, non-Hispanic/Latino; 1 American Indian or Alaska Native, non-Hispanic/Latino; 1 Asian, non-Hispanic/Latino; 2 Two or more races, non-Hispanic/Latino), 12 international. Average age 28. 103 applicants, 32% accepted, 16 enrolled. In 2013, 15 master's, 8 doctorates awarded. *Degree requirements:* For master's, thesis optional; for doctorate, comprehensive exam, thesis/dissertation, qualifying examination, preliminary examination. *Entrance requirements:* For master's, GRE General Test (minimum score 1000 combined verbal and quantitative), minimum undergraduate GPA of 3.0 or equivalent; for doctorate, GRE General Test (minimum score 1100 combined verbal and quantitative), minimum undergraduate GPA of 3.0 or equivalent; master's degree with minimum GPA of 3.25 (recommended). Additional exam requirements/recommendations for international students: Required—TOEFL (minimum score 77 iBT); Recommended—TWE. *Application deadline:* For fall admission, 4/30 for domestic and international students; for spring admission, 10/15 for domestic and international students. Applications are processed on a rolling basis. Application fee: $60 ($75 for international students). Electronic applications accepted. *Financial support:* Fellowships with partial tuition reimbursements, research assistantships with partial tuition reimbursements, teaching assistantships with partial tuition reimbursements, and Federal Work-Study available. Support available to part-time students. Financial award applicants required to submit FAFSA. *Faculty research:* Wellness, motivation, teaching effectiveness, learning and development. *Unit head:* Dr. Timothy P. Gavin, Head of the Graduate Program, 765-494-3178, Fax: 765-494-1239, E-mail: gavin1@purdue.edu. *Application contact:* Lisa Duncan, Graduate Contact, 765-494-3162, E-mail: llduncan@purdue.edu.
Website: http://www.purdue.edu/hhs/hk/.

Robert Morris University, Graduate Studies, School of Education and Social Sciences, Moon Township, PA 15108-1189. Offers business education (MS); education (Postbaccalaureate Certificate); instructional leadership (MS), including education, sport management; instructional management and leadership (PhD). *Accreditation:* Teacher Education Accreditation Council. Part-time and evening/weekend programs available. Postbaccalaureate distance learning degree programs offered (no on-campus study). *Faculty:* 20 full-time (9 women), 6 part-time/adjunct (3 women). *Students:* 203 part-time (127 women); includes 20 minority (11 Black or African American, non-Hispanic/Latino; 3 Asian, non-Hispanic/Latino; 2 Hispanic/Latino; 4 Two or more races, non-Hispanic/Latino), 4 international. Average age 26. 126 applicants, 44% accepted, 43 enrolled. In 2013, 102 master's, 6 doctorates awarded. *Degree requirements:* For doctorate, thesis/dissertation. *Entrance requirements:* Additional exam requirements/recommendations for international students: Required—TOEFL (minimum score 550 paper-based; 79 iBT). *Application deadline:* For fall admission, 7/1 priority date for domestic and international students; for spring admission, 11/1 priority date for domestic and international students. Applications are processed on a rolling basis. Application fee: $35. Electronic applications accepted. *Expenses:* Contact institution. *Unit head:* Dr. Mary Ann Rafoth, Dean, 412-397-3488, Fax: 412-397-2524, E-mail: rafoth@rmu.edu. *Application contact:* Assistant Dean, Graduate Admissions, 412-397-5200, Fax: 412-397-5915, E-mail: graduateadmissions@rmu.edu.
Website: http://www.rmu.edu/web/cms/schools/sess/.

Robert Morris University Illinois, Morris Graduate School of Management, Chicago, IL 60605. Offers accounting (MBA); accounting/finance (MBA); business analytics (MIS); design and media (MM); educational technology (MM); health care administration (MM); higher education administration (MM); human resource management (MBA); information security (MIS); information systems (MIS); law enforcement administration (MM); management (MBA); management/finance (MBA); management/human resource management (MBA); mobile computing (MIS); sports administration (MM). Part-time and evening/weekend programs available. *Faculty:* 12 full-time (5 women), 18 part-time/adjunct (4 women). *Students:* 240 full-time (128 women), 195 part-time (127 women); includes 242 minority (147 Black or African American, non-Hispanic/Latino; 2 American Indian or Alaska Native, non-Hispanic/Latino; 24 Asian, non-Hispanic/Latino; 63 Hispanic/Latino; 1 Native Hawaiian or other Pacific Islander, non-Hispanic/Latino; 5 Two or more races, non-Hispanic/Latino), 26 international. Average age 33. 210 applicants, 63% accepted, 116 enrolled. In 2013, 278 master's awarded. *Entrance requirements:* For master's, official transcripts, two letters of recommendation. Additional exam requirements/recommendations for international students: Required—TOEFL (minimum score 550 paper-based). *Application deadline:* Applications are processed on a rolling basis. Application fee: $20 ($100 for international students). Electronic applications accepted. *Expenses: Tuition:* Full-time $14,400; part-time $2400 per course. *Financial support:* In 2013–14, 488 students received support. Federal Work-Study and scholarships/grants available. Support available to part-time students. Financial award applicants required to submit FAFSA. *Unit head:* Kayed Akkawi, Dean for Morris Graduate School of Management, 312-935-6050, Fax: 312-935-6020, E-mail: kakkawi@robertmorris.edu. *Application contact:* Fernando Villeda, Dean of Graduate Enrollment, 312-935-6050, Fax: 312-935-6020, E-mail: fvilleda@robertmorris.edu.

St. Cloud State University, School of Graduate Studies, School of Health and Human Services, Department of Kinesiology, St. Cloud, MN 56301-4498. Offers exercise science (MS); sports management (MS). *Degree requirements:* For master's, thesis or alternative. *Entrance requirements:* For master's, GRE General Test, minimum overall GPA of 2.75 in previous undergraduate and graduate records or in last half of undergraduate work. Additional exam requirements/recommendations for international students: Required—Michigan English Language Assessment Battery; Recommended—TOEFL (minimum score 550 paper-based; 79 iBT), IELTS (minimum score 6.5). Electronic applications accepted.

St. John's University, College of Professional Studies, Department of Sport Management, Queens, NY 11439. Offers MPS. Part-time and evening/weekend programs available. *Students:* 59 full-time (24 women), 22 part-time (8 women); includes 26 minority (12 Black or African American, non-Hispanic/Latino; 1 American Indian or Alaska Native, non-Hispanic/Latino; 3 Asian, non-Hispanic/Latino; 9 Hispanic/Latino; 1 Two or more races, non-Hispanic/Latino), 13 international. Average age 26. 122 applicants, 76% accepted, 32 enrolled. In 2013, 22 master's awarded. *Degree requirements:* For master's, comprehensive exam, thesis optional, capstone project, internship. *Entrance requirements:* For master's, bachelor's degree from regionally-accredited college or university, minimum GPA of 3.0, 2 letters of recommendation, 300-word essay. Additional exam requirements/recommendations for international students: Required—TOEFL (minimum score 600 paper-based; 100 iBT), IELTS (minimum score 5.5). *Application deadline:* For fall admission, 5/1 priority date for domestic and international students; for spring admission, 11/1 priority date for domestic and international students. Applications are processed on a rolling basis. Application fee: $70. Electronic applications accepted. *Expenses: Tuition:* Full-time $19,800; part-time $1100 per credit. *Required fees:* $170 per semester. *Faculty research:* The Olympic Movement, sports economics, administration of intercollegiate athletics, sport management education. *Unit head:* Prof. Glenn Gerstner, Chair, 718-990-7474, E-mail: gerstneg@stjohns.edu. *Application contact:* Robert Medrano, Director of Graduate Admissions, 718-990-1601, Fax: 718-990-5686, E-mail: gradhelp@stjohns.edu.
Website: http://www.stjohns.edu/academics/schools-and-colleges/college-professional-studies/programs-and-majors/sport-management-masters-professional-studies.

Saint Leo University, Graduate Business Studies, Saint Leo, FL 33574-6665. Offers accounting (M Acc, MBA); business (MBA); health care management (MBA); human resource management (MBA); information security management (MBA); marketing (MBA); marketing research and social media analytics (MBA); project management (MBA); sport business (MBA). Part-time and evening/weekend programs available. Postbaccalaureate distance learning degree programs offered (no on-campus study). *Faculty:* 48 full-time (12 women), 61 part-time/adjunct (21 women). *Students:* 1,855 full-time (1,020 women); includes 810 minority (587 Black or African American, non-Hispanic/Latino; 7 American Indian or Alaska Native, non-Hispanic/Latino; 36 Asian, non-Hispanic/Latino; 161 Hispanic/Latino; 3 Native Hawaiian or other Pacific Islander, non-Hispanic/Latino; 16 Two or more races, non-Hispanic/Latino), 33 international. Average age 38. In 2013, 905 master's awarded. *Entrance requirements:* For master's, GMAT (minimum score 500 if applicant has less than 3.0 in the last two years of undergraduate study), bachelor's degree with minimum GPA of 3.0 in the last 60 hours of coursework from regionally-accredited college or university; 2 years of professional work experience; resume; 2 letters of recommendation. Additional exam requirements/recommendations for international students: Required—TOEFL (minimum score 550 paper-based; 80 iBT). *Application deadline:* For fall admission, 7/1 priority date for domestic and international students; for spring admission, 11/12 priority date for domestic students; 11/1 for international students. Applications are processed on a rolling basis. Application fee: $80. Electronic applications accepted. *Expenses: Tuition:* Full-time $12,114; part-time $673 per semester hour. Tuition and fees vary according to degree level, campus/location and program. *Financial support:* In 2013–14, 116 students received support. Career-related internships or fieldwork, Federal Work-Study, scholarships/grants, and health care benefits available. Financial award application deadline: 3/1; financial award applicants required to submit FAFSA. *Unit head:* Dr. Lorrie McGovern, Assistant Dean, Graduate Studies in Business, 352-588-7390, Fax: 352-588-8585, E-mail: mbaslu@saintleo.edu. *Application contact:* Joshua Stagner, Director of Graduate Admission, 800-707-8846, Fax: 352-588-7873, E-mail: grad.admissions@saintleo.edu.
Website: http://www.saintleo.edu/academics/graduate.aspx.

Saint Mary's College of California, School of Liberal Arts, Department of Kinesiology, Moraga, CA 94575. Offers sport management (MA); sport studies (MA). Part-time programs available. *Degree requirements:* For master's, thesis or special project. *Entrance requirements:* For master's, minimum GPA of 2.75, BA in physical education or related field, or professional experience. Electronic applications accepted. *Expenses:* Contact institution. *Faculty research:* Moral development in sport, applied motor learning, achievement motivation, sport history.

St. Thomas University, School of Business, Department of Management, Miami Gardens, FL 33054-6459. Offers accounting (MBA); general management (MSM, Certificate); health management (MBA, MSM, Certificate); human resource management (MBA, MSM, Certificate); international business (MBA, MIB, MSM, Certificate); justice administration (MSM, Certificate); management accounting (MSM, Certificate); public management (MSM, Certificate); sports administration (MS). Part-time and evening/weekend programs available. *Degree requirements:* For master's, comprehensive exam. *Entrance requirements:* For master's, interview, minimum GPA of 3.0 or GMAT. Additional exam requirements/recommendations for international students: Required—TOEFL (minimum score 550 paper-based; 79 iBT). Electronic applications accepted.

Sports Management

San Diego State University, Graduate and Research Affairs, College of Business Administration, Sports Business Management Program, San Diego, CA 92182. Offers MBA.

Seattle University, College of Arts and Sciences, Center for the Study of Sport and Exercise, Seattle, WA 98122-1090. Offers MSAL, JD/MSAL. Part-time and evening/weekend programs available. *Faculty:* 2 full-time (1 woman), 1 part-time/adjunct (0 women). *Students:* 2 full-time (1 woman), 37 part-time (22 women); includes 11 minority (1 Black or African American, non-Hispanic/Latino; 1 Asian, non-Hispanic/Latino; 5 Hispanic/Latino; 1 Native Hawaiian or other Pacific Islander, non-Hispanic/Latino; 3 Two or more races, non-Hispanic/Latino). Average age 26. 62 applicants, 45% accepted, 16 enrolled. In 2013, 22 master's awarded. *Degree requirements:* For master's, thesis or applied inquiry. *Entrance requirements:* For master's, GRE (Verbal, Quantitative, and Analytical), minimum GPA of 3.0, three letters of recommendation, essay, resume. Additional exam requirements/recommendations for international students: Required—TOEFL, IELTS. *Application deadline:* For fall admission, 2/15 for domestic and international students. Application fee: $55. Electronic applications accepted. *Financial support:* In 2013–14, 14 students received support. Research assistantships and scholarships/grants available. Financial award applicants required to submit FAFSA. *Faculty research:* Sport consumer behavior, strategic management of sport organizations, leadership in sport, organizational behavior, lifestyle sports. *Total annual research expenditures:* $1,000. *Unit head:* Dr. Dan Tripps, Director, 206-398-4605, E-mail: trippsd@seattleu.edu. *Application contact:* Janet Shandley, Associate Dean of Graduate Admissions, 206-296-5900, Fax: 206-298-5656, E-mail: grad_admissions@seattleu.edu.
Website: https://www.seattleu.edu/artsci/departments/sport-exercise/.

Seton Hall University, Stillman School of Business, Programs in Business Administration, South Orange, NJ 07079-2697. Offers accounting (MBA); finance (MBA); information technology management (MBA); international business (MBA); management (MBA); marketing (MBA); sport management (MBA); supply chain management (MBA). Part-time and evening/weekend programs available. *Faculty:* 32 full-time (6 women), 20 part-time/adjunct (3 women). *Students:* 67 full-time (23 women), 162 part-time (66 women); includes 28 minority (7 Black or African American, non-Hispanic/Latino; 7 Asian, non-Hispanic/Latino; 6 Hispanic/Latino; 8 Native Hawaiian or other Pacific Islander, non-Hispanic/Latino). Average age 31. 216 applicants, 28% accepted, 39 enrolled. In 2013, 139 master's awarded. *Degree requirements:* For master's, 20 hours of community service (Social Responsibility Project). *Entrance requirements:* For master's, GMAT, GRE or CPA, advanced degree from AACSB institution, MS in a business discipline, professional degree (MD, JD, PhD, DVM, DDS, etc.), minimum undergraduate GPA of 3.0. Additional exam requirements/recommendations for international students: Required—TOEFL (minimum score 102 iBT), IELTS or PTE. *Application deadline:* For fall admission, 5/31 priority date for domestic students, 3/31 priority date for international students; for spring admission, 10/31 priority date for domestic students, 9/30 priority date for international students. Applications are processed on a rolling basis. Application fee: $75. Electronic applications accepted. *Financial support:* In 2013–14, research assistantships with full tuition reimbursements (averaging $23,956 per year) were awarded; career-related internships or fieldwork, Federal Work-Study, scholarships/grants, and unspecified assistantships also available. Support available to part-time students. Financial award application deadline: 6/30; financial award applicants required to submit FAFSA. *Faculty research:* Sport, hedge funds, international business, legal issues, disclosure and branding. *Total annual research expenditures:* $68,000. *Unit head:* Dr. Joyce Strawser, Dean, 973-761-9013, Fax: 973-761-9217, E-mail: joyce.strawser@shu.edu. *Application contact:* Catherine Bianchi, Director of Graduate Admissions, 973-761-9262, Fax: 973-761-9208, E-mail: catherine.bianchi@shu.edu.
Website: http://www.shu.edu/academics/business.

Seton Hill University, Program in Business Administration, Greensburg, PA 15601. Offers accounting (MBA); entrepreneurship (MBA, Certificate); management (MBA); sports management (MBA). Part-time and evening/weekend programs available. *Faculty:* 9 full-time (3 women), 6 part-time/adjunct (1 woman). *Students:* 37 full-time (15 women), 52 part-time (34 women); includes 4 minority (3 Black or African American, non-Hispanic/Latino; 1 Hispanic/Latino), 8 international. Average age 30. 93 applicants, 47% accepted, 28 enrolled. In 2013, 15 master's awarded. *Entrance requirements:* For master's, resume, 3 letters of recommendation, personal statement, transcripts. Additional exam requirements/recommendations for international students: Required—TOEFL (minimum score 600 paper-based; 100 iBT), IELTS (minimum score 6.5). *Application deadline:* Applications are processed on a rolling basis. Application fee: $0. Electronic applications accepted. *Expenses: Tuition:* Full-time $14,220; part-time $790 per credit. *Required fees:* $700; $34 per credit. $50 per semester. *Financial support:* Federal Work-Study, scholarships/grants, and tuition discounts available. Financial award application deadline: 8/15. *Faculty research:* Entrepreneurship, leadership and strategy, knowledge management, sports management, human resources. *Unit head:* Dr. Douglas Nelson, Director, 724-830-4738, E-mail: dnelson@setonhill.edu. *Application contact:* Laurel Komarny, Program Counselor, 724-838-4209, E-mail: lkomarny@setonhill.edu.
Website: http://www.setonhill.edu/academics/graduate_programs/mba.

Sonoma State University, School of Science and Technology, Department of Kinesiology, Rohnert Park, CA 94928. Offers adapted physical education (MA); interdisciplinary (MA); interdisciplinary pre-occupational therapy (MA); lifetime physical activity (MA), including coach education, fitness and wellness; physical education (MA); pre-physical therapy (MA). Part-time programs available. *Faculty:* 5 full-time (3 women). *Students:* 1 full-time (0 women), 11 part-time (3 women); includes 2 minority (1 Hispanic/Latino; 1 Two or more races, non-Hispanic/Latino). Average age 29. *Degree requirements:* For master's, thesis, oral exam. *Entrance requirements:* For master's, minimum GPA of 2.8. Additional exam requirements/recommendations for international students: Required—TOEFL (minimum score 500 paper-based). *Application deadline:* For fall admission, 11/30 for domestic students; for spring admission, 9/1 for domestic students. Applications are processed on a rolling basis. Application fee: $55. *Expenses:* Tuition, state resident: full-time $8500. Tuition, nonresident: full-time $12,964. *Required fees:* $1762. *Financial support:* Career-related internships or fieldwork available. Financial award application deadline: 3/2; financial award applicants required to submit FAFSA. *Unit head:* Dr. Elaine McHugh, Chair, 707-664-2660, E-mail: elaine.mchugh@sonoma.edu. *Application contact:* Dr. Lauren Morimoto, Graduate Coordinator, 707-664-2479, E-mail: morimoto@sonoma.edu.
Website: http://www.sonoma.edu/kinesiology/.

Southeast Missouri State University, School of Graduate Studies, Harrison College of Business, Cape Girardeau, MO 63701-4799. Offers accounting (MBA); entrepreneurship (MBA); environmental management (MBA); financial management (MBA); general management (MBA); health administration (MBA); industrial management (MBA); international business (MBA); organizational management (MS); sport management (MBA). *Accreditation:* AACSB. Part-time and evening/weekend programs available. Postbaccalaureate distance learning degree programs offered (no on-campus study). *Faculty:* 27 full-time (7 women), 1 (woman) part-time/adjunct. *Students:* 59 full-time (27 women), 83 part-time (28 women); includes 10 minority (5 Black or African American, non-Hispanic/Latino; 3 Asian, non-Hispanic/Latino; 1 Hispanic/Latino; 1 Two or more races, non-Hispanic/Latino), 40 international. Average age 28. 77 applicants, 79% accepted, 48 enrolled. In 2013, 50 master's awarded. *Degree requirements:* For master's, variable foreign language requirement, comprehensive exam (for some programs), thesis or alternative, applied research project. *Entrance requirements:* For master's, GMAT or GRE, minimum undergraduate GPA of 2.5, C or better in prerequisite courses. Additional exam requirements/recommendations for international students: Required—TOEFL (minimum score 550 paper-based; 79 iBT), IELTS (minimum score 6), PTE (minimum score 53). *Application deadline:* For fall admission, 8/1 for domestic students, 6/1 for international students; for spring admission, 11/21 for domestic students, 10/1 for international students; for summer admission, 5/15 for domestic students. Applications are processed on a rolling basis. Application fee: $30 ($40 for international students). Electronic applications accepted. *Expenses:* Tuition, state resident: full-time $5139; part-time $285.50 per credit hour. Tuition, nonresident: full-time $9099; part-time $505.50 per credit hour. *Financial support:* In 2013–14, 52 students received support, including 12 teaching assistantships with full tuition reimbursements available (averaging $8,144 per year); career-related internships or fieldwork, Federal Work-Study, scholarships/grants, traineeships, tuition waivers (full), and unspecified assistantships also available. Financial award application deadline: 6/30; financial award applicants required to submit FAFSA. *Faculty research:* Ethics, corporate finance, generational difference, leadership, organizational justice. *Unit head:* Dr. Kenneth A. Heischmidt, Director, Graduate Business Studies, 573-651-2912, Fax: 573-651-5032, E-mail: kheischmidt@semo.edu. *Application contact:* Gail Amick, Admissions Specialist, 573-651-2590, Fax: 573-651-5936, E-mail: gamick@semo.edu.
Website: http://www.semo.edu/mba.

Southern Methodist University, Annette Caldwell Simmons School of Education and Human Development, Department of Allied Physiology and Wellness, Dallas, TX 75275. Offers sport management (MS). Program offered jointly with Cox School of Business. *Entrance requirements:* For master's, GMAT, resume, essays, transcripts from all colleges and universities attended, two references. Additional exam requirements/recommendations for international students: Required—TOEFL or PTE.

Southern Nazarene University, College of Professional and Graduate Studies, School of Kinesiology, Bethany, OK 73008. Offers sports management and administration (MA). *Entrance requirements:* For master's, baccalaureate degree from regionally-accredited college or university, official transcripts from each institution attended, three letters of recommendation, essay. *Unit head:* Stephane Shellenberger, Chair, 405-717-6225, Fax: 405-491-6302, E-mail: sshellen@snu.edu.
Website: http://snu.edu/school-of-kinesiology.

Southern New Hampshire University, School of Business, Manchester, NH 03106-1045. Offers accounting (MBA, MS, Graduate Certificate); accounting finance (MS); accounting/auditing (MS); accounting/forensic accounting (MS); accounting/taxation (MS); athletic administration (MBA, Graduate Certificate); business administration (IMBA, MBA, Certificate, Graduate Certificate), including accounting (Certificate), business administration (MBA), business information systems (Graduate Certificate), human resource management (Certificate); corporate social responsibility (MBA); entrepreneurship (MBA); finance (MBA, MS, Graduate Certificate); finance/corporate finance (MS); finance/investments and securities (MS); forensic accounting (MBA); healthcare informatics (MBA); healthcare management (MBA); human resource management (Graduate Certificate); information technology (MS, Graduate Certificate); information technology management (MBA); international business (Graduate Certificate); international business and information technology (Graduate Certificate); international finance (Graduate Certificate); international sport management (Graduate Certificate); justice studies (MBA); leadership of nonprofit organizations (Graduate Certificate); marketing (MBA, MS, Graduate Certificate); operations and project management (MS); operations and supply chain management (MBA, Graduate Certificate); organizational leadership (MS); project management (MBA, Graduate Certificate); Six Sigma (MBA); Six Sigma quality (Graduate Certificate); social media marketing (MBA); sport management (MBA, MS, Graduate Certificate); sustainability and environmental compliance (MBA); workplace conflict management (MBA); MBA/Certificate. *Accreditation:* ACBSP. Part-time and evening/weekend programs available. Postbaccalaureate distance learning degree programs offered (no on-campus study). Terminal master's awarded for partial completion of doctoral program. *Degree requirements:* For master's, one foreign language, comprehensive exam (for some programs), thesis or alternative. *Entrance requirements:* For master's, minimum GPA of 2.5. Additional exam requirements/recommendations for international students: Required—TOEFL (minimum score 500 paper-based). Electronic applications accepted.

Springfield College, Graduate Programs, Programs in Physical Education, Springfield, MA 01109-3797. Offers adapted physical education (M Ed, MPE, MS); advanced level coaching (M Ed, MPE, MS); athletic administration (M Ed, MPE, MS); general physical education (PhD, CAGS); health education licensure (MPE, MS); health education licensure program (M Ed); physical education licensure (MPE, MS); physical education licensure program (M Ed); teaching and administration (MS). Part-time programs available. *Faculty:* 33 full-time, 5 part-time/adjunct. *Students:* 52 full-time. 44 applicants, 86% accepted, 26 enrolled. In 2013, 22 master's, 4 doctorates awarded. *Degree requirements:* For master's, comprehensive exam, thesis (for some programs). *Entrance requirements:* For master's and doctorate, GRE General Test. Additional exam requirements/recommendations for international students: Required—TOEFL (minimum score 550 paper-based); Recommended—IELTS (minimum score 6). *Application deadline:* For fall admission, 1/15 priority date for domestic students, 1/15 for international students; for winter admission, 11/1 for domestic and international students; for spring admission, 11/1 for domestic and international students. Applications are processed on a rolling basis. Application fee: $50. Electronic applications accepted. *Expenses: Tuition:* Full-time $13,620; part-time $908 per credit. *Financial support:* Fellowships with partial tuition reimbursements, teaching assistantships with partial tuition reimbursements, career-related internships or fieldwork, Federal Work-Study, institutionally sponsored loans, and unspecified assistantships available. Financial award application deadline: 3/1; financial award applicants required to submit FAFSA. *Unit head:* Dr. Michelle Moosbrugger, Director, 413-748-3486, E-mail: mmoosbrugger@springfieldcollege.edu. *Application contact:* Evelyn Cohen, Associate Director of Graduate Admissions, 413-748-3479, Fax: 413-748-3694, E-mail: ecohen@springfieldcollege.edu.

Springfield College, Graduate Programs, Programs in Sport Management and Recreation, Springfield, MA 01109-3797. Offers recreational management (M Ed, MS); sport management (M Ed, MS); therapeutic recreational management (M Ed, MS). Part-time programs available. *Faculty:* 8 full-time, 2 part-time/adjunct. *Students:* 36 full-time. 43 applicants, 77% accepted, 21 enrolled. In 2013, 14 master's awarded. *Degree requirements:* For master's, comprehensive exam, research project. *Entrance requirements:* Additional exam requirements/recommendations for international students: Required—TOEFL (minimum score 550 paper-based); Recommended—IELTS (minimum score 6). *Application deadline:* For fall admission, 1/15 for domestic and international students; for winter admission, 11/1 for international students; for spring admission, 11/1 for domestic and international students. Applications are

processed on a rolling basis. Application fee: $50. Electronic applications accepted. *Expenses: Tuition:* Full-time $13,620; part-time $908 per credit. *Financial support:* Fellowships with partial tuition reimbursements, teaching assistantships with partial tuition reimbursements, career-related internships or fieldwork, Federal Work-Study, institutionally sponsored loans, and unspecified assistantships available. Financial award application deadline: 3/1; financial award applicants required to submit FAFSA. *Unit head:* Dr. Kevin McAllister, Director, 413-748-3476, Fax: 413-748-3685, E-mail: kmcallister@springfieldcollege.edu. *Application contact:* Evelyn Cohen, Associate Director of Graduate Admissions, 413-748-3479, Fax: 413-748-3694, E-mail: ecohen@springfieldcollege.edu.

State University of New York College at Cortland, Graduate Studies, School of Professional Studies, Department of Sport Management, Cortland, NY 13045. Offers international sport management (MS); sport management (MS). *Entrance requirements:* For master's, GMAT or GRE, 2 letters of recommendation. *Expenses:* Tuition, state resident: full-time $9870; part-time $411 per credit hour. Tuition, nonresident: full-time $18,350; part-time $765 per credit hour. *Required fees:* $1458; $65 per credit hour.

Syracuse University, Falk College of Sport and Human Dynamics, Program in Sport Venue and Event Management, Syracuse, NY 13244. Offers MS. *Students:* 17 full-time (10 women), 4 part-time (3 women); includes 4 minority (2 Black or African American, non-Hispanic/Latino; 1 Asian, non-Hispanic/Latino; 1 Two or more races, non-Hispanic/Latino), 6 international. Average age 25. 38 applicants, 47% accepted, 12 enrolled. *Entrance requirements:* For master's, GRE, undergraduate transcripts, three recommendations, resume, personal statement. Additional exam requirements/recommendations for international students: Required—TOEFL (minimum score 100 iBT). *Application deadline:* For fall admission, 3/15 for domestic students; for summer admission, 3/15 priority date for domestic and international students. Application fee: $75. Electronic applications accepted. *Financial support:* Application deadline: 1/1; applicants required to submit FAFSA. *Unit head:* Chad McEvoy, Graduate Program Director, 315-443-2630, Fax: 315-443-2562, E-mail: falk@syr.edu. *Application contact:* Felicia Otero, Director of Admissions, 315-443-5555, Fax: 315-443-1018, E-mail: falk@syr.edu.
Website: http://falk.syr.edu/SportManagement/Default.aspx.

Temple University, Fox School of Business, Doctoral Programs in Business, Philadelphia, PA 19122-6096. Offers accounting (PhD); entrepreneurship (PhD); finance (PhD); international business (PhD); management information systems (PhD); marketing (PhD); risk management and insurance (PhD); statistics (PhD); strategic management (PhD); tourism and sport (PhD). *Accreditation:* AACSB. *Degree requirements:* For doctorate, thesis/dissertation. *Entrance requirements:* For doctorate, GRE General Test, GMAT, minimum GPA of 3.0, master's degree. Additional exam requirements/recommendations for international students: Required—TOEFL (minimum score 600 paper-based; 100 iBT), IELTS (minimum score 7.5). Electronic applications accepted.

Temple University, School of Tourism and Hospitality Management, Program in Sport Business, Philadelphia, PA 19122-6096. Offers athletics administration (MS); recreation and event management (MS); sport analytics (MS); sport marketing and promotions (MS). Part-time programs available. *Faculty:* 12 full-time (2 women), 3 part-time/adjunct (1 woman). *Students:* 19 full-time (10 women), 7 part-time (4 women); includes 2 minority (both Black or African American, non-Hispanic/Latino). 54 applicants, 54% accepted, 20 enrolled. *Degree requirements:* For master's, thesis optional, internship or project. *Entrance requirements:* For master's, GRE General Test, GMAT, or MAT, bachelor's degree or equivalent with minimum GPA of 3.0, 500-word essay, 2 letters of recommendation, resume. Additional exam requirements/recommendations for international students: Required—TOEFL (minimum score 550 paper-based; 79 iBT), IELTS (minimum score 6.5). *Application deadline:* For fall admission, 3/1 priority date for domestic students, 1/15 priority date for international students; for spring admission, 8/15 priority date for domestic students, 6/30 priority date for international students. Applications are processed on a rolling basis. Application fee: $60. Electronic applications accepted. *Expenses:* Contact institution. *Financial support:* In 2013–14, 1 teaching assistantship with full tuition reimbursement (averaging $18,000 per year) was awarded. Financial award application deadline: 3/1; financial award applicants required to submit FAFSA. *Faculty research:* Industrial/organization management, corporate social responsibility, diversity/inclusion, sport/recreation for persons with disabilities, youth sport development, sport pricing, sport consumer behavior, marketing/advertising assessment, facility design and operation, participant sport behavior, mass participant sport events, brand evaluation, sport marketing communication, sport economics, recreation programming and assessment, non-profit development and management. *Unit head:* Dr. Joris Drayer, Associate Professor/Director of Programs in Sport and Recreation, 215-204-8701, Fax: 215-204-8705, E-mail: joris.drayer@temple.edu. *Application contact:* Michael J. Usino, Senior Associate Director of Recruitment, 215-204-3103, Fax: 215-204-8705, E-mail: musino@temple.edu.
Website: http://sthm.temple.edu/grad/explore-ma-sports.html.

Tennessee State University, The School of Graduate Studies and Research, College of Health Sciences, Department of Human Performance and Sports Sciences, Nashville, TN 37209-1561. Offers exercise science (MA Ed); sport administration (MA Ed). *Degree requirements:* For master's, thesis optional. *Entrance requirements:* For master's, GRE General Test or MAT.

Tennessee Technological University, College of Graduate Studies, College of Education, Department of Exercise Science, Physical Education and Wellness, Cookeville, TN 38505. Offers adapted physical education (MA); elementary/middle school physical education (MA); lifetime wellness (MA); sport management (MA). *Accreditation:* NCATE. Part-time programs available. Postbaccalaureate distance learning degree programs offered (no on-campus study). *Faculty:* 7 full-time (0 women). *Students:* 10 full-time (0 women), 38 part-time (11 women); includes 5 minority (all Black or African American, non-Hispanic/Latino). Average age 27. 38 applicants, 58% accepted, 20 enrolled. In 2013, 23 master's awarded. *Degree requirements:* For master's, comprehensive exam, thesis or alternative. *Entrance requirements:* For master's, MAT or GRE. Additional exam requirements/recommendations for international students: Required—TOEFL (minimum score 527 paper-based; 71 iBT), IELTS (minimum score 5.5), PTE (minimum score 48), or TOEIC (Test of English as an International Communication). *Application deadline:* For fall admission, 8/1 for domestic students, 5/1 for international students; for spring admission, 12/1 for domestic students, 10/1 for international students. Applications are processed on a rolling basis. Application fee: $35 ($40 for international students). Electronic applications accepted. *Expenses:* Tuition, state resident: full-time $9347; part-time $465 per credit hour. Tuition, nonresident: full-time $23,635; part-time $1152 per credit hour. *Financial support:* In 2013–14, fellowships (averaging $8,000 per year), 3 research assistantships (averaging $4,000 per year), 4 teaching assistantships (averaging $4,000 per year) were awarded; career-related internships or fieldwork also available. Financial award application deadline: 4/1. *Unit head:* Dr. John Steven Smith, Interim Chairperson, 931-372-3467, Fax: 931-372-6319, E-mail: jssmith@tntech.edu. *Application contact:* Shelia K. Kendrick, Coordinator of Graduate Studies, 931-372-3808, Fax: 931-372-3497, E-mail: skendrick@tntech.edu.

Texas A&M University, College of Education and Human Development, Department of Health and Kinesiology, College Station, TX 77843. Offers athletic training (MS); health education (M Ed, MS, Ed D, PhD); kinesiology (MS, PhD); sport management (MS). Part-time programs available. *Faculty:* 38. *Students:* 206 full-time (113 women), 71 part-time (38 women); includes 81 minority (35 Black or African American, non-Hispanic/Latino; 8 Asian, non-Hispanic/Latino; 33 Hispanic/Latino; 5 Two or more races, non-Hispanic/Latino), 43 international. Average age 29. 167 applicants, 71% accepted, 79 enrolled. In 2013, 68 master's, 16 doctorates awarded. *Degree requirements:* For master's, thesis (for some programs); for doctorate, comprehensive exam, thesis/dissertation. *Entrance requirements:* For master's and doctorate, GRE General Test. Additional exam requirements/recommendations for international students: Required—TOEFL. *Application deadline:* Applications are processed on a rolling basis. Application fee: $50 ($75 for international students). Electronic applications accepted. *Expenses:* Tuition, state resident: full-time $4078; part-time $226.55 per credit hour. Tuition, nonresident: full-time $10,450; part-time $580.55 per credit hour. *Required fees:* $2328; $278.50 per credit hour. $642.45 per semester. *Financial support:* Fellowships with partial tuition reimbursements, research assistantships, teaching assistantships, career-related internships or fieldwork, and institutionally sponsored loans available. Financial award application deadline: 2/15; financial award applicants required to submit FAFSA. *Unit head:* Dr. Richard Kreider, Head, 979-845-1333, Fax: 979-847-8987, E-mail: rkreider@hlkn.tamu.edu. *Application contact:* Christina Escamilla, Senior Academic Advisor I, 979-845-4530, E-mail: cescamil@tamu.edu.
Website: http://hlknweb.tamu.edu/.

Texas Woman's University, Graduate School, College of Health Sciences, Department of Kinesiology, Denton, TX 76201. Offers adapted physical education (MS, PhD); biomechanics (MS, PhD); coaching (MS); exercise physiology (MS, PhD); pedagogy (MS); sport management (MS, PhD). Part-time and evening/weekend programs available. *Faculty:* 11 full-time (5 women), 3 part-time/adjunct (2 women). *Students:* 48 full-time (35 women), 105 part-time (70 women); includes 42 minority (26 Black or African American, non-Hispanic/Latino; 2 American Indian or Alaska Native, non-Hispanic/Latino; 5 Asian, non-Hispanic/Latino; 9 Hispanic/Latino), 16 international. Average age 30. 51 applicants, 69% accepted, 25 enrolled. In 2013, 55 master's, 3 doctorates awarded. Terminal master's awarded for partial completion of doctoral program. *Degree requirements:* For master's, comprehensive exam, thesis or alternative; for doctorate, comprehensive exam, thesis/dissertation, qualifying exam. *Entrance requirements:* For master's, GRE General Test (biomechanics emphasis only), 2 letters of reference, curriculum vitae, interview (adapted physical education emphasis only); for doctorate, GRE General Test (biomechanics emphasis only), interview, 3 letters of reference, curriculum vitae. Additional exam requirements/recommendations for international students: Required—TOEFL (minimum score 550 paper-based; 79 iBT). *Application deadline:* For fall admission, 7/1 priority date for domestic students, 3/1 for international students; for spring admission, 11/1 priority date for domestic students, 7/1 for international students. Applications are processed on a rolling basis. Application fee: $50 ($75 for international students). Electronic applications accepted. *Expenses:* Tuition, state resident: full-time $4182; part-time $233.32 per credit hour. Tuition, nonresident: full-time $10,716; part-time $595.32 per credit hour. *Financial support:* In 2013–14, 46 students received support, including 7 research assistantships (averaging $10,659 per year), 14 teaching assistantships (averaging $10,659 per year); career-related internships or fieldwork, Federal Work-Study, institutionally sponsored loans, scholarships/grants, traineeships, health care benefits, and unspecified assistantships also available. Support available to part-time students. Financial award application deadline: 3/1; financial award applicants required to submit FAFSA. *Faculty research:* Exercise and Type 2 diabetes risk, bone mineral density and exercise in special populations, obesity in children, factors influencing sport consumer behavior and loyalty, roles and responsibilities of paraeducators in adapted physical education. *Total annual research expenditures:* $200,485. *Unit head:* Dr. Charlotte (Barney) Sanborn, Chair, 940-898-2575, Fax: 940-898-2581, E-mail: dnichols@twu.edu. *Application contact:* Dr. Samuel Wheeler, Assistant Director of Admissions, 940-898-3188, Fax: 940-898-3081, E-mail: wheelersr@twu.edu.
Website: http://www.twu.edu/kinesiology/.

Tiffin University, Program in Business Administration, Tiffin, OH 44883-2161. Offers finance (MBA); general management (MBA); healthcare administration (MBA); human resources (MBA); international business (MBA); leadership (MBA); marketing (MBA); sports management (MBA). *Accreditation:* ACBSP. Part-time and evening/weekend programs available. Postbaccalaureate distance learning degree programs offered (no on-campus study). *Entrance requirements:* For master's, minimum undergraduate GPA of 2.5, work experience. Additional exam requirements/recommendations for international students: Required—TOEFL (minimum score 550 paper-based; 79 iBT). Electronic applications accepted. *Faculty research:* Small business, executive development operations, research and statistical analysis, market research, management information systems.

Troy University, Graduate School, College of Health and Human Services, Program in Sport and Fitness Management, Troy, AL 36082. Offers MS. Part-time and evening/weekend programs available. *Faculty:* 15 full-time (4 women), 2 part-time/adjunct (1 woman). *Students:* 36 full-time (17 women), 69 part-time (18 women); includes 71 minority (37 Black or African American, non-Hispanic/Latino; 31 Hispanic/Latino; 3 Two or more races, non-Hispanic/Latino). Average age 28. 47 applicants, 91% accepted, 42 enrolled. In 2013, 24 master's awarded. *Degree requirements:* For master's, comprehensive exam, minimum GPA of 3.0, candidacy, research course. *Entrance requirements:* For master's, GRE (minimum score of 850 on old exam or 290 on new exam), GMAT (minimum score of 380), or MAT (minimum score of 385), bachelor's degree; minimum undergraduate GPA of 2.5 or 3.0 on last 30 semester hours, letter of recommendation. Additional exam requirements/recommendations for international students: Required—TOEFL (minimum score 523 paper-based; 70 iBT), IELTS (minimum score 6). *Application deadline:* Applications are processed on a rolling basis. Application fee: $50. Electronic applications accepted. *Expenses:* Tuition, state resident: full-time $6084; part-time $338 per credit hour. Tuition, nonresident: full-time $12,168; part-time $676 per credit hour. *Required fees:* $630; $35 per credit hour. $50 per semester. *Financial support:* Career-related internships or fieldwork and unspecified assistantships available. *Faculty research:* Sport marketing, fitness, sport law. *Unit head:* Dr. Anthony Dixon, Chairman, 334-808-6424, Fax: 334-670-3802, E-mail: adixon@troy.edu. *Application contact:* Brenda K. Campbell, Director of Graduate Admissions, 334-670-3178, Fax: 334-670-3733, E-mail: bcamp@troy.edu.

United States Sports Academy, Graduate Programs, Program in Sport Management, Daphne, AL 36526-7055. Offers MSS, Ed D. Part-time programs available. Postbaccalaureate distance learning degree programs offered (no on-campus study). *Degree requirements:* For master's, comprehensive exam, thesis optional; for doctorate, comprehensive exam, thesis/dissertation. *Entrance requirements:* For master's, GRE General Test, GMAT, or MAT, minimum GPA of 2.5, 3 letters of recommendation, resume; for doctorate, GRE General Test, GMAT, or MAT, master's degree, 3 letters of recommendation, resume. Additional exam requirements/recommendations for international students: Required—TOEFL (minimum score 500 paper-based). Electronic applications accepted. *Faculty research:* Sport law, leadership behavior, personnel evaluation.

Sports Management

The University of Alabama, Graduate School, College of Education, Department of Kinesiology, Tuscaloosa, AL 35487-0312. Offers alternative sport pedagogy (MA); exercise science (MA, PhD); human performance (MA); sport management (MA); sport pedagogy (MA, PhD). Part-time programs available. *Faculty:* 8 full-time (1 woman). *Students:* 58 full-time (18 women), 29 part-time (15 women); includes 15 minority (9 Black or African American, non-Hispanic/Latino; 1 Asian, non-Hispanic/Latino; 2 Hispanic/Latino; 3 Two or more races, non-Hispanic/Latino), 7 international. Average age 30. 74 applicants, 74% accepted, 32 enrolled. In 2013, 26 master's, 4 doctorates awarded. *Degree requirements:* For master's, comprehensive exam, thesis optional; for doctorate, comprehensive exam, thesis/dissertation. *Entrance requirements:* For master's and doctorate, GRE, MAT, minimum GPA of 3.0. Additional exam requirements/recommendations for international students: Required—TOEFL. *Application deadline:* Applications are processed on a rolling basis. Application fee: $50 ($60 for international students). Electronic applications accepted. *Expenses:* Tuition, state resident: full-time $9450. Tuition, nonresident: full-time $23,950. *Financial support:* In 2013–14, 14 students received support, including 26 teaching assistantships with full and partial tuition reimbursements available (averaging $12,366 per year); fellowships and research assistantships also available. Financial award applicants required to submit FAFSA. *Faculty research:* Race, gender and sexuality in sports; physical education teacher socialization; disability sports; physical activity and health; environmental physiology. *Unit head:* Dr. Matt Curtner-Smith, Department Head and Professor, 205-348-9209, Fax: 205-348-0867, E-mail: msmith@bamaed.ua.edu. *Application contact:* Dr. Kathy S. Wetzel, Assistant Dean for Student Services, 205-348-1154, Fax: 205-348-0080, E-mail: kwetzel@bamaed.ua.edu.
Website: http://education.ua.edu/academics/kine/.

The University of Alabama, Graduate School, College of Human Environmental Sciences, Program in Human Environmental Science, Tuscaloosa, AL 35487. Offers family financial planning and counseling (MS); interactive technology (MS); quality management (MS); restaurant and meeting management (MS); rural community health (MS); sport management (MS). *Faculty:* 1 full-time (0 women). *Students:* 55 full-time (34 women), 98 part-time (48 women); includes 41 minority (30 Black or African American, non-Hispanic/Latino; 2 American Indian or Alaska Native, non-Hispanic/Latino; 2 Asian, non-Hispanic/Latino; 2 Hispanic/Latino; 5 Two or more races, non-Hispanic/Latino), 1 international. Average age 34. 102 applicants, 69% accepted, 60 enrolled. In 2013, 88 master's awarded. *Degree requirements:* For master's, comprehensive exam. *Entrance requirements:* For master's, GRE (for some specializations), minimum GPA of 3.0. Additional exam requirements/recommendations for international students: Required—TOEFL. *Application deadline:* Applications are processed on a rolling basis. Application fee: $50 ($60 for international students). Electronic applications accepted. *Expenses:* Tuition, state resident: full-time $9450. Tuition, nonresident: full-time $23,950. *Faculty research:* Hospitality management, sports medicine education, technology and education. *Unit head:* Dr. Milla D. Boschung, Dean, 205-348-6250, Fax: 205-348-1786, E-mail: mboschun@ches.ua.edu. *Application contact:* Dr. Stuart Usdan, Associate Dean, 205-348-6150, Fax: 205-348-3789, E-mail: susdan@ches.ua.edu.

University of Alberta, Faculty of Graduate Studies and Research, Program in Business Administration, Edmonton, AB T6G 2E1, Canada. Offers international business (MBA); leisure and sport management (MBA); natural resources and energy (MBA); technology commercialization (MBA); MBA/LL B; MBA/M Ag; MBA/M Eng; MBA/MF; MBA/PhD. *Accreditation:* AACSB. Part-time and evening/weekend programs available. *Degree requirements:* For master's, thesis or alternative. *Entrance requirements:* For master's, GMAT. Additional exam requirements/recommendations for international students: Required—TOEFL (minimum score 600 paper-based). Electronic applications accepted. *Faculty research:* Natural resources and energy/management and policy/family enterprise/international business/healthcare research management.

University of Arkansas, Graduate School, College of Education and Health Professions, Department of Health, Human Performance and Recreation, Program in Recreation and Sports Management, Fayetteville, AR 72701-1201. Offers M Ed, Ed D. *Degree requirements:* For master's, thesis optional; for doctorate, thesis/dissertation. *Entrance requirements:* For doctorate, GRE General Test. Electronic applications accepted.

University of Central Florida, College of Business Administration, Program in Sport Business Management, Orlando, FL 32816. Offers MSBM. *Faculty:* 6 full-time (0 women), 1 (woman) part-time/adjunct. *Students:* 55 full-time (25 women), 2 part-time (0 women); includes 18 minority (11 Black or African American, non-Hispanic/Latino; 1 Asian, non-Hispanic/Latino; 6 Hispanic/Latino), 5 international. Average age 25. 42 applicants, 45% accepted, 14 enrolled. In 2013, 33 master's awarded. *Degree requirements:* For master's, thesis or alternative, internship. *Entrance requirements:* For master's, GMAT, minimum GPA of 3.0, letters of recommendation. Additional exam requirements/recommendations for international students: Required—TOEFL. *Application deadline:* For fall admission, 2/15 priority date for domestic students. Application fee: $30. Electronic applications accepted. *Financial support:* In 2013–14, 37 students received support, including 31 research assistantships with partial tuition reimbursements available (averaging $5,200 per year), 6 teaching assistantships (averaging $6,900 per year). *Unit head:* Dr. Richard Lapchick, Director, 407-823-4887, E-mail: richard.lapchick@ucf.edu. *Application contact:* Judy Ryder, Director, Graduate Admissions, 407-235-3916, Fax: 407-823-0219, E-mail: jryder@ucf.edu.
Website: http://www.bus.ucf.edu/sportbusiness/.

University of Colorado Denver, Business School, Master of Business Administration Program, Denver, CO 80217. Offers bioinnovation and entrepreneurship (MBA); business intelligence (MBA); business strategy (MBA); business to business marketing (MBA); business to consumer marketing (MBA); change management (MBA); corporate financial management (MBA); enterprise technology management (MBA); entrepreneurship (MBA); health administration (MBA), including financial management, health administration, health information technologies, international health management and policy; human resources management (MBA); international business (MBA); investment management (MBA); managing for sustainability (MBA); sports and entertainment management (MBA). *Accreditation:* AACSB. Part-time and evening/weekend programs available. Postbaccalaureate distance learning degree programs offered (no on-campus study). *Students:* 611 full-time (246 women), 144 part-time (58 women); includes 102 minority (14 Black or African American, non-Hispanic/Latino; 2 American Indian or Alaska Native, non-Hispanic/Latino; 38 Asian, non-Hispanic/Latino; 42 Hispanic/Latino; 6 Two or more races, non-Hispanic/Latino), 26 international. Average age 32. 330 applicants, 64% accepted, 125 enrolled. In 2013, 398 master's awarded. *Degree requirements:* For master's, 48 semester hours, including 30 of core courses, 3 in international business, and 15 in electives from over 50 other graduate business courses. *Entrance requirements:* For master's, GMAT, resume, official transcripts, essay, two letters of recommendation, financial statements (for international applicants). Additional exam requirements/recommendations for international students: Required—TOEFL (minimum score 560 paper-based; 83 iBT); Recommended—IELTS (minimum score 6.5). *Application deadline:* For fall admission, 4/15 priority date for domestic students, 3/15 priority date for international students; for spring admission, 10/15 priority date for domestic students, 9/15 priority date for international students. Applications are processed on a rolling basis. Application fee: $50 ($75 for international students). Electronic applications accepted. *Expenses:* Contact institution. *Financial support:* In 2013–14, 62 students received support. Fellowships, research assistantships, teaching assistantships, Federal Work-Study, institutionally sponsored loans, scholarships/grants, traineeships, and unspecified assistantships available. Financial award application deadline: 4/1; financial award applicants required to submit FAFSA. *Faculty research:* Marketing, management, entrepreneurship, finance, health administration. *Unit head:* Elizabeth Cooperman, Professor of Finance and Managing for Sustainability/MBA Program Director, 303-315-8422, E-mail: elizabeth.cooperman@ucdenver.edu. *Application contact:* Shelly Townley, Admissions Director, Graduate Programs, 303-315-8202, E-mail: shelly.townley@ucdenver.edu.
Website: http://www.ucdenver.edu/academics/colleges/business/degrees/mba/Pages/MBA.aspx.

University of Colorado Denver, Business School, Program in Management and Organization, Denver, CO 80217. Offers business strategy (MS); change and innovation (MS); enterprise technology management (MS); entrepreneurship and innovation (MS); global management (MS); human resources management (MS); leadership and management (MS); quantitative decision methods (MS); sports and entertainment management (MS); sustainability management (MS). *Accreditation:* AACSB. Part-time and evening/weekend programs available. Postbaccalaureate distance learning degree programs offered (no on-campus study). *Students:* 27 full-time (19 women), 14 part-time (7 women); includes 4 minority (1 Black or African American, non-Hispanic/Latino; 2 Hispanic/Latino; 1 Two or more races, non-Hispanic/Latino), 6 international. Average age 29. 38 applicants, 45% accepted, 8 enrolled. In 2013, 28 master's awarded. *Degree requirements:* For master's, 30 semester hours (12 of required courses, 12 of management electives, and 6 of free electives). *Entrance requirements:* For master's, GMAT, resume, two letters of recommendation, essay, financial statements (for international applicants). Additional exam requirements/recommendations for international students: Required—TOEFL (minimum score 537 paper-based; 75 iBT); Recommended—IELTS (minimum score 6.5). *Application deadline:* For fall admission, 4/15 for domestic students, 3/15 for international students; for spring admission, 10/15 for domestic students, 9/15 for international students. Applications are processed on a rolling basis. Application fee: $50 ($75 for international students). Electronic applications accepted. *Expenses:* Contact institution. *Financial support:* In 2013–14, 5 students received support. Fellowships, research assistantships, teaching assistantships, Federal Work-Study, institutionally sponsored loans, scholarships/grants, and traineeships available. Financial award application deadline: 4/1; financial award applicants required to submit FAFSA. *Faculty research:* Human resource management, management of catastrophe, turnaround strategies. *Unit head:* Dr. Kenneth Bettenhausen, Associate Professor/Director of MS in Management, 303-315-8425, E-mail: kenneth.bettenhausen@ucdenver.edu. *Application contact:* Shelly Townley, Admissions Director, Graduate Programs, 303-315-8202, E-mail: shelly.townley@ucdenver.edu.
Website: http://www.ucdenver.edu/academics/colleges/business/degrees/ms/management/Pages/Management.aspx.

University of Dallas, Graduate School of Management, Irving, TX 75062-4736. Offers accounting (MBA, MM, MS); business management (MBA, MM); corporate finance (MBA, MM); financial services (MBA); global business (MBA, MM); health services management (MBA, MM); human resource management (MBA, MM); information assurance (MBA, MM, MS); information technology (MBA, MM, MS); information technology service management (MBA, MM, MS); marketing management (MBA, MM); organization development (MBA, MM); project management (MBA, MM); sports and entertainment management (MBA, MM); strategic leadership (MBA, MM); supply chain management (MBA); supply chain management and market logistics (MM). *Accreditation:* ACBSP. Part-time and evening/weekend programs available. Postbaccalaureate distance learning degree programs offered (no on-campus study). *Entrance requirements:* Additional exam requirements/recommendations for international students: Required—TOEFL. Electronic applications accepted. *Expenses:* Contact institution.

University of Florida, Graduate School, College of Health and Human Performance, Department of Tourism, Recreation and Sport Management, Gainesville, FL 32611. Offers health and human performance (PhD), including recreation, parks and tourism (MS, PhD), sport management; recreation, parks and tourism (MS), including natural resource recreation, recreation, parks and tourism (MS, PhD), therapeutic recreation, tourism; sport management (MS); JD/MS; MSM/MS. *Faculty:* 7 full-time (5 women). *Students:* 64 full-time (27 women), 13 part-time (4 women); includes 11 minority (7 Black or African American, non-Hispanic/Latino; 1 Asian, non-Hispanic/Latino; 3 Hispanic/Latino), 27 international. Average age 27. 15 applicants, 40% accepted, 1 enrolled. In 2013, 51 master's, 4 doctorates awarded. *Degree requirements:* For master's, comprehensive exam (for some programs), thesis (for some programs); for doctorate, comprehensive exam, thesis/dissertation. *Entrance requirements:* For master's and doctorate, GRE General Test, minimum GPA of 3.0. Additional exam requirements/recommendations for international students: Required—TOEFL (minimum score 550 paper-based; 80 iBT), IELTS (minimum score 6). *Application deadline:* For fall admission, 3/1 for domestic students, 12/1 for international students; for spring admission, 10/15 for domestic students, 5/1 for international students. Applications are processed on a rolling basis. Application fee: $30. Electronic applications accepted. *Expenses:* Tuition, state resident: full-time $12,640. Tuition, nonresident: full-time $30,000. *Financial support:* In 2013–14, 27 students received support, including 10 research assistantships (averaging $15,850 per year), 20 teaching assistantships (averaging $11,840 per year); career-related internships or fieldwork, Federal Work-Study, and unspecified assistantships also available. Financial award application deadline: 2/1; financial award applicants required to submit FAFSA. *Faculty research:* Hospitality, natural resource management, sport management, tourism. *Unit head:* Michael Sagas, PhD, Department Chair and Professor, 352-294-1640, Fax: 352-392-7588, E-mail: msagas@hhp.ufl.edu. *Application contact:* Stephen M. Holland, PhD, Professor/Graduate Coordinator, 352-294-1669, Fax: 352-392-7588, E-mail: sholland@hhp.ufl.edu.
Website: http://www.hhp.ufl.edu/trsm/.

University of Florida, Graduate School, Warrington College of Business Administration, Hough Graduate School of Business, Programs in Business Administration, Gainesville, FL 32611. Offers business administration (MBA); competitive strategy (MBA); entrepreneurship (MBA); finance (MBA); global management (MBA); Graham-Buffett security analysis (MBA); human resource management (MBA); information systems and operations management (MBA); international studies (MBA); Latin American business (MBA); management (MBA); marketing (MBA); real estate (MBA); sports administration (MBA); JD/MBA; MBA/MS; MBA/PhD; MBA/Pharm D; MD/MBA. *Accreditation:* AACSB. Part-time and evening/weekend programs available. Postbaccalaureate distance learning degree programs offered. *Faculty:* 72 full-time (10 women), 29 part-time/adjunct (7 women). *Students:* 440 full-time (122 women), 472 part-time (159 women); includes 203 minority (43 Black or African American, non-Hispanic/Latino; 3 American Indian or Alaska Native, non-Hispanic/Latino; 64 Asian, non-Hispanic/Latino; 92 Hispanic/Latino; 1 Native Hawaiian or other Pacific Islander, non-Hispanic/Latino), 39 international. Average age 32. 568 applicants, 58% accepted, 261 enrolled. In 2013, 405 master's awarded. *Degree requirements:* For master's, capstone course. *Entrance requirements:* For master's,

GMAT (minimum score 465), minimum GPA of 3.0, interview. Additional exam requirements/recommendations for international students: Required—TOEFL (minimum score 550 paper-based; 80 iBT), IELTS (minimum score 6). *Application deadline:* For fall admission, 7/1 for domestic students, 1/1 for international students; for spring admission, 12/1 for domestic and international students. Applications are processed on a rolling basis. Application fee: $30. Electronic applications accepted. *Expenses:* Tuition, state resident: full-time $12,640. Tuition, nonresident: full-time $30,000. *Financial support:* In 2013–14, 24 students received support, including 24 teaching assistantships (averaging $6,143 per year); career-related internships or fieldwork, scholarships/grants, and unspecified assistantships also available. Support available to part-time students. Financial award applicants required to submit FAFSA. *Faculty research:* Accounting, finance, insurance, management, real estate, urban analysis marketing. *Unit head:* Alexander D. Sevilla, Assistant Dean/Director of MBA Program, 352-273-3252, Fax: 352-392-8791, E-mail: alex.sevilla@warrington.ufl.edu. *Application contact:* Andrew S. Lord, Senior Director of Admissions, 352-273-3241, Fax: 352-392-8791, E-mail: andrew.lord@warrington.ufl.edu.
Website: http://www.floridamba.ufl.edu/.

The University of Iowa, Graduate College, College of Liberal Arts and Sciences, Department of Health and Human Physiology, Iowa City, IA 52242-1316. Offers athletic training (MS); clinical exercise physiology (MS); health and human physiology (PhD); leisure studies (MA, PhD), including recreational sport management (PhD), therapeutic recreation (MA). *Degree requirements:* For master's, thesis optional, exam; for doctorate, comprehensive exam, thesis/dissertation. *Entrance requirements:* For master's and doctorate, GRE General Test, minimum GPA of 3.0. Additional exam requirements/recommendations for international students: Required—TOEFL (minimum score 600 paper-based; 100 iBT). Electronic applications accepted.

University of Louisville, Graduate School, College of Education and Human Development, Department of Health and Sport Sciences, Louisville, KY 40292-0001. Offers community health education (M Ed); exercise physiology (MS); health and physical education (MAT); sport administration (MS). Part-time and evening/weekend programs available. *Students:* 54 full-time (22 women), 11 part-time (9 women); includes 12 minority (6 Black or African American, non-Hispanic/Latino; 1 American Indian or Alaska Native, non-Hispanic/Latino; 1 Asian, non-Hispanic/Latino; 3 Hispanic/Latino; 1 Two or more races, non-Hispanic/Latino), 3 international. Average age 27. 91 applicants, 70% accepted, 40 enrolled. In 2013, 16 master's awarded. *Entrance requirements:* For master's, GRE General Test. Additional exam requirements/recommendations for international students: Required—TOEFL (minimum score 560 paper-based; 83 iBT). Application fee: $60. Electronic applications accepted. *Expenses:* Tuition, state resident: full-time $10,788; part-time $599 per credit hour. Tuition, nonresident: full-time $22,446; part-time $1247 per credit hour. *Required fees:* $196. Tuition and fees vary according to program and reciprocity agreements. *Financial support:* Fellowships, research assistantships, teaching assistantships, career-related internships or fieldwork, Federal Work-Study, scholarships/grants, health care benefits, and unspecified assistantships available. Financial award application deadline: 6/1; financial award applicants required to submit FAFSA. *Faculty research:* Impact of sports and sport marketing on society, factors associated with school and community health, cardiac and pulmonary rehabilitation, impact of participation in activities on student retention and graduation, strength and conditioning. *Unit head:* Dr. Anita Moorman, Chair, 502-852-0553, Fax: 502-852-4534, E-mail: amm@louisville.edu. *Application contact:* Libby Leggett, Director, Graduate Admissions, 502-852-3101, Fax: 502-852-6536, E-mail: gradadm@louisville.edu.
Website: http://www.louisville.edu/education/departments/hss.

University of Mary Hardin-Baylor, Graduate Studies in Exercise Science, Belton, TX 76513. Offers exercise science (MS Ed); sport administration (MS Ed). Part-time and evening/weekend programs available. *Faculty:* 7 full-time (2 women). *Students:* 10 full-time (6 women), 14 part-time (3 women); includes 5 minority (2 Black or African American, non-Hispanic/Latino; 3 Hispanic/Latino). Average age 27. 15 applicants, 73% accepted, 10 enrolled. In 2013, 8 master's awarded. *Degree requirements:* For master's, comprehensive exam. *Entrance requirements:* For master's, minimum GPA of 3.0. Additional exam requirements/recommendations for international students: Required—TOEFL (minimum score 550 paper-based; 80 iBT), IELTS (minimum score 6). *Application deadline:* For fall admission, 6/15 priority date for international students; for spring admission, 10/15 priority date for international students. Application fee: $35 ($135 for international students). *Expenses: Tuition:* Full-time $14,130; part-time $785 per credit hour. *Required fees:* $1350; $75 per credit hour. $50 per term. *Financial support:* Federal Work-Study, unspecified assistantships, and scholarships (for some active duty military personnel only) available. Support available to part-time students. Financial award application deadline: 6/1; financial award applicants required to submit FAFSA. *Unit head:* Dr. Colin Wilborn, Dean, Graduate School/Program Director, Master of Science in Education in Exercise Science Program/Associate Professor of Exercise Sport Science, 254-295-4488, E-mail: cwilborn@umhb.edu. *Application contact:* Melissa Ford, Director of Graduate Admissions, 254-295-4020, Fax: 254-295-5038, E-mail: mford@umhb.edu.
Website: http://www.graduate.umhb.edu/exss.

University of Massachusetts Amherst, Graduate School, Interdisciplinary Programs, Dual Degree Program in Business Administration and Sport Management, Amherst, MA 01003. Offers MBA/MS. Part-time programs available. *Students:* 22 full-time (9 women), 1 part-time (0 women); includes 1 minority (Two or more races, non-Hispanic/Latino), 7 international. Average age 25. 60 applicants, 30% accepted, 13 enrolled. *Entrance requirements:* Additional exam requirements/recommendations for international students: Required—TOEFL (minimum score 600 paper-based; 100 iBT), IELTS (minimum score 7). *Application deadline:* For fall admission, 2/1 for domestic and international students; for spring admission, 10/1 for domestic and international students. Applications are processed on a rolling basis. Application fee: $75. Electronic applications accepted. *Financial support:* Career-related internships or fieldwork, Federal Work-Study, scholarships/grants, traineeships, health care benefits, tuition waivers (full), and unspecified assistantships available. Support available to part-time students. Financial award application deadline: 2/1. *Unit head:* Dr. Stephen McKelvey, Graduate Program Director, 413-545-0471, Fax: 413-545-0642. *Application contact:* Lindsay DeSantis, Supervisor of Admissions, 413-545-0722, Fax: 413-577-0010, E-mail: gradadm@grad.umass.edu.
Website: http://www.isenberg.umass.edu/sportmgt/Dual_Degree/.

University of Massachusetts Amherst, Graduate School, Isenberg School of Management, Department of Sport Management, Amherst, MA 01003. Offers MS, MBA/MS. Part-time programs available. *Faculty:* 14 full-time (5 women). *Students:* 12 full-time (6 women), 7 part-time (2 women); includes 6 minority (1 Black or African American, non-Hispanic/Latino; 3 Asian, non-Hispanic/Latino; 1 Hispanic/Latino; 1 Two or more races, non-Hispanic/Latino), 4 international. Average age 26. 62 applicants, 32% accepted, 12 enrolled. In 2013, 14 master's awarded. Terminal master's awarded for partial completion of doctoral program. *Degree requirements:* For master's, thesis or alternative. *Entrance requirements:* For master's, GMAT or GRE General Test. Additional exam requirements/recommendations for international students: Required—TOEFL (minimum score 550 paper-based; 80 iBT), IELTS (minimum score 6.5). *Application deadline:* For fall admission, 2/1 for domestic and international students. Applications are processed on a rolling basis. Application fee: $75. Electronic applications accepted. *Financial support:* Fellowships with full and partial tuition reimbursements, research assistantships with full and partial tuition reimbursements, teaching assistantships with full and partial tuition reimbursements, career-related internships or fieldwork, Federal Work-Study, scholarships/grants, traineeships, health care benefits, tuition waivers (full and partial), and unspecified assistantships available. Support available to part-time students. Financial award application deadline: 2/1; financial award applicants required to submit FAFSA. *Unit head:* Dr. Stephen McKelvey, Graduate Program Director, 413-545-0471, Fax: 413-577-0642. *Application contact:* Lindsay DeSantis, Supervisor of Admissions, 413-545-0722, Fax: 413-577-0010, E-mail: gradadm@grad.umass.edu.
Website: http://www.isenberg.umass.edu/sportmgt/.

University of Massachusetts Amherst, Graduate School, Isenberg School of Management, Program in Management, Amherst, MA 01003. Offers accounting (PhD); business administration (MBA); entrepreneurship (MBA); finance (MBA, PhD); healthcare administration (MBA); hospitality and tourism management (PhD); management science (PhD); marketing (MBA, PhD); organization studies (PhD); sport management (PhD); strategic management (PhD); MBA/MS. *Accreditation:* AACSB. Part-time and evening/weekend programs available. Postbaccalaureate distance learning degree programs offered. *Faculty:* 68 full-time (14 women). *Students:* 140 full-time (59 women), 1,127 part-time (319 women); includes 229 minority (24 Black or African American, non-Hispanic/Latino; 2 American Indian or Alaska Native, non-Hispanic/Latino; 135 Asian, non-Hispanic/Latino; 51 Hispanic/Latino; 6 Native Hawaiian or other Pacific Islander, non-Hispanic/Latino; 11 Two or more races, non-Hispanic/Latino), 131 international. Average age 36. 828 applicants, 56% accepted, 351 enrolled. In 2013, 361 master's, 12 doctorates awarded. Terminal master's awarded for partial completion of doctoral program. *Degree requirements:* For doctorate, comprehensive exam, thesis/dissertation. *Entrance requirements:* For master's and doctorate, GMAT or GRE General Test. Additional exam requirements/recommendations for international students: Required—TOEFL (minimum score 550 paper-based; 80 iBT), IELTS (minimum score 6.5). *Application deadline:* For fall admission, 1/20 for domestic and international students. Applications are processed on a rolling basis. Application fee: $75. Electronic applications accepted. *Financial support:* Fellowships with full and partial tuition reimbursements, research assistantships with full and partial tuition reimbursements, teaching assistantships with full and partial tuition reimbursements, career-related internships or fieldwork, Federal Work-Study, scholarships/grants, traineeships, health care benefits, tuition waivers (full and partial), and unspecified assistantships available. Support available to part-time students. Financial award application deadline: 1/20; financial award applicants required to submit FAFSA. *Unit head:* Dr. John Wells, Chair, 413-545-7609, Fax: 413-577-2234. *Application contact:* Lindsay DeSantis, Supervisor of Admissions, 413-545-0722, Fax: 413-577-0010, E-mail: gradadm@grad.umass.edu.
Website: http://www.isenberg.umass.edu/.

University of Miami, Graduate School, School of Education and Human Development, Department of Kinesiology and Sport Sciences, Program in Sport Administration, Coral Gables, FL 33124. Offers MS Ed. Part-time and evening/weekend programs available. *Faculty:* 6 full-time (3 women), 5 part-time/adjunct (2 women). *Students:* 20 full-time (8 women), 6 part-time (0 women); includes 9 minority (6 Black or African American, non-Hispanic/Latino; 3 Hispanic/Latino), 3 international. Average age 23. 58 applicants, 29% accepted, 17 enrolled. In 2013, 20 master's awarded. *Degree requirements:* For master's, special project. *Entrance requirements:* For master's, GRE General Test. Additional exam requirements/recommendations for international students: Required—TOEFL (minimum score 550 paper-based; 80 iBT); Recommended—IELTS (minimum score 6.5). *Application deadline:* For fall admission, 10/1 for international students; for spring admission, 10/1 for international students. Applications are processed on a rolling basis. Application fee: $65. Electronic applications accepted. *Financial support:* In 2013–14, 11 students received support. Institutionally sponsored loans and scholarships/grants available. Financial award application deadline: 3/1; financial award applicants required to submit FAFSA. *Faculty research:* Constitutional procedural due process, legal liability, tort law, moral development in sports administration, ethics intervention. *Unit head:* Dr. Warren Whisenant, Associate Department Chairperson, 305-284-5622, Fax: 305-284-5168, E-mail: wwhisenant@miami.edu. *Application contact:* Lois Heffernan, Graduate Admissions Coordinator, 305-284-2167, Fax: 305-284-9395, E-mail: lheffernan@miami.edu.
Website: http://www.education.miami.edu/program/Programs.asp?Program_ID=18&Src=Graduate.

University of Michigan, Horace H. Rackham School of Graduate Studies, School of Kinesiology, Ann Arbor, MI 48109. Offers kinesiology (MS, PhD); sport management (AM). *Faculty:* 30 full-time (13 women). *Students:* 72 full-time (34 women); includes 32 minority (3 Black or African American, non-Hispanic/Latino; 22 Asian, non-Hispanic/Latino; 5 Hispanic/Latino; 2 Two or more races, non-Hispanic/Latino). 166 applicants, 42% accepted, 31 enrolled. In 2013, 17 master's, 11 doctorates awarded. Terminal master's awarded for partial completion of doctoral program. *Degree requirements:* For master's, thesis (for some programs); for doctorate, comprehensive exam, thesis/dissertation, oral defense of dissertation. *Entrance requirements:* For master's and doctorate, GRE General Test. Additional exam requirements/recommendations for international students: Required—TOEFL. *Application deadline:* For fall admission, 1/15 priority date for domestic students, 1/15 for international students. Applications are processed on a rolling basis. Application fee: $60 ($75 for international students). Electronic applications accepted. *Expenses:* Contact institution. *Financial support:* In 2013–14, 9 fellowships, 10 research assistantships, 8 teaching assistantships were awarded; Federal Work-Study, scholarships/grants, health care benefits, and unspecified assistantships also available. Financial award application deadline: 1/15. *Faculty research:* Motor development, exercise physiology, biomechanics, sport medicine, sport management. *Unit head:* Dr. Ketra L. Armstrong, Associate Dean for Graduate Programs and Faculty Affairs, 734-647-3027, Fax: 734-647-2808, E-mail: ketra@umich.edu. *Application contact:* Charlene F. Ruloff, Graduate Program Coordinator, 734-764-1343, Fax: 734-647-2808, E-mail: cruloff@umich.edu.
Website: http://www.kines.umich.edu/.

University of Minnesota, Twin Cities Campus, Graduate School, College of Education and Human Development, School of Kinesiology, Minneapolis, MN 55455-0213. Offers adapted physical education (MA, PhD); biomechanics (MA); biomechanics and neural control (PhD); coaching (Certificate); developmental adapted physical education (M Ed); exercise physiology (MA, PhD); human factors/ergonomics (MA, PhD); international/comparative sport (MA, PhD); kinesiology (M Ed, MA, MS, PhD); leisure services/management (MA, PhD); motor development (MA, PhD); motor learning/control (MA, PhD); outdoor education/recreation (MA, PhD); physical education (M Ed); recreation, park, and leisure studies (M Ed, MA, PhD); sport and exercise science (M Ed); sport management (M Ed, MA, PhD); sport psychology (MA, PhD); sport sociology (MA, PhD); therapeutic recreation (MA, PhD). Part-time programs available. *Faculty:* 14 full-time (6 women). *Students:* 140 full-time (51 women), 52 part-time (19 women); includes 18 minority (9 Black or African American, non-Hispanic/Latino; 1 American Indian or Alaska Native, non-Hispanic/Latino; 4 Asian, non-Hispanic/

Latino; 4 Hispanic/Latino), 25 international. Average age 29. 172 applicants, 51% accepted, 77 enrolled. In 2013, 89 master's, 11 doctorates, 13 other advanced degrees awarded. Terminal master's awarded for partial completion of doctoral program. *Degree requirements:* For master's, final oral exam; for doctorate, thesis/dissertation, preliminary written/oral exam, final oral exam. *Entrance requirements:* For master's, GRE or MAT, minimum GPA of 3.0; for doctorate, GRE or MAT, minimum GPA of 3.0, writing sample. Application fee: $75 ($95 for international students). *Financial support:* In 2013–14, 3 fellowships (averaging $22,667 per year), 8 research assistantships with full tuition reimbursements (averaging $849 per year), 41 teaching assistantships with full tuition reimbursements (averaging $12,766 per year) were awarded; career-related internships or fieldwork, Federal Work-Study, institutionally sponsored loans, and tuition waivers (full and partial) also available. Support available to part-time students. *Faculty research:* Exercise physiology; biochemical, molecular and nutritional aspects of exercise; sport training and performance; sport and exercise psychology; behavioral aspects of physical activity; youth sport science; gender and sport sociology; sports management; sports policy, marketing and law; motor development and disabilities; movement perception and action; movement neuroscience. *Total annual research expenditures:* $472,507. *Unit head:* Dr. Li Li Ji, Director, 612-624-9809, Fax: 612-626-7700, E-mail: llji@umn.edu. *Application contact:* Dr. Jennifer Engler, Assistant Dean, 612-626-2887, Fax: 612-626-7496, E-mail: engle009@umn.edu.

University of Nebraska at Kearney, Graduate Programs, College of Education, Department of Health, Physical Education, Recreation, and Leisure Studies, Kearney, NE 68849-0001. Offers general physical education (MA Ed), including recreation and leisure, sports administration; physical education exercise science (MA Ed); physical education master teacher (MA Ed), including pedagogy, special populations. Part-time and evening/weekend programs available. *Degree requirements:* For master's, comprehensive exam, thesis optional. *Entrance requirements:* For master's, GRE General Test, personal statement. Additional exam requirements/recommendations for international students: Required—TOEFL (minimum score 550 paper-based). Electronic applications accepted. *Faculty research:* Ergonomic aids, nutrition, motor development, sports pedagogy, applied behavior analysis.

University of New Brunswick Fredericton, School of Graduate Studies, Faculty of Business Administration, Fredericton, NB E3B 5A3, Canada. Offers business administration (MBA); engineering management (MBA); entrepreneurship (MBA); sports and recreation management (MBA); MBA/LL B. Part-time programs available. *Faculty:* 23 full-time (3 women), 5 part-time/adjunct (2 women). *Students:* 48 full-time (15 women), 31 part-time (12 women), 1 international. In 2013, 30 master's awarded. *Degree requirements:* For master's, thesis optional. *Entrance requirements:* For master's, GMAT (minimum score 550), minimum GPA of 3.0; 3-5 years of work experience; 3 letters of reference with at least one academic reference. Additional exam requirements/recommendations for international students: Required—TOEFL (minimum score 580 paper-based; 92 iBT) or IELTS (minimum score 7). *Application deadline:* For fall admission, 10/31 priority date for domestic and international students; for spring admission, 3/31 priority date for domestic and international students. Application fee: $50 Canadian dollars. Electronic applications accepted. *Financial support:* In 2013–14, 6 fellowships, 3 research assistantships (averaging $4,500 per year), 22 teaching assistantships (averaging $2,250 per year) were awarded. *Faculty research:* Entrepreneurship, finance, law, sport and recreation management, and engineering management. *Unit head:* Judy Roy, Director of Graduate Studies, 506-458-7307, Fax: 506-453-3561, E-mail: jroy@unb.ca. *Application contact:* Marilyn Davis, Acting Graduate Secretary, 506-453-4766, Fax: 506-453-3561, E-mail: mbacontact@unb.ca.
Website: http://go.unb.ca/gradprograms.

University of New Brunswick Fredericton, School of Graduate Studies, Faculty of Kinesiology, Fredericton, NB E3B 5A3, Canada. Offers exercise and sport science (M Sc); sport and recreation management (MBA); sport and recreation studies (MA). Part-time programs available. *Faculty:* 14 full-time (6 women), 1 part-time/adjunct (0 women). *Students:* 27 full-time (13 women), 5 part-time (1 woman). In 2013, 9 master's awarded. *Degree requirements:* For master's, thesis (for some programs). *Entrance requirements:* For master's, GMAT (minimum score of 550 for sport and recreation management program), minimum GPA of 3.0, written statement of research goals and interests. Additional exam requirements/recommendations for international students: Required—TOEFL (minimum score 92 iBT), IELTS (minimum score 7). *Application deadline:* For winter admission, 1/31 for domestic students; for spring admission, 3/31 for domestic students. Applications are processed on a rolling basis. Application fee: $50 Canadian dollars. Electronic applications accepted. *Financial support:* In 2013–14, 31 research assistantships, 61 teaching assistantships were awarded; fellowships with tuition reimbursements, career-related internships or fieldwork, and scholarships/grants also available. *Unit head:* Dr. Usha Kuruganti, Acting Director of Graduate Studies, 506-447-3101, Fax: 506-453-3511, E-mail: ukurugan@unb.ca. *Application contact:* Leslie Harquail, Graduate Secretary, 506-453-4575, Fax: 506-453-3511, E-mail: harquail@unb.ca.
Website: http://go.unb.ca/gradprograms.

University of New Haven, Graduate School, College of Business, Program in Business Administration, West Haven, CT 06516-1916. Offers accounting (MBA, Certificate), including CPA (MBA); business administration (MBA); business management (Certificate); business policy and strategic leadership (MBA); finance (MBA), including CFA; global marketing (MBA); human resource management (Certificate); human resources management (MBA); international business (Certificate); marketing (MBA, Certificate); sports management (MBA). Part-time and evening/weekend programs available. *Students:* 125 full-time (55 women), 88 part-time (30 women); includes 31 minority (16 Black or African American, non-Hispanic/Latino; 1 American Indian or Alaska Native, non-Hispanic/Latino; 8 Asian, non-Hispanic/Latino; 5 Hispanic/Latino; 1 Native Hawaiian or other Pacific Islander, non-Hispanic/Latino), 72 international. 196 applicants, 89% accepted, 72 enrolled. In 2013, 143 master's, 24 other advanced degrees awarded. *Degree requirements:* For master's, thesis optional. *Entrance requirements:* For master's, GMAT. Additional exam requirements/recommendations for international students: Required—TOEFL (minimum score 80 iBT), IELTS, PTE (minimum score 53). *Application deadline:* For fall admission, 5/31 for international students; for winter admission, 10/15 for international students; for spring admission, 1/15 for international students. Applications are processed on a rolling basis. Application fee: $75. Electronic applications accepted. Application fee is waived when completed online. *Expenses: Tuition:* Full-time $21,600; part-time $800 per credit hour. *Required fees:* $45 per trimester. *Financial support:* Research assistantships with partial tuition reimbursements, teaching assistantships with partial tuition reimbursements, career-related internships or fieldwork, Federal Work-Study, scholarships/grants, and unspecified assistantships available. Support available to part-time students. Financial award applicants required to submit FAFSA. *Unit head:* Dr. Armando Rodriguez, Director, 203-932-7372, E-mail: arodriguez@newhaven.edu. *Application contact:* Eloise Gormley, Director of Graduate Admissions, 203-932-7440, E-mail: gradinfo@newhaven.edu.
Website: http://www.newhaven.edu/7433/.

University of New Haven, Graduate School, College of Business, Program in Sports Management, West Haven, CT 06516-1916. Offers collegiate athletic administration (MS); facility management (MS); management of sports industries (Certificate); sports management (MS). Part-time and evening/weekend programs available. *Students:* 18 full-time (8 women), 8 part-time (0 women); includes 2 minority (1 Black or African American, non-Hispanic/Latino; 1 Asian, non-Hispanic/Latino), 8 international. 24 applicants, 83% accepted, 10 enrolled. In 2013, 11 master's awarded. *Entrance requirements:* For master's, GMAT. Additional exam requirements/recommendations for international students: Required—TOEFL (minimum score 80 iBT), IELTS, PTE (minimum score 53). *Application deadline:* For fall admission, 5/31 for international students; for winter admission, 10/15 for international students; for spring admission, 1/15 for international students. Applications are processed on a rolling basis. Application fee: $75. Electronic applications accepted. Application fee is waived when completed online. *Expenses: Tuition:* Full-time $21,600; part-time $800 per credit hour. *Required fees:* $45 per trimester. *Financial support:* Research assistantships with partial tuition reimbursements, teaching assistantships with partial tuition reimbursements, career-related internships or fieldwork, Federal Work-Study, scholarships/grants, and unspecified assistantships available. Support available to part-time students. Financial award applicants required to submit FAFSA. *Unit head:* Prof. Gil B. Fried, Chair, 203-932-7081, E-mail: gfried@newhaven.edu. *Application contact:* Eloise Gormley, Director of Graduate Admissions, 203-932-7440, E-mail: gradinfo@newhaven.edu.
Website: http://www.newhaven.edu/6851/.

University of New Mexico, Graduate School, College of Education, Department of Health, Exercise and Sports Sciences, Program in Physical Education, Albuquerque, NM 87131-2039. Offers adapted physical education (MS); curriculum and instruction (MS); exercise science (MS); generalist (MS); sports administration (MS). Part-time programs available. *Faculty:* 6 full-time (3 women). *Students:* 53 full-time (19 women), 27 part-time (14 women); includes 32 minority (3 Black or African American, non-Hispanic/Latino; 3 American Indian or Alaska Native, non-Hispanic/Latino; 2 Asian, non-Hispanic/Latino; 22 Hispanic/Latino; 2 Two or more races, non-Hispanic/Latino), 12 international. Average age 28. 48 applicants, 65% accepted, 23 enrolled. In 2013, 22 master's awarded. Terminal master's awarded for partial completion of doctoral program. *Degree requirements:* For master's, comprehensive exam, thesis optional. *Entrance requirements:* For master's, GRE, 3 letters of reference, minimum cumulative GPA of 3.0 in last 2 years of bachelor's degree, letter of intent. Additional exam requirements/recommendations for international students: Required—TOEFL (minimum score 550 paper-based). *Application deadline:* For fall admission, 3/1 priority date for domestic students; for spring admission, 11/1 priority date for domestic students. Application fee: $50. Electronic applications accepted. *Financial support:* In 2013–14, 57 students received support, including 1 fellowship (averaging $2,290 per year), 1 teaching assistantship with full tuition reimbursement available (averaging $11,294 per year); career-related internships or fieldwork, Federal Work-Study, institutionally sponsored loans, scholarships/grants, health care benefits, tuition waivers, and unspecified assistantships also available. Financial award application deadline: 3/1; financial award applicants required to submit FAFSA. *Faculty research:* Physical education pedagogy, sports psychology, sports administration, cardiac rehabilitation, sports physiology, physical fitness assessment, exercise prescription. *Total annual research expenditures:* $17,400. *Unit head:* Dr. Todd Seidler, Chair, 505-277-2783, Fax: 505-277-6227, E-mail: tseidler@unm.edu. *Application contact:* Monica Lopez, Department Office, 505-277-5151, Fax: 505-277-6227, E-mail: mllopez@unm.edu.
Website: http://coe.unm.edu/departments/hess/pe-teacher-education.html.

University of New Mexico, Graduate School, College of Education, Department of Health, Exercise and Sports Sciences, Program in Physical Education, Sports and Exercise Science, Albuquerque, NM 87131-2039. Offers curriculum and instruction (PhD); exercise science (PhD); sports administration (PhD). Part-time programs available. *Faculty:* 18 full-time (10 women). *Students:* 26 full-time (9 women), 17 part-time (5 women); includes 11 minority (3 Black or African American, non-Hispanic/Latino; 1 Asian, non-Hispanic/Latino; 6 Hispanic/Latino; 1 Native Hawaiian or other Pacific Islander, non-Hispanic/Latino), 7 international. Average age 34. 25 applicants, 36% accepted, 5 enrolled. In 2013, 4 doctorates awarded. *Degree requirements:* For doctorate, comprehensive exam, thesis/dissertation, inquiry skills, 24 credits in supporting area. *Entrance requirements:* For doctorate, GRE, letter of intent, 3 letters of reference, minimum cumulative GPA of 3.0 in last 2 years of bachelor's degree. Additional exam requirements/recommendations for international students: Required—TOEFL (minimum score 550 paper-based). *Application deadline:* For fall admission, 3/1 priority date for domestic students; for spring admission, 11/1 priority date for domestic students. Application fee: $50. Electronic applications accepted. *Financial support:* In 2013–14, 33 students received support, including 3 fellowships (averaging $2,290 per year), 16 teaching assistantships with full tuition reimbursements available (averaging $10,987 per year); career-related internships or fieldwork, Federal Work-Study, institutionally sponsored loans, scholarships/grants, health care benefits, tuition waivers, and unspecified assistantships also available. Financial award application deadline: 3/1; financial award applicants required to submit FAFSA. *Faculty research:* Facility risk management, physical education pedagogy practices, physiological adaptations to exercise, physiological adaptations to heat, sport leadership. *Total annual research expenditures:* $17,400. *Unit head:* Dr. Todd Seidler, Chair, 505-277-2783, Fax: 505-277-6227, E-mail: tseidler@unm.edu. *Application contact:* Monica Lopez, Program Office, 505-277-5151, Fax: 505-277-6227, E-mail: mllopez@unm.edu.
Website: http://coe.unm.edu/departments/hess/pe-teacher-education/physical-education-sports-and-exercise-science-phd.html.

The University of North Carolina at Chapel Hill, Graduate School, College of Arts and Sciences, Department of Exercise and Sport Science, Chapel Hill, NC 27599. Offers athletic training (MA); exercise physiology (MA); sport administration (MA). *Degree requirements:* For master's, comprehensive exam, thesis. *Entrance requirements:* For master's, GRE General Test, minimum GPA of 3.0. Additional exam requirements/recommendations for international students: Required—TOEFL (minimum score 550 paper-based). Electronic applications accepted. *Faculty research:* Mild head injury in sport, endocrine system's response to exercise, obesity and children, effect of aerobic exercise on cerebral bloodflow in elderly population.

University of Northern Colorado, Graduate School, College of Natural and Health Sciences, School of Sport and Exercise Science, Greeley, CO 80639. Offers exercise science (MS, PhD); sport administration (MS, PhD); sport pedagogy (MS, PhD). Part-time and evening/weekend programs available. *Degree requirements:* For master's, comprehensive exam; for doctorate, comprehensive exam, thesis/dissertation. *Entrance requirements:* For master's, 2 letters of recommendation, resume; for doctorate, GRE General Test, 3 letters of recommendation, resume. Electronic applications accepted.

University of North Florida, College of Education and Human Services, Department of Leadership, School Counseling and Sport Management, Jacksonville, FL 32224. Offers counselor education (M Ed), including school counseling; educational leadership (M Ed, Ed D), including athletic administration (M Ed), educational leadership, educational technology (M Ed), instructional leadership (M Ed). Part-time and evening/weekend programs available. *Faculty:* 16 full-time (8 women), 1 (woman) part-time/adjunct. *Students:* 76 full-time (59 women), 212 part-time (153 women); includes 91 minority (65 Black or African American, non-Hispanic/Latino; 1 American Indian or Alaska Native, non-Hispanic/Latino; 3 Asian, non-Hispanic/Latino; 13 Hispanic/Latino; 1 Native

Hawaiian or other Pacific Islander, non-Hispanic/Latino; 8 Two or more races, non-Hispanic/Latino), 6 international. Average age 35. 151 applicants, 60% accepted, 71 enrolled. In 2013, 59 master's, 12 doctorates awarded. *Degree requirements:* For doctorate, thesis/dissertation. *Entrance requirements:* For master's, GRE General Test, minimum GPA of 3.0 in last 60 hours, interview, 3 letters of recommendation; for doctorate, GRE General Test, master's degree, interview, 3 letters of recommendation, writing sample. Additional exam requirements/recommendations for international students: Required—TOEFL (minimum score 500 paper-based). *Application deadline:* For fall admission, 7/1 priority date for domestic students, 5/1 for international students; for spring admission, 11/1 priority date for domestic students, 10/1 for international students. Application fee: $30. Electronic applications accepted. *Expenses:* Tuition, state resident: full-time $9794; part-time $408.10 per credit hour. Tuition, nonresident: full-time $22,383; part-time $932.61 per credit hour. *Required fees:* $2020; $84.20 per credit hour. Tuition and fees vary according to course load and program. *Financial support:* In 2013–14, 49 students received support, including 8 research assistantships (averaging $2,573 per year); teaching assistantships, career-related internships or fieldwork, Federal Work-Study, scholarships/grants, tuition waivers (partial), and unspecified assistantships also available. Support available to part-time students. Financial award application deadline: 4/1; financial award applicants required to submit FAFSA. *Faculty research:* Counseling: ethics; lesbian, bisexual and transgender issues; educational leadership: school culture and climate; educational assessment and accountability; school safety and student discipline. *Total annual research expenditures:* $128,099. *Unit head:* Dr. Jennifer Kane, Chair, 904-620-2465, E-mail: jkane@unf.edu. *Application contact:* Dr. Amanda Pascale, Director, The Graduate School, 904-620-1360, Fax: 904-620-1362, E-mail: graduateschool@unf.edu.
Website: http://www.unf.edu/coehs/lscsm/.

University of North Texas, Robert B. Toulouse School of Graduate Studies, Denton, TN 76203-5017. Offers accounting (MS, PhD); applied anthropology (MA, MS); applied behavior analysis (Certificate); applied technology and performance improvement (M Ed, MS, PhD); art education (MA, PhD); art history (MA); art museum education (Certificate); arts leadership (Certificate); audiology (Au D); behavior analysis (MS); biochemistry and molecular biology (MS, PhD); biology (MA, MS, PhD); business (PhD); business computer information systems (PhD); chemistry (MS, PhD); clinical psychology (PhD); communication studies (MA, MS); computer engineering (MS); computer science (MS); computer science and engineering (PhD); counseling (M Ed, MS, PhD), including clinical mental health counseling (MS), college and university counseling (M Ed, MS), elementary school counseling (M Ed, MS), secondary school counseling (M Ed, MS); counseling psychology (PhD); creative writing (MA); criminal justice (MS); curriculum and instruction (M Ed, PhD), including curriculum studies (PhD), early childhood studies (PhD), language and literacy studies (PhD); decision sciences (MBA); design (MA, MFA), including fashion design (MFA), innovation studies, interior design (MFA); early childhood studies (MS); economics (MS); educational leadership (M Ed, Ed D, PhD); educational psychology (MS), including family studies, gifted and talented (MS, PhD), human development, learning and cognition, research, measurement and evaluation; educational research (PhD), including gifted and talented (MS, PhD), human development and family studies, psychological aspects of sports and exercise, research, measurement and statistics; electrical engineering (MS); emergency management (MPA); engineering systems (MS); English (MA, PhD); environmental science (MS, PhD); experimental psychology (PhD); finance (MBA, MS, PhD); financial management (MPA); French (MA); health psychology and behavioral medicine (PhD); health services management (MBA); higher education (M Ed, Ed D, PhD); history (MA, MS, PhD), including European history (PhD), military history (PhD), United States history (PhD); hospitality management (MS); human resources management (MPA); information science (MS, PhD); information technologies (MBA); information technology and decision sciences (MS); interdisciplinary studies (MA, MS); international sustainable tourism (MS); jazz studies (MM); journalism (MA, MJ, Graduate Certificate), including interactive and virtual digital communication (Graduate Certificate), narrative journalism (Graduate Certificate), public relations (Graduate Certificate); kinesiology (MS); learning technologies (MS, PhD); library science (MS); local government management (MPA); logistics and supply chain management (MBA, PhD); long-term care, senior housing, and aging services (MA, MS); management science (PhD); marketing (MBA, PhD); materials science and engineering (MS, PhD); mathematics (MA, PhD); merchandising (MS); music (MA, MM Ed, PhD), including ethnomusicology (MA), music education (MM Ed, PhD), music theory (MA, PhD), musicology (MA, PhD), performance (MA); nonprofit management (MPA); operations and supply chain management (MBA); performance (MM, DMA); philosophy (MA, PhD); physics (MS, PhD); political science (MA, MS, PhD); public administration and management (PhD), including emergency management, nonprofit management, public financial management, urban management; radio, television and film (MA, MFA); recreation, event and sport management (MS); rehabilitation counseling (MS, Certificate); sociology (MA, MS, PhD); Spanish (MA); special education (M Ed, PhD), including autism intervention (PhD), emotional/behavioral disorders (PhD), mild/moderate disabilities (PhD); speech-language pathology (MA, MS); strategic management (MBA); studio art (MFA); taxation (MS); teaching (M Ed); MBA/MS; MS/MPH; MSES/MBA. Part-time and evening/weekend programs available. Postbaccalaureate distance learning degree programs offered. *Faculty:* 661 full-time (213 women), 240 part-time/adjunct (144 women). *Students:* 3,106 full-time (1,620 women), 3,543 part-time (2,221 women); includes 1,740 minority (533 Black or African American, non-Hispanic/Latino; 15 American Indian or Alaska Native, non-Hispanic/Latino; 286 Asian, non-Hispanic/Latino; 746 Hispanic/Latino; 3 Native Hawaiian or other Pacific Islander, non-Hispanic/Latino; 157 Two or more races, non-Hispanic/Latino), 1,145 international. Average age 32. 6,289 applicants, 43% accepted, 1751 enrolled. In 2013, 1,778 master's, 239 doctorates, 10 other advanced degrees awarded. Terminal master's awarded for partial completion of doctoral program. *Degree requirements:* For master's, variable foreign language requirement, comprehensive exam (for some programs), thesis (for some programs); for doctorate, variable foreign language requirement, comprehensive exam (for some programs), thesis/dissertation; for other advanced degree, variable foreign language requirement, comprehensive exam (for some programs). *Entrance requirements:* For master's and doctorate, GRE, GMAT. Additional exam requirements/recommendations for international students: Required—TOEFL (minimum score 550 paper-based; 79 iBT). *Application deadline:* For fall admission, 7/15 for domestic students, 3/15 for international students; for spring admission, 11/15 for domestic students, 9/15 for international students; for summer admission, 5/1 for domestic students. Applications are processed on a rolling basis. Application fee: $60. Electronic applications accepted. *Financial support:* Fellowships with partial tuition reimbursements, research assistantships with partial tuition reimbursements, teaching assistantships, career-related internships or fieldwork, Federal Work-Study, institutionally sponsored loans, scholarships/grants, health care benefits, and library assistantships available. Support available to part-time students. Financial award applicants required to submit FAFSA. *Unit head:* Mark Wardell, Dean, 940-565-2383, E-mail: mark.wardell@unt.edu. *Application contact:* Toulouse School of Graduate Studies, 940-565-2383, Fax: 940-565-2141, E-mail: gradsch@unt.edu.
Website: http://tsgs.unt.edu/.

University of San Francisco, College of Arts and Sciences, Collegiate Athletics Program, San Francisco, CA 94117-1080. Offers MCA. Postbaccalaureate distance learning degree programs offered. *Entrance requirements:* For master's, baccalaureate degree from accredited institution; minimum undergraduate GPA of 2.7; written goal statement; two letters of recommendation; resume; official transcripts. Additional exam requirements/recommendations for international students: Required—TOEFL (minimum score 570 paper-based; 90 iBT). *Expenses: Tuition:* Full-time $21,150; part-time $1175 per unit. Tuition and fees vary according to course load, campus/location and program.

University of San Francisco, College of Arts and Sciences, Sport Management Program, San Francisco, CA 94117-1080. Offers MA. Evening/weekend programs available. *Faculty:* 5 full-time (1 woman), 9 part-time/adjunct (1 woman). *Students:* 189 full-time (77 women), 11 part-time (6 women); includes 61 minority (14 Black or African American, non-Hispanic/Latino; 15 Asian, non-Hispanic/Latino; 25 Hispanic/Latino; 7 Two or more races, non-Hispanic/Latino), 24 international. Average age 26. 201 applicants, 43% accepted, 72 enrolled. In 2013, 99 master's awarded. *Degree requirements:* For master's, thesis or alternative. *Entrance requirements:* For master's, interview, minimum GPA of 2.75. *Application deadline:* For spring admission, 9/1 for domestic students. Applications are processed on a rolling basis. Application fee: $55 ($65 for international students). *Expenses: Tuition:* Full-time $21,150; part-time $1175 per unit. Tuition and fees vary according to course load, campus/location and program. *Financial support:* In 2013–14, 33 students received support. Career-related internships or fieldwork, Federal Work-Study, and institutionally sponsored loans available. Financial award application deadline: 3/2; financial award applicants required to submit FAFSA. *Faculty research:* Media and sports, sports marketing, sports law, management and organization. *Unit head:* Dr. Daniel Rascher, Graduate Director, 415-422-2678, Fax: 415-422-6267. *Application contact:* Mark Landerghini, Information Contact, 415-422-5101, Fax: 415-422-2217, E-mail: asgraduate@usfca.edu.
Website: http://www.usfca.edu/artsci/sm/.

University of South Carolina, The Graduate School, College of Hospitality, Retail, and Sport Management, Department of Sport and Entertainment Management, Columbia, SC 29208. Offers live sport and entertainment events (MS); public assembly facilities management (MS). Part-time programs available. *Degree requirements:* For master's, comprehensive exam, thesis optional. *Entrance requirements:* For master's, GRE General Test or GMAT (preferred), minimum GPA of 3.0. Additional exam requirements/recommendations for international students: Required—TOEFL (minimum score 570 paper-based; 70 iBT). Electronic applications accepted. *Expenses:* Contact institution. *Faculty research:* Public assembly marketing, operations, box office, booking and scheduling, law/economic impacts.

University of Southern Mississippi, Graduate School, College of Health, School of Human Performance and Recreation, Hattiesburg, MS 39406-0001. Offers human performance (MS, PhD), including exercise physiology (PhD), human performance (MS), physical education (MS); interscholastic athletic administration (MS); recreation and leisure management (MS); sport administration (MS); sport and coaching education (MS); sport management (MS). Part-time and evening/weekend programs available. *Faculty:* 13 full-time (5 women). *Students:* 60 full-time (20 women), 43 part-time (9 women); includes 19 minority (13 Black or African American, non-Hispanic/Latino; 1 American Indian or Alaska Native, non-Hispanic/Latino; 2 Hispanic/Latino; 3 Two or more races, non-Hispanic/Latino), 4 international. Average age 29. 62 applicants, 77% accepted, 38 enrolled. In 2013, 39 master's, 1 doctorate awarded. *Degree requirements:* For master's, comprehensive exam, thesis optional; for doctorate, comprehensive exam, thesis/dissertation. *Entrance requirements:* For master's, GRE General Test, minimum GPA of 2.75 in last 60 hours; for doctorate, GRE General Test, minimum GPA of 3.5. Additional exam requirements/recommendations for international students: Required—TOEFL, IELTS. *Application deadline:* For fall admission, 3/1 priority date for domestic students, 3/1 for international students; for spring admission, 1/10 priority date for domestic and international students. Applications are processed on a rolling basis. Application fee: $50. Electronic applications accepted. *Financial support:* In 2013–14, 1 fellowship (averaging $16,000 per year), 6 research assistantships with full tuition reimbursements (averaging $7,492 per year), 5 teaching assistantships with full tuition reimbursements (averaging $7,330 per year) were awarded; career-related internships or fieldwork, Federal Work-Study, institutionally sponsored loans, scholarships/grants, health care benefits, and unspecified assistantships also available. Financial award application deadline: 3/15; financial award applicants required to submit FAFSA. *Faculty research:* Exercise physiology, health behaviors, resource management, activity interaction, site development. *Unit head:* Dr. Frederick Green, Director, 601-266-5379, Fax: 601-266-4445. *Application contact:* Dr. Trenton Gould, Graduate Coordinator, 601-266-5379, Fax: 601-266-4445.
Website: http://www.usm.edu/graduateschool/table.php.

University of South Florida, College of Business, Department of Business Administration, Tampa, FL 33620-9951. Offers business administration (MBA); executive business administration (EMBA); sport and entertainment management (MBA); MBA/MS. *Accreditation:* AACSB. Part-time and evening/weekend programs available. *Students:* 65 full-time (13 women); includes 21 minority (7 Black or African American, non-Hispanic/Latino; 4 Asian, non-Hispanic/Latino; 9 Hispanic/Latino; 1 Native Hawaiian or other Pacific Islander, non-Hispanic/Latino), 2 international. Average age 31. 46 applicants, 80% accepted, 33 enrolled. In 2013, 18 master's awarded. *Degree requirements:* For master's, comprehensive exam, thesis (for some programs). *Entrance requirements:* For master's, GMAT (preferred), GRE or MCAT, minimum GPA of 3.0 in upper-level bachelor's degree course work from regionally-accredited institution; recommendation letters; statement of purpose. Additional exam requirements/recommendations for international students: Required—TOEFL (minimum score 550 paper-based; 79 iBT) or IELTS (minimum score 6.5). *Application deadline:* For fall admission, 6/1 for domestic students, 1/2 for international students; for spring admission, 10/15 for domestic students, 6/1 for international students. Application fee: $30. *Financial support:* Scholarships/grants, health care benefits, and unspecified assistantships available. Financial award applicants required to submit FAFSA. *Faculty research:* Business communications; business intelligence; business process improvement; corporate governance; sustainability, ethics, and environmentally-friendly business practices; small business development; graduate education; women/minority business development; business planning; leadership. *Unit head:* Dr. Jacqueline Reck, Professor and Interim Dean, 813-974-6721, Fax: 813-974-6528, E-mail: jreck@usf.edu. *Application contact:* Irene Hurst, Director, MBA and EMBA Programs, 813-974-3335, Fax: 813-974-4518, E-mail: ihurst@usf.edu.
Website: http://business.usf.edu/.

The University of Tennessee, Graduate School, College of Education, Health and Human Sciences, Department of Exercise, Sport, and Leisure Studies, Knoxville, TN 37996. Offers exercise science (MS, PhD), including biomechanics/sports medicine, exercise physiology; recreation and leisure studies (MS); sport management (MS); sport studies (MS, PhD); therapeutic recreation (MS). Part-time and evening/weekend programs available. *Degree requirements:* For master's, thesis optional. *Entrance requirements:* For master's, minimum GPA of 2.7. Additional exam requirements/recommendations for international students: Required—TOEFL. Electronic applications accepted. *Expenses:* Tuition, state resident: full-time $9540; part-time $531 per credit

hour. Tuition, nonresident: full-time $27,728; part-time $1542 per credit hour. *Required fees:* $1404; $67 per credit hour.

University of the Incarnate Word, School of Graduate Studies and Research, H-E-B School of Business and Administration, Programs in Administration, San Antonio, TX 78209-6397. Offers adult education (MAA); communication arts (MAA); healthcare administration (MAA); instructional technology (MAA); nutrition (MAA); organizational development (MAA); sports management (MAA). Part-time and evening/weekend programs available. Postbaccalaureate distance learning degree programs offered (no on-campus study). *Faculty:* 20 full-time (10 women), 14 part-time/adjunct (6 women). *Students:* 31 full-time (22 women), 54 part-time (36 women); includes 61 minority (14 Black or African American, non-Hispanic/Latino; 1 Asian, non-Hispanic/Latino; 46 Hispanic/Latino), 6 international. Average age 31. 63 applicants, 68% accepted, 21 enrolled. In 2013, 35 master's awarded. *Degree requirements:* For master's, capstone. *Entrance requirements:* For master's, GRE, GMAT, undergraduate degree, minimum GPA of 2.5. Additional exam requirements/recommendations for international students: Required—TOEFL (minimum score 560 paper-based; 83 iBT). *Application deadline:* Applications are processed on a rolling basis. Application fee: $20. Electronic applications accepted. *Expenses: Tuition:* Part-time $815 per credit hour. *Required fees:* $86 per credit hour. One-time fee: $40 part-time. Tuition and fees vary according to degree level and program. *Financial support:* Federal Work-Study and scholarships/grants available. Financial award applicants required to submit FAFSA. *Unit head:* Dr. Mark Teachout, MAA Programs Director, 210-829-3177, Fax: 210-805-3564, E-mail: teachout@uiwtx.edu. *Application contact:* Andrea Cyterski-Acosta, Dean of Enrollment, 210-829-6005, Fax: 210-829-3921, E-mail: admis@uiwtx.edu.
Website: http://www.uiw.edu/maa/.

University of the Incarnate Word, School of Graduate Studies and Research, H-E-B School of Business and Administration, Programs in Business Administration, San Antonio, TX 78209-6397. Offers general business (MBA); international business (MBA); marketing (MBA); sports management (MBA). *Accreditation:* ACBSP. Part-time and evening/weekend programs available. Postbaccalaureate distance learning degree programs offered. *Faculty:* 20 full-time (10 women), 14 part-time/adjunct (6 women). *Students:* 95 full-time (33 women), 74 part-time (40 women); includes 93 minority (11 Black or African American, non-Hispanic/Latino; 1 American Indian or Alaska Native, non-Hispanic/Latino; 4 Asian, non-Hispanic/Latino; 71 Hispanic/Latino; 2 Native Hawaiian or other Pacific Islander, non-Hispanic/Latino; 4 Two or more races, non-Hispanic/Latino), 41 international. Average age 28. 183 applicants, 66% accepted, 51 enrolled. In 2013, 75 master's awarded. *Degree requirements:* For master's, capstone. *Entrance requirements:* For master's, GMAT (minimum score 450), undergraduate degree with minimum overall GPA of 2.5. Additional exam requirements/recommendations for international students: Required—TOEFL (minimum score 560 paper-based; 83 iBT). *Application deadline:* Applications are processed on a rolling basis. Application fee: $20. Electronic applications accepted. *Expenses: Tuition:* Part-time $815 per credit hour. *Required fees:* $86 per credit hour. One-time fee: $40 part-time. Tuition and fees vary according to degree level and program. *Financial support:* Federal Work-Study and scholarships/grants available. Financial award applicants required to submit FAFSA. *Unit head:* Dr. Jeannie Scott, Acting Dean, 210-283-5002, Fax: 210-805-3564, E-mail: scott@uiwtx.edu. *Application contact:* Andrea Cyterski-Acosta, Dean of Enrollment, 210-829-6005, Fax: 210-829-3921, E-mail: admis@uiwtx.edu.
Website: http://www.uiw.edu/mba/index.htm and http://www.uiw.edu/mba/admission.html.

University of the Incarnate Word, School of Graduate Studies and Research, School of Nursing and Health Professions, Programs in Sports Management, San Antonio, TX 78209-6397. Offers MS. Part-time and evening/weekend programs available. *Faculty:* 1 full-time (0 women). *Students:* 13 full-time (5 women), 8 part-time (3 women); includes 7 minority (4 Black or African American, non-Hispanic/Latino; 3 Hispanic/Latino), 3 international. Average age 26. 22 applicants, 86% accepted, 1 enrolled. In 2013, 9 master's awarded. *Degree requirements:* For master's, internship. *Entrance requirements:* For master's, GRE, letter of recommendation from professional in field. Additional exam requirements/recommendations for international students: Required—TOEFL (minimum score 560 paper-based; 83 iBT). *Application deadline:* Applications are processed on a rolling basis. Application fee: $20. Electronic applications accepted. *Expenses: Tuition:* Part-time $815 per credit hour. *Required fees:* $86 per credit hour. One-time fee: $40 part-time. Tuition and fees vary according to degree level and program. *Financial support:* Federal Work-Study and scholarships/grants available. Financial award applicants required to submit FAFSA. *Unit head:* Dr. Randall Griffiths, Assistant Professor, 210-829-2795, Fax: 210-829-3174, E-mail: rgriffit@uiwtx.edu. *Application contact:* Andrea Cyterski-Acosta, Dean of Enrollment, 210-829-6005, Fax: 210-829-3921, E-mail: admis@uiwtx.edu.
Website: http://www.uiw.edu/gradstudies/documents/mssportsmanagement.pdf.

University of the Southwest, Graduate Programs, Hobbs, NM 88240-9129. Offers business administration (MBA); curriculum and instruction (MSE); curriculum and instruction: bilingual (MSE); curriculum and instruction: TESOL (MSE); early childhood education (MSE); educational administration (MSE); mental health counseling (MSE); school counseling (MSE); special education (MSE); sports management (MBA). Part-time and evening/weekend programs available. Postbaccalaureate distance learning degree programs offered (no on-campus study). *Degree requirements:* For master's, comprehensive exam, thesis (for some programs). *Entrance requirements:* Additional exam requirements/recommendations for international students: Recommended—TOEFL. Electronic applications accepted.

University of Wisconsin–La Crosse, Graduate Studies, College of Science and Health, Department of Exercise and Sport Science, La Crosse, WI 54601-3742. Offers clinical exercise physiology (MS); human performance (MS), including applied sport science, human performance, strength and conditioning; physical education teaching (MS), including adapted physical education, adventure education, physical education teaching; special/adapted physical education (MS); sport administration (MS). Part-time and evening/weekend programs available. *Faculty:* 11 full-time (1 woman), 1 part-time/adjunct (0 women). *Students:* 45 full-time (17 women), 22 part-time (8 women); includes 4 minority (1 Black or African American, non-Hispanic/Latino; 1 American Indian or Alaska Native, non-Hispanic/Latino; 1 Asian, non-Hispanic/Latino; 1 Two or more races, non-Hispanic/Latino), 1 international. Average age 25. 107 applicants, 51% accepted, 41 enrolled. In 2013, 53 master's awarded. *Entrance requirements:* Additional exam requirements/recommendations for international students: Required—TOEFL (minimum score 550 paper-based; 79 iBT). Electronic applications accepted. *Financial support:* Research assistantships with partial tuition reimbursements, Federal Work-Study, scholarships/grants, health care benefits, and tuition waivers (partial) available. Support available to part-time students. Financial award application deadline: 3/15; financial award applicants required to submit FAFSA. *Unit head:* Mark Gibson, Chair, E-mail: mgibson@uwlax.edu. *Application contact:* Corey Sjoquist, Director of Admissions, 608-785-8939, E-mail: admissions@uwlax.edu.
Website: http://www.uwlax.edu/sah/ess/index.htm.

Valparaiso University, Graduate School, Program in Sports Administration, Valparaiso, IN 46383. Offers MS, JD/MS. Part-time and evening/weekend programs available. *Students:* 32 full-time (11 women), 6 part-time (2 women); includes 3 minority (2 Black or African American, non-Hispanic/Latino; 1 Hispanic/Latino), 4 international. Average age 24. In 2013, 16 master's awarded. *Entrance requirements:* For master's, minimum GPA of 3.0. Additional exam requirements/recommendations for international students: Required—TOEFL (minimum score 550 paper-based; 80 iBT), IELTS (minimum score 6). *Application deadline:* Applications are processed on a rolling basis. Application fee: $30 ($50 for international students). Electronic applications accepted. *Expenses: Tuition:* Full-time $10,350; part-time $575 per credit hour. *Required fees:* $378; $101 per term. Tuition and fees vary according to course load and program. *Financial support:* Available to part-time students. Applicants required to submit FAFSA. *Unit head:* Dr. Jennifer A. Ziegler, Dean, Graduate School and Continuing Education, 219-464-5313, Fax: 219-464-5381, E-mail: jennifer.ziegler@valpo.edu. *Application contact:* Jessica Choquette, Graduate Admissions Specialist, 219-464-5313, Fax: 219-464-5381, E-mail: jessica.choquette@valpo.edu.
Website: http://www.valpo.edu/grad/sportsad/.

Washington State University, Graduate School, College of Education, Department of Educational Leadership and Counseling Psychology, Program in Sport Management, Pullman, WA 99164. Offers MA. *Degree requirements:* For master's, comprehensive exam (for some programs), thesis (for some programs), oral and written exam. *Entrance requirements:* For master's, GRE General Test, minimum GPA of 3.0, 3 letters of recommendation, transcripts showing all college or university course work, statement of professional objectives, current curriculum vitae/resume. Additional exam requirements/recommendations for international students: Required—TOEFL (minimum score 550 paper-based; 80 iBT). Electronic applications accepted. *Faculty research:* Sport marketing, sport business decision-making process and power relationships, understanding of sport consumer behavior, socio-cultural issues related to sport, sport law.

Wayne State College, Department of Health, Human Performance and Sport, Wayne, NE 68787. Offers exercise science (MSE); organizational management (MS), including sport management. Part-time and evening/weekend programs available. *Degree requirements:* For master's, comprehensive exam, thesis optional. *Entrance requirements:* For master's, GRE General Test, minimum GPA of 3.0. Additional exam requirements/recommendations for international students: Required—TOEFL (minimum score 550 paper-based). Electronic applications accepted.

Wayne State University, College of Education, Division of Kinesiology, Health and Sports Studies, Detroit, MI 48202. Offers adapted physical education (Certificate); coaching (Certificate); elementary physical education (Certificate); exercise and sport science (M Ed); health education (M Ed, Certificate); kinesiology (M Ed, PhD), including exercise and sport science (PhD), physical education pedagogy (PhD); physical education (M Ed); secondary physical education (Certificate); sports administration (MA); wellness clinician/research (M Ed). Part-time programs available. *Students:* 42 full-time (27 women), 78 part-time (38 women); includes 43 minority (35 Black or African American, non-Hispanic/Latino; 1 Asian, non-Hispanic/Latino; 5 Hispanic/Latino; 2 Two or more races, non-Hispanic/Latino), 5 international. Average age 30. 120 applicants, 48% accepted, 30 enrolled. In 2013, 32 master's awarded. *Degree requirements:* For master's, thesis (for some programs); for doctorate, thesis/dissertation. *Entrance requirements:* For master's and doctorate, minimum undergraduate GPA of 3.0, undergraduate degree directly relating to the field of specialization being applied for, or undergraduate degree accompanied by extensive educational background in a closely-related field. Additional exam requirements/recommendations for international students: Required—TOEFL (minimum score 79 iBT), TWE (minimum score 5.5), Michigan English Language Assessment Battery (minimum score 85); Recommended—IELTS (minimum score 6.5). *Application deadline:* For fall admission, 6/1 priority date for domestic students, 5/1 priority date for international students; for winter admission, 10/1 priority date for domestic students, 9/1 priority date for international students; for spring admission, 2/1 priority date for domestic students, 1/1 priority date for international students. Applications are processed on a rolling basis. Application fee: $0. Electronic applications accepted. *Expenses:* Tuition, state resident: part-time $554.15 per credit. Tuition, nonresident: part-time $1200.35 per credit. *Required fees:* $42.15 per credit. $268.30 per semester. Tuition and fees vary according to course load and program. *Financial support:* In 2013–14, 22 students received support, including 4 fellowships with tuition reimbursements available (averaging $13,050 per year), 5 research assistantships with tuition reimbursements available (averaging $16,508 per year); career-related internships or fieldwork, Federal Work-Study, scholarships/grants, health care benefits, and unspecified assistantships also available. Support available to part-time students. Financial award application deadline: 3/31; financial award applicants required to submit FAFSA. *Faculty research:* Exercise and sport science, nutrition and physical activity interventions, school and community health, obesity prevention. *Total annual research expenditures:* $1.3 million. *Unit head:* Dr. Nate McCaughtry, Assistant Dean, Division of Kinesiology, Health and Sport Studies/Director, Center for School Health, 313-577-0014, Fax: 313-577-5002, E-mail: aj4391@wayne.edu. *Application contact:* Janice Green, Assistant Dean, 313-577-1605, E-mail: jwgreen@wayne.edu.
Website: http://coe.wayne.edu/kinesiology/index.php.

Webber International University, Graduate School of Business, Babson Park, FL 33827-0096. Offers accounting (MBA); management (MBA); security management (MBA); sports management (MBA). Part-time and evening/weekend programs available. *Degree requirements:* For master's, thesis or alternative. *Entrance requirements:* For master's, previous course work in financial and managerial accounting. Additional exam requirements/recommendations for international students: Required—TOEFL. *Faculty research:* Finance strategy, market research, investments, intranet.

Western Illinois University, School of Graduate Studies, College of Education and Human Services, Department of Kinesiology, Program in Sport Management, Macomb, IL 61455-1390. Offers MS. Part-time programs available. *Students:* 49 full-time (18 women), 7 part-time (4 women); includes 9 minority (6 Black or African American, non-Hispanic/Latino; 1 Hispanic/Latino; 2 Two or more races, non-Hispanic/Latino). Average age 24. In 2013, 32 master's awarded. *Entrance requirements:* For master's, minimum GPA of 3.0. Additional exam requirements/recommendations for international students: Required—TOEFL (minimum score 550 paper-based; 80 iBT). *Application deadline:* Applications are processed on a rolling basis. Application fee: $30. Electronic applications accepted. *Financial support:* In 2013–14, 31 students received support, including 26 research assistantships with full tuition reimbursements available (averaging $7,544 per year), 5 teaching assistantships with full tuition reimbursements available (averaging $8,688 per year). *Unit head:* Dr. Janet Wigglesworth, Chairperson, 309-298-1981. *Application contact:* Dr. Nancy Parsons, Associate Provost and Director of Graduate Studies, 309-298-1806, Fax: 309-298-2345, E-mail: grad-office@wiu.edu.
Website: http://wiu.edu/kinesiology.

Western Kentucky University, Graduate Studies, College of Health and Human Services, Department of Kinesiology, Recreation and Sport, Bowling Green, KY 42101. Offers athletic administration and coaching (MS); physical education (MS); recreation and sport administration (MS). Part-time and evening/weekend programs available. Postbaccalaureate distance learning degree programs offered. *Degree requirements:* For master's, comprehensive exam, thesis optional. *Entrance requirements:* For master's, GRE General Test, minimum GPA of 2.75. Additional exam requirements/

recommendations for international students: Required—TOEFL (minimum score 555 paper-based; 79 iBT). *Faculty research:* Orthopedic rehabilitation, fitness center coordination, heat acclimation, biomechanical and physiological parameters.

Western Michigan University, Graduate College, College of Education and Human Development, Department of Health, Physical Education and Recreation, Kalamazoo, MI 49008. Offers exercise and sports medicine (MS), including athletic training, exercise physiology; physical education (MA), including coaching sport performance, pedagogy, special physical education, sport management.

Western New England University, College of Business, Program in Business Administration, Springfield, MA 01119. Offers general business (MBA); sport management (MBA); JD/MBA; Pharm D/MBA. *Accreditation:* AACSB. Part-time and evening/weekend programs available. Postbaccalaureate distance learning degree programs offered (no on-campus study). *Faculty:* 20 full-time (7 women). *Students:* 123 part-time (51 women); includes 8 minority (2 Black or African American, non-Hispanic/Latino; 3 Asian, non-Hispanic/Latino; 2 Hispanic/Latino; 1 Two or more races, non-Hispanic/Latino), 7 international. Average age 31. 585 applicants. In 2013, 45 master's awarded. *Entrance requirements:* For master's, GMAT, official transcript, two letters of recommendation, essay, resume. Additional exam requirements/recommendations for international students: Required—TOEFL. *Application deadline:* Applications are processed on a rolling basis. Application fee: $30. Electronic applications accepted. Tuition and fees vary according to program. *Financial support:* Application deadline: 4/15; applicants required to submit FAFSA. *Unit head:* Dr. Julie Siciliano, Dean, 413-782-1224, E-mail: julie.siciliano@wne.edu. *Application contact:* Matthew Fox, Director of Recruiting and Marketing for Adult Learners, 413-782-1517, Fax: 413-782-1779, E-mail: study@wne.edu.

West Texas A&M University, College of Nursing and Health Sciences, Department of Sports and Exercise Sciences, Canyon, TX 79016-0001. Offers sport management (MS); sports and exercise sciences (MS). Part-time and evening/weekend programs available. *Degree requirements:* For master's, comprehensive exam, thesis optional. *Entrance requirements:* For master's, GRE General Test. Additional exam requirements/recommendations for international students: Required—TOEFL (minimum score 550 paper-based). Electronic applications accepted. *Faculty research:* American government, public administration, state and local government, international politics.

West Virginia University, School of Physical Education, Morgantown, WV 26506. Offers athletic coaching education (MS); athletic training (MS); physical education/teacher education (MS, PhD), including curriculum and instruction (PhD), motor behavior (PhD), physical education supervision (PhD); sport and exercise psychology (PhD); sport management (MS). *Degree requirements:* For doctorate, comprehensive exam, thesis/dissertation, oral exam. *Entrance requirements:* For master's, GRE or MAT, minimum GPA of 3.0; for doctorate, GRE General Test or MAT, minimum GPA of 3.5. Additional exam requirements/recommendations for international students: Required—TOEFL (minimum score 550 paper-based). Electronic applications accepted.

Faculty research: Sport psychosociology, teacher education, exercise psychology, counseling.

Wichita State University, Graduate School, College of Education, Department of Sport Management, Wichita, KS 67260. Offers M Ed. *Unit head:* Dr. Mark Vermillion, Chair, 316-978-5444, Fax: 316-978-5451, E-mail: mark.vermillion@wichita.edu. *Application contact:* Jordan Oleson, Admissions Coordinator, 316-978-3095, Fax: 316-978-3253, E-mail: jordan.oleson@wichita.edu.
Website: http://www.wichita.edu/sportmanagement.

Wingate University, Thayer School of Education, Wingate, NC 28174-0159. Offers community college leadership (Ed D); educational leadership (MA Ed, Ed D); elementary education (MA Ed, MAT); health and physical education (MA Ed); sport administration (MA Ed). *Accreditation:* NCATE. Part-time and evening/weekend programs available. *Degree requirements:* For master's, portfolio. *Entrance requirements:* For master's, GRE General Test or MAT, teaching certificate (MA Ed).

Winona State University, College of Education, Department of Education Leadership, Winona, MN 55987. Offers educational leadership (Ed S), including general superintendency, K-12 principalship; general school leadership (MS); K-12 principalship (MS); outdoor education/adventure-based leadership (MS); sports management (MS); teacher leadership (MS). *Accreditation:* NCATE. Part-time and evening/weekend programs available. *Degree requirements:* For master's, comprehensive exam, thesis optional; for Ed S, thesis optional.

Xavier University, College of Social Sciences, Health and Education, Department of Sports Studies, Cincinnati, OH 45207. Offers sport administration (M Ed). Part-time and evening/weekend programs available. *Faculty:* 2 full-time (1 woman), 5 part-time/adjunct (1 woman). *Students:* 34 full-time (11 women), 20 part-time (7 women); includes 12 minority (10 Black or African American, non-Hispanic/Latino; 2 Hispanic/Latino). Average age 27. 33 applicants, 100% accepted, 22 enrolled. In 2013, 38 master's awarded. *Degree requirements:* For master's, thesis optional, internship. *Entrance requirements:* For master's, GRE or MAT. Additional exam requirements/recommendations for international students: Required—TOEFL (minimum score 550 paper-based; 79 iBT). *Application deadline:* For fall admission, 2/15 priority date for domestic and international students; for spring admission, 9/15 priority date for domestic and international students. Applications are processed on a rolling basis. Application fee: $35. Electronic applications accepted. *Expenses: Tuition:* Part-time $594 per credit hour. *Required fees:* $3 per semester. *Financial support:* In 2013–14, 35 students received support. Applicants required to submit FAFSA. *Faculty research:* Coaching education, brand equity, strategic management, economic impact, place marketing. *Unit head:* Dr. Douglas Olberding, Chair, 513-745-1085, Fax: 513-745-4291, E-mail: olberdin@xavier.edu. *Application contact:* Roger Bosse, Graduate Services Director, 513-745-3357, Fax: 513-745-1048, E-mail: bosse@xavier.edu.
Website: http://www.xavier.edu/sport-administration/.

ACADEMIC AND PROFESSIONAL PROGRAMS IN SOCIAL WORK

Section 32
Social Work

This section contains a directory of institutions offering graduate work in social work, followed by in-depth entries submitted by institutions that chose to prepare detailed program descriptions. Additional information about programs listed in the directory but not augmented by an in-depth entry may be obtained by writing directly to the dean of a graduate school or chair of a department at the address given in the directory.

For programs offering related work, see also in this book *Allied Health* and *Education*. In another guide in this series:

Graduate Programs in the Humanities, Arts & Social Sciences
See *Criminology and Forensics, Family and Consumer Sciences, Psychology and Counseling,* and *Sociology, Anthropology, and Archaeology*

CONTENTS

Program Directories

Human Services	1694
Social Work	1699

Displays and Close-Ups

Adelphi University	1700, 1723
University at Buffalo, the State University of New York	1714, 1725
University of Pennsylvania	1718, 1727

Human Services

Abilene Christian University, Graduate School, College of Education and Human Services, Abilene, TX 79699-9100. Offers M Ed, MS, MSSW, Certificate, Post-Master's Certificate. *Accreditation:* Teacher Education Accreditation Council. *Faculty:* 5 full-time (1 woman), 12 part-time/adjunct (7 women). *Students:* 156 full-time (129 women), 51 part-time (35 women); includes 61 minority (23 Black or African American, non-Hispanic/Latino; 2 American Indian or Alaska Native, non-Hispanic/Latino; 2 Asian, non-Hispanic/Latino; 25 Hispanic/Latino; 9 Two or more races, non-Hispanic/Latino), 4 international. 272 applicants, 42% accepted, 99 enrolled. In 2013, 104 master's, 5 other advanced degrees awarded. *Degree requirements:* For master's, comprehensive exam (for some programs), thesis (for some programs), practicum. *Entrance requirements:* For master's, GRE. Additional exam requirements/recommendations for international students: Required—TOEFL (minimum score 550 paper-based; 90 iBT), IELTS (minimum score 6.5), PTE. *Application deadline:* For fall admission, 8/15 priority date for domestic students; for winter admission, 10/1 priority date for domestic students; for spring admission, 12/15 priority date for domestic students; for summer admission, 4/15 for domestic students. Applications are processed on a rolling basis. Application fee: $50. Electronic applications accepted. *Expenses: Tuition:* Full-time $17,100; part-time $950 per credit hour. *Financial support:* In 2013–14, 69 students received support. Career-related internships or fieldwork and scholarships/grants available. Financial award application deadline: 4/1; financial award applicants required to submit FAFSA. *Unit head:* Dr. Donnie Snider, Dean, 325-674-2700, E-mail: dcs03b@acu.edu. *Application contact:* Corey Patterson, Director of Graduate Admission and Recruiting, 325-674-6566, Fax: 325-674-6717, E-mail: gradinfo@acu.edu.

Albertus Magnus College, Master of Science in Human Services Program, New Haven, CT 06511-1189. Offers MS. Evening/weekend programs available. *Faculty:* 3 full-time (1 woman), 8 part-time/adjunct (5 women). *Students:* 26 full-time (25 women), 10 part-time (all women); includes 20 minority (17 Black or African American, non-Hispanic/Latino; 3 Hispanic/Latino). 14 applicants, 86% accepted, 9 enrolled. In 2013, 25 master's awarded. *Degree requirements:* For master's, thesis, internship, capstone thesis. *Entrance requirements:* For master's, minimum GPA of 2.8. *Application deadline:* For fall admission, 8/15 for domestic students; for spring admission, 1/15 for domestic students. Application fee: $50. Electronic applications accepted. *Financial support:* Applicants required to submit FAFSA. *Unit head:* Dr. Sean O'Connell, Interim Vice President for Academic Affairs, 203-777-8539, Fax: 203-777-3701, E-mail: soconnell@albertus.edu. *Application contact:* Dr. Ragaa Mazen, Director, 203-777-8574, Fax: 203-777-3701, E-mail: rmazen@albertus.edu.
Website: http://www.albertus.edu/masters-degrees/human-services/.

Andrews University, School of Graduate Studies, College of Arts and Sciences, Department of Behavioral Science, Berrien Springs, MI 49104. Offers international development (MSA). *Faculty:* 9 full-time (1 woman). *Students:* 13 full-time (11 women), 10 part-time (8 women); includes 13 minority (7 Black or African American, non-Hispanic/Latino; 1 American Indian or Alaska Native, non-Hispanic/Latino; 1 Asian, non-Hispanic/Latino; 4 Hispanic/Latino), 5 international. Average age 29. 30 applicants, 67% accepted, 5 enrolled. In 2013, 1 master's awarded. *Entrance requirements:* For master's, GRE. Additional exam requirements/recommendations for international students: Required—TOEFL (minimum score 550 paper-based). Application fee: $40. *Unit head:* Dr. Duane C. McBride, Chair, 269-471-3152. *Application contact:* Monica Wringer, Supervisor of Graduate Admission, 800-253-2874, Fax: 269-471-6321, E-mail: graduate@andrews.edu.

Bellevue University, Graduate School, College of Arts and Sciences, Bellevue, NE 68005-3098. Offers clinical counseling (MS); healthcare administration (MHA); human services (MA); international security and intelligence studies (MS); managerial communication (MA). Postbaccalaureate distance learning degree programs offered.

Boricua College, Program in Human Services, New York, NY 10032-1560. Offers MS. Program offered in Brooklyn and Manhattan. Evening/weekend programs available. *Degree requirements:* For master's, thesis. *Entrance requirements:* For master's, interview by the faculty.

Brandeis University, The Heller School for Social Policy and Management, Program in Nonprofit Management, Waltham, MA 02454-9110. Offers child, youth, and family management (MBA); health care management (MBA); social impact management (MBA); social policy and management (MBA); sustainable development (MBA); MBA/MA; MBA/MD. MBA/MD program offered in conjunction with Tufts University School of Medicine. *Accreditation:* AACSB. Part-time programs available. *Degree requirements:* For master's, team consulting project. *Entrance requirements:* For master's, GMAT (preferred) or GRE, 2 letters of recommendation, problem statement analysis, 3-5 years of professional experience. Additional exam requirements/recommendations for international students: Required—TOEFL (minimum score 600 paper-based; 100 iBT). Electronic applications accepted. *Expenses:* Contact institution. *Faculty research:* Health care; children and families; elder and disabled services; social impact management; organizations in the non-profit, for-profit, or public sector.

California State University, Sacramento, Office of Graduate Studies, College of Health and Human Services, Division of Social Work, Sacramento, CA 95819. Offers family and children's services (MSW); health care (MSW); mental health (MSW); social justice and corrections (MSW). *Accreditation:* CSWE. *Degree requirements:* For master's, thesis, research project, or comprehensive exam; writing proficiency exam. *Entrance requirements:* For master's, minimum GPA of 2.5 during previous 2 years of course work. Additional exam requirements/recommendations for international students: Required—TOEFL. *Application deadline:* For fall admission, 1/18 for domestic students, 3/1 for international students; for spring admission, 9/30 for international students. Applications are processed on a rolling basis. Application fee: $55. Electronic applications accepted. *Financial support:* Career-related internships or fieldwork and Federal Work-Study available. Support available to part-time students. Financial award application deadline: 3/1; financial award applicants required to submit FAFSA. *Unit head:* Dr. Dale Russell, Chair, 916-278-6943, E-mail: drussell@csus.edu. *Application contact:* Jose Martinez, Graduate Admissions Supervisor, 916-278-7871, E-mail: martinj@skymail.csus.edu.
Website: http://www.csus.edu/hhs/sw.

Capella University, School of Public Service Leadership, Doctoral Programs in Healthcare, Minneapolis, MN 55402. Offers criminal justice (PhD); emergency management (PhD); epidemiology (Dr PH); general health administration (DHA); general public administration (DPA); health advocacy and leadership (Dr PH); health care administration (PhD); health care leadership (DHA); health policy advocacy (DHA); multidisciplinary human services (PhD); nonprofit management and leadership (PhD); public safety leadership (PhD); social and community services (PhD).

Capella University, School of Public Service Leadership, Master's Programs in Healthcare, Minneapolis, MN 55402. Offers criminal justice (MS); emergency management (MS); general public health (MPH); gerontology (MS); health administration (MHA); health care operations (MHA); health management policy (MPH); health policy (MHA); homeland security (MS); multidisciplinary human sevrices (MS); public administration (MPA); public safety leadership (MS); social and community services (MS); social behavioral sciences (MPH); MS/MPA.

Carlos Albizu University, Miami Campus, Graduate Programs, Miami, FL 33172-2209. Offers clinical psychology (Psy D); entrepreneurship (MBA); exceptional student education (MS); human services (PhD); industrial/organizational psychology (MS); marriage and family therapy (MS); mental health counseling (MS); nonprofit management (MBA); organizational management (MBA); psychology (MS); school counseling (MS); teaching English as a second language (MS). *Accreditation:* APA. Part-time and evening/weekend programs available. *Faculty:* 26 full-time (20 women), 34 part-time/adjunct (16 women). *Students:* 416 full-time (335 women), 281 part-time (237 women); includes 604 minority (57 Black or African American, non-Hispanic/Latino; 1 American Indian or Alaska Native, non-Hispanic/Latino; 13 Asian, non-Hispanic/Latino; 533 Hispanic/Latino), 14 international. Average age 36. 176 applicants, 59% accepted, 96 enrolled. In 2013, 176 master's, 37 doctorates awarded. Terminal master's awarded for partial completion of doctoral program. *Degree requirements:* For master's, one foreign language, comprehensive exam, integrative project (MBA), research project (exceptional student education, teaching English as a second language); for doctorate, one foreign language, comprehensive exam, internship, project. *Entrance requirements:* For master's, 3 letters of recommendation, interview, minimum GPA of 3.0, resume, statement of purpose, official transcripts; for doctorate, 3 letters of recommendation, minimum GPA of 3.0, resume, interview, statement of purpose, official transcripts. Additional exam requirements/recommendations for international students: Required—Michigan Test of English Language Proficiency. *Application deadline:* For fall admission, 4/1 priority date for domestic students, 5/1 priority date for international students; for spring admission, 11/1 priority date for domestic students, 9/1 priority date for international students. Applications are processed on a rolling basis. Application fee: $50. Electronic applications accepted. *Expenses: Tuition:* Full-time $9360; part-time $520 per credit. *Required fees:* $298 per term. Tuition and fees vary according to course load, degree level and program. *Financial support:* In 2013–14, 62 students received support. Federal Work-Study, scholarships/grants, and tuition discounts available. Financial award application deadline: 6/1; financial award applicants required to submit FAFSA. *Faculty research:* Psychotherapy, forensic psychology, neuropsychology, marketing strategy, entrepreneurship, special education. *Unit head:* Peter M. Rubio, Interim Chancellor, 305-593-1223 Ext. 3120, Fax: 305-592-7930, E-mail: prubio@albizu.edu. *Application contact:* Vanessa Almendarez, Administrative Assistant, 305-593-1223 Ext. 3137, Fax: 305-593-1854, E-mail: valmendarez@albizu.edu.

Chestnut Hill College, School of Graduate Studies, Program in Administration of Human Services, Philadelphia, PA 19118-2693. Offers administration of human services (MS); leadership development (CAS). Part-time and evening/weekend programs available. *Faculty:* 3 full-time (2 women), 7 part-time/adjunct (5 women). *Students:* 11 full-time (10 women), 26 part-time (18 women); includes 20 minority (all Black or African American, non-Hispanic/Latino), 1 international. Average age 37. 10 applicants, 80% accepted. In 2013, 14 master's awarded. *Degree requirements:* For master's, special projects or internship. *Entrance requirements:* For master's, GRE General Test or MAT, 100 volunteer hours or 1 year of work-related human services experience, statement of professional goals, writing sample, letters of recommendation. Additional exam requirements/recommendations for international students: Required—TOEFL (minimum score 500 paper-based), IELTS (mnimum score 6.0), or TWE (minimum score 22). *Application deadline:* For fall admission, 7/1 for domestic and international students; for spring admission, 11/1 for domestic and international students; for summer admission, 4/1 for domestic and international students. Applications are processed on a rolling basis. *Expenses:* Contact institution. *Financial support:* Unspecified assistantships available. *Faculty research:* Best practices and trends in adult education degree programs, middle and late adulthood development, quality of living issues for older persons. *Unit head:* Dr. Barbara Hogan, Dean, School of Graduate Studies, 215-248-7120, Fax: 215-248-7161, E-mail: hoganb@chc.edu. *Application contact:* Jayne Mashett, Director of Admissions, School of Graduate Studies, 215-248-7020, Fax: 215-248-7161, E-mail: gradadmissions@chc.edu.
Website: http://www.chc.edu/Graduate/Programs/Masters/Administration_of_Human_Services/.

Concordia University Chicago, College of Graduate and Innovative Programs, Program in Human Services, River Forest, IL 60305-1499. Offers human services (MA), including administration, exercise science. Part-time and evening/weekend programs available. *Degree requirements:* For master's, comprehensive exam, thesis. *Entrance requirements:* For master's, minimum GPA of 2.9. Additional exam requirements/recommendations for international students: Required—TOEFL (minimum score 550 paper-based). Electronic applications accepted.

Concordia University Wisconsin, Graduate Programs, School of Human Services, Mequon, WI 53097-2402. Offers MOT, MSN, MSPT, MSRS, DPT.

Coppin State University, Division of Graduate Studies, Division of Arts and Sciences, Department of Social Sciences, Baltimore, MD 21216-3698. Offers human services administration (MS). Part-time and evening/weekend programs available. *Entrance requirements:* For master's, resume, references, interview.

Drury University, Graduate Programs in Education, Springfield, MO 65802. Offers elementary education (M Ed); gifted education (M Ed); human services (M Ed); instructional mathematics K-8 (M Ed); instructional technology (M Ed); middle school teaching (M Ed); secondary education (M Ed); special education (M Ed); special reading (M Ed). *Accreditation:* NCATE. Part-time and evening/weekend programs available. *Degree requirements:* For master's, thesis. *Entrance requirements:* For master's, GRE or MAT, minimum GPA of 2.75. Additional exam requirements/recommendations for international students: Required—TOEFL. Electronic applications accepted. *Faculty research:* Cultural enrichment, research skills, parental involvement relating to reading skills, reading strategies for mainstreaming children.

East Central University, School of Graduate Studies, Department of Human Resources, Ada, OK 74820-6899. Offers administration (MSHR); counseling (MSHR); criminal justice (MSHR); human services (MSHR); rehabilitation counseling (MSHR). *Accreditation:* CORE. Part-time and evening/weekend programs available. *Degree requirements:* For master's, thesis optional. *Entrance requirements:* For master's, GRE General Test, MAT, minimum GPA of 2.5. Electronic applications accepted.

Eastern Michigan University, Graduate School, College of Health and Human Services, Interdisciplinary Program in Health and Human Services, Ypsilanti, MI 48197. Offers community building (Graduate Certificate). Part-time and evening/weekend programs available. *Students:* 1 part-time (0 women), all international. Average age 25.

7 applicants, 14% accepted, 1 enrolled. In 2013, 4 Graduate Certificates awarded. *Entrance requirements:* Additional exam requirements/recommendations for international students: Required—TOEFL. Application fee: $35. *Expenses:* Tuition, state resident: full-time $12,300; part-time $466 per credit hour. Tuition, nonresident: full-time $23,159; part-time $918 per credit hour. *Required fees:* $71 per credit hour. $46 per semester. One-time fee: $100. Tuition and fees vary according to course level and degree level. *Unit head:* Dr. Marcia Bombyk, Program Coordinator, 734-487-4173, Fax: 734-487-8536, E-mail: marcia.bombyk@emich.edu. *Application contact:* Graduate Admissions, 734-487-2400, Fax: 734-487-6559, E-mail: graduate.admissions@emich.edu.

Eastern New Mexico University, Graduate School, College of Liberal Arts and Sciences, Department of Health and Human Services, Portales, NM 88130. Offers nursing (MSN); speech pathology and audiology (MS). *Accreditation:* ASHA. Part-time programs available. Postbaccalaureate distance learning degree programs offered (minimal on-campus study). *Degree requirements:* For master's, thesis optional, oral and written comprehensive exam, oral presentation of professional portfolio. *Entrance requirements:* For master's, GRE, three letters of recommendation, resume, two essays. Additional exam requirements/recommendations for international students: Required—TOEFL (minimum score 550 paper-based; 79 iBT), IELTS (minimum score 6). Electronic applications accepted.

Ferris State University, College of Education and Human Services, Big Rapids, MI 49307. Offers M Ed, MS, MSCJ, MSCTE. Part-time and evening/weekend programs available. Postbaccalaureate distance learning degree programs offered (minimal on-campus study). *Faculty:* 14 full-time (8 women), 9 part-time/adjunct (6 women). *Students:* 28 full-time (21 women), 125 part-time (69 women); includes 26 minority (16 Black or African American, non-Hispanic/Latino; 1 American Indian or Alaska Native, non-Hispanic/Latino; 1 Asian, non-Hispanic/Latino; 2 Hispanic/Latino; 6 Two or more races, non-Hispanic/Latino), 12 international. Average age 69. 33 applicants, 70% accepted, 19 enrolled. In 2013, 56 master's awarded. *Degree requirements:* For master's, comprehensive exam or thesis/dissertation, research paper or project. *Entrance requirements:* For master's, minimum GPA of 3.0. Additional exam requirements/recommendations for international students: Required—TOEFL (minimum score 500 paper-based; 61 iBT), IELTS. *Application deadline:* For fall admission, 7/1 priority date for domestic and international students; for winter admission, 12/15 for domestic and international students; for spring admission, 11/1 priority date for domestic and international students; for summer admission, 3/1 priority date for domestic and international students. Applications are processed on a rolling basis. Application fee: $30. Electronic applications accepted. Application fee is waived when completed online. *Financial support:* In 2013–14, 1 research assistantship (averaging $4,850 per year) was awarded; career-related internships or fieldwork, Federal Work-Study, scholarships/grants, and unspecified assistantships also available. Support available to part-time students. Financial award applicants required to submit FAFSA. *Faculty research:* Competency testing, teaching methodologies, assessment of teaching effectiveness, suicide prevention, women in education, special needs. *Unit head:* Steven Reifert, Interim Dean, 231-591-5080, Fax: 231-592-3792, E-mail: feifers@ferris.edu. *Application contact:* Dr. Kristen Salomonson, Dean, Enrollment Services/Director, Admissions and Records, 231-591-2100, Fax: 231-591-3944, E-mail: admissions@ferris.edu.

Georgia State University, Andrew Young School of Policy Studies, School of Social Work, Atlanta, GA 30294. Offers child welfare leadership (Certificate); community partnerships (MSW); forensic social work (Certificate). *Accreditation:* CSWE. Part-time programs available. *Faculty:* 13 full-time (9 women), 3 part-time/adjunct (0 women). *Students:* 97 full-time (89 women), 1 (woman) part-time; includes 51 minority (39 Black or African American, non-Hispanic/Latino; 3 Asian, non-Hispanic/Latino; 4 Hispanic/Latino; 5 Two or more races, non-Hispanic/Latino), 2 international. Average age 29. 120 applicants, 80% accepted, 43 enrolled. In 2013, 44 master's awarded. *Entrance requirements:* For master's, GRE; for Certificate, GRE. Additional exam requirements/recommendations for international students: Required—TOEFL (minimum score 550 paper-based; 100 iBT) or IELTS (minimum score 7). *Application deadline:* For fall admission, 2/1 priority date for domestic and international students. Application fee: $50. Electronic applications accepted. *Expenses: Tuition, area resident:* Full-time $4176; part-time $348 per credit hour. Tuition, state resident: full-time $14,544; part-time $1212 per credit hour. Tuition, nonresident: full-time $14,544; part-time $1212 per credit hour. Tuition and fees vary according to course load and program. *Financial support:* In 2013–14, research assistantships with tuition reimbursements (averaging $4,000 per year), teaching assistantships with tuition reimbursements (averaging $4,000 per year) were awarded; career-related internships or fieldwork, institutionally sponsored loans, scholarships/grants, tuition waivers, and unspecified assistantships also available. Financial award application deadline: 2/1; financial award applicants required to submit FAFSA. *Faculty research:* Community partnership, non-profit organizations, child welfare practice and policy, gerontological practice and policy, restorative justice. *Unit head:* Renanda Dear, Director of Student and Community Services, 404-413-1057, Fax: 404-413-1075, E-mail: rwood@gsu.edu. *Application contact:* Charisma Parker, Admissions Coordinator, 404-413-0030, Fax: 404-413-0023, E-mail: cparker28@gsu.edu.
Website: http://aysps.gsu.edu/socialwork.

Indiana University Northwest, School of Public and Environmental Affairs, Gary, IN 46408-1197. Offers criminal justice (MPA); environmental affairs (Graduate Certificate); health services (MPA); human services (MPA); nonprofit management (Certificate); public management (MPA). *Accreditation:* NASPAA (one or more programs are accredited). Part-time programs available. *Faculty:* 5 full-time (3 women). *Students:* 17 full-time (13 women), 73 part-time (49 women); includes 62 minority (48 Black or African American, non-Hispanic/Latino; 2 Asian, non-Hispanic/Latino; 12 Hispanic/Latino). Average age 38. 25 applicants, 92% accepted, 21 enrolled. In 2013, 27 master's, 26 other advanced degrees awarded. *Entrance requirements:* For master's, GRE General Test or GMAT, letters of recommendation. *Application deadline:* For fall admission, 8/15 priority date for domestic students. Applications are processed on a rolling basis. *Financial support:* Career-related internships or fieldwork, Federal Work-Study, and tuition waivers (partial) available. Support available to part-time students. Financial award application deadline: 3/1. *Faculty research:* Employment in income security policies, evidence in criminal justice, equal employment law, social welfare policy and welfare reform, public finance in developing countries. *Unit head:* Dr. Barbara Peat, Department Chair, 219-981-5645. *Application contact:* Tierra Jackson, Senior Secretary, 219-981-5616, E-mail: jacksoti@iun.edu.
Website: http://www.iun.edu/spea/index.htm.

Kansas State University, Graduate School, College of Human Ecology, School of Family Studies and Human Services, Manhattan, KS 66506. Offers communication sciences and disorders (MS); conflict resolution (Graduate Certificate); early childhood education (MS); family and community services (MS); family studies (MS, PhD); life span human development (MS, PhD); marriage and family therapy (MS, PhD); personal financial planning (MS, PhD, Graduate Certificate); youth development (MS, Graduate Certificate). *Accreditation:* AAMFT/COAMFTE; ASHA. Part-time programs available. Postbaccalaureate distance learning degree programs offered (no on-campus study). *Faculty:* 34 full-time (22 women), 11 part-time/adjunct (8 women). *Students:* 68 full-time (56 women), 131 part-time (86 women); includes 42 minority (19 Black or African American, non-Hispanic/Latino; 2 American Indian or Alaska Native, non-Hispanic/Latino; 4 Asian, non-Hispanic/Latino; 14 Hispanic/Latino; 1 Native Hawaiian or other Pacific Islander, non-Hispanic/Latino; 2 Two or more races, non-Hispanic/Latino), 3 international. Average age 31. 248 applicants, 29% accepted, 48 enrolled. In 2013, 35 master's, 7 doctorates awarded. *Degree requirements:* For master's, thesis or alternative. *Entrance requirements:* For master's, GRE, minimum GPA of 3.0 in last 2 years of undergraduate study; for doctorate, GRE. Additional exam requirements/recommendations for international students: Required—TOEFL (minimum score 600 paper-based). *Application deadline:* For fall admission, 2/1 priority date for domestic students, 1/1 priority date for international students; for spring admission, 10/1 priority date for domestic students, 8/1 priority date for international students; for summer admission, 2/1 priority date for domestic students, 12/1 priority date for international students. Applications are processed on a rolling basis. Application fee: $50 ($75 for international students). Electronic applications accepted. *Financial support:* In 2013–14, 63 students received support, including 45 research assistantships (averaging $13,500 per year), 18 teaching assistantships with full tuition reimbursements available (averaging $11,000 per year). Financial award application deadline: 3/1. *Faculty research:* Health and security of military families, personal and family risk assessment and evaluation, disorders of communication and swallowing, families and health. *Total annual research expenditures:* $14.9 million. *Unit head:* Dr. Maurice MacDonald, Director, 785-532-5510, Fax: 785-532-5505, E-mail: morey@ksu.edu. *Application contact:* Connie Fechter, Administrative Specialist, 785-532-5510, Fax: 785-532-5505, E-mail: fechter@ksu.edu.
Website: http://www.he.k-state.edu/fshs/.

Kent State University, Graduate School of Education, Health, and Human Services, Kent, OH 44242-0001. Offers M Ed, MA, MAT, MS, Au D, PhD, Ed S. *Accreditation:* NCATE. Part-time and evening/weekend programs available. Postbaccalaureate distance learning degree programs offered. *Faculty:* 200 full-time (124 women), 87 part-time/adjunct (61 women). *Students:* 919 full-time (690 women), 566 part-time (415 women); includes 184 minority (107 Black or African American, non-Hispanic/Latino; 9 American Indian or Alaska Native, non-Hispanic/Latino; 32 Asian, non-Hispanic/Latino; 13 Hispanic/Latino; 22 Native Hawaiian or other Pacific Islander, non-Hispanic/Latino; 1 Two or more races, non-Hispanic/Latino), 93 international. 1,519 applicants, 35% accepted. In 2013, 435 master's, 34 doctorates, 42 other advanced degrees awarded. *Degree requirements:* For master's, thesis (for some programs); for doctorate, comprehensive exam, thesis/dissertation. *Entrance requirements:* For doctorate and Ed S, GRE General Test. Additional exam requirements/recommendations for international students: Required—TOEFL (minimum score 550 paper-based; 80 iBT). *Application deadline:* Applications are processed on a rolling basis. Application fee: $30 ($60 for international students). Electronic applications accepted. *Financial support:* In 2013–14, 93 research assistantships with full tuition reimbursements (averaging $10,455 per year), 27 teaching assistantships (averaging $11,945 per year) were awarded; Federal Work-Study, scholarships/grants, unspecified assistantships, and 2 administrative assistantships (averaging $10,250 per year) also available. Financial award application deadline: 4/1; financial award applicants required to submit FAFSA. *Unit head:* Dr. Daniel Mahony, Dean, 330-672-2202, Fax: 330-672-3407, E-mail: dmahony@kent.edu. *Application contact:* Nancy Miller, Academic Program Coordinator, Office of Graduate Student Services, 330-672-2576, Fax: 330-672-9162, E-mail: nmiller1@kent.edu.
Website: http://www.kent.edu/ehhs/.

Lehigh University, College of Education, Program in Counseling Psychology, Bethlehem, PA 18015. Offers counseling and human services (M Ed); counseling psychology (PhD); elementary counseling with certification (M Ed); international counseling (M Ed, Certificate); secondary school counseling with certification (M Ed). *Accreditation:* APA (one or more programs are accredited). Part-time programs available. Postbaccalaureate distance learning degree programs offered (minimal on-campus study). *Faculty:* 6 full-time (4 women), 4 part-time/adjunct (3 women). *Students:* 50 full-time (43 women), 45 part-time (37 women); includes 14 minority (6 Black or African American, non-Hispanic/Latino; 2 Asian, non-Hispanic/Latino; 5 Hispanic/Latino; 1 Two or more races, non-Hispanic/Latino), 17 international. Average age 30. 177 applicants, 34% accepted, 25 enrolled. In 2013, 43 master's, 5 doctorates awarded. *Degree requirements:* For doctorate, comprehensive exam, thesis/dissertation. *Entrance requirements:* For master's, minimum GPA of 3.0, 2 letters of recommendation, essay, transcript; for doctorate, GRE General Test, 2 letters of recommendation, transcript, essay; for Certificate, minimum GPA of 3.0. Additional exam requirements/recommendations for international students: Required—TOEFL (minimum score 600 paper-based; 93 iBT). *Application deadline:* For fall admission, 2/15 for domestic students, 11/15 for international students; for winter admission, 2/1 for international students. Application fee: $65. Electronic applications accepted. Application fee is waived when completed online. *Financial support:* In 2013–14, 21 students received support, including 2 fellowships with full and partial tuition reimbursements available (averaging $16,000 per year), 6 research assistantships with partial tuition reimbursements available (averaging $9,000 per year); career-related internships or fieldwork, Federal Work-Study, institutionally sponsored loans, scholarships/grants, tuition waivers (full and partial), and unspecified assistantships also available. Financial award application deadline: 2/15; financial award applicants required to submit FAFSA. *Faculty research:* Maternal/infant attachment, multicultural training and counseling, career development and health interventions, intersection of identities. *Unit head:* Dr. Arnold R. Spokane, Director, 610-758-3257, Fax: 610-758-3227, E-mail: ars1@lehigh.edu. *Application contact:* Donna M. Johnson, Manager, Graduate Programs Admissions, 610-758-3231, Fax: 610-758-6223, E-mail: dmj4@lehigh.edu.
Website: http://coe.lehigh.edu/academics/disciplines/cp.

Liberty University, School of Health Sciences, Lynchburg, VA 24515. Offers biomedical sciences (MS); clinical mental health counseling (MA); global health (MPH); health promotion (MPH); human services (MA), including addictions and recovery, business, Christian ministry, criminal justice, crisis response and trauma, executive leadership, health and wellness, life coaching, marriage and family, military resilience; marriage and family therapy (MA); nurse educator (MS); nursing (MSN); nursing administration (MSN); nutrition (MPH); pastoral care and counseling (PhD); professional counseling (MA, PhD). *Students:* 2,830 full-time (2,293 women), 6,275 part-time (5,051 women); includes 1,677 minority (1,178 Black or African American, non-Hispanic/Latino; 19 American Indian or Alaska Native, non-Hispanic/Latino; 36 Asian, non-Hispanic/Latino; 278 Hispanic/Latino; 7 Native Hawaiian or other Pacific Islander, non-Hispanic/Latino; 159 Two or more races, non-Hispanic/Latino), 177 international. Average age 37. 9,147 applicants, 50% accepted, 2939 enrolled. In 2013, 2,618 master's, 11 doctorates awarded. *Degree requirements:* For master's, thesis (for some programs); for doctorate, thesis/dissertation. *Entrance requirements:* For doctorate, MAT or GRE, minimum GPA of 3.25 in master's program, 2-3 recommendations, writing samples (for some programs), letter of intent, professional vitae. Additional exam requirements/recommendations for international students: Required—TOEFL (minimum score 600 paper-based; 100 iBT). Application fee: $50. *Expenses: Tuition:* Full-time $9630; part-time $535 per credit hour. *Required fees:* $175 per term. One-time fee: $50. Tuition and fees vary according to course load, degree level, campus/location and program.

Application contact: Jay Bridge, Director of Admissions, 800-424-9595, Fax: 800-628-7977, E-mail: gradadmissions@liberty.edu.

Lincoln University, Graduate Programs, Philadelphia, PA 19104. Offers early childhood education (M Ed); educational leadership (M Ed); human resources (MSA), including finance, human resources management; human services (MHS); reading (MSR). Evening/weekend programs available. *Faculty:* 10 full-time (4 women), 34 part-time/adjunct (19 women). *Students:* 224 full-time (145 women), 115 part-time (74 women); includes 328 minority (311 Black or African American, non-Hispanic/Latino; 17 Hispanic/Latino). Average age 40. 237 applicants, 65% accepted, 64 enrolled. In 2013, 155 master's awarded. *Degree requirements:* For master's, thesis. *Entrance requirements:* For master's, working as full-time, paid staff member in the human services field, at least one year of paid experience in this field, and undergraduate degree in human services or a related field from an accredited institution (for MHS). *Application deadline:* For fall admission, 6/1 priority date for domestic and international students. Applications are processed on a rolling basis. Application fee: $50. *Expenses:* Tuition, state resident: full-time $10,106; part-time $567 per hour. Tuition, nonresident: full-time $17,636; part-time $949 per hour. *Financial support:* Application deadline: 8/1. *Unit head:* Dr. Cheryl Gooch, Dean, School of Humanities and Graduate Studies, 484-365-7664, E-mail: cgooch@lincoln.edu. *Application contact:* Jernice Lea, Director of Graduate Admissions, 215-590-8233, Fax: 215-387-3859, E-mail: jlea@lincoln.edu.
Website: http://www.lincoln.edu/academicaffairs/uc.html.

Lindenwood University, Graduate Programs, School of Human Services, St. Charles, MO 63301-1695. Offers nonprofit administration (MA); public administration (MPA). Part-time programs available. Postbaccalaureate distance learning degree programs offered (no on-campus study). *Faculty:* 3 full-time (1 woman), 2 part-time/adjunct (1 woman). *Students:* 26 full-time (18 women), 42 part-time (28 women); includes 35 minority (33 Black or African American, non-Hispanic/Latino; 1 American Indian or Alaska Native, non-Hispanic/Latino; 1 Two or more races, non-Hispanic/Latino), 4 international. Average age 35. 48 applicants, 63% accepted, 25 enrolled. In 2013, 11 master's awarded. *Degree requirements:* For master's, minimum cumulative GPA of 3.0, directed internship, capstone project. *Entrance requirements:* Additional exam requirements/recommendations for international students: Required—TOEFL (minimum score 550 paper-based; 80 iBT). *Application deadline:* For fall admission, 8/26 priority date for domestic and international students; for spring admission, 1/27 priority date for domestic and international students. Applications are processed on a rolling basis. Application fee: $30 ($100 for international students). Electronic applications accepted. *Expenses: Tuition:* Full-time $14,800; part-time $428 per credit hour. *Required fees:* $350. Tuition and fees vary according to course level and course load. *Financial support:* In 2013–14, 42 students received support. Career-related internships or fieldwork, institutionally sponsored loans, scholarships/grants, tuition waivers, and unspecified assistantships available. Financial award application deadline: 6/30; financial award applicants required to submit FAFSA. *Unit head:* Carla Mueller, Dean, 636-949-4731, E-mail: cmueller@lindenwood.edu. *Application contact:* Brett Barger, Dean of Evening Admissions and Extension Campuses, 636-949-4934, Fax: 636-949-4109, E-mail: adultadmissions@lindenwood.edu.
Website: http://www.lindenwood.edu/humanServices/.

Louisiana State University in Shreveport, College of Business, Education, and Human Development, Program in Human Services Administration, Shreveport, LA 71115-2399. Offers MS. Part-time and evening/weekend programs available. Postbaccalaureate distance learning degree programs offered (no on-campus study). *Students:* 3 full-time (2 women), 16 part-time (12 women); includes 7 minority (6 Black or African American, non-Hispanic/Latino; 1 Hispanic/Latino), 1 international. Average age 29. 7 applicants, 71% accepted, 1 enrolled. In 2013, 8 master's awarded. *Degree requirements:* For master's, final project. *Entrance requirements:* For master's, GRE, minimum GPA of 3.0 in last 2 undergraduate years, interview, recommendations. Additional exam requirements/recommendations for international students: Required—TOEFL (minimum score 550 paper-based; 80 iBT). *Application deadline:* For fall admission, 6/30 for domestic and international students; for spring admission, 11/30 for domestic and international students. Applications are processed on a rolling basis. Application fee: $10 ($20 for international students). *Expenses: Tuition, area resident:* Part-time $182 per credit hour. *Required fees:* $51. *Financial support:* In 2013–14, 2 research assistantships (averaging $3,780 per year) were awarded. *Unit head:* Dr. Helen Wise, Program Director, 318-797-5333, Fax: 318-797-5358, E-mail: helen.wise@lsus.edu. *Application contact:* Christianne Wojcik, Director of Academic Services, 318-797-5247, Fax: 318-798-4120, E-mail: christianne.wojcik@lsus.edu.

McDaniel College, Graduate and Professional Studies, Program in Human Services Management, Westminster, MD 21157-4390. Offers MS. *Accreditation:* NCATE. Evening/weekend programs available. *Degree requirements:* For master's, internship. *Entrance requirements:* For master's, 3 letters of reference. Additional exam requirements/recommendations for international students: Required—TOEFL.

Minnesota State University Mankato, College of Graduate Studies, College of Social and Behavioral Sciences, Department of Sociology and Corrections, Mankato, MN 56001. Offers sociology (MA); sociology: college teaching (MA); sociology: corrections (MS); sociology: human services planning and administration (MS). Part-time programs available. *Students:* 15 full-time (13 women), 16 part-time (10 women). *Degree requirements:* For master's, comprehensive exam, thesis or alternative. *Entrance requirements:* For master's, minimum GPA of 3.0 during previous 2 years, 3 letters of reference, resume. Additional exam requirements/recommendations for international students: Required—TOEFL. *Application deadline:* For fall admission, 7/1 priority date for domestic students; for spring admission, 11/1 for domestic students. Applications are processed on a rolling basis. Application fee: $40. Electronic applications accepted. *Financial support:* Research assistantships with full tuition reimbursements, teaching assistantships with full tuition reimbursements, career-related internships or fieldwork, Federal Work-Study, institutionally sponsored loans, and unspecified assistantships available. Support available to part-time students. Financial award application deadline: 3/15; financial award applicants required to submit FAFSA. *Faculty research:* Women's suffrage movements. *Unit head:* Dr. Barbara Carson, Chairperson, 507-389-1562. *Application contact:* 507-389-2321, E-mail: grad@mnsu.edu.
Website: http://sbs.mnsu.edu/soccorr/.

Minnesota State University Moorhead, Graduate Studies, College of Education and Human Services, Moorhead, MN 56563-0002. Offers counseling and student affairs (MS); curriculum and instruction (MS); educational leadership (MS, Ed S); nursing (MS); reading (MS); special education (MS); speech-language pathology (MS). *Accreditation:* NCATE. Part-time and evening/weekend programs available. *Degree requirements:* For master's, comprehensive exam, final oral exam, project or thesis. *Entrance requirements:* Additional exam requirements/recommendations for international students: Required—TOEFL. Electronic applications accepted.

Minnesota State University Moorhead, Graduate Studies, College of Social and Natural Sciences, Program in Public, Human Services, and Health Administration, Moorhead, MN 56563-0002. Offers MS. Part-time and evening/weekend programs available. *Degree requirements:* For master's, final oral exam, final project paper or thesis. *Entrance requirements:* For master's, GRE General Test, minimum GPA of 2.75. Additional exam requirements/recommendations for international students: Required—TOEFL (minimum score 550 paper-based). Electronic applications accepted.

Montana State University Billings, College of Allied Health Professions, Department of Rehabilitation and Human Services, Billings, MT 59101-0298. Offers MSRC. *Accreditation:* CORE. Part-time programs available. *Degree requirements:* For master's, thesis or professional paper and/or field experience. *Entrance requirements:* For master's, GRE General Test or MAT, minimum GPA of 3.0. *Application deadline:* For fall admission, 7/15 for international students; for spring admission, 12/1 for international students. Applications are processed on a rolling basis. Application fee: $40. *Expenses:* Tuition, state resident: full-time $2653.75; part-time $1718 per semester. Tuition, nonresident: full-time $7015; part-time $4640 per semester. *Required fees:* $2445; $444 per credit. *Financial support:* Teaching assistantships, career-related internships or fieldwork, Federal Work-Study, institutionally sponsored loans, scholarships/grants, tuition waivers (partial), and unspecified assistantships available. Support available to part-time students. Financial award application deadline: 5/1; financial award applicants required to submit FAFSA. *Unit head:* Terry Blackwell, Chair, 406-896-5834, E-mail: tblackwell@msubillings.edu. *Application contact:* David M. Sullivan, Graduate Studies Counselor, 406-657-2053, Fax: 406-657-2299, E-mail: dsullivan@msubillings.edu.

Murray State University, College of Education, Department of Educational Studies, Leadership and Counseling, Program in Human Development and Leadership, Murray, KY 42071. Offers MS. Part-time programs available. *Degree requirements:* For master's, thesis optional. *Entrance requirements:* Additional exam requirements/recommendations for international students: Required—TOEFL.

National Louis University, College of Arts and Sciences, Chicago, IL 60603. Offers adult education (Ed D); counseling and human services (MS); language and academic development (M Ed, Certificate); psychology (MA, PhD, Certificate); public policy (MA); written communication (MS, Certificate). Part-time and evening/weekend programs available. Postbaccalaureate distance learning degree programs offered (minimal on-campus study). *Degree requirements:* For master's and Certificate, comprehensive exam (for some programs), thesis (for some programs); for doctorate, thesis/dissertation. *Entrance requirements:* For master's, MAT or GRE, 3 professional or academic references, interview, minimum GPA of 3.0; for doctorate, GRE General Test, MAT, or Watson-Glaser Critical Thinking Appraisal, three professional or academic references, statement of academic and professional goals, 3 years of experience in field, interview, master's degree, resume, writing sample; for Certificate, GRE, MAT, or Watson-Glaser Critical Thinking Appraisal, three professional or academic references, statement of academic and professional goals, interview, minimum GPA of 3.0. Additional exam requirements/recommendations for international students: Required—Department of Language Studies Assessment or TOEFL (minimum score 550 paper-based; 79 iBT). Electronic applications accepted.

National University, Academic Affairs, School of Health and Human Services, La Jolla, CA 92037-1011. Offers clinical affairs (MS); clinical informatics (Certificate); clinical regulatory affairs (MS); health and life science analytics (MS); health coaching (Certificate); health informatics (MS); healthcare administration (MHA); nurse anesthesia (MS); nursing (MS), including forensic nursing, nursing administration, nursing informatics; nursing administration (Certificate); nursing informatics (Certificate); nursing practice (DNP); public health (MPH), including health promotion, healthcare administration, mental health. Part-time and evening/weekend programs available. Postbaccalaureate distance learning degree programs offered (no on-campus study). *Faculty:* 20 full-time (12 women), 27 part-time/adjunct (16 women). *Students:* 229 full-time (176 women), 89 part-time (52 women); includes 215 minority (58 Black or African American, non-Hispanic/Latino; 1 American Indian or Alaska Native, non-Hispanic/Latino; 68 Asian, non-Hispanic/Latino; 63 Hispanic/Latino; 8 Native Hawaiian or other Pacific Islander, non-Hispanic/Latino; 17 Two or more races, non-Hispanic/Latino), 18 international. Average age 33. 118 applicants, 100% accepted, 92 enrolled. In 2013, 29 master's awarded. *Degree requirements:* For master's, thesis (for some programs). *Entrance requirements:* For master's, interview, minimum GPA of 2.5. Additional exam requirements/recommendations for international students: Required—TOEFL (minimum score 550 paper-based; 79 iBT), IELTS (minimum score 6). *Application deadline:* Applications are processed on a rolling basis. Application fee: $60 ($65 for international students). Electronic applications accepted. *Expenses: Tuition:* Full-time $13,824; part-time $1728 per course. One-time fee: $160. *Financial support:* Career-related internships or fieldwork, institutionally sponsored loans, scholarships/grants, and tuition waivers (partial) available. Support available to part-time students. Financial award application deadline: 6/30; financial award applicants required to submit FAFSA. *Faculty research:* Nursing education, obesity prevention, workforce diversity. *Unit head:* School of Health and Human Services, 800-628-8648, E-mail: shhs@nu.edu. *Application contact:* Louis Cruz, Interim Vice President for Enrollment Services, 800-628-8648, E-mail: advisor@nu.edu.
Website: http://www.nu.edu/OurPrograms/SchoolOfHealthAndHumanServices.html.

New England College, Program in Community Mental Health Counseling, Henniker, NH 03242-3293. Offers human services (MS); mental health counseling (MS). Part-time and evening/weekend programs available. *Degree requirements:* For master's, internship.

Northeastern University, College of Professional Studies, Boston, MA 02115-5096. Offers applied nutrition (MS); commerce and economic development (MS); corporate and organizational communication (MS); digital media (MPS); geographic information technology (MPS); global studies and international affairs (MS); homeland security (MA); human services (MS); informatics (MPS); leadership (MS); nonprofit management (MS); project management (MS); regulatory affairs for drugs, biologics, and medical devices (MS); regulatory affairs of food and food industries (MS); respiratory care leadership (MS); technical communication (MS). Postbaccalaureate distance learning degree programs offered (no on-campus study).

Nova Southeastern University, Institute for the Study of Human Service, Health, and Justice, Fort Lauderdale, FL 33314-7796. Offers child protection (MHS); criminal justice (MS, PhD); developmental disabilities (MS); gerontology (MA). Part-time programs available. Postbaccalaureate distance learning degree programs offered (no on-campus study). *Faculty:* 5 full-time (4 women), 79 part-time/adjunct (41 women). *Students:* 72 full-time (45 women), 385 part-time (320 women); includes 293 minority (209 Black or African American, non-Hispanic/Latino; 1 American Indian or Alaska Native, non-Hispanic/Latino; 5 Asian, non-Hispanic/Latino; 71 Hispanic/Latino; 7 Two or more races, non-Hispanic/Latino). Average age 35. 425 applicants, 39% accepted, 153 enrolled. In 2013, 110 master's awarded. *Degree requirements:* For master's, thesis optional; for doctorate, thesis/dissertation. *Entrance requirements:* For master's, minimum GPA of 2.5, 2 letters of recommendation, 150-300 word personal statement; for doctorate, minimum GPA of 3.0 in master's program; master's degree; successfully defended master's thesis, GRE (minimum score of 300), or sample of published work from refereed publication in criminal justice field; personal statement; 3 letters of recommendation. *Application deadline:* For fall admission, 8/11 for domestic and international students; for winter admission, 12/22 for domestic and international students; for spring admission, 4/21 for domestic and international students; for summer admission, 4/27 for domestic and international students. Applications are processed on a rolling basis. Application fee: $50. Electronic applications accepted. *Financial support:*

Applicants required to submit FAFSA. *Unit head:* Dr. Kimberly Durham, Dean, 954-262-7001, Fax: 954-262-3220, E-mail: durham@nova.edu. *Application contact:* Russell Garner, Director of Administration and Student Services, 954-262-7001, E-mail: gradschool@nova.edu.
Website: http://www.nova.edu/humanservices/.

Pontifical Catholic University of Puerto Rico, College of Graduate Studies in Behavioral Science and Community Affairs, Ponce, PR 00717-0777. Offers clinical psychology (PhD, Psy D); clinical social work (MSW); criminology (MA); industrial psychology (PhD); psychology (PhD); public administration (MSS); rehabilitation counseling (MA). Part-time and evening/weekend programs available. *Degree requirements:* For master's, thesis; for doctorate, comprehensive exam, thesis/dissertation. *Entrance requirements:* For master's, EXADEP, GRE General Test, 3 letters of recommendation, interview, minimum GPA of 2.75.

Post University, Program in Human Services, Waterbury, CT 06723-2540. Offers human services (MS); human services/alcohol and drug counseling (MS); human services/clinical counseling (MS); human services/non-profit management (MS). Part-time and evening/weekend programs available. Postbaccalaureate distance learning degree programs offered.

Purdue University Calumet, Graduate Studies Office, School of Education, Program in Counseling, Hammond, IN 46323-2094. Offers human services (MS Ed); mental health counseling (MS Ed); school counseling (MS Ed). *Entrance requirements:* Additional exam requirements/recommendations for international students: Required—TOEFL.

Roberts Wesleyan College, Program in Social Work, Rochester, NY 14624-1997. Offers child and family practice (MSW); mental health practice (MSW). *Accreditation:* CSWE. *Entrance requirements:* For master's, minimum GPA of 2.75. *Application deadline:* For fall admission, 4/1 priority date for domestic students. Applications are processed on a rolling basis. Application fee: $35. *Expenses: Tuition:* Full-time $12,816; part-time $712 per credit hour. One-time fee: $300. Tuition and fees vary according to course load and program. *Financial support:* Fellowships, career-related internships or fieldwork, scholarships/grants, and tuition waivers (partial) available. Financial award applicants required to submit FAFSA. *Faculty research:* Religion and social work, family studies, values and ethics. *Unit head:* Dr. David Skiff, Chair, 585-594-6578, E-mail: skiffd@roberts.edu. *Application contact:* Beverly Keim, Graduate Admissions Coordinator, 585-594-6232, E-mail: keimb@roberts.edu.
Website: http://www.roberts.edu/graduate/programs/social-work-msw.aspx.

Rosemont College, Schools of Graduate and Professional Studies, Counseling Psychology Program, Rosemont, PA 19010-1699. Offers human services (MA); school counseling (MA). Part-time and evening/weekend programs available. *Degree requirements:* For master's, thesis or alternative, practicum. *Entrance requirements:* For master's, minimum undergraduate GPA of 3.0, 3 letters of recommendation. Additional exam requirements/recommendations for international students: Required—TOEFL. Electronic applications accepted. Application fee is waived when completed online. *Expenses:* Contact institution. *Faculty research:* Addictions counseling.

St. Joseph's College, New York, Graduate Programs, Program in Human Services Management and Leadership, Brooklyn, NY 11205-3688. Offers MS.

St. Mary's University, Graduate School, Department of Counseling and Human Services, San Antonio, TX 78228-8507. Offers community counseling (MA); counseling (Sp C); counseling education and supervision (PhD); marriage and family relations (Certificate); marriage and family therapy (MA, PhD); mental health (MA); mental health and substance abuse counseling (Certificate); substance abuse (MA). *Accreditation:* AAMFT/COAMFTE (one or more programs are accredited); ACA (one or more programs are accredited). Postbaccalaureate distance learning degree programs offered (minimal on-campus study). *Degree requirements:* For master's, comprehensive exam, internship; for doctorate, comprehensive exam, thesis/dissertation, internship. *Entrance requirements:* For master's, GRE General Test, MAT; for doctorate, GRE General Test, recommendation from employers, admissions committee and department faculty. Additional exam requirements/recommendations for international students: Required—TOEFL (minimum score 550 paper-based; 80 iBT). Electronic applications accepted. *Expenses:* Contact institution.

Sojourner-Douglass College, Graduate Program, Baltimore, MD 21205-1814. Offers human services (MASS); public administration (MASS); urban education (reading) (MASS). Part-time and evening/weekend programs available. *Degree requirements:* For master's, comprehensive exam, written proposal oral defense. *Entrance requirements:* For master's, Graduate Examination.

South Carolina State University, School of Graduate and Professional Studies, Department of Human Services, Orangeburg, SC 29117-0001. Offers counselor education (M Ed); rehabilitation counseling (MA). *Accreditation:* CORE. Part-time and evening/weekend programs available. *Faculty:* 9 full-time (6 women), 8 part-time/adjunct (5 women). *Students:* 107 full-time (74 women), 35 part-time (27 women); includes 135 minority (all Black or African American, non-Hispanic/Latino). Average age 31. 54 applicants, 93% accepted, 50 enrolled. In 2013, 54 master's awarded. *Degree requirements:* For master's, comprehensive exam (for some programs), departmental qualifying exam, internship. *Entrance requirements:* For master's, GRE, MAT, minimum GPA of 2.7. *Application deadline:* For fall admission, 6/15 priority date for domestic students, 6/15 for international students; for spring admission, 11/1 for domestic and international students. Applications are processed on a rolling basis. Application fee: $25. Electronic applications accepted. *Expenses:* Tuition, state resident: full-time $8906; part-time $543 per credit hour. Tuition, nonresident: full-time $18,040; part-time $1051 per credit hour. *Financial support:* In 2013–14, 35 students received support. Fellowships, career-related internships or fieldwork, institutionally sponsored loans, and unspecified assistantships available. Financial award application deadline: 6/1. *Faculty research:* Handicap, disability, rehabilitation evaluation, vocation. *Unit head:* Dr. Cassandra Sligh Conway, Chair, 803-536-7075, Fax: 803-533-3636, E-mail: csligh-dewalt@scsu.edu. *Application contact:* Curtis Foskey, Coordinator of Graduate Admissions, 803-536-8419, Fax: 803-536-8812, E-mail: cfoskey@scsu.edu.

Southeastern University, Department of Behavioral and Social Sciences, Lakeland, FL 33801-6099. Offers human services (MA); professional counseling (MS); school counseling (MS). Evening/weekend programs available.

Springfield College, Graduate Programs, Program in Human Services, Springfield, MA 01109-3797. Offers human services (MS), including community counseling psychology, mental health counseling, organizational management and leadership. Part-time and evening/weekend programs available. *Faculty:* 14 full-time (7 women), 73 part-time/adjunct (41 women). *Students:* 428 full-time (315 women); includes 305 minority (238 Black or African American, non-Hispanic/Latino; 1 Asian, non-Hispanic/Latino; 36 Hispanic/Latino; 30 Two or more races, non-Hispanic/Latino), 1 international. Average age 37. 490 applicants, 99% accepted, 428 enrolled. In 2013, 274 master's awarded. *Degree requirements:* For master's, comprehensive exam, thesis (for some programs), Community Action Research Project. *Entrance requirements:* Additional exam requirements/recommendations for international students: Required—TOEFL (minimum score 550 paper-based). *Application deadline:* For fall admission, 8/31 for domestic and international students; for winter admission, 11/1 for domestic and international students; for spring admission, 12/31 for domestic and international students; for summer admission, 4/30 for domestic and international students. Applications are processed on a rolling basis. Application fee: $40. Electronic applications accepted. *Expenses:* Contact institution. *Financial support:* Application deadline: 3/1; applicants required to submit FAFSA. *Unit head:* Dr. Robert J. Willey, Dean, 413-748-3982, E-mail: rwilley@springfieldcollege.edu. *Application contact:* Marisol Guevara, Director of Recruitment and Admissions, 413-748-3742, E-mail: mguevara@springfieldcollege.edu.
Website: http://www.springfieldcollege.edu/springfield-college-school-of-human-services/shs-programs/school-of-human-services-master-of-science-program/index.

Texas Southern University, College of Liberal Arts and Behavioral Sciences, Department of Human Services and Consumer Sciences, Houston, TX 77004-4584. Offers MS. Part-time and evening/weekend programs available. *Faculty:* 3 full-time (all women), 1 (woman) part-time/adjunct. *Students:* 14 full-time (11 women), 14 part-time (12 women); includes 27 minority (25 Black or African American, non-Hispanic/Latino; 1 Asian, non-Hispanic/Latino; 1 Hispanic/Latino). Average age 34. 17 applicants, 76% accepted, 7 enrolled. In 2013, 6 master's awarded. *Degree requirements:* For master's, comprehensive exam, thesis (for some programs). *Entrance requirements:* For master's, GRE General Test, minimum GPA of 2.5. Additional exam requirements/recommendations for international students: Required—TOEFL. *Application deadline:* For fall admission, 7/1 for domestic and international students; for spring admission, 11/1 for domestic and international students. Applications are processed on a rolling basis. Application fee: $50 ($75 for international students). Electronic applications accepted. *Financial support:* In 2013–14, 1 teaching assistantship (averaging $7,373 per year) was awarded; scholarships/grants and unspecified assistantships also available. Financial award application deadline: 5/1. *Faculty research:* Food radiation/food for space travel, adolescent parenting, gerontology/grandparenting. *Unit head:* Dr. Selina Ahmed, Interim Chair, 713-313-7636, Fax: 713-313-7228, E-mail: ahmed_sm@tsu.edu. *Application contact:* Dr. Gregory Maddox, Dean of the Graduate School, 713-313-7011 Ext. 4410, Fax: 713-639-1876, E-mail: maddox_gh@tsu.edu.
Website: http://www.tsu.edu/academics/colleges__schools/colabs/hscs/.

Thomas University, Department of Human Services, Thomasville, GA 31792-7499. Offers community counseling (MSCC); rehabilitation counseling (MRC). *Accreditation:* CORE. Part-time programs available. *Entrance requirements:* For master's, resume, 3 academic/professional references. Additional exam requirements/recommendations for international students: Required—TOEFL (minimum score 600 paper-based). Electronic applications accepted.

Universidad del Turabo, Graduate Programs, School of Social Sciences and Humanities, Programs in Public Affairs, Program in Human Services Administration, Gurabo, PR 00778-3030. Offers MPA. *Entrance requirements:* For master's, GRE, EXADEP, interview.

Université de Montréal, Faculty of Arts and Sciences, Programs in Applied Human Sciences, Montréal, QC H3C 3J7, Canada. Offers PhD. *Degree requirements:* For doctorate, thesis/dissertation, general exam. Electronic applications accepted.

University of Baltimore, Graduate School, The Yale Gordon College of Liberal Arts, Program in Human Services Administration, Baltimore, MD 21201-5779. Offers MS. Part-time and evening/weekend programs available. *Entrance requirements:* For master's, interview. Additional exam requirements/recommendations for international students: Required—TOEFL (minimum score 550 paper-based). Electronic applications accepted.

University of Bridgeport, School of Arts and Sciences, Department of Counseling, Bridgeport, CT 06604. Offers clinical mental health counseling (MS); college student personnel (MS); community counseling (MS); human resource development (MS); human service (MS). Part-time and evening/weekend programs available. *Faculty:* 7 full-time (4 women), 13 part-time/adjunct (7 women). *Students:* 28 full-time (22 women), 79 part-time (61 women); includes 60 minority (45 Black or African American, non-Hispanic/Latino; 11 Hispanic/Latino; 4 Two or more races, non-Hispanic/Latino), 3 international. Average age 34. 124 applicants, 46% accepted, 29 enrolled. In 2013, 26 master's awarded. *Degree requirements:* For master's, thesis, project. *Entrance requirements:* Additional exam requirements/recommendations for international students: Recommended—TOEFL (minimum score 550 paper-based; 80 iBT), IELTS (minimum score 6.5). *Application deadline:* For fall admission, 8/1 priority date for domestic and international students; for spring admission, 12/1 priority date for domestic and international students. Applications are processed on a rolling basis. Application fee: $50. Electronic applications accepted. *Expenses:* Contact institution. *Financial support:* In 2013–14, 27 students received support. Fellowships, research assistantships, teaching assistantships, career-related internships or fieldwork, Federal Work-Study, and institutionally sponsored loans available. Support available to part-time students. Financial award application deadline: 6/1; financial award applicants required to submit FAFSA. *Faculty research:* Corporate elder care programs. *Unit head:* Dr. Sara L. Connolly, Director, Division of Counseling and Human Resources, 203-576-4183, Fax: 203-576-4219, E-mail: sconnoll@bridgeport.edu. *Application contact:* Leanne Proctor, Director of Graduate Admissions, 203-576-4552, Fax: 203-576-4941, E-mail: admit@bridgeport.edu.

University of Central Missouri, The Graduate School, Warrensburg, MO 6409. Offers accountancy (MA); accounting (MBA); applied mathematics (MS); aviation safety (MA); biology (MS); business administration (MBA); career and technical education leadership (MS); college student personnel administration (MS); communication (MA); computer science (MS); counseling (MS); criminal justice (MS); educational leadership (Ed D); educational technology (MS); elementary and early childhood education (MSE); English (MA); environmental studies (MA); finance (MBA); history (MA); human services/educational technology (Ed S); human services/learning resources (Ed S); human services/professional counseling (Ed S); industrial hygiene (MS); industrial management (MS); information systems (MBA); information technology (MS); kinesiology (MS); library science and information services (MS); literacy education (MSE); marketing (MBA); mathematics (MS); music (MA); occupational safety management (MS); psychology (MS); rural family nursing (MS); school administration (MSE); social gerontology (MS); sociology (MA); special education (MSE); speech language pathology (MS); superintendency (Ed S); teaching (MAT); teaching English as a second language (MA); technology (MS); technology management (PhD); theatre (MA). Part-time programs available. *Faculty:* 233. *Students:* 890 full-time (396 women), 1,486 part-time (1,001 women); includes 192 minority (97 Black or African American, non-Hispanic/Latino; 9 American Indian or Alaska Native, non-Hispanic/Latino; 32 Asian, non-Hispanic/Latino; 40 Hispanic/Latino; 3 Native Hawaiian or other Pacific Islander, non-Hispanic/Latino; 11 Two or more races, non-Hispanic/Latino), 539 international. Average age 31. 1,953 applicants, 75% accepted. In 2013, 719 master's, 58 other advanced degrees awarded. *Degree requirements:* For master's and Ed S, comprehensive exam (for some programs), thesis (for some programs). *Entrance requirements:* Additional exam requirements/recommendations for international students: Required—TOEFL (minimum score 550 paper-based; 79 iBT). *Application deadline:* For fall admission, 6/1 for domestic students; for spring admission, 10/1 for domestic and international students. Applications are processed on a rolling basis. Application fee: $30 ($75 for international students). Electronic applications accepted. *Expenses:* Tuition, state resident: full-time $7326; part-time $276.25 per credit hour. Tuition, nonresident: full-time $13,956; part-

time $552.50 per credit hour. *Required fees:* $29 per credit hour. *Financial support:* In 2013–14, 118 students received support, including 271 research assistantships with full and partial tuition reimbursements available (averaging $7,500 per year), 109 teaching assistantships with full and partial tuition reimbursements available (averaging $7,500 per year); career-related internships or fieldwork, Federal Work-Study, scholarships/grants, and administrative and laboratory assistantships also available. Support available to part-time students. Financial award application deadline: 3/1; financial award applicants required to submit FAFSA. *Unit head:* Dr. Joseph Vaughn, Assistant Provost for Research/Dean, 660-543-4092, Fax: 660-543-4778, E-mail: vaughn@ucmo.edu. *Application contact:* Brittany Lawrence, Graduate Student Services Coordinator, 660-543-4621, Fax: 660-543-4778, E-mail: gradinfo@ucmo.edu.
Website: http://www.ucmo.edu/graduate/.

University of Colorado Colorado Springs, College of Education, Colorado Springs, CO 80933-7150. Offers counseling and human services (MA); curriculum and instruction (MA); educational administration (MA); educational leadership (MA, PhD); special education (MA). *Accreditation:* ACA; NCATE. Part-time and evening/weekend programs available. Postbaccalaureate distance learning degree programs offered (minimal on-campus study). *Faculty:* 25 full-time (17 women), 39 part-time/adjunct (29 women). *Students:* 220 full-time (146 women), 237 part-time (163 women); includes 86 minority (18 Black or African American, non-Hispanic/Latino; 3 American Indian or Alaska Native, non-Hispanic/Latino; 11 Asian, non-Hispanic/Latino; 46 Hispanic/Latino; 8 Two or more races, non-Hispanic/Latino), 16 international. Average age 35. 182 applicants, 88% accepted, 118 enrolled. In 2013, 140 master's, 8 doctorates awarded. *Degree requirements:* For master's, comprehensive exam, thesis or alternative, microcomputer proficiency; for doctorate, comprehensive exam, thesis/dissertation, research lab. *Entrance requirements:* For master's, GRE General Test. Additional exam requirements/recommendations for international students: Recommended—TOEFL. *Application deadline:* For fall admission, 2/28 priority date for domestic students, 2/28 for international students; for spring admission, 10/15 for domestic and international students. Applications are processed on a rolling basis. Application fee: $60 ($75 for international students). *Expenses:* Tuition, state resident: full-time $8882; part-time $1622 per course. Tuition, nonresident: full-time $17,435; part-time $3048 per course. One-time fee: $100. Tuition and fees vary according to course load, degree level, campus/location and program. *Financial support:* In 2013–14, 23 students received support, including 23 fellowships (averaging $1,577 per year); career-related internships or fieldwork, Federal Work-Study, and scholarships/grants also available. Support available to part-time students. Financial award application deadline: 3/1; financial award applicants required to submit FAFSA. *Faculty research:* Linguistically diverse education (LDE), educational policy, evidence-based reading and writing instruction, relational and social aggression, positive behavior supports (PBS), inclusive schooling, K-12 education policy. *Total annual research expenditures:* $136,574. *Unit head:* Dr. Mary Snyder, Dean, 719-255-3701, Fax: 719-262-4133, E-mail: msnyder3@uccs.edu. *Application contact:* Juliane Field, Director, 719-255-4526, Fax: 719-255-4110, E-mail: jfield@uccs.edu.
Website: http://www.uccs.edu/coe.

University of Great Falls, Graduate Studies, Program in Organization Management, Great Falls, MT 59405. Offers human development (MSM); management (MSM). Part-time and evening/weekend programs available. Postbaccalaureate distance learning degree programs offered (minimal on-campus study). *Degree requirements:* For master's, thesis optional. *Entrance requirements:* For master's, GRE General Test or MAT, 3 letters of recommendation. Additional exam requirements/recommendations for international students: Required—TOEFL (minimum score 500 paper-based). Electronic applications accepted.

University of Idaho, College of Graduate Studies, College of Education, Department of Leadership and Counseling, Boise, ID 83844-2282. Offers adult/organizational learning and leadership (MS, Ed S); educational leadership (M Ed, Ed S); rehabilitation counseling and human services (M Ed, MS); school counseling (M Ed, MS); special education (M Ed). *Faculty:* 13 full-time, 11 part-time/adjunct. *Students:* 58 full-time (39 women), 200 part-time (121 women). Average age 39. In 2013, 83 master's, 38 other advanced degrees awarded. *Entrance requirements:* Additional exam requirements/recommendations for international students: Required—TOEFL (minimum score 550 paper-based). *Application deadline:* Applications are processed on a rolling basis. Application fee: $60. Electronic applications accepted. *Expenses:* Tuition, state resident: full-time $5596; part-time $363 per credit hour. Tuition, nonresident: full-time $18,672; part-time $1089 per credit hour. *Financial support:* Applicants required to submit FAFSA. *Unit head:* Dr. Jeffrey Brooks, Chair, 208-364-4047, E-mail: mweitz@uidaho.edu. *Application contact:* Stephanie Thomas, Graduate Recruitment Coordinator, 208-885-4001, Fax: 208-885-4406, E-mail: gadms@uidaho.edu.
Website: http://www.uidaho.edu/ed/leadershipcounseling.

University of Illinois at Springfield, Graduate Programs, College of Education and Human Services, Program in Human Services, Springfield, IL 62703-5407. Offers alcohol and substance abuse (Graduate Certificate); alcoholism and substance abuse (MA); child and family services (MA); gerontology (MA); social services administration (MA). Part-time and evening/weekend programs available. Postbaccalaureate distance learning degree programs offered (no on-campus study). *Faculty:* 5 full-time (all women), 1 part-time/adjunct (0 women). *Students:* 20 full-time (17 women), 66 part-time (58 women); includes 32 minority (27 Black or African American, non-Hispanic/Latino; 3 Hispanic/Latino; 2 Two or more races, non-Hispanic/Latino). Average age 36. 61 applicants, 46% accepted, 23 enrolled. In 2013, 43 master's, 1 other advanced degree awarded. *Degree requirements:* For master's, internship; project or thesis. *Entrance requirements:* For master's, minimum undergraduate GPA of 3.0, 2 letters of recommendation, statement of intent. Additional exam requirements/recommendations for international students: Required—TOEFL (minimum score 500 paper-based; 61 iBT). Application fee: $60 ($75 for international students). Electronic applications accepted. *Expenses:* Tuition, state resident: full-time $7440. Tuition, nonresident: full-time $15,744. *Required fees:* $2985.60. *Financial support:* In 2013–14, fellowships with full tuition reimbursements (averaging $9,900 per year), research assistantships with full tuition reimbursements (averaging $9,550 per year), teaching assistantships with full tuition reimbursements (averaging $9,700 per year) were awarded; career-related internships or fieldwork, Federal Work-Study, scholarships/grants, health care benefits, and unspecified assistantships also available. Support available to part-time students. Financial award application deadline: 11/15. *Unit head:* Dr. Carolyn Peck, Program Administrator, 217-206-7577, Fax: 217-206-6775, E-mail: peck.carolyn@uis.edu. *Application contact:* Dr. Lynn Pardie, Office of Graduate Studies, 800-252-8533, Fax: 217-206-7623, E-mail: lpard1@uis.edu.
Website: http://www.uis.edu/humanservices.

University of Illinois at Urbana–Champaign, Graduate College, School of Social Work, Champaign, IL 61820. Offers advocacy, leadership, and social change (MSW); children, youth and family services (MSW); health care (MSW); mental health (MSW); school social work (MSW); social work (PhD). *Accreditation:* CSWE (one or more programs are accredited). *Students:* 259 (225 women). *Entrance requirements:* For master's and doctorate, minimum GPA of 3.0. Application fee: $75 ($90 for international students). *Unit head:* Wynne S. Korr, Dean, 217-333-2260, Fax: 217-244-5220, E-mail: wkorr@illinois.edu. *Application contact:* Cheryl M. Street, Admissions and Records Officer, 217-333-2261, Fax: 217-244-5220, E-mail: street@illinois.edu.
Website: http://socialwork.illinois.edu/.

University of Maryland, Baltimore County, Graduate School, College of Arts, Humanities and Social Sciences, Department of Psychology, Program in Human Services Psychology, Baltimore, MD 21250. Offers MA, PhD. *Faculty:* 14 full-time (5 women), 11 part-time/adjunct (4 women). *Students:* 73 full-time (61 women), 39 part-time (27 women); includes 28 minority (13 Black or African American, non-Hispanic/Latino; 6 Asian, non-Hispanic/Latino; 7 Hispanic/Latino; 2 Two or more races, non-Hispanic/Latino). Average age 25. 124 applicants, 17% accepted, 8 enrolled. In 2013, 21 master's, 8 doctorates awarded. *Degree requirements:* For master's, thesis; for doctorate, comprehensive exam, thesis/dissertation. *Entrance requirements:* For master's, GRE General Test, minimum GPA of 3.0; for doctorate, GRE General Test, GRE Subject Test, minimum GPA of 3.0. Additional exam requirements/recommendations for international students: Required—TOEFL. *Application deadline:* For fall admission, 12/1 for domestic and international students. Application fee: $50. Electronic applications accepted. One-time fee: $200 full-time. *Financial support:* In 2013–14, 4 students received support, including 3 fellowships with full and partial tuition reimbursements available (averaging $26,000 per year), 30 research assistantships with full and partial tuition reimbursements available (averaging $18,300 per year), 13 teaching assistantships with full and partial tuition reimbursements available (averaging $15,450 per year); career-related internships or fieldwork, Federal Work-Study, scholarships/grants, health care benefits, tuition waivers, and unspecified assistantships also available. Financial award application deadline: 3/1; financial award applicants required to submit FAFSA. *Faculty research:* Addictive behaviors, cardiovascular and cerebrovascular disease, family violence, pediatric psychology, community prevention. *Total annual research expenditures:* $282,103. *Unit head:* Dr. Lynnda Dahlquist, Director, 410-455-2567, Fax: 410-455-1055, E-mail: dahlquis@umbc.edu. *Application contact:* Nicole Mooney, Program Management Specialist, 410-455-2567, Fax: 410-455-1055, E-mail: psycdept@umbc.edu.

University of Massachusetts Boston, Office of Graduate Studies, College of Public and Community Service, Program in Human Services, Boston, MA 02125-3393. Offers MS. Part-time and evening/weekend programs available. *Degree requirements:* For master's, practicum, final project. *Entrance requirements:* For master's, MAT, GRE, minimum GPA of 2.75. *Faculty research:* Institutional and policy context of human services, ethics and social policy, public law and human services, social welfare, politics and human services.

University of Nebraska at Kearney, Graduate Programs, College of Business and Technology, Department of Business, Kearney, NE 68849-0001. Offers accounting (MBA); generalist (MBA); human resources (MBA); human services (MBA); marketing (MBA). *Accreditation:* AACSB. Part-time and evening/weekend programs available. *Degree requirements:* For master's, thesis optional. *Entrance requirements:* For master's, GMAT or GRE, letters of recommendation, work history, letter of interest, resume. Additional exam requirements/recommendations for international students: Required—TOEFL (minimum score 550 paper-based; 79 iBT). Electronic applications accepted. *Faculty research:* Small business financial management, employment law, expert systems, international trade and marketing, environmental economics.

University of Northern Iowa, Graduate College, College of Education, School of Health, Physical Education, and Leisure Services, Program in Leisure, Youth and Human Services, Cedar Falls, IA 50614. Offers MA, Ed D. *Students:* 28 full-time (20 women), 6 part-time (2 women); includes 7 minority (6 Black or African American, non-Hispanic/Latino; 1 Hispanic/Latino), 4 international. 20 applicants, 60% accepted, 9 enrolled. In 2013, 10 master's awarded. *Degree requirements:* For master's, comprehensive exam, thesis or alternative; for doctorate, thesis/dissertation. *Entrance requirements:* For master's, minimum GPA of 3.0; for doctorate, GRE, minimum GPA of 3.5. Additional exam requirements/recommendations for international students: Required—TOEFL (minimum score 500 paper-based; 61 iBT). *Application deadline:* Applications are processed on a rolling basis. Application fee: $50 ($70 for international students). Electronic applications accepted. *Financial support:* Career-related internships or fieldwork, Federal Work-Study, institutionally sponsored loans, tuition waivers (full), and unspecified assistantships available. Financial award application deadline: 2/1. *Unit head:* Dr. Julianne Gassman, Coordinator, 319-273-2264, Fax: 319-273-5958, E-mail: julianne.gassman@uni.edu. *Application contact:* Laurie S. Russell, Record Analyst, 319-273-2623, Fax: 319-273-2885, E-mail: laurie.russell@uni.edu.
Website: http://www.uni.edu/coe/departments/school-health-physical-education-leisure-services/leisure-youth-and-human-services-0.

University of Northwestern–St. Paul, Program in Human Services, St. Paul, MN 55113-1598. Offers family studies (MAHS). Part-time and evening/weekend programs available. Postbaccalaureate distance learning degree programs offered (no on-campus study). *Expenses: Tuition:* Full-time $8820; part-time $490 per credit.
Website: http://www.unwsp.edu/web/grad-studies/master-of-arts-in-human-services.

University of Oklahoma, College of Arts and Sciences, Department of Human Relations, Norman, OK 73019. Offers family relations (MHR); human relations licensure (Graduate Certificate). Part-time and evening/weekend programs available. Postbaccalaureate distance learning degree programs offered (minimal on-campus study). *Faculty:* 25 full-time (17 women), 4 part-time/adjunct (all women). *Students:* 329 full-time (218 women), 538 part-time (345 women); includes 392 minority (228 Black or African American, non-Hispanic/Latino; 35 American Indian or Alaska Native, non-Hispanic/Latino; 18 Asian, non-Hispanic/Latino; 78 Hispanic/Latino; 2 Native Hawaiian or other Pacific Islander, non-Hispanic/Latino; 31 Two or more races, non-Hispanic/Latino), 10 international. Average age 34. 298 applicants, 86% accepted, 159 enrolled. In 2013, 309 master's, 62 other advanced degrees awarded. *Degree requirements:* For master's, comprehensive exam, thesis optional. *Entrance requirements:* Additional exam requirements/recommendations for international students: Required—TOEFL (minimum score 79 iBT). *Application deadline:* For fall admission, 4/1 for domestic students, 3/1 for international students; for spring admission, 11/1 for domestic students, 9/1 for international students. Applications are processed on a rolling basis. Application fee: $50 ($100 for international students). Electronic applications accepted. *Expenses:* Tuition, state resident: full-time $4205; part-time $175.20 per credit hour. Tuition, nonresident: full-time $16,205; part-time $675.20 per credit hour. *Required fees:* $2745; $103.85 per credit hour. $126.50 per semester. *Financial support:* In 2013–14, 139 students received support, including 3 research assistantships with partial tuition reimbursements available (averaging $11,124 per year); career-related internships or fieldwork, scholarships/grants, and unspecified assistantships also available. Financial award application deadline: 6/1; financial award applicants required to submit FAFSA. *Faculty research:* Non-profit organizations, high risk youth, trauma, women's studies, impact of war on women and children. *Total annual research expenditures:* $53,235. *Unit head:* Dr. Wesley Long, Chair, 405-325-1756, Fax: 405-325-4402, E-mail: wlong@ou.edu. *Application contact:* Lawana Miller, Admissions Coordinator, 405-325-1756, Fax: 405-325-4402, E-mail: lmiller@ou.edu.
Website: http://www.ou.edu/cas/hr.

University of Oklahoma, College of Liberal Studies, Norman, OK 73019. Offers administrative leadership (MA Ed, Graduate Certificate); criminal justice (MS); liberal

studies (MA, MA Ed), including human and health services administration (MA Ed), integrated studies (MA), museum studies (MA Ed); prevention science (MPS). Part-time and evening/weekend programs available. Postbaccalaureate distance learning degree programs offered (no on-campus study). *Faculty:* 16 full-time (11 women), 2 part-time/adjunct (0 women). *Students:* 33 full-time (13 women), 562 part-time (262 women); includes 147 minority (57 Black or African American, non-Hispanic/Latino; 27 American Indian or Alaska Native, non-Hispanic/Latino; 7 Asian, non-Hispanic/Latino; 29 Hispanic/Latino; 2 Native Hawaiian or other Pacific Islander, non-Hispanic/Latino; 25 Two or more races, non-Hispanic/Latino), 2 international. Average age 36. 203 applicants, 94% accepted, 122 enrolled. In 2013, 161 master's, 27 other advanced degrees awarded. Terminal master's awarded for partial completion of doctoral program. *Degree requirements:* For master's, comprehensive exam (for some programs), thesis optional, practicum (for museum studies only); for Graduate Certificate, comprehensive exam (for some programs), thesis optional. *Entrance requirements:* For master's and Graduate Certificate, minimum cumulative GPA of 3.0 in previous undergraduate/graduate coursework. Additional exam requirements/recommendations for international students: Required—TOEFL (minimum score 79 iBT). *Application deadline:* For fall admission, 7/1 for domestic students, 1/1 for international students; for winter admission, 12/1 for domestic and international students; for spring admission, 5/1 for domestic and international students. Application fee: $50 ($100 for international students). Electronic applications accepted. *Expenses:* Tuition, state resident: full-time $4205; part-time $175.20 per credit hour. Tuition, nonresident: full-time $16,205; part-time $675.20 per credit hour. *Required fees:* $2745; $103.85 per credit hour. $126.50 per semester. *Financial support:* In 2013–14, 109 students received support. Career-related internships or fieldwork, Federal Work-Study, institutionally sponsored loans, scholarships/grants, health care benefits, and tuition waivers (partial) available. Support available to part-time students. Financial award application deadline: 6/1; financial award applicants required to submit FAFSA. *Faculty research:* Race, crime, and class inequality; human trafficking; textual analysis and early Christianity; drug policy implementation; professionalism in police practice; service-learning; Chinese cultural studies. *Total annual research expenditures:* $31,745. *Unit head:* Dr. James Pappas, Dean/Vice President of OU Outreach, 405-325-6361, Fax: 405-325-7132, E-mail: jpappas@ou.edu. *Application contact:* Missy Heinze, Recruitment Coordinator, 800-522-0559, Fax: 405-325-7132, E-mail: mheinze@ou.edu.
Website: http://www.ou.edu/cls/.

University of Phoenix–Minneapolis/St. Louis Park Campus, College of Human Services, St. Louis Park, MN 55426. Offers community counseling (MSC).

University of Phoenix–Puerto Rico Campus, College of Human Services, Guaynabo, PR 00968. Offers marriage and family counseling (MSC); mental health counseling (MSC). Evening/weekend programs available. *Degree requirements:* For master's, thesis (for some programs). *Entrance requirements:* For master's, Counselor Preparation Comprehensive Examination, minimum undergraduate GPA of 2.5, 3 years work experience. Additional exam requirements/recommendations for international students: Required—TOEFL (minimum score 550 paper-based; 79 iBT). Electronic applications accepted.

Upper Iowa University, Online Master's Programs, Fayette, IA 52142-1857. Offers accounting (MBA); corporate financial management (MBA); global business (MBA); health and human services (MPA); higher education administration (MHEA); homeland security (MPA); human resources management (MBA); justice administration (MPA); organizational development (MBA); public personnel management (MPA); quality management (MBA). MBA also available at Madison, WI campus. Part-time programs available. Postbaccalaureate distance learning degree programs offered (no on-campus study). *Degree requirements:* For master's, research project. *Entrance requirements:* For master's, GMAT, GRE, or minimum GPA of 2.7 during last 60 hours. Additional exam requirements/recommendations for international students: Required—TOEFL (minimum score 570 paper-based). Electronic applications accepted. *Faculty research:* Total quality management, CQI, teams, organization culture and climate, management.

Walden University, Graduate Programs, School of Social Work and Human Services, Minneapolis, MN 55401. Offers addictions (MSW); addictions and social work (DSW); children, families, and couples (MSW); clinical expertise (DSW); criminal justice (DSW); crisis and trauma (MSW); disaster, crisis, and intervention (DSW); forensic populations and settings (MSW); general program (MSW); human services (MS, PhD), including clinical social work (PhD), criminal justice, disaster, crisis and intervention, family studies and intervention strategies (PhD), family studies and interventions, general program, human services administration (PhD), human services and administration (MS), public health, social policy analysis and planning; medical social work (MSW, DSW); military families and culture (MSW); policy practice (DSW); social work (PhD), including addictions and social work, clinical expertise, disaster, crisis and intervention (MS, PhD), family studies and interventions (MS, PhD), medical social work, policy practice, social work administration; social work administration (DSW). Part-time and evening/weekend programs available. Postbaccalaureate distance learning degree programs offered (minimal on-campus study). *Faculty:* 11 full-time (7 women), 89 part-time/adjunct (60 women). *Students:* 906 full-time (794 women), 469 part-time (394 women); includes 930 minority (812 Black or African American, non-Hispanic/Latino; 14 American Indian or Alaska Native, non-Hispanic/Latino; 12 Asian, non-Hispanic/Latino; 61 Hispanic/Latino;

4 Native Hawaiian or other Pacific Islander, non-Hispanic/Latino; 27 Two or more races, non-Hispanic/Latino), 11 international. Average age 41. 673 applicants, 97% accepted, 555 enrolled. In 2013, 417 master's, 11 doctorates awarded. *Degree requirements:* For master's, residency (for some programs); for doctorate, thesis/dissertation, residency. *Entrance requirements:* For master's, bachelor's degree or higher; minimum GPA of 2.5; official transcripts; goal statement (for some programs); access to computer and Internet; for doctorate, master's degree or higher; three years of related professional or academic experience (preferred); minimum GPA of 3.0; goal statement and current resume (select programs); official transcripts; access to computer and Internet. Additional exam requirements/recommendations for international students: Required—TOEFL (minimum score 550 paper-based; 79 iBT), IELTS (minimum score 6.5), Michigan English Language Assessment Battery (minimum score 82), or PTE. *Application deadline:* Applications are processed on a rolling basis. Application fee: $0. Electronic applications accepted. *Expenses: Tuition:* Full-time $11,813.55; part-time $500 per credit. *Required fees:* $618.76. *Financial support:* Fellowships, Federal Work-Study, scholarships/grants, unspecified assistantships, and family tuition reduction, active duty/veteran tuition reduction, group tuition reduction, interest-free payment plans, employee tuition reduction available. Support available to part-time students. Financial award applicants required to submit FAFSA. *Unit head:* Dr. Savitri Dixon-Saxon, Associate Dean, 800-925-3368. *Application contact:* Jennifer Hall, Vice President of Enrollment Management, 866-4-WALDEN, E-mail: info@waldenu.edu. Website: http://www.waldenu.edu/colleges-schools/school-of-social-work-and-human-services/academic-programs.

Washburn University, School of Applied Studies, Department of Human Services, Topeka, KS 66621. Offers addiction counseling (MA). Evening/weekend programs available. *Faculty:* 4 full-time (3 women). *Students:* 14 full-time (12 women), 2 part-time (both women). Average age 40. *Entrance requirements:* For master's, minimum GPA of 3.0 in last 60 hours of coursework. Additional exam requirements/recommendations for international students: Required—TOEFL (minimum score 80 iBT). *Application deadline:* For fall admission, 5/1 for domestic students. Application fee: $35. *Expenses:* Tuition, state resident: full-time $5850; part-time $325 per credit hour. Tuition, nonresident: full-time $11,916; part-time $662 per credit hour. *Required fees:* $86; $43 per semester. Tuition and fees vary according to program. *Financial support:* Career-related internships or fieldwork, Federal Work-Study, institutionally sponsored loans, and scholarships/grants available. Financial award applicants required to submit FAFSA. *Faculty research:* Professional identity development in students, expressive therapeutic writing, prevention, community mental health, agency professional development, behavioral analysis, group living among the elderly, ethical identity development, higher education pedagogy, Morita therapy/anxiety disorders, ecological/contextual healing, post-trauma. *Unit head:* Dr. Brian Ogawa, Chair, 785-670-2116, Fax: 785-670-1027, E-mail: brian.ogawa@washburn.edu.
Website: http://www.washburn.edu/academics/college-schools/applied-studies/departments/human-services/.

West Virginia University, Eberly College of Arts and Sciences, School of Applied Social Sciences, Division of Social Work, Morgantown, WV 26506. Offers aging and health care (MSW); children and families (MSW); community mental health (MSW); community organization and social administration (MSW); direct (clinical) social work practice (MSW). *Accreditation:* CSWE. Part-time programs available. *Degree requirements:* For master's, fieldwork. *Entrance requirements:* For master's, GRE, minimum GPA of 2.75, 2 letters of reference. Additional exam requirements/recommendations for international students: Required—TOEFL. *Faculty research:* Rural and small town social work practice, gerontology, health and mental health, welfare reform, child welfare.

Wichita State University, Graduate School, Fairmount College of Liberal Arts and Sciences, School of Community Affairs, Wichita, KS 67260. Offers criminal justice (MA). Part-time programs available. *Unit head:* Dr. Michael Birzer, Director, 316-978-7200, Fax: 316-978-3626, E-mail: michael.birzer@wichita.edu. *Application contact:* Jordan Oleson, Admissions Coordinator, 316-978-3095, Fax: 316-978-3253, E-mail: jordan.oleson@wichita.edu.

Wilmington University, College of Social and Behavioral Sciences, New Castle, DE 19720-6491. Offers administration of human services (MS); administration of justice (MS); clinical mental health counseling (MS); homeland security (MS). *Accreditation:* ACA. Part-time and evening/weekend programs available. *Entrance requirements:* Additional exam requirements/recommendations for international students: Required—TOEFL (minimum score 500 paper-based). Electronic applications accepted.

Youngstown State University, Graduate School, Bitonte College of Health and Human Services, Department of Health Professions, Youngstown, OH 44555-0001. Offers health and human services (MHHS); public health (MPH). *Accreditation:* NAACLS. Part-time and evening/weekend programs available. *Degree requirements:* For master's, thesis optional. *Entrance requirements:* For master's, GRE General Test, minimum GPA of 3.0. Additional exam requirements/recommendations for international students: Required—TOEFL. *Faculty research:* Drug prevention, multiskilling in health care, organizational behavior, health care management, health behaviors, research management.

Social Work

Abilene Christian University, Graduate School, College of Education and Human Services, School of Social Work, Abilene, TX 79699-9100. Offers MSSW. *Accreditation:* CSWE. Part-time programs available. *Faculty:* 6 part-time/adjunct (2 women). *Students:* 30 full-time (25 women), 7 part-time (6 women); includes 11 minority (1 Black or African American, non-Hispanic/Latino; 6 Hispanic/Latino; 4 Two or more races, non-Hispanic/Latino), 1 international. 43 applicants, 49% accepted, 21 enrolled. In 2013, 13 master's awarded. *Degree requirements:* For master's, thesis. *Entrance requirements:* For master's, GRE if undergraduate GPA less than 3.0 or MAT. Additional exam requirements/recommendations for international students: Required—TOEFL (minimum score 550 paper-based; 90 iBT), IELTS (minimum score 6.5), PTE. *Application deadline:* For fall admission, 2/16 priority date for domestic students; for spring admission, 11/1 for domestic students. Applications are processed on a rolling basis. Application fee: $50. Electronic applications accepted. *Expenses: Tuition:* Full-time $17,100; part-time $950 per credit hour. *Financial support:* In 2013–14, 27 students received support, including 2 research assistantships with partial tuition reimbursements available (averaging $5,800 per year); career-related internships or fieldwork, Federal Work-Study, and tuition waivers (partial) also available. Financial award application deadline: 4/1; financial award applicants required to submit FAFSA. *Unit head:* Dr. Wayne Paris, MSSW

Director, 325-674-2072, Fax: 325-674-6525, E-mail: socialwork@acu.edu. *Application contact:* Corey Patterson, Director of Graduate Admission and Recruiting, 325-674-6566, Fax: 325-674-6717, E-mail: gradinfo@acu.edu.
Website: http://www.acu.edu/socialwork.

Adelphi University, School of Social Work, Garden City, NY 11530-0701. Offers social welfare (DSW); social work (MSW, PhD). *Accreditation:* CSWE (one or more programs are accredited). Part-time and evening/weekend programs available. *Faculty:* 24 full-time (17 women), 105 part-time/adjunct (82 women). *Students:* 442 full-time (391 women), 297 part-time (262 women); includes 342 minority (205 Black or African American, non-Hispanic/Latino; 17 Asian, non-Hispanic/Latino; 108 Hispanic/Latino; 2 Native Hawaiian or other Pacific Islander, non-Hispanic/Latino; 10 Two or more races, non-Hispanic/Latino), 8 international. Average age 33. 669 applicants, 68% accepted, 306 enrolled. In 2013, 303 master's, 6 doctorates awarded. *Degree requirements:* For master's, field internships; for doctorate, thesis/dissertation. *Entrance requirements:* For master's, minimum undergraduate GPA of 3.0, paid or volunteer work experience, 3 letters of recommendation, interview; for doctorate, GRE, MSW with minimum GPA of 3.3, 3 years of post-MSW work experience, 3 letters of reference, 3 examples of professional writing. Additional exam requirements/recommendations for international

Social Work

students: Required—TOEFL (minimum score 550 paper-based; 80 iBT). *Application deadline:* For fall admission, 4/1 for international students; for spring admission, 12/1 for domestic students, 11/1 for international students. Application fee: $50. Electronic applications accepted. *Expenses: Tuition:* Full-time $32,530; part-time $1010 per credit. *Required fees:* $1150. Tuition and fees vary according to degree level and program. *Financial support:* In 2013–14, 32 research assistantships with partial tuition reimbursements (averaging $3,341 per year) were awarded; career-related internships or fieldwork, Federal Work-Study, institutionally sponsored loans, scholarships/grants, traineeships, tuition waivers (full and partial), and unspecified assistantships also available. Financial award application deadline: 2/15; financial award applicants required to submit FAFSA. *Faculty research:* Services for rape victims, immigrant research methods, remarriage and step families, social health indicators. *Unit head:* Dr. Andrew Safyer, Dean, 516-877-4300, E-mail: asafyer@adelphi.edu. *Application contact:* Christine Murphy, Director of Admissions, 516-877-3050, Fax: 516-877-3039, E-mail: graduateadmissions@adelphi.edu.
Website: http://socialwork.adelphi.edu/.

See Display below and Close-Up on page 1723.

Alabama Agricultural and Mechanical University, School of Graduate Studies, School of Arts and Sciences, Department of Social Work, Huntsville, AL 35811. Offers MSW. *Accreditation:* CSWE. *Degree requirements:* For master's, thesis. *Entrance requirements:* For master's, GRE General Test, portfolio. Additional exam requirements/recommendations for international students: Required—TOEFL (minimum score 500 paper-based; 61 iBT). Electronic applications accepted.

Albany State University, College of Arts and Humanities, Albany, GA 31705-2717. Offers English education (M Ed); public administration (MPA), including community and economic development administration, criminal justice administration, general administration, health administration and policy, human resources management, public policy, water resources management; social work (MSW). Part-time programs available. *Degree requirements:* For master's, comprehensive exam, professional portfolio (for MPA), internship, capstone report. *Entrance requirements:* For master's, GRE, MAT, minimum GPA of 3.0, official transcript, pre-medical record/certificate of immunization, letters of reference. Electronic applications accepted. *Faculty research:* HIV prevention for minority students.

American Jewish University, Graduate School of Nonprofit Management, Program in Jewish Communal Studies, Bel Air, CA 90077-1599. Offers MAJCS. *Degree requirements:* For master's, thesis. *Entrance requirements:* For master's, GMAT or GRE General Test, interview.

Andrews University, School of Graduate Studies, College of Arts and Sciences, Department of Social Work, Berrien Springs, MI 49104. Offers MSW. *Accreditation:* CSWE. *Faculty:* 7 full-time (6 women), 1 (woman) part-time/adjunct. *Students:* 33 full-time (21 women), 10 part-time (7 women); includes 26 minority (20 Black or African American, non-Hispanic/Latino; 1 American Indian or Alaska Native, non-Hispanic/Latino; 3 Asian, non-Hispanic/Latino; 2 Hispanic/Latino), 4 international. Average age 34. 64 applicants, 48% accepted, 21 enrolled. In 2013, 26 master's awarded. *Entrance requirements:* For master's, GRE. Additional exam requirements/recommendations for international students: Required—TOEFL (minimum score 550 paper-based). *Application deadline:* Applications are processed on a rolling basis. Application fee: $40. *Unit head:* Dr. Curtis VanderWaal, Chair, 269-471-6196. *Application contact:* Monica Wringer, Supervisor of Graduate Admission, 800-253-2874, Fax: 269-471-6321, E-mail: graduate@andrews.edu.

Appalachian State University, Cratis D. Williams Graduate School, Department of Social Work, Boone, NC 28608. Offers MSW. *Accreditation:* CSWE. Part-time and evening/weekend programs available. Postbaccalaureate distance learning degree programs offered (no on-campus study). *Degree requirements:* For master's, comprehensive exam. *Entrance requirements:* For master's, GRE General Test, 3 letters of recommendation. Additional exam requirements/recommendations for international students: Required—TOEFL (minimum score 550 paper-based; 79 iBT), IELTS (minimum score 6.5). Electronic applications accepted. *Faculty research:* Community and organizational practice, individual and family.

Arizona State University at the Tempe campus, College of Public Programs, School of Social Work, Phoenix, AZ 85004-0689. Offers assessment of integrative health modalities (Graduate Certificate); gerontology and geriatric care (Graduate Certificate); Latino cultural competency (Graduate Certificate); social work (PhD); social work (advanced direct practice) (MSW); social work (planning, administration and community practice) (MSW); trauma and bereavement (Graduate Certificate); MPA/MSW. *Accreditation:* CSWE (one or more programs are accredited). Part-time programs available. Terminal master's awarded for partial completion of doctoral program. *Degree requirements:* For master's, thesis or alternative, capstone project, interactive Program of Study (iPOS) submitted before completing 50 percent of required credit hours; for doctorate, comprehensive exam, thesis/dissertation, interactive Program of Study (iPOS) submitted before completing 50 percent of required credit hours. *Entrance requirements:* For master's, GRE or MAT, minimum GPA of 3.2 or equivalent in last 2 years of work leading to bachelor's degree; for doctorate, GRE, minimum GPA of 3.0 or equivalent in last 2 years of work leading to bachelor's degree, 3 letters of recommendation, resume, samples of professional writing, personal statement. Additional exam requirements/recommendations for international students: Required—TOEFL, IELTS, or PTE. Electronic applications accepted. *Expenses:* Contact institution.

Arkansas State University, Graduate School, College of Nursing and Health Professions, Department of Social Work, Jonesboro, AR 72467. Offers addiction studies (Certificate); social work (MSW). *Accreditation:* CSWE. Part-time programs available. *Faculty:* 7 full-time (5 women). *Students:* 27 full-time (22 women), 37 part-time (33 women); includes 26 minority (24 Black or African American, non-Hispanic/Latino; 2 Hispanic/Latino). Average age 33. 63 applicants, 54% accepted, 33 enrolled. In 2013, 40 master's awarded. *Degree requirements:* For master's, comprehensive exam, thesis (for some programs). *Entrance requirements:* For master's, GRE or MAT, appropriate bachelor's degree, letters of reference, personal statement, resume, official transcript, immunization records. Additional exam requirements/recommendations for international students: Required—TOEFL (minimum score 550 paper-based; 79 iBT), IELTS (minimum score 6), PTE (minimum score 56). *Application deadline:* For fall admission, 3/1 for domestic and international students; for spring admission, 10/1 for domestic and international students. Applications are processed on a rolling basis. Application fee: $30 ($40 for international students). Electronic applications accepted. *Expenses:* Contact institution. *Financial support:* In 2013–14, 6 students received support. Career-related internships or fieldwork, scholarships/grants, and unspecified assistantships available. Financial award application deadline: 7/1; financial award applicants required to submit FAFSA. *Unit head:* Dr. Karen Allen, Chair, 870-972-3984, Fax: 870-972-3987, E-mail: kallen@astate.edu. *Application contact:* Vickey Ring, Graduate Admissions Coordinator, 870-972-3029, Fax: 870-972-3857, E-mail: vickeyring@astate.edu.
Website: http://www.astate.edu/college/conhp/departments/social-work/.

Asbury University, School of Graduate and Professional Studies, Master of Social Work Program, Wilmore, KY 40390-1198. Offers child and family services (MSW). *Accreditation:* CSWE. *Degree requirements:* For master's, comprehensive exam, 954 praticum hours completed in agency. *Entrance requirements:* For master's, prerequisite courses in psychology, sociology, and statistics. Additional exam requirements/recommendations for international students: Required—TOEFL. Electronic applications accepted. *Expenses:* Contact institution. *Faculty research:* Integration of faith and practice, survivors of family violence, program evaluation, cross-cultural counseling.

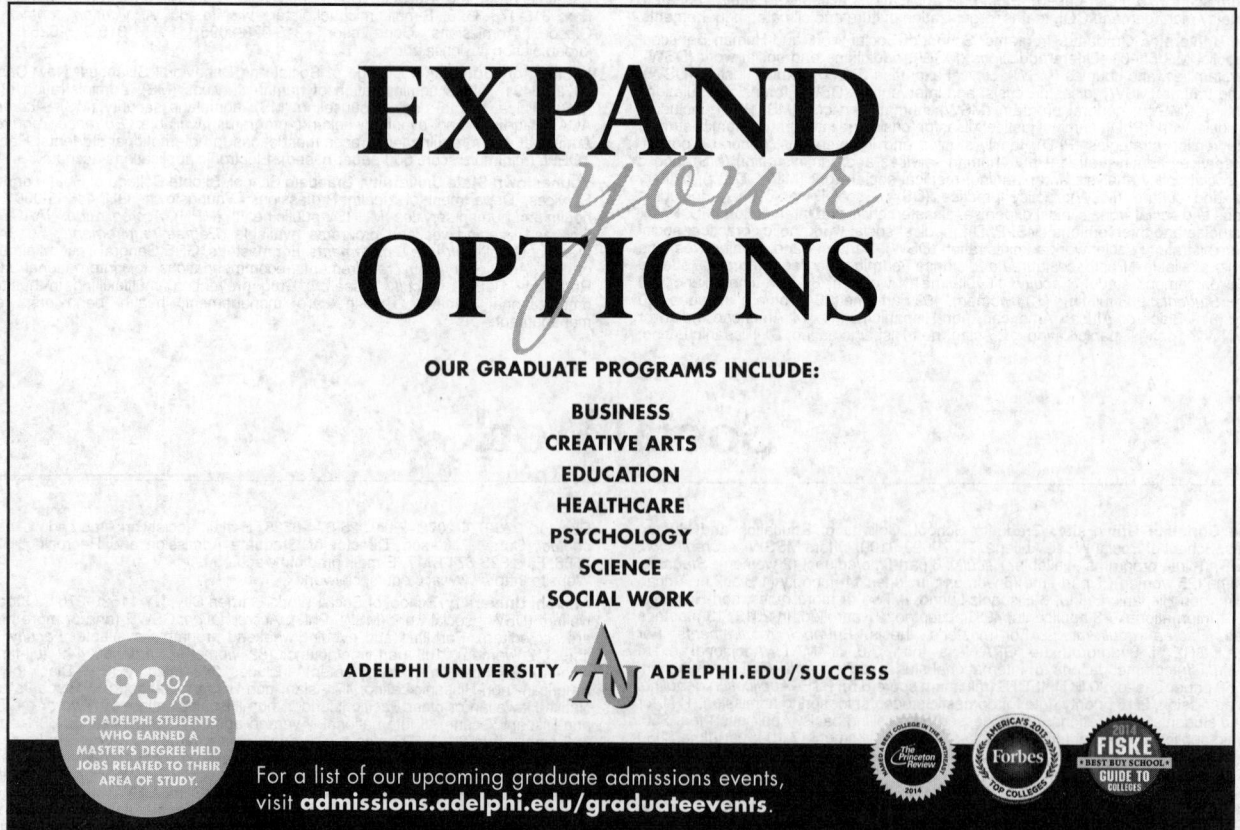

Assumption College, Graduate Studies, School Counseling Program, Worcester, MA 01609-1296. Offers school counseling (MA, CAGS); social worker/adjustment counselor (CAGS). Part-time and evening/weekend programs available. *Faculty:* 3 full-time (1 woman), 4 part-time/adjunct (all women). *Students:* 55 full-time (50 women), 15 part-time (13 women); includes 7 minority (1 Asian, non-Hispanic/Latino; 4 Hispanic/Latino; 1 Native Hawaiian or other Pacific Islander, non-Hispanic/Latino; 1 Two or more races, non-Hispanic/Latino). Average age 27. 37 applicants, 68% accepted, 17 enrolled. In 2013, 23 master's, 5 other advanced degrees awarded. *Degree requirements:* For master's, comprehensive exam, internship, practicum; for CAGS, comprehensive exam, practicum. *Entrance requirements:* For master's, 3 letters of recommendation, resume, interview, essay; for CAGS, 3 letters of recommendation, resume, essay, interview. Additional exam requirements/recommendations for international students: Required—TOEFL (minimum score 540 paper-based; 76 iBT), IELTS (minimum score 6). *Application deadline:* For fall and winter admission, 2/1 for domestic and international students; for summer admission, 2/1 for domestic students, 2/2 for international students. Application fee: $30. Electronic applications accepted. *Expenses: Tuition:* Full-time $10,098; part-time $561 per credit. *Required fees:* $20 per term. Full-time tuition and fees vary according to course load and program. *Financial support:* In 2013–14, 11 students received support. Tuition waivers (full and partial), unspecified assistantships, and institutional discounts available. Financial award application deadline: 5/1; financial award applicants required to submit FAFSA. *Faculty research:* Low dose stress reduction interventions for elementary school teachers. *Unit head:* Dr. Mary Ann Mariani, Director, 508-767-7087, Fax: 508-767-7263, E-mail: mmariani@assumption.edu. *Application contact:* Laura Lawrence, Graduate Programs Operations Manager, 508-767-7387, Fax: 508-767-7030, E-mail: graduate@assumption.edu. Website: http://graduate.assumption.edu/school-counseling/masterofarts.

Augsburg College, Program in Social Work, Minneapolis, MN 55454-1351. Offers MSW. *Accreditation:* CSWE. Part-time and evening/weekend programs available. *Degree requirements:* For master's, thesis optional. *Entrance requirements:* For master's, previous course work in human biology and statistics.

Aurora University, College of Professional Studies, School of Social Work, Aurora, IL 60506-4892. Offers MSW, DSW. *Accreditation:* CSWE. Part-time and evening/weekend programs available. *Degree requirements:* For master's, thesis optional; for doctorate, comprehensive exam, thesis/dissertation. *Entrance requirements:* For master's, minimum GPA of 3.0; for doctorate, GRE, MSW from CSWE-accredited school; minimum GPA of 3.0; at least 3 years of post-MSW social work experience; 3 letters of recommendation; writing sample in the area of clinical social work; personal interview. Additional exam requirements/recommendations for international students: Required—TOEFL (minimum score 550 paper-based). Electronic applications accepted. *Expenses:* Contact institution.

Austin Peay State University, College of Graduate Studies, College of Behavioral and Health Sciences, Department of Social Work, Clarksville, TN 37044. Offers MSW. Part-time and evening/weekend programs available. *Faculty:* 3 full-time (1 woman). *Students:* 23 full-time (21 women), 8 part-time (6 women); includes 11 minority (6 Black or African American, non-Hispanic/Latino; 1 Asian, non-Hispanic/Latino; 4 Two or more races, non-Hispanic/Latino). Average age 33. 26 applicants, 65% accepted, 17 enrolled. In 2013, 16 master's awarded. *Degree requirements:* For master's, internship of 400-500 hours. *Entrance requirements:* For master's, GRE General Test, letters of recommendation. Additional exam requirements/recommendations for international students: Required—TOEFL (minimum score 500 paper-based). *Application deadline:* For fall admission, 8/5 priority date for domestic students. Application fee: $25. *Expenses:* Tuition, state resident: full-time $7500; part-time $375 per credit hour. Tuition, nonresident: full-time $20,800; part-time $1040 per credit hour. *Required fees:* $1284; $64.20 per credit hour. *Financial support:* In 2013–14, research assistantships (averaging $6,500 per year) were awarded; career-related internships or fieldwork, Federal Work-Study, institutionally sponsored loans, scholarships/grants, and unspecified assistantships also available. Support available to part-time students. Financial award application deadline: 3/1; financial award applicants required to submit FAFSA. *Unit head:* Mary Fran Davis, Chair, 931-221-7730, Fax: 931-221-6440, E-mail: davism@apsu.edu. *Application contact:* June D. Lee, Graduate Coordinator, 800-859-4723, Fax: 931-221-7641, E-mail: gradadmissions@apsu.edu. Website: http://www.apsu.edu/socialwork/.

Azusa Pacific University, School of Behavioral and Applied Sciences, Department of Social Work, Azusa, CA 91702-7000. Offers MSW. *Accreditation:* CSWE.

Barry University, School of Social Work, Doctoral Program in Social Work, Miami Shores, FL 33161-6695. Offers PhD. Part-time and evening/weekend programs available. *Degree requirements:* For doctorate, thesis/dissertation. *Entrance requirements:* For doctorate, GRE, MSW from an accredited school of social work, 2 years of professional experience. Electronic applications accepted. *Faculty research:* Family and children services, homelessness, gerontology, school social work.

Barry University, School of Social Work, Master's Program in Social Work, Miami Shores, FL 33161-6695. Offers MSW. *Accreditation:* CSWE. Part-time and evening/weekend programs available. *Degree requirements:* For master's, fieldwork. *Entrance requirements:* For master's, minimum GPA of 3.0, minimum of 30 liberal arts credits. Additional exam requirements/recommendations for international students: Required—TOEFL (minimum score 550 paper-based). Electronic applications accepted. *Faculty research:* Family and children services, homelessness, gerontology, school social work.

Baylor University, School of Social Work, Waco, TX 76798-7320. Offers MSW, PhD, M Div/MSW, MSW/MBA, MTS/MSW. *Accreditation:* CSWE. Part-time programs available. Postbaccalaureate distance learning degree programs offered (minimal on-campus study). *Faculty:* 11 full-time (5 women), 13 part-time/adjunct (7 women). *Students:* 86 full-time (74 women), 12 part-time (11 women); includes 28 minority (7 Black or African American, non-Hispanic/Latino; 7 Asian, non-Hispanic/Latino; 11 Hispanic/Latino; 3 Two or more races, non-Hispanic/Latino), 10 international. Average age 27. 190 applicants, 72% accepted, 71 enrolled. In 2013, 68 master's awarded. *Degree requirements:* For master's, research project; for doctorate, comprehensive exam, thesis/dissertation. *Entrance requirements:* For master's, writing sample; for doctorate, GRE, writing sample. Additional exam requirements/recommendations for international students: Required—TOEFL (minimum score 550 paper-based; 80 iBT) or IELTS (minimum score 6.5). *Application deadline:* For spring admission, 3/15 for domestic and international students. Applications are processed on a rolling basis. Application fee: $45. Electronic applications accepted. *Expenses: Tuition:* Full-time $25,866; part-time $1437 per credit hour. *Required fees:* $2736; $152 per credit hour. Tuition and fees vary according to course load and program. *Financial support:* In 2013–14, 12 research assistantships with tuition reimbursements (averaging $6,800 per year) were awarded; career-related internships or fieldwork, Federal Work-Study, institutionally sponsored loans, scholarships/grants, traineeships, tuition waivers (full and partial), and unspecified assistantships also available. Support available to part-time students. Financial award application deadline: 6/1; financial award applicants required to submit FAFSA. *Faculty research:* Healthy marriage, family literacy, Alzheimer's and grief, congregational community service, clergy sexual abuse, older volunteers, military family support. *Total annual research expenditures:* $533,412. *Unit head:* Dr. Robin K. Rogers, Associate Dean for Graduate Studies, 254-710-4321, Fax: 254-710-6455,

E-mail: rob_rogers@baylor.edu. *Application contact:* Charletra Hurt, Director of Recruitment and Career Services, 254-710-4479, Fax: 254-710-6455, E-mail: charletra_hurt@baylor.edu. Website: http://www.baylor.edu/social_work/?_buref-661-48570.

Binghamton University, State University of New York, Graduate School, College of Community and Public Affairs, Department of Social Work, Vestal, NY 13850. Offers MSW. *Accreditation:* CSWE. Part-time and evening/weekend programs available. *Faculty:* 10 full-time (7 women), 4 part-time/adjunct (3 women). *Students:* 94 full-time (76 women), 49 part-time (44 women); includes 40 minority (20 Black or African American, non-Hispanic/Latino; 2 American Indian or Alaska Native, non-Hispanic/Latino; 5 Asian, non-Hispanic/Latino; 10 Hispanic/Latino; 3 Native Hawaiian or other Pacific Islander, non-Hispanic/Latino), 1 international. Average age 31. 161 applicants, 53% accepted, 66 enrolled. In 2013, 48 master's awarded. *Degree requirements:* For master's, thesis. *Entrance requirements:* For master's, GRE General Test. Additional exam requirements/recommendations for international students: Required—TOEFL (minimum score 550 paper-based; 80 iBT). *Application deadline:* For fall admission, 2/1 priority date for domestic and international students. Applications are processed on a rolling basis. Application fee: $75. Electronic applications accepted. *Financial support:* In 2013–14, 35 students received support. Career-related internships or fieldwork, Federal Work-Study, institutionally sponsored loans, scholarships/grants, health care benefits, and unspecified assistantships available. Financial award application deadline: 2/15; financial award applicants required to submit FAFSA. *Unit head:* Dr. Victoria Rizzo, Chairperson, 607-777-5683, E-mail: vrizzo@binghamton.edu. *Application contact:* Kishan Zuber, Recruiting and Admissions Coordinator, 607-777-2151, Fax: 607-777-2501, E-mail: kzuber@binghamton.edu.

Boise State University, College of Social Sciences and Public Affairs, School of Social Work, Boise, ID 83725-0399. Offers MSW. *Accreditation:* CSWE. Part-time programs available. *Entrance requirements:* For master's, GRE General Test, minimum GPA of 3.0. Electronic applications accepted.

Boston College, Graduate School of Social Work, Chestnut Hill, MA 02467-3800. Offers MSW, PhD, JD/MSW, MSW/MA, MSW/MBA. *Accreditation:* CSWE (one or more programs are accredited). Part-time programs available. *Faculty:* 27 full-time, 67 part-time/adjunct. *Students:* 399 full-time, 82 part-time; includes 121 minority (36 Black or African American, non-Hispanic/Latino; 5 American Indian or Alaska Native, non-Hispanic/Latino; 19 Asian, non-Hispanic/Latino; 37 Hispanic/Latino; 5 Native Hawaiian or other Pacific Islander, non-Hispanic/Latino; 19 Two or more races, non-Hispanic/Latino). 1,122 applicants, 51% accepted, 265 enrolled. In 2013, 218 master's, 9 doctorates awarded. *Degree requirements:* For master's, 2 internships; for doctorate, comprehensive exam, thesis/dissertation. *Entrance requirements:* For doctorate, GRE, master's degree. Additional exam requirements/recommendations for international students: Required—TOEFL (minimum score 550 paper-based; 80 iBT). *Application deadline:* For fall admission, 3/1 for domestic students. Application fee: $40. Electronic applications accepted. *Expenses:* Contact institution. *Financial support:* In 2013–14, 313 students received support, including 19 fellowships with full tuition reimbursements available (averaging $18,000 per year); career-related internships or fieldwork, Federal Work-Study, institutionally sponsored loans, scholarships/grants, traineeships, tuition waivers (partial), and unspecified assistantships also available. Support available to part-time students. Financial award applicants required to submit FAFSA. *Faculty research:* Well-being of children and families, health and mental health issues, aging and work, consumer-directed services, international social work practice. *Total annual research expenditures:* $3.7 million. *Application contact:* Dr. William Howard, Director of Admissions, 617-552-4024, Fax: 617-552-1690, E-mail: swadmit@bc.edu. Website: http://www.bc.edu/schools/gssw/.

Boston University, Graduate School of Arts and Sciences, Interdisciplinary Program in Sociology and Social Work, Boston, MA 02215. Offers PhD. *Students:* 21 full-time (17 women), 6 part-time (all women); includes 6 minority (1 Black or African American, non-Hispanic/Latino; 4 Asian, non-Hispanic/Latino; 1 Hispanic/Latino), 2 international. Average age 36. 38 applicants, 18% accepted, 2 enrolled. *Degree requirements:* For doctorate, one foreign language, comprehensive exam, thesis/dissertation, critical essay. *Entrance requirements:* For doctorate, GRE General Test or MAT, 3 letters of recommendation, scholarly writing sample. Additional exam requirements/recommendations for international students: Required—TOEFL (minimum score 550 paper-based; 84 iBT). *Application deadline:* For fall admission, 1/15 for domestic and international students. Application fee: $80. Electronic applications accepted. *Expenses: Tuition:* Full-time $43,970; part-time $1374 per credit hour. *Required fees:* $60 per semester. Tuition and fees vary according to class time, course level and program. *Financial support:* In 2013–14, 26 students received support, including 4 fellowships with full tuition reimbursements available (averaging $20,000 per year); career-related internships or fieldwork, Federal Work-Study, scholarships/grants, and health care benefits also available. Support available to part-time students. Financial award application deadline: 1/15; financial award applicants required to submit FAFSA. *Faculty research:* Mental health, child welfare, aging, substance abuse. *Unit head:* Ellen DeVoe, Director, 617-353-7885, Fax: 617-353-5612, E-mail: edevoe@bu.edu. *Application contact:* Dustin Stonecipher, Staff Coordinator, 617-353-9675, Fax: 617-353-5612, E-mail: dtstone@bu.edu. Website: http://www.bu.edu/ssw/academics/phd/.

Boston University, School of Social Work, Boston, MA 02215. Offers clinical practice with individuals, families, and groups (MSW); macro social work practice (MSW); social work (MSW); social work and sociology (PhD); D Min/MSW; M Div/MSW; MSW/Ed D; MSW/Ed M; MSW/MPH; MSW/MTS. *Accreditation:* CSWE (one or more programs are accredited). Part-time and evening/weekend programs available. Postbaccalaureate distance learning degree programs offered (minimal on-campus study). *Faculty:* 26 full-time (18 women), 43 part-time/adjunct (34 women). *Students:* 170 full-time (147 women), 442 part-time (396 women); includes 114 minority (40 Black or African American, non-Hispanic/Latino; 1 American Indian or Alaska Native, non-Hispanic/Latino; 19 Asian, non-Hispanic/Latino; 39 Hispanic/Latino; 15 Two or more races, non-Hispanic/Latino), 4 international. Average age 32. 937 applicants, 64% accepted, 179 enrolled. In 2013, 151 master's, 3 doctorates awarded. *Degree requirements:* For doctorate, one foreign language, thesis/dissertation, critical essay. *Entrance requirements:* For master's, GRE General Test or MAT (if GPA below 3.0), minimum GPA of 3.0; for doctorate, GRE General Test or MAT, writing sample. Additional exam requirements/recommendations for international students: Required—TOEFL (minimum score 577 paper-based; 91 iBT), IELTS (minimum score 6.5). *Application deadline:* For fall admission, 1/15 priority date for domestic students, 1/15 for international students. Application fee: $80. Electronic applications accepted. *Expenses:* Contact institution. *Financial support:* In 2013–14, 184 students received support. Career-related internships or fieldwork, Federal Work-Study, institutionally sponsored loans, and scholarships/grants available. Support available to part-time students. Financial award application deadline: 3/1; financial award applicants required to submit FAFSA. *Faculty research:* Aging, children and families, substance abuse and HIV, trauma and mental health, public health social work. *Total annual research expenditures:* $2.8 million. *Unit head:* Gail Steketee, Dean, 617-353-3760, Fax: 617-353-5612. *Application contact:* Ali

Social Work

Ailport, Admissions and Financial Aid Coordinator, 617-353-3750, Fax: 617-353-5612, E-mail: busswad@bu.edu. Website: http://www.bu.edu/ssw/.

Bridgewater State University, School of Graduate Studies, School of Arts and Sciences, Department of Social Work, Bridgewater, MA 02325-0001. Offers MSW. *Accreditation:* CSWE.

Brigham Young University, Graduate Studies, College of Family, Home, and Social Sciences, School of Social Work, Provo, UT 84602. Offers social work (MSW), including clinical practice, research. *Accreditation:* CSWE. *Faculty:* 8 full-time (3 women), 5 part-time/adjunct (4 women). *Students:* 80 full-time (52 women); includes 11 minority (1 Black or African American, non-Hispanic/Latino; 3 Asian, non-Hispanic/Latino; 3 Hispanic/Latino; 2 Native Hawaiian or other Pacific Islander, non-Hispanic/Latino; 2 Two or more races, non-Hispanic/Latino). Average age 27. 133 applicants, 35% accepted, 42 enrolled. In 2013, 36 master's awarded. *Degree requirements:* For master's, thesis optional. *Entrance requirements:* Additional exam requirements/recommendations for international students: Required—TOEFL (minimum score 580 paper-based; 85 iBT), IELTS (minimum score 7). *Application deadline:* For fall admission, 1/15 for domestic and international students. Application fee: $50. Electronic applications accepted. *Expenses: Tuition:* Full-time $6130; part-time $340 per credit hour. Tuition and fees vary according to program and student's religious affiliation. *Financial support:* In 2013–14, 48 students received support, including 48 fellowships with full and partial tuition reimbursements available (averaging $1,218 per year), 17 research assistantships (averaging $2,280 per year), 5 teaching assistantships (averaging $2,400 per year); career-related internships or fieldwork, tuition waivers (partial), and administrative aides, paid field practicum, AmeriCorps education awards also available. Financial award application deadline: 1/15. *Faculty research:* Poverty, adoptions, depression, spirituality, child welfare, marriage and family, American Indian child welfare, health care, mental health, mood disorders, substance abuse, women and gender. *Total annual research expenditures:* $100,000. *Unit head:* Dr. Gordon E. Limb, Director, 801-422-3282, Fax: 801-422-0624, E-mail: socialwork@byu.edu. *Application contact:* Nanci Shumpert, Graduate Secretary, 801-422-5681, Fax: 801-422-0624, E-mail: msw@byu.edu. Website: https://socialwork.byu.edu/Pages/Home.aspx.

Bryn Mawr College, Graduate School of Social Work and Social Research, Bryn Mawr, PA 19010. Offers MLSP, MSS, PhD. *Accreditation:* CSWE (one or more programs are accredited). Part-time and evening/weekend programs available. *Faculty:* 13 full-time (9 women), 11 part-time/adjunct (7 women). *Students:* 179 full-time (160 women), 33 part-time (27 women); includes 59 minority (38 Black or African American, non-Hispanic/Latino; 4 Asian, non-Hispanic/Latino; 14 Hispanic/Latino; 3 Two or more races, non-Hispanic/Latino), 4 international. Average age 33. 200 applicants, 81% accepted, 83 enrolled. In 2013, 106 master's, 1 doctorate awarded. *Degree requirements:* For master's, fieldwork; for doctorate, comprehensive exam, thesis/dissertation. *Entrance requirements:* For master's, interview, 3 letters of reference; for doctorate, GRE General Test, interview, 3 letters of reference, master's degree. Additional exam requirements/recommendations for international students: Required—TOEFL (minimum score 620 paper-based). *Application deadline:* For fall admission, 3/31 priority date for domestic and international students. Applications are processed on a rolling basis. Application fee: $50. Electronic applications accepted. *Expenses:* Contact institution. *Financial support:* In 2013–14, 183 students received support, including 11 fellowships with full and partial tuition reimbursements available (averaging $5,364 per year), 6 research assistantships with full and partial tuition reimbursements available (averaging $5,400 per year), 5 teaching assistantships with full and partial tuition reimbursements available (averaging $6,994 per year); career-related internships or fieldwork, Federal Work-Study, institutionally sponsored loans, scholarships/grants, tuition waivers (full and partial), and dissertation awards (for PhD) also available. Support available to part-time students. Financial award application deadline: 3/1; financial award applicants required to submit FAFSA. *Faculty research:* Ethical issues, children and adolescents, poverty, mental health, child and family welfare. *Total annual research expenditures:* $7.1 million. *Unit head:* Dr. Darlyne Bailey, Dean, 610-520-2610, Fax: 610-520-2613, E-mail: dbailey01@brynmawr.edu. *Application contact:* Diane D. Craw, Assistant to the Dean and Administrative Director, Social Work, 610-520-2612, Fax: 610-520-2613, E-mail: dcraw@brynmawr.edu.
Website: http://www.brynmawr.edu/socialwork.

California State University, Bakersfield, Division of Graduate Studies, School of Social Sciences and Education, Program in Social Work, Bakersfield, CA 93311. Offers MSW. *Accreditation:* CSWE. *Application deadline:* For fall admission, 2/1 for domestic students. Applications are processed on a rolling basis. Application fee: $55. *Unit head:* Dr. Jong Choi, Department Director, 661-654-3434, Fax: 661-665-6928, E-mail: jchoi6@csub.edu. *Application contact:* Debbie Blowers, Assistant Director of Admissions, 661-664-3381, E-mail: dblowers@csub.edu.
Website: http://www.csub.edu/socialwork/index.html.

California State University, Chico, Office of Graduate Studies, College of Behavioral and Social Sciences, School of Social Work, Chico, CA 95929-0722. Offers MSW. *Accreditation:* CSWE. Evening/weekend programs available. *Degree requirements:* For master's, thesis, project, or comprehensive exam. *Entrance requirements:* For master's, 3 letters of recommendation on departmental form, statement of purpose. Additional exam requirements/recommendations for international students: Required—TOEFL (minimum score 550 paper-based; 80 iBT), IELTS (minimum score 6.5), PTE (minimum score 59). Electronic applications accepted.

California State University, Dominguez Hills, College of Health, Human Services and Nursing, Program in Social Work, Carson, CA 90747-0001. Offers MSW. *Accreditation:* CSWE. Part-time and evening/weekend programs available. *Faculty:* 4 full-time (all women), 10 part-time/adjunct (6 women). *Students:* 133 full-time (104 women), 53 part-time (46 women); includes 155 minority (46 Black or African American, non-Hispanic/Latino; 8 Asian, non-Hispanic/Latino; 93 Hispanic/Latino; 8 Two or more races, non-Hispanic/Latino). Average age 32. 171 applicants, 66% accepted, 63 enrolled. In 2013, 63 master's awarded. *Degree requirements:* For master's, thesis. *Entrance requirements:* For master's, minimum GPA of 2.75 in last 60 units; 3 courses in behavioral science, 2 in humanities, 1 each in English composition, elementary statistics, and human biology. *Application deadline:* For fall admission, 4/30 for domestic students. Applications are processed on a rolling basis. *Expenses:* Tuition, state resident: full-time $6738. Tuition, nonresident: full-time $13,434. *Required fees:* $622. *Faculty research:* HIV/AIDS, community capacity, program evaluation. *Unit head:* Dr. Susan D. Einbinder, Acting Chair, 310-243-2349, E-mail: sdeinbinder@csudh.edu. *Application contact:* Susan Nakaoka, Director of Admissions, 310-243-2181, Fax: 310-217-6800, E-mail: snakaoka@csudh.edu.
Website: http://www4.csudh.edu/social-work/.

California State University, East Bay, Office of Academic Programs and Graduate Studies, College of Letters, Arts, and Social Sciences, Department of Social Work, Hayward, CA 94542-3000. Offers children, youth, and families (MSW); community mental health (MSW). *Accreditation:* CSWE. *Degree requirements:* For master's, comprehensive exam. *Entrance requirements:* For master's, minimum GPA of 2.8; courses in statistics and either human biology, physiology, or anatomy; liberal arts or social science baccalaureate; 3 letters of recommendation; personal statement; consent

to criminal background check; student professional liability insurance. Additional exam requirements/recommendations for international students: Required—TOEFL (minimum score 550 paper-based). Electronic applications accepted.

California State University, Fresno, Division of Graduate Studies, College of Health and Human Services, Department of Social Work Education, Fresno, CA 93740-8027. Offers MSW. *Accreditation:* CSWE. Part-time and evening/weekend programs available. *Degree requirements:* For master's, thesis or alternative. *Entrance requirements:* For master's, GRE General Test, minimum GPA of 2.5. Additional exam requirements/recommendations for international students: Required—TOEFL. Electronic applications accepted. *Faculty research:* Children at risk, international cooperation, child welfare training, nutrition.

California State University, Fullerton, Graduate Studies, College of Health and Human Development, Program of Social Work, Fullerton, CA 92834-9480. Offers MSW. *Accreditation:* CSWE. Part-time programs available. *Students:* 142 full-time (125 women); includes 91 minority (7 Black or African American, non-Hispanic/Latino; 10 Asian, non-Hispanic/Latino; 66 Hispanic/Latino; 8 Two or more races, non-Hispanic/Latino), 4 international. Average age 26. 410 applicants, 44% accepted, 115 enrolled. In 2013, 54 master's awarded. *Entrance requirements:* For master's, minimum GPA of 3.0 for last 60 semester or 90 quarter units. Application fee: $55. *Financial support:* Career-related internships or fieldwork, Federal Work-Study, institutionally sponsored loans, and scholarships/grants available. Support available to part-time students. Financial award application deadline: 3/1; financial award applicants required to submit FAFSA. *Unit head:* Dr. David Chenot, Director, 657-278-8610. *Application contact:* Admissions/Applications, 657-278-2371.
Website: http://hhd.fullerton.edu/msw.

California State University, Long Beach, Graduate Studies, College of Health and Human Services, Department of Social Work, Long Beach, CA 90840. Offers MSW. *Accreditation:* CSWE. Part-time and evening/weekend programs available. Postbaccalaureate distance learning degree programs offered (no on-campus study). *Degree requirements:* For master's, thesis. Electronic applications accepted.

California State University, Los Angeles, Graduate Studies, College of Health and Human Services, School of Social Work, Los Angeles, CA 90032-8530. Offers MSW. *Accreditation:* CSWE. *Faculty:* 33 full-time (25 women), 2 part-time/adjunct (both women). *Students:* 209 full-time (173 women), 45 part-time (41 women); includes 187 minority (14 Black or African American, non-Hispanic/Latino; 1 American Indian or Alaska Native, non-Hispanic/Latino; 18 Asian, non-Hispanic/Latino; 146 Hispanic/Latino; 8 Two or more races, non-Hispanic/Latino), 11 international. Average age 32. 722 applicants, 24% accepted, 113 enrolled. In 2013, 94 master's awarded. *Entrance requirements:* Additional exam requirements/recommendations for international students: Required—TOEFL (minimum score 500 paper-based). *Application deadline:* For fall admission, 5/1 for domestic and international students. Applications are processed on a rolling basis. Application fee: $55. *Financial support:* Application deadline: 3/1. *Unit head:* Dr. Dale Weaver, Chair, 323-343-4680, Fax: 323-343-5009, E-mail: dweaver@calstatela.edu. *Application contact:* Dr. Larry Fritz, Dean of Graduate Studies, 323-343-3820, Fax: 323-343-5653, E-mail: lfritz@calstatela.edu.
Website: http://www.calstatela.edu/dept/soc_work/index.htm.

California State University, Monterey Bay, College of Professional Studies, Health, Human Services and Public Policy Department, Seaside, CA 93955-8001. Offers public policy (MPP); social work (MSW). Part-time programs available. *Degree requirements:* For master's, internship. *Entrance requirements:* For master's, GRE, curriculum vitae, recommendations. Additional exam requirements/recommendations for international students: Required—TOEFL (minimum score 525 paper-based; 71 iBT). Electronic applications accepted. *Faculty research:* Social policy, health policy, politics and government.

California State University, Northridge, Graduate Studies, College of Social and Behavioral Sciences, Department of Social Work, Northridge, CA 91330. Offers MSW. Part-time programs available. *Entrance requirements:* For master's, GRE (if cumulative undergraduate GPA less than 3.0).

California State University, Northridge, Graduate Studies, The Tseng College of Extended Learning, Northridge, CA 91330. Offers business administration (Graduate Certificate); health administration (MPA); health education (MPH); knowledge management (MKM); music industry administration (MA); nonprofit-sector management (Graduate Certificate); public administration (MPA); public sector management and leadership (MPA); social work (MSW); taxation (MS); tourism, hospitality and recreation management (MS). *Entrance requirements:* For master's, GRE (if cumulative undergraduate GPA less than 3.0).

California State University, Sacramento, Office of Graduate Studies, College of Health and Human Services, Division of Social Work, Sacramento, CA 95819. Offers family and children's services (MSW); health care (MSW); mental health (MSW); social justice and corrections (MSW). *Accreditation:* CSWE. *Degree requirements:* For master's, thesis, research project, or comprehensive exam; writing proficiency exam. *Entrance requirements:* For master's, minimum GPA of 2.5 during previous 2 years of course work. Additional exam requirements/recommendations for international students: Required—TOEFL. *Application deadline:* For fall admission, 1/18 for domestic students, 3/1 for international students; for spring admission, 9/30 for international students. Applications are processed on a rolling basis. Application fee: $55. Electronic applications accepted. *Financial support:* Career-related internships or fieldwork and Federal Work-Study available. Support available to part-time students. Financial award application deadline: 3/1; financial award applicants required to submit FAFSA. *Unit head:* Dr. Dale Russell, Chair, 916-278-6943, E-mail: drussell@csus.edu. *Application contact:* Jose Martinez, Graduate Admissions Supervisor, 916-278-7871, E-mail: martinj@skymail.csus.edu.
Website: http://www.csus.edu/hhs/sw.

California State University, San Bernardino, Graduate Studies, College of Social and Behavioral Sciences, Department of Social Work, San Bernardino, CA 92407-2397. Offers MSW. *Accreditation:* CSWE. Part-time and evening/weekend programs available. *Students:* 133 full-time (113 women), 27 part-time (26 women); includes 86 minority (20 Black or African American, non-Hispanic/Latino; 3 Asian, non-Hispanic/Latino; 63 Hispanic/Latino), 1 international. Average age 29. 260 applicants, 44% accepted, 69 enrolled. In 2013, 57 master's awarded. *Degree requirements:* For master's, field practicum, research project. *Entrance requirements:* For master's, minimum GPA of 2.75 in last 2 years of course work, liberal arts background. *Application deadline:* For fall admission, 8/31 priority date for domestic students. Application fee: $55. *Financial support:* Fellowships, research assistantships, career-related internships or fieldwork, Federal Work-Study, institutionally sponsored loans, and stipends available. Support available to part-time students. Financial award application deadline: 5/1. *Faculty research:* Addiction, computers in social work practice, minority issues, gerontology. *Unit head:* Laurie Smith, Director/Associate Professor/Graduate Coordinator, 909-537-3837, Fax: 909-537-7029, E-mail: lasmith@csusb.edu. *Application contact:* Dr. Jeffrey Thompson, Dean of Graduate Studies, 909-537-5058, E-mail: jthompso@csusb.edu.

California State University, Stanislaus, College of Human and Health Sciences, Program in Social Work (MSW), Turlock, CA 95382. Offers MSW. *Accreditation:* CSWE.

Degree requirements: For master's, thesis. *Entrance requirements:* For master's, minimum GPA of 3.0, 3 letters of reference, personal statement. Electronic applications accepted. *Faculty research:* Mental health supervision, health issues on adulthood and aging, geriatric social work, effects of violence on children, rural mental health.

California University of Pennsylvania, School of Graduate Studies and Research, College of Education and Human Services, Department of Social Work, California, PA 15419-1394. Offers MSW. *Accreditation:* CSWE. Part-time programs available. *Degree requirements:* For master's, comprehensive exam. *Entrance requirements:* For master's, GRE, letters of reference. Additional exam requirements/recommendations for international students: Required—TOEFL. Electronic applications accepted. *Faculty research:* Social welfare and policy, housing and community development, health and mental health, Black Appalachian, aging.

Campbellsville University, Carver School of Social Work, Campbellsville, KY 42718-2799. Offers counseling (MA); social work (MA). *Accreditation:* CSWE. Part-time and evening/weekend programs available. Postbaccalaureate distance learning degree programs offered (minimal on-campus study). *Entrance requirements:* For master's, GRE. Electronic applications accepted.

Capella University, Harold Abel School of Social and Behavioral Science, Doctoral Programs in Counseling, Minneapolis, MN 55402. Offers general counselor education and supervision (PhD); general social work (DSW).

Carleton University, Faculty of Graduate Studies, Faculty of Public Affairs and Management, School of Social Work, Ottawa, ON K1S 5B6, Canada. Offers MSW. Part-time programs available. *Degree requirements:* For master's, thesis optional. *Entrance requirements:* For master's, basic research methods course. Additional exam requirements/recommendations for international students: Required—TOEFL. *Faculty research:* Social administration, program evaluation, history of Canadian social welfare, women's issues, education in social work.

Case Western Reserve University, Jack, Joseph and Morton Mandel School of Applied Social Sciences, Cleveland, OH 44106. Offers nonprofit management (MNO); social welfare (PhD); social work (MSSA); JD/MSSA; MSSA/MA; MSSA/MBA; MSSA/MNO. *Accreditation:* CSWE (one or more programs are accredited). Evening/weekend programs available. Postbaccalaureate distance learning degree programs offered (no on-campus study). *Faculty:* 40 full-time (23 women), 52 part-time/adjunct (34 women). *Students:* 310 full-time (255 women), 76 part-time (62 women); includes 106 minority (70 Black or African American, non-Hispanic/Latino; 3 American Indian or Alaska Native, non-Hispanic/Latino; 10 Asian, non-Hispanic/Latino; 11 Hispanic/Latino; 12 Two or more races, non-Hispanic/Latino), 27 international. Average age 30. 429 applicants, 81% accepted, 199 enrolled. In 2013, 136 master's, 3 doctorates awarded. *Degree requirements:* For master's, fieldwork; for doctorate, thesis/dissertation. *Entrance requirements:* For master's, GRE General Test, MAT, or minimum GPA of 2.7; for doctorate, GRE General Test. Additional exam requirements/recommendations for international students: Required—TOEFL (minimum score 557 paper-based, 90 iBT) or IELTS (minimum score 7). *Application deadline:* For fall admission, 4/18 for domestic students, 3/14 for international students; for spring admission, 11/22 for domestic students; for summer admission, 3/7 for domestic students. Applications are processed on a rolling basis. Application fee: $0. Electronic applications accepted. *Expenses:* Contact institution. *Financial support:* In 2013–14, 352 students received support, including 352 fellowships with full tuition reimbursements available (averaging $11,000 per year); career-related internships or fieldwork, Federal Work-Study, institutionally sponsored loans, scholarships/grants, tuition waivers (partial), and paid field placement (for MSSA students) also available. Support available to part-time students. Financial award application deadline: 4/30; financial award applicants required to submit FAFSA. *Faculty research:* Urban poverty, community social development, substance abuse, health, child welfare, aging, mental health. *Total annual research expenditures:* $3.8 million. *Unit head:* Dr. Grover Cleveland Gilmore, Dean, 216-368-2256, E-mail: msassdean@case.edu. *Application contact:* Richard Sigg, Admissions/Recruitment, 216-368-1655, Fax: 216-368-6624, E-mail: msassadmit@po.cwru.edu.
Website: http://msass.case.edu/.

The Catholic University of America, National Catholic School of Social Service, Washington, DC 20064. Offers MSW, PhD, MSW/JD. *Accreditation:* CSWE (one or more programs are accredited). Part-time programs available. *Faculty:* 15 full-time (13 women), 28 part-time/adjunct (22 women). *Students:* 177 full-time (153 women), 114 part-time (103 women); includes 68 minority (26 Black or African American, non-Hispanic/Latino; 5 Asian, non-Hispanic/Latino; 27 Hispanic/Latino; 10 Two or more races, non-Hispanic/Latino), 2 international. Average age 33. 252 applicants, 79% accepted, 117 enrolled. In 2013, 136 master's awarded. *Degree requirements:* For master's, comprehensive exam, thesis or alternative; for doctorate, comprehensive exam, thesis/dissertation, minimum GPA of 3.0. *Entrance requirements:* For master's, GRE or MAT (if undergraduate GPA less than 3.0), statement of purpose, official copies of academic transcripts, three letters of recommendation, resume; for doctorate, GRE, statement of purpose, official copies of academic transcripts, three letters of recommendation, resume, writing sample. Additional exam requirements/recommendations for international students: Required—TOEFL (minimum score 600 paper-based). *Application deadline:* For fall admission, 7/15 priority date for domestic students, 7/15 for international students; for spring admission, 12/1 priority date for domestic students, 10/15 for international students. Applications are processed on a rolling basis. Application fee: $55. Electronic applications accepted. *Expenses:* Contact institution. *Financial support:* Fellowships, research assistantships, teaching assistantships, Federal Work-Study, scholarships/grants, tuition waivers (full and partial), and unspecified assistantships available. Financial award application deadline: 2/1; financial award applicants required to submit FAFSA. *Faculty research:* International social development; spirituality and social work; advancement of children, youth, and families; global aging; community development and social justice; promotion of health; mental health well-being. *Total annual research expenditures:* $107,340. *Unit head:* Dr. Will Rainford, Dean, 202-319-5454, Fax: 202-319-5093, E-mail: zabora@cua.edu. *Application contact:* Andrew Woodall, Director of Graduate Admissions, 202-319-5057, Fax: 202-319-6533, E-mail: cua-admissions@cua.edu.
Website: http://ncsss.cua.edu.

Chicago State University, School of Graduate and Professional Studies, College of Arts and Sciences, Program in Social Work, Chicago, IL 60628. Offers MSW. *Accreditation:* CSWE. Electronic applications accepted.

Clark Atlanta University, School of Social Work, Atlanta, GA 30314. Offers MSW, PhD. *Accreditation:* CSWE (one or more programs are accredited). Part-time programs available. *Faculty:* 11 full-time (6 women), 21 part-time/adjunct (13 women). *Students:* 268 full-time (226 women), 85 part-time (72 women); includes 322 minority (316 Black or African American, non-Hispanic/Latino; 3 American Indian or Alaska Native, non-Hispanic/Latino; 1 Asian, non-Hispanic/Latino; 2 Hispanic/Latino), 3 international. Average age 32. 220 applicants, 91% accepted, 159 enrolled. In 2013, 90 master's, 6 doctorates awarded. Terminal master's awarded for partial completion of doctoral program. *Degree requirements:* For master's, one foreign language; for doctorate, one foreign language, comprehensive exam, thesis/dissertation. *Entrance requirements:* For master's, GRE General Test, minimum undergraduate GPA of 3.0; for doctorate, GRE General Test. Additional exam requirements/recommendations for international students: Required—TOEFL (minimum score 500 paper-based; 61 iBT). *Application deadline:* For fall admission, 4/1 for domestic and international students; for spring admission, 11/1 for domestic and international students. Applications are processed on a rolling basis. Application fee: $40 ($55 for international students). Electronic applications accepted. *Expenses: Tuition:* Full-time $14,616; part-time $812 per credit hour. *Required fees:* $706; $353 per semester. *Financial support:* Career-related internships or fieldwork, Federal Work-Study, scholarships/grants, and unspecified assistantships available. Support available to part-time students. Financial award application deadline: 4/30; financial award applicants required to submit FAFSA. *Unit head:* Dr. Vimala Pillari, Interim Dean, 404-880-8006, E-mail: rlyle@cau.edu. *Application contact:* Michelle Clark-Davis, Graduate Program Admissions, 404-880-6605, E-mail: cauadmissions@cau.edu.

Cleveland State University, College of Graduate Studies, College of Liberal Arts and Social Sciences, School of Social Work, Cleveland, OH 44115. Offers MSW. Program offered jointly with The University of Akron. *Accreditation:* CSWE. Part-time and evening/weekend programs available. Postbaccalaureate distance learning degree programs offered (no on-campus study). *Faculty:* 10 full-time (2 women), 8 part-time/adjunct (5 women). *Students:* 146 full-time (120 women), 73 part-time (66 women); includes 112 minority (101 Black or African American, non-Hispanic/Latino; 8 Hispanic/Latino; 3 Two or more races, non-Hispanic/Latino). Average age 37. 179 applicants, 43% accepted. In 2013, 78 master's awarded. *Entrance requirements:* For master's, 3 letters of reference. Additional exam requirements/recommendations for international students: Required—TOEFL (minimum score 525 paper-based); Recommended—IELTS (minimum score 6). *Application deadline:* For fall admission, 2/28 for domestic students. Application fee: $30. *Expenses:* Tuition, state resident: full-time $8335; part-time $521 per credit hour. Tuition, nonresident: full-time $15,670; part-time $979 per credit hour. *Required fees:* $50; $25 per semester. *Financial support:* In 2013–14, 15 students received support, including 10 research assistantships with full and partial tuition reimbursements available (averaging $3,480 per year); tuition waivers (full) also available. Financial award applicants required to submit FAFSA. *Faculty research:* Mental health, aging. *Total annual research expenditures:* $1.2 million. *Unit head:* Dr. Maggie Jackson, Director, 216-687-4599, Fax: 216-687-5590, E-mail: m.jackson@csuohio.edu. *Application contact:* Deborah L. Brown, Interim Assistant Director, Graduate Admissions, 216-523-7572, Fax: 216-687-5400, E-mail: d.l.brown@csuohio.edu.
Website: http://www.csuohio.edu/class/social-work/social-work.

The College at Brockport, State University of New York, School of Education and Human Services, Greater Rochester Collaborative Master of Social Work Program, Brockport, NY 14420-2997. Offers gerontology (AGC); interdisciplinary health practice (MSW). Program offered jointly with Nazareth College of Rochester. *Accreditation:* CSWE. Part-time programs available. *Faculty:* 3 full-time (all women), 4 part-time/adjunct (all women). *Students:* 50 full-time (44 women), 103 part-time (87 women); includes 29 minority (19 Black or African American, non-Hispanic/Latino; 1 American Indian or Alaska Native, non-Hispanic/Latino; 1 Asian, non-Hispanic/Latino; 3 Hispanic/Latino; 1 Native Hawaiian or other Pacific Islander, non-Hispanic/Latino; 4 Two or more races, non-Hispanic/Latino), 2 international. 131 applicants, 70% accepted, 59 enrolled. In 2013, 55 master's, 9 other advanced degrees awarded. *Degree requirements:* For master's, thesis or alternative. *Entrance requirements:* For master's, minimum GPA of 3.0, letters of recommendation; statement of objectives. Additional exam requirements/recommendations for international students: Required—TOEFL (minimum score 550 paper-based; 79 iBT), IELTS (minimum score 6.5). *Application deadline:* For fall admission, 1/15 priority date for domestic and international students. Application fee: $50. Electronic applications accepted. *Expenses:* Contact institution. *Financial support:* Federal Work-Study, scholarships/grants, and unspecified assistantships available. Support available to part-time students. Financial award application deadline: 3/15; financial award applicants required to submit FAFSA. *Faculty research:* Care giving, child welfare, gerontological social work, home-school-community partnerships, domestic violence. *Unit head:* Dr. Jason Dauenhauer, Director, 585-395-8450, Fax: 585-395-8603, E-mail: grcmsw@brockport.edu. *Application contact:* Brad Snyder, Coordinator of Admissions, 585-395-3845, Fax: 585-395-8603, E-mail: bsnyder@brockport.edu.
Website: http://www.brockport.edu/grcmsw.

The College of St. Scholastica, Graduate Studies, Department of Social Work, Duluth, MN 55811-4199. Offers MSW. Part-time programs available. *Students:* 20 full-time (15 women); includes 1 minority (American Indian or Alaska Native, non-Hispanic/Latino). Average age 32. *Application deadline:* Applications are processed on a rolling basis. Application fee: $0. Application fee is waived when completed online. Tuition and fees vary according to course load, program and student level. *Unit head:* Dr. Lee Gustafson, Chair, 218-723-7048, E-mail: lgustaf3@css.edu. *Application contact:* Lindsay Lahti, Director of Graduate and Extended Studies Recruitment, 218-723-2240, Fax: 218-733-2275, E-mail: llahti@css.edu.
Website: http://www.css.edu/Graduate/Masters-Doctoral-and-Professional-Programs/Areas-of-Study/Master-of-Social-Work.html.

Colorado State University, Graduate School, College of Health and Human Sciences, School of Social Work, Fort Collins, CO 80523-1586. Offers MSW, PhD. *Accreditation:* CSWE. Part-time and evening/weekend programs available. Postbaccalaureate distance learning degree programs offered (minimal on-campus study). *Faculty:* 9 full-time (all women), 2 part-time/adjunct (both women). *Students:* 69 full-time (60 women), 44 part-time (38 women); includes 12 minority (3 Black or African American, non-Hispanic/Latino; 1 American Indian or Alaska Native, non-Hispanic/Latino; 7 Hispanic/Latino; 1 Two or more races, non-Hispanic/Latino), 2 international. Average age 37. 118 applicants, 33% accepted, 21 enrolled. In 2013, 94 master's awarded. *Degree requirements:* For master's, variable foreign language requirement, thesis optional; for doctorate, variable foreign language requirement, comprehensive exam, thesis/dissertation. *Entrance requirements:* For master's, minimum GPA of 3.0, 400 hours of human service experience, bachelor's degree, 18 credits in social and behavioral sciences; for doctorate, minimum GPA of 3.0, two years of post-MSW experience, master's degree in social work, leadership potential, statistics course, resume, transcripts, 3 letters of recommendation, personal statement, interview. Additional exam requirements/recommendations for international students: Required—TOEFL (minimum score 550 paper-based; 80 iBT), IELTS (minimum score 6.5). *Application deadline:* For fall admission, 1/3 priority date for domestic and international students; for spring admission, 6/1 priority date for domestic and international students. Application fee: $50. Electronic applications accepted. *Expenses:* Contact institution. *Financial support:* In 2013–14, 3 students received support, including 1 research assistantship with partial tuition reimbursement available (averaging $22,032 per year), 2 teaching assistantships with partial tuition reimbursements available (averaging $2,391 per year); career-related internships or fieldwork, scholarships/grants, and unspecified assistantships also available. Financial award application deadline: 12/15. *Faculty research:* Psychopharmacology, youth corrections, gerontology, HIV/AIDS communities, rural communities. *Total annual research expenditures:* $857,343. *Unit head:* Dr. Audrey Shillington, School Director, 970-491-2378, Fax: 970-491-7280, E-mail: audrey.shillington@colostate.edu. *Application contact:* Peter Friedrichsen, MSW

Program Coordinator, 970-491-2536, Fax: 970-491-7280, E-mail: peter.friedrichsen@colostate.edu.
Website: http://www.ssw.chhs.colostate.edu/index.aspx.

Columbia University, School of Social Work, New York, NY 10027. Offers MSSW, PhD, JD/MS, MBA/MS, MPA/MS, MPH/MS, MS/M Div, MS/MA, MS/MS, MS/MS Ed. MS/MS Ed offered jointly with Bank Street College of Education; MS/M Div with Union Theological Seminary in New York; MS/MA with The Jewish Theological Seminary; MS/MS dual degree with the Graduate School of Architecture, Planning, and Preservation. *Accreditation:* CSWE (one or more programs are accredited). *Faculty:* 44 full-time (25 women), 129 part-time/adjunct (90 women). *Students:* 930 full-time (805 women), 38 part-time (30 women); includes 322 minority (89 Black or African American, non-Hispanic/Latino; 1 American Indian or Alaska Native, non-Hispanic/Latino; 84 Asian, non-Hispanic/Latino; 115 Hispanic/Latino; 1 Native Hawaiian or other Pacific Islander, non-Hispanic/Latino; 32 Two or more races, non-Hispanic/Latino), 122 international. Average age 26. 1,305 applicants, 77% accepted, 375 enrolled. In 2013, 418 master's, 16 doctorates awarded. *Degree requirements:* For doctorate, thesis/dissertation. *Entrance requirements:* For master's, 3 letters of reference; for doctorate, GRE General Test, 3 letters of recommendation. Additional exam requirements/recommendations for international students: Required—TOEFL (minimum score 577 paper-based; 98 iBT), IELTS (minimum score 7), TWE (minimum score 4). *Application deadline:* For fall admission, 12/1 priority date for domestic and international students; for winter admission, 10/15 for domestic students; for spring admission, 10/15 priority date for domestic and international students. Applications are processed on a rolling basis. Application fee: $65. Electronic applications accepted. *Expenses:* Contact institution. *Financial support:* In 2013–14, 668 students received support, including 3 fellowships (averaging $5,000 per year), 5 research assistantships with partial tuition reimbursements available, 2 teaching assistantships with partial tuition reimbursements available; career-related internships or fieldwork, Federal Work-Study, institutionally sponsored loans, scholarships/grants, health care benefits, and unspecified assistantships also available. Support available to part-time students. Financial award application deadline: 2/1; financial award applicants required to submit FAFSA. *Faculty research:* Advanced clinical practice; economic, social, and health inequities; diverse populations at risk; health and mental health; international social welfare. *Unit head:* Dr. Jeanette Takamura, Dean, 212-851-2289. *Application contact:* Debbie Lesperance, Director of Admissions, 212-851-2211, Fax: 212-851-2305, E-mail: dl635@columbia.edu.
Website: http://www.socialwork.columbia.edu.

Cornell University, Graduate School, Graduate Fields of Human Ecology, Field of Policy Analysis and Management, Ithaca, NY 14853-0001. Offers consumer policy (PhD); family and social welfare policy (PhD); health administration (MHA); health management and policy (PhD); public policy (PhD). *Faculty:* 33 full-time (12 women). *Students:* 66 full-time (39 women); includes 19 minority (2 Black or African American, non-Hispanic/Latino; 8 Asian, non-Hispanic/Latino; 5 Hispanic/Latino; 4 Two or more races, non-Hispanic/Latino), 9 international. Average age 25. 175 applicants, 30% accepted, 36 enrolled. In 2013, 26 master's, 2 doctorates awarded. *Degree requirements:* For master's, thesis; for doctorate, thesis/dissertation. *Entrance requirements:* For master's, GRE General Test or GMAT, 2 letters of recommendation; for doctorate, GRE General Test, 2 letters of recommendation. Additional exam requirements/recommendations for international students: Required—TOEFL (minimum score 550 paper-based; 77 iBT). *Application deadline:* For fall admission, 1/15 for domestic students. Application fee: $95. Electronic applications accepted. *Financial support:* In 2013–14, 16 students received support, including 3 fellowships with full and partial tuition reimbursements available, 2 research assistantships with full and partial tuition reimbursements available, 11 teaching assistantships with full and partial tuition reimbursements available; institutionally sponsored loans, scholarships/grants, health care benefits, tuition waivers (full and partial), and unspecified assistantships also available. Financial award applicants required to submit FAFSA. *Faculty research:* Health policy, family policy, social welfare policy, program evaluation, consumer policy. *Unit head:* Director of Graduate Studies, 607-255-7772. *Application contact:* Graduate Field Assistant, 607-255-7772, Fax: 607-255-4071, E-mail: pam_phd@cornell.edu.
Website: http://www.gradschool.cornell.edu/fields.php?id=69&a=2.

Dalhousie University, Faculty of Health Professions, School of Social Work, Halifax, NS B3H3J5, Canada. Offers MSW. Part-time programs available. Postbaccalaureate distance learning degree programs offered (minimal on-campus study). *Degree requirements:* For master's, thesis optional, field placement. *Entrance requirements:* For master's, bachelor's degree in social work, 2 years work experience in social work, minimum GPA of 3.0. Additional exam requirements/recommendations for international students: Required—TOEFL, IELTS, CANTEST, CAEL, or Michigan English Language Assessment Battery. Electronic applications accepted. *Expenses:* Contact institution. *Faculty research:* Family and child welfare, physical and mental health, public policy, elder abuse, violence against women, community practice.

Delaware State University, Graduate Programs, College of Education, Health and Public Policy, Department of Social Work, Program in Social Work, Dover, DE 19901-2277. Offers MSW. *Accreditation:* CSWE. Evening/weekend programs available. *Entrance requirements:* For master's, GRE, minimum GPA of 3.0 in major, 2.75 overall. Additional exam requirements/recommendations for international students: Required—TOEFL. Electronic applications accepted. *Faculty research:* Gerontology, human behavior, corrections, child welfare, adolescent behavior policy.

DePaul University, College of Liberal Arts and Social Sciences, Chicago, IL 60614. Offers Arabic (MA); Chinese (MA); English (MA); French (MA); German (MA); history (MA); interdisciplinary studies (MA, MS); international public service (MS); international studies (MA); Italian (MA); Japanese (MA); leadership and policy studies (MS); liberal studies (MA); new media studies (MA); nonprofit management (MNM); public administration (MPA); public health (MPH); public service management (MS); social work (MSW); sociology (MA); Spanish (MA); sustainable urban development (MA); women and gender studies (MA); writing and publishing (MA); writing, rhetoric, and discourse (MA); MA/PhD. Part-time and evening/weekend programs available. Postbaccalaureate distance learning degree programs offered (no on-campus study). *Faculty:* 75 full-time (38 women), 26 part-time/adjunct (15 women). *Students:* 539 full-time (382 women), 391 part-time (255 women); includes 302 minority (150 Black or African American, non-Hispanic/Latino; 30 Asian, non-Hispanic/Latino; 91 Hispanic/Latino; 1 Native Hawaiian or other Pacific Islander, non-Hispanic/Latino; 30 Two or more races, non-Hispanic/Latino), 33 international. Average age 29. In 2013, 419 master's awarded. Terminal master's awarded for partial completion of doctoral program. *Degree requirements:* For master's, variable foreign language requirement, comprehensive exam (for some programs), thesis (for some programs). *Application deadline:* Applications are processed on a rolling basis. Application fee: $40. Electronic applications accepted. Tuition and fees vary according to course level, course load and degree level. *Financial support:* Applicants required to submit FAFSA. *Unit head:* Dr. Charles Suchar, Dean, 773-325-7305. *Application contact:* Ann Spittle, Director of Graduate Admission, 773-325-7315, Fax: 312-476-3244, E-mail: graddepaul@depaul.edu.
Website: http://las.depaul.edu/.

Dominican University, Graduate School of Social Work, River Forest, IL 60305. Offers MSW. *Accreditation:* CSWE. Part-time programs available. *Faculty:* 8 full-time (5 women), 16 part-time/adjunct (10 women). *Students:* 96 full-time (82 women), 72 part-time (59 women); includes 82 minority (32 Black or African American, non-Hispanic/Latino; 1 American Indian or Alaska Native, non-Hispanic/Latino; 4 Asian, non-Hispanic/Latino; 44 Hispanic/Latino; 1 Two or more races, non-Hispanic/Latino), 2 international. Average age 32. 189 applicants, 43% accepted, 57 enrolled. In 2013, 70 master's awarded. *Entrance requirements:* For master's, minimum GPA of 2.75. Additional exam requirements/recommendations for international students: Required—TOEFL (minimum score 83 iBT); Recommended—IELTS (minimum score 7). *Application deadline:* For fall admission, 7/1 for domestic and international students; for spring admission, 11/1 for domestic and international students. Applications are processed on a rolling basis. Application fee: $25. Electronic applications accepted. *Expenses: Tuition:* Full-time $17,626; part-time $816 per credit hour. *Required fees:* $370; $90 per semester. Tuition and fees vary according to course load, degree level and program. *Financial support:* In 2013–14, 64 students received support, including 4 research assistantships (averaging $4,000 per year); Federal Work-Study, scholarships/grants, and unspecified assistantships also available. Financial award applicants required to submit FAFSA. *Faculty research:* Human trafficking, domestic violence, gerontology, school social work, child welfare. *Unit head:* Dr. Charles Stoops, Dean, 708-366-3316, E-mail: cstoops@dom.edu. *Application contact:* Kathy Clyburn, Assistant Dean, 708-771-5298, Fax: 708-366-3446, E-mail: kclyburn@dom.edu.
Website: http://socialwork.dom.edu/.

East Carolina University, Graduate School, College of Human Ecology, School of Social Work, Greenville, NC 27858-4353. Offers gerontology (Certificate); social work (MSW); substance abuse (Certificate). *Accreditation:* CSWE. Postbaccalaureate distance learning degree programs offered (no on-campus study). *Degree requirements:* For master's, comprehensive exam. *Entrance requirements:* For master's, GRE or MAT. Additional exam requirements/recommendations for international students: Required—TOEFL. *Expenses:* Tuition, state resident: full-time $4223. Tuition, nonresident: full-time $16,540. *Required fees:* $2184. *Faculty research:* Social research, gerontology, women's issues, social services in schools, human behavior.

Eastern Michigan University, Graduate School, College of Health and Human Services, School of Social Work, Ypsilanti, MI 48197. Offers family and children's services (MSW); mental health and chemical dependency (MSW); services to the aging (MSW). *Accreditation:* CSWE. Part-time and evening/weekend programs available. *Faculty:* 21 full-time (18 women). *Students:* 19 full-time (17 women), 203 part-time (168 women); includes 75 minority (65 Black or African American, non-Hispanic/Latino; 1 American Indian or Alaska Native, non-Hispanic/Latino; 1 Asian, non-Hispanic/Latino; 5 Hispanic/Latino; 3 Two or more races, non-Hispanic/Latino). Average age 35. 309 applicants, 36% accepted, 77 enrolled. In 2013, 68 master's awarded. *Entrance requirements:* Additional exam requirements/recommendations for international students: Required—TOEFL. *Application deadline:* For fall admission, 1/15 priority date for domestic students. Applications are processed on a rolling basis. Application fee: $35. *Expenses:* Tuition, state resident: full-time $12,300; part-time $466 per credit hour. Tuition, nonresident: full-time $23,159; part-time $918 per credit hour. *Required fees:* $71 per credit hour. $46 per semester. One-time fee: $100. Tuition and fees vary according to course level and degree level. *Financial support:* Fellowships, research assistantships with full tuition reimbursements, teaching assistantships with full tuition reimbursements, career-related internships or fieldwork, Federal Work-Study, institutionally sponsored loans, scholarships/grants, tuition waivers (partial), and unspecified assistantships available. Support available to part-time students. Financial award applicants required to submit FAFSA. *Unit head:* Dr. Lynn Nybell, Interim Director, 734-487-0393, Fax: 734-487-6832, E-mail: lnybell@emich.edu. *Application contact:* Julie Harkema, Admissions Coordinator, 734-487-4206, Fax: 734-487-6832, E-mail: jharkema@emich.edu.
Website: http://www.emich.edu/sw.

Eastern Washington University, Graduate Studies, College of Social and Behavioral Sciences and Social Work, School of Social Work, Cheney, WA 99004-2431. Offers MSW, MPA/MSW. *Accreditation:* CSWE. Part-time programs available. *Faculty:* 23 full-time (13 women). *Students:* 144 full-time (119 women), 122 part-time (89 women); includes 44 minority (5 Black or African American, non-Hispanic/Latino; 10 American Indian or Alaska Native, non-Hispanic/Latino; 8 Asian, non-Hispanic/Latino; 21 Hispanic/Latino). Average age 36. 163 applicants, 37% accepted, 61 enrolled. In 2013, 90 master's awarded. *Degree requirements:* For master's, comprehensive exam. *Entrance requirements:* For master's, minimum GPA of 3.0. *Application deadline:* Applications are processed on a rolling basis. Application fee: $50. *Financial support:* In 2013–14, 23 teaching assistantships with partial tuition reimbursements (averaging $7,000 per year) were awarded; career-related internships or fieldwork, Federal Work-Study, institutionally sponsored loans, scholarships/grants, health care benefits, tuition waivers (partial), and unspecified assistantships also available. Support available to part-time students. Financial award application deadline: 2/1; financial award applicants required to submit FAFSA. *Unit head:* Dr. Jim Perez, Interim Dean, 509-359-4863. *Application contact:* Diane Somerday, Program Coordinator, 509-359-6482.
Website: http://www.ewu.edu/csbssw/programs/social-work/social-work-degrees/msw.xml.

East Tennessee State University, School of Graduate Studies, College of Arts and Sciences, Department of Social Work, Johnson City, TN 37614. Offers MSW. *Accreditation:* CSWE. *Faculty:* 10 full-time (7 women), 6 part-time/adjunct (all women). *Students:* 70 full-time (56 women), 34 part-time (24 women); includes 21 minority (13 Black or African American, non-Hispanic/Latino; 5 Hispanic/Latino; 3 Two or more races, non-Hispanic/Latino), 1 international. Average age 34. 108 applicants, 61% accepted, 53 enrolled. In 2013, 36 master's awarded. *Degree requirements:* For master's, comprehensive exam, field practicum. *Entrance requirements:* For master's, minimum GPA of 2.75, 3.0 for last 60 hours; three letters of recommendation; resume. Additional exam requirements/recommendations for international students: Required—TOEFL (minimum score 550 paper-based; 79 iBT). *Application deadline:* For fall admission, 2/1 for domestic and international students. Application fee: $35 ($45 for international students). Electronic applications accepted. *Expenses:* Tuition, state resident: full-time $7900; part-time $395 per credit hour. Tuition, nonresident: full-time $21,960; part-time $1098 per credit hour. *Required fees:* $1345; $84 per credit hour. *Financial support:* In 2013–14, 25 students received support, including 8 research assistantships with full tuition reimbursements available (averaging $6,000 per year), teaching assistantships with full tuition reimbursements available (averaging $6,000 per year); career-related internships or fieldwork, institutionally sponsored loans, scholarships/grants, and unspecified assistantships also available. Financial award application deadline: 7/1; financial award applicants required to submit FAFSA. *Faculty research:* Social work education, domestic violence, factors that contribute to a quality therapeutic relationship, mental illness stigma. *Unit head:* Dr. Michael Smith, Chair, 423-439-6014, Fax: 423-439-6010, E-mail: smithml1@etsu.edu. *Application contact:* Kimberly Brockman, Graduate Specialist, 423-439-6165, Fax: 423-439-5624, E-mail: brockmank@etsu.edu.
Website: http://www.etsu.edu/socialwork/.

Edinboro University of Pennsylvania, College of Arts and Sciences, Department of Social Work, Edinboro, PA 16444. Offers MSW. *Accreditation:* CSWE. Evening/weekend programs available. *Degree requirements:* For master's, competency exam. Electronic applications accepted.

Fayetteville State University, Graduate School, Program in Social Work, Fayetteville, NC 28301-4298. Offers MSW. *Accreditation:* CSWE. *Faculty:* 12 full-time (7 women), 7 part-time/adjunct (2 women). *Students:* 122 full-time (112 women), 43 part-time (30 women); includes 119 minority (103 Black or African American, non-Hispanic/Latino; 3 American Indian or Alaska Native, non-Hispanic/Latino; 3 Asian, non-Hispanic/Latino; 5 Hispanic/Latino; 5 Two or more races, non-Hispanic/Latino). Average age 35. 56 applicants, 100% accepted, 56 enrolled. In 2013, 77 master's awarded. *Application deadline:* For fall admission, 1/15 for domestic students. Application fee: $40. *Unit head:* Dr. Terri Moore-Brown, Department Chair, 910-672-1853, E-mail: tmbrown@uncfsu.edu. *Application contact:* Katrina Hoffman, Graduate Admissions Officer, 910-672-1374, Fax: 910-672-1470, E-mail: khoffma1@uncfsu.edu.

Florida Agricultural and Mechanical University, Division of Graduate Studies, Research, and Continuing Education, College of Arts and Sciences, Department of History and Political Science, Program in Applied Social Science, Tallahassee, FL 32307-3200. Offers African American history (MASS); criminal justice (MASS); economics (MASS); history (MASS); political science (MASS); public administration (MASS); public management (MASS); social work (MASS); sociology (MASS). Part-time programs available. *Degree requirements:* For master's, thesis optional. *Entrance requirements:* For master's, GRE General Test, minimum GPA of 3.0. *Faculty research:* Southern history, black history, election trends, presidential history.

Florida Agricultural and Mechanical University, Division of Graduate Studies, Research, and Continuing Education, College of Arts and Sciences, Department of History and Political Science, Program in Social Work, Tallahassee, FL 32307-3200. Offers MSW. *Accreditation:* CSWE. *Entrance requirements:* For master's, GRE General Test, minimum GPA of 3.0, 3 letters of recommendation. Additional exam requirements/recommendations for international students: Required—TOEFL.

Florida Atlantic University, College of Design and Social Inquiry, School of Social Work, Boca Raton, FL 33431-0991. Offers MSW. *Accreditation:* CSWE. Part-time and evening/weekend programs available. *Faculty:* 19 full-time (12 women), 2 part-time/adjunct (1 woman). *Students:* 139 full-time (117 women), 128 part-time (108 women); includes 103 minority (51 Black or African American, non-Hispanic/Latino; 2 American Indian or Alaska Native, non-Hispanic/Latino; 3 Asian, non-Hispanic/Latino; 41 Hispanic/Latino; 6 Two or more races, non-Hispanic/Latino), 2 international. Average age 34. 317 applicants, 58% accepted, 126 enrolled. In 2013, 98 master's awarded. *Entrance requirements:* Additional exam requirements/recommendations for international students: Required—TOEFL (minimum score 500 paper-based; 61 iBT), IELTS (minimum score 6). *Application deadline:* For fall admission, 5/1 priority date for domestic students, 2/15 for international students. Applications are processed on a rolling basis. Application fee: $30. *Expenses:* Tuition, state resident: full-time $6660; part-time $370 per credit hour. Tuition, nonresident: full-time $18,450; part-time $1025 per credit hour. Tuition and fees vary according to course load. *Financial support:* Fellowships with tuition reimbursements, research assistantships with tuition reimbursements, career-related internships or fieldwork, Federal Work-Study, institutionally sponsored loans, and tuition waivers (partial) available. Financial award application deadline: 4/1. *Faculty research:* Child welfare, social work education. *Unit head:* Dr. Michele Hawkins, Director, 561-297-3234, Fax: 561-297-2866, E-mail: mhawkins@fau.edu. *Application contact:* Dr. Elwood Hamlin, II, Coordinator, 501-297-3234, E-mail: ehamlin@fau.edu.
Website: http://www.fau.edu/ssw/.

Florida Gulf Coast University, College of Professional Studies, Program in Social Work, Fort Myers, FL 33965-6565. Offers MSW. *Accreditation:* CSWE. Part-time and evening/weekend programs available. *Entrance requirements:* For master's, GRE General Test, MAT, minimum GPA of 3.0. Additional exam requirements/recommendations for international students: Required—TOEFL (minimum score 550 paper-based). Electronic applications accepted. *Faculty research:* Gerontology, clinical case management, domestic violence, homelessness, migrant workers.

Florida International University, Robert Stempel College of Public Health and Social Work, School of Social Work, Miami, FL 33199. Offers social welfare (PhD); social work (MSW). *Accreditation:* CSWE (one or more programs are accredited). Part-time and evening/weekend programs available. *Degree requirements:* For doctorate, comprehensive exam, thesis/dissertation. *Entrance requirements:* For master's, minimum undergraduate GPA of 3.0 in upper-level coursework; letters of recommendation; undergraduate courses in biology (including human biology), statistics, and social/behavioral science (12 credits); BSW from accredited program; for doctorate, GRE, minimum graduate GPA of 3.5, 3 letters of recommendation, resume, writing samples, 2 examples of scholarly work. Additional exam requirements/recommendations for international students: Required—TOEFL (minimum score 550 paper-based; 80 iBT). Electronic applications accepted.

Florida State University, The Graduate School, College of Social Work, Tallahassee, FL 32306. Offers clinical social work (MSW); social policy and administration (MSW); social work (PhD); JD/MSW; MPA/MSW; MS/MSW; MSW/MBA. *Accreditation:* CSWE (one or more programs are accredited). Part-time and evening/weekend programs available. Postbaccalaureate distance learning degree programs offered (no on-campus study). *Faculty:* 34 full-time (23 women). *Students:* 257 full-time (232 women), 244 part-time (217 women); includes 152 minority (107 Black or African American, non-Hispanic/Latino; 1 American Indian or Alaska Native, non-Hispanic/Latino; 3 Asian, non-Hispanic/Latino; 34 Hispanic/Latino; 7 Two or more races, non-Hispanic/Latino), 6 international. Average age 31. 310 applicants, 74% accepted, 156 enrolled. In 2013, 240 master's, 1 doctorate awarded. *Degree requirements:* For master's, thesis optional; for doctorate, comprehensive exam, thesis/dissertation. *Entrance requirements:* For master's, GRE General Test, minimum GPA of 3.0; for doctorate, GRE General Test, minimum GPA of 3.0. Additional exam requirements/recommendations for international students: Required—TOEFL (minimum score 80 iBT). *Application deadline:* For fall admission, 5/1 for domestic and international students; for winter admission, 3/1 for domestic and international students; for spring admission, 10/1 for domestic and international students. Applications are processed on a rolling basis. Application fee: $30. Electronic applications accepted. *Expenses:* Tuition, state resident: part-time $403.51 per credit hour. Tuition, nonresident: part-time $1004.85 per credit hour. *Required fees:* $75.81 per credit hour. One-time fee: $20 part-time. Tuition and fees vary according to course load, campus/location and student level. *Financial support:* In 2013–14, 40 students received support, including 1 fellowship (averaging $22,000 per year), 34 research assistantships (averaging $3,500 per year), 13 teaching assistantships (averaging $15,000 per year); career-related internships or fieldwork, scholarships/grants, health care benefits, tuition waivers (partial), and unspecified assistantships also available. Financial award application deadline: 5/1; financial award applicants required to submit FAFSA. *Faculty research:* Family violence, AIDS/HIV, aging, family therapy, substance abuse, criminal justice. *Total annual research expenditures:* $2.6 million. *Unit head:* Dr. Nicholas Mazza, Dean, 850-644-4752, Fax: 850-644-9750, E-mail: nfmazza@fsu.edu.

Application contact: Craig Stanley, Director of the MSW Program, 800-378-9550, Fax: 850-644-1201, E-mail: grad@csw.fsu.edu.
Website: http://csw.fsu.edu/.

Fordham University, Graduate School of Social Service, New York, NY 10023. Offers social work (MSW, PhD); JD/MSW. *Accreditation:* CSWE (one or more programs are accredited). Part-time and evening/weekend programs available. Postbaccalaureate distance learning degree programs offered (no on-campus study). *Degree requirements:* For master's, 1200 hours of field placement; for doctorate, comprehensive exam, thesis/dissertation. *Entrance requirements:* For master's, BA in liberal arts; for doctorate, GRE, master's degree in social work or related field. Additional exam requirements/recommendations for international students: Required—TOEFL (minimum score 575 paper-based; 90 iBT). Electronic applications accepted. *Expenses:* Contact institution. *Faculty research:* Aging, children and family, healthcare, domestic violence, substance abuse.

Gallaudet University, The Graduate School, Washington, DC 20002-3625. Offers ASL/English bilingual early childhood education: birth to 5 (Certificate); audiology (Au D); clinical psychology (PhD); critical studies in the education of deaf learners (PhD); deaf and hard of hearing infants, toddlers, and their families (Certificate); deaf education (Ed S); deaf education: advanced studies (MA); deaf education: special programs (MA); deaf history (Certificate); deaf studies (MA, Certificate); educating deaf students with disabilities (Certificate); education: teacher preparation (MA), including deaf education, early childhood education and deaf education, elementary education and deaf education, secondary education and deaf education; educational neuroscience (PhD); hearing, speech and language sciences (MS, PhD); international development (MA); interpretation (MA, PhD), including combined interpreting practice and research (MA), interpreting research (MA); linguistics (MA, PhD); mental health counseling (MA); peer mentoring (Certificate); public administration (MPA); school counseling (MA); school psychology (Psy S); sign language teaching (MA); social work (MSW); speech-language pathology (MS). Part-time programs available. *Faculty:* 55 full-time (37 women). *Students:* 361 full-time (279 women), 108 part-time (73 women); includes 98 minority (39 Black or African American, non-Hispanic/Latino; 1 American Indian or Alaska Native, non-Hispanic/Latino; 12 Asian, non-Hispanic/Latino; 36 Hispanic/Latino; 1 Native Hawaiian or other Pacific Islander, non-Hispanic/Latino; 9 Two or more races, non-Hispanic/Latino), 31 international. Average age 30. 602 applicants, 49% accepted, 177 enrolled. In 2013, 140 master's, 32 doctorates, 11 other advanced degrees awarded. Terminal master's awarded for partial completion of doctoral program. *Degree requirements:* For master's, comprehensive exam (for some programs), thesis optional; for doctorate, comprehensive exam, thesis/dissertation. *Entrance requirements:* For master's and doctorate, GRE General Test or MAT, letters of recommendation, interviews, goals statement, ASL proficiency interview, written English competency. Additional exam requirements/recommendations for international students: Required—TOEFL. *Application deadline:* For fall admission, 2/15 for domestic students. Applications are processed on a rolling basis. Application fee: $75. Electronic applications accepted. *Expenses:* Tuition: Full-time $14,774; part-time $821 per credit. *Required fees:* $198 per semester. *Financial support:* In 2013–14, 325 students received support. Fellowships, research assistantships, teaching assistantships, career-related internships or fieldwork, Federal Work-Study, scholarships/grants, tuition waivers (partial), and unspecified assistantships available. Support available to part-time students. Financial award applicants required to submit FAFSA. *Faculty research:* Bimodal bilingualism development, cochlear implants, telecommunications access, cancer genetics, linguistics, visual language and visual learning, advancement of avatar and robotics translation, algal productivity and physiology in the Anacostia River. *Unit head:* Dr. Carol J. Erting, Dean, Research, Graduate School, Continuing Studies, and International Programs, 202-651-5520, Fax: 202-651-5027, E-mail: carol.erting@gallaudet.edu. *Application contact:* Wednesday Luria, Coordinator of Prospective Graduate Student Services, 202-651-5400, Fax: 202-651-5295, E-mail: graduate.school@gallaudet.edu.
Website: http://www.gallaudet.edu/x26696.xml.

George Mason University, College of Health and Human Services, Department of Social Work, Fairfax, VA 22030. Offers MSW. *Accreditation:* CSWE. *Faculty:* 15 full-time (11 women), 31 part-time/adjunct (26 women). *Students:* 139 full-time (126 women), 37 part-time (28 women); includes 51 minority (23 Black or African American, non-Hispanic/Latino; 10 Asian, non-Hispanic/Latino; 17 Hispanic/Latino; 1 Native Hawaiian or other Pacific Islander, non-Hispanic/Latino). Average age 30. 292 applicants, 52% accepted, 75 enrolled. In 2013, 79 master's awarded. *Entrance requirements:* For master's, 2 official transcripts; expanded goals statement; resume; bachelor's degree with minimum GPA of 3.0; 30 undergraduate credits in liberal arts with English composition; history or government, social sciences and statistics; 3 letters of recommendation. Additional exam requirements/recommendations for international students: Required—TOEFL (minimum score 570 paper-based; 88 iBT), IELTS (minimum score 6.5), PTE. *Application deadline:* For fall admission, 1/15 priority date for domestic students. Application fee: $65 ($80 for international students). Electronic applications accepted. *Expenses:* Contact institution. *Financial support:* In 2013–14, 5 students received support, including 5 research assistantships with full and partial tuition reimbursements available (averaging $14,300 per year); teaching assistantships, career-related internships or fieldwork, Federal Work-Study, scholarships/grants, unspecified assistantships, and health care benefits for full-time research or teaching assistantship recipients) also available. Financial award application deadline: 3/1; financial award applicants required to submit FAFSA. *Faculty research:* Social work methods, child welfare, social work ethics, field education, supervision. *Total annual research expenditures:* $15,361. *Unit head:* Mike Wolf-Branigin, Interim Department Chair, 703-993-4229, Fax: 703-993-2193, E-mail: mwolfbra@gmu.edu. *Application contact:* Raleigh Contreras, Administrative Support Specialist, 703-993-4247, Fax: 703-993-2193, E-mail: rcontre2@gmu.edu.
Website: http://chhs.gmu.edu/socialwork/.

Georgia State University, Andrew Young School of Policy Studies, School of Social Work, Atlanta, GA 30294. Offers child welfare leadership (Certificate); community partnerships (MSW); forensic social work (Certificate). *Accreditation:* CSWE. Part-time programs available. *Faculty:* 13 full-time (9 women), 3 part-time/adjunct (0 women). *Students:* 97 full-time (89 women), 1 (woman) part-time; includes 51 minority (39 Black or African American, non-Hispanic/Latino; 3 Asian, non-Hispanic/Latino; 4 Hispanic/Latino; 5 Two or more races, non-Hispanic/Latino), 2 international. Average age 29. 120 applicants, 80% accepted, 43 enrolled. In 2013, 44 master's awarded. *Entrance requirements:* For master's, GRE; for Certificate, GRE. Additional exam requirements/recommendations for international students: Required—TOEFL (minimum score 550 paper-based; 100 iBT) or IELTS (minimum score 7). *Application deadline:* For fall admission, 2/1 priority date for domestic and international students. Application fee: $50. Electronic applications accepted. *Expenses: Tuition, area resident:* Full-time $4176; part-time $348 per credit hour. Tuition, state resident: full-time $14,544; part-time $1212 per credit hour. Tuition, nonresident: full-time $14,544; part-time $1212 per credit hour. Tuition and fees vary according to course load and program. *Financial support:* In 2013–14, research assistantships with tuition reimbursements (averaging $4,000 per year), teaching assistantships with tuition reimbursements (averaging $4,000 per year) were awarded; career-related internships or fieldwork, institutionally sponsored loans,

scholarships/grants, tuition waivers, and unspecified assistantships also available. Financial award application deadline: 2/1; financial award applicants required to submit FAFSA. *Faculty research:* Community partnership, non-profit organizations, child welfare practice and policy, gerontological practice and policy, restorative justice. *Unit head:* Renanda Dear, Director of Student and Community Services, 404-413-1057, Fax: 404-413-1075, E-mail: rwood@gsu.edu. *Application contact:* Charisma Parker, Admissions Coordinator, 404-413-0030, Fax: 404-413-0023, E-mail: cparker28@gsu.edu.
Website: http://aysps.gsu.edu/socialwork.

Governors State University, College of Health Professions, Program in Social Work, University Park, IL 60484. Offers MSW. *Accreditation:* CSWE.

The Graduate Center, City University of New York, Graduate Studies, Program in Social Welfare, New York, NY 10016-4039. Offers DSW, PhD. *Degree requirements:* For doctorate, thesis/dissertation, project, qualifying exam. *Entrance requirements:* For doctorate, MSW or equivalent, 3 years of post-master's work experience. Additional exam requirements/recommendations for international students: Required—TOEFL. Electronic applications accepted.

Grambling State University, School of Graduate Studies and Research, College of Professional Studies, School of Social Work, Grambling, LA 71245. Offers MSW. *Accreditation:* CSWE. Part-time programs available. *Faculty:* 4 full-time (3 women), 1 part-time/adjunct (0 women). *Students:* 67 full-time (58 women), 3 part-time (all women); includes 65 minority (64 Black or African American, non-Hispanic/Latino; 1 Hispanic/Latino), 2 international. Average age 29. In 2013, 27 master's awarded. *Degree requirements:* For master's, comprehensive exam, research project or thesis. *Entrance requirements:* For master's, GRE, minimum GPA of 3.0 on last degree, 36 hours in liberal arts, autobiography, interview. Additional exam requirements/recommendations for international students: Required—TOEFL (minimum score 500 paper-based; 62 iBT). *Application deadline:* For fall admission, 5/15 priority date for domestic and international students. Applications are processed on a rolling basis. Electronic applications accepted. *Financial support:* Research assistantships, health care benefits, tuition waivers (full and partial), and unspecified assistantships available. Financial award application deadline: 5/31; financial award applicants required to submit FAFSA. *Unit head:* Dr. Carolyn F. Hester, Acting Associate Dean, 318-274-3302, Fax: 318-274-3254, E-mail: hesterc@gram.edu. *Application contact:* Philis A. Burton, Administrative Assistant, 318-274-3304, Fax: 318-274-3254, E-mail: burtonp@gram.edu.
Website: http://www.gram.edu/academics/majors/professional%20studies/departments/social%20work/.

Grand Valley State University, College of Community and Public Service, School of Social Work, Allendale, MI 49401-9403. Offers MSW. *Accreditation:* CSWE. Part-time programs available. *Entrance requirements:* Additional exam requirements/recommendations for international students: Required—TOEFL. Electronic applications accepted. *Faculty research:* Drug addiction, aging, management, effectiveness of therapy.

Gratz College, Graduate Programs, Program in Jewish Communal Service, Melrose Park, PA 19027. Offers MA, Certificate, MSW/Certificate. MSW/Certificate offered jointly with University of Pennsylvania. Part-time and evening/weekend programs available. Postbaccalaureate distance learning degree programs offered. *Degree requirements:* For master's, one foreign language, internship.

Hawai`i Pacific University, College of Humanities and Social Sciences, Program in Social Work, Honolulu, HI 96813. Offers MSW. *Accreditation:* CSWE. Part-time and evening/weekend programs available. *Faculty:* 7 full-time (5 women), 2 part-time/adjunct (0 women). *Students:* 66 full-time (57 women), 20 part-time (15 women); includes 50 minority (9 Black or African American, non-Hispanic/Latino; 11 Asian, non-Hispanic/Latino; 11 Hispanic/Latino; 2 Native Hawaiian or other Pacific Islander, non-Hispanic/Latino; 17 Two or more races, non-Hispanic/Latino). Average age 33. 87 applicants, 61% accepted, 36 enrolled. In 2013, 32 master's awarded. *Financial support:* In 2013–14, 21 students received support. Career-related internships or fieldwork, Federal Work-Study, scholarships/grants, tuition waivers, and unspecified assistantships available. *Unit head:* Dr. Lorraine Marais, Director, 808-566-2475, E-mail: lmarais@hpu.edu. *Application contact:* Rumi Yoshida, Associate Director of Graduate Admissions, 808-543-8034, Fax: 808-544-0280, E-mail: grad@hpu.edu.
Website: http://www.hpu.edu/CHSS/SocialWork/index.html.

Howard University, School of Social Work, Washington, DC 20059. Offers MSW, PhD. *Accreditation:* CSWE (one or more programs are accredited). Part-time programs available. *Degree requirements:* For doctorate, comprehensive exam, thesis/dissertation, qualifying exam. *Entrance requirements:* For master's, minimum GPA of 2.5; for doctorate, GRE General Test, minimum GPA of 3.3, MSW or master's in related field. Additional exam requirements/recommendations for international students: Required—TOEFL. *Faculty research:* Infant mortality, child and family services, displaced populations, social work practice, domestic violence, black males, mental health.

Humboldt State University, Academic Programs, College of Professional Studies, Department of Social Work, Arcata, CA 95521-8299. Offers MSW. *Accreditation:* CSWE. *Entrance requirements:* For master's, 3 letters of recommendation. Additional exam requirements/recommendations for international students: Required—TOEFL (minimum score 500 paper-based).

Hunter College of the City University of New York, Graduate School, School of Social Work, New York, NY 10065-5085. Offers MSW, DSW. DSW offered jointly with Graduate School and University Center of the City University of New York. *Accreditation:* CSWE (one or more programs are accredited). *Faculty:* 30 full-time (14 women), 51 part-time/adjunct (33 women). *Students:* 780 full-time (656 women), 253 part-time (181 women); includes 511 minority (251 Black or African American, non-Hispanic/Latino; 4 American Indian or Alaska Native, non-Hispanic/Latino; 49 Asian, non-Hispanic/Latino; 207 Hispanic/Latino), 15 international. Average age 32. 1,410 applicants, 36% accepted, 296 enrolled. In 2013, 476 master's awarded. *Degree requirements:* For master's, major paper. *Entrance requirements:* Additional exam requirements/recommendations for international students: Required—TOEFL. *Application deadline:* For fall admission, 1/15 for domestic and international students. Applications are processed on a rolling basis. Application fee: $125. *Financial support:* In 2013–14, 120 fellowships (averaging $1,000 per year) were awarded; career-related internships or fieldwork, Federal Work-Study, and tuition waivers (partial) also available. Support available to part-time students. *Faculty research:* Child welfare, AIDS, homeless, aging, mental health. *Unit head:* Dr. Jacqueline B. Mondros, Dean/Professor, 212-452-7085, Fax: 212-452-7150, E-mail: jmondros@hunter.cuny.edu. *Application contact:* Raymond Montero, Coordinator of Admissions, 212-452-7005, E-mail: grad.socworkadvisor@hunter.cuny.edu.
Website: http://www.hunter.cuny.edu/socwork/.

Illinois State University, Graduate School, College of Arts and Sciences, School of Social Work, Normal, IL 61790-2200. Offers MSW. *Accreditation:* CSWE. *Faculty research:* Developing professional careers in child welfare, research and policy work for the Evan B. Donaldson Adoption Institute, evidence-based practice training pilot evaluation.

Indiana University East, School of Social Work, Richmond, IN 47374-1289. Offers MSW.

Indiana University Northwest, Division of Social Work, Gary, IN 46408-1197. Offers MSW. Part-time and evening/weekend programs available. *Faculty:* 1 full-time (0 women). *Students:* 27 full-time (24 women), 61 part-time (52 women); includes 32 minority (24 Black or African American, non-Hispanic/Latino; 1 American Indian or Alaska Native, non-Hispanic/Latino; 7 Hispanic/Latino). Average age 37. 21 applicants, 100% accepted, 15 enrolled. In 2013, 16 master's awarded. *Entrance requirements:* For master's, minimum GPA of 3.0. *Application deadline:* For fall admission, 2/1 for domestic students. *Expenses:* Contact institution. *Financial support:* Career-related internships or fieldwork, Federal Work-Study, and tuition waivers (partial) available. Support available to part-time students. Financial award application deadline: 6/1; financial award applicants required to submit FAFSA. *Faculty research:* Educational outcomes, generalist practice, homelessness. *Total annual research expenditures:* $1,000. *Unit head:* Dr. Darlene Lynch, Director, 219-980-6614, E-mail: darlynch@iun.edu. *Application contact:* Jennifer Anderson, Field Coordinator, 219-981-4201.
Website: http://www.iun.edu/social-work/msw-dgree/index.htm.

Indiana University–Purdue University Indianapolis, School of Social Work, Indianapolis, IN 46202-2896. Offers MSW, PhD, Certificate. *Accreditation:* CSWE (one or more programs are accredited). Part-time and evening/weekend programs available. *Faculty:* 40 full-time. *Students:* 352 full-time (296 women), 230 part-time (195 women); includes 103 minority (61 Black or African American, non-Hispanic/Latino; 7 Asian, non-Hispanic/Latino; 18 Hispanic/Latino; 17 Two or more races, non-Hispanic/Latino), 13 international. Average age 32. 277 applicants, 66% accepted, 125 enrolled. In 2013, 193 master's, 3 doctorates awarded. Terminal master's awarded for partial completion of doctoral program. *Degree requirements:* For master's, field practicum; for doctorate, thesis/dissertation, residential internship. *Entrance requirements:* For master's, minimum GPA of 2.5; course work in social behavior, statistics, research methodology, and human biology; for doctorate, GRE General Test. Additional exam requirements/recommendations for international students: Required—TOEFL. Application fee: $55 ($65 for international students). *Expenses:* Contact institution. *Financial support:* Fellowships with full tuition reimbursements, research assistantships with partial tuition reimbursements, teaching assistantships, Federal Work-Study, institutionally sponsored loans, scholarships/grants, and tuition waivers (partial) available. Support available to part-time students. Financial award applicants required to submit FAFSA. *Faculty research:* Social justice, institutional child welfare, mental health, aging, AIDS/HIV. *Total annual research expenditures:* $145,580. *Unit head:* Dr. Margaret Adamek, Dean, 317-274-6730, Fax: 317-274-8630. *Application contact:* Marlo Dale, Information Contact for MSW, 317-274-6966.
Website: http://socialwork.iu.edu/.

Indiana University South Bend, School of Social Work, South Bend, IN 46634-7111. Offers MSW. Part-time and evening/weekend programs available. *Faculty:* 4 full-time (2 women). *Students:* 31 full-time (30 women), 73 part-time (56 women); includes 16 minority (10 Black or African American, non-Hispanic/Latino; 1 Asian, non-Hispanic/Latino; 4 Hispanic/Latino; 1 Two or more races, non-Hispanic/Latino). Average age 35. 43 applicants, 79% accepted, 29 enrolled. In 2013, 31 master's awarded. *Application deadline:* For fall admission, 2/1 priority date for domestic students. *Expenses:* Contact institution. *Financial support:* Career-related internships or fieldwork and Federal Work-Study available. Support available to part-time students. Financial award application deadline: 3/1; financial award applicants required to submit FAFSA. *Unit head:* Dr. Carol Rippey Massat, Program Director, 574-520-4880, E-mail: cmassat@iupui.edu. *Application contact:* Diane Banic, Administrative Assistant, 574-520-4880, E-mail: dbanic@iusb.edu.
Website: https://www.iusb.edu/social-work/master.php.

Institute for Clinical Social Work, Graduate Programs, Chicago, IL 60601. Offers PhD. Part-time programs available. *Degree requirements:* For doctorate, thesis/dissertation, supervised practicum. *Entrance requirements:* For doctorate, 2 years of experience. *Faculty research:* Impact of AIDS on partners, effects of learning disabilities on children and families, clinical social work issues.

Inter American University of Puerto Rico, Metropolitan Campus, Graduate Programs, Program in Social Work, San Juan, PR 00919-1293. Offers advanced clinical services (MSW); advanced social work administration (MSW); clini al services (MSW); social work administration (MSW). *Accreditation:* CSWE. Evening/weekend programs available. *Degree requirements:* For master's, comprehensive exam. *Entrance requirements:* For master's, GRE or EXADEP, interview. Electronic applications accepted.

Jackson State University, Graduate School, School of Social Work, Jackson, MS 39217. Offers MSW, PhD. *Accreditation:* CSWE (one or more programs are accredited). Evening/weekend programs available. *Degree requirements:* For master's, comprehensive exam; for doctorate, comprehensive exam, thesis/dissertation. *Entrance requirements:* For master's, GRE General Test; for doctorate, MAT. Additional exam requirements/recommendations for international students: Required—TOEFL (minimum score 520 paper-based; 67 iBT).

Kean University, Nathan Weiss Graduate College, Program in Social Work, Union, NJ 07083. Offers MSW. *Accreditation:* CSWE. Part-time programs available. *Faculty:* 6 full-time (5 women). *Students:* 107 full-time (89 women), 2 part-time (both women); includes 61 minority (38 Black or African American, non-Hispanic/Latino; 2 Asian, non-Hispanic/Latino; 17 Hispanic/Latino; 4 Two or more races, non-Hispanic/Latino). Average age 30. 273 applicants, 37% accepted, 51 enrolled. In 2013, 50 master's awarded. *Degree requirements:* For master's, field work. *Entrance requirements:* For master's, baccalaureate degree; minimum cumulative GPA of 3.0, 3.5 on BSW including research courses; official transcripts; completion of at least 425 hours of field education at the BSW level; three letters of recommendation; professional resume/curriculum vitae; personal statement. Additional exam requirements/recommendations for international students: Required—TOEFL (minimum score 550 paper-based; 79 iBT). *Application deadline:* For fall admission, 6/1 for domestic students, 3/15 for international students. Applications are processed on a rolling basis. Application fee: $75 ($150 for international students). Electronic applications accepted. *Expenses:* Tuition, state resident: full-time $12,099; part-time $589 per credit. Tuition, nonresident: full-time $16,399; part-time $722 per credit. *Required fees:* $3050; $139 per credit. Part-time tuition and fees vary according to course level, course load, degree level and program. *Financial support:* In 2013–14, 6 research assistantships with full tuition reimbursements (averaging $3,713 per year) were awarded; unspecified assistantships also available. Financial award applicants required to submit FAFSA. *Unit head:* Dr. Josephine Norward, Program Coordinator, 908-737-4033, E-mail: jnorward@kean.edu. *Application contact:* Steven Koch, Admissions Counselor, 908-737-5924, E-mail: skoch@kean.edu.
Website: http://grad.kean.edu/msw.

Kennesaw State University, College of Health and Human Services, Program in Social Work, Kennesaw, GA 30144-5591. Offers MSW. *Accreditation:* CSWE. *Students:* 103 full-time (89 women), 5 part-time (all women); includes 28 minority (21 Black or African American, non-Hispanic/Latino; 1 Asian, non-Hispanic/Latino; 5 Hispanic/Latino; 1 Two or more races, non-Hispanic/Latino). Average age 31. 123 applicants, 51% accepted, 46

enrolled. In 2013, 37 master's awarded. *Entrance requirements:* For master's, GRE, criminal history check, minimum GPA of 2.75, 3 letters of recommendation, resume. Additional exam requirements/recommendations for international students: Required—TOEFL (minimum score 550 paper-based; 80 iBT), IELTS (minimum score 6). *Application deadline:* For fall admission, 3/15 for domestic and international students. Application fee: $60. Electronic applications accepted. *Expenses:* Tuition, state resident: full-time $4806; part-time $267 per semester hour. Tuition, nonresident: full-time $17,298; part-time $961 per semester hour. *Required fees:* $1834; $784.50 per semester. *Financial support:* In 2013–14, 2 research assistantships (averaging $8,000 per year) were awarded; unspecified assistantships also available. Financial award application deadline: 4/1; financial award applicants required to submit FAFSA. *Unit head:* Dr. Alan Kirk, Department Chair, 770-423-6630, E-mail: akirk@kennesaw.edu. *Application contact:* Rheanna Braun, Admissions Counselor, 770-423-6630, E-mail: ksugrad@kennesaw.edu.
Website: http://www.kennesaw.edu.

Kutztown University of Pennsylvania, College of Liberal Arts and Sciences, Program in Social Work, Kutztown, PA 19530-0730. Offers MSW. *Accreditation:* CSWE. Part-time and evening/weekend programs available. *Faculty:* 11 full-time (5 women). *Students:* 53 full-time (45 women), 18 part-time (14 women); includes 16 minority (7 Black or African American, non-Hispanic/Latino; 9 Hispanic/Latino), 4 international. Average age 30. 94 applicants, 48% accepted, 39 enrolled. In 2013, 22 master's awarded. *Degree requirements:* For master's, comprehensive exam. *Entrance requirements:* For master's, GRE. Additional exam requirements/recommendations for international students: Required—TOEFL (minimum score 550 paper-based; 79 iBT). *Application deadline:* For fall admission, 8/1 priority date for domestic and international students; for spring admission, 12/1 priority date for domestic and international students. Applications are processed on a rolling basis. Application fee: $35. Electronic applications accepted. *Expenses: Tuition, area resident:* Part-time $442 per credit. Tuition, state resident: part-time $442 per credit. Tuition, nonresident: part-time $663 per credit. *Required fees:* $80 per credit. *Financial support:* Career-related internships or fieldwork, Federal Work-Study, scholarships/grants, and unspecified assistantships available. Financial award application deadline: 3/1; financial award applicants required to submit FAFSA. *Unit head:* Dr. John Vafeas, Chairperson, 610-683-4235, E-mail: vafeas@kutztown.edu. *Application contact:* Kelly Hish, Admissions Clerk, 610-683-4200, Fax: 610-683-1393, E-mail: graduate@kutztown.edu.

Lakehead University, Graduate Studies, Gerontology Collaborative Program-Northern Educational Center for Aging and Health, Thunder Bay, ON P7B 5E1, Canada. Offers gerontology (M Ed, M Sc, MA, MSW). Part-time programs available. *Degree requirements:* For master's, thesis (for some programs). *Entrance requirements:* Additional exam requirements/recommendations for international students: Required—TOEFL. *Faculty research:* Integrated health information systems.

Lakehead University, Graduate Studies, School of Social Work, Thunder Bay, ON P7B 5E1, Canada. Offers gerontology (MSW); social work (MSW); women's studies (MSW). Part-time programs available. *Degree requirements:* For master's, thesis or project. *Entrance requirements:* For master's, minimum B average. Additional exam requirements/recommendations for international students: Required—TOEFL. *Faculty research:* Clinical psychology, social work and practice theory, long-term care, health care for frail elderly, women's studies.

Laurentian University, School of Graduate Studies and Research, School of Social Work, Sudbury, ON P3E 2C6, Canada. Offers MSW. Open only to French-speaking students. Part-time programs available. *Degree requirements:* For master's, thesis. *Faculty research:* Income security, poverty, violence against women, child poverty, effects of economic crisis on families.

Loma Linda University, School of Science and Technology, Department of Social Work and Social Ecology, Loma Linda, CA 92350. Offers social policy and research (PhD); social work (MSW). *Accreditation:* CSWE. *Degree requirements:* For master's, comprehensive exam, thesis optional; for doctorate, comprehensive exam, thesis/dissertation. *Entrance requirements:* For master's and doctorate, GRE General Test. Additional exam requirements/recommendations for international students: Required—TOEFL, Michigan English Language Assessment Battery. Electronic applications accepted.

Long Island University–LIU Post, School of Health Professions and Nursing, Master of Social Work Program, Brookville, NY 11548-1300. Offers alcohol and substance abuse (MSW); child and family welfare (MSW); forensic social work (MSW); gerontology (MSW); nonprofit management (MSW). *Accreditation:* CSWE.

Louisiana State University and Agricultural & Mechanical College, Graduate School, College of Human Sciences and Education, School of Social Work, Baton Rouge, LA 70803. Offers MSW, PhD. *Accreditation:* CSWE (one or more programs are accredited). Part-time programs available. *Faculty:* 16 full-time (12 women). *Students:* 178 full-time (154 women), 49 part-time (43 women); includes 59 minority (51 Black or African American, non-Hispanic/Latino; 1 American Indian or Alaska Native, non-Hispanic/Latino; 2 Asian, non-Hispanic/Latino; 2 Hispanic/Latino; 3 Two or more races, non-Hispanic/Latino), 3 international. Average age 28. 148 applicants, 77% accepted, 91 enrolled. In 2013, 113 master's, 3 doctorates awarded. *Degree requirements:* For master's, thesis, field instruction; for doctorate, comprehensive exam, thesis/dissertation. *Entrance requirements:* For master's and doctorate, GRE General Test, minimum GPA of 3.0. Additional exam requirements/recommendations for international students: Required—TOEFL (minimum score 550 paper-based; 79 iBT), IELTS (minimum score 6.5), or PTE (minimum score 59). *Application deadline:* For fall admission, 2/15 for domestic and international students. Application fee: $50 ($70 for international students). Electronic applications accepted. *Financial support:* In 2013–14, 182 students received support, including 3 fellowships (averaging $35,959 per year), 4 research assistantships with partial tuition reimbursements available (averaging $13,750 per year), 14 teaching assistantships with partial tuition reimbursements available (averaging $13,354 per year); career-related internships or fieldwork, Federal Work-Study, scholarships/grants, health care benefits, and unspecified assistantships also available. Support available to part-time students. Financial award applicants required to submit FAFSA. *Faculty research:* Child welfare, gerontology, addictions, mental health. *Total annual research expenditures:* $108,659. *Unit head:* Dr. Daphne Cain, Dean, 225-578-5875, Fax: 225-578-1357, E-mail: dscain@lsu.edu. *Application contact:* Denise Chiasson, Assistant Dean, 225-578-1234, Fax: 225-578-1357, E-mail: dchiass@lsu.edu.
Website: http://www.socialwork.lsu.edu/.

Loyola University Chicago, School of Social Work, Chicago, IL 60660. Offers MSW, PhD, PGC, JD/MSW, M Div/MSW, MJ/MSW, MSW/MA. *Accreditation:* CSWE (one or more programs are accredited). Part-time programs available. *Degree requirements:* For doctorate, comprehensive exam, thesis/dissertation. *Entrance requirements:* For master's, GRE; for doctorate, GRE or MAT. Additional exam requirements/recommendations for international students: Required—TOEFL (minimum score 550 paper-based; 79 iBT). *Expenses: Tuition:* Full-time $16,740; part-time $930 per credit. *Required fees:* $135 per semester. *Faculty research:* Aging, trauma, migration, poverty, substance abuse.

Marywood University, Academic Affairs, College of Health and Human Services, School of Social Work and Administrative Services, Scranton, PA 18509-1598. Offers gerontology (MS); health services administration (MHSA); public administration (MPA); social work (MSW). *Accreditation:* CSWE. *Entrance requirements:* Additional exam requirements/recommendations for international students: Required—TOEFL (minimum score 550 paper-based; 79 iBT). *Application deadline:* For fall admission, 4/1 priority date for domestic students, 3/31 priority date for international students; for spring admission, 11/1 priority date for domestic students, 8/31 priority date for international students. Applications are processed on a rolling basis. Application fee: $35. Electronic applications accepted. *Expenses:* Contact institution. *Financial support:* Research assistantships, career-related internships or fieldwork, scholarships/grants, and unspecified assistantships available. Support available to part-time students. Financial award application deadline: 6/30; financial award applicants required to submit FAFSA. *Faculty research:* Impaired professionals, ethics, child welfare, communities, professional gatekeeping. *Unit head:* Dr. Lloyd L. Lyter, Director, 570-348-6282 Ext. 2388, E-mail: lyter@marywood.edu. *Application contact:* Tammy Manka, Assistant Director of Graduate Admissions, 570-348-6211 Ext. 2322, E-mail: tmanka@marywood.edu.
Website: http://www.marywood.edu/ssw/.

Marywood University, Academic Affairs, Reap College of Education and Human Development, Doctoral Program in Human Development, Emphasis in Social Work, Scranton, PA 18509-1598. Offers PhD. *Entrance requirements:* Additional exam requirements/recommendations for international students: Required—TOEFL (minimum score 550 paper-based; 79 iBT). *Application deadline:* For fall admission, 1/30 priority date for domestic and international students. Application fee: $35. Electronic applications accepted. *Expenses:* Contact institution. *Financial support:* Career-related internships or fieldwork, scholarships/grants, and unspecified assistantships available. Support available to part-time students. Financial award application deadline: 6/30; financial award applicants required to submit FAFSA. *Unit head:* Dr. Timiko Tanaka, Director, 570-348-6279, E-mail: ktanaka@marywood.edu. *Application contact:* Tammy Manka, Assistant Director of Graduate Admissions, 570-348-6211 Ext. 2322, E-mail: tmanka@marywood.edu.
Website: http://www.marywood.edu/phd/specializations.html.

McGill University, Faculty of Graduate and Postdoctoral Studies, Faculty of Arts, School of Social Work, Montréal, QC H3A 2T5, Canada. Offers MSW, PhD, Diploma, MSW/LL B. PhD offered jointly with Université de Montréal.

McMaster University, School of Graduate Studies, Faculty of Social Sciences, School of Social Work, Hamilton, ON L8S 4M2, Canada. Offers analysis of social welfare policy (MSW); analysis of social work practice (MSW). Part-time programs available. *Entrance requirements:* For master's, minimum B+ average in final year, BSW from accredited program, half course each in introductory statistics and introductory social research methods. Additional exam requirements/recommendations for international students: Required—TOEFL (minimum score 580 paper-based). *Faculty research:* Health policy, income maintenance, child welfare, native issues, immigration policies, racism.

Memorial University of Newfoundland, School of Graduate Studies, School of Social Work, St. John's, NL A1C 5S7, Canada. Offers MSW. Part-time and evening/weekend programs available. *Degree requirements:* For master's, thesis optional, internship. *Entrance requirements:* For master's, BSW with a minimum of 2nd-class standing or equivalent. Electronic applications accepted. *Faculty research:* Violence, child abuse, sexual abuse, social policy, gerontology.

Metropolitan State University of Denver, School of Letters, Arts and Sciences, Denver, CO 80217-3362. Offers social work (MSW). *Degree requirements:* For master's, field work.

Michigan State University, The Graduate School, College of Social Science, School of Social Work, East Lansing, MI 48824. Offers clinical social work (MSW); organizational and community practice (MSW); social work (PhD). *Accreditation:* CSWE. Part-time programs available. Postbaccalaureate distance learning degree programs offered (minimal on-campus study). *Entrance requirements:* Additional exam requirements/recommendations for international students: Required—TOEFL. Electronic applications accepted.

Middle Tennessee State University, College of Graduate Studies, College of Behavioral and Health Sciences, Department of Social Work, Murfreesboro, TN 37132. Offers MSW. *Students:* 23 full-time (21 women), 19 part-time (18 women); includes 13 minority (9 Black or African American, non-Hispanic/Latino; 1 American Indian or Alaska Native, non-Hispanic/Latino; 3 Two or more races, non-Hispanic/Latino). 97 applicants, 76% accepted. In 2013, 18 master's awarded. *Entrance requirements:* Additional exam requirements/recommendations for international students: Required—TOEFL (minimum score 525 paper-based; 71 iBT), IELTS (minimum score 6). *Unit head:* Dr. Rebecca Smith, Chair, 615-898-2868, Fax: 615-898-5428, E-mail: rebecca.smith@mtsu.edu. *Application contact:* Dr. Michael D. Allen, Vice Provost for Research and Dean, 615-898-2840, Fax: 615-904-8020, E-mail: michael.allen@mtsu.edu.
Website: http://www.mtsu.edu/socialwork/.

Millersville University of Pennsylvania, College of Graduate and Professional Studies, School of Humanities and Social Sciences, Department of Social Work, Millersville, PA 17551-0302. Offers MSW. *Accreditation:* CSWE. Part-time programs available. *Faculty:* 9 full-time (7 women), 13 part-time/adjunct (11 women). *Students:* 51 full-time (42 women), 67 part-time (58 women); includes 23 minority (8 Black or African American, non-Hispanic/Latino; 1 American Indian or Alaska Native, non-Hispanic/Latino; 1 Asian, non-Hispanic/Latino; 11 Hispanic/Latino; 1 Native Hawaiian or other Pacific Islander, non-Hispanic/Latino; 1 Two or more races, non-Hispanic/Latino), 1 international. Average age 31. 43 applicants, 100% accepted, 43 enrolled. In 2013, 46 master's awarded. *Degree requirements:* For master's, field practicum. *Entrance requirements:* For master's, GRE or MAT (if GPA less than 2.8), 3 letters of recommendation, resume, goal statement, official transcripts. Additional exam requirements/recommendations for international students: Required—TOEFL (minimum score 550 paper-based, 79 iBT) or IELTS (minimum score 6). *Application deadline:* For fall admission, 2/1 for domestic and international students. Application fee: $40. Electronic applications accepted. *Expenses:* Tuition, state resident: full-time $7956; part-time $442 per credit. Tuition, nonresident: full-time $11,934; part-time $663 per credit. *Required fees:* $2196; $122 per credit. Tuition and fees vary according to course load. *Financial support:* In 2013–14, 18 students received support, including 18 research assistantships with full tuition reimbursements available (averaging $4,785 per year); institutionally sponsored loans and unspecified assistantships also available. Support available to part-time students. Financial award application deadline: 3/15; financial award applicants required to submit FAFSA. *Faculty research:* International social work; social justice advocacy; cultural competence; trauma-informed art therapy; mentoring. *Total annual research expenditures:* $25,000. *Unit head:* Dr. Karen M. Rice, Chair, 717-871-5297, Fax: 717-872-3959, E-mail: karen.rice@millersville.edu. *Application contact:* Dr. Victor S. DeSantis, Dean of College of Graduate and Professional Studies/Associate Provost for Civic and Community Engagement, 717-872-3099, Fax: 717-872-3453, E-mail: victor.desantis@millersville.edu.
Website: http://www.millersville.edu/socialwork/grad/index.php.

Social Work

Minnesota State University Mankato, College of Graduate Studies, College of Social and Behavioral Sciences, Department of Social Work, Mankato, MN 56001. Offers MSW. *Accreditation:* CSWE. *Students:* 38 full-time (32 women), 5 part-time (all women). *Entrance requirements:* Additional exam requirements/recommendations for international students: Required—TOEFL. *Application deadline:* For fall admission, 3/1 for domestic students. *Unit head:* Dr. Nancy Fitzsimons, Graduate Coordinator, 507-389-1287. *Application contact:* 507-389-2321, E-mail: grad@mnsu.edu.

Missouri State University, Graduate College, College of Health and Human Services, School of Social Work, Springfield, MO 65897. Offers MSW. *Accreditation:* CSWE. Part-time programs available. *Faculty:* 10 full-time (9 women), 10 part-time/adjunct (7 women). *Students:* 31 full-time (29 women), 67 part-time (59 women); includes 1 minority (Two or more races, non-Hispanic/Latino), 3 international. Average age 32. 42 applicants, 81% accepted, 34 enrolled. In 2013, 42 master's awarded. *Degree requirements:* For master's, comprehensive exam, thesis or alternative. *Entrance requirements:* For master's, GRE, minimum GPA of 3.0. Additional exam requirements/recommendations for international students: Required—TOEFL (minimum score 550 paper-based; 79 iBT). *Application deadline:* For fall admission, 2/15 priority date for domestic and international students. Application fee: $35 ($50 for international students). Electronic applications accepted. *Expenses:* Tuition: state resident: full-time $4500; part-time $250 per credit hour. Tuition, nonresident: full-time $9018; part-time $501 per credit hour. *Required fees:* $361 per semester. Tuition and fees vary according to course level, course load and program. *Financial support:* In 2013–14, 3 research assistantships with full tuition reimbursements (averaging $8,324 per year) were awarded; Federal Work-Study, institutionally sponsored loans, scholarships/grants, and unspecified assistantships also available. Financial award application deadline: 3/31; financial award applicants required to submit FAFSA. *Faculty research:* Child and family therapy, rural social work, adolescent social issues, domestic violence. *Unit head:* Carol Langer, Acting Director, 417-836-6953, Fax: 417-836-7688, E-mail: socialwork@missouristate.edu. *Application contact:* Misty Stewart, Coordinator of Graduate Recruitment, 417-836-6079, Fax: 417-836-6200, E-mail: mistystewart@missouristate.edu.
Website: http://www.missouristate.edu/swk/.

Monmouth University, The Graduate School, School of Social Work, West Long Branch, NJ 07764-1898. Offers clinical practice with families and children (MSW); international and community development (MSW); play therapy (Post-Master's Certificate). *Accreditation:* CSWE. Part-time and evening/weekend programs available. *Faculty:* 15 full-time (11 women), 17 part-time/adjunct (13 women). *Students:* 142 full-time (125 women), 120 part-time (106 women); includes 76 minority (45 Black or African American, non-Hispanic/Latino; 1 American Indian or Alaska Native, non-Hispanic/Latino; 4 Asian, non-Hispanic/Latino; 22 Hispanic/Latino; 1 Native Hawaiian or other Pacific Islander, non-Hispanic/Latino; 3 Two or more races, non-Hispanic/Latino), 2 international. Average age 30. 256 applicants, 92% accepted, 135 enrolled. In 2013, 91 master's awarded. *Degree requirements:* For master's, thesis, internship. *Entrance requirements:* For master's, minimum GPA of 3.0 in major, 2.75 overall with college course in English, math, biology, and psychology (preferred additional work in history, sociology, political science, anthropology, and economics); three department recommendation forms, autobiographical statement form; for Post-Master's Certificate, master's degree in medical or mental health discipline and eligibility for licensure in that discipline. Additional exam requirements/recommendations for international students: Required—TOEFL (minimum score 550 paper-based, 79 iBT), IELTS (minimum score 6) or Michigan English Language Assessment Battery (minimum score 77). *Application deadline:* For fall admission, 3/15 for domestic and international students. Applications are processed on a rolling basis. Application fee: $50. Electronic applications accepted. *Expenses:* Tuition: Part-time $1004 per credit hour. *Required fees:* $157 per semester. *Financial support:* In 2013–14, 145 students received support, including 137 fellowships (averaging $3,937 per year), 14 research assistantships (averaging $6,642 per year); career-related internships or fieldwork, scholarships/grants, and unspecified assistantships also available. Support available to part-time students. Financial award applicants required to submit FAFSA. *Faculty research:* Child welfare citizen participation, cultural diversity, diversity issues, employee help. *Unit head:* Dr. Rosemary Barbera, Program Director, 732-571-3606, Fax: 732-263-5217, E-mail: swdept@monmouth.edu. *Application contact:* Laure Vento-Cifelli, Associate Vice President of Undergraduate and Graduate Admission, 732-571-3452, Fax: 732-263-5123, E-mail: gradadm@monmouth.edu.
Website: http://www.monmouth.edu/school-of-social-work/master-of-social-work.aspx.

Morgan State University, School of Graduate Studies, School of Social Work, Baltimore, MD 21251. Offers MSW, PhD. *Accreditation:* CSWE. *Entrance requirements:* For doctorate, GRE.

Nazareth College of Rochester, Graduate Studies, Department of Social Work, Rochester, NY 14618-3790. Offers MSW. Program offered jointly with The College at Brockport, State University of New York. *Accreditation:* CSWE. *Entrance requirements:* For master's, minimum GPA of 3.0.

Newman University, School of Social Work, Wichita, KS 67213-2097. Offers MSW. *Accreditation:* CSWE. Postbaccalaureate distance learning degree programs offered (no on-campus study). *Faculty:* 8 full-time (4 women), 8 part-time/adjunct (5 women). *Students:* 56 full-time (49 women), 85 part-time (69 women); includes 43 minority (15 Black or African American, non-Hispanic/Latino; 5 American Indian or Alaska Native, non-Hispanic/Latino; 2 Asian, non-Hispanic/Latino; 17 Hispanic/Latino; 4 Two or more races, non-Hispanic/Latino). Average age 36. 142 applicants, 53% accepted, 50 enrolled. In 2013, 49 master's awarded. *Degree requirements:* For master's, comprehensive exam (for some programs), thesis optional, fieldwork. *Entrance requirements:* For master's, minimum GPA of 3.0, 3 letters of reference. Additional exam requirements/recommendations for international students: Required—TOEFL (minimum score 600 paper-based; 100 iBT). *Application deadline:* For fall admission, 8/15 for domestic students, 7/15 priority date for international students. Applications are processed on a rolling basis. Application fee: $25 ($40 for international students). *Expenses:* Contact institution. *Financial support:* Application deadline: 8/15; applicants required to submit FAFSA. *Unit head:* Dr. Gloria Hegge, Interim Director, 316-942-4291 Ext. 2436, Fax: 316-942-4483, E-mail: heggeg@newmanu.edu. *Application contact:* Linda Kay Sabala, Director of Graduate Admissions, 316-942-4291 Ext. 2230, Fax: 316-942-4483, E-mail: sabalal@newmanu.edu.

New Mexico Highlands University, Graduate Studies, School of Social Work, Las Vegas, NM 87701. Offers bilingual/bicultural clinical practice (MSW); clinical practice (MSW); government non-profit management (MSW). *Accreditation:* CSWE. Part-time programs available. *Faculty:* 19 full-time (9 women), 49 part-time/adjunct (32 women). *Students:* 65 full-time (34 women), 146 part-time (89 women); includes 137 minority (3 Black or African American, non-Hispanic/Latino; 9 American Indian or Alaska Native, non-Hispanic/Latino; 1 Asian, non-Hispanic/Latino; 120 Hispanic/Latino; 2 Native Hawaiian or other Pacific Islander, non-Hispanic/Latino; 2 Two or more races, non-Hispanic/Latino), 23 international. Average age 34. 259 applicants, 98% accepted, 148 enrolled. In 2013, 145 master's awarded. *Degree requirements:* For master's, comprehensive exam, thesis or alternative. *Entrance requirements:* For master's, minimum undergraduate GPA of 3.0. Additional exam requirements/recommendations

for international students: Required—TOEFL (minimum score 540 paper-based). *Application deadline:* For fall admission, 1/15 priority date for domestic students. Applications are processed on a rolling basis. Application fee: $15. *Expenses:* Tuition, state resident: full-time $4278; part-time $178 per credit hour. Tuition, nonresident: full-time $6716; part-time $281 per credit hour. One-time fee: $15. *Financial support:* Career-related internships or fieldwork, Federal Work-Study, institutionally sponsored loans, scholarships/grants, tuition waivers (partial), and unspecified assistantships available. Support available to part-time students. Financial award application deadline: 3/1; financial award applicants required to submit FAFSA. *Faculty research:* Treatment attrition among domestic violence batterers, children's health and mental health, Dejando Huellas: meeting the bilingual/bicultural needs of the Latino mental health patient, impact of culture on the therapeutic process, effects of generational gang involvement on adolescents' future. *Unit head:* Dr. Alfredo Garcia, Dean, 505-891-9053, Fax: 505-454-3290, E-mail: a_garcia@nmhu.edu. *Application contact:* LouAnn Romero, Administrative Assistant, Graduate Studies, 505-454-3087, E-mail: laromero@nmhu.edu.

New Mexico State University, Graduate School, College of Health and Social Services, School of Social Work, Las Cruces, NM 88003. Offers MSW. *Accreditation:* CSWE. Part-time and evening/weekend programs available. *Faculty:* 11 full-time (7 women), 13 part-time/adjunct (10 women). *Students:* 119 full-time (105 women), 35 part-time (31 women); includes 92 minority (6 Black or African American, non-Hispanic/Latino; 3 American Indian or Alaska Native, non-Hispanic/Latino; 1 Asian, non-Hispanic/Latino; 77 Hispanic/Latino; 5 Two or more races, non-Hispanic/Latino). Average age 31. 108 applicants, 77% accepted, 73 enrolled. In 2013, 62 master's awarded. *Degree requirements:* For master's, comprehensive exam, thesis optional, written exam. *Entrance requirements:* For master's, minimum cumulative GPA of 3.0. Additional exam requirements/recommendations for international students: Required—TOEFL (minimum score 550 paper-based; 79 iBT), IELTS (minimum score 6.5). *Application deadline:* For fall admission, 2/15 priority date for domestic and international students. Applications are processed on a rolling basis. Application fee: $40 ($50 for international students). Electronic applications accepted. *Expenses:* Tuition, state resident: full-time $5398; part-time $224.90 per credit. Tuition, nonresident: full-time $18,821; part-time $784.20 per credit. *Required fees:* $1310; $54.60 per credit. *Financial support:* In 2013–14, 53 students received support, including 2 research assistantships (averaging $12,196 per year), 13 teaching assistantships (averaging $8,130 per year); career-related internships or fieldwork, Federal Work-Study, traineeships, health care benefits, and unspecified assistantships also available. Financial award application deadline: 3/1. *Faculty research:* Attachment issues, border issues, substance abuse, sexual orientation, family diversity. *Total annual research expenditures:* $5,019. *Unit head:* Dr. Tina Hancock, Head, 575-646-3043, Fax: 575-646-4343, E-mail: thancock@nmsu.edu. *Application contact:* Dr. Ivan de la Rosa, Graduate Program Coordinator, 575-646-2143, Fax: 575-646-4116, E-mail: lilo@nmsu.edu.
Website: http://socialwork.nmsu.edu/.

New York University, Silver School of Social Work, New York, NY 10003. Offers MSW, PhD, MSW/JD, MSW/MA, MSW/MPA, MSW/MPH. *Accreditation:* CSWE (one or more programs are accredited). Part-time and evening/weekend programs available. *Faculty:* 46 full-time (36 women), 141 part-time/adjunct (95 women). *Students:* 744 full-time (654 women), 313 part-time (262 women); includes 380 minority (103 Black or African American, non-Hispanic/Latino; 1 American Indian or Alaska Native, non-Hispanic/Latino; 82 Asian, non-Hispanic/Latino; 65 Hispanic/Latino; 2 Native Hawaiian or other Pacific Islander, non-Hispanic/Latino; 127 Two or more races, non-Hispanic/Latino), 62 international. Average age 27. 1,542 applicants, 77% accepted, 439 enrolled. In 2013, 548 master's, 13 doctorates awarded. *Degree requirements:* For doctorate, comprehensive exam, thesis/dissertation. *Entrance requirements:* For master's, bachelor's degree; for doctorate, GRE, MSW. Additional exam requirements/recommendations for international students: Required—TOEFL, IELTS, TWE. *Application deadline:* For fall admission, 1/9 priority date for domestic and international students; for spring admission, 10/3 priority date for domestic and international students. Applications are processed on a rolling basis. Application fee: $60. Electronic applications accepted. *Expenses:* Contact institution. *Financial support:* In 2013–14, 995 students received support. Career-related internships or fieldwork, Federal Work-Study, scholarships/grants, health care benefits, tuition waivers (partial), and unspecified assistantships available. Support available to part-time students. Financial award application deadline: 3/1; financial award applicants required to submit FAFSA. *Faculty research:* Social welfare policies, public health, aging, mental health, substance abuse. *Unit head:* Dr. Lynn Videka, Dean, 212-998-5959, Fax: 212-995-4172. *Application contact:* Robert W. Sommo, Jr., Assistant Dean for Enrollment Services, 212-998-5910, Fax: 212-995-4171, E-mail: ssw.admissions@nyu.edu.
Website: http://www.socialwork.nyu.edu/.

Norfolk State University, School of Graduate Studies, School of Social Work, Norfolk, VA 23504. Offers MSW, PhD. *Accreditation:* CSWE (one or more programs are accredited). Part-time programs available. *Students:* 149 full-time (139 women), 36 part-time (31 women); includes 145 minority (137 Black or African American, non-Hispanic/Latino; 1 Asian, non-Hispanic/Latino; 4 Hispanic/Latino; 3 Two or more races, non-Hispanic/Latino), 1 international. Average age 34. In 2013, 62 master's, 1 doctorate awarded. *Degree requirements:* For doctorate, thesis/dissertation. *Entrance requirements:* For master's, minimum GPA of 2.7. Additional exam requirements/recommendations for international students: Required—TOEFL. *Application deadline:* For fall admission, 3/1 for domestic students; for spring admission, 10/1 for domestic students. Application fee: $30. *Financial support:* Fellowships, research assistantships, teaching assistantships, career-related internships or fieldwork, Federal Work-Study, scholarships/grants, traineeships, and unspecified assistantships available. Financial award applicants required to submit FAFSA. *Unit head:* Dr. Marvin Feit, Dean, 757-823-8668. *Application contact:* Margaret Kerekes, Coordinator, 757-823-8696, E-mail: mdkerekes@nsu.edu.

North Carolina Agricultural and Technical State University, School of Graduate Studies, College of Arts and Sciences, Department of Sociology and Social Work, Greensboro, NC 27411. Offers MSW. Joint program with The University of North Carolina at Greensboro. *Accreditation:* CSWE. Part-time and evening/weekend programs available. *Degree requirements:* For master's, comprehensive exam, qualifying exam. *Entrance requirements:* For master's, GRE General Test.

North Carolina State University, Graduate School, College of Humanities and Social Sciences, Department of Social Work, Raleigh, NC 27695. Offers MSW. *Accreditation:* CSWE.

Northern Kentucky University, Office of Graduate Programs, College of Education and Human Services, Program in Social Work, Highland Heights, KY 41099. Offers MSW. Part-time and evening/weekend programs available. *Faculty:* 9 full-time (8 women), 9 part-time/adjunct (6 women). *Students:* 125 full-time (109 women), 3 part-time (all women); includes 18 minority (14 Black or African American, non-Hispanic/Latino; 1 Asian, non-Hispanic/Latino; 1 Hispanic/Latino; 2 Two or more races, non-Hispanic/Latino), 1 international. Average age 32. 78 applicants, 65% accepted, 48 enrolled. In 2013, 13 master's awarded. *Entrance requirements:* For master's, GRE (minimum score of 1000), minimum GPA of 3.0; undergraduate courses in psychology,

sociology, and statistics with minimum C average; 3 letters of recommendation; essay; letter of intent; resume; interview, essay. Additional exam requirements/recommendations for international students: Required—TOEFL (minimum score 550 paper-based; 79 iBT); Recommended—IELTS (minimum score 6.5). *Application deadline:* For fall admission, 4/1 for domestic students, 6/1 for international students. Application fee: $40. Electronic applications accepted. *Expenses:* Tuition, state resident: full-time $4446; part-time $494 per credit hour. Tuition, nonresident: full-time $6885; part-time $765 per credit hour. *Required fees:* $72 per semester. One-time fee: $125.50. Part-time tuition and fees vary according to course load, degree level, program and reciprocity agreements. *Financial support:* In 2013–14, 27 students received support. Unspecified assistantships available. Financial award application deadline: 5/1. *Faculty research:* Children and families experiencing homelessness, team based learning and diversity, impact of mentoring, photovoice and barriers to college, family directed structural therapy. *Unit head:* Dr. Holly Riffe, MSW Director, 859-572-5609, Fax: 859-572-6592, E-mail: riffeh@nku.edu. *Application contact:* Dr. Christian Gamm, Director of Graduate Programs, 859-572-6364, Fax: 859-572-6670, E-mail: gammc1@nku.edu.
Website: http://coehs.nku.edu/gradprograms/msw.html.

Northwest Nazarene University, Graduate Studies, Program in Social Work, Nampa, ID 83686-5897. Offers addiction studies (MSW); clinical mental health practice (MSW); management, community planning and social administration (MSW); medical social work (MSW). *Accreditation:* CSWE. Part-time programs available. Postbaccalaureate distance learning degree programs offered (no on-campus study). *Faculty:* 10 full-time (6 women), 5 part-time/adjunct (4 women). *Students:* 129 full-time (97 women), 33 part-time (29 women); includes 23 minority (3 Black or African American, non-Hispanic/Latino; 1 American Indian or Alaska Native, non-Hispanic/Latino; 12 Hispanic/Latino; 7 Two or more races, non-Hispanic/Latino). Average age 27. 152 applicants, 54% accepted, 73 enrolled. In 2013, 54 master's awarded. *Degree requirements:* For master's, comprehensive exam. *Application deadline:* Applications are processed on a rolling basis. Application fee: $50. Electronic applications accepted. *Expenses: Tuition:* Part-time $565 per credit. *Unit head:* Dr. Lawanna Lancaster, Director, 208-467-8679, E-mail: msw@nnu.edu. *Application contact:* Jodie Engel, Program Assistant, 208-467-8679, Fax: 208-467-8879, E-mail: jrodriguez-engel@nnu.edu.

The Ohio State University, Graduate School, College of Social Work, Columbus, OH 43210. Offers MSW, PhD. *Accreditation:* CSWE (one or more programs are accredited). Part-time programs available. *Faculty:* 30. *Students:* 401 full-time (334 women), 84 part-time (76 women); includes 92 minority (53 Black or African American, non-Hispanic/Latino; 1 American Indian or Alaska Native, non-Hispanic/Latino; 6 Asian, non-Hispanic/Latino; 16 Hispanic/Latino; 16 Two or more races, non-Hispanic/Latino), 14 international. Average age 30. In 2013, 252 master's, 4 doctorates awarded. *Degree requirements:* For master's, thesis optional; for doctorate, thesis/dissertation. *Entrance requirements:* For master's, GRE. Additional exam requirements/recommendations for international students: Required—TOEFL (minimum score 550 paper-based; 79 iBT), Michigan English Language Assessment Battery (minimum score 82); Recommended—IELTS (minimum score 7). *Application deadline:* For fall admission, 12/13 priority date for domestic students, 11/30 priority date for international students; for winter admission, 12/1 for domestic students, 11/1 for international students; for spring admission, 3/1 for domestic students, 2/1 for international students. Applications are processed on a rolling basis. Application fee: $60 ($70 for international students). Electronic applications accepted. *Financial support:* Fellowships, research assistantships, teaching assistantships, Federal Work-Study, institutionally sponsored loans, and unspecified assistantships available. Support available to part-time students. *Unit head:* Tom Gregoire, Dean, 614-292-9426, E-mail: gregoire.5@osu.edu. *Application contact:* Graduate Admissions, 614-292-6031, Fax: 614-292-3656, E-mail: gradadmissions@osu.edu.
Website: http://csw.osu.edu/.

The Ohio State University at Lima, Graduate Programs, Lima, OH 45804. Offers early childhood education (M Ed); education (MA); middle childhood education (M Ed); social work (MSW). Part-time programs available. *Faculty:* 37. *Students:* 8 full-time (6 women), 8 part-time (7 women). Average age 31. Terminal master's awarded for partial completion of doctoral program. *Degree requirements:* For master's, comprehensive exam (for some programs), thesis (for some programs). *Entrance requirements:* For master's, GRE, minimum GPA of 3.0. Additional exam requirements/recommendations for international students: Required—TOEFL (minimum score 550 paper-based, 79 iBT), IELTS (minimum score 7), or Michigan English Language Assessment Battery (minimum score 82). *Application deadline:* For fall admission, 6/1 for domestic and international students; for spring admission, 10/15 for domestic and international students. Applications are processed on a rolling basis. Application fee: $60 ($70 for international students). Electronic applications accepted. *Financial support:* Application deadline: 2/15. *Unit head:* Dr. Gregory Rose, Interim Dean and Director, 419-995-8481, E-mail: rose.9@osu.edu. *Application contact:* Graduate Admissions, 614-292-9444, Fax: 614-292-3895, E-mail: gradadmissions@osu.edu.

The Ohio State University–Mansfield Campus, Graduate Programs, Mansfield, OH 44906-1599. Offers early childhood education (M Ed); education (MA); middle childhood education (M Ed); social work (MSW). Part-time programs available. *Faculty:* 40. *Students:* 18 full-time (17 women), 30 part-time (29 women). Average age 31. *Degree requirements:* For master's, comprehensive exam (for some programs), thesis (for some programs). *Entrance requirements:* For master's, GRE, minimum GPA of 3.0. Additional exam requirements/recommendations for international students: Required—TOEFL (minimum 550 paper-based, 79 iBT), IELTS (minimum score 7) or Michigan English Language Assessment Battery (minimum score 82). *Application deadline:* For fall admission, 6/1 for domestic and international students; for spring admission, 10/15 for domestic and international students. Applications are processed on a rolling basis. Application fee: $60 ($70 for international students). Electronic applications accepted. *Financial support:* Teaching assistantships with full tuition reimbursements, Federal Work-Study, and scholarships/grants available. Support available to part-time students. Financial award application deadline: 2/15. *Unit head:* Dr. Stephen M. Gavazzi, Dean and Director, 419-755-4221, Fax: 419-755-4241, E-mail: gavazzi.1@osu.edu. *Application contact:* Graduate Admissions, 614-292-9444, Fax: 614-292-3895, E-mail: gradadmissions@osu.edu.

The Ohio State University–Newark Campus, Graduate Programs, Newark, OH 43055-1797. Offers early/middle childhood education (M Ed); education - teaching and learning (MA); social work (MSW). Part-time programs available. *Faculty:* 53. *Students:* 10 full-time (9 women), 27 part-time (24 women); includes 3 minority (1 Black or African American, non-Hispanic/Latino; 2 Hispanic/Latino). Average age 35. Terminal master's awarded for partial completion of doctoral program. *Degree requirements:* For master's, comprehensive exam (for some programs), thesis (for some programs). *Entrance requirements:* For master's, GRE, minimum GPA of 3.0. Additional exam requirements/recommendations for international students: Required—TOEFL (minimum score 550 paper-based; 79 iBT), IELTS (minimum score 7), or Michigan English Language Assessment Battery (minimum score 82). *Application deadline:* For fall admission, 6/1 for domestic and international students; for spring admission, 10/15 for domestic students, 2/1 for international students. Applications are processed on a rolling basis.

Application fee: $60 ($70 for international students). Electronic applications accepted. *Financial support:* Application deadline: 2/15. *Unit head:* Dr. William L. MacDonald, Dean/Director, 740-366-9333 Ext. 330, E-mail: macdonald.24@osu.edu. *Application contact:* Graduate Admissions, 614-292-9444, Fax: 614-292-3985, E-mail: gradadmissions@osu.edu.

Ohio University, Graduate College, College of Health Sciences and Professions, Department of Social and Public Health, Program in Social Work, Athens, OH 45701-2979. Offers MSW. *Accreditation:* CSWE. Part-time programs available. *Degree requirements:* For master's, fieldwork. *Entrance requirements:* For master's, GRE General Test or minimum GPA of 3.0, liberal arts background with coursework in human biology, statistics, and three social science areas; paid or volunteer work in human services. Additional exam requirements/recommendations for international students: Required—TOEFL (minimum score 620 paper-based; 105 iBT) or IELTS (minimum score 7.5). Electronic applications accepted. *Faculty research:* Violence, families, rural life.

Our Lady of the Lake University of San Antonio, Worden School of Social Service, San Antonio, TX 78207-4689. Offers MSW. *Accreditation:* CSWE. Part-time programs available. Postbaccalaureate distance learning degree programs offered (no on-campus study). *Faculty:* 9 full-time (8 women), 19 part-time/adjunct (13 women). *Students:* 341 full-time (312 women), 120 part-time (112 women); includes 210 minority (84 Black or African American, non-Hispanic/Latino; 2 American Indian or Alaska Native, non-Hispanic/Latino; 5 Asian, non-Hispanic/Latino; 117 Hispanic/Latino; 2 Native Hawaiian or other Pacific Islander, non-Hispanic/Latino). Average age 35. 447 applicants, 71% accepted, 244 enrolled. In 2013, 29 master's awarded. *Degree requirements:* For master's, thesis optional, practicum. *Entrance requirements:* For master's, GRE General Test or MAT. Additional exam requirements/recommendations for international students: Required—TOEFL. *Application deadline:* For fall admission, 4/2 priority date for domestic and international students; for spring admission, 11/1 priority date for domestic and international students; for summer admission, 2/1 priority date for domestic and international students. Applications are processed on a rolling basis. Application fee: $25 ($50 for international students). Electronic applications accepted. *Expenses: Tuition:* Full-time $9120; part-time $760 per credit. *Required fees:* $698; $334 per trimester. Tuition and fees vary according to course load, degree level, campus/location and program. *Financial support:* Research assistantships, career-related internships or fieldwork, Federal Work-Study, institutionally sponsored loans, scholarships/grants, and tuition waivers (partial) available. Financial award application deadline: 4/15. *Faculty research:* Cross-cultural social work practice, mental health, adult literacy, spirituality, maternal health care, experiential learning. *Unit head:* Dr. Cora Le-Doux, Director, 210-434-6711 Ext. 2228, E-mail: cle-doux@lake.ollusa.edu. *Application contact:* Graduate Admission, 210-431-3961 Ext. 2314, Fax: 210-431-4013, E-mail: gradadm@lake.ollusa.edu.
Website: http://www.ollusa.edu/s/1190/ollu.aspx?sid=1190&gid=1&pgid=1757.

Park University, School of Graduate and Professional Studies, Kansas City, MO 54105. Offers adult education (M Ed); business and government leadership (Graduate Certificate); business, government, and global society (MPA); communication and leadership (MA); creative and life writing (Graduate Certificate); disaster and emergency management (MPA, Graduate Certificate); educational leadership (M Ed); finance (MBA, Graduate Certificate); general business (MBA); global business (Graduate Certificate); healthcare administration (MHA); healthcare services management and leadership (Graduate Certificate); international business (MBA); language and literacy (M Ed), including English for speakers of other languages, special reading teacher/literacy coach; leadership of international healthcare organizations (Graduate Certificate); management information systems (MBA, Graduate Certificate); music performance (ADP, Graduate Certificate), including cello (MM, ADP), piano (MM, ADP), viola (MM, ADP), violin (MM, ADP); nonprofit and community services management (MPA); nonprofit leadership (Graduate Certificate); performance (MM), including cello (MM, ADP), piano (MM, ADP), viola (MM, ADP), violin (MM, ADP); public management (MPA); social work (MSW); teacher leadership (M Ed), including curriculum and assessment, instructional leader. Part-time and evening/weekend programs available. Postbaccalaureate distance learning degree programs offered (no on-campus study). *Students:* 862 full-time (482 women); includes 55 minority (30 Black or African American, non-Hispanic/Latino; 2 American Indian or Alaska Native, non-Hispanic/Latino; 4 Asian, non-Hispanic/Latino; 14 Hispanic/Latino; 5 Two or more races, non-Hispanic/Latino), 141 international. Average age 34. 497 applicants, 62% accepted, 119 enrolled. In 2013, 281 master's, 14 other advanced degrees awarded. *Degree requirements:* For master's, comprehensive exam (for some programs), thesis (for some programs), internship (for some programs); exam (for some programs). *Entrance requirements:* For master's, GRE or GMAT (for some programs), teacher certification (for some M Ed programs), letters of recommendation, essay, resume (for some programs). Additional exam requirements/recommendations for international students: Required—TOEFL (minimum score 550 paper-based; 79 iBT), IELTS (minimum score 6). *Application deadline:* For fall admission, 8/1 priority date for domestic students, 7/15 priority date for international students; for spring admission, 1/1 priority date for domestic students, 11/1 priority date for international students. Applications are processed on a rolling basis. Application fee: $50 ($100 for international students). Electronic applications accepted. *Financial support:* In 2013–14, 2 research assistantships with full tuition reimbursements (averaging $15,760 per year) were awarded. Financial award applicants required to submit FAFSA. *Unit head:* Dr. Laurie Dipadova-Stocks, Dean of Graduate and Professional Studies, 816-559-5624, Fax: 816-472-1173, E-mail: ldipadovastocks@park.edu. *Application contact:* Judith Appollis, Director of Graduate Admissions and Internationalization, School of Graduate and Professional Studies, 816-559-5627, Fax: 816-472-1173, E-mail: gradschool@park.edu.
Website: http://www.park.edu/grad.

Phillips Theological Seminary, Programs in Theology, Tulsa, OK 74116. Offers administration of church agencies (M Div); campus ministry (M Div); church-related social work (M Div); college and seminary teaching (M Div); global mission work (M Div); institutional chaplaincy (M Div); ministerial vocations in Christian education (M Div); ministry (D Min), including parish ministry, pastoral counseling, practices of ministry; ministry and culture (MAMC), including Christian education, congregational leadership, history and practice of Christian spirituality; theology, ethics, and culture; ministry of music (M Div); pastoral care and counseling (M Div); pastoral ministry (M Div); theological studies (MTS). *Accreditation:* ATS. Part-time programs available. Postbaccalaureate distance learning degree programs offered (minimal on-campus study). *Degree requirements:* For master's, thesis (for some programs); for doctorate, thesis/dissertation. *Entrance requirements:* For master's, minimum GPA of 2.5; for doctorate, M Div, minimum GPA of 3.0. *Faculty research:* Biblical studies, historical studies, theology and culture, practical theology, theology and film.

Pontifical Catholic University of Puerto Rico, College of Graduate Studies in Behavioral Science and Community Affairs, Program in Clinical Social Work, Ponce, PR 00717-0777. Offers MSW. *Accreditation:* CSWE. Part-time and evening/weekend programs available. *Entrance requirements:* For master's, EXADEP, 3 letters of recommendation, interview, minimum GPA of 2.75.

Social Work

Portland State University, Graduate Studies, Graduate School of Social Work, Portland, OR 97207-0751. Offers social work (MSW); social work and social research (PhD). *Accreditation:* CSWE (one or more programs are accredited). Part-time programs available. *Faculty:* 30 full-time (20 women), 30 part-time/adjunct (19 women). *Students:* 392 full-time (315 women), 135 part-time (118 women); includes 141 minority (26 Black or African American, non-Hispanic/Latino; 15 American Indian or Alaska Native, non-Hispanic/Latino; 16 Asian, non-Hispanic/Latino; 66 Hispanic/Latino; 18 Two or more races, non-Hispanic/Latino), 4 international. Average age 35. 704 applicants, 36% accepted, 209 enrolled. In 2013, 229 master's, 7 doctorates awarded. *Degree requirements:* For doctorate, comprehensive exam, thesis/dissertation, residency. *Entrance requirements:* For master's, minimum GPA of 3.0 in upper-division course work or 2.75 overall; for doctorate, GRE General Test, 4 references. Additional exam requirements/recommendations for international students: Required—TOEFL (minimum score 550 paper-based). *Application deadline:* For fall admission, 2/1 for domestic and international students. Application fee: $50. *Expenses:* Tuition, state resident: full-time $9207; part-time $341 per credit. Tuition, nonresident: full-time $14,391; part-time $533 per credit. *Required fees:* $1263; $22 per credit. $98 per quarter. One-time fee: $150. Tuition and fees vary according to program. *Financial support:* In 2013–14, 3 research assistantships with full and partial tuition reimbursements (averaging $10,580 per year), 5 teaching assistantships with full and partial tuition reimbursements (averaging $12,337 per year) were awarded; career-related internships or fieldwork, Federal Work-Study, scholarships/grants, tuition waivers (partial), and unspecified assistantships also available. Support available to part-time students. Financial award application deadline: 3/1; financial award applicants required to submit FAFSA. *Faculty research:* Child welfare; child mental health; social welfare policies and services; work, family, and dependent care; adult mental health. *Total annual research expenditures:* $302,847. *Unit head:* Dr. Laura B Nissen, Dean, 503-725-3997, Fax: 503-725-5545, E-mail: nissen@pdx.edu. *Application contact:* Janet Putnam, Director of Student Affairs, 503-725-5021, Fax: 503-725-5545, E-mail: putnamj@pdx.edu.
Website: http://www.ssw.pdx.edu/.

Quinnipiac University, College of Arts and Sciences, Program in Social Work, Hamden, CT 06518-1940. Offers MSW. Part-time and evening/weekend programs available. *Faculty:* 4 full-time (all women), 4 part-time/adjunct (3 women). *Students:* 8 full-time (7 women), 3 part-time (all women). 14 applicants, 79% accepted, 10 enrolled. *Entrance requirements:* For master's, bachelor's degree with at least 20 semester credits in liberal arts and a course in statistics with a grade of C or better; minimum GPA of 3.0. Additional exam requirements/recommendations for international students: Required—TOEFL (minimum score 575 paper-based; 90 iBT), IELTS (minimum score 6.5). *Application deadline:* For fall admission, 7/30 priority date for domestic students, 4/15 for international students; for spring admission, 12/15 priority date for domestic students, 9/15 for international students. Applications are processed on a rolling basis. Application fee: $45. Electronic applications accepted. *Expenses: Tuition:* Part-time $920 per credit. *Required fees:* $37 per credit. *Financial support:* In 2013–14, 6 students received support. Career-related internships or fieldwork, Federal Work-Study, scholarships/grants, and unspecified assistantships available. Support available to part-time students. Financial award applicants required to submit FAFSA. *Faculty research:* Older adult sexuality, social work practice in health settings, gerontology and social work, adolescent sexuality, prevention programs in social work practice, international social work, evidence-based treatments for children and families, organizational practice, inter-professional education, curriculum development in social work education and inter-professional practice, stress reduction approaches in clinical practice and professional education. *Unit head:* Deborah Rejent, MSW Program Director, E-mail: deborah.rejent@quinnipiac.edu. *Application contact:* Office of Graduate Admissions, 800-462-1944, Fax: 203-582-3443, E-mail: graduate@quinnipiac.edu.
Website: http://www.quinnipiac.edu/msw.

Radford University, College of Graduate and Professional Studies, Waldron College of Health and Human Services, School of Social Work, Radford, VA 24142. Offers MSW. *Accreditation:* CSWE. Part-time programs available. *Faculty:* 9 full-time (7 women), 8 part-time/adjunct (5 women). *Students:* 73 full-time (64 women), 47 part-time (38 women); includes 24 minority (20 Black or African American, non-Hispanic/Latino; 1 Asian, non-Hispanic/Latino; 2 Hispanic/Latino; 1 Two or more races, non-Hispanic/Latino), 2 international. Average age 31. 73 applicants, 60% accepted, 31 enrolled. In 2013, 38 master's awarded. *Degree requirements:* For master's, comprehensive exam. *Entrance requirements:* For master's, minimum GPA of 2.75, 3.0 in last 60 hours of upper-division coursework; 3 letters of reference; personal essay; case study; previous experience in the field of human services; legal/military history form; resume; official transcripts. Additional exam requirements/recommendations for international students: Required—TOEFL (minimum score 550 paper-based; 79 iBT). *Application deadline:* For fall admission, 2/15 priority date for domestic students, 12/1 for international students; for spring admission, 7/1 for international students. Applications are processed on a rolling basis. Application fee: $50. Electronic applications accepted. *Expenses:* Tuition, state resident: full-time $6800; part-time $283 per credit hour. Tuition, nonresident: full-time $15,610; part-time $627 per credit hour. *Required fees:* $2944; $123 per credit hour. Tuition and fees vary according to program. *Financial support:* In 2013–14, 22 students received support, including 19 research assistantships (averaging $4,737 per year), 2 teaching assistantships with partial tuition reimbursements available (averaging $10,500 per year); career-related internships or fieldwork, Federal Work-Study, institutionally sponsored loans, scholarships/grants, and unspecified assistantships also available. Financial award application deadline: 3/1; financial award applicants required to submit FAFSA. *Unit head:* Dr. Diane Hodge, Interim Director, 540-831-7689, Fax: 540-831-7670, E-mail: dmhodge@radford.edu. *Application contact:* Rebecca Conner, Director, Graduate Enrollment, 540-831-6296, Fax: 540-831-6061, E-mail: gradcollege@radford.edu.
Website: http://www.radford.edu/content/wchs/home/social-work.html.

Rhode Island College, School of Graduate Studies, School of Social Work, Providence, RI 02908-1991. Offers MSW. *Accreditation:* CSWE. Part-time programs available. *Faculty:* 8 full-time (6 women), 12 part-time/adjunct (8 women). *Students:* 93 full-time (80 women), 121 part-time (99 women); includes 35 minority (23 Black or African American, non-Hispanic/Latino; 1 Asian, non-Hispanic/Latino; 11 Hispanic/Latino). Average age 31. In 2013, 65 master's awarded. *Entrance requirements:* For master's, official transcripts, personal statement, 3 letters of recommendation. Additional exam requirements/recommendations for international students: Recommended—TOEFL (minimum score 550 paper-based; 79 iBT). *Application deadline:* For fall admission, 2/1 for domestic students. Applications are processed on a rolling basis. Application fee: $50. *Expenses:* Contact institution. *Financial support:* Career-related internships or fieldwork, Federal Work-Study, scholarships/grants, health care benefits, and unspecified assistantships available. Support available to part-time students. Financial award application deadline: 5/15; financial award applicants required to submit FAFSA. *Unit head:* Dr. Sue Pearlmutter, Dean, 401-456-8042, E-mail: spearlmutter@ric.edu. *Application contact:* Graduate Studies, 401-456-8700.
Website: http://www.ric.edu/socialWork/.

The Richard Stockton College of New Jersey, School of Graduate and Continuing Studies, Program in Social Work, Galloway, NJ 08205-9441. Offers MSW. Evening/weekend programs available. *Faculty:* 8 full-time (5 women), 3 part-time/adjunct (all women). *Students:* 55 full-time (49 women), 9 part-time (8 women); includes 25 minority (14 Black or African American, non-Hispanic/Latino; 1 Asian, non-Hispanic/Latino; 9 Hispanic/Latino; 1 Native Hawaiian or other Pacific Islander, non-Hispanic/Latino). Average age 33. 142 applicants, 49% accepted, 38 enrolled. In 2013, 35 master's awarded. *Degree requirements:* For master's, thesis optional, field work. *Entrance requirements:* Additional exam requirements/recommendations for international students: Required—TOEFL. *Application deadline:* For fall admission, 2/1 for domestic and international students. Application fee: $50. Electronic applications accepted. *Expenses: Tuition, area resident:* Part-time $559 per credit. Tuition, state resident: part-time $559 per credit. Tuition, nonresident: part-time $861 per credit. *Required fees:* $168.23 per credit. $75 per semester. Tuition and fees vary according to course load and degree level. *Financial support:* In 2013–14, 12 students received support, including 7 research assistantships; fellowships, career-related internships or fieldwork, Federal Work-Study, scholarships/grants, and unspecified assistantships also available. Financial award application deadline: 3/1; financial award applicants required to submit FAFSA. *Unit head:* Dr. Diane Falk, Program Director, 609-626-3640, E-mail: gradschool@stockton.edu. *Application contact:* Tara Williams, Assistant Director of Graduate Enrollment Management, 609-626-3640, Fax: 609-626-6050, E-mail: gradschool@stockton.edu.
Website: http://www.stockton.edu/grad.

Roberts Wesleyan College, Program in Social Work, Rochester, NY 14624-1997. Offers child and family practice (MSW); mental health practice (MSW). *Accreditation:* CSWE. *Entrance requirements:* For master's, minimum GPA of 2.75. *Application deadline:* For fall admission, 4/1 priority date for domestic students. Applications are processed on a rolling basis. Application fee: $35. *Expenses: Tuition:* Full-time $12,816; part-time $712 per credit hour. One-time fee: $300. Tuition and fees vary according to course load and program. *Financial support:* Fellowships, career-related internships or fieldwork, scholarships/grants, and tuition waivers (partial) available. Financial award applicants required to submit FAFSA. *Faculty research:* Religion and social work, family studies, values and ethics. *Unit head:* Dr. David Skiff, Chair, 585-594-6578, E-mail: skiffd@roberts.edu. *Application contact:* Beverly Keim, Graduate Admissions Coordinator, 585-594-6232, E-mail: keimb@roberts.edu.
Website: http://www.roberts.edu/graduate/programs/social-work-msw.aspx.

Rutgers, The State University of New Jersey, New Brunswick, School of Social Work, Piscataway, NJ 08854-8097. Offers MSW, PhD, JD/MSW, M Div/MSW. *Accreditation:* CSWE (one or more programs are accredited). Part-time programs available. *Degree requirements:* For doctorate, comprehensive exam, thesis/dissertation. *Entrance requirements:* For doctorate, GRE General Test. Additional exam requirements/recommendations for international students: Required—TOEFL. Electronic applications accepted. *Faculty research:* Family theory, adolescent development, child and adolescent mental health delivery systems, poverty and employment policy.

St. Ambrose University, College of Education and Health Sciences, Program in Social Work, Davenport, IA 52803-2898. Offers MSW. *Accreditation:* CSWE. Part-time and evening/weekend programs available. *Degree requirements:* For master's, comprehensive exam (for some programs), thesis or alternative, integration projects. *Entrance requirements:* For master's, minimum GPA of 3.0, course work in statistics, bachelor's degree in liberal arts. Additional exam requirements/recommendations for international students: Required—TOEFL. Electronic applications accepted. *Faculty research:* Social work practice, cults/sects, family therapy, developmental disabilities.

St. Catherine University, Graduate Programs, Program in Social Work, St. Paul, MN 55105. Offers MSW. Program offered jointly with University of St. Thomas. *Accreditation:* CSWE. Part-time and evening/weekend programs available. *Degree requirements:* For master's, clinical research paper. *Entrance requirements:* For master's, minimum GPA of 3.0. Additional exam requirements/recommendations for international students: Required—Michigan English Language Assessment Battery or TOEFL (minimum score 600 paper-based; 100 iBT). *Expenses:* Contact institution.

St. Cloud State University, School of Graduate Studies, School of Health and Human Services, Department of Social Work, St. Cloud, MN 56301-4498. Offers MSW. *Accreditation:* CSWE. Part-time programs available. *Entrance requirements:* For master's, minimum GPA of 3.0.

Saint Leo University, Graduate Studies in Social Work, Saint Leo, FL 33574-6665. Offers advanced clinical practice (MSW). Postbaccalaureate distance learning degree programs offered (minimal on-campus study). *Faculty:* 6 full-time (5 women), 10 part-time/adjunct (9 women). *Students:* 109 full-time (93 women), 74 part-time (62 women); includes 71 minority (54 Black or African American, non-Hispanic/Latino; 1 Asian, non-Hispanic/Latino; 13 Hispanic/Latino; 3 Two or more races, non-Hispanic/Latino). Average age 37. In 2013, 48 master's awarded. *Entrance requirements:* For master's, GRE (minimum score 1000) or MAT (minimum score 410) if undergraduate GPA less than 3.0, 3 recommendations; minimum GPA of 3.0 in undergraduate work, resume, and personal statement (for regular two-year full-time MSW); BSW from CSWE-accredited program with minimum GPA of 3.25 in social work completed in the last 5 years and minimum B average in upper-level social work courses (for one-year full-time advanced standing MSW). *Application deadline:* For fall admission, 3/15 for domestic and international students. Application fee: $80. Electronic applications accepted. *Expenses:* Contact institution. *Financial support:* In 2013–14, 2 students received support. Career-related internships or fieldwork, Federal Work-Study, and health care benefits available. Financial award application deadline: 3/1. *Unit head:* Dr. Cindy Lee, Director of Graduate Studies in Social Work, 352-588-8869, Fax: 352-588-8289, E-mail: cindy.lee@saintleo.edu. *Application contact:* Joshua Stagner, Director of Graduate Admission, 800-707-8846, Fax: 352-588-7873, E-mail: grad.admissions@saintleo.edu.
Website: http://online.saintleo.edu/admissions/graduate/social-work-programs.aspx.

Saint Louis University, Graduate Education, College of Education and Public Service, School of Social Work, St. Louis, MO 63103-2097. Offers MSW. *Accreditation:* CSWE. Part-time programs available. *Entrance requirements:* For master's, minimum GPA of 3.0, letters of recommendation. Additional exam requirements/recommendations for international students: Required—TOEFL (minimum score 550 paper-based). *Expenses:* Contact institution. *Faculty research:* Gerontology, mental health issues, child welfare (especially abuse and neglect), social justice, and peace making, homelessness.

Salem State University, School of Graduate Studies, Program in Social Work, Salem, MA 01970-5353. Offers MSW. *Accreditation:* CSWE. Part-time and evening/weekend programs available. *Students:* 116 full-time (103 women), 116 part-time (101 women); includes 44 minority (9 Black or African American, non-Hispanic/Latino; 1 American Indian or Alaska Native, non-Hispanic/Latino; 6 Asian, non-Hispanic/Latino; 25 Hispanic/Latino; 3 Two or more races, non-Hispanic/Latino), 5 international. 241 applicants, 51% accepted, 73 enrolled. In 2013, 72 master's awarded. *Entrance requirements:* For master's, GRE, MAT. Additional exam requirements/recommendations for international students: Required—TOEFL (minimum score 550 paper-based; 80 iBT) or IELTS (minimum score 5.5). *Application deadline:* For fall admission, 2/15 for domestic students. Applications are processed on a rolling basis. Application fee: $50. *Financial support:* Career-related internships or fieldwork, Federal Work-Study, scholarships/

grants, and unspecified assistantships available. Support available to part-time students. Financial award application deadline: 5/1; financial award applicants required to submit FAFSA. *Application contact:* Dr. Lee A. Brossoit, Assistant Dean of Graduate Admissions, 978-542-6675, Fax: 978-542-7215, E-mail: lbrossoit@salemstate.edu.
Website: http://www.salemstate.edu/academics/schools/12457.php.

Salisbury University, Program in Social Work, Salisbury, MD 21801-6837. Offers MSW. *Accreditation:* CSWE. Part-time and evening/weekend programs available. Postbaccalaureate distance learning degree programs offered (no on-campus study). *Faculty:* 7 full-time (5 women), 23 part-time/adjunct (22 women). *Students:* 152 full-time (144 women), 36 part-time (31 women); includes 36 minority (27 Black or African American, non-Hispanic/Latino; 1 American Indian or Alaska Native, non-Hispanic/Latino; 1 Asian, non-Hispanic/Latino; 2 Hispanic/Latino; 5 Two or more races, non-Hispanic/Latino), 1 international. Average age 32. 222 applicants, 53% accepted, 116 enrolled. In 2013, 73 master's awarded. *Entrance requirements:* For master's, 3 letters of recommendation, resume, personal statement. Additional exam requirements/recommendations for international students: Required—TOEFL (minimum score 550 paper-based; 79 iBT), IELTS (minimum score 6.5). *Application deadline:* For fall admission, 2/3 for domestic and international students. Application fee: $50. Electronic applications accepted. *Expenses: Tuition, area resident:* Part-time $342 per credit hour. Tuition, state resident: part-time $342 per credit hour. Tuition, nonresident: part-time $631 per credit hour. *Required fees:* $76 per credit hour. Tuition and fees vary according to program. *Financial support:* In 2013–14, 25 students received support, including 2 teaching assistantships with full tuition reimbursements available (averaging $5,000 per year); career-related internships or fieldwork, institutionally sponsored loans, scholarships/grants, and unspecified assistantships also available. Support available to part-time students. Financial award application deadline: 3/1; financial award applicants required to submit FAFSA. *Faculty research:* Pediatric primary care and behavioral health integration, juvenile violence prediction and treatment, effective approaches to teaching theoretical content and theorizing skills assessing competency, domestic and intimate partner violence prevention, teaching effectiveness online and face-to-face using online and distance education. *Unit head:* Dr. Deborah Matthews, Chair of Department of Social Work, 410-548-3993, E-mail: damatthews@salisbury.edu. *Application contact:* Susan Mareski, Administrative Assistant, 410-677-5363, E-mail: smmareski@salisbury.edu.
Website: http://www.salisbury.edu/socialwork.

San Diego State University, Graduate and Research Affairs, College of Health and Human Services, School of Social Work, San Diego, CA 92182. Offers MSW, JD/MSW, MSW/MPH. JD/MSW offered jointly with California Western School of Law. *Accreditation:* CSWE. Part-time programs available. *Degree requirements:* For master's, comprehensive exam, thesis optional. *Entrance requirements:* For master's, GRE General Test. Additional exam requirements/recommendations for international students: Required—TOEFL. Electronic applications accepted. *Faculty research:* Child maltreatment, substance abuse, neighborhood studies, child welfare.

San Francisco State University, Division of Graduate Studies, College of Health and Social Sciences, School of Social Work, San Francisco, CA 94132-1722. Offers MSW. *Accreditation:* CSWE. Part-time programs available. *Students:* Average age 33. *Degree requirements:* For master's, thesis optional. *Application deadline:* Applications are processed on a rolling basis. *Financial support:* Career-related internships or fieldwork and Federal Work-Study available. *Unit head:* Dr. Eileen Levy, Director, 415-405-4084, E-mail: efl@sfsu.edu. *Application contact:* Prof. Sonja Lenz-Rashid, MSW Admissions Chair, 415-405-2459, E-mail: srlenz@sfsu.edu.
Website: http://socwork.sfsu.edu/.

San Jose State University, Graduate Studies and Research, College of Applied Sciences and Arts, School of Social Work, San Jose, CA 95192-0001. Offers MSW, Certificate. *Accreditation:* CSWE. Electronic applications accepted.

Savannah State University, Master of Social Work Program, Savannah, GA 31404. Offers MSW. *Accreditation:* CSWE. *Faculty:* 5 full-time (3 women), 2 part-time/adjunct (1 woman). *Students:* 84 full-time (71 women); includes 59 minority (56 Black or African American, non-Hispanic/Latino; 3 Hispanic/Latino). Average age 33. 51 applicants, 94% accepted, 36 enrolled. In 2013, 26 master's awarded. *Degree requirements:* For master's, field practicum, seminar course for each semester in field placement. *Entrance requirements:* For master's, GRE General Test (minimum score of 3.0 in analytical writing portion), minimum GPA of 2.8, degree from accredited institution with liberal arts courses, official transcripts, directed essay, 3 letters of recommendation. Additional exam requirements/recommendations for international students: Required—TOEFL. *Application deadline:* For fall admission, 5/23 for domestic students, 5/15 for international students; for spring admission, 10/31 for domestic students, 10/1 for international students. Applications are processed on a rolling basis. Application fee: $25. *Expenses:* Tuition, state resident: full-time $4482; part-time $187 per credit hour. Tuition, nonresident: full-time $16,660; part-time $694 per credit hour. *Required fees:* $1716; $858 per term. *Financial support:* Career-related internships or fieldwork, Federal Work-Study, institutionally sponsored loans, scholarships/grants, health care benefits, and unspecified assistantships available. Financial award applicants required to submit FAFSA. *Faculty research:* Clinical and administrative social work. *Unit head:* Dr. Juan Paz, Chair, 912-358-3288, E-mail: pazj@savannahstate.edu. *Application contact:* Dr. Shinaz Jindani, MSW Program Coordinator, 912-358-3251.
Website: http://www.savannahstate.edu/prospective-student/degrees-grad-sw.shtml.

Shippensburg University of Pennsylvania, School of Graduate Studies, College of Education and Human Services, Department of Social Work and Gerontology, Shippensburg, PA 17257-2299. Offers social work (MSW). *Accreditation:* CSWE. Part-time and evening/weekend programs available. *Faculty:* 6 full-time (5 women), 2 part-time/adjunct (1 woman). *Students:* 23 full-time (22 women), 32 part-time (30 women); includes 7 minority (4 Black or African American, non-Hispanic/Latino; 1 Asian, non-Hispanic/Latino; 1 Hispanic/Latino; 1 Two or more races, non-Hispanic/Latino). Average age 32. 63 applicants, 67% accepted, 32 enrolled. In 2013, 17 master's awarded. *Degree requirements:* For master's, thesis, field practicum. *Entrance requirements:* For master's, GRE or MAT (if GPA is below 2.8), 3 professional references; resume; written academic and professional statement; course work in human biology, economics, government/political science, psychology, sociology/anthropology and statistics. Additional exam requirements/recommendations for international students: Required—TOEFL (minimum score 580 paper-based); Recommended—IELTS (minimum score 6). *Application deadline:* For fall admission, 4/30 for international students; for spring admission, 9/30 for international students. Applications are processed on a rolling basis. Application fee: $45. Electronic applications accepted. *Expenses: Tuition, area resident:* Part-time $442 per credit. Tuition, state resident: part-time $442 per credit. Tuition, nonresident: part-time $663 per credit. *Required fees:* $127 per credit. *Financial support:* In 2013–14, 5 research assistantships with full tuition reimbursements (averaging $5,000 per year) were awarded; career-related internships or fieldwork, scholarships/grants, unspecified assistantships, and resident hall director and student payroll positions also available. Support available to part-time students. Financial award application deadline: 3/1; financial award applicants required to submit FAFSA. *Unit head:* Dr. Deborah F. Jacobs, Co-Director, MU-SU Master of Social Work Program, 717-477-1276, Fax: 717-477-4051, E-mail: dfjaco@ship.edu. *Application contact:* Jeremy R. Goshorn, Assistant Dean of Graduate Admissions, 717-477-1231, Fax: 717-477-4016, E-mail: jrgoshorn@ship.edu.
Website: http://www.ship.edu/social_work/.

Simmons College, School of Social Work, Boston, MA 02115. Offers assistive technology (MS Ed, Ed S); behavior analysis (MS, PhD, Ed S); education (MA, CAGS); language and literacy (MS Ed, Ed S); social work (MSW, PhD); special education (MS Ed), including moderate disabilities, severe disabilities; teaching (MAT), including elementary education, general education, high school education; teaching English as a second language (MA, CAGS); urban leadership (MSW); MSW/MBA. *Accreditation:* CSWE (one or more programs are accredited). Part-time programs available. Postbaccalaureate distance learning degree programs offered (no on-campus study). *Students:* 519 full-time (454 women), 703 part-time (604 women); includes 192 minority (61 Black or African American, non-Hispanic/Latino; 1 American Indian or Alaska Native, non-Hispanic/Latino; 35 Asian, non-Hispanic/Latino; 71 Hispanic/Latino; 2 Native Hawaiian or other Pacific Islander, non-Hispanic/Latino; 22 Two or more races, non-Hispanic/Latino), 16 international. 952 applicants, 66% accepted, 353 enrolled. In 2013, 159 master's, 2 doctorates awarded. Terminal master's awarded for partial completion of doctoral program. *Degree requirements:* For master's, thesis (for some programs); for doctorate, comprehensive exam (for some programs), thesis/dissertation (for some programs). *Entrance requirements:* For master's, GRE, MAT, MTEL (for different programs); for doctorate, GRE, BCBA Analyst Exam. Additional exam requirements/recommendations for international students: Required—TOEFL (minimum score 600 paper-based; 100 iBT). *Application deadline:* Applications are processed on a rolling basis. Application fee: $45. Electronic applications accepted. *Financial support:* Teaching assistantships and scholarships/grants available. *Unit head:* Dr. Stefan Krug, Dean, 617-521-3924. *Application contact:* Carlos D. Frontado, Director of Admissions, 617-521-3920, Fax: 617-521-3980, E-mail: ssw@simmons.edu.
Website: http://www.simmons.edu/ssw/.

Smith College, School for Social Work, Northampton, MA 01063. Offers MSW, PhD. *Accreditation:* CSWE (one or more programs are accredited). *Students:* 277 full-time (239 women), 59 part-time (43 women); includes 90 minority (25 Black or African American, non-Hispanic/Latino; 3 American Indian or Alaska Native, non-Hispanic/Latino; 13 Asian, non-Hispanic/Latino; 32 Hispanic/Latino; 17 Two or more races, non-Hispanic/Latino), 11 international. 467 applicants, 51% accepted, 139 enrolled. *Degree requirements:* For master's, thesis; for doctorate, thesis/dissertation. *Entrance requirements:* For doctorate, MAT. Additional exam requirements/recommendations for international students: Required—TOEFL. *Application deadline:* For fall admission, 2/21 for domestic students. Applications are processed on a rolling basis. Application fee: $60. *Expenses:* Contact institution. *Financial support:* In 2013–14, 227 students received support. Career-related internships or fieldwork, institutionally sponsored loans, and scholarships/grants available. Financial award application deadline: 3/20; financial award applicants required to submit FAFSA. *Faculty research:* Social work practice, human behavior in the social environment, social welfare policy, social work research. *Unit head:* Dr. Carolyn Jacobs, Dean/Professor, 413-585-7977, E-mail: cjacobs@smith.edu. *Application contact:* Irene Rodriguez Martin, Director of Enrollment Management and Continuing Education, 413-585-7960, Fax: 413-585-7994, E-mail: imartin@smith.edu.
Website: http://www.smith.edu/ssw/.

Southern Adventist University, School of Social Work, Collegedale, TN 37315-0370. Offers MSW. Postbaccalaureate distance learning degree programs offered.

Southern Connecticut State University, School of Graduate Studies, School of Health and Human Services, Department of Social Work, New Haven, CT 06515-1355. Offers MSW, MSW/MS. *Accreditation:* CSWE. Part-time and evening/weekend programs available. *Degree requirements:* For master's, thesis. *Entrance requirements:* For master's, minimum undergraduate QPA of 3.0 in graduate major field, interview. Electronic applications accepted. *Faculty research:* Social work practice; social service development; services for women, the aging, children, and families in educational and health care systems.

Southern Illinois University Carbondale, Graduate School, College of Education and Human Services, School of Social Work, Carbondale, IL 62901-4701. Offers MSW, JD/MSW. *Accreditation:* CSWE. *Faculty:* 10 full-time (6 women). *Students:* 104 full-time (80 women), 18 part-time (13 women); includes 29 minority (25 Black or African American, non-Hispanic/Latino; 1 American Indian or Alaska Native, non-Hispanic/Latino; 1 Asian, non-Hispanic/Latino; 2 Hispanic/Latino), 5 international. Average age 30. 61 applicants, 61% accepted, 32 enrolled. In 2013, 67 master's awarded. *Entrance requirements:* For master's, GRE General Test, minimum GPA of 2.7. Additional exam requirements/recommendations for international students: Required—TOEFL. *Application deadline:* For fall admission, 3/1 for domestic students. Applications are processed on a rolling basis. Application fee: $50. *Financial support:* In 2013–14, 19 students received support, including 6 research assistantships with full tuition reimbursements available; fellowships with full tuition reimbursements available, teaching assistantships with full tuition reimbursements available, career-related internships or fieldwork, and tuition waivers (full) also available. Financial award application deadline: 5/1. *Faculty research:* Service delivery systems, comparative race relations, advocacy research, gerontology, child welfare and health. *Unit head:* Dr. Elaine Jurkowski, Director of Graduate Studies, 618-453-2243, E-mail: etjurkow@siu.edu. *Application contact:* Judy Wright, Assistant to Graduate Director, 618-453-1202, Fax: 618-453-1219, E-mail: mmmjw@siu.edu.
Website: http://socialwork.siu.edu/.

Southern Illinois University Edwardsville, Graduate School, College of Arts and Sciences, Department of Social Work, Edwardsville, IL 62026. Offers school social work (MSW); social work (MSW). *Accreditation:* CSWE. Part-time and evening/weekend programs available. *Faculty:* 10 full-time (6 women). *Students:* 43 full-time (35 women), 26 part-time (24 women); includes 17 minority (11 Black or African American, non-Hispanic/Latino; 1 American Indian or Alaska Native, non-Hispanic/Latino; 2 Asian, non-Hispanic/Latino; 2 Hispanic/Latino; 1 Two or more races, non-Hispanic/Latino). 78 applicants, 58% accepted. In 2013, 32 master's awarded. *Degree requirements:* For master's, final exam, capstone course. *Entrance requirements:* Additional exam requirements/recommendations for international students: Required—TOEFL (minimum score 550 paper-based, 79 iBT), IELTS (minimum score 6.5), Michigan Test of English Language Proficiency or PTE. *Application deadline:* For fall admission, 2/15 for domestic and international students. Application fee: $30. Electronic applications accepted. *Expenses:* Tuition, state resident: full-time $3551. Tuition, nonresident: full-time $8378. *Financial support:* In 2013–14, 15 students received support, including 3 fellowships with full tuition reimbursements available (averaging $8,370 per year), 3 research assistantships with full tuition reimbursements available (averaging $9,585 per year), 9 teaching assistantships with full tuition reimbursements available (averaging $9,585 per year); institutionally sponsored loans, scholarships/grants, and unspecified assistantships also available. Financial award application deadline: 3/1; financial award applicants required to submit FAFSA. *Unit head:* Dr. Kathleen Tunney, Chair, 618-650-5428, E-mail: ktunney@siue.edu. *Application contact:* Dr. Bryan Duckham, Director, 618-650-3104, E-mail: bduckha@siue.edu.
Website: http://www.siue.edu/artsandsciences/socialwork/grad_msw.shtml.

Social Work

Southern University at New Orleans, School of Graduate Studies, New Orleans, LA 70126-1009. Offers criminal justice (MA); management information systems (MS); museum studies (MA); social work (MSW). *Accreditation:* CSWE. Part-time and evening/weekend programs available. *Degree requirements:* For master's, thesis. *Entrance requirements:* For master's, GRE/GMAT. Additional exam requirements/recommendations for international students: Required—TOEFL.

Spalding University, Graduate Studies, College of Social Sciences and Humanities, School of Social Work, Louisville, KY 40203-2188. Offers MSW. *Accreditation:* CSWE. Evening/weekend programs available. *Faculty:* 7 full-time (5 women), 4 part-time/adjunct (all women). *Students:* 43 full-time (36 women), 4 part-time (all women); includes 23 minority (17 Black or African American, non-Hispanic/Latino; 6 Two or more races, non-Hispanic/Latino). Average age 32. 47 applicants, 57% accepted, 22 enrolled. In 2013, 29 master's awarded. *Degree requirements:* For master's, thesis or alternative, project presentation. *Entrance requirements:* For master's, transcripts, letters of recommendation, personal essay, personal interview. Additional exam requirements/recommendations for international students: Required—TOEFL (minimum score 535 paper-based). *Application deadline:* For fall admission, 5/1 priority date for domestic students. Application fee: $30. *Expenses: Tuition:* Full-time $21,450. *Required fees:* $810. Tuition and fees vary according to course load, degree level, program and student level. *Financial support:* In 2013–14, 1 research assistantship (averaging $3,390 per year) was awarded; career-related internships or fieldwork, Federal Work-Study, and scholarships/grants also available. Financial award application deadline: 3/30; financial award applicants required to submit FAFSA. *Faculty research:* Addictions, spirituality, feminist studies, mental retardation, action research. *Unit head:* Dr. Kevin Borders, Interim Chair, 502-873-4482, E-mail: kborders@spalding.edu. *Application contact:* Angela Lucear, Administrative Assistant, 502-588-7183, Fax: 502-585-7158, E-mail: alucear@spalding.edu.
Website: http://spalding.edu/academics/social-work/.

Springfield College, Graduate Programs, School of Social Work, Springfield, MA 01109-3797. Offers advanced generalist (weekday and weekend) (MSW); advanced standing (MSW); JD/MSW. *Accreditation:* CSWE. Part-time programs available. *Faculty:* 12 full-time, 8 part-time/adjunct. *Students:* 214 full-time, 146 part-time. 288 applicants, 81% accepted, 155 enrolled. In 2013, 103 master's awarded. *Degree requirements:* For master's, comprehensive exam. *Entrance requirements:* Additional exam requirements/recommendations for international students: Required—TOEFL (minimum score 550 paper-based); Recommended—IELTS (minimum score 6). *Application deadline:* For fall admission, 3/1 for domestic and international students. Applications are processed on a rolling basis. Application fee: $50. Electronic applications accepted. *Expenses: Tuition:* Full-time $13,620; part-time $908 per credit. *Financial support:* Fellowships with partial tuition reimbursements, teaching assistantships with partial tuition reimbursements, career-related internships or fieldwork, Federal Work-Study, institutionally sponsored loans, and unspecified assistantships available. Financial award application deadline: 3/1; financial award applicants required to submit FAFSA. *Unit head:* Dr. Francine Vecchiolla, Dean, 413-748-3057, Fax: 413-748-3069, E-mail: fvecchiolla@springfieldcollege.edu. *Application contact:* Evelyn Cohen, Associate Director of Graduate Admissions, 413-748-3479, Fax: 413-748-3694, E-mail: ecohen@springfieldcollege.edu.

Stephen F. Austin State University, Graduate School, College of Applied Arts and Science, School of Social Work, Nacogdoches, TX 75962. Offers MSW. *Accreditation:* CSWE. *Degree requirements:* For master's, comprehensive exam, thesis optional. *Entrance requirements:* For master's, GRE General Test, interview. Additional exam requirements/recommendations for international students: Required—TOEFL (minimum score 550 paper-based).

Stony Brook University, State University of New York, Stony Brook University Medical Center, Health Sciences Center, School of Social Welfare, Doctoral Program in Social Welfare, Stony Brook, NY 11794. Offers PhD. *Faculty:* 14 full-time (8 women), 42 part-time/adjunct (24 women). *Students:* 26 full-time (21 women), 4 part-time (3 women); includes 7 minority (5 Black or African American, non-Hispanic/Latino; 1 Asian, non-Hispanic/Latino; 1 Two or more races, non-Hispanic/Latino), 1 international. 13 applicants, 38% accepted, 4 enrolled. In 2013, 3 doctorates awarded. *Degree requirements:* For doctorate, thesis/dissertation. *Entrance requirements:* For doctorate, GRE General Test, three letters of reference, personal statement, writing sample. Additional exam requirements/recommendations for international students: Required—TOEFL. *Application deadline:* For fall admission, 2/1 for domestic students. Application fee: $100. *Expenses:* Tuition, state resident: full-time $9870; part-time $411 per credit. Tuition, nonresident: full-time $18,350; part-time $765 per credit. *Financial support:* In 2013–14, 2 fellowships were awarded; teaching assistantships also available. Financial award application deadline: 2/1. *Unit head:* Dr. Frances L. Brisbane, Dean, 631-444-2139, Fax: 631-444-7565, E-mail: frances.brisbane@stonybrook.edu. *Application contact:* Jennifer Davidson, Coordinator, 631-444-8361, Fax: 631-444-7565, E-mail: jennifer.davidson@stonybrook.edu.
Website: http://socialwelfare.stonybrookmedicine.edu/.

Stony Brook University, State University of New York, Stony Brook University Medical Center, Health Sciences Center, School of Social Welfare, Master's Program in Social Work, Stony Brook, NY 11794. Offers MSW. *Accreditation:* CSWE. *Faculty:* 14 full-time (8 women), 42 part-time/adjunct (24 women). *Students:* 352 full-time (285 women), 15 part-time (14 women); includes 125 minority (52 Black or African American, non-Hispanic/Latino; 1 American Indian or Alaska Native, non-Hispanic/Latino; 11 Asian, non-Hispanic/Latino; 57 Hispanic/Latino; 4 Two or more races, non-Hispanic/Latino), 2 international. Average age 35. 527 applicants, 38% accepted, 195 enrolled. In 2013, 156 master's awarded. *Degree requirements:* For master's, project or thesis. *Entrance requirements:* For master's, interview. *Application deadline:* For fall admission, 2/1 for domestic students. Application fee: $100. *Expenses:* Tuition, state resident: full-time $9870; part-time $411 per credit. Tuition, nonresident: full-time $18,350; part-time $765 per credit. *Financial support:* Teaching assistantships available. Financial award application deadline: 3/1. *Unit head:* Dr. Frances L. Brisbane, Dean, 631-444-2139, Fax: 631-444-7565, E-mail: fbrisbane@notes.cc.sunysb.edu. *Application contact:* Kathy Albin, Director of Admission and Student Services, 631-444-3141, Fax: 631-444-7565, E-mail: kathleen.albin@stonybrook.edu.
Website: http://socialwelfare.stonybrookmedicine.edu/.

Syracuse University, Falk College of Sport and Human Dynamics, Dual Master's Program in Social Work and Marriage and Family Therapy, Syracuse, NY 13244. Offers MSW/MA. *Students:* 1 (woman) full-time. Average age 44. 7 applicants, 14% accepted. *Entrance requirements:* Additional exam requirements/recommendations for international students: Required—TOEFL or IELTS. *Application deadline:* For fall admission, 3/15 priority date for domestic and international students; for summer admission, 1/15 priority date for domestic students, 1/15 for international students. *Unit head:* Prof. Carrie Smith, Associate Professor/Director, School of Social Work, 315-443-5562, Fax: 315-443-2562, E-mail: falk@syr.edu. *Application contact:* Felicia Otero, Director of College Admissions, 315-443-5555, Fax: 315-443-2562, E-mail: falk@syr.edu.
Website: http://falk.syr.edu/SocialWork/MastersDual.aspx.

Syracuse University, Falk College of Sport and Human Dynamics, Program in Social Work, Syracuse, NY 13244. Offers MSW. *Accreditation:* CSWE. Part-time and evening/weekend programs available. *Students:* 127 full-time (117 women), 89 part-time (73 women); includes 41 minority (25 Black or African American, non-Hispanic/Latino; 2 American Indian or Alaska Native, non-Hispanic/Latino; 2 Asian, non-Hispanic/Latino; 9 Hispanic/Latino; 3 Two or more races, non-Hispanic/Latino), 3 international. Average age 31. 37 applicants, 76% accepted, 13 enrolled. In 2013, 88 master's awarded. *Degree requirements:* For master's, thesis or alternative, field placement. *Entrance requirements:* Additional exam requirements/recommendations for international students: Required—TOEFL (minimum score 100 iBT). *Application deadline:* For fall admission, 3/15 priority date for domestic and international students; for summer admission, 1/15 priority date for domestic and international students. Applications are processed on a rolling basis. Application fee: $75. Electronic applications accepted. *Financial support:* Fellowships with full tuition reimbursements, research assistantships with full and partial tuition reimbursements, teaching assistantships with full and partial tuition reimbursements, and tuition waivers available. Financial award application deadline: 1/1; financial award applicants required to submit FAFSA. *Faculty research:* Aging policy, healthcare, criminal justice, disability, rights of passage. *Unit head:* Dr. Carrie Smith, Acting Director, 315-443-5555, E-mail: falk@syr.edu. *Application contact:* Felicia Otero, Information Contact, 315-443-5555, E-mail: falk@syr.edu.
Website: http://falk.syr.edu/SocialWork/Default.aspx.

Temple University, College of Health Professions and Social Work, School of Social Work, Philadelphia, PA 19122. Offers MSW. *Accreditation:* CSWE. Part-time and evening/weekend programs available. *Faculty:* 29 full-time (14 women). *Students:* 354 full-time (295 women), 187 part-time (158 women); includes 199 minority (137 Black or African American, non-Hispanic/Latino; 17 Asian, non-Hispanic/Latino; 30 Hispanic/Latino; 15 Two or more races, non-Hispanic/Latino), 3 international. 534 applicants, 46% accepted, 120 enrolled. In 2013, 199 master's awarded. *Degree requirements:* For master's, internship, field practicum. *Entrance requirements:* For master's, minimum GPA of 3.0, 3 letters of recommendation, statement of goals, resume. Additional exam requirements/recommendations for international students: Required—TOEFL (minimum score 550 paper-based; 79 iBT). *Application deadline:* For fall admission, 3/15 priority date for domestic students, 2/15 for international students; for spring admission, 11/1 priority date for domestic students, 10/15 for international students; for summer admission, 3/15 for domestic students, 2/15 for international students. Applications are processed on a rolling basis. Application fee: $60. Electronic applications accepted. *Financial support:* In 2013–14, 6 research assistantships with full and partial tuition reimbursements (averaging $16,549 per year) were awarded; career-related internships or fieldwork, Federal Work-Study, scholarships/grants, traineeships, tuition waivers (partial), unspecified assistantships, and field assistantships also available. Support available to part-time students. Financial award application deadline: 1/1. *Faculty research:* Child welfare, alcoholism, social work practice, developmental disabilities, human sexuality, mental health services, health and corrections. *Total annual research expenditures:* $2.7 million. *Unit head:* Dr. Jeffrey Draine, Chair, 215-204-5443, Fax: 215-204-9606, E-mail: jetpak@temple.edu. *Application contact:* Erin Brocious, 215-204-1962, E-mail: erin.brocious@temple.edu.
Website: http://chpsw.temple.edu/ssa/home.

Tennessee State University, The School of Graduate Studies and Research, College of Public Service and Urban Affairs, Nashville, TN 37209-1561. Offers human resource management (MPS); public administration (MPA, PhD); social work (MSW); strategic leadership (MPS); training and development (MPS). *Accreditation:* NASPAA (one or more programs are accredited). Part-time and evening/weekend programs available. *Students:* 49 full-time (28 women), 108 part-time (67 women); includes 90 minority (86 Black or African American, non-Hispanic/Latino; 2 American Indian or Alaska Native, non-Hispanic/Latino; 1 Asian, non-Hispanic/Latino; 1 Hispanic/Latino). Average age 35. *Degree requirements:* For master's, comprehensive exam, thesis optional; for doctorate, comprehensive exam, thesis/dissertation. *Entrance requirements:* For master's, GRE General Test, minimum GPA of 2.5, writing sample; for doctorate, GRE General Test, minimum GPA of 3.25, writing sample. *Application deadline:* For fall admission, 3/1 priority date for domestic students. Application fee: $25. *Financial support:* Research assistantships and teaching assistantships available. Support available to part-time students. *Faculty research:* Total quality management and process improvement, national health care policy and administration, starting non-profit ventures, public service ethics, state education financing across the U.S. public. *Unit head:* Dr. Michael Harris, Dean, 615-963-7201, Fax: 615-963-7275, E-mail: mharris50@tnstate.edu. *Application contact:* Deborah Chisom, Director of Graduate Admissions, 615-963-5962, Fax: 615-963-5963, E-mail: dchiscom@tnstate.edu.
Website: http://www.tnstate.edu/cpsua/.

Texas A&M University–Commerce, Graduate School, College of Education and Human Services, Department of Social Work, Commerce, TX 75429-3011. Offers MSW. *Accreditation:* CSWE. *Entrance requirements:* For master's, GRE General Test. *Expenses:* Tuition, state resident: full-time $3630; part-time $2420 per year. Tuition, nonresident: full-time $9948; part-time $6632.16 per year. *Required fees:* $1006 per year. Tuition and fees vary according to course load.

Texas State University, Graduate School, College of Applied Arts, Program in Social Work, San Marcos, TX 78666. Offers MSW. *Accreditation:* CSWE. *Faculty:* 18 full-time (13 women), 2 part-time/adjunct (both women). *Students:* 117 full-time (104 women), 104 part-time (94 women); includes 92 minority (23 Black or African American, non-Hispanic/Latino; 2 Asian, non-Hispanic/Latino; 62 Hispanic/Latino; 5 Two or more races, non-Hispanic/Latino). Average age 32. 352 applicants, 35% accepted, 75 enrolled. In 2013, 116 master's awarded. *Degree requirements:* For master's, comprehensive exam. *Entrance requirements:* For master's, minimum GPA of 3.0 in last 60 hours of course work, 3 recommendation forms, curriculum vitae. Additional exam requirements/recommendations for international students: Required—TOEFL (minimum score 550 paper-based; 78 iBT). *Application deadline:* For fall admission, 6/15 priority date for domestic students, 6/1 for international students; for spring admission, 10/15 for domestic students, 10/1 for international students. Applications are processed on a rolling basis. Application fee: $40 ($90 for international students). Electronic applications accepted. *Expenses: Tuition,* state resident: full-time $6663; part-time $278 per credit hour. Tuition, nonresident: full-time $15,159; part-time $632 per credit hour. *Required fees:* $1872; $54 per credit hour. $306 per term. Tuition and fees vary according to course load. *Financial support:* In 2013–14, 160 students received support, including 9 research assistantships (averaging $11,603 per year), 2 teaching assistantships (averaging $11,425 per year); career-related internships or fieldwork, Federal Work-Study, institutionally sponsored loans, and unspecified assistantships also available. Support available to part-time students. Financial award application deadline: 4/1; financial award applicants required to submit FAFSA. *Unit head:* Dr. Angela Ausbrooks, MSW Program Coordinator, 512-245-9067, E-mail: aa16@txstate.edu. *Application contact:* Dr. Andrea Golato, Dean of the Graduate College, 512-245-2581, Fax: 512-245-8365, E-mail: gradcollege@txstate.edu.
Website: http://www.socialwork.txstate.edu.

Thompson Rivers University, Program in Social Work, Kamloops, BC V2C 0C8, Canada. Offers MSW.

Touro College, Graduate School of Social Work, New York, NY 10010. Offers MSW. *Students:* 101 full-time (80 women), 173 part-time (142 women); includes 122 minority (81 Black or African American, non-Hispanic/Latino; 2 American Indian or Alaska Native, non-Hispanic/Latino; 5 Asian, non-Hispanic/Latino; 30 Hispanic/Latino; 1 Native Hawaiian or other Pacific Islander, non-Hispanic/Latino; 3 Two or more races, non-Hispanic/Latino), 3 international. *Unit head:* Dr. Steven Huberman, Dean, 212-463-0400 Ext. 5269, E-mail: msw@touro.edu. *Application contact:* Dr. Bradley Karasik, Director of Recruitment, Admissions and Enrollment Management, 212-463-0400 Ext. 5630, Fax: 212-627-3693, E-mail: bradley.karasik@touro.edu.
Website: http://www.touro.edu/msw/.

Troy University, Graduate School, College of Education, Program in Counseling and Psychology, Troy, AL 36082. Offers agency counseling (Ed S); clinical mental health (MS); community counseling (MS, Ed S); corrections counseling (MS); rehabilitation counseling (MS); school psychology (MS, Ed S); school psychometry (MS); social service counseling (MS); student affairs counseling (MS); substance abuse counseling (MS). *Accreditation:* ACA; CORE; NCATE. Part-time and evening/weekend programs available. *Faculty:* 63 full-time (34 women), 4 part-time/adjunct (2 women). *Students:* 344 full-time (284 women), 616 part-time (502 women); includes 615 minority (520 Black or African American, non-Hispanic/Latino; 3 American Indian or Alaska Native, non-Hispanic/Latino; 5 Asian, non-Hispanic/Latino; 68 Hispanic/Latino; 19 Two or more races, non-Hispanic/Latino). Average age 34. 293 applicants, 88% accepted, 156 enrolled. In 2013, 253 master's awarded. *Degree requirements:* For master's, comprehensive exam, thesis. *Entrance requirements:* For master's, GRE (minimum score of 850 on old exam or 290 on new exam), GMAT (minimum score of 380), or MAT (minimum score of 385), bachelor's degree; minimum undergraduate GPA of 2.5 or 3.0 on last 30 semester hours, letter of recommendation. Additional exam requirements/recommendations for international students: Required—TOEFL (minimum score 523 paper-based; 70 iBT), IELTS (minimum score 6). *Application deadline:* Applications are processed on a rolling basis. Application fee: $50. Electronic applications accepted. *Expenses:* Tuition, state resident: full-time $6084; part-time $338 per credit hour. Tuition, nonresident: full-time $12,168; part-time $676 per credit hour. *Required fees:* $630; $35 per credit hour. $50 per semester. *Unit head:* Dr. Andrew Creamer, Chair, 334-670-3350, Fax: 334-670-3291, E-mail: drcreamer@troy.edu. *Application contact:* Brenda K. Campbell, Director of Graduate Admissions, 334-670-3178, Fax: 334-670-3733, E-mail: bcamp@troy.edu.

Tulane University, School of Social Work, New Orleans, LA 70118-5669. Offers MSW, JD/MSW, MSW/MPH. *Accreditation:* CSWE (one or more programs are accredited). Part-time programs available. *Degree requirements:* For master's, thesis. *Entrance requirements:* Additional exam requirements/recommendations for international students: Required—TOEFL. Electronic applications accepted.

Universidad del Este, Graduate School, Carolina, PR 00984. Offers accounting (MBA); adult education (M Ed); agribusiness (MBA); criminal justice and criminology (MA); curriculum and instruction - early education (M Ed); curriculum and instruction - elementary (M Ed); curriculum and instruction - English (M Ed); curriculum and instruction - Spanish (M Ed); human resources (MBA); information security management (MBA); information technology and Web business development (MBA); management (MBA); public policy (MPA); social work (MA), including clinical social work; special education (M Ed); strategic leadership (MBA). *Students:* 464 full-time (322 women), 669 part-time (499 women); all minorities (all Hispanic/Latino). Average age 35. 693 applicants, 61% accepted, 332 enrolled. In 2013, 228 master's awarded. *Unit head:* Jose R. Clintron, Dean, 787-257-7373 Ext. 3007, E-mail: ue_jcintron@suagm.edu. *Application contact:* Clotilde Santiago, Director of Admissions, 787-257-7373 Ext. 3400, E-mail: ue_csantiago@suagm.edu.

Université de Moncton, Faculty of Arts and Social Sciences, School of Social Work, Moncton, NB E1A 3E9, Canada. Offers MSW. *Degree requirements:* For master's, one foreign language, major paper. *Entrance requirements:* For master's, minimum GPA of 3.0. *Faculty research:* Burnout and education, mental health (institutionalization), unemployment's effect on youth, women and health services.

Université de Montréal, Faculty of Arts and Sciences, School of Social Service, Program in Social Administration, Montréal, QC H3C 3J7, Canada. Offers DESS. Electronic applications accepted.

Université de Sherbrooke, Faculty of Letters and Human Sciences, Department of Social Service, Sherbrooke, QC J1K 2R1, Canada. Offers MSS.

Université du Québec à Montréal, Graduate Programs, Program in Social Intervention, Montréal, QC H3C 3P8, Canada. Offers MA. Part-time programs available. *Degree requirements:* For master's, thesis. *Entrance requirements:* For master's, appropriate bachelor's degree or equivalent, proficiency in French.

Université du Québec en Abitibi-Témiscamingue, Graduate Programs, Program in Social Work, Rouyn-Noranda, QC J9X 5E4, Canada. Offers MSW.

Université du Québec en Outaouais, Graduate Programs, Program in Social Work, Gatineau, QC J8X 3X7, Canada. Offers MA. *Degree requirements:* For master's, thesis (for some programs).

Université Laval, Faculty of Social Sciences, School of Social Work, Programs in Social Work, Québec, QC G1K 7P4, Canada. Offers M Serv Soc, PhD. Terminal master's awarded for partial completion of doctoral program. *Degree requirements:* For master's, thesis (for some programs); for doctorate, comprehensive exam, thesis/dissertation. *Entrance requirements:* For master's and doctorate, knowledge of French, comprehension of written English. Electronic applications accepted.

University at Albany, State University of New York, School of Social Welfare, Albany, NY 12222-0001. Offers MSW, PhD, MSW/MA. *Accreditation:* CSWE (one or more programs are accredited). Part-time and evening/weekend programs available. *Degree requirements:* For doctorate, thesis/dissertation. *Entrance requirements:* For doctorate, GRE General Test. Additional exam requirements/recommendations for international students: Required—TOEFL (minimum score 550 paper-based). Electronic applications accepted. *Faculty research:* Welfare reform, homelessness, children and families, mental health, substance abuse.

University at Buffalo, the State University of New York, Graduate School, School of Social Work, Buffalo, NY 14260. Offers social welfare (PhD); social work (MSW); JD/MSW; MBA/MSW; MPH/MSW. *Accreditation:* CSWE (one or more programs are accredited). Part-time programs available. Postbaccalaureate distance learning degree programs offered (minimal on-campus study). *Faculty:* 24 full-time (17 women), 50 part-time/adjunct (39 women). *Students:* 290 full-time (247 women), 172 part-time (137 women); includes 62 minority (41 Black or African American, non-Hispanic/Latino; 3 American Indian or Alaska Native, non-Hispanic/Latino; 8 Asian, non-Hispanic/Latino; 8 Hispanic/Latino; 2 Native Hawaiian or other Pacific Islander, non-Hispanic/Latino), 28 international. Average age 30. 447 applicants, 75% accepted, 255 enrolled. In 2013, 181 master's, 5 doctorates awarded. *Median time to degree:* Of those who began their doctoral program in fall 2005, 100% received their degree in 8 years or less. *Degree requirements:* For master's, 900 hours of field work; for doctorate, comprehensive exam, thesis/dissertation. *Entrance requirements:* For master's, 24 credits of course work in liberal arts; for doctorate, GRE General Test, MSW or equivalent. Additional exam

requirements/recommendations for international students: Required—TOEFL (minimum score 600 paper-based; 100 iBT). *Application deadline:* For fall admission, 3/1 priority date for domestic and international students. Applications are processed on a rolling basis. Application fee: $75. Electronic applications accepted. *Financial support:* In 2013–14, 97 students received support, including 5 fellowships with full tuition reimbursements available (averaging $10,900 per year), 6 research assistantships with full tuition reimbursements available (averaging $15,000 per year), 7 teaching assistantships with full tuition reimbursements available (averaging $1,000 per year); Federal Work-Study, scholarships/grants, health care benefits, tuition waivers (partial), unspecified assistantships, and instructorships and research grants (for PhD students) also available. Financial award application deadline: 4/30; financial award applicants required to submit FAFSA. *Faculty research:* Trauma, substance abuse, child welfare, aging, human rights. *Total annual research expenditures:* $1.1 million. *Unit head:* Dr. Nancy J. Smyth, Dean, 716-645-3381, Fax: 716-645-3883, E-mail: sw-dean@buffalo.edu. *Application contact:* Maria Carey, Admissions Processor, 716-645-3381, Fax: 716-645-3456, E-mail: sw-info@buffalo.edu.
Website: http://www.socialwork.buffalo.edu.

See Display on next page and Close-Up on page 1725.

The University of Akron, Graduate School, College of Health Professions, School of Social Work, Akron, OH 44325. Offers MSW. *Accreditation:* CSWE. *Faculty:* 6 full-time (3 women), 51 part-time/adjunct (36 women). *Students:* 103 full-time (90 women), 23 part-time (19 women); includes 29 minority (20 Black or African American, non-Hispanic/Latino; 2 Asian, non-Hispanic/Latino; 5 Hispanic/Latino; 2 Two or more races, non-Hispanic/Latino), 1 international. Average age 31. 98 applicants, 44% accepted, 36 enrolled. In 2013, 54 master's awarded. *Entrance requirements:* For master's, undergraduate major in social work or related field, three letters of recommendation, essay. Additional exam requirements/recommendations for international students: Required—TOEFL (minimum score 550 paper-based; 79 iBT). *Application deadline:* For fall admission, 2/15 for domestic and international students. Application fee: $40 ($60 for international students). Electronic applications accepted. *Expenses:* Tuition, state resident: full-time $7430; part-time $412.80 per credit hour. Tuition, nonresident: full-time $12,722; part-time $706.80 per credit hour. *Required fees:* $53 per credit hour. $12 per semester. Tuition and fees vary according to course load and program. *Financial support:* In 2013–14, 9 teaching assistantships with full tuition reimbursements were awarded; Federal Work-Study also available. *Faculty research:* Spirituality and alternative healing, child welfare education and training, ethics and social work practice, evidence-based social work practice, social work continuing education. *Total annual research expenditures:* $13,052. *Unit head:* Dr. Timothy McCarragher, Director, 330-972-5976, E-mail: mccarra@uakron.edu. *Application contact:* Dr. Mark Tausig, Associate Dean, 330-972-6266, Fax: 330-972-6475, E-mail: mtausig@uakron.edu.
Website: http://www.uakron.edu/socialwork/.

The University of Alabama, Graduate School, School of Social Work, Tuscaloosa, AL 35487-0314. Offers MSW, PhD. *Accreditation:* CSWE (one or more programs are accredited). Postbaccalaureate distance learning degree programs offered (minimal on-campus study). *Faculty:* 28 full-time (22 women). *Students:* 304 full-time (263 women), 48 part-time (39 women); includes 125 minority (106 Black or African American, non-Hispanic/Latino; 1 American Indian or Alaska Native, non-Hispanic/Latino; 3 Asian, non-Hispanic/Latino; 8 Hispanic/Latino; 7 Two or more races, non-Hispanic/Latino), 9 international. Average age 30. 460 applicants, 47% accepted, 150 enrolled. In 2013, 203 master's, 3 doctorates awarded. *Degree requirements:* For doctorate, comprehensive exam, thesis/dissertation. *Entrance requirements:* For master's, GRE or MAT (if GPA less than 3.0), minimum GPA of 2.5; for doctorate, GRE, minimum GPA of 3.0. Additional exam requirements/recommendations for international students: Required—TOEFL (minimum score 79 iBT), IELTS. *Application deadline:* For fall admission, 2/1 priority date for domestic and international students; for spring admission, 9/1 priority date for domestic and international students; for summer admission, 9/1 priority date for domestic students, 2/1 priority date for international students. Applications are processed on a rolling basis. Application fee: $50 ($60 for international students). Electronic applications accepted. *Expenses:* Tuition, state resident: full-time $9450. Tuition, nonresident: full-time $23,950. *Financial support:* In 2013–14, 113 students received support, including 6 research assistantships with full tuition reimbursements available (averaging $12,744 per year), 5 teaching assistantships with full tuition reimbursements available (averaging $12,744 per year); career-related internships or fieldwork, scholarships/grants, traineeships, health care benefits, and unspecified assistantships also available. Financial award application deadline: 2/1; financial award applicants required to submit FAFSA. *Faculty research:* Children and adolescents at risk, trauma, gerontology, child welfare policy, health. *Total annual research expenditures:* $134,350. *Unit head:* Dr. Lucinda L. Roff, Dean, 205-348-3924, Fax: 205-348-9419, E-mail: lroff@sw.ua.edu. *Application contact:* Casey Barnes, Admissions Coordinator, 205-348-8413, Fax: 205-348-9419, E-mail: cbarnes@sw.ua.edu.
Website: http://www.socialwork.ua.edu/.

University of Alaska Anchorage, College of Health, School of Social Work, Anchorage, AK 99508. Offers clinical social work practice (Certificate); social work (MSW); social work management (Certificate). *Accreditation:* CSWE. Part-time and evening/weekend programs available. Postbaccalaureate distance learning degree programs offered (no on-campus study). *Degree requirements:* For master's, comprehensive exam (for some programs), thesis or alternative, research project. *Entrance requirements:* For master's, GRE General Test, writing sample. Additional exam requirements/recommendations for international students: Required—TOEFL (minimum score 550 paper-based). Electronic applications accepted. *Expenses:* Contact institution.

University of Arkansas, Graduate School, J. William Fulbright College of Arts and Sciences, School of Social Work, Fayetteville, AR 72701-1201. Offers MSW. *Accreditation:* CSWE. *Entrance requirements:* For master's, GRE General Test. Electronic applications accepted.

University of Arkansas at Little Rock, Graduate School, College of Professional Studies, School of Social Work, Program in Social Work, Little Rock, AR 72204-1099. Offers advanced direct practice (MSW); management and community practice (MSW). *Accreditation:* CSWE. *Entrance requirements:* For master's, GRE General Test or MAT. *Expenses:* Tuition, state resident: full-time $5690; part-time $284.50 per credit hour. Tuition, nonresident: full-time $13,030; part-time $651.50 per credit hour. *Required fees:* $1121; $672 per term. One-time fee: $40 full-time.

The University of British Columbia, Faculty of Arts and Faculty of Graduate Studies, School of Social Work, Vancouver, BC V6T 1Z2, Canada. Offers MSW, PhD. *Degree requirements:* For master's, thesis or essay; for doctorate, comprehensive exam, thesis/dissertation. *Entrance requirements:* For master's, BSW; for doctorate, MSW. Additional exam requirements/recommendations for international students: Required—TOEFL (minimum score 580 paper-based; 93 iBT). Electronic applications accepted. *Expenses:* Tuition, area resident: Full-time $8000 Canadian dollars. *Faculty research:* Gerontology, family resources, diversity, social inequality.

University of Calgary, Faculty of Graduate Studies, Faculty of Social Work, Calgary, AB T2N 1N4, Canada. Offers MSW, PhD, Postgraduate Diploma. *Degree requirements:*

Social Work

For master's, thesis (for some programs); for doctorate, thesis/dissertation, candidacy exam. *Entrance requirements:* For master's, BSW, minimum undergraduate GPA of 3.4 (1 year program), minimum GPA of 3.5 (2 year program); for doctorate, minimum graduate GPA of 3.5, MSW (preferred); for Postgraduate Diploma, MSW, minimum graduate GPA of 3.5. Additional exam requirements/recommendations for international students: Required—TOEFL (paper-based 550) or IELTS (7). Electronic applications accepted. *Faculty research:* Family violence, direct practice, gerontology, child welfare, community development.

University of California, Berkeley, Graduate Division, School of Social Welfare, Berkeley, CA 94720-1500. Offers MSW, PhD, MSW/PhD. *Accreditation:* CSWE (one or more programs are accredited). Terminal master's awarded for partial completion of doctoral program. *Degree requirements:* For master's, thesis optional; for doctorate, thesis/dissertation, qualifying exam. *Entrance requirements:* For master's and doctorate, GRE General Test, minimum GPA of 3.0, 3 letters of recommendation. Additional exam requirements/recommendations for international students: Required—TOEFL, TWE. *Faculty research:* Child welfare, law and social welfare, minority mental health, social welfare policy analysis, health services.

University of California, Los Angeles, Graduate Division, School of Public Affairs, Program in Social Welfare, Los Angeles, CA 90095. Offers MSW, PhD, JD/MSW. *Accreditation:* CSWE (one or more programs are accredited). *Degree requirements:* For master's, comprehensive exam, research project; for doctorate, thesis/dissertation, oral and written qualifying exams. *Entrance requirements:* For master's, GRE General Test, minimum GPA of 3.0; for doctorate, GRE General Test, minimum undergraduate GPA of 3.0. Additional exam requirements/recommendations for international students: Required—TOEFL. Electronic applications accepted.

University of Central Florida, College of Health and Public Affairs, School of Social Work, Orlando, FL 32816. Offers children's services (Certificate); military social work (Certificate); social work (MSW); social work administration (Certificate). *Accreditation:* CSWE. Part-time and evening/weekend programs available. *Faculty:* 19 full-time (16 women), 20 part-time/adjunct (14 women). *Students:* 252 full-time (219 women), 89 part-time (76 women); includes 147 minority (73 Black or African American, non-Hispanic/Latino; 4 Asian, non-Hispanic/Latino; 62 Hispanic/Latino; 8 Two or more races, non-Hispanic/Latino), 3 international. Average age 30. 271 applicants, 75% accepted, 142 enrolled. In 2013, 143 master's, 1 other advanced degree awarded. *Degree requirements:* For master's, thesis or alternative, field education. *Entrance requirements:* For master's, resume. Additional exam requirements/recommendations for international students: Required—TOEFL. *Application deadline:* For fall admission, 3/1 for domestic students. Application fee: $30. Electronic applications accepted. *Financial support:* In 2013–14, 4 students received support, including 1 fellowship with partial tuition reimbursement available (averaging $10,000 per year), 3 research assistantships with partial tuition reimbursements available (averaging $8,300 per year); career-related internships or fieldwork, Federal Work-Study, institutionally sponsored loans, and unspecified assistantships also available. Financial award application deadline: 3/1; financial award applicants required to submit FAFSA. *Unit head:* Dr. Bonnie Yegidis, Director, 407-823-2114, E-mail: bonnie.yegidis@ucf.edu. *Application contact:* Barbara Rodriguez Lamas, Director, Admissions and Student Services, 407-823-2766, Fax: 407-823-6442, E-mail: gradadmissions@ucf.edu.
Website: http://www.cohpa.ucf.edu/social/.

University of Chicago, School of Social Service Administration, Chicago, IL 60637. Offers social service administration (PhD); social work (AM); AM/M Div; MBA/AM; MPP/AM. *Accreditation:* CSWE (one or more programs are accredited). Part-time and evening/weekend programs available. *Faculty:* 34 full-time (21 women), 23 part-time/adjunct (15 women). *Students:* 466 full-time (378 women), 17 part-time (12 women); includes 119 minority (48 Black or African American, non-Hispanic/Latino; 5 American Indian or Alaska Native, non-Hispanic/Latino; 29 Asian, non-Hispanic/Latino; 26 Hispanic/Latino; 2 Native Hawaiian or other Pacific Islander, non-Hispanic/Latino; 9 Two or more races, non-Hispanic/Latino), 28 international. 747 applicants, 53% accepted, 207 enrolled. In 2013, 226 master's, 12 doctorates awarded. *Degree requirements:* For master's, 2 field placements; for doctorate, comprehensive exam, thesis/dissertation. *Entrance requirements:* For master's, 3 letters of recommendation; for doctorate, GRE General Test, writing sample, 4 letters of recommendation. Additional exam requirements/recommendations for international students: Required—TOEFL (minimum score 600 paper-based; 104 iBT), IELTS (minimum score 7). *Application deadline:* For fall admission, 1/15 priority date for domestic and international students. Applications are processed on a rolling basis. Application fee: $60 ($70 for international students). Electronic applications accepted. *Expenses:* Contact institution. *Financial support:* In 2013–14, 415 students received support, including 20 research assistantships with full and partial tuition reimbursements available (averaging $15,000 per year), 20 teaching assistantships with full and partial tuition reimbursements available (averaging $12,000 per year); fellowships, career-related internships or fieldwork, Federal Work-Study, institutionally sponsored loans, scholarships/grants, health care benefits, and unspecified assistantships also available. Support available to part-time students. Financial award application deadline: 4/15; financial award applicants required to submit FAFSA. *Faculty research:* Family treatment, mental health, the aged, child welfare, health administration. *Unit head:* Dr. Neil Guterman, Dean, 773-702-1420. *Application contact:* Laura Chavez Hardy, Director of Admissions, 773-702-1492, Fax: 773-834-4751, E-mail: lchardy@uchicago.edu.
Website: http://www.ssa.uchicago.edu/.

University of Cincinnati, Graduate School, School of Social Work, Cincinnati, OH 45221. Offers MSW. *Accreditation:* CSWE. Part-time programs available. *Entrance requirements:* Additional exam requirements/recommendations for international students: Required—TOEFL. Electronic applications accepted. *Faculty research:* Fatherhood, mediation, mental illness, child welfare, elderly.

University of Denver, Graduate School of Social Work, Denver, CO 80208-7100. Offers animal-assisted social work (Certificate); couples and family therapy (Certificate); social work (MSW, PhD); social work with Latinos/as (Certificate). Certificate in couples and family therapy offered in cooperation with the Denver Family Institute. *Accreditation:* CSWE (one or more programs are accredited). Part-time and evening/weekend programs available. *Faculty:* 29 full-time (20 women), 84 part-time/adjunct (70 women). *Students:* 488 full-time (438 women), 15 part-time (11 women); includes 83 minority (13 Black or African American, non-Hispanic/Latino; 4 American Indian or Alaska Native, non-Hispanic/Latino; 1 Asian, non-Hispanic/Latino; 56 Hispanic/Latino; 1 Native Hawaiian or other Pacific Islander, non-Hispanic/Latino; 8 Two or more races, non-Hispanic/Latino), 1 international. Average age 28. In 2013, 238 master's, 7 doctorates, 142 other advanced degrees awarded. *Degree requirements:* For doctorate, comprehensive exam, thesis/dissertation. *Entrance requirements:* For master's, bachelor's degree in social work (for advanced standing program only); 20 undergraduate semester hours in the arts and humanities, social/behavioral sciences, and biological sciences; for doctorate, master's degree in social work or in one of the social sciences with substantial professional experience in the social work field; two-years of post-master's practice experience (preferred). Additional exam requirements/recommendations for international students: Required—TOEFL (minimum score 587 paper-based; 95 iBT). *Application deadline:* For fall admission, 1/15 priority date for domestic students. Applications are processed on a rolling basis. Application fee: $65. Electronic applications accepted. *Financial support:* In 2013–14, 451 students received support, including 13 teaching assistantships with full and partial tuition reimbursements available (averaging $30,954 per year); Federal Work-Study, scholarships/grants, and

unspecified assistantships also available. Support available to part-time students. Financial award application deadline: 2/15; financial award applicants required to submit FAFSA. *Faculty research:* Child welfare, adolescent development, mental health, international development, gerontology. *Total annual research expenditures:* $4.2 million. *Unit head:* Dr. James Herbert Williams, Dean, 303-871-2203, E-mail: james.herbert@du.edu. *Application contact:* Colin Schneider, Director of Admission and Financial Aid, 303-871-3634, Fax: 303-871-2845, E-mail: gssw-admission@du.edu. Website: http://www.du.edu/socialwork/.

University of Georgia, School of Social Work, Athens, GA 30602. Offers MA, MSW, PhD, Certificate. *Accreditation:* CSWE (one or more programs are accredited). Part-time and evening/weekend programs available. *Degree requirements:* For master's, thesis or alternative; for doctorate, one foreign language, thesis/dissertation. *Entrance requirements:* For master's and doctorate, GRE General Test. Electronic applications accepted. *Faculty research:* Juvenile justice, substance abuse, civil rights and social justice, gerontology, social policy.

University of Guam, Office of Graduate Studies, College of Natural and Applied Sciences, Program in Social Work, Mangilao, GU 96923. Offers MSW.

University of Hawaii at Manoa, Graduate Division, School of Social Work, Honolulu, HI 96822. Offers social welfare (PhD); social work (MSW). *Accreditation:* CSWE (one or more programs are accredited). Part-time programs available. *Degree requirements:* For doctorate, comprehensive exam, thesis/dissertation. *Entrance requirements:* For doctorate, master's degree (MSW preferred), minimum GPA of 3.0. Additional exam requirements/recommendations for international students: Required—TOEFL (minimum score 560 paper-based; 83 iBT), IELTS (minimum score 5). *Faculty research:* Health, mental health, AIDS, substance abuse, rural health, community-based research, social policy.

University of Houston, Graduate School of Social Work, Houston, TX 77204. Offers MSW, PhD. *Accreditation:* CSWE (one or more programs are accredited). Part-time programs available. *Degree requirements:* For master's, 900 clock hours of field experience, integrative paper. *Entrance requirements:* For master's, GRE, minimum GPA of 3.0 in last 60 hours, bachelor's degree. Additional exam requirements/recommendations for international students: Required—TOEFL (minimum score 550 paper-based; 79 iBT). *Faculty research:* Health care, gerontology, political social work, mental health, children and families.

University of Illinois at Chicago, Graduate College, Jane Addams College of Social Work, Chicago, IL 60607-7128. Offers MSW, PhD. *Accreditation:* CSWE (one or more programs are accredited). Part-time programs available. *Faculty:* 25 full-time (16 women), 9 part-time/adjunct (7 women). *Students:* 375 full-time (321 women), 108 part-time (92 women); includes 210 minority (74 Black or African American, non-Hispanic/Latino; 21 Asian, non-Hispanic/Latino; 96 Hispanic/Latino; 19 Two or more races, non-Hispanic/Latino), 7 international. Average age 28. 1,011 applicants, 56% accepted, 275 enrolled. In 2013, 200 master's, 3 doctorates awarded. Terminal master's awarded for partial completion of doctoral program. *Degree requirements:* For doctorate, thesis/dissertation. *Entrance requirements:* For master's, GMAT, minimum GPA of 2.75; for doctorate, GRE General Test or MAT, minimum GPA of 2.75. Additional exam requirements/recommendations for international students: Required—TOEFL. *Application deadline:* For fall admission, 2/1 priority date for domestic and international students. Applications are processed on a rolling basis. Application fee: $40 ($50 for international students). Electronic applications accepted. *Expenses:* Tuition, state resident: full-time $11,066; part-time $3689 per term. Tuition, nonresident: full-time $23,064; part-time $7688 per term. *Required fees:* $3004; $1190 per term. Tuition and fees vary according to course level and program. *Financial support:* Fellowships with full tuition reimbursements, research assistantships with full tuition reimbursements, teaching assistantships with full tuition reimbursements, Federal Work-Study, scholarships/grants, traineeships, tuition waivers (full), and unspecified assistantships available. Financial award applicants required to submit FAFSA. *Unit head:* Dr. Creasie Finney Hairston, Dean, 312-996-3219. *Application contact:* Edward Potts, Director of Admissions and Financial Aid, 312-996-3218, E-mail: epotts@uic.edu. Website: http://www.uic.edu/jaddams/college/.

University of Illinois at Urbana–Champaign, Graduate College, School of Social Work, Champaign, IL 61820. Offers advocacy, leadership, and social change (MSW); children, youth and family services (MSW); health care (MSW); mental health (MSW); school social work (MSW); social work (PhD). *Accreditation:* CSWE (one or more programs are accredited). *Students:* 259 (225 women). *Entrance requirements:* For master's and doctorate, minimum GPA of 3.0. Application fee: $75 ($90 for international students). *Unit head:* Wynne S. Korr, Dean, 217-333-2260, Fax: 217-244-5220, E-mail: wkorr@illinois.edu. *Application contact:* Cheryl M. Street, Admissions and Records Officer, 217-333-2261, Fax: 217-244-5220, E-mail: street@illinois.edu. Website: http://socialwork.illinois.edu/.

The University of Iowa, Graduate College, College of Liberal Arts and Sciences, School of Social Work, Iowa City, IA 52242-1316. Offers MSW, PhD, JD/MSW, MSW/MA, MSW/MS, MSW/PhD. *Accreditation:* CSWE. *Degree requirements:* For master's, thesis optional; for doctorate, comprehensive exam, thesis/dissertation. *Entrance requirements:* For master's, minimum GPA of 3.0; for doctorate, GRE General Test, minimum GPA of 3.0. Additional exam requirements/recommendations for international students: Required—TOEFL (minimum score 600 paper-based; 100 iBT). Electronic applications accepted.

The University of Kansas, Graduate Studies, School of Social Welfare, Lawrence, KS 66045. Offers social work (MSW, PhD); JD/MSW. *Accreditation:* CSWE (one or more programs are accredited). Part-time programs available. Postbaccalaureate distance learning degree programs offered (minimal on-campus study). *Faculty:* 89. *Students:* 301 full-time (266 women), 80 part-time (69 women); includes 78 minority (31 Black or African American, non-Hispanic/Latino; 4 American Indian or Alaska Native, non-Hispanic/Latino; 3 Asian, non-Hispanic/Latino; 21 Hispanic/Latino; 19 Two or more races, non-Hispanic/Latino), 9 international. Average age 32. 352 applicants, 73% accepted, 194 enrolled. In 2013, 176 master's, 5 doctorates awarded. *Degree requirements:* For doctorate, comprehensive exam, thesis/dissertation. *Entrance requirements:* For master's, minimum GPA of 3.0, social work related experience, 3 letters of recommendation, student-issued transcripts from all previously attended schools regardless of degree status; for doctorate, GRE Quantitative and Verbal Tests, master's degree in social work or related field, minimum GPA of 3.5, personal statement, 3 letters of recommendation, completion of a statistics course with minimum B grade. Additional exam requirements/recommendations for international students: Required—TOEFL, IELTS accepted for MSW. *Application deadline:* For fall admission, 2/15 for domestic and international students. Application fee: $55 ($75 for international students). Electronic applications accepted. *Financial support:* Fellowships, research assistantships with full and partial tuition reimbursements, teaching assistantships with full and partial tuition reimbursements, Federal Work-Study, scholarships/grants, and tuition waivers (partial) available. Support available to part-time students. Financial award application deadline: 3/31; financial award applicants required to submit FAFSA. *Faculty research:* Poverty, child welfare, children's mental health, aging and long-term care, families and connections. *Unit head:* Tom McDonald, Interim Dean, 785-864-8959,

E-mail: t-mcdonald@ku.edu. *Application contact:* Becky Hofer, Director of Graduate Admissions, 785-864-8956, Fax: 785-864-5277, E-mail: bhofer@ku.edu. Website: http://www.socwel.ku.edu/.

University of Kentucky, Graduate School, College of Social Work, Lexington, KY 40506-0032. Offers MSW, PhD. *Degree requirements:* For master's, comprehensive exam; for doctorate, comprehensive exam, thesis/dissertation. *Entrance requirements:* For master's, GRE General Test, minimum undergraduate GPA of 2.75; for doctorate, GRE General Test, minimum undergraduate GPA of 3.0. Additional exam requirements/recommendations for international students: Required—TOEFL (minimum score 550 paper-based). Electronic applications accepted.

University of Louisville, Graduate School, Raymond A. Kent School of Social Work, Louisville, KY 40292-0001. Offers marriage and family therapy (PMC), including mental health; social work (MSSW, PhD), including alcohol and drug counseling (MSSW), gerontology (MSSW), marriage and family (PhD), school social work (MSSW). *Accreditation:* AAMFT/COAMFTE; CSWE (one or more programs are accredited). Part-time and evening/weekend programs available. *Students:* 309 full-time (260 women), 91 part-time (76 women); includes 124 minority (87 Black or African American, non-Hispanic/Latino; 1 American Indian or Alaska Native, non-Hispanic/Latino; 3 Asian, non-Hispanic/Latino; 21 Hispanic/Latino; 12 Two or more races, non-Hispanic/Latino), 8 international. Average age 32. 327 applicants, 67% accepted, 174 enrolled. In 2013, 131 master's, 2 doctorates awarded. *Degree requirements:* For doctorate, comprehensive exam, thesis/dissertation. *Entrance requirements:* For master's, GRE or minimum GPA of 2.75; for doctorate, GRE General Test, interview, writing sample. Additional exam requirements/recommendations for international students: Required—TOEFL (minimum score 550 paper-based; 79 iBT). *Application deadline:* For fall admission, 7/31 for domestic and international students. Applications are processed on a rolling basis. Application fee: $60. Electronic applications accepted. *Expenses:* Tuition, state resident: full-time $10,788; part-time $599 per credit hour. Tuition, nonresident: full-time $22,446; part-time $1247 per credit hour. *Required fees:* $196. Tuition and fees vary according to program and reciprocity agreements. *Financial support:* Research assistantships with full tuition reimbursements, teaching assistantships with full tuition reimbursements, Federal Work-Study, institutionally sponsored loans, scholarships/grants, health care benefits, and unspecified assistantships available. Support available to part-time students. Financial award application deadline: 5/15; financial award applicants required to submit FAFSA. *Faculty research:* Child welfare, substance abuse, gerontology, family functioning, health behavior. *Total annual research expenditures:* $2.5 million. *Unit head:* Dr. Terry Singer, Dean, 502-852-6402, Fax: 502-852-0422, E-mail: terry.singer@louisville.edu. *Application contact:* Libby Leggett, Director, Graduate Admissions, 502-852-3101, Fax: 502-852-6536, E-mail: gradadm@louisville.edu.
Website: http://www.louisville.edu/kent.

University of Maine, Graduate School, College of Natural Sciences, Forestry, and Agriculture, School of Social Work, Orono, ME 04469. Offers MSW. *Accreditation:* CSWE. Part-time and evening/weekend programs available. *Faculty:* 28 full-time (24 women), 3 part-time/adjunct (2 women). *Students:* 109 full-time (88 women), 2 part-time (both women); includes 6 minority (2 Black or African American, non-Hispanic/Latino; 2 American Indian or Alaska Native, non-Hispanic/Latino; 1 Asian, non-Hispanic/Latino; 1 Hispanic/Latino), 3 international. Average age 34. 50 applicants, 72% accepted, 31 enrolled. In 2013, 46 master's awarded. *Entrance requirements:* For master's, GRE General Test, MAT. Additional exam requirements/recommendations for international students: Required—TOEFL. *Application deadline:* For fall admission, 2/1 priority date for domestic students. Applications are processed on a rolling basis. Application fee: $65. Electronic applications accepted. *Expenses:* Tuition, state resident: full-time $7524. Tuition, nonresident: full-time $23,112. *Required fees:* $1970. *Financial support:* In 2013–14, 17 students received support. Application deadline: 3/1. *Faculty research:* Community mental health services, social welfare policy, disability studies, diversity, health policy. *Total annual research expenditures:* $62,033. *Unit head:* Dr. Gail Werrbach, Director, 207-581-2397, Fax: 207-581-2396. *Application contact:* Scott G. Delcourt, Associate Dean of the Graduate School, 207-581-3291, Fax: 207-581-3232, E-mail: graduate@maine.edu.
Website: http://www2.umaine.edu/graduate/.

The University of Manchester, School of Nursing, Midwifery and Social Work, Manchester, United Kingdom. Offers nursing (M Phil, PhD); social work (M Phil, PhD).

University of Manitoba, Faculty of Graduate Studies, Faculty of Social Work, Winnipeg, MB R3T 2N2, Canada. Offers MSW, PhD. *Degree requirements:* For master's, thesis or alternative.

University of Maryland, Baltimore, Graduate School, School of Social Work, Doctoral Program in Social Work, Baltimore, MD 21201. Offers PhD. Part-time programs available. *Degree requirements:* For doctorate, thesis/dissertation. *Entrance requirements:* For doctorate, GRE General Test, minimum GPA of 3.5, MSW. *Faculty research:* Social work research, social work teaching.

University of Maryland, Baltimore, Graduate School, School of Social Work, Master's Program in Social Work, Baltimore, MD 21201. Offers MSW, MBA/MSW, MSW/JD, MSW/MA, MSW/MPH. MSW/MA offered jointly with Baltimore Hebrew University; MBA/MSU with University of Maryland, College Park; MSW/MPH with The Johns Hopkins University. *Accreditation:* CSWE. *Entrance requirements:* For master's, minimum GPA of 3.0. Additional exam requirements/recommendations for international students: Required—TOEFL. Electronic applications accepted. *Faculty research:* Aging, families and children, health, mental health, social action and community development.

University of Maryland, College Park, Academic Affairs, Robert H. Smith School of Business, Combined MSW/MBA Program, College Park, MD 20742. Offers MSW/MBA. *Accreditation:* AACSB. *Students:* 2 full-time (both women). 8 applicants, 38% accepted, 1 enrolled. *Entrance requirements:* Additional exam requirements/recommendations for international students: Required—TOEFL. *Application deadline:* For fall admission, 12/15 priority date for domestic students, 12/15 for international students; for spring admission, 11/30 for domestic students, 6/1 for international students. Application fee: $75. *Expenses:* Tuition, state resident: full-time $10,314; part-time $573 per credit hour. Tuition, nonresident: full-time $22,248; part-time $1236 per credit. *Required fees:* $1446; $403.15 per semester. Tuition and fees vary according to program. *Financial support:* In 2013–14, 1 fellowship (averaging $79,151 per year) was awarded; research assistantships and teaching assistantships also available. *Unit head:* Dr. Anand Anandalingam, Dean, 301-405-2308, E-mail: ganand@umd.edu. *Application contact:* Dr. Charles A. Caramello, Dean of Graduate School, 301-405-0358, Fax: 301-314-9305, E-mail: ccaramel@umd.edu.

University of Michigan, School of Social Work, Ann Arbor, MI 48109. Offers MSW, PhD, MSW/JD, MSW/MBA, MSW/MPH, MSW/MPP, MSW/MSI, MSW/MUP. PhD offered through the Horace H. Rackham School of Graduate Studies. *Accreditation:* CSWE (one or more programs are accredited). *Faculty:* 55 full-time (33 women), 64 part-time/adjunct (44 women). *Students:* 649 full-time (537 women), 4 part-time (all women); includes 202 minority (79 Black or African American, non-Hispanic/Latino; 3 American Indian or Alaska Native, non-Hispanic/Latino; 30 Asian, non-Hispanic/Latino; 62 Hispanic/Latino; 28 Two or more races, non-Hispanic/Latino), 11 international.

Social Work

Average age 27. 1,496 applicants, 55% accepted, 368 enrolled. In 2013, 339 master's, 9 doctorates awarded. *Degree requirements:* For doctorate, oral defense of dissertation, preliminary exam. *Entrance requirements:* For master's, minimum of 20 academic semester credits in psychology, sociology, anthropology, economics, history, political science, government, and/or languages; for doctorate, GRE General Test. Additional exam requirements/recommendations for international students: Required—TOEFL (minimum score 600 paper-based; 100 iBT), IELTS (minimum score 7), Michigan English Language Assessment Battery (minimum score 85). *Application deadline:* For fall admission, 3/1 priority date for domestic students, 2/1 priority date for international students. Applications are processed on a rolling basis. Application fee: $75 ($90 for international students). Electronic applications accepted. *Expenses:* Contact institution. *Financial support:* In 2013–14, 607 students received support. Career-related internships or fieldwork, Federal Work-Study, scholarships/grants, traineeships, and unspecified assistantships available. Financial award application deadline: 3/15; financial award applicants required to submit FAFSA. *Faculty research:* Children and families, aging, community organization, health and mental health, policy and evaluation. *Total annual research expenditures:* $3.9 million. *Unit head:* Laura Lein, Dean, 734-764-5347, Fax: 734-764-9954, E-mail: leinl@umich.edu. *Application contact:* Timothy Colenback, Assistant Dean for Student Services, 734-936-0961, Fax: 734-936-1961, E-mail: timot@umich.edu.
Website: http://www.ssw.umich.edu/.

University of Minnesota, Duluth, Graduate School, College of Education and Human Service Professions, Department of Social Work, Duluth, MN 55812-2496. Offers MSW. *Accreditation:* CSWE. Part-time and evening/weekend programs available. Postbaccalaureate distance learning degree programs offered (minimal on-campus study). *Entrance requirements:* For master's, minimum GPA of 3.0. Additional exam requirements/recommendations for international students: Required—TOEFL (minimum score 550 paper-based). *Faculty research:* Domestic abuse, substance abuse, minority health, child welfare, gerontology.

University of Minnesota, Twin Cities Campus, Graduate School, College of Education and Human Development, School of Social Work, Minneapolis, MN 55455-0213. Offers MSW, PhD. *Accreditation:* CSWE (one or more programs are accredited). Part-time and evening/weekend programs available. Postbaccalaureate distance learning degree programs offered. *Faculty:* 23 full-time (14 women). *Students:* 244 full-time (208 women), 56 part-time (48 women); includes 76 minority (31 Black or African American, non-Hispanic/Latino; 6 American Indian or Alaska Native, non-Hispanic/Latino; 27 Asian, non-Hispanic/Latino; 11 Hispanic/Latino; 1 Native Hawaiian or other Pacific Islander, non-Hispanic/Latino), 8 international. Average age 31. 407 applicants, 57% accepted, 146 enrolled. In 2013, 145 master's, 10 doctorates awarded. *Degree requirements:* For doctorate, thesis/dissertation. *Entrance requirements:* For master's, minimum GPA of 3.0, 1 year of work experience; for doctorate, GRE, minimum GPA of 3.0, MSW. *Application deadline:* For fall admission, 1/15 for domestic students. Application fee: $75 ($95 for international students). *Financial support:* In 2013–14, 142 students received support, including 2 fellowships (averaging $22,500 per year), 28 research assistantships (averaging $10,470 per year), 2 teaching assistantships (averaging $7,515 per year); career-related internships or fieldwork, Federal Work-Study, institutionally sponsored loans, and tuition waivers (full and partial) also available. Support available to part-time students. Financial award applicants required to submit FAFSA. *Faculty research:* Mental health, clinical mental health, aging and disability, work with youth, family and community violence prevention, new American and immigrant populations, child welfare, youth leadership, community engagement, mediation and restitution, social justice. *Total annual research expenditures:* $4.2 million. *Unit head:* Dr. James Reinardy, Director, 612-624-3673, Fax: 612-624-3746, E-mail: jreinard@umn.edu. *Application contact:* Dr. Jennifer Engler, Assistant Dean, 612-626-2887, Fax: 612-626-7496, E-mail: engle009@umn.edu.
Website: http://www.cehd.umn.edu/ssw/.

University of Mississippi, Graduate School, School of Applied Sciences, Department of Social Work, Oxford, MS 38677. Offers MSW. *Accreditation:* CSWE. *Faculty:* 15 full-time (10 women), 6 part-time/adjunct (5 women). *Students:* 16 full-time (all women), 27 part-time (24 women); includes 22 minority (19 Black or African American, non-Hispanic/Latino; 1 Asian, non-Hispanic/Latino; 1 Hispanic/Latino; 1 Two or more races, non-Hispanic/Latino). Application fee: $40. *Unit head:* Dr. Carol Minor Boyd, Chair, 662-915-7336, Fax: 662-915-1288, E-mail: socialwk@olemiss.edu. *Application contact:* Dr. Christy M. Wyandt, Associate Dean, 662-915-7474, Fax: 662-915-7577, E-mail: cwyandt@olemiss.edu.
Website: http://www.olemiss.edu/depts/socialwork/.

University of Missouri, Graduate School, School of Social Work, Columbia, MO 65211. Offers gerontological social work (Certificate); military social work (Certificate); social work (MSW, PhD). *Accreditation:* CSWE. Part-time programs available. *Faculty:* 15 full-time (9 women). *Students:* 97 full-time (81 women), 78 part-time (68 women); includes 14 minority (6 Black or African American, non-Hispanic/Latino; 1 American Indian or Alaska Native, non-Hispanic/Latino; 3 Hispanic/Latino; 4 Two or more races, non-Hispanic/Latino), 2 international. Average age 31. 151 applicants, 62% accepted, 63 enrolled. In 2013, 87 master's, 1 doctorate, 12 other advanced degrees awarded. *Entrance requirements:* For master's, GRE General Test, minimum GPA of 3.0. Additional exam requirements/recommendations for international students: Required—TOEFL (minimum score 500 paper-based; 61 iBT). *Application deadline:* For fall admission, 1/15 priority date for domestic and international students. Applications are processed on a rolling basis. Application fee: $55 ($75 for international students). Electronic applications accepted. *Financial support:* Fellowships with tuition reimbursements, research assistantships with tuition reimbursements, teaching assistantships with tuition reimbursements, institutionally sponsored loans, scholarships/grants, health care benefits, and unspecified assistantships available. Support available to part-time students. *Faculty research:* Assessment of risk and resiliency factors in trauma populations, retirement, child welfare, parenting education, adolescent mood disorders, gerontology, rural practice, employee empowerment and involvement, children and youth, field education, substance use disorders in women, child welfare services and organization, maternal and child health, youth development and community betterment, international social work issues, epidemiology, etiology, prevention of health risk behaviors. *Unit head:* Dr. Marjorie Sable, Director, 573-882-0914, E-mail: sablem@missouri.edu. *Application contact:* Crystal Null, Administrative Assistant, 573-884-9385, E-mail: nullc@missouri.edu.
Website: http://ssw.missouri.edu/.

University of Missouri–Kansas City, College of Arts and Sciences, Department of Social Work, Kansas City, MO 64110-2499. Offers MSW. *Accreditation:* CSWE. Part-time and evening/weekend programs available. *Faculty:* 8 full-time (6 women), 10 part-time/adjunct (6 women). *Students:* 114 full-time (97 women), 55 part-time (48 women); includes 45 minority (35 Black or African American, non-Hispanic/Latino; 1 American Indian or Alaska Native, non-Hispanic/Latino; 5 Hispanic/Latino; 4 Two or more races, non-Hispanic/Latino), 4 international. Average age 32. 155 applicants, 52% accepted, 77 enrolled. In 2013, 46 master's awarded. *Entrance requirements:* For master's, minimum GPA of 3.0, 3 letters of reference. Additional exam requirements/recommendations for international students: Recommended—TOEFL (minimum score

550 paper-based; 80 iBT). *Application deadline:* For fall admission, 4/30 for domestic and international students; for spring admission, 12/1 for domestic and international students. Applications are processed on a rolling basis. Application fee: $45 ($50 for international students). *Expenses:* Tuition, state resident: full-time $6073; part-time $337.40 per credit hour. Tuition, nonresident: full-time $15,680; part-time $871.10 per credit hour. *Required fees:* $97.59 per credit hour. Full-time tuition and fees vary according to program. *Financial support:* In 2013–14, 5 research assistantships with partial tuition reimbursements (averaging $11,760 per year) were awarded; career-related internships or fieldwork and institutionally sponsored loans also available. Financial award application deadline: 3/1; financial award applicants required to submit FAFSA. *Faculty research:* Social justice, LGBT issues, deinstitutionalization, community collaboration and partnerships, evaluation of strengths model with addiction model. *Unit head:* Dr. Thomas Sandreczki, Interim Department Chair, 816-235-6308, E-mail: sandreczkit@umkc.edu. *Application contact:* Tamera Byland, Director of Admissions, 816-235-1111, Fax: 816-235-5544, E-mail: admit@umkc.edu.
Website: http://cas.umkc.edu/socialwork/.

University of Missouri–St. Louis, College of Arts and Sciences, School of Social Work, St. Louis, MO 63121. Offers gerontology (MS, Certificate); long term care administration (Certificate); social work (MSW). *Accreditation:* CSWE. *Faculty:* 10 full-time (8 women), 9 part-time/adjunct (6 women). *Students:* 73 full-time (65 women), 75 part-time (66 women); includes 27 minority (24 Black or African American, non-Hispanic/Latino; 1 Asian, non-Hispanic/Latino; 1 Hispanic/Latino; 1 Two or more races, non-Hispanic/Latino), 1 international. Average age 32. 155 applicants, 51% accepted, 50 enrolled. In 2013, 53 master's awarded. *Entrance requirements:* For master's, 3 letters of recommendation. Additional exam requirements/recommendations for international students: Required—TOEFL (minimum score 550 paper-based; 79 iBT), IELTS (minimum score 6.5). *Application deadline:* For fall admission, 2/15 for domestic and international students. Application fee: $50 ($40 for international students). Electronic applications accepted. *Expenses:* Tuition, state resident: full-time $7364; part-time $409.10 per credit hour. Tuition, nonresident: full-time $19,162; part-time $1008.50 per credit hour. *Financial support:* In 2013–14, 3 research assistantships with full and partial tuition reimbursements (averaging $6,750 per year), 7 teaching assistantships with full and partial tuition reimbursements (averaging $5,440 per year) were awarded. Financial award applicants required to submit FAFSA. *Faculty research:* Family violence, child abuse/neglect, immigration, community economic development. *Unit head:* Dr. Margaret Sherraden, Graduate Program Director, 314-516-6364, Fax: 314-516-5816, E-mail: socialwork@umsl.edu. *Application contact:* 314-516-5458, Fax: 314-516-6996, E-mail: gradadm@umsl.edu.
Website: http://www.umsl.edu/~socialwk/.

The University of Montana, Graduate School, College of Health Professions and Biomedical Sciences, School of Social Work, Missoula, MT 59812-0002. Offers MSW. *Accreditation:* CSWE.

University of Nebraska at Omaha, Graduate Studies, College of Public Affairs and Community Service, School of Social Work, Omaha, NE 68182. Offers MSW. *Accreditation:* CSWE. *Faculty:* 13 full-time (11 women). *Students:* 102 full-time (86 women), 86 part-time (78 women); includes 37 minority (13 Black or African American, non-Hispanic/Latino; 1 American Indian or Alaska Native, non-Hispanic/Latino; 2 Asian, non-Hispanic/Latino; 16 Hispanic/Latino; 5 Two or more races, non-Hispanic/Latino), 1 international. Average age 29. 151 applicants, 58% accepted, 73 enrolled. In 2013, 55 master's awarded. *Degree requirements:* For master's, comprehensive exam, thesis (for some programs). *Entrance requirements:* For master's, minimum GPA of 3.0, 3 letters of recommendation, resume, statement of purpose. Additional exam requirements/recommendations for international students: Required—TOEFL (minimum score 500 paper-based; 61 iBT), IELTS (minimum score 5.5), PTE (minimum score 44). *Application deadline:* For fall admission, 1/15 for domestic students. Applications are processed on a rolling basis. Application fee: $45. Electronic applications accepted. *Financial support:* In 2013–14, 8 students received support, including 4 research assistantships with tuition reimbursements available, 4 teaching assistantships with tuition reimbursements available; fellowships, career-related internships or fieldwork, Federal Work-Study, institutionally sponsored loans, scholarships/grants, tuition waivers (full), and unspecified assistantships also available. Support available to part-time students. Financial award application deadline: 3/1; financial award applicants required to submit FAFSA. *Unit head:* Dr. Amanda Randall, Director, 402-554-2791. *Application contact:* Dr. Peter Szto, Graduate Program Chair, 402-554-2330, E-mail: graduate@unomaha.edu.

University of Nevada, Las Vegas, Graduate College, Greenspun College of Urban Affairs, School of Social Work, Las Vegas, NV 89154-5032. Offers forensic social work (Advanced Certificate); social work (MSW); MSW/JD. *Accreditation:* CSWE. *Faculty:* 12 full-time (8 women), 16 part-time/adjunct (12 women). *Students:* 139 full-time (120 women), 47 part-time (40 women); includes 87 minority (37 Black or African American, non-Hispanic/Latino; 1 American Indian or Alaska Native, non-Hispanic/Latino; 9 Asian, non-Hispanic/Latino; 27 Hispanic/Latino; 1 Native Hawaiian or other Pacific Islander, non-Hispanic/Latino; 12 Two or more races, non-Hispanic/Latino), 10 international. Average age 34. 167 applicants, 59% accepted, 75 enrolled. In 2013, 65 master's awarded. *Degree requirements:* For master's, comprehensive exam, thesis optional. *Entrance requirements:* Additional exam requirements/recommendations for international students: Required—TOEFL (minimum score 550 paper-based; 80 iBT), IELTS (minimum score 7). *Application deadline:* For fall admission, 4/1 for domestic students, 5/1 for international students; for spring admission, 10/1 for international students. Application fee: $60 ($95 for international students). Electronic applications accepted. *Expenses:* Tuition, state resident: full-time $4752; part-time $264 per credit. Tuition, nonresident: full-time $18,662; part-time $554.50 per credit. *International tuition:* $18,952 full-time. *Required fees:* $532; $12 per credit. $266 per semester. One-time fee: $35. Tuition and fees vary according to course load and program. *Financial support:* In 2013–14, 9 students received support, including 5 research assistantships with partial tuition reimbursements available (averaging $10,146 per year), 4 teaching assistantships with partial tuition reimbursements available (averaging $10,000 per year); institutionally sponsored loans, scholarships/grants, health care benefits, and unspecified assistantships also available. Financial award application deadline: 3/1. *Faculty research:* Child welfare and juvenile justice, health and mental health, poverty and social justice, substance abuse, public policy. *Total annual research expenditures:* $484,864. *Unit head:* Dr. Joanne Thompson, Director/Professor, 702-895-0521, Fax: 702-895-4079, E-mail: joanne.thompson@unlv.edu. *Application contact:* Graduate College Admissions Evaluator, 702-895-3320, Fax: 702-895-4180, E-mail: gradcollege@unlv.edu.
Website: http://socialwork.unlv.edu/.

University of Nevada, Reno, Graduate School, Division of Health Sciences, School of Social Work, Reno, NV 89557. Offers MSW. *Accreditation:* CSWE. *Degree requirements:* For master's, thesis optional. *Entrance requirements:* For master's, GRE General Test, minimum GPA of 2.75, statistics course. Additional exam requirements/recommendations for international students: Required—TOEFL (minimum score 500 paper-based; 61 iBT), IELTS (minimum score 6). Electronic applications accepted.

Faculty research: Policy practice, poverty, women's issues, race and diversity, vulnerable family, social justice, social change, diversity.

University of New England, Westbrook College of Health Professions, Program in Social Work, Biddeford, ME 04005-9526. Offers MSW. *Accreditation:* CSWE. Part-time programs available. Postbaccalaureate distance learning degree programs offered (no on-campus study). *Faculty:* 18 full-time (15 women), 50 part-time/adjunct (40 women). *Students:* 661 full-time (598 women), 276 part-time (253 women); includes 213 minority (140 Black or African American, non-Hispanic/Latino; 10 American Indian or Alaska Native, non-Hispanic/Latino; 14 Asian, non-Hispanic/Latino; 32 Hispanic/Latino; 6 Native Hawaiian or other Pacific Islander, non-Hispanic/Latino; 11 Two or more races, non-Hispanic/Latino). Average age 35. 790 applicants, 51% accepted, 274 enrolled. In 2013, 119 master's awarded. *Degree requirements:* For master's, field internships. *Application deadline:* For fall admission, 4/1 for domestic students; for spring admission, 3/31 for domestic and international students. Applications are processed on a rolling basis. Application fee: $0. Electronic applications accepted. *Financial support:* Scholarships/grants available. Financial award application deadline: 5/1; financial award applicants required to submit FAFSA. *Unit head:* Dr. Danielle Wozniak, Director, School of Social Work, 207-221-4514, E-mail: dwozniak@une.edu. *Application contact:* Dr. Cynthia Forrest, Vice President for Student Affairs, 207-221-4225, Fax: 207-523-1925, E-mail: gradadmissions@une.edu.
Website: http://www.une.edu/wchp/socialwork/programs.

University of New Hampshire, Graduate School Manchester Campus, Manchester, NH 03101. Offers business administration (MBA); counseling (M Ed); education (M Ed, MAT); educational administration and supervision (M Ed, Ed S); information technology (MS); management of technology (MS); public administration (MPA); public health (MPH, Certificate); social work (MSW); software systems engineering (Certificate). Part-time and evening/weekend programs available. *Students:* 2 full-time (0 women), 5 part-time (0 women), 2 international. Average age 38. 6 applicants, 17% accepted, 1 enrolled. In 2013, 1 master's awarded. *Degree requirements:* For master's, thesis or alternative. *Entrance requirements:* Additional exam requirements/recommendations for international students: Required—TOEFL (minimum score 550 paper-based; 80 iBT). *Application deadline:* For fall admission, 6/1 for domestic students, 4/1 for international students; for spring admission, 12/1 for domestic students. Applications are processed on a rolling basis. Application fee: $65. Electronic applications accepted. *Expenses:* Tuition, state resident: full-time $13,500; part-time $750 per credit hour. Tuition, nonresident: full-time $26,200; part-time $1100 per credit hour. *Required fees:* $1741; $435.25 per term. Tuition and fees vary according to course level, course load, campus/location and program. *Financial support:* Fellowships, research assistantships, teaching assistantships, Federal Work-Study, scholarships/grants, health care benefits, and unspecified assistantships available. Support available to part-time students. Financial award application deadline: 3/1; financial award applicants required to submit FAFSA. *Unit head:* Candice Brown, Director, 603-641-4313, E-mail: unhm.gradcenter@unh.edu. *Application contact:* Graduate Admissions Office, 603-862-3000, Fax: 603-862-0275, E-mail: grad.school@unh.edu.
Website: http://www.gradschool.unh.edu/manchester/.

University of New Hampshire, Graduate School, School of Health and Human Services, Department of Social Work, Durham, NH 03824. Offers MSW, Postbaccalaureate Certificate. *Accreditation:* CSWE. Part-time programs available. *Faculty:* 11 full-time (8 women). *Students:* 124 full-time (105 women), 17 part-time (15 women); includes 7 minority (1 Black or African American, non-Hispanic/Latino; 3 Hispanic/Latino; 3 Two or more races, non-Hispanic/Latino), 2 international. Average age 32. 124 applicants, 61% accepted, 35 enrolled. In 2013, 40 master's awarded. *Entrance requirements:* Additional exam requirements/recommendations for international students: Required—TOEFL (minimum score 550 paper-based; 80 iBT). *Application deadline:* For fall admission, 2/1 for domestic and international students. Applications are processed on a rolling basis. Application fee: $65. Electronic applications accepted. *Expenses:* Tuition, state resident: full-time $13,500; part-time $750 per credit hour. Tuition, nonresident: full-time $26,200; part-time $1100 per credit hour. *Required fees:* $1741; $435.25 per term. Tuition and fees vary according to course level, course load, campus/location and program. *Financial support:* In 2013–14, 11 students received support, including 6 teaching assistantships; fellowships, research assistantships, career-related internships or fieldwork, Federal Work-Study, and scholarships/grants also available. Support available to part-time students. Financial award application deadline: 2/15. *Unit head:* Dr. Anne Broussard, Chairperson, 603-862-3953. *Application contact:* Kim Kelsey, Administrative Assistant, 603-862-0215, E-mail: kfrarie@cisunix.unh.edu.
Website: http://www.chhs.unh.edu/sw/graduate-programs.

The University of North Carolina at Chapel Hill, Graduate School, School of Social Work, Chapel Hill, NC 27599. Offers MSW, PhD, JD/MSW, MHA/MCRP, MPA/MSW, MSPH/MSW. *Accreditation:* CSWE (one or more programs are accredited). Part-time programs available. Terminal master's awarded for partial completion of doctoral program. *Degree requirements:* For doctorate, thesis/dissertation, qualifying exam. *Entrance requirements:* For master's and doctorate, GRE General Test, minimum GPA of 3.0. Electronic applications accepted. *Faculty research:* School success, risk and resiliency, welfare reform, aging, substance abuse.

The University of North Carolina at Charlotte, The Graduate School, College of Health and Human Services, Department of Social Work, Charlotte, NC 28223-0001. Offers MSW. *Accreditation:* CSWE. Part-time programs available. *Faculty:* 12 full-time (9 women), 9 part-time/adjunct (7 women). *Students:* 99 full-time (91 women), 4 part-time (all women); includes 35 minority (17 Black or African American, non-Hispanic/Latino; 1 American Indian or Alaska Native, non-Hispanic/Latino; 5 Asian, non-Hispanic/Latino; 7 Hispanic/Latino; 5 Two or more races, non-Hispanic/Latino). Average age 28. 119 applicants, 73% accepted, 50 enrolled. In 2013, 56 master's awarded. *Degree requirements:* For master's, thesis or alternative, practicum. *Entrance requirements:* For master's, GRE, minimum GPA of 2.7 overall, 3.0 in last 30 hours of course work. Additional exam requirements/recommendations for international students: Required—TOEFL (minimum score 557 paper-based; 83 iBT). *Application deadline:* For fall admission, 2/1 for domestic and international students; for spring admission, 11/1 for domestic students, 10/1 for international students. Application fee: $75. Electronic applications accepted. *Expenses:* Tuition, state resident: full-time $3522. Tuition, nonresident: full-time $16,051. *Required fees:* $2585. Tuition and fees vary according to course load and program. *Financial support:* In 2013–14, 8 students received support, including 6 research assistantships (averaging $2,531 per year), 1 teaching assistantship (averaging $1,650 per year); career-related internships or fieldwork, Federal Work-Study, institutionally sponsored loans, scholarships/grants, unspecified assistantships, and administrative assistantships also available. Support available to part-time students. Financial award application deadline: 4/1; financial award applicants required to submit FAFSA. *Faculty research:* The impact of violence on Latinos, intervention strategies, risk and resilience framework and feminist theory to guide social work interventions, analyzing evaluation data, qualitative analysis of faith-based social service programs, culturally competent practice with Latinas. *Total annual research expenditures:* $435,628. *Unit head:* Dr. Vivian Lord, Chair, 704-687-0752, Fax: 704-687-

2343, E-mail: vblord@uncc.edu. *Application contact:* Kathy B. Giddings, Director of Graduate Admissions, 704-687-5503, Fax: 704-687-1668, E-mail: gradadm@uncc.edu.
Website: http://socialwork.uncc.edu/master-social-work.

The University of North Carolina at Greensboro, Graduate School, School of Human Environmental Sciences, Department of Social Work, Greensboro, NC 27412-5001. Offers MSW. Program offered jointly with North Carolina Agricultural and Technical State University. *Accreditation:* CSWE. *Entrance requirements:* For master's, GRE General Test. Additional exam requirements/recommendations for international students: Required—TOEFL. Electronic applications accepted.

The University of North Carolina at Pembroke, Graduate Studies, Department of Social Work, Pembroke, NC 28372-1510. Offers MSW. Part-time programs available.

The University of North Carolina Wilmington, School of Social Work, Wilmington, NC 28403-3297. Offers MSW. *Accreditation:* CSWE. *Faculty:* 6 full-time (3 women). *Students:* 43 full-time (37 women); includes 6 minority (2 Black or African American, non-Hispanic/Latino; 4 Hispanic/Latino). Average age 29. 96 applicants, 49% accepted, 19 enrolled. In 2013, 15 master's awarded. *Degree requirements:* For master's, comprehensive exam, thesis or alternative. *Entrance requirements:* For master's, GMAT, GRE General Test. Additional exam requirements/recommendations for international students: Required—TOEFL (minimum score 550 paper-based; 79 iBT), IELTS (minimum score 6.5). *Application deadline:* For fall admission, 6/1 for domestic students, 3/15 for international students; for spring admission, 11/1 for domestic students, 10/1 for international students. Application fee: $60. *Expenses:* Tuition, state resident: full-time $4163. Tuition, nonresident: full-time $16,098. *Financial support:* In 2013–14, 13 teaching assistantships with full and partial tuition reimbursements (averaging $9,500 per year) were awarded. *Unit head:* Dr. Lori Messinger, Director, 910-962-3687, Fax: 910-962-7283, E-mail: messingerl@uncw.edu. *Application contact:* Dr. Stacey Kolomer, Graduate Coordinator, 910-962-2853, Fax: 910-962-7283, E-mail: kolomers@uncw.edu.
Website: http://www.uncw.edu/swk/.

University of North Dakota, Graduate School, College of Education and Human Development, School of Social Work, Grand Forks, ND 58202. Offers MSW. *Accreditation:* CSWE. *Degree requirements:* For master's, comprehensive exam, thesis or alternative. *Entrance requirements:* For master's, minimum GPA of 3.0. Additional exam requirements/recommendations for international students: Required—TOEFL (minimum score 550 paper-based; 79 iBT), IELTS (minimum score 6.5). Electronic applications accepted. *Faculty research:* Mental health, gerontology, chemical abuse, children and families.

University of Northern British Columbia, Office of Graduate Studies, Prince George, BC V2N 4Z9, Canada. Offers business administration (Diploma); community health science (M Sc); disability management (MA); education (M Ed); first nations studies (MA); gender studies (MA); history (MA); interdisciplinary studies (MA); international studies (MA); mathematical, computer and physical sciences (M Sc); natural resources and environmental studies (M Sc, MA, MNRES, PhD); political science (MA); psychology (M Sc, PhD); social work (MSW). Part-time and evening/weekend programs available. Postbaccalaureate distance learning degree programs offered (no on-campus study). *Degree requirements:* For master's, thesis; for doctorate, thesis/dissertation. *Entrance requirements:* For master's, GRE, minimum B average in undergraduate course work; for doctorate, candidacy exam, minimum A average in graduate course work.

University of Northern Iowa, Graduate College, College of Social and Behavioral Sciences, Department of Social Work, Cedar Falls, IA 50614. Offers MSW. *Accreditation:* CSWE. *Students:* 53 full-time (45 women), 4 part-time (3 women); includes 2 minority (1 Black or African American, non-Hispanic/Latino; 1 Hispanic/Latino), 2 international. 58 applicants, 33% accepted, 16 enrolled. In 2013, 33 master's awarded. *Entrance requirements:* For master's, minimum GPA of 3.0; 3 letters of recommendation; personal autobiographical statement. Additional exam requirements/recommendations for international students: Required—TOEFL (minimum score 500 paper-based; 61 iBT). *Application deadline:* For fall admission, 8/1 priority date for domestic students. Applications are processed on a rolling basis. Application fee: $50 ($70 for international students). Electronic applications accepted. *Financial support:* Application deadline: 2/1. *Unit head:* Dr. Cynthia L. Juby, Interim Department Head, 319-273-5845, Fax: 319-273-6976, E-mail: cynthia.juby@uni.edu. *Application contact:* Laurie S. Russell, Record Analyst, 319-273-2623, Fax: 319-273-2885, E-mail: laurie.russell@uni.edu.
Website: http://www.uni.edu/socialwork/.

University of Oklahoma, College of Arts and Sciences, School of Social Work, Norman, OK 73019. Offers social work (MSW), including administrative and community practice, direct practice. *Accreditation:* CSWE. Part-time and evening/weekend programs available. *Faculty:* 24 full-time (15 women), 9 part-time/adjunct (8 women). *Students:* 244 full-time (208 women), 120 part-time (100 women); includes 113 minority (53 Black or African American, non-Hispanic/Latino; 23 American Indian or Alaska Native, non-Hispanic/Latino; 5 Asian, non-Hispanic/Latino; 19 Hispanic/Latino; 13 Two or more races, non-Hispanic/Latino), 3 international. Average age 32. 198 applicants, 69% accepted, 106 enrolled. In 2013, 127 master's awarded. *Degree requirements:* For master's, comprehensive exam, thesis optional. *Entrance requirements:* For master's, bachelor's degree, minimum GPA of 3.0. Additional exam requirements/recommendations for international students: Required—TOEFL (minimum score 79 iBT). *Application deadline:* For fall admission, 2/1 for domestic and international students; for spring admission, 11/1 for domestic students, 9/1 for international students. Application fee: $50 ($100 for international students). Electronic applications accepted. *Expenses:* Tuition, state resident: full-time $4205; part-time $175.20 per credit hour. Tuition, nonresident: full-time $16,205; part-time $675.20 per credit hour. *Required fees:* $2745; $103.85 per credit hour. $126.50 per semester. *Financial support:* In 2013–14, 148 students received support, including 17 research assistantships with partial tuition reimbursements available (averaging $10,168 per year); career-related internships or fieldwork, scholarships/grants, and tuition waivers (full) also available. Support available to part-time students. Financial award application deadline: 6/1; financial award applicants required to submit FAFSA. *Faculty research:* Cultural considerations in delivery of social services, forensic trauma, improving adult outcomes for youth with disabilities, HIV/AIDS prevention with communities of color, child welfare issues. *Total annual research expenditures:* $36,021. *Unit head:* Dr. Julie Miller-Cribbs, Director, 405-325-2821, Fax: 405-325-4683, E-mail: jmcribbs@ou.edu. *Application contact:* Judy Meisner, Admission and Recruiting Specialist, 405-325-2821, Fax: 405-325-4683, E-mail: judith.a.meisner-1@ou.edu.
Website: http://ou.edu/socialwork.

University of Ottawa, Faculty of Graduate and Postdoctoral Studies, Faculty of Social Sciences, School of Social Work, Ottawa, ON K1N 6N5, Canada. Offers MSS. Program offered in French. *Degree requirements:* For master's, thesis or alternative. *Entrance requirements:* For master's, honors bachelor's degree or equivalent, minimum B average. Electronic applications accepted. *Faculty research:* Family-children, health.

University of Pennsylvania, School of Social Policy and Practice, Graduate Group on Social Welfare, Philadelphia, PA 19104. Offers PhD. *Degree requirements:* For

Social Work

doctorate, thesis/dissertation. *Entrance requirements:* For doctorate, GRE General Test, MSW or master's degree in related field. Additional exam requirements/recommendations for international students: Required—TOEFL (minimum score 600 paper-based; 100 iBT). Electronic applications accepted. *Faculty research:* Mental health, child welfare, organizational behavior, urban poverty, comparative social welfare.

University of Pennsylvania, School of Social Policy and Practice, Program in Social Work, Philadelphia, PA 19104. Offers MNPL, MSSP, MSW, DSW, JD/MSW, MSW/Certificate, MSW/MBA, MSW/MBE, MSW/MCP, MSW/MGA, MSW/MPH, MSW/MS Ed, MSW/MSC, MSW/PhD. *Accreditation:* CSWE. Part-time programs available. Terminal master's awarded for partial completion of doctoral program. *Degree requirements:* For master's, fieldwork; for doctorate, thesis/dissertation. *Entrance requirements:* For master's, GRE, GMAT, or LSAT (for MSSP or MNPL); for doctorate, GRE, MSW or master's degree in related field. Additional exam requirements/recommendations for international students: Required—TOEFL (minimum score 600 paper-based; 100 iBT). Electronic applications accepted. *Faculty research:* Homelessness, juvenile justice, mental health/children's mental health, child welfare, domestic and family violence.

See Display below and Close-Up on page 1727.

University of Pittsburgh, School of Social Work, Pittsburgh, PA 15260. Offers gerontology (Certificate); social work (MSW, PhD); M Div/MSW; MPA/MSW; MPH/PhD; MPIA/MSW; MSW/JD; MSW/MPH. *Accreditation:* CSWE (one or more programs are accredited). Part-time programs available. *Faculty:* 21 full-time (13 women), 40 part-time/adjunct (28 women). *Students:* 401 full-time (346 women), 162 part-time (135 women); includes 123 minority (61 Black or African American, non-Hispanic/Latino; 32 Asian, non-Hispanic/Latino; 18 Hispanic/Latino; 12 Two or more races, non-Hispanic/Latino). Average age 28. 672 applicants, 69% accepted, 199 enrolled. In 2013, 201 master's, 4 doctorates awarded. *Degree requirements:* For master's, practicum; for doctorate, comprehensive exam, thesis/dissertation; for Certificate, thesis. *Entrance requirements:* For master's, minimum QPA of 3.0, course work in statistics; for doctorate, GRE, MSW or related degree, course work in statistics. Additional exam requirements/recommendations for international students: Required—TOEFL (minimum score 600 paper-based; 100 iBT). *Application deadline:* For fall admission, 12/31 priority date for domestic and international students. Applications are processed on a rolling basis. Application fee: $40. Electronic applications accepted. *Expenses:* Tuition, state resident: full-time $19,964; part-time $807 per credit. Tuition, nonresident: full-time $32,686; part-time $1337 per credit. *Required fees:* $740; $200. Tuition and fees vary according to program. *Financial support:* In 2013–14, 231 students received support, including 9 teaching assistantships with full tuition reimbursements available (averaging $16,710 per year); fellowships, research assistantships with full tuition reimbursements available, career-related internships or fieldwork, institutionally sponsored loans, scholarships/grants, traineeships, tuition waivers (full), and unspecified assistantships also available. Financial award application deadline: 3/31; financial award applicants required to submit FAFSA. *Faculty research:* Mental health services research, child abuse and neglect, geriatrics, criminal justice race issues. *Unit head:* Dr. Larry E. Davis, Dean, 412-624-6304, Fax: 412-624-6323, E-mail: ledavis@pitt.edu. *Application contact:* Philip Mack, Director of Admissions, 412-624-6346, Fax: 412-624-6323, E-mail: psm8@pitt.edu.
Website: http://www.socialwork.pitt.edu.

University of Puerto Rico, Río Piedras Campus, College of Social Sciences, Graduate School of Social Work, San Juan, PR 00931-3300. Offers MSW, PhD. *Accreditation:* CSWE. Part-time programs available. *Degree requirements:* For master's, comprehensive exam, thesis; for doctorate, comprehensive exam, thesis/dissertation. *Entrance requirements:* For master's, PAEG or GRE, interview, minimum GPA of 3.0, letter of recommendation; for doctorate, PAEG or GRE, interview, minimum GPA of 3.0,

3 letters of recommendation, social work experience. *Faculty research:* Social work in Puerto Rico, Cuba, and the Dominican Republic; migration; poverty in Puerto Rico.

University of Regina, Faculty of Graduate Studies and Research, Faculty of Social Work, Regina, SK S4S 0A2, Canada. Offers indigenous social work (MISW); social work (MSW, PhD). PhD offered as a special case program. Part-time programs available. *Faculty:* 17 full-time (8 women), 7 part-time/adjunct (4 women). *Students:* 25 full-time (22 women), 50 part-time (46 women). 58 applicants, 40% accepted. In 2013, 16 master's awarded. *Degree requirements:* For master's, thesis; for doctorate, thesis/dissertation. *Entrance requirements:* For master's, BSW. Additional exam requirements/recommendations for international students: Required—TOEFL (minimum score 580 paper-based; 80 iBT), IELTS (minimum score 6.5). *Application deadline:* For fall admission, 1/31 for domestic and international students. Application fee: $100. Electronic applications accepted. *Expenses:* Contact institution. *Financial support:* In 2013–14, 1 research assistantship (averaging $5,500 per year), 4 teaching assistantships (averaging $2,356 per year) were awarded; fellowships, career-related internships or fieldwork, and scholarships/grants also available. Financial award application deadline: 6/15. *Faculty research:* Social policy analysis; social justice, human rights, and social work; family and child policies and programs; aging, society, and human service work; work, welfare, and social justice. *Unit head:* Dr. Judy White, Acting Dean, 306-664-7375, Fax: 306-664-7131, E-mail: judy.white@uregina.ca. *Application contact:* Dr. Ailsa Watkinson, Graduate Program Coordinator, 306-664-7374, E-mail: ailsa.watkinson@uregina.ca.
Website: http://www.uregina.ca/socialwork/.

University of St. Francis, College of Arts and Sciences, Joliet, IL 60435-6169. Offers advanced generalist forensic social work (Post-Master's Certificate); physician assistant practice (MS); social work (MSW). *Faculty:* 7 full-time (5 women), 1 (woman) part-time/adjunct. *Students:* 106 full-time (86 women), 22 part-time (20 women); includes 59 minority (21 Black or African American, non-Hispanic/Latino; 7 Asian, non-Hispanic/Latino; 26 Hispanic/Latino; 5 Two or more races, non-Hispanic/Latino). Average age 30. 88 applicants, 42% accepted, 28 enrolled. In 2013, 54 master's, 3 other advanced degrees awarded. *Entrance requirements:* Additional exam requirements/recommendations for international students: Required—TOEFL (minimum score 550 paper-based; 79 iBT). *Application deadline:* Applications are processed on a rolling basis. Application fee: $30. Electronic applications accepted. Application fee is waived when completed online. *Expenses:* Contact institution. *Financial support:* In 2013–14, 11 students received support. Scholarships/grants, tuition waivers (partial), and unspecified assistantships available. Support available to part-time students. Financial award applicants required to submit FAFSA. *Unit head:* Dr. Robert Kase, Dean, 815-740-3367, Fax: 815-740-6366. *Application contact:* Sandra Sloka, Director of Admissions for Graduate and Degree Completion Programs, 800-735-7500, Fax: 815-740-3431, E-mail: ssloka@stfrancis.edu.
Website: http://www.stfrancis.edu/academics/cas.

University of St. Thomas, Graduate Studies, School of Social Work, St. Paul, MN 55105-1096. Offers MSW. *Accreditation:* CSWE. Part-time and evening/weekend programs available. Postbaccalaureate distance learning degree programs offered (minimal on-campus study). *Faculty:* 25 full-time (20 women), 21 part-time/adjunct (15 women). *Students:* 84 full-time (70 women), 284 part-time (255 women); includes 35 minority (12 Black or African American, non-Hispanic/Latino; 8 Asian, non-Hispanic/Latino; 2 Hispanic/Latino; 13 Two or more races, non-Hispanic/Latino). Average age 32. 290 applicants, 83% accepted, 137 enrolled. In 2013, 141 master's awarded. *Degree requirements:* For master's, thesis, fieldwork. *Entrance requirements:* For master's, previous course work in developmental psychology, human biology, and statistics or research methods. Additional exam requirements/recommendations for international students: Required—TOEFL (minimum score 600 paper-based; 100 iBT). *Application*

deadline: For fall admission, 1/10 for domestic students. Application fee: $35. Electronic applications accepted. *Expenses:* Contact institution. *Financial support:* In 2013–14, 24 fellowships, 17 research assistantships were awarded; career-related internships or fieldwork, Federal Work-Study, institutionally sponsored loans, scholarships/grants, and unspecified assistantships also available. Support available to part-time students. Financial award application deadline: 7/1; financial award applicants required to submit FAFSA. *Faculty research:* Clinical supervision and practice, group work, child welfare and social work. *Unit head:* Dr. Barbara W. Shank, Dean and Professor, 651-962-5801, Fax: 651-962-5819, E-mail: bwshank@stthomas.edu. *Application contact:* Hannah Lehman, Graduate Admissions Counselor, 651-690-6185, Fax: 651-690-6549, E-mail: hclehman@stkate.edu.
Website: http://www.stthomas.edu/socialwork/.

University of South Africa, College of Human Sciences, Pretoria, South Africa. Offers adult education (M Ed); African languages (MA, PhD); African politics (MA, PhD); Afrikaans (MA, PhD); ancient history (MA, PhD); ancient Near Eastern studies (MA, PhD); anthropology (MA, PhD); applied linguistics (MA); Arabic (MA, PhD); archaeology (MA); art history (MA); Biblical archaeology (MA); Biblical studies (M Th, D Th, PhD); Christian spirituality (M Th, D Th); church history (M Th, D Th); classical studies (MA, PhD); clinical psychology (MA); communication (MA, PhD); comparative education (M Ed, Ed D); consulting psychology (D Admin, D Com, PhD); curriculum studies (M Ed, Ed D); development studies (M Admin, MA, D Admin, PhD); didactics (M Ed, Ed D); education (M Tech); education management (M Ed, Ed D); educational psychology (M Ed); English (MA); environmental education (M Ed); French (MA, PhD); German (MA, PhD); Greek (MA); guidance and counseling (M Ed); health studies (MA, PhD), including health sciences education (MA), health services management (MA), medical and surgical nursing science (critical care general) (MA), midwifery and neonatal nursing science (MA), trauma and emergency care (MA); history (MA, PhD); history of education (Ed D); inclusive education (M Ed, Ed D); information and communications technology policy and regulation (MA); information science (MA, MIS, PhD); international politics (MA, PhD); Islamic studies (MA, PhD); Italian (MA, PhD); Judaica (MA, PhD); linguistics (MA, PhD); mathematical education (M Ed); mathematics education (MA); missiology (M Th, D Th); modern Hebrew (MA, PhD); musicology (MA, MMus, D Mus, PhD); natural science education (M Ed); New Testament (M Th, D Th); Old Testament (D Th); pastoral therapy (M Th, D Th); philosophy (MA); philosophy of education (M Ed, Ed D); politics (MA, PhD); Portuguese (MA, PhD); practical theology (M Th, D Th); psychology (MA, MS, PhD); psychology of education (M Ed, Ed D); public health (MA); religious studies (MA, D Th, PhD); Romance languages (MA); Russian (MA, PhD); Semitic languages (MA, PhD); social behavior studies in HIV/AIDS (MA); social science (mental health) (MA); social science in development studies (MA); social science in psychology (MA); social science in social work (MA); social science in sociology (MA); social work (MSW, DSW, PhD); socio-education (M Ed, Ed D); sociolinguistics (MA); sociology (MA, PhD); Spanish (MA, PhD); systematic theology (M Th, D Th); TESOL (teaching English to speakers of other languages) (MA); theological ethics (M Th, D Th); theory of literature (MA, PhD); urban ministries (D Th); urban ministry (M Th).

University of South Carolina, The Graduate School, College of Social Work, Columbia, SC 29208. Offers MSW, PhD, JD/MSW, MSW/MPA, MSW/MPH. *Accreditation:* CSWE (one or more programs are accredited). Part-time programs available. *Degree requirements:* For master's, comprehensive exam; for doctorate, thesis/dissertation. *Entrance requirements:* For master's, GRE (minimum combined score 800), minimum undergraduate GPA of 3.0. Additional exam requirements/ recommendations for international students: Required—TOEFL (minimum score 570 paper-based). Electronic applications accepted. *Expenses:* Contact institution. *Faculty research:* Victimization, child abuse and neglect, families.

The University of South Dakota, Graduate School, School of Health Sciences, Vermillion, SD 57069-2390. Offers addiction studies (MA); alcohol and drug studies (Graduate Certificate); occupational therapy (MS); physical therapy (DPT); physician assistant studies (MS); social work (MSW). Part-time programs available. *Entrance requirements:* For master's, GRE General Test, GRE Subject Test. *Faculty research:* Occupational therapy, physical therapy, vision, pediatrics, geriatrics.

University of Southern California, Graduate School, School of Social Work, Los Angeles, CA 90089. Offers community organization, planning and administration (MSW); families and children (MSW); health (MSW); mental health (MSW); military social work and veterans services (MSW); older adults (MSW); public child welfare (MSW); school settings (MSW); social work (MSW, PhD); systems of mental illness recovery (MSW); work and life (MSW); JD/MSW; M Pl/MSW; MPA/MSW; MSW/MBA; MSW/MJCS; MSW/MS. *Accreditation:* CSWE (one or more programs are accredited). *Degree requirements:* For doctorate, comprehensive exam, thesis/dissertation, qualifying exam/publishable paper. *Entrance requirements:* For doctorate, GRE General Test. Additional exam requirements/recommendations for international students: Required—TOEFL (minimum score 600 paper-based; 100 iBT), ESL exam. Electronic applications accepted. *Faculty research:* Department of Defense Educational Activity, detection/treatment of depression among older adults, health/aging, psychosocial adaptation to extreme environments/man made disasters; mental health needs of older adults.

University of Southern Indiana, Graduate Studies, College of Liberal Arts, Program in Social Work, Evansville, IN 47712-3590. Offers MSW. *Accreditation:* CSWE. Part-time and evening/weekend programs available. *Faculty:* 6 full-time (2 women), 1 (woman) part-time/adjunct. *Students:* 55 full-time (48 women), 35 part-time (31 women); includes 8 minority (3 Black or African American, non-Hispanic/Latino; 1 Asian, non-Hispanic/ Latino; 1 Hispanic/Latino; 3 Two or more races, non-Hispanic/Latino), 1 international. Average age 30. 115 applicants, 58% accepted, 56 enrolled. In 2013, 49 master's awarded. *Entrance requirements:* For master's, minimum GPA of 2.5. Additional exam requirements/recommendations for international students: Required—TOEFL (minimum score 550 paper-based; 79 iBT), IELTS (minimum score 6). *Application deadline:* For fall admission, 2/1 for domestic and international students. Application fee: $40. Electronic applications accepted. *Expenses:* Tuition, state resident: full-time $5567; part-time $309 per credit hour. Tuition, nonresident: full-time $10,977; part-time $610 per credit. *Required fees:* $23 per semester. *Financial support:* In 2013–14, 7 students received support. Federal Work-Study, scholarships/grants, tuition waivers (full and partial), and unspecified assistantships available. Financial award application deadline: 3/1; financial award applicants required to submit FAFSA. *Unit head:* Dr. Vaughn DeCoster, Director, 812-465-7003, E-mail: vadecoster@usi.edu. *Application contact:* Dr. Mayola Rowser, Interim Director, Graduate Studies, 812-465-7016, Fax: 812-464-1956, E-mail: mrowser@usi.edu.
Website: http://www.usi.edu/liberalarts/master-of-social-work.

University of Southern Maine, College of Management and Human Service, School of Social Work, Portland, ME 04104-9300. Offers MSW. *Accreditation:* CSWE. Part-time and evening/weekend programs available. *Faculty:* 9 full-time (5 women), 1 part-time/ adjunct (0 women). *Students:* 38 full-time (31 women), 35 part-time (30 women); includes 7 minority (1 Black or African American, non-Hispanic/Latino; 3 American Indian or Alaska Native, non-Hispanic/Latino; 1 Asian, non-Hispanic/Latino; 1 Hispanic/ Latino; 1 Two or more races, non-Hispanic/Latino). Average age 32. 97 applicants, 55% accepted, 37 enrolled. In 2013, 39 master's awarded. *Entrance requirements:* For master's, GRE or MAT. *Application deadline:* For winter admission, 2/1 priority date for domestic students. Application fee: $65. Electronic applications accepted. *Expenses:* Tuition, state resident: part-time $380 per credit. Tuition, nonresident: part-time $1026 per credit. Part-time tuition and fees vary according to program. *Financial support:* Research assistantships available. *Faculty research:* Poverty and discrimination, aging, interpersonal violence, evaluation of interventions and effectiveness, child and adult mental health, social welfare history, diversity issues. *Unit head:* Dr. Susan Fineran, Professor/Director, 207-780-4227, E-mail: sfineran@usm.maine.edu. *Application contact:* Mary Sloan, Assistant Dean of Graduate Studies and Director of Graduate Admissions, 207-780-4386, E-mail: gradstudies@usm.maine.edu.
Website: http://www.usm.maine.edu/swo.

University of Southern Mississippi, Graduate School, College of Health, School of Social Work, Hattiesburg, MS 39406-0001. Offers MSW. *Accreditation:* CSWE. Part-time programs available. *Faculty:* 13 full-time (7 women). *Students:* 73 full-time (61 women), 69 part-time (66 women); includes 66 minority (55 Black or African American, non-Hispanic/Latino; 2 American Indian or Alaska Native, non-Hispanic/Latino; 1 Native Hawaiian or other Pacific Islander, non-Hispanic/Latino; 8 Two or more races, non-Hispanic/Latino). Average age 34. 49 applicants, 84% accepted, 28 enrolled. In 2013, 63 master's awarded. *Degree requirements:* For master's, comprehensive exam, thesis or alternative, practicum. *Entrance requirements:* For master's, GRE General Test, minimum GPA of 2.75 in last 60 hours. Additional exam requirements/recommendations for international students: Required—TOEFL, IELTS. *Application deadline:* For fall admission, 4/1 priority date for domestic and international students; for spring admission, 1/10 priority date for domestic and international students. Applications are processed on a rolling basis. Application fee: $50. Electronic applications accepted. *Financial support:* In 2013–14, 16 research assistantships with tuition reimbursements (averaging $7,600 per year), teaching assistantships with tuition reimbursements (averaging $7,600 per year) were awarded; career-related internships or fieldwork, Federal Work-Study, scholarships/grants, health care benefits, and unspecified assistantships also available. Financial award application deadline: 3/15; financial award applicants required to submit FAFSA. *Faculty research:* Delinquency prevention, risk and resiliency in youth, successful aging, women in social service management, social work and the law. *Unit head:* Dr. Tim Rehner, Director, 601-266-4171, Fax: 601-266-4165, E-mail: tim.rehner@usm.edu. *Application contact:* Dr. Thomas Osowski, Assistant Professor/MSW Coordinator, 601-266-4171, Fax: 601-266-4165, E-mail: tom.osowski@usm.edu.
Website: http://www.usm.edu/graduateschool/table.php.

University of South Florida, College of Behavioral and Community Sciences, School of Social Work, Tampa, FL 33620. Offers MSW, PhD, MSW/MPH. *Accreditation:* CSWE. Part-time and evening/weekend programs available. *Faculty:* 12 full-time (10 women), 17 part-time/adjunct (13 women). *Students:* 116 full-time (101 women), 44 part-time (39 women); includes 47 minority (19 Black or African American, non-Hispanic/Latino; 2 American Indian or Alaska Native, non-Hispanic/Latino; 4 Asian, non-Hispanic/Latino; 16 Hispanic/Latino; 6 Two or more races, non-Hispanic/Latino), 2 international. Average age 32. 264 applicants, 22% accepted, 30 enrolled. In 2013, 48 master's, 2 doctorates awarded. *Degree requirements:* For master's, thesis, comprehensive exam or capstone project; for doctorate, comprehensive exam, thesis/dissertation. *Entrance requirements:* For master's, GRE General Test, three letters of recommendation; 750-word biographical sketch; interview; field experience (preferred); for doctorate, GRE General Test (minimum preferred scores of 500 verbal and 500 quantitative on old scoring), minimum GPA of 3.0 in last two years of undergraduate work; master's degree in social work program with minimum GPA of 3.5; three letters of recommendation; statement of purpose, career goals, and research interests; professional/academic writing sample; interview. Additional exam requirements/recommendations for international students: Required—TOEFL (minimum score 550 paper-based; 79 iBT). *Application deadline:* For fall admission, 2/15 priority date for domestic students, 1/2 for international students. Applications are processed on a rolling basis. Application fee: $30. Electronic applications accepted. *Financial support:* In 2013–14, 1 student received support, including 1 research assistantship with tuition reimbursement available (averaging $9,001 per year); unspecified assistantships also available. Financial award application deadline: 3/15; financial award applicants required to submit FAFSA. *Faculty research:* Kinship care, child trauma, juvenile delinquency, end-of-life issues, aging issues, child welfare, health and mental health disparities among various populations, HIV/AIDS and sexual violence in Haiti, integrated behavioral health care, international social work practice. *Total annual research expenditures:* $46,894. *Unit head:* Dr. Bonnie Yegidis, Director and Professor, 813-974-1276, Fax: 813-974-4675, E-mail: byegidis@usf.edu. *Application contact:* Dr. Lisa Rapp, Associate Director and Associate Professor, 813-974-1809, Fax: 813-974-4675, E-mail: lrapp@usf.edu.
Website: http://www.cas.usf.edu/social_work/.

University of South Florida, University College/Distance Education, Tampa, FL 33620-9951. *Unit head:* Kathy Barnes, Interdisciplinary Programs Coordinator, 813-974-8031, Fax: 813-974-7061, E-mail: barnesk@usf.edu. *Application contact:* Karen Tylinski, Metro Initiatives, 813-974-9943, Fax: 813-974-7061, E-mail: ktylinsk@usf.edu.
Website: http://uc.usf.edu/.

The University of Tennessee, Graduate School, College of Social Work, Doctor of Social Work Program, Knoxville, TN 37996. Offers clinical practice and leadership (DSW). *Expenses:* Tuition, state resident: full-time $9540; part-time $531 per credit hour. Tuition, nonresident: full-time $27,728; part-time $1542 per credit hour. *Required fees:* $1404; $67 per credit hour.

The University of Tennessee, Graduate School, College of Social Work, Master of Science in Social Work Program, Knoxville, TN 37996. Offers evidenced-based interpersonal practice (MSSW); management leadership and community practice (MSSW). Part-time programs available. Postbaccalaureate distance learning degree programs offered (minimal on-campus study). *Expenses:* Tuition, state resident: full-time $9540; part-time $531 per credit hour. Tuition, nonresident: full-time $27,728; part-time $1542 per credit hour. *Required fees:* $1404; $67 per credit hour.

The University of Tennessee, Graduate School, College of Social Work, PhD in Social Work Program, Knoxville, TN 37996. Offers PhD. *Expenses:* Tuition, state resident: full-time $9540; part-time $531 per credit hour. Tuition, nonresident: full-time $27,728; part-time $1542 per credit hour. *Required fees:* $1404; $67 per credit hour.

The University of Texas at Arlington, Graduate School, School of Social Work, Arlington, TX 76019. Offers MSSW, PhD. *Accreditation:* CSWE (one or more programs are accredited). Part-time and evening/weekend programs available. Postbaccalaureate distance learning degree programs offered (no on-campus study). *Degree requirements:* For master's, thesis optional; for doctorate, comprehensive exam, thesis/dissertation. *Entrance requirements:* For master's, GRE General Test (if GPA less than 3.0), 3 letters of recommendation; for doctorate, GRE General Test (if GPA is below 3.4), minimum graduate GPA of 3.4. Additional exam requirements/recommendations for international students: Required—TOEFL (minimum score 550 paper-based). Electronic applications accepted. *Faculty research:* Community practice, administrative practice, mental health and children and families.

Social Work

The University of Texas at Austin, Graduate School, School of Social Work, Austin, TX 78712-1111. Offers MSSW, PhD. *Accreditation:* CSWE (one or more programs are accredited). Part-time programs available. *Degree requirements:* For doctorate, thesis/dissertation. *Entrance requirements:* For master's and doctorate, GRE General Test. Additional exam requirements/recommendations for international students: Required—TOEFL. *Faculty research:* Substance abuse, child welfare, gerontology, mental health, public policy.

The University of Texas at El Paso, Graduate School, College of Health Sciences, Social Work Program, El Paso, TX 79968-0001. Offers social work in the border region (MSW). Part-time programs available. *Entrance requirements:* For master's, statistics and biology, undergraduate degree from accredited university. Additional exam requirements/recommendations for international students: Required—TOEFL (minimum score 550 paper-based; 80 iBT). Electronic applications accepted. *Faculty research:* Immigration, trauma, health, farm workers, child welfare, mental health.

The University of Texas at San Antonio, College of Public Policy, Department of Social Work, San Antonio, TX 78249-0617. Offers MSW. *Accreditation:* CSWE. *Faculty:* 13 full-time (8 women), 7 part-time/adjunct (6 women). *Students:* 96 full-time (76 women), 136 part-time (115 women); includes 148 minority (23 Black or African American, non-Hispanic/Latino; 1 American Indian or Alaska Native, non-Hispanic/Latino; 5 Asian, non-Hispanic/Latino; 111 Hispanic/Latino; 2 Native Hawaiian or other Pacific Islander, non-Hispanic/Latino; 6 Two or more races, non-Hispanic/Latino), 1 international. Average age 31. 104 applicants, 86% accepted, 59 enrolled. In 2013, 67 master's awarded. *Entrance requirements:* For master's, GRE, bachelor's degree, three letters of recommendation, statement of purpose. Additional exam requirements/recommendations for international students: Required—TOEFL (minimum score 550 paper-based; 79 iBT), IELTS (minimum score 6.5). *Application deadline:* For fall admission, 7/1 for domestic students, 4/1 for international students; for spring admission, 11/1 for domestic students, 9/1 for international students. Application fee: $45 ($80 for international students). *Expenses:* Tuition, state resident: full-time $4671. Tuition, nonresident: full-time $8708. *International tuition:* $17,415 full-time. *Required fees:* $1924.60. Tuition and fees vary according to course load and degree level. *Unit head:* Dr. Martell Teasley, Department Chair, 210-458-3000, Fax: 210-458-3001, E-mail: martell.teasley@utsa.edu. *Application contact:* Robert Ambrosino, Graduate Advisor of Record, 210-458-2026, Fax: 210-458-2026, E-mail: robert.ambrosino@utsa.edu.
Website: http://copp.utsa.edu/social-work/home.

The University of Texas–Pan American, College of Health Sciences and Human Services, Department of Social Work, Edinburg, TX 78539. Offers MSSW. *Accreditation:* CSWE. Part-time programs available. *Entrance requirements:* For master's, minimum GPA of 3.0, basic statistics course completed within 5 years of admission. Additional exam requirements/recommendations for international students: Recommended—TOEFL (minimum score 500 paper-based). *Expenses:* Tuition, state resident: full-time $5986; part-time $333 per credit hour. Tuition, nonresident: full-time $12,358; part-time $687 per credit hour. *Required fees:* $782. Tuition and fees vary according to program. *Faculty research:* Child welfare, family violence, social justice, Hispanic traditional healing (curanderismo and spirituality), community development.

University of the Fraser Valley, Graduate Studies, Abbotsford, BC V2S 7M8, Canada. Offers criminal justice (MA); social work (MSW). Evening/weekend programs available. *Faculty:* 21 full-time (11 women). *Students:* 36 full-time (17 women), 9 part-time (all women). Average age 42. In 2013, 18 master's awarded. *Degree requirements:* For master's, thesis optional, major research paper. *Entrance requirements:* For master's, bachelor's degree, work experience in related field. Additional exam requirements/recommendations for international students: Recommended—TOEFL (minimum score 88 iBT), IELTS (minimum score 6.5), TWE. *Application deadline:* For fall admission, 1/31 priority date for domestic students, 4/1 priority date for international students; for winter admission, 9/30 priority date for domestic students, 10/1 priority date for international students; for spring admission, 12/31 priority date for domestic students, 2/1 priority date for international students. Application fee: $45 ($150 for international students). Electronic applications accepted. *Expenses:* Contact institution. *Financial support:* Research assistantships, scholarships/grants, health care benefits, and bursaries available. Financial award application deadline: 5/10. *Faculty research:* Criminal justice, criminology, social work, child welfare. *Unit head:* Dr. Adrienne Chan, Associate Vice President, Research, Engagement and Graduate Studies, 604-504-4074, Fax: 778-880-0356, E-mail: adrienne.chan@ufv.ca. *Application contact:* Educational Advisors, 604-854-4528, Fax: 604-855-7614, E-mail: advising@ufv.ca.
Website: http://www.ufv.ca/Graduate_Studies.htm.

The University of Toledo, College of Graduate Studies, College of Social Justice and Human Service, Department of Criminal Justice and Social Work, Toledo, OH 43606-3390. Offers child advocacy (Certificate); criminal justice (MA); elder law (Certificate); juvenile justice (Certificate); patient advocacy (Certificate); social work (MSW); JD/MA. *Accreditation:* CSWE. Part-time programs available. *Faculty:* 26. *Students:* 45 full-time (32 women), 76 part-time (67 women); includes 26 minority (11 Black or African American, non-Hispanic/Latino; 3 Asian, non-Hispanic/Latino; 9 Hispanic/Latino; 3 Two or more races, non-Hispanic/Latino). Average age 33. 97 applicants, 69% accepted, 48 enrolled. In 2013, 67 master's, 19 other advanced degrees awarded. *Degree requirements:* For master's, comprehensive exam, thesis. *Entrance requirements:* For master's and Certificate, minimum cumulative GPA of 2.7 for all previous academic work, letters of recommendation. Additional exam requirements/recommendations for international students: Required—TOEFL (minimum score 550 paper-based; 80 iBT). *Application deadline:* For fall admission, 1/15 priority date for domestic and international students. Applications are processed on a rolling basis. Application fee: $45 ($75 for international students). Electronic applications accepted. *Financial support:* In 2013–14, 2 research assistantships with full and partial tuition reimbursements (averaging $12,000 per year), 14 teaching assistantships with full and partial tuition reimbursements (averaging $8,300 per year) were awarded; Federal Work-Study, scholarships/grants, tuition waivers (full and partial), unspecified assistantships, and administrative assistantships also available. *Unit head:* Dr. Shanhe Jiang, Chair, 419-530-4329, E-mail: shanhe.jiang@utoledo.edu. *Application contact:* Graduate School Office, 419-530-4723, Fax: 419-530-4724, E-mail: grdsch@utnet.utoledo.edu.
Website: http://www.utoledo.edu/eduhshs/.

University of Toronto, School of Graduate Studies, Faculty of Social Work, Toronto, ON M5S 1A1, Canada. Offers MSW, PhD, MH Sc/MSW. Part-time programs available. *Degree requirements:* For doctorate, thesis/dissertation, oral exam/thesis defense. *Entrance requirements:* For master's, minimum mid-B average in final year of full-time study, 3 full courses in social sciences, experience in social services (recommended), 3 letters of reference, resume; for doctorate, MSW or equivalent, minimum B+ average, competency in basic statistical methods. Additional exam requirements/recommendations for international students: Required—TOEFL (minimum score 580 paper-based; 93 iBT); IELTS (minimum score 7), TWE (minimum score 5), or Michigan English Language Assessment Battery (minimum score 85). Electronic applications accepted. *Expenses:* Contact institution.

University of Utah, Graduate School, College of Social Work, Salt Lake City, UT 84112. Offers MSW, PhD, MSW/JD, MSW/MPA, MSW/MPH. *Accreditation:* CSWE (one or more programs are accredited). Part-time and evening/weekend programs available. Postbaccalaureate distance learning degree programs offered (minimal on-campus study). *Faculty:* 18 full-time (10 women), 35 part-time/adjunct (22 women). *Students:* 309 full-time (228 women), 36 part-time (19 women); includes 61 minority (7 Black or African American, non-Hispanic/Latino; 2 American Indian or Alaska Native, non-Hispanic/Latino; 3 Asian, non-Hispanic/Latino; 36 Hispanic/Latino; 2 Native Hawaiian or other Pacific Islander, non-Hispanic/Latino; 11 Two or more races, non-Hispanic/Latino), 7 international. Average age 34. 309 applicants, 69% accepted, 161 enrolled. In 2013, 224 master's, 10 doctorates awarded. *Degree requirements:* For master's, thesis or alternative; for doctorate, comprehensive exam, thesis/dissertation. *Entrance requirements:* For master's, GRE General Test or MAT (if cumulative GPA is below 3.0), minimum GPA of 3.0; for doctorate, GRE General Test. Additional exam requirements/recommendations for international students: Required—TOEFL (minimum score 600 paper-based; 100 iBT). *Application deadline:* For fall admission, 11/1 for domestic and international students. Application fee: $205. Electronic applications accepted. *Expenses:* Contact institution. *Financial support:* In 2013–14, 55 students received support, including 25 fellowships with partial tuition reimbursements available (averaging $15,000 per year), 24 research assistantships with full and partial tuition reimbursements available (averaging $15,000 per year), 6 teaching assistantships with partial tuition reimbursements available (averaging $5,000 per year); Federal Work-Study and institutionally sponsored loans also available. Support available to part-time students. Financial award application deadline: 3/15; financial award applicants required to submit FAFSA. *Faculty research:* Health, mental health, gerontology, child welfare, forensic social work, instructional social work. *Total annual research expenditures:* $265,538. *Unit head:* Dr. Jannah H. Mather, Dean, 801-581-6194, Fax: 801-585-3219, E-mail: jannah.mather@socwk.utah.edu. *Application contact:* Dr. Hank Liese, Associate Dean, 801-581-8828, Fax: 801-585-3219, E-mail: hank.liese@socwk.utah.edu.
Website: http://www.socwk.utah.edu/.

University of Vermont, Graduate College, College of Education and Social Services, Department of Social Work, Burlington, VT 05405. Offers MSW. *Accreditation:* CSWE. *Students:* 47 (37 women); includes 5 minority (1 Black or African American, non-Hispanic/Latino; 1 American Indian or Alaska Native, non-Hispanic/Latino; 2 Hispanic/Latino; 1 Two or more races, non-Hispanic/Latino). 82 applicants, 70% accepted, 22 enrolled. In 2013, 26 master's awarded. *Entrance requirements:* For master's, GRE General Test, resume. Additional exam requirements/recommendations for international students: Required—TOEFL (minimum score 550 paper-based; 80 iBT). *Application deadline:* For fall admission, 2/1 priority date for domestic students, 2/1 for international students. Applications are processed on a rolling basis. Application fee: $65. Electronic applications accepted. *Financial support:* Application deadline: 2/1. *Unit head:* Gary Widrick, Chair, 802-656-8800. *Application contact:* Susan Comerford, Coordinator, 802-656-8800.

University of Victoria, Faculty of Graduate Studies, Faculty of Human and Social Development, School of Social Work, Victoria, BC V8W 2Y2, Canada. Offers MSW. *Entrance requirements:* For master's, BSW. Additional exam requirements/recommendations for international students: Required—TOEFL (minimum score 575 paper-based), IELTS (minimum score 7). Electronic applications accepted. *Faculty research:* Women's issues, public policy formation and implementation, child welfare, First Nations, community development.

University of Victoria, Faculty of Graduate Studies, Faculty of Human and Social Development, Studies in Policy and Practice Program, Victoria, BC V8W 2Y2, Canada. Offers MA. Part-time programs available. *Degree requirements:* For master's, thesis. *Entrance requirements:* For master's, resume. Additional exam requirements/recommendations for international students: Required—TOEFL (minimum score 575 paper-based), IELTS (minimum score 7). Electronic applications accepted. *Faculty research:* Women's issues, public policy formation and implementation, health promotion and education, children, youth and families.

University of Washington, Graduate School, School of Social Work, Seattle, WA 98195. Offers MSW, PhD, MPH/MSW. *Accreditation:* CSWE (one or more programs are accredited). Evening/weekend programs available. Postbaccalaureate distance learning degree programs offered (minimal on-campus study). *Degree requirements:* For master's, thesis optional; for doctorate, thesis/dissertation. *Entrance requirements:* For master's, GRE General Test, minimum GPA of 3.0; for doctorate, master's degree, sample of scholarly work, minimum GPA of 3.0. Additional exam requirements/recommendations for international students: Required—TOEFL. *Faculty research:* Health and mental health; children, youth, and families; multicultural issues; reducing risk and enhancing protective factors in children; etrology of substance use.

University of Washington, Tacoma, Graduate Programs, Program in Social Work, Tacoma, WA 98402-3100. Offers advanced integrative practice (MSW); social work (MSW). Part-time and evening/weekend programs available. *Degree requirements:* For master's, completion of all 75 required credits with minimum cumulative GPA of 3.0, 2.7 in each course; degree completion within 6 years. *Entrance requirements:* For master's, baccalaureate degree from regionally-accredited institution, minimum GPA of 3.0 on most recent 90 quarter credit hours or 60 semester hours, resume, social service experience form, two essay question responses, criminal/conviction history and background check clearance, three letters of reference. Additional exam requirements/recommendations for international students: Required—TOEFL (minimum score 580 paper-based; 70 iBT). Electronic applications accepted. *Faculty research:* Domestic violence and prevention, LGBT issues, gerontological social work, transnational social work, child welfare-mental health.

University of West Florida, College of Professional Studies, School of Justice Studies and Social Work, Department of Social Work, Pensacola, FL 32514-5750. Offers MSW. Part-time and evening/weekend programs available. *Entrance requirements:* For master's, GRE or MAT, official transcripts; minimum undergraduate cumulative GPA of 3.0; academic preparation as demonstrated by quality and relevance of undergraduate degree major; letter of intent; 3 letters of recommendation; work experience as documented on the Social Work Supplemental Application. Additional exam requirements/recommendations for international students: Required—TOEFL (minimum score 550 paper-based). Electronic applications accepted.

University of Windsor, Faculty of Graduate Studies, Faculty of Arts and Social Sciences, School of Social Work, Windsor, ON N9B 3P4, Canada. Offers MSW. Part-time programs available. *Degree requirements:* For master's, thesis or alternative. *Entrance requirements:* For master's, minimum B+ average in last year of undergraduate study. Additional exam requirements/recommendations for international students: Required—TOEFL (minimum score 600 paper-based). Electronic applications accepted. *Faculty research:* Addiction, social policy analysis, gerontology and health care.

University of Wisconsin–Green Bay, Graduate Studies, Program in Social Work, Green Bay, WI 54311-7001. Offers MSW. *Accreditation:* CSWE. *Faculty:* 7 full-time (4 women), 9 part-time/adjunct (7 women). *Students:* 23 full-time (19 women), 28 part-time (22 women); includes 14 minority (4 Black or African American, non-Hispanic/Latino; 2 American Indian or Alaska Native, non-Hispanic/Latino; 2 Asian, non-Hispanic/Latino; 6 Hispanic/Latino). Average age 33. 28 applicants, 100% accepted, 27 enrolled. In 2013, 15 master's awarded. *Degree requirements:* For master's, thesis or alternative.

Entrance requirements: For master's, GRE, minimum GPA of 2.75. *Application deadline:* For fall admission, 8/1 priority date for domestic students; for spring admission, 11/1 priority date for domestic students. Applications are processed on a rolling basis. Application fee: $56. Electronic applications accepted. *Expenses:* Tuition, state resident: full-time $7640; part-time $424 per credit. Tuition, nonresident: full-time $16,772; part-time $932 per credit. *Required fees:* $1378. Full-time tuition and fees vary according to course load and reciprocity agreements. *Faculty research:* Child welfare. *Unit head:* Dr. Doreen Higgins, Coordinator, 920-465-2567, E-mail: higginsd@uwgb.edu. *Application contact:* Mary Valitchka, Graduate Studies Coordinator, 920-465-2143, Fax: 920-465-2043, E-mail: valitchm@uwgb.edu.
Website: http://www.uwgb.edu/graduate.

University of Wisconsin–Madison, Graduate School, College of Letters and Science, School of Social Work, Madison, WI 53706-1380. Offers social welfare (PhD); social work (MSW). *Accreditation:* CSWE (one or more programs are accredited). Terminal master's awarded for partial completion of doctoral program. *Degree requirements:* For doctorate, thesis/dissertation. *Entrance requirements:* For master's, minimum GPA of 3.0 on last 60 credits; for doctorate, GRE General Test, minimum GPA of 3.0 on last 60 credits. Electronic applications accepted. *Expenses:* Contact institution. *Faculty research:* Poverty, caregiving, child welfare, developmental disabilities, mental health, severe mental illnesses, adolescence, family, social policy, child support.

University of Wisconsin–Milwaukee, Graduate School, School of Social Welfare, Department of Social Work, Milwaukee, WI 53201-0413. Offers applied gerontology (Certificate); marriage and family therapy (Certificate); non-profit management (Certificate); social work (MSW, PhD). *Accreditation:* CSWE. Part-time programs available. *Faculty:* 14 full-time (8 women). *Students:* 186 full-time (165 women), 87 part-time (79 women); includes 63 minority (35 Black or African American, non-Hispanic/Latino; 1 American Indian or Alaska Native, non-Hispanic/Latino; 4 Asian, non-Hispanic/Latino; 4 Hispanic/Latino; 19 Two or more races, non-Hispanic/Latino), 2 international. Average age 30. 323 applicants, 56% accepted, 106 enrolled. In 2013, 123 master's awarded. *Degree requirements:* For master's, thesis or alternative. *Entrance requirements:* For doctorate, GRE, bachelor's degree. Additional exam requirements/recommendations for international students: Required—TOEFL (minimum score 550 paper-based; 79 iBT), IELTS (minimum score 6.5). *Application deadline:* For fall admission, 1/1 priority date for domestic students; for spring admission, 9/1 for domestic students. Applications are processed on a rolling basis. Application fee: $56 ($96 for international students). Electronic applications accepted. *Financial support:* In 2013–14, 5 fellowships, 4 research assistantships, 3 teaching assistantships were awarded; career-related internships or fieldwork, health care benefits, unspecified assistantships, and project assistantships also available. Support available to part-time students. Financial award application deadline: 4/15; financial award applicants required to submit FAFSA. *Unit head:* Deborah Padgett, Department Chair, 414-229-6452, E-mail: dpadgett@uwm.edu. *Application contact:* General Information Contact, 414-229-4982, Fax: 414-229-6967, E-mail: gradschool@uwm.edu.
Website: http://www.uwm.edu/Dept/SSW/sw/.

University of Wisconsin–Oshkosh, Graduate Studies, Department of Social Work, Oshkosh, WI 54901. Offers MSW. Program offered jointly with University of Wisconsin–Green Bay. *Accreditation:* CSWE. Part-time programs available. *Entrance requirements:* For master's, GRE, letters of recommendation, previous courses in statistics and human biology, work experience. Additional exam requirements/recommendations for international students: Required—TOEFL (minimum score 550 paper-based; 79 iBT).

University of Wyoming, College of Health Sciences, Division of Social Work, Laramie, WY 82071. Offers MSW. *Accreditation:* CSWE. *Degree requirements:* For master's, comprehensive exam, thesis or alternative. *Entrance requirements:* For master's, minimum GPA of 3.0. Additional exam requirements/recommendations for international students: Required—TOEFL. *Expenses:* Contact institution. *Faculty research:* Social work education, child welfare, mental health, diversity, school social work.

Valdosta State University, Department of Social Work, Valdosta, GA 31698. Offers MSW. *Accreditation:* CSWE. Part-time and evening/weekend programs available. Postbaccalaureate distance learning degree programs offered (minimal on-campus study). *Faculty:* 6 full-time (4 women). *Students:* 65 full-time (62 women), 40 part-time (31 women); includes 41 minority (34 Black or African American, non-Hispanic/Latino; 4 Hispanic/Latino; 3 Two or more races, non-Hispanic/Latino). Average age 25. 79 applicants, 49% accepted, 35 enrolled. In 2013, 32 master's awarded. *Degree requirements:* For master's, comprehensive exam, 5 practica. *Entrance requirements:* For master's, GRE General Test, MAT, minimum GPA of 3.0 in last 2 years of course work. Additional exam requirements/recommendations for international students: Required—TOEFL (minimum score 523 paper-based). *Application deadline:* For fall admission, 3/15 for domestic and international students. Applications are processed on a rolling basis. Application fee: $35. *Expenses:* Tuition, state resident: full-time $4140; part-time $230 per credit hour. Tuition, nonresident: full-time $14,904; part-time $828 per credit hour. *Required fees:* $995 per semester. Tuition and fees vary according to course load. *Financial support:* In 2013–14, 4 students received support, including 2 research assistantships with full tuition reimbursements available (averaging $3,652 per year); career-related internships or fieldwork, institutionally sponsored loans, scholarships/grants, and unspecified assistantships also available. Financial award application deadline: 7/1; financial award applicants required to submit FAFSA. *Unit head:* Dr. Mizanur Miah, Head, 229-249-4864, Fax: 229-245-4341, E-mail: mrmiah@valdosta.edu. *Application contact:* Rebecca Powers, Coordinator of Graduate Admissions, 229-333-5694, Fax: 229-245-3853, E-mail: rlwaters@valdosta.edu.
Website: http://www.valdosta.edu/colleges/education/social-work/.

Virginia Commonwealth University, Graduate School, School of Social Work, Doctoral Program in Social Work, Richmond, VA 23284-9005. Offers PhD. *Degree requirements:* For doctorate, comprehensive exam, thesis/dissertation. *Entrance requirements:* For doctorate, GRE General Test, MSW or related degree. Additional exam requirements/recommendations for international students: Required—TOEFL (minimum score 600 paper-based; 100 iBT). Electronic applications accepted.

Virginia Commonwealth University, Graduate School, School of Social Work, Master's Program in Social Work, Richmond, VA 23284-9005. Offers MSW, JD/MSW, MSW/M Div, MSW/MPH. *Accreditation:* CSWE. *Entrance requirements:* Additional exam requirements/recommendations for international students: Required—TOEFL (minimum score 600 paper-based; 100 iBT). Electronic applications accepted.

Walden University, Graduate Programs, School of Social Work and Human Services, Minneapolis, MN 55401. Offers addictions (MSW); addictions and social work (DSW); children, families, and couples (MSW); clinical expertise (DSW); criminal justice (DSW); crisis and trauma (MSW); disaster, crisis, and intervention (DSW); forensic populations and settings (MSW); general program (MSW); human services (MS, PhD), including clinical social work (PhD), criminal justice, disaster, crisis and intervention, family studies and intervention strategies (PhD), family studies and interventions, general program, human services administration (PhD), human services and administration (MS), public health, social policy analysis and planning; medical social work (MSW, DSW); military families and culture (MSW); policy practice (DSW); social work (PhD), including addictions and social work, clinical expertise, disaster, crisis and intervention (MS, PhD),

family studies and interventions (MS, PhD), medical social work, policy practice, social work administration; social work administration (DSW). Part-time and evening/weekend programs available. Postbaccalaureate distance learning degree programs offered (minimal on-campus study). *Faculty:* 11 full-time (7 women), 89 part-time/adjunct (60 women). *Students:* 906 full-time (794 women), 469 part-time (394 women); includes 930 minority (812 Black or African American, non-Hispanic/Latino; 14 American Indian or Alaska Native, non-Hispanic/Latino; 12 Asian, non-Hispanic/Latino; 61 Hispanic/Latino; 4 Native Hawaiian or other Pacific Islander, non-Hispanic/Latino; 27 Two or more races, non-Hispanic/Latino), 11 international. Average age 41. 673 applicants, 97% accepted, 555 enrolled. In 2013, 417 master's, 11 doctorates awarded. *Degree requirements:* For master's, residency (for some programs); for doctorate, thesis/dissertation, residency. *Entrance requirements:* For master's, bachelor's degree or higher; minimum GPA of 2.5; official transcripts; goal statement (for some programs); access to computer and Internet; for doctorate, master's degree or higher; three years of related professional or academic experience (preferred); minimum GPA of 3.0; goal statement and current resume (select programs); official transcripts; access to computer and Internet. Additional exam requirements/recommendations for international students: Required—TOEFL (minimum score 550 paper-based; 79 iBT), IELTS (minimum score 6.5), Michigan English Language Assessment Battery (minimum score 82), or PTE. *Application deadline:* Applications are processed on a rolling basis. Application fee: $0. Electronic applications accepted. *Expenses:* Tuition: Full-time $11,813.55; part-time $500 per credit. *Required fees:* $618.76. *Financial support:* Fellowships, Federal Work-Study, scholarships/grants, unspecified assistantships, and family tuition reduction, active duty/veteran tuition reduction, group tuition reduction, interest-free payment plans, employee tuition reduction available. Support available to part-time students. Financial award applicants required to submit FAFSA. *Unit head:* Dr. Savitri Dixon-Saxon, Associate Dean, 800-925-3368. *Application contact:* Jennifer Hall, Vice President of Enrollment Management, 866-4-WALDEN, E-mail: info@waldenu.edu. Website: http://www.waldenu.edu/colleges-schools/school-of-social-work-and-human-services/academic-programs.

Walla Walla University, Graduate School, Wilma Hepker School of Social Work and Sociology, College Place, WA 99324-1198. Offers social work (MSW). *Accreditation:* CSWE. Part-time programs available. *Entrance requirements:* For master's, minimum GPA of 2.75. Additional exam requirements/recommendations for international students: Required—TOEFL (minimum score 550 paper-based; 79 iBT). Electronic applications accepted.

Washburn University, School of Applied Studies, Department of Social Work, Topeka, KS 66621. Offers clinical social work (MSW); JD/MSW. *Accreditation:* CSWE. Part-time and evening/weekend programs available. *Faculty:* 7 full-time (3 women), 1 part-time/adjunct (0 women). *Students:* 64 full-time (58 women), 22 part-time (21 women). Average age 31. In 2013, 52 master's awarded. *Degree requirements:* For master's, practicum. *Entrance requirements:* For master's, coursework in human biology and cultural anthropology (or multiculturalism or human diversity). Additional exam requirements/recommendations for international students: Required—TOEFL (minimum score 80 iBT). *Application deadline:* For fall admission, 1/15 priority date for domestic and international students; for spring admission, 10/15 priority date for domestic and international students. Applications are processed on a rolling basis. Application fee: $25. *Expenses:* Tuition, state resident: full-time $5850; part-time $325 per credit hour. Tuition, nonresident: full-time $11,916; part-time $662 per credit hour. *Required fees:* $86; $43 per semester. Tuition and fees vary according to program. *Financial support:* Career-related internships or fieldwork, Federal Work-Study, institutionally sponsored loans, and scholarships/grants available. Support available to part-time students. Financial award applicants required to submit FAFSA. *Faculty research:* Trauma, multicultural issues, school social work, emotional intelligence, animal-assisted therapy. *Unit head:* Dr. Mark Kaufman, Chair, 785-670-2135, Fax: 785-670-1027, E-mail: mark.kaufman@washburn.edu. *Application contact:* Dr. Kimberly Harrison, MSW Program Director, 785-670-1957, Fax: 785-670-1027, E-mail: kimberly.harrison@washburn.edu.
Website: http://www.washburn.edu/academics/college-schools/applied-studies/departments/social-work/index.html.

Washington University in St. Louis, George Warren Brown School of Social Work, St. Louis, MO 63130. Offers Alaska native/American Indian studies (MSW); children, youth and families (MSW); gerontology (MSW); mental health (MSW); public health (MPA, MPH), including epidemiology/biostatistics (MPH), global health (MPA); social and economic development (MSW); social work (MSW, PhD), including health (MSW); JD/MSW; M Arch/MSW; MBA/MSW; MPH/MBA; MSW/M Div; MSW/MAPS; MSW/MJCS; MSW/MPH. MSW/M Div and MSW/MAPS offered jointly with Eden Theological Seminary. *Accreditation:* CSWE (one or more programs are accredited). *Faculty:* 42 full-time (24 women), 81 part-time/adjunct (49 women). *Students:* 298 full-time (263 women), 5 part-time (all women); includes 78 minority (32 Black or African American, non-Hispanic/Latino; 4 American Indian or Alaska Native, non-Hispanic/Latino; 18 Asian, non-Hispanic/Latino; 9 Hispanic/Latino; 2 Native Hawaiian or other Pacific Islander, non-Hispanic/Latino; 13 Two or more races, non-Hispanic/Latino), 47 international. Average age 26. 817 applicants, 62% accepted, 303 enrolled. In 2013, 239 master's, 5 doctorates awarded. *Degree requirements:* For master's, 60 credit hours (MSW), 52 credit hours (MPH); practicum; for doctorate, comprehensive exam, thesis/dissertation. *Entrance requirements:* For master's, GRE, GMAT, LSAT, or MCAT (public health), minimum GPA of 3.0; for doctorate, GRE, MA or MSW. Additional exam requirements/recommendations for international students: Required—TOEFL (minimum score 100 iBT). *Application deadline:* For fall admission, 3/1 priority date for domestic and international students. Applications are processed on a rolling basis. Application fee: $40. Electronic applications accepted. *Expenses:* Contact institution. *Financial support:* In 2013–14, 301 students received support. Fellowships, research assistantships, Federal Work-Study, institutionally sponsored loans, scholarships/grants, health care benefits, tuition waivers (partial), and unspecified assistantships available. Support available to part-time students. Financial award application deadline: 3/1; financial award applicants required to submit FAFSA. *Faculty research:* Mental health services, social development, child welfare, at-risk teens, autism, environmental health, health policy, health communications, obesity, violence and injury prevention, chronic disease prevention, poverty, public health, productive aging/gerontology, social work, civic engagement, school social work, program evaluation, health disparities. *Unit head:* Dr. Edward F. Lawlor, Dean/Professor, 314-935-6693, Fax: 314-935-8511, E-mail: elawlor@wustl.edu. *Application contact:* Leslie D. Duling, Admissions Counselor, 314-935-6694, Fax: 314-935-4859, E-mail: lduling@brownschool.wustl.edu.
Website: http://gwbweb.wustl.edu/.

Wayne State University, College of Liberal Arts and Sciences, Department of Political Science, Program in Public Administration, Detroit, MI 48202. Offers aging policy and management (MPA); criminal justice policy and management (MPA); economic development policy and management (MPA); health and human services policy and management (MPA); human and fiscal resource management (MPA); information technology management (MPA); nonprofit policy and management (MPA); organizational behavior and management (MPA); public budgeting and financial management (MPA); public policy analysis and program evaluation (MPA); social welfare policy and management (MPA); urban and metropolitan policy and management

(MPA). *Accreditation:* NASPAA. Evening/weekend programs available. *Students:* 11 full-time (5 women), 55 part-time (43 women); includes 20 minority (14 Black or African American, non-Hispanic/Latino; 2 Asian, non-Hispanic/Latino; 2 Hispanic/Latino; 2 Two or more races, non-Hispanic/Latino), 1 international. Average age 33. 83 applicants, 34% accepted, 17 enrolled. In 2013, 19 master's awarded. *Degree requirements:* For master's, comprehensive exam. *Entrance requirements:* For master's, GRE General Test, minimum undergraduate upper-division GPA of 3.0 or master's degree. Additional exam requirements/recommendations for international students: Required—TOEFL (minimum score 550 paper-based; 79 iBT), TWE (minimum score 5.5), Michigan English Language Assessment Battery (minimum score 85); Recommended—IELTS (minimum score 6.5). *Application deadline:* For fall admission, 6/1 priority date for domestic students, 5/1 priority date for international students; for winter admission, 10/1 priority date for domestic students, 9/1 priority date for international students; for spring admission, 2/1 priority date for domestic students, 1/1 priority date for international students. Applications are processed on a rolling basis. Application fee: $0. Electronic applications accepted. *Expenses:* Tuition, state resident: part-time $554.15 per credit. Tuition, nonresident: part-time $1200.35 per credit. *Required fees:* $42.15 per credit. $268.30 per semester. Tuition and fees vary according to course load and program. *Financial support:* In 2013–14, 21 students received support. Fellowships, teaching assistantships, scholarships/grants, and unspecified assistantships available. Financial award application deadline: 3/31; financial award applicants required to submit FAFSA. *Faculty research:* Urban politics, urban education, state administration. *Unit head:* Dr. Daniel Geller, Department Chair, 313-577-6328, E-mail: dgeller@wayne.edu. *Application contact:* Dr. Brady Baybeck, Associate Professor/Director, Graduate Program in Public Administration, E-mail: mpa@wayne.edu.
Website: http://clasweb.clas.wayne.edu/mpa.

Wayne State University, School of Social Work, Detroit, MI 48202. Offers alcohol and drug abuse studies (Certificate); disabilities (Certificate); gerontology (Certificate); social welfare research and evaluation (Certificate); social work (MSW, PhD); social work and gerontology (PhD); social work and infant mental health (MSW, PhD); social work practice with families and couples (Certificate). *Accreditation:* CSWE (one or more programs are accredited). Part-time and evening/weekend programs available. *Students:* 500 full-time (443 women), 119 part-time (103 women); includes 209 minority (164 Black or African American, non-Hispanic/Latino; 4 American Indian or Alaska Native, non-Hispanic/Latino; 9 Asian, non-Hispanic/Latino; 16 Hispanic/Latino; 2 Native Hawaiian or other Pacific Islander, non-Hispanic/Latino; 14 Two or more races, non-Hispanic/Latino), 21 international. Average age 32. 770 applicants, 37% accepted, 202 enrolled. In 2013, 301 master's, 2 doctorates, 17 other advanced degrees awarded. *Degree requirements:* For doctorate, thesis/dissertation. *Entrance requirements:* For master's, personal interest statement, resume, 3 references; for doctorate, GRE, resume, three letters of reference, personal statement, summary of relevant research and professional experience, writing sample; for Certificate, MSW or actively enrolled in advanced portion of MSW program. Additional exam requirements/recommendations for international students: Required—TOEFL (minimum score 550 paper-based; 79 iBT), TWE (minimum score 5.5), Michigan English Language Assessment Battery (minimum score 85); Recommended—IELTS (minimum score 6.5). *Application deadline:* For fall admission, 10/1 priority date for domestic and international students. Application fee: $0. Electronic applications accepted. *Expenses:* Tuition, state resident: part-time $554.15 per credit. Tuition, nonresident: part-time $1200.35 per credit. *Required fees:* $42.15 per credit. $268.30 per semester. Tuition and fees vary according to course load and program. *Financial support:* In 2013–14, 90 students received support, including 3 fellowships with tuition reimbursements available (averaging $15,541 per year), 2 research assistantships with tuition reimbursements available (averaging $16,508 per year); teaching assistantships with tuition reimbursements available, scholarships/grants, and unspecified assistantships also available. Financial award application deadline: 3/31; financial award applicants required to submit FAFSA. *Faculty research:* Child welfare, violence, adolescent dating, intimate partner and family violence, sexual assault, gerontology, long-term care, end of life issues, healthy aging, health care, behavioral health and infant mental health, community capacity building, innovation in community, leadership and policy. *Total annual research expenditures:* $484,660. *Unit head:* Dr. Cheryl Waites, Dean and Professor, 313-577-4401, Fax: 313-577-8770, E-mail: dv7029@wayne.edu. *Application contact:* Julie Alter-Kay, Director, Office of Admissions and Student Services, 313-577-4409, E-mail: j.alter-kay@wayne.edu.
Website: http://socialwork.wayne.edu/.

West Chester University of Pennsylvania, College of Business and Public Affairs, Department of Social Work, West Chester, PA 19383. Offers MSW. *Accreditation:* CSWE. Part-time and evening/weekend programs available. *Faculty:* 9 full-time (8 women), 7 part-time/adjunct (6 women). *Students:* 117 full-time (100 women), 51 part-time (45 women); includes 53 minority (45 Black or African American, non-Hispanic/Latino; 7 Hispanic/Latino; 1 Two or more races, non-Hispanic/Latino). Average age 31. 226 applicants, 75% accepted, 92 enrolled. In 2013, 53 master's awarded. *Degree requirements:* For master's, research paper. *Entrance requirements:* For master's, minimum GPA of 3.0 (in some cases applicants will be admitted on a provisional basis if GPA is lower than 3.0); personal statement of 3 to 5 pages clearly articulating professional goals; two letters of recommendation. Additional exam requirements/recommendations for international students: Required—TOEFL (minimum score 550 paper-based; 80 iBT). *Application deadline:* For fall admission, 4/15 priority date for domestic students, 3/15 for international students; for spring admission, 10/15 priority date for domestic students, 9/1 for international students. Applications are processed on a rolling basis. Application fee: $45. Electronic applications accepted. *Expenses:* Tuition, state resident: full-time $7956; part-time $442 per credit. Tuition, nonresident: full-time $11,934; part-time $663 per credit. *Required fees:* $2134.20; $106.24 per credit. Tuition and fees vary according to campus/location and program. *Financial support:* Unspecified assistantships available. Support available to part-time students. Financial award application deadline: 2/15; financial award applicants required to submit FAFSA. *Faculty research:* Trauma and disaster intervention; mental health recovery; traumatic brain injury; social work with older adults; substance use disorders; multicultural resources; grief, loss, and bereavement. *Unit head:* Dr. Page Buck, Chair and Graduate Coordinator, 610-430-4171, E-mail: pbuck@wcupa.edu. *Application contact:* Office of Graduate Studies, 610-436-2943, Fax: 610-436-2763, E-mail: gradstudy@wcupa.edu.
Website: http://www.wcupa.edu/_ACADEMICS/sch_sba/socialWork/default.asp.

Western Carolina University, Graduate School, College of Health and Human Sciences, Department of Social Work, Cullowhee, NC 28723. Offers MSW. *Accreditation:* CSWE. Part-time programs available. *Entrance requirements:* For master's, appropriate undergraduate major with minimum GPA of 3.0, 3 recommendations, resume. Additional exam requirements/recommendations for international students: Required—TOEFL (minimum score 550 paper-based; 79 iBT).

Western Kentucky University, Graduate Studies, College of Health and Human Services, Department of Social Work, Bowling Green, KY 42101. Offers MSW. *Accreditation:* CSWE. *Entrance requirements:* Additional exam requirements/recommendations for international students: Required—TOEFL (minimum score 555 paper-based; 79 iBT).

Western Michigan University, Graduate College, College of Health and Human Services, School of Social Work, Kalamazoo, MI 49008. Offers MSW. *Accreditation:* CSWE. Part-time programs available.

Western New Mexico University, Graduate Division, Department of Social Work, Silver City, NM 88062-0680. Offers MSW. Part-time programs available. Postbaccalaureate distance learning degree programs offered. Electronic applications accepted.

West Texas A&M University, College of Education and Social Sciences, Department of Psychology, Sociology and Social Work, Canyon, TX 79016-0001. Offers psychology (MA); social work (MS). Part-time and evening/weekend programs available. *Degree requirements:* For master's, comprehensive exam, thesis optional. *Entrance requirements:* For master's, GRE General Test, 3 letters of recommendation; interview; minimum GPA of 3.25 in psychology, 3.0 overall. Additional exam requirements/recommendations for international students: Required—TOEFL (minimum score 550 paper-based). Electronic applications accepted. *Faculty research:* Application of sociological principles to historical and contemporary analyses of social systems.

West Virginia University, Eberly College of Arts and Sciences, School of Applied Social Sciences, Division of Social Work, Morgantown, WV 26506. Offers aging and health care (MSW); children and families (MSW); community mental health (MSW); community organization and social administration (MSW); direct (clinical) social work practice (MSW). *Accreditation:* CSWE. Part-time programs available. *Degree requirements:* For master's, fieldwork. *Entrance requirements:* For master's, GRE, minimum GPA of 2.75, 2 letters of reference. Additional exam requirements/recommendations for international students: Required—TOEFL. *Faculty research:* Rural and small town social work practice, gerontology, health and mental health, welfare reform, child welfare.

Wheelock College, Graduate Programs, Division of Social Work, Boston, MA 02215-4176. Offers MSW. *Accreditation:* CSWE. *Degree requirements:* For master's, comprehensive exam, thesis. *Entrance requirements:* For master's, minimum GPA of 3.0; undergraduate course work in human biology, statistics. Additional exam requirements/recommendations for international students: Required—TOEFL. Electronic applications accepted.

Wichita State University, Graduate School, Fairmount College of Liberal Arts and Sciences, School of Social Work, Wichita, KS 67260. Offers MSW. *Accreditation:* CSWE. *Unit head:* Dr. Brien Bolin, Director, 316-978-7250, Fax: 316-978-3328, E-mail: brien.bolin@wichita.edu. *Application contact:* Jordan Oleson, Admissions Coordinator, 316-978-3095, Fax: 316-978-3253, E-mail: jordan.oleson@wichita.edu.

Widener University, School of Human Service Professions, Center for Social Work Education, Chester, PA 19013-5792. Offers MSW, PhD. *Accreditation:* CSWE. Part-time programs available. *Faculty:* 15 full-time (9 women), 16 part-time/adjunct (9 women). *Students:* 149 full-time (131 women), 210 part-time (185 women); includes 175 minority (137 Black or African American, non-Hispanic/Latino; 1 American Indian or Alaska Native, non-Hispanic/Latino; 5 Asian, non-Hispanic/Latino; 25 Hispanic/Latino; 2 Native Hawaiian or other Pacific Islander, non-Hispanic/Latino; 5 Two or more races, non-Hispanic/Latino), 1 international. Average age 33. 184 applicants, 95% accepted. In 2013, 117 master's awarded. *Degree requirements:* For master's, field practica. *Entrance requirements:* For master's, minimum GPA of 3.0. *Application deadline:* For fall admission, 3/1 for domestic students. Applications are processed on a rolling basis. Application fee: $25 ($300 for international students). Electronic applications accepted. *Expenses:* Contact institution. *Financial support:* In 2013–14, 11 students received support, including 6 fellowships; career-related internships or fieldwork, Federal Work-Study, institutionally sponsored loans, and unspecified assistantships also available. Support available to part-time students. Financial award applicants required to submit FAFSA. *Faculty research:* Clinical practice, clinical supervision, gerontology, child welfare, self-psychology. *Total annual research expenditures:* $85,000. *Unit head:* Dr. Paula T. Silver, Associate Dean and Director, 610-499-1150, Fax: 610-499-4617, E-mail: socialwork@widener.edu. *Application contact:* Jill L. Brinker, Secretary, 610-499-1513, Fax: 610-499-4617, E-mail: socialwork@widener.edu.

Wilfrid Laurier University, Faculty of Graduate and Postdoctoral Studies, Lyle S. Hallman Faculty of Social Work, Waterloo, ON N2L 3C5, Canada. Offers Aboriginal studies (MSW); community, policy, planning and organizations (MSW); critical social policy and organizational studies (PhD); individuals, families and groups (MSW); social work practice (individuals, families, groups and communities) (PhD); social work practice: individuals, families, groups and communities (PhD). Part-time programs available. *Degree requirements:* For master's, thesis optional; for doctorate, thesis/dissertation. *Entrance requirements:* For master's, course work in social science, research methodology, and statistics; honors BA with a minimum B average; for doctorate, master's degree in social work, minimum A- average. Additional exam requirements/recommendations for international students: Required—TOEFL (minimum score 89 iBT). Electronic applications accepted. *Expenses:* Contact institution.

Winthrop University, College of Arts and Sciences, Program in Social Work, Rock Hill, SC 29733. Offers MA. *Accreditation:* CSWE. *Entrance requirements:* For master's, GRE or MAT, minimum GPA of 3.0, 3 letters of recommendation, resume. Electronic applications accepted.

Yeshiva University, Wurzweiler School of Social Work, New York, NY 10033-3201. Offers MSW, PhD, MSW/Certificate. *Accreditation:* CSWE (one or more programs are accredited). Part-time and evening/weekend programs available. Terminal master's awarded for partial completion of doctoral program. *Degree requirements:* For master's, thesis, integrative essay; for doctorate, comprehensive exam, thesis/dissertation. *Entrance requirements:* For master's, interview, minimum GPA of 3.0, letters of reference; for doctorate, GRE, interview, letters of reference, writing sample, MSW, minimum of 2 years of professional social work experience. Additional exam requirements/recommendations for international students: Required—TOEFL (minimum score 577 paper-based). *Expenses:* Contact institution. *Faculty research:* Child abuse, AIDS, day care, non profits, gerontology.

York University, Faculty of Graduate Studies, Atkinson Faculty of Liberal and Professional Studies, Program in Social Work, Toronto, ON M3J 1P3, Canada. Offers MSW, PhD. Part-time and evening/weekend programs available. *Degree requirements:* For master's, thesis or alternative. Electronic applications accepted.

ADELPHI UNIVERSITY
School of Social Work

Programs of Study

The School of Social Work at Adelphi University offers programs leading to a Master of Social Work (M.S.W.), a Ph.D. in Social Work, and post-master's certificate programs in advanced trauma studies and treatment, addictions, bilingual school social work, and human resource management. Recently the school made the list in *U.S. News & World Report's 2013 Best Graduate Schools*.

The 64-credit M.S.W. program combines core courses in the foundations of social work with supervised field instruction, to give students experience in applying social work theories to professional practice. The program fosters an abiding commitment to professional values and social justice and equips students with knowledge and skills for social work practice with a wide range of clients and diverse communities. All first-year M.S.W. students are required to take 10 core courses in a set sequence. The plan of study in the first year includes eight courses plus a minimum of 600 hours of supervised field instruction. In their second year of study, students complete six required courses, two elective courses, plus 600 hours of field instruction in advanced, direct social work practice. In addition, M.S.W. students are eligible to enroll in a joint program with the Robert B. Willumstad School of Business leading to a certificate in human resource management that requires only 9 additional credits beyond the M.S.W.

The 51-credit Ph.D. in Social Work gives practitioners the skills and knowledge to effect significant change in social welfare policy and practice. The program emphasizes critical thinking and prepares students to develop knowledge for all methods of social work practice. Graduates are able to provide leadership in the profession as scholars, educators, researchers, and administrators in social agencies. Candidates can pursue doctoral study while they continue to work. Classes are offered one day a week in the late afternoon and early evening. Students must pass qualifying examinations that test mastery and integration of the first two years of study, and they must complete and successfully defend a dissertation that evidences original, independent research.

The interdisciplinary 16-credit certificate in bilingual education is for M.S.W. graduates who are bilingual and work, or plan to work, in a school setting that requires certification in bilingual education. The program consists of core courses that meet the bilingual certification requirements for pupil personnel service professionals mandated by the New York State Department of Education. Courses are offered jointly by the School of Social Work and the Ruth S. Ammon School of Education.

Research Facilities

The University's primary research holdings are at Swirbul Library and include 603,000 volumes (including bound periodicals and government publications); 786,000 items in microformats; 35,000 audiovisual items; and online access to more than 80,000 e-books, 76,000 electronic journal titles, and 265 research databases.

Value

Earning an Adelphi degree means joining a growing alumni network of more than 90,000. For the eighth straight year, Adelphi was designated a Best Buy by the *Fiske Guide to Colleges*, one of only 20 private universities nationwide to earn that distinction. *The Princeton Review* also named Adelphi a Best College in the Northeast, and *Forbes* magazine named Adelphi a Top College. According to payscale.com's 2013 College Education ROI rankings, Adelphi ranks in the top 15 percent of colleges and universities nationwide for return on investment. The numbers speak for themselves—91 percent of Adelphi undergraduates receive financial aid or scholarships.

Financial Aid

The School of Social Work offers various ways to help defray the cost of graduate study. These include scholarships, assistantships, agency tuition remission, and field-placement stipends. More information is available online at ecampus.adelphi.edu/sfs.

Cost of Study

For the 2014–15 academic year, the tuition rate is $990 per credit for the M.S.W. and $1,170 for the Ph.D. University fees range from $330 to $575 per semester.

Living and Housing Costs

The University assists single and married students in finding suitable accommodations whenever possible. The cost of living depends on the location and number of rooms rented.

Location

Located in historic Garden City, New York, just 23 miles from Manhattan, where students are able to take advantage of numerous cultural and internship opportunities, Adelphi's 75-acre suburban campus is known for the beauty of its landscape and architecture. The campus is a short walk from the Long Island Rail Road and is convenient to New York's major airports and several major highways. Off-campus centers are located in Manhattan, the Hudson Valley, and Suffolk County

The University and the School

Founded in 1896, Adelphi is a fully accredited, private university with nearly 8,000 undergraduate, graduate, and returning-adult students in the arts and sciences, business, clinical psychology, education, nursing, and social work. Students come from 40 states and 45 countries.

For more than 50 years, the School of Social Work has trained social work practitioners who are dedicated to improving the lives of individuals, families, groups, and communities. Through its many programs, the School has been a driving force for ethical social work practice and a strong advocate for social justice. The School is committed to the development of new knowledge that can inform the evolution of social policy, the organization and delivery of social services, and the profession's ability to intervene effectively with, and on behalf of, vulnerable, disenfranchised, and marginalized populations. The scholarship, research, and demonstration projects that the faculty members and graduate students are engaged in respond to the exigencies of contemporary life and contribute to social work's capacity to improve individuals' well-being. The School features small classes in a supportive environment that fosters a close and nurturing relationship between faculty members and students. Faculty members have extensive teaching experience and are recognized as leaders in their respective fields. The broad base of diverse students and professionals seeking advanced degrees enhances the classroom learning and enriches the educational experience for all.

Applying

Master's degree applicants should have a bachelor's degree with a strong science and liberal arts background; doctoral applicants should have an M.S.W. and at least three years' experience in the field. All applicants must submit a completed application, a $50 application fee, official college transcripts, and three letters of recommendation. Ph.D. applicants must also submit GRE scores and have a minimum 3.3 GPA. An interview is required. Application deadlines are July 15 for the fall semester and December 1 for the spring semester in the M.S.W. program, and April 1 for doctoral applications. .

Correspondence and Information

800-ADELPHI
socialwork.adelphi.edu

THE FACULTY AND THEIR RESEARCH

Wahiba Abu-Ras, Ph.D., Columbia University. Child welfare, oppression and diversity.

Julie Cooper Altman, Ph.D., University of Chicago. Engagement in child welfare services, client use of agency-initiated services, worker use of knowledge, impact of welfare reform, M.S.W. child welfare training outcomes.

Richard Belson, D.S.W., Adelphi University. Marriage and family therapy.

Roni Berger, Ph.D., Hebrew University (Jerusalem). Immigrants and refugees, qualitative and combined research methods, remarriage and stepfamilies, law guardianship.

Matthew Bogenschutz, M.S.W., University of Minnesota, Twin Cities. History and philosophy of social welfare.

Ellen Bogolub, Ph.D., Rutgers University. Families and divorce, child welfare.

Adelphi University

Diann Cameron-Kelly, Ph.D., Fordham University. Early childhood and family systems, civic engagement and civic duty, child and adolescent development.

Peter Chernack, D.S.W., Adelphi University. Evaluation of alternative models of field education, university-community partnerships, higher education leadership development.

Carol Cohen, D.S.W., CUNY. Social work with groups, agency-based practice, organizational and community practice.

CarolAnn Daniel, Ph.D., CUNY. Health, gender and Caribbean diaspora; qualitative methods; critical theory.

Beverly Araujo Dawson, Ph.D., University of Michigan. Impact of psychosocial stressors (discrimination and language barriers on the mental health of Latino immigrants), development of culturally competent interventions for Latino communities.

Judy Fenster, Ph.D., New York University. Substance abuse, social work education and curriculum.

Richard Francoeur, Ph.D., University of Pittsburgh. Social work practice, public health social work, practice evaluation.

Godfrey A. Gregg, Ph.D., New York University. Breast cancer, end-of-life issues, sexual orientation, thanatology.

Patricia Joyce, D.S.W., CUNY, Hunter. Trauma, incest, mental illness, nonoffending mothers of sexually abused children, cultural competence and PTSD, secondary trauma and ethnicity, psychoanalytic theory, professionals' constructions of clients, social welfare rhetoric, social process of treatment planning in agency practice.

Njeri Kagotho, Ph.D., University of Washington. Social welfare, research.

Tae Kuen Kim, Ph.D., University of Pennsylvania. Social welfare policy, applied statistics, comparative welfare study.

Stavroula Kyriakakis, Ph.D., University of Washington (St. Louis). Intimate partner violence in immigrant communities, domestic violence interventions.

Shannon Lane, Ph.D., University of Connecticut. Political social work, women's issues.

Roger Levin, Ph.D., New York University. Issues In social welfare, history and philosophy of social welfare.

Jennifer McClendon, Ph.D., University of Washington (St. Louis). Crisis intervention, organizational development.

Elizabeth Palley, Ph.D., Brandeis University. Disability and family policy, education policy.

Subadra Panchanadeswaran, Ph.D., University of Baltimore. Immigrant women's health, mental health and trauma, human behavior and theories.

Marilyn Paul, Ph.D., Adelphi University. Psychosocial issues confronting contemporary families, social work practice.

Laura Quiros, Ph.D., CUNY. Addiction and mental health, diversity and oppression, multicultural social work education.

Geoffrey Ream, Ph.D., Cornell University. Contextual mediators between adolescent sexuality and negative outcomes.

Ellen Rosenberg, D.S.W., Columbia. Social work assessment and diagnosis,

Philip Rozario, Ph.D., Washington (St. Louis). The well-being of caregivers of frail older adults, meaning in later life; successful and productive aging; long-term care issues of frail older adults.

Andrew Safyer, Ph.D., University of Michigan. At-risk youths and their families, ego psychology, defense mechanisms, narcissistic personality disorders.

Carol Sussal, D.S.W., Adelphi University. Social work practice with gay, lesbian, bisexual, and transgendered persons.

Bradley D. Zodikoff, Ph.D., Columbia University. Gerontology, geriatric mental health services, family caregiving, social work practice in healthcare, social work research methods.

School of Social Work Community Partnerships

Adelphi New York Statewide Breast Cancer Hotline & Support Program: The only comprehensive, university-based, breast cancer counseling program in New York State, the program supports, educates, and empowers breast cancer patients, professionals and the community.

Adelphi Hartford Partnership Program for Aging Education (HPPAE): Funded by the John A. Hartford Foundation through the New York Academy of Medicine, the HPPAE prepares master's students for practice and leadership roles in gerontology and geriatric mental health.

Geriatric Mental Health Needs Assessment Project: With funding from the Long Island Community Foundation, this needs assessment study helps identify specific barriers to geriatric mental healthcare on Long Island.

Investigators to Investors: Funded by the Department of Health and Human Services, Children's Bureau, this five-year project trains M.S.W. child-welfare professionals from the New York City Administration for Children's Services (ACS).

Long Island Center for Nonprofit Leadership: This University-based, community-driven leadership-development initiative responds to the immediate and long-term leadership crisis facing Long Island's nonprofit sector.

Primary Care Project on Immigrant Women: Funded by the New York Hospital Medical Center of Queens, this project seeks to increase the ability of primary-care medical residents to competently work cross-culturally with immigrant Muslim women.

Consistently ranked as one of the top programs in the nation, the School of Social Work is a strong advocate for social justice and a driving force for ethical social work practice.

The School of Social Work ensures that every graduate is grounded in both theory and practical experience—and thoroughly prepared to make an impact.

UNIVERSITY AT BUFFALO, THE STATE UNIVERSITY OF NEW YORK

School of Social Work

UB School of Social Work
University at Buffalo *The State University of New York*

Programs of Study

The University at Buffalo (UB) School of Social Work offers doctoral and master's degree programs that provide value, quality, and dynamic programming at an affordable price.

PhD in Social Welfare: UB's doctoral degree program focuses on interdisciplinary approaches to critical social problems, with the opportunity to develop an individualized course of study that utilizes the extensive resources of the University to meet the student's specific needs and interests. An MSW/PhD dual degree is now available.

Master of Social Work (MSW): UB's highly ranked MSW program integrates trauma-informed and human rights perspectives as a transformational lens to focus social work policy and practice. Students create a flexible and individualized advanced year curriculum, building on the core of their foundation year courses. The entire curriculum is rooted in an evidence-based practice approach to social work. For this reason, all students learn the critical skills to evaluate their practice in their foundation year.

Students can complete their MSW degree in two years (full time) or three years (part time). Those accepted into the advanced standing MSW program (see admission requirements) can complete their MSW degree in one year (full time) or one-and-a-half years (part time). An online MSW program option is now available.

Within the MSW program, students complete field placements to help make the transition from student to social work professional. Traditional MSW program students complete two field placements, and advanced standing MSW students complete one.

Dual-Degree Options: Joint and dual degrees are available in collaboration with the College of Arts and Sciences (BA/MSW), Law School (JD/MSW), School of Management (MBA/MSW), and the School of Public Health and Health Professions (MPH/MSW).

Research Facilities

The Buffalo Center for Social Research is the heart and hub of the knowledge-creation activities for the entire School, resulting in an exciting synergy of people and ideas. Whether it is a team of faculty members and students writing a grant, students analyzing data, interviewers conducting focus groups, student-led teams evaluating agency practice, or ideas being explored in a research seminar, all the work conducted has a common goal: research that makes a real-world impact.

Financial Aid

As a public institution, UB offers a world-class education at an affordable price. In addition to the many sources of funding available to students through federal (FAFSA) and state programs, the University at Buffalo is also an approved school under the Canada Student Loans Plan through the Ontario Student Assistance Program. Tuition scholarships, research stipends, and other means of financial support may be available to eligible students. The School of Social Work offers merit-based Dean's Admissions Awards to highly qualified applicants. A list of these programs, as well as UB scholarship and fellowship opportunities, is available at http://www.socialwork.buffalo.edu/msw/apply/funding.asp.

Cost of Study

Tuition for New York State residents is one-third to one-quarter the tuition of most private schools' tuition, and for non–New York State residents it is about half. For the 2013–14 academic year, full-time MSW program tuition per semester was $5,450 for New York State residents and $9,175 for nonresidents.

Living and Housing Costs

In addition to on-campus and off-campus housing available for graduate students, there is moderately priced housing readily available around the Amherst suburban campus. In order to accommodate the needs of as many students as possible, UB also offers gender-neutral housing in some of its dorms and apartments. More details regarding housing are available online at http://www.ub-housing.buffalo.edu.

Student Group

Rho Kappa is UB School of Social Work's chapter of the Phi Alpha Honor Society for Social Work. Phi Alpha fosters high standards of education for social workers and invites those who have attained excellence in scholarship and achievement in social work to become members. The School of Social Work also has its own Graduate School Association, an active subgroup of the University at Buffalo Graduate Student Association.

Student Outcomes

Over the last three years the average MSW student graduation rate was 89 percent. The MSW degree automatically entitles graduates to sit for the Licensed Master Social Worker (LMSW) exam. UB alumni have a first-time pass rate of 89 percent for the New York State LMSW exam and 94 percent for the Licensed Clinical Social Worker (LCSW) exam, both of which are above the New York State and national average.

Location

Buffalo is the second-largest city in New York; it prides itself on being a big city that feels like a small town. With world-class art galleries and museums, a citywide system of parks and green space, major and minor league sports teams, and a wide array of cultural and recreational elements, the area is a great place to study, work, and live.

The University and the School

UB is a premier research-intensive public university and a member of the Association of American Universities. As the largest, most comprehensive institution in the 64-campus State University of New York system, UB's research projects, creative activity, and dedicated people seek to positively impact the local and global community. The University at Buffalo School

University at Buffalo, the State University of New York

of Social Work is a highly ranked, CSWE-accredited graduate school offering MSW and PhD degrees, as well as continuing professional education.

Applying

For details on the application process for all programs, prospective students should visit www.socialwork.buffalo.edu/admissions.asp.

Correspondence and Information

School of Social Work
685 Baldy Hall
University at Buffalo, the State University of New York
Buffalo, New York 14260-1200
Phone: 716-645-3381 or 800-386-6129 (toll-free)
Fax: 716-645-3456
E-mail: sw-info@buffalo.edu
Website: http://www.socialwork.buffalo.edu

THE FACULTY AND THEIR RESEARCH

The faculty consists of a diverse community of scholars, teachers, and activists for change, with interests that span the globe from India to Canada, Pakistan to Korea, and the United States to the United Kingdom. Faculty members share a common passion for community-University partnerships in research and practice.

Faculty areas of interest include:
- Aging
- Children and youth
- Diversity and multicultural issues
- Domestic violence
- Gender and gender issues
- Mental health
- Poverty
- Substance abuse
- Trauma

inSocialWork is a podcast series of the University at Buffalo School of Social Work. The purpose of the series is to engage practitioners and researchers in lifelong learning and to promote research to practice and practice to research. *inSocialWork* features conversations with prominent social work professionals, interviews with cutting-edge researchers, and information on emerging trends and best practices in the field of social work. *inSocialWork* is available online at http://www.insocialwork.org.

Vibrant downtown Buffalo, New York during the summer.

Parker Hall on South Campus, home to the Buffalo Center for Social Research and Office of Continuing Education.

UNIVERSITY OF PENNSYLVANIA
School of Social Policy and Practice

Programs of Study

The School of Social Policy & Practice at the University of Pennsylvania offers the following degree programs: Master of Social Work (M.S.W.), Master of Science in Nonprofit Leadership (NPL), Master of Science in Social Policy (MSSP), Clinical Doctorate in Social Work (D.S.W.), and Doctor of Philosophy (Ph.D.) in Social Welfare. In addition, students can combine the M.S.W. with the Master of Bioethics (M.S.W./M.B.E.), the Master of Business Administration (M.S.W./M.B.A.), the Master of City Planning (M.S.W./M.C.P.), the Master of Science in Criminology (M.S.W./M.S.), the Master of Science in Education (M.S.W./M.S.Ed.), the Juris Doctor (M.S.W./J.D.), the Master of Public Administration (M.S.W./M.P.A.), the Master of Public Health (M.S.W./M.P.H.), the Master of Science in Social Policy (M.S.W./MSSP), and the Doctor of Philosophy (M.S.W./Ph.D.) degree program. The School also offers an M.S.W./Certificate in Jewish Communal Studies, an M.S.W./Certificate in Catholic, Christian, or Lutheran Social Ministry, and an M.S.W./Home-School Visitor Certificate. In addition, the M.S.W. program has the following certificate programs, concentrations and specializations: Child Well-Being and Child Welfare Specialization (CW2); Goldring Reentry Initiative (GRI); Penn Aging Certificate Fellows Program (PAC); Program in Mental Health Education Assessment, Recovery, and Leadership for Social Workers (P.E.A.R.L.S.) Fellowship Program; and the Global Human Rights Certificate.

The school offers an Advanced Standing M.S.W. program. This program is designed for exceptional B.S.W. students who have graduated from a CSWE-accredited B.S.W. program within the past five years. A limited number of students are accepted into this program. Students begin graduate studies in the summer, followed by two semesters of full-time study. After successful completion of the two required summer courses, plus a no-cost integrated practice seminar and field placement, students enter their advanced year of study.

The primary goal of the Master of Social Work program is to prepare social workers for leadership roles in developing and providing services to individuals, families, groups, communities, and organizations. Full-time (two-year) and part-time (three-year) courses of study are available.

The Master of Science in Nonprofit Leadership program is a full-time, rigorous one-year program designed for professionals who wish to assume leadership positions in business, foundations, government, or nonprofit organizations dedicated to social change. This program offers a part-time option in which students may complete the program requirements in five semesters or 2½ academic years.

The Master of Science in Social Policy program is designed to prepare students for leadership positions in analyzing and shaping social policy at the local, national, and international level. The MSSP program is a ten- to eleven-month program spanning three semesters of full-time study. Students may elect to extend the full-time program over a longer period of time or choose to pursue a part-time option. Individualized educational plans are developed for each option.

The Clinical Doctorate in Social Work program is intended for clinicians with at least two years of post-M.S.W. experience. Penn's clinical D.S.W. program differs from most doctoral programs in that it is a professional-practice degree, designed to prepare students for advanced clinical practice and university-level teaching. This program is an intensive, accelerated program that enables students to satisfy all degree requirements—course work and dissertation—in three years, without career disruption.

The Ph.D. in Social Welfare program prepares students to address a wide range of social problems related to human welfare. Most graduates of this doctoral program pursue leadership positions in public and private human services organizations or careers in postsecondary teaching and research.

Research Facilities

The School operates six research centers: the Center for High Impact Philanthropy; the Center for Mental Health and Aging (CMHA); the Field Center for Children's Policy, Practice, and Research; the Evelyn Jacobs Ortner Center on Family Violence; the Out-of-School Time Research Center; and the Program for Religion and Social Policy Research.

Financial Aid

Financial aid is based on merit and need and is available for all SP2 master's programs as well as the Clinical D.S.W. program. More than 85 percent of M.S.W. students receive financial aid. The School recognizes merit by offering a range of scholarships to those who qualify. The Ph.D. program provides aid in the form of merit fellowships and graduate assistantships, which enable students to gain teaching experience and to collaborate with members of the faculty on research projects.

Cost of Study

For academic year 2014–15, tuition and student fees for the full-time M.S.W. program are $43,326 per year. The cost per course unit for all part-time students, including tuition and student fees, is $5,354. Tuition and fees for the full-time NPL program are $53,224. Tuition and fees for the full-time MSSP program are $53,224. Tuition for the clinical D.S.W. program is calculated on a per-course basis; students must complete fourteen courses and the dissertation. Tuition and fees per course are $5,596. Students should expect that the per-course tuition will increase slightly for years two and three, as determined by the University. All students accepted into the Ph.D. program and who maintain their academic standing are eligible for financial

support, including full-tuition scholarships as well as fellowships or research assistantships for the three years of course work.

Living and Housing Costs

The estimated annual cost of living, including room and board, books, and miscellaneous (e.g., health insurance), for a single student is $26,425 for academic year 2014–15. On-campus living accommodations are available in Sansom Place, Penn's graduate student housing, and the neighborhoods surrounding Penn offer a wide variety of options in off-campus living accommodations.

Student Groups

The School is committed to recruiting a diverse student body, representing a wide range of age groups and educational, geographical, and ethnic backgrounds. The following student organizations are available within the School: Student Union, Association of Black Social Workers, Criminal Justice Bloc, Disabilities Special Interest Group, Jewish Social Work Alliance, Hispanic/Latino Alliance for Change and Equality, QSP2, Social Work Advocates for Immigrant Rights, SP2 School Social Group, Students for International Social Work, and United Community Clinic.

Student Outcomes

A 2013–14 survey of 2013 School of Social Policy & Practice alumni found that 71 percent of respondents had secured full-time, part-time, or temporary employment post-graduation. The average salary for full-time positions was $45,218. SP2 graduates find employment in—among many others—the fields of clinical practice, case management, and policy analysis/research. Alumni go on to work in hospitals, schools, private practices, government agencies, and nonprofits in Philadelphia, across the country, and around the globe.

Location

Penn's location in a major metropolitan area enhances the quality of its programs, research, and student life. Philadelphia is a thriving mix of ethnic neighborhoods, historic colonial streets, and contemporary architecture. With close to 100 institutions of higher learning, the city is a magnet for students from around the world. The city's cultural and recreational life has a world-class orchestra and opera, dozens of museums, four professional sports teams, art galleries, secondhand bookstores, jazz clubs, an Italian market, and a renowned international film festival. The city is conveniently located in the cradle of the metropolitan northeastern United States, within 2 hours of Baltimore, New York, and Washington, D.C.

The University and the Program

The University of Pennsylvania is a private Ivy League university with a long and distinguished history of education in social work. The University was founded by Benjamin Franklin and is the oldest university in the country. Penn's social work program, one of the oldest in the country, was established in 1908. The University has pioneered in the development of many professional fields of higher education in addition to social work, including city planning, nursing, medicine, law, education, veterinary medicine, dentistry, and business.

Applying

Applications to all master's programs open in September and are accepted on a rolling basis until their respective entering cohorts are filled.

Priority consideration is given to Advanced Standing M.S.W. applications received by January 15 and to all other M.S.W. program applications received by February 1. It is the School's policy to offer an interview to all M.S.W. applicants who meet minimal admission criteria. The interviews are primarily personal interviews; however, when geographic distance is a question, a Skype interview can be arranged. GRE scores are not required for admission to the M.S.W. program.

Priority consideration is given to NPL applicants whose applications are complete on or before March 15 and to MSSP applicants whose applications are complete on or before March 15. GRE scores are required for both NPL and MSSP applicants.

Applications to both doctoral programs open in September. The deadline for applications for admission to the Ph.D. program is December 15. The deadline for applications for admission to the Clinical D.S.W. program is March 1. All transcripts, official test scores, and letters of recommendation must be received by these deadlines.

TOEFL scores are required for all international applicants to all programs for whom English is not a first language and who have not completed a full-time, four-year undergraduate degree in the United States.

Correspondence and Information

Admissions Office
University of Pennsylvania School of Social Policy & Practice
3701 Locust Walk
Philadelphia, Pennsylvania 19104
Phone: 215-746-1934
E-mail: apply@sp2.upenn.edu
Website: http://www.sp2.upenn.edu

University of Pennsylvania

THE FACULTY AND THEIR RESEARCH AREAS

Joretha Bourjolly, Ph. D.
Associate Professor and Associate Dean, Academic Affairs; Ph.D., Bryn Mawr, 1996. Effects of chronic illness on individuals and family members as well, impact of racial and economic factors on the delivery of health care.

Ram A. Cnaan, Ph. D.
Professor; Ph.D., Pittsburgh, 1981. Social work research methods, faith-based social services and social policy, volunteerism and volunteer action, prisoners' reentry, international social development.

Dennis Culhane, Ph.D.
Professor; Ph.D., Boston College, 1990. Homelessness, housing policy, policy analysis research methods.

Ezekiel Dixon-Román, Ph.D.
Assistant Professor; Ph.D., Fordham, 2007. Sociology of education, cultural studies, quantitative methods, public policy.

Andrea M. Doyle, Ph.D., LCSW
Assistant Professor; Ph.D., Washington (Seattle), 2003. Dialectical behavioral therapy and psychodynamic approaches to clinical therapy, group work, measurement of clinical process.

Malitta Engstrom, Ph.D.
Assistant Professor; Ph.D., Columbia. Problematic substance use and its co-occurrence with victimization, HIV, incarceration and mental health concerns, multigenerational social work practice with families, grandparents caring for grandchildren.

Peter Frumkin, Ph.D.
Professor; Ph.D., Chicago, 1997; Philanthropy, nonprofit management, social entrepreneurship.

Antonio Garcia, Ph.D.
Assistant Professor; Ph.D., Washington (Seattle), 2010. Child welfare and services research; Latino youth and families; measurement and contextualization of racial/ethnic disparities; development and implementation of culturally congruent, evidence-based mental health services in child-serving systems of care.

Richard James Gelles, Ph.D.
Professor and Former Dean; Ph.D., New Hampshire, 1973. Child welfare, family violence, child abuse.

Zvi D. Gellis, Ph.D.
Professor; Ph.D., Toronto, 1999. Gerontology, geriatrics, evidence-based depression and anxiety interventions, integrated health and mental health care, telehealth interventions, randomized trials.

Toorjo (T. J.) Ghose, Ph.D.
Associate Professor; Ph.D., UCLA, 2005. Substance abuse, HIV/AIDS in developing countries, mental health service provision, welfare policy.

Johanna Greeson, Ph.D.
Assistant Professor; Ph.D., North Carolina at Chapel Hill, 2009. The transition to adulthood among youth who age out of foster care; natural mentoring and other supportive adult relationships for youth who age out of foster care; child traumatic stress; applied community-based intervention research and translation of research to practice; resiliency, risk, and protective factors; neurobiological mechanisms of resiliency-focused interventions; life course theory.

Chao Guo, Ph.D.
Associate Professor; Ph.D., USC, 2003. Intersection between nonprofit and voluntary action and government, representation in nonprofit organizations, nonprofit advocacy, nonprofit governance, collaboration within and across sectors, social entrepreneurship, volunteerism.

Femida Handy, Ph.D.
Professor, Ph.D., York, 1995. Nonprofit entrepreneurship and volunteerism, comparative and international aspects of the nonprofit and voluntary sector, social accounting.

Roberta Rehner Iversen, Ph.D.
Associate Professor; Ph.D., Bryn Mawr, 1991. Low-income families and economic mobility; poverty, welfare, and workforce development policies.

John L. Jackson, Ph.D.
Professor and Dean; Ph.D., Columbia, 2000. Ethnographic methods in media analysis; race theory and identity; globalization, transnationalism, and diaspora; religion, media, and modernity; social theory; urban studies and class formation; the politics and poetics of ethnography; cultural studies and performance theory; Africana studies and popular culture; U.S., Israel.

Kenwyn K. Smith, Ph.D.
Professor; Ph.D., Yale, 1974. Group and intergroup relations, organizational change, organizational politics, conflict management, impact of organizational dynamics on the health of employees.

Phyllis Solomon, Ph.D.
Professor; Ph.D., Case Western Reserve, 1978. Social work research methods, mental health policy and service delivery systems, severely mentally disabled persons and their families.

Susan Sorenson, Ph.D.
Professor; Ph.D., Cincinnati, 1985. Public health; epidemiology and prevention of violence, including homicide, suicide, sexual assault, child abuse, battering, and firearms.

Mark J. Stern, Ph.D.
Professor; Ph.D., York (England), 1980. Social welfare policy; social history and social welfare; poverty in the United States, 1900–present.

Allison Werner-Lin, Ph.D., M.A., Ed.M.
Assistant Professor; Ph.D., Chicago, 2006. Intersection of genomic discovery and family life, decision making about genetic testing and hereditary cancer risk management, genome-based health literacy, medical family therapy and psychoeducation, grief and bereavement, life cycle growth into adulthood.

Yin-Ling Irene Wong, Ph.D.
Associate Professor; Ph.D., Wisconsin, 1995. Social policy, homelessness, homelessness prevention and poverty research.

The passionate pursuit of social justice is the heart of SP2's mission.

SP2 faculty, students, staff, and alumni lead the University's Community Teamworks program, which organizes days of service and volunteer projects in and around West Philadelphia.

APPENDIXES

Institutional Changes
Since the 2014 Edition

Following is an alphabetical listing of institutions that have recently closed, merged with other institutions, or changed their names or status. In the case of a name change, the former name appears first, followed by the new name.

Alderson-Broaddus College (Philippi, WV): *name changed to Alderson Broaddus University*

American InterContinental University London (London, United Kingdom): *merged into Regent's University London (London, United Kingdom)*

The American University of Athens (Athens, Greece): *no longer accredited by agency recognized by USDE or CHEA*

Arizona State University (Tempe, AZ): *name changed to Arizona State University at the Tempe campus*

Armstrong Atlantic State University (Savannah, GA): *name changed to Armstrong State University*

The Art Institute of Dallas (Dallas, TX): *name changed to The Art Institute of Dallas, a campus of South University*

A.T. Still University of Health Sciences (Kirksville, MO): *name changed to A.T. Still University*

Bangor Theological Seminary (Bangor, ME): *closed*

BryanLGH College of Health Sciences (Lincoln, NE): *name changed to Bryan College of Health Sciences*

Caldwell College (Caldwell, NJ): *name changed to Caldwell University*

Calvary Baptist Theological Seminary (Landsdale, PA): *closed*

Catholic Theological Union at Chicago (Chicago, IL): *name changed to Catholic Theological Union*

Central Baptist Theological Seminary of Virginia Beach (Virginia Beach, VA): *name changed to Virginia Beach Theological Seminary*

Central State University (Wilberforce, OH): *no longer offers graduate degrees*

Chancellor University (Cleveland, OH): *closed*

Cleveland Chiropractic College–Kansas City Campus (Overland Park, KS): *name changed to Cleveland University–Kansas City*

Coe College (Cedar Rapids, IA): *no longer offers graduate degrees*

College of Mount St. Joseph (Cincinnati, OH): *name changed to Mount St. Joseph University*

Collège universitaire de Saint-Boniface (Saint-Boniface, MB, Canada): *name changed to Université de Saint-Boniface*

Colorado Technical University Sioux Falls (Sioux Falls, SD): *closed*

Conservatorio de Musica (San Juan, PR): *name changed to Conservatorio de Musica de Puerto Rico*

Conway School of Landscape Design (Conway, MA): *name changed to The Conway School*

Corcoran College of Art and Design (Washington, DC): *merged into a single entry for The George Washington University (Washington, DC)*

Davenport University (Warren, MI): *merged into a single entry for Davenport University (Grand Rapids, MI)*

DeVry University (Lincolnshire, IL): *closed*

Franklin College Switzerland (Sorengo, Switzerland): *name changed to Franklin University Switzerland*

Graduate School and University Center of the City University of New York (New York, NY): *name changed to The Graduate Center, City University of New York*

Gwynedd-Mercy College (Gwynedd Valley, PA): *name changed to Gwynedd Mercy University*

ICR Graduate School (Santee, CA): *name changed to Institute for Creation Research*

Instituto Tecnológico y de Estudios Superiores de Monterrey, Campus Mazatlán (Mazatlán, Mexico): *closed*

Jamestown College (Jamestown, ND): *name changed to University of Jamestown*

Jewish University of America (Skokie, IL): *closed*

The Johns Hopkins University (Baltimore, MD): *name changed to Johns Hopkins University*

King College (Bristol, TN): *name changed to King University*

Kona University (Kailua-Kona, HI): *no longer accredited by agency recognized by USDE or CHEA*

Laurel University, Spanish Academic Division (Miami, FL): *closed*

Logan University–College of Chiropractic (Chesterfield, MO): *name changed to Logan University*

Long Island University–Brooklyn Campus (Brooklyn, NY): *name changed to Long Island University–LIU Brooklyn*

Long Island University–C. W. Post Campus (Brookville, NY): *name changed to Long Island University–LIU Post*

Louisiana State University and Agricultural and Mechanical College (Baton Rouge, LA): *name changed to Louisiana State University and Agricultural & Mechanical College*

Maranatha Baptist Bible College (Watertown, WI): *name changed to Maranatha Baptist University*

Mars Hill College (Mars Hill, NC): *name changed to Mars Hill University*

Massachusetts College of Pharmacy and Health Sciences (Boston, MA): *name changed to MCPHS University*

Mount Mary College (Milwaukee, WI): *name changed to Mount Mary University*

Mount Sinai School of Medicine (New York, NY): *name changed to Icahn School of Medicine at Mount Sinai*

Newschool of Architecture & Design (San Diego, CA): *name changed to NewSchool of Architecture and Design*

North Shore–LIJ Graduate School of Molecular Medicine (Manhasset, NY): *name changed to Elmezzi Graduate School of Molecular Medicine*

Northwestern College (St. Paul, MN): *name changed to University of Northwestern–St. Paul*

Oglethorpe University (Atlanta, GA): *no longer offers graduate degrees*

Perelandra College (La Mesa, CA): *no longer accredited by agency recognized by USDE or CHEA*

Polytechnic Institute of New York University (Brooklyn, NY): *Polytechnic School of Engineering now profiled as a unit of New York University (New York, NY)*

Polytechnic Institute of NYU, Long Island Graduate Center (Melville, NY): *Polytechnic School of Engineering now profiled as a unit of New York University (New York, NY)*

Polytechnic Institute of NYU, Westchester Graduate Center (Hawthorne, NY): *Polytechnic School of Engineering now profiled as a unit of New York University (New York, NY)*

Regent's American College London (London, United Kingdom): *name changed to Regent's University London*

Rockford College (Rockford, IL): *name changed to Rockford University*

Schiller International University (Strasbourg, France): *closed*

Southern California College of Optometry (Fullerton, CA): *name changed to Marshall B. Ketchum University*

Spertus Institute of Jewish Studies (Chicago, IL): *name changed to Spertus Institute for Jewish Learning and Leadership*

Tai Sophia Institute (Laurel, MD): *name changed to Maryland University of Integrative Health*

Teacher Education University (Winter Park, FL): *no longer accredited by agency recognized by USDE or CHEA*

University of Atlanta (Atlanta, GA): *no longer accredited by agency recognized by USDE or CHEA*

University of Medicine and Dentistry of New Jersey (Newark, NJ): *merged into Rutgers School of Health Related Professions with programs at Rutgers, The State University of New Jersey, Camden (Camden, NJ); Rutgers, The State University of New Jersey, Newark (Newark, NJ); Rutgers, The State University of New Jersey, New Brunswick (Piscataway, NJ); and Rowan University (Glassboro, NJ)*

University of Phoenix–Central Florida Campus (Maitland, FL): *closed*

University of Phoenix–Fairfield County Campus (Norwalk, CT): *closed*

University of Phoenix–Harrisburg Campus (Harrisburg, PA): *closed*

University of Phoenix–Metro Detroit Campus (Troy, MI): *closed*

University of Phoenix–Northern Nevada Campus (Reno, NV): *closed*

University of Phoenix–Northern Virginia Campus (Reston, VA): *closed*

University of Phoenix–Phoenix Main Campus (Tempe, AZ): *name changed to University of Phoenix–Phoenix Campus*

University of Phoenix–Raleigh Campus (Raleigh, NC): *closed*

University of Phoenix–Richmond Campus (Richmond, VA): *name changed to University of Phoenix–Richmond-Virginia Beach Campus*

University of Phoenix–Washington Campus (Tukwila, WA): *name changed to University of Phoenix–Western Washington Campus*

University of Phoenix–West Michigan Campus (Walker, MI): *closed*

University of Puerto Rico, Río Piedras (San Juan, PR): *name changed to University of Puerto Rico, Río Piedras Campus*

The University of Tennessee Space Institute (Tullahoma, TN): *merged into a single entry for The University of Tennessee (Knoxville, TN)*

University of Tulsa (Tulsa, OK): *name changed to The University of Tulsa*

Victory University (Memphis, TN): *closed*

Western State University College of Law at Argosy University (Fullerton, CA): *name changed to Western State College of Law at Argosy University*

World Medicine Institute of Acupuncture and Herbal Medicine (Honolulu, HI): *name changed to World Medicine Institute*

Abbreviations Used in the Guides

The following list includes abbreviations of degree names used in the profiles in the 2015 edition of the guides. Because some degrees (e.g., Doctor of Education) can be abbreviated in more than one way (e.g., D.Ed. or Ed.D.), and because the abbreviations used in the guides reflect the preferences of the individual colleges and universities, the list may include two or more abbreviations for a single degree.

DEGREES

A Mus D	Doctor of Musical Arts
AC	Advanced Certificate
AD	Artist's Diploma
	Doctor of Arts
ADP	Artist's Diploma
Adv C	Advanced Certificate
Adv M	Advanced Master
AGC	Advanced Graduate Certificate
AGSC	Advanced Graduate Specialist Certificate
ALM	Master of Liberal Arts
AM	Master of Arts
AMBA	Accelerated Master of Business Administration
	Aviation Master of Business Administration
AMRS	Master of Arts in Religious Studies
APC	Advanced Professional Certificate
APMPH	Advanced Professional Master of Public Health
App Sc	Applied Scientist
App Sc D	Doctor of Applied Science
AstE	Astronautical Engineer
Au D	Doctor of Audiology
B Th	Bachelor of Theology
CAES	Certificate of Advanced Educational Specialization
CAGS	Certificate of Advanced Graduate Studies
CAL	Certificate in Applied Linguistics
CALS	Certificate of Advanced Liberal Studies
CAMS	Certificate of Advanced Management Studies
CAPS	Certificate of Advanced Professional Studies
CAS	Certificate of Advanced Studies
CASPA	Certificate of Advanced Study in Public Administration
CASR	Certificate in Advanced Social Research
CATS	Certificate of Achievement in Theological Studies
CBHS	Certificate in Basic Health Sciences
CBS	Graduate Certificate in Biblical Studies
CCJA	Certificate in Criminal Justice Administration
CCSA	Certificate in Catholic School Administration
CCTS	Certificate in Clinical and Translational Science
CE	Civil Engineer
CEM	Certificate of Environmental Management
CET	Certificate in Educational Technologies
CGS	Certificate of Graduate Studies
Ch E	Chemical Engineer
CM	Certificate in Management
CMH	Certificate in Medical Humanities
CMM	Master of Church Ministries

CMS	Certificate in Ministerial Studies
CNM	Certificate in Nonprofit Management
CPASF	Certificate Program for Advanced Study in Finance
CPC	Certificate in Professional Counseling
	Certificate in Publication and Communication
CPH	Certificate in Public Health
CPM	Certificate in Public Management
CPS	Certificate of Professional Studies
CScD	Doctor of Clinical Science
CSD	Certificate in Spiritual Direction
CSS	Certificate of Special Studies
CTS	Certificate of Theological Studies
CURP	Certificate in Urban and Regional Planning
D Admin	Doctor of Administration
D Arch	Doctor of Architecture
D Be	Doctor in Bioethics
D Com	Doctor of Commerce
D Couns	Doctor of Counseling
D Div	Doctor of Divinity
D Ed	Doctor of Education
D Ed Min	Doctor of Educational Ministry
D Eng	Doctor of Engineering
D Engr	Doctor of Engineering
D Ent	Doctor of Enterprise
D Env	Doctor of Environment
D Law	Doctor of Law
D Litt	Doctor of Letters
D Med Sc	Doctor of Medical Science
D Min	Doctor of Ministry
D Miss	Doctor of Missiology
D Mus	Doctor of Music
D Mus A	Doctor of Musical Arts
D Phil	Doctor of Philosophy
D Prof	Doctor of Professional Studies
D Ps	Doctor of Psychology
D Sc	Doctor of Science
D Sc D	Doctor of Science in Dentistry
D Sc IS	Doctor of Science in Information Systems
D Sc PA	Doctor of Science in Physician Assistant Studies
D Th	Doctor of Theology
D Th P	Doctor of Practical Theology
DA	Doctor of Accounting
	Doctor of Arts
DA Ed	Doctor of Arts in Education
DAH	Doctor of Arts in Humanities
DAOM	Doctorate in Acupuncture and Oriental Medicine
DAT	Doctorate of Athletic Training
DATH	Doctorate of Art Therapy
DBA	Doctor of Business Administration
DBH	Doctor of Behavioral Health
DBL	Doctor of Business Leadership
DBS	Doctor of Buddhist Studies
DC	Doctor of Chiropractic
DCC	Doctor of Computer Science
DCD	Doctor of Communications Design

DCL	Doctor of Civil Law	DPTSc	Doctor of Physical Therapy Science
	Doctor of Comparative Law	Dr DES	Doctor of Design
DCM	Doctor of Church Music	Dr NP	Doctor of Nursing Practice
DCN	Doctor of Clinical Nutrition	Dr PH	Doctor of Public Health
DCS	Doctor of Computer Science	Dr Sc PT	Doctor of Science in Physical Therapy
DDN	Diplôme du Droit Notarial	DRSc	Doctor of Regulatory Science
DDS	Doctor of Dental Surgery	DS	Doctor of Science
DE	Doctor of Education	DS Sc	Doctor of Social Science
	Doctor of Engineering	DSJS	Doctor of Science in Jewish Studies
DED	Doctor of Economic Development	DSL	Doctor of Strategic Leadership
DEIT	Doctor of Educational Innovation and Technology	DSW	Doctor of Social Work
		DTL	Doctor of Talmudic Law
DEL	Doctor of Executive Leadership	DV Sc	Doctor of Veterinary Science
DEM	Doctor of Educational Ministry	DVM	Doctor of Veterinary Medicine
DEPD	Diplôme Études Spécialisées	DWS	Doctor of Worship Studies
DES	Doctor of Engineering Science	EAA	Engineer in Aeronautics and Astronautics
DESS	Diplôme Études Supérieures Spécialisées	EASPh D	Engineering and Applied Science Doctor of Philosophy
DFA	Doctor of Fine Arts		
DGP	Diploma in Graduate and Professional Studies	ECS	Engineer in Computer Science
		Ed D	Doctor of Education
DH Ed	Doctor of Health Education	Ed DCT	Doctor of Education in College Teaching
DH Sc	Doctor of Health Sciences	Ed L D	Doctor of Education Leadership
DHA	Doctor of Health Administration	Ed M	Master of Education
DHCE	Doctor of Health Care Ethics	Ed S	Specialist in Education
DHL	Doctor of Hebrew Letters	Ed Sp	Specialist in Education
	Doctor of Hebrew Literature	EDB	Executive Doctorate in Business
DHS	Doctor of Health Science	EDM	Executive Doctorate in Management
DHSc	Doctor of Health Science	EE	Electrical Engineer
Dip CS	Diploma in Christian Studies	EJD	Executive Juris Doctor
DIT	Doctor of Industrial Technology	EMBA	Executive Master of Business Administration
DJ Ed	Doctor of Jewish Education	EMFA	Executive Master of Forensic Accounting
DJS	Doctor of Jewish Studies	EMHA	Executive Master of Health Administration
DLS	Doctor of Liberal Studies	EMIB	Executive Master of International Business
DM	Doctor of Management	EML	Executive Master of Leadership
	Doctor of Music	EMPA	Executive Master of Public Administration
DMA	Doctor of Musical Arts	EMS	Executive Master of Science
DMD	Doctor of Dental Medicine	EMTM	Executive Master of Technology Management
DME	Doctor of Music Education		
DMEd	Doctor of Music Education	Eng	Engineer
DMFT	Doctor of Marital and Family Therapy	Eng Sc D	Doctor of Engineering Science
DMH	Doctor of Medical Humanities	Engr	Engineer
DML	Doctor of Modern Languages	Ex Doc	Executive Doctor of Pharmacy
DMP	Doctorate in Medical Physics	Exec Ed D	Executive Doctor of Education
DMPNA	Doctor of Management Practice in Nurse Anesthesia	Exec MBA	Executive Master of Business Administration
		Exec MPA	Executive Master of Public Administration
DN Sc	Doctor of Nursing Science	Exec MPH	Executive Master of Public Health
DNAP	Doctor of Nurse Anesthesia Practice	Exec MS	Executive Master of Science
DNP	Doctor of Nursing Practice	G Dip	Graduate Diploma
DNP-A	Doctor of Nursing PracticeAnesthesia	GBC	Graduate Business Certificate
DNS	Doctor of Nursing Science	GCE	Graduate Certificate in Education
DO	Doctor of Osteopathy	GDM	Graduate Diploma in Management
DOT	Doctor of Occupational Therapy	GDPA	Graduate Diploma in Public Administration
DPA	Doctor of Public Administration	GDRE	Graduate Diploma in Religious Education
DPC	Doctor of Pastoral Counseling	GEMBA	Global Executive Master of Business Administration
DPDS	Doctor of Planning and Development Studies		
		GEMPA	Gulf Executive Master of Public Administration
DPH	Doctor of Public Health		
DPM	Doctor of Plant Medicine	GM Acc	Graduate Master of Accountancy
	Doctor of Podiatric Medicine	GMBA	Global Master of Business Administration
DPPD	Doctor of Policy, Planning, and Development	GP LL M	Global Professional Master of Laws
		GPD	Graduate Performance Diploma
DPS	Doctor of Professional Studies	GSS	Graduate Special Certificate for Students in Special Situations
DPT	Doctor of Physical Therapy		

IEMBA	International Executive Master of Business Administration
IM Acc	Integrated Master of Accountancy
IMA	Interdisciplinary Master of Arts
IMBA	International Master of Business Administration
IMES	International Master's in Environmental Studies
Ingeniero	Engineer
JCD	Doctor of Canon Law
JCL	Licentiate in Canon Law
JD	Juris Doctor
JSD	Doctor of Juridical Science
	Doctor of Jurisprudence
	Doctor of the Science of Law
JSM	Master of Science of Law
L Th	Licenciate in Theology
LL B	Bachelor of Laws
LL CM	Master of Laws in Comparative Law
LL D	Doctor of Laws
LL M	Master of Laws
LL M in Tax	Master of Laws in Taxation
LL M CL	Master of Laws (Common Law)
M Ac	Master of Accountancy
	Master of Accounting
	Master of Acupuncture
M Ac OM	Master of Acupuncture and Oriental Medicine
M Acc	Master of Accountancy
	Master of Accounting
M Acct	Master of Accountancy
	Master of Accounting
M Accy	Master of Accountancy
M Actg	Master of Accounting
M Acy	Master of Accountancy
M Ad	Master of Administration
M Ad Ed	Master of Adult Education
M Adm	Master of Administration
M Adm Mgt	Master of Administrative Management
M Admin	Master of Administration
M ADU	Master of Architectural Design and Urbanism
M Adv	Master of Advertising
M Aero E	Master of Aerospace Engineering
M AEST	Master of Applied Environmental Science and Technology
M Ag	Master of Agriculture
M Ag Ed	Master of Agricultural Education
M Agr	Master of Agriculture
M Anesth Ed	Master of Anesthesiology Education
M App Comp Sc	Master of Applied Computer Science
M App St	Master of Applied Statistics
M Appl Stat	Master of Applied Statistics
M Aq	Master of Aquaculture
M Arc	Master of Architecture
M Arch	Master of Architecture
M Arch I	Master of Architecture I
M Arch II	Master of Architecture II
M Arch E	Master of Architectural Engineering
M Arch H	Master of Architectural History
M Bioethics	Master in Bioethics
M Biomath	Master of Biomathematics
M Ch	Master of Chemistry

M Ch E	Master of Chemical Engineering
M Chem	Master of Chemistry
M Cl D	Master of Clinical Dentistry
M Cl Sc	Master of Clinical Science
M Comp	Master of Computing
M Comp Sc	Master of Computer Science
M Coun	Master of Counseling
M Dent	Master of Dentistry
M Dent Sc	Master of Dental Sciences
M Des	Master of Design
M Des S	Master of Design Studies
M Div	Master of Divinity
M Ec	Master of Economics
M Econ	Master of Economics
M Ed	Master of Education
M Ed T	Master of Education in Teaching
M En	Master of Engineering
	Master of Environmental Science
M En S	Master of Environmental Sciences
M Eng	Master of Engineering
M Eng Mgt	Master of Engineering Management
M Engr	Master of Engineering
M Ent	Master of Enterprise
M Env	Master of Environment
M Env Des	Master of Environmental Design
M Env E	Master of Environmental Engineering
M Env Sc	Master of Environmental Science
M Fin	Master of Finance
M Geo E	Master of Geological Engineering
M Geoenv E	Master of Geoenvironmental Engineering
M Geog	Master of Geography
M Hum	Master of Humanities
M Hum Svcs	Master of Human Services
M IBD	Master of Integrated Building Delivery
M IDST	Master's in Interdisciplinary Studies
M Kin	Master of Kinesiology
M Land Arch	Master of Landscape Architecture
M Litt	Master of Letters
M Mat SE	Master of Material Science and Engineering
M Math	Master of Mathematics
M Mech E	Master of Mechanical Engineering
M Med Sc	Master of Medical Science
M Mgmt	Master of Management
M Mgt	Master of Management
M Min	Master of Ministries
M Mtl E	Master of Materials Engineering
M Mu	Master of Music
M Mus	Master of Music
M Mus Ed	Master of Music Education
M Music	Master of Music
M Nat Sci	Master of Natural Science
M Oc E	Master of Oceanographic Engineering
M Pet E	Master of Petroleum Engineering
M Pharm	Master of Pharmacy
M Phil	Master of Philosophy
M Phil F	Master of Philosophical Foundations
M Pl	Master of Planning
M Plan	Master of Planning
M Pol	Master of Political Science
M Pr Met	Master of Professional Meteorology
M Prob S	Master of Probability and Statistics
M Psych	Master of Psychology

M Pub	Master of Publishing	MAB	Master of Agribusiness
M Rel	Master of Religion	MABC	Master of Arts in Biblical Counseling
M Sc	Master of Science		Master of Arts in Business Communication
M Sc A	Master of Science (Applied)	MABE	Master of Arts in Bible Exposition
M Sc AC	Master of Science in Applied Computing	MABL	Master of Arts in Biblical Languages
M Sc AHN	Master of Science in Applied Human Nutrition	MABM	Master of Agribusiness Management
		MABMH	bioethics and medical humanities
M Sc BMC	Master of Science in Biomedical Communications	MABS	Master of Arts in Biblical Studies
M Sc CS	Master of Science in Computer Science	MABT	Master of Arts in Bible Teaching
M Sc E	Master of Science in Engineering	MAC	Master of Accountancy
M Sc Eng	Master of Science in Engineering		Master of Accounting
M Sc Engr	Master of Science in Engineering		Master of Arts in Communication
M Sc F	Master of Science in Forestry		Master of Arts in Counseling
M Sc FE	Master of Science in Forest Engineering	MACC	Master of Arts in Christian Counseling
M Sc Geogr	Master of Science in Geography		Master of Arts in Clinical Counseling
M Sc N	Master of Science in Nursing	MACCM	Master of Arts in Church and Community Ministry
M Sc OT	Master of Science in Occupational Therapy	MACCT	Master of Accounting
M Sc P	Master of Science in Planning	MACD	Master of Arts in Christian Doctrine
M Sc Pl	Master of Science in Planning	MACE	Master of Arts in Christian Education
M Sc PT	Master of Science in Physical Therapy	MACFM	Master of Arts in Children's and Family Ministry
M Sc T	Master of Science in Teaching	MACH	Master of Arts in Church History
M SEM	Master of Sustainable Environmental Management	MACI	Master of Arts in Curriculum and Instruction
M Serv Soc	Master of Social Service	MACIS	Master of Accounting and Information Systems
M Soc	Master of Sociology	MACJ	Master of Arts in Criminal Justice
M Sp Ed	Master of Special Education	MACL	Master of Arts in Christian Leadership
M Stat	Master of Statistics	MACM	Master of Arts in Christian Ministries
M Sys E	Master of Systems Engineering		Master of Arts in Christian Ministry
M Sys Sc	Master of Systems Science		Master of Arts in Church Music
M Tax	Master of Taxation		Master of Arts in Counseling Ministries
M Tech	Master of Technology	MACN	Master of Arts in Counseling
M Th	Master of Theology	MACO	Master of Arts in Counseling
M Tox	Master of Toxicology	MAcOM	Master of Acupuncture and Oriental Medicine
M Trans E	Master of Transportation Engineering	MACP	Master of Arts in Christian Practice
M Urb	Master of Urban Planning		Master of Arts in Counseling Psychology
M Vet Sc	Master of Veterinary Science	MACS	Master of Applied Computer Science
MA	Master of Accounting		Master of Arts in Catholic Studies
	Master of Administration		Master of Arts in Christian Studies
	Master of Arts	MACSE	Master of Arts in Christian School Education
MA Comm	Master of Arts in Communication	MACT	Master of Arts in Christian Thought
MA Ed	Master of Arts in Education		Master of Arts in Communications and Technology
MA Ed Ad	Master of Arts in Educational Administration	MAD	Master of Art and Design
MA Ext	Master of Agricultural Extension	MAD-Crit	Master of Arts in Design Criticism
MA Islamic	Master of Arts in Islamic Studies	MADR	Master of Arts in Dispute Resolution
MA Min	Master of Arts in Ministry	MADS	Master of Animal and Dairy Science
MA Miss	Master of Arts in Missiology		Master of Applied Disability Studies
MA Past St	Master of Arts in Pastoral Studies	MAE	Master of Aerospace Engineering
MA Ph	Master of Arts in Philosophy		Master of Agricultural Economics
MA Psych	Master of Arts in Psychology		Master of Agricultural Education
MA Sc	Master of Applied Science		Master of Architectural Engineering
MA Sp	Master of Arts (Spirituality)		Master of Art Education
MA Th	Master of Arts in Theology		Master of Arts in Education
MA-R	Master of Arts (Research)		Master of Arts in English
MAA	Master of Administrative Arts	MAEd	Master of Arts Education
	Master of Applied Anthropology	MAEL	Master of Arts in Educational Leadership
	Master of Applied Arts	MAEM	Master of Arts in Educational Ministries
	Master of Arts in Administration	MAEN	Master of Arts in English
MAAA	Master of Arts in Arts Administration	MAEP	Master of Arts in Economic Policy
MAAAP	Master of Arts Administration and Policy		
MAAE	Master of Arts in Art Education		
MAAT	Master of Arts in Applied Theology		
	Master of Arts in Art Therapy		

MAES	Master of Arts in Environmental Sciences
MAET	Master of Arts in English Teaching
MAF	Master of Arts in Finance
MAFE	Master of Arts in Financial Economics
MAFLL	Master of Arts in Foreign Language and Literature
MAFM	Master of Accounting and Financial Management
MAFS	Master of Arts in Family Studies
MAG	Master of Applied Geography
MAGU	Master of Urban Analysis and Management
MAH	Master of Arts in Humanities
MAHA	Master of Arts in Humanitarian Assistance
	Master of Arts in Humanitarian Studies
MAHCM	Master of Arts in Health Care Mission
MAHG	Master of American History and Government
MAHL	Master of Arts in Hebrew Letters
MAHN	Master of Applied Human Nutrition
MAHSR	Master of Applied Health Services Research
MAIA	Master of Arts in International Administration
	Master of Arts in International Affairs
MAIB	Master of Arts in International Business
MAIDM	Master of Arts in Interior Design and Merchandising
MAIH	Master of Arts in Interdisciplinary Humanities
MAIOP	Master of Arts in Industrial/Organizational Psychology
MAIPCR	Master of Arts in International Peace and Conflict Management
MAIS	Master of Arts in Intercultural Studies
	Master of Arts in Interdisciplinary Studies
	Master of Arts in International Studies
MAIT	Master of Administration in Information Technology
	Master of Applied Information Technology
MAJ	Master of Arts in Journalism
MAJ Ed	Master of Arts in Jewish Education
MAJCS	Master of Arts in Jewish Communal Service
MAJE	Master of Arts in Jewish Education
MAJPS	Master of Arts in Jewish Professional Studies
MAJS	Master of Arts in Jewish Studies
MAL	Master in Agricultural Leadership
MALA	Master of Arts in Liberal Arts
MALD	Master of Arts in Law and Diplomacy
MALER	Master of Arts in Labor and Employment Relations
MALM	Master of Arts in Leadership Evangelical Mobilization
MALP	Master of Arts in Language Pedagogy
MALPS	Master of Arts in Liberal and Professional Studies
MALS	Master of Arts in Liberal Studies
MAM	Master of Acquisition Management
	Master of Agriculture and Management
	Master of Applied Mathematics
	Master of Arts in Ministry
	Master of Arts Management
	Master of Avian Medicine
MAMB	Master of Applied Molecular Biology
MAMC	Master of Arts in Mass Communication
	Master of Arts in Ministry and Culture

	Master of Arts in Ministry for a Multicultural Church
	Master of Arts in Missional Christianity
MAME	Master of Arts in Missions/Evangelism
MAMFC	Master of Arts in Marriage and Family Counseling
MAMFCC	Master of Arts in Marriage, Family, and Child Counseling
MAMFT	Master of Arts in Marriage and Family Therapy
MAMHC	Master of Arts in Mental Health Counseling
MAMI	Master of Arts in Missions
MAMS	Master of Applied Mathematical Sciences
	Master of Arts in Ministerial Studies
	Master of Arts in Ministry and Spirituality
MAMT	Master of Arts in Mathematics Teaching
MAN	Master of Applied Nutrition
MANT	Master of Arts in New Testament
MAOL	Master of Arts in Organizational Leadership
MAOM	Master of Acupuncture and Oriental Medicine
	Master of Arts in Organizational Management
MAOT	Master of Arts in Old Testament
MAP	Master of Applied Psychology
	Master of Arts in Planning
	Master of Psychology
	Master of Public Administration
MAP Min	Master of Arts in Pastoral Ministry
MAPA	Master of Arts in Public Administration
MAPC	Master of Arts in Pastoral Counseling
	Master of Arts in Professional Counseling
MAPE	Master of Arts in Political Economy
MAPM	Master of Arts in Pastoral Ministry
	Master of Arts in Pastoral Music
	Master of Arts in Practical Ministry
MAPP	Master of Arts in Public Policy
MAPPS	Master of Arts in Asia Pacific Policy Studies
MAPS	Master of Arts in Pastoral Counseling/Spiritual Formation
	Master of Arts in Pastoral Studies
	Master of Arts in Public Service
MAPT	Master of Practical Theology
MAPW	Master of Arts in Professional Writing
MAR	Master of Arts in Reading
	Master of Arts in Religion
Mar Eng	Marine Engineer
MARC	Master of Arts in Rehabilitation Counseling
MARE	Master of Arts in Religious Education
MARL	Master of Arts in Religious Leadership
MARS	Master of Arts in Religious Studies
MAS	Master of Accounting Science
	Master of Actuarial Science
	Master of Administrative Science
	Master of Advanced Study
	Master of Aeronautical Science
	Master of American Studies
	Master of Applied Science
	Master of Applied Statistics
	Master of Archival Studies
MASA	Master of Advanced Studies in Architecture
MASD	Master of Arts in Spiritual Direction
MASE	Master of Arts in Special Education

MASF	Master of Arts in Spiritual Formation
MASJ	Master of Arts in Systems of Justice
MASLA	Master of Advanced Studies in Landscape Architecture
MASM	Master of Aging Services Management
	Master of Arts in Specialized Ministries
MASP	Master of Applied Social Psychology
	Master of Arts in School Psychology
MASPAA	Master of Arts in Sports and Athletic Administration
MASS	Master of Applied Social Science
	Master of Arts in Social Science
MAST	Master of Arts in Science Teaching
MASW	Master of Aboriginal Social Work
MAT	Master of Arts in Teaching
	Master of Arts in Theology
	Master of Athletic Training
	Master's in Administration of Telecommunications
Mat E	Materials Engineer
MATCM	Master of Acupuncture and Traditional Chinese Medicine
MATDE	Master of Arts in Theology, Development, and Evangelism
MATDR	Master of Territorial Management and Regional Development
MATE	Master of Arts for the Teaching of English
MATESL	Master of Arts in Teaching English as a Second Language
MATESOL	Master of Arts in Teaching English to Speakers of Other Languages
MATF	Master of Arts in Teaching English as a Foreign Language/Intercultural Studies
MATFL	Master of Arts in Teaching Foreign Language
MATH	Master of Arts in Therapy
MATI	Master of Administration of Information Technology
MATL	Master of Arts in Teacher Leadership
	Master of Arts in Teaching of Languages
	Master of Arts in Transformational Leadership
MATM	Master of Arts in Teaching of Mathematics
MATS	Master of Arts in Theological Studies
	Master of Arts in Transforming Spirituality
MATSL	Master of Arts in Teaching a Second Language
MAUA	Master of Arts in Urban Affairs
MAUD	Master of Arts in Urban Design
MAURP	Master of Arts in Urban and Regional Planning
MAWSHP	Master of Arts in Worship
MAYM	Master of Arts in Youth Ministry
MB	Master of Bioinformatics
	Master of Biology
MBA	Master of Business Administration
MBA-AM	Master of Business Administration in Aviation Management
MBA-EP	Master of Business Administration–Experienced Professionals
MBA/MGPS	Master of Business Administration/Master of Global Policy Studies
MBAA	Master of Business Administration in Aviation

MBAE	Master of Biological and Agricultural Engineering
	Master of Biosystems and Agricultural Engineering
MBAH	Master of Business Administration in Health
MBAi	Master of Business Administration–International
MBAICT	Master of Business Administration in Information and Communication Technology
MBATM	Master of Business Administration in Technology Management
MBC	Master of Building Construction
MBE	Master of Bilingual Education
	Master of Bioengineering
	Master of Bioethics
	Master of Biological Engineering
	Master of Biomedical Engineering
	Master of Business and Engineering
	Master of Business Economics
	Master of Business Education
MBEE	Master in Biotechnology Enterprise and Entrepreneurship
MBET	Master of Business, Entrepreneurship and Technology
MBIOT	Master of Biotechnology
MBiotech	Master of Biotechnology
MBL	Master of Business Law
	Master of Business Leadership
MBLE	Master in Business Logistics Engineering
MBMI	Master of Biomedical Imaging and Signals
MBMSE	Master of Business Management and Software Engineering
MBOE	Master of Business Operational Excellence
MBS	Master of Biblical Studies
	Master of Biological Science
	Master of Biomedical Sciences
	Master of Bioscience
	Master of Building Science
	Master of Business and Science
MBST	Master of Biostatistics
MBT	Master of Biblical and Theological Studies
	Master of Biomedical Technology
	Master of Biotechnology
	Master of Business Taxation
MC	Master of Communication
	Master of Counseling
	Master of Cybersecurity
MC Ed	Master of Continuing Education
MC Sc	Master of Computer Science
MCA	Master of Arts in Applied Criminology
	Master of Commercial Aviation
MCAM	Master of Computational and Applied Mathematics
MCC	Master of Computer Science
MCCS	Master of Crop and Soil Sciences
MCD	Master of Communications Disorders
	Master of Community Development
MCE	Master in Electronic Commerce
	Master of Christian Education
	Master of Civil Engineering
	Master of Control Engineering
MCEM	Master of Construction Engineering Management

MCH	Master of Chemical Engineering
MCHE	Master of Chemical Engineering
MCIS	Master of Communication and Information Studies
	Master of Computer and Information Science
	Master of Computer Information Systems
MCIT	Master of Computer and Information Technology
MCJ	Master of Criminal Justice
MCJA	Master of Criminal Justice Administration
MCL	Master in Communication Leadership
	Master of Canon Law
	Master of Comparative Law
MCM	Master of Christian Ministry
	Master of Church Music
	Master of City Management
	Master of Communication Management
	Master of Community Medicine
	Master of Construction Management
	Master of Contract Management
	Master of Corporate Media
MCMP	Master of City and Metropolitan Planning
MCMS	Master of Clinical Medical Science
MCN	Master of Clinical Nutrition
MCOL	Master of Arts in Community and Organizational Leadership
MCP	Master of City Planning
	Master of Community Planning
	Master of Counseling Psychology
	Master of Cytopathology Practice
	Master of Science in Quality Systems and Productivity
MCPC	Master of Arts in Chaplaincy and Pastoral Care
MCPD	Master of Community Planning and Development
MCR	Master in Clinical Research
MCRP	Master of City and Regional Planning
MCRS	Master of City and Regional Studies
MCS	Master of Christian Studies
	Master of Clinical Science
	Master of Combined Sciences
	Master of Communication Studies
	Master of Computer Science
	Master of Consumer Science
MCSE	Master of Computer Science and Engineering
MCSL	Master of Catholic School Leadership
MCSM	Master of Construction Science/ Management
MCST	Master of Science in Computer Science and Information Technology
MCTP	Master of Communication Technology and Policy
MCTS	Master of Clinical and Translational Science
MCVS	Master of Cardiovascular Science
MD	Doctor of Medicine
MDA	Master of Development Administration
	Master of Dietetic Administration
MDB	Master of Design-Build
MDE	Master of Developmental Economics
	Master of Distance Education
	Master of the Education of the Deaf

MDH	Master of Dental Hygiene
MDM	Master of Design Methods
	Master of Digital Media
MDP	Master in Sustainable Development Practice
	Master of Development Practice
MDR	Master of Dispute Resolution
MDS	Master of Dental Surgery
	Master of Design Studies
ME	Master of Education
	Master of Engineering
	Master of Entrepreneurship
	Master of Evangelism
ME Sc	Master of Engineering Science
MEA	Master of Educational Administration
	Master of Engineering Administration
MEAP	Master of Environmental Administration and Planning
MEBT	Master in Electronic Business Technologies
MEC	Master of Electronic Commerce
MECE	Master of Electrical and Computer Engineering
Mech E	Mechanical Engineer
MED	Master of Education of the Deaf
MEDS	Master of Environmental Design Studies
MEE	Master in Education
	Master of Electrical Engineering
	Master of Energy Engineering
	Master of Environmental Engineering
MEEM	Master of Environmental Engineering and Management
MEENE	Master of Engineering in Environmental Engineering
MEEP	Master of Environmental and Energy Policy
MEERM	Master of Earth and Environmental Resource Management
MEH	Master in Humanistic Studies
	Master of Environmental Horticulture
MEHP	Master of Education in the Health Professions
MEHS	Master of Environmental Health and Safety
MEIM	Master of Entertainment Industry Management
MEL	Master of Educational Leadership
	Master of English Literature
MELP	Master of Environmental Law and Policy
MEM	Master of Ecosystem Management
	Master of Electricity Markets
	Master of Engineering Management
	Master of Environmental Management
	Master of Marketing
MEME	Master of Engineering in Manufacturing Engineering
	Master of Engineering in Mechanical Engineering
MENG	Master of Arts in English
MENVEGR	Master of Environmental Engineering
MEP	Master of Engineering Physics
MEPC	Master of Environmental Pollution Control
MEPD	Master of EducationNProfessional Development
	Master of Environmental Planning and Design
MER	Master of Employment Relations
MERE	Master of Entrepreneurial Real Estate

MES	Master of Education and Science	MGPS/MA	Master of Global Policy Studies/Master of Arts
	Master of Engineering Science	MGPS/MPH	Master of Global Policy Studies/Master of Public Health
	Master of Environment and Sustainability		
	Master of Environmental Science	MGREM	Master of Global Real Estate Management
	Master of Environmental Studies	MGS	Master of Gerontological Studies
	Master of Environmental Systems		Master of Global Studies
	Master of Special Education	MH	Master of Humanities
MESM	Master of Environmental Science and Management	MH Ed	Master of Health Education
		MH Sc	Master of Health Sciences
MET	Master of Educational Technology	MHA	Master of Health Administration
	Master of Engineering Technology		Master of Healthcare Administration
	Master of Entertainment Technology		Master of Hospital Administration
	Master of Environmental Toxicology		Master of Hospitality Administration
METM	Master of Engineering and Technology Management	MHAD	Master of Health Administration
		MHB	Master of Human Behavior
MEVE	Master of Environmental Engineering	MHCA	Master of Health Care Administration
MF	Master of Finance	MHCI	Master of Health Care Informatics
	Master of Forestry		Master of Human-Computer Interaction
MFA	Master of Fine Arts	MHCL	Master of Health Care Leadership
MFAM	Master in Food Animal Medicine	MHE	Master of Health Education
MFAS	Master of Fisheries and Aquatic Science		Master of Human Ecology
MFAW	Master of Fine Arts in Writing	MHE Ed	Master of Home Economics Education
MFC	Master of Forest Conservation	MHEA	Master of Higher Education Administration
MFCS	Master of Family and Consumer Sciences	MHHS	Master of Health and Human Services
MFE	Master of Financial Economics	MHI	Master of Health Informatics
	Master of Financial Engineering		Master of Healthcare Innovation
	Master of Forest Engineering	MHIIM	Master of Health Informatics and Information Management
MFG	Master of Functional Genomics		
MFHD	Master of Family and Human Development	MHIS	Master of Health Information Systems
MFM	Master of Financial Management	MHK	Master of Human Kinetics
	Master of Financial Mathematics	MHL	Master of Hebrew Literature
MFMS	Master's in Food Microbiology and Safety	MHM	Master of Healthcare Management
MFPE	Master of Food Process Engineering	MHMS	Master of Health Management Systems
MFR	Master of Forest Resources	MHP	Master of Health Physics
MFRC	Master of Forest Resources and Conservation		Master of Heritage Preservation
			Master of Historic Preservation
MFS	Master of Food Science	MHPA	Master of Heath Policy and Administration
	Master of Forensic Sciences	MHPE	Master of Health Professions Education
	Master of Forest Science	MHR	Master of Human Resources
	Master of Forest Studies	MHRD	Master in Human Resource Development
	Master of French Studies	MHRIR	Master of Human Resources and Industrial Relations
MFST	Master of Food Safety and Technology		
MFT	Master of Family Therapy	MHRLR	Master of Human Resources and Labor Relations
	Master of Food Technology		
MFWB	Master of Fishery and Wildlife Biology	MHRM	Master of Human Resources Management
MFWCB	Master of Fish, Wildlife and Conservation Biology	MHS	Master of Health Science
			Master of Health Sciences
MFWS	Master of Fisheries and Wildlife Sciences		Master of Health Studies
MFYCS	Master of Family, Youth and Community Sciences		Master of Hispanic Studies
			Master of Human Services
MG	Master of Genetics		Master of Humanistic Studies
MGA	Master of Global Affairs	MHSA	Master of Health Services Administration
	Master of Governmental Administration	MHSM	Master of Health Systems Management
MGC	Master of Genetic Counseling	MI	Master of Information
MGD	Master of Graphic Design		Master of Instruction
MGE	Master of Geotechnical Engineering	MI Arch	Master of Interior Architecture
MGEM	Master of Global Entrepreneurship and Management	MIA	Master of Interior Architecture
			Master of International Affairs
MGIS	Master of Geographic Information Science	MIAA	Master of International Affairs and Administration
	Master of Geographic Information Systems		
MGM	Master of Global Management	MIAM	Master of International Agribusiness Management
MGP	Master of Gestion de Projet		
MGPS	Master of Global Policy Studies		

MIAPD	Master of Interior Architecture and Product Design
MIB	Master of International Business
MIBA	Master of International Business Administration
MICM	Master of International Construction Management
MID	Master of Industrial Design
	Master of Industrial Distribution
	Master of Interior Design
	Master of International Development
MIDC	Master of Integrated Design and Construction
MIE	Master of Industrial Engineering
MIH	Master of Integrative Health
MIHTM	Master of International Hospitality and Tourism Management
MIJ	Master of International Journalism
MILR	Master of Industrial and Labor Relations
MiM	Master in Management
MIM	Master of Industrial Management
	Master of Information Management
	Master of International Management
MIMLAE	Master of International Management for Latin American Executives
MIMS	Master of Information Management and Systems
	Master of Integrated Manufacturing Systems
MIP	Master of Infrastructure Planning
	Master of Intellectual Property
	Master of International Policy
MIPA	Master of International Public Affairs
MIPER	Master of International Political Economy of Resources
MIPP	Master of International Policy and Practice
	Master of International Public Policy
MIPS	Master of International Planning Studies
MIR	Master of Industrial Relations
	Master of International Relations
MIRHR	Master of Industrial Relations and Human Resources
MIS	Master of Industrial Statistics
	Master of Information Science
	Master of Information Systems
	Master of Integrated Science
	Master of Interdisciplinary Studies
	Master of International Service
	Master of International Studies
MISE	Master of Industrial and Systems Engineering
MISKM	Master of Information Sciences and Knowledge Management
MISM	Master of Information Systems Management
MIT	Master in Teaching
	Master of Industrial Technology
	Master of Information Technology
	Master of Initial Teaching
	Master of International Trade
	Master of Internet Technology
MITA	Master of Information Technology Administration
MITM	Master of Information Technology and Management
MITO	Master of Industrial Technology and Operations

MJ	Master of Journalism
	Master of Jurisprudence
MJ Ed	Master of Jewish Education
MJA	Master of Justice Administration
MJM	Master of Justice Management
MJS	Master of Judicial Studies
	Master of Juridical Science
MKM	Master of Knowledge Management
ML	Master of Latin
ML Arch	Master of Landscape Architecture
MLA	Master of Landscape Architecture
	Master of Liberal Arts
MLAS	Master of Laboratory Animal Science
	Master of Liberal Arts and Sciences
MLAUD	Master of Landscape Architecture in Urban Development
MLD	Master of Leadership Development
MLE	Master of Applied Linguistics and Exegesis
MLER	Master of Labor and Employment Relations
MLHR	Master of Labor and Human Resources
MLI Sc	Master of Library and Information Science
MLIS	Master of Library and Information Science
	Master of Library and Information Studies
MLM	Master of Library Media
MLRHR	Master of Labor Relations and Human Resources
MLS	Master of Leadership Studies
	Master of Legal Studies
	Master of Liberal Studies
	Master of Library Science
	Master of Life Sciences
MLSP	Master of Law and Social Policy
MLT	Master of Language Technologies
MLTCA	Master of Long Term Care Administration
MM	Master of Management
	Master of Ministry
	Master of Missiology
	Master of Music
MM Ed	Master of Music Education
MM Sc	Master of Medical Science
MM St	Master of Museum Studies
MMA	Master of Marine Affairs
	Master of Media Arts
	Master of Musical Arts
MMAE	Master of Mechanical and Aerospace Engineering
MMAL	Master of Maritime Administration and Logistics
MMAS	Master of Military Art and Science
MMB	Master of Microbial Biotechnology
MMBA	Managerial Master of Business Administration
MMC	Master of Manufacturing Competitiveness
	Master of Mass Communications
	Master of Music Conducting
MMCM	Master of Music in Church Music
MMCSS	Master of Mathematical Computational and Statistical Sciences
MME	Master of Manufacturing Engineering
	Master of Mathematics Education
	Master of Mathematics for Educators
	Master of Mechanical Engineering
	Master of Medical Engineering

	Master of Mining Engineering	MNS	Master of Natural Science
	Master of Music Education	MO	Master of Oceanography
MMF	Master of Mathematical Finance	MOD	Master of Organizational Development
MMFT	Master of Marriage and Family Therapy	MOGS	Master of Oil and Gas Studies
MMG	Master of Management	MOH	Master of Occupational Health
MMH	Master of Management in Hospitality	MOL	Master of Organizational Leadership
	Master of Medical Humanities	MOM	Master of Oriental Medicine
MMI	Master of Management of Innovation	MOR	Master of Operations Research
MMIS	Master of Management Information Systems	MOT	Master of Occupational Therapy
MMM	Master of Manufacturing Management	MP	Master of Physiology
	Master of Marine Management		Master of Planning
	Master of Medical Management	MP Ac	Master of Professional Accountancy
MMME	Master of Metallurgical and Materials Engineering	MP Acc	Master of Professional Accountancy
			Master of Professional Accounting
MMP	Master of Management Practice		Master of Public Accounting
	Master of Marine Policy	MP Aff	Master of Public Affairs
	Master of Medical Physics	MP Aff/MPH	Master of Public Affairs/Master of Public Health
	Master of Music Performance		
MMPA	Master of Management and Professional Accounting	MP Th	Master of Pastoral Theology
		MPA	Master of Physician Assistant
MMQM	Master of Manufacturing Quality Management		Master of Professional Accountancy
			Master of Professional Accounting
MMR	Master of Marketing Research		Master of Public Administration
MMRM	Master of Marine Resources Management		Master of Public Affairs
MMS	Master of Management Science	MPAC	Master of Professional Accounting
	Master of Management Studies	MPAID	Master of Public Administration and International Development
	Master of Manufacturing Systems		
	Master of Marine Studies	MPAP	Master of Physician Assistant Practice
	Master of Materials Science		Master of Public Affairs and Politics
	Master of Medical Science	MPAS	Master of Physician Assistant Science
	Master of Medieval Studies		Master of Physician Assistant Studies
MMSE	Master of Manufacturing Systems Engineering	MPC	Master of Pastoral Counseling
			Master of Professional Communication
	Multidisciplinary Master of Science in Engineering		Master of Professional Counseling
MMSM	Master of Music in Sacred Music	MPCU	Master of Planning in Civic Urbanism
MMT	Master in Marketing	MPD	Master of Product Development
	Master of Music Teaching		Master of Public Diplomacy
	Master of Music Therapy	MPDS	Master of Planning and Development Studies
	Master's in Marketing Technology		
MMus	Master of Music	MPE	Master of Physical Education
MN	Master of Nursing		Master of Power Engineering
	Master of Nutrition	MPEM	Master of Project Engineering and Management
MN NP	Master of Nursing in Nurse Practitioner		
MNA	Master of Nonprofit Administration	MPH	Master of Public Health
	Master of Nurse Anesthesia	MPHE	Master of Public Health Education
MNAL	Master of Nonprofit Administration and Leadership	MPHTM	Master of Public Health and Tropical Medicine
MNAS	Master of Natural and Applied Science	MPI	Master of Product Innovation
MNCM	Master of Network and Communications Management	MPIA	Master in International Affairs
			Master of Public and International Affairs
MNE	Master of Network Engineering	MPM	Master of Pastoral Ministry
	Master of Nuclear Engineering		Master of Pest Management
MNL	Master in International Business for Latin America		Master of Policy Management
			Master of Practical Ministries
MNM	Master of Nonprofit Management		Master of Project Management
MNO	Master of Nonprofit Organization		Master of Public Management
MNPL	Master of Not-for-Profit Leadership	MPNA	Master of Public and Nonprofit Administration
MNpS	Master of Nonprofit Studies		
MNR	Master of Natural Resources	MPO	Master of Prosthetics and Orthotics
MNRES	Master of Natural Resources and Environmental Studies	MPOD	Master of Positive Organizational Development
MNRM	Master of Natural Resource Management	MPP	Master of Public Policy
MNRS	Master of Natural Resource Stewardship	MPPA	Master of Public Policy Administration

	Master of Public Policy and Administration
MPPAL	Master of Public Policy, Administration and Law
MPPM	Master of Public and Private Management
	Master of Public Policy and Management
MPPPM	Master of Plant Protection and Pest Management
MPRTM	Master of Parks, Recreation, and Tourism Management
MPS	Master of Pastoral Studies
	Master of Perfusion Science
	Master of Planning Studies
	Master of Political Science
	Master of Preservation Studies
	Master of Professional Studies
	Master of Public Service
MPSA	Master of Public Service Administration
MPSRE	Master of Professional Studies in Real Estate
MPT	Master of Pastoral Theology
	Master of Physical Therapy
	Master of Practical Theology
MPVM	Master of Preventive Veterinary Medicine
MPW	Master of Professional Writing
	Master of Public Works
MQM	Master of Quality Management
MQS	Master of Quality Systems
MR	Master of Recreation
	Master of Retailing
MRA	Master in Research Administration
MRC	Master of Rehabilitation Counseling
MRCP	Master of Regional and City Planning
	Master of Regional and Community Planning
MRD	Master of Rural Development
MRE	Master of Real Estate
	Master of Religious Education
MRED	Master of Real Estate Development
MREM	Master of Resource and Environmental Management
MRLS	Master of Resources Law Studies
MRM	Master of Resources Management
MRP	Master of Regional Planning
MRS	Master of Religious Studies
MRSc	Master of Rehabilitation Science
MS	Master of Science
MS Cmp E	Master of Science in Computer Engineering
MS Kin	Master of Science in Kinesiology
MS Acct	Master of Science in Accounting
MS Accy	Master of Science in Accountancy
MS Aero E	Master of Science in Aerospace Engineering
MS Ag	Master of Science in Agriculture
MS Arch	Master of Science in Architecture
MS Arch St	Master of Science in Architectural Studies
MS Bio E	Master of Science in Bioengineering
	Master of Science in Biomedical Engineering
MS Bm E	Master of Science in Biomedical Engineering
MS Ch E	Master of Science in Chemical Engineering
MS Chem	Master of Science in Chemistry
MS Cp E	Master of Science in Computer Engineering
MS Eco	Master of Science in Economics
MS Econ	Master of Science in Economics

MS Ed	Master of Science in Education
MS El	Master of Science in Educational Leadership and Administration
MS En E	Master of Science in Environmental Engineering
MS Eng	Master of Science in Engineering
MS Engr	Master of Science in Engineering
MS Env E	Master of Science in Environmental Engineering
MS Exp Surg	Master of Science in Experimental Surgery
MS Int A	Master of Science in International Affairs
MS Mat E	Master of Science in Materials Engineering
MS Mat SE	Master of Science in Material Science and Engineering
MS Met E	Master of Science in Metallurgical Engineering
MS Mgt	Master of Science in Management
MS Min	Master of Science in Mining
MS Min E	Master of Science in Mining Engineering
MS Mt E	Master of Science in Materials Engineering
MS Otal	Master of Science in Otalrynology
MS Pet E	Master of Science in Petroleum Engineering
MS Phys	Master of Science in Physics
MS Poly	Master of Science in Polymers
MS Psy	Master of Science in Psychology
MS Pub P	Master of Science in Public Policy
MS Sc	Master of Science in Social Science
MS Sp Ed	Master of Science in Special Education
MS Stat	Master of Science in Statistics
MS Surg	Master of Science in Surgery
MS Tax	Master of Science in Taxation
MS Tc E	Master of Science in Telecommunications Engineering
MS-R	Master of Science (Research)
MS/CAGS	Master of Science/Certificate of Advanced Graduate Studies
MSA	Master of School Administration
	Master of Science Administration
	Master of Science in Accountancy
	Master of Science in Accounting
	Master of Science in Administration
	Master of Science in Aeronautics
	Master of Science in Agriculture
	Master of Science in Anesthesia
	Master of Science in Architecture
	Master of Science in Aviation
	Master of Sports Administration
MSA Phy	Master of Science in Applied Physics
MSAA	Master of Science in Astronautics and Aeronautics
MSAAE	Master of Science in Aeronautical and Astronautical Engineering
MSABE	Master of Science in Agricultural and Biological Engineering
MSAC	Master of Science in Acupuncture
MSACC	Master of Science in Accounting
MSAE	Master of Science in Aeronautical Engineering
	Master of Science in Aerospace Engineering
	Master of Science in Applied Economics
	Master of Science in Applied Engineering
	Master of Science in Architectural Engineering
MSAH	Master of Science in Allied Health

MSAL	Master of Sport Administration and Leadership	MSCIT	Master of Science in Computer Information Technology
MSAM	Master of Science in Applied Mathematics	MSCJ	Master of Science in Criminal Justice
MSANR	Master of Science in Agriculture and Natural Resources Systems Management	MSCJA	Master of Science in Criminal Justice Administration
MSAPM	Master of Security Analysis and Portfolio Management	MSCJS	Master of Science in Crime and Justice Studies
MSAS	Master of Science in Applied Statistics	MSCLS	Master of Science in Clinical Laboratory Studies
	Master of Science in Architectural Studies	MSCM	Master of Science in Church Management
MSAT	Master of Science in Accounting and Taxation		Master of Science in Conflict Management
	Master of Science in Advanced Technology		Master of Science in Construction Management
	Master of Science in Athletic Training	MScM	Master of Science in Management
MSB	Master of Science in Bible	MSCM	Master of Supply Chain Management
	Master of Science in Biotechnology	MSCNU	Master of Science in Clinical Nutrition
	Master of Science in Business	MSCP	Master of Science in Clinical Psychology
	Master of Sustainable Business		Master of Science in Community Psychology
MSBA	Master of Science in Business Administration		Master of Science in Computer Engineering
	Master of Science in Business Analysis		Master of Science in Counseling Psychology
MSBAE	Master of Science in Biological and Agricultural Engineering	MSCPE	Master of Science in Computer Engineering
	Master of Science in Biosystems and Agricultural Engineering	MSCPharm	Master of Science in Pharmacy
MSBC	Master of Science in Building Construction	MSCPI	Master in Strategic Planning for Critical Infrastructures
MSBCB	bioinformatics and computational biology	MSCR	Master of Science in Clinical Research
MSBE	Master of Science in Biological Engineering	MSCRP	Master of Science in City and Regional Planning
	Master of Science in Biomedical Engineering		Master of Science in Community and Regional Planning
MSBENG	Master of Science in Bioengineering	MSCRP/MP Aff	Master of Science in Community and Regional Planning/Master of Public Affairs
MSBIT	Master of Science in Business Information Technology	MSCRP/MSSD	Master of Science in Community and Regional Planning/Master of Science in Sustainable Design
MSBM	Master of Sport Business Management	MSCRP/MSUD	Master of Science in Community and Regional Planning/Masters of Science in Urban Design
MSBME	Master of Science in Biomedical Engineering		
MSBMS	Master of Science in Basic Medical Science	MSCS	Master of Science in Clinical Science
MSBS	Master of Science in Biomedical Sciences		Master of Science in Computer Science
MSC	Master of Science in Commerce	MSCSD	Master of Science in Communication Sciences and Disorders
	Master of Science in Communication	MSCSE	Master of Science in Computer Science and Engineering
	Master of Science in Computers		
	Master of Science in Counseling	MSCTE	Master of Science in Career and Technical Education
	Master of Science in Criminology	MSD	Master of Science in Dentistry
MSCC	Master of Science in Christian Counseling		Master of Science in Design
	Master of Science in Community Counseling		Master of Science in Dietetics
MSCD	Master of Science in Communication Disorders	MSE	Master of Science Education
			Master of Science in Economics
	Master of Science in Community Development		Master of Science in Education
MSCE	Master of Science in Civil Engineering		Master of Science in Engineering
	Master of Science in Clinical Epidemiology		Master of Science in Engineering Management
	Master of Science in Computer Engineering		Master of Software Engineering
	Master of Science in Continuing Education		Master of Special Education
MSCEE	Master of Science in Civil and Environmental Engineering		Master of Structural Engineering
		MSECE	Master of Science in Electrical and Computer Engineering
MSCF	Master of Science in Computational Finance	MSED	Master of Sustainable Economic Development
MSCH	Master of Science in Chemical Engineering		
MSChE	Master of Science in Chemical Engineering	MSEE	Master of Science in Electrical Engineering
MSCI	Master of Science in Clinical Investigation		Master of Science in Environmental Engineering
	Master of Science in Curriculum and Instruction		
MSCIS	Master of Science in Computer and Information Systems	MSEH	Master of Science in Environmental Health
	Master of Science in Computer Information Science	MSEL	Master of Science in Educational Leadership
	Master of Science in Computer Information Systems		

MSEM	Master of Science in Engineering Management
	Master of Science in Engineering Mechanics
	Master of Science in Environmental Management
MSENE	Master of Science in Environmental Engineering
MSEO	Master of Science in Electro-Optics
MSEP	Master of Science in Economic Policy
MSEPA	Master of Science in Economics and Policy Analysis
MSES	Master of Science in Embedded Software Engineering
	Master of Science in Engineering Science
	Master of Science in Environmental Science
	Master of Science in Environmental Studies
MSESM	Master of Science in Engineering Science and Mechanics
MSET	Master of Science in Educational Technology
	Master of Science in Engineering Technology
MSEV	Master of Science in Environmental Engineering
MSEVH	Master of Science in Environmental Health and Safety
MSF	Master of Science in Finance
	Master of Science in Forestry
	Master of Spiritual Formation
MSFA	Master of Science in Financial Analysis
MSFAM	Master of Science in Family Studies
MSFCS	Master of Science in Family and Consumer Science
MSFE	Master of Science in Financial Engineering
MSFOR	Master of Science in Forestry
MSFP	Master of Science in Financial Planning
MSFS	Master of Science in Financial Sciences
	Master of Science in Forensic Science
MSFSB	Master of Science in Financial Services and Banking
MSFT	Master of Science in Family Therapy
MSGC	Master of Science in Genetic Counseling
MSH	Master of Science in Health
	Master of Science in Hospice
MSHA	Master of Science in Health Administration
MSHCA	Master of Science in Health Care Administration
MSHCI	Master of Science in Human Computer Interaction
MSHCPM	Master of Science in Health Care Policy and Management
MSHE	Master of Science in Health Education
MSHES	Master of Science in Human Environmental Sciences
MSHFID	Master of Science in Human Factors in Information Design
MSHFS	Master of Science in Human Factors and Systems
MSHI	Master of Science in Health Informatics
MSHP	Master of Science in Health Professions
	Master of Science in Health Promotion
MSHR	Master of Science in Human Resources
MSHRL	Master of Science in Human Resource Leadership
MSHRM	Master of Science in Human Resource Management
MSHROD	Master of Science in Human Resources and Organizational Development
MSHS	Master of Science in Health Science
	Master of Science in Health Services
	Master of Science in Health Systems
	Master of Science in Homeland Security
MSHT	Master of Science in History of Technology
MSI	Master of Science in Information
	Master of Science in Instruction
	Master of System Integration
MSIA	Master of Science in Industrial Administration
	Master of Science in Information Assurance and Computer Security
MSIB	Master of Science in International Business
MSIDM	Master of Science in Interior Design and Merchandising
MSIDT	Master of Science in Information Design and Technology
MSIE	Master of Science in Industrial Engineering
	Master of Science in International Economics
MSIEM	Master of Science in Information Engineering and Management
MSIID	Master of Science in Information and Instructional Design
MSIM	Master of Science in Information Management
	Master of Science in International Management
MSIMC	Master of Science in Integrated Marketing Communications
MSIR	Master of Science in Industrial Relations
MSIS	Master of Science in Information Science
	Master of Science in Information Studies
	Master of Science in Information Systems
	Master of Science in Interdisciplinary Studies
MSIS/MA	Master of Science in Information Studies/ Master of Arts
MSISE	Master of Science in Infrastructure Systems Engineering
MSISM	Master of Science in Information Systems Management
MSISPM	Master of Science in Information Security Policy and Management
MSIST	Master of Science in Information Systems Technology
MSIT	Master of Science in Industrial Technology
	Master of Science in Information Technology
	Master of Science in Instructional Technology
MSITM	Master of Science in Information Technology Management
MSJ	Master of Science in Journalism
	Master of Science in Jurisprudence
MSJC	Master of Social Justice and Criminology
MSJE	Master of Science in Jewish Education
MSJFP	Master of Science in Juvenile Forensic Psychology
MSJJ	Master of Science in Juvenile Justice
MSJPS	Master of Science in Justice and Public Safety
MSJS	Master of Science in Jewish Studies
MSK	Master of Science in Kinesiology
MSL	Master of School Leadership

	Master of Science in Leadership	MSOL	Master of Science in Organizational Leadership
	Master of Science in Limnology	MSOM	Master of Science in Operations Management
	Master of Strategic Leadership		Master of Science in Oriental Medicine
	Master of Studies in Law	MSOR	Master of Science in Operations Research
MSLA	Master of Science in Landscape Architecture	MSOT	Master of Science in Occupational Technology
	Master of Science in Legal Administration		Master of Science in Occupational Therapy
MSLD	Master of Science in Land Development	MSP	Master of Science in Pharmacy
MSLFS	Master of Science in Life Sciences		Master of Science in Planning
MSLP	Master of Speech-Language Pathology		Master of Science in Psychology
MSLS	Master of Science in Library Science		Master of Speech Pathology
MSLSCM	Master of Science in Logistics and Supply Chain Management	MSPA	Master of Science in Physician Assistant
			Master of Science in Professional Accountancy
MSLT	Master of Second Language Teaching	MSPAS	Master of Science in Physician Assistant Studies
MSM	Master of Sacred Ministry	MSPC	Master of Science in Professional Communications
	Master of Sacred Music		
	Master of School Mathematics		Master of Science in Professional Counseling
	Master of Science in Management	MSPE	Master of Science in Petroleum Engineering
	Master of Science in Organization Management	MSPG	Master of Science in Psychology
	Master of Security Management	MSPH	Master of Science in Public Health
MSMA	Master of Science in Marketing Analysis	MSPHR	Master of Science in Pharmacy
MSMAE	Master of Science in Materials Engineering	MSPM	Master of Science in Professional Management
MSMC	Master of Science in Mass Communications		Master of Science in Project Management
MSME	Master of Science in Mathematics Education	MSPNGE	Master of Science in Petroleum and Natural Gas Engineering
	Master of Science in Mechanical Engineering	MSPS	Master of Science in Pharmaceutical Science
MSMFE	Master of Science in Manufacturing Engineering		Master of Science in Political Science
MSMFT	Master of Science in Marriage and Family Therapy		Master of Science in Psychological Services
MSMIS	Master of Science in Management Information Systems	MSPT	Master of Science in Physical Therapy
		MSpVM	Master of Specialized Veterinary Medicine
MSMIT	Master of Science in Management and Information Technology	MSR	Master of Science in Radiology
			Master of Science in Reading
MSMLS	Master of Science in Medical Laboratory Science	MSRA	Master of Science in Recreation Administration
MSMOT	Master of Science in Management of Technology	MSRC	Master of Science in Resource Conservation
		MSRE	Master of Science in Real Estate
MSMS	Master of Science in Management Science		Master of Science in Religious Education
	Master of Science in Medical Sciences	MSRED	Master of Science in Real Estate Development
MSMSE	Master of Science in Manufacturing Systems Engineering	MSRLS	Master of Science in Recreation and Leisure Studies
	Master of Science in Material Science and Engineering	MSRMP	Master of Science in Radiological Medical Physics
	Master of Science in Mathematics and Science Education	MSRS	Master of Science in Rehabilitation Science
MSMT	Master of Science in Management and Technology	MSS	Master of Science in Software
			Master of Security Studies
MSMus	Master of Sacred Music		Master of Social Science
MSN	Master of Science in Nursing		Master of Social Services
MSN-R	Master of Science in Nursing (Research)		Master of Software Systems
MSNA	Master of Science in Nurse Anesthesia		Master of Sports Science
MSNE	Master of Science in Nuclear Engineering		Master of Strategic Studies
MSNED	Master of Science in Nurse Education	MSSA	Master of Science in Social Administration
MSNM	Master of Science in Nonprofit Management	MSSCP	Master of Science in Science Content and Process
MSNS	Master of Science in Natural Science		
	Master of Science in Nutritional Science	MSSD	Master of Science in Sustainable Design
MSOD	Master of Science in Organizational Development	MSSE	Master of Science in Software Engineering
MSOEE	Master of Science in Outdoor and Environmental Education		Master of Science in Space Education
			Master of Science in Special Education
MSOES	Master of Science in Occupational Ergonomics and Safety	MSSEM	Master of Science in Systems and Engineering Management
MSOH	Master of Science in Occupational Health		

MSSI	Master of Science in Security Informatics	MTOM	Master of Traditional Oriental Medicine
	Master of Science in Strategic Intelligence	MTP	Master of Transpersonal Psychology
MSSL	Master of Science in School Leadership	MTPC	Master of Technical and Professional Communication
	Master of Science in Strategic Leadership	MTR	Master of Translational Research
MSSLP	Master of Science in Speech-Language Pathology	MTS	Master of Theatre Studies
MSSM	Master of Science in Sports Medicine		Master of Theological Studies
MSSP	Master of Science in Social Policy	MTSC	Master of Technical and Scientific Communication
MSSPA	Master of Science in Student Personnel Administration	MTSE	Master of Telecommunications and Software Engineering
MSSS	Master of Science in Safety Science	MTT	Master in Technology Management
	Master of Science in Systems Science	MTX	Master of Taxation
MSST	Master of Science in Security Technologies	MUA	Master of Urban Affairs
MSSW	Master of Science in Social Work	MUCD	Master of Urban and Community Design
MSSWE	Master of Science in Software Engineering	MUD	Master of Urban Design
MST	Master of Science and Technology	MUDS	Master of Urban Design Studies
	Master of Science in Taxation	MUEP	Master of Urban and Environmental Planning
	Master of Science in Teaching	MUP	Master of Urban Planning
	Master of Science in Technology	MUPDD	Master of Urban Planning, Design, and Development
	Master of Science in Telecommunications		
	Master of Science Teaching	MUPP	Master of Urban Planning and Policy
MSTC	Master of Science in Technical Communication	MUPRED	Master of Urban Planning and Real Estate Development
	Master of Science in Telecommunications	MURP	Master of Urban and Regional Planning
MSTCM	Master of Science in Traditional Chinese Medicine		Master of Urban and Rural Planning
MSTE	Master of Science in Telecommunications Engineering	MURPL	Master of Urban and Regional Planning
	Master of Science in Transportation Engineering	MUS	Master of Urban Studies
		MUSA	Master of Urban Spatial Analytics
MSTM	Master of Science in Technical Management	MVM	Master of VLSI and Microelectronics
	Master of Science in Technology Management	MVP	Master of Voice Pedagogy
	Master of Science in Transfusion Medicine	MVPH	Master of Veterinary Public Health
MSTOM	Master of Science in Traditional Oriental Medicine	MVS	Master of Visual Studies
MSUD	Master of Science in Urban Design	MWC	Master of Wildlife Conservation
MSW	Master of Social Work	MWE	Master in Welding Engineering
MSWE	Master of Software Engineering	MWPS	Master of Wood and Paper Science
MSWREE	Master of Science in Water Resources and Environmental Engineering	MWR	Master of Water Resources
		MWS	Master of Women's Studies
MSX	Master of Science in Exercise Science		Master of Worship Studies
MT	Master of Taxation	MZS	Master of Zoological Science
	Master of Teaching	Nav Arch	Naval Architecture
	Master of Technology	Naval E	Naval Engineer
	Master of Textiles	ND	Doctor of Naturopathic Medicine
MTA	Master of Tax Accounting	NE	Nuclear Engineer
	Master of Teaching Arts	Nuc E	Nuclear Engineer
	Master of Tourism Administration	OD	Doctor of Optometry
MTCM	Master of Traditional Chinese Medicine	OTD	Doctor of Occupational Therapy
MTD	Master of Training and Development	PBME	Professional Master of Biomedical Engineering
MTE	Master in Educational Technology	PC	Performer's Certificate
MTESOL	Master in Teaching English to Speakers of Other Languages	PD	Professional Diploma
		PGC	Post-Graduate Certificate
MTHM	Master of Tourism and Hospitality Management	PGD	Postgraduate Diploma
		Ph L	Licentiate of Philosophy
MTI	Master of Information Technology	Pharm D	Doctor of Pharmacy
MTIM	Master of Trust and Investment Management	PhD	Doctor of Philosophy
		PhD Otal	Doctor of Philosophy in Otalrynology
MTL	Master of Talmudic Law	PhD Surg	Doctor of Philosophy in Surgery
MTM	Master of Technology Management	PhDEE	Doctor of Philosophy in Electrical Engineering
	Master of Telecommunications Management		
	Master of the Teaching of Mathematics	PMBA	Professional Master of Business Administration
MTMH	Master of Tropical Medicine and Hygiene	PMC	Post Master Certificate

PMD	Post-Master's Diploma		SMACT	Master of Science in Art, Culture and Technology
PMS	Professional Master of Science		SMBT	Master of Science in Building Technology
	Professional Master's		SP	Specialist Degree
Post-Doctoral MS	Post-Doctoral Master of Science		Sp C	Specialist in Counseling
Post-MSN Certificate	Post-Master of Science in Nursing Certificate		Sp Ed	Specialist in Education
PPDPT	Postprofessional Doctor of Physical Therapy		Sp LIS	Specialist in Library and Information Science
Pro-MS	Professional Science Master's		SPA	Specialist in Arts
PSM	Professional Master of Science		SPCM	Specialist in Church Music
	Professional Science Master's		Spec	Specialist's Certificate
Psy D	Doctor of Psychology		Spec M	Specialist in Music
Psy M	Master of Psychology		SPEM	Specialist in Educational Ministries
Psy S	Specialist in Psychology		Spt	Specialist Degree
Psya D	Doctor of Psychoanalysis		SPTH	Specialist in Theology
Rh D	Doctor of Rehabilitation		SSP	Specialist in School Psychology
S Psy S	Specialist in Psychological Services		STB	Bachelor of Sacred Theology
Sc D	Doctor of Science		STD	Doctor of Sacred Theology
Sc M	Master of Science		STL	Licentiate of Sacred Theology
SCCT	Specialist in Community College Teaching		STM	Master of Sacred Theology
ScDPT	Doctor of Physical Therapy Science		TDPT	Transitional Doctor of Physical Therapy
SD	Doctor of Science		Th D	Doctor of Theology
	Specialist Degree		Th M	Master of Theology
SJD	Doctor of Juridical Science		VMD	Doctor of Veterinary Medicine
SLPD	Doctor of Speech-Language Pathology		WEMBA	Weekend Executive Master of Business Administration
SM	Master of Science		XMA	Executive Master of Arts
SM Arch S	Master of Science in Architectural Studies			

INDEXES

Displays and Close-Ups

Adelphi University
    Business Administration and Management   70, 181
    Education   640, 727
    Social Work   1700, 1723
Embry-Riddle Aeronautical University–Daytona
    Business Administration/Aviation Management   616, 635
Fashion Institute of Technology
    Cosmetics and Fragrance Marketing and Management   507, 535
    Global Fashion Management   96, 183
Manhattanville College
    Business Administration and Management   185
    Education   674, 729
Monmouth University   116, 187
North Carolina State University
    Business Administration   120, 189
Northwestern University
    Education and Social Policy   682, 731
Pratt Institute
    Information and Library Science   1582, 1597

Syracuse University
    Library and Information Studies   1583, 1599
University at Buffalo, the State University of New York
    Social Work   1714, 1725
University of California, Los Angeles
    Business Administration and Management   145, 191
University of Kentucky
    Library and Information Science   1593, 1601
University of Oklahoma
    Business Administration and Management   158, 193
University of Ottawa
    Business Administration and Management   159, 195
University of Pennsylvania
    Education   712, 733
    Social Work   1718, 1727
The University of Texas at Dallas
    Business Administration and Management   168, 197
Vanderbilt University   721, 735

Directories and Subject Areas in This Book

Accounting	200	Industrial and Manufacturing Management	392
Actuarial Science	402	Information Studies	1580
Adult Education	950	Insurance	403
Advertising and Public Relations	308	Intellectual Property Law	1545
Agricultural Education	1248	International and Comparative Education	933
Archives/Archival Administration	1578	International Business	408
Art Education	1252	Investment Management	291
Athletic Training and Sports Medicine	1618	Kinesiology and Movement Studies	1641
Aviation Management	616	Law	1547
Business Administration and Management—General	70	Legal and Justice Studies	1567
Business Education	1266	Leisure Studies	1606
Community College Education	960	Library Science	1586
Computer Education	1270	Logistics	617
Counselor Education	1273	Management Information Systems	438
Curriculum and Instruction	738	Management Strategy and Policy	480
Developmental Education	1319	Marketing Research	533
Distance Education Development	777	Marketing	500
Early Childhood Education	963	Mathematics Education	1380
Education of Students with Severe/Multiple Disabilities	1128	Middle School Education	1066
Education of the Gifted	1129	Multilingual and Multicultural Education	1165
Educational Leadership and Administration	781	Museum Education	1410
Educational Measurement and Evaluation	861	Music Education	1411
Educational Media/Instructional Technology	871	Nonprofit Management	538
Educational Policy	906	Organizational Behavior	556
Educational Psychology	912	Organizational Management	560
Education—General	640	Physical Education	1653
Electronic Commerce	316	Project Management	584
Elementary Education	997	Quality Management	596
English as a Second Language	1136	Quantitative Analysis	600
English Education	1320	Reading Education	1433
Entertainment Management	340	Real Estate	608
Entrepreneurship	322	Recreation and Park Management	1608
Environmental Education	1340	Religious Education	1477
Environmental Law	1542	Science Education	1483
Exercise and Sports Science	1623	Secondary Education	1082
Facilities Management	341	Social Sciences Education	1512
Finance and Banking	247	Social Work	1699
Foreign Languages Education	1343	Special Education	1179
Foundations and Philosophy of Education	925	Sports Management	1672
Health Education	1358	Student Affairs	937
Health Law	1543	Supply Chain Management	622
Higher Education	1042	Sustainability Management	491
Home Economics Education	1378	Taxation	293
Hospitality Management	344	Transportation Management	632
Human Resources Development	356	Travel and Tourism	349
Human Resources Management	362	Urban Education	1241
Human Services	1694	Vocational and Technical Education	1530

Directories and Subject Areas in This Book

Directories and Subject Areas

Following is an alphabetical listing of directories and subject areas. Also listed are cross-references for subject area names not used in the directory structure of the guides, for example, "City and Regional Planning (*see* Urban and Regional Planning)."

Graduate Programs in the Humanities, Arts & Social Sciences

Addictions/Substance Abuse Counseling
Administration (*see* Arts Administration; Public Administration)
African-American Studies
African Languages and Literatures (*see* African Studies)
African Studies
Agribusiness (*see* Agricultural Economics and Agribusiness)
Agricultural Economics and Agribusiness
Alcohol Abuse Counseling (*see* Addictions/Substance Abuse Counseling)
American Indian/Native American Studies
American Studies
Anthropology
Applied Arts and Design—General
Applied Behavior Analysis
Applied Economics
Applied History (*see* Public History)
Applied Psychology
Applied Social Research
Arabic (*see* Near and Middle Eastern Languages)
Arab Studies (*see* Near and Middle Eastern Studies)
Archaeology
Architectural History
Architecture
Archives Administration (*see* Public History)
Area and Cultural Studies (*see* African-American Studies; African Studies; American Indian/Native American Studies; American Studies; Asian-American Studies; Asian Studies; Canadian Studies; Cultural Studies; East European and Russian Studies; Ethnic Studies; Folklore; Gender Studies; Hispanic Studies; Holocaust Studies; Jewish Studies; Latin American Studies; Near and Middle Eastern Studies; Northern Studies; Pacific Area/Pacific Rim Studies; Western European Studies; Women's Studies)
Art/Fine Arts
Art History
Arts Administration
Arts Journalism
Art Therapy
Asian-American Studies
Asian Languages
Asian Studies
Behavioral Sciences (*see* Psychology)
Bible Studies (*see* Religion; Theology)
Biological Anthropology
Black Studies (*see* African-American Studies)
Broadcasting (*see* Communication; Film, Television, and Video Production)
Broadcast Journalism
Building Science
Canadian Studies
Celtic Languages
Ceramics (*see* Art/Fine Arts)
Child and Family Studies
Child Development
Chinese
Chinese Studies (*see* Asian Languages; Asian Studies)
Christian Studies (*see* Missions and Missiology; Religion; Theology)
Cinema (*see* Film, Television, and Video Production)
City and Regional Planning (*see* Urban and Regional Planning)
Classical Languages and Literatures (*see* Classics)
Classics

Clinical Psychology
Clothing and Textiles
Cognitive Psychology (*see* Psychology—General; Cognitive Sciences)
Cognitive Sciences
Communication—General
Community Affairs (*see* Urban and Regional Planning; Urban Studies)
Community Planning (*see* Architecture; Environmental Design; Urban and Regional Planning; Urban Design; Urban Studies)
Community Psychology (*see* Social Psychology)
Comparative and Interdisciplinary Arts
Comparative Literature
Composition (*see* Music)
Computer Art and Design
Conflict Resolution and Mediation/Peace Studies
Consumer Economics
Corporate and Organizational Communication
Corrections (*see* Criminal Justice and Criminology)
Counseling (*see* Counseling Psychology; Pastoral Ministry and Counseling)
Counseling Psychology
Crafts (*see* Art/Fine Arts)
Creative Arts Therapies (*see* Art Therapy; Therapies—Dance, Drama, and Music)
Criminal Justice and Criminology
Cultural Anthropology
Cultural Studies
Dance
Decorative Arts
Demography and Population Studies
Design (*see* Applied Arts and Design; Architecture; Art/Fine Arts; Environmental Design; Graphic Design; Industrial Design; Interior Design; Textile Design; Urban Design)
Developmental Psychology
Diplomacy (*see* International Affairs)
Disability Studies
Drama Therapy (*see* Therapies—Dance, Drama, and Music)
Dramatic Arts (*see* Theater)
Drawing (*see* Art/Fine Arts)
Drug Abuse Counseling (*see* Addictions/Substance Abuse Counseling)
Drug and Alcohol Abuse Counseling (*see* Addictions/Substance Abuse Counseling)
East Asian Studies (*see* Asian Studies)
East European and Russian Studies
Economic Development
Economics
Educational Theater (*see* Theater; Therapies—Dance, Drama, and Music)
Emergency Management
English
Environmental Design
Ethics
Ethnic Studies
Ethnomusicology (*see* Music)
Experimental Psychology
Family and Consumer Sciences—General
Family Studies (*see* Child and Family Studies)
Family Therapy (*see* Child and Family Studies; Clinical Psychology; Counseling Psychology; Marriage and Family Therapy)
Filmmaking (*see* Film, Television, and Video Production)
Film Studies (*see* Film, Television, and Video Production)
Film, Television, and Video Production
Film, Television, and Video Theory and Criticism
Fine Arts (*see* Art/Fine Arts)
Folklore
Foreign Languages (*see* specific language)
Foreign Service (*see* International Affairs; International Development)
Forensic Psychology
Forensic Sciences
Forensics (*see* Speech and Interpersonal Communication)
French

Gender Studies
General Studies (see Liberal Studies)
Genetic Counseling
Geographic Information Systems
Geography
German
Gerontology
Graphic Design
Greek (see Classics)
Health Communication
Health Psychology
Hebrew (see Near and Middle Eastern Languages)
Hebrew Studies (see Jewish Studies)
Hispanic and Latin American Languages
Hispanic Studies
Historic Preservation
History
History of Art (see Art History)
History of Medicine
History of Science and Technology
Holocaust and Genocide Studies
Home Economics (see Family and Consumer Sciences—General)
Homeland Security
Household Economics, Sciences, and Management (see Family and Consumer Sciences—General)
Human Development
Humanities
Illustration
Industrial and Labor Relations
Industrial and Organizational Psychology
Industrial Design
Interdisciplinary Studies
Interior Design
International Affairs
International Development
International Economics
International Service (see International Affairs; International Development)
International Trade Policy
Internet and Interactive Multimedia
Interpersonal Communication (see Speech and Interpersonal Communication)
Interpretation (see Translation and Interpretation)
Islamic Studies (see Near and Middle Eastern Studies; Religion)
Italian
Japanese
Japanese Studies (see Asian Languages; Asian Studies; Japanese)
Jewelry (see Art/Fine Arts)
Jewish Studies
Journalism
Judaic Studies (see Jewish Studies; Religion)
Labor Relations (see Industrial and Labor Relations)
Landscape Architecture
Latin American Studies
Latin (see Classics)
Law Enforcement (see Criminal Justice and Criminology)
Liberal Studies
Lighting Design
Linguistics
Literature (see Classics; Comparative Literature; specific language)
Marriage and Family Therapy
Mass Communication
Media Studies
Medical Illustration
Medieval and Renaissance Studies
Metalsmithing (see Art/Fine Arts)
Middle Eastern Studies (see Near and Middle Eastern Studies)
Military and Defense Studies
Mineral Economics
Ministry (see Pastoral Ministry and Counseling; Theology)
Missions and Missiology
Motion Pictures (see Film, Television, and Video Production)
Museum Studies
Music
Musicology (see Music)
Music Therapy (see Therapies—Dance, Drama, and Music)

National Security
Native American Studies (see American Indian/Native American Studies)
Near and Middle Eastern Languages
Near and Middle Eastern Studies
Near Environment (see Family and Consumer Sciences)
Northern Studies
Organizational Psychology (see Industrial and Organizational Psychology)
Oriental Languages (see Asian Languages)
Oriental Studies (see Asian Studies)
Pacific Area/Pacific Rim Studies
Painting (see Art/Fine Arts)
Pastoral Ministry and Counseling
Philanthropic Studies
Philosophy
Photography
Playwriting (see Theater; Writing)
Policy Studies (see Public Policy)
Political Science
Population Studies (see Demography and Population Studies)
Portuguese
Printmaking (see Art/Fine Arts)
Product Design (see Industrial Design)
Psychoanalysis and Psychotherapy
Psychology—General
Public Administration
Public Affairs
Public History
Public Policy
Public Speaking (see Mass Communication; Rhetoric; Speech and Interpersonal Communication)
Publishing
Regional Planning (see Architecture; Urban and Regional Planning; Urban Design; Urban Studies)
Rehabilitation Counseling
Religion
Renaissance Studies (see Medieval and Renaissance Studies)
Rhetoric
Romance Languages
Romance Literatures (see Romance Languages)
Rural Planning and Studies
Rural Sociology
Russian
Scandinavian Languages
School Psychology
Sculpture (see Art/Fine Arts)
Security Administration (see Criminal Justice and Criminology)
Slavic Languages
Slavic Studies (see East European and Russian Studies; Slavic Languages)
Social Psychology
Social Sciences
Sociology
Southeast Asian Studies (see Asian Studies)
Soviet Studies (see East European and Russian Studies; Russian)
Spanish
Speech and Interpersonal Communication
Sport Psychology
Studio Art (see Art/Fine Arts)
Substance Abuse Counseling (see Addictions/Substance Abuse Counseling)
Survey Methodology
Sustainable Development
Technical Communication
Technical Writing
Telecommunications (see Film, Television, and Video Production)
Television (see Film, Television, and Video Production)
Textile Design
Textiles (see Clothing and Textiles; Textile Design)
Thanatology
Theater
Theater Arts (see Theater)
Theology
Therapies—Dance, Drama, and Music
Translation and Interpretation

Transpersonal and Humanistic Psychology
Urban and Regional Planning
Urban Design
Urban Planning (*see* Architecture; Urban and Regional Planning; Urban Design; Urban Studies)
Urban Studies
Video (*see* Film, Television, and Video Production)
Visual Arts (*see* Applied Arts and Design; Art/Fine Arts; Film, Television, and Video Production; Graphic Design; Illustration; Photography)
Western European Studies
Women's Studies
World Wide Web (*see* Internet and Interactive Multimedia)
Writing

Graduate Programs in the Biological/ Biomedical Sciences & Health-Related Medical Professions

Acupuncture and Oriental Medicine
Acute Care/Critical Care Nursing Administration (*see* Health Services Management and Hospital Administration; Nursing and Healthcare Administration; Pharmaceutical Administration)
Adult Nursing
Advanced Practice Nursing (*see* Family Nurse Practitioner Studies)
Allied Health—General
Allied Health Professions (*see* Clinical Laboratory Sciences/Medical Technology; Clinical Research; Communication Disorders; Dental Hygiene; Emergency Medical Services; Occupational Therapy; Physical Therapy; Physician Assistant Studies; Rehabilitation Sciences)
Allopathic Medicine
Anatomy
Anesthesiologist Assistant Studies
Animal Behavior
Bacteriology
Behavioral Sciences (*see* Biopsychology; Neuroscience; Zoology)
Biochemistry
Bioethics
Biological and Biomedical Sciences—General Biological Chemistry (*see* Biochemistry)
Biological Oceanography (*see* Marine Biology)
Biophysics
Biopsychology
Botany
Breeding (*see* Botany; Plant Biology; Genetics)
Cancer Biology/Oncology
Cardiovascular Sciences
Cell Biology
Cellular Physiology (*see* Cell Biology; Physiology)
Child-Care Nursing (*see* Maternal and Child/Neonatal Nursing)
Chiropractic
Clinical Laboratory Sciences/Medical Technology
Clinical Research
Community Health
Community Health Nursing
Computational Biology
Conservation (*see* Conservation Biology; Environmental Biology)
Conservation Biology
Crop Sciences (*see* Botany; Plant Biology)
Cytology (*see* Cell Biology)
Dental and Oral Surgery (*see* Oral and Dental Sciences)
Dental Assistant Studies (*see* Dental Hygiene)
Dental Hygiene
Dental Services (*see* Dental Hygiene)
Dentistry
Developmental Biology Dietetics (*see* Nutrition)
Ecology
Embryology (*see* Developmental Biology)
Emergency Medical Services
Endocrinology (*see* Physiology)
Entomology

Environmental Biology
Environmental and Occupational Health
Epidemiology
Evolutionary Biology
Family Nurse Practitioner Studies
Foods (*see* Nutrition)
Forensic Nursing
Genetics
Genomic Sciences
Gerontological Nursing
Health Physics/Radiological Health
Health Promotion
Health-Related Professions (*see* individual allied health professions)
Health Services Management and Hospital Administration
Health Services Research
Histology (*see* Anatomy; Cell Biology)
HIV/AIDS Nursing
Hospice Nursing
Hospital Administration (*see* Health Services Management and Hospital Administration)
Human Genetics
Immunology
Industrial Hygiene
Infectious Diseases
International Health
Laboratory Medicine (*see* Clinical Laboratory Sciences/Medical Technology; Immunology; Microbiology; Pathology)
Life Sciences (*see* Biological and Biomedical Sciences)
Marine Biology
Maternal and Child Health
Maternal and Child/Neonatal Nursing
Medical Imaging
Medical Microbiology
Medical Nursing (*see* Medical/Surgical Nursing)
Medical Physics
Medical/Surgical Nursing
Medical Technology (*see* Clinical Laboratory Sciences/Medical Technology)
Medical Sciences (*see* Biological and Biomedical Sciences)
Medical Science Training Programs (*see* Biological and Biomedical Sciences)
Medicinal and Pharmaceutical Chemistry
Medicinal Chemistry (*see* Medicinal and Pharmaceutical Chemistry)
Medicine (*see* Allopathic Medicine; Naturopathic Medicine; Osteopathic Medicine; Podiatric Medicine)
Microbiology
Midwifery (*see* Nurse Midwifery)
Molecular Biology
Molecular Biophysics
Molecular Genetics
Molecular Medicine
Molecular Pathogenesis
Molecular Pathology
Molecular Pharmacology
Molecular Physiology
Molecular Toxicology
Naturopathic Medicine
Neural Sciences (*see* Biopsychology; Neurobiology; Neuroscience)
Neurobiology
Neuroendocrinology (*see* Biopsychology; Neurobiology; Neuroscience; Physiology)
Neuropharmacology (*see* Biopsychology; Neurobiology; Neuroscience; Pharmacology)
Neurophysiology (*see* Biopsychology; Neurobiology; Neuroscience; Physiology)
Neuroscience
Nuclear Medical Technology (*see* Clinical Laboratory Sciences/ Medical Technology)
Nurse Anesthesia
Nurse Midwifery
Nurse Practitioner Studies (*see* Family Nurse Practitioner Studies)
Nursing Administration (*see* Nursing and Healthcare Administration)
Nursing and Healthcare Administration
Nursing Education
Nursing—General
Nursing Informatics

Nutrition

Occupational Health (see Environmental and Occupational Health; Occupational Health Nursing)

Occupational Health Nursing

Occupational Therapy

Oncology (see Cancer Biology/Oncology)

Oncology Nursing

Optometry

Oral and Dental Sciences

Oral Biology (see Oral and Dental Sciences)

Oral Pathology (see Oral and Dental Sciences)

Organismal Biology (see Biological and Biomedical Sciences; Zoology)

Oriental Medicine and Acupuncture (see Acupuncture and Oriental Medicine)

Orthodontics (see Oral and Dental Sciences)

Osteopathic Medicine

Parasitology

Pathobiology

Pathology

Pediatric Nursing

Pedontics (see Oral and Dental Sciences)

Perfusion

Pharmaceutical Administration

Pharmaceutical Chemistry (see Medicinal and Pharmaceutical Chemistry)

Pharmaceutical Sciences

Pharmacology

Pharmacy

Photobiology of Cells and Organelles (see Botany; Cell Biology; Plant Biology)

Physical Therapy

Physician Assistant Studies

Physiological Optics (see Vision Sciences)

Podiatric Medicine

Preventive Medicine (see Community Health and Public Health)

Physiological Optics (see Physiology)

Physiology

Plant Biology

Plant Molecular Biology

Plant Pathology

Plant Physiology

Pomology (see Botany; Plant Biology)

Psychiatric Nursing

Public Health—General

Public Health Nursing (see Community Health Nursing)

Psychiatric Nursing

Psychobiology (see Biopsychology)

Psychopharmacology (see Biopsychology; Neuroscience; Pharmacology)

Radiation Biology

Radiological Health (see Health Physics/Radiological Health)

Rehabilitation Nursing

Rehabilitation Sciences

Rehabilitation Therapy (see Physical Therapy)

Reproductive Biology

School Nursing

Sociobiology (see Evolutionary Biology)

Structural Biology

Surgical Nursing (see Medical/Surgical Nursing)

Systems Biology

Teratology

Therapeutics

Theoretical Biology (see Biological and Biomedical Sciences)

Therapeutics (see Pharmaceutical Sciences; Pharmacology; Pharmacy)

Toxicology

Transcultural Nursing

Translational Biology

Tropical Medicine (see Parasitology)

Veterinary Medicine

Veterinary Sciences

Virology

Vision Sciences

Wildlife Biology (see Zoology)

Women's Health Nursing

Zoology

Graduate Programs in the Physical Sciences, Mathematics, Agricultural Sciences, the Environment & Natural Resources

Acoustics

Agricultural Sciences

Agronomy and Soil Sciences

Analytical Chemistry

Animal Sciences

Applied Mathematics

Applied Physics

Applied Statistics

Aquaculture

Astronomy

Astrophysical Sciences (see Astrophysics; Atmospheric Sciences; Meteorology; Planetary and Space Sciences)

Astrophysics

Atmospheric Sciences

Biological Oceanography (see Marine Affairs; Marine Sciences; Oceanography)

Biomathematics

Biometry

Biostatistics

Chemical Physics

Chemistry

Computational Sciences

Condensed Matter Physics

Dairy Science (see Animal Sciences)

Earth Sciences (see Geosciences)

Environmental Management and Policy

Environmental Sciences

Environmental Studies (see Environmental Management and Policy)

Experimental Statistics (see Statistics)

Fish, Game, and Wildlife Management

Food Science and Technology

Forestry

General Science (see specific topics)

Geochemistry

Geodetic Sciences

Geological Engineering (see Geology)

Geological Sciences (see Geology)

Geology

Geophysical Fluid Dynamics (see Geophysics)

Geophysics

Geosciences

Horticulture

Hydrogeology

Hydrology

Inorganic Chemistry

Limnology

Marine Affairs

Marine Geology

Marine Sciences

Marine Studies (see Marine Affairs; Marine Geology; Marine Sciences; Oceanography)

Mathematical and Computational Finance

Mathematical Physics

Mathematical Statistics (see Applied Statistics; Statistics)

Mathematics

Meteorology

Mineralogy

Natural Resource Management (see Environmental Management and Policy; Natural Resources)

Natural Resources

Nuclear Physics (see Physics)

Ocean Engineering (see Marine Affairs; Marine Geology; Marine Sciences; Oceanography)

Oceanography

Optical Sciences

Optical Technologies (see Optical Sciences)

Optics (see Applied Physics; Optical Sciences; Physics)

Organic Chemistry

Paleontology
Paper Chemistry (*see* Chemistry)
Photonics
Physical Chemistry
Physics
Planetary and Space Sciences
Plant Sciences
Plasma Physics
Poultry Science (*see* Animal Sciences)
Radiological Physics (*see* Physics)
Range Management (*see* Range Science)
Range Science
Resource Management (*see* Environmental Management and Policy;
    Natural Resources)
Solid-Earth Sciences (*see* Geosciences)
Space Sciences (*see* Planetary and Space Sciences)
Statistics
Theoretical Chemistry
Theoretical Physics
Viticulture and Enology
Water Resources

Graduate Programs in Engineering & Applied Sciences

Aeronautical Engineering (*see* Aerospace/Aeronautical Engineering)
Aerospace/Aeronautical Engineering
Aerospace Studies (*see* Aerospace/Aeronautical Engineering)
Agricultural Engineering
Applied Mechanics (*see* Mechanics)
Applied Science and Technology
Architectural Engineering
Artificial Intelligence/Robotics
Astronautical Engineering (*see* Aerospace/Aeronautical Engineering)
Automotive Engineering
Aviation
Biochemical Engineering
Bioengineering
Bioinformatics
Biological Engineering (*see* Bioengineering)
Biomedical Engineering
Biosystems Engineering
Biotechnology
Ceramic Engineering (*see* Ceramic Sciences and Engineering)
Ceramic Sciences and Engineering
Ceramics (*see* Ceramic Sciences and Engineering)
Chemical Engineering
Civil Engineering
Computer and Information Systems Security
Computer Engineering
Computer Science
Computing Technology (*see* Computer Science)
Construction Engineering
Construction Management
Database Systems
Electrical Engineering
Electronic Materials
Electronics Engineering (*see* Electrical Engineering)
Energy and Power Engineering
Energy Management and Policy
Engineering and Applied Sciences
Engineering and Public Affairs (*see* Technology and Public Policy)
Engineering and Public Policy (*see* Energy Management and Policy;
    Technology and Public Policy)
Engineering Design
Engineering Management
Engineering Mechanics (*see* Mechanics)
Engineering Metallurgy (*see* Metallurgical Engineering and
    Metallurgy)
Engineering Physics
Environmental Design (*see* Environmental Engineering)
Environmental Engineering
Ergonomics and Human Factors

Financial Engineering
Fire Protection Engineering
Food Engineering (*see* Agricultural Engineering)
Game Design and Development
Gas Engineering (*see* Petroleum Engineering)
Geological Engineering
Geophysics Engineering (*see* Geological Engineering)
Geotechnical Engineering
Hazardous Materials Management
Health Informatics
Health Systems (*see* Safety Engineering; Systems Engineering)
Highway Engineering (*see* Transportation and Highway Engineering)
Human-Computer Interaction
Human Factors (*see* Ergonomics and Human Factors)
Hydraulics
Hydrology (*see* Water Resources Engineering)
Industrial Engineering (*see* Industrial/Management Engineering)
Industrial/Management Engineering
Information Science
Internet Engineering
Macromolecular Science (*see* Polymer Science and Engineering)
Management Engineering (*see* Engineering Management; Industrial/
    Management Engineering)
Management of Technology
Manufacturing Engineering
Marine Engineering (*see* Civil Engineering)
Materials Engineering
Materials Sciences
Mechanical Engineering
Mechanics
Medical Informatics
Metallurgical Engineering and Metallurgy
Metallurgy (*see* Metallurgical Engineering and Metallurgy)
Mineral/Mining Engineering
Modeling and Simulation
Nanotechnology
Nuclear Engineering
Ocean Engineering
Operations Research
Paper and Pulp Engineering
Petroleum Engineering
Pharmaceutical Engineering
Plastics Engineering (*see* Polymer Science and Engineering)
Polymer Science and Engineering
Public Policy (*see* Energy Management and Policy; Technology and
    Public Policy)
Reliability Engineering
Robotics (*see* Artificial Intelligence/Robotics)
Safety Engineering
Software Engineering
Solid-State Sciences (*see* Materials Sciences)
Structural Engineering
Surveying Science and Engineering
Systems Analysis (*see* Systems Engineering)
Systems Engineering
Systems Science
Technology and Public Policy
Telecommunications
Telecommunications Management
Textile Sciences and Engineering
Textiles (*see* Textile Sciences and Engineering)
Transportation and Highway Engineering
Urban Systems Engineering (*see* Systems Engineering)
Waste Management (*see* Hazardous Materials Management)
Water Resources Engineering

Graduate Programs in Business, Education, Information Studies, Law & Social Work

Accounting
Actuarial Science

Adult Education
Advertising and Public Relations
Agricultural Education
Alcohol Abuse Counseling (*see* Counselor Education)
Archival Management and Studies
Art Education
Athletics Administration (*see* Kinesiology and Movement Studies)
Athletic Training and Sports Medicine
Audiology (*see* Communication Disorders)
Aviation Management
Banking (*see* Finance and Banking)
Business Administration and Management—General
Business Education
Communication Disorders
Community College Education
Computer Education
Continuing Education (*see* Adult Education)
Counseling (*see* Counselor Education)
Counselor Education
Curriculum and Instruction
Developmental Education
Distance Education Development
Drug Abuse Counseling (*see* Counselor Education)
Early Childhood Education
Educational Leadership and Administration
Educational Measurement and Evaluation
Educational Media/Instructional Technology
Educational Policy
Educational Psychology
Education—General
Education of the Blind (*see* Special Education)
Education of the Deaf (*see* Special Education)
Education of the Gifted
Education of the Hearing Impaired (*see* Special Education)
Education of the Learning Disabled (*see* Special Education)
Education of the Mentally Retarded (*see* Special Education)
Education of the Physically Handicapped (*see* Special Education)
Education of Students with Severe/Multiple Disabilities
Education of the Visually Handicapped (*see* Special Education)
Electronic Commerce
Elementary Education
English as a Second Language
English Education
Entertainment Management
Entrepreneurship
Environmental Education
Environmental Law
Exercise and Sports Science
Exercise Physiology (*see* Kinesiology and Movement Studies)
Facilities and Entertainment Management
Finance and Banking
Food Services Management (*see* Hospitality Management)
Foreign Languages Education
Foundations and Philosophy of Education
Guidance and Counseling (*see* Counselor Education)
Health Education
Health Law
Hearing Sciences (*see* Communication Disorders)
Higher Education
Home Economics Education
Hospitality Management
Hotel Management (*see* Travel and Tourism)
Human Resources Development
Human Resources Management
Human Services
Industrial Administration (*see* Industrial and Manufacturing Management)
Industrial and Manufacturing Management
Industrial Education (*see* Vocational and Technical Education)
Information Studies
Instructional Technology (*see* Educational Media/Instructional Technology)
Insurance
Intellectual Property Law
International and Comparative Education
International Business

International Commerce (*see* International Business)
International Economics (*see* International Business)
International Trade (*see* International Business)
Investment and Securities (*see* Business Administration and Management; Finance and Banking; Investment Management)
Investment Management
Junior College Education (*see* Community College Education)
Kinesiology and Movement Studies
Law
Legal and Justice Studies
Leisure Services (*see* Recreation and Park Management)
Leisure Studies
Library Science
Logistics
Management (*see* Business Administration and Management)
Management Information Systems
Management Strategy and Policy
Marketing
Marketing Research
Mathematics Education
Middle School Education
Movement Studies (*see* Kinesiology and Movement Studies)
Multilingual and Multicultural Education
Museum Education
Music Education
Nonprofit Management
Nursery School Education (*see* Early Childhood Education)
Occupational Education (*see* Vocational and Technical Education)
Organizational Behavior
Organizational Management
Parks Administration (*see* Recreation and Park Management)
Personnel (*see* Human Resources Development; Human Resources Management; Organizational Behavior; Organizational Management; Student Affairs)
Philosophy of Education (*see* Foundations and Philosophy of Education)
Physical Education
Project Management
Public Relations (*see* Advertising and Public Relations)
Quality Management
Quantitative Analysis
Reading Education
Real Estate
Recreation and Park Management
Recreation Therapy (*see* Recreation and Park Management)
Religious Education
Remedial Education (*see* Special Education)
Restaurant Administration (*see* Hospitality Management)
Science Education
Secondary Education
Social Sciences Education
Social Studies Education (*see* Social Sciences Education)
Social Work
Special Education
Speech-Language Pathology and Audiology (*see* Communication Disorders)
Sports Management
Sports Medicine (*see* Athletic Training and Sports Medicine)
Sports Psychology and Sociology (*see* Kinesiology and Movement Studies)
Student Affairs
Substance Abuse Counseling (*see* Counselor Education)
Supply Chain Management
Sustainability Management
Systems Management (*see* Management Information Systems)
Taxation
Teacher Education (*see* specific subject areas)
Teaching English as a Second Language (*see* English as a Second Language)
Technical Education (*see* Vocational and Technical Education)
Transportation Management
Travel and Tourism
Urban Education
Vocational and Technical Education
Vocational Counseling (*see* Counselor Education)

NOTES

NOTES

NOTES

NOTES